THE PHILOSOPHER'S INDEX

1991 CUMULATIVE EDITION

VOLUME 25

RELATED PRODUCTS

Retrospective Editions:

The Philosopher's Index: A Retrospective Index to U.S. Publications from 1940 indexes approximately 15,000 philosophy articles from U.S. journals published from 1940–1966, and approximately 5,000 philosophy books published from 1940–1976. Supported by NEH Grant RT-23984-76-375.

Published in April 1978. 1,619 pages. Hardbound in three volumes. $295 (Individuals: $130). ISBN 0-912632-09-7.

The Philosopher's Index: A Retrospective Index to Non-U.S. English Language Publications from 1940 indexes approximately 12,000 philosophy articles published from 1940–1966, and approximately 5,000 philosophy books published from 1940–1978. Supported by NEH Grant RT-27265-77-1360.

Published in April 1980. 1,265 pages. Hardbound in three volumes. $280 (Individuals: $120). ISBN 0-912632-12-7.

CD-ROM and ON-LINE:

The Philosopher's Index is now available on CD-ROM from DIALOG OnDisc.© It contains information from 1940 to the present including over 150,000 articles, books, and contributions to anthologies.

The *Index* is also available on-line from DIALOG, File 57, and from DIALOG's low-cost, after-hours information retrieval service, KNOWLEDGE INDEX.

For additional information on these services, please call DIALOG at (800) 3-DIALOG, or write to: Dialog Information Services, Inc., Marketing Department, 3460 Hillview Avenue, Palo Alto, CA 94304, USA.

Search Aids:

The Philosopher's Index Thesaurus, Second Edition is more comprehensive and designed to assist users in searching the Philosopher's Index Database. This Edition adds many new subject descriptors and cross-references. A summary of indexing policies is also included.

Published in May 1992. 90 pages. $19. ISBN 0-912632-20-8.

***Searching the Philosopher's Index Database on* DIALOG** is a tutorial manual that explains the commands needed to do most searches through DIALOG or KNOWLEDGE INDEX. This manual describes the information contained in the Philosopher's Index Database and includes examples of basic and advanced searches.

Published in 1988. 63 pages. $15. ISBN 0-912632-50-X.

For additional information on products and services, please call the Philosophy Documentation Center at: (800) 444-2419 *or* (419) 372-2419 Fax: (419) 372-6987

The Philosopher's Index

An International Index To Philosophical Periodicals and Books

—25th Anniversary Volume—

1991 CUMULATIVE EDITION
VOLUME 25

Bowling Green State University, Bowling Green, OH 43403-0189, U.S.A.

PHILOSOPHY DOCUMENTATION CENTER

Mission Statement: The mission of the Philosophy Documentation Center is to serve philosophers, students, and others by providing them with reliable information, quality products and needed services.

The Center strives to fulfill its mission by 1) publishing and distributing philosophy indexes, directories, bibliographies, and scholarly journals; 2) providing a computer-searchable philosophy database; 3) publishing philosophy software; 4) offering typesetting and subscription fulfillment services; 5) renting mailing lists; and 6) providing convention exhibit services for philosophy journals and books.

THE PHILOSOPHER'S INDEX

Editor

Richard H. Lineback

Editorial Staff

Thomas Attig, Assistant Editor
Bowling Green State University
Mark Christensen, Assistant Editor
Lourdes College
Douglas D. Daye, Assistant Editor
Bowling Green State University
Robert Goodwin, Assistant Editor
Bowling Green State University
Cheedy JaJa, Assistant to the Editors
Bowling Green State University
Brenda Jubin, Assistant Editor
Yale University
Fred Miller, Assistant Editor
Bowling Green State University
Frederick Rickey, Assistant to the Editors
Bowling Green State University
René Ruiz, Assistant Editor
Bowling Green State University
Janet Stake, Assistant to the Editors
Bowling Green State University
Lynn Walkiewicz, Assistant Editor
Bowling Green State University
Robert Wolf, Assistant Editor
Southern Illinois University

Table of Contents

The Philosopher's Index

The Philosopher's Index, ISSN 0031-7993, a publication of the Philosophy Documentation Center, is a subject and author index with abstracts. Philosophy books and journals in English, French, German, Spanish, and Italian are indexed, along with selected books and journals in other languages and related interdisciplinary publications. This periodical is published quarterly and cumulated annually as a service to the philosophical community. Suggestions for improving this service are solicited and should be sent to the Editor.

Policies: Each quarterly issue of the *Index* includes the articles of journals and books that are received in the months prior to its publication. The dates on the journals indexed vary due to dissimilar publishing schedules and to delays encountered in overseas mailing.

The following factors are weighed in selecting journals to be indexed: 1) the purpose of the journal, 2) its circulation, and 3) recommendations from members of the philosophic community. Articles in interdisciplinary journals are indexed only if they are related to philosophy.

Most of the journal articles and books cited in *The Philosopher's Index* can be obtained from the Bowling Green State University Library, through the Inter-Library Loan Department. The library, though, requests that you first try to locate the articles and books through your local or regional library facilities.

Subscriptions should be mailed to *The Philosopher's Index*, Bowling Green State University, Bowling Green, Ohio 43403-0189. The 1992 subscription price (4 numbers) is $149 (Individuals $42). The price of single numbers, including back issues, is $40 (Individuals $12). An annual Cumulative Edition of *The Philosopher's Index* is published in the spring following the volume year. The 1992 Cumulative Edition is $155 (Individuals $51).

ISBN 0-912632-53-4

Abbreviations of Periodicals Indexed

(*Journal is no longer indexed and/or published. However, the abbreviation is included here for use in conjunction with DIALOG.)

*Abraxas**	*Abraxas*
Acta Phil Fennica	*Acta Philosophica Fennica*
*Agora**	*Agora*
Agr Human Values	*Agriculture and Human Values*
Aitia	*Aitia*
*Ajatus**	*Ajatus*
*Aletheia**	*Aletheia*
*Alg Log**	*Algebra and Logic*
Alg Ned Tijdschr Wijs	*Algemeen Nederlands Tijdschrift voor Wijsbegeerte*
Amer J Philo	*American Journal of Philology*
Amer J Theol Phil	*American Journal of Theology & Philosophy*
Amer Phil Quart	*American Philosophical Quarterly*
*An Cated Suarez**	*Anales de la Catedra Francisco Suarez*
An Seminar Metaf	*Anales del Seminario de Metafisica*
Analisis Filosof	*Analisis Filosofico*
Analysis	*Analysis*
Ancient Phil	*Ancient Philosophy*
*Ann Esth**	*Annales D'Esthétique*
Ann Fac Lett Filosof	*Annali della Facolta di Lettere e Filosofia*
Ann Univ Mariae Curie-Phil	*Annales Universitatis Mariae Curie-Skłodowska, Sectio I/Philosophia-Sociologia*
Annals Math Log	*Annals of Mathematical Logic (see Annals Pure Applied Log)*
Annals Pure Applied Log	*Annals of Pure and Applied Logic (formerly Annals of Mathematical Logic)*
Antioch Rev	*Antioch Review*
Anu Filosof	*Anuario Filosofico*
Apeiron	*Apeiron*
Applied Phil	*Applied Philosophy (see Int J Applied Phil)*
Aquinas	*Aquinas*
*Arch Begriff**	*Archiv für Begriffsgeschichte*
*Arch Filosof**	*Archivio di Filosofia*
Arch Gesch Phil	*Archiv für Geschichte der Philosophie*
*Arch Math Log**	*Archiv für Mathematische Logik und Grundlagen Forschung*
Arch Phil	*Archives de Philosophie*
Arch Rechts Soz	*Archiv für Rechts und Sozialphilosophie*
Arch Stor Cult	*Archivio di Storia della Cultura*
Argumentation	*Argumentation*
Aris Soc	*The Aristotelian Society: Supplementary Volume*
Asian J Phil	*The Asian Journal of Philosophy*
Asian Phil	*Asian Philosophy*
Augustin Stud	*Augustinian Studies*
Augustinus	*Augustinus*
Auslegung	*Auslegung*
Austl J Phil	*Australasian Journal of Philosophy*
Behavior Phil	*Behavior and Philosophy (formerly Behaviorism)*
Behaviorism	*Behaviorism (see Behavior Phil)*
Berkeley News	*Berkeley Newsletter*
Between Species	*Between the Species*
Bigaku	*Bigaku*
Bijdragen	*Bijdragen, Tijdschrift voor Filosofie en Theologie*
Bioethics	*Bioethics*
Bioethics Quart	*Bioethics Quarterly (see J Med Human)*
Biol Phil	*Biology & Philosophy*
Boll Centro Stud Vichiani	*Bollettino del Centro di Studi Vichiani*
*Boston Col Stud Phil**	*Boston College Studies in Philosophy*
*Brahmavadin**	*Brahmavadin*
Bridges	*Bridges: An Interdisciplinary Journal of Theology, Philosophy, History, and Science*
Brit J Aes	*The British Journal of Aesthetics*
Brit J Phil Sci	*British Journal for the Philosophy of Science*
Bull Hegel Soc Gt Brit	*Bulletin of the Hegel Society of Great Britain*
Bull Santayana Soc	*Overheard in Seville: Bulletin of the Santayana Society*
Bull Sect Log	*Bulletin of the Section of Logic*
Bull Soc Fr Phil	*Bulletin de la Société Française de Philosophie*
Bus Ethics Quart	*Business Ethics Quarterly*
Bus Prof Ethics J	*Business & Professional Ethics Journal*
Cad Hist Filosof Cie	*Cadernos de História e Filosofia da Ciência*
Can J Phil	*Canadian Journal of Philosophy*
*Can J Theol**	*Canadian Journal of Theology*
Can Phil Rev	*Canadian Philosophical Reviews*
Chin Stud Hist Phil	*Chinese Studies in History and Philosophy (see Chin Stud Phil)*
Chin Stud Phil	*Chinese Studies in Philosophy (formerly Chin Stud Hist Phil)*
*Cirpho**	*Cirpho Review*
*Cl Quart**	*The Classical Quarterly*

Clio	Clio
Club Voltaire*	Club Voltaire
Cogito	Cogito
Cognition	Cognition
Commun Cog	Communication and Cognition
Conceptus	Conceptus
Cont Phil	Contemporary Philosophy
Convivium*	Convivium
Crim Just Ethics	Criminal Justice Ethics
Crit Inquiry	Critical Inquiry
Crit Rev	Critical Review
Crit Texts	Critical Texts
Critica	Crítica
Cuad Etica	Cuadernos de Etica
Cuad Filosof	Cuadernos de Filosofía
Cult Herm	Cultural Hermeneutics (see Phil Soc Crit)
Dalhousie Rev*	Dalhousie Review
Dan Yrbk Phil*	Danish Yearbook of Philosophy
Darshan-Manjari	Darshan-Manjari
Darshana Int	Darshana International
De Phil	De Philosophia
Deut Vier Lit*	Deutsche Vierteljahresschrift für Literaturwissenschaft und Geistes Geschichte
Deut Z Phil	Deutsche Zeitschrift für Philosophie
Dialec Hum	Dialectics and Humanism
Dialectica	Dialectica
Dialogo Filosof	Dialogo Filosofico
Dialogos	Diálogos
Dialogue (Canada)	Dialogue: Canadian Philosophical Review—Revue Canadienne de Philosophie
Dialogue (PST)	Dialogue
Dialoog*	Dialoog
Dianoia	Diánoia
Diogenes	Diogenes
Dionysius	Dionysius
Diotima	Diotima
Discurso*	Discurso
Doctor Communis*	Doctor Communis
Econ Phil	Economics and Philosophy
Educ Filosof	Educação e Filosofia
Educ Phil Theor	Educational Philosophy and Theory
Educ Stud	Educational Studies
Educ Theor	Educational Theory
Eidos	Eidos
El Basilisco	El Basilisco
Ensay Estud*	Ensayos y Estudios
Environ Ethics	Environmental Ethics
Epistemologia	Epistemologia
Erkenntnis	Erkenntnis
Espiritu	Espíritu
Estetika	Estetika
Estud Filosof*	Estudios Filosóficos
Ethics	Ethics
Ethics Animals*	Ethics and Animals
Ethics Behavior	Ethics and Behavior
Ethics Med	Ethics and Medicine: A Christian Perspective on Issues in Bioethics
Ethos*	Ethos
Etud Phil*	Les Etudes Philosophiques
Etudes	Etudes
Etyka	Etyka
Euthanasia Rev*	The Euthanasia Review
Exer Pat*	Exercices de la Patience
Exist Psychiat*	Existential Psychiatry
Explor Knowl	Explorations in Knowledge
Faith Phil	Faith and Philosophy
Fem Stud	Feminist Studies
Filosofia	Filosofia
Filozof Cas	Filozoficky Casopis CSAV
Filozof Istraz	Filozofska Istrsazivanja
Found Lang	Foundations of Language (see Ling Phil)
Fran Stud	Franciscan Studies
Free Inq	Free Inquiry
Frei Z Phil Theol	Freiburger Zeitschrift für Philosophie und Theologie
Futurum*	Futurum
G Crit Filosof Ital	Giornale Critico della Filosofia Italiana
G Metaf	Giornale di Metafisica
Gnosis	Gnosis
Grad Fac Phil J	Graduate Faculty Philosophy Journal

Grazer Phil Stud	*Grazer Philosophische Studien*
Gregorianum	*Gregorianum*
*Grund Kyber Geist**	*Grundlagenstudien aus Kybernetik und Geisteswissenschaft*
Hastings Center Rep	*Hastings Center Report*
*Hastings Center Stud**	*Hastings Center Studies*
*Hegel-Jrbh**	*Hegel-Jahrbuch*
Hermathena	*Hermathena*
Heythrop J	*Heythrop Journal*
*Hibbert J**	*Hibbert Journal*
Hist Euro Ideas	*History of European Ideas*
Hist Phil Life Sci	*History and Philosophy of the Life Sciences*
Hist Phil Log	*History and Philosophy of Logic*
Hist Phil Quart	*History of Philosophy Quarterly*
Hist Polit Thought	*History of Political Thought*
Hist Theor	*History and Theory*
Hobbes Stud	*Hobbes Studies*
Horiz Phil	*Horizons Philosophiques*
*Human Context**	*The Human Context*
*Human Soc**	*Humanities in Society*
Human Stud	*Human Studies*
Humanist	*The Humanist*
Humanitas	*Humanitas*
*Humanitas (Mexico)**	*Humanitas*
Hume Stud	*Hume Studies*
Husserl Stud	*Husserl Studies*
Hypatia	*Hypatia*
Ideal Stud	*Idealistic Studies*
Il Protag	*Il Protagora*
Independ J Phil	*Independent Journal of Philosophy*
*Indian J Phil**	*Indian Journal of Philosophy*
*Indian Phil Cult**	*Indian Philosophy and Culture*
Indian Phil Quart	*Indian Philosophical Quarterly*
Inform Log	*Informal Logic*
Inquiry	*Inquiry*
*Int Dialog Z**	*Internationale Dialog Zeitschrift*
Int J Applied Phil	*International Journal of Applied Philosophy (formerly Applied Philosophy)*
Int J Moral Soc Stud	*International Journal of Moral and Social Studies*
Int J Phil Relig	*International Journal for Philosophy of Religion*
Int Log Rev	*International Logic Review*
Int Phil Quart	*International Philosophical Quarterly*
Int Stud Phil	*International Studies in Philosophy (formerly Studi Internazionali di Filosofia)*
Int Stud Phil Sci	*International Studies in the Philosophy of Science*
*Interchange**	*Interchange*
Interpretation	*Interpretation*
Irish Phil J	*Irish Philosophical Journal*
*ITA Humanidades**	*ITA Humanidades*
Iyyun	*Iyyun*
J Aes Art Crit	*The Journal of Aesthetics and Art Criticism*
J Aes Educ	*The Journal of Aesthetic Education*
J Agr Ethics	*Journal of Agricultural Ethics*
J Applied Phil	*Journal of Applied Philosophy*
J Brit Soc Phenomenol	*The Journal of the British Society for Phenomenology*
J Bus Ethics	*Journal of Business Ethics*
J Chin Phil	*Journal of Chinese Philosophy*
J Crit Anal	*The Journal of Critical Analysis*
*J Comp Syst**	*Journal of Computing Systems*
J Dharma	*Journal of Dharma*
*J Existent**	*Journal of Existentialism*
J Hellen Stud	*The Journal of Hellenic Studies*
J Hist Ideas	*Journal of the History of Ideas*
J Hist Phil	*Journal of the History of Philosophy*
*J Indian Acad Phil**	*Journal of the Indian Academy of Philosophy*
J Indian Counc Phil Res	*Journal of Indian Council of Philosophical Research*
J Indian Phil	*Journal of Indian Philosophy*
J Liber Stud	*The Journal of Libertarian Studies*
J Med Ethics	*Journal of Medical Ethics*
J Med Human	*The Journal of Medical Humanities (formerly The Journal of Medical Humanities and Bioethics)*
J Med Human Bioethics	*The Journal of Medical Humanities and Bioethics (formerly Bioethics Quarterly)*
J Med Phil	*The Journal of Medicine and Philosophy*
J Mind Behav	*The Journal of Mind and Behavior*
J Moral Educ	*Journal of Moral Education*
J Non-Classical Log	*The Journal of Non-Classical Logic*
J Phil	*The Journal of Philosophy*
*J Phil Assn**	*Journal of the Philosophical Association*
J Phil Educ	*Journal of Philosophy of Education (formerly Proceedings of the Philosophy of Education Society of Great Britain)*

J Phil Log	Journal of Philosophical Logic
J Phil Res	Journal of Philosophical Research (formerly Philosophy Research Archives)
J Phil Sport	Journal of the Philosophy of Sport
J Prag	Journal of Pragmatics
J Relig Ethics	Journal of Religious Ethics
J Semantics	Journal of Semantics
J Soc Biol Struct	Journal of Social and Biological Structures
J Soc Phil	Journal of Social Philosophy
J Speculative Phil	The Journal of Speculative Philosophy
J Sym Log	The Journal of Symbolic Logic
J Theor Crit Vis Arts*	The Journal of the Theory and Criticism of the Visual Arts
J Theor Soc Behav	Journal for the Theory of Social Behaviour
J Thought	Journal of Thought
J Value Inq	The Journal of Value Inquiry
J W Vir Phil Soc*	Journal of the West Virginia Philosophical Society
Kantstudien	Kant-Studien
Kennis Methode	Kennis en Methode
Kinesis	Kinesis
Kodikas/Code*	Kodikas/Code: An International Journal of Semiotics
Koelner Z Soz*	Koelner Zeitschrift für Soziologie und Sozial-Psychologie
Kriterion	Kriterion
Kursbuch*	Kursbuch
Laval Theol Phil	Laval Théologique et Philosophique
Law Phil	Law and Philosophy
Ling Phil	Linguistics and Philosophy (formerly Foundations of Language)
Listening	Listening: Journal of Religion and Culture
Locke News	The Locke Newsletter
Log Anal	Logique et Analyse
Logos (Italy)*	Logos
Logos (Mexico)	Logos
Logos (USA)	Logos
Magyar Filozof Szemle	Magyar Filozofiai Szemle
Main Currents*	Main Currents
Man Nature	Man and Nature/L'homme et la Nature
Man World	Man and World
Manuscrito	Manuscrito: Revista Internacional de Filosofia
Med Human Rev	Medical Humanities Review
Med Stud	Mediaeval Studies
Merkur*	Merkur
Metamedicine	Metamedicine (see Theor Med)
Metaphilosophy	Metaphilosophy
Method	Method: Journal of Lonergan Studies
Method Sci	Methodology and Science
Methodos*	Methodos
Midwest J Phil*	Midwestern Journal of Philosophy
Midwest Stud Phil	Midwest Studies in Philosophy
Mill News*	The Mill News Letter
Mind	Mind: A Quarterly Review of Philosophy
Mind Lang	Mind & Language
Mod Sch	The Modern Schoolman
Mod Theol	Modern Theology
Monist	The Monist
Music Man*	Music and Man
NAO	NAO Revista de la Cultura del Mediterráneo
Nat Forum	National Forum
Nature Syst*	Nature and System
Neue Hefte Phil	Neue Hefte für Philosophie
New Scholas	The New Scholasticism
New Vico Stud	New Vico Studies
Nietzsche-Stud	Nietzsche-Studien
Notre Dame J Form Log	Notre Dame Journal of Formal Logic
Notre Dame J Law Ethics	Notre Dame Journal of Law, Ethics & Public Policy
Nous	Noûs
Nouv Repub Lett	Nouvelles de la République des Lettres
Organon*	Organon
Owl Minerva	The Owl of Minerva
Pac Phil Forum*	Pacific Philosophical Forum (see Phil Forum (Dekalb)*)
Pac Phil Quart	Pacific Philosophical Quarterly (formerly The Personalist)
Pakistan Phil Congr*	Pakistan Philosophical Congress
Pakistan Phil J*	The Pakistan Philosophical Journal
Pat Med	Patristica et Mediaevalia
Pen Ling Oper*	Pensiero e Linguaggio in Operazioni
Pensamiento	Pensamiento
Personalist	The Personalist (see Pacific Philosophical Quarterly)
Personalist Forum	The Personalist Forum
Perspekt Phil*	Perspektiven der Philosophie

Petite Rev Phil	*La Petite Revue de Philosophie*
Phil Books	*Philosophical Books*
*Phil Context**	*Philosophy in Context*
Phil East West	*Philosophy East and West*
*Phil Educ Proc**	*Proceedings of the Far Western Philosophy of Education Society*
Phil Exch	*Philosophic Exchange*
Phil Forum	*The Philosophical Forum (formerly Philosophical Forum (Boston))*
Phil Forum (Boston)	*Philosophical Forum (see Phil Forum)*
*Phil Forum (Dekalb)**	*Philosophy Forum (formerly Pacific Philosophical Forum)*
Phil Inq	*Philosophical Inquiry*
Phil Invest	*Philosophical Investigations*
*Phil Jahr**	*Philosophisches Jahrbuch*
*Phil Ling**	*Philosophical Linguistics*
Phil Lit	*Philosophy and Literature*
Phil Log	*Philosophie et Logique*
Phil Math	*Philosophia Mathematica*
Phil Natur	*Philosophia Naturalis*
Phil Papers	*Philosophical Papers*
*Phil Perspekt**	*Philosophische Perspektiven*
Phil Phenomenol Res	*Philosophy and Phenomenological Research*
Phil Psych	*Philosophical Psychology*
Phil Pub Affairs	*Philosophy and Public Affairs*
Phil Quart	*Philosophical Quarterly*
*Phil Quart (India)**	*Philosophical Quarterly*
Phil Quart (Scotland)	*Philosophical Quarterly (see Phil Quart)*
Phil Reform	*Philosophia Reformata*
Phil Res Arch	*Philosophy Research Archives (see J Phil Res)*
Phil Rev	*The Philosophical Review*
Phil Rev (Taiwan)	*Philosophical Review*
Phil Rhet	*Philosophy and Rhetoric*
Phil Rundsch	*Philosophische Rundschau*
Phil Sci	*Philosophy of Science*
Phil Sci (Tucson)	*Philosophy in Science*
Phil Soc Act	*Philosophy and Social Action*
Phil Soc Crit	*Philosophy and Social Criticism (formerly Cultural Hermeneutics)*
Phil Soc Sci	*Philosophy of the Social Sciences*
Phil Stud	*Philosophical Studies*
Phil Stud (Ireland)	*Philosophical Studies*
Phil Stud Educ	*Philosophical Studies in Education*
*Phil Stud Japan**	*Philosophical Studies of Japan*
Phil Theol	*Philosophy and Theology*
Phil Today	*Philosophy Today*
Phil Topics	*Philosophical Topics (formerly Southwestern Journal of Philosophy)*
Philosophia (Athens)	*Philosophia*
Philosophia (Israel)	*Philosophia: Philosophical Quarterly of Israel*
Philosophica	*Philosophica*
Philosophica (Czechoslovakia)	*Philosophica: Zborník Univerzity Komenského*
Philosophica (India)	*Philosophica*
Philosophiques	*Philosophiques*
Philosophy	*Philosophy*
Phoenix	*Phoenix*
Phronesis	*Phronesis*
Polis	*Polis*
Polit Theor	*Political Theory*
*Poznan Stud**	*Poznań Studies in the Philosophy of the Sciences and Humanities*
*Prag Micro**	*Pragmatics Microfiche*
*Praxis**	*Praxis*
Praxis Int	*Praxis International*
*Problemos**	*Problemos*
Proc Amer Phil Ass	*Proceedings and Addresses of the American Philosophical Association*
Proc Aris Soc	*Proceedings of the Aristotelian Society*
Proc Boston Colloq Anc Phil	*Proceedings of the Boston Area Colloquium in Ancient Philosophy*
Proc Cath Phil Ass	*Proceedings of the American Catholic Philosophical Association*
Proc N Mex W Tex Phil Soc	*Proceedings of the New Mexico-West Texas Philosophical Society (see SW Phil Stud)*
Proc Phil Educ	*Philosophy of Education: Proceedings*
*Proc Phil Educ Soc Austrl**	*Proceedings of the Philosophy of Education Society of Australasia*
Proc Phil Educ Soc GB	*Proceedings of the Philosophy of Education Society of Great Britain (see J Phil Educ)*
Proc Phil Sci Ass	*Proceedings of the Biennial Meetings of the Philosophy of Science Association*
Proc S Atlantic Phil Educ Soc	*Proceedings of the South Atlantic Philosophy of Education Society*
Process Stud	*Process Studies*
Pub Affairs Quart	*Public Affairs Quarterly*
Quest	*Quest: Philosophical Discussions*
Rad Phil	*Radical Philosophy*
*Rad Phil News**	*Radical Philosopher's Newsjournal*
Ratio	*Ratio*
Ratio Juris	*Ratio Juris*

Reason Papers	*Reason Papers*
*Rechtstheor**	*Rechtstheorie*
*Relev Log News**	*Relevance Logic Newsletter*
Relig Hum	*Religious Humanism*
Relig Stud	*Religious Studies*
Rep Math Log	*Reports on Mathematical Logic*
Rep Phil	*Reports on Philosophy*
Res Phenomenol	*Research in Phenomenology*
*Rev Esth**	*Revue d'Esthétique*
*Rev Etud Augustin**	*Revue des Etudes Augustiniennes*
*Rev Exist Psych Psychiat**	*Review of Existential Psychology & Psychiatry*
Rev Filosof (Argentina)	*Revista de Filosofía*
*Rev Filosof (Argentina)**	*Revista de Filosofía: Publicación de la Asociación de Estudios Filosóficas*
Rev Filosof (Costa Rica)	*Revista de Filosofía de la Universidad de Costa Rica*
Rev Filosof (Mexico)	*Revista de Filosofía*
Rev Filosof (Romania)	*Revista de Filosofía (formerly Revista de Filosofie)*
*Rev Filosof (Spain)**	*Revista de Filosofie*
Rev Filosof (Venezuela)	*Revista de Filosofia*
Rev Filozof	*Revista de Filosofie (see Rev Filosof (Romania))*
Rev Int Phil	*Revue Internationale de Philosophie*
*Rev J Phil Soc Sci**	*Review Journal of Philosophy and Social Science*
Rev Latin de Filosof	*Revista Latinoamericana de Filosofía*
Rev Metaph	*The Review of Metaphysics*
Rev Metaph Morale	*Revue de Metaphysique et de Morale*
Rev Phil Fr	*Revue Philosophique de la France et de l'Etranger*
Rev Phil Louvain	*Revue Philosophique de Louvain*
Rev Port Filosof	*Revista Portuguesa de Filosofia*
Rev Sci Phil Theol	*Revue des Sciences Philosophiques et Theologiques*
*Rev Teilhard de Chardin**	*Revue Teilhard de Chardin*
Rev Theol Phil	*Revue de Théologie et de Philosophie*
Rev Thomiste	*Revue Thomiste*
*Rev Univ Ottawa**	*Revue de l'Université d'Ottawa*
Rev Ven Filosof	*Revista Venezolana de Filosofía*
*Rev World**	*Revolutionary World*
Riv Filosof	*Rivista di Filosofia*
Riv Filosof Neo-Scolas	*Rivista di Filosofia Neo-Scolastica*
Riv Int Filosof Diritto	*Rivista Internazionale di Filosofia del Diritto*
Riv Stud Croce	*Rivista di Studi Crociani*
Russell	*Russell*
S Afr J Phil	*South African Journal of Philosophy*
S J Phil	*The Southern Journal of Philosophy*
*Salzburger Jrbh Phil**	*Salzburger Jahrbuch für Philosophie*
Sapientia	*Sapientia*
Sapienza	*Sapienza*
Schopenhauer Jahr	*Schopenhauer-Jahrbuch*
Sci Tech Human Values	*Science, Technology, and Human Values*
Scientia	*Scientia*
*Second Order**	*Second Order*
Soc Epistem	*Social Epistemology*
Soc Indic Res	*Social Indicators Research*
Soc Phil Pol	*Social Philosophy and Policy*
*Soc Prax**	*Social Praxis: International and Interdisciplinary Journal of Social Thought*
Soc Theor Pract	*Social Theory and Practice*
Sophia (Australia)	*Sophia*
*Sophia (Italy)**	*Sophia*
Soviet Stud Phil	*Soviet Studies in Philosophy*
*Sowjet Ges Beitr**	*Sowjetwissenschaft Gesellschaftswissenschaftliche Beitraege*
*Soz Welt**	*Soziale Welt*
*Sprache Tech Zeit**	*Sprache im Technischen Zeitalter*
Stromata	*Stromata*
*Stud Gen**	*Studium Generale*
Stud Hist Phil Sci	*Studies in History and Philosophy of Science*
Stud Int Filosof	*Studi Internazionale di Filosofia (see Int Stud Phil)*
Stud Leibniz	*Studia Leibnitiana*
Stud Log	*Studia Logica*
Stud Phil (Switzerland)	*Studia Philosophica*
Stud Phil Christ	*Studia Philosophiae Christiane*
Stud Phil Educ	*Studies in Philosophy and Education*
Stud Phil Hist Phil	*Studies in Philosophy and the History of Philosophy*
Stud Soviet Tho	*Studies in Soviet Thought*
Stud Spinozana	*Studia Spinozana*
SW J Phil	*Southwestern Journal of Philosophy (see Phil Topics)*
SW Phil Rev	*Southwest Philosophy Review*
SW Phil Stud	*Southwest Philosophical Studies (formerly Proceedings of the New Mexico–West Texas Philosophical Society)*
*Syn Phil**	*Synthesis Philosophica*

Synthese	Synthese
Systematics*	Systematics
Teach Phil	Teaching Philosophy
Telos*	Telos
Teor Metod*	Teorie a Metoda
Teorema	Teorema
Teoresi*	Teoresi
Teoria	Teoria: Rivisa di Filosofia
Themata	Thémata Revista de Filosofia
Theol Phil*	Theologie und Philosophie
Theor Decis	Theory and Decision
Theor Med	Theoretical Medicine (formerly Metamedicine)
Theor Theor*	Theoria to Theory
Theoria	Theoria
Theoria (Spain)	Theoria
Thinking	Thinking: The Journal of Philosophy for Children
Thomist	The Thomist
Thought	Thought
Thought Pract*	Thought and Practice
Tijdschr Filosof	Tijdschrift voor Filosofie
Tijdschr Stud Verlich Denken	Tijdschrift voor de Studie van de Verlichting en van Het Vrije Denken
Topoi	Topoi
Traditio*	Traditio: Studies in Ancient and Medieval History, Thought and Religion
Trans Peirce Soc	Transactions of the Charles S. Peirce Society
Trans/Form/Acao	Trans/Form/Acao
Tribuene*	Tribuene
Tulane Stud Phil	Tulane Studies in Philosophy
Ultim Real Mean	Ultimate Reality and Meaning
Under J Phil*	Undergraduate Journal of Philosophy
Univ Human Rights*	Universal Human Rights
Univ Phil	Universitas Philosophica
Universitas*	Universitas
Utilitas	Utilitas: A Journal of Utilitarian Studies
Values Ethics Health Care*	Values and Ethics in Health Care
Vedanta Kesari*	Vedanta Kesari
Vera Lex	Vera Lex
Vivarium	Vivarium
Wiss Weis*	Wissenschaft und Weisheit
Wiss Welt*	Wissenschaft und Weltbild
Z Aes Allg Kunst*	Zeitschrift für Aesthetik und Allgemeine Kunstwissenschaft
Z Allg Wiss*	Zeitschrift für Allgemeine Wissenschaftstheorie
Z Math Log	Zeitschrift für Mathematische Logik und Grundlagen der Mathematik
Z Phil Forsch	Zeitschrift für Philosophische Forschung
Z Relig Geist*	Zeitschrift für Religions-und Geistesgeschichte
Z Soz*	Zeitschrift für Sozialpsychologie
Zygon	Zygon

Key to Abbreviations

Ag	August
ann	annual
Ap	April
bi-ann	biannually (2 x a year)
bi-enn	biennially (every 2 years)
bi-m	bi-monthly (every 2 months)
D	December
F.	February
irr	irregular
Ja	January
Je	June
Jl	July
mono	monograph
m	monthly
Mr	March
My	May
N	November
O	October
q	quarterly
S	September
semi-ann	semiannually (2 x a year)
semi-m	semimonthly (2 x a month)
Spr	Spring
Sum	Summer
supp	supplement
Wint	Winter
yr	year

List of Periodicals Indexed

Acta Philosophica Fennica. ISSN 0355-1792. (irr) Academic Bookstore, Keskuskatu 1, 00100 Helsinki, Finland

Agriculture and Human Values. ISSN 0889-048X. (q) Managing Editor, 370 ASB, University of Florida, Gainesville, FL 32611, USA

Aitia: Philosophy-Humanities Magazine. ISSN 0731-5880. (3 times a yr) Knapp Hall 15, SUNY at Farmingdale, Farmingdale, NY 11735, USA

Algemeen Nederlands Tijdschrift voor Wijsbegeerte. ISSN 0002-5275. (q) Van Gorcum, Postbus 43, 9400 AA Assen, The Netherlands

American Journal of Philology. ISSN 0002-9475. (q) The Johns Hopkins University Press, 701 West 40th Street, Suite 275, Baltimore, MD 21211, USA

American Journal of Theology & Philosophy. ISSN 0194-3448. (3 times a yr) W. Creighton Peden, Editor, Department of Philosophy, Augusta College, Augusta, GA 30910, USA

American Philosophical Quarterly. ISSN 0003-0481. (q) Philosophy Documentation Center, Bowling Green State University, Bowling Green, OH 43403-0189, USA

Anales del Seminario de Metafísica. ISSN 0580-8650. (ann) Editor, Universidad Complutense, Noviciado 3, 28015 Madrid, Spain

Analisis Filosofico. ISSN 0326-1301. (semi-ann) Bulnes 642, 1176 Buenos Aires, Argentina

Analysis. ISSN 0003-2638. (q) Basil Blackwell, 108 Cowley Road, Oxford OX41JF, England (or 3 Cambridge Center, Cambridge, MA 02142, USA)

Ancient Philosophy. ISSN 0740-2007. (semi-ann) Prof. Ronald Polansky, Duquesne University, Pittsburgh, PA 15282, USA

Annales Universitatis Mariae Curie-Skłodowskiej, Sectio 1/Philosophia-Sociologia. ISSN 0137-2025. (ann) Biuro Wydawnictw, Uniwersytet Marii Curie-Skłodowskiej, Pl. Marii Curie-Skłodowskiej 5, 20-031 Lublin, Poland

Annali della Facolta di Lettere e Filosofia. Pubblicazioni dell'Università di Studi di Bari, Palazzo Ateneo, 70100 Bari, Italy

Annals of Pure and Applied Logic. ISSN 0168-0072. Elsevier Science Publishers, Box 211, 1000 AE Amsterdam, The Netherlands

Antioch Review. ISSN 0003-5769. (q) P.O. Box 148, Yellow Springs, OH 45387, USA

Anuario Filosofico. ISSN 0066-5215. Service de Publicaciones de la Universidad de Navarra, S.A. Edificio Bibliotecas, Campus Universitario, 31080 Pamplona, Spain

Apeiron: A Journal of Ancient Philosophy and Science. ISSN 0003-6390. (q) Academic Printing and Publishing, P.O. Box 4834, Edmonton, Alberta, Canada T6E 5G7

Aquinas. ISSN 0003-7362. (3 times a yr) Pontificia Universita Lateranense, Piazza S. Giovanni in Laterano 4, 00120 Città del Vaticano, Vatican City State

Archiv für Geschichte der Philosophie. ISSN 0003-9101. (3 times a yr) Walter de Gruyter, Genthiner Str. 13, 1000 Berlin 30, Germany

Archiv für Rechts und Sozialphilosophie. ISSN 0001-2343. (q) Franz Steiner Verlag Wiesbaden GmbH, P.O.B. 101526, 7000 Stuttgart, Germany

Archives de Philosophie. ISSN 0003-9632. 72 rue des Saints-Pères, 75007 Paris, France

Archivio di Storia della Cultura. (ann) Morano Editore S.P.A., Vico S. Domenico Maggiore, 9-80134 Naples, Italy

Argumentation. ISSN 0920-427X. (q) Kluwer Academic Publishers, P.O. Box 358, Accord-Station, Hingham, MA 02018-0358, USA

The Aristotelian Society: Supplementary Volume. ISSN 0309-7013. (ann) Members: The Aristotelian Society, Department of Philosophy, Birkbeck College, University of London, Malet Street, London WC1E 7HX, England. Non-members: Basil Blackwell, 108 Cowley Road, Oxford OX4 1JF, England (or 3 Cambridge Center, Cambridge, MA 02142, USA)

The Asian Journal of Philosophy. (semi-ann) Prof. Tran Van Doan, Department of Philosophy, National Taiwan University, Roosevelt Road, Sec. 4, 10764 Taipei, Taiwan, Republic of China

Asian Philosophy. (semi-ann) Carfax Publishing Company, P.O. Box 25, Abingdon, Oxfordshire OX14 3UE, United Kingdom

Augustinian Studies. ISSN 0094-5323. (ann) Tolentine Hall, P.O. Box 98, Villanova University, Villanova, PA 19085, USA

Augustinus. ISSN 0004-802X. (q) P. José Oroz Reta, General Dávila 5, Madrid 28003, Spain

Auslegung: A Journal of Philosophy. ISSN 0733-4311. (semi-ann) Editors, Department of Philosophy, University of Kansas, Lawrence, KS 66045, USA

Australasian Journal of Philosophy. ISSN 0004-8402. (q) Robert Young, Editor, Department of Philosophy, La Trobe University, Bundoora, Victoria 3083, Australia

Behavior and Philosophy. (semi-ann) Boyd Printing, 49 Sheridan Avenue, Albany, NY 12210, USA

Berkeley Newsletter. ISSN 0332-026X. (ann) The Editor, Department of Philosophy, Trinity College, Dublin 2, Ireland

Between the Species: A Journal of Ethics. (q) Schweitzer Center, San Francisco Bay Institute, P.O. Box 254, Berkeley, CA 94701, USA

Bigaku. ISSN 0520-0962. (q) The Japanese Society for Aesthetics, c/o Faculty of Letters, University of Tokyo, Bunkyo-Ku, Tokyo, Japan

Bijdragen, Tijdschrift voor Filosofie en Theologie. ISSN 0006-2278. (q) Administratie Bijdragen, Krips Repro B.V., Postbus 106, 7940 AC Meppel, The Netherlands

Bioethics. ISSN 0269-9702. (q) Basil Blackwell, 108 Cowley Road, Oxford OX4 1JF, United Kingdom (or 3 Cambridge Center, Cambridge, MA 02142, USA)

Biology & Philosophy. ISSN 0169-3867. (q) Kluwer Academic Publishers, 101 Philip Drive, Norwell, MA 02061, USA

Bollettino del Centro di Studi Vichiani. ISSN 0392-7334. (ann) Bibliopolis, Edizioni di Filosofia e Scienze, SpA, Via Arangio Ruiz 83, 80122 Naples, Italy

Bridges: An Interdisciplinary Journal of Theology, Philosophy, History, and Science. ISSN 1042-2234. (semi-ann) Robert S. Frey, Editor, 5702 Yellow Rose Court, Columbia, MD 21045, USA

The British Journal of Aesthetics. ISSN 0007-0904. (q) Oxford University Press, Pinkhill House, Southfield Road, Eynsham, Oxford OX8 1JJ, England

British Journal for the Philosophy of Science. ISSN 0007-0882. (q) Oxford University Press, Pinkhill House, Southfield Road, Eynsham, Oxford OX8 1JJ, England

Bulletin de la Société Française de Philosophie. ISSN 0037-9352. (q) 12 rue Colbert, 75002 Paris, France

Bulletin of the Hegel Society of Great Britain. ISSN 0263-5232. (bi-ann) H. Williams, Department of International Politics, University College of Wales, Penglais Aberystwyth, Dyfed SY23 3DB, Great Britain

Bulletin of the Section of Logic.(q) Managing Editor, Grzegorz Malinowski, 8 Marca 8, 90-365 LAdź, Poland

Business Ethics Quarterly. ISSN 1052-150X. (q) Philosophy Documentation Center, Bowling Green State University, Bowling Green, OH 43403-0189, USA

Business & Professional Ethics Journal. ISSN 0277-2027. (q) Center for Applied Philosophy, 243 Dauer Hall, University of Florida, Gainesville, FL 32611, USA

Cadernos de História e Filosofia da Ciéncia. ISSN 0101-3424. (semi-ann) Editor, Centro de Lógica-Unicamp, C.P. 6133, 13.081 Campinas, São Paulo, Brazil

Canadian Journal of Philosophy. ISSN 0045-5091. (q) University of Calgary Press, 2500 University Drive NW, Calgary, Alberta, Canada T2N 1N4

Canadian Philosophical Reviews. ISSN 0228-491X. (m) Academic Printing and Publishing, Box 4834, Edmonton, Alberta, Canada T6E 5G7

Chinese Studies in Philosophy. ISSN 0023-8627. (q) M.E. Sharpe, 80 Business Park Drive, Armonk, NY 10504, USA

Clio. ISSN 0884-2043. (q) Indiana University-Purdue University, Fort Wayne, IN 46805, USA

Cogito. ISSN 0950-8864. (3 times a yr) Carfax Publishing Company, P.O. Box 25, Abingdon, Oxfordshire OX14 3UE, England

Cognition: International Journal of Cognitive Science. ISSN 0010-0277. (m) Elsevier Science Publishers, P.O. Box 211, 1000 AE Amsterdam, The Netherlands

Communication and Cognition. ISSN 0378-0880. (q) Blandijnberg 2, B-9000 Gent, Belgium

Conceptus: Zeitschrift für Philosophie. ISSN 0010-5155. (3 times a yr) Verband der Wissenschaftlichen Gesellschaften, Oesterreichs, Lindengasse 37, A-1070 Vienna, Austria

Contemporary Philosophy. (bi-m) P.O. Box 1373, Boulder, CO 80306, USA

Criminal Justice Ethics. ISSN 0731-129X. (semi-ann) The Institute for Criminal Justice Ethics, CUNY, John Jay College of Criminal Justice, 899 Tenth Avenue, New York, NY 10019, USA

Crítica: Revista Hispanoamericana de Filosofía. ISSN 0011-1503. (3 times a yr) Apartado 70-447, 04510 Mexico, DF, Mexico

Critical Inquiry. ISSN 0093-1896. (q) The University of Chicago, Wieboldt Hall 202, 1050 East 59th Street, Chicago, IL 60637, USA

Critical Review: An Interdisciplinary Journal. ISSN 0891-3811. (q) P.O. Box 14528, Dept. 26A, Chicago, IL 60614, USA

Critical Texts: A Review of Theory and Criticism. ISSN 0730-2304. (3 times a yr) Department of English and Comparative Literature, 602 Philosophy Hall, Columbia University, New York, NY 10027, USA

Cuadernos de Etica. ISSN 0326-9523. (semi-ann) Asociación Argentina de Investigaciones Eticas, Tte. Gral. J. D. Perón 2395-30 "6", 1040 Buenos Aires, Argentina

Cuadernos de Filosofía. ISSN 0590-1901. (semi-ann) Prof. Margarita Costa, Editor, Instituto de Filosofia, 25 de Mayo 217, 1002 Buenos Aires, Argentina

Darshan-Manjari: The Burdwan University Journal of Philosophy. (ann) Aminul Haque, Gopal Ch. Khan, Editors, Department of Philosophy, The University of Burdwan, Golabag, Burdwan 713104, India

De Philosophia. ISSN 0228-412X. Editor, Department of Philosophy, University of Ottawa, Ottawa, Ontario, Canada K1N 6N5

Deutsche Zeitschrift für Philosophie. ISSN 0012-1045. (m) VEB Deutscher Verlag der Wissenschaften, 1080 Berlin, Germany

Dialectica: Revue Internationale de Philosophie de la Connaissance. ISSN 0012-2017. (q) P.O. Box 1081, CH-2501 Bienne, Switzerland

Dialectics and Humanism. ISSN 0324-8275. (q) Foreign Trade Enterprise, Ars Polona, Krakowskie Przedmieście 7, 00-068 Warsaw, Poland

Dialogo Filosofico. ISSN 0213-1196. (3 times a yr) Apartado 121, 28770 Colmenar Viejo, Madrid, Spain

Diálogos. ISSN 0012-2122. (semi-ann) Box 21572, UPR Station, Río Piedras, PR 00931, USA

Dialogue. ISSN 0012-2246. (semi-ann) Phi Sigma Tau, Department of Philosophy, Marquette University, Milwaukee, WI 53233, USA

Dialogue: Canadian Philosophical Review-Revue Canadienne de Philosophie. ISSN 0012-2173. (q) Prof. Steven Davis, Editor, Department of Philosophy, Simon Fraser University, Burnaby, British Columbia, Canada V5A 1S6

Diánoia. ISSN 0185-2450. (ann) Instituto de Investigaciones Filosóficas, Dirección del Anuario de Filosofía, Circuito Mtro. Mario de la Cueva, Ciudad de la Investigación en Humanidades, Coyoacán 04510, Mexico, DF, Mexico

Diogenes. ISSN 0392-1921. (q) Berg Publishers Ltd., 150 Cowley Road, Oxford OX4 1JJ, United Kingdom

Dionysius. ISSN 0705-1085. (ann) Department of Classics, Dalhousie University, Halifax, Nova Scotia, Canada B3H 3J5

Diotima. (ann) Hellenic Society for Philosophical Studies, 40 Hypsilantou Street, Athens 11521, Greece

Economics and Philosophy. ISSN 0266-2671. (semi-ann) Cambridge University Press, 40 West 20th Street, New York, NY 10011, USA (or The Edinburgh Building, Shaftesbury Road, Cambridge CB2 2RU, England)

Educação e Filosofia. ISSN 0102-6801. (semi-ann) Revista "Educação e Filosofia", Universidade Federal de Uberlândia, Av. Universitaria, 155 C.P. 593, Campus Santa Monica, 38.400 Uberlândia MG, Brazil

Educational Philosophy and Theory. ISSN 0013-1857. (semi-ann) D.N. Aspin, Editor, Faculty of Education, Monash University, Clayton, Victoria 3168, Australia

Educational Studies. ISSN 0013-1946. (q) Richard LaBrecque, Editor, 131 Taylor Education Building, University of Kentucky, Lexington, KY 40506-0001, USA

Educational Theory. ISSN 0013-2004. (q) Education Building, University of Illinois, 1310 South 6th Street, Champaign, IL 61820, USA

Eidos: The Canadian Graduate Journal of Philosophy. ISSN 0707-2287. (semi-ann) Editors, Department of Philosophy, University of Waterloo, Waterloo, Ontario, Canada N2L 3G1

El Basilisco. ISSN 0210-0088. (q) Apartado 360, 33080 Oviedo, Spain

Environmental Ethics: An Interdisciplinary Journal Dedicated to the Philosophical Aspects of Environmental Problems. ISSN 0163-4275. (q) Department of Philosophy, The University of North Texas, P.O. Box 13496, Denton, TX 76203-3496, USA

Epistemologia: An Italian Journal for the Philosophy of Science. (semi-ann) Tilgher-Genova s.a.s., via Assarotti 52, 16122 Genova, Italy

Erkenntnis: An International Journal of Analytic Philosophy. ISSN 0165-0106. Kluwer Academic Publishers, 101 Philip Drive, Norwell, MA 02061, USA

Espíritu. ISSN 0014-0716. (ann) Durán y Bas Nr 9, Apartado 1382, 08080 Barcelona, Spain

Estetika. ISSN 0014-1291. (q) Kubon & Sagner GmbH, Hess-Str 39/41, Postfach 34 01 08, 8 München 34, Germany

Ethics: An International Journal of Social, Political, and Legal Philosophy. ISSN 0014-1704. (q) University of Chicago Press, P.O. Box 37005, Chicago, IL 60637, USA

Ethics and Behavior. (q) Journal Subscription Department, LEA, 365 Broadway, Hillsdale, NJ 07642, USA

Ethics and Medicine: A Christian Perspective on Issues in Bioethics. (3 times a yr) Rutherford House Periodicals, 127 Woodland Road, Wyncot, PA 19095, USA

Etudes. ISSN 0014-2263. (m) Jean-Yves Calvez, Rédacteur en chef, 14 rue d'Assas, 75006 Paris, France

Etyka. (semi-ann) Zaklad Etyki, Instytut Filozofii UW, Krakowskie Przedmescie 3, 00-326, Warsaw 64, Poland

Explorations in Knowledge. ISSN 0261-1376. (semi-ann) David Lamb, Sombourne Press, 294 Leigh Road, Chandlers Ford, Eastleigh, Hants S05 3AU, Great Britain

Faith and Philosophy. ISSN 0739-7046. (q) Michael Peterson, Managing Editor, Asbury College, Wilmore, KY 40390, USA

Feminist Studies. ISSN 0046-3663. (3 times a yr) Claire G. Moses, Women's Studies Program, University of Maryland, College Park, MD 20742, USA

Filosofia. ISSN 0015-1823. (q) Piazzo Statuto 26, 10144 Turin, Italy

Filozoficky Casopis CSAV. ISSN 0015-1831. (bi-m) Kubon & Sagner GmbH, Hess-Str 39/41, Postfach 34 01 08, 8 München 34, Germany

Filozofska Istraživanja. ISSN 0351-4706. Editor, Filozofski Fakultet, D. Salaja 3, p.p. 171, 41000 Zagreb, Yugoslavia

Franciscan Studies. ISSN 0080-5459. (ann) St. Bonaventure University, St. Bonaventure, NY 14778, USA

Free Inquiry. ISSN 0272-0701. (q) Paul Kurtz, Editor, Box 5, Central Park Station, Buffalo, NY 14215, USA

Freiburger Zeitschrift für Philosophie und Theologie. ISSN 0016-0725. (semi-ann) Editions St.-Paul, Perolles 42, CH-1700 Fribourg, Switzerland

Giornale Critico della Filosofia Italiana. ISSN 0017-0089. (q) LICOSA, SpA, Subscription Department, Via B. Fortini 120/10, 50125 Florence, Italy

Giornale di Metafisica. (3 times a yr) Tilgher-Genova s.a.s., via Assarotti 52, 16122 Genova, Italy

Gnosis: A Journal of Philosophic Interest. ISSN 0316-618X. (ann) Editor, Department of Philosophy, Concordia University, 1455 de Maisonneuve Boulevard West, Montreal, Quebec, Canada H3G 1M8

Graduate Faculty Philosophy Journal. ISSN 0093-4240. (semi-ann) Editor, Department of Philosophy, New School for Social Research, 65 Fifth Avenue, New York, NY 10003, USA

Grazer Philosophische Studien. ISSN 0165-9227. (ann) Humanities Press International, Atlantic Highlands, NJ 07716, USA

Gregorianum. ISSN 0017-4114. (q) 4 Piazza della Pilotta, 1-00187 Rome, Italy

Hastings Center Report. ISSN 0093-0334. (bi-m) The Hastings Center, 255 Elm Road, Briarcliff Manor, NY 10510, USA

Heidegger Studies. (ann) Duncker & Humblot GmbH, Postfach 41 03 29, 1000 Berlin 41, Germany

Hermathena: A Dublin University Review. ISSN 0018-0750. (semi-ann) The Editor, Trinity College, Dublin 2, Ireland

The Heythrop Journal. ISSN 0018-1196. (q) The Manager, 11 Cavendish Square, London W1M 0AN, England

History and Philosophy of Logic. ISSN 0144-5340. (semi-ann) Taylor & Francis, 4 John Street, London WC1N 2ET, England

History and Philosophy of the Life Sciences. ISSN 0391-9114. (semi-ann) Taylor & Francis, 1900 Frost Road, Suite 101, Bristol, PA 19007, USA (or Rankine Road, Basingstoke, Hants RG24 0PR, England)

History and Theory: Studies in the Philosophy of History. ISSN 0018-2656. (q) Julia Perkins, History and Theory, Wesleyan Station, Middletown, CT 06457, USA

History of European Ideas. ISSN 0191-6599. (bi-m) Pergamon Press, Headington Hill Hall, Oxford OX3 0BW, England

History of Philosophy Quarterly. ISSN 0740-0675. (q) Philosophy Documentation Center, Bowling Green State University, Bowling Green, OH 43403-0189, USA

History of Political Thought. ISSN 0143-781X. (q) Imprint Academic, 32 Haldon Road, Exeter EX4 4DZ, England

Hobbes Studies. (ann) Van Gorcum, P.O. Box 43, 9400 AA Assen, The Netherlands

Horizons Philosophiques. ISSN 0709-4469. (semi-ann) Service de l'Edition, College Edouard-Montpetit, 945 chemin Chambly, Longueuil, Quebec, Canada J4H 3M6

Human Studies: A Journal for Philosophy and the Social Sciences. ISSN 0163-8548. (q) Martinus Nijhoff Publishers, P.O. Box 322, 3300 AH Dordrecht, The Netherlands

The Humanist. ISSN 0018-7399. (bi-m) Lloyd L. Morain, Editor, American Humanist Assocation, 7 Harwood Drive, P.O. Box 146, Amherst, NY 14226-0146, USA

Hume Studies. ISSN 0319-7336. (semi-ann) Editor, Department of Philosophy, University of Western Ontario, London, Ontario, Canada N6A 3K7

Husserl Studies. ISSN 0167-9848. (q) Kluwer Academic Publishers, P.O. Box 322, 3300 AA Dordrecht, The Netherlands (or 101 Philip Drive, Norwell, MA 02061, USA)

Hypatia: A Journal of Feminist Philosophy. ISSN 0887-5367. (3 times a yr) Linda Lopez McAlister, Editor, University of South Florida, SOC 107, Tampa, FL 33620-8100, USA

Idealistic Studies: An International Philosophical Journal. ISSN 0046-8541. (3 times a yr) Walter Wright, Editor, Department of Philosophy, Clark University, Worcester, MA 01610, USA

Il Protagora. (semi-ann) via A. Gidiuli 19, 73100 Lecce, Italy

The Independent Journal of Philosophy. ISSN 0378-4789. (irr) George Elliott Tucker, Editor, 47 Van Winkle Street, Boston, MA 02124, USA

Indian Philosophical Quarterly. ISSN 0376-415X. The Editor, Department of Philosophy, University of Poona, Pune 411 007, India

Informal Logic. ISSN 0824-2577. (3 times a yr) Assistant to the Editors, Department of Philosophy, University of Windsor, Windsor, Ontario, Canada N9B 3P4

Inquiry: An Interdisciplinary Journal of Philosophy. ISSN 0020-174X. (q) Universitetsforlaget, P.O. Box 2959, Tøyen, 0608 Oslo 6, Norway

International Journal for Philosophy of Religion. ISSN 0020-7047. (q) Kluwer Academic Publishers, Distribution Centre, P.O. Box 322, 3300 AH Dordrecht, The Netherlands

International Journal of Applied Philosophy. ISSN 0739-098X. (semi-ann) Indian River Community College, Fort Pierce, FL 34981-5599, USA

International Journal of Moral and Social Studies. ISSN 0267-9655. (3 times a yr) Journals, One Harewood Row, London NW1 6SE, United Kingdom

International Logic Review. (semi-ann) Editor, via Belmeloro 3, 40126 Bologna, Italy

International Philosophical Quarterly. ISSN 0019-0365. (q) Vincent Potter, S.J., Fordham University, Bronx, NY 10458, USA

International Studies in Philosophy. ISSN 0270-5664. (3 times a yr) Scholars Press, P.O. Box 15288, Atlanta, GA 30333, USA

International Studies in the Philosophy of Science. ISSN 0269-8595. (3 times a yr) Carfax Publishing Company, P.O. Box 25, Abingdon, Oxfordshire OX14 3UE, England

Interpretation: A Journal of Political Philosophy. ISSN 0020-9635. (3 times a yr) Hilail Gildin, Editor-in-Chief, King Hall 101, Queens College, Flushing, NY 11367-0904, USA

Irish Philosophical Journal. ISSN 0266-9080. (semi-ann) Dr. Bernard Cullen, Editor, Department of Scholastic Philosophy, Queen's University, Belfast BT7 1NN, Northern Ireland

Iyyun: The Jerusalem Philosophical Quarterly. ISSN 0021-3306. (q) Manager, S.H. Bergman Centre for Philosophical Studies, Hebrew University of Jerusalem, Jerusalem 91905, Israel

Journal for the Theory of Social Behavior. ISSN 0021-8308. (q) Basil Blackwell, 108 Cowley Road, Oxford OX4 1JF, England (or 3 Cambridge Center, Cambridge, MA 02142, USA)

The Journal of Aesthetic Education. ISSN 0021-8510. (q) University of Illinois Press, 54 East Gregory Drive, Champaign, IL 61820, USA

The Journal of Aesthetics and Art Criticism. ISSN 0021-8529. (q) Donald W. Crawford, Editor, University of Wisconsin-Madision, 5145 H.C. White Hall, 600 North Park Street, Madison, WI 53706, USA

Journal of Agricultural Ethics. ISSN 0893-4282. (bi-ann) Room 039, MacKinnon Building, University of Guelph, Guelph, Ontario, Canada N1G 2W1

Journal of Applied Philosophy. ISSN 0264-3758. (bi-ann) Carfax Publishing Company, P.O. Box 25, Abingdon, Oxfordshire OX14 3UE, England

Journal of Business Ethics. ISSN 0167-4544. Kluwer Academic Publishers, 101 Philip Drive, Norwell, MA 02061, USA

Journal of Chinese Philosophy. ISSN 0301-8121. (q) Dialogue Publishing Company, P.O. Box 11071, Honolulu, HI 96828, USA

The Journal of Critical Analysis. ISSN 0022-0213. (q) The National Council for Critical Analysis, Shirley Schievella, P.O. Box 137, Port Jefferson, NY 11777, USA

Journal of Dharma. ISSN 0253-7222. (q) Center for the Study of World Religions, Dharmaram College, Bangalore 560029, India

The Journal of Hellenic Studies. ISSN 0075-4269. (ann) Secretary, The Hellenic Society, 31-34 Gordon Square, London WC1H 0PP, England

Journal of Indian Council of Philosophical Research. ISSN 0970-7794. (3 times a yr) Subscription Department, Motilal Banarsidass, Bungalow Road, Jawahar Nagar, Delhi 110007, India

Journal of Indian Philosophy. ISSN 0022-1791. Kluwer Academic Publishers, 101 Philip Drive, Norwell, MA 02061, USA

The Journal of Libertarian Studies. ISSN 0363-2873. (q) Center for Libertarian Studies, P.O. Box 4091, Burlingame, CA 94011, USA

Journal of Medical Ethics: The Journal of the Institute of Medical Ethics. ISSN 0306-6800. (q) Subscription Manager, Professional and Scientific Publications (JME), Tavistock House East, Tavistock Square, London WC1H 9JR, England (or Professional and Scientific Publications, 1172 Commonwealth Avenue, Boston, MA 02134, USA)

The Journal of Medical Humanities. ISSN 1041-3545. (q) Human Sciences Press, 233 Spring Street, New York, NY 10013, USA

The Journal of Medicine and Philosophy. ISSN 0360-5310. Kluwer Academic Publishers, 101 Philip Drive, Norwell, MA 02061, USA

The Journal of Mind and Behavior. ISSN 0271-0137. (q) Circulation Department, P.O. Box 522, Village Station, New York, NY 10014, USA

Journal of Moral Education. ISSN 0305-7240. (3 times a yr) Carfax Publishing Company, P.O. Box 25, Abingdon, Oxfordshire OX14 3UE, England

The Journal of Non-Classical Logic. (bi-ann) Centro de Lógica-Unicamp, C.P. 6133, 13.081 Campinas, São Paulo, Brazil

Journal of Philosophical Logic. ISSN 0022-3611. Kluwer Academic Publishers, 101 Philip Drive, Norwell, MA 02061, USA

Journal of Philosophical Research. ISSN 1053-8364. (ann) Philosophy Documentation Center, Bowling Green State University, Bowling Green, OH 43403-0189, USA

The Journal of Philosophy. ISSN 0022-362X. (m) 709 Philosophy Hall, Columbia University, New York, NY 10027, USA

Journal of Philosophy of Education. ISSN 0309-8249. (semi-ann) Carfax Publishing Company, P.O. Box 25, Abingdon, Oxfordshire OX14 3UE, England

Journal of Pragmatics. ISSN 0378-2166. (bi-m) Elsevier Science Publishers, P.O. Box 211, 1000 AE Amsterdam, The Netherlands

The Journal of Religious Ethics. ISSN 0384-9694. (semi-ann) Scholars Press, P.O. Box 15288, Atlanta, GA 30333, USA

Journal of Semantics. ISSN 0167-5133. (q) Oxford University Press, Pinkhill House, Southfield Road, Eynsham, Oxford OX8 1JJ, England

Journal of Social and Biological Structures. ISSN 01040-1750. (q) JAI Press, Inc., 55 Old Post Road-No. 2, Greenwich, CT 06836, USA (For England, Europe, Africa, and Asia: 118 Pentonville, Road, London N1 9JN, United Kingdom)

Journal of Social Philosophy. ISSN 0047-2786. (3 times a yr) Dr. Peter French, Editor, Trinity University, San Antonio, TX 78212, USA

The Journal of Speculative Philosophy. ISSN 0891-625X. (q) Pennsylvania State University Press, Suite C, 820 North University Drive, University Park, PA 16802, USA

The Journal of Symbolic Logic. ISSN 0022-4812. Association for Symbolic Logic, Department of Mathematics, University of Illinois, 1409 West Green Street, Urbana, IL 61801, USA

The Journal of the British Society for Phenomenology. ISSN 007-1773. (3 times a yr) Haigh & Hochland, JBSP Department, Precinct Centre, Manchester M13 9QA, England

Journal of the History of Ideas. ISSN 0022-5037. (q) Donald R. Kelley, Executive Editor, 442 Rush Rhees Library, University of Rochester, Rochester, NY 14627, USA

Journal of the History of Philosophy. ISSN 0022-5053. (q) Business Office, Department of Philosophy, Washington University, St. Louis, MO 63130, USA

Journal of the Philosophy of Sport. ISSN 0094-8705. (ann) Human Kinetics Publishers, Box 5076, Champaign, IL 61820-9971, USA

Journal of Thought. ISSN 0022-5231. (q) Dr. Robert M. Lang, Editor, College of Education, Leadership, and Educational Policy Studies, Northern Illinois University, Dekalb, IL 60115, USA

The Journal of Value Inquiry. ISSN 0022-5363. (q) Kluwer Academic Publishers, Spuiboulevard 50, 3300 AA Dordrecht, The Netherlands

Kant-Studien: Philosophische Zeitschrift der Kant-Gesellschaft. ISSN 0022-8877. (q) Walter de Gruyter, Genthiner Str. 13, 1000 Berlin 30, Germany

Kennis en Methode: Tijdschrift voor Wetenschapsfilosofie en Methodologie. ISSN 0165-1773. (q) Boompers, Box 58, 7940 AB Meppel, The Netherlands

Kinesis: Graduate Journal in Philosophy. ISSN 0023-1568. (semi-ann) Department of Philosophy, Southern Illinois University, Carbondale, IL 62901, USA

Kriterion: Revista de Filosofia. (bi-ann) Faculdade de Filosofia e Ciências Humanas, Rua Carangola, 288-sala 817, C.P. 253, 30350 Belo Horizonte, Brazil

Laval Théologique et Philosophique. ISSN 0023-9054. (3 times a yr) Service de Revues, Les Presses de l'Université Laval, C.P. 2447, Quebec, Canada G1K 7R4

Law and Philosophy: An International Journal for Jurisprudence and Legal Philosophy. ISSN 0167-5249. Kluwer Academic Publishers, 101 Philip Drive, Norwell, MA 02061, USA

Linguistics and Philosophy. ISSN 0165-0157. Kluwer Academic Publishers, 101 Philip Drive, Norwell, MA 02061, USA

Listening: Journal of Religion and Culture. ISSN 0024-4414. (3 times a yr) P.O. Box 1108, Route 53, Romeoville, IL 60441-2298, USA

The Locke Newsletter. ISSN 0307-2606. (ann) Roland Hall, Department of Philosophy, University of York, York, England

Logique et Analyse. ISSN 0024-5836. (q) Editions E. Nauwelaerts, 17 Kolonel Begaultlaan, B-3010 Leuven, Belgium

Logos: Philosophic Issues in Christian Perspective. ISSN 0276-5667. (ann) Department of Philosophy, Santa Clara University, Santa Clara, CA 95053, USA

Logos: Revista de Filosofía. ISSN 0185-6375. (3 times a yr) Apartado Postal 18-907, Colonia Tacubaya, Delegación Miguel Hidalgo, C.P. 11800, Mexico, DF, Mexico

Magyar Filozófiai Szemle. ISSN 0025-0090. (bi-m) Kultura, P.O. Box 149, H-1389 Budapest 62, Hungary

Man and Nature/L'homme et la Nature. (ann) Academic Printing and Publishing, P.O. Box 4834, South Edmonton, Alberta, Canada T6E 5G7

Man and World: An International Philosophical Review. ISSN 0025-1534. Martinus Nijhoff Publishers, P.O. Box 322, 3300 AH Dordrecht, The Netherlands

Manuscrito: Revista Internacional de Filosofia. ISSN 0100-6045. (bi-ann) Circulation Department, Centro de Lógica, Unicamp C.P. 6133, 13.081 Campinas, São Paulo, Brazil

Mediaeval Studies. ISSN 0076-5872. (ann) Dr. Ron B. Thomson, Director of Publications, Pontifical Institute of Mediaeval Studies, 59 Queen's Park Crescent East, Toronto, Ontario, Canada M5S 2C4

Medical Humanities Review. ISSN 0892-2772. (bi-ann) Institute for the Medical Humanities, University of Texas Medical Branch, Galveston, TX 77550, USA

Metaphilosophy. ISSN 0026-1068. Basil Blackwell, 108 Cowley Road, Oxford OX4 1JF, England (or 3 Cambridge Center, Cambridge, MA 02142, USA)

Method: Journal of Lonergan Studies. ISSN 0736-7392. (semi-ann) The Lonergan Institute, Boston College, Chestnut Hill, MA 02167, USA

Methodology and Science. ISSN 0543-6095. (q) Dr. P.H. Esser, Secretary and Editor, Beelslaan 20, 2012 PK Haarlem, The Netherlands

Midwest Studies in Philosophy. (ann) Dr. Theodore E. Uehling, Jr., Editor, Division of the Humanities, University of Minnesota, 112 Humanities Building, Morris, MN 56267, USA

Mind: A Quarterly Review of Philosophy. ISSN 0026-4423. (q) Oxford University Press, Pinkhill House, Southfield Road, Eynsham, Oxford OX8 1JJ, England

Mind & Language. ISSN 0268-1064. (q) Basil Blackwell, 108 Cowley Road, Oxford OX4 1JF, England (or 3 Cambridge Center, Cambridge, MA 02142, USA)

The Modern Schoolman: A Quarterly Journal of Philosophy. ISSN 0026-8402. (q) William C. Charron, Editor, Department of Philosophy, St. Louis University, St. Louis, MO 63103, USA

Modern Theology. ISSN 0266-7177. (q) Basil Blackwell, 108 Cowley Road, Oxford OX4 1JF, United Kingdom (or 3 Cambridge Center, Cambridge, MA 02142, USA)

The Monist: An International Quarterly Journal of General Philosophic Inquiry. ISSN 0026-9662. (q) P.O. Box 600, La Salle, IL 61301, USA

NAO Revista de la Cultura del Mediterráneo. (3 times a yr) Mansilla 3344, 1° C, 1425 Capital Federal, Argentina

National Forum: Phi Kappa Phi Journal. ISSN 0162-1831. (q) Subscription Department, 129 Quad Center, Auburn University, Auburn University, AL 36849, USA

Neue Hefte für Philosophie. ISSN H085-3917. (irr/ann) Vandenhoeck & Ruprecht, Postfach 3753, 3400 Göttingen, Germany

The New Scholasticism. ISSN 0028-6621. (q) Treasurer, The American Catholic Philosophical Association, Catholic University of America, Washington, DC 20064, USA

New Vico Studies. ISSN 0733-9542. (ann) Institute for Vico Studies, 69 Fifth Avenue, New York, NY 10003, USA (or Humanities Press International, 171 First Avenue, Atlantic Highlands, NJ 07716, USA)

Nietzsche-Studien. (ann) Walter de Gruyter, Genthiner Str. 13, 1000 Berlin, Germany

Notre Dame Journal of Formal Logic. ISSN 0029-4527. (q) Business Manager, University of Notre Dame, Box 5, Notre Dame, IN 46556, USA

Notre Dame Journal of Law, Ethics & Public Policy. (semi-ann) Zigad I. Naccasha, Managing Editor, University of Notre Dame, Notre Dame, IN 46556, USA

Noûs. ISSN 0029-4624. (q) Department of Philosophy, 126 Sycamore Hall, Indiana University, Bloomington, IN 47405, USA

Nouvelles de la République des Lettres. ISSN 0392-2332. (bi-ann) C.C. 1794767/01, Banca Commerciale Italiana, AG3 Naples, Italy

The Owl of Minerva. ISSN 0030-7580. (semi-ann) Department of Philosophy, Villanova University, Villanova, PA 19085, USA

Pacific Philosophical Quarterly. ISSN 0279-0750. (q) Expediters of the Printed Word, 515 Madison Avenue, New York, NY 10022, USA

Patristica et Mediaevalia. ISSN 0235-2280. (ann) Editor, Miembros del Centro de Estudios de Filosofía Medieval, 25 de Mayo 217, 2° Piso, 1002 Buenos Aires, Argentina

Pensamiento. ISSN 0031-4749. (q) Administración, Pablo Aranda 3, 28006 Madrid, Spain

The Personalist Forum. ISSN 0889-065X. Editor, Department of Philosophy, Furman University, Greenville, SC 29613, USA

Philosophia. ISSN 0031-8000. (ann) Editorial Office-Distribution, Research Center for Greek Philosophy, Academy of Athens, 14 Anagnostopoulou Street, Athens 106 73, Greece

Philosophia: Philosophical Quarterly of Israel. ISSN 0048-3893. (q) Bar-Ilan University, Subscriptions, Department of Philosophy, Ramat-Gan 52100, Israel

Philosophia Mathematica. ISSN 0031-8019. (semi-ann) J. Fang, Box 206, Wood Crossroad, VA 23190, USA

Philosophia Naturalis. ISSN 0031-8027. (bi-ann) Vittorio Klostermann GmbH, Postfach 90 06 01, Frauenlobstrasse 22, 6000 Frankfurt AM Main 90, Germany

Philosophia Reformata. ISSN 0031-8035. (q) Centrum voor Reformatorische Wijsbegeerte, P.O. Box 368, 3500 AJ Utrecht, The Netherlands

Philosophic Exchange: Annual Proceedings. ISSN 0193-5046. (ann) Center for Philosophic Exchange, SUNY at Brockport, Brockport, NY 14420, USA

Philosophica. ISSN 0379-8402. (semi-ann) Rozier 44, B-9000 Gent, Belgium

Philosophica. (q) 38A/10 Belgachia Road, Calcutta 700037, India

Philosophica: Zborník Univerzity Komenského. (ann) Dr. Miroslav Marcelli, Editor-in-Chief, Študijné a informačné stredisko Spoločenskovedných pracovísk Univerzity Komenského, Šafarikovo nám estie 6, 808 01 Bratislava, Czechoslovakia

Philosophical Books. ISSN 0031-8051. (q) Basil Blackwell, 108 Cowley Road, Oxford OX4 1JF, England (or 3 Cambridge Center, Cambridge, MA 02142, USA)

The Philosophical Forum. ISSN 0031-806X. (q) CUNY, Baruch College, Box 239, 17 Lexington Avenue, New York, NY 10010, USA

Philosophical Inquiry: An International Philosophical Quarterly. (q) Prof. D.Z. Andriopoulos, Editor, Department of Philosophy, Adelphi University, Garden City, Long Island, NY 11530, USA (or P.O. Box 3825, C.P. Athens, Greece)

Philosophical Investigations. ISSN 0190-0536. (q) Basil Blackwell, 108 Cowley Road, Oxford OX4 1JF, England (or 3 Cambridge Center, Cambridge, MA 02142, USA)

Philosophical Papers. ISSN 0556-8641. (3 times a yr) Department of Philosophy, Rhodes University, P.O. Box 94, Grahamstown 6140, South Africa

Philosophical Psychology. ISSN 0951-5089. (3 times a yr) Carfax Publishing Company, P.O. Box 25, Abingdon, Oxfordshire OX14 3UE, United Kingdom

Philosophical Quarterly. ISSN 0031-8094. (q) Basil Blackwell, 108 Cowley Road, Oxford OX4 1JF, England (or 3 Cambridge Center, Cambridge, MA 02142, USA)

Philosophical Review. (ann) Editor-in-Chief, Department of Philosophy, National Taiwan University, Taipei 10764, Taiwan, Republic of China

The Philosophical Review. ISSN 0031-8103. (q) 327 Goldwin Smith Hall, Cornell University, Ithaca, NY 14853, USA

Philosophical Studies. ISSN 0554-0739. (ann) Prof. Dermot Moran, Editor, Department of Philosophy, University College Dublin, Dublin 4, Ireland

Philosophical Studies: An International Journal for Philosophy in the Analytic Tradition. ISSN 0031-8116. Kluwer Academic Publishers, 101 Philip Drive, Norwell, MA 02061, USA

Philosophical Studies in Education: Proceedings of the Annual Meeting of the Ohio Valley Philosophy of Education Society. ISSN 0160-7561. (ann) Terence O'Connor, Indiana State University, Terre Haute, IN 47809, USA

Philosophical Topics. ISSN 0276-2080. (semi-ann) Christopher S. Hill, Editor, Department of Philosophy, University of Arkansas, Fayetteville, AR 72701, USA

Philosophie et Logique. ISSN 0035-4031. (q) Editura Academiei Republicii Socialiste Romania, Str. Gutenberg 3 bis, Sector 6, Bucaresti, Romania

Philosophiques. ISSN 0316-2923. (semi-ann) Les Editions Bellarmin, 165 rue Deslauriers, Saint-Laurent, Quebec, Canada H4N 2S4

Philosophische Rundschau: Zeitschrift für Philosophische Kritik. ISSN 0031-8159. (q) J.C.B. Mohr (Paul Siebeck), Postfach 2040, 7400 Tübingen, Germany

Philosophy. ISSN 0031-8191. (q plus 2 supps). Cambridge University Press, Edinburgh Building, Shaftesbury Road, Cambridge, CB2 2RU, England, (or 40 West 20th Street, New York, NY 10011, USA)

Philosophy and Literature. ISSN 0190-0013. (semi-ann) The Johns Hopkins University Press, 701 West 40th Street, Suite 275, Baltimore, MD 21211-2190, USA

Philosophy and Phenomenological Research. ISSN 0031-8205. (q) Brown University, Box 1947, Providence, RI 02912, USA

Philosophy and Public Affairs. ISSN 0048-3915. (q) The Johns Hopkins University Press, 701 West 40th Street, Suite 275, Baltimore, MD 21211-2190, USA

Philosophy and Rhetoric. ISSN 0031-8213. (q) Department of Philosophy, The Pennsylvania State University, University Park, PA 16802, USA

Philosophy and Social Action. ISSN 0377-2772. (q) Business Editor, M-120 Greater Kailash-I, New Delhi 110048, India

Philosophy and Social Criticism. ISSN 0191-4537. (q) David M. Rasmussen, Editor, P.O. Box 368, Lawrence, KS 66044, USA

Philosophy and Theology: Marquette University Quarterly. ISSN 0-87462-559-9. (q) A. Tallon, Department of Philosophy and Theology, Marquette University, Milwaukee, WI 53233, USA

Philosophy East and West. ISSN 0031-8221. (q) The University of Hawaii Press, 2840 Kolowalu Street, Honolulu, HI 96822, USA

Philosophy in Science. ISSN 0277-2434. (ann) Pachart Publishing House, 1130 San Lucas Circle, Tucson, AZ 85704, USA

Philosophy of Education: Proceedings of the Philosophy of Education Society. ISSN 8756-6575. (ann) Dr. Thomas W. Nelson, Managing Editor, Illinois State University, Normal, IL 61761, USA

Philosophy of Science. ISSN 0031-8248. (q) Executive Secretary, Philosophy of Science Association, Department of Philosophy, 114 Morrill Hall, Michigan State University, East Lansing, MI 48824-1036, USA

Philosophy of the Social Sciences. ISSN 0048-3931. (q) Sage Publications, 2455 Teller Road, Newbury Park, CA 91320, USA

Philosophy Today. ISSN 0031-8256. (q) DePaul University, 802 West Belden Avenue, Chicago, IL 60614, USA

Phoenix. ISSN 0031-8299. (q) J. Schutz, Editorial Assistant, Trinity College, Larkin 339, University of Toronto, Toronto, Ontario, Canada M5S 1H8

Phronesis: A Journal for Ancient Philosophy. ISSN 0031-8868. (3 times a yr) Van Gorcum, P.O. Box 43, 9400 AA Assen, The Netherlands

Polis. (semi-ann) P. P. Nicholson, Department of Politics, University of York, York YO1 5DD, United Kingdom (or Prof. Kent F. Moors, Department of Political Science, Duquesne University, Pittsburgh, PA 15282-0001, USA)

Political Theory. ISSN 0090-5917. (q) Sage Publications, 2455 Teller Road, Newbury Park, CA 91320, USA

Praxis International. ISSN 0260-8448. Basil Blackwell, 108 Cowley Road, Oxford OX4 1JF, England (or 3 Cambridge Center, Cambridge, MA 02142, USA)

Proceedings and Addresses of the American Philosophical Association. ISSN 0065-972X. (7 times a yr) The American Philosophical Association, University of Delaware, Newark, DE 19716, USA

Proceedings of the American Catholic Philosophical Association. ISSN 0065-7638. (ann) Treasurer, The American Catholic Philosophical Association, Catholic University of America, Washington, DC 20064, USA

Proceedings of the Aristotelian Society. ISSN 0066-7374. Basil Blackwell, 108 Cowley Road, Oxford OX4 1JF, England (distributes to institutions). The Aristotelian Society, Department of Philosophy, Birkbeck College, London WC1E 7HX, United Kingdom

Proceedings of the Biennial Meetings of the Philosophy of Science Association. ISSN 0270-8647. (ann) Philosophy of Science Association, 18 Morill Hall, Michigan State University, East Lansing, MI 48824-1036, USA

Proceedings of the Boston Area Colloquium in Ancient Philosophy. (ann) Co-publishing Program, University Press of America, 4720 Boston Way, Lanham, MD 20706, USA

Proceedings of the South Atlantic Philosophy of Education Society. (ann) Warren Strandberg, School of Education, Virginia Commonwealth University, Richmond, VA 23284-2020, USA

Process Studies. ISSN 0360-6503. (q) Center for Process Studies, 1325 North College Avenue, Claremont, CA 91711, USA

Public Affairs Quarterly. ISSN 0887-0373. (q) Philosophy Documentation Center, Bowling Green State University, Bowling Green, OH 43403-0189, USA

Quest: Philosophical Discussions. ISSN 1011-226X. (bi-ann) Circulation Manager, P.O. Box 9114, 9703 LC Groningen, The Netherlands

Radical Philosophy. (3 times a yr) Howard Feather, Thurrock Technical College, Woodview, Grays, Essex RM16 4YR, England

Ratio. ISSN 0034-0066. (semi-ann) Basil Blackwell, 108 Cowley Road, Oxford OX4 1JF, England (or 3 Cambridge Center, Cambridge, MA 02142, USA)

Ratio Juris: An International Journal of Jurisprudence and Philosophy of Law. ISSN 0952-1919. (3 times a year) Basil Blackwell, 3 Cambridge Center, Cambridge, MA 02142 USA

Reason Papers: A Journal of Interdisciplinary Normative Studies. ISSN 0363-1893. (ann) Department of Philosophy, Auburn University, Auburn University, AL 36849, USA

Religious Humanism. ISSN 0034-4095. (q) Fellowship of Religious Humanists, P.O. Box 278, Yellow Springs, OH 45387, USA

Religious Studies. ISSN 0034-4125. (q) Cambridge University Press, Edinburgh Building, Shaftesbury Road, Cambridge, CB2 2RU, United Kingdom (or 40 West 20th Street, New York, NY 10011, USA)

Reports on Mathematical Logic. ISSN 0137-2904. (ann) Centrala Handlu Zagranicznego "Ars Polona," ul. Krakowskie Przedmiescie 7, 00-068 Warsaw, Poland

Reports on Philosophy. ISSN 0324-8712. Elzbieta Paczkowska-Lagowska, Editor-in-Chief, Instytut Filozofii, ul. Grodzka 52, 31-044 Krakow, Poland

Research in Phenomenology. ISSN 0085-5553. (ann) Humanities Press International, Atlantic Highlands, NJ 07716, USA

The Review of Metaphysics. ISSN 0034-6632. (q) Catholic University of America, Washington, DC 20064, USA

Revista de Filosofía. ISSN 0185-3481. (3 times a yr) Universidad Iberoamericana, Prolongaciuon Paseo de la Reforma No. 880, Lomas de Santa Fe, 01210 Mexico, DF, Mexico

Revista de Filosofía. (semi-ann) Centro de Estidios Filosóficos, Edificio Viyaluz piso 8, Apartado 526, Maracaibo, Venezuela

Revista de Filosofía. (semi-ann) Centro de Estidios Filosóficos, Edificio Viyaluz piso 8, Apartado 526, Maracaibo, Venezuela

Revista de Filosofía: Publicatión de la Asociatión de Estudios Filosóficos. ISSN 0326-8160. (semi-ann) Marcelo Diego Boeri, ADEF C.C. 3758 Correo Central, 1000 Capital Federal, Argentina

Revista de Filosofía de la Universidad de Costa Rica. ISSN 0034-8252. (semi-ann) Editor, Universidad de Costa Rica, Apartado 75-2060, San José, Costa Rica

Revista de Filosofie. ISSN 0034-8260. (bi-m) Rompresfilatelia, Calea Victoriei 125, 79717 Bucharest, Romania

Revista Latinoamericana de Filosofía. ISSN 0325-0725. (3 times a yr) Box 1192, Birmingham, AL 35201, USA (or Casilla de Correo 5379, Correo Central, 1000 Buenos Aires, Argentina)

Revista Portuguesa de Filosofia. ISSN 0035-0400. (q) Faculdade de Filosofia, UCP, 4719 Braga , Portugal

Revista Venezolana de Filosofía. (semi-ann) Departamento de Filosofía, Apartado 80659, Caracas, Venezuela

Revue de Métaphysique et de Morale. ISSN 0035-1571. (q) 156 Avenue Parmentier, 75010 Paris, France

Revue de Théologie et de Philosophie. ISSN 0035-1784. (q) 7 ch. des Cèdres, CH-1004 Lausanne, Switzerland

Revue des Sciences Philosophiques et Théologiques. ISSN 0035-2209. (q) J. Vrin, 6 Place de la Sorbonne, 75005 Paris, France

Revue Internationale de Philosophie. ISSN 0048-8143. 2.000 FB. (q) Imprimérie Universa, rue Hoender 24, B-9230 Wetteren, Belgium

Revue Philosophique de la France et de L'etranger. ISSN 0035-3833. (q) Redaction de la Revue Philosophique, 12 rue Jean-de-Beauvais, 75005 Paris, France

Revue Philosophique de Louvain. ISSN 0035-3841. (q) Editions Peeters, B.P. 41, B-3000 Leuven, Belgium

Revue Thomiste: Revue Doctrinale de Théologie et de Philosophie. ISSN 0035-4295. (q) Ecole de Théologie, Avenue Lacordaire, Cedex, 31078 Toulouse, France

Rivista di Filosofia. ISSN 0035-6239. (q) Societa Editrice Il Mulino, Strada Maggiore 37, 40125 Bologna, Italy

Rivista di Filosofia Neo-Scolastica. ISSN 0035-6247. (q) Pubblicazioni dell'Universita Cattolica del Sacro Cuore, Vita e Pensiero, Largo A. Gemelli, 20123 Milan, Italy

Rivista di Studi Crociani. ISSN 0035-659X. (q) Presso la Societa di Storia Partia, Piazza Municipio, Maschio Angiolino, 80133 Naples, Italy

Rivista Internazionale di Filosofia del Diritto. (q) Casa Editrice Dott. A. Giuffre, via Busto Arsizio 40, 20151 Milan, Italy

Russell: Journal of the Bertrand Russell Archives. ISSN 0036-0163. (q) McMaster University Library Press, McMaster University, Hamilton, Ontario, Canada L8S 4L6

Sapientia. ISSN 0036-4703. (q) Bartolome Mitre 1869, 1039 Buenos Aires, Argentina

Sapienza. ISSN 0036-4711. (q) Vicoletto S. Pietro a Maiella, 4-80134 Naples, Italy

Schopenhauer-Jahrbuch. ISSN 0080-6935. (ann) Verlag Kramer, Bornheimer Landwehr 57a, Postfach 600445, 6000 Frankfurt 60, Germany

Science, Technology, and Human Values. ISSN 0162-2439. (q) Sage Publications, 2455 Teller Road, Newbury Park, CA 91320, USA

Scientia: An International Review of Scientific Synthesis. ISSN 0036-8687. (3 times a yr) via F. lli Bronzetti 20, 20129 Milan, Italy

Social Epistemology: A Journal of Knowledge, Culture, and Policy. ISSN 0269-1728. (q) Taylor and Francis, 1900 Frost Road, Suite 101, Bristol, PA 19007, USA (or Rankine Road, Basingstoke, Hants RG24 OPR, United Kingdom)

Social Indicators Research: An International and Interdisciplinary Journal for Quality-of-Life Measurement. ISSN 0303-8300. Kluwer Academic Publishers, 101 Philip Drive, Norwell, MA 02061, USA

Social Philosophy and Policy. ISSN 0265-0525. (semi-ann) Basil Blackwell, 108 Cowley Road, Oxford OX4 1JF, England (or 3 Cambridge Center, Cambridge, MA 02142, USA)

Social Theory and Practice. ISSN 0037-802X. (3 times a yr) Department of Philosophy R-36C, 203 Dodd Hall, The Florida State University, Tallahassee, FL 32306-1054, USA

Sophia. ISSN 0038-1527. (3 times a yr) School of Humanities, Deakin University, Victoria 3217, Australia

South African Journal of Philosophy. ISSN 0258-0136. (q) Bureau for Scientific Publications, P.O. Box 1758, Pretoria 0001, South Africa

The Southern Journal of Philosophy. ISSN 0038-4283. (q) Editor, Department of Philosophy, Memphis State University, Memphis, TN 38152, USA

Southwest Philosophical Studies. ISSN 0885-9310. (3 times a yr) Jack Weir, Co-Editor, Department of Philosophy, Hardin-Simmons University, Abilene, TX 79698, USA (or Joseph D. Stamey, Co-Editor, Department of Philosophy, McMurry University, Abilene, TX 79697, USA)

Southwest Philosophy Review. ISSN 0897-2346. (semi-ann) Department of Philosophy, University of Central Arkansas, Conway, AR 72302, USA

Soviet Studies in Philosophy. ISSN 0038-5883. (q) M.E. Sharpe, 80 Business Park Drive, Armonk, NY 10504, USA

Stromata. ISSN 0049-2353. (q) Universidad del Salvador, C.C. 10, 1663 San Miguel, Argentina

Studia Leibnitiana. ISSN 0039-3185. (semi-ann) Franz Steiner Verlag Wiesbaden GmbH, Postfach 101526, 7000 Stuttgart, Germany

Studia Logica. ISSN 0039-3215. Kluwer Academic Publishers, 101 Philip Drive, Norwell, MA 02061, USA

Studia Philosophiae Christiane. ISSN 0585-5470. (semi-ann) ATK, ul. Dewajtis 5, 01-653 Warsaw, Poland

Studia Philosophica. (ann) Helmut Holzhey and Jean-Pierre Leyvraz, Editors, Verlag Paul Haupt, Falkenplatz 11/14, CH-3001 Berne, Switzerland

Studia Spinozana. ISSN 0179-3896. (ann) Douglas J. Den Uyl, Bellarmine College, Newburg Road, Louisville, KY 40205, USA

Studies in History and Philosophy of Science. ISSN 0039-3681. (q) Pergamon Press, Maxwell House, Fairview Park, Elmsford, NY 10523, USA

Studies in Philosophy and Education. ISSN 0039-3746. (q) Kluwer Academic Publishers, P.O. Box 358, Accord Station, Hingham, MA 02018-0358, USA

Studies in Philosophy and the History of Philosophy. (irr) Catholic University of America Press, Washington, DC 20064, USA

Studies in Soviet Thought. ISSN 0039-3797. Kluwer Academic Publishers, 101 Philip Drive, Norwell, MA 02061, USA

Synthese: An International Journal for Epistemology, Methodology, and Philosophy of Science. ISSN 0039-7857. Kluwer Academic Publishers, 101 Philip Drive, Norwell, MA 02061, USA

Teaching Philosophy. ISSN 0145-5788. (q) Philosophy Documentation Center, Bowling Green State University, Bowling Green, OH 43403-0189, USA

Teorema. ISSN 0210-1602. (q) Apartado 61, 159, 28080 Madrid, Spain

Teoria: Rivista di Filosofia. (bi-ann) E.T.S., C.C.P. 12157566, Piazza Torricelli 4, 56100 Pisa, Italy

Theoretical Medicine: An International Journal for the Philosophy and Methodology of Medical Research and Practice. ISSN 0167-9902. Kluwer Academic Publishers, 101 Philip Drive, Norwell, MA 02061, USA

Theoria. ISSN 0495-4548. (3 times a yr) Plaza de Pio XII, 1, 6°, 1ª, Apartado 1.594, 20.080 San Sebastian, Spain

Theoria: A Swedish Journal of Philosophy. ISSN 0046-5825. (3 times a yr) Filosofiska Institution, Kungshuset i Lundagard, S-223 50 Lund, Sweden

Theory and Decision: An International Journal for Philosophy and Methodology of the Social Sciences. ISSN 0040-5833. Kluwer Academic Publishers, 101 Philip Drive, Norwell, MA 02061, USA

Thinking: The Journal of Philosophy for Children. ISSN 0190-3330. (q) The Institute for the Advancement of Philosophy for Children, Montclair State College, Upper Montclair, NJ 07043, USA

The Thomist. ISSN 0040-6325. (q) The Thomist Press, 487 Michigan Avenue NE, Washington, DC 20017, USA

Thought: A Review of Culture and Idea. ISSN 0040-6457. (q) Fordham University Press, Fordham University, Bronx, NY 10458, USA

Tijdschrift voor de Studie van de Verlichting en van Het Vrije Denken. ISSN 0774-1847. (q) Centrum voor de Studie van de Verlichting en van Het Vrije Denken, Vrije Universiteit Brussel, Pleinlaan 2-B416, 1050 Brussels, Belgium

Tijdschrift voor Filosofie. ISSN 0040-750X. (q) Kardinaal Mercierplein 2, B-3000 Leuven, Belgium

Thémata Revista de Filosofia. ISSN 0210-8365. (ann) Servicio de Publicaciones de la Universidad de Sevilla, C. San Fernando 4, E-41004, Sevilla C, Spain

Topoi: An International Review of Philosophy. ISSN 0167-7411. Kluwer Academic Publishers, 101 Philip Drive, Norwell, MA 02061, USA

Trans/Form/Ação. ISSN 0101-3173. (ann) Biblioteca Central da UNESP, Av. Vicente Ferreira, 1278 C.P. 603, 17500 Marilia, SP, Brazil

Transactions of the Charles S. Peirce Society: A Quarterly Journal in American Philosophy. ISSN 0009-1774. (q) Editor, Department of Philosophy, Baldy Hall, SUNY at Buffalo, Buffalo, NY 14260, USA

Tulane Studies in Philosophy. ISSN 0082-6776. (ann) Department of Philosophy, Tulane University, New Orleans, LA 70118, USA

Ultimate Reality and Meaning: Interdisciplinary Studies in the Philosophy of Understanding. ISSN 0709-549X. (q) University of Toronto Press, 5201 Dufferin Street, Downsview, Ontario, Canada M3H 5T8

Universitas Philosophica. (semi-ann) Facultad de Filosofía, Univeridad Javeriana, Carrera 7, No. 39-08, Bogota D.E. 2, Colombia

Utilitas: A Journal of Utilitarian Studies. (semi-ann) Oxford University Press, Pinkhill House, Southfield Road, Eynsham, Oxford OX8 1JJ, England

Vera Lex. (semi-ann) Prof. Virginia Black, Editor, Department of Philosophy and Religious Studies, Pace University, Pleasantville, NY 10570, USA

Vivarium: An International Journal for the Philosophy and Intellectual Life of the Middle Ages and Renaissance. ISSN 0042-7543. (semi-ann) E.J. Brill, Plantijnstr. 2, Postbus 9000, 2300 PA Leiden, The Netherlands

Zeitschrift für Mathematische Logik und Grundlagen der Mathematik. ISSN 0044-3050. (bi-m) Deutscher Verlag der Wissenschaften GmbH, Johannes-Dieckmann-Str 10, 1080 Berlin, Germany

Zeitschrift für Philosophische Forschung. ISSN 0044-3301. (q) Vittorio Klostermann GmbH, Postfach 90 06 01, 6000 Frankfurt AM Main 90, Germany

Zygon: Journal of Religion and Science. ISSN 0591-2385. (q) Karl E. Peters, Editor, Rollins College, Winter Park, FL 32789, USA

Guidance on the Use of the Subject Index

The Subject Index lists in alphabetical order the significant subject descriptors and proper names that describe the content of the articles and books indexed. Since titles are frequently misleading, the editors read each article and book to determine which subject headings accurately describe it. Each entry under a subject heading includes the complete title of the book or article and the author's name.

Subject entries fall into the following classes:

1) proper names, such as Quine, Kant, and Hegel;
2) nationalities, such as American and German;
3) historical periods, which are: ancient, medieval, renaissance, modern, nineteenth-century, and twentieth century;
4) major fields of philosophy, which are: aesthetics, axiology, education, epistemology, ethics, history, language, logic, metaphysics, philosophical anthropology, philosophy, political philosophy, religion, science, and social philosophy;
5) subdivisions of the major fields of philosophy, such as: utilitarianism, induction, realism, and nominalism;
6) other specific topics, such as grue, pain, paradox, and Turing-machine;
7) bibliographies, which are listed under "bibliographies," the person or subject, and the appropriate historical period.

The Subject Index is used like the index found in the back of a textbook. Scan the alphabetical listing of significant words until the desired subject is found. If the title confirms your interest, then locate the author's name, which occurs after the title, in the section entitled "Author Index with Abstracts." The title, in addition to suggesting the content of the article or book, indicates the language in which the document is written.

Although every effort is made to standardize subject headings, complete uniformity is impossible. Hence, check for various spellings of subject headings, particularly of proper names. Due consideration should be given to subject headings that sometimes are written with a space, a hyphen, or an umlaut. The following example illustrates some possibilities:

DE MORGAN
DE-MORGAN
DEMORGAN

Not only does the computer treat the above subject headings as different, but it may file other subject headings between them.

Generally, only the last names of famous philosophers are used as subject headings. Last names and first initials usually are used for other philosophers. The following list indicates who of two or more philosophers with the same last name is designated by last name only.

Alexander (Samuel)
Austin (J L)
Bacon (Francis)
Bradley (Francis H)
Brown (Thomas)
Butler (Joseph)
Collins (Anthony)
Darwin (Charles)
Eckhart (Meister)
Edwards (Jonathan)
Green (Thomas H)
Hartmann (Edward von)
Huxley (T H)
James (William)
Jung (Carl G)
Lewis (C I)
Mill (John Stuart)
Moore (G E)
Niebuhr (Reinhold)
Paul (Saint)
Price (Richard)
Russell (Bertrand)
Schiller (Friedrich)
Toynbee (Arnold)
Wolff (Christian)

ABSURD
El humanismo de Albert Camus. QUESADA, Anabelle.

ABSURDITY
Concerning the Absurdity of Life. SMITH, Quentin.

ABUSE
The Molested. MAY, William F.

ACADEMIA
Writing and the Moral Self. LANG, Berel.
"Approaching Ethical Questions: A University Perspective" in *Integrity in Health Care Institutions: Humane Environments for Teaching, Inquiry, and Healing*, STEINER, Daniel.
"Covenant, Leadership, and Value Formation in Academic Health Centers" in *Integrity in Health Care Institutions: Humane Environments for Teaching, Inquiry, and Healing*, BULGER, Roger J.
"Ethics of Method: Greasing the Machine and Telling Stories" in *Feminist Ethics*, TREBILCOT, Joyce.
"The Left Establishment" in *Perspectives on Ideas and Reality*, SCRUTON, Roger.
"The Revival of Community and the Public Obligation of Academic Health Centers" in *Integrity in Health Care Institutions: Humane Environments for Teaching, Inquiry, and Healing*, GREEN, Lawrence W.
"Values and Academic Health Centers: A Commentary and Recommendations" in *Integrity in Health Care Institutions: Humane Environments for Teaching, Inquiry, and Healing*, PELLEGRINO, Edmund D.
"Values and the Advance of Medical Science" in *Integrity in Health Care Institutions: Humane Environments for Teaching, Inquiry, and Healing*, FREDRICKSON, Donald S.
"Double Trouble": An Introduction. FRASER, Nancy.
An Ethical Justification of Women's Studies, Or What's a Nice Girl Like You Doing in a Place like This?. MC GRATH, Lynette.

ACADEMIC
"Methodische Aspekte des Kunstwissenschaftlichen Umgangs mit moderner Kunst" in *XIth International Congress in Aesthetics, Nottingham 1988*, LINGNER, Michael.
The Classical Roots of Hume's Skepticism. OLSHEWSKY, Thomas M.

ACADEMIC FREEDOM
Convictions. HOOK, Sidney.

ACCEPTANCE
Nomic Probability and the Foundations of Induction. POLLOCK, John L.
Acceptance Is Not Enough: A Critique of Hamblin. JOHNSON, Ralph H.
Acceptance Without Belief. MAHER, Patrick.
Belief, Acceptance, and Knowledge. RADFORD, Colin.
Rehabilitating Responsibility. GADEN, Gerry.
Theory Pursuit: Between Discovery and Acceptance. WHITT, Laurie Anne.

ACCIDENT(S)
Causes and Coincidences. OWENS, David.
On the Alleged Impossibility of a Science of Accidents in Aristotle. URBANAS, Alban.

ACCOUNTABILITY
Accountability and Responsibility in Research. WOOLF, Patricia K.
Rehabilitating Responsibility. GADEN, Gerry.
When Scientists are Wrong: Admitting Inadvertent Error in Research. LEIBEL, Wayne.

ACCOUNTING
An Axiomatic Basis of Accounting: A Structuralist Reconstruction. BALZER, Wolfgang and MATTESSICH, Richard.
Beyond Bean Counting: Establishing High Ethical Standards in the Public Accounting Profession. COHEN, Jeffrey R and PANT, Laurie W.
Establishing an Ethic of Accounting: A Response to Westra's Call for Government Employment of Auditors. WAPLES, Elain and SHAUB, Michael K.
Ethical Judgments on Selected Accounting Issues: An Empirical Study. STANGA, Keith G and TURPEN, Richard A.
The Evaluation of "Outcomes" of Accounting Ethics Education. LOEB, Stephen E.
Historical Perspectives: Development of the Codes of Ethics in the Legal, Medical and Accounting Professions. BACKOF, Jeanne F and MARTIN JR, Charles L.
Personal Morals and Professional Ethics: A Review and Empirical Examination of Public Accounting. BEETS, S Douglas.
Professional Ethics and Accounting Education: A Critique of the 8-Step Method. ARMSTRONG, Mary Beth.

ACHIEVEMENT(S)
The Hermeneutics of Life History: Personal Achievement and History in Gadamer, Habermas, and Erikson. WALLULIS, Jerald.
An Inquiry into the Meaning of Teacher Clarity in Recent Research and into the Value of the Research for the Teacher. CRABTREE, Walden.
Ten Types of Scientific Progress. KUKLA, Andre.

ACKERMANN, R
Instrumental Realism: The Interface between Philosophy of Science and Philosophy of Technology. IHDE, Don.

ACQUAINTANCE
Genuine Names and Knowledge by Acquaintance. DONNELLAN, Keith S.
A Theoretical Note on Simmel's Concept of Acquaintance. DOUBT, Keith.

ACQUISITION(S)
"Incremental Acquisition and a Parametrized Model of Grammar" in *Acting and Reflecting: The Interdisciplinary Turn in Philosophy*, CLARK, Robin.
Adquisición del lenguaje y antropología. FERNÁNDEZ, Teresa Bejarano.
Are Property Rights Problematic?. GAUS, Gerald F and LOMASKY, Loren E.

ACT UTILITARIANISM
Act-Utilitarian Prisoner's Dilemmas. RABINOWICZ, Wlodzimierz.
Hume's Ethics: Acts, Rules, Dispositions and Utility. SHIRLEY, Edward.
The Paradox of Group Beneficence. OTSUKA, Michael.

ACT(S)
see also Speech Act(s)
On the Problem of Empathy (Third Revised Edition). STEIN, Edith.
"Acts and Necessity in the Philosophy of John William Miller" in *The Philosophy of John William Miller*, DIEFENBECK, James A.
"The Nature of Acts: Moore on Husserl" in *The Analytic Tradition: Philosophical Quarterly Monographs, Volume 1*, KÜNNE, Wolfgang.
Conditional Intention. CARTWRIGHT, J P W.
La creencia y su conexión con los actos linguísticos. SAAB, Salma.
Deciding to Act. FIELDS, L.
Moral Goodness, Esteem, and Acting from Duty. LEMOS, Noah M.
A Note on Hooker's "Rule Consequentialism". CARSON, Tom.
Les objets de la sémiologie théâtrale: le texte et le spectacle. VIGEANT, Louise.
Tacit Consent. CARR, Craig L.
Thomas Aquinas and the Will: A Note on Interpretation. CROWE, Frederick.

ACTING
Willing and Acting in Husserl's Lectures on Ethics and Value Theory. NENON, Thomas J.

ACTION THEORY
Das Ich im deutschen Idealismus und das Selbst im Zen-Buddhist Fichte und Dogen. NAGASAWA, Kunihiko.
Intention, Agency and Criminal Liability: Philosophy of Action and the Criminal Law. DUFF, R A.
Die Moral der Vernunft Tanszendentale Handlungs-und Legitimationstheorie in der Philosophie Kants. SANDERMANN, Edmund.
Philosophical Perspectives, 3: Philosophy of Mind and Action Theory, 1989. TOMBERLIN, James E (ed).
Philosophical Perspectives, 4: Action Theory and Philosophy of Mind, 1990. TOMBERLIN, James E (ed).
The Philosophical Theology of John Duns Scotus. ADAMS, Marilyn McCord (ed).
The Philosophy of Action: An Introduction. MOYA, Carlos J.
Spuren der Macht. RÖTTGERS, Kurt.
Arational Actions. HURSTHOUSE, Rosalind.
Consciousness Naturalized: Supervenience Without Physical Determinism. SENCHUK, Dennis M.
Distant Action in Classical Electromagnetic Theory. MUNDY, Brent.
Hornsby's Puzzles: Rejoinder to Wreen and Hornsby. KOSROVANI, Emilio.
Intentional Single and Joint Action. TUOMELA, Raimo.
King Solomon and Everyman: A Problem in Coordinating Conflicting Moral Intuitions. RORTY, Amelie Oksenberg.
Krtapranasa and Akrtabhyagama: An Analysis, Defence and Rationale of the Buddhist Theory of Action. CHINCHORE, Mangala R.
The Problem of Other Cultures and Other Periods in Action Explanations. MARTIN, Rex.

ACTION(S)
After Principles. BARDEN, Garrett.
Being True to the World: Moral Realism and Practical Wisdom. JACOBS, Jonathan A.
Explaining Human Action. LENNON, Kathleen.
Mind in Action: Essays in the Philosophy of Mind. RORTY, Amelie Oksenberg.
Nietzsches Scheitern am Werk. HELLER, Edmund.
A Post-Modern Epistemology. SORRI, Mari.
Reading Habermas. RASMUSSEN, David M.
The Realm of Rights. THOMSON, Judith Jarvis.
Sound, Speech, and Music. BURROWS, David.
Weakness of the Will. GOSLING, Justin.
"Action, Inference, Belief, and Intention" in *Philosophical Perspectives, 4: Action Theory and Philosophy of Mind, 1990*, AUNE, Bruce.
"Action, Story, and History—On Rereading 'The Human Condition'" in *The Realm of Humanitas: Responses to the Writings of Hannah Arendt*, RICOEUR, Paul.
"Actions by Collectives" in *Philosophical Perspectives, 3: Philosophy of Mind and Action Theory, 1989*, TUOMELA, Raimo.
"Davidson on Explaining Intentional Actions" in *The Mind of Donald Davidson*, LANZ, Peter.
"Doing What One Ought to Do" in *Meaning and Method: Essays in Honor of Hilary Putnam*, PUTNAM, Ruth Anna.
"An Internalist Conception of Rational Action" in *Philosophical Perspectives, 4: Action Theory and Philosophy of Mind, 1990*, AUDI, Robert.

ACTION(S)

"On the Old Saw That Character Is Destiny" in Identity, Character, and Morality: Essays in Moral Psychology, MOODY-ADAMS, Michele.
"Practical Thinking, Reasons for Doing, and Intentional Action" in *Philosophical Perspectives, 4: Action Theory and Philosophy of Mind, 1990*, CASTAÑEDA, Héctor-Neri.
"Proximate Causation of Action" in *Philosophical Perspectives, 3: Philosophy of Mind and Action Theory, 1989*, BRAND, Myles.
"Reasons Explanation of Action: An Incompatibilist Account" in *Philosophical Perspectives, 3: Philosophy of Mind and Action Theory, 1989*, GINET, Carl.
"Seeing To It That: A Canonical Form for Agentives" in *Knowledge Representation and Defeasible Reasoning*, BELNAP JR, Nuel D and PERLOFF, Michael.
"The Theory of Structuration" in *Social Theory of Modern Societies: Anthony Giddens and His Critics*, THOMPSON, John B.
"Where There's a Will There's a Way: Kierkegaard's Theory of Action" in *Writing the Politics of Difference*, EVANS, C Stephen.
"Eigen Elements" Emerging from the Interaction of Two Knowing and Acting Subjects. VALLÉE, Robert.
Action and Explanation. MAJUMDAR, Aruna.
Action and Freedom. ROY, Pabitrakumar.
Akratic Action and the Practical Role of Better Judgment. MELE, Alfred R.
Character and Explanation in Aristotle's *Ethics* and *Poetics*. DESLAURIERS, Marguerite.
Concepts of "Action", "Structure" and "Power" in 'Critical Social Realism': A Positive and Reconstructive Critique. PATOMÄKI, Heikki.
Consequentialism: The Philosophical Dog That Does Not Bark?. HOLBROOK, Daniel.
Croce e la storia della cultura. TESSITORE, Fulvio.
Emotions and Responsibility. TURSKI, George.
Ethical Dimensions of Human Attitudes to Nature. BURES, Radim.
God and Man: Action and Reference in Hobbes. BERTMAN, Martin A.
Governance by Emotion. ALLEN, R T.
Habermas on Strategic and Communicative Action. JOHNSON, James.
Individuo y acción en el pensamiento griego. RODA, Roberto.
Inside World-Outside World: Epistemology on the Conscious Action of the Nervous System. DE JONG, B M.
The Insufficiency of Descartes' Provisional Morality. COOLIDGE JR, Francis P.
Intention, Cognitive Commitment, and Planning. AUDI, Robert.
The Intentional and the Intended. GARCIA, J L A.
Intentions, Actions, and Routines: A Problem in Krister Segerberg's Theory of Action. ELGESEM, Dag.
Intenzione e azione in Wittgenstein. RAINONE, Antonio.
La justificación práctica del principio de no contradicción en Aristóteles. CASSINI, A.
Man Not a Subject of Science?. SLEZAK, Peter.
Nietzsche and Post-Modernity. ERICKSON, Stephen A.
On 'High-Mindedness'. GARCIA, Jorge.
Origen y desembocadura de la acción: el sujeto inevitable. CRUZ, Manuel.
Prichard, Davidson and Action. GUSTAFSON, Don.
Προαιρεσις in Epictetus. DOBBIN, Robert.
El problema de la "acción intencional" en el conocimiento sensible. DELBOSCO, Héctor J.
Professor Von Wright on Action. DEWASHI, Mahadev.
El proyecto crítico de Kant. CHAVES, Carmen.
Purposive Intending. PINK, T L M.
Les représentations de l'action. SAINT SERNIN, Bertrand.
Responsibility: Repudiators Referring to the Divided Centre of Action in the Physical Agent (in Czechoslovakian). PEARS, D.
Roberts on Responsibility for Action and Character in the *Nicomachean Ethics*. BRICKHOUSE, Thomas C.
Le rôle de l'imagination dans le mouvement animal et l'action humaine chez Aristotle. DUGRÉ, François.
Searle on Natural Agency. BISHOP, John.
A Short Vindication of Reichenbach's "Event-Splitting". PFEIFER, Karl.
St Thomas on the Motives of Unjust Acts. WEITHMAN, Paul J.
Sujeto, acto y operación. GAMARRA, Daniel.
Le temps de l'action. BOYER, Alain.
We Will Do It: An Analysis of Group Intentions. TUOMELA, Raimo.
Weakness of Will and Rational Action. AUDI, Robert.
Yajna and the Doctrine of Karma: A Contradiction in Indian Thought about Action. KRISHNA, Daya.

ACTIVE EUTHANASIA

Euthanasia: Toward an Ethical Social Policy. THOMASMA, David C.

ACTIVISM

Active Citizenship as Political Obligation. SKILLEN, Tony.
Ecofeminist Theory and Grassroots Politics. LAHAR, Stephanie.
The Impact of Activist Pressures on Recombinant DNA Research. RABINO, Isaac.
Informed Consent or Informed Rejection of Pesticide Use: A Concept for Environmental Action. ORTON, David.

ACTIVITY(-TIES)

"Time and Thisness" in *Themes From Kaplan*, ADAMS, Robert Merrihew.
The Art of Philosophy. COOPER, Neil.
The Causal History of Computational Activity: Maudlin and Olympia. BARNES, Eric.
Noia, acedia ed epochè. BOTTANI, Livio.
Teleology and the Concepts of Causation. VON GLASERSFELD, Ernst.
The Operation of Values: Knowledge in the Conception of G H Mead (in Polish). HETMANSKI, Marek.

ACTOR(S)

"La 'présence' de l'acteur au théâtre" in *XIth International Congress in Aesthetics, Nottingham 1988*, SAISON, Maryvonne.

ACTUAL ENTITY(-TIES)

The Modes of Actuality. FORD, Lewis S.

ACTUALISM

Actualism, Ontological Commitment, and Possible World Semantics. MENZEL, Ch.

ACTUALITY

"A Reply to Gabriella Baptist's "Ways and Loci of Modality"" in *Essays on Hegel's Logic*, CHAFFIN, Deborah G.
"Ways and Loci of Modality" in *Essays on Hegel's Logic*, BAPTIST, Gabriella.
La "riabilitazione" della δυναμιζ e dell'ενεργεια in Heidegger. VOLPI, Franco.
Actual Preferences, Actual People. GOODIN, Robert E.
Actuality and Quantification. HAZEN, Allen.
Aristotelian and Whiteheadian Conceptions of Actuality: I. FETZ, Reto Luzius and FELT, James W.
Aspetti di attualità teoretica del pensiero procliano negli studi di Werner Beierwaltes. SCOTTI, Nicoletta.
Concentric Circles: An Exploration of Three Concepts in Process Metaphysics. AUXIER, Randall.
Dall'attualismo al tensionalismo. SIMONE, Aldo.
Gustavo Bontadini un metafisico per vocazione. LATORA, Salvatore.
Knowability, Actuality, and the Metaphysics of Context-Dependence. PERCIVAL, Philip.
On "Why is There Something Rather Than Nothing?". KUSCH, Martin.
Time, Actuality and Omniscience. LEFTOW, Brian.

ACZEL, P

Logics of Truth. TURNER, Raymond.

ADAMS, M

Ockham, Adams and Connotation: A Critical Notice of Marilyn Adams, *William Ockham*. SPADE, Paul Vincent.
Ontological Reductionism and Faith Versus Reason: A Critique of Adams on Ockham. FREDDOSO, Alfred J.

ADAPTATION

Causes, Proximate and Ultimate. FRANCIS, Richard C.
Fitness and Evolutionary Explanation: A Response. BYERLY, Henry C and MICHOD, Richard E.
On the Adaptations of Organisms and the Fitness of Types. ETTINGER, Lia and JABLONKA, Eva and MC LAUGHLIN, Peter.

ADDICTION

Rational Chocolate Addiction or How Chocolate Cures Irrationality. ELLIOTT, C S.

ADDITION

Reducts of (C,+,·) Which Contain +. MARKER, D and PILLAY, A.

ADDITIVITY

On the Completeness of a Certain System of Arithmetic of Whole Numbers in Which Addition Occurs as the Only Operation. PRESBURGER, Mojzesz and JACQUETTE, Dale.

ADEQUACY

Dummett's Ought from Is. GREEN, Karen.
A Second Copy Thesis in Hume?. PAPPAS, George S.

ADLER, A

The Authentic Self: Toward a Philosophy of Personality. LACENTRA, Walter.

ADLER, M

Freedom in the Modern World: Jacques Maritain, Yves R Simon, Mortimer J Adler. TORRE, Michael D (ed).
"Adler on Freedom" in *Freedom in the Modern World: Jacques Maritain, Yves R Simon, Mortimer J Adler*, MC INERNY, Ralph.
"Adler's *The Idea of Freedom*" in *Freedom in the Modern World: Jacques Maritain, Yves R Simon, Mortimer J Adler*, FITZGERALD, Desmond J.
"Democracy and Philosophy: On Yves R Simon and Mortimer J Adler" in *Freedom in the Modern World: Jacques Maritain, Yves R Simon, Mortimer J Adler*, ANASTAPLO, George.
"A Dialectical Version of Philosophical Discussion" in *Freedom in the Modern World: Jacques Maritain, Yves R Simon, Mortimer J Adler*, BIRD, Otto.
"Mr Adler and Matthew Arnold" in *Freedom in the Modern World: Jacques Maritain, Yves R Simon, Mortimer J Adler*, VAN DOREN, John.
"Recollections of Three Thinkers: Adler, Simon, and Maritain" in *Freedom in the Modern World: Jacques Maritain, Yves R Simon, Mortimer J Adler*, GALLAGHER, Donald A.
The Specific Features of Cognition Progress in Philosophy: Demonstrated by the Example of Max Adler (in German). MÖCKEL, Christian.

ADMINISTRATION

Philosophical Streets: New Approaches to Urbanism. CROW, Dennis (ed).
"Mario Bunge's Influence on the Administrative and Systems Sciences" in *Studies on Mario Bunge's "Treatise"*, MATTESSICH, Richard V.
Ethics and Educational Administration: Are Ethical Politics "Ethical"?. RUDDER, Charles F.

ADMISSIBILITY

Problems of Substitution and Admissibility in the Modal System Grz and in Intuitionistic Propositional Calculus. RYBAKOV, V V.

ADOLESCENTS

"Individuality and Collectivity: False Antonyms" in *Abeunt Studia in Mores: A Festschrift for Helga Doblin*, PYTOWSKA, Ewa.

ADOPTION

Abortion, Coercive Pregnancy, and Adoption. JAMES, David N.

ADORNO, T

Adorno's Aesthetic Theory: The Redemption of Illusion. ZUIDERVAART, Lambert.
Critical Theory and Philosophy. INGRAM, David.
Herrschaft und Versöhnung: Einführung in das Denken Theodor W Adornos. KAGER, Reinhard.
Models and Concepts of Ideology. RITSERT, Jürgen.
The Persistence of Modernity: Essays on Aesthetics, Ethics, and Postmodernism. WELLMER, Albrecht.
"Hegel and the Subversion of Systems: *Der Fall Adorno*" in *Writing the Politics of Difference*, DONOUGHO, Martin.
Adorno and the French Post-Structuralists on the Other of Reason. NUYEN, A T.
Announcement of the Endless in Horkheimer, Adorno and Habermas (in Serbo-Croatian). SIEBERT, Rudolf J.
The Avant Garde, Institutional and Critical Theories of Art. SNYMAN, Johan J.
Ist die Kantische Theorie eine Theorie entfremdeter Erkenntnis?. KERBER, Harald.
The Jargon of Authenticity: Adorno and Feminist Essentialism. PHELAN, Shane.
Die Metaphysik der Kritik: Zum Verhältnis von Metaphysik und Erfahrung bei Max Horkheimer und Theodor W Adorno. RECKI, Birgit.
Over Overdrijven. GRIFFIOEN, S.
The Theological Secret of Th W Adorno's Aesthetic Theory (in German). HOLZ, Hans Heinz.

ADVAITA VEDANTA

Advaita and Religious Language. GRIMES, John.
The Advaita Theory of Liberation. DAS, Bhupendra Chandra.
Karma and Reincarnation in Advaita Vedānta. SHARMA, Arvind.
Knowledge, Reason and Human Autonomy: A Review Article. KRISHNA, Daya.
Ramana Maharsi on the Theories of Creation in Advaita Vedānta. SHARMA, Arvind.
Some Problems in the Epistemology of Advaita. GRIMES, John.
The Word That Became the Absolute: Relevance of Sankara's Ontology of Language. GUPTA, Som Raj.

ADVERBIALS

Der sinnliche Gehalt der Wahrnehmung. SCHANTZ, Richard.

ADVERTISING

Choosing Social Responsibility Over Law: The *Soldier of Fortune* Classified Advertising Cases. TOMLINSON, Don E.
Doctors and Their Advertising. BURTON, Gene E.
Physical Environment Television Advertisement Themes: 1979 and 1989. PETERSON, Robin T.
Remarks on Marketing Ethics. BRENNAN, Bernard F.
Research Note On Equity and Ethics in State-Promotion of Agricultural Products. ADELAJA, Adesoji O and BRUMFIELD, Robin G.

ADVISING

The Philosopher as Insider and Outsider: How to Advise, Compromise, and Criticize. KAMM, Frances M.

AENESIDEMUS

Experience and Causal Explanation in Medical Empiricism. PENTZOPOULOU-VALALAS, Teresa.

AESTHETIC

Aesthetic Constraints on Theory Selection: A Critique of Laudan. MARTIN, James E.
Aesthetic Order. LORAND, Ruth.
Ein Husserlmanuskript über Ästhetik. SCARAMUZZA, Gabriele and SCHUHMANN, Karl.
Knowledge as Active, Aesthetic, and Hypothetical: A Pragmatic Interpretation of Whitehead's Cosmology. FRISINA, Warren G.

AESTHETIC EDUCATION

Aesthetic Education and Aesthetic Atmosphere (in Czechoslovakian). MATHAUSER, Zdenek.
The Substance of Aesthetic Education in the School (in Czechoslovakian). SABOUK, Sava.

AESTHETIC EXPERIENCE(S)

"Aesthetic Experience and Culture" in *XIth International Congress in Aesthetics, Nottingham 1988*, SCRUTON, Roger.
"Aesthetic Experience: Where Did We Go Wrong?" in *XIth International Congress in Aesthetics, Nottingham 1988*, FISHER, John.
"Try the Image—Temporality and Fullness in Aesthetic Experience" in *XIth International Congress in Aesthetics, Nottingham 1988*, JIMENEZ, Jose.
Criticism: Foundation and Recommendation for Teaching. HOLT JR, David K.
Discipline-Based Art Education: Conceptions and Misconceptions. EISNER, Elliot W.

AESTHETIC JUDGMENT

Adorno's Aesthetic Theory: The Redemption of Illusion. ZUIDERVAART, Lambert.
"Are There Aesthetic Qualities?" in *XIth International Congress in Aesthetics, Nottingham 1988*, SOMERVILLE, James.
Community and the Evil Poem. KEMAL, S.
El concepto de "conformidad a fines" en la Crítica del Juicio Estético. PÖLTNER, Günter.

AESTHETICS

see also Beauty, Creativity, Literature, Music, Poetry
"Also sprach Herakleitos". WOHLFART, Günter.
Against Architecture: The Writings of Georges Bataille. HOLLIER, Denis.
The Anatomy of Philosophical Style. LANG, Berel.
Art and Answerability: Early Philosophical Essays—M M Bakhtin. HOLQUIST, Michael (ed).
Ästhetik des Abschieds: Kritik der Moderne. EBELING, Hans.
Benjamin Constant and the Post-Revolutionary Mind. FONTANA, Biancamaria.
Contemplating Music—Source Readings in the Aesthetics of Music, Volume II: Import. KATZ, Ruth (ed).
The Dice-Playing God: Reflections on Life in a Post-Modern Age. KRIEGLSTEIN, Werner.
Diderot's Dream. ANDERSON, Wilda.
Estetica: Come Scienza dell'Espressione e Linguistica Generale. CROCE, Benedetto.
Herrschaft und Versöhnung: Einführung in das Denken Theodor W Adornos. KAGER, Reinhard.
The Ideas of Ayn Rand. MERRILL, Ronald E.
Kalkulierte Absurditäten. STRUB, Christian.
L'objet-peinture: Pour une théorie de la réception. PAQUIN, Nycole.
The Legacy of Hermann Cohen. KLUBACK, William.
Mimesis as Make-Believe: On the Foundations of the Representational Arts. WALTON, Kendall L.
Modernity, Aesthetics, and the Bounds of Art. MC CORMICK, Peter J.
Musical Aesthetics: A Historical Reader, Volume III, The Twentieth Century. LIPPMAN, Edward A (ed).
Nicolai Hartmann's New Ontology. WERKMEISTER, W H.
Nietzsche: A Frenzied Look. ACKERMANN, Robert John.
The Persistence of Modernity: Essays on Aesthetics, Ethics, and Postmodernism. WELLMER, Albrecht.
Phänomenologie als ästhetische Theorie. FELLMANN, Ferdinand.
Philosophical Streets: New Approaches to Urbanism. CROW, Dennis (ed).
Proust: The Creative Silence. CARANFA, Angelo.
Schellings Philosophie der Kunst: Göttliche Imagination und Ästhetische Einbildungskraft. BARTH, Bernhard.
Socialism, Feminism and Philosophy: A Radical Philosophy Reader. SAYERS, Sean (ed).
Style and Music: Theory, History, and Ideology. MEYER, Leonard B.
Velázquez et Goya. PIERRE, Christian (trans).
Wege aus der Moderne. WELSCH, Wolfgang (ed).
Wittgenstein, Ethics and Aesthetics: The View from Eternity. TILGHMAN, B R.
The World of the Imagination: Sum and Substance. BRANN, Eva T H.
XIth International Congress in Aesthetics, Nottingham 1988. WOODFIELD, Richard (ed).
"Chinese Aesthetics" in *Understanding the Chinese Mind: The Philosophical Roots*, WU, Kuang-Ming.
"Communication esthetique comme bonheur" in *XIth International Congress in Aesthetics, Nottingham 1988*, SASAKI, Kenichi.
"Creative Intuition in American Film: Maritain at the Movies" in *From Twilight to Dawn: The Cultural Vision of Jacques Maritain*, LAUDER, Robert E.
"*Pale Fire* Solved" in *Acting and Reflecting: The Interdisciplinary Turn in Philosophy*, CARRIER, David.
"Structure of Methodology of an Aesthetic Theorem" in *XIth International Congress in Aesthetics, Nottingham 1988*, KHANIN, Dmitry.
"...A Presence of Absence...". BATKIN, Norton.
"Art Nonsense" or the Nine Flavours. ANAND, Mulk Raj.
"Just for the Thrill": Sycophantizing Aristotle's *Poetics*. CARSON, Anne.
Aesthetic Appreciation and Human Katharsis. NIARCHOS, Constantine G.
Aesthetic Authority and Tradition: Nietzsche and the Greeks. STRONG, Tracy B.
Aesthetic Liberalism: Kant and the Ethics of Modernity. CASCARDI, Anthony J.

AESTHETICS

The Aesthetic Relation of Musical Performer and Audience. PUTMAN, Daniel.

Aesthetics and Art Education. SMITH, Peter.

Aesthetics and Natural Law in Newton's Methodology. JACQUETTE, Dale.

The Aesthetics of Imperfection. HAMILTON, Andy.

Aesthetics of T G Masaryk (in Czechoslovakian). HLAVACEK, Lubos.

Aesthetics of T G Masaryk II (in Czechoslovakian). HLAVACEK, Lubos.

Alternatives et questions dans la littérature romanesque. COMETTI, Jean-Pierre.

Anachronistic Themes and Literary Value: The Tempest. SKILLEAS, Ole Martin.

Aristotelian Mimesis Reevaluated. HALLIWELL, Stephen.

Aristotle and Nietzsche on Art as Imitation of Nature. DROST, Mark P.

Art and Aesthetics and the Crisis of Culture. MORAWSKI, Stefan.

Art and Craft. MOUNCE, H O.

Art and Morality in Plato: A Reappraisal. HALL, Robert W.

Art and Morality: On the Problem of Stating a Problem. HATTINGH, J P.

Art and Neurology: A Discussion. HALPIN, David M G and SORRELL, Martin.

Art and Philosophy: The Person in the Cybernetic Age. HETZLER, Florence M.

Art et cosmos. PASSERON, René.

Art et mystère. TAVARES DE MIRANDA, Maria.

Art for Existence's Sake: A Heideggerian Revision. SCHUMACHER, Paul J.

Art Works, But How?—Kant and Aesthetics/Heidegger and Truth. SYNNING, Ralph.

Art's Autonomy and Absolute Idealism: The Role of Aesthetics in Schelling's Philosophy (in Dutch). BRAECKMAN, A.

Art, Aesthetics, and the Pitfalls of Discipline-Based Art Education. ARNSTINE, Donald.

Art, Life and Reality. NOVITZ, David.

Art, Stance and Education. PUSCH, James.

El arte y la urbanidad de la razón. CORDUA, Carla.

Arte y significación. ECHAURI, Raul.

Artist and Peasant. XING-PEI, Fei.

Authenticity Again. SHARPE, R A.

Author's Position in Interpretation of a Work of Art (in Japanese). WATANABE, Hiroshi.

The Avant Garde, Institutional and Critical Theories of Art. SNYMAN, Johan J.

Bakhtin's Marxist Formalism. MC BRIDE, William Thomas.

The Beautiful, the Ugly, and the Tao. COLEMAN, Earle J.

Beauty and the Genealogy of Art Theory. CARROLL, Noël.

Beethoven's Ninth Symphony: The Sense of an Ending. SOLOMON, Maynard.

Boors and Bumpkins, Snobs and Snoots. GODLOVITCH, S.

Can Art Save Us? A Meditation on Gadamer. DEVEREAUX, Mary.

The Case Against Art: Wunderlich on Joyce. MAHAFFEY, Vicki.

Change and Development. MC LEOD, John.

Cognitive Art. LAUTER, H A.

Community and the Evil Poem. KEMAL, S.

Comprensión intercultural y arte. BERENSON, Frances.

El concepto de "conformidad a fines" en la Crítica del Juicio Estético. PÖLTNER, Günter.

Conditional Essences. HAIGHT, Mary R.

Copies, Reproducibility and Aesthetic Adequacy. CHANG, Briankle G.

The Core of Aesthetics. WOLLHEIM, Richard.

Un cosmos interprété. SPANTIDOU, Constantina.

Criticism: Foundation and Recommendation for Teaching. HOLT JR, David K.

Cuteness. MORREALL, John.

De quelques interprétations philosophiques de l'idée artisique d'interprétation. MOUTSOPOULOS, E.

The Death of the Author (as Producer). STOPFORD, John.

The Death of the Author: An Analytical Autopsy. LAMARQUE, Peter.

The Definition of 'Art'. ROWE, M W.

Die Wahrheit des literarischen Kunstwerks: R Ingardens Begriff des Quasi-Urteils (in Japanese). KAWAKAMI, Akitaka.

La diffusione del pensiero spagnolo contemporaneo nell'Italia di oggi. SAVIGNANO, Armando.

Edward Bullogh's Aesthetics and Aestheticism: Features of Reality to Be Experienced. BOULTING, Noel E.

The Empirical Author: Salman Rushdie's The Satanic Verses. CLOSE, Anthony.

La estética de la recepción desde la teoría platónica del arte. ORTIZ DE URBINA, Ricardo Sánchez.

Estetica e interrogazione. GARRONI, Emilio.

Experiencia de lo sublime y principios racionales. ARTOLA, José María.

A Fat Worm of Error?. MC GHEE, Michael.

La figure d'Héraclite dans la pensée du jeune Nietzsche. VOELKE, André-Jea.

Die Figuren des Menschlichen. MEYER, Michel.

Form and Funk: The Aesthetic Challenge of Popular Art. SHUSTERMAN, Richard.

Frontières des études littéraires: science de la littérature, science des discours. ANGENOT, Marc.

Functional and Procedural Definitions of Art. DAVIES, Stephen.

Glenn Gould: "architecteur" des Variations Goldberg. GUERTIN, Ghyslaine.

Der Harmonie-Gedanke im frühen Mittelalter. BEIERWALTES, Werner.

Hegel, Antigone, and the Possibility of Ecstatic Dialogue. WILLETT, Cynthia.

Hegel, Heidegger, and the Question of Art Today. GROSSMANN, Andreas.

The Hidden Order of Arts Education. ROSS, Malcolm.

Historizing contra fetishizing—The Progress of Modern Technology in W Benjamin's Aesthetic Reflexion (in German). WAGNER, Gerhard.

Horace's Ars Poetica and the Deconstructive Leech. HABIB, M A R.

Humanizing the Humanities: Some Reflections on George Steiner's "Brutal Paradox". KARIER, Clarence J.

Hume and the Paradox of Taste Again. WERTZ, S K.

Husserl—Bolzano II (in Czechoslovakian). BAYEROVA, Marie.

Hutcheson's Account of Beauty as a Response to Mandeville. MICHAEL, Emily and MICHAEL, Fred S.

Identifying Musical Works of Art. JACOBS, Jo Ellen.

Imitación y purificación en la estética de Aristóteles. CAPPELLETTI, Angel.

The Incoherence and Irrationality of Philosophers. RADFORD, Colin.

The Influence of Modernism on Art Education. MEESON, Philip.

Interart Analogy: Practice and Theory in Comparing the Arts. THOMAS, Troy.

Interprétation de l'art—Art de l'interprétation. TOMBRAS, Spyros.

Interprétation et philosophie de l'art. MARCONDES CÉSAR, Constança.

Interpretation of Art as a Philosophical Problem (in Czechoslovakian). MOKREJS, Antonin.

Interpreting Art. BLOCKER, H Gene.

Is King Lear Like the Pacific Ocean or the Washington Monument? Critical Pluralism and Literary Interpretation. PHELAN, James.

Is the Creative Process in Art a Form of Puzzle Solving?. LEDDY, Thomas.

Is the Post- in Postmodernism the Post- in Postcolonial?. APPIAH, Kwame Anthony.

Jean-Jacques Rousseau et Friedrich Schiller: le théâtre sous le feu des lumières. MATTE, Martin.

Ji Kang's "Sheng-wu-aile-lun": Concerning Its Logical Development (in Japanese). HARA, Masayuki.

Kansas, Oz, and the Function of Art. CONLON, James.

Kant über den Witz und Kants Witz. RITZEL, Wolfgang.

Kant und Wittgenstein. STETTER, Christian.

Kant's Apotheosis of Genius. QUINN, Timothy Sean.

Kants "Reflexionen zur Ästhetik": Zur Werkgeschichte der "Kritik der ästhetischen Urteilskraft". FRANK, Manfred.

Kants Kritik der Urteilskraft. RAYMAEKERS, Bart.

Kants Logik der Synthesis und die Schliessung einer "unübersehbaren Kluft". FUNKE, Gerhard.

Kierkegaard: Aesthetics and 'The Aesthetic'. PATTISON, George.

Kompensierte Moderne. LÖVENICH, F.

Kristeva and Holbein, Artist of Melancholy. LECHTE, John.

L'art comme pénétration d'un mystère. GOULA-MITACOU, Xéni.

L'interprétation comme art de création réitérée. SKOURIOTI, Athéna.

La communication de l'art (in Japanese). SHINOHARA, Motoaki.

Love, Friendship, and the Aesthetics of Character. NOVITZ, David.

El lugar de la crítica de arte. ORTIZ DE URBINA, Ricardo Sánchez.

M Heideggers Auslegung von Sophokles' "Oedipus Tyrannus" (in Japanese). SEKIGUCHI, Hiroshi.

Marxist Literary Aesthetics. MILLER, Seumas.

La metáfora en Aristóteles. GAMBRA, José Miguel.

Michael Polanyi's Aesthetics: A Phenomenological Study. BISWAS, Goutam.

Music in Hegel's Aesthetics: A Re-Evaluation. JOHNSON, Julian.

Music Performance and the Tools of the Trade. GODLOVITCH, Stan.

Music, Meaning, and the Art of Elocution. TROTT, Elizabeth Anne.

Nachahmung und Gestaltung—Baumgarten, Meditationes 73 (in Japanese). MATSUO, Hiroshi.

The Nagaraja: Symbol and Symbolism in Hindu Art and Iconography. DURAN, Jane.

Natural Generativity and Imitation. SARTWELL, Crispin.

Nature' Song. SALLIS, John.

Nomologie et anomie: lecture de deux antinomies. ZANETTI, Véronique.

A Note on Ruth Lorand's 'Free and Dependent Beauty: A Puzzling Issue'. LORD, Catherine.

Les objets de la sémiologie théâtrale: le texte et le spectacle. VIGEANT, Louise.

On Capturing Cities. GOODMAN, Nelson.

On Davies' Institutional Definition of Art. OPPY, Graham.

On Decadence. DURAN, Jane.

On the Historical Triviality of Art. STOLNITZ, Jerome.

The Ontology of Musical Works and the Authenticity of their Performances. DAVIES, Stephen.

Osservazioni sul bello naturale e sul bello artistico in filosofia. FRANCHI, Alfredo.

Panofsky, Polanyi, and Intrinsic Meaning. UN-CHOL, Shin.

The Parallel Fallacy: On Comparing Art and Science. TOPPER, David.

Perceptual Aspects of Art for the Blind. ARNHEIM, Rudolf.

Perennial Modernity: Forms as Aesthetic and Symbolic. MAQUET, Jacques.

AESTHETICS

Persons as Natural Works of Art. ALDRICH, Virgil.
Philosophical Prolegomena of Structural Thinking (in Czechoslovakian). CHVATIK, Kvetoslav.
Philosophy as an Art. LEVINSON, Jerrold.
Pictures and Depictions: A Consideration of Peacocke's Views. KEMP, G N.
Pierre Menard's *Don Quixote*. BAILEY, George.
Plato's Analogy between Painter and Poet. JANAWAY, Christopher.
Plato's *Statesman* Story: The Birth of Fiction Reconceived. TOMASI, John.
Poetry and Autonomy. SANKOWSKI, Edward.
Popular Art and Aesthetic Theory: Why the Muse Is Unembarrassed. ANDERSON, Richard L.
Post-Modern Pastiche. ROSE, Margaret A.
Post-Modernism as the Lesser Evil: Criticism and Agreement in Lyotard's "Widerstreit" ("Conflict") (in German). KRÜGER, Hans-Peter.
La problemática ética en el pensamiento de Husserl. IRIBARNE, Julia V.
Problems Concerning the Presence of the Composer in His Music (in Polish). BUCZEK, Barbara.
Qu'est-ce que l'expressionnisme allemand?. RICHARD, Lionel.
Quelques remarques sur la composition de la *Dialectique de la faculté de juger téléologique*. KOPPER, Joachim.
Questioning "the Romantic Ideology": Wordsworth. WOLFSON, Susan J.
Realism, Irrealism, and Ideology: A Critique of Nelson Goodman. MITCHELL, W J T.
Reason in Criticism. MIRI, Mrinal.
La réception de Spinoza dans la littérature néerlandaise. HENRARD, Roger.
La réflexion dans l'esthétique kantienne. LYOTARD, Jean-François.
Reply to the Symposiasts. WOLLHEIM, Richard.
Retrospections. GOODMAN, Nelson.
Revealing the Truth of Art. BOWIE, Andrew.
The Role of Music in Nietzsche's *Birth of Tragedy*. HECKMAN, Peter.
Scharfstein as a Metaphysician of Art (in Hebrew). LURIE, Yuval.
Schopenhauer en de kunst van het verzaken. DE MARTELAERE, Patricia.
Schopenhauers "objektives Interesse". NEYMEYR, Barbara.
The Scottish Influence on French Aesthetic Thought: Later Developments. MANNS, James W.
Seeing the Original. BASS, Walter.
Sémiologie visuelle, peinture et intertextualité. PAQUET, Bernard.
Sémiotique des "genres": Une théorie de la réception. PAQUIN, Nycole.
La sémiotique, les objets singuliers et la complexité. THÉRIEN, Gilles.
Sign, Symbol, and System. ELGIN, Catherine Z.
Space and Its Questions (in Czechoslovakian). PATOCKA, Jan.
Le statut sémiotique de la perspective dans l'oeuvre picturale. CARANI, Marie.
Storicità della poesia: estetica e storicismo in Francesco De Sanctis. GALASSO, Giuseppe.
Subjektivität, Allgemeingültigkeit und Apriorität des Geschmacksurteils bei Kant. BAUM, Manfred.
Le supplément poétique. WATTEYNE, Nathalie.
A Synthetic Formulation of Nietzsche's Aesthetic Model. JOVANOVSKI, Thomas.
Technique of Painting and Sociology of Picture (in Czechoslovakian). HLAVACEK, Josef.
Technological Progress and Architectural Response. WINTERS, Edward.
The "Presuppositions" and "Realizations" in Aesthetics of Zdenek Mathauser (in Czechoslovakian). SVATON, Vladimir.
The Heterogeneity of Poetic Language in Kristeva (in Japanese). NARUSE, Katsuji.
The Picture in Movement and in Response (in Czechoslovakian). JIRIK, Vlastimil.
The Problem of Cognition and Truth in Aesthetics (in Czechoslovakian). SINDELAR, Dusan.
The Status of Fiction: Between Nostalgia and Nihilism (in French). IMHOOF, Stefan.
The Strategy of Forced Reconciliation (in Serbo-Croatian). RAULET, Gérard.
The Theological Secret of Th W Adorno's Aesthetic Theory (in German). HOLZ, Hans Heinz.
Thèses sur le rôle de l'interprétation dans l'art. SEEL, Gerhard.
Three Assumptions that Influence Art Education: A Description and a Critique. RICHMOND, Stuart.
Tiempo, soledad y muerte: La encrucijada del poeta. RADCHIK, Laura.
To Catch a Thief: Chu Hsi (1130-1200) and the Hermeneutic Art. BERTHRONG, John.
To Umberto Eco's Criticism of Icon (in Czechoslovakian). HAMAN, Ales.
Transcendance ou présence?. PARAIN-VIAL, Jeanne.
The *Trés Riches Heures*: An Illuminated Manuscript in the Age of Mechanical Reproduction. CAMILLE, Michael.
Über das Geschmacksurteil und die künstlerische Freiheit bei Kant (in Japanese). UE, Satoko.
Understanding Performance Art: Art beyond Art. HEYD, Thomas.
Understanding the Message of the Work of Art. SPASSOVA, Pravda.
Usefulness in Literary History. SMALL, Ian and GUY, Josephine.
Values, the Environment and the Creative Act. THOMAS, John C.
Verdad e inteligibilidad: Los rasgos invariantes de la doctrina platónica de las ideas. LUIS DEL BARCO, José.
Vers une mise en signe de l'installation. RÉGIMBALD, Manon.
The Very Idea of Perfect Realism. FISHER, John Andrew.
Visual Fictions. CURRIE, Gregory.
Vom "Wahr-Lachen" der Moderne: Karl Valentins Semantik paradoxer Lebenswelten. GÖNNER, Gerhard.
What Goodman Leaves Out. ELGIN, Catherine Z.
What is Philosophy of Culture? (in Polish). NOWICKI, Andrzej.
What's It All About? The Critical Method of Analysis as Applied to Drama. CLEARY JR, Donald L.
Why Do I Love Thee? A Response to Nozick's Account of Romantic Love. SMITH, Tara.
Why is Kitsch Bad? (in Hebrew). KULKA, Tomas.
Why 'Art' Doesn't Have Two Senses. ROWE, M W.
William Wadsworth: Nature, Imagination, Ultimate Reality and Meaning. MAHONEY, John L.
Wittgenstein on Frazer's *Golden Bough*. COVEOS, Costis M.
Wittgenstein on Tolstoi's *What is Art?*. BEARDSMORE, R W.
Wollheim's Theory of Artist as Spectator: A Complication. OLDS, Clifton.
Zur Erkenntnistheorie des Ästhetischen: Schopenhauers Beziehung zu Kant. DÖRFLINGER, Bernd.
'I Heard a Plaintive Melody'. HANFLING, Oswald.

AFFIRMATION

Skepticism, Enigma and Integrity: Horizons of Affirmation in Nietzsche's Philosophy. HULL, Robert.

AFFIRMATIVE ACTION

Writing and the Moral Self. LANG, Berel.
Affirmative Action Revisited: Justice and Public Policy Considerations. VANTERPOOL, Rudolph V.
Affirmative Action Rhetoric. RADIN, Margaret Jane.
Change and Continuity in the Concept of Civil Rights: Thurgood Marshall and Affirmative Action. TUSHNET, Mark.
The Doctrine of Double Effect and Affirmative Action. JORDAN, Jeff.
The Message of Affirmative Action. HILL JR, Thomas E.

AFRICAN

African Philosophy: The Essential Readings. SEREQUEBERHAN, Tsenay.
I, We and Body: First Joint Symposium of Philosophers from Africa and from the Netherlands. KIMMERLE, Heinz (ed).
"The Discussion on Identity Among African Philosophers" in *I, We and Body: First Joint Symposium of Philosophers from Africa and from the Netherlands*, FENNEMA, J G.
"The Notion of Time in African Thinking: A Survey of Some Approaches" in *I, We and Body: First Joint Symposium of Philosophers from Africa and from the Netherlands*, VAN ZUYLEKOM, Ruud M.
"Oedipus and the Dogon: The Myth of Modernity Interrogated" in *I, We and Body: First Joint Symposium of Philosophers from Africa and from the Netherlands*, OOSTERLING, Henk A F.
"The Ontological Significance of 'I' and 'We' in African Philosophy" in *I, We and Body: First Joint Symposium of Philosophers from Africa and from the Netherlands*, NYASANI, Joseph M.
"Person and Community in African Thought" in *I, We and Body: First Joint Symposium of Philosophers from Africa and from the Netherlands*, GYEKYE, Kwame.
The African Liberation Struggle: A Hermeneutic Exploration of an African Historical-Political Horizon. SEREQUEBERHAN, Tsenay.
Bondedness, *Moyo* and *Umunthu* as the Elements of aChewa Spirituality: Organizing Logic and Principle of Life. SINDIMA, Harvey.
Cultural Fundamentals in Philosophy. ORUKA, H Odera.
Dr C Neugebauer's Critical Note on Ethnophilosophy in the Philosophical Discourse in Africa: Some Remarks. BEWAJI, J A I.
Hegel and Kant—A Refutation of their Racism. NEUGEBAUER, Christian.
Human Rights in the Context of Uganda's Political Experience. KIGONGO, J K.
Is the Post- in Postmodernism the Post- in Postcolonial?. APPIAH, Kwame Anthony.
Just War Theory and the ANC's Armed Struggle. MILLER, S R.
Karl Marx and African Emancipatory Thought: A Critique of Marx's Euro-centric Metaphysics. SEREQUEBERHAN, Tsenay.
Metaphysics, Religion and Yoruba Traditional Thought. OLADIPO, Olusegun.
Multinational Corporate Social Policy Process for Ethical Responsibility in Sub-Saharan Africa. PRATT, Cornelius B.
On African Feminism: Two Reasons for the Rejection of Feminism. KWAME, Safro.
Philosophy of African Intellectuals. WAMBA-DIA-WAMBA, Ernest.
Professional Education of African Americans: A Challenge to Ethical Thinking. HARRIS, William M.
A Response to A G A Bello's Methodological Preliminaries. ANYANWU, Kane C.
Self-Potential as a Yoruba Ultimate: A Further Contribution to URAM Yoruba Studies. LAWUYI, Olatunde B.
The Aristotelian Debate in African Philosophy: Miscellaneous Remarks on a Denied Discourse (in German). NEUGEBAUER, Christian.
Ultimate Reality and Meaning in Africa: Some Methodological Preliminaries—A Test Case. BELLO, A G A.
Umuntu Ngumuntu Ngabantu: An African Concept of Humanity. SHUTTE, Augustine.

AFRO-AMERICAN
"Unspeakable Things Unspoken: The Afro-American Presence in American Literature" in *The Tanner Lectures on Human Values, Volume XI*, MORRISON, Toni.
A Returning to the Source: The Philosophy of Alain Locke. BIRT, Robert E.

AFTERLIFE
"Keine festbegrenzte und Wahrhaft anschauliche Vorstelling". SCHREURS, Nico.
Cuestiones de sobrevivencia. MILLÁN, Gustavo Ortiz (trans) and SOSA, Ernest.
Identity, Transformation, and What Matters in Survival. MARTIN, Raymond.

AGAPE
The Ethical Thought of Martin Luther King. STERLING, Marvin C.

AGE OF REASON
see Enlightenment

AGENCY
Ethics with Aristotle. BROADIE, Sarah.
Fallen Freedom: Kant on Radical Evil and Moral Regeneration. MICHALSON JR, Gordon E.
How to Build a Conscious Machine. ANGEL, Leonard.
Intention, Agency and Criminal Liability: Philosophy of Action and the Criminal Law. DUFF, R A.
Kant's Theory of Freedom. ALLISON, Henry E.
The Philosophy of Action: An Introduction. MOYA, Carlos J.
"Aspects of Identity and Agency" in *Identity, Character, and Morality: Essays in Moral Psychology*, RORTY, Amélie Oksenberg and WONG, David.
"Intention and Personal Policies" in *Philosophical Perspectives, 3: Philosophy of Mind and Action Theory, 1989*, BRATMAN, Michael E.
An Abyss of Difference: Laing, Sartre and Jaspers. KIRSNER, Douglas.
Agency and Morality. BROOK, Richard.
Agency and Omniscience. KAPITAN, Tomis.
Agency and Probabilistic Causality. PRICE, Huw.
Before Refraining: Concepts for Agency. BELNAP JR, Nuel D.
Defining the Limits of Institutional Moral Agency in Health Care: A Response to Kevin Wildes. RIE, Michael A.
Emotions and Rationality. BERENSON, F M.
The Ethical Implications of the Straight-Commission Compensation System—An Agency Perspective. KURLAND, Nancy B.
Feminist Second Thoughts About Free Agency. BENSON, Paul.
Individual and Corporate Responsibility: Two Alternative Approaches. SURBER, Jere.
Intentional Single and Joint Action. TUOMELA, Raimo.
Locke on Personal Identity and the Trinity Controversy of the 1690s. WEDEKING, Gary.
Searle on Natural Agency. BISHOP, John.
Stit and the Language of Agency. PERLOFF, Michael.
Structure/Antistructure and Agency under Oppression. LUGONES, Maria C.

AGENT(S)
Thinking the Unthinkable: Meanings of the Holocaust. GOTTLIEB, Roger S (ed).
"Seeing To It That: A Canonical Form for Agentives" in *Knowledge Representation and Defeasible Reasoning*, BELNAP JR, Nuel D and PERLOFF, Michael.
Commentary: "Individual and Corporate Responsibility". FRENCH, Peter A.
Reason and Reality Revisited. PLUHAR, Evelyn.
Responsibility: Repudiators Referring to the Divided Centre of Action in the Physical Agent (in Czechoslovakian). PEARS, D.
Taking Role Moralities Seriously. WUESTE, Daniel E.
Two Kinds of Agent-Relativity. HUMBERSTONE, I L.

AGGREGATE(S)
Aggregation Theorems and Multidimensional Stochastic Choice Models. MARLEY, A A J.

AGGRESSION
The Anatomy of Aggression. LUPER-FOY, Steven.
Antropología y Agresión: notas para un análisis filosófico. FERNÁNDEZ TRESGUERRES, Alfonso.

AGING
Human Interests: Reflections on Philosophical Anthropology. RESCHER, Nicholas.
The Last Choice: Preemptive Suicide in Advanced Age. PRADO, C G.
"Human Rights, Population Again, and Intergenerational Equity" in *Meaning and Method: Essays in Honor of Hilary Putnam*, DANIELS, Norman.
Is Mandatory Retirement Unfair Age Discrimination?. WEDEKING, Gary A.
De natuurlijke ouderdom: een grenzeloze geschiedenis. BIJSTERVELD, Karin.

AGNOSTICISM
The Agnostic Fallacy. KEENE, G B.
Ignoramus, Ignorabimus!. BUENO, Gustavo.
Mansel's Agnosticism. FITZGERALD, Timothy.

AGONY
Freud: Uma Concepção Agónica da Educação. BARBOSA, Manuel.

AGREEMENT(S)
"Surrogate Motherhood Agreements: The Risks to Innocent Human Life" in *Beyond Baby M: Ethical Issues in New Reproductive Techniques*, BOPP JR, James.

AGRICULTURE
Agricultural Bioethics: Implications of Agricultural Biotechnology. GENDEL, Steven M (& other eds).
Shaping Genes: Ethics, Law and Science of Using Genetic Technology in Medicine and Agriculture. MACER, Darryl.
"Moral Responsibility, Values, and Making Decisions about Biotechnology" in *Agricultural Bioethics: Implications of Agricultural Biotechnology*, HOLLANDER, Rachelle D.
Agricultura, desarrollo y autonomía. BLATZ, Charlie.
Agricultural Practices, Ecology, and Ethics in the Third World. WESTRA, L S and BOWEN, K L and BEHE, B K.
Ethical Dilemmas Posed By Recent and Prospective Developments with Respect to Agricultural Research. JOHNSON, Glenn L.
Genetically Engineered Herbicide Resistance, Part Two. COMSTOCK, Gary.
Handsome Lake's Teachings: The Shift from Female to Male Agriculture in Iroquois Agriculture. HOLLY, Marilyn.
Moral Metaphysics, Moral Revolution, and Environmental Ethics. PADEN, Roger.
Research Note On Equity and Ethics in State-Promotion of Agricultural Products. ADELAJA, Adesoji O and BRUMFIELD, Robin G.

AIDS
The Crisis in Health Care: Ethical Issues. MC KENZIE, Nancy F (ed).
Enriching Business Ethics. WALTON, Clarence C (ed).
AIDS and 'Dirt': Reflections on the Ethics of Ritual Cleanliness. CHURCHILL, Larry R.
AIDS and the L-Word. DEVINE, Philip E.
AIDS and the Psycho-Social Disciplines: The Social Control of 'Dangerous' Behavior. KAPLAN, Mark S.
AIDS, Myth, and Ethics. SUNDSTRÖM, Per.
Ethical Challenges of HIV Infection in the Workplace. LEONARD, Arthur S.
Ethics, AIDS, and Community Responsibility. DOUARD, John.
HIV and the Obligation to Treat. SHELDON, Mark.
Mandatory AIDS Testing: The Legal, Ethical and Practical Issues. WERDEL, A Alyce.
Negotiating Criteria and Setting Limits: The Case of AIDS. CUTTER, Mary Ann Gardell.
No Time for an AIDS Backlash. MURPHY, Timothy F.
Noncompliance in AIDS Research. ARRAS, John D.

AIM(S)
Etica e morale: mira teleogica e prospettiva deontologica. RICOEUR, Paul.
On Primoratz's Definition of Terrorism. SINNOTT-ARMSTRONG, Walter.

AIRAKSINEN, T
On Häyry and Airaksinen's 'Hard and Soft Offers as Constraints'. DAY, J P.

AJZEN, I
Ethical Decision Making in the Medical Profession: An Application of the Theory of Planned Behavior. RANDALL, Donna M and GIBSON, Annetta M.

AKRASIA
Mind in Action: Essays in the Philosophy of Mind. RORTY, Amelie Oksenberg.
"Is Akratic Action Always Irrational?" in *Identity, Character, and Morality: Essays in Moral Psychology*, MC INTYRE, Alison.
Akratic Action and the Practical Role of Better Judgment. MELE, Alfred R.
On an Alleged Inconsistency in the Nicomachean Ethics (IX,4). MARTIN, C F J.
Plato and Davidson: Parts of the Soul and Weakness of Will. PENNER, Terrence M.

AL-FARABI
Aristotelian Logic and the Arabic Language in Alfarabi. ABED, Shukri B.
Al-Fârâbî lógico: su exposicón de la "Isagogé" de Porfirio. RAMÓN, Rafael.
Some Remarks on the Political Science of Maimonides and Farabi. BARTLETT, Robert (trans) and STRAUSS, Leo.

AL-KINDI
Al-Kindi's Psychology (in Hebrew). SCHWARZ, Dov.

ALBANIAN
The Concert: Mao's Panopticon. TALMOR, Sascha.

ALBARRACIN, A
Elementos dinámicos de la teoría celular. GONZÁLEZ RECIO, José Luis.

ALBERT OF SAXONY
Las proposiciones de relativo en Alberto de Sajonia. TALEGÓN, César.

ALBINUS
A Middle Platonic Reading of Plato's Theory of Recollection. SCHRENK, Lawrence P.
La transformation de la philosophie de Platon dans le "Prologos" d'Albinus. NETSCHKE-HENTSCHKE, Ada Babette.

ALBIRUNI
Karma and Rebirth in *Alberuni's India*. SHARMA, Arvind.

ALCIBIADES
Socrates and Alcibiades: Eros, Piety, and Politics. HOWLAND, Jacob A.

ALCOHOLISM
The Conceptual Bind in Defining the Volitional Component of Alcoholism. VATZ, Richard E and WEINBERG, Lee S.
Fingarette on the Disease Concept of Alcoholism. CORLETT, J Angelo.

ALEXANDER THE GREAT
The Moral Interpretation of the 'Second Preface' to Arrian's *Anabasis*. GRAY, V J.

ALGEBRA
see also Boolean Algebra
Algebraization of Paraconsistent Logic P[1]. LEWIN, R A and MIKENBERG, I F and SCHWARZE, M G.
An Almost General Splitting Theorem for Modal Logic. KRACHT, Marcus.
The Answer to Dziobiak's Question. PALASINSKI, Marek.
Arithmetizing Uniform *NC*. ALLEN, B.
B-Varieties with Normal Free Algebras. TEMBROWSKI, Bronislaw.
Boolean Products of CW—Algebras and Pseudo-Complementation. TORRENS, Antoni.
A Calculus for the Common Rules of.... RAUTENBERG, Wolfgan.
Cloture Intervallaire et Extension Logique d'une Relation. ILLE, Pierre.
A Complete Syntactical Characterization of the Intuitionistic Logic. SKURA, Tomasz.
Complexly Fractionated Syllogistic Quantifiers. PETERSON, Philip L.
Conductive $\aleph_0$-Categorical Theories. SCHMERL, James H.
Corrections to Some Results for BCK Logics and Algebras. BUNDER, M W.
The Correspondence between George Boole and Stanley Jevons, 1863-1864. GRATTAN-GUINNESS, I.
Decidable Fragments of Field Theories. TUNG, Shih-Ping.
Definability Theorems in Normal Extensions of the Provability Logic. MAKSIMOVA, Larisa L.
Differentially Algebraic Group Chunks. PILLAY, Anand.
Domain Theory in Logical Form. ABRAMSKY, Samson.
Elementary Theory of Free Heyting Algebras. IDZIAK, Pawel M.
Embedding Brouwer Algebras in the Medvedev Lattice. SORBI, Andrea.
Equational Subsystems. WEAVER, George.
F-Multipliers and the Localization of Hilbert Algebras. BUSNEAG, Dumitru.
Finite Axiomatizability and Theories with Trivial Algebraic Closure. MACPHERSON, Dugald.
$I\Delta_3$-Algebras. FIGALLO, Aldo V.
Information Functions with Applications. SZYMANEK, Krzysztof.
Intuitionistic Sentential Calculus with Identity. LUKOWSKI, Piotr.
Johan Jacob Ferguson, geb um 1630 im Haag(?), gest vor dem 24 November 1706, vermutlich am 6 Oktober 1691 in Amsterdam. VAN MAANEN, Jan A.
Jumping with Random Reals. BARTOSZYNSKI, Tomek and JUDAH, Haim.
Kernels in N-Normal Symmetric Heyting Algebras. GALLI, A and SAGASTUME, M.
λ-Definability on Free Algebras. ZAIONC, Marek.
Lukasiewicz Logic and Wajsberg Algebras. RODRIGUEZ, Antonio J and TORRENS, Antoni.
N-Normal Factors in Finite Symmetric Heyting Algebras. GALLI, Adriana C and SAGASTUME, Marta.
Nelson Algebras Through Heyting Ones[1]:1. SENDLEWSKI, Andrzej.
A Note on Matrices for Systems of Nonsense-Logics. HALKOWSKA, Katarzyna.
A Note on the Axiomatization of Equational Classes of *n*-Valued Lukasiewicz Algebras. ADAMS, M E and CIGNOLI, R.
Notes on Modal Definability. VAN BENTHEM, Johan.
An Omniscience Principle, the König Lemma and the Hahn-Banach Theorem. ISHIHARA, Hajime.
On a Theorem of Günter Asser. CALUDE, Cristian and SÂNTEAN, Lila.
On Pure Refutation Formulations of Sentential Logics. SKURA, Tomasz.
On Regular Modal Logics with Axiom.... SWIRYDOWICZ, Kazimierz.
On Some Operators on Pseudovarieties. GRACZYNSKA, Ewa.
On the Absoluteness of Types in Boolean Valued Lattices. NISHIMURA, Hirokazu.
On the Development of Paraconsistent Logic and Da Costa's Work. LOFFREDO D'OTTAVIANO, Itala M.
On the Structure of De Morgan Monoids with Corollaries on Relevant Logic and Theories. SLANEY, John K.
Operative versus Combinatory Spaces. IVANOV, Lyubomir.
The Priestley Duality for Wajsberg Algebras. MARTÍNEZ, N G.
Reducts of (C,+,·) Which Contain +. MARKER, D and PILLAY, A.
Relatively Congruence-Distributive Subquasivarieties of Filtral Varieties. CZELAKOWSKI, Janusz.
Schanuel's Conjecture and Free Exponential Rings. MACINTYRE, Angus.
Sheaves in Universal Algebra and Model Theory: Part I. IDZIAK, Pawel M.
Sheaves in Universal Algebra and Model Theory: Part II. IDZIAK, Pawel M.
Some Nonstandard Methods Applied to Distributive Lattices. GEHRKE, Mai and INSALL, Matt and KAISER, Klaus.
Some Remarks on the Algebraic Structure of the Medvedev Lattice. SORBI, Andrea.
Some Results about Borel Sets in Descriptive Set Theory of Hyperfinite Sets. ZIVALJEVIC, Bosko.
The Theory of Descriptions Revisited. PERUZZI, Alberto.
A Topological Interpretation of Diagonalizable Algebras. HAWRANEK, Jacek.
Tores et *p*-Groupes. BOROVIK, Aleksandr Vasilievich and POIZAT, Bruno Petrovich.

ALGORITHM(S)
Computability, Complexity, Logic. BÖRGER, E.
Do the Right Thing: Studies in Limited Rationality. RUSSELL, Stuart.
Logic Programming: Proceedings of the Seventh International Conference. WARREN, David H D (ed).
Categorical Grammars Determined from Linguistic Data by Unification. BUSZKOWSKI, Wojciech and PENN, Gerald.
On the Existence of Polynomial Time Algorithms for Interpolation Problems in Propositional Logic. DALHAUS, E and ISRAELI, A and MAKOWSKY, J A.
Ordering Pairwise Comparison Structures. DELVER, R and MONSUUR, H and STORCKEN, A J A.
Schanuel's Conjecture and Free Exponential Rings. MACINTYRE, Angus.
Some Improvements to Turner's Algorithm for Bracket Abstraction. BUNDER, M W.

ALIEN
Experience of the Alien in Husserl's Phenomenology. WALDENFELS, Bernhard.

ALIENATION
Controlling Technology: Contemporary Issues. THOMPSON, William B.
Existentialism. COOPER, David E.
Femininity and Domination: Studies in the Phenomenology of Oppression. BARTKY, Sandra Lee.
Marx's Radical Critique of Capitalist Society: A Reconstruction and Critical Evaluation. ARNOLD, N Scott.
The Meaning of Socialism. LUNTLEY, Michael.
Alienation, Schools, and Society. ZHANG, Wei Rose.
The Effects of Patrol Officers' Defensiveness Toward the Outside World on Their Ethical Orientations. SHERNOCK, Stan K.
Hacia un desarrollo de la cultura y una cultura del desarrollo. ROSALES, Amán.
Hegel, Marx, Nietzsche, and the Future of Self-Alienation. SCHACHT, Richard.
Ist die Kantische Theorie eine Theorie entfremdeter Erkenntnis?. KERBER, Harald.
Romanticism, Rationality and Alienation—the Triple-H-Theory Revisited. BRUNKHORST, Hauke.

ALLAIS, M
An Outline of My Main Contributions to Economic Science. ALLAIS, Maurice.

ALLEGORY(-RIES)
Dream and Culture: An Anthropological Study of the Western Intellectual Tradition. PARMAN, Susan.
Platos Idee des Guten. FERBER, Rafael.
"La réhabilitation de l'allégorie: baroque et modernité" in *XIth International Congress in Aesthetics, Nottingham 1988*, COURT, Raymond.

ALLISON, H
Two-Steps-in-One-Proof: The Structure of the Transcendental Deduction of the Categories. EVANS, J Claude.

ALLOCATION
Philosophical Foundations of Health Education. LAURA, Ronald S.
Community Values in Vermont Health Planning. WALLACE-BRODEUR, Paul H.
Giving Voice to the Pragmatic Majority in New Jersey. HILL, T Patrick.
Health Care in Common: Setting Priorities in Oregon. GARLAND, Michael J and HASNAIN, Romana.
Public Input Into Health Care Policy: Controversy and Contribution in California. COLBERT, Treacy.
A Vision of the Health Decisions Movement. CRAWSHAW, Ralph.

ALTERITY
Alterity, Identity, Image: Contributions Towards a Theoretical Perspective. CORBEY, R (ed).
Ontology and Alterity in Merleau-Ponty. JOHNSON, Galen A (ed).
"Alterity and the Paradox of Being" in *Ontology and Alterity in Merleau-Ponty*, FROMAN, Wayne J.
"Écart: Reply to Lefort's 'Flesh and Otherness'" in *Ontology and Alterity in Merleau-Ponty*, DILLON, Martin C.
"Merleau-Ponty and Deep Ecology" in *Ontology and Alterity in Merleau-Ponty*, LANGER, Monika.

ALTERNATIVE(S)
"Arbitrary Reasons" in *Doubting: Contemporary Perspectives on Skepticism*, LUPER-FOY, Steven.
"Common Security through Alternative Defense" in *In the Interest of Peace: A Spectrum of Philosophical Views*, HAMPSCH, George.
"A Defense of Dualism" in *The Case for Dualism*, FOSTER, John.

ALTERNATIVE(S)
"The Dynamics of Alternative Realities" in *Reconsidering Psychology: Perspectives from Continental Philosophy*, GLYNN, Simon.
Cultural Literacy: Posing Queer Questions. GREENE, Maxine.
The Range of Options. ZIMMERMAN, Michael J.

ALTHUSSER, L
"Louis Althusser and Joseph D Sneed: A Strange Encounter in Philosophy of Science?" in *Imre Lakatos and Theories of Scientific Change*, BALTAS, Aristides.
Dialogo sobre humanismo y Marxismo (primera parte). SILVA CAMARENA, Juan Manuel.

ALTRUISM
Morality—What's In It For Me?: A Historical Introduction to Ethics. NELSON, William N.
Other Selves: Philosophers on Friendship. PAKALUK, Michael (ed).
"Evolutionary Altruism and Psychological Egoism" in *Logic, Methodology and Philosophy of Science, VIII*, SOBER, Elliott.
Altruism and the Avoidance of Solipsism. CHONG, Kim-Chong.
Beyond Self-Interest and Altruism: A Reconstruction of Adam Smith's Theory of Human Conduct. KHALIL, Elias L.
The Economics of (Very) Primitive Societies. TULLOCK, Gordon.
Evolutionary Naturalistic Justifications of Morality: A Matter of Faith and Works. ROTTSCHAEFER, William A.
Friendship, Self-Love, and Concern for Others in Aristotle's Ethics. MC KERLIE, Dennis.
Myth and Morality: The Love Command. HEFNER, Philip.
The Natural History of Altruism. HUNT, Morton.
The Paradox of Aquinas's Altruism: From Self-Love to Love of Others. HAYDEN, R Mary.
Reproductive Gifts and Gift Giving: The Altruistic Woman. RAYMOND, Janice G.
Warum lebt der Mensch moralisch?. BURKHARDT, Cornelia and FRANKENHÄUSER, Gerald.

AMBIGUITY
Ambiguity, Generality, and Indeterminacy: Tests and Definitions. GILLON, Brendan S.
Ambiguity, Inductive Systems, and the Modeling of Subjective Probability Judgements. MONETA, Giovanni B.
La passione dell'essere: Viaggio lungo i sentieri del nulla. IANNOTTA, Daniella.

AMERICAN
see also Latin American
American Philosophy and the Romantic Tradition. GOODMAN, Russell B.
Liberalism and American Constitutional Law. SMITH, Rogers M.
Pragmatism: From Peirce to Davidson. MURPHY, John P.
Talking Philosophy: A Wordbook. SPARKES, A W.
"American Citizenship: The Quest for Inclusion" in *The Tanner Lectures on Human Values, Volume XI*, SHKLAR, Judith.
"The Philosophical Meaning of American Civilization in World History" in *Freedom in the Modern World: Jacques Maritain, Yves R Simon, Mortimer J Adler*, NOVAK, Michael.
The Case for a New American Pragmatism. LAVINE, Thelma Z.
A Comparison of Nigerian to American Views of Bribery and Extortion in International Commerce. TSALIKIS, John and NWACHUKWU, Osita.
The Enlightenment in American Law II: The Constitution. RECK, Andrew J.
Global Injustices. MC BRIDE, William L.
Heidegger at 100, in America. KOLB, David.
Images of the Environment in Corporate America. SKORPEN, Erling.
Individual and Social Morality in Japan and the United States: Rival Conceptions of the Self. MAC INTYRE, Alasdair.
Infiniti mondi e mondo nuovo: Conquista dell'America e critica della civilità europea in Giordano Bruno. RICCI, Saverio.
Jeffersonian Ethics in Foreign Affairs: John Quincy Adams and the Moral Sentiments of a Realist. RUSSELL, Greg.
Nietzsche in America: Fashion and Fascination. VAN DER WILL, Wilfried.
Philosophy for Children and Continental Philosophy. MARTENS, Ekkehard.
A Proposal for Health Care: Revolution Not Reform. BARNET, Robert J.
Social Science as Moral Philosophy?: Reflections on Alan Wolfe's *Whose Keeper?*. MASON, John R.
Souls Without Longing. PLATT, Michael.
The Problem of the History-Making Role of Ideas in American Historical Thought (in Polish). CABAJ, Jerzy.
Walt Whitman: Jacobin Poet of American Democracy. MOSHER, Michael.
Where Are All the Pragmatist Feminists?. SEIGFRIED, Charlene Haddock.
Wishful Thinking and the Budget Deficit. FRANKLIN, Daniel Paul.

AMERICAN PHILOSOPHICAL ASSOC
PES and the APA—An Impressionistic History. MACMILLAN, C J B.

AMMONIUS
The Trouble with Fragrance. ELLIS, John.

AMORAL
Amoralism—On the Limits of Moral Thinking. SANDOE, Peter.
Amoralism: Reply to Peter Sandoe. HARE, R M.
Hume on Divine Amorality. WALLS, Jerry L.

ANACHRONISM
Legitimate Anachronism as a Problem for Intellectual History and for Philosophy. DU TOIT, André.

ANALOGICAL ARGUMENT(S)
The Emergence of Analogy: Analogical Reasoning as a Constraint Satisfaction Process. VAN DORMAEL, Jan.

ANALOGY(-GIES)
The Immutability of God in the Theology of Hans Urs Von Balthasar. O'HANLON, G F.
Within Reason: A Guide to Non-Deductive Reasoning. BURBIDGE, John.
"Tommaso Campanella: L'ente e l'analogia nella *Universalis Philosophia*" in *Razionalitá critica: nella filosofia moderna*, LAMACCHIA, Ada.
Ecosystems as Circuits: Diagrams and the Limits of Physical Analogies. TAYLOR, Peter J and BLUM, Ann S.
The Emergence of Analogy: Analogical Reasoning as a Constraint Satisfaction Process. VAN DORMAEL, Jan.
Interart Analogy: Practice and Theory in Comparing the Arts. THOMAS, Troy.
Kant's First Analogy Revisited. BUESSEM, George E.
The Ontological Status of the Principle of the Excluded Middle. STRAUSS, Daniël F M.
Structural Analogies Between Physical Systems. KROES, Peter.

ANALYSIS
see also Linguistic Analysis
Causality in Sociological Research. KARPINSKI, Jakub.
Une introduction à l'analyse du discours argumentatif. MENDENHALL, Vance.
John Craige's Mathematical Principles of Christian Theology. NASH, Richard.
Philosophical Writing: An Introduction. MARTINICH, A P.
The Rhetoric of Berkeley's Philosophy. WALMSLEY, Peter.
Trois essais sur la pensée. THEAU, Jean.
"Analysis, Language, and Concepts: The Second Paradox of Analysis" in *Philosophical Perspectives, 4: Action Theory and Philosophy of Mind, 1990*, ACKERMAN, Felicia.
"Realism, Reference and Theory" in *Key Themes in Philosophy*, HARRÉ, Rom.
Account of a Philosophical Expedition in Search of the Elusive Paradigm (in Dutch). GOUWS, A S.
Analysis as a Method in Philosophy with Special Reference to A J Ayer. SRINIVAS, K.
The Context of Discourse: Let's Not Throw the Baby Out with the Bathwater. ABRAMS, Dominic and HOGG, Michael A.
Davidson's Paratactic Analysis of Mood. MILLER, Seumas.
Discourse: Definitions and Contradictions. PARKER, Ian.
Discourse: Noun, Verb or Social Practice?. POTTER, Jonathan (and others).
The Economic Analysis of Institutions. RICKETTS, Martin.
Emergenz Bausteine für eine Begriffsexplikation. STÖCKLER, Manfred.
Frege and the Analysis of Thoughts. GARAVASO, Pieranna.
G H Bantock as Educational Philosopher. BARRIE, John A.
Health Policy Analysis as Ideology and as Utopian Rhetoric. MILLER, Irwin.
L'explicite et l'implicite dans la conception du signe chez Hobbes. POLIAKOV, Igor.
Leibniz's "Analysis of Multitude and Phenomena into Unities and Reality". RUTHERFORD, Donald.
A Normative Theory of Teaching. POPP, Jerome.
A Problem Solving Interpretation of Argument Analysis. BERNSTEIN, David.
Real Things: Discourse, Context and Practice. PARKER, Ian.
Die Rolle der Philosophiegeschichte im "Neuen philosophischen Denken" in der UdSSR. VAN DER ZWEERDE, Evert.
Synthetic Mechanics Revisited. BURGESS, John P.
Verisimilitude Based on Concept Analysis. ORLOWSKA, Ewa.
Weak Axioms of Determinacy and Subsystems of Analysis II. TANAKA, Kazuyuki.
What's It All About? The Critical Method of Analysis as Applied to Drama. CLEARY JR, Donald L.

ANALYTIC
The Analytic Tradition: Philosophical Quarterly Monographs, Volume 1. BELL, David (ed).
Classics of Analytic Philosophy. AMMERMAN, Robert R (ed).
Epistemology and Skepticism: An Enquiry into the Nature of Epistemology. CHATALIAN, George.
Frege and Other Philosophers. DUMMETT, Michael.
Frege in Perspective. WEINER, Joan.
Has Semantics Rested on a Mistake?. WETTSTEIN, Howard.
Una lettura idealistica della "Analitica Trascendentale". BELLINI, Ornella.
Il Paradigma del Sapere. LENTINI, Luigi.
Philosophical Logic. STRAWSON, P F (ed).
Resurrecting Marx: The Analytical Marxists on Freedom, Exploitation, and Justice. GORDON, David.
"Analytic and Pragmatist Aesthetics" in *XIth International Congress in Aesthetics, Nottingham 1988*, SHUSTERMAN, Richard.
"Clarity" in *The Analytic Tradition: Philosophical Quarterly Monographs, Volume 1*, HART, W D.

ANALYTIC

"Does Analytic Aesthetics Rest on a Mistake?" in XIth International Congress in Aesthetics, Nottingham 1988, LUDEKING, K.
"Through a Glass Darkly: Vagueness in the Metaphysics of the Analytic Tradition" in *The Analytic Tradition: Philosophical Quarterly Monographs, Volume 1*, SACKS, Mark.
Context Principle, Fruitfulness of Logic and the Cognitive Value of Arithmetic in Frege. RUFFINO, Marco Antonio.
Dummett and the Origins of Analytical Philosophy, or the Philosophy of Thought vs Philosophy of Language (in German). DÖLLING, Evelyn and DÖLLING, Johannes.
De Kant-interpretatie van Evert Willem Beth. PEIJNENBURG, J.
The Moderns in an Introductory Analytic Course. DICKER, Georges.
Das neue (post-analytische) Interesse an der Präanalytischen Philosophie. NAGL, Ludwig.
Orlowska's Relevant Implications, Relevant Logics and Analytic Implication. GIAMBRONE, Steve.
Per un'analisi del discorso dichiarativo. CELANO, Bruno.
Prior's Disease. USBERTI, Gabriele.
Questions of "Analytical" and "Non-Analytical" Philosophy (in Serbo Croatian). JAKOVLJEVIC, Dragan.
Sobre cuatro obras de Mauricio Beuchot. PEÑA, Lorenzo.
Some Remarks on the Linguistic Turn. PERUZZI, Alberto.
Tautology: How Not to Use a Word. DREBEN, Burton and FLOYD, Juliet.
The Transcendental Method of Metaphysics of Coreth and Muck and Its Relation to Analytic Philosophy. RUNGGALDIER, Edmund.
Wittgenstein's Gift to Contemporary Analytic Philosophy of Religion. KELLENBERGER, J.

ANALYTIC STATEMENT(S)

Why are Definitions True?. SKIDMORE, Arthur.

ANALYTICITY

Analiticidad, empirismo y verdad necesaria. HERNÁNDEZ IGLESIAS, Manuel Angel.

ANAPHORA

Instantial Terms, Anaphora and Arbitrary Objects. KING, Jeffrey C.

ANARCHISM

Anarchism and Feminism. MOODY, Thomas E.
Aufklärung und Reform. SCHNEIDERS, Werner.
Métaphysique radicale. MARGOLIS, Joseph.
Sartre and Political Legitimacy. KNEE, Philip.

ANARCHY

Bertrand Russell. ALCARO, Mario.
Statism and Anarchy. SHATZ, Marshall (ed).
"Construindo a 'ordem anárquica". PIOZZI, Patrícia.

ANATOMY

The Anatomist and the Painter: The Continuity of Hume's *Treatise* and *Essays*. IMMERWAHR, John.

ANAXAGORAS

The Book of Anaxagoras. BRUMBAUGH, Robert S.

ANAXIMANDER

Cosmic Justice in Anaximander. ENGMANN, Joyce.

ANAXIMENES

Non-Technical *Pisteis* in Aristotle and Anaximenes. MIRHADY, David.

ANCIENT

see also Greek
"Also sprach Herakleitos". WOHLFART, Günter.
Aristotle on Sleep and Dreams. GALLOP, David (trans).
The Chain of Change: A Study of Aristotle's "Physics" VII. WARDY, Robert.
Chinese Texts and Philosophical Contexts. ROSEMONT JR, Henry (ed).
The Chronology of Plato's Dialogues. BRANDWOOD, Leonard.
Das Ethische in der Rhetorik des Aristoteles. WÖRNER, Markus Hilmar.
Geschichte, Freiheit und Struktur. RUMPEL, Roland.
The Great Goddess and the Aistian Mythical World. VYCINAS, Vincent.
Hellenic and Christian Studies. ARMSTRONG, A H.
Matter, Morals and Medicine: The Ancient Greek Origins of Science, Ethics and the Medical Profession. CARELLA, Michael Jerome.
Mystical Monotheism: A Study in Ancient Platonic Theology. KENNEY, John Peter.
Myth and Philosophy: A Contest of Truths. HATAB, Lawrence J.
On Duties: Cicero. GRIFFIN, M T (ed).
On Homosexuality: Lysis, Phaedrus, and Symposium. JOWETT, Benjamin (trans).
The Origins of Aristotelian Science. FEREJOHN, Michael.
Philosophy in World Perspective: A Comparative Hermeneutic of the Major Theories. DILWORTH, David A.
Philosophy of the Ancients. RICKEN, Friedo.
Philosophy's Journey: From the Presocratics to the Present (Second Edition). KOLENDA, Konstantin.
Plato's "Parmenides". MEINWALD, Constance C.
Platonic Piety. MORGAN, Michael L.
Platos Idee des Guten. FERBER, Rafael.
Psychology (Companions to Ancient Thought: 2). EVERSON, Stephen (ed).
Reflexion und Metareflexion bei Platon und Fichte. ZEHNPFENNIG, Barbara.
Socrates: An Annotated Bibliography. NAVIA, Luis E.
Zetetic Skepticism. UMPHREY, Stewart.
"Ancient Ethics" in *A Companion to Ethics*, LARUE, Gerald A.
"Ethics in Ancient Greece" in *A Companion to Ethics*, ROWE, Christopher.
"Roman Humanism" in *The Question of Humanism: Challenges and Possibilities*, BOOTH, Allan.
Accessible Hellenistic Philosophy. SHARPLES, R W.
L'aporia della kinesis in Aristotele. ROCCARO, Giuseppe.
The Appropriation of Significance: The Concept of *Kang-Tung*in the *I Ching*. TONG, Lik Kuen.
Aristotelian Mimesis Reevaluated. HALLIWELL, Stephen.
Aristotle and Protagoras: The Good Human Being as the Measure of Goods. GOTTLIEB, Paula.
Aristotle and the Spheres of Motivation: *De Anima* III. HUTCHINSON, D S.
Aristotle on Dialectic. HAMLYN, D W.
Aristotle on Justice, Equality and the Rule of Law. QUINN, Michael.
Aristotle on Personality and Some Implications for Friendship. REINER, Paula.
Aristotle on the Function of Man in Relation to Eudaimonia. HESTER, Marcus.
Aristotle's Apodeictic Syllogism. JOHNSTON, David.
Aristotle's Definition of Motion and its Ontological Implications. BRAGUE, Rémi and ADLER, Pierre and D'URSEL, Laurent.
Aristotle, the Direction Problem, and the Structure of the Sublunar Realm. KRONZ, Frederick.
The Book of Anaxagoras. BRUMBAUGH, Robert S.
Character and Explanation in Aristotle's *Ethics* and *Poetics*. DESLAURIERS, Marguerite.
The Contending Among the Hundred Schools of Thought During the Warring States Period. ZEHUA, Liu.
Cosmic Justice in Anaximander. ENGMANN, Joyce.
Death Is One of Two Things. RUDEBUSCH, George.
The Driving Ratio in Plato's Divided Line. DREHER, John Paul.
Eleatics Against Each Other (in Hungarian). KAMPIS, György.
L'epiglottide nell'antichità tra medicina e filosofia. REPICI, Luciana.
Eristic, Antilogic, Sophistic, Dialectic: Plato's Demarcation of Philosophy from Sophistry. NEHAMAS, Alexander.
Friendship, Self-Love, and Concern for Others in Aristotle's Ethics. MC KERLIE, Dennis.
From Pyrrhonism to Post-Modernism. GLIDDEN, David K.
The Good in Plato's *Gorgias*. WHITE, F C.
A Great Intellectual Current Worthy of National Pride. CHANGLU, Qiao.
Hamartia, Akrasia: Ignorance, and Blame in Aristotle's Philosophy. CYZYK, Mar.
Heraclitus: Heidegger's 1943 Lecture Held at Freiburg University. FRINGS, Manfred S.
Homer's Contest: Nietzsche on Politics and the State in Ancient Greece. SMITH, Bruce.
Individuo y acción en el pensamiento griego. RODA, Roberto.
Is Aristotle an Internal Realist? Nussbaum and the Divine Perspective. EARLS, C Anthony.
L'imagination au pouvoir. BODÉÜS, Richard.
Lucian: The Sale of Lives (in Hebrew). SCOLNICOV, Samuel (trans).
I metodi della metafisica platonico-accademica "generalizzante" ed "elementarizzante" nei libri "M" e "N".... CATTANEI, E.
A Middle Platonic Reading of Plato's Theory of Recollection. SCHRENK, Lawrence P.
Non-Technical *Pisteis* in Aristotle and Anaximenes. MIRHADY, David.
La notion de non-être dans l'histoire de la langue grecque archaïque. LÉTOUBLON, Françoise.
On Ancients and Moderns. CROPSEY, Joseph.
On the Alleged Impossibility of a Science of Accidents in Aristotle. URBANAS, Alban.
On the Form and Authenticity of the *Lysis*. TEJERA, V.
On the Functional Unity of the Four Dimensions of Thought in the *Book of Changes*. LIU, Shu-Hsien.
Ontologia e creazione in Filone Alessandrino: Dialogo con Giovanni Reale e Roberto Radice. MARTÍN, Josè Pablo.
Le origini dell'ateismo antico (quinta parte). ZEPPI, Stelio.
Osservazioni sul *Filebo*. MASI, Giuseppe.
Paideia Helénica. FREIRE, António.
Parental Nature and Stoic Οικειοσισ. BLUNDELL, Mary Whitlock.
Per una rilettura dei libri "M" e "N" della *Metafisica* di Aristotele alla luce delle "dottrine non scritte" di Platone. CATTANEI, Elisabetta.
Perception and Evaluation: Aristotle on the Moral Imagination. HANKINSON, R J.
Philosophical Anthropology in Greek Antiquity. GHOSE, A M.
Philosophie ancienne et médiévale. MC EVOY, James.
Plato and Archytas in the Seventh Letter. LLOYD, G E R.
Plato and Aristotle on Division and Definition. DESLAURIERS, Marguerite.
Plato's Gods. PEHRSON, C W P.
Plato's Line Revisited: The Pedagogy of Complete Reflection. WOOD, Robert E.
Plato's Reply to the 'Worst Difficulty' Argument of the *Parmenides*: *Sophist* 248a-249d. MC PHERRAN, Mark.

ANCIENT
Platonismo vivo: (Debate actual sobre Platón, la Academia y las Ideas). *JUÁREZ, Agustin Uña.*
Presencia de Grecia y de Roma clásicas en la Revolución francesa de 1789. RECIO GARCÍA, Tomás.
Προαιρεσις in Epictetus. DOBBIN, Robert.
Réflexiones sur l'idéee de la guerre dans la philosophie présocratique. FREUND, Julien.
Riflessioni sulla fondazione dell'assioma parmenideo. GRAZIANI, Andrea.
Roberts on Responsibility for Action and Character in the *Nicomachean Ethics*. BRICKHOUSE, Thomas C.
Le rôle de l'imagination dans le mouvement animal et l'action humaine chez Aristotle. DUGRÉ, François.
Scepticism and Relativity. BARNES, Jonathan.
The Seasonal Structure Underlying the Arrangement of the Hexagrams in the *Yijing*. ANDERSON, Allan W.
Self-Predication and Synonymy. SILVERMAN, Allan.
Semantica aristotelica e sillogistica modale. MARIANI, Mauro.
Sense-Experience and the Argument for Recollection in Plato's *Phaedo*. BEDU-ADDO, J T.
Simon and Socrates. BRUMBAUGH, Robert S.
Sir Karl Popper on Presocratic Philosophers (in Hungarian). STEIGER, Kornel.
Socrates and Asclepius: The Final Words. SANTILLI, Paul C.
Socrates' Critique of Cognitivism. MATSON, Wallace I and LEITE, Adam.
Socrates, the Craft Analogy, and Science. GRAHAM, Daniel W.
Socratic Reason and Socratic Revelation. MC PHERRAN, Mark L.
Some Observations About Plato's *Phaedo*. MASCHLER, Chaninah.
Sophoclean Logic (*Antigone* 175-81). O'SULLIVAN, Neil.
Le statut de l'argument dialectiques d'après *Réf soph* 11, 172a9-15. DORION, Louis-André.
Structural Motifs in the Arrangement of the 64 *Gua* in the *Zhouyi*. SCHULZ, Larry J.
Struttura e finalità dei dialoghi platonici: Che cosa significa "venire in soccorso al discorso"?. SZLEZÁK, Thomas A.
The Supremely Happy Life in Aristotle's *Nicomachean Ethics*. CURZER, Howard J.
La teoria aristotelica dell'apodissi. SAINATI, Vittorio.
The Heraclitus' Lesson (in Portuguese). SANTOS, M C A dos.
The Initial Form of Empiristic and Aprioristic Conception of Knowledge on the World (in Polish). MORAWIEC, E.
Theoria, Aisthesis, Mimesis and Doxa. MÉCHOULAN, Éric.
La transformation de la philosophie de Platon dans le "Prologos" d'Albinus. NETSCHKE-HENTSCHKE, Ada Babette.
Travail et nature dans l'Antiquité. MULLER, Robert.
The Truth about Lies in Plato's *Republic*. PAGE, Carl.
Two Varieties of Temperance in the *Gorgias*. CURZER, Howard J.
Unifying Plato: Charles Kahn on Platonic *Prolepsis*. GRISWOLD JR, Charles L.
The Unjust Treatment of Polemarchus. PAGE, Carl.
Variações sobre o *De Interpretatione*, de Aristóteles. ROSA, Joaquim Coelho.
Vlastos on the Unity of Virtue: Why Pauline Predication Will Not Save the Biconditionality Thesis. WAKEFIELD, Jerome C.
War Demokrits Weltbild mechanistisch und antiteleologisch?. HIRSCH, Ulrike.
The Wisdom of Plato's Aristophanes. SALMAN, Charles.
Yet More on *Meno* 82a-85d. FOWLER, D H.

ANDERSON, T
Response to Tyler Anderson. SMITH, Huston.

ANDROCENTRISM
Ecofeminism and Androcentric Epistemology. DURAN, Jane.

ANENCEPHALIC(S)
"Anencephalics as Organ Donors" in *Biomedical Ethics Reviews, 1989*, THOMASMA, David C.
"Should Abnormal Fetuses Be Brought to Term for the Sole Purpose of Providing Infant Transplant Organs?" in *Biomedical Ethics Reviews, 1989*, GRABER, Glenn C.

ANGELO, R
Growing Up on Screen—Images of Instruction. HANSEN, Karen.

ANGER
Anger as a Vice: A Maimonidean Critique of Aristotle's Ethics. FRANK, Daniel H.
What is Wrong With Wicked Feelings?. ROBERTS, Robert C.

ANGLO-AMERICAN
Anglo-American Philosophy of Law: An Introduction to Its Development and Outcome. LEVY, Beryl Harold.

ANGUISH
Existentialism. COOPER, David E.
Sartre on Anguish. JAMBOR, Mishka.

ANIMAL EXPERIMENTATION
Animal Experimentation: The Consensus Changes. LANGLEY, Gill (ed).
Animal Experimentation: The Moral Issue. BAIRD, Robert M (ed).
Biomedical Ethics Reviews, 1990. HUMBER, James M (ed).
Das Tier in der Moral. WOLF, Ursula.
"Federal Laws and Policies Governing Animal Research: Their History, Nature, and Adequacy" in *Biomedical Ethics Reviews, 1990*, ROLLIN, Bernard E.
"NIH Guidelines and Animal Welfare" in *Biomedical Ethics Reviews, 1990*, RUSSOW, Lilly-Marlene.
Animal Experimentation and the Argument from Limited Resources. FINK, Charles K.
The Distinction Between Equality in Moral Status and Deserving Equal Consideration. DE GRAZIA, David.
Response to Squadrito's "Commentary: Interests and Equal Moral Status". DE GRAZIA, David.

ANIMAL LIBERATION
Animal Experimentation: The Consensus Changes. LANGLEY, Gill (ed).
A Morally Deep World: An Essay on Moral Significance and Environmental Ethics. JOHNSON, Lawrence E.
Animal Liberation as a Valid Response to Structural Violence. LISZT, Amy.
Animal Liberators are Not Anti-Science. MAGEL, Charles.
A Clue for a Classical Realist Contribution to the Debate Over the Value of Animals. KLONOSKI, Richard J.
Response to Finsen's "Response to Lizst's Animal Liberation as a Valid Response to Structural Violence". LISZT, Amy.
Response to Lizst's "Animal Liberation as a Valid Response to Structural Violence". FINSEN, Susan.
Singer's Cookbook. JOHNSON, Edward.

ANIMAL RIGHTS
Animal Experimentation: The Consensus Changes. LANGLEY, Gill (ed).
Animal Experimentation: The Moral Issue. BAIRD, Robert M (ed).
A Morally Deep World: An Essay on Moral Significance and Environmental Ethics. JOHNSON, Lawrence E.
"Nothing of the Origin and Destiny of Cats": The Remainder of the Logos. ROSE, John M.
Animals in Biomedical Research: The Undermining Effect of the Rhetoric of the Besieged. GLUCK, John P and KUBACKI, Steven R.
Do Animals Feel Pain?. HARRISON, Peter.
Do Animals Have Rights?. MACHAN, Tibor R.
Ecofeminism and the Eating of Animals. ADAMS, Carol J.
Institutional Animal Care and Use Committees and the Moderate Position. STEPHENSON, Wendell.
The Moral Status of Animals and Their Use in Research: A Philosophical Review. DEGRAZIA, David.
Moral Theories, Impartiality, and the Status of Non-Rational, Sentient Beings. FILICE, Carlo.
On Utilitarianism and Utilitarian Attitudes. MILLER, Harlan B.
Prejudice and Progress in Animal and Environmental Protection. FOX, Michael W.
Pythagoras—The First Animal Rights Philosopher. VIOLIN, Mary Ann.
Reason and Reality Revisited. PLUHAR, Evelyn.
Reply to Stephenson on Biomedical Research. GENDIN, Sidney.
Souls and Sentientism. RYDER, Richard D.
Stewardship: Whose Creation Is It Anyway?. BARAD-ANDRADE, Judith.
Toward An Ecological Ethic of Care. CURTIN, Deane.
Your Daughter or Your Dog? A Feminist Assessment of the Animal Research Issue. SLICER, Deborah.

ANIMAL(S)
Animal Experimentation: The Consensus Changes. LANGLEY, Gill (ed).
Animal Experimentation: The Moral Issue. BAIRD, Robert M (ed).
Biomedical Ethics Reviews, 1987. HUMBER, James M (ed).
Existence et Subjectivité: Études de Psychologie Phénoménologique. THINÈS, Georges.
Das Tier in der Moral. WOLF, Ursula.
"The 'Frankenstein Thing': The Moral Impact of Genetic Engineering of Agricultural Animals" in *Agricultural Bioethics: Implications of Agricultural Biotechnology*, ROLLIN, B E.
"Am I Obsessed by Bobby? (Humanism of the Other Animal)" in *Re-Reading Levinas*, LLEWELYN, John.
"Animal Parts, Human Wholes: On the Use of Animals as a Source of Organs for Human Transplants" in *Biomedical Ethics Reviews, 1987*, FREY, R G.
"Animals as a Source of Human Transplant Organs" in *Biomedical Ethics Reviews, 1987*, NELSON, James L.
"Animals" in *A Companion to Ethics*, GRUEN, Lori.
"The Case against bGH" in *Agricultural Bioethics: Implications of Agricultural Biotechnology*, COMSTOCK, Gary L.
"Ordinary Animals, Language Animals and Verbal Tradition" in *Harré and His Critics*, REYNOLDS, Vernon.
"The Rights and Wrongs of Animal Use for Human Organ Transplant" in *Biomedical Ethics Reviews, 1987*, WERNER, Richard.
Animal Faith, Puritanism, and the Schutz-Gurwitsch Debate: A Commentary. LYMAN, Stanford M.
A Clue for a Classical Realist Contribution to the Debate Over the Value of Animals. KLONOSKI, Richard J.

ANIMAL(S)

Comment on Romain's "Feminist Reflections on Humans and Other Domestic Animals. RUD JR, Anthony G.
Commentary: Interests and Equal Moral Status. SQUADRITO, Kathy.
Concept Attribution in Nonhuman Animals. ALLEN, Collin and HAUSER, Marc D.
Descartes on Sensations and 'Animal Minds'. SENCERZ, Stefan.
The Distinction Between Equality in Moral Status and Deserving Equal Consideration. DE GRAZIA, David.
Do Animals Have Rights?. MACHAN, Tibor R.
Domesticated and Then Some. DURAN, Jane.
Faustian Phenomena: Teleology in Goethe's Interpretation of Plants and Animals. CORNELL, John F.
Feminist Reflections on Humans and Other Domestic Animals. ROMAIN, Dianne.
Harrison on Animal Pain. HOUSE, Ian.
Multiple Realities in Santayana's Last Puritan. VAITKUS, Steven.
Personal Identity and Brain Transplants. SNOWDON, P F.
Response to Squadrito's "Commentary: Interests and Equal Moral Status". DE GRAZIA, David.
So Animal a Human..., or the Moral Relevance of Being An Omnivore. GEORGE, Kathryn Paxton.
Species, Individuals, and Domestication: A Commentary on Jane Duran's "Domesticated and Then Some". VARNER, Gary E.
Stewardship: Whose Creation Is It Anyway?. BARAD-ANDRADE, Judith.
Thoughtful Brutes: The Ascription of Mental Predicates to Animals in Locke's "Essay". SQUADRITO, Kathleen.
Utilitarian Killing, Replacement, and Rights. PLUHAR, Evelyn.
Werkzeugproduktion im Tierreich und menschliche Werkzeugproduktion. BEURTON, Peter.
Why Personal Identity Is Animal Identity. CARTER, William R.

ANIMATION

Material Beings. VAN INWAGEN, Peter.
Machines as Persons?. CHERRY, Christopher.

ANKERSMIT, F

Historiography and Postmodernism: Reconsiderations. ZAGORIN, Perez.

ANOMALY(-LIES)

Anomalism, Supervenience, and Davidson on Content-Individuation. ROWLANDS, Mark.
An Anomaly in the D-N Model of Explanation. BLUM, Alex.
Functional Support for Anomalous Monism. EDWARDS, Jim.

ANOMIE

Nomologie et anomie: lecture de deux antinomies. ZANETTI, Véronique.

ANSCOMBE, E

Moral Obligation and Metaphysics. COOKE, Vincent M.

ANSCOMBE, G

Anscombian and Cartesian Scepticism. HAMILTON, Andy.
Ultimate Ends in Practical Reasoning. MAC DONALD, Scott.

ANSELM

God and Subjectivity. GALGAN, Gerald J.
The Caterus Objection. FORGIE, J William.
Foi et intelligence dans l'"unique arguments": Un plan pour "Proslogion II-IV". LABBÉ, Y.
In Defense of Anselm. ASPENSON, Steven S.
Libertad y necesidad en el 'Cur Deus Homo' de San Anselmo de Canterbury (segunda parte). CORTI, E C.
Offices and God. HUGLY, Philip and SAYWARD, Charles.

ANTHROPIC

Residual Natural Evil and Anthropic Reasoning. MC LEAN, Murdith.

ANTHROPOCENTRISM

Animal Experimentation: The Moral Issue. BAIRD, Robert M (ed).
Cosmos and Anthropos: A Philosophical Interpretation of the Anthropic Cosmological Principle. HARRIS, Errol E.
"Historia" de la naturaleza versus "Naturaleza" de la historia. LEAL, Fernando A.
Antirealism and Realist Claims of Invariance. ELDER, Crawford L.
Leopold's "Means and Ends in Wild Life Management". HARGROVE, Eugene C and CALLICOTT, J Baird.
Masaryk's "Anthropism" (in Czechoslovakian). NOVY, Lubomir.
Nietzsche's Environmental Ethics. HALLMAN, Max O.
What is the Explanandum of the Anthropic Principle?. WILSON, Patrick A.

ANTHROPOLOGY

Blaise Pascals: "Pensées" (1656-1662) Systematische 'Gedanken' über. KIRSCH, Ulrich.
Claude Lévi-Strauss. LEACH, Edmund.
David Hume: Historiker und Philosoph. LÜTHE, Rudolf.
Kierkegaards Phänomenologie der Freiheitserfahrung. DISSE, Jörg.
Teoria e interpretazione: Per un'epistemologia delle scienze umane. BORUTTI, Silvana.
Varieties of Social Explanation: An Introduction to the Philosophy of Social Science. LITTLE, Daniel.

"Oedipus and the Dogon: The Myth of Modernity Interrogated" in I, We and Body: First Joint Symposium of Philosophers from Africa and from the Netherlands, OOSTERLING, Henk A F.
Antropología del trabajo según la Encíclica "Laborem Excercens". QUESADA GUARDIA, Annabelle.
Antropología y Agresión: notas para un análisis filosófico. FERNÁNDEZ TRESGUERRES, Alfonso.
Aspectos antropológicos de la fecundación in vitro. CAFFARRA, Carlos.
Concepts of Culture: Lonergan and the Anthropologists. KLEIN, Dennis.
Evans-Pritchard on Persons and Their Cattle-Clocks: A Note on the Anthropological Account of Man. CHANDRA, Suresh.
History and Historical Anthropology. GOUREVITCH, Aron I.
La loi de vérité. POULAIN, Jacques.
La práctica tecnológica. HERRERA JIMÉNEZ, Rodolfo.
El principio antrópico. PEREZ DE LABORDA, A.
Recent Work on Ethical Relativism. STEWART, Robert M and THOMAS, Lynn L.
To the History of Glory and Fall of the Book "Civilization at the Crossroads" after August 1968 (in Czechoslovakian). SINDELAR, Jan.
Transcultural Dialogue and the Problem of the Concept of Ultimate Reality and Meaning. SINGLETON, Michael.
Zande Logic and Western Logic. JENNINGS, Richard C.

ANTHROPOMORPHISM

Do Animals Have Rights?. MACHAN, Tibor R.
Il problema teologico nel pensiero di Heidegger. PENATI, G.

ANTI-ART

"Anti-Art and Anti-Criticism—The Killers of Art or its Rescuers?" in XIth International Congress in Aesthetics, Nottingham 1988, SEPÄNMAA, Yrö.
"The New Anti-Aestheticism" in XIth International Congress in Aesthetics, Nottingham 1988, GOLASZEWSKA, Maria.

ANTI-SEMITISM

Thinking the Unthinkable: Meanings of the Holocaust. GOTTLIEB, Roger S (ed).

ANTIFOUNDATIONALISM

The Bellman's Map: Does Antifoundationalism Entail Incommensurability and Relativism?. CHURCHILL, John.

ANTINOMY(-MIES)

The Logical Structure of the First Antinomy. LOPARIC, Zeljko.
Nomologie et anomie: lecture de deux antinomies. ZANETTI, Véronique.
La primera antinomia kantiana: el origen y los límites del Universo. PUYAU, Hermes.
Saving Faith from Kant's Remarkable Antinomy. QUINN, Philip L.

ANTIQUITY

Die Wiederkehr im Unterschied. PEETZ, Siegbert.

ANTIREALISM

Anti-Realism and Skepticism in Ethics. SCHUELER, G F.
Anti-Realism Untouched. MELIA, Joseph.
Antirealism and Realist Claims of Invariance. ELDER, Crawford L.
Coherence, Anti-realism, and the Vienna Circle. YOUNG, James O.
Interpreting State Reduction from the Practices-up. CORDERO, Alberto.
The Logical Status of Modal Reductionism. MOSER, Paul K and VANDER NAT, Arnold.
The Participant Irrealist At Large in the Laboratory. HACKING, Ian.
Realism About What?. JONES, Roger.
Realisms. LEVIN, Michael.
Verificationism and Anti-Realism. ROGERSON, Kenneth.
'Just More Theory': A Manoeuvre in Putnam's Model-Theoretic Argument for Antirealism. TAYLOR, Barry.

ANTISCIENCE

A Historico-Philosophical Investigation of Anti-Science: The Phenomenological Encounter. RAINA, Dhruv.

ANXIETY

Readings in Existential Psychology and Psychiatry. HOELLER, Keith (ed).
What is History? And Other Late Unpublished Writings (The Collected Works of Eric Voegelin, Vol 28). HOLLWECK, Thomas A (ed).

APA

see American Philosophical Association

APARTHEID

Umuntu Ngumuntu Ngabantu: An African Concept of Humanity. SHUTTE, Augustine.

APATHY

A Case for Apathy. NEUMANN, Michael.

APE(S)

What Makes Us So Different from the Apes?. LAYNG, Tony.

APEL, K

"Linguistics as a Borderline Case" in Abeunt Studia in Mores: A Festschrift for Helga Doblin, MERRILL, Sarah A Bishop.
Ist die Kantische Theorie eine Theorie entfremdeter Erkenntnis?. KERBER, Harald.
La reivindicación de la racionalidad en K O Apel. SMILG VIDAL, Norberto.

APHASIA
Aphasia and Inner Language. LANTÉRI-LAURA, Georges and WALKER, R Scott.
Aphasia—The Worm's Eye View of a Philosophic Patient and the Medical Establishment. ALEXANDER, Edwin.

APHORISM(S)
Nietzsches Scheitern am Werk. HELLER, Edmund.
"Ruminations": Notes de lecture sur quelques aphorismes de Nietzsche. BLONDEL, Eric.

APOCALYPSE
Political Openings. WOOD, David.
Providence and Political Responsibility: The Nature of Praxis in an Age of Apocalypse. LAKELAND, Paul.

APOLOGETICS
Apology, Speculation, and Philosophy's Fate. VAN NESS, Peter H.
Filosofía cristiana y apologética en Mons Audino Rodríguez y Olmos. CATURELLI, Alberto.
Michel de Montaigne: La "nottola" dell'Umanesimo francese. LONGO, Margherita.

APPARITIONS
The Limits of Influence: Psychokinesis and the Philosophy of Science. BRAUDE, Stephen E (ed).
Contagious Folly: *An Adventure* and Its Skeptics. CASTLE, Terry.

APPEARANCE(S)
The Unity of Kant's "Critique of Pure Reason": Experience, Language, and Knowledge. WILLIAMS, T C.
"The Appearance of a Material Object" in *Philosophical Perspectives, 4: Action Theory and Philosophy of Mind, 1990*, O'SHAUGHNESSY, Brian.
Osservazioni sul bello naturale e sul bello artistico in filosofia. FRANCHI, Alfredo.

APPERCEPTION
Kant's Transcendental Psychology. KITCHER, Patricia.
The Unity of Understanding: A Study in Kantian Problems. SCHWYZER, Hubert.
"Apperception and Epistemic Responsibility" in *Central Themes in Early Modern Philosophy*, KITCHER, Patricia.
Der Gegenstand der Vorstellungen und die transzendentale Apperzeption. LÓPEZ-FERNÁNDEZ, Alvaro.
Kant in Hegels begtipsleer. DE VOS, L.

APPETITE(S)
The Many Appetites of Thomas Hobbes. HURLEY, Paul.

APPIAH, A
Realism Without Representation: A Response to Appiah. DEVITT, Michael.

APPLICATION(S)
A Companion to Ethics. SINGER, Peter (ed).
Negotation Games: Applying Game Theory to Bargaining and Arbitration. BRAMS, Steven J.
Philosophical Applications of Free Logic. LAMBERT, Karel (ed).
Philosophy: Theory and Practice. THIROUX, Jacques P.
Universalism versus Communitarianism: Contemporary Debates in Ethics. RASMUSSEN, David.
"Environmental Ethics" in *A Companion to Ethics*, ELLIOT, Robert.
Ecological Feminism and Ecosystem Ecology. WARREN, Karen J and CHENEY, Jim.
The Ethical Theory of Peter A Bertocci. PADGETT, Jack F.
Healthy Scepticism. FRANKLIN, James.
Island Biogeography, Species-Area Curves, and Statistical Errors: Applied Biology and Scientific Rationality. SHRADER-FRECHETTE, Kristin.
El principio de exclusión y sus aplicaciones. GARZÓN, León.
Remarks on Marketing Ethics. BRENNAN, Bernard F.

APPLIED ETHICS
Applying Ethics: A Text with Readings (Third Edition). OLEN, Jeffrey.
Kants Kategorischer Imperativ als Leitfaden humaner Praxis. NISTERS, Thomas.
"Abortion" in *A Companion to Ethics*, WARREN, Mary Anne.
"Animals" in *A Companion to Ethics*, GRUEN, Lori.
"Crime and Punishment" in *A Companion to Ethics*, TEN, C L.
"Euthanasia" in *A Companion to Ethics*, KUHSE, Helga.
"Personal Relationships" in *A Companion to Ethics*, LA FOLLETTE, Hugh.
"Politics and the Problem of Dirty Hands" in *A Companion to Ethics*, COADY, C A J.
"Sex" in *A Companion to Ethics*, BELLIOTTI, Raymond A.
"War and Peace" in *A Companion to Ethics*, MC MAHAN, Jeff.
"World Poverty" in *A Companion to Ethics*, DOWER, Nigel.
Applied Ethics and Meta-Philosophy. DAVSON-GALLE, Peter.
How Is Applied Philosophy to Be Applied?. KLINEFELTER, Donald S.
Is there an Ethics of Computing?. BROWN, Geoffrey.
The Market for Bodily Parts: A Response to Ruth Chadwick. TADD, G V.
Possibilities of Consensus: Toward Democratic Moral Discourse. JENNINGS, Bruce.
Rights-Talk Will Not Sort Out Child-Abuse: Comment on Archard on Parental Rights. MIDGLEY, Mary.
The Role of Moral Intuition in Applied Ethics: A Consideration of Positions of Peirce and Strike and Soltis. MC CARTHY, Christine.
Should Philosophy be Applied?. NESBITT, Winston.
Specifying Norms as a Way to Resolve Concrete Ethical Problems. RICHARDSON, Henry S.

APPLIED PHILOSOPHY
Applied Ethics and Meta-Philosophy. DAVSON-GALLE, Peter.
Homunculus Trouble, or, What Is Applied Philosophy?. MIDGLEY, Mary.
How Is Applied Philosophy to Be Applied?. KLINEFELTER, Donald S.
Should Philosophy be Applied?. NESBITT, Winston.

APPRAISAL(S)
Ethical Dilemmas in Performance Appraisal Revisited. LONGENECKER, Clinton and LUDWIG, Dean.

APPRECIATION
"Appreciation and Justification" in *XIth International Congress in Aesthetics, Nottingham 1988*, FEAGIN, Susan.
"The Principle of Transcendence and the Foundation of Axiology" in *Logic and Ethics*, GRZEGORCZYK, Andrzej.
DBAE: Complaints, Reminiscences, and Response. BROUDY, Harry S.

APPREHENSION
Tomás de Aquino: la aprehensión del acto de ser (II). GONZÁLEZ, Orestes J.

APPROPRIATION
When is Original Appropriation *Required*?. SCHMIDTZ, David.

APPROXIMATION
"Approximation and the Two Ideas of Truth" in *Studies on Mario Bunge's "Treatise"*, NOWAKOWA, Izabella and NOWAK, Leszek.
"Newtonianism Before and After the Einsteinian Revolution" in *Some Truer Method*, AGASSI, Joseph.
"Realism, Approximate Truth, and Philosophical Method" in *Scientific Theories*, BOYD, Richard.
Incommensurability and Recurrence: from Oresme to Simmel. SMALL, Robin.

AQUINAS
Discussioni sul neo-Tomismo: Per il progresso della Filosofia Cristiana. BLANDINO, Giovanni.
Ethical Practice in Clinical Medicine. ELLOS, William J.
Introduction to the Philosophy of Nature. HETZLER, Florence M.
Metaphysik als Metahistorik oder Hermeneutik des unreinen Denkens Die Philosophie Max Müllers. RUIZ-PESCE, Ramón Eduardo.
The Preface to Thomistic Metaphysics. KNASAS, John F X.
Swimming Against the Current in Contemporary Philosophy: Occasional Essays and Papers. VEATCH, Henry B.
Thomistic Papers, V. RUSSMAN, Thomas A (ed).
Towards a Christian Philosophy. OWENS, Joseph I.
The Vatican, the Law and the Human Embryo. COUGHLAN, Michael J.
"Adler's *The Idea of Freedom*" in *Freedom in the Modern World: Jacques Maritain, Yves R Simon, Mortimer J Adler*, FITZGERALD, Desmond J.
"Christianity, Humanism, and St Thomas Aquinas" in *The Question of Humanism: Challenges and Possibilities*, MC LAUGHLIN, R J.
"Faith and Goodness" in *The Philosophy in Christianity*, STUMP, Eleonore S.
"St Thomas and Medieval Humanism" in *The Question of Humanism: Challenges and Possibilities*, SYNAN, Edward A.
El "De Ente et Uno": una ontología agustiniana. MAGNAVACCA, Silvia.
"Sociátá" et "communion" chez saint Thomas d'Aquin. LA SOUJEOLE, Benoît-Dominique.
The Absolute in Morality and the Christian Conscience. FUCHS, Josef.
Amor y comunicación. FORMENT, Eudaldo.
La analogía del ser en Suárez. ROIG GIRONELLA, J.
Antropología en la Q D "De virtutibus in communi" de Santo Tomás. CORSO, Laura E.
Aquinas and the Deconstruction of History. KELLY, Eugene.
Aquinas on Almsgiving, Justice and Charity: An Interpretation and Reassessment. POPE, Stephen J.
Aquinas on Resolution in Metaphysics. TAVUZZI, Michael.
Aquinas versus Epistemological Criticism: A Case for Philosophy *in* Science. DEL RE, Giuseppe.
Aristotle and Aquinas on Indignation: From Nemesis to Theodicy. NERNEY, Gayne.
Compatibilities on the Idea of Law in Thomas Aquinas and Thomas Hobbes. FULLER, Timothy.
El concepto tradicional de verdad en Santo Tomás. FORMENT, Eudaldo.
El conocimiento de Dios en la exposición de Tomás de Aquino sobre el "De divinis nominibus" de D Areopagita. ANDEREGGEN, Ignacio E M.
Conocimientos negativo y conocimiento afirmativo de Dios en Santo Tomás y en Hegel. ANDEREGGEN, Ignacio E M.
La contrainte. NEUBERG, Marc.
La crisi dei fondamenti della scienza: Un recupero dell'ilemorfismo?. DEL RE, Giuseppe.
Decir lo mismo (Frege y Santo Tomás). SANGUINETI, Juan J.
La determinación de la esencia en X: Zubiri y Tomás de Aquino. SOTO, José Cercós.
Discussione di alcune questioni di cosmologia neo-tomista. BLANDINO, Giovanni.

AQUINAS

The Distinction between Res Significata and *Modus Significandi* in Aquinas's Theological Epistemology. ROCCA, Gregory.
Divine Irony and the Natural Law: Speculation and Edification in Aquinas. HIBBS, Thomas S.
Divine Reason and Virtue in St Thomas's Natural Law Theory. KILLORAN, John B.
La doctrina del don de San Agustín de Hipona. BELDA PLANS, Pilar.
Du libre arbitre selon s Thomas d'Aquin. CORBIN, Michel.
La eleccion de un maestro. VAN STEENBERGHEN, Fernand.
Establishing of the Object of Metaphysics—Separation (in Polish). MARYNIARCZYK, A.
La ética y los derechos humanos en la filosofía clásica. ALONSO, Luz García.
Los Factores Originales de la Sociedad en Tomás de Aquino. BEUCHOT, Mauricio.
Goerner on Thomistic Natural Law. HALL, Pamela.
Immateriality and the Domain of Thomistic Natural Philosophy. JOHNSON, Mark F.
La interpretación de Santo Tomás en García Morente. FORMENT, Eudaldo.
L'"irrisio fidei" chez Raymond Lulle et S Thomas D'Aquin. SERVERAT, Vincent.
L'origine première des choses. NICOLAS, Jean-Hervé.
L'unité-unicité de l'"esse" Thomiste. PASQUA, Hervé.
The Latin Avicenna as a Source of Thomas Aquinas's Metaphysics. WIPPEL, John F.
Materiality and Aquinas' Natural Philosophy: A Reply to Johnson. KNASAS, John F X.
The Modernity of St Thomas' Political Philosophy. WALTER, Edward.
La neoscolastica italiana dalle sue prime manifestazioni all'enciclica *Aeterni Patris*. ROSSI, G F.
No Rules without Virtues: No Virtues without Rules. BRAYBROOKE, David.
Un nouveau début à l'édition léonine des oeuvres de saint Thomas d'Aquin. HISSETTE, Roland.
Nuestra voluntad es "de Dios". FERNÁNDEZ BURILLO, Santiago A.
Nuestra voluntad es "de Dios". FERNÁNDEZ BURILLO, Santiago A.
Object and Intention in Moral Judgments According to Aquinas. FINNIS, John.
Omniscience, Immutability, and the Divine Mode of Knowing. SULLIVAN, Thomas D.
The Paradox of Aquinas's Altruism: From Self-Love to Love of Others. HAYDEN, R Mary.
El personalismo de Santo Tomás. FORMENT, Eudaldo.
Philosophers on Gender and Sexuality. VADAKKEMURIYIL, A.
Physique aristotélicienne et métaphysique thomiste. VERNIER, Jean-Marie.
Plato's *Parmenides* and St Thomas's Analysis of God as One and Trinity. KLEIN, Sherwin.
Postcriptum: La libertad como necesidad del bien, en San Agustín. PEGUEROLES, Juan.
Qué conocemos de dios? Hobbes versus Tomas. LUKAC DE STIER, María Liliana.
La question de l'être. LARIVÉ, Marc.
A Reading of Aquinas's Five Ways. FOGELIN, Robert J.
Reflexiones en torno a la sensibilidad externa. ALVAREZ-CASTELLANOS, Juan José Sánchez.
Le relazioni divine secondo S Tommaso d'Aquino: Riproposizione di un problema e prospettive di indagine. VENTIMIGLIA, Giovanni.
Response to Hall's "Goerner on Thomistic Natural Law". GOERNER, E A.
Sanction and the Law According to St Thomas Aquinas. HENLE, R J.
Santo Tomás y el desafío de la ética analítica contemporánea. MASSINI CORREAS, Carlos Ignacio.
Santo Tomás y la prostitución. PONFERRADA, Gustavo E.
The Scope of Deliberation: A Conflict in Aquinas. IRWIN, T H.
Sobre la naturaleza de los "derechos". HERNÁNDEZ, Héctor H.
St Augustine and the Second Way. KLUGE, Eike-Henner W.
St Thomas on the Motives of Unjust Acts. WEITHMAN, Paul J.
Substancia y sustantividad: Tomás de Aquino y X Zubiri. CERCÓS SOTO, José Luis.
Sujeto, acto y operación. GAMARRA, Daniel.
Super-yo y vida moral: Una valoración tomista de la hipótesis psicoanalítica. PITHOD, Abelardo.
La Teoría del conocimiento en Santo Tomás de Aquino. BEUCHOT, Mauricio.
Thomas Aquinas and Henry of Ghent on the Succession of Substantial Forms and the Origin of Human Life. WILSON, Gordon A.
Thomas Aquinas and the Renewal of Philosophy: Some Reflections on the Thomism of Mercier (in Dutch). STEEL, C.
Thomas Aquinas and the Will: A Note on Interpretation. CROWE, Frederick.
Thomas d'Aquin a-t-il tente d'exprimer le principe d'individuation à l'intérieur des proprietés.... CASPAR, Philippe.
Tomás de Aquino: la aprehensión del acto de ser (II). GONZÁLEZ, Orestes J.
El tránsito de la existencia al ser. KELZ, Carlos R.
El tratado de Ideología de Fray Zeferino Gonzalez. BUENO SÁNCHEZ, Gustavo.
Los tres estados de la esencia según Santo Tomás de Aquino. CASAUBÓN, Juan A.
Trinidad y ontología trascendental: Ideas en torno al libro IX del "De Trinitate" de S Agustín. RODRÍGUEZ VALLS, Francisco.
Ultimate Ends in Practical Reasoning. MAC DONALD, Scott.
Wainwright, Maritain and Aquinas on Transcendent Experiences. ROY, Louis.
What Can a Discursive Theory of Morality Learn from Aquinas?. RENTTO, Juha-Pekka.

ARAB

Al-Kindi's Psychology (in Hebrew). SCHWARZ, Dov.

ARABIC

Aristotelian Logic and the Arabic Language in Alfarabi. ABED, Shukri B.
Encounter on the Narrow Ridge: A Life of Martin Buber. FRIEDMAN, Maurice.
Ibn Rushd: Averroes. URVOY, Dominique.
Florilegi filosofici ed enciclopedie in Germania nella prima metà del Duecento. STURLESE, Loris.

ARATIONAL

Arational Actions. HURSTHOUSE, Rosalind.

ARBITRATION

Negotation Games: Applying Game Theory to Bargaining and Arbitration. BRAMS, Steven J.

ARCHEOLOGY

Critical Traditions in Contemporary Archaeology. PINSKY, Valerie (ed).
"Childe's Early Marxism" in *Critical Traditions in Contemporary Archaeology*, GATHERCOLE, Peter.
"Commentary: A Critical Role for the History of Archaeology" in *Critical Traditions in Contemporary Archaeology*, PINSKY, Valerie.
"Commentary: Common Knowledge and Archaeology" in *Critical Traditions in Contemporary Archaeology*, ZUBROW, Ezra.
"Dialectics, Critical Inquiry, and Archaeology" in *Critical Traditions in Contemporary Archaeology*, SAITTA, Dean J.
"Efficient Explanations and Efficient Behaviour" in *Critical Traditions in Contemporary Archaeology*, SALMON, Merrilee H.
"The History, Philosophy of Sociology of Archaeology: The Case of the Ancient Monuments Protection Act (1882)" in *Critical Traditions in Contemporary Archaeology*, MURRAY, Tim.
"Inference to the Best Explanation in Archaeology" in *Critical Traditions in Contemporary Archaeology*, HANEN, Marsha and KELLEY, Jane.
"The Interpretive Dilemma" in *Critical Traditions in Contemporary Archaeology*, WYLIE, Alison.
"Philosophical Lessons from the History of Stonehenge Studies" in *Critical Traditions in Contemporary Archaeology*, CHIPPINDALE, Christopher.
"Philosophy of Science and Archaeology" in *Critical Traditions in Contemporary Archaeology*, DUNNELL, Robert C.
"The Structure of American Theoretical Archaeology: A Preliminary Report" in *Critical Traditions in Contemporary Archaeology*, EMBREE, Lester.
Historical Continuity and Discontinuity in the Philosophy of Gadamer and Foucault (in Hungarian). UJLAKI, Gabriella.
On the Possibility of Lawful Explanation in Archaeology. SALMON, Merrilee H.

ARCHETYPE(S)

Archetypal Process: Self and Divine in Whitehead, Jung, and Hillman. GRIFFIN, David Ray (ed).
"Eternal Objects and Archetypes, Past and Depth: Response to Hopper" in *Archetypal Process: Self and Divine in Whitehead, Jung, and Hillman*, COBB JR, John B.
"Introduction: Archetypal Psychology and Process Philosophy" in *Archetypal Process: Self and Divine in Whitehead, Jung, and Hillman*, GRIFFIN, David Ray.
"Once More: The Cavern Beneath the Cave" in *Archetypal Process: Self and Divine in Whitehead, Jung, and Hillman*, HOPPER, Stanley R.

ARCHIMEDIAN POINT

The Balance of Consciousness: Eric Voegelin's Political Theory. KEULMAN, Kenneth.

ARCHITECTURE

Against Architecture: The Writings of Georges Bataille. HOLLIER, Denis.
Philosophical Events: Essays of the '80s. RAJCHMAN, John.
Philosophical Streets: New Approaches to Urbanism. CROW, Dennis (ed).
Unsere postmoderne Moderne (Second Edition). WELSCH, Wolfgang.
"*In Situ*: Beyond the Architectonics of the Modern" in *Postmodernism—Philosophy and the Arts (Continental Philosophy III)*, WATSON, Stephen H.
Foreign Bodies in Strange Places: A Note on Maurice Merleau-Ponty, Georges Bataille, and Architecture. KRELL, David Farrell.
Post-Modern Pastiche. ROSE, Margaret A.
Storicità tecnica e architettura. MAZZARELLA, Eugenio.
Technological Progress and Architectural Response. WINTERS, Edward.

ARCHYTAS

Plato and Archytas in the Seventh Letter. LLOYD, G E R.

ARENDT, H

The Realm of Humanitas: Responses to the Writings of Hannah Arendt. GARNER, Reuben (ed).

ARENDT, H

"Action, Story, and History—On Rereading 'The Human Condition'" in The Realm of Humanitas: Responses to the Writings of Hannah Arendt, RICOEUR, Paul.
"Arendt and Representative Democracy" in *The Realm of Humanitas: Responses to the Writings of Hannah Arendt*, KATEB, George.
"Authority, Authoritarianism, and Education" in *The Realm of Humanitas: Responses to the Writings of Hannah Arendt*, GARNER, Reuben.
"Democracy and the Political" in *The Realm of Humanitas: Responses to the Writings of Hannah Arendt*, WOLIN, Sheldon S.
"Hannah Arendt: la memoria come spazio del pensiero" in *Razionalitá critica: nella filosofia moderna*, FISTETTI, Francesco.
"Judging—The Actor and the Spectator" in *The Realm of Humanitas: Responses to the Writings of Hannah Arendt*, BERNSTEIN, Richard J.
"L'idée d'égalité et la notion moderne du droit" in *Égalité Uguaglianza*, RENAUT, Alain.
"Totalitarianism and Population Superfluity" in *The Realm of Humanitas: Responses to the Writings of Hannah Arendt*, RUBENSTEIN, Richard L.
Arendt and Benjamin on the Promise of History: A Network of Possibilities or One Apocalyptic Moment?. HONOHAN, Iseult.
Habermas and Arendt on the Philosopher's "Error": Tracking the Diabiological in Heidegger. BERNASCONI, Robert.
Hannah Arendt's Political Theory: Ethics and Enemies. DOSSA, Shiraz.
Over Overdrijven. GRIFFIOEN, S.
The Pariah as Hero: Hannah Arendt's Political Actor. RING, Jennifer.
The World of Human Community in Hanna Arendt's Work (in Czechoslovakian). KOUBA, Pavel.
Using Arendt and Heidegger to Consider Feminist Thinking on Women and Reproductive/Infertility Technologies. KLAWITER, Maren.

ARGUMENT(S)

Critical Reasoning (Third Edition). CEDERBLOM, Jerry.
Does God Exist? The Great Debate. MORELAND, J P.
The Elements of Reasoning. CONWAY, David.
Das Ethische in der Rhetorik des Aristoteles. WÖRNER, Markus Hilmar.
Une introduction à l'analyse du discours argumentatif. MENDENHALL, Vance.
Philosophical Writing: An Introduction. MARTINICH, A P.
Semantic Structures. JACKENDOFF, Ray.
Talking Philosophy: A Wordbook. SPARKES, A W.
Understanding Arguments: An Introduction to Informal Logic (Fourth Edition). FOGELIN, Robert J.
"Critical Thinking and Philosophy for Children: The Educational Value of Philosophy". LINDOP, Clive.
'*P*, Therefore, *P*' Without Circularity. SORENSEN, Roy A.
Can An Argument Be Both Valid and Invalid Too?. NEBLETT, William R.
Cherniak on Scientific Realism. BROWN, Harold I.
Consequentialism: The Philosophical Dog That Does Not Bark?. HOLBROOK, Daniel.
A Critical Look at Arguments for Food Irradiation. SMITH, Tony.
The Debate Over the So-Called Reality of Moral Dilemmas. STATMAN, Daniel.
Embryo Research and Abortion—the Arguments that Swayed Parliament. SHORT, David S.
Essentially Contested Concepts: The Ethics and Tactics of Argument. GARVER, Eugene.
Evaluating Arguments: The Premise-Conclusion Relation. BOWLES, George.
Gewirth and the Pain of Contradiction. DAVIS, Michael.
Hamblin on the Standard Treatment. JOHNSON, Ralph H.
Hobbes on Capital Punishment. HEYD, David.
The Inconspicious Role of Paraphrase. SHERRY, David.
Irony and Argument in *Dialogues*, XII. DAVIS, Scott.
Philosophical Culture in the Warsaw-Lvov School (in Polish). GLUCHOWSKI, Gerard.
Philosophy, Argument, and Narration. VERENE, Donald Phillip.
Quantifying Support. BLACK, John.
Should Philosophy be Applied?. NESBITT, Winston.
Students: A Source-Spot for Arguments. BERKOWITZ, Leonard J.
Towards a Research Agenda for Informal Logic and Critical Thinking. WEINSTEIN, Mark.
Transcendentalism About Content. DEVITT, Michael.

ARGUMENTATION

Within Reason: A Guide to Non-Deductive Reasoning. BURBIDGE, John.
Acceptance Is Not Enough: A Critique of Hamblin. JOHNSON, Ralph H.
Argumentation and Values (in French). BOREL, Marie-Jeanne.
Argumentation—Distributed or Monological?. BARTH, E M.
Aristotle on Dialectic. HAMLYN, D W.
Everyday Argumentation from a Speech Act Perspective. GROOTENDORST, Rob.
Habermas and Theological Ethics (in French). BÜHLER, Pierre.
Law: From Foundation to Argumentation. LEMPEREUR, Alain.
Logique et théorie de l'argumentation dans le "Guide de l'étudiant". LAFLEUR, Claude.
Meyer's Theory of Problematology. GOLDEN, James L and JAMISON, David L.
Occasions for Argumentation. HILPINEN, Risto.
Philosophical Argument and the Rhetorical Wedge. JOHNSTONE JR, Henry W.
The Place of Argumentation in the Theory of Reasoning. JOHNSON, Ralph H.
A Pragma-Dialectical Perspective on Norms. VAN EEMEREN, Frans H.
Pragma-Dialectics: A Radical Departure in Fallacy Theory. WOODS, John.
A Problem Solving Interpretation of Argument Analysis. BERNSTEIN, David.
Rhetoric and Argumentation: Relativism and Beyond. KIENPOINTNER, Manfred.
The Serious Play of Plato's *Euthydemus*. ROOCHNIK, David.

ARISTO

The Poetic Theory of the Stoic 'Aristo'. ASMIS, Elizabeth.

ARISTOCRACY

Not So Virtuous Republics: Montesquieu, Venice, and the Theory of Aristocratic Republicanism. CARRITHERS, David W.

ARISTOPHANES

El trilema de Aristófanes y los presupuestos normativos del diálgo crítico. MALIANDI, Ricardo.
The Wisdom of Plato's Aristophanes. SALMAN, Charles.

ARISTOTELIANISM

Aristotelian Logic. PARRY, William T.
"Aristotelian Social Democracy" in *Liberalism and the Good*, NUSSBAUM, Martha C.
A Brief Survey of Indian Buddhistic Logic (in Hungarian). FEHER, Judit.
Aristotelianism and the Origins of "Political Science" in the Twelfth Century. NEDERMAN, Cary J.
Azande Logic *Verus* Western Logic?. TRIPLETT, Timm.
Descartes und der reale Unterschied zwischen der Seele und dem Körper. IMLAY, Robert A.
Justice and Aristotelian Practical Reason. DAHL, Norman.
L'inspiration aristotélicienne de la métaphysique de Bergson. WASZKINEL, Romuald.
Scepticism and Relativity. BARNES, Jonathan.
Towards a Feminist Reassessment of Intellectual Virtue. BRAATEN, Jane.
Universalistische Ethik und Urteilskraft: ein aristotelischer Blick auf Kant. HÖFFE, Otfried.

ARISTOTELIANS

Aristotelian Logic and the Arabic Language in Alfarabi. ABED, Shukri B.
On Being an Aristotelian. MEYNELL, Hugo A.

ARISTOTLE

Aristotelis Ethica Evdemia. WALZER, R R (ed).
Aristotle on Sleep and Dreams. GALLOP, David (trans).
Aristotle's Psychology. ROBINSON, Daniel N.
The Chain of Change: A Study of Aristotle's "Physics" VII. WARDY, Robert.
Ethical Practice in Clinical Medicine. ELLOS, William J.
Ethics with Aristotle. BROADIE, Sarah.
Das Ethische in der Rhetorik des Aristoteles. WÖRNER, Markus Hilmar.
Le existentia de deo e le Immortalitate del Anima: Lineas de Philosophia del Esser. BLANDINO, Giovanni.
God and Subjectivity. GALGAN, Gerald J.
A Guided Tour of Selections from Aristotle's Nicomachean Ethics. BIFFLE, Christopher.
Ibn Rushd: Averroes. URVOY, Dominique.
Introduction to the Philosophy of Nature. HETZLER, Florence M.
An Invitation To Cognitive Science. LEIBER, Justin.
Methods and Problems in Greek Science: Selected Papers. LLOYD, G E R.
Morality—What's In It For Me?: A Historical Introduction to Ethics. NELSON, William N.
Myth and Philosophy: A Contest of Truths. HATAB, Lawrence J.
Of Memory, Reminiscence, and Writing: On the Verge. KRELL, David Farrell.
The Origins of Aristotelian Science. FEREJOHN, Michael.
A Philosophy of Morals. HELLER, Agnes.
The Preface to Thomistic Metaphysics. KNASAS, John F X.
The Recovery of the Soul: An Aristotelian Essay on Self-fulfilment. RANKIN, Kenneth.
Swimming Against the Current in Contemporary Philosophy: Occasional Essays and Papers. VEATCH, Henry B.
Towards a Christian Philosophy. OWENS, Joseph I.
Der Ursprung der Erziehungsziele in der Lehre von Plato, Aristoteles und Neill. EGGER, Paul.
"Aristotle's Philosophy of Mind" in *Psychology (Companions to Ancient Thought: 2)*, IRWIN, T H.
"A Reply to Cynthia Willett's "The Shadow of Hegel's *Science of Logic*" in *Essays on Hegel's Logic*, DI GIOVANNI, George.
"A Reply to Edward Halper's "Hegel and the Problem of the Differentia"" in *Essays on Hegel's Logic*, DONOUGHO, Martin.
"Were Plato and Aristotle Humanists?" in *The Question of Humanism: Challenges and Possibilities*, ANDIC, Martin.
"Just for the Thrill": Sycophantizing Aristotle's *Poetics*. CARSON, Anne.
"Nothing of the Origin and Destiny of Cats": The Remainder of the Logos. ROSE, John M.
La "riabilitazione" della δυναμιζ e dell'ενεργεια in Heidegger. VOLPI, Franco.

ARISTOTLE

Action or/and Dwelling. BOEDER, Heribert.
Algunas observaciones sobre la noción de *Pragma* en Aristóteles. FEMENÍAS, María Luisa.
La analogía del ser en Suárez. ROIG GIRONELLA, J.
Analyse d'un corpus iconographique rassemblé par Maxime Préaud ou Aristote et la mélancolie. FLEURY, Chantal.
Anger as a Vice: A Maimonidean Critique of Aristotle's Ethics. FRANK, Daniel H.
L'aporia della kinesis in Aristotele. ROCCARO, Giuseppe.
Aristippus Against Happiness. IRWIN, T H.
Aristote admet-il un infini en acte et en puissance en "Physique III, 4-8"?. CÔTÉ, Antoine.
Aristotele professore?. NATALI, Carlo.
Aristóteles desde Heidegger. CASARES, Angel J.
Aristotelian and Whiteheadian Conceptions of Actuality: I. FETZ, Reto Luzius and FELT, James W.
Aristotelian and Whiteheadian Conceptions of Actuality: II. FETZ, Reto Luzius and FELT, James W.
Aristotelian Contraries. BOGEN, James.
Aristotelian Essentialism. MATTHEWS, Gareth B.
Aristotelian Form and End. CURZER, Howard J.
Aristotelian Mimesis Reevaluated. HALLIWELL, Stephen.
Aristotle and Aquinas on Indignation: From Nemesis to Theodicy. NERNEY, Gayne.
Aristotle and Nietzsche on Art as Imitation of Nature. DROST, Mark P.
Aristotle and Protagoras: The Good Human Being as the Measure of Goods. GOTTLIEB, Paula.
Aristotle and the Spheres of Motivation: *De Anima* III. HUTCHINSON, D S.
Aristotle in Dante's Paradise. BOURBEAU, Marguerite.
Aristotle on Dialectic. HAMLYN, D W.
Aristotle on Justice, Equality and the Rule of Law. QUINN, Michael.
Aristotle on Personality and Some Implications for Friendship. REINER, Paula.
Aristotle on the Function of Man in Relation to Eudaimonia. HESTER, Marcus.
Aristotle or Nietzsche?. FRANKS, Joan M.
Aristotle's Account of Practical Reasoning as a Theoretical Base for Research on Teaching. NOEL, Jana.
Aristotle's Apodeictic Syllogism. JOHNSTON, David.
Aristotle's Causality Theory. ANDRIOPOULOS, D Z.
Aristotle's Definition of Motion and its Ontological Implications. BRAGUE, Rémi and ADLER, Pierre and D'URSEL, Laurent.
Aristotle's Motionless Soul. TWEEDALE, Martin.
Aristotle's Much Maligned *Megalopsychos*. CURZER, Howard J.
Aristotle's Technical Simulation and its Logic of Causal Relations. LOECK, Gisela.
Aristotle, the Direction Problem, and the Structure of the Sublunar Realm. KRONZ, Frederick.
El averroísmo de Juan de Sècheville. RODRÍGUEZ, Juan Acosta.
Being and Categorial Intuition. COBB-STEVENS, Richard.
Breves notas acerca de la *Política* de Aristóteles. ÁLVAREZ, Margarita Mauri.
Can Fiction Be Stranger Than Truth? An Aristotelian Answer. GALLOP, David.
Cantidad o ex-tensión?. BOLZÁN, J E.
Causality: Sankara and Aristotle. DHAVAMONY, Mariasusai.
Character and Explanation in Aristotle's *Ethics* and *Poetics*. DESLAURIERS, Marguerite.
Common Ground: Aristotle on Human and Divine Noetic Activity. MORGAN, Vance G.
La comprensión aristotélica del trabajo. INNERARITY, Carmen.
El concepto de substancia sensible en Aristóteles: Génesis histórica de la cuestión. BLAQUIER, Carlos P.
Contemplación y Dios en Aristóteles. DE KIRCHNER, Beatriz Bossi.
La contrainte. NEUBERG, Marc.
Does Aristotle Beg the Question in His Defense of the Principle of Non-Contradiction?. DEGNAN, Michael.
Du libre arbitre selon s Thomas d'Aquin. CORBIN, Michel.
The Emergence and Original Meaning of the Name 'Metaphysics'. REINER, Hans and ADLER, Pierre and PASKIN, David.
Éthique et Morale. RICOEUR, Paul.
Etica, retórica y política en la antropología aristotélica. MARTIN, Victor R.
Être et non-être chez Aristote: contraires ou contradictoires?. BERTI, Enrico.
Evolutionary Ethics and the Search for Predecessors: Kant, Hume, and All the Way Back to Aristotle?. RUSE, Michael.
External Creation and Eternal Production of the World According to Bonaventura (in Dutch). VAN VELDHUIJSEN, Peter.
Finalidad y dimensiones "kaíricas" de la estructura del ser. MOUTSOPOULOS, Evanghélos A.
Friendship and Education. WHITE, Patricia.
Friendship, Self-Love, and Concern for Others in Aristotle's Ethics. MC KERLIE, Dennis.
The Generation of Form in Aristotle. SHIELDS, Christopher.
Glose sur le prologue du traité "de l'âme" d'Aristote. VERNIER, Jean-Marie.
A Great Philosopher's Not So Great Account of Great Virtue: Aristotle's Treatment of 'Greatness of Soul'. CURZER, Howard J.
Hacia el saber del hombre: Dialéctica, lógica y ontológica en Aristóteles. MARÍN, Victor R.
Hamartia, Akrasia: Ignorance, and Blame in Aristotle's Philosophy. CYZYK, Mar.
Heidegger und die Frage um die Quelle des Grundbegriffes der Metaphysik (in Polish). ROZDZENSKI, R.
Idées de négations. CHIESA, Curzio.
Imitación y purificación en la estética de Aristóteles. CAPPELLETTI, Angel.
Impersonal Friends. WHITING, Jennifer E.
Is a Whole Identical to its Parts?. SCALTSAS, Theodore.
Is Aristotle an Internal Realist? Nussbaum and the Divine Perspective. EARLS, C Anthony.
Jivacide, Zombies and *Jivanmuktas*. HERMAN, A L.
La justificación práctica del principio de no contradicción en Aristóteles. CASSINI, A.
A Kantian View of Moral Luck. MOORE, A W.
L'être du non-être en perspective aristotélicienne. DE MURALT, André.
L'imagination au pouvoir. BODÉÜS, Richard.
Lenguaje y verdad en Aristóteles. RODRIGUEZ, M L.
Maimonides: A Natural Law Theorist?. LEVINE, Michael.
Making the Citizens Good: Aristotle's City and Its Contemporary Relevance. SIMPSON, Peter.
Metafisica e dialettica: quattro saggi sull'interpretazione hegeliana di Aristotele. FERRARIN, Alfredo.
La metáfora en Aristóteles. GAMBRA, José Miguel.
Metaphysik und Erfahrung. BUBNER, Rüdiger.
I metodi della metafisica platonico-accademica "generalizzante" ed "elementarizzante" nei libri "M" e "N".... CATTANEI, E.
Moral Theories, Impartiality, and the Status of Non-Rational, Sentient Beings. FILICE, Carlo.
La naturaleza como vida en la interpretación hegeliana de Aristóteles. BARROSO, Inmaculada Acosta.
Naturaleza, espíritu, finalidad. ALARCÓN, Enrique.
A New Reading of Aristotle's *Hyle*. POLIS, Dennis F.
Non-Technical *Pisteis* in Aristotle and Anaximenes. MIRHADY, David.
A Note on the Jural Relation. BUTLER, Ken.
The *Nous*-Body Problem in Aristotle. MODRAK, Deborah K W.
Nuestra voluntad es "de Dios". FERNÁNDEZ BURILLO, Santiago A.
On an Alleged Inconsistency in the Nicomachean Ethics (IX,4). MARTIN, C F J.
On Becoming A Moral Agent: From Aristotle to Harry Stottlemeier. PRITCHARD, Michael S.
On Being an Aristotelian. MEYNELL, Hugo A.
On the Alleged Impossibility of a Science of Accidents in Aristotle. URBANAS, Alban.
Ousia, Substratum, and Matter. SFEKAS, Stanley.
Partial Wholes. BARNES, Jonathan.
Per una rilettura dei libri "M" e "N" della *Metafisica* di Aristotele alla luce delle "dottrine non scritte" di Platone. CATTANEI, Elisabetta.
Perception and Evaluation: Aristotle on the Moral Imagination. HANKINSON, R J.
Philosophers on Gender and Sexuality. VADAKKEMURIYIL, A.
Physique aristotélicienne et métaphysique thomiste. VERNIER, Jean-Marie.
Plato and Aristotle on Division and Definition. DESLAURIERS, Marguerite.
Posibilidad e indeterminación: Aristóteles frente a Diodoro Crono. QUEVEDO, Amalia.
Potencia, finalidad y posibilidad en "Metafísica" IX, 3-4. GARCIA MARQUÉS, Alfonso.
Précis of "Whose Justice? Which Rationality?". MAC INTYRE, Alasdair.
La prétendue intuition de Dieu dans le De Coelo d'Aristote. BODÉÜS, Richard.
Προαιρεσις in Epictetus. DOBBIN, Robert.
Prudence: Aristotelian Perspectives on Practical Reason. HASLAM, Nick.
La question de l'être. LARIVÉ, Marc.
Referential Opacity in Aristotle. SPELLMAN, Lynne.
Reflections on Aristotle's Criticism of Forms. MOKASHI, Ashwini A.
Roberts on Responsibility for Action and Character in the *Nicomachean Ethics*. BRICKHOUSE, Thomas C.
Le rôle de l'imagination dans le mouvement animal et l'action humaine chez Aristotle. DUGRÉ, François.
The Role of Aristotle's *Praxis* Today. GUY, Alfred.
Semantica aristotelica e sillogistica modale. MARIANI, Mauro.
Le statut de l'argument dialectiques d'après *Réf soph* 11, 172a9-15. DORION, Louis-André.
Substances and Space-Time: What Aristotle Would Have Said to Einstein. MAUDLIN, Tim.
The Supremely Happy Life in Aristotle's *Nicomachean Ethics*. CURZER, Howard J.
Lo sviluppo degli studi logici nel pensiero tedesco della seconda metà dell'800. MANGIAGALLI, Maurizio.
Teleologie: Chance oder Belastung für die Philosophie?. PLEINES, Jürgen-Eckardt.
Teleology and the Concepts of Causation. VON GLASERSFELD, Ernst.

ARISTOTLE

La teoria aristotelica dell'apodissi. *SAINATI, Vittorio*.
The Aristotelian Debate in African Philosophy: Miscellaneous Remarks on a Denied Discourse (in German). NEUGEBAUER, Christian.
Thinking of Unity (in Dutch). AERTSEN, Jan A.
The Two Barbaras. THOM, Paul.
The Unity of Moral Virtues in Aristotle's *Nicomachean Ethics*. TELFER, Elizabeth.
Univocità dell'essere e intenzionalià del conoscere. ANTONELLI, Mauro.
Variações sobre o *De Interpretatione*, de Aristóteles. ROSA, Joaquim Coelho.
Virtue Ethics and the Appeal to Human Nature. WOODRUFF, Paul.
What Can a Discursive Theory of Morality Learn from Aquinas?. RENTTO, Juha-Pekka.

ARITHMETIC

Frege in Perspective. WEINER, Joan.
Parts of Classes. LEWIS, David.
A 1-Generic Degree Which Bounds a Minimal Degree. KUMABE, Masahiro.
Arithmetizing Uniform *NC*. ALLEN, B.
Bounded Arithmetic and the Polynomial Hierarchy. KRAJICEK, Jan and PUDLÁK, Pavel and TAKEUTI, Gaisi.
Context Principle, Fruitfulness of Logic and the Cognitive Value of Arithmetic in Frege. RUFFINO, Marco Antonio.
A Decidable Ehrenfeucht Theory with Exactly Two Hyperarithmetic Models. REED, R C.
The Degree of a Σ_n Cut. CHONG, C T and MOURAD, K J.
Derivability Conditions on Rosser's Provability Predicates. ARAI, Toshiyasu.
Enumerations of Turing Ideals with Applications. MARKER, David.
Equational Theory of Positive Numbers with Exponentiation is Not Finitely Axiomatizable. GUREVIC, R.
Exponentiation and Second-Order Bounded Arithmetic. KRAJICEK, Jan.
Extended Bar Induction in Applicative Theories. RENARDEL DE LAVALETTE, Gerard R.
Finite Kripke Models and Predicate Logics of Provability. ARTEMOV, Sergei and DZHAPARIDZE, Giorgie.
Incompleteness of a Free Arithmetic. BENCIVENGA, Ermanno.
The Interpretability Logic of Peano Arithmetic. BERARDUCCI, Alessandro.
Lifschitz' Realizability. VAN OOSTEN, Jaap.
Logical Equations and Admissible Rules of Inference with Parameters in Modal Provability Logics. RYBAKOV, V V.
The Meaning of Δυναμισ at *Timaeus* 31c. PRITCHARD, Paul.
Mojzesz Presburger: Life and Work. ZYGMUNT, Jan.
Nonstandard Arithmetic of Hilbert Subsets. YASUMOTO, Masahiro.
On Diophantine Equations Solvable in Models of Open Induction. OTERO, Margarita.
On the Completeness of a Certain System of Arithmetic of Whole Numbers in Which Addition Occurs as the Only Operation. PRESBURGER, Mojzesz and JACQUETTE, Dale.
Randomness by Design. DEMBSKI, William.
Sub-Arithmetical Ultrapowers: A Survey. MC LAUGHLIN, Thomas G.
When Is Arithmetic Possible?. MC COLM, Gregory L.

ARITHMETIZATION

"Logical and Philosophical Foundations for Arithmetical Logic" in *Physicalism in Mathematics*, GAUTHIER, Yvon.

ARIUS

"The Philosophy in Christianity: Arius and Athanasius" in *The Philosophy in Christianity*, WILES, Maurice.

ARMS RACE

"The Arms-Race Implications of Libertarian Capitalism" in *Issues in War and Peace: Philosophical Inquiries*, KUNKEL, Joseph.
"If Peace Were at Hand, How Would We Know It?" in *Issues in War and Peace: Philosophical Inquiries*, PARTRIDGE, Ernest.

ARMSTRONG, D

Is a Whole Identical to its Parts?. SCALTSAS, Theodore.
The Laws of Physics as Nomic Universals. ZYCINSKI, Jozef.
Phenomenal Qualities and the Nontransitivity of Matching. BURGESS, John A.

ARNAULD

Leibniz and Arnauld. SLEIGH JR, Robert C.
Malebranche versus Arnauld. COOK, Monte.

ARNESON, R

Difficulties with the Principle of Equal Opportunity for Welfare. CHRISTIANO, Thomas.

ARNOLD, M

"Mr Adler and Matthew Arnold" in *Freedom in the Modern World: Jacques Maritain, Yves R Simon, Mortimer J Adler*, VAN DOREN, John.

ARON, R

Sartre, Aron et le relativisme historique. BAUGH, Bruce.

ARRIAN

The Moral Interpretation of the 'Second Preface' to Arrian's *Anabasis*. GRAY, V J.

ART

Adorno's Aesthetic Theory: The Redemption of Illusion. ZUIDERVAART, Lambert.
Art and Answerability: Early Philosophical Essays—M M Bakhtin. HOLQUIST, Michael (ed).
Ästhetik des Abschieds: Kritik der Moderne. EBELING, Hans.
Creative Characters. YOUNG-BRUEHL, Elisabeth.
Echoes: After Heidegger. SALLIS, John.
L'objet-peinture: Pour une théorie de la réception. PAQUIN, Nycole.
Modernity, Aesthetics, and the Bounds of Art. MC CORMICK, Peter J.
Nietzsche (I and II): The Will to Power as Art, The Eternal Recurrence of the Same—Heidegger. KRELL, David Farrell (trans).
On Walter Benjamin: Critical Essays and Recollections. SMITH, Gary (ed).
Philosophical Events: Essays of the '80s. RAJCHMAN, John.
Philosophy of Sport. HYLAND, Drew A.
Postmodernism—Philosophy and the Arts (Continental Philosophy III). SILVERMAN, Hugh J (ed).
Schellings Philosophie der Kunst: Göttliche Imagination und Ästhetische Einbildungskraft. BARTH, Bernhard.
Wittgenstein, Ethics and Aesthetics: The View from Eternity. TILGHMAN, B R.
XIth International Congress in Aesthetics, Nottingham 1988. WOODFIELD, Richard (ed).
"Art and Democracy in Habermas" in *Writing the Politics of Difference*, PICHÉ, Claude.
"Art and Meaning" in *XIth International Congress in Aesthetics, Nottingham 1988*, DIFFEY, T J.
"The Avant Garde, Institutional and Critical Theories of Art" in *XIth International Congress in Aesthetics, Nottingham 1988*, SNYMAN, J J.
"Distance, Disinterest, and Autonomy: Gardens as a Challenge to the Theory of Art" in *XIth International Congress in Aesthetics, Nottingham 1988*, MILLER, Mara.
"Does Analytic Aesthetics Rest on a Mistake?" in *XIth International Congress in Aesthetics, Nottingham 1988*, LUDEKING, K.
"Exiles and Fugitives: The Maritain-Tate-Gordon Letters" in *From Twilight to Dawn: The Cultural Vision of Jacques Maritain*, DUNAWAY, John M.
"Experiencing Art" in *XIth International Congress in Aesthetics, Nottingham 1988*, ROBINSON, Jenefer.
"Imitation and Art" in *XIth International Congress in Aesthetics, Nottingham 1988*, SÖRBOM, Göran.
"Methodische Aspekte des Kunstwissenschaftlichen Umgangs mit moderner Kunst" in *XIth International Congress in Aesthetics, Nottingham 1988*, LINGNER, Michael.
"Nietzsche: Art and Existence" in *XIth International Congress in Aesthetics, Nottingham 1988*, DAVEY, J R N.
"Normative Aesthetics and Contemporary Art: Bürger's Critique of Adorno" in *XIth International Congress in Aesthetics, Nottingham 1988*, ZUIDERVAART, Lambert.
"Le Retour À La Figuration En Art Actuel: Tradition Et Innovation" in *XIth International Congress in Aesthetics, Nottingham 1988*, LANGLOIS, Monique.
"The Social Status of Art: Why the Institutional Approach is not Sufficient" in *XIth International Congress in Aesthetics, Nottingham 1988*, DZIEMIDOK, Bohdan.
"T E Wilkerson on Originality in Art and Morals" in *XIth International Congress in Aesthetics, Nottingham 1988*, SPECTOR, Arnold.
"Tradition as Innovation" in *XIth International Congress in Aesthetics, Nottingham 1988*, KUCZYNSKA, Alicja.
"Art Nonsense" or the Nine Flavours. ANAND, Mulk Raj.
Aesthetic Appreciation and Human Katharsis. NIARCHOS, Constantine G.
Aesthetics and Art Education. SMITH, Peter.
Análisis político-epistemológico de la obra de arte según Walter Benjamin. COMESAÑA, Santalices Gloria.
Aristotle and Nietzsche on Art as Imitation of Nature. DROST, Mark P.
Art and Aesthetics and the Crisis of Culture. MORAWSKI, Stefan.
Art and Censorship. SERRA, Richard.
Art and Craft. MOUNCE, H O.
Art and Morality in Plato: A Reappraisal. HALL, Robert W.
Art and Morality: On the Problem of Stating a Problem. HATTINGH, J P.
Art and Neurology: A Discussion. HALPIN, David M G and SORRELL, Martin.
Art and Philosophy: The Person in the Cybernetic Age. HETZLER, Florence M.
Art et cosmos. PASSERON, René.
Art et mystère. TAVARES DE MIRANDA, Maria.
Art for Existence's Sake: A Heideggerian Revision. SCHUMACHER, Paul J.
The Art of Philosophy. COOPER, Neil.
Art's Autonomy and Absolute Idealism: The Role of Aesthetics in Schelling's Philosophy (in Dutch). BRAECKMAN, A.
Art, Aesthetics, and the Pitfalls of Discipline-Based Art Education. ARNSTINE, Donald.
Art, Life and Reality. NOVITZ, David.
Art, Stance and Education. PUSCH, James.
Art, Truth and the Education of Subjectivity. HEPBURN, Ronald W.
Arte y conocimiento. ECHAURI, Raúl.

ART

ART CRITICISM

ART EDUCATION

ART HISTORY

ART OBJECT(S)

ART-FOR-ART'S SAKE

ARTIFACT(S)

ARTIFICIAL

ARTIFICIAL INSEMINATION

ARTIFICIAL INTELLIGENCE

ARTIFICIAL INTELLIGENCE
"Philosophy at Carnegie Mellon: Past, Present, Future" in Acting and Reflecting: The Interdisciplinary Turn in Philosophy, HAUGELAND, John.
"The Tetrad Project" in *Acting and Reflecting: The Interdisciplinary Turn in Philosophy*, SPIRTES, Peter and SCHEINES, Richard and GLYMOUR, Clark.
Artificial Intelligence and Wittgenstein. CASEY, Gerard.
Cognitive Science on a Wing and a Prayer. KEITH, William.
Cognitivism and Cognitive Science (in Portuguese). OLIVEIRA, M B de.
Dialogues in Natural Language with GURU, a Psychologic Inference Engine. COLBY, Kenneth M and COLBY, Peter M and STOLLER, Robert J.
Explanation—Opening Address. SMART, J J C.
Fear and Loathing (and Other Intentional States) in Searle's Chinese Room. JACQUETTE, Dale.
Logic and Artificial Intelligence: An Exposition. DE SWART, H C M.
Minds, Machines and Gödels Theorem (in German). RHEINWALD, Rosemarie.
Natural Problems and Artificial Intelligence. HENLEY, Tracy.
On the Impossibility of Artificial Intelligence. WEISS, Paul.
On the Purported Pragmatico-Semantic Foundation of Linguistics and AI Through Wittgenstein's Late Philosophy. LEINFELLNER-RUPERTSBERGER, Elisabeth.
Overloading Intentions for Efficient Practical Reasoning. POLLACK, Martha E.
El paradigma computacional aplicado al estudio de la vida. GUTIÉRREZ, Claudio.
Philosophische Anstösse in der computerunterstützten Intelligenz-Forschung. HRACHOVEC, Herbert.
Philosophy and Cognitive Science (in Czechoslovakian). PSTRUZINA, Karel.
Predication, Fiction, and Artificial Intelligence. RAPAPORT, William J.
Rationalism, Expertise and the Dreyfuses' Critique of AI Research. ROBINSON, William S.
Relevant Containment Logics and Certain Frame Problems of AI. SYLVAN, Richard.
Replies to My Computational Commentators. DIETRICH, Eric.
Représentation philosophique par réseau sémantique variable. BOSS, Gilbert and LONGEART, Maryvonne.
Technological Progress and Architectural Response. WINTERS, Edward.

ARTIFICIAL WOMB(S)
Artificial Means of Reproduction and Our Understanding of the Family. MACKLIN, Ruth.
The Artificial Womb—Patriarchal Bone or Technological Blessing?. HEDMAN, Carl.

ARTIST(S)
"Truth, Understanding and the Artist's Vision" in *XIth International Congress in Aesthetics, Nottingham 1988*, SAVILE, Anthony.
Artist and Peasant. XING-PEI, Fei.
Artists, Computer Programs and Performance. GODLOVITCH, A.
Kompensierte Moderne. LÖVENICH, F.
Kristeva and Holbein, Artist of Melancholy. LECHTE, John.
La communication de l'art (in Japanese). SHINOHARA, Motoaki.
Wollheim's Theory of Artist as Spectator: A Complication. OLDS, Clifton.

ARTISTIC
Osservazioni sul bello naturale e sul bello artistico in filosofia. FRANCHI, Alfredo.
Über das Geschmacksurteil und die künstlerische Freiheit bei Kant (in Japanese). UE, Satoko.

ARTS
The Humanities in the Nineties: A View From the Netherlands. ZÜRCHER, Erik (ed).
Mimesis as Make-Believe: On the Foundations of the Representational Arts. WALTON, Kendall L.
Aristotelian Mimesis Reevaluated. HALLIWELL, Stephen.
Change and Development. MC LEOD, John.
DBAE: Complaints, Reminiscences, and Response. BROUDY, Harry S.
Hutcheson's Account of Beauty as a Response to Mandeville. MICHAEL, Emily and MICHAEL, Fred S.
Interart Analogy: Practice and Theory in Comparing the Arts. THOMAS, Troy.
Progress in Mathematics and Other Arts. SEDZIWY, Stanislaw.

ASCETICISM
Nietzsche On Truth and Philosophy. CLARK, Maudemarie.
The Question of Ethics. SCOTT, Charles E.
Philosophical Asceiticism (in French). DE MONTICELLI, Roberta.

ASCLEPIUS
Socrates and Asclepius: The Final Words. SANTILLI, Paul C.

ASCRIPTION(S)
On Removing Puzzles About Belief Ascription. DEVITT, Michael.
On Respecting Puzzles About Belief Ascription (A Reply to Devitt). LYCAN, William G.

ASIAN
see also Oriental
India and the Theory of the Asiatic Mode of Production (in Hungarian). RENNER, Zsuzsanna.

ASPECT(S)
Metaphor and Aspect-Perception. KEMP, G Neville.

ASPIRATION(S)
Conception of Values in Polish Sociology (in Polish). STYK, Jozef.

ASSER, G
On a Theorem of Günter Asser. CALUDE, Cristian and SÂNTEAN, Lila.

ASSERTION(S)
"Convention and Assertion" in *The Mind of Donald Davidson*, ZILIAN, Hans Georg.
"Davidson on Assertion, Convention and Belief" in *The Mind of Donald Davidson*, PICARDI, Eva.
"The Ethical Root of Language" in *Logic and Ethics*, GORMALLY, M C.
"Introduction to A Logic of Assertions" in *Knowledge Representation and Defeasible Reasoning*, GILES, Robin.

ASSIMILATION
Two Models of Preferential Treatment for Working Mothers. BABER, H E.

ASSUMPTION(S)
Conclusion. GRIFFITHS, A Phillips.
The Need for Charity in Semantics. WARMBROD, Ken.
Telling Tales: Notes on Heidegger's "Career," the "Heidegger Affair," and the Assumptions of Narrativity. DAVIES, Paul.

ASTRONOMY
I Modelli l'Invenzione e la Conferma. PETRONI, Angelo Maria.
"Astronomical Improbability" in *Logic, Methodology and Philosophy of Science, VIII*, HACKING, Ian.

ASTROPHYSICS
"Astronomical Improbability" in *Logic, Methodology and Philosophy of Science, VIII*, HACKING, Ian.

ASYMMETRY
Change, Cause and Contradiction: A Defence of the Tenseless Theory of Time. LE POIDEVIN, Robin.
Causes and Laws: The Asymmetry Puzzle. BYERLY, Henry.
Epistemological Time Asymmetry. SAVITT, Steven F.
Response to Ehring's 'Papineau on Causal Asymmetry'. PAPINEAU, David.

ATHANASIUS
"The Philosophy in Christianity: Arius and Athanasius" in *The Philosophy in Christianity*, WILES, Maurice.

ATHEISM
see also Theism
Atheism, Ayn Rand, and other Heresies. SMITH, George H.
Does God Exist? The Great Debate. MORELAND, J P.
The Metaphysics of Religious Belief. SHOOMAN, A P.
The Self-Overcoming of Nihilism: Nishitani Keiji. PARKES, Graham (trans).
"The Newtonians and Deism" in *Essays on the Context, Nature, and Influence of Isaac Newton's Theology*, FORCE, James E.
Der "Atheist" und der "Theologe": Schopenhauer als Hörer Schleiermachers. REGEHLY, Thomas.
"Scientific Atheism" in the Era of Perestrojka. MELNICK, A James.
El ateísmo Freudeano. MARLASCA, Antonio.
Atheism, Theism and Big Bang Cosmology. SMITH, Quentin.
An Atheological Argument from Evil Natural Laws. SMITH, Quentin.
From Immanentism to Atheism. LY, Gabriel.
Hume Contra Spinoza?. KLEVER, Wim.
Naturalistic Ethics and the Argument from Evil. NELSON, Mark T.
Nietzsche's Use of Atheism. ROTH, Robin Alice.
Nihilism and the Impossibility of Political Philosophy. BASINSKI, Paul A.
L'odissea dell'ateismo e del nichilismo. FABRO, Cornelio.
Le origini dell'ateismo antico (quinta parte). ZEPPI, Stelio.
Plantinga and Probabilistic Atheism. CHRZAN, Keith.
The Problem of Atheism in Recent Soviet Publications. DAHM, Helmut.
Reason and Revelation in the Thought of Leo Strauss. COLMO, Christopher A.
The Unitarian Universalist Association: Humanism or Theism?. KURTZ, Paul and BULLOUGH, Vern L.

ATHLETICS
The Behavior of the NCAA: A Question of Ethics. STIEBER, John.

ATLANTIS
Plato's *Statesman* Story: The Birth of Fiction Reconceived. TOMASI, John.

ATOMIC PHYSICS
Quantum Physics and the Identity of Indiscernibles. FRENCH, Steven and REDHEAD, Michael.

ATOMISM
La interpretación russelliana de Leibniz y el atomismo metodológico de Moore. RODRÍGUEZ CONSUEGRA, Francisco.
The Philosophy of Logical Wholism. MC CARTY, David Charles.
Postilla. GALASSO, Giuseppe.
Wittgenstein's Critique of Mechanistic Atomism. MC DONOUGH, Richard.
Wittgenstein's Holism. PEARS, David.

ATONEMENT
In Defense of Anselm. ASPENSON, Steven S.

ATTEMPTING
Intention, Agency and Criminal Liability: Philosophy of Action and the Criminal Law. DUFF, R A.
"Attempting the Impossible" in *Liability and Responsibility*, WHITE, Alan R.

ATTITUDE(S)
The Difference Between Truth and Opinion: How the Misuse of Language Can Lead to Disaster. COONEY, Timothy J.
"Prolegomena to a Structural Theory of Belief and Other Attitudes" in *Propositional Attitudes: The Role of Content in Logic, Language, and Mind*, KAMP, Hans.
Attitudes, Leprechauns and Neutrinos: The Ontology of Behavioral Science. CHANDLER, Marthe.
Is the Skeptical Attitude the Attitude of a Skeptic?. PAPRZYCKA, Katarzyna.
The Problem of Unauthorized Welfare. VALLENTYNE, Peter.
Roderick Firth's Contribution to Ethics. BRANDT, R B.
Visual Fictions. CURRIE, Gregory.

ATTRIBUTE(S)
"Hegel's Criticism of Spinoza's Concept of the Absolute" in *Essays on Hegel's Logic*, BYRNE, Laura.
Classes and Attributes in Extended Modal Systems: Proceedings of the Colloquium in Modal and Many Valued Logic. MARCUS, Ruth Barcan.
Hume Contra Spinoza?. KLEVER, Wim.
What Are *Civil* Rights?. WEINREB, Lloyd L.

ATTRIBUTION
"Skepticism and Everyday Knowledge Attributions" in *Doubting: Contemporary Perspectives on Skepticism*, COHEN, Stewart.
Belief Attribution in Science: Folk Psychology under Theoretical Stress. TROUT, J D.

AUDI, R
Rationalism, Supervenience, and Moral Epistemology. KLAGGE, James.
The Separation of Church and State: Some Questions for Professor Audi. WEITHMAN, Paul J.

AUDIENCE
The Aesthetic Relation of Musical Performer and Audience. PUTMAN, Daniel.

AUDITOR(S)
Establishing an Ethic of Accounting: A Response to Westra's Call for Government Employment of Auditors. WAPLES, Elain and SHAUB, Michael K.
Some Unresolved Ethical Issues in Auditing. GUNZ, Sally and MC CUTCHEON, John.

AUGUSTINE
Grace, Politics and Desire: Essays on Augustine. MEYNELL, Hugo A (ed).
"Augustine and Poetic Exegesis" in *Grace, Politics and Desire: Essays on Augustine*, WESTRA, Haijo J.
"Augustine and the Norms of Authentic Conversion" in *Grace, Politics and Desire: Essays on Augustine*, MEYNELL, Hugo A.
"Augustine on Music" in *Grace, Politics and Desire: Essays on Augustine*, JORDAN, William.
"Augustine's Methods of Biblical Interpretation" in *Grace, Politics and Desire: Essays on Augustine*, HAMILTON, Gordon J.
"Augustine's Philosophy of Being" in *The Philosophy in Christianity*, STEAD, Christopher.
"The Background to Augustine's Denial of Religious Plurality" in *Grace, Politics and Desire: Essays on Augustine*, VANDERSPOEL, John.
"The Body and Human Values in Augustine of Hippo" in *Grace, Politics and Desire: Essays on Augustine*, MILES, Margaret R.
"Justice and Love in the Political Thought of St Augustine" in *Grace, Politics and Desire: Essays on Augustine*, PAREL, Anthony J.
"Love as Rhetorical Principle: The Relationship Between Content and Style in the Rhetoric of St Augustine" in *Grace, Politics and Desire: Essays on Augustine*, SUTHERLAND, Christine Mason.
"Memory and Scripture in the Conversion of Augustine" in *Grace, Politics and Desire: Essays on Augustine*, COWARD, Harold G.
"Predestination and Freedom in Augustine's Ethics" in *The Philosophy in Christianity*, O'DALY, Gerard.
"Two Converts: Augustine and Pascal" in *Grace, Politics and Desire: Essays on Augustine*, CHADBOURNE, Richard M.
La "memoria Dei" en el libro X de Las confesiones. PEGUEROLES, Juan.
Augustine's Theology of the Trinity: Its Relevance. CLARK, Mary T.
Las aventuras de la differencia (G Vattimo). PEGUEROLES, Juan.
El deseo infinito. PEGUEROLES, Juan.
El deseo y el amor en San Agustín. PEGUEROLES, Juan.
Dios y el hombre en San Agustin. PEGUEROLES, Juan.
The Emerging Tension Between Self and Society, As Exemplified in Augustine. THOMPSON JR, George B.
El hombre agustiniamo: Itinerario tras el ser de la existencia. MOLINA, Mario A.
La libertad como autodeterminaciín en san Agustín. GALINDO, José Antonio.
La libertad como búsqueda de la verdad en el joven Agustín. WEISMANN, F J.
Libertad como posibilidad, libertad como necesidad: Juliano y San Agustín. PEGUEROLES, Juan.
Metamorphoses: On the Limits of Thought. ALEXAKOS, Panos D.
La palabra interior: La filosofía del lenguaje en San Agustín. PEGUEROLES, Juan.
Porphyry's Criticism of Christianity and The Problem of Augustine's Platonism. EVANGELIOU, Christos.
Postcriptum: La libertad como necesidad del bien, en San Agustín. PEGUEROLES, Juan.
Rasgos de la communidad agustiniana según la 'Regula recepta'. ANOZ, José.
A Reflection on Saint Augustine's *Confessions*. BARKOVICH, Greg.
The Sacred, Secular, and Profane in Augustine's World of Shadows. SPENCER, Jon Michael.
San Agustín y la sexualidad conyugal. BURKE, Cormac.
Sant'Agostino e Hegel a confronto. CALEO, Marcello.
The Significance of the Moral Concept of Virtue in St Augustine's Ethics. TORCHIA, N Joseph.
St Augustine and the Second Way. KLUGE, Eike-Henner W.
Structure and Meaning in St Augustine's *Confessions*. CROSSON, Frederick J.
La teología de la historia en la "ciudad de Dios" (2). OROZ RETA, José (trans) and BAGET BOZZO, Giovanni.
La teología de la historia en la Ciudad de Dios. OROZ RETA, José (trans) and BAGET-BOZZO, Giovanni.
Tres grandes testigos de la luz interior: San Agustín, san Buenaventura y J Henry Newman. OROZ RETA, José.
Working with Wittgenstein's Builders. BIRSCH, Douglas and DORBOLO, Jon.

AUGUSTINISM
Homicide and Love. SMITH, Steven G.
Some Perspectives in Eriugenian Studies: Three Recent Studies. OTTEN, Willemien.
'Postmodern Critical Augustinianism': A Short *Summa* in Forty Two Responses to Unasked Questions. MILBANK, John.

AULARD, A
The Role of Memory in the Historiography of the French Revolution. HUTTON, Patrick H.

AUROBINDO GHOSE
Indian Thought Is a Systematic Body of Thought. SHAH, K J.
Sri Aurobindo and the Process of Physical Transformation. REDDY, V Ananda.

AUSTEN, J
Persuasion: Jane Austen's Philosophical Rhetoric. KASTELY, James L.

AUSTIN
Speech Acts and Literary Theory. PETREY, Sandy.
Response to Foulk's "In Defense of Cahn's Scamps". SILK, David.
Wittgenstein versus Hart: Two Models of Rules for Social and Legal Theory. HUND, John.

AUSTRALIAN
Land, Well-Being and Compensation. PARGETTER, Robert and YOUNG, Robert and BIGELOW, John.
North American, British and Australian Philosophy of Education from 1941 to 1991: Links, Trends, Prospects. BECK, Clive.

AUTHENTICITY
The Authentic Self: Toward a Philosophy of Personality. LACENTRA, Walter.
Chinese Buddhist Apocrypha. BUSWELL JR, Robert E (ed).
History and Spirit: An Inquiry into the Philosophy of Liberation. KOVEL, Joel.
On Walter Benjamin: Critical Essays and Recollections. SMITH, Gary (ed).
The Politics of Being: The Political Thought of Martin Heidegger. WOLIN, Richard.
Selbsttäuschung. LÖW-BEER, Martin.
Vulgarity and Authenticity: Dimensions of Otherness in the World of Jean-Paul Sartre. CHARMÉ, Stuart Zane.
"Augustine and the Norms of Authentic Conversion" in *Grace, Politics and Desire: Essays on Augustine*, MEYNELL, Hugo A.
"Authenticity, Conversion, and the City of Ends in Sartre's *Notebooks for an Ethics*" in *Writing the Politics of Difference*, ANDERSON, Thomas C.
Authenticity Again. SHARPE, R A.
Authenticity as Virtue (in Dutch). STRUYKER BOUDIER, C E M.
Authenticity: A Sartrean Perspective. CATALANO, Joseph.
Heidegger on the Self, Authenticity and Inauthenticity. MANSBACH, Abraham.
The Jargon of Authenticity: Adorno and Feminist Essentialism. PHELAN, Shane.
A Kierkegaardian Critique of Heidegger's Concept of Authenticity. BERTHOLD-BOND, Daniel.
Nietzsche on Authenticity. GOLOMB, Jacob.
On the Form and Authenticity of the *Lysis*. TEJERA, V.
The Ontology of Musical Works and the Authenticity of their Performances. DAVIES, Stephen.
Plato and Archytas in the Seventh Letter. LLOYD, G E R.
Riproposta di una teoria della soggettività in un'epoca di decostruzione del soggetto. LATORA, Salvatore.
Sartre and Our Identity as Individuals. DILMAN, Ilham.

AUTHOR(S)

Writers and Philosophers: A Sourcebook of Philosophical Influences on Literature. THOMAS, Edmund J.
The Death of the Author (as Producer). STOPFORD, John.
The Empirical Author: Salman Rushdie's *The Satanic Verses*. CLOSE, Anthony.

AUTHORITARIANISM

"Authority, Authoritarianism, and Education" in *The Realm of Humanitas: Responses to the Writings of Hannah Arendt*, GARNER, Reuben.

AUTHORITY(-TIES)

The Dice-Playing God: Reflections on Life in a Post-Modern Age. KRIEGLSTEIN, Werner.
Leviathan: Hobbes. TUCK, Richard (ed).
Relating Humanities and Social Thought (Science, Ideology, and Value, Volume 4). EDEL, Abraham.
Sacred Fragments: Recovering Theology for the Modern Jew. GILLMAN, Neil.
"Uguaglianza, riconoscimento del simile e principio d'autorità nell'ultimo Diderot" in *Égalité Uguaglianza*, GOGGI, Gianluigi.
Aesthetic Authority and Tradition: Nietzsche and the Greeks. STRONG, Tracy B.
Authority. WILLARD, Charles A.
Butler and the Authority of Conscience. O'BRIEN, Wendell.
Certainty and Authority. WINCH, Peter.
The Crisis of Authority. OLDS, Mason.
Democratic and Professional Authority in Education. WALKER, J C.
The Epistemology and Ethics of Consensus: Uses and Misuses of 'Ethical' Expertise. TONG, Rosemarie.
A Paradox About Authority. ODERBERG, David S.
Realism in the Authority of Law. BRIGHAM, John and HARRINGTON, Christine.

AUTHORSHIP

Art and Answerability: Early Philosophical Essays—M M Bakhtin. HOLQUIST, Michael (ed).
"Textual Responsibility" in *The Political Responsibility of Intellectuals*, LECERCLE, J J.
The Authorship of Faith. SESSIONS, W L.
The Authorship of the *Abstract* Revisited. NELSON, John O.
The Death of the Author: An Analytical Autopsy. LAMARQUE, Peter.
Erfurt, Ampl Q 70A: A Quaestiones-commentary on the Second Part of Alexander de Villa Dei's *Doctrinale*. KNEEPKENS, C H.
Intellectual Property and Copyright Ethics. ALFINO, Mark.
Richard Rufus of Cornwall and the Authorship of the *Scriptum super Metaphysicam*. NOONE, Timothy B.

AUTOBIOGRAPHY

The Anatomy of Philosophical Style. LANG, Berel.
"Mario Bunge's Life and Work" in *Studies on Mario Bunge's "Treatise"*, BUNGE, Mario.
Retrospections. GOODMAN, Nelson.
Self-Making and World-Making. BRUNER, Jerome.
Theory and Practice. POWELL, J Enoch.

AUTOMATA

Extension of Gurevich-Harrington's Restricted Memory Determinacy Theorem. YAKHNIS, Alexander and YAKHNIS, Vladimir.
Verification of Concurrent Programs: the Automata-Theoretic Framework. VARDI, Moshe Y.

AUTOMATION

Work, Inc.: A Philosophical Inquiry. BYRNE, Edmund F.

AUTOMORPHISM(S)

"Automorphisms of the Lattice of Recursively Enumerable Sets and Hyperhypersimple Sets" in *Logic, Methodology and Philosophy of Science, VIII*, HERRMANN, Eberhard.

AUTONOMY

see also Freedom, Liberty
Controlling Technology: Contemporary Issues. THOMPSON, William B.
The Crisis in Health Care: Ethical Issues. MC KENZIE, Nancy F (ed).
Fallen Freedom: Kant on Radical Evil and Moral Regeneration. MICHALSON JR, Gordon E.
Historia del nombrar: Dos episodios de la subjetividad. THIEBAUT, Carlos.
Human Goodness: Generosity and Courage. PYBUS, Elizabeth.
Kant's System of Rights. MULHOLLAND, Leslie A.
Kant's Theory of Freedom. ALLISON, Henry E.
Kierkegaards Phänomenologie der Freiheitserfahrung. DISSE, Jörg.
Moral Philosophy from Montaigne to Kant: An Anthology, Volume I & II. SCHNEEWIND, J B (ed).
Philosophy and Politics. HUNT, G M K (ed).
The Power of Ideology. MÉSZÁROS, István.
Self, Society, and Personal Choice. MEYERS, Diana T.
Suicide: Right or Wrong?. DONNELLY, John (ed).
Theory and Practice in Medical Ethics. GRABER, Glenn C.
"Citizenship and Autonomy" in *Social Theory of Modern Societies: Anthony Giddens and His Critics*, HELD, David.
Agricultura, desarrollo y autonomía. BLATZ, Charlie.
Are Pregnant Women Fetal Containers?. PURDY, Laura.
Art's Autonomy and Absolute Idealism: The Role of Aesthetics in Schelling's Philosophy (in Dutch). BRAECKMAN, A.
Authority and the Diffusion of Moral Expertise. MC MAHON, Christopher.
Autonomy and Personal History. CHRISTMAN, John.
Autonomy and Political Obligation in Kant. STERN, David S.
Autonomy and Quantum Physics: Nietzsche, Heidegger, and Heisenberg. SEIGFRIED, Hans.
Autonomy and the Common Weal. DANIS, Marion and CHURCHILL, Larry R.
Autonomy, Emotions and Desires: Some Problems Concerning R F Dearden's Account of Autonomy. STONE, Carolyn M.
Autonomy, Empathy, and Transcendence in Sophocles' *Antigone*: A Phenomenological Perspective. NISSIM-SABAT, Marilyn.
Autonomy, Liberalism and State Neutrality. MASON, Andrew D.
Basic Elements of the Concept of Individualism. WILKIE, Raymond.
Chronic Illness and the Physician-Patient Relationship. MOROS, Daniel A (and others).
Commentary— "Make Me Live": Autonomy and Terminal Illness. MISBIN, Robert I.
Community and Autonomy: Logically Incompatible Values?. MASON, Andrew.
The Consequences of Endorsing Sentimental Homicide. BARRY, Robert L.
Don Quijote: voluntad y representación. MURILLO, Roberto.
Emotions and Responsibility. TURSKI, George.
Empowering Teachers: Towards a Justification for Intervention. HARRIS, Kevin.
El ensimismamiento del poder: Maquiavelo y la ciencia política moderna. GARCIA, Romano.
Equal Opportunity and the Family. VALLENTYNE, Peter and LIPSON, Morry.
La filosofía transcendental: el destino de un proyecto ilustrado. FLAMARIQUE, Lourdes.
Fragmentos póstumos Friedrich Nietzsche. GIACOIA JUNIOR, Oswaldo.
Freedom and Autonomy: The Kantian Analytic and a Sartrean Critique. BEAVERS, Anthony.
Freedom Not to be Free: The Case of the Slavery Contract in J S Mill's *On Liberty*. ARCHARD, David.
The Futures of Physicians: Agency and Autonomy Reconsidered. SALMON, J Warren and WHITE, William and FEINGLASS, Joe.
The Irreducibly Clinical Character of Bioethics. WEAR, Stephen.
Kant's Search for the Philosopher's Stone. AXIOTIS, Ares.
Knowledge, Reason and Human Autonomy: A Review Article. KRISHNA, Daya.
The Limits of a Wish. RIE, Michael A.
Measuring the Quality of Life: Why, How and What?. HÄYRY, Matti.
Moral oder Klugheit? Überlegungen zur Gestalt der Autonomie des Politischen im Denken Kants. SCHMITZ, Heinz-Gerd.
Nietzsche as Instructor in Autonomy? Comments. FOWLER, Mark C.
Nietzsche contra Kant and the Problem of Autonomy. WHITE, Richard.
Nonautonomous Psychology. PETRIE, Bradford.
On Respect. BLUM, Alex.
Orchestrating Social Change: An Imperative in Care of the Chronically Ill. ROTH, Patricia A and HARRISON, Janet K.
El papel de la comunicación espontánea en los procesos de evolución social. RODRÍGUEZ HÖLKEMEYER, Patricia.
Peter Gardner on Religious Upbringing and the Liberal Ideal of Religious Autonomy. MC LAUGHLIN, T H.
The Pharmacist's Role in Patient Care. SCHULZ, Richard M and BRUSHWOOD, David B.
The Physician-Societal Relationship. CRELINSTEN, Gordon L.
Poetry and Autonomy. SANKOWSKI, Edward.
Private Defense. GORR, Michael.
Reassessing Autonomy in Long-Term Care. AGICH, George J.
Reconsidering the Wisdom of the Body. SULLIVAN, Mark D.
La revolución teórica del Príncipe de Maquiavelo. GIGLIOLI, Giovanna.
Scepticism and Autonomy. HOOKWAY, Christopher.

AVANT GARDE

"The Avant Garde, Institutional and Critical Theories of Art" in *XIth International Congress in Aesthetics, Nottingham 1988*, SNYMAN, J J.
The Avant Garde, Institutional and Critical Theories of Art. SNYMAN, Johan J.
On the Philosophy of the Czech Avant-garde, Part II (in Czechoslovakian). STROHS, S.
Understanding Performance Art: Art beyond Art. HEYD, Thomas.

AVERROES

Ibn Rushd: Averroes. URVOY, Dominique.

AVERROISM

"Christian Averroism, Fideism and the 'Two-fold Truth'" in *The Philosophy in Christianity*, BROWN, Stuart.
El averroísmo de Juan de Sècheville. RODRÍGUEZ, Juan Acosta.

AVICENNA

El autoconocimiento del alma según Avicena latino. OYARZABAL, Manuel.

AVICENNA
La distinción entre esencia y existencia en Avicena. IBÁÑEZ, Alejandro Herrera.
The Latin Avicenna as a Source of Thomas Aquinas's Metaphysics. WIPPEL, John F.

AWARENESS
see also Consciousness
Choiceless Awareness. SEN, Sanat Kumar.
What is the Price of a Rich Life?. MEYER, Zofia Golab.

AXELROD, R
The Inapplicability of Evolutionary Stable Strategy to the Prisoner's Dilemma. MARINOFF, Louis.

AXIOLOGY
see also Value(s)
Baffling Phenomena: And Other Studies in the Philosophy of Knowledge and Valuation. RESCHER, Nicholas.
Returning to Sils-Maria: A Commentary to Nietzsche's "Also sprach Zarathustra". WHITLOCK, Greg.
The Tanner Lectures on Human Values, Volume XI. PETERSON, Grethe B (ed).
The Tanner Lectures On Human Values, Volume XII. PETERSON, Grethe B (ed).
Axiology as the Form of Purity of Heart: A Reading Husserliana XXVIII. HART, James G.
Creative Value. ODDIE, Graham.
A Critical Examination of Scheler's Justification of the Existence of Values. MOOSA, Imtiaz.
A Dialogue on Value, I: Values and Relations. LACHS, John.
A Dialogue on Value, II: Why Is There Something Good, Not Simply Something?. KOHÁK, Erazim.
A Dialogue on Value, III: Is Everything Intrinsically Good?. LACHS, John.
Feminist Transformations of Moral Theory. HELD, Virginia.
La fondazione dei valori nell'assiologia critica di Nicola Petruzzellis. TURCO, Giovanni.
How Wide Is the Gap Between Facts and Values?. RESCHER, Nicholas.
Hume and Intrinsic Value. THOMAS, D A Lloyd.
Knowing and Valuing Fairness. HINTON, J M.
Laudan's Model of Axiological Change and the Bohr-Einstein Debate 77. FOLSE JR, Henry J.
Moral Dilemmas. MAC INTYRE, Alasdair.
Lo que no sabemos sobre los valores. INGARDEN, Roman.
Skepticism About Goodness and Rightness. GOLDMAN, Alan H.
La tecnología desde un punto de vista ético. RAMÍREZ, E Roy.
Thoughts on the Taxonomy and Semantics of Value Terms. MARIETTA JR, Don E.
Tradition and Its Value: A Contribution to the History of Polish Marxist Philosophical Thought (in Polish). GRADKOWSKI, Waldemar.
True and False Pleasures. LOVIBOND, Sabina.
Values, the Environment and the Creative Act. THOMAS, John C.

AXIOM OF CHOICE
The Dual Cantor-Bernstein Theorem and the Partition Principle. BANASCHEWSKI, Bernhard and MOORE, Gregory H.
An Equivalent of the Axiom of Choice in Finite Models of the Powerset Axiom. ABIAN, Alexander and AMIN, Wael A.
Equivalent Versions of a Weak Form of the Axiom of Choice. SHANNON, G.
Provable Forms of Martin's Axiom. SHANNON, Gary P.

AXIOM OF DETERMINACY
Weak Axioms of Determinacy and Subsystems of Analysis II. TANAKA, Kazuyuki.

AXIOM OF REDUCIBILITY
Was the Axiom of Reducibility a Principle of Logic?. LINSKY, Bernard.

AXIOM(S)
Algebraization of Paraconsistent Logic P^1. LEWIN, R A and MIKENBERG, I F and SCHWARZE, M G.
Axiomatization of 'Peircean' Branching-Time Logic. ZANARDO, Alberto.
Eine Bemerkung zu spektralen Darstellungen von ρ-stelligen Aufzählbaren. DEUTSCH, Michael.
The Cardinality of Powersets in Finite Models of the Powerset Axiom. ABIAN, Alexander and AMIN, Wael A.
Constructive Interpolation Theorems for $S2^0$ and S2. BARCA, Anne and MC ROBBIE, Michael.
Double Extension Set Theory. KISIELEWICZ, Andrzej.
First-Order Theories Without Axioms. STEPIEN, Teodor.
Gentzenization and Decidability of Some Contraction-Less Relevant Logics. BRADY, Ross T.
Grammar Logics. FARIÑAS DEL CERRO, Luis and PENTTONEN, Martti.
Hereditarily Finite Finsler Sets. BOOTH, David.
Intuitionistic Sentential Calculus with Classical Identity. LUKOWSKI, Piotr.
Intuitive Semantics for Some Three-Valued Logics Connected with Information, Contrariety and Subcontrariety. VAKARELOV, Dimitir.
Kantian and Non-Kantian Logics. PUGA, Leila Z and DA COSTA, Newton C A and CARNIELLI, Walter A.
The Logic of Lost Lingens. SEAGER, William.
More Axioms for the Set-Theoretic Hierarchy. POLLARD, Stephen.
Multiset Theory. BLIZARD, Wayne D.
On Regular Modal Logics with Axiom.... SWIRYDOWICZ, Kazimierz.
On Subsystems of the System J_1 of Arruda and Da Costa. URBAS, Igor.
Paraconsistency and the J-Systems of Arruda and da Costa. URBAS, Igor.
Peirced Clean Through. MEYER, Robert K.
Provable Forms of Martin's Axiom. SHANNON, Gary P.
Relevance and Paraconsistency—A New Approach, Part II: The Formal Systems. AVRON, Arnon.
Riflessioni sulla fondazione dell'assioma parmenideo. GRAZIANI, Andrea.
Routley-Meyer Type Semantics for Urquhart's C. MÉNDEZ, José M.
The Simple Substitution Property of Gödel's Intermediate Propositional Logics S_n's. SASAKI, Katsumi.
Single-Axiom Systems. STEPIEN, Teodor.
The Special Model Axiom in Nonstandard Analysis. ROSS, David.
A Strengthening of Scott's ZF-Minus-Extensionality Result. POLLARD, Stephen.
A Unification-Theoretic Method for Investigating the *k*-Provability Problem. FARMER, William.
The Union Axiom in Zermelo Set Theory. GONZÁLEZ, Carlos G.
Variations on da Costa *C* Systems and Dual-Intuitionistic Logics (I). SYLVAN, Richard.
Why are Definitions True?. SKIDMORE, Arthur.

AXIOMATIC
"An Axiomatic Basis as a Desired Form of a Physical Theory" in *Logic, Methodology and Philosophy of Science, VIII*, LUDWIG, G.
An Axiomatic Basis of Accounting: A Structuralist Reconstruction. BALZER, Wolfgang and MATTESSICH, Richard.
Prior's Disease. USBERTI, Gabriele.

AXIOMATICS
The Axiomatic Method: Its Origin and Purpose. AGASHE, S D.

AXIOMATIZABILITY
The Elementary Theory of the Natural Lattice is Finitely Axiomatizable. CEGIELSKI, Patrick.
Equational Theory of Positive Numbers with Exponentiation is Not Finitely Axiomatizable. GUREVIC, R.
Finite Axiomatizability and Theories with Trivial Algebraic Closure. MACPHERSON, Dugald.
Intorno all'autofondazione delle norme: Ragione formale e principio razionale tra logica e diritto. SCIACCA, Fabrizio.
Modal Counterparts of Medvedev Logic of Finite Problems Are Not Finitely Axiomatizable. SHEHTMAN, Valentin.
A Solution to a Problem of Urquhart. KRACHT, Marcus.

AXIOMATIZATION
The Axiomatization of Randomness. VAN LAMBALGEN, Michiel.
Axiomatization of the De Morgan Type Rules. HERRMANN, B.
Linear Axiomatics of Communicative Product-Free Lambek Calculus. ZIELONKA, Wojciech.
On Axiomatization of Many-Valued Logics Associated with Formalization of Plausible Reasonings. ANSHAKOV, O M and FINN, V K and SKVORTSOV, D P.

AYER
Analysis as a Method in Philosophy with Special Reference to A J Ayer. SRINIVAS, K.
Lenguaje y metafísica en Alfred J Ayer. BEUCHOT, Mauricio.

BACH, J
Glenn Gould: "archilecteur" *des Variations Goldberg*. GUERTIN, Ghyslaine.

BACHELARD
Bachelard and Scientific Realism. TIJIATTAS, Mary.

BACKWARD CAUSATION
Backwards Causation and the Permanence of the Past. ODDIE, Graham.
A Critique of Mellor's Argument against 'Backwards' Causation. RIGGS, Peter J.
Hornsby's Puzzles: Rejoinder to Wreen and Hornsby. KOSROVANI, Emilio.

BADRINATHJI
Dehātmavāda or the Body as Soul: Exploration of a Possibility within Nyāya Thought. LATH, Mukund (trans) and SHUKLA, Pandit Badrinath.

BAIER, A
Reply to Dahl, Baier and Schneewind. MAC INTYRE, Alasdair.

BAIRD, D
Factor Analysis, Information-Transforming Instruments, and Objectivity: A Reply and Discussion. MULAIK, Stanley A.

BAKHTIN, M
Art and Answerability: Early Philosophical Essays—M M Bakhtin. HOLQUIST, Michael (ed).
Bakhtin and the Epistemology of Discourse. THOMSON, Clive (ed).
"Dialogism in the Novel and Bakhtin's Theory of Culture" in *XIth International Congress in Aesthetics, Nottingham 1988*, SHEVTSOVA, Maria.
Bakhtin's Marxist Formalism. MC BRIDE, William Thomas.

BALABAN, O
The Role of Aristotle's *Praxis* Today. GUY, Alfred.

BAMBROUGH, R
Reply to the President: "Ethics and the Limits of Consistency". WILLIAMS, Bernard.
Wittgenstein on Names and Family Resemblances. HYMERS, Michael.

BANTOCK, G
G H Bantock as Educational Philosopher. BARRIE, John A.

BARBEY-D'AUREVILLY, J
L'inquiétante étrangeté de Jules Amédée Barbey d'Aurevilly. ROMEYER DHERBEY, Gilbert.

BARE PARTICULARS
Haecceitas and the Bare Particular. PARK, Woosuk.

BARGAINING
Negotation Games: Applying Game Theory to Bargaining and Arbitration. BRAMS, Steven J.
"A Bargaining Theory Approach to Default Provisions and Disclosure Rules in Contract Law" in *Liability and Responsibility*, COLEMAN, Jules L and HECKATHORN, Douglas D and MASER, Steven M.
Shrewd Bargaining on the Moral Frontier: Toward a Theory of Morality in Practice. DEES, J Gregory and CRAMPTON, Peter C.

BARINDUCTION
Extended Bar Induction in Applicative Theories. RENARDEL DE LAVALETTE, Gerard R.
Lifschitz' Realizability. VAN OOSTEN, Jaap.

BAROQUE
"La réhabilitation de l'allégorie: baroque et modernité" in *XIth International Congress in Aesthetics, Nottingham 1988*, COURT, Raymond.
Descartes e le "culture" barocche: Appunti su alcune recenti interpretazioni. LOJACONO, Ettore.

BARROW, J
Barrow and Tipler on the Anthropic Principle versus Divine Design. CRAIG, William Lane.

BARRY, B
A Theory of Social Justice?. HORTON, John.

BARTH
The Barth Legacy: New Athanasius or Origen Redivivus? A Response to T F Torrance. MULLER, Richard A.

BARTHES, R
"Roland Barthes et Umberto Eco à la Recherche du Roman Postmoderne" in *XIth International Congress in Aesthetics, Nottingham 1988*, ZNEPOLSKY, Ivahilo.
The Death of the Author (as Producer). STOPFORD, John.
The Death of the Author: An Analytical Autopsy. LAMARQUE, Peter.
La sémiotique, les objets singuliers et la complexité. THÉRIEN, Gilles.

BARTLEY, W
A Dilemma for Bartley's Pancritical Rationalism. HAUPTLI, Bruce W.

BASIC BELIEF(S)
The Crucial Disanalogies Between Properly Basic Belief and Belief in God. GRIGG, Richard.
Plantinga's Box. SESSIONS, William Lad.

BASIC NEED(S)
Development Aid: The Moral Obligation to Innovation. DUNDON, Stanislaus J.

BATAILLE, G
Against Architecture: The Writings of Georges Bataille. HOLLIER, Denis.
Foreign Bodies in Strange Places: A Note on Maurice Merleau-Ponty, Georges Bataille, and Architecture. KRELL, David Farrell.
The Joy of Transgression: Bataille and Kristeva. MARCHAK, Catherine.

BAUDELAIRE
On Walter Benjamin: Critical Essays and Recollections. SMITH, Gary (ed).
Kompensierte Moderne. LÖVENICH, F.

BAUM, L
Interpretation and the Social Reality of Law. GOLDFORD, Dennis.

BAXTER, D
The World-Shift Theory of Free Choice. DAVIS, Wayne A.

BAY, C
Libertad individual frente a determinación social. FRANCISCO PÉREZ, M.

BAYES
Experiment: Right or Wrong. FRANKLIN, Allan.
"Rationality and Objectivity in Science, *or* Tom Kuhn Meets Tom Bayes" in *Scientific Theories*, SALMON, Wesley C.
"Two Perspectives on Consensus for (Bayesian) Inference and Decisions" in *Knowledge Representation and Defeasible Reasoning*, SEIDENFELD, Teddy.
Bayes' Bayesianism. EARMAN, John.
Let's Razor Ockham's Razor. SOBER, Elliott.

BAYES RULE
A Fully Logical Inductive Logic. NOLT, John.

BAYESIANISM
Do the Right Thing: Studies in Limited Rationality. RUSSELL, Stuart.
The Dynamics of Rational Deliberation. SKYRMS, Brian.

Knowledge in Flux: Modeling the Dynamics of Epistemic States. GÄRDENFORS, Peter.
The Sweep of Probability. SCHLESINGER, George N.
"The Bayesian Alternative to the Methodology of Scientific Research Programmes" in *Imre Lakatos and Theories of Scientific Change*, URBACH, Peter.
"Bayesian Problems of Old Evidence" in *Scientific Theories*, EELLS, E.
"Fitting Your Theory to the Facts: Probably Not Such a Bad Thing After All" in *Scientific Theories*, HOWSON, Colin.
"Jeffrey's Rule, Passage of Experience, and *Neo*-Bayesianism" in *Knowledge Representation and Defeasible Reasoning*, PEARL, Judea.
Against Conditionalization. BACCHUS, Fahiem and KYBURG JR, Henry E and THALOS, Mariam.
Annabel and the Bookmaker: An Everyday Tale of Bayesian Folk. MILNE, Peter.
A Bayesian Proof of a Humean Principle. GILLIES, Donald.
A Dilemma for Subjective Bayesians—and How to Resolve It. MILNE, Peter.
Explaining Science. KORB, Kevin B.
The Geometry of Legal Principles. CHUAQUI, Rolando and MALITZ, Jerome.
The Last Word on Induction?. HOWSON, Colin.
On the Descriptive Adequacy of Levi's Decision Theory. MAHER, Patrick and KASHIMA, Yoshihisa.
Reply to Maher and Kashima: "On the Descriptive Adequacy of Levi's Decision Theory". LEVI, Isaac.
Theory of the Apparatus and Theory of the Phenomena: The Case of Low Dose Electron Microscopy. SWIJTINK, Zeno G.
The Turing-Good Weight of Evidence Function and Popper's Measure of the Severity of a Test. GILLIES, Donald.
Two Principles of Bayesian Epistemology. TALBOTT, W J.
Weights or the Value of Knowledge. RAMSEY, F P.
Why Scientists Gather Evidence. MAHER, Patrick.

BAYLE
Bayle, Leibniz, Hume and Reid on Extension, Composites and Simples. CUMMINS, Phillip.
El escepticismo crítico en el Diccionario de Bayle. ARROYO, Julián.

BEATRICE OF NAZARETH
"Beatrice of Nazareth" in *A History of Women Philosophers, Volume II: Medieval, Renaissance and Enlightenment, A.D. 500-1600*, WOLFSKEEL, Cornelia.

BEAUTIFUL
Análisis de la doctrina ética de las "observaciones sobre lo bello y sublime". GONZÁLEZ PORTA, Mario A.

BEAUTY
The Dialogues of Plato, Volume II. ALLEN, R E (trans).
Hellenic and Christian Studies. ARMSTRONG, A H.
"Beautiful Things and the Aesthetic Subject" in *XIth International Congress in Aesthetics, Nottingham 1988*, VAN DER SCHOOT, Albert.
"The New Anti-Aestheticism" in *XIth International Congress in Aesthetics, Nottingham 1988*, GOLASZEWSKA, Maria.
The Beautiful, the Ugly, and the Tao. COLEMAN, Earle J.
Beauty and the Genealogy of Art Theory. CARROLL, Noël.
Edward Bullogh's Aesthetics and Aestheticism: Features of Reality to Be Experienced. BOULTING, Noel E.
Hutcheson's Account of Beauty as a Response to Mandeville. MICHAEL, Emily and MICHAEL, Fred S.
Nietzsche's Genealogy: Of Beauty and Community. KEMAL, S.
A Note on Ruth Lorand's 'Free and Dependent Beauty: A Puzzling Issue'. LORD, Catherine.
Osservazioni sul bello naturale e sul bello artistico in filosofia. FRANCHI, Alfredo.
Remaking the She-Devil: A Critical Look at Feminist Approaches to Beauty. DAVIS, Kathy.

BECOMING
Being and Becoming: A Critique of Post-Modernism. CENTORE, F F.
Divenire, principio di causalità, affermazione teologica. SACCHI, Dario.
A Marxist Approach to the Concept of Being/Becoming Human. GOLUBOVIC, Zagorka.

BEDIENT, C
Reading Kristeva: A Response to Calvin Bedient. MOI, Toril.

BEETHOVEN
Beethoven's Ninth Symphony: The Sense of an Ending. SOLOMON, Maynard.

BEGGING THE QUESTION
'P, Therefore, P' Without Circularity. SORENSEN, Roy A.
Does Aristotle Beg the Question in His Defense of the Principle of Non-Contradiction?. DEGNAN, Michael.
On Begging the Question 'Who is N?'. PATTON, Thomas E.

BEGINNING
"Beginning" in *Essays on Hegel's Logic*, MAKER, William.
La pensée gonséthienne et le mouvement systémique. PEGUIRON, Nicolas.
Quantum Cosmology and the Beginning of the Universe. SMITH, Gerrit.

BEHAVIOR

Explaining Behavior: Reasons in a World of Causes. DRETSKE, Fred.
The Idea of a Social Science and its Relation to Philosophy (Second Edition). WINCH, Peter.
Linguistic Behaviour. BENNETT, Jonathan.
"Can the Mind Change the World?" in *Meaning and Method: Essays in Honor of Hilary Putnam*, BLOCK, Ned.
"An Empirical Interpretation of Ethogenics" in *Harré and His Critics*, ARGYLE, Michael.
"Folk Psychology and the Explanation of Human Behavior" in *Philosophical Perspectives, 3: Philosophy of Mind and Action Theory, 1989*, CHURCHLAND, Paul M.
"I Don't Know Why I Did It" in *Harré and His Critics*, CROWLE, Tony.
Behavior, Biology, and Information Theory. SENCHUK, Dennis M.
Behavioral Paradigm for a Psychological Resolution of the Free Will Issue. HARCUM, E Rae.
Corporate Codes of Conduct: A Collective Conscience and Continuum. RAIBORN, Cecily A and PAYNE, Dinah.
Corresponding Regressions, Procedural Evidence, and the Dialectics of Substantive Theory, Metaphysics, Methodology. CHAMBERS, William.
Developmental Constraints on Ethical Behaviour in Business. HARRIS, Claudia and BROWN, William.
Economic Theory and Human Behavior. MC NULTY, T Michael.
Inferring Formal Causation from Corresponding Regressions. CHAMBERS, William V.
Kritik der Soziobiologie des Menschen. KASPAR, Rudolf F.
Machines as Persons?. HANFLING, Oswald.
The Micro-Macro Problem in Collective Behavior: Reconciling Agency and Structure. LEE, Raymond L M.
Moral Behavior at Public Performances. OLDS, Mason.
Natural Problems and Artificial Intelligence. HENLEY, Tracy.
Philosophy and the Theory of Social Behaviour. HAMLYN, D W.
The Problematics of "Clarity" in Research of Teaching: A Response to Walden Crabtree. SCHULTZ, Frederick M.
Realism, Naturalism and Social Behaviour. OUTHWAITE, William.
Rehabilitating Responsibility. GADEN, Gerry.
Role Theory: A Reconstruction. VAN VONDEREN, Marijke L.
Secondary Reflection and Marcelian Anthropology. MICHAUD, Thomas A.
Teamwork. COHEN, Philip R and LEVESQUE, Hector J.
Untangling Cause, Necessity, Temporality, and Method: Response to Chamber's Method of Corresponding Regressions. WILLIAMS, Richard N.
What Makes Us So Different from the Apes?. LAYNG, Tony.
Why (Legal) Rules Often Fail to Control Human Behavior. CROMBAG, H F M.

BEHAVIORAL SCIENCES

see also Human Sciences
Attitudes, Leprechauns and Neutrinos: The Ontology of Behavioral Science. CHANDLER, Marthe.
Search for Beliefs to Live by Consistent with Science. SPERRY, R W.

BEHAVIORISM

Creativity in George Herbert Mead. GUNTER, Pete A Y (ed).
Mind and Cognition: A Reader. LYCAN, William G (ed).
Wittgenstein: Meaning and Mind, Volume 3 of an Analytical Commentary on Philosophical Investigations. HACKER, P M S.
Behaviourism, Neuroscience and Translational Indeterminacy. WARMBROD, Ken.
The Development of Wittgenstein's Views about the Other Minds Problem. TER HARK, M R M.
Lewis's Functionalism and Reductive Materialism. KERNOHAN, Andrew.
The Locked-In Syndrome and the Behaviorist Epistemology of Other Minds. KURTHEN, Martin (and others).

BEIERWALTES, W

Aspetti di attualità teoretica del pensiero procliano negli studi di Werner Beierwaltes. SCOTTI, Nicoletta.

BEING

see also Dasein, Existence, Ontology
Being and Becoming: A Critique of Post-Modernism. CENTORE, F F.
Echoes: After Heidegger. SALLIS, John.
God and Subjectivity. GALGAN, Gerald J.
The Great Goddess and the Aistian Mythical World. VYCINAS, Vincent.
History and the Paradoxes of Metaphysics in "Dantons Tod". TAYLOR, Rodney.
Inscriptions and Reflections: Essays in Philosophical Theology. SCHARLEMANN, Robert P.
Introduction to the Philosophy of Nature. HETZLER, Florence M.
Jean-Paul Sartre. HENGELBROCK, Jürgen.
The Many Dimensions of the Human Person. STEGER, E Ecker.
Metaphysik als Metahistorik oder Hermeneutik des unreinen Denkens Die Philosophie Max Müllers. RUIZ-PESCE, Ramón Eduardo.
Nicolai Hartmann's New Ontology. WERKMEISTER, W H.
The Origin of Thought. ROSMINI, Antonio.
Le Philosophie et les Passions. MEYER, Michel.
The Politics of Being: The Political Thought of Martin Heidegger. WOLIN, Richard.
Quest for Certainty: A Comparative Study of Heidegger and Sankara. GRIMES, John A.
The Question of God in Heidegger's Phenomenology. KOVACS, George.
Self and Non-Self: The Drigdrisyaviveka Attributed to Samkara. RAPHAEL (trans).
Strukturanthropologie "Der menschliche Mensch". ROMBACH, Heinrich.
"Alterity and the Paradox of Being" in *Ontology and Alterity in Merleau-Ponty*, FROMAN, Wayne J.
"Augustine's Philosophy of Being" in *The Philosophy in Christianity*, STEAD, Christopher.
"Between Being and Essence: Reflection's Logical Disguises" in *Essays on Hegel's Logic*, DAHLSTROM, Daniel O.
"Esserci e differenza ontologica in Heidegger" in *Razionalitá critica: nella filosofia moderna*, ESPOSITO, Costantino.
"Listening at the Abyss" in *Ontology and Alterity in Merleau-Ponty*, BURKE, Patrick.
"A Reply to Cynthia Willett's "The Shadow of Hegel's *Science of Logic*" in *Essays on Hegel's Logic*, DI GIOVANNI, George.
"The Shadow of Hegel's *Science of Logic*" in *Essays on Hegel's Logic*, WILLETT, Cynthia.
A "Con-versão" da Filosofia em Martin Heidegger. ESTÊVÃO, Carlos.
"Extrinsic Cognoscibility": A Seventeenth Century Supertranscendental Notion. DOYLE, John P.
La "riabilitazione" della δυναμιζ e dell'ενεργεια in Heidegger. VOLPI, Franco.
La analogía del ser en Suárez. ROIG GIRONELLA, J.
Aristóteles desde Heidegger. CASARES, Angel J.
Aristotelian and Whiteheadian Conceptions of Actuality: II. FETZ, Reto Luzius and FELT, James W.
Being and Categorial Intuition. COBB-STEVENS, Richard.
Condemned to Time: The Limits of Merleau-Ponty's Quest for Being. LOWRY, Atherton C.
L'essere mortale dei mortali: Un'analisi sul problema della morte nel pensiero del secondo Heidegger. CICCHESE, Gennaro.
Establishing of the Object of Metaphysics—Separation (in Polish). MARYNIARCZYK, A.
Être et non-être chez Aristote: contraires ou contradictoires?. BERTI, Enrico.
Finalidad y dimensiones "kaíricas" de la estructura del ser. MOUTSOPOULOS, Evanghélos A.
Fondamento e verità. CAMPANALE, Domenico.
Foreign Bodies in Strange Places: A Note on Maurice Merleau-Ponty, Georges Bataille, and Architecture. KRELL, David Farrell.
From the Phenomenology of Time Toward Process Metaphysics: Pragmatism and Heidegger. ROSENTHAL, Sandra B.
Heidegger and Myth: A Loop in the History of Being. HATAB, Lawrence J.
Heidegger and the Critique of the Understanding of Evil as Privatio Boni. CAPOBIANCO, Richard.
Heidegger e la duplicità del presente. PENZO, Maurizio.
Heidegger on Logic and Language: Some Aporiai. FAY, Thomas A.
Heidegger und die Frage um die Quelle des Grundbegriffes der Metaphysik (in Polish). ROZDZENSKI, R.
Heraclitus: Heidegger's 1943 Lecture Held at Freiburg University. FRINGS, Manfred S.
Hölderlin über Urteil und Sein. GRAESER, Andreas.
El hombre y el misterio del ser. TRIANA, Manuel.
Incarnation and Essentialization: A Reading of Heidegger. CAPUTO, John D.
Intersubjectivity without Subjectivism. SINGER, Beth J.
Is There a "Meaning" of Being? Against the Deconstructionist Reading of Heidegger. SCHALOW, Frank.
A Kierkegaardian Critique of Heidegger's Concept of Authenticity. BERTHOLD-BOND, Daniel.
L'être du non-être en perspective aristotélicienne. DE MURALT, André.
L'unité-unicité de l'"esse" Thomiste. PASQUA, Hervé.
M Heideggers Auslegung von Sophokles' "Oedipus Tyrannus" (in Japanese). SEKIGUCHI, Hiroshi.
Marxism as the Foundation of Philosophies of Science: *The Case of G Lukács' Ontology of Social Being*. TUCHANSKA, Barbara.
A Marxist Approach to the Concept of Being/Becoming Human. GOLUBOVIC, Zagorka.
Memory, Forgetfulness and the Disclosure of Being in Heidegger and Plotinus. BALES, Eugene F.
Metafisica e dialettica: quattro saggi sull'interpretazione hegeliana di Aristotele. FERRARIN, Alfredo.
The Metaphilosophy of Dialogue. KUCZYNSKI, Janusz.
Nature et liberté dans l'ontologie fondamentale de Heidegger. BRISART, Robert.
La noción de ser en Tomás de Sutton. ECHAURI, Raúl.
Note sulle recenti traduzioni di *Essere e tempo* in Francia. MARRATI, Paola.
Il paradosso del fondamento nella simbolica del gioco e sogno della libertà. MASULLO, Aldo.
La passione dell'essere: Viaggio lungo i sentieri del nulla. IANNOTTA, Daniella.
Porosity: Violence and the Question of Politics in Heidegger's *Introduction to Metaphysics*. MC NEILL, William.

BEING

La puissance d'être selon Tillich. GOUNELLE, André.
La question de l'être et du non-être des objets mathématiques chez Plotin et Jamblique. O'MEARA, Dominic.
La question de l'être. LARIVÉ, Marc.
Il rapporto Parmenide-Telesio dal Persio al Maranta. ARTESE, Luciano.
As relações entre o Deus da Razão e o Deus da Fé. RENAUD, Michel.
Riflessioni sulla fondazione dell'assioma parmenideo. GRAZIANI, Andrea.
Sartre's Being-for-Heidegger, Heidegger's Being-for-Sartre. MARTINOT, Steve.
El ser principial y Dios: Una observación a la teología de Maimónides. GARCÍA GONZÁLEZ, Juan.
Ser y Dios, entre filosofía y teología, en Heidegger y Siewerth. CABADA, Manuel.
El ser y el sentido: Notas husserlianas. PEGUEROLES, Juan.
Sobre la "Metafísica del bien y del mal". MELENDO, Tomás.
Spinoza, Heidegger, and the Ontological Argument. SINGER, Brent A.
Temporality and the Concept of Being. SHALOM, Albert.
Le temps du souffrir: Remarques critiques sur la phénoménologie de M Henry. PORÉE, Jérôme.
La théologie de Heidegger. CRÉTELLA, Henri.
Thinking (Beyond) Being. STENSTAD, Gail.
Thomas d'Aquin a-t-il tente d'exprimer le principe d'individuation à l'intérieur des proprietés.... CASPAR, Philippe.
Thought and Being in Kant and Hegel. HOULGATE, Stephen.
Thought Rhythym and Experience in *Der Satz vom Grund* (in Dutch). PEETERS, L.
El tránsito de la existencia al ser. KELZ, Carlos R.
Ultimate Double Binds. SCHÜRMANN, Reiner.
Univocità dell'essere e intenzionalià del conoscere. ANTONELLI, Mauro.
We Mortals. LINGIS, Alphonso.
Wege der Seinsfrage: Aus Anlass der 100. GANDER, Hans-Helmuth.
What Philosophy for Judaism and Christianity? (in French). DUPONCHEELE, Joseph.

BEING-IN-THE-WORLD

Being-in-the-World: A Commentary on Heidegger's "Being and Time", Division 1. DREYFUS, Hubert L.
Caminhos do Filosofar. MIRANDA, Maria do Carmo Tavares de.
Existentialism. COOPER, David E.
Getting the Subject Back into the World: Heidegger's Version. KERR, Fergus.
Sinn-Wahrheit-Ort: Tres etapas en el pensamiento de Heidegger. BERCIANO V, Modesto.

BELIEF(S)

see also Faith
Divine Nature and Human Language: Essays in Philosophical Theology. ALSTON, William P.
Experiment: Right or Wrong. FRANKLIN, Allan.
Explaining Behavior: Reasons in a World of Causes. DRETSKE, Fred.
False Consciousness. MEYERSON, Denise.
The Fragmentation of Reason. STICH, Stephen.
A Hindu Perspective on the Philosophy of Religion. SHARMA, Arvind.
Human Interests: Reflections on Philosophical Anthropology. RESCHER, Nicholas.
In Defense of Mystical Ideas: Support for Mystical Beliefs from a Purely Theoretical Viewpoint. CHAPMAN, Tobias.
John Craige's Mathematical Principles of Christian Theology. NASH, Richard.
Knowledge in Flux: Modeling the Dynamics of Epistemic States. GÄRDENFORS, Peter.
Linguistic Behaviour. BENNETT, Jonathan.
Metaphysical Delusion. COWLEY, Fraser.
L'ordine della certezza: Scientificità e persuasione in Descartes. BONICALZI, Francesca.
Philosophical Papers: F P Ramsey. MELLOR, D H (ed).
Philosophical Perspectives, 3: Philosophy of Mind and Action Theory, 1989. TOMBERLIN, James E (ed).
Representing and Reasoning With Probabilistic Knowledge: A Logical Approach to Probabilities. BACCHUS, Fahiem.
Der sinnliche Gehalt der Wahrnehmung. SCHANTZ, Richard.
"Belief Revision, Non-Monotonic Reasoning, and the Ramsey Test" in *Knowledge Representation and Defeasible Reasoning*, CROSS, Charles.
"Belief, Nominalism, and Quantification" in *Philosophical Perspectives, 4: Action Theory and Philosophy of Mind, 1990*, TOMBERLIN, James E.
"Beliefs About Mathematical Objects" in *Physicalism in Mathematics*, RESNIK, Michael D.
"Cognitive Access and Semantic Puzzle" in *Propositional Attitudes: The Role of Content in Logic, Language, and Mind*, OWENS, Joseph I.
"Davidson on Assertion, Convention and Belief" in *The Mind of Donald Davidson*, PICARDI, Eva.
"Dogmatism and Belief in French Cultural Life in the 1930s" in *From Twilight to Dawn: The Cultural Vision of Jacques Maritain*, SUTHER, Judith D.
"Hope" in *The Philosophy in Christianity*, SUTHERLAND, Stewart.
"Hysteria, Belief and Magic" in *Harré and His Critics*, TAYLOR, David.
"Illogical Belief" in *Philosophical Perspectives, 3: Philosophy of Mind and Action Theory, 1989*, SALMON, Nathan.
"Jeffrey's Rule, Passage of Experience, and *Neo*-Bayesianism" in *Knowledge Representation and Defeasible Reasoning*, PEARL, Judea.
"The Mode-of-Presentation Problem" in *Propositional Attitudes: The Role of Content in Logic, Language, and Mind*, SCHIFFER, Stephen.
"On the Characterization of Cognitive Progress" in *Imre Lakatos and Theories of Scientific Change*, HILPINEN, Risto.
"Pragmatism and Choosing to Believe" in *Reading Rorty*, HEAL, Jane.
"Prolegomena to a Structural Theory of Belief and Other Attitudes" in *Propositional Attitudes: The Role of Content in Logic, Language, and Mind*, KAMP, Hans.
"Reasons and Causes" in *Philosophical Perspectives, 3: Philosophy of Mind and Action Theory, 1989*, DRETSKE, Fred.
"Substitution Arguments and the Individuation of Beliefs" in *Meaning and Method: Essays in Honor of Hilary Putnam*, FODOR, Jerry A.
Acceptance Without Belief. MAHER, Patrick.
Annabel and the Bookmaker: An Everyday Tale of Bayesian Folk. MILNE, Peter.
Belief Attribution in Science: Folk Psychology under Theoretical Stress. TROUT, J D.
Belief, Acceptance, and Knowledge. RADFORD, Colin.
Belief, Contradiction, and the Logic of Self-Deception. DA COSTA, Newton C A and FRENCH, Steven.
Beliefs and Responsibility. ELLIOTT, Car.
Birth Defects: Traditional Beliefs Challenged by Scientific Explanations. DRYDEN, Richard.
Blanshard's Ethics of Belief and Metaphysical Postulates. PHILLIPS, Winfred George.
Can There Be Justified Philosophical Beliefs?. NIELSEN, Kai.
Clever Bookies and Coherent Beliefs. CHRISTENSEN, David.
Comments on Schiffer's *Remnants of Meaning*. RICHARD, Mark.
Conditionals and Monotonic Belief Revisions: the Success Postulate. ARLO COSTA, Horacio L.
Consumer Ethics: An Investigation of the Ethical Beliefs of Eldery Consumers. VITELL, Scott J and LUMPKIN, James R and RAWWAS, Mohammed Y A.
La creencia y su conexión con los actos linguísticos. SAAB, Salma.
A Critique of Genealogies. KIM, Chin-Tai.
Crossed Fingers and Praying Hands: Remarks on Religious Belief and Superstition. RAY, R J.
Davidson and the Sceptic: The Thumbnail Version. CRAIG, Edward.
De Re Desire. MARKIE, Peter and PATRICK, Timothy.
Dialogue and Doubt in Descartes' First Meditation. LINVILLE, Kent.
A Dilemma for Bartley's Pancritical Rationalism. HAUPTLI, Bruce W.
A Dilemma for Subjective Bayesians—and How to Resolve It. MILNE, Peter.
Doubt and Faith: Santayana and Kierkegaard on Fundamental Belief. SARTWELL, Crispin.
Doxastic Paradoxes Without Self-Reference. KOONS, Robert Charles.
Dretske on the Explanatory Role of Belief. BAKER, Lynne Rudder.
Educating Intelligent Believers and Unbelievers. NODDINGS, Nel.
Embedded Probabilities. DUBUCS, J.
Emotion and Belief. BORUAH, Bijoy H.
An Epistemic Analysis of Explanations and Causal Beliefs. GÄRDENFORS, Peter.
Epistemic Obligations and Doxastic Voluntarism. GOGGANS, Phil.
The Epistemological Significance of the Inner Witness of the Holy Spirit. ABRAHAM, William J.
Epistemology on Holiday. KAPLAN, Mark.
Evidence and Reasons for Belief. FOLEY, Richard.
Evil and the Proper Basicality of Belief in God. DRAPER, Paul.
Explanation—Opening Address. SMART, J J C.
Firth and the Ethics of Belief. CHISHOLM, Roderick M.
Flaw, Conformity of Critical Dialogue? (in French). BÜHLER, Pierre.
From Historical Marxisms to Historical Materialism: Toward the Theory of Ideology. MOCNIK, Rastko.
A General Possible Worlds Framework for Reasoning about Knowledge and Belief. WANSING, Heinrich.
How Beliefs Explain: Reply to Baker. DRETSKE, Fred.
How to Change Your Mind. MARTINS, João P and CRAVO, Maria R.
Hume and Belief in the Existence of an External World. COSTA, Michael J.
Hume on Practical Reason. ROBERTSON, John.
Internalism and Epistemically Responsible Belief. GRECO, John.
Interpretatie en filosofische methode. BUEKENS, Filip.
Is Kripke's Puzzle Really a Puzzle. CORLETT, J Angelo.
Kierkegaard on the Limits of Christian Epistemology. WISDO, David.
Knowledge is Merely True Belief. SARTWELL, Crispin.
The Logic of Lost Lingens. SEAGER, William.
The Many-Gods Objection and Pascal's Wager. JORDAN, Jeff.
Meaning Holism and Interpretability. TALMAGE, Catherine J L and MERCER, Mark.
Mental Causes. HEIL, John and MELE, Alfred.
Moore's Paradox Revisited. LINVILLE, Kent and RING, Merrill.
Morally Untenable Beliefs. BURKE, Richard J.
New Operators for Theory Change. HANSSON, Sven.

BELIEF(S)
The Normal Rewards of Success. WHYTE, J T.
Occasions for Argumentation. HILPINEN, Risto.
On Removing Puzzles About Belief Ascription. DEVITT, Michael.
On Respecting Puzzles About Belief Ascription (A Reply to Devitt). LYCAN, William G.
On the Irreducibility of the Will. GARCIA, J L A.
On the Logic of Conscious Belief. TOKARZ, Marek.
On the Nature and Norms of Theoretical Commitment. HORWICH, Paul.
The Paradox of Epistemology: A Defense of Naturalism. KETCHUM, Richard J.
Pascal on Self-Caused Belief. DAVIS, Stephen T.
Persons and the Intentional Stance. DIBRELL, William.
A Problem in the Foundations of Set Theory. MADDY, Penelope.
Proper Names, Cognitive Contents, and Beliefs. BRAUN, David M.
Purposive Intending. PINK, T L M.
Putnam on Kripke's Puzzle. GARRETT, Richard.
Rational Trust and Deferential Belief. NORRIS, Stephen P.
Reading the Darkness: Wittgenstein and Indoctrination. MC CARTY, Luise Prior and MC CARTY, David Charles.
Real Patterns. DENNETT, Daniel C.
Recent Obituaries of Epistemology. HAACK, Susan.
The Relational Theory of Belief (A Reply to Richard). SCHIFFER, Stephen.
Saving Psychological Solipsism. MALONEY, J Christopher.
Scientific Realism, Perceptual Beliefs, and Justification. OTTE, Richard.
Search for Beliefs to Live by Consistent with Science. SPERRY, R W.
Self-Notions. PERRY, John.
Some Dependence Relations of Empirical Belief. MALHERBE, Jeanette.
Some Revisionary Proposals About Belief and Believing. MARCUS, Ruth Barcan.
Swinburne on Credal Belief. MAITZEN, Stephen.
The Contradiction of Belief and Reason in the Middle Ages: the Case of Boetius de Dacia (in Hungarian). JOÓS, Ernest.
Toward a Pragmatic Conception of Religious Faith. GOLDING, Joshua L.
Truth and Teleology. PAPINEAU, David.
Two Methods of Constructing Contractions and Revisions of Knowledge Systems. ROTT, Hans.
Understanding the Question: Wittgenstein on Faith and Meaning. EISENSTEIN, Gabe.
Waiting for the Vanishing Shed. PHILLIPS, D Z.
When Fair Betting Odds are Not Degrees of Belief. SEIDENFELD, Teddy and SCHERVISH, M J and KADANE, J B.
Why We Should Care Whether Our Beliefs Are True. LYCAN, William G.
Wittgenstein's Lectures on Religious Belief. MARTIN, Michael.

BELIEVING
Understanding the Representational Mind. PERNER, Josef.
Freud's Warning to Potential Believers. EBISCH, Glen A.
Is Coming to Believe in God Reasonable or Unreasonable?. HERBERT, R T.

BELL, D
More about Thoughts. DUMMETT, Michael.

BELL, J
Hidden Locality, Conspiracy and Superluminal Signals. KRONZ, Frederick M.

BELLO
A Response to A G A Bello's Methodological Preliminaries. ANYANWU, Kane C.

BENACERRAF, P
Physicalism in Mathematics. IRVINE, Andrew D (ed).
"Epistemology and Nominalism" in *Physicalism in Mathematics*, BURGESS, John P.

BENEFICENCE
Medicine and Money: A Study of the Role of Beneficence in Health Care Cost Containment. MARSH, Frank H.
The Paradox of Group Beneficence. OTSUKA, Michael.
Process Metaphysics and Minimalism: Implications for Public Policy. KEFFER, Steven and KING, Sallie and KRAFT, Steven.

BENEFIT(S)
Whose Genome Project?. MACER, Darryl.

BENEVOLENCE
Benevolence and Resentment. STEPHENSON, Wendell.
La benevolencia como categoría fundamental de la Etica eudemonista. RODRÍGUEZ DUPLÁ, Leonardo.
La valenza della carità nelle forme della vita politica. PELLECCHIA, Pasquale.

BENJAMIN, W
On Walter Benjamin: Critical Essays and Recollections. SMITH, Gary (ed).
"The Question of Translatability: Benjamin, Derrida, Quine" in *Hermeneutics and the Poetic Motion, Translation Perspectives V—1990*, TURK, Horst.
Análisis político-epistemológico de la obra de arte según Walter Benjamin. COMESAÑA, Santalices Gloria.
Arendt and Benjamin on the Promise of History: A Network of Possibilities or One Apocalyptic Moment?. HONOHAN, Iseult.
The Death of the Author (as Producer). STOPFORD, John.
Historizing contra fetishizing—The Progress of Modern Technology in W Benjamin's Aesthetic Reflexion (in German). WAGNER, Gerhard.
El significado de lo teológico en Walter Benjamin. BOSCÁN, Antonio S.

BENNETT, J
Las criticas de J Bennett a la doctrina kantiana del esquematismo. JÁUREGUI, Claudia.

BENTHAM
The Legal-Rational State: A Comparison of Hobbes, Bentham and Kelsen. LEE, Keekok.
The Background to Bentham on Evidence. LEWIS, A D E.
Bentham, Science and the Construction of Jurisprudence. JACOBS, Struan.
Bentham, the Benthamites, and the Nineteenth-Century British Peace Movement. CONWAY, Stephen.
Utilitarian Strategies in Bentham and John Stuart Mill. KELLY, P J.

BERGER, P
Misconceptions of the Social Sciences. SEGAL, Robert A.

BERGMAN, H.
Toward the Death of Man. KLUBACK, William.

BERGMANN, G
Scotus, Frege, and Bergmann. PARK, Woosuk.

BERGSON
Bergsonism. DELEUZE, Gilles.
Experiential Method: Qualitative Research in the Humanities Using Metaphysics and Phenomenology. KIDD, James W.
Interpreting Evolution: Darwin and Teilhard de Chardin. BIRX, H James.
Toward the Death of Man. KLUBACK, William.
La dialéctica del deseo como realización de la identidad en Henri Bergson. ELÓSEGUI, María.
L'emozione creatrice: Il significato della morale nella prospettiva di Bergson. PESSINA, Adriano.
Henri Bergson and Postmodernism. MULDOON, Mark S.
Interpretación mundanel e identidad propia. GARCÍA-GÓMEZ, Jorge.
L'inspiration aristotélicienne de la métaphysique de Bergson. WASZKINEL, Romuald.
Les mathématiques, la biologie et le statut scientifique de la philosophie pour Bergson. SOULEZ, Philippe.

BERKELEY
Berkeley's Revolution in Vision. ATHERTON, Margaret.
Knowledge of the External World. AUNE, Bruce.
The Rhetoric of Berkeley's Philosophy. WALMSLEY, Peter.
"Berkeley and Malebranche on Causality and Volition" in *Central Themes in Early Modern Philosophy*, JOLLEY, Nicholas.
Berkeley and Common Sense Realism. PAPPAS, George S.
Berkeley's Anti-Abstractionism: Reply to Moked. GLOUBERMAN, Mark.
Berkeley's Arguments for Other Minds. FALKENSTEIN, Lorne.
Berkeley, Perception, and Identity. BAXTER, Donald L M.
Il caso "Siris", ovvero la "seconda filosofia" di George Berkeley vescovo di Cloyne. NERI, Luigi.
The Continuous and the Discrete: Leibniz Versus Berkeley. ANAPOLITANOS, D A.
Corpuscles, Mechanism, and Essentialism in Berkeley and Locke. ATHERTON, Margaret.
Hobbes, Berkeley y las ideas abstractas. ROBLES, José A.
A Note on Berkeley's Anti-Abstractionism. MOKED, Gabriel.
The Role of Perceptual Relativity in Berkeley's Philosophy. MUEHLMANN, Robert.
What Berkeley's Notions Are. LEE, Richard N.

BERLIN, I
"Die Geschichte hat kein Libretto": Zu Isaiah Berlins Begriff des Nationalismus. RITTER, Henning.
"Two Concepts of Liberty" Thirty Years Later: A Sartre-Inspired Critique. MC BRIDE, William L.
Conflicting Views of Liberalism. SKOBLE, Aeon James.
Response to Berlin and McBride. RENICK, Timothy M.

BERNARD, C
Reconsidering the Wisdom of the Body. SULLIVAN, Mark D.

BERNAYS, P
El cincuentenario de los *Grundlagen der Mathematik* de Hilbert y Bernays. RAGGIO, Andrés R.

BERTOCCI, P
Creative Insecurity and "Tiptoe Experiences". HOWIE, John.
The Ethical Theory of Peter A Bertocci. PADGETT, Jack F.
The Philosophical Achievement of Peter A Bertocci. RECK, Andrew J.

BET(S)
Against Conditionalization. BACCHUS, Fahiem and KYBURG JR, Henry E and THALOS, Mariam.

BETH, E
In the Service of Human Society: Formal, Information, or Anti-Logical?. BARTH, E M.
De Kant-interpretatie van Evert Willem Beth. PEIJNENBURG, J.

BETTING
Annabel and the Bookmaker: An Everyday Tale of Bayesian Folk. MILNE, Peter.
When Fair Betting Odds are Not Degrees of Belief. SEIDENFELD, Teddy and SCHERVISH, M J and KADANE, J B.

BEUCHOT, M
Sobre cuatro obras de Mauricio Beuchot. PEÑA, Lorenzo.

BEUYS, J
La démonstration mystifiante: Wittgenstein et Beuys. LA CHANCE, Michaël.

BHAGAVAD GITA
Philosophy of the "Gita". PATEL, Ramesh N.

BHARTRHARI
"Speech Versus Writing" in Derrida and Bhartrhari. COWARD, Harold G.

BHASKAR, R
Concepts of "Action", "Structure" and "Power" in 'Critical Social Realism': A Positive and Reconstructive Critique. PATOMÄKI, Heikki.
Educational Research and Bhaskar's Conception of Discovery. CORSON, David.

BIAS(ES)
Captives of Controversy: The Myth of the Neutral Social Researcher in Contemporary Scientific Controversies. SCOTT, Pam and RICHARDS, Evelleen and MARTIN, Brian.
Feminism and Epistemology. CHANDLER, John.
Marx and Russia. NAARDEN, Bruno.
Partialism and Parenthood. NELSON, James Lindemann.
Universality Biases: *How Theories About Human Nature Succeed*. HORNSTEIN, Gail A and STAR, Susan Leigh.

BIBLE
The Bible as Rhetoric: Studies in Biblical Persuasion and Credibility. WARNER, Martin (ed).
The Idea of Christian Charity: A Critique of Some Contemporary Conceptions. GRAHAM, Gordon.
Science versus Religion. CLEMENTS, Tad S.
"'Tales Artfully Spun'" in *The Bible as Rhetoric: Studies in Biblical Persuasion and Credibility*, TRIGG, Roger.
"'Truth' and 'Rhetoric' in the Pauline Epistles" in *The Bible as Rhetoric: Studies in Biblical Persuasion and Credibility*, KENNEDY, George.
"Augustine's Methods of Biblical Interpretation" in *Grace, Politics and Desire: Essays on Augustine*, HAMILTON, Gordon J.
"The Bible and the Rhetorical Sublime" in *The Bible as Rhetoric: Studies in Biblical Persuasion and Credibility*, POLAND, Lynn.
"Biblical Story and the Heroine" in *The Bible as Rhetoric: Studies in Biblical Persuasion and Credibility*, STOCKER, Margarita.
"History, Truth, and Narrative" in *The Bible as Rhetoric: Studies in Biblical Persuasion and Credibility*, SUTHERLAND, Stewart.
"Newton as a Bible Scholar" in *Essays on the Context, Nature, and Influence of Isaac Newton's Theology*, POPKIN, Richard H.
Biblical Narrative and the Theology of Metonymy. WARD, Graham.
Knowing Good and Evil. WILLIAMS, C J F.
Stewardship: Whose Creation Is It Anyway?. BARAD-ANDRADE, Judith.
The Structure of Philo's Commentary on the Pentateuch. THORNE, Gary W A.

BIBLIOGRAPHY
Bibliography of Bioethics, Volume 16. WALTERS, LeRoy (ed).
Exploring Phenomenology (Second Edition). STEWART, David.
Indexes to the Collected Works (Collected Works of John Stuart Mill, Vol XXXIII). ROBSON, John M (ed).
Philosophy Books, 1982-1986. MAY, Thomas (ed).
Russische Philosophie. GOERDT, Wilhelm.
Socrates: An Annotated Bibliography. NAVIA, Luis E.
Wittgenstein: A Bibliographical Guide. FRONGIA, Guido.
Writers and Philosophers: A Sourcebook of Philosophical Influences on Literature. THOMAS, Edmund J.
"Mario Bunge's Life and Work" in *Studies on Mario Bunge's "Treatise"*, BUNGE, Mario.
"A Miller Bibliography with a Brief Description of The Williams College Miller Archives" in *The Philosophy of John William Miller*, JOHNSTONE JR, Henry W.
"Selected Bibliography of Fred R Dallmayr" in *Life-World and Politics: Between Modernity and Postmodernity*, WHITE, Stephen K.
Angelo Camillo De Meis nell'episolario di Francesco Fiorentino. CACCIAPUOTI, Fabiana.
Bibliographie de Paul Ricoeur: Compléments (jusqu'en 1990). VANSINA, Frans.
Comprehensive Evolutionary Epistemology Bibliography. CZIKO, Gary A and CAMPBELL, Donald T.
Il dibattito italiano sullo statuto della filosofia politica: Contributo ad una bibliographia. BACCELLI, Luca.

BINET, A
Metaphors of Mind: Conceptions of the Nature of Intelligence. STERNBERG, Robert J.

BIOCHEMISTRY
Molecular Biology and the Unity of Science. KINCAID, Harold.

BIOETHICS
see also Medical Ethics
Agricultural Bioethics: Implications of Agricultural Biotechnology. GENDEL, Steven M (& other eds).
Bibliography of Bioethics, Volume 16. WALTERS, LeRoy (ed).
Biomedical Ethics Reviews, 1989. HUMBER, James M (ed).
Biomedical Ethics Reviews, 1990. HUMBER, James M (ed).
New Harvest: Transplanting Body Parts and Reaping the Benefits. KEYES, C Don (ed).
Shaping Genes: Ethics, Law and Science of Using Genetic Technology in Medicine and Agriculture. MACER, Darryl.
Taking Sides: Clashing Views on Controversial Bioethical Issues (Fourth Edition). LEVINE, Carol (ed).
Well and Good: Case Studies in Biomedical Ethics (Revised Edition). THOMAS, John E.
"Biotechnology and Bioethics" in *Agricultural Bioethics: Implications of Agricultural Biotechnology*, GENDEL, Steven M.
Bioethics Inside the Beltway: The Human Genome Project. JUENGST, Eric T.
Bioethics on Trial. CAPLAN, Arthur L.
CAHBI: Europe Needs a Universal Bioethical System. GUNNING, Karel.
Common-Sense Morality. BROCK, Dan.
Crazy Making: Embryos and Gestational Mothers. ANNAS, George J.
The Editor's Response to "The Embryo Debate: The Archbishop of York's Speech to the House of Lords". DE S CAMERON, Nigel M.
The Embryo Debate: The Archbishop of York's Speech to the House of Lords. THE ARCHBISHOP OF YORK.
The Enforcement of Moral Obligations to Potential Fetuses: Johnson Controls versus the UAW. WHITE, Ronald F.
Éthique et technique: bioéthique. KEMP, Peter.
Fetal Neural Transplantation: Placing the Ethical Debate within the Context of Society's Use of Human Material. JONES, D Gareth.
Filosofía desde la teoría causal de la referencia. NUBIOLA, Jaime.
New Creations? Commentary. BALK, Roger A.
New Creations? Commentary. FREEDMAN, Benjamin and GOULET, Marie-Claude.
New Creations? Commentary. MACER, Darryl.
The Pharmacist's Role in Patient Care. SCHULZ, Richard M and BRUSHWOOD, David B.
Possibilities of Consensus: Toward Democratic Moral Discourse. JENNINGS, Bruce.
The Prophetic and the Priestly. CHILDRESS, James F.
Reassessing Autonomy in Long-Term Care. AGICH, George J.
Rich Cases: The Ethics of Thick Description. DAVIS, Dena S.
Schopenhauers Idee einer rekonstruktiven Ethik (mit Anwendungen auf die moderne Medizin-Ethik). BIRNBACHER, Dieter.
Still Saving the Life of Ethics. SCHNEIDERMAN, Lawrence J.

BIOGRAPHY
Bertrand Russell: The Psychobiography of a Moralist. BRINK, Andrew.
Encounter on the Narrow Ridge: A Life of Martin Buber. FRIEDMAN, Maurice.
Freedom in the Modern World: Jacques Maritain, Yves R Simon, Mortimer J Adler. TORRE, Michael D (ed).
Hegel In His Time—Jacques D'Hondt. BURBIDGE, John (trans).
Jean-Jacques: The Early Life and Work of Jean-Jacques, 1712-1754. CRANSTON, Maurice.
The Noble Savage: Jean-Jacques Rousseau, 1754-1762. CRANSTON, Maurice.
The Politics of Being: The Political Thought of Martin Heidegger. WOLIN, Richard.
"Adler on Freedom" in *Freedom in the Modern World: Jacques Maritain, Yves R Simon, Mortimer J Adler*, MC INERNY, Ralph.
"Hélène Metzger: Eléments de biographie" in *Études sur/Studies on Hélène Metzger*, FREUDENTHAL, Gad.
"Introduction" in *Life-World and Politics: Between Modernity and Postmodernity*, WHITE, Stephen K.
"Miller: The Man and His Philosophy" in *The Philosophy of John William Miller*, FELL, Joseph P.
"'Congenial Vocation': J M Robson and the Mill Project" in *A Cultivated Mind: Essays On J S Mill Presented to John M Robson*, O'GRADY, Jean.
Heidegger's Apology: Biography as Philosophy and Ideology. KISIEL, Theodore.
Heidegger, pensador con biografía. RODRÍGUEZ, Ramón.
Heidegger: vita e distino—Sullo biografia heideggeriana di Hugo Ott. ESPOSITO, Costantino.
An Impatient Man and his Papers. HINTIKKA, Jaakko.
Is "The Theory of History" (1914) Collingwood's First Essay on the Philosophy of History?. PATRICK, James.
De jonge Wittgenstein (1889-1921): Denken als ethos. DE DIJN, H.
The Member for Westminster: Doctrinaire Philosopher, Party Hack, or Public Moralist?. COLLINI, Stefan.
Montinari and Nietzsche's Biography. HOLLINGDALE, R G.
Roderick Firth: His Life and Work. RAWLS, John.
Was Karl Marx a Social Scientist?. FLEW, Antony.

BIOLOGICAL WARFARE
Biotechnology and Warfare. REINIKAINEN, Pekka.
Treating the Troops. HOWE, Edmund G and MARTIN, Edward D.

BIOLOGY
see also Darwinism, Ecology, Evolution, Life
Evolution als Höherentwicklung des Bewusstseins. KUMMER, Christian.
The Nature of Politics. MASTERS, Roger D.
"Evolution—Matter of Fact or Metaphysical Idea?" in *Logic, Methodology and Philosophy of Science, VIII*, LÖTHER, Rolf.
"Teleology and the Relationship Between Biology and the Physical Sciences in the Nineteenth and Twentieth Centuries" in *Some Truer Method*, BEATTY, John.
Behavior, Biology, and Information Theory. SENCHUK, Dennis M.
Between Two Worlds: Humans in Nature and Culture. GARDINER, Robert W.
Biological Foundations of Prediction in an Unpredictable Environment. MARUSIC, M.
Biological Holism and the Evolution of Ethics. SHRADER-FRECHETTE, Kristin.
Biology and Ethics: Callicott Reconsidered. SHRADER-FRECHETTE, Kristin.
Biology and the Social Sciences. WILSON, Edward O.
Can Marxism Help Biology?. KASSIOLA, Joel.
Crypto-theologie: hoffentlich ein Ende: Reactie op Callebaut en Wachelder. SOONTIENS, Frans.
Cultural Evolution, Biology and Language: Empirical and Rational Criteria of Selection (in German). DORSCHEL, Andreas.
Does Representational Content Arise from Biological Function?. HALL, Richard J.
Erneuerung als Grundmechanismus der Evolution. EBELING, Werner.
Evolved Ethics Re-Examined: The Theory of Robert J Richards. WILLIAMS, Patricia.
Explanation in Biology. SMITH, John Maynard.
The Explanatory Tools of Theoretical Population Biology. COOPER, Gregory.
Functions As Selected Effects: The Conceptual Analyst's Defense. NEANDER, Karen.
Global Arguments for the Safety of Engineered Organisms. KLINE, David and GENDEL, Stephen M.
Island Biogeography, Species-Area Curves, and Statistical Errors: Applied Biology and Scientific Rationality. SHRADER-FRECHETTE, Kristin.
L'étude du vivant et la méthodologie ouverte. PILET, Paul-Emile.
Les mathématiques, la biologie et le statut scientifique de la philosophie pour Bergson. SOULEZ, Philippe.
Molecular Biology and the Unity of Science. KINCAID, Harold.
Moral und Biologie. RICHTER, Klaus.
Must Scientific Diagrams Be Eliminable? The Case of Path Analysis. GRIESEMER, James R.
The Neurophilosophy of Pain. GILLETT, G R.
On the Possibility of Directed Mutations in Bacteria: Statistical Analyses and Reductionist Strategies. SARKAR, Sahotra.
On the Uniqueness of Biological Research. PORTMANN, Adolph.
El paradigma computacional aplicado al estudio de la vida. GUTIÉRREZ, Claudio.
The Phenotype as the Level of Selection: Cave organisms as Model Systems. KANE, Thomas C and RICHARDSON, Robert C and FONG, Daniel W.
Pictorial Representation in Biology. TAYLOR, Peter J and BLUM, Ann S.
Il polipo di Trembley (1740) e la "catena delle verità": Note di ricerca. TODESCO, Fabio.
Recent Work in the Philosophy of Biology. STERELNY, Kim.
Reconsidering the Wisdom of the Body. SULLIVAN, Mark D.
Reduction and the Part/Whole Relation. KRECZ, Charles A.
Reply to Shrader-Frechette's "Biological Holism and the Evolution of Ethics". CALLICOTT, J Baird.
Self-Organization, Emergent Properties and the Unity of the World. ROTH, Gerhard and SCHWEGLER, Helmut.
A Semiotical Reflection on Biology, Living Signs and Artificial Life. EMMECHE, Claus.
Species, Higher Taxa, and the Units of Evolution. ERESHEFSKY, Marc.
Teleo-theologie und kein Ende: Reactie op Soontiens. CALLEBAUT, Werner and WACHELDER, J.
Theorie antireduktionistischer Argumente: Fallstudie Bohr. HOYNINGEN-HUENE, Paul.
Theory Structure and Theory Change in Contemporary Molecular Biology. CULP, Sylvia and KITCHER, Philip.
The Unity of the Natural Sciences: Comment on Portmann. VON UEXKUELL, Thure.
The Varieties of Self-Interest. EPSTEIN, Richard A.
Why the Anti-Reductionist Consensus Won't Survive: The Case of Classical Mendelian Genetics. WATERS, C Kenneth.

BIOMEDICAL RESEARCH
Animal Experimentation: The Moral Issue. BAIRD, Robert M (ed).
Institutional Animal Care and Use Committees and the Moderate Position. STEPHENSON, Wendell.
Reply to Stephenson on Biomedical Research. GENDIN, Sidney.

BIRGITTA, S
"Birgitta of Sweden" in *A History of Women Philosophers, Volume II: Medieval, Renaissance and Enlightenment, A.D. 500-1600*, WOLFSKEEL, Cornelia.

BIRTH
Dans quelle mesure et par quelles images les mythes grecs ont-ils symbolisé le néant?. RUDHARDT, Jean.

BIRTH DEFECTS
Birth Defects: Traditional Beliefs Challenged by Scientific Explanations. DRYDEN, Richard.
Monstrous Imagination: Progeny as Art in French Classicism. HUET, Marie-Hélène.

BLACK, M
Genuine Names and Knowledge by Acquaintance. DONNELLAN, Keith S.
The Inductive Support of Inductive Rules: Themes from Max Black. SANFORD, David H.
Max on Moore. STROLL, Avrum.
Meaning and Intention: Black Versus Grice. MARTINICH, A P.
Sur le vague en mathématiques. GRANGER, G G.
Wittgenstein's Holism. PEARS, David.

BLACKBURN, S
Antirealism and Realist Claims of Invariance. ELDER, Crawford L.
Blackburn on Filling in Space. RICE, Hugh.
Contents and Causes: A Reply to Blackburn. STURGEON, Nicholas L.

BLACKMAIL
A Comparison of Nigerian to American Views of Bribery and Extortion in International Commerce. TSALIKIS, John and NWACHUKWU, Osita.

BLACKS
Contemporary Perspectives on Masculinity: Men, Women, and Politics in Modern Society. CLATTERBAUGH, Kenneth.

BLAKE
"William Blake and the Romantic Perception of Humanism" in *The Question of Humanism: Challenges and Possibilities*, ABRAHAMS, Cecil.

BLAME
Between the Horns of the Negative-Positive Duty Debate. MALM, H M.
Explaining Without Blaming the Victim. ILLINGWORTH, Patricia M L.
Hamartia, Akrasia: Ignorance, and Blame in Aristotle's Philosophy. CYZYK, Mar.
Is Karl Marx to Blame for "Barracks Socialism"?. BUTENKO, A P.

BLANC, L
"The Origins of Some of Our Misconceptions" in *Perspectives on Ideas and Reality*, LUDASSY, Mária.

BLANCHOT, M
"A Fine Risk: Reading Blanchot Reading Levinas" in *Re-Reading Levinas*, DAVIES, Paul.

BLANSHARD, B
Blanshard on Philosophical Style. SMITH, John E.
Blanshard's Critique of Ethical Subjectivism. JOHNSON, Oliver A.
Blanshard's Ethics of Belief and Metaphysical Postulates. PHILLIPS, Winfred George.
Brand Blanshard and Gewirth: Ethics and Rights. HOWIE, John.
Reason and Reasonableness in the Philosophy of Brand Branshard. RECK, Andrew J.
Reflections on Blanshard, Reason, and Religion. FERRÉ, Frederick.

BLASPHEMY
The Satanic Novel: A Philosophical Dialogue on Blasphemy and Censorship. SPRIGGE, T L S.

BLINDNESS
An Oath of Silence: Wittgenstein's Philosophy of Religion. JOHNSON, Charles W.
Perceptual Aspects of Art for the Blind. ARNHEIM, Rudolf.

BLOCH, E
Hope and Its Hieroglyph: A Critical Decipherment of Ernst Bloch's "Principle of Hope". ROBERTS, Richard H.

BLOCH, L
"Léon Bloch et Hélène Metzger" in *Études sur/Studies on Hélène Metzger*, BLAY, Michel.

BLONDEL, M
Il dibattito sulla verità tra Blondel e Garrigou-Lagrange. BERTOLDI, Francesco.
Maurice Blondel's Moral Logic. LONG, Fiachra.
The Postmodern Flavor of Blondel's Method. LONG, Fiachra.

BLOOM, A
"Great Books, Democracy and Truth" in *Freedom in the Modern World: Jacques Maritain, Yves R Simon, Mortimer J Adler*, ADLER, Mortimer J.
Souls Without Longing. PLATT, Michael.

BLOOR, D
Azande Logic *Verus* Western Logic?. TRIPLETT, Timm.
The Strong Programme for the Sociology of Science, Reflexivity and Relativism. NOLA, Robert.

BLUMENBERG, H
Must We Return to Moral Realism?. ROSEN, Michael.
On Behalf of Skeptical Rhetoric. FALZER, Paul R.

BOBBIO, N
Bobbio e la scienza politica in Italia. MANCARELLA, Angelo.
La democracia de los antiguos y la de los modernos. YTURBE, Corina.
Norberto Bobbio ideologo del neoilluminismo: Per una rilettura di "Politica e cultura". QUARANTA, Mario.

BODY(-DIES)
see also Matter, Minds, Substance(s)
How to Build a Conscious Machine. ANGEL, Leonard.
L'objet-peinture: Pour une théorie de la réception. PAQUIN, Nycole.
Lesbian Philosophies and Cultures. ALLEN, Jeffner (ed).
Matter and Memory. BERGSON, Henri.
Mind-Body. MOULYN, Adrian C.
Nietzsche: The Body and Culture—Philosophy as a Philological Genealogy. BLONDEL, Eric.
Other Human Beings. COCKBURN, David.
A Post-Modern Epistemology. SORRI, Mari.
"The Body and Human Values in Augustine of Hippo" in *Grace, Politics and Desire: Essays on Augustine*, MILES, Margaret R.
"Docile Bodies, Rebellious Bodies" in *Writing the Politics of Difference*, BORDO, Susan.
"Flesh and Otherness" in *Ontology and Alterity in Merleau-Ponty*, LEFORT, Claude.
"Flesh as Otherness" in *Ontology and Alterity in Merleau-Ponty*, MADISON, Gary Brent.
"Mind and Body" in *Key Themes in Philosophy*, WILKES, K V.
"Nietzsche and Merleau-Ponty: The Body as Attitude" in *Abeunt Studia in Mores: A Festschrift for Helga Doblin*, ECKBLAD, Joyce.
The 'Body': A Husserlian Phenomenological Analysis. DAS, Paritosh Kumar.
Attitudes Towards the Body: Philosophy and Common Sense. WILLIAMSON, Colwyn.
Bodily Theory and Theory of the Body. GILES, James.
The Body as Understood in Contemporary Thought and Biblical Categories. VERGOTE, Antoine.
The Body Politic: Democratic Metaphors, Totalitarian Practices, Erotic Rebellions. BERGOFFEN, Debra B.
El conocimiento de los cuerpos según Malebranche (I). FERNANDEZ RODRIGUEZ, Jose Luis.
Le corps et ses langages: quelques perspectives de travail historique. COURTINE, Jean-Jacques.
Dehātmavāda or the Body as Soul: Exploration of a Possibility within Nyāya Thought. LATH, Mukund (trans) and SHUKLA, Pandit Badrinath.
Descartes und der reale Unterschied zwischen der Seele und dem Körper. IMLAY, Robert A.
The Discursive Formation of the Body in the History of Medicine. LEVIN, David Michael and SOLOMON, George F.
Disembodying 'Bodily' Sensations. COMBES, Richard.
L'epiglottide nell'antichità tra medicina e filosofia. REPICI, Luciana.
Functionalisme versus dubbelaspecttheorie: tertium datur. MACKOR, Anne Ruth.
The Inorganic Body and the Ambiguity of Freedom. COLLIER, Andrew.
Knowing through the Body. JOHNSON, Mark.
L'écriture réparatrice. HAREL, Simon.
The Market for Bodily Parts: A Response to Ruth Chadwick. TADD, G V.
The *Nous*-Body Problem in Aristotle. MODRAK, Deborah K W.
Per una filosofia del corpo. PELLECCHIA, Pasquale.
Phenomenalism and the Reality of Body in Leibniz's Later Philosophy. RUTHERFORD, Donald P.
The Real Distinction Between Mind and Body. YABLO, Stephen.
Searle's Oplossing voor het lichaam-geest probleem: ipse dixit—Een reactie op Anne Ruth Mackor. MEIJSING, Monica.
Some Recent Research on the Mind-Body Problem in Descartes. MILES, Murray.
Taoist Visions of the Body. KOHN, Livia.
Why Shouldn't We Be Able to Solve the Mind-Body Problem?. KIRK, Robert.
Why the Mind is Not in the Head But in the Society's Connectionist Network. FISCHER, Roland.

BOEHME
The Theosophic Discourse According to Jacob Boehme (in French). DEGHAYE, Pierre.

BOER, S
Object-Dependent Thoughts and Psychological Redundancy. NOONAN, Harold W.

BOETHIUS
The Dilemma of Freedom and Foreknowledge. ZAGZEBSKI, Linda Trinkaus.
Boethius and the Consolation of Philosophy, or, How to Be a Good Philosopher. BELSEY, Andrew.
Eternity and Simultaneity. LEFTOW, Brian.

BOGDANOV, A
Dialectical Perception: A Synthesis of Lenin and Bogdanov. WRIGHT, Edmond.

BOHM, D
Problema psicofísico y realidad cuántica en la física heterodoxa de David Bohm. MONSERRAT, Javier.

BOHR, N
Bohr's Idea of Complementarity and Plato's Philosophy. MAHOOTIAN, Farzad.
Independence from Future Theories: A Research Strategy in Quantum Theory. RUEGER, Alexander.
Metaphysical Awakening in Philosophy of Quantum Physics. FOLSE, Henry J.
Theorie antireduktionistischer Argumente: Fallstudie Bohr. HOYNINGEN-HUENE, Paul.

BOK, S
The Political Philosophy of Sissela Bok. FAREY, Caroline.

BOLTZMANN
Philosophical Objections to the Kinetic Theory. NYHOF, John.

BOLZANO
Bolzano's Contribution to Cognition and/or the Creation of Theory of Sets (in Czechoslovakian). VECERKA, Kazimir.
On Bolzano's Conception of the Essentials of Ethics and its Coherences (in Czechoslovakian). HALA, Vlastimil.

BONAVENTURE
External Creation and Eternal Production of the World According to Bonaventura (in Dutch). VAN VELDHUIJSEN, Peter.
Tres grandes testigos de la luz interior: San Agustín, san Buenaventura y J Henry Newman. OROZ RETA, José.

BONHOEFFER, D
The Search for an Ethical Sacrament: From Bonhoeffer to Critical Social Theory. FLOYD, Wayne Whitson.

BONJOUR, L
The Structure of Empirical Knowledge. DE PIERRIS, Graciela.

BONTADINI, G
Gustavo Bontadini un metafisico per vocazione. LATORA, Salvatore.

BONUCCI, F
Francesco Bonucci, tra medicina e filosofia. STORTI, Cinzia.

BOOK(S)
"Great Books, Democracy and Truth" in *Freedom in the Modern World: Jacques Maritain, Yves R Simon, Mortimer J Adler*, ADLER, Mortimer J.
Libri da salvare. POLC, Jaroslav.

BOOLE
The Correspondence between George Boole and Stanley Jevons, 1863-1864. GRATTAN-GUINNESS, I.

BOOLEAN ALGEBRA
Absolutely Independent Sets of Generation of Filters in Boolean Algebras. GRYGIEL, Joanna.
Boolean Algebras and Orbits of the Lattice of R.E. Sets Modulo the Finite Sets. CHOLAK, Peter.
Boolean Powers of Abelian Groups. EDA, Katsuya.
Connection Structures. BIACINO, Loredana and GERLA, Giangiacomo.
Finite Logics and the Simple Substitution Property. HOSOI, Tsutomu and SASAKI, Katsumi.
Indiscernibility and Identity in Probability Theory. ROEPER, Peter and LEBLANC, Hugues.
Lattice Nonembeddings and Initial Segments of the Recursively Enumerable Degrees. DOWNEY, Rod.
Modal Logics with *n*-ary Connectives. GHILARDI, S and MELONI, C G.
A Note on Complete Partitions in Boolean Algebras. SACHWANOWICZ, Wojciech.
A Note on Matrices for Systems of Nonsense-Logics. HALKOWSKA, Katarzyna.
Plain Semi-Post Algebras as a Poset-Based Generalization of Post Algebras and their Representability. CAT HO, Nguyen and RASIOWA, Helena.
The Problem of Properties in Quantum Mechanics. BUB, Jeffrey.
Semantic Holism. BELNAP JR, Nuel D and MASSEY, Gerald J.
Théories d'algébres de Boole munies d'idéaux distingués, II. TOURAILLE, Alain.
Two Hypergraph Theorems Equivalent to BPI. COWEN, Robert H.
Weakly Semirecursive Sets. JOCKUSCH JR, Carl G and OWINGS JR, James C.

BOON, L
Praktijkontwikkeling en wetenschappelijke (onderwijs)kunde: Een reactie op Boon e.a.. WARDEKKER, Wim.

BOREDOM
Noia, acedia ed epochè. BOTTANI, Livio.

BORGES, J
Pierre Menard's *Don Quixote*. BAILEY, George.

BORN, M
Born's Probabilistic Interpretation: A Case Study of 'Concepts in Flux'. BELLER, Mara.

BOSKOVIC, R
Attraction and Repulsion in Comprehension of Boskovic, Hegel and Engels (in Serbo-Croatian). STOILJKOVIC, Dragoslav.
Boskovic on His Own Theory of Forces: From a Sentence to the Theory of Natural Philosophy (in Serbo-Croatian). MARTINOVIC, Ivica.
Boskovic's Ideas on the Nature of Cognition Process (in Yugoslavian). DORDEVIC, Radomir.
Boskovic's Mathematical Conception of Continuity and the Differentiability of Function (in Serbo-Croatian). STIPANIC, Ernest.
Boskovic's Philosophical Understanding of Matter (in Serbo-Croatian). STOJKOVIC, Andrija B K.
Boskovic's Philosophy in the Evaluation of Franjo Markovic (1887): Origins and Results (in Serbo-Croatian). KUTLESA, Stipe.
Boskovic's Philosophy of Mathematics (in Serbo-Croatian). HOMANN, Frederick A.
Boskovic's Theory of Forces in His Treatise "De Continuitatis Lege" (in Serbo-Croatian). BRUNSKO, Zagorka.
From Boskovic's Supplements to the Poem of Benedikt Stay (in Serbo-Croatian). D'AGOSTINO, Salvo.
R J Boskovic's "Theoria" — A Sign Post to the Essence of the Modern Natural Science (in Serbo-Croatian). ZENKO, Franjo.
R J Boskovic's Philosophy of Space (in Serbo-Croatian). ROSSI, Arcangelo.
Ruder Boskovic as a Humanist and Scientist (in Serbo-Croatian). SUPEK, Ivan.
Some Characteristics of Boskovic's Scientific Methodology (in Serbo-Croatian). FESTINI, Heda.
The Gnoseological Aspect of Boskovic's "Theory of Natural Philosophy" (in Serbo-Croatian). ACIMOVIC, Mirko.
The Influence of Roger Boskovic on Bertrand Russell's Early Philosophy of Physics (in Serbo-Croatian). LEWIS, Albert C.
The Phenomenalism of Newton and Boskovic: A Comparative Study (in Serbo-Croatian). PRINCE, Augustus.

BOUDIER, C
Het scheppende en herscheppende woord: zijn blijvende actualiteit. DENGERINK, J D.

BOUNDARY(-RIES)
The Limits of Thought—and Beyond. PRIEST, Graham.
The No-Slip Condition of Fluid Dynamics. DAY, Michael A.

BOURGEOIS, W
On Saving the Phenomena and the Mice: A Reply to Bourgeois Concerning Van Fraassen's Image of Science. FOSS, Jeff.

BOWNE, B
Bowne and Peirce on the Logic of Religious Belief. ANDERSON, Douglas R.
James and Bowne on the Philosophy of Religious Experience. DOTTERER, Donald W.
Moral Laws in Borden P Bowne's *Principles of Ethics*. BURROW JR, Rufus.

BOYD, R
Glymour on Deoccamization and the Epistemology of Geometry. DURAN, Jane.
On Boyd. HACKING, Ian.

BOYLE
The Early Essays and Ethics of Robert Boyle. HARWOOD, John T (ed).
Does the Grisez-Finnis-Boyle Moral Philosophy Rest on a Mistake?. VEATCH, Henry and RAUTENBERG, Joseph.
The Impact of Science Studies on Political Philosophy. LATOUR, Bruno.

BRADLEY
Bradley and Lonergan's Relativist. TESKE, Roland.
Cook Wilson as Critic of Bradley. TACELLI, Ronald K.

BRAHMAN
Is the Central Upanishadic Teaching a Reductionist Thesis?. PULIGANDLA, Ramakrishna.

BRAIN
see also Mind, Minds
"Brains Don't Lie: They Don't Even Make Many Mistakes" in *Doubting: Contemporary Perspectives on Skepticism*, TYMOCZKO, Thomas.
"A New Visualization of the Mind-Brain Relationship" in *The Case for Dualism*, HARRISON, Stephen.
Churchland and the Talking Brain. MUKHERJI, Nirmalangshu.
Is the Brain a Digital Computer?. SEARLE, John R.
On the Impossibility of Artificial Intelligence. WEISS, Paul.
Personal Identity and Brain Transplants. SNOWDON, P F.
The Poverty of Neurophilosophy. STENT, Gunther S.
The Reductionist Ideal in Cognitive Psychology. MONTGOMERY, Richard.
Some Philosophical Aspects of Psychophysiology—Are There Any Elements of "Neurophilosophy"? (in German). RÜDIGER, Wolfgang.
Two Brains, Two Minds? Wigan's Theory of Mental Duality. PUCCETTI, Roland.

BRAIN DEATH
"Definition and Death" in *Biomedical Ethics Reviews, 1989*, O'NEIL, Rick.
"On Human Death" in *Biomedical Ethics Reviews, 1989*, HUMBER, James M.
Death and the Beginning of Life. IGLESIAS, Teresa.

BRAIN PROCESSES
Metaphors of Mind: Conceptions of the Nature of Intelligence. STERNBERG, Robert J.
"Thirty Five Years On—Is Consciousness Still a Brain Process?" in *The Mind of Donald Davidson*, PLACE, Ullin T.

BRAIN STATE(S)
Japan's Dilemma with the Definition of Death. KIMURA, Rihito.

BRANDON, R
The Phenotype as the Level of Selection: Cave organisms as Model Systems. KANE, Thomas C and RICHARDSON, Robert C and FONG, Daniel W.

BRANDT, R
Deugden en plichtsbesef. STEUTEL, J W.

BRAYBROOKE, D
Ethical Impressionism: A Response to Braybrooke. BONEVAC, Daniel.

BRAZILIAN
"Social Theory and Political Practice: Unger's Brazilian Journalism" in *Critique and Construction: A Symposium on Roberto Unger's "Politics"*, SIMON, William H.

BRENTANO
A Phenomenologically and Psychologically Based Concept of Ethics (in Czechoslovakian). BAYEROVA, M.
Brentano e Fichte negli scritti "minori" di E Husserl. BELLO, A Ales.
Univocità dell'essere e intenzionalià del conoscere. ANTONELLI, Mauro.

BRIBE(S)
A Comparison of Nigerian to American Views of Bribery and Extortion in International Commerce. TSALIKIS, John and NWACHUKWU, Osita.

BRIBERY
Toward a Theory of Bribery. DANLEY, John R.

BRIDGMAN, P
P W Bridgman's Operational Perspective on Physics: Part I—Origins and Development. MOYER, Albert E.

BRINK, C
Verisimilitude by Power Relations. ODDIE, Graham.

BRITISH
see also English
Patriarcha and Other Writings: Sir Robert Filmer. SOMMERVILLE, Johann P (ed).
Talking Philosophy: A Wordbook. SPARKES, A W.
"The History, Philosophy of Sociology of Archaeology: The Case of the Ancient Monuments Protection Act (1882)" in *Critical Traditions in Contemporary Archaeology*, MURRAY, Tim.
Bentham, the Benthamites, and the Nineteenth-Century British Peace Movement. CONWAY, Stephen.
John Stuart Mill and Royal India. MOORE, Robin J.
North American, British and Australian Philosophy of Education from 1941 to 1991: Links, Trends, Prospects. BECK, Clive.
Once Again the Ockhamist Statutes of 1339 and 1340: Some New Perspectives. THIJSSEN, J M M H.
Reforming Britain's National Health Service. KESSEL, Ros.

BRODY, B
Essentialism Old and New: Suarez and Brody. KRONEN, John D.

BROUWER, L
Brouwer's Intuitionism (Studies in the History and Philosophy of Mathematics, Vol 2). VAN STIGT, W P.
Brouwerian Intuitionism. DETLEFSEN, Michael.
The Ontological Status of the Principle of the Excluded Middle. STRAUSS, Daniël F M.

BRUNO
Il "De imaginum, signorum et idearum compositione" di Giordano Bruno, ed il significato filosofico .... STURLESE, Rita.
Bruno e la matematica a lui contemporanea: In margine al "De Minimo". AQUILECCHIA, Giovanni.
Considerazioni in margine a un'interpretazione di Bruno. MANZONI, Claudio.
The Hermetic Influence on the Rise of Modern Science. MITRA, Prabir.
Infiniti mondi e mondo nuovo: Conquista dell'America e critica della civilità europea in Giordano Bruno. RICCI, Saverio.

BRUNS, G
Gerald Bruns's Cavell. CREWE, Jonathan.
On Bruns, on Cavell. CONANT, James.

BUBER
Encounter on the Narrow Ridge: A Life of Martin Buber. FRIEDMAN, Maurice.

BUBNER, R
Over het morele en zedelijke handelen, toegelicht aan het instituut huwelijk. COBBEN, Paul.

BUCHNER
History and the Paradoxes of Metaphysics in "Dantons Tod". TAYLOR, Rodney.

BUDDHA
Chinese Buddhist Apocrypha. BUSWELL JR, Robert E (ed).
The Buddha as an Owner of Property and Permanent Resident in Medieval Indian Monasteries. SCHOPEN, Gregory.

BUDDHISM
Behind the Masks of God: An Essay Toward Comparative Theology. NEVILLE, Robert Cummings.
Celebrating Peace. ROUNER, Leroy S (ed).
Chinese Buddhist Apocrypha. BUSWELL JR, Robert E (ed).
Dialogue with the Other: The Inter-Religious Dialogue. TRACY, David.
The Law of Karma: A Philosophical Study. REICHENBACH, Bruce R.
Mind Only: A Philosophical and Doctrinal Analysis of the Vijñānavāda. WOOD, Thomas E.
"Buddhism, Sri Lanka, and the Prospects for Peace" in *Celebrating Peace*, SMART, Ninian.
"Buddhist Ethics" in *A Companion to Ethics*, DE SILVA, Padmasiri.
'Ontological Commitment' in the Context of the Buddhist Thought. MITTAL, Kewal Krisha.
A Brief Survey of Indian Buddhistic Logic (in Hungarian). FEHER, Judit.
The Buddha as an Owner of Property and Permanent Resident in Medieval Indian Monasteries. SCHOPEN, Gregory.
Buddhist Anthropology vis-à-vis Modern Philosophy and Contemporary Neurophysiology. BUGAULT, Guy.
Buddhist Approaches to Abortion. FLORIDA, R E.
Buddhist Views of Suicide and Euthanasia. BECKER, Carl B.
Death, Honor, and Loyalty: The Bushidō Ideal. HURST III, G Cameron.
Dharmakīrti on Inference and Properties. GANERI, Jonardon.
Heidegger und Schopenhauer. HECKER, Hellmuth.
Introduction to Dharmakīrti's Theory of Inference as Presented in *Pramānavarttika Svopajñavrtti* 1-10. HAYES, Richard P and GILLON, Brendan S.
Krtapranasa and Akrtabhyagama: An Analysis, Defence and Rationale of the Buddhist Theory of Action. CHINCHORE, Mangala R.
Lost Buddhist Texts: The Rationale of Their Reconstruction in Sanskrit. CHINCHORE, Mangala R.
The Nature of Buddhism. KLOSTERMAIER, Klaus.
Punyadāna or Transference of Merit—A Fiction. KRISHAN, Y.
Representative Realism and Absolute Reality. ENGLISH, Parker.
Self and Suffering: Deconstruction and Reflexive Definition in Buddhism and Christianity. MELLOR, Philip A.
The Self in Medieval Japanese Buddhism: Focusing on Dōgen. KIMURA, Kiyotaka.
Towards a Philosophy of Buddhist Religion. HOFFMAN, Frank J.

BUDGET(S)
Wishful Thinking and the Budget Deficit. FRANKLIN, Daniel Paul.

BUENO, G
Nota sobre la causalidad apotética a la escala psicológica. FUENTES ORTEGA, Juan Bautista.
Problemas en torno al concepto de "ciencias humanas" como ciencias con doble plano operatorio. ALVARGONZÁLEZ, David.

BUKHARIN, N
The Blackmail of the Single Alternative: Bukharin, Trotsky and Perestrojka. DAY, Richard B.

BULGARIAN
Bulgaria: The Romantic Period of the Opposition Continues. KANEV, Krassimir.

BULLOGH, E
Edward Bullogh's Aesthetics and Aestheticism: Features of Reality to Be Experienced. BOULTING, Noel E.

BULTMANN
Meaning, Truth and Realism in Bultmann and Lindbeck. FERGUSSON, David.

BUNGE, M
Studies on Mario Bunge's "Treatise". WEINGARTNER, Paul (ed).
"Mario Bunge's Life and Work" in *Studies on Mario Bunge's "Treatise"*, BUNGE, Mario.
"Mario Bunge's Realist Semantics: An Antidote against Incommensurability?" in *Studies on Mario Bunge's "Treatise"*, BARTELS, Andreas.
"The Non-Statement View: A Dialogue between Socrates and Theaetetus" in *Studies on Mario Bunge's "Treatise"*, WEINGARTNER, Paul.
"On Mario Bunge's Semantical Realism" in *Studies on Mario Bunge's "Treatise"*, FERRATER-MORA, José.
"On the Concept of 'a Language'" in *Studies on Mario Bunge's "Treatise"*, DILLINGER, Mike.
"Scientific Philosophical and Sociopolitical Aspects of the Work of Mario Bunge" in *Studies on Mario Bunge's "Treatise"*, ROSENTHAL, Erwin.
"The Significance of the *Treatise* in the Light of the Western Philosophical Tradition" in *Studies on Mario Bunge's "Treatise"*, CUPANI, Alberto.
Emergent Psychoneural Monism: Mario Bunge and the Body and Soul Problem (in German). MÖLLER, Wolfgang.
La investigación y las metodologías en las Ciencias Humanas. DACAL ALONSO, José Antonio.

BURBIDGE, J
"A Reply to John Burbidge's "Where is the Place of Understanding?"" in *Essays on Hegel's Logic*, HOULGATE, Stephen.

BURBULES, N
Irony and Method: Comments on Burbules on Dialogue. NEIMAN, Alven M.

BUREAUCRACY(-CIES)
On Bureaucracy and Science: A Response to Fuller. TWENEY, Ryan D.

BURGE, T
All the Difference in the World. CRANE, Tim.
Anti-Individualism and Privileged Access. MC KINSEY, Michael.
Must Psychology Be Individualistic?. EGAN, Frances.

BURGER, P
Understanding Performance Art: Art beyond Art. HEYD, Thomas.

BURIDAN
Buridan's Divided Modal Syllogistic. WILLING, Anthony.

BURKE
"The Existential Sublime: From Burke's Aesthetics to the Socio-Political" in *XIth International Congress in Aesthetics, Nottingham 1988*, CROWTHER, Paul.
Edmund Burke en zijn "Reflections on the Revolution in France". DE VALK, J M M.
Natural and Political Society in the Thought of Edmund Burke (in German). TSCHURENEV, Eva-Maria.
Puzzling Through Burke. HERZOG, Don.
The Skeptic's Burke: *Reflections on the Revolution in France,* 1790-1990. MOSHER, Michael A.
Strauss's Three Burkes: The Problem of Edmund Burke in *Natural Right and History*. LENZNER, Steven J.

BURLEY, W
The Real Difficulty with Burley's Realistic Semantics. FITZGERALD, Michael J.

BUSINESS
see also Corporation(s)
Ethics and the Defense Procurement System. LANSING, Paul and BURKARD, Kimberly.
The Ethics of Health Care as a Business. WERHANE, Patricia H.
Health Care as a Business: The Ethic of Hippocrates Versus the Ethic of Managed Care. WAYMACK, Mark H.
Justice: The Root of American Business Ideology and Ethics. MC GOWAN, Richard.
Medicine and Business: An Unhealthy Mix?. BROCK, Dan W.
Medicine as Business and Profession. AGICH, George J.
Physicians, Entrepreneurism and the Problem of Conflict of Interest. GREEN, Ronald M.

BUSINESS ETHICS
Business Ethics. SHAW, William H.
Enriching Business Ethics. WALTON, Clarence C (ed).
Essentials of Business Ethics. MADSEN, Peter (ed).
Good Intentions Aside: A Manager's Guide to Resolving Ethical Problems. NASH, Laura L.
Work, Inc.: A Philosophical Inquiry. BYRNE, Edmund F.
"Business Ethics" in *A Companion to Ethics*, SOLOMON, Robert C.
"Everyone's Doing It"—A Reply to Richard DeGeorge. GREEN, Ronald M.
Applying the Principles of Gestalt Theory to Teaching Ethics. HUNT, Eugene H and BULLIS, Ronald K.
Believing that Everyone Else is Less Ethical: Implications for Work Behavior and Ethics Instruction. TYSON, Thomas.
Beyond Bean Counting: Establishing High Ethical Standards in the Public Accounting Profession. COHEN, Jeffrey R and PANT, Laurie W.
Business and Environmental Ethics. HOFFMAN, W Michael.
Business and Professional Ethics: An Oxymoron?. PORTER, Jack Nusan.
Business Ethics and Extant Social Contracts. DUNFEE, Thomas W.
Business Ethics and Social Responsibility in Finance Instruction: An Abdication of Responsibility. HAWLEY, Delvin D.
Business Ethics and Stakeholder Analysis. GOODPASTER, Kenneth E.
The Business Ethics of Pharmacists: Conflicts Practices and Beliefs. VITELL, Scott J and RAWWAS, Mohammed Y A and FESTERVAND, Troy A.
The Cases *For* and *Against* Theological Approaches to Business Ethics. TRUNDLE JR, Robert C.
The Challenge of Global Ethics. BULLER, Paul F and KOHLS, John J and ANDERSON, Kenneth S.
Challenging the Egoistic Paradigm. BOWIE, Norman E.
Characteristics and Practices of "Christian-Based" Companies. IBRAHIM, Nabil A and RUE, Leslie W and MC DOUGALL, Patricia P and GREENE, G Robert.

BUSINESS ETHICS
A Comparison of Nigerian to American Views of Bribery and Extortion in International Commerce. TSALIKIS, John and NWACHUKWU, Osita.
Concerns of College Students Regarding Business Ethics: A Replication. PETERSON, Robert A and BELTRAMINI, Richard F and KOZMETSKY, George.
Consumer Ethics: An Investigation of the Ethical Beliefs of Eldery Consumers. VITELL, Scott J and LUMPKIN, James R and RAWWAS, Mohammed Y A.
Corporate Policy and the Ethics of Competitor Intelligence Gathering. PAINE, Lynn Sharp.
Corporate Social Responsibility and the Marketplace. COTTRILL, Melville T.
A Cross-Cultural Comparison of the Ethics of Business Students. LYSONSKI, Steven and GAIDIS, William.
Danger Signs of Unethical Behavior: How to Determine If Your Firm Is at Ethical Risk. COOKE, Robert Allan.
Defining the Ethical Standards of the High-Technology Industry. FIMBEL, Nancie and BURSTEIN, Jerome S.
Deride, Abide or Dissent: On the Ethics of Professional Conduct. HAUPTMAN, Robert and HILL, Fred.
Developmental Constraints on Ethical Behaviour in Business. HARRIS, Claudia and BROWN, William.
Differences in Moral Values Between Corporations. NYSTROM, Paul C.
Economic Efficiency and the Quality of Life. JACOBSEN, Rockney.
Economic Efficiency: A Paradigm for Business Ethics. STIEBER, John and PRIMEAUX, Patrick.
Economics and Ethics. REILLY, B J and KYJ, M J.
Economics, Ethics, and Tort Remedies: The Emerging Concept of Hedonic Value. KARNS, Jack E.
Epistemological Structures in Marketing: Paradigms, Metaphors, and Marketing Ethics. REIDENBACH, R Eric and ROBIN, Donald P.
The Ethical Decision-Making Processes of Information Systems Workers. PARADICE, David B and DEJOIE, Roy M.
The Ethical Implications of the Straight-Commission Compensation System—An Agency Perspective. KURLAND, Nancy B.
Ethical Judgments on Selected Accounting Issues: An Empirical Study. STANGA, Keith G and TURPEN, Richard A.
Ethical Myopia: The Case of "Framing" by Framing. SINGER, Alan E and LYSONSKI, Steven and SINGER, Ming and HAYES, David.
The Ethical Roots of Business. VOGEL, David.
Ethical Values of Individuals at Different Levels in the Organizational Hierarchy of a Single Firm. HARRIS, James R.
Ethics Committees. COHEN, Cynthia B (ed).
Ethics in Declining Organizations. LEMKE, Dwight K and SCHMINKE, Marshall.
The Ethics of Rent Control. HANLY, Ken.
Ethics, Education, and Corporate Leadership. BASSIRY, G R.
Ethics, Public Policy, and Managing Advanced Technologies: The Case of Electronic Surveillance. OTTENSMEYER, Edward J and HEROUX, Mark A.
Exit, Voice, and Ethics. KEELEY, Michael and GRAHAM, Jill W.
An Experimental Assessment of Alternative Teaching Approaches for Introductory Business Ethics. BURTON, Scot and JOHNSTON, Mark W and WILSON, Elizabeth J.
Exploring the Structure of Ethical Attributions as a Component of the Consumer Decision Model. WHALEN, Joel and PITTS, Robert E and WONG, John K.
Fostering Ethical Marketing Decisions. LACZNIAK, Gene R and MURPHY, Patrick E.
Goodwill, Going Concern, Stocks and Flows: A Prescription for Moral Analysis. SWANDA JR, John R.
Green and "Everybody's Doing It". DE GEORGE, Richard T.
In Defense of Sharks: Moral Issues in Hostile Liquidating Takeovers. ALMEDER, Robert and CAREY, David.
The Inadequacy of a Deontological Analysis of Peer Relations in Organizations. MARTIN, Robert M.
Increasing Applied Business Ethics Courses in Business School Curricula. SIMS, Ronald R and SIMS, Serbrenia J.
The Indefensibility of Insider Trading. WERHANE, Patricia H.
The Influence of Non-Anonymity Deriving from Feedback of Research Results on Marketing Professionals' Research Ethics. AKAAH, Ishmael P.
Insider Trading Revisited. MARTIN, Deryl W and PETERSON, Jeffrey H.
The Institutionalization of Organizational Ethics. SIMS, Ronald R.
International Marketing Ethics. LACZNIAK, Gene R and MURPHY, Patrick E.
The Law of Business Ethics and Social Responsibility. BURKE III, William T.
Marketing Ethics and Education: Some Empirical Findings. MERRITT, Sharyne.
The Moral Authority of Transnational Corporate Codes. FREDERICK, William C.
Morality and Ethics in Organizational Administration. ADELMAN, Howard.
Multinational Corporate Social Policy Process for Ethical Responsibility in Sub-Saharan Africa. PRATT, Cornelius B.
The Politics of Ethics: Socratic Questioning is Needed in the Marketplace. TRUNDLE, Robert.
Predictors of Ethical Decisions Regarding Insider Trading. TERPSTRA, David E and REYES, Mario G C and BOKOR, Donald W.
Preferential Hiring and the Question of Competence. PHILIPS, Michael.
Principled Moral Reasoning: Is It a Viable Approach to Promote Ethical Integrity?. WEBER, James and GREEN, Sharon.
Promoting Moral Growth Through Intra-Group Participation. NELSON, D R and OBREMSKI, T E.
A Proposal for Corporate Ethical Reform: The Ethical Dialogue Group. PAYNE, Stephen L.
A Reaction to Vogel's "The Ethical Roots of Business". MC MAHON, Thomas F.
Reactions to Ethical Dilemmas: A Study Pertaining to Certified Public Accounts. CLAYPOOL, G A and FETYKO, D F and PEARSON, M A.
The Relative Importance of Social Responsibility in Determining Organizational Effectiveness: Student Responses. KRAFT, Kenneth L.
The Relative Importance of Social Responsibility in Determining Organizational Effectiveness. KRAFT, Kenneth.
Remarks on Marketing Ethics. BRENNAN, Bernard F.
Risk, Commitment, and Project Abandonment. DEVANEY, Mike.
The Role of Ethics and Social Responsibility in Achieving Organizational Effectiveness: Students Versus Managers. KRAFT, Kenneth L and SINGHAPAKDI, Anusorn.
Shareholder Authorized Inside Trading: A Legal and Moral Analysis. SHAW, Bill.
Shrewd Bargaining on the Moral Frontier: Toward a Theory of Morality in Practice. DEES, J Gregory and CRAMPTON, Peter C.
Smoking in Public: A Moral Imperative for the Most Toxic of Environmental Wastes. LUDINGTON, David M.
Social Responsibility and Strategic Management: Toward an Enterprise Strategy Classification. MEZNAR, Martin B and CHRISMAN, James J and CARROLL, Archie B.
The Sociology of Knowledge: Toward an Existential View of Business Ethics. PHILLIPS, Nelson.
Socrates in Dallas: Managing the Facilities. CASTRO, Barry.
The Teaching of Business Ethics: A Survey of AACSB Member Schools. SCHOENFELDT, Lyle F and MC DONALD, Don M and YOUNGBLOOD, Stuart A.
When is "Everyone's Doing It" a Moral Justification?. GREEN, Ronald M.

BUTLER
Butler and the Authority of Conscience. O'BRIEN, Wendell.
Should Children Be Taught to Obey Their Conscience?. HUGHEN, Richard.
'Following Nature' in Butler's Sermons. BRINTON, Alan.

BYERLY, H
Adequacy Criteria for a Theory of Fitness. ROSENBERG, Alexander.
Byerly and Michod on Fitness. SMITH, John Maynard.
Commentary on Byerly and Michod. LENNOX, James G.
Commentary on the Paper by H C Byerly and R E Michod's "Fitness and Evolutionary Explanation". BRITO DA CUNHA, A.
Comments on "Fitness and Evolutionary Explanation". KLEINER, Scott A.
Natural Selection as Natural History. VAN DER STEEN, Wim J.
On Causality, Heritability and Fitness. ETTINGER, Lia and JABLONKA, Eva and FALK, Raphael.

CAFFARA, C
Christ, Moral Absolutes, and the Good: Recent Moral Theology. PINCKAERS, Servais.

CAHN, S
In Defense of Cahn's Scamps. FOULK, Gary.

CALCULUS
"Monotonic Solution of The Frame Problem in The Situation Calculus" in *Knowledge Representation and Defeasible Reasoning*, SCHUBERT, Lenhart.
Models for Inconsistent and Incomplete Differential Calculus. MORTENSEN, Chris.
Die Natur der Sprache: Von der Ontologie zur Technologie. HOTTOIS, Gilbert.
Parthood and Persistence. KAZMI, Ali Akhtar.
Remarks on Analogy. DA COSTA, Newton C A and SETTE, A M.

CALLEBAUT, W
Crypto-theologie: hoffentlich ein Ende: Reactie op Callebaut en Wachelder. SOONTIENS, Frans.

CALLICOTT, J
Biological Holism and the Evolution of Ethics. SHRADER-FRECHETTE, Kristin.
Biology and Ethics: Callicott Reconsidered. SHRADER-FRECHETTE, Kristin.
A Clue for a Classical Realist Contribution to the Debate Over the Value of Animals. KLONOSKI, Richard J.

CALVIN
The Assurance of Faith. WOLTERSTORFF, Nicholas.

CALVINISM
American Moralism and the Origin of Bioethics in the United States. JONSEN, Albert R.

CAMPANELLA
"Tommaso Campanella: L'ente e l'analogia nella *Universalis Philosophia*" in *Razionalitá critica: nella filosofia moderna*, LAMACCHIA, Ada.
Campanella's "Civitas Solis" Is Ruled by Love Without Emotion (in German). ZÖHRER-ERNST, Ulla.

CAMUS
"Camus Revisited: Neither Victim nor Executioner" in *In the Interest of Peace: A Spectrum of Philosophical Views*, BOVE, Laurence.
El humanismo de Albert Camus. QUESADA, Anabelle.
La inocencia y el mal en la obra de Albert Camus. JIMÉNEZ, Alexander.
Jivacide, Zombies and *Jivanmuktas*. HERMAN, A L.
The Nietzsche Temptation in the Thought of Albert Camus. DUVALL, William E.
Prometheus or Cain? Albert Camus's Account of the Western Quest for Justice. WARD, Bruce K.

CANADIAN
The Exclusion of Evidence Obtained by Constitutionally Impermissible Means in Canada. MC DONALD, David C.
Recent Canadian Work on Wittgenstein: 1980-1989. WILLIAMSON, George.
Uncertainty and the Shaping of Medical Decisions. BERESFORD, Eric B.

CANALS, F
Entorn del libre de F canals i Vidal: "Sobre la esencia del conocimiento". COLOMER, Eusebi.

CANETTI, E
Leben als Passion: Elias Canettis "Masse und Macht" als Beitrag zum Begreifen der Moderne. DIETZSCH, Steffen.

CANON(S)
Chinese Buddhist Apocrypha. BUSWELL JR, Robert E (ed).
The Case Against Art: Wunderlich on Joyce. MAHAFFEY, Vicki.

CANTOR
Le Kantisme de la théorie cantorienne de l'infini. BACHTA, Abdelkader.

CAPACITY(-TIES)
Kant's Transcendental Psychology. KITCHER, Patricia.
Patient Decision-Making Capacity and Risk. WICCLAIR, Mark R.
Resources, Capacities, and Ownership: The Workmanship Ideal and Distributive Justice. SHAPIRO, Ian.
Seeing Our Seeing and Knowing Our Knowing. BEN-ZEEV, Aaron.

CAPITAL PUNISHMENT
Hobbes on Capital Punishment. HEYD, David.

CAPITALISM
Interpreting Political Responsibility. DUNN, John.
Marx's Radical Critique of Capitalist Society: A Reconstruction and Critical Evaluation. ARNOLD, N Scott.
The Meaning of Socialism. LUNTLEY, Michael.
Morality and Modernity. POOLE, Ross.
Resurrecting Marx: The Analytical Marxists on Freedom, Exploitation, and Justice. GORDON, David.
"Postmodernism and (Post)Marxism" in *Postmodernism—Philosophy and the Arts (Continental Philosophy III)*, O'NEILL, J.
Alienation, Schools, and Society. ZHANG, Wei Rose.
Beyond Mourning and Melancholia on the Left. DUBIEL, Helmut.
Capitalismo, Socialidad y participación. PASSANITI, Daniel.
The Divided Machine: Capitalist Crisis and the Organization of Labor. TURCHETTO, Maria and ESPOSITO, Joan.
Economies of Time: On the Idea of Time in Marx's Political Economy. BOOTH, William James.
Entrepreneurial Philosophy (in German). HERDER-DORNEICH, Philipp.
The Ethical Roots of Business. VOGEL, David.
The Intellectuals at the End of History. BRUNKHORST, Hauke.
Market Order or Commanded Chaos. FLEW, Antony.
The New Consensus: II—The Democratic Welfare State. FRIEDMAN, Jeffrey.
The Differences Between the Capitalist and the Modern Society (in German). KRÜGER, Hans-Peter.

CAPITINI, A
Il pensiero di Aldo Capitini e la filosofia del neoidealismo. CESA, Claudio.

CAPLAN, A
The Evaluation of "Outcomes" of Accounting Ethics Education. LOEB, Stephen E.

CAPUTO, J
"Maritain and the Future of Reason" in *From Twilight to Dawn: The Cultural Vision of Jacques Maritain*, BOYLE, William J.
Radical Hermeneutics, Critical Theory, and the Political. DOODY, John A.
Las reglas del juego: consideraciones críticas sobre "Radical Hermeneutics" de John Caputo. PEÑA, Lorenzo.

CARACCIOLO, A
Selected Problems of Albert Caracciolo's Philosophy of Culture (in Polish). TECZA, Beata.

CARDINALITY
The Cardinality of Powersets in Finite Models of the Powerset Axiom. ABIAN, Alexander and AMIN, Wael A.
Unidimensional Theories are Superstable. HRUSHOVSKI, Ehud.

CARDINALS
The Complete 0. KANAMORI, Akihiro and AWERBUCH-FRIEDLANDER, Tamara.
Full Reflection of Stationary Sets Below $\aleph_\omega$. JECH, Thomas and SHELAH, Saharon.
A Hierarchy of Ramsey Cardinals. FENG, Qi.
Infinitary Combinatorics and Modal Logic. BLASS, A.
The Normal Depth of Filters on an Infinite Cardinal. DI PRISCO, C A and FULLER, M and HENLE, J M.
Partition Properties and Prikry Forcing on Simple Spaces. HENLE, J M.
Partitioning Pairs of Countable Sets of Ordinals. VELLEMAN, Dan.
Regressive Partition Relations, *n*-Subtle Cardinals, and Borel Diagonalization. KANAMORI, Akihiro.
Shelah's pcf Theory and Its Applications. BURKE, Maxim R and MAGIDOR, Menachem.
Some Results on Higher Suslin Trees. DAVID, R.
The Spectrum of Resplendency. BALDWIN, John T.
The Strength of the Failure of the Singular Cardinal Hypothesis. GITIK, Moti.
Successors of Singular Cardinals and Measurability Revisited. APTER, Arthur W.

CARDONA, C
Sobre la "Metafísica del bien y del mal". MELENDO, Tomás.

CARE
The 'Voice of Care': Implications for Bioethical Education. CARSE, Alisa L.
Feminist Fears in Ethics. NODDINGS, Nel.
Gilligan on Justice and Care: Two Interpretations. VREEKE, G J.
Husserl's Notion of Constitution in Heidegger's Treatment of Care. THOMAS, V C.
Nursing Responsibility for the Placebo Effect. CONNELLY, Robert J.
Separating Care and Cure: An Analysis of Historical and Contemporary Images of Nursing and Medicine. JECKER, Nancy S and SELF, Donnie J.

CARING
A Philosophy of Morals. HELLER, Agnes.
"Some Thoughts about 'Caring'" in *Feminist Ethics*, HOAGLAND, Sarah Lucia.
Caring About Nature: Feminist Ethics and the Environment. KING, Roger J H.
A Comment on Fry's "The Role of Caring in a Theory of Nursing Ethics". BOYER, Jeannine Ross and NELSON, James Lindemann.
Comment on Romain's "Feminist Reflections on Humans and Other Domestic Animals. RUD JR, Anthony G.
The Environmental Dependence of Dispositional Aims: Response to the Presidential Address. RAYWID, Mary Ann.
Feminist Reflections on Humans and Other Domestic Animals. ROMAIN, Dianne.
Her Terrain is Outside His "Domain". PEEPLES, S Elise.
Rational and Caring Teachers: How Dispositional Aims Shape Teacher Preparation. ARNSTINE, Barbara.
The Science of Caring. PUKA, Bill.
Toward An Ecological Ethic of Care. CURTIN, Deane.

CARNAP
"Carnap, Quine and the Rejection of Intuition" in *Perspectives on Quine*, CREATH, Richard.
Descriptions: Contemporary Philosophy and the Nyāya. SHAW, J L.
Did Kuhn Kill Logical Empiricism?. REISCH, George A.
How Not to Russell Carnap's *Aufbau*. RICHARDSON, Alan.
Logicism, Pragmatism and Metascience: Towards a Pancritical-Pragmatic Meta-Level Discourse. AXTELL, G S.
Persistent Propensities: Portrait of a Familiar Controversy. NORDMANN, Alfred.
Semantic Holism. BELNAP JR, Nuel D and MASSEY, Gerald J.
Wittgenstein y el fisicalismo. HALLER, Rudolf.

CARNOT, L
The Fundamental Hypotheses of Mechanics in Lazare N M Carnot's Thought (in Italian). DRAGO, Antonino and MANNO, Salvatore D.

CARR, D
Limning the Liminal: Carr and Ricoeur on Time and Narrative. PELLAUER, David.

CARTESIANISM
Human Consciousness. HANNAY, Alastair.
"Cognitive Access and Semantic Puzzle" in *Propositional Attitudes: The Role of Content in Logic, Language, and Mind*, OWENS, Joseph I.
"Epistemic Universalizability: From Skepticism to Infallibilism" in *Doubting: Contemporary Perspectives on Skepticism*, ADLER, Jonathan E.
"First-Person Access" in *Philosophical Perspectives, 4: Action Theory and Philosophy of Mind, 1990*, SHOEMAKER, Sydney.
"Klein on Certainty and Canonical Beliefs" in *Doubting: Contemporary Perspectives on Skepticism*, FELDMAN, Richard.

CARTESIANISM
"Maritain's American Illusions" in *From Twilight to Dawn: The Cultural Vision of Jacques Maritain*, MANCINI, Matthew J.
Against Cartesian Dualism: Strawson and Sartre on the Unity of Person. MUI, Constance.
Against Common Sense: Avoiding Cartesian Anxiety. BINEHAM, Jeffery L.
Anscombian and Cartesian Scepticism. HAMILTON, Andy.
Berkeley's Cartesian Anti-Abstractionism. GLOUBERMAN, Mark.
Cartesian Feminists. LONGACRE, Judith.
Cartesian Scepticism and Relevant Alternatives. SCHRECK, P A.
Certainty, the Cogito, and Cartesian Dualism. GLOUBERMAN, Mark.
The Cogito and the Diallelus. ZELLNER, Harold.
Heideggerian Retrieval of Cartesianism. ROY, Krishna.
Irreducible Dualisms and the Residue of Commonsense: On the Inevitability of Cartesian Anxiety. HIKINS, James W and CHERWITZ, Richard A.
Merleau-Ponty on the Cartesian "Dubito": A Critical Analysis. HUDAC, Michael C.
Paradigmas cartesianos. LOPARIC, Z.
Process Thought and the Spaciness of Mind. EDWARDS, Rem B.
Rediscovering Scepticism. BAILEY, Alan.
Vico in Voegelin. CAPORALI, Riccardo.
Was ist ein Polyhistor? Gehversuche auf einem verlassenen Terrain. JAUMANN, Herbert.

CARTWRIGHT, N
How Nancy Cartwright Tells the Truth. FRANKLIN, Allan.
Realism and the Collapse of the Wave-Packet. KRIPS, Henry.

CASATI, R
Lockes Qualitäten: Erwiderung auf Casati. KIENZLE, Bertram.

CASE STUDY(-DIES)
Medical Ethics in Practice. BARD, Terry R.
Well and Good: Case Studies in Biomedical Ethics (Revised Edition). THOMAS, John E.
Getting Down to Cases: The Revival of Casuistry in Bioethics. ARRAS, John D.
Legal Reasoning and Practical Political Education. STRAUBER, Ira.
The Noncompliant Substance Abuser: Commentary. CASSEL, Christine and LA PUMA, John.
Rich Cases: The Ethics of Thick Description. DAVIS, Dena S.

CASE(S)
Feminist Ethics and Case-Based Reasoning: A Marriage of Purpose. RIESBECK, Christopher K and MORPHIS, Maxine.
Privacy and Disclosure in Medical Genetics Examined in an Ethics of Care. WERTZ, Dorothy C and FLETCHER, John C.

CASSIRER
The Taming of Chance. HACKING, Ian.
Conditio sine qua non? Zuordnung in the Early Epistemologies of Cassirer and Schlick. RYCKMAN, Thomas.
Ernst Cassirer and Martin Heidegger: The Davos Debate. LYNCH, Dennis A.
Hegel as Advocate of Machiavelli (in German). JAMME, Christoph.
Man as the Animal Symbolism in the Conception of S Langer (in Polish). BYTNIEWSKI, Pawel.

CASTANEDA, H
Castañeda's Quasi-Indicators and the Tensed Theory of Time. SMITH, Quentin.
Whether Any Individual at all Could Have a Guise Structure. MILLER, Barry.

CASTE(S)
The Place of the Hidden Moon: Erotic Mysticism in the Vaisnava-sahajiyā Cult of Bengal. DIMOCK JR, Edward C.

CASTORIADIS, C
"Unger, Castoriadis, and the Romance of a National Future" in *Critique and Construction: A Symposium on Roberto Unger's "Politics"*, RORTY, Richard.

CASUISTRY
Ethics Committee Simulations. WINSTON, Morton.
Getting Down to Cases: The Revival of Casuistry in Bioethics. ARRAS, John D.
How Is Applied Philosophy to Be Applied?. KLINEFELTER, Donald S.

CATASTROPHE THEORY
Modernism's Two Eternities. GEORGIEFF, Andrey.

CATASTROPHISM
Conciencia de catástrofe, poder y libertad. DEI, H Daniel.

CATEGORICAL
Are Kantian Duties Categorical?. SCHOEMAN, Ferdinand.
Assessing Human Needs. JONES, John D.
Being and Categorial Intuition. COBB-STEVENS, Richard.
The Categorical Nature of Mathematical Cognition. NYSANBAYEV, A N and KADYRZHANOV, R K.
Conductive $\aleph_0$-Categorical Theories. SCHMERL, James H.
Does Reason Command Itself for Its Own Sake?. KRAENZEL, Frederick.

CATEGORICAL GRAMMAR(S)
Categorical Grammars Determined from Linguistic Data by Unification. BUSZKOWSKI, Wojciech and PENN, Gerald.

CATEGORICAL IMPERATIVE
Kant's System of Rights. MULHOLLAND, Leslie A.
Kants Kategorischer Imperativ als Leitfaden humaner Praxis. NISTERS, Thomas.
"Kantian Ethics" in *A Companion to Ethics*, O'NEILL, Onora.
Discourse and the Moral Point of View: Deriving a Dialogical Principle of Universalization. REHG, William.
Elogio critico dell'imperfezione. TUSA, Carlo.
The First Formulation of the Categorical Imperative as Literally a "Legislative" Metaphor. GREEN, Ronald M.
Maurice Blondel's Moral Logic. LONG, Fiachra.
On Kant's Conception of Science and the Critique of Practical Reason. KÖRNER, Stephan.

CATEGORICITY
Teoria e interpretazione: Per un'epistemologia delle scienze umane. BORUTTI, Silvana.
Stability for Pairs of Equivalence Relations. TOFFALORI, Carlo.

CATEGORY MISTAKE
Do Animals Have Rights?. MACHAN, Tibor R.

CATEGORY THEORY
Natural Complex versus Natural System. KHALIL, Elias L.
The Uses and Abuses of the History of Topos Theory. MC LARTY, Colin.

CATEGORY(-RIES)
Fallen Freedom: Kant on Radical Evil and Moral Regeneration. MICHALSON JR, Gordon E.
Nicolai Hartmann's New Ontology. WERKMEISTER, W H.
"Hegel and the Problem of the Differentia" in *Essays on Hegel's Logic*, HALPER, Edward.
"A Reply to Edward Halper's "Hegel and the Problem of the Differentia"" in *Essays on Hegel's Logic*, DONOUGHO, Martin.
"Vision and Mind" in *Logic, Methodology and Philosophy of Science, VIII*, GLEZER, Vadim D.
"Pathologies" in Two Syntactic Categories of Partial Maps. MONTAGNA, Franco.
Colimit Completions and the Effective Topos. ROBINSON, Edmund and ROSOLINI, Giuseppe.
Cuteness. MORREALL, John.
Domain Theory in Logical Form. ABRAMSKY, Samson.
An Existence Theorem for Recursion Categories. HELLER, Alex.
Intuitionistic Categorial Grammar. RANTA, Aarne.
Kants Schemata als Anwendungsbedingungen von Kategorien auf Anschauungen. LOHMAR, Dieter.
The Making and Molding of Child Abuse. HACKING, Ian.
Peirce's Logic of Discovery: Abduction and the Universal Categories. TURRISI, Patricia A.
Predication and Deduction in Aristotle: Aspirations to Completeness. SMITH, Robin.
Some Remarks on ω-Powers of Enumerated Sets and Their Applications to ω-Operations. ORLICKI, Andrzej.
Two-Steps-in-One-Proof: The Structure of the Transcendental Deduction of the Categories. EVANS, J Claude.

CATERUS, J
The Caterus Objection. FORGIE, J William.

CATHOLIC
Towards a Christian Philosophy. OWENS, Joseph I.
Antropología del trabajo según la Encíclica "Laborem Excercens". QUESADA GUARDIA, Annabelle.
Christ, Moral Absolutes, and the Good: Recent Moral Theology. PINCKAERS, Servais.
The Doctrine of Double Effect: Its Philosophical Viability. BOLE, Thomas.
Heidegger: vita e distino—Sullo biografia heideggeriana di Hugo Ott. ESPOSITO, Costantino.
History as Argument for Revision in Moral Theology. GRISEZ, Germain.

CATHOLICISM
The Vatican, the Law and the Human Embryo. COUGHLAN, Michael J.
"Catholicism and Liberalism—200 Years of Contest and Consensus" in *Liberalism and the Good*, LANGAN, John.
"Exiles and Fugitives: The Maritain-Tate-Gordon Letters" in *From Twilight to Dawn: The Cultural Vision of Jacques Maritain*, DUNAWAY, John M.
"World War II and the Anti-Democratic Impulse in Catholicism" in *From Twilight to Dawn: The Cultural Vision of Jacques Maritain*, HELLMAN, John.
Catholic and Marxist Views on Human Development. MC GOVERN, Arthur F.
Economic Rights: A Test Case for Catholic Social Teaching. MC CANN, Dennis P.
Etica del desarrollo: algunos principios y orientaciones a la luz de la docrina social de la Iglesia Católica. BRENES, Víctor.
Marriage is an Institution Created by God: A Philosophical Analysis. BOYLE, Joseph.
Medical Ethics in Ireland: A Decade of Change. DOOLEY, Dolores.
Religious Liberty, Religious Dissent and the Catholic Tradition. COWDIN, Daniel M.

CATHOLICISM

The Common European Home (in German). FEIEREIS, Konrad.
Ultramontanisme et gallicanisme engagentils deux visions de la société. BRESSOLETTE, Claude.

CATO

Cato's Letters, John Locke, and the Republican Paradigm. HAMOWY, Ronald.

CAUCHY, A

On Cauchy's Notion of Infinitesimal. CUTLAND, Nigel J (and others).

CAUSAL EXPLANATION

"Dubbing and Redubbing: The Vulnerability of Rigid Destination" in *Scientific Theories*, KUHN, Thomas S.
Aristotle's Technical Simulation and its Logic of Causal Relations. LOECK, Gisela.
Contrastive Explanations. LIPTON, Peter.
A Critique of Genealogies. KIM, Chin-Tai.
Experience and Causal Explanation in Medical Empiricism. PENTZOPOULOU-VALALAS, Teresa.
Explanation in Biology. SMITH, John Maynard.
How Nancy Cartwright Tells the Truth. FRANKLIN, Allan.
Nonbranching and Nontransitivity. EHRING, Douglas.

CAUSAL LAW(S)

Partitions, Probabilistic Causal Laws, and Simpson's Paradox. HARDCASTLE, Valerie Gray.

CAUSALITY

Causality in Sociological Research. KARPINSKI, Jakub.
Central Themes in Early Modern Philosophy. COVER, J A (ed).
Le existentia de deo e le Immortalitate del Anima: Lineas de Philosophia del Esser. BLANDINO, Giovanni.
The Idea of the Miraculous: The Challenge to Science and Religion. WILLIAMS, T C.
Leibniz and Arnauld. SLEIGH JR, Robert C.
Metaphysical Delusion. COWLEY, Fraser.
Philosophy and Cognitive Science. FETZER, James H.
The Philosophy of Action: An Introduction. MOYA, Carlos J.
A Progress of Sentiments: Reflections on Hume's "Treatise". BAIER, Annette C.
Science and Reason. KYBURG JR, Henry E.
"Berkeley and Malebranche on Causality and Volition" in *Central Themes in Early Modern Philosophy*, JOLLEY, Nicholas.
"Can the Mind Change the World?" in *Meaning and Method: Essays in Honor of Hilary Putnam*, BLOCK, Ned.
"Leibniz on Malebranche on Causality" in *Central Themes in Early Modern Philosophy*, SLEIGH JR, Robert C.
"Marxian Ideology and Causality" in *Perspectives on Ideas and Reality*, ROCKMORE, Tom.
"On a Causal Theory of Content" in *Philosophical Perspectives, 3: Philosophy of Mind and Action Theory, 1989*, BAKER, Lynne Rudder.
"Real Humean Causes" in *Central Themes in Early Modern Philosophy*, BAIER, Annette.
"Type Epiphenomenalism, Type Dualism, and the Causal Priority of the Physical" in *Philosophical Perspectives, 3: Philosophy of Mind and Action Theory, 1989*, MC LAUGHLIN, Brian P.
Action and Explanation. MAJUMDAR, Aruna.
Agency and Probabilistic Causality. PRICE, Huw.
Aristotle's Causality Theory. ANDRIOPOULOS, D Z.
Causal Propensities: Statistical Causality versus Aleatory Causality. SALMON, Wesley C.
The Causal Theory of Reference and Religious Language. HARRIS, James F.
Causalistico-Occasionalistic Dispute in Islam as Opposing of "Greek" and "Islamic" Spirit (in Serbo-Croatian). BUCAN, Daniel.
Causality Assessment in Epidemiology. VINEIS, Paolo.
Causality, Determinism and Objective Reality in Modern Physics. NARAYAN, S Shankar.
Causality: Sankara and Aristotle. DHAVAMONY, Mariasusai.
The Chicken and the Egg. TEICHMANN, Roger.
Conceptual Necessity, Causality and Self-Ascriptions of Sensation. KAUFMAN, Frederik.
Counterfactuals and the Complexity of Causal Notions. PIZZI, Claudio.
David Hume and the Mysterious Shroud of Turin. SCHOEN, Edward L.
Divenire, principio di causalità, affermazione teologica. SACCHI, Dario.
Emanating Causes: New Battle Lines for Natural Theology?. KING-FARLOW, John.
Explanation and Causality: Some Suggestions from Econometrics. GALAVOTTI, Maria Carla.
Externalist Theories of Perception. ALSTON, William P.
Filosofía desde la teoría causal de la referencia. NUBIOLA, Jaime.
Kitcher and Salmon's *Scientific Explanation*; and Salmon's *Four Decades of Scientific Explanation*. FETZER, James H.
The Limits of Explanation. SWINBURNE, Richard.
The Logic of Causal Inference: Econometrics and the Conditional Analysis of Causation. HOOVER, Kevin D.
Metaphysics of the Person, Determinism and Responsibility. FAY, Thomas A.
Monadic Marxism: A Critique of Elster's Methodological Individualism. MOGGACH, Douglas.
Nietzsche e Spinoza. BIUSO, Alberto G.
Nota sobre la causalidad apotética a la escala psicológica. FUENTES ORTEGA, Juan Bautista.
On the Causality of Sky. MISHRA, Aruna Ranjan.
Personal Identity and the Causal Continuity Requirement. ELLIOT, Robert.
Probabilistic Causality from a Dynamical Point of View. VON PLATO, Jan.
Probabilistic Causality: A Rejoinder to Ellery Eells. DUPRÉ, John.
Probability and Epistemology. PIENKOWSKI, M.
Relativité et quanta: leurs mutuelles exisgences et les corrélations d'Einstein-Podolsky-Rosen. COSTA DE BEAUREGARD, Olivier.
Response to Ehring's 'Papineau on Causal Asymmetry'. PAPINEAU, David.
Supervenience and Singular Causal Claims. WOODWARD, James.
Symptomatic Acts and the Value of Evidence in Causal Decision Theory. MAHER, Patrick.
Thoughts and Theses on Causality. TILANDER, A.
Wittgenstein's Indeterminism. SCHEER, Richard K.

CAUSATION

Change, Cause and Contradiction: A Defence of the Tenseless Theory of Time. LE POIDEVIN, Robin.
Explaining Behavior: Reasons in a World of Causes. DRETSKE, Fred.
Human Nature and Historical Knowledge: Hume, Hegel and Vico. POMPA, Leon.
Introduction to Metaphysics: The Fundamental Questions. SCHOEDINGER, Andrew B (ed).
Knowledge in Flux: Modeling the Dynamics of Epistemic States. GÄRDENFORS, Peter.
The Law of Karma: A Philosophical Study. REICHENBACH, Bruce R.
Philosophical Papers: F P Ramsey. MELLOR, D H (ed).
Probabilistic Causality. EELLS, Ellery.
The Secret Connexion: Causation, Realism, and David Hume. STRAWSON, Galen.
Varieties of Social Explanation: An Introduction to the Philosophy of Social Science. LITTLE, Daniel.
"Explanatory Exclusion and the Problem of Mental Causation" in *Information, Semantics and Epistemology*, KIM, Jaegwon.
"Mental Quausation" in *Philosophical Perspectives, 3: Philosophy of Mind and Action Theory, 1989*, HORGAN, Terence.
"Proximate Causation of Action" in *Philosophical Perspectives, 3: Philosophy of Mind and Action Theory, 1989*, BRAND, Myles.
"Risk, Causation, and Harm" in *Liability and Responsibility*, ROBINSON, Glen O.
"The Value of Knowledge" in *Scientific Theories*, SKYRMS, Brian.
The Antinomy of Perception: Merleau-Ponty and Causal Representation Theory. HASS, Lawrence.
The Causal Efficacy of Content. SEGAL, Gabriel and SOBER, Elliott.
Causation in the Philosophy of Mind. JACKSON, Frank and PETTIT, Philip.
Causation: Reductionism Versus Realism. TOOLEY, Michael.
Causes and Coincidences. OWENS, David.
Causing, Enabling, and Counterfactual Dependence. MACKIE, Penelope.
Coming To Be Without a Cause. SULLIVAN, T D.
Direct and Indirect Causes. SPOHN, Wolfgang.
Ensuring Two Bird Deaths with One Throw. LESLIE, John.
An Epistemic Analysis of Explanations and Causal Beliefs. GÄRDENFORS, Peter.
Explanation, Causation and Laws. EDGINGTON, Dorothy.
General Causation. SAPIRE, David.
How Beliefs Explain: Reply to Baker. DRETSKE, Fred.
How's and Why's: Causation Un-Locked. FRANKEL, Lois.
Hume and Physical Necessity. FLEW, Antony.
Hume and Thick Connexions. BLACKBURN, Simon.
Intentionalistic Explanations in the Social Sciences. SEARLE, John R.
Madden's Account of Necessity in Causation. LEVINE, Michael P.
Mental Causation and Non-Reductive Monism. MACDONALD, Cynthia and MACDONALD, Graham.
Mental Causes. HEIL, John and MELE, Alfred.
Miracles and Ghazali's First Theory of Causation. BAHLUL, Raja.
Motion, Causation, and the Causal Theory of Identity. EHRING, Douglas.
The Nature of Causation: A Singularist Account. TOOLEY, Michael.
Nonautonomous Psychology. PETRIE, Bradford.
Peirce's Realism, Intentionality and Final Causation. TURIANO, Mark.
Preemption, Direct Causation, and Identity. EHRING, Douglas.
The Problem of Causation and Time-Symmetry in Physics. BHARUCHA, Filita.
Search for Beliefs to Live by Consistent with Science. SPERRY, R W.
Singular Causation and Law. IRZIK, Gürol.
Sobre causación y unificación según Wesley Salmon. OLIVÉ, León.
Teleology and the Concepts of Causation. VON GLASERSFELD, Ernst.

CAUSE(S)

Yoga on War and Peace. TIGUNAIT, Pandit Rajmani.
"The Four Causes" in *Studies on Mario Bunge's "Treatise"*, ESPINOZA, Miguel.

CAUSE(S)
"Functional Explanations and Reasons as Causes" in *Philosophical Perspectives, 3: Philosophy of Mind and Action Theory, 1989*, SAYRE-MC CORD, Geoffrey.
"Reasons and Causes" in *Philosophical Perspectives, 3: Philosophy of Mind and Action Theory, 1989*, DRETSKE, Fred.
The Authorship of Faith. SESSIONS, W L.
The Causal History of Computational Activity: Maudlin and Olympia. BARNES, Eric.
Causal Independence in EPR Arguments. BUTTERFIELD, Jeremy.
Causes and Laws. ARMSTRONG, D M and HEATHCOTE, Adrian.
Causes and Laws: The Asymmetry Puzzle. BYERLY, Henry.
Causes, Proximate and Ultimate. FRANCIS, Richard C.
Dretske on the Explanatory Role of Belief. BAKER, Lynne Rudder.
Forms and Causes In Plato's *Phaedo*. BYRNE, Christopher.
Giacomo Andrea Giacomini: un clinico padovano tra Metafisica e Scienza. FEDERSPIL, Giovanni.
Hume on Probability. GOWER, Barry.
Narcissim Project and Corporate Decay: The Case of General Motors. SCHWARTZ, Howard S.
Newcomb's Problem, Prisoners' Dilemma, and Collective Action. HURLEY, S L.
Non-Dominance, Third Person and Non-Action Newcomb Problems, and Metatickles. SOBEL, Jordan Howard.
Origen y desembocadura de la acción: el sujeto inevitable. CRUZ, Manuel.
Le rôle des causes comme instruments de la définition. VALOIS, Raynald.
Some Versions of Newcomb's Problem Are Prisoners' Dilemmas. SOBEL, Jordan Howard.
Spinoza's Two Causal Chains. GILEAD, Amihud.
Untangling Cause, Necessity, Temporality, and Method: Response to Chamber's Method of Corresponding Regressions. WILLIAMS, Richard N.
What Happened in Eastern Europe in 1989?. CHIROT, Daniel.

CAVELL, S
Gerald Bruns's Cavell. CREWE, Jonathan.
On Bruns, on Cavell. CONANT, James.
Reply to Crewe and Conant. BRUNS, Gerald L.

CELAN, P
Ästhetik des Abschieds: Kritik der Moderne. EBELING, Hans.

CELL(S)
Elementos dinámicos de la teoría celular. GONZÁLEZ RECIO, José Luis.
From Presentation to Representation in E B Wilson's *The Cell*. MAIENSCHEIN, Jane.
New Creations? Commentary. BALK, Roger A.
New Creations? Commentary. MACER, Darryl.
Outrageous Fortune: Selling Other People's Cells. ANNAS, George J.

CENSORSHIP
The Political Ontology of Martin Heidegger. BOURDIEU, Pierre.
Art and Censorship. SERRA, Richard.
Artistic Freedom: An Art World Paradox. LANKFORD, E Louis.
The Satanic Novel: A Philosophical Dialogue on Blasphemy and Censorship. SPRIGGE, T L S.

CENTRAL AMERICAN
Las ideas en Centroamerica: De 1838 a 1970. ESTRADA, Olga C (ed).

CERTAINTY
Criteria of Certainty: Truth and Judgment in the English Enlightenment. COPE, Kevin L.
L'ordine della certezza: Scientificità e persuasione in Descartes. BONICALZI, Francesca.
Quest for Certainty: A Comparative Study of Heidegger and Sankara. GRIMES, John A.
An Anti-Sceptical Fugue. GILLETT, Grant.
Certain Hope. PHILLIPS GRIFFITHS, A.
Certainty, the Cogito, and Cartesian Dualism. GLOUBERMAN, Mark.
The Problem of Protocol Statements and Schlick's Concept of 'Konstatierungen'. ZHAI, Zhenming.
Reinventing Certainty: The Significance of Ian Hacking's Realism. GROSS, Alan G.
Wittgenstein escéptico?. CABANCHIK, Samuel.

CERTITUDE
"The Problem of Certitude: Reflections on the Grammar of Assent" in *Thomistic Papers, V*, SULLIVAN, Thomas D.

CHADWICK, R
The Market for Bodily Parts: A Response to Ruth Chadwick. TADD, G V.

CHAIN(S)
Il polipo di Trembley (1740) e la "catena delle verità": Note di ricerca. TODESCO, Fabio.
Provable Forms of Martin's Axiom. SHANNON, Gary P.
Some Descending Chains of Incomplete Model Logics. XU, Ming.

CHALASINSKI, J
The Conception of Culture According to Jozef Chalasinski (1904-1979) (in Polish). GRYKO, Czeslaw.

CHALLENGE(S)
The Question of Humanism: Challenges and Possibilities. GOICOECHEA, David (ed).
"Afterword: The Answer of Humanism" in *The Question of Humanism: Challenges and Possibilities*, MADIGAN, Tim.
Biological Foundations of Prediction in an Unpredictable Environment. MARUSIC, M.
The Challenge to Lakatos Restated. AKEROYD, F Michael.

CHALMERS, A
Chalmers on Method. GOWER, Barry.
In Defence of Unrepresentative Realism. TONGS, A R.

CHAMBERS
Untangling Cause, Necessity, Temporality, and Method: Response to Chamber's Method of Corresponding Regressions. WILLIAMS, Richard N.

CHANCE
see also Probability
The Taming of Chance. HACKING, Ian.
Azar y explicación: Algunas observaciones. PÉREZ RANSANZ, Ana Rosa.
Chance and Law in Irreversible Thermodynamics, Theoretical Biology and Theology. PEACOCKE, Arthur.
Hume on Probability. GOWER, Barry.
Natuurlijke selectie, doelgerichtheid en een uitzonderlijke samenloop van omstandigheden: Een kritiek op F Soontiëns. SLURINK, Pouwel.

CHANGE
see also Social Change
The Chain of Change: A Study of Aristotle's "Physics" VII. WARDY, Robert.
Change, Cause and Contradiction: A Defence of the Tenseless Theory of Time. LE POIDEVIN, Robin.
The Ontology of Physical Objects: Four-Dimensional Hunks of Matter. HELLER, Mark.
"Conceptual Change and the Progress of Science" in *Logic, Methodology and Philosophy of Science, VIII*, PEARCE, David.
Change and Development. MC LEOD, John.
Conditionals and Monotonic Belief Revisions: the Success Postulate. ARLO COSTA, Horacio L.
The Difference Between Real Change and *Mere* Cambridge Change. CLELAND, Carol E.
Do Not Despair: There is Life after Constructivism. BIJKER, Wieke.
Eradicating the Obvious. CLARK, Stephen R L.
Een gedesoriënteerde veranderingswetenschap. GASTELAARS, M.
Marx's Theory of Revolutionary Change. PANICHAS, George E and HOBART, Michael E.
The Meaning of Recent Changes in Eastern Europe. MARKOVIC, Mihailo.
Ontology and History. BARLINGAY, S S.
A Peep into Man's History: The Lessons for Today. SINGH, Ajai R and SINGH, Shakuntala A.
Plantinga's Box. SESSIONS, William Lad.
The Academic Lehrjahre of Novalis—A Period of Search for His Own View of History (in Polish). JAKUSZKO, Honorata.
Theory Structure and Theory Change in Contemporary Molecular Biology. CULP, Sylvia and KITCHER, Philip.
Time, Change and Contradiction. SMITH, Joseph Wayne.
Vectors and Change. BIGELOW, John and PARGETTER, Robert.

CHAOS
Beyond Natural Selection. WESSON, Robert.
The Difference Between Truth and Opinion: How the Misuse of Language Can Lead to Disaster. COONEY, Timothy J.
Chaos and Indeterminism. HOBBS, Jesse.
Chaos, History, and Narrative. REISCH, George A.
The Nature of Physical Reality. POLKINGHORNE, John C.
La philosophie du chaos. BOUTOT, Alain.

CHARACTER DEVELOPMENT
Government and Character. PINCOFFS, Edmund L.

CHARACTER TRAIT(S)
Mind in Action: Essays in the Philosophy of Mind. RORTY, Amelie Oksenberg.
"Aesthetic Reasons" in *XIth International Congress in Aesthetics, Nottingham 1988*, CHARLTON, William.
Aristotle on Personality and Some Implications for Friendship. REINER, Paula.
Moral Depth. KEKES, John.
Two Varieties of Temperance in the *Gorgias*. CURZER, Howard J.

CHARACTER(S)
Creative Characters. YOUNG-BRUEHL, Elisabeth.
Identity and Discrimination. WILLIAMSON, Timothy.
Identity, Character, and Morality: Essays in Moral Psychology. FLANAGAN, Owen (ed).
Shaping Character: Moral Education in the Christian College. HOLMES, Arthur F.
"Content, Character, and Nondescriptive Meaning" in *Themes From Kaplan*, ACKERMAN, Felicia.

CHARACTER(S)
"Natural Affection and Responsibility for Character: A Critique of Kantian Views of the Virtues" in *Identity, Character, and Morality: Essays in Moral Psychology*, TRIANOSKY, Gregory.
"On the Old Saw That Character Is Destiny" in *Identity, Character, and Morality: Essays in Moral Psychology*, MOODY-ADAMS, Michele.
"On the Primacy of Character" in *Identity, Character, and Morality: Essays in Moral Psychology*, WATSON, Gary.
"Trust, Affirmation, and Moral Character: A Critique of Kantian Morality" in *Identity, Character, and Morality: Essays in Moral Psychology*, THOMAS, Laurence.
"Virtue Theory" in *A Companion to Ethics*, PENCE, Greg.
Character and Explanation in Aristotle's *Ethics* and *Poetics*. DESLAURIERS, Marguerite.
Love, Friendship, and the Aesthetics of Character. NOVITZ, David.
Markets and Morals. SMITH, G W.
Perhaps by Skill Alone. MISSIMER, Connie.
Response to Smith's "Markets and Morals". LOCKE, Don.
Roberts on Responsibility for Action and Character in the *Nicomachean Ethics*. BRICKHOUSE, Thomas C.
What is it Like to be an Aardvark?. TIGHLMAN, B R.

CHARACTERISTICS
Other Selves: Philosophers on Friendship. PAKALUK, Michael (ed).
"Secular Humanism and Eupraxophy" in *The Question of Humanism: Challenges and Possibilities*, KURTZ, Paul.
Pavlov's View on the Inheritance of Acquired Characteristics .... WINDHOLZ, George and LAMAL, P A.
El personalismo cristiano de Emmanuel Mounier. ARAYA, Eval A.
Why Do I Love Thee? A Response to Nozick's Account of Romantic Love. SMITH, Tara.

CHARACTERIZING
On Capturing Cities. GOODMAN, Nelson.

CHARITY
The Idea of Christian Charity: A Critique of Some Contemporary Conceptions. GRAHAM, Gordon.
Aquinas on Almsgiving, Justice and Charity: An Interpretation and Reassessment. POPE, Stephen J.
Charity and Moral Imperatives. ODEGARD, Douglas.
Famine and Charity. WHELAN JR, John M.
The Need for Charity in Semantics. WARMBRŌD, Ken.

CHARRON, P
L'horizon philosophique de Pierre Charron. ADAM, Michel.

CHAUVINISM
In Defense of Human "Chauvinism": A Response to R Routley and V Routley. PASKE, Gerald H.

CHEMISTRY
"Un essai de vulgarisation" in *Études sur/Studies on Hélène Metzger*, BENSAUDE-VINCENT, Bernadette.
"Hélène Metzger et l'historiographie de la chimie du XVIIIe siècle" in *Études sur/Studies on Hélène Metzger*, CHRISTIE, John R R.
"Hélène Metzger et l'interprétation de la chimie du XVIIe siècle" in *Études sur/Studies on Hélène Metzger*, GOLINSKI, Jan.
Davy Refuted Lavoisier Not Lakatos. ZUCKER, Arthur.
How the Models of Chemistry Vie. HOFMANN, James R.
On Kant's Conception of Science and the Critique of Practical Reason. KÖRNER, Stephan.

CHEN, X
Light Problems: Reply to Chen. ACHINSTEIN, Peter.

CHERNIAK, C
Cherniak on Scientific Realism. BROWN, Harold I.

CHILD ABUSE
Child Abuse: Parental Rights and the Interests of the Child. ARCHARD, David.
The Making and Molding of Child Abuse. HACKING, Ian.
Rights-Talk Will Not Sort Out Child-Abuse: Comment on Archard on Parental Rights. MIDGLEY, Mary.

CHILDE, V
"Childe's Early Marxism" in *Critical Traditions in Contemporary Archaeology*, GATHERCOLE, Peter.

CHILDHOOD
"Friedrich Nichte" in *Looking After Nietzsche*, RICKELS, Laurence A.
Childhood Betrayed: A Personalist Analysis. HANINK, James.

CHILDREN
About Time: Inventing the Fourth Dimension. FRIEDMAN, William J.
Understanding the Representational Mind. PERNER, Josef.
"The Legacy of Baby Doe: Nurses' Ethical and Legal Obligations to Severely Handicapped Newborns" in *Biomedical Ethics Reviews, 1987*, MARTIN, Darlene Aulds.
"Critical Thinking and Philosophy for Children: The Educational Value of Philosophy". LINDOP, Clive.
The 'Disagreements' Approach to Inservicing Philosophy for Children. WOOLCOCK, Peter G.
Art, Stance and Education. PUSCH, James.
Chapter One of *Harry Stottlemeier's Discovery*: An Integrative Crucible of Critical and Creative Thinking. SASSEVILLE, Michel.
Child Abuse: Parental Rights and the Interests of the Child. ARCHARD, David.
Child Development and Research Ethics: A Changing Calculus of Concerns. THOMPSON, Ross A.
Coaching: Who Needs It and What is It?. GUIN, Philip.
The Community of Inquiry and the Development of Self-Esteem. LAGO, Juan Carlos.
The Design, Use and Evaluation of Philosophical Stories for Children. CHING-CHUNG, Chao.
Do Children Think Philosophically?. KITCHENER, Richard F.
Educating for Meaning. WELBY, Victoria.
Education and the Cultivation of Reflection. SCHNEIDER, Herbert W.
Environmental Ethics: What? Why? How?. SILVA, Catherine Young.
The Foundation of the Ability to Reach Conclusions—The Empirical Basis of Logic. GOLAB-MEYER, Zofia.
Friendship and Education. WHITE, Patricia.
How the Child Reasons. THAYER-BACON, Barbara.
If Children thought Like Adults. GAUKER, Christopher.
J S Mill's Concept of Maturity as the Criterion in Determining Children's Eligibility for Rights. KIM, Ki Su.
Logic and the Young Child. TENG, Yu-jen.
On Becoming A Moral Agent: From Aristotle to Harry Stottlemeier. PRITCHARD, Michael S.
The Paternalistic Attitude Toward Children. AVIRAM, Aharon.
Pedagogy of the Unimpressed: Philosophy for Children and the Adult Learner. TURGEON, Wendy.
Phenomenology and the Philosophy for Children Program. HAMRICK, William.
Philosophy for Children and Continental Philosophy. MARTENS, Ekkehard.
Philosophy is Also for the Young—At Least Possibly. LIPMAN, Matthew.
Rationality and Moral Status. BILOW, Scott H.
Reason and the Child. WEINSTEIN, Mark.
Response to Professor Kitchener's "Do Children Think Philosophically?". LIPMAN, Matthew.
The Role of Stories in a Community of Inquiry. HON-MING, Chen.
Small is Beautiful. THOMASON, Neil.
Some More Ideas About the Relation Between Philosophy for Children and Self-Esteem. GAZZARD, Ann.
Student Resistance in Philosophy for Children. LARDNER, A T.
The Subjection of Children. AVIRAM, Aharon.
Talking. VELASCO, Monica A.
Volunteering Children. MC DONNELL, Kevin.
What is the Price of a Rich Life?. MEYER, Zofia Golab.
Why Have Children?. ANSCOMBE, G E M.
William James and the Nature of Thinking: A Framework for Elfie. MELVILLE, Mary E.

CHILEAN
Conceptos centrales de la filosofía política en Chile democrático. COLLE, Reymond.

CHINESE
see also Buddhism, Confucianism, Taoism
Behind the Masks of God: An Essay Toward Comparative Theology. NEVILLE, Robert Cummings.
The Butterfly as Companion: Meditations on the First Three Chapters of the Chuang Tzu. WU, Kuang-Ming.
Chinese Buddhist Apocrypha. BUSWELL JR, Robert E (ed).
Chinese Texts and Philosophical Contexts. ROSEMONT JR, Henry (ed).
Demystifying Mentalities. LLOYD, G E R.
Law, Culture, and Values: Essays in Honor of Gray L Dorsey. VOJCANIN, Sava Alexander (ed).
New Dimensions of Confucian and Neo-Confucian Philosophy. CHENG, Chung-ying.
Understanding the Chinese Mind: The Philosophical Roots. ALLINSON, Robert E (ed).
"Chinese Aesthetics" in *Understanding the Chinese Mind: The Philosophical Roots*, WU, Kuang-Ming.
"The Chinese Case in a Philosophy of World Religions" in *Understanding the Chinese Mind: The Philosophical Roots*, NEVILLE, Robert C.
"Chinese Metaphysics as Non-Metaphysics: Confucian and Daoist Insights into the Nature of Reality" in *Understanding the Chinese Mind: The Philosophical Roots*, CHENG, Chung-ying.
"Classical Chinese Ethics" in *A Companion to Ethics*, HANSEN, Chad.
"The Fiduciary Relationship between Professionals and Clients: A Chinese Perspective" in *Ethics, Trust, and the Professions: Philosophical and Cultural Aspects*, QUI, Ren-zong.
"Imre Lakatos in China" in *Imre Lakatos and Theories of Scientific Change*, DAINIAN, Fan.
"Interpreting across Boundaries" in *Understanding the Chinese Mind: The Philosophical Roots*, SMITH, John E.
"Language in the Heart-mind" in *Understanding the Chinese Mind: The Philosophical Roots*, HANSEN, Chad.

CHINESE
"Marginalia Sino-logica" in *Understanding the Chinese Mind: The Philosophical Roots*, HARBSMEIER, Christoph.
"The Mass Noun Hypothesis and the Part-Whole Analysis of the White Horse Dialogue" in *Chinese Texts and Philosophical Contexts*, HARBSMEIER, Christoph.
"The Mencian Conception of *Ren xing*: Does it Mean 'Human Nature'?" in *Chinese Texts and Philosophical Contexts*, AMES, Roger T.
"On the Expression *Zai You*" in *Chinese Texts and Philosophical Contexts*, LAU, D C.
"On Understanding Chinese Philosophy: An Inquiry and a Proposal" in *Understanding the Chinese Mind: The Philosophical Roots*, SZE-KWANG, Lao.
"An Overview of the Chinese Mind" in *Understanding the Chinese Mind: The Philosophical Roots*, ALLINSON, Robert E.
"Philosophy of Technology in China" in *Philosophy of Technology*, DASHENG, Gao and TSING, Zou.
"Plasticity into Power: Two Crises in the History of France and China" in *Critique and Construction: A Symposium on Roberto Unger's "Politics"*, CLEARY, J C and HIGONNET, Patrice.
"Plurality and Unity in the Configuration of the Chinese People" in *The Tanner Lectures on Human Values, Volume XI*, XIAOTONG, Fei.
"Reflections and Replies" in *Chinese Texts and Philosophical Contexts*, GRAHAM, Angus C.
"Reflections on Chinese Language and Philosophy" in *Hermeneutics and the Poetic Motion, Translation Perspectives V—1990*, SOO, Francis.
"Should the Ancient Masters Value Reason?" in *Chinese Texts and Philosophical Contexts*, HANSEN, Chad.
"Some Notes on Morphology and Syntax in Classical Chinese" in *Chinese Texts and Philosophical Contexts*, PULLEYBLANK, Edwin G.
"Substance, Process, Phase: *Wuxing* in the *Huainanzi*" in *Chinese Texts and Philosophical Contexts*, MAJOR, John S.
"Who Compiled the *Chuang Tzu*?" in *Chinese Texts and Philosophical Contexts*, ROTH, Harold.
The Appropriation of Significance: The Concept of *Kang-Tung*in the *I Ching*. TONG, Lik Kuen.
Artist and Peasant. XING-PEI, Fei.
A Brief Discussion of One Aspect of the *Shangtong* Idea. YUANHUA, Wang.
Chen Que versus Huang Zongxi: Confucianism Faces Modern Times in the Seventeenth Century. STRUVE, Lynn A.
China's Importation of Western Psychiatry: Cultural Relativity and Mental Disorders. WOO, Deborah.
China's Traditional Mode of Thought and Science. DISHENG, Yang.
The Chinese Moral Ethos and the Concept of Individual Rights. TAO, Julia.
The Contending Among the Hundred Schools of Thought During the Warring States Period. ZEHUA, Liu.
A Critique of One Interpretation of Practical Materialism. DANSHEN, Huang.
Euthanasia in China: A Report. DA PU, Shi.
The Fate of Independent Thought in Traditional China. WHITE, Harry.
Freedom and Realms of Living. CI, Jiwei.
From Immanentism to Atheism. LY, Gabriel.
Fundamental Values in the Thought of Confucius and Mencius (in Polish). CYRANOWSKA, Maria.
A Great Intellectual Current Worthy of National Pride. CHANGLU, Qiao.
Is There a Distinction Between Reason and Emotion in Mencius?. WONG, David B.
Ji Kang's "Sheng-wu-aile-lun": Concerning Its Logical Development (in Japanese). HARA, Masayuki.
The Liberal Teachings of the Young Liang Qichao. QI, Feng.
Marx, Engels and Max Weber on Eastern Societies—With a Special Respect to China (in Hungarian). DRUCKER, György.
Montesquieu and China. HONGXUN, Hou.
Moral Reasoning in a Communist Chinese Society. WALKER, Lawrence J and MORAN, Thomas J.
Morality in Flux: Medical Ethics in the People's Republic of China. QIU, Ren-Zong.
Names, Actualities, and the Emergence of Essentialist Theories of Naming in Classical Chinese Thought. MAKEHAM, John.
The New Dimensions of Chinese Medical Ethics. MC GREAL, Ian Philip.
On the "Arriving at Principles from Numbers" Method of Thought in the Late-Ming, Early-Qing Period. WEIPING, Chen.
On the Concept of Freedom in the *I Ching*: A Deconstructionist View of Self-Cultivation. SCHULZ, Larry J and CUNNINGHAM, Thomas J.
On the Duality of China's Traditional Mode of Thought and the Difficulty of Transforming It. ZIHLIN, Li.
On the Functional Unity of the Four Dimensions of Thought in the *Book of Changes*. LIU, Shu-Hsien.
The Relevance of Confucian Ethics. CHUNG, Bongkil.
The Seasonal Structure Underlying the Arrangement of the Hexagrams in the *Yijing*. ANDERSON, Allan W.
The State of Studies on Western Philosophy in China. FANG-TONG, Liu.
Structural Motifs in the Arrangement of the 64 *Gua* in the *Zhouyi*. SCHULZ, Larry J.
Tang Junyi's Philosophical View of History and His Explanation of the Philosophy of Wang Chuanshan. SHAFU, Xiao.
Taoist Visions of the Body. KOHN, Livia.
The Theoretical Premises of Scientific Socialism and Its Mode of Thought. YUQUAN, Tao.
Traditional Chinese Culture: Contemporary Developments —Profound Selections from the Works of Fang Dongmei. GUOBAO, Jiang.

CHIPLEY, W
Critics and Historical Continuity. CARTER, John.
Dr Chipley's Warning. WHITE, Ronald.

CHISHOLM, R
Epistemic Justification: Essays in the Theory of Knowledge. ALSTON, William P.
Chisholm, Reid and the Problem of the Epistemic Surd. LEHRER, Keith.
Epistemology on Holiday. KAPLAN, Mark.

CHOICE(S)
see also Decision(s)
Gerechtigkeit, Wohlfahrt und Rationalität. SCHMIDT, Johannes.
Negotation Games: Applying Game Theory to Bargaining and Arbitration. BRAMS, Steven J.
A Philosophy of Morals. HELLER, Agnes.
Self, Society, and Personal Choice. MEYERS, Diana T.
Style and Music: Theory, History, and Ideology. MEYER, Leonard B.
"Being Is Better than Freedom" in *Freedom in the Modern World: Jacques Maritain, Yves R Simon, Mortimer J Adler*, DENNEHY, Raymond.
"Pragmatism and Choosing to Believe" in *Reading Rorty*, HEAL, Jane.
"Where There's a Will There's a Way: Kierkegaard's Theory of Action" in *Writing the Politics of Difference*, EVANS, C Stephen.
Aggregation of Preferences: The Fuzzy Case. BILLOT, Antoine.
Aggregation Theorems and Multidimensional Stochastic Choice Models. MARLEY, A A J.
Before Refraining: Concepts for Agency. BELNAP JR, Nuel D.
Choice Procedure Consistent with Similarity Relations. AIZPURUA, Jose Maria and NIETO, Jorge and URIARTE, Jose Ramon.
Communism: A Post-Mortem. BAUMAN, Zygmunt.
An Experimental Analysis of Risk Taking. DAHLBÄCK, Olof.
Freiheit und Bindung menschlicher Entscheidungen. KLEMENT, H W and RADERMACHER, F J.
Implications of Behavioral Consistency in Dynamic Choice Under Uncertainty. DARDANONI, Valentino.
In Praise of Clutter as a Necessary Part of the Feminist Perspective. AYIM, Maryann.
Independence of Irrelevant Alternatives in the Theory of Voting. BORDES, Georges and TIDEMAN, Nicolaus.
On a Moorean Solution to Instability Puzzles. KROON, Frederick W.
Oppression and Victimization; Choice and Responsibility. WENDELL, Susan.
Peter Gardner on Religious Upbringing and the Liberal Ideal of Religious Autonomy. MC LAUGHLIN, T H.
Reply to Maryann Ayim's "In Praise of Clutter as a Necessary Part of the Feminist Perspective". WENDELL, Susan.
Rome Inferences and Structural Opacity. MOORE, F C T.
Society as a Department Store. LEGUTKO, Ryszard.
Symptomatic Acts and the Value of Evidence in Causal Decision Theory. MAHER, Patrick.
The Freedom of Values and the Value of Freedom (in Czechoslovakian). SLEJSKA, D.

CHOMSKY, N
"How Natural Is Natural Language?" in *Logic, Methodology and Philosophy of Science, VIII*, KOSTER, Jan.
Cognitive Science on a Wing and a Prayer. KEITH, William.
Intentionality and Modern Philosophical Psychology, I: The Modern Reduction of Intentionality. LYONS, William.
On Rhetorical Strategies: *Verstehen Sie*?. SLEZAK, Peter.
Platón, el lenguaje y el marciano. ACERO, Juan José.
Response to Slezak: *Nein, Ich verstehe nicht*. KEITH, William.
Three Models of Competence: A Critical Evaluation of Chomsky. MUKHERJI, Arundhati.

CHONG-SAN
The Relevance of Confucian Ethics. CHUNG, Bongkil.

CHRIST
see also Jesus
Does Faith Create Its Own Objects?. MAC KINNON, Donald M.
Foundationalism and Peter's Confession. HESTER, Marcus.
Pre-existence and Personal Identity. FEENSTRA, Ronald J.
The Questioning of Values in Theology (in French). WIDMER, Gabriel-Ph.
Theology and the Necessity of Natures. ANGLIN, W S.

CHRISTIAN
Christian Faith and Historical Understanding (Second Edition). NASH, Ronald H.
Discussioni sul neo-Tomismo: Per il progresso della Filosofia Cristiana. BLANDINO, Giovanni.
John Dewey: Religious Faith and Democratic Humanism. ROCKEFELLER, Steven C.
Towards a Christian Philosophy. OWENS, Joseph I.

CHRISTIAN

"Christian Peacemakers in the Warmaking State" in *Celebrating Peace*, BERRIGAN, Daniel.
"Islam in European Thought" in *The Tanner Lectures on Human Values, Volume XI*, HOURANI, Albert.
"Teaching Peace in a Christian Context" in *Celebrating Peace*, GILLIGAN, John J.
La "Scuola di Padova" ed i problemi dell'ontologia italiana contemporanea. MANGIAGALLI, Maurizio.
The Absolute in Morality and the Christian Conscience. FUCHS, Josef.
Certain Hope. PHILLIPS GRIFFITHS, A.
Christelijke filosofie. WYLLEMAN, A.
Cuarenta años del "Instituto Filosófico de Balmesiana". FORMENT, Eudaldo.
Filosofia dell'esistenza e cristologia: La Weltanschauung cristiana di R Guardini. DI MARCO, Chiar.
Filosofía y Cristianismo (En el Centenario de Heidegger). CARDONA, Carlos.
Forgiveness: A Christian Model. ADAMS, Marilyn McCord.
Giustino Martire, il primo platonico cristiano. GIRGENTI, Giuseppe.
El lugar de la doctrina social de la reflexión teológico moral cristiana. BRIANCESCO, E.
Machiavelli's Notions of Justice: Text and Analysis. PAREL, A J.
Methodological Alternatives in Process Theology. BROWN, Delwin and GREEVE DAVANEY, Sheila.
Myth and Morality: The Love Command. HEFNER, Philip.
The Nature of Faith: Religious, Monotheistic, and Christian. YANDELL, Keith E.
Omnipotence Need Not Entail Omniscience. SONTAG, Frederick.
Plantinga's Box. SESSIONS, William Lad.
Process Theology as Empirical, Rational, and Speculative: Some Reflections on Method. GRIFFIN, David Ray.
Prometheus or Cain? Albert Camus's Account of the Western Quest for Justice. WARD, Bruce K.
La Querelle de la Moralité du Théâtre au XVIIe Siècle. FUMAROLI, M Marc.
Radical Theology, Postmodernity and Christian Life in the Void. COWDELL, Scott.
The Relevance of Historical Evidence for Christian Faith: A Critique of a Kierkegaardian View. EVANS, C Stephen.
Scientific Research and the Christian Faith. PETERS, Ted.
Self and Suffering: Deconstruction and Reflexive Definition in Buddhism and Christianity. MELLOR, Philip A.
Social Science as Moral Philosophy?: Reflections on Alan Wolfe's *Whose Keeper?*. MASON, John R.
Toward a Pragmatic Conception of Religious Faith. GOLDING, Joshua L.

CHRISTIAN ETHICS

Adam's Place in Nature: Respect or Domination?. NASH, Roger.
Characteristics and Practices of "Christian-Based" Companies. IBRAHIM, Nabil A and RUE, Leslie W and MC DOUGALL, Patricia P and GREENE, G Robert.
Response to 'Rescuing the Innocent'. GARDNER, G T G.
Response to 'Rescuing the Innocent'. MORROW, James.
Tradition and Ethics: Prospects in a Liberal Society. GUROIAN, Vigen.

CHRISTIAN HUMANISM

Is Anything Sacred? Christian Humanism and Christian Nihilism. CUPITT, Don.
L'horizon philosophique de Pierre Charron. ADAM, Michel.

CHRISTIANITY

'Religion' and the Religions in the English Enlightenment. HARRISON, Peter.
Behind the Masks of God: An Essay Toward Comparative Theology. NEVILLE, Robert Cummings.
The Call to Personhood. MC FADYEN, Alistair I.
Celebrating Peace. ROUNER, Leroy S (ed).
Dialogue with the Other: The Inter-Religious Dialogue. TRACY, David.
Does God Exist? The Great Debate. MORELAND, J P.
Escape from God. TURNER, Dean.
For Self-Examination: Judge for Yourself. HONG, Howard V (ed & trans).
For What May I Hope? Thinking with Kant and Kierkegaard. FENDT, Gene.
From Hegel to Nietzsche: The Revolution in Nineteenth-Century Thought. LÖWITH, Karl.
Hellenic and Christian Studies. ARMSTRONG, A H.
Hope and Its Hieroglyph: A Critical Decipherment of Ernst Bloch's "Principle of Hope". ROBERTS, Richard H.
How to Play Theological Ping-Pong: And Other Essays on Faith and Reason. ABRAHAM, William J (ed).
The Idea of Christian Charity: A Critique of Some Contemporary Conceptions. GRAHAM, Gordon.
John Craige's Mathematical Principles of Christian Theology. NASH, Richard.
Leibniz and Arnauld. SLEIGH JR, Robert C.
Nicholas of Cusa's de Pace Fidei and Cribratio Alkorani: Translation and Analysis. HOPKINS, Jasper.
The Philosophy in Christianity. VESEY, Godfrey (ed).
Returning to Sils-Maria: A Commentary to Nietzsche's "Also sprach Zarathustra". WHITLOCK, Greg.
The Self-Overcoming of Nihilism: Nishitani Keiji. PARKES, Graham (trans).
Shaping Character: Moral Education in the Christian College. HOLMES, Arthur F.
To Be at Home: Christianity, Civil Religion, and World Community. ROUNER, Leroy S.
Die Wiederkehr im Unterschied. PEETZ, Siegbert.
"Bernanosian Barbs and the Maritain's Marigny Lecture" in *From Twilight to Dawn: The Cultural Vision of Jacques Maritain*, BUSH, William.
"Calvary or the Slaughter-house" in *From Twilight to Dawn: The Cultural Vision of Jacques Maritain*, SCHALL, James V.
"Christian Ethics" in *A Companion to Ethics*, PRESTON, Ronald.
"Europe and Islam" in *The Tanner Lectures On Human Values, Volume XII*, LEWIS, Bernard.
"On Not Knowing too Much About God" in *The Philosophy in Christianity*, ARMSTRONG, A H.
"The Philosophy in Christianity: Arius and Athanasius" in *The Philosophy in Christianity*, WILES, Maurice.
"Reason in Mystery" in *The Philosophy in Christianity*, KRETZMANN, Norman.
"Reflections on Maritain's *Le Crépuscule de la Civilisation*" in *From Twilight to Dawn: The Cultural Vision of Jacques Maritain*, MC INERNY, Ralph.
"Truth and the Wisdom of Enduring" in *Phenomenology of the Truth Proper to Religion*, FARLEY, Edward.
"Keine festbegrenzte und Wahrhaft anschauliche Vorstelling". SCHREURS, Nico.
Allocution Made to a Magistrate. PAREL, A J (ed & trans) and MACHIAVELLI, Niccolò.
Augustine's Theology of the Trinity: Its Relevance. CLARK, Mary T.
Can the Discussion Partners Trust Each Other?. FÖLDESI, Tamás.
A Christian Philosopher in a "Broken World". VERBEKE, Gerard.
A Christian Response to Professor Zagorka Golubovic. ZADEMACH, Wieland.
Christians and Marxist Theory of Human Liberation. KOWALCZYK, Stanislaw.
Christians and Marxists in Dialogue Building Confidence in a Time of Crisis. WEST, Charles C.
The Community as Sacrament. LIDERBACH, Daniel.
Cristianesimo tragico, cristianesimo ludico: i due volti della fedeltà al Dio dialettico. GARGANO, Monica.
Da secularidade da Filosofia. COUTINHO, Jorge.
The Dialectic of National and Universal Commitments in Christian-Marxist Dialogue. WILL, James E.
Dialogue—A New Utopia?. GÓRNIAK-KOCIKOWSKA, Krystyna.
The Editor's Response to "The Embryo Debate: The Archbishop of York's Speech to the House of Lords". DE S CAMERON, Nigel M.
The Embryo Debate: The Archbishop of York's Speech to the House of Lords. THE ARCHBISHOP OF YORK.
Epistemología contemporánea y filosofía cristiana. ZANOTTI, Gabriel J.
Filosofía cristiana y apologética en Mons Audino Rodríguez y Olmos. CATURELLI, Alberto.
Franz Rosenzweig e Friedrich Meinecke. D'ANTUONO, Emilia.
Getting the Subject Back into the World: Heidegger's Version. KERR, Fergus.
Historicism and the Understanding of Theology in Troeltsch's Times (in German). NOWAK, Kurt.
The History of the Christian Philosophical Reflection on Peace. WASKIEWICZ, Hanna.
Humanismo y humanismo cristiano. DERISI, Octavio N.
A Hungarian Christian-Marxist Dialogue and Its Lessons. LUKÁCS, József.
Incarnational Anthropology. HALDANE, John.
Kierkegaard on the Limits of Christian Epistemology. WISDO, David.
Kierkegaard's Pragmatist Faith. EMMANUEL, Steven M.
Liberation Theology and the Interpretation of Political Violence. SONTAG, Frederick.
Lonergan's Method in Ethics and the Meaning of Human Sexuality. FRISBY, Mark E.
Marxisten und Christen für eine gerechte, friedliche Welt. NEHRING, Hartmut.
Method Divorced from Content in Theology: An Assessment of Lonergan's *Method in Theology*. REYNOLDS, Terrence.
Middle Knowledge and the Damnation of the Heathen: A Response to William Craig. HASKER, William.
The Nurture of War: "Just War" Theory's Contribution. SANTONI, Ronald E.
Pannenberg's Doctrine of God. O'DONNELL, John.
Persona y sociedad según Jacques Maritain. WASHBURN, Jimmy.
El personalismo cristiano de Emmanuel Mounier. ARAYA, Eval A.
Porphyry's Criticism of Christianity and The Problem of Augustine's Platonism. EVANGELIOU, Christos.
Rational Suicide and Christian Virtue. MAGUIRE, Daniel C.
Reinvigorating the International Christian-Marxist Dialogue. MOJZES, Paul.
Die Rolle des Individuums und seine Beteiligung an gesellschaftlichen Prozessen. SCHLIWA, Harald and ZEDDIES, Helmut.
Romano Guardini's Theological Critique of the Modern Age (in Dutch). VAN DER VLOET, J.
The Servant Species: Humanity as Priesthood. LINZEY, Andrew.

CHRISTIANITY
Some Reflections on Post-Marxism and Post-Christianity: A Response to Professor Arthur Mc Govern. STOJANOVIC, Svetozar.
Souls and Sentientism. RYDER, Richard D.
Le statut de la philosophie chez Étienne Gilson. PROUVOST, Géry.
Structure and Meaning in St Augustine's *Confessions*. CROSSON, Frederick J.
Sur le concept de Révélation. GABORIAU, Florent.
Technological Faith and Christian Doubt. FERRÉ, Frederick.
Tempo ed eternità: La filosofia narrante di F Rosenzweig. DI MARCO, Chiara.
The Common European Home (in German). FEIEREIS, Konrad.
Tradition and Interpretation. VAN BEECK, Frans Jozef.
Two Aspects of the Christian-Marxist Dialogue: A Protestant Response. FRITZSCHE, Helmut.
Ultramontanisme et gallicanisme engagentils deux visions de la société. BRESSOLETTE, Claude.
Vasilii Vasil'evich Rozanov: "My Soul Is Woven of Filth, Tenderness, and Grief". KUVAKIN, V A.
Das vergeistigte Glück: Gedanken zum christlichen Eudämonieverständnis. DEMMER, Klaus.
What Philosophy for Judaism and Christianity? (in French). DUPONCHEELE, Joseph.
Why Have Children?. ANSCOMBE, G E M.
'Postmodern Critical Augustinianism': A Short *Summa* in Forty Two Responses to Unasked Questions. MILBANK, John.

CHRISTIANO, T
A Defense of Equal Opportunity for Welfare. ARNESON, Richard J.

CHRISTOLOGY
Prefacing Pluralism: John Hick and the Mastery of Religion. LOUGHLIN, Gerard.
A Response to Gerard Loughlin's "Prefacing Pluralism: John Hick and the Mastery of Religion". HICK, John.

CHRONOLOGY
The Chronology of Plato's Dialogues. BRANDWOOD, Leonard.

CHU HSI
To Catch a Thief: Chu Hsi (1130-1200) and the Hermeneutic Art. BERTHRONG, John.

CHUANG TZU
The Butterfly as Companion: Meditations on the First Three Chapters of the Chuang Tzu. WU, Kuang-Ming.
The Beautiful, the Ugly, and the Tao. COLEMAN, Earle J.
Logic and Language in the *Chuang Tzu*. ALT, Wayne E.
Non-World Making in Chuang Tzu. WU, Kuang-Ming.
A Response to Kuang-Ming Wu's "Non-World-Making". FLEMING, Jesse.

CHURCH
The Crisis of Authority. OLDS, Mason.
Democracy and the Church-State Relationship. KAINZ, Howard.
Teología de la liberación y doctrina social de la Iglesia hoy. GALLI, C M.
Tradition and Interpretation. VAN BEECK, Frans Jozef.
Tycho's System and Galileo's *Dialogue*. MARGOLIS, Howard.

CHURCH'S THESIS
Lifschitz' Realizability. VAN OOSTEN, Jaap.

CHURCH, A
A Partial Functions Version of Church's Simple Theory of Types. FARMER, William M.

CHURCH, F
A New Humanism: A Response. COLLINS, Jacqueline A.
A New Humanism: A Response. DOERR, Edd.
A New Humanism: A Response. ERICSON, Edward L.
A New Humanism: A Response. HARRIS, W Edward.
A New Humanism: A Response. MAIN, William.
A New Humanism: A Response. PHIFER, Kenneth W.
A New Humanism: A Response. WILSON, Edwin H.

CHURCHILL, L
AIDS, Myth, and Ethics. SUNDSTRÖM, Per.

CHURCHLAND, P
Churchland and the Talking Brain. MUKHERJI, Nirmalangshu.
Churchland, Introspection, and Dualism. ZEMACH, Eddy M.
Observation: An Empirical Discussion. GILMAN, Daniel.
Qualia and Theory Reduction: A Criticism of Paul Churchland. BACHRACH, Jay E.

CHWISTEK, L
The Idea of Common Sense in the Philosophy of L Chwistek (in Polish). JOZEFCZUK, Grzegorz.

CICERO
On Duties: Cicero. GRIFFIN, M T (ed).
'Domina et Regina Virtutum': Justice and *Societas* in *De Officiis*. ATKINS, E M.
Cicero's Focus: From the Best Regime to the Model Statesman. NICGORSKI, Walter.
Nature, Justice, and Duty in the *Defensor Pacis*: Marsiglio of Padua's Ciceronian Impulse. NEDERMAN, Cary J.

CINEMA
see Film

CIRCULARITY
'*P*, Therefore, *P*' Without Circularity. SORENSEN, Roy A.
Circularity of Thought in Hegel's Logic. BALABAN, Oded.
The Inductive Support of Inductive Rules: Themes from Max Black. SANFORD, David H.

CITIZEN(S)
Government and Character. PINCOFFS, Edmund L.

CITIZENSHIP
"American Citizenship: The Quest for Inclusion" in *The Tanner Lectures on Human Values, Volume XI*, SHKLAR, Judith.
"Citizenship and Autonomy" in *Social Theory of Modern Societies: Anthony Giddens and His Critics*, HELD, David.
"Conscience, Citizenship, and the Nuclear State" in *In the Interest of Peace: A Spectrum of Philosophical Views*, WOODWARD, Beverly.
Active Citizenship as Political Obligation. SKILLEN, Tony.
Civic Education for Teachers. SCAHILL, John.
Community as Compulsion? A Reply to Skillen on Citizenship and the State. ELLIOT, Gregory and OSBORNE, Peter.
Mental Handicap and Citizenship. SPICKER, Paul.

CITY PLANNING
Philosophical Streets: New Approaches to Urbanism. CROW, Dennis (ed).

CITY(-TIES)
On Walter Benjamin: Critical Essays and Recollections. SMITH, Gary (ed).
Jean-Jacques Rousseau on the Physiogonomy of the Modern City. ELLISON, Charles E.
L'esthétique de John Dewey et le contexte urbain. GAVIN, William J.

CITY-STATE(S)
Das Ethische in der Rhetorik des Aristoteles. WÖRNER, Markus Hilmar.

CIVIL DISOBEDIENCE
Civil Disobedience in Focus. BEDAU, Hugo Adam (ed).
Die moderne Gesellschaft im Rechtsstaat. BAURMANN, Michael.
Ecosabotage and Civil Disobedience. MARTIN, Michael.
Humble Rebel Henry David Thoreau (in Czechoslovakian). JANAT, B.

CIVIL LAW(S)
Hegels Theorie des Gesetzes. BOGDANDY, Armin Von.

CIVIL LIBERTY(-TIES)
Civil Rights versus Civil Liberties: The Case of Discriminatory Verbal Harassment. GREY, Thomas.

CIVIL RIGHT(S)
John Locke: Segundo Tratado sobre el Gobierno Civil. MELLIZO, Carlos (trans).
Black and White Together: A Reconsideration. ALLEN, W B.
Change and Continuity in the Concept of Civil Rights: Thurgood Marshall and Affirmative Action. TUSHNET, Mark.
Civil Rights versus Civil Liberties: The Case of Discriminatory Verbal Harassment. GREY, Thomas.
Two Conceptions of Civil Rights. EPSTEIN, Richard A.
What Are *Civil* Rights?. WEINREB, Lloyd L.

CIVIL SOCIETY
Ethics, Politics, and Human Nature. PAUL, Ellen Frankel (ed).
John Locke: Segundo Tratado sobre el Gobierno Civil. MELLIZO, Carlos (trans).
The Political Philosophy of Michael Oakeshott. FRANCO, Paul.
"The Civil and the Sacred" in *The Tanner Lectures On Human Values, Volume XII*, GELLNER, Ernest.
The Changing Face of Civil Society in Eastern Europe. KOLARSKA-BOBINSKA, Lena.
Revolution, Civil Society and Democracy. ARATO, Andrew.
Tra Kant e Hegel: per una riaffermazione dell'antico concetto di società civile. MARINI, Giuliano.

CIVILIZATION(S)
From Twilight to Dawn: The Cultural Vision of Jacques Maritain. REDPATH, Peter A (ed).
L'Utopia di Fourier. TUNDO, Laura.
"Calvary or the Slaughter-house" in *From Twilight to Dawn: The Cultural Vision of Jacques Maritain*, SCHALL, James V.
"Maritain and the Future of Reason" in *From Twilight to Dawn: The Cultural Vision of Jacques Maritain*, BOYLE, William J.
"The Philosophy of Work and the Future of Civilization: Maritain, Weil and Simon" in *From Twilight to Dawn: The Cultural Vision of Jacques Maritain*, DOERING, Bernard.
Freud on Civilization and Neurosis. FLUXMAN, Tony.
Infiniti mondi e mondo nuovo: Conquista dell'America e critica della civilità europea in Giordano Bruno. RICCI, Saverio.
Paideia Helénica. FREIRE, António.

CLARITY
"Clarity" in *The Analytic Tradition: Philosophical Quarterly Monographs, Volume 1*, HART, W D.
An Inquiry into the Meaning of Teacher Clarity in Recent Research and into the Value of the Research for the Teacher. CRABTREE, Walden.
The Problematics of "Clarity" in Research of Teaching: A Response to Walden Crabtree. SCHULTZ, Frederick M.

CLARK, T
Art History in the Mirror Stage: Interpreting *Un Bar aux Folies Bergères*. CARRIER, David.

CLARKE
Connection Structures. BIACINO, Loredana and GERLA, Giangiacomo.
Consideraciones en torno a la polémica Leibniz-Clarke. PONCE ALBERCA, Carmen.

CLASS CONFLICT(S)
Dezelfde wateren aan nieuwe oevers: Alexis de Tocqueville en de Franse Revolutie. ZIJDERVELD, A C.

CLASS STRUGGLE
From Class Struggle to Struggle without Classes?. BALIBAR, Etienne.
Marxist Historians and the Question of Class in the French Revolution. AMARIGLIO, Jack and NORTON, Bruce.
The Politics and Morality of Unequal Exchange: Emmanuel and Roemer, Analysis and Synthesis. SCHWEICKART, David.

CLASS THEORY
Marx's Historical Understanding of the Proletariat and Class in 19th-Century England. MAZLISH, Bruce.

CLASS(ES)
see also Set(s)
Parts of Classes. LEWIS, David.
Philosophical Essays. CARTWRIGHT, Richard.
An Extension of Borel Determinacy. MARTIN, Donald A.
Generalizing Classical and Effective Model Theory in Theories of Operations and Classes. MANCOSU, Paolo.
A Note on the Axiomatization of Equational Classes of *n*-Valued Lukasiewicz Algebras. ADAMS, M E and CIGNOLI, R.
On the Lengths of Proofs of Set Theoretical Statements in Zermelo-Fraenkel Set Theory and Kelley-Morse Theory.... CORRADA, Manuel.
Real Numbers, Continued Fractions and Complexity Classes. LABHALLA, Salah and LOMBARDI, Henri.
Universal Structures in Power $\aleph_1$. MEKLER, Alan H.
When Is Arithmetic Possible?. MC COLM, Gregory L.

CLASSICAL PHYSICS
"Newton's Legacy" in *Some Truer Method*, PURRINGTON, Robert D and DURHAM, Frank.
Perspectives on Quantum Reality versus Classical Reality. HOME, Dipankar.

CLASSICISM
La Grecia "Tedesca" fra Nostalgia e Mito. FOLLIERO-METZ, Grazia Dolores.
Filosofía, hoy. CUÉLLAR, Hortensia.
Naturalized Epistemology Sublimated: Rapprochement without the Ruts. FULLER, Steve.
Never Say "Never"! On the Communication Problem between Intuitionism and Classicism. HELLMAN, Geoffrey.

CLASSICS
"Creative Intuition, Great Books, and Freedom of Intellect" in *Freedom in the Modern World: Jacques Maritain, Yves R Simon, Mortimer J Adler*, ROYAL, Robert.
"Great Books, Democracy and Truth" in *Freedom in the Modern World: Jacques Maritain, Yves R Simon, Mortimer J Adler*, ADLER, Mortimer J.

CLASSIFICATION
Classification by Comparison with Paradigms. EBERLE, Rolf.
Classifying Conditionals II. JACKSON, Frank.
A Critical Note on J S Mill's Classification of Fallacies. HON, Giora.
Entwurf eines Klassifikationsschemas für philosophische Positionen. WIMMER, Franz.
Is There Higher-Order Vagueness?. SAINSBURY, Mark.
Jackson Classifying Conditionals. DUDMAN, V H.
Jackson on Classifying Conditionals. LOWE, E J.
Names, Actualities, and the Emergence of Essentialist Theories of Naming in Classical Chinese Thought. MAKEHAM, John.
Negotiating Criteria and Setting Limits: The Case of AIDS. CUTTER, Mary Ann Gardell.
The Philosophical Significance of Psychological Differences Among Humans. LACHS, John.
Representations of the Natural System in the Nineteenth Century. O'HARA, Robert J.
Some Thoughts on Common Scents. ALMAGOR, Uri.
Über den Versuch einer philosophiegeschichtlichen Klassifikation der Lehre Nāgārjunas. TOMASCHITZ, Wolfgang.

CLAUSEWITZ, C
"Absolute Violence and the Idea of War" in *In the Interest of Peace: A Spectrum of Philosophical Views*, HOLMES, Robert.
Clausewitz ou l'oeuvre inachevée: l'esprit de la guerre. PHILONENKO, Alexis.

CLEAVE, J
On Cauchy's Notion of Infinitesimal. CUTLAND, Nigel J (and others).

CLEMENCY
Entitled to Clemency: Mercy in the Criminal Law. JOHNSON, Carla Ann Hage.

CLIENT(S)
Ethics, Trust, and the Professions: Philosophical and Cultural Aspects. PELLEGRINO, Edmund D (ed).
"The Fiduciary Relationship and the Nature of Professions" in *Ethics, Trust, and the Professions: Philosophical and Cultural Aspects*, SOKOLOWSKI, Robert.
"The Fiduciary Relationship between Professionals and Clients: A Chinese Perspective" in *Ethics, Trust, and the Professions: Philosophical and Cultural Aspects*, QUI, Ren-zong.
Informing Clients About Limits to Confidentiality. PIZZIMENTI, Lee Ann.

CLINICAL ETHICS
Conceptual Issues in Nursing Ethics Research. PENTICUFF, Joy Hinson.
Integrity and Compromise in Nursing Ethics. WINSLOW, Betty J and WINSLOW, Gerald R.
Nursing Ethics: Current State of the Art. FRY, Sara T.
Orchestrating Social Change: An Imperative in Care of the Chronically Ill. ROTH, Patricia A and HARRISON, Janet K.
Privacy and Disclosure in Medical Genetics Examined in an Ethics of Care. WERTZ, Dorothy C and FLETCHER, John C.
Toward An Expanded Vision of Clinical Ethics Education: From the Individual to the Institution. SOLOMON, Mildred Z (and others).

CLOCK(S)
Clocks and Time (in Czechoslovakian). DUBSKY, Ivan.

CLORE, G
Describing the Emotions: A Review of *The Cognitive Structure of Emotions* by Ortony, Clore and Collins. BEN-ZEEV, Aaron.

CLOSURE
"Are There Counterexamples to the Closure Principle?" in *Doubting: Contemporary Perspectives on Skepticism*, VOGEL, Jonathan.
Beethoven's Ninth Symphony: The Sense of an Ending. SOLOMON, Maynard.
Cartesian Scepticism and Relevant Alternatives. SCHRECK, P A.
Knowledge and Deductive Closure. WHITE, James L.

COALITION(S)
Experimental Studies of Interactive Decisions. RAPOPORT, Amnon.

COBB, J
"Language as Metaphorical: A Reply to John Cobb" in *Archetypal Process: Self and Divine in Whitehead, Jung, and Hillman*, HOPPER, Stanley R.

CODE OF CONDUCT
Personal Morals and Professional Ethics: A Review and Empirical Examination of Public Accounting. BEETS, S Douglas.

CODE(S)
Corporate Codes of Conduct: A Collective Conscience and Continuum. RAIBORN, Cecily A and PAYNE, Dinah.
Historical Perspectives: Development of the Codes of Ethics in the Legal, Medical and Accounting Professions. BACKOF, Jeanne F and MARTIN JR, Charles L.
Rights and Utilitarianism. EWIN, R E.
Thinking Like an Engineer: The Place of a Code of Ethics in the Practice of a Profession. DAVIS, Michael.

COERCION
Human Rights in the Context of Uganda's Political Experience. KIGONGO, J K.
Law and Psychiatry: The Problems That Will Not Go Away. SZASZ, Thomas.

COEXISTENCE
Marranos (Pigs), or from Coexistence to Toleration. SHELL, Marc.

COGITO
The Cogito and Hermeneutics: The Question of the Subject in Ricoeur. JERVOLINO, Domenico.
Certainty, the Cogito, and Cartesian Dualism. GLOUBERMAN, Mark.
The Cogito and the Diallelus. ZELLNER, Harold.
Le premier registre de Descartes. RODIS-LEWIS, Geneviève.
Was Descartes a Liar? Diagonal Doubt Defended. SLEZAK, Peter.

COGNITION
see also Knowing, Thinking
Has Semantics Rested on a Mistake?. WETTSTEIN, Howard.
How to Build a Person: A Prolegomenon. POLLOCK, John L.
In Praise of the Cognitive Emotions. SCHEFFLER, Israel.
Kant's Transcendental Psychology. KITCHER, Patricia.
Mind and Cognition: A Reader. LYCAN, William G (ed).
Phänomenologische Philosophie. STRÖKER, Elisabeth.
A Post-Modern Epistemology. SORRI, Mari.

COGNITION

Pour une philosophie du sens et de la valeur. VASSILIE-LEMENY, Sorin-Titus.
Reflexion und Metareflexion bei Platon und Fichte. ZEHNPFENNIG, Barbara.
Varieties of Moral Personality: Ethics and Psychological Realism. FLANAGAN, Owen.
The World of the Imagination: Sum and Substance. BRANN, Eva T H.
Zetetic Skepticism. UMPHREY, Stewart.
"The Ethics of Science as a Form of the Cognition of Science" in *Logic, Methodology and Philosophy of Science, VIII*, YUDIN, Boris G.
"Moral Responsibility and Moral Commitment: The Integration of Affect and Cognition" in *The Moral Domain: Essays in the Ongoing Discussion between Philosophy and the Social Sciences*, HASTE, Helen.
"On the Characterization of Cognitive Progress" in *Imre Lakatos and Theories of Scientific Change*, HILPINEN, Risto.
A priori et a posteriori dans la pratique cognitive: le modele de la regulation des couples ago-antagonistes. BERNARD-WEIL, E.
Bolzano's Contribution to Cognition and/or the Creation of Theory of Sets (in Czechoslovakian). VECERKA, Kazimir.
Boskovic's Ideas on the Nature of Cognition Process (in Yugoslavian). DORDEVIC, Radomir.
The Categorical Nature of Mathematical Cognition. NYSANBAYEV, A N and KADYRZHANOV, R K.
The Causal History of Computational Activity: Maudlin and Olympia. BARNES, Eric.
Cognitive Art. LAUTER, H A.
The Conative Function of the Other in *Les Mots et les Choses*. RACEVSKIS, Karlis.
Conscience de soi et langage intérieur: quelques spéculations. MORIN, Alain and EVERETT, James.
Descartes on Sensory Representation: A Study of the *Dioptrics*. MAC KENZIE, Ann Wilbur.
Discipline-Based Art Education: Heat and Light. SWANGER, David.
Epistemic Paternalism: Communication Control in Law and Society. GOLDMAN, Alvin I.
Hayden White: "Historicism" as Linguistic Relativism in Historiography (in Polish). POMORSKI, Jan.
Historical Relativism as a Manifestation of the Cognitive Activity of a Historian According to Collingwood (in Polish). ZDYBEL, Jolanta.
Husserl's Phenomenology of Knowledge and Cognition (in Polish). DEBOWSKI, Jozef.
If Children thought Like Adults. GAUKER, Christopher.
Is Connectionism Commonsense?. O'BRIEN, Gerard J.
Kant's Account of Intuition. FALKENSTEIN, Lorne.
Nietzsche's Arctic Zone of Cognition and Post-Structuralism. PARENT, David.
Non-Rational Cognitive Processes as Changes of Distinctions. HEYLIGHEN, Francis.
El problema del conocimiento en Pascal. CASTRO MÉNDEZ, Silvia.
Remarks on the Modularity of Mind. SHANNON, Benny.
Reply to McKinney on Lonergan: A Deconstruction. MARSH, James L.
The Operation of Values: Knowledge in the Conception of G H Mead (in Polish). HETMANSKI, Marek.
The Problem of Cognition and Truth in Aesthetics (in Czechoslovakian). SINDELAR, Dusan.
The Specific Features of Cognition Progress in Philosophy: Demonstrated by the Example of Max Adler (in German). MÖCKEL, Christian.
Three Realities and Two Discourses. TABORSKY, Edwina.
Le tournant cognitif en sémiotique. MEUNIER, Jean-Guy.

COGNITIVE

The Fragmentation of Reason. STICH, Stephen.
Kommunikations-Theoretische Schriften II: Symbolische Erkenntnis und Kommunikation. UNGEHEUER, Gerold (ed).
Reasoning and Revision in Hybrid Representation Systems. NEBEL, Bernhard.
"Cognitive Significance Without Cognitive Content" in *Themes From Kaplan*, WETTSTEIN, Howard.
"An Empirical Interpretation of Ethogenics" in *Harré and His Critics*, ARGYLE, Michael.
"Turning the Tables on Frege or How is it that 'Hesperus is Hesperus' is Trivial?" in *Philosophical Perspectives, 3: Philosophy of Mind and Action Theory, 1989*, WETTSTEIN, Howard.
"The Fragmentation of Reason": Précis of Two Chapters. STICH, Stephen P.
Common Ground: Aristotle on Human and Divine Noetic Activity. MORGAN, Vance G.
Evaluating Cognitive Strategies: A Reply to Cohen, Goldman, Harman, and Lycan. STICH, Stephen P.
Intention, Cognitive Commitment, and Planning. AUDI, Robert.
Kant's Diversity Theory: A Dissenting View. GLOUBERMAN, Mark.
Potenzialità conoscitive del Trascendentale di Husserl. O'DWYER BELLINETTI, Luciana.
Proper Names, Cognitive Contents, and Beliefs. BRAUN, David M.
Some Remarks on the Rationality of Induction. INDURKHYA, Bipin.
Die Sprachen und das Denken: Klein Bestandsaufnahme zum linguistischen Relativismus (Sapir-Whorf-Hypothese). FRANZEN, Winfried.
Stephen P Stich, "The Fragmentation of Reason". COHEN, L Jonathan.
Stephen P Stich, "The Fragmentation of Reason". GOLDMAN, Alvin I.

COGNITIVE PSYCHOLOGY

Acts of Meaning. BRUNER, Jerome.
Artificial Intelligence and Human Cognition. WAGMAN, Morton.
The Case for Dualism. SMYTHIES, John R (ed).
Consciousness and the Computational Mind. JACKENDOFF, Ray.
Explaining Behavior: Reasons in a World of Causes. DRETSKE, Fred.
Mind and Cognition: A Reader. LYCAN, William G (ed).
Understanding the Representational Mind. PERNER, Josef.
"Cognitive Psychology, Entrapment, and the Philosophy of Mind" in *The Case for Dualism*, GAULD, Alan.
"On the Nature of Theories: A Neurocomputational Perspective" in *Scientific Theories*, CHURCHLAND, Paul M.
Cognitive Psychology, Phenomenology, and the "Creative Tension of Voices". EVANS, Fred.
Describing the Emotions: A Review of *The Cognitive Structure of Emotions* by Ortony, Clore and Collins. BEN-ZEEV, Aaron.
Epistemology, Psychology, and Goldman. CORLETT, J Angelo.
Externalism and Marr's Theory of Vision. FRANCESCOTTI, Robert M.
Fear and Loathing (and Other Intentional States) in Searle's Chinese Room. JACQUETTE, Dale.
I Know What I Know, If You Know What I Mean. DURAN, Jane.
Individualism and Semantic Development. PATTERSON, Sarah.
Is the Creative Process in Art a Form of Puzzle Solving?. LEDDY, Thomas.
Parallel Governing. SCALTSAS, Theodore.
Personal Construct Theory as the Ground for a Rapproachment Between Psychology and Philosophy in Education. WARREN, W G.
The Reductionist Ideal in Cognitive Psychology. MONTGOMERY, Richard.
Social Epistemology and Social Cognition. CORLETT, J Angelo.
Social Epistemology and Social Cognitive Psychology. SCHMITT, Frederick.
Towards a Reasonable Version of Methodological Solipsism. ROWLANDS, Mark.
Whither Social Epistemology? A Reply to Fuller. SCHMAUS, Warren.
Who's the Horse? A Response to Corlett. HEYES, Cecilia.

COGNITIVE SCIENCE

Epistemics. DURAN, Jane.
Foundations of Cognitive Science: The Essential Readings. GARFIELD, Jay L.
An Invitation To Cognitive Science. LEIBER, Justin.
The Natural and the Normative: Theories of Spatial Perception from Kant to Helmholtz. HATFIELD, Gary.
Philosophy and Cognitive Science. FETZER, James H.
Sensations: A Defense of Type Materialism. HILL, Christopher S.
"Semantic Anorexia: On the Notion of 'Content' in Cognitive Science" in *Meaning and Method: Essays in Honor of Hilary Putnam*, ANTONY, Louise.
Against Logicist Cognitive Science. OAKSFORD, Mike and CHATER, Nick.
Cognitive Science on a Wing and a Prayer. KEITH, William.
Cognitivism and Cognitive Science (in Portuguese). OLIVEIRA, M B de.
Dialogues in Natural Language with GURU, a Psychologic Inference Engine. COLBY, Kenneth M and COLBY, Peter M and STOLLER, Robert J.
Eléments pour une "philosophie de la psychologie". PETIT, Jean-Luc.
Massively Parallel Distributed Processing and a Computationalist Foundation for Cognitive Science. LYNGZEIDETSON, Albert E.
Mental Misrepresentation. MALONEY, J Christopher.
Models of Memory: Wittgenstein and Cognitive Science. STERN, David G.
Narrow Content: Fodor's Folly. ADAMS, Fred and DREBUSHENKO, David and FULLER, Gary and STECKER, Robert.
On Rhetorical Strategies: *Verstehen Sie*?. SLEZAK, Peter.
Philosophical and Religious Implications of Cognitive Social Learning Theories of Personality. ROTTSCHAEFER, William A.
Philosophy and Cognitive Science (in Czechoslovakian). PSTRUZINA, Karel.
Response to Slezak: *Nein, Ich verstehe nicht*. KEITH, William.
Rules and Relations: Some Connectionist Implications for Cognitive Science and Language. CILLIERS, F P.
Stich, Content, Prediction, and Explanation in Cognitive Science. WALLIS, Charles S.
You Can Fool Some of the People All of the Time, Everything Else Being Equal; Hedged Laws and Psychological Explanation. FODOR, Jerry A.

COGNITIVISM

"Meaning—Norms and Objectivity" in *Logic and Ethics*, JACK, Julie.
À propos d'arguments qui s'ignorent. VIGNAUX, Georges.
Backgrounding Desire. PETTIT, Philip and SMITH, Michael.
Cognitivism and Cognitive Science (in Portuguese). OLIVEIRA, M B de.
Hume's Metaethical Cognitivism and the Natural Law Theory. GRAEFRATH, Bernd.
Is the Brain a Digital Computer?. SEARLE, John R.
Meaning and Value. SCHIFFER, Stephen.
Moral Epistemology and the Supervenience of Ethical Concepts. AUDI, Robert.
Socrates' Critique of Cognitivism. MATSON, Wallace I and LEITE, Adam.

COGNITIVISM
Who's Afraid of Virginia Woolf?. MATRAVERS, Derek.
Wittgenstein et le cognitivisme. OUELLET, Pierre.

COHEN, G
Explaining Historical Development: A Marxian Critique of Cohen's Historical Materialism. WARREN, Paul.
Two Qualms About Functionalist Marxism. DICKMAN, Joel.

COHEN, H
The Legacy of Hermann Cohen. KLUBACK, William.

COHEN, L
Belief, Acceptance, and Knowledge. RADFORD, Colin.

COHEN, M
Cohen on Einstein's Simultaneity *Gedankenexperiment*. WHITE, V Alan.

COHERENCE
The Dynamics of Rational Deliberation. SKYRMS, Brian.
"'Circular' Coherence and 'Absurd' Foundations" in *Truth and Interpretation: Perspectives on the Philosophy of Donald Davidson*, SOSA, Ernest.
"A Coherence Theory of Truth and Knowledge" in *Reading Rorty*, DAVIDSON, Donald.
"A Coherence Theory of Truth and Knowledge" in *Truth and Interpretation: Perspectives on the Philosophy of Donald Davidson*, DAVIDSON, Donald.
Coherence, Anti-realism, and the Vienna Circle. YOUNG, James O.
Correspondence, Consensus, and Coherence and the Rape of Democracy. PASK, Gordon.
A Critique of Plantinga's Theological Foundationalism. ZEIS, John.
Discourses on Political Violence: The Problem of Coherence. DU TOIT, A B.
Ethics and Coherence. DE GEORGE, Richard T.
Explanation—Opening Address. SMART, J J C.
The Foundationalist Justification of Epistemic Principles. REMEDIOS, F.
The Identity Theory of Truth. BALDWIN, Thomas.
Moral Truth and Coherence: Comments on Goldman. STEUP, M.
On Making a Coherence Theory of Truth True. SYLVAN, Richard.
On the Epistemic Status of Considered Moral Judgments. TIMMONS, Mark.
Same Human Being, Same Person?. THORNTON, Mark.
Sequencing Rules and Coherence in Discourse. TSUI, Amy B M.

COHN, P
Filosofía de la violencia. MAGGIOLO, Roberto Jiménez.

COLEMAN, J
Torts of Necessity: A Moral Theory of Compensation. KLEPPER, Howard.

COLERIDGE
Delicate Subjects: Romanticism, Gender, and the Ethics of Understanding. ELLISON, Julie.
G H Bantock as Educational Philosopher. BARRIE, John A.
Logic and Logos—The Search for Unity in Hegel and Coleridge: I, Alienation and the Logocentric Response. PERKINS, Mary Anne.
Logic and Logos—The Search for Unity in Hegel and Coleridge: II: The 'Otherness" of God. PERKINS, Mary Anne.
Logic and Logos—The Search for Unity in Hegel and Coleridge, III: A Different Logos. PERKINS, Mary Anne.

COLLECTION(S)
Collection and Division in the *Phaedrus* and *Statesman*. WEDIN, Michael V.

COLLECTIVE ACTION(S)
Foundations of Social Theory. COLEMAN, James S.
Rationality in Action: Contemporary Approaches. MOSER, Paul K (ed).
"Actions by Collectives" in *Philosophical Perspectives, 3: Philosophy of Mind and Action Theory, 1989*, TUOMELA, Raimo.
The Micro-Macro Problem in Collective Behavior: Reconciling Agency and Structure. LEE, Raymond L M.
Musical Time as a Practical Accomplishment: A Change in Tempo. WEEKS, P A D.
Newcomb's Problem, Prisoners' Dilemma, and Collective Action. HURLEY, S L.

COLLECTIVE(S)
"Heritage and Collective Responsibility" in *The Political Responsibility of Intellectuals*, JEDLICKI, Jerzy.
Aggregation of Preferences: The Fuzzy Case. BILLOT, Antoine.
Collectives and Collections. GILBERT, Paul.
Committees and Consensus: How Many Heads Are Better Than One?. CAWS, Peter.

COLLECTIVISM
Collectives and Collections. GILBERT, Paul.
German Collectivism and the Welfare State. NEAMAN, Elliot Yale.
What is the Problem Concerning Social Entities?. THOMPSON, J L.

COLLECTIVITY(-TIES)
"Individuality and Collectivity: False Antonyms" in *Abeunt Studia in Mores: A Festschrift for Helga Doblin*, PYTOWSKA, Ewa.

COLLEGE(S)
Shaping Character: Moral Education in the Christian College. HOLMES, Arthur F.

COLLINGWOOD
Art and Craft. MOUNCE, H O.
Collingwood and the Idea of Progress. VAN DER DUSSEN, W Jan.
Collingwood's Detective Image of the Historian and the Study of Hadrian's Wall. COUSE, G S.
Historical Relativism as a Manifestation of the Cognitive Activity of a Historian According to Collingwood (in Polish). ZDYBEL, Jolanta.
The Idea of History as a Scale of Forms. GOLDSTEIN, Leon J.
Is "The Theory of History" (1914) Collingwood's First Essay on the Philosophy of History?. PATRICK, James.
Progressive Traditionalism as the Spirit of Collingwood's Philosophy. KISSELL, Michael A.
Some Aspects of R G Collingwood's Doctrine of Absolute Presuppositions. SAARI, Heikki.
Was R G Collingwood the Author of "The Theory of History"?. CONNELLY, James.

COLLINS, A
Describing the Emotions: A Review of *The Cognitive Structure of Emotions* by Ortony, Clore and Collins. BEN-ZEEV, Aaron.

COLMO, C
Comment on Colmo's "Reason and Revelation in the Thought of Leo Strauss". LOWENTHAL, David.

COLONIALISM
Critical Fanonism. GATES JR, Henry Louis.
La imagen del indígena en el pensamiento colombiano del siglo XIX: La perspectiva de J M Samper. GÓMEZ-MULLER, Alfredo.
Is the Post- in Postmodernism the Post- in Postcolonial?. APPIAH, Kwame Anthony.
The Aristotelian Debate in African Philosophy: Miscellaneous Remarks on a Denied Discourse (in German). NEUGEBAUER, Christian.

COLOR
Colour: A Philosophical Introduction (Second Edition). WESTPHAL, Jonathan.
Cool Red. LEVINE, Joseph.
Descartes on Colour. COTTINGHAM, John.
The Dimension of Color. FÓTI, Véronique.
Hegel and Schopenhauer as Partisans of Goethe's Theory of Color. LAUXTERMANN, P F H.
On 'This is Red and This is Blue': *Tractatus* 6.3751. SAHU, Neelamani.
On Two Recent Accounts of Colour. MC GINN, Marie.
The Other European Science of Nature?. UBEROI, J P S.
Physicalist Theories of Color. BOGHOSSIAN, Paul A and VELLEMAN, J David.
Reply to Levine's "Cool Red". HARDIN, C L.
Reply to Teller's "Simpler Arguments Might Work Better". HARDIN, C L.
Simpler Arguments Might Work Better. TELLER, Davida Y.
Die Sprachen und das Denken: Klein Bestandsaufnahme zum linguistischen Relativismus (Sapir-Whorf-Hypothese). FRANZEN, Winfried.
What is Wrong in Inverting Spectra. CASATI, Roberto.
Wittgenstein and the Color Incompatibility Problem. JACQUETTE, Dale.
Wittgenstein's "Remarks on Colour". ERICKSON, Glenn W.

COMATOSE
The Locked-In Syndrome and the Behaviorist Epistemology of Other Minds. KURTHEN, Martin (and others).

COMBINATORICS
Infinitary Combinatorics and Modal Logic. BLASS, A.

COMBINATORY LOGIC
Corrections to Some Results for BCK Logics and Algebras. BUNDER, M W.
Some Improvements to Turner's Algorithm for Bracket Abstraction. BUNDER, M W.
Systems of Combinatory Logic Related to Quine's 'New Foundations'. HOLMES, M R.

COMEDY
Cristianesimo tragico, cristianesimo ludico: i due volti della fedeltà al Dio dialettico. GARGANO, Monica.
Vom "Wahr-Lachen" der Moderne: Karl Valentins Semantik paradoxer Lebenswelten. GÖNNER, Gerhard.

COMMAND(S)
L'interpretazione del conflitto fra norme nell'ultimo Kelsen. CELANO, Brun.
Validity and Satisfaction in Imperative Logic. SEGERBERG, Krister.

COMMANDMENT(S)
The Recent Revival of Divine Command Ethics. QUINN, Philip L.

COMMENSURABILITY
"Scientific Discovery and Commensurability of Meaning" in *Imre Lakatos and Theories of Scientific Change*, NERSESSIAN, Nancy J.
Commensurability as a Prerequisite of Rational Choice: An Examination of Sidgwick's Position. RICHARDSON, Henry S.

COMMENTARY(-RIES)
Introduction to the Philosophy of Nature. HETZLER, Florence M.
Russische Philosophie. GOERDT, Wilhelm.
Comments and Replies. TAYLOR, Charles.

COMMENTARY(-RIES)
Textual Deference. SMITH, Barry.
Theme and Commentary. GREEN, Thomas F.

COMMITMENT(S)
How to Play Theological Ping-Pong: And Other Essays on Faith and Reason. ABRAHAM, William J (ed).
"The Ethics of Social Commitment" in *Biomedical Ethics Reviews, 1990*, BAILLIE, Harold W and GARRETT, Thomas M.
"The Hungarian Intellectual and the Choice of Commitment or Neutrality" in *The Political Responsibility of Intellectuals*, MACLEAN, Ian (trans) and MOLNAR, Miklós.
"Integrity and Radical Change" in *Feminist Ethics*, DAVION, Victoria M.
The Dialectic of National and Universal Commitments in Christian-Marxist Dialogue. WILL, James E.
Four Dialogue Systems. MACKENZIE, Jim.
Inconsistent Commitment and Commitment to Inconsistencies. KRABBE, Erik C W.
Intention, Cognitive Commitment, and Planning. AUDI, Robert.
On Being Committed to Morality. NIELSEN, Kai.
Risk, Commitment, and Project Abandonment. DEVANEY, Mike.

COMMITTEE(S)
Committees and Consensus: How Many Heads Are Better Than One?. CAWS, Peter.
Consensus, Contracts, and Committees. MORENO, Jonathan D.

COMMODITY(-TIES)
"Obsolescence and Desire: Fashion and the Commodity Form" in *Postmodernism—Philosophy and the Arts (Continental Philosophy III)*, FAURSCHOU, Gail.
The Costs of Commercial Medicine. DOUGHERTY, Charles J.
The Ethics of Selectively Marketing the Health Maintenance Organization. WAYMACK, Mark H.
Freedom, Commodification, and the Alienation of Labor in Adam Smith's "Wealth of Nations". WERHANE, Patricia H.

COMMON GOOD
The Common Good, Human Rights and Education: A Need for Conceptual Reformulization. CRAIG, Robert P.
The Modernity of St Thomas' Political Philosophy. WALTER, Edward.
Rethinking the Commons. HERRING, Ronald J.

COMMON SENSE
Realism with a Human Face. PUTNAM, Hilary.
"Commonsense Reasoning, Social Change, and the Law" in *Critique and Construction: A Symposium on Roberto Unger's "Politics"*, VAN ZANDT, David E.
"Fission and the Facts" in *Philosophical Perspectives, 3: Philosophy of Mind and Action Theory, 1989*, JOHNSTON, Mark.
"Threading-the-Needle: The Case For and Against Common-Sense Realism". TIBBETTS, Paul.
Against Common Sense: Avoiding Cartesian Anxiety. BINEHAM, Jeffery L.
Berkeley and Common Sense Realism. PAPPAS, George S.
Causal Holism and Commonsense Psychology: A Reply to O'Brien. STICH, Stephen P.
Chisholm, Reid and the Problem of the Epistemic Surd. LEHRER, Keith.
Common Sense and the Foundations of Economic Theory: Duhem versus Robbins. SHEARMUR, Jeremy.
Education and the Emotions: The Relevance of the Russellian Perspective. MATTAI, Bansraj.
Irreducible Dualisms and the Residue of Commonsense: On the Inevitability of Cartesian Anxiety. HIKINS, James W and CHERWITZ, Richard A.
Is Connectionism Commonsense?. O'BRIEN, Gerard J.
Keith Lehrer and Thomas Reid. CHISHOLM, Roderick M.
Max on Moore. STROLL, Avrum.
Radical Critique, Scepticism and Commonsense. GAITA, Raimond.
The Idea of Common Sense in the Philosophy of L Chwistek (in Polish). JOZEFCZUK, Grzegorz.

COMMONWEALTH
Political Writings—John Milton. DZELZAINIS, Martin (ed).

COMMUNICATION
Alltagssprachliche Metakommunikation im Englischen und Deutschen. WELTE, Werner.
The Communicative Ethics Controversy. BENHABIB, Seyla (ed).
Dämonie und Gesellschaft. CATTEPOEL, Jan.
The Dice-Playing God: Reflections on Life in a Post-Modern Age. KRIEGLSTEIN, Werner.
Difference and Subjectivity: Dialogue and Personal Identity. JACQUES, Francis.
The Foundations of Linguistic Theory: Selected Writings of Roy Harris. LOVE, Nigel (ed).
Intentions in Communication. COHEN, Philip R (ed).
Irony and the Discourse of Modernity. BEHLER, Ernst.
Kommunikations-Theoretische Schriften II: Symbolische Erkenntnis und Kommunikation. UNGEHEUER, Gerold (ed).
Linguistic Behaviour. BENNETT, Jonathan.
Reading Habermas. RASMUSSEN, David M.
La sociedad sin hombres: Niklas Luhmann o la teoría como escándalo. IZUZQUIZA, Ignacio.
"Communication esthetique comme bonheur" in *XIth International Congress in Aesthetics, Nottingham 1988*, SASAKI, Kenichi.
"Davidson on Convention" in *The Mind of Donald Davidson*, JUTRONIC-TIHOMIROVIC, Dunja.
"Le kitsch en tant que valeur communicative" in *XIth International Congress in Aesthetics, Nottingham 1988*, STÉPHANOV, Ivan.
Amor y comunicación. FORMENT, Eudaldo.
Are There Cultural Universals?. WIREDU, Kwasi.
Author's Position in Interpretation of a Work of Art (in Japanese). WATANABE, Hiroshi.
La comunicación en la vida cotidiana. FÓSCOLO, Norma.
Conocimiento y comunicación: Algunas reflexiones sobre la vida social. SUANCES MARCOS, M.
Contents and Causes: A Reply to Blackburn. STURGEON, Nicholas L.
Cross-Cultural Philosophizing. RANLY, Ernest W.
L'epoché di Husserl in Ferruccio Rossi-Landi. PONZIO, Augusto.
La force du nombre: remarques autour de la notion de communauté. FAUCHER, Luc.
Habermas e o Terror Prático. LOPARIC, Zeljko.
Habermas et la théologie: Notes pour une discussion entre la théologie et la "Théorie de l'agir communicationnel". KISSLING, Christian.
Habermas on Strategic and Communicative Action. JOHNSON, James.
Intersubjectivity and Critical Consciousness: Remarks on Habermas's Theory of Communicative Action. WAGNER, Gerhard and ZIPPRIAN, Heinz.
L'Assertion dans les contextes épistémiques; garants objectaux et bases d'évaluation. MOULOUD, Noël.
La communication de l'art (in Japanese). SHINOHARA, Motoaki.
La loi de vérité. POULAIN, Jacques.
Never Say "Never"! On the Communication Problem between Intuitionism and Classicism. HELLMAN, Geoffrey.
Organizational Value Contention and Managerial Mindsets. LIEDTKA, Jeanne.
Pragmática del lenguaje y racionalidad comunicativa. DE ZAN, J.
Reply to Sturgeon's "Contents and Causes" A Reply to Blackburn. BLACKBURN, Simon.
Social Communication and Interest Relationships (in German). LUUTZ, Wolfgang.
System-Theoretical Bases of Social Theory (in German). LUHMANN, Niklas.
The Metacultural Hypothesis and the Foundations of Cultural Activity (in Polish). PORENA, Boris.
Die Theorie des kommunikativen Handelns in Diskussion. KISSLING, Christian.
Voix et Existence. DIAGNE, Oumar.

COMMUNICATIVE ETHICS
The Chief of Medicine. BRODY, Howard.
Ethical Expertise and Moral Maturity: Conflict or Complement?. MOSS, Lenny.
La metáfora como resolución de un problema comunicativo-lingüístico. FERNÁNDEZ, Teresa Bejaran.

COMMUNION
"Sociátá" et "communion" chez saint Thomas d'Aquin. LA SOUJEOLE, Benoît-Dominique.
Oratio Placabilis Deo Eriugena's Fragmentary Eucharistic Teaching. SMITH, R U.

COMMUNISM
see also Historical Materialism, Leninism, Marxism
Communism: A Post-Mortem. BAUMAN, Zygmunt.
Communism: The Philosophical Foundations. FLEW, Antony.
Die DDR und ihre Philosophen: Über Voraussetzungen einer Urteilsbildung. RUBEN, Peter.
Georg Lukács and Stalinism (in German). TIETZ, Udo.
The Ideas of Karl Marx at a Turning Point in Human Civilization. PANTIN, I and PLIMAK, E.
Kommunismus—Utopie und Wirklichkeit. HAVEMANN, Robert.
Marx and the Problem of Conflicting Models of History. BEST, Steven.
Marxism, Post-Marxism and the Implosion of Communism. STOJANOVIC, Svetozar.
Per l'Europa dopo il crollo della Cortina di Ferro. GRYGIEL, Stanislaw.
Reflections on the Eastern European Revolutions: The God that Failed. MAZLISH, Bruce.
Romania's Revolution and its Prospects. BRUCAN, Silviu.
Some Basic Problems of a Political Theory of Modern Socialism (in German). SEGERT, Dieter.
The Development of a Concept of Modern Socialism: Theses under Discussion (in German). BRIE, Michael.
The Party's Claim to Power: The Power of Knowledge in "Real Socialism" (in German). MARZ, Lutz.
The Pros and Cons of Trotsky's Marxism (in German). HEDELER, Wladislaw.
Was Marx a Socialist?. TSIPKO, A.
What Happened in Eastern Europe in 1989?. CHIROT, Daniel.

COMMUNIST(S)
Moral Reasoning in a Communist Chinese Society. WALKER, Lawrence J and MORAN, Thomas J.

COMMUNITARIAN
Theories of Criminal Justice: A Critical Reappraisal. ELLIS, Ralph D.

COMMUNITARIANISM
Rawls: "A Theory of Justice" and Its Critics. KUKATHAS, Chandran.
Universalism versus Communitarianism: Contemporary Debates in Ethics. RASMUSSEN, David.
Varieties of Moral Personality: Ethics and Psychological Realism. FLANAGAN, Owen.
Au-delà de la critique communautarienne du libéralisme? D'Alasdair MacIntyre à Stanley Hauerwas. VAN GERWEN, Jef.
Communitarianism and the Question of Tolerance. PASSERIN D'ENTRÈVES, Maurizio.
Discourse Ethics and the Communitarian Critique of Neo-Kantianism. REHG, William.
Ethics, AIDS, and Community Responsibility. DOUARD, John.
L'être de l'humain: Notes sur la tradition communautarienne. CHAUMONT, Jean-Michel.
La pensée de Rawls face au défi communautarien. IROEGBU, Pantaleon.
The Perils of Love: Why Women Need Rights. INGRAM, Attracta.
Stout on Relativism, Liberalism, and Communitarianism. QUIRK, Michael J.
Toward a Reconciliation of Liberalism and Communitarianism. ELLIS, Ralph D.

COMMUNITY LIVING
Community: The Tie That Binds. ROUSSEAU, Mary F.

COMMUNITY(-TIES)
Benjamin Constant and the Post-Revolutionary Mind. FONTANA, Biancamaria.
The Call to Personhood. MC FADYEN, Alistair I.
The Communicative Ethics Controversy. BENHABIB, Seyla (ed).
Community: The Tie That Binds. ROUSSEAU, Mary F.
History and Spirit: An Inquiry into the Philosophy of Liberation. KOVEL, Joel.
Ibn Rushd: Averroes. URVOY, Dominique.
Interpreting Political Responsibility. DUNN, John.
La intersubjectividad en Husserl, Volume I and II. IRIBARNE, Julia V.
Rawls: "A Theory of Justice" and Its Critics. KUKATHAS, Chandran.
To Be at Home: Christianity, Civil Religion, and World Community. ROUNER, Leroy S.
Work, Inc.: A Philosophical Inquiry. BYRNE, Edmund F.
"Liberty, Community, and Corrective Justice" in *Liability and Responsibility*, WEINRIB, Ernest J.
"Person and Community in African Thought" in *I, We and Body: First Joint Symposium of Philosophers from Africa and from the Netherlands*, GYEKYE, Kwame.
"Vocation, Friendship, and Community: Limitations of the Personal-Impersonal Framework" in *Identity, Character, and Morality: Essays in Moral Psychology*, BLUM, Lawrence A.
Against Human Rights. NELSON, John O.
Artist and Peasant. XING-PEI, Fei.
Community and Autonomy: Logically Incompatible Values?. MASON, Andrew.
Community and Neutrality in Critical Thought. HOSTETLER, Karl.
Community and the Evil Poem. KEMAL, S.
Community and Utopia: A Transcendental Deduction. POPOV, Stefan.
The Community as Sacrament. LIDERBACH, Daniel.
Community Responsibility and the Development of Oregon's Health Care Priorities. GARLAND, Michael J and HASNAIN, Romana.
Community Values in Vermont Health Planning. WALLACE-BRODEUR, Paul H.
Community, Law, and the Idiom and Rhetoric of Rights. MAC INTYRE, Alasdair.
Contemporary Ethics and Scheler's Phenomenology of Community. VACEK, Edward.
Giving Voice to the Pragmatic Majority in New Jersey. HILL, T Patrick.
Intersubjectivity without Subjectivism. SINGER, Beth J.
Josiah Royce: la metafisica della comunità. BUZZI GRASSI, Elisa.
L'esthétique de John Dewey et le contexte urbain. GAVIN, William J.
Lonergan's Recovery of the Notion of Natural Right: Introduction to a New Context for an Old Discussion. BRAIO, Frank Paul.
Nietzsche's Genealogy: Of Beauty and Community. KEMAL, S.
Public Input Into Health Care Policy: Controversy and Contribution in California. COLBERT, Treacy.
Punitive Damages: New Twists in Torts. WALTON, Clarence C.
Rasgos de la communidad agustiniana según la 'Regula recepta'. ANOZ, José.
Si la filosofía política es ciencia práctica. DONADÍO MAGGI, María C.
The World of Human Community in Hanna Arendt's Work (in Czechoslovakian). KOUBA, Pavel.
Towards a Feminist Reassessment of Intellectual Virtue. BRAATEN, Jane.
La valenza della carità nelle forme della vita politica. PELLECCHIA, Pasquale.
A Vision of the Health Decisions Movement. CRAWSHAW, Ralph.
Wittgenstein et l'institution du langage. SEYMOUR, Michel.

COMPACTNESS
Boolean Powers of Abelian Groups. EDA, Katsuya.
Constructive Compact Operators on a Hilbert Space. ISHIHARA, Hajime.
Definitions of Compact. HOWARD, Paul E.
Two Hypergraph Theorems Equivalent to BPI. COWEN, Robert H.

COMPARATIVE PHILOSOPHY
"Interpreting across Boundaries" in *Understanding the Chinese Mind: The Philosophical Roots*, SMITH, John E.
"Speech Versus Writing" in Derrida and Bhartrhari. COWARD, Harold G.
Comparative Dialectics: Nishida Kitarō's Logic of Place and Western Dialectical Thought. AXTELL, G S.
Emotion East and West: Introduction to a Comparative Philosophy. MARKS, Joel.
Indian Philosophy in the Context of World Philosophy. BHATTACHARYYA, Kalidas.
Indigenous Ends and Alien Means: A Footnote on Indian Renaissance. CHAUDHURI, Minakshi Ray.
A Peep into Man's History: The Lessons for Today. SINGH, Ajai R and SINGH, Shakuntala A.
Phenomenology and Indian Philosophy. SINGH, Navjyoti.
Problems of Understanding. MEHTA, J L.
Republic: 2. BANAJI, V F.
Science and Consciousness. WOJCIECHOWSKI, Jerzy A.
Traditional Chinese Culture: Contemporary Developments —Profound Selections from the Works of Fang Dongmei. GUOBAO, Jiang.
Virtue Ethics and Maori Ethics. PERRETT, Roy W and PATTERSON, John.

COMPARATIVE RELIGION
'Religion' and the Religions in the English Enlightenment. HARRISON, Peter.
"The Chinese Case in a Philosophy of World Religions" in *Understanding the Chinese Mind: The Philosophical Roots*, NEVILLE, Robert C.
Paul Tillich and Inter-religious Dialogue. FOERSTER, John.
Religions in the Balance. FENNER, Peter.

COMPARATIVE(S)
Behind the Masks of God: An Essay Toward Comparative Theology. NEVILLE, Robert Cummings.
First-Order Logics for Comparative Similarity. WILLIAMSON, Timothy.

COMPARATIVISM
Leibniz, Humboldt, and the Origins of Comparativism. DE MAURO, Tullio (ed).
"Comparatismo e grammatica comparata: Tipologia linguistica e forma grammaticale" in *Leibniz, Humboldt, and the Origins of Comparativism*, SWIGGERS, Pierre.
"Descent, Perfection and the Comparative Method Since Leibniz" in *Leibniz, Humboldt, and the Origins of Comparativism*, HOENIGSWALD, Henry M.
"Leibniz and Wilhelm von Humboldt and the History of Comparative Linguistics" in *Leibniz, Humboldt, and the Origins of Comparativism*, ROBINS, Robert H.
"Leibniz on Particles: Linguistic Form and Comparatism" in *Leibniz, Humboldt, and the Origins of Comparativism*, DASCAL, Marcelo.
"Representation and the Place of Linguistic Change before Comparative Grammar" in *Leibniz, Humboldt, and the Origins of Comparativism*, AUROUX, Sylvain.
"Die Säkularisierung des 'Tertium comparationis'" in *Leibniz, Humboldt, and the Origins of Comparativism*, BORSCHE, Tilman.
"Le voyage de 'Schreiten': Leibniz et les débuts du comparatisme finno-ougrien" in *Leibniz, Humboldt, and the Origins of Comparativism*, DROIXHE, Daniel.

COMPARISON(S)
Quest for Certainty: A Comparative Study of Heidegger and Sankara. GRIMES, John A.
"Da Humboldt ai neogrammatici: Continuità e fratture" in *Leibniz, Humboldt, and the Origins of Comparativism*, RAMAT, Paolo.
"Tradition and Convolution—Settings of Aesthetic Phenomena in the Third World" in *XIth International Congress in Aesthetics, Nottingham 1988*, ERZEN, Jale.
Account of a Philosophical Expedition in Search of the Elusive Paradigm (in Dutch). GOUWS, A S.
Classification by Comparison with Paradigms. EBERLE, Rolf.
Interart Analogy: Practice and Theory in Comparing the Arts. THOMAS, Troy.
Is Happiness Relative?. VEENHOVEN, Ruut.
Making Interpersonal Comparisons Coherently. BARRETT, Martin and HAUSMAN, Daniel.
On Comparison of Theories by Their Contents. WOLENSKI, Jan.
The Parallel Fallacy: On Comparing Art and Science. TOPPER, David.
Reductive and Nonreductive Simile Theories of Metaphor. TIRRELL, Lynne.
La storia universale come storia comparata in Max Weber. DI MARCO, Giuseppe Antonio.

COMPASSION
The Legacy of Hermann Cohen. KLUBACK, William.
Compassion. SNOW, Nancy E.
In Defense of Sentimentality. SOLOMON, Robert C.
Of One Mind or Two? Query on the Innate Good in Mencius. LAI, Whalen.

COMPATIBILISM
The Non-Reality of Free Will. DOUBLE, Richard.
"Klein on Certainty and Canonical Beliefs" in *Doubting: Contemporary Perspectives on Skepticism*, FELDMAN, Richard.
"When is the Will Free?" in *Philosophical Perspectives, 3: Philosophy of Mind and Action Theory, 1989*, VAN INWAGEN, Peter.
Free Will and Being a Victim. SMILANSKY, S.
The Free Will Defense and Determinism. SENNETT, James F.
Freedom, Necessity, and Laws of Nature as Relations between Universals. VIHVELIN, Kadri.
In Defence of Theological Compatibilism. FLINT, Thomas P.
Logic and the Free Will Problem. VAN INWAGEN, Peter.
The World-Shift Theory of Free Choice. DAVIS, Wayne A.

COMPATIBILITY
The Co-Existence of God and Evil. TRAU, Jane Mary.
The Dilemma of Freedom and Foreknowledge. ZAGZEBSKI, Linda Trinkaus.
Hume Revisited: A Problem With the Free Will Defense. MARKHAM, Ian.

COMPENSATION
Liability and Responsibility. FREY, R G (ed).
"Beyond Foreseeability: Consequential Damages in the Law of Contract" in *Liability and Responsibility*, EPSTEIN, Richard A.
"Theories of Compensation" in *Liability and Responsibility*, GOODIN, Robert E.
Commentary: When Opportunity Knocks. HYMAN, David A.
The Ethical Implications of the Straight-Commission Compensation System—An Agency Perspective. KURLAND, Nancy B.
Land, Well-Being and Compensation. PARGETTER, Robert and YOUNG, Robert and BIGELOW, John.
Moral Dilemmas, Compromise and Compensation. DAY, J P.
Property, Entitlement, and Remedy. PAUL, Jeffrey.
Torts of Necessity: A Moral Theory of Compensation. KLEPPER, Howard.

COMPETENCE
Deciding for Others: The Ethics of Surrogate Decision Making. BUCHANAN, Allen E.
"Semantics and Semantic Competence" in *Philosophical Perspectives, 3: Philosophy of Mind and Action Theory, 1989*, SOAMES, Scott.
Connectionism, Competence, and Explanation. CLARK, Andy.
Decisionmaking Competence and Risk—Comments on Wicclair. BROCK, Dan W.
Feminist Second Thoughts About Free Agency. BENSON, Paul.
Risk-Related Standard Inevitable in Assessing Competence—Comments on Wicclair. SKENE, Loane.

COMPETITION
Enriching Business Ethics. WALTON, Clarence C (ed).
The Anatomy of Aggression. LUPER-FOY, Steven.
Corporate Policy and the Ethics of Competitor Intelligence Gathering. PAINE, Lynn Sharp.
Role Differentiation Problems in Professional Ethics. WANGERIN, Paul T.

COMPLEMENTARITY
Art and Philosophy: The Person in the Cybernetic Age. HETZLER, Florence M.
Bohr's Idea of Complementarity and Plato's Philosophy. MAHOOTIAN, Farzad.
Relating Science and Theology with Complementarity: A Caution. SHARPE, Kevin J.
The Relation between Science and Theology: The Case for Complimentarity Revisited. REICH, K Helmut.

COMPLETENESS
see also Incompleteness
Computability, Complexity, Logic. BÖRGER, E.
Classification of Intermediate Predicate Logics Under the Type of Deductive Completeness. TAKANO, Mitio and YAMAKAMI, Tomoyuki.
Complementary Sentential Logics. VARZI, Achille C.
A Complete Deductive-System for Since-Until Branching-Time Logic. ZANARDO, Alberto.
Expressive Power and Semantic Completeness: Boolean Connectives in Modal Logic. HUMBERSTONE, I L.
Expressiveness and Completeness of an Interval Tense Logic. VENEMA, Yde.
An Extension of Ono's Completeness Result. SUZUKI, Nobu-Yuki.
Henkin's Completeness Proof: Forty Years Later. LEBLANC, Hugues and ROEPER, Peter and THAU, Michael and WEAVER, George.
An Integer-Valued Matrix Characteristic for Implicational *S5*. ULRICH, Dolph.
Is There Completeness in Mathematics after Gödel?. HINTIKKA, Jaakko.
Many-Valued Modal Logics: Uses and Predicate Calculus. OSTERMANN, Pascal.
Mojzesz Presburger: Life and Work. ZYGMUNT, Jan.
On the Completeness of a Certain System of Arithmetic of Whole Numbers in Which Addition Occurs as the Only Operation. PRESBURGER, Mojzesz and JACQUETTE, Dale.
Related Semantics for All Lewis, Lemmon and Feys' Modal Logics. SYLVAN, Richard.
Variations on da Costa *C* Systems and Dual-Intuitionistic Logics (I). SYLVAN, Richard.

COMPLEXITY
Computability, Complexity, Logic. BÖRGER, E.
Metaphysics of Natural Complexes (Second Edition). WALLACE, Kathleen (ed).
Complexity and Evolution: What Everybody Knows. MC SHEA, Daniel W.
The Complexity of Intrinsically R.E. Subsets of Existentially Decidable Models. CHISHOLM, John.
Coping with Complexity—Coping with Dialectics, in Theory and Practice (in German). THIEL, Rainer.
Randomness by Design. DEMBSKI, William.
Real Numbers, Continued Fractions and Complexity Classes. LABHALLA, Salah and LOMBARDI, Henri.
Why Natural Selection Leads to Complexity. BENZON, William L and HAYS, David G.

COMPOSER(S)
Problems Concerning the Presence of the Composer in His Music (in Polish). BUCZEK, Barbara.

COMPOSITE(S)
Bayle, Leibniz, Hume and Reid on Extension, Composites and Simples. CUMMINS, Phillip.

COMPOSITION
The Chronology of Plato's Dialogues. BRANDWOOD, Leonard.
Material Beings. VAN INWAGEN, Peter.
"Understanding and the Principle of Compositionality" in *Philosophical Perspectives, 4: Action Theory and Philosophy of Mind, 1990*, GRANDY, Richard E.
Is a Whole Identical to its Parts?. SCALTSAS, Theodore.
A Pieced Quilt: A Critical Discussion of Stephen Schiffer's *Remnants of Meaning*. ANTONY, Louise.
The Poetic Theory of the Stoic 'Aristo'. ASMIS, Elizabeth.

COMPREHENSION
Comprensión intercultural y arte. BERENSON, Frances.
Le satori dans le bouddhisme zen et la rationalité. HÉLAL, Georges.

COMPROMISE(S)
Institutional Integrity: Approval, Toleration and Holy War or 'Always True to You in My Fashion'. WILDES, Kevin W.
Integrity and Compromise in Nursing Ethics. WINSLOW, Betty J and WINSLOW, Gerald R.
Moral Dilemmas, Compromise and Compensation. DAY, J P.
The Philosopher as Insider and Outsider: How to Advise, Compromise, and Criticize. KAMM, Frances M.

COMPUTABILITY
Computability, Complexity, Logic. BÖRGER, E.

COMPUTATION
Do the Right Thing: Studies in Limited Rationality. RUSSELL, Stuart.
An Invitation To Cognitive Science. LEIBER, Justin.
"Neural Representation and Neural Computation" in *Philosophical Perspectives, 4: Action Theory and Philosophy of Mind, 1990*, CHURCHLAND, Patricia Smith and SEJNOWSKI, Terrence J.
The Causal History of Computational Activity: Maudlin and Olympia. BARNES, Eric.
Computation and Mathematical Empiricism. RESNIK, Michael D.
Domain Theory in Logical Form. ABRAMSKY, Samson.
Reasoning and Computation in Leibniz. SPRUIT, Leen and TAMBURRINI, Guglielmo.

COMPUTATIONAL COMPLEXITY
Complexity for Type-2 Relations. TOWNSEND, Mike.
Computational Structure of GPSG Models. RISTAD, Eric Sven.

COMPUTATIONAL MODEL(S)
Nomic Probability and the Foundations of Induction. POLLOCK, John L.
"Benefits to Moral Philosophy of the Computational Model of the Mind" in *Acting and Reflecting: The Interdisciplinary Turn in Philosophy*, HARMAN, Gilbert.
"The Computational Conception of Mind" in *Acting and Reflecting: The Interdisciplinary Turn in Philosophy*, SCOTT, Dana S.
Herbert Simon's Computational Models of Scientific Discovery. DOWNES, Stephen M.
How to Change Your Mind. MARTINS, João P and CRAVO, Maria R.
The Nature of Irony: Toward a Computational Model of Irony. LITTMAN, David C and MEY, Jacob L.

COMPUTATIONALISM
Replies to My Computational Commentators. DIETRICH, Eric.

COMPUTER ASSISTED INSTRUCTION
Computer Alternatives in the History of Philosophy Classroom. TESCHNER, George and MC CLUSKY, Frank.

COMPUTER SCIENCE
Intentions in Communication. COHEN, Philip R (ed).
Logic Programming: Proceedings of the Seventh International Conference. WARREN, David H D (ed).
Reasoning and Revision in Hybrid Representation Systems. NEBEL, Bernhard.

COMPUTER SCIENCE
Logic and Knowledge Representation. PETROV, V V and PEREVERZEV, V N.
On the Development of Paraconsistent Logic and Da Costa's Work. LOFFREDO D'OTTAVIANO, Itala M.

COMPUTER(S)
see also Artificial Intelligence
Logic Programming: Proceedings of the Seventh International Conference. WARREN, David H D (ed).
"Discussion: Progress in Philosophy" in *Acting and Reflecting: The Interdisciplinary Turn in Philosophy*, SIMON, Herbert A.
"Epistemology: Formal and Empirical" in *Acting and Reflecting: The Interdisciplinary Turn in Philosophy*, SIMON, Herbert.
"Machine Models for the Growth of Knowledge: Theory Nets in Prolog" in *Imre Lakatos and Theories of Scientific Change*, SNEED, Joseph D.
Artists, Computer Programs and Performance. GODLOVITCH, A.
Computers, Personal Data, and Theories of Technology: Comparative Approaches to Privacy Protection in the 1990s. BENNETT, Colin J.
Ends and Meaning in Machine-Like Systems. ATLAN, H.
Is the Brain a Digital Computer?. SEARLE, John R.
Is there an Ethics of Computing?. BROWN, Geoffrey.
On the Impossibility of Artificial Intelligence. WEISS, Paul.
El paradigma computacional aplicado al estudio de la vida. GUTIÉRREZ, Claudio.
Parallel Governing. SCALTSAS, Theodore.
Philosophische Anstösse in der computerunterstützten Intelligenz-Forschung. HRACHOVEC, Herbert.
Why the Standard View Is Standard: People, Not Machines, Understand Patients' Problems. MILLER, Randolph A.

CONANT, J
Reply to Crewe and Conant. BRUNS, Gerald L.

CONCEIVABILITY
Could I Conceive Being a Brain in a Vat?. COLLIER, John D.

CONCEPT(S)
see also Idea(s)
Foundations of Moral and Political Philosophy. PAUL, Ellen Frankel (ed).
Models and Concepts of Ideology. RITSERT, Jürgen.
The Unity of Kant's "Critique of Pure Reason": Experience, Language, and Knowledge. WILLIAMS, T C.
The Unity of Understanding: A Study in Kantian Problems. SCHWYZER, Hubert.
"Analysis, Language, and Concepts: The Second Paradox of Analysis" in *Philosophical Perspectives, 4: Action Theory and Philosophy of Mind, 1990*, ACKERMAN, Felicia.
"Concepts, Prototypes and Information" in *Information, Semantics and Epistemology*, GRANDY, Richard E.
"Frege, Concepts and the Design of Language" in *Information, Semantics and Epistemology*, HIGGINBOTHAM, James.
"Is There a Concept of Person in Greek Philosophy?" in *Psychology (Companions to Ancient Thought: 2)*, GILL, Christopher.
Aphasia—The Worm's Eye View of a Philosophic Patient and the Medical Establishment. ALEXANDER, Edwin.
Concept Attribution in Nonhuman Animals. ALLEN, Collin and HAUSER, Marc D.
Conceptos centrales de la filosofía política en Chile democrático. COLLE, Reymond.
Concepts of Process in Social Science Explanations. VAYDA, Andrew P and MC CAY, Bonnie J and EGHENTER, Cristina.
The Conditions of the Question: What Is Philosophy?. DELEUZE, Gilles.
The Dynamics of Concepts and Non-local Interactions. VAN LOOCKE, Philip R.
Essentially Contested Concepts: The Ethics and Tactics of Argument. GARVER, Eugene.
For One Concept of Liberty. BEEHLER, Rodger.
Frege and the Analysis of Thoughts. GARAVASO, Pieranna.
Is There Higher-Order Vagueness?. SAINSBURY, Mark.
Kant in Hegels begtipsleer. DE VOS, L.
L'identité personnelle et la source des concepts. SHALOM, Albert.
La logica di Hegel come testo filosofico (II). COSTA, Filippo.
More about Thoughts. DUMMETT, Michael.
On the Eliminatibility of Ideal Linguistic Entities. WYBRANIEC-SKARDOWSKA, Urszula.
The Praxiology of Perception: Visual Orientations and Practical Action. COULTER, Jeff and PARSONS, E D.
The Significance of the Moral Concept of Virtue in St Augustine's Ethics. TORCHIA, N Joseph.
The Structure of Self-Commentary in Hegel's Dialectical Logic. GASKINS, Richard H.
The Object and the Concept: Spinoza's Theory with Regard to the Development of Modern Natural Science (in German). GOLDENBAUM, Ursula.
Value Concepts and Preconventional, Conventional and Postconventional Morality (in Dutch). VOS, H M.
Verisimilitude Based on Concept Analysis. ORLOWSKA, Ewa.
Wittgenstein and Social Science. TRIGG, Roger.

CONCEPTION
Epistemology and Skepticism: An Enquiry into the Nature of Epistemology. CHATALIAN, George.
Bogdan Suchodolski's Philosophy of Culture (in Polish). TRUCHLINSKA, Bogumila.
Consciousness and Commissurotomy: III—Toward the Improvement of Alternative Conceptions. NATSOULAS, Thomas.
Perception and Neuroscience. GILLETT, Grant R.
The Academic Lehrjahre of Novalis—A Period of Search for His Own View of History (in Polish). JAKUSZKO, Honorata.

CONCEPTUAL ANALYSIS
A Conceptual Model of Corporate Moral Development. REIDENBACH, R Eric and ROBIN, Donald P.
Functions As Selected Effects: The Conceptual Analyst's Defense. NEANDER, Karen.
The Justification of Conceptual Development Claims. HAAFTEN, Wouter Van.

CONCEPTUAL SCHEME(S)
"The Third Dogma" in *Truth and Interpretation: Perspectives on the Philosophy of Donald Davidson*, KRAUT, Robert.
Getting to the Truth Through Conceptual Revolutions. KELLY, Kevin and GLYMOUR, Clark.
Goethe and Wittgenstein. ROWE, M W.
Sociology, Selection, and Success: A Critique of David Hull's Analysis of Science and Systematics. DONOGHUE, Michael J.
Two Kinds of Conceptual-Scheme Realism. CLAYTON, Philip.

CONCEPTUALISM
The Logical Status of Modal Reductionism. MOSER, Paul K and VANDER NAT, Arnold.

CONCEPTUALIZATION
The Avant Garde, Institutional and Critical Theories of Art. SNYMAN, Johan J.
Conceptual Idealism Revisited. RESCHER, Nicholas.
General Thinking Skills: Are There Such Things?. ANDREWS, John N.
The Nature of Buddhism. KLOSTERMAIER, Klaus.

CONCERN
Personal Concern and the Extension of Consciousness. SCHECHTMAN, Marya.

CONCESSION(S)
Doubting: Contemporary Perspectives on Skepticism. ROTH, Michael D (ed).

CONCLUSION(S)
Evaluating Arguments: The Premise-Conclusion Relation. BOWLES, George.

CONCRESCENCE
Efficient Causation Within Concrescence. FORD, Lewis S.

CONCRETE
"Abstract and Concrete in Hegel's Logic" in *Essays on Hegel's Logic*, GRIER, Philip T.
"A Reply to Philip Grier's "Abstract and Concrete in Hegel's Logic"" in *Essays on Hegel's Logic*, HARRIS, Errol E.

CONCRETENESS
The Concrete and the Abstract Science: Description versus Explanation. GUPTA, Amitabha.

CONCUPISCENCE
Grace, Politics and Desire: Essays on Augustine. MEYNELL, Hugo A (ed).

CONDITION(S)
Responsibility and Criminal Liability. SISTARE, C T.
Zetetic Skepticism. UMPHREY, Stewart.
"Kierkegaardian Faith: 'The Condition' and the 'Response'. FERREIRA, M Jamie.
Statistical Explanation, Probability, and Counteracting Conditions. GRIMES, Thomas R.

CONDITIONAL PROBABILITY
Logical Forms: An Introduction to Philosophical Logic. SAINSBURY, Mark.
"Conditionals and Conditional Probabilities: Three Triviality Theorems" in *Knowledge Representation and Defeasible Reasoning*, LEBLANC, Hugues and ROEPER, Peter.
Conditional Probabilities, Conditionalization, and Dutch Books. SOBEL, Jordan Howard.
Conditionalisation and Quantum Probabilities. MILNE, Peter.
Copi's Conditional Probability Problem. SINGH, Dasarath and SINGH, Kameshwar.
A Critique of Mellor's Argument against 'Backwards' Causation. RIGGS, Peter J.

CONDITIONAL(S)
see also Implication
The Dilemma of Freedom and Foreknowledge. ZAGZEBSKI, Linda Trinkaus.

CONDITIONAL(S)

Inference and Understanding: A Philosophical and Psychological Perspective. MANKTELOW, K I.
Knowledge in Flux: Modeling the Dynamics of Epistemic States. GÄRDENFORS, Peter.
"Conditionals and Conditional Probabilities: Three Triviality Theorems" in *Knowledge Representation and Defeasible Reasoning*, LEBLANC, Hugues and ROEPER, Peter.
"The Logic of Implication". BALZER, Noel.
Classifying Conditionals II. JACKSON, Frank.
Conditional Essences. HAIGHT, Mary R.
Conditional Intention. CARTWRIGHT, J P W.
Conditionals and Monotonic Belief Revisions: the Success Postulate. ARLO COSTA, Horacio L.
Conditionals, Quantification, and Strong Mathematical Induction. COHEN, Daniel H.
The Deduction Theorem in a Strict Functional Calculus of First Order Based on Strict Implication. MARCUS, Ruth Barcan.
Even and *Even If*. LYCAN, William G.
Even, Still and Counterfactuals. BARKER, Stephen.
The Gärdenfors Impossibility Theorem in Non-Monotonic Contexts. MAKINSON, David.
Grammar, Semantics and Conditionals. DUDMAN, V H.
Historical Necessity and Conditionals. NUTE, Donald.
Indicative Conditionals Are Truth-Functional. HANSON, William H.
Jackson Classifying Conditionals. DUDMAN, V H.
Jackson on Classifying Conditionals. LOWE, E J.
Pragmatic Conditional Reasoning: Context and Content Effects on the Interpretation of Causal Assertions. HILTON, Denis J.
Probabilistic Dependence Among Conditionals. LANCE, Mark.
Ratifiability, Game Theory, and the Principle of Independence of Irrelevant Alternatives. EELLS, Ellery and HARPER, William L.
Temporal Necessity and the Conditional. CROSS, Charles B.
We Will Do It: An Analysis of Group Intentions. TUOMELA, Raimo.
What is a Law of Nature? A Humean Answer. URBACH, Peter.

CONDITIONALISM

The Tragedy of Reason: Toward a Platonic Conception of Logos. ROOCHNIK, David.
Against Conditionalization. BACCHUS, Fahiem and KYBURG JR, Henry E and THALOS, Mariam.

CONDUCT

see also Action(s)
Are Physicians a "Delinquent Community"?: Issues in Professional Competence, Conduct, and Self-Regulation. SWAZEY, Judith P.
Are Physicians a "Delinquent Community"?: Issues in Professional Competence, Conduct, Self-Regulation: Comment. LAMMERS, Stephen E.
Understanding Professional Misconduct: The Moral Responsibilities of Professionals. NORTON, Thomas W.

CONFIDENTIALITY

Ethical Practice in Clinical Medicine. ELLOS, William J.
Medical Ethics for Physicians-in-Training. KANTOR, Jay E.
Informing Clients About Limits to Confidentiality. PIZZIMENTI, Lee Ann.

CONFIRMATION

see also Verification
The Sweep of Probability. SCHLESINGER, George N.
"Fitting Your Theory to the Facts: Probably Not Such a Bad Thing After All" in *Scientific Theories*, HOWSON, Colin.
Conservatism and Tacit Confirmation. ADLER, Jonathan E.
A Green Parrot is Just as Much a Red Herring as a White Shoe: A Note on Confirmation, Background Knowledge.... FRENCH, Steven.
The Irrelevance of Bootstrapping. CHRISTENSEN, David.
Is Confirmation Differential?. ERWIN, Edward and SIEGEL, Harvey.

CONFLICT OF INTEREST

Negotation Games: Applying Game Theory to Bargaining and Arbitration. BRAMS, Steven J.
The Ethical Implications of the Straight-Commission Compensation System—An Agency Perspective. KURLAND, Nancy B.
Physicians, Entrepreneurism and the Problem of Conflict of Interest. GREEN, Ronald M.
Some Unresolved Ethical Issues in Auditing. GUNZ, Sally and MC CUTCHEON, John.
Taking Positional Conflicts of Interest Seriously. DZIENKOWSKI, John S.
Truth, Neutrality, and Conflict of Interest. LICHTENBERG, Judith.

CONFLICT(S)

Moral Dilemmas. GOWANS, Christopher W (ed).
Natural Reasons: Personality and Polity. HURLEY, S L.
"Moral Conflict and Political Consensus" in *Liberalism and the Good*, GUTMANN, Amy and THOMPSON, Dennis.
"Obligation and Performance: A Kantian Account of Moral Conflict" in *Identity, Character, and Morality: Essays in Moral Psychology*, HERMAN, Barbara.
"The Rope of Violence and the Snake of Peace" in *Celebrating Peace*, LARSON, Gerald J.
The Business Ethics of Pharmacists: Conflicts Practices and Beliefs. VITELL, Scott J and RAWWAS, Mohammed Y A and FESTERVAND, Troy A.
Fools and Heretics. BAMBROUGH, Renford.
Is There a New Teacher Unionism?. URBAN, Wayne J.
Moral Conflicts in Kantian Ethics. MC CARTY, Richard.
Personal Construct Theory as the Ground for a Rapproachment Between Psychology and Philosophy in Education. WARREN, W G.
Problemas lógicos en el relativismo ético. CAMACHO, Luis A.
Why Democracy and Rights Do Not Mix. NELSON, John O.

CONFORMITY

El concepto de "conformidad a fines" en la Crítica del Juicio Estético. PÖLTNER, Günter.
Flaw, Conformity of Critical Dialogue? (in French). BÜHLER, Pierre.

CONFRONTATION

"What If They Gave a Crisis and Nobody Came: A Hermeneutical Analysis" in *In the Interest of Peace: A Spectrum of Philosophical Views*, HIRSCHBEIN, Ron.
Un confronto sempre attuale: Leggendo—A Lambertino, Psicoanalisi e morale in Freud. DOVOLICH, Claudia.

CONFUCIANISM

New Dimensions of Confucian and Neo-Confucian Philosophy. CHENG, Chung-ying.
Philosophy in World Perspective: A Comparative Hermeneutic of the Major Theories. DILWORTH, David A.
"The Concept of *Li* in Confucian Moral Theory" in *Understanding the Chinese Mind: The Philosophical Roots*, CUA, Antonio S.
"Hsun Tzu and Chuang Tzu" in *Chinese Texts and Philosophical Contexts*, NIVISON, David S.
Chen Que versus Huang Zongxi: Confucianism Faces Modern Times in the Seventeenth Century. STRUVE, Lynn A.
Freedom and Realms of Living. CI, Jiwei.
The Liberal Teachings of the Young Liang Qichao. QI, Feng.
Mencius' Criticism of Mohism: An Analysis of *Meng Tzu* 3A:5. SHUN, Kwong-Loi.
The Relevance of Confucian Ethics. CHUNG, Bongkil.
The Self in Confucian Ethics. SHUN, Kwong-Loi.
Two Ways of Morality: Confucian and Kantian. LEE, Kwang-Sae.

CONFUCIUS

Leben als Passion: Elias Canettis "Masse und Macht" als Beitrag zum Begreifen der Moderne. DIETZSCH, Steffen.
The Relevance of Confucian Ethics. CHUNG, Bongkil.

CONGRESS

Wishful Thinking and the Budget Deficit. FRANKLIN, Daniel Paul.

CONGRUENCE(S)

Congruenza, schematismo, sintesi: Prospettive leibniziane intorno al criterio di verità secondo Giambattista Vico. PINCHARD, Bruno.
Location and Range. SCHLESINGER, George N.
Sheaves in Universal Algebra and Model Theory: Part II. IDZIAK, Pawel M.

CONJUNCTION(S)

Why is Conjunctive Simplification Invalid?. THOMPSON, Bruce R.

CONNECTION(S)

Connection Structures. BIACINO, Loredana and GERLA, Giangiacomo.
Even, Still and Counterfactuals. BARKER, Stephen.
The Metamathematics-Popperian Epistemology Connection and its Relation to the Logic of Turing's Programme. BEAUSOLEIL, Jean-Roch.

CONNECTIONISM

Meaning and Mental Representation. CUMMINS, Robert.
The Representational Theory of Mind: An Introduction. STERELNY, Kim.
"Connectionism, Eliminativism and the Future of Folk Psychology" in *Philosophical Perspectives, 4: Action Theory and Philosophy of Mind, 1990*, RAMSEY, William and STICH, Stephen and GARON, Joseph.
Causal Holism and Commonsense Psychology: A Reply to O'Brien. STICH, Stephen P.
Connectionism, Competence, and Explanation. CLARK, Andy.
Connectionism, Modularity, and Tacit Knowledge. DAVIES, Martin.
Connectionist Minds. CLARK, Andy.
Is Connectionism Commonsense?. O'BRIEN, Gerard J.
Models of Memory: Wittgenstein and Cognitive Science. STERN, David G.
Rationalism, Expertise and the Dreyfuses' Critique of AI Research. ROBINSON, William S.

CONNECTIVE(S)

Philosophical Logic. STRAWSON, P F (ed).
"Introduction to A Logic of Assertions" in *Knowledge Representation and Defeasible Reasoning*, GILES, Robin.
Common Logic of Binary Connectives Has Finite Maximality Degree (Preliminary Report). RAUTENBERG, Wolfgang.
The Completeness of Provable Realizability. MINTS, G E.
Expressive Completeness and Decidability. SCHUMM, George and SHAPIRO, Stewart.
Expressive Power and Semantic Completeness: Boolean Connectives in Modal Logic. HUMBERSTONE, I L.

CONNECTIVE(S)
The Gärdenfors Impossibility Theorem in Non-Monotonic Contexts. MAKINSON, David.
Modal Logics with *n*-ary Connectives. GHILARDI, S and MELONI, C G.
Post's Functional Completeness Theorem. PELLETIER, Francis Jeffry and MARTIN, Norman M.
Semantic Holism is Seriously False. MASSEY, Gerald J.
Verification, Falsification, and the Logic of Enquiry. MILNE, Peter.

CONNEXIVE LOGIC
Why is Conjunctive Simplification Invalid?. THOMPSON, Bruce R.

CONNOTATION
Analyse critique de quelques modèles sémiotiques de l'idéologie (deuxième partie). TREMBLAY, Robert.
Ockham, Adams and Connotation: A Critical Notice of Marilyn Adams, *William Ockham*. SPADE, Paul Vincent.

CONSCIENCE
"Conscience, Citizenship, and the Nuclear State" in *In the Interest of Peace: A Spectrum of Philosophical Views*, WOODWARD, Beverly.
"Modernization of the Law of the *Prise de Conscience*" in *Freedom in the Modern World: Jacques Maritain, Yves R Simon, Mortimer J Adler*, CALIFANO, Joseph J.
'The Appearing God' in Hegel's *Phenomenology of Spirit*. JAMROS, Daniel P.
Butler and the Authority of Conscience. O'BRIEN, Wendell.
Conscience, Sympathy and the Foundation of Morality. CI, Jiwei.
The Ethics of Suspicion. BERNASCONI, Robert.
La Fenomenología aplicada a la Educación. GENÍS, Octavi Fullat.
Le paradoxe de la conscience erronáe d'Abálard à Karl Rahner. BELMANS, Théo G.
Should Children Be Taught to Obey Their Conscience?. HUGHEN, Richard.
Sobre la génesis de la conciencia de si mismo. BEJARANO, Teresa.
Synderesis, the Spark of Conscience, in the English Renaissance. GREENE, Robert A.

CONSCIENTIOUS OBJECTION
La "objeción de conciencia". BELARMINO, Pedro.
Matters of Conscience. SIMS, Pamela F.

CONSCIOUS
Trois essais sur la pensée. THEAU, Jean.
Conscious and Unconscious States. BEN-ZEEV, Aaron.
On the Logic of Conscious Belief. TOKARZ, Marek.

CONSCIOUSNESS
The Balance of Consciousness: Eric Voegelin's Political Theory. KEULMAN, Kenneth.
Bewusstsein und Natursein. CHO, Kah Kyung.
The Cogito and Hermeneutics: The Question of the Subject in Ricoeur. JERVOLINO, Domenico.
False Consciousness. MEYERSON, Denise.
Femininity and Domination: Studies in the Phenomenology of Oppression. BARTKY, Sandra Lee.
From Sentience To Symbols. PICKERING, John (ed).
How to Build a Conscious Machine. ANGEL, Leonard.
Human Nature and Historical Knowledge: Hume, Hegel and Vico. POMPA, Leon.
Das Ich im deutschen Idealismus und das Selbst im Zen-Buddhist Fichte und Dogen. NAGASAWA, Kunihiko.
Jean-Paul Sartre. HENGELBROCK, Jürgen.
Mannheim and Hungarian Marxism. GABEL, Joseph.
The Power of Consciousness and the Force of Circumstances in Sartre's Philosophy. BUSCH, Thomas W.
Sensations: A Defense of Type Materialism. HILL, Christopher S.
The Unity of Understanding: A Study in Kantian Problems. SCHWYZER, Hubert.
"Comment on David L Miller's 'Consciousness, the Attitude of the Individual and Perspectives'" in *Creativity in George Herbert Mead*, MORRIS, Charles.
"Comment on David L Miller's 'Consciousness, the Attitude of the Individual and Perspectives'" in *Creativity in George Herbert Mead*, DUNCAN, Hugh D.
"Comment on David L Miller's 'Consciousness, the Attitude of the Individual and Perspectives'" in *Creativity in George Herbert Mead*, LEE, Harold N.
"Comment on David L Miller's 'Consciousness, the Attitude of the Individual and Perspectives'" in *Creativity in George Herbert Mead*, RECK, Andrew J.
"Comment on David L Miller's 'Consciousness, the Attitude of the Individual and Perspectives'" in *Creativity in George Herbert Mead*, BROYER, John Albin.
"Consciousness, the Attitude of the Individual and Perspectives" in *Creativity in George Herbert Mead*, MILLER, David L.
"Response to Comments on 'Consciousness, the Attitude of the Individual and Perspectives'" in *Creativity in George Herbert Mead*, MILLER, David L.
"Thirty Five Years On—Is Consciousness Still a Brain Process?" in *The Mind of Donald Davidson*, PLACE, Ullin T.
"'I Am We' Consciousness and Dialog as Organizational Ethics Method". NIELSEN, Richard P.
The 'Body': A Husserlian Phenomenological Analysis. DAS, Paritosh Kumar.
Het belang van Husserls aanzet tot een fenomenologie van de bewustzijnsperspectieven. FREDERIX, Lode.
Conciencia de catástrofe, poder y libertad. DEI, H Daniel.
Consciousness and Commissurotomy: III—Toward the Improvement of Alternative Conceptions. NATSOULAS, Thomas.
Consciousness and the Practice of Science. CONRAD, Deborah.
Consciousness—From Behavioural Neurologist's Horizon. MUKHOPADHYAY, Asok Kumar.
Consciousness: Creative and Self-Creating. BUKALA, C R.
Eric Voegelin's View of History as a Drama of Transfiguration. HUGHES, Glenn.
Etwas ist in mir da—Zu Ulrich Posthast: Philosophisches Buch. WOLF, Ursula.
Hegel and the Overcoming of the Understanding. BAUR, Michael.
Hegel's Critical Theory and Feminist Concerns. HAYIM, Gila J.
Heidegger and Psychoanalysis: The Seminars in Zollikon. SCOTT, Charles E.
The Historical Consciousness of Man. MITSCHERLING, Jeff.
How Many Selves Make Me?. WILKES, Kathleen V.
Husserl's Time Perception (in Portuguese). PEREIRA JÚNIOR, A.
Inside World-Outside World: Epistemology on the Conscious Action of the Nervous System. DE JONG, B M.
Interpretación mundanel e identidad propia. GARCÍA-GÓMEZ, Jorge.
Is Neuroscience Relevant to Philosophy?. CHURCHLAND, Patricia Smith.
James and Freud. MYERS, Gerald E.
The Locked-In Syndrome and the Behaviorist Epistemology of Other Minds. KURTHEN, Martin (and others).
Meditation on the Two Consciousnesses and on the Three Worlds of Popper (in Hungarian). RADI, Peter.
Merleau-Ponty on Taking the Attitude of the Other. MATUSTIK, Martin J.
Must Thinking Bats be Conscious?. HANNA, Patricia.
Personal Concern and the Extension of Consciousness. SCHECHTMAN, Marya.
Persons and Human Beings. GARRETT, Brian.
Philosophie et mythologie dans la dernière philosophie de Schelling. MAESSCHALCK, Marc.
Pre-existence and Personal Identity. FEENSTRA, Ronald J.
Relationship Between Consciousness and Reality (in Serbo-Croatian). CUCULOVSKI, Ljubomir.
Role Taking, Corporeal Intersubjectivity, and Self: Mead and Merleau-Ponty. BOURGEOIS, Patrick L and ROSENTHAL, Sandra B.
Die Rolle des unglücklichen Bewusstseins in Hegels *Phänomenologie des Geistes*. STEWARD, Jon.
Sartre on Pre-Reflective Consciousness. AGRAWAL, M M.
Science and Consciousness. WOJCIECHOWSKI, Jerzy A.
Sensory Qualities and 'Homunctionalism': A Review Essay of W G Lycan's *Consciousness*. KOBES, Bernard W.
Souls and Sentientism. RYDER, Richard D.
Time, Self and Consciousness: Some Conceptual Patterns in the Context of Indian Thought. BALSLEV, Anindita.
A Unique Way of Existing: Merleau-Ponty and the Subject. SIEGEL, Jerrold.
Why Shouldn't We Be Able to Solve the Mind-Body Problem?. KIRK, Robert.
World History as the Progress of Consciousness: An Interpretation of Hegel's Philosophy of History. HOULGATE, Stephen.

CONSENSUS
Wahrheit—Diskurs—Demokratie: Studien zur "Konsensustheorie der Wahrheit". SCHEIT, Herbert.
Committees and Consensus: How Many Heads Are Better Than One?. CAWS, Peter.
Consensus in Panels and Committees: Conceptual and Ethical Issues. VEATCH, Robert M and MORENO, Jonathan D.
Consensus of Expertise: The Role of Consensus of Experts in Formulating Public Policy and Estimating Facts. VEATCH, Robert M.
Consensus, Contracts, and Committees. MORENO, Jonathan D.
Correspondence, Consensus, and Coherence and the Rape of Democracy. PASK, Gordon.
The Epistemology and Ethics of Consensus: Uses and Misuses of 'Ethical' Expertise. TONG, Rosemarie.
Possibilities of Consensus: Toward Democratic Moral Discourse. JENNINGS, Bruce.
Staat als Konsens mündiger Bürger? Zur Staatsansicht deutscher Vormärzliberaler. LIEPERT, Anita.
La teoría consensual de la verdad de Jürgen Habermas. BELARDINELLI, Sergio.

CONSENT
"Rights and Remedies in a Consent Theory of Contract" in *Liability and Responsibility*, BARNETT, Randy E.
Les enjeux égalitaires du consensus rationnel: Habermas et ses sources. MARCIL-LACOSTE, Louise.
Parental Obligations and the Ethics of Surrogacy: A Causal Perspective. NELSON, James Lindemann.

CONSENT
Siting, Justice, and Conceptions of Good. ENGLISH, Mary.
Tacit Consent. CARR, Craig L.

CONSEQUENCE(S)
"Winning Against and With the Opponent" in *Logic and Ethics*, HOLOWKA, Jacek.
A Calculus for the Common Rules of.... RAUTENBERG, Wolfgan.
The Deduction Theorem for Quantum Logic—Some Negative Results. MALINOWSKI, Jacek.
Expressive Power and Semantic Completeness: Boolean Connectives in Modal Logic. HUMBERSTONE, I L.
Die Folgen vorherrschender Moralkonzeptionen. POGGE, Thomas W.
Fostering Ethical Marketing Decisions. LACZNIAK, Gene R and MURPHY, Patrick E.
Logic Without Truth. ALCHOURRÓN, Carlos E and MARTINO, Antonio A.
Meaning as Grammar plus *Consequences*. DE QUEIROZ, Ruy J G B.
On Comparison of Theories by Their Contents. WOLENSKI, Jan.
On Theories of Non-Monotonic Consequence Operations II. FIJALKOWSKA, Dorota and FIJALKOWSKI, Jan.
Q-Consequence Operation. MALINOWSKI, Grzegorz.
Semantics without Reference. GAUKER, Christopher.
Single-Axiom Systems. STEPIEN, Teodor.
Smook on Logical and Extralogical Constants. HITCHCOCK, David and GEORGE, Rolf.
A Two-Valued Logic for Reasoning about Different Types of Consequence in Kleene's Three-Valued Logic. KONIKOWSKA, Beata.

CONSEQUENTIALISM
The Realm of Rights. THOMSON, Judith Jarvis.
"Consequentialism" in *A Companion to Ethics*, PETTIT, Philip.
"Utility and the Good" in *A Companion to Ethics*, GOODIN, Robert E.
The Compatability of Consequentialism with Deontological Convictions. FORREST, Peter.
Consequentialism and Self-Defeat. MOSER, Paul K.
Consequentialism and the Unforeseeable Future. NORCROSS, Alastair.
Consequentialism: The Philosophical Dog That Does Not Bark?. HOLBROOK, Daniel.
La estructura consecuencialista del utilitarismo. GUTIÉRREZ, Gilberto.
In Defense of Human "Chauvinism": A Response to R Routley and V Routley. PASKE, Gerald H.
The Morality of Killing and Causing Suffering: Reasons for Rejecting Peter Singer's Pluralistic Consequentialism. LANDMAN, Willem A.
A Note on Hooker's "Rule Consequentialism". CARSON, Tom.
Terrorism and Argument from Analogy. WALLACE, G.

CONSERVATION
The River of the Mother of God, and Other Essays by Aldo Leopold. FLADER, Susan L (ed).
El eslabón entre la conservación y el desarrollo sostenible: Maribel Gómez Mata. JANZEN, Daniel H.
Rethinking the Commons. HERRING, Ronald J.

CONSERVATISM
Contemporary Perspectives on Masculinity: Men, Women, and Politics in Modern Society. CLATTERBAUGH, Kenneth.
The Ideas of Ayn Rand. MERRILL, Ronald E.
Television and the Crisis of Democracy. KELLNER, Douglas.
"Conservative and Radical Critiques of Nuclear Policy" in *Issues in War and Peace: Philosophical Inquiries*, LITKE, Robert.
"Der geschlossne Handelsstaat"—Zur konservativen Kritik einer aufklärerischen Utopie. MARQUARDT, Jochen.
Conservatism and Tacit Confirmation. ADLER, Jonathan E.
Edmund Burke en zijn "Reflections on the Revolution in France". DE VALK, J M M.
Natural and Political Society in the Thought of Edmund Burke (in German). TSCHURENEV, Eva-Maria.
Puzzling Through Burke. HERZOG, Don.

CONSISTENCY
"Ethics and the Limits of Consistency" in *Logic and Ethics*, BAMBROUGH, Renford.
Congress, Consistency, and Environmental Law. LEMONS, John and BROWN, Donald A and VARNER, Gary E.
Double Standards, Racial Equality and the Right Reference Class. ADLER, Jonathan E.
Ethics and the Limits of Consistency. BAMBROUGH, Renford.
Implications of Behavioral Consistency in Dynamic Choice Under Uncertainty. DARDANONI, Valentino.
Inconsistent Commitment and Commitment to Inconsistencies. KRABBE, Erik C W.
Independence of Irrelevant Alternatives in the Theory of Voting. BORDES, Georges and TIDEMAN, Nicolaus.
Propositional Consistency Proofs. BUSS, S R.
The Quarrel Theorem: First Attempt to the Logic of Lie. MAJCHER, B.
Rationality, Consistency and Truth. FRENCH, Steven.
Relative Consistency and Accessible Domains. SIEG, Wilfried.
A Study of the Foundations of Ethical Decision Making of Clinical Medical Ethicists. SELF, Donnie J and SKEEL, Joy D.

CONSTANCY
The Cosmological Constant: Einstein's Greatest Mistake?. RAY, Christopher.

CONSTANT(S)
A Remark on Individual Constants. BLUM, Alex.

CONSTANT, B
Benjamin Constant and the Post-Revolutionary Mind. FONTANA, Biancamaria.

CONSTITUTION(S)
Hegels Theorie des Gesetzes. BOGDANDY, Armin Von.
Abortion: Privacy versus Liberty. GOULD, James.
Basic Rights and Constitutional Interpretation. LYONS, David.
Le critiche a Kelsen durante la Repubblica di Weimar. ROEHRSSEN, Carlo.
The Enlightenment in American Law II: The Constitution. RECK, Andrew J.
Neutrality Between Religion and Irreligion. LINDSAY, Ronald A.
Response to Lyons' "Basic Rights and Constitutional Interpretations". LUCKHARDT, Grant.
Rights and Structure in Constitutional Theory. MILLER, Geoffrey P.

CONSTITUTIONALISM
Liberalism and American Constitutional Law. SMITH, Rogers M.

CONSTRAINT(S)
Style and Music: Theory, History, and Ideology. MEYER, Leonard B.
The "No Crossing Constraint" in Autosegmental Phonology. COLEMAN, John and LOCAL, John.
Constrained Maximization. SOBEL, Jordan Howard.
La contrainte. NEUBERG, Marc.
The Emergence of Analogy: Analogical Reasoning as a Constraint Satisfaction Process. VAN DORMAEL, Jan.
Love Canal and the Ethics of Environmental Health. BRUMMER, James.
Settled Objectives and Rational Constraints. MC CANN, Hugh J.

CONSTRUCT(S)
La sociedad sin hombres: Niklas Luhmann o la teoría como escándalo. IZUZQUIZA, Ignacio.
Learning Disabilities: A Questionable Construct. KLATT, Heinz-Joachim.

CONSTRUCTION(S)
Language and "The Feminine" in Nietzsche and Heidegger. GRAYBEAL, Jean.
Constructing Strongly Equivalent Nonisomorphic Models for Unstable Theories. HYTTINEN, Tapani and TUURI, Heikki.
Constructions by Transfinitely Many Workers. KNIGHT, Julia F.
Historical Relativism as a Manifestation of the Cognitive Activity of a Historian According to Collingwood (in Polish). ZDYBEL, Jolanta.
The Making and Molding of Child Abuse. HACKING, Ian.
A Metatheorem for Constructions by Finitely Many Workers. KNIGHT, J F.
On a Complexity-Based Way of Constructivizing the Recursive Functions. KROON, F W and BURKHARD, W A.
On Making a Coherence Theory of Truth True. SYLVAN, Richard.

CONSTRUCTIONALISM
The Participant Irrealist At Large in the Laboratory. HACKING, Ian.
A Study of Ontology. FINE, Kit.

CONSTRUCTIVISM
Critique and Construction: A Symposium on Roberto Unger's "Politics". LOVIN, Robin W (ed).
Theories of Science in Society. COZZENS, Susan E (ed).
"Programmatic Thought and the Critique of the Social Disciplines" in *Critique and Construction: A Symposium on Roberto Unger's "Politics"*, TRUBEK, David M.
"Responsibility and Future Generations: A Constructivist Model" in *Philosophy of Technology*, SMITH, Janet Farrell.
"The Scientific Roots of Constructivist Epistemologies" in *Études sur/Studies on Hélène Metzger*, LÖWY, Ilana.
"When the Owl of Minerva Takes Flight at Dawn: Radical Constructivism in Social Theory" in *Critique and Construction: A Symposium on Roberto Unger's "Politics"*, BURNS, Robert P.
Autopoesis—Subject—Reality (in German). ZIEMKE, Axel and STÖBER, Konrad.
Constructive Compact Operators on a Hilbert Space. ISHIHARA, Hajime.
Constructive Interpolation Theorems for $S2^0$ and S2. BARCA, Anne and MC ROBBIE, Michael.
Constructive Modal Logics I. WIJESEKERA, Duminda.
A Constructive Version of Sperner's Lemma and Brouwer's Fixed Point Theorem. KHALIFA, A K.
A Constructivism Based on Classical Truth. MIGLIOLI, P (and others).
Contributi piagetiani ad una scienza della mente. BORELLA, Silvia.
Do Not Despair: There is Life after Constructivism. BIJKER, Wieke.
An Omniscience Principle, the König Lemma and the Hahn-Banach Theorem. ISHIHARA, Hajime.
The Problem of Reality. JACKENDOFF, Ray.
Remarks on Special Lattices and Related Constructive Logics with Strong Negation. PAGLIANI, Piero.

CONSTRUCTIVISM
Rights as Rhetoric: Nonsense on Stilts?. O'NEILL, William.
Topos Based Semantics for Constructive Logic with Strong Negation. KLUNDER, Barbara.
Wittgenstein, eskimo's en emoties. POTT, Heleen.

CONSULTATION
Authority and the Diffusion of Moral Expertise. MC MAHON, Christopher.
The Clinical Ethicist at the Bedside. LA PUMA, John and SCHIEDERMAYER, David L.
Ethics Consultation as Moral Engagement. MORENO, Jonathan D.
Why Philosophers Should Offer Ethics Consultations. THOMASMA, David C.

CONSUMER(S)
Markets, Managers and Theory in Education. HALLIDAY, John.
Consumer Ethics: An Investigation of the Ethical Beliefs of Eldery Consumers. VITELL, Scott J and LUMPKIN, James R and RAWWAS, Mohammed Y A.
The Costs of Commercial Medicine. DOUGHERTY, Charles J.
Exploring the Structure of Ethical Attributions as a Component of the Consumer Decision Model. WHALEN, Joel and PITTS, Robert E and WONG, John K.
State Education Service or Prisoner's Dilemma: The 'Hidden Hand' as Source of Education Policy. JONATHAN, R.
A Survey of Critical Theories of "Western Marxism". YUJIN, Zhao.

CONSUMPTION
El consumo como sistema ideológico. MÁRQUEZ FERNÁNDEZ, Alvaro B.

CONTACT(S)
The Chain of Change: A Study of Aristotle's "Physics" VII. WARDY, Robert.

CONTEMPLATION
"Tragic Action and Aesthetic Contempolation" in *XIth International Congress in Aesthetics, Nottingham 1988*, BOULLART, Karel.
The Supremely Happy Life in Aristotle's *Nicomachean Ethics*. CURZER, Howard J.

CONTEMPORARY
see also Twentieth
Amythia: Crisis in the Natural History of Western Culture. RUE, Loyal D.
Il Paradigma del Sapere. LENTINI, Luigi.
"Auto-da-Fé: Consequences of Pragmatism" in *Reading Rorty*, WILLIAMS, Bernard.
"Contemporary Deontology" in *A Companion to Ethics*, DAVIS, Nancy.
"Descartes, Rorty and the Mind-Body Fiction" in *Reading Rorty*, HORNSBY, Jennifer.
"Erweitert sich der Gegenstand der Zeitgenössischen Ästhetik?" in *XIth International Congress in Aesthetics, Nottingham 1988*, SIMEONOVA, Stanka.
"Feminist Ethics: Projects, Problems, Prospects" in *Feminist Ethics*, JAGGAR, Alison M.
"Let Me Accentuate the Positive" in *Reading Rorty*, QUINE, W V.
"Mirrors and Veils, Thoughts and Things: The Epistemological Problematic" in *Reading Rorty*, YOLTON, John W.
"Normative Aesthetics and Contemporary Art: Bürger's Critique of Adorno" in *XIth International Congress in Aesthetics, Nottingham 1988*, ZUIDERVAART, Lambert.
"Redefining Philosophy as Literature: Richard Rorty's 'Defence' of Literary Culture" in *Reading Rorty*, FISCHER, Michael.
"Le Retour À La Figuration En Art Actuel: Tradition Et Innovation" in *XIth International Congress in Aesthetics, Nottingham 1988*, LANGLOIS, Monique.
"Rorty's Talk-About" in *Reading Rorty*, HOUGHTON, David.
"Veritable Reflections" in *Reading Rorty*, VISION, Gerald.
Il "parlare commune" come lume storico-naturale della "riproduzione sociale". MININNI, Giuseppe.
Failure of a Renaissance (Why It Is Impossible to Remain a Marxist in East Central Europe). VAJDA, Mihaly.
Filosofía, hoy. CUÉLLAR, Hortensia.
Marxism in the USSR Today. FISK, Milton.
Nicola Abbagnano tra esistenzialismo e neoilluminismo. QUARTA, Antonio.
Philosophy of Science and the Persistent Narratives of Modernity. ROUSE, Joseph.
Recent Work on Ethical Relativism. STEWART, Robert M and THOMAS, Lynn L.
Scepticism: the Current Debate. ODEGARD, Douglas.
A Teologia e a Filosofia perante os desafios da Cultura Contemporânea. POLICARPO, J.

CONTENT
Meaning and Mental Representation. CUMMINS, Robert.
The Philosopher's Joke. WATSON, Richard A.
Propositional Attitudes: The Role of Content in Logic, Language, and Mind. ANDERSON, C Anthony (ed).
"'Narrow' Aspects of Intentionality and the Information - Theoretic Approach to Content" in *Information, Semantics and Epistemology*, FIELD, Hartry.
"Content and Norms in a Natural World" in *Information, Semantics and Epistemology*, PEACOCKE, Christopher.
"Content, Character, and Nondescriptive Meaning" in *Themes From Kaplan*, ACKERMAN, Felicia.
"Content, Context and Explanation" in *Information, Semantics and Epistemology*, STAMPE, Dennis W.
"Externalizing Content" in *The Mind of Donald Davidson*, POTRC, Matjaz.
"Fodor's Character" in *Information, Semantics and Epistemology*, SCHIFFER, Stephen.
"Individuals in Informational and Intentional Content" in *Information, Semantics and Epistemology*, PERRY, John.
"The Intentionality All-Stars" in *Philosophical Perspectives, 4: Action Theory and Philosophy of Mind, 1990*, HAUGELAND, John.
"Narrow Content" in *Propositional Attitudes: The Role of Content in Logic, Language, and Mind*, STALNAKER, Robert.
"On a Causal Theory of Content" in *Philosophical Perspectives, 3: Philosophy of Mind and Action Theory, 1989*, BAKER, Lynne Rudder.
"Perceptual Content" in *Themes From Kaplan*, PEACOCKE, Christopher.
"Semantic Anorexia: On the Notion of 'Content' in Cognitive Science" in *Meaning and Method: Essays in Honor of Hilary Putnam*, ANTONY, Louise.
"Semantic Innocence and Psychological Understanding" in *Philosophical Perspectives, 3: Philosophy of Mind and Action Theory, 1989*, HORNSBY, Jennifer.
Demonstrative Content: A Reply to John McDowell. PEACOCKE, Christopher.
Dretske on Knowledge and Content. GJELSVIK, Olav.
Externalism Revisited: Is There Such a Thing as Narrow Content?. JACOB, Pierre.
Information, Access, or Intimate Decisions About One's Action? The Content of Privacy. INNESS, Julie.
More about Thoughts. DUMMETT, Michael.
Multiple Personality and Irrationality. GILLETT, Grant R.
Music in Hegel's *Aesthetics*: A Re-Evaluation. JOHNSON, Julian.
Narrow Content: Fodor's Folly. ADAMS, Fred and DREBUSHENKO, David and FULLER, Gary and STECKER, Robert.
Perceptual Content in the Stoics. SORABJI, Richard.
The Status of Content Revisited. BOGHOSSIAN, Paul A.
Storicità della poesia: estetica e storicismo in Francesco De Sanctis. GALASSO, Giuseppe.
Thoughts. SMITH, David Woodruff.
Transcendentalism About Content. DEVITT, Michael.

CONTENT ANALYSIS
"Empirical Content" in *Truth and Interpretation: Perspectives on the Philosophy of Donald Davidson*, DAVIDSON, Donald.

CONTEXT(S)
The Foundations of Linguistic Theory: Selected Writings of Roy Harris. LOVE, Nigel (ed).
The Metaphysics of the "Tractatus". CARRUTHERS, Peter.
"Content, Context and Explanation" in *Information, Semantics and Epistemology*, STAMPE, Dennis W.
Knowability, Actuality, and the Metaphysics of Context-Dependence. PERCIVAL, Philip.
Pragmatic Conditional Reasoning: Context and Content Effects on the Interpretation of Causal Assertions. HILTON, Denis J.
Scandinavian Extraction Phenomena Revisited: Weak and Strong Generative Capacity. MILLER, Philip H.
Systems of Interpretation and the Function of the Metaphor. CRIDER, Cathleen and CIRILLO, Leonard.

CONTEXTUALISM
The Hermetic Influence on the Rise of Modern Science. MITRA, Prabir.
Universalistische Ethik und Urteilskraft: ein aristotelischer Blick auf Kant. HÖFFE, Otfried.

CONTINENTAL
Bewusstsein und Natursein. CHO, Kah Kyung.
Echoes: After Heidegger. SALLIS, John.
The Power of Consciousness and the Force of Circumstances in Sartre's Philosophy. BUSCH, Thomas W.
Reconsidering Psychology: Perspectives from Continental Philosophy. FAULCONER, James E (ed).
Writing the Politics of Difference. SILVERMAN, Hugh J (ed).
"The Future of Continental Philosophy" in *Writing the Politics of Difference*, STAMBAUGH, Joan.
"Translating the Differences: The Futures of Continental Philosophy" in *Writing the Politics of Difference*, WOOD, David.
La Fenomenología aplicada a la Educación. GENÍS, Octavi Fullat.
Philosophy for Children and Continental Philosophy. MARTENS, Ekkehard.

CONTINGENCY(-CIES)
Cálculo y ser (Aproximación a Leibniz). MARZOA, Felipe Martínez.
Discussioni sul neo-Tomismo: Per il progresso della Filosofia Cristiana. BLANDINO, Giovanni.
Leibniz and Arnauld. SLEIGH JR, Robert C.
Vernunft und Kontingenz: Rationalität und Ethos in der Phänomenologie. ORTH, Ernst Wolfgang (ed).

CONTINGENCY(-CIES)

"Freedom and Contingency" in *Life-World and Politics: Between Modernity and Postmodernity*, CONNOLLY, William E.
"Necessidade e contingência nos primeiros escritos de Nietzsche" in *Dinâmica do Pensar: Homenagem a Oswaldo Market*, NABAIS, Nuno.
"A Reply to Gabriella Baptist's "Ways and Loci of Modality"" in *Essays on Hegel's Logic*, CHAFFIN, Deborah G.
Contingency and Modal Logic. DEUTSCH, Harry.
Contingentie als uitgangspunt: Het denken van Richard Rorty. GEERTSEMA, H G.
El evento (ereignis) como concepto fundamental de la filosofía de Heidegger (1a parte). BERCIANO V, Modesto.
El evento (Ereignis) como concepto fundamental de la filosofía de Heidegger (2a parte). BERCIANO V, Modesto.
Explaining Necessity. MASON, Richard V.
Leibniz on Creation, Contingency and Per-Se Modality. MC NAMARA, Paul.
On the Logic of Contingent Relevant Implication: Conceptual Incoherence in the Intuitive Interpretation of *R*. LANCE, Mark.
Sartre and Political Legitimacy. KNEE, Philip.

CONTINGENT

The Contingent *A Priori*: Kripke's Two Types of Examples. GEIRSSON, Heimir.
Indeterminate Identity, Contingent Identity and Abelardian Predicates. NOONAN, Harold W.

CONTINUITY

"Continuity and Discontinuity in the Definition of a Disciplinary Field: The Case of XXth Century Physics" in *Imre Lakatos and Theories of Scientific Change*, CINI, Marcello.
Charles S Peirce's Theory of Infinitesimals. LEVY, Stephen H.
Continuità e discontinuità tra Husserl e Heidegger: genesi e sviluppo d una polemica filosofica. RIZZACASA, Aurelio.
Discussione di alcune questioni di cosmologia neo-tomista. BLANDINO, Giovanni.
Motion, Causation, and the Causal Theory of Identity. EHRING, Douglas.
On Some Paradoxes of the Infinite. ALLIS, Victor and KOETSIER, Teunis.
The Ontological Status of the Principle of the Excluded Middle. STRAUSS, Daniël F M.
Personal Concern and the Extension of Consciousness. SCHECHTMAN, Marya.
Personal Identity and Reductionism. GARRETT, Brian.
Personal Identity and the Causal Continuity Requirement. ELLIOT, Robert.
Personal Identity, Reincarnation, and Resurrection. IALACCI, Michael.
Recent Work on Naturalized Epistemology. MAFFIE, James.
Sur la méthode de Ferdinand Gonseth. VUILLEMIN, Jule.

CONTINUUM

Brouwer's Intuitionism (Studies in the History and Philosophy of Mathematics, Vol 2). VAN STIGT, W P.
"Tradition as Innovation" in *XIth International Congress in Aesthetics, Nottingham 1988*, KUCZYNSKA, Alicja.
The Borel Conjecture. JUDAH, Haim and SHELAH, Saharon and WOODIN, W H.
The Continuous and the Discrete: Leibniz Versus Berkeley. ANAPOLITANOS, D A.

CONTINUUM HYPOTHESIS

A Linear Continuum of Time. DOWDEN, Bradley H.

CONTRACEPTION

Abortion as the Illicit Method of Birth Control. KEILKOPF, Charles F.

CONTRACT(S)

Liability and Responsibility. FREY, R G (ed).
Moral Dealing: Contract, Ethics, and Reason. GAUTHIER, David.
"A Bargaining Theory Approach to Default Provisions and Disclosure Rules in Contract Law" in *Liability and Responsibility*, COLEMAN, Jules L and HECKATHORN, Douglas D and MASER, Steven M.
"Beyond Foreseeability: Consequential Damages in the Law of Contract" in *Liability and Responsibility*, EPSTEIN, Richard A.
"Rights and Remedies in a Consent Theory of Contract" in *Liability and Responsibility*, BARNETT, Randy E.
A Deontological Analysis of Peer Relations in Organizations. MOBERG, Dennis J and MEYER, Michael J.
Ethics and the Defense Procurement System. LANSING, Paul and BURKARD, Kimberly.
Individualism, Absolutism, and Contract in Hobbes' Political Theory. GROVER, Robinson A.
Insider Trading Revisited. MARTIN, Deryl W and PETERSON, Jeffrey H.
On Surrogacy: Morality, Markets, and Motherhood. MOODY-ADAMS, Michele M.
Role Morality as a Complex Instance of Ordinary Morality. ANDRE, Judith.

CONTRACTARIANISM

The Limits of Government: An Essay on the Public Goods Arguments. SCHMIDTZ, David.
Rawls: "A Theory of Justice" and Its Critics. KUKATHAS, Chandran.
"Arendt and Representative Democracy" in *The Realm of Humanitas: Responses to the Writings of Hannah Arendt*, KATEB, George.
Bargaining with the Not-Yet-Born: Gauthier's Contractarian Theory of Inter-Generational Justice and Its Limitations. DE-SHALIT, A.
Hobbes on Capital Punishment. HEYD, David.
Reading Hobbes in Other Words: Contractarian, Utilitarian, Game Theorist. HARDIN, Russell.
The Superfluity of the Original Position. DEN HARTOGH, G A.
Thomas Hobbes and the Contractarian Theory of Law. GAUTHIER, David.

CONTRACTION(S)

Knowledge in Flux: Modeling the Dynamics of Epistemic States. GÄRDENFORS, Peter.
Gentzenization and Decidability of Some Contraction-Less Relevant Logics. BRADY, Ross T.
Theory Contraction through Base Contraction. FUHRMANN, André.
Two Methods of Constructing Contractions and Revisions of Knowledge Systems. ROTT, Hans.

CONTRACTUALISM

Morality—What's In It For Me?: A Historical Introduction to Ethics. NELSON, William N.
Contractualism, Moral Motivation, and Practical Reason. FREEMAN, Samuel.
Gilbert Harman's Internalist Moral Relativism. POJMAN, Louis P.

CONTRADICTION

Change, Cause and Contradiction: A Defence of the Tenseless Theory of Time. LE POIDEVIN, Robin.
Leibniz' Position der Rationalität. KAEHLER, Klaus Erich.
"The Contradictory Character of Postmodernism" in *Postmodernism—Philosophy and the Arts (Continental Philosophy III)*, KUSPIT, Donald.
Belief, Contradiction, and the Logic of Self-Deception. DA COSTA, Newton C A and FRENCH, Steven.
Could God Make a Contradiction True?. GOLDSTICK, D.
Cultural Theory Looks at Identity and Contradiction. COCKS, Joan.
Gewirth and the Pain of Contradiction. DAVIS, Michael.
Inconsistent Commitment and Commitment to Inconsistencies. KRABBE, Erik C W.
Logic, Contradiction and Quantum Theory. SMITH, Joseph Wayne.
On the Status of Proofs by Contradiction in the XVIIth Century. MANCOSU, Paolo.
Premiss Tree Proofs and Logic of Contradiction. SIKIC, Zvonimir.
Psychology and Controversy. AGASSI, Joseph.
Rationality, Consistency and Truth. FRENCH, Steven.
Time, Change and Contradiction. SMITH, Joseph Wayne.
True Contradictions. PARSONS, Terence.

CONTRARIES

Aristotelian Contraries. BOGEN, James.
On Some Logically Equivalent Propositions. KELLY, Charles J.

CONTRARIETY

Intuitive Semantics for Some Three-Valued Logics Connected with Information, Contrariety and Subcontrariety. VAKARELOV, Dimitir.

CONTRAST(S)

A Note on Van Fraassen's Explanatory Contrastiveness. PAPRZYCKA, Katarzyna.

CONTROLS

Controlling Technology: Contemporary Issues. THOMPSON, William B.
Divine Knowledge and Divine Control: A Response to Gordon and Sadowsky. BASINGER, David.
Origen y desembocadura de la acción: el sujeto inevitable. CRUZ, Manuel.
The Primacy of the Political: Towards a Theory of National Integration. RAJAN, R Sundara.
Radin on Personhood and Rent Control. GREENBERG, Dan.
Siting, Justice, and Conceptions of Good. ENGLISH, Mary.

CONVENTION(S)

Morals, Motivation and Convention: Hume's Influential Doctrines. SNARE, Francis.
"Convention and Assertion" in *The Mind of Donald Davidson*, ZILIAN, Hans Georg.
"Davidson on Convention" in *The Mind of Donald Davidson*, JUTRONIC-TIHOMIROVIC, Dunja.
"Theories as Mere Conventions" in *Scientific Theories*, KYBURG JR, Henry E.
Conventional Foundationalism and the Origins of the Norms. CUDD, Ann E.
Conventions, règles et nécessité. VOIZARD, Alain.

CONVENTIONALISM

The Positivist Science of Law. LEE, Keekok.
"On Learning from the Mistakes of Positivists" in *Logic, Methodology and Philosophy of Science, VIII*, NERLICH, Graham.
"Realism, Conventionality, and 'Realism About'" in *Meaning and Method: Essays in Honor of Hilary Putnam*, BOYD, Richard.
Conventionalism in Physics. MORRIS, W T.
Equivalent Descriptions. BEN-MENAHEM, Yemima.
Geometrical and Physical Conventionalism of Henri Poincaré in Epistemological Formulation. GIEDYMIN, Jerzy.

COSMOLOGY
Devenir et génération chez Platon. HUBERT, Bernard.
Ethik zwischen globaler Verantwortung und spekulativer Weltschematik. JOOS, Egbert.
Falsification and Disconfirmation in Cosmology. ZYCINSKI, Joseph.
Die immerwährende Schöpfung als fundamentaler Seinsvorgang. KNAPPIK, G J.
In a Crazy Time the Crazy Come Out Well: Machiavelli and the Cosmology of His Day. BASU, Sammy.
Infiniti mondi e mondo nuovo: Conquista dell'America e critica della civiltà europea in Giordano Bruno. RICCI, Saverio.
The Interplay of Nature and Man in the *Periphyseon* of Johannes Scottus Eriugena. OTTEN, Willemien.
Knowledge as Active, Aesthetic, and Hypothetical: A Pragmatic Interpretation of Whitehead's Cosmology. FRISINA, Warren G.
The Logical Structure of the First Antinomy. LOPARIC, Zeljko.
More on Russell's Hypothesis. HINDERLITER, Hilton.
La pertinence du concept d'horizon de réalité en physique théorique contemporaine. COHEN-TANNOUDJI, Gilles.
Philosophical Elements in Penrose's and Hawking's Research in Contemporary Cosmology. DREES, Wim.
Plato, the History of Science and Our Understanding of Nature (in German). GLOY, Karen.
Quantum Cosmology and the Beginning of the Universe. SMITH, Gerrit.
Taoist Visions of the Body. KOHN, Livia.

COSMOS
Cosmos and Anthropos: A Philosophical Interpretation of the Anthropic Cosmological Principle. HARRIS, Errol E.
The Intelligible World-Animal in Plato's *Timaeus*. PARRY, Richard D.

COST(S)
The Health Crisis. SZUMSKI, Bonnie (ed).
Medicine and Money: A Study of the Role of Beneficence in Health Care Cost Containment. MARSH, Frank H.
The Futures of Physicians: Agency and Autonomy Reconsidered. SALMON, J Warren and WHITE, William and FEINGLASS, Joe.

COST-BENEFIT ANALYSIS
A Case for Apathy. NEUMANN, Michael.

COTTA, S
La via della pace: in merito ad un recente libro. ZANUSO, Francesca.

COTTINGHAM, J
Descartes on Sensations and 'Animal Minds'. SENCERZ, Stefan.

COUNSELING
The Idea of Christian Charity: A Critique of Some Contemporary Conceptions. GRAHAM, Gordon.
Philosophy and a Career in Counseling. ANGELETT, William.

COUNTEREXAMPLE(S)
"Are There Counterexamples to the Closure Principle?" in *Doubting: Contemporary Perspectives on Skepticism*, VOGEL, Jonathan.
The Persistence of Counterexample: Re-examining the Debate over Leibniz Law. LANDINI, Gregory and FOSTER, Thomas.

COUNTERFACTUAL(S)
"Counterfactual Reduction" in *Imre Lakatos and Theories of Scientific Change*, RANTALA, V.
Causing, Enabling, and Counterfactual Dependence. MACKIE, Penelope.
Comments on 'Nonlocal Influences and Possible Worlds'. STAPP, Henry P.
Contrafácticos. KVART, Igal and STELLINO, Ana Isabel.
Counterfactuals and the Complexity of Causal Notions. PIZZI, Claudio.
Even, Still and Counterfactuals. BARKER, Stephen.
Induction and Modality. JOHNSON, David.
Power, Liberty, and Counterfactual Conditionals in Hobbes' Thought. POLANSKY, Ronald and TORELL, Kurt.
A Reconstruction of Jeffrey's Notion of Ratifiability in Terms of Counterfactual Beliefs. SHIN, Hyung Song.
Tu scis regem sedere. D'ORS, Angel.

COURAGE
Human Goodness: Generosity and Courage. PYBUS, Elizabeth.
Beggars and Kings: Cowardice and Courage in Shakespeare's *Richard II*. JENSEN, Pamela K.

COURT(S)
Bioethics on Trial. CAPLAN, Arthur L.
The Moral Significance of Institutional Integrity. WEAR, Stephen.

COVERING LAW(S)
Explanation and Scientific Realism. GASPER, Philip.
How Nancy Cartwright Tells the Truth. FRANKLIN, Allan.
Why Friedman's Non-Monotonic Reasoning Defies Hempel's Covering Law Model. JANSSEN, M C W and TAN, Y H.

COWARDICE
Beggars and Kings: Cowardice and Courage in Shakespeare's *Richard II*. JENSEN, Pamela K.
Weakness of Will as a Species of Executive Cowardice. SWANTON, Christine.

CRAFT(S)
Art and Craft. MOUNCE, H O.
Socrates, the Craft Analogy, and Science. GRAHAM, Daniel W.

CRAIG, E
Unfair to Nozick. BRUECKNER, Anthony.

CRAIG, W
Craig, Mackie and the *Kalam* Cosmological Argument. OPPY, Graham.

CRAIGE, J
John Craige's Mathematical Principles of Christian Theology. NASH, Richard.

CRAMER, W
Zum Wandel der Metaphysik nach ihrem Ende. BUCHHEIM, Thomas.

CRANE, T
On Crane and Mellor's Argument Against Physicalism. ROBINSON, Don.
The Reason Why: Response to Crane. PAPINEAU, David.

CRAWFORD, M
The Influence of Non-Anonymity Deriving from Feedback of Research Results on Marketing Professionals' Research Ethics. AKAAH, Ishmael P.

CREATION
Die Aufhebung der Begriffs-philosophie. KRONABEL, Christoph.
Behind the Masks of God: An Essay Toward Comparative Theology. NEVILLE, Robert Cummings.
The Immutability of God in the Theology of Hans Urs Von Balthasar. O'HANLON, G F.
"Creation and Big Bang: The Word as Space of Creation" in *Science and Religion: One World-Changing Perspectives on Reality*, VAHANIAN, G.
Adam's Place in Nature: Respect or Domination?. NASH, Roger.
The Conditions of the Question: What Is Philosophy?. DELEUZE, Gilles.
La création *ex nihilo* en question. CERBELAUD, Dominique.
Creation in a Closed Universe, *Or Have Physicists Disproved the Existence of God?*. LE POIDEVIN, Robin.
Does Faith Create Its Own Objects?. MAC KINNON, Donald M.
External Creation and Eternal Production of the World According to Bonaventura (in Dutch). VAN VELDHUIJSEN, Peter.
Die immerwährende Schöpfung als fundamentaler Seinsvorgang. KNAPPIK, G J.
L'origine première des choses. NICOLAS, Jean-Hervé.
Leibniz on Creation, Contingency and Per-Se Modality. MC NAMARA, Paul.
Ontologia e creazione in Filone Alessandrino: Dialogo con Giovanni Reale e Roberto Radice. MARTÍN, Josè Pablo.
Ramana Maharsi on the Theories of Creation in Advaita Vedānta. SHARMA, Arvind.
Reply to Davies: Creation and Existence. VALLICELLA, William F.
Het scheppende en herscheppende woord: zijn blijvende actualiteit. DENGERINK, J D.
La teología de la creación y el problema de los orígenes. PODESTA, Gustavo.
True and False Pleasures. LOVIBOND, Sabina.
Why Didn't God Create the World Sooner?. LEFTOW, Brian.

CREATIONISM
Nine Talmudic Readings. ARONOWICZ, Annette (trans).
The Creationist Theory of Abrupt Appearances: A Critique. STRAHLER, Arthur N.
Stewardship: Whose Creation Is It Anyway?. BARAD-ANDRADE, Judith.

CREATIVE
Creative Value. ODDIE, Graham.
L'emozione creatrice: Il significato della morale nella prospettiva di Bergson. PESSINA, Adriano.

CREATIVE SUBJECT(S)
What is Philosophy of Culture? (in Polish). NOWICKI, Andrzej.

CREATIVITY
Behind the Masks of God: An Essay Toward Comparative Theology. NEVILLE, Robert Cummings.
Creative Characters. YOUNG-BRUEHL, Elisabeth.
Creativity in George Herbert Mead. GUNTER, Pete A Y (ed).
New Dimensions of Confucian and Neo-Confucian Philosophy. CHENG, Chung-ying.
"Inspiration and Creativity: An Extension" in *Archetypal Process: Self and Divine in Whitehead, Jung, and Hillman*, SLUSSER, Gerald H.
"Response to Comments on 'Consciousness, the Attitude of the Individual and Perspectives'" in *Creativity in George Herbert Mead*, MILLER, David L.
Consciousness: Creative and Self-Creating. BUKALA, C R.
Creative Insecurity and "Tiptoe Experiences". HOWIE, John.
Is Creativity Good?. HALPER, Edward.
Is Friedrich Nietzsche a Precursor to the Holistic Movement?. KREBBS JR, R Stephen.
Is the Creative Process in Art a Form of Puzzle Solving?. LEDDY, Thomas.
Thinking versus Thought. KRISHNA, Daya.
Universals and Creativity. WESTPHAL, Jonathan.

CREATOR
The Metaphysics of Religious Belief. SHOOMAN, A P.
"God as Creator" in *The Philosophy in Christianity*, WARD, Keith.

CREATURE(S)
Traité de la créature. VARET, Gilbert.

CREDIBILITY
The Credibility of Extraordinary Events. SCHLESINGER, George N.

CREED(S)
Swinburne on Credal Belief. MAITZEN, Stephen.

CREEL, R
Patripassianism, Theopaschitism and the Suffering of God. SAROT, Marcel.

CREWE, J
Reply to Crewe and Conant. BRUNS, Gerald L.

CRIME(S)
Responsibility and Criminal Liability. SISTARE, C T.
Crime, Minorities, and the Social Contract. LAWSON, Bill.
War and Crime. HOLYST, Brunon.

CRIMINAL JUSTICE
Theories of Criminal Justice: A Critical Reappraisal. ELLIS, Ralph D.
"Can Responsibility Be Diminished?" in *Liability and Responsibility*, KENNY, Anthony.
"Intention and Side-Effects" in *Liability and Responsibility*, FINNIS, John.
The Birth of the Death-Machine. MEGIVERN, James J.
Discretion, Punishment, and Juvenile Justice. SCHRAG, Francis.
The Exclusion of Evidence Obtained by Constitutionally Impermissible Means in Canada. MC DONALD, David C.
Gorr on Actus Reus. MURPHY, Jeffrie G.
A Note on the Death Penalty as the Best Bet. BAYLES, Michael D.
The Orthodox Model of the Criminal Offense. HUSAK, Douglas N.
Reply to Murphy and Husak. GORR, Michael.

CRIMINAL LAWS
Intention, Agency and Criminal Liability: Philosophy of Action and the Criminal Law. DUFF, R A.
The Actus Reus Requirement: A Qualified Defense. GORR, Michael.
Deconstructing Community Self-Paternalism. SCHONSHECK, Jonathan.
Entitled to Clemency: Mercy in the Criminal Law. JOHNSON, Carla Ann Hage.
Gorr on Actus Reus. MURPHY, Jeffrie G.
The Orthodox Model of the Criminal Offense. HUSAK, Douglas N.
Reply to Murphy and Husak. GORR, Michael.
Surrogate Motherhood. PROKOPIJEVIC, Miroslav.
Using the Market to Measure Deserved Punishment. DAVIS, Michael.

CRIMINOLOGY
Theories of Criminal Justice: A Critical Reappraisal. ELLIS, Ralph D.

CRISIS(ES)
Amythia: Crisis in the Natural History of Western Culture. RUE, Loyal D.
"Understanding the Cuban Missile Crisis: A Dialectical Approach" in *Issues in War and Peace: Philosophical Inquiries*, HIRSCHBEIN, Ron.
"What If They Gave a Crisis and Nobody Came: A Hermeneutical Analysis" in *In the Interest of Peace: A Spectrum of Philosophical Views*, HIRSCHBEIN, Ron.
Ka-Meh und das alte Neue—über epistemische Krise und Emanzipation. SANDKÜHLER, Hans Jörg.

CRITERIA
Beyond Numerical and Causal Accuracy: Expanding the Set of Justificational Criteria. RAMSEY, Jeffry L.
The Justification of Conceptual Development Claims. HAAFTEN, Wouter Van.
Locke's Account of Personal Identity. SCHRECK, P A.
Recent Obituaries of Epistemology. HAACK, Susan.
Religions in the Balance. FENNER, Peter.
Response to Wilkie's "Habits of the Heart". RAITZ, Keith L.
The Right to Self-Determination. BERG, Jonathan.
Wittgenstein on Criteria and Other Minds. TEMKIN, Jack.

CRITERIOLOGY
McDowell Against Criterial Knowledge. ROBINSON, Paul.

CRITICAL
Razionalitá critica: nella filosofia moderna. LAMACCHIA, Ada (ed).
Alternativen und Irrtum in der Kritischen Philosophie Kants. LOH, Werne.
Can Genealogy Be Critical? A Somewhat Unromantic Look at Nietzsche and Foucault. VISKER, Rudi.
Critical Marxism as an Historical Process of Society and Science (in German). SANDKÜHLER, Hans Jörg.
El trilema de Aristófanes y los presupuestos normativos del diálgo crítico. MALIANDI, Ricardo.

CRITICAL LEGAL STUDIES
"Retributive Hatred: An Essay on Criminal Liability and the Emotions" in *Liability and Responsibility*, MURPHY, Jeffrie G.
Critical Legal Studies and Liberalism: Understanding the Similarities and Differences. WAGNER DE CEW, Judith.
Dworkin, Habermas, and the CLS Movement on Moral Criticism in Law. INGRAM, David.

CRITICAL PHILOSOPHY
The Critical Problem of Knowledge. BLANDINO, Giovanni (ed).
Philosophical Fragments. FIRCHOW, Peter (trans).
"The Contradictory Character of Postmodernism" in *Postmodernism—Philosophy and the Arts (Continental Philosophy III)*, KUSPIT, Donald.
Nietzsche as Colleague. SCHACHT, Richard.

CRITICAL RATIONALISM
Moral und Politik aus der Sicht des Kritischen Rationalismus. SALAMUN, Kurt (ed).
El proyecto crítico de Kant. CHAVES, Carmen.

CRITICAL REALISM
Hume's Critical Realism: A Reply to Livingston. WILSON, Fred.

CRITICAL THEORY
After the Demise of the Tradition: Rorty, Critical Theory, and the Fate of Philosophy. NIELSEN, Kai.
Between Freiburg and Frankfurt: Toward a Critical Ontology. DALLMAYR, Fred R.
Il compito della filosofia: Saggio su Windelband. OLIVA, Rossella Bonito.
Critical Theory and Philosophy. INGRAM, David.
The Critique of Power: Reflective Stages in a Critical Social Theory. HONNETH, Axel.
The Dice-Playing God: Reflections on Life in a Post-Modern Age. KRIEGLSTEIN, Werner.
Hermeneutics and Critical Theory in Ethics and Politics. KELLY, Michael (ed).
Herrschaft und Versöhnung: Einführung in das Denken Theodor W Adornos. KAGER, Reinhard.
Ideals and Illusions: On Reconstruction and Deconstruction in Contemporary Critical Theory. MC CARTHY, Thomas.
Television and the Crisis of Democracy. KELLNER, Douglas.
"Jürgen Habermas fra 'teoria critica' e 'neo-illuminismo'" in *Razionalitá critica: nella filosofia moderna*, MONTANARI, Marcello.
"Postmodernism and Critical Theory" in *XIth International Congress in Aesthetics, Nottingham 1988*, ERJAVEC, Ales.
Deconstruction or Dialectics? (in Serbo-Croation). BRUNKHORST, Hauke.
Hegel's Critical Theory and Feminist Concerns. HAYIM, Gila J.
Hegel, Marx, and the Concept of Immanent Critique. BUCHWALTER, Andrew.
Die Metaphysik der Kritik: Zum Verhältnis von Metaphysik und Erfahrung bei Max Horkheimer und Theodor W Adorno. RECKI, Birgit.
Metaphysik und Metaphysikkritik. HARTMANN, Klaus.
Peter Dews' Logics of Disintegration: Poststructuralism/Critical Theory. BUTLER, Judith.
Radical Hermeneutics, Critical Theory, and the Political. DOODY, John A.
The Search for an Ethical Sacrament: From Bonhoeffer to Critical Social Theory. FLOYD, Wayne Whitson.
Society as an "Accidental Product of Human Activities": Max Horkheimer's Social Theory and Critique. BALOG, Andreas.

CRITICAL THINKING
Critical Reasoning (Third Edition). CEDERBLOM, Jerry.
Diderot's Dream. ANDERSON, Wilda.
Logic for an Overcast Tuesday. RAFALKO, Robert J.
"Critical Thinking and Philosophy for Children: The Educational Value of Philosophy". LINDOP, Clive.
Chapter One of *Harry Stottlemeier's Discovery*: An Integrative Crucible of Critical and Creative Thinking. SASSEVILLE, Michel.
Community and Neutrality in Critical Thought. HOSTETLER, Karl.
Critical Activity and Ethics: The Problem of Generalization. KANIOWSKI, Andrzej M.
Critical Thinking and Thinking Critically: Response to Siegel. FINOCCHIARO, Maurice A.
Do Children Think Philosophically?. KITCHENER, Richard F.
Educating Intelligent Believers and Unbelievers. NODDINGS, Nel.
Must Thinking Be Critical to Be Critical Thinking? Reply to Finocchiaro. SIEGEL, Harvey.
Thinking About Thinking: What Are We to Think?. CARBONE JR, Peter F.
Thirty Great Ways to Mess Up a Critical Thinking Test. FACIONE, Peter A.
Towards a Research Agenda for Informal Logic and Critical Thinking. WEINSTEIN, Mark.

CRITICISM
see also Literary Criticism, Textual Criticism
The Anatomy of Philosophical Style. LANG, Berel.
Explaining Religion: Criticism and Theory from Bodin to Freud. PREUS, J Samuel (ed).
Nine Talmudic Readings. ARONOWICZ, Annette (trans).
The Political Philosophy of Michael Oakeshott. FRANCO, Paul.
"Anti-Art and Anti-Criticism—The Killers of Art or its Rescuers?" in *XIth International Congress in Aesthetics, Nottingham 1988*, SEPÄNMAA, Yrö.
"David Ferry's Paradise of Form" in *Abeunt Studia in Mores: A Festschrift for Helga Doblin*, WEST, Philip.
"The Profundity of Music" in *XIth International Congress in Aesthetics, Nottingham 1988*, KIVY, Peter.

CRITICISM

The Case Against Art: Wunderlich on Joyce. MAHAFFEY, Vicki.
Charles Renouvier e le scuole di morale in Francia nel XIX secolo. ROSSI, Fabio.
Commentary: "Love Canal and the Ethics of Environmental Health". FESSENDEN-RADEN, June and BROWN JR, Stuart M.
A Critique of Mellor's Argument against 'Backwards' Causation. RIGGS, Peter J.
Cuteness. MORREALL, John.
Economists and Philosophers as Critics of the Free Enterprise System. ARNOLD, N Scott.
Healthy Scepticism. FRANKLIN, James.
Interpreting Art. BLOCKER, H Gene.
The Philosopher's Prism: Foucault, Feminism, and Critique. ALADJEM, Terry K.
Political Theory and Cultural Criticism: Towards a Theory of Cultural Politics. MACDONALD, Bradley J.
Qu'est-ce que la Critique? (Critique et *Aufklärung*). FOUCAULT, M Michel.
Relevance as an Explanation of Communication. ROBERTS, Lawrence D.
The Sources of Stalinism. TSIPKO, A.
Stopping the Thought That Stops Thought: Response to John Scahill. ENGEL, David.

CRITIQUE

Mothers of In(ter)vention: Women's Writing in Philosophy of Education. LEACH, Mary S.

CROCE

Bobbio e la scienza politica in Italia. MANCARELLA, Angelo.
Croce e la storia della cultura. TESSITORE, Fulvio.
Gramsci, Croce and the Italian Political Tradition. BELLAMY, Richard.
Hegel, Croce, Gentile: On the Idea of the "Ethical State". SANTORO, Liberato and CASALE, Giuseppe.
Note ad un recente libro sull'incontro-scontro tra Croce e Gentile. ANTISERI, Dario.
Postilla. GALASSO, Giuseppe.
Venti lettere inedite di Angelo Camillo De Meis a Bertrando Spaventa. RASCAGLIA, Maria.

CRUELTY

Alterity, Identity, Image: Contributions Towards a Theoretical Perspective. CORBEY, R (ed).

CRUSIUS

Crusius: un jalón olvidado en la ruta hacia el criticismo. ROLDÁN, Concha.

CRYSTAL(S)

"Hélène Metzger et la cristallographie" in *Études sur/Studies on Hélène Metzger*, BLONDEL, Christine.

CUBAN

"Understanding the Cuban Missile Crisis: A Dialectical Approach" in *Issues in War and Peace: Philosophical Inquiries*, HIRSCHBEIN, Ron.

CULPABILITY

"Cybernetics, Culpability, and Risk" in *Philosophy of Technology*, ANDERSON, Lyle V.
Culpabilidad, rito y ritualismo: Una aproprimación psicoanaliítica. RODRIGUEZ AMENABAR, S M.
Innocents and Innocence: Moral Puzzles of Professional Status and Culpable Conduct. SNOWDEN, John R.
Why Corporations Are Not Morally Responsible for Anything They Do. VELASQUEZ, Manuel G.

CULTURAL ANTHROPOLOGY

Los universales culturales. PASSMORE, John and GARCÍA MONSIVÁIS, Blanca.

CULTURAL CRITICISM

The Ironist's Cage. ROTH, Michael S.

CULTURAL DIVERSITY

An Ethical Justification of Women's Studies, Or What's a Nice Girl Like You Doing in a Place like This?. MC GRATH, Lynette.

CULTURAL OBJECT(S)

The Philatelic Commemoration of American Education. WILLERS, Jack Conrad.

CULTURAL PLURALISM

Democratic Individuality. GILBERT, Alan.
The Bright Side of Textbook Controversies. SCAHILL, John.
Feminist Theory, Plurality of Voices and Cultural Imperialism. HERNANDEZ, Adriana.

CULTURAL RELATIVISM

To Die or Not to Die?. BERGER, Arthur S (ed).
Existen los universales culturales?. WIREDU, Kwasi and GARCÍA MONSIVÁIS, Blanca.
International Marketing Ethics. LACZNIAK, Gene R and MURPHY, Patrick E.
Textbook Controversies and Community. WATRAS, Joseph.

CULTURE(S)

About Time: Inventing the Fourth Dimension. FRIEDMAN, William J.
Acts of Meaning. BRUNER, Jerome.
Amythia: Crisis in the Natural History of Western Culture. RUE, Loyal D.
Il compito della filosofia: Saggio su Windelband. OLIVA, Rossella Bonito.
The Devil and Secular Humanism: The Children of the Enlightenment. RADEST, Howard B.
Dream and Culture: An Anthropological Study of the Western Intellectual Tradition. PARMAN, Susan.
Empiricism and Subjectivity: An Essay on Hume's Theory of Human Nature. BOUNDAS, Constantin V (trans).
The Great Goddess and the Aistian Mythical World. VYCINAS, Vincent.
La Grecia "Tedesca" fra Nostalgia e Mito. FOLLIERO-METZ, Grazia Dolores.
I, We and Body: First Joint Symposium of Philosophers from Africa and from the Netherlands. KIMMERLE, Heinz (ed).
Ibn Rushd: Averroes. URVOY, Dominique.
Idea, mente, specie: Platonismo e scienza in Johannes Marcus Marci (1595-1667). MOCCHI, Giuliana.
Kierkegaard in Golden Age Denmark. KIRMMSE, Bruce H.
Law, Culture, and Values: Essays in Honor of Gray L Dorsey. VOJCANIN, Sava Alexander (ed).
Lesbian Philosophies and Cultures. ALLEN, Jeffner (ed).
Narrative in Culture: The Uses of Storytelling in the Sciences, Philosophy, and Literature. NASH, Christopher (ed).
Nietzsche: The Body and Culture—Philosophy as a Philological Genealogy. BLONDEL, Eric.
On Durkheim's Rules of Sociological Method. GANE, Mike.
The Other Side of Language: A Philosophy of Listening. FIUMARA, Gemma Corradi.
The Political Ontology of Martin Heidegger. BOURDIEU, Pierre.
Reflexões, 3: Filosofia Política Sociologia cultura Portuguesa Temas Literários. DE MELO, Romeu.
To Be at Home: Christianity, Civil Religion, and World Community. ROUNER, Leroy S.
Der Ursprung der Erziehungsziele in der Lehre von Plato, Aristoteles und Neill. EGGER, Paul.
"Aesthetic Experience and Culture" in *XIth International Congress in Aesthetics, Nottingham 1988*, SCRUTON, Roger.
"Culture and the Word" in *Hermeneutics and the Poetic Motion, Translation Perspectives V—1990*, SCHMIDT, Dennis J and GADAMER, Hans-Georg.
"Determinants of the Culture and Personality of Institutions" in *Integrity in Health Care Institutions: Humane Environments for Teaching, Inquiry, and Healing*, HAUGHTON, James G.
"Dialogism in the Novel and Bakhtin's Theory of Culture" in *XIth International Congress in Aesthetics, Nottingham 1988*, SHEVTSOVA, Maria.
"Intellectuals between Politics and Culture" in *The Political Responsibility of Intellectuals*, SZACKI, Jerzy.
"The Philosophy of Culture in Jacques Maritain" in *From Twilight to Dawn: The Cultural Vision of Jacques Maritain*, GALLAGHER, Donald A.
"The Position of Culture within Development" in *I, We and Body: First Joint Symposium of Philosophers from Africa and from the Netherlands*, KIMMERLE, Heinz.
Are There Cultural Universals?. WIREDU, Kwasi.
Art and Aesthetics and the Crisis of Culture. MORAWSKI, Stefan.
Bogdan Suchodolski's Philosophy of Culture (in Polish). TRUCHLINSKA, Bogumila.
Il carteggio Xavier Léon: corrispondenti italiana. QUILICI, Leana and RAGGHIANTI, Renzo.
Concepts of Culture: Lonergan and the Anthropologists. KLEIN, Dennis.
Consciousness for the Twenty-First Century. CSIKSZENTMIHALYI, Mihaly.
Croce e la storia della cultura. TESSITORE, Fulvio.
A Cross-Cultural Comparison of the Ethics of Business Students. LYSONSKI, Steven and GAIDIS, William.
Cross-Cultural Philosophizing. RANLY, Ernest W.
Cultural Evolution, Biology and Language: Empirical and Rational Criteria of Selection (in German). DORSCHEL, Andreas.
Cultural Fundamentals in Philosophy. ORUKA, H Odera.
Cultural Fundamentals in Philosophy: Obstacles in Philosophical Dialogues. ORUKA, Henry Odera.
Cultural Literacy: Posing Queer Questions. GREENE, Maxine.
Cultural Theory Looks at Identity and Contradiction. COCKS, Joan.
Culture as an Open System. VAN PEURSEN, C A.
Descartes e le "culture" barocche: Appunti su alcune recenti interpretazioni. LOJACONO, Ettore.
Dialogue and Understanding (in German). FRITZSCHE, Helmut.
Il dibattito sulla verità tra Blondel e Garrigou-Lagrange. BERTOLDI, Francesco.
The Effects of Patrol Officers' Defensiveness Toward the Outside World on Their Ethical Orientations. SHERNOCK, Stan K.
An Ethnomedical Perspective of Medical Ethics. FABREGA JR, Horacio.
Existen los universales culturales?. WIREDU, Kwasi and GARCÍA MONSIVÁIS, Blanca.
Filosofia e cultura ne "Il Politecnico" de E Vittorini. DE SIENA, Santa.
Form and Funk: The Aesthetic Challenge of Popular Art. SHUSTERMAN, Richard.
Form of Life in Wittgenstein's Later Work. GARVER, Newton.

CULTURE(S)

From Immanentism to Atheism. LY, Gabriel.

A Genetic Exploration of Women's Subjugation: The Adventures of a Gadfly. MITTRA, Aditya Barna.

Giuseppe De Luca e la polemica sulla moralità di Péguy. FIORENTINO, Fernando.

Goodbye and Farewell: Siegel versus Feyerabend. NORDMANN, Alfred.

Hacia un desarrollo de la cultura y una cultura del desarrollo. ROSALES, Amán.

Hayek's Theory of Cultural Evolution: An Evaluation in the Light of Vanberg's Critique. HODGSON, Geoffrey M.

The Historical Event as a Cultural Indicator: The Case of Judaism. NEUSNER, Jacob.

History and Historical Anthropology. GOUREVITCH, Aron I.

Humor, Schooling, and Cultural Intelligence: A Response to Pritscher. O'CONNOR, Terence.

The Impact of the French Revolution on the Development of Philosophy. NETOPILIK, Jakub.

The Importance of Cultural Pedagogy. MC DERMOTT, John J.

The Ins and Outs of Mysticism. HART, Kevin.

Italian Marxism and Philosophy of Culture (in Polish). PAPULI, Giovanni.

Izydora Dambska's Philosophy of Culture (in Polish). BOBER, Ireneusz.

Law and Culture: The Conception of Legal Culture (in Polish). GRYKO, Czeslaw.

Liberalism, Aboriginal Rights, and Cultural Minorities. DANLEY, John R.

Materiali per una storia dell'epistemologia in Italia. CASTELLANA, Mario.

Max Scheler: Theory of Forms of Knowledge and Perspective of Overcoming the Crisis of European Culture (in Polish). RUBA, Marek.

Metaphysics and Culture. LADRIÈRE, Jean.

A Naturalistic Theory of Archaic Moral Order. CAMPBELL, Donald.

Natuur en cultuur: de heuristische waarde van een dichotomie. WESTERMAN, Pauline.

Nietzsche and the Cultural Resonance of the 'Death of God'. ROBERTS, Richard H.

Norberto Bobbio ideologo del neoilluminismo: Per una rilettura di "Politica e cultura". QUARANTA, Mario.

Ontology and History. BARLINGAY, S S.

Philosophical Culture in the Warsaw-Lvov School (in Polish). GLUCHOWSKI, Gerard.

Philosophy of Culture and Its Place in the Scientific Achievement of Roman Ingarden (in Polish). MAJEWSKA, Zofia.

Philosophy of Culture in the Works of Szymon Starowolski (1588-1656) (in Polish). SZYDLOWSKI, Piotr.

Plural World of Contemporary Science and Philosophy (in Serbo-Croatian). LELAS, Srdjan.

Poetry and Autonomy. SANKOWSKI, Edward.

Political Culture and Institution Building: Democratic Evolution at Work and the Case of Poland. LAMENTOWICZ, Wojtek.

Political Theory and Cultural Criticism: Towards a Theory of Cultural Politics. MACDONALD, Bradley J.

The Politics of the Rule of Law. RAZ, Joseph.

Post-Modernism as the Lesser Evil: Criticism and Agreement in Lyotard's "Widerstreit" ("Conflict") (in German). KRÜGER, Hans-Peter.

Postmodernist Elitism and Postmodern Struggles. GROSSBERG, Lawrence.

A Problem for Radical (Onto-Theos) Pluralism. BILIMORIA, Purusottama.

The Problem of Other Cultures and Other Periods in Action Explanations. MARTIN, Rex.

Prologomena to Jozef Tischner's Philosophy of Culture (in Polish). WIECZOREK, Krzysztof.

Qu'est-ce que la Critique? (Critique et *Aufklärung*). FOUCAULT, M Michel.

Rationality, Culture and Values. CHATTOPADHYAYA, D P.

Reflections on the Nature of Ideology. VAN DOAN, Tran.

Religion and Cultural Evolution. MASSIMINI, Fausto and FAVE, Antonella Delle.

Restoring Cultural History: Beyond Gombrich. PAVUR, Claude N.

Rousseau intimiste et la fusion des cultures?. GRASSI, Marie-Claire.

Selected Problems of Albert Caracciolo's Philosophy of Culture (in Polish). TECZA, Beata.

Stereotypes and Group-Claims. HARVEY, J.

Study of Society and Polity: Scientific and Philosophical. CHATTOPADHYAYA, D P.

Swedish Model or Swedish Culture?. TRAGARDH, Lars.

A Teologia e a Filosofia perante os desafios da Cultura Contemporânea. POLICARPO, J.

The Concept of Environment from the Point of View of Philosophy of Culture (in Polish). CHYMUK, Maria.

The Conception of Culture According to Jozef Chalasinski (1904-1979) (in Polish). GRYKO, Czeslaw.

The Metacultural Hypothesis and the Foundations of Cultural Activity (in Polish). PORENA, Boris.

Walt Whitman and the Culture of Democracy. KATEB, George.

What is Philosophy of Culture? (in Polish). NOWICKI, Andrzej.

Wittgenstein on Frazer's *Golden Bough*. COVEOS, Costis M.

CUPITT, D

The A/Theology of Don Cupitt: A Theological Option in Our Post-Modern Age. TARBOX JR, Everett J.

CURING

Separating Care and Cure: An Analysis of Historical and Contemporary Images of Nursing and Medicine. JECKER, Nancy S and SELF, Donnie J.

CURRICULUM

Education as a Human Right: A Theory of Curriculum and Pedagogy. VANDENBERG, Donald.

In Praise of the Cognitive Emotions. SCHEFFLER, Israel.

Markets, Managers and Theory in Education. HALLIDAY, John.

Aristotele professore?. NATALI, Carlo.

Discipline-Based Art Education: Heat and Light. SWANGER, David.

The Hidden Order of Arts Education. ROSS, Malcolm.

Increasing Applied Business Ethics Courses in Business School Curricula. SIMS, Ronald R and SIMS, Serbrenia J.

The Influence of Modernism on Art Education. MEESON, Philip.

Liberal Education in an Unfree World. LA BRECQUE, Richard.

Moral Philosophy at West Point in the Nineteenth Century. SHIVE, Kenneth D.

The On-Going Deconstruction of Marxism-Leninism. BUCHHOLZ, Arnold and SWIDERSKI, E M.

Principled Moral Reasoning: Is It a Viable Approach to Promote Ethical Integrity?. WEBER, James and GREEN, Sharon.

CURVE(S)

The Curve Fitting Problem: A Solution. TURNEY, Peter.

CUT ELIMINATION

On Subsystems of the System J_1 of Arruda and Da Costa. URBAS, Igor.

Relevance and Paraconsistency—A New Approach, Part III: Cut-Free Gentzen-Type Systems. AVRON, Arnon.

CUTENESS

Cuteness. MORREALL, John.

CYBERNETICS

"Cybernetics, Culpability, and Risk" in *Philosophy of Technology*, ANDERSON, Lyle V.

"Eigen Elements" Emerging from the Interaction of Two Knowing and Acting Subjects. VALLÉE, Robert.

El paradigma de sistemas: posibilidades para una práctica social emancipadora. RODRÍGUEZ HÖLKEMEYER, Patricia.

CYLINDRIC ALGEBRAS

Cylindric Algebras with Terms. FELDMAN, Norman.

On Generalizations of a Theorem of Vaught. BIRÓ, Balázs.

Weak Cylindric Set Algebras and Weak Subdirect Indecomposability. ANDRÉKA, H and NÉMETI, I and THOMPSON, R J.

CYRENAIC(S)

"The Objective Appearance of Pyrrhonism" in *Psychology (Companions to Ancient Thought: 2)*, EVERSON, Stephen.

CZECHOSLOVAKIAN

On the Philosophy of the Czech Avant-garde, Part II (in Czechoslovakian). STROHS, S.

Responsibility in the Tradition of Czech Thought (in Czechoslovakian). ZUMR, J.

DA COSTA, N

On the Development of Paraconsistent Logic and Da Costa's Work. LOFFREDO D'OTTAVIANO, Itala M.

DAHL, N

Reply to Dahl, Baier and Schneewind. MAC INTYRE, Alasdair.

DAHL, T

Women's Law. DUXBURY, Neil.

DAILY LIFE

"Television and the Aesthetics of Everyday Life" in *XIth International Congress in Aesthetics, Nottingham 1988*, LUKACS, Anthony.

"Paramount Reality" in Schutz and Gurwitsch. KASSAB, Elizabeth Suzanne.

DAIMON

Shattering: Toward a Politics of Daimonic Life. KRELL, David Farrell.

Socratic Reason and Socratic Revelation. MC PHERRAN, Mark L.

DALLMAYR, F

Life-World and Politics: Between Modernity and Postmodernity. WHITE, Stephen K (ed).

"Introduction" in *Life-World and Politics: Between Modernity and Postmodernity*, WHITE, Stephen K.

"Rationality between Modernity and Postmodernity" in *Life-World and Politics: Between Modernity and Postmodernity*, SCHRAG, Calvin O.

"Selected Bibliography of Fred R Dallmayr" in *Life-World and Politics: Between Modernity and Postmodernity*, WHITE, Stephen K.

Encountering Dallmayr. KIVISTO, Peter.

Philosophy and Politics: On Fred Dallmayr's "Critical Encounters". MISGELD, Dieter.

A Response to My Critics. DALLMAYR, Fred.

DALY, M
Pour une interprétation féministe de l'idée chrétienne de Dieu. DION, Michel.

DAMBSKA, I
Izydora Dambska's Philosophy of Culture (in Polish). BOBER, Ireneusz.

DANCE
"Dance is a Performing Art" in *XIth International Congress in Aesthetics, Nottingham 1988*, MC FEE, Graham.
"Postmodernism in Dance: Dance, Discourse, Democracy" in *Postmodernism—Philosophy and the Arts (Continental Philosophy III)*, LEVIN, David Michael.

DANCY, J
Scepticism: Three Recently Presented Arguments Examined. DURRANT, Michael.

DANISH
Kierkegaard in Golden Age Denmark. KIRMMSE, Bruce H.

DANTE
Aristotle in Dante's Paradise. BOURBEAU, Marguerite.

DANTO, A
Historische Objektivitat. WEBERMAN, David.
Pierre Menard's *Don Quixote*. BAILEY, George.
Why the Problem of the External World is a Pseudo-Problem: Santayana and Danto. SHIRLEY, Edward S.

DARWIN
Interpreting Evolution: Darwin and Teilhard de Chardin. BIRX, H James.
"Teleology and the Relationship Between Biology and the Physical Sciences in the Nineteenth and Twentieth Centuries" in *Some Truer Method*, BEATTY, John.
Darwin's Long and Short Arguments. SINTONEN, Matti.
The Darwinian Synthesis: A Critique of the Rosenberg/Williams Argument. VAN BALEN, G.
Engels y Darwin en el origen del hombre: Elementos para una discusión. GALLARDO, Helio.
Evolutionary Ethics and the Search for Predecessors: Kant, Hume, and All the Way Back to Aristotle?. RUSE, Michael.
Evolutionary Naturalistic Justifications of Morality: A Matter of Faith and Works. ROTTSCHAEFER, William A.
On the Possibility of Directed Mutations in Bacteria: Statistical Analyses and Reductionist Strategies. SARKAR, Sahotra.
There's More Than One Way to Recognize a Darwinian: Lyell's Darwinism. RECKER, Doren.

DARWINISM
Beyond Natural Selection. WESSON, Robert.
De l'épistémologie à la politique: La philosophie de l'histoire de Karl R Popper. RUELLAND, Jacques G.
"The Significance of Evolution" in *A Companion to Ethics*, RUSE, Michael.
The Development of Otto's Thought 1898-1917. MINNEY, Robin.
The Elusiveness of Human Nature. SMITHURST, Michael.
Peirce and Evolution: Comment on O'Hear. GOMILA, Antoni.
Sociology, Selection, and Success: A Critique of David Hull's Analysis of Science and Systematics. DONOGHUE, Michael J.
There's More Than One Way to Recognize a Darwinian: Lyell's Darwinism. RECKER, Doren.

DASEIN
The Political Ontology of Martin Heidegger. BOURDIEU, Pierre.
The Question of Ethics. SCOTT, Charles E.
Dasein and Gelassenheit in Heidegger (in Czechoslovakian). PAUZA, M.
Dasein—Mitsein—Sprache: Heideggers Auffassung über das "Wesen der Sprache" in "Sein und Zeit". TIETZ, Udo.
Getting the Subject Back into the World: Heidegger's Version. KERR, Fergus.
Heideggers Bedeutung für die Psychologie. VON USLAR, Detlev.
Heideggers Denken und die Ökologie. PADRUTT, Hanspeter.
Incarnational Anthropology. HALDANE, John.
Martin Heidegger and the Place of Language. VAN RODEN ALLEN, Robert.
Reply to Vallicella: Heidegger and Idealism. SMITH, Quentin.
Sartre's Being-for-Heidegger, Heidegger's Being-for-Sartre. MARTINOT, Steve.
Shattering: Toward a Politics of Daimonic Life. KRELL, David Farrell.
Sinn-Wahrheit-Ort: Tres etapas en el pensamiento de Heidegger. BERCIANO V, Modesto.
The Time of the Political. BIRMINGHAM, Peg.

DATA
Causality in Sociological Research. KARPINSKI, Jakub.
Categorical Grammars Determined from Linguistic Data by Unification. BUSZKOWSKI, Wojciech and PENN, Gerald.
Computers, Personal Data, and Theories of Technology: Comparative Approaches to Privacy Protection in the 1990s. BENNETT, Colin J.
Logic and Artificial Intelligence: An Exposition. DE SWART, H C M.

DATABASE(S)
Logic Programming: Proceedings of the Seventh International Conference. WARREN, David H D (ed).

DAVIDSON, D
Donald Davidson. EVNINE, Simon.
The Mind of Donald Davidson. BRANDL, Johannes (ed).
Objectivity, Relativism, and Truth: Philosophical Papers, Volume 1. RORTY, Richard.
The Philosophy of Action: An Introduction. MOYA, Carlos J.
Pragmatism: From Peirce to Davidson. MURPHY, John P.
Truth and Interpretation: Perspectives on the Philosophy of Donald Davidson. LE PORE, Ernest (ed).
"'A Nice Derangement of Epitaphs': Some Comments on Davidson and Hacking" in *Truth and Interpretation: Perspectives on the Philosophy of Donald Davidson*, DUMMETT, Michael.
"Convention and Assertion" in *The Mind of Donald Davidson*, ZILIAN, Hans Georg.
"Davidson and Social Science" in *Truth and Interpretation: Perspectives on the Philosophy of Donald Davidson*, ROOT, Michael.
"Davidson on Assertion, Convention and Belief" in *The Mind of Donald Davidson*, PICARDI, Eva.
"Davidson on Convention" in *The Mind of Donald Davidson*, JUTRONIC-TIHOMIROVIC, Dunja.
"Davidson on Explaining Intentional Actions" in *The Mind of Donald Davidson*, LANZ, Peter.
"Davidson's Semantics and Computational Understanding of Language" in *The Mind of Donald Davidson*, BOJADZIEV, Damjan.
"Externalizing Content" in *The Mind of Donald Davidson*, POTRC, Matjaz.
"How to Turn the *Tractatus* Wittgenstein into (Almost) Donald Davidson" in *Truth and Interpretation: Perspectives on the Philosophy of Donald Davidson*, SMART, J J C.
"Indeterminacy of French Interpretation: Derrida and Davidson" in *Truth and Interpretation: Perspectives on the Philosophy of Donald Davidson*, WHEELER III, Samuel C.
"Meaning, Holism and Use" in *Truth and Interpretation: Perspectives on the Philosophy of Donald Davidson*, BILGRAMI, Akeel.
"The Metaphysics of Interpretation" in *Truth and Interpretation: Perspectives on the Philosophy of Donald Davidson*, ROVANE, Carol.
"On Davidson's "Saying That"" in *Truth and Interpretation: Perspectives on the Philosophy of Donald Davidson*, BURGE, Tyler.
"Ontological Relativity in Quine and Davidson" in *The Mind of Donald Davidson*, MALPAS, J E.
"The Parody of Conversation" in *Truth and Interpretation: Perspectives on the Philosophy of Donald Davidson*, HACKING, Ian.
"Pragmatism, Davidson and Truth" in *Truth and Interpretation: Perspectives on the Philosophy of Donald Davidson*, RORTY, Richard.
"Radical Interpretation and Epistemology" in *Truth and Interpretation: Perspectives on the Philosophy of Donald Davidson*, MC GINN, Colin.
"Radical Interpretation and Global Skepticism" in *Truth and Interpretation: Perspectives on the Philosophy of Donald Davidson*, KLEIN, Peter D.
"Some Remarks on Davidson's Theory of Truth" in *The Mind of Donald Davidson*, VARGA VON KIBÉD, Matthias.
"Testing Theories of Interpretation" in *Truth and Interpretation: Perspectives on the Philosophy of Donald Davidson*, VERMAZEN, Bruce.
"Thirty Five Years On—Is Consciousness Still a Brain Process?" in *The Mind of Donald Davidson*, PLACE, Ullin T.
"Translation Theories and the Decipherment of Linear B" in *Truth and Interpretation: Perspectives on the Philosophy of Donald Davidson*, WALLACE, John.
"Understanding Our Actual Scheme" in *The Mind of Donald Davidson*, SIITONEN, Arto.
"What Davidson Should Have Said" in *Information, Semantics and Epistemology*, LE PORE, Ernest and LOEWER, Barry.
"What Davidson Should Have Said" in *The Mind of Donald Davidson*, LE PORE, Ernest and LOEWER, Barry.
"What is Present to the Mind?" in *The Mind of Donald Davidson*, DAVIDSON, Donald.
"What is Wrong with the Building Block Theory of Language?" in *The Mind of Donald Davidson*, BRANDL, Johannes.
"Wittgenstein's Notion of Secondary Meaning and Davidson's Account of Metaphor—A Comparison" in *The Mind of Donald Davidson*, SCHULTE, Joachim.
Akratic Action and the Practical Role of Better Judgment. MELE, Alfred R.
Anomalism, Supervenience, and Davidson on Content-Individuation. ROWLANDS, Mark.
Apriorisme et théorie du choix rationnel. KAUFMANN, J Nicolas.
Belief, Desire and the Praxis of Reasoning. WILLIAMS, Stephen.
Davidson and the Sceptic: The Thumbnail Version. CRAIG, Edward.
Davidson's Paratactic Analysis of Mood. MILLER, Seumas.
Davidson's Transcendental Arguments. MAKER, William.
Davidson's Troubles with Supervenience. KLAGGE, James.
Holism and Indeterminacy. MALPAS, Jeff.
The Implications of Error for Davidsonian Charity. LARSON, David.
Interpretatie en filosofische methode. BUEKENS, Filip.
Is Davidson a Volitionist In Spite of Himself?. CLEVELAND, Timothy.
Logical Constants and the Glory of Truth-Conditional Semantics. LYCAN, William G.
On Saying That Again. HAND, Michael.

DAVIDSON, D
On the Propositional Attitudes. COLEMAN, Keith.
Plato and Davidson: Parts of the Soul and Weakness of Will. PENNER, Terrence M.
Prichard, Davidson and Action. GUSTAFSON, Don.
Rorty, Davidson and Truth. BAGHRAMIAN, Maria.
Seeing Metaphor as Seeing-as. TIRRELL, Lynne.
A Short Vindication of Reichenbach's "Event-Splitting". PFEIFER, Karl.
Truths without Facts. SEN, Pranab Kumar.
La verdad. ALVAREZ GÓMEZ, Mariano.

DAVIES, B
Reply to Davies: Creation and Existence. VALLICELLA, William F.

DAVIES, S
On Davies' Institutional Definition of Art. OPPY, Graham.

DAVIS, M
Davis and the Unfair-Advantage Theory of Punishment: A Critique. SCHEID, Don E.

DAVIS, N
Killing and Letting Die—Putting the Debate in Context. CHANDLER, John.

DAVY, H
"Romanticism and the Sciences" in *Romanticism and the Sciences*, KNIGHT, David.
Davy Refuted Lavoisier Not Lakatos. ZUCKER, Arthur.

DAY, J
In Defence of "Hard" Offers: A Reply to J P Day. HÄYRY, Matti and AIRAKSINEN, Timo.

DE BEAUVOIR
"Philosophy Becomes Autobiography: The Development of the Self in the Writings of Simone de Beauvoir" in *Writing the Politics of Difference*, PILARDI, Jo-Ann.
"El segundo sexo", vigencia y proyección. COMESAÑN SANTALICES, Gloria M.

DE CHARDIN, PIERRE TEILHARD
see Teilhard

DE GEORGE, R
"Everyone's Doing It"—A Reply to Richard DeGeorge. GREEN, Ronald M.

DE GRAZIA, D
Commentary: Interests and Equal Moral Status. SQUADRITO, Kathy.

DE LUCA, G
Giuseppe De Luca e la polemica sulla moralità di Péguy. FIORENTINO, Fernando.

DE MAN, P
Jacques Derrida's Response to the Call for Ethics. CHAMPAGNE, R A.
Paul de Man, Deconstruction, and Discipleship. ALLMAN, John.

DE MEIS, A
Venti lettere inedite di Angelo Camillo De Meis a Bertrando Spaventa. RASCAGLIA, Maria.

DE PAUL, M
The Highest Moral Knowledge and Internalism: Some Comments. LEMOS, Noah.

DE SANCTIS, F
Storicità della poesia: estetica e storicismo in Francesco De Sanctis. GALASSO, Giuseppe.

DE SOUSA, R
Transcending Paradigms. REY, George.

DE SUTTON, T
La noción de ser en Tomás de Sutton. ECHAURI, Raúl.

DEAN, W
Directions in Historicism: Language, Experience, and Pragmatic Adjudication. DAVANEY, Sheila Greeve.

DEARDEN, R
Autonomy, Emotions and Desires: Some Problems Concerning R F Dearden's Account of Autonomy. STONE, Carolyn M.

DEATH
Blaise Pascals: "Pensées" (1656-1662) Systematische 'Gedanken' über. KIRSCH, Ulrich.
Convictions. HOOK, Sidney.
Echoes: After Heidegger. SALLIS, John.
Le existentia de deo e le Immortalitate del Anima: Lineas de Philosophia del Esser. BLANDINO, Giovanni.
The Last Choice: Preemptive Suicide in Advanced Age. PRADO, C G.
The Metaphysics of Religious Belief. SHOOMAN, A P.
Suicide: Right or Wrong?. DONNELLY, John (ed).
Theory and Practice in Medical Ethics. GRABER, Glenn C.
"A imortalidade do escritor—Filosofia do pensar e da morte no jovem Feuerbach" in *Dinâmica do Pensar: Homenagem a Oswaldo Market*, SERRÃO, Adriana Veríssimo.
Arguing for Rational Suicide. HUMPHRY, Derek.
Conceptos filosóficos como sustrato del sentido de la muerte, desde la época prehispánica hasta la actual. DE LOS ANGELES IMAZ LIRA, María.
Death Is One of Two Things. RUDEBUSCH, George.
Death, Honor, and Loyalty: The Bushidō Ideal. HURST III, G Cameron.
L'essere mortale dei mortali: Un'analisi sul problema della morte nel pensiero del secondo Heidegger. CICCHESE, Gennaro.
Giacomo Andrea Giacomini: un clinico padovano tra Metafisica e Scienza. FEDERSPIL, Giovanni.
Japan's Dilemma with the Definition of Death. KIMURA, Rihito.
La mort de Socrate et la vie des machines. BEAUNE, Jean-Claude.
Philosophieren als Sein zum Tode: Zur Interpretation von Platons "Phaidon". FISCHER, Norbert.
Rational Suicide and Christian Virtue. MAGUIRE, Daniel C.
Some Observations About Plato's *Phaedo*. MASCHLER, Chaninah.
Some Puzzles About the Evil of Death. FELDMAN, Fred.
Tiempo, soledad y muerte: La encrucijada del poeta. RADCHIK, Laura.
We Mortals. LINGIS, Alphonso.
When Death Is at the Door. WINSLADE, William J.

DEATH PENALTY
Theories of Criminal Justice: A Critical Reappraisal. ELLIS, Ralph D.
The Birth of the Death-Machine. MEGIVERN, James J.
Capital Punishment and Realism. COCKBURN, David.
John Stuart Mill über die Todesstrafe. WOLF, Jean-Claude.
A Note on the Death Penalty as the Best Bet. BAYLES, Michael D.
Racial Bias, the Death Penalty, and Desert. MEYERS, Christopher.

DEBATE(S)
Essentially Contested Concepts: The Ethics and Tactics of Argument. GARVER, Eugene.

DEBT(S)
Ethical Issues in Bankruptcy: A Jewish Perspective. TAMARI, Meir.

DECADENCE
On Decadence. DURAN, Jane.

DECAY
Narcissim Project and Corporate Decay: The Case of General Motors. SCHWARTZ, Howard S.

DECENTRALIZATION
The Base Camp Paradox: A Reflection on the Place of Tâtonnement in General Equilibrium Theory. DE VROEY, Michel.
Parallel Governing. SCALTSAS, Theodore.

DECEPTION
Selbsttäuschung. LÖW-BEER, Martin.
Suspicion, Deception, and Concealment. ROSEN, Stanley.

DECIDABILITY
The Complexity of Intrinsically R.E. Subsets of Existentially Decidable Models. CHISHOLM, John.
Decidable and Enumerable Predicate Logics of Provability. DZHAPARIDZE, Giorgie.
A Decidable Ehrenfeucht Theory with Exactly Two Hyperarithmetic Models. REED, R C.
Decidable Fragments of Field Theories. TUNG, Shih-Ping.
Expressive Completeness and Decidability. SCHUMM, George and SHAPIRO, Stewart.
Gentzenization and Decidability of Some Contraction-Less Relevant Logics. BRADY, Ross T.
The Method of Axiomatic Rejection for the Intuitionistic Propositional Logic. DUTKIEWICZ, Rafal.

DECIDING
Deciding to Act. FIELDS, L.

DECISION ELEMENT(S)
"War, Omnicide, and Sanity: The Lesson of the Cuban Missile Crisis" in *Issues in War and Peace: Philosophical Inquiries*, SOMERVILLE, John.

DECISION PROCEDURE(S)
Baffling Phenomena: And Other Studies in the Philosophy of Knowledge and Valuation. RESCHER, Nicholas.
Do the Right Thing: Studies in Limited Rationality. RUSSELL, Stuart.
Experimental Studies of Interactive Decisions. RAPOPORT, Amnon.
"The Implications of Determinism" in *A Companion to Ethics*, YOUNG, Robert.
Business Ethics and Stakeholder Analysis. GOODPASTER, Kenneth E.
Commensurability as a Prerequisite of Rational Choice: An Examination of Sidgwick's Position. RICHARDSON, Henry S.
Exploring the Structure of Ethical Attributions as a Component of the Consumer Decision Model. WHALEN, Joel and PITTS, Robert E and WONG, John K.
The Ideal of Shared Decision Making Between Physicians and Patients. BROCK, Dan W.
An Integrative Model of Clinical-Ethical Decision Making. GRUNDSTEIN-AMADO, Rivka.
Negotiating Criteria and Setting Limits: The Case of AIDS. CUTTER, Mary Ann Gardell.
Organizational Value Contention and Managerial Mindsets. LIEDTKA, Jeanne.

DECISION PROCEDURE(S)

The Outranking Approach and the Foundations of Electre Methods. ROY, Bernard.
Problem Solving, Decision Making and Reflective Thinking. MERKLE, Patricia.
Utilitarianism and the Idea of Reflective Equilibrium. TERSMAN, Folke.
Weitere verschärfungen zu den Reduktionstypen.... DEUTSCH, Michael.

DECISION THEORY

The Dynamics of Rational Deliberation. SKYRMS, Brian.
Experimental Studies of Interactive Decisions. RAPOPORT, Amnon.
Probabilistic Causality. EELLS, Ellery.
Rationality in Action: Contemporary Approaches. MOSER, Paul K (ed).
"Decisions Without Ordering" in *Acting and Reflecting: The Interdisciplinary Turn in Philosophy*, SEIDENFELD, Teddy and SCHERVISH, M J.
"Defeasible Specification of Utilities" in *Knowledge Representation and Defeasible Reasoning*, LOUI, Ronald.
"The Value of Knowledge" in *Scientific Theories*, SKYRMS, Brian.
Eine Bemerkung zu spektralen Darstellungen von ρ-stelligen Aufzählbaren. DEUTSCH, Michael.
Co-ordination, Salience and Rationality. MILLER, Seumas.
A Comparative Study of Multiattribute Decision Making Methodologies. KARNI, Reuven and SANCHEZ, Pedro and TUMMALA, V M Rao.
Constrained Maximization. SOBEL, Jordan Howard.
Critical Interaction: Judgment, Decision, and the Social Testing of Moral Hypotheses. IANNONE, A P.
A Decision-Theoretic Reconstruction of *Roe v Wade*. LOCKHART, Ted.
Explaining Science. KORB, Kevin B.
Game Theory is Not a Useful Tool for the Political Scientist. BUNGE, Mario.
The Geometry of Legal Principles. CHUAQUI, Rolando and MALITZ, Jerome.
Independence of Irrelevant Alternatives in the Theory of Voting. BORDES, Georges and TIDEMAN, Nicolaus.
The Logic of Rational Play in Games of Perfect Information. BONANNO, Giacomo.
Mathematical Statistics and Metastatistical Analysis. RIVADULLA, Andrés.
McClennen's Early Cooperative Solution to the Prisoner's Dilemma. MAC INTOSH, Duncan.
The Mutual Investment Game: Peculiarities of Indifference. CUBITT, Robin P and HOLLIS, Martin.
Non-Dominance, Third Person and Non-Action Newcomb Problems, and Metatickles. SOBEL, Jordan Howard.
On the Descriptive Adequacy of Levi's Decision Theory. MAHER, Patrick and KASHIMA, Yoshihisa.
Ordering Pairwise Comparison Structures. DELVER, R and MONSUUR, H and STORCKEN, A J A.
The Outranking Approach and the Foundations of Electre Methods. ROY, Bernard.
The Pareto Rule and Strategic Voting. MAC INTYRE, Ian.
Predictors of Ethical Decisions Regarding Insider Trading. TERPSTRA, David E and REYES, Mario G C and BOKOR, Donald W.
The Ranking of Preference. RAWLING, Piers.
A Reconstruction of Jeffrey's Notion of Ratifiability in Terms of Counterfactual Beliefs. SHIN, Hyung Song.
Reply to Maher and Kashima: "On the Descriptive Adequacy of Levi's Decision Theory". LEVI, Isaac.
Some Versions of Newcomb's Problem Are Prisoners' Dilemmas. SOBEL, Jordan Howard.
Symptomatic Acts and the Value of Evidence in Causal Decision Theory. MAHER, Patrick.
Teoría general de las decisiones. DE LA SIENRA, Adolfo García.
The Value of Perfect Information in Non-linear Utility Theory. SCHLEE, Edward E.

DECISION(S)

Deciding for Others: The Ethics of Surrogate Decision Making. BUCHANAN, Allen E.
"Moral Balance: A Model of How People Arrive at Moral Decisions" in *The Moral Domain: Essays in the Ongoing Discussion between Philosophy and the Social Sciences*, NISAN, Mordecai.
"Two Perspectives on Consensus for (Bayesian) Inference and Decisions" in *Knowledge Representation and Defeasible Reasoning*, SEIDENFELD, Teddy.
"Eigen Elements" Emerging from the Interaction of Two Knowing and Acting Subjects. VALLÉE, Robert.
The Clinical Ethicist at the Bedside. LA PUMA, John and SCHIEDERMAYER, David L.
Clinical Judgment and Bioethics: The Decision Making Link. WRIGHT, Richard A.
Commentary—"Make Me Live": Autonomy and Terminal Illness. MILLER, David H.
Committees and Consensus: How Many Heads Are Better Than One?. CAWS, Peter.
Decisionmaking Competence and Risk—Comments on Wicclair. BROCK, Dan W.
Ethical Decision Making in the Medical Profession: An Application of the Theory of Planned Behavior. RANDALL, Donna M and GIBSON, Annetta M.
The Ethical Decision-Making Processes of Information Systems Workers. PARADICE, David B and DEJOIE, Roy M.
Ethical Myopia: The Case of "Framing" by Framing. SINGER, Alan E and LYSONSKI, Steven and SINGER, Ming and HAYES, David.
The Ethical Significance of Corporate Law. NESTERUK, Jeffrey.
Ethics Consultation as Moral Engagement. MORENO, Jonathan D.
Goodwill, Going Concern, Stocks and Flows: A Prescription for Moral Analysis. SWANDA JR, John R.
On Some Multiattribute Value Function Generalizations of the EQQ Model in the Context of Personal Inventory Decisions. TROUTT, Marvin D.
Patient Decision-Making Capacity and Risk. WICCLAIR, Mark R.
A Response to Brock and Skene. WICCLAIR, Mark R.
A Study of the Foundations of Ethical Decision Making of Clinical Medical Ethicists. SELF, Donnie J and SKEEL, Joy D.
Uncertainty and the Shaping of Medical Decisions. BERESFORD, Eric B.

DECLARATION OF INDEPENDENCE

The Enlightenment in American Law I: The Declaration of Independence. RECK, Andrew J.

DECLINE

Ethics in Declining Organizations. LEMKE, Dwight K and SCHMINKE, Marshall.

DECOMPOSITION

"A Dilworth Decomposition Theorem" in *Logic, Methodology and Philosophy of Science, VIII*, FOREMAN, Matthew.
The t-Variable Method in Gentzen-Style Automatic Theorem Proving. EDWALD, Tryggvi.

DECONSTRUCTION

Being and Becoming: A Critique of Post-Modernism. CENTORE, F F.
The Metaphysics of the "Tractatus". CARRUTHERS, Peter.
Nietzsche and the Question of Interpretation. SCHRIFT, Alan D.
Re-Reading Levinas. BERNASCONI, Robert (ed).
Swimming Against the Current in Contemporary Philosophy: Occasional Essays and Papers. VEATCH, Henry B.
Who Comes after the Subject?. CADAVA, Eduardo (ed).
"At This Very Moment in This Work Here I Am" in *Re-Reading Levinas*, DERRIDA, Jacques and BEREZDIVIN, Ruben.
"Deconstructing the Book of Job" in *The Bible as Rhetoric: Studies in Biblical Persuasion and Credibility*, CLINES, David.
"Freud, Husserl, Derrida: An Experiement" in *Phenomenology of the Truth Proper to Religion*, LOWE, Walter.
"Human Nature and Unnatural Humanisms" in *From Twilight to Dawn: The Cultural Vision of Jacques Maritain*, ROYAL, Robert.
"Nietzsche Medused" in *Looking After Nietzsche*, PAUTRAT, Bernard.
"Psychology after Philosophy" in *Reconsidering Psychology: Perspectives from Continental Philosophy*, POLKINGHORNE, Donald.
"Wholly Otherwise" in *Re-Reading Levinas*, CRITCHLEY, Simon (trans) and LEVINAS, Emmanuel.
Another Look at the Derrida-Searle Debate. ALFINO, Mark.
Aquinas and the Deconstruction of History. KELLY, Eugene.
Beyond the "Limits" of *Mundane Reason*. BOGEN, David.
But Suppose We Were to Take the Rectorial Address Seriously...Gérard Granel's *De l'université*. FYNSK, Christopher.
A Critique of Derrida's Hegel Deconstruction: Speech, Phonetic Writing, and Hieroglyphic Script in Logic, Law, Art. CUTROFELLO, Andrew.
De la matérialité du discours saisi dans l'institution. KREMER-MARIETTI, Angèle.
The De-Con-Struction of Reason. GLYNN, Simon.
Deconstructing Lonergan. MC KINNEY, Ronald H.
Deconstructing/Deconstructive Inquiry: The Politics of Knowing and Being Known. LATHER, Patti.
Deconstruction as Symbolic Play: Simmel/Derrida. WEINSTEIN, Deena and WEINSTEIN, Michael A.
Deconstruction or Dialectics? (in Serbo-Croation). BRUNKHORST, Hauke.
Derrida's huishouding. BERNS, Egidius.
Derrida's Other Conversation. DAVIES, Paul.
Derrida, Deconstruction and Nietzsche: The Tree of Knowledge and the Tree of Life. ZELECHOW, Bernard.
The Disorder of Things. MAJOR-POETZL, Pamela.
An Entropic Analysis of Postmodernism. MC KINNEY, Ronald H.
Les gisants et les pleureuses: Pour un tombeau de Michel Foucault. AUZIAS, Jean-Marie.
Hindu Doubts About God: Towards a Mīmāmsā Deconstruction. BILIMORIA, Purusottama.
Horace's *Ars Poetica* and the Deconstructive Leech. HABIB, M A R.
Jacques Derrida's Response to the Call for Ethics. CHAMPAGNE, R A.
Kant the Liberal, Kant the Anarchist: Rawls and Lyotard on Kantian Justice. MAY, Todd G.
Language and Political Agency: Derrida, Marx, and Bakhtin. EVANS, Fred.
Language, Physics, and Geology (and a Few Words on Theology). BROGAN, Jacqueline Vaught.

DECONSTRUCTION
A Little Daylight: A Reading of Derrida's "White Mythology". LAWLOR, Leonard.
Paul de Man, Deconstruction, and Discipleship. ALLMAN, John.
Politics and the Limits of Metaphysics: Heidegger, Ferry and Renaut, and Lyotard. FÓTI, Véronique M.
Le pouvoir de la différence. DELIVOYATSIS, Socratis.
Las reglas del juego: consideraciones críticas sobre "Radical Hermeneutics" de John Caputo. PEÑA, Lorenzo.
Reply to Marsh's "Reply to McKinney on Lonergan". MC KINNEY, Ronald H.
Response: "The Rooting and Uprooting of Reason: On *Spacings* by John Sallis". SALLIS, John.
The Rooting and Uprooting of Reason: On *Spacings* by John Sallis. MALY, Kenneth.
Sankara and Derrida on Philosophy of Language. COWARD, Harold.
The Early and Later Deconstruction in Derrida's Writings (in Hebrew). LANDAU, Iddo.
Two Reversibilities: Merleau-Ponty and Derrida. YOUNT, Mark.
The Worldly Self in Schutz: On Sighting, Citing, and Siting the Self. LANGSDORF, Lenore.

DECONSTRUCTIONISM
Ideals and Illusions: On Reconstruction and Deconstruction in Contemporary Critical Theory. MC CARTHY, Thomas.
A Dionysian Songbook: the Mysterious Singing. LEVINE, Elliott M.
Historiography and Postmodernism: Reconsiderations. ZAGORIN, Perez.
Is There a "Meaning" of Being? Against the Deconstructionist Reading of Heidegger. SCHALOW, Frank.
The Moral Ontology of Charles Taylor: Contra Deconstructivism. HOY, Terry.
Ms en abyme: Deconstruction and Feminism. ELAM, Diane.
Nietzsche in Derrida's *Spurs*: Deconstruction as Deracination. FREYDBERG, Bernard D.
On the Concept of Freedom in the *I Ching*: A Deconstructionist View of Self-Cultivation. SCHULZ, Larry J and CUNNINGHAM, Thomas J.

DEDEKIND
Eudoxos and Dedekind: On the Ancient Greek Theory of Ratios and its Relation to Modern Mathematics. STEIN, Howard.

DEDUCIBILITY
Gettier's Principle for Deducibility of Justification. BASU, Sandhya.

DEDUCTION
"Deductive Heuristics" in *Imre Lakatos and Theories of Scientific Change*, MUSGRAVE, Alan.
"The Deductive Model in Ethics" in *Logic and Ethics*, LAZARI-PAWLOWSKA, Ija.
The Agnostic Fallacy. KEENE, G B.
Causality Assessment in Epidemiology. VINEIS, Paolo.
Classification of Intermediate Predicate Logics Under the Type of Deductive Completeness. TAKANO, Mitio and YAMAKAMI, Tomoyuki.
Concerning F L Will's *Beyond Deduction*. SINGER, Marcus G.
Knowledge and Deductive Closure. WHITE, James L.
Predication and Deduction in Aristotle: Aspirations to Completeness. SMITH, Robin.
Two-Steps-in-One-Proof: The Structure of the Transcendental Deduction of the Categories. EVANS, J Claude.
Understanding Induction. MACNAMARA, John.

DEDUCTION THEOREM
The Deduction Theorem for Quantum Logic—Some Negative Results. MALINOWSKI, Jacek.

DEDUCTIVE-NOMOLOGICAL MODEL
Contrastive Explanations. LIPTON, Peter.
Explanation. REDHEAD, Michael.
How to Put Questions to Nature. SINTONEN, Matti.
The Limits of Explanation. SWINBURNE, Richard.

DEFEASIBILITY
Knowledge Representation and Defeasible Reasoning. KYBURG JR, Henry E (ed).
"Defeasible Logic and The Frame Problem" in *Knowledge Representation and Defeasible Reasoning*, NUTE, Donald.
"Defeasible Specification of Utilities" in *Knowledge Representation and Defeasible Reasoning*, LOUI, Ronald.
"A Framework for Reasoning with Defaults" in *Knowledge Representation and Defeasible Reasoning*, GEFFNER, Hector and PEARL, Judea.

DEFECT(S)
Arguments for Abortion of Abnormal Fetuses and the Moral Status of the Developing Embryo. SUTTON, Agneta.

DEFENSE
"Catastrophic Possibilities of Space-Based Defense" in *Philosophy of Technology*, BELLA, David.
"Common Security through Alternative Defense" in *In the Interest of Peace: A Spectrum of Philosophical Views*, HAMPSCH, George.
"Legitimate Defense and Strategic Defense" in *Issues in War and Peace: Philosophical Inquiries*, STERBA, James P.
"The Man in the Teflon Suit: A Flaw in the Argument for Strategic Defense" in *Issues in War and Peace: Philosophical Inquiries*, HOEKEMA, David.
Private Defense. GORR, Michael.
Self-Defence and National Defence. DE ROOSE, Frank.

DEFINABILITY
Boundedness Theorems for Dilators and Ptykes. KECHRIS, Alexander S.
Definability in Self-Referential Systems. SOBRINHO, J Zimbarg.
Definability Theorems in Normal Extensions of the Provability Logic. MAKSIMOVA, Larisa L.
λ-Definability on Free Algebras. ZAIONC, Marek.
The Monadic Second-Order Logic of Graphs IV: Definability Properties of Equational Graphs. COURCELLE, Bruno.
Notes on Modal Definability. VAN BENTHEM, Johan.
On Type Definable Subgroups of a Stable Group. NEWELSKI, Ludomir.

DEFINITE DESCRIPTIONS
Philosophical Essays. CARTWRIGHT, Richard.
"Definite Descriptions and the Ontological Argument" in *Philosophical Applications of Free Logic*, MANN, William E.
"A Theory of Definite Descriptions" in *Philosophical Applications of Free Logic*, LAMBERT, Karel.
Definite Descriptions and Definite Generics. OJEDA, Almerindo E.
Definite Descriptions. DANIELS, Charles B.
Intensional Identities. SLATER, B H.
On Rigidity and Persistence. WILLIAMSON, Timothy.
Russell on Ordinary Names and Synonymy. PINEAU, Lois.
Russell's Theory of Definite Descriptions. LAMBERT, Karel.

DEFINITENESS
Wanted Dead or Alive: Two Attempts to Solve Schrödinger's Paradox. ALBERT, David and LOEWER, Barry.

DEFINITION(S)
African Philosophy: The Essential Readings. SEREQUEBERHAN, Tsenay.
Aristotelian Logic and the Arabic Language in Alfarabi. ABED, Shukri B.
Civil Disobedience in Focus. BEDAU, Hugo Adam (ed).
The Elements of Reasoning. CONWAY, David.
Lesbian Philosophies and Cultures. ALLEN, Jeffner (ed).
Talking Philosophy: A Wordbook. SPARKES, A W.
"Definition and Death" in *Biomedical Ethics Reviews, 1989*, O'NEIL, Rick.
"Definition, Essence, and Understanding in Spinoza" in *Central Themes in Early Modern Philosophy*, PARKINSON, G H R.
"On Understanding Chinese Philosophy: An Inquiry and a Proposal" in *Understanding the Chinese Mind: The Philosophical Roots*, SZE-KWANG, Lao.
Against the Fantasts. THOMAS, J L H.
Ambiguity, Generality, and Indeterminacy: Tests and Definitions. GILLON, Brendan S.
The Community of Inquiry and the Development of Self-Esteem. LAGO, Juan Carlos.
Death and the Beginning of Life. IGLESIAS, Teresa.
The Definition of 'Art'. ROWE, M W.
La definizione di "retta" data da Euclide e le geometrie non-euclidee. BLANDINO, Giovanni.
The Emergence and Original Meaning of the Name 'Metaphysics'. REINER, Hans and ADLER, Pierre and PASKIN, David.
Formalization of Functionally Complete Propositional Calculus with the Functor of Implication.... LEJEWSKI, Czeslaw.
Glosses on Heidegger's Architectonic Word-Play. PRUFER, Thomas.
Information, Access, or Intimate Decisions About One's Action? The Content of Privacy. INNESS, Julie.
Japan's Dilemma with the Definition of Death. KIMURA, Rihito.
On Primoratz's Definition of Terrorism. SINNOTT-ARMSTRONG, Walter.
On the Nature of Rape. BOGART, J H.
Plato and Aristotle on Division and Definition. DESLAURIERS, Marguerite.
Propositional Relevance. BOWLES, George.
Reply to Gordon: Discourse at Work. CHMIELEWSKI, Philip J.
Le rôle des causes comme instruments de la définition. VALOIS, Raynald.
Some More Ideas About the Relation Between Philosophy for Children and Self-Esteem. GAZZARD, Ann.
Tendencias actuales en filosofía de la tecnología. CAMACHO, Luis.
Vacuous Truth. ALMEDER, Robert F.
What Are *Civil* Rights?. WEINREB, Lloyd L.
Why are Definitions True?. SKIDMORE, Arthur.

DEGENAAR, J
Legitimate Anachronism as a Problem for Intellectual History and for Philosophy. DU TOIT, André.
Reason and Imagination (in Dutch). VAN PEURSEN, C A.

DEGREE(S)
A 1-Generic Degree Which Bounds a Minimal Degree. KUMABE, Masahiro.
Common Logic of Binary Connectives Has Finite Maximality Degree (Preliminary Report). RAUTENBERG, Wolfgang.
The Degree of a Σ_n Cut. CHONG, C T and MOURAD, K J.
Degrees of Orderings Not Isomorphic to Recursive Linear Orderings. JOCKUSCH JR, Carl G and SOARE, Robert I.

DEGREE(S)

The Density of Infima in the Recursively Enumerable Degrees. SLAMAN, Theodore A.
First-Order Logics for Comparative Similarity. WILLIAMSON, Timothy.
Lattice Nonembeddings and Initial Segments of the Recursively Enumerable Degrees. DOWNEY, Rod.
Logics Preserving Degrees of Truth. NOWAK, Marek.
Minimal Degrees Recursive in 1-Generic Degrees. CHONG, C T and DOWNEY, R G.
Non-Bounding Construction. SHOENFIELD, J R.
On Restricted Forms of Enumeration Reducibility. WATSON, Phil.
Some Results on Bounded Truth-Table Degrees. DITCHEV, Angel V.
Weakly Semirecursive Sets. JOCKUSCH JR, Carl G and OWINGS JR, James C.

DEISM

Escape from God. TURNER, Dean.
Explaining Religion: Criticism and Theory from Bodin to Freud. PREUS, J Samuel (ed).
"The Newtonians and Deism" in *Essays on the Context, Nature, and Influence of Isaac Newton's Theology*, FORCE, James E.
"Polytheism, Deism, and Newton" in *Essays on the Context, Nature, and Influence of Isaac Newton's Theology*, POPKIN, Richard H.

DEL VECCHIO, G

A propósito del filósofo del derecho Giorgio del Vecchio. DI PIETRO, Alfredo.

DELEUZE, G

Patterns of Dissonance. BRAIDOTTI, Rosi.
Deleuze und Spinozas "Ethik". OITTINEN, Vesa.

DELIBERATION

The Dynamics of Rational Deliberation. SKYRMS, Brian.
Ethical Deliberations as Dramatic Rehearsal. CASPARY, William R.
The Scope of Deliberation: A Conflict in Aquinas. IRWIN, T H.

DELL'UTRI, M

Brains in a Vat, Language and Metalanguage. CASATI, Roberto and DOKIC, Jérome.

DELMINIO, G

"Il teatro della memoria di Giulio Camillo Delminio: un tentativo di riorganizzare il sapere nel Cinquecento" in *Razionalitá critica: nella filosofia moderna*, NARDELLI, Domenica.

DEMARCATION

Il Paradigma del Sapere. LENTINI, Luigi.
Compromiso Ontico y Teorías Científicas. MAYORGA, Alejandro and VARGAS, Celso.
Popper's Demarcation of Science Refuted. AGASSI, Joseph.

DEMENTIA

Nutrition, Hydration, and the Demented Elderly. POST, Stephen G.

DEMIURGE

The Intelligible World-Animal in Plato's *Timaeus*. PARRY, Richard D.

DEMOCRACY

Democratic Individuality. GILBERT, Alan.
The Devil and Secular Humanism: The Children of the Enlightenment. RADEST, Howard B.
John Dewey: Religious Faith and Democratic Humanism. ROCKEFELLER, Steven C.
Law, Culture, and Values: Essays in Honor of Gray L Dorsey. VOJCANIN, Sava Alexander (ed).
The Meaning of Socialism. LUNTLEY, Michael.
Die moderne Gesellschaft im Rechtsstaat. BAURMANN, Michael.
Moral und Politik aus der Sicht des Kritischen Rationalismus. SALAMUN, Kurt (ed).
New Reflections on the Revolution of Our Time. LACLAU, Ernesto.
Objectivity, Relativism, and Truth: Philosophical Papers, Volume 1. RORTY, Richard.
Political Theory in the Welfare State. LUHMANN, Niklas.
Television and the Crisis of Democracy. KELLNER, Douglas.
Wahrheit—Diskurs—Demokratie: Studien zur "Konsensustheorie der Wahrheit". SCHEIT, Herbert.
Writing the Politics of Difference. SILVERMAN, Hugh J (ed).
"Approaches to Democratic Equality: Maritain, Simon, and Kolnai" in *Freedom in the Modern World: Jacques Maritain, Yves R Simon, Mortimer J Adler*, HITTINGER, John P.
"Aristotelian Social Democracy" in *Liberalism and the Good*, NUSSBAUM, Martha C.
"Art and Democracy in Habermas" in *Writing the Politics of Difference*, PICHÉ, Claude.
"Democracy and Philosophy: On Yves R Simon and Mortimer J Adler" in *Freedom in the Modern World: Jacques Maritain, Yves R Simon, Mortimer J Adler*, ANASTAPLO, George.
"Democracy and the Political" in *The Realm of Humanitas: Responses to the Writings of Hannah Arendt*, WOLIN, Sheldon S.
"Democracy and the Threat of Nuclear Weapons" in *Issues in War and Peace: Philosophical Inquiries*, CHURCHILL, R Paul.
"Doing and Making in a Democracy: Dewey's Experience of Technology" in *Philosophy of Technology*, HICKMAN, Larry.
"Jacques Maritain and the Future of Democratic Authority" in *From Twilight to Dawn: The Cultural Vision of Jacques Maritain*, O'DONNELL, Charles P.
"L'égalité ambiguë: construction juridique ou déduction métaphysique?" in *Égalité Uguaglianza*, WUNENBURGER, Jean-Jacques.
"Maritain's American Illusions" in *From Twilight to Dawn: The Cultural Vision of Jacques Maritain*, MANCINI, Matthew J.
"Modern Democracy and Political Philosophy" in *Writing the Politics of Difference*, LEFORT, Claude.
"The Political Origins of Democracy" in *Writing the Politics of Difference*, HOWARD, Dick.
"Practical Reason and Social Democracy" in *Critique and Construction: A Symposium on Roberto Unger's "Politics"*, HAWTHORN, Geoffrey.
"The Priority of Democracy to Philosophy" in *Reading Rorty*, RORTY, Richard.
"Routine and Revolution" in *Critique and Construction: A Symposium on Roberto Unger's "Politics"*, SUNSTEIN, Cass R.
"World War II and the Anti-Democratic Impulse in Catholicism" in *From Twilight to Dawn: The Cultural Vision of Jacques Maritain*, HELLMAN, John.
"Yves R Simon's Contribution to a Structural Political Pluralism" in *Freedom in the Modern World: Jacques Maritain, Yves R Simon, Mortimer J Adler*, KOYZIS, David T.
Anotaciones en torno al poder de la democracia. MOLINA, Carlos.
Bobbio e la scienza politica in Italia. MANCARELLA, Angelo.
The Community of Inquiry Education for Democracy. SHARP, Ann Margaret.
Constitutional Democracy and the Legitimacy of Judicial Review. FREEMAN, Samuel.
La democracia ateniense. GÓMEZ ROBLEDO, Antonio.
La democracia de los antiguos y la de los modernos. YTURBE, Corina.
Democracy and Socialism: Philosophical *Aporiae*. CUNNINGHAM, Frank.
Democracy and the Church-State Relationship. KAINZ, Howard.
Democratic and Professional Authority in Education. WALKER, J C.
Dezelfde wateren aan nieuwe oevers: Alexis de Tocqueville en de Franse Revolutie. ZIJDERVELD, A C.
Educação e democracia: Subsídios para uma consciência educacional pluralizante. ARAÚJO, Alberto Filipe.
Emerson and the Inhibitions of Democracy. SHKLAR, Judith N.
The Epistemological Moral Relevance of Democracy. NINO, Carlos S.
Ethical Pluralism and the Role of Opposition in Democratic Politics. D'AGOSTINO, Fred.
Faith in the Open Society: The Limits of Hermeneutics. AGASSI, Joseph.
Los fundamentos discursivos de la democracia y los conflictos de intereses. GUARIGLIA, Osvaldo.
Gorbatschews "Erneurung des Sozialismus"—Ideologie in der Krise des Kommunismus. KUX, Ernst.
The Ideology of Intellectuals and the Chinese Student Protest Movement of 1989. CALHOUN, Craig.
Jean-Jacques Rousseau and the Fusion of Democratic Sovereignty with Aristocratic Government. CRANSTON, Maurice.
Legal Positivism and Democracy in the Twentieth Century. SQUELLA, Agustí.
Liberalismo e democrazia: la giustificazione estetica di Rorty. MARRONE, Pierpaolo.
Locke on Taxation and Suffrage. HUGHES, Martin.
Modelos elitarios de democracia. VERGARA ESTÉVEZ, Jorge.
The New Consensus: II—The Democratic Welfare State. FRIEDMAN, Jeffrey.
The Political Philosophy of Sissela Bok. FAREY, Caroline.
Possibilities of Consensus: Toward Democratic Moral Discourse. JENNINGS, Bruce.
Preferences and Politics. SUNSTEIN, Cass R.
Rediscovering the Left. HOWARD, Dick.
Renaissance of Democracy?. LEFORT, Claude and HARVEY, Robert.
Revolution, Civil Society and Democracy. ARATO, Andrew.
Die Rolle der Philosophiegeschichte im "Neuen philosophischen Denken" in der UdSSR. VAN DER ZWEERDE, Evert.
Strange Attractors: How Individualists Connect to Form Democratic Unity. ROSENBLUM, Nancy.
T G Masaryk—A Modern Thinker (in Czechoslovakian). OPAT, Jaroslav.
The Meaning of Discussions on Democratic Socialism in Czechoslovakia (in Czechoslovakian). KAMARYT, Jan.
Uguaglianza e temporalità nella "Democrazia in America". BAGLIONI, Emma.
The Unity of Human Rights in Western and Eastern Europe: Meditation about Human Rights. FÖLDESI, Tamás.
Walt Whitman and the Culture of Democracy. KATEB, George.
Walt Whitman: Jacobin Poet of American Democracy. MOSHER, Michael.
Why Democracy and Rights Do Not Mix. NELSON, John O.
The World Reconsidered: A Brief *AggiornamentoF* for Leftist Intellectuals. SKIRBEKK, Gunnar.
Zu Jürgen Habermas' Option für Fortschritt, Vernunft und Demokratie. BOGNER, Hagen.

DEMOCRATIC SOCIALISM
From Patriarchal Socialism to Socialist Democracy: Thoughts on a New Theory of Society. MOCEK, Reinhard.
Illusions and Visions: Models Of and In Modern Societies. MARZ, Lutz.

DEMOCRITUS
Vide et non-être chez Leucippe et Démocrite. VOELKE, André-Jean.
War Demokrits Weltbild mechanistisch und antiteleologisch?. HIRSCH, Ulrike.

DEMON(S)
Scepticism and Dreaming: Imploding the Demon. WRIGHT, Crispin.

DEMONSTRATION
Lo sviluppo degli studi logici nel pensiero tedesco della seconda metà dell'800. MANGIAGALLI, Maurizio.

DEMONSTRATIVES
The Origins of Aristotelian Science. FEREJOHN, Michael.
"Afterthoughts" in *Themes From Kaplan*, KAPLAN, David.
"Demonstratives: An Essay on the Semantics, Logic, Metaphysics, and Epistemology of Demonstratives" in *Themes From Kaplan*, KAPLAN, David.
Demonstrative Content: A Reply to John McDowell. PEACOCKE, Christopher.
Demonstrative Utterances. BERCKMANS, Paul.
On Kaplan's Logic of Demonstratives. CHAKRAVARTI, Sitansu S.

DENIAL
Doubting: Contemporary Perspectives on Skepticism. ROTH, Michael D (ed).
Need, Denial and Abandonment: Heidegger and the Turn. URPETH, James R.

DENNETT, D
Persons and the Intentional Stance. DIBRELL, William.
The Role of Homunculi in Psychology. WARD, Andrew.

DENOTING
Russell's Theory of Definite Descriptions. LAMBERT, Karel.

DEONTIC
Rights, Systems of Rights, and Unger's System of Rights: Part I. EIDENMÜLLER, Horst.

DEONTIC LOGIC
Logic and Ethics. GEACH, Peter (ed).
The Sweep of Probability. SCHLESINGER, George N.
"Deontic Logic and Imperative Logic" in *Logic and Ethics*, HARRISON, Jonathan.
"A Simpler Solution to the Paradoxes of Deontic Logic" in *Philosophical Perspectives, 4: Action Theory and Philosophy of Mind, 1990*, FELDMAN, Fred.
"Whatever Happened to Deontic Logic" in *Logic and Ethics*, GEACH, Peter.
A Case for a Heretical Deontic Semantics. EDELBERG, Walter.
Deontic Logic and Possible World Semantics: A Historical Sketch. WOLENSKI, Jan.
How Far Can Hume's Is-Ought Thesis Be Generalized?. SCHURZ, Gerhard.
Kantian and Non-Kantian Logics. PUGA, Leila Z and DA COSTA, Newton C A and CARNIELLI, Walter A.
Moral Relativism and Deontic Logic. HUGLY, Philip and SAYWARD, Charles.
The Revenger's Paradox. HANSSON, Sven Ove.
Underivability Results in Mixed Systems of Monadic Deontic Logic. GALVAN, Sergio.

DEONTOLOGICAL
The Inadequacy of a Deontological Analysis of Peer Relations in Organizations. MARTIN, Robert M.

DEONTOLOGICAL ETHICS
see also Categorical Imperative
"'Ought' Does Imply 'Can'". SAPONTZIS, Steve F.
In Defense of Human "Chauvinism": A Response to R Routley and V Routley. PASKE, Gerald H.

DEONTOLOGY
"Contemporary Deontology" in *A Companion to Ethics*, DAVIS, Nancy.
Agency and Morality. BROOK, Richard.
The Compatability of Consequentialism with Deontological Convictions. FORREST, Peter.
A Deontological Analysis of Peer Relations in Organizations. MOBERG, Dennis J and MEYER, Michael J.
Etica e morale: mira teleogica e prospettiva deontologica. RICOEUR, Paul.
Friendship: Mutual Apprenticeship in Moral Development. VOLBRECHT, Rose Mary.
On Lying and the Role of Content in Kant's Ethics. SEDGWICK, Sally.

DEPENDENCY
Natural Fetal Dependency States and Fetal Dependency Principles. HERBENICK, Raymond M.
Probabilistic Dependence Among Conditionals. LANCE, Mark.
Supervenience, Determination, and Dependency. GRIMES, Thomas.

DEPICTION(S)
Mimesis as Make-Believe: On the Foundations of the Representational Arts. WALTON, Kendall L.
The World of the Imagination: Sum and Substance. BRANN, Eva T H.
Pictures and Depictions: A Consideration of Peacocke's Views. KEMP, G N.

DEPTH
The Normal Depth of Filters on an Infinite Cardinal. DI PRISCO, C A and FULLER, M and HENLE, J M.
Towards a View of Time as Depth. ARGYROS, Alexander J.

DERIVABILITY
Derivability Conditions on Rosser's Provability Predicates. ARAI, Toshiyasu.
Underivability Results in Mixed Systems of Monadic Deontic Logic. GALVAN, Sergio.

DERKSEN, A
'Inference to the Best Explanation' of 'Inference to the Best Interpretation'? Een antwoord op Derksens ..... MOOIJ, A W M.

DERRIDA, J
Essays on Heidegger and Others: Philosophical Papers, Volume 2. RORTY, Richard.
French Philosophers in Conversation: Levinas, Schneider, Serres, Irigaray, Le Doeuff, Derrida. MORTLEY, Raoul.
Ideals and Illusions: On Reconstruction and Deconstruction in Contemporary Critical Theory. MC CARTHY, Thomas.
Irony and the Discourse of Modernity. BEHLER, Ernst.
L'objet-peinture: Pour une théorie de la réception. PAQUIN, Nycole.
Nietzsche and the Question of Interpretation. SCHRIFT, Alan D.
Of Memory, Reminiscence, and Writing: On the Verge. KRELL, David Farrell.
Patterns of Dissonance. BRAIDOTTI, Rosi.
A Philosophical Daybook: Post-Critical Investigations. POTEAT, William H.
Re-Reading Levinas. BERNASCONI, Robert (ed).
""Bois"—Derrida's Final Word on Levinas" in *Re-Reading Levinas*, CRITCHLEY, Simon.
"Freud, Husserl, Derrida: An Experiement" in *Phenomenology of the Truth Proper to Religion*, LOWE, Walter.
"Heidegger and Psychological Explanation: Taking Account of Derrida" in *Reconsidering Psychology: Perspectives from Continental Philosophy*, FAULCONER, James E.
"Indeterminacy of French Interpretation: Derrida and Davidson" in *Truth and Interpretation: Perspectives on the Philosophy of Donald Davidson*, WHEELER III, Samuel C.
"Merleau-Ponty and Derrida: Writing on Writing" in *Ontology and Alterity in Merleau-Ponty*, SILVERMAN, Hugh J.
"Merleau-Ponty and *l'Écriture*" in *Writing the Politics of Difference*, FROMAN, Wayne J.
"The Question of Translatability: Benjamin, Derrida, Quine" in *Hermeneutics and the Poetic Motion, Translation Perspectives V—1990*, TURK, Horst.
"Wholly Otherwise" in *Re-Reading Levinas*, CRITCHLEY, Simon (trans) and LEVINAS, Emmanuel.
"Speech Versus Writing" in Derrida and Bhartrhari. COWARD, Harold G.
Another Look at the Derrida-Searle Debate. ALFINO, Mark.
A Critique of Derrida's Hegel Deconstruction: Speech, Phonetic Writing, and Hieroglyphic Script in Logic, Law, Art. CUTROFELLO, Andrew.
Deconstructing Lonergan. MC KINNEY, Ronald H.
Deconstruction as Symbolic Play: Simmel/Derrida. WEINSTEIN, Deena and WEINSTEIN, Michael A.
Derrida's huishouding. BERNS, Egidius.
Derrida's Other Conversation. DAVIES, Paul.
Derrida, Deconstruction and Nietzsche: The Tree of Knowledge and the Tree of Life. ZELECHOW, Bernard.
Encountering Dallmayr. KIVISTO, Peter.
Genealogy and *Différance*. SCOTT, Charles E.
Jacques Derrida's Response to the Call for Ethics. CHAMPAGNE, R A.
Language and Political Agency: Derrida, Marx, and Bakhtin. EVANS, Fred.
Language, Physics, and Geology (and a Few Words on Theology). BROGAN, Jacqueline Vaught.
Language, Speech and Writing: Merleau-Ponty and Derrida on Saussure. FREE, George.
A Little Daylight: A Reading of Derrida's "White Mythology". LAWLOR, Leonard.
Nietzsche in Derrida's *Spurs*: Deconstruction as Deracination. FREYDBERG, Bernard D.
Philosophy and Politics: On Fred Dallmayr's "Critical Encounters". MISGELD, Dieter.
Political Openings. WOOD, David.
A Response to My Critics. DALLMAYR, Fred.
Sankara and Derrida on Philosophy of Language. COWARD, Harold.
Text and Technology. CROWELL, Steven Galt.
The Early and Later Deconstruction in Derrida's Writings (in Hebrew). LANDAU, Iddo.
Two Reversibilities: Merleau-Ponty and Derrida. YOUNT, Mark.

DESCARTES
The Anatomy of Philosophical Style. LANG, Berel.
Berkeley's Revolution in Vision. ATHERTON, Margaret.
Descartes Among the Scholastics. GRENE, Marjorie.
God and Subjectivity. GALGAN, Gerald J.
An Invitation To Cognitive Science. LEIBER, Justin.

DESCARTES

Knowledge of the External World. AUNE, Bruce.

Meditations on First Philosophy: A Bilingual Edition—René Descartes. HEFFERNAN, George (trans).

Modern Faith and Thought. THIELICKE, Helmut.

On True and False Ideas, New Objections to Descartes' Meditations and Descartes' Replies. ARNAULD, Antoine (trans).

L'ordine della certezza: Scientificità e persuasione in Descartes. BONICALZI, Francesca.

A Philosophical Daybook: Post-Critical Investigations. POTEAT, William H.

"Descartes on the Representationality of Sensation" in *Central Themes in Early Modern Philosophy,* WILSON, Margaret D.

"Descartes, Rorty and the Mind-Body Fiction" in *Reading Rorty,* HORNSBY, Jennifer.

"Radical Interpretation and Global Skepticism" in *Truth and Interpretation: Perspectives on the Philosophy of Donald Davidson,* KLEIN, Peter D.

"Spinoza and Descartes and the Existence of Extended Substance" in *Central Themes in Early Modern Philosophy,* WOOLHOUSE, R S.

The Alliance between Puritanism and Cartesian Logic at Harvard, 1687-1735. KENNEDY, Rick.

Der Begriff des Selbstbewusstseins bei Kant. GLOY, Karen.

Berkeley's Anti-Abstractionism: Reply to Moked. GLOUBERMAN, Mark.

Cartesian Passions and Cartesian Dualism. HOFFMAN, Paul.

Cartesian Syntax. ENGLEBRETSEN, George.

The Cogito and the Diallelus. ZELLNER, Harold.

Crítica de Heidegger al "intuicionalismo" cartesiano. FORMENT, Eudaldo.

The Dating of Rule IV-B in Descartes's *Regulae ad directionem ingenii.* VAN DE PITTE, Frederick P.

Descartes censuré par Huet. MALBREIL, Germain.

Descartes e le "culture" barocche: Appunti su alcune recenti interpretazioni. LOJACONO, Ettore.

Descartes et Corneille ou les démesures de l'*ego.* BEYSSADE, Jean-Marie.

Descartes on Colour. COTTINGHAM, John.

Descartes on Sensations and 'Animal Minds'. SENCERZ, Stefan.

Descartes on Sensory Representation: A Study of the *Dioptrics.* MAC KENZIE, Ann Wilbur.

Descartes und der reale Unterschied zwischen der Seele und dem Körper. IMLAY, Robert A.

Dialogue and Doubt in Descartes' First Meditation. LINVILLE, Kent.

The Dimension of Color. FÓTI, Véronique.

Die erkenntniskritische Wendung Descartes' als Konsequenz geschichtlicher Entwicklung des Leib-Seele-Dualismus. POHLENZ, G.

Ethics as Drawn from the Method. CARTER, Richard B.

Expectation, Modelling and Assent in the History of Optics—II. Kelper and Descartes. CROMBIE, A C.

The Fifth Meditation. EDELBERG, Walter.

Filosofía y fe en Descartes. FERNANDEZ, Javier.

Filósofos naúfragos. BALIÑAS, Carlos.

The Insufficiency of Descartes' Provisional Morality. COOLIDGE JR, Francis P.

Kant's Diversity Theory: A Dissenting View. GLOUBERMAN, Mark.

Malebranche and the Vision in God: A Note on *The Search After Truth,* III, 2, iii. NADLER, Steven.

Man Not a Subject of Science?. SLEZAK, Peter.

Metaphysik und Erfahrung. BUBNER, Rüdiger.

Le premier registre de Descartes. RODIS-LEWIS, Geneviève.

Radical Critique, Scepticism and Commonsense. GAITA, Raimond.

The Real Distinction Between Mind and Body. YABLO, Stephen.

Real Selves: Persons as a Substantial Kind. LOWE, E J.

Representation and the Freedom of the Will. STAMPE, Dennis W.

Scepticism and Dreaming: Imploding the Demon. WRIGHT, Crispin.

Les sens trompeurs: Usage cartésien d'un motif sceptique. CAVAILLÉ, Jean-Pierre.

Some Recent Research on the Mind-Body Problem in Descartes. MILES, Murray.

Thoughtful Brutes: The Ascription of Mental Predicates to Animals in Locke's "Essay". SQUADRITO, Kathleen.

Truth and Stability in Descartes' *Meditations.* BENNETT, Jonathan.

Two Cartesian Arguments for the Simplicity of the Soul. ZIMMERMAN, Dean W.

Was Descartes a Liar? Diagonal Doubt Defended. SLEZAK, Peter.

Why the Problem of the External World is a Pseudo-Problem: Santayana and Danto. SHIRLEY, Edward S.

DESCRIBING

Rich Cases: The Ethics of Thick Description. DAVIS, Dena S.

DESCRIPTION(S)

Aristotelian Logic and the Arabic Language in Alfarabi. ABED, Shukri B.

Meaning and Truth: The Essential Readings in Modern Semantics. GARFIELD, Jay L (ed).

"Has the Description Theory of Names Been Refuted?" in *Meaning and Method: Essays in Honor of Hilary Putnam,* KATZ, Jerrold J.

Churchland, Introspection, and Dualism. ZEMACH, Eddy M.

The Concrete and the Abstract Science: Description versus Explanation. GUPTA, Amitabha.

Conditional Essences. HAIGHT, Mary R.

Descriptions and Group Reference. MUKHERJI, Nirmalangshu.

Descriptions: Contemporary Philosophy and the Nyāya. SHAW, J L.

In Defence of Unrepresentative Realism. TONGS, A R.

Indefinite Descriptions: In Defense of Russell. LUDLOW, Peter and NEALE, Stephen.

On Begging the Question 'Who is N?'. PATTON, Thomas E.

Philosophy of Science: From Justification to Explanation. KANTOROVICH, Aharon.

Plato's Ontology and the Role of Mathematics in the Description of Nature. ZYCINSKI, Joseph.

The Theory of Descriptions Revisited. PERUZZI, Alberto.

DESCRIPTIVE MEANING

Reference and Pronominal Descriptions. WILSON, George M.

DESCRIPTIVE SET THEORY

Boundedness Theorems for Dilators and Ptykes. KECHRIS, Alexander S.

A Coding of the Countable Linear Orderings. DEHORNOY, Patrick.

From Discrete to Continuous Time. KEISLER, H Jerome.

Some Results about Borel Sets in Descriptive Set Theory of Hyperfinite Sets. ZIVALJEVIC, Bosko.

DESCRIPTIVES

Per un'analisi del discorso dichiarativo. CELANO, Bruno.

DESCRIPTIVISM

The Causal Theory of Reference and Religious Language. HARRIS, James F.

DESERT(S)

Racial Bias, the Death Penalty, and Desert. MEYERS, Christopher.

The Rights-Interpretation of Desert. GARCÍA, Jorge.

DESIGN

"Design Methodology: A Personal Statement" in *Philosophy of Technology,* GASPARSKI, Wojciech.

Randomness by Design. DEMBSKI, William.

A Reply to Mayo's Criticisms of Urbach's "Randomization and the Design of Experiments". URBACH, Peter.

DESIGN ARGUMENT

Barrow and Tipler on the Anthropic Principle versus Divine Design. CRAIG, William Lane.

Hume's Reproduction Parody of the Design Argument. DRAPER, Paul.

DESIRE(S)

Explaining Behavior: Reasons in a World of Causes. DRETSKE, Fred.

False Consciousness. MEYERSON, Denise.

Grace, Politics and Desire: Essays on Augustine. MEYNELL, Hugo A (ed).

History and Spirit: An Inquiry into the Philosophy of Liberation. KOVEL, Joel.

Lesbian Philosophies and Cultures. ALLEN, Jeffner (ed).

Rationality in Action: Contemporary Approaches. MOSER, Paul K (ed).

The Realizations of the Future: An Inquiry into the Authority of Praxis. ALLAN, George.

"The Body and Human Values in Augustine of Hippo" in *Grace, Politics and Desire: Essays on Augustine,* MILES, Margaret R.

"Hope" in *The Philosophy in Christianity,* SUTHERLAND, Stewart.

"Obsolescence and Desire: Fashion and the Commodity Form" in *Postmodernism—Philosophy and the Arts (Continental Philosophy III),* FAURSCHOU, Gail.

"Woman's Experience: Renaming the Dialectic of Desire and Recognition" in *Writing the Politics of Difference,* MILLS, Patricia J.

'Desire' in Yoga and Jung. COWARD, Harold.

Autonomy, Emotions and Desires: Some Problems Concerning R F Dearden's Account of Autonomy. STONE, Carolyn M.

Backgrounding Desire. PETTIT, Philip and SMITH, Michael.

De Re Desire. MARKIE, Peter and PATRICK, Timothy.

El deseo infinito. PEGUEROLES, Juan.

El deseo y el amor en San Agustín. PEGUEROLES, Juan.

Desire and Duty in Kant. GRIGG, Russell.

Evolution and Nostalgia in Hegel's Theory of Desire. BERTHOLD-BOND, Daniel.

The Faculty of Desire. LACHTERMAN, David.

Governance by Emotion. ALLEN, R T.

Hume on Practical Reason. ROBERTSON, John.

Irrational Desires. HUBIN, Donald C.

The Many Appetites of Thomas Hobbes. HURLEY, Paul.

Mental Causes. HEIL, John and MELE, Alfred.

Moral Responsibility, Psychiatric Disorders and Duress. ELLIOTT, Carl.

The Normal Rewards of Success. WHYTE, J T.

On the Irreducibility of the Will. GARCIA, J L A.

Persons and the Intentional Stance. DIBRELL, William.

Plato and Davidson: Parts of the Soul and Weakness of Will. PENNER, Terrence M.

Political Economy and Mimetic Desire: A Postmodernist Reading of "Babette's Feast". SHAPIRO, Michael J.

Rome Inferences and Structural Opacity. MOORE, F C T.

Sidgwick and Self-Interest. CRISP, Roger.

Spinoza's Materialist Ethics: The Education of Desire. RAVVEN, Heidi M.

DESIRE(S)

Universalizability and the Summing of Desires. PERSSON, Ingmar.
Universalizability and the Summing of Desires: Reply to Ingmar Persson. HARE, R M.
Wanting, Getting, Having. HUMBERSTONE, I L.

DESPAIR

Espoir et désespoir de la raison chez Kant. GRIMALDI, Nicolas.

DESPOTISM

Not So Virtuous Republics: Montesquieu, Venice, and the Theory of Aristocratic Republicanism. CARRITHERS, David W.

DESTINY

Algunos márgenes de la condición humana. MAS, Oscar.
El evento (ereignis) como concepto fundamental de la filosofía de Heidegger (1a parte). BERCIANO V, Modesto.

DESTRUCTION

Destruktion und Übersetzung: Zu den Aufgaben von Philosophiegeschichte nach Martin Heidegger. OPILIK, Klaus.

DESTUTT DE TRACY, A

De l'Idéologie comme correlat des termes idéologiste et idéologue. ZOLUA, Buenzey Maluenga.

DETERMINACY

The Equivalence of Determinacy and Iterated Sharps. DUBOSE, Derrick Albert.
An Extension of Borel Determinacy. MARTIN, Donald A.
Extension of Gurevich-Harrington's Restricted Memory Determinacy Theorem. YAKHNIS, Alexander and YAKHNIS, Vladimir.

DETERMINATION

Governance by Emotion. ALLEN, R T.
Supervenience, Determination, and Dependency. GRIMES, Thomas.

DETERMINISM

The Non-Reality of Free Will. DOUBLE, Richard.
Readings in Existential Psychology and Psychiatry. HOELLER, Keith (ed).
The Taming of Chance. HACKING, Ian.
"Determinism, Probability and Randomness in Classical Statistical Physics" in *Imre Lakatos and Theories of Scientific Change*, CLARK, Peter.
"Freedom and Determination: An Examination of Yves R Simon's Ontology of Freedom" in *Freedom in the Modern World: Jacques Maritain, Yves R Simon, Mortimer J Adler*, GREEN, Catherine.
"The Implications of Determinism" in *A Companion to Ethics*, YOUNG, Robert.
"Metaphysical Foundations of Freedom in the Social and Political Thought of Yves R Simon" in *Freedom in the Modern World: Jacques Maritain, Yves R Simon, Mortimer J Adler*, UDOIDEM, S Iniobong.
"Newton, Nonlinearity and Determinism" in *Some Truer Method*, DURHAM, Frank and PURRINGTON, Robert D.
"When is the Will Free?" in *Philosophical Perspectives, 3: Philosophy of Mind and Action Theory, 1989*, VAN INWAGEN, Peter.
Action and Explanation. MAJUMDAR, Aruna.
Causality Assessment in Epidemiology. VINEIS, Paolo.
Causality, Determinism and Objective Reality in Modern Physics. NARAYAN, S Shankar.
Chaos and Indeterminism. HOBBS, Jesse.
Comments on 'Nonlocal Influences and Possible Worlds'. STAPP, Henry P.
Conocimiento y determinismo. LAGUNILLA, Ana E Galán.
Consciousness Naturalized: Supervenience Without Physical Determinism. SENCHUK, Dennis M.
La création du Nouveau par le Hasard et par le temps: un vieux thème épicurien. LARGEAULT, Jean.
Determinism and the Experience of Freedom. DOUBLE, Richard.
A Determinist Dilemma. PERSSON, Ingmar.
Direct and Indirect Causes. SPOHN, Wolfgang.
Ensuring Two Bird Deaths with One Throw. LESLIE, John.
Ethics Without Free Will. SLOTE, Michael.
Fragility and Deterministic Modelling in the Exact Sciences. TAVAKOL, R K.
The Free Will Defense and Determinism. SENNETT, James F.
The Hole Truth. BUTTERFIELD, Jeremy.
Logic and the Free Will Problem. VAN INWAGEN, Peter.
Metaphysics of the Person, Determinism and Responsibility. FAY, Thomas A.
The Nature of Physical Reality. POLKINGHORNE, John C.
New Naturalism and Other Ethical Theories. SHENG, C L.
No Moral Responsibility Without Alternative Possibilities. WEBBER, May A.
La objetividad del azar en un mundo determinista. MARTÍNEZ, S.
On a Mainstay of Incompatibilism. BLUM, Alex.
On Relativity Theory and Openness of the Future. STEIN, Howard.
A Picture of the Self Which Supports the Moral Responsibility. ANDERSON, Susan Leigh.
The Problem of Moral Freedom and Nicolai Hartmann. PRASAD, Kamata.
Response to Slote's "Ethics Without Free Will". VAN INWAGEN, Peter.
Response to van Inwagen's "Logic and the Free Will Problem". SLOTE, Michael.
The World-Shift Theory of Free Choice. DAVIS, Wayne A.

DETERRENCE

Military Ethics: Looking Toward the Future. FOTION, Nicholas G.
Theories of Criminal Justice: A Critical Reappraisal. ELLIS, Ralph D.
"Deterrence or Disarmament: An Appraisal of Consequentialist Arguments" in *In the Interest of Peace: A Spectrum of Philosophical Views*, KUNKEL, Joseph.
"Moral Counterforce" in *In the Interest of Peace: A Spectrum of Philosophical Views*, LEE, Steven.
"Nuclear Space and Time" in *In the Interest of Peace: A Spectrum of Philosophical Views*, STAHL, Gary.
A Note on the Death Penalty as the Best Bet. BAYLES, Michael D.
Nuclear Stalemate: A Superior Escape from the Dilemmas of Deterrence. SCHONSHECK, Jonathan.
Retaliation Rationalized: Gauthier's Solution to the Deterrence Dilemma. MAC INTOSH, Duncan.
Schopenhauers Straftheorie und die aktuelle Strafzweckdiskussion. KÜPPER, Georg.

DEVARAJA, N

Some Problems in the Epistemology of Advaita. GRIMES, John.

DEVELOPMENT(S)

About Time: Inventing the Fourth Dimension. FRIEDMAN, William J.
Beyond Ethnocentrism: A Reconstruction of Marx's Concept of Science. MC KELVEY, Charles.
Fichte's Theory of Subjectivity. NEUHOUSER, Frederick.
La sociedad sin hombres: Niklas Luhmann o la teoría como escándalo. IZUZQUIZA, Ignacio.
Varieties of Moral Personality: Ethics and Psychological Realism. FLANAGAN, Owen.
Wisdom: Its Nature, Origins, and Development. STERNBERG, Robert J.
Wittgenstein, Ethics and Aesthetics: The View from Eternity. TILGHMAN, B R.
"The Development of Self-Consciousness: Baldwin, Mead, and Vygotsky" in *Reconsidering Psychology: Perspectives from Continental Philosophy*, MARKOVA, Ivana.
Agricultura, desarrollo y autonomía. BLATZ, Charlie.
Between Necessity and Superabundance: Meta-economic Reflections on Marxism. WALDENFELS, Bernhard.
Change and Development. MC LEOD, John.
The Community of Inquiry and the Development of Self-Esteem. LAGO, Juan Carlos.
Cuatro modelos de desarrollo costarricense: un análisis y evalución ética. CROCKER, David A.
El desarrollo como proceso: una investigación filosófica. DOWER, Nigel.
Development Aid: The Moral Obligation to Innovation. DUNDON, Stanislaus J.
The Development of Modern Mathematics and Plato's Parable of the Cave. MAURIN, Krzysztof.
El eslabón entre la conservación y el desarrollo sostenible: Maribel Gómez Mata. JANZEN, Daniel H.
Essai sur le développement historique de la voie phénoménologique. MAESSCHALCK, Marc.
Etica del desarrollo: algunos principios y orientaciones a la luz de la docrina social de la Iglesia Católica. BRENES, Víctor.
Explaining Historical Development: A Marxian Critique of Cohen's Historical Materialism. WARREN, Paul.
Hacia un desarrollo de la cultura y una cultura del desarrollo. ROSALES, Amán.
The Justification of Conceptual Development Claims. HAAFTEN, Wouter Van.
Lacan in Slovenia—An Interview with Slavoj Zizek and Renata Salecl. DEWS, Peter and OSBORNE, Peter.
Note ad un recente libro sull'incontro-scontro tra Croce e Gentile. ANTISERI, Dario.
Progress in Mathematics and Other Arts. SEDZIWY, Stanislaw.
Public Discourse in the Development of Educational Policy. CURREN, Randall R.
O Saber, a Ética e a Ação Social. CARDOSO D EOLIVEIRA, Roberto.
The Social Philosophy of Marxism: The Founders and the Present Day. SHEVCHENKO, V N.
Some More Ideas About the Relation Between Philosophy for Children and Self-Esteem. GAZZARD, Ann.
Some Reflections on Post-Marxism and Post-Christianity: A Response to Professor Arthur Mc Govern. STOJANOVIC, Svetozar.
Tareas y métodos en la ética del desarrollo. GOULET, Denis.
When Do People Begin?. GRISEZ, Germain.

DEVITT, M

Aberrations of a Sledgehammer: Reply to Devitt. LUNTLEY, Michael.
On Respecting Puzzles About Belief Ascription (A Reply to Devitt). LYCAN, William G.
Representations and Realism. APPIAH, Anthony.

DEVOTION(S)

The Bhakti Tradition in Hinduism—Bhakti Yoga an Overview. PILLAI, A S Narayana.
A Re-Examination of the Nature of Religion. BARUA, Archana.

DEWEY

American Philosophy and the Romantic Tradition. GOODMAN, Russell B.
Ethical Practice in Clinical Medicine. ELLOS, William J.
John Dewey: Religious Faith and Democratic Humanism. ROCKEFELLER, Steven C.
Pragmatism: From Peirce to Davidson. MURPHY, John P.
"Between Dewey and Gramsci: Unger's Emancipatory Experimentalism" in *Critique and Construction: A Symposium on Roberto Unger's "Politics"*, WEST, Cornel.
"Doing and Making in a Democracy: Dewey's Experience of Technology" in *Philosophy of Technology*, HICKMAN, Larry.
"The Human Person in American Pragmatism" in *The Question of Humanism: Challenges and Possibilities*, FRANCIS, Richard P.
"Workplace Democracy for Teachers: John Dewey's Contribution" in *Philosophy of Technology*, BYRNE, Edmund F.
"Event" in Dewey's Philosophy. DUFF, Barry E.
Burglars, Robber Barons, and the Good Life. PEKARSKY, Daniel.
Commentary on "Epistemology as Hypothesis". SLEEPER, R W.
A Comparison of John Dewey and Lawrence Kohlberg's Approach to Moral Education. SOCOSKI, Patrick M.
Contextualizing Knowledge: A Reply to "Dewey and the Theory of Knowledge". HICKMAN, Larry.
Dead Souls and Living Instruments. HICKMAN, Larry.
Dewey and the Theory of Knowledge. THAYER, H S.
Dewey, Indeterminacy, and the Spectator Theory of Knowledge. KULP, Christopher B.
Epistemology as Hypothesis. PUTNAM, Hilary and PUTNAM, Ruth Anna.
Ethical Deliberations as Dramatic Rehearsal. CASPARY, William R.
Habermas's Ontology of Learning: Reconstructing Dewey. YOUNG, R E.
L'esthétique de John Dewey et le contexte urbain. GAVIN, William J.
Problem Solving, Decision Making and Reflective Thinking. MERKLE, Patricia.
Reflections on Reflecting. PRITSCHER, Conrad.
Response to Merkle and Pritscher. SMITH, Phil.
The Tragic World of John Dewey. JACQUES, Robert A.
The Vanishing Subject of Contemporary Discourse: A Pragmatic Response. COLAPIETRO, Vincent M.

DEWS, P

Peter Dews' Logics of Disintegration: Poststructuralism/Critical Theory. BUTLER, Judith.

DHARMA

Chinese Buddhist Apocrypha. BUSWELL JR, Robert E (ed).
Social Reality and Moral Order. BARLINGAY, S S.

DHARMAKIRTI

Dharmakīrti on Inference and Properties. GANERI, Jonardon.
Introduction to Dharmakīrti's Theory of Inference as Presented in *Pramāṇavārttika Svopajñavṛtti* 1-10. HAYES, Richard P and GILLON, Brendan S.

DIAGNOSIS

Diagnosis Without Doctors. MAZOUÉ, James G.
Subjective Boundaries and Combinations in Psychiatric Diagnoses. MIROWSKY, John.
Toward the Obsolescence of the Schizophrenia Hypothesis. SARBIN, Theodore R.
Why the Standard View Is Standard: People, Not Machines, Understand Patients' Problems. MILLER, Randolph A.

DIAGONAL ARGUMENT

Fixed Points and Diagonal Method. NEGRI, Maurizio.
Was Descartes a Liar? Diagonal Doubt Defended. SLEZAK, Peter.

DIAGONALIZATION

Diagonalization and Fixed Points. TONELLA, Guido.
A Topological Interpretation of Diagonalizable Algebras. HAWRANEK, Jacek.

DIAGRAM(S)

Ecosystems as Circuits: Diagrams and the Limits of Physical Analogies. TAYLOR, Peter J and BLUM, Ann S.
From Presentation to Representation in E B Wilson's *The Cell*. MAIENSCHEIN, Jane.
Must Scientific Diagrams Be Eliminable? The Case of Path Analysis. GRIESEMER, James R.
Representations of the Natural System in the Nineteenth Century. O'HARA, Robert J.
Science in the Age of Mechanical Reproduction: Moral and Epistemic Relations Between Diagrams and Photographs. LYNCH, Michael.

DIALECTIC

Critique of Dialectical Reason, Volume 2: Jean-Paul Sartre. HOARE, Quintin (trans).
The Dice-Playing God: Reflections on Life in a Post-Modern Age. KRIEGLSTEIN, Werner.
Encyclopedia of the Philosophical Sciences in Outline and Critical Writings—G W F Hegel. BEHLER, Ernst (ed).
Hegel In His Time—Jacques D'Hondt. BURBIDGE, John (trans).
Herrschaft und Versöhnung: Einführung in das Denken Theodor W Adornos. KAGER, Reinhard.
Ideas, Principios y Dialectica. LAFUENTE, Maria Isabel.
Modernism as a Philosophical Problem: On the Dissatisfactions of European High Culture. PIPPIN, Robert B.
Negative Dialectics and the End of Philosophy. ERICKSON, Glenn W.
Overcoming Foundations: Studies in Systematic Philosophy. WINFIELD, Richard Dien.
"A Concise Theory of Dialectics" in *Harré and His Critics*, DE WAELE, Jean-Pierre.
"A Dialectical Version of Philosophical Discussion" in *Freedom in the Modern World: Jacques Maritain, Yves R Simon, Mortimer J Adler*, BIRD, Otto.
"Dialectics, Critical Inquiry, and Archaeology" in *Critical Traditions in Contemporary Archaeology*, SAITTA, Dean J.
"Kant, Hegel and the Possibility of a Speculative Logic" in *Essays on Hegel's Logic*, DUQUETTE, David A.
"Mr Adler and Matthew Arnold" in *Freedom in the Modern World: Jacques Maritain, Yves R Simon, Mortimer J Adler*, VAN DOREN, John.
"The Shadow of Hegel's *Science of Logic*" in *Essays on Hegel's Logic*, WILLETT, Cynthia.
"Understanding the Cuban Missile Crisis: A Dialectical Approach" in *Issues in War and Peace: Philosophical Inquiries*, HIRSCHBEIN, Ron.
Adorno and the French Post-Structuralists on the Other of Reason. NUYEN, A T.
An Alternative Logical Framework for Dialectical Reasoning in the Social and Policy Sciences. SABRE, Ru Michael.
Aristotle on Dialectic. HAMLYN, D W.
Comparative Dialectics: Nishida Kitarō's Logic of Place and Western Dialectical Thought. AXTELL, G S.
Conocimiento metodico y no metodico; so pretexto de una incursion acerca de la dialectica segun platon. SALA, J F A.
Coping with Complexity—Coping with Dialectics, in Theory and Practice (in German). THIEL, Rainer.
Cultural Literacy: Posing Queer Questions. GREENE, Maxine.
Deconstruction or Dialectics? (in Serbo-Croation). BRUNKHORST, Hauke.
El desaparecer de lo eterno en sí mismo: Una clave del pensamiento de Hegel. ALBIZU, Edgardo.
Desarrollos actuales de la epistemología dialéctica. MENDOZA, Celina A Lértora.
Dialectic and Diagonalization. KADVANY, John.
Dialectical Thinking in Metaphysics—Van Kues: Coincidental Thinking and the Problem of Idealistic Monism (in German). WINKLER, Norbert.
La dialettica come "dépasser" in Sartre. TOGNONATO, Claudio.
División y dialéctica en el *Fedro*. SANTA CRUZ, María Isabel.
Everyday Argumentation from a Speech Act Perspective. GROOTENDORST, Rob.
Hacia el saber del hombre: Dialéctica, lógica y ontológica en Aristóteles. MARÍN, Victor R.
Hegel, Antigone, and the Possibility of Ecstatic Dialogue. WILLETT, Cynthia.
Hegel, Logic, and Metaphysics. HARTSHORNE, Charles.
Hegel, Marx, Lukács: The Dialectic of Freedom and Necessity. DAY, Richard B.
Hegels Geschichtsphilosophie im Vergleich mit anderen Geschichtskonzeptionen. GLOY, Karen.
Das Imperiale an der Identitätsphilosophie: Spuren des Totalitären in der abendländischen Philosophie. MANSILLA, Hugo C F.
The Incoherence of Kant's Transcendental Dialectic: Specifying the Minimal Conditions for Dialectical Error. HERMAN, David J.
The Later Schelling's Conception of Dialectical Method, in Contradistinction to Hegel's. BEACH, Edward A.
Logique et métaphysique. POUBLANC, Franck.
Marx and Dialectics (in German). ADLER, Max.
Metafisica e dialettica: quattro saggi sull'interpretazione hegeliana di Aristotele. FERRARIN, Alfredo.
New Studies on Hegel's Philosophy of Law, versus on the Dialectics of Hegel and Marx (in Hungarian). GÖHLER, Gerhard.
On Some Unsettled Questions Touching the Character of Marxism, Especially as Philosophy. SUCHTING, W A.
On the Duality of China's Traditional Mode of Thought and the Difficulty of Transforming It. ZIHLIN, Li.
An Open Letter to Maxine Greene on "The Problem of Freedom in an Era of Ecological Interdependence". BOWERS, C A.
A Pragma-Dialectical Perspective on Norms. VAN EEMEREN, Frans H.
Pragma-Dialectics: A Radical Departure in Fallacy Theory. WOODS, John.
Reconstruction, Dialectic and Praxis. RIORDAN, Patrick.
Reply to McKinney on Lonergan: A Deconstruction. MARSH, James L.
Rethinking the Dialectic: A Social Semiotic Perspective for Educators. HAMMER, Rhonda and MC LAREN, Peter.
Socratic Pragmatics: Maieutic Dialogues. HANKE, Michael.
Le statut de l'argument dialectiques d'après *Réf soph* 11, 172a9-15. DORION, Louis-André.
The Structure of Self-Commentary in Hegel's Dialectical Logic. GASKINS, Richard H.
La subversion de l'"elenchos" juridique dans l'"Apologie de Socrate". DORION, Louis-André.

DIALECTIC
The Heterogeneity of Poetic Language in Kristeva (in Japanese). NARUSE, Katsuji.
The Theological Secret of Th W Adorno's Aesthetic Theory (in German). HOLZ, Hans Heinz.
Toward a Formalization of Dialectical Logic. THOMASON, Steven K.
Transcendental Idealism: The Dialectical Dimension. GLOUBERMAN, M.
Trotsky's Dialectic. THATCHER, Ian D.
Ways to See a Revolution and World Outlook: Alexander von Humboldt (in German). HERLITZIUS, Erwin.

DIALECTICAL MATERIALISM
see also Historical Materialism
Communism: The Philosophical Foundations. FLEW, Antony.
A Critique of Marx's Extension of the Principles of Dialectical Materialism into the Phenomena of Social Life. NYONG, Prince David.
A Critique of One Interpretation of Practical Materialism. DANSHEN, Huang.
Is It Practical Ontology or Is It the Dialectical Materialist Theory of Material Monism?. JINFU, Wang.
Marx's *Aufhebung* of Philosophy and the Foundations of Historical-Materialist Science. FRACCHIA, Joseph.
On J L Fischer's Reflections About Categories of Dialectic Materialism (in Czechoslovakian). TOSENOVSKY, Ludvik.
Todor Pavlov (1890-1977)—The Generalization of Reflection (in German). HOLZ, Hans Heinz.

DIALOGUE(S)
Bakhtin and the Epistemology of Discourse. THOMSON, Clive (ed).
The Chronology of Plato's Dialogues. BRANDWOOD, Leonard.
Dialogue with the Other: The Inter-Religious Dialogue. TRACY, David.
The Dialogues of Plato, Volume II. ALLEN, R E (trans).
Plato's "Parmenides". MEINWALD, Constance C.
Platonic Piety. MORGAN, Michael L.
The Rhetoric of Berkeley's Philosophy. WALMSLEY, Peter.
"Dialogue and Discourses" in *Writing the Politics of Difference*, WALDENFELS, Bernhard.
"'I Am We' Consciousness and Dialog as Organizational Ethics Method". NIELSEN, Richard P.
Can the Discussion Partners Trust Each Other?. FÖLDESI, Tamás.
Christians and Marxists in Dialogue Building Confidence in a Time of Crisis. WEST, Charles C.
Continuing the Conversation—A Reply to My Interlocutors. OLIVIER, G.
Dialogic Leadership as Ethics Action (Praxis) Method. NIELSEN, Richard P.
Dialogue and Understanding (in German). FRITZSCHE, Helmut.
Dialogue as a Way of Being Human. YIN, Lu-jun.
Four Dialogue Systems. MACKENZIE, Jim.
From Dialogue Rights to Property Rights. SHEARMUR, Jeremy.
Ground, Pivot, Motion: Ecofeminist Theory, Dialogics, and Literary Practice. MURPHY, Patrick.
A Hungarian Christian-Marxist Dialogue and Its Lessons. LUKÁCS, József.
Logics of Dialogue: A Necessary Multiplicity. MAIER, Robert.
The Metaphilosophy of Dialogue. KUCZYNSKI, Janusz.
The Occasion Fleeting: A Talk with Richard Selzer. JOSYPH, Peter.
Osservazioni sul *Filebo*. MASI, Giuseppe.
Paul Ricoeur e Gabriel Marcel. DE LOURDES SIRGADO GANHO, Maria.
Paul Tillich and Inter-religious Dialogue. FOERSTER, John.
A Proposal for Corporate Ethical Reform: The Ethical Dialogue Group. PAYNE, Stephen L.
Reinvigorating the International Christian-Marxist Dialogue. MOJZES, Paul.
Reply to Shearmur's "From Dialogue Rights to Property Rights". MICHELMAN, Frank.
Socratic Pragmatics: Maieutic Dialogues. HANKE, Michael.
Struttura e finalità dei dialoghi platonici: Che cosa significa "venire in soccorso al discorso"?. SZLEZÁK, Thomas A.
El trilema de Aristófanes y los presupuestos normativos del diálgo crítico. MALIANDI, Ricardo.
Unifying Plato: Charles Kahn on Platonic *Prolepsis*. GRISWOLD JR, Charles L.
Vers une Pédagogie du Dialogue. TONOIU, Vasile.

DICK, A
A Supplement to "David Hume to Alexander Dick: A New Letter". KLEMME, Heiner F.

DICKIE, G
The Avant Garde, Institutional and Critical Theories of Art. SNYMAN, Johan J.
On Davies' Institutional Definition of Art. OPPY, Graham.
Why 'Art' Doesn't Have Two Senses. ROWE, M W.

DICTATORSHIP
Statism and Anarchy. SHATZ, Marshall (ed).

DICTIONARY
Dictionary of Religion and Philosophy. MAC GREGOR, Geddes.
The Philosopher's Dictionary. MARTIN, Robert M.
Dictionaries and Proper Names. MARCONI, Diego.
El escepticismo crítico en el Diccionario de Bayle. ARROYO, Julián.
The Indeterminacy Thesis Reformulated. GEMES, Ken.

DIDEROT
Hegel's Intertextual Dialectic: Diderot's *Le Neveu de Rameau* in the *Phenomenology of Spirit*. PRICE, David W.

DIFFERANCE
Genealogy and *Différance*. SCOTT, Charles E.
Language and Political Agency: Derrida, Marx, and Bakhtin. EVANS, Fred.

DIFFERENCE
Difference and Subjectivity: Dialogue and Personal Identity. JACQUES, Francis.
Essentially Speaking: Feminism, Nature and Difference. FUSS, Diana.
La sociedad sin hombres: Niklas Luhmann o la teoría como escándalo. IZUZQUIZA, Ignacio.
"Identity and Difference in Liberalism" in *Liberalism and the Good*, CONNOLLY, William E.
"Sex, Gender, and the Politics of Difference" in *Writing the Politics of Difference*, KUYKENDALL, Eleanor H.
"Translating the Differences: The Futures of Continental Philosophy" in *Writing the Politics of Difference*, WOOD, David.
"Les utopies littéraires au XVIIIe siècle" in *Égalité Uguaglianza*, IMBROSCIO, Carmelina.
An Abyss of Difference: Laing, Sartre and Jaspers. KIRSNER, Douglas.
Las aventuras de la differencia (G Vattimo). PEGUEROLES, Juan.
Derrida's huishouding. BERNS, Egidius.
Just Can't Find the Words: How Expression is Achieved. KING, Debra W.
Mismidad y diferencia. COUTO-SOARES, Maria Luisa.
On the Issue of Sex Differences. ALLEN, Elizabeth.
Le pouvoir de la différence. DELIVOYATSIS, Socratis.
Rawls's Difference Principle and a Problem of Sacrifice. VOICE, Paul.
Reply to Marsh's "Reply to McKinney on Lonergan". MC KINNEY, Ronald H.

DIFFERENTIATION
Bergsonism. DELEUZE, Gilles.
"A Feminist Theory of Social Differentiation" in *Feminism/Postmodernism*, YEATMAN, Anna.
Différentielles et intégrales sociales chez Rousseau. BACHTA, Abdelkader.
Is Confirmation Differential?. ERWIN, Edward and SIEGEL, Harvey.
What are Discernible?. SCHLESINGER, George N.

DIGITAL
Dretske on Perception. HOROWITZ, Amir.

DIGNITY
La dignità dell'uomo da Kant a Hegel. PAOLINELLI, Marco.

DILATOR(S)
Boundedness Theorems for Dilators and Ptykes. KECHRIS, Alexander S.
A Strong Boundedness Theorem for Dilators. KECHRIS, Alexander S and WOODIN, W H.

DILEMMA(S)
Moral Dilemmas. GOWANS, Christopher W (ed).
"Against Tolerating the Intolerable" in *Logic and Ethics*, JACKSON, Jennifer.
"The Interpretive Dilemma" in *Critical Traditions in Contemporary Archaeology*, WYLIE, Alison.
A Comment on Maxwell's Resolution of the Wave/Particle Dilemma. SQUIRES, Euan J.
The Debate Over the So-Called Reality of Moral Dilemmas. STATMAN, Daniel.
A Determinist Dilemma. PERSSON, Ingmar.
Ethical Dilemmas in Performance Appraisal Revisited. LONGENECKER, Clinton and LUDWIG, Dean.
Ethical Dilemmas Posed By Recent and Prospective Developments with Respect to Agricultural Research. JOHNSON, Glenn L.
Genuine Moral Dilemmas and the Containment of Incoherence. PASKE, Gerald H.
Moral Dilemmas, Compromise and Compensation. DAY, J P.
Moral Dilemmas, Disjunctive Obligations, and Kant's Principle that 'Ought' Implies 'Can'. JACQUETTE, Dale.
Moral Dilemmas. MAC INTYRE, Alasdair.
More on Quine's Dilemma of Undetermination. GIBSON, Roger F.
Reactions to Ethical Dilemmas: A Study Pertaining to Certified Public Accounts. CLAYPOOL, G A and FETYKO, D F and PEARSON, M A.

DILTHEY
Bewusstsein und Natursein. CHO, Kah Kyung.
Hermeneutical Studies: Dilthey, Sophocles, and Plato. WILSON, Barrie A.
De la problématique diltheyenne à l'intégralisme de Jean Granier. AJERAR, Hassane.
Systematic Assumptions in Dilthey's Critique of Metaphysics. NENON, Thomas.

DIMENSIONAL ANALYSIS
The Ontology of Physical Objects: Four-Dimensional Hunks of Matter. HELLER, Mark.

DIODORUS CRONUS
Posibilidad e indeterminación: Aristóteles frente a Diodoro Crono. QUEVEDO, Amalia.

DIODOTUS
Rethinking the Diodotean Argument. JOHNSON, Laurie M.
DIONYSIAN
Nietzsche: A Frenzied Look. ACKERMANN, Robert John.
The Transfigurations of Intoxication: Nietzsche, Schopenhauer, and Dionysus. NUSSBAUM, Martha C.
DIONYSIUS
El conocimiento de Dios en la exposición de Tomás de Aquino sobre el "De divinis nominibus" de D Areopagita. ANDEREGGEN, Ignacio E M.
DIOPHANTINE EQUATION(S)
On Diophantine Equations Solvable in Models of Open Induction. OTERO, Margarita.
DIRECTIVE(S)
Cruzan and Caring for Others. LYNN, Joanne and GLOVER, Jacqueline.
Cruzan: No Rights Violated. ROBERTSON, John A.
DISABILITY
The Sanctity of Life and Substituted Judgement: The Case of Baby J. HORNETT, Stuart I.
DISADVANTAGE(S)
Learning Disabilities: A Questionable Construct. KLATT, Heinz-Joachim.
DISAGREEMENT(S)
Natural Reasons: Personality and Polity. HURLEY, S L.
"A Dialectical Version of Philosophical Discussion" in *Freedom in the Modern World: Jacques Maritain, Yves R Simon, Mortimer J Adler*, BIRD, Otto.
The 'Disagreements' Approach to Inservicing Philosophy for Children. WOOLCOCK, Peter G.
Disagreement in Philosophy. HELEN, Mercy and CHAKRAVARTI, Mihirvikash.
Paradigms, Populations and Problem-Fields: Approaches to Disagreement. ALLCHIN, Douglas.
DISARMAMENT
"Deterrence or Disarmament: An Appraisal of Consequentialist Arguments" in *In the Interest of Peace: A Spectrum of Philosophical Views*, KUNKEL, Joseph.
"Nuclear Abolition and the Fear of Cheating" in *In the Interest of Peace: A Spectrum of Philosophical Views*, PERKINS JR, Raymond.
DISASTER(S)
The Moral Responsibility of Corporate Executives for Disasters. BISHOP, John D.
DISCIPLE(S)
Paul de Man, Deconstruction, and Discipleship. ALLMAN, John.
DISCIPLINE(S)
"Continuity and Discontinuity in the Definition of a Disciplinary Field: The Case of XXth Century Physics" in *Imre Lakatos and Theories of Scientific Change*, CINI, Marcello.
Art, Aesthetics, and the Pitfalls of Discipline-Based Art Education. ARNSTINE, Donald.
Biology and the Social Sciences. WILSON, Edward O.
De lógica y matemática o donde situar el mundo matemático. DE LORENZO, Javier.
Division and Difference in the "Discipline" of Economics. AMARIGLIO, Jack and RESNICK, Stephen and WOLFF, Richard.
The Future of the Past: From the History of Historiography to Historiology. GRANDAZZI, Alexandre.
Ms en abyme: Deconstruction and Feminism. ELAM, Diane.
Philip Kitchers Soziobiologie-Kritik. VOLLMER, Gerhard.
Sociology: An Infirm Science. BUSINO, Giovanni and FERGUSON, Jeanne.
Theology and the Social Sciences—Discipline and Antidiscipline. MURPHY, Nancey.
Theology as the Queen (Bee) of the Disciplines?. VAUX, Kenneth.
DISCLOSURE(S)
Memory, Forgetfulness and the Disclosure of Being in Heidegger and Plotinus. BALES, Eugene F.
DISCORD
Scientia e fide. BLANDINO, Giovanni.
DISCOURSE
Bakhtin and the Epistemology of Discourse. THOMSON, Clive (ed).
The Communicative Ethics Controversy. BENHABIB, Seyla (ed).
Narrative in Culture: The Uses of Storytelling in the Sciences, Philosophy, and Literature. NASH, Christopher (ed).
Negative Dialectics and the End of Philosophy. ERICKSON, Glenn W.
Nietzsches Scheitern am Werk. HELLER, Edmund.
The Other Side of Language: A Philosophy of Listening. FIUMARA, Gemma Corradi.
The Potential of Modern Discourse: Musil, Peirce, and Perturbation. FINLAY, Marike.
Reading Habermas. RASMUSSEN, David M.
Spuren der Macht. RÖTTGERS, Kurt.
"Dialogue and Discourses" in *Writing the Politics of Difference*, WALDENFELS, Bernhard.
"The Metaphysic of Things and Discourse About Them" in *Reconsidering Psychology: Perspectives from Continental Philosophy*, WILLIAMS, Richard N.
A Contribution of the Conception of "Discursivity" and "Spontaneiti" of Thinking (in Czechoslovakian). BENYOVSZKY, Ladislav.
Constrained Discourse and Public Life. MOON, J Donald.
The Context of Discourse: Let's Not Throw the Baby Out with the Bathwater. ABRAMS, Dominic and HOGG, Michael A.
Critical Fanonism. GATES JR, Henry Louis.
Discourse and the Moral Point of View: Deriving a Dialogical Principle of Universalization. REHG, William.
Discourse Ethics and the Communitarian Critique of Neo-Kantianism. REHG, William.
Discourse: Definitions and Contradictions. PARKER, Ian.
Discourse: Noun, Verb or Social Practice?. POTTER, Jonathan (and others).
O discurso filosófico e a unidade da verdade nas primeiras obras de Paul Ricoeur. RENAUD, Michel.
Dr C Neugebauer's Critical Note on Ethnophilosophy in the Philosophical Discourse in Africa: Some Remarks. BEWAJI, J A I.
Gonseth et le discours théologique. MOREL, Bernard.
La metáfora como resolución de un problema comunicativo-lingüístico. FERNÁNDEZ, Teresa Bejaran.
A Moral Ideal for Everyone and No One. CONWAY, Daniel W.
Mothers of In(ter)vention: Women's Writing in Philosophy of Education. LEACH, Mary S.
Per un'analisi del discorso dichiarativo. CELANO, Bruno.
Possibility of Philosophical-Theological Discourse (in Serbo-Croatian). BELIC, Miljenko.
Pragmatique du discours et réciprocité de perspectives (A propos de Don Quichotte et Don Juan). GÓMEZ-MORIANA, Antonio.
Real Things: Discourse, Context and Practice. PARKER, Ian.
Una reflexión sobre el pensamiento científico técnico. CORONA, N A.
Sequencing Rules and Coherence in Discourse. TSUI, Amy B M.
A significação "crítica" de Le volontaire et l'involontaire. HENRIQUES, Fernanda.
Technology, Truth and Language: The Crisis of Theological Discourse. CROWLEY, Paul.
The Theosophic Discourse According to Jacob Boehme (in French). DEGHAYE, Pierre.
Three Realities and Two Discourses. TABORSKY, Edwina.
The Vanishing Subject of Contemporary Discourse: A Pragmatic Response. COLAPIETRO, Vincent M.
DISCOURSE ETHICS
A New Approach in Moral Theory (in Dutch). KETTNER, Matthias.
DISCOVERY
Herbert Simon's Computational Models of Scientific Discovery. DOWNES, Stephen M.
Philosophy of Science: From Justification to Explanation. KANTOROVICH, Aharon.
Theory Pursuit: Between Discovery and Acceptance. WHITT, Laurie Anne.
DISCRETION
Discretion, Punishment, and Juvenile Justice. SCHRAG, Francis.
Jurisprudential Oaks from Mythical Acorns: The Hart-Dworkin Debate Revisited. BOON LEONG PHANG, Andrew.
A Theoretical Note on Simmel's Concept of Acquaintance. DOUBT, Keith.
DISCRIMINATION
Identity and Discrimination. WILLIAMSON, Timothy.
"Equality, Discrimination and Preferential Treatment" in *A Companion to Ethics*, BOXILL, Bernard R.
"Higher-Order Discrimination" in *Identity, Character, and Morality: Essays in Moral Psychology*, PIPER, Adrian M S.
Civil Rights versus Civil Liberties: The Case of Discriminatory Verbal Harassment. GREY, Thomas.
The Ethics of Statistical Discrimination. MAITZEN, Stephen.
Is Mandatory Retirement Unfair Age Discrimination?. WEDEKING, Gary A.
Matters of Conscience. SIMS, Pamela F.
Racial Bias, the Death Penalty, and Desert. MEYERS, Christopher.
Why Markets Don't Stop Discrimination. SUNSTEIN, Cass R.
DISCURSIVE
The Discursive Formation of the Body in the History of Medicine. LEVIN, David Michael and SOLOMON, George F.
What Can a Discursive Theory of Morality Learn from Aquinas?. RENTTO, Juha-Pekka.
DISCURSIVE LOGIC
Une introduction à l'analyse du discours argumentatif. MENDENHALL, Vance.
DISEASE
Moral Theory and Medical Practice. FULFORD, K W M.
Fingarette on the Disease Concept of Alcoholism. CORLETT, J Angelo.
Geschiedenis als muurbloempje. PRINS, Ad.
The Temporality of Illness: Four Levels of Experience. TOOMBS, S Kay.

DISINTERESTEDNESS
A Fat Worm of Error?. MC GHEE, Michael.
DISJUNCTION
A Calculus for the Common Rules of.... RAUTENBERG, Wolfgan.
Macdonald on Type Reduction via Disjunction. ENDICOTT, Ronald P.
Relevance and Paraconsistency—A New Approach, Part II: The Formal Systems. AVRON, Arnon.
DISJUNCTIVE SYLLOGISM
The Irrelevance of Classical Logic. KEENE, G B.
DISORDER(S)
Delivering Hydrocephalic Fetuses. STRONG, Carson.
Note on Entropy, Disorder and Disorganization. DENBIGH, K G.
DISPOSITION(S)
The Environmental Dependence of Dispositional Aims: Response to the Presidential Address. RAYWID, Mary Ann.
Fostering the Disposition to be Rational. SIEGEL, Harvey.
Hume's Ethics: Acts, Rules, Dispositions and Utility. SHIRLEY, Edward.
Perhaps by Skill Alone. MISSIMER, Connie.
Persistent Propensities: Portrait of a Familiar Controversy. NORDMANN, Alfred.
Rational and Caring Teachers: How Dispositional Aims Shape Teacher Preparation. ARNSTINE, Barbara.
Real Dispositions in the Physical World. THOMPSON, Ian J.
DISSATISFACTION
Desacralization and the Disenchantment of the World. WENNEMANN, Daryl.
DISSENT
Psychology and Controversy. AGASSI, Joseph.
Religious Liberty, Religious Dissent and the Catholic Tradition. COWDIN, Daniel M.
DISSONANCE
Rediscovering the Left. HOWARD, Dick.
DISTINCTION(S)
The Ethics of Inarticulacy. KYMLICKA, Will.
The Incoherence of Kant's Transcendental Dialectic: Specifying the Minimal Conditions for Dialectical Error. HERMAN, David J.
Non-Rational Cognitive Processes as Changes of Distinctions. HEYLIGHEN, Francis.
Separating Care and Cure: An Analysis of Historical and Contemporary Images of Nursing and Medicine. JECKER, Nancy S and SELF, Donnie J.
DISTRIBUTION
The Crisis in Health Care: Ethical Issues. MC KENZIE, Nancy F (ed).
"On Fair Distribution of Indivisible Goods" in *Logic and Ethics*, SZANIAWSKI, Klemens.
Intermediate Quantifiers versus Percentages. CARNES, Robert D and PETERSON, Philip L.
Morals by Appropriation. FREEMAN, Samuel.
DISTRIBUTIVE JUSTICE
Baffling Phenomena: And Other Studies in the Philosophy of Knowledge and Valuation. RESCHER, Nicholas.
Gerechtigkeit, Wohlfahrt und Rationalität. SCHMIDT, Johannes.
What Is Justice? Classic and Contemporary Readings. SOLOMON, Robert C (ed).
Distributive Justice and Utility. GOLDSTICK, D.
Nozick et la stabilité des principes de justice distributive. BÉGIN, Luc.
Resources, Capacities, and Ownership: The Workmanship Ideal and Distributive Justice. SHAPIRO, Ian.
Siting, Justice, and Conceptions of Good. ENGLISH, Mary.
DIVERSITY
Continuity and Diversity in Philosophy of Education: An Introduction. BURBULES, Nicholas C.
Goodbye and Farewell: Siegel versus Feyerabend. NORDMANN, Alfred.
Kant's Diversity Theory: A Dissenting View. GLOUBERMAN, Mark.
Transition to Pragmatic Liberalism: Diversity, Contingency, and Social Solidarity. LINDGREN, Ralph.
DIVESTITURE
Principled Divestiture and Moral Integrity. CAHN, Steven M.
DIVINATION
On the Functional Unity of the Four Dimensions of Thought in the *Book of Changes*. LIU, Shu-Hsien.
DIVINE
The Dilemma of Freedom and Foreknowledge. ZAGZEBSKI, Linda Trinkaus.
Divine Nature and Human Language: Essays in Philosophical Theology. ALSTON, William P.
Fallen Freedom: Kant on Radical Evil and Moral Regeneration. MICHALSON JR, Gordon E.
"Divine Truth in Husserl and Kant: Some Issues in Phenomenological Theology" in *Phenomenology of the Truth Proper to Religion*, HART, James G.
"Jung and Whitehead on Self and Divine: The Necessity for Symbol and Myth" in *Archetypal Process: Self and Divine in Whitehead, Jung, and Hillman*, SLUSSER, Gerald H.
The Antinomy of Divine Necessity. SCHRADER, David E.
Common Ground: Aristotle on Human and Divine Noetic Activity. MORGAN, Vance G.
Divine Foresight and Human Moral Responsibility (in Hebrew). BAR-ON, A Zvie.
Divine Knowledge and Divine Control: A Response to Gordon and Sadowsky. BASINGER, David.
Divine Reason and Virtue in St Thomas's Natural Law Theory. KILLORAN, John B.
Francesco Bonucci, tra medicina e filosofia. STORTI, Cinzia.
Logic and Logos—The Search for Unity in Hegel and Coleridge, III: A Different Logos. PERKINS, Mary Anne.
Le relazioni divine secondo S Tommaso d'Aquino: Riproposizione di un problema e prospettive di indagine. VENTIMIGLIA, Giovanni.
Theology and the Necessity of Natures. ANGLIN, W S.
DIVINE IMPERATIVE(S)
The Recent Revival of Divine Command Ethics. QUINN, Philip L.
DIVINE RIGHT(S)
Politics Drawn From the Very Words of Holy Scripture—Jacques-Benigne Bossuet. RILEY, Patrick (ed).
DIVINE WILL
Plotin: Traité sur la liberté et la volonté de l'Un. LEROUX, Georges.
Freedom and the Free Will Defense. GALE, Richard M.
DIVINITY
Behind the Masks of God: An Essay Toward Comparative Theology. NEVILLE, Robert Cummings.
History and Spirit: An Inquiry into the Philosophy of Liberation. KOVEL, Joel.
Mystical Monotheism: A Study in Ancient Platonic Theology. KENNEY, John Peter.
The A/Theology of Don Cupitt: A Theological Option in Our Post-Modern Age. TARBOX JR, Everett J.
Freedom Is Our Divinity (in German). EHRHARDT, Walter E.
Our Inner Divinity: Humanism and the Spiritual Enterprise. ARISIAN, Khoren.
DIVISIBILITY
Some Features of Hume's Conception of Space. FRASCA-SPADA, Marina.
DIVISION
Collection and Division in the *Phaedrus* and *Statesman*. WEDIN, Michael V.
División y dialéctica en el *Fedro*. SANTA CRUZ, María Isabel.
Plato and Aristotle on Division and Definition. DESLAURIERS, Marguerite.
DOCTOR-PATIENT RELATIONSHIP
Ethical Practice in Clinical Medicine. ELLOS, William J.
Medical Work in America: Essays on Health Care. FREIDSON, Eliot.
"Facts and Values in the Physician-Patient Relationship" in *Ethics, Trust, and the Professions: Philosophical and Cultural Aspects*, BROCK, Dan W.
"The Phenomenon of Trust and the Patient-Physician Relationship" in *Ethics, Trust, and the Professions: Philosophical and Cultural Aspects*, ZANER, Richard M.
Anencephalic Infants and Special Relationships. JECKER, Nancy S.
The Chief of Medicine. BRODY, Howard.
Chronic Illness and the Physician-Patient Relationship. MOROS, Daniel A (and others).
Consumer Sovereignty versus Informed Consent: Saying No to Requests to "Do Everything" for Dying Patients. WEBER, Leonard.
The Costs of Commercial Medicine. DOUGHERTY, Charles J.
Diagnosis Without Doctors. MAZOUÉ, James G.
Doctors and Their Advertising. BURTON, Gene E.
The Limits of a Wish. RIE, Michael A.
Uninformed Consent. MARCUS, Ruth Barcan and KUCKLICK, B and BERCOVITCH, S.
DOCTRINE(S)
The Philosophy in Christianity. VESEY, Godfrey (ed).
A Contribution to the Discussion of the Doctrinal Preconditions of the Deformation of Socialism. KOLODII, A F.
El lugar de la doctrina social de la reflexión teológico moral cristiana. BRIANCESCO, E.
Marranos (Pigs), or from Coexistence to Toleration. SHELL, Marc.
DOCUMENT(S)
Literacy as Disempowerment: The Role of Documentary Texts. DE CASTELL, Suzanne.
DOGEN
Das Ich im deutschen Idealismus und das Selbst im Zen-Buddhist Fichte und Dogen. NAGASAWA, Kunihiko.
The Self in Medieval Japanese Buddhism: Focusing on Dōgen. KIMURA, Kiyotaka.
DOGMA
"Two Dogmas of Kantian Aesthetics" in *XIth International Congress in Aesthetics, Nottingham 1988*, ZANGWILL, Nick.
Fools and Heretics. BAMBROUGH, Renford.

DOGMATISM
"Dogmatism and Belief in French Cultural Life in the 1930s" in *From Twilight to Dawn: The Cultural Vision of Jacques Maritain*, SUTHER, Judith D.
"God's World and Man Becoming: How Can Science Possibly Help Us Transcend Dogmatism?" in *Science and Religion: One World-Changing Perspectives on Reality*, VAN DER VEKEN, J.
Fichte on Skepticism. BREAZEALE, Daniel.
The Critical and the Dogmatic Tendency of Phenomenological Philosophy (in Czechoslovakian). CIBULKA, Josef.

DOMAIN(S)
Domain Theory in Logical Form. ABRAMSKY, Samson.
Her Terrain is Outside His "Domain". PEEPLES, S Elise.
Wofür sind wir verantworlich?. NEUMAIER, Otto.

DOMINATION
Femininity and Domination: Studies in the Phenomenology of Oppression. BARTKY, Sandra Lee.
Domination and Moral Struggle: the Philosophical Heritage of Marxism Reviewed. HONNETH, Axel.
Feminism and Ecology: On the Domination of Nature. MILLS, Patricia Jagentowicz.
Some Thoughts About Heterosexualism. HOAGLAND, Sarah Lucia.

DONAGAN, A
Abortion in Rape Cases. BEABOUT, Greg.

DONATISM
La doctrina del don de San Agustín de Hipona. BELDA PLANS, Pilar.

DONNELLAN, K
On Begging the Question 'Who is N?'. PATTON, Thomas E.

DOSTOYEVSKY
F M Dostoievsky (1821-1881): Great Existentialist-Psychiatrist. ESSER, P H.

DOUBLE EFFECT
"Intention and Side-Effects" in *Liability and Responsibility*, FINNIS, John.
The Doctrine of Double Effect and Affirmative Action. JORDAN, Jeff.
The Doctrine of Double Effect: Its Philosophical Viability. BOLE, Thomas.
Tooley and the Trolley. FISCHER, John Martin.

DOUBLE JEOPARDY
On Leo Katz, Double Jeopardy, and the Blockburger Test. LOCKE, Lawrence A.

DOUBT
Doubting: Contemporary Perspectives on Skepticism. ROTH, Michael D (ed).
Meditations on First Philosophy: A Bilingual Edition—René Descartes. HEFFERNAN, George (trans).
Metaphysical Delusion. COWLEY, Fraser.
Dialogue and Doubt in Descartes' First Meditation. LINVILLE, Kent.
Doubt and Faith: Santayana and Kierkegaard on Fundamental Belief. SARTWELL, Crispin.
Merleau-Ponty on the Cartesian "Dubito": A Critical Analysis. HUDAC, Michael C.
Technological Faith and Christian Doubt. FERRÉ, Frederick.

DOVE, P
The Neglected Background of Radical Liberalism: P E Dove's Theory of Property. CUNLIFFE, John.

DOXASTIC LOGIC
On the Logic of Conscious Belief. TOKARZ, Marek.

DOXOGRAPHY
Externalist Theories of Perception. ALSTON, William P.
The Logic of Lost Lingens. SEAGER, William.

DRAMA
Hegel, Antigone, and the Possibility of Ecstatic Dialogue. WILLETT, Cynthia.
Interpreting *Interpretations*. GROSSMAN, Morris.
What Good is Irony?. LEVINSON, Henry S.
What's It All About? The Critical Method of Analysis as Applied to Drama. CLEARY JR, Donald L.

DREAM(S)
Aristotle on Sleep and Dreams. GALLOP, David (trans).
Dream and Culture: An Anthropological Study of the Western Intellectual Tradition. PARMAN, Susan.
"Metaphor, Dreamwork and Irrationality" in *Truth and Interpretation: Perspectives on the Philosophy of Donald Davidson*, CAVELL, Marcia.
Moral Dreams and Practical Realities. LINZEY, Andrew.
The Quest for Transformational Experience. BULKLEY, Kelly.

DREAMING
Scepticism and Dreaming: Imploding the Demon. WRIGHT, Crispin.

DRETSKE, F
"Information and the Mental" in *Truth and Interpretation: Perspectives on the Philosophy of Donald Davidson*, PUTNAM, Hilary.
Dretske on Knowledge and Content. GJELSVIK, Olav.
Dretske on Perception. HOROWITZ, Amir.
Gettier's Principle for Deducibility of Justification. BASU, Sandhya.

DRUG(S)
Biomedical Ethics Reviews, 1987. HUMBER, James M (ed).
"The Case against bGH" in *Agricultural Bioethics: Implications of Agricultural Biotechnology*, COMSTOCK, Gary L.
"The Case for Physician-Dispensed Drugs" in *Biomedical Ethics Reviews, 1989*, IRVINE, William B.
"Ethical Issues in Prescribing Drugs for the Aged and the Dying" in *Biomedical Ethics Reviews, 1987*, HOFFMASTER, Barry and BACHRACH, Sarah.
"The Ethics of Physicians Dispensing Drugs for Profit" in *Biomedical Ethics Reviews, 1989*, KNOWLTON, Calvin H.
"Prescribing Drugs for the Aged and Dying" in *Biomedical Ethics Reviews, 1987*, YEZZI, Ron.
"Should Physicians Dispense Drugs for a Profit?" in *Biomedical Ethics Reviews, 1989*, WEINSTEIN, Michael P.
Ethical Considerations and Ramifications of the 1989 Generic Drug Scandal. HEACOCK, Marian V and ORVIS, Gregory P.
Geschiedenis als muurbloempje. PRINS, Ad.
The Political Economy of Tardive Dyskinesia: Asymmetries in Power and Responsibility. COHEN, David and MC CUBBIN, Michael.
Psychoactive Drug Prescribing in Japan: Epistemological and Bioethical Considerations. SAKAI, Akio.
A Response to 'Psychoactive Drug Prescribing in Japan'. COVERDALE, John.
Response to Dr Sakai's 'Psychoactive Drug Prescribing in Japan'. RITCHIE, Karen.

DRYDEN
Criteria of Certainty: Truth and Judgment in the English Enlightenment. COPE, Kevin L.

DUALISM
see also Body(-dies), Minds
Bergsonism. DELEUZE, Gilles.
The Case for Dualism. SMYTHIES, John R (ed).
David Hume's Theory of Mind. FLAGE, Daniel E.
Evolution als Höherentwicklung des Bewusstseins. KUMMER, Christian.
Other Human Beings. COCKBURN, David.
A Philosophical Daybook: Post-Critical Investigations. POTEAT, William H.
Psychology (Companions to Ancient Thought: 2). EVERSON, Stephen (ed).
Self and Non-Self: The Drigdrisyaviveka Attributed to Samkara. RAPHAEL (trans).
Sensations: A Defense of Type Materialism. HILL, Christopher S.
"A Comment on Three Topics in Volume 7 of the *Treatise*: Teleology, the Mind-Body Problem, and Health and Disease" in *Studies on Mario Bunge's "Treatise"*, DUBROVSKY, Bernardo.
"A Defense of Dualism" in *The Case for Dualism*, FOSTER, John.
"Descartes, Rorty and the Mind-Body Fiction" in *Reading Rorty*, HORNSBY, Jennifer.
"Dualism: A Parapsychological Perspective" in *The Case for Dualism*, BELOFF, John.
"A Dualist Account of Embodiment" in *The Case for Dualism*, ROBINSON, Howard.
"In Defense of the Demon" in *The Case for Dualism*, HARRISON, Jonathan.
"Mario Bunge on the Mind-Body Problem and Ontology: Critical Examinations" in *Studies on Mario Bunge's "Treatise"*, KUROSAKI, Hiroshi.
"The Mind-Body Problem" in *The Case for Dualism*, SMYTHIES, John R.
"Personal Identity and the Mind-Body Problem" in *The Case for Dualism*, MADELL, Geoffrey.
"Plotinus and Soul-Body Dualism" in *Psychology (Companions to Ancient Thought: 2)*, EMILSSON, Eyjólfur K.
"Reply to Dretske's 'Does Meaning Matter?'" in *Information, Semantics and Epistemology*, FODOR, Jerry A.
"Tackling the Mind" in *Studies on Mario Bunge's "Treatise"*, SHEA, William R.
"Type Epiphenomenalism, Type Dualism, and the Causal Priority of the Physical" in *Philosophical Perspectives, 3: Philosophy of Mind and Action Theory, 1989*, MC LAUGHLIN, Brian P.
"Ways of Establishing Harmony" in *Information, Semantics and Epistemology*, DENNETT, Daniel C.
Against Cartesian Dualism: Strawson and Sartre on the Unity of Person. MUI, Constance.
Against Common Sense: Avoiding Cartesian Anxiety. BINEHAM, Jeffery L.
Cartesian Passions and Cartesian Dualism. HOFFMAN, Paul.
Certainty, the Cogito, and Cartesian Dualism. GLOUBERMAN, Mark.
Churchland, Introspection, and Dualism. ZEMACH, Eddy M.
Contextualizing Knowledge: A Reply to "Dewey and the Theory of Knowledge". HICKMAN, Larry.
Die erkenntniskritische Wendung Descartes' als Konsequenz geschichtlicher Entwicklung des Leib-Seele-Dualismus. POHLENZ, G.
Irreducible Dualisms and the Residue of Commonsense: On the Inevitability of Cartesian Anxiety. HIKINS, James W and CHERWITZ, Richard A.
On the Duality of China's Traditional Mode of Thought and the Difficulty of Transforming It. ZIHLIN, Li.
Personal Identity and the Idea of a Human Being. MADELL, Geoffrey.
Le premier registre de Descartes. RODIS-LEWIS, Geneviève.

DUALISM
The Quest for Transformational Experience. BULKLEY, Kelly.
The Real Distinction Between Mind and Body. YABLO, Stephen.
Replies to My Computational Commentators. DIETRICH, Eric.
Sustaining Non-Rationalized Practices: Body-Mind, Power and Situational Ethics—Interview with Hubert and Stuart Dreyfus. FLYVBJERG, Bent.
Two Cartesian Arguments for the Simplicity of the Soul. ZIMMERMAN, Dean W.
The Unavoidability of Gender. SCHEMAN, Naomi.
What is it Like to be an Aardvark?. TIGHLMAN, B R.

DUALITY(-TIES)
Heidegger e la duplicità del presente. PENZO, Maurizio.
Nelson Algebras Through Heyting Ones^1:1. SENDLEWSKI, Andrzej.
The Priestley Duality for Wajsberg Algebras. MARTÍNEZ, N G.
Two Brains, Two Minds? Wigan's Theory of Mental Duality. PUCCETTI, Roland.

DUCHAMP, M
Philosophical Events: Essays of the '80s. RAJCHMAN, John.

DUDMAN, V
Classifying Conditionals II. JACKSON, Frank.

DUFF, A
Duff and the Wager. JORDAN, Jeff.

DUMMETT, M
Abstract Singular Reference: A Dilemma for Dummett. MILLER, Alexander.
Dummett and the Origins of Analytical Philosophy, or the Philosophy of Thought vs Philosophy of Language (in German). DÖLLING, Evelyn and DÖLLING, Johannes.
Dummett's Ought from Is. GREEN, Karen.
The Task of a Theory of Meaning. SAYRE, Patricia.
Verificationism and Anti-Realism. ROGERSON, Kenneth.

DUNS SCOTUS
The Philosophical Theology of John Duns Scotus. ADAMS, Marilyn McCord (ed).
Algunas consideraciones sobre la substancia en la metafísica de Juan Duns Escoto. BEUCHOT, Mauricio.
The Condemnation of 1277: Another Light on Scotist Ethics. INGHAM, Mary E.
Dicendum est eum non esse hominem: Ein mögliches frühes Zeugnis für die anthropologische Gewichtung.... KÖHLER, Theodor Wolfram.
Haecceitas and the Bare Particular. PARK, Woosuk.
Peirce's Haecceitism. DI LEO, Jeffrey R.
Scotus, Frege, and Bergmann. PARK, Woosuk.

DURAN, J
Species, Individuals, and Domestication: A Commentary on Jane Duran's "Domesticated and Then Some". VARNER, Gary E.

DURATION
see also Time
Bergsonism. DELEUZE, Gilles.

DURESS
Moral Responsibility, Psychiatric Disorders and Duress. ELLIOTT, Carl.

DURKHEIM
On Durkheim's Rules of Sociological Method. GANE, Mike.
The Taming of Chance. HACKING, Ian.

DUSSEL, E
Filosofía de la liberación como nuevo pensamiento a partir de los oprimidos y como de-strucción (2a parte). AÑIZAR, Humberto Encarnación.
Origins and Tendencies of the Philosophy of Liberation in Latin American Thought: A Critique of Dussel's Ethics. SCHUTTE, Ofelia.

DUTCH
The Humanities in the Nineties: A View From the Netherlands. ZÜRCHER, Erik (ed).
A Case Against Dutch Euthanasia. FENIGSEN, Richard.
Clever Bookies and Coherent Beliefs. CHRISTENSEN, David.
Het Dialectisch Humanistisch Grondmotief van Natuur en Vrijheid in de Pedagogiek als Wetenschap. OUWENDORP, C.
Een gedesoriënteerde veranderingswetenschap. GASTELAARS, M.
Has the Study of Philosophy at Dutch Universities Changed under Economic and Political Pressures?. VAN DER MEULEN, Barend and LEYDESDORFF, Loet.
La réception de Spinoza dans la littérature néerlandaise. HENRARD, Roger.
Welke natuur is het beschermen waard?. VAN DER WINDT, Henny J and HARBERS, Hans.
Wetenschapsontwikkeling en kundes. BOON, Louis (and others).

DUTTON, D
Misreading Rorty. KOLENDA, Konstantin.

DUTY(-TIES)
see also Obligation(s)
Moral Dilemmas. GOWANS, Christopher W (ed).
The Realm of Rights. THOMSON, Judith Jarvis.
"An Ethic of Prima Facie Duties" in *A Companion to Ethics*, DANCY, Jonathan.
"Friendship and Duty: Some Difficult Relations" in *Identity, Character, and Morality: Essays in Moral Psychology*, STOCKER, Michael.
"Pacifism, Duty, and Supererogation" in *In the Interest of Peace: A Spectrum of Philosophical Views*, CADY, Duane L.
Advocacy of Just Health Policies as Professional Duty: Cultural Biases and Ethical Responsibilities. CRANDALL, Lee A.
Are Kantian Duties Categorical?. SCHOEMAN, Ferdinand.
Between the Horns of the Negative-Positive Duty Debate. MALM, H M.
Categorical Requirements: Kant and Hume on the Idea of Duty. WIGGINS, David.
A Critique of Kantian Arguments Against Emotions as Moral Motives. OAKLEY, Justin.
Desire and Duty in Kant. GRIGG, Russell.
Directions of Justification in the Negative-Positive Duty Debate. MALM, H M.
Duties to Friends. PASSELL, Dan.
Duty and Inclination: The Phenomenological Value Ethics of Hans Reiner. GÖRTZEN, René.
Generosity: A Duty Without a Right. STITH, Richard.
Justification in the 20th Century. PLANTINGA, Alvin.
Kant and the Origins of Totalitarianism. SIEBERS, Tobin.
Loyalty: The Police. EWIN, R E.
Moral Goodness, Esteem, and Acting from Duty. LEMOS, Noah M.
The Moral Status of the Corporation. EWIN, R E.
Nature, Justice, and Duty in the *Defensor Pacis*: Marsiglio of Padua's Ciceronian Impulse. NEDERMAN, Cary J.
On Law and Morality: A Dialogue. VON WRIGHT, Georg Henrik.
Partialism and Parenthood. NELSON, James Lindemann.
The Professional's Dilemma: Choosing Between Service and Success. MC DOWELL, Banks.
Property Rights and Preservationist Duties. GOODIN, Robert E.
Relative Duties in the Law. WELLMAN, Carl.
Supererogation and the Fulfillment of Duty. MELLEMA, Gregory.
What is Virtue Ethics All About?. TRIANOSKY, Gregory.

DWORKIN, R
Descent into Subjectivity: Studies of Rawls, Dworkin and Unger in the Context of Modern Thought. MURPHY JR, Cornelius F.
Dworkin and His Critics: The Relevance of Ethical Theory in Philosophy of Law. BALL, Stephen W.
Dworkin, Habermas, and the CLS Movement on Moral Criticism in Law. INGRAM, David.
La elusión mediante sociedades a la luz de los principios constitucionales. RUIZ ZAPATERO, Guillermo.
Equality. MILLER, David.
Jurisprudential Oaks from Mythical Acorns: The Hart-Dworkin Debate Revisited. BOON LEONG PHANG, Andrew.
Legal Positivism, Social Rules, and *Riggs* versus *Palmer*. BEEHLER, Rodger.
Protestant Hermeneutics and the Rule of Law: Gadamer and Dworkin. HENLEY, Kenneth.
Skepticism and Legal Interpretation. NATHAN, Daniel O.
Taking Rights Seriously in the Abortion Case. DWORKIN, Ronald.
Toward a Reconciliation of Liberalism and Communitarianism. ELLIS, Ralph D.
Whose Right? Ronald Dworkin, Women, and Pornographers. LANGTON, Rae.

DYING
see also Death
The Crisis in Health Care: Ethical Issues. MC KENZIE, Nancy F (ed).
Ethical Practice in Clinical Medicine. ELLOS, William J.
"Ethical Issues in Prescribing Drugs for the Aged and the Dying" in *Biomedical Ethics Reviews, 1987*, HOFFMASTER, Barry and BACHRACH, Sarah.
"Prescribing Drugs for the Aged and Dying" in *Biomedical Ethics Reviews, 1987*, YEZZI, Ron.
Consumer Sovereignty versus Informed Consent: Saying No to Requests to "Do Everything" for Dying Patients. WEBER, Leonard.

DYNAMIC LOGIC
Dynamic Predicate Logic. GROENENDIJK, Jeroen and STOKHOF, Martin.

DYNAMICS
The Dynamics of Rational Deliberation. SKYRMS, Brian.
"The Dynamics of Alternative Realities" in *Reconsidering Psychology: Perspectives from Continental Philosophy*, GLYNN, Simon.
"Probability in Dynamical Systems" in *Logic, Methodology and Philosophy of Science, VIII*, VON PLATO, Jan.
The Theory of Legal Dynamics Reconsidered. WEINBERGER, Ota.

DYNAMISM
Spuren der Macht. RÖTTGERS, Kurt.

EAST EUROPEAN
The Changing Face of Civil Society in Eastern Europe. KOLARSKA-BOBINSKA, Lena.
Failure of a Renaissance (Why It Is Impossible to Remain a Marxist in East Central Europe). VAJDA, Mihaly.
Illusions and Visions: Models Of and In Modern Societies. MARZ, Lutz.

EAST EUROPEAN
The Meaning of Recent Changes in Eastern Europe. MARKOVIC, Mihailo.
Romania's Revolution and its Prospects. BRUCAN, Silviu.
The Welfare State: What is Left?. PRYCHITKO, David L.
What Happened in Eastern Europe in 1989?. CHIROT, Daniel.
The World Reconsidered: A Brief *AggiornamentoF* for Leftist Intellectuals. SKIRBEKK, Gunnar.

EASTERN
see Oriental

EASTERN PHILOSOPHY
see Oriental

ECCLESIOLOGY
The Critical Problem of Knowledge. BLANDINO, Giovanni (ed).
"The Credibility of Ecclesiastical Teaching on the Morality of War" in *Celebrating Peace*, YODER, John H.

ECKERMANN, J
"Namely, Eckermann" in *Looking After Nietzsche*, RONELL, Avital.

ECKHART
Meister Eckhart and the Neoplatonic Heritage: The Thinker's Way to God. WOODS, Richard.

ECO, U
"Roland Barthes et Umberto Eco à la Recherche du Roman Postmoderne" in *XIth International Congress in Aesthetics, Nottingham 1988*, ZNEPOLSKY, Ivahilo.
The Doubts about Post-Modernism (in Czechoslovakian). AJVAZ, Michal.
To Umberto Eco's Criticism of Icon (in Czechoslovakian). HAMAN, Ales.

ECOLOGY
A Morally Deep World: An Essay on Moral Significance and Environmental Ethics. JOHNSON, Lawrence E.
The River of the Mother of God, and Other Essays by Aldo Leopold. FLADER, Susan L (ed).
"Marxism, Humanism, and Ecology" in *The Question of Humanism: Challenges and Possibilities*, LAWLER, James and ORUDJEV, Zaid.
"Merleau-Ponty and Deep Ecology" in *Ontology and Alterity in Merleau-Ponty*, LANGER, Monika.
Agricultural Practices, Ecology, and Ethics in the Third World. WESTRA, L S and BOWEN, K L and BEHE, B K.
Algunas consecuencias del panenteismo krausista: ecología y mujer. MENÉNDEZ UREÑA, Enrique.
A Candidate Paradigm for Human Ecology. BAPAT, Jyotsna.
Deep Ecology versus Ecofeminism: Healthy Differences or Incompatible Philosophies?. SESSIONS, Robert.
Ecofeminism and Androcentric Epistemology. DURAN, Jane.
Ecofeminist Theory and Grassroots Politics. LAHAR, Stephanie.
Ecological Feminism and Ecosystem Ecology. WARREN, Karen J and CHENEY, Jim.
Ecosabotage and Civil Disobedience. MARTIN, Michael.
Ecosocialism—Utopian and Scientific. HAYWARD, Tim.
Expecting Nature's Best: Optimality Models and Perfect Adaptation. HOLCOMB, H R.
Feminism and Ecology: On the Domination of Nature. MILLS, Patricia Jagentowicz.
Global Arguments for the Safety of Engineered Organisms. KLINE, David and GENDEL, Stephen M.
Ground, Pivot, Motion: Ecofeminist Theory, Dialogics, and Literary Practice. MURPHY, Patrick.
Heideggers Denken und die Ökologie. PADRUTT, Hanspeter.
Intentionality and the Ecological Approach. LOOREN DE JONG, H.
Island Biogeography, Species-Area Curves, and Statistical Errors: Applied Biology and Scientific Rationality. SHRADER-FRECHETTE, Kristin.
Kann in O Höffes Ethik der politischen Gerechtigkeit eine ökologische Ethik aufgehoben werden?. WETZEL, Manfred.
An Open Letter to Maxine Greene on "The Problem of Freedom in an Era of Ecological Interdependence". BOWERS, C A.
Physical Environment Television Advertisement Themes: 1979 and 1989. PETERSON, Robin T.
The Pot at the End of the Rainbow: Political Myth and the Ecological Crisis. DOYLE, Timothy.
Some Fundamental Aspects of Socioecological Theory and Policy, Part I (in German). OPIELKA, Michael.
Some Fundamental Aspects of Socioecological Theory and Policy, Part II (in German). OPIELKA, Michael.
Utilitaristische Ethik als Antwort auf die ökologische Krise. WOLF, Jean-Claude.
The Values of a Habitat. PARKER, Kelly.
Welke natuur is het beschermen waard?. VAN DER WINDT, Henny J and HARBERS, Hans.
What is the Price of a Rich Life?. MEYER, Zofia Golab.
Your Daughter or Your Dog? A Feminist Assessment of the Animal Research Issue. SLICER, Deborah.

ECONOMICS
Aspectos Metodológicos de la Investigación Científica. GONZÁLEZ, Wenceslao J (ed).
Beyond Ethnocentrism: A Reconstruction of Marx's Concept of Science. MC KELVEY, Charles.
A Cultivated Mind: Essays On J S Mill Presented to John M Robson. LAINE, Michael (ed).
The Death of Industrial Civilization. KASSIOLA, Joel Jay.
Earthbound: Introductory Essays in Environmental Ethics. REGAN, Tom (ed).
Gerechtigkeit, Wohlfahrt und Rationalität. SCHMIDT, Johannes.
Intelligibility in Science. DILWORTH, Craig (ed).
Interpreting Political Responsibility. DUNN, John.
Kierkegaard in Golden Age Denmark. KIRMMSE, Bruce H.
Medicine and Money: A Study of the Role of Beneficence in Health Care Cost Containment. MARSH, Frank H.
The Power of Ideology. MÉSZÁROS, István.
"Are Economic Kinds Natural?" in *Scientific Theories*, NELSON, Alan.
"Are There Economic Laws?" in *Studies on Mario Bunge's "Treatise"*, BARCELÓ, Alfons.
"Falsificationism Looked at from an 'Economic' Point of View" in *Imre Lakatos and Theories of Scientific Change*, RADNITZKY, Gerard.
"Miller on Economics" in *The Philosophy of John William Miller*, BROCKWAY, George P.
"Utility". BROOME, John.
Adam Smith and Social Justice: The Ethical Basis of *The Wealth of Nations*. OSSAR, Jacob.
African Famine: New Economic and Ethical Perspectives. LUCAS JR, George R.
Agricultura, desarrollo y autonomía. BLATZ, Charlie.
The Base Camp Paradox: A Reflection on the Place of Tâtonnement in General Equilibrium Theory. DE VROEY, Michel.
Between Necessity and Superabundance: Meta-economic Reflections on Marxism. WALDENFELS, Bernhard.
Beyond Malthusianism: Demography and Technology in John Stuart Mill's Stationary State. KURFIRST, Robert.
Biology and the Social Sciences. WILSON, Edward O.
Common Sense and the Foundations of Economic Theory: Duhem versus Robbins. SHEARMUR, Jeremy.
The Conflation of Productivity and Efficiency in Economics and Economic History. SINGH, Harinder and FRANTZ, Roger.
Division and Difference in the "Discipline" of Economics. AMARIGLIO, Jack and RESNICK, Stephen and WOLFF, Richard.
The Economic Analysis of Institutions. RICKETTS, Martin.
An Economic Model of Scientific Activity and Truth Acquisition. GOLDMAN, Alvin I and SHAKED, Moshe.
Economic Rights: A Test Case for Catholic Social Teaching. MC CANN, Dennis P.
Economic Theory and Human Behavior. MC NULTY, T Michael.
Economics and Ethics. REILLY, B J and KYJ, M J.
Economics, Ethics, and Tort Remedies: The Emerging Concept of Hedonic Value. KARNS, Jack E.
Economie in de spiegel van de natuurwetenschappen. KUIPERS, Theo A F.
Economists and Philosophers as Critics of the Free Enterprise System. ARNOLD, N Scott.
Ecosocialism—Utopian and Scientific. HAYWARD, Tim.
Entrepreneurial Philosophy (in German). HERDER-DORNEICH, Philipp.
The Ethics of Health Care as a Business. WERHANE, Patricia H.
German Collectivism and the Welfare State. NEAMAN, Elliot Yale.
Hermeneutics: A Protreptic. JOHNSON, Gregory R.
How to Get Rid of Your Expensive Philosopher of Science and Still Keep Control Over the Fuzzing Conversation of Mankind. VISKER, Rudi.
The Humanism of Economics or Economizing on Humanism?. RIUMIN, V A.
The Ideas of Karl Marx at a Turning Point in Human Civilization. PANTIN, I and PLIMAK, E.
The Impact of the French Revolution on the Development of Philosophy. NETOPILIK, Jakub.
Jevons's Applications of Utilitarian Theory to Economic Policy. PEART, Sandra J.
Keynesian Uncertainty and the Weight of Arguments. RUNDE, Jochen.
The Logic of Causal Inference: Econometrics and the Conditional Analysis of Causation. HOOVER, Kevin D.
Medicine as Business and Profession. AGICH, George J.
Metaphysics, MSRP and Economics. GLASS, J C and JOHNSON, W.
Once Again Pure Exchange Economies: A Critical View Towards the Structuralistic Reconstructions by Balzer & Stegmüller. REQUATE, Till.
An Outline of My Main Contributions to Economic Science. ALLAIS, Maurice.
Pisces Economicus: The Fish as Econontic Man. BOULIER, Bryan L and GOLDFARB, Robert S.
Political Economy and Mimetic Desire: A Postmodernist Reading of "Babette's Feast". SHAPIRO, Michael J.
Prediction and Explanation in Economics. SWAMIDASAN, Nalini.
Rational Chocolate Addiction or How Chocolate Cures Irrationality. ELLIOTT, C S.
Rationality, Culture and Values. CHATTOPADHYAYA, D P.

ECONOMICS

Response to W J Norman's "Has Rational Economic Man a Heart". LA CASSE, Chantale and ROSS, Don.
Self-Interest and the New Bashing of Economics. KIRZNER, Israel M.
The Differences Between the Capitalist and the Modern Society (in German). KRÜGER, Hans-Peter.
The Meaning of Discussions on Democratic Socialism in Czechoslovakia (in Czechoslovakian). KAMARYT, Jan.
Values, the Environment and the Creative Act. THOMAS, John C.
Was heisst "sich in der Gesellschaft orientieren"?. BÖHME, Gernot.
The Welfare State: What is Left?. PRYCHITKO, David L.
Why Markets Don't Stop Discrimination. SUNSTEIN, Cass R.
Wie van de drie: Wil de ware wetenschapsonderzoeker opstaan?. BIJSTERVELD, Karin and MESMAN, Jessica.

ECONOMY

Economic Efficiency: A Paradigm for Business Ethics. STIEBER, John and PRIMEAUX, Patrick.
Economies of Time: On the Idea of Time in Marx's Political Economy. BOOTH, William James.
Once Again Pure Exchange Economies: A Critical View Towards the Structuralistic Reconstructions by Balzer & Stegmüller. REQUATE, Till.
Rationality, Economic Action and Scarcity (in Hungarian). FEKETE, László.
The Legacy of Hamann—Thinking, Language and Economy (in Hungarian). RATHMANN, János.

ECOSYSTEM(S)

A Morally Deep World: An Essay on Moral Significance and Environmental Ethics. JOHNSON, Lawrence E.
Conciencia de catástrofe, poder y libertad. DEI, H Daniel.
Ecosystems as Circuits: Diagrams and the Limits of Physical Analogies. TAYLOR, Peter J and BLUM, Ann S.

ECSTASY

Echoes: After Heidegger. SALLIS, John.
"The Language of Ecstasy and the Ecstasy of Language" in *The Bible as Rhetoric: Studies in Biblical Persuasion and Credibility*, BARRETT, Cyril.

ECUMENISM

The Balance of Consciousness: Eric Voegelin's Political Theory. KEULMAN, Kenneth.

EDIFICATION

Divine Irony and the Natural Law: Speculation and Edification in Aquinas. HIBBS, Thomas S.

EDUCATION

see also Moral Education
Abeunt Studia in Mores: A Festschrift for Helga Doblin. MERRILL, Sarah A Bishop (ed).
Convictions. HOOK, Sidney.
Education as a Human Right: A Theory of Curriculum and Pedagogy. VANDENBERG, Donald.
Égalité Uguaglianza. FERRARI, Jean (ed).
Freedom in the Modern World: Jacques Maritain, Yves R Simon, Mortimer J Adler. TORRE, Michael D (ed).
French Philosophers in Conversation: Levinas, Schneider, Serres, Irigaray, Le Doeuff, Derrida. MORTLEY, Raoul.
The Humanities in the Nineties: A View From the Netherlands. ZÜRCHER, Erik (ed).
In Praise of the Cognitive Emotions. SCHEFFLER, Israel.
Markets, Managers and Theory in Education. HALLIDAY, John.
Moralische Verbindlichkeit oder Erziehung. LANGEWAND, Alfred.
Philosophical Foundations of Health Education. LAURA, Ronald S.
Platonic Piety. MORGAN, Michael L.
Relating Humanities and Social Thought (Science, Ideology, and Value, Volume 4). EDEL, Abraham.
The River of the Mother of God, and Other Essays by Aldo Leopold. FLADER, Susan L (ed).
Shaping Character: Moral Education in the Christian College. HOLMES, Arthur F.
Strukturanthropologie "Der menschliche Mensch". ROMBACH, Heinrich.
Der Ursprung der Erziehungsziele in der Lehre von Plato, Aristoteles und Neill. EGGER, Paul.
"Authority, Authoritarianism, and Education" in *The Realm of Humanitas: Responses to the Writings of Hannah Arendt*, GARNER, Reuben.
"The Hospital-Academic Health Center Interface: The Community of Practice and the Community of Learning" in *Integrity in Health Care Institutions: Humane Environments for Teaching, Inquiry, and Healing*, RABKIN, Mitchell T.
"John Mill's Education: Fact, Fiction, and Myth" in *A Cultivated Mind: Essays On J S Mill Presented to John M Robson*, STILLINGER, Jack.
"Maritain, Simon, and Vichy's Elite Schools" in *Freedom in the Modern World: Jacques Maritain, Yves R Simon, Mortimer J Adler*, HELLMAN, John.
"Parallels on Work, Theory and Practice in Yves R Simon and John Paul II" in *Freedom in the Modern World: Jacques Maritain, Yves R Simon, Mortimer J Adler*, GUEGUEN, John A.
"A Return to the Crossroads: A Maritainian View of the New Educational Reformers" in *From Twilight to Dawn: The Cultural Vision of Jacques Maritain*, HANCOCK, Curtis L.
"Una uguale educazione?" in *Égalité Uguaglianza*, PANCERA, Carlo.
"Critical Thinking and Philosophy for Children: The Educational Value of Philosophy". LINDOP, Clive.
"Does Metaphysics Really Matter for Practice?" It Depends on the Practitioner. GARRISON, James W.
"Event" in Dewey's Philosophy. DUFF, Barry E.
"Excellence, Equity, and Equality" Clarified. GREEN, Thomas F.
"Faith" in a Broad Sense as a Goal in Promoting Human Development. BECK, Clive.
The "New" Scholars in Philosophy of Education, 1976-1986. QUANTZ, Richard A.
"Working in America": A New Approach for the Humanities. SESSIONS, Robert.
The 'Teacher as Midwife': New Wine in Old Skins?. SANCHEZ, Karen L.
The 'Voice of Care': Implications for Bioethical Education. CARSE, Alisa L.
Aesthetic Education and Aesthetic Atmosphere (in Czechoslovakian). MATHAUSER, Zdenek.
Aesthetics and Art Education. SMITH, Peter.
AIDS and 'Dirt': Reflections on the Ethics of Ritual Cleanliness. CHURCHILL, Larry R.
Alienation, Schools, and Society. ZHANG, Wei Rose.
Aristotele professore?. NATALI, Carlo.
Aristotle's Account of Practical Reasoning as a Theoretical Base for Research on Teaching. NOEL, Jana.
Art and Morality in Plato: A Reappraisal. HALL, Robert W.
Art, Aesthetics, and the Pitfalls of Discipline-Based Art Education. ARNSTINE, Donald.
Art, Stance and Education. PUSCH, James.
Art, Truth and the Education of Subjectivity. HEPBURN, Ronald W.
Autonomy, Emotions and Desires: Some Problems Concerning R F Dearden's Account of Autonomy. STONE, Carolyn M.
Basal Readers—'Dominant But Dead' versus Gadamer and Language for Understanding. WIRTH, Arthur G.
Belief as a Condition of Knowledge: The Need for a Philosophical Perspective in Higher Education Reform. BRELL JR, Carl D.
The Bright Side of Textbook Controversies. SCAHILL, John.
Burglars, Robber Barons, and the Good Life. PEKARSKY, Daniel.
But Suppose We Were to Take the Rectorial Address Seriously...Gérard Granel's *De l'université*. FYNSK, Christopher.
Cartesian Feminists. LONGACRE, Judith.
Chapter One of *Harry Stottlemeier's Discovery*: An Integrative Crucible of Critical and Creative Thinking. SASSEVILLE, Michel.
Civic Education for Teachers. SCAHILL, John.
The Classroom as a Model of the World. STURGEON, Kareen B.
Coherent Programs in Teacher Education: When Are They Educational?. FLODEN, Robert E and BUCHMANN, Margret.
The Common Good, Human Rights and Education: A Need for Conceptual Reformulization. CRAIG, Robert P.
Community and Neutrality in Critical Thought. HOSTETLER, Karl.
The Community of Inquiry Education for Democracy. SHARP, Ann Margaret.
A Comparison of John Dewey and Lawrence Kohlberg's Approach to Moral Education. SOCOSKI, Patrick M.
A Comprehensive and Comprehensible Survey of Modern Philosophy. PEROVICH JR, Anthony.
Computer Alternatives in the History of Philosophy Classroom. TESCHNER, George and MC CLUSKY, Frank.
Concerning the Interests of Insects. GROSSINGER, Robin.
Connecting *Techne* and *Praxis* in Teaching. HOSTETLER, Karl.
Continuity and Diversity in Philosophy of Education: An Introduction. BURBULES, Nicholas C.
A Critical Review of *The Moral Dimensions of Teaching*. LISMAN, C David.
Critics and Historical Continuity. CARTER, John.
Cultural Literacy: Posing Queer Questions. GREENE, Maxine.
DBAE: Complaints, Reminiscences, and Response. BROUDY, Harry S.
The Dead Horse Phenomenon in Educational Theory. ROBENSTINE, Clark.
Deconstructing/Deconstructive Inquiry: The Politics of Knowing and Being Known. LATHER, Patti.
Democratic and Professional Authority in Education. WALKER, J C.
Het Dialectisch Humanistisch Grondmotief van Natuur en Vrijheid in de Pedagogiek als Wetenschap. OUWENDORP, C.
Difference as Deficit. REAGAN, Timothy.
The Difference-Deficit Debate: Theoretical Smokescreen for a Conservative Ambush. MC DADE, Laurie A.
Discipline-Based Art Education: Conceptions and Misconceptions. EISNER, Elliot W.
Discipline-Based Art Education: Heat and Light. SWANGER, David.
Do the Right Thing. SUTTLE, Bruce B.
Dr Chipley's Warning. WHITE, Ronald.
Educação e democracia: Subsídios para uma consciência educacional pluralizante. ARAÚJO, Alberto Filipe.
Educating for Meaning. WELBY, Victoria.
Educating Intelligent Believers and Unbelievers. NODDINGS, Nel.

EDUCATION

Educating-Increasing Intelligence Levels by Developing a Sense of Humor. PRITSCHER, Conrad.
Education and the Cultivation of Reflection. SCHNEIDER, Herbert W.
Education and the Emotions: The Relevance of the Russellian Perspective. MATTAI, Bansraj.
Education for Judgment. JAMES, William.
Educational Research and Bhaskar's Conception of Discovery. CORSON, David.
Educational Research in Mexico. SANCHEZ-PUENTES, Ricardo.
Emile's Education. SHAVER, Robert.
Emotions, Education and Time. DE SOUSA, Ronald.
Empowering Teachers: Towards a Justification for Intervention. HARRIS, Kevin.
The Environmental Dependence of Dispositional Aims: Response to the Presidential Address. RAYWID, Mary Ann.
Epistemology and Political Rationality. FUTERNICK, Ken.
Equal Educational Opportunity as a Public Policy. BUNTING, I A.
Essay on the Notion of Reading. ROSE, Rebecca Fine (trans) and WEIL, Simone and TESSIN, Timothy.
Ethical Deliberations as Dramatic Rehearsal. CASPARY, William R.
Ethics and Educational Administration: Are Ethical Politics "Ethical"?. RUDDER, Charles F.
Ethics Committee Simulations. WINSTON, Morton.
Ethics in Educational Policy Analysis. WILLERS, Jack Conrad.
Ethics, Education, and Corporate Leadership. BASSIRY, G R.
La ética/moral en el Bachillerato español: Estado de la cuestión. GARCÍA LÓPEZ, Tomás.
The Evaluation of "Outcomes" of Accounting Ethics Education. LOEB, Stephen E.
The Expression of Experience: Code's Critique of Gilligan's Abortion Study. PITT, Alice.
Fabricas o escuelas de Filosofia?. DÍAZ, Adolfo García.
Fostering the Disposition to be Rational. SIEGEL, Harvey.
The Foundations of Professionalism: Fifty Years of the Philosophy of Education Society in Retrospect. GIARELLI, James M and CHAMBLISS, J J.
Freud: Uma Concepção Agónica da Educação. BARBOSA, Manuel.
Friendship and Education. WHITE, Patricia.
Friendship and Education. WHITE, Patricia.
G H Bantock as Educational Philosopher. BARRIE, John A.
Een gedesoriënteerde veranderingswetenschap. GASTELAARS, M.
General Thinking Skills: Are There Such Things?. ANDREWS, John N.
Getting Down to Cases: The Revival of Casuistry in Bioethics. ARRAS, John D.
The Goals of Science Education. MARTIN, Michael.
Growing Up on Screen—Images of Instruction. HANSEN, Karen.
Habermas's Ontology of Learning: Reconstructing Dewey. YOUNG, R E.
Has the Study of Philosophy at Dutch Universities Changed under Economic and Political Pressures?. VAN DER MEULEN, Barend and LEYDESDORFF, Loet.
Help in Finding Missing Premises. DONN, Mike.
The Higher Level Skills: Tomorrow's 'Basics'. EDUC COMMISSION OF STATES.
History of Modern Philosophy as an Issues-Based Introductory Course. DIXON, Nicholas.
How Teachers Know. STENGEL, Barbara S.
How the Child Reasons. THAYER-BACON, Barbara.
Humor, Schooling, and Cultural Intelligence: A Response to Pritscher. O'CONNOR, Terence.
The Importance of Cultural Pedagogy. MC DERMOTT, John J.
In Defense of Cahn's Scamps. FOULK, Gary.
Increasing Applied Business Ethics Courses in Business School Curricula. SIMS, Ronald R and SIMS, Serbrenia J.
An Inquiry into the Meaning of Teacher Clarity in Recent Research and into the Value of the Research for the Teacher. CRABTREE, Walden.
Irony and Method: Comments on Burbules on Dialogue. NEIMAN, Alven M.
The Irreducibly Clinical Character of Bioethics. WEAR, Stephen.
Is Collaborative Research Exploitative?. LADWIG, James G.
Is Philosophy Detrimental to Mathematics Education?. LUZZATTO, Stefano.
Is There a New Teacher Unionism?. URBAN, Wayne J.
J S Mill and Indian Education. ZASTOUPIL, Lynn.
J S Mill's Concept of Maturity as the Criterion in Determining Children's Eligibility for Rights. KIM, Ki Su.
Justice: The Root of American Business Ideology and Ethics. MC GOWAN, Richard.
The Justification of "English". MEYNELL, Hugo A.
The Justification of Conceptual Development Claims. HAAFTEN, Wouter Van.
Kant, Pestalozzi and the Role of Ideology in Educational Thought. ADAMS, Ian.
Kennen en kunnen: Een repliek op Wardekker. HARBERS, Hans.
Kierkegaard's Mirror. ROSENOW, Eliyahu.
Knowledge Growth and Teaching: Towards a Genetic Foundation for Teachers' Knowledge. ORTON, Robert E.
La Fenomenología aplicada a la Educación. GENÍS, Octavi Fullat.
Learning Anew from Old Arguments. BIEL, Joseph.
Learning Disabilities: A Questionable Construct. KLATT, Heinz-Joachim.
Liberal Education in an Unfree World. LA BRECQUE, Richard.
Lifelong Education: The Institutionalisation of an Illiberal and Regressive Ideology. BAGNALL, Richard G.
Making Student Groups Work: "To Teach is to Learn Twice". THOMASON, Neil.
Marketing Ethics and Education: Some Empirical Findings. MERRITT, Sharyne.
Meaningful Existence, Embodiment and Physical Education. WHITEHEAD, Margaret.
Method and Message: Commentary on the Future of Philosophy of Education. DENTON, David E.
Moral Education: Realistically Speaking. VOKEY, Daniel.
Moral Reasoning in a Communist Chinese Society. WALKER, Lawrence J and MORAN, Thomas J.
Moral Skepticism and Moral Education. BARCALOW, Emmett.
Morality and Religion: Necessary Bedfellows in Education?. LOSITO, William F.
Mothers of In(ter)vention: Women's Writing in Philosophy of Education. LEACH, Mary S.
Must the State Justify Its Educational Policies?. HESLEP, Robert D.
A Normative Theory of Teaching. POPP, Jerome.
North American, British and Australian Philosophy of Education from 1941 to 1991: Links, Trends, Prospects. BECK, Clive.
Note ad un recente libro sull'incontro-scontro tra Croce e Gentile. ANTISERI, Dario.
Of *Praxis* and *Techne* and Cabbages and Kings. GREEN, Joe L.
On the Form and Authenticity of the *Lysis*. TEJERA, V.
The On-Going Deconstruction of Marxism-Leninism. BUCHHOLZ, Arnold and SWIDERSKI, E M.
An Open Letter to Maxine Greene on "The Problem of Freedom in an Era of Ecological Interdependence". BOWERS, C A.
P4C as "Pre-Secondary" Philosophy. DUPUIS, Adrian M and THOMPSON, A Gray.
P4C: A Remedy for Education. MOSTERT, Pieter.
Paideia Helénica. FREIRE, António.
The Paradox of Indoctrination: A Hermeneutical Solution. GARRISON, James W.
The Paternalistic Attitude Toward Children. AVIRAM, Aharon.
Personal Construct Theory as the Ground for a Rapproachment Between Psychology and Philosophy in Education. WARREN, W G.
PES and School Reform. TOZER, Steven.
PES and the APA—An Impressionistic History. MACMILLAN, C J B.
Peter Gardner on Religious Upbringing and the Liberal Ideal of Religious Autonomy. MC LAUGHLIN, T H.
Phenomenology and the Philosophy for Children Program. HAMRICK, William.
The Philatelic Commemoration of American Education. WILLERS, Jack Conrad.
The Philosopher as Hero. DUHAN, Laura.
Philosophically Useful Kibitzing. PRATTE, Richard.
Philosophy for Children and Continental Philosophy. MARTENS, Ekkehard.
Philosophy in the *"Gymnasium:"* European Observations and Recommendations. VAN DER LEEUW, Karel and MOSTERT, Pieter.
Philosophy is Also for the Young—At Least Possibly. LIPMAN, Matthew.
Philosophy, Education, and Public Practice. GIARELLI, James M.
The Physiology of Moral Maturity. HEMMING, James.
Political Self-Education of the English Working Class. PEPPERELL, Keith C.
The Politics of Knowledge. SPRING, Joel.
The Politics of Professionalism. FARBER, Paul.
Postmodern Metaphors for Teacher Education?. STONE, Lynda.
The Power of Hegemony vis-à-vis the Marketplace of Ideas: Response to Orton. BROSIO, Richard A.
Practical Reasoning in Teaching: A Response to Jana Noel. PENDLEBURY, Shirley.
Praktijkontwikkeling en wetenschappelijke (onderwijs)kunde: Een reactie op Boon e.a.. WARDEKKER, Wim.
The Priority of Excellence Reconsidered. BULL, Barry L.
Problem Solving, Decision Making and Reflective Thinking. MERKLE, Patricia.
The Problematics of "Clarity" in Research of Teaching: A Response to Walden Crabtree. SCHULTZ, Frederick M.
Professional Education of African Americans: A Challenge to Ethical Thinking. HARRIS, William M.
Professional Ethics and Accounting Education: A Critique of the 8-Step Method. ARMSTRONG, Mary Beth.
Professions and Professionalism. DOWNIE, R S.
Public Discourse in the Development of Educational Policy. CURREN, Randall R.
The Question of Responsibility in the Context of Instructional Technology. TAYLOR, William and KONSTANTELLOU, Eva.
Rational and Caring Teachers: How Dispositional Aims Shape Teacher Preparation. ARNSTINE, Barbara.

EDUCATION

Rational Trust and Deferential Belief. NORRIS, Stephen P.
Re-Viewing the Political Structure of Knowledge. LEACH, Mary S.
Reading the Darkness: Wittgenstein and Indoctrination. MC CARTY, Luise Prior and MC CARTY, David Charles.
Reason and the Child. WEINSTEIN, Mark.
Reclaiming Virtue: Philosophy in the Field of Educational Technology. BELLAND, John and SMITH, Phillip L.
Reflections on Reflecting. PRITSCHER, Conrad.
Rehabilitating Responsibility. GADEN, Gerry.
Remarks about the Idea of the University (in Dutch). ROSSOUW, H W.
A Response to Beck, Giarelli/Chambliss, Leach, Tozer, and Macmillan. GREENE, Maxine.
Response to Donald Vandenberg's "Co-intentional Pedagogy". GREENE, Maxine.
Response to Foulk's "In Defense of Cahn's Scamps". SILK, David.
Response to Merkle and Pritscher. SMITH, Phil.
Response to Robenstine's "The Dead Horse Phenomenon in Educational Theory". BROSIO, Richard.
Response to the Presidential Address: Willer's "Ethics in Educational Policy Analysis". DRAKE, William E.
Restoring Cultural History: Beyond Gombrich. PAVUR, Claude N.
Rethinking the Dialectic: A Social Semiotic Perspective for Educators. HAMMER, Rhonda and MC LAREN, Peter.
Retrieving Husserl from His Legacy. FUCHS, Wolfgang.
The Role of Moral Intuition in Applied Ethics: A Consideration of Positions of Peirce and Strike and Soltis. MC CARTHY, Christine.
The School and the Home: Partners or Pariahs—A Response to Kennedy on Home Schools. ENGEL, David E.
Sex, Drugs and Rock 'n Roll: Youth, Instruction and Experience in Contemporary American Film. ANGELO, Richard.
Should Children Be Taught to Obey Their Conscience?. HUGHEN, Richard.
Silvio Spaventa e Antonio Labriola, gli 'aspetti-pedagogici'. DE CUMIS, Nicola Siciliani.
Similarity According to Jen-Jen. HSENG-HONG, Yeh.
Small is Beautiful. THOMASON, Neil.
Social Science Knowledge and Explanations in Educational Studies. DALE, Michael.
Socrates in Dallas: Managing the Facilities. CASTRO, Barry.
Some Clarifications and Cautions Essential for Good Philosophy of Science Teaching. DAVSON-GALLE, Peter.
Some More Ideas About the Relation Between Philosophy for Children and Self-Esteem. GAZZARD, Ann.
Souls Without Longing. PLATT, Michael.
Special Problems in Teaching Modern Philosophy. PHILLIPS, Hollibert.
State Education Service or Prisoner's Dilemma: The 'Hidden Hand' as Source of Education Policy. JONATHAN, R.
Stereotypes and Group-Claims. HARVEY, J.
Stopping the Thought That Stops Thought: Response to John Scahill. ENGEL, David.
Structural Violence and Fallible Plans: A Case Study in Philosophy and Educational Planning. MOULDER, J.
The Subject in Feminism. BRAIDOTTI, Rosi.
The Subjection of Children. AVIRAM, Aharon.
Talking. VELASCO, Monica A.
The Teacher as Judge: A Brief Sketch of Two Fairness Principles. KATZ, Michael S.
Teaching Acts: An Unfinished Story. MC EWAN, Hunter.
Teaching by Questioning. WHALLEY, Michael.
Teaching Clinical Ethics in the Residency Years: Preparing Competent Professionals. FORROW, Lachlan and ARNOLD, Robert M and FRADER, Joel.
Teaching Ethics in the Health Care Setting, Part I. COUTTS, Mary Carrington.
Teaching Feminist Ethics as Male Consciousness-Raising. WALTON, Barbara J.
Teaching Johnny to Think. SANDERS, James and MC PECK, John.
The Teaching of Business Ethics: A Survey of AACSB Member Schools. SCHOENFELDT, Lyle F and MC DONALD, Don M and YOUNGBLOOD, Stuart A.
Teaching Philosophy: Skills and Mentalities. RICHARD, Arsene.
Telling Stories About Teaching. MACMILLAN, C J B.
The Tensions Between Education and Development. GARDNER, Howard.
Textbook Controversies and Community. WATRAS, Joseph.
The Substance of Aesthetic Education in the School (in Czechoslovakian). SABOUK, Sava.
Theme and Commentary. GREEN, Thomas F.
Thinking About Home Schooling: Some Historical, Philosophical, and Cultural Reasons. KENNEDY, David.
Thinking About Thinking: What Are We to Think?. CARBONE JR, Peter F.
Tipos de lectura, tipos de texto. PEREDA, Carlos.
Toward a Rationale for Literary Literacy. BOGDAN, Deanne.
Toward An Expanded Vision of Clinical Ethics Education: From the Individual to the Institution. SOLOMON, Mildred Z (and others).
Transcending Paradigms. REY, George.
Varieties of Educational Dialogue. BURBULES, Nicholas C.
Warnings on Resistance and the Language of Possibility: Gramsci and a Pedagogy from the Surreal. SENESE, Guy B.
Wetenschapsontwikkeling en kundes. BOON, Louis (and others).
What is the Price of a Rich Life?. MEYER, Zofia Golab.
What Makes Practice Educational?. HOGAN, Pádraig.
Whose Education Is It Anyway?. TAMIR, Yael.
William James and the Nature of Thinking: A Framework for Elfie. MELVILLE, Mary E.

EDUCATIONAL THEORY(-RIES)

Education as a Human Right: A Theory of Curriculum and Pedagogy. VANDENBERG, Donald.
Continuity and Diversity in Philosophy of Education: An Introduction. BURBULES, Nicholas C.
Educational Research in Mexico. SANCHEZ-PUENTES, Ricardo.
Lifelong Education: The Institutionalisation of an Illiberal and Regressive Ideology. BAGNALL, Richard G.
North American, British and Australian Philosophy of Education from 1941 to 1991: Links, Trends, Prospects. BECK, Clive.
Personal Construct Theory as the Ground for a Rapproachment Between Psychology and Philosophy in Education. WARREN, W G.
Reclaiming Virtue: Philosophy in the Field of Educational Technology. BELLAND, John and SMITH, Phillip L.

EDWARDS, P

In Defence of Heidegger. JANUSZ, Sharon and WEBSTER, Glenn.

EELLS, E

Probabilistic Causality: A Rejoinder to Ellery Eells. DUPRÉ, John.

EFFECTIVENESS

Colimit Completions and the Effective Topos. ROBINSON, Edmund and ROSOLINI, Giuseppe.
Effective Model Theory versus Recursive Model Theory. CHISHOLM, John.
The Role of Ethics and Social Responsibility in Achieving Organizational Effectiveness: Students Versus Managers. KRAFT, Kenneth L and SINGHAPAKDI, Anusorn.

EFFICACY

"Reply to Dretske's 'Does Meaning Matter?'" in *Information, Semantics and Epistemology*, FODOR, Jerry A.
The Causal Efficacy of Content. SEGAL, Gabriel and SOBER, Elliott.
Normas, sistemas jurídicos y eficacia. NAVARRO, Pablo Eugenio.
Vico: dalla collocazione storica all'efficiacia teoretica. FRANCHINI, Raffaello.

EFFICIENCY

"Efficient Explanations and Efficient Behaviour" in *Critical Traditions in Contemporary Archaeology*, SALMON, Merrilee H.
The Conflation of Productivity and Efficiency in Economics and Economic History. SINGH, Harinder and FRANTZ, Roger.
Economic Efficiency: A Paradigm for Business Ethics. STIEBER, John and PRIMEAUX, Patrick.
Economists and Philosophers as Critics of the Free Enterprise System. ARNOLD, N Scott.
An Outline of My Main Contributions to Economic Science. ALLAIS, Maurice.
Productivity and X-Efficiency: A Reply to Singh and Frantz. SARAYDAR, Edward.

EFFICIENT CAUSE(S)

Le existentia de deo e le Immortalitate del Anima: Lineas de Philosophia del Esser. BLANDINO, Giovanni.
Efficient Causation Within Concrescence. FORD, Lewis S.
General Causation. SAPIRE, David.

EGALITARIANISM

Democratic Individuality. GILBERT, Alan.
Gerechtigkeit, Wohlfahrt und Rationalität. SCHMIDT, Johannes.
"Uguaglianza, riconoscimento del simile e principio d'autorità nell'ultimo Diderot" in *Égalité Uguaglianza*, GOGGI, Gianluigi.
"La 'grande illusion' du XVIIIe siècle" in *Égalité Uguaglianza*, ROSSO, Corrado.
Response to Miller's "Equality". MINOGUE, K.

EGO

see also Self(-ves)
Jean-Paul Sartre. HENGELBROCK, Jürgen.
Mind-Body. MOULYN, Adrian C.
The Concept of Ego in Husserl's Philosophy. DAS, Paritosh Kumar.

EGOISM

Living the Good Life: An Introduction to Moral Philosophy. GRAHAM, Gordon.
Moral Philosophy from Montaigne to Kant: An Anthology, Volume I & II. SCHNEEWIND, J B (ed).
Other Selves: Philosophers on Friendship. PAKALUK, Michael (ed).
The Self-Overcoming of Nihilism: Nishitani Keiji. PARKES, Graham (trans).
"Egoism" in *A Companion to Ethics*, BAIER, Kurt.
"Rational Egoism, Self, and Others" in *Identity, Character, and Morality: Essays in Moral Psychology*, BRINK, David O.
Challenging the Egoistic Paradigm. BOWIE, Norman E.

EGOISM
An Economic Model of Scientific Activity and Truth Acquisition. GOLDMAN, Alvin I and SHAKED, Moshe.
Friendship, Self-Love, and Concern for Others in Aristotle's Ethics. MC KERLIE, Dennis.
Pride, Hypocrisy and Civility in Mandeville's Social and Historical Theory. DICKEY, Laurence.
Rileggendo Marx: "diritti" e "bisogni". BADALONI, Nicola.
Schopenhauers Entwurf einer asketischen Tugendethik. WOLF, Jean-Claude.

EHRING, D
Response to Ehring's 'Papineau on Causal Asymmetry'. PAPINEAU, David.

EIDETIC
La Fenomenología aplicada a la Educación. GENÍS, Octavi Fullat.
On the Paradoxical Inception and Motivation of Transcendental Philosophy in Plato and Husserl. HOPKINS, Burt C.

EIGEN, M
Evolution als Höherentwicklung des Bewusstseins. KUMMER, Christian.

EIGHTEENTH CENTURY
see Modern

EINSTEIN
L'inertie et l'espace-temps absolu de Newton à Einstein. GHINS, Michel.
Science and Reason. KYBURG JR, Henry E.
"Newtonianism Before and After the Einsteinian Revolution" in *Some Truer Method*, AGASSI, Joseph.
Cohen on Einstein's Simultaneity *Gedankenexperiment*. WHITE, V Alan.
Constructing or Completing Physical Geometry?. CARRIER, Martin.
The Cosmological Constant: Einstein's Greatest Mistake?. RAY, Christopher.
On the Nature of Einstein's Realism. POLIKAROV, Azaria.
P W Bridgman's Operational Perspective on Physics: Part I—Origins and Development. MOYER, Albert E.
Substances and Space-Time: What Aristotle Would Have Said to Einstein. MAUDLIN, Tim.

ELDERLY
Deciding for Others: The Ethics of Surrogate Decision Making. BUCHANAN, Allen E.
Medicine and Money: A Study of the Role of Beneficence in Health Care Cost Containment. MARSH, Frank H.
Consumer Ethics: An Investigation of the Ethical Beliefs of Eldery Consumers. VITELL, Scott J and LUMPKIN, James R and RAWWAS, Mohammed Y A.
Nutrition, Hydration, and the Demented Elderly. POST, Stephen G.
Reassessing Autonomy in Long-Term Care. AGICH, George J.

ELEATIC
Eleatics Against Each Other (in Hungarian). KAMPIS, György.

ELECTIONS
Bulgaria: The Romantic Period of the Opposition Continues. KANEV, Krassimir.
Ethical Considerations Regarding Public Opinion Polling During Election Campaigns. MICHALOS, Alex C.

ELECTRODYNAMICS
L'inertie et l'espace-temps absolu de Newton à Einstein. GHINS, Michel.

ELEMENT(S)
Philosophical Elements in Penrose's and Hawking's Research in Contemporary Cosmology. DREES, Wim.
Il rapporto Parmenide-Telesio dal Persio al Maranta. ARTESE, Luciano.

ELEMENTARY
The Elementary Theory of the Natural Lattice is Finitely Axiomatizable. CEGIELSKI, Patrick.

ELEMENTARY EDUCATION
Philosophy is Also for the Young—At Least Possibly. LIPMAN, Matthew.

ELEMENTARY EQUIVALENCE
Many-Sorted Elementary Equivalence. DZIERZGOWSKI, Daniel.

ELIADE, M
Is Anything Sacred? Christian Humanism and Christian Nihilism. CUPITT, Don.
Misconceptions of the Social Sciences. SEGAL, Robert A.

ELIMINATION
The Sweep of Probability. SCHLESINGER, George N.
The Last Word on Elimination of Quantifiers in Modules. GUTE, Hans B and REUTER, K K.
On the Eliminatibility of Ideal Linguistic Entities. WYBRANIEC-SKARDOWSKA, Urszula.
Reduction, Elimination, and the Mental. SCHWARTZ, Justin.
Relative Elimination of Quantifiers for Henselian Valued Fields. BASARAB, Serban A.

ELIMINATIVISM
Mind and Cognition: A Reader. LYCAN, William G (ed).
"Connectionism, Eliminativism and the Future of Folk Psychology" in *Philosophical Perspectives, 4: Action Theory and Philosophy of Mind, 1990*, RAMSEY, William and STICH, Stephen and GARON, Joseph.
"Non-Scientific Realism" about Propositional Attitudes as a Response to Eliminativist Arguments. HANNAN, Barbara.
Belief Attribution in Science: Folk Psychology under Theoretical Stress. TROUT, J D.
Causal Holism and Commonsense Psychology: A Reply to O'Brien. STICH, Stephen P.
Connectionist Minds. CLARK, Andy.
Eliminative Materialism and Substantive Commitments. NELSON, Mark T.
Functionalism, the Absent Qualia Objection and Eliminativism. AVERILL, Edward Wilson.
Is Connectionism Commonsense?. O'BRIEN, Gerard J.
The Status of Content Revisited. BOGHOSSIAN, Paul A.
Where Does the Self-Refutation Objection Take Us?. RAMSEY, William.

ELITISM
Relating Humanities and Social Thought (Science, Ideology, and Value, Volume 4). EDEL, Abraham.
"Maritain, Simon, and Vichy's Elite Schools" in *Freedom in the Modern World: Jacques Maritain, Yves R Simon, Mortimer J Adler*, HELLMAN, John.
Elites and Systematic Change in Hungary. SZALAI, Erzsebet.
Postmodernist Elitism and Postmodern Struggles. GROSSBERG, Lawrence.

ELLERMAN, D
Note on a Paper of D P Ellerman. PAALMAN-DE MIRANDA, Aïda B.

ELLIPSIS
Ellipsis and Higher-Order Unification. DALRYMPLE, Mary and SHIEBER, Stuart M and PEREIRA, Fernando C N.

ELLIS, B
Ellis, Epistemic Values, and the Problem of Induction. VOLLRATH, John.

ELLUL, J
Desacralization and the Disenchantment of the World. WENNEMANN, Daryl.

ELSTER, J
Methodological Individualism and Marx: Some Remarks on Jon Elster, Game Theory, and Other Things. WOLFF, Robert Paul.
Monadic Marxism: A Critique of Elster's Methodological Individualism. MOGGACH, Douglas.
Rational Choice Theory Considered as Psychology and Moral Philosophy. MONGIN, Philippe.

EMANCIPATION
Heidegger and Emancipation. OLIVIER, G.
Ka-Meh und das alte Neue—über epistemische Krise und Emanzipation. SANDKÜHLER, Hans Jörg.
The Perversion of Emancipation into Repression (in German). SCHMIDT, Hartwig.
Wissen und Emanzipation. SANDKÜHLER, Hans Jörg.

EMBEDDING
Embeddability, Syntax, and Semantics in Accounts of Scientific Theories. TURNEY, Peter.
Embedded Probabilities. DUBUCS, J.

EMBODIMENT
A Post-Modern Epistemology. SORRI, Mari.
"A Dualist Account of Embodiment" in *The Case for Dualism*, ROBINSON, Howard.
Meaningful Existence, Embodiment and Physical Education. WHITEHEAD, Margaret.

EMBRYO(S)
The Vatican, the Law and the Human Embryo. COUGHLAN, Michael J.
Arguments for Abortion of Abnormal Fetuses and the Moral Status of the Developing Embryo. SUTTON, Agneta.
Aristotle's Technical Simulation and its Logic of Causal Relations. LOECK, Gisela.
The Editor's Response to "The Embryo Debate: The Archbishop of York's Speech to the House of Lords". DE S CAMERON, Nigel M.
The Embryo Debate: The Archbishop of York's Speech to the House of Lords. THE ARCHBISHOP OF YORK.
Embryo Research and Abortion—the Arguments that Swayed Parliament. SHORT, David S.
The Ethics of *Ex Utero* Research on Spare 'Non-Viable' IVF Human Embryos. BAYLIS, Françoise E.
Hydatidiform Moles and Teratomas Confirm the Human Identity of the Preimplantation Embryo. SUAREZ, Antoine.
Quale statuto per l'embrione umano?. COMPAGNONI, Francesco.
The Status of Frozen Embryos. ANDERSON, Susan Leigh.
Who or What is the Preembryo?. MC CORMICK, Richard A.
Whose Life is it Anyway?. TRUSTED, Jennifer.
Zygotes, Souls, Substances, and Persons. BOLE III, Thomas J.

EMBRYOLOGY
Human Fertilisation and Embryology. DE S CAMERON, Nigel M.
Identity and Status of the Human Embryo. SPAGNOLA, Antonio G.
Philosophische Uberlegungen zu "Menschenwürde" und Fortpflanzungs-Medizin. SCHÖNE-SEIFERT, Bettina.

EMERGENCE
"Emergent Evolution and the Level Structure of Reality" in *Studies on Mario Bunge's "Treatise"*, BLITZ, David.
"The Four Causes" in *Studies on Mario Bunge's "Treatise"*, ESPINOZA, Miguel.
Emergent Psychoneural Monism: Mario Bunge and the Body and Soul Problem (in German). MÖLLER, Wolfgang.
Emergenz Bausteine für eine Begriffsexplikation. STÖCKLER, Manfred.

EMERGENTISM
"Mind-Dust or Magic? Panpsychism Versus Emergence" in *Philosophical Perspectives, 4: Action Theory and Philosophy of Mind, 1990*, VAN CLEVE, James.
Self-Organization, Emergent Properties and the Unity of the World. ROTH, Gerhard and SCHWEGLER, Helmut.

EMERSON
American Philosophy and the Romantic Tradition. GOODMAN, Russell B.
East-West Philosophy in Nineteenth-Century America: Emerson and Hinduism. GOODMAN, Russell B.
Emerson and Nietzsche's 'Beyond-Man'. STACK, George J.
Emerson and the Inhibitions of Democracy. SHKLAR, Judith N.
George Kateb's Ahistorical Emersonianism. MARX, Leo.

EMMANUEL, A
The Politics and Morality of Unequal Exchange: Emmanuel and Roemer, Analysis and Synthesis. SCHWEICKART, David.

EMOTION(S)
see also Feeling(s)
Contemplating Music—Source Readings in the Aesthetics of Music, Volume II: Import. KATZ, Ruth (ed).
David Hume: Historiker und Philosoph. LÜTHE, Rudolf.
In Praise of the Cognitive Emotions. SCHEFFLER, Israel.
Love's Knowledge: Essays on Philosophy and Literature. NUSSBAUM, Martha C.
Mind in Action: Essays in the Philosophy of Mind. RORTY, Amelie Oksenberg.
Le Philosophie et les Passions. MEYER, Michel.
"Hume and Moral Emotions" in *Identity, Character, and Morality: Essays in Moral Psychology*, LIND, Marcia.
"The Place of Emotions in Kantian Morality" in *Identity, Character, and Morality: Essays in Moral Psychology*, SHERMAN, Nancy.
"What Emotions Are About" in *Philosophical Perspectives, 4: Action Theory and Philosophy of Mind, 1990*, BAIER, Annette C.
"What's Wrong with Bitterness?" in *Feminist Ethics*, MC FALL, Lynne.
Autonomy, Emotions and Desires: Some Problems Concerning R F Dearden's Account of Autonomy. STONE, Carolyn M.
Burning Passions. NEILL, Alex and RIDLEY, Aaron.
The Celebration of Emotion: Vallabha's Ontology of Affective Experience. TIMM, Jeffrey R.
A Critique of Kantian Arguments Against Emotions as Moral Motives. OAKLEY, Justin.
David Wong on Emotions in Mencius. IHARA, Craig K.
Describing the Emotions: A Review of *The Cognitive Structure of Emotions* by Ortony, Clore and Collins. BEN-ZEEV, Aaron.
A Determinist Dilemma. PERSSON, Ingmar.
Discipline-Based Art Education: Heat and Light. SWANGER, David.
Education and the Emotions: The Relevance of the Russellian Perspective. MATTAI, Bansraj.
Emotion and Belief. BORUAH, Bijoy H.
Emotion East and West: Introduction to a Comparative Philosophy. MARKS, Joel.
Emotions and Rationality. BERENSON, F M.
Emotions and Responsibility. TURSKI, George.
Emotions, Education and Time. DE SOUSA, Ronald.
Emotions, Feelings and Contexts: A Reply to Robert Kraut. SOLOMON, Robert C.
L'emozione creatrice: Il significato della morale nella prospettiva di Bergson. PESSINA, Adriano.
Envy and Jealousy. BEN-ZEEV, Aaron.
Errors of an Ill-Reasoning Reason: The Disparagement of Emotions in the Moral Life. LAURITZEN, Paul.
Governance by Emotion. ALLEN, R T.
In Defense of Sentimentality. SOLOMON, Robert C.
The Incoherence and Irrationality of Philosophers. RADFORD, Colin.
Is There a Distinction Between Reason and Emotion in Mencius?. WONG, David B.
Ji Kang's "Sheng-wu-aile-lun": Concerning Its Logical Development (in Japanese). HARA, Masayuki.
Just Can't Find the Words: How Expression is Achieved. KING, Debra W.
Moral Experience and Justification. SINNOTT-ARMSTRONG, Walter.
The Notion of *Klesa* and Its Bearing on the Yoga Analysis of Mind. BALSLEV, Anindita N.
Reason and Emotion. FRICKER, Miranda.
Response to Craig Ihara's Discussion. WONG, David B.
Sartre and James on the Role of the Body in Emotion. BAUGH, Bruce.
Transcending Paradigms. REY, George.
What is this Thing Called 'Love'?. BERENSON, Frances.
Who's Afraid of Virginia Woolf?. MATRAVERS, Derek.
Wittgenstein on Emotion. PATEL, Kartikeya C.
Wittgenstein, eskimo's en emoties. POTT, Heleen.

EMOTIVE
The Philosophical Basis of Rational-Emotive Therapy (RET). ELLIS, Albert.

EMOTIVISM
Blanshard's Critique of Ethical Subjectivism. JOHNSON, Oliver A.

EMPATHY
On the Problem of Empathy (Third Revised Edition). STEIN, Edith.
Autonomy, Empathy, and Transcendence in Sophocles' *Antigone*: A Phenomenological Perspective. NISSIM-SABAT, Marilyn.

EMPIRE(S)
John Stuart Mill and Royal India. MOORE, Robin J.

EMPIRICAL
Structures in Mathematical Theories: Reports of the San Sebastian International Symposium, 1990. DÍEZ, Amparo (ed).
"Some Reflections on Empirical Psychology: Toward an Interpretive Psychology" in *Reconsidering Psychology: Perspectives from Continental Philosophy*, KOCKELMANS, Joseph J.
"Difficoltà" con Simmel: Considerazioni in margine ad un convegno. LANDKAMMER, Joachim.
The Empirical Author: Salman Rushdie's *The Satanic Verses*. CLOSE, Anthony.
Empirical Equivalence and Undetermination. LAUDAN, Larry and LEPLIN, Jarrett.
Kant's Theory of Empirical Judgment and Modern Semantics. HANNA, Robert.
On Empirical Interpretation. MUNDY, Brent.
What is Empirical in Mathematics?. PETERSON, Philip L.

EMPIRICAL KNOWLEDGE
On the Nature of Einstein's Realism. POLIKAROV, Azaria.
The Possibilities of Scepticisms: Philosophy and Theology without Apology. JACKSON, Timothy P.
Some Dependence Relations of Empirical Belief. MALHERBE, Jeanette.
The Structure of Empirical Knowledge. DE PIERRIS, Graciela.
The Initial Form of Empiristic and Aprioristic Conception of Knowledge on the World (in Polish). MORAWIEC, E.

EMPIRICISM
see also Pragmatism
Criteria of Certainty: Truth and Judgment in the English Enlightenment. COPE, Kevin L.
Empiricism and Subjectivity: An Essay on Hume's Theory of Human Nature. BOUNDAS, Constantin V (trans).
Ideas, Principios y Dialectica. LAFUENTE, Maria Isabel.
Knowledge of the External World. AUNE, Bruce.
Sacred Fragments: Recovering Theology for the Modern Jew. GILLMAN, Neil.
Scientific Theories. SAVAGE, C Wade (ed).
"Contrastive Empiricism" in *Scientific Theories*, SOBER, Elliott.
"Doing Without Meaning" in *Perspectives on Quine*, QUINTON, Anthony.
"Empirical Content" in *Truth and Interpretation: Perspectives on the Philosophy of Donald Davidson*, DAVIDSON, Donald.
"Rebuilding the Ship while Sailing on the Water" in *Perspectives on Quine*, HAACK, Susan.
"Three Indeterminacies" in *Perspectives on Quine*, QUINE, W V.
"Understanding Our Actual Scheme" in *The Mind of Donald Davidson*, SIITONEN, Arto.
Analiticidad, empirismo y verdad necesaria. HERNÁNDEZ IGLESIAS, Manuel Angel.
Are All False Theories Equally False? A Remark on David Miller's Problem and Geometric Conventionalism. MORMANN, Thomas.
Der Begriff der Bewegung bei Kant: Über den Grundbegriff der Empirie und die empirischen Begriffe. HOFFMANN, Thomas Sören.
Believing What We Do Not See: The Case Against van Fraassen's Conception of Observation. DOBSON, Andrew.
Compromiso Ontico y Teorías Científicas. MAYORGA, Alejandro and VARGAS, Celso.
Computation and Mathematical Empiricism. RESNIK, Michael D.
Conditio sine qua non? Zuordnung in the Early Epistemologies of Cassirer and Schlick. RYCKMAN, Thomas.
Current Trends in the Philosophy of Medicine. POTTER, Robert Lyman.
Empirical Tests are Only Auxiliary Devices. LAI, Tyrone.
Empirical Theology: A Revisable Tradition. DEAN, William.
Empiricism versus Realism: High Points in the Debate During the Past 150 Years. DILWORTH, Craig.
Epistemologia e teoria politica. ZOLO, Danilo.

EMPIRICISM
Experience and Causal Explanation in Medical Empiricism. PENTZOPOULOU-VALALAS, Teresa.
The Experience of Value and Theological Argumentation. DEVENISH, Philip E.
The Foundation of the Ability to Reach Conclusions—The Empirical Basis of Logic. GOLAB-MEYER, Zofia.
James and Bowne on the Philosophy of Religious Experience. DOTTERER, Donald W.
Logic and Empiricism. BOSTOCK, David.
Medicine in John Locke's Philosophy. SANCHEZ-GONZALEZ, Miguel A.
Methodological, Epistemological, and Ontological Motifs in the Thought of Reinhold Niebuhr. AYERS, Robert H.
Moral Epistemology and the Supervenience of Ethical Concepts. AUDI, Robert.
Naturalism and Scepticism. BELL, Martin and MC GINN, Marie.
Platonism from an Empiricist Point of View. LUCE, Lila.
Process Theology as Empirical, Rational, and Speculative: Some Reflections on Method. GRIFFIN, David Ray.
Reduction, Elimination, and the Mental. SCHWARTZ, Justin.
Semantica della "Vorstellung" e valore della teoria in *Erkenntnis und Irrtum* di Ernst Mach. BELLOMO, Andrea.
Lo statuo della filosofia politica nel dibattito italiano. BACCELLI, Luca.
Lo sviluppo degli studi logici nel pensiero tedesco della seconda metà dell' '800. MANGIAGALLI, Maurizio.
Testing for Convergent Realism. ARONSON, Jerrold L.
Two Dogmas of Neo-Empiricism: The "Theory-Informity" of Observation and the Quine-Duhem Thesis. GREENWOOD, John D.
Was Kant a Nativist?. FALKENSTEIN, Lorne.

EMPLOYEE(S)
Ethical Dilemmas in Performance Appraisal Revisited. LONGENECKER, Clinton and LUDWIG, Dean.
Information Privacy and Performance Appraisal: An Examination of Employee Perceptions and Reactions. MOSSHOLDER, Kevin W and GILES, William F and WESOLOWSKI, Mark A.

EMPLOYER(S)
Hidden Agendas. FRIEDMAN, Robert.

EMPLOYMENT
A Deontological Analysis of Peer Relations in Organizations. MOBERG, Dennis J and MEYER, Michael J.
Words on Work. GRAY, C B.

EMPOWERMENT
The Meaning of Socialism. LUNTLEY, Michael.
Democratic and Professional Authority in Education. WALKER, J C.
Literacy as Disempowerment: The Role of Documentary Texts. DE CASTELL, Suzanne.
Response to "Literacy as Disempowerment". RAITZ, Keith L.

ENABLING
Causing, Enabling, and Counterfactual Dependence. MACKIE, Penelope.
Politics in Hobbes' Mechanics: The Social as Enabling. LYNCH, William T.

ENCULTURATION
Recent Work on Ethical Relativism. STEWART, Robert M and THOMAS, Lynn L.

ENCYCLOPEDIA(S)
Ka-Meh und das alte Neue—über epistemische Krise und Emanzipation. SANDKÜHLER, Hans Jörg.
Wissen und Emanzipation. SANDKÜHLER, Hans Jörg.

END(S)
see also Teleology
Aristotelian Form and End. CURZER, Howard J.
Consequentialism: The Philosophical Dog That Does Not Bark?. HOLBROOK, Daniel.
Ultimate Ends in Practical Reasoning. MAC DONALD, Scott.

ENEMY(-MIES)
"Loving One's Enemies" in *In the Interest of Peace: A Spectrum of Philosophical Views*, GAN, Barry.

ENERGY
Ethics and Energy Supplement. STEVENSON, Mark.

ENFORCEMENT
Corporate Codes of Conduct: A Collective Conscience and Continuum. RAIBORN, Cecily A and PAYNE, Dinah.
The Enforcement of Moral Obligations to Potential Fetuses: Johnson Controls versus the UAW. WHITE, Ronald F.

ENGELS
Collected Works, Volume 26, Engels: 1882-1889. ENGELS, Frederick.
Hegel In His Time—Jacques D'Hondt. BURBIDGE, John (trans).
Attraction and Repulsion in Comprehension of Boskovic, Hegel and Engels (in Serbo-Croatian). STOILJKOVIC, Dragoslav.
Engels y Darwin en el origen del hombre: Elementos para una discusión. GALLARDO, Helio.
The Ideas of Karl Marx at a Turning Point in Human Civilization. PANTIN, I and PLIMAK, E.
The Intellectual Compatibility of Marx and Engels. HUNLEY, J D.
Marx's Historical Understanding of the Proletariat and Class in 19th-Century England. MAZLISH, Bruce.
Marx, Engels and Max Weber on Eastern Societies—With a Special Respect to China (in Hungarian). DRUCKER, György.
Notes sur utopie et marxisme. ARANTES, Urias Corrêa.

ENGINEERING
How to Build a Conscious Machine. ANGEL, Leonard.
Codes of Ethics and the Moral Education of Engineers. LUEGENBIEHL, Heinz C.
Commentary on Layton's "Engineering Needs a Loyal Opposition". ANDERSON, Robert M (and others).
Commentary: "Codes of Ethics and the Moral Education of Engineers". PUKA, Bill.
Engineers and Management: The Challenge of the Challenger Incident. WERHANE, Patricia H.
Management's Hat Trick: Misuse of "Engineering Judgment" in the Challenger Incident. HERKERT, Joseph R.
Thinking Like an Engineer: The Place of a Code of Ethics in the Practice of a Profession. DAVIS, Michael.

ENGLISH
see also British
'Religion' and the Religions in the English Enlightenment. HARRISON, Peter.
Alltagssprachliche Metakommunikation im Englischen und Deutschen. WELTE, Werner.
Events in the Semantics of English: A Study in Subatomic Semantics. PARSONS, Terence.
Writing and the Moral Self. LANG, Berel.
"From Sectarian Radical to National Possession" in *A Cultivated Mind: Essays On J S Mill Presented to John M Robson*, COLLINI, Stefan.
David Hume on Religion in England. ROTH, Robert J.
Hobbes, Jacobo I y el derecho inglés. RIBEIRO, Renato Janine.
Political Self-Education of the English Working Class. PEPPERELL, Keith C.

ENJOYMENT
Jean-Jacques Rousseau et Friedrich Schiller: le théâtre sous le feu des lumières. MATTE, Martin.

ENLIGHTENMENT
see also Modern
'Religion' and the Religions in the English Enlightenment. HARRISON, Peter.
Criteria of Certainty: Truth and Judgment in the English Enlightenment. COPE, Kevin L.
The Devil and Secular Humanism: The Children of the Enlightenment. RADEST, Howard B.
Diderot's Dream. ANDERSON, Wilda.
Idea, mente, specie: Platonismo e scienza in Johannes Marcus Marci (1595-1667). MOCCHI, Giuliana.
The Noble Savage: Jean-Jacques Rousseau, 1754-1762. CRANSTON, Maurice.
"Edward Gibbon in History: Aspects of the Text in 'The History of the Decline and Fall of the Roman Empire'" in *The Tanner Lectures on Human Values, Volume XI*, POCOCK, J G A.
"An Old Question Raised Yet Again: Is Kant an Enlightenment Humanist?" in *The Question of Humanism: Challenges and Possibilities*, LUIK, John.
"Zarathustra and Enlightenment Humanism" in *The Question of Humanism: Challenges and Possibilities*, GOICOECHEA, David.
"Der geschlossne Handelsstaat"—Zur konservativen Kritik einer aufklärerischen Utopie. MARQUARDT, Jochen.
The Ambivalence of the Idea of Equality in the French Enlightenment. CHISICK, Harvey.
Aufklärung und Reform. SCHNEIDERS, Werner.
The Enlightenment in American Law I: The Declaration of Independence. RECK, Andrew J.
The Enlightenment in American Law II: The Constitution. RECK, Andrew J.
Ethics in Current Affairs: The Theme of the Enlightenment in Michel Foucault (in German). SCHMID, Wilhelm.
Glasnost and Enlightenment. OLSON, Alan M.
Justice, Redistribution, and the Family. POST, Stephen G.
Radical Enlightenment and Freethinkers (in German). POTT, Martin.
Zu Grundfragen des Toleranzproblems in Vergangenheit und Gegenwart. WOLLGAST, Siegfried.

ENQUIRY
see Inquiry

ENTAILMENT
'Is' Therefore 'Ought'. VERMA, Roop Rekha.
Material Implication and Entailment. CENIZA, Claro R.
Note on a Paper of D P Ellerman. PAALMAN-DE MIRANDA, Aïda B.
Problems of the Notions of 'Entailment' and 'Material Implication'. MULAY, Sharmila R.

ENTHYMEME(S)
Help in Finding Missing Premises. DONN, Mike.
Smook on Logical and Extralogical Constants. HITCHCOCK, David and GEORGE, Rolf.

ENTITLEMENT
Robert Nozick: Property, Justice, and the Minimal State. WOLFF, Jonathan.
"Rights and Remedies in a Consent Theory of Contract" in *Liability and Responsibility*, BARNETT, Randy E.
Nozick on Social Justice. AGARWALA, Binod Kumar.
Nozick's Identity Crisis. LUCY, W N R.
Property, Entitlement, and Remedy. PAUL, Jeffrey.

ENTITY(-TIES)
Accent on *One*: Entity and Identity. BOLINGER, Dwight.
Aristotelian and Whiteheadian Conceptions of Actuality: I. FETZ, Reto Luzius and FELT, James W.
On the Eliminatibility of Ideal Linguistic Entities. WYBRANIEC-SKARDOWSKA, Urszula.
On the Individuation of Events. CLELAND, Carol.
Time and Identity. HARPER, A W J.
Vom Sein zur Selbstreferentialität: Überlegungen zur Theorie autopoietischer Systeme Niklas Luhmanns. GRIPP-HAGELSTANGE, Helga.
Whether Any Individual at all Could Have a Guise Structure. MILLER, Barry.

ENTRAPMENT
"Cognitive Psychology, Entrapment, and the Philosophy of Mind" in *The Case for Dualism*, GAULD, Alan.

ENTREPRENEURSHIP
Atheism, Ayn Rand, and other Heresies. SMITH, George H.

ENTROPY
Complexity and Evolution: What Everybody Knows. MC SHEA, Daniel W.
An Entropic Analysis of Postmodernism. MC KINNEY, Ronald H.
The Many Faces of Irreversibility. DENBIGH, K G.
Note on Entropy, Disorder and Disorganization. DENBIGH, K G.

ENUMERATION
Decidable and Enumerable Predicate Logics of Provability. DZHAPARIDZE, Giorgie.
Malebranche and the Vision in God: A Note on *The Search After Truth*, III, 2, iii. NADLER, Steven.
On Restricted Forms of Enumeration Reducibility. WATSON, Phil.

ENUNCIATION
La oposición de los enunciados "estrictamente" particulares en perspectiva trivalente. OFFENBERGER, Niels.

ENVIRONMENT(S)
Beyond Natural Selection. WESSON, Robert.
A Morally Deep World: An Essay on Moral Significance and Environmental Ethics. JOHNSON, Lawrence E.
"From Nuclear Winter to Hiroshima: Nuclear Weapons and the Environment" in *Issues in War and Peace: Philosophical Inquiries*, GAY, William.
"Reconsidering Psychology" in *Reconsidering Psychology: Perspectives from Continental Philosophy*, FAULCONER, James E and WILLIAMS, Richard N.
Between Two Worlds: Humans in Nature and Culture. GARDINER, Robert W.
Biological Foundations of Prediction in an Unpredictable Environment. MARUSIC, M.
A Candidate Paradigm for Human Ecology. BAPAT, Jyotsna.
The Environmental Dependence of Dispositional Aims: Response to the Presidential Address. RAYWID, Mary Ann.
Fostering the Disposition to be Rational. SIEGEL, Harvey.
How to Change Your Mind. MARTINS, João P and CRAVO, Maria R.
Images of the Environment in Corporate America. SKORPEN, Erling.
Medio ambiente y derecho. ROMERO, Jorge Enrique.
El pensamiento de Heidegger y Marcuse en relación con la ecología. ARRIETA, Jeannette and HAYLING, Annie.
Response to Sapontzis's Reply. WEIR, Jack.
Rethinking the Commons. HERRING, Ronald J.
Smoking in Public: A Moral Imperative for the Most Toxic of Environmental Wastes. LUDINGTON, David M.
The Concept of Environment from the Point of View of Philosophy of Culture (in Polish). CHYMUK, Maria.
The Values of a Habitat. PARKER, Kelly.
Values, the Environment and the Creative Act. THOMAS, John C.

ENVIRONMENTAL ETHICS
Business Ethics. SHAW, William H.
Earthbound: Introductory Essays in Environmental Ethics. REGAN, Tom (ed).
Essentials of Business Ethics. MADSEN, Peter (ed).
A Morally Deep World: An Essay on Moral Significance and Environmental Ethics. JOHNSON, Lawrence E.
The River of the Mother of God, and Other Essays by Aldo Leopold. FLADER, Susan L (ed).
"Environmental Ethics" in *A Companion to Ethics*, ELLIOT, Robert.
Adam's Place in Nature: Respect or Domination?. NASH, Roger.
Agricultural Practices, Ecology, and Ethics in the Third World. WESTRA, L S and BOWEN, K L and BEHE, B K.
Beyond Naturalism: A Reconstruction of Daoist Environmental Ethics. PEERENBOOM, Randall P.
Business and Environmental Ethics. HOFFMAN, W Michael.
The Classroom as a Model of the World. STURGEON, Kareen B.
Commentary: "Love Canal and the Ethics of Environmental Health". FESSENDEN-RADEN, June and BROWN JR, Stuart M.
Concerning the Interests of Insects. GROSSINGER, Robin.
Environmental Ethics and the Case for Hunting. KING, Roger J H.
Environmental Ethics: What? Why? How?. SILVA, Catherine Young.
El eslabón entre la conservación y el desarrollo sostenible: Maribel Gómez Mata. JANZEN, Daniel H.
Ethical Dimensions of Human Attitudes to Nature. BURES, Radim.
Ethics and Energy Supplement. STEVENSON, Mark.
Ethics and Instrumentalism: A Response to Janna Thompson. PLUMWOOD, Val.
Farming Salmon Ethically. NEEDHAM, E A and LEHMAN, Hugh.
Has the History of Philosophy Ruined the Environment?. ATTFIELD, Robin.
How to Construe Nature: Environmental Ethics and the Interpretation of Nature. KING, Roger J H.
Informed Consent or Informed Rejection of Pesticide Use: A Concept for Environmental Action. ORTON, David.
Love Canal and the Ethics of Environmental Health. BRUMMER, James.
Means and Ends in Wild Life Management. LEOPOLD, Aldo.
Moral Metaphysics, Moral Revolution, and Environmental Ethics. PADEN, Roger.
Moral Planes and Intrinsic Values. ANDERSON, James C.
Multinational Corporate Social Policy Process for Ethical Responsibility in Sub-Saharan Africa. PRATT, Cornelius B.
Natural Law and the Environment. BROWN, Montague.
Nietzsche's Environmental Ethics. HALLMAN, Max O.
No Holism without Pluralism. VARNER, Gary E.
Prejudice and Progress in Animal and Environmental Protection. FOX, Michael W.
Process Metaphysics and Minimalism: Implications for Public Policy. KEFFER, Steven and KING, Sallie and KRAFT, Steven.
The Quest for Transformational Experience. BULKLEY, Kelly.
The Servant Species: Humanity as Priesthood. LINZEY, Andrew.
Utilitaristische Ethik als Antwort auf die ökologische Krise. WOLF, Jean-Claude.

ENVIRONMENTALISM
Biological Holism and the Evolution of Ethics. SHRADER-FRECHETTE, Kristin.
Caring About Nature: Feminist Ethics and the Environment. KING, Roger J H.
Deep Ecology versus Ecofeminism: Healthy Differences or Incompatible Philosophies?. SESSIONS, Robert.
Loving Your Mother: On the Woman-Nature Relationship. ROACH, Catherine.
Nature, Self, and Gender: Feminism, Environmental Philosophy, and the Critique of Rationalism. PLUMWOOD, Val.
Reply to Shrader-Frechette's "Biological Holism and the Evolution of Ethics". CALLICOTT, J Baird.
Spiritual Values and "The Goddess". BRANDEN, Victoria.
Toward An Ecological Ethic of Care. CURTIN, Deane.
Welke natuur is het beschermen waard?. VAN DER WINDT, Henny J and HARBERS, Hans.

ENVY
Envy and Jealousy. BEN-ZEEV, Aaron.
What is Wrong With Wicked Feelings?. ROBERTS, Robert C.

EPICTETUS
Morality—What's In It For Me?: A Historical Introduction to Ethics. NELSON, William N.
Προαιρεσις in Epictetus. DOBBIN, Robert.

EPICUREANISM
Vegetarianism and Virtue: On Gassendi's Epicurean Defense. MICHAEL, Emily.

EPICUREANS
Moral Philosophy from Montaigne to Kant: An Anthology, Volume I & II. SCHNEEWIND, J B (ed).
Some Puzzles About the Evil of Death. FELDMAN, Fred.

EPICURUS
"Epicurus' Philosophy of Mind" in *Psychology (Companions to Ancient Thought: 2)*, ANNAS, Julia.
Accessible Hellenistic Philosophy. SHARPLES, R W.
Zur inhaltlichen Bedeutung des Hegelschen "Schemas der Naturphilosophie" in den Epikurstudien des jungen Marx. MIELKE, Dietmar.

EPIDEMIC(S)
Causality Assessment in Epidemiology. VINEIS, Paolo.

EPIGENESIS
Epigenetic Landscaping: Waddington's Use of Cell Fate Bifurcation Diagrams. GILBERT, Scott F.
Taking Mathematics Seriously?. ZYCINSKI, Joseph.

EPIPHENOMENALISM
"Type Epiphenomenalism, Type Dualism, and the Causal Priority of the Physical" in *Philosophical Perspectives, 3: Philosophy of Mind and Action Theory, 1989*, MC LAUGHLIN, Brian P.

EPIPHENOMENALISM
Better the Union Theory. HONDERICH, Ted.
Epiphenomenalism and Machines: A Discussion of Van Rooijen's Critique of Popper. PECNJAK, Davor.

EPISTEMIC
Knowledge in Flux: Modeling the Dynamics of Epistemic States. GÄRDENFORS, Peter.
"Epistemological Pacifism" in *In the Interest of Peace: A Spectrum of Philosophical Views*, BURKE, Richard.
"The Intelligibility of Scepticism" in *The Analytic Tradition: Philosophical Quarterly Monographs, Volume 1*, SKORUPSKI, John.
"Scientific Method and the Objectivity of Epistemic Value Judgments" in *Logic, Methodology and Philosophy of Science, VIII*, SHRADER-FRECHETTE, Kristin.
Aesthetic Constraints on Theory Selection: A Critique of Laudan. MARTIN, James E.
Ellis, Epistemic Values, and the Problem of Induction. VOLLRATH, John.
Epistemic Obligations and Doxastic Voluntarism. GOGGANS, Phil.
Epistemology, Psychology, and Goldman. CORLETT, J Angelo.
The Foundationalist Justification of Epistemic Principles. REMEDIOS, F.
Ideal Rationality and Handwaving. RICHTER, Reed.
On the Epistemic Status of Considered Moral Judgments. TIMMONS, Mark.
On the Epistemic Value of Moral Experience. TOLHURST, William.
Rhetoric as Praxis: An Alternative to the Epistemic Approach. ZHAO, Shanyang.
Social Epistemics and Social Psychology. GOLDMAN, Alvin.
Telling It Like It Was: Historical Narratives on Their Own Terms. NORMAN, Andrew P.
Truth in Epistemology. STURGEON, Scott.
What is Social about Social Epistemics?. MAFFIE, James.
Who's the Horse? A Response to Corlett. HEYES, Cecilia.

EPISTEMIC LOGIC
A General Possible Worlds Framework for Reasoning about Knowledge and Belief. WANSING, Heinrich.

EPISTEMOLOGY
see also Action(s), Empiricism, Idealism, Imagination, Knowledge, Memory, Perception, Rationalism, Realism, Scepticism, Truth(s)
Acting and Reflecting: The Interdisciplinary Turn in Philosophy. SIEG, Wilfried (ed).
American Philosophy and the Romantic Tradition. GOODMAN, Russell B.
Artificial Intelligence and Human Cognition. WAGMAN, Morton.
Baffling Phenomena: And Other Studies in the Philosophy of Knowledge and Valuation. RESCHER, Nicholas.
Bakhtin and the Epistemology of Discourse. THOMSON, Clive (ed).
Brouwer's Intuitionism (Studies in the History and Philosophy of Mathematics, Vol 2). VAN STIGT, W P.
Il compito della filosofia: Saggio su Windelband. OLIVA, Rossella Bonito.
Core Questions in Philosophy: A Text With Readings. SOBER, Elliott.
The Critical Problem of Knowledge. BLANDINO, Giovanni (ed).
De l'épistémologie à la politique: La philosophie de l'histoire de Karl R Popper. RUELLAND, Jacques G.
Doubting: Contemporary Perspectives on Skepticism. ROTH, Michael D (ed).
Epistemic Justification: Essays in the Theory of Knowledge. ALSTON, William P.
Epistemics. DURAN, Jane.
Epistemology and Skepticism: An Enquiry into the Nature of Epistemology. CHATALIAN, George.
Experiment: Right or Wrong. FRANKLIN, Allan.
Expressionism in Philosophy: Spinoza. DELEUZE, Gilles.
Feminism/Postmodernism. NICHOLSON, Linda J (ed).
The Fragmentation of Reason. STICH, Stephen.
George Santayana y la Ironia de la Materia. IZUZQUIZA, Ignacio.
Human Nature and Historical Knowledge: Hume, Hegel and Vico. POMPA, Leon.
The Ideas of Ayn Rand. MERRILL, Ronald E.
Information, Semantics and Epistemology. VILLANUEVA, Enrique (ed).
Knowledge in Flux: Modeling the Dynamics of Epistemic States. GÄRDENFORS, Peter.
Knowledge in Perspective: Selected Essays in Epistemology. SOSA, Ernest.
Knowledge of the External World. AUNE, Bruce.
Knowledge, Fiction, and Imagination. NOVITZ, David.
Leibniz' Position der Rationalität. KAEHLER, Klaus Erich.
Meditations on First Philosophy: A Bilingual Edition—René Descartes. HEFFERNAN, George (trans).
The Mind of Donald Davidson. BRANDL, Johannes (ed).
The Moral Animus of David Hume. SIEBERT, Donald T.
Moral und Politik aus der Sicht des Kritischen Rationalismus. SALAMUN, Kurt (ed).
The Natural and the Normative: Theories of Spatial Perception from Kant to Helmholtz. HATFIELD, Gary.
Nomic Probability and the Foundations of Induction. POLLOCK, John L.
L'ordine della certezza: Scientificità e persuasione in Descartes. BONICALZI, Francesca.
Overcoming Foundations: Studies in Systematic Philosophy. WINFIELD, Richard Dien.
Il Paradigma del Sapere. LENTINI, Luigi.
Perspectives on Ideas and Reality. NYÍRI, J C (ed).
Philosophical Perspectives, 3: Philosophy of Mind and Action Theory, 1989. TOMBERLIN, James E (ed).
The Philosophical Theology of John Duns Scotus. ADAMS, Marilyn McCord (ed).
Philosophical Writings: A Selection—William of Ockham. BOEHNER, Philotheus (ed & trans).
Philosophische Hermeneutik. INEICHEN, Hans.
A Post-Modern Epistemology. SORRI, Mari.
The Potential of Modern Discourse: Musil, Peirce, and Perturbation. FINLAY, Marike.
Reading Rorty. MALACHOWSKI, Alan (ed).
Reasoning and Revision in Hybrid Representation Systems. NEBEL, Bernhard.
Reasons and Experience. MILLAR, Alan.
Reflexion und Metareflexion bei Platon und Fichte. ZEHNPFENNIG, Barbara.
Scientific Theories. SAVAGE, C Wade (ed).
The Secret Connexion: Causation, Realism, and David Hume. STRAWSON, Galen.
The Social Horizon of Knowledge. BUCZKOWSKI, Piotr (ed).
Teoria e interpretazione: Per un'epistemologia delle scienze umane. BORUTTI, Silvana.
Thinking Philosophically: An Introduction to Philosophy with Readings. GUSMANO, Joseph J.
Whose Science? Whose Knowledge? Thinking from Women's Lives. HARDING, Sandra.
Wisdom: Its Nature, Origins, and Development. STERNBERG, Robert J.
"'Circular' Coherence and 'Absurd' Foundations" in *Truth and Interpretation: Perspectives on the Philosophy of Donald Davidson*, SOSA, Ernest.
"Against Instrumentalism" in *Studies on Mario Bunge's "Treatise"*, VOLLMER, Gerhard.
"Commentary: Common Knowledge and Archaeology" in *Critical Traditions in Contemporary Archaeology*, ZUBROW, Ezra.
"The Conditions of Thought" in *The Mind of Donald Davidson*, DAVIDSON, Donald.
"Deep Epistemology Without Foundations (in Language)" in *Reading Rorty*, MALACHOWSKI, Alan R.
"Effective Epistemology, Psychology, and Artificial Intelligence" in *Acting and Reflecting: The Interdisciplinary Turn in Philosophy*, KELLY, Kevin.
"Epistemology and Nominalism" in *Physicalism in Mathematics*, BURGESS, John P.
"Epistemology: Formal and Empirical" in *Acting and Reflecting: The Interdisciplinary Turn in Philosophy*, SIMON, Herbert.
"Julian of Norwich" in *A History of Women Philosophers, Volume II: Medieval, Renaissance and Enlightenment, A.D. 500-1600*, EVASDAUGHTER, Elizabeth N.
"Mario Bunge on Epistemology" in *Studies on Mario Bunge's "Treatise"*, BUNGE, Mario.
"Mirrors and Veils, Thoughts and Things: The Epistemological Problematic" in *Reading Rorty*, YOLTON, John W.
"On Relativism" in *Studies on Mario Bunge's "Treatise"*, BOUDON, Raymond.
"Our Perception of the External World" in *Key Themes in Philosophy*, TILES, J E.
"The Problem of the External World" in *Key Themes in Philosophy*, HAMLYN, D W.
"Radical Interpretation and Epistemology" in *Truth and Interpretation: Perspectives on the Philosophy of Donald Davidson*, MC GINN, Colin.
"Rebuilding the Ship while Sailing on the Water" in *Perspectives on Quine*, HAACK, Susan.
"Rorty in the Epistemological Tradition" in *Reading Rorty*, TAYLOR, Charles.
"The Scientific Roots of Constructivist Epistemologies" in *Études sur/Studies on Hélène Metzger*, LÖWY, Ilana.
"Difficoltà" con Simmel: Considerazioni in margine ad un convegno. LANDKAMMER, Joachim.
"Eigen Elements" Emerging from the Interaction of Two Knowing and Acting Subjects. VALLÉE, Robert.
"Inhabiting" in the *Phenomenology of Perception*. WEINER, Scott E.
Das "objektive Denken" in Schellings Naturphilosophie. BUCHHEIM, Thomas.
"Phénoménologie" de l'expression. CHAUVIRE, Christiane.
"Sigma": conoscenza e metodo. SAVA, Gabriella.
"The Fragmentation of Reason": Précis of Two Chapters. STICH, Stephen P.
'Rules' and 'Knowledge'. HARRISON III, Frank R.
'Seventeen' Subtleties in Plato's *Theaetetus*. FOGELMAN, Brian D and HUTCHINSON, D S.
A Brief Survey of Indian Buddhistic Logic (in Hungarian). FEHER, Judit.
A priori et a posteriori dans la pratique cognitive: le modele de la regulation des couples ago-antagonistes. BERNARD-WEIL, E.
The A Priori in Phenomenology and the Legacy of Logical Empiricism. BLOSSER, Philip.
Action and Explanation. MAJUMDAR, Aruna.

EPISTEMOLOGY

Against Common Sense: Avoiding Cartesian Anxiety. BINEHAM, Jeffery L.
Against Conditionalization. BACCHUS, Fahiem and KYBURG JR, Henry E and THALOS, Mariam.
The Agnostic Fallacy. KEENE, G B.
Akratic Action and the Practical Role of Better Judgment. MELE, Alfred R.
Algunas observaciones sobre la noción de *Pragma* en Aristóteles. FEMENÍAS, María Luisa.
Alle origini della riflessione di Leopold von Ranke sulla storia: K F Bachmann e J G Fichte. GHELARDI, Maurizio.
Alternativen und Irrtum in der Kritischen Philosophie Kants. LOH, Werne.
Análisis político-epistemológico de la obra de arte según Walter Benjamin. COMESAÑA, Santalices Gloria.
Analiticidad, empirismo y verdad necesaria. HERNÁNDEZ IGLESIAS, Manuel Angel.
Anti-Realism and Skepticism in Ethics. SCHUELER, G F.
An Anti-Sceptical Fugue. GILLETT, Grant.
The Antinomy of Perception: Merleau-Ponty and Causal Representation Theory. HASS, Lawrence.
Aportes para el debate en torno a la teología de la liberción. RUBIOLO, E.
Apriorisme et théorie du choix rationnel. KAUFMANN, J Nicolas.
Arte y conocimiento. ECHAURI, Raúl.
Aspects of the Problem of Reference (1): Phenomenology, Hermeneutics and Deconstruction. RAJAN, R Sundara.
The Assurance of Faith. WOLTERSTORFF, Nicholas.
Authority. WILLARD, Charles A.
Autopoesis—Subject—Reality (in German). ZIEMKE, Axel and STÖBER, Konrad.
Bachelard and Scientific Realism. TIJIATTAS, Mary.
Der Begriff des Selbstbewusstseins bei Kant. GLOY, Karen.
Het belang van Husserls aanzet tot een fenomenologie van de bewustzijnsperspectieven. FREDERIX, Lode.
Belief, Acceptance, and Knowledge. RADFORD, Colin.
Belief, Contradiction, and the Logic of Self-Deception. DA COSTA, Newton C A and FRENCH, Steven.
Belief, Desire and the Praxis of Reasoning. WILLIAMS, Stephen.
Believing What We Do Not See: The Case Against van Fraassen's Conception of Observation. DOBSON, Andrew.
Brouwerian Intuitionism. DETLEFSEN, Michael.
Buddhist Anthropology vis-à-vis Modern Philosophy and Contemporary Neurophysiology. BUGAULT, Guy.
Can Knowledge Occur Unknowingly?. CHAUDHURI, Manjusree.
Can There Be Justified Philosophical Beliefs?. NIELSEN, Kai.
Capacidad de la mente humana para alcanzar el ser de las cosas, hasta el mismo *Esse subsistens* (II). DERISI, Octavio N.
El carácter inmanente del conocimiento. SEGURA, Carmen.
Cartesian Scepticism and Relevant Alternatives. SCHRECK, P A.
Cartesian Skepticism and Inference to the Best Explanation. VOGEL, Jonathan.
The Causal Efficacy of Content. SEGAL, Gabriel and SOBER, Elliott.
Ce que Ferdinand Gonseth a d'important à dire à l'épistémologie contemporaine. JORGE, Maria M A.
Certainty, the Cogito, and Cartesian Dualism. GLOUBERMAN, Mark.
Chisholm, Reid and the Problem of the Epistemic Surd. LEHRER, Keith.
Cientificidad y Romanticismo: Acerca de las relaciones entre cientismo, gnosticismo y romanticismo. KOSLOWSKI, Peter.
Classification by Comparison with Paradigms. EBERLE, Rolf.
Clever Bookies and Coherent Beliefs. CHRISTENSEN, David.
Closing the Chinese Room. WEISS, Thomas.
The Cogito and the Diallelus. ZELLNER, Harold.
Coherence, Anti-realism, and the Vienna Circle. YOUNG, James O.
Commentary on "Epistemology as Hypothesis". SLEEPER, R W.
Comments on Schiffer's *Remnants of Meaning*. RICHARD, Mark.
Comprehensive Evolutionary Epistemology Bibliography. CZIKO, Gary A and CAMPBELL, Donald T.
El concepto de Filosofia y conocimiento en Ludwig Wittgenstein. ESPARZA-BRACHO, Jesús.
El concepto de verdad en la física moderna. ROMERO BARÓ, José María.
El concepto tradicional de verdad en Santo Tomás. FORMENT, Eudaldo.
Conceptual Necessity, Causality and Self-Ascriptions of Sensation. KAUFMAN, Frederik.
Conditio sine qua non? Zuordnung in the Early Epistemologies of Cassirer and Schlick. RYCKMAN, Thomas.
El conocimiento de los cuerpos según Malebranche (I). FERNANDEZ RODRIGUEZ, Jose Luis.
Conocimiento metodico y no metodico; so pretexto de una incursion acerca de la dialectica segun platon. SALA, J F A.
Conocimiento y comunicación: Algunas reflexiones sobre la vida social. SUANCES MARCOS, M.
Conocimiento y determinismo. LAGUNILLA, Ana E Galán.
Consciousness and Introspective Knowledge. CARLOYE, Jack C.
Consciousness and Synchronic Identity. MATHESON, Carl.
Conservatism and Tacit Confirmation. ADLER, Jonathan E.
Considerazioni sul problema della conoscenza. BACCARI, Luciano.
Contextualizing Knowledge: A Reply to "Dewey and the Theory of Knowledge". HICKMAN, Larry.
Cook Wilson as Critic of Bradley. TACELLI, Ronald K.
Cool Red. LEVINE, Joseph.
Correspondence, Consensus, and Coherence and the Rape of Democracy. PASK, Gordon.
La cosmologia tra filosofia ed empirologia. PELLECCHIA, Pasquale.
Could Someone Else Have Had My Headache?. STONE, Jim.
Crítica de Heidegger al "intuicionalismo" cartesiano. FORMENT, Eudaldo.
A Critique of Jayarasi's Critique of Perception. MOHANTA, D K.
A Critique of Plantinga's Theological Foundationalism. ZEIS, John.
The Crucial Disanalogies Between Properly Basic Belief and Belief in God. GRIGG, Richard.
La cuestión del Método de una filosofía latinoamericana. SCANNONE, J C.
Davidson and the Sceptic: The Thumbnail Version. CRAIG, Edward.
Davidson's Transcendental Arguments. MAKER, William.
De Re Desire. MARKIE, Peter and PATRICK, Timothy.
Defending the Tradition. NIELSEN, Kai.
The Degeneration of Popper's Theory of Demarcation. GRÜNBAUM, Adolf.
Deleuze und Spinozas "Ethik". OITTINEN, Vesa.
Desarrollos actuales de la epistemología dialéctica. MENDOZA, Celina A Lértora.
Determinism and the Experience of Freedom. DOUBLE, Richard.
Dewey and the Theory of Knowledge. THAYER, H S.
Dewey, Indeterminacy, and the Spectator Theory of Knowledge. KULP, Christopher B.
Dharmakirti on Inference and Properties. GANERI, Jonardon.
A Dilemma of Late Life Memory. MC KEE, Patrick.
Dimensions of Observability. KOSSO, Peter.
Directions of Justification in the Negative-Positive Duty Debate. MALM, H M.
Una discussione di epistemologia. BLANDINO, Giovanni and FEDERSPIL, G.
The Distinction between *Res Significata* and *Modus Significandi* in Aquinas's Theological Epistemology. ROCCA, Gregory.
División y dialéctica en el *Fedro*. SANTA CRUZ, María Isabel.
Doubt and Faith: Santayana and Kierkegaard on Fundamental Belief. SARTWELL, Crispin.
Doxastic Paradoxes Without Self-Reference. KOONS, Robert Charles.
Dravya, Guna and *Paryāya* in Jaina Thought. SONI, Jayandra.
Dretske on Knowledge and Content. GJELSVIK, Olav.
Dretske on Perception. HOROWITZ, Amir.
Dummett's Ought from Is. GREEN, Karen.
The Dynamics of Concepts and Non-local Interactions. VAN LOOCKE, Philip R.
An Economic Model of Scientific Activity and Truth Acquisition. GOLDMAN, Alvin I and SHAKED, Moshe.
Editologie et Scientificite. BAUDET, Jean C.
Eléments pour une "philosophie de la psychologie". PETIT, Jean-Luc.
Eléments pour une philosophie de l'expression. UCCIANI, Louis.
Embedded Probabilities. DUBUCS, J.
The Emergence of Analogy: Analogical Reasoning as a Constraint Satisfaction Process. VAN DORMAEL, Jan.
Emotion and Belief. BORUAH, Bijoy H.
Empiricism versus Realism: High Points in the Debate During the Past 150 Years. DILWORTH, Craig.
Entorn del libre de F canals i Vidal: "Sobre la esencia del conocimiento". COLOMER, Eusebi.
Entwurf eines Klassifikationsschemas für philosophische Positionen. WIMMER, Franz.
Epistemic Internalism's Dilemma. HETHERINGTON, Stephen Cade.
Epistemic Justification and Psychological Realism. TAYLOR, James E.
Epistemic Leaks and Epistemic Meltdowns: A Response to William Morris on Scepticism with Regard to Reason. KARLSSON, Mikael M.
Epistemic Norms and Evolutionary Success. CLARKE, Murray.
Epistemic Obligations and Doxastic Voluntarism. GOGGANS, Phil.
Epistemic Paternalism: Communication Control in Law and Society. GOLDMAN, Alvin I.
Epistemología contemporánea y filosofía cristiana. ZANOTTI, Gabriel J.
Epistemologia e teoria politica. ZOLO, Danilo.
The Epistemological Significance of Transformative Religious Experiences: A Kierkegaardian Exploration. EVANS, C Stephen.
Epistemological Structures in Marketing: Paradigms, Metaphors, and Marketing Ethics. REIDENBACH, R Eric and ROBIN, Donald P.
Epistemological Time Asymmetry. SAVITT, Steven F.
Épistémologie et questionnement: le modèle en tant que forme de l'interrogation scientifique. BORUTTI, Silvana.
Epistemology and Political Rationality. FUTERNICK, Ken.
Epistemology as Hypothesis. PUTNAM, Hilary and PUTNAM, Ruth Anna.
The Epistemology of J M Keynes. O'DONNELL, Rod.
Epistemology on Holiday. KAPLAN, Mark.
Epistemology, Practical Research, and Human Subjects. ROSS, Murray and SELMAN, Mark.
Epistemology, Psychology, and Goldman. CORLETT, J Angelo.
Die erkenntniskritische Wendung Descartes' als Konsequenz geschichtlicher Entwicklung des Leib-Seele-Dualismus. POHLENZ, G.

EPISTEMOLOGY

Ernst Cassirer and Martin Heidegger: The Davos Debate. LYNCH, Dennis A.
El escepticismo crítico en el Diccionario de Bayle. ARROYO, Julián.
Espoir et désespoir de la raison chez Kant. GRIMALDI, Nicolas.
Estetica e interrogazione. GARRONI, Emilio.
Estrategias metacientíficas: Parte II. HIDALGO TUÑÓN, Alberto.
The Ethics Behind the Absence of Ethics in Alfred Schutz's Thought. BARBER, Michael.
Etwas ist in mir da—Zu Ulrich Posthast: Philosophisches Buch. WOLF, Ursula.
Evaluating Cognitive Strategies: A Reply to Cohen, Goldman, Harman, and Lycan. STICH, Stephen P.
Evidence and Reasons for Belief. FOLEY, Richard.
Explanation and Causality: Some Suggestions from Econometrics. GALAVOTTI, Maria Carla.
Explanation in Physical Theory. CLARK, Peter.
Externalist Theories of Perception. ALSTON, William P.
The Fallibility Paradox. LEHRER, Keith and KIM, Kihyeon.
Farewell to the Tradition: Doing without Metaphysics and Epistemology. NIELSEN, Kai.
Feminism and Epistemology. CHANDLER, John.
Feminism and Philosophy of Science. LONGINO, Helen E.
Feminism and Relativism. RUSSELL, Denise.
The Fifth Meditation. EDELBERG, Walter.
Firth and the Ethics of Belief. CHISHOLM, Roderick M.
Firth's Critique of Epistemological Rule-Utilitarianism. SHOPE, Robert K.
Fisiormorfismo de la razón versus racionalismo. PACHO, Julián.
Fools and Heretics. BAMBROUGH, Renford.
For Anil Gupta. HART, W D.
Foundationalism and Peter's Confession. HESTER, Marcus.
Foundationalism, Holism, or Hegel?. STERN, David S.
The Foundationalist Justification of Epistemic Principles. REMEDIOS, F.
From Russell to Quine: Basic Statements, Foundationalism, Truth, and Other Myths. LINDBERG, Jordan J.
Gadamer's Concrete Universal. KERBY, Anthony Paul.
Der Gegenstand der Vorstellungen und die transzendentale Apperzeption. LÓPEZ-FERNÁNDEZ, Alvaro.
General Causation. SAPIRE, David.
Geometrical and Physical Conventionalism of Henri Poincaré in Epistemological Formulation. GIEDYMIN, Jerzy.
Gettier's Principle for Deducibility of Justification. BASU, Sandhya.
Getting to the Truth Through Conceptual Revolutions. KELLY, Kevin and GLYMOUR, Clark.
Glymour on Deoccamization and the Epistemology of Geometry. DURAN, Jane.
Gonseth et le discours théologique. MOREL, Bernard.
Gottlob Frege, lettere a Wittgenstein. PENCO, Carlo and PARODI, Alessandra.
Hattiangadi's Theory of Scientific Problems and the Structure of Standard Epistemologies. GIUNTI, Marco.
Healthy Scepticism. FRANKLIN, James.
Heraclitus: Heidegger's 1944 Lecture Held at Freiburg University. FRINGS, Manfred S.
Herbert Spiegelberg 1904-1990. SCHUHMANN, Karl.
Herméneutique et épistémologie Gadamer entre Heidegger et Hegel. ROCKMORE, Tom.
Historical Continuity and Discontinuity in the Philosophy of Gadamer and Foucault (in Hungarian). UJLAKI, Gabriella.
Hobbes, Berkeley y las ideas abstractas. ROBLES, José A.
Hölderlin über Urteil und Sein. GRAESER, Andreas.
How Do Scientific Explanations Explain?. KINOSHITA, Joyce.
How Not to Russell Carnap's *Aufbau*. RICHARDSON, Alan.
How to Change Your Mind. MARTINS, João P and CRAVO, Maria R.
Hume's Critical Realism: A Reply to Livingston. WILSON, Fred.
Hume's Rejection of the Theory of Ideas. WRIGHT, John P.
Hume, Reid and Innate Ideas: A Response to John P Wright. GALLIE, Roger D.
I Know What I Know, If You Know What I Mean. DURAN, Jane.
The Identity Theory of Truth. BALDWIN, Thomas.
If Children thought Like Adults. GAUKER, Christopher.
If There Is a God, Any Experience Which Seems to Be of God, Will Be Genuine. LEVINE, Michael P.
The Immanence of Thought: Hegel's Critique of Foundationalism. STERN, David S.
In Defence of Reincarnation. DANIELS, Charles B.
In Defense of Southern Fundamentalism. HORGAN, Terence and GRAHAM, George.
In What Way is Abductive Inference Creative?. KAPITAN, Tomis.
Individualism and Semantic Development. PATTERSON, Sarah.
Induction and Modality. JOHNSON, David.
Induction and Stochastic Independence. AGASSI, Joseph.
The Inference to the Best Explanation. BEN-MENAHEM, Y.
Ingarden und Husserls transzendentaler Idealismus. HAEFLIGER, Gregor.
El innatismo de Leibniz. HERRERA, Alejandro.
Inside World-Outside World: Epistemology on the Conscious Action of the Nervous System. DE JONG, B M.
Institutional Mental Health and Social Control: The Ravages of Epistemological Hubris. FARBER, Seth.
Insularity and the Persistence of Perceptual Illusion. CAM, Philip.
Intention, Cognitive Commitment, and Planning. AUDI, Robert.
Intentionality and Modern Philosophical Psychology—II: The Return to Representation. LYONS, Willia.
Intentionality and the Public World: Husserl's Treatment of Objectivity in the Cartesian Meditations. ARP, Kristana.
Interdisciplinary Epistemology. BODEN, Margaret A.
Internalism and Epistemically Responsible Belief. GRECO, John.
Irrational Desires. HUBIN, Donald C.
Is Coming to Believe in God Reasonable or Unreasonable?. HERBERT, R T.
Is Davidson a Volitionist In Spite of Himself?. CLEVELAND, Timothy.
Is Knowledge Socially Determined? A Critique. CHAUDHURY, Mahasweta.
Is Kripke's Puzzle Really a Puzzle. CORLETT, J Angelo.
Ist die Kantische Theorie eine Theorie entfremdeter Erkenntnis?. KERBER, Harald.
Justification in the 20th Century. PLANTINGA, Alvin.
Justification, Truth, Goals, and Pragmatism: Comments on Stich's "Fragmentation of Reason". HARMAN, Gilbert.
Ka-Meh und das alte Neue—über epistemische Krise und Emanzipation. SANDKÜHLER, Hans Jörg.
Kant in Hegels begtipsleer. DE VOS, L.
Kant's First Analogy Revisited. BUESSEM, George E.
Kants Begriff der synthetischen Urteile a priori. ROS, Arno.
Kants *Kritik der Urteilskraft*. RAYMAEKERS, Bart.
Kants Schemata als Anwendungsbedingungen von Kategorien auf Anschauungen. LOHMAR, Dieter.
Kants Theorie der Gegenstandserkenntnis und Schopenhauers Lehre vom Ding an sich. BAUMANN, Lutz.
Kants Theorie der geometrischen Erkenntnis und die nichteuklikische Geometrie. SCHIRN, Matthias.
Keith Lehrer and Thomas Reid. CHISHOLM, Roderick M.
Kierkegaard on the Limits of Christian Epistemology. WISDO, David.
Kinds of Truth and Psychoanalysis as a Myth: Some Epistemological Remarks on the Freudian Model (in Italian). BORUTTI, Silvana.
Knowing through the Body. JOHNSON, Mark.
Knowledge and Deductive Closure. WHITE, James L.
Knowledge as Active, Aesthetic, and Hypothetical: A Pragmatic Interpretation of Whitehead's Cosmology. FRISINA, Warren G.
Knowledge is Merely True Belief. SARTWELL, Crispin.
Knowledge, Reason and Human Autonomy: A Review Article. KRISHNA, Daya.
L'affirmation de l'existence de Dieu selon Austin Farrer. HENDERSON, Edward H.
L'Assertion dans les contextes épistémiques; garants objectaux et bases d'évaluation. MOULOUD, Noël.
L'écriture réparatrice. HAREL, Simon.
L'épistémologie mathématique de Gonseth dans la perspective du pragmatisme de Peirce. HEINZMANN, Gerhard.
L'étude du vivant et la méthodologie ouverte. PILET, Paul-Emile.
L'identité personnelle et la source des concepts. SHALOM, Albert.
The Later Schelling's Conception of Dialectical Method, in Contradistinction to Hegel's. BEACH, Edward A.
Levels of Knowledge in the *Theaetetus*. DORTER, Kenneth.
Los límites de mi lenguaje—los límites de mi mundo. KLOYBER, Christian.
The Locked-In Syndrome and the Behaviorist Epistemology of Other Minds. KURTHEN, Martin (and others).
Logic and Empiricism. BOSTOCK, David.
Logic and Language in the *Chuang Tzu*. ALT, Wayne E.
Lonergan's Performative Transcendental Argument Against Scepticism. REHG, William R.
Macdonald on Type Reduction via Disjunction. ENDICOTT, Ronald P.
Making Noises in Counterpoint or Chorus: Putnam's Rejection of Relativism. JOHNSON, Jeffery L.
Malebranche versus Arnauld. COOK, Monte.
La matemática: certeza y verdad. CAÑÓN LOYES, Camino.
Materiali per una storia dell'epistemologia in Italia. CASTELLANA, Mario.
A Mathematical A Priorist Answers Philip Kitcher. NORTON-SMITH, Thomas M.
Max on Moore. STROLL, Avrum.
Max Scheler's Analysis of Illusions, Idols, and Ideologies. IBANA, Rainier R A.
Meaning as Grammar plus *Consequences*. DE QUEIROZ, Ruy J G B.
The Meaning of Meaning. HELLER, Michael.
Meno, the Slave-Boy, and the *Elenchos*. BENSON, Hugh H.
Merleau-Ponty on the Cartesian "Dubito": A Critical Analysis. HUDAC, Michael C.
Metafisica todavia? (conclusión). SANABRIA, José Rubén.
Metaphysical Realism and Psychologistic Semantics. HORGAN, Terence.
Methodological, Epistemological, and Ontological Motifs in the Thought of Reinhold Niebuhr. AYERS, Robert H.
Meyer's Theory of Problematology. GOLDEN, James L and JAMISON, David L.
Mismidad y diferencia. COUTO-SOARES, Maria Luisa.

EPISTEMOLOGY

Modest A Priori Knowledge. SUMMERFIELD, Donna M.
Moore's Paradox Revisited. LINVILLE, Kent and RING, Merrill.
Moral Epistemology and the Supervenience of Ethical Concepts. AUDI, Robert.
Moral Scepticism and Inductive Scepticism. BLACK, Robert.
More on Quine's Dilemma of Undetermination. GIBSON, Roger F.
Ms en abyme: Deconstruction and Feminism. ELAM, Diane.
Myself. WILLIAMS, C J F.
Names, Actualities, and the Emergence of Essentialist Theories of Naming in Classical Chinese Thought. MAKEHAM, John.
Naturalism and Scepticism. BELL, Martin and MC GINN, Marie.
Naturalized Epistemology Sublimated: Rapprochement without the Ruts. FULLER, Steve.
The Nature and Significance of Intuition: A View Based on a Core Idea Held by S Radhakrishnan. FITZ, Hope K.
Das neue (post-analytische) Interesse an der Präanalytischen Philosophie. NAGL, Ludwig.
A New Interpretation of Russell's Multiple-Relation Theory of Judgment. LANDINI, Gregory.
Newcomb's Problem, Prisoners' Dilemma, and Collective Action. HURLEY, S L.
Nominalism and Abstract Reference. MORELAND, J P.
Non-Dominance, Third Person and Non-Action Newcomb Problems, and Metatickles. SOBEL, Jordan Howard.
The Normal Rewards of Success. WHYTE, J T.
Normativity and the Very Idea of Moral Epistemology. COPP, David.
Note on a Paper of D P Ellerman. PAALMAN-DE MIRANDA, Aïda B.
A Note on Verisimilitude and Relativization to Problems. MONGIN, Philippe.
Notes on the Specification of "Meaning" in Schutz. EMBREE, Lester.
Objectivity and Growth of Knowledge. CHAUDHURY, Mahasweta.
Objet et communauté transcendantale: autour d'un fragment du dernier Husserl. BENOIST, J.
La objetividad y la distinción ciencia/ética. PUTNAM, Hilary and MURILLO, Lorena.
Obligation and Knowledge (in French). SCHULTHESS, Daniel.
Observation: An Empirical Discussion. GILMAN, Daniel.
Omniscience, Immutability, and the Divine Mode of Knowing. SULLIVAN, Thomas D.
On "Why is There Something Rather Than Nothing?". KUSCH, Martin.
On 'This is Red and This is Blue': *Tractatus* 6.3751. SAHU, Neelamani.
On a Moorean Solution to Instability Puzzles. KROON, Frederick W.
On Appealing to the Evidence. PHILLIPS, Hollibert E.
On Being an Aristotelian. MEYNELL, Hugo A.
On Empirical Interpretation. MUNDY, Brent.
On Falsificationist Interpretations of Peirce. SULLIVAN, Patrick F.
On Husserl's Theory of the Constitution of Objectiving Meaning (in Czechoslovakian). ZATKA, V.
On Induction and Properties. ZABLUDOWSKI, Andrzej.
On Knowing and Naming. BEARDS, Andrew.
On Making a Coherence Theory of Truth True. SYLVAN, Richard.
On Naturalizing Epistemology. ALMEDER, Robert.
On Removing Puzzles About Belief Ascription. DEVITT, Michael.
On Respecting Puzzles About Belief Ascription (A Reply to Devitt). LYCAN, William G.
On the "Arriving at Principles from Numbers" Method of Thought in the Late-Ming, Early-Qing Period. WEIPING, Chen.
On the Aim of Scientific Theories in Relating to the World: A Defence of the Semantic Account. BAUR, Michael.
On the Concept of Mímésis (in Czechoslovakian). VEJRAZKA, Michal.
On the Dearth of Philosophical Contributions to Medicine. YARBOROUGH, Mark.
On the Irreducibility of the Will. GARCIA, J L A.
On the Nature and Norms of Theoretical Commitment. HORWICH, Paul.
On the Nature of Einstein's Realism. POLIKAROV, Azaria.
On the Paradoxical Inception and Motivation of Transcendental Philosophy in Plato and Husserl. HOPKINS, Burt C.
On the Phenomenon of Marginality in Epistemology: Gonseth and his Tradition. WITKOWSKI, Lech.
On the Question of Nietzsche's "Scientism". GALLO, Beverly E.
On the Source of the Eternal Truths. BEACH, Edward A (trans) and VON SCHELLING, F W J.
On Two Recent Accounts of Colour. MC GINN, Marie.
The Ontology of Mental Images. HOLBROOK, Daniel.
The Other European Science of Nature?. UBEROI, J P S.
The Outranking Approach and the Foundations of Electre Methods. ROY, Bernard.
Overloading Intentions for Efficient Practical Reasoning. POLLACK, Martha E.
The Paradox of Epistemology: A Defense of Naturalism. KETCHUM, Richard J.
Peirce's Logic of Discovery: Abduction and the Universal Categories. TURRISI, Patricia A.
Penny Pinching and Backward Induction. HOLLIS, Martin.
La pensée gonséthienne et le mouvement systémique. PEGUIRON, Nicolas.
Per un'analisi del discorso dichiarativo. CELANO, Bruno.
Perceptual Content in the Stoics. SORABJI, Richard.
Philosophers as Professional Relativists: Canadian Philosophical Association Presidential Address 1990. BUTTS, Robert E.
Philosophical Hermeneutics and its Meaning for Philosophy. PAGE, Carl.
Philosophical Hierarchies and Lyotard's Dichotomies. SASSOWER, Raphael and OGAZ, Charla Phyllis.
Philosophical Reminiscences with Reflections on Firth's Work. PUTNAM, Hilary.
La philosophie des sciences de Hertz et le Tractatus. LEROUX, Jean.
Plantinga's Box. SESSIONS, William Lad.
Por um novo modelo de saber: Problemática do discurso Filosófico-Teológico. DINIS, Alfredo.
The Possibilities of Scepticisms: Philosophy and Theology without Apology. JACKSON, Timothy P.
The Poverty of Naturalistic Moral Realism: Comments on Timmons. HOLMGREN, Margaret.
Practical Intuition and Rhetorical Example. SCHOLLMEIER, Paul.
Pragmatics and Pragmatism. SULLIVAN, Patrick F.
The Praxiology of Perception: Visual Orientations and Practical Action. COULTER, Jeff and PARSONS, E D.
Predication and Logic of Language (II). GANGADEAN, Ashok.
Prediction and Explanation in Economics. SWAMIDASAN, Nalini.
A Problem in the Foundations of Set Theory. MADDY, Penelope.
The Problem of Protocol Statements and Schlick's Concept of 'Konstatierungen'. ZHAI, Zhenming.
El problema de la "acción intencional" en el conocimiento sensible. DELBOSCO, Héctor J.
El problema del conocimiento en Pascal. CASTRO MÉNDEZ, Silvia.
Problemas en torno al concepto de "ciencias humanas" como ciencias con doble plano operatorio. ALVARGONZÁLEZ, David.
Problématicité, rationalité et interrogativité. CARRILHO, Manuel Mari.
Le problématologique devant la faculté de juger. PARRET, Herman.
Problèmes de l'expression. ROSSET, Clément.
Purposive Intending. PINK, T L M.
Putnam's Realism and Relativity: An Uneasy Balance. THROOP, William and DORAN, Katheryn.
Qualia and Theory Reduction: A Criticism of Paul Churchland. BACHRACH, Jay E.
Le questionnement, comme synthèse de l'humain. LEMPEREUR, Alain.
Radical Critique, Scepticism and Commonsense. GAITA, Raimond.
La ragione e i valori nella determinazione delle norme. CORTESE, Roberto.
Rāmānuja's Hermeneutics of the *Upanisads* in Comparison with Sankara's Interpretation. SAWAI, Yoshitsugu.
The Range of Options. ZIMMERMAN, Michael J.
Rationalism, Supervenience, and Moral Epistemology. KLAGGE, James.
Rationality and Reasonableness. BURBULES, Nicholas C.
Rationality, Reasons, and the Sociology of Knowledge (in Serbo-Croatian). KAISER, Matthias.
A Reading of Aquinas's Five Ways. FOGELIN, Robert J.
The Real Difficulty with Burley's Realistic Semantics. FITZGERALD, Michael J.
Reasoning and Computation in Leibniz. SPRUIT, Leen and TAMBURRINI, Guglielmo.
Recent Obituaries of Epistemology. HAACK, Susan.
Recent Work on Naturalized Epistemology. MAFFIE, James.
Reconsidering the Wisdom of the Body. SULLIVAN, Mark D.
A Reconstruction of Jeffrey's Notion of Ratifiability in Terms of Counterfactual Beliefs. SHIN, Hyung Song.
Rediscovering Scepticism. BAILEY, Alan.
Reflexiones en torno a la sensibilidad externa. ALVAREZ-CASTELLANOS, Juan José Sánchez.
Rejoining *Alētheia* and Truth: or Truth Is a Five-Letter Word. HATAB, Lawrence J.
The Relational Theory of Belief (A Reply to Richard). SCHIFFER, Stephen.
Renaissance Ideas and the Idea of the Renaissance. TRINKAUS, Charles.
Replies and Comments. PUTNAM, Hilary.
Reply to Levine's "Cool Red". HARDIN, C L.
Reply to Teller's "Simpler Arguments Might Work Better". HARDIN, C L.
Reply to Wilson's "Shadows on the Cave Wall: Philosophy and Visual Science". HARDIN, C L.
Representative Realism and Absolute Reality. ENGLISH, Parker.
Rescuing Natural Law Theory from the Rationalists. DENNEHY, Raymond.
A Response to Gerard Loughlin's "Prefacing Pluralism: John Hick and the Mastery of Religion". HICK, John.
A Restoration of Popperian Inductive Scepticism. MILLER, David.
Retaliation Rationalized: Gauthier's Solution to the Deterrence Dilemma. MAC INTOSH, Duncan.
Roderick Firth's Contribution to Ethics. BRANDT, R B.
Roderick Firth: His Life and Work. RAWLS, John.
Le rôle des causes comme instruments de la définition. VALOIS, Raynald.
The Role of Perceptual Relativity in Berkeley's Philosophy. MUEHLMANN, Robert.
Die Rolle des unglücklichen Bewusstseins in Hegels *Phänomenologie des Geistes*. STEWARD, Jon.

EPISTEMOLOGY

Rorty, Davidson and Truth. BAGHRAMIAN, Maria.
Rousseau et Kant: A propos de la genèse de la théorie kantienne des idées. PICHÉ, Claude.
Sankara on Reason, Scriptural Authority and Self-Knowledge. UPADHYAYA, K N.
Sartre and James on the Role of the Body in Emotion. BAUGH, Bruce.
Le satori dans le bouddhisme zen et la rationalité. HÉLAL, Georges.
Saying Good-bye to Historical Truth. SPENCE, Donald P.
Scepticism and Autonomy. HOOKWAY, Christopher.
Scepticism and Dreaming: Imploding the Demon. WRIGHT, Crispin.
Scepticism: the Current Debate. ODEGARD, Douglas.
Schematism and Schemata: Kant and the P.D.P.. VAN DE VIJVER, Gertrudis.
Schopenhauer und Fichtes Schrift "Die Bestimmung des Menschen". DECHER, Friedhelm.
Science and Art: The New Golem From the Transdisciplinary to an Ultra-disciplinary Epistemology. BERGER, René.
Scientific Knowledge and Human Happiness. ROY, Krishna.
Scientific Method and the Study of Society. NARASIMHAN, R.
Scientific Realism and Postmodern Philosophy. MURPHY, Nancey.
The Search for an Elusive *A Priori*. CAPEK, Milic.
A Second Copy Thesis in Hume?. PAPPAS, George S.
Seeing in the Mind's Eye. BORUAH, Bijoy H.
Seeing Our Seeing and Knowing Our Knowing. BEN-ZEEV, Aaron.
A Sellarsian Hume?. LIVINGSTON, Donald.
Sensations and Judgments of Perception: Diagnosis and Rehabilitation of Some of Kant's Misleading Examples. KOTZIN, Rhoda and BAUMGÄRTNER, Järg.
Sensory Qualities and 'Homunctionalism': A Review Essay of W G Lycan's *Consciousness*. KOBES, Bernard W.
Shadows on the Cave Wall: Philosophy and Visual Science. WILSON, Hugh R.
Simpler Arguments Might Work Better. TELLER, Davida Y.
Skepticism, Enigma and Integrity: Horizons of Affirmation in Nietzsche's Philosophy. HULL, Robert.
Sobre el alcance de una "ciencia media" entre las ciencias humanas estrictas y los saberes prácticos positivos. BUENO, Gustavo.
Sobre el conocimiento tecnológico. VILLORO, Luis.
Social Epistemics and Social Psychology. GOLDMAN, Alvin.
Social Epistemology and Social Cognition. CORLETT, J Angelo.
Social Epistemology and Social Cognitive Psychology. SCHMITT, Frederick.
Social Epistemology and the Brave New World of Science and Technology Studies. FULLER, Steve.
Social Space as a Determinant of "Collective Thinking" (in Polish). SYMOTIUK, Stefan.
Sociology of Knowledge with Special Reference to Karl Popper. MANDAL, Sunil Baran.
Soggettività e autocoscienza: Prospettive e problemi in Dieter Henrich. CELANO, Bruno.
Solving the Problem of Induction Using a Values-Based Epistemology. ELLIS, Brian.
Some Dependence Relations of Empirical Belief. MALHERBE, Jeanette.
Some Philosophical Directions Towards a Simple Theory of the Self. MANN, David W.
Some Problems in the Epistemology of Advaita. GRIMES, John.
Some Recent Work in Epistemology. MOSER, Paul K.
Some Reflections on Husserl's Approach to the Problem of Transcendence. DHAR, Benulal.
Some Revisionary Proposals About Belief and Believing. MARCUS, Ruth Barcan.
Some Versions of Newcomb's Problem Are Prisoners' Dilemmas. SOBEL, Jordan Howard.
Starting Thought From Women's Lives: Eight Resources for Maximizing Objectivity. HARDING, Sandra.
Staving Off Catastrophe: A Critical Notice of Jerry Fodor's *Psychosemantics*. JONES, Todd and MULAIRE, Edmond and STICH, Stephen.
Stephen P Stich, "The Fragmentation of Reason". COHEN, L Jonathan.
Stephen P Stich, "The Fragmentation of Reason". GOLDMAN, Alvin I.
Stereotypes and Group-Claims. HARVEY, J.
Stit and the Language of Agency. PERLOFF, Michael.
The Strong Programme for the Sociology of Science, Reflexivity and Relativism. NOLA, Robert.
Structural Representation and Surrogative Reasoning. SWOYER, Chris.
The Structure of Empirical Knowledge. DE PIERRIS, Graciela.
Sur le vague en mathématiques. GRANGER, G G.
La teoría de la ciencia de Guillermo de Ockham: una imagen prospectiva. LARRE, Olga and BOLZÁN, J E.
La Teoría del conocimiento en Santo Tomás de Aquino. BEUCHOT, Mauricio.
The Text of the Nyāya-Sūtras: Some Problems. KRISHNA, Daya.
The Idea of Common Sense in the Philosophy of L Chwistek (in Polish). JOZEFCZUK, Grzegorz.
The Initial Form of Empiristic and Aprioristic Conception of Knowledge on the World (in Polish). MORAWIEC, E.
The Object and the Concept: Spinoza's Theory with Regard to the Development of Modern Natural Science (in German). GOLDENBAUM, Ursula.
The Operation of Values: Knowledge in the Conception of G H Mead (in Polish). HETMANSKI, Marek.
The Oscillation of the Concept of Reason in Michel Foucault (in German). BENJOWSKI, Regina.
The Specific Features of Cognition Progress in Philosophy: Demonstrated by the Example of Max Adler (in German). MÖCKEL, Christian.
Theoretical Explanation and Errors of Measurement. FORGE, John.
The Theory of Triple Perception. SARMA, Rajendra Nath.
A Thinker's Agency in Thinking. NAMBIAR, Sankaran.
Thinking versus Thought. KRISHNA, Daya.
Thoughts and Feelings and Things: A New Psychiatric Epistemology. HUNDERT, Edward M.
Three Notions of Judgement (in Czechoslovakian). KOTATKO, Petr.
Three Realities and Two Discourses. TABORSKY, Edwina.
Time, Actuality and Omniscience. LEFTOW, Brian.
Le tournant cognitif en sémiotique. MEUNIER, Jean-Guy.
Towards a Reasonable Version of Methodological Solipsism. ROWLANDS, Mark.
Towards a Research Agenda for Informal Logic and Critical Thinking. WEINSTEIN, Mark.
Transzendentale Argumente pragmatisch relativiert: Über fundamentale Optionen in der Philosophie. LAUENER, Henri.
El tratado de Ideología de Fray Zeferino Gonzalez. BUENO SÁNCHEZ, Gustavo.
El trilema de Aristófanes y los presupuestos normativos del diálgo crítico. MALIANDI, Ricardo.
Tropes and Laws. FUHRMANN, André.
The Trouble With Goldman's Reliabilism. GLEB, Gary.
Truth and Language-World Connections. GROVER, Dorothy.
Truth and Stability in Descartes' *Meditations*. BENNETT, Jonathan.
Truth in Epistemology. STURGEON, Scott.
Truth, Justification and the Inescapability of Epistemology: Comments on Copp. RUSSELL, Bruce.
Truth, Method, and Objectivity: *Husserl and Gadamer on Scientific Method*. NUYEN, A T.
Truths without Facts. SEN, Pranab Kumar.
Der Übergang vom Bestimmt-Bestimmenden zum freien Schema in Kants Kritik der Urteilskraft. KAULBACH, Friedrich.
Unamuno: De la decepción de la verdad, a la apología de la veracidad. SILVA CAMARENA, Juan Manuel.
The Unavoidability of Gender. SCHEMAN, Naomi.
Univocità dell'essere e intenzionalià del conoscere. ANTONELLI, Mauro.
Uno sguardo sulla filosofia americana contemporanea. CENTRONE, Marino.
Vacuous Truth. ALMEDER, Robert F.
The Value-Ought of Self-Realization: A Phenomenological Approach. VELASSERRY, Sebastian.
Verbum-Signum: La définition du langage chez s Augustin et Nicolas de Cues. HENNIGFELD, Jochem.
Verdad e inteligibilidad: Los rasgos invariables de la doctrina platónica de las ideas. LUIS DEL BARCO, José.
Verificationism and Anti-Realism. ROGERSON, Kenneth.
Verisimilitude by Power Relations. ODDIE, Graham.
Vérité à Faire: Merleau-Ponty's Question Concerning Truth. WALDENFELS, Bernhard.
Vers une mise en signe de l'installation. RÉGIMBALD, Manon.
Une version de l'épistémologie gonséthienne: le béton et les cailloux. BONSACK, François.
Was ist ein Polyhistor? Gehversuche auf einem verlassenen Terrain. JAUMANN, Herbert.
Was Kant a Nativist?. FALKENSTEIN, Lorne.
Was Moore a Positivist?. O'CONNOR, David.
What is Empirical in Mathematics?. PETERSON, Philip L.
What is so Practical about Theory? Lewin Revisited. SANDELANDS, Lloyd E.
What is Social about Social Epistemics?. MAFFIE, James.
What is the Logical Form of Probability Assignment in Quantum Mechanics?. HALPIN, John F.
What Putnam Should Have Said: An Alternative Reply to Rorty. HARTZ, Carolyn G.
Whither Social Epistemology? A Reply to Fuller. SCHMAUS, Warren.
Who's the Horse? A Response to Corlett. HEYES, Cecilia.
Why Friedman's Non-Monotonic Reasoning Defies Hempel's Covering Law Model. JANSSEN, M C W and TAN, Y H.
Why We Should Care Whether Our Beliefs Are True. LYCAN, William G.
Wittgenstein and Social Science. TRIGG, Roger.
Wittgenstein escéptico?. CABANCHIK, Samuel.
Wittgenstein on Emotion. PATEL, Kartikeya C.
Zum Verbleib der Königsberger Kant-Handschriften: Funde und Desiderate. STARK, Werner.

EQUAL OPPORTUNITY
A Defense of Equal Opportunity for Welfare. ARNESON, Richard J.
Equal Educational Opportunity as a Public Policy. BUNTING, I A.
Equal Opportunity and the Family. VALLENTYNE, Peter and LIPSON, Morry.

EQUALITY
see also Egalitarianism
Convictions. HOOK, Sidney.
Égalité Uguaglianza. FERRARI, Jean (ed).
"Approaches to Democratic Equality: Maritain, Simon, and Kolnai" in *Freedom in the Modern World: Jacques Maritain, Yves R Simon, Mortimer J Adler*, HITTINGER, John P.
"Egalité ou fraternité" in *Égalité Uguaglianza*, OPPICI, Patrizia.
"Equality, Discrimination and Preferential Treatment" in *A Companion to Ethics*, BOXILL, Bernard R.
"Equality" in *Philosophy and Politics*, MILLER, David.
"Foundations of Liberal Equality" in *The Tanner Lectures on Human Values, Volume XI*, DWORKIN, Ronald.
"L'égalité ambiguë: construction juridique ou déduction métaphysique?" in *Égalité Uguaglianza*, WUNENBURGER, Jean-Jacques.
"L'égalité des droits en 1789" in *Égalité Uguaglianza*, GOYARD-FABRE, Simone.
"L'égalité en 1789" in *Égalité Uguaglianza*, D'HONDT, Jacques.
"L'idée d'égalité et la notion moderne du droit" in *Égalité Uguaglianza*, RENAUT, Alain.
"Response to Miller's 'Equality'" in *Philosophy and Politics*, MINOGUE, Kenneth.
"Una uguale educazione?" in *Égalité Uguaglianza*, PANCERA, Carlo.
"Les utopies littéraires au XVIIIe siècle" in *Égalité Uguaglianza*, IMBROSCIO, Carmelina.
The Ambivalence of the Idea of Equality in the French Enlightenment. CHISICK, Harvey.
Aristotle on Justice, Equality and the Rule of Law. QUINN, Michael.
Bobbio e la scienza politica in Italia. MANCARELLA, Angelo.
Challenge: Subjectivist Naturalism. FOLDVARY, Fred E.
Commentary: Interests and Equal Moral Status. SQUADRITO, Kathy.
Conclusion. GRIFFITHS, A Phillips.
Difficulties with the Principle of Equal Opportunity for Welfare. CHRISTIANO, Thomas.
The Distinction Between Equality in Moral Status and Deserving Equal Consideration. DE GRAZIA, David.
Equality. MILLER, David.
Ethics, AIDS, and Community Responsibility. DOUARD, John.
The Homogeneous Form of Logic Programs with Equality. DEMOPOULOS, William.
Libertad, Igualdad, Fraternidad. BUENO, Gustavo.
Not So Virtuous Republics: Montesquieu, Venice, and the Theory of Aristocratic Republicanism. CARRITHERS, David W.
Perelman et la philosophie anglo-saxonne. MARCIL-LACOSTE, Louise.
Plural But Equal: Group Identity and Voluntary Integration. ROBACK, Jennifer.
Response to Miller's "Equality". MINOGUE, K.
Rethinking the Family. KYMLICKA, Will.
Self-Ownership, Equality, and the Structure of Property Rights. CHRISTMAN, John.
Was Marx a Socialist?. TSIPKO, A.

EQUATION(S)
"Problems of Admissibility and Substitution, Logical Equations and Restricted Theories of Free Algebras" in *Logic, Methodology and Philosophy of Science, VIII*, RYBAKOV, V V.
The Curve Fitting Problem: A Solution. TURNEY, Peter.
Equational Subsystems. WEAVER, George.
Equational Theory of Positive Numbers with Exponentiation is Not Finitely Axiomatizable. GUREVIC, R.
Logical Equations and Admissible Rules of Inference with Parameters in Modal Provability Logics. RYBAKOV, V V.
The Monadic Second-Order Logic of Graphs IV: Definability Properties of Equational Graphs. COURCELLE, Bruno.
A Note on Popper's Equation of Simplicity with Falsifiability. TURNEY, Peter.
A Note on the Axiomatization of Equational Classes of *n*-Valued Lukasiewicz Algebras. ADAMS, M E and CIGNOLI, R.

EQUILIBRIUM
The Dynamics of Rational Deliberation. SKYRMS, Brian.
"Are Economic Kinds Natural?" in *Scientific Theories*, NELSON, Alan.
"What Are General Equilibrium Theories?" in *Acting and Reflecting: The Interdisciplinary Turn in Philosophy*, HAUSMAN, Dan.
The Base Camp Paradox: A Reflection on the Place of Tâtonnement in General Equilibrium Theory. DE VROEY, Michel.
Binary 2 x 2 Games. FISHBURN, Peter C and KILGOUR, D Marc.
The Logic of Rational Play in Games of Perfect Information. BONANNO, Giacomo.

EQUITY
"Excellence, Equity, and Equality" Clarified. GREEN, Thomas F.
Rawlsian Nash Solutions. FABELLA, Raul V.
Research Note On Equity and Ethics in State-Promotion of Agricultural Products. ADELAJA, Adesoji O and BRUMFIELD, Robin G.

EQUIVALENCE
Empirical Equivalence and Undetermination. LAUDAN, Larry and LEPLIN, Jarrett.
Maximal R.E. Equivalence Relations. CARROLL, Jeffrey S.
The Minimal and Semiminimal Notions of Truth. FOX, J.
On Some Logically Equivalent Propositions. KELLY, Charles J.
Stability for Pairs of Equivalence Relations. TOFFALORI, Carlo.

EQUIVOCATION
Equivocation in The Surprise Exam Paradox. FERGUSON, Kenneth G.

ERIGENA
Apophasis and Metaphysics in the *Periphyseon* of John Scottus Eriugena. CARABINE, Deirdre.
Cusanus and Eriugena. BEIERWALTES, Werner.
Emanating Causes: New Battle Lines for Natural Theology?. KING-FARLOW, John.
The Interplay of Nature and Man in the *Periphyseon* of Johannes Scottus Eriugena. OTTEN, Willemien.
John Scottus Eriugena: Recent Works of Consultation. MC EVOY, James J.
Oratio Placabilis Deo Eriugena's Fragmentary Eucharistic Teaching. SMITH, R U.
Some Perspectives in Eriugenian Studies: Three Recent Studies. OTTEN, Willemien.

ERIKSON, E
The Hermeneutics of Life History: Personal Achievement and History in Gadamer, Habermas, and Erikson. WALLULIS, Jerald.

EROS
The Dialogues of Plato, Volume II. ALLEN, R E (trans).
Schopenhauers Wille und Platons Eros. VOIGTLÄNDER, Hanns-Dieter.

EROTETICS
Implied Questions. WISNIEWSKI, Andrzej.

EROTICISM
The Place of the Hidden Moon: Erotic Mysticism in the Vaisnava-sahajiyā Cult of Bengal. DIMOCK JR, Edward C.

ERROR(S)
A Critical Note on J S Mill's Classification of Fallacies. HON, Giora.
The Incoherence of Kant's Transcendental Dialectic: Specifying the Minimal Conditions for Dialectical Error. HERMAN, David J.
Theoretical Explanation and Errors of Measurement. FORGE, John.

ESCAPISM
Escape from God. TURNER, Dean.
The Rationality of Escapism and Self Deception. LONGEWAY, John L.

ESCHATOLOGY
Beyond the Big Bang: Quantum Cosmologies and God. DREES, Willem B.

ESSE
The Preface to Thomistic Metaphysics. KNASAS, John F X.
Action or/and Dwelling. BOEDER, Heribert.
El tránsito de la existencia al ser. KELZ, Carlos R.

ESSENCE(S)
see also Form(s)
Aristotelian Logic and the Arabic Language in Alfarabi. ABED, Shukri B.
Cálculo y ser (Aproximación a Leibniz). MARZOA, Felipe Martínez.
Philosophical Essays. CARTWRIGHT, Richard.
Pour une philosophie du sens et de la valeur. VASSILIE-LEMENY, Sorin-Titus.
"Between Being and Essence: Reflection's Logical Disguises" in *Essays on Hegel's Logic*, DAHLSTROM, Daniel O.
"Definition, Essence, and Understanding in Spinoza" in *Central Themes in Early Modern Philosophy*, PARKINSON, G H R.
"Essence and Subversion in Hegel and Heidegger" in *Writing the Politics of Difference*, MC CUMBER, John.
Conditional Essences. HAIGHT, Mary R.
La determinación de la esencia en X: Zubiri y Tomás de Aquino. SOTO, José Cercós.
La distinción entre esencia y existencia en Avicena. IBÁÑEZ, Alejandro Herrera.
La esencia metafísica de Dios. DERISI, Octavio N.
Forbes's Branching Conception of Possible Worlds. MILLS, Eugene.
The Latin Avicenna as a Source of Thomas Aquinas's Metaphysics. WIPPEL, John F.
Locke on Real Essence. OWEN, David W D.
On the Problem of the Essence of Truth in the Natural Sciences (in Dutch). KOCKELMANS, J.
R J Boskovic's "Theoria" — A Sign Post to the Essence of the Modern Natural Science (in Serbo-Croatian). ZENKO, Franjo.
Los tres estados de la esencia según Santo Tomás de Aquino. CASAUBÓN, Juan A.
The World Essence. BIGELOW, John.

ESSENTIALISM

Essentially Speaking: Feminism, Nature and Difference. FUSS, Diana.
Metaphysics: A Contemporary Introduction. POST, John F.
"Merleau-Ponty and Hegel: Radical Essentialism" in *Ontology and Alterity in Merleau-Ponty*, FLAY, Joseph C.
Aristotelian Essentialism. MATTHEWS, Gareth B.
Corpuscles, Mechanism, and Essentialism in Berkeley and Locke. ATHERTON, Margaret.
Essentialism Old and New: Suarez and Brody. KRONEN, John D.
The Hole Truth. BUTTERFIELD, Jeremy.
Incarnation and Essentialization: A Reading of Heidegger. CAPUTO, John D.
The Jargon of Authenticity: Adorno and Feminist Essentialism. PHELAN, Shane.
Leibniz on Superessentialism and World-Bound Individuals. COVER, Jan A.
Modal Logic. MARCUS, Ruth Barcan.
The Myth of the Essential Indexical. MILLIKAN, Ruth.
Names, Actualities, and the Emergence of Essentialist Theories of Naming in Classical Chinese Thought. MAKEHAM, John.
Processes, Substances, and Leibniz's Epistemology: A Case for Essentialism in Contemporary Physics. PIRO, Francesco.

ESTHETICS

see Aesthetics

ETERNAL

On the Logic of Eternal Knowledge. KELLY, Charles J.
Spinoza on the Eternity of the Human Mind. LUCASH, Frank.

ETERNAL OBJECT(S)

"Eternal Objects and Archetypes, Past and Depth: Response to Hopper" in *Archetypal Process: Self and Divine in Whitehead, Jung, and Hillman*, COBB JR, John B.

ETERNAL RECURRENCE

Nietzsche (I and II): The Will to Power as Art, The Eternal Recurrence of the Same—Heidegger. KRELL, David Farrell (trans).
Nietzsche On Truth and Philosophy. CLARK, Maudemarie.
The Self-Overcoming of Nihilism: Nishitani Keiji. PARKES, Graham (trans).
Incommensurability and Recurrence: from Oresme to Simmel. SMALL, Robin.
Vie et totalité chez Nietzsche. HAAR, Michel.

ETERNALITY

External Creation and Eternal Production of the World According to Bonaventura (in Dutch). VAN VELDHUIJSEN, Peter.

ETERNITY

The Immutability of God in the Theology of Hans Urs Von Balthasar. O'HANLON, G F.
Eternity and Simultaneity. LEFTOW, Brian.
Modernism's Two Eternities. GEORGIEFF, Andrey.
A Problem for the Eternity Solution. WIDERKER, David.
Tempo ed eternità: La filosofia narrante di F Rosenzweig. DI MARCO, Chiara.
Temporality Revisited: Kierkegaard and the Transitive Character of Time. SCHALOW, Frank.
Why Didn't God Create the World Sooner?. LEFTOW, Brian.
William of Auvergne and the Eternity of the World. TESKE, Roland J.

ETHICAL

Ethical Considerations and Ramifications of the 1989 Generic Drug Scandal. HEACOCK, Marian V and ORVIS, Gregory P.
Ethical Deliberations as Dramatic Rehearsal. CASPARY, William R.
Hegel, Croce, Gentile: On the Idea of the "Ethical State". SANTORO, Liberato and CASALE, Giuseppe.

ETHICAL NATURALISM

"Natur" als Massstab menschlichen Handelns. BIRNBACHER, Dieter.
Linguistic Intuitions and Varieties of Ethical Naturalism. BALL, Stephen W.

ETHICAL THEORY(-RIES)

Morality in Practice (Third Edition). STERBA, James P.
Dworkin and His Critics: The Relevance of Ethical Theory in Philosophy of Law. BALL, Stephen W.
New Naturalism and Other Ethical Theories. SHENG, C L.
On the Alleged Methodological Infirmity of Ethics. MOODY-ADAMS, Michele M.
Santo Tomás y el desafío de la ética analítica contemporánea. MASSINI CORREAS, Carlos Ignacio.

ETHICS

see also Altruism, Bioethics, Business Ethics, Christian Ethics, Happiness, Humanism, Idealism, Justice, Medical Ethics, Metaethics, Moral(s), Normative Ethics, Political Phil, Social Phil
After Principles. BARDEN, Garrett.
Agricultural Bioethics: Implications of Agricultural Biotechnology. GENDEL, Steven M (& other eds).
Animal Experimentation: The Consensus Changes. LANGLEY, Gill (ed).
Animal Experimentation: The Moral Issue. BAIRD, Robert M (ed).
Applying Ethics: A Text with Readings (Third Edition). OLEN, Jeffrey.
Aristotelis Ethica Evdemia. WALZER, F R (ed).
An Audience for Moral Philosophy?. EDELMAN, John T.
Being True to the World: Moral Realism and Practical Wisdom. JACOBS, Jonathan A.
Beyond Baby M: Ethical Issues in New Reproductive Techniques. BARTELS, Dianne M (ed).
Bibliography of Bioethics, Volume 16. WALTERS, LeRoy (ed).
Biomedical Ethics Reviews, 1987. HUMBER, James M (ed).
Biomedical Ethics Reviews, 1989. HUMBER, James M (ed).
Biomedical Ethics Reviews, 1990. HUMBER, James M (ed).
Blaise Pascals: "Pensées" (1656-1662) Systematische 'Gedanken' über. KIRSCH, Ulrich.
Business Ethics. SHAW, William H.
Chinese Texts and Philosophical Contexts. ROSEMONT JR, Henry (ed).
Civil Disobedience in Focus. BEDAU, Hugo Adam (ed).
The Communicative Ethics Controversy. BENHABIB, Seyla (ed).
A Companion to Ethics. SINGER, Peter (ed).
Conduct and Character: Readings in Moral Theory. TIMMONS, Mark.
Core Questions in Philosophy: A Text With Readings. SOBER, Elliott.
The Crisis in Health Care: Ethical Issues. MC KENZIE, Nancy F (ed).
Dämonie und Gesellschaft. CATTEPOEL, Jan.
David Hume: Historiker und Philosoph. LÜTHE, Rudolf.
Deciding for Others: The Ethics of Surrogate Decision Making. BUCHANAN, Allen E.
Delicate Subjects: Romanticism, Gender, and the Ethics of Understanding. ELLISON, Julie.
The Devil and Secular Humanism: The Children of the Enlightenment. RADEST, Howard B.
Does God Exist? The Great Debate. MORELAND, J P.
The Early Essays and Ethics of Robert Boyle. HARWOOD, John T (ed).
Earthbound: Introductory Essays in Environmental Ethics. REGAN, Tom (ed).
Empiricism and Subjectivity: An Essay on Hume's Theory of Human Nature. BOUNDAS, Constantin V (trans).
Enriching Business Ethics. WALTON, Clarence C (ed).
Essays on Heidegger and Others: Philosophical Papers, Volume 2. RORTY, Richard.
Essentials of Business Ethics. MADSEN, Peter (ed).
Ethical Practice in Clinical Medicine. ELLOS, William J.
Ethics in Nursing: An Anthology. PENCE, Terry.
Ethics with Aristotle. BROADIE, Sarah.
Ethics Without God (Revised Edition). NIELSEN, Kai.
Ethics, Politics, and Human Nature. PAUL, Ellen Frankel (ed).
Ethics, Trust, and the Professions: Philosophical and Cultural Aspects. PELLEGRINO, Edmund D (ed).
Das Ethische in der Rhetorik des Aristoteles. WÖRNER, Markus Hilmar.
Euthanasia: Toward an Ethical Social Policy. THOMASMA, David C.
Existentialism. COOPER, David E.
Expressionism in Philosophy: Spinoza. DELEUZE, Gilles.
Fallen Freedom: Kant on Radical Evil and Moral Regeneration. MICHALSON JR, Gordon E.
Feminist Ethics. CARD, Claudia (ed).
For Self-Examination: Judge for Yourself. HONG, Howard V (ed & trans).
Franz Rosenzweig: Existentielles Denken und gelebte Bewährung. SCHMIED-KOWARZIK, Wolfdietrich.
Fundamentals of Philosophy (Third Edition). STEWART, David.
Gerechtigkeit, Wohlfahrt und Rationalität. SCHMIDT, Johannes.
Good and Evil: An Absolute Conception. GAITA, Raimond.
Good Intentions Aside: A Manager's Guide to Resolving Ethical Problems. NASH, Laura L.
A Guided Tour of Selections from Aristotle's Nicomachean Ethics. BIFFLE, Christopher.
Hegel: o la rebelión contra el límite. IZUZQUIZA, Ignacio.
Hermeneutics and Critical Theory in Ethics and Politics. KELLY, Michael (ed).
Historia del nombrar: Dos episodios de la subjetividad. THIEBAUT, Carlos.
Hobbes. TUCK, Richard.
How Should I Live? Philosophical Conversations About Moral Life. FEEZELL, Randolph M.
How to Play Theological Ping-Pong: And Other Essays on Faith and Reason. ABRAHAM, William J (ed).
Human Goodness: Generosity and Courage. PYBUS, Elizabeth.
Hume's Place in Moral Philosophy. CAPALDI, Nicholas.
The Idea of Christian Charity: A Critique of Some Contemporary Conceptions. GRAHAM, Gordon.
The Ideas of Ayn Rand. MERRILL, Ronald E.
Identity, Character, and Morality: Essays in Moral Psychology. FLANAGAN, Owen (ed).
Integrity in Health Care Institutions: Humane Environments for Teaching, Inquiry, and Healing. BULGER, Ruth Ellen (ed).
Introduction to Philosophy: Classical and Contemporary Readings. POJMAN, Louis P.
The Legacy of Hermann Cohen. KLUBACK, William.
Lesbian Philosophies and Cultures. ALLEN, Jeffner (ed).
Liability and Responsibility. FREY, R G (ed).
Liberalism and the Good. DOUGLASS, R Bruce (ed).
The Limits of Government: An Essay on the Public Goods Arguments. SCHMIDTZ, David.

ETHICS

Living the Good Life: An Introduction to Moral Philosophy. GRAHAM, Gordon.
Logic and Ethics. GEACH, Peter (ed).
Matter, Morals and Medicine: The Ancient Greek Origins of Science, Ethics and the Medical Profession. CARELLA, Michael Jerome.
Max Scheler's Concept of the Person: An Ethics of Humanism. PERRIN, Ron.
Meaning and Method: Essays in Honor of Hilary Putnam. BOOLOS, George (ed).
Medical Ethics for Physicians-in-Training. KANTOR, Jay E.
Medical Ethics in Practice. BARD, Terry R.
Michel Foucault's Force of Flight: Towards an Ethics for Thought. BERNAUER, James W.
Military Ethics: Looking Toward the Future. FOTION, Nicholas G.
Moral Dealing: Contract, Ethics, and Reason. GAUTHIER, David.
Moral Dilemmas. GOWANS, Christopher W (ed).
The Moral Domain: Essays in the Ongoing Discussion between Philosophy and the Social Sciences. WREN, Thomas E (ed).
Moral Philosophy from Montaigne to Kant: An Anthology, Volume I & II. SCHNEEWIND, J B (ed).
Moral Philosophy: Theories, Skills, and Applications. FALIKOWSKI, Anthony F.
Moral Theory and Medical Practice. FULFORD, K W M.
Moralische Verbindlichkeit oder Erziehung. LANGEWAND, Alfred.
Morality in Practice (Third Edition). STERBA, James P.
Morality—What's In It For Me?: A Historical Introduction to Ethics. NELSON, William N.
A Morally Deep World: An Essay on Moral Significance and Environmental Ethics. JOHNSON, Lawrence E.
Nation und Ethos: Die Moral des Patriotismus. KLUXEN-PYTA, Donate.
New Dimensions of Confucian and Neo-Confucian Philosophy. CHENG, Chung-ying.
New Harvest: Transplanting Body Parts and Reaping the Benefits. KEYES, C Don (ed).
Nicolai Hartmann's New Ontology. WERKMEISTER, W H.
Nonviolence in Theory and Practice. HOLMES, Robert L.
Other Selves: Philosophers on Friendship. PAKALUK, Michael (ed).
Overcoming Foundations: Studies in Systematic Philosophy. WINFIELD, Richard Dien.
The Persistence of Modernity: Essays on Aesthetics, Ethics, and Postmodernism. WELLMER, Albrecht.
Philosophical Perspectives on Newtonian Science. BRICKER, Phillip (ed).
The Philosophical Theology of John Duns Scotus. ADAMS, Marilyn McCord (ed).
A Philosophy of Morals. HELLER, Agnes.
Philosophy: An Introduction Through Literature. KLEIMAN, L (ed).
Pour une philosophie du sens et de la valeur. VASSILIE-LEMENY, Sorin-Titus.
Principles of Ethics. ROSMINI, Antonio.
The Question of Ethics. SCOTT, Charles E.
Re-Reading Levinas. BERNASCONI, Robert (ed).
Reading Habermas. RASMUSSEN, David M.
Realism with a Human Face. PUTNAM, Hilary.
The Realm of Rights. THOMSON, Judith Jarvis.
Reasons for Living: A Basic Ethics. PORTER, Burton F.
Relating Humanities and Social Thought (Science, Ideology, and Value, Volume 4). EDEL, Abraham.
The River of the Mother of God, and Other Essays by Aldo Leopold. FLADER, Susan L (ed).
Shaping Genes: Ethics, Law and Science of Using Genetic Technology in Medicine and Agriculture. MACER, Darryl.
Studies on Mario Bunge's "Treatise". WEINGARTNER, Paul (ed).
Suicide: Right or Wrong?. DONNELLY, John (ed).
Swimming Against the Current in Contemporary Philosophy: Occasional Essays and Papers. VEATCH, Henry B.
Taking Sides: Clashing Views on Controversial Bioethical Issues (Fourth Edition). LEVINE, Carol (ed).
Theory and Practice in Medical Ethics. GRABER, Glenn C.
Thinking Philosophically: An Introduction to Philosophy with Readings. GUSMANO, Joseph J.
Das Tier in der Moral. WOLF, Ursula.
To Die or Not to Die?. BERGER, Arthur S (ed).
Universalism versus Communitarianism: Contemporary Debates in Ethics. RASMUSSEN, David.
Varieties of Moral Personality: Ethics and Psychological Realism. FLANAGAN, Owen.
The Vatican, the Law and the Human Embryo. COUGHLAN, Michael J.
Well and Good: Case Studies in Biomedical Ethics (Revised Edition). THOMAS, John E.
Who Comes after the Subject?. CADAVA, Eduardo (ed).
Wittgenstein, Ethics and Aesthetics: The View from Eternity. TILGHMAN, B R.
"Approaching Ethical Questions: A University Perspective" in *Integrity in Health Care Institutions: Humane Environments for Teaching, Inquiry, and Healing*, STEINER, Daniel.
"Authenticity, Conversion, and the City of Ends in Sartre's *Notebooks for an Ethics*" in *Writing the Politics of Difference*, ANDERSON, Thomas C.
"Basic Needs, Legitimate Wants and Political Legitimacy in Mario Bunge's Conception of Ethics" in *Studies on Mario Bunge's "Treatise"*, GARZÓN-VALDÉS, Ernesto.
"Ethical Implications of Newtonian Science" in *Philosophical Perspectives on Newtonian Science*, HARRIS, Errol.
"Ethics and Science" in *Logic, Methodology and Philosophy of Science, VIII*, AGAZZI, Evandro.
"Ethics IP5: Shared Attributes and the Basis of Spinoza's Monism" in *Central Themes in Early Modern Philosophy*, GARRETT, Don.
"The Ethics of Science as a Form of the Cognition of Science" in *Logic, Methodology and Philosophy of Science, VIII*, YUDIN, Boris G.
"The Face and Reading: Immediacy and Mediation" in *Re-Reading Levinas*, CRITCHLEY, Simon (trans) and GREISCH, Jean.
"Heloise" in *A History of Women Philosophers, Volume II: Medieval, Renaissance and Enlightenment, A.D. 500-1600*, WAITHE, Mary Ellen.
"Integrity, Humaneness, and Institutions in Secular Pluralist Societies" in *Integrity in Health Care Institutions: Humane Environments for Teaching, Inquiry, and Healing*, ENGELHARDT JR, H Tristram.
"Levinas's Ethical Discourse between Individuation and Universality" in *Re-Reading Levinas*, CIARAMELLI, Fabio.
"Love and Perfect Coincidence in a Sartrean Ethics" in *Writing the Politics of Difference*, BELL, Linda A.
"Mario Bunge on Ethics" in *Studies on Mario Bunge's "Treatise"*, BUNGE, Mario.
"Medical Institutions and Their Moral Constraints" in *Integrity in Health Care Institutions: Humane Environments for Teaching, Inquiry, and Healing*, TOULMIN, Stephen.
"Modern Ethical Theory and Newtonian Science: Comments on Errol Harris" in *Philosophical Perspectives on Newtonian Science*, GRIER, Philip T.
"One-Way Traffic: The Ontology of Decolonization and its Ethics" in *Ontology and Alterity in Merleau-Ponty*, BERNASCONI, Robert.
"Predestination and Freedom in Augustine's Ethics" in *The Philosophy in Christianity*, O'DALY, Gerard.
"Soviet Ethics and New Thinking" in *In the Interest of Peace: A Spectrum of Philosophical Views*, GUSEYNOV, A A.
"Utilitarian Ethics and Superpower Negotiations: Lost Opportunities for Nuclear Peace" in *In the Interest of Peace: A Spectrum of Philosophical Views*, LACKEY, Douglas.
"Virtue, The Missing Link to the Last Volume of the *Treatise*" in *Studies on Mario Bunge's "Treatise"*, FORMAN, Frank.
"What Does Philosophy Add to Nuclear Discussions? An Introductory Essay" in *Issues in War and Peace: Philosophical Inquiries*, KUNKEL, Joseph and KLEIN, Kenneth.
"Which Values are Conducive to Human Survival? A Bunge-Test of Bunge-Ethics" in *Studies on Mario Bunge's "Treatise"*, ZECHA, Gerhard.
"'Making the Human' in Sartre's Unpublished Dialectical Ethics" in *Writing the Politics of Difference*, BOWMAN, Elizabeth A and STONE, Robert V.
Los "Derechos Humanos". BELARMINO, Pedro.
"Everyone's Doing It"—A Reply to Richard DeGeorge. GREEN, Ronald M.
"Hume and Hume's Connexions". KLEMME, Heiner.
"Is" and "Ought": A Different Connection. JOHNSON, Oliver A.
"Natur" als Massstab menschlichen Handelns. BIRNBACHER, Dieter.
The "New" Scholars in Philosophy of Education, 1976-1986. QUANTZ, Richard A.
"Nothing of the Origin and Destiny of Cats": The Remainder of the Logos. ROSE, John M.
La "objeción de conciencia". BELARMINO, Pedro.
"Ruminations": Notes de lecture sur quelques aphorismes de Nietzsche. BLONDEL, Eric.
"Seeing Things". PIPER, Adrian M S.
"Utility". BROOME, John.
"Voir vivre, sans vivre": Extraits du *Journal Intime*. AMIEL, H F.
"'I Am We' Consciousness and Dialog as Organizational Ethics Method". NIELSEN, Richard P.
"'Ought' Does Imply 'Can'". SAPONTZIS, Steve F.
"'Why Be Moral?' and Reforming Selves". WILLIAMSON, A Mark.
'Domina et Regina Virtutum': Justice and *Societas* in *De Officiis*. ATKINS, E M.
'Fetal Rights'? An Attempt to Render Plausible a Conservative Response. HODAPP, Paul.
'Is' Therefore 'Ought'. VERMA, Roop Rekha.
'Pride Produces the Idea of Self': Hume on Moral Agency. RORTY, Amélie.
'Queerness' and the Objectivity of Value: A Response to J L Mackie. SPOERL, Joseph.
'Too Busy for Ethics'. SELBY, G Raymond.
The 'Voice of Care': Implications for Bioethical Education. CARSE, Alisa L.
A New Approach in Moral Theory (in Dutch). KETTNER, Matthias.
A Phenomenologically and Psychologically Based Concept of Ethics (in Czechoslovakian). BAYEROVA, M.
Abortion as the Illicit Method of Birth Control. KEILKOPF, Charles F.
Abortion in Rape Cases. BEABOUT, Greg.
The Absolute in Morality and the Christian Conscience. FUCHS, Josef.
Accountability and Responsibility in Research. WOOLF, Patricia K.

ETHICS

Achilles' Revenge. DAKO, Martin.
Act-Utilitarian Prisoner's Dilemmas. RABINOWICZ, Wlodzimierz.
Actual Preferences, Actual People. GOODIN, Robert E.
Adam Smith and Social Justice: The Ethical Basis of *The Wealth of Nations*. OSSAR, Jacob.
Adam's Place in Nature: Respect or Domination?. NASH, Roger.
Adapting Kohlberg to Enhance the Assessment of Manager's Moral Reasoning. WEBER, James.
Advocacy of Just Health Policies as Professional Duty: Cultural Biases and Ethical Responsibilities. CRANDALL, Lee A.
Aesthetic Liberalism: Kant and the Ethics of Modernity. CASCARDI, Anthony J.
Agency and Morality. BROOK, Richard.
Agent-Action Judgements. TILLEY, John J.
Agricultura, desarrollo y autonomía. BLATZ, Charlie.
Agricultural Practices, Ecology, and Ethics in the Third World. WESTRA, L S and BOWEN, K L and BEHE, B K.
AIDS and 'Dirt': Reflections on the Ethics of Ritual Cleanliness. CHURCHILL, Larry R.
AIDS, Myth, and Ethics. SUNDSTRÖM, Per.
An Alternative to Property Rights in Human Tissue. SWAIN, Margaret S and MARUSYK, Randy W.
The Ambiguity of Political Virtue: A Response to Wolgast. LEVINSON, Sanford.
American Moralism and the Origin of Bioethics in the United States. JONSEN, Albert R.
Amor y comunicación. FORMENT, Eudaldo.
Amoralism—On the Limits of Moral Thinking. SANDOE, Peter.
Amoralism: Reply to Peter Sandoe. HARE, R M.
Amour de l'être et ambition de gloire: le spinozisme de Vauvenargues. BOVE, Laurent.
Análisis de la doctrina ética de las "observaciones sobre lo bello y sublime". GONZÁLEZ PORTA, Mario A.
Anencephalic Infants and Special Relationships. JECKER, Nancy S.
Anger as a Vice: A Maimonidean Critique of Aristotle's Ethics. FRANK, Daniel H.
Animal Experimentation and the Argument from Limited Resources. FINK, Charles K.
Animal Liberation as a Valid Response to Structural Violence. LISZT, Amy.
Animal Liberators are Not Anti-Science. MAGEL, Charles.
Animals in Biomedical Research: The Undermining Effect of the Rhetoric of the Besieged. GLUCK, John P and KUBACKI, Steven R.
Anti-Realism and Skepticism in Ethics. SCHUELER, G F.
Antropología en la Q D "De virtutibus in communi" de Santo Tomás. CORSO, Laura E.
Applied Ethics and Meta-Philosophy. DAVSON-GALLE, Peter.
Applying the Principles of Gestalt Theory to Teaching Ethics. HUNT, Eugene H and BULLIS, Ronald K.
Arational Actions. HURSTHOUSE, Rosalind.
Are Kantian Duties Categorical?. SCHOEMAN, Ferdinand.
Are Physicians a "Delinquent Community"?: Issues in Professional Competence, Conduct, and Self-Regulation. SWAZEY, Judith P.
Are Physicians a "Delinquent Community"?: Issues in Professional Competence, Conduct, Self-Regulation: Comment. LAMMERS, Stephen E.
Are Pregnant Women Fetal Containers?. PURDY, Laura.
Arguing for Rational Suicide. HUMPHRY, Derek.
An Argument for Utilitarianism: A Defence. NG, Yew-Kwang and SINGER, Peter.
Arguments for Abortion of Abnormal Fetuses and the Moral Status of the Developing Embryo. SUTTON, Agneta.
Aristippus Against Happiness. IRWIN, T H.
Aristotle or Nietzsche?. FRANKS, Joan M.
Aristotle's Much Maligned *Megalopsychos*. CURZER, Howard J.
Artificial Means of Reproduction and Our Understanding of the Family. MACKLIN, Ruth.
Authenticity: A Sartrean Perspective. CATALANO, Joseph.
Autonomy and Personal History. CHRISTMAN, John.
Backgrounding Desire. PETTIT, Philip and SMITH, Michael.
The Behavior of the NCAA: A Question of Ethics. STIEBER, John.
Being a Realist about Relativism (In Ethics). SAYRE-MC CORD, Geoffrey.
Beliefs and Responsibility. ELLIOTT, Car.
Believing that Everyone Else is Less Ethical: Implications for Work Behavior and Ethics Instruction. TYSON, Thomas.
Benevolence and Resentment. STEPHENSON, Wendell.
La benevolencia como categoría fundamental de la Etica eudemonista. RODRÍGUEZ DUPLÁ, Leonardo.
Between the Horns of the Negative-Positive Duty Debate. MALM, H M.
Between Two Worlds: Humans in Nature and Culture. GARDINER, Robert W.
Beyond Bean Counting: Establishing High Ethical Standards in the Public Accounting Profession. COHEN, Jeffrey R and PANT, Laurie W.
Beyond Naturalism: A Reconstruction of Daoist Environmental Ethics. PEERENBOOM, Randall P.
Bioethics Inside the Beltway: The Human Genome Project. JUENGST, Eric T.
Biological Holism and the Evolution of Ethics. SHRADER-FRECHETTE, Kristin.
The Biological Justification of Ethics: A Best-Case Scenario. ROSENBERG, Alexander.
Biology and Ethics: Callicott Reconsidered. SHRADER-FRECHETTE, Kristin.
Birth Defects: Traditional Beliefs Challenged by Scientific Explanations. DRYDEN, Richard.
The Birth of the Death-Machine. MEGIVERN, James J.
Blanshard's Critique of Ethical Subjectivism. JOHNSON, Oliver A.
Blanshard's Ethics of Belief and Metaphysical Postulates. PHILLIPS, Winfred George.
Brand Blanshard and Gewirth: Ethics and Rights. HOWIE, John.
Buddhist Approaches to Abortion. FLORIDA, R E.
Buddhist Views of Suicide and Euthanasia. BECKER, Carl B.
Business and Environmental Ethics. HOFFMAN, W Michael.
Business and Professional Ethics: An Oxymoron?. PORTER, Jack Nusan.
Business Ethics and Extant Social Contracts. DUNFEE, Thomas W.
Business Ethics and Social Responsibility in Finance Instruction: An Abdication of Responsibility. HAWLEY, Delvin D.
Business Ethics and Stakeholder Analysis. GOODPASTER, Kenneth E.
The Business Ethics of Pharmacists: Conflicts Practices and Beliefs. VITELL, Scott J and RAWWAS, Mohammed Y A and FESTERVAND, Troy A.
CAHBI: Europe Needs a Universal Bioethical System. GUNNING, Karel.
Can Art Save Us? A Meditation on Gadamer. DEVEREAUX, Mary.
Can Whistleblowing Be FULLY Legitimated? A Theoretical Discussion. DANDEKAR, Natalie.
A Case Against Dutch Euthanasia. FENIGSEN, Richard.
The Case of the Unmitigated Blackguard or Saving Kant's Moral Feelings. EARLS, Anthony.
The Cases *For* and *Against* Theological Approaches to Business Ethics. TRUNDLE JR, Robert C.
Categorical Requirements: Kant and Hume on the Idea of Duty. WIGGINS, David.
The Challenge of Global Ethics. BULLER, Paul F and KOHLS, John J and ANDERSON, Kenneth S.
Challenge: Subjectivist Naturalism. FOLDVARY, Fred E.
Challenging the Egoistic Paradigm. BOWIE, Norman E.
Character and Explanation in Aristotle's *Ethics* and *Poetics*. DESLAURIERS, Marguerite.
Characteristics and Practices of "Christian-Based" Companies. IBRAHIM, Nabil A and RUE, Leslie W and MC DOUGALL, Patricia P and GREENE, G Robert.
Charity and Moral Imperatives. ODEGARD, Douglas.
Charles Renouvier e le scuole di morale in Francia nel XIX secolo. ROSSI, Fabio.
The Chief of Medicine. BRODY, Howard.
Child Development and Research Ethics: A Changing Calculus of Concerns. THOMPSON, Ross A.
Chronic Illness and the Physician-Patient Relationship. MOROS, Daniel A (and others).
Chronic Illness and the Temporal Structure of Human Life. DOUARD, John W.
The Classroom as a Model of the World. STURGEON, Kareen B.
The Clinical Ethicist at the Bedside. LA PUMA, John and SCHIEDERMAYER, David L.
Clinical Judgment and Bioethics: The Decision Making Link. WRIGHT, Richard A.
A Clue for a Classical Realist Contribution to the Debate Over the Value of Animals. KLONOSKI, Richard J.
Co-ordination, Salience and Rationality. MILLER, Seumas.
Codes of Ethics and the Moral Education of Engineers. LUEGENBIEHL, Heinz C.
Commensurability as a Prerequisite of Rational Choice: An Examination of Sidgwick's Position. RICHARDSON, Henry S.
A Comment on Fry's "The Role of Caring in a Theory of Nursing Ethics". BOYER, Jeannine Ross and NELSON, James Lindemann.
Comment on Romain's "Feminist Reflections on Humans and Other Domestic Animals. RUD JR, Anthony G.
A Comment on the Argument Between Gewirth and his Critics. ROSS, Steven.
Commentary on Layton's "Engineering Needs a Loyal Opposition". ANDERSON, Robert M (and others).
Commentary: "Codes of Ethics and the Moral Education of Engineers". PUKA, Bill.
Commentary: "Individual and Corporate Responsibility". FRENCH, Peter A.
Commentary: "Love Canal and the Ethics of Environmental Health". FESSENDEN-RADEN, June and BROWN JR, Stuart M.
Commentary: "The University and Industrial Research: Selling Out?". CAMPBELL, L Leon.
Commentary: Interests and Equal Moral Status. SQUADRITO, Kathy.
Comments and Replies. TAYLOR, Charles.

ETHICS

Comments: "A Moral Ideal for Everyone and No One". HUNT, Lester.
Committees and Consensus: How Many Heads Are Better Than One?. CAWS, Peter.
Community and Autonomy: Logically Incompatible Values?. MASON, Andrew.
Community Responsibility and the Development of Oregon's Health Care Priorities. GARLAND, Michael J and HASNAIN, Romana.
The Compatability of Consequentialism with Deontological Convictions. FORREST, Peter.
The Compatibility of Justice and Kindness. PUTMAN, Daniel.
Conceptos religiosos y vida religiosa. BASSOLS, Alejandro Tomasini.
Conceptual Issues in Nursing Ethics Research. PENTICUFF, Joy Hinson.
A Conceptual Model of Corporate Moral Development. REIDENBACH, R Eric and ROBIN, Donald P.
Concerning the Interests of Insects. GROSSINGER, Robin.
Concerns of College Students Regarding Business Ethics: A Replication. PETERSON, Robert A and BELTRAMINI, Richard F and KOZMETSKY, George.
Conciencia de catástrofe, poder y libertad. DEI, H Daniel.
Conquering Chance. HENRY-HERMANN, Grete.
Conscience, Sympathy and the Foundation of Morality. CI, Jiwei.
Consensus in Panels and Committees: Conceptual and Ethical Issues. VEATCH, Robert M and MORENO, Jonathan D.
Consensus of Expertise: The Role of Consensus of Experts in Formulating Public Policy and Estimating Facts. VEATCH, Robert M.
Consensus, Contracts, and Committees. MORENO, Jonathan D.
Consequentialism and Self-Defeat. MOSER, Paul K.
Consequentialism and the Unforeseeable Future. NORCROSS, Alastair.
Consequentialism: The Philosophical Dog That Does Not Bark?. HOLBROOK, Daniel.
Constrained Maximization. SOBEL, Jordan Howard.
Consumer Ethics: An Investigation of the Ethical Beliefs of Eldery Consumers. VITELL, Scott J and LUMPKIN, James R and RAWWAS, Mohammed Y A.
Consumer Sovereignty versus Informed Consent: Saying No to Requests to "Do Everything" for Dying Patients. WEBER, Leonard.
Contemporary Ethics and Scheler's Phenomenology of Community. VACEK, Edward.
Contents and Causes: A Reply to Blackburn. STURGEON, Nicholas L.
Contestation and Consensus: The Morality of Abortion in Japan. LA FLEUR, William R.
Contractualism, Moral Motivation, and Practical Reason. FREEMAN, Samuel.
La contrainte. NEUBERG, Marc.
Corporate Codes of Conduct: A Collective Conscience and Continuum. RAIBORN, Cecily A and PAYNE, Dinah.
Corporate Policy and the Ethics of Competitor Intelligence Gathering. PAINE, Lynn Sharp.
Corporate Social Responsibility and the Marketplace. COTTRILL, Melville T.
The Costs of Commercial Medicine. DOUGHERTY, Charles J.
Crazy Making: Embryos and Gestational Mothers. ANNAS, George J.
La crítica kantiana a la virtud como término medio. MAURI, Margarita.
Critical Activity and Ethics: The Problem of Generalization. KANIOWSKI, Andrzej M.
A Critique of Kantian Arguments Against Emotions as Moral Motives. OAKLEY, Justin.
A Cross-Cultural Comparison of the Ethics of Business Students. LYSONSKI, Steven and GAIDIS, William.
Cuatro modelos de desarrollo costarricense: un análisis y evalución ética. CROCKER, David A.
Danger Signs of Unethical Behavior: How to Determine If Your Firm Is at Ethical Risk. COOKE, Robert Allan.
De las maravillas acerca de lo uno y lo múltiple o sobre los avatares del amor neoplatónico en Baruch de Espinosa. ALBIAC, Gabriel.
Death and the Beginning of Life. IGLESIAS, Teresa.
Death, Honor, and Loyalty: The Bushidō Ideal. HURST III, G Cameron.
The Debate Over the So-Called Reality of Moral Dilemmas. STATMAN, Daniel.
A Decision-Theoretic Reconstruction of *Roe v Wade*. LOCKHART, Ted.
Decisionmaking Competence and Risk—Comments on Wicclair. BROCK, Dan W.
A Defense of Ethical Noncognitivism. COBURN, Robert C.
Defining the Ethical Standards of the High-Technology Industry. FIMBEL, Nancie and BURSTEIN, Jerome S.
Defining the Limits of Institutional Moral Agency in Health Care: A Response to Kevin Wildes. RIE, Michael A.
Delivering Hydrocephalic Fetuses. STRONG, Carson.
A Deontological Analysis of Peer Relations in Organizations. MOBERG, Dennis J and MEYER, Michael J.
Deride, Abide or Dissent: On the Ethics of Professional Conduct. HAUPTMAN, Robert and HILL, Fred.
El deseo infinito. PEGUEROLES, Juan.
El deseo y el amor en San Agustín. PEGUEROLES, Juan.
Development Aid: The Moral Obligation to Innovation. DUNDON, Stanislaus J.
Developmental Constraints on Ethical Behaviour in Business. HARRIS, Claudia and BROWN, William.
Dialogic Leadership as Ethics Action (Praxis) Method. NIELSEN, Richard P.
Differences in Moral Values Between Corporations. NYSTROM, Paul C.
Directions of Justification in the Negative-Positive Duty Debate. MALM, H M.
Discourse and the Moral Point of View: Deriving a Dialogical Principle of Universalization. REHG, William.
Discourse Ethics and the Communitarian Critique of Neo-Kantianism. REHG, William.
Discovering Right and Wrong: A Realist Response to Gauthier's Morals by Agreement. GENOVA, A C.
Discretion, Punishment, and Juvenile Justice. SCHRAG, Francis.
La distinción entre intereses subjetivos y objetivos y su importancia para la Etica. PATZIG, Günther.
The Distinction Between Equality in Moral Status and Deserving Equal Consideration. DE GRAZIA, David.
Divine Foresight and Human Moral Responsibility (in Hebrew). BAR-ON, A Zvie.
Divine Reason and Virtue in St Thomas's Natural Law Theory. KILLORAN, John B.
Do Animals Feel Pain?. HARRISON, Peter.
Do Animals Have Rights?. MACHAN, Tibor R.
Doctors and Their Advertising. BURTON, Gene E.
Doctors' Rights and Patients' Obligations. MARSHALL, Sandra E.
The Doctrine of Double Effect: Its Philosophical Viability. BOLE, Thomas.
Does Prescriptivism Imply Naturalism?. KANTHAMANI, A.
Does Reason Command Itself for Its Own Sake?. KRAENZEL, Frederick.
Does the Grisez-Finnis-Boyle Moral Philosophy Rest on a Mistake?. VEATCH, Henry and RAUTENBERG, Joseph.
Domesticated and Then Some. DURAN, Jane.
Du fondement de la loi morale, une éthique de la raison ou du sentiment?. DAVAL, R.
Due note: Ritorni Rosminiani—Il momento di Ugo Spirito. PAOLETTI, Laura.
Duties to Friends. PASSELL, Dan.
Duty and Inclination: The Phenomenological Value Ethics of Hans Reiner. GÖRTZEN, René.
Economic Efficiency and the Quality of Life. JACOBSEN, Rockney.
Economic Efficiency: A Paradigm for Business Ethics. STIEBER, John and PRIMEAUX, Patrick.
Economic Theory and Human Behavior. MC NULTY, T Michael.
Economics and Ethics. REILLY, B J and KYJ, M J.
Economics, Ethics, and Tort Remedies: The Emerging Concept of Hedonic Value. KARNS, Jack E.
Ecosabotage and Civil Disobedience. MARTIN, Michael.
The Editor's Response to "The Embryo Debate: The Archbishop of York's Speech to the House of Lords". DE S CAMERON, Nigel M.
Elogio critico dell'imperfezione. TUSA, Carlo.
The Embryo Debate: The Archbishop of York's Speech to the House of Lords. THE ARCHBISHOP OF YORK.
Embryo Research and Abortion—the Arguments that Swayed Parliament. SHORT, David S.
L'emozione creatrice: Il significato della morale nella prospettiva di Bergson. PESSINA, Adriano.
Empowering Teachers: Towards a Justification for Intervention. HARRIS, Kevin.
Un enfoque Kantiano sobre el aborto. HARE, R M.
The Enforcement of Moral Obligations to Potential Fetuses: Johnson Controls versus the UAW. WHITE, Ronald F.
Engineers and Management: The Challenge of the Challenger Incident. WERHANE, Patricia H.
Environmental Ethics and the Case for Hunting. KING, Roger J H.
Epistemological Structures in Marketing: Paradigms, Metaphors, and Marketing Ethics. REIDENBACH, R Eric and ROBIN, Donald P.
The Epistemology and Ethics of Consensus: Uses and Misuses of 'Ethical' Expertise. TONG, Rosemarie.
Errors of an Ill-Reasoning Reason: The Disparagement of Emotions in the Moral Life. LAURITZEN, Paul.
El eslabón entre la conservación y el desarrollo sostenible: Maribel Gómez Mata. JANZEN, Daniel H.
Establishing an Ethic of Accounting: A Response to Westra's Call for Government Employment of Auditors. WAPLES, Elain and SHAUB, Michael K.
La estructura consecuencialista del utilitarismo. GUTIÉRREZ, Gilberto.
Ethical Challenges of HIV Infection in the Workplace. LEONARD, Arthur S.
Ethical Considerations and Ramifications of the 1989 Generic Drug Scandal. HEACOCK, Marian V and ORVIS, Gregory P.
Ethical Considerations for the Forensic Engineer Serving as an Expert Witness. CARPER, Kenneth L.
Ethical Considerations Regarding Public Opinion Polling During Election Campaigns. MICHALOS, Alex C.
Ethical Decision Making in the Medical Profession: An Application of the Theory of Planned Behavior. RANDALL, Donna M and GIBSON, Annetta M.
The Ethical Decision-Making Processes of Information Systems Workers. PARADICE, David B and DEJOIE, Roy M.

ETHICS

Ethical Dilemmas in Performance Appraisal Revisited. LONGENECKER, Clinton and LUDWIG, Dean.
Ethical Dilemmas Posed By Recent and Prospective Developments with Respect to Agricultural Research. JOHNSON, Glenn L.
Ethical Dimensions of Human Attitudes to Nature. BURES, Radim.
Ethical Expertise and Moral Maturity: Conflict or Complement?. MOSS, Lenny.
The Ethical Implications of the Straight-Commission Compensation System—An Agency Perspective. KURLAND, Nancy B.
Ethical Impressionism: A Response to Braybrooke. BONEVAC, Daniel.
Ethical Issues in Bankruptcy: A Jewish Perspective. TAMARI, Meir.
Ethical Judgments on Selected Accounting Issues: An Empirical Study. STANGA, Keith G and TURPEN, Richard A.
The Ethical Limitations of the Market. ANDERSON, Elizabeth.
Ethical Myopia: The Case of "Framing" by Framing. SINGER, Alan E and LYSONSKI, Steven and SINGER, Ming and HAYES, David.
The Ethical Roots of Business. VOGEL, David.
The Ethical Significance of Corporate Law. NESTERUK, Jeffrey.
The Ethical Theory of Peter A Bertocci. PADGETT, Jack F.
The Ethical Thought of Martin Luther King. STERLING, Marvin C.
Ethical Values of Individuals at Different Levels in the Organizational Hierarchy of a Single Firm. HARRIS, James R.
Ethics and Advocacy in Forecasting for Public Policy. WACHS, Martin.
Ethics and Coherence. DE GEORGE, Richard T.
Ethics and Educational Administration: Are Ethical Politics "Ethical"?. RUDDER, Charles F.
Ethics and Energy Supplement. STEVENSON, Mark.
Ethics and Instrumentalism: A Response to Janna Thompson. PLUMWOOD, Val.
Ethics and News. MACHAMER, Peter K and BOYLAN, Barbara.
Ethics and Politics (in German). EWALD, François.
Ethics and the Defense Procurement System. LANSING, Paul and BURKARD, Kimberly.
Ethics and the Limits of Consistency. BAMBROUGH, Renford.
Ethics and the Professional Responsibility of Lawyers. KIPNIS, Kenneth.
Ethics and the Professional Responsibility of Lawyers (Commentary). LENNERTZ, James E.
Ethics as Drawn from the Method. CARTER, Richard B.
The Ethics Behind the Absence of Ethics in Alfred Schutz's Thought. BARBER, Michael.
Ethics Committees: From Ethical Comfort to Ethical Cover. ANNAS, George J.
Ethics Consultation as Moral Engagement. MORENO, Jonathan D.
Ethics in Current Affairs: The Theme of the Enlightenment in Michel Foucault (in German). SCHMID, Wilhelm.
Ethics in Declining Organizations. LEMKE, Dwight K and SCHMINKE, Marshall.
Ethics in Educational Policy Analysis. WILLERS, Jack Conrad.
The Ethics of Conversion Therapy. MURPHY, Timothy F.
The Ethics of Corporate Health Insurance. LIGHT, Donald W.
The Ethics of *Ex Utero* Research on Spare 'Non-Viable' IVF Human Embryos. BAYLIS, Françoise E.
The Ethics of Health Care as a Business. WERHANE, Patricia H.
The Ethics of Inarticulacy. KYMLICKA, Will.
The Ethics of Mechanical Restraints. MOSS, Robert J and LA PUMA, John.
The Ethics of Postmodernism. GIBBONS, Michael T.
The Ethics of Rent Control. HANLY, Ken.
The Ethics of Selectively Marketing the Health Maintenance Organization. WAYMACK, Mark H.
The Ethics of Statistical Discrimination. MAITZEN, Stephen.
The Ethics of Suspicion. BERNASCONI, Robert.
Ethics Without Free Will. SLOTE, Michael.
Ethics Without Morality. BROWNE, Derek.
Ethics, AIDS, and Community Responsibility. DOUARD, John.
Ethics, Education, and Corporate Leadership. BASSIRY, G R.
Ethics, Public Policy, and Human Fetal Tissue Transplantation. CHILDRESS, James F.
Ethics, Public Policy, and Managing Advanced Technologies: The Case of Electronic Surveillance. OTTENSMEYER, Edward J and HEROUX, Mark A.
Éthique et Morale. RICOEUR, Paul.
Éthique et technique: bioéthique. KEMP, Peter.
An Ethnomedical Perspective of Medical Ethics. FABREGA JR, Horacio.
La ética como conciencia en el subdesarrollo. RAMÍREZ, E Roy.
La ética de Adam Smith: un utilitarismo de la simpatía. TASSET, José L.
Etica e morale: mira teleogica e prospettiva deontologica. RICOEUR, Paul.
Ética sin raíces. VARGAS, Alberto.
La ética y los derechos humanos en la filosofía clásica. ALONSO, Luz García.
Etica, retórica y política en la antropología aristotélica. MARTIN, Victor R.
La ética/moral en el Bachillerato español: Estado de la cuestión. GARCÍA LÓPEZ, Tomás.
The Evaluation of "Outcomes" of Accounting Ethics Education. LOEB, Stephen E.
Evolutionary Ethics and the Search for Predecessors: Kant, Hume, and All the Way Back to Aristotle?. RUSE, Michael.
Evolved Ethics Re-Examined: The Theory of Robert J Richards. WILLIAMS, Patricia.
Exit, Voice, and Ethics. KEELEY, Michael and GRAHAM, Jill W.
An Experimental Assessment of Alternative Teaching Approaches for Introductory Business Ethics. BURTON, Scot and JOHNSTON, Mark W and WILSON, Elizabeth J.
Exploring the Structure of Ethical Attributions as a Component of the Consumer Decision Model. WHALEN, Joel and PITTS, Robert E and WONG, John K.
External and Now-For-Then Preferences in Hare's Theory. HAJDIN, Mane.
Famine and Charity. WHELAN JR, John M.
Fanaticism: Reply to Thomas Wetterström. HARE, R M.
Farming Salmon Ethically. NEEDHAM, E A and LEHMAN, Hugh.
Feminist Ethics and Case-Based Reasoning: A Marriage of Purpose. RIESBECK, Christopher K and MORPHIS, Maxine.
Feminist Fears in Ethics. NODDINGS, Nel.
Feminist Reflections on Humans and Other Domestic Animals. ROMAIN, Dianne.
Fetal Neural Transplantation: Placing the Ethical Debate within the Context of Society's Use of Human Material. JONES, D Gareth.
La filosofia civile di Pasquale Villari. URBINATI, Nadia.
Filosofía de la violencia. MAGGIOLO, Roberto Jiménez.
Filosofía y teoría general de sistemas en el pensamiento de A Rapoport. SAXE FERNÁNDEZ, Eduardo E.
Filosofía, justicia y amor. LEVINAS, E and EZCURRA, Alicia Villar.
The First Formulation of the Categorical Imperative as Literally a "Legislative" Metaphor. GREEN, Ronald M.
Firth and the Ethics of Belief. CHISHOLM, Roderick M.
Florilegi filosofici ed enciclopedie in Germania nella prima metà del Duecento. STURLESE, Loris.
Die Folgen vorherrschender Moralkonzeptionen. POGGE, Thomas W.
Forgiveness: A Christian Model. ADAMS, Marilyn McCord.
Fostering Ethical Marketing Decisions. LACZNIAK, Gene R and MURPHY, Patrick E.
Four Perspectives on Moral Judgement: The Rational Principles of Jesus and Kant. PALMQUIST, Stephen R.
Free Will and Being a Victim. SMILANSKY, S.
Freedom and Autonomy: The Kantian Analytic and a Sartrean Critique. BEAVERS, Anthony.
Freedom and Realms of Living. CI, Jiwei.
Friedrich Schleiermacher und die Praktische Philosophie. TROWITZSCH, Michael.
Friendship and Education. WHITE, Patricia.
Friendship: Mutual Apprenticeship in Moral Development. VOLBRECHT, Rose Mary.
Fundamental Values in the Thought of Confucius and Mencius (in Polish). CYRANOWSKA, Maria.
The Futures of Physicians: Agency and Autonomy Reconsidered. SALMON, J Warren and WHITE, William and FEINGLASS, Joe.
G E Moore on the Values of Whole and Parts: A Critique. PAL, Jagat.
Generosity: A Duty Without a Right. STITH, Richard.
Genetically Engineered Herbicide Resistance, Part Two. COMSTOCK, Gary.
Genuine Moral Dilemmas and the Containment of Incoherence. PASKE, Gerald H.
Getting Down to Cases: The Revival of Casuistry in Bioethics. ARRAS, John D.
Gewirth and the Pain of Contradiction. DAVIS, Michael.
Gilbert Harman's Internalist Moral Relativism. POJMAN, Louis P.
Gilligan on Justice and Care: Two Interpretations. VREEKE, G J.
Giuseppe De Luca e la polemica sulla moralità di Péguy. FIORENTINO, Fernando.
Going Nowhere: Nagel on Normative Objectivity. FRIEDMAN, Marilyn.
Goodwill, Going Concern, Stocks and Flows: A Prescription for Moral Analysis. SWANDA JR, John R.
A Great Philosopher's Not So Great Account of Great Virtue: Aristotle's Treatment of 'Greatness of Soul'. CURZER, Howard J.
The Greatness and Limits of Kant's Practical Philosophy. HÖSLE, Vittorio.
Green and "Everybody's Doing It". DE GEORGE, Richard T.
Habermas and Theological Ethics (in French). BÜHLER, Pierre.
Habermas e o Terror Prático. LOPARIC, Zeljko.
Hacia un desarrollo de la cultura y una cultura del desarrollo. ROSALES, Amán.
Hare on Prudence. RABINOWICZ, Wlodzimierz.
Harrison on Animal Pain. HOUSE, Ian.
Has the History of Philosophy Ruined the Environment?. ATTFIELD, Robin.
Heads, Feds, and Beds: Ethical Dilemmas in the Delivery of Medical Care. WILLIAMS, Arthur R.
Health Care as a Business: The Ethic of Hippocrates Versus the Ethic of Managed Care. WAYMACK, Mark H.
Health Policy Analysis as Ideology and as Utopian Rhetoric. MILLER, Irwin.
Hegel's Critique of Liberalism and Natural Law: Reconstructing Ethical Life. GARZA JR, Abel.
Heidegger's Rector's Address: A Loss of the Question of Ethics. SCOTT, Charles.

ETHICS

Hide-and-Seek or Show-and-Tell? Emerging Issues of Informed Consent. HAAS, Leonard J.
The Highest Moral Knowledge and Internalism: Some Comments. LEMOS, Noah.
The Highest Moral Knowledge and the Truth Behind Internalism. DE PAUL, Michael R.
Historical Perspectives on the Morality of Virtue. WHITE, Richard.
Historical Perspectives: Development of the Codes of Ethics in the Legal, Medical and Accounting Professions. BACKOF, Jeanne F and MARTIN JR, Charles L.
HIV and the Obligation to Treat. SHELDON, Mark.
How Is Applied Philosophy to Be Applied?. KLINEFELTER, Donald S.
How to Construe Nature: Environmental Ethics and the Interpretation of Nature. KING, Roger J H.
Human Fertilisation and Embryology. DE S CAMERON, Nigel M.
Human Nature Technologically Revisited. ENGELHARDT JR, H Tristram.
Human Rights and Nietzsche. MINEAU, André.
The Humanism of Economics or Economizing on Humanism?. RIUMIN, V A.
Humanismo y humanismo cristiano. DERISI, Octavio N.
Hume's Ethics: Acts, Rules, Dispositions and Utility. SHIRLEY, Edward.
Hume's Metaethical Cognitivism and the Natural Law Theory. GRAEFRATH, Bernd.
Hungarian Philosophy: Its Ideas, an Historiographical Foundations (in Hungarian). STEINDLER, Larry.
Hydatidiform Moles and Teratomas Confirm the Human Identity of the Preimplantation Embryo. SUAREZ, Antoine.
Ideal and Morality (in German). JACOBS, Wilhelm G.
The Ideal of Shared Decision Making Between Physicians and Patients. BROCK, Dan W.
Identity and Status of the Human Embryo. SPAGNOLA, Antonio G.
Ignatian Discernment: A Philosophical Analysis. HUGHES, Gerard J.
Images of the Environment in Corporate America. SKORPEN, Erling.
Impersonal Friends. WHITING, Jennifer E.
The Importance of Being Human. DIAMOND, Cora.
In Defense of Human "Chauvinism": A Response to R Routley and V Routley. PASKE, Gerald H.
In Defense of Sharks: Moral Issues in Hostile Liquidating Takeovers. ALMEDER, Robert and CAREY, David.
Increasing Applied Business Ethics Courses in Business School Curricula. SIMS, Ronald R and SIMS, Serbrenia J.
The Indefensibility of Insider Trading. WERHANE, Patricia H.
Indirect Utilisme. ROSIER, Theo.
Individual and Corporate Responsibility: Two Alternative Approaches. SURBER, Jere.
Individual and Social Morality in Japan and the United States: Rival Conceptions of the Self. MAC INTYRE, Alasdair.
The Influence of Non-Anonymity Deriving from Feedback of Research Results on Marketing Professionals' Research Ethics. AKAAH, Ishmael P.
Information, Access, or Intimate Decisions About One's Action? The Content of Privacy. INNESS, Julie.
Informing the Public: Ethics, Policy Making, and Objectivity in News Reporting. IANNONE, A Pablo.
Innocents and Innocence: Moral Puzzles of Professional Status and Culpable Conduct. SNOWDEN, John R.
Insider Trading Revisited. MARTIN, Deryl W and PETERSON, Jeffrey H.
Institutional Animal Care and Use Committees and the Moderate Position. STEPHENSON, Wendell.
Institutional Integrity: Approval, Toleration and Holy War or 'Always True to You in My Fashion'. WILDES, Kevin W.
The Institutionalization of Organizational Ethics. SIMS, Ronald R.
An Integrative Model of Clinical-Ethical Decision Making. GRUNDSTEIN-AMADO, Rivka.
Integrity and Compromise in Nursing Ethics. WINSLOW, Betty J and WINSLOW, Gerald R.
Intellectual Property and Copyright Ethics. ALFINO, Mark.
International Marketing Ethics. LACZNIAK, Gene R and MURPHY, Patrick E.
Intimacy: A General Orientation in Japanese Religious Values. KASULIS, Thomas P.
The Irreducibly Clinical Character of Bioethics. WEAR, Stephen.
Is IVF Good Medicine?. CONNOR, Pauline.
Is there an Ethics of Computing?. BROWN, Geoffrey.
Is Utilitarianism Useless?. HAUSMAN, Daniel M.
An Issue in Corporate Social Responsibility: An Experiential Approach to Establish the Value of Human Life. DALTON, Dan R and COSIER, Richard A.
Jacques Derrida's Response to the Call for Ethics. CHAMPAGNE, R A.
Japanese Ethics: Beyond Good and Evil. WARGO, Robert J J.
Jeffersonian Ethics in Foreign Affairs: John Quincy Adams and the Moral Sentiments of a Realist. RUSSELL, Greg.
Just Causes. BLACKBURN, Simon.
Just Looking: Voyeurism and the Grounds of Privacy. NATHAN, Daniel O.
Justice in Preferential Hiring. SINGER, M S and SINGER, A E.
Justice: The Root of American Business Ideology and Ethics. MC GOWAN, Richard.
Justified Limits on Refusing Intervention. CHERVENAK, Frank A and MC CULLOUGH, Laurence B.
K J Shah's 'Philosophy, Religion, Morality, Spirituality: Some Issues'. GHOSE, A M.
Kann in O Höffes Ethik der politischen Gerechtigkeit eine ökologische Ethik aufgehoben werden?. WETZEL, Manfred.
Kant and the Origins of Totalitarianism. SIEBERS, Tobin.
Kant's Search for the Philosopher's Stone. AXIOTIS, Ares.
Kant, Teleology, and Sexual Ethics. COOKE, Vincent M.
A Kantian View of Moral Luck. MOORE, A W.
Kierkegaard's Mirror. ROSENOW, Eliyahu.
Kierkegaardian Transitions: Paradox and Pathos. FERREIRA, M Jamie.
Killing and Letting Die—Putting the Debate in Context. CHANDLER, John.
King Solomon and Everyman: A Problem in Coordinating Conflicting Moral Intuitions. RORTY, Amelie Oksenberg.
Kinship and Moral Relativity. PARGETTER, Robert.
Knowing When to Stop: The Limits of Medicine. JECKER, Nancy S.
Kohlberg and Piaget: Differences and Similarities. KAVATHATZOPOULOS, Iordanis.
The Law of Business Ethics and Social Responsibility. BURKE III, William T.
Law, Morality, and *la Reconquista*. CORDERO, Ronald A.
Leopold's "Means and Ends in Wild Life Management". HARGROVE, Eugene C and CALLICOTT, J Baird.
Le lezioni di Husserl sull'etica e sulla teoria del valore. DONNICI, Rocco.
La libertad como búsqueda de la verdad en el joven Agustín. WEISMANN, F J.
The Limits of a Wish. RIE, Michael A.
Linguistic Intuitions and Varieties of Ethical Naturalism. BALL, Stephen W.
Living a Life and the Problem of Existential Impossibility. LÖW-BEER, Martin.
La loi du Styx, Leibniz et la politique du bonheur. LE LANNOU, Jean-Michel.
Love Canal and the Ethics of Environmental Health. BRUMMER, James.
Lucian: The Sale of Lives (in Hebrew). SCOLNICOV, Samuel (trans).
El lugar de la doctrina social de la reflexión teológico moral cristiana. BRIANCESCO, E.
Machiavellianism Revisited. NELSON, George and GILBERTSON, Diana.
MacIntyre and the Indispensability of Tradition. SCHNEEWIND, J B.
MacIntyre on Hume. BAIER, Annette C.
MacIntyre, Tradition, and the Christian Philosopher. HIBBS, Thomas S.
Maimonides: A Natural Law Theorist?. LEVINE, Michael.
Management's Hat Trick: Misuse of "Engineering Judgment" in the Challenger Incident. HERKERT, Joseph R.
Mandatory AIDS Testing: The Legal, Ethical and Practical Issues. WERDEL, A Alyce.
The Many Appetites of Thomas Hobbes. HURLEY, Paul.
Mapping the Human Genome: Some Thoughts for Those Who Say "There Should Be A Law On It". SKENE, Loane.
Market Mechanisms and Principles of Justice. LOEWY, Erich H.
Marketing Ethics and Education: Some Empirical Findings. MERRITT, Sharyne.
Marketing Ethics: Some Dimensions of the Challenge. CAMENISCH, Paul F.
The Marxian Ethics. SARKER, Sunil Kumar.
Maternal Rights, Fetal Harms: Commentary. KINLAW, Kathy.
Maternal Rights, Fetal Harms: Commentary. STRONG, Carson.
McClennen's Early Cooperative Solution to the Prisoner's Dilemma. MAC INTOSH, Duncan.
Meaning, Truth Conditions and the Internal Point of View: The Ethical Dilemma. GOOSSENS, Charles.
Measuring the Quality of Life: Why, How and What?. HÄYRY, Matti.
Medical Futility, Medical Necessity: The - Problem - Without - A - Name. CALLAHAN, Daniel.
Medicine and Business: An Unhealthy Mix?. BROCK, Dan W.
Medicine as Business and Profession. AGICH, George J.
Mencius and the Mind-Dependence of Morality: An Analysis of Meng Tzu 6A: 4-5. SHUN, Kwong-Loi.
Merleau-Ponty's Phenomenology of Sympathy. MATUSTIK, Martin J.
Metaphysical Conundrums at the Root of Moral Disagreement. MC DERMOTT, John M.
Metaphysik und Erfahrung in Kants Grundlegung der Ethik. CRAMER, Konrad.
The Misuse of Maternal Mortality Statistics in the Abortion Debate. BECKWITH, Francis J.
The Molested. MAY, William F.
Moore's Moral Rules. PERKINS JR, Ray.
The Moral Authority of Transnational Corporate Codes. FREDERICK, William C.
Moral Conflicts in Kantian Ethics. MC CARTY, Richard.
Moral Depth. KEKES, John.
Moral Dilemmas, Compromise and Compensation. DAY, J P.
Moral Dreams and Practical Realities. LINZEY, Andrew.
Moral Epistemology and the Supervenience of Ethical Concepts. AUDI, Robert.
La moral existencial de G Marcel. MAÑERO, Salvador.
Moral Experience and Justification. SINNOTT-ARMSTRONG, Walter.
Moral Goodness, Esteem, and Acting from Duty. LEMOS, Noah M.
A Moral Ideal for Everyone and No One. CONWAY, Daniel W.

ETHICS

Moral Imagination, Objectivity, and Practical Wisdom. JACOBS, Jonathan.
Moral Laws in Borden P Bowne's *Principles of Ethics*. BURROW JR, Rufus.
Moral Metaphysics, Moral Revolution, and Environmental Ethics. PADEN, Roger.
Moral Obligation and Metaphysics. COOKE, Vincent M.
Moral Philosophy at West Point in the Nineteenth Century. SHIVE, Kenneth D.
Moral Planes and Intrinsic Values. ANDERSON, James C.
Moral Relativism and Deontic Logic. HUGLY, Philip and SAYWARD, Charles.
The Moral Responsibility of Corporate Executives for Disasters. BISHOP, John D.
The Moral Significance of Institutional Integrity. WEAR, Stephen.
Moral Skepticism and the Dangerous Maybe: Reconsidering Mackie's *Ethics*. METCALFE, John F.
Moral Skepticism. COPP, David.
The Moral Status of Animals and Their Use in Research: A Philosophical Review. DEGRAZIA, David.
The Moral Status of the Corporation. EWIN, R E.
Moral Theories, Impartiality, and the Status of Non-Rational, Sentient Beings. FILICE, Carlo.
Moral Truth and Coherence: Comments on Goldman. STEUP, M.
Moral und Biologie. RICHTER, Klaus.
Moral und Verwirklichung. KLEINGELD, Paulien.
Moral y política en Kant. PÉREZ ESTÉVEZ, Antonio.
Moraliteiten: Recente ethische publikaties in Vlaanderen en Nederland. STRUYKER BOUDIER, C E M.
Morality and Ethics in Organizational Administration. ADELMAN, Howard.
A Morality Based on Trust: Some Reflections on Japanese Morality. YAMAMOTO, Yutaka.
The Morality of a Free Market for Transplant Organs. NELSON, Mark T.
The Morality of Feminism. SEVENHUIJSEN, Selma.
The Morality of Killing and Causing Suffering: Reasons for Rejecting Peter Singer's Pluralistic Consequentialism. LANDMAN, Willem A.
Morally Untenable Beliefs. BURKE, Richard J.
La mort de Socrate et la vie des machines. BEAUNE, Jean-Claude.
Ms en abyme: Deconstruction and Feminism. ELAM, Diane.
Multinational Corporate Social Policy Process for Ethical Responsibility in Sub-Saharan Africa. PRATT, Cornelius B.
Murphy and Mercy. ADLER, Jacob.
Must We Return to Moral Realism?. ROSEN, Michael.
Narcissim Project and Corporate Decay: The Case of General Motors. SCHWARTZ, Howard S.
Natural Fetal Dependency States and Fetal Dependency Principles. HERBENICK, Raymond M.
The Natural History of Altruism. HUNT, Morton.
Natural Law and the Environment. BROWN, Montague.
Natural Law, Skepticism, and Methods of Ethics. SCHNEEWIND, J B.
Natural Problems and Artificial Intelligence. HENLEY, Tracy.
Natural Virtues, Natural Vices. BAIER, Annette C.
Naturalism, Freedom and Ethics in Spinoza. DE DIJN, Herman.
Naturalistic Ethics and the Argument from Evil. NELSON, Mark T.
The Nature of Moral Facts. ROSS, Steven.
Necesidad y existencia del código de moral profesional. MUÑOZ BARQUERO, Elizabeth.
Negotiating Criteria and Setting Limits: The Case of AIDS. CUTTER, Mary Ann Gardell.
New Creations? Commentary. BALK, Roger A.
New Creations? Commentary. FREEDMAN, Benjamin and GOULET, Marie-Claude.
New Creations? Commentary. MACER, Darryl.
The New Dimensions of Chinese Medical Ethics. MC GREAL, Ian Philip.
New Directions in Nursing Home Ethics. COLLOPY, Bart and BOYLE, Philip and JENNINGS, Bruce.
New Naturalism and Other Ethical Theories. SHENG, C L.
Nietzsche contra Kant and the Problem of Autonomy. WHITE, Richard.
Nietzsche's Environmental Ethics. HALLMAN, Max O.
No Holism without Pluralism. VARNER, Gary E.
No Moral Responsibility Without Alternative Possibilities. WEBBER, May A.
No Rules without Virtues: No Virtues without Rules. BRAYBROOKE, David.
The Noncompliant Substance Abuser: Commentary. CASSEL, Christine and LA PUMA, John.
The Noncompliant Substance Abuser: Commentary. STELL, Lance K.
Normativity and the Very Idea of Moral Epistemology. COPP, David.
Norms and Values. HANSSON, Sven Ove.
A Note on Hooker's "Rule Consequentialism". CARSON, Tom.
A Note on the Death Penalty as the Best Bet. BAYLES, Michael D.
Nueva modernidad adveniente y cultura emergente en América Latina. SCANNONE, J C.
Nurses and Physicians on Nutritional Support: A Comparison. LIASCHENKO, Joan and DAVIS, Anne J.
Nursing Ethics: Current State of the Art. FRY, Sara T.
Nursing Responsibility for the Placebo Effect. CONNELLY, Robert J.
Nutrition, Hydration, and the Demented Elderly. POST, Stephen G.
Object and Intention in Moral Judgments According to Aquinas. FINNIS, John.
The Objectivity of Moral Values: The Search in a Wrong Place. BANERJEE, Hiranmoy.
La objetividad y la distinción ciencia/ética. PUTNAM, Hilary and MURILLO, Lorena.
Of One Mind or Two? Query on the Innate Good in Mencius. LAI, Whalen.
On 'High-Mindedness'. GARCIA, Jorge.
On an Alleged Inconsistency in the Nicomachean Ethics (IX,4). MARTIN, C F J.
On Being Committed to Morality. NIELSEN, Kai.
On Bolzano's Conception of the Essentials of Ethics and its Coherences (in Czechoslovakian). HALA, Vlastimil.
On Excluding Something from Our Gathering: The Lack of Moral Standing of Non-Sentient Entities. LANDMAN, Willem A.
On Intuitions. WETTERSTRÖM, Thomas.
On Lying and the Role of Content in Kant's Ethics. SEDGWICK, Sally.
On Respect. BLUM, Alex.
On Squeamishness: A Response to Galston. FISHKIN, James S.
On Surrogacy: Morality, Markets, and Motherhood. MOODY-ADAMS, Michele M.
On the Alleged Methodological Infirmity of Ethics. MOODY-ADAMS, Michele M.
On the Epistemic Status of Considered Moral Judgments. TIMMONS, Mark.
On the Epistemic Value of Moral Experience. TOLHURST, William.
On the Genuine Queerness of Moral Properties and Facts. GARNER, Richard T.
On the Nature of Rape. BOGART, J H.
On the Teachability of ARETé in Plato (in Czechoslovakian). MOURAL, Josef.
On Utilitarianism and Utilitarian Attitudes. MILLER, Harlan B.
On Wittgenstein's Transcendental Ethics. PRASAD, Rajendra.
One Man's Reflection on a Masculine Role in Feminist Ethics: Epistemic versus Political Privilege. BOYD, Dwight.
The Open Question Argument. PAL, Jagat.
Orchestrating Social Change: An Imperative in Care of the Chronically Ill. ROTH, Patricia A and HARRISON, Janet K.
The Oregon Medicaid Experiment: Is It Just Enough?. FLECK, Leonard M.
The Oregon Priority-Setting Exercise: Quality of Life and Public Policy. HADORN, David C.
Organizational Value Contention and Managerial Mindsets. LIEDTKA, Jeanne.
Origins and Tendencies of the Philosophy of Liberation in Latin American Thought: A Critique of Dussel's Ethics. SCHUTTE, Ofelia.
Over het morele en zedelijke handelen, toegelicht aan het instituut huwelijk. COBBEN, Paul.
The Overdue Death of a Feminist Chameleon: Taking a Stand on Surrogacy Arrangements. TONG, Rosemarie.
Parental Obligations and the Ethics of Surrogacy: A Causal Perspective. NELSON, James Lindemann.
Partial Wholes. BARNES, Jonathan.
Partialism and Parenthood. NELSON, James Lindemann.
Paths to a Postmodern Ethics and Politics: A Reply to Gibbons. WHITE, Stephen K.
Patient Decision-Making Capacity and Risk. WICCLAIR, Mark R.
Perelman et la philosophie anglo-saxonne. MARCIL-LACOSTE, Louise.
Personal Morals and Professional Ethics: A Review and Empirical Examination of Public Accounting. BEETS, S Douglas.
El personalismo de Santo Tomás. FORMENT, Eudaldo.
Pharaoh's Magicians: The Ethics and Efficacy of Human Fetal Tissue Transplants. BARRY, Robert and KESLER, Darrel.
The Pharmacist's Role in Patient Care. SCHULZ, Richard M and BRUSHWOOD, David B.
Philosophical Reminiscences with Reflections on Firth's Work. PUTNAM, Hilary.
Philosophy within the Activity of the Nagyszombat (Trnava) University (in Hungarian). ORAVCOVÀ, Mariana.
Physical Environment Television Advertisement Themes: 1979 and 1989. PETERSON, Robin T.
Physical Possibility and Potentiality in Ethics. COVEY, Edward.
The Physician-Societal Relationship. CRELINSTEN, Gordon L.
Physicians, Entrepreneurism and the Problem of Conflict of Interest. GREEN, Ronald M.
A Picture of the Self Which Supports the Moral Responsibility. ANDERSON, Susan Leigh.
The Pincovian Persuasion: Six Problems in Virtue Ethics (A Free Response to Seung). BUDZISZEWSKI, J.
Piper's Criteria of Theory Selection. POSTOW, B C.
Plato and Davidson: Parts of the Soul and Weakness of Will. PENNER, Terrence M.
The Politics and Morality of Unequal Exchange: Emmanuel and Roemer, Analysis and Synthesis. SCHWEICKART, David.
The Politics of Ethics: Socratic Questioning is Needed in the Marketplace. TRUNDLE, Robert.
Possibilities of Consensus: Toward Democratic Moral Discourse. JENNINGS, Bruce.

ETHICS

Postcriptum: La libertad como necesidad del bien, en San Agustín. PEGUEROLES, Juan.
The Potential of Medicine as a Resource for Philosophy. FULFORD, K W M.
The Poverty of Naturalistic Moral Realism: Comments on Timmons. HOLMGREN, Margaret.
Predictors of Ethical Decisions Regarding Insider Trading. TERPSTRA, David E and REYES, Mario G C and BOKOR, Donald W.
Preferential Hiring and the Question of Competence. PHILIPS, Michael.
Prejudice and Progress in Animal and Environmental Protection. FOX, Michael W.
La prima e seconda edizione della "Geschichte des Materialismus" di Friedrich Albert Lange. COGNETTI, Giuseppe.
The Principle of Relevant Similarity. LEWIS, Gary W.
Principled Divestiture and Moral Integrity. CAHN, Steven M.
Principled Moral Reasoning: Is It a Viable Approach to Promote Ethical Integrity?. WEBER, James and GREEN, Sharon.
Privacy and Disclosure in Medical Genetics Examined in an Ethics of Care. WERTZ, Dorothy C and FLETCHER, John C.
A Problem for Radical (Onto-Theos) Pluralism. BILIMORIA, Purusottama.
The Problem of Moral Freedom and Nicolai Hartmann. PRASAD, Kamata.
El problema de la culpa y del "otro" en Heidegger y Siewerth. CABADA, Manuel.
Problemas lógicos en el relativismo ético. CAMACHO, Luis A.
Professional Education of African Americans: A Challenge to Ethical Thinking. HARRIS, William M.
Professional Ethics and Accounting Education: A Critique of the 8-Step Method. ARMSTRONG, Mary Beth.
The Professional's Dilemma: Choosing Between Service and Success. MC DOWELL, Banks.
Professions and Professionalism. DOWNIE, R S.
The Profit Motive and the Moral Assessment of Health Care Institutions. DANIELS, Norman.
Promoting Moral Growth Through Intra-Group Participation. NELSON, D R and OBREMSKI, T E.
Proof and Sanction in Mill's Utilitarianism. COHEN, Stephen.
The Prophetic and the Priestly. CHILDRESS, James F.
A Proposal for Corporate Ethical Reform: The Ethical Dialogue Group. PAYNE, Stephen L.
A Proposal for Health Care: Revolution Not Reform. BARNET, Robert J.
Prudence and Past Preferences; Reply to Wlodizimierz Rabinowicz. HARE, R M.
La prudencia (II). DERISI, Octavio N.
Psychiatry, Religious Conversion, and Medical Ethics. POST, Stephen G.
Psychoactive Drug Prescribing in Japan: Epistemological and Bioethical Considerations. SAKAI, Akio.
Psychology and Standards of Reasonable Expectation. SCHOEMAN, Ferdinand.
Public and Private Morality. SHAIDA, S A.
Public Relations: The Empiricial Research on Practitioner Ethics. PRATT, Cornelius B.
Punishment and Loss of Moral Standing. MORRIS, Christopher W.
Punishment and the Utilitarian Criterion of Right and Wrong. SCHALLER, Walter E.
Punitive Damages: New Twists in Torts. WALTON, Clarence C.
Putnam's Moral Objectivism. TIMMONS, Mark.
Pyrrhonism's Arguments Against Value. MC PHERRAN, Mark L.
Pythagoras—The First Animal Rights Philosopher. VIOLIN, Mary Ann.
The Quest for Transformational Experience. BULKLEY, Kelly.
The Question of Ethics in Foucault's Thought. SCOTT, Charles E.
The Range of Options. ZIMMERMAN, Michael J.
Rationalism, Supervenience, and Moral Epistemology. KLAGGE, James.
Rationality and Moral Status. BILOW, Scott H.
Rawls's Difference Principle and a Problem of Sacrifice. VOICE, Paul.
La razón ética. CARRACEDO, Jose Rubio.
A Reaction to Vogel's "The Ethical Roots of Business". MC MAHON, Thomas F.
Reactions to Ethical Dilemmas: A Study Pertaining to Certified Public Accounts. CLAYPOOL, G A and FETYKO, D F and PEARSON, M A.
Reason and Reality Revisited. PLUHAR, Evelyn.
The Reasonableness of Moral Reasons. TRUNDLE, Robert.
The Recent Revival of Divine Command Ethics. QUINN, Philip L.
Recent Work on Ethical Relativism. STEWART, Robert M and THOMAS, Lynn L.
Recognizing Suffering. CASSELL, Eric J.
Reforming Britain's National Health Service. KESSEL, Ros.
The Regulation of Virtue: Cross-Currents in Professional Ethics. JENNINGS, Bruce.
La reivindicación de la racionalidad en K O Apel. SMILG VIDAL, Norberto.
The Relative Importance of Social Responsibility in Determining Organizational Effectiveness: Student Responses. KRAFT, Kenneth L.
The Relative Importance of Social Responsibility in Determining Organizational Effectiveness. KRAFT, Kenneth.
The Relevance of Confucian Ethics. CHUNG, Bongkil.
Remarks on Marketing Ethics. BRENNAN, Bernard F.
Reply to Dahl, Baier and Schneewind. MAC INTYRE, Alasdair.
Reply to Shrader-Frechette's "Biological Holism and the Evolution of Ethics". CALLICOTT, J Baird.
Reply to Stephenson on Biomedical Research. GENDIN, Sidney.
Reply to Sturgeon's "Contents and Causes" A Reply to Blackburn. BLACKBURN, Simon.
Reply to the President: "Ethics and the Limits of Consistency". WILLIAMS, Bernard.
Reply to Weir: Unnecessary Fear, Nutrition, and Vegetarianism. SAPONTZIS, Steve F.
Les représentations de l'action. SAINT SERNIN, Bertrand.
Research Note On Equity and Ethics in State-Promotion of Agricultural Products. ADELAJA, Adesoji O and BRUMFIELD, Robin G.
Respect for Donor Choice and the Uniform Anatomical Gift Act. EDINGER, Walter.
A Response to 'Psychoactive Drug Prescribing in Japan'. COVERDALE, John.
A Response to Brock and Skene. WICCLAIR, Mark R.
Response to Dr Sakai's 'Psychoactive Drug Prescribing in Japan'. RITCHIE, Karen.
Response to Finsen's "Response to Lizst's Animal Liberation as a Valid Response to Structural Violence". LISZT, Amy.
Response to Lizst's "Animal Liberation as a Valid Response to Structural Violence". FINSEN, Susan.
Response to Sapontzis's Reply. WEIR, Jack.
Response to Squadrito's "Commentary: Interests and Equal Moral Status". DE GRAZIA, David.
Response to the Presidential Address: Willer's "Ethics in Educational Policy Analysis". DRAKE, William E.
Response to 'Rescuing the Innocent'. GARDNER, G T G.
Response to 'Rescuing the Innocent'. MORROW, James.
Response: Subjective Values and Objective Values. MACHAN, Tibor R.
Responsibility As a Moral Principle? A Critical Reflection on Hans Jonas' Ethics of Responsibility? (in German). KETTNER, Matthias.
Rhetoric and Ethics: Adam Smith on Theorizing about the Moral Sentiments. GRISWOLD JR, Charles L.
The Rhythms of Gratitude: Historical Developments and Philosophical Concerns. STEWART-ROBERTSON, Charles.
Rich Cases: The Ethics of Thick Description. DAVIS, Dena S.
Rights and Utilitarianism. EWIN, R E.
The Rights-Interpretation of Desert. GARCÍA, Jorge.
Risk, Commitment, and Project Abandonment. DEVANEY, Mike.
Risk-Related Standard Inevitable in Assessing Competence—Comments on Wicclair. SKENE, Loane.
Roderick Firth's Contribution to Ethics. BRANDT, R B.
Role Morality as a Complex Instance of Ordinary Morality. ANDRE, Judith.
The Role of Ethics and Social Responsibility in Achieving Organizational Effectiveness: Students Versus Managers. KRAFT, Kenneth L and SINGHAPAKDI, Anusorn.
Rome Inferences and Structural Opacity. MOORE, F C T.
Russell and the Ethical Concern of Wittgenstein's *Tractatus*. IGLESIAS, Teresa.
O Saber, a Ética e a Ação Social. CARDOSO D EOLIVEIRA, Roberto.
San Agustín y la sexualidad conyugal. BURKE, Cormac.
The Sanctity of Life and Substituted Judgement: The Case of Baby J. HORNETT, Stuart I.
Santo Tomás y el desafío de la ética analítica contemporánea. MASSINI CORREAS, Carlos Ignacio.
Santo Tomás y la prostitución. PONFERRADA, Gustavo E.
Sartre and the Objectivity of Values (in French). FRIEDLI, Serge.
Schopenhauers Entwurf einer asketischen Tugendethik. WOLF, Jean-Claude.
Schopenhauers Idee einer rekonstruktiven Ethik (mit Anwendungen auf die moderne Medizin-Ethik). BIRNBACHER, Dieter.
The Scope of Deliberation: A Conflict in Aquinas. IRWIN, T H.
The Self in Confucian Ethics. SHUN, Kwong-Loi.
Self, Society, and Kantian Impersonality. SORELL, Tom.
Sense, Passions and Morals in Hume and Kant. NUYEN, A T.
Separating Care and Cure: An Analysis of Historical and Contemporary Images of Nursing and Medicine. JECKER, Nancy S and SELF, Donnie J.
The Servant Species: Humanity as Priesthood. LINZEY, Andrew.
Setting Floating Limits: Functional Status Care Categories as National Policy. THOMASMA, David C.
Sex and Virtue. PUTMAN, D.
Shareholder Authorized Inside Trading: A Legal and Moral Analysis. SHAW, Bill.
Should Basic Care Get Priority? Doubts about Rationing the Oregon Way. VEATCH, Robert M.
Should Ethical Concerns Regulate Science? The European Experience with the Human Genome Project. RIX, Bo Andreassen.
Should Philosophy be Applied?. NESBITT, Winston.
Shrewd Bargaining on the Moral Frontier: Toward a Theory of Morality in Practice. DEES, J Gregory and CRAMPTON, Peter C.
Sidgwick and Self-Interest. CRISP, Roger.
The Significance of a Wish. ACKERMAN, Felicia.

ETHICS

The Significance of the Moral Concept of Virtue in St Augustine's Ethics. TORCHIA, N Joseph.
Sincerity and Japanese Values. REASONER, Paul.
Singer's Cookbook. JOHNSON, Edward.
Smoking in Public: A Moral Imperative for the Most Toxic of Environmental Wastes. LUDINGTON, David M.
So Animal a Human..., or the Moral Relevance of Being An Omnivore. GEORGE, Kathryn Paxton.
Sobre el gusto y la verdad práctica. ARREGUI, Jorge Vicente.
Social Science as Moral Philosophy?: Reflections on Alan Wolfe's *Whose Keeper*?. MASON, John R.
The Sociology of Knowledge: Toward an Existential View of Business Ethics. PHILLIPS, Nelson.
Socrates in Dallas: Managing the Facilities. CASTRO, Barry.
Solipsism in Kant's Practical Philosophy and the Discourse of Ethics. KUHLMANN, Wolfgang.
Some Remarks about Ethical Universalism. MOSER, Shia.
Some Unresolved Ethical Issues in Auditing. GUNZ, Sally and MC CUTCHEON, John.
Souls and Sentientism. RYDER, Richard D.
Speaking About the Unspeakable: Genocide and Philosophy. FREEMAN, Michael.
Species, Individuals, and Domestication: A Commentary on Jane Duran's "Domesticated and Then Some". VARNER, Gary E.
Specifying Norms as a Way to Resolve Concrete Ethical Problems. RICHARDSON, Henry S.
Spinoza's Materialist Ethics: The Education of Desire. RAVVEN, Heidi M.
Spinoza's Two Theories of Morality. LUCASH, Frank.
St Thomas on the Motives of Unjust Acts. WEITHMAN, Paul J.
The Status of Frozen Embryos. ANDERSON, Susan Leigh.
Still Saving the Life of Ethics. SCHNEIDERMAN, Lawrence J.
A Study of the Foundations of Ethical Decision Making of Clinical Medical Ethicists. SELF, Donnie J and SKEEL, Joy D.
Sturgeon's Defence of Moral Realism. JOBE, Evan K.
Su alcuni aspetti del neoilluminismo di L Geymonat. STOMEO, Anna.
The Subjection of Children. AVIRAM, Aharon.
Supererogation and the Fulfillment of Duty. MELLEMA, Gregory.
The Supremely Happy Life in Aristotle's *Nicomachean Ethics*. CURZER, Howard J.
Taking Positional Conflicts of Interest Seriously. DZIENKOWSKI, John S.
Taking Role Moralities Seriously. WUESTE, Daniel E.
Tareas y métodos en la ética del desarrollo. GOULET, Denis.
Taylor's Waking Dream: No One's Reply. CLARK, Stephen R L.
Teaching Clinical Ethics in the Residency Years: Preparing Competent Professionals. FORROW, Lachlan and ARNOLD, Robert M and FRADER, Joel.
Teaching Ethics in the Health Care Setting, Part I. COUTTS, Mary Carrington.
Teaching Feminist Ethics as Male Consciousness-Raising. WALTON, Barbara J.
The Teaching of Business Ethics: A Survey of AACSB Member Schools. SCHOENFELDT, Lyle F and MC DONALD, Don M and YOUNGBLOOD, Stuart A.
La tecnología desde un punto de vista ético. RAMÍREZ, E Roy.
Telling Stories: Creative Literature and Ethics. RADEY, Charles.
Le temps du souffrir: Remarques critiques sur la phénoménologie de M Henry. PORÉE, Jérôme.
Terrorism and Argument from Analogy. WALLACE, G.
The Evil Beyond Good and Evil (in German). BOLZ, Norbert.
The Superfluity of the Original Position. DEN HARTOGH, G A.
Theorizing about Morals. WALLACE, Jim.
Thinking Like an Engineer: The Place of a Code of Ethics in the Practice of a Profession. DAVIS, Michael.
Thinking the Other Without Violence? An Analysis of the Relation Between the Philosophy of Lévinas and Feminism. MANNING, Robert J S.
To Tell a Good Tale: Kierkegaardian Reflections on Moral Narrative and Moral Truth. TURNER, Jeffrey S.
Tooley and the Trolley. FISCHER, John Martin.
Toughness as a Political Virtue. GALSTON, William.
Toward a Theory of Bribery. DANLEY, John R.
Toward An Ecological Ethic of Care. CURTIN, Deane.
Toward An Expanded Vision of Clinical Ethics Education: From the Individual to the Institution. SOLOMON, Mildred Z (and others).
Treating the Troops. HOWE, Edmund G and MARTIN, Edward D.
Truth, Justification and the Inescapability of Epistemology: Comments on Copp. RUSSELL, Bruce.
Truth, Neutrality, and Conflict of Interest. LICHTENBERG, Judith.
Two Models of Preferential Treatment for Working Mothers. BABER, H E.
Two Ways of Morality: Confucian and Kantian. LEE, Kwang-Sae.
Ultimate Ends in Practical Reasoning. MAC DONALD, Scott.
Uncertainty and the Shaping of Medical Decisions. BERESFORD, Eric B.
Understanding Professional Misconduct: The Moral Responsibilities of Professionals. NORTON, Thomas W.
Ungeklärte Fragen im Dialog zwischen Glaube und Naturwissenschaft. FISCHER, Johannes.
The Unity of Moral Virtues in Aristotle's *Nicomachean Ethics*. TELFER, Elizabeth.
The Unity of the Vices. JACOBS, Jonathan and ZEIS, John.
Universalistische Ethik und Urteilskraft: ein aristotelischer Blick auf Kant. HÖFFE, Otfried.
Universalizability and the Summing of Desires. PERSSON, Ingmar.
Universalizability and the Summing of Desires: Reply to Ingmar Persson. HARE, R M.
The University and Industrial Research: Selling Out?. HILL, Judith M.
Unnecessary Pain, Nutrition, and Vegetarianism. WEIR, Jack.
Utilitarian Killing, Replacement, and Rights. PLUHAR, Evelyn.
Utilitarian Strategies in Bentham and John Stuart Mill. KELLY, P J.
Utilitarianism and the 'Punishment' of the Innocent: The General Problem. SMILANSKY, Saul.
Utilitarianism and the Idea of Reflective Equilibrium. TERSMAN, Folke.
Utilitaristische Ethik als Antwort auf die ökologische Krise. WOLF, Jean-Claude.
Value Concepts and Preconventional, Conventional and Postconventional Morality (in Dutch). VOS, H M.
The Values of a Habitat. PARKER, Kelly.
The Vatican's Dilemma: On the Morality of IVF and the Incarnation. DUCHARME, Howard.
Vegetarianism and Virtue: On Gassendi's Epicurean Defense. MICHAEL, Emily.
La vie, ou le point de rupture: Schopenhauer-Nietzsche. UCCIANI, Louis.
Violence: Can It Be Ethical?. FRINGS, Manfred.
Virtue Ethics and Maori Ethics. PERRETT, Roy W and PATTERSON, John.
Virtue Ethics and the Appeal to Human Nature. WOODRUFF, Paul.
The Virtue of a Representative. WOLGAST, Elizabeth.
Virtues and Rules. ROBERTS, Robert C.
Virtues and Values: A Platonic Account. SEUNG, T K.
Volunteering Children. MC DONNELL, Kevin.
Waiting for a New St Benedict: Alasdair MacIntyre and the Theory and Practice of Journalism. LAMBETH, Edmund B.
Warum lebt der Mensch moralisch?. BURKHARDT, Cornelia and FRANKENHÄUSER, Gerald.
Weakness of Will as a Species of Executive Cowardice. SWANTON, Christine.
Welcome 'Ethical Stress': A Humean Analysis and A Practical Proposal. MERRILL, Sarah A.
Welfarism and Utilitarianism: A Rehabilitation. NG, Yew-Kwang.
Wertfreiheit und Ethik in den Sozial-und Naturwissenschaften. ZIMMERMANN, Rolf.
What Can a Discursive Theory of Morality Learn from Aquinas?. RENTTO, Juha-Pekka.
What is Virtue Ethics All About?. TRIANOSKY, Gregory.
What is Wrong With Wicked Feelings?. ROBERTS, Robert C.
What Makes Practice Educational?. HOGAN, Pádraig.
When Death Is at the Door. WINSLADE, William J.
When is "Everyone's Doing It" a Moral Justification?. GREEN, Ronald M.
When Is Home Care Medically Necessary? Commentary. FORROW, Lachlan.
When Is Home Care Medically Necessary? Commentary. DANIELS, Norman and SABIN, James E.
When Scientists are Wrong: Admitting Inadvertent Error in Research. LEIBEL, Wayne.
Who are "We"? Ambiguities of the Modern Self. SKINNER, Quentin.
Who or What is the Preembryo?. MC CORMICK, Richard A.
Whose Education Is It Anyway?. TAMIR, Yael.
Whose Right? Ronald Dworkin, Women, and Pornographers. LANGTON, Rae.
Why Corporations Are Not Morally Responsible for Anything They Do. VELASQUEZ, Manuel G.
Why Philosophers Should Offer Ethics Consultations. THOMASMA, David C.
Wille, Willkür, and the Imputability of Immoral Actions. HUDSON, Hud.
Willing and Acting in Husserl's Lectures on Ethics and Value Theory. NENON, Thomas J.
Willkür und Wille bei Kant. STEKELER-WEITHOFER, Pirmin.
Wofür sind wir verantworlich?. NEUMAIER, Otto.
Wovor und wodurch sind wir verantworlich? Die Instanzen der Verantwortung. MAIER, Maria.
Zygotes, Souls, Substances, and Persons. BOLE III, Thomas J.

ETHICS COMMITTEES

Medical Ethics in Practice. BARD, Terry R.
Consensus in Panels and Committees: Conceptual and Ethical Issues. VEATCH, Robert M and MORENO, Jonathan D.
Ethics Committee Simulations. WINSTON, Morton.
Ethics Committees. COHEN, Cynthia B (ed).
Ethics Committees: From Ethical Comfort to Ethical Cover. ANNAS, George J.

ETHNICITY

African Philosophy: The Essential Readings. SEREQUEBERHAN, Tsenay.
"But Would That Still Be Me?" Notes on Gender, "Race," Ethnicity, as Sources of "Identity". APPIAH, Anthony.
Plural But Equal: Group Identity and Voluntary Integration. ROBACK, Jennifer.

ETHNOCENTRISM
Feminist Ethics. CARD, Claudia (ed).
To the History of Glory and Fall of the Book "Civilization at the Crossroads" after August 1968 (in Czechoslovakian). SINDELAR, Jan.

ETHOS
Vernunft und Kontingenz: Rationalität und Ethos in der Phänomenologie. ORTH, Ernst Wolfgang (ed).
Argumentation and Values (in French). BOREL, Marie-Jeanne.
Éthique et Morale. RICOEUR, Paul.

ETIQUETTE
Moral Behavior at Public Performances. OLDS, Mason.

ETYMOLOGY
"The Mencian Conception of *Ren xing*: Does it Mean 'Human Nature'?" in *Chinese Texts and Philosophical Contexts*, AMES, Roger T.
"On the Expression *Zai You*" in *Chinese Texts and Philosophical Contexts*, LAU, D C.

EUCKEN, R
Phänomenologie als ästhetische Theorie. FELLMANN, Ferdinand.

EUCLID
La definizione di "retta" data da Euclide e le geometrie non-euclidee. BLANDINO, Giovanni.

EUCLIDEAN GEOMETRY
How Euclidean Geometry Has Misled Metaphysics. NERLICH, Graham.

EUDAIMONISM
Blaise Pascals: "Pensées" (1656-1662) Systematische 'Gedanken' über. KIRSCH, Ulrich.
Das Ethische in der Rhetorik des Aristoteles. WÖRNER, Markus Hilmar.
Aristotle on the Function of Man in Relation to Eudaimonia. HESTER, Marcus.
Friendship, Self-Love, and Concern for Others in Aristotle's Ethics. MC KERLIE, Dennis.

EUDOXUS
Eudoxos and Dedekind: On the Ancient Greek Theory of Ratios and its Relation to Modern Mathematics. STEIN, Howard.

EUGENICS
Science and Moral Values. VOLLRATH, John.

EUROPEAN
The Great Goddess and the Aistian Mythical World. VYCINAS, Vincent.
Philosophie Juridique Européenne. TRIGEAUD, Jean-Marc.
"Islam in European Thought" in *The Tanner Lectures on Human Values, Volume XI*, HOURANI, Albert.
"Liberal Ideas and Reality: Central Europe 1848-49" in *Perspectives on Ideas and Reality*, GERGELY, András.
"Professional Organizations and Professional Ethics: A European View" in *Ethics, Trust, and the Professions: Philosophical and Cultural Aspects*, SASS, Hans-Martin.
CAHBI: Europe Needs a Universal Bioethical System. GUNNING, Karel.
Infiniti mondi e mondo nuovo: Conquista dell'America e critica della civilità europea in Giordano Bruno. RICCI, Saverio.
Max Scheler: Theory of Forms of Knowledge and Perspective of Overcoming the Crisis of European Culture (in Polish). RUBA, Marek.
Per una storia dell'idea di Europa: Riflessioni storiografiche. BALDASSARRE, Mariarosa.
Philosophy in the *"Gymnasium:"* European Observations and Recommendations. VAN DER LEEUW, Karel and MOSTERT, Pieter.
The Common European Home (in German). FEIEREIS, Konrad.
Wissen und Emanzipation. SANDKÜHLER, Hans Jörg.

EUTHANASIA
Convictions. HOOK, Sidney.
Euthanasia: Toward an Ethical Social Policy. THOMASMA, David C.
In Partnership with God: Contemporary Jewish Law and Ethics. SHERWIN, Byron L.
The Last Choice: Preemptive Suicide in Advanced Age. PRADO, C G.
Medical Ethics for Physicians-in-Training. KANTOR, Jay E.
Das Tier in der Moral. WOLF, Ursula.
To Die or Not to Die?. BERGER, Arthur S (ed).
"Euthanasia" in *A Companion to Ethics*, KUHSE, Helga.
Arguing for Rational Suicide. HUMPHRY, Derek.
Bioethics on Trial. CAPLAN, Arthur L.
Buddhist Views of Suicide and Euthanasia. BECKER, Carl B.
A Case Against Dutch Euthanasia. FENIGSEN, Richard.
The Consequences of Endorsing Sentimental Homicide. BARRY, Robert L.
Euthanasia in China: A Report. DA PU, Shi.
Missouri Stands Alone. COLBY, William H.
Nutrition, Hydration, and the Demented Elderly. POST, Stephen G.
When Death Is at the Door. WINSLADE, William J.

EVALUATION(S)
Critical Reasoning (Third Edition). CEDERBLOM, Jerry.
"Has Popper Been a Good Thing?" in *Imre Lakatos and Theories of Scientific Change*, PAPINEAU, David.
"Identity and Strong and Weak Evaluation" in *Identity, Character, and Morality: Essays in Moral Psychology*, FLANAGAN, Owen.
"On the Logic of Practical Evaluation" in *Logic and Ethics*, KÖRNER, Stephan.
"The Fragmentation of Reason": Précis of Two Chapters. STICH, Stephen P.
Axiology as the Form of Purity of Heart: A Reading Husserliana XXVIII. HART, James G.
Evaluating Arguments: The Premise-Conclusion Relation. BOWLES, George.
The Evaluation of "Outcomes" of Accounting Ethics Education. LOEB, Stephen E.
Expecting Nature's Best: Optimality Models and Perfect Adaptation. HOLCOMB, H R.
The Message of Affirmative Action. HILL JR, Thomas E.
Society as an "Accidental Product of Human Activities": Max Horkheimer's Social Theory and Critique. BALOG, Andreas.

EVALUATIVE
Bogdan Suchodolski's Philosophy of Culture (in Polish). TRUCHLINSKA, Bogumila.
Religions in the Balance. FENNER, Peter.

EVANS-PRITCHARD, E
Evans-Pritchard on Persons and Their Cattle-Clocks: A Note on the Anthropological Account of Man. CHANDRA, Suresh.

EVENT(S)
Events in the Semantics of English: A Study in Subatomic Semantics. PARSONS, Terence.
"Event" in Dewey's Philosophy. DUFF, Barry E.
Direct and Indirect Causes. SPOHN, Wolfgang.
Four Thousand Ships Passed Through the Lock: Object-Induced Measure Functions on Events. KRIFKA, Manfred.
The Historical Event as a Cultural Indicator: The Case of Judaism. NEUSNER, Jacob.
On the Individuation of Events. CLELAND, Carol.
A Short Vindication of Reichenbach's "Event-Splitting". PFEIFER, Karl.

EVIDENCE
Human Nature and Historical Knowledge: Hume, Hegel and Vico. POMPA, Leon.
The Limits of Influence: Psychokinesis and the Philosophy of Science. BRAUDE, Stephen E (ed).
"Bayesian Problems of Old Evidence" in *Scientific Theories*, EELLS, E.
The Background to Bentham on Evidence. LEWIS, A D E.
Epistemic Paternalism: Communication Control in Law and Society. GOLDMAN, Alvin I.
Evidence and Reasons for Belief. FOLEY, Richard.
The Evidence for Reincarnation. COCKBURN, David.
The Evidence of Experience. SCOTT, Joan W.
Evil and the Proper Basicality of Belief in God. DRAPER, Paul.
The Irrelevance of Bootstrapping. CHRISTENSEN, David.
Non-professional Judicial Reasoning. TAPANI KLAMI, Hannu.
On Appealing to the Evidence. PHILLIPS, Hollibert E.
Probability Out of Court: Notes on 'Guilt Beyond Reasonable Doubt'. COHEN, Stephen and BERSTEN, Michael.
Reasonable Evidence of Reasonableness. KELMAN, Mark.
The Relevance of Historical Evidence for Christian Faith: A Critique of a Kierkegaardian View. EVANS, C Stephen.
Richard Rufus of Cornwall and the Authorship of the *Scriptum super Metaphysicam*. NOONE, Timothy B.
Scientific Evidence: Creating and Evaluating Experimental Instruments and Research Techniques. BECHTEL, William.
Two Souls in One Body. HACKING, Ian.
Whewell's Developmental Psychologism: A Victorian Account of Scientific Progress. METCALFE, John F.
Why Scientists Gather Evidence. MAHER, Patrick.

EVIDENTIALISM
Evidence and Legal Reasoning: On the Intertwinement of the Probable and the Reasonable. KLAMI, Hannua Tapani (and others).
Foundationalism and Peter's Confession. HESTER, Marcus.

EVIL
The Co-Existence of God and Evil. TRAU, Jane Mary.
Fallen Freedom: Kant on Radical Evil and Moral Regeneration. MICHALSON JR, Gordon E.
Good and Evil: An Absolute Conception. GAITA, Raimond.
The Law of Karma: A Philosophical Study. REICHENBACH, Bruce R.
The Legacy of Hermann Cohen. KLUBACK, William.
Spirit and Existence: A Philosophy Inquiry into the Meaning of Spiritual Existence. GELVEN, Michael.
"The Problem of Evil in Proto-Ethical Idealism: J W Miller's Ethics in Historical Context" in *The Philosophy of John William Miller*, TYMAN, Stephen.
An Atheological Argument from Evil Natural Laws. SMITH, Quentin.
Cristianesimo tragico, cristianesimo ludico: i due volti della fedeltà al Dio dialettico. GARGANO, Monica.
Etica e diritto penale nella filosofia attualistica. RICCIO, Stefano.
Evil and the Proper Basicality of Belief in God. DRAPER, Paul.
Freedom and the Free Will Defense. GALE, Richard M.
God and Gratuitous Evil: A Reply to Yandell. CHRZAN, Keith.

EVIL

God's Ability to Will Moral Evil. BROWN, Robert F.
Heidegger and the Critique of the Understanding of Evil as Privatio Boni. CAPOBIANCO, Richard.
Hume Revisited: A Problem With the Free Will Defense. MARKHAM, Ian.
La inocencia y el mal en la obra de Albert Camus. JIMÉNEZ, Alexander.
Japanese Ethics: Beyond Good and Evil. WARGO, Robert J J.
Middle Knowledge and the Soteriological Problem of Evil. HUNT, David P.
Moral Depth. KEKES, John.
Moral Imagination, Objectivity, and Practical Wisdom. JACOBS, Jonathan.
Naturalistic Ethics and the Argument from Evil. NELSON, Mark T.
Plantinga and Probabilistic Atheism. CHRZAN, Keith.
Residual Natural Evil and Anthropic Reasoning. MC LEAN, Murdith.
Response to Gale's "Freedom and the Free Will Defense". HUMBER, James M.
Some Puzzles About the Evil of Death. FELDMAN, Fred.
The Evil Beyond Good and Evil (in German). BOLZ, Norbert.
Whitehead and Genuine Evil. BARINEAU, R Maurice.

EVIL DEMON ARGUMENT

"Arbitrary Reasons" in *Doubting: Contemporary Perspectives on Skepticism*, LUPER-FOY, Steven.

EVIL(S)

American Slavery and the Holocaust: Their Ideologies Compared. THOMAS, Laurence.
Traité de la créature. VARET, Gilbert.

EVOLUTION

see also Darwinism
Beyond Natural Selection. WESSON, Robert.
Cosmos and Anthropos: A Philosophical Interpretation of the Anthropic Cosmological Principle. HARRIS, Errol E.
Evolution als Höherentwicklung des Bewusstseins. KUMMER, Christian.
Evolution: Probleme und neue Aspekte ihrer Theorie. SCHEFFCZYK, Leo (ed).
Evolutionary Instability: Logical and Material Aspects of a Unified Theory of Biosocial Evolution. GEIGER, Gebhard.
The Fragmentation of Reason. STICH, Stephen.
Interpreting Evolution: Darwin and Teilhard de Chardin. BIRX, H James.
"Emergent Evolution and the Level Structure of Reality" in *Studies on Mario Bunge's "Treatise"*, BLITZ, David.
"Evolution—Matter of Fact or Metaphysical Idea?" in *Logic, Methodology and Philosophy of Science, VIII*, LÖTHER, Rolf.
"Evolutionary Altruism and Psychological Egoism" in *Logic, Methodology and Philosophy of Science, VIII*, SOBER, Elliott.
"Is There Anything We Should Not Want to Know?" in *Logic, Methodology and Philosophy of Science, VIII*, GÄRDENFORS, Peter.
"Modest Realism, Experience and Evolution" in *Harré and His Critics*, MANICAS, Peter.
The Biological Justification of Ethics: A Best-Case Scenario. ROSENBERG, Alexander.
Breve examen científico y filosófico de la teoría de la evolución. FALGUERAS, Ignacio.
Chance and Law in Irreversible Thermodynamics, Theoretical Biology and Theology. PEACOCKE, Arthur.
The Changing Nature of the Social Sciences. MASTERS, Roger D.
The Chicken and the Egg. TEICHMANN, Roger.
Commentary on Byerly and Michod. LENNOX, James G.
Commentary on the Paper by H C Byerly and R E Michod's "Fitness and Evolutionary Explanation". BRITO DA CUNHA, A.
Complexity and Evolution: What Everybody Knows. MC SHEA, Daniel W.
Consciousness for the Twenty-First Century. CSIKSZENTMIHALYI, Mihaly.
The Creationist Theory of Abrupt Appearances: A Critique. STRAHLER, Arthur N.
Cultural Evolution, Biology and Language: Empirical and Rational Criteria of Selection (in German). DORSCHEL, Andreas.
Darwin's Long and Short Arguments. SINTONEN, Matti.
The Darwinian Synthesis: A Critique of the Rosenberg/Williams Argument. VAN BALEN, G.
David Hull's Evolutionary Model for the Progress and Process of Science. OLDROYD, David.
Différentielles et intégrales sociales chez Rousseau. BACHTA, Abdelkader.
Does Representational Content Arise from Biological Function?. HALL, Richard J.
Elites and Systematic Change in Hungary. SZALAI, Erzsebet.
Epigenetic Landscaping: Waddington's Use of Cell Fate Bifurcation Diagrams. GILBERT, Scott F.
Erneuerung als Grundmechanismus der Evolution. EBELING, Werner.
Evolution and Nostalgia in Hegel's Theory of Desire. BERTHOLD-BOND, Daniel.
Evolution, "Typology" and "Population Thinking". GREENE, Marjorie.
Expecting Nature's Best: Optimality Models and Perfect Adaptation. HOLCOMB, H R.
Fitness and Evolutionary Explanation. BYERLY, Henry C and MICHOD, Richard E.
Fitness and Evolutionary Explanation: A Response. BYERLY, Henry C and MICHOD, Richard E.

How Did Morality Evolve?. IRONS, William.
Die immerwährende Schöpfung als fundamentaler Seinsvorgang. KNAPPIK, G J.
Is Karma Evolutionary?. KRISHAN, Y.
Una Metafísica estructural de la evolución. CONILL, Jesús.
Myth and Morality: The Love Command. HEFNER, Philip.
A Naturalistic Theory of Archaic Moral Order. CAMPBELL, Donald.
Natuurlijke selectie, doelgerichtheid en een uitzonderlijke samenloop van omstandigheden: Een kritiek op F Soontiëns. SLURINK, Pouwel.
El papel de la comunicación espontánea en los procesos de evolución social. RODRÍGUEZ HÖLKEMEYER, Patricia.
El paradigma de sistemas: posibilidades para una prácica social emancipadora. RODRÍGUEZ HÖLKEMEYER, Patricia.
Peirce and Evolution: Comment on O'Hear. GOMILA, Antoni.
The Phenotype as the Level of Selection: Cave organisms as Model Systems. KANE, Thomas C and RICHARDSON, Robert C and FONG, Daniel W.
Philosophy and Cognitive Science (in Czechoslovakian). PSTRUZINA, Karel.
The Physiology of Moral Maturity. HEMMING, James.
Political Culture and Institution Building: Democratic Evolution at Work and the Case of Poland. LAMENTOWICZ, Wojtek.
Por um novo modelo de saber: Problemática do discurso Filosófico-Teológico. DINIS, Alfredo.
Rationality, Culture and Values. CHATTOPADHYAYA, D P.
Religion and Cultural Evolution. MASSIMINI, Fausto and FAVE, Antonella Delle.
Representations of the Natural System in the Nineteenth Century. O'HARA, Robert J.
Reward, Punishment, and the Strategy of Evolution. SCHRADER, Malcolm E.
The Semantic Approach to Evolutionary Theory. ERESHEFSKY, Marc.
Species, Higher Taxa, and the Units of Evolution. ERESHEFSKY, Marc.
Sulla posizione dell'uomo nella natura. SEIDL, Horst.
The Process of Evolution in a Holistic World (in German). SOSCHINKA, Hans-Ulrich.
What Is This Stuff Called Fitness?. OLLASON, J G.
What Makes Us So Different from the Apes?. LAYNG, Tony.
Why Natural Selection Leads to Complexity. BENZON, William L and HAYS, David G.

EVOLUTIONARY EPISTEMOLOGY

Comprehensive Evolutionary Epistemology Bibliography. CZIKO, Gary A and CAMPBELL, Donald T.
Conceptual Selection. HULL, David L.
On Naturalizing Epistemology. ALMEDER, Robert.
On the Possibility of Directed Mutations in Bacteria: Statistical Analyses and Reductionist Strategies. SARKAR, Sahotra.
Scientific Pluralism and the Plurality of the Sciences: Comments on David Hull's *Science as a Process*. DUPRÉ, John.

EVOLUTIONARY ETHICS

"The Significance of Evolution" in *A Companion to Ethics*, RUSE, Michael.
"Natur" als Massstab menschlichen Handelns. BIRNBACHER, Dieter.
The Changing Nature of the Social Sciences. MASTERS, Roger D.
Evolutionary Ethics and the Search for Predecessors: Kant, Hume, and All the Way Back to Aristotle?. RUSE, Michael.
Evolutionary Naturalistic Justifications of Morality: A Matter of Faith and Works. ROTTSCHAEFER, William A.
Evolved Ethics Re-Examined: The Theory of Robert J Richards. WILLIAMS, Patricia.
The Origins of Morality: An Essay in Philosophical Anthropology. OLDENQUIST, Andrew.
Warum lebt der Mensch moralisch?. BURKHARDT, Cornelia and FRANKENHÄUSER, Gerald.

EVOLUTIONISM

Hayek's Theory of Cultural Evolution: An Evaluation in the Light of Vanberg's Critique. HODGSON, Geoffrey M.
Marx and the Problem of Conflicting Models of History. BEST, Steven.
Theory and Reality in the Work of Jean Henry Fabre. YAVETZ, Ido.

EXAMINATION(S)

Enumerations of Turing Ideals with Applications. MARKER, David.

EXAMPLE(S)

Against the Fantasts. THOMAS, J L H.
The Contingent *A Priori*: Kripke's Two Types of Examples. GEIRSSON, Heimir.
Practical Intuition and Rhetorical Example. SCHOLLMEIER, Paul.

EXCELLENCE

Variações sobre o *De Interpretatione*, de Aristóteles. ROSA, Joaquim Coelho.

EXCHANGE(S)

Once Again Pure Exchange Economies: A Critical View Towards the Structuralistic Reconstructions by Balzer & Stegmüller. REQUATE, Till.
Shareholder Authorized Inside Trading: A Legal and Moral Analysis. SHAW, Bill.

EXCLUDED MIDDLE

Intuitionistic Mathematics and Wittgenstein. GONZALEZ, Wenceslao J.
The Ontological Status of the Principle of the Excluded Middle. STRAUSS, Daniël F M.

EXCLUSION

Feminist Theory and the Politics of Inclusion. FISHER, Linda.

EXCLUSION PRINCIPLE

El principio de exclusión y sus aplicaciones. GARZÓN, León.

EXCLUSIONARY RULE

The Exclusion of Evidence Obtained by Constitutionally Impermissible Means in Canada. MC DONALD, David C.
Law and Exclusionary Reasons. ALEXANDER, Larry.

EXECUTIVE(S)

The Moral Responsibility of Corporate Executives for Disasters. BISHOP, John D.
Weakness of Will as a Species of Executive Cowardice. SWANTON, Christine.

EXEGESIS

"Augustine and Poetic Exegesis" in *Grace, Politics and Desire: Essays on Augustine*, WESTRA, Haijo J.
The Literal Sense of Scripture. WILLIAMS, Rowan.
The Structure of Philo's Commentary on the Pentateuch. THORNE, Gary W A.

EXEMPLIFICATION

Makin on the Ontological Argument. OPPY, Graham.

EXISTENCE

see also Being, Dasein, Ontology, Reality
The Balance of Consciousness: Eric Voegelin's Political Theory. KEULMAN, Kenneth.
Cálculo y ser (Aproximación a Leibniz). MARZOA, Felipe Martínez.
Caminhos do Filosofar. MIRANDA, Maria do Carmo Tavares de.
The Co-Existence of God and Evil. TRAU, Jane Mary.
Does God Exist? The Great Debate. MORELAND, J P.
Existence et Subjectivité: Études de Psychologie Phénoménologique. THINÈS, Georges.
In Defense of Mystical Ideas: Support for Mystical Beliefs from a Purely Theoretical Viewpoint. CHAPMAN, Tobias.
La intersubjectividad en Husserl, Volume I and II. IRIBARNE, Julia V.
Material Beings. VAN INWAGEN, Peter.
Metaphysics: A Contemporary Introduction. POST, John F.
Mind Only: A Philosophical and Doctrinal Analysis of the Vijñānavāda. WOOD, Thomas E.
The Ontology of Physical Objects: Four-Dimensional Hunks of Matter. HELLER, Mark.
An Outline of the Philosophy of Knowledge and Science. BLANDINO, Giovanni.
Published Essays, 1966-1985 (The Collected Works of Eric Voegelin, Volume 12). SANDOZ, Ellis (ed).
The Self-Overcoming of Nihilism: Nishitani Keiji. PARKES, Graham (trans).
Spirit and Existence: A Philosophy Inquiry into the Meaning of Spiritual Existence. GELVEN, Michael.
"Arguments for the Existence of God" in *Key Themes in Philosophy*, SWINBURNE, R G.
"Nietzsche: Art and Existence" in *XIth International Congress in Aesthetics, Nottingham 1988*, DAVEY, J R N.
"Predicates of Pure Existence: Newton on God's Space and Time" in *Philosophical Perspectives on Newtonian Science*, MC GUIRE, J E.
"Referring to Things That No Longer Exist" in *Philosophical Perspectives, 4: Action Theory and Philosophy of Mind, 1990*, CHISHOLM, Roderick M.
"Travels in the Postmodern: Making Sense of the Logical" in *Feminism/Postmodernism*, PROBYN, Elspeth.
The Antinomy of Divine Necessity. SCHRADER, David E.
Art for Existence's Sake: A Heideggerian Revision. SCHUMACHER, Paul J.
The Chicken and the Egg. TEICHMANN, Roger.
Coming To Be Without a Cause. SULLIVAN, T D.
Contingency and Modal Logic. DEUTSCH, Harry.
La dimostrazione "a posteriori" dell'esistenza di Dio nella filosofia di Leibniz. NICOLOSI, Salvatore.
A Disproof of the Existence of God. WEEKS, Ian.
La distinción entre esencia y existencia en Avicena. IBÁÑEZ, Alejandro Herrera.
The Existence of Non-Existence of Things which are Not in the Mind. POMERANTZ, Alfred.
Filosofia dell'esistenza e cristologia: La Weltanschauung cristiana di R Guardini. DI MARCO, Chiar.
Foi et intelligence dans l'"unique arguments": Un plan pour "Proslogion II-IV". LABBÉ, Y.
Heidegger's Attempt at Rehousing Man Through the *Kehre des Denkens*. RAUCHE, G A.
Hume and Belief in the Existence of an External World. COSTA, Michael J.
Hume on the Idea of Existence. CUMMINS, Phillip D.
In Defence of Heidegger. JANUSZ, Sharon and WEBSTER, Glenn.
Is Coming to Believe in God Reasonable or Unreasonable?. HERBERT, R T.
Kierkegaard irrazionalista? Filosofi e filosofie nella interpretazione del filosofo danese. FRANCHI, Alfredo.
L'affirmation de l'existence de Dieu selon Austin Farrer. HENDERSON, Edward H.
The Latin Avicenna as a Source of Thomas Aquinas's Metaphysics. WIPPEL, John F.
Not Over Yet: Prior's 'Thank Goodness' Argument'. KIERNAN-LEWIS, Delmas.
L'odissea dell'ateismo e del nichilismo. FABRO, Cornelio.
On "Why is There Something Rather Than Nothing?". KUSCH, Martin.
On Wishing there were Unicorns. CLARK, Stephen R L.
Reply to Davies: Creation and Existence. VALLICELLA, William F.
Reply to Smith: The Question of Idealism. VALLICELLA, William F.
A significação "crítica" de Le volontaire et l'involontaire. HENRIQUES, Fernanda.
Simultaneity, Conventionality and Existence. PETKOV, Vesselin.
St Augustine and the Second Way. KLUGE, Eike-Henner W.
Visione in Dio e visione di Dio nella filosofia di Malebranche. NICOLOSI, Salvatore.
The What and the How. ALMOG, Joseph.

EXISTENTIAL

A Philosophy of Morals. HELLER, Agnes.
"The Existential Sublime: From Burke's Aesthetics to the Socio-Political" in *XIth International Congress in Aesthetics, Nottingham 1988*, CROWTHER, Paul.
The *Sinnsfrage* and the *Seinsfrage*. PROTEVI, John.

EXISTENTIALISM

see also Alienation, Being, Death, Essence(s), Existence, Nihilism
Critique of Dialectical Reason, Volume 2: Jean-Paul Sartre. HOARE, Quintin (trans).
Dämonie und Gesellschaft. CATTEPOEL, Jan.
Existentialism. COOPER, David E.
Exploring Phenomenology (Second Edition). STEWART, David.
For Self-Examination: Judge for Yourself. HONG, Howard V (ed & trans).
Franz Rosenzweig: Existentielles Denken und gelebte Bewährung. SCHMIED-KOWARZIK, Wolfdietrich.
Geschichte, Freiheit und Struktur. RUMPEL, Roland.
Historische Objektivitat. WEBERMAN, David.
Jean-Paul Sartre. HENGELBROCK, Jürgen.
Kierkegaards Phänomenologie der Freiheitserfahrung. DISSE, Jörg.
Living the Good Life: An Introduction to Moral Philosophy. GRAHAM, Gordon.
Phenomenology of the Truth Proper to Religion. GUERRIÈRE, Daniel (ed).
The Power of Consciousness and the Force of Circumstances in Sartre's Philosophy. BUSCH, Thomas W.
The Question of God in Heidegger's Phenomenology. KOVACS, George.
Readings in Existential Psychology and Psychiatry. HOELLER, Keith (ed).
Sacred Fragments: Recovering Theology for the Modern Jew. GILLMAN, Neil.
Vulgarity and Authenticity: Dimensions of Otherness in the World of Jean-Paul Sartre. CHARMÉ, Stuart Zane.
Authenticity: A Sartrean Perspective. CATALANO, Joseph.
Dasein—Mitsein—Sprache: Heideggers Auffassung über das "Wesen der Sprache" in "Sein und Zeit". TIETZ, Udo.
F M Dostoievsky (1821-1881): Great Existentialist-Psychiatrist. ESSER, P H.
Fault-Lines in Kierkegaard and Hawthorne: *The Sickness unto Death* and "Ethan Brand". BENOIT, Raymond.
From Nothingness to No-thing-ness: the Roots of Ferry and Renaut's Humanism. BARBIERO, Daniel.
Heideggers Bedeutung für die Psychologie. VON USLAR, Detlev.
Hierofanías: Una retrospectiva de la obra de Ludwig Schajowicz. KERKHOFF, Manfred.
Husserl's Notion of Constitution in Heidegger's Treatment of Care. THOMAS, V C.
Das Individuum, die Politik und die Philosophie. GRUNWALD, Sabine.
Marcel on the Problem of Freedom. SUGUMAR, Devaki.
Nietzsche on Authenticity. GOLOMB, Jacob.
La passione dell'essere: Viaggio lungo i sentieri del nulla. IANNOTTA, Daniella.
Le pouvoir, existential de l'être humain. SCHÜSSLER, Werner.
Psychanalyse et existentialisme: A propos de la théorie lacanienne de la subjectivité. VAN HAUTE, P.
Sartre and his Successors: Existential Marxism and Postmodernism at Our *Fin de Siecle*. MC BRIDE, William L.
Sartre on Anguish. JAMBOR, Mishka.
The Sociology of Knowledge: Toward an Existential View of Business Ethics. PHILLIPS, Nelson.
Tareas y métodos en la ética del desarrollo. GOULET, Denis.
The Foundations of Franz Rosenzweig's Theory of Knowledge (in Hebrew). AMIR, Yehoyada.
Viktor Emil Frankl médico y filósofo. ALEGRÍA, Hernando Muciño.

EXIT

Exit, Voice, and Ethics. KEELEY, Michael and GRAHAM, Jill W.

EXPECTATION(S)
Bayes' Bayesianism. EARMAN, John.
Psychology and Standards of Reasonable Expectation. SCHOEMAN, Ferdinand.

EXPERIENCE(S)
see also Aesthetic Experience(s)
The Critical Problem of Knowledge. BLANDINO, Giovanni (ed).
David Hume: Historiker und Philosoph. LÜTHE, Rudolf.
Experiential Method: Qualitative Research in the Humanities Using Metaphysics and Phenomenology. KIDD, James W.
Human Consciousness. HANNAY, Alastair.
Identity and Discrimination. WILLIAMSON, Timothy.
In Defense of Mystical Ideas: Support for Mystical Beliefs from a Purely Theoretical Viewpoint. CHAPMAN, Tobias.
John Dewey: Religious Faith and Democratic Humanism. ROCKEFELLER, Steven C.
Logic in the Husserlian Context. TITO, Johanna Maria.
The Political Philosophy of Michael Oakeshott. FRANCO, Paul.
A Post-Modern Epistemology. SORRI, Mari.
Published Essays, 1966-1985 (The Collected Works of Eric Voegelin, Volume 12). SANDOZ, Ellis (ed).
Reasons and Experience. MILLAR, Alan.
The Unity of Kant's "Critique of Pure Reason": Experience, Language, and Knowledge. WILLIAMS, T C.
"Cultural Tradition, Historical Experience, and Social Change: The Limits of Convergence" in *The Tanner Lectures on Human Values, Volume XI*, EISENSTADT, S N.
"Experiencing Art" in *XIth International Congress in Aesthetics, Nottingham 1988*, ROBINSON, Jenefer.
"The Intrinsic Quality of Experience" in *Philosophical Perspectives, 4: Action Theory and Philosophy of Mind, 1990*, HARMAN, Gilbert.
"Modest Realism, Experience and Evolution" in *Harré and His Critics*, MANICAS, Peter.
"A noção de experiência nos diálogos platónicos" in *Dinâmica do Pensar: Homenagem a Oswaldo Market*, SANTOS, José Trindade.
"Event" in Dewey's Philosophy. DUFF, Barry E.
"Seeing Things". PIPER, Adrian M S.
The Argument from Religious Experience: A Narrowing of Alternatives. KETCHUM, Richard.
Bodily Theory and Theory of the Body. GILES, James.
Consciousness and Synchronic Identity. MATHESON, Carl.
Cool Red. LEVINE, Joseph.
Dall'attualismo al tensionalismo. SIMONE, Aldo.
The De-Con-Struction of Reason. GLYNN, Simon.
Desacralization and the Disenchantment of the World. WENNEMANN, Daryl.
Divenire, principio di causalità, affermazione teologica. SACCHI, Dario.
È possibile un'esperienza di Dio?. CAVADI, Augusto.
Edward Bullogh's Aesthetics and Aestheticism: Features of Reality to Be Experienced. BOULTING, Noel E.
The Evidence of Experience. SCOTT, Joan W.
Experience and Causal Explanation in Medical Empiricism. PENTZOPOULOU-VALALAS, Teresa.
Experience of the Alien in Husserl's Phenomenology. WALDENFELS, Bernhard.
Externalism and Experience. MC CULLOCH, Gregory.
Filosofia dell'esistenza e cristologia: La Weltanschauung cristiana di R Guardini. DI MARCO, Chiar.
From the Phenomenology of Time Toward Process Metaphysics: Pragmatism and Heidegger. ROSENTHAL, Sandra B.
Gustavo Bontadini un metafisico per vocazione. LATORA, Salvatore.
Hamanns Metakritik im ersten Entwurf. BAYER, Oswald.
Juicios de percepción y de experiencia en Kant. FERNÁNDEZ, Alvaro López.
The Justification of Kepler's Ellipse. BAIGRIE, Brian S.
Lezioni di filosofia della scienza di Guilio Preti. LECIS, Pier Luigi.
Metaphysik und Erfahrung in Kants Grundlegung der Ethik. CRAMER, Konrad.
Metaphysik und Erfahrung. BUBNER, Rüdiger.
On the Epistemic Value of Moral Experience. TOLHURST, William.
Philosophical Asceiticism (in French). DE MONTICELLI, Roberta.
Piper's Criteria of Theory Selection. POSTOW, B C.
Qualia and Theory Reduction: A Criticism of Paul Churchland. BACHRACH, Jay E.
The Reformed Subjectivist Principle Revisited. FORD, Lewis S.
Relativism, Ineffability, and the Appeal to Experience: A Reply to the Myth Makers. BARNES, L Philip.
Reply to Levine's "Cool Red". HARDIN, C L.
Scepticism: Three Recently Presented Arguments Examined. DURRANT, Michael.
Sense-Experience and the Argument for Recollection in Plato's *Phaedo*. BEDU-ADDO, J T.
Sex, Drugs and Rock 'n Roll: Youth, Instruction and Experience in Contemporary American Film. ANGELO, Richard.
The Subject of Experience. GILLETT, Grant.
Le supplément poétique. WATTEYNE, Nathalie.
Die Verfehlung des Themas "Metaphysik und Erfahrung". WIEHL, Reiner.
Wanted Dead or Alive: Two Attempts to Solve Schrödinger's Paradox. ALBERT, David and LOEWER, Barry.
What is it Like to be an Aardvark?. TIGHLMAN, B R.

EXPERIMENT(S)
Experiment: Right or Wrong. FRANKLIN, Allan.
"Reason and Experiment in Newton's *Opticks*: Comments on Peter Achinstein" in *Philosophical Perspectives on Newtonian Science*, HUGHES, R I G.
Can a Theory-Laden Observation Test the Theory?. FRANKLIN, A (and others).
On the Locus of Medical Discovery. REINES, Brandon P.
The Participant Irrealist At Large in the Laboratory. HACKING, Ian.
Reproducibility as a Methodological Imperative in Experimental Research. HONES, Michael.

EXPERIMENTAL
"Experimental Realism" in *Harré and His Critics*, ARONSON, Jerry.
"Newton's Corpuscular Query and Experimental Philosophy" in *Philosophical Perspectives on Newtonian Science*, ACHINSTEIN, Peter.
Is History and Philosophy of Science Withering on the Vine?. FULLER, Steve W.
Scientific Evidence: Creating and Evaluating Experimental Instruments and Research Techniques. BECHTEL, William.

EXPERIMENTALISM
L'étude du vivant et la méthodologie ouverte. PILET, Paul-Emile.

EXPERIMENTATION
The Crisis in Health Care: Ethical Issues. MC KENZIE, Nancy F (ed).
"The Psychoanalytic Enterprise in Scientific Perspective" in *Scientific Theories*, GRÜNBAUM, Adolf.
Hacking's Experimental Argument for Realism. HOLCOMB III, Harmon R.
Probabilistic Causality from a Dynamical Point of View. VON PLATO, Jan.
A Reply to Mayo's Criticisms of Urbach's "Randomization and the Design of Experiments". URBACH, Peter.
Scientific Realism and Experimental Practice in High-Energy Physics. HONES, Michael J.
Uninformed Consent. MARCUS, Ruth Barcan and KUCKLICK, B and BERCOVITCH, S.
Volunteering Children. MC DONNELL, Kevin.

EXPERT(S)
Bioethics on Trial. CAPLAN, Arthur L.

EXPERTISE
Consensus of Expertise: The Role of Consensus of Experts in Formulating Public Policy and Estimating Facts. VEATCH, Robert M.
The Epistemology and Ethics of Consensus: Uses and Misuses of 'Ethical' Expertise. TONG, Rosemarie.

EXPLANATION
see also Causal Explanation
Criteria of Certainty: Truth and Judgment in the English Enlightenment. COPE, Kevin L.
Critical Traditions in Contemporary Archaeology. PINSKY, Valerie (ed).
Explaining Religion: Criticism and Theory from Bodin to Freud. PREUS, J Samuel (ed).
Intelligibility in Science. DILWORTH, Craig (ed).
Knowledge in Flux: Modeling the Dynamics of Epistemic States. GÄRDENFORS, Peter.
The Metaphysics of Religious Belief. SHOOMAN, A P.
Varieties of Social Explanation: An Introduction to the Philosophy of Social Science. LITTLE, Daniel.
"Content, Context and Explanation" in *Information, Semantics and Epistemology*, STAMPE, Dennis W.
"Efficient Explanations and Efficient Behaviour" in *Critical Traditions in Contemporary Archaeology*, SALMON, Merrilee H.
"Explanation and Understanding in the Science of Human Behavior" in *Reconsidering Psychology: Perspectives from Continental Philosophy*, SCHRAG, Calvin O.
"Folk Psychology and the Explanation of Human Behavior" in *Philosophical Perspectives, 3: Philosophy of Mind and Action Theory, 1989*, CHURCHLAND, Paul M.
"Functional Explanations and Reasons as Causes" in *Philosophical Perspectives, 3: Philosophy of Mind and Action Theory, 1989*, SAYRE-MC CORD, Geoffrey.
"Inference to the Best Explanation in Archaeology" in *Critical Traditions in Contemporary Archaeology*, HANEN, Marsha and KELLEY, Jane.
"Meaning and Explanation" in *Themes From Kaplan*, MORAVCSIK, Julius.
"Mechanism, Purpose, and Explanatory Exclusion" in *Philosophical Perspectives, 3: Philosophy of Mind and Action Theory, 1989*, KIM, Jaegwon.
"Ways of Establishing Harmony" in *Information, Semantics and Epistemology*, DENNETT, Daniel C.
Action and Explanation. MAJUMDAR, Aruna.
An Anomaly in the D-N Model of Explanation. BLUM, Alex.

EXPLANATION

Assessing Functional Explanations in the Social Sciences. KINCAID, Harold.

Azar y explicación: Algunas observaciones. PÉREZ RANSANZ, Ana Rosa.

Cartesian Skepticism and Inference to the Best Explanation. VOGEL, Jonathan.

Causal Propensities: Statistical Causality versus Aleatory Causality. SALMON, Wesley C.

Causes and Coincidences. OWENS, David.

Ceteris Paribus Laws. SCHIFFER, Stephen.

The Chromosome Theory of Mendelian Inheritance: Explanation and Realism in Theory Construction. VICEDO, Marga.

Concepts of Process in Social Science Explanations. VAYDA, Andrew P and MC CAY, Bonnie J and EGHENTER, Cristina.

The Concrete and the Abstract Science: Description versus Explanation. GUPTA, Amitabha.

Connectionism, Competence, and Explanation. CLARK, Andy.

Contents and Causes: A Reply to Blackburn. STURGEON, Nicholas L.

Contrastive Explanations. LIPTON, Peter.

Does Representational Content Arise from Biological Function?. HALL, Richard J.

Dretske on the Explanatory Role of Belief. BAKER, Lynne Rudder.

An Epistemic Analysis of Explanations and Causal Beliefs. GÄRDENFORS, Peter.

Explanation and Causality: Some Suggestions from Econometrics. GALAVOTTI, Maria Carla.

Explanation and Scientific Realism. GASPER, Philip.

Explanation and the Theory of Questions. CROSS, Charles B.

Explanation and Understanding in Social Science. SKORUPSKI, John.

Explanation in Biology. SMITH, John Maynard.

Explanation in Physical Theory. CLARK, Peter.

Explanation, Causation and Laws. EDGINGTON, Dorothy.

Explanation—Opening Address. SMART, J J C.

Explanation-Explication Conflict in Transformational Grammar. DAS GUPTA, Amitabha.

Explanation. REDHEAD, Michael.

The Explanatory Tools of Theoretical Population Biology. COOPER, Gregory.

Fitness and Evolutionary Explanation. BYERLY, Henry C and MICHOD, Richard E.

Fitness and Evolutionary Explanation: A Response. BYERLY, Henry C and MICHOD, Richard E.

A Genetic Exploration of Women's Subjugation: The Adventures of a Gadfly. MITTRA, Aditya Barna.

How Beliefs Explain: Reply to Baker. DRETSKE, Fred.

How Do Scientific Explanations Explain?. KINOSHITA, Joyce.

How to Put Questions to Nature. SINTONEN, Matti.

How's and Why's: Causation Un-Locked. FRANKEL, Lois.

Independence from Future Theories: A Research Strategy in Quantum Theory. RUEGER, Alexander.

The Inference to the Best Explanation. BEN-MENAHEM, Y.

Intentionalistic Explanations in the Social Sciences. SEARLE, John R.

Just Causes. BLACKBURN, Simon.

Kitcher and Salmon's *Scientific Explanation*; and Salmon's *Four Decades of Scientific Explanation*. FETZER, James H.

Limited Explanations. CLARK, Stephen R L.

The Limits of Explanation. SWINBURNE, Richard.

Mathematical Modelling and Constrastive Explanation. MORTON, Adam.

The Metaphoric Structure of Sociological Explanation. CORRADI, Consuelo.

More on Russell's Hypothesis. HINDERLITER, Hilton.

A Note on Van Fraassen's Explanatory Contrastiveness. PAPRZYCKA, Katarzyna.

Philosophy of Science: From Justification to Explanation. KANTOROVICH, Aharon.

Prediction and Explanation in Economics. SWAMIDASAN, Nalini.

Preemption, Direct Causation, and Identity. EHRING, Douglas.

The Problem of Other Cultures and Other Periods in Action Explanations. MARTIN, Rex.

Rational Choice Theory Considered as Psychology and Moral Philosophy. MONGIN, Philippe.

Real Dispositions in the Physical World. THOMPSON, Ian J.

The Real Meaning of 'Meaning'. CARTER, Alan.

Reply to Sturgeon's "Contents and Causes" A Reply to Blackburn. BLACKBURN, Simon.

Scientific Explanation: Causation *and* Unification. SALMON, Wesley C.

The Semantic Approach to Evolutionary Theory. ERESHEFSKY, Marc.

Singular Causation and Law. IRZIK, Gürol.

Singular Explanation and the Social Sciences. RUBEN, David-Hillel.

Social Science Knowledge and Explanations in Educational Studies. DALE, Michael.

Statistical Explanation, Probability, and Counteracting Conditions. GRIMES, Thomas R.

Stich, Content, Prediction, and Explanation in Cognitive Science. WALLIS, Charles S.

Theoretical Explanation and Errors of Measurement. FORGE, John.

Tipos ideales en historia. TOZZI, María Verónica.

What is so Practical about Theory? Lewin Revisited. SANDELANDS, Lloyd E.

What is the Explanandum of the Anthropic Principle?. WILSON, Patrick A.

Wittgenstein on Freud's 'Abominable Mess'. CIOFFI, Frank.

You Can Fool Some of the People All of the Time, Everything Else Being Equal; Hedged Laws and Psychological Explanation. FODOR, Jerry A.

EXPLICATION

Doxology and the History of Philosophy. NORMORE, Calvin G.

Explanation-Explication Conflict in Transformational Grammar. DAS GUPTA, Amitabha.

EXPLOITATION

Marx's Radical Critique of Capitalist Society: A Reconstruction and Critical Evaluation. ARNOLD, N Scott.

Resurrecting Marx: The Analytical Marxists on Freedom, Exploitation, and Justice. GORDON, David.

From Class Struggle to Struggle without Classes?. BALIBAR, Etienne.

Is Collaborative Research Exploitative?. LADWIG, James G.

Nietzsche's Environmental Ethics. HALLMAN, Max O.

The Politics and Morality of Unequal Exchange: Emmanuel and Roemer, Analysis and Synthesis. SCHWEICKART, David.

EXPORTATION

A Notorious Affair Called Exportation. BURDICK, Howard.

EXPRESSIBILITY

Mathematical Expressibility, Perceptual Relativity, and Secondary Qualities. PEREBOOM, Derk.

EXPRESSION(S)

Contemplating Music—Source Readings in the Aesthetics of Music, Volume II: Import. KATZ, Ruth (ed).

Estetica: Come Scienza dell'Espressione e Linguistica Generale. CROCE, Benedetto.

"Phénoménologie" de l'expression. CHAUVIRE, Christiane.

Eléments pour une philosophie de l'expression. UCCIANI, Louis.

Expressions versus Numbers. WETZEL, Linda.

Just Can't Find the Words: How Expression is Achieved. KING, Debra W.

Musical Time as a Practical Accomplishment: A Change in Tempo. WEEKS, P A D.

Problèmes de l'expression. ROSSET, Clément.

Vérité à Faire: Merleau-Ponty's Question Concerning Truth. WALDENFELS, Bernhard.

Wittgenstein on Tolstoi's *What is Art*?. BEARDSMORE, R W.

EXPRESSIONISM

Expressionism in Philosophy: Spinoza. DELEUZE, Gilles.

Qu'est-ce que l'expressionnisme allemand?. RICHARD, Lionel.

EXPRESSIVENESS

Expressive Completeness and Decidability. SCHUMM, George and SHAPIRO, Stewart.

EXTENSION

"On the Existence of End Extensions of Models of Bounded Induction" in *Logic, Methodology and Philosophy of Science, VIII*, WILKIE, A.

About Prikry Generic Extensions. SURESON, Claude.

Bayle, Leibniz, Hume and Reid on Extension, Composites and Simples. CUMMINS, Phillip.

Cloture Intervallaire et Extension Logique d'une Relation. ILLE, Pierre.

Double Extension Set Theory. KISIELEWICZ, Andrzej.

Effective Extensions of Partial Orders. KUMAR ROY, Dev.

Some Extensions of Built-Upness on Systems of Fundamental Sequences. KADOTA, Noriya.

Zeno's Paradox of Extension. MC KIE, John R.

EXTENSIONALITY

"Why Intensionalists Ought Not Be Fregeans" in *Truth and Interpretation: Perspectives on the Philosophy of Donald Davidson*, KATZ, Jerrold J.

Extensionality, Underdetermination and Indeterminacy. SOLOMON, Miriam.

New Semantics for the Extensional but Hyper-Intensional Part..... BRESSAN, Aldo.

EXTERNAL WORLD

Knowledge of the External World. AUNE, Bruce.

"Our Perception of the External World" in *Key Themes in Philosophy*, TILES, J E.

"The Problem of the External World" in *Key Themes in Philosophy*, HAMLYN, D W.

How Not to Russell Carnap's *Aufbau*. RICHARDSON, Alan.

Scepticism: The External World and Meaning. BAR-ON, Dorit.

Why the Problem of the External World is a Pseudo-Problem: Santayana and Danto. SHIRLEY, Edward S.

EXTERNALISM

Epistemic Justification: Essays in the Theory of Knowledge. ALSTON, William P.

Knowledge in Perspective: Selected Essays in Epistemology. SOSA, Ernest.

The Mind of Donald Davidson. BRANDL, Johannes (ed).

"The Conditions of Thought" in *The Mind of Donald Davidson*, DAVIDSON, Donald.

"Externalizing Content" in *The Mind of Donald Davidson*, POTRC, Matjaz.

"Skepticism and Rationality" in *Doubting: Contemporary Perspectives on Skepticism*, FOLEY, Richard.

EXTERNALISM
Boors and Bumpkins, Snobs and Snoots. GODLOVITCH, S.
Externalism and Experience. MC CULLOCH, Gregory.
Externalism and Marr's Theory of Vision. FRANCESCOTTI, Robert M.
Externalism Revisited: Is There Such a Thing as Narrow Content?. JACOB, Pierre.
Externalist Theories of Perception. ALSTON, William P.

FABRE, J
Theory and Reality in the Work of Jean Henry Fabre. YAVETZ, Ido.

FACT(S)
Being True to the World: Moral Realism and Practical Wisdom. JACOBS, Jonathan A.
Morals, Motivation and Convention: Hume's Influential Doctrines. SNARE, Francis.
"Fact and Fiction" in *Reading Rorty*, CLARK, Michael.
"Facts and Values in the Physician-Patient Relationship" in *Ethics, Trust, and the Professions: Philosophical and Cultural Aspects*, BROCK, Dan W.
"Reason, Spontaneity, and the *Li*—A Confucian Critique of Graham's Solution to the Problem of Fact and Value" in *Chinese Texts and Philosophical Contexts*, FINGARETTE, Herbert.
"Who Chooses?" in *Chinese Texts and Philosophical Contexts*, ROSEMONT JR, Henry.
'Is' Therefore 'Ought'. VERMA, Roop Rekha.
How Wide Is the Gap Between Facts and Values?. RESCHER, Nicholas.
The Nature of Moral Facts. ROSS, Steven.
On Judicial Ascertainment of Facts. VARGA, Csaba.
Preconditions of Predication: From Qualia to Quantum Mechanics. FORSTER, Malcolm.
Questioni di filosofia politica. VECA, Salvatore.
La ragione e i valori nella determinazione delle norme. CORTESE, Roberto.
Truths without Facts. SEN, Pranab Kumar.

FACULTY(-TIES)
The Faculty of Desire. LACHTERMAN, David.

FAILURE(S)
"The Justification of Negation as Failure" in *Logic, Methodology and Philosophy of Science, VIII*, FINE, Kit.
Market Order or Commanded Chaos. FLEW, Antony.
Risk, Commitment, and Project Abandonment. DEVANEY, Mike.

FAIRNESS
"On Fair Distribution of Indivisible Goods" in *Logic and Ethics*, SZANIAWSKI, Klemens.
Do the Right Thing. SUTTLE, Bruce B.
Four Arguments Against Political Obligations from Gratitude. KLOSKO, George.
Games, Fairness, and Rawls's *A Theory of Justice*. LADEN, Anthony.
Justice in Preferential Hiring. SINGER, M S and SINGER, A E.
The Justification of Justice as Fairness: A Two Stage Process. VAGGALIS, Ted.
Knowing and Valuing Fairness. HINTON, J M.
Nozick on Rights and Minimal State. AGARWALA, Binod Kumar.
The Teacher as Judge: A Brief Sketch of Two Fairness Principles. KATZ, Michael S.
Testing Fairmindedness. FISHER, Alec.

FAITH
see also Belief(s)
Being and Becoming: A Critique of Post-Modernism. CENTORE, F F.
Blaise Pascals: "Pensées" (1656-1662) Systematische 'Gedanken' über. KIRSCH, Ulrich.
Christian Faith and Historical Understanding (Second Edition). NASH, Ronald H.
For What May I Hope? Thinking with Kant and Kierkegaard. FENDT, Gene.
How to Play Theological Ping-Pong: And Other Essays on Faith and Reason. ABRAHAM, William J (ed).
Human Interests: Reflections on Philosophical Anthropology. RESCHER, Nicholas.
Inscriptions and Reflections: Essays in Philosophical Theology. SCHARLEMANN, Robert P.
Thomistic Papers, V. RUSSMAN, Thomas A (ed).
"Faith and Goodness" in *The Philosophy in Christianity*, STUMP, Eleonore S.
"Faith and Rationality" in *Key Themes in Philosophy*, BARRETT, D C.
"A Faith of True Proportions: Reply to Sullivan" in *Thomistic Papers, V*, RUSSMAN, Thomas A.
"Kierkegaard's Phenomenology of Faith as Suffering" in *Writing the Politics of Difference*, WESTPHAL, Merold.
"A Reply to Russman's 'A Faith of True Proportions'" in *Thomistic Papers, V*, SULLIVAN, Thomas D.
"Faith" in a Broad Sense as a Goal in Promoting Human Development. BECK, Clive.
"Kierkegaardian Faith: 'The Condition' and the 'Response'. FERREIRA, M Jamie.
Animal Faith, Puritanism, and the Schutz-Gurwitsch Debate: A Commentary. LYMAN, Stanford M.
The Assurance of Faith. WOLTERSTORFF, Nicholas.
The Authorship of Faith. SESSIONS, W L.
La crisi dei fondamenti della scienza: Un recupero dell'ilemorfismo?. DEL RE, Giuseppe.
Da secularidade da Filosofia. COUTINHO, Jorge.
Does Faith Create Its Own Objects?. MAC KINNON, Donald M.
Doubt and Faith: Santayana and Kierkegaard on Fundamental Belief. SARTWELL, Crispin.
Down to Earth and Up to Religion: Kantian Idealism in Light of Kierkegaard's Leap of Faith. PERL, Paul.
L'emozione creatrice: Il significato della morale nella prospettiva di Bergson. PESSINA, Adriano.
Faith and Reason: Reflections on MacIntyre's 'Tradition-constituted Enquiry'. MARKHAM, Ian.
Faith and the Possibility of Private Meaning. GURREY, Charles S.
The Faith Dimension of Humanism. EARLES, Beverley.
Faith in the Open Society: The Limits of Hermeneutics. AGASSI, Joseph.
Filosofía y fe en Descartes. FERNANDEZ, Javier.
Flaw, Conformity of Critical Dialogue? (in French). BÜHLER, Pierre.
Foi et intelligence dans l'"unique arguments": Un plan pour "Proslogion II-IV". LABBÉ, Y.
Jewish Faith and the Holocaust. COHN-SHERBOK, Dan.
Kierkegaard's Pragmatist Faith. EMMANUEL, Steven M.
The Knight of Faith. ADAMS, Robert Merrihew.
L'"irrisio fidei" chez Raymond Lulle et S Thomas D'Aquin. SERVERAT, Vincent.
Masaryk's Religious Thinking (in Czechoslovakian). FUNDA, Otakar A.
Multiple Realities in Santayana's Last Puritan. VAITKUS, Steven.
The Nature of Faith: Religious, Monotheistic, and Christian. YANDELL, Keith E.
A New Humanism. CHURCH, F Forrester.
Ontological Reductionism and Faith Versus Reason: A Critique of Adams on Ockham. FREDDOSO, Alfred J.
El proyecto crítico de Kant. CHAVES, Carmen.
A Reflection on Saint Augustine's *Confessions*. BARKOVICH, Greg.
As relações entre o Deus da Razão e o Deus da Fé. RENAUD, Michel.
The Relevance of Historical Evidence for Christian Faith: A Critique of a Kierkegaardian View. EVANS, C Stephen.
Sant'Agostino e Hegel a confronto. CALEO, Marcello.
Saving Faith from Kant's Remarkable Antinomy. QUINN, Philip L.
Scientia e fide. BLANDINO, Giovanni.
Technological Faith and Christian Doubt. FERRÉ, Frederick.
The Philosophical Invariables of Masaryk's Thinking (in Czechoslovakian). SROVNAL, Jindrich.
Toward a Pragmatic Conception of Religious Faith. GOLDING, Joshua L.
Understanding the Question: Wittgenstein on Faith and Meaning. EISENSTEIN, Gabe.
Ungeklärte Fragen im Dialog zwischen Glaube und Naturwissenschaft. FISCHER, Johannes.
Verità di ragione e verità di fede. MESSINESE, Leonardo.
Would Hegel Have Liked to Burn Down All the Churches and Replace Them with Philosophical Academies?. LUFT, Eric V D.

FALLACY(-CIES)
The Elements of Reasoning. CONWAY, David.
'*P*, Therefore, *P*' Without Circularity. SORENSEN, Roy A.
Authority. WILLARD, Charles A.
A Critical Note on J S Mill's Classification of Fallacies. HON, Giora.
Hamblin on the Standard Treatment. JOHNSON, Ralph H.
The Pragmatic Fallacy. SALMON, Nathan.

FALLIBILISM
Pragma-Dialectics: A Radical Departure in Fallacy Theory. WOODS, John.

FALLIBILITY
Experiment: Right or Wrong. FRANKLIN, Allan.
The Fallibility Paradox. LEHRER, Keith and KIM, Kihyeon.

FALSE
False Consciousness. MEYERSON, Denise.
Mannheim and Hungarian Marxism. GABEL, Joseph.
Are All False Theories Equally False? A Remark on David Miller's Problem and Geometric Conventionalism. MORMANN, Thomas.

FALSIFIABILITY
The Degeneration of Popper's Theory of Demarcation. GRÜNBAUM, Adolf.
Una discussione di epistemologia. BLANDINO, Giovanni and FEDERSPIL, G.
A Kuhnian Model of Falsifiability. STONE, Mark A.
A Note on Popper's Equation of Simplicity with Falsifiability. TURNEY, Peter.

FALSIFICATION
A Hindu Perspective on the Philosophy of Religion. SHARMA, Arvind.
"Falsificationism Looked at from an 'Economic' Point of View" in *Imre Lakatos and Theories of Scientific Change*, RADNITZKY, Gerard.
Assessing Human Needs. JONES, John D.
Falsification and Disconfirmation in Cosmology. ZYCINSKI, Joseph.
On Falsificationist Interpretations of Peirce. SULLIVAN, Patrick F.
Research Programmes and Empirical Results. AKEROYD, F M.
Verification, Falsification and Cancellation in KT. WILLIAMSON, Timothy.
Verification, Falsification, and the Logic of Enquiry. MILNE, Peter.

FAMILY
Euthanasia: Toward an Ethical Social Policy. THOMASMA, David C.
To Die or Not to Die?. BERGER, Arthur S (ed).
"Mill's Second Prize in the Lottery of Life" in *A Cultivated Mind: Essays On J S Mill Presented to John M Robson*, ROBSON, Ann P.
"Surrogacy and the Family: Social and Value Considerations" in *Beyond Baby M: Ethical Issues in New Reproductive Techniques*, ASCH, Adrienne.
Artificial Means of Reproduction and Our Understanding of the Family. MACKLIN, Ruth.
Do These Feminists Like Women?. SOMMERS, Christina.
Equal Opportunity and the Family. VALLENTYNE, Peter and LIPSON, Morry.
Justice, Redistribution, and the Family. POST, Stephen G.
Rousseau's Political Defense of the Sex-Roled Family. WEISS, Penny.

FAMILY RESEMBLANCE(S)
On Boyd. HACKING, Ian.
Wittgenstein on Names and Family Resemblances. HYMERS, Michael.

FAMINE
African Famine: New Economic and Ethical Perspectives. LUCAS JR, George R.
Famine and Charity. WHELAN JR, John M.

FANATICISM
The Other Nietzsche: Criticism of Moral Utopia (in German). MAURER, Reinhart.

FANFANI, A
Capitalismo, Socialidad y participación. PASSANITI, Daniel.

FANG, D
Traditional Chinese Culture: Contemporary Developments —Profound Selections from the Works of Fang Dongmei. GUOBAO, Jiang.

FANON, F
Critical Fanonism. GATES JR, Henry Louis.

FANTASY
Against the Fantasts. THOMAS, J L H.

FARABI
see Al-Farabi

FARBER, M
Phenomenology as Cooperative Task: Husserl-Farber Correspondence during 1936-37. CHO, Kah Kyung.

FARIAS, V
Heidegger After Farias. ROCKMORE, Tom.

FARMING
Farming Salmon Ethically. NEEDHAM, E A and LEHMAN, Hugh.

FARRER, A
L'affirmation de l'existence de Dieu selon Austin Farrer. HENDERSON, Edward H.

FASCISM
"World War II and the Anti-Democratic Impulse in Catholicism" in *From Twilight to Dawn: The Cultural Vision of Jacques Maritain*, HELLMAN, John.
Nietzsche and Fascism. WILLIAMS, Howard.

FASHION
"The Limits and Possibilities of Fashion in Painting" in *XIth International Congress in Aesthetics, Nottingham 1988*, WINTERS, E J.
"Obsolescence and Desire: Fashion and the Commodity Form" in *Postmodernism—Philosophy and the Arts (Continental Philosophy III)*, FAURSCHOU, Gail.

FATALISM
The Law of Karma: A Philosophical Study. REICHENBACH, Bruce R.

FATE
Das Verhängnis Erste Philosophie. EBELING, Hans.

FAUSTIAN
Faustian Phenomena: Teleology in Goethe's Interpretation of Plants and Animals. CORNELL, John F.

FEAR
Yoga on War and Peace. TIGUNAIT, Pandit Rajmani.
Emotions, Feelings and Contexts: A Reply to Robert Kraut. SOLOMON, Robert C.
The Incoherence and Irrationality of Philosophers. RADFORD, Colin.

FEDIER, F
Note sulle recenti traduzioni di *Essere e tempo* in Francia. MARRATI, Paola.

FEELING(S)
see also Emotion(s)
Musical Aesthetics: A Historical Reader, Volume III, The Twentieth Century. LIPPMAN, Edward A (ed).
The Case of the Unmitigated Blackguard or Saving Kant's Moral Feelings. EARLS, Anthony.
A Critical Examination of Scheler's Justification of the Existence of Values. MOOSA, Imtiaz.
Emotions, Feelings and Contexts: A Reply to Robert Kraut. SOLOMON, Robert C.
What is Wrong With Wicked Feelings?. ROBERTS, Robert C.

FEINBERG, J
Prohibiting Immorality. WESTMORELAND, Robert.
The Rights-Interpretation of Desert. GARCÍA, Jorge.

FELICITY
The Early Essays and Ethics of Robert Boyle. HARWOOD, John T (ed).

FEMININE
Language and "The Feminine" in Nietzsche and Heidegger. GRAYBEAL, Jean.
Re-Reading Levinas. BERNASCONI, Robert (ed).
"Antigone's Dilemma" in *Re-Reading Levinas*, CHANTER, Tina.
"Ethics and the Feminine" in *Re-Reading Levinas*, CHALIER, Catherine.
"Questions to Emmanuel Levinas: On the Divinity of Love" in *Re-Reading Levinas*, WHITFORD, Margaret (trans) and IRIGARAY, Luce.

FEMININITY
Femininity and Domination: Studies in the Phenomenology of Oppression. BARTKY, Sandra Lee.
Self, Society, and Personal Choice. MEYERS, Diana T.

FEMINISM
see also Woman, Women
Abeunt Studia in Mores: A Festschrift for Helga Doblin. MERRILL, Sarah A Bishop (ed).
Bakhtin and the Epistemology of Discourse. THOMSON, Clive (ed).
Contemporary Perspectives on Masculinity: Men, Women, and Politics in Modern Society. CLATTERBAUGH, Kenneth.
Delicate Subjects: Romanticism, Gender, and the Ethics of Understanding. ELLISON, Julie.
Essentially Speaking: Feminism, Nature and Difference. FUSS, Diana.
Ethics, Politics, and Human Nature. PAUL, Ellen Frankel (ed).
Femininity and Domination: Studies in the Phenomenology of Oppression. BARTKY, Sandra Lee.
Feminism/Postmodernism. NICHOLSON, Linda J (ed).
Feminist Ethics. CARD, Claudia (ed).
French Philosophers in Conversation: Levinas, Schneider, Serres, Irigaray, Le Doeuff, Derrida. MORTLEY, Raoul.
Patterns of Dissonance. BRAIDOTTI, Rosi.
Socialism, Feminism and Philosophy: A Radical Philosophy Reader. SAYERS, Sean (ed).
Whose Science? Whose Knowledge? Thinking from Women's Lives. HARDING, Sandra.
Writing the Politics of Difference. SILVERMAN, Hugh J (ed).
"Biblical Story and the Heroine" in *The Bible as Rhetoric: Studies in Biblical Persuasion and Credibility*, STOCKER, Margarita.
"Docile Bodies, Rebellious Bodies" in *Writing the Politics of Difference*, BORDO, Susan.
"Ethics of Method: Greasing the Machine and Telling Stories" in *Feminist Ethics*, TREBILCOT, Joyce.
"The Feistiness of Feminism" in *Feminist Ethics*, CARD, Claudia.
"Feminism and Peace Theory: Women as Nurturers versus Women as Public Citizens" in *In the Interest of Peace: A Spectrum of Philosophical Views*, DUHAN, Laura.
"Feminism, Science, and the Anti-Enlightenment Critiques" in *Feminism/Postmodernism*, HARDING, Sandra.
"Feminist Ethics: Projects, Problems, Prospects" in *Feminist Ethics*, JAGGAR, Alison M.
"A Feminist Theory of Social Differentiation" in *Feminism/Postmodernism*, YEATMAN, Anna.
"Gender Trouble, Feminist Theory, and Psychoanalytic Discourse" in *Feminism/Postmodernism*, BUTLER, Judith.
"The Idea of a Female Ethic" in *A Companion to Ethics*, GRIMSHAW, Jean.
"Marie le Jars de Gournay" in *A History of Women Philosophers, Volume II: Medieval, Renaissance and Enlightenment, A.D. 500-1600*, ZEDLER, Beatrice H.
"On the Logic of Pluralist Feminism" in *Feminist Ethics*, LUGONES, Maria C.
"Postmodernism and Other Skepticisms" in *Feminist Ethics*, PIERCE, Christine.
"Rationality, Relativism, Feminism" in *Writing the Politics of Difference*, WINANT, Terry.
"Reconnecting: A Reply to Robert Moore" in *Archetypal Process: Self and Divine in Whitehead, Jung, and Hillman*, KELLER, Catherine.
"A Response to *Lesbian Ethics*: Why Ethics?" in *Feminist Ethics*, FRYE, Marilyn.
"Social Criticism without Philosophy: An Encounter between Feminism and Postmodernism" in *Feminism/Postmodernism*, FRASER, Nancy and NICHOLSON, Linda J.
"Some Thoughts about 'Caring'" in *Feminist Ethics*, HOAGLAND, Sarah Lucia.
"Travels in the Postmodern: Making Sense of the Logical" in *Feminism/Postmodernism*, PROBYN, Elspeth.
"What's Wrong with Bitterness?" in *Feminist Ethics*, MC FALL, Lynne.
"Double Trouble": An Introduction. FRASER, Nancy.

FEMINISM
"El segundo sexo", vigencia y proyección. COMESAÑN SANTALICES, Gloria M.
"They Lived Happily Ever After": Sommers on Women and Marriage. FRIEDMAN, Marilyn.
"To Illuminate Your Trace": Self in Late Modern Feminist Theology. KELLER, Catherine.
Anarchism and Feminism. MOODY, Thomas E.
The Artificial Womb—Patriarchal Bone or Technological Blessing?. HEDMAN, Carl.
The Baby with a Gun: A Feminist Inquiry Into Plausibility, Certainty and Context in Moral Education. THOMPSON, Audrey.
Campanella's "Civitas Solis" Is Ruled by Love Without Emotion (in German). ZÖHRER-ERNST, Ulla.
Caring About Nature: Feminist Ethics and the Environment. KING, Roger J H.
Cartesian Feminists. LONGACRE, Judith.
Comment on Romain's "Feminist Reflections on Humans and Other Domestic Animals. RUD JR, Anthony G.
The Crisis in Psychoanalysis: Resolution Through Husserlian Phenomenology and Feminism. NISSIM-SABAT, Marilyn.
Cultural Theory Looks at Identity and Contradiction. COCKS, Joan.
Deep Ecology versus Ecofeminism: Healthy Differences or Incompatible Philosophies?. SESSIONS, Robert.
Disarming the Baby with the Gun: Reply to Audrey Thompson. GLASS, Ronald David.
Do These Feminists Like Women?. SOMMERS, Christina.
Does Sommers Like Women? More on Liberalism, Gender Hierarchy, and Scarlett O'Hara. FRIEDMAN, Marilyn.
Ecofeminism and Androcentric Epistemology. DURAN, Jane.
Ecofeminism and the Eating of Animals. ADAMS, Carol J.
Ecofeminist Theory and Grassroots Politics. LAHAR, Stephanie.
Ecological Feminism and Ecosystem Ecology. WARREN, Karen J and CHENEY, Jim.
Environmental Ethics and the Case for Hunting. KING, Roger J H.
An Ethical Justification of Women's Studies, Or What's a Nice Girl Like You Doing in a Place like This?. MC GRATH, Lynette.
Feminism and Ecology: On the Domination of Nature. MILLS, Patricia Jagentowicz.
Feminism and Epistemology. CHANDLER, John.
Feminism and Philosophy of Science. LONGINO, Helen E.
Feminism and Pluralism in Contemporary Theology. STENGER, Mary Ann.
Feminism and Relativism. RUSSELL, Denise.
Feminist Ethics and Case-Based Reasoning: A Marriage of Purpose. RIESBECK, Christopher K and MORPHIS, Maxine.
Feminist Fears in Ethics. NODDINGS, Nel.
Feminist Philosophy and the Genetic Fallacy. CROUCH, Margaret A.
Feminist Reflections on Humans and Other Domestic Animals. ROMAIN, Dianne.
The Feminist Revelation. SOMMERS, Christina.
Feminist Second Thoughts About Free Agency. BENSON, Paul.
Feminist Spirituality as a Path to Humanism. FRANKEL, Lois.
Feminist Theory and Its Discontents. TRESS, Daryl Mc Gowan.
Feminist Theory and the Politics of Inclusion. FISHER, Linda.
Feminist Theory, Plurality of Voices and Cultural Imperialism. HERNANDEZ, Adriana.
Feminist Transformations of Moral Theory. HELD, Virginia.
A Genetic Exploration of Women's Subjugation: The Adventures of a Gadfly. MITTRA, Aditya Barna.
Ground, Pivot, Motion: Ecofeminist Theory, Dialogics, and Literary Practice. MURPHY, Patrick.
Hegel's Critical Theory and Feminist Concerns. HAYIM, Gila J.
Historicisms New and Old: "Charles Dickens" Meets Marxism, Feminism, and West Coast Foucault. NEWTON, Judith.
History as Geneology: Wittgenstein and the Feminist Deconstruction of Objectivity. LAMPSHIRE, Wendy L.
How to Construe Nature: Environmental Ethics and the Interpretation of Nature. KING, Roger J H.
I Love Myself When I am Laughing: A New Paradigm for Sex. DAVIS, Karen Elizabeth.
The Jargon of Authenticity: Adorno and Feminist Essentialism. PHELAN, Shane.
L'homme n'est pas l'humain. BOUCHARD, Guy.
Loving Your Mother: On the Woman-Nature Relationship. ROACH, Catherine.
The Morality of Feminism. SEVENHUIJSEN, Selma.
Motherhood and the Possibility of a Contemporary Discourse for Women. GREY, Mary.
Mothers of In(ter)vention: Women's Writing in Philosophy of Education. LEACH, Mary S.
Ms en abyme: Deconstruction and Feminism. ELAM, Diane.
Nature, Self, and Gender: Feminism, Environmental Philosophy, and the Critique of Rationalism. PLUMWOOD, Val.
Nietzsche and the Woman Question. DIETHE, Carol.
Nietzsche in Derrida's *Spurs*: Deconstruction as Deracination. FREYDBERG, Bernard D.
Nietzsche on Woman. THOMPSON, J L.
On African Feminism: Two Reasons for the Rejection of Feminism. KWAME, Safro.
On the Empirical Status of Radical Feminism: A Reply to Schedler. MUI, Constance L.
One Man's Reflection on a Masculine Role in Feminist Ethics: Epistemic versus Political Privilege. BOYD, Dwight.
The Philosopher's Prism: Foucault, Feminism, and Critique. ALADJEM, Terry K.
Postcritical Religion and the Latent Freud. KEISER, R Melvin.
Pour une interprétation féministe de l'idée chrétienne de Dieu. DION, Michel.
Reason and Emotion. FRICKER, Miranda.
Reconstructing the Subject: Feminism, Modernism, and Postmodernism. HEKMAN, Susan.
Remaking the She-Devil: A Critical Look at Feminist Approaches to Beauty. DAVIS, Kathy.
A Response to Beck, Giarelli/Chambliss, Leach, Tozer, and Macmillan. GREENE, Maxine.
Rethinking Feminist Humanism. STRAUS, Nina Pelikan.
Rethinking the Family. KYMLICKA, Will.
Revealing Gendered Texts. FREELAND, Cynthia A.
Sartre and Sexism. BARNES, Hazel E.
Starting Thought From Women's Lives: Eight Resources for Maximizing Objectivity. HARDING, Sandra.
The Subject in Feminism. BRAIDOTTI, Rosi.
Teaching Feminist Ethics as Male Consciousness-Raising. WALTON, Barbara J.
Thinking the Other Without Violence? An Analysis of the Relation Between the Philosophy of Lévinas and Feminism. MANNING, Robert J S.
Toward A Value-Laden Theory: Feminism and Social Science. BERNICK, Susan E.
Toward An Ecological Ethic of Care. CURTIN, Deane.
Towards a Feminist Reassessment of Intellectual Virtue. BRAATEN, Jane.
Twenty Years Since *Women and Madness*: Toward a Feminist Institute of Mental Health and Healing. CHESLER, Phyllis.
The Unavoidability of Gender. SCHEMAN, Naomi.
Using Arendt and Heidegger to Consider Feminist Thinking on Women and Reproductive/Infertility Technologies. KLAWITER, Maren.
The Vita Femina and Truth. BURNEY-DAVIS, Terri and KREBBS, R Stephen.
Where Are All the Pragmatist Feminists?. SEIGFRIED, Charlene Haddock.
Women's Law. DUXBURY, Neil.
Your Daughter or Your Dog? A Feminist Assessment of the Animal Research Issue. SLICER, Deborah.

FENELON, F
Filosofia e ascesi nel Seicento: Il caso francese. BOSCO, Domenico.

FENNER, D
Quantum Realism: A Reply to Professor Fenner. BENNETT, Barbara J.

FERDINAND THE CATHOLIC
The Foxy Prophet: Machiavelli versus Machiavelli on Ferdinand the Catholic. ANDREW, Edward.

FERGUSON
Johan Jacob Ferguson, geb um 1630 im Haag(?), gest vor dem 24 November 1706, vermutlich am 6 Oktober 1691 in Amsterdam. VAN MAANEN, Jan A.

FERRY, D
"David Ferry's Paradise of Form" in *Abeunt Studia in Mores: A Festschrift for Helga Doblin*, WEST, Philip.

FESSARD, G
Gabriel Marcel na correspondência com Gaston Fessard. CABRAL, Roque.

FETISHISM
Historizing contra fetishizing—The Progress of Modern Technology in W Benjamin's Aesthetic Reflexion (in German). WAGNER, Gerhard.
L'écriture réparatrice. HAREL, Simon.

FETUS(ES)
"Anencephalics as Organ Donors" in *Biomedical Ethics Reviews, 1989*, THOMASMA, David C.
"Should Abnormal Fetuses Be Brought to Term for the Sole Purpose of Providing Infant Transplant Organs?" in *Biomedical Ethics Reviews, 1989*, GRABER, Glenn C.
'Fetal Rights'? An Attempt to Render Plausible a Conservative Response. HODAPP, Paul.
Are Pregnant Women Fetal Containers?. PURDY, Laura.
Delivering Hydrocephalic Fetuses. STRONG, Carson.
The Enforcement of Moral Obligations to Potential Fetuses: Johnson Controls versus the UAW. WHITE, Ronald F.
Ethics, Public Policy, and Human Fetal Tissue Transplantation. CHILDRESS, James F.
Fetal Neural Transplantation: Placing the Ethical Debate within the Context of Society's Use of Human Material. JONES, D Gareth.
Law Without Values: Do the Unborn Have to Wait for a Consensus?. VACCARI, Michael A.
Maternal Rights, Fetal Harms: Commentary. KINLAW, Kathy.

FETUS(ES)
Maternal Rights, Fetal Harms: Commentary. STRONG, Carson.
Natural Fetal Dependency States and Fetal Dependency Principles. HERBENICK, Raymond M.
Pharaoh's Magicians: The Ethics and Efficacy of Human Fetal Tissue Transplants. BARRY, Robert and KESLER, Darrel.
Philosophische Uberlegungen zu "Menschenwürde" und Fortpflanzungs-Medizin. SCHÖNE-SEIFERT, Bettina.

FEUERBACH
God and Subjectivity. GALGAN, Gerald J.
"A imortalidade do escritor—Filosofia do pensar e da morte no jovem Feuerbach" in *Dinâmica do Pensar: Homenagem a Oswaldo Market*, SERRÁO, Adriana Veríssimo.
Escaping from Reality or Coming to Terms with It—What is Religion? (in German). POLLACK, Detlef.

FEYERABEND, P
The Social Horizon of Knowledge. BUCZKOWSKI, Piotr (ed).
"Beyond Objectivity and Relativism: Feyerabend's 'Two Argumentative Chains' and Sociology" in *The Social Horizon of Knowledge*, JARY, David.
Goodbye and Farewell: Siegel versus Feyerabend. NORDMANN, Alfred.
Positivism and the Pragmatic Theory of Observation. OBERDAN, Thomas.
Scientific Rationality—A Rethinking. CHAUDHURY, Mahasweta.

FICHTE
Fichte's Theory of Subjectivity. NEUHOUSER, Frederick.
Das Ich im deutschen Idealismus und das Selbst im Zen-Buddhist Fichte und Dogen. NAGASAWA, Kunihiko.
Moralische Verbindlichkeit oder Erziehung. LANGEWAND, Alfred.
Reflexion und Metareflexion bei Platon und Fichte. ZEHNPFENNIG, Barbara.
"O inimigo da liberdade: sobre o sentido do materialismo para Fichte" in *Dinâmica do Pensar: Homenagem a Oswaldo Market*, BARATA-MOURA, José.
"Kant and Fichte: An Ethics of Self-Respect in Individualism" in *Abeunt Studia in Mores: A Festschrift for Helga Doblin*, ECKBLAD, Joyce.
"Romantic Philosophy and Organization of the Disciplines: the Founding of the Humboldt University of Berlin" in *Romanticism and the Sciences*, SHAFFER, Elinor S.
"Der geschlossne Handelsstaat"—Zur konservativen Kritik einer aufklärerischen Utopie. MARQUARDT, Jochen.
Anerkennung: Fichtes Grundlegungen des Rechtsgrundes. JANKE, Wolfgang.
Brentano e Fichte negli scritti "minori" di E Husserl. BELLO, A Ales.
Fichte on Skepticism. BREAZEALE, Daniel.
Schopenhauer und Fichtes Schrift "Die Bestimmung des Menschen". DECHER, Friedhelm.
Von der dreifachen Vollendung des Deutschen Idealismus und der unvollendeten metaphysischen Wahrheit. JANKE, Wolfgang.

FICTION(S)
Fictions of Reality in the Age of Hume and Johnson. DAMROSCH, Leo.
Knowledge, Fiction, and Imagination. NOVITZ, David.
Mimesis as Make-Believe: On the Foundations of the Representational Arts. WALTON, Kendall L.
"Fact and Fiction" in *Reading Rorty*, CLARK, Michael.
"Illocutionary Pretence Inside and Outside Fiction" in *XIth International Congress in Aesthetics, Nottingham 1988*, TSOHATZIDIS, S L.
"Make-Believe, Ontology and Point of View" in *XIth International Congress in Aesthetics, Nottingham 1988*, LAMARQUE, Peter.
Can Fiction Be Stranger Than Truth? An Aristotelian Answer. GALLOP, David.
Deceptive Comfort: The Power of Kafka's Stories. BENNETT, Jane.
Fictional Objects in Literature and Mental Representations. BACHRACH, Jay E.
Henry James and the Paradox of Literary Mastery. BLAIR, Sara.
The Incoherence and Irrationality of Philosophers. RADFORD, Colin.
Plato's *Statesman* Story: The Birth of Fiction Reconceived. TOMASI, John.
Predication, Fiction, and Artificial Intelligence. RAPAPORT, William J.
Tendencias actuales en filosofía de la tecnología. CAMACHO, Luis.
The Status of Fiction: Between Nostalgia and Nihilism (in French). IMHOOF, Stefan.
Visual Fictions. CURRIE, Gregory.
Who's Afraid of Virginia Woolf?. MATRAVERS, Derek.

FICTIONALITY
Mathematics and Oliver Twist. MADDY, Penelope.
Mathematics Without Truth (A Reply to Maddy). FIELD, Hartry.

FIDEISM
"Christian Averroism, Fideism and the 'Two-fold Truth'" in *The Philosophy in Christianity*, BROWN, Stuart.
Fideísmo y autoritarismo en Lutero. CAPPELLETTI, Angel.

FIDELITY
A intersubjectividade em Gabriel Marcel. MORUJÁO, Alexandre Fradique.

FIELD THEORY
Distant Action in Classical Electromagnetic Theory. MUNDY, Brent.
Prolegomenon to a Proper Interpretation of Quantum Field Theory. TELLER, Paul.

FIELD(S)
Decidable Fragments of Field Theories. TUNG, Shih-Ping.
Differentially Algebraic Group Chunks. PILLAY, Anand.
On the Angular Component Map Modulo *P*. PAS, Johan.
Relative Elimination of Quantifiers for Henselian Valued Fields. BASARAB, Serban A.
Schanuel's Conjecture and Free Exponential Rings. MACINTYRE, Angus.

FIELD, H
Physicalism in Mathematics. IRVINE, Andrew D (ed).
"Field and Fregean Platonism" in *Physicalism in Mathematics*, WRIGHT, Crispin.
"Knowledge of Mathematical Objects" in *Physicalism in Mathematics*, PAPINEAU, David.
"The Logic of Physical Theory" in *Physicalism in Mathematics*, URQUHART, Alasdair.
"Nominalism" in *Physicalism in Mathematics*, HALE, Bob.
"Physicalism, Reductionism and Hilbert" in *Physicalism in Mathematics*, HALLETT, Michael.
"Physicalistic Platonism" in *Physicalism in Mathematics*, MADDY, Penelope.
Mathematics and Oliver Twist. MADDY, Penelope.
Truth and Language-World Connections. GROVER, Dorothy.

FIFTEENTH CENTURY
see Renaissance

FILM
"Creative Intuition in American Film: Maritain at the Movies" in *From Twilight to Dawn: The Cultural Vision of Jacques Maritain*, LAUDER, Robert E.
"Filming: Inscriptions of *Denken*" in *Postmodernism—Philosophy and the Arts (Continental Philosophy III)*, WURZER, Wilhelm S and SILVERMAN, Hugh J.
Growing Up on Screen—Images of Instruction. HANSEN, Karen.
Kansas, Oz, and the Function of Art. CONLON, James.
Sex, Drugs and Rock 'n Roll: Youth, Instruction and Experience in Contemporary American Film. ANGELO, Richard.
Visual Fictions. CURRIE, Gregory.

FILON OF ALEXANDRIA
Ontologia e creazione in Filone Alessandrino: Dialogo con Giovanni Reale e Roberto Radice. MARTÍN, Josè Pablo.

FILTER(S)
Absolutely Independent Sets of Generation of Filters in Boolean Algebras. GRYGIEL, Joanna.
Full Reflection of Stationary Sets Below $\aleph_\omega$. JECH, Thomas and SHELAH, Saharon.
A Hierarchy of Ramsey Cardinals. FENG, Qi.
The Normal Depth of Filters on an Infinite Cardinal. DI PRISCO, C A and FULLER, M and HENLE, J M.
Relatively Congruence-Distributive Subquasivarieties of Filtral Varieties. CZELAKOWSKI, Janusz.

FINALITY
Le existentia de deo e le Immortalitate del Anima: Lineas de Philosophia del Esser. BLANDINO, Giovanni.
Nietzsche e Spinoza. BIUSO, Alberto G.

FINANCE
A Thinker's Guide to Living Well. BRADFORD, Dennis E.
Business Ethics and Social Responsibility in Finance Instruction: An Abdication of Responsibility. HAWLEY, Delvin D.

FINE ART(S)
"The Concept of Fine Art: A Critique" in *XIth International Congress in Aesthetics, Nottingham 1988*, LORD, C.

FINE, A
Comment: Selective Anti-Realism. MC MULLIN, Ernan.
Contemporary Shapes of Scientific Realism (in Czechoslovakian). PARUSNIKOVA, Zuzana.
Fine's "Shaky Game" (and Why Noa is No Ark for Science). SCHLAGEL, Richard H.

FINE, K
Instantial Terms, Anaphora and Arbitrary Objects. KING, Jeffrey C.

FINITE
"Finite Idealism: The Midworld and Its History" in *The Philosophy of John William Miller*, CORRINGTON, Robert S.
Finite Axiomatizability and Theories with Trivial Algebraic Closure. MACPHERSON, Dugald.
Finite Logics and the Simple Substitution Property. HOSOI, Tsutomu and SASAKI, Katsumi.
Hereditarily Finite Finsler Sets. BOOTH, David.
The Idea of Transcendence. COBURN, Robert C.
A Metatheorem for Constructions by Finitely Many Workers. KNIGHT, J F.
Modal Counterparts of Medvedev Logic of Finite Problems Are Not Finitely Axiomatizable. SHEHTMAN, Valentin.
N-Normal Factors in Finite Symmetric Heyting Algebras. GALLI, Adriana C and SAGASTUME, Marta.

FINITE MODEL PROPERTY
A Solution to a Problem of Urquhart. KRACHT, Marcus.

FINKLESTEIN, D
Logic, Contradiction and Quantum Theory. SMITH, Joseph Wayne.

FINNIS, J
Does the Grisez-Finnis-Boyle Moral Philosophy Rest on a Mistake?. VEATCH, Henry and RAUTENBERG, Joseph.

FINNISH
Gelehrter zwischen Romantik und Hegelianismus in Finnland—Johan Vilhelm Snellman (1806-1881). HÄNTSCH, Carola.

FINSEN, S
Response to Finsen's "Response to Lizst's Animal Liberation as a Valid Response to Structural Violence". LISZT, Amy.

FIRST CAUSE
'What Place, then, for a creator?': Hawking on God and Creation. CRAIG, William Lane.

FIRST ORDER THEORY(-RIES)
First-Order Theories Without Axioms. STEPIEN, Teodor.
The Undecidability of *k*-Provability. BUSS, Samuel R.

FIRST PHILOSOPHY
God and Subjectivity. GALGAN, Gerald J.

FIRST PRINCIPLE(S)
Introduction to the Philosophy of Nature. HETZLER, Florence M.

FIRTH, R
Firth and the Ethics of Belief. CHISHOLM, Roderick M.
Firth's Critique of Epistemological Rule-Utilitarianism. SHOPE, Robert K.
Philosophical Reminiscences with Reflections on Firth's Work. PUTNAM, Hilary.
Roderick Firth's Contribution to Ethics. BRANDT, R B.
Roderick Firth: His Life and Work. RAWLS, John.

FISCHER, J
On J L Fischer's Reflections About Categories of Dialectic Materialism (in Czechoslovakian). TOSENOVSKY, Ludvik.

FISHER, R
On the Necessity for Random Sampling. JOHNSTONE, D J.

FISHKIN, J
Equal Opportunity and the Family. VALLENTYNE, Peter and LIPSON, Morry.

FISSION
"Fission and the Facts" in *Philosophical Perspectives, 3: Philosophy of Mind and Action Theory, 1989*, JOHNSTON, Mark.
Identity, Transformation, and What Matters in Survival. MARTIN, Raymond.

FITNESS
Adequacy Criteria for a Theory of Fitness. ROSENBERG, Alexander.
Byerly and Michod on Fitness. SMITH, John Maynard.
Commentary on Byerly and Michod. LENNOX, James G.
Commentary on the Paper by H C Byerly and R E Michod's "Fitness and Evolutionary Explanation". BRITO DA CUNHA, A.
Comments on "Fitness and Evolutionary Explanation". KLEINER, Scott A.
Fitness and Evolutionary Explanation. BYERLY, Henry C and MICHOD, Richard E.
Fitness and Evolutionary Explanation: A Response. BYERLY, Henry C and MICHOD, Richard E.
Natural Selection as Natural History. VAN DER STEEN, Wim J.
On Causality, Heritability and Fitness. ETTINGER, Lia and JABLONKA, Eva and FALK, Raphael.
On the Adaptations of Organisms and the Fitness of Types. ETTINGER, Lia and JABLONKA, Eva and MC LAUGHLIN, Peter.
Persistent Propensities: Portrait of a Familiar Controversy. NORDMANN, Alfred.
What Is This Stuff Called Fitness?. OLLASON, J G.

FIXED POINT(S)
"Degrees of Functions with No Fixed Points" in *Logic, Methodology and Philosophy of Science, VIII*, JOCKUSCH JR, Carl G.
A Constructive Version of Sperner's Lemma and Brouwer's Fixed Point Theorem. KHALIFA, A K.
Fixed Points and Diagonal Method. NEGRI, Maurizio.
The Homogeneous Form of Logic Programs with Equality. DEMOPOULOS, William.
A Note on Some Extension Results. MONTAGNA, Franco and SOMMARUGA, Giovanni.

FLAND, R
El tratado de las obligaciones dialógicas en la Edad Media: el caso de Robert Fland. BEUCHOT, Mauricio.

FLECK, L
Thomas S Kuhn and L Fleck: Two Sociologists of Science. FLURI, Philippe H.

FLETCHER, J
Principle Monism and Action Descriptions: Situationism and its Critics Revisited. PINCHES, Charles.

FODOR, J
The Representational Theory of Mind: An Introduction. STERELNY, Kim.
Connectionist Minds. CLARK, Andy.
Intentionality and Modern Philosophical Psychology, I: The Modern Reduction of Intentionality. LYONS, William.
Mental Misrepresentation. MALONEY, J Christopher.
Modularity of Mind Revisited. BENNETT, Laura J.
Must Psychology Be Individualistic?. EGAN, Frances.
Narrow Content: Fodor's Folly. ADAMS, Fred and DREBUSHENKO, David and FULLER, Gary and STECKER, Robert.
Remarks on the Modularity of Mind. SHANNON, Benny.

FOGELIN, R
Fogelin on Hume on Miracles. FLEW, Antony.

FOLDUARY, F
Response: Subjective Values and Objective Values. MACHAN, Tibor R.

FOLK PSYCHOLOGY
"Connectionism, Eliminativism and the Future of Folk Psychology" in *Philosophical Perspectives, 4: Action Theory and Philosophy of Mind, 1990*, RAMSEY, William and STICH, Stephen and GARON, Joseph.
"Folk Psychology and the Explanation of Human Behavior" in *Philosophical Perspectives, 3: Philosophy of Mind and Action Theory, 1989*, CHURCHLAND, Paul M.
Belief Attribution in Science: Folk Psychology under Theoretical Stress. TROUT, J D.
Functional Support for Anomalous Monism. EDWARDS, Jim.
In Defense of Southern Fundamentalism. HORGAN, Terence and GRAHAM, George.

FOOD
A Critical Look at Arguments for Food Irradiation. SMITH, Tony.

FOOT, P
Knowing and Valuing Fairness. HINTON, J M.

FORBES, G
Forbes's Branching Conception of Possible Worlds. MILLS, Eugene.

FORCE(S)
"Camus Revisited: Neither Victim nor Executioner" in *In the Interest of Peace: A Spectrum of Philosophical Views*, BOVE, Laurence.
"Moral Counterforce" in *In the Interest of Peace: A Spectrum of Philosophical Views*, LEE, Steven.
"On the Deep Structure of Violence" in *In the Interest of Peace: A Spectrum of Philosophical Views*, LITKE, Robert.
"Philosophical Perspectives on Newtonian Science" in *Philosophical Perspectives on Newtonian Science*, HUGHES, R I G.
Boskovic on His Own Theory of Forces: From a Sentence to the Theory of Natural Philosophy (in Serbo-Croatian). MARTINOVIC, Ivica.
Boskovic's Theory of Forces in His Treatise "De Continuitatis Lege" (in Serbo-Croatian). BRUNSKO, Zagorka.
Giacomo Andrea Giacomini: un clinico padovano tra Metafisica e Scienza. FEDERSPIL, Giovanni.

FORCING
About Prikry Generic Extensions. SURESON, Claude.
Effective Model Theory versus Recursive Model Theory. CHISHOLM, John.
Full Reflection of Stationary Sets Below $\aleph_\omega$. JECH, Thomas and SHELAH, Saharon.
The Kunen-Miller Chart (Lebesgue Measure, the Baire Property, Laver Reals and Preservation Theorems for Forcing). JUDAH, Haim and SHELAH, Saharon.
Partition Properties and Prikry Forcing on Simple Spaces. HENLE, J M.
Some Results on Higher Suslin Trees. DAVID, R.
Successors of Singular Cardinals and Measurability Revisited. APTER, Arthur W.

FORECASTING
Ethics and Advocacy in Forecasting for Public Policy. WACHS, Martin.

FOREIGN POLICY
Jeffersonian Ethics in Foreign Affairs: John Quincy Adams and the Moral Sentiments of a Realist. RUSSELL, Greg.

FOREKNOWLEDGE
The Dilemma of Freedom and Foreknowledge. ZAGZEBSKI, Linda Trinkaus.
"Beyond Foreseeability: Consequential Damages in the Law of Contract" in *Liability and Responsibility*, EPSTEIN, Richard A.
"Foreknowledge and the Vulnerability of God" in *The Philosophy in Christianity*, LUCAS, J R.
Foreknowledge, Middle Knowledge and "Nearby" Worlds. DAVISON, Scott A.
A New Foreknowledge Dilemma. ZAGZEBSKI, Linda.
A Problem for the Eternity Solution. WIDERKER, David.
Providence, Freedom and Human Destiny. TALBOTT, Thomas.

FORGERY(-RIES)
Simon and Socrates. BRUMBAUGH, Robert S.

FORGIVENESS
Forgiveness: A Christian Model. ADAMS, Marilyn McCord.

FORM(S)

see also Essence(s), Idea(s)
Introduction to the Philosophy of Nature. HETZLER, Florence M.
Linguistic Behaviour. BENNETT, Jonathan.
The Philosopher's Joke. WATSON, Richard A.
Philosophie Juridique Européenne. TRIGEAUD, Jean-Marc.
Plato's "Parmenides". MEINWALD, Constance C.
The Political Ontology of Martin Heidegger. BOURDIEU, Pierre.
Aristotelian Form and End. CURZER, Howard J.
Aristotelian Syllogisms and Generalized Quantifiers. WESTERSTAHL, Dag.
Form of Life in Wittgenstein's Later Work. GARVER, Newton.
Forms and Causes In Plato's *Phaedo*. BYRNE, Christopher.
The Generation of Form in Aristotle. SHIELDS, Christopher.
The Idea of History as a Scale of Forms. GOLDSTEIN, Leon J.
The Intelligible World-Animal in Plato's *Timaeus*. PARRY, Richard D.
Kant e o problema da origem das representações elementares: apontamentos. MARQUES, U R de Azevedo.
Levels of Knowledge in the *Theaetetus*. DORTER, Kenneth.
Linguistic Forms and Social Obligations: A Critique of the Doctrine of Literal Expression in Searle. BOGEN, David.
Music in Hegel's *Aesthetics*: A Re-Evaluation. JOHNSON, Julian.
Nachahmung und Gestaltung—Baumgarten, *Meditationes* 73 (in Japanese). MATSUO, Hiroshi.
On Plato's Theory of the *Metheksis* of Ideas. JIYUAN, Yu.
On the Form and Authenticity of the *Lysis*. TEJERA, V.
Origen de la inversión kantiana del binomio materia-forma. SOTO BRUNA, Maria Jesus.
Perennial Modernity: Forms as Aesthetic and Symbolic. MAQUET, Jacques.
Philosophical Scepticism: An Intelligible Challenge. GRUNDY, Jeremy.
The Recurring Problem of the Third Man. HALES, Steven D.
Reflections on Aristotle's Criticism of Forms. MOKASHI, Ashwini A.
Self-Predication and Synonymy. SILVERMAN, Allan.
Thoughts and Feelings and Things: A New Psychiatric Epistemology. HUNDERT, Edward M.
Wittgenstein on Logical Form and Kantian Geometry. SUMMERFIELD, Donna M.

FORMAL CAUSE

Inferring Formal Causation from Corresponding Regressions. CHAMBERS, William V.

FORMAL LANGUAGE(S)

Computability, Complexity, Logic. BÖRGER, E.
A Formal Representation of Declaration-Related Legal Relations. HANSSON, Sven Ove.

FORMAL LOGIC

Una lettura idealistica della "Analitica Trascendentale". BELLINI, Ornella.
Logical Forms: An Introduction to Philosophical Logic. SAINSBURY, Mark.
"On the Logic of Practical Evaluation" in *Logic and Ethics*, KÖRNER, Stephan.
In the Service of Human Society: Formal, Information, or Anti-Logical?. BARTH, E M.
Trotsky's Dialectic. THATCHER, Ian D.

FORMAL STRUCTURE(S)

General Causation. SAPIRE, David.

FORMAL SYSTEM(S)

The Mind's I Has Two Eyes. MARTIN, J E and ENGLEMAN, K H.

FORMALISM

Reasoning and Revision in Hybrid Representation Systems. NEBEL, Bernhard.
Bakhtin's Marxist Formalism. MC BRIDE, William Thomas.
Formalisme et intuitionnisme en philosophie des mathématiques. LARGEAULT, Jean.
On Some Alleged Difficulties in the Interpretation of Quantum Mechanics. DIEKS, Dennis.
Philosophical Reflections on the Foundations of Mathematics. COUTURE, Jocelyne and LAMBEK, Joachim.

FORMALIZATION

Toward a Formalization of Dialectical Logic. THOMASON, Steven K.

FORMATION

The Discursive Formation of the Body in the History of Medicine. LEVIN, David Michael and SOLOMON, George F.
The Formation of the Modern State: A Reconstruction of Max Weber's Arguments. AXTMANN, Roland.
El proceso de formación de la clase obrera de las minas en Asturias. MORADIELLOS, Enrique.

FORMULA(S)

The Completeness of Provable Realizability. MINTS, G E.
On Simplicity of Formulas. KRYNICKI, Michal and SZCZERBA, Leslaw.
On the Structure of De Morgan Monoids with Corollaries on Relevant Logic and Theories. SLANEY, John K.
Propositional Consistency Proofs. BUSS, S R.
Tree Proofs for Syllogistic. SIMONS, Peter M.

FORTUNE

In a Crazy Time the Crazy Come Out Well: Machiavelli and the Cosmology of His Day. BASU, Sammy.

FOUCAULT, M

Essays on Heidegger and Others: Philosophical Papers, Volume 2. RORTY, Richard.
Ideals and Illusions: On Reconstruction and Deconstruction in Contemporary Critical Theory. MC CARTHY, Thomas.
Michel Foucault's Force of Flight: Towards an Ethics for Thought. BERNAUER, James W.
Patterns of Dissonance. BRAIDOTTI, Rosi.
Philosophical Events: Essays of the '80s. RAJCHMAN, John.
The Question of Ethics. SCOTT, Charles E.
"Docile Bodies, Rebellious Bodies" in *Writing the Politics of Difference*, BORDO, Susan.
"Foucault and the Question of Humanism" in *The Question of Humanism: Challenges and Possibilities*, SCOTT, Charles E.
Acceptance of Others and Concern for Oneself (in French). MULLER, Denis.
Can Genealogy Be Critical? A Somewhat Unromantic Look at Nietzsche and Foucault. VISKER, Rudi.
The Conative Function of the Other in *Les Mots et les Choses*. RACEVSKIS, Karlis.
De la matérialité du discours saisi dans l'institution. KREMER-MARIETTI, Angèle.
The Death of the Author: An Analytical Autopsy. LAMARQUE, Peter.
Deceptive Comfort: The Power of Kafka's Stories. BENNETT, Jane.
The Disorder of Things. MAJOR-POETZL, Pamela.
Ethics and Politics (in German). EWALD, François.
Ethics in Current Affairs: The Theme of the Enlightenment in Michel Foucault (in German). SCHMID, Wilhelm.
Footprints in the Snow. SEERVELD, Calvin.
Foucault and The Referent. LUNN, Forrest.
Foucault et la psychothérapie. DREYFUS, Hubert L.
Foucault's Critique of Heidegger. HILL, R Kevin.
Foucault, Nietzsche, History: Two Modes of the Genealogical Method. SAX, Benjamin C.
Foucault: Making a Difference. LILLY, Reginald.
Les gisants et les pleureuses: Pour un tombeau de Michel Foucault. AUZIAS, Jean-Marie.
Historical Continuity and Discontinuity in the Philosophy of Gadamer and Foucault (in Hungarian). UJLAKI, Gabriella.
Historicisms New and Old: "Charles Dickens" Meets Marxism, Feminism, and West Coast Foucault. NEWTON, Judith.
I Love Myself When I am Laughing: A New Paradigm for Sex. DAVIS, Karen Elizabeth.
Literature and Language After the Death of God. STEIN, A L.
Michel Foucault: From the Humanities to Political Thought (in German). SEITTER, Walter.
The Moral Ontology of Charles Taylor: Contra Deconstructivism. HOY, Terry.
Nietzsche and Foucault on *Ursprung* and Genealogy. COOK, Deborah.
On the Genealogical Method: Nietzsche and Foucault. SAX, Benjamin C.
The Philosopher's Prism: Foucault, Feminism, and Critique. ALADJEM, Terry K.
Le pouvoir de la différence. DELIVOYATSIS, Socratis.
Power, Knowledge and Freedom: The Meaning of Foucault's Threefold Break with the History of Ideas (in German). ENGLER, Wolfgang.
Le problème politique chez Sartre et Foucault. KNEE, Phili.
The Question of Ethics in Foucault's Thought. SCOTT, Charles E.
The Oscillation of the Concept of Reason in Michel Foucault (in German). BENJOWSKI, Regina.

FOULK, G

Response to Foulk's "In Defense of Cahn's Scamps". SILK, David.

FOUNDATION(S)

David Hume and the Problem of Reason. DANFORD, John W.
Foundations of Moral and Political Philosophy. PAUL, Ellen Frankel (ed).
Foundations of Social Theory. COLEMAN, James S.
Overcoming Foundations: Studies in Systematic Philosophy. WINFIELD, Richard Dien.
Wittgenstein's Lectures on the Foundations of Mathematics, Cambridge 1939. DIAMOND, Cora (ed).
"Beyond Signifiers" in *Writing the Politics of Difference*, DILLON, Martin C.
"Deep Epistemology Without Foundations (in Language)" in *Reading Rorty*, MALACHOWSKI, Alan R.
"Foundations of Liberal Equality" in *The Tanner Lectures on Human Values, Volume XI*, DWORKIN, Ronald.
Communism: The Philosophical Foundations. FLEW, Antony.
La fondazione dei valori nell'assiologia critica di Nicola Petruzzellis. TURCO, Giovanni.
The Foundation of the Ability to Reach Conclusions—The Empirical Basis of Logic. GOLAB-MEYER, Zofia.
Friends and Enemies of Liberalism. ARCHARD, David.
Matrix Representation of Husserl's Part-Whole-Foundation Theory. BLECKSMITH, Richard and NULL, Gilbert.
Il paradosso del fondamento nella simbolica del gioco e sogno della libertà. MASULLO, Aldo.
The Concept of "Foundation" in Schelling (in Hungarian). VETO, Miklos.

FOUNDATIONALISM
Epistemic Justification: Essays in the Theory of Knowledge. ALSTON, William P.
Knowledge in Perspective: Selected Essays in Epistemology. SOSA, Ernest.
Reasons and Experience. MILLAR, Alan.
"'Circular' Coherence and 'Absurd' Foundations" in *Truth and Interpretation: Perspectives on the Philosophy of Donald Davidson*, SOSA, Ernest.
"Foundational Physics and Empiricist Critique" in *Scientific Theories*, SKLAR, Lawrence.
"Foundationalism and Foundation in Strauss and Maritain" in *From Twilight to Dawn: The Cultural Vision of Jacques Maritain*, ASSELIN, D T.
"Philosophy and the Sciences" in *Acting and Reflecting: The Interdisciplinary Turn in Philosophy*, SUPPES, Patrick.
Alvin Plantinga and Natural Theology. BROWN, Hunter.
Conventional Foundationalism and the Origins of the Norms. CUDD, Ann E.
A Critique of Plantinga's Theological Foundationalism. ZEIS, John.
The Crucial Disanalogies Between Properly Basic Belief and Belief in God. GRIGG, Richard.
Davidson's Transcendental Arguments. MAKER, William.
Deconstructing Lonergan. MC KINNEY, Ronald H.
Defending the Tradition. NIELSEN, Kai.
Factor Analysis, Information-Transforming Instruments, and Objectivity: A Reply and Discussion. MULAIK, Stanley A.
Farewell to the Tradition: Doing without Metaphysics and Epistemology. NIELSEN, Kai.
Foundationalism and Peter's Confession. HESTER, Marcus.
Foundationalism, Holism, or Hegel?. STERN, David S.
The Foundationalist Justification of Epistemic Principles. REMEDIOS, F.
From Russell to Quine: Basic Statements, Foundationalism, Truth, and Other Myths. LINDBERG, Jordan J.
The Immanence of Thought: Hegel's Critique of Foundationalism. STERN, David S.
Kitcher and Kant. BHAVE, S M.
Knowing through the Body. JOHNSON, Mark.
The Moral Ontology of Charles Taylor: Contra Deconstructivism. HOY, Terry.
Moral Skepticism and Moral Education. BARCALOW, Emmett.
Realism, Anti-Foundationalism and the Enthusiasm for Natural Kinds. BOYD, Richard.
Recent Obituaries of Epistemology. HAACK, Susan.

FOURIER, C
L'Utopia di Fourier. TUNDO, Laura.

FRACTION(S)
Real Numbers, Continued Fractions and Complexity Classes. LABHALLA, Salah and LOMBARDI, Henri.

FRAGMENT(S)
Philosophical Fragments. FIRCHOW, Peter (trans).

FRAIBERG, S
Perceptual Aspects of Art for the Blind. ARNHEIM, Rudolf.

FRAME OF REFERENCE
Essai sur le thème du réferentiel. ORY, André.
Vers une Pédagogie du Dialogue. TONOIU, Vasile.

FRAME(S)
"The Frame Problem and Relevant Predication" in *Knowledge Representation and Defeasible Reasoning*, DUNN, J Michael.
"Monotonic Solution of The Frame Problem in The Situation Calculus" in *Knowledge Representation and Defeasible Reasoning*, SCHUBERT, Lenhart.
Ethical Myopia: The Case of "Framing" by Framing. SINGER, Alan E and LYSONSKI, Steven and SINGER, Ming and HAYES, David.
Every World Can See a Reflexive World. HUGHES, G E.
Kripke Bundles for Intermediate Predicate Logics and Kripke Frames for Intuitionistic Modal Logics. SUZUKI, Nobu-Yuki.
A Lemma in the Logic of Action. SURENDONK, Timothy J.
Relevant Containment Logics and Certain Frame Problems of AI. SYLVAN, Richard.

FRAMEWORK(S)
Conceptual Issues in Nursing Ethics Research. PENTICUFF, Joy Hinson.

FRANCO-FERRAZ, M
On Franco-Ferraz, Theism and the Theatre of the Mind. BADÍA-CABRERA, Miguel A.

FRANK, M
Revealing the Truth of Art. BOWIE, Andrew.

FRANKFURT SCHOOL
Between Freiburg and Frankfurt: Toward a Critical Ontology. DALLMAYR, Fred R.
Freud, Marxism and the Frankfurt School (in Serbo-Croation). FLEGO, Gvozden.
The Hopeless Realist (in Serbo-Croatian). WIGGERHAUS, Rolf.

FRANKFURT, H
No Moral Responsibility Without Alternative Possibilities. WEBBER, May A.

FRANKL, V
Viktor Emil Frankl médico y filósofo. ALEGRÍA, Hernando Muciño.

FRANTZ, R
Productivity and X-Efficiency: A Reply to Singh and Frantz. SARAYDAR, Edward.

FRASER, J
Towards a View of Time as Depth. ARGYROS, Alexander J.

FRATERNITY
"Egalité ou fraternité" in *Égalité Uguaglianza*, OPPICI, Patrizia.

FRAUD
Accountability and Responsibility in Research. WOOLF, Patricia K.
Ethics and the Defense Procurement System. LANSING, Paul and BURKARD, Kimberly.
Morality and Ethics in Organizational Administration. ADELMAN, Howard.
Predictors of Ethical Decisions Regarding Insider Trading. TERPSTRA, David E and REYES, Mario G C and BOKOR, Donald W.
Shareholder Authorized Inside Trading: A Legal and Moral Analysis. SHAW, Bill.
When Scientists are Wrong: Admitting Inadvertent Error in Research. LEIBEL, Wayne.

FREE
B-Varieties with Normal Free Algebras. TEMBROWSKI, Bronislaw.
Feminist Second Thoughts About Free Agency. BENSON, Paul.
λ-Definability on Free Algebras. ZAIONC, Marek.
A Note on Ruth Lorand's 'Free and Dependent Beauty: A Puzzling Issue'. LORD, Catherine.
Schanuel's Conjecture and Free Exponential Rings. MACINTYRE, Angus.

FREE CHOICE
Foreknowledge, Middle Knowledge and "Nearby" Worlds. DAVISON, Scott A.
Hell, This Isn't Necessary After All. WALTERS, Kerry S.
Providence, Freedom and Human Destiny. TALBOTT, Thomas.
The Passing On of Values (in French). PIGUET, J-Claude.
The World-Shift Theory of Free Choice. DAVIS, Wayne A.

FREE ENTERPRISE
Economists and Philosophers as Critics of the Free Enterprise System. ARNOLD, N Scott.

FREE LOGIC
Philosophical Applications of Free Logic. LAMBERT, Karel (ed).
"Free Part—Whole Theory" in *Philosophical Applications of Free Logic*, SIMONS, Peter M.
"Problems of Admissibility and Substitution, Logical Equations and Restricted Theories of Free Algebras" in *Logic, Methodology and Philosophy of Science, VIII*, RYBAKOV, V V.
"A Theory of Definite Descriptions" in *Philosophical Applications of Free Logic*, LAMBERT, Karel.
A Basic Free Logic. WU, Kathleen Johnson.
Incompleteness of a Free Arithmetic. BENCIVENGA, Ermanno.
The Theory of Descriptions Revisited. PERUZZI, Alberto.

FREE MARKET(S)
The Ethics of Rent Control. HANLY, Ken.
The Morality of a Free Market for Transplant Organs. NELSON, Mark T.
State Education Service or Prisoner's Dilemma: The 'Hidden Hand' as Source of Education Policy. JONATHAN, R.
Why Markets Don't Stop Discrimination. SUNSTEIN, Cass R.

FREE RIDER(S)
On Being Committed to Morality. NIELSEN, Kai.

FREE SPEECH
Free Speech, Free Exchange, and Rawlsian Liberalism. SHAPIRO, Daniel.

FREE THOUGHT
"Creative Intuition, Great Books, and Freedom of Intellect" in *Freedom in the Modern World: Jacques Maritain, Yves R Simon, Mortimer J Adler*, ROYAL, Robert.
Considerazioni in margine a un'interpretazione di Bruno. MANZONI, Claudio.

FREE WILL
see also Determinism
Key Themes in Philosophy. GRIFFITHS, A Phillips (ed).
The Non-Reality of Free Will. DOUBLE, Richard.
"Is Free Will Incompatible with Something or Other?" in *Key Themes in Philosophy*, GRIFFITHS, A Phillips.
"Responsibility and 'Free Will'" in *Key Themes in Philosophy*, VESEY, Godfrey.
"When is the Will Free?" in *Philosophical Perspectives, 3: Philosophy of Mind and Action Theory, 1989*, VAN INWAGEN, Peter.
Action and Freedom. ROY, Pabitrakumar.
Baur's "Conversation with Gadamer" and "Contribution to the Gadamer-Lonergan Discussion": A Reaction. LAWRENCE, Fred.
Behavioral Paradigm for a Psychological Resolution of the Free Will Issue. HARCUM, E Rae.
The Condemnation of 1277: Another Light on Scotist Ethics. INGHAM, Mary E.

FREE WILL

Creative Value. ODDIE, Graham.
Don Quijote: voluntad y representación. MURILLO, Roberto.
Empirical and Philosophical Reactions to Harcum's "Behavioral Paradigm for a Psychological Resolution of ...". POLLIO, Howard R and HENLEY, Tracy.
Ethics Without Free Will. SLOTE, Michael.
Free Will and Being a Victim. SMILANSKY, S.
The Free Will Defense and Determinism. SENNETT, James F.
Freedom and the Free Will Defense. GALE, Richard M.
Freedom, Necessity, and Laws of Nature as Relations between Universals. VIHVELIN, Kadri.
From Philosophical Psychology to Philosophical Anthropology (in Dutch). VERGOTE, A.
Hume Revisited: A Problem With the Free Will Defense. MARKHAM, Ian.
Logic and the Free Will Problem. VAN INWAGEN, Peter.
A New Foreknowledge Dilemma. ZAGZEBSKI, Linda.
No Moral Responsibility Without Alternative Possibilities. WEBBER, May A.
Parity for the Theoretical Ghosts and Gremlins: Response to Pollio/Henley and Rychlak. HARCUM, E Rae.
The Poverty of Neurophilosophy. STENT, Gunther S.
A Problem for the Eternity Solution. WIDERKER, David.
Response to Gale's "Freedom and the Free Will Defense". HUMBER, James M.
Response to Slote's "Ethics Without Free Will". VAN INWAGEN, Peter.
Response to van Inwagen's "Logic and the Free Will Problem". SLOTE, Michael.
Some Theoretical and Methodological Questions Concerning Harcum's Proposed Resolution of the Free Will Issue. RYCHLAK, Joseph F.
Thomas Aquinas and the Will: A Note on Interpretation. CROWE, Frederick.
Why Plantinga Must Move from Defense to Theodicy. WALLS, Jerry L.
Wille, Willkür, and the Imputability of Immoral Actions. HUDSON, Hud.
Willkür und Wille bei Kant. STEKELER-WEITHOFER, Pirmin.
The World-Shift Theory of Free Choice. DAVIS, Wayne A.

FREEDOM

see also Liberty
Democratic Individuality. GILBERT, Alan.
The Dilemma of Freedom and Foreknowledge. ZAGZEBSKI, Linda Trinkaus.
Existentialism. COOPER, David E.
Freedom in the Modern World: Jacques Maritain, Yves R Simon, Mortimer J Adler. TORRE, Michael D (ed).
Geschichte, Freiheit und Struktur. RUMPEL, Roland.
Hegel: o la rebelión contra el límite. IZUZQUIZA, Ignacio.
Hegels Theorie des Gesetzes. BOGDANDY, Armin Von.
Hellenic and Christian Studies. ARMSTRONG, A H.
Ideas, Principios y Dialectica. LAFUENTE, Maria Isabel.
Inscriptions and Reflections: Essays in Philosophical Theology. SCHARLEMANN, Robert P.
Jean-Paul Sartre. HENGELBROCK, Jürgen.
Kant's System of Rights. MULHOLLAND, Leslie A.
Kant's Theory of Freedom. ALLISON, Henry E.
Kierkegaards Phänomenologie der Freiheitserfahrung. DISSE, Jörg.
Leibniz and Arnauld. SLEIGH JR, Robert C.
The Many Dimensions of the Human Person. STEGER, E Ecker.
The Meaning of Socialism. LUNTLEY, Michael.
Overcoming Foundations: Studies in Systematic Philosophy. WINFIELD, Richard Dien.
The Philosophy of Money: Georg Simmel (Second Edition). FRISBY, David (ed & trans).
Plotin: Traité sur la liberté et la volonté de l'Un. LEROUX, Georges.
Plotinus and Freedom: A Meditation on Enneads 6:8. WESTRA, Laura.
The Political Philosophy of Michael Oakeshott. FRANCO, Paul.
The Power of Consciousness and the Force of Circumstances in Sartre's Philosophy. BUSCH, Thomas W.
Quest for Certainty: A Comparative Study of Heidegger and Sankara. GRIMES, John A.
Resurrecting Marx: The Analytical Marxists on Freedom, Exploitation, and Justice. GORDON, David.
The Taming of Chance. HACKING, Ian.
"Adler on Freedom" in *Freedom in the Modern World: Jacques Maritain, Yves R Simon, Mortimer J Adler*, MC INERNY, Ralph.
"Adler's *The Idea of Freedom*" in *Freedom in the Modern World: Jacques Maritain, Yves R Simon, Mortimer J Adler*, FITZGERALD, Desmond J.
"Being Is Better than Freedom" in *Freedom in the Modern World: Jacques Maritain, Yves R Simon, Mortimer J Adler*, DENNEHY, Raymond.
"Freedom and Contingency" in *Life-World and Politics: Between Modernity and Postmodernity*, CONNOLLY, William E.
"Freedom and Determination: An Examination of Yves R Simon's Ontology of Freedom" in *Freedom in the Modern World: Jacques Maritain, Yves R Simon, Mortimer J Adler*, GREEN, Catherine.
"Freedom and Economic Organization in a Democracy" in *Freedom in the Modern World: Jacques Maritain, Yves R Simon, Mortimer J Adler*, NELSON, Ralph.
"Freedom and Practical Rationality in the Thought of Yves R Simon" in *Freedom in the Modern World: Jacques Maritain, Yves R Simon, Mortimer J Adler*, MULVANEY, Robert J.
"The Freedoms of Man and Their Relation to God" in *Freedom in the Modern World: Jacques Maritain, Yves R Simon, Mortimer J Adler*, TORRE, Michael D.
"The Individual's Horizon and Valuation" in *The Social Horizon of Knowledge*, FALKIEWICZ, Andrzej.
"Liberalism and Liberty: The Fragility of a Tradition" in *Key Themes in Philosophy*, GRAHAM, Keith.
"Metaphysical Foundations of Freedom in the Social and Political Thought of Yves R Simon" in *Freedom in the Modern World: Jacques Maritain, Yves R Simon, Mortimer J Adler*, UDOIDEM, S Iniobong.
"Predestination and Freedom in Augustine's Ethics" in *The Philosophy in Christianity*, O'DALY, Gerard.
"Prudence as the Cornerstone of the Contemporary Thomistic Philosophy of Freedom" in *Freedom in the Modern World: Jacques Maritain, Yves R Simon, Mortimer J Adler*, MAHONEY, Marianne.
"Schelling and the Origins of His *Naturphilosophie*" in *Romanticism and the Sciences*, MORGAN, S R.
Action and Freedom. ROY, Pabitrakumar.
Alle origini della riflessione di Leopold von Ranke sulla storia: K F Bachmann e J G Fichte. GHELARDI, Maurizio.
Are Property Rights Problematic?. GAUS, Gerald F and LOMASKY, Loren E.
Artistic Freedom: An Art World Paradox. LANKFORD, E Louis.
Aspects of Freedom. WOOD, Robert E.
Autonomy and Personal History. CHRISTMAN, John.
Basic Rights and Constitutional Interpretation. LYONS, David.
Ein Bedürfnis nach Schelling. BRAUN, Hermann.
Brand Blanshard and Gewirth: Ethics and Rights. HOWIE, John.
A Comment on the Argument Between Gewirth and his Critics. ROSS, Steven.
Consciousness Naturalized: Supervenience Without Physical Determinism. SENCHUK, Dennis M.
Descartes et Corneille ou les démesures de l'*ego*. BEYSSADE, Jean-Marie.
Determinism and the Experience of Freedom. DOUBLE, Richard.
Las disonancias de la libertad (I). INNERARITY, Daniel.
Du libre arbitre selon s Thomas d'Aquin. CORBIN, Michel.
El enigma de la libertad humana en Gabriel Marcel. O'CALLAGHAN, Paul.
Ensuring Two Bird Deaths with One Throw. LESLIE, John.
The Ethics of Suspicion. BERNASCONI, Robert.
Existencia de Dios y libertad humana. HERRERA, J Jesús.
Foreknowledge, Middle Knowledge and "Nearby" Worlds. DAVISON, Scott A.
Freedom and Autonomy: The Kantian Analytic and a Sartrean Critique. BEAVERS, Anthony.
Freedom and Happiness in Kant's Political Philosophy. HELLER, Agnes.
Freedom and Human Nature. FLEW, Antony.
Freedom and Realms of Living. CI, Jiwei.
Freedom Is Our Divinity (in German). EHRHARDT, Walter E.
Freedom Not to be Free: The Case of the Slavery Contract in J S Mill's *On Liberty*. ARCHARD, David.
Freiheit und Bindung menschlicher Entscheidungen. KLEMENT, H W and RADERMACHER, F J.
Hegel, Marx, Lukács: The Dialectic of Freedom and Necessity. DAY, Richard B.
Hegels Geschichtsphilosophie im Vergleich mit anderen Geschichtskonzeptionen. GLOY, Karen.
Human Rights and Freedom: Is Kant Relevant to the Current Discussion?. SCHWEIDLER, Walter.
Ideal and Morality (in German). JACOBS, Wilhelm G.
In Defence of Theological Compatibilism. FLINT, Thomas P.
The Inorganic Body and the Ambiguity of Freedom. COLLIER, Andrew.
Kant: del derecho de libertad a la exigencia racional del Estado. PASTORE, Romano.
Kantian Freedom Naturalized. MELCHERT, Norman.
Knowledge as Bondage: An Unconventional Approach. SEN, Sanat Kumar.
La libertad como autodeterminaciín en san Agustín. GALINDO, José Antonio.
La libertad como búsqueda de la verdad en el joven Agustín. WEISMANN, F J.
Libertad como posibilidad, libertad como necesidad: Juliano y San Agustín. PEGUEROLES, Juan.
Libertad individual frente a determinación social. FRANCISCO PÉREZ, M.
Marcel on the Problem of Freedom. SUGUMAR, Devaki.
Metaphysical Conundrums at the Root of Moral Disagreement. MC DERMOTT, John M.
Moral Imagination, Freedom, and the Humanities. KEKES, John.
Naturalism, Freedom and Ethics in Spinoza. DE DIJN, Herman.
On a Mainstay of Incompatibilism. BLUM, Alex.
On Social Rights. SANDU, Gabriel and KUOKKANEN, Martti.
On the Concept of Freedom in the *I Ching*: A Deconstructionist View of Self-Cultivation. SCHULZ, Larry J and CUNNINGHAM, Thomas J.
An Open Letter to Maxine Greene on "The Problem of Freedom in an Era of Ecological Interdependence". BOWERS, C A.

FREEDOM
Perestrojka der Philosophie?. IGNATOW, Assen.
Die Perestrojka in der Sowjetischen Philosophie: Mythos oder Realität. BYKOVA, M.
Plotino: la libertad como primer principio. DE GARAY, Jesús.
Political Freedom. TULLY, James.
Post-Liberalism versus Temperate Liberalism. JACOBS, Struan.
Postcriptum: La libertad como necesidad del bien, en San Agustín. PEGUEROLES, Juan.
Power, Knowledge and Freedom: The Meaning of Foucault's Threefold Break with the History of Ideas (in German). ENGLER, Wolfgang.
Les présupposés métaphysiques de la "lisibilité" de l'être. KÜHN, Rolf.
The Problem of Moral Freedom and Nicolai Hartmann. PRASAD, Kamata.
Racionalidad y libertad. FERNÁNDEZ DEL VALLE, Agustín Basave.
Representation and the Freedom of the Will. STAMPE, Dennis W.
Response to Berlin and McBride. RENICK, Timothy M.
Response to Stampe's "Representation and the Freedom of the Will". GIBSON, Martha I.
The Rule of Law in *The German Constitution*. HANCE, Allen S.
Sartre and Political Legitimacy. KNEE, Philip.
Sartre on Anguish. JAMBOR, Mishka.
Sartre on Surpassing the Given. BUSCH, Thomas W.
Schelling's Treatise on the Essence of Human Freedom and Heidegger's Thought. FROMAN, Wayne J.
Social Reality and Moral Order. BARLINGAY, S S.
Tenets of Freedom. BLUM, Alex.
The Freedom of Values and the Value of Freedom (in Czechoslovakian). SLEJSKA, D.
The Perversion of Emancipation into Repression (in German). SCHMIDT, Hartwig.
The Philosophy of Responsibility (in German). SCHRÖDER, Richard.
Über das Geschmacksurteil und die künstlerische Freiheit bei Kant (in Japanese). UE, Satoko.
Wille, Willkür, and the Imputability of Immoral Actions. HUDSON, Hud.
Willkür und Wille bei Kant. STEKELER-WEITHOFER, Pirmin.
The World of Man and Man in the World in Light of the New Philosophical Thinking. DZHAKHAIA, L G.

FREETHINKERS
Radical Enlightenment and Freethinkers (in German). POTT, Martin.

FREGE
Aspectos Metodológicos de la Investigación Científica. GONZÁLEZ, Wenceslao J (ed).
Frege and Other Philosophers. DUMMETT, Michael.
Frege in Perspective. WEINER, Joan.
Has Semantics Rested on a Mistake?. WETTSTEIN, Howard.
The Logical Basis of Metaphysics. DUMMETT, Michael.
Mathematics and the Image of Reason. TILES, Mary E.
Pulling up the Ladder: The Metaphysical Roots of Wittgenstein's Tractatus. BROCKHAUS, Richard R.
Themes From Kaplan. ALMOG, Joseph (ed).
"Cognitive Significance Without Cognitive Content" in *Themes From Kaplan*, WETTSTEIN, Howard.
"Field and Fregean Platonism" in *Physicalism in Mathematics*, WRIGHT, Crispin.
"Frege and Popper: Two Critics of Psychologism" in *Imre Lakatos and Theories of Scientific Change*, CURRIE, G.
"Frege on Sense and Linguistic Meaning" in *The Analytic Tradition: Philosophical Quarterly Monographs, Volume 1*, BURGE, Tyler.
"Frege, Concepts and the Design of Language" in *Information, Semantics and Epistemology*, HIGGINBOTHAM, James.
"Neo-Fregean Thoughts" in *Philosophical Perspectives, 3: Philosophy of Mind and Action Theory, 1989*, BOËR, Steven E.
"On Davidson's "Saying That"" in *Truth and Interpretation: Perspectives on the Philosophy of Donald Davidson*, BURGE, Tyler.
"Referência e valor cognitivo" in *Dinâmica do Pensar: Homenagem a Oswaldo Market*, BRANQUINHO, João.
"The Reverse Frege Puzzle" in *Philosophical Perspectives, 3: Philosophy of Mind and Action Theory, 1989*, YAGISAWA, Takashi.
"Singular Propositions, Abstract Constituents, and Propositional Attitudes" in *Themes From Kaplan*, ZALTA, Edward N.
"Thought and Perception: The Views of Two Philosophical Innovators" in *The Analytic Tradition: Philosophical Quarterly Monographs, Volume 1*, DUMMETT, Michael.
"Turning the Tables on Frege or How is it that 'Hesperus is Hesperus' is Trivial?" in *Philosophical Perspectives, 3: Philosophy of Mind and Action Theory, 1989*, WETTSTEIN, Howard.
"What Is Abstraction and What Is It Good For?" in *Physicalism in Mathematics*, SIMONS, Peter.
"Why Intensionalists Ought Not Be Fregeans" in *Truth and Interpretation: Perspectives on the Philosophy of Donald Davidson*, KATZ, Jerrold J.
Blind Grasping and Fregean Senses. SCHWEIZER, Paul.
Context Principle, Fruitfulness of Logic and the Cognitive Value of Arithmetic in Frege. RUFFINO, Marco Antonio.
Decir lo mismo (Frege y Santo Tomás). SANGUINETI, Juan J.
Descriptions: Contemporary Philosophy and the Nyāya. SHAW, J L.
Direct Reference, Meaning, and Thought. RECANATI, François.
Frege and Husserl on Number. TIESZEN, Richard.
Frege and the Analysis of Thoughts. GARAVASO, Pieranna.
Frege, Informative Identities, and Logicism. MILNE, Peter.
Frege-Russell Semantics?. WETTSTEIN, Howard.
Gottlob Frege, lettere a Wittgenstein. PENCO, Carlo and PARODI, Alessandra.
The Indispensability of *Sinn*. FORBES, Graeme.
Predication and Logic of Language (I). GANGADEAN, Ashok.
Predication and Logic of Language (II). GANGADEAN, Ashok.
Problems with the Fregean Interpretation of Husserl. BROWN, Charles S.
Psychologism Reconsidered. AACH, John.
Reflexiones en torno a la oración oblicua. MUÑOZ, Angel and CAROSIO, Alba.
Scotus, Frege, and Bergmann. PARK, Woosuk.
Sentidos, referencias y concepto en Frege. MARTINEZ FREIRE, P.
Sobre la semántica de los nombres propios. SCHIRN, Matthias.
Some Remarks on the Linguistic Turn. PERUZZI, Alberto.
Thoughts Which Only I Can Think. WILLIAMS, C J F.
Vagueness, Natural Language and Logic. BERKELEY, Istvan S N.
Wittgenstein sobre la noción de regla en Frege. PADILLA GÁLVEZ, Jesús.

FREIRE, P
The Master-Slave Dialectic in Latin America: The Social Criticism of Zea, Freire, and Roig. SCHUTTE, Ofelia M.

FRENCH
Diderot's Dream. ANDERSON, Wilda.
Égalité Uguaglianza. FERRARI, Jean (ed).
French Philosophers in Conversation: Levinas, Schneider, Serres, Irigaray, Le Doeuff, Derrida. MORTLEY, Raoul.
Locke and French Materialism. YOLTON, John W.
Models and Concepts of Ideology. RITSERT, Jürgen.
On Durkheim's Rules of Sociological Method. GANE, Mike.
Who Comes after the Subject?. CADAVA, Eduardo (ed).
"Egalité ou fraternité" in *Égalité Uguaglianza*, OPPICI, Patrizia.
"La femme intellectuelle au XVIIIe siècle ou l'inégalité des sexes" in *Égalité Uguaglianza*, GEFFRIAUD-ROSSO, Jeannette.
"John Stuart Mill and France" in *A Cultivated Mind: Essays On J S Mill Presented to John M Robson*, FILIPIUK, Marion.
"L'égalité en 1789" in *Égalité Uguaglianza*, D'HONDT, Jacques.
"Plasticity into Power: Two Crises in the History of France and China" in *Critique and Construction: A Symposium on Roberto Unger's "Politics"*, CLEARY, J C and HIGONNET, Patrice.
"Una uguale educazione?" in *Égalité Uguaglianza*, PANCERA, Carlo.
"La 'grande illusion' du XVIIIe siècle" in *Égalité Uguaglianza*, ROSSO, Corrado.
The Ambivalence of the Idea of Equality in the French Enlightenment. CHISICK, Harvey.
The Birth of the Death-Machine. MEGIVERN, James J.
Cent ans de philosophie à l'Institut Supérieur de Philosophie. LADRIÈRE, Jean.
De l'Idéologie comme correlat des termes idéologiste et idéologue. ZOLUA, Buenzey Maluenga.
Gabriel Marcel na correspondência com Gaston Fessard. CABRAL, Roque.
Note sulle recenti traduzioni di *Essere e tempo* in Francia. MARRATI, Paola.
Qu'est-ce que l'expressionnisme allemand?. RICHARD, Lionel.
La Querelle de la Moralité du Théâtre au XVIIe Siècle. FUMAROLI, M Marc.
Réflexion sur l'état actuel et les perspectives de l'enseignement de la philosophie en France. DERRIDA, Jacques and BOURGEOIS, Bernard.
The Scottish Influence on French Aesthetic Thought: Later Developments. MANNS, James W.
Las Sociedades de Pensamiento y la Revolución Francesa. RHENÁN SEGURA, Jorge.
Ultramontanisme et gallicanisme engagentils deux visions de la société. BRESSOLETTE, Claude.

FRENCH REVOLUTION
Dezelfde wateren aan nieuwe oevers: Alexis de Tocqueville en de Franse Revolutie. ZIJDERVELD, A C.
Edmund Burke en zijn "Reflections on the Revolution in France". DE VALK, J M M.
The Impact of the French Revolution on the Development of Philosophy. NETOPILIK, Jakub.
Joseph de Maistre en de Revolutie. VAN BELLINGEN, Jozef.
Justus Möser: De Revolutie en de grondslagen van de moderne staat. WALRAVENS, Else.
Kant y la Revolución Francesa. PÉREZ ESTÉVEZ, Antonio.
Kant's visie op de Franse Revolutie en op de grondslagen van het recht. VAN DER WAL, G A.
Libertad, Igualdad, Fraternidad. BUENO, Gustavo.
Marxist Historians and the Question of Class in the French Revolution. AMARIGLIO, Jack and NORTON, Bruce.
Over leesbaarheid en maakbaarheid van de geschiedenis. WEYEMBERGH, Maurice.
Presencia de Grecia y de Roma clásicas en la Revolución francesa de 1789. RECIO GARCÍA, Tomás.

FRENCH REVOLUTION
The Role of Memory in the Historiography of the French Revolution. HUTTON, Patrick H.
Sartre's onuitgevoerde project: de Robespierre-biografie. DETHIER, Hubert.
Zwischen Enttäuschung und Versöhnung: Hegel, die deutsche Misere und die Französiche Revolution. ARNDT, Andreas.

FRENCH, P
Why Corporations Are Not Morally Responsible for Anything They Do. VELASQUEZ, Manuel G.

FREUD
Alterity, Identity, Image: Contributions Towards a Theoretical Perspective. CORBEY, R (ed).
The Authentic Self: Toward a Philosophy of Personality. LACENTRA, Walter.
The Kernel of Truth in Freud. LAWTON, Philip.
Of Memory, Reminiscence, and Writing: On the Verge. KRELL, David Farrell.
"Freud, Husserl, Derrida: An Experiement" in *Phenomenology of the Truth Proper to Religion*, LOWE, Walter.
"Friedrich Nichte" in *Looking After Nietzsche*, RICKELS, Laurence A.
"On Becoming a Subject: Lacan's Rereading of Freud" in *Reconsidering Psychology: Perspectives from Continental Philosophy*, BERGOFFEN, Debra B.
"The Psychoanalytic Enterprise in Scientific Perspective" in *Scientific Theories*, GRÜNBAUM, Adolf.
"His Majesty Is a Baby?" A Critical Response to Peter Hammond Schwartz. SPRINGBORG, Patricia.
The "Tally Argument" and the Validation of Psychoanalysis. RICHARDSON, Robert C.
'Inference to the Best Explanation' of 'Inference to the Best Interpretation'? Een antwoord op Derksens ..... MOOIJ, A W M.
A Contribution to the Early History of Psychoanalysis (in Serbo-Croatian). MACHO, Thomas H.
El ateísmo Freudeano. MARLASCA, Antonio.
Comments on Freud and Wittgenstein, and on Adolf Grünbaum's "Foundations of Psychoanalysis". FISCHER, Kurt Rudolf.
Un confronto sempre attuale: Leggendo—A Lambertino, Psicoanalisi e morale in Freud. DOVOLICH, Claudia.
Did Freud Develop a Social Philosophy? (in Serbo-Croatian). FLEGO, Gvozden.
Freud and the Question of Truth (in Serbo-Croatian). GÖRLICH, Bernard.
Freud Contra Sartre: Repression or Self-Deception?. MIRVISH, Adrian.
Freud devait-il choisir entre les deux conceptions du symbole que lui attribue Lévi-Strauss?. CHARRON, Ghyslain.
Freud on Civilization and Neurosis. FLUXMAN, Tony.
Freud's Warning to Potential Believers. EBISCH, Glen A.
Freud, Marxism and the Frankfurt School (in Serbo-Croation). FLEGO, Gvozden.
Freud: Uma Concepção Agónica da Educação. BARBOSA, Manuel.
Hegel, Nietzsche, and Freud on Madness and the Unconscious. BERTHOLD-BOND, Daniel.
Is Grünbaum's Critique of Habermas' Understanding Freud Definite? (in Serbo-Croatian). NAGL, Ludwig.
James and Freud. MYERS, Gerald E.
Lacan Between Freud and Heidegger (in Serbo-Croatian). VETTER, Helmut.
Misconceptions of the Social Sciences. SEGAL, Robert A.
Phenomenology and Psychoanalysis: The Hermeneutical Mediation. RAJAN, R Sundara.
A Philosophical Resistance to Freud. SACHS, David.
Postcritical Religion and the Latent Freud. KEISER, R Melvin.
Repression of Sexuality in Philosophy and the Return of the Repressed in Freud's Psychoanalysis (in Serbo-Croatian). KORDIC, Radoman.
Wittgenstein on Freud's 'Abominable Mess'. CIOFFI, Frank.

FRIEDMAN, M
Prediction and Explanation in Economics. SWAMIDASAN, Nalini.
Unification, Realism and Inference. MORRISON, Margaret.
Why Friedman's Non-Monotonic Reasoning Defies Hempel's Covering Law Model. JANSSEN, M C W and TAN, Y H.

FRIENDSHIP
Abeunt Studia in Mores: A Festschrift for Helga Doblin. MERRILL, Sarah A Bishop (ed).
Other Selves: Philosophers on Friendship. PAKALUK, Michael (ed).
"The Classical Conception of Friendship" in *Abeunt Studia in Mores: A Festschrift for Helga Doblin*, FOX, William.
"The Emergence of Morality in Personal Relationships" in *The Moral Domain: Essays in the Ongoing Discussion between Philosophy and the Social Sciences*, KELLER, Monika.
"Friendship and Duty: Some Difficult Relations" in *Identity, Character, and Morality: Essays in Moral Psychology*, STOCKER, Michael.
"Vocation, Friendship, and Community: Limitations of the Personal-Impersonal Framework" in *Identity, Character, and Morality: Essays in Moral Psychology*, BLUM, Lawrence A.
"Amicus plato, sed magis amica veritas" (Notas sobre el conflicto amistad-verdad). CARRETERO, Joaquín M.
Amor y comunicación. FORMENT, Eudaldo.
Aristotle on Personality and Some Implications for Friendship. REINER, Paula.
Duties to Friends. PASSELL, Dan.
Friendship and Education. WHITE, Patricia.
Friendship and Education. WHITE, Patricia.
Friendship, Self-Love, and Concern for Others in Aristotle's Ethics. MC KERLIE, Dennis.
Friendship: Mutual Apprenticeship in Moral Development. VOLBRECHT, Rose Mary.
Impersonal Friends. WHITING, Jennifer E.
Love, Friendship, and the Aesthetics of Character. NOVITZ, David.
The Unjust Treatment of Polemarchus. PAGE, Carl.

FROMM
Dialogo sobre humanismo y Marxismo (primera parte). SILVA CAMARENA, Juan Manuel.
Vida y Resurrección en el pensamiento de Erich Fromm. CHAVES, Flory.

FRY, S
A Comment on Fry's "The Role of Caring in a Theory of Nursing Ethics". BOYER, Jeannine Ross and NELSON, James Lindemann.

FRYDMAN, S
Sawa Frydman: A Polish Legal Realist. MOS, Urszula.

FULLER, M
Delicate Subjects: Romanticism, Gender, and the Ethics of Understanding. ELLISON, Julie.

FULLER, S
The Importance of Asking the Right Questions. PATTERSON, Dennis.
On Bureaucracy and Science: A Response to Fuller. TWENEY, Ryan D.
Social Science-Based Understandings of Science: Reflections on Fuller. KRUGLANSKI, Arie W.
The Uses of Humanistic History. PORTER, Theodore M.
Whither Social Epistemology? A Reply to Fuller. SCHMAUS, Warren.

FULMER, G
The Limits of Power. TALIAFERRO, Charles.

FUNCTION(S)
see also Recursive Function(s)
"Degrees of Functions with No Fixed Points" in *Logic, Methodology and Philosophy of Science, VIII*, JOCKUSCH JR, Carl G.
"Free Sets for Commutative Families of Functions" in *Logic, Methodology and Philosophy of Science, VIII*, ABRAHAM, Uri.
"Polarized Partition Relations and Almost-Disjoint Functions" in *Logic, Methodology and Philosophy of Science, VIII*, BAUMGARTNER, James E.
Aristotle on the Function of Man in Relation to Eudaimonia. HESTER, Marcus.
Codes of Ethics and the Moral Education of Engineers. LUEGENBIEHL, Heinz C.
Complexity for Type-2 Relations. TOWNSEND, Mike.
A Constructive Version of Sperner's Lemma and Brouwer's Fixed Point Theorem. KHALIFA, A K.
Does Representational Content Arise from Biological Function?. HALL, Richard J.
The Equivalence of Determinacy and Iterated Sharps. DUBOSE, Derrick Albert.
Functions As Selected Effects: The Conceptual Analyst's Defense. NEANDER, Karen.
Indiscernibility and Identity in Probability Theory. ROEPER, Peter and LEBLANC, Hugues.
Information Functions with Applications. SZYMANEK, Krzysztof.
Kansas, Oz, and the Function of Art. CONLON, James.
Marketing Ethics: Some Dimensions of the Challenge. CAMENISCH, Paul F.
An Omniscience Principle, the König Lemma and the Hahn-Banach Theorem. ISHIHARA, Hajime.
A Partial Functions Version of Church's Simple Theory of Types. FARMER, William M.
Shelah's pcf Theory and Its Applications. BURKE, Maxim R and MAGIDOR, Menachem.
Some Extensions of Built-Upness on Systems of Fundamental Sequences. KADOTA, Noriya.
Some Results about Borel Sets in Descriptive Set Theory of Hyperfinite Sets. ZIVALJEVIC, Bosko.
The Strength of the Failure of the Singular Cardinal Hypothesis. GITIK, Moti.
Sub-Arithmetical Ultrapowers: A Survey. MC LAUGHLIN, Thomas G.

FUNCTIONAL ANALYSIS
The Functional Conception of Culture and the Explanation of the Value-Shaping Process (in Polish). BROZI, Krzysztof J.

FUNCTIONAL COMPLETENESS
Characterization of Prime Numbers in Lukasiewicz's Logical Matrix. KARPENKO, Alexander S.
Expressive Completeness and Decidability. SCHUMM, George and SHAPIRO, Stewart.
Expressiveness and Completeness of an Interval Tense Logic. VENEMA, Yde.
Formalization of Functionally Complete Propositional Calculus with the Functor of Implication.... LEJEWSKI, Czeslaw.

FUNCTIONAL COMPLETENESS

Post's Functional Completeness Theorem. PELLETIER, Francis Jeffry and MARTIN, Norman M.

FUNCTIONAL(S)

Complexity for Type-2 Relations. TOWNSEND, Mike.
Functional and Procedural Definitions of Art. DAVIES, Stephen.
Jumps of Nontrivial Splittings of Recursively Enumerable Sets. INGRASSIA, Michael A and LEMPP, Steffen.

FUNCTIONALISM

Explaining Human Action. LENNON, Kathleen.
How to Build a Person: A Prolegomenon. POLLOCK, John L.
Mind and Cognition: A Reader. LYCAN, William G (ed).
The Representational Theory of Mind: An Introduction. STERELNY, Kim.
Sensations: A Defense of Type Materialism. HILL, Christopher S.
"The Intrinsic Quality of Experience" in *Philosophical Perspectives, 4: Action Theory and Philosophy of Mind, 1990*, HARMAN, Gilbert.
Analytic Functionalism and the Reduction of Phenomenal States. LEVIN, Janet.
Assessing Functional Explanations in the Social Sciences. KINCAID, Harold.
Causes, Proximate and Ultimate. FRANCIS, Richard C.
Closing the Chinese Room. WEISS, Thomas.
Cognitivism and Cognitive Science (in Portuguese). OLIVEIRA, M B de.
Fear and Loathing (and Other Intentional States) in Searle's Chinese Room. JACQUETTE, Dale.
Functional Support for Anomalous Monism. EDWARDS, Jim.
Functionalism's Impotence. WECKERT, J.
Functionalism, the Absent Qualia Objection and Eliminativism. AVERILL, Edward Wilson.
Lewis's Functionalism and Reductive Materialism. KERNOHAN, Andrew.
Sensory Qualities and 'Homunctionalism': A Review Essay of W G Lycan's *Consciousness*. KOBES, Bernard W.
Two Qualms About Functionalist Marxism. DICKMAN, Joel.

FUNDAMENTALISM

Franz Rosenzweig: Existentielles Denken und gelebte Bewährung. SCHMIED-KOWARZIK, Wolfdietrich.
Kierkegaards Phänomenologie der Freiheitserfahrung. DISSE, Jörg.
"Newton and Fundamentalism, II" in *Essays on the Context, Nature, and Influence of Isaac Newton's Theology*, POPKIN, Richard H.
"Et la religion le remplit de fureur...". BOULAD-AYOUB, Josiane.
A Heideggerian Analysis of Fundamentalism: A Brief Discussion. O'CONNELL, Colin.
In Defense of Southern Fundamentalism. HORGAN, Terence and GRAHAM, George.

FUNDING

Has the Study of Philosophy at Dutch Universities Changed under Economic and Political Pressures?. VAN DER MEULEN, Barend and LEYDESDORFF, Loet.
The University and Industrial Research: Selling Out?. HILL, Judith M.

FUTURE

Baffling Phenomena: And Other Studies in the Philosophy of Knowledge and Valuation. RESCHER, Nicholas.
Evolution: Probleme und neue Aspekte ihrer Theorie. SCHEFFCZYK, Leo (ed).
The Realizations of the Future: An Inquiry into the Authority of Praxis. ALLAN, George.
Returning to Sils-Maria: A Commentary to Nietzsche's "Also sprach Zarathustra". WHITLOCK, Greg.
Consequentialism and the Unforeseeable Future. NORCROSS, Alastair.
Future Individuals. TEICHMANN, Roger.
How Would an *Übermensch* Regard His Past and Future?. MC INERNEY, Peter K.
On Relativity Theory and Openness of the Future. STEIN, Howard.
Real Possibility. DEUTSCH, Harry.

FUTURE GENERATION(S)

Earthbound: Introductory Essays in Environmental Ethics. REGAN, Tom (ed).
"Responsibility and Future Generations: A Constructivist Model" in *Philosophy of Technology*, SMITH, Janet Farrell.
Bargaining with the Not-Yet-Born: Gauthier's Contractarian Theory of Inter-Generational Justice and Its Limitations. DE-SHALIT, A.

FUZZY SETS

Note on the Integration of Prototype Theory and Fuzzy-Set Theory. FUHRMANN, G.

GADAMER, H

Hermeneutics and the Poetic Motion, Translation Perspectives V—1990. SCHMIDT, Dennis J (ed).
The Hermeneutics of Life History: Personal Achievement and History in Gadamer, Habermas, and Erikson. WALLULIS, Jerald.
Historische Objektivitat. WEBERMAN, David.
The Other Side of Language: A Philosophy of Listening. FIUMARA, Gemma Corradi.
Philosophical Hermeneutics and Literary Theory. WEINSHEIMER, Joel.
Philosophische Hermeneutik. INEICHEN, Hans.
"Bold Counsels and Carpenters: Pagan Translation" in *Hermeneutics and the Poetic Motion, Translation Perspectives V—1990*, LEAVEY JR, John P.
"The Exemplary Status of Translating" in *Hermeneutics and the Poetic Motion, Translation Perspectives V—1990*, SCHMIDT, Lawrence K.
Basal Readers—'Dominant But Dead' versus Gadamer and Language for Understanding. WIRTH, Arthur G.
Baur's "Conversation with Gadamer" and "Contribution to the Gadamer-Lonergan Discussion": A Reaction. LAWRENCE, Fred.
Can Art Save Us? A Meditation on Gadamer. DEVEREAUX, Mary.
Derrida's Other Conversation. DAVIES, Paul.
Footprints in the Snow. SEERVELD, Calvin.
Gadamer over 'Vermittlung': de Hegeliaanse draad in zijn hermeneutiek. VAN DER HOEVEN, J.
Gadamer's Concrete Universal. KERBY, Anthony Paul.
Herméneutique et épistémologie Gadamer entre Heidegger et Hegel. ROCKMORE, Tom.
The Historical Consciousness of Man. MITSCHERLING, Jeff.
Historical Continuity and Discontinuity in the Philosophy of Gadamer and Foucault (in Hungarian). UJLAKI, Gabriella.
L'universalisation de l'herméneutique chez Hans-Georg Gadamer. GRONDIN, Jean.
Ontología hermenéutica y reflexión filológica: el acceso a la filosofía de H G Gadamer. DOMINGO, Agustín.
Philosophical Hermeneutics and its Meaning for Philosophy. PAGE, Carl.
Protestant Hermeneutics and the Rule of Law: Gadamer and Dworkin. HENLEY, Kenneth.
To Catch a Thief: Chu Hsi (1130-1200) and the Hermeneutic Art. BERTHRONG, John.
Les trois sortes d'universalité dans l'herméneutique de H G Gadamer. MARGOLIS, Joseph.
Truth, Method, and Objectivity: *Husserl and Gadamer on Scientific Method*. NUYEN, A T.

GAIA HYPOTHESIS

Nature as Personal. DOMBROWSKI, Daniel A.

GALE, R

Response to Gale's "Freedom and the Free Will Defense". HUMBER, James M.

GALEN

Methods and Problems in Greek Science: Selected Papers. LLOYD, G E R.

GALILEO

The Drama of Galileo, The Past and the Present. VOISE, Waldemar.
La filosofia: in soccorso de' governi. COLAPIETRA, Raffaele.
Scientia e fide. BLANDINO, Giovanni.
Tycho's System and Galileo's *Dialogue*. MARGOLIS, Howard.

GALSTON, W

On Squeamishness: A Response to Galston. FISHKIN, James S.

GAME THEORY

Do the Right Thing: Studies in Limited Rationality. RUSSELL, Stuart.
Experimental Studies of Interactive Decisions. RAPOPORT, Amnon.
Negotation Games: Applying Game Theory to Bargaining and Arbitration. BRAMS, Steven J.
Rationality in Action: Contemporary Approaches. MOSER, Paul K (ed).
"Winning Against and With the Opponent" in *Logic and Ethics*, HOLOWKA, Jacek.
Binary 2 x 2 Games. FISHBURN, Peter C and KILGOUR, D Marc.
Choice Procedure Consistent with Similarity Relations. AIZPURUA, Jose Maria and NIETO, Jorge and URIARTE, Jose Ramon.
Discovering Right and Wrong: A Realist Response to Gauthier's Morals by Agreement. GENOVA, A C.
Duff and the Wager. JORDAN, Jeff.
The Economic Analysis of Institutions. RICKETTS, Martin.
The Economics of (Very) Primitive Societies. TULLOCK, Gordon.
An Experimental Analysis of Risk Taking. DAHLBÄCK, Olof.
Game Theory is Not a Useful Tool for the Political Scientist. BUNGE, Mario.
Games, Fairness, and Rawls's *A Theory of Justice*. LADEN, Anthony.
The Inapplicability of Evolutionary Stable Strategy to the Prisoner's Dilemma. MARINOFF, Louis.
Is Collaborative Research Exploitative?. LADWIG, James G.
The Logic of Rational Play in Games of Perfect Information. BONANNO, Giacomo.
Methodological Individualism and Marx: Some Remarks on Jon Elster, Game Theory, and Other Things. WOLFF, Robert Paul.
The Mutual Investment Game: Peculiarities of Indifference. CUBITT, Robin P and HOLLIS, Martin.
A Note on the Permutationally Convex Games. ALIDAEE, Bahram.
On Judicial Ascertainment of Facts. VARGA, Csaba.
Penny Pinching and Backward Induction. HOLLIS, Martin.
Ratifiability, Game Theory, and the Principle of Independence of Irrelevant Alternatives. EELLS, Ellery and HARPER, William L.
Reading Hobbes in Other Words: Contractarian, Utilitarian, Game Theorist. HARDIN, Russell.

GAME(S)
see also Language Game(s)
Introduction Critique au Droit Naturel. HERVADA, Javier.
The Equivalence of Determinacy and Iterated Sharps. DUBOSE, Derrick Albert.
An Extension of Borel Determinacy. MARTIN, Donald A.
Extension of Gurevich-Harrington's Restricted Memory Determinacy Theorem. YAKHNIS, Alexander and YAKHNIS, Vladimir.
Notions of Relative Ubiquity for Invariant Sets of Relational Structures. BANKSTON, Paul and RUITENBURG, Wim.
On Scott and Karp Trees of Uncountable Models. HYTTINEN, Tapani and VÄÄNÄNEN, Jouko.
Preservation by Homomorphisms and Infinitary Languages. HYTTINEN, Tapani.
The Newcomb Paradox as a Poker Game (in Hebrew). SPECTOR, Raz.
Weak Axioms of Determinacy and Subsystems of Analysis II. TANAKA, Kazuyuki.

GANDHI
"Gandhi's Quest for a Nonviolent Political Philosophy" in *Celebrating Peace*, PAREKH, Bhikhu.
"Toward Understanding the Pragmatics of Absolute Pacifism" in *In the Interest of Peace: A Spectrum of Philosophical Views*, KOHL, Marvin.

GANGESA
Gangesa and Transfer of Meaning. SAHA, Sukharanjan.

GAOS, J
El conocimiento del singular en José Gaos. LLANO, Carlos.
Introducción a la filosofía de Gaos. SALMERÓN, Fernando.

GARAVASO, P
Some Objections To Garavaso's Wittgenstein. HUMPHREY, John A.

GARCIA MORENTE, M
La interpretación de Santo Tomás en García Morente. FORMENT, Eudaldo.

GARDEN(S)
"Distance, Disinterest, and Autonomy: Gardens as a Challenge to the Theory of Art" in *XIth International Congress in Aesthetics, Nottingham 1988*, MILLER, Mara.

GARDENFORS, P
Theory Revision and Probability. SCHLECHTA, Karl.
Two Methods of Constructing Contractions and Revisions of Knowledge Systems. ROTT, Hans.

GARDNER, P
Peter Gardner on Religious Upbringing and the Liberal Ideal of Religious Autonomy. MC LAUGHLIN, T H.

GARRIGOU-LAGRANGE, R
Il dibattito sulla verità tra Blondel e Garrigou-Lagrange. BERTOLDI, Francesco.

GARRISON, J
Comments of Garrison on Greene: Does Metaphysics Really Matter for Practice?. NEIMAN, Alven M.

GASSENDI
Vegetarianism and Virtue: On Gassendi's Epicurean Defense. MICHAEL, Emily.

GAUTHIER, D
"'Why Be Moral?' and Reforming Selves". WILLIAMSON, A Mark.
Bargaining with the Not-Yet-Born: Gauthier's Contractarian Theory of Inter-Generational Justice and Its Limitations. DE-SHALIT, A.
Can There Be Justified Philosophical Beliefs?. NIELSEN, Kai.
Constrained Maximization. SOBEL, Jordan Howard.
Discovering Right and Wrong: A Realist Response to Gauthier's Morals by Agreement. GENOVA, A C.
McClennen's Early Cooperative Solution to the Prisoner's Dilemma. MAC INTOSH, Duncan.
Morals by Appropriation. FREEMAN, Samuel.
Ownership as Theft. GRUNEBAUM, James O.
Retaliation Rationalized: Gauthier's Solution to the Deterrence Dilemma. MAC INTOSH, Duncan.

GEMES, K
Induction and Stochastic Independence. AGASSI, Joseph.

GENDER
Creative Characters. YOUNG-BRUEHL, Elisabeth.
Delicate Subjects: Romanticism, Gender, and the Ethics of Understanding. ELLISON, Julie.
Femininity and Domination: Studies in the Phenomenology of Oppression. BARTKY, Sandra Lee.
Self, Society, and Personal Choice. MEYERS, Diana T.
Varieties of Moral Personality: Ethics and Psychological Realism. FLANAGAN, Owen.
Vulgarity and Authenticity: Dimensions of Otherness in the World of Jean-Paul Sartre. CHARMÉ, Stuart Zane.
"Feminism, Postmodernism, and Gender-Scepticism" in *Feminism/ Postmodernism*, BORDO, Susan.
"Gender and Moral Luck" in *Identity, Character, and Morality: Essays in Moral Psychology*, CARD, Claudia.
"Gender and the Complexity of Moral Voices" in *Feminist Ethics*, MOODY-ADAMS, Michele M.
"Gender Trouble, Feminist Theory, and Psychoanalytic Discourse" in *Feminism/Postmodernism*, BUTLER, Judith.
"The Idea of a Female Ethic" in *A Companion to Ethics*, GRIMSHAW, Jean.
"Sex, Gender, and the Politics of Difference" in *Writing the Politics of Difference*, KUYKENDALL, Eleanor H.
"But Would That Still Be Me?" Notes on Gender, "Race," Ethnicity, as Sources of "Identity". APPIAH, Anthony.
Concerns of College Students Regarding Business Ethics: A Replication. PETERSON, Robert A and BELTRAMINI, Richard F and KOZMETSKY, George.
A Different Different Voice: On the Feminist Challenge in Moral Theory. ROONEY, Phyllis.
Do These Feminists Like Women?. SOMMERS, Christina.
Does Sommers Like Women? More on Liberalism, Gender Hierarchy, and Scarlett O'Hara. FRIEDMAN, Marilyn.
Ethical Judgments on Selected Accounting Issues: An Empirical Study. STANGA, Keith G and TURPEN, Richard A.
Feminism and Philosophy of Science. LONGINO, Helen E.
Feminist Fears in Ethics. NODDINGS, Nel.
Feminist Philosophy and the Genetic Fallacy. CROUCH, Margaret A.
Gendered Reason: Sex Metaphor and Conceptions of Reason. ROONEY, Phyllis.
Incorporating Gender Issues in Modern Philosophy. IMMERWAHR, John.
Irigaray on Subjectivity. SCHUTTE, Ofelia.
Jean-Jacques Rousseau, Sexist?. THOMAS, Paul.
The Lesbian, the Mother, the Heterosexual Lover: Irigaray's Recodings of Difference. HOLMLUND, Christine.
The Morality of Feminism. SEVENHUIJSEN, Selma.
Mothers of In(ter)vention: Women's Writing in Philosophy of Education. LEACH, Mary S.
Philosophers on Gender and Sexuality. VADAKKEMURIYIL, A.
Revealing Gendered Texts. FREELAND, Cynthia A.
The Unavoidability of Gender. SCHEMAN, Naomi.

GENE(S)
The Chromosome Theory of Mendelian Inheritance: Explanation and Realism in Theory Construction. VICEDO, Marga.
Dementia Praecox as a Failure of Neoteny. BEMPORAD, Jules R.
Realism and Simplicity in the Castle-East Debate on the Stability of the Hereditary Units. VICEDO, Marga.

GENEALOGY
Michel Foucault's Force of Flight: Towards an Ethics for Thought. BERNAUER, James W.
Nietzsche: The Body and Culture—Philosophy as a Philological Genealogy. BLONDEL, Eric.
Beauty and the Genealogy of Art Theory. CARROLL, Noël.
Can Genealogy Be Critical? A Somewhat Unromantic Look at Nietzsche and Foucault. VISKER, Rudi.
A Critique of Genealogies. KIM, Chin-Tai.
Foucault, Nietzsche, History: Two Modes of the Genealogical Method. SAX, Benjamin C.
Foucault: Making a Difference. LILLY, Reginald.
Genealogy and *Différance*. SCOTT, Charles E.
History and Historical Anthropology. GOUREVITCH, Aron I.
Nietzsche and Foucault on *Ursprung* and Genealogy. COOK, Deborah.
Nietzsche and the Critique of Oppositional Thinking. SCHRIFT, Alan D.
Nietzsche's Genealogy: Of Beauty and Community. KEMAL, S.
On the Genealogical Method: Nietzsche and Foucault. SAX, Benjamin C.
The Question of Ethics in Foucault's Thought. SCOTT, Charles E.

GENERAL RELATIVITY
L'inertie et l'espace-temps absolu de Newton à Einstein. GHINS, Michel.

GENERAL WILL
Kant's System of Rights. MULHOLLAND, Leslie A.
Différentielles et intégrales sociales chez Rousseau. BACHTA, Abdelkader.
Rousseau, the General Will, and Individual Liberty. KAIN, Philip J.

GENERALITY
Ambiguity, Generality, and Indeterminacy: Tests and Definitions. GILLON, Brendan S.
Meinongian Theories of Generality. SANTAMBROGIO, Marco.

GENERALIZATION(S)
see also Induction
Critical Reasoning (Third Edition). CEDERBLOM, Jerry.
Critical Activity and Ethics: The Problem of Generalization. KANIOWSKI, Andrzej M.
Green and "Everybody's Doing It". DE GEORGE, Richard T.
Instantial Terms, Anaphora and Arbitrary Objects. KING, Jeffrey C.
I metodi della metafisica platonico-accademica "generalizzante" ed "elementarizzante" nei libri "M" e "N".... CATTANEI, E.
A Truth-Functional Logic for Near-Universal Generalizations. CARLSTROM, Ian F.
When is "Everyone's Doing It" a Moral Justification?. GREEN, Ronald M.

GENERATION
Absolutely Independent Sets of Generation of Filters in Boolean Algebras. GRYGIEL, Joanna.
The Generation of Form in Aristotle. SHIELDS, Christopher.

GENERATIVE
Dialogue on Science, Society, and the Generative Order. BOHM, D and KELLY, Sean.
Natural Generativity and Imitation. SARTWELL, Crispin.

GENERIC
A 1-Generic Degree Which Bounds a Minimal Degree. KUMABE, Masahiro.
About Prikry Generic Extensions. SURESON, Claude.
Definite Descriptions and Definite Generics. OJEDA, Almerindo E.

GENEROSITY
Human Goodness: Generosity and Courage. PYBUS, Elizabeth.
Pour une philosophie du sens et de la valeur. VASSILIE-LEMENY, Sorin-Titus.
Generosity: A Duty Without a Right. STITH, Richard.

GENESIS
"The World Could Not Contain the Books" in *The Bible as Rhetoric: Studies in Biblical Persuasion and Credibility*, EDWARDS, Michael.

GENET, J
Writing the Revolution—The Politics of Truth in Genet's *Prisoner of Love*. CRITCHLEY, Simon.

GENETIC ENGINEERING
Ethics, Politics, and Human Nature. PAUL, Ellen Frankel (ed).
Shaping Genes: Ethics, Law and Science of Using Genetic Technology in Medicine and Agriculture. MACER, Darryl.
"The 'Frankenstein Thing': The Moral Impact of Genetic Engineering of Agricultural Animals" in *Agricultural Bioethics: Implications of Agricultural Biotechnology*, ROLLIN, B E.
Genetically Engineered Herbicide Resistance, Part Two. COMSTOCK, Gary.
Global Arguments for the Safety of Engineered Organisms. KLINE, David and GENDEL, Stephen M.
Human Nature Technologically Revisited. ENGELHARDT JR, H Tristram.
The Impact of Activist Pressures on Recombinant DNA Research. RABINO, Isaac.
New Creations? Commentary. BALK, Roger A.
New Creations? Commentary. MACER, Darryl.

GENETIC EXPLANATION(S)
Birth Defects: Traditional Beliefs Challenged by Scientific Explanations. DRYDEN, Richard.

GENETIC FALLACY
A Critique of Genealogies. KIM, Chin-Tai.
Feminist Philosophy and the Genetic Fallacy. CROUCH, Margaret A.

GENETIC SCREENING
Genetics, Neuroscience, and Biotechnology. LAPPÈ, Marc.

GENETICS
Beyond Natural Selection. WESSON, Robert.
Adequacy Criteria for a Theory of Fitness. ROSENBERG, Alexander.
Bioethics Inside the Beltway: The Human Genome Project. JUENGST, Eric T.
Byerly and Michod on Fitness. SMITH, John Maynard.
Les combinaisons de la vie, l'organisation du vivant, le réseau du soi. LIVET, Pierre.
Comments on "Fitness and Evolutionary Explanation". KLEINER, Scott A.
Genetics, Neuroscience, and Biotechnology. LAPPÈ, Marc.
Life and Cognition. FROLOV, Ivan T.
On Causality, Heritability and Fitness. ETTINGER, Lia and JABLONKA, Eva and FALK, Raphael.
Privacy and Disclosure in Medical Genetics Examined in an Ethics of Care. WERTZ, Dorothy C and FLETCHER, John C.
Quale statuto per l'embrione umano?. COMPAGNONI, Francesco.
Should Ethical Concerns Regulate Science? The European Experience with the Human Genome Project. RIX, Bo Andreassen.
What Is This Stuff Called Fitness?. OLLASON, J G.
Whose Genome Project?. MACER, Darryl.
Why the Anti-Reductionist Consensus Won't Survive: The Case of Classical Mendelian Genetics. WATERS, C Kenneth.

GENIUS
"Genius in Romantic Natural Philosophy" in *Romanticism and the Sciences*, SCHAFFER, Simon.
Kant's Apotheosis of Genius. QUINN, Timothy Sean.

GENOCIDE
Understanding War: A Philosophical Inquiry. MC MURTRY, John.
Speaking About the Unspeakable: Genocide and Philosophy. FREEMAN, Michael.

GENOVA, A
More on Quine's Dilemma of Undetermination. GIBSON, Roger F.

GENRE
Sémiotique des "genres": Une théorie de la réception. PAQUIN, Nycole.

GENTILE
Dall'attualismo al tensionalismo. SIMONE, Aldo.
Etica e diritto penale nella filosofia attualistica. RICCIO, Stefano.
Gentile e gli 'epigoni" dell'hegelismo napoletano: il carteggio con Sebastiano Maturi. SAVORELLI, Alessandro.
Gramsci, Gentile and the Theory of the Ethical State in Italy. SCHECTER, Darrow.
Hegel, Croce, Gentile: On the Idea of the "Ethical State". SANTORO, Liberato and CASALE, Giuseppe.
Note ad un recente libro sull'incontro-scontro tra Croce e Gentile. ANTISERI, Dario.
Venti lettere inedite di Angelo Camillo De Meis a Bertrando Spaventa. RASCAGLIA, Maria.

GENTZEN CALCULUS
On Subsystems of the System J_1 of Arruda and Da Costa. URBAS, Igor.

GEOMETRY
"First-Order Spacetime Geometry" in *Logic, Methodology and Philosophy of Science, VIII*, GOLDBLATT, Robert.
The Axiomatic Method: Its Origin and Purpose. AGASHE, S D.
Bruno e la matematica a lui contemporanea: In margine al "De Minimo". AQUILECCHIA, Giovanni.
Constructing or Completing Physical Geometry?. CARRIER, Martin.
La definizione di "retta" data da Euclide e le geometrie non-euclidee. BLANDINO, Giovanni.
The Development of Moral Reasoning and the Foundations of Geometry. MACNAMARA, John.
Dialectic and Diagonalization. KADVANY, John.
The Driving Ratio in Plato's Divided Line. DREHER, John Paul.
Geometrical and Physical Conventionalism of Henri Poincaré in Epistemological Formulation. GIEDYMIN, Jerzy.
Glymour on Deoccamization and the Epistemology of Geometry. DURAN, Jane.
Kants Theorie der geometrischen Erkenntnis und die nichteuklikische Geometrie. SCHIRN, Matthias.
Nuove ricerche sul 'Liber metaphysicus' *di Giambattista Vico*. CACCIATORE, Giuseppe.
On the Status of Proofs by Contradiction in the XVIIth Century. MANCOSU, Paolo.
Some Features of Hume's Conception of Space. FRASCA-SPADA, Marina.
Sur la méthode de Ferdinand Gonseth. VUILLEMIN, Jule.
Synthetic Mechanics Revisited. BURGESS, John P.
Wittgenstein on Logical Form and Kantian Geometry. SUMMERFIELD, Donna M.
Yet More on *Meno* 82a-85d. FOWLER, D H.

GEOPHYSICS
On the Objectivity of the Laws of Physics. HAMAN, Krzysztof E.

GERIATRICS
"Ethical Issues in Prescribing Drugs for the Aged and the Dying" in *Biomedical Ethics Reviews, 1987*, HOFFMASTER, Barry and BACHRACH, Sarah.
"Prescribing Drugs for the Aged and Dying" in *Biomedical Ethics Reviews, 1987*, YEZZI, Ron.
De natuurlijke ouderdom: een grenzeloze geschiedenis. BIJSTERVELD, Karin.

GERMAN
Alltagssprachliche Metakommunikation im Englischen und Deutschen. WELTE, Werner.
Dinâmica do Pensar: Homenagem a Oswaldo Market. FAC LETRAS UNIV LISBOA (ed).
From Hegel to Nietzsche: The Revolution in Nineteenth-Century Thought. LÖWITH, Karl.
La Grecia "Tedesca" fra Nostalgia e Mito. FOLLIERO-METZ, Grazia Dolores.
On Walter Benjamin: Critical Essays and Recollections. SMITH, Gary (ed).
Phänomenologie als ästhetische Theorie. FELLMANN, Ferdinand.
Published Essays, 1966-1985 (The Collected Works of Eric Voegelin, Volume 12). SANDOZ, Ellis (ed).
Reflexion und Metareflexion bei Platon und Fichte. ZEHNPFENNIG, Barbara.
Schellings Philosophie der Kunst: Göttliche Imagination und Ästhetische Einbildungskraft. BARTH, Bernhard.
"Conceptions of Peace" in *Celebrating Peace*, RENDTORFF, Trutz.
"The Cultural Dynamics of Philosophical Aesthetics" in *XIth International Congress in Aesthetics, Nottingham 1988*, PAETZOLD, Heinz.
"Historical Consciousness in the German Romantic *Naturforschung*" in *Romanticism and the Sciences*, VON ENGELHARDT, Dietrich and SALAZAR, Christine.
"Theology and the Sciences in the German Romantic Period" in *Romanticism and the Sciences*, GREGORY, Frederick.
Die DDR und ihre Philosophen: Über Voraussetzungen einer Urteilsbildung. RUBEN, Peter.
Het Dialectisch Humanistisch Grondmotief van Natuur en Vrijheid in de Pedagogiek als Wetenschap. OUWENDORP, C.
Florilegi filosofici ed enciclopedie in Germania nella prima metà del Duecento. STURLESE, Loris.

GERMAN
Fundamental Question of Philosophy: Remarks on the Pending Philosophical Reappraisal of the Past in the GDR (in German). SCHRÖDER, Richard.
Future through Self-Organization (in German). ARTZT, M.
German Collectivism and the Welfare State. NEAMAN, Elliot Yale.
Hegel, Spengler, and the Enigma of World History: Progress or Decline?. FARRENKOPF, John.
Heidegger's Rector's Address: A Loss of the Question of Ethics. SCOTT, Charles.
Illusions and Visions: Models Of and In Modern Societies. MARZ, Lutz.
Kant in Russia: The Initial Phase (continued). NEMETH, Thomas.
Michel Foucault: From the Humanities to Political Thought (in German). SEITTER, Walter.
Die Philosophie im einen Deutschland. HENRICH, Dieter.
The Post-Modern Challenge: From Marx to Nietzsche in the West German Alternative and Green Movement. BETZ, Hans-Georg.
Radical Enlightenment and Freethinkers (in German). POTT, Martin.
Sociologie in de Weimarrepubliek. HABERMAS, Jürgen.
Lo sviluppo degli studi logici nel pensiero tedesco della seconda metà dell' '800. MANGIAGALLI, Maurizio.
The Enticing Thing About Stalinism (in German). PÄTZOLT, Harald.
Views on Nietzsche in the GDR (in Hungarian). BOGNAR, Laszlo.
Von der dreifachen Vollendung des Deutschen Idealismus und der unvollendeten metaphysischen Wahrheit. JANKE, Wolfgang.
Welchen Platz kann die Philosophie künftig in unserem Lande beanspruchen und vor welchen Aufgaben steht sie?. RÜDIGER, Wolfgang.
Wissenschaftsphilosophie in der DDR—Versuch einer kritischen Betrachtung. HÖRZ, Herbert.
Zwischen Enttäuschung und Versöhnung: Hegel, die deutsche Misere und die Französiche Revolution. ARNDT, Andreas.

GERONTOLOGY
Aktuelle Aufgaben interdisziplinärer Bedürfnisforschung aus psychologischer Sicht. WOLF, Edith.
A Dilemma of Late Life Memory. MC KEE, Patrick.
New Directions in Nursing Home Ethics. COLLOPY, Bart and BOYLE, Philip and JENNINGS, Bruce.

GESTALT
Applying the Principles of Gestalt Theory to Teaching Ethics. HUNT, Eugene H and BULLIS, Ronald K.

GESTURE(S)
Gestualità e mito: i due caratteri distintivi della lingua originaria secondo Vico. CANTELLI, Gianfranco.

GETTIER, E
Gettier's Principle for Deducibility of Justification. BASU, Sandhya.

GEWIRTH, A
Brand Blanshard and Gewirth: Ethics and Rights. HOWIE, John.
A Comment on the Argument Between Gewirth and his Critics. ROSS, Steven.
Gewirth and the Pain of Contradiction. DAVIS, Michael.
Reason and Reality Revisited. PLUHAR, Evelyn.

GEYMONAT, L
Su alcuni aspetti del neoilluminismo di L Geymonat. STOMEO, Anna.

GHAZALI
Miracles and Ghazali's First Theory of Causation. BAHLUL, Raja.

GIACOMINI, G
Giacomo Andrea Giacomini: un clinico padovano tra Metafisica e Scienza. FEDERSPIL, Giovanni.

GIANNINI, H
La obra de Humberto Giannini: Un modo diferente de filosofar. ECHEVERRÍA, José.

GIARELLI, J
Philosophically Useful Kibitzing. PRATTE, Richard.

GIBBON, E
"Edward Gibbon in History: Aspects of the Text in 'The History of the Decline and Fall of the Roman Empire'" in *The Tanner Lectures on Human Values, Volume XI*, POCOCK, J G A.

GIBBONS, M
Paths to a Postmodern Ethics and Politics: A Reply to Gibbons. WHITE, Stephen K.

GIBSON, J
"Why Do Things Look as They Do?" Some Gibsonian Answers to Koffka's Question. NATSOULAS, Thomas.
The Praxiology of Perception: Visual Orientations and Practical Action. COULTER, Jeff and PARSONS, E D.

GIDDENS, A
Social Theory of Modern Societies: Anthony Giddens and His Critics. HELD, David (ed).
"Citizenship and Autonomy" in *Social Theory of Modern Societies: Anthony Giddens and His Critics*, HELD, David.
"Hermeneutics and Modern Social Theory" in *Social Theory of Modern Societies: Anthony Giddens and His Critics*, BAUMAN, Zygmunt.
"Models of Historical Trajectory: An Assessment of Gidden's Critique of Marxism" in *Social Theory of Modern Societies: Anthony Giddens and His Critics*, WRIGHT, Erik Olin.
"A Reply to My Critics" in *Social Theory of Modern Societies: Anthony Giddens and His Critics*, GIDDENS, Anthony.
"Social Theory as Critique" in *Social Theory of Modern Societies: Anthony Giddens and His Critics*, BERNSTEIN, Richard J.
"The Theory of Structuration" in *Social Theory of Modern Societies: Anthony Giddens and His Critics*, THOMPSON, John B.
Concepts of "Action", "Structure" and "Power" in 'Critical Social Realism': A Positive and Reconstructive Critique. PATOMÄKI, Heikki.

GIERE, R
Explaining Science. KORB, Kevin B.

GIFT(S)
Reproductive Gifts and Gift Giving: The Altruistic Woman. RAYMOND, Janice G.

GILBERT
Co-ordination, Salience and Rationality. MILLER, Seumas.

GILL, C
Plato's *Statesman* Story: The Birth of Fiction Reconceived. TOMASI, John.

GILLIGAN, C
The 'Voice of Care': Implications for Bioethical Education. CARSE, Alisa L.
A Different Different Voice: On the Feminist Challenge in Moral Theory. ROONEY, Phyllis.
The Expression of Experience: Code's Critique of Gilligan's Abortion Study. PITT, Alice.
Gilligan on Justice and Care: Two Interpretations. VREEKE, G J.
Her Terrain is Outside His "Domain". PEEPLES, S Elise.
Rethinking Feminist Humanism. STRAUS, Nina Pelikan.
The Science of Caring. PUKA, Bill.

GILSON
From Unity to Pluralism: The Internal Evolution of Thomism. MC COOL, Gerald A.
"Does Gilson Theologize Thomistic Metaphysics?" in *Thomistic Papers, V*, KNASAS, John F X.
"Gilson's Use of History In Philosophy" in *Thomistic Papers, V*, MAURER, Armand A.
Le statut de la philosophie chez Étienne Gilson. PROUVOST, Géry.
Thinking of Unity (in Dutch). AERTSEN, Jan A.

GIVING
Aquinas on Almsgiving, Justice and Charity: An Interpretation and Reassessment. POPE, Stephen J.
The Rhythms of Gratitude: Historical Developments and Philosophical Concerns. STEWART-ROBERTSON, Charles.

GLOBAL
The Challenge of Global Ethics. BULLER, Paul F and KOHLS, John J and ANDERSON, Kenneth S.
The Classroom as a Model of the World. STURGEON, Kareen B.
Global Injustices. MC BRIDE, William L.
Global Responsibility. AGASSI, Joseph.
La tecnología desde un punto de vista ético. RAMÍREZ, E Roy.
Tendencias actuales en filosofía de la tecnología. CAMACHO, Luis.

GLOBAL WARMING
Ethics and Energy Supplement. STEVENSON, Mark.

GLORY
Amour de l'être et ambition de gloire: le spinozisme de Vauvenargues. BOVE, Laurent.
Leviathan, King of the Proud. SHAVER, Robert.

GLYMOUR, C
Glymour on Deoccamization and the Epistemology of Geometry. DURAN, Jane.
The Irrelevance of Bootstrapping. CHRISTENSEN, David.

GNOSEOLOGY
Ce que Ferdinand Gonseth a d'important à dire à l'épistémologie contemporaine. JORGE, Maria M A.
The Gnoseological Aspect of Boskovic's "Theory of Natural Philosophy" (in Serbo-Croatian). ACIMOVIC, Mirko.

GNOSTICISM
Toward the Death of Man. KLUBACK, William.
Cientificidad y Romanticismo: Acerca de las relaciones entre cientismo, gnosticismo y romanticismo. KOSLOWSKI, Peter.

GOAL(S)
A Case for Apathy. NEUMANN, Michael.

GOD
see also Absolute, Atheism, Ontological Proof
'Religion' and the Religions in the English Enlightenment. HARRISON, Peter.
Amythia: Crisis in the Natural History of Western Culture. RUE, Loyal D.

GOD

Behind the Masks of God: An Essay Toward Comparative Theology. NEVILLE, Robert Cummings.
Being and Becoming: A Critique of Post-Modernism. CENTORE, F F.
Beyond the Big Bang: Quantum Cosmologies and God. DREES, Willem B.
The Call to Personhood. MC FADYEN, Alistair I.
The Co-Existence of God and Evil. TRAU, Jane Mary.
Discussioni sul neo-Tomismo: Per il progresso della Filosofia Cristiana. BLANDINO, Giovanni.
Divine Nature and Human Language: Essays in Philosophical Theology. ALSTON, William P.
Does God Exist? The Great Debate. MORELAND, J P.
Empiricism and Subjectivity: An Essay on Hume's Theory of Human Nature. BOUNDAS, Constantin V (trans).
Encounter on the Narrow Ridge: A Life of Martin Buber. FRIEDMAN, Maurice.
Ethics Without God (Revised Edition). NIELSEN, Kai.
Le existentia de deo e le Immortalitate del Anima: Lineas de Philosophia del Esser. BLANDINO, Giovanni.
God and Subjectivity. GALGAN, Gerald J.
Hellenic and Christian Studies. ARMSTRONG, A H.
A Hindu Perspective on the Philosophy of Religion. SHARMA, Arvind.
History and the Paradoxes of Metaphysics in "Dantons Tod". TAYLOR, Rodney.
The Idea of Christian Charity: A Critique of Some Contemporary Conceptions. GRAHAM, Gordon.
The Immutability of God in the Theology of Hans Urs Von Balthasar. O'HANLON, G F.
Inscriptions and Reflections: Essays in Philosophical Theology. SCHARLEMANN, Robert P.
John Dewey: Religious Faith and Democratic Humanism. ROCKEFELLER, Steven C.
Kierkegaards Phänomenologie der Freiheitserfahrung. DISSE, Jörg.
Locke and French Materialism. YOLTON, John W.
The Metaphysics of Religious Belief. SHOOMAN, A P.
Metaphysics: A Contemporary Introduction. POST, John F.
On True and False Ideas, New Objections to Descartes' Meditations and Descartes' Replies. ARNAULD, Antoine (trans).
Philosophy of the "Gita". PATEL, Ramesh N.
The Preface to Thomistic Metaphysics. KNASAS, John F X.
Published Essays, 1966-1985 (The Collected Works of Eric Voegelin, Volume 12). SANDOZ, Ellis (ed).
The Question of God in Heidegger's Phenomenology. KOVACS, George.
Sacred Fragments: Recovering Theology for the Modern Jew. GILLMAN, Neil.
Towards a Christian Philosophy. OWENS, Joseph I.
The Transcendental Temptation: A Critique of Religion and the Paranormal. KURTZ, Paul.
What is History? And Other Late Unpublished Writings (The Collected Works of Eric Voegelin, Vol 28). HOLLWECK, Thomas A (ed).
"'Where Two Are to Become One': Mysticism and Monism" in *The Philosophy in Christianity*, JANTZEN, Grace M.
"Arguments for the Existence of God" in *Key Themes in Philosophy*, SWINBURNE, R G.
"Could God Become Man?" in *The Philosophy in Christianity*, SWINBURNE, Richard.
"Faith and Rationality" in *Key Themes in Philosophy*, BARRETT, D C.
"Foreknowledge and the Vulnerability of God" in *The Philosophy in Christianity*, LUCAS, J R.
"The Freedoms of Man and Their Relation to God" in *Freedom in the Modern World: Jacques Maritain, Yves R Simon, Mortimer J Adler*, TORRE, Michael D.
"God as Creator" in *The Philosophy in Christianity*, WARD, Keith.
"God as the Ideal: The All-of-Monads and the All-Consciousness" in *Phenomenology of the Truth Proper to Religion*, LAYCOCK, Steven W.
"How Could Ethics Depend on Religion?" in *A Companion to Ethics*, BERG, Jonathan.
"On Not Knowing too Much About God" in *The Philosophy in Christianity*, ARMSTRONG, A H.
"The Peace of God" in *Celebrating Peace*, MINEAR, Paul S.
"Predicates of Pure Existence: Newton on God's Space and Time" in *Philosophical Perspectives on Newtonian Science*, MC GUIRE, J E.
"Thomism and Divine Absolute Power" in *Thomistic Papers, V*, KENNEDY, Leonard A.
"Lest Anyone Should Fall": A Middle Knowledge Perspective on Perseverance and Apostolic Warnings. CRAIG, William Lane.
La "memoria Dei" en el libro X de Las confesiones. PEGUEROLES, Juan.
'The Appearing God' in Hegel's *Phenomenology of Spirit*. JAMROS, Daniel P.
Analisi fenomenologica del concetto di religione. MONDIN, Battista.
The Antinomy of Divine Necessity. SCHRADER, David E.
The Argument from Religious Experience: A Narrowing of Alternatives. KETCHUM, Richard.
An Atheological Argument from Evil Natural Laws. SMITH, Quentin.
Augustine's Theology of the Trinity: Its Relevance. CLARK, Mary T.
Auschwitz, Morality and the Suffering of God. SAROT, Marcel.
The Authorship of Faith. SESSIONS, W L.
A Case Against Theistic Morality. VARMA, Ved Prakash.
Choosing Religious Languages: A Note on Two 'Proofs' of God's Existence. SAPADIN, Eugene.
The Condemnation of 1277: Another Light on Scotist Ethics. INGHAM, Mary E.
El conocimiento de Dios en la exposición de Tomás de Aquino sobre el "De divinis nominibus" de D Areopagita. ANDEREGGEN, Ignacio E M.
Conocimientos negativo y conocimiento afirmativo de Dios en Santo Tomás y en Hegel. ANDEREGGEN, Ignacio E M.
Contemplación y Dios en Aristóteles. DE KIRCHNER, Beatriz Bossi.
Could God Make a Contradiction True?. GOLDSTICK, D.
Craig, Mackie and the *Kalam* Cosmological Argument. OPPY, Graham.
Creation in a Closed Universe, *Or* Have Physicists Disproved the Existence of God?. LE POIDEVIN, Robin.
Cristianesimo tragico, cristianesimo ludico: i due volti della fedeltà al Dio dialettico. GARGANO, Monica.
The Crucial Disanalogies Between Properly Basic Belief and Belief in God. GRIGG, Richard.
La cuestión de Dios en el pensar de Heidegger. FORNET-BETANCOURT, Raúl.
Dialectical Thinking in Metaphysics—Van Kues: Coincidental Thinking and the Problem of Idealistic Monism (in German). WINKLER, Norbert.
Dieu tout-puissant et souffrant. RICHARD, Jean.
La dimostrazione "a posteriori" dell'esistenza di Dio nella filosofia di Leibniz. NICOLOSI, Salvatore.
Dios y el hombre en San Agustin. PEGUEROLES, Juan.
Discovering God in Western Civilization. BRESLAUER, S Daniel.
A Disproof of the Existence of God. WEEKS, Ian.
The Distinction between *Res Significata* and *Modus Significandi* in Aquinas's Theological Epistemology. ROCCA, Gregory.
Divine Unity and Superfluous Synonymity. LEVINE, Michael P.
La doctrina del don de San Agustín de Hipona. BELDA PLANS, Pilar.
Du libre arbitre selon s Thomas d'Aquin. CORBIN, Michel.
È possibile un'esperienza di Dio?. CAVADI, Augusto.
The Epistemological Significance of Transformative Religious Experiences: A Kierkegaardian Exploration. EVANS, C Stephen.
La esencia metafísica de Dios. DERISI, Octavio N.
L'essere mortale dei mortali: Un'analisi sul problema della morte nel pensiero del secondo Heidegger. CICCHESE, Gennaro.
Eternity and Simultaneity. LEFTOW, Brian.
Evil and the Proper Basicality of Belief in God. DRAPER, Paul.
Existencia de Dios y libertad humana. HERRERA, J Jesús.
Festrede zum 300: Geburstag von Gottfried Wilhelm Leibniz am 1 Juli 1946 in der Aula der Universitat Leipzig. GADAMER, Hans-Georg.
La fondazione dei valori nell'assiologia critica di Nicola Petruzzellis. TURCO, Giovanni.
Foreknowledge, Middle Knowledge and "Nearby" Worlds. DAVISON, Scott A.
Foundationalism and Peter's Confession. HESTER, Marcus.
Freedom and the Free Will Defense. GALE, Richard M.
Freedom Is Our Divinity (in German). EHRHARDT, Walter E.
God and Gratuitous Evil: A Reply to Yandell. CHRZAN, Keith.
God and Man: Action and Reference in Hobbes. BERTMAN, Martin A.
God and Real Time. CRAIG, William Lane.
God's Ability to Will Moral Evil. BROWN, Robert F.
Godsverduistering en Godsdienstfilosofie. DE BOER, Th.
Godsverduistering en Godsdienstfilosofie. VAN DER HOEVEN, J.
Gustavo Bontadini un metafisico per vocazione. LATORA, Salvatore.
Hindu Doubts About God: Towards a Mīmāṃsā Deconstruction. BILIMORIA, Purusottama.
How Can We Speak of God? How Can We Speak of Anything. FORREST, Peter.
Hume on Divine Amorality. WALLS, Jerry L.
Hume's *Dialogues* and the Redefinition of the Philosophy of Religion. SCHNER, George.
If There Is a God, Any Experience Which Seems to Be of God, Will Be Genuine. LEVINE, Michael P.
Die immerwährende Schöpfung als fundamentaler Seinsvorgang. KNAPPIK, G J.
In Defense of Anselm. ASPENSON, Steven S.
Is Coming to Believe in God Reasonable or Unreasonable?. HERBERT, R T.
Is There a Natural Law?. WALDSTEIN, Wolfgang.
Kenny and Religious Experiences. JORDAN, J.
Kierkegaard irrazionalista? Filosofi e filosofie nella interpretazione del filosofo danese. FRANCHI, Alfredo.
Kierkegaard on Theistic Proof. STERN, Kenneth.
Kierkegaard, Nietzsche, and the Death of God. NASH, Ronald H.
L'affirmation de l'existence de Dieu selon Austin Farrer. HENDERSON, Edward H.
L'origine première des choses. NICOLAS, Jean-Hervé.
L'unité-unicité de l'"esse" Thomiste. PASQUA, Hervé.
The Latin Avicenna as a Source of Thomas Aquinas's Metaphysics. WIPPEL, John F.

GOD
The Limits of Power. TALIAFERRO, Charles.
Literature and Language After the Death of God. STEIN, A L.
Logic and Logos—The Search for Unity in Hegel and Coleridge: II: The 'Otherness" of God. PERKINS, Mary Anne.
Il Logos come immagine di Dio in Filone di Alessandria. BELLETTI, Bruno.
Malebranche and the Vision in God: A Note on *The Search After Truth*, III, 2, iii. NADLER, Steven.
Marriage is an Institution Created by God: A Philosophical Analysis. BOYLE, Joseph.
Middle Knowledge and the Damnation of the Heathen: A Response to William Craig. HASKER, William.
Middle Knowledge and the Soteriological Problem of Evil. HUNT, David P.
The Modal Ontological Argument and the Necessary A Posteriori. FORGIE, J W.
A New Foreknowledge Dilemma. ZAGZEBSKI, Linda.
Nietzsche and the Cultural Resonance of the 'Death of God'. ROBERTS, Richard H.
Nietzsche's Use of Atheism. ROTH, Robin Alice.
El nombre propio de Dios. PONFERRADA, Gustavo E.
Nuestra voluntad es "de Dios". FERNÁNDEZ BURILLO, Santiago A.
Nuestra voluntad es "de Dios". FERNÁNDEZ BURILLO, Santiago A.
Offices and God. HUGLY, Philip and SAYWARD, Charles.
Omnipotence Need Not Entail Omniscience. SONTAG, Frederick.
Omniscience, Immutability, and the Divine Mode of Knowing. SULLIVAN, Thomas D.
On the Logic of Eternal Knowledge. KELLY, Charles J.
Ontologia e creazione in Filone Alessandrino: Dialogo con Giovanni Reale e Roberto Radice. MARTÍN, Josè Pablo.
The Other Comes to Teach Me: A Review of Recent Levinas Publications. GIBBS, Robert.
Pannenberg's Doctrine of God. O'DONNELL, John.
Patripassianism, Theopaschitism and the Suffering of God. SAROT, Marcel.
Il pensiero di Aldo Capitini e la filosofia del neoidealismo. CESA, Claudio.
Per l'Europa dopo il crollo della Cortina di Ferro. GRYGIEL, Stanislaw.
The Philosophical Achievement of Peter A Bertocci. RECK, Andrew J.
Philosophy and Religion (in Dutch). DHONDT, U.
Plato's *Parmenides* and St Thomas's Analysis of God as One and Trinity. KLEIN, Sherwin.
Possibility of Dialogic Encounter of Religious and Philosophical Humanitas (in Serbo-Croatian). SKLEDAR, Nikola.
Pour une interprétation féministe de l'idée chrétienne de Dieu. DION, Michel.
La prétendue intuition de Dieu dans le De Coelo d'Aristote. BODÉÜS, Richard.
Il problema teologico nel pensiero di Heidegger. PENATI, G.
Protecting God: The Lexical Formation of Trinitarian Language. BARRIGAR, Christian J.
Providence, Freedom and Human Destiny. TALBOTT, Thomas.
Quantum Physics, Philosophy, and the Image of God: Insights from Wolfgang Pauli. LAURIKAINEN, K V.
Qué conocemos de dios? Hobbes versus Tomas. LUKAC DE STIER, María Liliana.
The Recent Revival of Divine Command Ethics. QUINN, Philip L.
A Reflection on Saint Augustine's *Confessions*. BARKOVICH, Greg.
As relações entre o Deus da Razão e o Deus da Fé. RENAUD, Michel.
El reloj de Dios (Glosas provisionales a un principio leibniziano). MUÑOZ, Jacobo.
Reply to Davies: Creation and Existence. VALLICELLA, William F.
Reply to Lowenthal. COLMO, Christopher A.
Response to Gale's "Freedom and the Free Will Defense". HUMBER, James M.
Rilievi di struttura sul *De deo abscondito* di Nicola Cusano. DELCÒ, Alessandro.
Sant'Agostino e Hegel a confronto. CALEO, Marcello.
Het scheppende en herscheppende woord: zijn blijvende actualiteit. DENGERINK, J D.
El ser principial y Dios: Una observación a la teología de Maimónides. GARCÍA GONZÁLEZ, Juan.
Ser y Dios, entre filosofía y teología, en Heidegger y Siewerth. CABADA, Manuel.
Speech, Sin and the Word of God (in Dutch). GESTRICH, Christof.
Spinoza's Two Causal Chains. GILEAD, Amihud.
St Augustine and the Second Way. KLUGE, Eike-Henner W.
Struttura e finalità dei dialoghi platonici: Che cosa significa "venire in soccorso al discorso"?. SZLEZÁK, Thomas A.
Sur quelques textes de Spinoza relatifs à la notion de loi. PREPOSIET, Jean.
Time, Actuality and Omniscience. LEFTOW, Brian.
La toute-puissance du Dieu du théisme dans le champ de la perversion. ANSALDI, Jean.
Unamuno y el problema de Dios. FORMENT, Eudaldo.
Understanding the Question: Wittgenstein on Faith and Meaning. EISENSTEIN, Gabe.
Vasilii Vasil'evich Rozanov: "My Soul Is Woven of Filth, Tenderness, and Grief". KUVAKIN, V A.
Das vergeistigte Glück: Gedanken zum christlichen Eudämonieverständnis. DEMMER, Klaus.
Viktor Emil Frankl médico y filósofo. ALEGRÍA, Hernando Muciño.
Visione in Dio e visione di Dio nella filosofia di Malebranche. NICOLOSI, Salvatore.
Whitehead and Genuine Evil. BARINEAU, R Maurice.
Why Didn't God Create the World Sooner?. LEFTOW, Brian.
Why Natural Theology, Still, Yet?. HUTCHINGS, Patrick.
Why Plantinga Must Move from Defense to Theodicy. WALLS, Jerry L.
Wittgenstein's Gift to Contemporary Analytic Philosophy of Religion. KELLENBERGER, J.
X Zubiri in Roma: Natura, Storia, Dio. JAVIERRE ORTAS, A M.
'Following Nature' in Butler's Sermons. BRINTON, Alan.
'What Place, then, for a creator?': Hawking on God and Creation. CRAIG, William Lane.

GODDESS(ES)
The Great Goddess and the Aistian Mythical World. VYCINAS, Vincent.
Spiritual Values and "The Goddess". BRANDEN, Victoria.

GODEL
see Goedel

GODS
Hegel and the Gods of Greece (in Hungarian). KERENYI, Karoly.
The Many-Gods Objection and Pascal's Wager. JORDAN, Jeff.
Plato's Gods. PEHRSON, C W P.

GODWIN
Moraliteit en magie. LESAGE, Dieter.

GOEBEL, R
Zeeman-Göbel Topologies. HEATHCOTE, Adrian.

GOEDEL
Gödel's Theorem in Focus. SHANKER, S G (ed).
Is There Completeness in Mathematics after Gödel?. HINTIKKA, Jaakko.
The Relevance of Gödel's Theorem to Husserl's *Formal and Transcendental Logic*. BOULOS, Pierre J.

GOEDEL THEOREM(S)
Gödel's Theorem in Focus. SHANKER, S G (ed).
Massively Parallel Distributed Processing and a Computationalist Foundation for Cognitive Science. LYNGZEIDETSON, Albert E.
Minds, Machines and Gödels Theorem (in German). RHEINWALD, Rosemarie.
On an Alleged Refutation of Hilbert's Program Using Gödel's First Incompleteness Theorem. DETLEFSEN, Michael.
'Just More Theory': A Manoeuvre in Putnam's Model-Theoretic Argument for Antirealism. TAYLOR, Barry.

GOETHE
Goethe, Kant, and Hegel: Volume I, Discovering the Mind. KAUFMANN, Walter.
On Walter Benjamin: Critical Essays and Recollections. SMITH, Gary (ed).
"Namely, Eckermann" in *Looking After Nietzsche*, RONELL, Avital.
"Romanticism and the Sciences" in *Romanticism and the Sciences*, KNIGHT, David.
Faustian Phenomena: Teleology in Goethe's Interpretation of Plants and Animals. CORNELL, John F.
Goethe and Wittgenstein. ROWE, M W.
Hegel and Schopenhauer as Partisans of Goethe's Theory of Color. LAUXTERMANN, P F H.
The Other European Science of Nature?. UBEROI, J P S.
Wittgenstein's "Remarks on Colour". ERICKSON, Glenn W.

GOETZ, S
The "Kalam" Cosmological Argument and the Hypothesis of a Quiescent Universe. CRAIG, William Lane.

GOFFMAN, E
The Metaphoric Structure of Sociological Explanation. CORRADI, Consuelo.

GOLDMAN, A
Epistemology, Psychology, and Goldman. CORLETT, J Angelo.
Moral Truth and Coherence: Comments on Goldman. STEUP, M.
Social Epistemology and Social Cognitive Psychology. SCHMITT, Frederick.
The Trouble With Goldman's Reliabilism. GLEB, Gary.
What is Social about Social Epistemics?. MAFFIE, James.

GOLDSMITH, O
Tory History Incognito: Hume's *History of England* in Goldsmith's *History of England*. KENNELLY, Laura B.

GOLEM
In Partnership with God: Contemporary Jewish Law and Ethics. SHERWIN, Byron L.
Science and Art: The New Golem From the Transdisciplinary to an Ultra-disciplinary Epistemology. BERGER, René.

GOLUBOVIC, Z
A Christian Response to Professor Zagorka Golubovic. ZADEMACH, Wieland.
Dialogue as a Way of Being Human. YIN, Lu-jun.

GOMBRICH, E
Restoring Cultural History: Beyond Gombrich. PAVUR, Claude N.

GONSETH, F
Ce que Ferdinand Gonseth a d'important à dire à l'épistémologie contemporaine. JORGE, Maria M A.
Essai sur le thème du réferentiel. ORY, André.
Gonseth et le discours théologique. MOREL, Bernard.
L'épistémologie mathématique de Gonseth dans la perspective du pragmatisme de Peirce. HEINZMANN, Gerhard.
L'étude du vivant et la méthodologie ouverte. PILET, Paul-Emile.
On the Phenomenon of Marginality in Epistemology: Gonseth and his Tradition. WITKOWSKI, Lech.
La pensée gonséthienne et le mouvement systémique. PEGUIRON, Nicolas.
La pertinence du concept d'horizon de réalité en physique théorique contemporaine. COHEN-TANNOUDJI, Gilles.
La philosophie ouverte de F Gonseth aboutit-elle à une conception réaliste ou relativiste. LAUENER, Henri.
Sur la méthode de Ferdinand Gonseth. VUILLEMIN, Jule.
Vers une Pédagogie du Dialogue. TONOIU, Vasile.
Une version de l'épistémologie gonséthienne: le béton et les cailloux. BONSACK, François.

GONZALEZ, F
El tratado de Ideología de Fray Zeferino Gonzalez. BUENO SÁNCHEZ, Gustavo.

GOOD
see also Evil(s), Virtue(s)
After Principles. BARDEN, Garrett.
The Co-Existence of God and Evil. TRAU, Jane Mary.
Hegel: o la rebelión contra el límite. IZUZQUIZA, Ignacio.
Liberalism and the Good. DOUGLASS, R Bruce (ed).
Moral Pluralism and Legal Neutrality. SADURSKI, Wojciech.
Platos Idee des Guten. FERBER, Rafael.
Reflexion und Metareflexion bei Platon und Fichte. ZEHNPFENNIG, Barbara.
Returning to Sils-Maria: A Commentary to Nietzsche's "Also sprach Zarathustra". WHITLOCK, Greg.
The Tragedy of Reason: Toward a Platonic Conception of Logos. ROOCHNIK, David.
"Bringing the Good Back In" in *Liberalism and the Good*, SULLIVAN, William M.
"The Search for a Defensible Good: The Emerging Dilemma of Liberalism" in *Liberalism and the Good*, DOUGLASS, R Bruce and MARA, Gerald M.
"Utility and the Good" in *A Companion to Ethics*, GOODIN, Robert E.
Aristotle and Protagoras: The Good Human Being as the Measure of Goods. GOTTLIEB, Paula.
Death Is One of Two Things. RUDEBUSCH, George.
A Dialogue on Value, I: Values and Relations. LACHS, John.
A Dialogue on Value, II: Why Is There Something Good, Not Simply Something?. KOHÁK, Erazim.
A Dialogue on Value, III: Is Everything Intrinsically Good?. LACHS, John.
The Ethics of Inarticulacy. KYMLICKA, Will.
Etica e diritto penale nella filosofia attualistica. RICCIO, Stefano.
The Good in Plato's *Gorgias*. WHITE, F C.
Japanese Ethics: Beyond Good and Evil. WARGO, Robert J J.
Liberalism: Political Success, Moral Failure?. SIMPSON, Peter.
Moral Depth. KEKES, John.
Moral und Verwirklichung. KLEINGELD, Paulien.
The Open Question Argument. PAL, Jagat.
Play and the Theory of Basic Human Goods. CELANO, Anthony J.
Sidgwick and Self-Interest. CRISP, Roger.
Siting, Justice, and Conceptions of Good. ENGLISH, Mary.
Spinoza's Two Theories of Morality. LUCASH, Frank.
The Evil Beyond Good and Evil (in German). BOLZ, Norbert.

GOOD LIFE
Das Ethische in der Rhetorik des Aristoteles. WÖRNER, Markus Hilmar.
Living the Good Life: An Introduction to Moral Philosophy. GRAHAM, Gordon.

GOOD SAMARITANISM
Community as Compulsion? A Reply to Skillen on Citizenship and the State. ELLIOT, Gregory and OSBORNE, Peter.

GOODMAN, N
Cognitive Art. LAUTER, H A.
The Core of Aesthetics. WOLLHEIM, Richard.
Realism, Irrealism, and Ideology: A Critique of Nelson Goodman. MITCHELL, W J T.
Self-Making and World-Making. BRUNER, Jerome.
Truth. ULLIAN, Joseph S.
What Goodman Leaves Out. ELGIN, Catherine Z.

GOODNESS
The Dialogues of Plato, Volume II. ALLEN, R E (trans).
Good and Evil: An Absolute Conception. GAITA, Raimond.
Human Goodness: Generosity and Courage. PYBUS, Elizabeth.
"Faith and Goodness" in *The Philosophy in Christianity*, STUMP, Eleonore S.
Moral Goodness, Esteem, and Acting from Duty. LEMOS, Noah M.
Of One Mind or Two? Query on the Innate Good in Mencius. LAI, Whalen.
On Law and Morality: A Dialogue. VON WRIGHT, Georg Henrik.
Skepticism About Goodness and Rightness. GOLDMAN, Alan H.

GOODS
"Equality" in *Philosophy and Politics*, MILLER, David.
"On Fair Distribution of Indivisible Goods" in *Logic and Ethics*, SZANIAWSKI, Klemens.
The Anatomy of Aggression. LUPER-FOY, Steven.
The Ethical Limitations of the Market. ANDERSON, Elizabeth.

GOODWILL
Kants Kategorischer Imperativ als Leitfaden humaner Praxis. NISTERS, Thomas.

GORBACHEV, M
The Blackmail of the Single Alternative: Bukharin, Trotsky and Perestrojka. DAY, Richard B.
Gorbatschews "Erneurung des Sozialismus"—Ideologie in der Krise des Kommunismus. KUX, Ernst.
The Ideological Impasse of Gorbachev's Perestrojka. KRIZAN, Mojmir.
Lenin, Gorbachev, and 'National-Statehood': Can Leninism Countenance the New Soviet Federal Order?. GLEASON, Gregory.
Perestrojka der Philosophie?. IGNATOW, Assen.

GORDON, D
Divine Knowledge and Divine Control: A Response to Gordon and Sadowsky. BASINGER, David.
Reply to Gordon: Discourse at Work. CHMIELEWSKI, Philip J.

GORSKI, P
Theology and the Social Sciences—Discipline and Antidiscipline. MURPHY, Nancey.

GORZ, A
Gorz on Work and Liberation. SAYERS, Sean.

GOSPEL(S)
"The Fourth Gospel's Art of Rational Persuasion" in *The Bible as Rhetoric: Studies in Biblical Persuasion and Credibility*, WARNER, Martin.
"The World Could Not Contain the Books" in *The Bible as Rhetoric: Studies in Biblical Persuasion and Credibility*, EDWARDS, Michael.
Middle Knowledge and the Damnation of the Heathen: A Response to William Craig. HASKER, William.

GOSSIP
A Theoretical Note on Simmel's Concept of Acquaintance. DOUBT, Keith.

GOULD, G
"Glenn Gould: La technologie au service d'une nouvelle définition de la musique" in *XIth International Congress in Aesthetics, Nottingham 1988*, GUERTIN, Ghyslaine.
Glenn Gould: "archilecteur" *des Variations Goldberg*. GUERTIN, Ghyslaine.

GOVERNANCE
Parallel Governing. SCALTSAS, Theodore.
Some Remarks on the Political Science of Maimonides and Farabi. BARTLETT, Robert (trans) and STRAUSS, Leo.

GOVERNMENT REGULATION(S)
"Infertility and the Role of the Federal Government" in *Beyond Baby M: Ethical Issues in New Reproductive Techniques*, ELLIS, Gary.
Government and Character. PINCOFFS, Edmund L.

GOVERNMENT(S)
Benjamin Constant and the Post-Revolutionary Mind. FONTANA, Biancamaria.
The Limits of Government: An Essay on the Public Goods Arguments. SCHMIDTZ, David.
Television and the Crisis of Democracy. KELLNER, Douglas.
Alexander Hamilton: The Separation of Powers. PRATT, Ronald L.
Art and Censorship. SERRA, Richard.
Ethics and the Defense Procurement System. LANSING, Paul and BURKARD, Kimberly.
La filosofia: in soccorso de' governi. COLAPIETRA, Raffaele.

GOWER, B
How to Defend Science Against Scepticism: A Reply to Barry Gower. CHALMERS, Alan.

GOYA, F
Velázquez et Goya. PIERRE, Christian (trans).

GRACE
San Ignacio de Loyola y el humanismo. GARCÍA-MATEO, Rogelio.

GRACIA, J
Sobre la individualidad. CATES, Lynn.

GRADATION(S)
Sulla posizione dell'uomo nella natura. SEIDL, Horst.

GRAHAM, A
"Reason, Spontaneity, and the *Li*—A Confucian Critique of Graham's Solution to the Problem of Fact and Value" in *Chinese Texts and Philosophical Contexts*, FINGARETTE, Herbert.
"Who Chooses?" in *Chinese Texts and Philosophical Contexts*, ROSEMONT JR, Henry.

GRAMMAR(S)
Logic Programming: Proceedings of the Seventh International Conference. WARREN, David H D (ed).

GRAMMAR(S)
Saggio di semantica. BRÉAL, Michel.
Writing and the Moral Self. LANG, Berel.
"Comparatismo e grammatica comparata: Tipologia linguistica e forma grammaticale" in *Leibniz, Humboldt, and the Origins of Comparativism*, SWIGGERS, Pierre.
"Incremental Acquisition and a Parametrized Model of Grammar" in *Acting and Reflecting: The Interdisciplinary Turn in Philosophy*, CLARK, Robin.
"Linguistics: What's Wrong with 'The Right View'" in *Philosophical Perspectives, 3: Philosophy of Mind and Action Theory, 1989*, DEVITT, Michael and STERELNY, Kim.
"Translation Theories and the Decipherment of Linear B" in *Truth and Interpretation: Perspectives on the Philosophy of Donald Davidson*, WALLACE, John.
Computational Structure of GPSG Models. RISTAD, Eric Sven.
Erfurt, Ampl Q 70A: A Quaestiones-commentary on the Second Part of Alexander de Villa Dei's *Doctrinale*. KNEEPKENS, C H.
Grammaire et Liturgie dans les "Sophismes" du XIIIe Siècle. ROSIER, Irène and ROY, Bruno.
Grammar Logics. FARIÑAS DEL CERRO, Luis and PENTTONEN, Martti.
Grammar, Semantics and Conditionals. DUDMAN, V H.
Grammatica e diritto: Una normatività fragile?. VITALE, Vincenzo.
Intuitionistic Categorial Grammar. RANTA, Aarne.
Meaning as Grammar plus *Consequences*. DE QUEIROZ, Ruy J G B.
Philosophy: Sections 86-93 (pp 405-35) of the So-Called "Big Typescript" (Catalog Number 213)—Ludwig Wittgenstein. WITTGENSTEIN, Ludwig and NYMAN, Heikki.
Phrase Structure Parameters. FODOR, Janet Dean and CRAIN, Stephen.
Scandinavian Extraction Phenomena Revisited: Weak and Strong Generative Capacity. MILLER, Philip H.
Syntax and Pragmatics: Apartheid or Integration?. BOLKESTEIN, A Machtelt.
Virtues and Rules. ROBERTS, Robert C.

GRAMSCI, A
Gramsci, Croce and the Italian Political Tradition. BELLAMY, Richard.
Gramsci, Gentile and the Theory of the Ethical State in Italy. SCHECTER, Darrow.
El lugar de las superestructuras y los intelectuales en la filosofía política de Gramsci. RUIZ, Angel.
Two Views of the Revolution: Gramsci and Sorel, 1916-1920. SCHECTER, Darrow.
Warnings on Resistance and the Language of Possibility: Gramsci and a Pedagogy from the Surreal. SENESE, Guy B.

GRANIER, J
De la problématique diltheyenne à l'intégralisme de Jean Granier. AJERAR, Hassane.

GRAPH(S)
The Monadic Second-Order Logic of Graphs IV: Definability Properties of Equational Graphs. COURCELLE, Bruno.
Two Hypergraph Theorems Equivalent to BPI. COWEN, Robert H.
Valency, Adicity, and Adity in Peirce's MS 482. BURCH, Robert W.
Why Are Graphs so Central in Science?. KROHN, Roger.

GRASSI, B
Critica della filosofia zoologica per Battista Grassi. MESCHIARI, Alberto.

GRATITUDE
Four Arguments Against Political Obligations from Gratitude. KLOSKO, George.
The Rhythms of Gratitude: Historical Developments and Philosophical Concerns. STEWART-ROBERTSON, Charles.

GRAVITY
"Kant and Newton: Why Gravity Is Essential to Matter" in *Philosophical Perspectives on Newtonian Science*, FRIEDMAN, Michael.
La cosmologia tra filosofia ed empirologia. PELLECCHIA, Pasquale.
Quantum Gravity: Some Philosophical Reflections. ALTEKAR, E V.

GRAY, J
'One Very Simple Principle'. RILEY, Jonathan.
Post-Liberalism versus Temperate Liberalism. JACOBS, Struan.

GREATNESS
A Great Philosopher's Not So Great Account of Great Virtue: Aristotle's Treatment of 'Greatness of Soul'. CURZER, Howard J.

GREEK
see also Ancient
Aristotle on Sleep and Dreams. GALLOP, David (trans).
Demystifying Mentalities. LLOYD, G E R.
La Grecia "Tedesca" fra Nostalgia e Mito. FOLLIERO-METZ, Grazia Dolores.
Hellenic and Christian Studies. ARMSTRONG, A H.
Jurisculture, Volume I: Greece and Rome. DORSEY, Gray L.
Matter, Morals and Medicine: The Ancient Greek Origins of Science, Ethics and the Medical Profession. CARELLA, Michael Jerome.
Methods and Problems in Greek Science: Selected Papers. LLOYD, G E R.
Mystical Monotheism: A Study in Ancient Platonic Theology. KENNEY, John Peter.
Myth and Philosophy: A Contest of Truths. HATAB, Lawrence J.
Nietzsche: A Frenzied Look. ACKERMANN, Robert John.
Philosophy of the Ancients. RICKEN, Friedo.
Plato's "Parmenides". MEINWALD, Constance C.
"Ethics in Ancient Greece" in *A Companion to Ethics*, ROWE, Christopher.
"Greek Medical Models of Mind" in *Psychology (Companions to Ancient Thought: 2)*, HANKINSON, R J.
"Is There a Concept of Person in Greek Philosophy?" in *Psychology (Companions to Ancient Thought: 2)*, GILL, Christopher.
"O mito de Narciso" in *Dinâmica do Pensar: Homenagem a Oswaldo Market*, NUNES CORREIA, Carlos João.
"Poetic Revenge and Modern Totalitarianism" in *From Twilight to Dawn: The Cultural Vision of Jacques Maritain*, REDPATH, Peter A.
Dans quelle mesure et par quelles images les mythes grecs ont-ils symbolisé le néant?. RUDHARDT, Jean.
La democracia ateniense. GÓMEZ ROBLEDO, Antonio.
Dialectic and Diagonalization. KADVANY, John.
The Epic Hero as Politico. CAMPBELL, Blair.
Ethics Without Morality. BROWNE, Derek.
From Truth to 'Alhieia to Opening and Rapture. MALY, Kenneth.
Hegel and the Gods of Greece (in Hungarian). KERENYI, Karoly.
Heidegger and Myth: A Loop in the History of Being. HATAB, Lawrence J.
Heracles and the Passage from Nature to Culture in G Vico's *La Scienza Nuova*. MIUCCIO, Giuliana.
Heraclitus: Heidegger's 1944 Lecture Held at Freiburg University. FRINGS, Manfred S.
Homer's Contest: Nietzsche on Politics and the State in Ancient Greece. SMITH, Bruce.
Idéalisme ou réalisme?. LARGEAULT, Jean.
Individuo y acción en el pensamiento griego. RODA, Roberto.
La logique du mythe et la question du non-être. COULOUBARITSIS, Lambros.
La notion de non-être dans l'histoire de la langue grecque archaïque. LÉTOUBLON, Françoise.
Paideia Helénica. FREIRE, António.
Philosophical Anthropology in Greek Antiquity. GHOSE, A M.
Theoria, Aisthesis, Mimesis and Doxa. MÉCHOULAN, Éric.
Verbum-Signum: La définition du langage chez s Augustin et Nicolas de Cues. HENNIGFELD, Jochem.
Yet More on *Meno* 82a-85d. FOWLER, D H.

GREEN, R
Green and "Everybody's Doing It". DE GEORGE, Richard T.

GREENE, M
Comments of Garrison on Greene: Does Metaphysics Really Matter for Practice?. NEIMAN, Alven M.

GREENHOUSE EFFECT
Ethics and Energy Supplement. STEVENSON, Mark.

GREGORY OF NYSSA
El deseo infinito. PEGUEROLES, Juan.

GRICE, H
A Dilemma for Sentential Dualism. MOSER, Paul K.
Formulation of Grice's Three Intentions. LENKA, Laxminarayan.
A Pragmatic Analysis of Tautological Utterances. WARD, Gregory L and HIRSCHBERG, Julia.

GRICE, P
Meaning and Intention: Black Versus Grice. MARTINICH, A P.

GRIEF
Entre el duelo y la melancolia. SILVA CAMARENA, Juan Manuel.

GRIGOREV, A
Two Conservative Views of Nationality and Personality: A A Grigor'ev and K N Leont'ev. DOWLER, E W.

GRISEZ, G
Does the Grisez-Finnis-Boyle Moral Philosophy Rest on a Mistake?. VEATCH, Henry and RAUTENBERG, Joseph.

GROSSETESTE
William of Auvergne and the Eternity of the World. TESKE, Roland J.

GROUNDING
Fonti diritto e regole. DE GIACOMO, Claudio.
Comments of Garrison on Greene: Does Metaphysics Really Matter for Practice?. NEIMAN, Alven M.
Two Ways of Grounding Meaning. GERRARD, Steve.

GROUP(S)
Experimental Studies of Interactive Decisions. RAPOPORT, Amnon.
"Ethics in Small-Scale Societies" in *A Companion to Ethics*, SILBERBAUER, George.
Boolean Powers of Abelian Groups. EDA, Katsuya.
Contagious Folly: *An Adventure* and Its Skeptics. CASTLE, Terry.
Descriptions and Group Reference. MUKHERJI, Nirmalangshu.
Differentially Algebraic Group Chunks. PILLAY, Anand.
An Existence Theorem for Recursion Categories. HELLER, Alex.
Grupo de Piaget y estructuras afines. GONZÁLEZ CARLOMÁN, Antonio.

GROUP(S)
Making Student Groups Work: "To Teach is to Learn Twice". THOMASON, Neil.
On the Angular Component Map Modulo *P*. PAS, Johan.
On Type Definable Subgroups of a Stable Group. NEWELSKI, Ludomir.
Small is Beautiful. THOMASON, Neil.
Social Movements and Individual Identity: A Critique of Freud on the Psychology of Groups. WARTENBERG, Thomas E.
Tores et *p*-Groupes. BOROVIK, Aleksandr Vasilievich and POIZAT, Bruno Petrovich.
We Will Do It: An Analysis of Group Intentions. TUOMELA, Raimo.
Weakly Minimal Groups of Unbounded Exponent. LOVEYS, James.

GROWTH
Objectivity and Growth of Knowledge. CHAUDHURY, Mahasweta.

GRUENBAUM, A
The "Tally Argument" and the Validation of Psychoanalysis. RICHARDSON, Robert C.
The Degeneration of Popper's Theory of Demarcation. GRÜNBAUM, Adolf.
Zeno's Paradox of Extension. MC KIE, John R.

GUARDINI, R
Filosofia dell'esistenza e cristologia: La Weltanschauung cristiana di R Guardini. DI MARCO, Chiar.
Romano Guardini's Theological Critique of the Modern Age (in Dutch). VAN DER VLOET, J.

GUILT
El problema de la culpa y del "otro" en Heidegger y Siewerth. CABADA, Manuel.
Punishment and the Utilitarian Criterion of Right and Wrong. SCHALLER, Walter E.
Work and Family: Should Parents Feel Guilty?. PAINE, Lynn Sharp.

GUNTHER, A
Die Aufhebung der Begriffs-philosophie. KRONABEL, Christoph.

GUPTA, A
For Anil Gupta. HART, W D.
Logics of Truth. TURNER, Raymond.

GURVITCH
Libertad individual frente a determinación social. FRANCISCO PÉREZ, M.

GURWITSCH, A
Reflections on the Schutz-Gurwitsch Correspondence. LANDGREBE, Ludwig.

GUTOWSKI, P
Response to Piotr Gutowski's "Charles Hartshorne's Rationalism". HARTSHORNE, Charles.

GUY, A
La filosofía iberoamericana en la obra de Alain Guy. CATURELLI, Alberto.
Filósofo hispanista. FORMENT, Eudaldo.

HABERMAS, J
Between Freiburg and Frankfurt: Toward a Critical Ontology. DALLMAYR, Fred R.
Critical Theory and Philosophy. INGRAM, David.
Essays on Heidegger and Others: Philosophical Papers, Volume 2. RORTY, Richard.
Hermeneutics and Critical Theory in Ethics and Politics. KELLY, Michael (ed).
The Hermeneutics of Life History: Personal Achievement and History in Gadamer, Habermas, and Erikson. WALLULIS, Jerald.
Historische Objektivitat. WEBERMAN, David.
Philosophical Events: Essays of the '80s. RAJCHMAN, John.
Philosophische Hermeneutik. INEICHEN, Hans.
Reading Habermas. RASMUSSEN, David M.
Wahrheit—Diskurs—Demokratie: Studien zur "Konsensustheorie der Wahrheit". SCHEIT, Herbert.
"Art and Democracy in Habermas" in *Writing the Politics of Difference*, PICHÉ, Claude.
"Beyond Freud and Piaget: Biographical Worlds—Interpersonal Self" in *The Moral Domain: Essays in the Ongoing Discussion between Philosophy and the Social Sciences*, NOAM, Gil G.
"Jürgen Habermas fra 'teoria critica' e 'neo-illuminismo'" in *Razionalitá critica: nella filosofia moderna*, MONTANARI, Marcello.
"Linguistics as a Borderline Case" in *Abeunt Studia in Mores: A Festschrift for Helga Doblin*, MERRILL, Sarah A Bishop.
A New Approach in Moral Theory (in Dutch). KETTNER, Matthias.
A Post-Metaphysical Moral: An Introduction to the Moral Theory of Jürgen Habermas (in French). HUNYADI, Mark.
Announcement of the Endless in Horkheimer, Adorno and Habermas (in Serbo-Croatian). SIEBERT, Rudolf J.
A Candidate Paradigm for Human Ecology. BAPAT, Jyotsna.
Dialogue and Understanding (in German). FRITZSCHE, Helmut.
Discourse and the Moral Point of View: Deriving a Dialogical Principle of Universalization. REHG, William.
Discourse Ethics and the Communitarian Critique of Neo-Kantianism. REHG, William.
Dworkin, Habermas, and the CLS Movement on Moral Criticism in Law. INGRAM, David.
Les enjeux égalitaires du consensus rationnel: Habermas et ses sources. MARCIL-LACOSTE, Louise.
The Enlightenment—a Stranded Project? Habermas on Nietzsche as a 'Turning Point' to Postmodernity. NAGL, Ludwig.
Footprints in the Snow. SEERVELD, Calvin.
Los fundamentos discursivos de la democracia y los conflictos de intereses. GUARIGLIA, Osvaldo.
Habermas and Arendt on the Philosopher's "Error": Tracking the Diabiological in Heidegger. BERNASCONI, Robert.
Habermas and Solidarity. FUNK, Nanette.
Habermas and Theological Ethics (in French). BÜHLER, Pierre.
Habermas e o Terror Prático. LOPARIC, Zeljko.
Habermas et la théologie: Notes pour une discussion entre la théologie et la "Théorie de l'agir communicationnel". KISSLING, Christian.
Habermas on Heidegger's *Being and Time*. SCHARFF, Robert C.
Habermas on Strategic and Communicative Action. JOHNSON, James.
Habermas's Ontology of Learning: Reconstructing Dewey. YOUNG, R E.
Havel and Habermas on Identity and Revolution. MATUSTIK, Martin J.
Intersubjectivity and Critical Consciousness: Remarks on Habermas's Theory of Communicative Action. WAGNER, Gerhard and ZIPPRIAN, Heinz.
Is Grünbaum's Critique of Habermas' Understanding Freud Definite? (in Serbo-Croatian). NAGL, Ludwig.
Ist die Kantische Theorie eine Theorie entfremdeter Erkenntnis?. KERBER, Harald.
Nueva modernidad adveniente y cultura emergente en América Latina. SCANNONE, J C.
Providence and Political Responsibility: The Nature of Praxis in an Age of Apocalypse. LAKELAND, Paul.
Radical Hermeneutics, Critical Theory, and the Political. DOODY, John A.
Reply to Chmielewski: Cooperation by Definition. GORDON, David.
La teoría consensual de la verdad de Jürgen Habermas. BELARDINELLI, Sergio.
Die Theorie des kommunikativen Handelns in Diskussion. KISSLING, Christian.
Zu Jürgen Habermas' Option für Fortschritt, Vernunft und Demokratie. BOGNER, Hagen.

HABIT(S)
The Potential of Modern Discourse: Musil, Peirce, and Perturbation. FINLAY, Marike.
A Thinker's Guide to Living Well. BRADFORD, Dennis E.
"Inhabiting" in the *Phenomenology of Perception*. WEINER, Scott E.
Antropología en la Q D "De virtutibus in communi" de Santo Tomás. CORSO, Laura E.
L'Habitude, activité fondatrice de l'existence actuelle dans la philosophie de Spinoza. BOVE, Lauren.

HACKING, I
Instrumental Realism: The Interface between Philosophy of Science and Philosophy of Technology. IHDE, Don.
"'A Nice Derangement of Epitaphs': Some Comments on Davidson and Hacking" in *Truth and Interpretation: Perspectives on the Philosophy of Donald Davidson*, DUMMETT, Michael.
Hacking's Experimental Argument for Realism. HOLCOMB III, Harmon R.
Realism, Anti-Foundationalism and the Enthusiasm for Natural Kinds. BOYD, Richard.
Reinventing Certainty: The Significance of Ian Hacking's Realism. GROSS, Alan G.

HADEWYCH OF ANTWERP
"Hadewych of Antwerp" in *A History of Women Philosophers, Volume II: Medieval, Renaissance and Enlightenment, A.D. 500-1600*, WOLFSKEEL, Cornelia.

HALL, P
Response to Hall's "Goerner on Thomistic Natural Law". GOERNER, E A.

HALLDEN-COMPLETENESS
Some Syntactical Properties of Intermediate Predicate Logics. SUZUKI, Nobu-Yuki.

HAMANN
Hamanns Metakritik im ersten Entwurf. BAYER, Oswald.
The Legacy of Hamann—Thinking, Language and Economy (in Hungarian). RATHMANN, János.

HAMBLIN, C
Acceptance Is Not Enough: A Critique of Hamblin. JOHNSON, Ralph H.
Hamblin on the Standard Treatment. JOHNSON, Ralph H.

HAMILTON
Alexander Hamilton: The Separation of Powers. PRATT, Ronald L.
The Inapplicability of Evolutionary Stable Strategy to the Prisoner's Dilemma. MARINOFF, Louis.

HANDICAPPED
Mental Handicap and Citizenship. SPICKER, Paul.

HAPPINESS
see also Pleasure(s)
Blaise Pascals: "Pensées" (1656-1662) Systematische 'Gedanken' über. KIRSCH, Ulrich.
Ethics with Aristotle. BROADIE, Sarah.
Glück und Lebenssinn: Eine religionsphilosophische Untersuchung. DRESCHER, Johannes.
A Guided Tour of Selections from Aristotle's Nicomachean Ethics. BIFFLE, Christopher.
Human Interests: Reflections on Philosophical Anthropology. RESCHER, Nicholas.
L'Utopia di Fourier. TUNDO, Laura.
"Communication esthetique comme bonheur" in *XIth International Congress in Aesthetics, Nottingham 1988*, SASAKI, Kenichi.
"Maritain and Happiness in Modern Thomism" in *From Twilight to Dawn: The Cultural Vision of Jacques Maritain*, HUDSON, Deal W.
Aristippus Against Happiness. IRWIN, T H.
Freedom and Happiness in Kant's Political Philosophy. HELLER, Agnes.
The Greatest Happiness Principle. SPRIGGE, T L S.
Indirect Utilisme. ROSIER, Theo.
Is Happiness Relative?. VEENHOVEN, Ruut.
Scientific Knowledge and Human Happiness. ROY, Krishna.
The Supremely Happy Life in Aristotle's *Nicomachean Ethics*. CURZER, Howard J.

HARCUM, E
Empirical and Philosophical Reactions to Harcum's "Behavioral Paradigm for a Psychological Resolution of ...". POLLIO, Howard R and HENLEY, Tracy.
Some Theoretical and Methodological Questions Concerning Harcum's Proposed Resolution of the Free Will Issue. RYCHLAK, Joseph F.

HARDIN, L
Simpler Arguments Might Work Better. TELLER, Davida Y.

HARE, R
Amoralism—On the Limits of Moral Thinking. SANDOE, Peter.
Does Prescriptivism Imply Naturalism?. KANTHAMANI, A.
External and Now-For-Then Preferences in Hare's Theory. HAJDIN, Mane.
Hare on Prudence. RABINOWICZ, Wlodzimierz.
The Objectivity of Moral Values: The Search in a Wrong Place. BANERJEE, Hiranmoy.
On Intuitions. WETTERSTRÖM, Thomas.
Universalizability and the Summing of Desires. PERSSON, Ingmar.

HARM(S)
The Realm of Rights. THOMSON, Judith Jarvis.
"Risk, Causation, and Harm" in *Liability and Responsibility*, ROBINSON, Glen O.
'One Very Simple Principle'. RILEY, Jonathan.
AIDS and the L-Word. DEVINE, Philip E.
Between the Horns of the Negative-Positive Duty Debate. MALM, H M.
Cruzan: No Rights Violated. ROBERTSON, John A.
Just Looking: Voyeurism and the Grounds of Privacy. NATHAN, Daniel O.
On the Nature of Rape. BOGART, J H.
Punishment and Loss of Moral Standing. MORRIS, Christopher W.
The Punishment of Attempts. NUYEN, A T.
Surrogate Motherhood. PROKOPIJEVIC, Miroslav.

HARMAN, G
Agent-Action Judgements. TILLEY, John J.
Belief, Desire and the Praxis of Reasoning. WILLIAMS, Stephen.
Gilbert Harman's Internalist Moral Relativism. POJMAN, Louis P.

HARMONY
L'Utopia di Fourier. TUNDO, Laura.
"Ways of Establishing Harmony" in *Information, Semantics and Epistemology*, DENNETT, Daniel C.
Der Harmonie-Gedanke im frühen Mittelalter. BEIERWALTES, Werner.
Verità di ragione e verità di fede. MESSINESE, Leonardo.
La via della pace: in merito ad un recente libro. ZANUSO, Francesca.

HARRE, R
Harré and His Critics. BHASKAR, Roy (ed).
"Are Selves Real?" in *Harré and His Critics*, JENSEN, Uffe J.
"Introduction: Realism and Human Being" in *Harré and His Critics*, BHASKAR, Roy.
"The Realism of the Symbolic" in *Harré and His Critics*, SMITH, Charles W.
"Rom Harré: Realism and the Turn to Social Constructionism" in *Harré and His Critics*, SHOTTER, John.

HARRIS, R
The Foundations of Linguistic Theory: Selected Writings of Roy Harris. LOVE, Nigel (ed).

HARRIS, W
W T Harris' Philosophy as Personalism. LAUDER, Robert E.

HARRISON, P
Harrison on Animal Pain. HOUSE, Ian.

HART, H
H L A Hart and the "Open Texture" of Language. BIX, Brian.
Interpretation and the Social Reality of Law. GOLDFORD, Dennis.
Jurisprudential Oaks from Mythical Acorns: The Hart-Dworkin Debate Revisited. BOON LEONG PHANG, Andrew.
Wittgenstein versus Hart: Two Models of Rules for Social and Legal Theory. HUND, John.

HARTMANN, N
Nicolai Hartmann's New Ontology. WERKMEISTER, W H.
The Problem of Moral Freedom and Nicolai Hartmann. PRASAD, Kamata.

HARTSHORNE, C
Charles Hartshorne's Rationalism. GUTOWSKI, Piotr.
Response to Piotr Gutowski's "Charles Hartshorne's Rationalism". HARTSHORNE, Charles.

HASIDISM
Encounter on the Narrow Ridge: A Life of Martin Buber. FRIEDMAN, Maurice.

HATE
"Retributive Hatred: An Essay on Criminal Liability and the Emotions" in *Liability and Responsibility*, MURPHY, Jeffrie G.

HATTIANGADI, J
Hattiangadi's Theory of Scientific Problems and the Structure of Standard Epistemologies. GIUNTI, Marco.

HAVEL, V
Havel and Habermas on Identity and Revolution. MATUSTIK, Martin J.
The Intellectual in the Post Modern Age: East/West Contrasts. BAYARD, Caroline.

HAVING
Wanting, Getting, Having. HUMBERSTONE, I L.

HAWKING, S
Beyond the Big Bang: Quantum Cosmologies and God. DREES, Willem B.
Cosmology and Religion. JAKI, Stanley.
Creation in a Closed Universe, *Or* Have Physicists Disproved the Existence of God?. LE POIDEVIN, Robin.
Philosophical Elements in Penrose's and Hawking's Research in Contemporary Cosmology. DREES, Wim.
'What Place, then, for a creator?': Hawking on God and Creation. CRAIG, William Lane.

HAWTHORNE, N
Fault-Lines in Kierkegaard and Hawthorne: *The Sickness unto Death* and "Ethan Brand". BENOIT, Raymond.

HAYEK, F
From Dialogue Rights to Property Rights. SHEARMUR, Jeremy.
From Intersubjectivity through Epistemology to Property: Rejoinder to Michelman. SHEARMUR, Jeremy.
Hayek's Theory of Cultural Evolution: An Evaluation in the Light of Vanberg's Critique. HODGSON, Geoffrey M.
Hermeneutics: A Protreptic. JOHNSON, Gregory R.
How Individualistic Is Methodological Individualism?. MADISON, G B.
Reply to Shearmur's "From Dialogue Rights to Property Rights". MICHELMAN, Frank.

HAYRY, M
On Häyry and Airaksinen's 'Hard and Soft Offers as Constraints'. DAY, J P.

HEALING
An Ethnomedical Perspective of Medical Ethics. FABREGA JR, Horacio.
The Stilling of the *Aufhebung: Streit* in "The Origin of the Work of Art". PROTEVI, John.

HEALTH
The Health Crisis. SZUMSKI, Bonnie (ed).
A Thinker's Guide to Living Well. BRADFORD, Dennis E.
"A Comment on Three Topics in Volume 7 of the *Treatise*: Teleology, the Mind-Body Problem, and Health and Disease" in *Studies on Mario Bunge's "Treatise"*, DUBROVSKY, Bernardo.
The Ethics of Corporate Health Insurance. LIGHT, Donald W.
The Theme of Health in Nietzsche's Thought. LETTERI, Mark.

HEALTH CARE
The Crisis in Health Care: Ethical Issues. MC KENZIE, Nancy F (ed).
The Health Crisis. SZUMSKI, Bonnie (ed).
Integrity in Health Care Institutions: Humane Environments for Teaching, Inquiry, and Healing. BULGER, Ruth Ellen (ed).
Medical Ethics in Practice. BARD, Terry R.
Medical Work in America: Essays on Health Care. FREIDSON, Eliot.
Medicine and Money: A Study of the Role of Beneficence in Health Care Cost Containment. MARSH, Frank H.
Philosophical Foundations of Health Education. LAURA, Ronald S.
Theory and Practice in Medical Ethics. GRABER, Glenn C.
To Die or Not to Die?. BERGER, Arthur S (ed).
"Approaching Ethical Questions: A University Perspective" in *Integrity in Health Care Institutions: Humane Environments for Teaching, Inquiry, and Healing*, STEINER, Daniel.
"Can National Health Insurance Solve the Crisis in Health Care?" in *Biomedical Ethics Reviews, 1990*, IRVINE, William B.

HEALTH CARE
"Covenant, Leadership, and Value Formation in Academic Health Centers" in *Integrity in Health Care Institutions: Humane Environments for Teaching, Inquiry, and Healing*, BULGER, Roger J.
"Determinants of the Culture and Personality of Institutions" in *Integrity in Health Care Institutions: Humane Environments for Teaching, Inquiry, and Healing*, HAUGHTON, James G.
"The Hospital-Academic Health Center Interface: The Community of Practice and the Community of Learning" in *Integrity in Health Care Institutions: Humane Environments for Teaching, Inquiry, and Healing*, RABKIN, Mitchell T.
"Integrity, Humaneness, and Institutions in Secular Pluralist Societies" in *Integrity in Health Care Institutions: Humane Environments for Teaching, Inquiry, and Healing*, ENGELHARDT JR, H Tristram.
"Medical Institutions and Their Moral Constraints" in *Integrity in Health Care Institutions: Humane Environments for Teaching, Inquiry, and Healing*, TOULMIN, Stephen.
"The Politics of Trust in American Health Care" in *Ethics, Trust, and the Professions: Philosophical and Cultural Aspects*, FOX, Daniel M.
"The Revival of Community and the Public Obligation of Academic Health Centers" in *Integrity in Health Care Institutions: Humane Environments for Teaching, Inquiry, and Healing*, GREEN, Lawrence W.
"Values and Academic Health Centers: A Commentary and Recommendations" in *Integrity in Health Care Institutions: Humane Environments for Teaching, Inquiry, and Healing*, PELLEGRINO, Edmund D.
Advocacy of Just Health Policies as Professional Duty: Cultural Biases and Ethical Responsibilities. CRANDALL, Lee A.
Chronic Illness and the Temporal Structure of Human Life. DOUARD, John W.
Commentary: When Opportunity Knocks. BERENSON, Robert A.
Community Responsibility and the Development of Oregon's Health Care Priorities. GARLAND, Michael J and HASNAIN, Romana.
Consumer Sovereignty versus Informed Consent: Saying No to Requests to "Do Everything" for Dying Patients. WEBER, Leonard.
Defining the Limits of Institutional Moral Agency in Health Care: A Response to Kevin Wildes. RIE, Michael A.
Democracy and Justice in Health Policy. JENNINGS, Bruce.
Desperately Seeking Science: The Creation of Knowledge in Family Practice. GOLDSTEIN, Jared.
Doctors and Their Advertising. BURTON, Gene E.
The Ethics of Health Care as a Business. WERHANE, Patricia H.
Heads, Feds, and Beds: Ethical Dilemmas in the Delivery of Medical Care. WILLIAMS, Arthur R.
Health Care as a Business: The Ethic of Hippocrates Versus the Ethic of Managed Care. WAYMACK, Mark H.
Health Policy Analysis as Ideology and as Utopian Rhetoric. MILLER, Irwin.
An Integrative Model of Clinical-Ethical Decision Making. GRUNDSTEIN-AMADO, Rivka.
Judaism, Justice, and Access to Health Care. MACKLER, Aaron L.
The Limits of a Wish. RIE, Michael A.
Market Mechanisms and Principles of Justice. LOEWY, Erich H.
Medical Futility, Medical Necessity: The - Problem - Without - A - Name. CALLAHAN, Daniel.
Medicine and Business: An Unhealthy Mix?. BROCK, Dan W.
The Moral Significance of Institutional Integrity. WEAR, Stephen.
The Oregon Medicaid Experiment: Is It Just Enough?. FLECK, Leonard M.
The Profit Motive and the Moral Assessment of Health Care Institutions. DANIELS, Norman.
A Proposal for Health Care: Revolution Not Reform. BARNET, Robert J.
Reassessing Autonomy in Long-Term Care. AGICH, George J.
Reforming Britain's National Health Service. KESSEL, Ros.
Setting Floating Limits: Functional Status Care Categories as National Policy. THOMASMA, David C.
Should Basic Care Get Priority? Doubts about Rationing the Oregon Way. VEATCH, Robert M.
The Significance of a Wish. ACKERMAN, Felicia.
Surrogate Decisionmaking and Other Matters. GREENLAW, Jane.
Teaching Ethics in the Health Care Setting, Part I. COUTTS, Mary Carrington.
When Is Home Care Medically Necessary? Commentary. FORROW, Lachlan.
When Is Home Care Medically Necessary? Commentary. DANIELS, Norman and SABIN, James E.
Wie van de drie: Wil de ware wetenschapsonderzoeker opstaan?. BIJSTERVELD, Karin and MESMAN, Jessica.

HEALTH EDUCATION
Philosophical Foundations of Health Education. LAURA, Ronald S.

HEART
Axiology as the Form of Purity of Heart: A Reading Husserliana XXVIII. HART, James G.

HEBREO, L
De las maravillas acerca de lo uno y lo múltiple o sobre los avatares del amor neoplatónico en Baruch de Espinosa. ALBIAC, Gabriel.

HEBREW
Scharfstein as a Metaphysician of Art (in Hebrew). LURIE, Yuval.

HEDONISM
see also Happiness
Living the Good Life: An Introduction to Moral Philosophy. GRAHAM, Gordon.
The Greatest Happiness Principle. SPRIGGE, T L S.
Kant's Psychological Hedonism. GRIFFITHS, A Phillips.
Some Puzzles About the Evil of Death. FELDMAN, Fred.

HEELAN, P
Instrumental Realism: The Interface between Philosophy of Science and Philosophy of Technology. IHDE, Don.

HEGEL
Essays on Hegel's Logic. DI GIOVANNI, George (ed).
Goethe, Kant, and Hegel: Volume I, Discovering the Mind. KAUFMANN, Walter.
Hegel In His Time—Jacques D'Hondt. BURBIDGE, John (trans).
Hegel: o la rebelión contra el límite. IZUZQUIZA, Ignacio.
Hegels Theorie des Gesetzes. BOGDANDY, Armin Von.
History and the Paradoxes of Metaphysics in "Dantons Tod". TAYLOR, Rodney.
Human Nature and Historical Knowledge: Hume, Hegel and Vico. POMPA, Leon.
Irony and the Discourse of Modernity. BEHLER, Ernst.
Una lettura idealistica della "Analitica Trascendentale". BELLINI, Ornella.
Modern Faith and Thought. THIELICKE, Helmut.
Of Memory, Reminiscence, and Writing: On the Verge. KRELL, David Farrell.
Overcoming Foundations: Studies in Systematic Philosophy. WINFIELD, Richard Dien.
Published Essays, 1966-1985 (The Collected Works of Eric Voegelin, Volume 12). SANDOZ, Ellis (ed).
The Self-Overcoming of Nihilism: Nishitani Keiji. PARKES, Graham (trans).
"Abstract and Concrete in Hegel's Logic" in *Essays on Hegel's Logic*, GRIER, Philip T.
"Essence and Subversion in Hegel and Heidegger" in *Writing the Politics of Difference*, MC CUMBER, John.
"Hegel and the Problem of the Differentia" in *Essays on Hegel's Logic*, HALPER, Edward.
"Hegel and the Subversion of Systems: *Der Fall Adorno*" in *Writing the Politics of Difference*, DONOUGHO, Martin.
"Hegel e a linguagem: estudo em forma de prefácio ou introdução" in *Dinâmica do Pensar: Homenagem a Oswaldo Market*, POMBO, Olga.
"Hegel's Criticism of Spinoza's Concept of the Absolute" in *Essays on Hegel's Logic*, BYRNE, Laura.
"Love between Us" in *Who Comes after the Subject?*, IRIGARAY, Luce.
"Merleau-Ponty and Hegel: Radical Essentialism" in *Ontology and Alterity in Merleau-Ponty*, FLAY, Joseph C.
"The Method of Hegel's *Science of Logic*" in *Essays on Hegel's Logic*, WINFIELD, Richard Dien.
"Subversion of System/Systems of Subversion" in *Writing the Politics of Difference*, SHAPIRO, Gary.
"Ways and Loci of Modality" in *Essays on Hegel's Logic*, BAPTIST, Gabriella.
'The Appearing God' in Hegel's *Phenomenology of Spirit*. JAMROS, Daniel P.
Ancora una discussione su Hegel: logica, storia, fenomenologia. NUZZO, Angelica.
Après Weil, avec Weil: Une lecture de Gilbert Kirscher. LABARRIÈRE, Pierre-Jean.
Attraction and Repulsion in Comprehension of Boskovic, Hegel and Engels (in Serbo-Croatian). STOILJKOVIC, Dragoslav.
A Brief Discussion of One Aspect of the *Shangtong* Idea. YUANHUA, Wang.
Circularity of Thought in Hegel's Logic. BALABAN, Oded.
Conocimientos negativo y conocimiento afirmativo de Dios en Santo Tomás y en Hegel. ANDEREGGEN, Ignacio E M.
A Critique of Derrida's Hegel Deconstruction: Speech, Phonetic Writing, and Hieroglyphic Script in Logic, Law, Art. CUTROFELLO, Andrew.
De l'Idéologie comme correlat des termes idéologiste et idéologue. ZOLUA, Buenzey Maluenga.
El desaparecer de lo eterno en sí mismo: Una clave del pensamiento de Hegel. ALBIZU, Edgardo.
La dignità dell'uomo da Kant a Hegel. PAOLINELLI, Marco.
Las disonancias de la libertad (I). INNERARITY, Daniel.
Erneuerung als Grundmechanismus der Evolution. EBELING, Werner.
Evolution and Nostalgia in Hegel's Theory of Desire. BERTHOLD-BOND, Daniel.
Foucault: Making a Difference. LILLY, Reginald.
Foundationalism, Holism, or Hegel?. STERN, David S.
From Hegel to Lukacs: The Problem of Ontology from the Point of View of Social and Natural Theory (in German). MOCEK, Reinhard.
Gadamer over 'Vermittlung': de Hegeliaanse draad in zijn hermeneutiek. VAN DER HOEVEN, J.
Glasnost and Enlightenment. OLSON, Alan M.
Hegel and Kant—A Refutation of their Racism. NEUGEBAUER, Christian.
Hegel and Schopenhauer as Partisans of Goethe's Theory of Color. LAUXTERMANN, P F H.

HEGEL

Hegel and the Gods of Greece (in Hungarian). KERENYI, Karoly.
Hegel and the Humean Problem of Induction. SUCHTING, W A.
Hegel and the Overcoming of the Understanding. BAUR, Michael.
Hegel as Advocate of Machiavelli (in German). JAMME, Christoph.
Hegel's Critical Theory and Feminist Concerns. HAYIM, Gila J.
Hegel's Critique of Liberalism and Natural Law: Reconstructing Ethical Life. GARZA JR, Abel.
Hegel's Intertextual Dialectic: Diderot's *Le Neveu de Rameau* in the *Phenomenology of Spirit*. PRICE, David W.
Hegel's Legend of Self-Determination. KAMAL, Muhammad.
Hegel's *Logic* and Marx's Early Development. PRINCIPE, Michael A.
Hegel, Antigone, and the Possibility of Ecstatic Dialogue. WILLETT, Cynthia.
Hegel, Croce, Gentile: On the Idea of the "Ethical State". SANTORO, Liberato and CASALE, Giuseppe.
Hegel, Heidegger, and the Question of Art Today. GROSSMANN, Andreas.
Hegel, Logic, and Metaphysics. HARTSHORNE, Charles.
Hegel, Marx, and the Concept of Immanent Critique. BUCHWALTER, Andrew.
Hegel, Marx, Lukács: The Dialectic of Freedom and Necessity. DAY, Richard B.
Hegel, Marx, Nietzsche, and the Future of Self-Alienation. SCHACHT, Richard.
Hegel, Nietzsche, and Freud on Madness and the Unconscious. BERTHOLD-BOND, Daniel.
Hegel, Spengler, and the Enigma of World History: Progress or Decline?. FARRENKOPF, John.
Hegel: fenomenología del espíritu. MONTOYA, Rocío Basurto.
Hegels Geschichtsphilosophie im Vergleich mit anderen Geschichtskonzeptionen. GLOY, Karen.
Hermeneutic or Metaphysical Hegelianism? Kojève's Dilemma. REDDING, Paul.
Herméneutique et épistémologie Gadamer entre Heidegger et Hegel. ROCKMORE, Tom.
Hölderlin über Urteil und Sein. GRAESER, Andreas.
The Immanence of Thought: Hegel's Critique of Foundationalism. STERN, David S.
Das Imperiale an der Identitätsphilosophie: Spuren des Totalitären in der abendländischen Philosophie. MANSILLA, Hugo C F.
Ist die Naturphilosophie eine abgelegte Gestalt des modernen Geistes. WAHSNER, Renate.
Kant in Hegels begtipsleer. DE VOS, L.
The Later Schelling's Conception of Dialectical Method, in Contradistinction to Hegel's. BEACH, Edward A.
Logic and Logos—The Search for Unity in Hegel and Coleridge: I, Alienation and the Logocentric Response. PERKINS, Mary Anne.
Logic and Logos—The Search for Unity in Hegel and Coleridge: II: The 'Otherness" of God. PERKINS, Mary Anne.
Logic and Logos—The Search for Unity in Hegel and Coleridge, III: A Different Logos. PERKINS, Mary Anne.
La logica di Hegel come testo filosofico (II). COSTA, Filippo.
Marx and Dialectics (in German). ADLER, Max.
Marx's 'Critique of Hegel's *Philosophy of Right*'. JACKSON, M W.
The Master-Slave Dialectic in Latin America: The Social Criticism of Zea, Freire, and Roig. SCHUTTE, Ofelia M.
Metafisica e dialettica: quattro saggi sull'interpretazione hegeliana di Aristotele. FERRARIN, Alfredo.
Metaphysik und Metaphysikkritik. HARTMANN, Klaus.
Music in Hegel's *Aesthetics*: A Re-Evaluation. JOHNSON, Julian.
La naturaleza como vida en la interpretación hegeliana de Aristóteles. BARROSO, Inmaculada Acosta.
New Studies on Hegel's Philosophy of Law, versus on the Dialectics of Hegel and Marx (in Hungarian). GÖHLER, Gerhard.
Orthodoxy or Atheism? Remarks on the New Edition of Hegel's Lectures on Religion (in Hungarian). MOLNÁR, László M.
Over het morele en zedelijke handelen, toegelicht aan het instituut huwelijk. COBBEN, Paul.
Providence and Political Responsibility: The Nature of Praxis in an Age of Apocalypse. LAKELAND, Paul.
La recepción de la "crítica de la razón pura" en el joven Hegel. DEL CARMEN PAREDES MARTIN, M.
Rethinking Politics: Carl Schmitt vs Hegel. WINFIELD, Richard Dien.
The Return of the Initiate: Hegel on Bread and Wine. AUXIER, Randall E.
Rileggendo Marx: "diritti" e "bisogni". BADALONI, Nicola.
Die Rolle des unglücklichen Bewusstseins in Hegels *Phänomenologie des Geistes*. STEWARD, Jon.
The Rule of Law in *The German Constitution*. HANCE, Allen S.
Sant'Agostino e Hegel a confronto. CALEO, Marcello.
Schattenseiten der Hegelei: Fallsbeispiel—Lassalles Hegel-Rhapsodie. BEYER, Wilhelm Raimund.
Schelling on Hegel: From his Lectures in Munich and Berlin (in Hungarian). FEHÉR, I.
Schopenhauer and Hegel (in Hebrew). SIGAD, Ran.
The Stilling of the *Aufhebung: Streit* in "The Origin of the Work of Art". PROTEVI, John.
The Structure of Self-Commentary in Hegel's Dialectical Logic. GASKINS, Richard H.
Teleologie: Chance oder Belastung für die Philosophie?. PLEINES, Jürgen-Eckardt.
The Beginning and Structure of the "Phaenomenology of Mind" (in Hungarian). PÖGGELER, Otto.
The Notion of Sublime in Kant and Hegel: A Psycho-Analytical Reading (in Serbo-Croatian). ZIZEK, Slavoj.
The Perversion of Emancipation into Repression (in German). SCHMIDT, Hartwig.
Theorising Ideas: *Idee* and *Vorstellung* from Kant to Hegel to Marx. CRISTAUDO, Wayne.
Thought and Being in Kant and Hegel. HOULGATE, Stephen.
Time in Hegel's *Phenomenology of Spirit*. FLAY, Joseph C.
Tra Kant e Hegel: per una riaffermazione dell'antico concetto di società civile. MARINI, Giuliano.
Von der dreifachen Vollendung des Deutschen Idealismus und der unvollendeten metaphysischen Wahrheit. JANKE, Wolfgang.
World History as the Progress of Consciousness: An Interpretation of Hegel's Philosophy of History. HOULGATE, Stephen.
Would Hegel Have Liked to Burn Down All the Churches and Replace Them with Philosophical Academies?. LUFT, Eric V D.
Zur inhaltlichen Bedeutung des Hegelschen "Schemas der Naturphilosophie" in den Epikurstudien des jungen Marx. MIELKE, Dietmar.
Zwischen Enttäuschung und Versöhnung: Hegel, die deutsche Misere und die Französiche Revolution. ARNDT, Andreas.

HEGELIANISM

A "Realizacção da Razão": Um Programa Hegeliano?. BARATA-MOURA, José.
Against Architecture: The Writings of Georges Bataille. HOLLIER, Denis.
Hope and Its Hieroglyph: A Critical Decipherment of Ernst Bloch's "Principle of Hope". ROBERTS, Richard H.
"The Role of Publicity in the Disintegration of the Hegelian School" in *Perspectives on Ideas and Reality*, SZÍVÓS, Mihály.
Adorno and the French Post-Structuralists on the Other of Reason. NUYEN, A T.
Gelehrter zwischen Romantik und Hegelianismus in Finnland—Johan Vilhelm Snellman (1806-1881). HÄNTSCH, Carola.
Gentile e gli 'epigoni" dell'hegelismo napoletano: il carteggio con Sebastiano Maturi. SAVORELLI, Alessandro.
Schattenseiten der Hegelei: Fallsbeispiel—Lassalles Hegel-Rhapsodie. BEYER, Wilhelm Raimund.
Why Should a Dialectician Learn to Count to Four?. ZIZEK, Slavoj.

HEGEMONY

Television and the Crisis of Democracy. KELLNER, Douglas.

HEIDEGGER

The Anatomy of Philosophical Style. LANG, Berel.
Being and Becoming: A Critique of Post-Modernism. CENTORE, F F.
Being-in-the-World: A Commentary on Heidegger's "Being and Time", Division 1. DREYFUS, Hubert L.
Between Freiburg and Frankfurt: Toward a Critical Ontology. DALLMAYR, Fred R.
Bewusstsein und Natursein. CHO, Kah Kyung.
The Cogito and Hermeneutics: The Question of the Subject in Ricoeur. JERVOLINO, Domenico.
Echoes: After Heidegger. SALLIS, John.
Essays on Heidegger and Others: Philosophical Papers, Volume 2. RORTY, Richard.
Instrumental Realism: The Interface between Philosophy of Science and Philosophy of Technology. IHDE, Don.
Language and "The Feminine" in Nietzsche and Heidegger. GRAYBEAL, Jean.
Looking After Nietzsche. RICKELS, Laurence A (ed).
Metaphysik als Metahistorik oder Hermeneutik des unreinen Denkens Die Philosophie Max Müllers. RUIZ-PESCE, Ramón Eduardo.
Nietzsche and the Question of Interpretation. SCHRIFT, Alan D.
Of Memory, Reminiscence, and Writing: On the Verge. KRELL, David Farrell.
The Other Side of Language: A Philosophy of Listening. FIUMARA, Gemma Corradi.
Phänomenologische Philosophie. STRÖKER, Elisabeth.
Philosophische Hermeneutik. INEICHEN, Hans.
The Political Ontology of Martin Heidegger. BOURDIEU, Pierre.
The Politics of Being: The Political Thought of Martin Heidegger. WOLIN, Richard.
Quest for Certainty: A Comparative Study of Heidegger and Sankara. GRIMES, John A.
The Question of Ethics. SCOTT, Charles E.
The Question of God in Heidegger's Phenomenology. KOVACS, George.
Reconsidering Psychology: Perspectives from Continental Philosophy. FAULCONER, James E (ed).
The Self-Overcoming of Nihilism: Nishitani Keiji. PARKES, Graham (trans).
Das Verhängnis Erste Philosophie. EBELING, Hans.
"Essence and Subversion in Hegel and Heidegger" in *Writing the Politics of Difference*, MC CUMBER, John.

HEIDEGGER

"Esserci e differenza ontologica in Heidegger" in *Razionalitá critica: nella filosofia moderna*, ESPOSITO, Costantino.
"Heidegger and Psychological Explanation: Taking Account of Derrida" in *Reconsidering Psychology: Perspectives from Continental Philosophy*, FAULCONER, James E.
"Heidegger and the Problem of World" in *Reconsidering Psychology: Perspectives from Continental Philosophy*, RICHARDSON, William J.
"Heidegger's Way In, Through, and Out of Politics: The Story of His Rectorate" in *Perspectives on Ideas and Reality*, FEHÉR, István M.
"Heidegger: What Is Called Humanism?" in *The Question of Humanism: Challenges and Possibilities*, BROWN, Richard S G.
L' "altro inizio" della filosofia: I *Beiträge zur Philosophie* di Heidegger. SAMONÀ, Leonardo.
"As Real As It Gets...": Ricoeur and Narrativity. KELLNER, Hans.
A "Con-versão" da Filosofia em Martin Heidegger. ESTÊVÁO, Carlos.
"Das Wort sie sollen lassen stahn": Zur Edition und Interpretation philosophischer Texte, erläutert am B Kants. BRANDT, Reinhard.
"Nothing of the Origin and Destiny of Cats": The Remainder of the Logos. ROSE, John M.
La "riabilitazione" della δυναμιζ e dell'ενεργεια in Heidegger. VOLPI, Franco.
Action or/and Dwelling. BOEDER, Heribert.
The Ambivalent Unthought of the Overman and the Duality of Heidegger's Political Thinking. HAAR, Michel.
The Anomaly of World: From Scheler to Heidegger. SCHALOW, Frank.
Aristóteles desde Heidegger. CASARES, Angel J.
Art and Morality: On the Problem of Stating a Problem. HATTINGH, J P.
Art for Existence's Sake: A Heideggerian Revision. SCHUMACHER, Paul J.
Art Works, But How?—Kant and Aesthetics/Heidegger and Truth. SYNNING, Ralph.
Autonomy and Quantum Physics: Nietzsche, Heidegger, and Heisenberg. SEIGFRIED, Hans.
But Suppose We Were to Take the Rectorial Address Seriously...Gérard Granel's *De l'université*. FYNSK, Christopher.
Changing the Subject: Heidegger, "the" National and Epochal. SCHMIDT, Dennis J.
Constituição do sentido e justificação da validade: Heidegger e o problema da filosofia transcendental. APEL, Karl-Otto.
Continuità e discontinuità tra Husserl e Heidegger: genesi e sviluppo d una polemica filosofica. RIZZACASA, Aurelio.
Crítica de Heidegger al "intuicionalismo" cartesiano. FORMENT, Eudaldo.
La cuestión de Dios en el pensar de Heidegger. FORNET-BETANCOURT, Raúl.
Dasein and Gelassenheit in Heidegger (in Czechoslovakian). PAUZA, M.
Dasein—Mitsein—Sprache: Heideggers Auffassung über das "Wesen der Sprache" in "Sein und Zeit". TIETZ, Udo.
Destruktion und Übersetzung: Zu den Aufgaben von Philosophiegeschichte nach Martin Heidegger. OPILIK, Klaus.
A determinação heideggeriana de fenómeno em *Sein und Zeit* como superação do "cepticismo metódico". DAS NEVES, Jorge César.
Die Wissenschaft denkt nicht. SALANSKIS, Jean-Michel.
The Doubleness of the Unthought of the Overman: Ambiguities of Heideggerian Political Thought. HAAR, Michel.
L'epocalità metafisica di Nietzsche: "Sentiero interrotto" della filosofia heideggeriana. TRAVERSO, Patrizia.
Ernst Cassirer and Martin Heidegger: The Davos Debate. LYNCH, Dennis A.
A essência da técnica segundo Heidegger. RENAUD, Michel.
L'essere mortale dei mortali: Un'analisi sul problema della morte nel pensiero del secondo Heidegger. CICCHESE, Gennaro.
The Ethics of Postmodernism. GIBBONS, Michael T.
El evento (ereignis) como concepto fundamental de la filosofía de Heidegger (1a parte). BERCIANO V, Modesto.
El evento (Ereignis) como concepto fundamental de la filosofía de Heidegger (2a parte). BERCIANO V, Modesto.
Filosofía y Cristianismo (En el Centenario de Heidegger). CARDONA, Carlos.
Foucault's Critique of Heidegger. HILL, R Kevin.
From Nothingness to No-thing-ness: the Roots of Ferry and Renaut's Humanism. BARBIERO, Daniel.
From the Phenomenology of Time Toward Process Metaphysics: Pragmatism and Heidegger. ROSENTHAL, Sandra B.
Getting the Subject Back into the World: Heidegger's Version. KERR, Fergus.
Glosses on Heidegger's Architectonic Word-Play. PRUFER, Thomas.
Habermas and Arendt on the Philosopher's "Error": Tracking the Diabiological in Heidegger. BERNASCONI, Robert.
Habermas on Heidegger's *Being and Time*. SCHARFF, Robert C.
Hegel, Heidegger, and the Question of Art Today. GROSSMANN, Andreas.
Heidegger After Farias. ROCKMORE, Tom.
Heidegger and Emancipation. OLIVIER, G.
Heidegger and Myth: A Loop in the History of Being. HATAB, Lawrence J.
Heidegger and Nietzsche—Thinkers of the 'Between'? (in Dutch). GOOSEN, D P.
Heidegger and Psychoanalysis: The Seminars in Zollikon. SCOTT, Charles E.
Heidegger and the Critique of the Understanding of Evil as Privatio Boni. CAPOBIANCO, Richard.
Heidegger and the Japanese Connection. BILIMORIA, Purusottama.
Heidegger and the Temporal Constitution of the *A Priori*. SCHALOW, Frank.
Heidegger at 100, in America. KOLB, David.
Heidegger e la duplicità del presente. PENZO, Maurizio.
Heidegger e o Oriente ou da Extrema In-diferença Ocidental. DO CARMO SILVA, Carlos Henrique.
Heidegger en la filosofía española: La eficacia de Heidegger en las filosofías de Ortega y Zubiri. RAMOS, Antonio Pintor.
Heidegger on Logic and Language: Some Aporiai. FAY, Thomas A.
Heidegger on Nietzsche and Nihilism (in Czechoslovakian). MAJOR, L.
Heidegger on the Self, Authenticity and Inauthenticity. MANSBACH, Abraham.
Heidegger und die Frage um die Quelle des Grundbegriffes der Metaphysik (in Polish). ROZDZENSKI, R.
Heidegger und Schopenhauer. HECKER, Hellmuth.
Heidegger's Apology: Biography as Philosophy and Ideology. KISIEL, Theodore.
Heidegger's Attempt at Rehousing Man Through the *Kehre des Denkens*. RAUCHE, G A.
Heidegger's *Kampf*: The Difficulty of Life. CAPUTO, John D.
Heidegger's Rector's Address: A Loss of the Question of Ethics. SCOTT, Charles.
Heidegger, pensador con biografía. RODRÍGUEZ, Ramón.
Heidegger: vita e distino—Sullo biografia heideggeriana di Hugo Ott. ESPOSITO, Costantino.
A Heideggerian Analysis of Fundamentalism: A Brief Discussion. O'CONNELL, Colin.
Heideggerian Retrieval of Cartesianism. ROY, Krishna.
Heideggers "logische Untersuchungen". OUDEMANS, Th C W.
Heideggers Bedeutung für die Psychologie. VON USLAR, Detlev.
Heideggers Denken und die Ökologie. PADRUTT, Hanspeter.
Heraclitus: Heidegger's 1943 Lecture Held at Freiburg University. FRINGS, Manfred S.
Heraclitus: Heidegger's 1944 Lecture Held at Freiburg University. FRINGS, Manfred S.
Herméneutique et épistémologie Gadamer entre Heidegger et Hegel. ROCKMORE, Tom.
Husserl's Notion of Constitution in Heidegger's Treatment of Care. THOMAS, V C.
In Defence of Heidegger. JANUSZ, Sharon and WEBSTER, Glenn.
Incarnation and Essentialization: A Reading of Heidegger. CAPUTO, John D.
Incarnational Anthropology. HALDANE, John.
Is There a "Meaning" of Being? Against the Deconstructionist Reading of Heidegger. SCHALOW, Frank.
Jacques Derrida's Response to the Call for Ethics. CHAMPAGNE, R A.
A Kierkegaardian Critique of Heidegger's Concept of Authenticity. BERTHOLD-BOND, Daniel.
L'herméneutique dans la "phènoménologie comme telle". GREISCH, Jean.
Lacan Between Freud and Heidegger (in Serbo-Croatian). VETTER, Helmut.
Logos and the Place of the Other. BIRMINGHAM, Peg E.
M Heideggers Auslegung von Sophokles' "Oedipus Tyrannus" (in Japanese). SEKIGUCHI, Hiroshi.
Martin Heidegger and the Place of Language. VAN RODEN ALLEN, Robert.
Memory, Forgetfulness and the Disclosure of Being in Heidegger and Plotinus. BALES, Eugene F.
Need, Denial and Abandonment: Heidegger and the Turn. URPETH, James R.
Nietzsche and Heidegger. LAWRENCE, Joseph P.
Nietzsche, Heidegger, and the Critique of Humanism. HODGE, Joanna.
Noia, acedia ed epochè. BOTTANI, Livio.
Note sulle recenti traduzioni di *Essere e tempo* in Francia. MARRATI, Paola.
On Behalf of Skeptical Rhetoric. FALZER, Paul R.
On Heidegger and National Socialism: A Triple Turn?. ROCKMORE, Tom.
Paths to a Postmodern Ethics and Politics: A Reply to Gibbons. WHITE, Stephen K.
El pensamiento de Heidegger y Marcuse en relación con la ecología. ARRIETA, Jeannette and HAYLING, Annie.
Philosophieren als Sein zum Tode: Zur Interpretation von Platons "Phaidon". FISCHER, Norbert.
The Physics of Modern Perception: Beyond Body and World. BARRY JR, James.
Political Openings. WOOD, David.
Politics and the Limits of Metaphysics: Heidegger, Ferry and Renaut, and Lyotard. FÓTI, Véronique M.
Porosity: Violence and the Question of Politics in Heidegger's *Introduction to Metaphysics*. MC NEILL, William.
El problema de la culpa y del "otro" en Heidegger y Siewerth. CABADA, Manuel.
Il problema teologico nel pensiero di Heidegger. PENATI, G.
Prolegomena to an Understanding of Heidegger's Turn. GRONDIN, Jean.
Reconstructing the Political. JANICAUD, Dominique.
Rejoining *Alētheia* and Truth: or Truth Is a Five-Letter Word. HATAB, Lawrence J.
Reply to Vallicella: Heidegger and Idealism. SMITH, Quentin.
Réponses à quelques questions. MARION, Jean-Luc.

HEIDEGGER

Retreat from Radicality: Pöggeler on Heidegger's Politics. EDLER, Frank H W.
Sartre's Being-for-Heidegger, Heidegger's Being-for-Sartre. MARTINOT, Steve.
Schelling's Treatise on the Essence of Human Freedom and Heidegger's Thought. FROMAN, Wayne J.
Ser y Dios, entre filosofía y teología, en Heidegger y Siewerth. CABADA, Manuel.
Shattering: Toward a Politics of Daimonic Life. KRELL, David Farrell.
Sinn-Wahrheit-Ort: Tres etapas en el pensamiento de Heidegger. BERCIANO V, Modesto.
The *Sinnsfrage* and the *Seinsfrage*. PROTEVI, John.
Sobre la "Metafísica del bien y del mal". MELENDO, Tomás.
Spinoza, Heidegger, and the Ontological Argument. SINGER, Brent A.
Squaring the Hermeneutical Circle. ROSEN, Stanley.
The Stilling of the *Aufhebung: Streit* in "The Origin of the Work of Art". PROTEVI, John.
Storicità tecnica e architettura. MAZZARELLA, Eugenio.
The Subject of Hermeneutics and the Hermeneutics of the Subject. RICHARDSON, William.
Sur l'habitation poétique de l'homme. PIERSON, Dominique.
Telling Tales: Notes on Heidegger's "Career," the "Heidegger Affair," and the Assumptions of Narrativity. DAVIES, Paul.
Le temps du souffrir: Remarques critiques sur la phénoménologie de M Henry. PORÉE, Jérôme.
Text and Technology. CROWELL, Steven Galt.
La théologie de Heidegger. CRÉTELLA, Henri.
Thinking (Beyond) Being. STENSTAD, Gail.
Thought Rhythym and Experience in *Der Satz vom Grund* (in Dutch). PEETERS, L.
The Time of the Political. BIRMINGHAM, Peg.
Ultimate Double Binds. SCHÜRMANN, Reiner.
Using Arendt and Heidegger to Consider Feminist Thinking on Women and Reproductive/Infertility Technologies. KLAWITER, Maren.
Die Verfehlung des Themas "Metaphysik und Erfahrung". WIEHL, Reiner.
Wege der Seinsfrage: Aus Anlass der 100. GANDER, Hans-Helmuth.

HEIDEMA, J

Verisimilitude by Power Relations. ODDIE, Graham.

HEINE, H

Schattenseiten der Hegelei: Fallsbeispiel—Lassalles Hegel-Rhapsodie. BEYER, Wilhelm Raimund.

HEISENBERG

The Potential of Modern Discourse: Musil, Peirce, and Perturbation. FINLAY, Marike.
Autonomy and Quantum Physics: Nietzsche, Heidegger, and Heisenberg. SEIGFRIED, Hans.

HEISIG, J

"Imaginal Soul and Ideational Spirit: A Response to James Heisig" in *Archetypal Process: Self and Divine in Whitehead, Jung, and Hillman*, WINQUIST, Charles E.

HELD, V

The Moral Foundations of Intangible Property. CHILD, James W.

HELIOCENTRIC

Por um novo modelo de saber: Problemática do discurso Filosófico-Teológico. DINIS, Alfredo.

HELL

Hell, This Isn't Necessary After All. WALTERS, Kerry S.

HELLENISM

Nietzsche: A Frenzied Look. ACKERMANN, Robert John.
Accessible Hellenistic Philosophy. SHARPLES, R W.
Aristippus Against Happiness. IRWIN, T H.

HELMHOLTZ

The Natural and the Normative: Theories of Spatial Perception from Kant to Helmholtz. HATFIELD, Gary.

HELOISE

"Heloise" in *A History of Women Philosophers, Volume II: Medieval, Renaissance and Enlightenment, A.D. 500-1600*, WAITHE, Mary Ellen.

HEMPEL

Azar y explicación: Algunas observaciones. PÉREZ RANSANZ, Ana Rosa.
Chaos, History, and Narrative. REISCH, George A.
Explanation, Causation and Laws. EDGINGTON, Dorothy.
Horwich, Hempel, and Hypothetico-Deductivism. GEMES, Ken.
How Do Scientific Explanations Explain?. KINOSHITA, Joyce.
On Empirical Interpretation. MUNDY, Brent.
On the Possibility of Lawful Explanation in Archaeology. SALMON, Merrilee H.
Singular Explanation and the Social Sciences. RUBEN, David-Hillel.
Why Friedman's Non-Monotonic Reasoning Defies Hempel's Covering Law Model. JANSSEN, M C W and TAN, Y H.

HENKIN, L

Henkin's Completeness Proof: Forty Years Later. LEBLANC, Hugues and ROEPER, Peter and THAU, Michael and WEAVER, George.

HENRICH, D

Soggettività e autocoscienza: Prospettive e problemi in Dieter Henrich. CELANO, Bruno.
Two-Steps-in-One-Proof: The Structure of the Transcendental Deduction of the Categories. EVANS, J Claude.

HENRY OF GHENT

Thomas Aquinas and Henry of Ghent on the Succession of Substantial Forms and the Origin of Human Life. WILSON, Gordon A.

HENRY, M

Grandeur et limites du *Marx* de Michel Henry. CANTIN, Serge.
Le temps du souffrir: Remarques critiques sur la phénoménologie de M Henry. PORÉE, Jérôme.

HERACLITUS

"Also sprach Herakleitos". WOHLFART, Günter.
"Heraclitus' Theory of Soul and Its Antecedents" in *Psychology (Companions to Ancient Thought: 2)*, SCHOFIELD, Malcolm.
La figure d'Héraclite dans la pensée du jeune Nietzsche. VOELKE, André-Jea.
Heraclitus: Heidegger's 1943 Lecture Held at Freiburg University. FRINGS, Manfred S.
Heraclitus: Heidegger's 1944 Lecture Held at Freiburg University. FRINGS, Manfred S.
The Heraclitus' Lesson (in Portuguese). SANTOS, M C A dos.

HERBART

Moralische Verbindlichkeit oder Erziehung. LANGEWAND, Alfred.
Het Dialectisch Humanistisch Grondmotief van Natuur en Vrijheid in de Pedagogiek als Wetenschap. OUWENDORP, C.

HEREDITY

Beyond Natural Selection. WESSON, Robert.
The Darwinian Synthesis: A Critique of the Rosenberg/Williams Argument. VAN BALEN, G.
Hereditarily Finite Finsler Sets. BOOTH, David.

HERITAGE

"Heritage and Collective Responsibility" in *The Political Responsibility of Intellectuals*, JEDLICKI, Jerzy.

HERMENEUTICS

African Philosophy: The Essential Readings. SEREQUEBERHAN, Tsenay.
Being-in-the-World: A Commentary on Heidegger's "Being and Time", Division 1. DREYFUS, Hubert L.
The Cogito and Hermeneutics: The Question of the Subject in Ricoeur. JERVOLINO, Domenico.
Dialogue with the Other: The Inter-Religious Dialogue. TRACY, David.
Hermeneutical Studies: Dilthey, Sophocles, and Plato. WILSON, Barrie A.
Hermeneutics and Critical Theory in Ethics and Politics. KELLY, Michael (ed).
Hermeneutics and the Poetic Motion, Translation Perspectives V—1990. SCHMIDT, Dennis J (ed).
The Hermeneutics of Life History: Personal Achievement and History in Gadamer, Habermas, and Erikson. WALLULIS, Jerald.
Markets, Managers and Theory in Education. HALLIDAY, John.
Modernity, Aesthetics, and the Bounds of Art. MC CORMICK, Peter J.
Nietzsche and the Question of Interpretation. SCHRIFT, Alan D.
Nine Talmudic Readings. ARONOWICZ, Annette (trans).
Phenomenology of the Truth Proper to Religion. GUERRIÈRE, Daniel (ed).
Philosophical Hermeneutics and Literary Theory. WEINSHEIMER, Joel.
Philosophische Hermeneutik. INEICHEN, Hans.
Philosophy in World Perspective: A Comparative Hermeneutic of the Major Theories. DILWORTH, David A.
Velázquez et Goya. PIERRE, Christian (trans).
"Augustine's Methods of Biblical Interpretation" in *Grace, Politics and Desire: Essays on Augustine*, HAMILTON, Gordon J.
"The Exemplary Status of Translating" in *Hermeneutics and the Poetic Motion, Translation Perspectives V—1990*, SCHMIDT, Lawrence K.
"Filosofia e hermenêutica" in *Dinâmica do Pensar: Homenagem a Oswaldo Market*, GONÇALVES, Joaquim Cerqueira.
"Hermeneutics and Modern Social Theory" in *Social Theory of Modern Societies: Anthony Giddens and His Critics*, BAUMAN, Zygmunt.
"Ideology and Religion: A Hermeneutic Conflict" in *Phenomenology of the Truth Proper to Religion*, KEARNEY, Richard.
"Philosophy and the Mirage of Hermeneutics" in *Reading Rorty*, HOLÓWKA, Jacek.
"Pontos de vista—exercício hermenêutico sobre um excerto da *Monadologia*" in *Dinâmica do Pensar: Homenagem a Oswaldo Market*, RIBEIRO FERREIRA, Maria Luisa.
"Radical Hermeneutics and Religious Truth: The Case of Sheehan and Schillebeeckx" in *Phenomenology of the Truth Proper to Religion*, CAPUTO, John D.
"The Secularization of Philosophy" in *Writing the Politics of Difference*, VATTIMO, Gianni.
"Das Wort sie sollen lassen stahn": Zur Edition und Interpretation philosophischer Texte, erläutert am B Kants. BRANDT, Reinhard.
(Post-) Metaphysik und (Post-) Moderne: Zur Sache des "schwachen Denkens". FRÜCHTL, Josef.

HERMENEUTICS
Anachronistic Themes and Literary Value: *The Tempest*. SKILLEAS, Ole Martin.
Aspects of the Problem of Reference (1): Phenomenology, Hermeneutics and Deconstruction. RAJAN, R Sundara.
Aspects of the Problem of Reference (I). RAJAN, R Sundara.
Beyond Realism: Nietzsche's New Infinite. CONWAY, Daniel W.
Biblical Hermeneutics and the Search for Religious Truth (in French). THEISSEN, Gerd.
Cultural Literacy: Posing Queer Questions. GREENE, Maxine.
De la problématique diltheyenne à l'intégralisme de Jean Granier. AJERAR, Hassane.
Derrida's Other Conversation. DAVIES, Paul.
A Dialogic Interpretation of Hume's *Dialogues*. SESSIONS, William Lad.
Die Wissenschaft denkt nicht. SALANSKIS, Jean-Michel.
Encountering Dallmayr. KIVISTO, Peter.
Explanation and Understanding in Social Science. SKORUPSKI, John.
Faith in the Open Society: The Limits of Hermeneutics. AGASSI, Joseph.
Gadamer over 'Vermittlung': de Hegeliaanse draad in zijn hermeneutiek. VAN DER HOEVEN, J.
Gadamer's Concrete Universal. KERBY, Anthony Paul.
Heideggerian Retrieval of Cartesianism. ROY, Krishna.
Heideggers "logische Untersuchungen". OUDEMANS, Th C W.
Hermeneutic Phenomenology and Taoism. KIDD, James W.
Hermenêutica e Estruturalismo. ROCHA, Acílio Estanqueiro.
Hermeneutics (in Hungarian). SCHREITER, Jörg.
Hermeneutics: A Protreptic. JOHNSON, Gregory R.
Herméneutique et épistémologie Gadamer entre Heidegger et Hegel. ROCKMORE, Tom.
The Historical Consciousness of Man. MITSCHERLING, Jeff.
Historical Continuity and Discontinuity in the Philosophy of Gadamer and Foucault (in Hungarian). UJLAKI, Gabriella.
How Individualistic Is Methodological Individualism?. MADISON, G B.
Is Grünbaum's Critique of Habermas' Understanding Freud Definite? (in Serbo-Croatian). NAGL, Ludwig.
L'herméneutique dans la "phènoménologie comme telle". GREISCH, Jean.
L'universalisation de l'herméneutique chez Hans-Georg Gadamer. GRONDIN, Jean.
A lógica do sentido na filosofia hermenêutica. COSTA, Miguel Dias.
Man and Hermeneutics. ROY, Krishna.
Metaphysics and Culture. LADRIÈRE, Jean.
Montinari and Nietzsche's Biography. HOLLINGDALE, R G.
Mystical Experience, Hermeneutics, and Rationality. SHEAR, Jonathan.
Nietzsche and the Philosophy of Scientific Power: Will to Power as Constructive Interpretation. BABICH, Babette E.
Nietzsche as Colleague. SCHACHT, Richard.
Nietzsche's "Will to Power" Nachlass. HELLER, Peter.
Ontología hermenéutica y reflexión filológica: el acceso a la filosofía de H G Gadamer. DOMINGO, Agustín.
The Paradox of Indoctrination: A Hermeneutical Solution. GARRISON, James W.
Philosophical Hermeneutics and its Meaning for Philosophy. PAGE, Carl.
Philosophy and Politics: On Fred Dallmayr's "Critical Encounters". MISGELD, Dieter.
The Postmodern Flavor of Blondel's Method. LONG, Fiachra.
Presentism and the Indeterminacy of Translation. HARDCASTLE, Gary L.
Protestant Hermeneutics and the Rule of Law: Gadamer and Dworkin. HENLEY, Kenneth.
Qu'est-ce qu'interpréter?. MERCIER, André.
Radical Hermeneutics, Critical Theory, and the Political. DOODY, John A.
Rāmānuja's Hermeneutics of the *Upanisads* in Comparison with Sankara's Interpretation. SAWAI, Yoshitsugu.
Las reglas del juego: consideraciones críticas sobre "Radical Hermeneutics" de John Caputo. PEÑA, Lorenzo.
Squaring the Hermeneutical Circle. ROSEN, Stanley.
The Subject of Hermeneutics and the Hermeneutics of the Subject. RICHARDSON, William.
La théologie de Heidegger. CRÉTELLA, Henri.
To Catch a Thief: Chu Hsi (1130-1200) and the Hermeneutic Art. BERTHRONG, John.
Les trois sortes d'universalité dans l'herméneutique de H G Gadamer. MARGOLIS, Joseph.
Why the Mind is Not in the Head But in the Society's Connectionist Network. FISCHER, Roland.

HERMETIC
The Hermetic Influence on the Rise of Modern Science. MITRA, Prabir.

HERO(ES)
Emerson and the Inhibitions of Democracy. SHKLAR, Judith N.
The Epic Hero as Politico. CAMPBELL, Blair.
The Philosopher as Hero. DUHAN, Laura.

HEROINE
"Biblical Story and the Heroine" in *The Bible as Rhetoric: Studies in Biblical Persuasion and Credibility*, STOCKER, Margarita.

HERRAD OF HOHENBOURG
"Herrad of Hohenbourg" in *A History of Women Philosophers, Volume II: Medieval, Renaissance and Enlightenment, A.D. 500-1600*, GIBSON, Joan.

HERTZ
Pulling up the Ladder: The Metaphysical Roots of Wittgenstein's Tractatus. BROCKHAUS, Richard R.
La philosophie des sciences de Hertz et le Tractatus. LEROUX, Jean.

HERZBERGER, H
Logics of Truth. TURNER, Raymond.

HETERONOMY
Philosophy of History is Heternomous Philosophy (in German). SCHULTE, Christoph.

HETEROSEXISM
Some Thoughts About Heterosexualism. HOAGLAND, Sarah Lucia.

HETTINGER, E
Trade Secrets and the Justification of Intellectual Property: A Comment on Hettinger. PAINE, Lynn Sharp.

HEURISTICS
Education as a Human Right: A Theory of Curriculum and Pedagogy. VANDENBERG, Donald.
"Deductive Heuristics" in *Imre Lakatos and Theories of Scientific Change*, MUSGRAVE, Alan.
Heuristics and the Generalized Correspondence Principle. RADDER, Hans.
Kant's Doctrine of Heuristics: An Interpretation of the Ideas of Reason. GRACYK, Theodore A.
Rethinking the Dialectic: A Social Semiotic Perspective for Educators. HAMMER, Rhonda and MC LAREN, Peter.

HEXTER, J
Pride and the Meaning of *Utopia*. MOULAKIS, Athanasios.

HICK, J
A Certain 'Politics of Speech': 'Religious Pluralism' in the Age of the McDonald's Hamburger. SURIN, Kenneth.
Hick and Saints: Is Saint-Production a Valid Test?. PENTZ, Rebecca.
Prefacing Pluralism: John Hick and the Mastery of Religion. LOUGHLIN, Gerard.
Relativism, Ineffability, and the Appeal to Experience: A Reply to the Myth Makers. BARNES, L Philip.
A Religious Theory of Religion: Critical Notice. BYRNE, Peter.

HICKS, J
Prediction and Explanation in Economics. SWAMIDASAN, Nalini.

HIDDEN VARIABLE(S)
Hidden Locality, Conspiracy and Superluminal Signals. KRONZ, Frederick M.

HIDDENNESS
Rilievi di struttura sul *De deo abscondito* di Nicola Cusano. DELCÒ, Alessandro.

HIERARCHY(-CHIES)
Almost Hugeness and a Related Notion. BARBANEL, Julius.
Bounded Arithmetic and the Polynomial Hierarchy. KRAJICEK, Jan and PUDLÁK, Pavel and TAKEUTI, Gaisi.
Bounds in Weak Truth-Table Reducibility. HABART, Karol.
A Hierarchy of Ramsey Cardinals. FENG, Qi.
More Axioms for the Set-Theoretic Hierarchy. POLLARD, Stephen.
Some Extensions of Built-Upness on Systems of Fundamental Sequences. KADOTA, Noriya.

HIGHER EDUCATION
Belief as a Condition of Knowledge: The Need for a Philosophical Perspective in Higher Education Reform. BRELL JR, Carl D.

HIGHER ORDER LOGICS
Exponentiation and Second-Order Bounded Arithmetic. KRAJICEK, Jan.
Inductive Types and Type Constraints in the Second-Order Lambda Calculus. MENDLER, Nax Paul.
The Monadic Second-Order Logic of Graphs IV: Definability Properties of Equational Graphs. COURCELLE, Bruno.
A Partial Functions Version of Church's Simple Theory of Types. FARMER, William M.
Supervenience, Goodness and Higher-Order Universals. ODDIE, Graham.

HILBERT, D
Brouwer's Intuitionism (Studies in the History and Philosophy of Mathematics, Vol 2). VAN STIGT, W P.
Mathematics and the Image of Reason. TILES, Mary E.
"Physicalism, Reductionism and Hilbert" in *Physicalism in Mathematics*, HALLETT, Michael.
"Reflections on Hilbert's Program" in *Acting and Reflecting: The Interdisciplinary Turn in Philosophy*, SIEG, Wilfried.
El cincuentenario de los *Grundlagen der Mathematik* de Hilbert y Bernays. RAGGIO, Andrés R.
Formalisme et intuitionnisme en philosophie des mathématiques. LARGEAULT, Jean.

HILBERT, D
On an Alleged Refutation of Hilbert's Program Using Gödel's First Incompleteness Theorem. DETLEFSEN, Michael.
Relative Consistency and Accessible Domains. SIEG, Wilfried.

HILDEGARD OF BINGEN
"Hildegard of Bingen" in *A History of Women Philosophers, Volume II: Medieval, Renaissance and Enlightenment, A.D. 500-1600*, GÖSSMANN, Elisabeth and BEST, Katherine.

HILLMAN, J
Archetypal Process: Self and Divine in Whitehead, Jung, and Hillman. GRIFFIN, David Ray (ed).
"Back of 'Back to Beyond' and Creeping Dichotomism" in *Archetypal Process: Self and Divine in Whitehead, Jung, and Hillman*, CASEY, Edward S.
"Imaginal Soul and Ideational Spirit: A Response to James Heisig" in *Archetypal Process: Self and Divine in Whitehead, Jung, and Hillman*, WINQUIST, Charles E.
"A Metaphysical Psychology to Un-Locke Our Ailing World" in *Archetypal Process: Self and Divine in Whitehead, Jung, and Hillman*, GRIFFIN, David Ray.
"The Mystique of the Nonrational and a New Spirituality" in *Archetypal Process: Self and Divine in Whitehead, Jung, and Hillman*, HEISIG, James W.
"Once More: The Cavern Beneath the Cave" in *Archetypal Process: Self and Divine in Whitehead, Jung, and Hillman*, HOPPER, Stanley R.
"Psychocosmetics and the Underworld Connection" in *Archetypal Process: Self and Divine in Whitehead, Jung, and Hillman*, KELLER, Catherine.
"A Riposte" in *Archetypal Process: Self and Divine in Whitehead, Jung, and Hillman*, HEISIG, James W.

HILMY, S
Stephen Hilmy on Matters of Method and Style. COVEOS, Costis M.

HINDU
A Hindu Perspective on the Philosophy of Religion. SHARMA, Arvind.
East-West Philosophy in Nineteenth-Century America: Emerson and Hinduism. GOODMAN, Russell B.
Hindu Doubts About God: Towards a Mīmāmsā Deconstruction. BILIMORIA, Purusottama.
The *Nagaraja*: Symbol and Symbolism in Hindu Art and Iconography. DURAN, Jane.

HINDUISM
Celebrating Peace. ROUNER, Leroy S (ed).
The Law of Karma: A Philosophical Study. REICHENBACH, Bruce R.
Philosophy of the "Gita". PATEL, Ramesh N.
The Bhakti Tradition in Hinduism—Bhakti Yoga an Overview. PILLAI, A S Narayana.
Jivacide, Zombies and *Jivanmuktas*. HERMAN, A L.
Karma and Rebirth in *Alberuni's India*. SHARMA, Arvind.
Karma and Reincarnation in Advaita Vedānta. SHARMA, Arvind.
Philosophy and the Sociology of Knowledge: An Investigation into the Nature of Orthodoxy (Astikya) in Hindu Thought. SHARMA, Arvind.

HINTIKKA, J
Deontic Logic and Possible World Semantics: A Historical Sketch. WOLENSKI, Jan.
De Kant-interpretatie van Evert Willem Beth. PEIJNENBURG, J.
On the Ontology of Branching Quantifiers. PATTON, Thomas.
The Philosophy of Logical Wholism. MC CARTY, David Charles.
A Very Short Guide to Understanding Wittgenstein. RESNICK, Larry.
Wittgenstein's Phenomenology Revisited. GIER, Nicholas F.

HINTIKKA, M
A Very Short Guide to Understanding Wittgenstein. RESNICK, Larry.

HISTORICAL MATERIALISM
see also Dialectical Materialism
Mannheim and Hungarian Marxism. GABEL, Joseph.
Marxism and Philosophy in the Twentieth Century: A Defense of Vulgar Marxism. HUDELSON, Richard.
"Models of Historical Trajectory: An Assessment of Gidden's Critique of Marxism" in *Social Theory of Modern Societies: Anthony Giddens and His Critics*, WRIGHT, Erik Olin.
Arendt and Benjamin on the Promise of History: A Network of Possibilities or One Apocalyptic Moment?. HONOHAN, Iseult.
Engels y Darwin en el origen del hombre: Elementos para una discusión. GALLARDO, Helio.
European Counterimages: Problems of Periodization and Historical Memory. DINER, Dan.
Explaining Historical Development: A Marxian Critique of Cohen's Historical Materialism. WARREN, Paul.
From Historical Marxisms to Historical Materialism: Toward the Theory of Ideology. MOCNIK, Rastko.
Marx, Nietzsche, and the "New Class". EVANS, Fred.
On Some Unsettled Questions Touching the Character of Marxism, Especially as Philosophy. SUCHTING, W A.
On the Coherence of Historical Materialism. NIELSEN, Kai.
Philosophiehistorische Forschung und historischer Materialismus. THOM, Martina.

HISTORICAL RELATIVISM
Dionysian and Apollonian Pathos of Distance: A New Image of World History. BROWN, David H.

HISTORICISM
"Some Aspects of Hélène Metzger's Philosophy of Science" in *Études sur/Studies on Hélène Metzger*, CARRIER, Martin.
Directions in Historicism: Language, Experience, and Pragmatic Adjudication. DAVANEY, Sheila Greeve.
The Evidence of Experience. SCOTT, Joan W.
Historicism and Phenomenology (in Czechoslovakian). CIBULKA, J.
Historicism and the Understanding of Theology in Troeltsch's Times (in German). NOWAK, Kurt.
Historicisms New and Old: "Charles Dickens" Meets Marxism, Feminism, and West Coast Foucault. NEWTON, Judith.
Historizing contra fetishizing—The Progress of Modern Technology in W Benjamin's Aesthetic Reflexion (in German). WAGNER, Gerhard.
History, Historicism, Narratives: Identity in the Philosophy of History of Karl Popper. PARLEJ, Piotr.
The Ironist's Cage. ROTH, Michael S.
Storicità della poesia: estetica e storicismo in Francesco De Sanctis. GALASSO, Giuseppe.

HISTORICITY
The Balance of Consciousness: Eric Voegelin's Political Theory. KEULMAN, Kenneth.
Evolution: Probleme und neue Aspekte ihrer Theorie. SCHEFFCZYK, Leo (ed).
The Politics of Being: The Political Thought of Martin Heidegger. WOLIN, Richard.
Giustino Martire, il primo platonico cristiano. GIRGENTI, Giuseppe.
Legitimate Anachronism as a Problem for Intellectual History and for Philosophy. DU TOIT, André.
Post-Modern Pastiche. ROSE, Margaret A.
Storicità tecnica e architettura. MAZZARELLA, Eugenio.
The Time of the Political. BIRMINGHAM, Peg.

HISTORIOGRAPHY
Myth and Modern Philosophy. DANIEL, Stephen H.
Philosophische Hermeneutik. INEICHEN, Hans.
Footprints in the Snow. SEERVELD, Calvin.
The Future of the Past: From the History of Historiography to Historiology. GRANDAZZI, Alexandre.
G H Bantock as Educational Philosopher. BARRIE, John A.
Heracles and the Passage from Nature to Culture in G Vico's *La Scienza Nuova*. MIUCCIO, Giuliana.
The Hermetic Influence on the Rise of Modern Science. MITRA, Prabir.
Historiography and Postmodernism: Reconsiderations. ZAGORIN, Perez.
History as Geneology: Wittgenstein and the Feminist Deconstruction of Objectivity. LAMPSHIRE, Wendy L.
Per una storia dell'idea di Europa: Riflessioni storiografiche. BALDASSARRE, Mariarosa.
Persistent Propensities: Portrait of a Familiar Controversy. NORDMANN, Alfred.
Reply to Professor Zagorin's "Historiography and Postmodernism: Reconsideration". ANKERSMIT, Frank R.
The Role of Memory in the Historiography of the French Revolution. HUTTON, Patrick H.
The Concept of History in the Renaissance (in Hungarian). RASZLAI, Tibor.
The Problem of the History-Making Role of Ideas in American Historical Thought (in Polish). CABAJ, Jerzy.

HISTORY
A "Realizacção da Razão": Um Programa Hegeliano?. BARATA-MOURA, José.
'Religion' and the Religions in the English Enlightenment. HARRISON, Peter.
Adorno's Aesthetic Theory: The Redemption of Illusion. ZUIDERVAART, Lambert.
African Philosophy: The Essential Readings. SEREQUEBERHAN, Tsenay.
Alltagssprachliche Metakommunikation im Englischen und Deutschen. WELTE, Werner.
The Anatomy of Philosophical Style. LANG, Berel.
Aspectos Metodológicos de la Investigación Científica. GONZÁLEZ, Wenceslao J (ed).
Caminhos do Filosofar. MIRANDA, Maria do Carmo Tavares de.
Christian Faith and Historical Understanding (Second Edition). NASH, Ronald H.
Collected Works, Volume 26, Engels: 1882-1889. ENGELS, Frederick.
A Companion to Ethics. SINGER, Peter (ed).
The Concept of Objectivity: An Approximation. BUTLER, Kenneth G.
Contemplating Music—Source Readings in the Aesthetics of Music, Volume II: Import. KATZ, Ruth (ed).
Criteria of Certainty: Truth and Judgment in the English Enlightenment. COPE, Kevin L.
Critical Traditions in Contemporary Archaeology. PINSKY, Valerie (ed).

HISTORY

Critique of Dialectical Reason, Volume 2: Jean-Paul Sartre. HOARE, Quintin (trans).
David Hume and the Problem of Reason. DANFORD, John W.
David Hume: Historiker und Philosoph. LÜTHE, Rudolf.
De l'épistémologie à la politique: La philosophie de l'histoire de Karl R Popper. RUELLAND, Jacques G.
Democratic Individuality. GILBERT, Alan.
Dream and Culture: An Anthropological Study of the Western Intellectual Tradition. PARMAN, Susan.
Experiment: Right or Wrong. FRANKLIN, Allan.
Explaining Religion: Criticism and Theory from Bodin to Freud. PREUS, J Samuel (ed).
From Hegel to Nietzsche: The Revolution in Nineteenth-Century Thought. LÖWITH, Karl.
Geschichte, Freiheit und Struktur. RUMPEL, Roland.
Hegel In His Time—Jacques D'Hondt. BURBIDGE, John (trans).
The Hermeneutics of Life History: Personal Achievement and History in Gadamer, Habermas, and Erikson. WALLULIS, Jerald.
Herrschaft und Versöhnung: Einführung in das Denken Theodor W Adornos. KAGER, Reinhard.
Historische Objektivitat. WEBERMAN, David.
History and Spirit: An Inquiry into the Philosophy of Liberation. KOVEL, Joel.
History and the Paradoxes of Metaphysics in "Dantons Tod". TAYLOR, Rodney.
A History of Women Philosophers, Volume II: Medieval, Renaissance and Enlightenment, A.D. 500-1600. WAITHE, Mary Ellen (ed).
Human Nature and Historical Knowledge: Hume, Hegel and Vico. POMPA, Leon.
The Humanities in the Nineties: A View From the Netherlands. ZÜRCHER, Erik (ed).
Ibn Rushd: Averroes. URVOY, Dominique.
Interpreting Evolution: Darwin and Teilhard de Chardin. BIRX, H James.
La intersubjectividad en Husserl, Volume I and II. IRIBARNE, Julia V.
Introduction Critique au Droit Naturel. HERVADA, Javier.
An Invitation To Cognitive Science. LEIBER, Justin.
Kierkegaard in Golden Age Denmark. KIRMMSE, Bruce H.
The Legacy of Hermann Cohen. KLUBACK, William.
Metaphysik als Metahistorik oder Hermeneutik des unreinen Denkens Die Philosophie Max Müllers. RUIZ-PESCE, Ramón Eduardo.
Modern Faith and Thought. THIELICKE, Helmut.
Modernity, Aesthetics, and the Bounds of Art. MC CORMICK, Peter J.
The Moral Animus of David Hume. SIEBERT, Donald T.
Moral Dilemmas. GOWANS, Christopher W (ed).
Morality—What's In It For Me?: A Historical Introduction to Ethics. NELSON, William N.
Musical Aesthetics: A Historical Reader, Volume III, The Twentieth Century. LIPPMAN, Edward A (ed).
Nation und Ethos: Die Moral des Patriotismus. KLUXEN-PYTA, Donate.
The Natural and the Normative: Theories of Spatial Perception from Kant to Helmholtz. HATFIELD, Gary.
Negative Dialectics and the End of Philosophy. ERICKSON, Glenn W.
Nietzsche: A Frenzied Look. ACKERMANN, Robert John.
On Durkheim's Rules of Sociological Method. GANE, Mike.
Other Selves: Philosophers on Friendship. PAKALUK, Michael (ed).
Perspectives on Ideas and Reality. NYÍRI, J C (ed).
Philosophical Events: Essays of the '80s. RAJCHMAN, John.
Philosophical Hermeneutics and Literary Theory. WEINSHEIMER, Joel.
Le Philosophie et les Passions. MEYER, Michel.
Philosophy in World Perspective: A Comparative Hermeneutic of the Major Theories. DILWORTH, David A.
The Philosophy of John William Miller. FELL, Joseph P (ed).
Philosophy of Technology. DURBIN, Paul T (ed).
Philosophy of the Ancients. RICKEN, Friedo.
A Post-Modern Epistemology. SORRI, Mari.
Published Essays, 1966-1985 (The Collected Works of Eric Voegelin, Volume 12). SANDOZ, Ellis (ed).
The Realizations of the Future: An Inquiry into the Authority of Praxis. ALLAN, George.
Relating Humanities and Social Thought (Science, Ideology, and Value, Volume 4). EDEL, Abraham.
Science and Religion: One World-Changing Perspectives on Reality. FENNEMA, Jan (ed).
Structures in Mathematical Theories: Reports of the San Sebastian International Symposium, 1990. DÍEZ, Amparo (ed).
Style and Music: Theory, History, and Ideology. MEYER, Leonard B.
The Tanner Lectures on Human Values, Volume XI. PETERSON, Grethe B (ed).
Theories of Criminal Justice: A Critical Reappraisal. ELLIS, Ralph D.
Universalism versus Communitarianism: Contemporary Debates in Ethics. RASMUSSEN, David.
Untersuchungen zur Theorie des hypothetischen Urteils. LINNEWEBER-LAMMERSKITTEN, Helmut.
Der Ursprung der Erziehungsziele in der Lehre von Plato, Aristoteles und Neill. EGGER, Paul.
The Vatican, the Law and the Human Embryo. COUGHLAN, Michael J.
Vico: A Study of the 'New Science' (Second Edition). POMPA, Leon.
Weakness of the Will. GOSLING, Justin.
What is History? And Other Late Unpublished Writings (The Collected Works of Eric Voegelin, Vol 28). HOLLWECK, Thomas A (ed).
Whose Science? Whose Knowledge? Thinking from Women's Lives. HARDING, Sandra.
Die Wiederkehr im Unterschied. PEETZ, Siegbert.
Wittgenstein: A Bibliographical Guide. FRONGIA, Guido.
"Commentary: A Critical Role for the History of Archaeology" in *Critical Traditions in Contemporary Archaeology*, PINSKY, Valerie.
"Edward Gibbon in History: Aspects of the Text in 'The History of the Decline and Fall of the Roman Empire'" in *The Tanner Lectures on Human Values, Volume XI*, POCOCK, J G A.
"Gilson's Use of History In Philosophy" in *Thomistic Papers, V*, MAURER, Armand A.
"Historical Consciousness in the German Romantic *Naturforschung*" in *Romanticism and the Sciences*, VON ENGELHARDT, Dietrich and SALAZAR, Christine.
"Historical Interaction between Science and Religion" in *Science and Religion: One World-Changing Perspectives on Reality*, PEDERSEN, O.
"History and Mimesis" in *Looking After Nietzsche*, LACOUE-LABARTHE, Philippe.
"History and Rhetoric in the Prophets" in *The Bible as Rhetoric: Studies in Biblical Persuasion and Credibility*, BARTON, John.
"The History, Philosophy of Sociology of Archaeology: The Case of the Ancient Monuments Protection Act (1882)" in *Critical Traditions in Contemporary Archaeology*, MURRAY, Tim.
"Interpretation and Overinterpretation: World, History, Texts" in *The Tanner Lectures On Human Values, Volume XII*, ECO, Umberto.
"Liberal Ideas and Reality: Central Europe 1848-49" in *Perspectives on Ideas and Reality*, GERGELY, András.
"Literature, History, and What Men Learn" in *The Philosophy of John William Miller*, ELIAS, Robert H.
"On Understanding Chinese Philosophy: An Inquiry and a Proposal" in *Understanding the Chinese Mind: The Philosophical Roots*, SZE-KWANG, Lao.
"Philosophical Lessons from the History of Stonehenge Studies" in *Critical Traditions in Contemporary Archaeology*, CHIPPINDALE, Christopher.
"The Philosophical Meaning of American Civilization in World History" in *Freedom in the Modern World: Jacques Maritain, Yves R Simon, Mortimer J Adler*, NOVAK, Michael.
"Remarks on Experience in Metaphysics" in *Thomistic Papers, V*, GILSON, Etienne.
"Science, Conscience, and Public Policy: Historical Reflections on Controversial Reproductive Issues" in *Beyond Baby M: Ethical Issues in New Reproductive Techniques*, EYLER, John.
"Seek and Ye Might Find" in *Scientific Theories*, CAPLAN, Arthur L.
"Some Considerations on the Study of the History of Seventeenth-Century Science" in *Études sur/Studies on Hélène Metzger*, SCHMITT, Charles B.
"War, Omnicide, and Sanity: The Lesson of the Cuban Missile Crisis" in *Issues in War and Peace: Philosophical Inquiries*, SOMERVILLE, John.
"Why Must History Always Be Rewritten?" in *Perspectives on Ideas and Reality*, LAKATOS, László.
"As Real As It Gets...": Ricoeur and Narrativity. KELLNER, Hans.
"Construindo a 'ordem anárquica". PIOZZI, Patrícia.
"Die Geschichte hat kein Libretto": Zu Isaiah Berlins Begriff des Nationalismus. RITTER, Henning.
"Historia" de la naturaleza *versus* "Naturaleza" de la historia. LEAL, Fernando A.
Aesthetics and Natural Law in Newton's Methodology. JACQUETTE, Dale.
The African Liberation Struggle: A Hermeneutic Exploration of an African Historical-Political Horizon. SEREQUEBERHAN, Tsenay.
The Alliance between Puritanism and Cartesian Logic at Harvard, 1687-1735. KENNEDY, Rick.
The Ambivalence of the Idea of Equality in the French Enlightenment. CHISICK, Harvey.
Anachronistic Themes and Literary Value: *The Tempest*. SKILLEAS, Ole Martin.
Ancora una discussione su Hegel: logica, storia, fenomenologia. NUZZO, Angelica.
Angelo Camillo De Meis nell'episolario di Francesco Fiorentino. CACCIAPUOTI, Fabiana.
Aquinas and the Deconstruction of History. KELLY, Eugene.
Arendt and Benjamin on the Promise of History: A Network of Possibilities or One Apocalyptic Moment?. HONOHAN, Iseult.
Art History in the Mirror Stage: Interpreting *Un Bar aux Folies Bergères*. CARRIER, David.
Autonomy and Personal History. CHRISTMAN, John.
The Barth Legacy: New Athanasius or Origen Redivivus? A Response to T F Torrance. MULLER, Richard A.
Basic Elements of the Concept of Individualism. WILKIE, Raymond.
The Body as Understood in Contemporary Thought and Biblical Categories. VERGOTE, Antoine.
Changing the Subject: Heidegger, "the" National and Epochal. SCHMIDT, Dennis J.

HISTORY

Chaos, History, and Narrative. REISCH, George A.
Charles Renouvier e le scuole di morale in Francia nel XIX secolo. ROSSI, Fabio.
Collingwood and the Idea of Progress. VAN DER DUSSEN, W Jan.
Collingwood's Detective Image of the Historian and the Study of Hadrian's Wall. COUSE, G S.
The Comeuppance of Science and Technology. CLEVELAND, Harlan.
Comme en un miroir: quelques remarques historiques sur l'arbitraire du signe. LATRAVERSE, François.
La conceptión tolstoiana de la historia. MARÍN CASANOVA, Jose A.
Conceptos filosóficos como sustrato del sentido de la muerte, desde la época prehispánica hasta la actual. DE LOS ANGELES IMAZ LIRA, María.
Le corps et ses langages: quelques perspectives de travail historique. COURTINE, Jean-Jacques.
Critical Marxism as an Historical Process of Society and Science (in German). SANDKÜHLER, Hans Jörg.
Critics and Historical Continuity. CARTER, John.
Croce e la storia della cultura. TESSITORE, Fulvio.
Cultural Fundamentals in Philosophy: Obstacles in Philosophical Dialogues. ORUKA, Henry Odera.
David Hume on Religion in England. ROTH, Robert J.
De lógica y matemática o donde situar el mundo matemático. DE LORENZO, Javier.
La democracia de los antiguos y la de los modernos. YTURBE, Corina.
Desarrollos actuales de la epistemología dialéctica. MENDOZA, Celina A Lértora.
Destruktion und Übersetzung: Zu den Aufgaben von Philosophiegeschichte nach Martin Heidegger. OPILIK, Klaus.
Dialogue or Mutual Accusations?. SAGATOVSKII, V N.
Dionysian and Apollonian Pathos of Distance: A New Image of World History. BROWN, David H.
Discovering God in Western Civilization. BRESLAUER, S Daniel.
East-West Philosophy in Nineteenth-Century America: Emerson and Hinduism. GOODMAN, Russell B.
La eleccion de un maestro. VAN STEENBERGHEN, Fernand.
The Emergence and Original Meaning of the Name 'Metaphysics'. REINER, Hans and ADLER, Pierre and PASKIN, David.
The Enlightenment in American Law I: The Declaration of Independence. RECK, Andrew J.
Eradicating the Obvious. CLARK, Stephen R L.
Eric Voegelin's View of History as a Drama of Transfiguration. HUGHES, Glenn.
Ethics and Politics (in German). EWALD, François.
Foucault, Nietzsche, History: Two Modes of the Genealogical Method. SAX, Benjamin C.
Franz Rosenzweig e Friedrich Meinecke. D'ANTUONO, Emilia.
The Future of the Past: From the History of Historiography to Historiology. GRANDAZZI, Alexandre.
Hayden White: "Historicism" as Linguistic Relativism in Historiography (in Polish). POMORSKI, Jan.
Healthy Scepticism. FRANKLIN, James.
Hegel, Spengler, and the Enigma of World History: Progress or Decline?. FARRENKOPF, John.
Hegels Geschichtsphilosophie im Vergleich mit anderen Geschichtskonzeptionen. GLOY, Karen.
Heracles and the Passage from Nature to Culture in G Vico's *La Scienza Nuova*. MIUCCIO, Giuliana.
Hermeneutics (in Hungarian). SCHREITER, Jörg.
Historia de la filosofía: para qué?. TOMASINI, Alejandro.
The Historical Event as a Cultural Indicator: The Case of Judaism. NEUSNER, Jacob.
Historical Relativism as a Manifestation of the Cognitive Activity of a Historian According to Collingwood (in Polish). ZDYBEL, Jolanta.
Historiography and Postmodernism: Reconsiderations. ZAGORIN, Perez.
History and Historical Anthropology. GOUREVITCH, Aron I.
History and Ontology: A Reading of Nietzsche's Second "Untimely Meditation". BAMBACH, Charles R.
The History of Philosophy, Inside and Out. MATHIEN, Thomas.
History, Differential Equations, and the Problem of Narration. MC CLOSKEY, Donald N.
History, Historicism, Narratives: Identity in the Philosophy of History of Karl Popper. PARLEJ, Piotr.
History, Indian Science and Policy-Making: A Philosophical Review. BHARGAVI, V and SUBRAMANIAM, K.
History, Lying, and Moral Responsibility. PORK, Andrus.
Hobbes and the Myth of "Final War". PASQUALUCCI, Paolo.
Hume's *Dialogues* and the Redefinition of the Philosophy of Religion. SCHNER, George.
Husserl and the Japanese. WELTON, Donn.
The Idea of History as a Scale of Forms. GOLDSTEIN, Leon J.
Las ideas en Centroamerica: De 1838 a 1970. ESTRADA, Olga C (ed).
Immateriality and the Domain of Thomistic Natural Philosophy. JOHNSON, Mark F.
An Impatient Man and his Papers. HINTIKKA, Jaakko.
The Intellectuals at the End of History. BRUNKHORST, Hauke.
Is "The Theory of History" (1914) Collingwood's First Essay on the Philosophy of History?. PATRICK, James.
Jan Hus und Thomas Müntzer—ein philosophiehistorischer Vergleich (in Czechoslovakian). KOLESNYK, Alexander.
Jeffersonian Ethics in Foreign Affairs: John Quincy Adams and the Moral Sentiments of a Realist. RUSSELL, Greg.
Kant et l'histoire de la philosophie la vision problématologique. TIMMERMANS, Benoît.
L'histoire de la philosophie et son temps. DECLÈVE, Henri.
Life and Cognition. FROLOV, Ivan T.
Limning the Liminal: Carr and Ricoeur on Time and Narrative. PELLAUER, David.
Locke, Lockean Ideas, and the Glorious Revolution. SCHWOERER, Lois G.
Marranos (Pigs), or from Coexistence to Toleration. SHELL, Marc.
Marx and Dialectics (in German). ADLER, Max.
Marx and the Problem of Conflicting Models of History. BEST, Steven.
Marx's *Aufhebung* of Philosophy and the Foundations of Historical-Materialist Science. FRACCHIA, Joseph.
Marx's Historical Understanding of the Proletariat and Class in 19th-Century England. MAZLISH, Bruce.
Marx's Theory of Revolutionary Change. PANICHAS, George E and HOBART, Michael E.
Marxist Historians and the Question of Class in the French Revolution. AMARIGLIO, Jack and NORTON, Bruce.
Materiali per una storia dell'epistemologia in Italia. CASTELLANA, Mario.
Métaphysique radicale. MARGOLIS, Joseph.
The Methodologies of Social History: A Critical Survey and Defense of Structurism. LLOYD, Christopher.
Mnêmê, anámnêsis, mnêmosynê: Sull'identità dell'uomo storico. MICCOLI, Paolo.
Modernism's Two Eternities. GEORGIEFF, Andrey.
Il mondo Il soggetto Lo smarrimento. INCARDONA, Nunzio.
The Moral Interpretation of the 'Second Preface' to Arrian's *Anabasis*. GRAY, V J.
The Moral Status of Animals and Their Use in Research: A Philosophical Review. DEGRAZIA, David.
Moral und Verwirklichung. KLEINGELD, Paulien.
MYSL' and the Intuitivist Debate in the Early 1920s. NETHERCOTT, Frances.
Neo-Sophistic Rhetorical Criticism or the Historical Reconstruction of Sophistic Doctrines?. SCHIAPPA, Edward.
Nietzsche and Foucault on *Ursprung* and Genealogy. COOK, Deborah.
Nietzsche and Post-Modernity. ERICKSON, Stephen A.
Nietzsche in Derrida's *Spurs*: Deconstruction as Deracination. FREYDBERG, Bernard D.
The Nietzsche Temptation in the Thought of Albert Camus. DUVALL, William E.
Nietzsche, Heidegger, and the Critique of Humanism. HODGE, Joanna.
Note ad un recente libro sull'incontro-scontro tra Croce e Gentile. ANTISERI, Dario.
On Ancients and Moderns. CROPSEY, Joseph.
On Bureaucracy and Science: A Response to Fuller. TWENEY, Ryan D.
On the Locus of Medical Discovery. REINES, Brandon P.
On the Phenomenon of Marginality in Epistemology: Gonseth and his Tradition. WITKOWSKI, Lech.
Ontology and History. BARLINGAY, S S.
Over leesbaarheid en maakbaarheid van de geschiedenis. WEYEMBERGH, Maurice.
Para una metahistoria del narrativisimo. GUARIGLIA, Osvaldo.
Paradojas del Romanticismo. KERKHOFF, Manfred.
A Peep into Man's History: The Lessons for Today. SINGH, Ajai R and SINGH, Shakuntala A.
Per una filosofia del corpo. PELLECCHIA, Pasquale.
Per una storia dell'idea di Europa: Riflessioni storiografiche. BALDASSARRE, Mariarosa.
Philosophy of African Intellectuals. WAMBA-DIA-WAMBA, Ernest.
Philosophy of History is Heternomous Philosophy (in German). SCHULTE, Christoph.
Pierre Menard's *Don Quixote*. BAILEY, George.
Plato's *Statesman* Story: The Birth of Fiction Reconceived. TOMASI, John.
Post-Holocaust Theodicy: Images of Deity, History, and Humanity. FREY, Robert Seitz.
The Postmodern Posture. KHANIN, Dmitry.
Power, Knowledge and Freedom: The Meaning of Foucault's Threefold Break with the History of Ideas (in German). ENGLER, Wolfgang.
La prima e seconda edizione della "Geschichte des Materialismus" di Friedrich Albert Lange. COGNETTI, Giuseppe.
La prima edizione sovietica di Solov'ev. MASTROIANNI, Giovanni.
Progressive Traditionalism as the Spirit of Collingwood's Philosophy. KISSELL, Michael A.
A Reaction to Vogel's "The Ethical Roots of Business". MC MAHON, Thomas F.
Reflections on the Philosophy of Hitlerism. HAND, Seán (trans) and LEVINAS, Emmanuel.
Reflexiones en torno a la metodología de la historia de la filosofía. BENÍTEZ, Laura.

HISTORY

The Relevance of Historical Evidence for Christian Faith: A Critique of a Kierkegaardian View. EVANS, C Stephen.
Renaissance Ideas and the Idea of the Renaissance. TRINKAUS, Charles.
Reply to Professor Zagorin's "Historiography and Postmodernism: Reconsideration". ANKERSMIT, Frank R.
Réponses à quelques questions. MARION, Jean-Luc.
Representations of the Natural System in the Nineteenth Century. O'HARA, Robert J.
Restoring Cultural History: Beyond Gombrich. PAVUR, Claude N.
A Returning to the Source: The Philosophy of Alain Locke. BIRT, Robert E.
La revolución teórica del Príncipe de Maquiavelo. GIGLIOLI, Giovanna.
Richard Rorty and the Image of Modernity. BRADLEY, James.
The Role of Memory in the Historiography of the French Revolution. HUTTON, Patrick H.
Romanticism and Modernity. LARMORE, Charles.
Ruminations of a Slow-witted Mind. PIKE, Burton (trans) and LUFT, David S and MUSIL, Robert.
Saying Good-bye to Historical Truth. SPENCE, Donald P.
Het scheppende en herscheppende woord: zijn blijvende actualiteit. DENGERINK, J D.
Social Epistemology and the Brave New World of Science and Technology Studies. FULLER, Steve.
Some Remarks on a Historical Theory of Justice and its Application to Ireland. MC KIM, Robert.
La storia universale come storia comparata in Max Weber. DI MARCO, Giuseppe Antonio.
Strauss's Three Burkes: The Problem of Edmund Burke in *Natural Right and History*. LENZNER, Steven J.
Lo sviluppo degli studi logici nel pensiero tedesco della seconda metà dell' '800. MANGIAGALLI, Maurizio.
Telling It Like It Was: Historical Narratives on Their Own Terms. NORMAN, Andrew P.
La teología de la historia en la "ciudad de Dios" (2). OROZ RETA, José (trans) and BAGET BOZZO, Giovanni.
La teología de la historia en la Ciudad de Dios. OROZ RETA, José (trans) and BAGET-BOZZO, Giovanni.
The Academic Lehrjahre of Novalis—A Period of Search for His Own View of History (in Polish). JAKUSZKO, Honorata.
The Freedom of Values and the Value of Freedom (in Czechoslovakian). SLEJSKA, D.
The Strategy of Forced Reconciliation (in Serbo-Croatian). RAULET, Gérard.
Thomas Hobbes and the Contractarian Theory of Law. GAUTHIER, David.
Tipos ideales en historia. TOZZI, María Verónica.
Tory History Incognito: Hume's *History of England* in Goldsmith's *History of England*. KENNELLY, Laura B.
Travaux récents sur la pensée du XIIIe siècle. VAN STEENBERGHEN, Fernand.
Two Designs of Universal History. KANTOR, K M.
Uguaglianza e temporalità nella "Democrazia in America". BAGLIONI, Emma.
The Unity of Theory and Practice in Historical Perspective. KRANCBERG, Sigmund.
Usefulness in Literary History. SMALL, Ian and GUY, Josephine.
The Uses and Abuses of the History of Topos Theory. MC LARTY, Colin.
The Uses of Humanistic History. PORTER, Theodore M.
Vasilii Vasil'evich Rozanov: "My Soul Is Woven of Filth, Tenderness, and Grief". KUVAKIN, V A.
Vico: dalla collocazione storica all'efficiacia teoretica. FRANCHINI, Raffaello.
Was ist ein Polyhistor? Gehversuche auf einem verlassenen Terrain. JAUMANN, Herbert.
Was R G Collingwood the Author of "The Theory of History"?. CONNELLY, James.
What Goodman Leaves Out. ELGIN, Catherine Z.
What Makes Practice Educational?. HOGAN, Pádraig.
World History as the Progress of Consciousness: An Interpretation of Hegel's Philosophy of History. HOULGATE, Stephen.
X Zubiri in Roma: Natura, Storia, Dio. JAVIERRE ORTAS, A M.

HISTORY OF IDEAS

Russische Philosophie. GOERDT, Wilhelm.
Spuren der Macht. RÖTTGERS, Kurt.
Thomistic Papers, V. RUSSMAN, Thomas A (ed).
"Great Books, Democracy and Truth" in *Freedom in the Modern World: Jacques Maritain, Yves R Simon, Mortimer J Adler*, ADLER, Mortimer J.
Aristotelianism and the Origins of "Political Science" in the Twelfth Century. NEDERMAN, Cary J.
Historical Perspectives on the Morality of Virtue. WHITE, Richard.
Nietzsche in America: Fashion and Fascination. VAN DER WILL, Wilfried.
The Rhythms of Gratitude: Historical Developments and Philosophical Concerns. STEWART-ROBERTSON, Charles.
Seven Types of Obloquy: Travesties of Marxism. GERAS, Norman.

HISTORY OF PHILOSOPHY

see also Ancient, Medieval, Modern, Nineteenth, Twentieth
Philosophy's Journey: From the Presocratics to the Present (Second Edition). KOLENDA, Konstantin.
Computer Alternatives in the History of Philosophy Classroom. TESCHNER, George and MC CLUSKY, Frank.
Doxology and the History of Philosophy. NORMORE, Calvin G.
Filosofía e historia de la filosofía. BEUCHOT, Mauricio.
Has the History of Philosophy Ruined the Environment?. ATTFIELD, Robin.
Historia de la filosofía: para qué?. TOMASINI, Alejandro.
The History of Philosophy, Inside and Out. MATHIEN, Thomas.
Ockham, Adams and Connotation: A Critical Notice of Marilyn Adams, *William Ockham*. SPADE, Paul Vincent.
Reflexiones en torno a la metodología de la historia de la filosofía. BENÍTEZ, Laura.
Relevancia de la historia de la filosofía para la filosofía. NATHAN, Elia.

HISTORY OF SCIENCE

Particles and Waves: Historical Essays in the Philosophy of Science. ACHINSTEIN, Peter.
"Bridge Structures and the Borderline Between the Internal and External History of Science" in *Imre Lakatos and Theories of Scientific Change*, GÄHDE, Ulrich.
Is History and Philosophy of Science Withering on the Vine?. FULLER, Steve W.
Scientific Racism in the Philosophy of Science: Some Historical Examples. UEBEL, Thomas E.
Social Science-Based Understandings of Science: Reflections on Fuller. KRUGLANSKI, Arie W.
Whither Social Epistemology? A Reply to Fuller. SCHMAUS, Warren.

HITLER

Heidegger: vita e distino—Sullo biografia heideggeriana di Hugo Ott. ESPOSITO, Costantino.

HIV

Duty to Treat or Right to Refuse?. DANIELS, Norman.

HMO

The Ethics of Selectively Marketing the Health Maintenance Organization. WAYMACK, Mark H.
When Is Home Care Medically Necessary? Commentary. FORROW, Lachlan.
When Is Home Care Medically Necessary? Commentary. DANIELS, Norman and SABIN, James E.

HOBBES

An Audience for Moral Philosophy?. EDELMAN, John T.
Hobbes. TUCK, Richard.
The Legal-Rational State: A Comparison of Hobbes, Bentham and Kelsen. LEE, Keekok.
Moral Dealing: Contract, Ethics, and Reason. GAUTHIER, David.
Morality—What's In It For Me?: A Historical Introduction to Ethics. NELSON, William N.
Nature and Politics: Liberalism in the Philosophies of Hobbes, Locke, and Rousseau. RAPACZYNSKI, Andrzej.
The Positivist Science of Law. LEE, Keekok.
Thomas Hobbes' Theory of Obligation: A Modern Interpretation. FORSBERG, Ralph P.
"Hobbes e as metáforas do Estado" in *Dinâmica do Pensar: Homenagem a Oswaldo Market*, DOS SANTOS, Leonel Ribeiro.
I "systemata subordinata" e il problema della partecipazione in Hobbes. SORGI, Giuseppe.
1668 Appendix to Leviathan. WRIGHT, George (trans) and HOBBES, Thomas.
Compatibilities on the Idea of Law in Thomas Aquinas and Thomas Hobbes. FULLER, Timothy.
From Precision to Peace: Hobbes and Political Language. MINOGUE, Kenneth.
God and Man: Action and Reference in Hobbes. BERTMAN, Martin A.
Hobbes and the Myth of "Final War". PASQUALUCCI, Paolo.
Hobbes and the Philosophy of International Relations. RAMOSE, Mogobe B.
Hobbes on Capital Punishment. HEYD, David.
Hobbes y la apología moderna del artificio. BOVERO, Michelangelo.
Hobbes' Science of Human Nature. SACKSTEDER, William.
Hobbes, Berkeley y las ideas abstractas. ROBLES, José A.
Hobbes, Jacobo I y el derecho inglés. RIBEIRO, Renato Janine.
The Impact of Science Studies on Political Philosophy. LATOUR, Bruno.
Individualism, Absolutism, and Contract in Hobbes' Political Theory. GROVER, Robinson A.
King Lear and Natural Law. YOUNG, R V.
L'explicite et l'implicite dans la conception du signe chez Hobbes. POLIAKOV, Igor.
Leviathan, King of the Proud. SHAVER, Robert.
The Many Appetites of Thomas Hobbes. HURLEY, Paul.
Ein neu gefundener Brief von Leibniz an Lambert van Velthuysen: Mit einer Einführung von Albert Heinekamp. HEIN, Isolde.
Politica e diritto in Hobbes. BAGLIONI, Emma.
Politics in Hobbes' Mechanics: The Social as Enabling. LYNCH, William T.
Power, Liberty, and Counterfactual Conditionals in Hobbes' Thought. POLANSKY, Ronald and TORELL, Kurt.
Pride, Hypocrisy and Civility in Mandeville's Social and Historical Theory. DICKEY, Laurence.

HOBBES
Prudence and Providence: On Hobbes's Theory of Practical Reason. HANCE, Allen S.
Qué conocemos de dios? Hobbes versus Tomas. LUKAC DE STIER, María Liliana.
Reading Hobbes in Other Words: Contractarian, Utilitarian, Game Theorist. HARDIN, Russell.
Sovranità e obbedienza. CATANIA, Alfonso.
The Symmetry Enigma in Hobbes. HAJI, Ishtiyaque.
Thomas Hobbes and the Contractarian Theory of Law. GAUTHIER, David.

HOEFFE, O
Kann in O Höffes Ethik der politischen Gerechtigkeit eine ökologische Ethik aufgehoben werden?. WETZEL, Manfred.
Neuvermessung des Rechts- und Staatsdiskurses: Zu Otfried Höffes Theorie der Politischen Gerechtigkeit. SITTER-LIVER, Beat.

HOHFELD, W
Relative Duties in the Law. WELLMAN, Carl.

HOLBEIN, H
Kristeva and Holbein, Artist of Melancholy. LECHTE, John.

HOLDERLIN
Ästhetik des Abschieds: Kritik der Moderne. EBELING, Hans.
Hölderlin über Urteil und Sein. GRAESER, Andreas.

HOLISM
Cosmos and Anthropos: A Philosophical Interpretation of the Anthropic Cosmological Principle. HARRIS, Errol E.
Donald Davidson. EVNINE, Simon.
Ethics, Politics, and Human Nature. PAUL, Ellen Frankel (ed).
The Health Crisis. SZUMSKI, Bonnie (ed).
Mind-Body. MOULYN, Adrian C.
A Morally Deep World: An Essay on Moral Significance and Environmental Ethics. JOHNSON, Lawrence E.
Philosophical Foundations of Health Education. LAURA, Ronald S.
"The Development of Self-Consciousness: Baldwin, Mead, and Vygotsky" in *Reconsidering Psychology: Perspectives from Continental Philosophy*, MARKOVA, Ivana.
"Holism and Naturalized Epistemology Confronted with the Problem of Truth" in *Perspectives on Quine*, LAUENER, Henri.
"Meaning, Holism and Use" in *Truth and Interpretation: Perspectives on the Philosophy of Donald Davidson*, BILGRAMI, Akeel.
"The Parody of Conversation" in *Truth and Interpretation: Perspectives on the Philosophy of Donald Davidson*, HACKING, Ian.
"Theories as Mere Conventions" in *Scientific Theories*, KYBURG JR, Henry E.
The "Middle Wittgenstein": From Logical Atomism to Practical Holism. STERN, David G.
Biological Holism and the Evolution of Ethics. SHRADER-FRECHETTE, Kristin.
A Clue for a Classical Realist Contribution to the Debate Over the Value of Animals. KLONOSKI, Richard J.
Dummett's Ought from Is. GREEN, Karen.
An Entropic Analysis of Postmodernism. MC KINNEY, Ronald H.
Foundationalism, Holism, or Hegel?. STERN, David S.
Hobbes and the Philosophy of International Relations. RAMOSE, Mogobe B.
Holism and Indeterminacy. MALPAS, Jeff.
Holism and Measurement (in Serbo-Croatian). BALZER, Wolfgang.
Holism and Nonseparability. HEALEY, Richard A.
Indeterminacy, Empirical Evidence, and Methodological Pluralism. ROUSE, Joseph.
Is Friedrich Nietzsche a Precursor to the Holistic Movement?. KREBBS JR, R Stephen.
Meaning Holism and Interpretability. TALMAGE, Catherine J L and MERCER, Mark.
No Holism without Pluralism. VARNER, Gary E.
Over de ambivalente rol van de theoriegeladenheidsthese in Rorty's 'overwinning' van de traditie. KRIBBE, Pamela.
The Philosophy of Logical Wholism. MC CARTY, David Charles.
Play of the Whole of Wholes (in Czechoslovakian). AXELOS, Kostas.
Reply to Shrader-Frechette's "Biological Holism and the Evolution of Ethics". CALLICOTT, J Baird.
Semantic Holism is Seriously False. MASSEY, Gerald J.
Semantic Holism. BELNAP JR, Nuel D and MASSEY, Gerald J.
The Process of Evolution in a Holistic World (in German). SOSCHINKA, Hans-Ulrich.
The World as a Whole and the World of Man (in Czechoslovakian). PATOCKA, Jan.
Wittgenstein's Holism. PEARS, David.

HOLLAND, A
Whose Life is it Anyway?. TRUSTED, Jennifer.

HOLOCAUST
Thinking the Unthinkable: Meanings of the Holocaust. GOTTLIEB, Roger S (ed).
American Slavery and the Holocaust: Their Ideologies Compared. THOMAS, Laurence.

Auschwitz, Morality and the Suffering of God. SAROT, Marcel.
Jewish Faith and the Holocaust. COHN-SHERBOK, Dan.
Post-Holocaust Theodicy: Images of Deity, History, and Humanity. FREY, Robert Seitz.

HOLY
Our Inner Divinity: Humanism and the Spiritual Enterprise. ARISIAN, Khoren.

HOLY SPIRIT
The Epistemological Significance of the Inner Witness of the Holy Spirit. ABRAHAM, William J.

HOME
The School and the Home: Partners or Pariahs—A Response to Kennedy on Home Schools. ENGEL, David E.
Thinking About Home Schooling: Some Historical, Philosophical, and Cultural Reasons. KENNEDY, David.

HOMER
The Epic Hero as Politico. CAMPBELL, Blair.

HOMOMORPHISM(S)
Cylindric Algebras with Terms. FELDMAN, Norman.
The Monadic Second-Order Logic of Graphs IV: Definability Properties of Equational Graphs. COURCELLE, Bruno.
On the Structure of De Morgan Monoids with Corollaries on Relevant Logic and Theories. SLANEY, John K.
Preservation by Homomorphisms and Infinitary Languages. HYTTINEN, Tapani.

HOMONYMY
Plato and the Senses of Words. BLACKSON, Thomas A.

HOMOPHOBIA
Some Thoughts About Heterosexualism. HOAGLAND, Sarah Lucia.

HOMOSEXUALITY
Alterity, Identity, Image: Contributions Towards a Theoretical Perspective. CORBEY, R (ed).
Contemporary Perspectives on Masculinity: Men, Women, and Politics in Modern Society. CLATTERBAUGH, Kenneth.
On Homosexuality: Lysis, Phaedrus, and Symposium. JOWETT, Benjamin (trans).
The Ethics of Conversion Therapy. MURPHY, Timothy F.

HOMUNCULUS(-LI)
The Role of Homunculi in Psychology. WARD, Andrew.

HONDERICH, T
"Information and the Mental" in *Truth and Interpretation: Perspectives on the Philosophy of Donald Davidson*, PUTNAM, Hilary.

HONESTY
"Why Honesty Is a Hard Virtue" in *Identity, Character, and Morality: Essays in Moral Psychology*, BAIER, Annette C.

HONOR
Death, Honor, and Loyalty: The Bushidō Ideal. HURST III, G Cameron.
Leviathan, King of the Proud. SHAVER, Robert.

HOOK, S
"The Russell-Hook Debates of 1958: Arguments from the Extremes on Nuclear War and the Soviet Union" in *In the Interest of Peace: A Spectrum of Philosophical Views*, GAY, William.
Pragmatic Naturalism: The Philosophy of Sidney Hook (1902-1989). KURTZ, Paul.

HOOKER, B
A Note on Hooker's "Rule Consequentialism". CARSON, Tom.

HOPE
Evolution: Probleme und neue Aspekte ihrer Theorie. SCHEFFCZYK, Leo (ed).
For What May I Hope? Thinking with Kant and Kierkegaard. FENDT, Gene.
Glück und Lebenssinn: Eine religionsphilosophische Untersuchung. DRESCHER, Johannes.
Hope and Its Hieroglyph: A Critical Decipherment of Ernst Bloch's "Principle of Hope". ROBERTS, Richard H.
Rorty's Humanistic Pragmatism: Philosophy Democratized. KOLENDA, Konstantin.
"Hope" in *The Philosophy in Christianity*, SUTHERLAND, Stewart.
Certain Hope. PHILLIPS GRIFFITHS, A.
O discurso filosófico e a unidade da verdade nas primeiras obras de Paul Ricoeur. RENAUD, Michel.
Espoir et désespoir de la raison chez Kant. GRIMALDI, Nicolas.
G Marcel: a dimensão metafísica da esperança. DA COSTA FREITAS, Manuel Barbosa.
Hope: Its Essence and Forms (in Polish). SYMOTIUK, Stefan.
Never say "Never say 'Never'": A Reply to Nicholas Gier. REEDER, Harry P.
Toward a Pragmatic Conception of Religious Faith. GOLDING, Joshua L.

HOPF, M
Arthur Schopenhauer als Staatsdenker. WÜRKNER, Joachim.

HOPING
The Intentional and the Intended. GARCIA, J L A.

HOPPER, S
"Eternal Objects and Archetypes, Past and Depth: Response to Hopper" in *Archetypal Process: Self and Divine in Whitehead, Jung, and Hillman*, COBB JR, John B.

HORACE
Horace's *Ars Poetica* and the Deconstructive Leech. HABIB, M A R.

HORKHEIMER, M
Critical Theory and Philosophy. INGRAM, David.
Announcement of the Endless in Horkheimer, Adorno and Habermas (in Serbo-Croatian). SIEBERT, Rudolf J.
Crisis of Modernity and Process Thought in Max Horkheimer's Early Work (in Serbo-Croatian). FILANDRA, Sacir.
Die Metaphysik der Kritik: Zum Verhältnis von Metaphysik und Erfahrung bei Max Horkheimer und Theodor W Adorno. RECKI, Birgit.
Society as an "Accidental Product of Human Activities": Max Horkheimer's Social Theory and Critique. BALOG, Andreas.

HORNSBY, J
Hornsby's Puzzles: Rejoinder to Wreen and Hornsby. KOSROVANI, Emilio.

HORWICH, P
Horwich, Hempel, and Hypothetico-Deductivism. GEMES, Ken.
On Russell's Principle of Induction. DA COSTA, Newton C A and FRENCH, Steven.

HOSPICE(S)
Comment on Hospice of Washington's Policy. ROBERTSON, John A.

HOSPITAL(S)
"Hospitals as Humane Corporations" in *Integrity in Health Care Institutions: Humane Environments for Teaching, Inquiry, and Healing*, REISER, Stanley Joel.

HOSTOS, E
La "Moral Social" de Eugenio María de Hostos. GONZÁLEZ, José Emilio.

HOWE, E
Treating the Troops: A Commentary. ANNAS, George J and GRODIN, Michael A.
Treating the Troops: A Commentary. LEVINE, Robert J.

HUET, P
Descartes censuré par Huet. MALBREIL, Germain.

HULL, D
David Hull's Evolutionary Model for the Progress and Process of Science. OLDROYD, David.
Scientific Pluralism and the Plurality of the Sciences: Comments on David Hull's *Science as a Process*. DUPRÉ, John.
Sociology, Selection, and Success: A Critique of David Hull's Analysis of Science and Systematics. DONOGHUE, Michael J.

HUMAN CONDITION
Human Interests: Reflections on Philosophical Anthropology. RESCHER, Nicholas.
"The Philosophy of Culture in Jacques Maritain" in *From Twilight to Dawn: The Cultural Vision of Jacques Maritain*, GALLAGHER, Donald A.
Algunos márgenes de la condición humana. MAS, Oscar.
Ethical Considerations Regarding Public Opinion Polling During Election Campaigns. MICHALOS, Alex C.
Vico, pensatore antimoderno: L'interpretazione di Eric Voegelin. ZANETTI, Gianfrancesco.

HUMAN CONSCIOUSNESS
Artificial Intelligence and Human Cognition. WAGMAN, Morton.
Human Consciousness. HANNAY, Alastair.
An Invitation To Cognitive Science. LEIBER, Justin.
The Science of the Mind (Second Edition). FLANAGAN, Owen.

HUMAN DEVELOPMENT
Catholic and Marxist Views on Human Development. MC GOVERN, Arthur F.
Developmental Constraints on Ethical Behaviour in Business. HARRIS, Claudia and BROWN, William.
The Physiology of Moral Maturity. HEMMING, James.
Sex and Virtue. PUTMAN, D.
The Tensions Between Education and Development. GARDNER, Howard.

HUMAN EXISTENCE
Proust: The Creative Silence. CARANFA, Angelo.
"Unger's *Politics* and the Appraisal of Political Possibility" in *Critique and Construction: A Symposium on Roberto Unger's "Politics"*, DUNN, John.
Eric Voegelin's View of History as a Drama of Transfiguration. HUGHES, Glenn.
El hombre agustiniamo: Itinerario tras el ser de la existencia. MOLINA, Mario A.
An Issue in Corporate Social Responsibility: An Experiential Approach to Establish the Value of Human Life. DALTON, Dan R and COSIER, Richard A.
La realtà umana nel pensiero di Xavier Zubiri. QUINTÁS, Alfonso López and NICOLOSI, Mauro.
Scientific Time and the Temporal Sense of Human Existence: Merleau-Ponty and Mead. BOURGEOIS, Patrick L and ROSENTHAL, Sandra B.

HUMAN GENOME
Mapping the Human Genome: Some Thoughts for Those Who Say "There Should Be A Law On It". SKENE, Loane.
Should Ethical Concerns Regulate Science? The European Experience with the Human Genome Project. RIX, Bo Andreassen.
Whose Genome Project?. MACER, Darryl.

HUMAN NATURE
The Balance of Consciousness: Eric Voegelin's Political Theory. KEULMAN, Kenneth.
David Hume's Theory of Mind. FLAGE, Daniel E.
Empiricism and Subjectivity: An Essay on Hume's Theory of Human Nature. BOUNDAS, Constantin V (trans).
Ethics, Politics, and Human Nature. PAUL, Ellen Frankel (ed).
Human Goodness: Generosity and Courage. PYBUS, Elizabeth.
Human Nature and Historical Knowledge: Hume, Hegel and Vico. POMPA, Leon.
Introduction Critique au Droit Naturel. HERVADA, Javier.
Leviathan: Hobbes. TUCK, Richard (ed).
The Nature of Politics. MASTERS, Roger D.
Le Philosophie et les Passions. MEYER, Michel.
Réflexions sur les passions. HUME, David.
Socialism, Feminism and Philosophy: A Radical Philosophy Reader. SAYERS, Sean (ed).
"Human Suffering and Our Post-Civilized Cultural Mind: A Maritainian Analysis" in *From Twilight to Dawn: The Cultural Vision of Jacques Maritain*, CALIFANO, Joseph J.
"A Return to the Crossroads: A Maritainian View of the New Educational Reformers" in *From Twilight to Dawn: The Cultural Vision of Jacques Maritain*, HANCOCK, Curtis L.
"Historia" de la naturaleza *versus* "Naturaleza" de la historia. LEAL, Fernando A.
A propósito del filósofo del derecho Giorgio del Vecchio. DI PIETRO, Alfredo.
Against Human Rights. NELSON, John O.
Alle origini della riflessione di Leopold von Ranke sulla storia: K F Bachmann e J G Fichte. GHELARDI, Maurizio.
The Biological Justification of Ethics: A Best-Case Scenario. ROSENBERG, Alexander.
Christians and Marxist Theory of Human Liberation. KOWALCZYK, Stanislaw.
Common Ground: Aristotle on Human and Divine Noetic Activity. MORGAN, Vance G.
Conclusion. GRIFFITHS, A Phillips.
The Elusiveness of Human Nature. SMITHURST, Michael.
The Feminist Revelation. SOMMERS, Christina.
Freedom and Human Nature. FLEW, Antony.
Hobbes' Science of Human Nature. SACKSTEDER, William.
Human Nature Technologically Revisited. ENGELHARDT JR, H Tristram.
Human Nature, Social Engineering, and the Reemergence of Civil Society. RAU, Zbigniew.
The Interplay of Nature and Man in the *Periphyseon* of Johannes Scottus Eriugena. OTTEN, Willemien.
Lonergan's Recovery of the Notion of Natural Right: Introduction to a New Context for an Old Discussion. BRAIO, Frank Paul.
Making the Citizens Good: Aristotle's City and Its Contemporary Relevance. SIMPSON, Peter.
Natural Virtues, Natural Vices. BAIER, Annette C.
Nietzsche contra Rousseau: Goethe versus Catilina?. BLONDEL, Eric.
Nietzsche e Spinoza. BIUSO, Alberto G.
Nietzsche on Human Nature. SCHACHT, Richard.
The Origins of Morality: An Essay in Philosophical Anthropology. OLDENQUIST, Andrew.
Parental Nature and Stoic Οικειωσισ. BLUNDELL, Mary Whitlock.
Partial Wholes. BARNES, Jonathan.
The Philosophical Significance of Psychological Differences Among Humans. LACHS, John.
Response to W J Norman's "Has Rational Economic Man a Heart". LA CASSE, Chantale and ROSS, Don.
Some Reflections on Post-Marxism and Post-Christianity: A Response to Professor Arthur Mc Govern. STOJANOVIC, Svetozar.
Two Aspects of the Christian-Marxist Dialogue: A Protestant Response. FRITZSCHE, Helmut.
Universality Biases: *How Theories About Human Nature Succeed*. HORNSTEIN, Gail A and STAR, Susan Leigh.
The Varieties of Self-Interest. EPSTEIN, Richard A.
Virtue Ethics and the Appeal to Human Nature. WOODRUFF, Paul.
The Worldly Self in Schutz: On Sighting, Citing, and Siting the Self. LANGSDORF, Lenore.

HUMAN RELATIONS
Bertrand Russell: The Psychobiography of a Moralist. BRINK, Andrew.
How Did Morality Evolve?. IRONS, William.
Solitude. KOCH, Philip J.
Voix et Existence. DIAGNE, Oumar.

HUMAN RIGHTS
Education as a Human Right: A Theory of Curriculum and Pedagogy. VANDENBERG, Donald.
"Human Rights, Population Again, and Intergenerational Equity" in *Meaning and Method: Essays in Honor of Hilary Putnam*, DANIELS, Norman.

HUMAN RIGHTS

Los "Derechos Humanos". BELARMINO, Pedro.
'Fetal Rights'? An Attempt to Render Plausible a Conservative Response. HODAPP, Paul.
Against Human Rights. NELSON, John O.
The Common Good, Human Rights and Education: A Need for Conceptual Reformulization. CRAIG, Robert P.
La ética y los derechos humanos en la filosofía clásica. ALONSO, Luz García.
Generosity: A Duty Without a Right. STITH, Richard.
Human Rights and Nietzsche. MINEAU, André.
Human Rights in the Context of Uganda's Political Experience. KIGONGO, J K.
The Juncture of Law and Morality in Prohibitions Against Torture. MARAN, Rita.
Some Remarks on Respect and Human Rights. BARNES, Annette.
The Unity of Human Rights in Western and Eastern Europe: Meditation about Human Rights. FÖLDESI, Tamás.
Universalismo o eurocentrismo. SPAEMANN, Robert.

HUMAN SCIENCES

Teoria e interpretazione: Per un'epistemologia delle scienze umane. BORUTTI, Silvana.
Elements of a Wittgensteinian Philosophy of the Human Sciences. SCHATZKI, Theodore R.
Hobbes' Science of Human Nature. SACKSTEDER, William.
La investigación y las metodologías en las Ciencias Humanas. DACAL ALONSO, José Antonio.
Problemas en torno al concepto de "ciencias humanas" como ciencias con doble plano operatorio. ALVARGONZÁLEZ, David.
Sobre el alcance de una "ciencia media" entre las ciencias humanas estrictas y los saberes prácticos positivos. BUENO, Gustavo.

HUMAN SUBJECT(S)

Science and Moral Values. VOLLRATH, John.
Considerazioni sul problema della conoscenza. BACCARI, Luciano.
Epistemology, Practical Research, and Human Subjects. ROSS, Murray and SELMAN, Mark.
The Self and Social Criticism. HARVEY, Charles W.
Uninformed Consent. MARCUS, Ruth Barcan and KUCKLICK, B and BERCOVITCH, S.

HUMAN(S)

see also Man, Person(s)
Beyond Natural Selection. WESSON, Robert.
The Difference Between Truth and Opinion: How the Misuse of Language Can Lead to Disaster. COONEY, Timothy J.
Divine Nature and Human Language: Essays in Philosophical Theology. ALSTON, William P.
Evolutionary Instability: Logical and Material Aspects of a Unified Theory of Biosocial Evolution. GEIGER, Gebhard.
Explaining Human Action. LENNON, Kathleen.
Fallen Freedom: Kant on Radical Evil and Moral Regeneration. MICHALSON JR, Gordon E.
Other Human Beings. COCKBURN, David.
Das Tier in der Moral. WOLF, Ursula.
"Conclusion" in *Philosophy and Politics*, GRIFFITHS, A Phillips.
"Human Order in the Natural Universe: Rediscovering Russell's Social Philosophy" in *Perspectives on Ideas and Reality*, MEZEI, György Iván.
"Human Symbols as Functioning Objects: A First Look at John William Miller's Contribution to Semiotics" in *The Philosophy of John William Miller*, COLAPIETRO, Vincent M.
"Introduction: Realism and Human Being" in *Harré and His Critics*, BHASKAR, Roy.
"Ordinary Animals, Language Animals and Verbal Tradition" in *Harré and His Critics*, REYNOLDS, Vernon.
"Perception and Human Reality" in *Harré and His Critics*, GRENE, Marjorie.
Antropología y Agresión: notas para un análisis filosófico. FERNÁNDEZ TRESGUERRES, Alfonso.
Assessing Human Needs. JONES, John D.
Between Two Worlds: Humans in Nature and Culture. GARDINER, Robert W.
A Christian Response to Professor Zagorka Golubovic. ZADEMACH, Wieland.
Dialogue as a Way of Being Human. YIN, Lu-jun.
La dignità dell'uomo da Kant a Hegel. PAOLINELLI, Marco.
Dios y el hombre en San Agustin. PEGUEROLES, Juan.
Economic Theory and Human Behavior. MC NULTY, T Michael.
Ethical Dimensions of Human Attitudes to Nature. BURES, Radim.
Ética sin raíces. VARGAS, Alberto.
Fetal Neural Transplantation: Placing the Ethical Debate within the Context of Society's Use of Human Material. JONES, D Gareth.
Freiheit und Bindung menschlicher Entscheidungen. KLEMENT, H W and RADERMACHER, F J.
Functionalisme versus dubbelaspecttheorie: tertium datur. MACKOR, Anne Ruth.
The Importance of Being Human. DIAMOND, Cora.
The Importance of Being Human. MC NAUGHTON, David.
Kritik der Soziobiologie des Menschen. KASPAR, Rudolf F.
The Lover-Beloved Relationship Reconsidered. HOLMES, Richard and DANIEL, Mano.
Man as the Animal Symbolism in the Conception of S Langer (in Polish). BYTNIEWSKI, Pawel.
A Marxist Approach to the Concept of Being/Becoming Human. GOLUBOVIC, Zagorka.
Nietzsche and Post-Modernity. ERICKSON, Stephen A.
La persona humana: Síntesis de la concepción antropológica de K Wojtyla. JIMÉNEZ GUERRERO, A.
Personal Identity and the Idea of a Human Being. MADELL, Geoffrey.
Play and the Theory of Basic Human Goods. CELANO, Anthony J.
Real Human Persons. DONAGAN, Alan.
Response to Diamond. MC NAUGHTON, David.
Response to McNaughton. DIAMOND, Cora.
El ser perfectible de la persona humana. JIMÉNEZ GUERRERO, A.
The Servant Species: Humanity as Priesthood. LINZEY, Andrew.
Spinoza on the Eternity of the Human Mind. LUCASH, Frank.
The World of Human Community in Hanna Arendt's Work (in Czechoslovakian). KOUBA, Pavel.
The Values of a Habitat. PARKER, Kelly.
Werkzeugproduktion im Tierreich und menschliche Werkzeugproduktion. BEURTON, Peter.
What Makes Us So Different from the Apes?. LAYNG, Tony.
Whose Life is it Anyway?. TRUSTED, Jennifer.

HUMANENESS

"Hospitals as Humane Corporations" in *Integrity in Health Care Institutions: Humane Environments for Teaching, Inquiry, and Healing*, REISER, Stanley Joel.

HUMANISM

Community: The Tie That Binds. ROUSSEAU, Mary F.
The Devil and Secular Humanism: The Children of the Enlightenment. RADEST, Howard B.
Diderot's Dream. ANDERSON, Wilda.
Ethics Without God (Revised Edition). NIELSEN, Kai.
From Twilight to Dawn: The Cultural Vision of Jacques Maritain. REDPATH, Peter A (ed).
John Dewey: Religious Faith and Democratic Humanism. ROCKEFELLER, Steven C.
Max Scheler's Concept of the Person: An Ethics of Humanism. PERRIN, Ron.
The Question of Humanism: Challenges and Possibilities. GOICOECHEA, David (ed).
Realism with a Human Face. PUTNAM, Hilary.
Rorty's Humanistic Pragmatism: Philosophy Democratized. KOLENDA, Konstantin.
Socialism, Feminism and Philosophy: A Radical Philosophy Reader. SAYERS, Sean (ed).
Toward the Death of Man. KLUBACK, William.
"Acting Human in Our Time" in *The Question of Humanism: Challenges and Possibilities*, ADAMCZEWSKI, Zygmunt.
"Afterword: The Answer of Humanism" in *The Question of Humanism: Challenges and Possibilities*, MADIGAN, Tim.
"Calvary or the Slaughter-house" in *From Twilight to Dawn: The Cultural Vision of Jacques Maritain*, SCHALL, James V.
"Christianity, Humanism, and St Thomas Aquinas" in *The Question of Humanism: Challenges and Possibilities*, MC LAUGHLIN, R J.
"Existentialism, Humanism, and Positivism" in *The Question of Humanism: Challenges and Possibilities*, HAYES, Calvin.
"Foucault and the Question of Humanism" in *The Question of Humanism: Challenges and Possibilities*, SCOTT, Charles E.
"Heidegger: What Is Called Humanism?" in *The Question of Humanism: Challenges and Possibilities*, BROWN, Richard S G.
"Human Nature and Unnatural Humanisms" in *From Twilight to Dawn: The Cultural Vision of Jacques Maritain*, ROYAL, Robert.
"The Human Person in American Pragmatism" in *The Question of Humanism: Challenges and Possibilities*, FRANCIS, Richard P.
"The Inevitability of Humanism" in *The Question of Humanism: Challenges and Possibilities*, NICHOLSON, Graeme.
"Kierkegaard's Teleological Humanism" in *The Question of Humanism: Challenges and Possibilities*, PERKINS, Robert L.
"Marxism, Humanism, and Ecology" in *The Question of Humanism: Challenges and Possibilities*, LAWLER, James and ORUDJEV, Zaid.
"The Modern Spirit and the Paradox of Humanism" in *The Question of Humanism: Challenges and Possibilities*, DORTER, Kenneth.
"An Old Question Raised Yet Again: Is Kant an Enlightenment Humanist?" in *The Question of Humanism: Challenges and Possibilities*, LUIK, John.
"The Philosophy of Culture in Jacques Maritain" in *From Twilight to Dawn: The Cultural Vision of Jacques Maritain*, GALLAGHER, Donald A.
"Psychiatry as Scientific Humanism: A Program Inspired by Roberto Unger's *Passion*" in *Critique and Construction: A Symposium on Roberto Unger's "Politics"*, HOBSON, J Allan.
"Pyrrhonism and the Concept of a Common Human Nature in Eighteenth-Century Aesthetic Thought" in *The Question of Humanism: Challenges and Possibilities*, CARDY, Michael.

HUMANISM

"Reflections on Maritain's *Le Crépuscule de la Civilisation*" in *From Twilight to Dawn: The Cultural Vision of Jacques Maritain*, MC INERNY, Ralph.
"Roman Humanism" in *The Question of Humanism: Challenges and Possibilities*, BOOTH, Allan.
"Sartre and the Humanism of Spontaneity" in *The Question of Humanism: Challenges and Possibilities*, HORNYANSKY, Monica C.
"Secular Humanism and Eupraxophy" in *The Question of Humanism: Challenges and Possibilities*, KURTZ, Paul.
"St Thomas and Medieval Humanism" in *The Question of Humanism: Challenges and Possibilities*, SYNAN, Edward A.
"Were Plato and Aristotle Humanists?" in *The Question of Humanism: Challenges and Possibilities*, ANDIC, Martin.
"What Is Renaissance Humanism?" in *The Question of Humanism: Challenges and Possibilities*, ANDIC, Martin.
"What Now Little Man? Comedy, Tragedy, and the Politics of Antihumanism" in *The Question of Humanism: Challenges and Possibilities*, AJZENSTAT, Samuel.
"William Blake and the Romantic Perception of Humanism" in *The Question of Humanism: Challenges and Possibilities*, ABRAHAMS, Cecil.
"Zarathustra and Enlightenment Humanism" in *The Question of Humanism: Challenges and Possibilities*, GOICOECHEA, David.
"The 'Humanism' and the Humanism of Karl Marx" in *The Question of Humanism: Challenges and Possibilities*, GOLDSTICK, Danny.
Cato's Letters, John Locke, and the Republican Paradigm. HAMOWY, Ronald.
Condiciones del surgimiento y desarrollo de la Psicología Humanista. CARPINTERO, Helio and MAYOR, Luis and ZALBIDEA, M A.
Considerazioni in margine a un'interpretazione di Bruno. MANZONI, Claudio.
La crisi dei fondamenti della scienza: Un recupero dell'ilemorfismo?. DEL RE, Giuseppe.
Dialogo sobre humanismo y Marxismo (primera parte). SILVA CAMARENA, Juan Manuel.
The Faith Dimension of Humanism. EARLES, Beverley.
Feminist Spirituality as a Path to Humanism. FRANKEL, Lois.
Freud's Warning to Potential Believers. EBISCH, Glen A.
From Nothingness to No-thing-ness: the Roots of Ferry and Renaut's Humanism. BARBIERO, Daniel.
The Humanism of Economics or Economizing on Humanism?. RIUMIN, V A.
El humanismo de Albert Camus. QUESADA, Anabelle.
Humanismo y humanismo cristiano. DERISI, Octavio N.
Humanist Religion for the Troubled. RUSTERHOLTZ, Wallace P.
Is History and Philosophy of Science Withering on the Vine?. FULLER, Steve W.
Masaryk's Religious Thinking (in Czechoslovakian). FUNDA, Otakar A.
Michel de Montaigne: La "nottola" dell'Umanesimo francese. LONGO, Margherita.
A New Humanism. CHURCH, F Forrester.
A New Humanism: A Response. COLLINS, Jacqueline A.
A New Humanism: A Response. DOERR, Edd.
A New Humanism: A Response. ERICSON, Edward L.
A New Humanism: A Response. HARRIS, W Edward.
A New Humanism: A Response. MAIN, William.
A New Humanism: A Response. PHIFER, Kenneth W.
A New Humanism: A Response. WILSON, Edwin H.
Nietzsche, Heidegger, and the Critique of Humanism. HODGE, Joanna.
Our Inner Divinity: Humanism and the Spiritual Enterprise. ARISIAN, Khoren.
The Problem of Atheism in Recent Soviet Publications. DAHM, Helmut.
Renaissance Humanism and the Religious Culture of the First Jesuits. O'MALLEY, John W.
Restoring Cultural History: Beyond Gombrich. PAVUR, Claude N.
Rethinking Feminist Humanism. STRAUS, Nina Pelikan.
Scientific Humanism and Religion. WILSON, Edward O.
T G Masaryk—A Modern Thinker (in Czechoslovakian). OPAT, Jaroslav.
The Concept of History in the Renaissance (in Hungarian). RASZLAI, Tibor.
The Unitarian Universalist Association: Humanism or Theism?. KURTZ, Paul and BULLOUGH, Vern L.
The Uses of Humanistic History. PORTER, Theodore M.

HUMANIST(S)

Educação para valores e maturidade pessoal do educador. ROCHA, Filipe.
Ruder Boskovic as a Humanist and Scientist (in Serbo-Croatian). SUPEK, Ivan.

HUMANITIES

Convictions. HOOK, Sidney.
Experiential Method: Qualitative Research in the Humanities Using Metaphysics and Phenomenology. KIDD, James W.
The Humanities in the Nineties: A View From the Netherlands. ZÜRCHER, Erik (ed).
Relating Humanities and Social Thought (Science, Ideology, and Value, Volume 4). EDEL, Abraham.
Swimming Against the Current in Contemporary Philosophy: Occasional Essays and Papers. VEATCH, Henry B.
"Working in America": A New Approach for the Humanities. SESSIONS, Robert.
The Importance of Cultural Pedagogy. MC DERMOTT, John J.
Michel Foucault: From the Humanities to Political Thought (in German). SEITTER, Walter.
Moral Imagination, Freedom, and the Humanities. KEKES, John.
The Relationship Between the Humanities and the Natural and Technical Sciences (in German). PACHO, Julián.

HUMANITY

A "Realizacção da Razão": Um Programa Hegeliano?. BARATA-MOURA, José.
Understanding War: A Philosophical Inquiry. MC MURTRY, John.
Wittgenstein, Ethics and Aesthetics: The View from Eternity. TILGHMAN, B R.
Dialogue—A New Utopia?. GÓRNIAK-KOCIKOWSKA, Krystyna.
A Great Intellectual Current Worthy of National Pride. CHANGLU, Qiao.
Logic and Logos—The Search for Unity in Hegel and Coleridge, III: A Different Logos. PERKINS, Mary Anne.
Man and Hermeneutics. ROY, Krishna.
The Metaphilosophy of Dialogue. KUCZYNSKI, Janusz.
Mnêmê, anámnêsis, mnêmosynê: Sull'identità dell'uomo storico. MICCOLI, Paolo.
Possibility of Dialogic Encounter of Religious and Philosophical Humanitas (in Serbo-Croatian). SKLEDAR, Nikola.
Umuntu Ngumuntu Ngabantu: An African Concept of Humanity. SHUTTE, Augustine.
Vida y Resurrección en el pensamiento de Erich Fromm. CHAVES, Flory.

HUMANIZATION

Humanizing the Humanities: Some Reflections on George Steiner's "Brutal Paradox". KARIER, Clarence J.

HUMANNESS

Aspects of Freedom. WOOD, Robert E.

HUMBOLDT

Leibniz, Humboldt, and the Origins of Comparativism. DE MAURO, Tullio (ed).
"'Lautform, innere Sprachform, Form der Sprachen'" in *Leibniz, Humboldt, and the Origins of Comparativism*, BARBA, Mario.
"Da Humboldt ai neogrammatici: Continuità e fratture" in *Leibniz, Humboldt, and the Origins of Comparativism*, RAMAT, Paolo.
"Humboldt et Leibniz: Le concept intérieur de la linguistique" in *Leibniz, Humboldt, and the Origins of Comparativism*, TRABANT, Jürgen.
"Leibniz and Wilhelm von Humboldt and the History of Comparative Linguistics" in *Leibniz, Humboldt, and the Origins of Comparativism*, ROBINS, Robert H.
"The Philosophical and Anthropological Place of Wilhelm von Humboldt's Linguistic Typology" in *Leibniz, Humboldt, and the Origins of Comparativism*, DI CESARE, Donatella.
"Romantic Philosophy and Organization of the Disciplines: the Founding of the Humboldt University of Berlin" in *Romanticism and the Sciences*, SHAFFER, Elinor S.
"Wilhelm von Humboldt und das Problem der Schrift" in *Leibniz, Humboldt, and the Origins of Comparativism*, STETTER, Christian.
Ways to See a Revolution and World Outlook: Alexander von Humboldt (in German). HERLITZIUS, Erwin.

HUME

David Hume and the Problem of Reason. DANFORD, John W.
David Hume's Theory of Mind. FLAGE, Daniel E.
David Hume: Historiker und Philosoph. LÜTHE, Rudolf.
Essays on the Context, Nature, and Influence of Isaac Newton's Theology. FORCE, James E (ed).
Fictions of Reality in the Age of Hume and Johnson. DAMROSCH, Leo.
Human Nature and Historical Knowledge: Hume, Hegel and Vico. POMPA, Leon.
Hume's Place in Moral Philosophy. CAPALDI, Nicholas.
The Idea of the Miraculous: The Challenge to Science and Religion. WILLIAMS, T C.
Knowledge of the External World. AUNE, Bruce.
The Moral Animus of David Hume. SIEBERT, Donald T.
Moral Dealing: Contract, Ethics, and Reason. GAUTHIER, David.
Morality—What's In It For Me?: A Historical Introduction to Ethics. NELSON, William N.
Morals, Motivation and Convention: Hume's Influential Doctrines. SNARE, Francis.
A Progress of Sentiments: Reflections on Hume's "Treatise". BAIER, Annette C.
Reasons and Experience. MILLAR, Alan.
Réflexions sur les passions. HUME, David.
The Secret Connexion: Causation, Realism, and David Hume. STRAWSON, Galen.
"The Breakdown of the Newtonian Synthesis of Science and Religion: Hume, Newton, and the Royal Society" in *Essays on the Context, Nature, and Influence of Isaac Newton's Theology*, FORCE, James E.
"Hume and Moral Emotions" in *Identity, Character, and Morality: Essays in Moral Psychology*, LIND, Marcia.
"Hume's Interest in Newton and Science" in *Essays on the Context, Nature, and Influence of Isaac Newton's Theology*, FORCE, James E.

HUME
"Real Humean Causes" in *Central Themes in Early Modern Philosophy*, BAIER, Annette.
"Hume and Hume's Connexions". KLEMME, Heiner.
'Pride Produces the Idea of Self': Hume on Moral Agency. RORTY, Amélie.
Action and Freedom. ROY, Pabitrakumar.
The Anatomist and the Painter: The Continuity of Hume's *Treatise* and *Essays*. IMMERWAHR, John.
The Authorship of the *Abstract* Revisited. NELSON, John O.
A Bayesian Proof of a Humean Principle. GILLIES, Donald.
Bayle, Leibniz, Hume and Reid on Extension, Composites and Simples. CUMMINS, Phillip.
Categorical Requirements: Kant and Hume on the Idea of Duty. WIGGINS, David.
The Classical Roots of Hume's Skepticism. OLSHEWSKY, Thomas M.
Coming To Be Without a Cause. SULLIVAN, T D.
El cuádruple problema de la inducción: Crítica de la solución popperiana del problema de Hume. GARCÍA NORRO, Juan José.
David Hume and the Mysterious Shroud of Turin. SCHOEN, Edward L.
David Hume on Religion in England. ROTH, Robert J.
David Hume's *Dialogues Concerning Natural Religion*: Otherness in History and in Text. MANNING, Robert J S.
David Hume's Theology of Liberation. BARRUS, Roger M.
A Dialogic Interpretation of Hume's *Dialogues*. SESSIONS, William Lad.
Discovering Right and Wrong: A Realist Response to Gauthier's Morals by Agreement. GENOVA, A C.
Emanating Causes: New Battle Lines for Natural Theology?. KING-FARLOW, John.
Epistemic Leaks and Epistemic Meltdowns: A Response to William Morris on Scepticism with Regard to Reason. KARLSSON, Mikael M.
Evolutionary Ethics and the Search for Predecessors: Kant, Hume, and All the Way Back to Aristotle?. RUSE, Michael.
Fogelin on Hume on Miracles. FLEW, Antony.
Fragmented Selves and the Problem of Ownership. BRENNAN, Andrew.
Freedom, Necessity, and Laws of Nature as Relations between Universals. VIHVELIN, Kadri.
Hegel and the Humean Problem of Induction. SUCHTING, W A.
Hume and Belief in the Existence of an External World. COSTA, Michael J.
Hume and Intrinsic Value. THOMAS, D A Lloyd.
Hume and Pascal: Pyrrhonism versus Nature. MAIA NETO, José R.
Hume and Physical Necessity. FLEW, Antony.
Hume and the Paradox of Taste Again. WERTZ, S K.
Hume and Thick Connexions. BLACKBURN, Simon.
Hume Contra Spinoza?. KLEVER, Wim.
Hume on Divine Amorality. WALLS, Jerry L.
Hume on Practical Reason. ROBERTSON, John.
Hume on Probability. GOWER, Barry.
Hume on Responsibility and Punishment. RUSSELL, Paul.
Hume on the Idea of Existence. CUMMINS, Phillip D.
Hume Revisited: A Problem With the Free Will Defense. MARKHAM, Ian.
Hume's "Of Miracles," Peirce, and the Balancing of Likelihoods. MERRILL, Kenneth R.
Hume's Critical Realism: A Reply to Livingston. WILSON, Fred.
Hume's *Dialogues* and the Redefinition of the Philosophy of Religion. SCHNER, George.
Hume's Ethics: Acts, Rules, Dispositions and Utility. SHIRLEY, Edward.
Hume's Metaethical Cognitivism and the Natural Law Theory. GRAEFRATH, Bernd.
Hume's Rejection of the Theory of Ideas. WRIGHT, John P.
Hume's Reproduction Parody of the Design Argument. DRAPER, Paul.
Hume's Theorem on Testimony Sufficient to Establish a Miracle. SOBEL, Jordan Howard.
Hume, Reid and Innate Ideas: A Response to John P Wright. GALLIE, Roger D.
Husserl and Hume: Overcrowding Scepticism?. MURPHY, Richard T.
Induction and Modality. JOHNSON, David.
Irony and Argument in *Dialogues*, XII. DAVIS, Scott.
Irrational Desires. HUBIN, Donald C.
The Laws of Physics as Nomic Universals. ZYCINSKI, Jozef.
MacIntyre on Hume. BAIER, Annette C.
Natural Virtues, Natural Vices. BAIER, Annette C.
Naturalism and Scepticism. BELL, Martin and MC GINN, Marie.
On Franco-Ferraz, Theism and the Theatre of the Mind. BADÍA-CABRERA, Miguel A.
Popper on Induction. SWANN, Andrew J.
Précis of "Whose Justice? Which Rationality?". MAC INTYRE, Alasdair.
A Second Copy Thesis in Hume?. PAPPAS, George S.
A Sellarsian Hume?. LIVINGSTON, Donald.
Sense, Passions and Morals in Hume and Kant. NUYEN, A T.
Some Features of Hume's Conception of Space. FRASCA-SPADA, Marina.
Some Remarks on the Rationality of Induction. INDURKHYA, Bipin.
A Supplement to "David Hume to Alexander Dick: A New Letter". KLEMME, Heiner F.
Tory History Incognito: Hume's *History of England* in Goldsmith's *History of England*. KENNELLY, Laura B.
Utility and Morality: Adam Smith's Critique of Hume. MARTIN, Marie A.
Welcome 'Ethical Stress': A Humean Analysis and A Practical Proposal. MERRILL, Sarah A.
What is a Law of Nature? A Humean Answer. URBACH, Peter.

HUMILITY
A New Humanism. CHURCH, F Forrester.
On Respect. BLUM, Alex.

HUMOR
The Philosopher's Joke. WATSON, Richard A.
Educating-Increasing Intelligence Levels by Developing a Sense of Humor. PRITSCHER, Conrad.
Humor, Schooling, and Cultural Intelligence: A Response to Pritscher. O'CONNOR, Terence.
Kant über den Witz und Kants Witz. RITZEL, Wolfgang.
A New Humanism. CHURCH, F Forrester.

HUNGARIAN
Mannheim and Hungarian Marxism. GABEL, Joseph.
"The Hungarian Intellectual and the Choice of Commitment or Neutrality" in *The Political Responsibility of Intellectuals*, MACLEAN, Ian (trans) and MOLNAR, Miklós.
A Hungarian Christian-Marxist Dialogue and Its Lessons. LUKÁCS, József.
Hungarian Philosophy: Its Ideas, an Historiographical Foundations (in Hungarian). STEINDLER, Larry.
Philosophy within the Activity of the Nagyszombat (Trnava) University (in Hungarian). ORAVCOVÀ, Mariana.
The Reception of Nietzsche in Hungary between the Two World Wars (in Hungarian). KISS, Endre.

HUNTING
Environmental Ethics and the Case for Hunting. KING, Roger J H.

HUS, J
Jan Hus und Thomas Müntzer—ein philosophiehistorischer Vergleich (in Czechoslovakian). KOLESNYK, Alexander.

HUSSERL
Bewusstsein und Natursein. CHO, Kah Kyung.
Exploring Phenomenology (Second Edition). STEWART, David.
La intersubjectividad en Husserl, Volume I and II. IRIBARNE, Julia V.
Logic in the Husserlian Context. TITO, Johanna Maria.
Phänomenologie als ästhetische Theorie. FELLMANN, Ferdinand.
Phänomenologische Philosophie. STRÖKER, Elisabeth.
The Power of Consciousness and the Force of Circumstances in Sartre's Philosophy. BUSCH, Thomas W.
Vernunft und Kontingenz: Rationalität und Ethos in der Phänomenologie. ORTH, Ernst Wolfgang (ed).
"Divine Truth in Husserl and Kant: Some Issues in Phenomenological Theology" in *Phenomenology of the Truth Proper to Religion*, HART, James G.
"Freud, Husserl, Derrida: An Experiement" in *Phenomenology of the Truth Proper to Religion*, LOWE, Walter.
"Imaginação e imaginário: Para além de Husserl" in *Dinâmica do Pensar: Homenagem a Oswaldo Market*, SARAIVA, Maria Manuela.
"The Nature of Acts: Moore on Husserl" in *The Analytic Tradition: Philosophical Quarterly Monographs, Volume 1*, KÜNNE, Wolfgang.
"Thought and Perception: The Views of Two Philosophical Innovators" in *The Analytic Tradition: Philosophical Quarterly Monographs, Volume 1*, DUMMETT, Michael.
"Il y a" et phénoménologie dans la pensée du jeune Lévinas. LANNOY, Jean-Luc.
The 'Body': A Husserlian Phenomenological Analysis. DAS, Paritosh Kumar.
A Phenomenologically and Psychologically Based Concept of Ethics (in Czechoslovakian). BAYEROVA, M.
The A Priori in Phenomenology and the Legacy of Logical Empiricism. BLOSSER, Philip.
The Anomaly of World: From Scheler to Heidegger. SCHALOW, Frank.
Aspects of the Problem of Reference (II). RAJAN, R Sundara.
Axiology as the Form of Purity of Heart: A Reading Husserliana XXVIII. HART, James G.
Being and Categorial Intuition. COBB-STEVENS, Richard.
Het belang van Husserls aanzet tot een fenomenologie van de bewustzijnsperspectieven. FREDERIX, Lode.
Brentano e Fichte negli scritti "minori" di E Husserl. BELLO, A Ales.
The Concept of Ego in Husserl's Philosophy. DAS, Paritosh Kumar.
Contemporary Shapes of Scientific Realism (in Czechoslovakian). PARUSNIKOVA, Zuzana.
Continuità e discontinuità tra Husserl e Heidegger: genesi e sviluppo d una polemica filosofica. RIZZACASA, Aurelio.
The Crisis in Psychoanalysis: Resolution Through Husserlian Phenomenology and Feminism. NISSIM-SABAT, Marilyn.
A determinação heideggeriana de fenómeno em *Sein und Zeit* como superação do "cepticismo metódico". DAS NEVES, Jorge César.
Ein Husserlmanuskript über Ästhetik. SCARAMUZZA, Gabriele and SCHUHMANN, Karl.
L'epoché di Husserl in Ferruccio Rossi-Landi. PONZIO, Augusto.
Essai sur le développement historique de la voie phénoménologique. MAESSCHALCK, Marc.

HUSSERL
Experience of the Alien in Husserl's Phenomenology. WALDENFELS, Bernhard.
Frege and Husserl on Number. TIESZEN, Richard.
The Genesis of Wittgenstein's Later Philosophy in His Failure as a Phenomenologist. HALLETT, Garth.
Heidegger e la duplicità del presente. PENZO, Maurizio.
Heidegger: vita e distino—Sullo biografia heideggeriana di Hugo Ott. ESPOSITO, Costantino.
Herbert Spiegelberg 1904-1990. SCHUHMANN, Karl.
Husserl and Hume: Overcrowding Scepticism?. MURPHY, Richard T.
Husserl and the Japanese. WELTON, Donn.
Husserl's Concept of Philosophy. SCHUHMANN, Karl.
Husserl's Notion of Constitution in Heidegger's Treatment of Care. THOMAS, V C.
Husserl's Phenomenology of Knowledge and Cognition (in Polish). DEBOWSKI, Jozef.
Husserl's Philosophy of Science and the Semantic Approach. MORMANN, Thomas.
Husserl's Presuppositionless Philosophy. REED-DOWNING, Teresa.
Husserl's Time Perception (in Portuguese). PEREIRA JÚNIOR, A.
Husserl's Yearbook. SCHUHMANN, Karl.
Husserl—Bolzano II (in Czechoslovakian). BAYEROVA, Marie.
Ingarden und Husserls transzendentaler Idealismus. HAEFLIGER, Gregor.
Intentionality and the Public World: Husserl's Treatment of Objectivity in the Cartesian Meditations. ARP, Kristana.
Interpretación mundanel e identidad propia. GARCÍA-GÓMEZ, Jorge.
Le lezioni di Husserl sull'etica e sulla teoria del valore. DONNICI, Rocco.
Man, History, and Philosophy in Husserl's Crisis of European Sciences (in Czechoslovakian). MAJOR, L.
Matrix Representation of Husserl's Part-Whole-Foundation Theory. BLECKSMITH, Richard and NULL, Gilbert.
Nature et liberté dans l'ontologie fondamentale de Heidegger. BRISART, Robert.
Noema and Meaning in Husserl. FOLLESDAL, Dagfinn.
Objet et communauté transcendantale: autour d'un fragment du dernier Husserl. BENOIST, J.
On Husserl's Theory of the Constitution of Objectiving Meaning (in Czechoslovakian). ZATKA, V.
On the Paradoxical Inception and Motivation of Transcendental Philosophy in Plato and Husserl. HOPKINS, Burt C.
Il pensiero dello "Stato" in Husserl: recenti problemi critici. FALCIONI, Daniela.
Phänomenologie und Monadologie: Husserl und Leibniz. CRISTIN, Renato.
Phenomenology and Psychoanalysis: The Hermeneutical Mediation. RAJAN, R Sundara.
Phenomenology and Scientific Realism: Husserl's Critique of Galileo. SOFFER, Gail.
Phenomenology as Cooperative Task: Husserl-Farber Correspondence during 1936-37. CHO, Kah Kyung.
Potenzialità conoscitive del Trascendentale di Husserl. O'DWYER BELLINETTI, Luciana.
La problemática ética en el pensamiento de Husserl. IRIBARNE, Julia V.
Problems with the Fregean Interpretation of Husserl. BROWN, Charles S.
Psychologism Reconsidered. AACH, John.
Quatre principes de la phénoménologie. HENRY, Michel.
Reflections on the Schutz-Gurwitsch Correspondence. LANDGREBE, Ludwig.
The Relevance of Gödel's Theorem to Husserl's *Formal and Transcendental Logic*. BOULOS, Pierre J.
Réponses à quelques questions. MARION, Jean-Luc.
Retrieving Husserl from His Legacy. FUCHS, Wolfgang.
El ser y el sentido: Notas husserlianas. PEGUEROLES, Juan.
Las situaciones objetivas en las *Investigaciones Lógicas* de Edmundo Husserl. MULLIGAN, Kevin.
Some Reflections on Husserl's Approach to the Problem of Transcendence. DHAR, Benulal.
Some Remarks on the Linguistic Turn. PERUZZI, Alberto.
The Concept of Sense in Merleau-Ponty (in Czechoslovakian). SIVAK, Jozef.
The Critical and the Dogmatic Tendency of Phenomenological Philosophy (in Czechoslovakian). CIBULKA, Josef.
Truth, Method, and Objectivity: *Husserl and Gadamer on Scientific Method*. NUYEN, A T.
Willing and Acting in Husserl's Lectures on Ethics and Value Theory. NENON, Thomas J.
Wo lag der Fehler der kategorialen Repräsentation? Zu Sinn und Reichweite einer Selbstkritik Husserls. LOHMAR, Dieter.

HUTCHESON, F
Hutcheson's Account of Beauty as a Response to Mandeville. MICHAEL, Emily and MICHAEL, Fred S.

HUYGENS
"Foils for Newton: Comments on Howard Stein" in *Philosophical Perspectives on Newtonian Science*, ARTHUR, Richard.
"On Locke, 'the Great Huygenius, and the Incomparable Mr. Newton'" in *Philosophical Perspectives on Newtonian Science*, STEIN, Howard.

HYDRATION
Nutrition, Hydration, and the Demented Elderly. POST, Stephen G.

HYLOMORPHISM
The Recovery of the Soul: An Aristotelian Essay on Self-fulfilment. RANKIN, Kenneth.

HYPNOSIS
Hypnosis and the Philosophy of Mind. HAIGHT, Mary.

HYPOTHESIS(-SES)
Experiment: Right or Wrong. FRANKLIN, Allan.
Experimental Methods and Conceptual Confusion: An Investigation into R L Gregory's Theory of Perception. HACKER, P M S.
Hypotheses, Probability, and Waves. ACHINSTEIN, Peter.
Is Confirmation Differential?. ERWIN, Edward and SIEGEL, Harvey.
John Stuart Mill on Induction and Hypothesis. JACOBS, Struan.
Let's Razor Ockham's Razor. SOBER, Elliott.
The Fundamental Hypotheses of Mechanics in Lazare N M Carnot's Thought (in Italian). DRAGO, Antonino and MANNO, Salvatore D.

HYPOTHETICAL(S)
Untersuchungen zur Theorie des hypothetischen Urteils. LINNEWEBER-LAMMERSKITTEN, Helmut.
Assessing Human Needs. JONES, John D.

HYPOTHETICO-DEDUCTIVE
Darwin's Long and Short Arguments. SINTONEN, Matti.
Horwich, Hempel, and Hypothetico-Deductivism. GEMES, Ken.
The Irrelevance of Bootstrapping. CHRISTENSEN, David.
Truth, Content, and the Hypothetico-Deductive Method. GRIMES, Thomas R.

HYSTERIA
"Hysteria, Belief and Magic" in *Harré and His Critics*, TAYLOR, David.

I
Das Ich im deutschen Idealismus und das Selbst im Zen-Buddhist Fichte und Dogen. NAGASAWA, Kunihiko.
Anscombian and Cartesian Scepticism. HAMILTON, Andy.
Thoughts Which Only I Can Think. WILLIAMS, C J F.

I CHING
The Appropriation of Significance: The Concept of *Kang-Tung*in the *I Ching*. TONG, Lik Kuen.
On the Concept of Freedom in the *I Ching*: A Deconstructionist View of Self-Cultivation. SCHULZ, Larry J and CUNNINGHAM, Thomas J.
The Seasonal Structure Underlying the Arrangement of the Hexagrams in the *Yijing*. ANDERSON, Allan W.

IBN-AL'ARABI
Ibn 'Arabi o la renovación espiritual del sufismo. SERRANO RAMÍREZ, Jose M.

ICON(S)
To Umberto Eco's Criticism of Icon (in Czechoslovakian). HAMAN, Ales.

ICONOGRAPHY
The *Nagaraja*: Symbol and Symbolism in Hindu Art and Iconography. DURAN, Jane.

IDEA(S)
see also Concept(s)
Cálculo y ser (Aproximación a Leibniz). MARZOA, Felipe Martínez.
David Hume's Theory of Mind. FLAGE, Daniel E.
Idea, mente, specie: Platonismo e scienza in Johannes Marcus Marci (1595-1667). MOCCHI, Giuliana.
Ideas, Principios y Dialectica. LAFUENTE, Maria Isabel.
Locke and French Materialism. YOLTON, John W.
Metaphysical Delusion. COWLEY, Fraser.
On True and False Ideas, New Objections to Descartes' Meditations and Descartes' Replies. ARNAULD, Antoine (trans).
The Origin of Thought. ROSMINI, Antonio.
Perspectives on Ideas and Reality. NYÍRI, J C (ed).
Platos Idee des Guten. FERBER, Rafael.
Bringing Things About. DIEFENBECK, James A.
Cook Wilson as Critic of Bradley. TACELLI, Ronald K.
La filosofía de la ciencia en Platón: Una introducción. PEREZ DE LABORDA, Alfonso.
Hume Contra Spinoza?. KLEVER, Wim.
Hume on the Idea of Existence. CUMMINS, Phillip D.
Hume's Rejection of the Theory of Ideas. WRIGHT, John P.
Kant e o problema da origem das representações elementares: apontamentos. MARQUES, U R de Azevedo.
Meditation on the Two Consciousnesses and on the Three Worlds of Popper (in Hungarian). RADI, Peter.
On Plato's Theory of the *Metheksis* of Ideas. JIYUAN, Yu.
Remarks about the Idea of the University (in Dutch). ROSSOUW, H W.
Rousseau et Kant: A propos de la genèse de la théorie kantienne des idées. PICHÉ, Claude.
A Second Copy Thesis in Hume?. PAPPAS, George S.
The Problem of the History-Making Role of Ideas in American Historical Thought (in Polish). CABAJ, Jerzy.

IDEA(S)

Theorising Ideas: *Idee* and *Vorstellung* from Kant to Hegel to Marx. CRISTAUDO, Wayne.
Verdad e inteligibilidad: Los rasgos invariables de la teoría platónica de las ideas. LUIS DEL BARCO, José.
Verdad e inteligibilidad: Los rasgos invariables de la doctrina platónica de las ideas. LUIS DEL BARCO, José.
The Way of Ideas: A Retrospective. YOLTON, John W.
What Berkeley's Notions Are. LEE, Richard N.
The Word as Will and Idea: Semantics in the *Tractatus*. COHEN, Daniel H.

IDEAL(S)

Blaise Pascals: "Pensées" (1656-1662) Systematische 'Gedanken' über. KIRSCH, Ulrich.
Community: The Tie That Binds. ROUSSEAU, Mary F.
To Be at Home: Christianity, Civil Religion, and World Community. ROUNER, Leroy S.
"God as the Ideal: The All-of-Monads and the All-Consciousness" in *Phenomenology of the Truth Proper to Religion*, LAYCOCK, Steven W.
"The Pursuit of Ideals and the Legitimation of Means" in *Perspectives on Ideas and Reality*, GARVER, Newton.
The Answer to Dziobiak's Question. PALASINSKI, Marek.
Comments on a Question of Wolniewicz. HAWRANEK, Jacek.
Enumerations of Turing Ideals with Applications. MARKER, David.
Goethe and Wittgenstein. ROWE, M W.
How Ideas Became Meanings: Locke and the Foundations of Semantic Theory. HANNA, Robert.
Ideal and Morality (in German). JACOBS, Wilhelm G.
Ideal Rationality and Handwaving. RICHTER, Reed.
Love in *Thus Spoke Zarathustra*. LEVITT, Tom.
A Moral Ideal for Everyone and No One. CONWAY, Daniel W.
On the Existence of Large *p*-Ideals. JUST, Winfried (and others).
Ramsey Ultrafilters and the Reaping Number—Con(r < u). GOLDSTERN, M and SHELAH, S.
Théories d'algébres de Boole munies d'idéaux distingués, II. TOURAILLE, Alain.
Two Hypergraph Theorems Equivalent to BPI. COWEN, Robert H.

IDEALISM

Donald Davidson. EVNINE, Simon.
Kant's Model of the Mind: A New Interpretation of Transcendental Idealism. WAXMAN, Wayne.
Una lettura idealistica della "Analitica Trascendentale". BELLINI, Ornella.
Max Scheler's Concept of the Person: An Ethics of Humanism. PERRIN, Ron.
Mind Only: A Philosophical and Doctrinal Analysis of the Vijñānavāda. WOOD, Thomas E.
Modernism as a Philosophical Problem: On the Dissatisfactions of European High Culture. PIPPIN, Robert B.
Phänomenologie als ästhetische Theorie. FELLMANN, Ferdinand.
Philosophie Juridique Européenne. TRIGEAUD, Jean-Marc.
The Philosophy of John William Miller. FELL, Joseph P (ed).
Reflexion und Metareflexion bei Platon und Fichte. ZEHNPFENNIG, Barbara.
Schellings Philosophie der Kunst: Göttliche Imagination und Ästhetische Einbildungskraft. BARTH, Bernhard.
The Unity of Kant's "Critique of Pure Reason": Experience, Language, and Knowledge. WILLIAMS, T C.
"Finite Idealism: The Midworld and Its History" in *The Philosophy of John William Miller*, CORRINGTON, Robert S.
"The Problem of Evil in Proto-Ethical Idealism: J W Miller's Ethics in Historical Context" in *The Philosophy of John William Miller*, TYMAN, Stephen.
La "Scuola di Padova" ed i problemi dell'ontologia italiana contemporanea. MANGIAGALLI, Maurizio.
Art's Autonomy and Absolute Idealism: The Role of Aesthetics in Schelling's Philosophy (in Dutch). BRAECKMAN, A.
Baur's "Conversation with Gadamer" and "Contribution to the Gadamer-Lonergan Discussion": A Reaction. LAWRENCE, Fred.
Ein Bedürfnis nach Schelling. BRAUN, Hermann.
Het belang van Husserls aanzet tot een fenomenologie van de bewustzijnsperspectieven. FREDERIX, Lode.
Berkeley and Common Sense Realism. PAPPAS, George S.
Can Peirce Be a Pragmaticist and an Idealist?. PETERSON, John.
Collingwood and the Idea of Progress. VAN DER DUSSEN, W Jan.
Collingwood's Detective Image of the Historian and the Study of Hadrian's Wall. COUSE, G S.
Conceptual Idealism Revisited. RESCHER, Nicholas.
Dead Souls and Living Instruments. HICKMAN, Larry.
Di cose grammaticali: Un itinerario campanelliano. ALUNNI, Charles.
Down to Earth and Up to Religion: Kantian Idealism in Light of Kierkegaard's Leap of Faith. PERL, Paul.
The Ethical Thought of Martin Luther King. STERLING, Marvin C.
Gentile e gli 'epigoni" dell'hegelismo napoletano: il carteggio con Sebastiano Maturi. SAVORELLI, Alessandro.
The Idea of History as a Scale of Forms. GOLDSTEIN, Leon J.
Idéalisme ou réalisme?. LARGEAULT, Jean.
El idealismo alemán como mitología de la razón. INNERARITY, Daniel.
Ingarden und Husserls transzendentaler Idealismus. HAEFLIGER, Gregor.
Is "The Theory of History" (1914) Collingwood's First Essay on the Philosophy of History?. PATRICK, James.
Is Transcendental Idealism Coherent?. BALDNER, Kent.
Kants Logik der Synthesis und die Schliessung einer "unübersehbaren Kluft". FUNKE, Gerhard.
The Limits of Thought—and Beyond. PRIEST, Graham.
On the Source of the Eternal Truths. BEACH, Edward A (trans) and VON SCHELLING, F W J.
Il pensiero di Aldo Capitini e la filosofia del neoidealismo. CESA, Claudio.
Pensiero e trascendenza. SANCIPRIANO, Mario.
La prima e seconda edizione della "Geschichte des Materialismus" di Friedrich Albert Lange. COGNETTI, Giuseppe.
Progressive Traditionalism as the Spirit of Collingwood's Philosophy. KISSELL, Michael A.
Realism, Idealism and Quantum Mechanics. LIST, C J.
Reply to Smith: The Question of Idealism. VALLICELLA, William F.
Reply to Vallicella: Heidegger and Idealism. SMITH, Quentin.
Representative Realism and Absolute Reality. ENGLISH, Parker.
The Role of Kant's Refutation of Idealism. HYMERS, Michael.
Schopenhauer und Fichtes Schrift "Die Bestimmung des Menschen". DECHER, Friedhelm.
Lo statuo della filosofia politica nel dibattito italiano. BACCELLI, Luca.
Strawson and the Refutation of Idealism. STEINHOFF, Gordon.
Transcendental Idealism: The Dialectical Dimension. GLOUBERMAN, M.
Die Verfehlung des Themas "Metaphysik und Erfahrung". WIEHL, Reiner.
Von der dreifachen Vollendung des Deutschen Idealismus und der unvollendeten metaphysischen Wahrheit. JANKE, Wolfgang.
Was R G Collingwood the Author of "The Theory of History"?. CONNELLY, James.

IDEALIZATION

Intelligibility in Science. DILWORTH, Craig (ed).
On the Eliminatibility of Ideal Linguistic Entities. WYBRANIEC-SKARDOWSKA, Urszula.

IDEATION

Dictionaries and Proper Names. MARCONI, Diego.

IDENTIFICATION

Compassion. SNOW, Nancy E.
Kripke on Theoretical Identifications: A Rejoinder to Perrick. BUXTON, James.
The Role of Perceptual Relativity in Berkeley's Philosophy. MUEHLMANN, Robert.

IDENTITY

see also Personal Identity
Alterity, Identity, Image: Contributions Towards a Theoretical Perspective. CORBEY, R (ed).
Essentially Speaking: Feminism, Nature and Difference. FUSS, Diana.
Identity and Discrimination. WILLIAMSON, Timothy.
Identity, Character, and Morality: Essays in Moral Psychology. FLANAGAN, Owen (ed).
Material Beings. VAN INWAGEN, Peter.
Nation und Ethos: Die Moral des Patriotismus. KLUXEN-PYTA, Donate.
The Ontology of Physical Objects: Four-Dimensional Hunks of Matter. HELLER, Mark.
Philosophical Essays. CARTWRIGHT, Richard.
Saussure: Signs, System, and Arbitrariness. HOLDCROFT, David.
To Be at Home: Christianity, Civil Religion, and World Community. ROUNER, Leroy S.
"Aspects of Identity and Agency" in *Identity, Character, and Morality: Essays in Moral Psychology*, RORTY, Amélie Oksenberg and WONG, David.
"The Contradictory Character of Postmodernism" in *Postmodernism—Philosophy and the Arts (Continental Philosophy III)*, KUSPIT, Donald.
"The Discussion on Identity Among African Philosophers" in *I, We and Body: First Joint Symposium of Philosophers from Africa and from the Netherlands*, FENNEMA, J G.
"Feminism, Postmodernism, and Gender-Scepticism" in *Feminism/Postmodernism*, BORDO, Susan.
"Filming: Inscriptions of *Denken*" in *Postmodernism—Philosophy and the Arts (Continental Philosophy III)*, WURZER, Wilhelm S and SILVERMAN, Hugh J.
"Identity and Difference in Liberalism" in *Liberalism and the Good*, CONNOLLY, William E.
"Identity and Strong and Weak Evaluation" in *Identity, Character, and Morality: Essays in Moral Psychology*, FLANAGAN, Owen.
"Social Criticism without Philosophy: An Encounter between Feminism and Postmodernism" in *Feminism/Postmodernism*, FRASER, Nancy and NICHOLSON, Linda J.
"But Would That Still Be Me?" Notes on Gender, "Race," Ethnicity, as Sources of "Identity". APPIAH, Anthony.
'Pride Produces the Idea of Self': Hume on Moral Agency. RORTY, Amélie.
Accent on *One*: Entity and Identity. BOLINGER, Dwight.
Berkeley, Perception, and Identity. BAXTER, Donald L M.
Causation in the Philosophy of Mind. JACKSON, Frank and PETTIT, Philip.

IDENTITY
Consciousness and Synchronic Identity. MATHESON, Carl.
Cultural Theory Looks at Identity and Contradiction. COCKS, Joan.
Deciding to Act. FIELDS, L.
La dialéctica del deseo como realización de la identidad en Henri Bergson. ELÓSEGUI, María.
Filosofía e identidad nacional en Honduras. ROMERO, Ramón.
Forbes's Branching Conception of Possible Worlds. MILLS, Eugene.
Frege, Informative Identities, and Logicism. MILNE, Peter.
Havel and Habermas on Identity and Revolution. MATUSTIK, Martin J.
History, Historicism, Narratives: Identity in the Philosophy of History of Karl Popper. PARLEJ, Piotr.
Hydatidiform Moles and Teratomas Confirm the Human Identity of the Preimplantation Embryo. SUAREZ, Antoine.
IΔ_3-Algebras. FIGALLO, Aldo V.
Identifying Musical Works of Art. JACOBS, Jo Ellen.
Identity and Status of the Human Embryo. SPAGNOLA, Antonio G.
Identity and Subjectivity (in Serbo-Croatian). FRANK, Manfred.
The Identity of Individuals in a Strict Functional Calculus of Second Order. MARCUS, Ruth Barcan.
The Identity Theory of Truth. BALDWIN, Thomas.
Identity, Transformation, and What Matters in Survival. MARTIN, Raymond.
Imagination and the Sense of Identity. HERTZBERG, Lars.
Das Imperiale an der Identitätsphilosophie: Spuren des Totalitären in der abendländischen Philosophie. MANSILLA, Hugo C F.
In Defence of Reincarnation. DANIELS, Charles B.
Indeterminate Identity, Contingent Identity and Abelardian Predicates. NOONAN, Harold W.
Indiscernibility and Identity in Probability Theory. ROEPER, Peter and LEBLANC, Hugues.
Intensional Identities. SLATER, B H.
An Intersubjective Concept of Individuality. HABERMAS, Jürgen.
Intuitionistic Sentential Calculus with Classical Identity. LUKOWSKI, Piotr.
Intuitionistic Sentential Calculus with Identity. LUKOWSKI, Piotr.
L'identité personnelle et la source des concepts. SHALOM, Albert.
The Lesbian, the Mother, the Heterosexual Lover: Irigaray's Recodings of Difference. HOLMLUND, Christine.
Location and Range. SCHLESINGER, George N.
A Modal Argument for Narrow Content. FODOR, Jerry A.
Modal Logic. MARCUS, Ruth Barcan.
Narrative Identity. RICOEUR, Paul.
Nature et fonction de la Mémoire dans À la recherche du temps perdu. ZÉPHIR, Jacques J.
Nonbranching and Nontransitivity. EHRING, Douglas.
On Defining Identity. SAVELLOS, Elias E.
On the Individuation of Events. CLELAND, Carol.
Parthood and Persistence. KAZMI, Ali Akhtar.
Personal Concern and the Extension of Consciousness. SCHECHTMAN, Marya.
PES and the APA—An Impressionistic History. MACMILLAN, C J B.
Political Openings. WOOD, David.
Preemption, Direct Causation, and Identity. EHRING, Douglas.
Principia Individuationis. DENKEL, Arda.
Recognizing Suffering. CASSELL, Eric J.
Referential Opacity in Aristotle. SPELLMAN, Lynne.
Relative Identity and Locke's Principle of Individuation. UZGALIS, William L.
Riproposta di una teoria della soggettività in un'epoca di decostruzione del soggetto. LATORA, Salvatore.
Salmon on the A Priori. BERTOLET, Rod.
Time and Identity. HARPER, A W J.
Vague Identity and Vague Objects. GARRETT, Brian.
Whether Any Individual at all Could Have a Guise Structure. MILLER, Barry.
Why Indeed? Papineau on Supervenience. CRANE, Tim.
Zygotes, Souls, Substances, and Persons. BOLE III, Thomas J.

IDENTITY THEORY
Historia del nombrar: Dos episodios de la subjetividad. THIEBAUT, Carlos.
The Recovery of the Soul: An Aristotelian Essay on Self-fulfilment. RANKIN, Kenneth.
Better the Union Theory. HONDERICH, Ted.
Motion, Causation, and the Causal Theory of Identity. EHRING, Douglas.
Purposive Intending. PINK, T L M.
Substance: Prolegomena to a Realist Theory of Identity. AYERS, Michael.

IDEOLOGY(-GIES)
Dämonie und Gesellschaft. CATTEPOEL, Jan.
False Consciousness. MEYERSON, Denise.
Issues in War and Peace: Philosophical Inquiries. KUNKEL, Joseph (ed).
Mannheim and Hungarian Marxism. GABEL, Joseph.
Models and Concepts of Ideology. RITSERT, Jürgen.
Moral Dealing: Contract, Ethics, and Reason. GAUTHIER, David.
Philosophy and the Spontaneous Philosophy of the Scientists and Other Essays. ELLIOTT, Gregory (ed).
The Power of Ideology. MÉSZÁROS, István.
The Savage Anomaly: The Power of Spinoza's Metaphysics and Politics. NEGRI, Antonio.
Vernunft und Kontingenz: Rationalität und Ethos in der Phänomenologie. ORTH, Ernst Wolfgang (ed).
"The Defence of a Social System Against Its Ideology: A Case Study" in *The Social Horizon of Knowledge*, NOWAK, Leszek.
"Ideology and Religion: A Hermeneutic Conflict" in *Phenomenology of the Truth Proper to Religion*, KEARNEY, Richard.
"Marxian Ideology and Causality" in *Perspectives on Ideas and Reality*, ROCKMORE, Tom.
"Remarks on the Structure of Social Consciousness" in *The Social Horizon of Knowledge*, BUCZKOWSKI, Piotr.
Analyse critique de quelques modèles sémiotiques de l'idéologie (deuxième partie). TREMBLAY, Robert.
The Blackmail of the Single Alternative: Bukharin, Trotsky and Perestrojka. DAY, Richard B.
Bulgaria: The Romantic Period of the Opposition Continues. KANEV, Krassimir.
Christians and Marxists in Dialogue Building Confidence in a Time of Crisis. WEST, Charles C.
De l'Idéologie comme correlat des termes idéologiste et idéologue. ZOLUA, Buenzey Maluenga.
The Dead Horse Phenomenon in Educational Theory. ROBENSTINE, Clark.
Enlightenment Psychology and Political Reaction in Plato's Social Philosophy: an Ideological Contradiction?. BRYANT, Joseph M.
From Historical Marxisms to Historical Materialism: Toward the Theory of Ideology. MOCNIK, Rastko.
Gorbatschews "Erneurung des Sozialismus"—Ideologie in der Krise des Kommunismus. KUX, Ernst.
Health Policy Analysis as Ideology and as Utopian Rhetoric. MILLER, Irwin.
Heidegger's Apology: Biography as Philosophy and Ideology. KISIEL, Theodore.
The Ideological Impasse of Gorbachev's Perestrojka. KRIZAN, Mojmir.
The Ideology of Intellectuals and the Chinese Student Protest Movement of 1989. CALHOUN, Craig.
The Influence of Modernism on Art Education. MEESON, Philip.
Justice: The Root of American Business Ideology and Ethics. MC GOWAN, Richard.
Kant, Pestalozzi and the Role of Ideology in Educational Thought. ADAMS, Ian.
Legitimate Anachronism as a Problem for Intellectual History and for Philosophy. DU TOIT, André.
Marx and Perestroika. ROCKMORE, Tom.
Marxism, Post-Marxism and the Implosion of Communism. STOJANOVIC, Svetozar.
Marxist Literary Aesthetics. MILLER, Seumas.
Max Scheler's Analysis of Illusions, Idols, and Ideologies. IBANA, Rainier R A.
The Pot at the End of the Rainbow: Political Myth and the Ecological Crisis. DOYLE, Timothy.
The Principle of Unity of Theory and Practice in Marxism: A Critique. DIMITRAKOS, D.
Realism, Irrealism, and Ideology: A Critique of Nelson Goodman. MITCHELL, W J T.
Reflections on the Nature of Ideology. VAN DOAN, Tran.
Response to Robenstine's "The Dead Horse Phenomenon in Educational Theory". BROSIO, Richard.
El tratado de Ideología de Fray Zeferino Gonzalez. BUENO SÁNCHEZ, Gustavo.

IF
Grammar, Semantics and Conditionals. DUDMAN, V H.

IGNATIUS OF LOYOLA
Ignatian Discernment: A Philosophical Analysis. HUGHES, Gerard J.
Renaissance Humanism and the Religious Culture of the First Jesuits. O'MALLEY, John W.
San Ignacio de Loyola y el humanismo. GARCÍA-MATEO, Rogelio.

IGNORANCE
Hamartia, Akrasia: Ignorance, and Blame in Aristotle's Philosophy. CYZYK, Mar.
Ignoramus, Ignorabimus!. BUENO, Gustavo.

IHARA, C
Response to Craig Ihara's Discussion. WONG, David B.

ILLICH, I
La critique du modèle industriel comme histoire de la rareté: Une introduction à la pensée d'Ivan Illich. ACHTERHUIS, Hans.
Le genre vernaculaire ou la nostalgie de la tradition: A propos d'Ivan Illich. KWASCHIN, Sylvie.

ILLNESS(ES)
Moral Theory and Medical Practice. FULFORD, K W M.
Chronic Illness and the Physician-Patient Relationship. MOROS, Daniel A (and others).
Chronic Illness and the Temporal Structure of Human Life. DOUARD, John W.
Orchestrating Social Change: An Imperative in Care of the Chronically Ill. ROTH, Patricia A and HARRISON, Janet K.

ILLOCUTIONARY ACT(S)

Meaning and Speech Acts: Volume I, Principles of Language Use. VANDERVEKEN, Daniel.
Meaning and Speech Acts: Volume II, Formal Semantics of Success and Satisfaction. VANDERVEKEN, Daniel.
"Illocutionary Pretence Inside and Outside Fiction" in *XIth International Congress in Aesthetics, Nottingham 1988*, TSOHATZIDIS, S L.

ILLOCUTIONARY FORCE(S)

In Defense of Cahn's Scamps. FOULK, Gary.
Is There More to Speech Acts Than Illocutionary Force and Propositional Content?. HAJDIN, Mane.
Response to Foulk's "In Defense of Cahn's Scamps". SILK, David.

ILLOGICAL

"Illogical Belief" in *Philosophical Perspectives, 3: Philosophy of Mind and Action Theory, 1989*, SALMON, Nathan.

ILLUSION(S)

Escaping from Reality or Coming to Terms with It—What is Religion? (in German). POLLACK, Detlef.
Insularity and the Persistence of Perceptual Illusion. CAM, Philip.
Max Scheler's Analysis of Illusions, Idols, and Ideologies. IBANA, Rainier R A.
Philosophy and Wisdom. MC KEE, Patrick.

ILLUSTRATION(S)

Creative Characters. YOUNG-BRUEHL, Elisabeth.

IMAGE(S)

Alterity, Identity, Image: Contributions Towards a Theoretical Perspective. CORBEY, R (ed).
L'objet-peinture: Pour une théorie de la réception. PAQUIN, Nycole.
"L'image de l'homme dans la théorie kantienne du génie" in *XIth International Congress in Aesthetics, Nottingham 1988*, LABRADA, Antonia.
"Responses" in *Archetypal Process: Self and Divine in Whitehead, Jung, and Hillman*, HILLMAN, James.
"Try the Image—Temporality and Fullness in Aesthetic Experience" in *XIth International Congress in Aesthetics, Nottingham 1988*, JIMENEZ, Jose.
La imaginación creadora en el pensamiento de Gastón Bachelard. CASTILLO, Roberto.
The Ontology of Mental Images. HOLBROOK, Daniel.
Reinterpreting Images. SLEZAK, Peter.
Sellar's Two Images of the World. AUNE, Bruce.
Sémiotique des "genres": Une théorie de la réception. PAQUIN, Nycole.

IMAGERY

"Heiligsprechung des Imaginären: Das Imaginäre in Cornelius Castoriadis' Gesellschaftstheorie" in *The Social Horizon of Knowledge*, LÖVENICH, Friedhelm.

IMAGINATION

Being True to the World: Moral Realism and Practical Wisdom. JACOBS, Jonathan A.
Echoes: After Heidegger. SALLIS, John.
French Philosophers in Conversation: Levinas, Schneider, Serres, Irigaray, Le Doeuff, Derrida. MORTLEY, Raoul.
Kant's Model of the Mind: A New Interpretation of Transcendental Idealism. WAXMAN, Wayne.
Knowledge, Fiction, and Imagination. NOVITZ, David.
Love's Knowledge: Essays on Philosophy and Literature. NUSSBAUM, Martha C.
The Moral Animus of David Hume. SIEBERT, Donald T.
Il Paradigma del Sapere. LENTINI, Luigi.
Schellings Philosophie der Kunst: Göttliche Imagination und Ästhetische Einbildungskraft. BARTH, Bernhard.
Wittgenstein: Meaning and Mind, Volume 3 of an Analytical Commentary on Philosophical Investigations. HACKER, P M S.
The World of the Imagination: Sum and Substance. BRANN, Eva T H.
"Imaginação e imaginário: Para além de Husserl" in *Dinâmica do Pensar: Homenagem a Oswaldo Market*, SARAIVA, Maria Manuela.
"Imaginal Soul and Ideational Spirit: A Response to James Heisig" in *Archetypal Process: Self and Divine in Whitehead, Jung, and Hillman*, WINQUIST, Charles E.
Il "De imaginum, signorum et idearum compositione" di Giordano Bruno, ed il significato filosofico .... STURLESE, Rita.
La imaginación creadora en el pensamiento de Gastón Bachelard. CASTILLO, Roberto.
Imagination and the Sense of Identity. HERTZBERG, Lars.
Imitación y purificación en la estética de Aristóteles. CAPPELLETTI, Angel.
Kierkegaardian Transitions: Paradox and Pathos. FERREIRA, M Jamie.
L'imagination au pouvoir. BODÉÜS, Richard.
Metodi e immagini della scienza nel "Centro di studi metodologici" di Torino (1945-1952). QUARTA, Antonio.
Moral Imagination, Freedom, and the Humanities. KEKES, John.
Moral Imagination, Objectivity, and Practical Wisdom. JACOBS, Jonathan.
The Ontology of Mental Images. HOLBROOK, Daniel.
Perception and Evaluation: Aristotle on the Moral Imagination. HANKINSON, R J.
A Problem for Intuitionism: The Apparent Possibility of Performing Infinitely Many Tasks in a Finite Time. MOORE, A W.
Reason and Imagination (in Dutch). VAN PEURSEN, C A.
Response: "The Rooting and Uprooting of Reason: On *Spacings* by John Sallis". SALLIS, John.
Le rôle de l'imagination dans le mouvement animal et l'action humaine chez Aristotle. DUGRÉ, François.
William Wadsworth: Nature, Imagination, Ultimate Reality and Meaning. MAHONEY, John L.

IMAGING

The World of the Imagination: Sum and Substance. BRANN, Eva T H.

IMITATION

"Imitation and Art" in *XIth International Congress in Aesthetics, Nottingham 1988*, SÖRBOM, Göran.
Nachahmung und Gestaltung—Baumgarten, *Meditationes* 73 (in Japanese). MATSUO, Hiroshi.
Natural Generativity and Imitation. SARTWELL, Crispin.

IMMANENCE

Expressionism in Philosophy: Spinoza. DELEUZE, Gilles.
Il Logos come immagine di Dio in Filone di Alessandria. BELLETTI, Bruno.

IMMANENTISM

From Immanentism to Atheism. LY, Gabriel.

IMMATERIAL

La esencia metafísica de Dios. DERISI, Octavio N.

IMMATERIALISM

Berkeley's Revolution in Vision. ATHERTON, Margaret.
Berkeley's Arguments for Other Minds. FALKENSTEIN, Lorne.
Il caso "Siris", ovvero la "seconda filosofia" di George Berkeley vescovo di Cloyne. NERI, Luigi.

IMMIGRATION

Law, Morality, and *la Reconquista*. CORDERO, Ronald A.

IMMORALITY

Ethics in Declining Organizations. LEMKE, Dwight K and SCHMINKE, Marshall.
Prohibiting Immorality. WESTMORELAND, Robert.
Wille, Willkür, and the Imputability of Immoral Actions. HUDSON, Hud.

IMMORTALITY

Le existentia de deo e le Immortalitate del Anima: Lineas de Philosophia del Esser. BLANDINO, Giovanni.
A Hindu Perspective on the Philosophy of Religion. SHARMA, Arvind.
The Metaphysics of Religious Belief. SHOOMAN, A P.
The Place of the Hidden Moon: Erotic Mysticism in the Vaisnava-sahajiyā Cult of Bengal. DIMOCK JR, Edward C.
Published Essays, 1966-1985 (The Collected Works of Eric Voegelin, Volume 12). SANDOZ, Ellis (ed).
"In Defense of the Demon" in *The Case for Dualism*, HARRISON, Jonathan.
Temporality and the Concept of Being. SHALOM, Albert.

IMMUNITY

The Making of a Nuclear Peace: The Task of Today's Just War Theorists. SICHOL, Marcia W.

IMMUTABILITY

The Immutability of God in the Theology of Hans Urs Von Balthasar. O'HANLON, G F.
Omniscience, Immutability, and the Divine Mode of Knowing. SULLIVAN, Thomas D.

IMPARTIALITY

see also Objectivity
"The Social Self and the Partiality Debates" in *Feminist Ethics*, FRIEDMAN, Marilyn.
Constructing Justice. GIBBARD, Allan.
A Theory of Social Justice?. HORTON, John.

IMPERATIVE LOGIC

"Deontic Logic and Imperative Logic" in *Logic and Ethics*, HARRISON, Jonathan.
A Lemma in the Logic of Action. SURENDONK, Timothy J.
Validity and Satisfaction in Imperative Logic. SEGERBERG, Krister.

IMPERATIVES

see also Command(s)
Charity and Moral Imperatives. ODEGARD, Douglas.
Does Reason Command Itself for Its Own Sake?. KRAENZEL, Frederick.
The Revenger's Paradox. HANSSON, Sven Ove.

IMPERFECTION

Elogio critico dell'imperfezione. TUSA, Carlo.

IMPLICATION

Untersuchungen zur Theorie des hypothetischen Urteils. LINNEWEBER-LAMMERSKITTEN, Helmut.
"Truth-Value of Ethical Statements" in *Logic and Ethics*, PRZELECKI, Marian.
"The Logic of Implication". BALZER, Noel.
Conditionals, Quantification, and Strong Mathematical Induction. COHEN, Daniel H.

IMPLICATION
Corrections to Some Results for BCK Logics and Algebras. BUNDER, M W.
$I\Delta_3$-Algebras. FIGALLO, Aldo V.
Implied Questions. WISNIEWSKI, Andrzej.
An Integer-Valued Matrix Characteristic for Implicational *S5*. ULRICH, Dolph.
L'interpretazione costruttiva dell'implicazione. MORICONI, Enrico.
A Note on Some Property of Purely Implicational Proportional Calculi. PRUCNAL, Tadeuss.
Orlowska's Relevant Implications, Relevant Logics and Analytic Implication. GIAMBRONE, Steve.
Peirced Clean Through. MEYER, Robert K.
La philosophie du chaos. BOUTOT, Alain.
Russell, Logicism, and the Choice of Logical Constants. BYRD, Michael.

IMPLICATURE
A Pragmatic Analysis of Tautological Utterances. WARD, Gregory L and HIRSCHBERG, Julia.

IMPOSSIBILITY
"Attempting the Impossible" in *Liability and Responsibility*, WHITE, Alan R.
The Agnostic Fallacy. KEENE, G B.
The Gärdenfors Impossibility Theorem in Non-Monotonic Contexts. MAKINSON, David.
Variações sobre o *De Interpretatione*, de Aristóteles. ROSA, Joaquim Coelho.

IMPOSSIBLE NUMBERS
The Logic of Impossible Quantities. SHERRY, David.

IMPRESSION(S)
Hume on the Idea of Existence. CUMMINS, Phillip D.

IMPRESSIONISM
Ethical Impressionism: A Response to Braybrooke. BONEVAC, Daniel.

IMPROVISATION
The Aesthetics of Imperfection. HAMILTON, Andy.

IN VITRO FERTILIZATION
"Arguing with Success: Is In Vitro Fertilization Research or Therapy?" in *Beyond Baby M: Ethical Issues in New Reproductive Techniques*, CAPLAN, Arthur L.
Aspectos antropológicos de la fecundación in vitro. CAFFARRA, Carlos.
Crazy Making: Embryos and Gestational Mothers. ANNAS, George J.
Is IVF Good Medicine?. CONNOR, Pauline.
The Vatican's Dilemma: On the Morality of IVF and the Incarnation. DUCHARME, Howard.

INCARNATION
"Could God Become Man?" in *The Philosophy in Christianity*, SWINBURNE, Richard.
In Defense of Anselm. ASPENSON, Steven S.
Incarnation and Essentialization: A Reading of Heidegger. CAPUTO, John D.
Incarnational Anthropology. HALDANE, John.
The Vatican's Dilemma: On the Morality of IVF and the Incarnation. DUCHARME, Howard.

INCEST
The Molested. MAY, William F.

INCLINATION(S)
The Scope of Deliberation: A Conflict in Aquinas. IRWIN, T H.

INCLUSION
Feminist Theory and the Politics of Inclusion. FISHER, Linda.

INCOHERENCE
Genuine Moral Dilemmas and the Containment of Incoherence. PASKE, Gerald H.

INCOME
Why Surfers Should Be Fed: The Liberal Case for an Unconditional Basic Income. VAN PARIJS, Philippe.

INCOMMENSURABILITY
Science and Relativism: Some Key Controversies in the Philosophy of Science. LAUDAN, Larry.
"On Incommensurability" in *Imre Lakatos and Theories of Scientific Change*, BALZER, W.
"Partial Interpretation, Meaning Variance, and Incommensurability" in *Imre Lakatos and Theories of Scientific Change*, ODDIE, Graham.
Belief, Desire and the Praxis of Reasoning. WILLIAMS, Stephen.
The Bellman's Map: Does Antifoundationalism Entail Incommensurability and Relativism?. CHURCHILL, John.
Incommensurability and Recurrence: from Oresme to Simmel. SMALL, Robin.
Incommensurability and the Indeterminacy of Translation. SANKEY, Howard.
Kuhn's Conception of Incommensurability. HOYNINGEN-HUENE, Paul.
Local Incommensurability and Communicability. CHEN, Xiang.
Translation Failure Between Theories. SANKEY, Howard.

INCOMPATIBILISM
"Reasons Explanation of Action: An Incompatibilist Account" in *Philosophical Perspectives, 3: Philosophy of Mind and Action Theory, 1989*, GINET, Carl.
On a Mainstay of Incompatibilism. BLUM, Alex.

INCOMPATIBILITY
Community and Autonomy: Logically Incompatible Values?. MASON, Andrew.
Frege, Informative Identities, and Logicism. MILNE, Peter.
Wittgenstein and the Color Incompatibility Problem. JACQUETTE, Dale.

INCOMPLETENESS
see also Completeness
Gödel's Theorem in Focus. SHANKER, S G (ed).
Fictional Incompleteness as Vagueness. SORENSEN, Roy A.
Incompleteness of a Free Arithmetic. BENCIVENGA, Ermanno.
Models for Inconsistent and Incomplete Differential Calculus. MORTENSEN, Chris.
On an Alleged Refutation of Hilbert's Program Using Gödel's First Incompleteness Theorem. DETLEFSEN, Michael.
The Relevance of Gödel's Theorem to Husserl's *Formal and Transcendental Logic*. BOULOS, Pierre J.
Some Descending Chains of Incomplete Model Logics. XU, Ming.
Unbounded Operators and the Incompleteness of Quantum Mechanics. HEATHCOTE, Adrian.

INCONSISTENCY
Four Dialogue Systems. MACKENZIE, Jim.
The Justification of Conceptual Development Claims. HAAFTEN, Wouter Van.
Models for Inconsistent and Incomplete Differential Calculus. MORTENSEN, Chris.
Theory Contraction through Base Contraction. FUHRMANN, André.

INCONTINENCE
Ethics with Aristotle. BROADIE, Sarah.
Weakness of Will and Rational Action. AUDI, Robert.

INDEFINITE TERM(S)
"Bare Plurals as Plural Indefinite Noun Phrases" in *Knowledge Representation and Defeasible Reasoning*, GILLON, Brendan.
Indefinite Descriptions: In Defense of Russell. LUDLOW, Peter and NEALE, Stephen.

INDEPENDENCE
"Informational Independence as a Semantical Phenomenon" in *Logic, Methodology and Philosophy of Science, VIII*, HINTIKKA, Jaakko and SANDU, Gabriel.
"Liberal Man" in *Philosophy and Politics*, MENDUS, Susan.
Absolutely Independent Sets of Generation of Filters in Boolean Algebras. GRYGIEL, Joanna.
The Axiomatization of Randomness. VAN LAMBALGEN, Michiel.
Challenge: Subjectivist Naturalism. FOLDVARY, Fred E.
Liberal Man. MENDUS, Susan.
The Union Axiom in Zermelo Set Theory. GONZÁLEZ, Carlos G.

INDETERMINACY
"Indeterminacy and Mental States" in *Perspectives on Quine*, FOLLESDAL, Dagfinn.
"The Refutation of Indeterminacy" in *Perspectives on Quine*, KATZ, Jerrold.
"Three Indeterminacies" in *Perspectives on Quine*, QUINE, W V.
Ambiguity, Generality, and Indeterminacy: Tests and Definitions. GILLON, Brendan S.
Behaviourism, Neuroscience and Translational Indeterminacy. WARMBRŌD, Ken.
Critical Legal Studies and Liberalism: Understanding the Similarities and Differences. WAGNER DE CEW, Judith.
Dewey, Indetermincy, and the Spectator Theory of Knowledge. KULP, Christopher B.
Extensionality, Underdetermination and Indeterminacy. SOLOMON, Miriam.
Holism and Indeterminacy. MALPAS, Jeff.
Incommensurability and the Indeterminacy of Translation. SANKEY, Howard.
The Indeterminacy Thesis Reformulated. GEMES, Ken.
Indeterminacy, Empirical Evidence, and Methodological Pluralism. ROUSE, Joseph.
Mechanism and Indeterminacy: Reply to MacIntosh. WARMBRŌD, Ken.
Onderbepaaldheid van theorie en onbepaaldheid van vertaling: Enige ontwikkelingen in Quine's filosofie. PERRICK, M.
Posibilidad e indeterminación: Aristóteles frente a Diodoro Crono. QUEVEDO, Amalia.
Presentism and the Indeterminacy of Translation. HARDCASTLE, Gary L.
The Uses of Rhetoric: Indeterminacy in Legal Reasoning, Practical Thinking and Interpretation of Literary Figures. OLMSTED, Wendy Raudenbush.
Visual Perception and the Wages of Indeterminacy. MONTGOMERY, Richard.

INDETERMINATE
Indeterminate Identity, Contingent Identity and Abelardian Predicates. NOONAN, Harold W.

INDETERMINISM
Chaos and Indeterminism. HOBBS, Jesse.
Wittgenstein's Indeterminism. SCHEER, Richard K.

INDEXICAL(S)
"Demonstratives: An Essay on the Semantics, Logic, Metaphysics, and Epistemology of Demonstratives" in *Themes From Kaplan*, KAPLAN, David.

INDEXICAL(S)
Logic and Language in the *Chuang Tzu*. ALT, Wayne E.
The Logic of Lost Lingens. SEAGER, William.
The Myth of the Essential Indexical. MILLIKAN, Ruth.

INDEXICALITY
Indexicality: The Transparent Subjective Mechanism for Encountering a World. CASTAÑEDA, Héctor-Neri.

INDIAN
see also Buddhism, Hinduism
Philosophy of the "Gita". PATEL, Ramesh N.
The Place of the Hidden Moon: Erotic Mysticism in the Vaisnava-sahajiyā Cult of Bengal. DIMOCK JR, Edward C.
Self and Non-Self: The Drigdrisyaviveka Attributed to Samkara. RAPHAEL (trans).
Yoga on War and Peace. TIGUNAIT, Pandit Rajmani.
The Yoga-Sūtra of Patañjali: A New Translation and Commentary. FEUERSTEIN, Georg.
"Indian Ethics" in *A Companion to Ethics*, BILIMORIA, Purusottama.
"The Rope of Violence and the Snake of Peace" in *Celebrating Peace*, LARSON, Gerald J.
A Brief Survey of Indian Buddhistic Logic (in Hungarian). FEHER, Judit.
Advaita and Religious Language. GRIMES, John.
The Bhakti Tradition in Hinduism—Bhakti Yoga an Overview. PILLAI, A S Narayana.
The Biographies of Siddhasena (II). GRANOFF, Phyllis.
Buddhist Anthropology vis-à-vis Modern Philosophy and Contemporary Neurophysiology. BUGAULT, Guy.
Can Knowledge Occur Unknowingly?. CHAUDHURI, Manjusree.
The Celebration of Emotion: Vallabha's Ontology of Affective Experience. TIMM, Jeffrey R.
A Critique of Jayarasi's Critique of Perception. MOHANTA, D K.
Dehātmavāda or the Body as Soul: Exploration of a Possibility within Nyāya Thought. LATH, Mukund (trans) and SHUKLA, Pandit Badrinath.
Dravya, Guna and *Paryāya* in Jaina Thought. SONI, Jayandra.
Gangesa and Transfer of Meaning. SAHA, Sukharanjan.
History, Indian Science and Policy-Making: A Philosophical Review. BHARGAVI, V and SUBRAMANIAM, K.
In Search of a Theory of Truth in Nyāya. SAHA, Sukharanjan.
India and the Theory of the Asiatic Mode of Production (in Hungarian). RENNER, Zsuzsanna.
Indian Philosophy in the Context of World Philosophy. BHATTACHARYYA, Kalidas.
Indian Thought Is a Systematic Body of Thought. SHAH, K J.
Indigenous Ends and Alien Means: A Footnote on Indian Renaissance. CHAUDHURI, Minakshi Ray.
Is Karma Evolutionary?. KRISHAN, Y.
Isvarakrsna's Two-Level-Perception: Propositional and Non-Propositional. CLEAR, Edeltraud Harzer.
J S Mill and Indian Education. ZASTOUPIL, Lynn.
John Stuart Mill and Royal India. MOORE, Robin J.
K J Shah's 'Philosophy, Religion, Morality, Spirituality: Some Issues'. GHOSE, A M.
Krtapranasa and Akrtabhyagama: An Analysis, Defence and Rationale of the Buddhist Theory of Action. CHINCHORE, Mangala R.
Man and Hermeneutics. ROY, Krishna.
Metaphor in the Language of Religion. PANDHARIPANDE, Rajeshwari.
The Notion of *Klesa* and Its Bearing on the Yoga Analysis of Mind. BALSLEV, Anindita N.
On the Causality of Sky. MISHRA, Aruna Ranjan.
A Peep into Man's History: The Lessons for Today. SINGH, Ajai R and SINGH, Shakuntala A.
Phenomenology and Indian Philosophy. SINGH, Navjyoti.
Philosophical and Normative Dimensions and Aspects of the Idea of Renaissance. GREGORIOS, Paulos Mar.
Philosophy and the Sociology of Knowledge: An Investigation into the Nature of Orthodoxy (Astikya) in Hindu Thought. SHARMA, Arvind.
Philosophy, Religion, Morality, Spirituality: Some Issues. SHAH, K J.
The Primacy of the Political: Towards a Theory of National Integration. RAJAN, R Sundara.
Professor Matilal on Some Topics of Indian Philosophy. BHATTACHARYYA, Sibajiban.
Punyadāna or Transference of Merit—A Fiction. KRISHAN, Y.
Ramana Maharsi on the Theories of Creation in Advaita Vedānta. SHARMA, Arvind.
Rāmānuja's Hermeneutics of the *Upanisads* in Comparison with Sankara's Interpretation. SAWAI, Yoshitsugu.
Re-understanding Indian Philosophy. BARLINGAY, S S.
Reflections on Ideas of Social Philosophy and Indian Code of Conduct. DASGUPTA, Manashi.
Republic: 2. BANAJI, V F.
Respect for Persons and Self-Respect: Western and Indian. GHOSH-DASTIDAR, Koyeli.
Respect for Privacy: Western and Indian. GHOSH-DASTIDAR, Koyeli.
Sankara and Derrida on Philosophy of Language. COWARD, Harold.
Search for Indian Traditional Paradigm of Society. SHARMA, K N.
Social Reality and Moral Order. BARLINGAY, S S.
Some Problems in the Epistemology of Advaita. GRIMES, John.
The Text of the Nyāya-Sūtras: Some Problems. KRISHNA, Daya.
The Theory of Triple Perception. SARMA, Rajendra Nath.
Time, Self and Consciousness: Some Conceptual Patterns in the Context of Indian Thought. BALSLEV, Anindita.
Tolerance in Indian Culture and Its Philosophical Basis. DRAVID, N S.
The Value-Ought of Self-Realization: A Phenomenological Approach. VELASSERRY, Sebastian.
The Word That Became the Absolute: Relevance of Sankara's Ontology of Language. GUPTA, Som Raj.
Yajna and the Doctrine of Karma: A Contradiction in Indian Thought about Action. KRISHNA, Daya.

INDIANS
From Brahma to a Blade of Grass. COLLINS, Alfred.

INDICATIVES
Indicative Conditionals Are Truth-Functional. HANSON, William H.

INDICATOR(S)
Castañeda's Quasi-Indicators and the Tensed Theory of Time. SMITH, Quentin.
The Historical Event as a Cultural Indicator: The Case of Judaism. NEUSNER, Jacob.
Myself. WILLIAMS, C J F.

INDIFFERENCE
The Sweep of Probability. SCHLESINGER, George N.

INDIGNATION
Aristotle and Aquinas on Indignation: From Nemesis to Theodicy. NERNEY, Gayne.

INDIRECT DISCOURSE
"Speaker Plans, Linguistic Contexts, and Indirect Speech Acts" in *Knowledge Representation and Defeasible Reasoning*, MC CAFFERTY, Andrew.
Kierkegaard's Mirror. ROSENOW, Eliyahu.
Remnants of Schiffer's Principle [P]. SEYMOUR, Daniel.

INDISCERNIBILITY
Indiscernibility and Identity in Probability Theory. ROEPER, Peter and LEBLANC, Hugues.

INDISCERNIBLES
Leibniz and Strawson: A New Essay in Descriptive Metaphysics. BROWN, Clifford.
Principia Individuationis. DENKEL, Arda.
Quantum Physics and the Identity of Indiscernibles. FRENCH, Steven and REDHEAD, Michael.
What are Discernible?. SCHLESINGER, George N.

INDIVIDUAL(S)
see also Person(s)
Benjamin Constant and the Post-Revolutionary Mind. FONTANA, Biancamaria.
Foundations of Social Theory. COLEMAN, James S.
Leibniz and Arnauld. SLEIGH JR, Robert C.
Le Philosophie et les Passions. MEYER, Michel.
Robert Nozick: Property, Justice, and the Minimal State. WOLFF, Jonathan.
"Consciousness, the Attitude of the Individual and Perspectives" in *Creativity in George Herbert Mead*, MILLER, David L.
"The Individual's Horizon and Valuation" in *The Social Horizon of Knowledge*, FALKIEWICZ, Andrzej.
"Individuals in Informational and Intentional Content" in *Information, Semantics and Epistemology*, PERRY, John.
"Liberalism and Liberty: The Fragility of a Tradition" in *Key Themes in Philosophy*, GRAHAM, Keith.
"Markets and Morals" in *Philosophy and Politics*, SMITH, G W.
"Vocation, Friendship, and Community: Limitations of the Personal-Impersonal Framework" in *Identity, Character, and Morality: Essays in Moral Psychology*, BLUM, Lawrence A.
'Why Did It Happen to Me?'. THOMAS, J L H.
Aristotle's Much Maligned *Megalopsychos*. CURZER, Howard J.
Aspects of Freedom. WOOD, Robert E.
Autonomy and Political Obligation in Kant. STERN, David S.
Las dos grandes paradojas?. SERRANO, Augusto.
Le droit de l'État et le devoir de l'individu. PFERSMANN, Otto.
Future Individuals. TEICHMANN, Roger.
Individual and Corporate Responsibility: Two Alternative Approaches. SURBER, Jere.
Individual and Social Morality in Japan and the United States: Rival Conceptions of the Self. MAC INTYRE, Alasdair.
Individuo y acción en el pensamiento griego. RODA, Roberto.
Das Individuum, die Politik und die Philosophie. GRUNWALD, Sabine.
Josiah Royce: la metafisica della comunità. BUZZI GRASSI, Elisa.
Leibniz on Superessentialism and World-Bound Individuals. COVER, Jan A.
Libre spéculation sur le rapport du vivant et du social. TOSEL, André.

INDIVIDUAL(S)

Modernity, the Individual and Rationality in Marxism (Surrealism and Revolution). CLOUDSLEY, Tim.
Nietzsche on Woman. THOMPSON, J L.
Parthood and Persistence. KAZMI, Ali Akhtar.
Reward, Punishment, and the Strategy of Evolution. SCHRADER, Malcolm E.
Die Rolle des Individuums und seine Beteiligung an gesellschaftlichen Prozessen. SCHLIWA, Harald and ZEDDIES, Helmut.
Rousseau, the General Will, and Individual Liberty. KAIN, Philip J.
Self-Conscious Individual versus Social Soul: The Rationale of Wittgenstein's Discussion of Rule Following. SAVIGNY, Eike V.
Social Epistemology and Social Cognition. CORLETT, J Angelo.
Some Remarks on Respect and Human Rights. BARNES, Annette.
Teamwork. COHEN, Philip R and LEVESQUE, Hector J.
The Passing On of Values (in French). PIGUET, J-Claude.
Whether Any Individual at all Could Have a Guise Structure. MILLER, Barry.
Who's the Horse? A Response to Corlett. HEYES, Cecilia.

INDIVIDUALISM

Explaining Human Action. LENNON, Kathleen.
The Representational Theory of Mind: An Introduction. STERELNY, Kim.
Thomas Hobbes' Theory of Obligation: A Modern Interpretation. FORSBERG, Ralph P.
"Individualism and Artificial Intelligence" in *Philosophical Perspectives, 4: Action Theory and Philosophy of Mind, 1990*, KOBES, Bernard W.
"Libertarianism" in *Philosophy and Politics*, BARRY, Norman P.
"On What's in the Head" in *Philosophical Perspectives, 3: Philosophy of Mind and Action Theory, 1989*, STALNAKER, Robert.
Anti-Individualism and Privileged Access. MC KINSEY, Michael.
Basic Elements of the Concept of Individualism. WILKIE, Raymond.
Burgeoning Skepticism. DE VRIES, Willem.
Conflicting Views of Liberalism. SKOBLE, Aeon James.
Externalism Revisited: Is There Such a Thing as Narrow Content?. JACOB, Pierre.
Festrede zum 300: Geburstag von Gottfried Wilhelm Leibniz am 1 Juli 1946 in der Aula der Universitat Leipzig. GADAMER, Hans-Georg.
How Individualistic Is Methodological Individualism?. MADISON, G B.
Individualism and Semantic Development. PATTERSON, Sarah.
Individualism, Absolutism, and Contract in Hobbes' Political Theory. GROVER, Robinson A.
Libertarianism. BARRY, Norman.
The Micro-Macro Problem in Collective Behavior: Reconciling Agency and Structure. LEE, Raymond L M.
Monadic Marxism: A Critique of Elster's Methodological Individualism. MOGGACH, Douglas.
Must Psychology Be Individualistic?. EGAN, Frances.
Response to Wilkie's "Habits of the Heart". RAITZ, Keith L.
Ruben and the Metaphysics of the Social World. TUOMELA, Raimo.
Social Movements and Individual Identity: A Critique of Freud on the Psychology of Groups. WARTENBERG, Thomas E.
Staat als Konsens mündiger Bürger? Zur Staatsansicht deutscher Vormärzliberaler. LIEPERT, Anita.
Strange Attractors: How Individualists Connect to Form Democratic Unity. ROSENBLUM, Nancy.

INDIVIDUALITY

The Call to Personhood. MC FADYEN, Alistair I.
Il compito della filosofia: Saggio su Windelband. OLIVA, Rossella Bonito.
Democratic Individuality. GILBERT, Alan.
Difference and Subjectivity: Dialogue and Personal Identity. JACQUES, Francis.
Good and Evil: An Absolute Conception. GAITA, Raimond.
Mind in Action: Essays in the Philosophy of Mind. RORTY, Amelie Oksenberg.
"Individuality and Collectivity: False Antonyms" in *Abeunt Studia in Mores: A Festschrift for Helga Doblin*, PYTOWSKA, Ewa.
"Reconsidering Psychology" in *Reconsidering Psychology: Perspectives from Continental Philosophy*, FAULCONER, James E and WILLIAMS, Richard N.
A Brief Discussion of One Aspect of the *Shangtong* Idea. YUANHUA, Wang.
George Kateb's Ahistorical Emersonianism. MARX, Leo.
Heidegger on the Self, Authenticity and Inauthenticity. MANSBACH, Abraham.
An Intersubjective Concept of Individuality. HABERMAS, Jürgen.
Kierkegaard's Mirror. ROSENOW, Eliyahu.
L'ontogenèse de l'individu: ses aspects scientifiques et philosophiques. BERNIER, Réjane.
Real Human Persons. DONAGAN, Alan.
Sobre la individualidad. CATES, Lynn.
Sulla matrice della teoria della sostanza nel *Discorso di metafisica* di Leibniz. DELCÓ, Alessandro.

INDIVIDUATION

Behind the Masks of God: An Essay Toward Comparative Theology. NEVILLE, Robert Cummings.
"Substitution Arguments and the Individuation of Beliefs" in *Meaning and Method: Essays in Honor of Hilary Putnam*, FODOR, Jerry A.
Anomalism, Supervenience, and Davidson on Content-Individuation. ROWLANDS, Mark.
El conocimiento del singular en José Gaos. LLANO, Carlos.
Ethics and Instrumentalism: A Response to Janna Thompson. PLUMWOOD, Val.
On the Individuation of Events. CLELAND, Carol.
Peirce's Haecceitism. DI LEO, Jeffrey R.
Relative Identity and Locke's Principle of Individuation. UZGALIS, William L.
Thomas d'Aquin a-t-il tente d'exprimer le principe d'individuation à l'intérieur des proprietés.... CASPAR, Philippe.

INDIVISIBILITY

"On Fair Distribution of Indivisible Goods" in *Logic and Ethics*, SZANIAWSKI, Klemens.

INDOCTRINATION

Bringing Things About. DIEFENBECK, James A.
The Paradox of Indoctrination: A Hermeneutical Solution. GARRISON, James W.
Reading the Darkness: Wittgenstein and Indoctrination. MC CARTY, Luise Prior and MC CARTY, David Charles.

INDUCTION

Logic, Methodology and Philosophy of Science, VII. MARCUS, Ruth Barcan (ed).
Nomic Probability and the Foundations of Induction. POLLOCK, John L.
The Positivist Science of Law. LEE, Keekok.
Probabilistic Causality. EELLS, Ellery.
Science and Reason. KYBURG JR, Henry E.
The Sweep of Probability. SCHLESINGER, George N.
"Inexact and Inductive Reasoning" in *Logic, Methodology and Philosophy of Science, VIII*, PARIS, J and VENCOVSKÁ, A.
"On the Existence of End Extensions of Models of Bounded Induction" in *Logic, Methodology and Philosophy of Science, VIII*, WILKIE, A.
Bayes' Bayesianism. EARMAN, John.
Conditionals, Quantification, and Strong Mathematical Induction. COHEN, Daniel H.
El cuádruple problema de la inducción: Crítica de la solución popperiana del problema de Hume. GARCÍA NORRO, Juan José.
Ellis, Epistemic Values, and the Problem of Induction. VOLLRATH, John.
Hegel and the Humean Problem of Induction. SUCHTING, W A.
Induction and Modality. JOHNSON, David.
The Inductive Support of Inductive Rules: Themes from Max Black. SANFORD, David H.
Inductive Types and Type Constraints in the Second-Order Lambda Calculus. MENDLER, Nax Paul.
John Stuart Mill on Induction and Hypothesis. JACOBS, Struan.
The Last Word on Induction?. HOWSON, Colin.
On Diophantine Equations Solvable in Models of Open Induction. OTERO, Margarita.
On Falsificationist Interpretations of Peirce. SULLIVAN, Patrick F.
On Induction and Properties. ZABLUDOWSKI, Andrzej.
On Metainductive Sentences. TRIVEDI, Saam.
On Russell's Principle of Induction. DA COSTA, Newton C A and FRENCH, Steven.
Popper on Induction. SWANN, Andrew J.
Preconditions of Predication: From Qualia to Quantum Mechanics. FORSTER, Malcolm.
Remarks on Analogy. DA COSTA, Newton C A and SETTE, A M.
Solving the Problem of Induction Using a Values-Based Epistemology. ELLIS, Brian.
Some Further Reflections on the Popper-Miller 'Disproof' of Probabilistic Induction. HOWSON, C.
Some New Double Induction and Superinduction Principles. SMULLYAN, Raymond M.
Some Remarks on the Rationality of Induction. INDURKHYA, Bipin.
A Suspicious Feature of the Popper/Miller Argument. GOOD, I J.
Swann versus Popper on Induction: An Arbitration. SETTLE, Tom.
Two Problems of Induction?. O'NEILL, John.
Understanding Induction. MACNAMARA, John.
When Is Arithmetic Possible?. MC COLM, Gregory L.

INDUCTIVE LOGIC

La Logica Simbolica: nella produzione scientifica in lingua russa (1961-1983). PENNINO, Luciano.
Ambiguity, Inductive Systems, and the Modeling of Subjective Probability Judgements. MONETA, Giovanni B.
Assessing Inductive Logics Empirically. SMOKLER, Howard.
A Fully Logical Inductive Logic. NOLT, John.
Pragmatic Truth and the Logic of Induction. DA COSTA, Newton C A and FRENCH, Steven.
Probability Logic in the Twentieth Century. HAILPERIN, Theodore.

INDUCTIVISM

Induction and Stochastic Independence. AGASSI, Joseph.
On the Alleged Impossibility of Inductive Probability. EELLS, Ellery.
A Refutation of Popperian Inductive Scepticism. GEMES, Ken.
A Restoration of Popperian Inductive Scepticism. MILLER, David.

INDUCTIVISM
Scepticism: Three Recently Presented Arguments Examined. DURRANT, Michael.

INDUSTRIALISM
The Death of Industrial Civilization. KASSIOLA, Joel Jay.
La critique du modèle industriel comme histoire de la rareté: Une introduction à la pensée d'Ivan Illich. ACHTERHUIS, Hans.
Maîtrise, marché et société industrielle. VAN PARIJS, Philippe.

INDUSTRIALIZATION
Le modèle industriel comme modèle énergétique. BERTEN, André.

INDUSTRY
Commentary: "The University and Industrial Research: Selling Out?". CAMPBELL, L Leon.
Defining the Ethical Standards of the High-Technology Industry. FIMBEL, Nancie and BURSTEIN, Jerome S.
The Relative Importance of Social Responsibility in Determining Organizational Effectiveness. KRAFT, Kenneth.
The University and Industrial Research: Selling Out?. HILL, Judith M.

INEFFABILITY
Il doppio volto dell'ineffabile in L Wittgenstein. TODISCO, Orlando.
Relativism, Ineffability, and the Appeal to Experience: A Reply to the Myth Makers. BARNES, L Philip.

INEQUALITY
"La femme intellectuelle au XVIIIe siècle ou l'inégalité des sexes" in *Égalité Uguaglianza*, GEFFRIAUD-ROSSO, Jeannette.
"Undressing Baby Bell" in *Harré and His Critics*, REDHEAD, Michael L G.
Nietzsche's Case for Inequality. GOETHALS, Susanne C.

INERTIA
La cosmologia tra filosofia ed empirologia. PELLECCHIA, Pasquale.
The Fundamental Hypotheses of Mechanics in Lazare N M Carnot's Thought (in Italian). DRAGO, Antonino and MANNO, Salvatore D.

INFALLIBILITY
"Epistemic Compatibilism and Canonical Beliefs" in *Doubting: Contemporary Perspectives on Skepticism*, KLEIN, Peter D.

INFERENCE RULE(S)
Nomic Probability and the Foundations of Induction. POLLOCK, John L.
Axiomatization of the De Morgan Type Rules. HERRMANN, B.
A Basic Free Logic. WU, Kathleen Johnson.
A Calculus for the Common Rules of.... RAUTENBERG, Wolfgan.
A Complete Syntactical Characterization of the Intuitionistic Logic. SKURA, Tomasz.
A Constructivism Based on Classical Truth. MIGLIOLI, P (and others).
First-Order Theories Without Axioms. STEPIEN, Teodor.
Linear Axiomatics of Communicative Product-Free Lambek Calculus. ZIELONKA, Wojciech.
Logical Constants as Punctuation Marks. DOSEN, Kosta.
Logical Equations and Admissible Rules of Inference with Parameters in Modal Provability Logics. RYBAKOV, V V.
Natural Deduction in Normal Modal Logic. HAWTHORN, John.
On Pure Refutation Formulations of Sentential Logics. SKURA, Tomasz.
Q-Consequence Operation. MALINOWSKI, Grzegorz.
Relevance and Paraconsistency—A New Approach, Part III: Cut-Free Gentzen-Type Systems. AVRON, Arnon.
Single-Axiom Systems. STEPIEN, Teodor.
The t-Variable Method in Gentzen-Style Automatic Theorem Proving. EDWALD, Tryggvi.

INFERENCE(S)
Inference and Understanding: A Philosophical and Psychological Perspective. MANKTELOW, K I.
Meaning and Speech Acts: Volume I, Principles of Language Use. VANDERVEKEN, Daniel.
What If...? Toward Excellence in Reasoning. HINTIKKA, Jaakko.
"Action, Inference, Belief, and Intention" in *Philosophical Perspectives, 4: Action Theory and Philosophy of Mind, 1990*, AUNE, Bruce.
"A Framework for Reasoning with Defaults" in *Knowledge Representation and Defeasible Reasoning*, GEFFNER, Hector and PEARL, Judea.
"Inference to the Best Explanation in Archaeology" in *Critical Traditions in Contemporary Archaeology*, HANEN, Marsha and KELLEY, Jane.
"Two Perspectives on Consensus for (Bayesian) Inference and Decisions" in *Knowledge Representation and Defeasible Reasoning*, SEIDENFELD, Teddy.
Cartesian Skepticism and Inference to the Best Explanation. VOGEL, Jonathan.
Dharmakirti on Inference and Properties. GANERI, Jonardon.
Dialogues in Natural Language with GURU, a Psychologic Inference Engine. COLBY, Kenneth M and COLBY, Peter M and STOLLER, Robert J.
Experimental Methods and Conceptual Confusion: An Investigation into R L Gregory's Theory of Perception. HACKER, P M S.
A Fully Logical Inductive Logic. NOLT, John.
Hypothesis Tests and Confidence Intervals in the Single Case. JOHNSTONE, D J.
In What Way is Abductive Inference Creative?. KAPITAN, Tomis.
The Inconspicuous Role of Paraphrase. SHERRY, David.
The Inference to the Best Explanation. BEN-MENAHEM, Y.
Introduction to Dharmakirti's Theory of Inference as Presented in *Pramānavārttika Svopajñavrtti* 1-10. HAYES, Richard P and GILLON, Brendan S.
Logics Preserving Degrees of Truth. NOWAK, Marek.
Mathematical Statistics and Metastatistical Analysis. RIVADULLA, Andrés.
Prior's Disease. USBERTI, Gabriele.
Rome Inferences and Structural Opacity. MOORE, F C T.
Unification, Realism and Inference. MORRISON, Margaret.

INFERTILITY
"Infertility and the Role of the Federal Government" in *Beyond Baby M: Ethical Issues in New Reproductive Techniques*, ELLIS, Gary.

INFINITARY CONCEPT(S)
Constructions by Transfinitely Many Workers. KNIGHT, Julia F.
Preservation by Homomorphisms and Infinitary Languages. HYTTINEN, Tapani.

INFINITARY LOGIC
Generalizing Classical and Effective Model Theory in Theories of Operations and Classes. MANCOSU, Paolo.
A Strong Boundedness Theorem for Dilators. KECHRIS, Alexander S and WOODIN, W H.

INFINITE
Las paradojas del Infinito. BOLZANO, Bernard.
The Savage Anomaly: The Power of Spinoza's Metaphysics and Politics. NEGRI, Antonio.
Aristote admet-il un infini en acte et en puissance en "Physique III, 4-8"?. CÔTÉ, Antoine.
The Infinite Apparatus in the Quantum Theory of Measurement. ROBINSON, Don.
On Some Paradoxes of the Infinite. ALLIS, Victor and KOETSIER, Teunis.
Plotinus and the *Apeiron* of Plato's *Parmenides*. HEISER, John H.
A Problem for Intuitionism: The Apparent Possibility of Performing Infinitely Many Tasks in a Finite Time. MOORE, A W.

INFINITESIMAL(S)
Charles S Peirce's Theory of Infinitesimals. LEVY, Stephen H.
On Cauchy's Notion of Infinitesimal. CUTLAND, Nigel J (and others).

INFINITIVE(S)
A Generalized Quantifier Logic for Naked Infinitives. VAN DER DOES, Jaap.

INFINITY
Infinity in Mathematics: Is Cantor Necessary?. FEFERMAN, Solomon.
The Limits of Thought—and Beyond. PRIEST, Graham.
Sur la méthode de Ferdinand Gonseth. VUILLEMIN, Jule.
The Problem of Infinity in Kant's Works (in German). RÖD, Wolfgang.

INFLUENCE(S)
"Tradition, Influence and Innovation" in *XIth International Congress in Aesthetics, Nottingham 1988*, HERMEREN, Goran.
Artist and Peasant. XING-PEI, Fei.
Heidegger and the Japanese Connection. BILIMORIA, Purusottama.
Kant in Russia: The Initial Phase (continued). NEMETH, Thomas.
Marx and Russia. NAARDEN, Bruno.
On the Historical Triviality of Art. STOLNITZ, Jerome.
The State of Studies on Western Philosophy in China. FANG-TONG, Liu.

INFORMAL LOGIC
Understanding Arguments: An Introduction to Informal Logic (Fourth Edition). FOGELIN, Robert J.
Evaluating Arguments: The Premise-Conclusion Relation. BOWLES, George.
In the Service of Human Society: Formal, Information, or Anti-Logical?. BARTH, E M.
Perhaps by Skill Alone. MISSIMER, Connie.
Quantifying Support. BLACK, John.
Smook on Logical and Extralogical Constants. HITCHCOCK, David and GEORGE, Rolf.
Students: A Source-Spot for Arguments. BERKOWITZ, Leonard J.
Testing Fairmindedness. FISHER, Alec.
Towards a Research Agenda for Informal Logic and Critical Thinking. WEINSTEIN, Mark.

INFORMATION
Information, Semantics and Epistemology. VILLANUEVA, Enrique (ed).
"'Narrow' Aspects of Intentionality and the Information - Theoretic Approach to Content" in *Information, Semantics and Epistemology*, FIELD, Hartry.
"Concepts, Prototypes and Information" in *Information, Semantics and Epistemology*, GRANDY, Richard E.
"Individuals in Informational and Intentional Content" in *Information, Semantics and Epistemology*, PERRY, John.
"Information and the Mental" in *Truth and Interpretation: Perspectives on the Philosophy of Donald Davidson*, PUTNAM, Hilary.
"Informational Independence as a Semantical Phenomenon" in *Logic, Methodology and Philosophy of Science, VIII*, HINTIKKA, Jaakko and SANDU, Gabriel.

INFORMATION
"Mario Bunge's Ontology as a Formal Foundation for Information Systems Concepts" in *Studies on Mario Bunge's "Treatise"*, WAND, Yair and WEBER, Ron.
"Some Marxism Themes in the Age of Information" in *Perspectives on Ideas and Reality*, NYÍRI, J C.
Commentary—"Make Me Live": Autonomy and Terminal Illness. MILLER, David H.
Dimensions of Observability. KOSSO, Peter.
Double Standards, Racial Equality and the Right Reference Class. ADLER, Jonathan E.
Dretske on Perception. HOROWITZ, Amir.
The Ethical Decision-Making Processes of Information Systems Workers. PARADICE, David B and DEJOIE, Roy M.
Freiheit und Bindung menschlicher Entscheidungen. KLEMENT, H W and RADERMACHER, F J.
Information Functions with Applications. SZYMANEK, Krzysztof.
Information Privacy and Performance Appraisal: An Examination of Employee Perceptions and Reactions. MOSSHOLDER, Kevin W and GILES, William F and WESOLOWSKI, Mark A.
Informational Property: Logorights. SCHULMAN, J Neil.
Language in Action. VAN BENTHEM, Johan.
Many-Valued Modal Logics: Uses and Predicate Calculus. OSTERMANN, Pascal.
Marketing Ethics: Some Dimensions of the Challenge. CAMENISCH, Paul F.
A Semiotical Reflection on Biology, Living Signs and Artificial Life. EMMECHE, Claus.
Sociedad informatizada y poder político. RICHARDS, Edgardo.
The Value of Perfect Information in Non-linear Utility Theory. SCHLEE, Edward E.

INFORMATION THEORY
Evolution als Höherentwicklung des Bewusstseins. KUMMER, Christian.
"Information Theory and the *Treatise*: Towards a New Understanding" in *Studies on Mario Bunge's "Treatise"*, KARY, Michael.
Aesthetic Order. LORAND, Ruth.
Behavior, Biology, and Information Theory. SENCHUK, Dennis M.

INFORMED CONSENT
Deciding for Others: The Ethics of Surrogate Decision Making. BUCHANAN, Allen E.
Medical Ethics for Physicians-in-Training. KANTOR, Jay E.
Hide-and-Seek or Show-and-Tell? Emerging Issues of Informed Consent. HAAS, Leonard J.
Informed Consent or Informed Rejection of Pesticide Use: A Concept for Environmental Action. ORTON, David.
Outrageous Fortune: Selling Other People's Cells. ANNAS, George J.
Risk-Related Standard Inevitable in Assessing Competence—Comments on Wicclair. SKENE, Loane.
Uninformed Consent. MARCUS, Ruth Barcan and KUCKLICK, B and BERCOVITCH, S.

INFORMING
The Chief of Medicine. BRODY, Howard.

INGARDEN, R
"Ingarden et la musique: Actualité de la pensée musicale de Roman Ingarden" in *XIth International Congress in Aesthetics, Nottingham 1988*, SMOJE, Dujka.
Ingarden und Husserls transzendentaler Idealismus. HAEFLIGER, Gregor.
Philosophy of Culture and Its Place in the Scientific Achievement of Roman Ingarden (in Polish). MAJEWSKA, Zofia.

INHIBITION(S)
Emerson and the Inhibitions of Democracy. SHKLAR, Judith N.

INJUSTICE
see also Justice
Justice in Preferential Hiring. SINGER, M S and SINGER, A E.

INNATE IDEA(S)
Hume, Reid and Innate Ideas: A Response to John P Wright. GALLIE, Roger D.

INNATENESS
On the Issue of Sex Differences. ALLEN, Elizabeth.

INNATISM
El innatismo de Leibniz. HERRERA, Alejandro.

INNOCENCE
Innocents and Innocence: Moral Puzzles of Professional Status and Culpable Conduct. SNOWDEN, John R.
La inocencia y el mal en la obra de Albert Camus. JIMÉNEZ, Alexander.
Private Defense. GORR, Michael.
Utilitarianism and the 'Punishment' of the Innocent: The General Problem. SMILANSKY, Saul.

INNOVATION(S)
Style and Music: Theory, History, and Ideology. MEYER, Leonard B.
"Innovation and Tradition in Post-Modernism" in *XIth International Congress in Aesthetics, Nottingham 1988*, ROSE, Margaret A.
"Tradition, Innovation, Kunstrezeption und Kuntswirkung—zu einigen Problemen" in *XIth International Congress in Aesthetics, Nottingham 1988*, ERHARD, John.
Development Aid: The Moral Obligation to Innovation. DUNDON, Stanislaus J.

INORGANIC
Romanticism and the Sciences. CUNNINGHAM, Andrew (ed).
The Inorganic Body and the Ambiguity of Freedom. COLLIER, Andrew.

INQUIRY
Zetetic Skepticism. UMPHREY, Stewart.
The Community of Inquiry Education for Democracy. SHARP, Ann Margaret.
The Role of Stories in a Community of Inquiry. HON-MING, Chen.

INQUISITION
The Foxy Prophet: Machiavelli versus Machiavelli on Ferdinand the Catholic. ANDREW, Edward.

INSANITY
"Can Responsibility Be Diminished?" in *Liability and Responsibility*, KENNY, Anthony.
The Ethico-Legal Meaning of Voluntary. BOURKE, Vernon J.

INSECT(S)
Concerning the Interests of Insects. GROSSINGER, Robin.

INSECURITY
Creative Insecurity and "Tiptoe Experiences". HOWIE, John.

INSIDER TRADING
The Indefensibility of Insider Trading. WERHANE, Patricia H.
Insider Trading Revisited. MARTIN, Deryl W and PETERSON, Jeffrey H.
Predictors of Ethical Decisions Regarding Insider Trading. TERPSTRA, David E and REYES, Mario G C and BOKOR, Donald W.

INSPIRATION
"Inspiration and Creativity: An Extension" in *Archetypal Process: Self and Divine in Whitehead, Jung, and Hillman*, SLUSSER, Gerald H.

INSTANT(S)
Before Refraining: Concepts for Agency. BELNAP JR, Nuel D.
Concerted Instant-Interval Temporal Semantics I: Temporal Ontologies. BOCHMAN, Alexander.
Concerted Instant-Interval Temporal Semantics II: Temporal Valuations and Logics of Change. BOCHMAN, Alexander.

INSTANTIATION
Instantial Terms, Anaphora and Arbitrary Objects. KING, Jeffrey C.

INSTITUTION(S)
Integrity in Health Care Institutions: Humane Environments for Teaching, Inquiry, and Healing. BULGER, Ruth Ellen (ed).
"Determinants of the Culture and Personality of Institutions" in *Integrity in Health Care Institutions: Humane Environments for Teaching, Inquiry, and Healing*, HAUGHTON, James G.
"Institutions and the Shaping of Character" in *Integrity in Health Care Institutions: Humane Environments for Teaching, Inquiry, and Healing*, COLES, Robert.
"Integrity, Humaneness, and Institutions in Secular Pluralist Societies" in *Integrity in Health Care Institutions: Humane Environments for Teaching, Inquiry, and Healing*, ENGELHARDT JR, H Tristram.
"Medical Institutions and Their Moral Constraints" in *Integrity in Health Care Institutions: Humane Environments for Teaching, Inquiry, and Healing*, TOULMIN, Stephen.
Aspects of Freedom. WOOD, Robert E.
De la matérialité du discours saisi dans l'institution. KREMER-MARIETTI, Angèle.
Defining the Limits of Institutional Moral Agency in Health Care: A Response to Kevin Wildes. RIE, Michael A.
The Economic Analysis of Institutions. RICKETTS, Martin.
Ethics Committees: From Ethical Comfort to Ethical Cover. ANNAS, George J.
Measuring the Success of Science. NIINILUOTO, Ilkka.
The Moral Significance of Institutional Integrity. WEAR, Stephen.
The Philosophy of the Welfare State. BARRY, Norman P.
Political Culture and Institution Building: Democratic Evolution at Work and the Case of Poland. LAMENTOWICZ, Wojtek.
Political Freedom. TULLY, James.
The Profit Motive and the Moral Assessment of Health Care Institutions. DANIELS, Norman.
The Reconstruction of Institutions. COLAPIETRO, Vincent M.
The Sociology of Knowledge: Toward an Existential View of Business Ethics. PHILLIPS, Nelson.
Sociology, Selection, and Success: A Critique of David Hull's Analysis of Science and Systematics. DONOGHUE, Michael J.
Taking Role Moralities Seriously. WUESTE, Daniel E.
Toward An Expanded Vision of Clinical Ethics Education: From the Individual to the Institution. SOLOMON, Mildred Z (and others).
What is the Problem Concerning Social Entities?. THOMPSON, J L.

INSTITUTIONALIZATION
Deinstitutionalization: Cycles of Despair. SCULL, Andrew.
The Institutionalization of Organizational Ethics. SIMS, Ronald R.

INTENSION
The Real Meaning of 'Meaning'. CARTER, Alan.

INTENSIONAL LOGIC
"Russellian Intensional Logic" in *Themes From Kaplan*, ANDERSON, C Anthony.
Extending Montague's System: A Three Valued Intensional Logic. ALVES, E H and GUERZONI, J A D.
Was the Axiom of Reducibility a Principle of Logic?. LINSKY, Bernard.

INTENSIONALITY
Meaning and Truth: The Essential Readings in Modern Semantics. GARFIELD, Jay L (ed).
"Intensionality and the Paradox of the Name Relation" in *Themes From Kaplan*, CHURCH, Alonzo.
"Why Intensionalists Ought Not Be Fregeans" in *Truth and Interpretation: Perspectives on the Philosophy of Donald Davidson*, KATZ, Jerrold J.
Intensional Identities. SLATER, B H.
Intensionality and Boundedness. MORRILL, Glyn.

INTENTION(S)
Explaining Human Action. LENNON, Kathleen.
The Fragmentation of Reason. STICH, Stephen.
Intention, Agency and Criminal Liability: Philosophy of Action and the Criminal Law. DUFF, R A.
Intentions in Communication. COHEN, Philip R (ed).
Linguistic Behaviour. BENNETT, Jonathan.
Mind in Action: Essays in the Philosophy of Mind. RORTY, Amelie Oksenberg.
Plotinus and Freedom: A Meditation on Enneads 6:8. WESTRA, Laura.
The Recovery of the Soul: An Aristotelian Essay on Self-fulfilment. RANKIN, Kenneth.
Wittgenstein and Contemporary Philosophy of Language. RUNDLE, Bede.
"Action, Inference, Belief, and Intention" in *Philosophical Perspectives, 4: Action Theory and Philosophy of Mind, 1990*, AUNE, Bruce.
"Intention and Personal Policies" in *Philosophical Perspectives, 3: Philosophy of Mind and Action Theory, 1989*, BRATMAN, Michael E.
"Intention and Side-Effects" in *Liability and Responsibility*, FINNIS, John.
The Actus Reus Requirement: A Qualified Defense. GORR, Michael.
Agency and Omniscience. KAPITAN, Tomis.
Avoiding the Fly Bottle. KOLENDA, Konstantin.
Conditional Intention. CARTWRIGHT, J P W.
A Critical Examination of Scheler's Justification of the Existence of Values. MOOSA, Imtiaz.
A Dilemma for Sentential Dualism. MOSER, Paul K.
Externalism Revisited: Is There Such a Thing as Narrow Content?. JACOB, Pierre.
He Doesn't Really Want to Try. ADAMS, Frederick.
Homicide and Love. SMITH, Steven G.
In Defence of "Hard" Offers: A Reply to J P Day. HÄYRY, Matti and AIRAKSINEN, Timo.
Individualism and Semantic Development. PATTERSON, Sarah.
Intention, Cognitive Commitment, and Planning. AUDI, Robert.
The Intentional and the Intended. GARCIA, J L A.
Intentions, Actions, and Routines: A Problem in Krister Segerberg's Theory of Action. ELGESEM, Dag.
Intenzione e azione in Wittgenstein. RAINONE, Antonio.
L'interpretazione del conflitto fra norme nell'ultimo Kelsen. CELANO, Brun.
Is Davidson a Volitionist In Spite of Himself?. CLEVELAND, Timothy.
Killing and Letting Die—Putting the Debate in Context. CHANDLER, John.
Meaning and Intention: Black Versus Grice. MARTINICH, A P.
Nuclear Deterrence and the Morality of Intentions. KULTGEN, John.
Object and Intention in Moral Judgments According to Aquinas. FINNIS, John.
On 'High-Mindedness'. GARCIA, Jorge.
On Häyry and Airaksinen's 'Hard and Soft Offers as Constraints'. DAY, J P.
Overloading Intentions for Efficient Practical Reasoning. POLLACK, Martha E.
A Philosophical Resistance to Freud. SACHS, David.
The Punishment of Attempts. NUYEN, A T.
Purposive Intending. PINK, T L M.
Retaliation Rationalized: Gauthier's Solution to the Deterrence Dilemma. MAC INTOSH, Duncan.
Seeing Metaphor as Seeing-as. TIRRELL, Lynne.
Settled Objectives and Rational Constraints. MC CANN, Hugh J.
Teamwork. COHEN, Philip R and LEVESQUE, Hector J.
We Will Do It: An Analysis of Group Intentions. TUOMELA, Raimo.

INTENTIONAL
"Davidson on Explaining Intentional Actions" in *The Mind of Donald Davidson*, LANZ, Peter.
All the Difference in the World. CRANE, Tim.
Intentionalistic Explanations in the Social Sciences. SEARLE, John R.
El problema de la "acción intencional" en el conocimiento sensible. DELBOSCO, Héctor J.

INTENTIONALISM
Persons and the Intentional Stance. DIBRELL, William.
Thoughts. SMITH, David Woodruff.

INTENTIONALITY
Explaining Behavior: Reasons in a World of Causes. DRETSKE, Fred.
Foundations of Cognitive Science: The Essential Readings. GARFIELD, Jay L.
Human Consciousness. HANNAY, Alastair.
The Philosophy of Action: An Introduction. MOYA, Carlos J.
Responsibility and Criminal Liability. SISTARE, C T.
"'Narrow' Aspects of Intentionality and the Information - Theoretic Approach to Content" in *Information, Semantics and Epistemology*, FIELD, Hartry.
"The Heart of the Mind: Intentionality versus Intelligence" in *The Case for Dualism*, PUCCETTI, Roland.
"The Intentionality All-Stars" in *Philosophical Perspectives, 4: Action Theory and Philosophy of Mind, 1990*, HAUGELAND, John.
Aspects of the Problem of Reference (1): Phenomenology, Hermeneutics and Deconstruction. RAJAN, R Sundara.
Aspects of the Problem of Reference (I). RAJAN, R Sundara.
Aspects of the Problem of Reference (II). RAJAN, R Sundara.
Closing the Chinese Room. WEISS, Thomas.
Consciousness: Creative and Self-Creating. BUKALA, C R.
Dummett and the Origins of Analytical Philosophy, or the Philosophy of Thought vs Philosophy of Language (in German). DÖLLING, Evelyn and DÖLLING, Johannes.
Emotion and Belief. BORUAH, Bijoy H.
Ethics in Educational Policy Analysis. WILLERS, Jack Conrad.
Formulation of Grice's Three Intentions. LENKA, Laxminarayan.
The Intentional and the Intended. GARCIA, J L A.
Intentional Single and Joint Action. TUOMELA, Raimo.
Intentionality and Modern Philosophical Psychology, I: The Modern Reduction of Intentionality. LYONS, William.
Intentionality and Modern Philosophical Psychology—II: The Return to Representation. LYONS, Willia.
Intentionality and the Ecological Approach. LOOREN DE JONG, H.
Intentionality and the Public World: Husserl's Treatment of Objectivity in the Cartesian Meditations. ARP, Kristana.
Mencius and the Mind-Dependence of Morality: An Analysis of Meng Tzu 6A: 4-5. SHUN, Kwong-Loi.
Mental Causes. HEIL, John and MELE, Alfred.
Michael Polanyi's Aesthetics: A Phenomenological Study. BISWAS, Goutam.
Il paradosso del fondamento nella simbolica del gioco e sogno della libertà. MASULLO, Aldo.
Peirce's Realism, Intentionality and Final Causation. TURIANO, Mark.
Philosophical Asceiticism (in French). DE MONTICELLI, Roberta.
Physicalism and Intentional Attitudes. MOSER, Paul K.
The Problem of Reality. JACKENDOFF, Ray.
Problems with the Fregean Interpretation of Husserl. BROWN, Charles S.
Professor Von Wright on Action. DEWASHI, Mahadev.
Putting One's Foot in One's Head—Part I: Why. PERLIS, Donald.
Univocità dell'essere e intenzionalià del conoscere. ANTONELLI, Mauro.

INTERACTION(S)
Experimental Studies of Interactive Decisions. RAPOPORT, Amnon.
The Other Side of Language: A Philosophy of Listening. FIUMARA, Gemma Corradi.
Causal Propensities: Statistical Causality versus Aleatory Causality. SALMON, Wesley C.
Dimensions of Observability. KOSSO, Peter.
Some Recent Research on the Mind-Body Problem in Descartes. MILES, Murray.

INTERACTIONISM
Language and Metaphysics: The Ontology of Metaphor. HAUSMAN, Carl R.
Van Rooijen and Mayr versus Popper: Is the Universe Causally Closed?. SETTLE, Tom.

INTERDEPENDENCE
The Challenge of Global Ethics. BULLER, Paul F and KOHLS, John J and ANDERSON, Kenneth S.
Varieties of Pluralism in a Polyphonic Society. RORTY, Amelie Oksenberg.

INTERDISCIPLINARY
Narrative in Culture: The Uses of Storytelling in the Sciences, Philosophy, and Literature. NASH, Christopher (ed).
Interdisciplinary Epistemology. BODEN, Margaret A.
Science and Art: The New Golem From the Transdisciplinary to an Ultra-disciplinary Epistemology. BERGER, René.

INTEREST(S)
"On the Conception of the Common Interest: Between Procedure and Substance" in *Hermeneutics and Critical Theory in Ethics and Politics*, GOULD, Carol C.
"The Physician's Knowledge and the Patient's Best Interest" in *Ethics, Trust, and the Professions: Philosophical and Cultural Aspects*, BUCHANAN, Allen E.
La distinción entre intereses subjetivos y objetivos y su importancia para la Etica. PATZIG, Günther.
Schopenhauers "objektives Interesse". NEYMEYR, Barbara.

INTERMEDIATE LOGICS
Classification of Intermediate Predicate Logics Under the Type of Deductive Completeness. TAKANO, Mitio and YAMAKAMI, Tomoyuki.
An Extension of Ono's Completeness Result. SUZUKI, Nobu-Yuki.
Intermediate Predicate Logics Determined by Ordinals. MINARI, Pierluigi and TAKANO, Mitio and ONO, Hiroakira.
Kripke Bundles for Intermediate Predicate Logics and Kripke Frames for Intuitionistic Modal Logics. SUZUKI, Nobu-Yuki.
On Certain Normalizable Natural Deduction Formulations of Some Propositional Intermediate Logics. BORICIC, Branislav R.
The Simple Substitution Property of Gödel's Intermediate Propositional Logics S_n's. SASAKI, Katsumi.
Some Syntactical Properties of Intermediate Predicate Logics. SUZUKI, Nobu-Yuki.

INTERNAL
Realism with a Human Face. PUTNAM, Hilary.
Is Aristotle an Internal Realist? Nussbaum and the Divine Perspective. EARLS, C Anthony.

INTERNAL RELATION(S)
Relevant Predication 2: Intrinsic Properties and Internal Relations. DUNN, J Michael.

INTERNALISM
Epistemic Justification: Essays in the Theory of Knowledge. ALSTON, William P.
Knowledge in Perspective: Selected Essays in Epistemology. SOSA, Ernest.
"An Internalist Conception of Rational Action" in *Philosophical Perspectives, 4: Action Theory and Philosophy of Mind, 1990*, AUDI, Robert.
"Skepticism and Rationality" in *Doubting: Contemporary Perspectives on Skepticism*, FOLEY, Richard.
Epistemic Internalism's Dilemma. HETHERINGTON, Stephen Cade.
Epistemic Norms and Evolutionary Success. CLARKE, Murray.
Gilbert Harman's Internalist Moral Relativism. POJMAN, Louis P.
The Highest Moral Knowledge and Internalism: Some Comments. LEMOS, Noah.
The Highest Moral Knowledge and the Truth Behind Internalism. DE PAUL, Michael R.
Internalism and Epistemically Responsible Belief. GRECO, John.
Justification in the 20th Century. PLANTINGA, Alvin.
On the Genuine Queerness of Moral Properties and Facts. GARNER, Richard T.
Putting One's Foot in One's Head—Part I: Why. PERLIS, Donald.
Scepticism: The External World and Meaning. BAR-ON, Dorit.
Thoughts. SMITH, David Woodruff.

INTERNATIONAL
International Marketing Ethics. LACZNIAK, Gene R and MURPHY, Patrick E.
Reinvigorating the International Christian-Marxist Dialogue. MOJZES, Paul.

INTERNATIONAL RELATION(S)
In the Interest of Peace: A Spectrum of Philosophical Views. KLEIN, Kenneth H (ed).
"Skepticism and International Affairs: Toward a New Realism" in *Issues in War and Peace: Philosophical Inquiries*, GROARKE, Leo.
"What If They Gave a Crisis and Nobody Came: A Hermeneutical Analysis" in *In the Interest of Peace: A Spectrum of Philosophical Views*, HIRSCHBEIN, Ron.
Hobbes and the Philosophy of International Relations. RAMOSE, Mogobe B.

INTERNATIONALISM
Some Remarks about Ethical Universalism. MOSER, Shia.

INTERPERSONAL
Is Utilitarianism Useless?. HAUSMAN, Daniel M.
Making Interpersonal Comparisons Coherently. BARRETT, Martin and HAUSMAN, Daniel.

INTERPERSONAL RELATION(S)
The Call to Personhood. MC FADYEN, Alistair I.
Difference and Subjectivity: Dialogue and Personal Identity. JACQUES, Francis.
"Personal Relationships" in *A Companion to Ethics*, LA FOLLETTE, Hugh.

INTERPOLATION
On the Existence of Polynomial Time Algorithms for Interpolation Problems in Propositional Logic. DALHAUS, E and ISRAELI, A and MAKOWSKY, J A.

INTERPRETATION
see also Hermeneutics
The Chronology of Plato's Dialogues. BRANDWOOD, Leonard.
Hellenic and Christian Studies. ARMSTRONG, A H.
Hermeneutical Studies: Dilthey, Sophocles, and Plato. WILSON, Barrie A.
L'objet-peinture: Pour une théorie de la réception. PAQUIN, Nycole.
Meaning and Mental Representation. CUMMINS, Robert.
Meaning and Speech Acts: Volume I, Principles of Language Use. VANDERVEKEN, Daniel.
Modernity, Aesthetics, and the Bounds of Art. MC CORMICK, Peter J.
Nietzsche and the Question of Interpretation. SCHRIFT, Alan D.
Nine Talmudic Readings. ARONOWICZ, Annette (trans).
Philosophical Hermeneutics and Literary Theory. WEINSHEIMER, Joel.
Philosophy of the "Gita". PATEL, Ramesh N.
Teoria e interpretazione: Per un'epistemologia delle scienze umane. BORUTTI, Silvana.
Velázquez et Goya. PIERRE, Christian (trans).
Wittgenstein: A Bibliographical Guide. FRONGIA, Guido.
"'A Nice Derangement of Epitaphs': Some Comments on Davidson and Hacking" in *Truth and Interpretation: Perspectives on the Philosophy of Donald Davidson*, DUMMETT, Michael.
"Indeterminacy of French Interpretation: Derrida and Davidson" in *Truth and Interpretation: Perspectives on the Philosophy of Donald Davidson*, WHEELER III, Samuel C.
"Interpretation and Overinterpretation: World, History, Texts" in *The Tanner Lectures On Human Values, Volume XII*, ECO, Umberto.
"The Metaphysics of Interpretation" in *Truth and Interpretation: Perspectives on the Philosophy of Donald Davidson*, ROVANE, Carol.
"A Nice Derangement of Epitaphs" in *Truth and Interpretation: Perspectives on the Philosophy of Donald Davidson*, DAVIDSON, Donald.
"On Interpreting J W Miller" in *The Philosophy of John William Miller*, GAHRINGER, Robert E.
"*Pale Fire* Solved" in *Acting and Reflecting: The Interdisciplinary Turn in Philosophy*, CARRIER, David.
"Partial Interpretation, Meaning Variance, and Incommensurability" in *Imre Lakatos and Theories of Scientific Change*, ODDIE, Graham.
"A Postmodern Language in Art" in *Postmodernism—Philosophy and the Arts (Continental Philosophy III)*, OLKOWSKI-LAETZ, Dorothea.
"Radical Interpretation and Epistemology" in *Truth and Interpretation: Perspectives on the Philosophy of Donald Davidson*, MC GINN, Colin.
"Radical Interpretation and Global Skepticism" in *Truth and Interpretation: Perspectives on the Philosophy of Donald Davidson*, KLEIN, Peter D.
"Responsibility and the Act of Interpretation: The Case of Law" in *The Political Responsibility of Intellectuals*, MACLEAN, Ian.
"Testing Theories of Interpretation" in *Truth and Interpretation: Perspectives on the Philosophy of Donald Davidson*, VERMAZEN, Bruce.
"The Third Dogma" in *Truth and Interpretation: Perspectives on the Philosophy of Donald Davidson*, KRAUT, Robert.
"Translation Theories and the Decipherment of Linear B" in *Truth and Interpretation: Perspectives on the Philosophy of Donald Davidson*, WALLACE, John.
"Truth in Meaning" in *Truth and Interpretation: Perspectives on the Philosophy of Donald Davidson*, LE PORE, Ernest.
"Vagueness, Logic and Interpretation" in *The Analytic Tradition: Philosophical Quarterly Monographs, Volume 1*, HOOKWAY, Christopher.
"Art Nonsense" or the Nine Flavours. ANAND, Mulk Raj.
"Das Wort sie sollen lassen stahn": Zur Edition und Interpretation philosophischer Texte, erläutert am B Kants. BRANDT, Reinhard.
Aesthetic Appreciation and Human Katharsis. NIARCHOS, Constantine G.
Art et cosmos. PASSERON, René.
Art et mystère. TAVARES DE MIRANDA, Maria.
Author's Position in Interpretation of a Work of Art (in Japanese). WATANABE, Hiroshi.
Congress, Consistency, and Environmental Law. LEMONS, John and BROWN, Donald A and VARNER, Gary E.
Un cosmos interprété. SPANTIDOU, Constantina.
De quelques interprétations philosophiques de l'idée artisique d'interprétation. MOUTSOPOULOS, E.
Doxology and the History of Philosophy. NORMORE, Calvin G.
The Drama of Galileo, The Past and the Present. VOISE, Waldemar.
Dynamic Predicate Logic. GROENENDIJK, Jeroen and STOKHOF, Martin.
Foucault's Critique of Heidegger. HILL, R Kevin.
History and Historical Anthropology. GOUREVITCH, Aron I.
Holism and Nonseparability. HEALEY, Richard A.
The Implications of Error for Davidsonian Charity. LARSON, David.
In Defence of "Hard" Offers: A Reply to J P Day. HÄYRY, Matti and AIRAKSINEN, Timo.
Interpretatie en filosofische methode. BUEKENS, Filip.
Interpretation and Theory in the Natural and the Human Sciences: Comments on Kuhn and Taylor. LACEY, Hugh.
Interprétation de l'art—Art de l'interprétation. TOMBRAS, Spyros.
Interprétation et philosophie de l'art. MARCONDES CÉSAR, Constança.
Interpretation of Relevant Logics in a Logic of Ternary Relations. ORLOWSKA, Ewa.
The Interpretation of Texts, People and Other Artifacts. DENNETT, Daniel C.
Interpreting Art. BLOCKER, H Gene.
Interpreting *Interpretations*. GROSSMAN, Morris.
Is *King Lear* Like the Pacific Ocean or the Washington Monument? Critical Pluralism and Literary Interpretation. PHELAN, James.
Josiah Royce: la metafisica della comunità. BUZZI GRASSI, Elisa.
Kinds of Truth and Psychoanalysis as a Myth: Some Epistemological Remarks on the Freudian Model (in Italian). BORUTTI, Silvana.
L'art comme pénétration d'un mystère. GOULA-MITACOU, Xéni.
L'interprétation comme art de création réitérée. SKOURIOTI, Athéna.
Legal Reasoning and Practical Political Education. STRAUBER, Ira.
Meaning Holism and Interpretability. TALMAGE, Catherine J L and MERCER, Mark.

INTERPRETATION
On Empirical Interpretation. MUNDY, Brent.
On Heidegger and National Socialism: A Triple Turn?. ROCKMORE, Tom.
On the Coherence of Historical Materialism. NIELSEN, Kai.
On the Logic of Contingent Relevant Implication: Conceptual Incoherence in the Intuitive Interpretation of *R*. LANCE, Mark.
An Open Letter to Maxine Greene on "The Problem of Freedom in an Era of Ecological Interdependence". BOWERS, C A.
The Pragmatist Sieve of Concepts: Description versus Interpretation. SEIGFRIED, Charlene Haddock.
Qu'est-ce qu'interpréter?. MERCIER, André.
The Rational Law-Maker and the Pragmatics of Legal Interpretation. DASCAL, Marcelo and WRÓBLEWSKI, Jerzy.
Reading Nietzsche. RISSER, James.
Response to Lyons' "Basic Rights and Constitutional Interpretations". LUCKHARDT, Grant.
Retreat from Radicality: Pöggeler on Heidegger's Politics. EDLER, Frank H W.
The *Rezeptionsgeschichte* of the Paris Manuscripts. MAIDAN, Michael.
Sawa Frydman: A Polish Legal Realist. MOS, Urszula.
Skepticism and Legal Interpretation. NATHAN, Daniel O.
Socrates and Asclepius: The Final Words. SANTILLI, Paul C.
Le statut de l'argument dialectiques d'après *Réf soph* 11, 172a9-15. DORION, Louis-André.
A Strengthening of Scott's ZF-Minus-Extensionality Result. POLLARD, Stephen.
Sul controllo nel procedimento di determinazione dei principi dell'ordinamento. COSTANZO, Angelo.
Systems of Interpretation and the Function of the Metaphor. CRIDER, Cathleen and CIRILLO, Leonard.
Thèses sur le rôle de l'interprétation dans l'art. SEEL, Gerhard.
Three Assumptions that Influence Art Education: A Description and a Critique. RICHMOND, Stuart.
Tradition and Interpretation. VAN BEECK, Frans Jozef.
Transcendance ou présence?. PARAIN-VIAL, Jeanne.
Truth in Interpretation: The Case of Psychoanalysis. ROTH, Paul A.
Understanding the Message of the Work of Art. SPASSOVA, Pravda.
The Uses of Rhetoric: Indeterminacy in Legal Reasoning, Practical Thinking and Interpretation of Literary Figures. OLMSTED, Wendy Raudenbush.
What's It All About? The Critical Method of Analysis as Applied to Drama. CLEARY JR, Donald L.
Why Are Graphs so Central in Science?. KROHN, Roger.
Work and Text. CURRIE, Gregory.
Zu einem "der tiefsten philosophischen Probleme". SIEGWART, Geo.

INTERPRETATIVE
"The Interpretive Dilemma" in *Critical Traditions in Contemporary Archaeology*, WYLIE, Alison.
"Some Reflections on Empirical Psychology: Toward an Interpretive Psychology" in *Reconsidering Psychology: Perspectives from Continental Philosophy*, KOCKELMANS, Joseph J.
The Interpretability Logic of Peano Arithmetic. BERARDUCCI, Alessandro.
Interpretation of Art as a Philosophical Problem (in Czechoslovakian). MOKREJS, Antonin.

INTERPRETATIVE SYSTEM(S)
Discourse: Noun, Verb or Social Practice?. POTTER, Jonathan (and others).

INTERROGATIVE LOGIC
What If...? Toward Excellence in Reasoning. HINTIKKA, Jaakko.

INTERSUBJECTIVITY
see also Other Minds
La intersubjectividad en Husserl, Volume I and II. IRIBARNE, Julia V.
Ontology and Alterity in Merleau-Ponty. JOHNSON, Galen A (ed).
"Two Texts on Merleau-Ponty by Emmanuel Levinas" in *Ontology and Alterity in Merleau-Ponty*, SMITH, Michael B.
"'I Am We' Consciousness and Dialog as Organizational Ethics Method". NIELSEN, Richard P.
From Intersubjectivity through Epistemology to Property: Rejoinder to Michelman. SHEARMUR, Jeremy.
Going Nowhere: Nagel on Normative Objectivity. FRIEDMAN, Marilyn.
An Intersubjective Concept of Individuality. HABERMAS, Jürgen.
A intersubjectividade em Gabriel Marcel. MORUJÁO, Alexandre Fradique.
Intersubjectivity and Critical Consciousness: Remarks on Habermas's Theory of Communicative Action. WAGNER, Gerhard and ZIPPRIAN, Heinz.
Il pensiero dello "Stato" in Husserl: recenti problemi critici. FALCIONI, Daniela.
Role Taking, Corporeal Intersubjectivity, and Self: Mead and Merleau-Ponty. BOURGEOIS, Patrick L and ROSENTHAL, Sandra B.
Umuntu Ngumuntu Ngabantu: An African Concept of Humanity. SHUTTE, Augustine.

INTERVAL(S)
Cloture Intervallaire et Extension Logique d'une Relation. ILLE, Pierre.
Concerted Instant-Interval Temporal Semantics I: Temporal Ontologies. BOCHMAN, Alexander.
Concerted Instant-Interval Temporal Semantics II: Temporal Valuations and Logics of Change. BOCHMAN, Alexander.
Expressiveness and Completeness of an Interval Tense Logic. VENEMA, Yde.

INTERVENTION
Empowering Teachers: Towards a Justification for Intervention. HARRIS, Kevin.
Justified Limits on Refusing Intervention. CHERVENAK, Frank A and MC CULLOUGH, Laurence B.

INTERVIEW(S)
Richard Rorty: An Interview (in Hebrew). KULKA, Tomas.

INTIMACY
Information, Access, or Intimate Decisions About One's Action? The Content of Privacy. INNESS, Julie.
The Molested. MAY, William F.

INTRINSIC
Panofsky, Polanyi, and Intrinsic Meaning. UN-CHOL, Shin.
Relevant Predication 2: Intrinsic Properties and Internal Relations. DUNN, J Michael.

INTRINSIC VALUE(S)
A Dialogue on Value, III: Is Everything Intrinsically Good?. LACHS, John.
Ethics and Instrumentalism: A Response to Janna Thompson. PLUMWOOD, Val.
Hume and Intrinsic Value. THOMAS, D A Lloyd.
Thoughts on the Taxonomy and Semantics of Value Terms. MARIETTA JR, Don E.

INTROSPECTION
The Way of Ideas: A Retrospective. YOLTON, John W.

INTUITION
Bergsonism. DELEUZE, Gilles.
Kant's Model of the Mind: A New Interpretation of Transcendental Idealism. WAXMAN, Wayne.
"Carnap, Quine and the Rejection of Intuition" in *Perspectives on Quine*, CREATH, Richard.
Cultural Fundamentals in Philosophy. ORUKA, H Odera.
The Epistemology of J M Keynes. O'DONNELL, Rod.
Fanaticism: Reply to Thomas Wetterström. HARE, R M.
Hacking's Experimental Argument for Realism. HOLCOMB III, Harmon R.
Kant on Concepts and Intuitions in the Mathematical Sciences. FRIEDMAN, Michael.
Kant's Account of Intuition. FALKENSTEIN, Lorne.
Kants Schemata als Anwendungsbedingungen von Kategorien auf Anschauungen. LOHMAR, Dieter.
The Nature and Significance of Intuition: A View Based on a Core Idea Held by S Radhakrishnan. FITZ, Hope K.
Practical Intuition and Rhetorical Example. SCHOLLMEIER, Paul.
Response to Squadrito's "Commentary: Interests and Equal Moral Status". DE GRAZIA, David.
La teoria hegeliana dell'autocoscienza e della sua razionalità. VARNIER, Giuseppe.

INTUITIONISM
Brouwer's Intuitionism (Studies in the History and Philosophy of Mathematics, Vol 2). VAN STIGT, W P.
"Intuitionism" in *A Companion to Ethics*, DANCY, Jonathan.
Colimit Completions and the Effective Topos. ROBINSON, Edmund and ROSOLINI, Giuseppe.
A Complete Syntactical Characterization of the Intuitionistic Logic. SKURA, Tomasz.
Crítica de Heidegger al "intuicionalismo" cartesiano. FORMENT, Eudaldo.
Dummett's Ought from Is. GREEN, Karen.
Elementary Theory of Free Heyting Algebras. IDZIAK, Pawel M.
Embedding Brouwer Algebras in the Medvedev Lattice. SORBI, Andrea.
Extended Bar Induction in Applicative Theories. RENARDEL DE LAVALETTE, Gerard R.
Information Functions with Applications. SZYMANEK, Krzysztof.
L'interpretazione costruttiva dell'implicazione. MORICONI, Enrico.
Intuitionism and Vagueness. SCHWARTZ, Stephen P and THROOP, William.
Intuitionistic Mathematics and Wittgenstein. GONZALEZ, Wenceslao J.
Kernels in N-Normal Symmetric Heyting Algebras. GALLI, A and SAGASTUME, M.
Lifschitz' Realizability. VAN OOSTEN, Jaap.
Never Say "Never"! On the Communication Problem between Intuitionism and Classicism. HELLMAN, Geoffrey.
Philosophical Reflections on the Foundations of Mathematics. COUTURE, Jocelyne and LAMBEK, Joachim.
A Problem for Intuitionism: The Apparent Possibility of Performing Infinitely Many Tasks in a Finite Time. MOORE, A W.
Some Remarks on the Algebraic Structure of the Medvedev Lattice. SORBI, Andrea.

INTUITIONISTIC LOGIC
Brouwer's Intuitionism (Studies in the History and Philosophy of Mathematics, Vol 2). VAN STIGT, W P.

INTUITIONISTIC LOGIC
Brouwerian Intuitionism. DETLEFSEN, Michael.
The Completeness of Provable Realizability. MINTS, G E.
Finite Logics and the Simple Substitution Property. HOSOI, Tsutomu and SASAKI, Katsumi.
Intuitionistic Categorial Grammar. RANTA, Aarne.
Intuitionistic Sentential Calculus with Classical Identity. LUKOWSKI, Piotr.
Intuitionistic Sentential Calculus with Identity. LUKOWSKI, Piotr.
Kripke Bundles for Intermediate Predicate Logics and Kripke Frames for Intuitionistic Modal Logics. SUZUKI, Nobu-Yuki.
The Method of Axiomatic Rejection for the Intuitionistic Propositional Logic. DUTKIEWICZ, Rafal.
Modal Counterparts of Medvedev Logic of Finite Problems Are Not Finitely Axiomatizable. SHEHTMAN, Valentin.
Nelson Algebras Through Heyting Ones^1:1. SENDLEWSKI, Andrzej.
Non-Commutative Intuitionistic Linear Logic. ABRUSCI, V Michele.
Problems of Substitution and Admissibility in the Modal System Grz and in Intuitionistic Propositional Calculus. RYBAKOV, V V.
Remarks on Special Lattices and Related Constructive Logics with Strong Negation. PAGLIANI, Piero.
Some Modifications of the Gödel Translation of Classical Intuitionistic Logic. BORICIC, Branislav.
Lo sviluppo degli studi logici nel pensiero tedesco della seconda metà dell'800. MANGIAGALLI, Maurizio.
There are Denumerably Many Ternary Intuitionistic Sheffer Functions. CUBRIC, Djordje.
Truth Table Logic with a Survey of Embeddability Results. TENNANT, Neil.
Variations on da Costa C Systems and Dual-Intuitionistic Logics (I). SYLVAN, Richard.

INTUITIONS
The Non-Reality of Free Will. DOUBLE, Richard.
Being and Categorial Intuition. COBB-STEVENS, Richard.
Linguistic Intuitions and Varieties of Ethical Naturalism. BALL, Stephen W.
On Intuitions. WETTERSTRÖM, Thomas.

INVARIANCE
Antirealism and Realist Claims of Invariance. ELDER, Crawford L.
Causal Paradoxes in Special Relativity. ARNTZENIUS, Frank.

INVENTION
Practicing the Arts of Rhetoric: Tradition and Invention. FARRELL, Thomas B.

INVERSION
What is Wrong in Inverting Spectra. CASATI, Roberto.

INVESTIGATION(S)
Wittgenstein, Ethics and Aesthetics: The View from Eternity. TILGHMAN, B R.
La investigación y las metodologías en las Ciencias Humanas. DACAL ALONSO, José Antonio.

INVOLUNTARY ACTION(S)
Beliefs and Responsibility. ELLIOTT, Car.

INWARDNESS
On the Uniqueness of Biological Research. PORTMANN, Adolph.
The Unity of the Natural Sciences: Comment on Portmann. VON UEXKUELL, Thure.

IRIGARAY, L
Essentially Speaking: Feminism, Nature and Difference. FUSS, Diana.
Patterns of Dissonance. BRAIDOTTI, Rosi.
Irigaray on Subjectivity. SCHUTTE, Ofelia.
The Lesbian, the Mother, the Heterosexual Lover: Irigaray's Recodings of Difference. HOLMLUND, Christine.

IRISH
Medical Ethics in Ireland: A Decade of Change. DOOLEY, Dolores.
Some Remarks on a Historical Theory of Justice and its Application to Ireland. MC KIM, Robert.

IRONY
Irony and the Discourse of Modernity. BEHLER, Ernst.
"Hegel's *Science of Logic*: Ironies of the Understanding" in *Essays on Hegel's Logic*, FLAY, Joseph C.
Beyond the "Limits" of *Mundane Reason*. BOGEN, David.
Boethius and the Consolation of Philosophy, or, How to Be a Good Philosopher. BELSEY, Andrew.
F M Dostoievsky (1821-1881): Great Existentialist-Psychiatrist. ESSER, P H.
From Philosophy to Politics: On Nietzsche's Ironic Metaphysics of Will to Power. PARENS, Erik.
Interpreting *Interpretations*. GROSSMAN, Morris.
The Ironist's Cage. ROTH, Michael S.
Irony and Argument in *Dialogues*, XII. DAVIS, Scott.
Irony and Method: Comments on Burbules on Dialogue. NEIMAN, Alven M.
The Irony of Richard Rorty and the Question of Political Judgment. WEISLOGEL, Eric L.
The Nature of Irony: Toward a Computational Model of Irony. LITTMAN, David C and MEY, Jacob L.
On Taking Socratic Irony Seriously (in Hebrew). SCOLNICOV, Samuel.
The Unbearable Seriousness of Irony. FERRARA, Alessandro.
What Good is Irony?. LEVINSON, Henry S.

IRRATIONAL
"The Mystique of the Nonrational and a New Spirituality" in *Archetypal Process: Self and Divine in Whitehead, Jung, and Hillman*, HEISIG, James W.
The Development of Otto's Thought 1898-1917. MINNEY, Robin.

IRRATIONALISM
Bergsonism. DELEUZE, Gilles.

IRRATIONALITY
Rationality in Action: Contemporary Approaches. MOSER, Paul K (ed).
Weakness of the Will. GOSLING, Justin.
"Metaphor, Dreamwork and Irrationality" in *Truth and Interpretation: Perspectives on the Philosophy of Donald Davidson*, CAVELL, Marcia.
The Incoherence and Irrationality of Philosophers. RADFORD, Colin.
Irrational Desires. HUBIN, Donald C.
Multiple Personality and Irrationality. GILLETT, Grant R.
Rational Chocolate Addiction or How Chocolate Cures Irrationality. ELLIOTT, C S.
Reason, Rationality and the Irrational. NAYAK, G C.

IRREVERSIBILITY
Irreversibility and Statistical Mechanics: A New Approach?. BATTERMAN, Robert W.
The Many Faces of Irreversibility. DENBIGH, K G.

IS
"The Study of Moral Development: A Bridge over the "Is-Ought" Gap" in *The Moral Domain: Essays in the Ongoing Discussion between Philosophy and the Social Sciences*, BOYD, Dwight R.
"Is" and "Ought": A Different Connection. JOHNSON, Oliver A.
'Is' Therefore 'Ought'. VERMA, Roop Rekha.
How Far Can Hume's Is-Ought Thesis Be Generalized?. SCHURZ, Gerhard.
On 'This is Red and This is Blue': *Tractatus* 6.3751. SAHU, Neelamani.

ISIDORE OF SEVILLE
Comentario a las "Sentencias" de Isidoro de Sevilla. ORTEGA MUÑOZ, Juan F.

ISLAM
Ibn Rushd: Averroes. URVOY, Dominique.
Nicholas of Cusa's de Pace Fidei and Cribratio Alkorani: Translation and Analysis. HOPKINS, Jasper.
The Tanner Lectures On Human Values, Volume XII. PETERSON, Grethe B (ed).
"Europe and Islam" in *The Tanner Lectures On Human Values, Volume XII*, LEWIS, Bernard.
"Islam in European Thought" in *The Tanner Lectures on Human Values, Volume XI*, HOURANI, Albert.
"Islamic Ethics" in *A Companion to Ethics*, NANJI, Azim.
Al-Fârâbî lógico: su exposicón de la "Isagogé" de Porfirio. RAMÓN, Rafael.
Causalistico-Occasionalistic Dispute in Islam as Opposing of "Greek" and "Islamic" Spirit (in Serbo-Croatian). BUCAN, Daniel.

ISOLATION
Species as Historical Individuals. KLUGE, Arnold G.

ISOMORPHISM
Constructing Strongly Equivalent Nonisomorphic Models for Unstable Theories. HYTTINEN, Tapani and TUURI, Heikki.
Degrees of Orderings Not Isomorphic to Recursive Linear Orderings. JOCKUSCH JR, Carl G and SOARE, Robert I.

ISRAEL
Nine Talmudic Readings. ARONOWICZ, Annette (trans).

ISRAELI
Philosophy in Israel (in Hungarian). WEILER, Gershon.

ISSUE(S)
Applying Ethics: A Text with Readings (Third Edition). OLEN, Jeffrey.

ISVARAKRSHANA
Isvarakrsna's Two-Level-Perception: Propositional and Non-Propositional. CLEAR, Edeltraud Harzer.

ITALIAN
Pour l'histoire de la fortune de Montesquieu en Italie (1789-1945). FELICE, Domenico.
Razionalitá critica: nella filosofia moderna. LAMACCHIA, Ada (ed).
Scienza, Filosofia e Religione tra '600 e '700 in Italia. PREDAVAL MAGRINI, Maria Vittoria (ed).
"Il 'Giornale de' Letterati' e le 'scienze della vita': dibattiti e interventi" in *Scienza, Filosofia e Religione tra '600 e '700 in Italia*, BOARETTI, Tiziano.
"L'Accademia delle scienze di Bologna: l'edizione del primo tomo dei 'Commentarii' (1731)" in *Scienza, Filosofia e Religione tra '600 e '700 in Italia*, DE ZAN, Mauro.
"Il corpuscolarismo italiano nel 'Giornale de' Letterati' di Roma (1668-1681)" in *Scienza, Filosofia e Religione tra '600 e '700 in Italia*, LOPICCOLI, Fiorella.
"Filosofia e politica in Giammaria Ortes" in *Scienza, Filosofia e Religione tra '600 e '700 in Italia*, GIACOTTO, Paolo.

ITALIAN

"Giovanni Gualberto (Alberto) De Soria e la 'Cosmologia'" in *Scienza, Filosofia e Religione tra '600 e '700 in Italia*, PONZELLINI, Ornella.
"Pier Caterino Zeno le vicende culturali del 'Giornale de' Letterati d'Italia'" in *Scienza, Filosofia e Religione tra '600 e '700 in Italia*, GENERALI, Dario.
Il dibattito italiano sullo statuto della filosofia politica: Contributo ad una bibliographia. BACCELLI, Luca.
La diffusione del pensiero spagnolo contemporaneo nell'Italia di oggi. SAVIGNANO, Armando.
La disputa sulle origini della neoscolastica italiana: Salvatore Roselli, Vincenzo Buzzetti e Gaetano Sanseverino. SCHMIDINGER, H M.
Gramsci, Croce and the Italian Political Tradition. BELLAMY, Richard.
Gramsci, Gentile and the Theory of the Ethical State in Italy. SCHECTER, Darrow.
Italian Marxism and Philosophy of Culture (in Polish). PAPULI, Giovanni.
La neoscolastica italiana dalle sue prime manifestazioni all'enciclica *Aeterni Patris*. ROSSI, G F.
Lo statuo della filosofia politica nel dibattito italiano. BACCELLI, Luca.
Sulla semiotizzazione dell' "a priori": Rossi-Landi e Hjelmslev. CAPUTO, Cosimo.
Il volgarizzamento del "De Rerum natura" di Bernardino Telesio a opera di Francesco Martelli. PIEROZZI, Letizia and SCAPPARONE, Elisabetta.

ITERATION

Iteration Again. BOOLOS, George.

JACKSON, F

Jackson Classifying Conditionals. DUDMAN, V H.
Jackson on Classifying Conditionals. LOWE, E J.

JACOBEAN

Walt Whitman: Jacobin Poet of American Democracy. MOSHER, Michael.
Why Should a Dialectician Learn to Count to Four?. ZIZEK, Slavoj.

JAINISM

Dravya, Guna and *Paryāya* in Jaina Thought. SONI, Jayandra.

JAKOBSON, R

Metaphor, Literalism, and the Non-Verbal Arts. BREDIN, Hugh.

JAMES

American Philosophy and the Romantic Tradition. GOODMAN, Russell B.
Dialogue with the Other: The Inter-Religious Dialogue. TRACY, David.
Ethical Practice in Clinical Medicine. ELLOS, William J.
Experiential Method: Qualitative Research in the Humanities Using Metaphysics and Phenomenology. KIDD, James W.
Pragmatism: From Peirce to Davidson. MURPHY, John P.
Analisi fenomenologica del concetto di religione. MONDIN, Battista.
Blanshard on Philosophical Style. SMITH, John E.
Consideraciones en torno al concepto de verdad según el pragmatismo. GORDILLO, Lourdes.
James and Bowne on the Philosophy of Religious Experience. DOTTERER, Donald W.
James and Freud. MYERS, Gerald E.
James, Rationality and Religious Belief. WAINWRIGHT, W J.
Das neue (post-analytische) Interesse an der Präanalytischen Philosophie. NAGL, Ludwig.
Pascal on Self-Caused Belief. DAVIS, Stephen T.
The Pragmatist Sieve of Concepts: Description versus Interpretation. SEIGFRIED, Charlene Haddock.
Sartre and James on the Role of the Body in Emotion. BAUGH, Bruce.
William James and the Nature of Thinking: A Framework for Elfie. MELVILLE, Mary E.
William James's Theory of Mind. COOPER, W E.

JAMES, H

Henry James and the Paradox of Literary Mastery. BLAIR, Sara.

JANSENISM

American Moralism and the Origin of Bioethics in the United States. JONSEN, Albert R.

JAPANESE

see also Buddhism
Das Ich im deutschen Idealismus und das Selbst im Zen-Buddhist Fichte und Dogen. NAGASAWA, Kunihiko.
"Fiduciary Relationships and the Medical Profession: A Japanese Point of View" in *Ethics, Trust, and the Professions: Philosophical and Cultural Aspects*, KIMURA, Rihito.
"Murasaki Shikibu" in *A History of Women Philosophers, Volume II: Medieval, Renaissance and Enlightenment, A.D. 500-1600*, WAITHE, Mary Ellen.
"'Tradition' et 'Innovation' dans la musique" in *XIth International Congress in Aesthetics, Nottingham 1988*, TAMBA, Akira.
Buddhist Views of Suicide and Euthanasia. BECKER, Carl B.
Contestation and Consensus: The Morality of Abortion in Japan. LA FLEUR, William R.
Death, Honor, and Loyalty: The Bushidō Ideal. HURST III, G Cameron.
Heidegger and the Japanese Connection. BILIMORIA, Purusottama.
Husserl and the Japanese. WELTON, Donn.
Individual and Social Morality in Japan and the United States: Rival Conceptions of the Self. MAC INTYRE, Alasdair.
Intimacy: A General Orientation in Japanese Religious Values. KASULIS, Thomas P.
Japan's Dilemma with the Definition of Death. KIMURA, Rihito.
Japanese Ethics: Beyond Good and Evil. WARGO, Robert J J.
A Morality Based on Trust: Some Reflections on Japanese Morality. YAMAMOTO, Yutaka.
Psychoactive Drug Prescribing in Japan: Epistemological and Bioethical Considerations. SAKAI, Akio.
A Response to 'Psychoactive Drug Prescribing in Japan'. COVERDALE, John.
Response to Dr Sakai's 'Psychoactive Drug Prescribing in Japan'. RITCHIE, Karen.
The Self in Medieval Japanese Buddhism: Focusing on Dōgen. KIMURA, Kiyotaka.
Sincerity and Japanese Values. REASONER, Paul.

JARRETT, J

Jarrett Completeness and Superluminal Signals. KRONZ, Frederick M.

JASPERS

Toward the Death of Man. KLUBACK, William.
An Abyss of Difference: Laing, Sartre and Jaspers. KIRSNER, Douglas.
Glasnost and Enlightenment. OLSON, Alan M.

JAYARASI

A Critique of Jayarasi's Critique of Perception. MOHANTA, D K.

JEALOUSY

Envy and Jealousy. BEN-ZEEV, Aaron.

JEFFERSON

The Enlightenment in American Law I: The Declaration of Independence. RECK, Andrew J.

JEFFREY, R

A Reconstruction of Jeffrey's Notion of Ratifiability in Terms of Counterfactual Beliefs. SHIN, Hyung Song.

JESUS

see also Christ
Four Perspectives on Moral Judgement: The Rational Principles of Jesus and Kant. PALMQUIST, Stephen R.
Verily, Nietzsche's Judgment of Jesus. ROTH, Robin A.

JEVONS, W

The Correspondence between George Boole and Stanley Jevons, 1863-1864. GRATTAN-GUINNESS, I.
Jevons's Applications of Utilitarian Theory to Economic Policy. PEART, Sandra J.

JEWISH

see also Judaism
In Partnership with God: Contemporary Jewish Law and Ethics. SHERWIN, Byron L.
The Realm of Humanitas: Responses to the Writings of Hannah Arendt. GARNER, Reuben (ed).
Sacred Fragments: Recovering Theology for the Modern Jew. GILLMAN, Neil.
Thinking the Unthinkable: Meanings of the Holocaust. GOTTLIEB, Roger S (ed).
"The Face of Truth in Rosenzweig, Levinas, and Jewish Mysticism" in *Phenomenology of the Truth Proper to Religion*, COHEN, Richard A.
Ethical Issues in Bankruptcy: A Jewish Perspective. TAMARI, Meir.
Jewish Faith and the Holocaust. COHN-SHERBOK, Dan.
Some Observations on the Influence of Christian Scholastic Authors on Jewish Thinkers in the 13th and 14th Century. REEDIJK, Wim M.
Wittgenstein on Jews: Some Counter-Examples. WASSERMANN, Gerhard D.

JOHN OF SALISBURY

Salisburian Stakes: The Uses of 'Tyranny' in John of Salisbury's *Policraticus*. FORHAN, Kate Langdon.

JOHN OF ST THOMAS

El problema de los universales en Juan de Santo Tomás en Juan de Santo Tomás. BEUCHOT, Mauricio.

JOHN OF THE CROSS

Algunos giros en torno a san Juan de la Cruz. VALDIVIA, Benjamín.

JOHN PAUL II

"Parallels on Work, Theory and Practice in Yves R Simon and John Paul II" in *Freedom in the Modern World: Jacques Maritain, Yves R Simon, Mortimer J Adler*, GUEGUEN, John A.

JOHNSON, M

Materiality and Aquinas' Natural Philosophy: A Reply to Johnson. KNASAS, John F X.

JOHNSON, S

Fictions of Reality in the Age of Hume and Johnson. DAMROSCH, Leo.

JONAS, H

Ethik zwischen globaler Verantwortung und spekulativer Weltschematik. JOOS, Egbert.
Responsibility As a Moral Principle? A Critical Reflection on Hans Jonas' Ethics of Responsibility? (in German). KETTNER, Matthias.

JONSEN, A

Getting Down to Cases: The Revival of Casuistry in Bioethics. ARRAS, John D.

JORGENSEN, J

Logic Without Truth. ALCHOURRÓN, Carlos E and MARTINO, Antonio A.

JOURNALISM

"Social Theory and Political Practice: Unger's Brazilian Journalism" in *Critique and Construction: A Symposium on Roberto Unger's "Politics"*, SIMON, William H.

Truth, Neutrality, and Conflict of Interest. LICHTENBERG, Judith.

Waiting for a New St Benedict: Alasdair MacIntyre and the Theory and Practice of Journalism. LAMBETH, Edmund B.

JUDAISM

Encounter on the Narrow Ridge: A Life of Martin Buber. FRIEDMAN, Maurice.

Franz Rosenzweig: Existentielles Denken und gelebte Bewährung. SCHMIED-KOWARZIK, Wolfdietrich.

In Partnership with God: Contemporary Jewish Law and Ethics. SHERWIN, Byron L.

Nine Talmudic Readings. ARONOWICZ, Annette (trans).

"Jewish Ethics" in *A Companion to Ethics*, KELLNER, Menachem.

"Science and Religion—the Jewish Position" in *Science and Religion: One World-Changing Perspectives on Reality*, BLOEMENDAL, M.

Discovering God in Western Civilization. BRESLAUER, S Daniel.

The Historical Event as a Cultural Indicator: The Case of Judaism. NEUSNER, Jacob.

Judaism, Justice, and Access to Health Care. MACKLER, Aaron L.

Spinoza en de geopenbaarde godsdienst. DE DIJN, H.

Tempo ed eternità: La filosofia narrante di F Rosenzweig. DI MARCO, Chiara.

The Foundations of Franz Rosenzweig's Theory of Knowledge (in Hebrew). AMIR, Yehoyada.

What Philosophy for Judaism and Christianity? (in French). DUPONCHEELE, Joseph.

JUDEO-CHRISTIAN

Le existentia de deo e le Immortalitate del Anima: Lineas de Philosophia del Esser. BLANDINO, Giovanni.

JUDEO-CHRISTIAN TRADITION

The Co-Existence of God and Evil. TRAU, Jane Mary.

Dream and Culture: An Anthropological Study of the Western Intellectual Tradition. PARMAN, Susan.

Science versus Religion. CLEMENTS, Tad S.

JUDGE(S)

Do the Right Thing. SUTTLE, Bruce B.

Interpretation and the Social Reality of Law. GOLDFORD, Dennis.

Non-professional Judicial Reasoning. TAPANI KLAMI, Hannu.

Reply to Lowenthal. COLMO, Christopher A.

The Teacher as Judge: A Brief Sketch of Two Fairness Principles. KATZ, Michael S.

JUDGING

"Judging—The Actor and the Spectator" in *The Realm of Humanitas: Responses to the Writings of Hannah Arendt*, BERNSTEIN, Richard J.

JUDGMENT(S)

see also Aesthetic Judgment, Moral Judgment(s)

The Anatomy of Judgment. REGAL, Philip J.

Human Goodness: Generosity and Courage. PYBUS, Elizabeth.

Kant's Transcendental Psychology. KITCHER, Patricia.

Logic in the Husserlian Context. TITO, Johanna Maria.

The Preface to Thomistic Metaphysics. KNASAS, John F X.

The Unity of Kant's "Critique of Pure Reason": Experience, Language, and Knowledge. WILLIAMS, T C.

Untersuchungen zur Theorie des hypothetischen Urteils. LINNEWEBER-LAMMERSKITTEN, Helmut.

Weakness of the Will. GOSLING, Justin.

"How to Reason About Value Judgments" in *Key Themes in Philosophy*, CLARK, Stephen R L.

"Value Judgments and Normative Claims" in *Key Themes in Philosophy*, SINGER, Marcus G.

"A voz prometida: Sobre a imaginação na *Kritik der Urteilskraft*" in *Dinâmica do Pensar: Homenagem a Oswaldo Market*, MOLDER, Maria Filomena.

Akratic Action and the Practical Role of Better Judgment. MELE, Alfred R.

Constrained Discourse and Public Life. MOON, J Donald.

A Dilemma of Late Life Memory. MC KEE, Patrick.

Double Standards, Racial Equality and the Right Reference Class. ADLER, Jonathan E.

Education for Judgment. JAMES, William.

Ethics and Educational Administration: Are Ethical Politics "Ethical"?. RUDDER, Charles F.

A Fat Worm of Error?. MC GHEE, Michael.

Hölderlin über Urteil und Sein. GRAESER, Andreas.

Judgment and Rationality in Lyotard's Discursive Archipelago. HENDLEY, Steven.

Kant's Apotheosis of Genius. QUINN, Timothy Sean.

Kant's Theory of Empirical Judgment and Modern Semantics. HANNA, Robert.

Kants "Reflexionen zur Ästhetik": Zur Werkgeschichte der "Kritik der ästhetischen Urteilskraft". FRANK, Manfred.

Kants Begriff der synthetischen Urteile a priori. ROS, Arno.

Kants *Kritik der Urteilskraft*. RAYMAEKERS, Bart.

MacIntyre on Hume. BAIER, Annette C.

A New Interpretation of Russell's Multiple-Relation Theory of Judgment. LANDINI, Gregory.

Nietzschean Perspectivism and the Logic of Practical Reason. REDDING, Paul.

Les présupposés métaphysiques de la "lisibilité" de l'être. KÜHN, Rolf.

Le problématologique devant la faculté de juger. PARRET, Herman.

Quelques remarques sur la composition de la *Dialectique de la faculté de juger téléologique*. KOPPER, Joachim.

La réflexion dans l'esthétique kantienne. LYOTARD, Jean-François.

Three Notions of Judgement (in Czechoslovakian). KOTATKO, Petr.

Der Übergang vom Bestimmt-Bestimmenden zum freien Schema in Kants Kritik der Urteilskraft. KAULBACH, Friedrich.

Universalistische Ethik und Urteilskraft: ein aristotelischer Blick auf Kant. HÖFFE, Otfried.

Zur Erkenntnistheorie des Ästhetischen: Schopenhauers Beziehung zu Kant. DÖRFLINGER, Bernd.

JUDICIARY

Moral Pluralism and Legal Neutrality. SADURSKI, Wojciech.

Black and White Together: A Reconsideration. ALLEN, W B.

Constitutional Democracy and the Legitimacy of Judicial Review. FREEMAN, Samuel.

Does Strict Judicial Scrutiny Involve the *Tu Quoque* Fallacy?. SCHEDLER, George.

Justification et justice procédurale. DUHAMEL, André.

Law: From Foundation to Argumentation. LEMPEREUR, Alain.

Non-professional Judicial Reasoning. TAPANI KLAMI, Hannu.

On Judicial Ascertainment of Facts. VARGA, Csaba.

JULIAN

Libertad como posibilidad, libertad como necesidad: Juliano y San Agustín. PEGUEROLES, Juan.

JULIAN OF NORWICH

"Julian of Norwich" in *A History of Women Philosophers, Volume II: Medieval, Renaissance and Enlightenment, A.D. 500-1600*, EVASDAUGHTER, Elizabeth N.

JUMP(S)

Jumping with Random Reals. BARTOSZYNSKI, Tomek and JUDAH, Haim.

Jumps of Nontrivial Splittings of Recursively Enumerable Sets. INGRASSIA, Michael A and LEMPP, Steffen.

JUNG

Archetypal Process: Self and Divine in Whitehead, Jung, and Hillman. GRIFFIN, David Ray (ed).

"Jung and Whitehead on Self and Divine: The Necessity for Symbol and Myth" in *Archetypal Process: Self and Divine in Whitehead, Jung, and Hillman*, SLUSSER, Gerald H.

"The Necessity for Symbol and Myth: A Literary Amplification" in *Archetypal Process: Self and Divine in Whitehead, Jung, and Hillman*, SELLERY, J'Nan Morse.

"Psychocosmetics and the Underworld Connection" in *Archetypal Process: Self and Divine in Whitehead, Jung, and Hillman*, KELLER, Catherine.

'Desire' in Yoga and Jung. COWARD, Harold.

JUNGER, E

Nietzsche and Ernst Jünger: From Nihilism to Totalitarianism. OHANA, David.

JURIDICAL

Fonti diritto e regole. DE GIACOMO, Claudio.

Introduction Critique au Droit Naturel. HERVADA, Javier.

Philosophie Juridique Européenne. TRIGEAUD, Jean-Marc.

"L'égalité ambiguë: construction juridique ou déduction métaphysique?" in *Égalité Uguaglianza*, WUNENBURGER, Jean-Jacques.

"L'égalité des droits en 1789" in *Égalité Uguaglianza*, GOYARD-FABRE, Simone.

The Background to Bentham on Evidence. LEWIS, A D E.

Conceptions of Justification in Legal Discourse. WROBLEWSKI, Jerzy.

La subversion de l'"elenchos" juridique dans l'"Apologie de Socrate". DORION, Louis-André.

JURISPRUDENCE

see also Law

Die moderne Gesellschaft im Rechtsstaat. BAURMANN, Michael.

Philosophy of Law: An Introduction to Jurisprudence (Revised Edition). MURPHY, Jeffrie G.

Bentham, Science and the Construction of Jurisprudence. JACOBS, Struan.

The Concept of Jurisprudence. ALEXY, Robert and DREIER, Ralf.

Dworkin and His Critics: The Relevance of Ethical Theory in Philosophy of Law. BALL, Stephen W.

JURISPRUDENCE
Jurisprudential Oaks from Mythical Acorns: The Hart-Dworkin Debate Revisited. BOON LEONG PHANG, Andrew.
Natural Law Theory: The Link Between its Descriptive Strength and its Prescriptive Strength. BRAYBROOKE, David.
Paradigms of Legal Science. JORI, Mario.
Soggetto e senso del diritto nell'esperienza giuridica moderna: appunti in tema di positività. FIASCHI, Giovanni.
What Is Jurisprudence About? Theories, Definitions, Concepts, or Conceptions of Law?. BAYLES, Michael D.

JUST WAR
The Making of a Nuclear Peace: The Task of Today's Just War Theorists. SICHOL, Marcia W.
Understanding War: A Philosophical Inquiry. MC MURTRY, John.
Just War Theory and the ANC's Armed Struggle. MILLER, S R.
Just War Theory: The Case of South Africa. MILLER, S R.
The Nurture of War: "Just War" Theory's Contribution. SANTONI, Ronald E.
On the Morality of Waging War Against the State. MILLER, Seumas.

JUSTICE
see also Distributive Justice
The Anatomy of Judgment. REGAL, Philip J.
Civil Disobedience in Focus. BEDAU, Hugo Adam (ed).
Introduction Critique au Droit Naturel. HERVADA, Javier.
John Locke: Segundo Tratado sobre el Gobierno Civil. MELLIZO, Carlos (trans).
Justice and the Good Life. DWORKIN, Ronald.
Justice: Alternative Political Perspectives (Second Edition). STERBA, James P (ed).
The Law of Karma: A Philosophical Study. REICHENBACH, Bruce R.
The Meaning of Socialism. LUNTLEY, Michael.
Moral Dealing: Contract, Ethics, and Reason. GAUTHIER, David.
Morals, Motivation and Convention: Hume's Influential Doctrines. SNARE, Francis.
The Nature of Politics. MASTERS, Roger D.
Philosophical Foundations of Health Education. LAURA, Ronald S.
Philosophie Juridique Européenne. TRIGEAUD, Jean-Marc.
Philosophy of Law (Fourth Edition). FEINBERG, Joel.
Philosophy: An Introduction Through Literature. KLEIMAN, L (ed).
Policraticus. NEDERMAN, Cary J (ed & trans).
Rawls: "A Theory of Justice" and Its Critics. KUKATHAS, Chandran.
Reading Rawls: Critical Studies on Rawls' 'A Theory of Justice'. DANIELS, Norman (ed).
Resurrecting Marx: The Analytical Marxists on Freedom, Exploitation, and Justice. GORDON, David.
Robert Nozick: Property, Justice, and the Minimal State. WOLFF, Jonathan.
Science and Moral Values. VOLLRATH, John.
Self, Society, and Personal Choice. MEYERS, Diana T.
What Is Justice? Classic and Contemporary Readings. SOLOMON, Robert C (ed).
"Justice and Love in the Political Thought of St Augustine" in *Grace, Politics and Desire: Essays on Augustine*, PAREL, Anthony J.
"Justice and Solidarity: On the Discussion Concerning Stage 6" in *The Moral Domain: Essays in the Ongoing Discussion between Philosophy and the Social Sciences*, HABERMAS, Jürgen.
"Justice in the Flesh" in *Ontology and Alterity in Merleau-Ponty*, LEVIN, David Michael.
"Liberty, Community, and Corrective Justice" in *Liability and Responsibility*, WEINRIB, Ernest J.
"National Health Insurance: How Just Must We Be?" in *Biomedical Ethics Reviews, 1990*, FLECK, Leonard M.
"Pacifism and Revolution" in *In the Interest of Peace: A Spectrum of Philosophical Views*, DONAGHY, John.
"Peace Through Justice: A Practical Reconciliation of Opposing Conceptions of Justice" in *In the Interest of Peace: A Spectrum of Philosophical Views*, STERBA, James.
"Punishment and Self-Defense" in *Liability and Responsibility*, FLETCHER, George P.
'Domina et Regina Virtutum': Justice and *Societas* in *De Officiis*. ATKINS, E M.
The 'Voice of Care': Implications for Bioethical Education. CARSE, Alisa L.
Adam Smith and Social Justice: The Ethical Basis of *The Wealth of Nations*. OSSAR, Jacob.
Affirmative Action Revisited: Justice and Public Policy Considerations. VANTERPOOL, Rudolph V.
Allocution Made to a Magistrate. PAREL, A J (ed & trans) and MACHIAVELLI, Niccolò.
Animal Liberators are Not Anti-Science. MAGEL, Charles.
Aquinas on Almsgiving, Justice and Charity: An Interpretation and Reassessment. POPE, Stephen J.
Aristotle on Justice, Equality and the Rule of Law. QUINN, Michael.
Bargaining with the Not-Yet-Born: Gauthier's Contractarian Theory of Inter-Generational Justice and Its Limitations. DE-SHALIT, A.
The Compatibility of Justice and Kindness. PUTMAN, Daniel.
Constructing Justice. GIBBARD, Allan.
Cosmic Justice in Anaximander. ENGMANN, Joyce.
Deficiencies in Contemporary Theories of Justice. LÖTTER, H P P.
Democracy and Justice in Health Policy. JENNINGS, Bruce.
Entitled to Clemency: Mercy in the Criminal Law. JOHNSON, Carla Ann Hage.
Filosofía, justicia y amor. LEVINAS, E and EZCURRA, Alicia Villar.
Free Speech, Free Exchange, and Rawlsian Liberalism. SHAPIRO, Daniel.
Games, Fairness, and Rawls's *A Theory of Justice*. LADEN, Anthony.
Gilligan on Justice and Care: Two Interpretations. VREEKE, G J.
Judaism, Justice, and Access to Health Care. MACKLER, Aaron L.
Justice and Aristotelian Practical Reason. DAHL, Norman.
Justice, Redistribution, and the Family. POST, Stephen G.
Justice: The Root of American Business Ideology and Ethics. MC GOWAN, Richard.
Justification et justice procédurale. DUHAMEL, André.
The Justification of Justice as Fairness: A Two Stage Process. VAGGALIS, Ted.
Kann in O Höffes Ethik der politischen Gerechtigkeit eine ökologische Ethik aufgehoben werden?. WETZEL, Manfred.
Kant the Liberal, Kant the Anarchist: Rawls and Lyotard on Kantian Justice. MAY, Todd G.
Lyotard's "Kantian Socialism". GEIMAN, Kevin Paul.
Machiavelli's Notions of Justice: Text and Analysis. PAREL, A J.
Market Mechanisms and Principles of Justice. LOEWY, Erich H.
Marxisten und Christen für eine gerechte, friedliche Welt. NEHRING, Hartmut.
Murphy and Mercy. ADLER, Jacob.
Nature, Justice, and Duty in the *Defensor Pacis*: Marsiglio of Padua's Ciceronian Impulse. NEDERMAN, Cary J.
Neuvermessung des Rechts- und Staatsdiskurses: Zu Otfried Höffes Theorie der Politischen Gerechtigkeit. SITTER-LIVER, Beat.
A Note on the Jural Relation. BUTLER, Ken.
Nozick on Social Justice. AGARWALA, Binod Kumar.
Nozick's Identity Crisis. LUCY, W N R.
Philosophy: Sections 86-93 (pp 405-35) of the So-Called "Big Typescript" (Catalog Number 213)—Ludwig Wittgenstein. WITTGENSTEIN, Ludwig and NYMAN, Heikki.
Politica e diritto in Hobbes. BAGLIONI, Emma.
Political Justice in Post-Communist Societies: The Case of Hungary. BENCE, György.
Précis of "Whose Justice? Which Rationality?". MAC INTYRE, Alasdair.
Propriété de soi et propriété du monde extérieur. COUTURE, Jocelyne.
Punishment and Loss of Moral Standing. MORRIS, Christopher W.
Reforming Britain's National Health Service. KESSEL, Ros.
Rethinking the Diodotean Argument. JOHNSON, Laurie M.
Should Basic Care Get Priority? Doubts about Rationing the Oregon Way. VEATCH, Robert M.
Some Remarks on a Historical Theory of Justice and its Application to Ireland. MC KIM, Robert.
St Thomas on the Motives of Unjust Acts. WEITHMAN, Paul J.
The Superfluity of the Original Position. DEN HARTOGH, G A.
A Theory of Social Justice?. HORTON, John.
Two Concepts of Justice. CHAKRAVARTI, A.
The Unjust Treatment of Polemarchus. PAGE, Carl.
Utilitarian Strategies in Bentham and John Stuart Mill. KELLY, P J.

JUSTIFIABILITY
The Concept of Objectivity: An Approximation. BUTLER, Kenneth G.
Ecosabotage and Civil Disobedience. MARTIN, Michael.
Whose Education Is It Anyway?. TAMIR, Yael.

JUSTIFICATION
Civil Disobedience in Focus. BEDAU, Hugo Adam (ed).
Epistemic Justification: Essays in the Theory of Knowledge. ALSTON, William P.
Epistemics. DURAN, Jane.
Foundations of Moral and Political Philosophy. PAUL, Ellen Frankel (ed).
Issues in War and Peace: Philosophical Inquiries. KUNKEL, Joseph (ed).
Knowledge in Perspective: Selected Essays in Epistemology. SOSA, Ernest.
Reasons and Experience. MILLAR, Alan.
Universalism versus Communitarianism: Contemporary Debates in Ethics. RASMUSSEN, David.
"Appreciation and Justification" in *XIth International Congress in Aesthetics, Nottingham 1988*, FEAGIN, Susan.
"How Not to Defend Liberal Institutions" in *Liberalism and the Good*, BARRY, Brian.
"Illogical Belief" in *Philosophical Perspectives, 3: Philosophy of Mind and Action Theory, 1989*, SALMON, Nathan.
"Responsibility and 'Free Will'" in *Key Themes in Philosophy*, VESEY, Godfrey.
L' "altro inizio" della filosofia: I *Beiträge zur Philosophie* di Heidegger. SAMONÀ, Leonardo.
"Everyone's Doing It"—A Reply to Richard DeGeorge. GREEN, Ronald M.
The Argument from Religious Experience: A Narrowing of Alternatives. KETCHUM, Richard.
Argumentation—Distributed or Monological?. BARTH, E M.

JUSTIFICATION
Beyond Numerical and Causal Accuracy: Expanding the Set of Justificational Criteria. RAMSEY, Jeffry L.
Can There Be Justified Philosophical Beliefs?. NIELSEN, Kai.
Can Utilitarianism Be Salvaged as a Theory for Social Choice?. VAN ASPEREN, G M.
Conceptions of Justification in Legal Discourse. WROBLEWSKI, Jerzy.
Conservatism and Tacit Confirmation. ADLER, Jonathan E.
Deconstructing Community Self-Paternalism. SCHONSHECK, Jonathan.
El desarrollo como proceso: una investigación filosófica. DOWER, Nigel.
Directions of Justification in the Negative-Positive Duty Debate. MALM, H M.
Epistemic Internalism's Dilemma. HETHERINGTON, Stephen Cade.
Epistemic Justification and Psychological Realism. TAYLOR, James E.
Epistemic Norms and Evolutionary Success. CLARKE, Murray.
Epistemology on Holiday. KAPLAN, Mark.
The Ethics of Statistical Discrimination. MAITZEN, Stephen.
The Fallibility Paradox. LEHRER, Keith and KIM, Kihyeon.
The Foundationalist Justification of Epistemic Principles. REMEDIOS, F.
Gettier's Principle for Deducibility of Justification. BASU, Sandhya.
How is Philosophy Possible?. SCHICK JR, Theodore W.
How Wide Is the Gap Between Facts and Values?. RESCHER, Nicholas.
The Importance of Being Human. MC NAUGHTON, David.
Institutional Animal Care and Use Committees and the Moderate Position. STEPHENSON, Wendell.
Internalism and Epistemically Responsible Belief. GRECO, John.
Justice in Preferential Hiring. SINGER, M S and SINGER, A E.
The Justification for Relevance Logic. BAGHRAMIAN, Maria.
Justification in the 20th Century. PLANTINGA, Alvin.
The Justification of Justice as Fairness: A Two Stage Process. VAGGALIS, Ted.
Justification, Truth, Goals, and Pragmatism: Comments on Stich's "Fragmentation of Reason". HARMAN, Gilbert.
Kant on Justification in Transcendental Philosophy. PEREBOOM, Derk.
Liberal Education in an Unfree World. LA BRECQUE, Richard.
Liberalismo e democrazia: la giustificazione estetica di Rorty. MARRONE, Pierpaolo.
Mathematics and Philosophy: The Story of a Misunderstanding. ROTA, GianCarlo.
The Message of Affirmative Action. HILL JR, Thomas E.
Modest A Priori Knowledge. SUMMERFIELD, Donna M.
Moral Experience and Justification. SINNOTT-ARMSTRONG, Walter.
Moral Skepticism and Moral Education. BARCALOW, Emmett.
Moral Skepticism. COPP, David.
Non-professional Judicial Reasoning. TAPANI KLAMI, Hannu.
Normativity and the Very Idea of Moral Epistemology. COPP, David.
Occasions for Argumentation. HILPINEN, Risto.
On Falsificationist Interpretations of Peirce. SULLIVAN, Patrick F.
On the Alleged Methodological Infirmity of Ethics. MOODY-ADAMS, Michele M.
Philosophy of Science: From Justification to Explanation. KANTOROVICH, Aharon.
Recent Obituaries of Epistemology. HAACK, Susan.
The Right to Self-Determination. BERG, Jonathan.
Scientific Realism, Perceptual Beliefs, and Justification. OTTE, Richard.
Should Philosophy be Applied?. NESBITT, Winston.
Sobre justificación y verdad: respuesta a León Olivé. VILLORO, Luis.
Some Dependence Relations of Empirical Belief. MALHERBE, Jeanette.
Some Recent Work in Epistemology. MOSER, Paul K.
Taking Role Moralities Seriously. WUESTE, Daniel E.
The Trouble With Goldman's Reliabilism. GLEB, Gary.
Truth in Epistemology. STURGEON, Scott.
Truth, Justification and the Inescapability of Epistemology: Comments on Copp. RUSSELL, Bruce.
Utilitarianism and the Idea of Reflective Equilibrium. TERSMAN, Folke.

JUVENILE(S)
Discretion, Punishment, and Juvenile Justice. SCHRAG, Francis.

KADARE, I
The Concert: Mao's Panopticon. TALMOR, Sascha.

KAFKA
Deceptive Comfort: The Power of Kafka's Stories. BENNETT, Jane.
Metamorphoses: On the Limits of Thought. ALEXAKOS, Panos D.

KALAM
The "Kalam" Cosmological Argument and the Hypothesis of a Quiescent Universe. CRAIG, William Lane.

KANGER, S
Deontic Logic and Possible World Semantics: A Historical Sketch. WOLENSKI, Jan.

KANT
Ästhetik des Abschieds: Kritik der Moderne. EBELING, Hans.
Between Freiburg and Frankfurt: Toward a Critical Ontology. DALLMAYR, Fred R.
The Communicative Ethics Controversy. BENHABIB, Seyla (ed).
Dinâmica do Pensar: Homenagem a Oswaldo Market. FAC LETRAS UNIV LISBOA (ed).
Fallen Freedom: Kant on Radical Evil and Moral Regeneration. MICHALSON JR, Gordon E.
For What May I Hope? Thinking with Kant and Kierkegaard. FENDT, Gene.
Frege and Other Philosophers. DUMMETT, Michael.
Goethe, Kant, and Hegel: Volume I, Discovering the Mind. KAUFMANN, Walter.
The Idea of the Miraculous: The Challenge to Science and Religion. WILLIAMS, T C.
Ideas, Principios y Dialectica. LAFUENTE, Maria Isabel.
Kant's Model of the Mind: A New Interpretation of Transcendental Idealism. WAXMAN, Wayne.
Kant's System of Rights. MULHOLLAND, Leslie A.
Kant's Theory of Freedom. ALLISON, Henry E.
Kant's Transcendental Psychology. KITCHER, Patricia.
Kants Kategorischer Imperativ als Leitfaden humaner Praxis. NISTERS, Thomas.
Knowledge of the External World. AUNE, Bruce.
Una lettura idealistica della "Analitica Trascendentale". BELLINI, Ornella.
Max Scheler's Concept of the Person: An Ethics of Humanism. PERRIN, Ron.
Modern Faith and Thought. THIELICKE, Helmut.
Moral Dealing: Contract, Ethics, and Reason. GAUTHIER, David.
Die Moral der Vernunft Tanszendentale Handlungs-und Legitimationstheorie in der Philosophie Kants. SANDERMANN, Edmund.
Moralische Verbindlichkeit oder Erziehung. LANGEWAND, Alfred.
Morality—What's In It For Me?: A Historical Introduction to Ethics. NELSON, William N.
The Natural and the Normative: Theories of Spatial Perception from Kant to Helmholtz. HATFIELD, Gary.
The Persistence of Modernity: Essays on Aesthetics, Ethics, and Postmodernism. WELLMER, Albrecht.
A Philosophy of Morals. HELLER, Agnes.
The Unity of Kant's "Critique of Pure Reason": Experience, Language, and Knowledge. WILLIAMS, T C.
The Unity of Understanding: A Study in Kantian Problems. SCHWYZER, Hubert.
Das Verhängnis Erste Philosophie. EBELING, Hans.
"The 'Essential Properties' of Matter, Space, and Time: Comments on Michael Friedman" in *Philosophical Perspectives on Newtonian Science*, DI SALLE, Robert.
"Apperception and Epistemic Responsibility" in *Central Themes in Early Modern Philosophy*, KITCHER, Patricia.
"Divine Truth in Husserl and Kant: Some Issues in Phenomenological Theology" in *Phenomenology of the Truth Proper to Religion*, HART, James G.
"Kant and Fichte: An Ethics of Self-Respect in Individualism" in *Abeunt Studia in Mores: A Festschrift for Helga Doblin*, ECKBLAD, Joyce.
"Kant and Newton: Why Gravity Is Essential to Matter" in *Philosophical Perspectives on Newtonian Science*, FRIEDMAN, Michael.
"Kantian and Phenomenological Traditions in Psychological Aesthetics" in *XIth International Congress in Aesthetics, Nottingham 1988*, ALLESCH, Christian.
"Kantian Ethics" in *A Companion to Ethics*, O'NEILL, Onora.
"L'image de l'homme dans la théorie kantienne du génie" in *XIth International Congress in Aesthetics, Nottingham 1988*, LABRADA, Antonia.
"Maimon, crítico de Kant" in *Dinâmica do Pensar: Homenagem a Oswaldo Market*, FERREIRA, Manuel Carmo.
"Natural Affection and Responsibility for Character: A Critique of Kantian Views of the Virtues" in *Identity, Character, and Morality: Essays in Moral Psychology*, TRIANOSKY, Gregory.
"Nota acerca da recepção de Kant no pensamento filosófico português" in *Dinâmica do Pensar: Homenagem a Oswaldo Market*, DA GAMA CAEIRO, Francisco.
"Obligation and Performance: A Kantian Account of Moral Conflict" in *Identity, Character, and Morality: Essays in Moral Psychology*, HERMAN, Barbara.
"An Old Question Raised Yet Again: Is Kant an Enlightenment Humanist?" in *The Question of Humanism: Challenges and Possibilities*, LUIK, John.
"Pacifism, Duty, and Supererogation" in *In the Interest of Peace: A Spectrum of Philosophical Views*, CADY, Duane L.
"The Place of Emotions in Kantian Morality" in *Identity, Character, and Morality: Essays in Moral Psychology*, SHERMAN, Nancy.
"A Reply to David Duquette's "Kant, Hegel and the Possibility of a Speculative Logic"" in *Essays on Hegel's Logic*, PINKARD, Terry.
"Trust, Affirmation, and Moral Character: A Critique of Kantian Morality" in *Identity, Character, and Morality: Essays in Moral Psychology*, THOMAS, Laurence.
"Two Dogmas of Kantian Aesthetics" in *XIth International Congress in Aesthetics, Nottingham 1988*, ZANGWILL, Nick.
"Übergang e antecipação em Kant" in *Dinâmica do Pensar: Homenagem a Oswaldo Market*, MARQUES, António.
"A voz prometida: Sobre a imaginação na *Kritik der Urteilskraft*" in *Dinâmica do Pensar: Homenagem a Oswaldo Market*, MOLDER, Maria Filomena.
"Das Wort sie sollen lassen stahn": Zur Edition und Interpretation philosophischer Texte, erläutert am B Kants. BRANDT, Reinhard.

KANT

"Seeing Things". PIPER, Adrian M S.
A Contribution of the Conception of "Discursivity" and "Spontaneiti" of Thinking (in Czechoslovakian). BENYOVSZKY, Ladislav.
Alternativen und Irrtum in der Kritischen Philosophie Kants. LOH, Werne.
Análisis de la doctrina ética de las "observaciones sobre lo bello y sublime". GONZÁLEZ PORTA, Mario A.
An Antinomy in Kelsen's Pure Theory of Law. BULYGIN, Eugenio.
Apriorische Einsicht und metaphysische Notwendigkeit: Eine Auseinandersetzung mit Kripkes Kant-Kritik. WENDEL, Hans Jürgen.
Are Kantian Duties Categorical?. SCHOEMAN, Ferdinand.
Art Works, But How?—Kant and Aesthetics/Heidegger and Truth. SYNNING, Ralph.
El arte y la urbanidad de la razón. CORDUA, Carla.
Autonomy and Political Obligation in Kant. STERN, David S.
Die Bedeutung der Mathematik Für die Philosophie Schopenhauers. RADBRUCH, Knut.
Der Begriff der Bewegung bei Kant: Über den Grundbegriff der Empirie und die empirischen Begriffe. HOFFMANN, Thomas Sören.
Der Begriff des Selbstbewusstseins bei Kant. GLOY, Karen.
Eine bisher unbeachtete Quelle des "Streits der Fakultäten". SELBACH, Ralf.
Capacidad de la mente humana para alcanzar el ser de las cosas, hasta el mismo *Esse subsistens* (II). DERISI, Octavio N.
The Case of the Unmitigated Blackguard or Saving Kant's Moral Feelings. EARLS, Anthony.
Categorical Requirements: Kant and Hume on the Idea of Duty. WIGGINS, David.
Community and the Evil Poem. KEMAL, S.
Community and Utopia: A Transcendental Deduction. POPOV, Stefan.
El concepto de "conformidad a fines" en la Crítica del Juicio Estético. PÖLTNER, Günter.
Conceptual Idealism Revisited. RESCHER, Nicholas.
Construction and the Role of Schematism in Kant's Philosophy of Mathematics (also in Portuguese). WINTERBOURNE, A T.
La crítica kantiana a la virtud como término medio. MAURI, Margarita.
Las criticas de J Bennett a la doctrina kantiana del esquematismo. JÁUREGUI, Claudia.
A Critique of Kantian Arguments Against Emotions as Moral Motives. OAKLEY, Justin.
Davidson's Transcendental Arguments. MAKER, William.
Desire and Duty in Kant. GRIGG, Russell.
The Development of Otto's Thought 1898-1917. MINNEY, Robin.
Het Dialectisch Humanistisch Grondmotief van Natuur en Vrijheid in de Pedagogiek als Wetenschap. OUWENDORP, C.
La dignità dell'uomo da Kant a Hegel. PAOLINELLI, Marco.
Does Reason Command Itself for Its Own Sake?. KRAENZEL, Frederick.
Down to Earth and Up to Religion: Kantian Idealism in Light of Kierkegaard's Leap of Faith. PERL, Paul.
Elogio critico dell'imperfezione. TUSA, Carlo.
Un enfoque Kantiano sobre el aborto. HARE, R M.
Ernst Cassirer and Martin Heidegger: The Davos Debate. LYNCH, Dennis A.
Errors of an Ill-Reasoning Reason: The Disparagement of Emotions in the Moral Life. LAURITZEN, Paul.
Espoir et désespoir de la raison chez Kant. GRIMALDI, Nicolas.
Evolutionary Ethics and the Search for Predecessors: Kant, Hume, and All the Way Back to Aristotle?. RUSE, Michael.
Experiencia de lo sublime y principios racionales. ARTOLA, José María.
The Faculty of Desire. LACHTERMAN, David.
A Fat Worm of Error?. MC GHEE, Michael.
La filosofía transcendental: el destino de un proyecto ilustrado. FLAMARIQUE, Lourdes.
The First Formulation of the Categorical Imperative as Literally a "Legislative" Metaphor. GREEN, Ronald M.
Die Folgen vorherrschender Moralkonzeptionen. POGGE, Thomas W.
Four Perspectives on Moral Judgement: The Rational Principles of Jesus and Kant. PALMQUIST, Stephen R.
Freedom and Autonomy: The Kantian Analytic and a Sartrean Critique. BEAVERS, Anthony.
Freedom and Happiness in Kant's Political Philosophy. HELLER, Agnes.
From Philosophical Psychology to Philosophical Anthropology (in Dutch). VERGOTE, A.
Der Gegenstand der Vorstellungen und die transzendentale Apperzeption. LÓPEZ-FERNÁNDEZ, Alvaro.
The Greatness and Limits of Kant's Practical Philosophy. HÖSLE, Vittorio.
Hamanns Metakritik im ersten Entwurf. BAYER, Oswald.
Hegel and Kant—A Refutation of their Racism. NEUGEBAUER, Christian.
Human Rights and Freedom: Is Kant Relevant to the Current Discussion?. SCHWEIDLER, Walter.
Hume's Rejection of the Theory of Ideas. WRIGHT, John P.
The Immanence of Thought: Hegel's Critique of Foundationalism. STERN, David S.
The Inadequacy of a Deontological Analysis of Peer Relations in Organizations. MARTIN, Robert M.
The Incoherence of Kant's Transcendental Dialectic: Specifying the Minimal Conditions for Dialectical Error. HERMAN, David J.
La influencia de Rousseau en el pensamiento de Kant. DE LOS ANGELES GIRALT, María.
Ist die Kantische Theorie eine Theorie entfremdeter Erkenntnis?. KERBER, Harald.
Jugement juridique et jugement pratique: de Kant à la philosophie du langage. LENOBLE, J and BERTEN, A.
Juicios de percepción y de experiencia en Kant. FERNÁNDEZ, Alvaro López.
Kant and Conceptual Semantics: A Sketch. POSY, Carl J.
Kant and the Origins of Totalitarianism. SIEBERS, Tobin.
Kant e o problema da origem das representações elementares: apontamentos. MARQUES, U R de Azevedo.
Kant en de mogelijkheid van de metafysica als wetenschap. PERRICK, M.
Kant et l'histoire de la philosophie la vision problématologique. TIMMERMANS, Benoît.
Kant in Hegels begtipsleer. DE VOS, L.
Kant in Russia: The Initial Phase (continued). NEMETH, Thomas.
Kant on Concepts and Intuitions in the Mathematical Sciences. FRIEDMAN, Michael.
Kant on Justification in Transcendental Philosophy. PEREBOOM, Derk.
Kant the Liberal, Kant the Anarchist: Rawls and Lyotard on Kantian Justice. MAY, Todd G.
Kant über den Witz und Kants Witz. RITZEL, Wolfgang.
Kant und Wittgenstein. STETTER, Christian.
Kant y la Revolución Francesa. PÉREZ ESTÉVEZ, Antonio.
Kant's Account of Intuition. FALKENSTEIN, Lorne.
Kant's Apotheosis of Genius. QUINN, Timothy Sean.
Kant's Diversity Theory: A Dissenting View. GLOUBERMAN, Mark.
Kant's Doctrine of Heuristics: An Interpretation of the Ideas of Reason. GRACYK, Theodore A.
Kant's First Analogy Revisited. BUESSEM, George E.
Kant's Psychological Hedonism. GRIFFITHS, A Phillips.
Kant's Search for the Philosopher's Stone. AXIOTIS, Ares.
Kant's Theory of Empirical Judgment and Modern Semantics. HANNA, Robert.
Kant's Theory of Peace and the Main Aspects of the Recent Discussion Surrounding It (in German). ZAHN, Manfred.
Kant's visie op de Franse Revolutie en op de grondslagen van het recht. VAN DER WAL, G A.
Kant, Mendelssohn, Lambert, and the Subjectivity of Time. FALKENSTEIN, Lorne.
Kant, Pestalozzi and the Role of Ideology in Educational Thought. ADAMS, Ian.
Kant, Teleology, and Sexual Ethics. COOKE, Vincent M.
Kant: del derecho de libertad a la exigencia racional del Estado. PASTORE, Romano.
Kantian Freedom Naturalized. MELCHERT, Norman.
A Kantian View of Moral Luck. MOORE, A W.
Le Kantisme de la théorie cantorienne de l'infini. BACHTA, Abdelkader.
Kants "Reflexionen zur Ästhetik": Zur Werkgeschichte der "Kritik der ästhetischen Urteilskraft". FRANK, Manfred.
Kants Begriff der synthetischen Urteile a priori. ROS, Arno.
Kants *Kritik der Urteilskraft*. RAYMAEKERS, Bart.
Kants Logik der Synthesis und die Schliessung einer "unübersehbaren Kluft". FUNKE, Gerhard.
Kants Schemata als Anwendungsbedingungen von Kategorien auf Anschauungen. LOHMAR, Dieter.
Kants Theorie der Gegenstandserkenntnis und Schopenhauers Lehre vom Ding an sich. BAUMANN, Lutz.
Kants Theorie der geometrischen Erkenntnis und die nichteuklikische Geometrie. SCHIRN, Matthias.
Kitcher and Kant. BHAVE, S M.
Locke on Mathematical Knowledge. CICOVACKI, Predrag.
Logic and Ontology. BROWNING, Douglas.
The Logical Structure of the First Antinomy. LOPARIC, Zeljko.
Lyotard's "Kantian Socialism". GEIMAN, Kevin Paul.
Metaphysik und Erfahrung in Kants Grundlegung der Ethik. CRAMER, Konrad.
Metaphysik und Erfahrung. BUBNER, Rüdiger.
Metaphysik und Metaphysikkritik. HARTMANN, Klaus.
Moral Conflicts in Kantian Ethics. MC CARTY, Richard.
Moral Dilemmas, Disjunctive Obligations, and Kant's Principle that 'Ought' Implies 'Can'. JACQUETTE, Dale.
Moral oder Klugheit? Überlegungen zur Gestalt der Autonomie des Politischen im Denken Kants. SCHMITZ, Heinz-Gerd.
Moral Theories, Impartiality, and the Status of Non-Rational, Sentient Beings. FILICE, Carlo.
Moral und Verwirklichung. KLEINGELD, Paulien.
Moral y política en Kant. PÉREZ ESTÉVEZ, Antonio.
Natural Law, Skepticism, and Methods of Ethics. SCHNEEWIND, J B.
Nature' Song. SALLIS, John.
Nietzsche as Instructor in Autonomy? Comments. FOWLER, Mark C.
Nietzsche contra Kant and the Problem of Autonomy. WHITE, Richard.
Nomologie et anomie: lecture de deux antinomies. ZANETTI, Véronique.
A Note on Ruth Lorand's 'Free and Dependent Beauty: A Puzzling Issue'. LORD, Catherine.

KANT
On Bolzano's Conception of the Essentials of Ethics and its Coherences (in Czechoslovakian). HALA, Vlastimil.
On Kant's Conception of Science and the Critique of Practical Reason. KÖRNER, Stephan.
On Lying and the Role of Content in Kant's Ethics. SEDGWICK, Sally.
On the Source of the Eternal Truths. BEACH, Edward A (trans) and VON SCHELLING, F W J.
Origen de la inversión kantiana del binomio materia-forma. SOTO BRUNA, Maria Jesus.
Over het morele en zedelijke handelen, toegelicht aan het instituut huwelijk. COBBEN, Paul.
Philosophische Uberlegungen zu "Menschenwürde" und Fortpflanzungs-Medizin. SCHÖNE-SEIFERT, Bettina.
Philosophy of History is Heternomous Philosophy (in German). SCHULTE, Christoph.
Practical Reason or Metapreferences? An Undogmatic Defense of Kantian Morality. NIDA-RÜMELIN, Julian.
La primera antinomia kantiana: el origen y los límites del Universo. PUYAU, Hermes.
El proyecto crítico de Kant. CHAVES, Carmen.
Der psychophysische Materialismus in der Perspektive Kants und Wittgensteins. MENDONÇA, W P.
Quelques remarques sur la composition de la *Dialectique de la faculté de juger téléologique*. KOPPER, Joachim.
La réflexion dans l'esthétique kantienne. LYOTARD, Jean-François.
Retaliatory Punishment as a Categorical Imperative. HÖFFE, Ottfried.
The Role of Kant's Refutation of Idealism. HYMERS, Michael.
Rousseau et Kant: A propos de la genèse de la théorie kantienne des idées. PICHÉ, Claude.
Saving Faith from Kant's Remarkable Antinomy. QUINN, Philip L.
Schematism and Schemata: Kant and the P.D.P.. VAN DE VIJVER, Gertrudis.
The Search for an Elusive *A Priori*. CAPEK, Milic.
Sensations and Judgments of Perception: Diagnosis and Rehabilitation of Some of Kant's Misleading Examples. KOTZIN, Rhoda and BAUMGÄRTNER, Järg.
Sense, Passions and Morals in Hume and Kant. NUYEN, A T.
Solipsism in Kant's Practical Philosophy and the Discourse of Ethics. KUHLMANN, Wolfgang.
Sophia and the Devil: Kant in the Face of Russian Religious Metaphysics. AKHUTIN, A V.
La speranza nel giusnaturalismo. TUSA, Carlo.
Squaring the Hermeneutical Circle. ROSEN, Stanley.
Strawson and the Refutation of Idealism. STEINHOFF, Gordon.
Su alcuni aspetti del neoilluminismo di L Geymonat. STOMEO, Anna.
The Subject of Experience. GILLETT, Grant.
Subjektivität, Allgemeingültigkeit und Apriorität des Geschmacksurteils bei Kant. BAUM, Manfred.
Teleologie: Chance oder Belastung für die Philosophie?. PLEINES, Jürgen-Eckardt.
The Notion of Sublime in Kant and Hegel: A Psycho-Analytical Reading (in Serbo-Croatian). ZIZEK, Slavoj.
The Philosophical Invariables of Masaryk's Thinking (in Czechoslovakian). SROVNAL, Jindrich.
The Problem of Infinity in Kant's Works (in German). RÖD, Wolfgang.
Theorising Ideas: *Idee* and *Vorstellung* from Kant to Hegel to Marx. CRISTAUDO, Wayne.
Thought and Being in Kant and Hegel. HOULGATE, Stephen.
Tra Kant e Hegel: per una riaffermazione dell'antico concetto di società civile. MARINI, Giuliano.
Transcendental Idealism: The Dialectical Dimension. GLOUBERMAN, M.
El tratado de Ideología de Fray Zeferino Gonzalez. BUENO SÁNCHEZ, Gustavo.
Two-Steps-in-One-Proof: The Structure of the Transcendental Deduction of the Categories. EVANS, J Claude.
Über das Geschmacksurteil und die künstlerische Freiheit bei Kant (in Japanese). UE, Satoko.
Der Übergang vom Bestimmt-Bestimmenden zum freien Schema in Kants Kritik der Urteilskraft. KAULBACH, Friedrich.
Universalistische Ethik und Urteilskraft: ein aristotelischer Blick auf Kant. HÖFFE, Otfried.
Verlichtingsfilosofie twee eeuwen later; J F Lyotard als postmoderne Kant. VAN PEPERSTRATEN, Frans.
Was Kant a Nativist?. FALKENSTEIN, Lorne.
Wie kaatst moet de bal verwachten. MERTENS, T.
Willkür und Wille bei Kant. STEKELER-WEITHOFER, Pirmin.
Wittgenstein on Logical Form and Kantian Geometry. SUMMERFIELD, Donna M.
Zum Verbleib der Königsberger Kant-Handschriften: Funde und Desiderate. STARK, Werner.
Zum Wandel der Metaphysik nach ihrem Ende. BUCHHEIM, Thomas.
Zur Erkenntnistheorie des Ästhetischen: Schopenhauers Beziehung zu Kant. DÖRFLINGER, Bernd.

KANTIANISM
Modernism as a Philosophical Problem: On the Dissatisfactions of European High Culture. PIPPIN, Robert B.
Morality and Modernity. POOLE, Ross.
Nietzsche On Truth and Philosophy. CLARK, Maudemarie.
Realism with a Human Face. PUTNAM, Hilary.
"Davidson and Social Science" in *Truth and Interpretation: Perspectives on the Philosophy of Donald Davidson*, ROOT, Michael.
"The Metaphysics of Interpretation" in *Truth and Interpretation: Perspectives on the Philosophy of Donald Davidson*, ROVANE, Carol.
Bradley and Lonergan's Relativist. TESKE, Roland.
Conditio sine qua non? Zuordnung in the Early Epistemologies of Cassirer and Schlick. RYCKMAN, Thomas.
The Doctrine of Double Effect: Its Philosophical Viability. BOLE, Thomas.
Mansel's Agnosticism. FITZGERALD, Timothy.
La recepción de la "crítica de la razón pura" en el joven Hegel. DEL CARMEN PAREDES MARTIN, M.
Schopenhauer und Fichtes Schrift "Die Bestimmung des Menschen". DECHER, Friedhelm.
Self, Society, and Kantian Impersonality. SORELL, Tom.
Two Ways of Morality: Confucian and Kantian. LEE, Kwang-Sae.

KAPLAN, D
Themes From Kaplan. ALMOG, Joseph (ed).
"Direct Reference, the Semantics of Thinking, and Guise Theory" in *Themes From Kaplan*, CASTAÑEDA, Héctor-Neri.
"Introduction" in *Themes From Kaplan*, MARCUS, Ruth Barcan.
"On Direct Reference" in *Themes From Kaplan*, DEUTSCH, Harry.
"Singular Propositions, Abstract Constituents, and Propositional Attitudes" in *Themes From Kaplan*, ZALTA, Edward N.
"Why Singular Propositions?" in *Themes From Kaplan*, CHISHOLM, Roderick M.
Demonstrative Utterances. BERCKMANS, Paul.
Making Sense of Words. MC CULLOCH, Gregory.
On Kaplan's Logic of Demonstratives. CHAKRAVARTI, Sitansu S.
On the Propositional Attitudes. COLEMAN, Keith.

KARMA
The Law of Karma: A Philosophical Study. REICHENBACH, Bruce R.
Self and Non-Self: The Drigdrisyaviveka Attributed to Samkara. RAPHAEL (trans).
Is Karma Evolutionary?. KRISHAN, Y.
Karma and Rebirth in *Alberuni's India*. SHARMA, Arvind.
Karma and Reincarnation in Advaita Vedānta. SHARMA, Arvind.
Punyadāna or Transference of Merit—A Fiction. KRISHAN, Y.
Re-understanding Indian Philosophy. BARLINGAY, S S.
Yajna and the Doctrine of Karma: A Contradiction in Indian Thought about Action. KRISHNA, Daya.

KASHIMA, Y
Reply to Maher and Kashima: "On the Descriptive Adequacy of Levi's Decision Theory". LEVI, Isaac.

KASPER, W
Alvin Plantinga and Natural Theology. BROWN, Hunter.

KATEB, G
George Kateb's Ahistorical Emersonianism. MARX, Leo.
Strange Attractors: How Individualists Connect to Form Democratic Unity. ROSENBLUM, Nancy.
Whitman and Memory: A Response to Kateb. BROMWICH, David.

KATZ, J
Teorías de verdad y teorías del significado. VARGAS, Celso.

KATZ, L
On Leo Katz, Double Jeopardy, and the Blockburger Test. LOCKE, Lawrence A.

KAUFMAN, G
Directions in Historicism: Language, Experience, and Pragmatic Adjudication. DAVANEY, Sheila Greeve.

KAVKA, G
The Symmetry Enigma in Hobbes. HAJI, Ishtiyaque.

KEITH, W
On Rhetorical Strategies: *Verstehen Sie*?. SLEZAK, Peter.

KELLER, C
"Psychocosmetics: A Jungian Response" in *Archetypal Process: Self and Divine in Whitehead, Jung, and Hillman*, MOORE, Robert L.

KELSEN, H
The Legal-Rational State: A Comparison of Hobbes, Bentham and Kelsen. LEE, Keekok.
An Antinomy in Kelsen's Pure Theory of Law. BULYGIN, Eugenio.
Le critiche a Kelsen durante la Repubblica di Weimar. ROEHRSSEN, Carlo.
L'interpretazione del conflitto fra norme nell'ultimo Kelsen. CELANO, Brun.
On Ideal Form, Empowering Norms, and "Normative Functions". PAULSON, Stanley L.
La ragione e i valori nella determinazione delle norme. CORTESE, Roberto.
Sobre la naturaleza de los "derechos". HERNÁNDEZ, Héctor H.
The Theory of Legal Dynamics Reconsidered. WEINBERGER, Ota.

KENNY, A
Kenny and Religious Experiences. JORDAN, J.
A Reading of Aquinas's Five Ways. FOGELIN, Robert J.

KEPLER
I Modelli l'Invenzione e la Conferma. PETRONI, Angelo Maria.
Expectation, Modelling and Assent in the History of Optics: Part I—Alhazen and the Medieval Tradition. CROMBIE, A C.
Expectation, Modelling and Assent in the History of Optics—II. Kelper and Descartes. CROMBIE, A C.
The Justification of Kepler's Ellipse. BAIGRIE, Brian S.

KEYNES, J
The Epistemology of J M Keynes. O'DONNELL, Rod.
Keynesian Uncertainty and the Weight of Arguments. RUNDE, Jochen.
Mr Keynes on Probability. RAMSEY, F P.
Not Very Likely: A Reply to Ramsey. WATT, D E.
Probability Logic in the Twentieth Century. HAILPERIN, Theodore.

KIENZLE, B
Primary and Secondary Qualities: A Reply to Kienzle. CASATI, Roberto.

KIERKEGAARD
For Self-Examination: Judge for Yourself. HONG, Howard V (ed & trans).
For What May I Hope? Thinking with Kant and Kierkegaard. FENDT, Gene.
Kierkegaard in Golden Age Denmark. KIRMMSE, Bruce H.
Kierkegaards Phänomenologie der Freiheitserfahrung. DISSE, Jörg.
Modern Faith and Thought. THIELICKE, Helmut.
Works of Love? Reflections on "Works of Love". FENDT, Gene.
"Kierkegaard's Phenomenology of Faith as Suffering" in *Writing the Politics of Difference*, WESTPHAL, Merold.
"Kierkegaard's Stages on Life's Way: How Many Are There?" in *Writing the Politics of Difference*, MICHELSEN, John M.
"Kierkegaard's Teleological Humanism" in *The Question of Humanism: Challenges and Possibilities*, PERKINS, Robert L.
"Where There's a Will There's a Way: Kierkegaard's Theory of Action" in *Writing the Politics of Difference*, EVANS, C Stephen.
"Kierkegaardian Faith: 'The Condition' and the 'Response'. FERREIRA, M Jamie.
Doubt and Faith: Santayana and Kierkegaard on Fundamental Belief. SARTWELL, Crispin.
Down to Earth and Up to Religion: Kantian Idealism in Light of Kierkegaard's Leap of Faith. PERL, Paul.
The Epistemological Significance of Transformative Religious Experiences: A Kierkegaardian Exploration. EVANS, C Stephen.
Faith and the Possibility of Private Meaning. GURREY, Charles S.
Fault-Lines in Kierkegaard and Hawthorne: *The Sickness unto Death* and "Ethan Brand". BENOIT, Raymond.
Kierkegaard irrazionalista? Filosofi e filosofie nella interpretazione del filosofo danese. FRANCHI, Alfredo.
Kierkegaard on the Limits of Christian Epistemology. WISDO, David.
Kierkegaard on Theistic Proof. STERN, Kenneth.
Kierkegaard's Mirror. ROSENOW, Eliyahu.
Kierkegaard's Pragmatist Faith. EMMANUEL, Steven M.
Kierkegaard, Nietzsche, and the Death of God. NASH, Ronald H.
Kierkegaard: Aesthetics and 'The Aesthetic'. PATTISON, George.
A Kierkegaardian Critique of Heidegger's Concept of Authenticity. BERTHOLD-BOND, Daniel.
Kierkegaardian Transitions: Paradox and Pathos. FERREIRA, M Jamie.
The Knight of Faith. ADAMS, Robert Merrihew.
Noia, acedia ed epochè. BOTTANI, Livio.
The Relevance of Historical Evidence for Christian Faith: A Critique of a Kierkegaardian View. EVANS, C Stephen.
Temporality Revisited: Kierkegaard and the Transitive Character of Time. SCHALOW, Frank.
To Tell a Good Tale: Kierkegaardian Reflections on Moral Narrative and Moral Truth. TURNER, Jeffrey S.

KILLING
Death and the Beginning of Life. IGLESIAS, Teresa.
Killing and Letting Die—Putting the Debate in Context. CHANDLER, John.
The Morality of Killing and Causing Suffering: Reasons for Rejecting Peter Singer's Pluralistic Consequentialism. LANDMAN, Willem A.
Utilitarian Killing, Replacement, and Rights. PLUHAR, Evelyn.

KILVINGTON, R
Tu scis regem sedere. D'ORS, Angel.

KIM, J
Disjunctive Laws and Supervenience. SEAGER, William.

KIND(S)
Two Kinds of Naming in the *Sophist*. STOUGH, Charlotte.

KINDNESS
The Compatibility of Justice and Kindness. PUTMAN, Daniel.

KINETIC THEORY
Particles and Waves: Historical Essays in the Philosophy of Science. ACHINSTEIN, Peter.
Philosophical Objections to the Kinetic Theory. NYHOF, John.

KING, M
The Ethical Thought of Martin Luther King. STERLING, Marvin C.
El pensamiento filosófico de Martin Luther King, Jr. STERLING, Marvin C.

KING, P
Buridan's Divided Modal Syllogistic. WILLING, Anthony.

KINSHIP
Kinship and Moral Relativity. PARGETTER, Robert.
A Structuralist Rousseau: On the Anthropology of Claude Lévi-Strauss. HONNETH, Axel.

KITARO, N
Comparative Dialectics: Nishida Kitarō's Logic of Place and Western Dialectical Thought. AXTELL, G S.

KITCHENER, R
Response to Professor Kitchener's "Do Children Think Philosophically?". LIPMAN, Matthew.

KITCHER, P
Kitcher and Kant. BHAVE, S M.
Kitcher's Circumlocutionary Structuralism. HAND, Michael.
A Mathematical A Priorist Answers Philip Kitcher. NORTON-SMITH, Thomas M.

KITSCH
"Le kitsch en tant que valeur communicative" in *XIth International Congress in Aesthetics, Nottingham 1988*, STÉPHANOV, Ivan.
Why is Kitsch Bad? (in Hebrew). KULKA, Tomas.

KLEIN, P
Knowledge and Deductive Closure. WHITE, James L.

KNITTER, P
Relativism, Ineffability, and the Appeal to Experience: A Reply to the Myth Makers. BARNES, L Philip.

KNOWING
Jurisculture, Volume I: Greece and Rome. DORSEY, Gray L.
Can Knowledge Occur Unknowingly?. CHAUDHURI, Manjusree.
La esencia metafísica de Dios. DERISI, Octavio N.
Hegel and the Humean Problem of Induction. SUCHTING, W A.
How Teachers Know. STENGEL, Barbara S.
Knowing and Valuing Fairness. HINTON, J M.
Omniscience, Immutability, and the Divine Mode of Knowing. SULLIVAN, Thomas D.
On Knowing and Naming. BEARDS, Andrew.
Seeing Our Seeing and Knowing Our Knowing. BEN-ZEEV, Aaron.

KNOWLEDGE
see also Epistemology
Artificial Intelligence: Its Scope and Limits. FETZER, James H.
Die Aufhebung der Begriffs-philosophie. KRONABEL, Christoph.
Baffling Phenomena: And Other Studies in the Philosophy of Knowledge and Valuation. RESCHER, Nicholas.
Beyond Ethnocentrism: A Reconstruction of Marx's Concept of Science. MC KELVEY, Charles.
The Concept of Objectivity: An Approximation. BUTLER, Kenneth G.
The Critical Problem of Knowledge. BLANDINO, Giovanni (ed).
The Critique of Power: Reflective Stages in a Critical Social Theory. HONNETH, Axel.
David Hume: Historiker und Philosoph. LÜTHE, Rudolf.
The Dice-Playing God: Reflections on Life in a Post-Modern Age. KRIEGLSTEIN, Werner.
Donald Davidson. EVNINE, Simon.
The Dynamics of Rational Deliberation. SKYRMS, Brian.
Education as a Human Right: A Theory of Curriculum and Pedagogy. VANDENBERG, Donald.
Empiricism and Subjectivity: An Essay on Hume's Theory of Human Nature. BOUNDAS, Constantin V (trans).
Epistemic Justification: Essays in the Theory of Knowledge. ALSTON, William P.
Epistemology and Skepticism: An Enquiry into the Nature of Epistemology. CHATALIAN, George.
Historische Objektivitat. WEBERMAN, David.
Human Goodness: Generosity and Courage. PYBUS, Elizabeth.
Human Nature and Historical Knowledge: Hume, Hegel and Vico. POMPA, Leon.
Ibn Rushd: Averroes. URVOY, Dominique.
Introduction to Philosophy: Classical and Contemporary Readings. POJMAN, Louis P.
Knowledge in Flux: Modeling the Dynamics of Epistemic States. GÄRDENFORS, Peter.
Knowledge in Perspective: Selected Essays in Epistemology. SOSA, Ernest.
Knowledge of the External World. AUNE, Bruce.
Knowledge Representation and Defeasible Reasoning. KYBURG JR, Henry E (ed).
Knowledge, Fiction, and Imagination. NOVITZ, David.
The Many Dimensions of the Human Person. STEGER, E Ecker.
Mathematics and the Image of Reason. TILES, Mary E.
Metaphors of Mind: Conceptions of the Nature of Intelligence. STERNBERG, Robert J.

KNOWLEDGE

Metaphysical Delusion. COWLEY, Fraser.
Methods and Problems in Greek Science: Selected Papers. LLOYD, G E R.
Negative Dialectics and the End of Philosophy. ERICKSON, Glenn W.
Nietzsche (III and IV): The Will to Power as Knowledge and as Metaphysics—Heidegger. KRELL, David Farrell (ed).
On Durkheim's Rules of Sociological Method. GANE, Mike.
L'ordine della certezza: Scientificità e persuasione in Descartes. BONICALZI, Francesca.
The Origins of Aristotelian Science. FEREJOHN, Michael.
An Outline of the Philosophy of Knowledge and Science. BLANDINO, Giovanni.
Overcoming Foundations: Studies in Systematic Philosophy. WINFIELD, Richard Dien.
Phänomenologische Philosophie. STRÖKER, Elisabeth.
Philosophical Papers: F P Ramsey. MELLOR, D H (ed).
Philosophy: An Introduction Through Literature. KLEIMAN, L (ed).
Platonic Piety. MORGAN, Michael L.
A Post-Modern Epistemology. SORRI, Mari.
The Potential of Modern Discourse: Musil, Peirce, and Perturbation. FINLAY, Marike.
Pragmatism: From Peirce to Davidson. MURPHY, John P.
Principles of Ethics. ROSMINI, Antonio.
Reasoning and Revision in Hybrid Representation Systems. NEBEL, Bernhard.
Representing and Reasoning With Probabilistic Knowledge: A Logical Approach to Probabilities. BACCHUS, Fahiem.
Responsibility and Criminal Liability. SISTARE, C T.
Rorty's Humanistic Pragmatism: Philosophy Democratized. KOLENDA, Konstantin.
Science and Relativism: Some Key Controversies in the Philosophy of Science. LAUDAN, Larry.
The Social Horizon of Knowledge. BUCZKOWSKI, Piotr (ed).
Theories of Science in Society. COZZENS, Susan E (ed).
Understanding the Representational Mind. PERNER, Josef.
The Unity of Kant's "Critique of Pure Reason": Experience, Language, and Knowledge. WILLIAMS, T C.
Whose Science? Whose Knowledge? Thinking from Women's Lives. HARDING, Sandra.
Wisdom: Its Nature, Origins, and Development. STERNBERG, Robert J.
Zetetic Skepticism. UMPHREY, Stewart.
"A Coherence Theory of Truth and Knowledge" in *Reading Rorty*, DAVIDSON, Donald.
"A Coherence Theory of Truth and Knowledge" in *Truth and Interpretation: Perspectives on the Philosophy of Donald Davidson*, DAVIDSON, Donald.
"The Conditions of Thought" in *The Mind of Donald Davidson*, DAVIDSON, Donald.
"Doing What One Ought to Do" in *Meaning and Method: Essays in Honor of Hilary Putnam*, PUTNAM, Ruth Anna.
"Everyday Knowledge as Representation of Reality" in *The Social Horizon of Knowledge*, MARUSZEWSKI, Tomasz.
"The Fiduciary Relationship and the Nature of Professions" in *Ethics, Trust, and the Professions: Philosophical and Cultural Aspects*, SOKOLOWSKI, Robert.
"The Four Causes" in *Studies on Mario Bunge's "Treatise"*, ESPINOZA, Miguel.
"Is There Anything We Should Not Want to Know?" in *Logic, Methodology and Philosophy of Science, VIII*, GÄRDENFORS, Peter.
"Machine Models for the Growth of Knowledge: Theory Nets in Prolog" in *Imre Lakatos and Theories of Scientific Change*, SNEED, Joseph D.
"Skepticism and Everyday Knowledge Attributions" in *Doubting: Contemporary Perspectives on Skepticism*, COHEN, Stewart.
"La trahison de la trahison des clercs" in *The Political Responsibility of Intellectuals*, GELLNER, Ernest.
"Two Roads to Skepticism" in *Doubting: Contemporary Perspectives on Skepticism*, MOSER, Paul K.
"The Value of Knowledge" in *Scientific Theories*, SKYRMS, Brian.
"Event" in Dewey's Philosophy. DUFF, Barry E.
"Sigma": conoscenza e metodo. SAVA, Gabriella.
'Rules' and 'Knowledge'. HARRISON III, Frank R.
'Seventeen' Subtleties in Plato's *Theaetetus*. FOGELMAN, Brian D and HUTCHINSON, D S.
Aesthetic Authority and Tradition: Nietzsche and the Greeks. STRONG, Tracy B.
An Anti-Sceptical Fugue. GILLETT, Grant.
Arte y conocimiento. ECHAURI, Raúl.
Autopoesis—Subject—Reality (in German). ZIEMKE, Axel and STÖBER, Konrad.
Belief as a Condition of Knowledge: The Need for a Philosophical Perspective in Higher Education Reform. BRELL JR, Carl D.
Belief, Acceptance, and Knowledge. RADFORD, Colin.
Beyond the Real/Apparent World: From Signs to Imaging in Nietzsche. WATSON, James R.
Boskovic's Philosophy in the Evaluation of Franjo Markovic (1887): Origins and Results (in Serbo-Croatian). KUTLESA, Stipe.
Bringing Things About. DIEFENBECK, James A.
Burgeoning Skepticism. DE VRIES, Willem.
Capacidad de la mente humana para alcanzar el ser de las cosas, hasta el mismo *Esse subsistens* (II). DERISI, Octavio N.
El carácter inmanente del conocimiento. SEGURA, Carmen.
Ceteris Paribus Laws. SCHIFFER, Stephen.
Cientificidad y Romanticismo: Acerca de las relaciones entre cientismo, gnosticismo y romanticismo. KOSLOWSKI, Peter.
El concepto de Filosofia y conocimiento en Ludwig Wittgenstein. ESPARZA-BRACHO, Jesús.
El conocimiento de los cuerpos según Malebranche (I). FERNANDEZ RODRIGUEZ, Jose Luis.
Conocimiento metodico y no metodico; so pretexto de una incursion acerca de la dialectica segun platon. SALA, J F A.
Conocimiento y comunicación: Algunas reflexiones sobre la vida social. SUANCES MARCOS, M.
Conocimiento y determinismo. LAGUNILLA, Ana E Galán.
Consciousness and Introspective Knowledge. CARLOYE, Jack C.
A Critique of Plantinga's Theological Foundationalism. ZEIS, John.
The Dead Horse Phenomenon in Educational Theory. ROBENSTINE, Clark.
Derrida, Deconstruction and Nietzsche: The Tree of Knowledge and the Tree of Life. ZELECHOW, Bernard.
Desperately Seeking Science: The Creation of Knowledge in Family Practice. GOLDSTEIN, Jared.
Dewey and the Theory of Knowledge. THAYER, H S.
Dewey, Indeterminacy, and the Spectator Theory of Knowledge. KULP, Christopher B.
Di cose grammaticali: Un itinerario campanelliano. ALUNNI, Charles.
Divine Knowledge and Divine Control: A Response to Gordon and Sadowsky. BASINGER, David.
Dretske on Knowledge and Content. GJELSVIK, Olav.
The Driving Ratio in Plato's Divided Line. DREHER, John Paul.
Editologie et Scientificite. BAUDET, Jean C.
The Enlightenment—a Stranded Project? Habermas on Nietzsche as a 'Turning Point' to Postmodernity. NAGL, Ludwig.
Entorn del libre de F canals i Vidal: "Sobre la esencia del conocimiento". COLOMER, Eusebi.
The Epistemology of J M Keynes. O'DONNELL, Rod.
Epistemology on Holiday. KAPLAN, Mark.
Ernst Mach and the Elimination of Subjectivity. HAMILTON, Andy.
Falsification and Disconfirmation in Cosmology. ZYCINSKI, Joseph.
Feminism and Epistemology. CHANDLER, John.
The Fifth Meditation. EDELBERG, Walter.
La filosofía de la ciencia en Platón: Una introducción. PEREZ DE LABORDA, Alfonso.
Fisiormorfismo de la razón versus racionalismo. PACHO, Julián.
Foucault and The Referent. LUNN, Forrest.
Foundationalism, Holism, or Hegel?. STERN, David S.
Friedrich Nietzsche and Classical Philology Today. IRMSCHER, Johannes.
From Presentation to Representation in E B Wilson's *The Cell*. MAIENSCHEIN, Jane.
Los fundamentos de la especulación metafísica sobre el conocimiento. SACCHI, Mario E.
A General Possible Worlds Framework for Reasoning about Knowledge and Belief. WANSING, Heinrich.
Giambattista Vico and the Quarrel between the Ancients and the Moderns. LEVINE, Joseph M.
Grundlegende Aspekte zur Problematik von Erkenntnis und Praxis. FORSCHE, Joachim.
The Highest Moral Knowledge and Internalism: Some Comments. LEMOS, Noah.
The Highest Moral Knowledge and the Truth Behind Internalism. DE PAUL, Michael R.
How to Change Your Mind. MARTINS, João P and CRAVO, Maria R.
Hume's Rejection of the Theory of Ideas. WRIGHT, John P.
Husserl's Phenomenology of Knowledge and Cognition (in Polish). DEBOWSKI, Jozef.
I Know What I Know, If You Know What I Mean. DURAN, Jane.
Ignoramus, Ignorabimus!. BUENO, Gustavo.
La imaginación creadora en el pensamiento de Gastón Bachelard. CASTILLO, Roberto.
The Immanence of Thought: Hegel's Critique of Foundationalism. STERN, David S.
Insularity and the Persistence of Perceptual Illusion. CAM, Philip.
Irigaray on Subjectivity. SCHUTTE, Ofelia.
Ist die Kantische Theorie eine Theorie entfremdeter Erkenntnis?. KERBER, Harald.
Justification in the 20th Century. PLANTINGA, Alvin.
Kant on Justification in Transcendental Philosophy. PEREBOOM, Derk.
Kant's Doctrine of Heuristics: An Interpretation of the Ideas of Reason. GRACYK, Theodore A.
Kennen en kunnen: Een repliek op Wardekker. HARBERS, Hans.
Knowability, Actuality, and the Metaphysics of Context-Dependence. PERCIVAL, Philip.
Knowing Good and Evil. WILLIAMS, C J F.

KNOWLEDGE
Knowing through the Body. JOHNSON, Mark.
Knowledge and Deductive Closure. WHITE, James L.
Knowledge as Bondage: An Unconventional Approach. SEN, Sanat Kumar.
Knowledge Growth and Teaching: Towards a Genetic Foundation for Teachers' Knowledge. ORTON, Robert E.
Knowledge is Merely True Belief. SARTWELL, Crispin.
Knowledge, Belief and Revelation: A Reply to Patrick Lee. HOITENGA JR, Dewey J.
Knowledge, Reason and Human Autonomy: A Review Article. KRISHNA, Daya.
Kripke Semantics for Knowledge Representation Logics. ORLOWSKA, Ewa.
Levels of Knowledge in the *Theaetetus*. DORTER, Kenneth.
Locke on Mathematical Knowledge. CICOVACKI, Predrag.
Logic and Knowledge Representation. PETROV, V V and PEREVERZEV, V N.
Logics of Dialogue: A Necessary Multiplicity. MAIER, Robert.
Marx's *Aufhebung* of Philosophy and the Foundations of Historical-Materialist Science. FRACCHIA, Joseph.
A Mathematical A Priorist Answers Philip Kitcher. NORTON-SMITH, Thomas M.
McDowell Against Criterial Knowledge. ROBINSON, Paul.
Meaning in a Realist Perspective. THERON, Stephen.
Meno, the Slave-Boy, and the *Elenchos*. BENSON, Hugh H.
Middle Knowledge and the Soteriological Problem of Evil. HUNT, David P.
Modest A Priori Knowledge. SUMMERFIELD, Donna M.
The Nature of Buddhism. KLOSTERMAIER, Klaus.
Nietzsche: The Divination Paradigm of Knowledge in Western Culture. BULHOF, Ilse N.
Obligation and Knowledge (in French). SCHULTHESS, Daniel.
On the Concept of Mímésis (in Czechoslovakian). VEJRAZKA, Michal.
On the Logic of Eternal Knowledge. KELLY, Charles J.
An Oscillatory Model of the Growth of Scientific Knowledge. AKEROYD, F Michael.
Paradigms of Legal Science. JORI, Mario.
Penny Pinching and Backward Induction. HOLLIS, Martin.
La pensée gonséthienne et le mouvement systémique. PEGUIRON, Nicolas.
Philosophers as Professional Relativists: Canadian Philosophical Association Presidential Address 1990. BUTTS, Robert E.
Philosophizing. PALMA, A B.
Plato's Analogy between Painter and Poet. JANAWAY, Christopher.
The Politics of Knowledge. SPRING, Joel.
The Power of Hegemony vis-à-vis the Marketplace of Ideas: Response to Orton. BROSIO, Richard A.
Power, Knowledge and Freedom: The Meaning of Foucault's Threefold Break with the History of Ideas (in German). ENGLER, Wolfgang.
Praktijkontwikkeling en wetenschappelijke (onderwijs)kunde: Een reactie op Boon e.a.. WARDEKKER, Wim.
Probability and Epistemology. PIENKOWSKI, M.
El problema de la "acción intencional" en el conocimiento sensible. DELBOSCO, Héctor J.
Re-Viewing the Political Structure of Knowledge. LEACH, Mary S.
Reflexiones en torno a la sensibilidad externa. ALVAREZ-CASTELLANOS, Juan José Sánchez.
Richard Rorty and the Image of Modernity. BRADLEY, James.
Rilievi di struttura sul *De deo abscondito* di Nicola Cusano. DELCÒ, Alessandro.
O Saber, a Ética e a Ação Social. CARDOSO D EOLIVEIRA, Roberto.
Scepticism: the Current Debate. ODEGARD, Douglas.
Science and Art: The New Golem From the Transdisciplinary to an Ultra-disciplinary Epistemology. BERGER, René.
Science and Consciousness. WOJCIECHOWSKI, Jerzy A.
Science in the Age of Mechanical Reproduction: Moral and Epistemic Relations Between Diagrams and Photographs. LYNCH, Michael.
The Search for an Elusive *A Priori*. CAPEK, Milic.
A Second Copy Thesis in Hume?. PAPPAS, George S.
Semantica della "Vorstellung" e valore della teoria in *Erkenntnis und Irrtum* di Ernst Mach. BELLOMO, Andrea.
A significação "crítica" de Le volontaire et l'involontaire. HENRIQUES, Fernanda.
Silvio Spaventa e Antonio Labriola, gli 'aspetti-pedagogici'. DE CUMIS, Nicola Siciliani.
Sobre el conocimiento tecnológico. VILLORO, Luis.
Social Epistemology and Social Cognition. CORLETT, J Angelo.
Social Science Knowledge and Explanations in Educational Studies. DALE, Michael.
Socrates' Critique of Cognitivism. MATSON, Wallace I and LEITE, Adam.
Some Features of Hume's Conception of Space. FRASCA-SPADA, Marina.
Some Recent Work in Epistemology. MOSER, Paul K.
La Teoría del conocimiento en Santo Tomás de Aquino. BEUCHOT, Mauricio.
The Foundations of Franz Rosenzweig's Theory of Knowledge (in Hebrew). AMIR, Yehoyada.
The Operation of Values: Knowledge in the Conception of G H Mead (in Polish). HETMANSKI, Marek.
The Specific Features of Cognition Progress in Philosophy: Demonstrated by the Example of Max Adler (in German). MÖCKEL, Christian.
Three Realities and Two Discourses. TABORSKY, Edwina.
Two Methods of Constructing Contractions and Revisions of Knowledge Systems. ROTT, Hans.
Two Principles of Bayesian Epistemology. TALBOTT, W J.
Unfair to Nozick. BRUECKNER, Anthony.
Was ist ein Polyhistor? Gehversuche auf einem verlassenen Terrain. JAUMANN, Herbert.
Weights or the Value of Knowledge. RAMSEY, F P.
Wetenschapsontwikkeling en kundes. BOON, Louis (and others).
What is so Practical about Theory? Lewin Revisited. SANDELANDS, Lloyd E.
Whewell's Developmental Psychologism: A Victorian Account of Scientific Progress. METCALFE, John F.
Why Friedman's Non-Monotonic Reasoning Defies Hempel's Covering Law Model. JANSSEN, M C W and TAN, Y H.
Wissen und Emanzipation. SANDKÜHLER, Hans Jörg.
Wittgenstein and Social Science. TRIGG, Roger.
Wittgenstein escéptico?. CABANCHIK, Samuel.
Zur Erkenntnistheorie des Ästhetischen: Schopenhauers Beziehung zu Kant. DÖRFLINGER, Bernd.

KOCHEN, S
Kochen's Interpretation of Quantum Mechanics. ARNTZENIUS, Frank.

KOERTGE, N
Metaphysics, MSRP and Economics. GLASS, J C and JOHNSON, W.

KOFFKA, K
"Why Do Things Look as They Do?" Some Gibsonian Answers to Koffka's Question. NATSOULAS, Thomas.

KOHAK, E
Nature as Personal. DOMBROWSKI, Daniel A.

KOHLBERG, L
"Beyond Freud and Piaget: Biographical Worlds—Interpersonal Self" in *The Moral Domain: Essays in the Ongoing Discussion between Philosophy and the Social Sciences*, NOAM, Gil G.
"The Emergence of Morality in Personal Relationships" in *The Moral Domain: Essays in the Ongoing Discussion between Philosophy and the Social Sciences*, KELLER, Monika.
"Justice and Solidarity: On the Discussion Concerning Stage 6" in *The Moral Domain: Essays in the Ongoing Discussion between Philosophy and the Social Sciences*, HABERMAS, Jürgen.
"The Majesty and Mystery of Kohlberg's Stage 6" in *The Moral Domain: Essays in the Ongoing Discussion between Philosophy and the Social Sciences*, PUKA, Bill.
Adapting Kohlberg to Enhance the Assessment of Manager's Moral Reasoning. WEBER, James.
A Comparison of John Dewey and Lawrence Kohlberg's Approach to Moral Education. SOCOSKI, Patrick M.
The Development of Moral Reasoning and the Foundations of Geometry. MACNAMARA, John.
Gilligan on Justice and Care: Two Interpretations. VREEKE, G J.
Kohlberg and Piaget: Differences and Similarities. KAVATHATZOPOULOS, Iordanis.
Moral Reasoning in a Communist Chinese Society. WALKER, Lawrence J and MORAN, Thomas J.
Promoting Moral Growth Through Intra-Group Participation. NELSON, D R and OBREMSKI, T E.
The Science of Caring. PUKA, Bill.
The Tensions Between Education and Development. GARDNER, Howard.
Die Theorie der moralischen Entwicklung von Lawrence Kohlberg und seiner Schule und die Moraltheologie. BUCHER, Anton.

KOJEVE, A
Hermeneutic or Metaphysical Hegelianism? Kojève's Dilemma. REDDING, Paul.
The Ironist's Cage. ROTH, Michael S.

KOLMOGOROV, A
The Autonomy of Probability Theory (Notes on Kolmogorov, Rényi, and Popper). LEBLANC, Hugues.
El azar objetivo como medida matemática de desorden. MARTÍNEZ, Sergio.

KOLNAI, A
"Approaches to Democratic Equality: Maritain, Simon, and Kolnai" in *Freedom in the Modern World: Jacques Maritain, Yves R Simon, Mortimer J Adler*, HITTINGER, John P.

KRAUSE, K
Algunas consecuencias del panenteismo krausista: ecología y mujer. MENÉNDEZ UREÑA, Enrique.

KRAUT, R
Emotions, Feelings and Contexts: A Reply to Robert Kraut. SOLOMON, Robert C.

KRIPKE, S
The Looking-Glass Self: An Examination of Self-Awareness. CANFIELD, John.

KRIPKE, S
The Metaphysics of Meaning. KATZ, Jerrold J.
Apriorische Einsicht und metaphysische Notwendigkeit: Eine Auseinandersetzung mit Kripkes Kant-Kritik. WENDEL, Hans Jürgen.
Conditional Essences. HAIGHT, Mary R.
The Contingent *A Priori*: Kripke's Two Types of Examples. GEIRSSON, Heimir.
Deontic Logic and Possible World Semantics: A Historical Sketch. WOLENSKI, Jan.
The Extent of Russell's Modal Views. MAGNELL, Thomas.
La force du nombre: remarques autour de la notion de communauté. FAUCHER, Luc.
Getting Rule-Following Straight. WONG, James.
Is Kripke's Puzzle Really a Puzzle. CORLETT, J Angelo.
Kripke on Theoretical Identifications: A Rejoinder to Perrick. BUXTON, James.
Logics of Truth. TURNER, Raymond.
McGinn on Concept Scepticism and Kripke's Sceptical Argument. SARTORELLI, Joseph.
On Knowing and Naming. BEARDS, Andrew.
On Removing Puzzles About Belief Ascription. DEVITT, Michael.
Putnam on Kripke's Puzzle. GARRETT, Richard.
Reglas, comunidades y juicios. ZALABARDO, José Luis.
Rule-Scepticism: Kripkean Understanding in Wittgenstein's Perspective. BEHERA, Satrughna.
Sobre la semántica de los nombres propios. SCHIRN, Matthias.
Units of Measurement and Natural Kinds: Some Kripkean Considerations. VAN BRAKEL, J.
A Very Short Guide to Understanding Wittgenstein. RESNICK, Larry.
Wittgenstein et l'institution du langage. SEYMOUR, Michel.

KRISHNAMURTI
Choiceless Awareness. SEN, Sanat Kumar.
Fragmentation, Meditation and Transformation: The Teachings of J Krishnamurti. NARAYANA MOORTY, J S R L.
Knowledge as Bondage: An Unconventional Approach. SEN, Sanat Kumar.

KRISTEVA, J
Language and "The Feminine" in Nietzsche and Heidegger. GRAYBEAL, Jean.
How I Slugged It Out with Toril Moi and Stayed Awake. BEDIENT, Calvin.
The Joy of Transgression: Bataille and Kristeva. MARCHAK, Catherine.
Kristeva and Holbein, Artist of Melancholy. LECHTE, John.
Motherhood and the Possibility of a Contemporary Discourse for Women. GREY, Mary.
Reading Kristeva: A Response to Calvin Bedient. MOI, Toril.
The Heterogeneity of Poetic Language in Kristeva (in Japanese). NARUSE, Katsuji.

KROKER, A
The Postmodern Posture. KHANIN, Dmitry.

KRYLOV, N
Irreversibility and Statistical Mechanics: A New Approach?. BATTERMAN, Robert W.

KUHN, T
Aspectos Metodológicos de la Investigación Científica. GONZÁLEZ, Wenceslao J (ed).
"Metzger, Kuhn, and Eighteenth-Century Disciplinary History" in *Études sur/Studies on Hélène Metzger*, MELHADO, Evan M.
"Rationality and Objectivity in Science, *or* Tom Kuhn Meets Tom Bayes" in *Scientific Theories*, SALMON, Wesley C.
"Scientific Revolutions and Scientific Rationality: The Case of the Elderly Holdout" in *Scientific Theories*, WORRALL, John.
Account of a Philosophical Expedition in Search of the Elusive Paradigm (in Dutch). GOUWS, A S.
Did Kuhn Kill Logical Empiricism?. REISCH, George A.
Estrategias metacientíficas: Parte II. HIDALGO TUÑÓN, Alberto.
Incommensurability and the Indeterminacy of Translation. SANKEY, Howard.
Interpretation and Theory in the Natural and the Human Sciences: Comments on Kuhn and Taylor. LACEY, Hugh.
Kuhn's Conception of Incommensurability. HOYNINGEN-HUENE, Paul.
A Kuhnian Model of Falsifiability. STONE, Mark A.
Local Incommensurability and Communicability. CHEN, Xiang.
Modelos de cambio científico en la filosofía actual de la ciencia. STRÖKER, Elisabeth.
Objectivity and Growth of Knowledge. CHAUDHURY, Mahasweta.
Observation: An Empirical Discussion. GILMAN, Daniel.
Paradigmas cartesianos. LOPARIC, Z.
Rejection Without Acceptance. MATHESON, Carl A and KLINE, A David.
Thomas S Kuhn and L Fleck: Two Sociologists of Science. FLURI, Philippe H.
Three Accounts of Paradigm Shift. MUKHERJEE, Nilratan.
Two Dogmas of Neo-Empiricism: The "Theory-Informity" of Observation and the Quine-Duhem Thesis. GREENWOOD, John D.
Why Scientists Gather Evidence. MAHER, Patrick.

KUZNECOV, A
La Logica Simbolica: nella produzione scientifica in lingua russa (1961-1983). PENNINO, Luciano.

KYMLICKA, W
Liberalism, Aboriginal Rights, and Cultural Minorities. DANLEY, John R.

LABEL(S)
A Theorem on Labelled Trees and the Limits of Its Provability. PFEIFFER, Helmut.

LABOR
Controlling Technology: Contemporary Issues. THOMPSON, William B.
Marx's Radical Critique of Capitalist Society: A Reconstruction and Critical Evaluation. ARNOLD, N Scott.
"Action, Story, and History—On Rereading 'The Human Condition'" in *The Realm of Humanitas: Responses to the Writings of Hannah Arendt*, RICOEUR, Paul.
Antropología del trabajo según la Encíclica "Laborem Excercens". QUESADA GUARDIA, Annabelle.
The Divided Machine: Capitalist Crisis and the Organization of Labor. TURCHETTO, Maria and ESPOSITO, Joan.
Freedom, Commodification, and the Alienation of Labor in Adam Smith's "Wealth of Nations". WERHANE, Patricia H.
Rationality and Social Labor in Marx. KHALIL, Elias L.

LABRIOLA, A
Silvio Spaventa e Antonio Labriola, gli 'aspetti-pedagogici'. DE CUMIS, Nicola Siciliani.

LACAN, J
"On Becoming a Subject: Lacan's Rereading of Freud" in *Reconsidering Psychology: Perspectives from Continental Philosophy*, BERGOFFEN, Debra B.
The Body Politic: Democratic Metaphors, Totalitarian Practices, Erotic Rebellions. BERGOFFEN, Debra B.
Lacan Between Freud and Heidegger (in Serbo-Croatian). VETTER, Helmut.
Psychanalyse et existentialisme: À propos de la théorie lacanienne de la subjectivité. VAN HAUTE, P.

LAING, R
An Abyss of Difference: Laing, Sartre and Jaspers. KIRSNER, Douglas.

LAKATOS, I
Imre Lakatos and Theories of Scientific Change. GAVROGLU, Kostas (ed).
"Bridge Structures and the Borderline Between the Internal and External History of Science" in *Imre Lakatos and Theories of Scientific Change*, GÄHDE, Ulrich.
"A Critical Consideration of the Lakatosian Concepts: 'Mature' and 'Immature' Science" in *Imre Lakatos and Theories of Scientific Change*, METAXOPOULOS, Emilio.
"Imre Lakatos in China" in *Imre Lakatos and Theories of Scientific Change*, DAINIAN, Fan.
"Lakatos on the Evaluation of Scientific Theories" in *Imre Lakatos and Theories of Scientific Change*, AVGELIS, Nikolaos.
"Methodological Sophisticationism: A Degenerating Project" in *Imre Lakatos and Theories of Scientific Change*, PERA, Marcello.
"Proofs and Refutations: A Reassessment" in *Imre Lakatos and Theories of Scientific Change*, ANAPOLITANOS, D A.
The Challenge to Lakatos Restated. AKEROYD, F Michael.
Davy Refuted Lavoisier Not Lakatos. ZUCKER, Arthur.
Estrategias metacientíficas: Parte II. HIDALGO TUÑÓN, Alberto.
From the Logic of Mathematical Discovery to the Methodology of Scientific Research Programmes. YUXIN, Zheng.
Metaphysics, MSRP and Economics. GLASS, J C and JOHNSON, W.
Objectivity and Growth of Knowledge. CHAUDHURY, Mahasweta.
Research Programmes and Empirical Results. AKEROYD, F M.
Three Accounts of Paradigm Shift. MUKHERJEE, Nilratan.

LAMBDA CALCULUS
Inductive Types and Type Constraints in the Second-Order Lambda Calculus. MENDLER, Nax Paul.
Kripke-Style Models for Typed Lambda Calculus. MITCHELL, John C and MOGGI, Eugenio.
λ-Definability on Free Algebras. ZAIONC, Marek.
Some Improvements to Turner's Algorithm for Bracket Abstraction. BUNDER, M W.
Uniform Proofs as a Foundation for Logic Programming. MILLER, Dale and NADATHUR, Gopalan and PFENNING, Frank and SCEDROV, Andre.

LAMBERT
Kommunikations-Theoretische Schriften II: Symbolische Erkenntnis und Kommunikation. UNGEHEUER, Gerold (ed).
Kant, Mendelssohn, Lambert, and the Subjectivity of Time. FALKENSTEIN, Lorne.
Quantum Physics and Logical Truth (in Italian). GIANNETTO, Enrico.

LAND
The River of the Mother of God, and Other Essays by Aldo Leopold. FLADER, Susan L (ed).
Land Rights and Aboriginal Sovereignty. THOMPSON, Janna.
Land, Well-Being and Compensation. PARGETTER, Robert and YOUNG, Robert and BIGELOW, John.

LANGE

La prima e seconda edizione della "Geschichte des Materialismus" di Friedrich Albert Lange. COGNETTI, Giuseppe.

LANGER, S

Man as the Animal Symbolism in the Conception of S Langer (in Polish). BYTNIEWSKI, Pawel.

LANGUAGE

see also Linguistics, Semantics
"Also sprach Herakleitos". WOHLFART, Günter.
Alltagssprachliche Metakommunikation im Englischen und Deutschen. WELTE, Werner.
The Anatomy of Judgment. REGAL, Philip J.
Aristotelian Logic and the Arabic Language in Alfarabi. ABED, Shukri B.
Artificial Intelligence and Human Cognition. WAGMAN, Morton.
Brouwer's Intuitionism (Studies in the History and Philosophy of Mathematics, Vol 2). VAN STIGT, W P.
Chinese Texts and Philosophical Contexts. ROSEMONT JR, Henry (ed).
Classics of Analytic Philosophy. AMMERMAN, Robert R (ed).
The Cogito and Hermeneutics: The Question of the Subject in Ricoeur. JERVOLINO, Domenico.
The Communicative Ethics Controversy. BENHABIB, Seyla (ed).
Community: The Tie That Binds. ROUSSEAU, Mary F.
Consciousness and the Computational Mind. JACKENDOFF, Ray.
Creative Characters. YOUNG-BRUEHL, Elisabeth.
The Difference Between Truth and Opinion: How the Misuse of Language Can Lead to Disaster. COONEY, Timothy J.
Divine Nature and Human Language: Essays in Philosophical Theology. ALSTON, William P.
Donald Davidson. EVNINE, Simon.
Essays on Heidegger and Others: Philosophical Papers, Volume 2. RORTY, Richard.
Events in the Semantics of English: A Study in Subatomic Semantics. PARSONS, Terence.
Existence et Subjectivité: Études de Psychologie Phénoménologique. THINÈS, Georges.
Fictions of Reality in the Age of Hume and Johnson. DAMROSCH, Leo.
The Foundations of Linguistic Theory: Selected Writings of Roy Harris. LOVE, Nigel (ed).
Frege and Other Philosophers. DUMMETT, Michael.
Frege in Perspective. WEINER, Joan.
French Philosophers in Conversation: Levinas, Schneider, Serres, Irigaray, Le Doeuff, Derrida. MORTLEY, Raoul.
From Sentience To Symbols. PICKERING, John (ed).
Has Semantics Rested on a Mistake?. WETTSTEIN, Howard.
Hermeneutical Studies: Dilthey, Sophocles, and Plato. WILSON, Barrie A.
A Hindu Perspective on the Philosophy of Religion. SHARMA, Arvind.
Identity and Discrimination. WILLIAMSON, Timothy.
In Defense of Mystical Ideas: Support for Mystical Beliefs from a Purely Theoretical Viewpoint. CHAPMAN, Tobias.
Inference and Understanding: A Philosophical and Psychological Perspective. MANKTELOW, K I.
Information, Semantics and Epistemology. VILLANUEVA, Enrique (ed).
Inscriptions and Reflections: Essays in Philosophical Theology. SCHARLEMANN, Robert P.
Intentions in Communication. COHEN, Philip R (ed).
Kalkulierte Absurditäten. STRUB, Christian.
Kommunikations-Theoretische Schriften II: Symbolische Erkenntnis und Kommunikation. UNGEHEUER, Gerold (ed).
Language and "The Feminine" in Nietzsche and Heidegger. GRAYBEAL, Jean.
Leibniz's Philosophy of Logic and Language (Second Edition). ISHIGURO, Hide.
Leibniz, Humboldt, and the Origins of Comparativism. DE MAURO, Tullio (ed).
Linguistic Behaviour. BENNETT, Jonathan.
The Logical Basis of Metaphysics. DUMMETT, Michael.
The Looking-Glass Self: An Examination of Self-Awareness. CANFIELD, John.
Meaning and Method: Essays in Honor of Hilary Putnam. BOOLOS, George (ed).
Meaning and Speech Acts: Volume I, Principles of Language Use. VANDERVEKEN, Daniel.
Meaning and Speech Acts: Volume II, Formal Semantics of Success and Satisfaction. VANDERVEKEN, Daniel.
Meaning and Truth: The Essential Readings in Modern Semantics. GARFIELD, Jay L (ed).
Metaphysical Delusion. COWLEY, Fraser.
The Metaphysics of Meaning. KATZ, Jerrold J.
Metaphysics: A Contemporary Introduction. POST, John F.
Mind and Cognition: A Reader. LYCAN, William G (ed).
The Mind of Donald Davidson. BRANDL, Johannes (ed).
Myth and Modern Philosophy. DANIEL, Stephen H.
Negative Dialectics and the End of Philosophy. ERICKSON, Glenn W.
New Dimensions of Confucian and Neo-Confucian Philosophy. CHENG, Chung-ying.
Nietzsche and the Question of Interpretation. SCHRIFT, Alan D.
Nietzsche On Truth and Philosophy. CLARK, Maudemarie.
The Ontology of Physical Objects: Four-Dimensional Hunks of Matter. HELLER, Mark.
The Other Side of Language: A Philosophy of Listening. FIUMARA, Gemma Corradi.
An Outline of the Philosophy of Knowledge and Science. BLANDINO, Giovanni.
Perspectives on Quine. BARRETT, Robert (ed).
Phänomenologische Philosophie. STRÖKER, Elisabeth.
A Philosophical Daybook: Post-Critical Investigations. POTEAT, William H.
Philosophical Essays. CARTWRIGHT, Richard.
Philosophical Hermeneutics and Literary Theory. WEINSHEIMER, Joel.
Philosophical Perspectives, 3: Philosophy of Mind and Action Theory, 1989. TOMBERLIN, James E (ed).
Philosophy and Cognitive Science. FETZER, James H.
A Post-Modern Epistemology. SORRI, Mari.
Postmodernism—Philosophy and the Arts (Continental Philosophy III). SILVERMAN, Hugh J (ed).
Properties as Processes: A Synoptic Study of Wilfried Sellars' Nominalism. SEIBT, Johanna.
Propositional Attitudes: The Role of Content in Logic, Language, and Mind. ANDERSON, C Anthony (ed).
Reading Rorty. MALACHOWSKI, Alan (ed).
The Rhetoric of Berkeley's Philosophy. WALMSLEY, Peter.
Rorty's Humanistic Pragmatism: Philosophy Democratized. KOLENDA, Konstantin.
Saggio di semantica. BRÉAL, Michel.
Saussure: Signs, System, and Arbitrariness. HOLDCROFT, David.
Semantic Structures. JACKENDOFF, Ray.
Speech Acts and Literary Theory. PETREY, Sandy.
Structures in Mathematical Theories: Reports of the San Sebastian International Symposium, 1990. DÍEZ, Amparo (ed).
Swimming Against the Current in Contemporary Philosophy: Occasional Essays and Papers. VEATCH, Henry B.
Talking Philosophy: A Wordbook. SPARKES, A W.
Teoria e interpretazione: Per un'epistemologia delle scienze umane. BORUTTI, Silvana.
Themes From Kaplan. ALMOG, Joseph (ed).
Three Great Traditions. PEDERSEN, Olaf.
Trois essais sur la pensée. THÉAU, Jean.
Truth and Interpretation: Perspectives on the Philosophy of Donald Davidson. LE PORE, Ernest (ed).
Understanding Arguments: An Introduction to Informal Logic (Fourth Edition). FOGELIN, Robert J.
The Unity of Kant's "Critique of Pure Reason": Experience, Language, and Knowledge. WILLIAMS, T C.
The Unity of Understanding: A Study in Kantian Problems. SCHWYZER, Hubert.
Wahrheit—Diskurs—Demokratie: Studien zur "Konsensustheorie der Wahrheit". SCHEIT, Herbert.
Wittgenstein and Contemporary Philosophy of Language. RUNDLE, Bede.
Writing and the Moral Self. LANG, Berel.
Writing the Politics of Difference. SILVERMAN, Hugh J (ed).
"'A Nice Derangement of Epitaphs': Some Comments on Davidson and Hacking" in *Truth and Interpretation: Perspectives on the Philosophy of Donald Davidson*, DUMMETT, Michael.
"'Vulgaris opinio babelica': Sui fondamenti storico-teorici della pluralità delle lingue nel pensiero di Leibniz" in *Leibniz, Humboldt, and the Origins of Comparativism*, GENSINI, Stefano.
"Analysis, Language, and Concepts: The Second Paradox of Analysis" in *Philosophical Perspectives, 4: Action Theory and Philosophy of Mind, 1990*, ACKERMAN, Felicia.
"At This Very Moment in This Work Here I Am" in *Re-Reading Levinas*, DERRIDA, Jacques and BEREZDIVIN, Ruben.
"A Central Problem for a Speech-Dispositional Account of Logic and Language" in *Perspectives on Quine*, BERGER, Alan.
"Davidson's Semantics and Computational Understanding of Language" in *The Mind of Donald Davidson*, BOJADZIEV, Damjan.
"Facts That Don't Matter" in *Meaning and Method: Essays in Honor of Hilary Putnam*, ELGIN, Catherine Z.
"Frege, Concepts and the Design of Language" in *Information, Semantics and Epistemology*, HIGGINBOTHAM, James.
"Hegel e a linguagem: estudo em forma de prefácio ou introdução" in *Dinâmica do Pensar: Homenagem a Oswaldo Market*, POMBO, Olga.
"How the Fable Becomes a World" in *Looking After Nietzsche*, CANNING, Peter.
"How to Turn the *Tractatus* Wittgenstein into (Almost) Donald Davidson" in *Truth and Interpretation: Perspectives on the Philosophy of Donald Davidson*, SMART, J J C.
"Incremental Acquisition and a Parametrized Model of Grammar" in *Acting and Reflecting: The Interdisciplinary Turn in Philosophy*, CLARK, Robin.
"Language as Metaphorical: A Reply to John Cobb" in *Archetypal Process: Self and Divine in Whitehead, Jung, and Hillman*, HOPPER, Stanley R.
"Language in the Heart-mind" in *Understanding the Chinese Mind: The Philosophical Roots*, HANSEN, Chad.

LANGUAGE

"The Language of Ecstasy and the Ecstasy of Language" in *The Bible as Rhetoric: Studies in Biblical Persuasion and Credibility*, BARRETT, Cyril.
"Mario Bunge on Semantics" in *Studies on Mario Bunge's "Treatise"*, BUNGE, Mario.
"Meaning, Holism and Use" in *Truth and Interpretation: Perspectives on the Philosophy of Donald Davidson*, BILGRAMI, Akeel.
"The Meanings of Logical Constants" in *Truth and Interpretation: Perspectives on the Philosophy of Donald Davidson*, HARMAN, Gilbert.
"Merleau-Ponty and *l'Écriture*" in *Writing the Politics of Difference*, FROMAN, Wayne J.
"On the Concept of 'a Language'" in *Studies on Mario Bunge's "Treatise"*, DILLINGER, Mike.
"On the Old Saw That Character Is Destiny" in *Identity, Character, and Morality: Essays in Moral Psychology*, MOODY-ADAMS, Michele.
"Ordinary Animals, Language Animals and Verbal Tradition" in *Harré and His Critics*, REYNOLDS, Vernon.
"The Otherness of Words: Joyce, Bakhtin, Heidegger" in *Postmodernism—Philosophy and the Arts (Continental Philosophy III)*, BRUNS, Gerald L.
"The Parody of Conversation" in *Truth and Interpretation: Perspectives on the Philosophy of Donald Davidson*, HACKING, Ian.
"Partial Truths about Partial Truth" in *Studies on Mario Bunge's "Treatise"*, MARQUIS, Jean-Pierre.
"Postmodern Language" in *Postmodernism—Philosophy and the Arts (Continental Philosophy III)*, SCOTT, Charles E.
"Psychology after Philosophy" in *Reconsidering Psychology: Perspectives from Continental Philosophy*, POLKINGHORNE, Donald.
"Quine as a Member of the Tradition of the Universality of Language" in *Perspectives on Quine*, HINTIKKA, Jaakko.
"Referência e valor cognitivo" in *Dinâmica do Pensar: Homenagem a Oswaldo Market*, BRANQUINHO, João.
"Reflections and Replies" in *Chinese Texts and Philosophical Contexts*, GRAHAM, Angus C.
"The Refutation of Indeterminacy" in *Perspectives on Quine*, KATZ, Jerrold.
"The Reverse Frege Puzzle" in *Philosophical Perspectives, 3: Philosophy of Mind and Action Theory, 1989*, YAGISAWA, Takashi.
"The Scientist as 'Homo Loquens'" in *Harré and His Critics*, HARRIS, Roy.
"Seeing To It That: A Canonical Form for Agentives" in *Knowledge Representation and Defeasible Reasoning*, BELNAP JR, Nuel D and PERLOFF, Michael.
"Sex, Gender, and the Politics of Difference" in *Writing the Politics of Difference*, KUYKENDALL, Eleanor H.
"Some Remarks on Davidson's Theory of Truth" in *The Mind of Donald Davidson*, VARGA VON KIBÉD, Matthias.
"The Source of the Concept of Truth" in *Meaning and Method: Essays in Honor of Hilary Putnam*, DUMMETT, Michael.
"The Third Dogma" in *Truth and Interpretation: Perspectives on the Philosophy of Donald Davidson*, KRAUT, Robert.
"Turning the Tables on Frege or How is it that 'Hesperus is Hesperus' is Trivial?" in *Philosophical Perspectives, 3: Philosophy of Mind and Action Theory, 1989*, WETTSTEIN, Howard.
"Two Conceptions of Philosophy" in *Perspectives on Quine*, STRAWSON, P F.
"Weighing Anchor: Postmodern Journeys from the Life-World" in *Life-World and Politics: Between Modernity and Postmodernity*, SHAPIRO, Michael J.
"What a Truth Theory Need Not Tell Us" in *Truth and Interpretation: Perspectives on the Philosophy of Donald Davidson*, GRANDY, Richard E.
"What Davidson Should Have Said" in *The Mind of Donald Davidson*, LE PORE, Ernest and LOEWER, Barry.
"What is Wrong with the Building Block Theory of Language?" in *The Mind of Donald Davidson*, BRANDL, Johannes.
"Wilhelm von Humboldt und das Problem der Schrift" in *Leibniz, Humboldt, and the Origins of Comparativism*, STETTER, Christian.
"Wittgenstein's Notion of Secondary Meaning and Davidson's Account of Metaphor—A Comparison" in *The Mind of Donald Davidson*, SCHULTE, Joachim.
"As Real As It Gets...": Ricoeur and Narrativity. KELLNER, Hans.
A "Con-versão" da Filosofia em Martin Heidegger. ESTÊVÃO, Carlos.
"Das Wort sie sollen lassen stahn": Zur Edition und Interpretation philosophischer Texte, erläutert am B Kants. BRANDT, Reinhard.
"Il y a" et phénoménologie dans la pensée du jeune Lévinas. LANNOY, Jean-Luc.
"Le signe en défaut". ROBIN, Régine.
The "Middle Wittgenstein": From Logical Atomism to Practical Holism. STERN, David G.
The "No Crossing Constraint" in Autosegmental Phonology. COLEMAN, John and LOCAL, John.
À propos d'arguments qui s'ignorent. VIGNAUX, Georges.
Abstract Singular Reference: A Dilemma for Dummett. MILLER, Alexander.
Accent on *One*: Entity and Identity. BOLINGER, Dwight.
Account of a Philosophical Expedition in Search of the Elusive Paradigm (in Dutch). GOUWS, A S.
Actualism, Ontological Commitment, and Possible World Semantics. MENZEL, Ch.
Adquisición del lenguaje y antropología. FERNÁNDEZ, Teresa Bejarano.
Advaita and Religious Language. GRIMES, John.
All the Difference in the World. CRANE, Tim.
Ambiguity, Generality, and Indeterminacy: Tests and Definitions. GILLON, Brendan S.
Anachronistic Themes and Literary Value: *The Tempest*. SKILLEAS, Ole Martin.
Analyse critique de quelques modèles sémiotiques de l'idéologie (deuxième partie). TREMBLAY, Robert.
Another Look at the Derrida-Searle Debate. ALFINO, Mark.
Anscombian and Cartesian Scepticism. HAMILTON, Andy.
Aphasia and Inner Language. LANTÉRI-LAURA, Georges and WALKER, R Scott.
Aphasia—The Worm's Eye View of a Philosophic Patient and the Medical Establishment. ALEXANDER, Edwin.
The Application of Montague Translations in Universal Research and Typology. TENT, Katrin.
La apuesta literaria de Nietzsche. MONTORO, Marcial Moreno.
Are There Cultural Universals?. WIREDU, Kwasi.
Art and Neurology: A Discussion. HALPIN, David M G and SORRELL, Martin.
Aspects of the Problem of Reference (I). RAJAN, R Sundara.
Aspects of the Problem of Reference (II). RAJAN, R Sundara.
Authenticity as Virtue (in Dutch). STRUYKER BOUDIER, C E M.
Author, Writer, Text: *The Will to Power*. MAGNUS, Bernd.
Avoiding the Fly Bottle. KOLENDA, Konstantin.
Basal Readers—'Dominant But Dead' versus Gadamer and Language for Understanding. WIRTH, Arthur G.
Behaviourism, Neuroscience and Translational Indeterminacy. WARMBRŌD, Ken.
Beyond the "Limits" of *Mundane Reason*. BOGEN, David.
Beyond the Real/Apparent World: From Signs to Imaging in Nietzsche. WATSON, James R.
Blanshard on Philosophical Style. SMITH, John E.
Blind Grasping and Fregean Senses. SCHWEIZER, Paul.
Brains in a Vat, Language and Metalanguage. CASATI, Roberto and DOKIC, Jérome.
Can Fiction Be Stranger Than Truth? An Aristotelian Answer. GALLOP, David.
Cartesian Syntax. ENGLEBRETSEN, George.
Castañeda's Quasi-Indicators and the Tensed Theory of Time. SMITH, Quentin.
A Certain 'Politics of Speech': 'Religious Pluralism' in the Age of the McDonald's Hamburger. SURIN, Kenneth.
Churchland and the Talking Brain. MUKHERJI, Nirmalangshu.
Circularity of Thought in Hegel's Logic. BALABAN, Oded.
Cognitive Psychology, Phenomenology, and the "Creative Tension of Voices". EVANS, Fred.
Cognitive Science on a Wing and a Prayer. KEITH, William.
Comme en un miroir: quelques remarques historiques sur l'arbitraire du signe. LATRAVERSE, François.
Commentary on "Epistemology as Hypothesis". SLEEPER, R W.
Computational Structure of GPSG Models. RISTAD, Eric Sven.
La condición pública del lenguaje y la autoridad de la primera persona. ROLLINS, Mark.
Connectionism, Modularity, and Tacit Knowledge. DAVIES, Martin.
Constructive Modal Logics I. WIJESEKERA, Duminda.
The Context of Discourse: Let's Not Throw the Baby Out with the Bathwater. ABRAMS, Dominic and HOGG, Michael A.
Conventions, règles et nécessité. VOIZARD, Alain.
Le corps et ses langages: quelques perspectives de travail historique. COURTINE, Jean-Jacques.
Cultural Evolution, Biology and Language: Empirical and Rational Criteria of Selection (in German). DORSCHEL, Andreas.
Dasein—Mitsein—Sprache: Heideggers Auffassung über das "Wesen der Sprache" in "Sein und Zeit". TIETZ, Udo.
Davidson's Paratactic Analysis of Mood. MILLER, Seumas.
Deciding to Act. FIELDS, L.
Decir lo mismo (Frege y Santo Tomás). SANGUINETI, Juan J.
Deconstruction as Symbolic Play: Simmel/Derrida. WEINSTEIN, Deena and WEINSTEIN, Michael A.
Defending the Tradition. NIELSEN, Kai.
Definability in Self-Referential Systems. SOBRINHO, J Zimbarg.
Definite Descriptions and Definite Generics. OJEDA, Almerindo E.
La démonstration mystifiante: Wittgenstein et Beuys. LA CHANCE, Michaël.
Demonstrative Utterances. BERCKMANS, Paul.
Derrida's huishouding. BERNS, Egidius.
El desaparecer de lo eterno en sí mismo: Una clave del pensamiento de Hegel. ALBIZU, Edgardo.
Dialectic and Diagonalization. KADVANY, John.
Dialogues in Natural Language with GURU, a Psychologic Inference Engine. COLBY, Kenneth M and COLBY, Peter M and STOLLER, Robert J.
Dictionaries and Proper Names. MARCONI, Diego.
Did Kuhn Kill Logical Empiricism?. REISCH, George A.
Did Plato Coin *Rhētorikē*?. SCHIAPPA, Edward.

LANGUAGE
Difference as Deficit. REAGAN, Timothy.
The Difference-Deficit Debate: Theoretical Smokescreen for a Conservative Ambush. MC DADE, Laurie A.
Différentielles et intégrales sociales chez Rousseau. BACHTA, Abdelkader.
A Dilemma for Bartley's Pancritical Rationalism. HAUPTLI, Bruce W.
A Dilemma for Sentential Dualism. MOSER, Paul K.
Dire e ascoltare nella tipologia del "sofista", del "filosof-re" e del pensatore socratico. MARCHETTI, Giancarlo.
Direct Reference, Meaning, and Thought. RECANATI, François.
Discourse: Definitions and Contradictions. PARKER, Ian.
Discourse: Noun, Verb or Social Practice?. POTTER, Jonathan (and others).
Distorted Tradition: Etymological Observations about the Misuse of Some Philosophical Terms in Modern Indian English. DE SANTIS, Stefano.
Does Wittgenstein's Concept of Language Game Patterns Come Up with a Solution to the Platonic Problem ... (in German). LÜTTERFELDS, Wilhelm.
Il doppio volto dell'ineffabile in L Wittgenstein. TODISCO, Orlando.
Dummett and the Origins of Analytical Philosophy, or the Philosophy of Thought vs Philosophy of Language (in German). DÖLLING, Evelyn and DÖLLING, Johannes.
Dynamic Predicate Logic. GROENENDIJK, Jeroen and STOKHOF, Martin.
Elements of Speech Act Theory in the Work of Thomas Reid. SCHUHMANN, Karl and SMITH, Barry.
Ellipsis and Higher-Order Unification. DALRYMPLE, Mary and SHIEBER, Stuart M and PEREIRA, Fernando C N.
The Enlightenment—a Stranded Project? Habermas on Nietzsche as a 'Turning Point' to Postmodernity. NAGL, Ludwig.
L'epoché di Husserl in Ferruccio Rossi-Landi. PONZIO, Augusto.
Even and *Even If*. LYCAN, William G.
Even, Still and Counterfactuals. BARKER, Stephen.
Everyday Argumentation from a Speech Act Perspective. GROOTENDORST, Rob.
The Exile of Literature: Poetry and the Politics of the Other(s). MURPHY, Bruce F.
Explanation-Explication Conflict in Transformational Grammar. DAS GUPTA, Amitabha.
Extensionality, Underdetermination and Indeterminacy. SOLOMON, Miriam.
Fondamento e verità. CAMPANALE, Domenico.
La force du nombre: remarques autour de la notion de communauté. FAUCHER, Luc.
Form of Life in Wittgenstein's Later Work. GARVER, Newton.
The Formal Language L_t and Topological Products. BERTOSSI, L E.
Formulation of Grice's Three Intentions. LENKA, Laxminarayan.
Foucault and The Referent. LUNN, Forrest.
Foucault's Critique of Heidegger. HILL, R Kevin.
Foucault, Nietzsche, History: Two Modes of the Genealogical Method. SAX, Benjamin C.
Four Thousand Ships Passed Through the Lock: Object-Induced Measure Functions on Events. KRIFKA, Manfred.
Frege-Russell Semantics?. WETTSTEIN, Howard.
Friedrich Nietzsche and Classical Philology Today. IRMSCHER, Johannes.
From Precision to Peace: Hobbes and Political Language. MINOGUE, Kenneth.
From What Can't Be Said To What Isn't Known. MC KINNON, Christine.
Future Individuals. TEICHMANN, Roger.
Gangesa and Transfer of Meaning. SAHA, Sukharanjan.
A Generalization of the Adequacy Theorem for the Quasi-Senses. BONOTTO, Cinzia.
The Genesis of Wittgenstein's Later Philosophy in His Failure as a Phenomenologist. HALLETT, Garth.
Genuine Names and Knowledge by Acquaintance. DONNELLAN, Keith S.
Gestualità e mito: i due caratteri distintivi della lingua originaria secondo Vico. CANTELLI, Gianfranco.
Glosses on Heidegger's Architectonic Word-Play. PRUFER, Thomas.
Grammaire et Liturgie dans les "Sophismes" du XIIIe Siècle. ROSIER, Irène and ROY, Bruno.
Grammar, Semantics and Conditionals. DUDMAN, V H.
Habermas et la théologie: Notes pour une discussion entre la théologie et la "Théorie de l'agir communicationnel". KISSLING, Christian.
Hegel's Intertextual Dialectic: Diderot's *Le Neveu de Rameau* in the *Phenomenology of Spirit*. PRICE, David W.
Heidegger on Logic and Language: Some Aporiai. FAY, Thomas A.
Heideggers "logische Untersuchungen". OUDEMANS, Th C W.
Herméneutique et épistémologie Gadamer entre Heidegger et Hegel. ROCKMORE, Tom.
The Historical Consciousness of Man. MITSCHERLING, Jeff.
How Ideas Became Meanings: Locke and the Foundations of Semantic Theory. HANNA, Robert.
Il y a vingt-cinq ans la sémiotique.... KHOURI, Nadia.
The Implications of Error for Davidsonian Charity. LARSON, David.
In Defence of "Hard" Offers: A Reply to J P Day. HÄYRY, Matti and AIRAKSINEN, Timo.
In Defence of Unrepresentative Realism. TONGS, A R.
In Defense of Plato: A Short Polemic. ROOCHNIK, David.
Indefinite Descriptions: In Defense of Russell. LUDLOW, Peter and NEALE, Stephen.
The Indeterminacy Thesis Reformulated. GEMES, Ken.
Indeterminacy, Empirical Evidence, and Methodological Pluralism. ROUSE, Joseph.
Indeterminate Identity, Contingent Identity and Abelardian Predicates. NOONAN, Harold W.
Indexicality: The Transparent Subjective Mechanism for Encountering a World. CASTAÑEDA, Héctor-Neri.
The Indispensability of *Sinn*. FORBES, Graeme.
The Ins and Outs of Mysticism. HART, Kevin.
Intensionality and Boundedness. MORRILL, Glyn.
Intentionality and Modern Philosophical Psychology—II: The Return to Representation. LYONS, Willia.
The Interpretation of Texts, People and Other Artifacts. DENNETT, Daniel C.
Interpreting *Interpretations*. GROSSMAN, Morris.
Interpreting Sophistical Rhetoric: A Response to Schiappa. POULAKOS, John.
Intuitionistic Categorial Grammar. RANTA, Aarne.
The Irony of Richard Rorty and the Question of Political Judgment. WEISLOGEL, Eric L.
Irreducible Dualisms and the Residue of Commonsense: On the Inevitability of Cartesian Anxiety. HIKINS, James W and CHERWITZ, Richard A.
Is There More to Speech Acts Than Illocutionary Force and Propositional Content?. HAJDIN, Mane.
De jonge Wittgenstein (1889-1921): Denken als ethos. DE DIJN, H.
The Joy of Transgression: Bataille and Kristeva. MARCHAK, Catherine.
Just Can't Find the Words: How Expression is Achieved. KING, Debra W.
Kant und Wittgenstein. STETTER, Christian.
L'Appel et le Phénomène. LARUELLE, François.
L'Assertion dans les contextes épistémiques; garants objectaux et bases d'évaluation. MOULOUD, Noël.
L'explicite et l'implicite dans la conception du signe chez Hobbes. POLIAKOV, Igor.
L'homme n'est pas l'humain. BOUCHARD, Guy.
L'inquiétante étrangeté de Jules Amédée Barbey d'Aurevilly. ROMEYER DHERBEY, Gilbert.
L'universalisation de l'herméneutique chez Hans-Georg Gadamer. GRONDIN, Jean.
Language and Conversation. GAITA, Raimond.
Language and Metaphysics: The Ontology of Metaphor. HAUSMAN, Carl R.
Language and Political Agency: Derrida, Marx, and Bakhtin. EVANS, Fred.
Language in Action. VAN BENTHEM, Johan.
The Language of Thought: No Syntax Without Semantics. CRANE, Tim.
Language, Logic and Reality. DEVARAJA, N K.
Language, Physics, and Geology (and a Few Words on Theology). BROGAN, Jacqueline Vaught.
Language, Speech and Writing: Merleau-Ponty and Derrida on Saussure. FREE, George.
The Last Word on *Philosophical Investigations* 43a. SAVIGNY, Eike V.
Later Wittgenstein on Objectivity of Rules. BEHERA, Sathrughna.
Law: From Foundation to Argumentation. LEMPEREUR, Alain.
Lenguaje y metafísica en Alfred J Ayer. BEUCHOT, Mauricio.
Lenguaje y verdad en Aristóteles. RODRIGUEZ, M L.
The Lesbian, the Mother, the Heterosexual Lover: Irigaray's Recodings of Difference. HOLMLUND, Christine.
Libri da salvare. POLC, Jaroslav.
Los límites de mi lenguaje—los límites de mi mundo. KLOYBER, Christian.
Il linguaggio ideologico della rivoluzione. MATHIEU, Vittorio.
Literature and Language After the Death of God. STEIN, A L.
Logic and Language in the *Chuang Tzu*. ALT, Wayne E.
Logics of Dialogue: A Necessary Multiplicity. MAIER, Robert.
La loi de vérité. POULAIN, Jacques.
Lost Buddhist Texts: The Rationale of Their Reconstruction in Sanskrit. CHINCHORE, Mangala R.
Malcolm on Wittgenstein on Rules. MOSER, Paul K.
Martin Heidegger and the Place of Language. VAN RODEN ALLEN, Robert.
Marx, Nietzsche, and the "New Class". EVANS, Fred.
Meaning and Intention: Black Versus Grice. MARTINICH, A P.
Meaning Holism and Interpretability. TALMAGE, Catherine J L and MERCER, Mark.
Meaning, Understanding and Translation. STROUD, Barry.
Meinongian Theories of Generality. SANTAMBROGIO, Marco.
Merleau-Ponty on Taking the Attitude of the Other. MATUSTIK, Martin J.
Metaphor and the Varieties of Lexical Meaning. HINTIKKA, Jaakko and SANDU, Gabriel.
Metaphor in the Language of Religion. PANDHARIPANDE, Rajeshwari.
Metaphor, Literalism, and the Non-Verbal Arts. BREDIN, Hugh.
Misreading Rorty. KOLENDA, Konstantin.
Moore's Paradox Revisited. LINVILLE, Kent and RING, Merrill.
The Myth of the Essential Indexical. MILLIKAN, Ruth.
Die Natur der Sprache: Von der Ontologie zur Technologie. HOTTOIS, Gilbert.
The Nature of Irony: Toward a Computational Model of Irony. LITTMAN, David C and MEY, Jacob L.

LANGUAGE

Necessary A Posteriori Truth. SWINBURNE, Richard.
The Need for Charity in Semantics. WARMBROD, Ken.
Neo-Sophistic Rhetorical Criticism or the Historical Reconstruction of Sophistic Doctrines?. SCHIAPPA, Edward.
Never say "Never say 'Never'": A Reply to Nicholas Gier. REEDER, Harry P.
Nietzsche and Foucault on *Ursprung* and Genealogy. COOK, Deborah.
Nietzsche and the Critique of Oppositional Thinking. SCHRIFT, Alan D.
Nietzsche and the Woman Question. DIETHE, Carol.
Nietzsche's Arctic Zone of Cognition and Post-Structuralism. PARENT, David.
Nietzsche: The Divination Paradigm of Knowledge in Western Culture. BULHOF, Ilse N.
Nombres y objetos en el *Tractatus*. VALDÉS, Margarita M.
Nonrules and Plausibility: An Illustration in Pragmatic Theory. POWELL, Mava Jo.
Not Every Object of a Sign has Being. PAPE, Helmut.
Note sulle recenti traduzioni di *Essere e tempo* in Francia. MARRATI, Paola.
Noun Phrases, Quantifiers, and Generic Names. LOWE, E J.
Observar un aspecto. GIANOTTI, José Arthur.
On 'This is Red and This is Blue': *Tractatus* 6.3751. SAHU, Neelamani.
On Häyry and Airaksinen's 'Hard and Soft Offers as Constraints'. DAY, J P.
On Husserl's Theory of the Constitution of Objectiving Meaning (in Czechoslovakian). ZATKA, V.
On Metainductive Sentences. TRIVEDI, Saam.
On Negation. KOKTOVÁ, Eva.
On Rhetorical Strategies: *Verstehen Sie*?. SLEZAK, Peter.
On Saying That Again. HAND, Michael.
On the Genealogical Method: Nietzsche and Foucault. SAX, Benjamin C.
On the Purported Pragmatico-Semantic Foundation of Linguistics and AI Through Wittgenstein's Late Philosophy. LEINFELLNER-RUPERTSBERGER, Elisabeth.
Onderbepaaldheid van theorie en onbepaaldheid van vertaling: Enige ontwikkelingen in Quine's filosofie. PERRICK, M.
Opacidad y presuposición. ARANOVICH, Raúl.
La palabra interior: La filosofía del lenguaje en San Agustín. PEGUEROLES, Juan.
Parody and the Argument from Probability in the *Apology*. LEWIS, Thomas J.
Persuasion: Jane Austen's Philosophical Rhetoric. KASTELY, James L.
Philosophical Argument and the Rhetorical Wedge. JOHNSTONE JR, Henry W.
Philosophical Hierarchies and Lyotard's Dichotomies. SASSOWER, Raphael and OGAZ, Charla Phyllis.
A Philosophical Resistance to Freud. SACHS, David.
Philosophical Scepticism: An Intelligible Challenge. GRUNDY, Jeremy.
La philosophie des sciences de Hertz et le Tractatus. LEROUX, Jean.
Philosophy, Argument, and Narration. VERENE, Donald Phillip.
Philosophy: Sections 86-93 (pp 405-35) of the So-Called "Big Typescript" (Catalog Number 213)—Ludwig Wittgenstein. WITTGENSTEIN, Ludwig and NYMAN, Heikki.
Phrase Structure Parameters. FODOR, Janet Dean and CRAIN, Stephen.
Phrases nominales énonciatives et phrases verbales. STAHL, Gérold.
Physicalism and Intentional Attitudes. MOSER, Paul K.
A Pieced Quilt: A Critical Discussion of Stephen Schiffer's *Remnants of Meaning*. ANTONY, Louise.
Plato and the Senses of Words. BLACKSON, Thomas A.
Platón, el lenguaje y el marciano. ACERO, Juan José.
The Poetic Theory of the Stoic 'Aristo'. ASMIS, Elizabeth.
Practicing the Arts of Rhetoric: Tradition and Invention. FARRELL, Thomas B.
A Pragma-Dialectical Perspective on Norms. VAN EEMEREN, Frans H.
A Pragmatic Analysis of Tautological Utterances. WARD, Gregory L and HIRSCHBERG, Julia.
Pragmatic Conditional Reasoning: Context and Content Effects on the Interpretation of Causal Assertions. HILTON, Denis J.
The Pragmatic Fallacy. SALMON, Nathan.
Pragmatic Principles and Language. BHAT, P R.
Pragmática del lenguaje y racionalidad comunicativa. DE ZAN, J.
Pragmatique du discours et réciprocité de perspectives (A propos de Don Quichotte et Don Juan). GÓMEZ-MORIANA, Antonio.
Predication and Logic of Language (I). GANGADEAN, Ashok.
Predication and Logic of Language (II). GANGADEAN, Ashok.
Preservation by Homomorphisms and Infinitary Languages. HYTTINEN, Tapani.
Process Vagueness. SORENSEN, Roy A.
Pronouns and Propositional Attitudes. SOAMES, Scott.
Proper Names, Cognitive Contents, and Beliefs. BRAUN, David M.
Protecting God: The Lexical Formation of Trinitarian Language. BARRIGAR, Christian J.
Putnam on Kripke's Puzzle. GARRETT, Richard.
Quine on Theory and Language. TANJI, Nobuharu.
Quine's Relativism. HUGLY, Philip and SAYWARD, Charles.
Rationality, Correlativity, and the Language of Process. HALL, David Lynn and AMES, Roger T.
Reading Kristeva: A Response to Calvin Bedient. MOI, Toril.
Real Things: Discourse, Context and Practice. PARKER, Ian.
Reductive and Nonreductive Simile Theories of Metaphor. TIRRELL, Lynne.
Reference and Pronominal Descriptions. WILSON, George M.
References in Narrative Text. WIEBE, Janyce M.
Reflections on the Usage of the Terms "Logic" and "Logical". PAUL, Gregor.
Una reflexión sobre el pensamiento científico técnico. CORONA, N A.
Las reglas del juego: consideraciones críticas sobre "Radical Hermeneutics" de John Caputo. PEÑA, Lorenzo.
Rejoining *Alētheia* and Truth: or Truth Is a Five-Letter Word. HATAB, Lawrence J.
Relevance as an Explanation of Communication. ROBERTS, Lawrence D.
Religion in Wittgenstein's Mirror. PHILLIPS, D Z.
Remarques sur l'analyse des termes mentaux chez Wittgenstein. BERNIER, Paul.
Reply to Gordon: Discourse at Work. CHMIELEWSKI, Philip J.
Représentation philosophique par réseau sémantique variable. BOSS, Gilbert and LONGEART, Maryvonne.
Response to Slezak: *Nein, Ich verstehe nicht*. KEITH, William.
Response: "The Rooting and Uprooting of Reason: On *Spacings* by John Sallis". SALLIS, John.
Rhetoric and Argumentation: Relativism and Beyond. KIENPOINTNER, Manfred.
The Rhetoric of Martianus Capella and Anselm de Besate in the Tradition of Menippean Satire. BENNETT, Beth S.
Role Theory: A Reconstruction. VAN VONDEREN, Marijke L.
Romanticism, Rationality and Alienation—the Triple-H-Theory Revisited. BRUNKHORST, Hauke.
The Rooting and Uprooting of Reason: On *Spacings* by John Sallis. MALY, Kenneth.
Rule-Scepticism: Kripkean Understanding in Wittgenstein's Perspective. BEHERA, Satrughna.
Rules and Relations: Some Connectionist Implications for Cognitive Science and Language. CILLIERS, F P.
Russell and the Ethical Concern of Wittgenstein's *Tractatus*. IGLESIAS, Teresa.
Russell on Ordinary Names and Synonymy. PINEAU, Lois.
Russell's Theory of Definite Descriptions. LAMBERT, Karel.
Sankara and Derrida on Philosophy of Language. COWARD, Harold.
Scandinavian Extraction Phenomena Revisited: Weak and Strong Generative Capacity. MILLER, Philip H.
Schelling's Treatise on the Essence of Human Freedom and Heidegger's Thought. FROMAN, Wayne J.
Schellings metaphysikkritische Sprachphilosophie. ROSENAU, Hartmut.
Scientific Realism and Postmodern Philosophy. MURPHY, Nancey.
Seeing Metaphor as Seeing-as. TIRRELL, Lynne.
Self-Making and World-Making. BRUNER, Jerome.
Semantics and Supervenience. BONEVAC, Daniel.
Sequencing Rules and Coherence in Discourse. TSUI, Amy B M.
The Significance of Rights Language. GOLDING, Martin P.
The *Sinnsfrage* and the *Seinsfrage*. PROTEVI, John.
Sobre la semántica de los nombres propios. SCHIRN, Matthias.
Socratic Pragmatics: Maieutic Dialogues. HANKE, Michael.
Some Problems of Legal Language. KNAPP, Viktor.
Some Revisionary Proposals About Belief and Believing. MARCUS, Ruth Barcan.
The Sorites Paradox and Higher-Order Vagueness. BURGESS, John A.
Die Sprachen und das Denken: Klein Bestandsaufnahme zum linguistischen Relativismus (Sapir-Whorf-Hypothese). FRANZEN, Winfried.
The Stilling of the *Aufhebung: Streit* in "The Origin of the Work of Art". PROTEVI, John.
Stit and the Language of Agency. PERLOFF, Michael.
Sulla semiotizzazione dell' "a priori": Rossi-Landi e Hjelmslev. CAPUTO, Cosimo.
Le supplément poétique. WATTEYNE, Nathalie.
Sur l'habitation poétique de l'homme. PIERSON, Dominique.
Syntactic Form and Textual Rhetoric: The Cognitive Basis for Certain Pragmatic Principles. PRIDEAUX, Gary D.
Syntax and Pragmatics: Apartheid or Integration?. BOLKESTEIN, A Machtelt.
Systems of Interpretation and the Function of the Metaphor. CRIDER, Cathleen and CIRILLO, Leonard.
Tait-Systems for Fragments of *Lm*. COLUMBUS, Joachim.
The Task of a Theory of Meaning. SAYRE, Patricia.
Technology, Truth and Language: The Crisis of Theological Discourse. CROWLEY, Paul.
La teoría consensual de la verdad de Jürgen Habermas. BELARDINELLI, Sergio.
La teoría de la suposición y los idiomas modernos. KNABENSCHUCH DE PORTA, Sabine.
La teoría del significado como uso en Wittgenstein. HERRERA, Alejandro.
Teorías de verdad y teorías del significado. VARGAS, Celso.
Text and Technology. CROWELL, Steven Galt.
The Legacy of Hamann—Thinking, Language and Economy (in Hungarian). RATHMANN, János.

LANGUAGE

Die Theorie des kommunikativen Handelns in Diskussion. KISSLING, Christian.
Thinking (Beyond) Being. STENSTAD, Gail.
Thought and Language. SAHA, Sukharanjan.
Thoughts Which Only I Can Think. WILLIAMS, C J F.
Three Models of Competence: A Critical Evaluation of Chomsky. MUKHERJI, Arundhati.
Thus Spoke Rorty: The Perils of Narrative Self-Creation. CONWAY, Daniel W.
Time and Propositions. SMITH, Quentin.
Toward a Rationale for Literary Literacy. BOGDAN, Deanne.
Les trois sortes d'universalité dans l'herméneutique de H G Gadamer. MARGOLIS, Joseph.
True Contradictions. PARSONS, Terence.
Truth and Language-World Connections. GROVER, Dorothy.
Truth and Understanding. HIGGINBOTHAM, James.
Truth. ULLIAN, Joseph S.
Two Kinds of Agent-Relativity. HUMBERSTONE, I L.
Two Kinds of Naming in the *Sophist*. STOUGH, Charlotte.
Two Ways of Grounding Meaning. GERRARD, Steve.
A Unification-Theoretic Method for Investigating the *k*-Provability Problem. FARMER, William.
Uniform Proofs as a Foundation for Logic Programming. MILLER, Dale and NADATHUR, Gopalan and PFENNING, Frank and SCEDROV, Andre.
Units of Measurement and Natural Kinds: Some Kripkean Considerations. VAN BRAKEL, J.
Universal Sentences: Russell, Wittgenstein, Prior, and the Nyāya. SHAW, J L.
Universals and Creativity. WESTPHAL, Jonathan.
The Uses of Rhetoric: Indeterminacy in Legal Reasoning, Practical Thinking and Interpretation of Literary Figures. OLMSTED, Wendy Raudenbush.
Vacuity. RAMER, Alexis Manaster.
Vague Identity and Vague Objects. GARRETT, Brian.
Vague Objects. ZEMACH, Eddy M.
Verbum-Signum: La définition du langage chez s Augustin et Nicolas de Cues. HENNIGFELD, Jochem.
Une version de l'épistémologie gonséthienne: le béton et les cailloux. BONSACK, François.
Vico: dalla collocazione storica all'efficiacia teoretica. FRANCHINI, Raffaello.
Visual Perception and the Wages of Indeterminacy. MONTGOMERY, Richard.
Il volgarizzamento del "De Rerum natura" di Bernardino Telesio a opera di Francesco Martelli. PIEROZZI, Letizia and SCAPPARONE, Elisabetta.
The Way of Ideas: A Retrospective. YOLTON, John W.
Wege der Seinsfrage: Aus Anlass der 100. GANDER, Hans-Helmuth.
What Good is Irony?. LEVINSON, Henry S.
Wittgenstein and "Mad Pain". KELLY, Michael Lee.
Wittgenstein and Marx—Some Methodological Remarks (in German). RAATZSCH, Richard.
Wittgenstein and Psychology. SHOTTER, John.
Wittgenstein and the Color Incompatibility Problem. JACQUETTE, Dale.
Wittgenstein and the Transmission of Traditions. O'HEAR, Anthony.
Wittgenstein et l'institution du langage. SEYMOUR, Michel.
Wittgenstein et le cognitivisme. OUELLET, Pierre.
Wittgenstein on Criteria and Other Minds. TEMKIN, Jack.
Wittgenstein's Account of Rule-Following. PEARS, David.
Wittgenstein's Holism. PEARS, David.
Wittgenstein's Influence: Meaning, Mind and Method. GRAYLING, A C.
Wittgenstein, Strawson y la no-posesión. BARINGOLTZ, Eleonora.
The Word as Will and Idea: Semantics in the *Tractatus*. COHEN, Daniel H.
Words like Faces (in Dutch). LESAGE, D.
Work and Text. CURRIE, Gregory.
Working with Wittgenstein's Builders. BIRSCH, Douglas and DORBOLO, Jon.
Writing the Revolution—The Politics of Truth in Genet's *Prisoner of Love*. CRITCHLEY, Simon.

LANGUAGE ACT(S)

Il linguaggio ideologico della rivoluzione. MATHIEU, Vittorio.

LANGUAGE GAME(S)

"Translation and Language Games" in *Hermeneutics and the Poetic Motion, Translation Perspectives V—1990*, ROSE, Marilyn Gaddis.
"The Wittgenstein-Problem in Sociology or: the 'Linguistic Turn' as a Pirouette" in *The Social Horizon of Knowledge*, RITSERT, Jürgen.
Does Wittgenstein's Concept of Language Game Patterns Come Up with a Solution to the Platonic Problem ... (in German). LÜTTERFELDS, Wilhelm.
Four Dialogue Systems. MACKENZIE, Jim.
The Last Word on *Philosophical Investigations* 43a. SAVIGNY, Eike V.
Observar un aspecto. GIANOTTI, José Arthur.
Qué miden los juegos de lenguaje?. LORENZ, Kuno.

LAPLACE

A Theory of Probability. REEVES, T V.

LARGE CARDINALS

Almost Hugeness and a Related Notion. BARBANEL, Julius.

LASAULX, E

Die Wiederkehr im Unterschied. PEETZ, Siegbert.

LASSALLE

Schattenseiten der Hegelei: Fallsbeispiel—Lassalles Hegel-Rhapsodie. BEYER, Wilhelm Raimund.

LATIN

Il volgarizzamento del "De Rerum natura" di Bernardino Telesio a opera di Francesco Martelli. PIEROZZI, Letizia and SCAPPARONE, Elisabetta.

LATIN AMERICAN

La contribución de la filosofía al cambio social en América Latina. FORNET-BETANCOURT, Raúl.
Cuatro modelos de desarrollo costarricense: un análisis y evalución ética. CROCKER, David A.
La cuestión del Método de una filosofía latinoamericana. SCANNONE, J C.
Etica del desarrollo: algunos principios y orientaciones a la luz de la docrina social de la Iglesia Católica. BRENES, Víctor.
La filosofía iberoamericana en la obra de Alain Guy. CATURELLI, Alberto.
Filosofía latinoamericana: Posibilidad o realidad?. BETANCOURT, Raúl Fornet.
Law, Morality, and *la Reconquista*. CORDERO, Ronald A.
The Master-Slave Dialectic in Latin America: The Social Criticism of Zea, Freire, and Roig. SCHUTTE, Ofelia M.
Medio ambiente y derecho. ROMERO, Jorge Enrique.
Origins and Tendencies of the Philosophy of Liberation in Latin American Thought: A Critique of Dussel's Ethics. SCHUTTE, Ofelia.
Para una teoría latinoamericana de las relaciones de la ciencia con la literatura: la cienciapoesía. CATALÁ, Rafael.

LATOUR, B

Na de sociale wending het roer nogmaals om. LATOUR, Bruno.
Natuur en cultuur: de heuristische waarde van een dichotomie. WESTERMAN, Pauline.
De natuurlijke ouderdom: een grenzeloze geschiedenis. BIJSTERVELD, Karin.

LATTICE(S)

An Almost General Splitting Theorem for Modal Logic. KRACHT, Marcus.
Boolean Algebras and Orbits of the Lattice of R.E. Sets Modulo the Finite Sets. CHOLAK, Peter.
Boolean Products of CW—Algebras and Pseudo-Complementation. TORRENS, Antoni.
Comments on a Question of Wolniewicz. HAWRANEK, Jacek.
Correction to "Undecidability of $L(F_\infty)$ and Other Lattices of R.E. Substructures" (Corrigendum). DOWNEY, Rod.
The Deduction Theorem for Quantum Logic—Some Negative Results. MALINOWSKI, Jacek.
The Elementary Theory of the Natural Lattice is Finitely Axiomatizable. CEGIELSKI, Patrick.
Embedding Brouwer Algebras in the Medvedev Lattice. SORBI, Andrea.
F-Multipliers and the Localization of Hilbert Algebras. BUSNEAG, Dumitru.
Lattice Nonembeddings and Initial Segments of the Recursively Enumerable Degrees. DOWNEY, Rod.
Maximal R.E. Equivalence Relations. CARROLL, Jeffrey S.
Mechanical Proof Procedures for Many-Valued Lattice-Based Logic Programming. SUBRAHMANIAN, V S.
A Note on the Axiomatization of Equational Classes of *n*-Valued Lukasiewicz Algebras. ADAMS, M E and CIGNOLI, R.
On Some Operators on Pseudovarieties. GRACZYNSKA, Ewa.
On the Absoluteness of Types in Boolean Valued Lattices. NISHIMURA, Hirokazu.
Plain Semi-Post Algebras as a Poset-Based Generalization of Post Algebras and their Representability. CAT HO, Nguyen and RASIOWA, Helena.
The Priestley Duality for Wajsberg Algebras. MARTÍNEZ, N G.
A Question About Semilattices. WOLNIEWICZ, Boguslaw.
Relatively Congruence-Distributive Subquasivarieties of Filtral Varieties. CZELAKOWSKI, Janusz.
Remarks on Special Lattices and Related Constructive Logics with Strong Negation. PAGLIANI, Piero.
Sheaves in Universal Algebra and Model Theory: Part II. IDZIAK, Pawel M.
Some Nonstandard Methods Applied to Distributive Lattices. GEHRKE, Mai and INSALL, Matt and KAISER, Klaus.
Some Remarks on the Algebraic Structure of the Medvedev Lattice. SORBI, Andrea.
There are Denumerably Many Ternary Intuitionistic Sheffer Functions. CUBRIC, Djordje.
Universal Structures in Power $\aleph_1$. MEKLER, Alan H.

LAUDAN, L

Aesthetic Constraints on Theory Selection: A Critique of Laudan. MARTIN, James E.
Between Rationalism and Relativism: On Larry Laudan's Model of Scientific Rationality. GROBLER, Adam.
Fix It and Be Damned: A Reply to Laudan. WORRALL, John.
Laudan's Model of Axiological Change and the Bohr-Einstein Debate 77. FOLSE JR, Henry J.
Pavlov's View on the Inheritance of Acquired Characteristics .... WINDHOLZ, George and LAMAL, P A.

LAUDAN, L
Ten Types of Scientific Progress. KUKLA, Andre.
Testing for Convergent Realism. ARONSON, Jerrold L.
LAVIN, M
The Principle of Relevant Similarity. LEWIS, Gary W.
LAVOISIER
Davy Refuted Lavoisier Not Lakatos. ZUCKER, Arthur.
LAW
see also Jurisprudence, Justice, Property(-ties), Punishment, Right(s)
Anglo-American Philosophy of Law: An Introduction to Its Development and Outcome. LEVY, Beryl Harold.
Community: The Tie That Binds. ROUSSEAU, Mary F.
Critique and Construction: A Symposium on Roberto Unger's "Politics". LOVIN, Robin W (ed).
Descent into Subjectivity: Studies of Rawls, Dworkin and Unger in the Context of Modern Thought. MURPHY JR, Cornelius F.
Hegels Theorie des Gesetzes. BOGDANDY, Armin Von.
In Partnership with God: Contemporary Jewish Law and Ethics. SHERWIN, Byron L.
Intention, Agency and Criminal Liability: Philosophy of Action and the Criminal Law. DUFF, R A.
Jurisculture, Volume I: Greece and Rome. DORSEY, Gray L.
Law, Culture, and Values: Essays in Honor of Gray L Dorsey. VOJCANIN, Sava Alexander (ed).
The Legal-Rational State: A Comparison of Hobbes, Bentham and Kelsen. LEE, Keekok.
Liberalism and American Constitutional Law. SMITH, Rogers M.
Medicine and Money: A Study of the Role of Beneficence in Health Care Cost Containment. MARSH, Frank H.
Die moderne Gesellschaft im Rechtsstaat. BAURMANN, Michael.
Die Moral der Vernunft Tanszendentale Handlungs-und Legitimationstheorie in der Philosophie Kants. SANDERMANN, Edmund.
Moral Pluralism and Legal Neutrality. SADURSKI, Wojciech.
New Harvest: Transplanting Body Parts and Reaping the Benefits. KEYES, C Don (ed).
Philosophy of Law (Fourth Edition). FEINBERG, Joel.
Philosophy of Law: An Introduction to Jurisprudence (Revised Edition). MURPHY, Jeffrie G.
The Positivist Science of Law. LEE, Keekok.
Practical Reason and Norms. RAZ, Joseph.
Reading Habermas. RASMUSSEN, David M.
The Realm of Rights. THOMSON, Judith Jarvis.
Responsibility and Criminal Liability. SISTARE, C T.
Shaping Genes: Ethics, Law and Science of Using Genetic Technology in Medicine and Agriculture. MACER, Darryl.
The Vatican, the Law and the Human Embryo. COUGHLAN, Michael J.
"Are There Economic Laws?" in *Studies on Mario Bunge's "Treatise"*, BARCELÓ, Alfons.
"A Bargaining Theory Approach to Default Provisions and Disclosure Rules in Contract Law" in *Liability and Responsibility*, COLEMAN, Jules L and HECKATHORN, Douglas D and MASER, Steven M.
"Commonsense Reasoning, Social Change, and the Law" in *Critique and Construction: A Symposium on Roberto Unger's "Politics"*, VAN ZANDT, David E.
"Responsibility and the Act of Interpretation: The Case of Law" in *The Political Responsibility of Intellectuals*, MACLEAN, Ian.
"Degenerate Law": Jurists and Nazism. LA TORRE, Massimo.
The 'Artificial Reason' of the Law. BICKENBACH, Jerome E.
Anerkennung: Fichtes Grundlegungen des Rechtsgrundes. JANKE, Wolfgang.
An Antinomy in Kelsen's Pure Theory of Law. BULYGIN, Eugenio.
The Background to Bentham on Evidence. LEWIS, A D E.
Bentham, Science and the Construction of Jurisprudence. JACOBS, Struan.
Causes and Laws: The Asymmetry Puzzle. BYERLY, Henry.
Choosing Social Responsibility Over Law: The *Soldier of Fortune* Classified Advertising Cases. TOMLINSON, Don E.
Community, Law, and the Idiom and Rhetoric of Rights. MAC INTYRE, Alasdair.
The Concept of Jurisprudence. ALEXY, Robert and DREIER, Ralf.
Conclusion: Legal Institutions and Limitations to Cognition and Power. O'BRIEN, James.
Controverses autour de l'ontologie du droit. DE MUNCK, Jean.
Corporate Codes of Conduct: A Collective Conscience and Continuum. RAIBORN, Cecily A and PAYNE, Dinah.
Critical Legal Studies and Liberalism: Understanding the Similarities and Differences. WAGNER DE CEW, Judith.
Le critiche a Kelsen durante la Repubblica di Weimar. ROEHRSSEN, Carlo.
Czeslaw Znamierowski's Conception of Constitutive Rules. CZEPITA, Stanislaw.
Una discussione di epistemologia. BLANDINO, Giovanni and FEDERSPIL, G.
Dworkin, Habermas, and the CLS Movement on Moral Criticism in Law. INGRAM, David.
La elusión mediante sociedades a la luz de los principios constitucionales. RUIZ ZAPATERO, Guillermo.
The Epistemological Moral Relevance of Democracy. NINO, Carlos S.
The Ethical Significance of Corporate Law. NESTERUK, Jeffrey.
The Ethico-Legal Meaning of Voluntary. BOURKE, Vernon J.
Ethics Committees: From Ethical Comfort to Ethical Cover. ANNAS, George J.
Etica e diritto penale nella filosofia attualistica. RICCIO, Stefano.
Evidence and Legal Reasoning: On the Intertwinement of the Probable and the Reasonable. KLAMI, Hannua Tapani (and others).
Exploring Extreme Violence (Torture). MACHAN, Tibor R.
From Dialogue Rights to Property Rights. SHEARMUR, Jeremy.
The Geometry of Legal Principles. CHUAQUI, Rolando and MALITZ, Jerome.
Grammatica e diritto: Una normatività fragile?. VITALE, Vincenzo.
H L A Hart and the "Open Texture" of Language. BIX, Brian.
Historical Perspectives on the Morality of Virtue. WHITE, Richard.
Hobbes, Jacobo I y el derecho inglés. RIBEIRO, Renato Janine.
The Importance of Asking the Right Questions. PATTERSON, Dennis.
The Institution of Law. BANKOWSKI, Zenon.
Interpretation and the Social Reality of Law. GOLDFORD, Dennis.
John Stuart Mill über die Todesstrafe. WOLF, Jean-Claude.
Jugement juridique et jugement pratique: de Kant à la philosophie du langage. LENOBLE, J and BERTEN, A.
L'institution juridique: imposition et interprétation. SÈVE, René.
Law and Culture: The Conception of Legal Culture (in Polish). GRYKO, Czeslaw.
Law and Exclusionary Reasons. ALEXANDER, Larry.
Law and Psychiatry: The Problems That Will Not Go Away. SZASZ, Thomas.
The Law of Business Ethics and Social Responsibility. BURKE III, William T.
Law Without Values: Do the Unborn Have to Wait for a Consensus?. VACCARI, Michael A.
Law, Morality, and *la Reconquista*. CORDERO, Ronald A.
Law: From Foundation to Argumentation. LEMPEREUR, Alain.
Le locutoire et l'illocutoire dans les énonciations relatives aux normes juridiques. AMSELEK, Paul.
La loi de vérité. POULAIN, Jacques.
La loi du Styx, Leibniz et la politique du bonheur. LE LANNOU, Jean-Michel.
La loi et ses législateurs ou les avatars du théologico-politique. TOSEL, André.
Medical Ethics in Ireland: A Decade of Change. DOOLEY, Dolores.
Medio ambiente y derecho. ROMERO, Jorge Enrique.
Natural Fetal Dependency States and Fetal Dependency Principles. HERBENICK, Raymond M.
New Studies on Hegel's Philosophy of Law, versus on the Dialectics of Hegel and Marx (in Hungarian). GÖHLER, Gerhard.
Non-professional Judicial Reasoning. TAPANI KLAMI, Hannu.
Non-Technical *Pisteis* in Aristotle and Anaximenes. MIRHADY, David.
Der Normgeltungsbegriff als probabilistischer Begriff: Zur Logik des soziologischen Normbegriffs. LÜBBE, Weyma.
On Ideal Form, Empowering Norms, and "Normative Functions". PAULSON, Stanley L.
On Law and Morality: A Dialogue. VON WRIGHT, Georg Henrik.
On Leo Katz, Double Jeopardy, and the Blockburger Test. LOCKE, Lawrence A.
On Scholarly Developments in Legal Semiotics. JACKSON, Bernard S.
On Surrogacy: Morality, Markets, and Motherhood. MOODY-ADAMS, Michele M.
On the Nature of Rape. BOGART, J H.
Paradigms of Legal Science. JORI, Mario.
The Persistence of Counterexample: Re-examining the Debate over Leibniz Law. LANDINI, Gregory and FOSTER, Thomas.
The Politics of the Rule of Law. RAZ, Joseph.
Probability Out of Court: Notes on 'Guilt Beyond Reasonable Doubt'. COHEN, Stephen and BERSTEN, Michael.
Protestant Hermeneutics and the Rule of Law: Gadamer and Dworkin. HENLEY, Kenneth.
Punitive Damages: New Twists in Torts. WALTON, Clarence C.
Realism in the Authority of Law. BRIGHAM, John and HARRINGTON, Christine.
Relative Duties in the Law. WELLMAN, Carl.
Response to 'Rescuing the Innocent'. GARDNER, G T G.
Response to 'Rescuing the Innocent'. MORROW, James.
Retaliatory Punishment as a Categorical Imperative. HÖFFE, Ottfried.
The Rule of Law in *The German Constitution*. HANCE, Allen S.
Sanction and the Law According to St Thomas Aquinas. HENLE, R J.
The Sanctity of Life and Substituted Judgement: The Case of Baby J. HORNETT, Stuart I.
Schopenhauers Straftheorie und die aktuelle Strafzweckdiskussion. KÜPPER, Georg.
Singular Causation and Law. IRZIK, Gürol.
Sovranità e obbedienza. CATANIA, Alfonso.
La speranza nel giusnaturalismo. TUSA, Carlo.
Sul controllo nel procedimento di determinazione dei principi dell'ordinamento. COSTANZO, Angelo.

LAW
Sur quelques textes de Spinoza relatifs à la notion de loi. PREPOSIET, Jean.
Surrogate Decisionmaking and Other Matters. GREENLAW, Jane.
Tacit Consent. CARR, Craig L.
Taking Rights Seriously in the Abortion Case. DWORKIN, Ronald.
Thomas Hobbes and the Contractarian Theory of Law. GAUTHIER, David.
Toward a Narrative Conception of Legal Discourse. PATTERSON, Dennis.
Trade Secrets and the Justification of Intellectual Property: A Comment on Hettinger. PAINE, Lynn Sharp.
Two Forms of Moral Responsibility. SANKOWSKI, Edward.
Ultimate Double Binds. SCHÜRMANN, Reiner.
What Is Jurisprudence About? Theories, Definitions, Concepts, or Conceptions of Law?. BAYLES, Michael D.
Why (Legal) Rules Often Fail to Control Human Behavior. CROMBAG, H F M.
Why Narrative Is Not Enough. FULLER, Steve.
Women's Law. DUXBURY, Neil.
Women, Madness, and Special Defences in the Law. BOETZKES, Elisabeth and TURNER, Susan (Guerin) and SOBSTYL, Edrie.

LAWLIKE PROPOSITION(S)
What is a Law of Nature? A Humean Answer. URBACH, Peter.

LAWS
see also Natural Law(s)
The Law of Karma: A Philosophical Study. REICHENBACH, Bruce R.
"Federal Laws and Policies Governing Animal Research: Their History, Nature, and Adequacy" in *Biomedical Ethics Reviews, 1990*, ROLLIN, Bernard E.
"NIH Guidelines and Animal Welfare" in *Biomedical Ethics Reviews, 1990*, RUSSOW, Lilly-Marlene.
Algunas reflexiones sobre la doctrina platónica de los preámbulos de las *Leyes*. GARCÍA MÁYNEZ, Eduardo.
Aristotle on Justice, Equality and the Rule of Law. QUINN, Michael.
Causes and Laws. ARMSTRONG, D M and HEATHCOTE, Adrian.
Ceteris Paribus Laws. SCHIFFER, Stephen.
Compatibilities on the Idea of Law in Thomas Aquinas and Thomas Hobbes. FULLER, Timothy.
Cruzan and Caring for Others. LYNN, Joanne and GLOVER, Jacqueline.
Disjunctive Laws and Supervenience. SEAGER, William.
Freedom, Necessity, and Laws of Nature as Relations between Universals. VIHVELIN, Kadri.
A Hostage to Technology. CRANFORD, Ronald E.
How Can They?. BUSALACCHI, Pete.
The Juncture of Law and Morality in Prohibitions Against Torture. MARAN, Rita.
The Laws of Physics as Nomic Universals. ZYCINSKI, Jozef.
Missouri Stands Alone. COLBY, William H.
Nancy Cruzan in China. ANNAS, George J.
The Nature of Causation: A Singularist Account. TOOLEY, Michael.
On the Objectivity of the Laws of Physics. HAMAN, Krzysztof E.
Paternalistic Laws. GOLDMAN, Alan H and GOLDMAN, Michael N.
Spinoza—Beyond Hobbes and Rousseau. GEISMANN, Georg.
Structural Analogies Between Physical Systems. KROES, Peter.
What is a Law of Nature? A Humean Answer. URBACH, Peter.
The World Essence. BIGELOW, John.
The World of Man and Man in the World in Light of the New Philosophical Thinking. DZHAKHAIA, L G.
You Can Fool Some of the People All of the Time, Everything Else Being Equal; Hedged Laws and Psychological Explanation. FODOR, Jerry A.

LAWYER(S)
"Degenerate Law": Jurists and Nazism. LA TORRE, Massimo.
The Ambiguity of Political Virtue: A Response to Wolgast. LEVINSON, Sanford.
Ethics and the Professional Responsibility of Lawyers. KIPNIS, Kenneth.
Ethics and the Professional Responsibility of Lawyers (Commentary). LENNERTZ, James E.
Smith Against the Ethicists. LUBAN, David.
Taking Positional Conflicts of Interest Seriously. DZIENKOWSKI, John S.

LAYTON, E
Commentary on Layton's "Engineering Needs a Loyal Opposition". ANDERSON, Robert M (and others).

LAZEROWITZ, M
Disagreement in Philosophy. HELEN, Mercy and CHAKRAVARTI, Mihirvikash.

LE DOEUFF, M
French Philosophers in Conversation: Levinas, Schneider, Serres, Irigaray, Le Doeuff, Derrida. MORTLEY, Raoul.

LEADERSHIP
Good Intentions Aside: A Manager's Guide to Resolving Ethical Problems. NASH, Laura L.
Business and Environmental Ethics. HOFFMAN, W Michael.
Dialogic Leadership as Ethics Action (Praxis) Method. NIELSEN, Richard P.

LEARNING
On Durkheim's Rules of Sociological Method. GANE, Mike.
"Learnability of Semantic Theory" in *Truth and Interpretation: Perspectives on the Philosophy of Donald Davidson*, MATTHEWS, Robert J.
"Learning and Meaning" in *Perspectives on Quine*, ULLIAN, Joseph S.
Belief as a Condition of Knowledge: The Need for a Philosophical Perspective in Higher Education Reform. BRELL JR, Carl D.
Emotions, Education and Time. DE SOUSA, Ronald.
Habermas's Ontology of Learning: Reconstructing Dewey. YOUNG, R E.
Learning Disabilities: A Questionable Construct. KLATT, Heinz-Joachim.
Rational Trust and Deferential Belief. NORRIS, Stephen P.
Sustaining Non-Rationalized Practices: Body-Mind, Power and Situational Ethics—Interview with Hubert and Stuart Dreyfus. FLYVBJERG, Bent.
The Thought That Learning Is by Ordeal: An Original Essay. WOODRUFF, Paul B.

LEARNING THEORY
Reflections on Reflecting. PRITSCHER, Conrad.

LECTURE(S)
Wittgenstein's Lectures on the Foundations of Mathematics, Cambridge 1939. DIAMOND, Cora (ed).

LEFT
"The Left Establishment" in *Perspectives on Ideas and Reality*, SCRUTON, Roger.
Beyond Mourning and Melancholia on the Left. DUBIEL, Helmut.

LEGAL
Anglo-American Philosophy of Law: An Introduction to Its Development and Outcome. LEVY, Beryl Harold.
Enriching Business Ethics. WALTON, Clarence C (ed).
Fonti diritto e regole. DE GIACOMO, Claudio.
To Die or Not to Die?. BERGER, Arthur S (ed).
"Can Responsibility Be Diminished?" in *Liability and Responsibility*, KENNY, Anthony.
Ethical Considerations and Ramifications of the 1989 Generic Drug Scandal. HEACOCK, Marian V and ORVIS, Gregory P.
For One Concept of Liberty. BEEHLER, Rodger.
A Formal Representation of Declaration-Related Legal Relations. HANSSON, Sven Ove.
Historical Perspectives: Development of the Codes of Ethics in the Legal, Medical and Accounting Professions. BACKOF, Jeanne F and MARTIN JR, Charles L.
Is There a Natural Law?. WALDSTEIN, Wolfgang.
L'institution juridique: imposition et interprétation. SÈVE, René.
Sawa Frydman: A Polish Legal Realist. MOS, Urszula.
Skepticism and Legal Interpretation. NATHAN, Daniel O.
Some Problems of Legal Language. KNAPP, Viktor.

LEGAL ETHICS
Ethics and the Professional Responsibility of Lawyers. KIPNIS, Kenneth.
Ethics and the Professional Responsibility of Lawyers (Commentary). LENNERTZ, James E.
Smith Against the Ethicists. LUBAN, David.

LEGAL POSITIVISM
Anglo-American Philosophy of Law: An Introduction to Its Development and Outcome. LEVY, Beryl Harold.
The Legal-Rational State: A Comparison of Hobbes, Bentham and Kelsen. LEE, Keekok.
The Positivist Science of Law. LEE, Keekok.
Legal Positivism and Democracy in the Twentieth Century. SQUELLA, Agustí.
Legal Positivism, Social Rules, and *Riggs* versus *Palmer*. BEEHLER, Rodger.
Neuvermessung des Rechts- und Staatsdiskurses: Zu Otfried Höffes Theorie der Politischen Gerechtigkeit. SITTER-LIVER, Beat.
Women, Madness, and Special Defences in the Law. BOETZKES, Elisabeth and TURNER, Susan (Guerin) and SOBSTYL, Edrie.

LEGAL REASONING
Artificial Intelligence and Human Cognition. WAGMAN, Morton.
"Attempting the Impossible" in *Liability and Responsibility*, WHITE, Alan R.
Conceptions of Justification in Legal Discourse. WROBLEWSKI, Jerzy.
A Decision-Theoretic Reconstruction of *Roe v Wade*. LOCKHART, Ted.
Evidence and Legal Reasoning: On the Intertwinement of the Probable and the Reasonable. KLAMI, Hannua Tapani (and others).
Legal Reasoning and Practical Political Education. STRAUBER, Ira.
Mapping the Human Genome: Some Thoughts for Those Who Say "There Should Be A Law On It". SKENE, Loane.
Paradigms of Legal Science. JORI, Mario.
The Rational Law-Maker and the Pragmatics of Legal Interpretation. DASCAL, Marcelo and WRÓBLEWSKI, Jerzy.
The Theory of Legal Dynamics Reconsidered. WEINBERGER, Ota.
Twice Told Tales: A Reply to Schlesinger. COHEN, L Jonathan.

LEGAL RIGHT(S)
The Exclusion of Evidence Obtained by Constitutionally Impermissible Means in Canada. MC DONALD, David C.
The Overdue Death of a Feminist Chameleon: Taking a Stand on Surrogacy Arrangements. TONG, Rosemarie.

LEGAL SYSTEM(S)
Law, Culture, and Values: Essays in Honor of Gray L Dorsey. VOJCANIN, Sava Alexander (ed).
Normas, sistemas jurídicos y eficacia. NAVARRO, Pablo Eugenio.
On Judicial Ascertainment of Facts. VARGA, Csaba.
Sul controllo nel procedimento di determinazione dei principi dell'ordinamento. COSTANZO, Angelo.
The Theory of Legal Dynamics Reconsidered. WEINBERGER, Ota.

LEGALITY
Animal Liberation as a Valid Response to Structural Violence. LISZT, Amy.

LEGALIZATION
Euthanasia in China: A Report. DA PU, Shi.

LEGISLATION
Animal Experimentation: The Consensus Changes. LANGLEY, Gill (ed).
Black and White Together: A Reconsideration. ALLEN, W B.
Congress, Consistency, and Environmental Law. LEMONS, John and BROWN, Donald A and VARNER, Gary E.
Does Strict Judicial Scrutiny Involve the *Tu Quoque* Fallacy?. SCHEDLER, George.
The First Formulation of the Categorical Imperative as Literally a "Legislative" Metaphor. GREEN, Ronald M.
The Patient Self-Determination Act. MC CLOSKEY, Elizabeth Leibold.
The Politics of the Rule of Law. RAZ, Joseph.
Prohibiting Immorality. WESTMORELAND, Robert.

LEGISLATOR(S)
La loi et ses législateurs ou les avatars du théologico-politique. TOSEL, André.

LEGISLATURE
Jean-Jacques Rousseau and the Fusion of Democratic Sovereignty with Aristocratic Government. CRANSTON, Maurice.

LEGITIMACY
Wahrheit—Diskurs—Demokratie: Studien zur "Konsensustheorie der Wahrheit". SCHEIT, Herbert.
"Basic Needs, Legitimate Wants and Political Legitimacy in Mario Bunge's Conception of Ethics" in *Studies on Mario Bunge's "Treatise"*, GARZÓN-VALDÉS, Ernesto.
"Legitimate Defense and Strategic Defense" in *Issues in War and Peace: Philosophical Inquiries*, STERBA, James P.
"Mario Bunge on Ethics" in *Studies on Mario Bunge's "Treatise"*, BUNGE, Mario.
"The State and Legitimacy" in *Key Themes in Philosophy*, BARRY, Norman.
Can Whistleblowing Be FULLY Legitimated? A Theoretical Discussion. DANDEKAR, Natalie.
How is Philosophy Possible?. SCHICK JR, Theodore W.
Telling It Like It Was: Historical Narratives on Their Own Terms. NORMAN, Andrew P.

LEGITIMATION
Die moderne Gesellschaft im Rechtsstaat. BAURMANN, Michael.
Die Moral der Vernunft Tanszendentale Handlungs-und Legitimationstheorie in der Philosophie Kants. SANDERMANN, Edmund.
Political Theory in the Welfare State. LUHMANN, Niklas.
"The Pursuit of Ideals and the Legitimation of Means" in *Perspectives on Ideas and Reality*, GARVER, Newton.

LEHRER, K
Keith Lehrer and Thomas Reid. CHISHOLM, Roderick M.

LEIBNIZ
Cálculo y ser (Aproximación a Leibniz). MARZOA, Felipe Martínez.
Kommunikations-Theoretische Schriften II: Symbolische Erkenntnis und Kommunikation. UNGEHEUER, Gerold (ed).
Leibniz and Arnauld. SLEIGH JR, Robert C.
Leibniz and Strawson: A New Essay in Descriptive Metaphysics. BROWN, Clifford.
Leibniz' Position der Rationalität. KAEHLER, Klaus Erich.
Leibniz's Philosophy of Logic and Language (Second Edition). ISHIGURO, Hide.
Leibniz, Humboldt, and the Origins of Comparativism. DE MAURO, Tullio (ed).
"'Vulgaris opinio babelica': Sui fondamenti storico-teorici della pluralità delle lingue nel pensiero di Leibniz" in *Leibniz, Humboldt, and the Origins of Comparativism*, GENSINI, Stefano.
"Descent, Perfection and the Comparative Method Since Leibniz" in *Leibniz, Humboldt, and the Origins of Comparativism*, HOENIGSWALD, Henry M.
"Humboldt et Leibniz: Le concept intérieur de la linguistique" in *Leibniz, Humboldt, and the Origins of Comparativism*, TRABANT, Jürgen.
"Leibniz and Locke on the Knowledge of Necessary Truths" in *Central Themes in Early Modern Philosophy*, BOLTON, Martha Brandt.
"Leibniz and the Philosophical Analysis of Science" in *Logic, Methodology and Philosophy of Science, VIII*, DUCHESNEAU, François.
"Leibniz and Wilhelm von Humboldt and the History of Comparative Linguistics" in *Leibniz, Humboldt, and the Origins of Comparativism*, ROBINS, Robert H.
"Leibniz on Malebranche on Causality" in *Central Themes in Early Modern Philosophy*, SLEIGH JR, Robert C.
"Leibniz on Particles: Linguistic Form and Comparatism" in *Leibniz, Humboldt, and the Origins of Comparativism*, DASCAL, Marcelo.
"Pontos de vista—exercício hermenêutico sobre um excerto da *Monadologia*" in *Dinâmica do Pensar: Homenagem a Oswaldo Market*, RIBEIRO FERREIRA, Maria Luisa.
"Le voyage de 'Schreiten': Leibniz et les débuts du comparatisme finno-ougrien" in *Leibniz, Humboldt, and the Origins of Comparativism*, DROIXHE, Daniel.
Bayle, Leibniz, Hume and Reid on Extension, Composites and Simples. CUMMINS, Phillip.
Congruenza, schematismo, sintesi: Prospettive leibniziane intorno al criterio di verità secondo Giambattista Vico. PINCHARD, Bruno.
Consideraciones en torno a la polémica Leibniz-Clarke. PONCE ALBERCA, Carmen.
The Continuous and the Discrete: Leibniz Versus Berkeley. ANAPOLITANOS, D A.
La dimostrazione "a posteriori" dell'esistenza di Dio nella filosofia di Leibniz. NICOLOSI, Salvatore.
Festrede zum 300: Geburstag von Gottfried Wilhelm Leibniz am 1 Juli 1946 in der Aula der Universitat Leipzig. GADAMER, Hans-Georg.
How Euclidean Geometry Has Misled Metaphysics. NERLICH, Graham.
El innatismo de Leibniz. HERRERA, Alejandro.
La interpretación russelliana de Leibniz y el atomismo metodológico de Moore. RODRÍGUEZ CONSUEGRA, Francisco.
Johan Jacob Ferguson, geb um 1630 im Haag(?), gest vor dem 24 November 1706, vermutlich am 6 Oktober 1691 in Amsterdam. VAN MAANEN, Jan A.
Kant and Conceptual Semantics: A Sketch. POSY, Carl J.
Leibniz on Creation, Contingency and Per-Se Modality. MC NAMARA, Paul.
Leibniz on Superessentialism and World-Bound Individuals. COVER, Jan A.
Leibniz's "Analysis of Multitude and Phenomena into Unities and Reality". RUTHERFORD, Donald.
Lógica y metafísica de Leibniz: Principales líneas de interpretación durante el siglo XX. HEINEKAMP, A and SCHUPP, F.
La loi du Styx, Leibniz et la politique du bonheur. LE LANNOU, Jean-Michel.
Die Natur der Sprache: Von der Ontologie zur Technologie. HOTTOIS, Gilbert.
Naturalism, Freedom and Ethics in Spinoza. DE DIJN, Herman.
Ein neu gefundener Brief von Leibniz an Lambert van Velthuysen: Mit einer Einführung von Albert Heinekamp. HEIN, Isolde.
The Persistence of Counterexample: Re-examining the Debate over Leibniz Law. LANDINI, Gregory and FOSTER, Thomas.
Phänomenologie und Monadologie: Husserl und Leibniz. CRISTIN, Renato.
Phenomenalism and the Reality of Body in Leibniz's Later Philosophy. RUTHERFORD, Donald P.
Le premier registre de Descartes. RODIS-LEWIS, Geneviève.
Principia Individuationis. DENKEL, Arda.
Processes, Substances, and Leibniz's Epistemology: A Case for Essentialism in Contemporary Physics. PIRO, Francesco.
Reasoning and Computation in Leibniz. SPRUIT, Leen and TAMBURRINI, Guglielmo.
El reloj de Dios (Glosas provisionales a un principio leibniziano). MUÑOZ, Jacobo.
Spontaneity and the Generation of Rational Beings in Leibniz's Theory of Biological Reproduction. FOUKE, Daniel C.
La substance composée chez Leibniz. CHAZERANS, Jean-François.
Sulla matrice della teoria della sostanza nel *Discorso di metafisica* di Leibniz. DELCÓ, Alessandro.
La tensione tra possibilità e necessità nell'argomento ontologico di Leibniz. NICOLOSI, Salvatore.
Truth at a World is a Modality. LINSKY, Bernard.
Universalität des Prinzips vom zureichenden Grund. NICOLÁS, Juan A.
What was Leibniz's Problem about Relations?. BURDICK, Howard.
Whitehead and Leibniz: Conflict and Convergence. MOONEY, Tim.

LENGTH
On the Lengths of Proofs of Set Theoretical Statements in Zermelo-Fraenkel Set Theory and Kelley-Morse Theory.... CORRADA, Manuel.

LENIN
Philosophy and the Spontaneous Philosophy of the Scientists and Other Essays. ELLIOTT, Gregory (ed).
Toward the Death of Man. KLUBACK, William.
Dialectical Perception: A Synthesis of Lenin and Bogdanov. WRIGHT, Edmond.
Fundamental Question of Philosophy: Remarks on the Pending Philosophical Reappraisal of the Past in the GDR (in German). SCHRÖDER, Richard.
Grundlegende Aspekte zur Problematik von Erkenntnis und Praxis. FORSCHE, Joachim.
The Ideological Impasse of Gorbachev's Perestrojka. KRIZAN, Mojmir.
Lenin, Gorbachev, and 'National-Statehood': Can Leninism Countenance the New Soviet Federal Order?. GLEASON, Gregory.
The Social Philosophy of Marxism: The Founders and the Present Day. SHEVCHENKO, V N.
The Development of a Concept of Modern Socialism: Theses under Discussion (in German). BRIE, Michael.
The Pros and Cons of Trotsky's Marxism (in German). HEDELER, Wladislaw.

LENINISM
Lenin and Philosophy: Should We Not Pose This Problem Anew?. VOLODIN, A.

LEON, X
Il carteggio Xavier Léon: corrispondenti italiana. QUILICI, Leana and RAGGHIANTI, Renzo.

LEONTIEV
Two Conservative Views of Nationality and Personality: A A Grigor'ev and K N Leont'ev. DOWLER, E W.

LEOPOLD, A
Leopold's "Means and Ends in Wild Life Management". HARGROVE, Eugene C and CALLICOTT, J Baird.

LEPORE, E
On Saying That Again. HAND, Michael.

LESBIAN
Lesbian Philosophies and Cultures. ALLEN, Jeffner (ed).
"A Response to *Lesbian Ethics*: Why *Ethics*?" in *Feminist Ethics*, FRYE, Marilyn.

LESSING
Modern Faith and Thought. THIELICKE, Helmut.
La polémica sobre el espinosismo de Lessing. FERNÁNDEZ LORENZO, Manuel.

LETTER(S)
Additional Letters (Collected Works of John Stuart Mill, Volume XXXII). ROBSON, John M (ed).
Plato and Archytas in the Seventh Letter. LLOYD, G E R.
Unpublished Correspondence between Russell and Wittgenstein. MC GUINNESS, B F and VON WRIGHT, G H.

LEUCIPPUS
Vide et non-être chez Leucippe et Démocrite. VOELKE, André-Jean.

LEVEL(S)
Une version de l'épistémologie gonséthienne: le béton et les cailloux. BONSACK, François.

LEVI, I
On the Descriptive Adequacy of Levi's Decision Theory. MAHER, Patrick and KASHIMA, Yoshihisa.

LEVI-STRAUSS, C
Claude Lévi-Strauss. LEACH, Edmund.
Freud devait-il choisir entre les deux conceptions du symbole que lui attribue Lévi-Strauss?. CHARRON, Ghyslain.
A Structuralist Rousseau: On the Anthropology of Claude Lévi-Strauss. HONNETH, Axel.

LEVINAS, E
French Philosophers in Conversation: Levinas, Schneider, Serres, Irigaray, Le Doeuff, Derrida. MORTLEY, Raoul.
Phänomenologische Philosophie. STRÖKER, Elisabeth.
Re-Reading Levinas. BERNASCONI, Robert (ed).
""Bois"—Derrida's Final Word on Levinas" in *Re-Reading Levinas*, CRITCHLEY, Simon.
"321 CONTACT: Textuality, the Other, Death" in *Re-Reading Levinas*, BEREZDIVIN, Ruben.
"Am I Obsessed by Bobby? (Humanism of the Other Animal)" in *Re-Reading Levinas*, LLEWELYN, John.
"Antigone's Dilemma" in *Re-Reading Levinas*, CHANTER, Tina.
"At This Very Moment in This Work Here I Am" in *Re-Reading Levinas*, DERRIDA, Jacques and BEREZDIVIN, Ruben.
"Ethics and the Feminine" in *Re-Reading Levinas*, CHALIER, Catherine.
"The Face and Reading: Immediacy and Mediation" in *Re-Reading Levinas*, CRITCHLEY, Simon (trans) and GREISCH, Jean.
"The Face of Truth in Rosenzweig, Levinas, and Jewish Mysticism" in *Phenomenology of the Truth Proper to Religion*, COHEN, Richard A.
"A Fine Risk: Reading Blanchot Reading Levinas" in *Re-Reading Levinas*, DAVIES, Paul.
"Levinas's Ethical Discourse between Individuation and Universality" in *Re-Reading Levinas*, CIARAMELLI, Fabio.
"One-Way Traffic: The Ontology of Decolonization and its Ethics" in *Ontology and Alterity in Merleau-Ponty*, BERNASCONI, Robert.
"Presentation" in *Re-Reading Levinas*, PEPERZAK, Adriaan.
"Questions to Emmanuel Levinas: On the Divinity of Love" in *Re-Reading Levinas*, WHITFORD, Margaret (trans) and IRIGARAY, Luce.
"Skepticism in the Face of Philosophy" in *Re-Reading Levinas*, BERNASCONI, Robert.
"Two Texts on Merleau-Ponty by Emmanuel Levinas" in *Ontology and Alterity in Merleau-Ponty*, SMITH, Michael B.
"Who Suffers?" in *Re-Reading Levinas*, O'CONNOR, Noreen.
"Il y a" et phénoménologie dans la pensée du jeune Lévinas. LANNOY, Jean-Luc.
The Ethics of Suspicion. BERNASCONI, Robert.
Filosofía, justicia y amor. LEVINAS, E and EZCURRA, Alicia Villar.
The Other Comes to Teach Me: A Review of Recent Levinas Publications. GIBBS, Robert.
Thinking the Other Without Violence? An Analysis of the Relation Between the Philosophy of Lévinas and Feminism. MANNING, Robert J S.

LEVINE, J
Reply to Levine's "Cool Red". HARDIN, C L.

LEVY-BRUHL, L
Lucien, Lévy-Bruhl: Una introduzione (di C Prandi). IANNOTTA, Daniella.

LEWIS
A Functional Calculus of First Order Based on Strict Implication. MARCUS, Ruth Barcan.
Truth at a World is a Modality. LINSKY, Bernard.

LEWIS, D
Conventional Foundationalism and the Origins of the Norms. CUDD, Ann E.
Could This Be Magic?. JUBIEN, Michael.
Is a Whole Identical to its Parts?. SCALTSAS, Theodore.
Lewis's Functionalism and Reductive Materialism. KERNOHAN, Andrew.
Modal Realism Without Counterparts. HALE, Susan C.
Reply of a Mad Dog. MILLER, Richard B.
Supervenience and Singular Causal Claims. WOODWARD, James.
Wittgenstein and "Mad Pain". KELLY, Michael Lee.

LIABILITY
Intention, Agency and Criminal Liability: Philosophy of Action and the Criminal Law. DUFF, R A.
Responsibility and Criminal Liability. SISTARE, C T.
The Actus Reus Requirement: A Qualified Defense. GORR, Michael.
Gorr on Actus Reus. MURPHY, Jeffrie G.
The Orthodox Model of the Criminal Offense. HUSAK, Douglas N.
Reply to Murphy and Husak. GORR, Michael.
Two Forms of Moral Responsibility. SANKOWSKI, Edward.

LIANG, Q
The Liberal Teachings of the Young Liang Qichao. QI, Feng.

LIAR
The Logic of the Liar from the Standpoint of the Aristotelian Syllogistic. KELLY, Charles J.

LIAR'S PARADOX
For Anil Gupta. HART, W D.
Liar Syllogisms and Related Paradoxes. SLATER, B H.
The Quarrel Theorem: First Attempt to the Logic of Lie. MAJCHER, B.

LIBERAL ARTS
The Anatomy of Judgment. REGAL, Philip J.

LIBERAL EDUCATION
"Poetic Revenge and Modern Totalitarianism" in *From Twilight to Dawn: The Cultural Vision of Jacques Maritain*, REDPATH, Peter A.
Liberal Education in an Unfree World. LA BRECQUE, Richard.

LIBERALISM
Critique and Construction: A Symposium on Roberto Unger's "Politics". LOVIN, Robin W (ed).
Descent into Subjectivity: Studies of Rawls, Dworkin and Unger in the Context of Modern Thought. MURPHY JR, Cornelius F.
The Devil and Secular Humanism: The Children of the Enlightenment. RADEST, Howard B.
Interpreting Political Responsibility. DUNN, John.
John Dewey: Religious Faith and Democratic Humanism. ROCKEFELLER, Steven C.
Justice and the Good Life. DWORKIN, Ronald.
Liberalism and American Constitutional Law. SMITH, Rogers M.
Liberalism and the Good. DOUGLASS, R Bruce (ed).
The Meaning of Socialism. LUNTLEY, Michael.
Mill and Liberalism (Second Edition). COWLING, Maurice.
Moral Pluralism and Legal Neutrality. SADURSKI, Wojciech.
Morality and Modernity. POOLE, Ross.
Philosophy and Politics. HUNT, G M K (ed).
Varieties of Moral Personality: Ethics and Psychological Realism. FLANAGAN, Owen.
"'Lopp'd and Bound': How Liberal Theory Obscures the Goods of Liberal Practices" in *Liberalism and the Good*, SALKEVER, Stephen G.
"Bringing the Good Back In" in *Liberalism and the Good*, SULLIVAN, William M.
"Catholicism and Liberalism—200 Years of Contest and Consensus" in *Liberalism and the Good*, LANGAN, John.
"Conversational Politics: Rorty's Pragmatist Apology for Liberalism" in *Reading Rorty*, BURROWS, Jo.
"Foundations of Liberal Equality" in *The Tanner Lectures on Human Values, Volume XI*, DWORKIN, Ronald.
"How Not to Defend Liberal Institutions" in *Liberalism and the Good*, BARRY, Brian.
"Identity and Difference in Liberalism" in *Liberalism and the Good*, CONNOLLY, William E.
"Is Liberalism Good Enough?" in *Liberalism and the Good*, SCHMITZ, Kenneth L.
"Liberal Ideas and Reality: Central Europe 1848-49" in *Perspectives on Ideas and Reality*, GERGELY, András.

LIBERALISM

"Liberal Man" in *Philosophy and Politics*, MENDUS, Susan.
"Liberalism and Liberty: The Fragility of a Tradition" in *Key Themes in Philosophy*, GRAHAM, Keith.
"Neutralities" in *Liberalism and the Good*, ACKERMAN, Bruce A.
"The Problem of Liberalism and the Good" in *Liberalism and the Good*, RICHARDSON, Henry S.
"Response to Mendus's 'Liberal Man'" in *Philosophy and Politics*, BINNS, Peter.
"The Search for a Defensible Good: The Emerging Dilemma of Liberalism" in *Liberalism and the Good*, DOUGLASS, R Bruce and MARA, Gerald M.
Aesthetic Liberalism: Kant and the Ethics of Modernity. CASCARDI, Anthony J.
AIDS and the L-Word. DEVINE, Philip E.
Au-delà de la critique communautarienne du libéralisme? D'Alasdair MacIntyre à Stanley Hauerwas. VAN GERWEN, Jef.
Autonomy, Liberalism and State Neutrality. MASON, Andrew D.
The Base Camp Paradox: A Reflection on the Place of Tâtonnement in General Equilibrium Theory. DE VROEY, Michel.
Communitarianism and the Question of Tolerance. PASSERIN D'ENTRÈVES, Maurizio.
Conflicting Views of Liberalism. SKOBLE, Aeon James.
Critical Legal Studies and Liberalism: Understanding the Similarities and Differences. WAGNER DE CEW, Judith.
David Hume's Theology of Liberation. BARRUS, Roger M.
Do These Feminists Like Women?. SOMMERS, Christina.
Does Sommers Like Women? More on Liberalism, Gender Hierarchy, and Scarlett O'Hara. FRIEDMAN, Marilyn.
Free Speech, Free Exchange, and Rawlsian Liberalism. SHAPIRO, Daniel.
Friends and Enemies of Liberalism. ARCHARD, David.
Hegel's Critique of Liberalism and Natural Law: Reconstructing Ethical Life. GARZA JR, Abel.
J G A Pocock's Republicanism and Political Theory: A Critique and Reinterpretation. SHAPIRO, Ian.
Kant the Liberal, Kant the Anarchist: Rawls and Lyotard on Kantian Justice. MAY, Todd G.
Law Without Values: Do the Unborn Have to Wait for a Consensus?. VACCARI, Michael A.
Liberal Man. MENDUS, Susan.
The Liberal Teachings of the Young Liang Qichao. QI, Feng.
Liberalism, Aboriginal Rights, and Cultural Minorities. DANLEY, John R.
Liberalism: Political Success, Moral Failure?. SIMPSON, Peter.
Liberalismo e democrazia: la giustificazione estetica di Rorty. MARRONE, Pierpaolo.
Marx's 'Critique of Hegel's *Philosophy of Right*'. JACKSON, M W.
Misreading Rorty. KOLENDA, Konstantin.
The Neglected Background of Radical Liberalism: P E Dove's Theory of Property. CUNLIFFE, John.
The Paternalistic Attitude Toward Children. AVIRAM, Aharon.
La pensée de Rawls face au défi communautarien. IROEGBU, Pantaleon.
The Philosophy of the Welfare State. BARRY, Norman P.
Post-Liberalism versus Temperate Liberalism. JACOBS, Struan.
Preferences and Politics. SUNSTEIN, Cass R.
Le projet de John Rawls. LAMBERT, Roger.
Rationality, Economic Action and Scarcity (in Hungarian). FEKETE, László.
Rawls, Sandel and the Self. CANEY, S.
Recent Work in Political Philosophy. GRAHAM, Gordon.
Reflections on the Philosophy of Hitlerism. HAND, Seán (trans) and LEVINAS, Emmanuel.
Response to Mendus's "Liberal Man". BINNS, Peter.
Rethinking Politics: Carl Schmitt vs Hegel. WINFIELD, Richard Dien.
Rethinking the Family. KYMLICKA, Will.
Rousseau's Liberalism. SORENSEN, L R.
Society as a Department Store. LEGUTKO, Ryszard.
Speaking About the Unspeakable: Genocide and Philosophy. FREEMAN, Michael.
Staat als Konsens mündiger Bürger? Zur Staatsansicht deutscher Vormärzliberaler. LIEPERT, Anita.
Stout on Relativism, Liberalism, and Communitarianism. QUIRK, Michael J.
Thus Spoke Rorty: The Perils of Narrative Self-Creation. CONWAY, Daniel W.
Toward a Reconciliation of Liberalism and Communitarianism. ELLIS, Ralph D.
Toward One Santayana: Recent Scholarship. KERR-LAWSON, Angus.
Tradition and Ethics: Prospects in a Liberal Society. GUROIAN, Vigen.
Transition to Pragmatic Liberalism: Diversity, Contingency, and Social Solidarity. LINDGREN, Ralph.
Who are "We"? Ambiguities of the Modern Self. SKINNER, Quentin.
Why Surfers Should Be Fed: The Liberal Case for an Unconditional Basic Income. VAN PARIJS, Philippe.

LIBERATION

History and Spirit: An Inquiry into the Philosophy of Liberation. KOVEL, Joel.
The Law of Karma: A Philosophical Study. REICHENBACH, Bruce R.
"The Humanistic Implications of Liberation Theology: Juan Luis Segundo and Karl Marx" in *The Question of Humanism: Challenges and Possibilities*, HEWITT, Marsha A.
The Advaita Theory of Liberation. DAS, Bhupendra Chandra.
The African Liberation Struggle: A Hermeneutic Exploration of an African Historical-Political Horizon. SEREQUEBERHAN, Tsenay.
Christians and Marxist Theory of Human Liberation. KOWALCZYK, Stanislaw.
Cuestiones actuales de epistemología teológica: Aportes de la teología de la liberación. SCANNONE, J C.
David Hume's Theology of Liberation. BARRUS, Roger M.
Filosofía de la liberación como nuevo pensamiento a partir de los oprimidos y como de-strucción (2a parte). ANÍZAR, Humberto Encarnación.
Gorz on Work and Liberation. SAYERS, Sean.
Liberation Theology and the Interpretation of Political Violence. SONTAG, Frederick.
Origins and Tendencies of the Philosophy of Liberation in Latin American Thought: A Critique of Dussel's Ethics. SCHUTTE, Ofelia.

LIBERATION THEOLOGY

Hope and Its Hieroglyph: A Critical Decipherment of Ernst Bloch's "Principle of Hope". ROBERTS, Richard H.
Aportes para el debate en torno a la teología de la liberción. RUBIOLO, E.
Filosofía de la liberación como nuevo pensamiento a partir de los oprimidos y como de-strucción (3a parte). ANÍZAR, Humberto Encarnación.
Teología de la liberación y doctrina social de la Iglesia hoy. GALLI, C M.
Theology of Liberation and Marxism (in Serbo-Croation). ORSOLIC, Marko.

LIBERTARIANISM

The Ideas of Ayn Rand. MERRILL, Ronald E.
Rawls: "A Theory of Justice" and Its Critics. KUKATHAS, Chandran.
Robert Nozick: Property, Justice, and the Minimal State. WOLFF, Jonathan.
"The Arms-Race Implications of Libertarian Capitalism" in *Issues in War and Peace: Philosophical Inquiries*, KUNKEL, Joseph.
"The Flaws in Sen's Case Against Paretian Libertarianism" in *Acting and Reflecting: The Interdisciplinary Turn in Philosophy*, PRESSLER, Jonathan.
"Libertarianism" in *Philosophy and Politics*, BARRY, Norman P.
"Peace Through Justice: A Practical Reconciliation of Opposing Conceptions of Justice" in *In the Interest of Peace: A Spectrum of Philosophical Views*, STERBA, James.
Arthur Schopenhauer als Staatsdenker. WÜRKNER, Joachim.
Determinism and the Experience of Freedom. DOUBLE, Richard.
Free Will and Being a Victim. SMILANSKY, S.
Libertarianism. BARRY, Norman.
Marxism and Contemporary Political Philosophy. COHEN, G A.
The New Consensus: II—The Democratic Welfare State. FRIEDMAN, Jeffrey.
Nozick et la stabilité des principes de justice distributive. BÉGIN, Luc.
A Picture of the Self Which Supports the Moral Responsibility. ANDERSON, Susan Leigh.
Society as a Department Store. LEGUTKO, Ryszard.
Two Conceptions of Civil Rights. EPSTEIN, Richard A.
Why Negative Rights Only?. JORDAN, Jeff.

LIBERTY

Benjamin Constant and the Post-Revolutionary Mind. FONTANA, Biancamaria.
Philosophy of Law (Fourth Edition). FEINBERG, Joel.
Political Writings—John Milton. DZELZAINIS, Martin (ed).
The Realm of Rights. THOMSON, Judith Jarvis.
"Liberty, Community, and Corrective Justice" in *Liability and Responsibility*, WEINRIB, Ernest J.
"Religion and *On Liberty*" in *A Cultivated Mind: Essays On J S Mill Presented to John M Robson*, HAMBURGER, Joseph.
"Two Concepts of Liberty" Thirty Years Later: A Sartre-Inspired Critique. MC BRIDE, William L.
"Voir vivre, sans vivre": Extraits du *Journal Intime*. AMIEL, H F.
'One Very Simple Principle'. RILEY, Jonathan.
Abortion: Privacy versus Liberty. GOULD, James.
The Basic Right to Liberty. PANICHAS, George E.
Bertrand Russell and Liberty: A Question Revisited. PADIA, Chandrakala.
La filosofia civile di Pasquale Villari. URBINATI, Nadia.
For One Concept of Liberty. BEEHLER, Rodger.
Freedom, Commodification, and the Alienation of Labor in Adam Smith's "Wealth of Nations". WERHANE, Patricia H.
Humanity, Morality, and Liberty. DUBCEK, Alexander A.
El idealismo alemán como mitología de la razón. INNERARITY, Daniel.
Libertad y necesidad en el 'Cur Deus Homo' de San Anselmo de Canterbury (segunda parte). CORTI, E C.
Libertad, Igualdad, Fraternidad. BUENO, Gustavo.
La loi du Styx, Leibniz et la politique du bonheur. LE LANNOU, Jean-Michel.
Per una nuova edizione della *Epistola* lockiana sulla tolleranza. MONTUORI, Mario.
Power, Liberty, and Counterfactual Conditionals in Hobbes' Thought. POLANSKY, Ronald and TORELL, Kurt.
Racionalidad y libertad. FERNÁNDEZ DEL VALLE, Agustín Basave.
Response to Berlin and McBride. RENICK, Timothy M.
Rousseau, the General Will, and Individual Liberty. KAIN, Philip J.
Zu Grundfragen des Toleranzproblems in Vergangenheit und Gegenwart. WOLLGAST, Siegfried.

LIE(S)

History, Lying, and Moral Responsibility. PORK, Andrus.
The Quarrel Theorem: First Attempt to the Logic of Lie. MAJCHER, B.

LIFE

Euthanasia: Toward an Ethical Social Policy. THOMASMA, David C.
Le existentia de deo e le Immortalitate del Anima: Lineas de Philosophia del Esser. BLANDINO, Giovanni.
New Harvest: Transplanting Body Parts and Reaping the Benefits. KEYES, C Don (ed).
The Noble Savage: Jean-Jacques Rousseau, 1754-1762. CRANSTON, Maurice.
The Vatican, the Law and the Human Embryo. COUGHLAN, Michael J.
"Il 'Giornale de' Letterati' e le 'scienze della vita': dibattiti e interventi" in *Scienza, Filosofia e Religione tra '600 e '700 in Italia*, BOARETTI, Tiziano.
"Kierkegaard's Stages on Life's Way: How Many Are There?" in *Writing the Politics of Difference*, MICHELSEN, John M.
"Voir vivre, sans vivre": Extraits du *Journal Intime*. AMIEL, H F.
Art, Life and Reality. NOVITZ, David.
Bondedness, *Moyo* and *Umunthu* as the Elements of aChewa Spirituality: Organizing Logic and Principle of Life. SINDIMA, Harvey.
Les combinaisons de la vie, l'organisation du vivant, le réseau du soi. LIVET, Pierre.
Concerning the Absurdity of Life. SMITH, Quentin.
Dall'attualismo al tensionalismo. SIMONE, Aldo.
Ética sin raíces. VARGAS, Alberto.
Francesco Bonucci, tra medicina e filosofia. STORTI, Cinzia.
Giacomo Andrea Giacomini: un clinico padovano tra Metafisica e Scienza. FEDERSPIL, Giovanni.
Heidegger's *Kampf*: The Difficulty of Life. CAPUTO, John D.
Law Without Values: Do the Unborn Have to Wait for a Consensus?. VACCARI, Michael A.
Love in *Thus Spoke Zarathustra*. LEVITT, Tom.
Philosophical Scepticism: An Intelligible Challenge. GRUNDY, Jeremy.
Porphyry and the Intelligible Triad. EDWARDS, M J.
Psychoanalysis: A Form of Life?. BREARLEY, Michael.
Sulla posizione dell'uomo nella natura. SEIDL, Horst.
Sur l'habitation poétique de l'homme. PIERSON, Dominique.
Thomas Aquinas and Henry of Ghent on the Succession of Substantial Forms and the Origin of Human Life. WILSON, Gordon A.
Vida y Resurrección en el pensamiento de Erich Fromm. CHAVES, Flory.
La vie, ou le point de rupture: Schopenhauer-Nietzsche. UCCIANI, Louis.

LIFE STYLE(S)

Reasons for Living: A Basic Ethics. PORTER, Burton F.
A Thinker's Guide to Living Well. BRADFORD, Dennis E.
Form of Life in Wittgenstein's Later Work. GARVER, Newton.

LIFE WORLD

Between Freiburg and Frankfurt: Toward a Critical Ontology. DALLMAYR, Fred R.
Life-World and Politics: Between Modernity and Postmodernity. WHITE, Stephen K (ed).
"Introduction" in *Life-World and Politics: Between Modernity and Postmodernity*, WHITE, Stephen K.
"Life-World: Variations on a Theme" in *Life-World and Politics: Between Modernity and Postmodernity*, DALLMAYR, Fred R.
"Weighing Anchor: Postmodern Journeys from the Life-World" in *Life-World and Politics: Between Modernity and Postmodernity*, SHAPIRO, Michael J.
"Paramount Reality" in Schutz and Gurwitsch. KASSAB, Elizabeth Suzanne.
El paradigma de sistemas: posibilidades para una prácica social emancipadora. RODRÍGUEZ HÖLKEMEYER, Patricia.

LIGHT

Particles and Waves: Historical Essays in the Philosophy of Science. ACHINSTEIN, Peter.
"Una uguale educazione?" in *Égalité Uguaglianza*, PANCERA, Carlo.
Conventionalism in Physics. MORRIS, W T.
Ethics as Drawn from the Method. CARTER, Richard B.

LIMITS

"Ethics and the Limits of Consistency" in *Logic and Ethics*, BAMBROUGH, Renford.
"From Leviathan to Lilliput" in *Celebrating Peace*, TOULMIN, Stephen.
Algunos márgenes de la condición humana. MAS, Oscar.
Animal Experimentation and the Argument from Limited Resources. FINK, Charles K.
The Ethical Limitations of the Market. ANDERSON, Elizabeth.
Knowing When to Stop: The Limits of Medicine. JECKER, Nancy S.
The Limits of Power. TALIAFERRO, Charles.

LINDBECK, G

Meaning, Truth and Realism in Bultmann and Lindbeck. FERGUSSON, David.

LINE

La definizione di "retta" data da Euclide e le geometrie non-euclidee. BLANDINO, Giovanni.

LINEAR

"Newton, Nonlinearity and Determinism" in *Some Truer Method*, DURHAM, Frank and PURRINGTON, Robert D.
A Coding of the Countable Linear Orderings. DEHORNOY, Patrick.
Degrees of Orderings Not Isomorphic to Recursive Linear Orderings. JOCKUSCH JR, Carl G and SOARE, Robert I.
Linear Axiomatics of Communicative Product-Free Lambek Calculus. ZIELONKA, Wojciech.
A Linear Continuum of Time. DOWDEN, Bradley H.
Non-Commutative Intuitionistic Linear Logic. ABRUSCI, V Michele.
On the Quasi-Ordering of Borel Linear Orders Under Embeddability. LOUVEAU, Alain and SAINT-RAYMOND, Jean.

LINGUISTIC ANALYSIS

Classics of Analytic Philosophy. AMMERMAN, Robert R (ed).
The "No Crossing Constraint" in Autosegmental Phonology. COLEMAN, John and LOCAL, John.
Computational Structure of GPSG Models. RISTAD, Eric Sven.
Four Thousand Ships Passed Through the Lock: Object-Induced Measure Functions on Events. KRIFKA, Manfred.
Notes on the Specification of "Meaning" in Schutz. EMBREE, Lester.
Process Vagueness. SORENSEN, Roy A.
References in Narrative Text. WIEBE, Janyce M.
Terrorism and Argument from Analogy. WALLACE, G.
The Heterogeneity of Poetic Language in Kristeva (in Japanese). NARUSE, Katsuji.

LINGUISTIC RULE(S)

The Foundations of Linguistic Theory: Selected Writings of Roy Harris. LOVE, Nigel (ed).

LINGUISTICS

Abeunt Studia in Mores: A Festschrift for Helga Doblin. MERRILL, Sarah A Bishop (ed).
Alltagssprachliche Metakommunikation im Englischen und Deutschen. WELTE, Werner.
The Difference Between Truth and Opinion: How the Misuse of Language Can Lead to Disaster. COONEY, Timothy J.
Estetica: Come Scienza dell'Espressione e Linguistica Generale. CROCE, Benedetto.
The Foundations of Linguistic Theory: Selected Writings of Roy Harris. LOVE, Nigel (ed).
Kalkulierte Absurditäten. STRUB, Christian.
Kommunikations-Theoretische Schriften II: Symbolische Erkenntnis und Kommunikation. UNGEHEUER, Gerold (ed).
Linguistic Behaviour. BENNETT, Jonathan.
The Metaphysics of Meaning. KATZ, Jerrold J.
Philosophische Hermeneutik. INEICHEN, Hans.
Properties as Processes: A Synoptic Study of Wilfried Sellars' Nominalism. SEIBT, Johanna.
Saussure: Signs, System, and Arbitrariness. HOLDCROFT, David.
Semantic Structures. JACKENDOFF, Ray.
Understanding the Chinese Mind: The Philosophical Roots. ALLINSON, Robert E (ed).
"'Lautform, innere Sprachform, Form der Sprachen'" in *Leibniz, Humboldt, and the Origins of Comparativism*, BARBA, Mario.
"Comparatismo e grammatica comparata: Tipologia linguistica e forma grammaticale" in *Leibniz, Humboldt, and the Origins of Comparativism*, SWIGGERS, Pierre.
"Da Humboldt ai neogrammatici: Continuità e fratture" in *Leibniz, Humboldt, and the Origins of Comparativism*, RAMAT, Paolo.
"Humboldt et Leibniz: Le concept intérieur de la linguistique" in *Leibniz, Humboldt, and the Origins of Comparativism*, TRABANT, Jürgen.
"Linguistics as a Borderline Case" in *Abeunt Studia in Mores: A Festschrift for Helga Doblin*, MERRILL, Sarah A Bishop.
"Linguistics: What's Wrong with 'The Right View'" in *Philosophical Perspectives, 3: Philosophy of Mind and Action Theory, 1989*, DEVITT, Michael and STERELNY, Kim.
"On the Concept of 'a Language'" in *Studies on Mario Bunge's "Treatise"*, DILLINGER, Mike.
"The Philosophical and Anthropological Place of Wilhelm von Humboldt's Linguistic Typology" in *Leibniz, Humboldt, and the Origins of Comparativism*, DI CESARE, Donatella.
"The Place of Friedrich Schlegel in the Development of Historical-Comparative Linguistics" in *Leibniz, Humboldt, and the Origins of Comparativism*, KOERNER, Konrad.
"The Problem of Linguistic Empowerment" in *Abeunt Studia in Mores: A Festschrift for Helga Doblin*, MERRILL, Sarah A Bishop.
"Representation and the Place of Linguistic Change before Comparative Grammar" in *Leibniz, Humboldt, and the Origins of Comparativism*, AUROUX, Sylvain.
"Die Säkularisierung des 'Tertium comparationis'" in *Leibniz, Humboldt, and the Origins of Comparativism*, BORSCHE, Tilman.
"Three Indeterminacies" in *Perspectives on Quine*, QUINE, W V.
Aristotelian Contraries. BOGEN, James.
Il carteggio Xavier Léon: corrispondenti italiana. QUILICI, Leana and RAGGHIANTI, Renzo.

LINGUISTICS
La creencia y su conexión con los actos linguísticos. SAAB, Salma.
Disjoint Reference into NP. SELLS, Peter.
Linguistic Forms and Social Obligations: A Critique of the Doctrine of Literal Expression in Searle. BOGEN, David.
Linguistic Intuitions and Varieties of Ethical Naturalism. BALL, Stephen W.
Never say "Never say 'Never'": A Reply to Nicholas Gier. REEDER, Harry P.
On the Purported Pragmatico-Semantic Foundation of Linguistics and AI Through Wittgenstein's Late Philosophy. LEINFELLNER-RUPERTSBERGER, Elisabeth.
The Potential of Medicine as a Resource for Philosophy. FULFORD, K W M.
Reference and Pronominal Descriptions. WILSON, George M.
Sobre la no paradoja de un cretense. WILSON, Jack L.
Some Problems of Legal Language. KNAPP, Viktor.
Die Sprachen und das Denken: Klein Bestandsaufnahme zum linguistischen Relativismus (Sapir-Whorf-Hypothese). FRANZEN, Winfried.
Teorías de verdad y teorías del significado. VARGAS, Celso.
Therapeutic Professions and the Diffusion of Deficit. GERGEN, Kenneth J.

LIPPS, H
Wittgenstein, Hans Lipps y los supuestos de la predicación. LÁZARO, Ramón Castilla.

LIST, F
"Die Geschichte hat kein Libretto": Zu Isaiah Berlins Begriff des Nationalismus. RITTER, Henning.

LISTENING
The Other Side of Language: A Philosophy of Listening. FIUMARA, Gemma Corradi.
Dire e ascoltare nella tipologia del "sofista", del "filosof-re" e del pensatore socratico. MARCHETTI, Giancarlo.

LISZT, A
Response to Lizst's "Animal Liberation as a Valid Response to Structural Violence". FINSEN, Susan.

LITERACY
Cultural Literacy: Posing Queer Questions. GREENE, Maxine.
Literacy as Disempowerment: The Role of Documentary Texts. DE CASTELL, Suzanne.
Response to "Literacy as Disempowerment". RAITZ, Keith L.
Toward a Rationale for Literary Literacy. BOGDAN, Deanne.

LITERAL
The Literal Sense of Scripture. WILLIAMS, Rowan.

LITERARY
The Rhetoric of Berkeley's Philosophy. WALMSLEY, Peter.
Works of Love? Reflections on "Works of Love". FENDT, Gene.
"Les utopies littéraires au XVIIIe siècle" in *Égalité Uguaglianza*, IMBROSCIO, Carmelina.
Die Wahrheit des literarischen Kunstwerks: R Ingardens Begriff des Quasi-Urteils (in Japanese). KAWAKAMI, Akitaka.
Toward a Rationale for Literary Literacy. BOGDAN, Deanne.
Usefulness in Literary History. SMALL, Ian and GUY, Josephine.

LITERARY CRITICISM
The Bible as Rhetoric: Studies in Biblical Persuasion and Credibility. WARNER, Martin (ed).
Creative Characters. YOUNG-BRUEHL, Elisabeth.
On Walter Benjamin: Critical Essays and Recollections. SMITH, Gary (ed).
"'Tales Artfully Spun'" in *The Bible as Rhetoric: Studies in Biblical Persuasion and Credibility*, TRIGG, Roger.
"The Bible and the Rhetorical Sublime" in *The Bible as Rhetoric: Studies in Biblical Persuasion and Credibility*, POLAND, Lynn.
"The World Could Not Contain the Books" in *The Bible as Rhetoric: Studies in Biblical Persuasion and Credibility*, EDWARDS, Michael.
Author, Writer, Text: *The Will to Power*. MAGNUS, Bernd.
Derrida's huishouding. BERNS, Egidius.
The Empirical Author: Salman Rushdie's *The Satanic Verses*. CLOSE, Anthony.
Is *King Lear* Like the Pacific Ocean or the Washington Monument? Critical Pluralism and Literary Interpretation. PHELAN, James.
Marxist Literary Aesthetics. MILLER, Seumas.
Reason in Criticism. MIRI, Mrinal.

LITERARY FORM(S)
On Franco-Ferraz, Theism and the Theatre of the Mind. BADÍA-CABRERA, Miguel A.

LITERARY THEORY
Myth and Modern Philosophy. DANIEL, Stephen H.
Philosophical Hermeneutics and Literary Theory. WEINSHEIMER, Joel.
Speech Acts and Literary Theory. PETREY, Sandy.
Frontières des études littéraires: science de la littérature, science des discours. ANGENOT, Marc.
Ground, Pivot, Motion: Ecofeminist Theory, Dialogics, and Literary Practice. MURPHY, Patrick.
The Moral Interpretation of the 'Second Preface' to Arrian's *Anabasis*. GRAY, V J.
The Status of Fiction: Between Nostalgia and Nihilism (in French). IMHOOF, Stefan.

LITERATURE
see also Fiction(s)
American Philosophy and the Romantic Tradition. GOODMAN, Russell B.
The Anatomy of Philosophical Style. LANG, Berel.
Delicate Subjects: Romanticism, Gender, and the Ethics of Understanding. ELLISON, Julie.
Fictions of Reality in the Age of Hume and Johnson. DAMROSCH, Leo.
History and the Paradoxes of Metaphysics in "Dantons Tod". TAYLOR, Rodney.
The Humanities in the Nineties: A View From the Netherlands. ZÜRCHER, Erik (ed).
Kalkulierte Absurditäten. STRUB, Christian.
Knowledge, Fiction, and Imagination. NOVITZ, David.
Lesbian Philosophies and Cultures. ALLEN, Jeffner (ed).
Love's Knowledge: Essays on Philosophy and Literature. NUSSBAUM, Martha C.
Narrative in Culture: The Uses of Storytelling in the Sciences, Philosophy, and Literature. NASH, Christopher (ed).
The Philosopher's Joke. WATSON, Richard A.
Proust: The Creative Silence. CARANFA, Angelo.
Romanticism and the Sciences. CUNNINGHAM, Andrew (ed).
The Tanner Lectures on Human Values, Volume XI. PETERSON, Grethe B (ed).
Time-Travel for Beginners and Other Stories. HARRISON, Jonathan.
Unsere postmoderne Moderne (Second Edition). WELSCH, Wolfgang.
The World of the Imagination: Sum and Substance. BRANN, Eva T H.
Writers and Philosophers: A Sourcebook of Philosophical Influences on Literature. THOMAS, Edmund J.
"Back to the Future" in *Postmodernism—Philosophy and the Arts (Continental Philosophy III)*, TAYLOR, Mark C.
"How to Recognise Metaphors in Literature" in *XIth International Congress in Aesthetics, Nottingham 1988*, ELOVAARA, Raili.
"Literature and Philosophy at the Crossroads: Proustian Subjects" in *Writing the Politics of Difference*, MC DONALD, Christie.
"Literature, History, and What Men Learn" in *The Philosophy of John William Miller*, ELIAS, Robert H.
"The Otherness of Words: Joyce, Bakhtin, Heidegger" in *Postmodernism—Philosophy and the Arts (Continental Philosophy III)*, BRUNS, Gerald L.
"Redefining Philosophy as Literature: Richard Rorty's 'Defence' of Literary Culture" in *Reading Rorty*, FISCHER, Michael.
"La tematica della follia tra Umanesimo nordico e Umanesimo latino: l'*Encomium Moriae* di Erasmo da Rotterdam" in *Razionalitá critica: nella filosofia moderna*, CASTELLANO, Veneranda.
"Unspeakable Things Unspoken: The Afro-American Presence in American Literature" in *The Tanner Lectures on Human Values, Volume XI*, MORRISON, Toni.
Alternatives et questions dans la littérature romanesque. COMETTI, Jean-Pierre.
Anachronistic Themes and Literary Value: *The Tempest*. SKILLEAS, Ole Martin.
Can Fiction Be Stranger Than Truth? An Aristotelian Answer. GALLOP, David.
Fictional Objects in Literature and Mental Representations. BACHRACH, Jay E.
Die Figuren des Menschlichen. MEYER, Michel.
Frontières des études littéraires: science de la littérature, science des discours. ANGENOT, Marc.
Gerald Bruns's Cavell. CREWE, Jonathan.
Giambattista Vico and the Quarrel between the Ancients and the Moderns. LEVINE, Joseph M.
Hegel's Intertextual Dialectic: Diderot's *Le Neveu de Rameau* in the *Phenomenology of Spirit*. PRICE, David W.
Henry James and the Paradox of Literary Mastery. BLAIR, Sara.
In Defense of Sentimentality. SOLOMON, Robert C.
The Justification of "English". MEYNELL, Hugo A.
The Last Utopia: Entropy and Revolution in the Poetics of Evgeny Zamjatin. SICHER, Efraim.
Los límites de mi lenguaje—los límites de mi mundo. KLOYBER, Christian.
Literature and Language After the Death of God. STEIN, A L.
On Bruns, on Cavell. CONANT, James.
Para una teoría latinoamericana de las relaciones de la ciencia con la literatura: la cienciapoesía. CATALÁ, Rafael.
Persuasion: Jane Austen's Philosophical Rhetoric. KASTELY, James L.
Questioning "the Romantic Ideology": Wordsworth. WOLFSON, Susan J.
La réception de Spinoza dans la littérature néerlandaise. HENRARD, Roger.
Revealing Gendered Texts. FREELAND, Cynthia A.
Schopenhauersche Weltsicht und totalitäre Humanität im Werke Thomas Manns. KRISTIANSEN, Borge.
Self-Making and World-Making. BRUNER, Jerome.
Teaching Ethics in the Health Care Setting, Part I. COUTTS, Mary Carrington.
Telling Stories: Creative Literature and Ethics. RADEY, Charles.
Toward a Rationale for Literary Literacy. BOGDAN, Deanne.
The Uses of Rhetoric: Indeterminacy in Legal Reasoning, Practical Thinking and Interpretation of Literary Figures. OLMSTED, Wendy Raudenbush.

LITURGY

Grammaire et Liturgie dans les "Sophismes" du XIIle Siècle. ROSIER, Irène and ROY, Bruno.
Tradition and Ethics: Prospects in a Liberal Society. GUROIAN, Vigen.

LIVING WILL(S)

Deciding for Others: The Ethics of Surrogate Decision Making. BUCHANAN, Allen E.
To Die or Not to Die?. BERGER, Arthur S (ed).

LIVINGSTON, D

Hume's Critical Realism: A Reply to Livingston. WILSON, Fred.

LLEWELLYN, K

Conclusion: Legal Institutions and Limitations to Cognition and Power. O'BRIEN, James.

LLOYD, H

Young and Lloyd on the Particle Theory of Light: A Response to Achinstein. CHEN, Xiang.

LOCATION

"Travels in the Postmodern: Making Sense of the Logical" in *Feminism/Postmodernism*, PROBYN, Elspeth.
Causal Independence in EPR Arguments. BUTTERFIELD, Jeremy.
Disembodying 'Bodily' Sensations. COMBES, Richard.
Realismo e fenomenismo nella fisica moderna. BLANDINO, Giovanni.

LOCKE

Criteria of Certainty: Truth and Judgment in the English Enlightenment. COPE, Kevin L.
Interpreting Political Responsibility. DUNN, John.
John Locke: Segundo Tratado sobre el Gobierno Civil. MELLIZO, Carlos (trans).
Knowledge of the External World. AUNE, Bruce.
Locke and French Materialism. YOLTON, John W.
Nature and Politics: Liberalism in the Philosophies of Hobbes, Locke, and Rousseau. RAPACZYNSKI, Andrzej.
Questions Concerning the Law of Nature: John Locke. CLAY, Jenny Strauss (ed & trans).
Reasons and Experience. MILLAR, Alan.
The Secret Connexion: Causation, Realism, and David Hume. STRAWSON, Galen.
"Foils for Newton: Comments on Howard Stein" in *Philosophical Perspectives on Newtonian Science*, ARTHUR, Richard.
"Leibniz and Locke on the Knowledge of Necessary Truths" in *Central Themes in Early Modern Philosophy*, BOLTON, Martha Brandt.
"On Locke, 'the Great Huygenius, and the Incomparable Mr. Newton'" in *Philosophical Perspectives on Newtonian Science*, STEIN, Howard.
The Assurance of Faith. WOLTERSTORFF, Nicholas.
Cato's Letters, John Locke, and the Republican Paradigm. HAMOWY, Ronald.
Corpuscles, Mechanism, and Essentialism in Berkeley and Locke. ATHERTON, Margaret.
Crime, Minorities, and the Social Contract. LAWSON, Bill.
Fragmented Selves and the Problem of Ownership. BRENNAN, Andrew.
How Ideas Became Meanings: Locke and the Foundations of Semantic Theory. HANNA, Robert.
How's and Why's: Causation Un-Locked. FRANKEL, Lois.
Locke on Mathematical Knowledge. CICOVACKI, Predrag.
Locke on Personal Identity and the Trinity Controversy of the 1690s. WEDEKING, Gary.
Locke on Personal Identity. WINKLER, Kenneth P.
Locke on Real Essence. OWEN, David W D.
Locke on Taxation and Suffrage. HUGHES, Martin.
Locke on the Ontology of Matter, Living Things and Persons. CHAPPELL, Vere.
Locke's Account of Personal Identity. SCHRECK, P A.
Locke, Lockean Ideas, and the Glorious Revolution. SCHWOERER, Lois G.
Lockes Qualitäten: Erwiderung auf Casati. KIENZLE, Bertram.
Medicine in John Locke's Philosophy. SANCHEZ-GONZALEZ, Miguel A.
The Moral Foundations of Intangible Property. CHILD, James W.
Ousia, Substratum, and Matter. SFEKAS, Stanley.
Per una nuova edizione della *Epistola* lockiana sulla tolleranza. MONTUORI, Mario.
Persons and Human Beings. GARRETT, Brian.
Political Freedom. TULLY, James.
Primary and Secondary Qualities: A Reply to Kienzle. CASATI, Roberto.
Relative Identity and Locke's Principle of Individuation. UZGALIS, William L.
Same Human Being, Same Person?. THORNTON, Mark.
Thoughtful Brutes: The Ascription of Mental Predicates to Animals in Locke's "Essay". SQUADRITO, Kathleen.
Tully's Locke. DEN HARTOGH, Govert.
The Way of Ideas: A Retrospective. YOLTON, John W.
When is Original Appropriation *Required*?. SCHMIDTZ, David.

LOCKE, A

A Returning to the Source: The Philosophy of Alain Locke. BIRT, Robert E.

LOEWER, B

On Saying That Again. HAND, Michael.

LOGIC

see also Deontic Logic, Infinitary Logic, Informal Logic, Intuitionistic Logic, Many-Valued Logics, Modal Logic, Predicate Logic, Proof(s), Propositional Logic, Relevant Logics, Tense Logic
Acting and Reflecting: The Interdisciplinary Turn in Philosophy. SIEG, Wilfried (ed).
The Analytic Tradition: Philosophical Quarterly Monographs, Volume 1. BELL, David (ed).
Aristotelian Logic and the Arabic Language in Alfarabi. ABED, Shukri B.
Aristotelian Logic. PARRY, William T.
The Big Questions: A Short Introduction to Philosophy (Third Edition). SOLOMON, Robert C.
Brouwer's Intuitionism (Studies in the History and Philosophy of Mathematics, Vol 2). VAN STIGT, W P.
Clear Thinking: A Practical Introduction. RUCHLIS, Hy.
Computability, Complexity, Logic. BÖRGER, E.
Core Questions in Philosophy: A Text With Readings. SOBER, Elliott.
Critical Reasoning (Third Edition). CEDERBLOM, Jerry.
The Elements of Reasoning. CONWAY, David.
Encyclopedia of the Philosophical Sciences in Outline and Critical Writings—G W F Hegel. BEHLER, Ernst (ed).
Essays on Hegel's Logic. DI GIOVANNI, George (ed).
Events in the Semantics of English: A Study in Subatomic Semantics. PARSONS, Terence.
Experimental Studies of Interactive Decisions. RAPOPORT, Amnon.
Frege in Perspective. WEINER, Joan.
Fundamentals of Philosophy (Third Edition). STEWART, David.
Gödel's Theorem in Focus. SHANKER, S G (ed).
Hegel: o la rebelión contra el límite. IZUZQUIZA, Ignacio.
Hegels Theorie des Gesetzes. BOGDANDY, Armin Von.
Identity and Discrimination. WILLIAMSON, Timothy.
Imre Lakatos and Theories of Scientific Change. GAVROGLU, Kostas (ed).
In Defense of Mystical Ideas: Support for Mystical Beliefs from a Purely Theoretical Viewpoint. CHAPMAN, Tobias.
Inference and Understanding: A Philosophical and Psychological Perspective. MANKTELOW, K I.
Une introduction à l'analyse du discours argumentatif. MENDENHALL, Vance.
John Craige's Mathematical Principles of Christian Theology. NASH, Richard.
Leibniz' Position der Rationalität. KAEHLER, Klaus Erich.
Logic for an Overcast Tuesday. RAFALKO, Robert J.
Logic in the Husserlian Context. TITO, Johanna Maria.
Logic Programming: Proceedings of the Seventh International Conference. WARREN, David H D (ed).
Logic, Methodology and Philosophy of Science, VIII. FENSTAD, J E (ed).
Logic, Methodology and Philosophy of Science, VII. MARCUS, Ruth Barcan (ed).
La Logica Simbolica: nella produzione scientifica in lingua russa (1961-1983). PENNINO, Luciano.
The Logical Basis of Metaphysics. DUMMETT, Michael.
Logical Forms: An Introduction to Philosophical Logic. SAINSBURY, Mark.
Mathematics and the Image of Reason. TILES, Mary E.
Meaning and Method: Essays in Honor of Hilary Putnam. BOOLOS, George (ed).
Meaning and Speech Acts: Volume I, Principles of Language Use. VANDERVEKEN, Daniel.
Meaning and Speech Acts: Volume II, Formal Semantics of Success and Satisfaction. VANDERVEKEN, Daniel.
The Metaphysics of Meaning. KATZ, Jerrold J.
The Metaphysics of the "Tractatus". CARRUTHERS, Peter.
I Modelli l'Invenzione e la Conferma. PETRONI, Angelo Maria.
Nomic Probability and the Foundations of Induction. POLLOCK, John L.
The Origins of Aristotelian Science. FEREJOHN, Michael.
Las paradojas del Infinito. BOLZANO, Bernard.
Parts of Classes. LEWIS, David.
Phänomenologie als ästhetische Theorie. FELLMANN, Ferdinand.
Philosophical Applications of Free Logic. LAMBERT, Karel (ed).
Philosophical Logic. STRAWSON, P F (ed).
Philosophical Papers: F P Ramsey. MELLOR, D H (ed).
Philosophical Writings: A Selection—William of Ockham. BOEHNER, Philotheus (ed & trans).
Probabilistic Causality. EELLS, Ellery.
Propositional Attitudes: The Role of Content in Logic, Language, and Mind. ANDERSON, C Anthony (ed).
Pulling up the Ladder: The Metaphysical Roots of Wittgenstein's Tractatus. BROCKHAUS, Richard R.
Rationality in Action: Contemporary Approaches. MOSER, Paul K (ed).
Reasoning and Revision in Hybrid Representation Systems. NEBEL, Bernhard.
Representing and Reasoning With Probabilistic Knowledge: A Logical Approach to Probabilities. BACCHUS, Fahiem.
Semantic Structures. JACKENDOFF, Ray.
Structures in Mathematical Theories: Reports of the San Sebastian International Symposium, 1990. DÍEZ, Amparo (ed).

LOGIC

The Sweep of Probability. SCHLESINGER, George N.
Themes From Kaplan. ALMOG, Joseph (ed).
Understanding Arguments: An Introduction to Informal Logic (Fourth Edition). FOGELIN, Robert J.
Untersuchungen zur Theorie des hypothetischen Urteils. LINNEWEBER-LAMMERSKITTEN, Helmut.
What If...? Toward Excellence in Reasoning. HINTIKKA, Jaakko.
Within Reason: A Guide to Non-Deductive Reasoning. BURBIDGE, John.
The World of the Imagination: Sum and Substance. BRANN, Eva T H.
"Afterthoughts" in *Themes From Kaplan*, KAPLAN, David.
"A Central Problem for a Speech-Dispositional Account of Logic and Language" in *Perspectives on Quine*, BERGER, Alan.
"Deductive Heuristics" in *Imre Lakatos and Theories of Scientific Change*, MUSGRAVE, Alan.
"Defeasible Logic and The Frame Problem" in *Knowledge Representation and Defeasible Reasoning*, NUTE, Donald.
"Demonstratives: An Essay on the Semantics, Logic, Metaphysics, and Epistemology of Demonstratives" in *Themes From Kaplan*, KAPLAN, David.
"Introduction to A Logic of Assertions" in *Knowledge Representation and Defeasible Reasoning*, GILES, Robin.
"Is Existence What Existential Quantification Expresses?" in *Perspectives on Quine*, ORENSTEIN, Alex.
"Logic and Pragmatic Truth" in *Logic, Methodology and Philosophy of Science, VIII*, DA COSTA, Newton C A.
"Logic and the World" in *Themes From Kaplan*, ALMOG, Joseph.
"Logic in Russell's Logicism" in *The Analytic Tradition: Philosophical Quarterly Monographs, Volume 1*, HYLTON, Peter.
"The Logic of Physical Theory" in *Physicalism in Mathematics*, URQUHART, Alasdair.
"Logical and Philosophical Foundations for Arithmetical Logic" in *Physicalism in Mathematics*, GAUTHIER, Yvon.
"The Logical Ideas of N A Vasiliev and Modern Logic" in *Logic, Methodology and Philosophy of Science, VIII*, SMIRNOV, V A.
"Marginalia Sino-logica" in *Understanding the Chinese Mind: The Philosophical Roots*, HARBSMEIER, Christoph.
"Mario Bunge's Philosophy of Logic and Mathematics" in *Studies on Mario Bunge's "Treatise"*, MIRÓ, Francisco.
"The Meanings of Logical Constants" in *Truth and Interpretation: Perspectives on the Philosophy of Donald Davidson*, HARMAN, Gilbert.
"A New Normative Theory of Probabilistic Logic" in *Knowledge Representation and Defeasible Reasoning*, ALELIUNAS, Romas.
"On Incommensurability" in *Imre Lakatos and Theories of Scientific Change*, BALZER, W.
"The Problem of De Re Modality" in *Themes From Kaplan*, FINE, Kit.
"Quine" in *Perspectives on Quine*, DREBEN, Burton.
"Reflections on Hilbert's Program" in *Acting and Reflecting: The Interdisciplinary Turn in Philosophy*, SIEG, Wilfried.
"The Standard of Equality of Numbers" in *Meaning and Method: Essays in Honor of Hilary Putnam*, BOOLOS, George.
"Vagueness, Logic and Interpretation" in *The Analytic Tradition: Philosophical Quarterly Monographs, Volume 1*, HOOKWAY, Christopher.
Un "mapa de ontologías". PEREDA, Carlos.
"Pathologies" in Two Syntactic Categories of Partial Maps. MONTAGNA, Franco.
"Sigma": conoscenza e metodo. SAVA, Gabriella.
"The Logic of Implication". BALZER, Noel.
'*P*, Therefore, *P*' Without Circularity. SORENSEN, Roy A.
A 1-Generic Degree Which Bounds a Minimal Degree. KUMABE, Masahiro.
A Brief Survey of Indian Buddhistic Logic (in Hungarian). FEHER, Judit.
About Prikry Generic Extensions. SURESON, Claude.
Absolutely Independent Sets of Generation of Filters in Boolean Algebras. GRYGIEL, Joanna.
Acceptance Is Not Enough: A Critique of Hamblin. JOHNSON, Ralph H.
Actuality and Quantification. HAZEN, Allen.
Aesthetic Order. LORAND, Ruth.
Against Conditionalization. BACCHUS, Fahiem and KYBURG JR, Henry E and THALOS, Mariam.
Aggregation Theorems and Multidimensional Stochastic Choice Models. MARLEY, A A J.
Al-Fârâbî lógico: su exposicón de la "Isagogé" de Porfirio. RAMÓN, Rafael.
Algebraization of Paraconsistent Logic P^1. LEWIN, R A and MIKENBERG, I F and SCHWARZE, M G.
The Alliance between Puritanism and Cartesian Logic at Harvard, 1687-1735. KENNEDY, Rick.
An Almost General Splitting Theorem for Modal Logic. KRACHT, Marcus.
Almost Hugeness and a Related Notion. BARBANEL, Julius.
Ambiguity, Inductive Systems, and the Modeling of Subjective Probability Judgements. MONETA, Giovanni B.
Ancora una discussione su Hegel: logica, storia, fenomenologia. NUZZO, Angelica.
Annabel and the Bookmaker: An Everyday Tale of Bayesian Folk. MILNE, Peter.
The Answer to Dziobiak's Question. PALASINSKI, Marek.
Anti-Realism Untouched. MELIA, Joseph.
Après Weil, avec Weil: Une lecture de Gilbert Kirscher. LABARRIÈRE, Pierre-Jean.
Una aproximación ontológica a la realidad fisica. HÜBNER, Adolf.
Argumentation—Distributed or Monological?. BARTH, E M.
Aristotelian Contraries. BOGEN, James.
Aristotelian Syllogisms and Generalized Quantifiers. WESTERSTAHL, Dag.
Arithmetizing Uniform *NC*. ALLEN, B.
Assessing Inductive Logics Empirically. SMOKLER, Howard.
The Autonomy of Probability Theory (Notes on Kolmogorov, Rényi, and Popper). LEBLANC, Hugues.
An Axiomatic Basis of Accounting: A Structuralist Reconstruction. BALZER, Wolfgang and MATTESSICH, Richard.
The Axiomatization of Randomness. VAN LAMBALGEN, Michiel.
Axiomatization of the De Morgan Type Rules. HERRMANN, B.
Axiomatization of 'Peircean' Branching-Time Logic. ZANARDO, Alberto.
Azande Logic *Verus* Western Logic?. TRIPLETT, Timm.
El azar objetivo como medida matemática de desorden. MARTÍNEZ, Sergio.
B-Varieties with Normal Free Algebras. TEMBROWSKI, Bronislaw.
A Basic Free Logic. WU, Kathleen Johnson.
A Bayesian Proof of a Humean Principle. GILLIES, Donald.
Eine Bemerkung zu spektralen Darstellungen von ρ-stelligen Aufzählbaren. DEUTSCH, Michael.
Bondedness, *Moyo* and *Umunthu* as the Elements of aChewa Spirituality: Organizing Logic and Principle of Life. SINDIMA, Harvey.
Boolean Algebras and Orbits of the Lattice of R.E. Sets Modulo the Finite Sets. CHOLAK, Peter.
Boolean Powers of Abelian Groups. EDA, Katsuya.
Boolean Products of CW—Algebras and Pseudo-Complementation. TORRENS, Antoni.
The Borel Conjecture. JUDAH, Haim and SHELAH, Saharon and WOODIN, W H.
Boskovic's Mathematical Conception of Continuity and the Differentiability of Function (in Serbo-Croatian). STIPANIC, Ernest.
Boskovic's Philosophy of Mathematics (in Serbo-Croatian). HOMANN, Frederick A.
Bounded Arithmetic and the Polynomial Hierarchy. KRAJICEK, Jan and PUDLÁK, Pavel and TAKEUTI, Gaisi.
Boundedness Theorems for Dilators and Ptykes. KECHRIS, Alexander S.
Bounds in Weak Truth-Table Reducibility. HABART, Karol.
Brains in a Vat, Language and Metalanguage. CASATI, Roberto and DOKIC, Jérome.
Brouwerian Intuitionism. DETLEFSEN, Michael.
Buridan's Divided Modal Syllogistic. WILLING, Anthony.
A Calculus for the Common Rules of.... RAUTENBERG, Wolfgan.
Can An Argument Be Both Valid and Invalid Too?. NEBLETT, William R.
Can There Be a Possible World in Which Memory Is Unreliable?. LEUNG, Edwin Sing Choe.
Cantidad o ex-tensión?. BOLZÁN, J E.
The Cardinality of Powersets in Finite Models of the Powerset Axiom. ABIAN, Alexander and AMIN, Wael A.
Cartesian Syntax. ENGLEBRETSEN, George.
A Case for a Heretical Deontic Semantics. EDELBERG, Walter.
Categorical Grammars Determined from Linguistic Data by Unification. BUSZKOWSKI, Wojciech and PENN, Gerald.
The Categorical Nature of Mathematical Cognition. NYSANBAYEV, A N and KADYRZHANOV, R K.
Causes and Laws. ARMSTRONG, D M and HEATHCOTE, Adrian.
Characterization of Prime Numbers in Lukasiewicz's Logical Matrix. KARPENKO, Alexander S.
Charles S Peirce's Theory of Infinitesimals. LEVY, Stephen H.
Circularity of Thought in Hegel's Logic. BALABAN, Oded.
Classes and Attributes in Extended Modal Systems: Proceedings of the Colloquium in Modal and Many Valued Logic. MARCUS, Ruth Barcan.
Classification of Intermediate Predicate Logics Under the Type of Deductive Completeness. TAKANO, Mitio and YAMAKAMI, Tomoyuki.
Classifying Conditionals II. JACKSON, Frank.
Cloture Intervallaire et Extension Logique d'une Relation. ILLE, Pierre.
A Coding of the Countable Linear Orderings. DEHORNOY, Patrick.
Colimit Completions and the Effective Topos. ROBINSON, Edmund and ROSOLINI, Giuseppe.
Comments on a Question of Wolniewicz. HAWRANEK, Jacek.
Common Logic of Binary Connectives Has Finite Maximality Degree (Preliminary Report). RAUTENBERG, Wolfgang.
Complementary Sentential Logics. VARZI, Achille C.
The Complete 0. KANAMORI, Akihiro and AWERBUCH-FRIEDLANDER, Tamara.
A Complete Deductive-System for Since-Until Branching-Time Logic. ZANARDO, Alberto.
A Complete Syntactical Characterization of the Intuitionistic Logic. SKURA, Tomasz.
The Completeness of Provable Realizability. MINTS, G E.
Complexity for Type-2 Relations. TOWNSEND, Mike.
The Complexity of Intrinsically R.E. Subsets of Existentially Decidable Models. CHISHOLM, John.

LOGIC

Complexly Fractionated Syllogistic Quantifiers. PETERSON, Philip L.
Computation and Mathematical Empiricism. RESNIK, Michael D.
Concerted Instant-Interval Temporal Semantics I: Temporal Ontologies. BOCHMAN, Alexander.
Concerted Instant-Interval Temporal Semantics II: Temporal Valuations and Logics of Change. BOCHMAN, Alexander.
Conditional Probabilities, Conditionalization, and Dutch Books. SOBEL, Jordan Howard.
Conditionals and Monotonic Belief Revisions: the Success Postulate. ARLO COSTA, Horacio L.
Conditionals, Quantification, and Strong Mathematical Induction. COHEN, Daniel H.
Conductive $\aleph_0$-Categorical Theories. SCHMERL, James H.
Connection Structures. BIACINO, Loredana and GERLA, Giangiacomo.
Constructing Strongly Equivalent Nonisomorphic Models for Unstable Theories. HYTTINEN, Tapani and TUURI, Heikki.
Construction and the Role of Schematism in Kant's Philosophy of Mathematics (also in Portuguese). WINTERBOURNE, A T.
Constructions by Transfinitely Many Workers. KNIGHT, Julia F.
Constructive Compact Operators on a Hilbert Space. ISHIHARA, Hajime.
Constructive Interpolation Theorems for $S2^0$ and S2. BARCA, Anne and MC ROBBIE, Michael.
Constructive Modal Logics I. WIJESEKERA, Duminda.
A Constructive Version of Sperner's Lemma and Brouwer's Fixed Point Theorem. KHALIFA, A K.
A Constructivism Based on Classical Truth. MIGLIOLI, P (and others).
Context Principle, Fruitfulness of Logic and the Cognitive Value of Arithmetic in Frege. RUFFINO, Marco Antonio.
Contingency and Modal Logic. DEUTSCH, Harry.
The Contingent *A Priori*: Kripke's Two Types of Examples. GEIRSSON, Heimir.
Contrafácticos. KVART, Igal and STELLINO, Ana Isabel.
Copi's Conditional Probability Problem. SINGH, Dasarath and SINGH, Kameshwar.
Correction to "Undecidability of $L(F_\infty)$ and Other Lattices of R.E. Substructures" (Corrigendum). DOWNEY, Rod.
Corrections to Some Results for BCK Logics and Algebras. BUNDER, M W.
The Correspondence between George Boole and Stanley Jevons, 1863-1864. GRATTAN-GUINNESS, I.
Corroboration and Conditional Positive Relevance. WAGNER, Carl G.
Could This Be Magic?. JUBIEN, Michael.
The Credibility of Extraordinary Events. SCHLESINGER, George N.
La creencia y su conexión con los actos linguísticos. SAAB, Salma.
A Critical Note on J S Mill's Classification of Fallacies. HON, Giora.
Cylindric Algebras with Terms. FELDMAN, Norman.
De lógica y matemática o donde situar el mundo matemático. DE LORENZO, Javier.
Decidable and Enumerable Predicate Logics of Provability. DZHAPARIDZE, Giorgie.
A Decidable Ehrenfeucht Theory with Exactly Two Hyperarithmetic Models. REED, R C.
Decidable Fragments of Field Theories. TUNG, Shih-Ping.
Decir lo mismo (Frege y Santo Tomás). SANGUINETI, Juan J.
The Deduction Theorem for Quantum Logic—Some Negative Results. MALINOWSKI, Jacek.
The Deduction Theorem in a Strict Functional Calculus of First Order Based on Strict Implication. MARCUS, Ruth Barcan.
Definability in Self-Referential Systems. SOBRINHO, J Zimbarg.
Definability Theorems in Normal Extensions of the Provability Logic. MAKSIMOVA, Larisa L.
Definite Descriptions. DANIELS, Charles B.
Definitions of Compact. HOWARD, Paul E.
La definizione di "retta" data da Euclide e le geometrie non-euclidee. BLANDINO, Giovanni.
The Degree of a Σ_n Cut. CHONG, C T and MOURAD, K J.
Degrees of Orderings Not Isomorphic to Recursive Linear Orderings. JOCKUSCH JR, Carl G and SOARE, Robert I.
The Density of Infima in the Recursively Enumerable Degrees. SLAMAN, Theodore A.
Deontic Logic and Possible World Semantics: A Historical Sketch. WOLENSKI, Jan.
Derivability Conditions on Rosser's Provability Predicates. ARAI, Toshiyasu.
El desaparecer de lo eterno en sí mismo: Una clave del pensamiento de Hegel. ALBIZU, Edgardo.
Descriptions: Contemporary Philosophy and the Nyāya. SHAW, J L.
Dharmakirti on Inference and Properties. GANERI, Jonardon.
Diagonalization and Fixed Points. TONELLA, Guido.
Differentially Algebraic Group Chunks. PILLAY, Anand.
A Dilemma for Subjective Bayesians—and How to Resolve It. MILNE, Peter.
Disjoint Reference into NP. SELLS, Peter.
Disjunctive Laws and Supervenience. SEAGER, William.
Does Aristotle Beg the Question in His Defense of the Principle of Non-Contradiction?. DEGNAN, Michael.
Domain Theory in Logical Form. ABRAMSKY, Samson.
Double Extension Set Theory. KISIELEWICZ, Andrzej.
Dretske on the Explanatory Role of Belief. BAKER, Lynne Rudder.
The Dual Cantor-Bernstein Theorem and the Partition Principle. BANASCHEWSKI, Bernhard and MOORE, Gregory H.
Duff and the Wager. JORDAN, Jeff.
The Dynamics of Concepts and Non-local Interactions. VAN LOOCKE, Philip R.
Effective Extensions of Partial Orders. KUMAR ROY, Dev.
Effective Model Theory versus Recursive Model Theory. CHISHOLM, John.
Elementary Theory of Free Heyting Algebras. IDZIAK, Pawel M.
The Elementary Theory of the Natural Lattice is Finitely Axiomatizable. CEGIELSKI, Patrick.
Ellis, Epistemic Values, and the Problem of Induction. VOLLRATH, John.
Embeddability, Syntax, and Semantics in Accounts of Scientific Theories. TURNEY, Peter.
Embedding Brouwer Algebras in the Medvedev Lattice. SORBI, Andrea.
En busca del contenido físico de la regla de Luders. MARTÍNEZ, Sergio and MURILLO, Lorena.
Enumerations of Turing Ideals with Applications. MARKER, David.
Epistemological Time Asymmetry. SAVITT, Steven F.
Equational Subsystems. WEAVER, George.
Equational Theory of Positive Numbers with Exponentiation is Not Finitely Axiomatizable. GUREVIC, R.
The Equivalence of Determinacy and Iterated Sharps. DUBOSE, Derrick Albert.
An Equivalent of the Axiom of Choice in Finite Models of the Powerset Axiom. ABIAN, Alexander and AMIN, Wael A.
Equivalent Versions of a Weak Form of the Axiom of Choice. SHANNON, G.
Equivocation in The Surprise Exam Paradox. FERGUSON, Kenneth G.
Erasing and Redrawing the Number Line: An Exercise in Rationality. SPARROW, Edward G.
Essentially Contested Concepts: The Ethics and Tactics of Argument. GARVER, Eugene.
Estructura lógica y ontología en el *Tractatus*. MARTÍNEZ, Sergio.
Eudoxos and Dedekind: On the Ancient Greek Theory of Ratios and its Relation to Modern Mathematics. STEIN, Howard.
Evaluating Arguments: The Premise-Conclusion Relation. BOWLES, George.
Even and *Even If*. LYCAN, William G.
Every World Can See a Reflexive World. HUGHES, G E.
An Existence Theorem for Recursion Categories. HELLER, Alex.
Exponentiation and Second-Order Bounded Arithmetic. KRAJICEK, Jan.
Expressions versus Numbers. WETZEL, Linda.
Expressive Completeness and Decidability. SCHUMM, George and SHAPIRO, Stewart.
Expressive Power and Semantic Completeness: Boolean Connectives in Modal Logic. HUMBERSTONE, I L.
Expressiveness and Completeness of an Interval Tense Logic. VENEMA, Yde.
Extended Bar Induction in Applicative Theories. RENARDEL DE LAVALETTE, Gerard R.
Extending Montague's System: A Three Valued Intensional Logic. ALVES, E H and GUERZONI, J A D.
An Extension of Borel Determinacy. MARTIN, Donald A.
Extension of Gurevich-Harrington's Restricted Memory Determinacy Theorem. YAKHNIS, Alexander and YAKHNIS, Vladimir.
An Extension of Ono's Completeness Result. SUZUKI, Nobu-Yuki.
The Extent of Russell's Modal Views. MAGNELL, Thomas.
F-Multipliers and the Localization of Hilbert Algebras. BUSNEAG, Dumitru.
Fictional Incompleteness as Vagueness. SORENSEN, Roy A.
Filosofía desde la teoría causal de la referencia. NUBIOLA, Jaime.
Finite Axiomatizability and Theories with Trivial Algebraic Closure. MACPHERSON, Dugald.
Finite Kripke Models and Predicate Logics of Provability. ARTEMOV, Sergei and DZHAPARIDZE, Giorgie.
Finite Logics and the Simple Substitution Property. HOSOI, Tsutomu and SASAKI, Katsumi.
Finite Support Iteration and Strong Measure Zero Sets. PAWLIKOWSKI, Janusz.
First-Order Logics for Comparative Similarity. WILLIAMSON, Timothy.
First-Order Theories Without Axioms. STEPIEN, Teodor.
Fixed Points and Diagonal Method. NEGRI, Maurizio.
Forbes's Branching Conception of Possible Worlds. MILLS, Eugene.
The Formal Language L_t and Topological Products. BERTOSSI, L E.
Formalization of Functionally Complete Propositional Calculus with the Functor of Implication.... LEJEWSKI, Czeslaw.
Formatives. ENGLEBRETSEN, George.
The Foundation of the Ability to Reach Conclusions—The Empirical Basis of Logic. GOLAB-MEYER, Zofia.
Four Dialogue Systems. MACKENZIE, Jim.
Four Thousand Ships Passed Through the Lock: Object-Induced Measure Functions on Events. KRIFKA, Manfred.
Frege and Husserl on Number. TIESZEN, Richard.
Frege and the Analysis of Thoughts. GARAVASO, Pieranna.
Frege, Informative Identities, and Logicism. MILNE, Peter.

LOGIC

From Discrete to Continuous Time. KEISLER, H Jerome.
From the Logic of Mathematical Discovery to the Methodology of Scientific Research Programmes. YUXIN, Zheng.
Full Reflection of Stationary Sets Below $\aleph_\omega$. JECH, Thomas and SHELAH, Saharon.
A Fully Logical Inductive Logic. NOLT, John.
A Functional Calculus of First Order Based on Strict Implication. MARCUS, Ruth Barcan.
The Gärdenfors Impossibility Theorem in Non-Monotonic Contexts. MAKINSON, David.
General Canonical Models for Graded Normal Logics (Graded Modalities IV). CERRATO, C.
A General Possible Worlds Framework for Reasoning about Knowledge and Belief. WANSING, Heinrich.
A Generalization of the Adequacy Theorem for the Quasi-Senses. BONOTTO, Cinzia.
A Generalized Quantifier Logic for Naked Infinitives. VAN DER DOES, Jaap.
Generalizing Classical and Effective Model Theory in Theories of Operations and Classes. MANCOSU, Paolo.
Gentzenization and Decidability of Some Contraction-Less Relevant Logics. BRADY, Ross T.
Genuine Moral Dilemmas and the Containment of Incoherence. PASKE, Gerald H.
Grammar Logics. FARIÑAS DEL CERRO, Luis and PENTTONEN, Martti.
A Green Parrot is Just as Much a Red Herring as a White Shoe: A Note on Confirmation, Background Knowledge.... FRENCH, Steven.
Grupo de Piaget y estructuras afines. GONZÁLEZ CARLOMÁN, Antonio.
Hamblin on the Standard Treatment. JOHNSON, Ralph H.
Hegel and the Humean Problem of Induction. SUCHTING, W A.
Hegel's *Logic* and Marx's Early Development. PRINCIPE, Michael A.
Hegel, Logic, and Metaphysics. HARTSHORNE, Charles.
Heidegger on Logic and Language: Some Aporiai. FAY, Thomas A.
Heideggers "logische Untersuchungen". OUDEMANS, Th C W.
Henkin's Completeness Proof: Forty Years Later. LEBLANC, Hugues and ROEPER, Peter and THAU, Michael and WEAVER, George.
Heraclitus: Heidegger's 1944 Lecture Held at Freiburg University. FRINGS, Manfred S.
Hereditarily Finite Finsler Sets. BOOTH, David.
A Hierarchy of Ramsey Cardinals. FENG, Qi.
Historical Necessity and Conditionals. NUTE, Donald.
History and Neo-Sophistic Criticism: A Reply to Poulakos. SCHIAPPA, Edward.
The Homogeneous Form of Logic Programs with Equality. DEMOPOULOS, William.
Hornsby's Puzzles: Rejoinder to Wreen and Hornsby. KOSROVANI, Emilio.
How Beliefs Explain: Reply to Baker. DRETSKE, Fred.
How Far Can Hume's Is-Ought Thesis Be Generalized?. SCHURZ, Gerhard.
How *Not* to Become a Millian Heir. SALMON, Nathan.
Hume on Probability. GOWER, Barry.
Hume's Theorem on Testimony Sufficient to Establish a Miracle. SOBEL, Jordan Howard.
Husserl's Philosophy of Science and the Semantic Approach. MORMANN, Thomas.
$I\Delta_3$-Algebras. FIGALLO, Aldo V.
Ideal Rationality and Handwaving. RICHTER, Reed.
The Identity of Individuals in a Strict Functional Calculus of Second Order. MARCUS, Ruth Barcan.
Implications of Behavioral Consistency in Dynamic Choice Under Uncertainty. DARDANONI, Valentino.
Implied Questions. WISNIEWSKI, Andrzej.
In Search of a Theory of Truth in Nyāya. SAHA, Sukharanjan.
In the Service of Human Society: Formal, Information, or Anti-Logical?. BARTH, E M.
The Inapplicability of Evolutionary Stable Strategy to the Prisoner's Dilemma. MARINOFF, Louis.
Incompleteness of a Free Arithmetic. BENCIVENGA, Ermanno.
Inconsistent Commitment and Commitment to Inconsistencies. KRABBE, Erik C W.
The Inconspicious Role of Paraphrase. SHERRY, David.
Indian Philosophy in the Context of World Philosophy. BHATTACHARYYA, Kalidas.
Indicative Conditionals Are Truth-Functional. HANSON, William H.
Indiscernibility and Identity in Probability Theory. ROEPER, Peter and LEBLANC, Hugues.
The Indispensability of *Sinn*. FORBES, Graeme.
The Inductive Support of Inductive Rules: Themes from Max Black. SANFORD, David H.
Inductive Types and Type Constraints in the Second-Order Lambda Calculus. MENDLER, Nax Paul.
Infinitary Combinatorics and Modal Logic. BLASS, A.
Infinity in Mathematics: Is Cantor Necessary?. FEFERMAN, Solomon.
Information Functions with Applications. SZYMANEK, Krzysztof.
Instantial Terms, Anaphora and Arbitrary Objects. KING, Jeffrey C.
An Integer-Valued Matrix Characteristic for Implicational *S5*. ULRICH, Dolph.
Intensional Identities. SLATER, B H.
Intensional Paradoxes. PRIEST, Graham.
Intermediate Predicate Logics Determined by Ordinals. MINARI, Pierluigi and TAKANO, Mitio and ONO, Hiroakira.
Intermediate Quantifiers versus Percentages. CARNES, Robert D and PETERSON, Philip L.
The Interpretability Logic of Peano Arithmetic. BERARDUCCI, Alessandro.
Interpretación mundanel e identidad propia. GARCÍA-GÓMEZ, Jorge.
Interpretation of Relevant Logics in a Logic of Ternary Relations. ORLOWSKA, Ewa.
L'interpretazione costruttiva dell'implicazione. MORICONI, Enrico.
Intorno all'autofondazione delle norme: Ragione formale e principio razionale tra logica e diritto. SCIACCA, Fabrizio.
Introduction to Dharmakīrti's Theory of Inference as Presented in *Pramānavārttika Svopajñavrtti* 1-10. HAYES, Richard P and GILLON, Brendan S.
Intuitionism and Vagueness. SCHWARTZ, Stephen P and THROOP, William.
Intuitionistic Mathematics and Wittgenstein. GONZALEZ, Wenceslao J.
Intuitionistic Sentential Calculus with Classical Identity. LUKOWSKI, Piotr.
Intuitionistic Sentential Calculus with Identity. LUKOWSKI, Piotr.
Intuitive Semantics for Some Three-Valued Logics Connected with Information, Contrariety and Subcontrariety. VAKARELOV, Dimitir.
The Irrelevance of Classical Logic. KEENE, G B.
Is Philosophy Detrimental to Mathematics Education?. LUZZATTO, Stefano.
Is There Completeness in Mathematics after Gödel?. HINTIKKA, Jaakko.
Is There Higher-Order Vagueness?. SAINSBURY, Mark.
Iteration Again. BOOLOS, George.
Jackson Classifying Conditionals. DUDMAN, V H.
Jackson on Classifying Conditionals. LOWE, E J.
John Stuart Mill on Induction and Hypothesis. JACOBS, Struan.
Jumping with Random Reals. BARTOSZYNSKI, Tomek and JUDAH, Haim.
Jumps of Nontrivial Splittings of Recursively Enumerable Sets. INGRASSIA, Michael A and LEMPP, Steffen.
La justificación práctica del principio de no contradicción en Aristóteles. CASSINI, A.
The Justification for Relevance Logic. BAGHRAMIAN, Maria.
Kant and Conceptual Semantics: A Sketch. POSY, Carl J.
Kant on Concepts and Intuitions in the Mathematical Sciences. FRIEDMAN, Michael.
Kant's Diversity Theory: A Dissenting View. GLOUBERMAN, Mark.
De Kant-interpretatie van Evert Willem Beth. PEIJNENBURG, J.
Kantian and Non-Kantian Logics. PUGA, Leila Z and DA COSTA, Newton C A and CARNIELLI, Walter A.
Le Kantisme de la théorie cantorienne de l'infini. BACHTA, Abdelkader.
Kernels in N-Normal Symmetric Heyting Algebras. GALLI, A and SAGASTUME, M.
Kitcher's Circumlocutionary Structuralism. HAND, Michael.
Knowability, Actuality, and the Metaphysics of Context-Dependence. PERCIVAL, Philip.
Kripke Bundles for Intermediate Predicate Logics and Kripke Frames for Intuitionistic Modal Logics. SUZUKI, Nobu-Yuki.
Kripke on Theoretical Identifications: A Rejoinder to Perrick. BUXTON, James.
Kripke Semantics for Knowledge Representation Logics. ORLOWSKA, Ewa.
Kripke-Style Models for Typed Lambda Calculus. MITCHELL, John C and MOGGI, Eugenio.
The Kunen-Miller Chart (Lebesgue Measure, the Baire Property, Laver Reals and Preservation Theorems for Forcing). JUDAH, Haim and SHELAH, Saharon.
λ-Definability on Free Algebras. ZAIONC, Marek.
La estructura de la ética y la moral. HARE, Richard N and BRASH, Jorge.
Language in Action. VAN BENTHEM, Johan.
Language, Logic and Reality. DEVARAJA, N K.
The Last Word on Elimination of Quantifiers in Modules. GUTE, Hans B and REUTER, K K.
Lattice Nonembeddings and Initial Segments of the Recursively Enumerable Degrees. DOWNEY, Rod.
A Lemma in the Logic of Action. SURENDONK, Timothy J.
Liar Syllogisms and Related Paradoxes. SLATER, B H.
Lifschitz' Realizability. VAN OOSTEN, Jaap.
Linear Axiomatics of Communicative Product-Free Lambek Calculus. ZIELONKA, Wojciech.
A Linear Continuum of Time. DOWDEN, Bradley H.
Locke on Mathematical Knowledge. CICOVACKI, Predrag.
Logic and Artificial Intelligence: An Exposition. DE SWART, H C M.
Logic and Empiricism. BOSTOCK, David.
Logic and Knowledge Representation. PETROV, V V and PEREVERZEV, V N.
Logic and Ontology. BROWNING, Douglas.
Logic and the Free Will Problem. VAN INWAGEN, Peter.
Logic and the Young Child. TENG, Yu-jen.
The Logic of Causal Inference: Econometrics and the Conditional Analysis of Causation. HOOVER, Kevin D.
The Logic of Impossible Quantities. SHERRY, David.

LOGIC

The Logic of Lost Lingens. SEAGER, William.
The Logic of Rational Play in Games of Perfect Information. BONANNO, Giacomo.
The Logic of the Liar from the Standpoint of the Aristotelian Syllogistic. KELLY, Charles J.
Logic Without Truth. ALCHOURRÓN, Carlos E and MARTINO, Antonio A.
Logic, Contradiction and Quantum Theory. SMITH, Joseph Wayne.
La logica di Hegel come testo filosofico (II). COSTA, Filippo.
Lógica y metafísica de Leibniz: Principales líneas de interpretación durante el siglo XX. HEINEKAMP, A and SCHUPP, F.
Logical Constants Across Varying Types. VAN BENTHEM, Johan.
Logical Constants and the Glory of Truth-Conditional Semantics. LYCAN, William G.
Logical Constants as Punctuation Marks. DOSEN, Kosta.
Logical Equations and Admissible Rules of Inference with Parameters in Modal Provability Logics. RYBAKOV, V V.
Logical Form and Radical Interpretation. MC CARTHY, Tim.
The Logical Status of Modal Reductionism. MOSER, Paul K and VANDER NAT, Arnold.
El logicismo russelliano: su significado filosófico. RODRÍGUEZ CONSUEGRA, Francisco.
Logics of Dialogue: A Necessary Multiplicity. MAIER, Robert.
Logics of Truth. TURNER, Raymond.
Logics Preserving Degrees of Truth. NOWAK, Marek.
Logique et théorie de l'argumentation dans le "Guide de l'étudiant". LAFLEUR, Claude.
Lukasiewicz Logic and Wajsberg Algebras. RODRIGUEZ, Antonio J and TORRENS, Antoni.
Making Sense of Words. MC CULLOCH, Gregory.
Many-Sorted Elementary Equivalence. DZIERZGOWSKI, Daniel.
Many-Valued Modal Logics: Uses and Predicate Calculus. OSTERMANN, Pascal.
Material Implication and Entailment. CENIZA, Claro R.
Mathematical Expressibility, Perceptual Relativity, and Secondary Qualities. PEREBOOM, Derk.
Mathematical Physics and Elementary Logic. MUNDY, Brent.
Mathematical Statistics and Metastatistical Analysis. RIVADULLA, Andrés.
Mathematics and Oliver Twist. MADDY, Penelope.
Mathematics and Philosophy: The Story of a Misunderstanding. ROTA, GianCarlo.
Mathematics Without Truth (A Reply to Maddy). FIELD, Hartry.
Matrix Representation of Husserl's Part-Whole-Foundation Theory. BLECKSMITH, Richard and NULL, Gilbert.
Maurice Blondel's Moral Logic. LONG, Fiachra.
Maximal R.E. Equivalence Relations. CARROLL, Jeffrey S.
McGinn on Concept Scepticism and Kripke's Sceptical Argument. SARTORELLI, Joseph.
Meaning in a Realist Perspective. THERON, Stephen.
The Meaning of Δυναμισ at *Timaeus* 31c. PRITCHARD, Paul.
Meanings in Ordinary Language and in Mathematics. THOMAS, R S D.
Mechanical Proof Procedures for Many-Valued Lattice-Based Logic Programming. SUBRAHMANIAN, V S.
Mechanism and Indeterminacy: Reply to MacIntosh. WARMBRŌD, Ken.
Metalogic and Modality. FIELD, Hartry.
The Metamathematics-Popperian Epistemology Connection and its Relation to the Logic of Turing's Programme. BEAUSOLEIL, Jean-Roch.
Metaphor and Aspect-Perception. KEMP, G Neville.
A Metatheorem for Constructions by Finitely Many Workers. KNIGHT, J F.
The Method of Axiomatic Rejection for the Intuitionistic Propositional Logic. DUTKIEWICZ, Rafal.
Minimal Degrees Recursive in 1-Generic Degrees. CHONG, C T and DOWNEY, R G.
Modal Counterparts of Medvedev Logic of Finite Problems Are Not Finitely Axiomatizable. SHEHTMAN, Valentin.
The Modal Logic of Pure Provability. BUSS, Samuel R.
Modal Logic. MARCUS, Ruth Barcan.
Modal Logics with n-ary Connectives. GHILARDI, S and MELONI, C G.
Modality and Mellor's McTaggart. CRESSWELL, M J.
Models for Inconsistent and Incomplete Differential Calculus. MORTENSEN, Chris.
Models for Relevant Modal Logics. FUHRMANN, André.
Mojzesz Presburger: Life and Work. ZYGMUNT, Jan.
The Monadic Second-Order Logic of Graphs IV: Definability Properties of Equational Graphs. COURCELLE, Bruno.
Moral Dilemmas, Disjunctive Obligations, and Kant's Principle that 'Ought' Implies 'Can'. JACQUETTE, Dale.
Moral Scepticism and Inductive Scepticism. BLACK, Robert.
More about Thoughts. DUMMETT, Michael.
More Axioms for the Set-Theoretic Hierarchy. POLLARD, Stephen.
Mr Keynes on Probability. RAMSEY, F P.
Multiset Theory. BLIZARD, Wayne D.
The Mutual Investment Game: Peculiarities of Indifference. CUBITT, Robin P and HOLLIS, Martin.
N-Normal Factors in Finite Symmetric Heyting Algebras. GALLI, Adriana C and SAGASTUME, Marta.
Natural Deduction in Normal Modal Logic. HAWTHORN, John.
Necessary A Posteriori Truth. SWINBURNE, Richard.
Negative Membership. BLIZARD, Wayne D.
Nelson Algebras Through Heyting Ones^1:1. SENDLEWSKI, Andrzej.
Never Say "Never"! On the Communication Problem between Intuitionism and Classicism. HELLMAN, Geoffrey.
New Operators for Theory Change. HANSSON, Sven.
New Semantics for the Extensional but Hyper-Intensional Part..... BRESSAN, Aldo.
Non-Bounding Construction. SHOENFIELD, J R.
Non-Commutative Intuitionistic Linear Logic. ABRUSCI, V Michele.
Nonstandard Arithmetic of Hilbert Subsets. YASUMOTO, Masahiro.
The Normal Depth of Filters on an Infinite Cardinal. DI PRISCO, C A and FULLER, M and HENLE, J M.
Not Very Likely: A Reply to Ramsey. WATT, D E.
A Note on Complete Partitions in Boolean Algebras. SACHWANOWICZ, Wojciech.
A Note on Matrices for Systems of Nonsense-Logics. HALKOWSKA, Katarzyna.
A Note on Schrödinger's Cat and the Unexpected Hanging Paradox. HOLTZMANN, Jack M.
A Note on Some Extension Results. MONTAGNA, Franco and SOMMARUGA, Giovanni.
A Note on Some Property of Purely Implicational Proportional Calculi. PRUCNAL, Tadeuss.
A Note on the Axiomatization of Equational Classes of n-Valued Lukasiewicz Algebras. ADAMS, M E and CIGNOLI, R.
Note on the Integration of Prototype Theory and Fuzzy-Set Theory. FUHRMANN, G.
A Note on the Permutationally Convex Games. ALIDAEE, Bahram.
A Note on Van Fraassen's Explanatory Contrastiveness. PAPRZYCKA, Katarzyna.
Notes on Modal Definability. VAN BENTHEM, Johan.
Notions of Relative Ubiquity for Invariant Sets of Relational Structures. BANKSTON, Paul and RUITENBURG, Wim.
A Notorious Affair Called Exportation. BURDICK, Howard.
Noun Phrases, Quantifiers, and Generic Names. LOWE, E J.
Occasions for Argumentation. HILPINEN, Risto.
Omitting Types for Stable CCC Theories. NEWELSKI, Ludomir.
An Omniscience Principle, the König Lemma and the Hahn-Banach Theorem. ISHIHARA, Hajime.
On a Complexity-Based Way of Constructivizing the Recursive Functions. KROON, F W and BURKHARD, W A.
On a Mainstay of Incompatibilism. BLUM, Alex.
On a Theorem of Günter Asser. CALUDE, Cristian and SÂNTEAN, Lila.
On an Alleged Refutation of Hilbert's Program Using Gödel's First Incompleteness Theorem. DETLEFSEN, Michael.
On Axiomatization of Many-Valued Logics Associated with Formalization of Plausible Reasonings. ANSHAKOV, O M and FINN, V K and SKVORTSOV, D P.
On Begging the Question 'Who is N?'. PATTON, Thomas E.
On Certain Normalizable Natural Deduction Formulations of Some Propositional Intermediate Logics. BORICIC, Branislav R.
On Comparison of Theories by Their Contents. WOLENSKI, Jan.
On Defining Identity. SAVELLOS, Elias E.
On Diophantine Equations Solvable in Models of Open Induction. OTERO, Margarita.
On Falsificationist Interpretations of Peirce. SULLIVAN, Patrick F.
On Generalizations of a Theorem of Vaught. BIRÓ, Balázs.
On Kaplan's Logic of Demonstratives. CHAKRAVARTI, Sitansu S.
On Making a Coherence Theory of Truth True. SYLVAN, Richard.
On Omniscience and a 'Set of All Truths': A Reply to Bringsjord. GRIM, Patrick.
On Pure Refutation Formulations of Sentential Logics. SKURA, Tomasz.
On Regular Modal Logics with Axiom.... SWIRYDOWICZ, Kazimierz.
On Restricted Forms of Enumeration Reducibility. WATSON, Phil.
On Rigidity and Persistence. WILLIAMSON, Timothy.
On Russell's Principle of Induction. DA COSTA, Newton C A and FRENCH, Steven.
On Scott and Karp Trees of Uncountable Models. HYTTINEN, Tapani and VÄÄNÄNEN, Jouko.
On Simplicity of Formulas. KRYNICKI, Michal and SZCZERBA, Leslaw.
On Some Logically Equivalent Propositions. KELLY, Charles J.
On Some Multiattribute Value Function Generalizations of the EQQ Model in the Context of Personal Inventory Decisions. TROUTT, Marvin D.
On Some Operators on Pseudovarieties. GRACZYNSKA, Ewa.
On Some Paradoxes of the Infinite. ALLIS, Victor and KOETSIER, Teunis.
On Subsystems of the System J_1 of Arruda and Da Costa. URBAS, Igor.
On the Absoluteness of Types in Boolean Valued Lattices. NISHIMURA, Hirokazu.
On the Alleged Impossibility of a Science of Accidents in Aristotle. URBANAS, Alban.
On the Angular Component Map Modulo *P*. PAS, Johan.

LOGIC

On the Completeness of a Certain System of Arithmetic of Whole Numbers in Which Addition Occurs as the Only Operation. PRESBURGER, Mojzesz and JACQUETTE, Dale.
On the Descriptive Adequacy of Levi's Decision Theory. MAHER, Patrick and KASHIMA, Yoshihisa.
On the Development of Paraconsistent Logic and Da Costa's Work. LOFFREDO D'OTTAVIANO, Itala M.
On the Eliminatibility of Ideal Linguistic Entities. WYBRANIEC-SKARDOWSKA, Urszula.
On the Existence of Large p-Ideals. JUST, Winfried (and others).
On the Existence of Polynomial Time Algorithms for Interpolation Problems in Propositional Logic. DALHAUS, E and ISRAELI, A and MAKOWSKY, J A.
On the Form and Authenticity of the *Lysis*. TEJERA, V.
On the Lengths of Proofs of Set Theoretical Statements in Zermelo-Fraenkel Set Theory and Kelley-Morse Theory.... CORRADA, Manuel.
On the Logic of Conscious Belief. TOKARZ, Marek.
On the Logic of Contingent Relevant Implication: Conceptual Incoherence in the Intuitive Interpretation of *R*. LANCE, Mark.
On the Logic of Eternal Knowledge. KELLY, Charles J.
On the Methodology of Possible World Semantics, I: Correspondence Theory. PEARCE, David and WANSING, Heinrich.
On the Necessity for Random Sampling. JOHNSTONE, D J.
On the Ontology of Branching Quantifiers. PATTON, Thomas.
On the Propositional Attitudes. COLEMAN, Keith.
On the Quasi-Ordering of Borel Linear Orders Under Embeddability. LOUVEAU, Alain and SAINT-RAYMOND, Jean.
On the Status of Proofs by Contradiction in the XVIIth Century. MANCOSU, Paolo.
On the Structure of De Morgan Monoids with Corollaries on Relevant Logic and Theories. SLANEY, John K.
On Theories of Non-Monotonic Consequence Operations II. FIJALKOWSKA, Dorota and FIJALKOWSKI, Jan.
On Type Definable Subgroups of a Stable Group. NEWELSKI, Ludomir.
The Ontological Status of the Principle of the Excluded Middle. STRAUSS, Daniël F M.
Operative versus Combinatory Spaces. IVANOV, Lyubomir.
La oposición de los enunciados "estrictamente" particulares en perspectiva trivalente. OFFENBERGER, Niels.
Ordering Pairwise Comparison Structures. DELVER, R and MONSUUR, H and STORCKEN, A J A.
The Ordertype of β-R.E. Sets. SUTNER, Klaus.
Orlowska's Relevant Implications, Relevant Logics and Analytic Implication. GIAMBRONE, Steve.
Paraconsistency and the J-Systems of Arruda and da Costa. URBAS, Igor.
The Paradox of Epistemology: A Defense of Naturalism. KETCHUM, Richard J.
The Pareto Rule and Strategic Voting. MAC INTYRE, Ian.
A Partial Functions Version of Church's Simple Theory of Types. FARMER, William M.
Partition Properties and Prikry Forcing on Simple Spaces. HENLE, J M.
Partitioning Pairs of Countable Sets of Ordinals. VELLEMAN, Dan.
Peirced Clean Through. MEYER, Robert K.
Perhaps by Skill Alone. MISSIMER, Connie.
Philosophical Reflections on the Foundations of Mathematics. COUTURE, Jocelyne and LAMBEK, Joachim.
The Philosophy of Logical Wholism. MC CARTY, David Charles.
The Place of Argumentation in the Theory of Reasoning. JOHNSON, Ralph H.
Plain Semi-Post Algebras as a Poset-Based Generalization of Post Algebras and their Representability. CAT HO, Nguyen and RASIOWA, Helena.
Platonism and Anti-Platonism in Nicholas of Cusa's Philosophy of Mathematics. HÖSLE, Vittorio.
Platonism from an Empiricist Point of View. LUCE, Lila.
Popper on Induction. SWANN, Andrew J.
Post's Functional Completeness Theorem. PELLETIER, Francis Jeffry and MARTIN, Norman M.
Pot Bites Kettle: A Reply to Miller. LYCAN, William G.
Pragma-Dialectics: A Radical Departure in Fallacy Theory. WOODS, John.
Pragmatic Truth and the Logic of Induction. DA COSTA, Newton C A and FRENCH, Steven.
Pragmática del lenguaje y racionalidad comunicativa. DE ZAN, J.
Predication and Logic of Language (I). GANGADEAN, Ashok.
Premiss Tree Proofs and Logic of Contradiction. SIKIC, Zvonimir.
Preservation by Homomorphisms and Infinitary Languages. HYTTINEN, Tapani.
The Priestley Duality for Wajsberg Algebras. MARTÍNEZ, N G.
Prior's Disease. USBERTI, Gabriele.
A Priority and Ways of Grasping a Proposition. WONG, Kai-Yee.
The Prisoner's *Other* Dilemma. ZALCMAN, Lawrence.
Probabilistic Dependence Among Conditionals. LANCE, Mark.
Probability Logic in the Twentieth Century. HAILPERIN, Theodore.
A Problem for Intuitionism: The Apparent Possibility of Performing Infinitely Many Tasks in a Finite Time. MOORE, A W.
A Problem in the Foundations of Set Theory. MADDY, Penelope.
A Problem Solving Interpretation of Argument Analysis. BERNSTEIN, David.
El problema de los universales en Juan de Santo Tomás en Juan de Santo Tomás. BEUCHOT, Mauricio.
Problems of Substitution and Admissibility in the Modal System Grz and in Intuitionistic Propositional Calculus. RYBAKOV, V V.
Problems of the Notions of 'Entailment' and 'Material Implication'. MULAY, Sharmila R.
Professor Matilal on Some Topics of Indian Philosophy. BHATTACHARYYA, Sibajiban.
The Progressive and the Imperfective Paradox. LASCARIDES, Alex.
Projective Subsets of Separable Metric Spaces. MILLER, Arnold W.
Las proposiciones de relativo en Alberto de Sajonia. TALEGÓN, César.
Propositional Consistency Proofs. BUSS, S R.
Propositional Functions and Families of Types. SMITH, Jan M.
Propositional Relevance. BOWLES, George.
Provable Forms of Martin's Axiom. SHANNON, Gary P.
Psychologism Reconsidered. AACH, John.
Q-Consequence Operation. MALINOWSKI, Grzegorz.
Quantifying Support. BLACK, John.
The Quarrel Theorem: First Attempt to the Logic of Lie. MAJCHER, B.
Qué miden los juegos de lenguaje?. LORENZ, Kuno.
A Question About Semilattices. WOLNIEWICZ, Boguslaw.
Quine's Relativism. HUGLY, Philip and SAYWARD, Charles.
Ramsey Ultrafilters and the Reaping Number—Con(r $<$ u). GOLDSTERN, M and SHELAH, S.
Randomness by Design. DEMBSKI, William.
Rationality of p-Adic Poincaré Series: Uniformity in p. MACINTYRE, Angus.
Rationality, Consistency and Truth. FRENCH, Steven.
Rationality, Correlativity, and the Language of Process. HALL, David Lynn and AMES, Roger T.
Rawlsian Nash Solutions. FABELLA, Raul V.
Real Numbers, Continued Fractions and Complexity Classes. LABHALLA, Salah and LOMBARDI, Henri.
Real Possibility. DEUTSCH, Harry.
Recursive Surreal Numbers. HARKLEROAD, Leon.
Reducts of (C,+,·) Which Contain +. MARKER, D and PILLAY, A.
Reflections on the Usage of the Terms "Logic" and "Logical". PAUL, Gregor.
Reflexiones en torno a la oración oblicua. MUÑOZ, Angel and CAROSIO, Alba.
A Refutation of Popperian Inductive Scepticism. GEMES, Ken.
Reglas, comunidades y juicios. ZALABARDO, José Luis.
Regressive Partition Relations, n-Subtle Cardinals, and Borel Diagonalization. KANAMORI, Akihiro.
Related Semantics for All Lewis, Lemmon and Feys' Modal Logics. SYLVAN, Richard.
The Relation between Science and Theology: The Case for Complimentarity Revisited. REICH, K Helmut.
Relations and Sixteenth-Century Mexican Logic. REDMOND, Walter.
Relative Consistency and Accessible Domains. SIEG, Wilfried.
Relative Elimination of Quantifiers for Henselian Valued Fields. BASARAB, Serban A.
Relatively Congruence-Distributive Subquasivarieties of Filtral Varieties. CZELAKOWSKI, Janusz.
Relativized Gödel Speed-Up and the Degree of Succinctness of Representations. SOLOMON, Martin K.
Relevance and Paraconsistency—A New Approach. AVRON, A.
Relevance and Paraconsistency—A New Approach, Part II: The Formal Systems. AVRON, Arnon.
Relevance and Paraconsistency—A New Approach, Part III: Cut-Free Gentzen-Type Systems. AVRON, Arnon.
The Relevance of Gödel's Theorem to Husserl's *Formal and Transcendental Logic*. BOULOS, Pierre J.
Relevant Containment Logics and Certain Frame Problems of AI. SYLVAN, Richard.
A Remark on Individual Constants. BLUM, Alex.
Remarks on Analogy. DA COSTA, Newton C A and SETTE, A M.
Remarks on Special Lattices and Related Constructive Logics with Strong Negation. PAGLIANI, Piero.
Remnants of Schiffer's Principle [P]. SEYMOUR, Daniel.
Reply of a Mad Dog. MILLER, Richard B.
Reply to Maher and Kashima: "On the Descriptive Adequacy of Levi's Decision Theory". LEVI, Isaac.
Reply to Smith: The Question of Idealism. VALLICELLA, William F.
Response to van Inwagen's "Logic and the Free Will Problem". SLOTE, Michael.
The Revenger's Paradox. HANSSON, Sven Ove.
Rhetoric and Argumentation: Relativism and Beyond. KIENPOINTNER, Manfred.
The Rhetoric of Opposition in Thomas More's *Utopia*: Giving Form to Competing Philosophies. WEGEMER, Gerard.
Rich Models. ALBERT, Michael H and GROSSBERG, Rami P.
Routley-Meyer Type Semantics for Urquhart's C. MÉNDEZ, José M.
Russell and the Ethical Concern of Wittgenstein's *Tractatus*. IGLESIAS, Teresa.

LOGIC

Russell, Logicism, and the Choice of Logical Constants. BYRD, Michael.
Salmon on the A Priori. BERTOLET, Rod.
Schanuel's Conjecture and Free Exponential Rings. MACINTYRE, Angus.
Semantic Holism is Seriously False. MASSEY, Gerald J.
Semantic Holism. BELNAP JR, Nuel D and MASSEY, Gerald J.
Semantics without Reference. GAUKER, Christopher.
Sentidos, referencias y concepto en Frege. MARTINEZ FREIRE, P.
Set Theoretic Properties of Loeb Measure. MILLER, Arnold W.
Sheaves in Universal Algebra and Model Theory: Part I. IDZIAK, Pawel M.
Sheaves in Universal Algebra and Model Theory: Part II. IDZIAK, Pawel M.
Shelah's pcf Theory and Its Applications. BURKE, Maxim R and MAGIDOR, Menachem.
A Short Vindication of Reichenbach's "Event-Splitting". PFEIFER, Karl.
The Simple Substitution Property of Gödel's Intermediate Propositional Logics S_n's. SASAKI, Katsumi.
La simplicidad en el *Tractatus*. ANSCOMBE, G E M.
Single-Axiom Systems. STEPIEN, Teodor.
Las situaciones objetivas en las *Investigaciones Lógicas* de Edmundo Husserl. MULLIGAN, Kevin.
Small Sets. HAZEN, A P.
Smook on Logical and Extralogical Constants. HITCHCOCK, David and GEORGE, Rolf.
Sobre la no paradoja de un cretense. WILSON, Jack L.
Sobre los universales. DÍAZ, Adolfo García.
Sobre tópicos y términos primitivos de la intensión. SARABIA, Jaime.
A Solution to a Problem of Urquhart. KRACHT, Marcus.
Some Descending Chains of Incomplete Model Logics. XU, Ming.
Some Extensions of Built-Upness on Systems of Fundamental Sequences. KADOTA, Noriya.
Some Further Reflections on the Popper-Miller 'Disproof' of Probabilistic Induction. HOWSON, C.
Some Improvements to Turner's Algorithm for Bracket Abstraction. BUNDER, M W.
Some Modal Logics Based on a Three-Valued Logic. MORIKAWA, Osamu.
Some Modifications of the Gödel Translation of Classical Intuitionistic Logic. BORICIC, Branislav.
Some New Double Induction and Superinduction Principles. SMULLYAN, Raymond M.
Some Nonstandard Methods Applied to Distributive Lattices. GEHRKE, Mai and INSALL, Matt and KAISER, Klaus.
Some Objections To Garavaso's Wittgenstein. HUMPHREY, John A.
Some Remarks on the Algebraic Structure of the Medvedev Lattice. SORBI, Andrea.
Some Remarks on the Linguistic Turn. PERUZZI, Alberto.
Some Remarks on ω-Powers of Enumerated Sets and Their Applications to ω-Operations. ORLICKI, Andrzej.
Some Results about Borel Sets in Descriptive Set Theory of Hyperfinite Sets. ZIVALJEVIC, Bosko.
Some Results on Bounded Truth-Table Degrees. DITCHEV, Angel V.
Some Results on Higher Suslin Trees. DAVID, R.
Some Syntactical Properties of Intermediate Predicate Logics. SUZUKI, Nobu-Yuki.
Sophoclean Logic (*Antigone* 175-81). O'SULLIVAN, Neil.
The Sorites Paradox and Higher-Order Vagueness. BURGESS, John A.
The Special Model Axiom in Nonstandard Analysis. ROSS, David.
The Spectrum of Resplendency. BALDWIN, John T.
Stability for Pairs of Equivalence Relations. TOFFALORI, Carlo.
Straight Talk about Sets. JUBIEN, Michael.
The Strength of the Failure of the Singular Cardinal Hypothesis. GITIK, Moti.
A Strengthening of Scott's ZF-Minus-Extensionality Result. POLLARD, Stephen.
A Strong Boundedness Theorem for Dilators. KECHRIS, Alexander S and WOODIN, W H.
The Structuralist View of Mathematical Objects. PARSONS, Charles.
Structure and Ontology. SHAPIRO, Stewart.
The Structure of Self-Commentary in Hegel's Dialectical Logic. GASKINS, Richard H.
The Structure of the Models of Decidable Monadic Theories of Graphs. SEESE, D.
Students: A Source-Spot for Arguments. BERKOWITZ, Leonard J.
A Study of Ontology. FINE, Kit.
Sub-Arithmetical Ultrapowers: A Survey. MC LAUGHLIN, Thomas G.
Successors of Singular Cardinals and Measurability Revisited. APTER, Arthur W.
Supervenience, Goodness and Higher-Order Universals. ODDIE, Graham.
Sur la méthode de Ferdinand Gonseth. VUILLEMIN, Jule.
Lo sviluppo degli studi logici nel pensiero tedesco della seconda metà dell'800. MANGIAGALLI, Maurizio.
Lo sviluppo degli studi logici nel pensiero tedesco della seconda metà dell' '800. MANGIAGALLI, Maurizio.
Synthetic Mechanics Revisited. BURGESS, John P.
Systems of Combinatory Logic Related to Quine's 'New Foundations'. HOLMES, M R.
The t-Variable Method in Gentzen-Style Automatic Theorem Proving. EDWALD, Tryggvi.
Tait-Systems for Fragments of *Lm*. COLUMBUS, Joachim.
Tautology: How Not to Use a Word. DREBEN, Burton and FLOYD, Juliet.
Taxonomies of Model-Theoretically Defined Topological Properties. BANKSTON, Paul.
Temporal Necessity and the Conditional. CROSS, Charles B.
La teoría de la suposición y los idiomas modernos. KNABENSCHUCH DE PORTA, Sabine.
La teoría de las cualidades sensibles en la *Summula Philosophiae Naturalis* atribuida a Guillermo de Ockham. LARRE, Olga L.
Teoría general de las decisiones. DE LA SIENRA, Adolfo García.
Testing Fairmindedness. FISHER, Alec.
The Text of the Nyāya-Sūtras: Some Problems. KRISHNA, Daya.
A Theorem on Labelled Trees and the Limits of Its Provability. PFEIFFER, Helmut.
Théories d'algébres de Boole munies d'idéaux distingués, II. TOURAILLE, Alain.
Theory Contraction through Base Contraction. FUHRMANN, André.
The Theory of Descriptions Revisited. PERUZZI, Alberto.
Theory Revision and Probability. SCHLECHTA, Karl.
There are Denumerably Many Ternary Intuitionistic Sheffer Functions. CUBRIC, Djordje.
Thirty Great Ways to Mess Up a Critical Thinking Test. FACIONE, Peter A.
This Article Should Not Be Rejected by *Mind*. LARAUDOGOITIA, Jon Perez.
Three Notions of Judgement (in Czechoslovakian). KOTATKO, Petr.
A Topological Interpretation of Diagonalizable Algebras. HAWRANEK, Jacek.
Topos Based Semantics for Constructive Logic with Strong Negation. KLUNDER, Barbara.
Tores et *p*-Groupes. BOROVIK, Aleksandr Vasilievich and POIZAT, Bruno Petrovich.
Toward a Formalization of Dialectical Logic. THOMASON, Steven K.
Towards a Modal-Structural Interpretation of Set Theory. HELLMAN, Geoffrey.
Towards a Research Agenda for Informal Logic and Critical Thinking. WEINSTEIN, Mark.
Tractatus: Críticas al logicismo. NUÑO, Juan A.
Transparent Approach to Logical Necessity and Possibility. MATERNA, P.
El tratado de las obligaciones dialógicas en la Edad Media: el caso de Robert Fland. BEUCHOT, Mauricio.
Tree Proofs for Syllogistic. SIMONS, Peter M.
True Contradictions. PARSONS, Terence.
Truth at a World is a Modality. LINSKY, Bernard.
Truth Table Logic with a Survey of Embeddability Results. TENNANT, Neil.
A Truth-Functional Logic for Near-Universal Generalizations. CARLSTROM, Ian F.
Tu scis regem sedere. D'ORS, Angel.
The Turing-Good Weight of Evidence Function and Popper's Measure of the Severity of a Test. GILLIES, Donald.
The Two Barbaras. THOM, Paul.
Two Hypergraph Theorems Equivalent to BPI. COWEN, Robert H.
Two Methods of Constructing Contractions and Revisions of Knowledge Systems. ROTT, Hans.
Two Principles of Bayesian Epistemology. TALBOTT, W J.
A Two-Valued Logic for Reasoning about Different Types of Consequence in Kleene's Three-Valued Logic. KONIKOWSKA, Beata.
Ultimate Reality and Meaning in Africa: Some Methodological Preliminaries—A Test Case. BELLO, A G A.
Undecidability and Initial Segments of the (R.E.) TT-Degrees. HAUGHT, Christine Ann and SHORE, Richard A.
The Undecidability of *k*-Provability. BUSS, Samuel R.
Underivability Results in Mixed Systems of Monadic Deontic Logic. GALVAN, Sergio.
Understanding Induction. MACNAMARA, John.
Understanding the System Construction in Logic. DAS, Ramesh Chandra.
Unfair to Nozick. BRUECKNER, Anthony.
Unidimensional Theories are Superstable. HRUSHOVSKI, Ehud.
A Unification-Theoretic Method for Investigating the *k*-Provability Problem. FARMER, William.
Uniform Proofs as a Foundation for Logic Programming. MILLER, Dale and NADATHUR, Gopalan and PFENNING, Frank and SCEDROV, Andre.
The Union Axiom in Zermelo Set Theory. GONZÁLEZ, Carlos G.
Universal Structures in Power $\aleph_1$. MEKLER, Alan H.
Universals and Predication of Species. PETERSON, John.
Upward Directedness of the Rudin-Keisler Ordering of *P*-Points. LAFLAMME, Claude.
The Uses and Abuses of the History of Topos Theory. MC LARTY, Colin.
Vague Identity and Vague Objects. GARRETT, Brian.
Vague Objects. ZEMACH, Eddy M.
Vagueness, Natural Language and Logic. BERKELEY, Istvan S N.
Valency, Adicity, and Adity in Peirce's MS 482. BURCH, Robert W.
Validity and Practical Reasoning. MITCHELL, David.
Validity and Satisfaction in Imperative Logic. SEGERBERG, Krister.
The Value of Perfect Information in Non-linear Utility Theory. SCHLEE, Edward E.
Variations on da Costa *C* Systems and Dual-Intuitionistic Logics (I). SYLVAN, Richard.

LOGIC
Varying Modal Theories. LUCAS, T and LAVENDHOMME, R.
La verdad. ALVAREZ GÓMEZ, Mariano.
Verification of Concurrent Programs: the Automata-Theoretic Framework. VARDI, Moshe Y.
Verification, Falsification and Cancellation in KT. WILLIAMSON, Timothy.
Verification, Falsification, and the Logic of Enquiry. MILNE, Peter.
Verisimilitude Based on Concept Analysis. ORLOWSKA, Ewa.
Verisimilitude by Power Relations: A Response to Oddie. BRINK, Chris and HEIDEMA, Johannes.
Was the Axiom of Reducibility a Principle of Logic?. LINSKY, Bernard.
Weak Axioms of Determinacy and Subsystems of Analysis II. TANAKA, Kazuyuki.
Weak Cylindric Set Algebras and Weak Subdirect Indecomposability. ANDRÉKA, H and NÉMETI, I and THOMPSON, R J.
Weakly Minimal Groups of Unbounded Exponent. LOVEYS, James.
Weakly Semirecursive Sets. JOCKUSCH JR, Carl G and OWINGS JR, James C.
Weights or the Value of Knowledge. RAMSEY, F P.
Weitere verschärfungen zu den Reduktionstypen.... DEUTSCH, Michael.
What is Empirical in Mathematics?. PETERSON, Philip L.
What was Leibniz's Problem about Relations?. BURDICK, Howard.
When Fair Betting Odds are Not Degrees of Belief. SEIDENFELD, Teddy and SCHERVISH, M J and KADANE, J B.
When Is Arithmetic Possible?. MC COLM, Gregory L.
Where Do Natural Numbers Come From?. HODES, Harold T.
Why are Definitions True?. SKIDMORE, Arthur.
Why is Conjunctive Simplification Invalid?. THOMPSON, Bruce R.
Wilhelm von Ockham: Das Risiko, mittelalterlich zu denken. PERLER, Dominik.
Wittgenstein on 2, 2, 2...: The Opening of Remarks on the Foundations of Mathematics. FLOYD, Juliet.
Wittgenstein on Logical Form and Kantian Geometry. SUMMERFIELD, Donna M.
Wittgenstein on Mathematical Proof. WRIGHT, Crispin.
Wittgenstein sobre la noción de regla en Frege. PADILLA GÁLVEZ, Jesús.
Wittgenstein's "Remarks on Colour". ERICKSON, Glenn W.
Wittgenstein's Philosophies of Mathematics. GERRARD, Steve.
Wittgenstein, Hans Lipps y los supuestos de la predicación. LÁZARO, Ramón Castilla.
You and She. WILLIAMS, C J F.
Zande Logic and Western Logic. JENNINGS, Richard C.
'Just More Theory': A Manoeuvre in Putnam's Model-Theoretic Argument for Antirealism. TAYLOR, Barry.

LOGICAL ANALYSIS
Can An Argument Be Both Valid and Invalid Too?. NEBLETT, William R.
Quantum Physics and Logical Truth (in Italian). GIANNETTO, Enrico.

LOGICAL ATOMISM
The "Middle Wittgenstein": From Logical Atomism to Practical Holism. STERN, David G.
Wittgenstein and the Color Incompatibility Problem. JACQUETTE, Dale.

LOGICAL CONSTANT(S)
Formatives. ENGLEBRETSEN, George.
Logical Constants Across Varying Types. VAN BENTHEM, Johan.
Logical Constants and the Glory of Truth-Conditional Semantics. LYCAN, William G.
Logical Constants as Punctuation Marks. DOSEN, Kosta.
Logical Form and Radical Interpretation. MC CARTHY, Tim.
Russell, Logicism, and the Choice of Logical Constants. BYRD, Michael.
Smook on Logical and Extralogical Constants. HITCHCOCK, David and GEORGE, Rolf.

LOGICAL EMPIRICISM
see also Logical Positivism
The A Priori in Phenomenology and the Legacy of Logical Empiricism. BLOSSER, Philip.
Did Kuhn Kill Logical Empiricism?. REISCH, George A.
Epistemological Structures in Marketing: Paradigms, Metaphors, and Marketing Ethics. REIDENBACH, R Eric and ROBIN, Donald P.
How Not to Russell Carnap's *Aufbau*. RICHARDSON, Alan.

LOGICAL FORM
Logical Form and Radical Interpretation. MC CARTHY, Tim.

LOGICAL IMPOSSIBILITY
Could God Make a Contradiction True?. GOLDSTICK, D.

LOGICAL POSITIVISM
Classics of Analytic Philosophy. AMMERMAN, Robert R (ed).
Ethical Dilemmas Posed By Recent and Prospective Developments with Respect to Agricultural Research. JOHNSON, Glenn L.
Paradigmas cartesianos. LOPARIC, Z.
Positivism and the Pragmatic Theory of Observation. OBERDAN, Thomas.
The Problem of Protocol Statements and Schlick's Concept of 'Konstatierungen'. ZHAI, Zhenming.

LOGICAL THEORY
"Negative Values" in *Logic and Ethics*, ELZENBERG, H.
Argumentation—Distributed or Monological?. BARTH, E M.
Occasions for Argumentation. HILPINEN, Risto.
The Place of Argumentation in the Theory of Reasoning. JOHNSON, Ralph H.

LOGICISM
Mathematics and the Image of Reason. TILES, Mary E.
"Logic in Russell's Logicism" in *The Analytic Tradition: Philosophical Quarterly Monographs, Volume 1*, HYLTON, Peter.
Against Logicist Cognitive Science. OAKSFORD, Mike and CHATER, Nick.
Frege, Informative Identities, and Logicism. MILNE, Peter.
L'interpretazione costruttiva dell'implicazione. MORICONI, Enrico.
Logicism, Pragmatism and Metascience: Towards a Pancritical-Pragmatic Meta-Level Discourse. AXTELL, G S.
El logicismo russelliano: su significado filosófico. RODRÍGUEZ CONSUEGRA, Francisco.
Philosophical Reflections on the Foundations of Mathematics. COUTURE, Jocelyne and LAMBEK, Joachim.
Russell, Logicism, and the Choice of Logical Constants. BYRD, Michael.
Tractatus: Críticas al logicismo. NUÑO, Juan A.

LOGOCENTRISM
Essays on Heidegger and Others: Philosophical Papers, Volume 2. RORTY, Richard.

LOGOS
The Tragedy of Reason: Toward a Platonic Conception of Logos. ROOCHNIK, David.
"Logos and Trinity: Patterns of Platonist Influence on Early Christianity" in *The Philosophy in Christianity*, DILLON, John.
"Λογοσ ε Ομονοια: algumas considerações em torno da razão sofística" in *Dinâmica do Pensar: Homenagem a Oswaldo Market*, VAZ PINTO, Maria José.
"Presentation" in *Re-Reading Levinas*, PEPERZAK, Adriaan.
Heidegger on Logic and Language: Some Aporiai. FAY, Thomas A.
Heraclitus: Heidegger's 1944 Lecture Held at Freiburg University. FRINGS, Manfred S.
Logic and Logos—The Search for Unity in Hegel and Coleridge: I, Alienation and the Logocentric Response. PERKINS, Mary Anne.
Logic and Logos—The Search for Unity in Hegel and Coleridge, III: A Different Logos. PERKINS, Mary Anne.
Logos and the Place of the Other. BIRMINGHAM, Peg E.
Il Logos come immagine di Dio in Filone di Alessandria. BELLETTI, Bruno.
Télos y arché: La physis del logos. INCARDONA, Nunzio.

LOMBARD
Causing, Enabling, and Counterfactual Dependence. MACKIE, Penelope.

LONERGAN, B
The Authentic Self: Toward a Philosophy of Personality. LACENTRA, Walter.
"'I Am We' Consciousness and Dialog as Organizational Ethics Method". NIELSEN, Richard P.
Baur's "Conversation with Gadamer" and "Contribution to the Gadamer-Lonergan Discussion": A Reaction. LAWRENCE, Fred.
Bradley and Lonergan's Relativist. TESKE, Roland.
Concepts of Culture: Lonergan and the Anthropologists. KLEIN, Dennis.
Deconstructing Lonergan. MC KINNEY, Ronald H.
Learning from Lonergan at Eleven. DALY, T V.
Lonergan's Method in Ethics and the Meaning of Human Sexuality. FRISBY, Mark E.
Lonergan's Performative Transcendental Argument Against Scepticism. REHG, William R.
Lonergan's Recovery of the Notion of Natural Right: Introduction to a New Context for an Old Discussion. BRAIO, Frank Paul.
Method Divorced from Content in Theology: An Assessment of Lonergan's *Method in Theology*. REYNOLDS, Terrence.
Praxis and Ultimate Reality: Intellectual, Moral and Religious Conversion as Radical Political Conversion. MARSH, James L.
Reconstruction, Dialectic and Praxis. RIORDAN, Patrick.
Reply to Marsh's "Reply to McKinney on Lonergan". MC KINNEY, Ronald H.
Reply to McKinney on Lonergan: A Deconstruction. MARSH, James L.
Thomas Aquinas and the Will: A Note on Interpretation. CROWE, Frederick.

LORAND, R
A Note on Ruth Lorand's 'Free and Dependent Beauty: A Puzzling Issue'. LORD, Catherine.

LOSEV, A
La prima edizione sovietica di Solov'ev. MASTROIANNI, Giovanni.

LOTTER, H
Continuing the Conversation—A Reply to My Interlocutors. OLIVIER, G.

LOTZE
Phänomenologie als ästhetische Theorie. FELLMANN, Ferdinand.

LOUGHLIN, G
A Response to Gerard Loughlin's "Prefacing Pluralism: John Hick and the Mastery of Religion". HICK, John.

LOVE
see also Eros
The Authentic Self: Toward a Philosophy of Personality. LACENTRA, Walter.
For What May I Hope? Thinking with Kant and Kierkegaard. FENDT, Gene.
Love's Knowledge: Essays on Philosophy and Literature. NUSSBAUM, Martha C.
The Many Dimensions of the Human Person. STEGER, E Ecker.
On Homosexuality: Lysis, Phaedrus, and Symposium. JOWETT, Benjamin (trans).
Other Selves: Philosophers on Friendship. PAKALUK, Michael (ed).
L'Utopia di Fourier. TUNDO, Laura.
"Justice and Love in the Political Thought of St Augustine" in *Grace, Politics and Desire: Essays on Augustine*, PAREL, Anthony J.
"Love and Perfect Coincidence in a Sartrean Ethics" in *Writing the Politics of Difference*, BELL, Linda A.
"Love as Rhetorical Principle: The Relationship Between Content and Style in the Rhetoric of St Augustine" in *Grace, Politics and Desire: Essays on Augustine*, SUTHERLAND, Christine Mason.
"Love between Us" in *Who Comes after the Subject?*, IRIGARAY, Luce.
"Mechtild of Magdeburg" in *A History of Women Philosophers, Volume II: Medieval, Renaissance and Enlightenment, A.D. 500-1600*, GIBSON, Joan.
"Questions to Emmanuel Levinas: On the Divinity of Love" in *Re-Reading Levinas*, WHITFORD, Margaret (trans) and IRIGARAY, Luce.
Amor y comunicación. FORMENT, Eudaldo.
Amour de l'être et ambition de gloire: le spinozisme de Vauvenargues. BOVE, Laurent.
Aristotle in Dante's Paradise. BOURBEAU, Marguerite.
Campanella's "Civitas Solis" Is Ruled by Love Without Emotion (in German). ZÖHRER-ERNST, Ulla.
Cuestiones actuales de epistemología teológica: Aportes de la teología de la liberación. SCANNONE, J C.
De las maravillas acerca de lo uno y lo múltiple o sobre los avatares del amor neoplatónico en Baruch de Espinosa. ALBIAC, Gabriel.
El deseo y el amor en San Agustín. PEGUEROLES, Juan.
Filosofía, justicia y amor. LEVINAS, E and EZCURRA, Alicia Villar.
Homicide and Love. SMITH, Steven G.
In Defence of Graded Love. LAI, Whalen.
Love in *Thus Spoke Zarathustra*. LEVITT, Tom.
Love, Friendship, and the Aesthetics of Character. NOVITZ, David.
The Perils of Love: Why Women Need Rights. INGRAM, Attracta.
What is this Thing Called 'Love'?. BERENSON, Frances.
Why Do I Love Thee? A Response to Nozick's Account of Romantic Love. SMITH, Tara.
The Wisdom of Plato's Aristophanes. SALMAN, Charles.

LOVELOCK, J
Nature as Personal. DOMBROWSKI, Daniel A.

LOVIBOND, S
Moral Realism and the Meaning of Life. MARGOLIS, Joseph.

LOVING
The Lover-Beloved Relationship Reconsidered. HOLMES, Richard and DANIEL, Mano.

LOWE, E
Classifying Conditionals II. JACKSON, Frank.

LOWENTHAL, D
Reply to Lowenthal. COLMO, Christopher A.

LOYALTY
Anotaciones en torno al poder de la democracia. MOLINA, Carlos.
Death, Honor, and Loyalty: The Bushidō Ideal. HURST III, G Cameron.
The Effects of Patrol Officers' Defensiveness Toward the Outside World on Their Ethical Orientations. SHERNOCK, Stan K.
Loyalty: The Police. EWIN, R E.

LUCIAN
Lucian: The Sale of Lives (in Hebrew). SCOLNICOV, Samuel (trans).

LUCK
Blaise Pascals: "Pensées" (1656-1662) Systematische 'Gedanken' über. KIRSCH, Ulrich.
Human Interests: Reflections on Philosophical Anthropology. RESCHER, Nicholas.
"Gender and Moral Luck" in *Identity, Character, and Morality: Essays in Moral Psychology*, CARD, Claudia.
Dretske on Knowledge and Content. GJELSVIK, Olav.
A Kantian View of Moral Luck. MOORE, A W.
Luck. RESCHER, Nicholas.

LUDERS, G
En busca del contenido físico de la regla de Luders. MARTÍNEZ, Sergio and MURILLO, Lorena.

LUEGENBIEHL, H
Commentary: "Codes of Ethics and the Moral Education of Engineers". PUKA, Bill.

LUHMANN, N
La sociedad sin hombres: Niklas Luhmann o la teoría como escándalo. IZUZQUIZA, Ignacio.
Das Verhängnis Erste Philosophie. EBELING, Hans.
Bestandserhaltung oder Kritik oder: Weder Bestandserhaltung noch Kritik—Die Intention der Systemtheorie Niklas Luhmanns. POLLACK, Detlef.
Vom Sein zur Selbstreferentialität: Überlegungen zur Theorie autopoietischer Systeme Niklas Luhmanns. GRIPP-HAGELSTANGE, Helga.

LUKACS, G
Mannheim and Hungarian Marxism. GABEL, Joseph.
From Hegel to Lukacs: The Problem of Ontology from the Point of View of Social and Natural Theory (in German). MOCEK, Reinhard.
Georg Lukács and Stalinism (in German). TIETZ, Udo.
Hegel, Marx, Lukács: The Dialectic of Freedom and Necessity. DAY, Richard B.
Lukács on the Ontology of Social Existence and Marx's Understanding of Society (in German). LENDVAI, Ferenc L.
Marxism as the Foundation of Philosophies of Science: *The Case of G Lukács' Ontology of Social Being*. TUCHANSKA, Barbara.
What is Ultimate in George Lukács's Ontology?. JOÓS, Ernest.

LUKES, S
Deceptive Comfort: The Power of Kafka's Stories. BENNETT, Jane.

LULL
L'"irrisio fidei" chez Raymond Lulle et S Thomas D'Aquin. SERVERAT, Vincent.

LUTHER
Fideísmo y autoritarismo en Lutero. CAPPELLETTI, Angel.

LUTZ, C
The Celebration of Emotion: Vallabha's Ontology of Affective Experience. TIMM, Jeffrey R.

LYCAN, W
Logical Form and Radical Interpretation. MC CARTHY, Tim.
On Removing Puzzles About Belief Ascription. DEVITT, Michael.
Sensory Qualities and 'Homunctionalism': A Review Essay of W G Lycan's *Consciousness*. KOBES, Bernard W.
Some New Directions in the Philosophy of Mind. THOMAS, Janice.

LYING
"The Ethical Root of Language" in *Logic and Ethics*, GORMALLY, M C.
On Lying and the Role of Content in Kant's Ethics. SEDGWICK, Sally.
The Political Philosophy of Sissela Bok. FAREY, Caroline.
Les sens trompeurs: Usage cartésien d'un motif sceptique. CAVAILLÉ, Jean-Pierre.
The Truth about Lies in Plato's *Republic*. PAGE, Carl.

LYOTARD, J
Essays on Heidegger and Others: Philosophical Papers, Volume 2. RORTY, Richard.
"Translation and Language Games" in *Hermeneutics and the Poetic Motion, Translation Perspectives V—1990*, ROSE, Marilyn Gaddis.
The Intellectual in the Post Modern Age: East/West Contrasts. BAYARD, Caroline.
Judgment and Rationality in Lyotard's Discursive Archipelago. HENDLEY, Steven.
Lyotard's "Kantian Socialism". GEIMAN, Kevin Paul.
Nietzsche and the Critique of Oppositional Thinking. SCHRIFT, Alan D.
Philosophical Hierarchies and Lyotard's Dichotomies. SASSOWER, Raphael and OGAZ, Charla Phyllis.
Post-Modernism as the Lesser Evil: Criticism and Agreement in Lyotard's "Widerstreit" ("Conflict") (in German). KRÜGER, Hans-Peter.
Verlichtingsfilosofie twee eeuwen later; J F Lyotard als postmoderne Kant. VAN PEPERSTRATEN, Frans.

MACCORMICK, D
The Institution of Law. BANKOWSKI, Zenon.

MACDONALD, C
Macdonald on Type Reduction via Disjunction. ENDICOTT, Ronald P.

MACER, D
New Creations? Commentary. BALK, Roger A.

MACH
"Phenomenalism, Relativity and Atoms: Rehabilitating Ernst Mach's Philosophy of Science" in *Logic, Methodology and Philosophy of Science, VIII*, WOLTERS, Gereon.
Ernst Mach and the Elimination of Subjectivity. HAMILTON, Andy.
Ernst Mach Leaves "The Church of Physics". BLACKMORE, John.
Scientific Racism in the Philosophy of Science: Some Historical Examples. UEBEL, Thomas E.
Self-Notions. PERRY, John.
Semantica della "Vorstellung" e valore della teoria in *Erkenntnis und Irrtum* di Ernst Mach. BELLOMO, Andrea.

MACHADO, A
Tiempo, soledad y muerte: La encrucijada del poeta. RADCHIK, Laura.

MACHAN, T
Against Human Rights. NELSON, John O.

MACHIAVELLI
El ensimismamiento del poder: Maquiavelo y la ciencia política moderna. GARCIA, Romano.
The Foxy Prophet: Machiavelli versus Machiavelli on Ferdinand the Catholic. ANDREW, Edward.
Hegel as Advocate of Machiavelli (in German). JAMME, Christoph.
In a Crazy Time the Crazy Come Out Well: Machiavelli and the Cosmology of His Day. BASU, Sammy.
Machiavelli's Notions of Justice: Text and Analysis. PAREL, A J.
Machiavelli's Sisters: Women and "the Conversation" of Political Theory. ZERILLI, Linda M G.
Machiavellianism Revisited. NELSON, George and GILBERTSON, Diana.
La revolución teórica del Príncipe de Maquiavelo. GIGLIOLI, Giovanna.

MACHINE(S)
Artificial Intelligence: Its Scope and Limits. FETZER, James H.
How to Build a Conscious Machine. ANGEL, Leonard.
Philosophy and Cognitive Science. FETZER, James H.
Ends and Meaning in Machine-Like Systems. ATLAN, H.
Epiphenomenalism and Machines: A Discussion of Van Rooijen's Critique of Popper. PECNJAK, Davor.
Functionalisme versus dubbelaspecttheorie: tertium datur. MACKOR, Anne Ruth.
Machines as Persons?. CHERRY, Christopher.
Machines as Persons?. HANFLING, Oswald.
Massively Parallel Distributed Processing and a Computationalist Foundation for Cognitive Science. LYNGZEIDETSON, Albert E.
The Mind's I Has Two Eyes. MARTIN, J E and ENGLEMAN, K H.

MACINTOSH, D
Mechanism and Indeterminacy: Reply to MacIntosh. WARMBRŌD, Ken.

MACINTOSH, J
In Defence of Reincarnation. DANIELS, Charles B.
The Possibility of Reincarnation. NOONAN, Harold W.

MACINTYRE, A
Aristotle or Nietzsche?. FRANKS, Joan M.
Faith and Reason: Reflections on MacIntyre's 'Tradition-constituted Enquiry'. MARKHAM, Ian.
MacIntyre and the Indispensability of Tradition. SCHNEEWIND, J B.
MacIntyre on Hume. BAIER, Annette C.
MacIntyre, Tradition, and the Christian Philosopher. HIBBS, Thomas S.
Virtues and Values: A Platonic Account. SEUNG, T K.
Waiting for a New St Benedict: Alasdair MacIntyre and the Theory and Practice of Journalism. LAMBETH, Edmund B.

MACKIE, J
'Queerness' and the Objectivity of Value: A Response to J L Mackie. SPOERL, Joseph.
Craig, Mackie and the *Kalam* Cosmological Argument. OPPY, Graham.
Moral Scepticism and Inductive Scepticism. BLACK, Robert.
Moral Skepticism and the Dangerous Maybe: Reconsidering Mackie's *Ethics*. METCALFE, John F.
On the Genuine Queerness of Moral Properties and Facts. GARNER, Richard T.
Representative Realism and Absolute Reality. ENGLISH, Parker.
Universe Indexed Properties and the Fate of the Ontological Argument. SENNETT, James F.

MACKOR, A
Searle's Oplossing voor het lichaam-geest probleem: ipse dixit—Een reactie op Anne Ruth Mackor. MEIJSING, Monica.

MADDEN, E
Madden's Account of Necessity in Causation. LEVINE, Michael P.

MADDY, P
Mathematics Without Truth (A Reply to Maddy). FIELD, Hartry.

MADNESS
Michel Foucault's Force of Flight: Towards an Ethics for Thought. BERNAUER, James W.
"La tematica della follia tra Umanesimo nordico e Umanesimo latino: l'*Encomium Moriae* di Erasmo da Rotterdam" in *Razionalitá critica: nella filosofia moderna*, CASTELLANO, Veneranda.
Hegel, Nietzsche, and Freud on Madness and the Unconscious. BERTHOLD-BOND, Daniel.
Women, Madness, and Special Defences in the Law. BOETZKES, Elisabeth and TURNER, Susan (Guerin) and SOBSTYL, Edrie.

MAGIC
"Hysteria, Belief and Magic" in *Harré and His Critics*, TAYLOR, David.

MAGNITUDE(S)
Are All False Theories Equally False? A Remark on David Miller's Problem and Geometric Conventionalism. MORMANN, Thomas.

MAHER, P
Reply to Maher and Kashima: "On the Descriptive Adequacy of Levi's Decision Theory". LEVI, Isaac.

MAHONEY, J
History as Argument for Revision in Moral Theology. GRISEZ, Germain.

MAIMON
"Maimon, crítico de Kant" in *Dinâmica do Pensar: Homenagem a Oswaldo Market*, FERREIRA, Manuel Carmo.

MAIMONIDES
Essays on the Context, Nature, and Influence of Isaac Newton's Theology. FORCE, James E (ed).
"The Crisis of Polytheism and the Answers of Vossius, Cudworth, and Newton" in *Essays on the Context, Nature, and Influence of Isaac Newton's Theology*, POPKIN, Richard H.
"Some Further Comments on Newton and Maimonides" in *Essays on the Context, Nature, and Influence of Isaac Newton's Theology*, POPKIN, Richard H.
Anger as a Vice: A Maimonidean Critique of Aristotle's Ethics. FRANK, Daniel H.
Maimonides: A Natural Law Theorist?. LEVINE, Michael.
El ser principial y Dios: Una observación a la teología de Maimónides. GARCÍA GONZÁLEZ, Juan.
Some Remarks on the Political Science of Maimonides and Farabi. BARTLETT, Robert (trans) and STRAUSS, Leo.

MAISTRE, J
Joseph de Maistre en de Revolutie. VAN BELLINGEN, Jozef.

MAKIN, S
Makin on the Ontological Argument. OPPY, Graham.

MAKINSON, D
Theory Revision and Probability. SCHLECHTA, Karl.

MALCOLM, N
Can Knowledge Occur Unknowingly?. CHAUDHURI, Manjusree.
Malcolm on Wittgenstein on Rules. MOSER, Paul K.

MALE(S)
On Homosexuality: Lysis, Phaedrus, and Symposium. JOWETT, Benjamin (trans).
One Man's Reflection on a Masculine Role in Feminist Ethics: Epistemic versus Political Privilege. BOYD, Dwight.

MALEBRANCHE
Berkeley's Revolution in Vision. ATHERTON, Margaret.
"Berkeley and Malebranche on Causality and Volition" in *Central Themes in Early Modern Philosophy*, JOLLEY, Nicholas.
"Leibniz on Malebranche on Causality" in *Central Themes in Early Modern Philosophy*, SLEIGH JR, Robert C.
El conocimiento de los cuerpos según Malebranche (I). FERNANDEZ RODRIGUEZ, Jose Luis.
Malebranche and the Vision in God: A Note on *The Search After Truth*, III, 2, iii. NADLER, Steven.
Malebranche versus Arnauld. COOK, Monte.
Visione in Dio e visione di Dio nella filosofia di Malebranche. NICOLOSI, Salvatore.

MALTHUS
African Famine: New Economic and Ethical Perspectives. LUCAS JR, George R.

MAN
see also Human(s), Individual(s), Person(s), Philosophical Anthropology
Strukturanthropologie "Der menschliche Mensch". ROMBACH, Heinrich.
"Could God Become Man?" in *The Philosophy in Christianity*, SWINBURNE, Richard.
"The Freedoms of Man and Their Relation to God" in *Freedom in the Modern World: Jacques Maritain, Yves R Simon, Mortimer J Adler*, TORRE, Michael D.
"L'image de l'homme dans la théorie kantienne du génie" in *XIth International Congress in Aesthetics, Nottingham 1988*, LABRADA, Antonia.
"Philosophy, Science and Man" in *Logic, Methodology and Philosophy of Science, VIII*, FEDOSEYEV, Pyotr.
Il "parlare commune" come lume storico-naturale della "riproduzione sociale". MININNI, Giuseppe.
The 'Gay Science' of Nietzsche (in Dutch). ESTERHUYSE, Willie.
Hacia el saber del hombre: Dialéctica, lógica y ontológica en Aristóteles. MARÍN, Victor R.
Heidegger and Emancipation. OLIVIER, G.
Heidegger's Attempt at Rehousing Man Through the *Kehre des Denkens*. RAUCHE, G A.
Hobbes y la apología moderna del artificio. BOVERO, Michelangelo.
Liberal Man. MENDUS, Susan.
Man Not a Subject of Science?. SLEZAK, Peter.
Nicola Abbagnano tra esistenzialismo e neoilluminismo. QUARTA, Antonio.
Per una filosofia del corpo. PELLECCHIA, Pasquale.
Su alcuni aspetti del neoilluminismo di L Geymonat. STOMEO, Anna.
Sur l'habitation poétique de l'homme. PIERSON, Dominique.
La tarea cósmica del hombre según Teilhard de Chardin. PATIÑO, Joel Rodríguez.
The Man as Subject of the Philosophy (in Hungarian). RICOEUR, Paul.

MAN
The Scheme of the Game of Man and World (Towards the Formation of the Planetary Man) (in Hungarian). AXELOS, Kostas.
The World as a Whole and the World of Man (in Czechoslovakian). PATOCKA, Jan.
La valenza della carità nelle forme della vita politica. PELLECCHIA, Pasquale.

MANAGEMENT
Good Intentions Aside: A Manager's Guide to Resolving Ethical Problems. NASH, Laura L.
Adapting Kohlberg to Enhance the Assessment of Manager's Moral Reasoning. WEBER, James.
Believing that Everyone Else is Less Ethical: Implications for Work Behavior and Ethics Instruction. TYSON, Thomas.
Business Ethics and Stakeholder Analysis. GOODPASTER, Kenneth E.
Corporate Policy and the Ethics of Competitor Intelligence Gathering. PAINE, Lynn Sharp.
Differences in Moral Values Between Corporations. NYSTROM, Paul C.
Economics and Ethics. REILLY, B J and KYJ, M J.
Engineers and Management: The Challenge of the Challenger Incident. WERHANE, Patricia H.
Ethical Dilemmas in Performance Appraisal Revisited. LONGENECKER, Clinton and LUDWIG, Dean.
Exploring the Structure of Ethical Attributions as a Component of the Consumer Decision Model. WHALEN, Joel and PITTS, Robert E and WONG, John K.
Goodwill, Going Concern, Stocks and Flows: A Prescription for Moral Analysis. SWANDA JR, John R.
Leopold's "Means and Ends in Wild Life Management". HARGROVE, Eugene C and CALLICOTT, J Baird.
Luck. RESCHER, Nicholas.
Machiavellianism Revisited. NELSON, George and GILBERTSON, Diana.
Management's Hat Trick: Misuse of "Engineering Judgment" in the Challenger Incident. HERKERT, Joseph R.
Means and Ends in Wild Life Management. LEOPOLD, Aldo.
Public Relations: The Empiricial Research on Practitioner Ethics. PRATT, Cornelius B.
The Relative Importance of Social Responsibility in Determining Organizational Effectiveness: Student Responses. KRAFT, Kenneth L.
The Relative Importance of Social Responsibility in Determining Organizational Effectiveness. KRAFT, Kenneth.
Social Responsibility and Strategic Management: Toward an Enterprise Strategy Classification. MEZNAR, Martin B and CHRISMAN, James J and CARROLL, Archie B.

MANDEVILLE
Hutcheson's Account of Beauty as a Response to Mandeville. MICHAEL, Emily and MICHAEL, Fred S.
Pride, Hypocrisy and Civility in Mandeville's Social and Historical Theory. DICKEY, Laurence.

MANET, E
Art History in the Mirror Stage: Interpreting *Un Bar aux Folies Bergères*. CARRIER, David.

MANKIND
see also Humanity
How to Get Rid of Your Expensive Philosopher of Science and Still Keep Control Over the Fuzzing Conversation of Mankind. VISKER, Rudi.

MANN, T
Schopenhauersche Weltsicht und totalitäre Humanität im Werke Thomas Manns. KRISTIANSEN, Borge.

MANNHEIM, K
Mannheim and Hungarian Marxism. GABEL, Joseph.
Sociologie in de Weimarrepubliek. HABERMAS, Jürgen.

MANSEL
Mansel's Agnosticism. FITZGERALD, Timothy.

MANUSCRIPT(S)
The *Trés Riches Heures*: An Illuminated Manuscript in the Age of Mechanical Reproduction. CAMILLE, Michael.
Zum Verbleib der Königsberger Kant-Handschriften: Funde und Desiderate. STARK, Werner.

MANY-SORTED LOGIC(S)
Many-Sorted Elementary Equivalence. DZIERZGOWSKI, Daniel.

MANY-VALUED LOGICS
Boolean Products of CW—Algebras and Pseudo-Complementation. TORRENS, Antoni.
Characterization of Prime Numbers in Lukasiewicz's Logical Matrix. KARPENKO, Alexander S.
Extending Montague's System: A Three Valued Intensional Logic. ALVES, E H and GUERZONI, J A D.
$I\Delta_3$-Algebras. FIGALLO, Aldo V.
Intuitive Semantics for Some Three-Valued Logics Connected with Information, Contrariety and Subcontrariety. VAKARELOV, Dimitir.
Lukasiewicz Logic and Wajsberg Algebras. RODRIGUEZ, Antonio J and TORRENS, Antoni.
Many-Valued Modal Logics: Uses and Predicate Calculus. OSTERMANN, Pascal.
Mechanical Proof Procedures for Many-Valued Lattice-Based Logic Programming. SUBRAHMANIAN, V S.
A Note on Matrices for Systems of Nonsense-Logics. HALKOWSKA, Katarzyna.
A Note on the Axiomatization of Equational Classes of *n*-Valued Lukasiewicz Algebras. ADAMS, M E and CIGNOLI, R.
On Axiomatization of Many-Valued Logics Associated with Formalization of Plausible Reasonings. ANSHAKOV, O M and FINN, V K and SKVORTSOV, D P.
Peirced Clean Through. MEYER, Robert K.
Plain Semi-Post Algebras as a Poset-Based Generalization of Post Algebras and their Representability. CAT HO, Nguyen and RASIOWA, Helena.
The Priestley Duality for Wajsberg Algebras. MARTÍNEZ, N G.
Routley-Meyer Type Semantics for Urquhart's C. MÉNDEZ, José M.
Some Modal Logics Based on a Three-Valued Logic. MORIKAWA, Osamu.
Tait-Systems for Fragments of L*m*. COLUMBUS, Joachim.
A Two-Valued Logic for Reasoning about Different Types of Consequence in Kleene's Three-Valued Logic. KONIKOWSKA, Beata.

MAP(S)
"Pathologies" in Two Syntactic Categories of Partial Maps. MONTAGNA, Franco.
On the Angular Component Map Modulo *P*. PAS, Johan.

MARCEL
Toward the Death of Man. KLUBACK, William.
El enigma de la libertad humana en Gabriel Marcel. O'CALLAGHAN, Paul.
G Marcel: a dimensão metafísica da esperança. DA COSTA FREITAS, Manuel Barbosa.
Gabriel Marcel na correspondência com Gaston Fessard. CABRAL, Roque.
El hombre y el misterio del ser. TRIANA, Manuel.
A intersubjectividade em Gabriel Marcel. MORUJÁO, Alexandre Fradique.
Marcel on the Problem of Freedom. SUGUMAR, Devaki.
La moral existencial de G Marcel. MAÑERO, Salvador.
Paul Ricoeur e Gabriel Marcel. DE LOURDES SIRGADO GANHO, Maria.
Secondary Reflection and Marcelian Anthropology. MICHAUD, Thomas A.

MARCI, J
Idea, mente, specie: Platonismo e scienza in Johannes Marcus Marci (1595-1667). MOCCHI, Giuliana.

MARCUS AURELIUS
Partial Wholes. BARNES, Jonathan.

MARCUSE, H
Critical Theory and Philosophy. INGRAM, David.
El pensamiento de Heidegger y Marcuse en relación con la ecología. ARRIETA, Jeannette and HAYLING, Annie.
Political Errors (in Serbo-Croatian). NOERR, Gunzelin Schmid.

MARECHAL, J
From Unity to Pluralism: The Internal Evolution of Thomism. MC COOL, Gerald A.

MARGIN(S)
Algunos márgenes de la condición humana. MAS, Oscar.
On the Phenomenon of Marginality in Epistemology: Gonseth and his Tradition. WITKOWSKI, Lech.

MARGINALITY
The Evidence of Experience. SCOTT, Joan W.
Starting Thought From Women's Lives: Eight Resources for Maximizing Objectivity. HARDING, Sandra.

MARGOLIS, J
Comprensión intercultural y arte. BERENSON, Frances.

MARIE DE GOURNAY
"Marie le Jars de Gournay" in *A History of Women Philosophers, Volume II: Medieval, Renaissance and Enlightenment, A.D. 500-1600*, ZEDLER, Beatrice H.

MARIOLOGY
"Birgitta of Sweden" in *A History of Women Philosophers, Volume II: Medieval, Renaissance and Enlightenment, A.D. 500-1600*, WOLFSKEEL, Cornelia.

MARITAIN
Freedom in the Modern World: Jacques Maritain, Yves R Simon, Mortimer J Adler. TORRE, Michael D (ed).
From Twilight to Dawn: The Cultural Vision of Jacques Maritain. REDPATH, Peter A (ed).
From Unity to Pluralism: The Internal Evolution of Thomism. MC COOL, Gerald A.
The Preface to Thomistic Metaphysics. KNASAS, John F X.
"Approaches to Democratic Equality: Maritain, Simon, and Kolnai" in *Freedom in the Modern World: Jacques Maritain, Yves R Simon, Mortimer J Adler*, HITTINGER, John P.
"Creative Intuition, Great Books, and Freedom of Intellect" in *Freedom in the Modern World: Jacques Maritain, Yves R Simon, Mortimer J Adler*, ROYAL, Robert.

MARITAIN

"Maritain, Simon, and Vichy's Elite Schools" in *Freedom in the Modern World: Jacques Maritain, Yves R Simon, Mortimer J Adler*, HELLMAN, John.
"Modernization of the Law of the *Prise de Conscience*" in *Freedom in the Modern World: Jacques Maritain, Yves R Simon, Mortimer J Adler*, CALIFANO, Joseph J.
"Nominalism, Usury, and Bourgeois Man" in *Freedom in the Modern World: Jacques Maritain, Yves R Simon, Mortimer J Adler*, MANCINI, Matthew J.
"Recollections of Three Thinkers: Adler, Simon, and Maritain" in *Freedom in the Modern World: Jacques Maritain, Yves R Simon, Mortimer J Adler*, GALLAGHER, Donald A.
Persona y sociedad según Jacques Maritain. WASHBURN, Jimmy.
Rescuing Natural Law Theory from the Rationalists. DENNEHY, Raymond.
Wainwright, Maritain and Aquinas on Transcendent Experiences. ROY, Louis.

MARKET(S)

Markets, Managers and Theory in Education. HALLIDAY, John.
Philosophy and Politics. HUNT, G M K (ed).
"Markets and Morals" in *Philosophy and Politics*, SMITH, G W.
"Response to Smith's 'Markets and Morals'" in *Philosophy and Politics*, LOCKE, Don.
Corporate Social Responsibility and the Marketplace. COTTRILL, Melville T.
The Ethical Limitations of the Market. ANDERSON, Elizabeth.
Markets and Morals. SMITH, G W.
On Surrogacy: Morality, Markets, and Motherhood. MOODY-ADAMS, Michele M.
An Outline of My Main Contributions to Economic Science. ALLAIS, Maurice.
Property in Science and the Market. O'NEILL, John.
Response to Smith's "Markets and Morals". LOCKE, Don.
Self-Interest and the New Bashing of Economics. KIRZNER, Israel M.
Shareholder Authorized Inside Trading: A Legal and Moral Analysis. SHAW, Bill.
Using the Market to Measure Deserved Punishment. DAVIS, Michael.

MARKET, O

Dinâmica do Pensar: Homenagem a Oswaldo Market. FAC LETRAS UNIV LISBOA (ed).
"Entrevista com o Professor Oswaldo Market Conduzida por" in *Dinâmica do Pensar: Homenagem a Oswaldo Market*, MARQUES, António and MOLDER, Filomena and NABAIS, Nuno.

MARKETING

Danger Signs of Unethical Behavior: How to Determine If Your Firm Is at Ethical Risk. COOKE, Robert Allan.
Epistemological Structures in Marketing: Paradigms, Metaphors, and Marketing Ethics. REIDENBACH, R Eric and ROBIN, Donald P.
The Ethics of Selectively Marketing the Health Maintenance Organization. WAYMACK, Mark H.
Fostering Ethical Marketing Decisions. LACZNIAK, Gene R and MURPHY, Patrick E.
The Influence of Non-Anonymity Deriving from Feedback of Research Results on Marketing Professionals' Research Ethics. AKAAH, Ishmael P.
International Marketing Ethics. LACZNIAK, Gene R and MURPHY, Patrick E.
Marketing Ethics and Education: Some Empirical Findings. MERRITT, Sharyne.
Marketing Ethics: Some Dimensions of the Challenge. CAMENISCH, Paul F.
Remarks on Marketing Ethics. BRENNAN, Bernard F.

MARKOVIC, F

Boskovic's Philosophy in the Evaluation of Franjo Markovic (1887): Origins and Results (in Serbo-Croatian). KUTLESA, Stipe.

MARR, D

Externalism and Marr's Theory of Vision. FRANCESCOTTI, Robert M.

MARRIAGE

"They Lived Happily Ever After": Sommers on Women and Marriage. FRIEDMAN, Marilyn.
Lonergan's Method in Ethics and the Meaning of Human Sexuality. FRISBY, Mark E.
Marriage is an Institution Created by God: A Philosophical Analysis. BOYLE, Joseph.
Over het morele en zedelijke handelen, toegelicht aan het instituut huwelijk. COBBEN, Paul.
San Agustín y la sexualidad conyugal. BURKE, Cormac.

MARSH, J

Reply to Marsh's "Reply to McKinney on Lonergan". MC KINNEY, Ronald H.

MARSHALL, T

"Citizenship and Autonomy" in *Social Theory of Modern Societies: Anthony Giddens and His Critics*, HELD, David.

MARSILIUS OF INGHEN

Erfurt, Ampl Q 70A: A Quaestiones-commentary on the Second Part of Alexander de Villa Dei's *Doctrinale*. KNEEPKENS, C H.

MARSILIUS OF PADUA

Marsilius on Rights. TIERNEY, Brian.
Nature, Justice, and Duty in the *Defensor Pacis*: Marsiglio of Padua's Ciceronian Impulse. NEDERMAN, Cary J.

MARTIN, E

Treating the Troops: A Commentary. ANNAS, George J and GRODIN, Michael A.
Treating the Troops: A Commentary. LEVINE, Robert J.

MARTIRE, G

Giustino Martire, il primo platonico cristiano. GIRGENTI, Giuseppe.

MARX

Beyond Ethnocentrism: A Reconstruction of Marx's Concept of Science. MC KELVEY, Charles.
Collected Works, Volume 26, Engels: 1882-1889. ENGELS, Frederick.
False Consciousness. MEYERSON, Denise.
Hegel In His Time—Jacques D'Hondt. BURBIDGE, John (trans).
Marx's Radical Critique of Capitalist Society: A Reconstruction and Critical Evaluation. ARNOLD, N Scott.
Resurrecting Marx: The Analytical Marxists on Freedom, Exploitation, and Justice. GORDON, David.
"The Humanistic Implications of Liberation Theology: Juan Luis Segundo and Karl Marx" in *The Question of Humanism: Challenges and Possibilities*, HEWITT, Marsha A.
"The 'Humanism' and the Humanism of Karl Marx" in *The Question of Humanism: Challenges and Possibilities*, GOLDSTICK, Danny.
"Die Geschichte hat kein Libretto": Zu Isaiah Berlins Begriff des Nationalismus. RITTER, Henning.
A proposito di Stato e totaliarismo nel pensiero di Marx. SIENA, Robertomaria.
Ein Bedürfnis nach Schelling. BRAUN, Hermann.
The Categorical Nature of Mathematical Cognition. NYSANBAYEV, A N and KADYRZHANOV, R K.
Communism: The Philosophical Foundations. FLEW, Antony.
Coping with Complexity—Coping with Dialectics, in Theory and Practice (in German). THIEL, Rainer.
A Critique of Marx's Extension of the Principles of Dialectical Materialism into the Phenomena of Social Life. NYONG, Prince David.
De l'Idéologie comme correlat des termes idéologiste et idéologue. ZOLUA, Buenzey Maluenga.
Economie in de spiegel van de natuurwetenschappen. KUIPERS, Theo A F.
Economies of Time: On the Idea of Time in Marx's Political Economy. BOOTH, William James.
Erneuerung als Grundmechanismus der Evolution. EBELING, Werner.
Grandeur et limites du *Marx* de Michel Henry. CANTIN, Serge.
Habermas and Solidarity. FUNK, Nanette.
Hegel's *Logic* and Marx's Early Development. PRINCIPE, Michael A.
Hegel, Marx, and the Concept of Immanent Critique. BUCHWALTER, Andrew.
Hegel, Marx, Lukács: The Dialectic of Freedom and Necessity. DAY, Richard B.
Hegel, Marx, Nietzsche, and the Future of Self-Alienation. SCHACHT, Richard.
The Ideas of Karl Marx at a Turning Point in Human Civilization. PANTIN, I and PLIMAK, E.
The Ideological Impasse of Gorbachev's Perestrojka. KRIZAN, Mojmir.
India and the Theory of the Asiatic Mode of Production (in Hungarian). RENNER, Zsuzsanna.
The Intellectual Compatibility of Marx and Engels. HUNLEY, J D.
Is Karl Marx to Blame for "Barracks Socialism"?. BUTENKO, A P.
Ist die Naturphilosophie eine abgelegte Gestalt des modernen Geistes. WAHSNER, Renate.
Karl Marx and African Emancipatory Thought: A Critique of Marx's Euro-centric Metaphysics. SEREQUEBERHAN, Tsenay.
Markets and Morals. SMITH, G W.
Marx and Dialectics (in German). ADLER, Max.
Marx and Perestroika. ROCKMORE, Tom.
Marx and Russia. NAARDEN, Bruno.
Marx and the Problem of Conflicting Models of History. BEST, Steven.
Marx as a Social Historian. MAHON, Joseph.
Marx's 'Critique of Hegel's *Philosophy of Right*'. JACKSON, M W.
Marx's *Aufhebung* of Philosophy and the Foundations of Historical-Materialist Science. FRACCHIA, Joseph.
Marx's Historical Understanding of the Proletariat and Class in 19th-Century England. MAZLISH, Bruce.
Marx's Theory of Revolutionary Change. PANICHAS, George E and HOBART, Michael E.
Marx, Engels and Max Weber on Eastern Societies—With a Special Respect to China (in Hungarian). DRUCKER, György.
Marx, Nietzsche, and the "New Class". EVANS, Fred.
Marxism, Post-Marxism and the Implosion of Communism. STOJANOVIC, Svetozar.
The Marxist Conception of Tradition. STEPANYANTS, Marietta.
Methodological Individualism and Marx: Some Remarks on Jon Elster, Game Theory, and Other Things. WOLFF, Robert Paul.
Modernity, the Individual and Rationality in Marxism (Surrealism and Revolution). CLOUDSLEY, Tim.

MARX

New Studies on Hegel's Philosophy of Law, versus on the Dialectics of Hegel and Marx (in Hungarian). GÖHLER, Gerhard.
Notes sur utopie et marxisme. ARANTES, Urias Corrêa.
On Marx's Conception of Rationality. MULLICK, Mohini.
On the Coherence of Historical Materialism. NIELSEN, Kai.
Philosophiehistorische Forschung und historischer Materialismus. THOM, Martina.
The Post-Modern Challenge: From Marx to Nietzsche in the West German Alternative and Green Movement. BETZ, Hans-Georg.
Rationality and Social Labor in Marx. KHALIL, Elias L.
Rediscovering the Left. HOWARD, Dick.
Response to Robenstine's "The Dead Horse Phenomenon in Educational Theory". BROSIO, Richard.
The *Rezeptionsgeschichte* of the Paris Manuscripts. MAIDAN, Michael.
Rileggendo Marx: "diritti" e "bisogni". BADALONI, Nicola.
Die Rolle des Individuums und seine Beteiligung an gesellschaftlichen Prozessen. SCHLIWA, Harald and ZEDDIES, Helmut.
The Social Philosophy of Marxism: The Founders and the Present Day. SHEVCHENKO, V N.
Superestructura ideológica de las relaciones sociales. MÁRQUEZ FERNÁNDEZ, Alvaro B.
Theorising Ideas: *Idee* and *Vorstellung* from Kant to Hegel to Marx. CRISTAUDO, Wayne.
Two Qualms About Functionalist Marxism. DICKMAN, Joel.
The Unity of Theory and Practice in Historical Perspective. KRANCBERG, Sigmund.
Was Karl Marx a Social Scientist?. FLEW, Antony.
Was Marx a Socialist?. TSIPKO, A.
Werkzeugproduktion im Tierreich und menschliche Werkzeugproduktion. BEURTON, Peter.
Wittgenstein and Marx—Some Methodological Remarks (in German). RAATZSCH, Richard.
Zur inhaltlichen Bedeutung des Hegelschen "Schemas der Naturphilosophie" in den Epikurstudien des jungen Marx. MIELKE, Dietmar.
Zwischen Enttäuschung und Versöhnung: Hegel, die deutsche Misere und die Französiche Revolution. ARNDT, Andreas.

MARXISM

Art and Answerability: Early Philosophical Essays—M M Bakhtin. HOLQUIST, Michael (ed).
Between Freiburg and Frankfurt: Toward a Critical Ontology. DALLMAYR, Fred R.
Beyond Ethnocentrism: A Reconstruction of Marx's Concept of Science. MC KELVEY, Charles.
De l'épistémologie à la politique: La philosophie de l'histoire de Karl R Popper. RUELLAND, Jacques G.
False Consciousness. MEYERSON, Denise.
Hope and Its Hieroglyph: A Critical Decipherment of Ernst Bloch's "Principle of Hope". ROBERTS, Richard H.
Mannheim and Hungarian Marxism. GABEL, Joseph.
Marxism and Philosophy in the Twentieth Century: A Defense of Vulgar Marxism. HUDELSON, Richard.
Models and Concepts of Ideology. RITSERT, Jürgen.
Philosophy and the Spontaneous Philosophy of the Scientists and Other Essays. ELLIOTT, Gregory (ed).
Resurrecting Marx: The Analytical Marxists on Freedom, Exploitation, and Justice. GORDON, David.
Socialism, Feminism and Philosophy: A Radical Philosophy Reader. SAYERS, Sean (ed).
"Childe's Early Marxism" in *Critical Traditions in Contemporary Archaeology*, GATHERCOLE, Peter.
"The Defence of a Social System Against Its Ideology: A Case Study" in *The Social Horizon of Knowledge*, NOWAK, Leszek.
"Dialectics, Critical Inquiry, and Archaeology" in *Critical Traditions in Contemporary Archaeology*, SAITTA, Dean J.
"Louis Althusser and Joseph D Sneed: A Strange Encounter in Philosophy of Science?" in *Imre Lakatos and Theories of Scientific Change*, BALTAS, Aristides.
"Marx Against Morality" in *A Companion to Ethics*, WOOD, Allen.
"Marxian Ideology and Causality" in *Perspectives on Ideas and Reality*, ROCKMORE, Tom.
"Marxism and Nuclear Deterrence" in *Issues in War and Peace: Philosophical Inquiries*, HAMPSCH, George H.
"Marxism, Humanism, and Ecology" in *The Question of Humanism: Challenges and Possibilities*, LAWLER, James and ORUDJEV, Zaid.
"Models of Historical Trajectory: An Assessment of Gidden's Critique of Marxism" in *Social Theory of Modern Societies: Anthony Giddens and His Critics*, WRIGHT, Erik Olin.
"Postmodernism and (Post)Marxism" in *Postmodernism—Philosophy and the Arts (Continental Philosophy III)*, O'NEILL, J.
"Scientific Philosophical and Sociopolitical Aspects of the Work of Mario Bunge" in *Studies on Mario Bunge's "Treatise"*, ROSENTHAL, Erwin.
"Some Marxism Themes in the Age of Information" in *Perspectives on Ideas and Reality*, NYÍRI, J C.
Alienation, Schools, and Society. ZHANG, Wei Rose.
Art and Aesthetics and the Crisis of Culture. MORAWSKI, Stefan.
Bakhtin's Marxist Formalism. MC BRIDE, William Thomas.
Between Necessity and Superabundance: Meta-economic Reflections on Marxism. WALDENFELS, Bernhard.
Can Marxism Help Biology?. KASSIOLA, Joel.
Can the Discussion Partners Trust Each Other?. FÖLDESI, Tamás.
Catholic and Marxist Views on Human Development. MC GOVERN, Arthur F.
Christians and Marxist Theory of Human Liberation. KOWALCZYK, Stanislaw.
Christians and Marxists in Dialogue Building Confidence in a Time of Crisis. WEST, Charles C.
Critical Activity and Ethics: The Problem of Generalization. KANIOWSKI, Andrzej M.
Critical Marxism as an Historical Process of Society and Science (in German). SANDKÜHLER, Hans Jörg.
A Critique of Marx's Extension of the Principles of Dialectical Materialism into the Phenomena of Social Life. NYONG, Prince David.
A Critique of One Interpretation of Practical Materialism. DANSHEN, Huang.
Die DDR und ihre Philosophen: Über Voraussetzungen einer Urteilsbildung. RUBEN, Peter.
Democracy and Socialism: Philosophical *Aporiae*. CUNNINGHAM, Frank.
The Dialectic of National and Universal Commitments in Christian-Marxist Dialogue. WILL, James E.
Dialogo sobre humanismo y Marxismo (primera parte). SILVA CAMARENA, Juan Manuel.
Dialogue—A New Utopia?. GÓRNIAK-KOCIKOWSKA, Krystyna.
The Divided Machine: Capitalist Crisis and the Organization of Labor. TURCHETTO, Maria and ESPOSITO, Joan.
Division and Difference in the "Discipline" of Economics. AMARIGLIO, Jack and RESNICK, Stephen and WOLFF, Richard.
Domination and Moral Struggle: the Philosophical Heritage of Marxism Reviewed. HONNETH, Axel.
European Counterimages: Problems of Periodization and Historical Memory. DINER, Dan.
An Examination of Marxist Doctrine in the Traditions of Russian Religious Philosophy. STEPANOVA, E A.
Explaining Historical Development: A Marxian Critique of Cohen's Historical Materialism. WARREN, Paul.
Failure of a Renaissance (Why It Is Impossible to Remain a Marxist in East Central Europe). VAJDA, Mihaly.
Freud, Marxism and the Frankfurt School (in Serbo-Croation). FLEGO, Gvozden.
From Class Struggle to Struggle without Classes?. BALIBAR, Etienne.
From Hegel to Lukacs: The Problem of Ontology from the Point of View of Social and Natural Theory (in German). MOCEK, Reinhard.
From Historical Marxisms to Historical Materialism: Toward the Theory of Ideology. MOCNIK, Rastko.
From Patriarchal Socialism to Socialist Democracy: Thoughts on a New Theory of Society. MOCEK, Reinhard.
Fundamental Question of Philosophy: Remarks on the Pending Philosophical Reappraisal of the Past in the GDR (in German). SCHRÖDER, Richard.
Georg Lukács and Stalinism (in German). TIETZ, Udo.
Global Injustices. MC BRIDE, William L.
Gramsci, Gentile and the Theory of the Ethical State in Italy. SCHECTER, Darrow.
Grundlegende Aspekte zur Problematik von Erkenntnis und Praxis. FORSCHE, Joachim.
Historicisms New and Old: "Charles Dickens" Meets Marxism, Feminism, and West Coast Foucault. NEWTON, Judith.
Historizing contra fetishizing—The Progress of Modern Technology in W Benjamin's Aesthetic Reflexion (in German). WAGNER, Gerhard.
A Hungarian Christian-Marxist Dialogue and Its Lessons. LUKÁCS, József.
Is It Practical Ontology or Is It the Dialectical Materialist Theory of Material Monism?. JINFU, Wang.
Italian Marxism and Philosophy of Culture (in Polish). PAPULI, Giovanni.
J G A Pocock's Republicanism and Political Theory: A Critique and Reinterpretation. SHAPIRO, Ian.
Ka-Meh und das alte Neue—über epistemische Krise und Emanzipation. SANDKÜHLER, Hans Jörg.
Kommunismus—Utopie und Wirklichkeit. HAVEMANN, Robert.
Lenin and Philosophy: Should We Not Pose This Problem Anew?. VOLODIN, A.
Liberation Theology and the Interpretation of Political Violence. SONTAG, Frederick.
El lugar de las superestructuras y los intelectuales en la filosofía política de Gramsci. RUIZ, Angel.
Lukács on the Ontology of Social Existence and Marx's Understanding of Society (in German). LENDVAI, Ferenc L.
Marx and Dialectics (in German). ADLER, Max.
The Marxian Ethics. SARKER, Sunil Kumar.
Marxism and Contemporary Political Philosophy. COHEN, G A.
Marxism and Social Change: Some Theoretical Reflections. TRIPATHY, Laxman Kumar.

MARXISM

Marxism as the Foundation of Philosophies of Science: *The Case of G Lukács' Ontology of Social Being*. TUCHANSKA, Barbara.
Marxism in the USSR Today. FISK, Milton.
Marxism, Post-Marxism and the Implosion of Communism. STOJANOVIC, Svetozar.
El marxismo, ciencia, ideología, gnosis?. BESANÇON, Alain.
A Marxist Approach to the Concept of Being/Becoming Human. GOLUBOVIC, Zagorka.
Marxist Literary Aesthetics. MILLER, Seumas.
Marxisten und Christen für eine gerechte, friedliche Welt. NEHRING, Hartmut.
Die Metaphysik der Kritik: Zum Verhältnis von Metaphysik und Erfahrung bei Max Horkheimer und Theodor W Adorno. RECKI, Birgit.
Monadic Marxism: A Critique of Elster's Methodological Individualism. MOGGACH, Douglas.
Notes sur utopie et marxisme. ARANTES, Urias Corrêa.
On J L Fischer's Reflections About Categories of Dialectic Materialism (in Czechoslovakian). TOSENOVSKY, Ludvik.
On Marx's Conception of Rationality. MULLICK, Mohini.
On Some Unsettled Questions Touching the Character of Marxism, Especially as Philosophy. SUCHTING, W A.
On the Philosophy of the Czech Avant-garde, Part II (in Czechoslovakian). STROHS, S.
The On-Going Deconstruction of Marxism-Leninism. BUCHHOLZ, Arnold and SWIDERSKI, E M.
Die Philosophie im einen Deutschland. HENRICH, Dieter.
Possibility of Dialogic Encounter of Religious and Philosophical Humanitas (in Serbo-Croatian). SKLEDAR, Nikola.
Post-Modernism as the Lesser Evil: Criticism and Agreement in Lyotard's "Widerstreit" ("Conflict") (in German). KRÜGER, Hans-Peter.
The Principle of Unity of Theory and Practice in Marxism: A Critique. DIMITRAKOS, D.
The Problem of Atheism in Recent Soviet Publications. DAHM, Helmut.
Problemas lógicos en el relativismo ético. CAMACHO, Luis A.
Recent Work on Ethical Relativism. STEWART, Robert M and THOMAS, Lynn L.
Reflections on the Eastern European Revolutions: The God that Failed. MAZLISH, Bruce.
Reinvigorating the International Christian-Marxist Dialogue. MOJZES, Paul.
Responsibility—A Challenge in Terms of Philosophy (in German). RÖSEBERG, Ulrich.
Revolution, Civil Society and Democracy. ARATO, Andrew.
Sartre and his Successors: Existential Marxism and Postmodernism at Our *Fin de Siecle*. MC BRIDE, William L.
Sartre's onuitgevoerde project: de Robespierre-biografie. DETHIER, Hubert.
Self-Management in the Context of the Disintegration of "Reali-Existing" Socialism. STANOJEVIC, Miroslav.
Seven Types of Obloquy: Travesties of Marxism. GERAS, Norman.
Some Aspects of the Relationship Between the Theory of Socialism and the Perception of an Era (in German). BRIE, André (and others).
Some Basic Problems of a Political Theory of Modern Socialism (in German). SEGERT, Dieter.
Some Reflections on Post-Marxism and Post-Christianity: A Response to Professor Arthur Mc Govern. STOJANOVIC, Svetozar.
The Sources of Stalinism. TSIPKO, A.
The State of Studies on Western Philosophy in China. FANG-TONG, Liu.
Subjectivisation as Control or Resistance: An Examination of Reformation Theology and Marxism. PATTMAN, Rob.
A Survey of Critical Theories of "Western Marxism". YUJIN, Zhao.
Tareas y métodos en la ética del desarrollo. GOULET, Denis.
The Common European Home (in German). FEIEREIS, Konrad.
The Development of a Concept of Modern Socialism: Theses under Discussion (in German). BRIE, Michael.
The Differences Between the Capitalist and the Modern Society (in German). KRÜGER, Hans-Peter.
The Enticing Thing About Stalinism (in German). PÄTZOLT, Harald.
The Party's Claim to Power: The Power of Knowledge in "Real Socialism" (in German). MARZ, Lutz.
The Pros and Cons of Trotsky's Marxism (in German). HEDELER, Wladislaw.
The Specific Features of Cognition Progress in Philosophy: Demonstrated by the Example of Max Adler (in German). MÖCKEL, Christian.
The Theological Secret of Th W Adorno's Aesthetic Theory (in German). HOLZ, Hans Heinz.
Theology of Liberation and Marxism (in Serbo-Croation). ORSOLIC, Marko.
The Theoretical Premises of Scientific Socialism and Its Mode of Thought. YUQUAN, Tao.
Thoughts on the Future of Marxism. LEVINE, Andrew.
Todor Pavlov (1890-1977)—The Generalization of Reflection (in German). HOLZ, Hans Heinz.
Trotsky's Dialectic. THATCHER, Ian D.
Two Aspects of the Christian-Marxist Dialogue: A Protestant Response. FRITZSCHE, Helmut.
Two Designs of Universal History. KANTOR, K M.
Two Views of the Revolution: Gramsci and Sorel, 1916-1920. SCHECTER, Darrow.
The Unity of Theory and Practice in Historical Perspective. KRANCBERG, Sigmund.
Welchen Platz kann die Philosophie künftig in unserem Lande beanspruchen und vor welchen Aufgaben steht sie?. RÜDIGER, Wolfgang.
Wissenschaftsphilosophie in der DDR—Versuch einer kritischen Betrachtung. HÖRZ, Herbert.

MARXIST(S)

"Between Dewey and Gramsci: Unger's Emancipatory Experimentalism" in *Critique and Construction: A Symposium on Roberto Unger's "Politics"*, WEST, Cornel.
The Dead Horse Phenomenon in Educational Theory. ROBENSTINE, Clark.
Law and Culture: The Conception of Legal Culture (in Polish). GRYKO, Czeslaw.
Marxist Historians and the Question of Class in the French Revolution. AMARIGLIO, Jack and NORTON, Bruce.

MASARYK, T

Aesthetics of T G Masaryk (in Czechoslovakian). HLAVACEK, Lubos.
Aesthetics of T G Masaryk II (in Czechoslovakian). HLAVACEK, Lubos.
Masaryk's "Anthropism" (in Czechoslovakian). NOVY, Lubomir.
Masaryk's Religious Thinking (in Czechoslovakian). FUNDA, Otakar A.
T G Masaryk—A Modern Thinker (in Czechoslovakian). OPAT, Jaroslav.
The Philosophical Invariables of Masaryk's Thinking (in Czechoslovakian). SROVNAL, Jindrich.

MASCULINITY

Contemporary Perspectives on Masculinity: Men, Women, and Politics in Modern Society. CLATTERBAUGH, Kenneth.

MASLOW, A

The Authentic Self: Toward a Philosophy of Personality. LACENTRA, Walter.

MASS

Adventures of the Concept of Mass and Matter. HELLER, Michael.
Form and Funk: The Aesthetic Challenge of Popular Art. SHUSTERMAN, Richard.

MASS TERM(S)

"The Mass Noun Hypothesis and the Part-Whole Analysis of the White Horse Dialogue" in *Chinese Texts and Philosophical Contexts*, HARBSMEIER, Christoph.

MASSES

"The Intellectuals and the Imitation of the Masses" in *The Political Responsibility of Intellectuals*, LOCK, Grahame.
Leben als Passion: Elias Canettis "Masse und Macht" als Beitrag zum Begreifen der Moderne. DIETZSCH, Steffen.

MASTURBATION

Dr Chipley's Warning. WHITE, Ronald.

MATCHING

Phenomenal Qualities and the Nontransitivity of Matching. BURGESS, John A.

MATERIAL IMPLICATION

Material Implication and Entailment. CENIZA, Claro R.
Problems of the Notions of 'Entailment' and 'Material Implication'. MULAY, Sharmila R.

MATERIAL OBJECT(S)

Material Beings. VAN INWAGEN, Peter.
"The Appearance of a Material Object" in *Philosophical Perspectives, 4: Action Theory and Philosophy of Mind, 1990*, O'SHAUGHNESSY, Brian.
Parthood and Persistence. KAZMI, Ali Akhtar.

MATERIALISM

see also Dialectical Materialism, Historical Materialism, Matter
Diderot's Dream. ANDERSON, Wilda.
George Santayana y la Ironia de la Materia. IZUZQUIZA, Ignacio.
The Idea of the Miraculous: The Challenge to Science and Religion. WILLIAMS, T C.
Locke and French Materialism. YOLTON, John W.
The Many Dimensions of the Human Person. STEGER, E Ecker.
Sensations: A Defense of Type Materialism. HILL, Christopher S.
Thomas Hobbes' Theory of Obligation: A Modern Interpretation. FORSBERG, Ralph P.
"Aristotle's Philosophy of Mind" in *Psychology (Companions to Ancient Thought: 2)*, IRWIN, T H.
"O inimigo da liberdade: sobre o sentido do materialismo para Fichte" in *Dinâmica do Pensar: Homenagem a Oswaldo Market*, BARATA-MOURA, José.
"What Is the 'Subjectivity' of the Mental?" in *Philosophical Perspectives, 4: Action Theory and Philosophy of Mind, 1990*, LYCAN, William G.
"Non-Scientific Realism" about Propositional Attitudes as a Response to Eliminativist Arguments. HANNAN, Barbara.
A Critique of One Interpretation of Practical Materialism. DANSHEN, Huang.
Eliminative Materialism and Substantive Commitments. NELSON, Mark T.
Entwurf eines Klassifikationsschemas für philosophische Positionen. WIMMER, Franz.
Lenin and Philosophy: Should We Not Pose This Problem Anew?. VOLODIN, A.

MATERIALISM

L'odissea dell'ateismo e del nichilismo. FABRO, Cornelio.
Over de ambivalente rol van de theoriegeladenheidsthese in Rorty's 'overwinning' van de traditie. KRIBBE, Pamela.
La prima e seconda edizione della "Geschichte des Materialismus" di Friedrich Albert Lange. COGNETTI, Giuseppe.
La prima edizione sovietica di Solov'ev. MASTROIANNI, Giovanni.
Der psychophysische Materialismus in der Perspektive Kants und Wittgensteins. MENDONÇA, W P.
Radical Enlightenment and Freethinkers (in German). POTT, Martin.
Spinoza's Materialist Ethics: The Education of Desire. RAVVEN, Heidi M.
Substrative Materialism. KERR-LAWSON, Angus.
Tecnología y sociedad. HERRERA, Rodolfo.
The Hopeless Realist (in Serbo-Croatian). WIGGERHAUS, Rolf.
Two Qualms About Functionalist Marxism. DICKMAN, Joel.
Where Does the Self-Refutation Objection Take Us?. RAMSEY, William.

MATERIALITY

Introducing Persons: Theories and Arguments in the Philosophy of Mind. CARRUTHERS, Peter.
Materiality and Aquinas' Natural Philosophy: A Reply to Johnson. KNASAS, John F X.

MATHEMATICS

see also Algebra, Geometry
Brouwer's Intuitionism (Studies in the History and Philosophy of Mathematics, Vol 2). VAN STIGT, W P.
The Chain of Change: A Study of Aristotle's "Physics" VII. WARDY, Robert.
Computability, Complexity, Logic. BÖRGER, E.
Foundations of Social Theory. COLEMAN, James S.
Frege and Other Philosophers. DUMMETT, Michael.
Frege in Perspective. WEINER, Joan.
Gödel's Theorem in Focus. SHANKER, S G (ed).
John Craige's Mathematical Principles of Christian Theology. NASH, Richard.
Logic, Methodology and Philosophy of Science, VIII. FENSTAD, J E (ed).
Logic, Methodology and Philosophy of Science, VII. MARCUS, Ruth Barcan (ed).
The Logical Basis of Metaphysics. DUMMETT, Michael.
Mathematics and the Image of Reason. TILES, Mary E.
Las paradojas del Infinito. BOLZANO, Bernard.
Parts of Classes. LEWIS, David.
Philosophical Papers: F P Ramsey. MELLOR, D H (ed).
Physicalism in Mathematics. IRVINE, Andrew D (ed).
Science and Reason. KYBURG JR, Henry E.
Some Truer Method. DURHAM, Frank (ed).
Structures in Mathematical Theories: Reports of the San Sebastian International Symposium, 1990. DÍEZ, Amparo (ed).
Theories of Science in Society. COZZENS, Susan E (ed).
Three Great Traditions. PEDERSEN, Olaf.
Wittgenstein's Lectures on the Foundations of Mathematics, Cambridge 1939. DIAMOND, Cora (ed).
"Beliefs About Mathematical Objects" in *Physicalism in Mathematics*, RESNIK, Michael D.
"Criticisms of the Usual Rationale for Validity in Mathematics" in *Physicalism in Mathematics*, DAVIS, Chandler.
"Knowledge of Mathematical Objects" in *Physicalism in Mathematics*, PAPINEAU, David.
"Making a World of Precision: Newton and the Construction of a Quantitiative World View" in *Some Truer Method*, WESTFALL, Richard S.
"Mario Bunge's Philosophy of Logic and Mathematics" in *Studies on Mario Bunge's "Treatise"*, MIRÓ, Francisco.
"Mathematics and Modality" in *Meaning and Method: Essays in Honor of Hilary Putnam*, FIELD, Hartry.
"Modal-Structural Mathematics" in *Physicalism in Mathematics*, HELLMAN, Geoffrey.
"Newton's 'Mathematical Way' a Century After the *Principia*" in *Some Truer Method*, HANKINS, Thomas L.
"Nominalism" in *Physicalism in Mathematics*, HALE, Bob.
"On the Relationship Between Mathematics and Physics" in *Studies on Mario Bunge's "Treatise"*, GARCÍA-SUCRE, Máximo.
"Ontological Commitment: Thick and Thin" in *Meaning and Method: Essays in Honor of Hilary Putnam*, HODES, Harold T.
"Π In the Sky" in *Physicalism in Mathematics*, BROWN, James Robert.
"Proofs and Refutations: A Reassessment" in *Imre Lakatos and Theories of Scientific Change*, ANAPOLITANOS, D A.
"Quine" in *Perspectives on Quine*, DREBEN, Burton.
"Reflections on Hilbert's Program" in *Acting and Reflecting: The Interdisciplinary Turn in Philosophy*, SIEG, Wilfried.
A Note on the Nature of Mathematical Thinking (in Polish). LUBANSKI, M.
Argumentation—Distributed or Monological?. BARTH, E M.
El azar objetivo como medida matemática de desorden. MARTÍNEZ, Sergio.
Die Bedeutung der Mathematik Für die Philosophie Schopenhauers. RADBRUCH, Knut.
Boskovic's Mathematical Conception of Continuity and the Differentiability of Function (in Serbo-Croatian). STIPANIC, Ernest.
Boskovic's Philosophy of Mathematics (in Serbo-Croatian). HOMANN, Frederick A.
Brouwerian Intuitionism. DETLEFSEN, Michael.
Bruno e la matematica a lui contemporanea: In margine al "De Minimo". AQUILECCHIA, Giovanni.
Il carteggio Xavier Léon: corrispondenti italiana. QUILICI, Leana and RAGGHIANTI, Renzo.
The Categorical Nature of Mathematical Cognition. NYSANBAYEV, A N and KADYRZHANOV, R K.
Charles S Peirce's Theory of Infinitesimals. LEVY, Stephen H.
El cincuentenario de los *Grundlagen der Mathematik* de Hilbert y Bernays. RAGGIO, Andrés R.
Computation and Mathematical Empiricism. RESNIK, Michael D.
The Concept of Mathematical Truth. ROTA, Gian-Carlo.
Construction and the Role of Schematism in Kant's Philosophy of Mathematics (also in Portuguese). WINTERBOURNE, A T.
The Continuous and the Discrete: Leibniz Versus Berkeley. ANAPOLITANOS, D A.
The Dating of Rule IV-B in Descartes's *Regulae ad directionem ingenii*. VAN DE PITTE, Frederick P.
De lógica y matemática o donde situar el mundo matemático. DE LORENZO, Javier.
The Development of Modern Mathematics and Plato's Parable of the Cave. MAURIN, Krzysztof.
Dialectic and Diagonalization. KADVANY, John.
Erasing and Redrawing the Number Line: An Exercise in Rationality. SPARROW, Edward G.
Estructuras y representaciones. DE LA SIENRA, Adolfo García.
Eudoxos and Dedekind: On the Ancient Greek Theory of Ratios and its Relation to Modern Mathematics. STEIN, Howard.
Expressions versus Numbers. WETZEL, Linda.
Filosofía y teoría general de sistemas en el pensamiento de A Rapoport. SAXE FERNÁNDEZ, Eduardo E.
Formalisme et intuitionnisme en philosophie des mathématiques. LARGEAULT, Jean.
Frege and Husserl on Number. TIESZEN, Richard.
From the Logic of Mathematical Discovery to the Methodology of Scientific Research Programmes. YUXIN, Zheng.
Generalizing Classical and Effective Model Theory in Theories of Operations and Classes. MANCOSU, Paolo.
Der Harmonie-Gedanke im frühen Mittelalter. BEIERWALTES, Werner.
Husserl's Philosophy of Science and the Semantic Approach. MORMANN, Thomas.
Infinity in Mathematics: Is Cantor Necessary?. FEFERMAN, Solomon.
Intorno all'autofondazione delle norme: Ragione formale e principio razionale tra logica e diritto. SCIACCA, Fabrizio.
Intuitionistic Mathematics and Wittgenstein. GONZALEZ, Wenceslao J.
Is Philosophy Detrimental to Mathematics Education?. LUZZATTO, Stefano.
Is There Completeness in Mathematics after Gödel?. HINTIKKA, Jaakko.
Johan Jacob Ferguson, geb um 1630 im Haag(?), gest vor dem 24 November 1706, vermutlich am 6 Oktober 1691 in Amsterdam. VAN MAANEN, Jan A.
Kant on Concepts and Intuitions in the Mathematical Sciences. FRIEDMAN, Michael.
Le Kantisme de la théorie cantorienne de l'infini. BACHTA, Abdelkader.
Kitcher and Kant. BHAVE, S M.
Kitcher's Circumlocutionary Structuralism. HAND, Michael.
L'épistémologie mathématique de Gonseth dans la perspective du pragmatisme de Peirce. HEINZMANN, Gerhard.
Locke on Mathematical Knowledge. CICOVACKI, Predrag.
Logic and Empiricism. BOSTOCK, David.
The Logic of Impossible Quantities. SHERRY, David.
La matemática: certeza y verdad. CAÑÓN LOYES, Camino.
A Mathematical A Priorist Answers Philip Kitcher. NORTON-SMITH, Thomas M.
Mathematical Expressibility, Perceptual Relativity, and Secondary Qualities. PEREBOOM, Derk.
Mathematical Modelling and Constrastive Explanation. MORTON, Adam.
Mathematical Physics and Elementary Logic. MUNDY, Brent.
Mathematical Statistics and Metastatistical Analysis. RIVADULLA, Andrés.
Mathematics and Oliver Twist. MADDY, Penelope.
Mathematics and Philosophy: The Story of a Misunderstanding. ROTA, GianCarlo.
Mathematics Without Truth (A Reply to Maddy). FIELD, Hartry.
Mathématiques et ontologie: les symétries en physique. BOUTOT, Alain.
Les mathématiques, la biologie et le statut scientifique de la philosophie pour Bergson. SOULEZ, Philippe.
Die Mathematisierung als Konstruktion theoretischer Denkformen in der Abfolge naturwissenschaftlicher Weltbilder. GÖTTLICHER, Gerd.
The Meaning of Mathematical Expressions: Does Philosophy Shed Any Light on Psychology?. ERNEST, Paul.
Meanings in Ordinary Language and in Mathematics. THOMAS, R S D.
The Measurement Problem: Some "Solutions". ALBERT, David Z and LOEWER, Barry.
Metalogic and Modality. FIELD, Hartry.

MATHEMATICS
Never Say "Never"! On the Communication Problem between Intuitionism and Classicism. HELLMAN, Geoffrey.
Un nouveau début à l'édition léonine des oeuvres de saint Thomas d'Aquin. HISSETTE, Roland.
On Cauchy's Notion of Infinitesimal. CUTLAND, Nigel J (and others).
On Some Alleged Difficulties in the Interpretation of Quantum Mechanics. DIEKS, Dennis.
On the "Arriving at Principles from Numbers" Method of Thought in the Late-Ming, Early-Qing Period. WEIPING, Chen.
On the Status of Proofs by Contradiction in the XVIIth Century. MANCOSU, Paolo.
Philosophical Reflections on the Foundations of Mathematics. COUTURE, Jocelyne and LAMBEK, Joachim.
La philosophie du chaos. BOUTOT, Alain.
Plato's Ontology and the Role of Mathematics in the Description of Nature. ZYCINSKI, Joseph.
Platonism and Anti-Platonism in Nicholas of Cusa's Philosophy of Mathematics. HÖSLE, Vittorio.
Platonism from an Empiricist Point of View. LUCE, Lila.
A Problem for Intuitionism: The Apparent Possibility of Performing Infinitely Many Tasks in a Finite Time. MOORE, A W.
Progress in Mathematics and Other Arts. SEDZIWY, Stanislaw.
La question de l'être et du non-être des objets mathématiques chez Plotin et Jamblique. O'MEARA, Dominic.
Relative Consistency and Accessible Domains. SIEG, Wilfried.
Représentation structurelle de la relation partie-tout. STAHL, Gérold.
Small Sets. HAZEN, A P.
Sobre la no paradoja de un cretense. WILSON, Jack L.
Some Objections To Garavaso's Wittgenstein. HUMPHREY, John A.
Straight Talk about Sets. JUBIEN, Michael.
The Structuralist View of Mathematical Objects. PARSONS, Charles.
Structure and Ontology. SHAPIRO, Stewart.
Sur le vague en mathématiques. GRANGER, G G.
Taking Mathematics Seriously?. ZYCINSKI, Joseph.
Tractatus: Críticas al logicismo. NUÑO, Juan A.
Uno sguardo sulla filosofia americana contemporanea. CENTRONE, Marino.
What is Empirical in Mathematics?. PETERSON, Philip L.
Where Do Natural Numbers Come From?. HODES, Harold T.
Wittgenstein on 2, 2, 2...: The Opening of Remarks on the Foundations of Mathematics. FLOYD, Juliet.
Wittgenstein on Mathematical Proof. WRIGHT, Crispin.
Wittgenstein's Philosophies of Mathematics. GERRARD, Steve.
Yet More on *Meno* 82a-85d. FOWLER, D H.

MATHEMATIZATION
Quantum Physics and Logical Truth (in Italian). GIANNETTO, Enrico.
Vacuity. RAMER, Alexis Manaster.

MATILAL, B
Professor Matilal on Some Topics of Indian Philosophy. BHATTACHARYYA, Sibajiban.

MATRIARCHY
The Great Goddess and the Aistian Mythical World. VYCINAS, Vincent.

MATRIX(-CES)
Characterization of Prime Numbers in Lukasiewicz's Logical Matrix. KARPENKO, Alexander S.
Diagonalization and Fixed Points. TONELLA, Guido.
Fixed Points and Diagonal Method. NEGRI, Maurizio.
An Integer-Valued Matrix Characteristic for Implicational *S*5. ULRICH, Dolph.
A Note on Matrices for Systems of Nonsense-Logics. HALKOWSKA, Katarzyna.
Paraconsistency and the J-Systems of Arruda and da Costa. URBAS, Igor.
Q-Consequence Operation. MALINOWSKI, Grzegorz.
Some Modal Logics Based on a Three-Valued Logic. MORIKAWA, Osamu.

MATTER
see also Materialism, Substance(s)
Evolutionary Instability: Logical and Material Aspects of a Unified Theory of Biosocial Evolution. GEIGER, Gebhard.
George Santayana y la Ironia de la Materia. IZUZQUIZA, Ignacio.
Introduction to the Philosophy of Nature. HETZLER, Florence M.
Locke and French Materialism. YOLTON, John W.
Matter and Memory. BERGSON, Henri.
"The 'Essential Properties' of Matter, Space, and Time: Comments on Michael Friedman" in *Philosophical Perspectives on Newtonian Science*, DI SALLE, Robert.
"Kant and Newton: Why Gravity Is Essential to Matter" in *Philosophical Perspectives on Newtonian Science*, FRIEDMAN, Michael.
"Philosophical Perspectives on Newtonian Science" in *Philosophical Perspectives on Newtonian Science*, HUGHES, R I G.
Adventures of the Concept of Mass and Matter. HELLER, Michael.
Aristotelian and Whiteheadian Conceptions of Actuality: I. FETZ, Reto Luzius and FELT, James W.
Boskovic's Philosophical Understanding of Matter (in Serbo-Croatian). STOJKOVIC, Andrija B K.
Discussione di alcune questioni di cosmologia neo-tomista. BLANDINO, Giovanni.
A New Theory of the Relationship of Mind and Matter. BOHM, David.
Origen de la inversión kantiana del binomio materia-forma. SOTO BRUNA, Maria Jesus.
Thomas d'Aquin a-t-il tente d'exprimer le principe d'individuation à l'intérieur des proprietés.... CASPAR, Philippe.

MATTIEU, V
La speranza nel giusnaturalismo. TUSA, Carlo.

MATURATION
"A Critical Consideration of the Lakatosian Concepts: 'Mature' and 'Immature' Science" in *Imre Lakatos and Theories of Scientific Change*, METAXOPOULOS, Emilio.

MATURITY
J S Mill's Concept of Maturity as the Criterion in Determining Children's Eligibility for Rights. KIM, Ki Su.
Postcritical Religion and the Latent Freud. KEISER, R Melvin.

MAUDLIN, T
The Causal History of Computational Activity: Maudlin and Olympia. BARNES, Eric.

MAUTHNER, F
Los límites de mi lenguaje—los límites de mi mundo. KLOYBER, Christian.

MAXIM(S)
Kant's Theory of Freedom. ALLISON, Henry E.
Kants Kategorischer Imperativ als Leitfaden humaner Praxis. NISTERS, Thomas.
A Philosophy of Morals. HELLER, Agnes.

MAXIMALITY
Common Logic of Binary Connectives Has Finite Maximality Degree (Preliminary Report). RAUTENBERG, Wolfgang.

MAXIMIZATION
The Biological Justification of Ethics: A Best-Case Scenario. ROSENBERG, Alexander.
Constrained Maximization. SOBEL, Jordan Howard.
The Paradox of Group Beneficence. OTSUKA, Michael.

MAXWELL
Particles and Waves: Historical Essays in the Philosophy of Science. ACHINSTEIN, Peter.
A Comment on Maxwell's Resolution of the Wave/Particle Dilemma. SQUIRES, Euan J.
On Relativity Theory and Openness of the Future. STEIN, Howard.

MAY, H
The Enlightenment in American Law II: The Constitution. RECK, Andrew J.

MAYO, D
A Reply to Mayo's Criticisms of Urbach's "Randomization and the Design of Experiments". URBACH, Peter.

MAYR, E
Van Rooijen and Mayr versus Popper: Is the Universe Causally Closed?. SETTLE, Tom.

MCBRIDE, W
Response to Berlin and McBride. RENICK, Timothy M.

MCCLENNEN, E
McClennen's Early Cooperative Solution to the Prisoner's Dilemma. MAC INTOSH, Duncan.

MCCLOSKEY, D
How to Get Rid of Your Expensive Philosopher of Science and Still Keep Control Over the Fuzzing Conversation of Mankind. VISKER, Rudi.

MCCULLOCH, G
Better the Union Theory. HONDERICH, Ted.

MCDOUGALL, W
Hypnosis and the Philosophy of Mind. HAIGHT, Mary.

MCDOWELL, J
Demonstrative Content: A Reply to John McDowell. PEACOCKE, Christopher.
McDowell Against Criterial Knowledge. ROBINSON, Paul.
True and False Pleasures. LOVIBOND, Sabina.

MCGEE, V
Probabilistic Dependence Among Conditionals. LANCE, Mark.

MCGINN, C
McGinn on Concept Scepticism and Kripke's Sceptical Argument. SARTORELLI, Joseph.
Why Shouldn't We Be Able to Solve the Mind-Body Problem?. KIRK, Robert.

MCGUINNESS, B
De jonge Wittgenstein (1889-1921): Denken als ethos. DE DIJN, H.

MCTAGGART
Modality and Mellor's McTaggart. CRESSWELL, M J.
Worlds Enough for Time. BIGELOW, John.

MEAD
Creativity in George Herbert Mead. GUNTER, Pete A Y (ed).
"Comment on David L Miller's 'Consciousness, the Attitude of the Individual and Perspectives'" in *Creativity in George Herbert Mead*, MORRIS, Charles.
"Comment on David L Miller's 'Consciousness, the Attitude of the Individual and Perspectives'" in *Creativity in George Herbert Mead*, DUNCAN, Hugh D.
"Comment on David L Miller's 'Consciousness, the Attitude of the Individual and Perspectives'" in *Creativity in George Herbert Mead*, LEE, Harold N.
"Comment on David L Miller's 'Consciousness, the Attitude of the Individual and Perspectives'" in *Creativity in George Herbert Mead*, RECK, Andrew J.
"Comment on David L Miller's 'Consciousness, the Attitude of the Individual and Perspectives'" in *Creativity in George Herbert Mead*, BROYER, John Albin.
"Consciousness, the Attitude of the Individual and Perspectives" in *Creativity in George Herbert Mead*, MILLER, David L.
"Response to Comments on 'Consciousness, the Attitude of the Individual and Perspectives'" in *Creativity in George Herbert Mead*, MILLER, David L.
Role Taking, Corporeal Intersubjectivity, and Self: Mead and Merleau-Ponty. BOURGEOIS, Patrick L and ROSENTHAL, Sandra B.
Scientific Time and the Temporal Sense of Human Existence: Merleau-Ponty and Mead. BOURGEOIS, Patrick L and ROSENTHAL, Sandra B.
The Operation of Values: Knowledge in the Conception of G H Mead (in Polish). HETMANSKI, Marek.

MEAN(S)
"The Pursuit of Ideals and the Legitimation of Means" in *Perspectives on Ideas and Reality*, GARVER, Newton.

MEANING
see also Referring, Semantics
Acts of Meaning. BRUNER, Jerome.
The Dice-Playing God: Reflections on Life in a Post-Modern Age. KRIEGLSTEIN, Werner.
The Foundations of Linguistic Theory: Selected Writings of Roy Harris. LOVE, Nigel (ed).
Frege and Other Philosophers. DUMMETT, Michael.
Good and Evil: An Absolute Conception. GAITA, Raimond.
Has Semantics Rested on a Mistake?. WETTSTEIN, Howard.
Information, Semantics and Epistemology. VILLANUEVA, Enrique (ed).
The Kernel of Truth in Freud. LAWTON, Philip.
The Logical Basis of Metaphysics. DUMMETT, Michael.
Meaning and Mental Representation. CUMMINS, Robert.
Meaning and Speech Acts: Volume I, Principles of Language Use. VANDERVEKEN, Daniel.
Meaning and Speech Acts: Volume II, Formal Semantics of Success and Satisfaction. VANDERVEKEN, Daniel.
Meaning and Truth: The Essential Readings in Modern Semantics. GARFIELD, Jay L (ed).
The Metaphysics of Meaning. KATZ, Jerrold J.
Musical Aesthetics: A Historical Reader, Volume III, The Twentieth Century. LIPPMAN, Edward A (ed).
Philosophical Essays. CARTWRIGHT, Richard.
Philosophical Logic. STRAWSON, P F (ed).
The Question of Humanism: Challenges and Possibilities. GOICOECHEA, David (ed).
The Secret Connexion: Causation, Realism, and David Hume. STRAWSON, Galen.
Semantic Structures. JACKENDOFF, Ray.
Truth and Interpretation: Perspectives on the Philosophy of Donald Davidson. LE PORE, Ernest (ed).
Wittgenstein and Contemporary Philosophy of Language. RUNDLE, Bede.
Wittgenstein: Meaning and Mind, Volume 3 of an Analytical Commentary on Philosophical Investigations. HACKER, P M S.
"Art and Meaning" in *XIth International Congress in Aesthetics, Nottingham 1988*, DIFFEY, T J.
"Content, Character, and Nondescriptive Meaning" in *Themes From Kaplan*, ACKERMAN, Felicia.
"Does Meaning Matter?" in *Information, Semantics and Epistemology*, DRETSKE, Frederick.
"Doing Without Meaning" in *Perspectives on Quine*, QUINTON, Anthony.
"Facts That Don't Matter" in *Meaning and Method: Essays in Honor of Hilary Putnam*, ELGIN, Catherine Z.
"Frege on Sense and Linguistic Meaning" in *The Analytic Tradition: Philosophical Quarterly Monographs, Volume 1*, BURGE, Tyler.
"Immanent and Transcendent Approaches to the Theory of Meaning" in *Perspectives on Quine*, HARMAN, Gilbert.
"Learning and Meaning" in *Perspectives on Quine*, ULLIAN, Joseph S.
"Linguistic Theory and Davidson's Program in Semantics" in *Truth and Interpretation: Perspectives on the Philosophy of Donald Davidson*, HIGGINBOTHAM, James.
"Meaning and Explanation" in *Themes From Kaplan*, MORAVCSIK, Julius.
"Meaning, Holism and Use" in *Truth and Interpretation: Perspectives on the Philosophy of Donald Davidson*, BILGRAMI, Akeel.
"Meaning, Truth and Evidence" in *Perspectives on Quine*, DAVIDSON, Donald.
"Meanings Just Ain't in the Head" in *Meaning and Method: Essays in Honor of Hilary Putnam*, DEVITT, Michael.
"The Meanings of Logical Constants" in *Truth and Interpretation: Perspectives on the Philosophy of Donald Davidson*, HARMAN, Gilbert.
"A Nice Derangement of Epitaphs" in *Truth and Interpretation: Perspectives on the Philosophy of Donald Davidson*, DAVIDSON, Donald.
"On Some Thought Experiments about Mind and Meaning" in *Propositional Attitudes: The Role of Content in Logic, Language, and Mind*, WALLACE, John and MASON, H E.
"Scientific Discovery and Commensurability of Meaning" in *Imre Lakatos and Theories of Scientific Change*, NERSESSIAN, Nancy J.
"A Study in Comparative Semantics" in *Propositional Attitudes: The Role of Content in Logic, Language, and Mind*, LE PORE, Ernest and LOEWER, Barry.
"Substitution Arguments and the Individuation of Beliefs" in *Meaning and Method: Essays in Honor of Hilary Putnam*, FODOR, Jerry A.
"Truth in Meaning" in *Truth and Interpretation: Perspectives on the Philosophy of Donald Davidson*, LE PORE, Ernest.
"What Davidson Should Have Said" in *The Mind of Donald Davidson*, LE PORE, Ernest and LOEWER, Barry.
"What is Wrong with the Building Block Theory of Language?" in *The Mind of Donald Davidson*, BRANDL, Johannes.
"Utility". BROOME, John.
Blind Grasping and Fregean Senses. SCHWEIZER, Paul.
Comments on Schiffer's *Remnants of Meaning*. RICHARD, Mark.
Die Wahrheit des literarischen Kunstwerks: R Ingardens Begriff des Quasi-Urteils (in Japanese). KAWAKAMI, Akitaka.
Direct Reference, Meaning, and Thought. RECANATI, François.
Educating for Meaning. WELBY, Victoria.
Ends and Meaning in Machine-Like Systems. ATLAN, H.
Essay on the Notion of Reading. ROSE, Rebecca Fine (trans) and WEIL, Simone and TESSIN, Timothy.
Fondamento e verità. CAMPANALE, Domenico.
Gangesa and Transfer of Meaning. SAHA, Sukharanjan.
Genuine Names and Knowledge by Acquaintance. DONNELLAN, Keith S.
How Beliefs Explain: Reply to Baker. DRETSKE, Fred.
How Ideas Became Meanings: Locke and the Foundations of Semantic Theory. HANNA, Robert.
How *Not* to Become a Millian Heir. SALMON, Nathan.
Is There a "Meaning" of Being? Against the Deconstructionist Reading of Heidegger. SCHALOW, Frank.
The Last Word on *Philosophical Investigations* 43a. SAVIGNY, Eike V.
McGinn on Concept Scepticism and Kripke's Sceptical Argument. SARTORELLI, Joseph.
Meaning and Intention: Black Versus Grice. MARTINICH, A P.
Meaning and Value. SCHIFFER, Stephen.
Meaning as Grammar plus *Consequences*. DE QUEIROZ, Ruy J G B.
Meaning Holism and Interpretability. TALMAGE, Catherine J L and MERCER, Mark.
Meaning in a Realist Perspective. THERON, Stephen.
The Meaning of Mathematical Expressions: Does Philosophy Shed Any Light on Psychology?. ERNEST, Paul.
The Meaning of Meaning. HELLER, Michael.
Meaning, Truth and Realism in Bultmann and Lindbeck. FERGUSSON, David.
Meaning, Truth Conditions and the Internal Point of View: The Ethical Dilemma. GOOSSENS, Charles.
Meaning, Understanding and Translation. STROUD, Barry.
Meanings in Ordinary Language and in Mathematics. THOMAS, R S D.
Metaphor and the Varieties of Lexical Meaning. HINTIKKA, Jaakko and SANDU, Gabriel.
Michael Polanyi's Aesthetics: A Phenomenological Study. BISWAS, Goutam.
Music, Meaning, and the Art of Elocution. TROTT, Elizabeth Anne.
Nietzsche's Metaperspectivism. ROTH, Robin Alice.
Noema and Meaning in Husserl. FOLLESDAL, Dagfinn.
Nonrules and Plausibility: An Illustration in Pragmatic Theory. POWELL, Mava Jo.
Notes on the Specification of "Meaning" in Schutz. EMBREE, Lester.
Observar un aspecto. GIANOTTI, José Arthur.
On Husserl's Theory of the Constitution of Objectiving Meaning (in Czechoslovakian). ZATKA, V.
On the Genealogical Method: Nietzsche and Foucault. SAX, Benjamin C.
The Open Question Argument. PAL, Jagat.
Panofsky, Polanyi, and Intrinsic Meaning. UN-CHOL, Shin.
A Philosophical Resistance to Freud. SACHS, David.
A Pieced Quilt: A Critical Discussion of Stephen Schiffer's *Remnants of Meaning*. ANTONY, Louise.
Pride and the Meaning of *Utopia*. MOULAKIS, Athanasios.
The Progressive and the Imperfective Paradox. LASCARIDES, Alex.

MEANING
The Real Meaning of 'Meaning'. CARTER, Alan.
Reflection in Politics and the Question of a Political Subject (in Czechoslovakian). HEJDANEK, Ladislav.
The Relational Theory of Belief (A Reply to Richard). SCHIFFER, Stephen.
Remnants of Schiffer's Principle [P]. SEYMOUR, Daniel.
Response to Lyons' "Basic Rights and Constitutional Interpretations". LUCKHARDT, Grant.
Scepticism: The External World and Meaning. BAR-ON, Dorit.
Sentidos, referencias y concepto en Frege. MARTINEZ FREIRE, P.
The *Sinnsfrage* and the *Seinsfrage*. PROTEVI, John.
State-Spaces and Meaning Relations Among Predicates. ARNTZENIUS, Frank.
Structure and Meaning in St Augustine's *Confessions*. CROSSON, Frederick J.
The Task of a Theory of Meaning. SAYRE, Patricia.
The Temporality of Illness: Four Levels of Experience. TOOMBS, S Kay.
La teoría del significado como uso en Wittgenstein. HERRERA, Alejandro.
Transcultural Dialogue and the Problem of the Concept of Ultimate Reality and Meaning. SINGLETON, Michael.
Truth and Understanding. HIGGINBOTHAM, James.
Two Ways of Grounding Meaning. GERRARD, Steve.
What is Ultimate in George Lukács's Ontology?. JOÓS, Ernest.
William Wadsworth: Nature, Imagination, Ultimate Reality and Meaning. MAHONEY, John L.
Wittgenstein's Account of Rule-Following. PEARS, David.
Wittgenstein's Influence: Meaning, Mind and Method. GRAYLING, A C.
Wo lag der Fehler der kategorialen Repräsentation? Zu Sinn und Reichweite einer Selbstkritik Husserls. LOHMAR, Dieter.
Words like Faces (in Dutch). LESAGE, D.

MEANING OF LIFE
Human Interests: Reflections on Philosophical Anthropology. RESCHER, Nicholas.
Jivacide, Zombies and *Jivanmuktas*. HERMAN, A L.
Living a Life and the Problem of Existential Impossibility. LÖW-BEER, Martin.

MEANINGFULNESS
Independent Evidence of Religion. D'SOUZA, Felix.

MEASURE
"Real Quantities and Their Sensible Measures" in *Philosophical Perspectives on Newtonian Science*, SKLAR, Lawrence.
The Borel Conjecture. JUDAH, Haim and SHELAH, Saharon and WOODIN, W H.
The Complete 0. KANAMORI, Akihiro and AWERBUCH-FRIEDLANDER, Tamara.
Finite Support Iteration and Strong Measure Zero Sets. PAWLIKOWSKI, Janusz.
A Hierarchy of Ramsey Cardinals. FENG, Qi.
Jumping with Random Reals. BARTOSZYNSKI, Tomek and JUDAH, Haim.
The Kunen-Miller Chart (Lebesgue Measure, the Baire Property, Laver Reals and Preservation Theorems for Forcing). JUDAH, Haim and SHELAH, Saharon.
Set Theoretic Properties of Loeb Measure. MILLER, Arnold W.

MEASUREMENT
Science and Reason. KYBURG JR, Henry E.
Embedding and Uniqueness in Relationist Theories. MUNDY, Brent.
En busca del contenido físico de la regla de Luders. MARTÍNEZ, Sergio and MURILLO, Lorena.
Holism and Measurement (in Serbo-Croatian). BALZER, Wolfgang.
The Infinite Apparatus in the Quantum Theory of Measurement. ROBINSON, Don.
Is Utilitarianism Useless?. HAUSMAN, Daniel M.
The Measurement Problem: Some "Solutions". ALBERT, David Z and LOEWER, Barry.
Measuring the Success of Science. NIINILUOTO, Ilkka.
The Philosophy of Quantum Mechanics. BUB, Jeffrey.
Simultaneity, Conventionality and Existence. PETKOV, Vesselin.
Theoretical Explanation and Errors of Measurement. FORGE, John.
Units of Measurement and Natural Kinds: Some Kripkean Considerations. VAN BRAKEL, J.

MECHANICS
see also Quantum Mechanics
Pulling up the Ladder: The Metaphysical Roots of Wittgenstein's Tractatus. BROCKHAUS, Richard R.
Some Truer Method. DURHAM, Frank (ed).
"Newton's 'Mathematical Way' a Century After the *Principia*" in *Some Truer Method*, HANKINS, Thomas L.
"Newton's Method and Newton's Style" in *Some Truer Method*, COHEN, I Bernard.
Politics in Hobbes' Mechanics: The Social as Enabling. LYNCH, William T.
Synthetic Mechanics Revisited. BURGESS, John P.
The Fundamental Hypotheses of Mechanics in Lazare N M Carnot's Thought (in Italian). DRAGO, Antonino and MANNO, Salvatore D.
Whitehead and Leibniz: Conflict and Convergence. MOONEY, Tim.

MECHANISM
"Mechanism, Purpose, and Explanatory Exclusion" in *Philosophical Perspectives, 3: Philosophy of Mind and Action Theory, 1989*, KIM, Jaegwon.
The Conditions of Fruitfulness of Theorizing About Mechanisms in Social Science. STINCHCOMBE, Arthur L.
Corpuscles, Mechanism, and Essentialism in Berkeley and Locke. ATHERTON, Margaret.
How's and Why's: Causation Un-Locked. FRANKEL, Lois.
Mechanism and Indeterminacy: Reply to MacIntosh. WARMBROD, Ken.
Minds, Machines and Gödels Theorem (in German). RHEINWALD, Rosemarie.

MECHANISTIC MATERIALISM
War Demokrits Weltbild mechanistisch und antiteleologisch?. HIRSCH, Ulrike.
Wittgenstein's Critique of Mechanistic Atomism. MC DONOUGH, Richard.

MECHTILD OF MAGDEBURG
"Mechtild of Magdeburg" in *A History of Women Philosophers, Volume II: Medieval, Renaissance and Enlightenment, A.D. 500-1600*, GIBSON, Joan.

MEDIA
Already Punished Enough. HUSAK, Douglas N.
Ethics and News. MACHAMER, Peter K and BOYLAN, Barbara.
Informing the Public: Ethics, Policy Making, and Objectivity in News Reporting. IANNONE, A Pablo.
Presidential Campaigns, Television News and Voter Turnout. WALTER, Edward.

MEDIATION
Das Ich im deutschen Idealismus und das Selbst im Zen-Buddhist Fichte und Dogen. NAGASAWA, Kunihiko.
Gadamer over 'Vermittlung': de Hegeliaanse draad in zijn hermeneutiek. VAN DER HOEVEN, J.

MEDICAID
Community Responsibility and the Development of Oregon's Health Care Priorities. GARLAND, Michael J and HASNAIN, Romana.
The Oregon Medicaid Experiment: Is It Just Enough?. FLECK, Leonard M.

MEDICAL ETHICS
see also Abortion, Bioethics, Euthanasia
Beyond Baby M: Ethical Issues in New Reproductive Techniques. BARTELS, Dianne M (ed).
Bibliography of Bioethics, Volume 16. WALTERS, LeRoy (ed).
Biomedical Ethics Reviews, 1989. HUMBER, James M (ed).
The Crisis in Health Care: Ethical Issues. MC KENZIE, Nancy F (ed).
Deciding for Others: The Ethics of Surrogate Decision Making. BUCHANAN, Allen E.
Ethical Practice in Clinical Medicine. ELLOS, William J.
Ethics in Nursing: An Anthology. PENCE, Terry.
Euthanasia: Toward an Ethical Social Policy. THOMASMA, David C.
The Last Choice: Preemptive Suicide in Advanced Age. PRADO, C G.
Matter, Morals and Medicine: The Ancient Greek Origins of Science, Ethics and the Medical Profession. CARELLA, Michael Jerome.
Medical Ethics for Physicians-in-Training. KANTOR, Jay E.
Medical Ethics in Practice. BARD, Terry R.
Medicine and Money: A Study of the Role of Beneficence in Health Care Cost Containment. MARSH, Frank H.
Moral Theory and Medical Practice. FULFORD, K W M.
Theory and Practice in Medical Ethics. GRABER, Glenn C.
Well and Good: Case Studies in Biomedical Ethics (Revised Edition). THOMAS, John E.
"Fiduciary Relationships and the Medical Profession: A Japanese Point of View" in *Ethics, Trust, and the Professions: Philosophical and Cultural Aspects*, KIMURA, Rihito.
"Values and the Advance of Medical Science" in *Integrity in Health Care Institutions: Humane Environments for Teaching, Inquiry, and Healing*, FREDRICKSON, Donald S.
"Values in Teaching and Learning: A Student-Teacher Dialogue" in *Integrity in Health Care Institutions: Humane Environments for Teaching, Inquiry, and Healing*, DUNN, Kim and BULGER, Ruth Ellen.
'Too Busy for Ethics'. SELBY, G Raymond.
The 'Voice of Care': Implications for Bioethical Education. CARSE, Alisa L.
Abortion as the Illicit Method of Birth Control. KEILKOPF, Charles F.
AIDS and 'Dirt': Reflections on the Ethics of Ritual Cleanliness. CHURCHILL, Larry R.
An Alternative to Property Rights in Human Tissue. SWAIN, Margaret S and MARUSYK, Randy W.
American Moralism and the Origin of Bioethics in the United States. JONSEN, Albert R.
Anencephalic Infants and Special Relationships. JECKER, Nancy S.
Animals in Biomedical Research: The Undermining Effect of the Rhetoric of the Besieged. GLUCK, John P and KUBACKI, Steven R.
Are Pregnant Women Fetal Containers?. PURDY, Laura.
Aspectos antropológicos de la fecundación in vitro. CAFFARRA, Carlos.
Autonomy and the Common Weal. DANIS, Marion and CHURCHILL, Larry R.

MEDICAL ETHICS

Birth Defects: Traditional Beliefs Challenged by Scientific Explanations. DRYDEN, Richard.
Buddhist Views of Suicide and Euthanasia. BECKER, Carl B.
The Chief of Medicine. BRODY, Howard.
The Clinical Ethicist at the Bedside. LA PUMA, John and SCHIEDERMAYER, David L.
Clinical Judgment and Bioethics: The Decision Making Link. WRIGHT, Richard A.
Comment on Hospice of Washington's Policy. ROBERTSON, John A.
Commentary— "Make Me Live": Autonomy and Terminal Illness. MISBIN, Robert I.
Commentary—"Make Me Live": Autonomy and Terminal Illness. MILLER, David H.
Community Values in Vermont Health Planning. WALLACE-BRODEUR, Paul H.
Consumer Sovereignty versus Informed Consent: Saying No to Requests to "Do Everything" for Dying Patients. WEBER, Leonard.
Contestation and Consensus: The Morality of Abortion in Japan. LA FLEUR, William R.
The Costs of Commercial Medicine. DOUGHERTY, Charles J.
Cruzan and Caring for Others. LYNN, Joanne and GLOVER, Jacqueline.
Cruzan: No Rights Violated. ROBERTSON, John A.
Death and the Beginning of Life. IGLESIAS, Teresa.
Decisionmaking Competence and Risk—Comments on Wicclair. BROCK, Dan W.
Delivering Hydrocephalic Fetuses. STRONG, Carson.
Democracy and Justice in Health Policy. JENNINGS, Bruce.
Development of an Institutional Policy on Artificial Hydration and Nutrition. KOSHUTA, Monica A and SCHMITZ, Phyllis J and LYNN, Joanne.
Diagnosis Without Doctors. MAZOUÉ, James G.
Doctors and Their Advertising. BURTON, Gene E.
Doctors' Rights and Patients' Obligations. MARSHALL, Sandra E.
Duty to Treat or Right to Refuse?. DANIELS, Norman.
Ethical Decision Making in the Medical Profession: An Application of the Theory of Planned Behavior. RANDALL, Donna M and GIBSON, Annetta M.
Ethics Committees. COHEN, Cynthia B (ed).
Ethics Committees: From Ethical Comfort to Ethical Cover. ANNAS, George J.
The Ethics of *Ex Utero* Research on Spare 'Non-Viable' IVF Human Embryos. BAYLIS, Françoise E.
The Ethics of Mechanical Restraints. MOSS, Robert J and LA PUMA, John.
The Ethics of Selectively Marketing the Health Maintenance Organization. WAYMACK, Mark H.
Ethics, AIDS, and Community Responsibility. DOUARD, John.
An Ethnomedical Perspective of Medical Ethics. FABREGA JR, Horacio.
The Futures of Physicians: Agency and Autonomy Reconsidered. SALMON, J Warren and WHITE, William and FEINGLASS, Joe.
Getting Down to Cases: The Revival of Casuistry in Bioethics. ARRAS, John D.
Giving Voice to the Pragmatic Majority in New Jersey. HILL, T Patrick.
Health Care in Common: Setting Priorities in Oregon. GARLAND, Michael J and HASNAIN, Romana.
Historical Perspectives: Development of the Codes of Ethics in the Legal, Medical and Accounting Professions. BACKOF, Jeanne F and MARTIN JR, Charles L.
HIV and the Obligation to Treat. SHELDON, Mark.
A Hostage to Technology. CRANFORD, Ronald E.
How Can They?. BUSALACCHI, Pete.
The Ideal of Shared Decision Making Between Physicians and Patients. BROCK, Dan W.
An Integrative Model of Clinical-Ethical Decision Making. GRUNDSTEIN-AMADO, Rivka.
The Irreducibly Clinical Character of Bioethics. WEAR, Stephen.
Is IVF Good Medicine?. CONNOR, Pauline.
Judaism, Justice, and Access to Health Care. MACKLER, Aaron L.
Justified Limits on Refusing Intervention. CHERVENAK, Frank A and MC CULLOUGH, Laurence B.
Killing Machines. ANNAS, George J.
Maternal Rights, Fetal Harms: Commentary. KINLAW, Kathy.
Maternal Rights, Fetal Harms: Commentary. STRONG, Carson.
Medical Ethics in Ireland: A Decade of Change. DOOLEY, Dolores.
Medicine as Business and Profession. AGICH, George J.
Missouri Stands Alone. COLBY, William H.
Morality in Flux: Medical Ethics in the People's Republic of China. QIU, Ren-Zong.
La mort de Socrate et la vie des machines. BEAUNE, Jean-Claude.
Nancy Cruzan in China. ANNAS, George J.
Natural Fetal Dependency States and Fetal Dependency Principles. HERBENICK, Raymond M.
Negotiating Criteria and Setting Limits: The Case of AIDS. CUTTER, Mary Ann Gardell.
The New Dimensions of Chinese Medical Ethics. MC GREAL, Ian Philip.
No Time for an AIDS Backlash. MURPHY, Timothy F.
Noncompliance in AIDS Research. ARRAS, John D.
The Noncompliant Substance Abuser: Commentary. CASSEL, Christine and LA PUMA, John.
The Noncompliant Substance Abuser: Commentary. STELL, Lance K.
Nurses and Physicians on Nutritional Support: A Comparison. LIASCHENKO, Joan and DAVIS, Anne J.
On Taking Substituted Judgment Seriously. BARON, Charles.
The Oregon Priority-Setting Exercise: Quality of Life and Public Policy. HADORN, David C.
Outrageous Fortune: Selling Other People's Cells. ANNAS, George J.
Patient Decision-Making Capacity and Risk. WICCLAIR, Mark R.
The Patient Self-Determination Act. MC CLOSKEY, Elizabeth Leibold.
Physicians, Entrepreneurism and the Problem of Conflict of Interest. GREEN, Ronald M.
Psychiatry, Religious Conversion, and Medical Ethics. POST, Stephen G.
Public Input Into Health Care Policy: Controversy and Contribution in California. COLBERT, Treacy.
Respect for Donor Choice and the Uniform Anatomical Gift Act. EDINGER, Walter.
Response to 'Rescuing the Innocent'. GARDNER, G T G.
Response to 'Rescuing the Innocent'. MORROW, James.
The Sanctity of Life and Substituted Judgement: The Case of Baby J. HORNETT, Stuart I.
Schopenhauers Idee einer rekonstruktiven Ethik (mit Anwendungen auf die moderne Medizin-Ethik). BIRNBACHER, Dieter.
Still Saving the Life of Ethics. SCHNEIDERMAN, Lawrence J.
A Study of the Foundations of Ethical Decision Making of Clinical Medical Ethicists. SELF, Donnie J and SKEEL, Joy D.
Surrogate Decisionmaking and Other Matters. GREENLAW, Jane.
Teaching Clinical Ethics in the Residency Years: Preparing Competent Professionals. FORROW, Lachlan and ARNOLD, Robert M and FRADER, Joel.
Telling Stories: Creative Literature and Ethics. RADEY, Charles.
A Vision of the Health Decisions Movement. CRAWSHAW, Ralph.
When Death Is at the Door. WINSLADE, William J.
Who or What is the Preembryo?. MC CORMICK, Richard A.
Why Philosophers Should Offer Ethics Consultations. THOMASMA, David C.

MEDICAL SCHOOL(S)

AIDS and 'Dirt': Reflections on the Ethics of Ritual Cleanliness. CHURCHILL, Larry R.

MEDICINE

Animal Experimentation: The Consensus Changes. LANGLEY, Gill (ed).
Matter, Morals and Medicine: The Ancient Greek Origins of Science, Ethics and the Medical Profession. CARELLA, Michael Jerome.
Methods and Problems in Greek Science: Selected Papers. LLOYD, G E R.
Moral Theory and Medical Practice. FULFORD, K W M.
Philosophical Foundations of Health Education. LAURA, Ronald S.
Shaping Genes: Ethics, Law and Science of Using Genetic Technology in Medicine and Agriculture. MACER, Darryl.
"Medical Techniques for Assisted Reproduction" in *Beyond Baby M: Ethical Issues in New Reproductive Techniques*, TAGATZ, George.
"Oliva Sabuco de Nantes Barrera" in *A History of Women Philosophers, Volume II: Medieval, Renaissance and Enlightenment, A.D. 500-1600*, WAITHE, Mary Ellen.
Aktuelle Aufgaben interdisziplinärer Bedürfnisforschung aus psychologischer Sicht. WOLF, Edith.
A Case Against Dutch Euthanasia. FENIGSEN, Richard.
Current Trends in the Philosophy of Medicine. POTTER, Robert Lyman.
The Discursive Formation of the Body in the History of Medicine. LEVIN, David Michael and SOLOMON, George F.
L'epiglottide nell'antichità tra medicina e filosofia. REPICI, Luciana.
The Ethico-Legal Meaning of Voluntary. BOURKE, Vernon J.
Francesco Bonucci, tra medicina e filosofia. STORTI, Cinzia.
Geschiedenis als muurbloempje. PRINS, Ad.
The Irreducibly Clinical Character of Bioethics. WEAR, Stephen.
Knowing When to Stop: The Limits of Medicine. JECKER, Nancy S.
The Locked-In Syndrome and the Behaviorist Epistemology of Other Minds. KURTHEN, Martin (and others).
Medical Critique [Krytyka Lekarska]: A Journal of Medicine and Philosophy—1897-1907. LÖWY, Ilana.
Medicine as Business and Profession. AGICH, George J.
Medicine in John Locke's Philosophy. SANCHEZ-GONZALEZ, Miguel A.
The Occasion Fleeting: A Talk with Richard Selzer. JOSYPH, Peter.
On the Dearth of Philosophical Contributions to Medicine. YARBOROUGH, Mark.
On the Locus of Medical Discovery. REINES, Brandon P.
Philosophische Uberlegungen zu "Menschenwürde" und Fortpflanzungs-Medizin. SCHÖNE-SEIFERT, Bettina.
The Potential of Medicine as a Resource for Philosophy. FULFORD, K W M.
Recognizing Suffering. CASSELL, Eric J.
The Temporality of Illness: Four Levels of Experience. TOOMBS, S Kay.
Uncertainty and the Shaping of Medical Decisions. BERESFORD, Eric B.
Viktor Emil Frankl médico y filósofo. ALEGRÍA, Hernando Muciño.

MEDICINE

Why the Standard View Is Standard: People, Not Machines, Understand Patients' Problems. MILLER, Randolph A.
Wie van de drie: Wil de ware wetenschapsonderzoeker opstaan?. BIJSTERVELD, Karin and MESMAN, Jessica.

MEDIEVAL

A History of Women Philosophers, Volume II: Medieval, Renaissance and Enlightenment, A.D. 500-1600. WAITHE, Mary Ellen (ed).
Ibn Rushd: Averroes. URVOY, Dominique.
The Philosophical Theology of John Duns Scotus. ADAMS, Marilyn McCord (ed).
Philosophical Writings: A Selection—William of Ockham. BOEHNER, Philotheus (ed & trans).
Philosophy's Journey: From the Presocratics to the Present (Second Edition). KOLENDA, Konstantin.
Policraticus. NEDERMAN, Cary J (ed & trans).
The Preface to Thomistic Metaphysics. KNASAS, John F X.
"Beatrice of Nazareth" in *A History of Women Philosophers, Volume II: Medieval, Renaissance and Enlightenment, A.D. 500-1600*, WOLFSKEEL, Cornelia.
"Birgitta of Sweden" in *A History of Women Philosophers, Volume II: Medieval, Renaissance and Enlightenment, A.D. 500-1600*, WOLFSKEEL, Cornelia.
"Catherine of Siena" in *A History of Women Philosophers, Volume II: Medieval, Renaissance and Enlightenment, A.D. 500-1600*, WOLFSKEEL, Cornelia.
"Hadewych of Antwerp" in *A History of Women Philosophers, Volume II: Medieval, Renaissance and Enlightenment, A.D. 500-1600*, WOLFSKEEL, Cornelia.
"Heloise" in *A History of Women Philosophers, Volume II: Medieval, Renaissance and Enlightenment, A.D. 500-1600*, WAITHE, Mary Ellen.
"Herrad of Hohenbourg" in *A History of Women Philosophers, Volume II: Medieval, Renaissance and Enlightenment, A.D. 500-1600*, GIBSON, Joan.
"Hildegard of Bingen" in *A History of Women Philosophers, Volume II: Medieval, Renaissance and Enlightenment, A.D. 500-1600*, GÖSSMANN, Elisabeth and BEST, Katherine.
"Julian of Norwich" in *A History of Women Philosophers, Volume II: Medieval, Renaissance and Enlightenment, A.D. 500-1600*, EVASDAUGHTER, Elizabeth N.
"Mechtild of Magdeburg" in *A History of Women Philosophers, Volume II: Medieval, Renaissance and Enlightenment, A.D. 500-1600*, GIBSON, Joan.
"Medieval and Renaissance Ethics" in *A Companion to Ethics*, HALDANE, John.
"Murasaki Shikibu" in *A History of Women Philosophers, Volume II: Medieval, Renaissance and Enlightenment, A.D. 500-1600*, WAITHE, Mary Ellen.
"St Thomas and Medieval Humanism" in *The Question of Humanism: Challenges and Possibilities*, SYNAN, Edward A.
Al-Fârâbî lógico: su exposicón de la "Isagogé" de Porfirio. RAMÓN, Rafael.
Al-Kindi's Psychology (in Hebrew). SCHWARZ, Dov.
Apophasis and Metaphysics in the *Periphyseon* of John Scottus Eriugena. CARABINE, Deirdre.
Aristotelianism and the Origins of "Political Science" in the Twelfth Century. NEDERMAN, Cary J.
El averroísmo de Juan de Sècheville. RODRÍGUEZ, Juan Acosta.
Buridan's Divided Modal Syllogistic. WILLING, Anthony.
Comentario a las "Sentencias" de Isidoro de Sevilla. ORTEGA MUÑOZ, Juan F.
La crisi dei fondamenti della scienza: Un recupero dell'ilemorfismo?. DEL RE, Giuseppe.
Cusanus and Eriugena. BEIERWALTES, Werner.
Erfurt, Ampl Q 70A: A Quaestiones-commentary on the Second Part of Alexander de Villa Dei's *Doctrinale*. KNEEPKENS, C H.
Florilegi filosofici ed enciclopedie in Germania nella prima metà del Duecento. STURLESE, Loris.
Giustino Martire, il primo platonico cristiano. GIRGENTI, Giuseppe.
Grammaire et Liturgie dans les "Sophismes" du XIIIe Siècle. ROSIER, Irène and ROY, Bruno.
Der Harmonie-Gedanke im frühen Mittelalter. BEIERWALTES, Werner.
The Interplay of Nature and Man in the *Periphyseon* of Johannes Scottus Eriugena. OTTEN, Willemien.
La interpretación de Santo Tomás en García Morente. FORMENT, Eudaldo.
John Scottus Eriugena: Recent Works of Consultation. MC EVOY, James J.
Libertad y necesidad en el 'Cur Deus Homo' de San Anselmo de Canterbury (segunda parte). CORTI, E C.
Logique et théorie de l'argumentation dans le "Guide de l'étudiant". LAFLEUR, Claude.
The Modernity of St Thomas' Political Philosophy. WALTER, Edward.
Un nouveau début à l'édition léonine des oeuvres de saint Thomas d'Aquin. HISSETTE, Roland.
Ockham, Adams and Connotation: A Critical Notice of Marilyn Adams, *William Ockham*. SPADE, Paul Vincent.
Once Again the Ockhamist Statutes of 1339 and 1340: Some New Perspectives. THIJSSEN, J M M H.
Philosophie ancienne et médiévale. MC EVOY, James.
A Reaction to Vogel's "The Ethical Roots of Business". MC MAHON, Thomas F.
A Reflection on Saint Augustine's *Confessions*. BARKOVICH, Greg.
Le relazioni divine secondo S Tommaso d'Aquino: Riproposizione di un problema e prospettive di indagine. VENTIMIGLIA, Giovanni.
The Rhetoric of Martianus Capella and Anselm de Besate in the Tradition of Menippean Satire. BENNETT, Beth S.
Some Observations on the Influence of Christian Scholastic Authors on Jewish Thinkers in the 13th and 14th Century. REEDIJK, Wim M.
Le statut de la philosophie chez Étienne Gilson. PROUVOST, Géry.
The Contradiction of Belief and Reason in the Middle Ages: the Case of Boetius de Dacia (in Hungarian). JOÓS, Ernest.
Tomás de Aquino: la aprehensión del acto de ser (II). GONZÁLEZ, Orestes J.
Travaux récents sur la pensée du XIIIe siècle. VAN STEENBERGHEN, Fernand.
Two Anonymous 12th-Century Tracts on Universals. DIJS, Judith.
Verbum-Signum: La définition du langage chez s Augustin et Nicolas de Cues. HENNIGFELD, Jochem.
Wilhelm von Ockham: Das Risiko, mittelalterlich zu denken. PERLER, Dominik.

MEDITATION

The Butterfly as Companion: Meditations on the First Three Chapters of the Chuang Tzu. WU, Kuang-Ming.
From Sentience To Symbols. PICKERING, John (ed).
The Relevance of Meditative Thinking. ERICKSON, Stephen A.

MEHRING, F

Critical Marxism as an Historical Process of Society and Science (in German). SANDKÜHLER, Hans Jörg.

MEINECKE, F

Franz Rosenzweig e Friedrich Meinecke. D'ANTUONO, Emilia.

MEINONG

Meinongian Theories of Generality. SANTAMBROGIO, Marco.
On Wishing there were Unicorns. CLARK, Stephen R L.

MELANCHOLY

Analyse d'un corpus iconographique rassemblé par Maxime Préaud ou Aristote et la mélancolie. FLEURY, Chantal.
Entre el duelo y la melancolia. SILVA CAMARENA, Juan Manuel.
Kristeva and Holbein, Artist of Melancholy. LECHTE, John.

MELLOR, D

A Critique of Mellor's Argument against 'Backwards' Causation. RIGGS, Peter J.
Modality and Mellor's McTaggart. CRESSWELL, M J.
On Crane and Mellor's Argument Against Physicalism. ROBINSON, Don.

MEMBERSHIP

Negative Membership. BLIZARD, Wayne D.

MEMORY

About Time: Inventing the Fourth Dimension. FRIEDMAN, William J.
Aristotle's Psychology. ROBINSON, Daniel N.
Bergsonism. DELEUZE, Gilles.
Matter and Memory. BERGSON, Henri.
Of Memory, Reminiscence, and Writing: On the Verge. KRELL, David Farrell.
An Outline of the Philosophy of Knowledge and Science. BLANDINO, Giovanni.
"Hannah Arendt: la memoria come spazio del pensiero" in *Razionalitá critica: nella filosofia moderna*, FISTETTI, Francesco.
"Memory and Scripture in the Conversion of Augustine" in *Grace, Politics and Desire: Essays on Augustine*, COWARD, Harold G.
Il "De imaginum, signorum et idearum compositione" di Giordano Bruno, ed il significato filosofico .... STURLESE, Rita.
Can There Be a Possible World in Which Memory Is Unreliable?. LEUNG, Edwin Sing Choe.
A Dilemma of Late Life Memory. MC KEE, Patrick.
Is Kripke's Puzzle Really a Puzzle. CORLETT, J Angelo.
Locke's Account of Personal Identity. SCHRECK, P A.
Memory, Forgetfulness and the Disclosure of Being in Heidegger and Plotinus. BALES, Eugene F.
Mnêmê, anámnêsis, mnêmosynê: Sull'identità dell'uomo storico. MICCOLI, Paolo.
Models of Memory: Wittgenstein and Cognitive Science. STERN, David G.
Nature et fonction de la Mémoire dans À la recherche du temps perdu. ZÉPHIR, Jacques J.
The Role of Memory in the Historiography of the French Revolution. HUTTON, Patrick H.
Whitman and Memory: A Response to Kateb. BROMWICH, David.

MEN

Contemporary Perspectives on Masculinity: Men, Women, and Politics in Modern Society. CLATTERBAUGH, Kenneth.

MENCIUS

David Wong on Emotions in Mencius. IHARA, Craig K.

MENCIUS
In Defence of Graded Love. LAI, Whalen.
Is There a Distinction Between Reason and Emotion in Mencius?. WONG, David B.
Mencius and the Mind-Dependence of Morality: An Analysis of Meng Tzu 6A: 4-5. SHUN, Kwong-Loi.
Mencius' Criticism of Mohism: An Analysis of *Meng Tzu* 3A:5. SHUN, Kwong-Loi.
Of One Mind or Two? Query on the Innate Good in Mencius. LAI, Whalen.
Response to Craig Ihara's Discussion. WONG, David B.
The Self in Confucian Ethics. SHUN, Kwong-Loi.

MENDELSSOHN
Kant, Mendelssohn, Lambert, and the Subjectivity of Time. FALKENSTEIN, Lorne.

MENDUS, S
"Response to Mendus's 'Liberal Man'" in *Philosophy and Politics*, BINNS, Peter.
Response to Mendus's "Liberal Man". BINNS, Peter.

MENTAL
"Explanatory Exclusion and the Problem of Mental Causation" in *Information, Semantics and Epistemology*, KIM, Jaegwon.
"Reply to Dretske's 'Does Meaning Matter?'" in *Information, Semantics and Epistemology*, FODOR, Jerry A.
"What Is the 'Subjectivity' of the Mental?" in *Philosophical Perspectives, 4: Action Theory and Philosophy of Mind, 1990*, LYCAN, William G.
Macdonald on Type Reduction via Disjunction. ENDICOTT, Ronald P.
Mental Causation and Non-Reductive Monism. MACDONALD, Cynthia and MACDONALD, Graham.
Multiple Personality and Irrationality. GILLETT, Grant R.
On Naturalizing the Semantics of Mental Representation. SILVERS, Stuart.
Philosophical Asceiticism (in French). DE MONTICELLI, Roberta.
The Reason Why: Response to Crane. PAPINEAU, David.
Reduction, Elimination, and the Mental. SCHWARTZ, Justin.
Seeing Our Seeing and Knowing Our Knowing. BEN-ZEEV, Aaron.
Why Indeed? Papineau on Supervenience. CRANE, Tim.

MENTAL EVENT(S)
"Information and the Mental" in *Truth and Interpretation: Perspectives on the Philosophy of Donald Davidson*, PUTNAM, Hilary.
"Mental Quausation" in *Philosophical Perspectives, 3: Philosophy of Mind and Action Theory, 1989*, HORGAN, Terence.
The Causal Efficacy of Content. SEGAL, Gabriel and SOBER, Elliott.
The Neurophilosophy of Pain. GILLETT, G R.
Qualia and Theory Reduction: A Criticism of Paul Churchland. BACHRACH, Jay E.

MENTAL HEALTH
China's Importation of Western Psychiatry: Cultural Relativity and Mental Disorders. WOO, Deborah.
Hide-and-Seek or Show-and-Tell? Emerging Issues of Informed Consent. HAAS, Leonard J.
Institutional Mental Health and Social Control: The Ravages of Epistemological Hubris. FARBER, Seth.
Twenty Years Since *Women and Madness*: Toward a Feminist Institute of Mental Health and Healing. CHESLER, Phyllis.

MENTAL ILLNESS
Creative Characters. YOUNG-BRUEHL, Elisabeth.
Deinstitutionalization: Cycles of Despair. SCULL, Andrew.
Mental Handicap and Citizenship. SPICKER, Paul.
Subjective Boundaries and Combinations in Psychiatric Diagnoses. MIROWSKY, John.
Therapeutic Professions and the Diffusion of Deficit. GERGEN, Kenneth J.

MENTAL IMAGE(S)
Meaning and Mental Representation. CUMMINS, Robert.
Thinking of Something. FITCH, Gregory.

MENTAL OBJECT(S)
Berkeley's Cartesian Anti-Abstractionism. GLOUBERMAN, Mark.
Wittgenstein: Representaciones y pensamientos. RABOSSI, Eduardo.

MENTAL PROCESS(ES)
Concept Attribution in Nonhuman Animals. ALLEN, Collin and HAUSER, Marc D.
Mental Misrepresentation. MALONEY, J Christopher.
Staving Off Catastrophe: A Critical Notice of Jerry Fodor's *Psychosemantics*. JONES, Todd and MULAIRE, Edmond and STICH, Stephen.
The Subject of Experience. GILLETT, Grant.
Thoughtful Brutes: The Ascription of Mental Predicates to Animals in Locke's "Essay". SQUADRITO, Kathleen.

MENTAL STATES
Demystifying Mentalities. LLOYD, G E R.
How to Build a Person: A Prolegomenon. POLLOCK, John L.
Human Consciousness. HANNAY, Alastair.
"Indeterminacy and Mental States" in *Perspectives on Quine*, FOLLESDAL, Dagfinn.
"Narrow Content" in *Propositional Attitudes: The Role of Content in Logic, Language, and Mind*, STALNAKER, Robert.
"On What's in the Head" in *Philosophical Perspectives, 3: Philosophy of Mind and Action Theory, 1989*, STALNAKER, Robert.
"Personal References" in *Information, Semantics and Epistemology*, LOAR, Brian.
"Phenomenal States" in *Philosophical Perspectives, 4: Action Theory and Philosophy of Mind, 1990*, LOAR, Brian.
The Celebration of Emotion: Vallabha's Ontology of Affective Experience. TIMM, Jeffrey R.
Consciousness and Introspective Knowledge. CARLOYE, Jack C.
David Wong on Emotions in Mencius. IHARA, Craig K.
Functionalism's Impotence. WECKERT, J.
Por qué los estados mentales no son clases naturales?. HANSBERG, Olbeth.
The Problem of Reality. JACKENDOFF, Ray.
Remarques sur l'analyse des termes mentaux chez Wittgenstein. BERNIER, Paul.
Response to Craig Ihara's Discussion. WONG, David B.
Towards a Reasonable Version of Methodological Solipsism. ROWLANDS, Mark.

MENTALISM
Externalism and Marr's Theory of Vision. FRANCESCOTTI, Robert M.
Intenzione e azione in Wittgenstein. RAINONE, Antonio.
Process Thought and the Spaciness of Mind. EDWARDS, Rem B.
Words like Faces (in Dutch). LESAGE, D.

MENZEL, C
The Limits of Power. TALIAFERRO, Charles.

MERCIER, D
Désiré Mercier et les débuts de l'Institut de Philosophie. AUBERT, Roger.
Thomas Aquinas and the Renewal of Philosophy: Some Reflections on the Thomism of Mercier (in Dutch). STEEL, C.

MERCY
Entitled to Clemency: Mercy in the Criminal Law. JOHNSON, Carla Ann Hage.
Murphy and Mercy. ADLER, Jacob.

MEREOLOGY
Parts of Classes. LEWIS, David.
"Free Part—Whole Theory" in *Philosophical Applications of Free Logic*, SIMONS, Peter M.
Definite Descriptions and Definite Generics. OJEDA, Almerindo E.
Is a Whole Identical to its Parts?. SCALTSAS, Theodore.
Matrix Representation of Husserl's Part-Whole-Foundation Theory. BLECKSMITH, Richard and NULL, Gilbert.
Pot Bites Kettle: A Reply to Miller. LYCAN, William G.

MERIT
Punyadāna or Transference of Merit—A Fiction. KRISHAN, Y.

MERKLE, P
Response to Merkle and Pritscher. SMITH, Phil.

MERLEAU-PONTY
Ontology and Alterity in Merleau-Ponty. JOHNSON, Galen A (ed).
Phänomenologische Philosophie. STRÖKER, Elisabeth.
"Alterity and the Paradox of Being" in *Ontology and Alterity in Merleau-Ponty*, FROMAN, Wayne J.
"Écart: Reply to Lefort's 'Flesh and Otherness'" in *Ontology and Alterity in Merleau-Ponty*, DILLON, Martin C.
"Flesh and Otherness" in *Ontology and Alterity in Merleau-Ponty*, LEFORT, Claude.
"Flesh as Otherness" in *Ontology and Alterity in Merleau-Ponty*, MADISON, Gary Brent.
"Justice in the Flesh" in *Ontology and Alterity in Merleau-Ponty*, LEVIN, David Michael.
"Listening at the Abyss" in *Ontology and Alterity in Merleau-Ponty*, BURKE, Patrick.
"Merleau-Ponty and Deep Ecology" in *Ontology and Alterity in Merleau-Ponty*, LANGER, Monika.
"Merleau-Ponty and Derrida: Writing on Writing" in *Ontology and Alterity in Merleau-Ponty*, SILVERMAN, Hugh J.
"Merleau-Ponty and Hegel: Radical Essentialism" in *Ontology and Alterity in Merleau-Ponty*, FLAY, Joseph C.
"Merleau-Ponty and *l'Écriture*" in *Writing the Politics of Difference*, FROMAN, Wayne J.
"Nietzsche and Merleau-Ponty: The Body as Attitude" in *Abeunt Studia in Mores: A Festschrift for Helga Doblin*, ECKBLAD, Joyce.
"One-Way Traffic: The Ontology of Decolonization and its Ethics" in *Ontology and Alterity in Merleau-Ponty*, BERNASCONI, Robert.
"Situation and Suspicion in the Thought of Merleau-Ponty" in *Ontology and Alterity in Merleau-Ponty*, WESTPHAL, Merold.
"Two Texts on Merleau-Ponty by Emmanuel Levinas" in *Ontology and Alterity in Merleau-Ponty*, SMITH, Michael B.
"'On How We are and How We Are not to Return to the Things Themselves'" in *Ontology and Alterity in Merleau-Ponty*, WATSON, Stephen.

MERLEAU-PONTY

"Inhabiting" in the *Phenomenology of Perception*. WEINER, Scott E.

The Antinomy of Perception: Merleau-Ponty and Causal Representation Theory. HASS, Lawrence.

Condemned to Time: The Limits of Merleau-Ponty's Quest for Being. LOWRY, Atherton C.

Dialogo sobre humanismo y Marxismo (primera parte). SILVA CAMARENA, Juan Manuel.

The Dimension of Color. FÓTI, Véronique.

Foreign Bodies in Strange Places: A Note on Maurice Merleau-Ponty, Georges Bataille, and Architecture. KRELL, David Farrell.

Language, Speech and Writing: Merleau-Ponty and Derrida on Saussure. FREE, George.

Merleau-Ponty on Taking the Attitude of the Other. MATUSTIK, Martin J.

Merleau-Ponty on the Cartesian "Dubito": A Critical Analysis. HUDAC, Michael C.

Merleau-Ponty's Phenomenology of Sympathy. MATUSTIK, Martin J.

Nature et liberté dans l'ontologie fondamentale de Heidegger. BRISART, Robert.

The Physics of Modern Perception: Beyond Body and World. BARRY JR, James.

Role Taking, Corporeal Intersubjectivity, and Self: Mead and Merleau-Ponty. BOURGEOIS, Patrick L and ROSENTHAL, Sandra B.

Scientific Time and the Temporal Sense of Human Existence: Merleau-Ponty and Mead. BOURGEOIS, Patrick L and ROSENTHAL, Sandra B.

The Concept of Sense in Merleau-Ponty (in Czechoslovakian). SIVAK, Jozef.

Two Reversibilities: Merleau-Ponty and Derrida. YOUNT, Mark.

A Unique Way of Existing: Merleau-Ponty and the Subject. SIEGEL, Jerrold.

Vérité à Faire: Merleau-Ponty's Question Concerning Truth. WALDENFELS, Bernhard.

METAETHICS

"Intuitionism" in *A Companion to Ethics*, DANCY, Jonathan.

"Method and Moral Theory" in *A Companion to Ethics*, JAMIESON, Dale.

"Morality and Psychological Development" in *A Companion to Ethics*, THOMAS, Laurence.

"Naturalism" in *A Companion to Ethics*, PIGDEN, Charles R.

"The Possibility of Convergence between Moral Psychology and Metaethics" in *The Moral Domain: Essays in the Ongoing Discussion between Philosophy and the Social Sciences*, WREN, Thomas E.

"Realism" in *A Companion to Ethics*, SMITH, Michael.

"Relativism" in *A Companion to Ethics*, WONG, David B.

"Subjectivism" in *A Companion to Ethics*, RACHELS, James.

"Universal Prescriptivism" in *A Companion to Ethics*, HARE, R M.

"Seeing Things". PIPER, Adrian M S.

Hume's Metaethical Cognitivism and the Natural Law Theory. GRAEFRATH, Bernd.

La estructura de la ética y la moral. HARE, Richard N and BRASH, Jorge.

The Open Question Argument. PAL, Jagat.

The Principle of Relevant Similarity. LEVVIS, Gary W.

METALANGUAGE

Brains in a Vat, Language and Metalanguage. CASATI, Roberto and DOKIC, Jérome.

METALOGIC

Metalogic and Modality. FIELD, Hartry.

METAMATHEMATICS

The Metamathematics-Popperian Epistemology Connection and its Relation to the Logic of Turing's Programme. BEAUSOLEIL, Jean-Roch.

Relative Consistency and Accessible Domains. SIEG, Wilfried.

METAPHILOSOPHY

Alltagssprachliche Metakommunikation im Englischen und Deutschen. WELTE, Werner.

Applied Ethics and Meta-Philosophy. DAVSON-GALLE, Peter.

Apuntes para un nuevo ámbito de la filosofía. RAMOS, Francisco José.

Filosofía y rebeldía. INNERARITY, Daniel.

METAPHOR(S)

Against Architecture: The Writings of Georges Bataille. HOLLIER, Denis.

Amythia: Crisis in the Natural History of Western Culture. RUE, Loyal D.

The Cogito and Hermeneutics: The Question of the Subject in Ricoeur. JERVOLINO, Domenico.

Demystifying Mentalities. LLOYD, G E R.

Essays on Heidegger and Others: Philosophical Papers, Volume 2. RORTY, Richard.

In Praise of the Cognitive Emotions. SCHEFFLER, Israel.

Kalkulierte Absurditäten. STRUB, Christian.

Knowledge, Fiction, and Imagination. NOVITZ, David.

Metaphors of Mind: Conceptions of the Nature of Intelligence. STERNBERG, Robert J.

Myth and Modern Philosophy. DANIEL, Stephen H.

Nietzsche and the Question of Interpretation. SCHRIFT, Alan D.

Nietzsche: The Body and Culture—Philosophy as a Philological Genealogy. BLONDEL, Eric.

Philosophical Hermeneutics and Literary Theory. WEINSHEIMER, Joel.

The Rhetoric of Berkeley's Philosophy. WALMSLEY, Peter.

"How to Recognise Metaphors in Literature" in *XIth International Congress in Aesthetics, Nottingham 1988*, ELOVAARA, Raili.

"Language as Metaphorical: A Reply to John Cobb" in *Archetypal Process: Self and Divine in Whitehead, Jung, and Hillman*, HOPPER, Stanley R.

"Metaphor, Dreamwork and Irrationality" in *Truth and Interpretation: Perspectives on the Philosophy of Donald Davidson*, CAVELL, Marcia.

"Metaphoric Architectures" in *Looking After Nietzsche*, KOFMAN, Sarah.

AIDS and 'Dirt': Reflections on the Ethics of Ritual Cleanliness. CHURCHILL, Larry R.

Aspects of the Problem of Reference (I). RAJAN, R Sundara.

Biblical Narrative and the Theology of Metonymy. WARD, Graham.

The Body Politic: Democratic Metaphors, Totalitarian Practices, Erotic Rebellions. BERGOFFEN, Debra B.

Gendered Reason: Sex Metaphor and Conceptions of Reason. ROONEY, Phyllis.

History, Differential Equations, and the Problem of Narration. MC CLOSKEY, Donald N.

Language and Metaphysics: The Ontology of Metaphor. HAUSMAN, Carl R.

A Little Daylight: A Reading of Derrida's "White Mythology". LAWLOR, Leonard.

Meanings in Ordinary Language and in Mathematics. THOMAS, R S D.

La metáfora como resolución de un problema comunicativo-lingüístico. FERNÁNDEZ, Teresa Bejaran.

La metáfora en Aristóteles. GAMBRA, José Miguel.

Metaphor and Aspect-Perception. KEMP, G Neville.

Metaphor and Pluralism. MAC CORMAC, Earl R.

Metaphor and the Varieties of Lexical Meaning. HINTIKKA, Jaakko and SANDU, Gabriel.

Metaphor in the Language of Religion. PANDHARIPANDE, Rajeshwari.

Metaphor, Literalism, and the Non-Verbal Arts. BREDIN, Hugh.

The Metaphoric Structure of Sociological Explanation. CORRADI, Consuelo.

Reductive and Nonreductive Simile Theories of Metaphor. TIRRELL, Lynne.

Seeing Metaphor as Seeing-as. TIRRELL, Lynne.

The *Sinnsfrage* and the *Seinsfrage*. PROTEVI, John.

Systems of Interpretation and the Function of the Metaphor. CRIDER, Cathleen and CIRILLO, Leonard.

METAPHYSICIAN(S)

Scharfstein as a Metaphysician of Art (in Hebrew). LURIE, Yuval.

METAPHYSICS

see also Being, Causation, Change, Determinism, Essence(s), Existence, Existentialism, Idealism, Materialism, Naturalism, Ontology, Philosophical Anthropology, Pluralism, Religion, Substance(s)

"Also sprach Herakleitos". WOHLFART, Günter.

About Time: Inventing the Fourth Dimension. FRIEDMAN, William J.

Acts of Meaning. BRUNER, Jerome.

Aristotle's Psychology. ROBINSON, Daniel N.

Artificial Intelligence: Its Scope and Limits. FETZER, James H.

Ästhetik des Abschieds: Kritik der Moderne. EBELING, Hans.

The Authentic Self: Toward a Philosophy of Personality. LACENTRA, Walter.

The Balance of Consciousness: Eric Voegelin's Political Theory. KEULMAN, Kenneth.

Being-in-the-World: A Commentary on Heidegger's "Being and Time", Division 1. DREYFUS, Hubert L.

Bergsonism. DELEUZE, Gilles.

Berkeley's Revolution in Vision. ATHERTON, Margaret.

Between Freiburg and Frankfurt: Toward a Critical Ontology. DALLMAYR, Fred R.

Bewusstsein und Natursein. CHO, Kah Kyung.

Beyond the Big Bang: Quantum Cosmologies and God. DREES, Willem B.

The Butterfly as Companion: Meditations on the First Three Chapters of the Chuang Tzu. WU, Kuang-Ming.

Cálculo y ser (Aproximación a Leibniz). MARZOA, Felipe Martínez.

Caminhos do Filosofar. MIRANDA, Maria do Carmo Tavares de.

The Case for Dualism. SMYTHIES, John R (ed).

Change, Cause and Contradiction: A Defence of the Tenseless Theory of Time. LE POIDEVIN, Robin.

Classics of Analytic Philosophy. AMMERMAN, Robert R (ed).

The Cogito and Hermeneutics: The Question of the Subject in Ricoeur. JERVOLINO, Domenico.

Il compito della filosofia: Saggio su Windelband. OLIVA, Rossella Bonito.

The Concept of Objectivity: An Approximation. BUTLER, Kenneth G.

Cosmos and Anthropos: A Philosophical Interpretation of the Anthropic Cosmological Principle. HARRIS, Errol E.

David Hume's Theory of Mind. FLAGE, Daniel E.

The Dialogues of Plato, Volume II. ALLEN, R E (trans).

Dinâmica do Pensar: Homenagem a Oswaldo Market. FAC LETRAS UNIV LISBOA (ed).

Discussioni sul neo-Tomismo: Per il progresso della Filosofia Cristiana. BLANDINO, Giovanni.

Do the Right Thing: Studies in Limited Rationality. RUSSELL, Stuart.

Donald Davidson. EVNINE, Simon.

Encyclopedia of the Philosophical Sciences in Outline and Critical Writings—G W F Hegel. BEHLER, Ernst (ed).

Essays on Hegel's Logic. DI GIOVANNI, George (ed).

METAPHYSICS

Existence et Subjectivité: Études de Psychologie Phénoménologique. THINÈS, Georges.
Le existentia de deo e le Immortalitate del Anima: Lineas de Philosophia del Esser. BLANDINO, Giovanni.
Existentialism. COOPER, David E.
Experiential Method: Qualitative Research in the Humanities Using Metaphysics and Phenomenology. KIDD, James W.
Explaining Behavior: Reasons in a World of Causes. DRETSKE, Fred.
Explaining Human Action. LENNON, Kathleen.
Exploring Phenomenology (Second Edition). STEWART, David.
False Consciousness. MEYERSON, Denise.
From Sentience To Symbols. PICKERING, John (ed).
Fundamentals of Philosophy (Third Edition). STEWART, David.
George Santayana y la Ironia de la Materia. IZUZQUIZA, Ignacio.
Geschichte, Freiheit und Struktur. RUMPEL, Roland.
God and Subjectivity. GALGAN, Gerald J.
Goethe, Kant, and Hegel: Volume I, Discovering the Mind. KAUFMANN, Walter.
History and the Paradoxes of Metaphysics in "Dantons Tod". TAYLOR, Rodney.
How to Build a Person: A Prolegomenon. POLLOCK, John L.
Human Consciousness. HANNAY, Alastair.
I, We and Body: First Joint Symposium of Philosophers from Africa and from the Netherlands. KIMMERLE, Heinz (ed).
Ideals and Illusions: On Reconstruction and Deconstruction in Contemporary Critical Theory. MC CARTHY, Thomas.
The Immutability of God in the Theology of Hans Urs Von Balthasar. O'HANLON, G F.
In Defense of Mystical Ideas: Support for Mystical Beliefs from a Purely Theoretical Viewpoint. CHAPMAN, Tobias.
Introducing Persons: Theories and Arguments in the Philosophy of Mind. CARRUTHERS, Peter.
Introduction to Metaphysics: The Fundamental Questions. SCHOEDINGER, Andrew B (ed).
Introduction to the Philosophy of Nature. HETZLER, Florence M.
Kant's Model of the Mind: A New Interpretation of Transcendental Idealism. WAXMAN, Wayne.
Kant's Theory of Freedom. ALLISON, Henry E.
Knowledge Representation and Defeasible Reasoning. KYBURG JR, Henry E (ed).
Leibniz and Arnauld. SLEIGH JR, Robert C.
Leibniz and Strawson: A New Essay in Descriptive Metaphysics. BROWN, Clifford.
Leibniz' Position der Rationalität. KAEHLER, Klaus Erich.
Una lettura idealistica della "Analitica Trascendentale". BELLINI, Ornella.
Locke and French Materialism. YOLTON, John W.
The Logical Basis of Metaphysics. DUMMETT, Michael.
Material Beings. VAN INWAGEN, Peter.
Matter and Memory. BERGSON, Henri.
Meditations on First Philosophy: A Bilingual Edition—René Descartes. HEFFERNAN, George (trans).
Metaphors of Mind: Conceptions of the Nature of Intelligence. STERNBERG, Robert J.
Metaphysical Delusion. COWLEY, Fraser.
The Metaphysics of Meaning. KATZ, Jerrold J.
Metaphysics of Natural Complexes (Second Edition). WALLACE, Kathleen (ed).
The Metaphysics of Religious Belief. SHOOMAN, A P.
The Metaphysics of the "Tractatus". CARRUTHERS, Peter.
Metaphysics: A Contemporary Introduction. POST, John F.
Metaphysik als Metahistorik oder Hermeneutik des unreinen Denkens Die Philosophie Max Müllers. RUIZ-PESCE, Ramón Eduardo.
Mind and Cognition: A Reader. LYCAN, William G (ed).
Mind in Action: Essays in the Philosophy of Mind. RORTY, Amelie Oksenberg.
Mind Only: A Philosophical and Doctrinal Analysis of the Vijñānavāda. WOOD, Thomas E.
Mind-Body. MOULYN, Adrian C.
Die Moral der Vernunft Tanszendentale Handlungs-und Legitimationstheorie in der Philosophie Kants. SANDERMANN, Edmund.
Negative Dialectics and the End of Philosophy. ERICKSON, Glenn W.
New Dimensions of Confucian and Neo-Confucian Philosophy. CHENG, Chung-ying.
Nicolai Hartmann's New Ontology. WERKMEISTER, W H.
Nietzsche (III and IV): The Will to Power as Knowledge and as Metaphysics—Heidegger. KRELL, David Farrell (ed).
Nietzsche On Truth and Philosophy. CLARK, Maudemarie.
Nietzsche: The Body and Culture—Philosophy as a Philological Genealogy. BLONDEL, Eric.
The Non-Reality of Free Will. DOUBLE, Richard.
Of Memory, Reminiscence, and Writing: On the Verge. KRELL, David Farrell.
On the Problem of Empathy (Third Revised Edition). STEIN, Edith.
The Ontology of Physical Objects: Four-Dimensional Hunks of Matter. HELLER, Mark.
The Origin of Thought. ROSMINI, Antonio.
Other Human Beings. COCKBURN, David.
The Other Side of Language: A Philosophy of Listening. FIUMARA, Gemma Corradi.
Phänomenologie als ästhetische Theorie. FELLMANN, Ferdinand.
Phänomenologische Philosophie. STRÖKER, Elisabeth.
Philosophical Perspectives, 3: Philosophy of Mind and Action Theory, 1989. TOMBERLIN, James E (ed).
Philosophical Perspectives, 4: Action Theory and Philosophy of Mind, 1990. TOMBERLIN, James E (ed).
The Philosophical Theology of John Duns Scotus. ADAMS, Marilyn McCord (ed).
Philosophical Writings: A Selection—William of Ockham. BOEHNER, Philotheus (ed & trans).
The Philosophy of Action: An Introduction. MOYA, Carlos J.
Philosophy of the "Gita". PATEL, Ramesh N.
Physicalism in Mathematics. IRVINE, Andrew D (ed).
The Place of the Hidden Moon: Erotic Mysticism in the Vaisnava-sahajiyā Cult of Bengal. DIMOCK JR, Edward C.
Plato's "Parmenides". MEINWALD, Constance C.
Plotin: Traité sur la liberté et la volonté de l'Un. LEROUX, Georges.
Plotinus and Freedom: A Meditation on Enneads 6:8. WESTRA, Laura.
Pragmatism: From Peirce to Davidson. MURPHY, John P.
The Preface to Thomistic Metaphysics. KNASAS, John F X.
Pulling up the Ladder: The Metaphysical Roots of Wittgenstein's Tractatus. BROCKHAUS, Richard R.
Quest for Certainty: A Comparative Study of Heidegger and Sankara. GRIMES, John A.
The Question of God in Heidegger's Phenomenology. KOVACS, George.
The Question of Humanism: Challenges and Possibilities. GOICOECHEA, David (ed).
Realism with a Human Face. PUTNAM, Hilary.
Reconsidering Psychology: Perspectives from Continental Philosophy. FAULCONER, James E (ed).
The Recovery of the Soul: An Aristotelian Essay on Self-fulfilment. RANKIN, Kenneth.
The Representational Theory of Mind: An Introduction. STERELNY, Kim.
The Savage Anomaly: The Power of Spinoza's Metaphysics and Politics. NEGRI, Antonio.
Science and Religion: One World-Changing Perspectives on Reality. FENNEMA, Jan (ed).
The Science of the Mind (Second Edition). FLANAGAN, Owen.
Scientific Theories. SAVAGE, C Wade (ed).
Selbsttäuschung. LÖW-BEER, Martin.
Self and Non-Self: The Drigdrisyaviveka Attributed to Samkara. RAPHAEL (trans).
The Self-Overcoming of Nihilism: Nishitani Keiji. PARKES, Graham (trans).
Sensations: A Defense of Type Materialism. HILL, Christopher S.
Der sinnliche Gehalt der Wahrnehmung. SCHANTZ, Richard.
Sound, Speech, and Music. BURROWS, David.
Spirit and Existence: A Philosophy Inquiry into the Meaning of Spiritual Existence. GELVEN, Michael.
Strukturanthropologie "Der menschliche Mensch". ROMBACH, Heinrich.
Studies on Mario Bunge's "Treatise". WEINGARTNER, Paul (ed).
Swimming Against the Current in Contemporary Philosophy: Occasional Essays and Papers. VEATCH, Henry B.
The Taming of Chance. HACKING, Ian.
Thinking Philosophically: An Introduction to Philosophy with Readings. GUSMANO, Joseph J.
Toward the Death of Man. KLUBACK, William.
The Tragedy of Reason: Toward a Platonic Conception of Logos. ROOCHNIK, David.
Understanding the Chinese Mind: The Philosophical Roots. ALLINSON, Robert E (ed).
Understanding the Representational Mind. PERNER, Josef.
The Unity of Kant's "Critique of Pure Reason": Experience, Language, and Knowledge. WILLIAMS, T C.
The Unity of Understanding: A Study in Kantian Problems. SCHWYZER, Hubert.
Das Verhängnis Erste Philosophie. EBELING, Hans.
Vico: A Study of the 'New Science' (Second Edition). POMPA, Leon.
Weakness of the Will. GOSLING, Justin.
"Back of 'Back to Beyond' and Creeping Dichotomism" in *Archetypal Process: Self and Divine in Whitehead, Jung, and Hillman*, CASEY, Edward S.
"Back to Beyond: On Cosmology" in *Archetypal Process: Self and Divine in Whitehead, Jung, and Hillman*, HILLMAN, James.
"Chinese Metaphysics as Non-Metaphysics: Confucian and Daoist Insights into the Nature of Reality" in *Understanding the Chinese Mind: The Philosophical Roots*, CHENG, Chung-ying.
"The Computational Conception of Mind" in *Acting and Reflecting: The Interdisciplinary Turn in Philosophy*, SCOTT, Dana S.
"Evolution—Matter of Fact or Metaphysical Idea?" in *Logic, Methodology and Philosophy of Science, VIII*, LÖTHER, Rolf.
"Giovanni Gualberto (Alberto) De Soria e la 'Cosmologia'" in *Scienza, Filosofia e Religione tra '600 e '700 in Italia*, PONZELLINI, Ornella.

METAPHYSICS

"Invidious Contrasts within Theory" in *Meaning and Method: Essays in Honor of Hilary Putnam*, SKLAR, Lawrence.
"The Metaphysic of Things and Discourse About Them" in *Reconsidering Psychology: Perspectives from Continental Philosophy*, WILLIAMS, Richard N.
"A Metaphysical Psychology to Un-Locke Our Ailing World" in *Archetypal Process: Self and Divine in Whitehead, Jung, and Hillman*, GRIFFIN, David Ray.
"The Metaphysics of Interpretation" in *Truth and Interpretation: Perspectives on the Philosophy of Donald Davidson*, ROVANE, Carol.
"Natural Kinds" in *Perspectives on Quine*, HACKING, Ian.
"Philosophy and the Mirage of Hermeneutics" in *Reading Rorty*, HOLÓWKA, Jacek.
"Through a Glass Darkly: Vagueness in the Metaphysics of the Analytic Tradition" in *The Analytic Tradition: Philosophical Quarterly Monographs, Volume 1*, SACKS, Mark.
L' "altro inizio" della filosofia: I *Beiträge zur Philosophie* di Heidegger. SAMONÀ, Leonardo.
"But Would That Still Be Me?" Notes on Gender, "Race," Ethnicity, as Sources of "Identity". APPIAH, Anthony.
El "De Ente et Uno": una ontología agustiniana. MAGNAVACCA, Silvia.
"Does Metaphysics Really Matter for Practice?" It Depends on the Practitioner. GARRISON, James W.
"Extrinsic Cognoscibility": A Seventeenth Century Supertranscendental Notion. DOYLE, John P.
La "memoria Dei" en el libro X de Las confesiones. PEGUEROLES, Juan.
"Paramount Reality" in Schutz and Gurwitsch. KASSAB, Elizabeth Suzanne.
"Sobria ebrietas": Nietzsche y las perpleijidades del espíritu. CRUZ CRUZ, Jua.
"Threading-the-Needle: The Case For and Against Common-Sense Realism". TIBBETTS, Paul.
"To Illuminate Your Trace": Self in Late Modern Feminist Theology. KELLER, Catherine.
"Why Do Things Look as They Do?" Some Gibsonian Answers to Koffka's Question. NATSOULAS, Thomas.
The 'Body': A Husserlian Phenomenological Analysis. DAS, Paritosh Kumar.
The 'Gay Science' of Nietzsche (in Dutch). ESTERHUYSE, Willie.
The 'New' Nietzsche. COOPER, David E.
'Ontological Commitment' in the Context of the Buddhist Thought. MITTAL, Kewal Krisha.
(Post-) Metaphysik und (Post-) Moderne: Zur Sache des "schwachen Denkens". FRÜCHTL, Josef.
A Contribution of the Conception of "Discursivity" and "Spontaneiti" of Thinking (in Czechoslovakian). BENYOVSZKY, Ladislav.
A Post-Metaphysical Moral: An Introduction to the Moral Theory of Jürgen Habermas (in French). HUNYADI, Mark.
Aberrations of a Sledgehammer: Reply to Devitt. LUNTLEY, Michael.
Aberrations of the Realism Debate. DEVITT, Michael.
An Abyss of Difference: Laing, Sartre and Jaspers. KIRSNER, Douglas.
Acerca de uma tese ricoeuriana. SUMARES, Manuel.
Action and Freedom. ROY, Pabitrakumar.
Adorno and the French Post-Structuralists on the Other of Reason. NUYEN, A T.
The Advaita Theory of Liberation. DAS, Bhupendra Chandra.
Against Cartesian Dualism: Strawson and Sartre on the Unity of Person. MUI, Constance.
Against the Fantasts. THOMAS, J L H.
Agency and Omniscience. KAPITAN, Tomis.
Algunas consecuencias del panenteismo krausista: ecología y mujer. MENÉNDEZ UREÑA, Enrique.
Algunas consideraciones sobre la substancia en la metafísica de Juan Duns Escoto. BEUCHOT, Mauricio.
An Alleged Analogy Between Numbers and Propositions. CRANE, Tim.
Altruism and the Avoidance of Solipsism. CHONG, Kim-Chong.
An Ambiguity in Parfit's Theory of Personal Identity. CURZER, Howard.
La analogía del ser en Suárez. ROIG GIRONELLA, J.
Analytic Functionalism and the Reduction of Phenomenal States. LEVIN, Janet.
The Anatomist and the Painter: The Continuity of Hume's *Treatise* and *Essays*. IMMERWAHR, John.
Anomalism, Supervenience, and Davidson on Content-Individuation. ROWLANDS, Mark.
The Anomaly of World: From Scheler to Heidegger. SCHALOW, Frank.
Anti-Individualism and Privileged Access. MC KINSEY, Michael.
Antirealism and Realist Claims of Invariance. ELDER, Crawford L.
Apophasis and Metaphysics in the *Periphyseon* of John Scottus Eriugena. CARABINE, Deirdre.
L'aporia della kìnesis in Aristotele. ROCCARO, Giuseppe.
Approaches to the Theory of Purusarthas. RAJAN, R Sundara.
Apriorische Einsicht und metaphysische Notwendigkeit: Eine Auseinandersetzung mit Kripkes Kant-Kritik. WENDEL, Hans Jürgen.
Aquinas on Resolution in Metaphysics. TAVUZZI, Michael.
Are There Cultural Universals?. WIREDU, Kwasi.
Aristote admet-il un infini en acte et en puissance en "Physique III, 4-8"?. CÔTÉ, Antoine.
Aristóteles desde Heidegger. CASARES, Angel J.
Aristotelian and Whiteheadian Conceptions of Actuality: I. FETZ, Reto Luzius and FELT, James W.
Aristotelian and Whiteheadian Conceptions of Actuality: II. FETZ, Reto Luzius and FELT, James W.
Aristotelian Contraries. BOGEN, James.
Aristotelian Essentialism. MATTHEWS, Gareth B.
Aristotelian Form and End. CURZER, Howard J.
Aristotle's Causality Theory. ANDRIOPOULOS, D Z.
Aristotle's Motionless Soul. TWEEDALE, Martin.
Aristotle's Technical Simulation and its Logic of Causal Relations. LOECK, Gisela.
Artificial Intelligence and Wittgenstein. CASEY, Gerard.
Artists, Computer Programs and Performance. GODLOVITCH, A.
Aspects of Freedom. WOOD, Robert E.
Aspetti di attualità teoretica del pensiero procliano negli studi di Werner Beierwaltes. SCOTTI, Nicoletta.
Atheism, Theism and Big Bang Cosmology. SMITH, Quentin.
Attitudes Towards the Body: Philosophy and Common Sense. WILLIAMSON, Colwyn.
Attitudes, Leprechauns and Neutrinos: The Ontology of Behavioral Science. CHANDLER, Marthe.
Autonomy, Empathy, and Transcendence in Sophocles' *Antigone*: A Phenomenological Perspective. NISSIM-SABAT, Marilyn.
Las aventuras de la differencia (G Vattimo). PEGUEROLES, Juan.
Avoiding the Fly Bottle. KOLENDA, Konstantin.
Backwards Causation and the Permanence of the Past. ODDIE, Graham.
Baur's "Conversation with Gadamer" and "Contribution to the Gadamer-Lonergan Discussion": A Reaction. LAWRENCE, Fred.
Bayle, Leibniz, Hume and Reid on Extension, Composites and Simples. CUMMINS, Phillip.
Ein Bedürfnis nach Schelling. BRAUN, Hermann.
Before Refraining: Concepts for Agency. BELNAP JR, Nuel D.
Der Begriff der Bewegung bei Kant: Über den Grundbegriff der Empirie und die empirischen Begriffe. HOFFMANN, Thomas Sören.
Being and Categorial Intuition. COBB-STEVENS, Richard.
The Bellman's Map: Does Antifoundationalism Entail Incommensurability and Relativism?. CHURCHILL, John.
Berkeley's Anti-Abstractionism: Reply to Moked. GLOUBERMAN, Mark.
Berkeley's Arguments for Other Minds. FALKENSTEIN, Lorne.
Berkeley's Cartesian Anti-Abstractionism. GLOUBERMAN, Mark.
Berkeley, Perception, and Identity. BAXTER, Donald L M.
Better the Union Theory. HONDERICH, Ted.
Beyond Realism: Nietzsche's New Infinite. CONWAY, Daniel W.
Bibliographie de Paul Ricoeur: Compléments (jusqu'en 1990). VANSINA, Frans.
The Biographies of Siddhasena (II). GRANOFF, Phyllis.
Blackburn on Filling in Space. RICE, Hugh.
Blanshard's Ethics of Belief and Metaphysical Postulates. PHILLIPS, Winfred George.
Bodily Theory and Theory of the Body. GILES, James.
The Body as Understood in Contemporary Thought and Biblical Categories. VERGOTE, Antoine.
Bolzano's Contribution to Cognition and/or the Creation of Theory of Sets (in Czechoslovakian). VECERKA, Kazimir.
The Book of Anaxagoras. BRUMBAUGH, Robert S.
A Brief Discussion of One Aspect of the *Shangtong* Idea. YUANHUA, Wang.
Bringing Things About. DIEFENBECK, James A.
Burgeoning Skepticism. DE VRIES, Willem.
Burning Passions. NEILL, Alex and RIDLEY, Aaron.
Can There Be a Possible World in Which Memory Is Unreliable?. LEUNG, Edwin Sing Choe.
Cartesian Passions and Cartesian Dualism. HOFFMAN, Paul.
Il caso "Siris", ovvero la "seconda filosofia" di George Berkeley vescovo di Cloyne. NERI, Luigi.
The Causal History of Computational Activity: Maudlin and Olympia. BARNES, Eric.
Causal Holism and Commonsense Psychology: A Reply to O'Brien. STICH, Stephen P.
Causalistico-Occasionalistic Dispute in Islam as Opposing of "Greek" and "Islamic" Spirit (in Serbo-Croatian). BUCAN, Daniel.
Causality: Sankara and Aristotle. DHAVAMONY, Mariasusai.
Causation in the Philosophy of Mind. JACKSON, Frank and PETTIT, Philip.
Causation: Reductionism Versus Realism. TOOLEY, Michael.
Causes and Coincidences. OWENS, David.
Causing, Enabling, and Counterfactual Dependence. MACKIE, Penelope.
The Celebration of Emotion: Vallabha's Ontology of Affective Experience. TIMM, Jeffrey R.
Ceteris Paribus Laws. SCHIFFER, Stephen.
Charles Hartshorne's Rationalism. GUTOWSKI, Piotr.
Chen Que versus Huang Zongxi: Confucianism Faces Modern Times in the Seventeenth Century. STRUVE, Lynn A.
The Chicken and the Egg. TEICHMANN, Roger.
China's Traditional Mode of Thought and Science. DISHENG, Yang.
Choosing Religious Languages: A Note on Two 'Proofs' of God's Existence. SAPADIN, Eugene.

METAPHYSICS

Churchland, Introspection, and Dualism. ZEMACH, Eddy M.
Clocks and Time (in Czechoslovakian). DUBSKY, Ivan.
Cognitive Psychology, Phenomenology, and the "Creative Tension of Voices". EVANS, Fred.
Collection and Division in the *Phaedrus* and *Statesman*. WEDIN, Michael V.
Comment on Huston Smith's Review of *The Essential Writings of Frithiof Schuon*. ANDERSON, Tyson.
Comment: Selective Anti-Realism. MC MULLIN, Ernan.
Commentary on "Epistemology as Hypothesis". SLEEPER, R W.
Commentary on Sayre-McCord's 'Being a Realist about Relativism'. WONG, David B.
Comments of Garrison on Greene: Does Metaphysics Really Matter for Practice?. NEIMAN, Alven M.
Common Ground: Aristotle on Human and Divine Noetic Activity. MORGAN, Vance G.
Comparative Dialectics: Nishida Kitarō's *Logic of Place and Western Dialectical Thought*. AXTELL, G S.
Compromiso Ontico y Teorías Científicas. MAYORGA, Alejandro and VARGAS, Celso.
Concentric Circles: An Exploration of Three Concepts in Process Metaphysics. AUXIER, Randall.
Concept Attribution in Nonhuman Animals. ALLEN, Collin and HAUSER, Marc D.
The Concept of Ego in Husserl's Philosophy. DAS, Paritosh Kumar.
The Concept of Mathematical Truth. ROTA, Gian-Carlo.
El concepto de substancia sensible en Aristóteles: Génesis histórica de la cuestión. BLAQUIER, Carlos P.
Conceptual Idealism Revisited. RESCHER, Nicholas.
Concerning the Absurdity of Life. SMITH, Quentin.
Condemned to Time: The Limits of Merleau-Ponty's Quest for Being. LOWRY, Atherton C.
Conditional Intention. CARTWRIGHT, J P W.
Connectionist Minds. CLARK, Andy.
El conocimiento de Dios en la exposición de Tomás de Aquino sobre el "De divinis nominibus" de D Areopagita. ANDEREGGEN, Ignacio E M.
El conocimiento de los cuerpos según Malebranche (I). FERNANDEZ RODRIGUEZ, Jose Luis.
El conocimiento del singular en José Gaos. LLANO, Carlos.
Conocimiento y determinismo. LAGUNILLA, Ana E Galán.
Conocimientos negativo y conocimiento afirmativo de Dios en Santo Tomás y en Hegel. ANDEREGGEN, Ignacio E M.
Conscious and Unconscious States. BEN-ZEEV, Aaron.
Consciousness Naturalized: Supervenience Without Physical Determinism. SENCHUK, Dennis M.
Consciousness—From Behavioural Neurologist's Horizon. MUKHOPADHYAY, Asok Kumar.
Consciousness: Creative and Self-Creating. BUKALA, C R.
Consideraciones en torno a la polémica Leibniz-Clarke. PONCE ALBERCA, Carmen.
Contemplación y Dios en Aristóteles. DE KIRCHNER, Beatriz Bossi.
The Contending Among the Hundred Schools of Thought During the Warring States Period. ZEHUA, Liu.
The Continuous and the Discrete: Leibniz Versus Berkeley. ANAPOLITANOS, D A.
Conventional Foundationalism and the Origins of the Norms. CUDD, Ann E.
Corpuscles, Mechanism, and Essentialism in Berkeley and Locke. ATHERTON, Margaret.
La cosmologia tra filosofia ed empirologia. PELLECCHIA, Pasquale.
Could I Conceive Being a Brain in a Vat?. COLLIER, John D.
Could Someone Else Have Had My Headache?. STONE, Jim.
La création du Nouveau par le Hasard et par le temps: un vieux thème épicurien. LARGEAULT, Jean.
Creation in a Closed Universe, *Or* Have Physicists Disproved the Existence of God?. LE POIDEVIN, Robin.
The Creationist Theory of Abrupt Appearances: A Critique. STRAHLER, Arthur N.
Critical Thinking and Thinking Critically: Response to Siegel. FINOCCHIARO, Maurice A.
Las criticas de J Bennett a la doctrina kantiana del esquematismo. JÁUREGUI, Claudia.
Crusius: un jalón olvidado en la ruta hacia el criticismo. ROLDÁN, Concha.
La cuestión de Dios en el pensar de Heidegger. FORNET-BETANCOURT, Raúl.
Cuestiones de sobrevivencia. MILLÁN, Gustavo Ortiz (trans) and SOSA, Ernest.
Dall'attualismo al tensionalismo. SIMONE, Aldo.
Dans quelle mesure et par quelles images les mythes grecs ont-ils symbolisé le néant?. RUDHARDT, Jean.
Dasein—Mitsein—Sprache: Heideggers Auffassung über das "Wesen der Sprache" in "Sein und Zeit". TIETZ, Udo.
David Wong on Emotions in Mencius. IHARA, Craig K.
Davidson's Troubles with Supervenience. KLAGGE, James.
The De-Con-Struction of Reason. GLYNN, Simon.
Dead Souls and Living Instruments. HICKMAN, Larry.
The Deconstruction of Time. LLEWELYN, John.
A Defence of the New Tenseless Theory of Time. OAKLANDER, L Nathan.
Defending the Tradition. NIELSEN, Kai.
Dehātmavāda or the Body as Soul: Exploration of a Possibility within Nyāya Thought. LATH, Mukund (trans) and SHUKLA, Pandit Badrinath.
Demonstrative Content: A Reply to John McDowell. PEACOCKE, Christopher.
Descartes censuré par Huet. MALBREIL, Germain.
Descartes on Colour. COTTINGHAM, John.
Descartes on Sensations and 'Animal Minds'. SENCERZ, Stefan.
Descartes on Sensory Representation: A Study of the *Dioptrics*. MAC KENZIE, Ann Wilbur.
Descartes und der reale Unterschied zwischen der Seele und dem Körper. IMLAY, Robert A.
Descriptions and Group Reference. MUKHERJI, Nirmalangshu.
La determinación de la esencia en X: Zubiri y Tomás de Aquino. SOTO, José Cercós.
A Determinist Dilemma. PERSSON, Ingmar.
The Development of Wittgenstein's Views about the Other Minds Problem. TER HARK, M R M.
Devenir et génération chez Platon. HUBERT, Bernard.
Dialectical Thinking in Metaphysics—Van Kues: Coincidental Thinking and the Problem of Idealistic Monism (in German). WINKLER, Norbert.
Die Wissenschaft denkt nicht. SALANSKIS, Jean-Michel.
The Difference Between Real Change and *Mere* Cambridge Change. CLELAND, Carol E.
The Dimension of Color. FÓTI, Véronique.
A Dionysian Songbook: the Mysterious Singing. LEVINE, Elliott M.
Dios y el hombre en San Agustin. PEGUEROLES, Juan.
Discussione di alcune questioni di cosmologia neo-tomista. BLANDINO, Giovanni.
Disembodying 'Bodily' Sensations. COMBES, Richard.
Las disonancias de la libertad (I). INNERARITY, Daniel.
A Disproof of the Existence of God. WEEKS, Ian.
La distinción entre esencia y existencia en Avicena. IBÁÑEZ, Alejandro Herrera.
Divenire, principio di causalità, affermazione teologica. SACCHI, Dario.
Divided Minds. HIRSCH, Eli.
La doctrina del don de San Agustín de Hipona. BELDA PLANS, Pilar.
Du libre arbitre selon s Thomas d'Aquin. CORBIN, Michel.
Efficient Causation Within Concrescence. FORD, Lewis S.
Eliminative Materialism and Substantive Commitments. NELSON, Mark T.
Emanating Causes: New Battle Lines for Natural Theology?. KING-FARLOW, John.
The Emergence and Original Meaning of the Name 'Metaphysics'. REINER, Hans and ADLER, Pierre and PASKIN, David.
Emergent Psychoneural Monism: Mario Bunge and the Body and Soul Problem (in German). MÖLLER, Wolfgang.
Emotions, Feelings and Contexts: A Reply to Robert Kraut. SOLOMON, Robert C.
El enigma de la libertad humana en Gabriel Marcel. O'CALLAGHAN, Paul.
Ensuring Two Bird Deaths with One Throw. LESLIE, John.
An Entropic Analysis of Postmodernism. MC KINNEY, Ronald H.
L'epocalità metafisica di Nietzsche: "Sentiero interrotto" della filosofia heideggeriana. TRAVERSO, Patrizia.
Ernst Mach and the Elimination of Subjectivity. HAMILTON, Andy.
Essai sur le développement historique de la voie phénoménologique. MAESSCHALCK, Marc.
Essentialism Old and New: Suarez and Brody. KRONEN, John D.
Establishing of the Object of Metaphysics—Separation (in Polish). MARYNIARCZYK, A.
Estructuras y representaciones. DE LA SIENRA, Adolfo García.
Être et non-être chez Aristote: contraires ou contradictoires?. BERTI, Enrico.
El evento (ereignis) como concepto fundamental de la filosofía de Heidegger (1a parte). BERCIANO V, Modesto.
El evento (Ereignis) como concepto fundamental de la filosofía de Heidegger (2a parte). BERCIANO V, Modesto.
The Evidence for Reincarnation. COCKBURN, David.
Examen del "ahora". HUÉSCAR, Antonio R.
The Existence of Non-Existence of Things which are Not in the Mind. POMERANTZ, Alfred.
Existencia de Dios y libertad humana. HERRERA, J Jesús.
Experience and Causal Explanation in Medical Empiricism. PENTZOPOULOU-VALALAS, Teresa.
Experimental Methods and Conceptual Confusion: An Investigation into R L Gregory's Theory of Perception. HACKER, P M S.
Explaining Necessity. MASON, Richard V.
External Creation and Eternal Production of the World According to Bonaventura (in Dutch). VAN VELDHUIJSEN, Peter.
Externalism and Experience. MC CULLOCH, Gregory.
Externalism Revisited: Is There Such a Thing as Narrow Content?. JACOB, Pierre.
Farewell to the Tradition: Doing without Metaphysics and Epistemology. NIELSEN, Kai.
Festrede zum 300: Geburstag von Gottfried Wilhelm Leibniz am 1 Juli 1946 in der Aula der Universitat Leipzig. GADAMER, Hans-Georg.

METAPHYSICS

Fictional Objects in Literature and Mental Representations. BACHRACH, Jay E.
Filosofía, hoy. CUÉLLAR, Hortensia.
Filósofos naúfragos. BALIÑAS, Carlos.
Finalidad y dimensiones "kaíricas" de la estructura del ser. MOUTSOPOULOS, Evanghélos A.
Finding Ourselves: Personal Identity and the Limits of Possible-World Arguments. BECK, Simon.
Finitude Rediscovered. BARBER, Michael.
Fogelin on Hume on Miracles. FLEW, Antony.
Foreign Bodies in Strange Places: A Note on Maurice Merleau-Ponty, Georges Bataille, and Architecture. KRELL, David Farrell.
Forms and Causes In Plato's *Phaedo*. BYRNE, Christopher.
Foucault: Making a Difference. LILLY, Reginald.
Fragmented Selves and the Problem of Ownership. BRENNAN, Andrew.
The Free Will Defense and Determinism. SENNETT, James F.
Freedom and the Free Will Defense. GALE, Richard M.
Freedom, Necessity, and Laws of Nature as Relations between Universals. VIHVELIN, Kadri.
Freud Contra Sartre: Repression or Self-Deception?. MIRVISH, Adrian.
From Brahma to a Blade of Grass. COLLINS, Alfred.
From Philosophy to Politics: On Nietzsche's Ironic Metaphysics of Will to Power. PARENS, Erik.
From Philosophy to Politics: On Nietzsche's Ironic Metaphysics of Will to Power. PARENS, Erik.
From Pyrrhonism to Post-Modernism. GLIDDEN, David K.
From the Phenomenology of Time Toward Process Metaphysics: Pragmatism and Heidegger. ROSENTHAL, Sandra B.
From Truth to 'Alhieia to Opening and Rapture. MALY, Kenneth.
Functionalism's Impotence. WECKERT, J.
Functionalisme versus dubbelaspecttheorie: tertium datur. MACKOR, Anne Ruth.
Los fundamentos de la especulación metafísica sobre el conocimiento. SACCHI, Mario E.
G E Moore on the Values of Whole and Parts: A Critique. PAL, Jagat.
Gelehrter zwischen Romantik und Hegelianismus in Finnland—Johan Vilhelm Snellman (1806-1881). HÄNTSCH, Carola.
The Generation of Form in Aristotle. SHIELDS, Christopher.
Glasnost and Enlightenment. OLSON, Alan M.
Glose sur le prologue du traité "de l'âme" d'Aristote. VERNIER, Jean-Marie.
God and Man: Action and Reference in Hobbes. BERTMAN, Martin A.
God and Real Time. CRAIG, William Lane.
Governance by Emotion. ALLEN, R T.
Gustavo Bontadini un metafisico per vocazione. LATORA, Salvatore.
Habermas on Heidegger's *Being and Time*. SCHARFF, Robert C.
Haecceitas and the Bare Particular. PARK, Woosuk.
Hamanns Metakritik im ersten Entwurf. BAYER, Oswald.
He Doesn't Really Want to Try. ADAMS, Frederick.
He Wants to Try. MELE, Alfred R.
Hegel and Schopenhauer as Partisans of Goethe's Theory of Color. LAUXTERMANN, P F H.
Hegel and the Overcoming of the Understanding. BAUR, Michael.
Hegel, Logic, and Metaphysics. HARTSHORNE, Charles.
Hegel, Marx, Lukács: The Dialectic of Freedom and Necessity. DAY, Richard B.
Hegel, Nietzsche, and Freud on Madness and the Unconscious. BERTHOLD-BOND, Daniel.
Hegel: fenomenología del espíritu. MONTOYA, Rocío Basurto.
Heidegger and Myth: A Loop in the History of Being. HATAB, Lawrence J.
Heidegger and Nietzsche—Thinkers of the 'Between'? (in Dutch). GOOSEN, D P.
Heidegger and Psychoanalysis: The Seminars in Zollikon. SCOTT, Charles E.
Heidegger and the Critique of the Understanding of Evil as Privatio Boni. CAPOBIANCO, Richard.
Heidegger and the Temporal Constitution of the *A Priori*. SCHALOW, Frank.
Heidegger on the Self, Authenticity and Inauthenticity. MANSBACH, Abraham.
Heidegger und die Frage um die Quelle des Grundbegriffes der Metaphysik (in Polish). ROZDZENSKI, R.
Heidegger und Schopenhauer. HECKER, Hellmuth.
Heidegger's Attempt at Rehousing Man Through the *Kehre des Denkens*. RAUCHE, G A.
A Heideggerian Analysis of Fundamentalism: A Brief Discussion. O'CONNELL, Colin.
Heideggerian Retrieval of Cartesianism. ROY, Krishna.
Heideggers Bedeutung für die Psychologie. VON USLAR, Detlev.
Henri Bergson and Postmodernism. MULDOON, Mark S.
Hermeneutic Phenomenology and Taoism. KIDD, James W.
An Historical Sketch of Pluralism. RECK, Andrew J.
Historicism and Phenomenology (in Czechoslovakian). CIBULKA, J.
History and Ontology: A Reading of Nietzsche's Second "Untimely Meditation". BAMBACH, Charles R.
Holism and Indeterminacy. MALPAS, Jeff.
Holism and Nonseparability. HEALEY, Richard A.
El hombre y el misterio del ser. TRIANA, Manuel.
Hope: Its Essence and Forms (in Polish). SYMOTIUK, Stefan.
How Euclidean Geometry Has Misled Metaphysics. NERLICH, Graham.
How Would an *Übermensch* Regard His Past and Future?. MC INERNEY, Peter K.
How's and Why's: Causation Un-Locked. FRANKEL, Lois.
Hume and Physical Necessity. FLEW, Antony.
Hume and Thick Connexions. BLACKBURN, Simon.
Hume Contra Spinoza?. KLEVER, Wim.
Hume on Practical Reason. ROBERTSON, John.
Hume on the Idea of Existence. CUMMINS, Phillip D.
Husserl and Hume: Overcrowding Scepticism?. MURPHY, Richard T.
Husserl's Concept of Philosophy. SCHUHMANN, Karl.
Husserl's Notion of Constitution in Heidegger's Treatment of Care. THOMAS, V C.
Husserl's Phenomenology of Knowledge and Cognition (in Polish). DEBOWSKI, Jozef.
Husserl's Time Perception (in Portuguese). PEREIRA JÚNIOR, A.
Husserl—Bolzano II (in Czechoslovakian). BAYEROVA, Marie.
Hypnosis and the Philosophy of Mind. HAIGHT, Mary.
The Idea of Transcendence. COBURN, Robert C.
Idéalisme ou réalisme?. LARGEAULT, Jean.
Ideas de mundo en el *Tractatus*. ROJO, Roberto.
Idées de négations. CHIESA, Curzio.
Identity, Transformation, and What Matters in Survival. MARTIN, Raymond.
La imaginación creadora en el pensamiento de Gastón Bachelard. CASTILLO, Roberto.
Immateriality and the Domain of Thomistic Natural Philosophy. JOHNSON, Mark F.
Das Imperiale an der Identitätsphilosophie: Spuren des Totalitären in der abendländischen Philosophie. MANSILLA, Hugo C F.
In Defence of Graded Love. LAI, Whalen.
Incarnation and Essentialization: A Reading of Heidegger. CAPUTO, John D.
Incarnational Anthropology. HALDANE, John.
The Incoherence of Kant's Transcendental Dialectic: Specifying the Minimal Conditions for Dialectical Error. HERMAN, David J.
Incommensurability and Recurrence: from Oresme to Simmel. SMALL, Robin.
The Inorganic Body and the Ambiguity of Freedom. COLLIER, Andrew.
The Integral Self: Systematic Illusion or Inescapable Task?. COLAPIETRO, Vincent M.
The Intelligible World-Animal in Plato's *Timaeus*. PARRY, Richard D.
The Intentional and the Intended. GARCIA, J L A.
Intentions, Actions, and Routines: A Problem in Krister Segerberg's Theory of Action. ELGESEM, Dag.
La interpretación russelliana de Leibniz y el atomismo metodológico de Moore. RODRÍGUEZ CONSUEGRA, Francisco.
Interpretatie en filosofische methode. BUEKENS, Filip.
An Intersubjective Concept of Individuality. HABERMAS, Jürgen.
Intersubjectivity without Subjectivism. SINGER, Beth J.
Is a Whole Identical to its Parts?. SCALTSAS, Theodore.
Is Connectionism Commonsense?. O'BRIEN, Gerard J.
Is Creativity Good?. HALPER, Edward.
Is Friedrich Nietzsche a Precursor to the Holistic Movement?. KREBBS JR, R Stephen.
Is Karma Evolutionary?. KRISHAN, Y.
Is Neuroscience Relevant to Philosophy?. CHURCHLAND, Patricia Smith.
Is the Brain a Digital Computer?. SEARLE, John R.
Is the Central Upanishadic Teaching a Reductionist Thesis?. PULIGANDLA, Ramakrishna.
Is the Skeptical Attitude the Attitude of a Skeptic?. PAPRZYCKA, Katarzyna.
Is There a "Meaning" of Being? Against the Deconstructionist Reading of Heidegger. SCHALOW, Frank.
Is There a Distinction Between Reason and Emotion in Mencius?. WONG, David B.
Is Transcendental Idealism Coherent?. BALDNER, Kent.
Ist die Naturphilosophie eine abgelegte Gestalt des modernen Geistes. WAHSNER, Renate.
Ist die Naturphilosophie eine abgelegte Gestalt des modernen Geistes?. WAHSNER, Renate.
Isvarakrsna's Two-Level-Perception: Propositional and Non-Propositional. CLEAR, Edeltraud Harzer.
James and Freud. MYERS, Gerald E.
Japanese Ethics: Beyond Good and Evil. WARGO, Robert J J.
Jivacide, Zombies and *Jivanmuktas*. HERMAN, A L.
John Wyclif's Metaphysics of Scriptural Integrity in the *De Veritate Sacrae Scripturae*. TRESKO, Michael.
Josiah Royce: la metafisica della comunità. BUZZI GRASSI, Elisa.
Juicios de percepción y de experiencia en Kant. FERNÁNDEZ, Alvaro López.
La justificación práctica del principio de no contradicción en Aristóteles. CASSINI, A.
Kant e o problema da origem das representações elementares: apontamentos. MARQUES, U R de Azevedo.

METAPHYSICS

Kant en de mogelijkheid van de metafysica als wetenschap. PERRICK, M.
Kant et l'histoire de la philosophie la vision problématologique. TIMMERMANS, Benoît.
Kant's Diversity Theory: A Dissenting View. GLOUBERMAN, Mark.
Kant's Doctrine of Heuristics: An Interpretation of the Ideas of Reason. GRACYK, Theodore A.
Kant's Theory of Empirical Judgment and Modern Semantics. HANNA, Robert.
Kant, Mendelssohn, Lambert, and the Subjectivity of Time. FALKENSTEIN, Lorne.
Kant: del derecho de libertad a la exigencia racional del Estado. PASTORE, Romano.
Kantian Freedom Naturalized. MELCHERT, Norman.
Karl Marx and African Emancipatory Thought: A Critique of Marx's Euro-centric Metaphysics. SEREQUEBERHAN, Tsenay.
Karma and Rebirth in *Alberuni's India*. SHARMA, Arvind.
Kenny and Religious Experiences. JORDAN, J.
A Kierkegaardian Critique of Heidegger's Concept of Authenticity. BERTHOLD-BOND, Daniel.
Knowability, Actuality, and the Metaphysics of Context-Dependence. PERCIVAL, Philip.
Krtapranasa and Akrtabhyagama: An Analysis, Defence and Rationale of the Buddhist Theory of Action. CHINCHORE, Mangala R.
L'affirmation de l'existence de Dieu selon Austin Farrer. HENDERSON, Edward H.
L'Appel et le Phénomène. LARUELLE, François.
L'être du non-être en perspective aristotélicienne. DE MURALT, André.
L'Habitude, activité fondatrice de l'existence actuelle dans la philosophie de Spinoza. BOVE, Lauren.
L'herméneutique dans la "phènoménologie comme telle". GREISCH, Jean.
L'horizon philosophique de Pierre Charron. ADAM, Michel.
L'inspiration aristotélicienne de la métaphysique de Bergson. WASZKINEL, Romuald.
L'ontogenèse de l'individu: ses aspects scientifiques et philosophiques. BERNIER, Réjane.
L'origine première des choses. NICOLAS, Jean-Hervé.
L'unité-unicité de l'"esse" Thomiste. PASQUA, Hervé.
Language and Metaphysics: The Ontology of Metaphor. HAUSMAN, Carl R.
The Language of Thought: No Syntax Without Semantics. CRANE, Tim.
Leibniz on Creation, Contingency and Per-Se Modality. MC NAMARA, Paul.
Leibniz on Superessentialism and World-Bound Individuals. COVER, Jan A.
Lenguaje y metafísica en Alfred J Ayer. BEUCHOT, Mauricio.
Lenguaje y verdad en Aristóteles. RODRIGUEZ, M L.
La libertad como autodeterminaciín en san Agustín. GALINDO, José Antonio.
Libertad como posibilidad, libertad como necesidad: Juliano y San Agustín. PEGUEROLES, Juan.
Libertad y necesidad en el 'Cur Deus Homo' de San Anselmo de Canterbury (segunda parte). CORTI, E C.
The Limits of Power. TALIAFERRO, Charles.
The Limits of Thought—and Beyond. PRIEST, Graham.
A Little Daylight: A Reading of Derrida's "White Mythology". LAWLOR, Leonard.
Locke on Personal Identity and the Trinity Controversy of the 1690s. WEDEKING, Gary.
Locke on Personal Identity. WINKLER, Kenneth P.
Locke on Real Essence. OWEN, David W D.
Locke on the Ontology of Matter, Living Things and Persons. CHAPPELL, Vere.
Lockes Qualitäten: Erwiderung auf Casati. KIENZLE, Bertram.
Logic and Logos—The Search for Unity in Hegel and Coleridge: I, Alienation and the Logocentric Response. PERKINS, Mary Anne.
Logic and Logos—The Search for Unity in Hegel and Coleridge, III: A Different Logos. PERKINS, Mary Anne.
Logic and Ontology. BROWNING, Douglas.
Logic and the Free Will Problem. VAN INWAGEN, Peter.
Lógica y metafísica de Leibniz: Principales líneas de interpretación durante el siglo XX. HEINEKAMP, A and SCHUPP, F.
The Logical Structure of the First Antinomy. LOPARIC, Zeljko.
La logique du mythe et la question du non-être. COULOUBARITSIS, Lambros.
Logique et métaphysique. POUBLANC, Franck.
Madden's Account of Necessity in Causation. LEVINE, Michael P.
Man Not a Subject of Science?. SLEZAK, Peter.
Martin Heidegger and the Place of Language. VAN RODEN ALLEN, Robert.
Materiality and Aquinas' Natural Philosophy: A Reply to Johnson. KNASAS, John F X.
The Matrix of Personality: A Whiteheadian Corroboration of Harry Stack Sullivan's Interpersonal Theory of Psychiatry. REGAN, Thomas J.
McDowell Against Criterial Knowledge. ROBINSON, Paul.
Meaning and Value. SCHIFFER, Stephen.
Meaning in a Realist Perspective. THERON, Stephen.
Meaning, Truth Conditions and the Internal Point of View: The Ethical Dilemma. GOOSSENS, Charles.
Meaningful Existence, Embodiment and Physical Education. WHITEHEAD, Margaret.
Meditation on the Two Consciousnesses and on the Three Worlds of Popper (in Hungarian). RADI, Peter.
Memory, Forgetfulness and the Disclosure of Being in Heidegger and Plotinus. BALES, Eugene F.
Mental Causation and Non-Reductive Monism. MACDONALD, Cynthia and MACDONALD, Graham.
Mental Causes. HEIL, John and MELE, Alfred.
Merleau-Ponty's Phenomenology of Sympathy. MATUSTIK, Martin J.
Metafísica de la vocación. AGUAYO CRUZ, Enrique Ignacio.
Metafisica e dialettica: quattro saggi sull'interpretazione hegeliana di Aristotele. FERRARIN, Alfredo.
Una Metafísica estructural de la evolución. CONILL, Jesús.
Metafísica todavía? (conclusión). SANABRIA, José Rubén.
Metamorphoses: On the Limits of Thought. ALEXAKOS, Panos D.
Metaphor and Pluralism. MAC CORMAC, Earl R.
Metaphor, Literalism, and the Non-Verbal Arts. BREDIN, Hugh.
Metaphysical Awakening in Philosophy of Quantum Physics. FOLSE, Henry J.
Metaphysical Conundrums at the Root of Moral Disagreement. MC DERMOTT, John M.
Metaphysics and Culture. LADRIÈRE, Jean.
Metaphysics of the Person, Determinism and Responsibility. FAY, Thomas A.
Metaphysics, MSRP and Economics. GLASS, J C and JOHNSON, W.
Metaphysics, Pragmatic Truth and the Underdetermination of Theories. PEREIRA JR, Alfredo and FRENCH, Steven.
Metaphysics, Religion and Yoruba Traditional Thought. OLADIPO, Olusegun.
Die Metaphysik der Kritik: Zum Verhältnis von Metaphysik und Erfahrung bei Max Horkheimer und Theodor W Adorno. RECKI, Birgit.
Metaphysik und Erfahrung in Kants Grundlegung der Ethik. CRAMER, Konrad.
Metaphysik und Erfahrung. BUBNER, Rüdiger.
Metaphysik und Metaphysikkritik. HARTMANN, Klaus.
Métaphysique radicale. MARGOLIS, Joseph.
I metodi della metafisica platonico-accademica "generalizante" ed "elementarizzante" nei libri "M" e "N".... CATTANEI, E.
Middle Knowledge and the Soteriological Problem of Evil. HUNT, David P.
The Mind's I Has Two Eyes. MARTIN, J E and ENGLEMAN, K H.
Minds, Machines and Gödels Theorem (in German). RHEINWALD, Rosemarie.
The Minimal and Semiminimal Notions of Truth. FOX, J.
Miracles and Ghazali's First Theory of Causation. BAHLUL, Raja.
A Modal Argument for Narrow Content. FODOR, Jerry A.
The Modal Ontological Argument and the Necessary A Posteriori. FORGIE, J W.
Modal Realism Without Counterparts. HALE, Susan C.
The Modes of Actuality. FORD, Lewis S.
Il mondo Il soggetto Lo smarrimento. INCARDONA, Nunzio.
Montaigne's 'Des Cannibales' and Natural Sources of Virtue. HOROWITZ, Maryanne Cline.
Moral Obligation and Metaphysics. COOKE, Vincent M.
Moral Realism and the Meaning of Life. MARGOLIS, Joseph.
Motion, Causation, and the Causal Theory of Identity. EHRING, Douglas.
Le mouvement phénoménologique. TAMINIAUX, Jacques.
Multiple Realities in Santayana's Last Puritan. VAITKUS, Steven.
Musical Time as a Practical Accomplishment: A Change in Tempo. WEEKS, P A D.
Must Thinking Bats be Conscious?. HANNA, Patricia.
Must Thinking Be Critical to Be Critical Thinking? Reply to Finocchiaro. SIEGEL, Harvey.
Mystical Experience, Hermeneutics, and Rationality. SHEAR, Jonathan.
Mythe et raison: Propos contemporains. FONTAINE-DE VISSCHER, Luce.
Narrow Content: Fodor's Folly. ADAMS, Fred and DREBUSHENKO, David and FULLER, Gary and STECKER, Robert.
La naturaleza como vida en la interpretación hegeliana de Aristóteles. BARROSO, Inmaculada Acosta.
Naturaleza, espíritu, finalidad. ALARCÓN, Enrique.
Naturalized Epistemology Sublimated: Rapprochement without the Ruts. FULLER, Steve.
Nature as Personal. DOMBROWSKI, Daniel A.
Nature et fonction de la Mémoire dans À la recherche du temps perdu. ZÉPHIR, Jacques J.
Nature et liberté dans l'ontologie fondamentale de Heidegger. BRISART, Robert.
The Nature of a Person-Stage. MC INERNEY, Peter K.
The Nature of Buddhism. KLOSTERMAIER, Klaus.
The Nature of Causation: A Singularist Account. TOOLEY, Michael.
The Neurophilosophy of Pain. GILLETT, G R.
A New Foreknowledge Dilemma. ZAGZEBSKI, Linda.
A New Reading of Aristotle's *Hyle*. POLIS, Dennis F.
Nietzsche and Ernst Jünger: From Nihilism to Totalitarianism. OHANA, David.
Nietzsche and Foucault on *Ursprung* and Genealogy. COOK, Deborah.

METAPHYSICS

Nietzsche and Heidegger. LAWRENCE, Joseph P.
Nietzsche and Post-Modernity. ERICKSON, Stephen A.
Nietzsche and the Philosophy of Scientific Power: Will to Power as Constructive Interpretation. BABICH, Babette E.
Nietzsche as Instructor in Autonomy? Comments. FOWLER, Mark C.
Nietzsche contra Kant and the Problem of Autonomy. WHITE, Richard.
Nietzsche on Authenticity. GOLOMB, Jacob.
Nietzsche's Arctic Zone of Cognition and Post-Structuralism. PARENT, David.
Nietzschean Perspectivism and the Logic of Practical Reason. REDDING, Paul.
La noción de ser en Tomás de Sutton. ECHAURI, Raúl.
Noema and Meaning in Husserl. FOLLESDAL, Dagfinn.
Noia, acedia ed epochè. BOTTANI, Livio.
El nombre propio de Dios. PONFERRADA, Gustavo E.
Non-World Making in Chuang Tzu. WU, Kuang-Ming.
Nonautonomous Psychology. PETRIE, Bradford.
Nonbranching and Nontransitivity. EHRING, Douglas.
Not Over Yet: Prior's 'Thank Goodness' Argument'. KIERNAN-LEWIS, Delmas.
A Note on Berkeley's Anti-Abstractionism. MOKED, Gabriel.
Notes sur une référence fugitive: Schopenhauer lecteur de Plotin. UCCIANI, Louis.
La notion de non-être dans l'histoire de la langue grecque archaïque. LÉTOUBLON, Françoise.
The Notion of *Klesa* and Its Bearing on the Yoga Analysis of Mind. BALSLEV, Anindita N.
The *Nous*-Body Problem in Aristotle. MODRAK, Deborah K W.
Nuestra voluntad es "de Dios". FERNÁNDEZ BURILLO, Santiago A.
Nuestra voluntad es "de Dios". FERNÁNDEZ BURILLO, Santiago A.
Nuove ricerche sul 'Liber metaphysicus' *di Giambattista Vico*. CACCIATORE, Giuseppe.
Object-Dependent Thoughts and Psychological Redundancy. NOONAN, Harold W.
Objective and Subjective Aspects of Pain. GRAHEK, Nikola.
Offices and God. HUGLY, Philip and SAYWARD, Charles.
On Being an Aristotelian. MEYNELL, Hugo A.
On Boyd. HACKING, Ian.
On Crane and Mellor's Argument Against Physicalism. ROBINSON, Don.
On Naturalizing the Semantics of Mental Representation. SILVERS, Stuart.
On Plato's Theory of the *Metheksis* of Ideas. JIYUAN, Yu.
On the Causality of Sky. MISHRA, Aruna Ranjan.
On the Concept of Freedom in the *I Ching*: A Deconstructionist View of Self-Cultivation. SCHULZ, Larry J and CUNNINGHAM, Thomas J.
On the Functional Unity of the Four Dimensions of Thought in the *Book of Changes*. LIU, Shu-Hsien.
On the Impossibility of Artificial Intelligence. WEISS, Paul.
On the Individuation of Events. CLELAND, Carol.
On the Logic of Eternal Knowledge. KELLY, Charles J.
On Wishing there were Unicorns. CLARK, Stephen R L.
Origen de la inversión kantiana del binomio materia-forma. SOTO BRUNA, Maria Jesus.
Origen y desembocadura de la acción: el sujeto inevitable. CRUZ, Manuel.
Ousia, Substratum, and Matter. SFEKAS, Stanley.
Il paradosso del fondamento nella simbolica del gioco e sogno della libertà. MASULLO, Aldo.
Parthood and Persistence. KAZMI, Ali Akhtar.
Partitions, Probabilistic Causal Laws, and Simpson's Paradox. HARDCASTLE, Valerie Gray.
La passione dell'essere: Viaggio lungo i sentieri del nulla. IANNOTTA, Daniella.
Peirce's Realism, Intentionality and Final Causation. TURIANO, Mark.
Pensiero e trascendenza. SANCIPRIANO, Mario.
Per una filosofia del corpo. PELLECCHIA, Pasquale.
Per una rilettura dei libri "M" e "N" della *Metafisica* di Aristotele alla luce delle "dottrine non scritte" di Platone. CATTANEI, Elisabetta.
Personal Concern and the Extension of Consciousness. SCHECHTMAN, Marya.
Personal Identity and Rebirth. STOEBER, Michael.
Personal Identity and Reductionism. GARRETT, Brian.
Personal Identity and the Causal Continuity Requirement. ELLIOT, Robert.
Personal Identity, Reincarnation, and Resurrection. IALACCI, Michael.
Persons and Human Beings. GARRETT, Brian.
Persons and the Intentional Stance. DIBRELL, William.
Phänomenologie und Monadologie: Husserl und Leibniz. CRISTIN, Renato.
Phenomenal Qualities and the Nontransitivity of Matching. BURGESS, John A.
Phenomenalism and the Reality of Body in Leibniz's Later Philosophy. RUTHERFORD, Donald P.
Phenomenology and Indian Philosophy. SINGH, Navjyoti.
Phenomenology and Psychoanalysis: The Hermeneutical Mediation. RAJAN, R Sundara.
Phenomenology and Scientific Realism: Husserl's Critique of Galileo. SOFFER, Gail.
Phenomenology as Cooperative Task: Husserl-Farber Correspondence during 1936-37. CHO, Kah Kyung.
Philosophical and Normative Dimensions and Aspects of the Idea of Renaissance. GREGORIOS, Paulos Mar.
Philosophical Asceiticism (in French). DE MONTICELLI, Roberta.
Die Philosophie im einen Deutschland. HENRICH, Dieter.
Philosophy and the Sociology of Knowledge: An Investigation into the Nature of Orthodoxy (Astikya) in Hindu Thought. SHARMA, Arvind.
Physical Possibility and Potentiality in Ethics. COVEY, Edward.
Physicalist Theories of Color. BOGHOSSIAN, Paul A and VELLEMAN, J David.
The Physics of Modern Perception: Beyond Body and World. BARRY JR, James.
Physique aristotélicienne et métaphysique thomiste. VERNIER, Jean-Marie.
Piecemeal Realism. FINE, Arthur.
Play of the Whole of Wholes (in Czechoslovakian). AXELOS, Kostas.
Plotino: la libertad como primer principio. DE GARAY, Jesús.
Plotinus and the *Apeiron* of Plato's *Parmenides*. HEISER, John H.
Politics and the Limits of Metaphysics: Heidegger, Ferry and Renaut, and Lyotard. FÓTI, Véronique M.
Porphyry and the Intelligible Triad. EDWARDS, M J.
Posibilidad e indeterminación: Aristóteles frente a Diodoro Crono. QUEVEDO, Amalia.
The Possibility of Reincarnation. NOONAN, Harold W.
The Postmodern Flavor of Blondel's Method. LONG, Fiachra.
Potencia, finalidad y posibilidad en "Metafísica" IX, 3-4. GARCIA MARQUÉS, Alfonso.
The Poverty of Neurophilosophy. STENT, Gunther S.
The Practical Importance of Personal Identity. DOEPKE, F.
The Pragmatist Sieve of Concepts: Description versus Interpretation. SEIGFRIED, Charlene Haddock.
Pre-existence and Personal Identity. FEENSTRA, Ronald J.
Preemption, Direct Causation, and Identity. EHRING, Douglas.
Les présupposés métaphysiques de la "lisibilité" de l'être. KÜHN, Rolf.
Primary and Secondary Qualities: A Reply to Kienzle. CASATI, Roberto.
Principia Individuationis. DENKEL, Arda.
Principio de Razón o fundamento de Amor. MENDEZ, J R.
Probabilistic Physics and the Metaphysics of Time. SHANKS, Niall.
A Problem for the Eternity Solution. WIDERKER, David.
The Problem of Reality. JACKENDOFF, Ray.
The Problem of Theoretical Self-Reflexivity in Peirce and Santayana. DILWORTH, David A.
The Problem of Who: Multiple Personality, Personal Identity and the Double Brain. APTER, Andrew.
Problems with the Fregean Interpretation of Husserl. BROWN, Charles S.
Process Thought and the Spaciness of Mind. EDWARDS, Rem B.
Processes, Substances, and Leibniz's Epistemology: A Case for Essentialism in Contemporary Physics. PIRO, Francesco.
Professor Von Wright on Action. DEWASHI, Mahadev.
Prolegomena to an Understanding of Heidegger's Turn. GRONDIN, Jean.
Psychanalyse et existentialisme: A propos de la théorie lacanienne de la subjectivité. VAN HAUTE, P.
Psychoanalysis: A Form of Life?. BREARLEY, Michael.
Der psychophysische Materialismus in der Perspektive Kants und Wittgensteins. MENDONÇA, W P.
Putnam's Realism and Relativity: An Uneasy Balance. THROOP, William and DORAN, Katheryn.
Putting One's Foot in One's Head—Part I: Why. PERLIS, Donald.
Quale statuto per l'embrione umano?. COMPAGNONI, Francesco.
Qualities and Qualia: What's in the Mind?. SHOEMAKER, Sydney.
Quantum Physics, Philosophy, and the Image of God: Insights from Wolfgang Pauli. LAURIKAINEN, K V.
Quantum Realism: A Reply to Professor Fenner. BENNETT, Barbara J.
Quatre principes de la phénoménologie. HENRY, Michel.
Qué conocemos de dios? Hobbes versus Tomas. LUKAC DE STIER, María Liliana.
La question de l'être et du non-être des objets mathématiques chez Plotin et Jamblique. O'MEARA, Dominic.
La question de l'être. LARIVÉ, Marc.
The Real Distinction Between Mind and Body. YABLO, Stephen.
Real Human Persons. DONAGAN, Alan.
Real Patterns. DENNETT, Daniel C.
Realism Without Representation: A Response to Appiah. DEVITT, Michael.
Realism, Anti-Foundationalism and the Enthusiasm for Natural Kinds. BOYD, Richard.
Realisms. LEVIN, Michael.
Reason and Imagination (in Dutch). VAN PEURSEN, C A.
Reason and Reasonableness in the Philosophy of Brand Branshard. RECK, Andrew J.
The Reason Why: Response to Crane. PAPINEAU, David.
The Recurring Problem of the Third Man. HALES, Steven D.
The Reductionist Ideal in Cognitive Psychology. MONTGOMERY, Richard.
Referential Opacity in Aristotle. SPELLMAN, Lynne.
Reflection in Politics and the Question of a Political Subject (in Czechoslovakian). HEJDANEK, Ladislav.

METAPHYSICS

Reflections on Aristotle's Criticism of Forms. MOKASHI, Ashwini A.
Reflections on Blanshard, Reason, and Religion. FERRÉ, Frederick.
The Reformed Subjectivist Principle Revisited. FORD, Lewis S.
Las reglas del juego: consideraciones críticas sobre "Radical Hermeneutics" de John Caputo. PEÑA, Lorenzo.
Reinterpreting Images. SLEZAK, Peter.
Relationism and Temporal Topology. LE POIDEVIN, Robin.
Relationship Between Consciousness and Reality (in Serbo-Croatian). CUCULOVSKI, Ljubomir.
Relative Identity and Locke's Principle of Individuation. UZGALIS, William L.
Relevant Predication 2: Intrinsic Properties and Internal Relations. DUNN, J Michael.
Religion, Nothingness, and the Challenge of Post-Modern Thought: An Introduction to the Philosophy of K Nishitani. JAMES, George A.
El reloj de Dios (Glosas provisionales a un principio leibniziano). MUÑOZ, Jacobo.
Replies to My Computational Commentators. DIETRICH, Eric.
Reply to Davies: Creation and Existence. VALLICELLA, William F.
Reply to Huston Smith. ANDERSON, Tyson.
Reply to Smith: The Question of Idealism. VALLICELLA, William F.
Reply to Vallicella: Heidegger and Idealism. SMITH, Quentin.
Réponses à quelques questions. MARION, Jean-Luc.
Representation and the Freedom of the Will. STAMPE, Dennis W.
The Representational Content of Musical Experience. DE BELLIS, Mark.
Representations and Realism. APPIAH, Anthony.
Republic: 2. BANAJI, V F.
Response to Craig Ihara's Discussion. WONG, David B.
Response to Gale's "Freedom and the Free Will Defense". HUMBER, James M.
A Response to Kuang-Ming Wu's "Non-World-Making". FLEMING, Jesse.
Response to Piotr Gutowski's "Charles Hartshorne's Rationalism". HARTSHORNE, Charles.
Response to Stampe's "Representation and the Freedom of the Will". GIBSON, Martha I.
Response to Tyler Anderson. SMITH, Huston.
Riflessioni sulla fondazione dell'assioma parmenideo. GRAZIANI, Andrea.
The Role of Kant's Refutation of Idealism. HYMERS, Michael.
The Role of Subjectivity in the Realism of Thomas Nagel and Jean-Paul Sartre. WIDER, Kathleen.
Role Taking, Corporeal Intersubjectivity, and Self: Mead and Merleau-Ponty. BOURGEOIS, Patrick L and ROSENTHAL, Sandra B.
Russell on Pastness. KENYON, Timothy A.
Same Human Being, Same Person?. THORNTON, Mark.
Sartre on Anguish. JAMBOR, Mishka.
Sartre on Pre-Reflective Consciousness. AGRAWAL, M M.
Sartre on Surpassing the Given. BUSCH, Thomas W.
Sartre's Being-for-Heidegger, Heidegger's Being-for-Sartre. MARTINOT, Steve.
Sartre, Aron et le relativisme historique. BAUGH, Bruce.
Saving Psychological Solipsism. MALONEY, J Christopher.
Scepticism: The External World and Meaning. BAR-ON, Dorit.
Schellings metaphysikkritische Sprachphilosophie. ROSENAU, Hartmut.
Schopenhauer en de kunst van het verzaken. DE MARTELAERE, Patricia.
Schopenhauers Wille und Platons Eros. VOIGTLÄNDER, Hanns-Dieter.
Science and Consciousness. WOJCIECHOWSKI, Jerzy A.
Scientific Time and the Temporal Sense of Human Existence: Merleau-Ponty and Mead. BOURGEOIS, Patrick L and ROSENTHAL, Sandra B.
Scotus, Frege, and Bergmann. PARK, Woosuk.
Searle on Natural Agency. BISHOP, John.
Searle's Oplossing voor het lichaam-geest probleem: ipse dixit—Een reactie op Anne Ruth Mackor. MEIJSING, Monica.
The Seasonal Structure Underlying the Arrangement of the Hexagrams in the *Yijing*. ANDERSON, Allan W.
Secondary Reflection and Marcelian Anthropology. MICHAUD, Thomas A.
Self-Notions. PERRY, John.
Self-Synthesis, Self-Knowledge, and Skepticism. MAZOUÉ, James G.
Les sens trompeurs: Usage cartésien d'un motif sceptique. CAVAILLÉ, Jean-Pierre.
El sentido del Universo en José Vasconcelos (2a parte). PATIÑO, Joel Rodríguez.
El sentido del Universo en José Vasconcelos. PATIÑO, Joel Rodríguez.
El ser principial y Dios: Una observación a la teología de Maimónides. GARCÍA GONZÁLEZ, Juan.
Ser y Dios, entre filosofía y teología, en Heidegger y Siewerth. CABADA, Manuel.
El ser y el sentido: Notas husserlianas. PEGUEROLES, Juan.
Settled Objectives and Rational Constraints. MC CANN, Hugh J.
El significado de lo teológico en Walter Benjamin. BOSCÁN, Antonio S.
Simbolismo y metafísica. MUÑOZ TRIGUERO, Isidro.
Sinn-Wahrheit-Ort: Tres etapas en el pensamiento de Heidegger. BERCIANO V, Modesto.
Small Sets. HAZEN, A P.
Sobre justificación y verdad: respuesta a León Olivé. VILLORO, Luis.
Sobre la "Metafísica del bien y del mal". MELENDO, Tomás.
Sobre la individualidad. CATES, Lynn.
Sobre le estructura dinámica de la realidad. MONSERRAT, Javier.
Social Reality and Moral Order. BARLINGAY, S S.
Some Aspects of R G Collingwood's Doctrine of Absolute Presuppositions. SAARI, Heikki.
Some New Directions in the Philosophy of Mind. THOMAS, Janice.
Some Philosophical Aspects of Psychophysiology—Are There Any Elements of "Neurophilosophy"? (in German). RÜDIGER, Wolfgang.
Some Puzzles About the Evil of Death. FELDMAN, Fred.
Some Recent Research on the Mind-Body Problem in Descartes. MILES, Murray.
Some Remarks on the Rationality of Induction. INDURKHYA, Bipin.
Some Self-Centric Tendencies in Sankara Advaita. JHINGRAN, Saral.
Sophia and the Devil: Kant in the Face of Russian Religious Metaphysics. AKHUTIN, A V.
Spinoza on the Eternity of the Human Mind. LUCASH, Frank.
Spinoza's Two Causal Chains. GILEAD, Amihud.
Spinoza, Heidegger, and the Ontological Argument. SINGER, Brent A.
Spinoza—Beyond Hobbes and Rousseau. GEISMANN, Georg.
Spontaneity and the Generation of Rational Beings in Leibniz's Theory of Biological Reproduction. FOUKE, Daniel C.
Squaring the Hermeneutical Circle. ROSEN, Stanley.
Sri Aurobindo and the Process of Physical Transformation. REDDY, V Ananda.
Strawson and the Refutation of Idealism. STEINHOFF, Gordon.
Structural Motifs in the Arrangement of the 64 *Gua* in the *Zhouyi*. SCHULZ, Larry J.
Structure/Antistructure and Agency under Oppression. LUGONES, Maria C.
A Study of Ontology. FINE, Kit.
Subject en zelfervaring. BERNET, R.
The Subject of Experience. GILLETT, Grant.
Subject-Object Theories. BAHM, Archie J.
Substance and Selfhood. LOWE, E J.
La substance composée chez Leibniz. CHAZERANS, Jean-François.
Substance: Prolegomena to a Realist Theory of Identity. AYERS, Michael.
Substances and Space-Time: What Aristotle Would Have Said to Einstein. MAUDLIN, Tim.
Substancia y sustantividad: Tomás de Aquino y X Zubiri. CERCÓS SOTO, José Luis.
Substrative Materialism. KERR-LAWSON, Angus.
Le sujet en dernier appel. MARION, Jean Luc.
Sujeto, acto y operación. GAMARRA, Daniel.
Sulla matrice della teoria della sostanza nel *Discorso di metafisica* di Leibniz. DELCÓ, Alessandro.
Supervenience Is a Two-Way Street. MILLER, Richard B.
Supervenience, Determination, and Dependency. GRIMES, Thomas.
Sur le fragment des trois ordres de Blaise Pascal. CHIBAUDEL, Pierre.
Sur quelques textes de Spinoza relatifs à la notion de loi. PREPOSIET, Jean.
Sur une façon stoïcienne de ne pas être. BRUNSCHWIG, Jacques.
Systematic Assumptions in Dilthey's Critique of Metaphysics. NENON, Thomas.
Taoist Visions of the Body. KOHN, Livia.
La tarea cósmica del hombre según Teilhard de Chardin. PATIÑO, Joel Rodríguez.
Teamwork. COHEN, Philip R and LEVESQUE, Hector J.
Teleologie: Chance oder Belastung für die Philosophie?. PLEINES, Jürgen-Eckardt.
Teleology and the Concepts of Causation. VON GLASERSFELD, Ernst.
Telesio e la cultura napoletana. STURLESE, Rita.
Télos y arché: La physis del logos. INCARDONA, Nunzio.
Tempo ed eternità: La filosofia narrante di F Rosenzweig. DI MARCO, Chiara.
Temporality and the Concept of Being. SHALOM, Albert.
Temporality Revisited: Kierkegaard and the Transitive Character of Time. SCHALOW, Frank.
Le temps du souffrir: Remarques critiques sur la phénoménologie de M Henry. PORÉE, Jérôme.
La teología de la creación y el problema de los orígenes. PODESTA, Gustavo.
La teología de la historia en la "ciudad de Dios" (2). OROZ RETA, José (trans) and BAGET BOZZO, Giovanni.
La teoría del tiempo en Ockham y la autenticidad de la *Summulae in Libros Physicorum*. LARRE, Olga L and BOLZÁN, J E.
The Text of the Nyāya-Sūtras: Some Problems. KRISHNA, Daya.
The Concept of Sense in Merleau-Ponty (in Czechoslovakian). SIVAK, Jozef.
The Critical and the Dogmatic Tendency of Phenomenological Philosophy (in Czechoslovakian). CIBULKA, Josef.
The Doubts about Post-Modernism (in Czechoslovakian). AJVAZ, Michal.
The Heraclitus' Lesson (in Portuguese). SANTOS, M C A dos.
The Man as Subject of the Philosophy (in Hungarian). RICOEUR, Paul.
The Problem of Infinity in Kant's Works (in German). RÖD, Wolfgang.
The Scheme of the Game of Man and World (Towards the Formation of the Planetary Man) (in Hungarian). AXELOS, Kostas.
The World as a Whole and the World of Man (in Czechoslovakian). PATOCKA, Jan.

METAPHYSICS

The Theory of Triple Perception. SARMA, Rajendra Nath.
Thinking of Something. FITCH, Gregory.
Thinking of Unity (in Dutch). AERTSEN, Jan A.
Thomas Aquinas and Henry of Ghent on the Succession of Substantial Forms and the Origin of Human Life. WILSON, Gordon A.
Thomas Aquinas and the Will: A Note on Interpretation. CROWE, Frederick.
Thomas d'Aquin a-t-il tente d'exprimer le principe d'individuation à l'intérieur des proprietés.... CASPAR, Philippe.
Thought and Being in Kant and Hegel. HOULGATE, Stephen.
Thought Rhythym and Experience in *Der Satz vom Grund* (in Dutch). PEETERS, L.
The Thought That Learning Is by Ordeal: An Original Essay. WOODRUFF, Paul B.
Thoughtful Brutes: The Ascription of Mental Predicates to Animals in Locke's "Essay". SQUADRITO, Kathleen.
Thoughts Which Only I Can Think. WILLIAMS, C J F.
Thoughts. SMITH, David Woodruff.
Thus Spoke Rorty: The Perils of Narrative Self-Creation. CONWAY, Daniel W.
Time and Identity. HARPER, A W J.
Time, Actuality and Omniscience. LEFTOW, Brian.
Time, Change and Contradiction. SMITH, Joseph Wayne.
Time, Self and Consciousness: Some Conceptual Patterns in the Context of Indian Thought. BALSLEV, Anindita.
Time-Travel and Topology. MAUDLIN, Tim.
Towards a View of Time as Depth. ARGYROS, Alexander J.
A Tradition of Natural Kinds. HACKING, Ian.
The Tragic World of John Dewey. JACQUES, Robert A.
Transcendental Idealism: The Dialectical Dimension. GLOUBERMAN, M.
The Transcendental Method of Metaphysics of Coreth and Muck and Its Relation to Analytic Philosophy. RUNGGALDIER, Edmund.
Transcultural Dialogue and the Problem of the Concept of Ultimate Reality and Meaning. SINGLETON, Michael.
La transformation de la philosophie de Platon dans le "Prologos" d'Albinus. NETSCHKE-HENTSCHKE, Ada Babette.
El tránsito de la existencia al ser. KELZ, Carlos R.
Travaux récents sur la pensée du XIIIe siècle. VAN STEENBERGHEN, Fernand.
Los tres estados de la esencia según Santo Tomás de Aquino. CASAUBÓN, Juan A.
Tres grandes testigos de la luz interior: San Agustín, san Buenaventura y J Henry Newman. OROZ RETA, José.
Trinidad y ontología trascendental: Ideas en torno al libro IX del "De Trinitate" de S Agustín. RODRÍGUEZ VALLS, Francisco.
The Trouble with Fragrance. ELLIS, John.
Two Kinds of Naming in the *Sophist*. STOUGH, Charlotte.
Two Reversibilities: Merleau-Ponty and Derrida. YOUNT, Mark.
Types of Pluralism. WATSON, Walter.
Unamuno y el problema de Dios. FORMENT, Eudaldo.
Universalität des Prinzips vom zureichenden Grund. NICOLÁS, Juan A.
Universality Biases: *How Theories About Human Nature Succeed*. HORNSTEIN, Gail A and STAR, Susan Leigh.
Vague Objects. TYE, Michael.
The Vanishing Subject of Contemporary Discourse: A Pragmatic Response. COLAPIETRO, Vincent M.
Verdad e inteligibilidad: Los rasgos invariables de la teoría platónica de las ideas. LUIS DEL BARCO, José.
Die Verfehlung des Themas "Metaphysik und Erfahrung". WIEHL, Reiner.
Verificationism and Anti-Realism. ROGERSON, Kenneth.
The Very Idea of Perfect Realism. FISHER, John Andrew.
Vide et non-être chez Leucippe et Démocrite. VOELKE, André-Jean.
Vie et totalité chez Nietzsche. HAAR, Michel.
Von der dreifachen Vollendung des Deutschen Idealismus und der unvollendeten metaphysischen Wahrheit. JANKE, Wolfgang.
Wahnbildung und Wirklichkeit des Willens. GRÄTZEL, Stephan.
Wanting, Getting, Having. HUMBERSTONE, I L.
Was Moore a Positivist?. O'CONNOR, David.
The Way of Ideas: A Retrospective. YOLTON, John W.
We Will Do It: An Analysis of Group Intentions. TUOMELA, Raimo.
Weakness of Will and Rational Action. AUDI, Robert.
The What and the How. ALMOG, Joseph.
What Berkeley's Notions Are. LEE, Richard N.
What is it Like to be an Aardvark?. TIGHLMAN, B R.
What is Ultimate in George Lukács's Ontology?. JOÓS, Ernest.
What is Wrong in Inverting Spectra. CASATI, Roberto.
When Do People Begin?. GRISEZ, Germain.
Whether Any Individual at all Could Have a Guise Structure. MILLER, Barry.
Whitehead and Leibniz: Conflict and Convergence. MOONEY, Tim.
Who's Afraid of Virginia Woolf?. MATRAVERS, Derek.
Why Indeed? Papineau on Supervenience. CRANE, Tim.
Why not Naturalistic Psychology?. GARRETT, Richard and GRAHAM, George.
Why Personal Identity Is Animal Identity. CARTER, William R.
Why Pluralism Now?. GARVER, Eugene.
Why Shouldn't We Be Able to Solve the Mind-Body Problem?. KIRK, Robert.
Why the Mind is Not in the Head But in the Society's Connectionist Network. FISCHER, Roland.
Why the Problem of the External World is a Pseudo-Problem: Santayana and Danto. SHIRLEY, Edward S.
Wilhelm von Ockham: Das Risiko, mittelalterlich zu denken. PERLER, Dominik.
William James's Theory of Mind. COOPER, W E.
William of Auvergne and the Eternity of the World. TESKE, Roland J.
Wittgenstein and Psychology. SHOTTER, John.
Wittgenstein on Freud's 'Abominable Mess'. CIOFFI, Frank.
Wittgenstein y el fisicalismo. HALLER, Rudolf.
Wittgenstein's Critique of Mechanistic Atomism. MC DONOUGH, Richard.
Wittgenstein's Indeterminism. SCHEER, Richard K.
Wittgenstein's Phenomenology Revisited. GIER, Nicholas F.
Wittgenstein: la tentación de lo místico. CABRERA, Isabel.
Wittgenstein: Representaciones y pensamientos. RABOSSI, Eduardo.
The World Essence. BIGELOW, John.
The World-Shift Theory of Free Choice. DAVIS, Wayne A.
The Worldly Self in Schutz: On Sighting, Citing, and Siting the Self. LANGSDORF, Lenore.
Worlds Enough for Time. BIGELOW, John.
X Zubiri in Roma: Natura, Storia, Dio. JAVIERRE ORTAS, A M.
Yajna and the Doctrine of Karma: A Contradiction in Indian Thought about Action. KRISHNA, Daya.
You Can Fool Some of the People All of the Time, Everything Else Being Equal; Hedged Laws and Psychological Explanation. FODOR, Jerry A.
Zeno's Paradox of Extension. MC KIE, John R.
Zum Wandel der Metaphysik nach ihrem Ende. BUCHHEIM, Thomas.
Zur inhaltlichen Bedeutung des Hegelschen "Schemas der Naturphilosophie" in den Epikurstudien des jungen Marx. MIELKE, Dietmar.
'What Place, then, for a creator?': Hawking on God and Creation. CRAIG, William Lane.

METAPSYCHOLOGY

Psychoanalysis, Scientific Method, and Philosophy. HOOK, Sidney (ed).

METASCIENCE

Estrategias metacientíficas: Parte II. HIDALGO TUÑÓN, Alberto.
Logicism, Pragmatism and Metascience: Towards a Pancritical-Pragmatic Meta-Level Discourse. AXTELL, G S.

METATHEORY

La teoría consensual de la verdad de Jürgen Habermas. BELARDINELLI, Sergio.

METHOD(S)

see also Scientific Method
Bergsonism. DELEUZE, Gilles.
Essays on Hegel's Logic. DI GIOVANNI, George (ed).
Experiential Method: Qualitative Research in the Humanities Using Metaphysics and Phenomenology. KIDD, James W.
On Durkheim's Rules of Sociological Method. GANE, Mike.
Some Truer Method. DURHAM, Frank (ed).
"Ethics of Method: Greasing the Machine and Telling Stories" in *Feminist Ethics*, TREBILCOT, Joyce.
"Method and the Authority of Science" in *Key Themes in Philosophy*, TILES, Mary.
"The Method of Hegel's *Science of Logic*" in *Essays on Hegel's Logic*, WINFIELD, Richard Dien.
"Newton's Method and Newton's Style" in *Some Truer Method*, COHEN, I Bernard.
"Strong and Weak Methods" in *Logic, Methodology and Philosophy of Science, VIII*, FILKORN, Vojtech.
"Where is the Place of Understanding?" in *Essays on Hegel's Logic*, BURBIDGE, John.
Brentano e Fichte negli scritti "minori" di E Husserl. BELLO, A Ales.
Chalmers on Method. GOWER, Barry.
Critica della filosofia zoologica per Battista Grassi. MESCHIARI, Alberto.
La cuestión del Método de una filosofía latinoamericana. SCANNONE, J C.
Descartes e le "culture" barocche: Appunti su alcune recenti interpretazioni. LOJACONO, Ettore.
Dialogic Leadership as Ethics Action (Praxis) Method. NIELSEN, Richard P.
An Experimental Assessment of Alternative Teaching Approaches for Introductory Business Ethics. BURTON, Scot and JOHNSTON, Mark W and WILSON, Elizabeth J.
La investigación y las metodologías en las Ciencias Humanas. DACAL ALONSO, José Antonio.
Irony and Method: Comments on Burbules on Dialogue. NEIMAN, Alven M.
Method and Message: Commentary on the Future of Philosophy of Education. DENTON, David E.
Method Divorced from Content in Theology: An Assessment of Lonergan's *Method in Theology*. REYNOLDS, Terrence.
I metodi della metafisica platonico-accademica "generalizzante" ed "elementarizzante" nei libri "M" e "N".... CATTANEI, E.
Nuove ricerche sul 'Liber metaphysicus' *di Giambattista Vico*. CACCIATORE, Giuseppe.

METHOD(S)

Philosophy: Sections 86-93 (pp 405-35) of the So-Called "Big Typescript" (Catalog Number 213)—Ludwig Wittgenstein. WITTGENSTEIN, Ludwig and NYMAN, Heikki.
Prior's Disease. USBERTI, Gabriele.
Special Problems in Teaching Modern Philosophy. PHILLIPS, Hollibert.
Stephen Hilmy on Matters of Method and Style. COVEOS, Costis M.
Truth, Content, and the Hypothetico-Deductive Method. GRIMES, Thomas R.
Varieties of Educational Dialogue. BURBULES, Nicholas C.

METHODOLOGICAL INDIVIDUALISM

Varieties of Social Explanation: An Introduction to the Philosophy of Social Science. LITTLE, Daniel.
How Individualistic Is Methodological Individualism?. MADISON, G B.
Methodological Individualism and Marx: Some Remarks on Jon Elster, Game Theory, and Other Things. WOLFF, Robert Paul.
What is the Problem Concerning Social Entities?. THOMPSON, J L.

METHODOLOGY

Acting and Reflecting: The Interdisciplinary Turn in Philosophy. SIEG, Wilfried (ed).
African Philosophy: The Essential Readings. SEREQUEBERHAN, Tsenay.
David Hume: Historiker und Philosoph. LÜTHE, Rudolf.
Foundations of Moral and Political Philosophy. PAUL, Ellen Frankel (ed).
Ibn Rushd: Averroes. URVOY, Dominique.
Ideas, Principios y Dialectica. LAFUENTE, Maria Isabel.
Imre Lakatos and Theories of Scientific Change. GAVROGLU, Kostas (ed).
La intersubjectividad en Husserl, Volume I and II. IRIBARNE, Julia V.
Logic, Methodology and Philosophy of Science, VIII. FENSTAD, J E (ed).
Logic, Methodology and Philosophy of Science, VII. MARCUS, Ruth Barcan (ed).
Michel Foucault's Force of Flight: Towards an Ethics for Thought. BERNAUER, James W.
The Power of Ideology. MÉSZÁROS, István.
Reading Rawls: Critical Studies on Rawls' 'A Theory of Justice'. DANIELS, Norman (ed).
"The Bayesian Alternative to the Methodology of Scientific Research Programmes" in *Imre Lakatos and Theories of Scientific Change*, URBACH, Peter.
"Commentary: A Critical Role for the History of Archaeology" in *Critical Traditions in Contemporary Archaeology*, PINSKY, Valerie.
"A Critical Consideration of the Lakatosian Concepts: 'Mature' and 'Immature' Science" in *Imre Lakatos and Theories of Scientific Change*, METAXOPOULOS, Emilio.
"Design Methodology: A Personal Statement" in *Philosophy of Technology*, GASPARSKI, Wojciech.
"Falsificationism Looked at from an 'Economic' Point of View" in *Imre Lakatos and Theories of Scientific Change*, RADNITZKY, Gerard.
"Has Popper Been a Good Thing?" in *Imre Lakatos and Theories of Scientific Change*, PAPINEAU, David.
"Impact of Global Modelling on Modern Methodology of Science" in *Logic, Methodology and Philosophy of Science, VIII*, GVISHIANI, J M.
"Lakatos on the Evaluation of Scientific Theories" in *Imre Lakatos and Theories of Scientific Change*, AVGELIS, Nikolaos.
"Many-Particle Physics: Calculational Complications That Become a Blessing for Methodology" in *Imre Lakatos and Theories of Scientific Change*, GOUDAROULIS, Yorgos.
"Methodological Sophisticationism: A Degenerating Project" in *Imre Lakatos and Theories of Scientific Change*, PERA, Marcello.
"Methodology and Ontology" in *Imre Lakatos and Theories of Scientific Change*, SMART, J J C.
"The Methodology of Scientific Research Programmes: A Retrospect" in *Imre Lakatos and Theories of Scientific Change*, WATKINS, John.
"The Methodology of Scientific Research Programmes and Some Developments in High Energy Physics" in *Imre Lakatos and Theories of Scientific Change*, GAVROGLU, Kostas.
"On Stories, Peacemaking, and Philosophical Method: Toward a Pluralistic Account of Non-Violence" in *Issues in War and Peace: Philosophical Inquiries*, BOVE, Laurence.
"Philosophy of Science and the Technological Dimension of Science" in *Imre Lakatos and Theories of Scientific Change*, KROES, Peter.
"The Structure of American Theoretical Archaeology: A Preliminary Report" in *Critical Traditions in Contemporary Archaeology*, EMBREE, Lester.
"Structure of Methodology of an Aesthetic Theorem" in *XIth International Congress in Aesthetics, Nottingham 1988*, KHANIN, Dmitry.
"Sigma": conoscenza e metodo. SAVA, Gabriella.
Analysis as a Method in Philosophy with Special Reference to A J Ayer. SRINIVAS, K.
Beyond Numerical and Causal Accuracy: Expanding the Set of Justificational Criteria. RAMSEY, Jeffry L.
Collingwood's Detective Image of the Historian and the Study of Hadrian's Wall. COUSE, G S.
A Comparative Study of Multiattribute Decision Making Methodologies. KARNI, Reuven and SANCHEZ, Pedro and TUMMALA, V M Rao.
Corresponding Regressions, Procedural Evidence, and the Dialectics of Substantive Theory, Metaphysics, Methodology. CHAMBERS, William.
Falsification and Disconfirmation in Cosmology. ZYCINSKI, Joseph.
Fix It and Be Damned: A Reply to Laudan. WORRALL, John.
Friendship and Education. WHITE, Patricia.
From the Logic of Mathematical Discovery to the Methodology of Scientific Research Programmes. YUXIN, Zheng.
General Thinking Skills: Are There Such Things?. ANDREWS, John N.
If It Aint's Broke, Don't Fix It. LAUDAN, Larry.
Indeterminacy, Empirical Evidence, and Methodological Pluralism. ROUSE, Joseph.
Is Scientific Methodology Interestingly Atemporal?. CUSHING, James T.
Logic and Ontology. BROWNING, Douglas.
Methodological Alternatives in Process Theology. BROWN, Delwin and GREEVE DAVANEY, Sheila.
Methodological, Epistemological, and Ontological Motifs in the Thought of Reinhold Niebuhr. AYERS, Robert H.
The Methodologies of Social History: A Critical Survey and Defense of Structurism. LLOYD, Christopher.
Modularity of Mind Revisited. BENNETT, Laura J.
On the Alleged Methodological Infirmity of Ethics. MOODY-ADAMS, Michele M.
On the Locus of Medical Discovery. REINES, Brandon P.
On the Methodology of Possible World Semantics, I: Correspondence Theory. PEARCE, David and WANSING, Heinrich.
On Tolerance (in French). DÜRRENMATT, Friedrich and BÜHLER, Pierre.
Philosophizing. PALMA, A B.
Philosophy of Science and the Persistent Narratives of Modernity. ROUSE, Joseph.
Por um novo modelo de saber: Problemática do discurso Filosófico-Teológico. DINIS, Alfredo.
Process Theology as Empirical, Rational, and Speculative: Some Reflections on Method. GRIFFIN, David Ray.
Realism and Simplicity in the Castle-East Debate on the Stability of the Hereditary Units. VICEDO, Marga.
Reflexiones en torno a la metodología de la historia de la filosofía. BENÍTEZ, Laura.
Reproducibility as a Methodological Imperative in Experimental Research. HONES, Michael.
A Response to A G A Bello's Methodological Preliminaries. ANYANWU, Kane C.
Le sens de la révolution méthodologique introduite par Rousseau dans la science politique. GOYARD-FABRE, Simone.
La storia universale come storia comparata in Max Weber. DI MARCO, Giuseppe Antonio.
Thomas S Kuhn and L Fleck: Two Sociologists of Science. FLURI, Philippe H.
Thoughts on the Future of Marxism. LEVINE, Andrew.
Towards a Reasonable Version of Methodological Solipsism. ROWLANDS, Mark.
Ultimate Reality and Meaning in Africa: Some Methodological Preliminaries—A Test Case. BELLO, A G A.
Understanding Science: A Two-Level Reflection. DAS GUPTA, Amitabha.

METONYMY

Biblical Narrative and the Theology of Metonymy. WARD, Graham.

METRICS

Projective Subsets of Separable Metric Spaces. MILLER, Arnold W.

METZGER, H

Études sur/Studies on Hélène Metzger. FREUDENTHAL, Gad.
"Le Centre international de synthèse dans les années trente" in *Études sur/Studies on Hélène Metzger*, GEMELLI, Giuliana.
"Epistémologie des sciences de la nature et herméneutique de l'histoire des sciences selon H Metzger" in *Études sur/Studies on Hélène Metzger*, FREUDENTHAL, Gad.
"Hélène Metzger et l'historiographie de la chimie du XVIIIe siècle" in *Études sur/Studies on Hélène Metzger*, CHRISTIE, John R R.
"Hélène Metzger et l'interprétation de la chimie du XVIIe siècle" in *Études sur/Studies on Hélène Metzger*, GOLINSKI, Jan.
"Hélène Metzger et la cristallographie" in *Études sur/Studies on Hélène Metzger*, BLONDEL, Christine.
"Hélène Metzger et la théorie corpusculaire des stahliens au XVIIIe siècle" in *Études sur/Studies on Hélène Metzger*, KUBBINGA, Henk H.
"Hélène Metzger: Eléments de biographie" in *Études sur/Studies on Hélène Metzger*, FREUDENTHAL, Gad.
"History of Science and Criticism of Positivism" in *Études sur/Studies on Hélène Metzger*, HEIDELBERGER, Michael.
"Léon Bloch et Hélène Metzger" in *Études sur/Studies on Hélène Metzger*, BLAY, Michel.
"Metzger, Kuhn, and Eighteenth-Century Disciplinary History" in *Études sur/Studies on Hélène Metzger*, MELHADO, Evan M.
"Some Aspects of Hélène Metzger's Philosophy of Science" in *Études sur/Studies on Hélène Metzger*, CARRIER, Martin.
"Some Considerations on the Study of the History of Seventeenth-Century Science" in *Études sur/Studies on Hélène Metzger*, SCHMITT, Charles B.
"Visages de Van Helmont, depuis Hélène Metzger jusqu'aà Walter Pagel" in *Études sur/Studies on Hélène Metzger*, HALLEUX, Robert.

MEXICAN
Conceptos filosóficos como sustrato del sentido de la muerte, desde la época prehispánica hasta la actual. DE LOS ANGELES IMAZ LIRA, María.
Educational Research in Mexico. SANCHEZ-PUENTES, Ricardo.
Relations and Sixteenth-Century Mexican Logic. REDMOND, Walter.

MEYER, M
Épistémologie et questionnement: le modële en tant que forme de l'interrogation scientifique. BORUTTI, Silvana.
Meyer's Theory of Problematology. GOLDEN, James L and JAMISON, David L.
Le problématologique devant la faculté de juger. PARRET, Herman.

MEYSING, M
Functionalisme versus dubbelaspecttheorie: tertium datur. MACKOR, Anne Ruth.

MICHELET, J
The Role of Memory in the Historiography of the French Revolution. HUTTON, Patrick H.

MICHELMAN, F
From Intersubjectivity through Epistemology to Property: Rejoinder to Michelman. SHEARMUR, Jeremy.

MICHOD, R
Adequacy Criteria for a Theory of Fitness. ROSENBERG, Alexander.
Byerly and Michod on Fitness. SMITH, John Maynard.
Commentary on Byerly and Michod. LENNOX, James G.
Commentary on the Paper by H C Byerly and R E Michod's "Fitness and Evolutionary Explanation". BRITO DA CUNHA, A.
Comments on "Fitness and Evolutionary Explanation". KLEINER, Scott A.
Natural Selection as Natural History. VAN DER STEEN, Wim J.
On Causality, Heritability and Fitness. ETTINGER, Lia and JABLONKA, Eva and FALK, Raphael.

MIEHOTTE, A
Existence et Subjectivité: Études de Psychologie Phénoménologique. THINÈS, Georges.

MILITARY
Bertrand Russell. ALCARO, Mario.
Military Ethics: Looking Toward the Future. FOTION, Nicholas G.
Understanding War: A Philosophical Inquiry. MC MURTRY, John.
Moral Philosophy at West Point in the Nineteenth Century. SHIVE, Kenneth D.
Treating the Troops. HOWE, Edmund G and MARTIN, Edward D.
Treating the Troops: A Commentary. ANNAS, George J and GRODIN, Michael A.
Treating the Troops: A Commentary. LEVINE, Robert J.

MILL
Additional Letters (Collected Works of John Stuart Mill, Volume XXXII). ROBSON, John M (ed).
A Cultivated Mind: Essays On J S Mill Presented to John M Robson. LAINE, Michael (ed).
Indexes to the Collected Works (Collected Works of John Stuart Mill, Vol XXXIII). ROBSON, John M (ed).
Mill and Liberalism (Second Edition). COWLING, Maurice.
The Positivist Science of Law. LEE, Keekok.
"From Sectarian Radical to National Possession" in *A Cultivated Mind: Essays On J S Mill Presented to John M Robson*, COLLINI, Stefan.
"John Mill's Education: Fact, Fiction, and Myth" in *A Cultivated Mind: Essays On J S Mill Presented to John M Robson*, STILLINGER, Jack.
"John Stuart Mill and France" in *A Cultivated Mind: Essays On J S Mill Presented to John M Robson*, FILIPIUK, Marion.
"John Stuart Mill and the East India Company" in *A Cultivated Mind: Essays On J S Mill Presented to John M Robson*, LLOYD, Trevor.
"John Stuart Mill and the Experience of Political Engagement" in *A Cultivated Mind: Essays On J S Mill Presented to John M Robson*, KINZER, Bruce L.
"Mill's Second Prize in the Lottery of Life" in *A Cultivated Mind: Essays On J S Mill Presented to John M Robson*, ROBSON, Ann P.
"Religion and *On Liberty*" in *A Cultivated Mind: Essays On J S Mill Presented to John M Robson*, HAMBURGER, Joseph.
"Sense and Sensibility in Mill's Political Thought" in *A Cultivated Mind: Essays On J S Mill Presented to John M Robson*, RYAN, Alan.
"'Congenial Vocation': J M Robson and the Mill Project" in *A Cultivated Mind: Essays On J S Mill Presented to John M Robson*, O'GRADY, Jean.
'One Very Simple Principle'. RILEY, Jonathan.
Beyond Malthusianism: Demography and Technology in John Stuart Mill's Stationary State. KURFIRST, Robert.
A Critical Note on J S Mill's Classification of Fallacies. HON, Giora.
Freedom Not to be Free: The Case of the Slavery Contract in J S Mill's *On Liberty*. ARCHARD, David.
Hypotheses, Probability, and Waves. ACHINSTEIN, Peter.
J S Mill and Indian Education. ZASTOUPIL, Lynn.
J S Mill's Concept of Maturity as the Criterion in Determining Children's Eligibility for Rights. KIM, Ki Su.
John Stuart Mill and Royal India. MOORE, Robin J.
John Stuart Mill on Induction and Hypothesis. JACOBS, Struan.
John Stuart Mill über die Todesstrafe. WOLF, Jean-Claude.
Markets and Morals. SMITH, G W.
The Member for Westminster: Doctrinaire Philosopher, Party Hack, or Public Moralist?. COLLINI, Stefan.
Post-Liberalism versus Temperate Liberalism. JACOBS, Struan.
Proof and Sanction in Mill's Utilitarianism. COHEN, Stephen.
Punishment and the Utilitarian Criterion of Right and Wrong. SCHALLER, Walter E.
A Tradition of Natural Kinds. HACKING, Ian.
Utilitarian Strategies in Bentham and John Stuart Mill. KELLY, P J.

MILL, H
"Mill's Second Prize in the Lottery of Life" in *A Cultivated Mind: Essays On J S Mill Presented to John M Robson*, ROBSON, Ann P.

MILLER, D
"Response to Miller's 'Equality'" in *Philosophy and Politics*, MINOGUE, Kenneth.
Are All False Theories Equally False? A Remark on David Miller's Problem and Geometric Conventionalism. MORMANN, Thomas.
On the Alleged Impossibility of Inductive Probability. EELLS, Ellery.
Response to Miller's "Equality". MINOGUE, K.
The Rights-Interpretation of Desert. GARCÍA, Jorge.
Some Further Reflections on the Popper-Miller 'Disproof' of Probabilistic Induction. HOWSON, C.
A Suspicious Feature of the Popper/Miller Argument. GOOD, I J.

MILLER, J
The Philosophy of John William Miller. FELL, Joseph P (ed).
"Acts and Necessity in the Philosophy of John William Miller" in *The Philosophy of John William Miller*, DIEFENBECK, James A.
"The Fatality of Thought" in *The Philosophy of John William Miller*, JOHNSTONE JR, Henry W.
"Literature, History, and What Men Learn" in *The Philosophy of John William Miller*, ELIAS, Robert H.
"Making the Moral World" in *The Philosophy of John William Miller*, STAHL, Gary.
"A Miller Bibliography with a Brief Description of The Williams College Miller Archives" in *The Philosophy of John William Miller*, JOHNSTONE JR, Henry W.
"Miller on Economics" in *The Philosophy of John William Miller*, BROCKWAY, George P.
"Miller: The Man and His Philosophy" in *The Philosophy of John William Miller*, FELL, Joseph P.
"On Interpreting J W Miller" in *The Philosophy of John William Miller*, GAHRINGER, Robert E.
"When the Truth Is in the Telling" in *The Philosophy of John William Miller*, STROUT, Cushing.

MILLER, R
Pot Bites Kettle: A Reply to Miller. LYCAN, William G.

MIMAMSA
Hindu Doubts About God: Towards a Mīmāmsā Deconstruction. BILIMORIA, Purusottama.
The Theory of Triple Perception. SARMA, Rajendra Nath.

MIMESIS
Echoes: After Heidegger. SALLIS, John.
Mimesis as Make-Believe: On the Foundations of the Representational Arts. WALTON, Kendall L.
"History and Mimesis" in *Looking After Nietzsche*, LACOUE-LABARTHE, Philippe.
"Just for the Thrill": Sycophantizing Aristotle's *Poetics*. CARSON, Anne.
Aristotelian Mimesis Reevaluated. HALLIWELL, Stephen.
On the Concept of Mímésis (in Czechoslovakian). VEJRAZKA, Michal.
Political Economy and Mimetic Desire: A Postmodernist Reading of "Babette's Feast". SHAPIRO, Michael J.
Popular Art and Aesthetic Theory: Why the Muse Is Unembarrassed. ANDERSON, Richard L.
Theoria, Aisthesis, Mimesis and Doxa. MÉCHOULAN, Éric.
The Time of the Political. BIRMINGHAM, Peg.

MIND
see also Soul(s), Spirit(s)
Acting and Reflecting: The Interdisciplinary Turn in Philosophy. SIEG, Wilfried (ed).
Artificial Intelligence and Human Cognition. WAGMAN, Morton.
Classics of Analytic Philosophy. AMMERMAN, Robert R (ed).
David Hume's Theory of Mind. FLAGE, Daniel E.
Donald Davidson. EVNINE, Simon.
Epistemics. DURAN, Jane.
Evolution als Höherentwicklung des Bewusstseins. KUMMER, Christian.
Explaining Behavior: Reasons in a World of Causes. DRETSKE, Fred.
From Sentience To Symbols. PICKERING, John (ed).
Goethe, Kant, and Hegel: Volume I, Discovering the Mind. KAUFMANN, Walter.
How to Build a Person: A Prolegomenon. POLLOCK, John L.
Introduction to Philosophy: Classical and Contemporary Readings. POJMAN, Louis P.

MIND

Kant's Model of the Mind: A New Interpretation of Transcendental Idealism. WAXMAN, Wayne.
Key Themes in Philosophy. GRIFFITHS, A Phillips (ed).
Leibniz' Position der Rationalität. KAEHLER, Klaus Erich.
Matter and Memory. BERGSON, Henri.
Metaphors of Mind: Conceptions of the Nature of Intelligence. STERNBERG, Robert J.
Metaphysik als Metahistorik oder Hermeneutik des unreinen Denkens Die Philosophie Max Müllers. RUIZ-PESCE, Ramón Eduardo.
Mind and Cognition: A Reader. LYCAN, William G (ed).
Mind in Action: Essays in the Philosophy of Mind. RORTY, Amelie Oksenberg.
Mind Only: A Philosophical and Doctrinal Analysis of the Vijñānavāda. WOOD, Thomas E.
Mind-Body. MOULYN, Adrian C.
The Natural and the Normative: Theories of Spatial Perception from Kant to Helmholtz. HATFIELD, Gary.
Of Memory, Reminiscence, and Writing: On the Verge. KRELL, David Farrell.
Phänomenologie als ästhetische Theorie. FELLMANN, Ferdinand.
Philosophical Perspectives, 3: Philosophy of Mind and Action Theory, 1989. TOMBERLIN, James E (ed).
Philosophical Perspectives, 4: Action Theory and Philosophy of Mind, 1990. TOMBERLIN, James E (ed).
Philosophy and Cognitive Science. FETZER, James H.
The Philosophy of Action: An Introduction. MOYA, Carlos J.
Propositional Attitudes: The Role of Content in Logic, Language, and Mind. ANDERSON, C Anthony (ed).
Psychology (Companions to Ancient Thought: 2). EVERSON, Stephen (ed).
The Representational Theory of Mind: An Introduction. STERELNY, Kim.
The Science of the Mind (Second Edition). FLANAGAN, Owen.
Selbsttäuschung. LÖW-BEER, Martin.
Sensations: A Defense of Type Materialism. HILL, Christopher S.
Truth and Interpretation: Perspectives on the Philosophy of Donald Davidson. LE PORE, Ernest (ed).
Understanding the Representational Mind. PERNER, Josef.
Wittgenstein: Meaning and Mind, Volume 3 of an Analytical Commentary on Philosophical Investigations. HACKER, P M S.
"Are There Alternatives?" in *Acting and Reflecting: The Interdisciplinary Turn in Philosophy*, NEWELL, Allen.
"The Basis of Lawful Behavior: Rules or Connections" in *Acting and Reflecting: The Interdisciplinary Turn in Philosophy*, MC CLELLAND, Jay.
"Benefits to Moral Philosophy of the Computational Model of the Mind" in *Acting and Reflecting: The Interdisciplinary Turn in Philosophy*, HARMAN, Gilbert.
"Can the Mind Change the World?" in *Meaning and Method: Essays in Honor of Hilary Putnam*, BLOCK, Ned.
"Cognitive Psychology, Entrapment, and the Philosophy of Mind" in *The Case for Dualism*, GAULD, Alan.
"The Computational Conception of Mind" in *Acting and Reflecting: The Interdisciplinary Turn in Philosophy*, SCOTT, Dana S.
"Discussion: Progress in Philosophy" in *Acting and Reflecting: The Interdisciplinary Turn in Philosophy*, SIMON, Herbert A.
"Epicurus' Philosophy of Mind" in *Psychology (Companions to Ancient Thought: 2)*, ANNAS, Julia.
"First-Person Access" in *Philosophical Perspectives, 4: Action Theory and Philosophy of Mind, 1990*, SHOEMAKER, Sydney.
"The Heart of the Mind: Intentionality versus Intelligence" in *The Case for Dualism*, PUCCETTI, Roland.
"The Intrinsic Quality of Experience" in *Philosophical Perspectives, 4: Action Theory and Philosophy of Mind, 1990*, HARMAN, Gilbert.
"Inverted Earth" in *Philosophical Perspectives, 4: Action Theory and Philosophy of Mind, 1990*, BLOCK, Ned.
"Language in the Heart-mind" in *Understanding the Chinese Mind: The Philosophical Roots*, HANSEN, Chad.
"Mind and Body" in *Key Themes in Philosophy*, WILKES, K V.
"Mind-Dust or Magic? Panpsychism Versus Emergence" in *Philosophical Perspectives, 4: Action Theory and Philosophy of Mind, 1990*, VAN CLEVE, James.
"A New Visualization of the Mind-Brain Relationship" in *The Case for Dualism*, HARRISON, Stephen.
"On Some Thought Experiments about Mind and Meaning" in *Propositional Attitudes: The Role of Content in Logic, Language, and Mind*, WALLACE, John and MASON, H E.
"An Overview of the Chinese Mind" in *Understanding the Chinese Mind: The Philosophical Roots*, ALLINSON, Robert E.
"The Reverse Frege Puzzle" in *Philosophical Perspectives, 3: Philosophy of Mind and Action Theory, 1989*, YAGISAWA, Takashi.
"What Emotions Are About" in *Philosophical Perspectives, 4: Action Theory and Philosophy of Mind, 1990*, BAIER, Annette C.
"What is Present to the Mind?" in *The Mind of Donald Davidson*, DAVIDSON, Donald.
An Alleged Analogy Between Numbers and Propositions. CRANE, Tim.
Anti-Individualism and Privileged Access. MC KINSEY, Michael.
Burgeoning Skepticism. DE VRIES, Willem.
Causation in the Philosophy of Mind. JACKSON, Frank and PETTIT, Philip.
Connectionist Minds. CLARK, Andy.
Conscious and Unconscious States. BEN-ZEEV, Aaron.
Contributi piagetiani ad una scienza della mente. BORELLA, Silvia.
Descartes on Sensory Representation: A Study of the *Dioptrics*. MAC KENZIE, Ann Wilbur.
Editologie et Scientificite. BAUDET, Jean C.
Eliminative Materialism and Substantive Commitments. NELSON, Mark T.
Emergent Psychoneural Monism: Mario Bunge and the Body and Soul Problem (in German). MÖLLER, Wolfgang.
The Existence of Non-Existence of Things which are Not in the Mind. POMERANTZ, Alfred.
Externalism and Experience. MC CULLOCH, Gregory.
Functionalism's Impotence. WECKERT, J.
Hypnosis and the Philosophy of Mind. HAIGHT, Mary.
Ji Kang's "Sheng-wu-aile-lun": Concerning Its Logical Development (in Japanese). HARA, Masayuki.
Keith Lehrer and Thomas Reid. CHISHOLM, Roderick M.
Massively Parallel Distributed Processing and a Computationalist Foundation for Cognitive Science. LYNGZEIDETSON, Albert E.
Mencius and the Mind-Dependence of Morality: An Analysis of Meng Tzu 6A: 4-5. SHUN, Kwong-Loi.
The Mind's I Has Two Eyes. MARTIN, J E and ENGLEMAN, K H.
A New Theory of the Relationship of Mind and Matter. BOHM, David.
Philosophische Anstösse in der computerunterstützten Intelligenz-Forschung. HRACHOVEC, Herbert.
Philosophy and Cognitive Science (in Czechoslovakian). PSTRUZINA, Karel.
A Pieced Quilt: A Critical Discussion of Stephen Schiffer's *Remnants of Meaning*. ANTONY, Louise.
Porphyry and the Intelligible Triad. EDWARDS, M J.
The Poverty of Neurophilosophy. STENT, Gunther S.
The Problem of Theoretical Self-Reflexivity in Peirce and Santayana. DILWORTH, David A.
Problems with the Fregean Interpretation of Husserl. BROWN, Charles S.
Putting One's Foot in One's Head—Part I: Why. PERLIS, Donald.
The Real Distinction Between Mind and Body. YABLO, Stephen.
The Reductionist Ideal in Cognitive Psychology. MONTGOMERY, Richard.
Remarks on the Modularity of Mind. SHANNON, Benny.
Some New Directions in the Philosophy of Mind. THOMAS, Janice.
Some Philosophical Aspects of Psychophysiology—Are There Any Elements of "Neurophilosophy"? (in German). RÜDIGER, Wolfgang.
Some Recent Research on the Mind-Body Problem in Descartes. MILES, Murray.
Spinoza on the Eternity of the Human Mind. LUCASH, Frank.
Sur le fragment des trois ordres de Blaise Pascal. CHIBAUDEL, Pierre.
The Contradiction of Belief and Reason in the Middle Ages: the Case of Boetius de Dacia (in Hungarian). JOÓS, Ernest.
Transcending Paradigms. REY, George.
Two Brains, Two Minds? Wigan's Theory of Mental Duality. PUCCETTI, Roland.
What is Wrong in Inverting Spectra. CASATI, Roberto.
Why not Naturalistic Psychology?. GARRETT, Richard and GRAHAM, George.
Why Shouldn't We Be Able to Solve the Mind-Body Problem?. KIRK, Robert.
Why the Mind is Not in the Head But in the Society's Connectionist Network. FISCHER, Roland.
William James's Theory of Mind. COOPER, W E.
Wittgenstein's Influence: Meaning, Mind and Method. GRAYLING, A C.

MINDS

see also Other Minds
How to Build a Conscious Machine. ANGEL, Leonard.
Other Human Beings. COCKBURN, David.
Analytic Functionalism and the Reduction of Phenomenal States. LEVIN, Janet.
Concept Attribution in Nonhuman Animals. ALLEN, Collin and HAUSER, Marc D.
Divided Minds. HIRSCH, Eli.
Functionalisme versus dubbelaspecttheorie: tertium datur. MACKOR, Anne Ruth.
Minds, Machines and Gödels Theorem (in German). RHEINWALD, Rosemarie.
Searle's Oplossing voor het lichaam-geest probleem: ipse dixit—Een reactie op Anne Ruth Mackor. MEIJSING, Monica.

MINIMAL LOGIC

The Minimal and Semiminimal Notions of Truth. FOX, J.

MINIMALISM

Robert Nozick: Property, Justice, and the Minimal State. WOLFF, Jonathan.
Process Metaphysics and Minimalism: Implications for Public Policy. KEFFER, Steven and KING, Sallie and KRAFT, Steven.

MINORITY(-TIES)

Crime, Minorities, and the Social Contract. LAWSON, Bill.
Liberalism, Aboriginal Rights, and Cultural Minorities. DANLEY, John R.

MIRACLE(S)
The Idea of the Miraculous: The Challenge to Science and Religion. WILLIAMS, T C.
The Metaphysics of Religious Belief. SHOOMAN, A P.
A Bayesian Proof of a Humean Principle. GILLIES, Donald.
David Hume and the Mysterious Shroud of Turin. SCHOEN, Edward L.
Fogelin on Hume on Miracles. FLEW, Antony.
Hume's "Of Miracles," Peirce, and the Balancing of Likelihoods. MERRILL, Kenneth R.
Hume's Theorem on Testimony Sufficient to Establish a Miracle. SOBEL, Jordan Howard.
Miracles and Ghazali's First Theory of Causation. BAHLUL, Raja.
Wittgenstein's Critique of Mechanistic Atomism. MC DONOUGH, Richard.

MIRROR THEORY(-RIES)
Persons as Natural Works of Art. ALDRICH, Virgil.

MISOLOGY
Nietzsche: The Body and Culture—Philosophy as a Philological Genealogy. BLONDEL, Eric.

MISTAKE(S)
False Consciousness. MEYERSON, Denise.

MODAL LOGIC
Leibniz's Philosophy of Logic and Language (Second Edition). ISHIGURO, Hide.
La Logica Simbolica: nella produzione scientifica in lingua russa (1961-1983). PENNINO, Luciano.
"Quine on Quantifying In" in *Propositional Attitudes: The Role of Content in Logic, Language, and Mind*, FINE, Kit.
Actuality and Quantification. HAZEN, Allen.
An Almost General Splitting Theorem for Modal Logic. KRACHT, Marcus.
Anti-Realism Untouched. MELIA, Joseph.
Before Refraining: Concepts for Agency. BELNAP JR, Nuel D.
Classes and Attributes in Extended Modal Systems: Proceedings of the Colloquium in Modal and Many Valued Logic. MARCUS, Ruth Barcan.
Constructive Interpolation Theorems for $S2^0$ and S2. BARCA, Anne and MC ROBBIE, Michael.
Constructive Modal Logics I. WIJESEKERA, Duminda.
Contingency and Modal Logic. DEUTSCH, Harry.
Decidable and Enumerable Predicate Logics of Provability. DZHAPARIDZE, Giorgie.
Definability Theorems in Normal Extensions of the Provability Logic. MAKSIMOVA, Larisa L.
Every World Can See a Reflexive World. HUGHES, G E.
Expressive Power and Semantic Completeness: Boolean Connectives in Modal Logic. HUMBERSTONE, I L.
The Extent of Russell's Modal Views. MAGNELL, Thomas.
Finite Kripke Models and Predicate Logics of Provability. ARTEMOV, Sergei and DZHAPARIDZE, Giorgie.
A Functional Calculus of First Order Based on Strict Implication. MARCUS, Ruth Barcan.
General Canonical Models for Graded Normal Logics (Graded Modalities IV). CERRATO, C.
A Generalization of the Adequacy Theorem for the Quasi-Senses. BONOTTO, Cinzia.
Grammar Logics. FARIÑAS DEL CERRO, Luis and PENTTONEN, Martti.
How Far Can Hume's Is-Ought Thesis Be Generalized?. SCHURZ, Gerhard.
The Identity of Individuals in a Strict Functional Calculus of Second Order. MARCUS, Ruth Barcan.
Infinitary Combinatorics and Modal Logic. BLASS, A.
An Integer-Valued Matrix Characteristic for Implicational *S*5. ULRICH, Dolph.
Intensional Identities. SLATER, B H.
The Interpretability Logic of Peano Arithmetic. BERARDUCCI, Alessandro.
Kripke Bundles for Intermediate Predicate Logics and Kripke Frames for Intuitionistic Modal Logics. SUZUKI, Nobu-Yuki.
Kripke on Theoretical Identifications: A Rejoinder to Perrick. BUXTON, James.
Kripke Semantics for Knowledge Representation Logics. ORLOWSKA, Ewa.
Logical Equations and Admissible Rules of Inference with Parameters in Modal Provability Logics. RYBAKOV, V V.
The Logical Status of Modal Reductionism. MOSER, Paul K and VANDER NAT, Arnold.
Many-Valued Modal Logics: Uses and Predicate Calculus. OSTERMANN, Pascal.
Modal Counterparts of Medvedev Logic of Finite Problems Are Not Finitely Axiomatizable. SHEHTMAN, Valentin.
The Modal Logic of Pure Provability. BUSS, Samuel R.
Modal Logic. MARCUS, Ruth Barcan.
Modal Logics with *n*-ary Connectives. GHILARDI, S and MELONI, C G.
Models for Relevant Modal Logics. FUHRMANN, André.
Natural Deduction in Normal Modal Logic. HAWTHORN, John.
New Semantics for the Extensional but Hyper-Intensional Part..... BRESSAN, Aldo.
A Note on Some Extension Results. MONTAGNA, Franco and SOMMARUGA, Giovanni.
Notes on Modal Definability. VAN BENTHEM, Johan.
On a Mainstay of Incompatibilism. BLUM, Alex.
On Regular Modal Logics with Axiom.... SWIRYDOWICZ, Kazimierz.
On Rigidity and Persistence. WILLIAMSON, Timothy.
Problems of Substitution and Admissibility in the Modal System Grz and in Intuitionistic Propositional Calculus. RYBAKOV, V V.
Related Semantics for All Lewis, Lemmon and Feys' Modal Logics. SYLVAN, Richard.
A Solution to a Problem of Urquhart. KRACHT, Marcus.
Some Descending Chains of Incomplete Model Logics. XU, Ming.
Some Modal Logics Based on a Three-Valued Logic. MORIKAWA, Osamu.
The Theory of Descriptions Revisited. PERUZZI, Alberto.
Toward a Formalization of Dialectical Logic. THOMASON, Steven K.
Towards a Modal-Structural Interpretation of Set Theory. HELLMAN, Geoffrey.
The Two Barbaras. THOM, Paul.
Underivability Results in Mixed Systems of Monadic Deontic Logic. GALVAN, Sergio.
Varying Modal Theories. LUCAS, T and LAVENDHOMME, R.
Verification, Falsification and Cancellation in KT. WILLIAMSON, Timothy.

MODAL REALISM
Pot Bites Kettle: A Reply to Miller. LYCAN, William G.

MODAL SYLLOGISMS
Buridan's Divided Modal Syllogistic. WILLING, Anthony.

MODAL THEORY
Identity and Discrimination. WILLIAMSON, Timothy.
"Modal-Structural Mathematics" in *Physicalism in Mathematics*, HELLMAN, Geoffrey.
How *Not* to Become a Millian Heir. SALMON, Nathan.
The Modal Ontological Argument and the Necessary A Posteriori. FORGIE, J W.
Modal Realism Without Counterparts. HALE, Susan C.
A Priority and Ways of Grasping a Proposition. WONG, Kai-Yee.
Stit and the Language of Agency. PERLOFF, Michael.
Towards a Modal-Structural Interpretation of Set Theory. HELLMAN, Geoffrey.

MODALITY
Good and Evil: An Absolute Conception. GAITA, Raimond.
Nicolai Hartmann's New Ontology. WERKMEISTER, W H.
The Recovery of the Soul: An Aristotelian Essay on Self-fulfilment. RANKIN, Kenneth.
Saggio di semantica. BRÉAL, Michel.
"A Backward Look at Quine's Animadversions on Modalities" in *Perspectives on Quine*, MARCUS, Ruth Barcan.
"Mathematics and Modality" in *Meaning and Method: Essays in Honor of Hilary Putnam*, FIELD, Hartry.
"The Problem of De Re Modality" in *Themes From Kaplan*, FINE, Kit.
"Ways and Loci of Modality" in *Essays on Hegel's Logic*, BAPTIST, Gabriella.
Actualism, Ontological Commitment, and Possible World Semantics. MENZEL, Ch.
Buridan's Divided Modal Syllogistic. WILLING, Anthony.
Explaining Necessity. MASON, Richard V.
General Canonical Models for Graded Normal Logics (Graded Modalities IV). CERRATO, C.
Induction and Modality. JOHNSON, David.
Metalogic and Modality. FIELD, Hartry.
Modality and Mellor's McTaggart. CRESSWELL, M J.
Reply of a Mad Dog. MILLER, Richard B.
Semantica aristotelica e sillogistica modale. MARIANI, Mauro.
A Study of Ontology. FINE, Kit.
Truth at a World is a Modality. LINSKY, Bernard.
Verification, Falsification and Cancellation in KT. WILLIAMSON, Timothy.
The What and the How. ALMOG, Joseph.

MODE(S)
Cartesian Passions and Cartesian Dualism. HOFFMAN, Paul.
The No-Slip Condition of Fluid Dynamics. DAY, Michael A.
Real Selves: Persons as a Substantial Kind. LOWE, E J.

MODEL THEORY
"Truth-Value of Ethical Statements" in *Logic and Ethics*, PRZELECKI, Marian.
Effective Model Theory versus Recursive Model Theory. CHISHOLM, John.
Generalizing Classical and Effective Model Theory in Theories of Operations and Classes. MANCOSU, Paolo.
Where Do Natural Numbers Come From?. HODES, Harold T.

MODEL(S)
Adorno's Aesthetic Theory: The Redemption of Illusion. ZUIDERVAART, Lambert.
Artificial Intelligence: Its Scope and Limits. FETZER, James H.
Causality in Sociological Research. KARPINSKI, Jakub.
Evolution: Probleme und neue Aspekte ihrer Theorie. SCHEFFCZYK, Leo (ed).
Experimental Studies of Interactive Decisions. RAPOPORT, Amnon.
Inscriptions and Reflections: Essays in Philosophical Theology. SCHARLEMANN, Robert P.

MODEL(S)

Models and Concepts of Ideology. RITSERT, Jürgen.
L'ordine della certezza: Scientificità e persuasione in Descartes. BONICALZI, Francesca.
"The Deductive Model in Ethics" in *Logic and Ethics*, LAZARI-PAWLOWSKA, Ija.
"Greek Medical Models of Mind" in *Psychology (Companions to Ancient Thought: 2)*, HANKINSON, R J.
"On the Existence of End Extensions of Models of Bounded Induction" in *Logic, Methodology and Philosophy of Science, VIII*, WILKIE, A.
A priori et a posteriori dans la pratique cognitive: le modele de la regulation des couples ago-antagonistes. BERNARD-WEIL, E.
About Prikry Generic Extensions. SURESON, Claude.
An Anomaly in the D-N Model of Explanation. BLUM, Alex.
Autonomy and Personal History. CHRISTMAN, John.
The Axiomatic Method: Its Origin and Purpose. AGASHE, S D.
Axiomatization of 'Peircean' Branching-Time Logic. ZANARDO, Alberto.
Boolean Products of CW—Algebras and Pseudo-Complementation. TORRENS, Antoni.
The Borel Conjecture. JUDAH, Haim and SHELAH, Saharon and WOODIN, W H.
Cicero's Focus: From the Best Regime to the Model Statesman. NICGORSKI, Walter.
The Complete 0. KANAMORI, Akihiro and AWERBUCH-FRIEDLANDER, Tamara.
The Complexity of Intrinsically R.E. Subsets of Existentially Decidable Models. CHISHOLM, John.
A Decidable Ehrenfeucht Theory with Exactly Two Hyperarithmetic Models. REED, R C.
Definability in Self-Referential Systems. SOBRINHO, J Zimbarg.
Definitions of Compact. HOWARD, Paul E.
The Degree of a Σ_n Cut. CHONG, C T and MOURAD, K J.
Enumerations of Turing Ideals with Applications. MARKER, David.
The Equivalence of Determinacy and Iterated Sharps. DUBOSE, Derrick Albert.
An Equivalent of the Axiom of Choice in Finite Models of the Powerset Axiom. ABIAN, Alexander and AMIN, Wael A.
Every World Can See a Reflexive World. HUGHES, G E.
Expectation, Modelling and Assent in the History of Optics: Part I—Alhazen and the Medieval Tradition. CROMBIE, A C.
Expecting Nature's Best: Optimality Models and Perfect Adaptation. HOLCOMB, H R.
Exponentiation and Second-Order Bounded Arithmetic. KRAJICEK, Jan.
Expressive Power and Semantic Completeness: Boolean Connectives in Modal Logic. HUMBERSTONE, I L.
Finite Support Iteration and Strong Measure Zero Sets. PAWLIKOWSKI, Janusz.
First-Order Logics for Comparative Similarity. WILLIAMSON, Timothy.
Full Reflection of Stationary Sets Below $\aleph_\omega$. JECH, Thomas and SHELAH, Saharon.
General Canonical Models for Graded Normal Logics (Graded Modalities IV). CERRATO, C.
The Homogeneous Form of Logic Programs with Equality. DEMOPOULOS, William.
How the Models of Chemistry Vie. HOFMANN, James R.
Incompleteness of a Free Arithmetic. BENCIVENGA, Ermanno.
An Integrative Model of Clinical-Ethical Decision Making. GRUNDSTEIN-AMADO, Rivka.
Intermediate Predicate Logics Determined by Ordinals. MINARI, Pierluigi and TAKANO, Mitio and ONO, Hiroakira.
Interpretation of Relevant Logics in a Logic of Ternary Relations. ORLOWSKA, Ewa.
Kripke Semantics for Knowledge Representation Logics. ORLOWSKA, Ewa.
Kripke-Style Models for Typed Lambda Calculus. MITCHELL, John C and MOGGI, Eugenio.
The Last Word on Elimination of Quantifiers in Modules. GUTE, Hans B and REUTER, K K.
The Meaning of Meaning. HELLER, Michael.
Le modèle industriel comme modèle énergétique. BERTEN, André.
Models for Inconsistent and Incomplete Differential Calculus. MORTENSEN, Chris.
Models for Relevant Modal Logics. FUHRMANN, André.
Multiset Theory. BLIZARD, Wayne D.
A Note on Some Extension Results. MONTAGNA, Franco and SOMMARUGA, Giovanni.
Omitting Types for Stable CCC Theories. NEWELSKI, Ludomir.
On Diophantine Equations Solvable in Models of Open Induction. OTERO, Margarita.
On Generalizations of a Theorem of Vaught. BIRÓ, Balázs.
On Scott and Karp Trees of Uncountable Models. HYTTINEN, Tapani and VÄÄNÄNEN, Jouko.
On Simplicity of Formulas. KRYNICKI, Michal and SZCZERBA, Leslaw.
On the Angular Component Map Modulo *P*. PAS, Johan.
The Outranking Approach and the Foundations of Electre Methods. ROY, Bernard.
Related Semantics for All Lewis, Lemmon and Feys' Modal Logics. SYLVAN, Richard.
Relative Elimination of Quantifiers for Henselian Valued Fields. BASARAB, Serban A.
Rich Models. ALBERT, Michael H and GROSSBERG, Rami P.
Sociology: An Infirm Science. BUSINO, Giovanni and FERGUSON, Jeanne.
Some Modal Logics Based on a Three-Valued Logic. MORIKAWA, Osamu.
The Special Model Axiom in Nonstandard Analysis. ROSS, David.
The Spectrum of Resplendency. BALDWIN, John T.
Stability for Pairs of Equivalence Relations. TOFFALORI, Carlo.
The Structure of the Models of Decidable Monadic Theories of Graphs. SEESE, D.
Successors of Singular Cardinals and Measurability Revisited. APTER, Arthur W.
Taxonomies of Model-Theoretically Defined Topological Properties. BANKSTON, Paul.
Three Models of Competence: A Critical Evaluation of Chomsky. MUKHERJI, Arundhati.
Tipos ideales en historia. TOZZI, María Verónica.
Unidimensional Theories are Superstable. HRUSHOVSKI, Ehud.
Universal Structures in Power $\aleph_1$. MEKLER, Alan H.
Upward Directedness of the Rudin-Keisler Ordering of *P*-Points. LAFLAMME, Claude.
Variations on da Costa *C* Systems and Dual-Intuitionistic Logics (I). SYLVAN, Richard.
Varying Modal Theories. LUCAS, T and LAVENDHOMME, R.
Voix et Existence. DIAGNE, Oumar.
'Just More Theory': A Manoeuvre in Putnam's Model-Theoretic Argument for Antirealism. TAYLOR, Barry.

MODELING

"Impact of Global Modelling on Modern Methodology of Science" in *Logic, Methodology and Philosophy of Science, VIII*, GVISHIANI, J M.
Fragility and Deterministic Modelling in the Exact Sciences. TAVAKOL, R K.
Mathematical Modelling and Constrastive Explanation. MORTON, Adam.

MODERATION

"Pragmatic Pacifism: A Methodology for Gaining the Ear of the Warist" in *In the Interest of Peace: A Spectrum of Philosophical Views*, SMITHKA, Paula.

MODERN

Anglo-American Philosophy of Law: An Introduction to Its Development and Outcome. LEVY, Beryl Harold.
Berkeley's Revolution in Vision. ATHERTON, Margaret.
Cálculo y ser (Aproximación a Leibniz). MARZOA, Felipe Martínez.
Central Themes in Early Modern Philosophy. COVER, J A (ed).
Il compito della filosofia: Saggio su Windelband. OLIVA, Rossella Bonito.
Criteria of Certainty: Truth and Judgment in the English Enlightenment. COPE, Kevin L.
David Hume and the Problem of Reason. DANFORD, John W.
David Hume: Historiker und Philosoph. LÜTHE, Rudolf.
Descartes Among the Scholastics. GRENE, Marjorie.
Diderot's Dream. ANDERSON, Wilda.
Égalité Uguaglianza. FERRARI, Jean (ed).
Empiricism and Subjectivity: An Essay on Hume's Theory of Human Nature. BOUNDAS, Constantin V (trans).
Études sur/Studies on Hélène Metzger. FREUDENTHAL, Gad.
Expressionism in Philosophy: Spinoza. DELEUZE, Gilles.
Fallen Freedom: Kant on Radical Evil and Moral Regeneration. MICHALSON JR, Gordon E.
Fichte's Theory of Subjectivity. NEUHOUSER, Frederick.
Hegel In His Time—Jacques D'Hondt. BURBIDGE, John (trans).
Hume's Place in Moral Philosophy. CAPALDI, Nicholas.
Idea, mente, specie: Platonismo e scienza in Johannes Marcus Marci (1595-1667). MOCCHI, Giuliana.
Ideas, Principios y Dialectica. LAFUENTE, Maria Isabel.
Jean-Jacques: The Early Life and Work of Jean-Jacques, 1712-1754. CRANSTON, Maurice.
Kants Kategorischer Imperativ als Leitfaden humaner Praxis. NISTERS, Thomas.
Meditations on First Philosophy: A Bilingual Edition—René Descartes. HEFFERNAN, George (trans).
Mill and Liberalism (Second Edition). COWLING, Maurice.
The Moral Animus of David Hume. SIEBERT, Donald T.
Moral Philosophy from Montaigne to Kant: An Anthology, Volume I & II. SCHNEEWIND, J B (ed).
On True and False Ideas, New Objections to Descartes' Meditations and Descartes' Replies. ARNAULD, Antoine (trans).
Philosophy in World Perspective: A Comparative Hermeneutic of the Major Theories. DILWORTH, David A.
Philosophy's Journey: From the Presocratics to the Present (Second Edition). KOLENDA, Konstantin.
A Progress of Sentiments: Reflections on Hume's "Treatise". BAIER, Annette C.
Questions Concerning the Law of Nature: John Locke. CLAY, Jenny Strauss (ed & trans).

MODERN

Réflexions sur les passions. HUME, David.
The Rhetoric of Berkeley's Philosophy. WALMSLEY, Peter.
The Savage Anomaly: The Power of Spinoza's Metaphysics and Politics. NEGRI, Antonio.
Scienza, Filosofia e Religione tra '600 e '700 in Italia. PREDAVAL MAGRINI, Maria Vittoria (ed).
L'Utopia di Fourier. TUNDO, Laura.
"Il 'Giornale de' Letterati' e le 'scienze della vita': dibattiti e interventi" in *Scienza, Filosofia e Religione tra '600 e '700 in Italia*, BOARETTI, Tiziano.
"L'Accademia delle scienze di Bologna: l'edizione del primo tomo dei 'Commentarii' (1731)" in *Scienza, Filosofia e Religione tra '600 e '700 in Italia*, DE ZAN, Mauro.
"Il corpuscolarismo italiano nel 'Giornale de' Letterati' di Roma (1668-1681)" in *Scienza, Filosofia e Religione tra '600 e '700 in Italia*, LOPICCOLI, Fiorella.
"Egalité ou fraternité" in *Égalité Uguaglianza*, OPPICI, Patrizia.
"La femme intellectuelle au XVIIIe siècle ou l'inégalité des sexes" in *Égalité Uguaglianza*, GEFFRIAUD-ROSSO, Jeannette.
"Filosofia e politica in Giammaria Ortes" in *Scienza, Filosofia e Religione tra '600 e '700 in Italia*, GIACOTTO, Paolo.
"Giovanni Gualberto (Alberto) De Soria e la 'Cosmologia'" in *Scienza, Filosofia e Religione tra '600 e '700 in Italia*, PONZELLINI, Ornella.
"Hélène Metzger et l'historiographie de la chimie du XVIIIe siècle" in *Études sur/Studies on Hélène Metzger*, CHRISTIE, John R R.
"Hélène Metzger et l'interprétation de la chimie du XVIIe siècle" in *Études sur/Studies on Hélène Metzger*, GOLINSKI, Jan.
"Hélène Metzger et la théorie corpusculaire des stahliens au XVIIIe siècle" in *Études sur/Studies on Hélène Metzger*, KUBBINGA, Henk H.
"L'égalité ambiguë: construction juridique ou déduction métaphysique?" in *Égalité Uguaglianza*, WUNENBURGER, Jean-Jacques.
"L'égalité des droits en 1789" in *Égalité Uguaglianza*, GOYARD-FABRE, Simone.
"L'égalité en 1789" in *Égalité Uguaglianza*, D'HONDT, Jacques.
"L'idée d'égalité et la notion moderne du droit" in *Égalité Uguaglianza*, RENAUT, Alain.
"Methodische Aspekte des Kunstwissenschaftlichen Umgangs mit moderner Kunst" in *XIth International Congress in Aesthetics, Nottingham 1988*, LINGNER, Michael.
"Metzger, Kuhn, and Eighteenth-Century Disciplinary History" in *Études sur/Studies on Hélène Metzger*, MELHADO, Evan M.
"Modern Moral Philosophy" in *A Companion to Ethics*, SCHNEEWIND, J B.
"Pier Caterino Zeno le vicende culturali del 'Giornale de' Letterati d'Italia'" in *Scienza, Filosofia e Religione tra '600 e '700 in Italia*, GENERALI, Dario.
"Poetic Revenge and Modern Totalitarianism" in *From Twilight to Dawn: The Cultural Vision of Jacques Maritain*, REDPATH, Peter A.
"The Social Contract Tradition" in *A Companion to Ethics*, KYMLICKA, Will.
"Some Considerations on the Study of the History of Seventeenth-Century Science" in *Études sur/Studies on Hélène Metzger*, SCHMITT, Charles B.
"Uguaglianza, riconoscimento del simile e principio d'autorità nell'ultimo Diderot" in *Égalité Uguaglianza*, GOGGI, Gianluigi.
"Una uguale educazione?" in *Égalité Uguaglianza*, PANCERA, Carlo.
"Les utopies littéraires au XVIIIe siècle" in *Égalité Uguaglianza*, IMBROSCIO, Carmelina.
"La 'grande illusion' du XVIIIe siècle" in *Égalité Uguaglianza*, ROSSO, Corrado.
"Extrinsic Cognoscibility": A Seventeenth Century Supertranscendental Notion. DOYLE, John P.
(Post-) Metaphysik und (Post-) Moderne: Zur Sache des "schwachen Denkens". FRÜCHTL, Josef.
The Authorship of the *Abstract* Revisited. NELSON, John O.
Berkeley and Common Sense Realism. PAPPAS, George S.
Butler and the Authority of Conscience. O'BRIEN, Wendell.
Il caso "Siris", ovvero la "seconda filosofia" di George Berkeley vescovo di Cloyne. NERI, Luigi.
Chen Que versus Huang Zongxi: Confucianism Faces Modern Times in the Seventeenth Century. STRUVE, Lynn A.
A Comprehensive and Comprehensible Survey of Modern Philosophy. PEROVICH JR, Anthony.
Congruenza, schematismo, sintesi: Prospettive leibniziane intorno al criterio di verità secondo Giambattista Vico. PINCHARD, Bruno.
Crusius: un jalón olvidado en la ruta hacia el criticismo. ROLDÁN, Concha.
The Dating of Rule IV-B in Descartes's *Regulae ad directionem ingenii*. VAN DE PITTE, Frederick P.
Descartes e le "culture" barocche: Appunti su alcune recenti interpretazioni. LOJACONO, Ettore.
Dialogue and Doubt in Descartes' First Meditation. LINVILLE, Kent.
La dignità dell'uomo da Kant a Hegel. PAOLINELLI, Marco.
La dimostrazione "a posteriori" dell'esistenza di Dio nella filosofia di Leibniz. NICOLOSI, Salvatore.
The Faculty of Desire. LACHTERMAN, David.
Fichte on Skepticism. BREAZEALE, Daniel.
The Fifth Meditation. EDELBERG, Walter.
La filosofía transcendental: el destino de un proyecto ilustrado. FLAMARIQUE, Lourdes.
Filosofía, hoy. CUÉLLAR, Hortensia.
The Formation of the Modern State: A Reconstruction of Max Weber's Arguments. AXTMANN, Roland.
Gestualità e mito: i due caratteri distintivi della lingua originaria secondo Vico. CANTELLI, Gianfranco.
The Greatness and Limits of Kant's Practical Philosophy. HÖSLE, Vittorio.
Hegel, Heidegger, and the Question of Art Today. GROSSMANN, Andreas.
History of Modern Philosophy as an Issues-Based Introductory Course. DIXON, Nicholas.
Hobbes y la apología moderna del artificio. BOVERO, Michelangelo.
Hume and Belief in the Existence of an External World. COSTA, Michael J.
Hume's Theorem on Testimony Sufficient to Establish a Miracle. SOBEL, Jordan Howard.
Incorporating Gender Issues in Modern Philosophy. IMMERWAHR, John.
The Insufficiency of Descartes' Provisional Morality. COOLIDGE JR, Francis P.
Jean-Jacques Rousseau on the Physiogonomy of the Modern City. ELLISON, Charles E.
Kant's Account of Intuition. FALKENSTEIN, Lorne.
Kant's First Analogy Revisited. BUESSEM, George E.
Kant's Psychological Hedonism. GRIFFITHS, A Phillips.
Kant's Search for the Philosopher's Stone. AXIOTIS, Ares.
Kant's Theory of Empirical Judgment and Modern Semantics. HANNA, Robert.
Least Parts and Greatest Wholes Variations on a Theme in Spinoza. SACKSTEDER, William.
Leibniz's "Analysis of Multitude and Phenomena into Unities and Reality". RUTHERFORD, Donald.
Locke's Account of Personal Identity. SCHRECK, P A.
Michel de Montaigne: La "nottola" dell'Umanesimo francese. LONGO, Margherita.
The Moderns in an Introductory Analytic Course. DICKER, Georges.
On Ancients and Moderns. CROPSEY, Joseph.
Per una nuova edizione della *Epistola* lockiana sulla tolleranza. MONTUORI, Mario.
The Persistence of Counterexample: Re-examining the Debate over Leibniz Law. LANDINI, Gregory and FOSTER, Thomas.
Philosophy and the Rise of Modern Science. SALMON, Wesley.
La polémica sobre el espinosismo de Lessing. FERNÁNDEZ LORENZO, Manuel.
Il polipo di Trembley (1740) e la "catena delle verità": Note di ricerca. TODESCO, Fabio.
Postilla. GALASSO, Giuseppe.
Power, Liberty, and Counterfactual Conditionals in Hobbes' Thought. POLANSKY, Ronald and TORELL, Kurt.
Le premier registre de Descartes. RODIS-LEWIS, Geneviève.
El proyecto crítico de Kant. CHAVES, Carmen.
Rationality, Economic Action and Scarcity (in Hungarian). FEKETE, László.
Rosmini interprete della Rivoluzione francese e di Rousseau. BOTTO, Evandro.
Scientific Realism and Postmodern Philosophy. MURPHY, Nancey.
Las Sociedades de Pensamiento y la Revolución Francesa. RHENÁN SEGURA, Jorge.
Special Problems in Teaching Modern Philosophy. PHILLIPS, Hollibert.
Spinoza's Materialist Ethics: The Education of Desire. RAVVEN, Heidi M.
Spinoza—Beyond Hobbes and Rousseau. GEISMANN, Georg.
Sulla matrice della teoria della sostanza nel *Discorso di metafisica* di Leibniz. DELCÓ, Alessandro.
A Supplement to "David Hume to Alexander Dick: A New Letter". KLEMME, Heiner F.
La teoría de la suposición y los idiomas modernos. KNABENSCHUCH DE PORTA, Sabine.
The Differences Between the Capitalist and the Modern Society (in German). KRÜGER, Hans-Peter.
Two-Steps-in-One-Proof: The Structure of the Transcendental Deduction of the Categories. EVANS, J Claude.
Verlichtingsfilosofie twee eeuwen later; J F Lyotard als postmoderne Kant. VAN PEPERSTRATEN, Frans.
Visione in Dio e visione di Dio nella filosofia di Malebranche. NICOLOSI, Salvatore.
Was Spinoza a Marrano of Reason?. POPKIN, Richard H.
Wie kaatst moet de bal verwachten. MERTENS, T.
Wissen und Emanzipation. SANDKÜHLER, Hans Jörg.

MODERNISM

Ästhetik des Abschieds: Kritik der Moderne. EBELING, Hans.
Modernism as a Philosophical Problem: On the Dissatisfactions of European High Culture. PIPPIN, Robert B.
The Persistence of Modernity: Essays on Aesthetics, Ethics, and Postmodernism. WELLMER, Albrecht.
Reading Habermas. RASMUSSEN, David M.
Wittgenstein, Ethics and Aesthetics: The View from Eternity. TILGHMAN, B R.
"False Universality" in *Critique and Construction: A Symposium on Roberto Unger's "Politics"*, GALSTON, William A.

MODERNISM

"Postmodernism in Dance: Dance, Discourse, Democracy" in *Postmodernism—Philosophy and the Arts (Continental Philosophy III)*, LEVIN, David Michael.
Art History in the Mirror Stage: Interpreting *Un Bar aux Folies Bergères*. CARRIER, David.
The Influence of Modernism on Art Education. MEESON, Philip.
Kansas, Oz, and the Function of Art. CONLON, James.
Kompensierte Moderne. LÖVENICH, F.
Modernism's Two Eternities. GEORGIEFF, Andrey.
Modernité et postmodernité: un enjeu politique?. BERTEN, André.
Nueva modernidad adveniente y cultura emergente en América Latina. SCANNONE, J C.
The Postmodern Posture. KHANIN, Dmitry.
Reconstructing the Subject: Feminism, Modernism, and Postmodernism. HEKMAN, Susan.

MODERNITY

Irony and the Discourse of Modernity. BEHLER, Ernst.
The Legal-Rational State: A Comparison of Hobbes, Bentham and Kelsen. LEE, Keekok.
Modernity, Aesthetics, and the Bounds of Art. MC CORMICK, Peter J.
Morality and Modernity. POOLE, Ross.
The Tanner Lectures On Human Values, Volume XII. PETERSON, Grethe B (ed).
Unsere postmoderne Moderne (Second Edition). WELSCH, Wolfgang.
Wege aus der Moderne. WELSCH, Wolfgang (ed).
"Poetry and Modernity" in *The Tanner Lectures On Human Values, Volume XII*, PAZ, Octavio.
"Religion and the Making of Society" in *Critique and Construction: A Symposium on Roberto Unger's "Politics"*, DAVIS, Charles.
Aesthetic Liberalism: Kant and the Ethics of Modernity. CASCARDI, Anthony J.
The Case for a New American Pragmatism. LAVINE, Thelma Z.
Crisis of Modernity and Process Thought in Max Horkheimer's Early Work (in Serbo-Croatian). FILANDRA, Sacir.
Heidegger and Emancipation. OLIVIER, G.
The Life of Order and the Order of Life: Eric Voegelin on Modernity and the Problem of Philosophical Anthropology. LEVY, David J.
Modernity, the Individual and Rationality in Marxism (Surrealism and Revolution). CLOUDSLEY, Tim.
Perennial Modernity: Forms as Aesthetic and Symbolic. MAQUET, Jacques.
Philosophy of Science and the Persistent Narratives of Modernity. ROUSE, Joseph.
Principio de Razón o fundamento de Amor. MENDEZ, J R.
Richard Rorty and the Image of Modernity. BRADLEY, James.
Romano Guardini's Theological Critique of the Modern Age (in Dutch). VAN DER VLOET, J.
Romanticism and Modernity. LARMORE, Charles.
Soggettività e autocoscienza: Prospettive e problemi in Dieter Henrich. CELANO, Bruno.
Storicità tecnica e architettura. MAZZARELLA, Eugenio.
Vico, pensatore antimoderno: L'interpretazione di Eric Voegelin. ZANETTI, Gianfrancesco.

MODIFIER(S)

Events in the Semantics of English: A Study in Subatomic Semantics. PARSONS, Terence.

MODULARITY

Connectionism, Modularity, and Tacit Knowledge. DAVIES, Martin.
Modularity of Mind Revisited. BENNETT, Laura J.
Remarks on the Modularity of Mind. SHANNON, Benny.

MOHANTY, J

Phenomenology and Indian Philosophy. SINGH, Navjyoti.

MOHISM

Mencius' Criticism of Mohism: An Analysis of *Meng Tzu* 3A:5. SHUN, Kwong-Loi.

MOI, T

How I Slugged It Out with Toril Moi and Stayed Awake. BEDIENT, Calvin.

MOKED, G

Berkeley's Anti-Abstractionism: Reply to Moked. GLOUBERMAN, Mark.

MOKSA

The Advaita Theory of Liberation. DAS, Bhupendra Chandra.

MOLINA

The Dilemma of Freedom and Foreknowledge. ZAGZEBSKI, Linda Trinkaus.

MOMENT(S)

Why Should a Dialectician Learn to Count to Four?. ZIZEK, Slavoj.

MONADIC

Monadic Marxism: A Critique of Elster's Methodological Individualism. MOGGACH, Douglas.
The Structure of the Models of Decidable Monadic Theories of Graphs. SEESE, D.

MONADOLOGY

Festrede zum 300: Geburstag von Gottfried Wilhelm Leibniz am 1 Juli 1946 in der Aula der Universitat Leipzig. GADAMER, Hans-Georg.
Phänomenologie und Monadologie: Husserl und Leibniz. CRISTIN, Renato.
Phenomenalism and the Reality of Body in Leibniz's Later Philosophy. RUTHERFORD, Donald P.

MONARCHY

Patriarcha and Other Writings: Sir Robert Filmer. SOMMERVILLE, Johann P (ed).
Politics Drawn From the Very Words of Holy Scripture—Jacques-Benigne Bossuet. RILEY, Patrick (ed).
"His Majesty Is a Baby?" A Critical Response to Peter Hammond Schwartz. SPRINGBORG, Patricia.
The Contending Among the Hundred Schools of Thought During the Warring States Period. ZEHUA, Liu.
Rejoinder to Springborg's "His Majesty Is a Baby?" A Critical Response to Peter Hammond Schwartz. SCHWARTZ, Peter Hammond.

MONEY

The Philosophy of Money: Georg Simmel (Second Edition). FRISBY, David (ed & trans).

MONISM

Mind-Body. MOULYN, Adrian C.
"'Where Two Are to Become One': Mysticism and Monism" in *The Philosophy in Christianity*, JANTZEN, Grace M.
"Ethics IP5: Shared Attributes and the Basis of Spinoza's Monism" in *Central Themes in Early Modern Philosophy*, GARRETT, Don.
Dialectical Thinking in Metaphysics—Van Kues: Coincidental Thinking and the Problem of Idealistic Monism (in German). WINKLER, Norbert.
Emergent Psychoneural Monism: Mario Bunge and the Body and Soul Problem (in German). MÖLLER, Wolfgang.
Functional Support for Anomalous Monism. EDWARDS, Jim.
Is It Practical Ontology or Is It the Dialectical Materialist Theory of Material Monism?. JINFU, Wang.
Mental Causation and Non-Reductive Monism. MACDONALD, Cynthia and MACDONALD, Graham.
No Holism without Pluralism. VARNER, Gary E.
Principle Monism and Action Descriptions: Situationism and its Critics Revisited. PINCHES, Charles.
William James's Theory of Mind. COOPER, W E.

MONOTHEISM

The Legacy of Hermann Cohen. KLUBACK, William.
Mystical Monotheism: A Study in Ancient Platonic Theology. KENNEY, John Peter.
The Transcendental Temptation: A Critique of Religion and the Paranormal. KURTZ, Paul.
Creation, Creativity and Necessary Being. HUGHES, Martin.
The Nature of Faith: Religious, Monotheistic, and Christian. YANDELL, Keith E.

MONOTONIC

Conditionals and Monotonic Belief Revisions: the Success Postulate. ARLO COSTA, Horacio L.
The Gärdenfors Impossibility Theorem in Non-Monotonic Contexts. MAKINSON, David.

MONTAGUE GRAMMAR

The Application of Montague Translations in Universal Research and Typology. TENT, Katrin.
Extending Montague's System: A Three Valued Intensional Logic. ALVES, E H and GUERZONI, J A D.

MONTAGUE, R

Deontic Logic and Possible World Semantics: A Historical Sketch. WOLENSKI, Jan.

MONTAIGNE

"Marie le Jars de Gournay" in *A History of Women Philosophers, Volume II: Medieval, Renaissance and Enlightenment, A.D. 500-1600*, ZEDLER, Beatrice H.
"Pyrrhonism and the Concept of a Common Human Nature in Eighteenth-Century Aesthetic Thought" in *The Question of Humanism: Challenges and Possibilities*, CARDY, Michael.
Michel de Montaigne: La "nottola" dell'Umanesimo francese. LONGO, Margherita.
Montaigne's 'Des Cannibales' and Natural Sources of Virtue. HOROWITZ, Maryanne Cline.
Sovranità e obbedienza. CATANIA, Alfonso.

MONTESQUIEU

Pour l'histoire de la fortune de Montesquieu en Italie (1789-1945). FELICE, Domenico.
Montesquieu and China. HONGXUN, Hou.
Not So Virtuous Republics: Montesquieu, Venice, and the Theory of Aristocratic Republicanism. CARRITHERS, David W.

MONTINARI, M

Montinari and Nietzsche's Biography. HOLLINGDALE, R G.
Nietzsche as Colleague. SCHACHT, Richard.

MOOD(S)

Davidson's Paratactic Analysis of Mood. MILLER, Seumas.

MOORE

"Moore and Philosophical Skepticism" in *The Analytic Tradition: Philosophical Quarterly Monographs, Volume 1*, BALDWIN, Thomas.
"The Nature of Acts: Moore on Husserl" in *The Analytic Tradition: Philosophical Quarterly Monographs, Volume 1*, KÜNNE, Wolfgang.
G E Moore on the Values of Whole and Parts: A Critique. PAL, Jagat.
Intorno all'autofondazione delle norme: Ragione formale e principio razionale tra logica e diritto. SCIACCA, Fabrizio.
Max on Moore. STROLL, Avrum.
Moore's Moral Rules. PERKINS JR, Ray.
The Open Question Argument. PAL, Jagat.
Was Moore a Positivist?. O'CONNOR, David.

MOORE, R

"Reconnecting: A Reply to Robert Moore" in *Archetypal Process: Self and Divine in Whitehead, Jung, and Hillman*, KELLER, Catherine.

MORAL

After Principles. BARDEN, Garrett.
Being True to the World: Moral Realism and Practical Wisdom. JACOBS, Jonathan A.
The Moral Animus of David Hume. SIEBERT, Donald T.
Die Moral der Vernunft Tanszendentale Handlungs-und Legitimationstheorie in der Philosophie Kants. SANDERMANN, Edmund.
Moral Dilemmas. GOWANS, Christopher W (ed).
"Moral Conflict and Political Consensus" in *Liberalism and the Good*, GUTMANN, Amy and THOMPSON, Dennis.
"The Necessity for Cooperation between Philosophical and Empirical Research" in *The Moral Domain: Essays in the Ongoing Discussion between Philosophy and the Social Sciences*, TUGENDHAT, Ernst.
"Is" and "Ought": A Different Connection. JOHNSON, Oliver A.
Backgrounding Desire. PETTIT, Philip and SMITH, Michael.
Commentary on Sayre-McCord's 'Being a Realist about Relativism'. WONG, David B.
Commentary: Interests and Equal Moral Status. SQUADRITO, Kathy.
The Compatability of Consequentialism with Deontological Convictions. FORREST, Peter.
A Critique of Kantian Arguments Against Emotions as Moral Motives. OAKLEY, Justin.
Defining the Limits of Institutional Moral Agency in Health Care: A Response to Kevin Wildes. RIE, Michael A.
Differences in Moral Values Between Corporations. NYSTROM, Paul C.
The Distinction Between Equality in Moral Status and Deserving Equal Consideration. DE GRAZIA, David.
Do Animals Feel Pain?. HARRISON, Peter.
The Enforcement of Moral Obligations to Potential Fetuses: Johnson Controls versus the UAW. WHITE, Ronald F.
Ethics Consultation as Moral Engagement. MORENO, Jonathan D.
Éthique et Morale. RICOEUR, Paul.
Die Folgen vorherrschender Moralkonzeptionen. POGGE, Thomas W.
Green and "Everybody's Doing It". DE GEORGE, Richard T.
The Highest Moral Knowledge and Internalism: Some Comments. LEMOS, Noah.
The Highest Moral Knowledge and the Truth Behind Internalism. DE PAUL, Michael R.
History, Lying, and Moral Responsibility. PORK, Andrus.
Ignatian Discernment: A Philosophical Analysis. HUGHES, Gerard J.
The Importance of Being Human. MC NAUGHTON, David.
Institutional Integrity: Approval, Toleration and Holy War or 'Always True to You in My Fashion'. WILDES, Kevin W.
A Kantian View of Moral Luck. MOORE, A W.
Knowing Good and Evil. WILLIAMS, C J F.
Moral Conflicts in Kantian Ethics. MC CARTY, Richard.
Moral Dilemmas, Compromise and Compensation. DAY, J P.
Moral Dilemmas, Disjunctive Obligations, and Kant's Principle that 'Ought' Implies 'Can'. JACQUETTE, Dale.
Moral Dreams and Practical Realities. LINZEY, Andrew.
Moral Epistemology and the Supervenience of Ethical Concepts. AUDI, Robert.
La moral existencial de G Marcel. MAÑERO, Salvador.
Moral Experience and Justification. SINNOTT-ARMSTRONG, Walter.
The Moral Foundations of Intangible Property. CHILD, James W.
Moral Goodness, Esteem, and Acting from Duty. LEMOS, Noah M.
A Moral Ideal for Everyone and No One. CONWAY, Daniel W.
Moral Imagination, Freedom, and the Humanities. KEKES, John.
Moral Planes and Intrinsic Values. ANDERSON, James C.
Moral Relativism and Deontic Logic. HUGLY, Philip and SAYWARD, Charles.
Moral Skepticism and the Dangerous Maybe: Reconsidering Mackie's *Ethics*. METCALFE, John F.
Moral Truth and Coherence: Comments on Goldman. STEUP, M.
Moral und Verwirklichung. KLEINGELD, Paulien.
Moral y política en Kant. PÉREZ ESTÉVEZ, Antonio.
The Nature of Moral Facts. ROSS, Steven.
Normativity and the Very Idea of Moral Epistemology. COPP, David.
On Excluding Something from Our Gathering: The Lack of Moral Standing of Non-Sentient Entities. LANDMAN, Willem A.
On the Epistemic Value of Moral Experience. TOLHURST, William.
On the Genuine Queerness of Moral Properties and Facts. GARNER, Richard T.
Praxis and Ultimate Reality: Intellectual, Moral and Religious Conversion as Radical Political Conversion. MARSH, James L.
La prudencia (II). DERISI, Octavio N.
The Role of Moral Intuition in Applied Ethics: A Consideration of Positions of Peirce and Strike and Soltis. MC CARTHY, Christine.
Sturgeon's Defence of Moral Realism. JOBE, Evan K.
The Subjection of Children. AVIRAM, Aharon.
The Other Nietzsche: Criticism of Moral Utopia (in German). MAURER, Reinhart.
To Tell a Good Tale: Kierkegaardian Reflections on Moral Narrative and Moral Truth. TURNER, Jeffrey S.
The Unity of Moral Virtues in Aristotle's *Nicomachean Ethics*. TELFER, Elizabeth.

MORAL AGENT(S)

"Some Advantages of Virtue Ethics" in *Identity, Character, and Morality: Essays in Moral Psychology*, SLOTE, Michael.
'Pride Produces the Idea of Self': Hume on Moral Agency. RORTY, Amélie.
Authority and the Diffusion of Moral Expertise. MC MAHON, Christopher.
The Chinese Moral Ethos and the Concept of Individual Rights. TAO, Julia.
The Moral Status of the Corporation. EWIN, R E.
On Becoming A Moral Agent: From Aristotle to Harry Stottlemeier. PRITCHARD, Michael S.
Rationality and Moral Status. BILOW, Scott H.

MORAL ARGUMENT

Just War Theory and the ANC's Armed Struggle. MILLER, S R.
The Morality of a Free Market for Transplant Organs. NELSON, Mark T.
Punishment and Loss of Moral Standing. MORRIS, Christopher W.

MORAL CODE(S)

Commentary: "Codes of Ethics and the Moral Education of Engineers". PUKA, Bill.
The Moral Authority of Transnational Corporate Codes. FREDERICK, William C.
Reflections on Ideas of Social Philosophy and Indian Code of Conduct. DASGUPTA, Manashi.

MORAL DEVELOPMENT

Aristotelis Ethica Evdemia. WALZER, R R (ed).
The Moral Domain: Essays in the Ongoing Discussion between Philosophy and the Social Sciences. WREN, Thomas E (ed).
"The Emergence of Morality in Personal Relationships" in *The Moral Domain: Essays in the Ongoing Discussion between Philosophy and the Social Sciences*, KELLER, Monika.
"Institutions and the Shaping of Character" in *Integrity in Health Care Institutions: Humane Environments for Teaching, Inquiry, and Healing*, COLES, Robert.
"Justice and Solidarity: On the Discussion Concerning Stage 6" in *The Moral Domain: Essays in the Ongoing Discussion between Philosophy and the Social Sciences*, HABERMAS, Jürgen.
"The Majesty and Mystery of Kohlberg's Stage 6" in *The Moral Domain: Essays in the Ongoing Discussion between Philosophy and the Social Sciences*, PUKA, Bill.
"The Study of Moral Development: A Bridge over the "Is-Ought" Gap" in *The Moral Domain: Essays in the Ongoing Discussion between Philosophy and the Social Sciences*, BOYD, Dwight R.
"Values in Teaching and Learning: A Student-Teacher Dialogue" in *Integrity in Health Care Institutions: Humane Environments for Teaching, Inquiry, and Healing*, DUNN, Kim and BULGER, Ruth Ellen.
"Faith" in a Broad Sense as a Goal in Promoting Human Development. BECK, Clive.
Burglars, Robber Barons, and the Good Life. PEKARSKY, Daniel.
A Conceptual Model of Corporate Moral Development. REIDENBACH, R Eric and ROBIN, Donald P.
The Development of Moral Reasoning and the Foundations of Geometry. MACNAMARA, John.
Friendship: Mutual Apprenticeship in Moral Development. VOLBRECHT, Rose Mary.
Her Terrain is Outside His "Domain". PEEPLES, S Elise.
Promoting Moral Growth Through Intra-Group Participation. NELSON, D R and OBREMSKI, T E.
The Science of Caring. PUKA, Bill.
The Functional Conception of Culture and the Explanation of the Value-Shaping Process (in Polish). BROZI, Krzysztof J.
Die Theorie der moralischen Entwicklung von Lawrence Kohlberg und seiner Schule und die Moraltheologie. BUCHER, Anton.

MORAL EDUCATION

Education as a Human Right: A Theory of Curriculum and Pedagogy. VANDENBERG, Donald.
Shaping Character: Moral Education in the Christian College. HOLMES, Arthur F.
The Baby with a Gun: A Feminist Inquiry Into Plausibility, Certainty and Context in Moral Education. THOMPSON, Audrey.

MORAL EDUCATION

Codes of Ethics and the Moral Education of Engineers. LUEGENBIEHL, Heinz C.
A Comparison of John Dewey and Lawrence Kohlberg's Approach to Moral Education. SOCOSKI, Patrick M.
Deugden en plichtsbesef. STEUTEL, J W.
Disarming the Baby with the Gun: Reply to Audrey Thompson. GLASS, Ronald David.
The Goals of Science Education. MARTIN, Michael.
Moral Education: Realistically Speaking. VOKEY, Daniel.
Moral Skepticism and Moral Education. BARCALOW, Emmett.

MORAL JUDGMENT(S)

Being True to the World: Moral Realism and Practical Wisdom. JACOBS, Jonathan A.
Hume's Place in Moral Philosophy. CAPALDI, Nicholas.
The Persistence of Modernity: Essays on Aesthetics, Ethics, and Postmodernism. WELLMER, Albrecht.
"Beyond Freud and Piaget: Biographical Worlds—Interpersonal Self" in *The Moral Domain: Essays in the Ongoing Discussion between Philosophy and the Social Sciences*, NOAM, Gil G.
"Moral Balance: A Model of How People Arrive at Moral Decisions" in *The Moral Domain: Essays in the Ongoing Discussion between Philosophy and the Social Sciences*, NISAN, Mordecai.
"The Return of Stage 6: Its Principle and Moral Point of View" in *The Moral Domain: Essays in the Ongoing Discussion between Philosophy and the Social Sciences*, BOYD, Dwight R and KOHLBERG, Lawrence and LEVINE, Charles.
Agent-Action Judgements. TILLEY, John J.
Amoralism—On the Limits of Moral Thinking. SANDOE, Peter.
Amoralism: Reply to Peter Sandoe. HARE, R M.
Authority and the Diffusion of Moral Expertise. MC MAHON, Christopher.
Critical Interaction: Judgment, Decision, and the Social Testing of Moral Hypotheses. IANNONE, A P.
A Defense of Ethical Noncognitivism. COBURN, Robert C.
Ethical Judgments on Selected Accounting Issues: An Empirical Study. STANGA, Keith G and TURPEN, Richard A.
Four Perspectives on Moral Judgement: The Rational Principles of Jesus and Kant. PALMQUIST, Stephen R.
Medical Futility, Medical Necessity: The - Problem - Without - A - Name. CALLAHAN, Daniel.
Moral Judgment. ROBERTSON, Emily.
Moral Pluralism. WOLGAST, Elizabeth.
No Rules without Virtues: No Virtues without Rules. BRAYBROOKE, David.
Object and Intention in Moral Judgments According to Aquinas. FINNIS, John.
On Squeamishness: A Response to Galston. FISHKIN, James S.
On the Epistemic Status of Considered Moral Judgments. TIMMONS, Mark.
The Poverty of Naturalistic Moral Realism: Comments on Timmons. HOLMGREN, Margaret.
Response to Slote's "Ethics Without Free Will". VAN INWAGEN, Peter.
The Rhythms of Gratitude: Historical Developments and Philosophical Concerns. STEWART-ROBERTSON, Charles.
Should Basic Care Get Priority? Doubts about Rationing the Oregon Way. VEATCH, Robert M.
The Significance of a Wish. ACKERMAN, Felicia.
Sturgeon's Defence of Moral Realism. JOBE, Evan K.
The Unity of the Vices. JACOBS, Jonathan and ZEIS, John.

MORAL LAWS

The Case of the Unmitigated Blackguard or Saving Kant's Moral Feelings. EARLS, Anthony.
Du fondement de la loi morale, une éthique de la raison ou du sentiment?. DAVAL, R.
Moral Laws in Borden P Bowne's *Principles of Ethics*. BURROW JR, Rufus.

MORAL POINT OF VIEW

"On Subjective Appreciation of Objective Moral Points" in *Logic and Ethics*, SRZEDNICKI, J.
Moraliteit en magie. LESAGE, Dieter.

MORAL PRINCIPLE(S)

David Hume and the Problem of Reason. DANFORD, John W.
Science and Moral Values. VOLLRATH, John.
"Modern Moral Philosophy" in *A Companion to Ethics*, SCHNEEWIND, J B.
Ethical Impressionism: A Response to Braybrooke. BONEVAC, Daniel.
The Ethical Thought of Martin Luther King. STERLING, Marvin C.
Personal Morals and Professional Ethics: A Review and Empirical Examination of Public Accounting. BEETS, S Douglas.
The Principle of Relevant Similarity. LEVVIS, Gary W.
Taylor's Waking Dream: No One's Reply. CLARK, Stephen R L.
Who are "We"? Ambiguities of the Modern Self. SKINNER, Quentin.

MORAL PSYCHOLOGY

Aristotle's Psychology. ROBINSON, Daniel N.
Identity, Character, and Morality: Essays in Moral Psychology. FLANAGAN, Owen (ed).
Varieties of Moral Personality: Ethics and Psychological Realism. FLANAGAN, Owen.
"Against the Neglect of "Content" in the Moral Theories of Kohlberg and Habermas" in *The Moral Domain: Essays in the Ongoing Discussion between Philosophy and the Social Sciences*, DöBERT, Rainer.
"The Possibility of Convergence between Moral Psychology and Metaethics" in *The Moral Domain: Essays in the Ongoing Discussion between Philosophy and the Social Sciences*, WREN, Thomas E.
Aristotle and the Spheres of Motivation: *De Anima* III. HUTCHINSON, D S.
Aristotle's Apodeictic Syllogism. JOHNSTON, David.
Compassion. SNOW, Nancy E.
Perception and Evaluation: Aristotle on the Moral Imagination. HANKINSON, R J.
Promoting Moral Growth Through Intra-Group Participation. NELSON, D R and OBREMSKI, T E.
Le rôle de l'imagination dans le mouvement animal et l'action humaine chez Aristotle. DUGRÉ, François.
Die Theorie der moralischen Entwicklung von Lawrence Kohlberg und seiner Schule und die Moraltheologie. BUCHER, Anton.

MORAL REASONING

Applying Ethics: A Text with Readings (Third Edition). OLEN, Jeffrey.
David Hume and the Problem of Reason. DANFORD, John W.
Logic and Ethics. GEACH, Peter (ed).
Moral Philosophy: Theories, Skills, and Applications. FALIKOWSKI, Anthony F.
"Deontic Logic and Imperative Logic" in *Logic and Ethics*, HARRISON, Jonathan.
"Ethics and the Limits of Consistency" in *Logic and Ethics*, BAMBROUGH, Renford.
"The Majesty and Mystery of Kohlberg's Stage 6" in *The Moral Domain: Essays in the Ongoing Discussion between Philosophy and the Social Sciences*, PUKA, Bill.
"Moral Responsibility and Moral Commitment: The Integration of Affect and Cognition" in *The Moral Domain: Essays in the Ongoing Discussion between Philosophy and the Social Sciences*, HASTE, Helen.
"Whatever Happened to Deontic Logic" in *Logic and Ethics*, GEACH, Peter.
Achilles' Revenge. DAKO, Martin.
Adapting Kohlberg to Enhance the Assessment of Manager's Moral Reasoning. WEBER, James.
Consensus, Contracts, and Committees. MORENO, Jonathan D.
The Expression of Experience: Code's Critique of Gilligan's Abortion Study. PITT, Alice.
External and Now-For-Then Preferences in Hare's Theory. HAJDIN, Mane.
Famine and Charity. WHELAN JR, John M.
Generosity: A Duty Without a Right. STITH, Richard.
Kohlberg and Piaget: Differences and Similarities. KAVATHATZOPOULOS, Iordanis.
La estructura de la ética y la moral. HARE, Richard N and BRASH, Jorge.
Moral Reasoning in a Communist Chinese Society. WALKER, Lawrence J and MORAN, Thomas J.
Physical Possibility and Potentiality in Ethics. COVEY, Edward.
Principled Moral Reasoning: Is It a Viable Approach to Promote Ethical Integrity?. WEBER, James and GREEN, Sharon.
Privacy and Disclosure in Medical Genetics Examined in an Ethics of Care. WERTZ, Dorothy C and FLETCHER, John C.
La razón ética. CARRACEDO, Jose Rubio.
The Reasonableness of Moral Reasons. TRUNDLE, Robert.
Specifying Norms as a Way to Resolve Concrete Ethical Problems. RICHARDSON, Henry S.
Terrorism and Argument from Analogy. WALLACE, G.
When is "Everyone's Doing It" a Moral Justification?. GREEN, Ronald M.

MORAL REPROACH

Toward a Theory of Bribery. DANLEY, John R.

MORAL RESPONSIBILITY(-TIES)

Beliefs and Responsibility. ELLIOTT, Car.
Commentary: "Individual and Corporate Responsibility". FRENCH, Peter A.
Divine Foresight and Human Moral Responsibility (in Hebrew). BAR-ON, A Zvie.
Engineers and Management: The Challenge of the Challenger Incident. WERHANE, Patricia H.
Explaining Without Blaming the Victim. ILLINGWORTH, Patricia M L.
Individual and Corporate Responsibility: Two Alternative Approaches. SURBER, Jere.
Management's Hat Trick: Misuse of "Engineering Judgment" in the Challenger Incident. HERKERT, Joseph R.
The Moral Responsibility of Corporate Executives for Disasters. BISHOP, John D.
A Picture of the Self Which Supports the Moral Responsibility. ANDERSON, Susan Leigh.
The Regulation of Virtue: Cross-Currents in Professional Ethics. JENNINGS, Bruce.
Two Forms of Moral Responsibility. SANKOWSKI, Edward.
Understanding Professional Misconduct: The Moral Responsibilities of Professionals. NORTON, Thomas W.

MORAL RESPONSIBILITY(-TIES)
Why Corporations Are Not Morally Responsible for Anything They Do. VELASQUEZ, Manuel G.
Wofür sind wir verantworlich?. NEUMAIER, Otto.

MORAL SENSE
"Hume and Hume's Connexions". KLEMME, Heiner.

MORAL SENTIMENT(S)
The Anatomist and the Painter: The Continuity of Hume's *Treatise* and *Essays*. IMMERWAHR, John.

MORAL SITUATION(S)
The Big Questions: A Short Introduction to Philosophy (Third Edition). SOLOMON, Robert C.
Morality in Practice (Third Edition). STERBA, James P.
Varieties of Moral Personality: Ethics and Psychological Realism. FLANAGAN, Owen.
The Ambiguity of Political Virtue: A Response to Wolgast. LEVINSON, Sanford.
Integrity and Compromise in Nursing Ethics. WINSLOW, Betty J and WINSLOW, Gerald R.
Tooley and the Trolley. FISCHER, John Martin.

MORAL THEORY(-RIES)
see also Ethical Theory(-ries)
An Audience for Moral Philosophy?. EDELMAN, John T.
Business Ethics. SHAW, William H.
Conduct and Character: Readings in Moral Theory. TIMMONS, Mark.
Foundations of Moral and Political Philosophy. PAUL, Ellen Frankel (ed).
Gerechtigkeit, Wohlfahrt und Rationalität. SCHMIDT, Johannes.
How Should I Live? Philosophical Conversations About Moral Life. FEEZELL, Randolph M.
Hume's Place in Moral Philosophy. CAPALDI, Nicholas.
Moral Philosophy from Montaigne to Kant: An Anthology, Volume I & II. SCHNEEWIND, J B (ed).
Moral Philosophy: Theories, Skills, and Applications. FALIKOWSKI, Anthony F.
Moral Theory and Medical Practice. FULFORD, K W M.
A Morally Deep World: An Essay on Moral Significance and Environmental Ethics. JOHNSON, Lawrence E.
Philosophy of Law: An Introduction to Jurisprudence (Revised Edition). MURPHY, Jeffrie G.
"The Concept of *Li* in Confucian Moral Theory" in *Understanding the Chinese Mind: The Philosophical Roots*, CUA, Antonio S.
"Higher-Order Discrimination" in *Identity, Character, and Morality: Essays in Moral Psychology*, PIPER, Adrian M S.
"Method and Moral Theory" in *A Companion to Ethics*, JAMIESON, Dale.
"Nuclear Deterrence and the Limits of Moral Theory" in *Issues in War and Peace: Philosophical Inquiries*, WERNER, Richard.
"Why Terrorism Is Morally Problematic" in *Feminist Ethics*, BAR ON, Bat-Ami.
"Seeing Things". PIPER, Adrian M S.
A New Approach in Moral Theory (in Dutch). KETTNER, Matthias.
Comments and Replies. TAYLOR, Charles.
The Common Good, Human Rights and Education: A Need for Conceptual Reformulization. CRAIG, Robert P.
A Different Different Voice: On the Feminist Challenge in Moral Theory. ROONEY, Phyllis.
Does the Grisez-Finnis-Boyle Moral Philosophy Rest on a Mistake?. VEATCH, Henry and RAUTENBERG, Joseph.
Errors of an Ill-Reasoning Reason: The Disparagement of Emotions in the Moral Life. LAURITZEN, Paul.
The Ethics of Inarticulacy. KYMLICKA, Will.
Feminist Transformations of Moral Theory. HELD, Virginia.
Kinship and Moral Relativity. PARGETTER, Robert.
Living a Life and the Problem of Existential Impossibility. LÖW-BEER, Martin.
Moral Dilemmas. MAC INTYRE, Alasdair.
Moral Metaphysics, Moral Revolution, and Environmental Ethics. PADEN, Roger.
Moral Pluralism. WOLGAST, Elizabeth.
Moral Skepticism. COPP, David.
Piper's Criteria of Theory Selection. POSTOW, B C.
The Problem of Unauthorized Welfare. VALLENTYNE, Peter.
Rhetoric and Ethics: Adam Smith on Theorizing about the Moral Sentiments. GRISWOLD JR, Charles L.
Taylor's Waking Dream: No One's Reply. CLARK, Stephen R L.
Virtues and Values: A Platonic Account. SEUNG, T K.

MORAL(S)
Kants Kategorischer Imperativ als Leitfaden humaner Praxis. NISTERS, Thomas.
Moral und Politik aus der Sicht des Kritischen Rationalismus. SALAMUN, Kurt (ed).
Morals, Motivation and Convention: Hume's Influential Doctrines. SNARE, Francis.
A Philosophy of Morals. HELLER, Agnes.
"Gender and Moral Luck" in *Identity, Character, and Morality: Essays in Moral Psychology*, CARD, Claudia.
"Hume and Moral Emotions" in *Identity, Character, and Morality: Essays in Moral Psychology*, LIND, Marcia.
"Maritain's Account of the Social Sciences" in *From Twilight to Dawn: The Cultural Vision of Jacques Maritain*, NELSON, Ralph.
"Moral Relativism and Strict Universalism" in *The Moral Domain: Essays in the Ongoing Discussion between Philosophy and the Social Sciences*, NUNNER-WINKLER, Gertrud.
"On the Primacy of Character" in *Identity, Character, and Morality: Essays in Moral Psychology*, WATSON, Gary.
"Response to Smith's 'Markets and Morals'" in *Philosophy and Politics*, LOCKE, Don.
"T E Wilkerson on Originality in Art and Morals" in *XIth International Congress in Aesthetics, Nottingham 1988*, SPECTOR, Arnold.
"Trust, Affirmation, and Moral Character: A Critique of Kantian Morality" in *Identity, Character, and Morality: Essays in Moral Psychology*, THOMAS, Laurence.
Christ, Moral Absolutes, and the Good: Recent Moral Theology. PINCKAERS, Servais.
Envy and Jealousy. BEN-ZEEV, Aaron.
Epistemology as Hypothesis. PUTNAM, Hilary and PUTNAM, Ruth Anna.
Genuine Moral Dilemmas and the Containment of Incoherence. PASKE, Gerald H.
History as Argument for Revision in Moral Theology. GRISEZ, Germain.
La inocencia y el mal en la obra de Albert Camus. JIMÉNEZ, Alexander.
Least Parts and Greatest Wholes Variations on a Theme in Spinoza. SACKSTEDER, William.
El lugar de la doctrina social de la reflexión teológico moral cristiana. BRIANCESCO, E.
Markets and Morals. SMITH, G W.
Moore's Moral Rules. PERKINS JR, Ray.
Moral Obligation and Metaphysics. COOKE, Vincent M.
Moral oder Klugheit? Überlegungen zur Gestalt der Autonomie des Politischen im Denken Kants. SCHMITZ, Heinz-Gerd.
Necesidad y existencia del código de moral profesional. MUÑOZ BARQUERO, Elizabeth.
The Objectivity of Moral Values: The Search in a Wrong Place. BANERJEE, Hiranmoy.
Philosophy, Religion, Morality, Spirituality: Some Issues. SHAH, K J.
The Problem of Moral Freedom and Nicolai Hartmann. PRASAD, Kamata.
Public and Private Morality. SHAIDA, S A.
Response to Smith's "Markets and Morals". LOCKE, Don.
Sartre and the Objectivity of Values (in French). FRIEDLI, Serge.
Sense, Passions and Morals in Hume and Kant. NUYEN, A T.
The Significance of the Moral Concept of Virtue in St Augustine's Ethics. TORCHIA, N Joseph.
Social Reality and Moral Order. BARLINGAY, S S.
Theorizing about Morals. WALLACE, Jim.
Virtues and Rules. ROBERTS, Robert C.

MORALISM
Hannah Arendt's Political Theory: Ethics and Enemies. DOSSA, Shiraz.

MORALITY
Amythia: Crisis in the Natural History of Western Culture. RUE, Loyal D.
An Audience for Moral Philosophy?. EDELMAN, John T.
Bertrand Russell: The Psychobiography of a Moralist. BRINK, Andrew.
The Communicative Ethics Controversy. BENHABIB, Seyla (ed).
Democratic Individuality. GILBERT, Alan.
Diderot's Dream. ANDERSON, Wilda.
The Difference Between Truth and Opinion: How the Misuse of Language Can Lead to Disaster. COONEY, Timothy J.
The Early Essays and Ethics of Robert Boyle. HARWOOD, John T (ed).
Ethics Without God (Revised Edition). NIELSEN, Kai.
Ethics, Politics, and Human Nature. PAUL, Ellen Frankel (ed).
Feminist Ethics. CARD, Claudia (ed).
Glück und Lebenssinn: Eine religionsphilosophische Untersuchung. DRESCHER, Johannes.
Good and Evil: An Absolute Conception. GAITA, Raimond.
Hobbes. TUCK, Richard.
Human Goodness: Generosity and Courage. PYBUS, Elizabeth.
Human Interests: Reflections on Philosophical Anthropology. RESCHER, Nicholas.
In Partnership with God: Contemporary Jewish Law and Ethics. SHERWIN, Byron L.
Kant's Theory of Freedom. ALLISON, Henry E.
Love's Knowledge: Essays on Philosophy and Literature. NUSSBAUM, Martha C.
Marx's Radical Critique of Capitalist Society: A Reconstruction and Critical Evaluation. ARNOLD, N Scott.
Max Scheler's Concept of the Person: An Ethics of Humanism. PERRIN, Ron.
Moral Philosophy from Montaigne to Kant: An Anthology, Volume I & II. SCHNEEWIND, J B (ed).
Moral Pluralism and Legal Neutrality. SADURSKI, Wojciech.
Moralische Verbindlichkeit oder Erziehung. LANGEWAND, Alfred.
Morality and Modernity. POOLE, Ross.

MORALITY

Morality—What's In It For Me?: A Historical Introduction to Ethics. NELSON, William N.
Nation und Ethos: Die Moral des Patriotismus. KLUXEN-PYTA, Donate.
Nietzsche: A Frenzied Look. ACKERMANN, Robert John.
The Non-Reality of Free Will. DOUBLE, Richard.
Le Philosophie et les Passions. MEYER, Michel.
Philosophy and Politics. HUNT, G M K (ed).
Philosophy of the "Gita". PATEL, Ramesh N.
Réflexions sur les passions. HUME, David.
Rorty's Humanistic Pragmatism: Philosophy Democratized. KOLENDA, Konstantin.
Socialism, Feminism and Philosophy: A Radical Philosophy Reader. SAYERS, Sean (ed).
The Taming of Chance. HACKING, Ian.
Das Tier in der Moral. WOLF, Ursula.
Time-Travel for Beginners and Other Stories. HARRISON, Jonathan.
Understanding the Chinese Mind: The Philosophical Roots. ALLINSON, Robert E (ed).
Understanding War: A Philosophical Inquiry. MC MURTRY, John.
Wittgenstein, Ethics and Aesthetics: The View from Eternity. TILGHMAN, B R.
Writing and the Moral Self. LANG, Berel.
"The 'Frankenstein Thing': The Moral Impact of Genetic Engineering of Agricultural Animals" in *Agricultural Bioethics: Implications of Agricultural Biotechnology*, ROLLIN, B E.
"Acting Human in Our Time" in *The Question of Humanism: Challenges and Possibilities*, ADAMCZEWSKI, Zygmunt.
"Are There Virtues Inherent in a Profession?" in *Ethics, Trust, and the Professions: Philosophical and Cultural Aspects*, MEILAENDER, Gilbert.
"Benefits to Moral Philosophy of the Computational Model of the Mind" in *Acting and Reflecting: The Interdisciplinary Turn in Philosophy*, HARMAN, Gilbert.
"Biting the Bullet: Rorty on Private and Public Morality" in *Reading Rorty*, GUIGNON, Charles B and HILEY, David R.
"The Credibility of Ecclesiastical Teaching on the Morality of War" in *Celebrating Peace*, YODER, John H.
"Doing What One Ought to Do" in *Meaning and Method: Essays in Honor of Hilary Putnam*, PUTNAM, Ruth Anna.
"Exposing Warism" in *Issues in War and Peace: Philosophical Inquiries*, CADY, Duane L.
"Gender and the Complexity of Moral Voices" in *Feminist Ethics*, MOODY-ADAMS, Michele M.
"Making the Moral World" in *The Philosophy of John William Miller*, STAHL, Gary.
"Markets and Morals" in *Philosophy and Politics*, SMITH, G W.
"Moral Counterforce" in *In the Interest of Peace: A Spectrum of Philosophical Views*, LEE, Steven.
"The Moral Life of a Pragmatist" in *Identity, Character, and Morality: Essays in Moral Psychology*, PUTNAM, Ruth Anna.
"Nuclearism and Sexism: Overcoming Their Shared Metaphysical Basis" in *Issues in War and Peace: Philosophical Inquiries*, SMITHKA, Paula.
"Obligation and Performance: A Kantian Account of Moral Conflict" in *Identity, Character, and Morality: Essays in Moral Psychology*, HERMAN, Barbara.
"Patriotism and the Pursuit of Peace" in *In the Interest of Peace: A Spectrum of Philosophical Views*, NATHANSON, Stephen.
"The Place of Emotions in Kantian Morality" in *Identity, Character, and Morality: Essays in Moral Psychology*, SHERMAN, Nancy.
La "Moral Social" de Eugenio María de Hostos. GONZÁLEZ, José Emilio.
"'Why Be Moral?' and Reforming Selves". WILLIAMSON, A Mark.
The 'New' Nietzsche. COOPER, David E.
'Too Busy for Ethics'. SELBY, G Raymond.
A Post-Metaphysical Moral: An Introduction to the Moral Theory of Jürgen Habermas (in French). HUNYADI, Mark.
Agency and Morality. BROOK, Richard.
Approaches to the Theory of Purusarthas. RAJAN, R Sundara.
Aristotle or Nietzsche?. FRANKS, Joan M.
Art and Censorship. SERRA, Richard.
Art and Morality in Plato: A Reappraisal. HALL, Robert W.
Art and Morality: On the Problem of Stating a Problem. HATTINGH, J P.
Auschwitz, Morality and the Suffering of God. SAROT, Marcel.
Can Whistleblowing Be FULLY Legitimated? A Theoretical Discussion. DANDEKAR, Natalie.
A Case Against Theistic Morality. VARMA, Ved Prakash.
Categorical Requirements: Kant and Hume on the Idea of Duty. WIGGINS, David.
Charles Renouvier e le scuole di morale in Francia nel XIX secolo. ROSSI, Fabio.
Common-Sense Morality. BROCK, Dan.
Community and the Evil Poem. KEMAL, S.
Conclusion. GRIFFITHS, A Phillips.
Un confronto sempre attuale: Leggendo—A Lambertino, Psicoanalisi e morale in Freud. DOVOLICH, Claudia.
Conscience, Sympathy and the Foundation of Morality. CI, Jiwei.
Contractualism, Moral Motivation, and Practical Reason. FREEMAN, Samuel.
A Critical Review of *The Moral Dimensions of Teaching*. LISMAN, C David.
The Debate Over the So-Called Reality of Moral Dilemmas. STATMAN, Daniel.
Desire and Duty in Kant. GRIGG, Russell.
Dworkin, Habermas, and the CLS Movement on Moral Criticism in Law. INGRAM, David.
Education and the Emotions: The Relevance of the Russellian Perspective. MATTAI, Bansraj.
Education for Judgment. JAMES, William.
Ethical Expertise and Moral Maturity: Conflict or Complement?. MOSS, Lenny.
The Ethics of Corporate Health Insurance. LIGHT, Donald W.
Ethics Without Morality. BROWNE, Derek.
An Ethnomedical Perspective of Medical Ethics. FABREGA JR, Horacio.
Etica e diritto penale nella filosofia attualistica. RICCIO, Stefano.
La ética/moral en el Bachillerato español: Estado de la cuestión. GARCÍA LÓPEZ, Tomás.
An Examination of Marxist Doctrine in the Traditions of Russian Religious Philosophy. STEPANOVA, E A.
God's Ability to Will Moral Evil. BROWN, Robert F.
Goodwill, Going Concern, Stocks and Flows: A Prescription for Moral Analysis. SWANDA JR, John R.
Hamartia, Akrasia: Ignorance, and Blame in Aristotle's Philosophy. CYZYK, Mar.
Henry James and the Paradox of Literary Mastery. BLAIR, Sara.
Historical Perspectives on the Morality of Virtue. WHITE, Richard.
How Did Morality Evolve?. IRONS, William.
Humanity, Morality, and Liberty. DUBCEK, Alexander A.
Ideal and Morality (in German). JACOBS, Wilhelm G.
Impersonal Friends. WHITING, Jennifer E.
The Importance of Being Human. DIAMOND, Cora.
La influencia de Rousseau en el pensamiento de Kant. DE LOS ANGELES GIRALT, María.
The Insufficiency of Descartes' Provisional Morality. COOLIDGE JR, Francis P.
John Rawls: de l'autonomie morale à la fiction de contrat social. RICOEUR, Paul.
The Juncture of Law and Morality in Prohibitions Against Torture. MARAN, Rita.
Kierkegaard: Aesthetics and 'The Aesthetic'. PATTISON, George.
King Solomon and Everyman: A Problem in Coordinating Conflicting Moral Intuitions. RORTY, Amelie Oksenberg.
Law, Morality, and *la Reconquista*. CORDERO, Ronald A.
Lucien, Lévy-Bruhl: Una introduzione (di C Prandi). IANNOTTA, Daniella.
Luck. RESCHER, Nicholas.
The Making and Molding of Child Abuse. HACKING, Ian.
The Many Appetites of Thomas Hobbes. HURLEY, Paul.
Maurice Blondel's Moral Logic. LONG, Fiachra.
Metaphysics and Culture. LADRIÈRE, Jean.
The Misuse of Maternal Mortality Statistics in the Abortion Debate. BECKWITH, Francis J.
Moral Behavior at Public Performances. OLDS, Mason.
Moral Depth. KEKES, John.
Moral Laws in Borden P Bowne's *Principles of Ethics*. BURROW JR, Rufus.
Moral Realism and the Meaning of Life. MARGOLIS, Joseph.
Moral Skepticism. COPP, David.
Moral und Biologie. RICHTER, Klaus.
Moraliteiten: Recente ethische publikaties in Vlaanderen en Nederland. STRUYKER BOUDIER, C E M.
Morality and Ethics in Organizational Administration. ADELMAN, Howard.
Morality and Religion: Necessary Bedfellows in Education?. LOSITO, William F.
The Morality of Feminism. SEVENHUIJSEN, Selma.
Morally Untenable Beliefs. BURKE, Richard J.
Morals by Appropriation. FREEMAN, Samuel.
Myth and Morality: The Love Command. HEFNER, Philip.
Natural Law, Skepticism, and Methods of Ethics. SCHNEEWIND, J B.
Nietzsche and Fascism. WILLIAMS, Howard.
Nietzsche as Instructor in Autonomy? Comments. FOWLER, Mark C.
Nietzsche contra Rousseau: Goethe versus Catilina?. BLONDEL, Eric.
Nuclear Deterrence and the Morality of Intentions. KULTGEN, John.
On Being Committed to Morality. NIELSEN, Kai.
On Law and Morality: A Dialogue. VON WRIGHT, Georg Henrik.
The Origins of Morality: An Essay in Philosophical Anthropology. OLDENQUIST, Andrew.
Partialism and Parenthood. NELSON, James Lindemann.
Pascal, etica, politica, socialità. DEREGIBUS, Arturo.
Peter Winch, *Simone Weil: The Just Balance*. WILLIAMS, Rowan.
The Physiology of Moral Maturity. HEMMING, James.
The Politics of Ethics: Socratic Questioning is Needed in the Marketplace. TRUNDLE, Robert.
The Possibilities of Scepticisms: Philosophy and Theology without Apology. JACKSON, Timothy P.

MORALITY

Prudence and Providence: On Hobbes's Theory of Practical Reason. HANCE, Allen S.
Punitive Damages: New Twists in Torts. WALTON, Clarence C.
Putnam's Moral Objectivism. TIMMONS, Mark.
The Range of Options. ZIMMERMAN, Michael J.
A Rational Choice Theory of Punishment. STERBA, James P.
Rationality, Economic Action and Scarcity (in Hungarian). FEKETE, László.
Reply to the President: "Ethics and the Limits of Consistency". WILLIAMS, Bernard.
Reply to Weir: Unnecessary Fear, Nutrition, and Vegetarianism. SAPONTZIS, Steve F.
Rescuing Natural Law Theory from the Rationalists. DENNEHY, Raymond.
Response to Sapontzis's Reply. WEIR, Jack.
Rights and Utilitarianism. EWIN, R E.
Role Morality as a Complex Instance of Ordinary Morality. ANDRE, Judith.
Schopenhauers Entwurf einer asketischen Tugendethik. WOLF, Jean-Claude.
The Self in Confucian Ethics. SHUN, Kwong-Loi.
Self, Society, and Kantian Impersonality. SORELL, Tom.
Shrewd Bargaining on the Moral Frontier: Toward a Theory of Morality in Practice. DEES, J Gregory and CRAMPTON, Peter C.
Socrates' Critique of Cognitivism. MATSON, Wallace I and LEITE, Adam.
Spinoza's Two Theories of Morality. LUCASH, Frank.
Subject en zelfervaring. BERNET, R.
Super-yo y vida moral: Una valoración tomista de la hipótesis psicoanalítica. PITHOD, Abelardo.
Synderesis, the Spark of Conscience, in the English Renaissance. GREENE, Robert A.
T G Masaryk—A Modern Thinker (in Czechoslovakian). OPAT, Jaroslav.
Taking Role Moralities Seriously. WUESTE, Daniel E.
Theme and Commentary. GREEN, Thomas F.
The Truth about Lies in Plato's *Republic*. PAGE, Carl.
Two Ways of Morality: Confucian and Kantian. LEE, Kwang-Sae.
Unnecessary Pain, Nutrition, and Vegetarianism. WEIR, Jack.
Utility and Morality: Adam Smith's Critique of Hume. MARTIN, Marie A.
Values, the Environment and the Creative Act. THOMAS, John C.
Das vergeistigte Glück: Gedanken zum christlichen Eudämonieverständnis. DEMMER, Klaus.
The Virtue of a Representative. WOLGAST, Elizabeth.
Virtue Theory and Abortion. HURSTHOUSE, Rosalind.
Warum lebt der Mensch moralisch?. BURKHARDT, Cornelia and FRANKENHÄUSER, Gerald.
What Can a Discursive Theory of Morality Learn from Aquinas?. RENTTO, Juha-Pekka.
Wie kaatst moet de bal verwachten. MERTENS, T.

MORE, T

Utopia: Sir Thomas More. LOGAN, George M (ed).
Pride and the Meaning of *Utopia*. MOULAKIS, Athanasios.
The Rhetoric of Opposition in Thomas More's *Utopia*: Giving Form to Competing Philosophies. WEGEMER, Gerard.

MORPHOLOGY

"Some Notes on Morphology and Syntax in Classical Chinese" in *Chinese Texts and Philosophical Contexts*, PULLEYBLANK, Edwin G.
Critica della filosofia zoologica per Battista Grassi. MESCHIARI, Alberto.
L'ontogenèse de l'individu: ses aspects scientifiques et philosophiques. BERNIER, Réjane.

MORRIS, T

The Limits of Power. TALIAFERRO, Charles.

MORRIS, W

Epistemic Leaks and Epistemic Meltdowns: A Response to William Morris on Scepticism with Regard to Reason. KARLSSON, Mikael M.

MORTALITY

The Misuse of Maternal Mortality Statistics in the Abortion Debate. BECKWITH, Francis J.
We Mortals. LINGIS, Alphonso.

MOSER, J

Justus Möser: De Revolutie en de grondslagen van de moderne staat. WALRAVENS, Else.

MOSER, P

"Justifying Beliefs: The Dream Hypothesis and Gratuitous Entities" in *Doubting: Contemporary Perspectives on Skepticism*, BAR-ON, Dorit.

MOSES

The Structure of Philo's Commentary on the Pentateuch. THORNE, Gary W A.

MOTHERHOOD

"Recreating Motherhood: Ideology and Technology in American Society" in *Beyond Baby M: Ethical Issues in New Reproductive Techniques*, ROTHMAN, Barbara Katz.
Do These Feminists Like Women?. SOMMERS, Christina.
Motherhood and the Possibility of a Contemporary Discourse for Women. GREY, Mary.
On the Empirical Status of Radical Feminism: A Reply to Schedler. MUI, Constance L.
Two Models of Preferential Treatment for Working Mothers. BABER, H E.

MOTHERSILL, M

Hume and the Paradox of Taste Again. WERTZ, S K.

MOTION(S)

"Absolute Time versus Absolute Motion: Comments on Lawrence Sklar" in *Philosophical Perspectives on Newtonian Science*, BRICKER, Phillip.
L'aporia della kinesis in Aristotele. ROCCARO, Giuseppe.
Aristotle's Definition of Motion and its Ontological Implications. BRAGUE, Rémi and ADLER, Pierre and D'URSEL, Laurent.
Aristotle, the Direction Problem, and the Structure of the Sublunar Realm. KRONZ, Frederick.
Der Begriff der Bewegung bei Kant: Über den Grundbegriff der Empirie und die empirischen Begriffe. HOFFMANN, Thomas Sören.
The Difference Between Real Change and *Mere* Cambridge Change. CLELAND, Carol E.
La dimostrazione "a posteriori" dell'esistenza di Dio nella filosofia di Leibniz. NICOLOSI, Salvatore.
From Boskovic's Supplements to the Poem of Benedikt Stay (in Serbo-Croatian). D'AGOSTINO, Salvo.
Motion, Causation, and the Causal Theory of Identity. EHRING, Douglas.
R J Boskovic's Philosophy of Space (in Serbo-Croatian). ROSSI, Arcangelo.
Shadows on the Cave Wall: Philosophy and Visual Science. WILSON, Hugh R.
The Heraclitus' Lesson (in Portuguese). SANTOS, M C A dos.

MOTIVATION(S)

Escape from God. TURNER, Dean.
Explaining Behavior: Reasons in a World of Causes. DRETSKE, Fred.
Explaining Human Action. LENNON, Kathleen.
Morals, Motivation and Convention: Hume's Influential Doctrines. SNARE, Francis.
Selbsttäuschung. LÖW-BEER, Martin.
Aristotle and the Spheres of Motivation: *De Anima* III. HUTCHINSON, D S.
Backgrounding Desire. PETTIT, Philip and SMITH, Michael.
Contractualism, Moral Motivation, and Practical Reason. FREEMAN, Samuel.
Deugden en plichtsbesef. STEUTEL, J W.
Penny Pinching and Backward Induction. HOLLIS, Martin.
Subjectivisation as Control or Resistance: An Examination of Reformation Theology and Marxism. PATTMAN, Rob.

MOTIVE(S)

False Consciousness. MEYERSON, Denise.
A Critique of Kantian Arguments Against Emotions as Moral Motives. OAKLEY, Justin.
The Profit Motive and the Moral Assessment of Health Care Institutions. DANIELS, Norman.
La speranza nel giusnaturalismo. TUSA, Carlo.

MOUNIER, E

El personalismo cristiano de Emmanuel Mounier. ARAYA, Eval A.

MOVEMENT(S)

Contemporary Perspectives on Masculinity: Men, Women, and Politics in Modern Society. CLATTERBAUGH, Kenneth.
Mind-Body. MOULYN, Adrian C.
Business and Environmental Ethics. HOFFMAN, W Michael.
Theory of Social Movements: Theory *for* Social Movements?. ROOTES, C A.
Thinking About Home Schooling: Some Historical, Philosophical, and Cultural Reasons. KENNEDY, David.
Thought Rhythym and Experience in *Der Satz vom Grund* (in Dutch). PEETERS, L.

MOZART

Mozart and Santayana and the Interface Between Music and Philosophy. DILWORTH, David A.

MULLER, A

"Der geschlossne Handelsstaat"—Zur konservativen Kritik einer aufklärerischen Utopie. MARQUARDT, Jochen.

MULLER, M

Metaphysik als Metahistorik oder Hermeneutik des unreinen Denkens Die Philosophie Max Müllers. RUIZ-PESCE, Ramón Eduardo.

MULTINATIONAL CORPORATION(S)

The Challenge of Global Ethics. BULLER, Paul F and KOHLS, John J and ANDERSON, Kenneth S.
The Moral Authority of Transnational Corporate Codes. FREDERICK, William C.
Multinational Corporate Social Policy Process for Ethical Responsibility in Sub-Saharan Africa. PRATT, Cornelius B.

MULTIPLE PERSONALITY(-TIES)

How Many Selves Make Me?. CLARK, Stephen R L.
How Many Selves Make Me?. WILKES, Kathleen V.
Multiple Personality and Irrationality. GILLETT, Grant R.
The Problem of Who: Multiple Personality, Personal Identity and the Double Brain. APTER, Andrew.
Two Souls in One Body. HACKING, Ian.

MULTIPLICITY
How Many Selves Make Me?. CLARK, Stephen R L.
Sulla matrice della teoria della sostanza nel *Discorso di metafisica* di Leibniz. DELCÓ, Alessandro.

MULTISET(S)
Multiset Theory. BLIZARD, Wayne D.
Negative Membership. BLIZARD, Wayne D.

MUNTZER, T
Jan Hus und Thomas Müntzer—ein philosophiehistorischer Vergleich (in Czechoslovakian). KOLESNYK, Alexander.
Theologie und Sozialvorstellungen bei Thomas Müuntzer (in Czechoslovakian). LAUBE, Adolf.

MURDER
Homicide and Love. SMITH, Steven G.

MURDOCH, I
Faith and the Possibility of Private Meaning. GURREY, Charles S.

MURPHY, J
Entitled to Clemency: Mercy in the Criminal Law. JOHNSON, Carla Ann Hage.
Murphy and Mercy. ADLER, Jacob.

MURRAY, J
Neuhaus and Murray on Natural Law and American Politics. LAWLER, Peter A.

MUSEUM(S)
Philosophical Events: Essays of the '80s. RAJCHMAN, John.

MUSIC
Consciousness and the Computational Mind. JACKENDOFF, Ray.
Contemplating Music—Source Readings in the Aesthetics of Music, Volume II: Import. KATZ, Ruth (ed).
Musical Aesthetics: A Historical Reader, Volume III, The Twentieth Century. LIPPMAN, Edward A (ed).
Proust: The Creative Silence. CARANFA, Angelo.
Sound, Speech, and Music. BURROWS, David.
Style and Music: Theory, History, and Ideology. MEYER, Leonard B.
XIth International Congress in Aesthetics, Nottingham 1988. WOODFIELD, Richard (ed).
"The Art of Forgetfulness, Schopenhauer and Contemporary Repetitive Music" in *XIth International Congress in Aesthetics, Nottingham 1988*, DE MUL, Jos.
"Augustine on Music" in *Grace, Politics and Desire: Essays on Augustine*, JORDAN, William.
"Glenn Gould: La technologie au service d'une nouvelle définition de la musique" in *XIth International Congress in Aesthetics, Nottingham 1988*, GUERTIN, Ghyslaine.
"Ingarden et la musique: Actualité de la pensée musicale de Roman Ingarden" in *XIth International Congress in Aesthetics, Nottingham 1988*, SMOJE, Dujka.
"The Profundity of Music" in *XIth International Congress in Aesthetics, Nottingham 1988*, KIVY, Peter.
"'Tradition' et 'Innovation' dans la musique" in *XIth International Congress in Aesthetics, Nottingham 1988*, TAMBA, Akira.
The Aesthetic Relation of Musical Performer and Audience. PUTMAN, Daniel.
The Aesthetics of Imperfection. HAMILTON, Andy.
Authenticity Again. SHARPE, R A.
Beethoven's Ninth Symphony: The Sense of an Ending. SOLOMON, Maynard.
Glenn Gould: "archilecteur" *des Variations Goldberg*. GUERTIN, Ghyslaine.
Der Harmonie-Gedanke im frühen Mittelalter. BEIERWALTES, Werner.
Identifying Musical Works of Art. JACOBS, Jo Ellen.
Ji Kang's "Sheng-wu-aile-lun": Concerning Its Logical Development (in Japanese). HARA, Masayuki.
Mozart and Santayana and the Interface Between Music and Philosophy. DILWORTH, David A.
Music in Hegel's *Aesthetics*: A Re-Evaluation. JOHNSON, Julian.
Music, Meaning, and the Art of Elocution. TROTT, Elizabeth Anne.
Musical Time as a Practical Accomplishment: A Change in Tempo. WEEKS, P A D.
The Ontology of Musical Works and the Authenticity of their Performances. DAVIES, Stephen.
Problems Concerning the Presence of the Composer in His Music (in Polish). BUCZEK, Barbara.
The Representational Content of Musical Experience. DE BELLIS, Mark.
The Role of Music in Nietzsche's *Birth of Tragedy*. HECKMAN, Peter.
The Metacultural Hypothesis and the Foundations of Cultural Activity (in Polish). PORENA, Boris.
'I Heard a Plaintive Melody'. HANFLING, Oswald.

MUSICOLOGY
Music Performance and the Tools of the Trade. GODLOVITCH, Stan.

MUSIL, R
The Potential of Modern Discourse: Musil, Peirce, and Perturbation. FINLAY, Marike.

MUTATION
On the Possibility of Directed Mutations in Bacteria: Statistical Analyses and Reductionist Strategies. SARKAR, Sahotra.

MUTUALITY
"Against Tolerating the Intolerable" in *Logic and Ethics*, JACKSON, Jennifer.
Constructing Justice. GIBBARD, Allan.

MYSTERY(-RIES)
Spirit and Existence: A Philosophy Inquiry into the Meaning of Spiritual Existence. GELVEN, Michael.
"Reason in Mystery" in *The Philosophy in Christianity*, KRETZMANN, Norman.
El hombre y el misterio del ser. TRIANA, Manuel.

MYSTIC(S)
How to Build a Conscious Machine. ANGEL, Leonard.
The Ins and Outs of Mysticism. HART, Kevin.
Wittgenstein: la tentación de lo místico. CABRERA, Isabel.

MYSTICAL EXPERIENCE(S)
Mystical Experience, Hermeneutics, and Rationality. SHEAR, Jonathan.
San Ignacio de Loyola y el humanismo. GARCÍA-MATEO, Rogelio.

MYSTICISM
Caminhos do Filosofar. MIRANDA, Maria do Carmo Tavares de.
Dialogue with the Other: The Inter-Religious Dialogue. TRACY, David.
A History of Women Philosophers, Volume II: Medieval, Renaissance and Enlightenment, A.D. 500-1600. WAITHE, Mary Ellen (ed).
In Defense of Mystical Ideas: Support for Mystical Beliefs from a Purely Theoretical Viewpoint. CHAPMAN, Tobias.
Mystical Monotheism: A Study in Ancient Platonic Theology. KENNEY, John Peter.
The Place of the Hidden Moon: Erotic Mysticism in the Vaisnava-sahajiyā Cult of Bengal. DIMOCK JR, Edward C.
"'Where Two Are to Become One': Mysticism and Monism" in *The Philosophy in Christianity*, JANTZEN, Grace M.
"Beatrice of Nazareth" in *A History of Women Philosophers, Volume II: Medieval, Renaissance and Enlightenment, A.D. 500-1600*, WOLFSKEEL, Cornelia.
"Catherine of Siena" in *A History of Women Philosophers, Volume II: Medieval, Renaissance and Enlightenment, A.D. 500-1600*, WOLFSKEEL, Cornelia.
"The Face of Truth in Rosenzweig, Levinas, and Jewish Mysticism" in *Phenomenology of the Truth Proper to Religion*, COHEN, Richard A.
"Hadewych of Antwerp" in *A History of Women Philosophers, Volume II: Medieval, Renaissance and Enlightenment, A.D. 500-1600*, WOLFSKEEL, Cornelia.
"Hildegard of Bingen" in *A History of Women Philosophers, Volume II: Medieval, Renaissance and Enlightenment, A.D. 500-1600*, GÖSSMANN, Elisabeth and BEST, Katherine.
Algunos giros en torno a san Juan de la Cruz. VALDIVIA, Benjamín.
La démonstration mystifiante: Wittgenstein et Beuys. LA CHANCE, Michaël.
Il doppio volto dell'ineffabile in L Wittgenstein. TODISCO, Orlando.
Filosofia e ascesi nel Seicento: Il caso francese. BOSCO, Domenico.
La filosofía mística de Russell y lo indecible en el *Tractatus*. TOMASINI BASSOLS, Alejandro.
The Ins and Outs of Mysticism. HART, Kevin.
Logique et métaphysique. POUBLANC, Franck.
Meister Eckhart and the Neoplatonic Heritage: The Thinker's Way to God. WOODS, Richard.
An Oath of Silence: Wittgenstein's Philosophy of Religion. JOHNSON, Charles W.
Tres grandes testigos de la luz interior: San Agustín, san Buenaventura y J Henry Newman. OROZ RETA, José.
Wainwright, Maritain and Aquinas on Transcendent Experiences. ROY, Louis.

MYTH(S)
Amythia: Crisis in the Natural History of Western Culture. RUE, Loyal D.
Claude Lévi-Strauss. LEACH, Edmund.
The Great Goddess and the Aistian Mythical World. VYCINAS, Vincent.
The Legacy of Hermann Cohen. KLUBACK, William.
Myth and Modern Philosophy. DANIEL, Stephen H.
Myth and Philosophy: A Contest of Truths. HATAB, Lawrence J.
The Transcendental Temptation: A Critique of Religion and the Paranormal. KURTZ, Paul.
What is History? And Other Late Unpublished Writings (The Collected Works of Eric Voegelin, Vol 28). HOLLWECK, Thomas A (ed).
"The Necessity for Symbol and Myth: A Literary Amplification" in *Archetypal Process: Self and Divine in Whitehead, Jung, and Hillman*, SELLERY, J'Nan Morse.
"Oedipus and the Dogon: The Myth of Modernity Interrogated" in *I, We and Body: First Joint Symposium of Philosophers from Africa and from the Netherlands*, OOSTERLING, Henk A F.
AIDS, Myth, and Ethics. SUNDSTRÖM, Per.
Gestualità e mito: i due caratteri distintivi della lingua originaria secondo Vico. CANTELLI, Gianfranco.
Heidegger and Myth: A Loop in the History of Being. HATAB, Lawrence J.

MYTH(S)
Heracles and the Passage from Nature to Culture in G Vico's *La Scienza Nuova*. MIUCCIO, Giuliana.
Kinds of Truth and Psychoanalysis as a Myth: Some Epistemological Remarks on the Freudian Model (in Italian). BORUTTI, Silvana.
Mnêmê, anámnêsis, mnêmosynê: Sull'identità dell'uomo storico. MICCOLI, Paolo.
Myth and Morality: The Love Command. HEFNER, Philip.
Mythe et raison: Propos contemporains. FONTAINE-DE VISSCHER, Luce.
The Pot at the End of the Rainbow: Political Myth and the Ecological Crisis. DOYLE, Timothy.
The Return of the Initiate: Hegel on Bread and Wine. AUXIER, Randall E.
Vico in Voegelin. CAPORALI, Riccardo.

MYTHOLOGY
Three Great Traditions. PEDERSEN, Olaf.
Culture as an Open System. VAN PEURSEN, C A.
Dans quelle mesure et par quelles images les mythes grecs ont-ils symbolisé le néant?. RUDHARDT, Jean.
La logique du mythe et la question du non-être. COULOUBARITSIS, Lambros.
Die Perestrojka in der Sowjetischen Philosophie: Mythos oder Realität. BYKOVA, M.
Philosophie et mythologie dans la dernière philosophie de Schelling. MAESSCHALCK, Marc.

MYTILENAEAN
Rethinking the Diodotean Argument. JOHNSON, Laurie M.

NAGARJUNA
Über den Versuch einer philosophiegeschichtlichen Klassifikation der Lehre Nāgārjunas. TOMASCHITZ, Wolfgang.

NAGEL, E
The Logic of Impossible Quantities. SHERRY, David.
Why the Anti-Reductionist Consensus Won't Survive: The Case of Classical Mendelian Genetics. WATERS, C Kenneth.

NAGEL, T
Altruism and the Avoidance of Solipsism. CHONG, Kim-Chong.
Concerning the Absurdity of Life. SMITH, Quentin.
Going Nowhere: Nagel on Normative Objectivity. FRIEDMAN, Marilyn.
Must Thinking Bats be Conscious?. HANNA, Patricia.
The Role of Subjectivity in the Realism of Thomas Nagel and Jean-Paul Sartre. WIDER, Kathleen.
Self, Society, and Kantian Impersonality. SORELL, Tom.
What is it Like to be an Aardvark?. TIGHLMAN, B R.

NAME(S)
Wittgenstein and Contemporary Philosophy of Language. RUNDLE, Bede.
"Has the Description Theory of Names Been Refuted?" in *Meaning and Method: Essays in Honor of Hilary Putnam*, KATZ, Jerrold J.
"Intensionality and the Paradox of the Name Relation" in *Themes From Kaplan*, CHURCH, Alonzo.
The Indispensability of *Sinn*. FORBES, Graeme.
El nombre propio de Dios. PONFERRADA, Gustavo E.
Nombres y objetos en el *Tractatus*. VALDÉS, Margarita M.
Noun Phrases, Quantifiers, and Generic Names. LOWE, E J.
Proper Names, Cognitive Contents, and Beliefs. BRAUN, David M.
Russell on Ordinary Names and Synonymy. PINEAU, Lois.
Wittgenstein on Names and Family Resemblances. HYMERS, Michael.

NAMING
"The Problem of Linguistic Empowerment" in *Abeunt Studia in Mores: A Festschrift for Helga Doblin*, MERRILL, Sarah A Bishop.
Frege-Russell Semantics?. WETTSTEIN, Howard.
Genuine Names and Knowledge by Acquaintance. DONNELLAN, Keith S.
L'Appel et le Phénomène. LARUELLE, François.
Names, Actualities, and the Emergence of Essentialist Theories of Naming in Classical Chinese Thought. MAKEHAM, John.
On Knowing and Naming. BEARDS, Andrew.
Le sujet en dernier appel. MARION, Jean-Luc.
Two Kinds of Naming in the *Sophist*. STOUGH, Charlotte.

NARCISSISM
"O mito de Narciso" in *Dinâmica do Pensar: Homenagem a Oswaldo Market*, NUNES CORREIA, Carlos João.
"His Majesty Is a Baby?" A Critical Response to Peter Hammond Schwartz. SPRINGBORG, Patricia.
Narcissim Project and Corporate Decay: The Case of General Motors. SCHWARTZ, Howard S.
Rejoinder to Springborg's "His Majesty Is a Baby?" A Critical Response to Peter Hammond Schwartz. SCHWARTZ, Peter Hammond.

NARRATIVE
Dialogue with the Other: The Inter-Religious Dialogue. TRACY, David.
Narrative in Culture: The Uses of Storytelling in the Sciences, Philosophy, and Literature. NASH, Christopher (ed).
"The Fourth Gospel's Art of Rational Persuasion" in *The Bible as Rhetoric: Studies in Biblical Persuasion and Credibility*, WARNER, Martin.
"As Real As It Gets...": Ricoeur and Narrativity. KELLNER, Hans.
Biblical Narrative and the Theology of Metonymy. WARD, Graham.
Chaos, History, and Narrative. REISCH, George A.
History, Differential Equations, and the Problem of Narration. MC CLOSKEY, Donald N.
History, Historicism, Narratives: Identity in the Philosophy of History of Karl Popper. PARLEJ, Piotr.
Limning the Liminal: Carr and Ricoeur on Time and Narrative. PELLAUER, David.
Narrative Identity. RICOEUR, Paul.
Para una metahistoria del narrativisimo. GUARIGLIA, Osvaldo.
Philosophy, Argument, and Narration. VERENE, Donald Phillip.
References in Narrative Text. WIEBE, Janyce M.
Reply to Professor Zagorin's "Historiography and Postmodernism: Reconsideration". ANKERSMIT, Frank R.
Saying Good-bye to Historical Truth. SPENCE, Donald P.
Teaching Acts: An Unfinished Story. MC EWAN, Hunter.
Telling It Like It Was: Historical Narratives on Their Own Terms. NORMAN, Andrew P.
Telling Stories About Teaching. MACMILLAN, C J B.
Telling Tales: Notes on Heidegger's "Career," the "Heidegger Affair," and the Assumptions of Narrativity. DAVIES, Paul.
To Tell a Good Tale: Kierkegaardian Reflections on Moral Narrative and Moral Truth. TURNER, Jeffrey S.
Toward a Narrative Conception of Legal Discourse. PATTERSON, Dennis.
Truth in Interpretation: The Case of Psychoanalysis. ROTH, Paul A.
Why Narrative Is Not Enough. FULLER, Steve.

NASH, J
Rawlsian Nash Solutions. FABELLA, Raul V.

NATION(S)
"Nation and Universe" in *The Tanner Lectures on Human Values, Volume XI*, WALZER, Michael.
"War and the Nation-State in Social Theory" in *Social Theory of Modern Societies: Anthony Giddens and His Critics*, SHAW, Martin.
Cuatro modelos de desarrollo costarricense: un análisis y evalución ética. CROCKER, David A.
La ética como conciencia en el subdesarrollo. RAMÍREZ, E Roy.
El factor prelógico en el desarrollo de América Latina: El teorema del preconsciente colectivo. MANSILLA, H C F.
Lenin, Gorbachev, and 'National-Statehood': Can Leninism Countenance the New Soviet Federal Order?. GLEASON, Gregory.

NATIONAL
Setting Floating Limits: Functional Status Care Categories as National Policy. THOMASMA, David C.

NATIONAL HEALTH PROGRAM(S)
Biomedical Ethics Reviews, 1990. HUMBER, James M (ed).
"Can National Health Insurance Solve the Crisis in Health Care?" in *Biomedical Ethics Reviews, 1990*, IRVINE, William B.
"The Ethics of Social Commitment" in *Biomedical Ethics Reviews, 1990*, BAILLIE, Harold W and GARRETT, Thomas M.
"The Moral Case for National Health Insurance" in *Biomedical Ethics Reviews, 1990*, DOUGHERTY, Charles J.
"National Health Insurance: An Ethical Assessment" in *Biomedical Ethics Reviews, 1990*, DYCK, Arthur J and DE LANEY, James S.
"National Health Insurance: How Just Must We Be?" in *Biomedical Ethics Reviews, 1990*, FLECK, Leonard M.

NATIONAL SECURITY
Self-Defence and National Defence. DE ROOSE, Frank.

NATIONAL SOCIALISM
The Politics of Being: The Political Thought of Martin Heidegger. WOLIN, Richard.
Heidegger at 100, in America. KOLB, David.
Reflections on the Philosophy of Hitlerism. HAND, Seán (trans) and LEVINAS, Emmanuel.
Ruminations of a Slow-witted Mind. PIKE, Burton (trans) and LUFT, David S and MUSIL, Robert.

NATIONALISM
Morality and Modernity. POOLE, Ross.
Nation und Ethos: Die Moral des Patriotismus. KLUXEN-PYTA, Donate.
"Human Survival and the Limits of National Sovereignty" in *In the Interest of Peace: A Spectrum of Philosophical Views*, WINSTON, Morton.
"Die Geschichte hat kein Libretto": Zu Isaiah Berlins Begriff des Nationalismus. RITTER, Henning.
The Dialectic of National and Universal Commitments in Christian-Marxist Dialogue. WILL, James E.
Filosofía e identidad nacional en Honduras. ROMERO, Ramón.
The World Reconsidered: A Brief *AggiornamentoF* for Leftist Intellectuals. SKIRBEKK, Gunnar.

NATIONALITY
Two Conservative Views of Nationality and Personality: A A Grigor'ev and K N Leont'ev. DOWLER, E W.

NATIVE AMERICAN(S)
Handsome Lake's Teachings: The Shift from Female to Male Agriculture in Iroquois Agriculture. HOLLY, Marilyn.

NATIVISM
Was Kant a Nativist?. FALKENSTEIN, Lorne.

NATURAL
Osservazioni sul bello naturale e sul bello artistico in filosofia. FRANCHI, Alfredo.
Residual Natural Evil and Anthropic Reasoning. MC LEAN, Murdith.
Unifying Plato: Charles Kahn on Platonic *Prolepsis*. GRISWOLD JR, Charles L.

NATURAL DEDUCTION
A Basic Free Logic. WU, Kathleen Johnson.
Logical Constants as Punctuation Marks. DOSEN, Kosta.
Natural Deduction in Normal Modal Logic. HAWTHORN, John.
On Certain Normalizable Natural Deduction Formulations of Some Propositional Intermediate Logics. BORICIC, Branislav R.
On the Logic of Contingent Relevant Implication: Conceptual Incoherence in the Intuitive Interpretation of *R*. LANCE, Mark.

NATURAL HISTORY
The History of Philosophy, Inside and Out. MATHIEN, Thomas.

NATURAL KINDS
"Are Economic Kinds Natural?" in *Scientific Theories*, NELSON, Alan.
"Natural Kinds" in *Perspectives on Quine*, HACKING, Ian.
Realism, Anti-Foundationalism and the Enthusiasm for Natural Kinds. BOYD, Richard.
A Tradition of Natural Kinds. HACKING, Ian.
Understanding Induction. MACNAMARA, John.
Units of Measurement and Natural Kinds: Some Kripkean Considerations. VAN BRAKEL, J.

NATURAL LANGUAGE(S)
Events in the Semantics of English: A Study in Subatomic Semantics. PARSONS, Terence.
Meaning and Speech Acts: Volume I, Principles of Language Use. VANDERVEKEN, Daniel.
Meaning and Speech Acts: Volume II, Formal Semantics of Success and Satisfaction. VANDERVEKEN, Daniel.
"How Natural Is Natural Language?" in *Logic, Methodology and Philosophy of Science, VIII*, KOSTER, Jan.
"Learnability of Semantic Theory" in *Truth and Interpretation: Perspectives on the Philosophy of Donald Davidson*, MATTHEWS, Robert J.
"Understanding and the Principle of Compositionality" in *Philosophical Perspectives, 4: Action Theory and Philosophy of Mind, 1990*, GRANDY, Richard E.
Dialogues in Natural Language with GURU, a Psychologic Inference Engine. COLBY, Kenneth M and COLBY, Peter M and STOLLER, Robert J.
Ellipsis and Higher-Order Unification. DALRYMPLE, Mary and SHIEBER, Stuart M and PEREIRA, Fernando C N.
Predication, Fiction, and Artificial Intelligence. RAPAPORT, William J.
Teorías de verdad y teorías del significado. VARGAS, Celso.
Vagueness, Natural Language and Logic. BERKELEY, Istvan S N.

NATURAL LAW(S)
Anglo-American Philosophy of Law: An Introduction to Its Development and Outcome. LEVY, Beryl Harold.
Hobbes. TUCK, Richard.
The Idea of the Miraculous: The Challenge to Science and Religion. WILLIAMS, T C.
Kant's System of Rights. MULHOLLAND, Leslie A.
Moral Philosophy from Montaigne to Kant: An Anthology, Volume I & II. SCHNEEWIND, J B (ed).
Questions Concerning the Law of Nature: John Locke. CLAY, Jenny Strauss (ed & trans).
Swimming Against the Current in Contemporary Philosophy: Occasional Essays and Papers. VEATCH, Henry B.
Thomas Hobbes' Theory of Obligation: A Modern Interpretation. FORSBERG, Ralph P.
"Foundationalism and Foundation in Strauss and Maritain" in *From Twilight to Dawn: The Cultural Vision of Jacques Maritain*, ASSELIN, D T.
"Natural Law" in *A Companion to Ethics*, BUCKLE, Stephen.
"Philosophical Perspectives on Newtonian Science" in *Philosophical Perspectives on Newtonian Science*, HUGHES, R I G.
Abortion as the Illicit Method of Birth Control. KEILKOPF, Charles F.
Aesthetics and Natural Law in Newton's Methodology. JACQUETTE, Dale.
An Atheological Argument from Evil Natural Laws. SMITH, Quentin.
Boskovic's Theory of Forces in His Treatise "De Continuitatis Lege" (in Serbo-Croatian). BRUNSKO, Zagorka.
David Hume and the Mysterious Shroud of Turin. SCHOEN, Edward L.
Divine Irony and the Natural Law: Speculation and Edification in Aquinas. HIBBS, Thomas S.
Divine Reason and Virtue in St Thomas's Natural Law Theory. KILLORAN, John B.
Goerner on Thomistic Natural Law. HALL, Pamela.
Hegel's Critique of Liberalism and Natural Law: Reconstructing Ethical Life. GARZA JR, Abel.
Hume's Metaethical Cognitivism and the Natural Law Theory. GRAEFRATH, Bernd.

Is There a Natural Law?. WALDSTEIN, Wolfgang.
King Lear and Natural Law. YOUNG, R V.
Maimonides: A Natural Law Theorist?. LEVINE, Michael.
Montaigne's 'Des Cannibales' and Natural Sources of Virtue. HOROWITZ, Maryanne Cline.
Natural Law and the Environment. BROWN, Montague.
Natural Law Theory: The Link Between its Descriptive Strength and its Prescriptive Strength. BRAYBROOKE, David.
Natural Law, Skepticism, and Methods of Ethics. SCHNEEWIND, J B.
Natuur en cultuur: de heuristische waarde van een dichotomie. WESTERMAN, Pauline.
Neuhaus and Murray on Natural Law and American Politics. LAWLER, Peter A.
Nuclear Deterrence and the Morality of Intentions. KULTGEN, John.
Rescuing Natural Law Theory from the Rationalists. DENNEHY, Raymond.
Response to Hall's "Goerner on Thomistic Natural Law". GOERNER, E A.
Rousseau's Liberalism. SORENSEN, L R.
Tropes and Laws. FUHRMANN, André.
Wetten en verhalen. KWA, Chunglin.

NATURAL LIGHT
Il "parlare commune" come lume storico-naturale della "riproduzione sociale". MININNI, Giuseppe.

NATURAL NUMBER(S)
Where Do Natural Numbers Come From?. HODES, Harold T.

NATURAL PHILOSOPHY
"Genius in Romantic Natural Philosophy" in *Romanticism and the Sciences*, SCHAFFER, Simon.
Boskovic on His Own Theory of Forces: From a Sentence to the Theory of Natural Philosophy (in Serbo-Croatian). MARTINOVIC, Ivica.
Consideraciones en torno a la polémica Leibniz-Clarke. PONCE ALBERCA, Carmen.
Eleatics Against Each Other (in Hungarian). KAMPIS, György.
Filósofos naúfragos. BALIÑAS, Carlos.
Immateriality and the Domain of Thomistic Natural Philosophy. JOHNSON, Mark F.
Ist die Naturphilosophie eine abgelegte Gestalt des modernen Geistes. WAHSNER, Renate.
Materiality and Aquinas' Natural Philosophy: A Reply to Johnson. KNASAS, John F X.
The Gnoseological Aspect of Boskovic's "Theory of Natural Philosophy" (in Serbo-Croatian). ACIMOVIC, Mirko.

NATURAL RESOURCES
Rethinking the Commons. HERRING, Ronald J.

NATURAL RIGHT(S)
Introduction Critique au Droit Naturel. HERVADA, Javier.
Les "droits naturels" et les "titres" selon Robert Nozick. SWEET, William.
Anerkennung: Fichtes Grundlegungen des Rechtsgrundes. JANKE, Wolfgang.
Lonergan's Recovery of the Notion of Natural Right: Introduction to a New Context for an Old Discussion. BRAIO, Frank Paul.
Rousseau's Liberalism. SORENSEN, L R.
Soggetto e senso del diritto nell'esperienza giuridica moderna: appunti in tema di positività. FIASCHI, Giovanni.
Spinoza en het ontstaan van de staat. VERBEEK, Bruno.
Strauss's Three Burkes: The Problem of Edmund Burke in *Natural Right and History*. LENZNER, Steven J.

NATURAL SCIENCES
The Chain of Change: A Study of Aristotle's "Physics" VII. WARDY, Robert.
"Epistémologie des sciences de la nature et herméneutique de l'histoire des sciences selon H Metzger" in *Études sur/Studies on Hélène Metzger*, FREUDENTHAL, Gad.
"Historical Consciousness in the German Romantic *Naturforschung*" in *Romanticism and the Sciences*, VON ENGELHARDT, Dietrich and SALAZAR, Christine.
"Reconciling Concepts between Natural Science and Theology" in *Science and Religion: One World-Changing Perspectives on Reality*, WEIDLICH, W.
A proposito dell'interesse di Dilthey per l'antropologia cinquecentesca. ORSUCCI, Andrea.
A Conjecture Concerning the Ranking of the Sciences. HUMPHREYS, Paul.
Conquering Chance. HENRY-HERMANN, Grete.
A Crucial Distinction: Initial Data and Law Application Instances. FLICHMAN, Eduardo.
Economie in de spiegel van de natuurwetenschappen. KUIPERS, Theo A F.
Die Mathematisierung als Konstruktion theoretischer Denkformen in der Abfolge naturwissenschaftlicher Weltbilder. GÖTTLICHER, Gerd.
On the Problem of the Essence of Truth in the Natural Sciences (in Dutch). KOCKELMANS, J.
R J Boskovic's "Theoria" — A Sign Post to the Essence of the Modern Natural Science (in Serbo-Croatian). ZENKO, Franjo.
Scientism, Interpretation, and Criticism. GORSKI, Philip S.
Social Science Knowledge and Explanations in Educational Studies. DALE, Michael.

NATURAL SCIENCES

The Relationship Between the Humanities and the Natural and Technical Sciences (in German). PACHO, Julián.

Ungeklärte Fragen im Dialog zwischen Glaube und Naturwissenschaft. FISCHER, Johannes.

The Unity of the Natural Sciences: Comment on Portmann. VON UEXKUELL, Thure.

Wertfreiheit und Ethik in den Sozial-und Naturwissenschaften. ZIMMERMANN, Rolf.

NATURAL SELECTION

The Biological Justification of Ethics: A Best-Case Scenario. ROSENBERG, Alexander.

Darwin's Long and Short Arguments. SINTONEN, Matti.

The Darwinian Synthesis: A Critique of the Rosenberg/Williams Argument. VAN BALEN, G.

Fitness and Evolutionary Explanation. BYERLY, Henry C and MICHOD, Richard E.

Functions As Selected Effects: The Conceptual Analyst's Defense. NEANDER, Karen.

Natural Selection as Natural History. VAN DER STEEN, Wim J.

Recent Work in the Philosophy of Biology. STERELNY, Kim.

What Is This Stuff Called Fitness?. OLLASON, J G.

Why Natural Selection Leads to Complexity. BENZON, William L and HAYS, David G.

NATURAL THEOLOGY

'Religion' and the Religions in the English Enlightenment. HARRISON, Peter.

Discussioni sul neo-Tomismo: Per il progresso della Filosofia Cristiana. BLANDINO, Giovanni.

"A Revived Natural Theology" in *Science and Religion: One World-Changing Perspectives on Reality*, POLKINGHORNE, J C.

Alvin Plantinga and Natural Theology. BROWN, Hunter.

David Hume's *Dialogues Concerning Natural Religion*: Otherness in History and in Text. MANNING, Robert J S.

A Dialogic Interpretation of Hume's *Dialogues*. SESSIONS, William Lad.

Emanating Causes: New Battle Lines for Natural Theology?. KING-FARLOW, John.

Why Natural Theology, Still, Yet?. HUTCHINGS, Patrick.

NATURALISM

The Devil and Secular Humanism: The Children of the Enlightenment. RADEST, Howard B.

Foundations of Moral and Political Philosophy. PAUL, Ellen Frankel (ed).

Good and Evil: An Absolute Conception. GAITA, Raimond.

The Metaphysics of Meaning. KATZ, Jerrold J.

Perspectives on Quine. BARRETT, Robert (ed).

The Positivist Science of Law. LEE, Keekok.

"Does Meaning Matter?" in *Information, Semantics and Epistemology*, DRETSKE, Frederick.

"Naturalism" in *A Companion to Ethics*, PIGDEN, Charles R.

"Needs and Values" in *Logic and Ethics*, WOLNIEWICZ, Boguslaw.

Aberrations of the Realism Debate. DEVITT, Michael.

Beyond Naturalism: A Reconstruction of Daoist Environmental Ethics. PEERENBOOM, Randall P.

Challenge: Subjectivist Naturalism. FOLDVARY, Fred E.

Does Prescriptivism Imply Naturalism?. KANTHAMANI, A.

Intentionality and the Ecological Approach. LOOREN DE JONG, H.

Kinship and Moral Relativity. PARGETTER, Robert.

Must We Return to Moral Realism?. ROSEN, Michael.

Naturalism and Scepticism. BELL, Martin and MC GINN, Marie.

Naturalism, Freedom and Ethics in Spinoza. DE DIJN, Herman.

Naturalistic Ethics and the Argument from Evil. NELSON, Mark T.

A Naturalistic Theory of Archaic Moral Order. CAMPBELL, Donald.

Naturalized Epistemology Sublimated: Rapprochement without the Ruts. FULLER, Steve.

New Naturalism and Other Ethical Theories. SHENG, C L.

On Franco-Ferraz, Theism and the Theatre of the Mind. BADÍA-CABRERA, Miguel A.

On Naturalizing the Semantics of Mental Representation. SILVERS, Stuart.

The Paradox of Epistemology: A Defense of Naturalism. KETCHUM, Richard J.

Philosophical and Religious Implications of Cognitive Social Learning Theories of Personality. ROTTSCHAEFER, William A.

Politica e diritto in Hobbes. BAGLIONI, Emma.

Pragmatic Naturalism: The Philosophy of Sidney Hook (1902-1989). KURTZ, Paul.

Realism, Naturalism and Social Behaviour. OUTHWAITE, William.

Searle on Natural Agency. BISHOP, John.

Spinoza en de geopenbaarde godsdienst. DE DIJN, H.

Zande Logic and Western Logic. JENNINGS, Richard C.

NATURALISTIC FALLACY

The Positivist Science of Law. LEE, Keekok.

"Natur" als Massstab menschlichen Handelns. BIRNBACHER, Dieter.

Evolved Ethics Re-Examined: The Theory of Robert J Richards. WILLIAMS, Patricia.

Metaphysik und Erfahrung in Kants Grundlegung der Ethik. CRAMER, Konrad.

NATURALISTIC PSYCHOLOGY

Why not Naturalistic Psychology?. GARRETT, Richard and GRAHAM, George.

NATURALIZED EPISTEMOLOGY

Epistemics. DURAN, Jane.

"Genetic Explanation in *The Roots of Reference*" in *Perspectives on Quine*, PARSONS, Charles.

"Holism and Naturalized Epistemology Confronted with the Problem of Truth" in *Perspectives on Quine*, LAUENER, Henri.

"On the Nature of Theories: A Neurocomputational Perspective" in *Scientific Theories*, CHURCHLAND, Paul M.

"Why and How to Naturalize Epistemology" in *Perspectives on Quine*, KOPPELBERG, Dirk.

Epistemic Justification and Psychological Realism. TAYLOR, James E.

Epistemic Norms and Evolutionary Success. CLARKE, Murray.

On Naturalizing Epistemology. ALMEDER, Robert.

Recent Work on Naturalized Epistemology. MAFFIE, James.

NATURE

Die Aufhebung der Begriffs-philosophie. KRONABEL, Christoph.

Divine Nature and Human Language: Essays in Philosophical Theology. ALSTON, William P.

Encyclopedia of the Philosophical Sciences in Outline and Critical Writings—G W F Hegel. BEHLER, Ernst (ed).

Evolution als Höherentwicklung des Bewusstseins. KUMMER, Christian.

George Santayana y la Ironia de la Materia. IZUZQUIZA, Ignacio.

Introduction Critique au Droit Naturel. HERVADA, Javier.

Introduction to the Philosophy of Nature. HETZLER, Florence M.

Metaphysics of Natural Complexes (Second Edition). WALLACE, Kathleen (ed).

Mind Only: A Philosophical and Doctrinal Analysis of the Vijñānavāda. WOOD, Thomas E.

Nature and Politics: Liberalism in the Philosophies of Hobbes, Locke, and Rousseau. RAPACZYNSKI, Andrzej.

Nicolai Hartmann's New Ontology. WERKMEISTER, W H.

A Progress of Sentiments: Reflections on Hume's "Treatise". BAIER, Annette C.

Socialism, Feminism and Philosophy: A Radical Philosophy Reader. SAYERS, Sean (ed).

Towards a Christian Philosophy. OWENS, Joseph I.

"Schelling and the Origins of His *Naturphilosophie*" in *Romanticism and the Sciences*, MORGAN, S R.

"Construindo a 'ordem anárquica". PIOZZI, Patrícia.

"Historia" de la naturaleza *versus* "Naturaleza" de la historia. LEAL, Fernando A.

"Natur" als Massstab menschlichen Handelns. BIRNBACHER, Dieter.

Das "objektive Denken" in Schellings Naturphilosophie. BUCHHEIM, Thomas.

A proposito dell'interesse di Dilthey per l'antropologia cinquecentesca. ORSUCCI, Andrea.

Adam's Place in Nature: Respect or Domination?. NASH, Roger.

Alle origini della riflessione di Leopold von Ranke sulla storia: K F Bachmann e J G Fichte. GHELARDI, Maurizio.

Aristotle and Nietzsche on Art as Imitation of Nature. DROST, Mark P.

Between Two Worlds: Humans in Nature and Culture. GARDINER, Robert W.

Boskovic on His Own Theory of Forces: From a Sentence to the Theory of Natural Philosophy (in Serbo-Croatian). MARTINOVIC, Ivica.

Caring About Nature: Feminist Ethics and the Environment. KING, Roger J H.

Il caso "Siris", ovvero la "seconda filosofia" di George Berkeley vescovo di Cloyne. NERI, Luigi.

Causes and Laws. ARMSTRONG, D M and HEATHCOTE, Adrian.

Las dos grandes paradojas?. SERRANO, Augusto.

Ethical Dimensions of Human Attitudes to Nature. BURES, Radim.

Feminism and Ecology: On the Domination of Nature. MILLS, Patricia Jagentowicz.

Hermeneutic or Metaphysical Hegelianism? Kojève's Dilemma. REDDING, Paul.

How to Construe Nature: Environmental Ethics and the Interpretation of Nature. KING, Roger J H.

How to Put Questions to Nature. SINTONEN, Matti.

Hume and Pascal: Pyrrhonism versus Nature. MAIA NETO, José R.

Images of the Environment in Corporate America. SKORPEN, Erling.

Ist die Naturphilosophie eine abgelegte Gestalt des modernen Geistes. WAHSNER, Renate.

Ist die Naturphilosophie eine abgelegte Gestalt des modernen Geistes?. WAHSNER, Renate.

Kantian Freedom Naturalized. MELCHERT, Norman.

The Lakatos Award Lecture: The Nature of Reality. REDHEAD, Michael.

The Laws of Physics as Nomic Universals. ZYCINSKI, Jozef.

Le promeneur solitaire: Rousseau and the Emergence of the Post-Social Self. GAUTHIER, David.

NATURE
Libri da salvare. POLC, Jaroslav.
Location and Range. SCHLESINGER, George N.
Loving Your Mother: On the Woman-Nature Relationship. ROACH, Catherine.
Natural and Political Society in the Thought of Edmund Burke (in German). TSCHURENEV, Eva-Maria.
La naturaleza como vida en la interpretación hegeliana de Aristóteles. BARROSO, Inmaculada Acosta.
La naturaleza y la historia como fundamento para un concepto renovada de razón. PADILLA, Leonel Eduardo.
Nature as Personal. DOMBROWSKI, Daniel A.
The Nature of Buddhism. KLOSTERMAIER, Klaus.
Nature' Song. SALLIS, John.
Nature, Self, and Gender: Feminism, Environmental Philosophy, and the Critique of Rationalism. PLUMWOOD, Val.
Natuur en cultuur: de heuristische waarde van een dichotomie. WESTERMAN, Pauline.
Nuestra voluntad es "de Dios". FERNÁNDEZ BURILLO, Santiago A.
Offices and God. HUGLY, Philip and SAYWARD, Charles.
Plato's Ontology and the Role of Mathematics in the Description of Nature. ZYCINSKI, Joseph.
Plato, the History of Science and Our Understanding of Nature (in German). GLOY, Karen.
Il rapporto Parmenide-Telesio dal Persio al Maranta. ARTESE, Luciano.
Responsibility As a Moral Principle? A Critical Reflection on Hans Jonas' Ethics of Responsibility? (in German). KETTNER, Matthias.
Rights and Rights Violators: A New Approach to the Nature of Rights. GERT, Heather J.
Sulla posizione dell'uomo nella natura. SEIDL, Horst.
Sur quelques textes de Spinoza relatifs à la notion de loi. PREPOSIET, Jean.
Theology and the Necessity of Natures. ANGLIN, W S.
Travail et nature dans l'Antiquité. MULLER, Robert.
Two Problems of Induction?. O'NEILL, John.
The Values of a Habitat. PARKER, Kelly.
Vie et totalité chez Nietzsche. HAAR, Michel.
Virtue Ethics and the Appeal to Human Nature. WOODRUFF, Paul.
Waiting for the Vanishing Shed. PHILLIPS, D Z.
Ways to See a Revolution and World Outlook: Alexander von Humboldt (in German). HERLITZIUS, Erwin.
Welke natuur is het beschermen waard?. VAN DER WINDT, Henny J and HARBERS, Hans.
Wetten en verhalen. KWA, Chunglin.
William Wadsworth: Nature, Imagination, Ultimate Reality and Meaning. MAHONEY, John L.
X Zubiri in Roma: Natura, Storia, Dio. JAVIERRE ORTAS, A M.
Zu einem "der tiefsten philosophischen Probleme". SIEGWART, Geo.
Zur inhaltlichen Bedeutung des Hegelschen "Schemas der Naturphilosophie" in den Epikurstudien des jungen Marx. MIELKE, Dietmar.
'Following Nature' in Butler's Sermons. BRINTON, Alan.

NAZISM
Encounter on the Narrow Ridge: A Life of Martin Buber. FRIEDMAN, Maurice.
The Political Ontology of Martin Heidegger. BOURDIEU, Pierre.
Thinking the Unthinkable: Meanings of the Holocaust. GOTTLIEB, Roger S (ed).
"Degenerate Law": Jurists and Nazism. LA TORRE, Massimo.
Heidegger After Farias. ROCKMORE, Tom.
Heidegger's Apology: Biography as Philosophy and Ideology. KISIEL, Theodore.
On Heidegger and National Socialism: A Triple Turn?. ROCKMORE, Tom.
Prague: le cimetière. BRETON, Stanislas.
Prolegomena to an Understanding of Heidegger's Turn. GRONDIN, Jean.
Retreat from Radicality: Pöggeler on Heidegger's Politics. EDLER, Frank H W.
Ruminations of a Slow-witted Mind. PIKE, Burton (trans) and LUFT, David S and MUSIL, Robert.
The Search for an Ethical Sacrament: From Bonhoeffer to Critical Social Theory. FLOYD, Wayne Whitson.
The Subject of Hermeneutics and the Hermeneutics of the Subject. RICHARDSON, William.

NECESSARY BEING
Creation, Creativity and Necessary Being. HUGHES, Martin.

NECESSARY TRUTH(S)
Central Themes in Early Modern Philosophy. COVER, J A (ed).
"Leibniz and Locke on the Knowledge of Necessary Truths" in *Central Themes in Early Modern Philosophy*, BOLTON, Martha Brandt.
Analiticidad, empirismo y verdad necesaria. HERNÁNDEZ IGLESIAS, Manuel Angel.
Explaining Necessity. MASON, Richard V.

NECESSITY(-TIES)
The Dilemma of Freedom and Foreknowledge. ZAGZEBSKI, Linda Trinkaus.
Ideas, Principios y Dialectica. LAFUENTE, Maria Isabel.
Jean-Paul Sartre. HENGELBROCK, Jürgen.
Leibniz and Arnauld. SLEIGH JR, Robert C.
A Progress of Sentiments: Reflections on Hume's "Treatise". BAIER, Annette C.
Towards a Christian Philosophy. OWENS, Joseph I.
"Acts and Necessity in the Philosophy of John William Miller" in *The Philosophy of John William Miller*, DIEFENBECK, James A.
"Necessidade e contingência nos primeiros escritos de Nietzsche" in *Dinâmica do Pensar: Homenagem a Oswaldo Market*, NABAIS, Nuno.
"Quantification, Time, and Necessity" in *Philosophical Applications of Free Logic*, COCCHIARELLA, Nino B.
The Antinomy of Divine Necessity. SCHRADER, David E.
Apriorische Einsicht und metaphysische Notwendigkeit: Eine Auseinandersetzung mit Kripkes Kant-Kritik. WENDEL, Hans Jürgen.
Between Necessity and Superabundance: Meta-economic Reflections on Marxism. WALDENFELS, Bernhard.
The Caterus Objection. FORGIE, J William.
Classes and Attributes in Extended Modal Systems: Proceedings of the Colloquium in Modal and Many Valued Logic. MARCUS, Ruth Barcan.
Conceptual Necessity, Causality and Self-Ascriptions of Sensation. KAUFMAN, Frederik.
Explaining Necessity. MASON, Richard V.
Hegel, Marx, Lukács: The Dialectic of Freedom and Necessity. DAY, Richard B.
Historical Necessity and Conditionals. NUTE, Donald.
Hume and Physical Necessity. FLEW, Antony.
Kants Begriff der synthetischen Urteile a priori. ROS, Arno.
Leibniz on Creation, Contingency and Per-Se Modality. MC NAMARA, Paul.
Libertad y necesidad en el 'Cur Deus Homo' de San Anselmo de Canterbury (segunda parte). CORTI, E C.
Madden's Account of Necessity in Causation. LEVINE, Michael P.
Necessary A Posteriori Truth. SWINBURNE, Richard.
Temporal Necessity and the Conditional. CROSS, Charles B.
La tensione tra possibilità e necessità nell'argomento ontologico di Leibniz. NICOLOSI, Salvatore.
Theology and the Necessity of Natures. ANGLIN, W S.
Torts of Necessity: A Moral Theory of Compensation. KLEPPER, Howard.
Transparent Approach to Logical Necessity and Possibility. MATERNA, P.
When Is Home Care Medically Necessary? Commentary. FORROW, Lachlan.
When Is Home Care Medically Necessary? Commentary. DANIELS, Norman and SABIN, James E.
World History as the Progress of Consciousness: An Interpretation of Hegel's Philosophy of History. HOULGATE, Stephen.

NEED(S)
"Needs and Values" in *Logic and Ethics*, WOLNIEWICZ, Boguslaw.
Aktuelle Aufgaben interdisziplinärer Bedürfnisforschung aus psychologischer Sicht. WOLF, Edith.
Assessing Human Needs. JONES, John D.
Need, Denial and Abandonment: Heidegger and the Turn. URPETH, James R.
Rileggendo Marx: "diritti" e "bisogni". BADALONI, Nicola.

NEGATION
The Origins of Aristotelian Science. FEREJOHN, Michael.
"The Justification of Negation as Failure" in *Logic, Methodology and Philosophy of Science, VIII*, FINE, Kit.
Idées de négations. CHIESA, Curzio.
Kernels in N-Normal Symmetric Heyting Algebras. GALLI, A and SAGASTUME, M.
Nelson Algebras Through Heyting Ones^1:1. SENDLEWSKI, Andrzej.
On Negation. KOKTOVÁ, Eva.
On Some Logically Equivalent Propositions. KELLY, Charles J.
Remarks on Special Lattices and Related Constructive Logics with Strong Negation. PAGLIANI, Piero.
Topos Based Semantics for Constructive Logic with Strong Negation. KLUNDER, Barbara.
Why is Conjunctive Simplification Invalid?. THOMPSON, Bruce R.

NEGATIVE
Herrschaft und Versöhnung: Einführung in das Denken Theodor W Adornos. KAGER, Reinhard.
Negative Dialectics and the End of Philosophy. ERICKSON, Glenn W.
"Negative Values" in *Logic and Ethics*, ELZENBERG, H.
Apophasis and Metaphysics in the *Periphyseon* of John Scottus Eriugena. CARABINE, Deirdre.
For One Concept of Liberty. BEEHLER, Rodger.
La logica di Hegel come testo filosofico (II). COSTA, Filippo.
Negative Membership. BLIZARD, Wayne D.
Why Negative Rights Only?. JORDAN, Jeff.

NEGOTIATION
Negotation Games: Applying Game Theory to Bargaining and Arbitration. BRAMS, Steven J.

NEGRU, I
La Logica Simbolica: nella produzione scientifica in lingua russa (1961-1983). PENNINO, Luciano.

NEILL, A

Der Ursprung der Erziehungsziele in der Lehre von Plato, Aristoteles und Neill. EGGER, Paul.

NELSON, L

Conquering Chance. HENRY-HERMANN, Grete.

NEO-CONFUCIANISM

New Dimensions of Confucian and Neo-Confucian Philosophy. CHENG, Chung-ying.

To Catch a Thief: Chu Hsi (1130-1200) and the Hermeneutic Art. BERTHRONG, John.

NEO-KANTIANISM

Discourse Ethics and the Communitarian Critique of Neo-Kantianism. REHG, William.

NEO-PLATONISM

Philosophy of the Ancients. RICKEN, Friedo.

Plotin: Traité sur la liberté et la volonté de l'Un. LEROUX, Georges.

"On Not Knowing too Much About God" in *The Philosophy in Christianity*, ARMSTRONG, A H.

Aspetti di attualità teoretica del pensiero procliano negli studi di Werner Beierwaltes. SCOTTI, Nicoletta.

La filosofia: in soccorso de' governi. COLAPIETRA, Raffaele.

Meister Eckhart and the Neoplatonic Heritage: The Thinker's Way to God. WOODS, Richard.

Postilla. GALASSO, Giuseppe.

Vico in Voegelin. CAPORALI, Riccardo.

NEO-THOMISM

Discussioni sul neo-Tomismo: Per il progresso della Filosofia Cristiana. BLANDINO, Giovanni.

The Preface to Thomistic Metaphysics. KNASAS, John F X.

Cent ans de philosophie à l'Institut Supérieur de Philosophie. LADRIÈRE, Jean.

Désiré Mercier et les débuts de l'Institut de Philosophie. AUBERT, Roger.

NEONATE(S)

Medicine and Money: A Study of the Role of Beneficence in Health Care Cost Containment. MARSH, Frank H.

NEOSCHOLASTICISM

Die Aufhebung der Begriffs-philosophie. KRONABEL, Christoph.

La "Scuola di Padova" ed i problemi dell'ontologia italiana contemporanea. MANGIAGALLI, Maurizio.

La disputa sulle origini della neoscolastica italiana: Salvatore Roselli, Vincenzo Buzzetti e Gaetano Sanseverino. SCHMIDINGER, H M.

La neoscolastica italiana dalle sue prime manifestazioni all'enciclica *Aeterni Patris*. ROSSI, G F.

Pensiero e trascendenza. SANCIPRIANO, Mario.

NERVOUS SYSTEM

Inside World-Outside World: Epistemology on the Conscious Action of the Nervous System. DE JONG, B M.

NESBITT, W

Applied Ethics and Meta-Philosophy. DAVSON-GALLE, Peter.

NETHERLANDS

Moraliteiten: Recente ethische publikaties in Vlaanderen en Nederland. STRUYKER BOUDIER, C E M.

NEUGEBAUER, C

Dr C Neugebauer's Critical Note on Ethnophilosophy in the Philosophical Discourse in Africa: Some Remarks. BEWAJI, J A I.

NEUHAUS, R

Neuhaus and Murray on Natural Law and American Politics. LAWLER, Peter A.

NEUROBIOLOGY

Genetics, Neuroscience, and Biotechnology. LAPPÈ, Marc.

The Poverty of Neurophilosophy. STENT, Gunther S.

NEUROLOGY

Art and Neurology: A Discussion. HALPIN, David M G and SORRELL, Martin.

Consciousness—From Behavioural Neurologist's Horizon. MUKHOPADHYAY, Asok Kumar.

NEUROPHYSIOLOGY

"Vision and Mind" in *Logic, Methodology and Philosophy of Science, VIII*, GLEZER, Vadim D.

Buddhist Anthropology vis-à-vis Modern Philosophy and Contemporary Neurophysiology. BUGAULT, Guy.

Is Neuroscience Relevant to Philosophy?. CHURCHLAND, Patricia Smith.

Some Philosophical Aspects of Psychophysiology—Are There Any Elements of "Neurophilosophy"? (in German). RÜDIGER, Wolfgang.

NEUROPSYCHOLOGY

"On the Nature of Theories: A Neurocomputational Perspective" in *Scientific Theories*, CHURCHLAND, Paul M.

NEUROSCIENCE

Perception and Neuroscience. GILLETT, Grant R.

NEUROSES

Freud on Civilization and Neurosis. FLUXMAN, Tony.

NEUTRAL MONISM

David Hume's Theory of Mind. FLAGE, Daniel E.

NEUTRALITY

Moral Pluralism and Legal Neutrality. SADURSKI, Wojciech.

"Neutralities" in *Liberalism and the Good*, ACKERMAN, Bruce A.

Autonomy, Liberalism and State Neutrality. MASON, Andrew D.

Community and Neutrality in Critical Thought. HOSTETLER, Karl.

Logical Constants Across Varying Types. VAN BENTHEM, Johan.

Neutrality Between Religion and Irreligion. LINDSAY, Ronald A.

Religious Commitment and Secular Reason: A Reply to Professor Weithman. AUDI, Robert.

The Separation of Church and State: Some Questions for Professor Audi. WEITHMAN, Paul J.

Truth, Neutrality, and Conflict of Interest. LICHTENBERG, Judith.

NEW TESTAMENT

"'In the Sermon Which I Have Just Completed, Wherever I Said Aristotle, I Meant Saint Paul'" in *The Bible as Rhetoric: Studies in Biblical Persuasion and Credibility*, JASPER, David.

"The Peace of God" in *Celebrating Peace*, MINEAR, Paul S.

NEWCOMB'S PARADOX

Newcomb's Problem, Prisoners' Dilemma, and Collective Action. HURLEY, S L.

Non-Dominance, Third Person and Non-Action Newcomb Problems, and Metatickles. SOBEL, Jordan Howard.

Some Versions of Newcomb's Problem Are Prisoners' Dilemmas. SOBEL, Jordan Howard.

The Newcomb Paradox as a Poker Game (in Hebrew). SPECTOR, Raz.

NEWMAN, J

"The Problem of Certitude: Reflections on the Grammar of Assent" in *Thomistic Papers, V*, SULLIVAN, Thomas D.

Tres grandes testigos de la luz interior: San Agustín, san Buenaventura y J Henry Newman. OROZ RETA, José.

NEWS

Ethics and News. MACHAMER, Peter K and BOYLAN, Barbara.

Informing the Public: Ethics, Policy Making, and Objectivity in News Reporting. IANNONE, A Pablo.

NEWTON

Essays on the Context, Nature, and Influence of Isaac Newton's Theology. FORCE, James E (ed).

L'inertie et l'espace-temps absolu de Newton à Einstein. GHINS, Michel.

Particles and Waves: Historical Essays in the Philosophy of Science. ACHINSTEIN, Peter.

Philosophical Perspectives on Newtonian Science. BRICKER, Phillip (ed).

Science and Reason. KYBURG JR, Henry E.

Some Truer Method. DURHAM, Frank (ed).

"The 'Essential Properties' of Matter, Space, and Time: Comments on Michael Friedman" in *Philosophical Perspectives on Newtonian Science*, DI SALLE, Robert.

"Absolute Time versus Absolute Motion: Comments on Lawrence Sklar" in *Philosophical Perspectives on Newtonian Science*, BRICKER, Phillip.

"The Breakdown of the Newtonian Synthesis of Science and Religion: Hume, Newton, and the Royal Society" in *Essays on the Context, Nature, and Influence of Isaac Newton's Theology*, FORCE, James E.

"The Crisis of Polytheism and the Answers of Vossius, Cudworth, and Newton" in *Essays on the Context, Nature, and Influence of Isaac Newton's Theology*, POPKIN, Richard H.

"Ethical Implications of Newtonian Science" in *Philosophical Perspectives on Newtonian Science*, HARRIS, Errol.

"Foils for Newton: Comments on Howard Stein" in *Philosophical Perspectives on Newtonian Science*, ARTHUR, Richard.

"Hume's Interest in Newton and Science" in *Essays on the Context, Nature, and Influence of Isaac Newton's Theology*, FORCE, James E.

"Kant and Newton: Why Gravity Is Essential to Matter" in *Philosophical Perspectives on Newtonian Science*, FRIEDMAN, Michael.

"Making a World of Precision: Newton and the Construction of a Quantitiative World View" in *Some Truer Method*, WESTFALL, Richard S.

"Modern Ethical Theory and Newtonian Science: Comments on Errol Harris" in *Philosophical Perspectives on Newtonian Science*, GRIER, Philip T.

"Newton and Fundamentalism, II" in *Essays on the Context, Nature, and Influence of Isaac Newton's Theology*, POPKIN, Richard H.

"Newton as a Bible Scholar" in *Essays on the Context, Nature, and Influence of Isaac Newton's Theology*, POPKIN, Richard H.

"Newton on Space and Time: Comments on J E McGuire" in *Philosophical Perspectives on Newtonian Science*, CARRIERO, John.

"Newton's 'Mathematical Way' a Century After the *Principia*" in *Some Truer Method*, HANKINS, Thomas L.

"Newton's Corpuscular Query and Experimental Philosophy" in *Philosophical Perspectives on Newtonian Science*, ACHINSTEIN, Peter.

"Newton's God of Dominion: The Unity of Newton's Theological, Scientific, and Political Thought" in *Essays on the Context, Nature, and Influence of Isaac Newton's Theology*, FORCE, James E.

NEWTON
"Newton's Legacy" in *Some Truer Method*, PURRINGTON, Robert D and DURHAM, Frank.
"Newton's Method and Newton's Style" in *Some Truer Method*, COHEN, I Bernard.
"Newton, Nonlinearity and Determinism" in *Some Truer Method*, DURHAM, Frank and PURRINGTON, Robert D.
"Newtonianism Before and After the Einsteinian Revolution" in *Some Truer Method*, AGASSI, Joseph.
"On Locke, 'the Great Huygenius, and the Incomparable Mr. Newton'" in *Philosophical Perspectives on Newtonian Science*, STEIN, Howard.
"Philosophical Perspectives on Newtonian Science" in *Philosophical Perspectives on Newtonian Science*, HUGHES, R I G.
"Polytheism, Deism, and Newton" in *Essays on the Context, Nature, and Influence of Isaac Newton's Theology*, POPKIN, Richard H.
"Predicates of Pure Existence: Newton on God's Space and Time" in *Philosophical Perspectives on Newtonian Science*, MC GUIRE, J E.
"Real Quantities and Their Sensible Measures" in *Philosophical Perspectives on Newtonian Science*, SKLAR, Lawrence.
"Reason and Experiment in Newton's *Opticks*: Comments on Peter Achinstein" in *Philosophical Perspectives on Newtonian Science*, HUGHES, R I G.
"Sir Isaac Newton, 'Gentleman of Wide Swallow'? Newton and the Latitudinarians" in *Essays on the Context, Nature, and Influence of Isaac Newton's Theology*, FORCE, James E.
"Some Further Comments on Newton and Maimonides" in *Essays on the Context, Nature, and Influence of Isaac Newton's Theology*, POPKIN, Richard H.
"Transcending Newton's Legacy" in *Some Truer Method*, STAPP, Henry P.
Adventures of the Concept of Mass and Matter. HELLER, Michael.
Aesthetics and Natural Law in Newton's Methodology. JACQUETTE, Dale.
Il caso "Siris", ovvero la "seconda filosofia" di George Berkeley vescovo di Cloyne. NERI, Luigi.
Consideraciones en torno a la polémica Leibniz-Clarke. PONCE ALBERCA, Carmen.
From Boskovic's Supplements to the Poem of Benedikt Stay (in Serbo-Croatian). D'AGOSTINO, Salvo.
The Justification of Kepler's Ellipse. BAIGRIE, Brian S.
The Fundamental Hypotheses of Mechanics in Lazare N M Carnot's Thought (in Italian). DRAGO, Antonino and MANNO, Salvatore D.
The Phenomenalism of Newton and Boskovic: A Comparative Study (in Serbo-Croatian). PRINCE, Augustus.

NEWTONIANS
"Léon Bloch et Hélène Metzger" in *Études sur/Studies on Hélène Metzger*, BLAY, Michel.
Connectionism, Competence, and Explanation. CLARK, Andy.

NEYMAN, J
Hypothesis Tests and Confidence Intervals in the Single Case. JOHNSTONE, D J.

NICHOLAS OF CUSA
Cusanus and Eriugena. BEIERWALTES, Werner.
Dialectical Thinking in Metaphysics—Van Kues: Coincidental Thinking and the Problem of Idealistic Monism (in German). WINKLER, Norbert.
Platonism and Anti-Platonism in Nicholas of Cusa's Philosophy of Mathematics. HÖSLE, Vittorio.
Rilievi di struttura sul *De deo abscondito* di Nicola Cusano. DELCÒ, Alessandro.

NIEBUHR
Methodological, Epistemological, and Ontological Motifs in the Thought of Reinhold Niebuhr. AYERS, Robert H.

NIELSEN, W
On the Coherence of Historical Materialism. NIELSEN, Kai.

NIETZSCHE
"Also sprach Herakleitos". WOHLFART, Günter.
The Anatomy of Philosophical Style. LANG, Berel.
Being and Becoming: A Critique of Post-Modernism. CENTORE, F F.
Bewusstsein und Natursein. CHO, Kah Kyung.
The Ideas of Ayn Rand. MERRILL, Ronald E.
Irony and the Discourse of Modernity. BEHLER, Ernst.
Language and "The Feminine" in Nietzsche and Heidegger. GRAYBEAL, Jean.
Looking After Nietzsche. RICKELS, Laurence A (ed).
Nietzsche (I and II): The Will to Power as Art, The Eternal Recurrence of the Same—Heidegger. KRELL, David Farrell (trans).
Nietzsche (III and IV): The Will to Power as Knowledge and as Metaphysics—Heidegger. KRELL, David Farrell (ed).
Nietzsche and the Question of Interpretation. SCHRIFT, Alan D.
Nietzsche On Truth and Philosophy. CLARK, Maudemarie.
Nietzsche: A Frenzied Look. ACKERMANN, Robert John.
Nietzsche: The Body and Culture—Philosophy as a Philological Genealogy. BLONDEL, Eric.
Nietzsches Scheitern am Werk. HELLER, Edmund.
Of Memory, Reminiscence, and Writing: On the Verge. KRELL, David Farrell.
The Question of Ethics. SCOTT, Charles E.
Returning to Sils-Maria: A Commentary to Nietzsche's "Also sprach Zarathustra". WHITLOCK, Greg.
The Self-Overcoming of Nihilism: Nishitani Keiji. PARKES, Graham (trans).
"Friedrich Nichte" in *Looking After Nietzsche*, RICKELS, Laurence A.
"History and Mimesis" in *Looking After Nietzsche*, LACOUE-LABARTHE, Philippe.
"How the Fable Becomes a World" in *Looking After Nietzsche*, CANNING, Peter.
"The Mechanized Philosopher" in *Looking After Nietzsche*, KITTLER, Friedrich.
"Metaphoric Architectures" in *Looking After Nietzsche*, KOFMAN, Sarah.
"Namely, Eckermann" in *Looking After Nietzsche*, RONELL, Avital.
"Necessidade e contingência nos primeiros escritos de Nietzsche" in *Dinâmica do Pensar: Homenagem a Oswaldo Market*, NABAIS, Nuno.
"Nietzsche and Merleau-Ponty: The Body as Attitude" in *Abeunt Studia in Mores: A Festschrift for Helga Doblin*, ECKBLAD, Joyce.
"Nietzsche Medused" in *Looking After Nietzsche*, PAUTRAT, Bernard.
"Nietzsche's Thesis on Teleology" in *Looking After Nietzsche*, NANCY, Jean-Luc.
"Nietzsche: Art and Existence" in *XIth International Congress in Aesthetics, Nottingham 1988*, DAVEY, J R N.
"Postmodern Language" in *Postmodernism—Philosophy and the Arts (Continental Philosophy III)*, SCOTT, Charles E.
"Zarathustra and Enlightenment Humanism" in *The Question of Humanism: Challenges and Possibilities*, GOICOECHEA, David.
"Ruminations": Notes de lecture sur quelques aphorismes de Nietzsche. BLONDEL, Eric.
"Sobria ebrietas": Nietzsche y las perpleijidades del espíritu. CRUZ CRUZ, Jua.
The 'Gay Science' of Nietzsche (in Dutch). ESTERHUYSE, Willie.
The 'New' Nietzsche. COOPER, David E.
Aesthetic Authority and Tradition: Nietzsche and the Greeks. STRONG, Tracy B.
The Ambivalent Unthought of the Overman and the Duality of Heidegger's Political Thinking. HAAR, Michel.
La apuesta literaria de Nietzsche. MONTORO, Marcial Moreno.
Aristotle and Nietzsche on Art as Imitation of Nature. DROST, Mark P.
Aristotle or Nietzsche?. FRANKS, Joan M.
Author, Writer, Text: *The Will to Power*. MAGNUS, Bernd.
Autonomy and Quantum Physics: Nietzsche, Heidegger, and Heisenberg. SEIGFRIED, Hans.
Beyond Realism: Nietzsche's New Infinite. CONWAY, Daniel W.
Can Genealogy Be Critical? A Somewhat Unromantic Look at Nietzsche and Foucault. VISKER, Rudi.
Comments: "A Moral Ideal for Everyone and No One". HUNT, Lester.
A Critique of Genealogies. KIM, Chin-Tai.
Deleuze und Spinozas "Ethik". OITTINEN, Vesa.
Derrida, Deconstruction and Nietzsche: The Tree of Knowledge and the Tree of Life. ZELECHOW, Bernard.
Dionysian and Apollonian Pathos of Distance: A New Image of World History. BROWN, David H.
A Dionysian Songbook: the Mysterious Singing. LEVINE, Elliott M.
The Doubleness of the Unthought of the Overman: Ambiguities of Heideggerian Political Thought. HAAR, Michel.
Emerson and Nietzsche's 'Beyond-Man'. STACK, George J.
The Enlightenment—a Stranded Project? Habermas on Nietzsche as a 'Turning Point' to Postmodernity. NAGL, Ludwig.
L'epocalità metafisica di Nietzsche: "Sentiero interrotto" della filosofia heideggeriana. TRAVERSO, Patrizia.
La figure d'Héraclite dans la pensée du jeune Nietzsche. VOELKE, André-Jea.
Foucault, Nietzsche, History: Two Modes of the Genealogical Method. SAX, Benjamin C.
Fragmentos póstumos Friedrich Nietzsche. GIACOIA JUNIOR, Oswaldo.
Friedrich Nietzsche and Classical Philology Today. IRMSCHER, Johannes.
From Philosophy to Politics: On Nietzsche's Ironic Metaphysics of Will to Power. PARENS, Erik.
From Philosophy to Politics: On Nietzsche's Ironic Metaphysics of Will to Power. PARENS, Erik.
Ghost Story (in German). SAUTET, Marc.
Hegel, Marx, Nietzsche, and the Future of Self-Alienation. SCHACHT, Richard.
Hegel, Nietzsche, and Freud on Madness and the Unconscious. BERTHOLD-BOND, Daniel.
Heidegger and Nietzsche—Thinkers of the 'Between'? (in Dutch). GOOSEN, D P.
Heidegger on Nietzsche and Nihilism (in Czechoslovakian). MAJOR, L.
Heidegger und Schopenhauer. HECKER, Hellmuth.
Hierofanías: Una retrospectiva de la obra de Ludwig Schajowicz. KERKHOFF, Manfred.
History and Ontology: A Reading of Nietzsche's Second "Untimely Meditation". BAMBACH, Charles R.
Homer's Contest: Nietzsche on Politics and the State in Ancient Greece. SMITH, Bruce.

NIETZSCHE

How Would an *Übermensch* Regard His Past and Future?. MC INERNEY, Peter K.
Human Rights and Nietzsche. MINEAU, André.
Is Creativity Good?. HALPER, Edward.
Is Friedrich Nietzsche a Precursor to the Holistic Movement?. KREBBS JR, R Stephen.
Kierkegaard, Nietzsche, and the Death of God. NASH, Ronald H.
Kompensierte Moderne. LÖVENICH, F.
Love in *Thus Spoke Zarathustra*. LEVITT, Tom.
Marx, Nietzsche, and the "New Class". EVANS, Fred.
Montinari and Nietzsche's Biography. HOLLINGDALE, R G.
A Moral Ideal for Everyone and No One. CONWAY, Daniel W.
Need, Denial and Abandonment: Heidegger and the Turn. URPETH, James R.
Nietzsche and Ernst Jünger: From Nihilism to Totalitarianism. OHANA, David.
Nietzsche and Fascism. WILLIAMS, Howard.
Nietzsche and Foucault on *Ursprung* and Genealogy. COOK, Deborah.
Nietzsche and Heidegger. LAWRENCE, Joseph P.
Nietzsche and Pessimism: The Metaphysics Hypostatised. CAUCHI, Francesca.
Nietzsche and Post-Modernity. ERICKSON, Stephen A.
Nietzsche and the Critique of Oppositional Thinking. SCHRIFT, Alan D.
Nietzsche and the Cultural Resonance of the 'Death of God'. ROBERTS, Richard H.
Nietzsche and the Philosophy of Scientific Power: Will to Power as Constructive Interpretation. BABICH, Babette E.
Nietzsche and the Woman Question. DIETHE, Carol.
Nietzsche as Colleague. SCHACHT, Richard.
Nietzsche as Instructor in Autonomy? Comments. FOWLER, Mark C.
Nietzsche contra Kant and the Problem of Autonomy. WHITE, Richard.
Nietzsche contra Rousseau: Goethe versus Catilina?. BLONDEL, Eric.
Nietzsche e Spinoza. BIUSO, Alberto G.
Nietzsche in America: Fashion and Fascination. VAN DER WILL, Wilfried.
Nietzsche in Derrida's *Spurs*: Deconstruction as Deracination. FREYDBERG, Bernard D.
Nietzsche on Authenticity. GOLOMB, Jacob.
Nietzsche on Human Nature. SCHACHT, Richard.
Nietzsche on Woman. THOMPSON, J L.
The Nietzsche Temptation in the Thought of Albert Camus. DUVALL, William E.
Nietzsche's "Will to Power" Nachlass. HELLER, Peter.
Nietzsche's Arctic Zone of Cognition and Post-Structuralism. PARENT, David.
Nietzsche's Case for Inequality. GOETHALS, Susanne C.
Nietzsche's Environmental Ethics. HALLMAN, Max O.
Nietzsche's Genealogy: Of Beauty and Community. KEMAL, S.
Nietzsche's Metaperspectivism. ROTH, Robin Alice.
Nietzsche's Use of Atheism. ROTH, Robin Alice.
Nietzsche, Heidegger, and the Critique of Humanism. HODGE, Joanna.
Nietzsche, Socrates and Pragmatism. RORTY, Richard.
Nietzsche: Moralist or Immoralist?—The Verdict of the European Protestant Theologians in the First World War. BAILEY, Charles E.
Nietzsche: The Divination Paradigm of Knowledge in Western Culture. BULHOF, Ilse N.
Nietzschean Perspectivism and the Logic of Practical Reason. REDDING, Paul.
Nihilism and the Impossibility of Political Philosophy. BASINSKI, Paul A.
On the Genealogical Method: Nietzsche and Foucault. SAX, Benjamin C.
On the Question of Nietzsche's "Scientism". GALLO, Beverly E.
Para una metahistoria del narrativisimo. GUARIGLIA, Osvaldo.
The Post-Modern Challenge: From Marx to Nietzsche in the West German Alternative and Green Movement. BETZ, Hans-Georg.
Reading Nietzsche. RISSER, James.
The Role of Music in Nietzsche's *Birth of Tragedy*. HECKMAN, Peter.
Skepticism, Enigma and Integrity: Horizons of Affirmation in Nietzsche's Philosophy. HULL, Robert.
Squaring the Hermeneutical Circle. ROSEN, Stanley.
Suspicion, Deception, and Concealment. ROSEN, Stanley.
A Synthetic Formulation of Nietzsche's Aesthetic Model. JOVANOVSKI, Thomas.
The Evil Beyond Good and Evil (in German). BOLZ, Norbert.
The Other Nietzsche: Criticism of Moral Utopia (in German). MAURER, Reinhart.
The Reception of Nietzsche in Hungary between the Two World Wars (in Hungarian). KISS, Endre.
The Theme of Health in Nietzsche's Thought. LETTERI, Mark.
Thus Spoke Rorty: The Perils of Narrative Self-Creation. CONWAY, Daniel W.
The Transfigurations of Intoxication: Nietzsche, Schopenhauer, and Dionysus. NUSSBAUM, Martha C.
Troeltsch and Nietzsche: Critical Reflections on Ernst Troeltsch's Portrayal of Nietzsche (in German). SCHÜSSLER, Ingeborg.
Verily, Nietzsche's Judgment of Jesus. ROTH, Robin A.
Vie et totalité chez Nietzsche. HAAR, Michel.
La vie, ou le point de rupture: Schopenhauer-Nietzsche. UCCIANI, Louis.
Views on Nietzsche in the GDR (in Hungarian). BOGNAR, Laszlo.
The Vita Femina and Truth. BURNEY-DAVIS, Terri and KREBBS, R Stephen.

NIGERIAN

A Comparison of Nigerian to American Views of Bribery and Extortion in International Commerce. TSALIKIS, John and NWACHUKWU, Osita.
Metaphysics, Religion and Yoruba Traditional Thought. OLADIPO, Olusegun.

NIHILISM

Education as a Human Right: A Theory of Curriculum and Pedagogy. VANDENBERG, Donald.
Looking After Nietzsche. RICKELS, Laurence A (ed).
Modernism as a Philosophical Problem: On the Dissatisfactions of European High Culture. PIPPIN, Robert B.
Morality and Modernity. POOLE, Ross.
Returning to Sils-Maria: A Commentary to Nietzsche's "Also sprach Zarathustra". WHITLOCK, Greg.
The Self-Overcoming of Nihilism: Nishitani Keiji. PARKES, Graham (trans).
A Dionysian Songbook: the Mysterious Singing. LEVINE, Elliott M.
L'epocalità metafisica di Nietzsche: "Sentiero interrotto" della filosofia heideggeriana. TRAVERSO, Patrizia.
Heidegger on Nietzsche and Nihilism (in Czechoslovakian). MAJOR, L.
Hierofanías: Una retrospectiva de la obra de Ludwig Schajowicz. KERKHOFF, Manfred.
El humanismo de Albert Camus. QUESADA, Anabelle.
Is Anything Sacred? Christian Humanism and Christian Nihilism. CUPITT, Don.
Is Friedrich Nietzsche a Precursor to the Holistic Movement?. KREBBS JR, R Stephen.
Kierkegaard, Nietzsche, and the Death of God. NASH, Ronald H.
Nietzsche and Ernst Jünger: From Nihilism to Totalitarianism. OHANA, David.
Nietzsche and Heidegger. LAWRENCE, Joseph P.
Nihilism and the Impossibility of Political Philosophy. BASINSKI, Paul A.
L'odissea dell'ateismo e del nichilismo. FABRO, Cornelio.
La passione dell'essere: Viaggio lungo i sentieri del nulla. IANNOTTA, Daniella.
Prometheus or Cain? Albert Camus's Account of the Western Quest for Justice. WARD, Bruce K.
Troeltsch and Nietzsche: Critical Reflections on Ernst Troeltsch's Portrayal of Nietzsche (in German). SCHÜSSLER, Ingeborg.

NIINILUOTO, I

The Credibility of Extraordinary Events. SCHLESINGER, George N.

NINETEENTH

Additional Letters (Collected Works of John Stuart Mill, Volume XXXII). ROBSON, John M (ed).
American Philosophy and the Romantic Tradition. GOODMAN, Russell B.
Benjamin Constant and the Post-Revolutionary Mind. FONTANA, Biancamaria.
A Cultivated Mind: Essays On J S Mill Presented to John M Robson. LAINE, Michael (ed).
For Self-Examination: Judge for Yourself. HONG, Howard V (ed & trans).
For What May I Hope? Thinking with Kant and Kierkegaard. FENDT, Gene.
Frege in Perspective. WEINER, Joan.
From Hegel to Nietzsche: The Revolution in Nineteenth-Century Thought. LÖWITH, Karl.
Hegel: o la rebelión contra el límite. IZUZQUIZA, Ignacio.
Hegels Theorie des Gesetzes. BOGDANDY, Armin Von.
Indexes to the Collected Works (Collected Works of John Stuart Mill, Vol XXXIII). ROBSON, John M (ed).
The Kernel of Truth in Freud. LAWTON, Philip.
Kierkegaard in Golden Age Denmark. KIRMMSE, Bruce H.
Kierkegaards Phänomenologie der Freiheitserfahrung. DISSE, Jörg.
Looking After Nietzsche. RICKELS, Laurence A (ed).
Nietzsche (I and II): The Will to Power as Art, The Eternal Recurrence of the Same—Heidegger. KRELL, David Farrell (trans).
Nietzsche (III and IV): The Will to Power as Knowledge and as Metaphysics—Heidegger. KRELL, David Farrell (ed).
Nietzsche and the Question of Interpretation. SCHRIFT, Alan D.
Nietzsche: A Frenzied Look. ACKERMANN, Robert John.
Nietzsches Scheitern am Werk. HELLER, Edmund.
Philosophical Fragments. FIRCHOW, Peter (trans).
Returning to Sils-Maria: A Commentary to Nietzsche's "Also sprach Zarathustra". WHITLOCK, Greg.
Statism and Anarchy. SHATZ, Marshall (ed).
Die Wiederkehr im Unterschied. PEETZ, Siegbert.
Works of Love? Reflections on "Works of Love". FENDT, Gene.
'The Appearing God' in Hegel's *Phenomenology of Spirit*. JAMROS, Daniel P.
Ancora una discussione su Hegel: logica, storia, fenomenologia. NUZZO, Angelica.
Charles Renouvier e le scuole di morale in Francia nel XIX secolo. ROSSI, Fabio.

NINETEENTH
Critica della filosofia zoologica per Battista Grassi. MESCHIARI, Alberto.
La disputa sulle origini della neoscolastica italiana: Salvatore Roselli, Vincenzo Buzzetti e Gaetano Sanseverino. SCHMIDINGER, H M.
Dr Chipley's Warning. WHITE, Ronald.
Due note: Ritorni Rosminiani—Il momento di Ugo Spirito. PAOLETTI, Laura.
Empiricism versus Realism: High Points in the Debate During the Past 150 Years. DILWORTH, Craig.
Evolution and Nostalgia in Hegel's Theory of Desire. BERTHOLD-BOND, Daniel.
Experience of the Alien in Husserl's Phenomenology. WALDENFELS, Bernhard.
F M Dostoievsky (1821-1881): Great Existentialist-Psychiatrist. ESSER, P H.
Fault-Lines in Kierkegaard and Hawthorne: *The Sickness unto Death* and "Ethan Brand". BENOIT, Raymond.
Fragmentos póstumos Friedrich Nietzsche. GIACOIA JUNIOR, Oswaldo.
From Philosophy to Politics: On Nietzsche's Ironic Metaphysics of Will to Power. PARENS, Erik.
Hegel's Legend of Self-Determination. KAMAL, Muhammad.
Hegel's *Logic* and Marx's Early Development. PRINCIPE, Michael A.
Hegel, Logic, and Metaphysics. HARTSHORNE, Charles.
Heidegger and the Japanese Connection. BILIMORIA, Purusottama.
Husserl's Presuppositionless Philosophy. REED-DOWNING, Teresa.
The Intellectual Compatibility of Marx and Engels. HUNLEY, J D.
Le lezioni di Husserl sull'etica e sulla teoria del valore. DONNICI, Rocco.
Love in *Thus Spoke Zarathustra*. LEVITT, Tom.
Montinari and Nietzsche's Biography. HOLLINGDALE, R G.
Moral Philosophy at West Point in the Nineteenth Century. SHIVE, Kenneth D.
La neoscolastica italiana dalle sue prime manifestazioni all'enciclica *Aeterni Patris*. ROSSI, G F.
Nietzsche and Pessimism: The Metaphysics Hypostatised. CAUCHI, Francesca.
Nietzsche e Spinoza. BIUSO, Alberto G.
Nietzsche's Case for Inequality. GOETHALS, Susanne C.
Nietzsche's Use of Atheism. ROTH, Robin Alice.
Orthodoxy or Atheism? Remarks on the New Edition of Hegel's Lectures on Religion (in Hungarian). MOLNÁR, László M.
Peirce's Haecceitism. DI LEO, Jeffrey R.
Political Self-Education of the English Working Class. PEPPERELL, Keith C.
La prima e seconda edizione della "Geschichte des Materialismus" di Friedrich Albert Lange. COGNETTI, Giuseppe.
Reading Nietzsche. RISSER, James.
Schelling on Hegel: From his Lectures in Munich and Berlin (in Hungarian). FEHÉR, I.
Het Schellingonderzoek op nieuwe wegen. BRAECKMAN, A.
Schopenhauer and Hegel (in Hebrew). SIGAD, Ran.
The Scottish Influence on French Aesthetic Thought: Later Developments. MANNS, James W.
Semantica della "Vorstellung" e valore della teoria in *Erkenntnis und Irrtum* di Ernst Mach. BELLOMO, Andrea.
Las situaciones objetivas en las *Investigaciones Lógicas* de Edmundo Husserl. MULLIGAN, Kevin.
Skepticism, Enigma and Integrity: Horizons of Affirmation in Nietzsche's Philosophy. HULL, Robert.
La storia universale come storia comparata in Max Weber. DI MARCO, Giuseppe Antonio.
Suspicion, Deception, and Concealment. ROSEN, Stanley.
Lo sviluppo degli studi logici nel pensiero tedesco della seconda metà dell' '800. MANGIAGALLI, Maurizio.
La teoria hegeliana dell'autocoscienza e della sua razionalità. VARNIER, Giuseppe.
The Beginning and Structure of the "Phaenomenology of Mind" (in Hungarian). PÖGGELER, Otto.
The Concept of "Foundation" in Schelling (in Hungarian). VETO, Miklos.
The Theme of Health in Nietzsche's Thought. LETTERI, Mark.
Time in Hegel's *Phenomenology of Spirit*. FLAY, Joseph C.
Tory History Incognito: Hume's *History of England* in Goldsmith's *History of England*. KENNELLY, Laura B.
Towards a Potential-Pragmatic Account of Peirce's Theory of Truth. SFENDONI-MENTZOU, Demetra.
Tra Kant e Hegel: per una riaffermazione dell'antico concetto di società civile. MARINI, Giuliano.
The Transfigurations of Intoxication: Nietzsche, Schopenhauer, and Dionysus. NUSSBAUM, Martha C.

NIRVANA
Mind Only: A Philosophical and Doctrinal Analysis of the Vijñānavāda. WOOD, Thomas E.

NISHITANI, K
Religion, Nothingness, and the Challenge of Post-Modern Thought: An Introduction to the Philosophy of K Nishitani. JAMES, George A.

NOBLE SAVAGE
Diderot's Dream. ANDERSON, Wilda.

NOEL, J
Practical Reasoning in Teaching: A Response to Jana Noel. PENDLEBURY, Shirley.

NOEMA
Noema and Meaning in Husserl. FOLLESDAL, Dagfinn.

NOETHER, E
Mathématiques et ontologie: les symétries en physique. BOUTOT, Alain.

NOMINALISM
Physicalism in Mathematics. IRVINE, Andrew D (ed).
Properties as Processes: A Synoptic Study of Wilfried Sellars' Nominalism. SEIBT, Johanna.
"Belief, Nominalism, and Quantification" in *Philosophical Perspectives, 4: Action Theory and Philosophy of Mind, 1990*, TOMBERLIN, James E.
"Epistemology and Nominalism" in *Physicalism in Mathematics*, BURGESS, John P.
"The Logic of Physical Theory" in *Physicalism in Mathematics*, URQUHART, Alasdair.
"Nominalism, Usury, and Bourgeois Man" in *Freedom in the Modern World: Jacques Maritain, Yves R Simon, Mortimer J Adler*, MANCINI, Matthew J.
"Nominalism" in *Physicalism in Mathematics*, HALE, Bob.
"Physicalistic Platonism" in *Physicalism in Mathematics*, MADDY, Penelope.
Fideísmo y autoritarismo en Lutero. CAPPELLETTI, Angel.
Nominalism and Abstract Reference. MORELAND, J P.
Once Again the Ockhamist Statutes of 1339 and 1340: Some New Perspectives. THIJSSEN, J M M H.
Two Anonymous 12th-Century Tracts on Universals. DIJS, Judith.
Universals and Predication of Species. PETERSON, John.

NOMOLOGICAL
Nomic Probability and the Foundations of Induction. POLLOCK, John L.

NON-EUCLIDEAN
Kants Theorie der geometrischen Erkenntnis und die nichteuklikische Geometrie. SCHIRN, Matthias.

NONBEING
Être et non-être chez Aristote: contraires ou contradictoires?. BERTI, Enrico.
Fondamento e verità. CAMPANALE, Domenico.
L'être du non-être en perspective aristotélicienne. DE MURALT, André.
La logique du mythe et la question du non-être. COULOUBARITSIS, Lambros.
La notion de non-être dans l'histoire de la langue grecque archaïque. LÉTOUBLON, Françoise.
La question de l'être et du non-être des objets mathématiques chez Plotin et Jamblique. O'MEARA, Dominic.
Riflessioni sulla fondazione dell'assioma parmenideo. GRAZIANI, Andrea.
Sur une façon stoïcienne de ne pas être. BRUNSCHWIG, Jacques.
Vide et non-être chez Leucippe et Démocrite. VOELKE, André-Jean.

NONCOGNITIVISM
A Defense of Ethical Noncognitivism. COBURN, Robert C.

NONCOMBATANT(S)
The Making of a Nuclear Peace: The Task of Today's Just War Theorists. SICHOL, Marcia W.

NONCOMPLIANCE
Noncompliance in AIDS Research. ARRAS, John D.

NONCONTRADICTION
Does Aristotle Beg the Question in His Defense of the Principle of Non-Contradiction?. DEGNAN, Michael.
La justificación práctica del principio de no contradicción en Aristóteles. CASSINI, A.
Naturaleza, espíritu, finalidad. ALARCÓN, Enrique.
Variações sobre o *De Interpretatione*, de Aristóteles. ROSA, Joaquim Coelho.

NONCOOPERATION
Binary 2 x 2 Games. FISHBURN, Peter C and KILGOUR, D Marc.

NONEXISTENCE
The Existence of Non-Existence of Things which are Not in the Mind. POMERANTZ, Alfred.

NONIDENTITY
The Recurring Problem of the Third Man. HALES, Steven D.

NONMONOTONIC
"Non-Monotonic Reasoning by Axiomatic Extensions" in *Logic, Methodology and Philosophy of Science, VIII*, JÄGER, Gerhard.
On Theories of Non-Monotonic Consequence Operations II. FIJALKOWSKA, Dorota and FIJALKOWSKI, Jan.

NONMORAL
Hume's Place in Moral Philosophy. CAPALDI, Nicholas.

NONSENSE
Moore's Paradox Revisited. LINVILLE, Kent and RING, Merrill.
A Note on Matrices for Systems of Nonsense-Logics. HALKOWSKA, Katarzyna.

NONSTANDARD ANALYSIS
Set Theoretic Properties of Loeb Measure. MILLER, Arnold W.
Some Nonstandard Methods Applied to Distributive Lattices. GEHRKE, Mai and INSALL, Matt and KAISER, Klaus.
The Special Model Axiom in Nonstandard Analysis. ROSS, David.

NONSTANDARD MODELS
Nonstandard Arithmetic of Hilbert Subsets. YASUMOTO, Masahiro.
Sub-Arithmetical Ultrapowers: A Survey. MC LAUGHLIN, Thomas G.

NONVIOLENCE
Civil Disobedience in Focus. BEDAU, Hugo Adam (ed).
Nonviolence in Theory and Practice. HOLMES, Robert L.
Yoga on War and Peace. TIGUNAIT, Pandit Rajmani.
"Gandhi's Quest for a Nonviolent Political Philosophy" in *Celebrating Peace*, PAREKH, Bhikhu.
"Loving One's Enemies" in *In the Interest of Peace: A Spectrum of Philosophical Views*, GAN, Barry.
"Nonviolent Resistance as the Moral Equivalent of War" in *In the Interest of Peace: A Spectrum of Philosophical Views*, CHURCHILL, R Paul.
"Toward Understanding the Pragmatics of Absolute Pacifism" in *In the Interest of Peace: A Spectrum of Philosophical Views*, KOHL, Marvin.
El pensamiento filosófico de Martin Luther King, Jr. STERLING, Marvin C.

NORM(S)
The Communicative Ethics Controversy. BENHABIB, Seyla (ed).
Intelligibility in Science. DILWORTH, Craig (ed).
Die Moral der Vernunft Tanszendentale Handlungs-und Legitimationstheorie in der Philosophie Kants. SANDERMANN, Edmund.
Practical Reason and Norms. RAZ, Joseph.
Wahrheit—Diskurs—Demokratie: Studien zur "Konsensustheorie der Wahrheit". SCHEIT, Herbert.
"Content and Norms in a Natural World" in *Information, Semantics and Epistemology*, PEACOCKE, Christopher.
"Meaning—Norms and Objectivity" in *Logic and Ethics*, JACK, Julie.
"Rationality and Social Norms" in *Logic, Methodology and Philosophy of Science, VIII*, ELSTER, Jon.
An Antinomy in Kelsen's Pure Theory of Law. BULYGIN, Eugenio.
Business Ethics and Extant Social Contracts. DUNFEE, Thomas W.
Conventional Foundationalism and the Origins of the Norms. CUDD, Ann E.
Éthique et Morale. RICOEUR, Paul.
Etica e morale: mira teleogica e prospettiva deontologica. RICOEUR, Paul.
Logic Without Truth. ALCHOURRÓN, Carlos E and MARTINO, Antonio A.
New Operators for Theory Change. HANSSON, Sven.
Normas, sistemas jurídicos y eficacia. NAVARRO, Pablo Eugenio.
Der Normgeltungsbegriff als probabilistischer Begriff: Zur Logik des soziologischen Normbegriffs. LÜBBE, Weyma.
Norms and Values. HANSSON, Sven Ove.
On Ideal Form, Empowering Norms, and "Normative Functions". PAULSON, Stanley L.
On the Nature and Norms of Theoretical Commitment. HORWICH, Paul.
Protective Norms as a Basis for Cooperation between Non-Privileged Constituencies. HEDMAN, Carl.
La ragione e i valori nella determinazione delle norme. CORTESE, Roberto.
Specifying Norms as a Way to Resolve Concrete Ethical Problems. RICHARDSON, Henry S.

NORMAL
B-Varieties with Normal Free Algebras. TEMBROWSKI, Bronislaw.
General Canonical Models for Graded Normal Logics (Graded Modalities IV). CERRATO, C.
Kernels in N-Normal Symmetric Heyting Algebras. GALLI, A and SAGASTUME, M.
N-Normal Factors in Finite Symmetric Heyting Algebras. GALLI, Adriana C and SAGASTUME, Marta.

NORMALIZATION
On Certain Normalizable Natural Deduction Formulations of Some Propositional Intermediate Logics. BORICIC, Branislav R.

NORMAN, W
Response to W J Norman's "Has Rational Economic Man a Heart". LA CASSE, Chantale and ROSS, Don.

NORMATIVE
Epistemics. DURAN, Jane.
Fonti diritto e regole. DE GIACOMO, Claudio.
"Biosemantics and the Normative Properties of Thought" in *Philosophical Perspectives, 3: Philosophy of Mind and Action Theory, 1989*, FORBES, Graeme.
"The Deductive Model in Ethics" in *Logic and Ethics*, LAZARI-PAWLOWSKA, Ija.
"Does Meaning Matter?" in *Information, Semantics and Epistemology*, DRETSKE, Frederick.
"Normative Aesthetics and Contemporary Art: Bürger's Critique of Adorno" in *XIth International Congress in Aesthetics, Nottingham 1988*, ZUIDERVAART, Lambert.
"Research Programmes and Paradigms as Dialogue Structures" in *Imre Lakatos and Theories of Scientific Change*, KOUTOUGOS, Aris.
"The Return of Stage 6: Its Principle and Moral Point of View" in *The Moral Domain: Essays in the Ongoing Discussion between Philosophy and the Social Sciences*, BOYD, Dwight R and KOHLBERG, Lawrence and LEVINE, Charles.
Feminist Second Thoughts About Free Agency. BENSON, Paul.
Firth and the Ethics of Belief. CHISHOLM, Roderick M.
The Morality of Killing and Causing Suffering: Reasons for Rejecting Peter Singer's Pluralistic Consequentialism. LANDMAN, Willem A.
A Normative Theory of Teaching. POPP, Jerome.
Normativity and the Very Idea of Moral Epistemology. COPP, David.
Si la filosofía política es ciencia práctica. DONADÍO MAGGI, María C.
Some Recent Work in Epistemology. MOSER, Paul K.
Stephen P Stich, "The Fragmentation of Reason". GOLDMAN, Alvin I.
Wovor und wodurch sind wir verantworlich? Die Instanzen der Verantwortung. MAIER, Maria.

NORMATIVE DISCOURSE
A Pragma-Dialectical Perspective on Norms. VAN EEMEREN, Frans H.

NORMATIVE ETHICS
Reasons for Living: A Basic Ethics. PORTER, Burton F.
Universalism versus Communitarianism: Contemporary Debates in Ethics. RASMUSSEN, David.
"Natural Law" in *A Companion to Ethics*, BUCKLE, Stephen.
A New Approach in Moral Theory (in Dutch). KETTNER, Matthias.
Acceptance of Others and Concern for Oneself (in French). MULLER, Denis.
Can Utilitarianism Be Salvaged as a Theory for Social Choice?. VAN ASPEREN, G M.
Common-Sense Morality. BROCK, Dan.
Virtue Ethics and Maori Ethics. PERRETT, Roy W and PATTERSON, John.

NORMATIVE JUDGMENT(S)
Critical Interaction: Judgment, Decision, and the Social Testing of Moral Hypotheses. IANNONE, A P.
A Decision-Theoretic Reconstruction of *Roe v Wade*. LOCKHART, Ted.
Deconstructing Community Self-Paternalism. SCHONSHECK, Jonathan.
Going Nowhere: Nagel on Normative Objectivity. FRIEDMAN, Marilyn.
La speranza nel giusnaturalismo. TUSA, Carlo.

NORTH AMERICAN
North American, British and Australian Philosophy of Education from 1941 to 1991: Links, Trends, Prospects. BECK, Clive.

NOTATIONALITY
The Aesthetics of Imperfection. HAMILTON, Andy.

NOTHING
"The Shadow of Hegel's *Science of Logic*" in *Essays on Hegel's Logic*, WILLETT, Cynthia.

NOTHINGNESS
Behind the Masks of God: An Essay Toward Comparative Theology. NEVILLE, Robert Cummings.
Jean-Paul Sartre. HENGELBROCK, Jürgen.
Los fundamentos de la especulación metafísica sobre el conocimiento. SACCHI, Mario E.
Heidegger und die Frage um die Quelle des Grundbegriffes der Metaphysik (in Polish). ROZDZENSKI, R.
Nothingness and Responsibility (in Czechoslovakian). HEJDANEK, L.
Religion, Nothingness, and the Challenge of Post-Modern Thought: An Introduction to the Philosophy of K Nishitani. JAMES, George A.
We Mortals. LINGIS, Alphonso.

NOTION(S)
Cálculo y ser (Aproximación a Leibniz). MARZOA, Felipe Martínez.
"Fodor's Character" in *Information, Semantics and Epistemology*, SCHIFFER, Stephen.
Self-Notions. PERRY, John.
What Berkeley's Notions Are. LEE, Richard N.

NOUMENALISM
The Unity of Kant's "Critique of Pure Reason": Experience, Language, and Knowledge. WILLIAMS, T C.

NOUN PHRASE(S)
Noun Phrases, Quantifiers, and Generic Names. LOWE, E J.
Phrases nominales énonciatives et phrases verbales. STAHL, Gérold.

NOUN(S)
"Bare Plurals as Plural Indefinite Noun Phrases" in *Knowledge Representation and Defeasible Reasoning*, GILLON, Brendan.

NOUS
The *Nous*-Body Problem in Aristotle. MODRAK, Deborah K W.

NOVALIS
The Academic Lehrjahre of Novalis—A Period of Search for His Own View of History (in Polish). JAKUSZKO, Honorata.

NOVEL
"Dialogism in the Novel and Bakhtin's Theory of Culture" in *XIth International Congress in Aesthetics, Nottingham 1988*, SHEVTSOVA, Maria.
"'Aufbruch oder Schwanengesang'?" in *XIth International Congress in Aesthetics, Nottingham 1988*, KRENZLIN, Norbert.

NOVEL

"They Read Novels, Don't They?" Using Novels in Teaching Philosophy. BOWLDEN, Larry S.
Alternatives et questions dans la littérature romanesque. COMETTI, Jean-Pierre.
The Concert: Mao's Panopticon. TALMOR, Sascha.
The Satanic Novel: A Philosophical Dialogue on Blasphemy and Censorship. SPRIGGE, T L S.

NOW

Examen del "ahora". HUÉSCAR, Antonio R.

NOZICK, R

Robert Nozick: Property, Justice, and the Minimal State. WOLFF, Jonathan.
Les "droits naturels" et les "titres" selon Robert Nozick. SWEET, William.
No Moral Responsibility Without Alternative Possibilities. WEBBER, May A.
Nozick et la stabilité des principes de justice distributive. BÉGIN, Luc.
Nozick on Rights and Minimal State. AGARWALA, Binod Kumar.
Nozick on Social Justice. AGARWALA, Binod Kumar.
Nozick's Identity Crisis. LUCY, W N R.
Property, Entitlement, and Remedy. PAUL, Jeffrey.
Self-Synthesis, Self-Knowledge, and Skepticism. MAZOUÉ, James G.
Unfair to Nozick. BRUECKNER, Anthony.
Why Do I Love Thee? A Response to Nozick's Account of Romantic Love. SMITH, Tara.

NUCLEAR DETERRENCE

"Marxism and Nuclear Deterrence" in *Issues in War and Peace: Philosophical Inquiries*, HAMPSCH, George H.
"Nuclear Deterrence and the Limits of Moral Theory" in *Issues in War and Peace: Philosophical Inquiries*, WERNER, Richard.
"Political Theology and the Ethics of Peace" in *Celebrating Peace*, MOLTMANN, Jürgen.
Nuclear Deterrence and the Morality of Intentions. KULTGEN, John.

NUCLEAR WAR

The Making of a Nuclear Peace: The Task of Today's Just War Theorists. SICHOL, Marcia W.
"Conscience, Citizenship, and the Nuclear State" in *In the Interest of Peace: A Spectrum of Philosophical Views*, WOODWARD, Beverly.
"Deterrence or Disarmament: An Appraisal of Consequentialist Arguments" in *In the Interest of Peace: A Spectrum of Philosophical Views*, KUNKEL, Joseph.
"Experiencing the Death of Humanity" in *Issues in War and Peace: Philosophical Inquiries*, GINSBERG, Robert.
"Nuclearism and Sexism: Overcoming Their Shared Metaphysical Basis" in *Issues in War and Peace: Philosophical Inquiries*, SMITHKA, Paula.
"The Russell-Hook Debates of 1958: Arguments from the Extremes on Nuclear War and the Soviet Union" in *In the Interest of Peace: A Spectrum of Philosophical Views*, GAY, William.
"Skepticism and International Affairs: Toward a New Realism" in *Issues in War and Peace: Philosophical Inquiries*, GROARKE, Leo.
"What Does Philosophy Add to Nuclear Discussions? An Introductory Essay" in *Issues in War and Peace: Philosophical Inquiries*, KUNKEL, Joseph and KLEIN, Kenneth.

NUCLEAR WASTE(S)

Congress, Consistency, and Environmental Law. LEMONS, John and BROWN, Donald A and VARNER, Gary E.

NUCLEAR WEAPON(S)

Military Ethics: Looking Toward the Future. FOTION, Nicholas G.
"Conservative and Radical Critiques of Nuclear Policy" in *Issues in War and Peace: Philosophical Inquiries*, LITKE, Robert.
"Democracy and the Threat of Nuclear Weapons" in *Issues in War and Peace: Philosophical Inquiries*, CHURCHILL, R Paul.
"From Nuclear Winter to Hiroshima: Nuclear Weapons and the Environment" in *Issues in War and Peace: Philosophical Inquiries*, GAY, William.
"Nuclear Abolition and the Fear of Cheating" in *In the Interest of Peace: A Spectrum of Philosophical Views*, PERKINS JR, Raymond.
"On the Implications of Sociobiology for Nuclear Weapons Policy" in *Issues in War and Peace: Philosophical Inquiries*, SCHONSHECK, Jonathan.
"Strategy: A New Era?" in *The Tanner Lectures On Human Values, Volume XII*, LUTTWAK, Edward N.
Nuclear Stalemate: A Superior Escape from the Dilemmas of Deterrence. SCHONSHECK, Jonathan.

NULL CLASS

Small Sets. HAZEN, A P.

NUMBER THEORY

Rationality of *p*-Adic Poincaré Series: Uniformity in *p*. MACINTYRE, Angus.

NUMBER(S)

see also Cardinals, Ordinals
Frege in Perspective. WEINER, Joan.
"The Standard of Equality of Numbers" in *Meaning and Method: Essays in Honor of Hilary Putnam*, BOOLOS, George.
An Alleged Analogy Between Numbers and Propositions. CRANE, Tim.
Arithmetizing Uniform *NC*. ALLEN, B.
A Constructive Version of Sperner's Lemma and Brouwer's Fixed Point Theorem. KHALIFA, A K.
Equational Theory of Positive Numbers with Exponentiation is Not Finitely Axiomatizable. GUREVIC, R.
Erasing and Redrawing the Number Line: An Exercise in Rationality. SPARROW, Edward G.
Expressions versus Numbers. WETZEL, Linda.
Frege and Husserl on Number. TIESZEN, Richard.
Mathematics and Oliver Twist. MADDY, Penelope.
The Meaning of Δυναμισ at *Timaeus* 31c. PRITCHARD, Paul.
On the "Arriving at Principles from Numbers" Method of Thought in the Late-Ming, Early-Qing Period. WEIPING, Chen.
On the Completeness of a Certain System of Arithmetic of Whole Numbers in Which Addition Occurs as the Only Operation. PRESBURGER, Mojzesz and JACQUETTE, Dale.
Ramsey Ultrafilters and the Reaping Number—Con($\mathbf{r} < \mathbf{u}$). GOLDSTERN, M and SHELAH, S.

NURSE(S)

Biomedical Ethics Reviews, 1987. HUMBER, James M (ed).
"The Legacy of Baby Doe: Nurses' Ethical and Legal Obligations to Severely Handicapped Newborns" in *Biomedical Ethics Reviews, 1987*, MARTIN, Darlene Aulds.
"The Nurse's Role: Responsibilities and Rights" in *Biomedical Ethics Reviews, 1987*, FOWLER, Marsha D M.
Nurses and Physicians on Nutritional Support: A Comparison. LIASCHENKO, Joan and DAVIS, Anne J.
Nursing Ethics: Current State of the Art. FRY, Sara T.

NURSING

Ethics in Nursing: An Anthology. PENCE, Terry.
A Comment on Fry's "The Role of Caring in a Theory of Nursing Ethics". BOYER, Jeannine Ross and NELSON, James Lindemann.
Conceptual Issues in Nursing Ethics Research. PENTICUFF, Joy Hinson.
Nursing Responsibility for the Placebo Effect. CONNELLY, Robert J.

NURSING HOME(S)

New Directions in Nursing Home Ethics. COLLOPY, Bart and BOYLE, Philip and JENNINGS, Bruce.

NUSSBAUM, M

Rethinking Feminist Humanism. STRAUS, Nina Pelikan.

NUTRITION

Comment on Hospice of Washington's Policy. ROBERTSON, John A.
Development of an Institutional Policy on Artificial Hydration and Nutrition. KOSHUTA, Monica A and SCHMITZ, Phyllis J and LYNN, Joanne.
Nurses and Physicians on Nutritional Support: A Comparison. LIASCHENKO, Joan and DAVIS, Anne J.
Nutrition, Hydration, and the Demented Elderly. POST, Stephen G.
Reply to Weir: Unnecessary Fear, Nutrition, and Vegetarianism. SAPONTZIS, Steve F.
Response to Sapontzis's Reply. WEIR, Jack.
Unnecessary Pain, Nutrition, and Vegetarianism. WEIR, Jack.

NYAYA

A Critique of Jayarasi's Critique of Perception. MOHANTA, D K.
Dehātmavāda or the Body as Soul: Exploration of a Possibility within Nyāya Thought. LATH, Mukund (trans) and SHUKLA, Pandit Badrinath.
In Search of a Theory of Truth in Nyāya. SAHA, Sukharanjan.
On the Causality of Sky. MISHRA, Aruna Ranjan.

O'BRIEN, W

The Making of a Nuclear Peace: The Task of Today's Just War Theorists. SICHOL, Marcia W.

O'HEAR, A

Peirce and Evolution: Comment on O'Hear. GOMILA, Antoni.

OAKESHOTT, M

The Political Philosophy of Michael Oakeshott. FRANCO, Paul.

OATH(S)

Non-Technical *Pisteis* in Aristotle and Anaximenes. MIRHADY, David.

OBEDIENCE

Leviathan: Hobbes. TUCK, Richard (ed).
L'interpretazione del conflitto fra norme nell'ultimo Kelsen. CELANO, Brun.
Method and Message: Commentary on the Future of Philosophy of Education. DENTON, David E.
Sovranità e obbedienza. CATANIA, Alfonso.

OBJECT(S)

Human Consciousness. HANNAY, Alastair.
L'objet-peinture: Pour une théorie de la réception. PAQUIN, Nycole.
Mathematics and the Image of Reason. TILES, Mary E.
The Secret Connexion: Causation, Realism, and David Hume. STRAWSON, Galen.
Self and Non-Self: The Drigdrisyaviveka Attributed to Samkara. RAPHAEL (trans).
The Unity of Understanding: A Study in Kantian Problems. SCHWYZER, Hubert.
"Beliefs About Mathematical Objects" in *Physicalism in Mathematics*, RESNIK, Michael D.

OBLIGATION(S)
Obligation and Knowledge (in French). SCHULTHESS, Daniel.
Parental Obligations and the Ethics of Surrogacy: A Causal Perspective. NELSON, James Lindemann.
The Professional's Dilemma: Choosing Between Service and Success. MC DOWELL, Banks.
The Revenger's Paradox. HANSSON, Sven Ove.
Some Recent Work in Epistemology. MOSER, Paul K.
El tratado de las obligaciones dialógicas en la Edad Media: el caso de Robert Fland. BEUCHOT, Mauricio.
Tu scis regem sedere. D'ORS, Angel.
Work and Family: Should Parents Feel Guilty?. PAINE, Lynn Sharp.

OBSCENITY
Artistic Freedom: An Art World Paradox. LANKFORD, E Louis.

OBSERVABILITY
Dimensions of Observability. KOSSO, Peter.

OBSERVABLES
On Saving the Phenomena and the Mice: A Reply to Bourgeois Concerning Van Fraassen's Image of Science. FOSS, Jeff.

OBSERVATION SENTENCE(S)
Quine on Theory and Language. TANJI, Nobuharu.

OBSERVATION(S)
Science and Reason. KYBURG JR, Henry E.
"Contrastive Empiricism" in *Scientific Theories*, SOBER, Elliott.
Believing What We Do Not See: The Case Against van Fraassen's Conception of Observation. DOBSON, Andrew.
Can a Theory-Laden Observation Test the Theory?. FRANKLIN, A (and others).
Una discussione di epistemologia. BLANDINO, Giovanni and FEDERSPIL, G.
Externalism and Experience. MC CULLOCH, Gregory.
Observation: An Empirical Discussion. GILMAN, Daniel.
Positivism and the Pragmatic Theory of Observation. OBERDAN, Thomas.

OCCASIONALISM
Causalistico-Occasionalistic Dispute in Islam as Opposing of "Greek" and "Islamic" Spirit (in Serbo-Croatian). BUCAN, Daniel.

OCCIDENTAL
Geschichte, Freiheit und Struktur. RUMPEL, Roland.
The Relevance of Meditative Thinking. ERICKSON, Stephen A.
Respect for Persons and Self-Respect: Western and Indian. GHOSH-DASTIDAR, Koyeli.
Respect for Privacy: Western and Indian. GHOSH-DASTIDAR, Koyeli.
The State of Studies on Western Philosophy in China. FANG-TONG, Liu.
Über den Versuch einer philosophiegeschichtlichen Klassifikation der Lehre Nāgārjunas. TOMASCHITZ, Wolfgang.

OCKHAM
The Dilemma of Freedom and Foreknowledge. ZAGZEBSKI, Linda Trinkaus.
Philosophical Writings: A Selection—William of Ockham. BOEHNER, Philotheus (ed & trans).
Marsilius on Rights. TIERNEY, Brian.
A New Foreknowledge Dilemma. ZAGZEBSKI, Linda.
Ockham, Adams and Connotation: A Critical Notice of Marilyn Adams, *William Ockham*. SPADE, Paul Vincent.
Once Again the Ockhamist Statutes of 1339 and 1340: Some New Perspectives. THIJSSEN, J M M H.
Ontological Reductionism and Faith Versus Reason: A Critique of Adams on Ockham. FREDDOSO, Alfred J.
La teoría de la ciencia de Guillermo de Ockham: una imagen prospectiva. LARRE, Olga and BOLZÁN, J E.
La teoría de las cualidades sensibles en la *Summula Philosophiae Naturalis* atribuida a Guillermo de Ockham. LARRE, Olga L.
La teoría del tiempo en Ockham y la autenticidad de la *Summulae in Libros Physicorum*. LARRE, Olga L and BOLZÁN, J E.
Wilhelm von Ockham: Das Risiko, mittelalterlich zu denken. PERLER, Dominik.

ODDIE, G
Verisimilitude by Power Relations: A Response to Oddie. BRINK, Chris and HEIDEMA, Johannes.

OGDEN, S
The Experience of Value and Theological Argumentation. DEVENISH, Philip E.

OKIN, S
Rethinking the Family. KYMLICKA, Will.

OLD TESTAMENT
"Deconstructing the Book of Job" in *The Bible as Rhetoric: Studies in Biblical Persuasion and Credibility*, CLINES, David.
"History and Rhetoric in the Prophets" in *The Bible as Rhetoric: Studies in Biblical Persuasion and Credibility*, BARTON, John.
The Structure of Philo's Commentary on the Pentateuch. THORNE, Gary W A.

OLIVE, L
Sobre justificación y verdad: respuesta a León Olivé. VILLORO, Luis.

OLIVIER, G
Interrupting Olivier's Socio-Political Conversation: Another Postmodern Proposal. ALLEN, J G.
Olivier's Postmodern Proposal: A Few Comments. LÖTTER, H P P.
A Response to Olivier's Postmodern, but Pre-South African Proposal. ROSSOUW, G.

OMISSION(S)
Between the Horns of the Negative-Positive Duty Debate. MALM, H M.

OMNIPOTENCE
Dieu tout-puissant et souffrant. RICHARD, Jean.
Omnipotence Need Not Entail Omniscience. SONTAG, Frederick.
La toute-puissance du Dieu du théisme dans le champ de la perversion. ANSALDI, Jean.

OMNISCIENCE
Mind Only: A Philosophical and Doctrinal Analysis of the Vijñānavāda. WOOD, Thomas E.
Agency and Omniscience. KAPITAN, Tomis.
Divine Foresight and Human Moral Responsibility (in Hebrew). BAR-ON, A Zvie.
In Defence of Theological Compatibilism. FLINT, Thomas P.
Omnipotence Need Not Entail Omniscience. SONTAG, Frederick.
Omniscience, Immutability, and the Divine Mode of Knowing. SULLIVAN, Thomas D.
On Omniscience and a 'Set of All Truths': A Reply to Bringsjord. GRIM, Patrick.
Time, Actuality and Omniscience. LEFTOW, Brian.

OMNIVORE
So Animal a Human..., or the Moral Relevance of Being An Omnivore. GEORGE, Kathryn Paxton.

ONE
Plotin: Traité sur la liberté et la volonté de l'Un. LEROUX, Georges.
Accent on *One*: Entity and Identity. BOLINGER, Dwight.
Thinking of Unity (in Dutch). AERTSEN, Jan A.

ONTOLOGICAL COMMITMENT(S)
"Ontological Commitment: Thick and Thin" in *Meaning and Method: Essays in Honor of Hilary Putnam*, HODES, Harold T.
'Ontological Commitment' in the Context of the Buddhist Thought. MITTAL, Kewal Krisha.

ONTOLOGICAL DIFFERENCE
Natural Complex versus Natural System. KHALIL, Elias L.

ONTOLOGICAL PROOF
The Caterus Objection. FORGIE, J William.
Creation, Creativity and Necessary Being. HUGHES, Martin.
Makin on the Ontological Argument. OPPY, Graham.
The Modal Ontological Argument and the Necessary A Posteriori. FORGIE, J W.
Spinoza, Heidegger, and the Ontological Argument. SINGER, Brent A.
La tensione tra possibilità e necessità nell'argomento ontologico di Leibniz. NICOLOSI, Salvatore.
Universe Indexed Properties and the Fate of the Ontological Argument. SENNETT, James F.
Visione in Dio e visione di Dio nella filosofia di Malebranche. NICOLOSI, Salvatore.

ONTOLOGICAL RELATIVITY
"Ontological Relativity in Quine and Davidson" in *The Mind of Donald Davidson*, MALPAS, J E.

ONTOLOGY
see also Being, Dasein, Existence, Metaphysics
Being-in-the-World: A Commentary on Heidegger's "Being and Time", Division 1. DREYFUS, Hubert L.
Between Freiburg and Frankfurt: Toward a Critical Ontology. DALLMAYR, Fred R.
Dinâmica do Pensar: Homenagem a Oswaldo Market. FAC LETRAS UNIV LISBOA (ed).
Echoes: After Heidegger. SALLIS, John.
Expressionism in Philosophy: Spinoza. DELEUZE, Gilles.
French Philosophers in Conversation: Levinas, Schneider, Serres, Irigaray, Le Doeuff, Derrida. MORTLEY, Raoul.
George Santayana y la Ironia de la Materia. IZUZQUIZA, Ignacio.
Hegel: o la rebelión contra el límite. IZUZQUIZA, Ignacio.
History and the Paradoxes of Metaphysics in "Dantons Tod". TAYLOR, Rodney.
Hope and Its Hieroglyph: A Critical Decipherment of Ernst Bloch's "Principle of Hope". ROBERTS, Richard H.
I, We and Body: First Joint Symposium of Philosophers from Africa and from the Netherlands. KIMMERLE, Heinz (ed).
Leibniz and Strawson: A New Essay in Descriptive Metaphysics. BROWN, Clifford.
The Many Dimensions of the Human Person. STEGER, E Ecker.
Metaphysics of Natural Complexes (Second Edition). WALLACE, Kathleen (ed).
Mimesis as Make-Believe: On the Foundations of the Representational Arts. WALTON, Kendall L.

ONTOLOGY

New Dimensions of Confucian and Neo-Confucian Philosophy. CHENG, Chung-ying.
Nicolai Hartmann's New Ontology. WERKMEISTER, W H.
Ontology and Alterity in Merleau-Ponty. JOHNSON, Galen A (ed).
The Ontology of Physical Objects: Four-Dimensional Hunks of Matter. HELLER, Mark.
Philosophical Applications of Free Logic. LAMBERT, Karel (ed).
Philosophical Essays. CARTWRIGHT, Richard.
Philosophical Logic. STRAWSON, P F (ed).
Plotin: Traité sur la liberté et la volonté de l'Un. LEROUX, Georges.
The Political Ontology of Martin Heidegger. BOURDIEU, Pierre.
Quest for Certainty: A Comparative Study of Heidegger and Sankara. GRIMES, John A.
The Question of God in Heidegger's Phenomenology. KOVACS, George.
The Savage Anomaly: The Power of Spinoza's Metaphysics and Politics. NEGRI, Antonio.
Works of Love? Reflections on "Works of Love". FENDT, Gene.
"Commentary: Common Knowledge and Archaeology" in *Critical Traditions in Contemporary Archaeology*, ZUBROW, Ezra.
"Definite Descriptions and the Ontological Argument" in *Philosophical Applications of Free Logic*, MANN, William E.
"Entrevista com o Professor Oswaldo Market Conduzida por" in *Dinâmica do Pensar: Homenagem a Oswaldo Market*, MARQUES, António and MOLDER, Filomena and NABAIS, Nuno.
"Esserci e differenza ontologica in Heidegger" in *Razionalitá critica: nella filosofia moderna*, ESPOSITO, Costantino.
"Filosofia e hermenêutica" in *Dinâmica do Pensar: Homenagem a Oswaldo Market*, GONÇALVES, Joaquim Cerqueira.
"Invidious Contrasts within Theory" in *Meaning and Method: Essays in Honor of Hilary Putnam*, SKLAR, Lawrence.
"Listening at the Abyss" in *Ontology and Alterity in Merleau-Ponty*, BURKE, Patrick.
"Make-Believe, Ontology and Point of View" in *XIth International Congress in Aesthetics, Nottingham 1988*, LAMARQUE, Peter.
"Mario Bunge on Ontology" in *Studies on Mario Bunge's "Treatise"*, BUNGE, Mario.
"Mario Bunge on the Mind-Body Problem and Ontology: Critical Examinations" in *Studies on Mario Bunge's "Treatise"*, KUROSAKI, Hiroshi.
"Mario Bunge's Ontology as a Formal Foundation for Information Systems Concepts" in *Studies on Mario Bunge's "Treatise"*, WAND, Yair and WEBER, Ron.
"Methodology and Ontology" in *Imre Lakatos and Theories of Scientific Change*, SMART, J J C.
"On the System" in *Studies on Mario Bunge's "Treatise"*, BOCHENSKI, Joseph M.
"The Ontological Significance of 'I' and 'We' in African Philosophy" in *I, We and Body: First Joint Symposium of Philosophers from Africa and from the Netherlands*, NYASANI, Joseph M.
"Ontology and Its Discontent" in *Studies on Mario Bunge's "Treatise"*, AGASSI, Joseph.
"Quine's Physicalism" in *Perspectives on Quine*, STROUD, Barry.
"Rorty, Realism and the Idea of Freedom" in *Reading Rorty*, BHASKAR, Roy.
"Tackling the Mind" in *Studies on Mario Bunge's "Treatise"*, SHEA, William R.
El "De Ente et Uno": una ontología agustiniana. MAGNAVACCA, Silvia.
Un "mapa de ontologías". PEREDA, Carlos.
La "Scuola di Padova" ed i problemi dell'ontologia italiana contemporanea. MANGIAGALLI, Maurizio.
Actualism, Ontological Commitment, and Possible World Semantics. MENZEL, Ch.
Una aproximación ontológica a la realidad fisica. HÜBNER, Adolf.
Aquinas versus Epistemological Criticism: A Case for Philosophy *in* Science. DEL RE, Giuseppe.
Aristotle's Definition of Motion and its Ontological Implications. BRAGUE, Rémi and ADLER, Pierre and D'URSEL, Laurent.
Attitudes, Leprechauns and Neutrinos: The Ontology of Behavioral Science. CHANDLER, Marthe.
Comparative Dialectics: Nishida Kitarō's Logic of Place and Western Dialectical Thought. AXTELL, G S.
Concerted Instant-Interval Temporal Semantics I: Temporal Ontologies. BOCHMAN, Alexander.
Condemned to Time: The Limits of Merleau-Ponty's Quest for Being. LOWRY, Atherton C.
Controverses autour de l'ontologie du droit. DE MUNCK, Jean.
Cosmology and Religion. JAKI, Stanley.
A Dialogue on Value, II: Why Is There Something Good, Not Simply Something?. KOHÁK, Erazim.
Die Wissenschaft denkt nicht. SALANSKIS, Jean-Michel.
Estructura lógica y ontología en el *Tractatus*. MARTÍNEZ, Sergio.
Estructuras y representaciones. DE LA SIENRA, Adolfo García.
Foucault's Critique of Heidegger. HILL, R Kevin.
From Hegel to Lukacs: The Problem of Ontology from the Point of View of Social and Natural Theory (in German). MOCEK, Reinhard.
Habermas on Heidegger's *Being and Time*. SCHARFF, Robert C.
Habermas's Ontology of Learning: Reconstructing Dewey. YOUNG, R E.
Hacia el saber del hombre: Dialéctica, lógica y ontológica en Aristóteles. MARÍN, Victor R.
Heidegger and the Temporal Constitution of the *A Priori*. SCHALOW, Frank.
A Heideggerian Analysis of Fundamentalism: A Brief Discussion. O'CONNELL, Colin.
History and Ontology: A Reading of Nietzsche's Second "Untimely Meditation". BAMBACH, Charles R.
El hombre y el misterio del ser. TRIANA, Manuel.
How Euclidean Geometry Has Misled Metaphysics. NERLICH, Graham.
The Institution of Law. BANKOWSKI, Zenon.
Is It Practical Ontology or Is It the Dialectical Materialist Theory of Material Monism?. JINFU, Wang.
L'ontogenèse de l'individu: ses aspects scientifiques et philosophiques. BERNIER, Réjane.
Language and Metaphysics: The Ontology of Metaphor. HAUSMAN, Carl R.
Locke on the Ontology of Matter, Living Things and Persons. CHAPPELL, Vere.
Logic and Ontology. BROWNING, Douglas.
La loi du Styx, Leibniz et la politique du bonheur. LE LANNOU, Jean-Michel.
Lukács on the Ontology of Social Existence and Marx's Understanding of Society (in German). LENDVAI, Ferenc L.
Marxism as the Foundation of Philosophies of Science: *The Case of G Lukács' Ontology of Social Being*. TUCHANSKA, Barbara.
Mathématiques et ontologie: les symétries en physique. BOUTOT, Alain.
Metaphysical Awakening in Philosophy of Quantum Physics. FOLSE, Henry J.
Metaphysik und Metaphysikkritik. HARTMANN, Klaus.
Methodological, Epistemological, and Ontological Motifs in the Thought of Reinhold Niebuhr. AYERS, Robert H.
The Modes of Actuality. FORD, Lewis S.
Die Natur der Sprache: Von der Ontologie zur Technologie. HOTTOIS, Gilbert.
Nietzsche and Heidegger. LAWRENCE, Joseph P.
Non-World Making in Chuang Tzu. WU, Kuang-Ming.
Not Every Object of a Sign has Being. PAPE, Helmut.
Not Over Yet: Prior's 'Thank Goodness' Argument'. KIERNAN-LEWIS, Delmas.
On the Causality of Sky. MISHRA, Aruna Ranjan.
On the Ontology of Branching Quantifiers. PATTON, Thomas.
Ontologia e creazione in Filone Alessandrino: Dialogo con Giovanni Reale e Roberto Radice. MARTÍN, Josè Pablo.
Ontología hermenéutica y reflexión filológica: el acceso a la filosofía de H G Gadamer. DOMINGO, Agustín.
Ontology and History. BARLINGAY, S S.
The Ontology of Musical Works and the Authenticity of their Performances. DAVIES, Stephen.
Phenomenology and Scientific Realism: Husserl's Critique of Galileo. SOFFER, Gail.
Philosophical Hermeneutics and its Meaning for Philosophy. PAGE, Carl.
Philosophy and Religion (in Dutch). DHONDT, U.
Pluralistic Ontology and Theory Reduction in the Physical Sciences. ROHRLICH, Fritz.
Porphyry and the Intelligible Triad. EDWARDS, M J.
Realisms. LEVIN, Michael.
A Response to Kuang-Ming Wu's "Non-World-Making". FLEMING, Jesse.
Sartre on Surpassing the Given. BUSCH, Thomas W.
Scotus, Frege, and Bergmann. PARK, Woosuk.
Structure and Ontology. SHAPIRO, Stewart.
A Study of Ontology. FINE, Kit.
Lo sviluppo degli studi logici nel pensiero tedesco della seconda metà dell' '800. MANGIAGALLI, Maurizio.
Tropes and Laws. FUHRMANN, André.
Two Anonymous 12th-Century Tracts on Universals. DIJS, Judith.
Ungeklärte Fragen im Dialog zwischen Glaube und Naturwissenschaft. FISCHER, Johannes.
The What and the How. ALMOG, Joseph.
What is Ultimate in George Lukács's Ontology?. JOÓS, Ernest.
Wilhelm von Ockham: Das Risiko, mittelalterlich zu denken. PERLER, Dominik.

OPEN TEXTURE

H L A Hart and the "Open Texture" of Language. BIX, Brian.

OPERATION(S)

After Principles. BARDEN, Garrett.
Logics Preserving Degrees of Truth. NOWAK, Marek.
On Theories of Non-Monotonic Consequence Operations II. FIJALKOWSKA, Dorota and FIJALKOWSKI, Jan.
Q-Consequence Operation. MALINOWSKI, Grzegorz.
Some Remarks on ω-Powers of Enumerated Sets and Their Applications to ω-Operations. ORLICKI, Andrzej.

OPERATIONALISM

P W Bridgman's Operational Perspective on Physics: Part I—Origins and Development. MOYER, Albert E.

OPERATOR(S)
Constructive Compact Operators on a Hilbert Space. ISHIHARA, Hajime.
The Homogeneous Form of Logic Programs with Equality. DEMOPOULOS, William.
On a Theorem of Günter Asser. CALUDE, Cristian and SÂNTEAN, Lila.
On Restricted Forms of Enumeration Reducibility. WATSON, Phil.
On Some Operators on Pseudovarieties. GRACZYNSKA, Ewa.
A Two-Valued Logic for Reasoning about Different Types of Consequence in Kleene's Three-Valued Logic. KONIKOWSKA, Beata.
Unbounded Operators and the Incompleteness of Quantum Mechanics. HEATHCOTE, Adrian.

OPINION(S)
The Difference Between Truth and Opinion: How the Misuse of Language Can Lead to Disaster. COONEY, Timothy J.

OPPORTUNISM
Machiavellianism Revisited. NELSON, George and GILBERTSON, Diana.

OPPORTUNITY(-TIES)
Difficulties with the Principle of Equal Opportunity for Welfare. CHRISTIANO, Thomas.

OPPOSITION
Political Theory in the Welfare State. LUHMANN, Niklas.
Ethical Pluralism and the Role of Opposition in Democratic Politics. D'AGOSTINO, Fred.
Heidegger and Nietzsche—Thinkers of the 'Between'? (in Dutch). GOOSEN, D P.
Nietzsche and the Critique of Oppositional Thinking. SCHRIFT, Alan D.
The Rhetoric of Opposition in Thomas More's *Utopia*: Giving Form to Competing Philosophies. WEGEMER, Gerard.

OPPRESSION
Femininity and Domination: Studies in the Phenomenology of Oppression. BARTKY, Sandra Lee.
In Praise of Clutter as a Necessary Part of the Feminist Perspective. AYIM, Maryann.
Oppression and Victimization; Choice and Responsibility. WENDELL, Susan.
Reply to Maryann Ayim's "In Praise of Clutter as a Necessary Part of the Feminist Perspective". WENDELL, Susan.
Structure/Antistructure and Agency under Oppression. LUGONES, Maria C.

OPTICS
Expectation, Modelling and Assent in the History of Optics: Part I—Alhazen and the Medieval Tradition. CROMBIE, A C.
Expectation, Modelling and Assent in the History of Optics—II. Kelper and Descartes. CROMBIE, A C.

OPTIMALITY
Expecting Nature's Best: Optimality Models and Perfect Adaptation. HOLCOMB, H R.

OPTIMISM
The Tragic World of John Dewey. JACQUES, Robert A.

ORAL TRADITION
A Philosophical Daybook: Post-Critical Investigations. POTEAT, William H.

ORDER
"Human Order in the Natural Universe: Rediscovering Russell's Social Philosophy" in *Perspectives on Ideas and Reality*, MEZEI, György Iván.
Aesthetic Order. LORAND, Ruth.
Dialogue on Science, Society, and the Generative Order. BOHM, D and KELLY, Sean.
Effective Extensions of Partial Orders. KUMAR ROY, Dev.
Equivalent Versions of a Weak Form of the Axiom of Choice. SHANNON, G.
Intersubjectivity without Subjectivism. SINGER, Beth J.
On the Quasi-Ordering of Borel Linear Orders Under Embeddability. LOUVEAU, Alain and SAINT-RAYMOND, Jean.
The Ordertype of β-R.E. Sets. SUTNER, Klaus.
Sul controllo nel procedimento di determinazione dei principi dell'ordinamento. COSTANZO, Angelo.
Sur le fragment des trois ordres de Blaise Pascal. CHIBAUDEL, Pierre.
Unifying Plato: Charles Kahn on Platonic *Prolepsis*. GRISWOLD JR, Charles L.

ORDERING
"Decisions Without Ordering" in *Acting and Reflecting: The Interdisciplinary Turn in Philosophy*, SEIDENFELD, Teddy and SCHERVISH, M J.
A Coding of the Countable Linear Orderings. DEHORNOY, Patrick.
Degrees of Orderings Not Isomorphic to Recursive Linear Orderings. JOCKUSCH JR, Carl G and SOARE, Robert I.
On Scott and Karp Trees of Uncountable Models. HYTTINEN, Tapani and VÄÄNÄNEN, Jouko.
Upward Directedness of the Rudin-Keisler Ordering of *P*-Points. LAFLAMME, Claude.
Verisimilitude by Power Relations: A Response to Oddie. BRINK, Chris and HEIDEMA, Johannes.

ORDINALS
The Complete 0. KANAMORI, Akihiro and AWERBUCH-FRIEDLANDER, Tamara.
Intermediate Predicate Logics Determined by Ordinals. MINARI, Pierluigi and TAKANO, Mitio and ONO, Hiroakira.
Partitioning Pairs of Countable Sets of Ordinals. VELLEMAN, Dan.
A Theorem on Labelled Trees and the Limits of Its Provability. PFEIFFER, Helmut.
Weak Cylindric Set Algebras and Weak Subdirect Indecomposability. ANDRÉKA, H and NÉMETI, I and THOMPSON, R J.

ORDINARY LANGUAGE
Alltagssprachliche Metakommunikation im Englischen und Deutschen. WELTE, Werner.
Il "parlare commune" come lume storico-naturale della "riproduzione sociale". MININNI, Giuseppe.
Meanings in Ordinary Language and in Mathematics. THOMAS, R S D.
Wittgenstein and Marx—Some Methodological Remarks (in German). RAATZSCH, Richard.

ORGAN DONOR(S)
"Anencephalics as Organ Donors" in *Biomedical Ethics Reviews, 1989*, THOMASMA, David C.
"Should Abnormal Fetuses Be Brought to Term for the Sole Purpose of Providing Infant Transplant Organs?" in *Biomedical Ethics Reviews, 1989*, GRABER, Glenn C.
Anencephalic Infants and Special Relationships. JECKER, Nancy S.
Respect for Donor Choice and the Uniform Anatomical Gift Act. EDINGER, Walter.

ORGAN TRANSPLANT(S)
"Animal Parts, Human Wholes: On the Use of Animals as a Source of Organs for Human Transplants" in *Biomedical Ethics Reviews, 1987*, FREY, R G.
"Animals as a Source of Human Transplant Organs" in *Biomedical Ethics Reviews, 1987*, NELSON, James L.
"The Rights and Wrongs of Animal Use for Human Organ Transplant" in *Biomedical Ethics Reviews, 1987*, WERNER, Richard.
An Alternative to Property Rights in Human Tissue. SWAIN, Margaret S and MARUSYK, Randy W.
The Market for Bodily Parts: A Response to Ruth Chadwick. TADD, G V.
The Morality of a Free Market for Transplant Organs. NELSON, Mark T.
Respect for Donor Choice and the Uniform Anatomical Gift Act. EDINGER, Walter.
Schopenhauers Idee einer rekonstruktiven Ethik (mit Anwendungen auf die moderne Medizin-Ethik). BIRNBACHER, Dieter.

ORGANIC
Romanticism and the Sciences. CUNNINGHAM, Andrew (ed).
The Tragic World of John Dewey. JACQUES, Robert A.

ORGANICISM
Whitehead and Leibniz: Conflict and Convergence. MOONEY, Tim.

ORGANISM
On the Adaptations of Organisms and the Fitness of Types. ETTINGER, Lia and JABLONKA, Eva and MC LAUGHLIN, Peter.
On the Uniqueness of Biological Research. PORTMANN, Adolph.
Reconsidering the Wisdom of the Body. SULLIVAN, Mark D.
The Reformed Subjectivist Principle Revisited. FORD, Lewis S.

ORGANIZATION(S)
Medical Work in America: Essays on Health Care. FREIDSON, Eliot.
"Work in Organizations as Social Activity" in *Harré and His Critics*, RODRIGUEZ LOPEZ, Jose Luis.
Commentary on Layton's "Engineering Needs a Loyal Opposition". ANDERSON, Robert M (and others).
A Deontological Analysis of Peer Relations in Organizations. MOBERG, Dennis J and MEYER, Michael J.
The Divided Machine: Capitalist Crisis and the Organization of Labor. TURCHETTO, Maria and ESPOSITO, Joan.
Ethical Values of Individuals at Different Levels in the Organizational Hierarchy of a Single Firm. HARRIS, James R.
Ethics in Declining Organizations. LEMKE, Dwight K and SCHMINKE, Marshall.
Exit, Voice, and Ethics. KEELEY, Michael and GRAHAM, Jill W.
Fostering Ethical Marketing Decisions. LACZNIAK, Gene R and MURPHY, Patrick E.
Future through Self-Organization (in German). ARTZT, M.
The Institutionalization of Organizational Ethics. SIMS, Ronald R.
Machiavellianism Revisited. NELSON, George and GILBERTSON, Diana.
Natural and Political Society in the Thought of Edmund Burke (in German). TSCHURENEV, Eva-Maria.
Organizational Value Contention and Managerial Mindsets. LIEDTKA, Jeanne.
El papel de la comunicación espontánea en los procesos de evolución social. RODRÍGUEZ HÖLKEMEYER, Patricia.
PES and School Reform. TOZER, Steven.
PES and the APA—An Impressionistic History. MACMILLAN, C J B.
Public Relations: The Empiricial Research on Practitioner Ethics. PRATT, Cornelius B.
Réflexion sur l'état actuel et les perspectives de l'enseignement de la philosophie en France. DERRIDA, Jacques and BOURGEOIS, Bernard.

ORGANIZATION(S)
The Relative Importance of Social Responsibility in Determining Organizational Effectiveness: Student Responses. KRAFT, Kenneth L.
The Rights of Organizations. GORDLEY, James.
The Process of Evolution in a Holistic World (in German). SOSCHINKA, Hans-Ulrich.
Understanding Professional Misconduct: The Moral Responsibilities of Professionals. NORTON, Thomas W.

ORIENTAL
see also Chinese, Indian
Bewusstsein und Natursein. CHO, Kah Kyung.
Philosophy in World Perspective: A Comparative Hermeneutic of the Major Theories. DILWORTH, David A.
Boston University Studies in Philosophy and Religion, Volumes 1-10. SMART, Ninian.
Heidegger e o Oriente ou da Extrema In-diferença Ocidental. DO CARMO SILVA, Carlos Henrique.
Idéalisme ou réalisme?. LARGEAULT, Jean.
The Marxist Conception of Tradition. STEPANYANTS, Marietta.
The Relevance of Meditative Thinking. ERICKSON, Stephen A.

ORIGEN
Nature as Personal. DOMBROWSKI, Daniel A.

ORIGIN(S)
Matter, Morals and Medicine: The Ancient Greek Origins of Science, Ethics and the Medical Profession. CARELLA, Michael Jerome.
"Ancient Ethics" in *A Companion to Ethics*, LARUE, Gerald A.
"The Origin of Ethics" in *A Companion to Ethics*, MIDGLEY, Mary.
"Le voyage de 'Schreiten': Leibniz et les débuts du comparatisme finno-ougrien" in *Leibniz, Humboldt, and the Origins of Comparativism*, DROIXHE, Daniel.
L'aporia della kìnesis in Aristotele. ROCCARO, Giuseppe.
La disputa sulle origini della neoscolastica italiana: Salvatore Roselli, Vincenzo Buzzetti e Gaetano Sanseverino. SCHMIDINGER, H M.
Language, Physics, and Geology (and a Few Words on Theology). BROGAN, Jacqueline Vaught.
Nietzsche's Metaperspectivism. ROTH, Robin Alice.
La primera antinomia kantiana: el origen y los límites del Universo. PUYAU, Hermes.
Rilievi di struttura sul *De deo abscondito* di Nicola Cusano. DELCÒ, Alessandro.
La teología de la creación y el problema de los orígenes. PODESTA, Gustavo.
Teorías físicas sobre el origen del Universo. GRATTON, Fausto T L.
Thomas Aquinas and Henry of Ghent on the Succession of Substantial Forms and the Origin of Human Life. WILSON, Gordon A.
Traité de la créature. VARET, Gilbert.

ORIGINAL SIN
The Interplay of Nature and Man in the *Periphyseon* of Johannes Scottus Eriugena. OTTEN, Willemien.

ORIGINALITY
Acerca de uma tese ricoeuriana. SUMARES, Manuel.
The Fate of Independent Thought in Traditional China. WHITE, Harry.
Seeing the Original. BASS, Walter.

ORLOWSKA, E
Orlowska's Relevant Implications, Relevant Logics and Analytic Implication. GIAMBRONE, Steve.

ORTEGA
Examen del "ahora". HUÉSCAR, Antonio R.
Filósofos naúfragos. BALIÑAS, Carlos.
Heidegger en la filosofia española: La eficacia de Heidegger en las filosofías de Ortega y Zubiri. RAMOS, Antonio Pintor.

ORTES, G
"Filosofia e politica in Giammaria Ortes" in *Scienza, Filosofia e Religione tra '600 e '700 in Italia*, GIACOTTO, Paolo.

ORTHODOXY
Russische Philosophie. GOERDT, Wilhelm.
Philosophy and the Sociology of Knowledge: An Investigation into the Nature of Orthodoxy (Astikya) in Hindu Thought. SHARMA, Arvind.

ORTONY, A
Describing the Emotions: A Review of *The Cognitive Structure of Emotions* by Ortony, Clore and Collins. BEN-ZEEV, Aaron.

OSHERON, D
Note on the Integration of Prototype Theory and Fuzzy-Set Theory. FUHRMANN, G.

OSTENSIVE COMMUNICATION
Relevance as an Explanation of Communication. ROBERTS, Lawrence D.

OTHER MINDS
Sensations: A Defense of Type Materialism. HILL, Christopher S.
Berkeley's Arguments for Other Minds. FALKENSTEIN, Lorne.
The Development of Wittgenstein's Views about the Other Minds Problem. TER HARK, M R M.
McDowell Against Criterial Knowledge. ROBINSON, Paul.
Wittgenstein on Criteria and Other Minds. TEMKIN, Jack.

OTHER(S)
Alterity, Identity, Image: Contributions Towards a Theoretical Perspective. CORBEY, R (ed).
Difference and Subjectivity: Dialogue and Personal Identity. JACQUES, Francis.
Existentialism. COOPER, David E.
La intersubjectividad en Husserl, Volume I and II. IRIBARNE, Julia V.
Le Philosophie et les Passions. MEYER, Michel.
"321 CONTACT: Textuality, the Other, Death" in *Re-Reading Levinas*, BEREZDIVIN, Ruben.
"Experience of the Other: Between Appropriation and Disappropriation" in *Life-World and Politics: Between Modernity and Postmodernity*, WALDENFELS, Bernhard.
"Rational Egoism, Self, and Others" in *Identity, Character, and Morality: Essays in Moral Psychology*, BRINK, David O.
Acceptance of Others and Concern for Oneself (in French). MULLER, Denis.
Bodily Theory and Theory of the Body. GILES, James.
The Conative Function of the Other in *Les Mots et les Choses*. RACEVSKIS, Karlis.
The Ethics Behind the Absence of Ethics in Alfred Schutz's Thought. BARBER, Michael.
The Integral Self: Systematic Illusion or Inescapable Task?. COLAPIETRO, Vincent M.
Logos and the Place of the Other. BIRMINGHAM, Peg E.
Merleau-Ponty on Taking the Attitude of the Other. MATUSTIK, Martin J.
The Other Comes to Teach Me: A Review of Recent Levinas Publications. GIBBS, Robert.
El problema de la culpa y del "otro" en Heidegger y Siewerth. CABADA, Manuel.
Thinking the Other Without Violence? An Analysis of the Relation Between the Philosophy of Lévinas and Feminism. MANNING, Robert J S.

OTHERNESS
Vulgarity and Authenticity: Dimensions of Otherness in the World of Jean-Paul Sartre. CHARMÉ, Stuart Zane.
"Écart: Reply to Lefort's 'Flesh and Otherness'" in *Ontology and Alterity in Merleau-Ponty*, DILLON, Martin C.
"Flesh and Otherness" in *Ontology and Alterity in Merleau-Ponty*, LEFORT, Claude.
"Flesh as Otherness" in *Ontology and Alterity in Merleau-Ponty*, MADISON, Gary Brent.
"Justice in the Flesh" in *Ontology and Alterity in Merleau-Ponty*, LEVIN, David Michael.
The Ethics of Postmodernism. GIBBONS, Michael T.
Logic and Logos—The Search for Unity in Hegel and Coleridge: II: The 'Otherness" of God. PERKINS, Mary Anne.

OTTO, R
The Development of Otto's Thought 1898-1917. MINNEY, Robin.

OTTO, W
Hegel and the Gods of Greece (in Hungarian). KERENYI, Karoly.
Mythe et raison: Propos contemporains. FONTAINE-DE VISSCHER, Luce.

OUGHT
Hume's Place in Moral Philosophy. CAPALDI, Nicholas.
"The Necessity for Cooperation between Philosophical and Empirical Research" in *The Moral Domain: Essays in the Ongoing Discussion between Philosophy and the Social Sciences*, TUGENDHAT, Ernst.
"The Study of Moral Development: A Bridge over the "Is-Ought" Gap" in *The Moral Domain: Essays in the Ongoing Discussion between Philosophy and the Social Sciences*, BOYD, Dwight R.
"Is" and "Ought": A Different Connection. JOHNSON, Oliver A.
"'Ought' Does Imply 'Can'". SAPONTZIS, Steve F.
'Is' Therefore 'Ought'. VERMA, Roop Rekha.
How Far Can Hume's Is-Ought Thesis Be Generalized?. SCHURZ, Gerhard.
The Value-Ought of Self-Realization: A Phenomenological Approach. VELASSERRY, Sebastian.

OVERMAN
The Ambivalent Unthought of the Overman and the Duality of Heidegger's Political Thinking. HAAR, Michel.
The Doubleness of the Unthought of the Overman: Ambiguities of Heideggerian Political Thought. HAAR, Michel.

OWENS, D
Disjunctive Laws and Supervenience. SEAGER, William.

OWENS, J
The Preface to Thomistic Metaphysics. KNASAS, John F X.

OWNERSHIP
Could Someone Else Have Had My Headache?. STONE, Jim.
Is there an Ethics of Computing?. BROWN, Geoffrey.
Marxism and Contemporary Political Philosophy. COHEN, G A.
Ownership as Theft. GRUNEBAUM, James O.

OWNERSHIP
Principled Divestiture and Moral Integrity. CAHN, Steven M.
Resources, Capacities, and Ownership: The Workmanship Ideal and Distributive Justice. SHAPIRO, Ian.
Self-Ownership and the Right of Property. MACK, Eric.
Self-Ownership, Equality, and the Structure of Property Rights. CHRISTMAN, John.
Some Philosophical Directions Towards a Simple Theory of the Self. MANN, David W.

PACIFISM
Bertrand Russell. ALCARO, Mario.
In the Interest of Peace: A Spectrum of Philosophical Views. KLEIN, Kenneth H (ed).
Military Ethics: Looking Toward the Future. FOTION, Nicholas G.
Nonviolence in Theory and Practice. HOLMES, Robert L.
"Epistemological Pacifism" in *In the Interest of Peace: A Spectrum of Philosophical Views*, BURKE, Richard.
"Loving One's Enemies" in *In the Interest of Peace: A Spectrum of Philosophical Views*, GAN, Barry.
"Pacifism and Revolution" in *In the Interest of Peace: A Spectrum of Philosophical Views*, DONAGHY, John.
"Pacifism, Duty, and Supererogation" in *In the Interest of Peace: A Spectrum of Philosophical Views*, CADY, Duane L.
"Pragmatic Pacifism: A Methodology for Gaining the Ear of the Warist" in *In the Interest of Peace: A Spectrum of Philosophical Views*, SMITHKA, Paula.
"Toward Understanding the Pragmatics of Absolute Pacifism" in *In the Interest of Peace: A Spectrum of Philosophical Views*, KOHL, Marvin.

PADGETT, A
God and Real Time. CRAIG, William Lane.

PAGEL, W
"Visages de Van Helmont, depuis Hélène Metzger jusqu'aà Walter Pagel" in *Études sur/Studies on Hélène Metzger*, HALLEUX, Robert.

PAIDEIA
Paideia Helénica. FREIRE, António.

PAIN(S)
Animal Experimentation: The Consensus Changes. LANGLEY, Gill (ed).
Do Animals Feel Pain?. HARRISON, Peter.
Harrison on Animal Pain. HOUSE, Ian.
The Neurophilosophy of Pain. GILLETT, G R.
Objective and Subjective Aspects of Pain. GRAHEK, Nikola.
Reply to Weir: Unnecessary Fear, Nutrition, and Vegetarianism. SAPONTZIS, Steve F.
The Temporality of Illness: Four Levels of Experience. TOOMBS, S Kay.
Unnecessary Pain, Nutrition, and Vegetarianism. WEIR, Jack.
Wittgenstein and "Mad Pain". KELLY, Michael Lee.

PAINTER(S)
Velázquez et Goya. PIERRE, Christian (trans).
The Anatomist and the Painter: The Continuity of Hume's *Treatise* and *Essays*. IMMERWAHR, John.
Plato's Analogy between Painter and Poet. JANAWAY, Christopher.

PAINTING
L'objet-peinture: Pour une théorie de la réception. PAQUIN, Nycole.
"The Limits and Possibilities of Fashion in Painting" in *XIth International Congress in Aesthetics, Nottingham 1988*, WINTERS, E J.
Horace's *Ars Poetica* and the Deconstructive Leech. HABIB, M A R.
Philosophy as an Art. LEVINSON, Jerrold.
Reply to the Symposiasts. WOLLHEIM, Richard.
Sémiologie visuelle, peinture et intertextualité. PAQUET, Bernard.
Technique of Painting and Sociology of Picture (in Czechoslovakian). HLAVACEK, Josef.

PANENTHEISM
Algunas consecuencias del panenteismo krausista: ecología y mujer. MENÉNDEZ UREÑA, Enrique.

PANNENBERG, W
Pannenberg's Doctrine of God. O'DONNELL, John.

PANOFSKY, E
Panofsky, Polanyi, and Intrinsic Meaning. UN-CHOL, Shin.
Le statut sémiotique de la perspective dans l'oeuvre picturale. CARANI, Marie.

PANPSYCHISM
"Mind-Dust or Magic? Panpsychism Versus Emergence" in *Philosophical Perspectives, 4: Action Theory and Philosophy of Mind, 1990*, VAN CLEVE, James.
William James's Theory of Mind. COOPER, W E.

PANTHEISM
Die Aufhebung der Begriffs-philosophie. KRONABEL, Christoph.
A proposito dell'interesse di Dilthey per l'antropologia cinquecentesca. ORSUCCI, Andrea.
Divine Unity and Superfluous Synonymity. LEVINE, Michael P.
Le origini dell'ateismo antico (quinta parte). ZEPPI, Stelio.

PAPACY
Ultramontanisme et gallicanisme engagentils deux visions de la société. BRESSOLETTE, Claude.

PAPAL AUTHORITY
The Crisis of Authority. OLDS, Mason.

PAPINEAU, D
Why Indeed? Papineau on Supervenience. CRANE, Tim.

PARABLE(S)
In Defence of Graded Love. LAI, Whalen.

PARACONSISTENT LOGICS
Algebraization of Paraconsistent Logic P^1. LEWIN, R A and MIKENBERG, I F and SCHWARZE, M G.
Intensional Paradoxes. PRIEST, Graham.
Kantian and Non-Kantian Logics. PUGA, Leila Z and DA COSTA, Newton C A and CARNIELLI, Walter A.
Models for Inconsistent and Incomplete Differential Calculus. MORTENSEN, Chris.
On Subsystems of the System J_1 of Arruda and Da Costa. URBAS, Igor.
On the Development of Paraconsistent Logic and Da Costa's Work. LOFFREDO D'OTTAVIANO, Itala M.
Paraconsistency and the J-Systems of Arruda and da Costa. URBAS, Igor.
Relevance and Paraconsistency—A New Approach. AVRON, A.
Relevance and Paraconsistency—A New Approach, Part II: The Formal Systems. AVRON, Arnon.
Toward a Formalization of Dialectical Logic. THOMASON, Steven K.
Variations on da Costa *C* Systems and Dual-Intuitionistic Logics (I). SYLVAN, Richard.

PARADIGM(S)
The Balance of Consciousness: Eric Voegelin's Political Theory. KEULMAN, Kenneth.
Euthanasia: Toward an Ethical Social Policy. THOMASMA, David C.
Explaining Religion: Criticism and Theory from Bodin to Freud. PREUS, J Samuel (ed).
Il Paradigma del Sapere. LENTINI, Luigi.
"Dubbing and Redubbing: The Vulnerability of Rigid Destination" in *Scientific Theories*, KUHN, Thomas S.
"Professional Paradigms" in *Ethics, Trust, and the Professions: Philosophical and Cultural Aspects*, LANGAN, John.
Account of a Philosophical Expedition in Search of the Elusive Paradigm (in Dutch). GOUWS, A S.
Behavioral Paradigm for a Psychological Resolution of the Free Will Issue. HARCUM, E Rae.
A Candidate Paradigm for Human Ecology. BAPAT, Jyotsna.
Classification by Comparison with Paradigms. EBERLE, Rolf.
Emotions, Education and Time. DE SOUSA, Ronald.
I Love Myself When I am Laughing: A New Paradigm for Sex. DAVIS, Karen Elizabeth.
A Kuhnian Model of Falsifiability. STONE, Mark A.
Orchestrating Social Change: An Imperative in Care of the Chronically Ill. ROTH, Patricia A and HARRISON, Janet K.
Paradigms, Populations and Problem-Fields: Approaches to Disagreement. ALLCHIN, Douglas.
Search for Beliefs to Live by Consistent with Science. SPERRY, R W.
Search for Indian Traditional Paradigm of Society. SHARMA, K N.
Thomas S Kuhn and L Fleck: Two Sociologists of Science. FLURI, Philippe H.
Three Accounts of Paradigm Shift. MUKHERJEE, Nilratan.
Transcending Paradigms. REY, George.

PARADOX(ES)
Identity and Discrimination. WILLIAMSON, Timothy.
Las paradojas del Infinito. BOLZANO, Bernard.
"The Modern Spirit and the Paradox of Humanism" in *The Question of Humanism: Challenges and Possibilities*, DORTER, Kenneth.
"A Simpler Solution to the Paradoxes of Deontic Logic" in *Philosophical Perspectives, 4: Action Theory and Philosophy of Mind, 1990*, FELDMAN, Fred.
Achilles' Revenge. DAKO, Martin.
Aesthetic Education and Aesthetic Atmosphere (in Czechoslovakian). MATHAUSER, Zdenek.
Beyond the "Limits" of *Mundane Reason*. BOGEN, David.
Causal Paradoxes in Special Relativity. ARNTZENIUS, Frank.
Doxastic Paradoxes Without Self-Reference. KOONS, Robert Charles.
Equivocation in The Surprise Exam Paradox. FERGUSON, Kenneth G.
The Fallibility Paradox. LEHRER, Keith and KIM, Kihyeon.
Fictional Incompleteness as Vagueness. SORENSEN, Roy A.
Humanizing the Humanities: Some Reflections on George Steiner's "Brutal Paradox". KARIER, Clarence J.
Hume and the Paradox of Taste Again. WERTZ, S K.
Intensional Paradoxes. PRIEST, Graham.
Kierkegaardian Transitions: Paradox and Pathos. FERREIRA, M Jamie.
The Logic of the Liar from the Standpoint of the Aristotelian Syllogistic. KELLY, Charles J.
Material Implication and Entailment. CENIZA, Claro R.

PASSION(S)
see also Emotion(s)
Le Philosophie et les Passions. MEYER, Michel.
A Progress of Sentiments: Reflections on Hume's "Treatise". BAIER, Annette C.
Réflexions sur les passions. HUME, David.
Weakness of the Will. GOSLING, Justin.
Burning Passions. NEILL, Alex and RIDLEY, Aaron.
Cartesian Passions and Cartesian Dualism. HOFFMAN, Paul.
Ethics as Drawn from the Method. CARTER, Richard B.
Feminist Theory and Its Discontents. TRESS, Daryl Mc Gowan.
Nietzsche e Spinoza. BIUSO, Alberto G.
Sense, Passions and Morals in Hume and Kant. NUYEN, A T.
The Transfigurations of Intoxication: Nietzsche, Schopenhauer, and Dionysus. NUSSBAUM, Martha C.

PAST
Backwards Causation and the Permanence of the Past. ODDIE, Graham.
How Would an *Übermensch* Regard His Past and Future?. MC INERNEY, Peter K.

PASTICHE
Post-Modern Pastiche. ROSE, Margaret A.

PASTORAL
The Idea of Christian Charity: A Critique of Some Contemporary Conceptions. GRAHAM, Gordon.

PATANJALI
'Desire' in Yoga and Jung. COWARD, Harold.
The Notion of *Klesa* and Its Bearing on the Yoga Analysis of Mind. BALSLEV, Anindita N.

PATERNALISM
Deciding for Others: The Ethics of Surrogate Decision Making. BUCHANAN, Allen E.
Die moderne Gesellschaft im Rechtsstaat. BAURMANN, Michael.
The Artificial Womb—Patriarchal Bone or Technological Blessing?. HEDMAN, Carl.
Deconstructing Community Self-Paternalism. SCHONSHECK, Jonathan.
The Paternalistic Attitude Toward Children. AVIRAM, Aharon.
Paternalistic Laws. GOLDMAN, Alan H and GOLDMAN, Michael N.
The Physician-Societal Relationship. CRELINSTEN, Gordon L.

PATIENT RIGHTS
Autonomy and the Common Weal. DANIS, Marion and CHURCHILL, Larry R.
Commentary— "Make Me Live": Autonomy and Terminal Illness. MISBIN, Robert I.
Commentary—"Make Me Live": Autonomy and Terminal Illness. MILLER, David H.
Hide-and-Seek or Show-and-Tell? Emerging Issues of Informed Consent. HAAS, Leonard J.
The Limits of a Wish. RIE, Michael A.
Measuring the Quality of Life: Why, How and What?. HÄYRY, Matti.
The Noncompliant Substance Abuser: Commentary. STELL, Lance K.
The Patient Self-Determination Act. MC CLOSKEY, Elizabeth Leibold.
The Pharmacist's Role in Patient Care. SCHULZ, Richard M and BRUSHWOOD, David B.

PATIENT(S)
Theory and Practice in Medical Ethics. GRABER, Glenn C.
To Die or Not to Die?. BERGER, Arthur S (ed).
"The Physician's Knowledge and the Patient's Best Interest" in *Ethics, Trust, and the Professions: Philosophical and Cultural Aspects*, BUCHANAN, Allen E.
Desperately Seeking Science: The Creation of Knowledge in Family Practice. GOLDSTEIN, Jared.
Doctors' Rights and Patients' Obligations. MARSHALL, Sandra E.
The Ideal of Shared Decision Making Between Physicians and Patients. BROCK, Dan W.
Knowing When to Stop: The Limits of Medicine. JECKER, Nancy S.
Patient Decision-Making Capacity and Risk. WICCLAIR, Mark R.
The Physician-Societal Relationship. CRELINSTEN, Gordon L.
A Response to Brock and Skene. WICCLAIR, Mark R.
Rich Cases: The Ethics of Thick Description. DAVIS, Dena S.

PATOCKA, J
The Picture in Movement and in Response (in Czechoslovakian). JIRIK, Vlastimil.

PATRIARCHY
Femininity and Domination: Studies in the Phenomenology of Oppression. BARTKY, Sandra Lee.
Patriarcha and Other Writings: Sir Robert Filmer. SOMMERVILLE, Johann P (ed).
Patterns of Dissonance. BRAIDOTTI, Rosi.
From Patriarchal Socialism to Socialist Democracy: Thoughts on a New Theory of Society. MOCEK, Reinhard.

PATRIOTISM
"Patriotism and the Pursuit of Peace" in *In the Interest of Peace: A Spectrum of Philosophical Views*, NATHANSON, Stephen.

PATRONAGE
Theories of Science in Society. COZZENS, Susan E (ed).

PATTERN(S)
Real Patterns. DENNETT, Daniel C.

PATTERSON, D
Why Narrative Is Not Enough. FULLER, Steve.

PAUL, R
Testing Fairmindedness. FISHER, Alec.

PAULI, W
El principio de exclusión y sus aplicaciones. GARZÓN, León.
Quantum Physics, Philosophy, and the Image of God: Insights from Wolfgang Pauli. LAURIKAINEN, K V.

PAVLOV
Pavlov's View on the Inheritance of Acquired Characteristics .... WINDHOLZ, George and LAMAL, P A.
Todor Pavlov (1890-1977)—The Generalization of Reflection (in German). HOLZ, Hans Heinz.

PEACE
Celebrating Peace. ROUNER, Leroy S (ed).
In the Interest of Peace: A Spectrum of Philosophical Views. KLEIN, Kenneth H (ed).
Issues in War and Peace: Philosophical Inquiries. KUNKEL, Joseph (ed).
The Making of a Nuclear Peace: The Task of Today's Just War Theorists. SICHOL, Marcia W.
The Moral Animus of David Hume. SIEBERT, Donald T.
Understanding War: A Philosophical Inquiry. MC MURTRY, John.
Yoga on War and Peace. TIGUNAIT, Pandit Rajmani.
"Buddhism, Sri Lanka, and the Prospects for Peace" in *Celebrating Peace*, SMART, Ninian.
"Christian Peacemakers in the Warmaking State" in *Celebrating Peace*, BERRIGAN, Daniel.
"Conceptions of Peace" in *Celebrating Peace*, RENDTORFF, Trutz.
"Early Advocates of Lasting World Peace: Utopians or Realists?" in *Celebrating Peace*, BOK, Sissela.
"Experiencing the Death of Humanity" in *Issues in War and Peace: Philosophical Inquiries*, GINSBERG, Robert.
"Feminism and Peace Theory: Women as Nurturers versus Women as Public Citizens" in *In the Interest of Peace: A Spectrum of Philosophical Views*, DUHAN, Laura.
"If Peace Were at Hand, How Would We Know It?" in *Issues in War and Peace: Philosophical Inquiries*, PARTRIDGE, Ernest.
"On Stories, Peacemaking, and Philosophical Method: Toward a Pluralistic Account of Non-Violence" in *Issues in War and Peace: Philosophical Inquiries*, BOVE, Laurence.
"Patriotism and the Pursuit of Peace" in *In the Interest of Peace: A Spectrum of Philosophical Views*, NATHANSON, Stephen.
"The Peace of God" in *Celebrating Peace*, MINEAR, Paul S.
"Peace Through Justice: A Practical Reconciliation of Opposing Conceptions of Justice" in *In the Interest of Peace: A Spectrum of Philosophical Views*, STERBA, James.
"Poetic Vision and the Hope for Peace" in *Celebrating Peace*, LEVERTOV, Denise.
"Political Theology and the Ethics of Peace" in *Celebrating Peace*, MOLTMANN, Jürgen.
"The Rope of Violence and the Snake of Peace" in *Celebrating Peace*, LARSON, Gerald J.
"Teaching Peace in a Christian Context" in *Celebrating Peace*, GILLIGAN, John J.
"Utilitarian Ethics and Superpower Negotiations: Lost Opportunities for Nuclear Peace" in *In the Interest of Peace: A Spectrum of Philosophical Views*, LACKEY, Douglas.
"War and Peace" in *A Companion to Ethics*, MC MAHAN, Jeff.
"What Does Philosophy Add to Nuclear Discussions? An Introductory Essay" in *Issues in War and Peace: Philosophical Inquiries*, KUNKEL, Joseph and KLEIN, Kenneth.
Bentham, the Benthamites, and the Nineteenth-Century British Peace Movement. CONWAY, Stephen.
The History of the Christian Philosophical Reflection on Peace. WASKIEWICZ, Hanna.
Kant's Theory of Peace and the Main Aspects of the Recent Discussion Surrounding It (in German). ZAHN, Manfred.
Marxisten und Christen für eine gerechte, friedliche Welt. NEHRING, Hartmut.
La via della pace: in merito ad un recente libro. ZANUSO, Francesca.

PEACOCKE, C
Pictures and Depictions: A Consideration of Peacocke's Views. KEMP, G N.
The Representational Content of Musical Experience. DE BELLIS, Mark.

PEDAGOGY
Education as a Human Right: A Theory of Curriculum and Pedagogy. VANDENBERG, Donald.
Moralische Verbindlichkeit oder Erziehung. LANGEWAND, Alfred.

PEDAGOGY

"Values in Teaching and Learning: A Student-Teacher Dialogue" in *Integrity in Health Care Institutions: Humane Environments for Teaching, Inquiry, and Healing*, DUNN, Kim and BULGER, Ruth Ellen.
Coaching: Who Needs It and What is It?. GUIN, Philip.
Comments: "A Moral Ideal for Everyone and No One". HUNT, Lester.
DBAE: Complaints, Reminiscences, and Response. BROUDY, Harry S.
Education for Judgment. JAMES, William.
Feminist Theory, Plurality of Voices and Cultural Imperialism. HERNANDEZ, Adriana.
The Importance of Cultural Pedagogy. MC DERMOTT, John J.
Knowledge Growth and Teaching: Towards a Genetic Foundation for Teachers' Knowledge. ORTON, Robert E.
Pedagogy of the Unimpressed: Philosophy for Children and the Adult Learner. TURGEON, Wendy.
Plato's Line Revisited: The Pedagogy of Complete Reflection. WOOD, Robert E.
The Power of Hegemony vis-à-vis the Marketplace of Ideas: Response to Orton. BROSIO, Richard A.
Response to Donald Vandenberg's "Co-intentional Pedagogy". GREENE, Maxine.
Silvio Spaventa e Antonio Labriola, gli 'aspetti-pedagogici'. DE CUMIS, Nicola Siciliani.
Teaching Acts: An Unfinished Story. MC EWAN, Hunter.
Thirty Great Ways to Mess Up a Critical Thinking Test. FACIONE, Peter A.
Warnings on Resistance and the Language of Possibility: Gramsci and a Pedagogy from the Surreal. SENESE, Guy B.

PEGUY, C

Giuseppe De Luca e la polemica sulla moralità di Péguy. FIORENTINO, Fernando.

PEIRCE

The Potential of Modern Discourse: Musil, Peirce, and Perturbation. FINLAY, Marike.
Pragmatism: From Peirce to Davidson. MURPHY, John P.
Bowne and Peirce on the Logic of Religious Belief. ANDERSON, Douglas R.
Can Peirce Be a Pragmaticist and an Idealist?. PETERSON, John.
Charles S Peirce's Theory of Infinitesimals. LEVY, Stephen H.
Hume's "Of Miracles," Peirce, and the Balancing of Likelihoods. MERRILL, Kenneth R.
In What Way is Abductive Inference Creative?. KAPITAN, Tomis.
Josiah Royce: la metafisica della comunità. BUZZI GRASSI, Elisa.
L'épistémologie mathématique de Gonseth dans la perspective du pragmatisme de Peirce. HEINZMANN, Gerhard.
Das neue (post-analytische) Interesse an der Präanalytischen Philosophie. NAGL, Ludwig.
Not Every Object of a Sign has Being. PAPE, Helmut.
On Falsificationist Interpretations of Peirce. SULLIVAN, Patrick F.
Peirce and Evolution: Comment on O'Hear. GOMILA, Antoni.
Peirce's Haecceitism. DI LEO, Jeffrey R.
Peirce's Logic of Discovery: Abduction and the Universal Categories. TURRISI, Patricia A.
Peirce's Realism, Intentionality and Final Causation. TURIANO, Mark.
Pragmatics and Pragmatism. SULLIVAN, Patrick F.
The Problem of Theoretical Self-Reflexivity in Peirce and Santayana. DILWORTH, David A.
The Role of Moral Intuition in Applied Ethics: A Consideration of Positions of Peirce and Strike and Soltis. MC CARTHY, Christine.
Santayana's Peirce. HOUSER, Nathan.
A Semiotical Reflection on Biology, Living Signs and Artificial Life. EMMECHE, Claus.
La sémiotique, les objets singuliers et la complexité. THÉRIEN, Gilles.
Substrative Materialism. KERR-LAWSON, Angus.
Towards a Potential-Pragmatic Account of Peirce's Theory of Truth. SFENDONI-MENTZOU, Demetra.
Valency, Adicity, and Adity in Peirce's MS 482. BURCH, Robert W.
Vers une mise en signe de l'installation. RÉGIMBALD, Manon.

PELLETIER, F

Vacuity. RAMER, Alexis Manaster.

PENAL LAW(S)

The Birth of the Death-Machine. MEGIVERN, James J.
Retaliatory Punishment as a Categorical Imperative. HÖFFE, Ottfried.

PENROSE, R

Philosophical Elements in Penrose's and Hawking's Research in Contemporary Cosmology. DREES, Wim.

PEOPLE(S)

Actual Preferences, Actual People. GOODIN, Robert E.
The Interpretation of Texts, People and Other Artifacts. DENNETT, Daniel C.

PEPPER, S

Metaphor and Pluralism. MAC CORMAC, Earl R.

PERCEPTION

see also Sense Data
About Time: Inventing the Fourth Dimension. FRIEDMAN, William J.
Aristotle's Psychology. ROBINSON, Daniel N.
Berkeley's Revolution in Vision. ATHERTON, Margaret.
David Hume's Theory of Mind. FLAGE, Daniel E.
Instrumental Realism: The Interface between Philosophy of Science and Philosophy of Technology. IHDE, Don.
Kant's Transcendental Psychology. KITCHER, Patricia.
Love's Knowledge: Essays on Philosophy and Literature. NUSSBAUM, Martha C.
Mathematics and the Image of Reason. TILES, Mary E.
The Natural and the Normative: Theories of Spatial Perception from Kant to Helmholtz. HATFIELD, Gary.
Proust: The Creative Silence. CARANFA, Angelo.
Der sinnliche Gehalt der Wahrnehmung. SCHANTZ, Richard.
"Our Perception of the External World" in *Key Themes in Philosophy*, TILES, J E.
"Perception and Human Reality" in *Harré and His Critics*, GRENE, Marjorie.
"Perception and Reality" in *Information, Semantics and Epistemology*, SOSA, Ernest.
"A Perception of Reality with an East-Nilotic People" in *I, We and Body: First Joint Symposium of Philosophers from Africa and from the Netherlands*, STOKS, Hans.
"Perceptual Content" in *Themes From Kaplan*, PEACOCKE, Christopher.
"The Problem of the External World" in *Key Themes in Philosophy*, HAMLYN, D W.
"Thought and Perception: The Views of Two Philosophical Innovators" in *The Analytic Tradition: Philosophical Quarterly Monographs, Volume 1*, DUMMETT, Michael.
"Inhabiting" in the *Phenomenology of Perception*. WEINER, Scott E.
"Why Do Things Look as They Do?" Some Gibsonian Answers to Koffka's Question. NATSOULAS, Thomas.
The Antinomy of Perception: Merleau-Ponty and Causal Representation Theory. HASS, Lawrence.
Berkeley, Perception, and Identity. BAXTER, Donald L M.
Cognitive Psychology, Phenomenology, and the "Creative Tension of Voices". EVANS, Fred.
Consciousness and Introspective Knowledge. CARLOYE, Jack C.
A Critique of Jayarasi's Critique of Perception. MOHANTA, D K.
Descartes on Sensory Representation: A Study of the *Dioptrics*. MAC KENZIE, Ann Wilbur.
Dialectical Perception: A Synthesis of Lenin and Bogdanov. WRIGHT, Edmond.
Dretske on Perception. HOROWITZ, Amir.
The Existence of Non-Existence of Things which are Not in the Mind. POMERANTZ, Alfred.
Experimental Methods and Conceptual Confusion: An Investigation into R L Gregory's Theory of Perception. HACKER, P M S.
Externalist Theories of Perception. ALSTON, William P.
A Generalized Quantifier Logic for Naked Infinitives. VAN DER DOES, Jaap.
La imaginación creadora en el pensamiento de Gastón Bachelard. CASTILLO, Roberto.
Insularity and the Persistence of Perceptual Illusion. CAM, Philip.
Isvarakrsna's Two-Level-Perception: Propositional and Non-Propositional. CLEAR, Edeltraud Harzer.
Juicios de percepción y de experiencia en Kant. FERNÁNDEZ, Alvaro López.
Keith Lehrer and Thomas Reid. CHISHOLM, Roderick M.
Kenny and Religious Experiences. JORDAN, J.
Malebranche versus Arnauld. COOK, Monte.
Mathematical Expressibility, Perceptual Relativity, and Secondary Qualities. PEREBOOM, Derk.
Metaphor and Aspect-Perception. KEMP, G Neville.
Objective and Subjective Aspects of Pain. GRAHEK, Nikola.
On the Epistemic Value of Moral Experience. TOLHURST, William.
On Two Recent Accounts of Colour. MC GINN, Marie.
Perception and Evaluation: Aristotle on the Moral Imagination. HANKINSON, R J.
Perception and Neuroscience. GILLETT, Grant R.
Perceptual Aspects of Art for the Blind. ARNHEIM, Rudolf.
Perceptual Content in the Stoics. SORABJI, Richard.
Persons as Natural Works of Art. ALDRICH, Virgil.
The Physics of Modern Perception: Beyond Body and World. BARRY JR, James.
The Praxiology of Perception: Visual Orientations and Practical Action. COULTER, Jeff and PARSONS, E D.
Professor Matilal on Some Topics of Indian Philosophy. BHATTACHARYYA, Sibajiban.
The Role of Perceptual Relativity in Berkeley's Philosophy. MUEHLMANN, Robert.
Scientific Realism, Perceptual Beliefs, and Justification. OTTE, Richard.
Seeing in the Mind's Eye. BORUAH, Bijoy H.
Seeing the Original. BASS, Walter.
Sensations and Judgments of Perception: Diagnosis and Rehabilitation of Some of Kant's Misleading Examples. KOTZIN, Rhoda and BAUMGÄRTNER, Järg.
Some Aspects of the Relationship Between the Theory of Socialism and the Perception of an Era (in German). BRIE, André (and others).

PERCEPTION
Some Thoughts on Common Scents. ALMAGOR, Uri.
The Theory of Triple Perception. SARMA, Rajendra Nath.
Visual Perception and the Wages of Indeterminacy. MONTGOMERY, Richard.

PERELMAN, C
Perelman et la philosophie anglo-saxonne. MARCIL-LACOSTE, Louise.

PERENNIAL PHILOSOPHY
Comment on Huston Smith's Review of *The Essential Writings of Frithiof Schuon. ANDERSON, Tyson.*
Reply to Huston Smith. ANDERSON, Tyson.
Response to Tyler Anderson. SMITH, Huston.

PERESTROIKA
The Humanism of Economics or Economizing on Humanism?. RIUMIN, V A.
Marx and Perestroika. ROCKMORE, Tom.

PERFECTIBILITY
El ser perfectible de la persona humana. JIMÉNEZ GUERRERO, A.

PERFECTION
Evolution: Probleme und neue Aspekte ihrer Theorie. SCHEFFCZYK, Leo (ed).
The Philosopher's Joke. WATSON, Richard A.
Filosofia e ascesi nel Seicento: Il caso francese. BOSCO, Domenico.
Hegels Geschichtsphilosophie im Vergleich mit anderen Geschichtskonzeptionen. GLOY, Karen.
Plotinus and the *Apeiron* of Plato's *Parmenides*. HEISER, John H.

PERFORMANCE(S)
The Aesthetic Relation of Musical Performer and Audience. PUTMAN, Daniel.
Artists, Computer Programs and Performance. GODLOVITCH, A.
Authenticity Again. SHARPE, R A.
Identifying Musical Works of Art. JACOBS, Jo Ellen.
Moral Behavior at Public Performances. OLDS, Mason.
Music Performance and the Tools of the Trade. GODLOVITCH, Stan.
The Ontology of Musical Works and the Authenticity of their Performances. DAVIES, Stephen.
Understanding Performance Art: Art beyond Art. HEYD, Thomas.

PERFORMATIVES
Speech Acts and Literary Theory. PETREY, Sandy.

PERFORMING ART(S)
"Dance is a Performing Art" in *XIth International Congress in Aesthetics, Nottingham 1988*, MC FEE, Graham.

PERIODIZATION
European Counterimages: Problems of Periodization and Historical Memory. DINER, Dan.

PERISHING
Cosmic Justice in Anaximander. ENGMANN, Joyce.

PERKINS, D
Is the Creative Process in Art a Form of Puzzle Solving?. LEDDY, Thomas.

PERMANENCE
Backwards Causation and the Permanence of the Past. ODDIE, Graham.

PERMUTATION(S)
Logical Constants Across Varying Types. VAN BENTHEM, Johan.
A Note on the Permutationally Convex Games. ALIDAEE, Bahram.

PERRICK, M
Kripke on Theoretical Identifications: A Rejoinder to Perrick. BUXTON, James.

PERSEVERANCE
"Lest Anyone Should Fall": A Middle Knowledge Perspective on Perseverance and Apostolic Warnings. CRAIG, William Lane.

PERSISTENCE
On Rigidity and Persistence. WILLIAMSON, Timothy.

PERSON(S)
see also Human(s), Individual(s)
The Call to Personhood. MC FADYEN, Alistair I.
How to Build a Person: A Prolegomenon. POLLOCK, John L.
Introducing Persons: Theories and Arguments in the Philosophy of Mind. CARRUTHERS, Peter.
The Looking-Glass Self: An Examination of Self-Awareness. CANFIELD, John.
Max Scheler's Concept of the Person: An Ethics of Humanism. PERRIN, Ron.
Medical Ethics for Physicians-in-Training. KANTOR, Jay E.
Metaphysik als Metahistorik oder Hermeneutik des unreinen-Denkens Die Philosophie Max Müllers. RUIZ-PESCE, Ramón Eduardo.
Mind in Action: Essays in the Philosophy of Mind. RORTY, Amelie Oksenberg.
Rawls: "A Theory of Justice" and Its Critics. KUKATHAS, Chandran.
Selbsttäuschung. LÖW-BEER, Martin.
The Vatican, the Law and the Human Embryo. COUGHLAN, Michael J.
"Is There a Concept of Person in Greek Philosophy?" in *Psychology (Companions to Ancient Thought: 2)*, GILL, Christopher.
"On Human Death" in *Biomedical Ethics Reviews, 1989*, HUMBER, James M.
"Person and Community in African Thought" in *I, We and Body: First Joint Symposium of Philosophers from Africa and from the Netherlands*, GYEKYE, Kwame.
"Personal References" in *Information, Semantics and Epistemology*, LOAR, Brian.
"Philosophy and Artificial Intelligence" in *Philosophical Perspectives, 4: Action Theory and Philosophy of Mind, 1990*, POLLOCK, John L.
"The Poetics of Personhood" in *Reading Rorty*, HOLLIS, Martin.
I "systemata subordinata" e il problema della partecipazione in Hobbes. SORGI, Giuseppe.
Altruism and the Avoidance of Solipsism. CHONG, Kim-Chong.
Arguments for Abortion of Abnormal Fetuses and the Moral Status of the Developing Embryo. SUTTON, Agneta.
Art and Philosophy: The Person in the Cybernetic Age. HETZLER, Florence M.
Childhood Betrayed: A Personalist Analysis. HANINK, James.
Consciousness and Commissurotomy: III—Toward the Improvement of Alternative Conceptions. NATSOULAS, Thomas.
Cuestiones de sobrevivencia. MILLÁN, Gustavo Ortiz (trans) and SOSA, Ernest.
La dignità dell'uomo da Kant a Hegel. PAOLINELLI, Marco.
Evans-Pritchard on Persons and Their Cattle-Clocks: A Note on the Anthropological Account of Man. CHANDRA, Suresh.
How Many Selves Make Me?. CLARK, Stephen R L.
Hydatidiform Moles and Teratomas Confirm the Human Identity of the Preimplantation Embryo. SUAREZ, Antoine.
Imagination and the Sense of Identity. HERTZBERG, Lars.
Living a Life and the Problem of Existential Impossibility. LÖW-BEER, Martin.
Machines as Persons?. CHERRY, Christopher.
Machines as Persons?. HANFLING, Oswald.
Moraliteit en magie. LESAGE, Dieter.
La naturaleza y la historia como fundamento para un concepto renovada de razón. PADILLA, Leonel Eduardo.
The Nature of a Person-Stage. MC INERNEY, Peter K.
Persona y sociedad según Jacques Maritain. WASHBURN, Jimmy.
El personalismo cristiano de Emmanuel Mounier. ARAYA, Eval A.
Persons and Human Beings. GARRETT, Brian.
Persons as Natural Works of Art. ALDRICH, Virgil.
Quale statuto per l'embrione umano?. COMPAGNONI, Francesco.
Radin on Personhood and Rent Control. GREENBERG, Dan.
Real Selves: Persons as a Substantial Kind. LOWE, E J.
La realtà umana nel pensiero di Xavier Zubiri. QUINTÁS, Alfonso López and NICOLOSI, Mauro.
Recognizing Suffering. CASSELL, Eric J.
Respect for Persons and Self-Respect: Western and Indian. GHOSH-DASTIDAR, Koyeli.
Riproposta di una teoria della soggettività in un'epoca di decostruzione del soggetto. LATORA, Salvatore.
Same Human Being, Same Person?. THORNTON, Mark.
The Status of Frozen Embryos. ANDERSON, Susan Leigh.
When Do People Begin?. GRISEZ, Germain.
Zygotes, Souls, Substances, and Persons. BOLE III, Thomas J.

PERSONAL IDENTITY
see also Identity
The Case for Dualism. SMYTHIES, John R (ed).
David Hume's Theory of Mind. FLAGE, Daniel E.
Deciding for Others: The Ethics of Surrogate Decision Making. BUCHANAN, Allen E.
Difference and Subjectivity: Dialogue and Personal Identity. JACQUES, Francis.
Introduction to Metaphysics: The Fundamental Questions. SCHOEDINGER, Andrew B (ed).
The Looking-Glass Self: An Examination of Self-Awareness. CANFIELD, John.
Material Beings. VAN INWAGEN, Peter.
Other Human Beings. COCKBURN, David.
Philosophy: An Introduction Through Literature. KLEIMAN, L (ed).
"Fission and the Facts" in *Philosophical Perspectives, 3: Philosophy of Mind and Action Theory, 1989*, JOHNSTON, Mark.
"Personal Identity and the Mind-Body Problem" in *The Case for Dualism*, MADELL, Geoffrey.
An Ambiguity in Parfit's Theory of Personal Identity. CURZER, Howard.
Bodily Theory and Theory of the Body. GILES, James.
Divided Minds. HIRSCH, Eli.
Finding Ourselves: Personal Identity and the Limits of Possible-World Arguments. BECK, Simon.
Fragmented Selves and the Problem of Ownership. BRENNAN, Andrew.
Locke on Personal Identity and the Trinity Controversy of the 1690s. WEDEKING, Gary.
Locke on Personal Identity. WINKLER, Kenneth P.

PERSONAL IDENTITY
Locke's Account of Personal Identity. SCHRECK, P A.
Nature as Personal. DOMBROWSKI, Daniel A.
Nozick's Identity Crisis. LUCY, W N R.
Personal Identity and Brain Transplants. SNOWDON, P F.
Personal Identity and Rebirth. STOEBER, Michael.
Personal Identity and Reductionism. GARRETT, Brian.
Personal Identity and the Causal Continuity Requirement. ELLIOT, Robert.
Personal Identity and the Idea of a Human Being. MADELL, Geoffrey.
Personal Identity, Reincarnation, and Resurrection. IALACCI, Michael.
Persons and the Intentional Stance. DIBRELL, William.
The Possibility of Reincarnation. NOONAN, Harold W.
The Practical Importance of Personal Identity. DOEPKE, F.
Pre-existence and Personal Identity. FEENSTRA, Ronald J.
The Problem of Who: Multiple Personality, Personal Identity and the Double Brain. APTER, Andrew.
Real Human Persons. DONAGAN, Alan.
Sartre and Our Identity as Individuals. DILMAN, Ilham.
The Subject of Experience. GILLETT, Grant.
Who are "We"? Ambiguities of the Modern Self. SKINNER, Quentin.
Why Personal Identity Is Animal Identity. CARTER, William R.

PERSONAL KNOWLEDGE
The Hermeneutics of Life History: Personal Achievement and History in Gadamer, Habermas, and Erikson. WALLULIS, Jerald.

PERSONAL RELATIONS
How Can They?. BUSALACCHI, Pete.
The Inadequacy of a Deontological Analysis of Peer Relations in Organizations. MARTIN, Robert M.
On Taking Substituted Judgment Seriously. BARON, Charles.

PERSONALISM
Artists, Computer Programs and Performance. GODLOVITCH, A.
Bowne and Peirce on the Logic of Religious Belief. ANDERSON, Douglas R.
Childhood Betrayed: A Personalist Analysis. HANINK, James.
The Ethical Theory of Peter A Bertocci. PADGETT, Jack F.
James and Bowne on the Philosophy of Religious Experience. DOTTERER, Donald W.
Moral Laws in Borden P Bowne's *Principles of Ethics*. BURROW JR, Rufus.
El personalismo de Santo Tomás. FORMENT, Eudaldo.
Personalist and Pragmatist Persons. STUHR, John J.
The Philosophical Achievement of Peter A Bertocci. RECK, Andrew J.
W T Harris' Philosophy as Personalism. LAUDER, Robert E.

PERSONALITY
The Authentic Self: Toward a Philosophy of Personality. LACENTRA, Walter.
Natural Reasons: Personality and Polity. HURLEY, S L.
Aristotle on Personality and Some Implications for Friendship. REINER, Paula.
Elogio critico dell'imperfezione. TUSA, Carlo.
Izydora Dambska's Philosophy of Culture (in Polish). BOBER, Ireneusz.
Nietzsche and Pessimism: The Metaphysics Hypostatised. CAUCHI, Francesca.
Two Conservative Views of Nationality and Personality: A A Grigor'ev and K N Leont'ev. DOWLER, E W.

PERSPECTIVE(S)
Enriching Business Ethics. WALTON, Clarence C (ed).
Boston University Studies in Philosophy and Religion, Volumes 1-10. SMART, Ninian.
The Nature of Causation: A Singularist Account. TOOLEY, Michael.
Nietzsche's "Will to Power" Nachlass. HELLER, Peter.
Pragmatique du discours et réciprocité de perspectives (A propos de Don Quichotte et Don Juan). GÓMEZ-MORIANA, Antonio.

PERSPECTIVISM
Baffling Phenomena: And Other Studies in the Philosophy of Knowledge and Valuation. RESCHER, Nicholas.
Nietzsche On Truth and Philosophy. CLARK, Maudemarie.
Nietzsche's Metaperspectivism. ROTH, Robin Alice.
Nietzschean Perspectivism and the Logic of Practical Reason. REDDING, Paul.

PERSSON, I
Universalizability and the Summing of Desires: Reply to Ingmar Persson. HARE, R M.

PERSUASION
"The Fourth Gospel's Art of Rational Persuasion" in *The Bible as Rhetoric: Studies in Biblical Persuasion and Credibility*, WARNER, Martin.
The Epistemology and Ethics of Consensus: Uses and Misuses of 'Ethical' Expertise. TONG, Rosemarie.
Is Coming to Believe in God Reasonable or Unreasonable?. HERBERT, R T.
Persuasion: Jane Austen's Philosophical Rhetoric. KASTELY, James L.
Philosophical Argument and the Rhetorical Wedge. JOHNSTONE JR, Henry W.

PERVERSION(S)
"Closing Up the Corpses: Diseases of Sexuality and the Emergence of the Psychiatric Style of Reasoning" in *Meaning and Method: Essays in Honor of Hilary Putnam*, DAVIDSON, Arnold I.

PESSIMISM
Nietzsche and Pessimism: The Metaphysics Hypostatised. CAUCHI, Francesca.

PESTALOZZI
Kant, Pestalozzi and the Role of Ideology in Educational Thought. ADAMS, Ian.

PESTICIDE(S)
Genetically Engineered Herbicide Resistance, Part Two. COMSTOCK, Gary.
Informed Consent or Informed Rejection of Pesticide Use: A Concept for Environmental Action. ORTON, David.

PETRUZZELLIS, N
La fondazione dei valori nell'assiologia critica di Nicola Petruzzellis. TURCO, Giovanni.

PHARMACOLOGY
Geschiedenis als muurbloempje. PRINS, Ad.

PHARMACY
The Business Ethics of Pharmacists: Conflicts Practices and Beliefs. VITELL, Scott J and RAWWAS, Mohammed Y A and FESTERVAND, Troy A.
The Pharmacist's Role in Patient Care. SCHULZ, Richard M and BRUSHWOOD, David B.

PHENOMENA
"Newton's Corpuscular Query and Experimental Philosophy" in *Philosophical Perspectives on Newtonian Science*, ACHINSTEIN, Peter.
"Phenomenal States" in *Philosophical Perspectives, 4: Action Theory and Philosophy of Mind, 1990*, LOAR, Brian.
"Inhabiting" in the *Phenomenology of Perception*. WEINER, Scott E.
A determinação heideggeriana de fenómeno em *Sein und Zeit* como superação do "cepticismo metódico". DAS NEVES, Jorge César.
Disembodying 'Bodily' Sensations. COMBES, Richard.
On Saving the Phenomena and the Mice: A Reply to Bourgeois Concerning Van Fraassen's Image of Science. FOSS, Jeff.
Theory of the Apparatus and Theory of the Phenomena: The Case of Low Dose Electron Microscopy. SWIJTINK, Zeno G.
Willing and Acting in Husserl's Lectures on Ethics and Value Theory. NENON, Thomas J.

PHENOMENALISM
Identity and Discrimination. WILLIAMSON, Timothy.
Knowledge of the External World. AUNE, Bruce.
Der sinnliche Gehalt der Wahrnehmung. SCHANTZ, Richard.
"Phenomenalism, Relativity and Atoms: Rehabilitating Ernst Mach's Philosophy of Science" in *Logic, Methodology and Philosophy of Science, VIII*, WOLTERS, Gereon.
"Why Do Things Look as They Do?" Some Gibsonian Answers to Koffka's Question. NATSOULAS, Thomas.
Analytic Functionalism and the Reduction of Phenomenal States. LEVIN, Janet.
Ernst Mach and the Elimination of Subjectivity. HAMILTON, Andy.
The Persistence of Counterexample: Re-examining the Debate over Leibniz Law. LANDINI, Gregory and FOSTER, Thomas.
Phenomenalism and the Reality of Body in Leibniz's Later Philosophy. RUTHERFORD, Donald P.
The Phenomenalism of Newton and Boskovic: A Comparative Study (in Serbo-Croatian). PRINCE, Augustus.

PHENOMENOLOGY
Acts of Meaning. BRUNER, Jerome.
Bewusstsein und Natursein. CHO, Kah Kyung.
The Cogito and Hermeneutics: The Question of the Subject in Ricoeur. JERVOLINO, Domenico.
Consciousness and the Computational Mind. JACKENDOFF, Ray.
Existence et Subjectivité: Études de Psychologie Phénoménologique. THINÈS, Georges.
Existentialism. COOPER, David E.
Experiential Method: Qualitative Research in the Humanities Using Metaphysics and Phenomenology. KIDD, James W.
Exploring Phenomenology (Second Edition). STEWART, David.
Geschichte, Freiheit und Struktur. RUMPEL, Roland.
Glück und Lebenssinn: Eine religionsphilosophische Untersuchung. DRESCHER, Johannes.
Historische Objektivitat. WEBERMAN, David.
La intersubjectividad en Husserl, Volume I and II. IRIBARNE, Julia V.
Jean-Paul Sartre. HENGELBROCK, Jürgen.
Life-World and Politics: Between Modernity and Postmodernity. WHITE, Stephen K (ed).
Logic in the Husserlian Context. TITO, Johanna Maria.
Max Scheler's Concept of the Person: An Ethics of Humanism. PERRIN, Ron.
Metaphysics: A Contemporary Introduction. POST, John F.
Musical Aesthetics: A Historical Reader, Volume III, The Twentieth Century. LIPPMAN, Edward A (ed).
Myth and Philosophy: A Contest of Truths. HATAB, Lawrence J.
On the Problem of Empathy (Third Revised Edition). STEIN, Edith.

PHENOMENOLOGY

On Walter Benjamin: Critical Essays and Recollections. SMITH, Gary (ed).
Phänomenologie als ästhetische Theorie. FELLMANN, Ferdinand.
Phänomenologische Philosophie. STRÖKER, Elisabeth.
Phenomenology of the Truth Proper to Religion. GUERRIÈRE, Daniel (ed).
The Power of Consciousness and the Force of Circumstances in Sartre's Philosophy. BUSCH, Thomas W.
Proust: The Creative Silence. CARANFA, Angelo.
The Question of God in Heidegger's Phenomenology. KOVACS, George.
Reconsidering Psychology: Perspectives from Continental Philosophy. FAULCONER, James E (ed).
Sound, Speech, and Music. BURROWS, David.
Strukturanthropologie "Der menschliche Mensch". ROMBACH, Heinrich.
Vernunft und Kontingenz: Rationalität und Ethos in der Phänomenologie. ORTH, Ernst Wolfgang (ed).
"Kantian and Phenomenological Traditions in Psychological Aesthetics" in *XIth International Congress in Aesthetics, Nottingham 1988*, ALLESCH, Christian.
"Life-World as Depth of Soul: Phenomenology and Psychoanalysis" in *Reconsidering Psychology: Perspectives from Continental Philosophy*, ROMANYSHYN, Robert.
"Phenomenologies and Religious Truth" in *Phenomenology of the Truth Proper to Religion*, WESTPHAL, Merold.
"Situation and Suspicion in the Thought of Merleau-Ponty" in *Ontology and Alterity in Merleau-Ponty*, WESTPHAL, Merold.
"Il y a" et phénoménologie dans la pensée du jeune Lévinas. LANNOY, Jean-Luc.
"Phénoménologie" de l'expression. CHAUVIRE, Christiane.
A Phenomenologically and Psychologically Based Concept of Ethics (in Czechoslovakian). BAYEROVA, M.
The A Priori in Phenomenology and the Legacy of Logical Empiricism. BLOSSER, Philip.
Analisi fenomenologica del concetto di religione. MONDIN, Battista.
Ancora una discussione su Hegel: logica, storia, fenomenologia. NUZZO, Angelica.
The Anomaly of World: From Scheler to Heidegger. SCHALOW, Frank.
Aspects of the Problem of Reference (1): Phenomenology, Hermeneutics and Deconstruction. RAJAN, R Sundara.
Aspects of the Problem of Reference (II). RAJAN, R Sundara.
Autonomy, Empathy, and Transcendence in Sophocles' *Antigone*: A Phenomenological Perspective. NISSIM-SABAT, Marilyn.
Het belang van Husserls aanzet tot een fenomenologie van de bewustzijnsperspectieven. FREDERIX, Lode.
Brentano e Fichte negli scritti "minori" di E Husserl. BELLO, A Ales.
Clocks and Time (in Czechoslovakian). DUBSKY, Ivan.
Cognitive Psychology, Phenomenology, and the "Creative Tension of Voices". EVANS, Fred.
The Concept of Ego in Husserl's Philosophy. DAS, Paritosh Kumar.
Contemporary Ethics and Scheler's Phenomenology of Community. VACEK, Edward.
Continuità e discontinuità tra Husserl e Heidegger: genesi e sviluppo d una polemica filosofica. RIZZACASA, Aurelio.
The Crisis in Psychoanalysis: Resolution Through Husserlian Phenomenology and Feminism. NISSIM-SABAT, Marilyn.
Current Trends in the Philosophy of Medicine. POTTER, Robert Lyman.
A determinação heideggeriana de fenómeno em *Sein und Zeit* como superação do "cepticismo metódico". DAS NEVES, Jorge César.
The Dimension of Color. FÓTI, Véronique.
Duty and Inclination: The Phenomenological Value Ethics of Hans Reiner. GÖRTZEN, René.
Ein Husserlmanuskript über Ästhetik. SCARAMUZZA, Gabriele and SCHUHMANN, Karl.
The Epistemological Significance of the Inner Witness of the Holy Spirit. ABRAHAM, William J.
Essai sur le développement historique de la voie phénoménologique. MAESSCHALCK, Marc.
Experience of the Alien in Husserl's Phenomenology. WALDENFELS, Bernhard.
Foucault: Making a Difference. LILLY, Reginald.
The Genesis of Wittgenstein's Later Philosophy in His Failure as a Phenomenologist. HALLETT, Garth.
Hegel's Intertextual Dialectic: Diderot's *Le Neveu de Rameau* in the *Phenomenology of Spirit*. PRICE, David W.
Hegel: fenomenología del espíritu. MONTOYA, Rocío Basurto.
Heideggers Denken und die Ökologie. PADRUTT, Hanspeter.
Herbert Spiegelberg 1904-1990. SCHUHMANN, Karl.
Hermeneutic Phenomenology and Taoism. KIDD, James W.
Hermeneutics: A Protreptic. JOHNSON, Gregory R.
Historicism and Phenomenology (in Czechoslovakian). CIBULKA, J.
A Historico-Philosophical Investigation of Anti-Science: The Phenomenological Encounter. RAINA, Dhruv.
Hope: Its Essence and Forms (in Polish). SYMOTIUK, Stefan.
Husserl's Concept of Philosophy. SCHUHMANN, Karl.
Husserl's Phenomenology of Knowledge and Cognition (in Polish). DEBOWSKI, Jozef.
Husserl's Presuppositionless Philosophy. REED-DOWNING, Teresa.
Husserl's Time Perception (in Portuguese). PEREIRA JÚNIOR, A.
Husserl—Bolzano II (in Czechoslovakian). BAYEROVA, Marie.
In Defence of Graded Love. LAI, Whalen.
Ingarden und Husserls transzendentaler Idealismus. HAEFLIGER, Gregor.
Intentionality and the Public World: Husserl's Treatment of Objectivity in the Cartesian Meditations. ARP, Kristana.
L'Appel et le Phénomène. LARUELLE, François.
L'herméneutique dans la "phènoménologie comme telle". GREISCH, Jean.
L'inspiration aristotélicienne de la métaphysique de Bergson. WASZKINEL, Romuald.
La Fenomenología aplicada a la Educación. GENÍS, Octavi Fullat.
Lezioni di filosofia della scienza di Guilio Preti. LECIS, Pier Luigi.
Le lezioni di Husserl sull'etica e sulla teoria del valore. DONNICI, Rocco.
Man, History, and Philosophy in Husserl's Crisis of European Sciences (in Czechoslovakian). MAJOR, L.
Max Scheler's Analysis of Illusions, Idols, and Ideologies. IBANA, Rainier R A.
Meaningful Existence, Embodiment and Physical Education. WHITEHEAD, Margaret.
Merleau-Ponty on Taking the Attitude of the Other. MATUSTIK, Martin J.
Merleau-Ponty's Phenomenology of Sympathy. MATUSTIK, Martin J.
Michael Polanyi's Aesthetics: A Phenomenological Study. BISWAS, Goutam.
Le mouvement phénoménologique. TAMINIAUX, Jacques.
Nature et liberté dans l'ontologie fondamentale de Heidegger. BRISART, Robert.
Never say "Never say 'Never'": A Reply to Nicholas Gier. REEDER, Harry P.
Never say "Never": A Response to Reeder's "Wittgenstein Never Was a Phenomenologist". GIER, Nicholas F.
Objet et communauté transcendantale: autour d'un fragment du dernier Husserl. BENOIST, J.
Phänomenologie und Monadologie: Husserl und Leibniz. CRISTIN, Renato.
Phenomenal Qualities and the Nontransitivity of Matching. BURGESS, John A.
Phenomenology and Indian Philosophy. SINGH, Navjyoti.
Phenomenology and Psychoanalysis: The Hermeneutical Mediation. RAJAN, R Sundara.
Phenomenology and Scientific Realism: Husserl's Critique of Galileo. SOFFER, Gail.
Phenomenology and the Philosophy for Children Program. HAMRICK, William.
Phenomenology as Cooperative Task: Husserl-Farber Correspondence during 1936-37. CHO, Kah Kyung.
Philosophical Anthropology: What, Why and How. SCHACHT, Richard.
La problemática ética en el pensamiento de Husserl. IRIBARNE, Julia V.
Progressive Traditionalism as the Spirit of Collingwood's Philosophy. KISSELL, Michael A.
Quatre principes de la phénoménologie. HENRY, Michel.
Reflections on the Schutz-Gurwitsch Correspondence. LANDGREBE, Ludwig.
Réponses à quelques questions. MARION, Jean-Luc.
Retrieving Husserl from His Legacy. FUCHS, Wolfgang.
The Rooting and Uprooting of Reason: On *Spacings* by John Sallis. MALY, Kenneth.
Sartre, Aron et le relativisme historique. BAUGH, Bruce.
Social Apriori of Responsibility in Scheler's Phenomenology (in Serbo-Croatian). VEAUTHIER, Frank W.
Solitude. KOCH, Philip J.
Some Reflections on Husserl's Approach to the Problem of Transcendence. DHAR, Benulal.
Subject en zelfervaring. BERNET, R.
Le sujet en dernier appel. MARION, Jean-Luc.
The Temporality of Illness: Four Levels of Experience. TOOMBS, S Kay.
Le temps du souffrir: Remarques critiques sur la phénoménologie de M Henry. PORÉE, Jérôme.
The Beginning and Structure of the "Phaenomenology of Mind" (in Hungarian). PÖGGELER, Otto.
The Concept of Sense in Merleau-Ponty (in Czechoslovakian). SIVAK, Jozef.
The Critical and the Dogmatic Tendency of Phenomenological Philosophy (in Czechoslovakian). CIBULKA, Josef.
Time in Hegel's *Phenomenology of Spirit*. FLAY, Joseph C.
Two Reversibilities: Merleau-Ponty and Derrida. YOUNT, Mark.
A Unique Way of Existing: Merleau-Ponty and the Subject. SIEGEL, Jerrold.
Die Verfehlung des Themas "Metaphysik und Erfahrung". WIEHL, Reiner.
Wittgenstein's Phenomenology Revisited. GIER, Nicholas F.

PHILO

Il Logos come immagine di Dio in Filone di Alessandria. BELLETTI, Bruno.
The Structure of Philo's Commentary on the Pentateuch. THORNE, Gary W A.

PHILODEMUS

The Poetic Theory of the Stoic 'Aristo'. ASMIS, Elizabeth.

PHILOLOGY

"Also sprach Herakleitos". WOHLFART, Günter.

PHILOLOGY

Nietzsche: The Body and Culture—Philosophy as a Philological Genealogy. BLONDEL, Eric.
Nietzsches Scheitern am Werk. HELLER, Edmund.
Die Wiederkehr im Unterschied. PEETZ, Siegbert.
Did Plato Coin *Rhētorikē*?. SCHIAPPA, Edward.
Friedrich Nietzsche and Classical Philology Today. IRMSCHER, Johannes.
Ontología hermenéutica y reflexión filológica: el acceso a la filosofía de H G Gadamer. DOMINGO, Agustín.

PHILOSOPHER(S)

Art and Philosophy: The Person in the Cybernetic Age. HETZLER, Florence M.
Die DDR und ihre Philosophen: Über Voraussetzungen einer Urteilsbildung. RUBEN, Peter.
Homunculus Trouble, or, What Is Applied Philosophy?. MIDGLEY, Mary.
MacIntyre, Tradition, and the Christian Philosopher. HIBBS, Thomas S.
The Philosopher as Hero. DUHAN, Laura.
The Philosopher as Insider and Outsider: How to Advise, Compromise, and Criticize. KAMM, Frances M.
Philosophers as Professional Relativists: Canadian Philosophical Association Presidential Address 1990. BUTTS, Robert E.
Why Philosophers Should Offer Ethics Consultations. THOMASMA, David C.

PHILOSOPHICAL ANTHROPOLOGY

Difference and Subjectivity: Dialogue and Personal Identity. JACQUES, Francis.
Dream and Culture: An Anthropological Study of the Western Intellectual Tradition. PARMAN, Susan.
History and the Paradoxes of Metaphysics in "Dantons Tod". TAYLOR, Rodney.
Human Interests: Reflections on Philosophical Anthropology. RESCHER, Nicholas.
The Looking-Glass Self: An Examination of Self-Awareness. CANFIELD, John.
The Many Dimensions of the Human Person. STEGER, E Ecker.
Strukturanthropologie "Der menschliche Mensch". ROMBACH, Heinrich.
Der Ursprung der Erziehungsziele in der Lehre von Plato, Aristoteles und Neill. EGGER, Paul.
Das Verhängnis Erste Philosophie. EBELING, Hans.
Adquisición del lenguaje y antropología. FERNÁNDEZ, Teresa Bejarano.
Analyse d'un corpus iconographique rassemblé par Maxime Préaud ou Aristote et la mélancolie. FLEURY, Chantal.
El autoconocimiento del alma según Avicena latino. OYARZABAL, Manuel.
Catholic and Marxist Views on Human Development. MC GOVERN, Arthur F.
A Christian Response to Professor Zagorka Golubovic. ZADEMACH, Wieland.
Conceptos filosóficos como sustrato del sentido de la muerte, desde la época prehispánica hasta la actual. DE LOS ANGELES IMAZ LIRA, María.
Culture as an Open System. VAN PEURSEN, C A.
Dicendum est eum non esse hominem: Ein mögliches frühes Zeugnis für die anthropologische Gewichtung.... KÖHLER, Theodor Wolfram.
Emerson and Nietzsche's 'Beyond-Man'. STACK, George J.
Etica, retórica y política en la antropología aristotélica. MARTIN, Victor R.
Evans-Pritchard on Persons and Their Cattle-Clocks: A Note on the Anthropological Account of Man. CHANDRA, Suresh.
Freud: Uma Concepção Agónica da Educação. BARBOSA, Manuel.
From Brahma to a Blade of Grass. COLLINS, Alfred.
From Philosophical Psychology to Philosophical Anthropology (in Dutch). VERGOTE, A.
El hombre agustiniamo: Itinerario tras el ser de la existencia. MOLINA, Mario A.
The Life of Order and the Order of Life: Eric Voegelin on Modernity and the Problem of Philosophical Anthropology. LEVY, David J.
Man as the Animal Symbolism in the Conception of S Langer (in Polish). BYTNIEWSKI, Pawel.
A Marxist Approach to the Concept of Being/Becoming Human. GOLUBOVIC, Zagorka.
On the Duality of China's Traditional Mode of Thought and the Difficulty of Transforming It. ZIHLIN, Li.
The Origins of Morality: An Essay in Philosophical Anthropology. OLDENQUIST, Andrew.
La persona humana: Síntesis de la concepción antropológica de K Wojtyla. JIMÉNEZ GUERRERO, A.
Philosophical Anthropology in Greek Antiquity. GHOSE, A M.
Philosophical Anthropology: What, Why and How. SCHACHT, Richard.
The Philosophical Significance of Psychological Differences Among Humans. LACHS, John.
El principio antrópico. PEREZ DE LABORDA, A.
Le progrès: De la temporalité historico-anthropothéologique et symbolique. HOTTOIS, Guy.
La realtà umana nel pensiero di Xavier Zubiri. QUINTÁS, Alfonso López and NICOLOSI, Mauro.
Search for Indian Traditional Paradigm of Society. SHARMA, K N.
El ser perfectible de la persona humana. JIMÉNEZ GUERRERO, A.
El ser y el sentido: Notas husserlianas. PEGUEROLES, Juan.
A Structuralist Rousseau: On the Anthropology of Claude Lévi-Strauss. HONNETH, Axel.
Sulla posizione dell'uomo nella natura. SEIDL, Horst.
Traditional Chinese Culture: Contemporary Developments —Profound Selections from the Works of Fang Dongmei. GUOBAO, Jiang.
Traité de la créature. VARET, Gilbert.
Los universales culturales. PASSMORE, John and GARCÍA MONSIVÁIS, Blanca.

PHILOSOPHICAL PSYCHOLOGY

Human Consciousness. HANNAY, Alastair.
From Philosophical Psychology to Philosophical Anthropology (in Dutch). VERGOTE, A.
Philosophische Anstösse in der computerunterstützten Intelligenz-Forschung. HRACHOVEC, Herbert.
Some Philosophical Aspects of Psychophysiology—Are There Any Elements of "Neurophilosophy"? (in German). RÜDIGER, Wolfgang.

PHILOSOPHIZING

Boethius and the Consolation of Philosophy, or, How to Be a Good Philosopher. BELSEY, Andrew.
Dr C Neugebauer's Critical Note on Ethnophilosophy in the Philosophical Discourse in Africa: Some Remarks. BEWAJI, J A I.

PHILOSOPHY

see also Metaphilosophy, Process Philosophy
African Philosophy: The Essential Readings. SEREQUEBERHAN, Tsenay.
After the Demise of the Tradition: Rorty, Critical Theory, and the Fate of Philosophy. NIELSEN, Kai.
American Philosophy and the Romantic Tradition. GOODMAN, Russell B.
The Analytic Tradition: Philosophical Quarterly Monographs, Volume 1. BELL, David (ed).
The Bible as Rhetoric: Studies in Biblical Persuasion and Credibility. WARNER, Martin (ed).
The Big Questions: A Short Introduction to Philosophy (Third Edition). SOLOMON, Robert C.
The Butterfly as Companion: Meditations on the First Three Chapters of the Chuang Tzu. WU, Kuang-Ming.
Convictions. HOOK, Sidney.
Core Questions in Philosophy: A Text With Readings. SOBER, Elliott.
Delicate Subjects: Romanticism, Gender, and the Ethics of Understanding. ELLISON, Julie.
Dictionary of Religion and Philosophy. MAC GREGOR, Geddes.
Does God Exist? The Great Debate. MORELAND, J P.
Frege and Other Philosophers. DUMMETT, Michael.
Fundamentals of Philosophy (Third Edition). STEWART, David.
La Grecia "Tedesca" fra Nostalgia e Mito. FOLLIERO-METZ, Grazia Dolores.
The Hermeneutics of Life History: Personal Achievement and History in Gadamer, Habermas, and Erikson. WALLULIS, Jerald.
The Humanities in the Nineties: A View From the Netherlands. ZÜRCHER, Erik (ed).
Das Ich im deutschen Idealismus und das Selbst im Zen-Buddhist Fichte und Dogen. NAGASAWA, Kunihiko.
The Idea of a Social Science and its Relation to Philosophy (Second Edition). WINCH, Peter.
Introduction to Philosophy: Classical and Contemporary Readings. POJMAN, Louis P.
Key Themes in Philosophy. GRIFFITHS, A Phillips (ed).
Lesbian Philosophies and Cultures. ALLEN, Jeffner (ed).
Library Research Guide to Philosophy: Illustrated Search Strategy and Sources. LIST, Charles J.
Love's Knowledge: Essays on Philosophy and Literature. NUSSBAUM, Martha C.
Modernism as a Philosophical Problem: On the Dissatisfactions of European High Culture. PIPPIN, Robert B.
Myth and Modern Philosophy. DANIEL, Stephen H.
Myth and Philosophy: A Contest of Truths. HATAB, Lawrence J.
New Dimensions of Confucian and Neo-Confucian Philosophy. CHENG, Chung-ying.
The Philosopher's Dictionary. MARTIN, Robert M.
The Philosopher's Joke. WATSON, Richard A.
Philosophical Writing: An Introduction. MARTINICH, A P.
Philosophy Books, 1982-1986. MAY, Thomas (ed).
The Philosophy in Christianity. VESEY, Godfrey (ed).
Philosophy's Journey: From the Presocratics to the Present (Second Edition). KOLENDA, Konstantin.
Philosophy: An Introduction Through Literature. KLEIMAN, L (ed).
Philosophy: Theory and Practice. THIROUX, Jacques P.
Psychoanalysis, Scientific Method, and Philosophy. HOOK, Sidney (ed).
Published Essays, 1966-1985 (The Collected Works of Eric Voegelin, Volume 12). SANDOZ, Ellis (ed).
Razionalitá critica: nella filosofia moderna. LAMACCHIA, Ada (ed).
Russische Philosophie. GOERDT, Wilhelm.
Socialism, Feminism and Philosophy: A Radical Philosophy Reader. SAYERS, Sean (ed).

PHILOSOPHY

Talking Philosophy: A Wordbook. SPARKES, A W.
A Thinker's Guide to Living Well. BRADFORD, Dennis E.
Thinking Philosophically: An Introduction to Philosophy with Readings. GUSMANO, Joseph J.
Thomistic Papers, V. RUSSMAN, Thomas A (ed).
Time-Travel for Beginners and Other Stories. HARRISON, Jonathan.
Towards a Christian Philosophy. OWENS, Joseph I.
The Transcendental Temptation: A Critique of Religion and the Paranormal. KURTZ, Paul.
Understanding the Chinese Mind: The Philosophical Roots. ALLINSON, Robert E (ed).
Unsere postmoderne Moderne (Second Edition). WELSCH, Wolfgang.
What is History? And Other Late Unpublished Writings (The Collected Works of Eric Voegelin, Vol 28). HOLLWECK, Thomas A (ed).
The World of the Imagination: Sum and Substance. BRANN, Eva T H.
Writers and Philosophers: A Sourcebook of Philosophical Influences on Literature. THOMAS, Edmund J.
The Yoga-Sūtra of Patañjali: A New Translation and Commentary. FEUERSTEIN, Georg.
"Discussion: Progress in Philosophy" in *Acting and Reflecting: The Interdisciplinary Turn in Philosophy*, SIMON, Herbert A.
"Does Philosophy 'Leave Everything as it is'? Even Theology?" in *The Philosophy in Christianity*, BAMBROUGH, Renford.
"How Should Psychologists Define Morality? or, The Negative Side Effects of Philosophy's Influence on Psychology" in *The Moral Domain: Essays in the Ongoing Discussion between Philosophy and the Social Sciences*, BLASI, Augusto.
"Impressions of Philosophy" in *Acting and Reflecting: The Interdisciplinary Turn in Philosophy*, SCHWARTZ, Thomas.
"Mario Bunge on his *Treatise* as a Philosophy" in *Studies on Mario Bunge's "Treatise"*, BUNGE, Mario.
"Miller: The Man and His Philosophy" in *The Philosophy of John William Miller*, FELL, Joseph P.
"New Tasks for the Philosophy of Physics" in *Harré and His Critics*, ROCHE, John F.
"Philosophy and the Academy" in *Acting and Reflecting: The Interdisciplinary Turn in Philosophy*, GLYMOUR, Clark.
"Philosophy and the Sciences" in *Acting and Reflecting: The Interdisciplinary Turn in Philosophy*, SUPPES, Patrick.
"Rationality Unbound" in *Acting and Reflecting: The Interdisciplinary Turn in Philosophy*, LEVI, Isaac.
"Reflections on Chinese Language and Philosophy" in *Hermeneutics and the Poetic Motion, Translation Perspectives V—1990*, SOO, Francis.
"The Significance of the *Treatise* in the Light of the Western Philosophical Tradition" in *Studies on Mario Bunge's "Treatise"*, CUPANI, Alberto.
"Speech Versus Writing" in Derrida and Bhartrhari. COWARD, Harold G.
"They Read Novels, Don't They?" Using Novels in Teaching Philosophy. BOWLDEN, Larry S.
The 'Disagreements' Approach to Inservicing Philosophy for Children. WOOLCOCK, Peter G.
Accessible Hellenistic Philosophy. SHARPLES, R W.
Analysis as a Method in Philosophy with Special Reference to A J Ayer. SRINIVAS, K.
Apology, Speculation, and Philosophy's Fate. VAN NESS, Peter H.
Après Weil, avec Weil: Une lecture de Gilbert Kirscher. LABARRIÈRE, Pierre-Jean.
Una aproximación ontológica a la realidad fisica. HÜBNER, Adolf.
Apuntes para un nuevo ámbito de la filosofía. RAMOS, Francisco José.
The Art of Philosophy. COOPER, Neil.
Die Bedeutung der Mathematik Für die Philosophie Schopenhauers. RADBRUCH, Knut.
Beyond Realism: Nietzsche's New Infinite. CONWAY, Daniel W.
Boethius and the Consolation of Philosophy, or, How to Be a Good Philosopher. BELSEY, Andrew.
Boskovic's Philosophy in the Evaluation of Franjo Markovic (1887): Origins and Results (in Serbo-Croatian). KUTLESA, Stipe.
Bradley and Lonergan's Relativist. TESKE, Roland.
Buchphilosophie und philosophische Praxis. RÖTTGERS, Kurt.
Can Peirce Be a Pragmaticist and an Idealist?. PETERSON, John.
The Case for a New American Pragmatism. LAVINE, Thelma Z.
Cent ans de philosophie à l'Institut Supérieur de Philosophie. LADRIÈRE, Jean.
Changing the Subject: Heidegger, "the" National and Epochal. SCHMIDT, Dennis J.
Chaos, History, and Narrative. REISCH, George A.
Christelijke filosofie. WYLLEMAN, A.
A Christian Philosopher in a "Broken World". VERBEKE, Gerard.
Coaching: Who Needs It and What is It?. GUIN, Philip.
Comments on Freud and Wittgenstein, and on Adolf Grünbaum's "Foundations of Psychoanalysis". FISCHER, Kurt Rudolf.
Concerning F L Will's *Beyond Deduction*. SINGER, Marcus G.
The Conditions of the Question: What Is Philosophy?. DELEUZE, Gilles.
The Conflation of Productivity and Efficiency in Economics and Economic History. SINGH, Harinder and FRANTZ, Roger.
Conquering Chance. HENRY-HERMANN, Grete.
Continuing the Conversation—A Reply to My Interlocutors. OLIVIER, G.
Contributi piagetiani ad una scienza della mente. BORELLA, Silvia.
A Critique of Genealogies. KIM, Chin-Tai.
Cuarenta años del "Instituto Filosófico de Balmesiana". FORMENT, Eudaldo.
Cultural Fundamentals in Philosophy. ORUKA, H Odera.
Cultural Fundamentals in Philosophy: Obstacles in Philosophical Dialogues. ORUKA, Henry Odera.
Current Trends in the Philosophy of Medicine. POTTER, Robert Lyman.
Deconstructing Lonergan. MC KINNEY, Ronald H.
Defending the Tradition. NIELSEN, Kai.
Derrida, Deconstruction and Nietzsche: The Tree of Knowledge and the Tree of Life. ZELECHOW, Bernard.
The Design, Use and Evaluation of Philosophical Stories for Children. CHING-CHUNG, Chao.
Désiré Mercier et les débuts de l'Institut de Philosophie. AUBERT, Roger.
Dialogue on Science, Society, and the Generative Order. BOHM, D and KELLY, Sean.
Disagreement in Philosophy. HELEN, Mercy and CHAKRAVARTI, Mihirvikash.
Distorted Tradition: Etymological Observations about the Misuse of Some Philosophical Terms in Modern Indian English. DE SANTIS, Stefano.
Do Children Think Philosophically?. KITCHENER, Richard F.
Doxology and the History of Philosophy. NORMORE, Calvin G.
Dr C Neugebauer's Critical Note on Ethnophilosophy in the Philosophical Discourse in Africa: Some Remarks. BEWAJI, J A I.
Drawing the Cave and Teaching the Divided Line. SCHONSHECK, Jonathan.
Les effets de la perestroïka dans les *Voprosy filosofii*. DENNES, Maryse.
The Emergence and Original Meaning of the Name 'Metaphysics'. REINER, Hans and ADLER, Pierre and PASKIN, David.
Emotion East and West: Introduction to a Comparative Philosophy. MARKS, Joel.
Entrance Strategies for Philosophy. FOGG, Walter L.
Entrepreneurial Philosophy (in German). HERDER-DORNEICH, Philipp.
Entwurf eines Klassifikationsschemas für philosophische Positionen. WIMMER, Franz.
Environmental Ethics: What? Why? How?. SILVA, Catherine Young.
Eristic, Antilogic, Sophistic, Dialectic: Plato's Demarcation of Philosophy from Sophistry. NEHAMAS, Alexander.
Fabricas o escuelas de Filosofia?. DÍAZ, Adolfo García.
Filosofia e cultura ne "Il Politecnico" de E Vittorini. DE SIENA, Santa.
Filosofía e historia de la filosofía. BEUCHOT, Mauricio.
La filosofía iberoamericana en la obra de Alain Guy. CATURELLI, Alberto.
Filosofía latinoamericana: Posibilidad o realidad?. BETANCOURT, Raúl Fornet.
La filosofía transcendental: el destino de un proyecto ilustrado. FLAMARIQUE, Lourdes.
Filosofía y Cristianismo (En el Centenario de Heidegger). CARDONA, Carlos.
Filosofía y rebeldía. INNERARITY, Daniel.
Filosofía, justicia y amor. LEVINAS, E and EZCURRA, Alicia Villar.
La filosofia: in soccorso de' governi. COLAPIETRA, Raffaele.
Filósofo hispanista. FORMENT, Eudaldo.
Francesco Bonucci, tra medicina e filosofia. STORTI, Cinzia.
Fundamental Question of Philosophy: Remarks on the Pending Philosophical Reappraisal of the Past in the GDR (in German). SCHRÖDER, Richard.
Fundamental Values in the Thought of Confucius and Mencius (in Polish). CYRANOWSKA, Maria.
Gerald Bruns's Cavell. CREWE, Jonathan.
A Global Point of View on Russell's Philosophy. RODRÍGUEZ-CONSUEGRA, Francisco.
Godsverduistering en Godsdienstfilosofie. DE BOER, Th.
Godsverduistering en Godsdienstfilosofie. VAN DER HOEVEN, J.
Goethe and Wittgenstein. ROWE, M W.
The Greatness and Limits of Kant's Practical Philosophy. HÖSLE, Vittorio.
Has the Study of Philosophy at Dutch Universities Changed under Economic and Political Pressures?. VAN DER MEULEN, Barend and LEYDESDORFF, Loet.
Hegel and Kant—A Refutation of their Racism. NEUGEBAUER, Christian.
Heidegger en la filosofia española: La eficacia de Heidegger en las filosofías de Ortega y Zubiri. RAMOS, Antonio Pintor.
An Historical Sketch of Pluralism. RECK, Andrew J.
The History of Philosophy, Inside and Out. MATHIEN, Thomas.
History, Differential Equations, and the Problem of Narration. MC CLOSKEY, Donald N.
Homunculus Trouble, or, What Is Applied Philosophy?. MIDGLEY, Mary.
How is Philosophy Possible?. SCHICK JR, Theodore W.
Hume's *Dialogues* and the Redefinition of the Philosophy of Religion. SCHNER, George.
Hungarian Philosophy: Its Ideas, an Historiographical Foundations (in Hungarian). STEINDLER, Larry.
Husserl's Concept of Philosophy. SCHUHMANN, Karl.
Husserl's Yearbook. SCHUHMANN, Karl.
Identity and Subjectivity (in Serbo-Croatian). FRANK, Manfred.

PHILOSOPHY
Incorporating Gender Issues in Modern Philosophy. IMMERWAHR, John.
Indian Philosophy in the Context of World Philosophy. BHATTACHARYYA, Kalidas.
Indian Thought Is a Systematic Body of Thought. SHAH, K J.
Das Individuum, die Politik und die Philosophie. GRUNWALD, Sabine.
Intentionality and Modern Philosophical Psychology, I: The Modern Reduction of Intentionality. LYONS, William.
Interrupting Olivier's Socio-Political Conversation: Another Postmodern Proposal. ALLEN, J G.
Is Grünbaum's Critique of Habermas' Understanding Freud Definite? (in Serbo-Croatian). NAGL, Ludwig.
Is Neuroscience Relevant to Philosophy?. CHURCHLAND, Patricia Smith.
Is Philosophy Detrimental to Mathematics Education?. LUZZATTO, Stefano.
Jan Hus und Thomas Müntzer—ein philosophiehistorischer Vergleich (in Czechoslovakian). KOLESNYK, Alexander.
Kant et l'histoire de la philosophie la vision problématologique. TIMMERMANS, Benoît.
Kant in Russia: The Initial Phase (continued). NEMETH, Thomas.
Kant on Justification in Transcendental Philosophy. PEREBOOM, Derk.
L'histoire de la philosophie et son temps. DECLÈVE, Henri.
Learning Anew from Old Arguments. BIEL, Joseph.
Lucian: The Sale of Lives (in Hebrew). SCOLNICOV, Samuel (trans).
Luck. RESCHER, Nicholas.
Making Student Groups Work: "To Teach is to Learn Twice". THOMASON, Neil.
Mathematics and Philosophy: The Story of a Misunderstanding. ROTA, GianCarlo.
Mencius' Criticism of Mohism: An Analysis of *Meng Tzu* 3A:5. SHUN, Kwong-Loi.
The Moderns in an Introductory Analytic Course. DICKER, Georges.
Il mondo Il soggetto Lo smarrimento. INCARDONA, Nunzio.
Mozart and Santayana and the Interface Between Music and Philosophy. DILWORTH, David A.
MYSL' and the Intuitivist Debate in the Early 1920s. NETHERCOTT, Frances.
Nietzsche as Colleague. SCHACHT, Richard.
Nietzsche on Human Nature. SCHACHT, Richard.
Nietzsche's Metaperspectivism. ROTH, Robin Alice.
Olivier's Postmodern Proposal: A Few Comments. LÖTTER, H P P.
On Ancients and Moderns. CROPSEY, Joseph.
On Becoming A Moral Agent: From Aristotle to Harry Stottlemeier. PRITCHARD, Michael S.
On Behalf of Skeptical Rhetoric. FALZER, Paul R.
On Bruns, on Cavell. CONANT, James.
On Tolerance (in French). DÜRRENMATT, Friedrich and BÜHLER, Pierre.
Ontología hermenéutica y reflexión filológica: el acceso a la filosofía de H G Gadamer. DOMINGO, Agustín.
P4C as "Pre-Secondary" Philosophy. DUPUIS, Adrian M and THOMPSON, A Gray.
P4C: A Remedy for Education. MOSTERT, Pieter.
Pascal critique des philosophes, Pascal philosophe. BOUCHILLOUX, Hélène.
Paul de Man, Deconstruction, and Discipleship. ALLMAN, John.
Pedagogy of the Unimpressed: Philosophy for Children and the Adult Learner. TURGEON, Wendy.
Philosophical Culture in the Warsaw-Lvov School (in Polish). GLUCHOWSKI, Gerard.
Philosophical Prolegomena of Structural Thinking (in Czechoslovakian). CHVATIK, Kvetoslav.
Philosophically Useful Kibitzing. PRATTE, Richard.
Philosophie ancienne et médiévale. MC EVOY, James.
Philosophie et religion. TROISFONTAINES, Claude.
Philosophie et société. BERTEN, André.
Die Philosophie im einen Deutschland. HENRICH, Dieter.
Philosophiehistorische Forschung und historischer Materialismus. THOM, Martina.
Philosophieren als Sein zum Tode: Zur Interpretation von Platons "Phaidon". FISCHER, Norbert.
Philosophizing. PALMA, A B.
Philosophy and the Rise of Modern Science. SALMON, Wesley.
Philosophy and the Theory of Social Behaviour. HAMLYN, D W.
Philosophy and Wisdom. MC KEE, Patrick.
Philosophy in Israel (in Hungarian). WEILER, Gershon.
Philosophy in the *"Gymnasium:"* European Observations and Recommendations. VAN DER LEEUW, Karel and MOSTERT, Pieter.
Philosophy in the *Big Typescript*: Philosophy as Trivial. LUCKHARDT, C Grant.
Philosophy is Also for the Young—At Least Possibly. LIPMAN, Matthew.
Philosophy of African Intellectuals. WAMBA-DIA-WAMBA, Ernest.
Philosophy within the Activity of the Nagyszombat (Trnava) University (in Hungarian). ORAVCOVÀ, Mariana.
Philosophy, Education, and Public Practice. GIARELLI, James M.
Philosophy: Sections 86-93 (pp 405-35) of the So-Called "Big Typescript" (Catalog Number 213)—Ludwig Wittgenstein. WITTGENSTEIN, Ludwig and NYMAN, Heikki.
Pisces Economicus: The Fish as Econontic Man. BOULIER, Bryan L and GOLDFARB, Robert S.
Plural World of Contemporary Science and Philosophy (in Serbo-Croatian). LELAS, Srdjan.
Possibility of Philosophical-Theological Discourse (in Serbo-Croatian). BELIC, Miljenko.
Pragmatic Naturalism: The Philosophy of Sidney Hook (1902-1989). KURTZ, Paul.
Professor Matilal on Some Topics of Indian Philosophy. BHATTACHARYYA, Sibajiban.
Questions of "Analytical" and "Non-Analytical" Philosophy (in Serbo Croatian). JAKOVLJEVIC, Dragan.
Re-understanding Indian Philosophy. BARLINGAY, S S.
Realism, Naturalism and Social Behaviour. OUTHWAITE, William.
La recepción de la "crítica de la razón pura" en el joven Hegel. DEL CARMEN PAREDES MARTIN, M.
Réflexion sur l'état actuel et les perspectives de l'enseignement de la philosophie en France. DERRIDA, Jacques and BOURGEOIS, Bernard.
The Relevance of Meditative Thinking. ERICKSON, Stephen A.
Relevancia de la historia de la filosofía para la filosofía. NATHAN, Elia.
Reply to Crewe and Conant. BRUNS, Gerald L.
Reply to Lowenthal. COLMO, Christopher A.
Reply to McKinney on Lonergan: A Deconstruction. MARSH, James L.
A Response to Olivier's Postmodern, but Pre-South African Proposal. ROSSOUW, G.
Response to Professor Kitchener's "Do Children Think Philosophically?". LIPMAN, Matthew.
Responsibility—A Challenge in Terms of Philosophy (in German). RÖSEBERG, Ulrich.
A Returning to the Source: The Philosophy of Alain Locke. BIRT, Robert E.
Revealing Gendered Texts. FREELAND, Cynthia A.
Rhetoric as Praxis: An Alternative to the Epistemic Approach. ZHAO, Shanyang.
Richard Rorty: An Interview (in Hebrew). KULKA, Tomas.
The Role of Stories in a Community of Inquiry. HON-MING, Chen.
Romanticism and Modernity. LARMORE, Charles.
The Serious Play of Plato's *Euthydemus*. ROOCHNIK, David.
Sobre cuatro obras de Mauricio Beuchot. PEÑA, Lorenzo.
Solipsism in Kant's Practical Philosophy and the Discourse of Ethics. KUHLMANN, Wolfgang.
The State of Studies on Western Philosophy in China. FANG-TONG, Liu.
The Status of Content Revisited. BOGHOSSIAN, Paul A.
Student Resistance in Philosophy for Children. LARDNER, A T.
Study of Society and Polity: Scientific and Philosophical. CHATTOPADHYAYA, D P.
Teaching Philosophy: Skills and Mentalities. RICHARD, Arsene.
Textual Deference. SMITH, Barry.
The Man as Subject of the Philosophy (in Hungarian). RICOEUR, Paul.
The Newcomb Paradox as a Poker Game (in Hebrew). SPECTOR, Raz.
The Notion of Sublime in Kant and Hegel: A Psycho-Analytical Reading (in Serbo-Croatian). ZIZEK, Slavoj.
La théologie de Heidegger. CRÉTELLA, Henri.
Theorising Ideas: *Idee* and *Vorstellung* from Kant to Hegel to Marx. CRISTAUDO, Wayne.
Tolerance in Indian Culture and Its Philosophical Basis. DRAVID, N S.
Transcendentalism About Content. DEVITT, Michael.
Trotsky's Dialectic. THATCHER, Ian D.
Types of Pluralism. WATSON, Walter.
Über den Versuch einer philosophiegeschichtlichen Klassifikation der Lehre Nāgārjunas. TOMASCHITZ, Wolfgang.
Uno sguardo sulla filosofia americana contemporanea. CENTRONE, Marino.
Unpublished Correspondence between Russell and Wittgenstein. MC GUINNESS, B F and VON WRIGHT, G H.
Viktor Emil Frankl médico y filósofo. ALEGRÍA, Hernando Muciño.
Voix et Existence. DIAGNE, Oumar.
Welchen Platz kann die Philosophie künftig in unserem Lande beanspruchen und vor welchen Aufgaben steht sie?. RÜDIGER, Wolfgang.
What is this Thing Called 'Love'?. BERENSON, Frances.
Why Pluralism Now?. GARVER, Eugene.
Wissenschaftsphilosophie in der DDR—Versuch einer kritischen Betrachtung. HÖRZ, Herbert.
Words on Work. GRAY, C B.

PHILOSOPHY OF EDUCATION
see Education

PHILOSOPHY OF HISTORY
see History

PHILOSOPHY OF LANGUAGES
see Languages

PHILOSOPHY OF LAW
see Law

PHYSICS
"Physics, Life and Mind" in *Science and Religion: One World-Changing Perspectives on Reality*, GIERER, A.
"Projections Are a Law of Nature" in *Studies on Mario Bunge's "Treatise"*, BURGOS, María Esther.
"Realism and Classicism, or Something More? Some Comments on Mario Bunge's Philosophy of Quantum Mechanics" in *Studies on Mario Bunge's "Treatise"*, STÖCKLER, Manfred.
"Reality and Probability in Mario Bunge's *Treatise*" in *Studies on Mario Bunge's "Treatise"*, PATY, Michel.
"The Rediscovery of Time" in *Logic, Methodology and Philosophy of Science, VIII*, PRIGOGINE, Ilya.
"Transcending Newton's Legacy" in *Some Truer Method*, STAPP, Henry P.
Adventures of the Concept of Mass and Matter. HELLER, Michael.
Aristotle, the Direction Problem, and the Structure of the Sublunar Realm. KRONZ, Frederick.
An Attempt at Interpretation of the Thomistic Hylomorphic Theory in View of Contemporary Physics. JANIK, J A.
Born's Probabilistic Interpretation: A Case Study of 'Concepts in Flux'. BELLER, Mara.
Boskovic's Philosophy in the Evaluation of Franjo Markovic (1887): Origins and Results (in Serbo-Croatian). KUTLESA, Stipe.
A Causal Interaction Constraint on the Initial Singularity?. STOEGER, W R and HELLER, Michael.
Comment: Selective Anti-Realism. MC MULLIN, Ernan.
El concepto de verdad en la física moderna. ROMERO BARÓ, José María.
Conquering Chance. HENRY-HERMANN, Grete.
Conventionalism in Physics. MORRIS, W T.
The Cosmological Constant: Einstein's Greatest Mistake?. RAY, Christopher.
Dewey, Indeterminacy, and the Spectator Theory of Knowledge. KULP, Christopher B.
Ernst Mach Leaves "The Church of Physics". BLACKMORE, John.
Explanation. REDHEAD, Michael.
Fine's "Shaky Game" (and Why Noa is No Ark for Science). SCHLAGEL, Richard H.
Física y Semántica en la filosofía de Quine. FUSTEGUERAS, Aurelio P.
Irreversibility and Statistical Mechanics: A New Approach?. BATTERMAN, Robert W.
Is Scientific Methodology Interestingly Atemporal?. CUSHING, James T.
The Justification of Kepler's Ellipse. BAIGRIE, Brian S.
Light Problems: Reply to Chen. ACHINSTEIN, Peter.
Mathematical Physics and Elementary Logic. MUNDY, Brent.
Die Mathematisierung als Konstruktion theoretischer Denkformen in der Abfolge naturwissenschaftlicher Weltbilder. GÖTTLICHER, Gerd.
The No-Slip Condition of Fluid Dynamics. DAY, Michael A.
On Kant's Conception of Science and the Critique of Practical Reason. KÖRNER, Stephan.
On the Objectivity of the Laws of Physics. HAMAN, Krzysztof E.
On the Origin of Spin in Relativity. SACHS, Mendel.
P W Bridgman's Operational Perspective on Physics: Part I—Origins and Development. MOYER, Albert E.
The Physics of Modern Perception: Beyond Body and World. BARRY JR, James.
Physique aristotélicienne et métaphysique thomiste. VERNIER, Jean-Marie.
Plato, the History of Science and Our Understanding of Nature (in German). GLOY, Karen.
Probabilistic Physics and the Metaphysics of Time. SHANKS, Niall.
The Problem of Causation and Time-Symmetry in Physics. BHARUCHA, Filita.
Problema psicofísico y realidad cuántica en la física heterodoxa de David Bohm. MONSERRAT, Javier.
Real Dispositions in the Physical World. THOMPSON, Ian J.
Realism About What?. JONES, Roger.
Realismo e fenomenismo nella fisica moderna. BLANDINO, Giovanni.
The Reason Why: Response to Crane. PAPINEAU, David.
Relationism and Temporal Topology. LE POIDEVIN, Robin.
Scientific Realism and Experimental Practice in High-Energy Physics. HONES, Michael J.
La teoria aristotelica dell'apodissi. SAINATI, Vittorio.
Teorías físicas sobre el origen del Universo. GRATTON, Fausto T L.
The Influence of Roger Boskovic on Bertrand Russell's Early Philosophy of Physics (in Serbo-Croatian). LEWIS, Albert C.
Theorie antireduktionistischer Argumente: Fallstudie Bohr. HOYNINGEN-HUENE, Paul.
Wetten en verhalen. KWA, Chunglin.
Young and Lloyd on the Particle Theory of Light: A Response to Achinstein. CHEN, Xiang.

PHYSIOLOGY
The Neurophilosophy of Pain. GILLETT, G R.
The Physiology of Moral Maturity. HEMMING, James.

PIAGET
Metaphors of Mind: Conceptions of the Nature of Intelligence. STERNBERG, Robert J.
Contributi piagetiani ad una scienza della mente. BORELLA, Silvia.
Do Children Think Philosophically?. KITCHENER, Richard F.
Grupo de Piaget y estructuras afines. GONZÁLEZ CARLOMÁN, Antonio.
How the Child Reasons. THAYER-BACON, Barbara.
Interdisciplinary Epistemology. BODEN, Margaret A.
Kohlberg and Piaget: Differences and Similarities. KAVATHATZOPOULOS, Iordanis.

PICHT, G
The Philosophy of Responsibility (in German). SCHRÖDER, Richard.

PICTURE(S)
Pictorial Representation in Biology. TAYLOR, Peter J and BLUM, Ann S.
Pictures and Depictions: A Consideration of Peacocke's Views. KEMP, G N.
Technique of Painting and Sociology of Picture (in Czechoslovakian). HLAVACEK, Josef.
The Picture in Movement and in Response (in Czechoslovakian). JIRIK, Vlastimil.

PIETY
Platonic Piety. MORGAN, Michael L.
Crusius: un jalón olvidado en la ruta hacia el criticismo. ROLDÁN, Concha.
A Dialogic Interpretation of Hume's *Dialogues*. SESSIONS, William Lad.
Socrates and Alcibiades: Eros, Piety, and Politics. HOWLAND, Jacob A.

PIKE, N
God's Ability to Will Moral Evil. BROWN, Robert F.

PINCOFFS, E
Virtues and Values: A Platonic Account. SEUNG, T K.

PIPER, A
Piper's Criteria of Theory Selection. POSTOW, B C.

PISAN, C
"Roswitha of Gandersheim, Christine Pisan, Margaret More Roper and Teresa of Avila" in *A History of Women Philosophers, Volume II: Medieval, Renaissance and Enlightenment, A.D. 500-1600*, WAITHE, Mary Ellen.

PITY
Schopenhauers Entwurf einer asketischen Tugendethik. WOLF, Jean-Claude.

PLACEBO(S)
Nursing Responsibility for the Placebo Effect. CONNELLY, Robert J.

PLANCK, M
Ernst Mach Leaves "The Church of Physics". BLACKMORE, John.

PLANET(S)
Tycho's System and Galileo's *Dialogue*. MARGOLIS, Howard.

PLANNING
Intention, Cognitive Commitment, and Planning. AUDI, Robert.
Overloading Intentions for Efficient Practical Reasoning. POLLACK, Martha E.
Structural Violence and Fallible Plans: A Case Study in Philosophy and Educational Planning. MOULDER, J.

PLANT(S)
Faustian Phenomena: Teleology in Goethe's Interpretation of Plants and Animals. CORNELL, John F.

PLANTINGA, A
Alvin Plantinga and Natural Theology. BROWN, Hunter.
A Critique of Plantinga's Theological Foundationalism. ZEIS, John.
The Crucial Disanalogies Between Properly Basic Belief and Belief in God. GRIGG, Richard.
The Free Will Defense and Determinism. SENNETT, James F.
Plantinga and Probabilistic Atheism. CHRZAN, Keith.
Plantinga's Box. SESSIONS, William Lad.
Plantinga, Pluralism and Justified Religious Belief. BASINGER, David.
Universe Indexed Properties and the Fate of the Ontological Argument. SENNETT, James F.
Why Plantinga Must Move from Defense to Theodicy. WALLS, Jerry L.

PLASTICITY
"Plasticity into Power: Two Crises in the History of France and China" in *Critique and Construction: A Symposium on Roberto Unger's "Politics"*, CLEARY, J C and HIGONNET, Patrice.

PLATO
An Audience for Moral Philosophy?. EDELMAN, John T.
The Chronology of Plato's Dialogues. BRANDWOOD, Leonard.
The Dialogues of Plato, Volume II. ALLEN, R E (trans).
Ethical Practice in Clinical Medicine. ELLOS, William J.
Hermeneutical Studies: Dilthey, Sophocles, and Plato. WILSON, Barrie A.
Idea, mente, specie: Platonismo e scienza in Johannes Marcus Marci (1595-1667). MOCCHI, Giuliana.
An Invitation To Cognitive Science. LEIBER, Justin.
Love's Knowledge: Essays on Philosophy and Literature. NUSSBAUM, Martha C.
Methods and Problems in Greek Science: Selected Papers. LLOYD, G E R.
Mystical Monotheism: A Study in Ancient Platonic Theology. KENNEY, John Peter.
Myth and Philosophy: A Contest of Truths. HATAB, Lawrence J.

PLATO

Of Memory, Reminiscence, and Writing: On the Verge. KRELL, David Farrell.
On Homosexuality: Lysis, Phaedrus, and Symposium. JOWETT, Benjamin (trans).
Plato's "Parmenides". MEINWALD, Constance C.
Platonic Piety. MORGAN, Michael L.
Platos Idee des Guten. FERBER, Rafael.
Reflexion und Metareflexion bei Platon und Fichte. ZEHNPFENNIG, Barbara.
Der Ursprung der Erziehungsziele in der Lehre von Plato, Aristoteles und Neill. EGGER, Paul.
Zetetic Skepticism. UMPHREY, Stewart.
"A noção de experiência nos diálogos platónicos" in *Dinâmica do Pensar: Homenagem a Oswaldo Market*, SANTOS, José Trindade.
"Plato's Theory of Mind" in *Psychology (Companions to Ancient Thought: 2)*, LOVIBOND, Sabina.
"Were Plato and Aristotle Humanists?" in *The Question of Humanism: Challenges and Possibilities*, ANDIC, Martin.
'Seventeen' Subtleties in Plato's *Theaetetus*. FOGELMAN, Brian D and HUTCHINSON, D S.
Algunas reflexiones sobre la doctrina platónica de los preámbulos de las *Leyes*. GARCÍA MÁYNEZ, Eduardo.
Aristotle and the Spheres of Motivation: *De Anima* III. HUTCHINSON, D S.
Art and Morality in Plato: A Reappraisal. HALL, Robert W.
Aspetti di attualità teoretica del pensiero procliano negli studi di Werner Beierwaltes. SCOTTI, Nicoletta.
Bohr's Idea of Complementarity and Plato's Philosophy. MAHOOTIAN, Farzad.
Collection and Division in the *Phaedrus* and *Statesman*. WEDIN, Michael V.
Conocimiento metodico y no metodico; so pretexto de una incursion acerca de la dialectica segun platon. SALA, J F A.
De las maravillas acerca de lo uno y lo múltiple o sobre los avatares del amor neoplatónico en Baruch de Espinosa. ALBIAC, Gabriel.
The Development of Modern Mathematics and Plato's Parable of the Cave. MAURIN, Krzysztof.
Devenir et génération chez Platon. HUBERT, Bernard.
Did Plato Coin *Rhetorike*?. SCHIAPPA, Edward.
Dire e ascoltare nella tipologia del "sofista", del "filosof-re" e del pensatore socratico. MARCHETTI, Giancarlo.
División y dialéctica en el *Fedro*. SANTA CRUZ, María Isabel.
Does Wittgenstein's Concept of Language Game Patterns Come Up with a Solution to the Platonic Problem ... (in German). LÜTTERFELDS, Wilhelm.
Drawing the Cave and Teaching the Divided Line. SCHONSHECK, Jonathan.
The Driving Ratio in Plato's Divided Line. DREHER, John Paul.
Enlightenment Psychology and Political Reaction in Plato's Social Philosophy: an Ideological Contradiction?. BRYANT, Joseph M.
L'epiglottide nell'antichità tra medicina e filosofia. REPICI, Luciana.
Eristic, Antilogic, Sophistic, Dialectic: Plato's Demarcation of Philosophy from Sophistry. NEHAMAS, Alexander.
La estética de la recepción desde la teoría platónica del arte. ORTIZ DE URBINA, Ricardo Sánchez.
La filosofía de la ciencia en Platón: Una introducción. PEREZ DE LABORDA, Alfonso.
Finalidad y dimensiones "kaíricas" de la estructura del ser. MOUTSOPOULOS, Evanghélos A.
Forms and Causes In Plato's *Phaedo*. BYRNE, Christopher.
In Defense of Plato: A Short Polemic. ROOCHNIK, David.
The Intelligible World-Animal in Plato's *Timaeus*. PARRY, Richard D.
Is a Whole Identical to its Parts?. SCALTSAS, Theodore.
Levels of Knowledge in the *Theaetetus*. DORTER, Kenneth.
The Meaning of Δυναμισ at *Timaeus* 31c. PRITCHARD, Paul.
Meno, the Slave-Boy, and the *Elenchos*. BENSON, Hugh H.
I metodi della metafisica platonico-accademica "generalizzante" ed "elementarizzante" nei libri "M" e "N".... CATTANEI, E.
A Middle Platonic Reading of Plato's Theory of Recollection. SCHRENK, Lawrence P.
A Note on the Jural Relation. BUTLER, Ken.
On Plato's Theory of the *Metheksis* of Ideas. JIYUAN, Yu.
On the Paradoxical Inception and Motivation of Transcendental Philosophy in Plato and Husserl. HOPKINS, Burt C.
On the Teachability of ARETé in Plato (in Czechoslovakian). MOURAL, Josef.
Osservazioni sul *Filebo*. MASI, Giuseppe.
Per una rilettura dei libri "M" e "N" della *Metafisica* di Aristotele alla luce delle "dottrine non scritte" di Platone. CATTANEI, Elisabetta.
Philosophers on Gender and Sexuality. VADAKKEMURIYIL, A.
Philosophieren als Sein zum Tode: Zur Interpretation von Platons "Phaidon". FISCHER, Norbert.
Plato and Archytas in the Seventh Letter. LLOYD, G E R.
Plato and Aristotle on Division and Definition. DESLAURIERS, Marguerite.
Plato and Davidson: Parts of the Soul and Weakness of Will. PENNER, Terrence M.
Plato and the Senses of Words. BLACKSON, Thomas A.
Plato's Analogy between Painter and Poet. JANAWAY, Christopher.
Plato's Gods. PEHRSON, C W P.
Plato's Line Revisited: The Pedagogy of Complete Reflection. WOOD, Robert E.
Plato's Ontology and the Role of Mathematics in the Description of Nature. ZYCINSKI, Joseph.
Plato's *Parmenides* and St Thomas's Analysis of God as One and Trinity. KLEIN, Sherwin.
Plato's Reply to the 'Worst Difficulty' Argument of the *Parmenides*: *Sophist* 248a-249d. MC PHERRAN, Mark.
Plato's *Statesman* Story: The Birth of Fiction Reconceived. TOMASI, John.
Plato's Three Waves and the Question of Utopia. HYLAND, Drew A.
Plato, the History of Science and Our Understanding of Nature (in German). GLOY, Karen.
Platón, el lenguaje y el marciano. ACERO, Juan José.
Platonismo vivo: (Debate actual sobre Platón, la Academia y las Ideas). JUÁREZ, Agustin Uña.
Plotinus and the *Apeiron* of Plato's *Parmenides*. HEISER, John H.
The Recurring Problem of the Third Man. HALES, Steven D.
Reflections on Aristotle's Criticism of Forms. MOKASHI, Ashwini A.
Schopenhauers Wille und Platons Eros. VOIGTLÄNDER, Hanns-Dieter.
Self-Predication and Synonymy. SILVERMAN, Allan.
Sense-Experience and the Argument for Recollection in Plato's *Phaedo*. BEDU-ADDO, J T.
The Serious Play of Plato's *Euthydemus*. ROOCHNIK, David.
Socrates and Asclepius: The Final Words. SANTILLI, Paul C.
Some Observations About Plato's *Phaedo*. MASCHLER, Chaninah.
Struttura e finalità dei dialoghi platonici: Che cosa significa "venire in soccorso al discorso"?. SZLEZÁK, Thomas A.
La subversion de l'"elenchos" juridique dans l'"Apologie de Socrate". DORION, Louis-André.
Suspicion, Deception, and Concealment. ROSEN, Stanley.
La teoria aristotelica dell'apodissi. SAINATI, Vittorio.
Thinking of Unity (in Dutch). AERTSEN, Jan A.
La transformation de la philosophie de Platon dans le "Prologos" d'Albinus. NETSCHKE-HENTSCHKE, Ada Babette.
The Truth about Lies in Plato's *Republic*. PAGE, Carl.
Two Kinds of Naming in the *Sophist*. STOUGH, Charlotte.
Unifying Plato: Charles Kahn on Platonic *Prolepsis*. GRISWOLD JR, Charles L.
Varieties of Educational Dialogue. BURBULES, Nicholas C.
Verdad e inteligibilidad: Los rasgos invariables de la teoría platónica de las ideas. LUIS DEL BARCO, José.
Verdad e inteligibilidad: Los rasgos invariantes de la doctrina platónica de las ideas. LUIS DEL BARCO, José.
Verdad e inteligibilidad: Los rasgos invariables de la doctrina platónica de las ideas. LUIS DEL BARCO, José.
Weaving and Practical Politics In Plato's *Statesman*. COLE, Eve Browning.
The Wisdom of Plato's Aristophanes. SALMAN, Charles.
Yet More on *Meno* 82a-85d. FOWLER, D H.

PLATONISM

De l'épistémologie à la politique: La philosophie de l'histoire de Karl R Popper. RUELLAND, Jacques G.
Gödel's Theorem in Focus. SHANKER, S G (ed).
Hellenic and Christian Studies. ARMSTRONG, A H.
Platonic Piety. MORGAN, Michael L.
The Tragedy of Reason: Toward a Platonic Conception of Logos. ROOCHNIK, David.
"Field and Fregean Platonism" in *Physicalism in Mathematics*, WRIGHT, Crispin.
"The Intellectuals and the Imitation of the Masses" in *The Political Responsibility of Intellectuals*, LOCK, Grahame.
"Logos and Trinity: Patterns of Platonist Influence on Early Christianity" in *The Philosophy in Christianity*, DILLON, John.
"Π In the Sky" in *Physicalism in Mathematics*, BROWN, James Robert.
"Physicalistic Platonism" in *Physicalism in Mathematics*, MADDY, Penelope.
"What Is Abstraction and What Is It Good For?" in *Physicalism in Mathematics*, SIMONS, Peter.
Cusanus and Eriugena. BEIERWALTES, Werner.
Giustino Martire, il primo platonico cristiano. GIRGENTI, Giuseppe.
The Laws of Physics as Nomic Universals. ZYCINSKI, Jozef.
Mathematics and Oliver Twist. MADDY, Penelope.
Metalogic and Modality. FIELD, Hartry.
Philosophical Reflections on the Foundations of Mathematics. COUTURE, Jocelyne and LAMBEK, Joachim.
Platonism and Anti-Platonism in Nicholas of Cusa's Philosophy of Mathematics. HÖSLE, Vittorio.
Platonism from an Empiricist Point of View. LUCE, Lila.
Platonismo vivo: (Debate actual sobre Platón, la Academia y las Ideas). JUÁREZ, Agustin Uña.
Porphyry's Criticism of Christianity and The Problem of Augustine's Platonism. EVANGELIOU, Christos.
Taylor's Waking Dream: No One's Reply. CLARK, Stephen R L.
Virtues and Values: A Platonic Account. SEUNG, T K.

PLAUSIBILITY

Nonrules and Plausibility: An Illustration in Pragmatic Theory. POWELL, Mava Jo.
On Axiomatization of Many-Valued Logics Associated with Formalization of Plausible Reasonings. ANSHAKOV, O M and FINN, V K and SKVORTSOV, D P.

PLAY
Play and the Theory of Basic Human Goods. CELANO, Anthony J.
Play of the Whole of Wholes (in Czechoslovakian). AXELOS, Kostas.

PLEASURE(S)
Ethics with Aristotle. BROADIE, Sarah.
Approaches to the Theory of Purusarthas. RAJAN, R Sundara.
A Fat Worm of Error?. MC GHEE, Michael.
True and False Pleasures. LOVIBOND, Sabina.

PLOTINUS
Hellenic and Christian Studies. ARMSTRONG, A H.
Mystical Monotheism: A Study in Ancient Platonic Theology. KENNEY, John Peter.
Plotinus and Freedom: A Meditation on Enneads 6:8. WESTRA, Laura.
"Plotinus and Soul-Body Dualism" in *Psychology (Companions to Ancient Thought: 2)*, EMILSSON, Eyjólfur K.
L'aspect rationnel et l'aspect religieux de la philosophie de Plotin. BRUNNER, Fernand.
Memory, Forgetfulness and the Disclosure of Being in Heidegger and Plotinus. BALES, Eugene F.
Notes sur une référence fugitive: Schopenhauer lecteur de Plotin. UCCIANI, Louis.
Plotino: la libertad como primer principio. DE GARAY, Jesús.
Plotinus and the *Apeiron* of Plato's *Parmenides*. HEISER, John H.
La question de l'être et du non-être des objets mathématiques chez Plotin et Jamblique. O'MEARA, Dominic.
Thinking of Unity (in Dutch). AERTSEN, Jan A.

PLURALISM
An Audience for Moral Philosophy?. EDELMAN, John T.
Enriching Business Ethics. WALTON, Clarence C (ed).
Moral Pluralism and Legal Neutrality. SADURSKI, Wojciech.
Moral und Politik aus der Sicht des Kritischen Rationalismus. SALAMUN, Kurt (ed).
Varieties of Social Explanation: An Introduction to the Philosophy of Social Science. LITTLE, Daniel.
"On the Logic of Pluralist Feminism" in *Feminist Ethics*, LUGONES, Maria C.
"Yves R Simon's Contribution to a Structural Political Pluralism" in *Freedom in the Modern World: Jacques Maritain, Yves R Simon, Mortimer J Adler*, KOYZIS, David T.
A Certain 'Politics of Speech': 'Religious Pluralism' in the Age of the McDonald's Hamburger. SURIN, Kenneth.
Conceptual Selection. HULL, David L.
Defining the Limits of Institutional Moral Agency in Health Care: A Response to Kevin Wildes. RIE, Michael A.
Democracy and Socialism: Philosophical *Aporiae*. CUNNINGHAM, Frank.
Difference as Deficit. REAGAN, Timothy.
The Difference-Deficit Debate: Theoretical Smokescreen for a Conservative Ambush. MC DADE, Laurie A.
Educação para valores e maturidade pessoal do educador. ROCHA, Filipe.
Ethical Pluralism and the Role of Opposition in Democratic Politics. D'AGOSTINO, Fred.
Ethics and Coherence. DE GEORGE, Richard T.
Feminism and Pluralism in Contemporary Theology. STENGER, Mary Ann.
Hick and Saints: Is Saint-Production a Valid Test?. PENTZ, Rebecca.
An Historical Sketch of Pluralism. RECK, Andrew J.
Institutional Integrity: Approval, Toleration and Holy War or 'Always True to You in My Fashion'. WILDES, Kevin W.
Is *King Lear* Like the Pacific Ocean or the Washington Monument? Critical Pluralism and Literary Interpretation. PHELAN, James.
Metaphor and Pluralism. MAC CORMAC, Earl R.
Moral Pluralism. WOLGAST, Elizabeth.
Mozart and Santayana and the Interface Between Music and Philosophy. DILWORTH, David A.
No Holism without Pluralism. VARNER, Gary E.
Plantinga, Pluralism and Justified Religious Belief. BASINGER, David.
Plural But Equal: Group Identity and Voluntary Integration. ROBACK, Jennifer.
Pluralistic Ontology and Theory Reduction in the Physical Sciences. ROHRLICH, Fritz.
Prefacing Pluralism: John Hick and the Mastery of Religion. LOUGHLIN, Gerard.
A Problem for Radical (Onto-Theos) Pluralism. BILIMORIA, Purusottama.
Questioni di filosofia politica. VECA, Salvatore.
Relevant Predication 2: Intrinsic Properties and Internal Relations. DUNN, J Michael.
A Religious Theory of Religion: Critical Notice. BYRNE, Peter.
The School and the Home: Partners or Pariahs—A Response to Kennedy on Home Schools. ENGEL, David E.
Scientific Pluralism and the Plurality of the Sciences: Comments on David Hull's *Science as a Process*. DUPRÉ, John.
Types of Pluralism. WATSON, Walter.
Varieties of Pluralism in a Polyphonic Society. RORTY, Amelie Oksenberg.
Virtue Theory and Abortion. HURSTHOUSE, Rosalind.
Why Pluralism Now?. GARVER, Eugene.

PLURALITY
Lesbian Philosophies and Cultures. ALLEN, Jeffner (ed).
Unsere postmoderne Moderne (Second Edition). WELSCH, Wolfgang.
"The Background to Augustine's Denial of Religious Plurality" in *Grace, Politics and Desire: Essays on Augustine*, VANDERSPOEL, John.
"Bare Plurals as Plural Indefinite Noun Phrases" in *Knowledge Representation and Defeasible Reasoning*, GILLON, Brendan.
"Plurality and Unity in the Configuration of the Chinese People" in *The Tanner Lectures on Human Values, Volume XI*, XIAOTONG, Fei.
Educação e democracia: Subsídios para uma consciência educacional pluralizante. ARAÚJO, Alberto Filipe.

POCOCK, J
J G A Pocock's Republicanism and Political Theory: A Critique and Reinterpretation. SHAPIRO, Ian.

POET(S)
Plato's Analogy between Painter and Poet. JANAWAY, Christopher.
Walt Whitman and the Culture of Democracy. KATEB, George.

POETICS
The Butterfly as Companion: Meditations on the First Three Chapters of the Chuang Tzu. WU, Kuang-Ming.
"Augustine and Poetic Exegesis" in *Grace, Politics and Desire: Essays on Augustine*, WESTRA, Haijo J.
"My Poetic World Versus the Real, Scientific World" in *XIth International Congress in Aesthetics, Nottingham 1988*, PASKOW, Alan.
"The Poetics of Personhood" in *Reading Rorty*, HOLLIS, Martin.
The Poetic Theory of the Stoic 'Aristo'. ASMIS, Elizabeth.
Sur l'habitation poétique de l'homme. PIERSON, Dominique.

POETRY
Existence et Subjectivité: Études de Psychologie Phénoménologique. THINÈS, Georges.
Myth and Philosophy: A Contest of Truths. HATAB, Lawrence J.
"Poetic Vision and the Hope for Peace" in *Celebrating Peace*, LEVERTOV, Denise.
"Poetry and Modernity" in *The Tanner Lectures On Human Values, Volume XII*, PAZ, Octavio.
"Just for the Thrill": Sycophantizing Aristotle's *Poetics*. CARSON, Anne.
The Exile of Literature: Poetry and the Politics of the Other(s). MURPHY, Bruce F.
Gerald Bruns's Cavell. CREWE, Jonathan.
Giuseppe De Luca e la polemica sulla moralità di Péguy. FIORENTINO, Fernando.
Horace's *Ars Poetica* and the Deconstructive Leech. HABIB, M A R.
How I Slugged It Out with Toril Moi and Stayed Awake. BEDIENT, Calvin.
On Bruns, on Cavell. CONANT, James.
Poetry and Autonomy. SANKOWSKI, Edward.
Reading Kristeva: A Response to Calvin Bedient. MOI, Toril.
Reply to Crewe and Conant. BRUNS, Gerald L.
Storicità della poesia: estetica e storicismo in Francesco De Sanctis. GALASSO, Giuseppe.
Le supplément poétique. WATTEYNE, Nathalie.

POINCARE
Geometrical and Physical Conventionalism of Henri Poincaré in Epistemological Formulation. GIEDYMIN, Jerzy.

POINT OF VIEW
"Make-Believe, Ontology and Point of View" in *XIth International Congress in Aesthetics, Nottingham 1988*, LAMARQUE, Peter.
Meaning, Truth Conditions and the Internal Point of View: The Ethical Dilemma. GOOSSENS, Charles.
Wittgenstein: On Seeing Problems from a Religious Point of View. HIGH, Dallas M.

POINT(S)
Upward Directedness of the Rudin-Keisler Ordering of *P*-Points. LAFLAMME, Claude.

POLANYI, M
Michael Polanyi's Aesthetics: A Phenomenological Study. BISWAS, Goutam.
Panofsky, Polanyi, and Intrinsic Meaning. UN-CHOL, Shin.

POLEMARCHUS
The Unjust Treatment of Polemarchus. PAGE, Carl.

POLEMICS
Continuità e discontinuità tra Husserl e Heidegger: genesi e sviluppo d una polemica filosofica. RIZZACASA, Aurelio.

POLICE
The Effects of Patrol Officers' Defensiveness Toward the Outside World on Their Ethical Orientations. SHERNOCK, Stan K.
Loyalty: The Police. EWIN, R E.

POLICY ANALYSIS
Response to the Presidential Address: Willer's "Ethics in Educational Policy Analysis". DRAKE, William E.

POLICY(-CIES)
see also Public Policy(-cies)
"Conservative and Radical Critiques of Nuclear Policy" in *Issues in War and Peace: Philosophical Inquiries*, LITKE, Robert.

POLICY(-CIES)

"Federal Laws and Policies Governing Animal Research: Their History, Nature, and Adequacy" in *Biomedical Ethics Reviews, 1990*, ROLLIN, Bernard E.
"Intention and Personal Policies" in *Philosophical Perspectives, 3: Philosophy of Mind and Action Theory, 1989*, BRATMAN, Michael E.
"Judgment and Policy: The Two-Step in Mandated Science and Technology" in *Philosophy of Technology*, LEVY, Edwin.
"Theories of Compensation" in *Liability and Responsibility*, GOODIN, Robert E.
Advocacy of Just Health Policies as Professional Duty: Cultural Biases and Ethical Responsibilities. CRANDALL, Lee A.
An Alternative Logical Framework for Dialectical Reasoning in the Social and Policy Sciences. SABRE, Ru Michael.
Burglars, Robber Barons, and the Good Life. PEKARSKY, Daniel.
Democracy and Justice in Health Policy. JENNINGS, Bruce.
Development of an Institutional Policy on Artificial Hydration and Nutrition. KOSHUTA, Monica A and SCHMITZ, Phyllis J and LYNN, Joanne.
Ethics and Educational Administration: Are Ethical Politics "Ethical"?. RUDDER, Charles F.
Ethics in Educational Policy Analysis. WILLERS, Jack Conrad.
Has the Study of Philosophy at Dutch Universities Changed under Economic and Political Pressures?. VAN DER MEULEN, Barend and LEYDESDORFF, Loet.
History, Indian Science and Policy-Making: A Philosophical Review. BHARGAVI, V and SUBRAMANIAM, K.
Informing the Public: Ethics, Policy Making, and Objectivity in News Reporting. IANNONE, A Pablo.
Is Mandatory Retirement Unfair Age Discrimination?. WEDEKING, Gary A.
Lifelong Education: The Institutionalisation of an Illiberal and Regressive Ideology. BAGNALL, Richard G.
The Logic of Causal Inference: Econometrics and the Conditional Analysis of Causation. HOOVER, Kevin D.
Must the State Justify Its Educational Policies?. HESLEP, Robert D.
Olivier's Postmodern Proposal: A Few Comments. LÖTTER, H P P.
Public Discourse in the Development of Educational Policy. CURREN, Randall R.
Setting Floating Limits: Functional Status Care Categories as National Policy. THOMASMA, David C.

POLIS

Making the Citizens Good: Aristotle's City and Its Contemporary Relevance. SIMPSON, Peter.

POLISH

"Power and Wisdom: The Expert as Mediating Figure in Contemporary Polish History" in *The Political Responsibility of Intellectuals*, KURCZEWSKI, Jacek.
Conception of Values in Polish Sociology (in Polish). STYK, Jozef.
Medical Critique [Krytyka Lekarska]: A Journal of Medicine and Philosophy—1897-1907. LÖWY, Ilana.

POLITICAL ACTION(S)

Political Theory in the Welfare State. LUHMANN, Niklas.
"Gandhi's Quest for a Nonviolent Political Philosophy" in *Celebrating Peace*, PAREKH, Bhikhu.
Arendt and Benjamin on the Promise of History: A Network of Possibilities or One Apocalyptic Moment?. HONOHAN, Iseult.
Critical Interaction: Judgment, Decision, and the Social Testing of Moral Hypotheses. IANNONE, A P.
The Impact of Activist Pressures on Recombinant DNA Research. RABINO, Isaac.
Language and Political Agency: Derrida, Marx, and Bakhtin. EVANS, Fred.
Logos and the Place of the Other. BIRMINGHAM, Peg E.
The Pariah as Hero: Hannah Arendt's Political Actor. RING, Jennifer.
Toughness as a Political Virtue. GALSTON, William.

POLITICAL PARTY(-TIES)

Bulgaria: The Romantic Period of the Opposition Continues. KANEV, Krassimir.
Conceptos centrales de la filosofía política en Chile democrático. COLLE, Reymond.
Lacan in Slovenia—An Interview with Slavoj Zizek and Renata Salecl. DEWS, Peter and OSBORNE, Peter.
Romania's Revolution and its Prospects. BRUCAN, Silviu.
Spiritual Values and "The Goddess". BRANDEN, Victoria.

POLITICAL PHIL

see also Authority(-ties), Communism, Democracy, Ethics, Freedom, Liberalism, Libertarianism, Right(s), Social Phil, Society(-ties), State(s), Utopia
Anglo-American Philosophy of Law: An Introduction to Its Development and Outcome. LEVY, Beryl Harold.
Collected Works, Volume 26, Engels: 1882-1889. ENGELS, Frederick.
Critique and Construction: A Symposium on Roberto Unger's "Politics". LOVIN, Robin W (ed).
Democratic Individuality. GILBERT, Alan.
Femininity and Domination: Studies in the Phenomenology of Oppression. BARTKY, Sandra Lee.
Fonti diritto e regole. DE GIACOMO, Claudio.
Foundations of Moral and Political Philosophy. PAUL, Ellen Frankel (ed).
Hobbes. TUCK, Richard.
In the Interest of Peace: A Spectrum of Philosophical Views. KLEIN, Kenneth H (ed).
Interpreting Political Responsibility. DUNN, John.
John Locke: Segundo Tratado sobre el Gobierno Civil. MELLIZO, Carlos (trans).
Justice: Alternative Political Perspectives (Second Edition). STERBA, James P (ed).
Kant's System of Rights. MULHOLLAND, Leslie A.
Law, Culture, and Values: Essays in Honor of Gray L Dorsey. VOJCANIN, Sava Alexander (ed).
The Legal-Rational State: A Comparison of Hobbes, Bentham and Kelsen. LEE, Keekok.
Leviathan: Hobbes. TUCK, Richard (ed).
Liberalism and American Constitutional Law. SMITH, Rogers M.
Liberalism and the Good. DOUGLASS, R Bruce (ed).
Life-World and Politics: Between Modernity and Postmodernity. WHITE, Stephen K (ed).
The Limits of Government: An Essay on the Public Goods Arguments. SCHMIDTZ, David.
Marx's Radical Critique of Capitalist Society: A Reconstruction and Critical Evaluation. ARNOLD, N Scott.
The Meaning of Socialism. LUNTLEY, Michael.
Mill and Liberalism (Second Edition). COWLING, Maurice.
Die moderne Gesellschaft im Rechtsstaat. BAURMANN, Michael.
Moral Pluralism and Legal Neutrality. SADURSKI, Wojciech.
Morals, Motivation and Convention: Hume's Influential Doctrines. SNARE, Francis.
Nation und Ethos: Die Moral des Patriotismus. KLUXEN-PYTA, Donate.
Nature and Politics: Liberalism in the Philosophies of Hobbes, Locke, and Rousseau. RAPACZYNSKI, Andrzej.
The Nature of Politics. MASTERS, Roger D.
New Reflections on the Revolution of Our Time. LACLAU, Ernesto.
On Duties: Cicero. GRIFFIN, M T (ed).
Patriarcha and Other Writings: Sir Robert Filmer. SOMMERVILLE, Johann P (ed).
Philosophie Juridique Européenne. TRIGEAUD, Jean-Marc.
Philosophy and Politics. HUNT, G M K (ed).
Philosophy of Law (Fourth Edition). FEINBERG, Joel.
Philosophy of Law: An Introduction to Jurisprudence (Revised Edition). MURPHY, Jeffrie G.
Policraticus. NEDERMAN, Cary J (ed & trans).
The Political Ontology of Martin Heidegger. BOURDIEU, Pierre.
The Political Philosophy of Michael Oakeshott. FRANCO, Paul.
The Political Responsibility of Intellectuals. MACLEAN, Ian (ed).
Political Theory in the Welfare State. LUHMANN, Niklas.
Political Writings—John Milton. DZELZAINIS, Martin (ed).
Political Writings—Kant. REISS, Hans (ed).
Politics Drawn From the Very Words of Holy Scripture—Jacques-Benigne Bossuet. RILEY, Patrick (ed).
The Positivist Science of Law. LEE, Keekok.
Pour l'histoire de la fortune de Montesquieu en Italie (1789-1945). FELICE, Domenico.
Practical Reason and Norms. RAZ, Joseph.
Questions Concerning the Law of Nature: John Locke. CLAY, Jenny Strauss (ed & trans).
Rawls: "A Theory of Justice" and Its Critics. KUKATHAS, Chandran.
Reading Rawls: Critical Studies on Rawls' 'A Theory of Justice'. DANIELS, Norman (ed).
Reflexões, 3: Filosofia Política Sociologia cultura Portuguesa Temas Literários. DE MELO, Romeu.
Resurrecting Marx: The Analytical Marxists on Freedom, Exploitation, and Justice. GORDON, David.
Robert Nozick: Property, Justice, and the Minimal State. WOLFF, Jonathan.
Self, Society, and Personal Choice. MEYERS, Diana T.
Statism and Anarchy. SHATZ, Marshall (ed).
The Tanner Lectures on Human Values, Volume XI. PETERSON, Grethe B (ed).
Television and the Crisis of Democracy. KELLNER, Douglas.
Theories of Criminal Justice: A Critical Reappraisal. ELLIS, Ralph D.
Thinking Philosophically: An Introduction to Philosophy with Readings. GUSMANO, Joseph J.
Thomas Hobbes' Theory of Obligation: A Modern Interpretation. FORSBERG, Ralph P.
Universalism versus Communitarianism: Contemporary Debates in Ethics. RASMUSSEN, David.
Utopia: Sir Thomas More. LOGAN, George M (ed).
Wege aus der Moderne. WELSCH, Wolfgang (ed).
What Is Justice? Classic and Contemporary Readings. SOLOMON, Robert C (ed).
"Basic Needs, Legitimate Wants and Political Legitimacy in Mario Bunge's Conception of Ethics" in *Studies on Mario Bunge's "Treatise"*, GARZÓN-VALDÉS, Ernesto.

POLITICAL PHIL

"Filosofia e politica in Giammaria Ortes" in *Scienza, Filosofia e Religione tra '600 e '700 in Italia*, GIACOTTO, Paolo.
"Notes on a Neglected Masterpiece, II: Theological-Political Treatise as a Prolegomenon to the Ethics" in *Central Themes in Early Modern Philosophy*, CURLEY, Edwin.
"The Priority of Democracy to Philosophy" in *Reading Rorty*, RORTY, Richard.
"Degenerate Law": Jurists and Nazism. LA TORRE, Massimo.
"Der geschlossne Handelsstaat"—Zur konservativen Kritik einer aufklärerischen Utopie. MARQUARDT, Jochen.
Les "droits naturels" et les "titres" selon Robert Nozick. SWEET, William.
"His Majesty Is a Baby?" A Critical Response to Peter Hammond Schwartz. SPRINGBORG, Patricia.
I "systemata subordinata" e il problema della partecipazione in Hobbes. SORGI, Giuseppe.
'One Very Simple Principle'. RILEY, Jonathan.
1668 Appendix to Leviathan. WRIGHT, George (trans) and HOBBES, Thomas.
A propósito del filósofo del derecho Giorgio del Vecchio. DI PIETRO, Alfredo.
A proposito di Stato e totaliarismo nel pensiero di Marx. SIENA, Robertomaria.
Abortion: Privacy versus Liberty. GOULD, James.
Active Citizenship as Political Obligation. SKILLEN, Tony.
The Actus Reus Requirement: A Qualified Defense. GORR, Michael.
Aesthetics and Natural Law in Newton's Methodology. JACQUETTE, Dale.
Affirmative Action Revisited: Justice and Public Policy Considerations. VANTERPOOL, Rudolph V.
The African Liberation Struggle: A Hermeneutic Exploration of an African Historical-Political Horizon. SEREQUEBERHAN, Tsenay.
Against Human Rights. NELSON, John O.
AIDS and the L-Word. DEVINE, Philip E.
Alexander Hamilton: The Separation of Powers. PRATT, Ronald L.
Algunas reflexiones sobre la doctrina platónica de los preámbulos de las *Leyes*. GARCÍA MÁYNEZ, Eduardo.
Allocution Made to a Magistrate. PAREL, A J (ed & trans) and MACHIAVELLI, Niccolò.
Already Punished Enough. HUSAK, Douglas N.
Anerkennung: Fichtes Grundlegungen des Rechtsgrundes. JANKE, Wolfgang.
Angelo Camillo De Meis nell'episolario di Francesco Fiorentino. CACCIAPUOTI, Fabiana.
Anotaciones en torno al poder de la democracia. MOLINA, Carlos.
An Antinomy in Kelsen's Pure Theory of Law. BULYGIN, Eugenio.
Aquinas and the Deconstruction of History. KELLY, Eugene.
Are Property Rights Problematic?. GAUS, Gerald F and LOMASKY, Loren E.
Aristotelianism and the Origins of "Political Science" in the Twelfth Century. NEDERMAN, Cary J.
Art and Censorship. SERRA, Richard.
Arthur Schopenhauer als Staatsdenker. WÜRKNER, Joachim.
Artistic Freedom: An Art World Paradox. LANKFORD, E Louis.
Au-delà de la critique communautarienne du libéralisme? D'Alasdair MacIntyre à Stanley Hauerwas. VAN GERWEN, Jef.
Aufklärung und Reform. SCHNEIDERS, Werner.
Autonomy and Political Obligation in Kant. STERN, David S.
Autonomy, Liberalism and State Neutrality. MASON, Andrew D.
The Background to Bentham on Evidence. LEWIS, A D E.
Bargaining with the Not-Yet-Born: Gauthier's Contractarian Theory of Inter-Generational Justice and Its Limitations. DE-SHALIT, A.
The Base Camp Paradox: A Reflection on the Place of Tâtonnement in General Equilibrium Theory. DE VROEY, Michel.
Beggars and Kings: Cowardice and Courage in Shakespeare's *Richard II*. JENSEN, Pamela K.
Bentham, Science and the Construction of Jurisprudence. JACOBS, Struan.
Bertrand Russell and Liberty: A Question Revisited. PADIA, Chandrakala.
Beyond Mourning and Melancholia on the Left. DUBIEL, Helmut.
The Blackmail of the Single Alternative: Bukharin, Trotsky and Perestrojka. DAY, Richard B.
Bobbio e la scienza politica in Italia. MANCARELLA, Angelo.
Breves notas acerca de la *Política* de Aristóteles. ÁLVAREZ, Margarita Mauri.
The Buddha as an Owner of Property and Permanent Resident in Medieval Indian Monasteries. SCHOPEN, Gregory.
Bulgaria: The Romantic Period of the Opposition Continues. KANEV, Krassimir.
Cato's Letters, John Locke, and the Republican Paradigm. HAMOWY, Ronald.
Certainty and Authority. WINCH, Peter.
The Changing Face of Civil Society in Eastern Europe. KOLARSKA-BOBINSKA, Lena.
Cicero's Focus: From the Best Regime to the Model Statesman. NICGORSKI, Walter.
Communism: A Post-Mortem. BAUMAN, Zygmunt.
Communism: The Philosophical Foundations. FLEW, Antony.
Compatibilities on the Idea of Law in Thomas Aquinas and Thomas Hobbes. FULLER, Timothy.
Computers, Personal Data, and Theories of Technology: Comparative Approaches to Privacy Protection in the 1990s. BENNETT, Colin J.
The Concept of Jurisprudence. ALEXY, Robert and DREIER, Ralf.
Conceptions of Justification in Legal Discourse. WROBLEWSKI, Jerzy.
Conceptos centrales de la filosofía política en Chile democrático. COLLE, Reymond.
Conclusion. GRIFFITHS, A Phillips.
Conclusion: Legal Institutions and Limitations to Cognition and Power. O'BRIEN, James.
Conflicting Views of Liberalism. SKOBLE, Aeon James.
Congress, Consistency, and Environmental Law. LEMONS, John and BROWN, Donald A and VARNER, Gary E.
Constitutional Democracy and the Legitimacy of Judicial Review. FREEMAN, Samuel.
The Contending Among the Hundred Schools of Thought During the Warring States Period. ZEHUA, Liu.
A Contribution to the Discussion of the Doctrinal Preconditions of the Deformation of Socialism. KOLODII, A F.
Coping with Complexity—Coping with Dialectics, in Theory and Practice (in German). THIEL, Rainer.
Critical Legal Studies and Liberalism: Understanding the Similarities and Differences. WAGNER DE CEW, Judith.
Critical Synthesis on the Uses and Justifications for the Regulations of Intellectual Property. SNAPPER, John.
Le critiche a Kelsen durante la Repubblica di Weimar. ROEHRSSEN, Carlo.
A Critique of Marx's Extension of the Principles of Dialectical Materialism into the Phenomena of Social Life. NYONG, Prince David.
A Critique of One Interpretation of Practical Materialism. DANSHEN, Huang.
Czeslaw Znamierowski's Conception of Constitutive Rules. CZEPITA, Stanislaw.
David Hume's Theology of Liberation. BARRUS, Roger M.
Davis and the Unfair-Advantage Theory of Punishment: A Critique. SCHEID, Don E.
Die DDR und ihre Philosophen: Über Voraussetzungen einer Urteilsbildung. RUBEN, Peter.
De l'Idéologie comme correlat des termes idéologiste et idéologue. ZOLUA, Buenzey Maluenga.
Deceptive Comfort: The Power of Kafka's Stories. BENNETT, Jane.
Deconstructing Community Self-Paternalism. SCHONSHECK, Jonathan.
Deficiencies in Contemporary Theories of Justice. LÖTTER, H P P.
La democracia ateniense. GÓMEZ ROBLEDO, Antonio.
La democracia de los antiguos y la de los modernos. YTURBE, Corina.
Democracy and Socialism: Philosophical *Aporiae*. CUNNINGHAM, Frank.
Los derechos de la mujer, legalidad y realidad. COMESAÑA, Santalices Gloria.
Dezelfde wateren aan nieuwe oevers: Alexis de Tocqueville en de Franse Revolutie. ZIJDERVELD, A C.
Dialogue or Mutual Accusations?. SAGATOVSKII, V N.
Il dibattito italiano sullo statuto della filosofia politica: Contributo ad una bibliographia. BACCELLI, Luca.
Discourses on Political Violence: The Problem of Coherence. DU TOIT, A B.
The Divided Machine: Capitalist Crisis and the Organization of Labor. TURCHETTO, Maria and ESPOSITO, Joan.
Divine Irony and the Natural Law: Speculation and Edification in Aquinas. HIBBS, Thomas S.
Does Strict Judicial Scrutiny Involve the *Tu Quoque* Fallacy?. SCHEDLER, George.
Le droit de l'État et le devoir de l'individu. PFERSMANN, Otto.
Dworkin and His Critics: The Relevance of Ethical Theory in Philosophy of Law. BALL, Stephen W.
Dworkin, Habermas, and the CLS Movement on Moral Criticism in Law. INGRAM, David.
Economies of Time: On the Idea of Time in Marx's Political Economy. BOOTH, William James.
Economists and Philosophers as Critics of the Free Enterprise System. ARNOLD, N Scott.
Edmund Burke en zijn "Reflections on the Revolution in France". DE VALK, J M M.
Elites and Systematic Change in Hungary. SZALAI, Erzsebet.
La elusión mediante sociedades a la luz de los principios constitucionales. RUIZ ZAPATERO, Guillermo.
Emerson and the Inhibitions of Democracy. SHKLAR, Judith N.
The Enlightenment in American Law II: The Constitution. RECK, Andrew J.
El ensimismamiento del poder: Maquiavelo y la ciencia política moderna. GARCIA, Romano.
Entitled to Clemency: Mercy in the Criminal Law. JOHNSON, Carla Ann Hage.
Entrepreneurial Philosophy (in German). HERDER-DORNEICH, Philipp.
The Epic Hero as Politico. CAMPBELL, Blair.
Epistemologia e teoria politica. ZOLO, Danilo.
The Epistemological Moral Relevance of Democracy. NINO, Carlos S.
Equality. MILLER, David.
Ethical Pluralism and the Role of Opposition in Democratic Politics. D'AGOSTINO, Fred.
Ethics and Politics (in German). EWALD, François.

POLITICAL PHIL

Ethics and the Professional Responsibility of Lawyers. KIPNIS, Kenneth.
Etica e diritto penale nella filosofia attualistica. RICCIO, Stefano.
European Counterimages: Problems of Periodization and Historical Memory. DINER, Dan.
Evidence and Legal Reasoning: On the Intertwinement of the Probable and the Reasonable. KLAMI, Hannua Tapani (and others).
The Exclusion of Evidence Obtained by Constitutionally Impermissible Means in Canada. MC DONALD, David C.
Explaining Historical Development: A Marxian Critique of Cohen's Historical Materialism. WARREN, Paul.
Feminist Second Thoughts About Free Agency. BENSON, Paul.
La filosofia civile di Pasquale Villari. URBINATI, Nadia.
Filosofía de la liberación como nuevo pensamiento a partir de los oprimidos y como de-strucción (2a parte). ANIZAR, Humberto Encarnación.
Filosofía e identidad nacional en Honduras. ROMERO, Ramón.
For One Concept of Liberty. BEEHLER, Rodger.
A Formal Representation of Declaration-Related Legal Relations. HANSSON, Sven Ove.
The Formation of the Modern State: A Reconstruction of Max Weber's Arguments. AXTMANN, Roland.
Four Arguments Against Political Obligations from Gratitude. KLOSKO, George.
The Foxy Prophet: Machiavelli versus Machiavelli on Ferdinand the Catholic. ANDREW, Edward.
Freedom and Happiness in Kant's Political Philosophy. HELLER, Agnes.
Freedom and Human Nature. FLEW, Antony.
Freedom Is Our Divinity (in German). EHRHARDT, Walter E.
Friends and Enemies of Liberalism. ARCHARD, David.
From Dialogue Rights to Property Rights. SHEARMUR, Jeremy.
From Intersubjectivity through Epistemology to Property: Rejoinder to Michelman. SHEARMUR, Jeremy.
From Patriarchal Socialism to Socialist Democracy: Thoughts on a New Theory of Society. MOCEK, Reinhard.
From Philosophy to Politics: On Nietzsche's Ironic Metaphysics of Will to Power. PARENS, Erik.
From Precision to Peace: Hobbes and Political Language. MINOGUE, Kenneth.
From Propaganda to "Oeffentlichkeit" in Eastern Europe: Four Models of the Public Space Under State Socialism. SUKOSD, Miklos.
Los fundamentos discursivos de la democracia y los conflictos de intereses. GUARIGLIA, Osvaldo.
Game Theory is Not a Useful Tool for the Political Scientist. BUNGE, Mario.
Georg Lukács and Stalinism (in German). TIETZ, Udo.
George Kateb's Ahistorical Emersonianism. MARX, Leo.
German Collectivism and the Welfare State. NEAMAN, Elliot Yale.
Goerner on Thomistic Natural Law. HALL, Pamela.
Gorbatschews "Erneurung des Sozialismus"—Ideologie in der Krise des Kommunismus. KUX, Ernst.
Gorr on Actus Reus. MURPHY, Jeffrie G.
Grammatica e diritto: Una normatività fragile?. VITALE, Vincenzo.
Gramsci, Croce and the Italian Political Tradition. BELLAMY, Richard.
Gramsci, Gentile and the Theory of the Ethical State in Italy. SCHECTER, Darrow.
Grandeur et limites du *Marx* de Michel Henry. CANTIN, Serge.
H L A Hart and the "Open Texture" of Language. BIX, Brian.
Hannah Arendt's Political Theory: Ethics and Enemies. DOSSA, Shiraz.
Havel and Habermas on Identity and Revolution. MATUSTIK, Martin J.
Hegel as Advocate of Machiavelli (in German). JAMME, Christoph.
Hegel, Marx, and the Concept of Immanent Critique. BUCHWALTER, Andrew.
Hobbes and the Myth of "Final War". PASQUALUCCI, Paolo.
Hobbes and the Philosophy of International Relations. RAMOSE, Mogobe B.
Hobbes, Jacobo I y el derecho inglés. RIBEIRO, Renato Janine.
Homer's Contest: Nietzsche on Politics and the State in Ancient Greece. SMITH, Bruce.
Human Rights in the Context of Uganda's Political Experience. KIGONGO, J K.
The Humanism of Economics or Economizing on Humanism?. RIUMIN, V A.
Humble Rebel Henry David Thoreau (in Czechoslovakian). JANAT, B.
Hume on Responsibility and Punishment. RUSSELL, Paul.
El idealismo alemán como mitología de la razón. INNERARITY, Daniel.
The Ideas of Karl Marx at a Turning Point in Human Civilization. PANTIN, I and PLIMAK, E.
The Ideological Impasse of Gorbachev's Perestrojka. KRIZAN, Mojmir.
The Ideology of Intellectuals and the Chinese Student Protest Movement of 1989. CALHOUN, Craig.
Illusions and Visions: Models Of and In Modern Societies. MARZ, Lutz.
The Impact of Science Studies on Political Philosophy. LATOUR, Bruno.
The Importance of Asking the Right Questions. PATTERSON, Dennis.
In a Crazy Time the Crazy Come Out Well: Machiavelli and the Cosmology of His Day. BASU, Sammy.
Individualism, Absolutism, and Contract in Hobbes' Political Theory. GROVER, Robinson A.
Das Individuum, die Politik und die Philosophie. GRUNWALD, Sabine.
The Institution of Law. BANKOWSKI, Zenon.
The Intellectuals at the End of History. BRUNKHORST, Hauke.
Interpretation and the Social Reality of Law. GOLDFORD, Dennis.
The Ironist's Cage. ROTH, Michael S.
The Irony of Richard Rorty and the Question of Political Judgment. WEISLOGEL, Eric L.
Is It Practical Ontology or Is It the Dialectical Materialist Theory of Material Monism?. JINFU, Wang.
Is Karl Marx to Blame for "Barracks Socialism"?. BUTENKO, A P.
J G A Pocock's Republicanism and Political Theory: A Critique and Reinterpretation. SHAPIRO, Ian.
Jean-Jacques Rousseau and the Fusion of Democratic Sovereignty with Aristocratic Government. CRANSTON, Maurice.
Jean-Jacques Rousseau, Sexist?. THOMAS, Paul.
Jeffersonian Ethics in Foreign Affairs: John Quincy Adams and the Moral Sentiments of a Realist. RUSSELL, Greg.
John Rawls: de l'autonomie morale à la fiction de contrat social. RICOEUR, Paul.
John Stuart Mill and Royal India. MOORE, Robin J.
John Stuart Mill über die Todesstrafe. WOLF, Jean-Claude.
Joseph de Maistre en de Revolutie. VAN BELLINGEN, Jozef.
The Juncture of Law and Morality in Prohibitions Against Torture. MARAN, Rita.
Jurisprudential Oaks from Mythical Acorns: The Hart-Dworkin Debate Revisited. BOON LEONG PHANG, Andrew.
Just War Theory and the ANC's Armed Struggle. MILLER, S R.
Just War Theory: The Case of South Africa. MILLER, S R.
Justice Powell and the Parochial Schools Case: A Case for Judicial Statesmanship. WALTMAN, Jerold.
Justification et justice procédurale. DUHAMEL, André.
Justus Möser: De Revolutie en de grondslagen van de moderne staat. WALRAVENS, Else.
Kann in O Höffes Ethik der politischen Gerechtigkeit eine ökologische Ethik aufgehoben werden?. WETZEL, Manfred.
Kant the Liberal, Kant the Anarchist: Rawls and Lyotard on Kantian Justice. MAY, Todd G.
Kant y la Revolución Francesa. PÉREZ ESTÉVEZ, Antonio.
Kant's Theory of Peace and the Main Aspects of the Recent Discussion Surrounding It (in German). ZAHN, Manfred.
Kant's visie op de Franse Revolutie en op de grondslagen van het recht. VAN DER WAL, G A.
Kant: del derecho de libertad a la exigencia racional del Estado. PASTORE, Romano.
Kommunismus—Utopie und Wirklichkeit. HAVEMANN, Robert.
L'être de l'humain: Notes sur la tradition communautarienne. CHAUMONT, Jean-Michel.
Lacan in Slovenia—An Interview with Slavoj Zizek and Renata Salecl. DEWS, Peter and OSBORNE, Peter.
Land Rights and Aboriginal Sovereignty. THOMPSON, Janna.
Land, Well-Being and Compensation. PARGETTER, Robert and YOUNG, Robert and BIGELOW, John.
Langage privé et communauté: Kripke et Wittgenstein. DUMOUCHEL, Paul.
Law and Exclusionary Reasons. ALEXANDER, Larry.
Law Without Values: Do the Unborn Have to Wait for a Consensus?. VACCARI, Michael A.
Legal Positivism and Democracy in the Twentieth Century. SQUELLA, Agustí.
Legal Positivism, Social Rules, and *Riggs* versus *Palmer*. BEEHLER, Rodger.
Legal Reasoning and Practical Political Education. STRAUBER, Ira.
Legitimate Anachronism as a Problem for Intellectual History and for Philosophy. DU TOIT, André.
Lenin and Philosophy: Should We Not Pose This Problem Anew?. VOLODIN, A.
Lenin, Gorbachev, and 'National-Statehood': Can Leninism Countenance the New Soviet Federal Order?. GLEASON, Gregory.
Leviathan, King of the Proud. SHAVER, Robert.
Liberal Man. MENDUS, Susan.
The Liberal Teachings of the Young Liang Qichao. QI, Feng.
Liberalism: Political Success, Moral Failure?. SIMPSON, Peter.
Libertad, Igualdad, Fraternidad. BUENO, Gustavo.
Libertarianism. BARRY, Norman.
Locke on Taxation and Suffrage. HUGHES, Martin.
La loi et ses législateurs ou les avatars du théologico-politique. TOSEL, André.
El lugar de las superestructuras y los intelectuales en la filosofía política de Gramsci. RUIZ, Angel.
Machiavelli's Notions of Justice: Text and Analysis. PAREL, A J.
Market Order or Commanded Chaos. FLEW, Antony.
Markets and Morals. SMITH, G W.
Marsilius on Rights. TIERNEY, Brian.
Marx and Perestroika. ROCKMORE, Tom.
Marx, Nietzsche, and the "New Class". EVANS, Fred.
Marxism and Contemporary Political Philosophy. COHEN, G A.
Marxism and Social Change: Some Theoretical Reflections. TRIPATHY, Laxman Kumar.

POLITICAL PHIL

Marxism as the Foundation of Philosophies of Science: *The Case of G Lukács' Ontology of Social Being*. TUCHANSKA, Barbara.
Marxism in the USSR Today. FISK, Milton.
Marxism, Post-Marxism and the Implosion of Communism. STOJANOVIC, Svetozar.
El marxismo, ciencia, ideología, gnosis?. BESANÇON, Alain.
The Marxist Conception of Tradition. STEPANYANTS, Marietta.
The Master-Slave Dialectic in Latin America: The Social Criticism of Zea, Freire, and Roig. SCHUTTE, Ofelia M.
The Meaning of Recent Changes in Eastern Europe. MARKOVIC, Mihailo.
Medio ambiente y derecho. ROMERO, Jorge Enrique.
The Member for Westminster: Doctrinaire Philosopher, Party Hack, or Public Moralist?. COLLINI, Stefan.
Mental Handicap and Citizenship. SPICKER, Paul.
Michel Foucault: From the Humanities to Political Thought (in German). SEITTER, Walter.
Modelos elitarios de democracia. VERGARA ESTÉVEZ, Jorge.
The Modernity of St Thomas' Political Philosophy. WALTER, Edward.
Montesquieu and China. HONGXUN, Hou.
The Moral Foundations of Intangible Property. CHILD, James W.
Moral oder Klugheit? Überlegungen zur Gestalt der Autonomie des Politischen im Denken Kants. SCHMITZ, Heinz-Gerd.
Natural and Political Society in the Thought of Edmund Burke (in German). TSCHURENEV, Eva-Maria.
Natural Law Theory: The Link Between its Descriptive Strength and its Prescriptive Strength. BRAYBROOKE, David.
Nature, Justice, and Duty in the *Defensor Pacis*: Marsiglio of Padua's Ciceronian Impulse. NEDERMAN, Cary J.
Natuur en cultuur: de heuristische waarde van een dichotomie. WESTERMAN, Pauline.
The Neglected Background of Radical Liberalism: P E Dove's Theory of Property. CUNLIFFE, John.
Ein neu gefundener Brief von Leibniz an Lambert van Velthuysen: Mit einer Einführung von Albert Heinekamp. HEIN, Isolde.
Neutrality Between Religion and Irreligion. LINDSAY, Ronald A.
Neuvermessung des Rechts- und Staatsdiskurses: Zu Otfried Höffes Theorie der Politischen Gerechtigkeit. SITTER-LIVER, Beat.
The New Consensus: II—The Democratic Welfare State. FRIEDMAN, Jeffrey.
New Studies on Hegel's Philosophy of Law, versus on the Dialectics of Hegel and Marx (in Hungarian). GÖHLER, Gerhard.
Nietzsche's Genealogy: Of Beauty and Community. KEMAL, S.
Nietzsche: Moralist or Immoralist?—The Verdict of the European Protestant Theologians in the First World War. BAILEY, Charles E.
Nihilism and the Impossibility of Political Philosophy. BASINSKI, Paul A.
Non-professional Judicial Reasoning. TAPANI KLAMI, Hannu.
Norberto Bobbio ideologo del neoilluminismo: Per una rilettura di "Politica e cultura". QUARANTA, Mario.
Normas, sistemas jurídicos y eficacia. NAVARRO, Pablo Eugenio.
Not So Virtuous Republics: Montesquieu, Venice, and the Theory of Aristocratic Republicanism. CARRITHERS, David W.
Note ad un recente libro sull'incontro-scontro tra Croce e Gentile. ANTISERI, Dario.
Notes sur utopie et marxisme. ARANTES, Urias Corrêa.
Nozick et la stabilité des principes de justice distributive. BÉGIN, Luc.
Nozick on Rights and Minimal State. AGARWALA, Binod Kumar.
Nozick on Social Justice. AGARWALA, Binod Kumar.
Nozick's Identity Crisis. LUCY, W N R.
Nuclear Deterrence and the Morality of Intentions. KULTGEN, John.
Nuclear Stalemate: A Superior Escape from the Dilemmas of Deterrence. SCHONSHECK, Jonathan.
On Ideal Form, Empowering Norms, and "Normative Functions". PAULSON, Stanley L.
On Judicial Ascertainment of Facts. VARGA, Csaba.
On Law and Morality: A Dialogue. VON WRIGHT, Georg Henrik.
On Leo Katz, Double Jeopardy, and the Blockburger Test. LOCKE, Lawrence A.
On Marx's Conception of Rationality. MULLICK, Mohini.
On Scholarly Developments in Legal Semiotics. JACKSON, Bernard S.
On Social Rights. SANDU, Gabriel and KUOKKANEN, Martti.
On Some Unsettled Questions Touching the Character of Marxism, Especially as Philosophy. SUCHTING, W A.
The Orthodox Model of the Criminal Offense. HUSAK, Douglas N.
Over leesbaarheid en maakbaarheid van de geschiedenis. WEYEMBERGH, Maurice.
Ownership as Theft. GRUNEBAUM, James O.
Paradigms of Legal Science. JORI, Mario.
A Paradox About Authority. ODERBERG, David S.
Parallel Governing. SCALTSAS, Theodore.
The Pariah as Hero: Hannah Arendt's Political Actor. RING, Jennifer.
Pascal, etica, politica, socialità. DEREGIBUS, Arturo.
Paternalistic Laws. GOLDMAN, Alan H and GOLDMAN, Michael N.
Paths to a Postmodern Ethics and Politics: A Reply to Gibbons. WHITE, Stephen K.
La pensée de Rawls face au défi communautarien. IROEGBU, Pantaleon.
Per una nuova edizione della *Epistola* lockiana sulla tolleranza. MONTUORI, Mario.
Perelman et la philosophie anglo-saxonne. MARCIL-LACOSTE, Louise.
Perestrojka der Philosophie?. IGNATOW, Assen.
Die Perestrojka in der Sowjetischen Philosophie: Mythos oder Realität. BYKOVA, M.
The Philosophy of the Welfare State. BARRY, Norman P.
Plato's Three Waves and the Question of Utopia. HYLAND, Drew A.
Politica e diritto in Hobbes. BAGLIONI, Emma.
Political Culture and Institution Building: Democratic Evolution at Work and the Case of Poland. LAMENTOWICZ, Wojtek.
Political Errors (in Serbo-Croatian). NOERR, Gunzelin Schmid.
Political Freedom. TULLY, James.
Political Justice in Post-Communist Societies: The Case of Hungary. BENCE, György.
The Political Philosophy of Sissela Bok. FAREY, Caroline.
Political Theory and Cultural Criticism: Towards a Theory of Cultural Politics. MACDONALD, Bradley J.
The Politics of the Rule of Law. RAZ, Joseph.
Post-Liberalism versus Temperate Liberalism. JACOBS, Struan.
The Post-Modern Challenge: From Marx to Nietzsche in the West German Alternative and Green Movement. BETZ, Hans-Georg.
Prague: le cimetière. BRETON, Stanislas.
Praxis and Ultimate Reality: Intellectual, Moral and Religious Conversion as Radical Political Conversion. MARSH, James L.
Preferences and Politics. SUNSTEIN, Cass R.
Presencia de Grecia y de Roma clásicas en la Revolución francesa de 1789. RECIO GARCÍA, Tomás.
Pride and the Meaning of *Utopia*. MOULAKIS, Athanasios.
The Primacy of the Political: Towards a Theory of National Integration. RAJAN, R Sundara.
Prisoners' Rights and Correctional Privatization: A Legal and Ethical Analysis. THOMAS, Charles W.
Private Defense. GORR, Michael.
Probability Out of Court: Notes on 'Guilt Beyond Reasonable Doubt'. COHEN, Stephen and BERSTEN, Michael.
Prohibiting Immorality. WESTMORELAND, Robert.
Le projet de John Rawls. LAMBERT, Roger.
Property in Science and the Market. O'NEILL, John.
Property, Entitlement, and Remedy. PAUL, Jeffrey.
Propriété de soi et propriété du monde extérieur. COUTURE, Jocelyne.
Protestant Hermeneutics and the Rule of Law: Gadamer and Dworkin. HENLEY, Kenneth.
Prudence and Providence: On Hobbes's Theory of Practical Reason. HANCE, Allen S.
Public and Private Morality. SHAIDA, S A.
The Punishment of Attempts. NUYEN, A T.
Puzzling Through Burke. HERZOG, Don.
Questioni di filosofia politica. VECA, Salvatore.
Radin on Personhood and Rent Control. GREENBERG, Dan.
A Rational Choice Theory of Punishment. STERBA, James P.
The Rational Law-Maker and the Pragmatics of Legal Interpretation. DASCAL, Marcelo and WRÓBLEWSKI, Jerzy.
Reading Hobbes in Other Words: Contractarian, Utilitarian, Game Theorist. HARDIN, Russell.
Realism in the Authority of Law. BRIGHAM, John and HARRINGTON, Christine.
Reason and Revelation in the Thought of Leo Strauss. COLMO, Christopher A.
Reasonable Evidence of Reasonableness. KELMAN, Mark.
Recent Work in Political Philosophy. GRAHAM, Gordon.
Rediscovering the Left. HOWARD, Dick.
Reflection in Politics and the Question of a Political Subject (in Czechoslovakian). HEJDANEK, Ladislav.
Reflections on Ideas of Social Philosophy and Indian Code of Conduct. DASGUPTA, Manashi.
Reflections on the Eastern European Revolutions: The God that Failed. MAZLISH, Bruce.
Rejoinder to Springborg's "His Majesty Is a Baby?" A Critical Response to Peter Hammond Schwartz. SCHWARTZ, Peter Hammond.
Relative Duties in the Law. WELLMAN, Carl.
La religión en la constitución de los Estados Unidos de América. PÉREZ ESTÉVEZ, Antonio.
Religious Commitment and Secular Reason: A Reply to Professor Weithman. AUDI, Robert.
Religious Liberty, Religious Dissent and the Catholic Tradition. COWDIN, Daniel M.
Renaissance Ideas and the Idea of the Renaissance. TRINKAUS, Charles.
Reply to Murphy and Husak. GORR, Michael.
Reply to Shearmur's "From Dialogue Rights to Property Rights". MICHELMAN, Frank.
Resources, Capacities, and Ownership: The Workmanship Ideal and Distributive Justice. SHAPIRO, Ian.
Response to Hall's "Goerner on Thomistic Natural Law". GOERNER, E A.

POLITICAL PHIL

Response to Mendus's "Liberal Man". BINNS, Peter.
Response to Miller's "Equality". MINOGUE, K.
Response to Powell's "Theory and Practice". SKIDELSKY, Robert.
Response to Smith's "Markets and Morals". LOCKE, Don.
Retaliatory Punishment as a Categorical Imperative. HÖFFE, Ottfried.
Rethinking the Diodotean Argument. JOHNSON, Laurie M.
La revolución teórica del Príncipe de Maquiavelo. GIGLIOLI, Giovanna.
Revolution, Civil Society and Democracy. ARATO, Andrew.
The Right to Self-Determination. BERG, Jonathan.
Rights, Systems of Rights, and Unger's System of Rights: Part I. EIDENMÜLLER, Horst.
Rileggendo Marx: "diritti" e "bisogni". BADALONI, Nicola.
The Role of Aristotle's *Praxis* Today. GUY, Alfred.
Die Rolle der Philosophiegeschichte im "Neuen philosophischen Denken" in der UdSSR. VAN DER ZWEERDE, Evert.
Romania's Revolution and its Prospects. BRUCAN, Silviu.
Rosmini interprete della Rivoluzione francese e di Rousseau. BOTTO, Evandro.
Rousseau's Liberalism. SORENSEN, L R.
Rousseau's Political Defense of the Sex-Roled Family. WEISS, Penny.
Rousseau, the General Will, and Individual Liberty. KAIN, Philip J.
The Rule of Law in *The German Constitution*. HANCE, Allen S.
Salisburian Stakes: The Uses of 'Tyranny' in John of Salisbury's *Policraticus*. FORHAN, Kate Langdon.
Sanction and the Law According to St Thomas Aquinas. HENLE, R J.
Sartre and his Successors: Existential Marxism and Postmodernism at Our *Fin de Siecle*. MC BRIDE, William L.
Sartre and Political Legitimacy. KNEE, Philip.
Sartre's onuitgevoerde project: de Robespierre-biografie. DETHIER, Hubert.
Sawa Frydman: A Polish Legal Realist. MOS, Urszula.
Schattenseiten der Hegelei: Fallsbeispiel—Lassalles Hegel-Rhapsodie. BEYER, Wilhelm Raimund.
Schopenhauers Straftheorie und die aktuelle Strafzweckdiskussion. KÜPPER, Georg.
Schopenhauersche Weltsicht und totalitäre Humanität im Werke Thomas Manns. KRISTIANSEN, Borge.
Self-Management in the Context of the Disintegration of "Reali-Existing" Socialism. STANOJEVIC, Miroslav.
Self-Ownership and the Right of Property. MACK, Eric.
Self-Ownership, Equality, and the Structure of Property Rights. CHRISTMAN, John.
The Separation of Church and State: Some Questions for Professor Audi. WEITHMAN, Paul J.
Si la filosofía política es ciencia práctica. DONADÍO MAGGI, María C.
The Significance of Rights Language. GOLDING, Martin P.
The Skeptic's Burke: *Reflections on the Revolution in France,* 1790-1990. MOSHER, Michael A.
Skepticism and Legal Interpretation. NATHAN, Daniel O.
Smith Against the Ethicists. LUBAN, David.
Sobre la naturaleza de los "derechos". HERNÁNDEZ, Héctor H.
Social Criticism and Political Philosophy. BARRY, Brian.
Society as a Department Store. LEGUTKO, Ryszard.
Socrates and Alcibiades: Eros, Piety, and Politics. HOWLAND, Jacob A.
Soggetto e senso del diritto nell'esperienza giuridica moderna: appunti in tema di positività. FIASCHI, Giovanni.
Some Basic Problems of a Political Theory of Modern Socialism (in German). SEGERT, Dieter.
Some Remarks on the Political Science of Maimonides and Farabi. BARTLETT, Robert (trans) and STRAUSS, Leo.
The Sources of Stalinism. TSIPKO, A.
Sovranità e obbedienza. CATANIA, Alfonso.
La speranza nel giusnaturalismo. TUSA, Carlo.
Spinoza en het ontstaan van de staat. VERBEEK, Bruno.
Spinoza—Beyond Hobbes and Rousseau. GEISMANN, Georg.
Staat als Konsens mündiger Bürger? Zur Staatsansicht deutscher Vormärzliberaler. LIEPERT, Anita.
Lo statuo della filosofia politica nel dibattito italiano. BACCELLI, Luca.
Strange Attractors: How Individualists Connect to Form Democratic Unity. ROSENBLUM, Nancy.
Strauss's Three Burkes: The Problem of Edmund Burke in *Natural Right and History*. LENZNER, Steven J.
Study of Society and Polity: Scientific and Philosophical. CHATTOPADHYAYA, D P.
Sul controllo nel procedimento di determinazione dei principi dell'ordinamento. COSTANZO, Angelo.
Sur l'éthique et la rationalité de l'État social. MARION, Normand.
Surrogate Motherhood. PROKOPIJEVIC, Miroslav.
A Survey of Critical Theories of "Western Marxism". YUJIN, Zhao.
Swedish Model or Swedish Culture?. TRAGARDH, Lars.
The Symmetry Enigma in Hobbes. HAJI, Ishtiyaque.
Taking Rights Seriously in the Abortion Case. DWORKIN, Ronald.
The Development of a Concept of Modern Socialism: Theses under Discussion (in German). BRIE, Michael.
The Freedom of Values and the Value of Freedom (in Czechoslovakian). SLEJSKA, D.
The Party's Claim to Power: The Power of Knowledge in "Real Socialism" (in German). MARZ, Lutz.
The Philosophical Invariables of Masaryk's Thinking (in Czechoslovakian). SROVNAL, Jindrich.
The Pros and Cons of Trotsky's Marxism (in German). HEDELER, Wladislaw.
Theology of Liberation and Marxism (in Serbo-Croation). ORSOLIC, Marko.
The Theoretical Premises of Scientific Socialism and Its Mode of Thought. YUQUAN, Tao.
Theory and Practice. POWELL, J Enoch.
The Theory of Legal Dynamics Reconsidered. WEINBERGER, Ota.
Thomas Hobbes and the Contractarian Theory of Law. GAUTHIER, David.
Thoughts on the Future of Marxism. LEVINE, Andrew.
Torts of Necessity: A Moral Theory of Compensation. KLEPPER, Howard.
Toward a Narrative Conception of Legal Discourse. PATTERSON, Dennis.
Transition to Pragmatic Liberalism: Diversity, Contingency, and Social Solidarity. LINDGREN, Ralph.
Treatment and Rehabilitation as a Mode of Punishment. MARTIN, Rex.
Tully's Locke. DEN HARTOGH, Govert.
Twice Told Tales: A Reply to Schlesinger. COHEN, L Jonathan.
Two Concepts of Justice. CHAKRAVARTI, A.
Two Conservative Views of Nationality and Personality: A A Grigor'ev and K N Leont'ev. DOWLER, E W.
Two Forms of Moral Responsibility. SANKOWSKI, Edward.
Two Views of the Revolution: Gramsci and Sorel, 1916-1920. SCHECTER, Darrow.
Unamuno y la Revolución de Octubre. ROBLES, Laureano.
The Unity of Human Rights in Western and Eastern Europe: Meditation about Human Rights. FÖLDESI, Tamás.
Universalismo o eurocentrismo. SPAEMANN, Robert.
Utility and Morality: Adam Smith's Critique of Hume. MARTIN, Marie A.
La valenza della carità nelle forme della vita politica. PELLECCHIA, Pasquale.
Venti lettere inedite di Angelo Camillo De Meis a Bertrando Spaventa. RASCAGLIA, Maria.
La via della pace: in merito ad un recente libro. ZANUSO, Francesca.
Vico, pensatore antimoderno: L'interpretazione di Eric Voegelin. ZANETTI, Gianfrancesco.
Walt Whitman and the Culture of Democracy. KATEB, George.
Walt Whitman: Jacobin Poet of American Democracy. MOSHER, Michael.
Was Marx a Socialist?. TSIPKO, A.
Ways to See a Revolution and World Outlook: Alexander von Humboldt (in German). HERLITZIUS, Erwin.
Weaving and Practical Politics In Plato's *Statesman*. COLE, Eve Browning.
The Welfare State: What is Left?. PRYCHITKO, David L.
Welke natuur is het beschermen waard?. VAN DER WINDT, Henny J and HARBERS, Hans.
What Happened in Eastern Europe in 1989?. CHIROT, Daniel.
What Is Jurisprudence About? Theories, Definitions, Concepts, or Conceptions of Law?. BAYLES, Michael D.
When is Original Appropriation *Required*?. SCHMIDTZ, David.
Whitman and Memory: A Response to Kateb. BROMWICH, David.
Why (Legal) Rules Often Fail to Control Human Behavior. CROMBAG, H F M.
Why Democracy and Rights Do Not Mix. NELSON, John O.
Why Narrative Is Not Enough. FULLER, Steve.
Why Should a Dialectician Learn to Count to Four?. ZIZEK, Slavoj.
Wie kaatst moet de bal verwachten. MERTENS, T.
Wishful Thinking and the Budget Deficit. FRANKLIN, Daniel Paul.
Women's Law. DUXBURY, Neil.
Women, Madness, and Special Defences in the Law. BOETZKES, Elisabeth and TURNER, Susan (Guerin) and SOBSTYL, Edrie.
The World of Man and Man in the World in Light of the New Philosophical Thinking. DZHAKHAIA, L G.
The World Reconsidered: A Brief *AggiornamentoF* for Leftist Intellectuals. SKIRBEKK, Gunnar.
Zu Jürgen Habermas' Option für Fortschritt, Vernunft und Demokratie. BOGNER, Hagen.
Zwischen Enttäuschung und Versöhnung: Hegel, die deutsche Misere und die Französiche Revolution. ARNDT, Andreas.

POLITICAL SCIENCE

David Hume and the Problem of Reason. DANFORD, John W.
Die moderne Gesellschaft im Rechtsstaat. BAURMANN, Michael.
Russische Philosophie. GOERDT, Wilhelm.
Wahrheit—Diskurs—Demokratie: Studien zur "Konsensustheorie der Wahrheit". SCHEIT, Herbert.
Aristotelianism and the Origins of "Political Science" in the Twelfth Century. NEDERMAN, Cary J.
Can Marxism Help Biology?. KASSIOLA, Joel.
Le sens de la révolution méthodologique introduite par Rousseau dans la science politique. GOYARD-FABRE, Simone.
Si la filosofía política es ciencia práctica. DONADÍO MAGGI, María C.
Some Remarks on the Political Science of Maimonides and Farabi. BARTLETT, Robert (trans) and STRAUSS, Leo.
Lo statuo della filosofia politica nel dibattito italiano. BACCELLI, Luca.
Thinking About Home Schooling: Some Historical, Philosophical, and Cultural Reasons. KENNEDY, David.

POLITICAL STRUCTURES

Political Theory in the Welfare State. LUHMANN, Niklas.
"Human Nature and Unnatural Humanisms" in *From Twilight to Dawn: The Cultural Vision of Jacques Maritain*, ROYAL, Robert.
I "systemata subordinata" e il problema della partecipazione in Hobbes. SORGI, Giuseppe.
Anarchism and Feminism. MOODY, Thomas E.
Political Freedom. TULLY, James.
The Politics of Knowledge. SPRING, Joel.
The Pot at the End of the Rainbow: Political Myth and the Ecological Crisis. DOYLE, Timothy.
Presidential Campaigns, Television News and Voter Turnout. WALTER, Edward.
Re-Viewing the Political Structure of Knowledge. LEACH, Mary S.
Uguaglianza e temporalità nella "Democrazia in America". BAGLIONI, Emma.

POLITICAL THEORY

Foundations of Moral and Political Philosophy. PAUL, Ellen Frankel (ed).
Gerechtigkeit, Wohlfahrt und Rationalität. SCHMIDT, Johannes.
The Political Philosophy of Michael Oakeshott. FRANCO, Paul.
Political Theory in the Welfare State. LUHMANN, Niklas.
Political Writings—Kant. REISS, Hans (ed).
"Conclusion" in *Philosophy and Politics*, GRIFFITHS, A Phillips.
"Radical Politics in a New Key?" in *Critique and Construction: A Symposium on Roberto Unger's "Politics"*, JUDT, Tony.
"Response to Skidelsky's 'Theory and Practice'" in *Philosophy and Politics*, SKIDELSKY, Robert.
"Theory and Practice" in *Philosophy and Politics*, POWELL, J Enoch.
"Unger, Castoriadis, and the Romance of a National Future" in *Critique and Construction: A Symposium on Roberto Unger's "Politics"*, RORTY, Richard.
Alexander Hamilton: The Separation of Powers. PRATT, Ronald L.
The Doubleness of the Unthought of the Overman: Ambiguities of Heideggerian Political Thought. HAAR, Michel.
Epistemologia e teoria politica. ZOLO, Danilo.
Hannah Arendt's Political Theory: Ethics and Enemies. DOSSA, Shiraz.
Jean-Jacques Rousseau on the Physiogonomy of the Modern City. ELLISON, Charles E.
Just War Theory and the ANC's Armed Struggle. MILLER, S R.
Machiavelli's Sisters: Women and "the Conversation" of Political Theory. ZERILLI, Linda M G.
Marx's 'Critique of Hegel's *Philosophy of Right*'. JACKSON, M W.
Ms en abyme: Deconstruction and Feminism. ELAM, Diane.
Neuhaus and Murray on Natural Law and American Politics. LAWLER, Peter A.
The Pariah as Hero: Hannah Arendt's Political Actor. RING, Jennifer.
Puzzling Through Burke. HERZOG, Don.
A Theory of Social Justice?. HORTON, John.
The Unity of Theory and Practice in Historical Perspective. KRANCBERG, Sigmund.
Warnings on Resistance and the Language of Possibility: Gramsci and a Pedagogy from the Surreal. SENESE, Guy B.

POLITICALIZATION

The Political Responsibility of Intellectuals. MACLEAN, Ian (ed).
The Politics of Ethics: Socratic Questioning is Needed in the Marketplace. TRUNDLE, Robert.

POLITICS

Adorno's Aesthetic Theory: The Redemption of Illusion. ZUIDERVAART, Lambert.
An Audience for Moral Philosophy?. EDELMAN, John T.
The Balance of Consciousness: Eric Voegelin's Political Theory. KEULMAN, Kenneth.
Benjamin Constant and the Post-Revolutionary Mind. FONTANA, Biancamaria.
Bertrand Russell. ALCARO, Mario.
The Call to Personhood. MC FADYEN, Alistair I.
Controlling Technology: Contemporary Issues. THOMPSON, William B.
Critical Theory and Philosophy. INGRAM, David.
A Cultivated Mind: Essays On J S Mill Presented to John M Robson. LAINE, Michael (ed).
Dämonie und Gesellschaft. CATTEPOEL, Jan.
De l'épistémologie à la politique: La philosophie de l'histoire de Karl R Popper. RUELLAND, Jacques G.
The Death of Industrial Civilization. KASSIOLA, Joel Jay.
Descent into Subjectivity: Studies of Rawls, Dworkin and Unger in the Context of Modern Thought. MURPHY JR, Cornelius F.
Essentially Speaking: Feminism, Nature and Difference. FUSS, Diana.
Das Ethische in der Rhetorik des Aristoteles. WÖRNER, Markus Hilmar.
Expressionism in Philosophy: Spinoza. DELEUZE, Gilles.
Femininity and Domination: Studies in the Phenomenology of Oppression. BARTKY, Sandra Lee.
Feminism/Postmodernism. NICHOLSON, Linda J (ed).
Fictions of Reality in the Age of Hume and Johnson. DAMROSCH, Leo.
From Hegel to Nietzsche: The Revolution in Nineteenth-Century Thought. LÖWITH, Karl.
Grace, Politics and Desire: Essays on Augustine. MEYNELL, Hugo A (ed).
Hegel In His Time—Jacques D'Hondt. BURBIDGE, John (trans).
Hermeneutics and Critical Theory in Ethics and Politics. KELLY, Michael (ed).
Hobbes. TUCK, Richard.
How to Play Theological Ping-Pong: And Other Essays on Faith and Reason. ABRAHAM, William J (ed).
Idea, mente, specie: Platonismo e scienza in Johannes Marcus Marci (1595-1667). MOCCHI, Giuliana.
Ideals and Illusions: On Reconstruction and Deconstruction in Contemporary Critical Theory. MC CARTHY, Thomas.
The Ideas of Ayn Rand. MERRILL, Ronald E.
Kierkegaard in Golden Age Denmark. KIRMMSE, Bruce H.
Marxism and Philosophy in the Twentieth Century: A Defense of Vulgar Marxism. HUDELSON, Richard.
Moral und Politik aus der Sicht des Kritischen Rationalismus. SALAMUN, Kurt (ed).
Nature and Politics: Liberalism in the Philosophies of Hobbes, Locke, and Rousseau. RAPACZYNSKI, Andrzej.
Philosophical Streets: New Approaches to Urbanism. CROW, Dennis (ed).
Platonic Piety. MORGAN, Michael L.
The Political Ontology of Martin Heidegger. BOURDIEU, Pierre.
The Political Philosophy of Michael Oakeshott. FRANCO, Paul.
Political Writings—John Milton. DZELZAINIS, Martin (ed).
The Politics of Being: The Political Thought of Martin Heidegger. WOLIN, Richard.
Postmodernism—Philosophy and the Arts (Continental Philosophy III). SILVERMAN, Hugh J (ed).
The River of the Mother of God, and Other Essays by Aldo Leopold. FLADER, Susan L (ed).
The Savage Anomaly: The Power of Spinoza's Metaphysics and Politics. NEGRI, Antonio.
Understanding War: A Philosophical Inquiry. MC MURTRY, John.
Writing and the Moral Self. LANG, Berel.
"Antigone's Daughters Reconsidered: Continuing Reflections on Women, Politics, and Power" in *Life-World and Politics: Between Modernity and Postmodernity*, ELSHTAIN, Jean Bethke.
"Heidegger's Way In, Through, and Out of Politics: The Story of His Rectorate" in *Perspectives on Ideas and Reality*, FEHÉR, István M.
"Intellectuals between Politics and Culture" in *The Political Responsibility of Intellectuals*, SZACKI, Jerzy.
"John Stuart Mill and the Experience of Political Engagement" in *A Cultivated Mind: Essays On J S Mill Presented to John M Robson*, KINZER, Bruce L.
"Justice and Love in the Political Thought of St Augustine" in *Grace, Politics and Desire: Essays on Augustine*, PAREL, Anthony J.
"Moral Conflict and Political Consensus" in *Liberalism and the Good*, GUTMANN, Amy and THOMPSON, Dennis.
"Newton's God of Dominion: The Unity of Newton's Theological, Scientific, and Political Thought" in *Essays on the Context, Nature, and Influence of Isaac Newton's Theology*, FORCE, James E.
"The Political Irresponsibility of Intellectuals" in *The Political Responsibility of Intellectuals*, TAMÁS, G M.
"The Political Origins of Democracy" in *Writing the Politics of Difference*, HOWARD, Dick.
"The Political Responsibility of Intellectuals" in *The Political Responsibility of Intellectuals*, MONTEFIORE, Alan.
"Politics and the Problem of Dirty Hands" in *A Companion to Ethics*, COADY, C A J.
"The Politics of Trust in American Health Care" in *Ethics, Trust, and the Professions: Philosophical and Cultural Aspects*, FOX, Daniel M.
"Politics, Technology and the Responsibility of the Intellectuals" in *The Political Responsibility of Intellectuals*, LEVY, David J.
"The Problem of Liberalism and the Good" in *Liberalism and the Good*, RICHARDSON, Henry S.
"Sense and Sensibility in Mill's Political Thought" in *A Cultivated Mind: Essays On J S Mill Presented to John M Robson*, RYAN, Alan.
"Situation and Suspicion in the Thought of Merleau-Ponty" in *Ontology and Alterity in Merleau-Ponty*, WESTPHAL, Merold.
"Et la religion le remplit de fureur...". BOULAD-AYOUB, Josiane.
The "New" Scholars in Philosophy of Education, 1976-1986. QUANTZ, Richard A.
The Ambivalent Unthought of the Overman and the Duality of Heidegger's Political Thinking. HAAR, Michel.
Análisis político-epistemológico de la obra de arte según Walter Benjamin. COMESAÑA, Santalices Gloria.
The Body Politic: Democratic Metaphors, Totalitarian Practices, Erotic Rebellions. BERGOFFEN, Debra B.
Breves notas acerca de la *Política* de Aristóteles. ÁLVAREZ, Margarita Mauri.
A Certain 'Politics of Speech': 'Religious Pluralism' in the Age of the McDonald's Hamburger. SURIN, Kenneth.
Constrained Discourse and Public Life. MOON, J Donald.
Deconstructing/Deconstructive Inquiry: The Politics of Knowing and Being Known. LATHER, Patti.
Division and Difference in the "Discipline" of Economics. AMARIGLIO, Jack and RESNICK, Stephen and WOLFF, Richard.
Ecofeminist Theory and Grassroots Politics. LAHAR, Stephanie.

POLITICS
Ecosocialism—Utopian and Scientific. HAYWARD, Tim.
Enlightenment Psychology and Political Reaction in Plato's Social Philosophy: an Ideological Contradiction?. BRYANT, Joseph M.
Epistemology and Political Rationality. FUTERNICK, Ken.
Ethics and Politics (in German). EWALD, François.
Etica, retórica y política en la antropología aristotélica. MARTIN, Victor R.
The Exile of Literature: Poetry and the Politics of the Other(s). MURPHY, Bruce F.
Feminist Theory and the Politics of Inclusion. FISHER, Linda.
Filosofia e cultura ne "Il Politecnico" de E Vittorini. DE SIENA, Santa.
Filosofía e identidad nacional en Honduras. ROMERO, Ramón.
From Philosophy to Politics: On Nietzsche's Ironic Metaphysics of Will to Power. PARENS, Erik.
Habermas and Arendt on the Philosopher's "Error": Tracking the Diabiological in Heidegger. BERNASCONI, Robert.
Hannah Arendt's Political Theory: Ethics and Enemies. DOSSA, Shiraz.
Human Rights and Nietzsche. MINEAU, André.
Human Rights in the Context of Uganda's Political Experience. KIGONGO, J K.
The Impact of the French Revolution on the Development of Philosophy. NETOPILIK, Jakub.
Das Individuum, die Politik und die Philosophie. GRUNWALD, Sabine.
Lacan in Slovenia—An Interview with Slavoj Zizek and Renata Salecl. DEWS, Peter and OSBORNE, Peter.
Michel Foucault: From the Humanities to Political Thought (in German). SEITTER, Walter.
Moral y política en Kant. PÉREZ ESTÉVEZ, Antonio.
Nietzsche and Fascism. WILLIAMS, Howard.
Norberto Bobbio ideologo del neoilluminismo: Per una rilettura di "Politica e cultura". QUARANTA, Mario.
On Heidegger and National Socialism: A Triple Turn?. ROCKMORE, Tom.
On Squeamishness: A Response to Galston. FISHKIN, James S.
Osservazioni sul *Filebo*. MASI, Giuseppe.
Poetry and Autonomy. SANKOWSKI, Edward.
La polémica sobre el espinosismo de Lessing. FERNÁNDEZ LORENZO, Manuel.
Politica e diritto in Hobbes. BAGLIONI, Emma.
Political Culture and Institution Building: Democratic Evolution at Work and the Case of Poland. LAMENTOWICZ, Wojtek.
Political Self-Education of the English Working Class. PEPPERELL, Keith C.
Political Theory and Cultural Criticism: Towards a Theory of Cultural Politics. MACDONALD, Bradley J.
Politics and the Limits of Metaphysics: Heidegger, Ferry and Renaut, and Lyotard. FÓTI, Véronique M.
Politics in Hobbes' Mechanics: The Social as Enabling. LYNCH, William T.
The Politics of Ethics: Socratic Questioning is Needed in the Marketplace. TRUNDLE, Robert.
The Politics of Professionalism. FARBER, Paul.
Porosity: Violence and the Question of Politics in Heidegger's *Introduction to Metaphysics*. MC NEILL, William.
Problemas conceptuales y políticas de desarrollo tecnológico. QUINTANILLA, Miguel Ángel.
Le problème politique chez Sartre et Foucault. KNEE, Phili.
Reason and Emotion. FRICKER, Miranda.
Reconstructing the Political. JANICAUD, Dominique.
Reflection in Politics and the Question of a Political Subject (in Czechoslovakian). HEJDANEK, Ladislav.
A Response to Olivier's Postmodern, but Pre-South African Proposal. ROSSOUW, G.
Rethinking Politics: Carl Schmitt vs Hegel. WINFIELD, Richard Dien.
Retreat from Radicality: Pöggeler on Heidegger's Politics. EDLER, Frank H W.
La revolución teórica del Príncipe de Maquiavelo. GIGLIOLI, Giovanna.
Seven Types of Obloquy: Travesties of Marxism. GERAS, Norman.
Shattering: Toward a Politics of Daimonic Life. KRELL, David Farrell.
Sociedad informatizada y poder político. RICHARDS, Edgardo.
Las Sociedades de Pensamiento y la Revolución Francesa. RHENÁN SEGURA, Jorge.
Some Fundamental Aspects of Socioecological Theory and Policy, Part I (in German). OPIELKA, Michael.
Some Fundamental Aspects of Socioecological Theory and Policy, Part II (in German). OPIELKA, Michael.
Spinoza en de geopenbaarde godsdienst. DE DIJN, H.
Telling Tales: Notes on Heidegger's "Career," the "Heidegger Affair," and the Assumptions of Narrativity. DAVIES, Paul.
Toughness as a Political Virtue. GALSTON, William.
The Virtue of a Representative. WOLGAST, Elizabeth.
What Makes Practice Educational?. HOGAN, Pádraig.
Writing the Revolution—The Politics of Truth in Genet's *Prisoner of Love*. CRITCHLEY, Simon.

POLLOCK, J
Epistemic Norms and Evolutionary Success. CLARKE, Murray.

POLLUTION
Earthbound: Introductory Essays in Environmental Ethics. REGAN, Tom (ed).

POLYNOMIALS
Bounded Arithmetic and the Polynomial Hierarchy. KRAJICEK, Jan and PUDLÁK, Pavel and TAKEUTI, Gaisi.
Nonstandard Arithmetic of Hilbert Subsets. YASUMOTO, Masahiro.
On the Existence of Polynomial Time Algorithms for Interpolation Problems in Propositional Logic. DALHAUS, E and ISRAELI, A and MAKOWSKY, J A.

POLYTHEISM
"The Crisis of Polytheism and the Answers of Vossius, Cudworth, and Newton" in *Essays on the Context, Nature, and Influence of Isaac Newton's Theology*, POPKIN, Richard H.
"Polytheism, Deism, and Newton" in *Essays on the Context, Nature, and Influence of Isaac Newton's Theology*, POPKIN, Richard H.

POOR
The Futility of Psychotherapy. ALBEE, George W.

POP ART
Form and Funk: The Aesthetic Challenge of Popular Art. SHUSTERMAN, Richard.

POPE, A
Criteria of Certainty: Truth and Judgment in the English Enlightenment. COPE, Kevin L.
Partial Wholes. BARNES, Jonathan.

POPPER
De l'épistémologie à la politique: La philosophie de l'histoire de Karl R Popper. RUELLAND, Jacques G.
Imre Lakatos and Theories of Scientific Change. GAVROGLU, Kostas (ed).
Moral und Politik aus der Sicht des Kritischen Rationalismus. SALAMUN, Kurt (ed).
"Frege and Popper: Two Critics of Psychologism" in *Imre Lakatos and Theories of Scientific Change*, CURRIE, G.
"Has Popper Been a Good Thing?" in *Imre Lakatos and Theories of Scientific Change*, PAPINEAU, David.
"Method and the Authority of Science" in *Key Themes in Philosophy*, TILES, Mary.
"Popper's Propensities: An Ontological Interpretation of Probability" in *Imre Lakatos and Theories of Scientific Change*, SFENDONI-MENTZOU, D.
The Autonomy of Probability Theory (Notes on Kolmogorov, Rényi, and Popper). LEBLANC, Hugues.
El azar objetivo como medida matemática de desorden. MARTÍNEZ, Sergio.
Compromiso Ontico y Teorías Científicas. MAYORGA, Alejandro and VARGAS, Celso.
El cuádruple problema de la inducción: Crítica de la solución popperiana del problema de Hume. GARCÍA NORRO, Juan José.
The Degeneration of Popper's Theory of Demarcation. GRÜNBAUM, Adolf.
Empirical Tests are Only Auxiliary Devices. LAI, Tyrone.
Estrategias metacientíficas: Parte II. HIDALGO TUÑÓN, Alberto.
History, Historicism, Narratives: Identity in the Philosophy of History of Karl Popper. PARLEJ, Piotr.
Induction and Stochastic Independence. AGASSI, Joseph.
Is Knowledge Socially Determined? A Critique. CHAUDHURY, Mahasweta.
Meditation on the Two Consciousnesses and on the Three Worlds of Popper (in Hungarian). RADI, Peter.
The Metamathematics-Popperian Epistemology Connection and its Relation to the Logic of Turing's Programme. BEAUSOLEIL, Jean-Roch.
Modelos de cambio científico en la filosofía actual de la ciencia. STRÖKER, Elisabeth.
A Note on Popper's Equation of Simplicity with Falsifiability. TURNEY, Peter.
A Note on Verisimilitude and Relativization to Problems. MONGIN, Philippe.
Objectivity and Growth of Knowledge. CHAUDHURY, Mahasweta.
On Comparison of Theories by Their Contents. WOLENSKI, Jan.
On the Alleged Impossibility of Inductive Probability. EELLS, Ellery.
On the Other Side of the Open Science (in Serbo-Croatian). POLSEK, Darko.
Popper on Induction. SWANN, Andrew J.
Popper's Demarcation of Science Refuted. AGASSI, Joseph.
A Refutation of Popperian Inductive Scepticism. GEMES, Ken.
A Restoration of Popperian Inductive Scepticism. MILLER, David.
Science and Truthlikeness. PANDIT, G L.
Scientific Rationality—A Rethinking. CHAUDHURY, Mahasweta.
Sir Karl Popper on Presocratic Philosophers (in Hungarian). STEIGER, Kornel.
Sociology of Knowledge with Special Reference to Karl Popper. MANDAL, Sunil Baran.
Some Further Reflections on the Popper-Miller 'Disproof' of Probabilistic Induction. HOWSON, C.
A Suspicious Feature of the Popper/Miller Argument. GOOD, I J.
Swann versus Popper on Induction: An Arbitration. SETTLE, Tom.
Three Accounts of Paradigm Shift. MUKHERJEE, Nilratan.
The Turing-Good Weight of Evidence Function and Popper's Measure of the Severity of a Test. GILLIES, Donald.
Two Problems of Induction?. O'NEILL, John.
Van Rooijen and Mayr versus Popper: Is the Universe Causally Closed?. SETTLE, Tom.
Verisimilitude Based on Concept Analysis. ORLOWSKA, Ewa.
Why Scientists Gather Evidence. MAHER, Patrick.

POPULAR CULTURE
Popular Art and Aesthetic Theory: Why the Muse Is Unembarrassed. ANDERSON, Richard L.
A Re-Examination of the Nature of Religion. BARUA, Archana.

POPULATION
Probabilistic Causality. EELLS, Ellery.
African Famine: New Economic and Ethical Perspectives. LUCAS JR, George R.
Evolution, "Typology" and "Population Thinking". GREENE, Marjorie.
The Explanatory Tools of Theoretical Population Biology. COOPER, Gregory.
Jean-Jacques Rousseau on the Physiogonomy of the Modern City. ELLISON, Charles E.
Paradigms, Populations and Problem-Fields: Approaches to Disagreement. ALLCHIN, Douglas.

POPULATION CONTROL(S)
"Totalitarianism and Population Superfluity" in *The Realm of Humanitas: Responses to the Writings of Hannah Arendt*, RUBENSTEIN, Richard L.

POPULATION DYNAMICS
Evolutionary Instability: Logical and Material Aspects of a Unified Theory of Biosocial Evolution. GEIGER, Gebhard.

PORNOGRAPHY
Whose Right? Ronald Dworkin, Women, and Pornographers. LANGTON, Rae.

PORPHYRY
Porphyry and the Intelligible Triad. EDWARDS, M J.
Porphyry's Criticism of Christianity and The Problem of Augustine's Platonism. EVANGELIOU, Christos.

PORTMANN, A
The Unity of the Natural Sciences: Comment on Portmann. VON UEXKUELL, Thure.

PORTUGUESE
"Nota acerca da recepção de Kant no pensamento filosófico português" in *Dinâmica do Pensar: Homenagem a Oswaldo Market*, DA GAMA CAEIRO, Francisco.
Educação e democracia: Subsídios para uma consciência educacional pluralizante. ARAÚJO, Alberto Filipe.
Educação para valores e maturidade pessoal do educador. ROCHA, Filipe.

POSITIVISM
see also Logical Positivism
De l'épistémologie à la politique: La philosophie de l'histoire de Karl R Popper. RUELLAND, Jacques G.
Hegels Theorie des Gesetzes. BOGDANDY, Armin Von.
Philosophie Juridique Européenne. TRIGEAUD, Jean-Marc.
The Positivist Science of Law. LEE, Keekok.
Realism with a Human Face. PUTNAM, Hilary.
Science and Relativism: Some Key Controversies in the Philosophy of Science. LAUDAN, Larry.
"Existentialism, Humanism, and Positivism" in *The Question of Humanism: Challenges and Possibilities*, HAYES, Calvin.
"History of Science and Criticism of Positivism" in *Études sur/Studies on Hélène Metzger*, HEIDELBERGER, Michael.
"Louis Althusser and Joseph D Sneed: A Strange Encounter in Philosophy of Science?" in *Imre Lakatos and Theories of Scientific Change*, BALTAS, Aristides.
"On Learning from the Mistakes of Positivists" in *Logic, Methodology and Philosophy of Science, VIII*, NERLICH, Graham.
"Difficoltà" con Simmel: Considerazioni in margine ad un convegno. LANDKAMMER, Joachim.
China's Importation of Western Psychiatry: Cultural Relativity and Mental Disorders. WOO, Deborah.
Educação e democracia: Subsídios para uma consciência educacional pluralizante. ARAÚJO, Alberto Filipe.
La filosofia civile di Pasquale Villari. URBINATI, Nadia.
On the Question of Nietzsche's "Scientism". GALLO, Beverly E.
Philosophical Objections to the Kinetic Theory. NYHOF, John.
Su alcuni aspetti del neoilluminismo di L Geymonat. STOMEO, Anna.
Tareas y métodos en la ética del desarrollo. GOULET, Denis.
Was Moore a Positivist?. O'CONNOR, David.

POSSIBILITY(-TIES)
Cálculo y ser (Aproximación a Leibniz). MARZOA, Felipe Martínez.
Zetetic Skepticism. UMPHREY, Stewart.
"Catastrophic Possibilities of Space-Based Defense" in *Philosophy of Technology*, BELLA, David.
Concentric Circles: An Exploration of Three Concepts in Process Metaphysics. AUXIER, Randall.
Le Kantisme de la théorie cantorienne de l'infini. BACHTA, Abdelkader.
Posibilidad e indeterminación: Aristóteles frente a Diodoro Crono. QUEVEDO, Amalia.
Real Possibility. DEUTSCH, Harry.
La tensione tra possibilità e necessità nell'argomento ontologico di Leibniz. NICOLOSI, Salvatore.
Transparent Approach to Logical Necessity and Possibility. MATERNA, P.
Warnings on Resistance and the Language of Possibility: Gramsci and a Pedagogy from the Surreal. SENESE, Guy B.

POSSIBLE WORLD(S)
Cálculo y ser (Aproximación a Leibniz). MARZOA, Felipe Martínez.
Meaning and Truth: The Essential Readings in Modern Semantics. GARFIELD, Jay L (ed).
Can There Be a Possible World in Which Memory Is Unreliable?. LEUNG, Edwin Sing Choe.
A Case for a Heretical Deontic Semantics. EDELBERG, Walter.
Comments on 'Nonlocal Influences and Possible Worlds'. STAPP, Henry P.
Could This Be Magic?. JUBIEN, Michael.
Deontic Logic and Possible World Semantics: A Historical Sketch. WOLENSKI, Jan.
Every World Can See a Reflexive World. HUGHES, G E.
Forbes's Branching Conception of Possible Worlds. MILLS, Eugene.
Is the Skeptical Attitude the Attitude of a Skeptic?. PAPRZYCKA, Katarzyna.
Jackson on Classifying Conditionals. LOWE, E J.
Kripke-Style Models for Typed Lambda Calculus. MITCHELL, John C and MOGGI, Eugenio.
Leibniz on Superessentialism and World-Bound Individuals. COVER, Jan A.
Metaphor and the Varieties of Lexical Meaning. HINTIKKA, Jaakko and SANDU, Gabriel.
Modal Realism Without Counterparts. HALE, Susan C.
Nonlocal Influences and Possible Worlds—A Stapp in the Wrong Direction. CLIFTON, Robert K and BUTTERFIELD, Jeremy N and REDHEAD, Michael L G.
On "Why is There Something Rather Than Nothing?". KUSCH, Martin.
On the Methodology of Possible World Semantics, I: Correspondence Theory. PEARCE, David and WANSING, Heinrich.
Reply of a Mad Dog. MILLER, Richard B.
Temporal Necessity and the Conditional. CROSS, Charles B.
Truth at a World is a Modality. LINSKY, Bernard.
Varying Modal Theories. LUCAS, T and LAVENDHOMME, R.
The World Essence. BIGELOW, John.

POST ALGEBRA(S)
Plain Semi-Post Algebras as a Poset-Based Generalization of Post Algebras and their Representability. CAT HO, Nguyen and RASIOWA, Helena.

POST, E
Post's Functional Completeness Theorem. PELLETIER, Francis Jeffry and MARTIN, Norman M.

POSTCOMMUNISM
Political Justice in Post-Communist Societies: The Case of Hungary. BENCE, György.

POSTHAST, U
Etwas ist in mir da—Zu Ulrich Posthast: Philosophisches Buch. WOLF, Ursula.

POSTMODERNISM
Adorno's Aesthetic Theory: The Redemption of Illusion. ZUIDERVAART, Lambert.
After the Demise of the Tradition: Rorty, Critical Theory, and the Fate of Philosophy. NIELSEN, Kai.
Against Architecture: The Writings of Georges Bataille. HOLLIER, Denis.
Bakhtin and the Epistemology of Discourse. THOMSON, Clive (ed).
Being and Becoming: A Critique of Post-Modernism. CENTORE, F F.
The Dice-Playing God: Reflections on Life in a Post-Modern Age. KRIEGLSTEIN, Werner.
Essays on Heidegger and Others: Philosophical Papers, Volume 2. RORTY, Richard.
Essentially Speaking: Feminism, Nature and Difference. FUSS, Diana.
Feminism/Postmodernism. NICHOLSON, Linda J (ed).
Hermeneutics and the Poetic Motion, Translation Perspectives V—1990. SCHMIDT, Dennis J (ed).
Irony and the Discourse of Modernity. BEHLER, Ernst.
Language and "The Feminine" in Nietzsche and Heidegger. GRAYBEAL, Jean.
Life-World and Politics: Between Modernity and Postmodernity. WHITE, Stephen K (ed).
Looking After Nietzsche. RICKELS, Laurence A (ed).
Myth and Modern Philosophy. DANIEL, Stephen H.
Objectivity, Relativism, and Truth: Philosophical Papers, Volume 1. RORTY, Richard.
Overcoming Foundations: Studies in Systematic Philosophy. WINFIELD, Richard Dien.
The Persistence of Modernity: Essays on Aesthetics, Ethics, and Postmodernism. WELLMER, Albrecht.
Philosophical Events: Essays of the '80s. RAJCHMAN, John.
Philosophical Streets: New Approaches to Urbanism. CROW, Dennis (ed).
A Post-Modern Epistemology. SORRI, Mari.
Postmodernism—Philosophy and the Arts (Continental Philosophy III). SILVERMAN, Hugh J (ed).
Reading Habermas. RASMUSSEN, David M.
Realism with a Human Face. PUTNAM, Hilary.
Rorty's Humanistic Pragmatism: Philosophy Democratized. KOLENDA, Konstantin.

POSTMODERNISM

Strukturanthropologie "Der menschliche Mensch". ROMBACH, Heinrich.
Unsere postmoderne Moderne (Second Edition). WELSCH, Wolfgang.
Wege aus der Moderne. WELSCH, Wolfgang (ed).
XIth International Congress in Aesthetics, Nottingham 1988. WOODFIELD, Richard (ed).
"Art of the Untruth? On Post Modern Visual Art" in *XIth International Congress in Aesthetics, Nottingham 1988*, KAULINGFREKS, Ruud.
"Back to the Future" in *Postmodernism—Philosophy and the Arts (Continental Philosophy III)*, TAYLOR, Mark C.
"The Contradictory Character of Postmodernism" in *Postmodernism—Philosophy and the Arts (Continental Philosophy III)*, KUSPIT, Donald.
"The Cultural Dynamics of Philosophical Aesthetics" in *XIth International Congress in Aesthetics, Nottingham 1988*, PAETZOLD, Heinz.
"Feminism, Postmodernism, and Gender-Scepticism" in *Feminism/Postmodernism*, BORDO, Susan.
"Filming: Inscriptions of *Denken*" in *Postmodernism—Philosophy and the Arts (Continental Philosophy III)*, WURZER, Wilhelm S and SILVERMAN, Hugh J.
"*In Situ*: Beyond the Architectonics of the Modern" in *Postmodernism—Philosophy and the Arts (Continental Philosophy III)*, WATSON, Stephen H.
"Innovation and Tradition in Post-Modernism" in *XIth International Congress in Aesthetics, Nottingham 1988*, ROSE, Margaret A.
"Lucid Intervals: Postmodernism and Photography" in *Postmodernism—Philosophy and the Arts (Continental Philosophy III)*, WEISS, Allen S.
"The Otherness of Words: Joyce, Bakhtin, Heidegger" in *Postmodernism—Philosophy and the Arts (Continental Philosophy III)*, BRUNS, Gerald L.
"A Postmodern Language in Art" in *Postmodernism—Philosophy and the Arts (Continental Philosophy III)*, OLKOWSKI-LAETZ, Dorothea.
"Postmodern Language" in *Postmodernism—Philosophy and the Arts (Continental Philosophy III)*, SCOTT, Charles E.
"Postmodernism and (Post)Marxism" in *Postmodernism—Philosophy and the Arts (Continental Philosophy III)*, O'NEILL, J.
"Postmodernism and Critical Theory" in *XIth International Congress in Aesthetics, Nottingham 1988*, ERJAVEC, Ales.
"Postmodernism and Other Skepticisms" in *Feminist Ethics*, PIERCE, Christine.
"Postmodernism and Theater" in *Postmodernism—Philosophy and the Arts (Continental Philosophy III)*, MC GLYNN, Fred.
"Postmodernism in Dance: Dance, Discourse, Democracy" in *Postmodernism—Philosophy and the Arts (Continental Philosophy III)*, LEVIN, David Michael.
"Rationality between Modernity and Postmodernity" in *Life-World and Politics: Between Modernity and Postmodernity*, SCHRAG, Calvin O.
"Roland Barthes et Umberto Eco à la Recherche du Roman Postmoderne" in *XIth International Congress in Aesthetics, Nottingham 1988*, ZNEPOLSKY, Ivahilo.
"Weighing Anchor: Postmodern Journeys from the Life-World" in *Life-World and Politics: Between Modernity and Postmodernity*, SHAPIRO, Michael J.
A Post-Metaphysical Moral: An Introduction to the Moral Theory of Jürgen Habermas (in French). HUNYADI, Mark.
The A/Theology of Don Cupitt: A Theological Option in Our Post-Modern Age. TARBOX JR, Everett J.
Biblical Hermeneutics and the Search for Religious Truth (in French). THEISSEN, Gerd.
Communism: A Post-Mortem. BAUMAN, Zygmunt.
The Death of the Author: An Analytical Autopsy. LAMARQUE, Peter.
Deconstructing/Deconstructive Inquiry: The Politics of Knowing and Being Known. LATHER, Patti.
Deconstruction or Dialectics? (in Serbo-Croation). BRUNKHORST, Hauke.
Empirical Theology: A Revisable Tradition. DEAN, William.
Encountering Dallmayr. KIVISTO, Peter.
The Enlightenment—a Stranded Project? Habermas on Nietzsche as a 'Turning Point' to Postmodernity. NAGL, Ludwig.
An Entropic Analysis of Postmodernism. MC KINNEY, Ronald H.
The Ethics of Postmodernism. GIBBONS, Michael T.
The Exile of Literature: Poetry and the Politics of the Other(s). MURPHY, Bruce F.
Filosofía, hoy. CUÉLLAR, Hortensia.
From Pyrrhonism to Post-Modernism. GLIDDEN, David K.
Henri Bergson and Postmodernism. MULDOON, Mark S.
Historiography and Postmodernism: Reconsiderations. ZAGORIN, Perez.
The Intellectual in the Post Modern Age: East/West Contrasts. BAYARD, Caroline.
Interrupting Olivier's Socio-Political Conversation: Another Postmodern Proposal. ALLEN, J G.
Is the Post- in Postmodernism the Post- in Postcolonial?. APPIAH, Kwame Anthony.
Kants "Reflexionen zur Ästhetik": Zur Werkgeschichte der "Kritik der ästhetischen Urteilskraft". FRANK, Manfred.
Marx's *Aufhebung* of Philosophy and the Foundations of Historical-Materialist Science. FRACCHIA, Joseph.
Modernité et postmodernité: un enjeu politique?. BERTEN, André.
Na de sociale wending het roer nogmaals om. LATOUR, Bruno.
Nietzsche on Human Nature. SCHACHT, Richard.
Nueva modernidad adveniente y cultura emergente en América Latina. SCANNONE, J C.
Paths to a Postmodern Ethics and Politics: A Reply to Gibbons. WHITE, Stephen K.
Philosophical Hierarchies and Lyotard's Dichotomies. SASSOWER, Raphael and OGAZ, Charla Phyllis.
Die Philosophie im einen Deutschland. HENRICH, Dieter.
Philosophy and Politics: On Fred Dallmayr's "Critical Encounters". MISGELD, Dieter.
Political Economy and Mimetic Desire: A Postmodernist Reading of "Babette's Feast". SHAPIRO, Michael J.
The Post-Modern Challenge: From Marx to Nietzsche in the West German Alternative and Green Movement. BETZ, Hans-Georg.
Post-Modern Pastiche. ROSE, Margaret A.
Post-Modernism as the Lesser Evil: Criticism and Agreement in Lyotard's "Widerstreit" ("Conflict") (in German). KRÜGER, Hans-Peter.
Postmodern Metaphors for Teacher Education?. STONE, Lynda.
The Postmodern Posture. KHANIN, Dmitry.
Postmodernist Elitism and Postmodern Struggles. GROSSBERG, Lawrence.
Radical Theology, Postmodernity and Christian Life in the Void. COWDELL, Scott.
Reconstructing the Subject: Feminism, Modernism, and Postmodernism. HEKMAN, Susan.
Religion, Nothingness, and the Challenge of Post-Modern Thought: An Introduction to the Philosophy of K Nishitani. JAMES, George A.
Reply to McKinney on Lonergan: A Deconstruction. MARSH, James L.
Reply to Professor Zagorin's "Historiography and Postmodernism: Reconsideration". ANKERSMIT, Frank R.
A Response to My Critics. DALLMAYR, Fred.
A Response to Olivier's Postmodern, but Pre-South African Proposal. ROSSOUW, G.
Sartre and his Successors: Existential Marxism and Postmodernism at Our *Fin de Siecle*. MC BRIDE, William L.
Scientific Realism and Postmodern Philosophy. MURPHY, Nancey.
Speaking About the Unspeakable: Genocide and Philosophy. FREEMAN, Michael.
The Doubts about Post-Modernism (in Czechoslovakian). AJVAZ, Michal.
The Strategy of Forced Reconciliation (in Serbo-Croatian). RAULET, Gérard.
The Theosophic Discourse According to Jacob Boehme (in French). DEGHAYE, Pierre.
The *Trés Riches Heures*: An Illuminated Manuscript in the Age of Mechanical Reproduction. CAMILLE, Michael.
The Unbearable Seriousness of Irony. FERRARA, Alessandro.
Verlichtingsfilosofie twee eeuwen later; J F Lyotard als postmoderne Kant. VAN PEPERSTRATEN, Frans.
'Postmodern Critical Augustinianism': A Short *Summa* in Forty Two Responses to Unasked Questions. MILBANK, John.

POSTSTRUCTURALISM

Against Architecture: The Writings of Georges Bataille. HOLLIER, Denis.
Philosophical Events: Essays of the '80s. RAJCHMAN, John.
Works of Love? Reflections on "Works of Love". FENDT, Gene.
Adorno and the French Post-Structuralists on the Other of Reason. NUYEN, A T.
Discourse: Definitions and Contradictions. PARKER, Ian.
Nietzsche's Arctic Zone of Cognition and Post-Structuralism. PARENT, David.
Peter Dews' Logics of Disintegration: Poststructuralism/Critical Theory. BUTLER, Judith.

POTENCY(-CIES)

La "riabilitazione" della δυναμιζ e dell'ενεργεια in Heidegger. VOLPI, Franco.
Potencia, finalidad y posibilidad en "Metafísica" IX, 3-4. GARCIA MARQUÉS, Alfonso.

POTENTIALITY

'Fetal Rights'? An Attempt to Render Plausible a Conservative Response. HODAPP, Paul.
Concentric Circles: An Exploration of Three Concepts in Process Metaphysics. AUXIER, Randall.
Physical Possibility and Potentiality in Ethics. COVEY, Edward.
Potenzialità conoscitive del Trascendentale di Husserl. O'DWYER BELLINETTI, Luciana.
Self-Potential as a Yoruba Ultimate: A Further Contribution to URAM Yoruba Studies. LAWUYI, Olatunde B.

POULAKOS, J

History and Neo-Sophistic Criticism: A Reply to Poulakos. SCHIAPPA, Edward.

POVERTY

The Idea of Christian Charity: A Critique of Some Contemporary Conceptions. GRAHAM, Gordon.
"World Poverty" in *A Companion to Ethics*, DOWER, Nigel.

POWELL, J

"Response to Skidelsky's 'Theory and Practice'" in *Philosophy and Politics*, SKIDELSKY, Robert.
Response to Powell's "Theory and Practice". SKIDELSKY, Robert.

POWELL, L
Justice Powell and the Parochial Schools Case: A Case for Judicial Statesmanship. WALTMAN, Jerold.
POWER(S)
The Critique of Power: Reflective Stages in a Critical Social Theory. HONNETH, Axel.
Negotation Games: Applying Game Theory to Bargaining and Arbitration. BRAMS, Steven J.
The Power of Ideology. MÉSZÁROS, István.
The Savage Anomaly: The Power of Spinoza's Metaphysics and Politics. NEGRI, Antonio.
Spuren der Macht. RÖTTGERS, Kurt.
"Antigone's Daughters Reconsidered: Continuing Reflections on Women, Politics, and Power" in *Life-World and Politics: Between Modernity and Postmodernity*, ELSHTAIN, Jean Bethke.
"From Leviathan to Lilliput" in *Celebrating Peace*, TOULMIN, Stephen.
"Power and Wisdom: The Expert as Mediating Figure in Contemporary Polish History" in *The Political Responsibility of Intellectuals*, KURCZEWSKI, Jacek.
"Thomism and Divine Absolute Power" in *Thomistic Papers, V*, KENNEDY, Leonard A.
Alexander Hamilton: The Separation of Powers. PRATT, Ronald L.
The Cardinality of Powersets in Finite Models of the Powerset Axiom. ABIAN, Alexander and AMIN, Wael A.
Concepts of "Action", "Structure" and "Power" in 'Critical Social Realism': A Positive and Reconstructive Critique. PATOMÄKI, Heikki.
Le critiche a Kelsen durante la Repubblica di Weimar. ROEHRSSEN, Carlo.
Deceptive Comfort: The Power of Kafka's Stories. BENNETT, Jane.
El ensimismamiento del poder: Maquiavelo y la ciencia política moderna. GARCIA, Romano.
Ethics in Current Affairs: The Theme of the Enlightenment in Michel Foucault (in German). SCHMID, Wilhelm.
Éthique et technique: bioéthique. KEMP, Peter.
Feminist Theory and Its Discontents. TRESS, Daryl Mc Gowan.
Foucault, Nietzsche, History: Two Modes of the Genealogical Method. SAX, Benjamin C.
In Defence of Theological Compatibilism. FLINT, Thomas P.
L'imagination au pouvoir. BODÉÜS, Richard.
The Limits of Power. TALIAFERRO, Charles.
Nietzsche and the Philosophy of Scientific Power: Will to Power as Constructive Interpretation. BABICH, Babette E.
Nietzsche's "Will to Power" Nachlass. HELLER, Peter.
The Philosopher's Prism: Foucault, Feminism, and Critique. ALADJEM, Terry K.
Le pouvoir, existential de l'être humain. SCHÜSSLER, Werner.
The Power of Hegemony vis-à-vis the Marketplace of Ideas: Response to Orton. BROSIO, Richard A.
Power, Knowledge and Freedom: The Meaning of Foucault's Threefold Break with the History of Ideas (in German). ENGLER, Wolfgang.
Power, Liberty, and Counterfactual Conditionals in Hobbes' Thought. POLANSKY, Ronald and TORELL, Kurt.
The Question of Ethics in Foucault's Thought. SCOTT, Charles E.
Reflections on the Nature of Ideology. VAN DOAN, Tran.
Sheaves in Universal Algebra and Model Theory: Part I. IDZIAK, Pawel M.
Some Remarks on ω-Powers of Enumerated Sets and Their Applications to ω-Operations. ORLICKI, Andrzej.
Subjectivisation as Control or Resistance: An Examination of Reformation Theology and Marxism. PATTMAN, Rob.
Verily, Nietzsche's Judgment of Jesus. ROTH, Robin A.
PRACTICAL
Philosophy of Technology. DURBIN, Paul T (ed).
"On the Logic of Practical Evaluation" in *Logic and Ethics*, KÖRNER, Stephan.
Friedrich Schleiermacher und die Praktische Philosophie. TROWITZSCH, Michael.
The Greatness and Limits of Kant's Practical Philosophy. HÖSLE, Vittorio.
How Teachers Know. STENGEL, Barbara S.
Practical Intuition and Rhetorical Example. SCHOLLMEIER, Paul.
Solipsism in Kant's Practical Philosophy and the Discourse of Ethics. KUHLMANN, Wolfgang.
The Theoretical Premises of Scientific Socialism and Its Mode of Thought. YUQUAN, Tao.
PRACTICAL REASON
Das Ethische in der Rhetorik des Aristoteles. WÖRNER, Markus Hilmar.
Practical Reason and Norms. RAZ, Joseph.
Toward the Death of Man. KLUBACK, William.
Universalism versus Communitarianism: Contemporary Debates in Ethics. RASMUSSEN, David.
"Freedom and Practical Rationality in the Thought of Yves R Simon" in *Freedom in the Modern World: Jacques Maritain, Yves R Simon, Mortimer J Adler*, MULVANEY, Robert J.
"Practical Reason and Social Democracy" in *Critique and Construction: A Symposium on Roberto Unger's "Politics"*, HAWTHORN, Geoffrey.
Aristotle's Account of Practical Reasoning as a Theoretical Base for Research on Teaching. NOEL, Jana.
Belief, Desire and the Praxis of Reasoning. WILLIAMS, Stephen.
The Case of the Unmitigated Blackguard or Saving Kant's Moral Feelings. EARLS, Anthony.
Certainty and Authority. WINCH, Peter.
Contractualism, Moral Motivation, and Practical Reason. FREEMAN, Samuel.
Feminist Ethics and Case-Based Reasoning: A Marriage of Purpose. RIESBECK, Christopher K and MORPHIS, Maxine.
Hume on Practical Reason. ROBERTSON, John.
Jugement juridique et jugement pratique: de Kant à la philosophie du langage. LENOBLE, J and BERTEN, A.
Justice and Aristotelian Practical Reason. DAHL, Norman.
The Many Appetites of Thomas Hobbes. HURLEY, Paul.
Nietzschean Perspectivism and the Logic of Practical Reason. REDDING, Paul.
Obligation and Knowledge (in French). SCHULTHESS, Daniel.
On Kant's Conception of Science and the Critique of Practical Reason. KÖRNER, Stephan.
Over het morele en zedelijke handelen, toegelicht aan het instituut huwelijk. COBBEN, Paul.
Practical Reason or Metapreferences? An Undogmatic Defense of Kantian Morality. NIDA-RÜMELIN, Julian.
Practical Reasoning in Teaching: A Response to Jana Noel. PENDLEBURY, Shirley.
Prudence and Providence: On Hobbes's Theory of Practical Reason. HANCE, Allen S.
Prudence: Aristotelian Perspectives on Practical Reason. HASLAM, Nick.
Ultimate Ends in Practical Reasoning. MAC DONALD, Scott.
Validity and Practical Reasoning. MITCHELL, David.
What Can a Discursive Theory of Morality Learn from Aquinas?. RENTTO, Juha-Pekka.
PRACTICAL WISDOM
Aristotelis Ethica Evdemia. WALZER, R R (ed).
Being True to the World: Moral Realism and Practical Wisdom. JACOBS, Jonathan A.
A Philosophy of Morals. HELLER, Agnes.
The Environmental Dependence of Dispositional Aims: Response to the Presidential Address. RAYWID, Mary Ann.
Fostering the Disposition to be Rational. SIEGEL, Harvey.
Moral Imagination, Objectivity, and Practical Wisdom. JACOBS, Jonathan.
PRACTICALITY
Man, History, and Philosophy in Husserl's Crisis of European Sciences (in Czechoslovakian). MAJOR, L.
The Practical Importance of Personal Identity. DOEPKE, F.
PRACTICE
An Inquiry into the Meaning of Teacher Clarity in Recent Research and into the Value of the Research for the Teacher. CRABTREE, Walden.
Response to Powell's "Theory and Practice". SKIDELSKY, Robert.
What Makes Practice Educational?. HOGAN, Pádraig.
PRACTICE(S)
Markets, Managers and Theory in Education. HALLIDAY, John.
Moral Theory and Medical Practice. FULFORD, K W M.
"'Lopp'd and Bound': How Liberal Theory Obscures the Goods of Liberal Practices" in *Liberalism and the Good*, SALKEVER, Stephen G.
"The Hospital-Academic Health Center Interface: The Community of Practice and the Community of Learning" in *Integrity in Health Care Institutions: Humane Environments for Teaching, Inquiry, and Healing*, RABKIN, Mitchell T.
"Theory and Practice" in *Philosophy and Politics*, POWELL, J Enoch.
"Does Metaphysics Really Matter for Practice?" It Depends on the Practitioner. GARRISON, James W.
Burglars, Robber Barons, and the Good Life. PEKARSKY, Daniel.
The Business Ethics of Pharmacists: Conflicts Practices and Beliefs. VITELL, Scott J and RAWWAS, Mohammed Y A and FESTERVAND, Troy A.
Coaching: Who Needs It and What is It?. GUIN, Philip.
Ethics and the Limits of Consistency. BAMBROUGH, Renford.
Philosophy, Education, and Public Practice. GIARELLI, James M.
Practicing the Arts of Rhetoric: Tradition and Invention. FARRELL, Thomas B.
The Principle of Unity of Theory and Practice in Marxism: A Critique. DIMITRAKOS, D.
Religion in Wittgenstein's Mirror. PHILLIPS, D Z.
Response to the Presidential Address: Willer's "Ethics in Educational Policy Analysis". DRAKE, William E.
Theory and Practice. POWELL, J Enoch.
The Unity of Theory and Practice in Historical Perspective. KRANCBERG, Sigmund.
Waiting for a New St Benedict: Alasdair MacIntyre and the Theory and Practice of Journalism. LAMBETH, Edmund B.
Waiting for the Vanishing Shed. PHILLIPS, D Z.
PRAGMATIC
Ästhetik des Abschieds: Kritik der Moderne. EBELING, Hans.
Glück und Lebenssinn: Eine religionsphilosophische Untersuchung. DRESCHER, Johannes.

PRAGMATIC

Moralische Verbindlichkeit oder Erziehung. LANGEWAND, Alfred.
Nation und Ethos: Die Moral des Patriotismus. KLUXEN-PYTA, Donate.
"Analytic and Pragmatist Aesthetics" in *XIth International Congress in Aesthetics, Nottingham 1988*, SHUSTERMAN, Richard.
"Logic and Pragmatic Truth" in *Logic, Methodology and Philosophy of Science, VIII*, DA COSTA, Newton C A.
The Assurance of Faith. WOLTERSTORFF, Nicholas.
Metaphysics, Pragmatic Truth and the Underdetermination of Theories. PEREIRA JR, Alfredo and FRENCH, Steven.
Pragmatic Conditional Reasoning: Context and Content Effects on the Interpretation of Causal Assertions. HILTON, Denis J.
Pragmatic Naturalism: The Philosophy of Sidney Hook (1902-1989). KURTZ, Paul.
Pragmatic Truth and the Logic of Induction. DA COSTA, Newton C A and FRENCH, Steven.
Pragmática del lenguaje y racionalidad comunicativa. DE ZAN, J.
Transition to Pragmatic Liberalism: Diversity, Contingency, and Social Solidarity. LINDGREN, Ralph.
The Values of a Habitat. PARKER, Kelly.

PRAGMATICISM

Can Peirce Be a Pragmaticist and an Idealist?. PETERSON, John.
Das neue (post-analytische) Interesse an der Präanalytischen Philosophie. NAGL, Ludwig.

PRAGMATICS

Alltagssprachliche Metakommunikation im Englischen und Deutschen. WELTE, Werner.
Kants Kategorischer Imperativ als Leitfaden humaner Praxis. NISTERS, Thomas.
Meaning and Truth: The Essential Readings in Modern Semantics. GARFIELD, Jay L (ed).
Die Moral der Vernunft Tanszendentale Handlungs-und Legitimationstheorie in der Philosophie Kants. SANDERMANN, Edmund.
Wahrheit—Diskurs—Demokratie: Studien zur "Konsensustheorie der Wahrheit". SCHEIT, Herbert.
Everyday Argumentation from a Speech Act Perspective. GROOTENDORST, Rob.
I Know What I Know, If You Know What I Mean. DURAN, Jane.
Law: From Foundation to Argumentation. LEMPEREUR, Alain.
Nonrules and Plausibility: An Illustration in Pragmatic Theory. POWELL, Mava Jo.
A Pragma-Dialectical Perspective on Norms. VAN EEMEREN, Frans H.
Pragma-Dialectics: A Radical Departure in Fallacy Theory. WOODS, John.
The Pragmatic Fallacy. SALMON, Nathan.
Pragmatic Principles and Language. BHAT, P R.
Pragmatics and Pragmatism. SULLIVAN, Patrick F.
Pragmatique du discours et réciprocité de perspectives (A propos de Don Quichotte et Don Juan). GÓMEZ-MORIANA, Antonio.
Predication and Logic of Language (II). GANGADEAN, Ashok.
The Rational Law-Maker and the Pragmatics of Legal Interpretation. DASCAL, Marcelo and WRÓBLEWSKI, Jerzy.
Socratic Pragmatics: Maieutic Dialogues. HANKE, Michael.
Syntactic Form and Textual Rhetoric: The Cognitive Basis for Certain Pragmatic Principles. PRIDEAUX, Gary D.
Syntax and Pragmatics: Apartheid or Integration?. BOLKESTEIN, A Machtelt.
Towards a Potential-Pragmatic Account of Peirce's Theory of Truth. SFENDONI-MENTZOU, Demetra.

PRAGMATISM

After the Demise of the Tradition: Rorty, Critical Theory, and the Fate of Philosophy. NIELSEN, Kai.
The Fragmentation of Reason. STICH, Stephen.
In Praise of the Cognitive Emotions. SCHEFFLER, Israel.
John Dewey: Religious Faith and Democratic Humanism. ROCKEFELLER, Steven C.
Objectivity, Relativism, and Truth: Philosophical Papers, Volume 1. RORTY, Richard.
Perspectives on Quine. BARRETT, Robert (ed).
Pragmatism: From Peirce to Davidson. MURPHY, John P.
Reading Rorty. MALACHOWSKI, Alan (ed).
Rorty's Humanistic Pragmatism: Philosophy Democratized. KOLENDA, Konstantin.
Science and Relativism: Some Key Controversies in the Philosophy of Science. LAUDAN, Larry.
"Auto-da-Fé: Consequences of Pragmatism" in *Reading Rorty*, WILLIAMS, Bernard.
"The Human Person in American Pragmatism" in *The Question of Humanism: Challenges and Possibilities*, FRANCIS, Richard P.
"The Moral Life of a Pragmatist" in *Identity, Character, and Morality: Essays in Moral Psychology*, PUTNAM, Ruth Anna.
"Pragmatism and Choosing to Believe" in *Reading Rorty*, HEAL, Jane.
"Pragmatism, Davidson and Truth" in *Truth and Interpretation: Perspectives on the Philosophy of Donald Davidson*, RORTY, Richard.
"Pragmatism, *Praxis*, and the Technological" in *Philosophy of Technology*, MARGOLIS, Joseph.
Accent on *One*: Entity and Identity. BOLINGER, Dwight.
Bowne and Peirce on the Logic of Religious Belief. ANDERSON, Douglas R.
The Case for a New American Pragmatism. LAVINE, Thelma Z.
Consideraciones en torno al concepto de verdad según el pragmatismo. GORDILLO, Lourdes.
Contextualizing Knowledge: A Reply to "Dewey and the Theory of Knowledge". HICKMAN, Larry.
Dead Souls and Living Instruments. HICKMAN, Larry.
Directions in Historicism: Language, Experience, and Pragmatic Adjudication. DAVANEY, Sheila Greeve.
From the Phenomenology of Time Toward Process Metaphysics: Pragmatism and Heidegger. ROSENTHAL, Sandra B.
The Importance of Asking the Right Questions. PATTERSON, Dennis.
In What Way is Abductive Inference Creative?. KAPITAN, Tomis.
Justification, Truth, Goals, and Pragmatism: Comments on Stich's "Fragmentation of Reason". HARMAN, Gilbert.
Kierkegaard's Pragmatist Faith. EMMANUEL, Steven M.
Knowledge as Active, Aesthetic, and Hypothetical: A Pragmatic Interpretation of Whitehead's Cosmology. FRISINA, Warren G.
L'épistémologie mathématique de Gonseth dans la perspective du pragmatisme de Peirce. HEINZMANN, Gerhard.
Logicism, Pragmatism and Metascience: Towards a Pancritical-Pragmatic Meta-Level Discourse. AXTELL, G S.
Das neue (post-analytische) Interesse an der Präanalytischen Philosophie. NAGL, Ludwig.
Nietzsche, Socrates and Pragmatism. RORTY, Richard.
Over de ambivalente rol van de theoriegeladenheidsthese in Rorty's 'overwinning' van de traditie. KRIBBE, Pamela.
Personalist and Pragmatist Persons. STUHR, John J.
La philosophie ouverte de F Gonseth aboutit-elle à une conception réaliste ou relativiste. LAUENER, Henri.
Positivism and the Pragmatic Theory of Observation. OBERDAN, Thomas.
The Potential of Medicine as a Resource for Philosophy. FULFORD, K W M.
Pragmatics and Pragmatism. SULLIVAN, Patrick F.
The Pragmatist Sieve of Concepts: Description versus Interpretation. SEIGFRIED, Charlene Haddock.
Problématicité, rationalité et interrogativité. CARRILHO, Manuel Mari.
Rorty, Davidson and Truth. BAGHRAMIAN, Maria.
The Vanishing Subject of Contemporary Discourse: A Pragmatic Response. COLAPIETRO, Vincent M.
Where Are All the Pragmatist Feminists?. SEIGFRIED, Charlene Haddock.

PRAXIOLOGY

The Praxiology of Perception: Visual Orientations and Practical Action. COULTER, Jeff and PARSONS, E D.

PRAXIS

Hope and Its Hieroglyph: A Critical Decipherment of Ernst Bloch's "Principle of Hope". ROBERTS, Richard H.
The Realizations of the Future: An Inquiry into the Authority of Praxis. ALLAN, George.
"Pragmatism, *Praxis*, and the Technological" in *Philosophy of Technology*, MARGOLIS, Joseph.
"Just for the Thrill": Sycophantizing Aristotle's *Poetics*. CARSON, Anne.
A priori et a posteriori dans la pratique cognitive: le modele de la regulation des couples ago-antagonistes. BERNARD-WEIL, E.
Buchphilosophie und philosophische Praxis. RÖTTGERS, Kurt.
Connecting *Techne* and *Praxis* in Teaching. HOSTETLER, Karl.
Dialogue as a Way of Being Human. YIN, Lu-jun.
Grundlegende Aspekte zur Problematik von Erkenntnis und Praxis. FORSCHE, Joachim.
Kennen en kunnen: Een repliek op Wardekker. HARBERS, Hans.
Marx and the Problem of Conflicting Models of History. BEST, Steven.
Of *Praxis* and *Techne* and Cabbages and Kings. GREEN, Joe L.
Praktijkontwikkeling en wetenschappelijke (onderwijs)kunde: Een reactie op Boon e.a.. WARDEKKER, Wim.
Praxis and Ultimate Reality: Intellectual, Moral and Religious Conversion as Radical Political Conversion. MARSH, James L.
Reconstruction, Dialectic and Praxis. RIORDAN, Patrick.
Rhetoric as Praxis: An Alternative to the Epistemic Approach. ZHAO, Shanyang.
The Role of Aristotle's *Praxis* Today. GUY, Alfred.
The Unity of Theory and Practice in Historical Perspective. KRANCBERG, Sigmund.

PREAUD, M

Analyse d'un corpus iconographique rassemblé par Maxime Préaud ou Aristote et la mélancolie. FLEURY, Chantal.

PRECEPT(S)

Comments: "A Moral Ideal for Everyone and No One". HUNT, Lester.

PRECOGNITION

The Limits of Influence: Psychokinesis and the Philosophy of Science. BRAUDE, Stephen E (ed).

PREDESTINATION
"Predestination and Freedom in Augustine's Ethics" in *The Philosophy in Christianity*, O'DALY, Gerard.

PREDICATE LOGIC
Actuality and Quantification. HAZEN, Allen.
Classification of Intermediate Predicate Logics Under the Type of Deductive Completeness. TAKANO, Mitio and YAMAKAMI, Tomoyuki.
Decidable and Enumerable Predicate Logics of Provability. DZHAPARIDZE, Giorgie.
Dynamic Predicate Logic. GROENENDIJK, Jeroen and STOKHOF, Martin.
An Extension of Ono's Completeness Result. SUZUKI, Nobu-Yuki.
Finite Kripke Models and Predicate Logics of Provability. ARTEMOV, Sergei and DZHAPARIDZE, Giorgie.
First-Order Logics for Comparative Similarity. WILLIAMSON, Timothy.
How Far Can Hume's Is-Ought Thesis Be Generalized?. SCHURZ, Gerhard.
The Inconspicious Role of Paraphrase. SHERRY, David.
Intermediate Predicate Logics Determined by Ordinals. MINARI, Pierluigi and TAKANO, Mitio and ONO, Hiroakira.
Kripke Bundles for Intermediate Predicate Logics and Kripke Frames for Intuitionistic Modal Logics. SUZUKI, Nobu-Yuki.
On Defining Identity. SAVELLOS, Elias E.
Single-Axiom Systems. STEPIEN, Teodor.
Some Modifications of the Gödel Translation of Classical Intuitionistic Logic. BORICIC, Branislav.
Some Syntactical Properties of Intermediate Predicate Logics. SUZUKI, Nobu-Yuki.
Tait-Systems for Fragments of *Lm*. COLUMBUS, Joachim.
A Truth-Functional Logic for Near-Universal Generalizations. CARLSTROM, Ian F.

PREDICATE(S)
Aristotelian Syllogisms and Generalized Quantifiers. WESTERSTAHL, Dag.
Eine Bemerkung zu spektralen Darstellungen von ρ-stelligen Aufzählbaren. DEUTSCH, Michael.
Derivability Conditions on Rosser's Provability Predicates. ARAI, Toshiyasu.
Formatives. ENGLEBRETSEN, George.
On Defining Identity. SAVELLOS, Elias E.
Remarks on Analogy. DA COSTA, Newton C A and SETTE, A M.
State-Spaces and Meaning Relations Among Predicates. ARNTZENIUS, Frank.

PREDICATION
Kalkulierte Absurditäten. STRUB, Christian.
The Origins of Aristotelian Science. FEREJOHN, Michael.
Philosophical Logic. STRAWSON, P F (ed).
Plato's "Parmenides". MEINWALD, Constance C.
"The Frame Problem and Relevant Predication" in *Knowledge Representation and Defeasible Reasoning*, DUNN, J Michael.
Aristotelian Contraries. BOGEN, James.
Kant and Conceptual Semantics: A Sketch. POSY, Carl J.
Ousia, Substratum, and Matter. SFEKAS, Stanley.
Preconditions of Predication: From Qualia to Quantum Mechanics. FORSTER, Malcolm.
Predication and Deduction in Aristotle: Aspirations to Completeness. SMITH, Robin.
Predication and Logic of Language (I). GANGADEAN, Ashok.
Predication and Logic of Language (II). GANGADEAN, Ashok.
Predication and Physical Law. SCHEIBE, Erhard.
Predication, Fiction, and Artificial Intelligence. RAPAPORT, William J.
The Problem of Properties in Quantum Mechanics. BUB, Jeffrey.
Relevant Predication 2: Intrinsic Properties and Internal Relations. DUNN, J Michael.
Universals and Predication of Species. PETERSON, John.
Wittgenstein, Hans Lipps y los supuestos de la predicación. LÁZARO, Ramón Castilla.

PREDICTABILITY
The Philosophy of Action: An Introduction. MOYA, Carlos J.
What Is Wrong with the Miracle Argument?. CARRIER, Martin.

PREDICTION
Science and Reason. KYBURG JR, Henry E.
Biological Foundations of Prediction in an Unpredictable Environment. MARUSIC, M.
A Fully Logical Inductive Logic. NOLT, John.
Jarrett Completeness and Superluminal Signals. KRONZ, Frederick M.
A Note on Schrödinger's Cat and the Unexpected Hanging Paradox. HOLTZMANN, Jack M.
Plural World of Contemporary Science and Philosophy (in Serbo-Croatian). LELAS, Srdjan.
Prediction and Explanation in Economics. SWAMIDASAN, Nalini.
The Roles of Predictions in Science and Religion. SCHOEN, Edward L.
Singular Causation and Law. IRZIK, Gürol.
Stich, Content, Prediction, and Explanation in Cognitive Science. WALLIS, Charles S.

PREEXISTENCE
Pre-existence and Personal Identity. FEENSTRA, Ronald J.

PREFERENCE LOGIC
Aggregation of Preferences: The Fuzzy Case. BILLOT, Antoine.

PREFERENCE(S)
The Last Choice: Preemptive Suicide in Advanced Age. PRADO, C G.
Natural Reasons: Personality and Polity. HURLEY, S L.
"Equality, Discrimination and Preferential Treatment" in *A Companion to Ethics*, BOXILL, Bernard R.
Act-Utilitarian Prisoner's Dilemmas. RABINOWICZ, Wlodzimierz.
Actual Preferences, Actual People. GOODIN, Robert E.
An Argument for Utilitarianism: A Defence. NG, Yew-Kwang and SINGER, Peter.
Choice Procedure Consistent with Similarity Relations. AIZPURUA, Jose Maria and NIETO, Jorge and URIARTE, Jose Ramon.
A Comparative Study of Multiattribute Decision Making Methodologies. KARNI, Reuven and SANCHEZ, Pedro and TUMMALA, V M Rao.
External and Now-For-Then Preferences in Hare's Theory. HAJDIN, Mane.
Fanaticism: Reply to Thomas Wetterström. HARE, R M.
On Intuitions. WETTERSTRÖM, Thomas.
Practical Reason or Metapreferences? An Undogmatic Defense of Kantian Morality. NIDA-RÜMELIN, Julian.
Preferences and Politics. SUNSTEIN, Cass R.
Prudence and Past Preferences; Reply to Wlodizimierz Rabinowicz. HARE, R M.
The Ranking of Preference. RAWLING, Piers.
Time Preference. ZIFF, Paul.

PREFERENTIAL HIRING
Justice in Preferential Hiring. SINGER, M S and SINGER, A E.
Preferential Hiring and the Question of Competence. PHILIPS, Michael.

PREGNANCY
Abortion, Coercive Pregnancy, and Adoption. JAMES, David N.
Are Pregnant Women Fetal Containers?. PURDY, Laura.

PREJUDICE(S)
Prejudice and Progress in Animal and Environmental Protection. FOX, Michael W.
Racial Bias, the Death Penalty, and Desert. MEYERS, Christopher.
Wittgenstein on Jews: Some Counter-Examples. WASSERMANN, Gerhard D.

PREMISE(S)
Evaluating Arguments: The Premise-Conclusion Relation. BOWLES, George.
Help in Finding Missing Premises. DONN, Mike.
Premiss Tree Proofs and Logic of Contradiction. SIKIC, Zvonimir.

PRERATIONAL
Sartre on Pre-Reflective Consciousness. AGRAWAL, M M.

PRESBURGER, J
Mojzesz Presburger: Life and Work. ZYGMUNT, Jan.

PRESCRIPTION
Biomedical Ethics Reviews, 1987. HUMBER, James M (ed).
Grammatica e diritto: Una normatività fragile?. VITALE, Vincenzo.
Per un'analisi del discorso dichiarativo. CELANO, Bruno.
Psychoactive Drug Prescribing in Japan: Epistemological and Bioethical Considerations. SAKAI, Akio.
A Response to 'Psychoactive Drug Prescribing in Japan'. COVERDALE, John.
Response to Dr Sakai's 'Psychoactive Drug Prescribing in Japan'. RITCHIE, Karen.

PRESCRIPTIVISM
"Universal Prescriptivism" in *A Companion to Ethics*, HARE, R M.
Does Prescriptivism Imply Naturalism?. KANTHAMANI, A.

PRESENCE
"La 'présence' de l'acteur au théâtre" in *XIth International Congress in Aesthetics, Nottingham 1988*, SAISON, Maryvonne.
"...A Presence of Absence...". BATKIN, Norton.
Dasein—Mitsein—Sprache: Heideggers Auffassung über das "Wesen der Sprache" in "Sein und Zeit". TIETZ, Udo.

PRESENT
Heidegger e la duplicità del presente. PENZO, Maurizio.

PRESERVATION
Property Rights and Preservationist Duties. GOODIN, Robert E.

PRESIDENCY
Presidential Campaigns, Television News and Voter Turnout. WALTER, Edward.

PRESOCRATICS
"Also sprach Herakleitos". WOHLFART, Günter.
Methods and Problems in Greek Science: Selected Papers. LLOYD, G E R.
Philosophy in World Perspective: A Comparative Hermeneutic of the Major Theories. DILWORTH, David A.
Philosophy of the Ancients. RICKEN, Friedo.
Réflexiones sur l'idéee de la guerre dans la philosophie présocratique. FREUND, Julien.
Sir Karl Popper on Presocratic Philosophers (in Hungarian). STEIGER, Kornel.
Suspicion, Deception, and Concealment. ROSEN, Stanley.

PRESUPPOSITION(S)
Husserl's Presuppositionless Philosophy. REED-DOWNING, Teresa.
Some Aspects of R G Collingwood's Doctrine of Absolute Presuppositions. SAARI, Heikki.
The "Presuppositions" and "Realizations" in Aesthetics of Zdenek Mathauser (in Czechoslovakian). SVATON, Vladimir.
Understanding Induction. MACNAMARA, John.

PRETENSE(S)
"Illocutionary Pretence Inside and Outside Fiction" in *XIth International Congress in Aesthetics, Nottingham 1988*, TSOHATZIDIS, S L.

PRETI, G
Lezioni di filosofia della scienza di Guilio Preti. LECIS, Pier Luigi.

PREVENTION
The Futility of Psychotherapy. ALBEE, George W.
The Moral Responsibility of Corporate Executives for Disasters. BISHOP, John D.

PRICE(S)
The Behavior of the NCAA: A Question of Ethics. STIEBER, John.

PRICHARD, H
Prichard, Davidson and Action. GUSTAFSON, Don.

PRIDE
'Pride Produces the Idea of Self': Hume on Moral Agency. RORTY, Amélie.
Pride and the Meaning of *Utopia*. MOULAKIS, Athanasios.
What is Wrong With Wicked Feelings?. ROBERTS, Robert C.

PRIGOGINE, I
Why Natural Selection Leads to Complexity. BENZON, William L and HAYS, David G.

PRIMACY
"An Ethic of Prima Facie Duties" in *A Companion to Ethics*, DANCY, Jonathan.

PRIMARY QUALITY(-TIES)
Lockes Qualitäten: Erwiderung auf Casati. KIENZLE, Bertram.
Primary and Secondary Qualities: A Reply to Kienzle. CASATI, Roberto.
Primary Qualities are Secondary Qualities Too. PRIEST, Graham.

PRIME MATTER
An Attempt at Interpretation of the Thomistic Hylomorphic Theory in View of Contemporary Physics. JANIK, J A.
A New Reading of Aristotle's *Hyle*. POLIS, Dennis F.

PRIME NUMBER(S)
Characterization of Prime Numbers in Lukasiewicz's Logical Matrix. KARPENKO, Alexander S.

PRIMITIVE
Working with Wittgenstein's Builders. BIRSCH, Douglas and DORBOLO, Jon.

PRIMORATZ, I
On Primoratz's Definition of Terrorism. SINNOTT-ARMSTRONG, Walter.

PRINCIPLE(S)
"Are There Counterexamples to the Closure Principle?" in *Doubting: Contemporary Perspectives on Skepticism*, VOGEL, Jonathan.
"Metaepistemology and Skepticism" in *Doubting: Contemporary Perspectives on Skepticism*, FUMERTON, Richard.
"Remarks on Experience in Metaphysics" in *Thomistic Papers, V*, GILSON, Etienne.
Applying the Principles of Gestalt Theory to Teaching Ethics. HUNT, Eugene H and BULLIS, Ronald K.
A Bayesian Proof of a Humean Principle. GILLIES, Donald.
Buddhist Approaches to Abortion. FLORIDA, R E.
The Chicken and the Egg. TEICHMANN, Roger.
Double Standards, Racial Equality and the Right Reference Class. ADLER, Jonathan E.
La elusión mediante sociedades a la luz de los principios constitucionales. RUIZ ZAPATERO, Guillermo.
Experiencia de lo sublime y principios racionales. ARTOLA, José María.
Four Perspectives on Moral Judgement: The Rational Principles of Jesus and Kant. PALMQUIST, Stephen R.
The Greatest Happiness Principle. SPRIGGE, T L S.
Quatre principes de la phénoménologie. HENRY, Michel.
Relevance as an Explanation of Communication. ROBERTS, Lawrence D.
Some New Double Induction and Superinduction Principles. SMULLYAN, Raymond M.
Syntactic Form and Textual Rhetoric: The Cognitive Basis for Certain Pragmatic Principles. PRIDEAUX, Gary D.
La teoria aristotelica dell'apodissi. SAINATI, Vittorio.
Two Principles of Bayesian Epistemology. TALBOTT, W J.

PRIOR, A
Contingency and Modal Logic. DEUTSCH, Harry.
Not Over Yet: Prior's 'Thank Goodness' Argument'. KIERNAN-LEWIS, Delmas.
Universal Sentences: Russell, Wittgenstein, Prior, and the Nyāya. SHAW, J L.

PRIORITY
Probabilistic Causality. EELLS, Ellery.
Medical Futility, Medical Necessity: The - Problem - Without - A - Name. CALLAHAN, Daniel.
The Oregon Priority-Setting Exercise: Quality of Life and Public Policy. HADORN, David C.

PRISON(S)
Prisoners' Rights and Correctional Privatization: A Legal and Ethical Analysis. THOMAS, Charles W.

PRISONER'S DILEMMA
Experimental Studies of Interactive Decisions. RAPOPORT, Amnon.
Rationality in Action: Contemporary Approaches. MOSER, Paul K (ed).
"Winning Against and With the Opponent" in *Logic and Ethics*, HOLOWKA, Jacek.
Act-Utilitarian Prisoner's Dilemmas. RABINOWICZ, Wlodzimierz.
Believing that Everyone Else is Less Ethical: Implications for Work Behavior and Ethics Instruction. TYSON, Thomas.
The Inapplicability of Evolutionary Stable Strategy to the Prisoner's Dilemma. MARINOFF, Louis.
McClennen's Early Cooperative Solution to the Prisoner's Dilemma. MAC INTOSH, Duncan.
The Mutual Investment Game: Peculiarities of Indifference. CUBITT, Robin P and HOLLIS, Martin.
Newcomb's Problem, Prisoners' Dilemma, and Collective Action. HURLEY, S L.
The Prisoner's *Other* Dilemma. ZALCMAN, Lawrence.
Some Versions of Newcomb's Problem Are Prisoners' Dilemmas. SOBEL, Jordan Howard.
The Symmetry Enigma in Hobbes. HAJI, Ishtiyaque.

PRISONER(S)
Capital Punishment and Realism. COCKBURN, David.
Prisoners' Rights and Correctional Privatization: A Legal and Ethical Analysis. THOMAS, Charles W.

PRITSCHER, C
Humor, Schooling, and Cultural Intelligence: A Response to Pritscher. O'CONNOR, Terence.
Response to Merkle and Pritscher. SMITH, Phil.

PRIVACY
Wittgenstein: Meaning and Mind, Volume 3 of an Analytical Commentary on Philosophical Investigations. HACKER, P M S.
Abortion: Privacy versus Liberty. GOULD, James.
Computers, Personal Data, and Theories of Technology: Comparative Approaches to Privacy Protection in the 1990s. BENNETT, Colin J.
Information Privacy and Performance Appraisal: An Examination of Employee Perceptions and Reactions. MOSSHOLDER, Kevin W and GILES, William F and WESOLOWSKI, Mark A.
Information, Access, or Intimate Decisions About One's Action? The Content of Privacy. INNESS, Julie.
Is there an Ethics of Computing?. BROWN, Geoffrey.
Just Looking: Voyeurism and the Grounds of Privacy. NATHAN, Daniel O.
Liberal Man. MENDUS, Susan.
Respect for Privacy: Western and Indian. GHOSH-DASTIDAR, Koyeli.
Richard Rorty and the Image of Modernity. BRADLEY, James.

PRIVATE
Kierkegaard in Golden Age Denmark. KIRMMSE, Bruce H.
Must Thinking Bats be Conscious?. HANNA, Patricia.
Private Defense. GORR, Michael.
Public and Private Morality. SHAIDA, S A.
The Unbearable Seriousness of Irony. FERRARA, Alessandro.

PRIVATE LANGUAGE(S)
Wittgenstein: Meaning and Mind, Volume 3 of an Analytical Commentary on Philosophical Investigations. HACKER, P M S.
La condición pública del lenguaje y la autoridad de la primera persona. ROLLINS, Mark.
Faith and the Possibility of Private Meaning. GURREY, Charles S.
La force du nombre: remarques autour de la notion de communauté. FAUCHER, Luc.
Language and Conversation. GAITA, Raimond.

PRIVATION
Heidegger and the Critique of the Understanding of Evil as Privatio Boni. CAPOBIANCO, Richard.

PRIVATIZATION
Prisoners' Rights and Correctional Privatization: A Legal and Ethical Analysis. THOMAS, Charles W.

PRIVILEGE(S)
The Case Against Art: Wunderlich on Joyce. MAHAFFEY, Vicki.

PRIVILEGED ACCESS
Anti-Individualism and Privileged Access. MC KINSEY, Michael.

PROBABILISM
Explaining Science. KORB, Kevin B.
A Green Parrot is Just as Much a Red Herring as a White Shoe: A Note on Confirmation, Background Knowledge.... FRENCH, Steven.

PROBABILISM

The Last Word on Induction?. HOWSON, Colin.
Der Normgeltungsbegriff als probabilistischer Begriff: Zur Logik des soziologischen Normbegriffs. LÜBBE, Weyma.
On the Alleged Impossibility of Inductive Probability. EELLS, Ellery.
Quantum Propension Theory: A Testable Resolution of the Wave/Particle Dilemma. MAXWELL, Nicholas.
Response to Ehring's 'Papineau on Causal Asymmetry'. PAPINEAU, David.

PROBABILITY

John Craige's Mathematical Principles of Christian Theology. NASH, Richard.
Logic, Methodology and Philosophy of Science, VII. MARCUS, Ruth Barcan (ed).
Nomic Probability and the Foundations of Induction. POLLOCK, John L.
Philosophical Papers: F P Ramsey. MELLOR, D H (ed).
Probabilistic Causality. EELLS, Ellery.
Representing and Reasoning With Probabilistic Knowledge: A Logical Approach to Probabilities. BACCHUS, Fahiem.
Science and Reason. KYBURG JR, Henry E.
The Sweep of Probability. SCHLESINGER, George N.
The Taming of Chance. HACKING, Ian.
"Astronomical Improbability" in *Logic, Methodology and Philosophy of Science, VIII*, HACKING, Ian.
"A Framework for Reasoning with Defaults" in *Knowledge Representation and Defeasible Reasoning*, GEFFNER, Hector and PEARL, Judea.
"The Interface Between Statistics and the Philosophy of Science" in *Logic, Methodology and Philosophy of Science, VIII*, GOOD, I J.
"Jeffrey's Rule, Passage of Experience, and *Neo*-Bayesianism" in *Knowledge Representation and Defeasible Reasoning*, PEARL, Judea.
"A New Normative Theory of Probabilistic Logic" in *Knowledge Representation and Defeasible Reasoning*, ALELIUNAS, Romas.
"Popper's Propensities: An Ontological Interpretation of Probability" in *Imre Lakatos and Theories of Scientific Change*, SFENDONI-MENTZOU, D.
"Probability in Dynamical Systems" in *Logic, Methodology and Philosophy of Science, VIII*, VON PLATO, Jan.
"Reality and Probability in Mario Bunge's *Treatise*" in *Studies on Mario Bunge's "Treatise"*, PATY, Michel.
"Undressing Baby Bell" in *Harré and His Critics*, REDHEAD, Michael L G.
Agency and Probabilistic Causality. PRICE, Huw.
Ambiguity, Inductive Systems, and the Modeling of Subjective Probability Judgements. MONETA, Giovanni B.
The Autonomy of Probability Theory (Notes on Kolmogorov, Rényi, and Popper). LEBLANC, Hugues.
Bayes' Bayesianism. EARMAN, John.
Born's Probabilistic Interpretation: A Case Study of 'Concepts in Flux'. BELLER, Mara.
Classifying Conditionals II. JACKSON, Frank.
Conditionalisation and Quantum Probabilities. MILNE, Peter.
The Credibility of Extraordinary Events. SCHLESINGER, George N.
Direct and Indirect Causes. SPOHN, Wolfgang.
Duff and the Wager. JORDAN, Jeff.
Embedded Probabilities. DUBUCS, J.
An Epistemic Analysis of Explanations and Causal Beliefs. GÄRDENFORS, Peter.
Evidence and Legal Reasoning: On the Intertwinement of the Probable and the Reasonable. KLAMI, Hannua Tapani (and others).
Finite Kripke Models and Predicate Logics of Provability. ARTEMOV, Sergei and DZHAPARIDZE, Giorgie.
A Fully Logical Inductive Logic. NOLT, John.
General Causation. SAPIRE, David.
The Geometry of Legal Principles. CHUAQUI, Rolando and MALITZ, Jerome.
Hume on Probability. GOWER, Barry.
Hypotheses, Probability, and Waves. ACHINSTEIN, Peter.
Hypothesis Tests and Confidence Intervals in the Single Case. JOHNSTONE, D J.
Indiscernibility and Identity in Probability Theory. ROEPER, Peter and LEBLANC, Hugues.
Is Confirmation Differential?. ERWIN, Edward and SIEGEL, Harvey.
Jackson Classifying Conditionals. DUDMAN, V H.
Keynesian Uncertainty and the Weight of Arguments. RUNDE, Jochen.
Kitcher and Salmon's *Scientific Explanation*; and Salmon's *Four Decades of Scientific Explanation*. FETZER, James H.
Mr Keynes on Probability. RAMSEY, F P.
Not Very Likely: A Reply to Ramsey. WATT, D E.
On the Descriptive Adequacy of Levi's Decision Theory. MAHER, Patrick and KASHIMA, Yoshihisa.
On the Necessity for Random Sampling. JOHNSTONE, D J.
Partitions, Probabilistic Causal Laws, and Simpson's Paradox. HARDCASTLE, Valerie Gray.
Plantinga and Probabilistic Atheism. CHRZAN, Keith.
Pragmatic Truth and the Logic of Induction. DA COSTA, Newton C A and FRENCH, Steven.
Probabilistic Causality from a Dynamical Point of View. VON PLATO, Jan.
Probabilistic Causality: A Rejoinder to Ellery Eells. DUPRÉ, John.
Probabilistic Dependence Among Conditionals. LANCE, Mark.
Probabilistic Physics and the Metaphysics of Time. SHANKS, Niall.
Probability and Epistemology. PIENKOWSKI, M.
Probability Logic in the Twentieth Century. HAILPERIN, Theodore.
Probability Out of Court: Notes on 'Guilt Beyond Reasonable Doubt'. COHEN, Stephen and BERSTEN, Michael.
Quantifying Support. BLACK, John.
Quantum Physics, Philosophy, and the Image of God: Insights from Wolfgang Pauli. LAURIKAINEN, K V.
Randomness and Probability in Dynamical Theories: On the Proposals of the Prigogine School. BATTERMAN, Robert.
La rationalité du théisme: la philosophie de la religion de Richard Swinburne. PADGETT, Alan G.
Some Further Reflections on the Popper-Miller 'Disproof' of Probabilistic Induction. HOWSON, C.
Statistical Explanation, Probability, and Counteracting Conditions. GRIMES, Thomas R.
A Suspicious Feature of the Popper/Miller Argument. GOOD, I J.
A Theory of Probability. REEVES, T V.
Theory Revision and Probability. SCHLECHTA, Karl.
Weights or the Value of Knowledge. RAMSEY, F P.
What is the Logical Form of Probability Assignment in Quantum Mechanics?. HALPIN, John F.
When Fair Betting Odds are Not Degrees of Belief. SEIDENFELD, Teddy and SCHERVISH, M J and KADANE, J B.

PROBLEM SOLVING

Artificial Intelligence and Human Cognition. WAGMAN, Morton.
A Problem Solving Interpretation of Argument Analysis. BERNSTEIN, David.
Problem Solving, Decision Making and Reflective Thinking. MERKLE, Patricia.

PROBLEM(S)

Nietzsche On Truth and Philosophy. CLARK, Maudemarie.
Philosophy of Technology. DURBIN, Paul T (ed).
Reasons for Living: A Basic Ethics. PORTER, Burton F.
Der Ursprung der Erziehungsziele in der Lehre von Plato, Aristoteles und Neill. EGGER, Paul.
"Heidegger and the Problem of World" in *Reconsidering Psychology: Perspectives from Continental Philosophy*, RICHARDSON, William J.
"Personal Identity and the Mind-Body Problem" in *The Case for Dualism*, MADELL, Geoffrey.
"The Problem of Certitude: Reflections on the Grammar of Assent" in *Thomistic Papers, V*, SULLIVAN, Thomas D.
Agency and Probabilistic Causality. PRICE, Huw.
The Curve Fitting Problem: A Solution. TURNEY, Peter.
Hattiangadi's Theory of Scientific Problems and the Structure of Standard Epistemologies. GIUNTI, Marco.
Holism and Indeterminacy. MALPAS, Jeff.
Libertarianism. BARRY, Norman.
The Life of Order and the Order of Life: Eric Voegelin on Modernity and the Problem of Philosophical Anthropology. LEVY, David J.
Mapping the Human Genome: Some Thoughts for Those Who Say "There Should Be A Law On It". SKENE, Loane.
Metaphysical Conundrums at the Root of Moral Disagreement. MC DERMOTT, John M.
Meyer's Theory of Problematology. GOLDEN, James L and JAMISON, David L.
Modal Counterparts of Medvedev Logic of Finite Problems Are Not Finitely Axiomatizable. SHEHTMAN, Valentin.
The *Nous*-Body Problem in Aristotle. MODRAK, Deborah K W.
Paradigms, Populations and Problem-Fields: Approaches to Disagreement. ALLCHIN, Douglas.
Relating Science and Theology with Complementarity: A Caution. SHARPE, Kevin J.
Rhetoric as Praxis: An Alternative to the Epistemic Approach. ZHAO, Shanyang.
What was Leibniz's Problem about Relations?. BURDICK, Howard.

PROCEDURE(S)

Functional and Procedural Definitions of Art. DAVIES, Stephen.

PROCESS PHILOSOPHY

Baffling Phenomena: And Other Studies in the Philosophy of Knowledge and Valuation. RESCHER, Nicholas.
"Introduction: Archetypal Psychology and Process Philosophy" in *Archetypal Process: Self and Divine in Whitehead, Jung, and Hillman*, GRIFFIN, David Ray.
Aristotelian and Whiteheadian Conceptions of Actuality: II. FETZ, Reto Luzius and FELT, James W.
Crisis of Modernity and Process Thought in Max Horkheimer's Early Work (in Serbo-Croatian). FILANDRA, Sacir.
Efficient Causation Within Concrescence. FORD, Lewis S.
The Matrix of Personality: A Whiteheadian Corroboration of Harry Stack Sullivan's Interpersonal Theory of Psychiatry. REGAN, Thomas J.

PROCESS PHILOSOPHY

Process Metaphysics and Minimalism: Implications for Public Policy. KEFFER, Steven and KING, Sallie and KRAFT, Steven.

Process Thought and the Spaciness of Mind. EDWARDS, Rem B.

Whitehead and Genuine Evil. BARINEAU, R Maurice.

PROCESS THEOLOGY

Archetypal Process: Self and Divine in Whitehead, Jung, and Hillman. GRIFFIN, David Ray (ed).

The Experience of Value and Theological Argumentation. DEVENISH, Philip E.

Methodological Alternatives in Process Theology. BROWN, Delwin and GREEVE DAVANEY, Sheila.

Process Theology as Empirical, Rational, and Speculative: Some Reflections on Method. GRIFFIN, David Ray.

PROCESS(ES)

Explaining Behavior: Reasons in a World of Causes. DRETSKE, Fred.

Properties as Processes: A Synoptic Study of Wilfried Sellars' Nominalism. SEIBT, Johanna.

Speech Acts and Literary Theory. PETREY, Sandy.

Causal Propensities: Statistical Causality versus Aleatory Causality. SALMON, Wesley C.

Concepts of Process in Social Science Explanations. VAYDA, Andrew P and MC CAY, Bonnie J and EGHENTER, Cristina.

David Hull's Evolutionary Model for the Progress and Process of Science. OLDROYD, David.

Deciding to Act. FIELDS, L.

El desarrollo como proceso: una investigación filosófica. DOWER, Nigel.

From Discrete to Continuous Time. KEISLER, H Jerome.

Language in Action. VAN BENTHEM, Johan.

Rationality, Correlativity, and the Language of Process. HALL, David Lynn and AMES, Roger T.

Retrospections. GOODMAN, Nelson.

Stephen P Stich, "The Fragmentation of Reason". COHEN, L Jonathan.

Stephen P Stich, "The Fragmentation of Reason". GOLDMAN, Alvin I.

Uguaglianza e temporalità nella "Democrazia in America". BAGLIONI, Emma.

PRODUCT(S)

An Existence Theorem for Recursion Categories. HELLER, Alex.

The Formal Language L_t and Topological Products. BERTOSSI, L E.

PRODUCTION

Marx's Radical Critique of Capitalist Society: A Reconstruction and Critical Evaluation. ARNOLD, N Scott.

Connecting *Techne* and *Praxis* in Teaching. HOSTETLER, Karl.

El consumo como sistema ideológico. MÁRQUEZ FERNÁNDEZ, Alvaro B.

India and the Theory of the Asiatic Mode of Production (in Hungarian). RENNER, Zsuzsanna.

Market Order or Commanded Chaos. FLEW, Antony.

Nozick on Social Justice. AGARWALA, Binod Kumar.

Reply to Chmielewski: Cooperation by Definition. GORDON, David.

Sociedad informatizada y poder político. RICHARDS, Edgardo.

PRODUCTIVITY

The Conflation of Productivity and Efficiency in Economics and Economic History. SINGH, Harinder and FRANTZ, Roger.

Productivity and X-Efficiency: A Reply to Singh and Frantz. SARAYDAR, Edward.

Werkzeugproduktion im Tierreich und menschliche Werkzeugproduktion. BEURTON, Peter.

PROFANE

The Sacred, Secular, and Profane in Augustine's World of Shadows. SPENCER, Jon Michael.

PROFESSION(S)

Ethics, Trust, and the Professions: Philosophical and Cultural Aspects. PELLEGRINO, Edmund D (ed).

Medical Work in America: Essays on Health Care. FREIDSON, Eliot.

"The Fiduciary Relationship and the Nature of Professions" in *Ethics, Trust, and the Professions: Philosophical and Cultural Aspects*, SOKOLOWSKI, Robert.

PROFESSIONAL CODE(S)

Codes of Ethics and the Moral Education of Engineers. LUEGENBIEHL, Heinz C.

Commentary: "Codes of Ethics and the Moral Education of Engineers". PUKA, Bill.

Establishing an Ethic of Accounting: A Response to Westra's Call for Government Employment of Auditors. WAPLES, Elain and SHAUB, Michael K.

Ethical Considerations for the Forensic Engineer Serving as an Expert Witness. CARPER, Kenneth L.

Innocents and Innocence: Moral Puzzles of Professional Status and Culpable Conduct. SNOWDEN, John R.

The Professional's Dilemma: Choosing Between Service and Success. MC DOWELL, Banks.

Truth, Neutrality, and Conflict of Interest. LICHTENBERG, Judith.

PROFESSIONAL ETHICS

Ethics, Trust, and the Professions: Philosophical and Cultural Aspects. PELLEGRINO, Edmund D (ed).

"Are There Virtues Inherent in a Profession?" in *Ethics, Trust, and the Professions: Philosophical and Cultural Aspects*, MEILAENDER, Gilbert.

"Professional Organizations and Professional Ethics: A European View" in *Ethics, Trust, and the Professions: Philosophical and Cultural Aspects*, SASS, Hans-Martin.

"Professional Paradigms" in *Ethics, Trust, and the Professions: Philosophical and Cultural Aspects*, LANGAN, John.

"Professions, Professors, and Competing Obligations" in *Ethics, Trust, and the Professions: Philosophical and Cultural Aspects*, GOROVITZ, Samuel.

"Trust and Distrust in Professional Ethics" in *Ethics, Trust, and the Professions: Philosophical and Cultural Aspects*, PELLEGRINO, Edmund D.

Are Physicians a "Delinquent Community"?: Issues in Professional Competence, Conduct, and Self-Regulation. SWAZEY, Judith P.

Are Physicians a "Delinquent Community"?: Issues in Professional Competence, Conduct, Self-Regulation: Comment. LAMMERS, Stephen E.

Business and Professional Ethics: An Oxymoron?. PORTER, Jack Nusan.

Child Development and Research Ethics: A Changing Calculus of Concerns. THOMPSON, Ross A.

Commentary: When Opportunity Knocks. BERENSON, Robert A.

Commentary: When Opportunity Knocks. HYMAN, David A.

Deride, Abide or Dissent: On the Ethics of Professional Conduct. HAUPTMAN, Robert and HILL, Fred.

Engineers and Management: The Challenge of the Challenger Incident. WERHANE, Patricia H.

Ethical Considerations for the Forensic Engineer Serving as an Expert Witness. CARPER, Kenneth L.

Ethics and Advocacy in Forecasting for Public Policy. WACHS, Martin.

Ethics and News. MACHAMER, Peter K and BOYLAN, Barbara.

Ethics and the Professional Responsibility of Lawyers. KIPNIS, Kenneth.

Ethics and the Professional Responsibility of Lawyers (Commentary). LENNERTZ, James E.

Health Care as a Business: The Ethic of Hippocrates Versus the Ethic of Managed Care. WAYMACK, Mark H.

Informing Clients About Limits to Confidentiality. PIZZIMENTI, Lee Ann.

Management's Hat Trick: Misuse of "Engineering Judgment" in the Challenger Incident. HERKERT, Joseph R.

Necesidad y existencia del código de moral profesional. MUÑOZ BARQUERO, Elizabeth.

Personal Morals and Professional Ethics: A Review and Empirical Examination of Public Accounting. BEETS, S Douglas.

Professional Ethics and Accounting Education: A Critique of the 8-Step Method. ARMSTRONG, Mary Beth.

Reactions to Ethical Dilemmas: A Study Pertaining to Certified Public Accounts. CLAYPOOL, G A and FETYKO, D F and PEARSON, M A.

The Regulation of Virtue: Cross-Currents in Professional Ethics. JENNINGS, Bruce.

Role Differentiation Problems in Professional Ethics. WANGERIN, Paul T.

Some Unresolved Ethical Issues in Auditing. GUNZ, Sally and MC CUTCHEON, John.

Taking Positional Conflicts of Interest Seriously. DZIENKOWSKI, John S.

The Teaching of Business Ethics: A Survey of AACSB Member Schools. SCHOENFELDT, Lyle F and MC DONALD, Don M and YOUNGBLOOD, Stuart A.

Thinking Like an Engineer: The Place of a Code of Ethics in the Practice of a Profession. DAVIS, Michael.

Understanding Professional Misconduct: The Moral Responsibilities of Professionals. NORTON, Thomas W.

Waiting for a New St Benedict: Alasdair MacIntyre and the Theory and Practice of Journalism. LAMBETH, Edmund B.

PROFESSIONAL(S)

"The Fiduciary Relationship between Professionals and Clients: A Chinese Perspective" in *Ethics, Trust, and the Professions: Philosophical and Cultural Aspects*, QUI, Ren-zong.

"Fiduciary Relationships and the Medical Profession: A Japanese Point of View" in *Ethics, Trust, and the Professions: Philosophical and Cultural Aspects*, KIMURA, Rihito.

"Is Trust of Professionals a Coherent Concept?" in *Ethics, Trust, and the Professions: Philosophical and Cultural Aspects*, VEATCH, Robert M.

Continuity and Diversity in Philosophy of Education: An Introduction. BURBULES, Nicholas C.

Philosophers as Professional Relativists: Canadian Philosophical Association Presidential Address 1990. BUTTS, Robert E.

Professional Education of African Americans: A Challenge to Ethical Thinking. HARRIS, William M.

PROFESSIONALISM

"Nourishing Professionalism" in *Ethics, Trust, and the Professions: Philosophical and Cultural Aspects*, FREIDSON, Eliot.

Advocacy of Just Health Policies as Professional Duty: Cultural Biases and Ethical Responsibilities. CRANDALL, Lee A.

PROFESSIONALISM
Art, Truth and the Education of Subjectivity. HEPBURN, Ronald W.
The Foundations of Professionalism: Fifty Years of the Philosophy of Education Society in Retrospect. GIARELLI, James M and CHAMBLISS, J J.
PES and the APA—An Impressionistic History. MACMILLAN, C J B.
The Politics of Professionalism. FARBER, Paul.
Professional Ethics and Accounting Education: A Critique of the 8-Step Method. ARMSTRONG, Mary Beth.
Professions and Professionalism. DOWNIE, R S.
A Response to Beck, Giarelli/Chambliss, Leach, Tozer, and Macmillan. GREENE, Maxine.

PROFESSOR(S)
"Professions, Professors, and Competing Obligations" in *Ethics, Trust, and the Professions: Philosophical and Cultural Aspects*, GOROVITZ, Samuel.

PROFIT(S)
"The Ethics of Physicians Dispensing Drugs for Profit" in *Biomedical Ethics Reviews, 1989*, KNOWLTON, Calvin H.
"Should Physicians Dispense Drugs for a Profit?" in *Biomedical Ethics Reviews, 1989*, WEINSTEIN, Michael P.
Economic Efficiency and the Quality of Life. JACOBSEN, Rockney.
The Indefensibility of Insider Trading. WERHANE, Patricia H.
Outrageous Fortune: Selling Other People's Cells. ANNAS, George J.
The Profit Motive and the Moral Assessment of Health Care Institutions. DANIELS, Norman.

PROGRAM(S)
"The Justification of Negation as Failure" in *Logic, Methodology and Philosophy of Science, VIII*, FINE, Kit.
Coherent Programs in Teacher Education: When Are They Educational?. FLODEN, Robert E and BUCHMANN, Margret.
The Homogeneous Form of Logic Programs with Equality. DEMOPOULOS, William.
Propositional Functions and Families of Types. SMITH, Jan M.
Should Ethical Concerns Regulate Science? The European Experience with the Human Genome Project. RIX, Bo Andreassen.
Uniform Proofs as a Foundation for Logic Programming. MILLER, Dale and NADATHUR, Gopalan and PFENNING, Frank and SCEDROV, Andre.
Verification of Concurrent Programs: the Automata-Theoretic Framework. VARDI, Moshe Y.

PROGRAMMING
Logic Programming: Proceedings of the Seventh International Conference. WARREN, David H D (ed).
Language in Action. VAN BENTHEM, Johan.

PROGRESS
Evolution: Probleme und neue Aspekte ihrer Theorie. SCHEFFCZYK, Leo (ed).
Science and Relativism: Some Key Controversies in the Philosophy of Science. LAUDAN, Larry.
"Bernanosian Barbs and the Maritain's Marigny Lecture" in *From Twilight to Dawn: The Cultural Vision of Jacques Maritain*, BUSH, William.
"Conceptual Change and the Progress of Science" in *Logic, Methodology and Philosophy of Science, VIII*, PEARCE, David.
Beyond Malthusianism: Demography and Technology in John Stuart Mill's Stationary State. KURFIRST, Robert.
The Changing Nature of the Social Sciences. MASTERS, Roger D.
Collingwood and the Idea of Progress. VAN DER DUSSEN, W Jan.
Complexity and Evolution: What Everybody Knows. MC SHEA, Daniel W.
David Hull's Evolutionary Model for the Progress and Process of Science. OLDROYD, David.
Hegel, Spengler, and the Enigma of World History: Progress or Decline?. FARRENKOPF, John.
An Oscillatory Model of the Growth of Scientific Knowledge. AKEROYD, F Michael.
PES and School Reform. TOZER, Steven.
Prejudice and Progress in Animal and Environmental Protection. FOX, Michael W.
Le progrès: De la temporalité historico-anthropothéologique et symbolique. HOTTOIS, Guy.
Progress in Mathematics and Other Arts. SEDZIWY, Stanislaw.
Research Programmes and Empirical Results. AKEROYD, F M.
Scientific Instruments, Scientific Progress and the Cyclotron. BAIRD, Davis and FAUST, Thomas.
Some Aspects of the Relationship Between the Theory of Socialism and the Perception of an Era (in German). BRIE, André (and others).
Technological Progress and Architectural Response. WINTERS, Edward.
Ten Types of Scientific Progress. KUKLA, Andre.
Zu Jürgen Habermas' Option für Fortschritt, Vernunft und Demokratie. BOGNER, Hagen.

PROHIBITION
Prohibiting Immorality. WESTMORELAND, Robert.

PROJECT(S)
Per una filosofia del corpo. PELLECCHIA, Pasquale.

PROJECTIBILITY
Projective Subsets of Separable Metric Spaces. MILLER, Arnold W.

PROJECTION
Contents and Causes: A Reply to Blackburn. STURGEON, Nicholas L.
Just Causes. BLACKBURN, Simon.

PROLETARIAT
"L'égalité en 1789" in *Égalité Uguaglianza*, D'HONDT, Jacques.
Hegel's *Logic* and Marx's Early Development. PRINCIPE, Michael A.
Marx's Historical Understanding of the Proletariat and Class in 19th-Century England. MAZLISH, Bruce.

PRONOMINALIZATION
Reference and Pronominal Descriptions. WILSON, George M.

PRONOUN(S)
Writing and the Moral Self. LANG, Berel.
Disjoint Reference into NP. SELLS, Peter.
Pronouns and Propositional Attitudes. SOAMES, Scott.
You and She. WILLIAMS, C J F.

PROOF THEORY
Against Logicist Cognitive Science. OAKSFORD, Mike and CHATER, Nick.

PROOF(S)
Computability, Complexity, Logic. BÖRGER, E.
Demystifying Mentalities. LLOYD, G E R.
Logic Programming: Proceedings of the Seventh International Conference. WARREN, David H D (ed).
"Proofs and Refutations: A Reassessment" in *Imre Lakatos and Theories of Scientific Change*, ANAPOLITANOS, D A.
La dimostrazione "a posteriori" dell'esistenza di Dio nella filosofia di Leibniz. NICOLOSI, Salvatore.
A Disproof of the Existence of God. WEEKS, Ian.
Henkin's Completeness Proof: Forty Years Later. LEBLANC, Hugues and ROEPER, Peter and THAU, Michael and WEAVER, George.
Intuitionistic Mathematics and Wittgenstein. GONZALEZ, Wenceslao J.
Kierkegaard on Theistic Proof. STERN, Kenneth.
Mechanical Proof Procedures for Many-Valued Lattice-Based Logic Programming. SUBRAHMANIAN, V S.
Nonlocal Influences and Possible Worlds—A Stapp in the Wrong Direction. CLIFTON, Robert K and BUTTERFIELD, Jeremy N and REDHEAD, Michael L G.
On Russell's Principle of Induction. DA COSTA, Newton C A and FRENCH, Steven.
On the Lengths of Proofs of Set Theoretical Statements in Zermelo-Fraenkel Set Theory and Kelley-Morse Theory.... CORRADA, Manuel.
On the Status of Proofs by Contradiction in the XVIIth Century. MANCOSU, Paolo.
Premiss Tree Proofs and Logic of Contradiction. SIKIC, Zvonimir.
Proof and Sanction in Mill's Utilitarianism. COHEN, Stephen.
Propositional Consistency Proofs. BUSS, S R.
Tree Proofs for Syllogistic. SIMONS, Peter M.
The Undecidability of *k*-Provability. BUSS, Samuel R.
Uniform Proofs as a Foundation for Logic Programming. MILLER, Dale and NADATHUR, Gopalan and PFENNING, Frank and SCEDROV, Andre.
Wittgenstein on Mathematical Proof. WRIGHT, Crispin.

PROPAGANDA
Nietzsche: Moralist or Immoralist?—The Verdict of the European Protestant Theologians in the First World War. BAILEY, Charles E.

PROPER NAME(S)
Philosophical Logic. STRAWSON, P F (ed).
Dictionaries and Proper Names. MARCONI, Diego.
Not Every Object of a Sign has Being. PAPE, Helmut.
On Begging the Question 'Who is N?'. PATTON, Thomas E.
Sobre la semántica de los nombres propios. SCHIRN, Matthias.
Words like Faces (in Dutch). LESAGE, D.

PROPERTY(-TIES)
Interpreting Political Responsibility. DUNN, John.
Kant's System of Rights. MULHOLLAND, Leslie A.
Leibniz and Arnauld. SLEIGH JR, Robert C.
The Limits of Government: An Essay on the Public Goods Arguments. SCHMIDTZ, David.
Plato's "Parmenides". MEINWALD, Constance C.
Properties as Processes: A Synoptic Study of Wilfried Sellars' Nominalism. SEIBT, Johanna.
The Realm of Rights. THOMSON, Judith Jarvis.
Robert Nozick: Property, Justice, and the Minimal State. WOLFF, Jonathan.
"The 'Essential Properties' of Matter, Space, and Time: Comments on Michael Friedman" in *Philosophical Perspectives on Newtonian Science*, DI SALLE, Robert.
An Alternative to Property Rights in Human Tissue. SWAIN, Margaret S and MARUSYK, Randy W.
Are Property Rights Problematic?. GAUS, Gerald F and LOMASKY, Loren E.
The Caterus Objection. FORGIE, J William.
Critical Synthesis on the Uses and Justifications for the Regulations of Intellectual Property. SNAPPER, John.

PROPERTY(-TIES)

Dharmakirti on Inference and Properties. GANERI, Jonardon.
The Difference Between Real Change and *Mere* Cambridge Change. CLELAND, Carol E.
From Dialogue Rights to Property Rights. SHEARMUR, Jeremy.
From Intersubjectivity through Epistemology to Property: Rejoinder to Michelman. SHEARMUR, Jeremy.
How Can We Speak of God? How Can We Speak of Anything. FORREST, Peter.
The Importance of Being Human. DIAMOND, Cora.
Informational Property: Logorights. SCHULMAN, J Neil.
Intellectual Property and Copyright Ethics. ALFINO, Mark.
Macdonald on Type Reduction via Disjunction. ENDICOTT, Ronald P.
Meaning and Value. SCHIFFER, Stephen.
A Modal Argument for Narrow Content. FODOR, Jerry A.
The Moral Foundations of Intangible Property. CHILD, James W.
Morals by Appropriation. FREEMAN, Samuel.
The Neglected Background of Radical Liberalism: P E Dove's Theory of Property. CUNLIFFE, John.
On Induction and Properties. ZABLUDOWSKI, Andrzej.
On Negation. KOKTOVÁ, Eva.
Ownership as Theft. GRUNEBAUM, James O.
The Problem of Properties in Quantum Mechanics. BUB, Jeffrey.
Property in Science and the Market. O'NEILL, John.
Property Rights and Preservationist Duties. GOODIN, Robert E.
Property, Entitlement, and Remedy. PAUL, Jeffrey.
Qualities and Qualia: What's in the Mind?. SHOEMAKER, Sydney.
Relevant Predication 2: Intrinsic Properties and Internal Relations. DUNN, J Michael.
Reply to Shearmur's "From Dialogue Rights to Property Rights". MICHELMAN, Frank.
Response to Diamond. MC NAUGHTON, David.
Response to McNaughton. DIAMOND, Cora.
Ruben and the Metaphysics of the Social World. TUOMELA, Raimo.
Self-Ownership and the Right of Property. MACK, Eric.
Self-Ownership, Equality, and the Structure of Property Rights. CHRISTMAN, John.
A Short Vindication of Reichenbach's "Event-Splitting". PFEIFER, Karl.
Some Problems of Legal Language. KNAPP, Viktor.
Substances and Space-Time: What Aristotle Would Have Said to Einstein. MAUDLIN, Tim.
Taxonomies of Model-Theoretically Defined Topological Properties. BANKSTON, Paul.
Trade Secrets and the Justification of Intellectual Property: A Comment on Hettinger. PAINE, Lynn Sharp.
The Trouble with Fragrance. ELLIS, John.
Tully's Locke. DEN HARTOGH, Govert.
What are Discernible?. SCHLESINGER, George N.
When is Original Appropriation *Required*?. SCHMIDTZ, David.
The World Essence. BIGELOW, John.

PROPHET(S)

The Foxy Prophet: Machiavelli versus Machiavelli on Ferdinand the Catholic. ANDREW, Edward.

PROPORTION

Osservazioni sul *Filebo*. MASI, Giuseppe.

PROPORTIONALITY

The Making of a Nuclear Peace: The Task of Today's Just War Theorists. SICHOL, Marcia W.
Private Defense. GORR, Michael.

PROPOSITION(S)

see also Sentence(s), Statement(s)
After Principles. BARDEN, Garrett.
Meaning and Speech Acts: Volume I, Principles of Language Use. VANDERVEKEN, Daniel.
Meaning and Speech Acts: Volume II, Formal Semantics of Success and Satisfaction. VANDERVEKEN, Daniel.
The Metaphysics of the "Tractatus". CARRUTHERS, Peter.
Philosophical Essays. CARTWRIGHT, Richard.
Representing and Reasoning With Probabilistic Knowledge: A Logical Approach to Probabilities. BACCHUS, Fahiem.
"Tense and Singular Propositions" in *Themes From Kaplan*, SALMON, Nathan.
"Time and Thisness" in *Themes From Kaplan*, ADAMS, Robert Merrihew.
"Why Singular Propositions?" in *Themes From Kaplan*, CHISHOLM, Roderick M.
An Alleged Analogy Between Numbers and Propositions. CRANE, Tim.
Could This Be Magic?. JUBIEN, Michael.
From What Can't Be Said To What Isn't Known. MC KINNON, Christine.
How *Not* to Become a Millian Heir. SALMON, Nathan.
Intensional Paradoxes. PRIEST, Graham.
The Meaning of Meaning. HELLER, Michael.
Mr Keynes on Probability. RAMSEY, F P.
Myself. WILLIAMS, C J F.
A New Interpretation of Russell's Multiple-Relation Theory of Judgment. LANDINI, Gregory.
Not Very Likely: A Reply to Ramsey. WATT, D E.
On 'This is Red and This is Blue': *Tractatus* 6.3751. SAHU, Neelamani.
On Some Logically Equivalent Propositions. KELLY, Charles J.
Perceptual Content in the Stoics. SORABJI, Richard.
Process Vagueness. SORENSEN, Roy A.
Propositional Functions and Families of Types. SMITH, Jan M.
Propositional Relevance. BOWLES, George.
Reflexiones en torno a la oración oblicua. MUÑOZ, Angel and CAROSIO, Alba.
Regressive Partition Relations, *n*-Subtle Cardinals, and Borel Diagonalization. KANAMORI, Akihiro.
Salmon on the A Priori. BERTOLET, Rod.
La simplicidad en el *Tractatus*. ANSCOMBE, G E M.
Sobre la no paradoja de un cretense. WILSON, Jack L.
Time and Propositions. SMITH, Quentin.
Verisimilitude by Power Relations: A Response to Oddie. BRINK, Chris and HEIDEMA, Johannes.

PROPOSITIONAL ATTITUDES

Propositional Attitudes: The Role of Content in Logic, Language, and Mind. ANDERSON, C Anthony (ed).
Pulling up the Ladder: The Metaphysical Roots of Wittgenstein's Tractatus. BROCKHAUS, Richard R.
"Direct Reference and Propositional Attitudes" in *Themes From Kaplan*, SOAMES, Scott.
"On Some Thought Experiments about Mind and Meaning" in *Propositional Attitudes: The Role of Content in Logic, Language, and Mind*, WALLACE, John and MASON, H E.
"Physicalism" in *Philosophical Perspectives, 4: Action Theory and Philosophy of Mind, 1990*, SCHIFFER, Stephen.
"Singular Propositions, Abstract Constituents, and Propositional Attitudes" in *Themes From Kaplan*, ZALTA, Edward N.
"A Study in Comparative Semantics" in *Propositional Attitudes: The Role of Content in Logic, Language, and Mind*, LE PORE, Ernest and LOEWER, Barry.
The Definition of 'Art'. ROWE, M W.
Making Sense of Words. MC CULLOCH, Gregory.
Mental Misrepresentation. MALONEY, J Christopher.
On the Propositional Attitudes. COLEMAN, Keith.
Pronouns and Propositional Attitudes. SOAMES, Scott.
Wanting, Getting, Having. HUMBERSTONE, I L.

PROPOSITIONAL FUNCTION(S)

Is There More to Speech Acts Than Illocutionary Force and Propositional Content?. HAJDIN, Mane.

PROPOSITIONAL LOGIC

Axiomatization of the De Morgan Type Rules. HERRMANN, B.
Complementary Sentential Logics. VARZI, Achille C.
Formalization of Functionally Complete Propositional Calculus with the Functor of Implication.... LEJEWSKI, Czeslaw.
Intuitionistic Sentential Calculus with Classical Identity. LUKOWSKI, Piotr.
Linear Axiomatics of Communicative Product-Free Lambek Calculus. ZIELONKA, Wojciech.
Mojzesz Presburger: Life and Work. ZYGMUNT, Jan.
A Note on Some Property of Purely Implicational Proportional Calculi. PRUCNAL, Tadeuss.
On Certain Normalizable Natural Deduction Formulations of Some Propositional Intermediate Logics. BORICIC, Branislav R.
On Pure Refutation Formulations of Sentential Logics. SKURA, Tomasz.
On the Existence of Polynomial Time Algorithms for Interpolation Problems in Propositional Logic. DALHAUS, E and ISRAELI, A and MAKOWSKY, J A.
A Priority and Ways of Grasping a Proposition. WONG, Kai-Yee.
Problems of Substitution and Admissibility in the Modal System Grz and in Intuitionistic Propositional Calculus. RYBAKOV, V V.
Propositional Consistency Proofs. BUSS, S R.
The Simple Substitution Property of Gödel's Intermediate Propositional Logics S_n's. SASAKI, Katsumi.
Lo sviluppo degli studi logici nel pensiero tedesco della seconda metà dell'800. MANGIAGALLI, Maurizio.

PROSTITUTION

Santo Tomás y la prostitución. PONFERRADA, Gustavo E.

PROTAGORAS

Aristotle and Protagoras: The Good Human Being as the Measure of Goods. GOTTLIEB, Paula.

PROTECTION

Computers, Personal Data, and Theories of Technology: Comparative Approaches to Privacy Protection in the 1990s. BENNETT, Colin J.
Protective Norms as a Basis for Cooperation between Non-Privileged Constituencies. HEDMAN, Carl.

PROTESTANT

Heidegger: vita e distino—Sullo biografia heideggeriana di Hugo Ott. ESPOSITO, Costantino.

PROTESTANTISM
"Conceptions of Peace" in *Celebrating Peace*, RENDTORFF, Trutz.
Two Aspects of the Christian-Marxist Dialogue: A Protestant Response. FRITZSCHE, Helmut.
Why Should a Dialectician Learn to Count to Four?. ZIZEK, Slavoj.

PROTOCOL(S)
The Problem of Protocol Statements and Schlick's Concept of 'Konstatierungen'. ZHAI, Zhenming.

PROTOTYPE(S)
"Concepts, Prototypes and Information" in *Information, Semantics and Epistemology*, GRANDY, Richard E.
Note on the Integration of Prototype Theory and Fuzzy-Set Theory. FUHRMANN, G.

PROUST
Proust: The Creative Silence. CARANFA, Angelo.
"Literature and Philosophy at the Crossroads: Proustian Subjects" in *Writing the Politics of Difference*, MC DONALD, Christie.
Nature et fonction de la Mémoire dans À la recherche du temps perdu. ZÉPHIR, Jacques J.

PROVABILITY
The Agnostic Fallacy. KEENE, G B.
Decidable and Enumerable Predicate Logics of Provability. DZHAPARIDZE, Giorgie.
Definability Theorems in Normal Extensions of the Provability Logic. MAKSIMOVA, Larisa L.
Derivability Conditions on Rosser's Provability Predicates. ARAI, Toshiyasu.
Exponentiation and Second-Order Bounded Arithmetic. KRAJICEK, Jan.
Henkin's Completeness Proof: Forty Years Later. LEBLANC, Hugues and ROEPER, Peter and THAU, Michael and WEAVER, George.
The Interpretability Logic of Peano Arithmetic. BERARDUCCI, Alessandro.
Logical Equations and Admissible Rules of Inference with Parameters in Modal Provability Logics. RYBAKOV, V V.
The Modal Logic of Pure Provability. BUSS, Samuel R.
A Note on Some Extension Results. MONTAGNA, Franco and SOMMARUGA, Giovanni.
A Unification-Theoretic Method for Investigating the *k*-Provability Problem. FARMER, William.

PROVIDENCE
Providence and Political Responsibility: The Nature of Praxis in an Age of Apocalypse. LAKELAND, Paul.
Providence, Freedom and Human Destiny. TALBOTT, Thomas.

PROXIMITY
Moraliteit en magie. LESAGE, Dieter.

PRUDENCE
"Prudence as the Cornerstone of the Contemporary Thomistic Philosophy of Freedom" in *Freedom in the Modern World: Jacques Maritain, Yves R Simon, Mortimer J Adler*, MAHONEY, Marianne.
Hare on Prudence. RABINOWICZ, Wlodzimierz.
Of One Mind or Two? Query on the Innate Good in Mencius. LAI, Whalen.
Prudence and Past Preferences; Reply to Wlodizimierz Rabinowicz. HARE, R M.
Prudence and Providence: On Hobbes's Theory of Practical Reason. HANCE, Allen S.
Prudence: Aristotelian Perspectives on Practical Reason. HASLAM, Nick.
La prudencia (II). DERISI, Octavio N.

PSYCHIATRY
Moral Theory and Medical Practice. FULFORD, K W M.
New Harvest: Transplanting Body Parts and Reaping the Benefits. KEYES, C Don (ed).
Readings in Existential Psychology and Psychiatry. HOELLER, Keith (ed).
"Closing Up the Corpses: Diseases of Sexuality and the Emergence of the Psychiatric Style of Reasoning" in *Meaning and Method: Essays in Honor of Hilary Putnam*, DAVIDSON, Arnold I.
"Psychiatry as Scientific Humanism: A Program Inspired by Roberto Unger's *Passion*" in *Critique and Construction: A Symposium on Roberto Unger's "Politics"*, HOBSON, J Allan.
China's Importation of Western Psychiatry: Cultural Relativity and Mental Disorders. WOO, Deborah.
Dementia Praecox as a Failure of Neoteny. BEMPORAD, Jules R.
F M Dostoievsky (1821-1881): Great Existentialist-Psychiatrist. ESSER, P H.
Institutional Mental Health and Social Control: The Ravages of Epistemological Hubris. FARBER, Seth.
Law and Psychiatry: The Problems That Will Not Go Away. SZASZ, Thomas.
The Matrix of Personality: A Whiteheadian Corroboration of Harry Stack Sullivan's Interpersonal Theory of Psychiatry. REGAN, Thomas J.
Moral Responsibility, Psychiatric Disorders and Duress. ELLIOTT, Carl.
Psychiatry, Religious Conversion, and Medical Ethics. POST, Stephen G.
Psychoactive Drug Prescribing in Japan: Epistemological and Bioethical Considerations. SAKAI, Akio.
A Response to 'Psychoactive Drug Prescribing in Japan'. COVERDALE, John.
Response to Dr Sakai's 'Psychoactive Drug Prescribing in Japan'. RITCHIE, Karen.
Some Philosophical Directions Towards a Simple Theory of the Self. MANN, David W.
Subjective Boundaries and Combinations in Psychiatric Diagnoses. MIROWSKY, John.
Thoughts and Feelings and Things: A New Psychiatric Epistemology. HUNDERT, Edward M.
Toward the Obsolescence of the Schizophrenia Hypothesis. SARBIN, Theodore R.

PSYCHICAL DISTANCE
Edward Bullogh's Aesthetics and Aestheticism: Features of Reality to Be Experienced. BOULTING, Noel E.

PSYCHICALISM
The Idea of the Miraculous: The Challenge to Science and Religion. WILLIAMS, T C.

PSYCHOANALYSIS
Bertrand Russell: The Psychobiography of a Moralist. BRINK, Andrew.
Creative Characters. YOUNG-BRUEHL, Elisabeth.
Dialogue with the Other: The Inter-Religious Dialogue. TRACY, David.
French Philosophers in Conversation: Levinas, Schneider, Serres, Irigaray, Le Doeuff, Derrida. MORTLEY, Raoul.
From Sentience To Symbols. PICKERING, John (ed).
The Kernel of Truth in Freud. LAWTON, Philip.
New Reflections on the Revolution of Our Time. LACLAU, Ernesto.
Patterns of Dissonance. BRAIDOTTI, Rosi.
Psychoanalysis, Scientific Method, and Philosophy. HOOK, Sidney (ed).
Selbsttäuschung. LÖW-BEER, Martin.
Teoria e interpretazione: Per un'epistemologia delle scienze umane. BORUTTI, Silvana.
Thinking the Unthinkable: Meanings of the Holocaust. GOTTLIEB, Roger S (ed).
"Gender Trouble, Feminist Theory, and Psychoanalytic Discourse" in *Feminism/Postmodernism*, BUTLER, Judith.
"Life-World as Depth of Soul: Phenomenology and Psychoanalysis" in *Reconsidering Psychology: Perspectives from Continental Philosophy*, ROMANYSHYN, Robert.
"The Psychoanalytic Enterprise in Scientific Perspective" in *Scientific Theories*, GRÜNBAUM, Adolf.
"Who Suffers?" in *Re-Reading Levinas*, O'CONNOR, Noreen.
The "Tally Argument" and the Validation of Psychoanalysis. RICHARDSON, Robert C.
'Inference to the Best Explanation' of 'Inference to the Best Interpretation'? Een antwoord op Derksens ..... MOOIJ, A W M.
A Contribution to the Early History of Psychoanalysis (in Serbo-Croatian). MACHO, Thomas H.
El ateísmo Freudeano. MARLASCA, Antonio.
Comments on Freud and Wittgenstein, and on Adolf Grünbaum's "Foundations of Psychoanalysis". FISCHER, Kurt Rudolf.
Un confronto sempre attuale: Leggendo—A Lambertino, Psicoanalisi e morale in Freud. DOVOLICH, Claudia.
The Crisis in Psychoanalysis: Resolution Through Husserlian Phenomenology and Feminism. NISSIM-SABAT, Marilyn.
Culpabilidad, rito y ritualismo: Una aproprimación psicoanalítica. RODRIGUEZ AMENABAR, S M.
The Degeneration of Popper's Theory of Demarcation. GRÜNBAUM, Adolf.
Freud and the Question of Truth (in Serbo-Croatian). GÖRLICH, Bernard.
Heidegger and Psychoanalysis: The Seminars in Zollikon. SCOTT, Charles E.
Kristeva and Holbein, Artist of Melancholy. LECHTE, John.
L'écriture réparatrice. HAREL, Simon.
Phenomenology and Psychoanalysis: The Hermeneutical Mediation. RAJAN, R Sundara.
Psychanalyse et existentialisme: A propos de la théorie lacanienne de la subjectivité. VAN HAUTE, P.
Psychoanalysis: A Form of Life?. BREARLEY, Michael.
Psychoanalysis: Acceptance and Overcoming of the Philosophical Heritage (in Serbo-Croatian). JOVANOVIC, Gordana.
Super-yo y vida moral: Una valoración tomista de la hipótesis psicoanalítica. PITHOD, Abelardo.
Truth in Interpretation: The Case of Psychoanalysis. ROTH, Paul A.
Wittgenstein on Freud's 'Abominable Mess'. CIOFFI, Frank.

PSYCHOEPISTEMOLOGY
Epistemology as Hypothesis. PUTNAM, Hilary and PUTNAM, Ruth Anna.

PSYCHOKINESIS
The Limits of Influence: Psychokinesis and the Philosophy of Science. BRAUDE, Stephen E (ed).

PSYCHOLIGISM
Whewell's Developmental Psychologism: A Victorian Account of Scientific Progress. METCALFE, John F.

PSYCHOLINGUISTICS
On the Locus of Medical Discovery. REINES, Brandon P.

PSYCHOLOGICAL EGOISM
"Evolutionary Altruism and Psychological Egoism" in *Logic, Methodology and Philosophy of Science, VIII*, SOBER, Elliott.

PSYCHOLOGICAL EGOISM
A Different Different Voice: On the Feminist Challenge in Moral Theory. ROONEY, Phyllis.

PSYCHOLOGISM
Pulling up the Ladder: The Metaphysical Roots of Wittgenstein's Tractatus. BROCKHAUS, Richard R.
"Frege and Popper: Two Critics of Psychologism" in *Imre Lakatos and Theories of Scientific Change*, CURRIE, G.
Husserl and Hume: Overcrowding Scepticism?. MURPHY, Richard T.
Metaphysical Realism and Psychologistic Semantics. HORGAN, Terence.
Psychologism Reconsidered. AACH, John.

PSYCHOLOGY
see also Behaviorism, Psychiatry, Psychoanalysis
Archetypal Process: Self and Divine in Whitehead, Jung, and Hillman. GRIFFIN, David Ray (ed).
Aristotle's Psychology. ROBINSON, Daniel N.
Dämonie und Gesellschaft. CATTEPOEL, Jan.
Existence et Subjectivité: Études de Psychologie Phénoménologique. THINÈS, Georges.
Explaining Human Action. LENNON, Kathleen.
Foundations of Cognitive Science: The Essential Readings. GARFIELD, Jay L.
The Fragmentation of Reason. STICH, Stephen.
From Sentience To Symbols. PICKERING, John (ed).
Inference and Understanding: A Philosophical and Psychological Perspective. MANKTELOW, K I.
Intentions in Communication. COHEN, Philip R (ed).
Kant's Transcendental Psychology. KITCHER, Patricia.
Kommunikations-Theoretische Schriften II: Symbolische Erkenntnis und Kommunikation. UNGEHEUER, Gerold (ed).
Logic in the Husserlian Context. TITO, Johanna Maria.
The Many Dimensions of the Human Person. STEGER, E Ecker.
Metaphors of Mind: Conceptions of the Nature of Intelligence. STERNBERG, Robert J.
Michel Foucault's Force of Flight: Towards an Ethics for Thought. BERNAUER, James W.
Mimesis as Make-Believe: On the Foundations of the Representational Arts. WALTON, Kendall L.
Mind in Action: Essays in the Philosophy of Mind. RORTY, Amelie Oksenberg.
The Moral Domain: Essays in the Ongoing Discussion between Philosophy and the Social Sciences. WREN, Thomas E (ed).
The Natural and the Normative: Theories of Spatial Perception from Kant to Helmholtz. HATFIELD, Gary.
Psychology (Companions to Ancient Thought: 2). EVERSON, Stephen (ed).
Readings in Existential Psychology and Psychiatry. HOELLER, Keith (ed).
Reconsidering Psychology: Perspectives from Continental Philosophy. FAULCONER, James E (ed).
The Science of the Mind (Second Edition). FLANAGAN, Owen.
Selbsttäuschung. LÖW-BEER, Martin.
Strukturanthropologie "Der menschliche Mensch". ROMBACH, Heinrich.
Varieties of Moral Personality: Ethics and Psychological Realism. FLANAGAN, Owen.
Wisdom: Its Nature, Origins, and Development. STERNBERG, Robert J.
Works of Love? Reflections on "Works of Love". FENDT, Gene.
The World of the Imagination: Sum and Substance. BRANN, Eva T H.
"Back to Beyond: On Cosmology" in *Archetypal Process: Self and Divine in Whitehead, Jung, and Hillman*, HILLMAN, James.
"Beyond Freud and Piaget: Biographical Worlds—Interpersonal Self" in *The Moral Domain: Essays in the Ongoing Discussion between Philosophy and the Social Sciences*, NOAM, Gil G.
"Effective Epistemology, Psychology, and Artificial Intelligence" in *Acting and Reflecting: The Interdisciplinary Turn in Philosophy*, KELLY, Kevin.
"Experience of the Other: Between Appropriation and Disappropriation" in *Life-World and Politics: Between Modernity and Postmodernity*, WALDENFELS, Bernhard.
"Explanation and Understanding in the Science of Human Behavior" in *Reconsidering Psychology: Perspectives from Continental Philosophy*, SCHRAG, Calvin O.
"Heidegger and Psychological Explanation: Taking Account of Derrida" in *Reconsidering Psychology: Perspectives from Continental Philosophy*, FAULCONER, James E.
"How Should Psychologists Define Morality? or, The Negative Side Effects of Philosophy's Influence on Psychology" in *The Moral Domain: Essays in the Ongoing Discussion between Philosophy and the Social Sciences*, BLASI, Augusto.
"Introduction: Archetypal Psychology and Process Philosophy" in *Archetypal Process: Self and Divine in Whitehead, Jung, and Hillman*, GRIFFIN, David Ray.
"Joining the Resistance: Psychology, Politics, Girls, and Women" in *The Tanner Lectures On Human Values, Volume XII*, GILLIGAN, Carol.
"The Metaphysic of Things and Discourse About Them" in *Reconsidering Psychology: Perspectives from Continental Philosophy*, WILLIAMS, Richard N.
"A Metaphysical Psychology to Un-Locke Our Ailing World" in *Archetypal Process: Self and Divine in Whitehead, Jung, and Hillman*, GRIFFIN, David Ray.
"Morality and Psychological Development" in *A Companion to Ethics*, THOMAS, Laurence.
"Psychocosmetics and the Underworld Connection" in *Archetypal Process: Self and Divine in Whitehead, Jung, and Hillman*, KELLER, Catherine.
"Psychocosmetics: A Jungian Response" in *Archetypal Process: Self and Divine in Whitehead, Jung, and Hillman*, MOORE, Robert L.
"Psychology after Philosophy" in *Reconsidering Psychology: Perspectives from Continental Philosophy*, POLKINGHORNE, Donald.
"Reconnecting: A Reply to Robert Moore" in *Archetypal Process: Self and Divine in Whitehead, Jung, and Hillman*, KELLER, Catherine.
"Reconsidering Psychology" in *Reconsidering Psychology: Perspectives from Continental Philosophy*, FAULCONER, James E and WILLIAMS, Richard N.
"Responses" in *Archetypal Process: Self and Divine in Whitehead, Jung, and Hillman*, HILLMAN, James.
"A Riposte" in *Archetypal Process: Self and Divine in Whitehead, Jung, and Hillman*, HEISIG, James W.
"Some Reflections on Empirical Psychology: Toward an Interpretive Psychology" in *Reconsidering Psychology: Perspectives from Continental Philosophy*, KOCKELMANS, Joseph J.
"Non-Scientific Realism" about Propositional Attitudes as a Response to Eliminativist Arguments. HANNAN, Barbara.
"Phénoménologie" de l'expression. CHAUVIRE, Christiane.
'Desire' in Yoga and Jung. COWARD, Harold.
A Phenomenologically and Psychologically Based Concept of Ethics (in Czechoslovakian). BAYEROVA, M.
Against Logicist Cognitive Science. OAKSFORD, Mike and CHATER, Nick.
Aktuelle Aufgaben interdisziplinärer Bedürfnisforschung aus psychologischer Sicht. WOLF, Edith.
Al-Kindi's Psychology (in Hebrew). SCHWARZ, Dov.
Already Punished Enough. HUSAK, Douglas N.
Anti-Individualism and Privileged Access. MC KINSEY, Michael.
Behavioral Paradigm for a Psychological Resolution of the Free Will Issue. HARCUM, E Rae.
Biology and the Social Sciences. WILSON, Edward O.
Causal Holism and Commonsense Psychology: A Reply to O'Brien. STICH, Stephen P.
Ceteris Paribus Laws. SCHIFFER, Stephen.
Churchland and the Talking Brain. MUKHERJI, Nirmalangshu.
Condiciones del surgimiento y desarrollo de la Psicología Humanista. CARPINTERO, Helio and MAYOR, Luis and ZALBIDEA, M A.
Consciousness for the Twenty-First Century. CSIKSZENTMIHALYI, Mihaly.
Contagious Folly: *An Adventure* and Its Skeptics. CASTLE, Terry.
Deinstitutionalization: Cycles of Despair. SCULL, Andrew.
The Development of Moral Reasoning and the Foundations of Geometry. MACNAMARA, John.
The Development of Otto's Thought 1898-1917. MINNEY, Robin.
Discourse: Definitions and Contradictions. PARKER, Ian.
Discourse: Noun, Verb or Social Practice?. POTTER, Jonathan (and others).
The Dynamics of Concepts and Non-local Interactions. VAN LOOCKE, Philip R.
Eléments pour une "philosophie de la psychologie". PETIT, Jean-Luc.
Empirical and Philosophical Reactions to Harcum's "Behavioral Paradigm for a Psychological Resolution of ...". POLLIO, Howard R and HENLEY, Tracy.
Enlightenment Psychology and Political Reaction in Plato's Social Philosophy: an Ideological Contradiction?. BRYANT, Joseph M.
Envy and Jealousy. BEN-ZEEV, Aaron.
Epistemic Justification and Psychological Realism. TAYLOR, James E.
Foucault et la psychothérapie. DREYFUS, Hubert L.
From Brahma to a Blade of Grass. COLLINS, Alfred.
Heideggers Bedeutung für die Psychologie. VON USLAR, Detlev.
If Children thought Like Adults. GAUKER, Christopher.
Institutional Mental Health and Social Control: The Ravages of Epistemological Hubris. FARBER, Seth.
Intentionality and Modern Philosophical Psychology, I: The Modern Reduction of Intentionality. LYONS, William.
Intentionality and Modern Philosophical Psychology—II: The Return to Representation. LYONS, Willia.
Intentionality and the Ecological Approach. LOOREN DE JONG, H.
Interdisciplinary Epistemology. BODEN, Margaret A.
Is Connectionism Commonsense?. O'BRIEN, Gerard J.
Is History and Philosophy of Science Withering on the Vine?. FULLER, Steve W.
James and Freud. MYERS, Gerald E.
Kant's Psychological Hedonism. GRIFFITHS, A Phillips.
L'ontogenèse de l'individu: ses aspects scientifiques et philosophiques. BERNIER, Réjane.
Lewis's Functionalism and Reductive Materialism. KERNOHAN, Andrew.
Love, Friendship, and the Aesthetics of Character. NOVITZ, David.
The Meaning of Mathematical Expressions: Does Philosophy Shed Any Light on Psychology?. ERNEST, Paul.

PSYCHOLOGY
Must Psychology Be Individualistic?. EGAN, Frances.
The Nature of a Person-Stage. MC INERNEY, Peter K.
A New Theory of the Relationship of Mind and Matter. BOHM, David.
Nietzsche and Pessimism: The Metaphysics Hypostatised. CAUCHI, Francesca.
Nonautonomous Psychology. PETRIE, Bradford.
Nota sobre la causalidad apotética a la escala psicológica. FUENTES ORTEGA, Juan Bautista.
Object-Dependent Thoughts and Psychological Redundancy. NOONAN, Harold W.
On Bureaucracy and Science: A Response to Fuller. TWENEY, Ryan D.
El paradigma computacional aplicado al estudio de la vida. GUTIÉRREZ, Claudio.
Parity for the Theoretical Ghosts and Gremlins: Response to Pollio/Henley and Rychlak. HARCUM, E Rae.
Philosophical and Religious Implications of Cognitive Social Learning Theories of Personality. ROTTSCHAEFER, William A.
The Philosophical Significance of Psychological Differences Among Humans. LACHS, John.
Physicalism and Intentional Attitudes. MOSER, Paul K.
The Political Economy of Tardive Dyskinesia: Asymmetries in Power and Responsibility. COHEN, David and MC CUBBIN, Michael.
Postcritical Religion and the Latent Freud. KEISER, R Melvin.
The Problem of Who: Multiple Personality, Personal Identity and the Double Brain. APTER, Andrew.
Problema psicofísico y realidad cuántica en la física heterodoxa de David Bohm. MONSERRAT, Javier.
Prudence: Aristotelian Perspectives on Practical Reason. HASLAM, Nick.
La psychologie de 1850 à 1950. FOUCAULT, Michel.
Psychologism Reconsidered. AACH, John.
Psychology and Controversy. AGASSI, Joseph.
Psychology and Standards of Reasonable Expectation. SCHOEMAN, Ferdinand.
Der psychophysische Materialismus in der Perspektive Kants und Wittgensteins. MENDONÇA, W P.
Rational Choice Theory Considered as Psychology and Moral Philosophy. MONGIN, Philippe.
The Rationality of Escapism and Self Deception. LONGEWAY, John L.
Religion and Cultural Evolution. MASSIMINI, Fausto and FAVE, Antonella Delle.
The Role of Homunculi in Psychology. WARD, Andrew.
Social Movements and Individual Identity: A Critique of Freud on the Psychology of Groups. WARTENBERG, Thomas E.
Some Theoretical and Methodological Questions Concerning Harcum's Proposed Resolution of the Free Will Issue. RYCHLAK, Joseph F.
Staving Off Catastrophe: A Critical Notice of Jerry Fodor's *Psychosemantics*. JONES, Todd and MULAIRE, Edmond and STICH, Stephen.
Stereotypes and Group-Claims. HARVEY, J.
The Tensions Between Education and Development. GARDNER, Howard.
The Enticing Thing About Stalinism (in German). PÄTZOLT, Harald.
The Functional Conception of Culture and the Explanation of the Value-Shaping Process (in Polish). BROZI, Krzysztof J.
Therapeutic Professions and the Diffusion of Deficit. GERGEN, Kenneth J.
Thoughts and Theses on Causality. TILANDER, A.
Twenty Years Since *Women and Madness*: Toward a Feminist Institute of Mental Health and Healing. CHESLER, Phyllis.
Two Souls in One Body. HACKING, Ian.
Where Does the Self-Refutation Objection Take Us?. RAMSEY, William.
Why not Naturalistic Psychology?. GARRETT, Richard and GRAHAM, George.
Why Shouldn't We Be Able to Solve the Mind-Body Problem?. KIRK, Robert.
Wittgenstein and Psychology. SHOTTER, John.
Wittgenstein, eskimo's en emoties. POTT, Heleen.
You Can Fool Some of the People All of the Time, Everything Else Being Equal; Hedged Laws and Psychological Explanation. FODOR, Jerry A.

PSYCHOTHERAPY
Encounter on the Narrow Ridge: A Life of Martin Buber. FRIEDMAN, Maurice.
Intelligibility in Science. DILWORTH, Craig (ed).
Readings in Existential Psychology and Psychiatry. HOELLER, Keith (ed).
Foucault et la psychothérapie. DREYFUS, Hubert L.
The Futility of Psychotherapy. ALBEE, George W.

PTOLEMY
Methods and Problems in Greek Science: Selected Papers. LLOYD, G E R.

PUBLIC
Kierkegaard in Golden Age Denmark. KIRMMSE, Bruce H.
"Excellence, Equity, and Equality" Clarified. GREEN, Thomas F.
From Propaganda to "Oeffentlichkeit" in Eastern Europe: Four Models of the Public Space Under State Socialism. SUKOSD, Miklos.
Philosophy, Education, and Public Practice. GIARELLI, James M.
The Priority of Excellence Reconsidered. BULL, Barry L.
Public and Private Morality. SHAIDA, S A.
The Unbearable Seriousness of Irony. FERRARA, Alessandro.

PUBLIC GOOD
The Limits of Government: An Essay on the Public Goods Arguments. SCHMIDTZ, David.
Government and Character. PINCOFFS, Edmund L.

PUBLIC HARM
La Querelle de la Moralité du Théâtre au XVIIe Siècle. FUMAROLI, M Marc.

PUBLIC HEALTH
Commentary: "Love Canal and the Ethics of Environmental Health". FESSENDEN-RADEN, June and BROWN JR, Stuart M.
Love Canal and the Ethics of Environmental Health. BRUMMER, James.

PUBLIC INTEREST(S)
Public Discourse in the Development of Educational Policy. CURREN, Randall R.

PUBLIC OFFICIAL(S)
Toward a Theory of Bribery. DANLEY, John R.

PUBLIC OPINION
Political Theory in the Welfare State. LUHMANN, Niklas.
Ethical Considerations Regarding Public Opinion Polling During Election Campaigns. MICHALOS, Alex C.
No Time for an AIDS Backlash. MURPHY, Timothy F.

PUBLIC POLICY(-CIES)
Foundations of Moral and Political Philosophy. PAUL, Ellen Frankel (ed).
Theories of Science in Society. COZZENS, Susan E (ed).
"Essential Ethical Considerations for Public Policy on Assisted Reproduction" in *Beyond Baby M: Ethical Issues in New Reproductive Techniques*, TAUER, Carol.
Affirmative Action Revisited: Justice and Public Policy Considerations. VANTERPOOL, Rudolph V.
Consensus in Panels and Committees: Conceptual and Ethical Issues. VEATCH, Robert M and MORENO, Jonathan D.
Consensus of Expertise: The Role of Consensus of Experts in Formulating Public Policy and Estimating Facts. VEATCH, Robert M.
Deinstitutionalization: Cycles of Despair. SCULL, Andrew.
Equal Educational Opportunity as a Public Policy. BUNTING, I A.
Ethics and Advocacy in Forecasting for Public Policy. WACHS, Martin.
Ethics, Public Policy, and Human Fetal Tissue Transplantation. CHILDRESS, James F.
Ethics, Public Policy, and Managing Advanced Technologies: The Case of Electronic Surveillance. OTTENSMEYER, Edward J and HEROUX, Mark A.
The Oregon Priority-Setting Exercise: Quality of Life and Public Policy. HADORN, David C.

PUBLIC RELATIONS
Constrained Discourse and Public Life. MOON, J Donald.
Public Relations: The Empiricial Research on Practitioner Ethics. PRATT, Cornelius B.

PUBLICATION(S)
Continuity and Diversity in Philosophy of Education: An Introduction. BURBULES, Nicholas C.
Moraliteiten: Recente ethische publikaties in Vlaanderen en Nederland. STRUYKER BOUDIER, C E M.
MYSL' and the Intuitivist Debate in the Early 1920s. NETHERCOTT, Frances.
Recent Canadian Work on Wittgenstein: 1980-1989. WILLIAMSON, George.

PUBLICITY
Television and the Crisis of Democracy. KELLNER, Douglas.
"The Role of Publicity in the Disintegration of the Hegelian School" in *Perspectives on Ideas and Reality*, SZÍVÓS, Mihály.

PUFENDORF
Natuur en cultuur: de heuristische waarde van een dichotomie. WESTERMAN, Pauline.

PUNCTUATION
Logical Constants as Punctuation Marks. DOSEN, Kosta.

PUNISHMENT
Liability and Responsibility. FREY, R G (ed).
The Limits of Government: An Essay on the Public Goods Arguments. SCHMIDTZ, David.
Die moderne Gesellschaft im Rechtsstaat. BAURMANN, Michael.
Moral Pluralism and Legal Neutrality. SADURSKI, Wojciech.
Philosophy of Law (Fourth Edition). FEINBERG, Joel.
Theories of Criminal Justice: A Critical Reappraisal. ELLIS, Ralph D.
"Crime and Punishment" in *A Companion to Ethics*, TEN, C L.
"A New Theory of Retribution" in *Liability and Responsibility*, HAMPTON, Jean.
"Punishment and Self-Defense" in *Liability and Responsibility*, FLETCHER, George P.
Already Punished Enough. HUSAK, Douglas N.
Davis and the Unfair-Advantage Theory of Punishment: A Critique. SCHEID, Don E.

PUNISHMENT
Discretion, Punishment, and Juvenile Justice. SCHRAG, Francis.
Hume on Responsibility and Punishment. RUSSELL, Paul.
John Stuart Mill über die Todesstrafe. WOLF, Jean-Claude.
Punishment and Loss of Moral Standing. MORRIS, Christopher W.
Punishment and the Utilitarian Criterion of Right and Wrong. SCHALLER, Walter E.
The Punishment of Attempts. NUYEN, A T.
A Rational Choice Theory of Punishment. STERBA, James P.
Retaliatory Punishment as a Categorical Imperative. HÖFFE, Ottfried.
Rethinking the Diodotean Argument. JOHNSON, Laurie M.
Reward, Punishment, and the Strategy of Evolution. SCHRADER, Malcolm E.
Schopenhauers Straftheorie und die aktuelle Strafzweckdiskussion. KÜPPER, Georg.
Treatment and Rehabilitation as a Mode of Punishment. MARTIN, Rex.
Using the Market to Measure Deserved Punishment. DAVIS, Michael.
Utilitarianism and the 'Punishment' of the Innocent: The General Problem. SMILANSKY, Saul.

PURIFICATION
Imitación y purificación en la estética de Aristóteles. CAPPELLETTI, Angel.

PURITANISM
The Alliance between Puritanism and Cartesian Logic at Harvard, 1687-1735. KENNEDY, Rick.
American Moralism and the Origin of Bioethics in the United States. JONSEN, Albert R.
Animal Faith, Puritanism, and the Schutz-Gurwitsch Debate: A Commentary. LYMAN, Stanford M.

PURITY
Axiology as the Form of Purity of Heart: A Reading Husserliana XXVIII. HART, James G.

PURPOSE(S)
The Philosophy of Money: Georg Simmel (Second Edition). FRISBY, David (ed & trans).
"Mechanism, Purpose, and Explanatory Exclusion" in *Philosophical Perspectives, 3: Philosophy of Mind and Action Theory, 1989*, KIM, Jaegwon.
Liberal Education in an Unfree World. LA BRECQUE, Richard.
Professor Von Wright on Action. DEWASHI, Mahadev.
Struttura e finalità dei dialoghi platonici: Che cosa significa "venire in soccorso al discorso"?. SZLEZÁK, Thomas A.

PURPOSIVENESS
Empiricism and Subjectivity: An Essay on Hume's Theory of Human Nature. BOUNDAS, Constantin V (trans).

PUTNAM, H
Meaning and Method: Essays in Honor of Hilary Putnam. BOOLOS, George (ed).
"Brains Don't Lie: They Don't Even Make Many Mistakes" in *Doubting: Contemporary Perspectives on Skepticism*, TYMOCZKO, Thomas.
"Doing What One Ought to Do" in *Meaning and Method: Essays in Honor of Hilary Putnam*, PUTNAM, Ruth Anna.
"Meanings Just Ain't in the Head" in *Meaning and Method: Essays in Honor of Hilary Putnam*, DEVITT, Michael.
"Perception and Revolution: 'The Princess Casamassima' and the Political Imagination" in *Meaning and Method: Essays in Honor of Hilary Putnam*, NUSSBAUM, Martha C.
All the Difference in the World. CRANE, Tim.
Brains in a Vat, Language and Metalanguage. CASATI, Roberto and DOKIC, Jérome.
Consciousness and Introspective Knowledge. CARLOYE, Jack C.
Contemporary Shapes of Scientific Realism (in Czechoslovakian). PARUSNIKOVA, Zuzana.
Contingentie als uitgangspunt: Het denken van Richard Rorty. GEERTSEMA, H G.
Could I Conceive Being a Brain in a Vat?. COLLIER, John D.
Equivalent Descriptions. BEN-MENAHEM, Yemima.
Farewell to the Tradition: Doing without Metaphysics and Epistemology. NIELSEN, Kai.
Intuitionism and Vagueness. SCHWARTZ, Stephen P and THROOP, William.
Logic, Contradiction and Quantum Theory. SMITH, Joseph Wayne.
Making Noises in Counterpoint or Chorus: Putnam's Rejection of Relativism. JOHNSON, Jeffery L.
On Knowing and Naming. BEARDS, Andrew.
Putnam and Truth (in Serbo-Croatian). JAKIC, Mirko.
Putnam on Kripke's Puzzle. GARRETT, Richard.
Putnam's Moral Objectivism. TIMMONS, Mark.
Putnam's Realism and Relativity: An Uneasy Balance. THROOP, William and DORAN, Katheryn.
The Real Meaning of 'Meaning'. CARTER, Alan.
Uno sguardo sulla filosofia americana contemporanea. CENTRONE, Marino.
What Putnam Should Have Said: An Alternative Reply to Rorty. HARTZ, Carolyn G.
Zu einem "der tiefsten philosophischen Probleme". SIEGWART, Geo.
'Just More Theory': A Manoeuvre in Putnam's Model-Theoretic Argument for Antirealism. TAYLOR, Barry.

PUZZLE(S)
Learning from Lonergan at Eleven. DALY, T V.
On Respecting Puzzles About Belief Ascription (A Reply to Devitt). LYCAN, William G.

PYRRHONISM
"The Objective Appearance of Pyrrhonism" in *Psychology (Companions to Ancient Thought: 2)*, EVERSON, Stephen.
"Pyrrhonism and the Concept of a Common Human Nature in Eighteenth-Century Aesthetic Thought" in *The Question of Humanism: Challenges and Possibilities*, CARDY, Michael.
The Classical Roots of Hume's Skepticism. OLSHEWSKY, Thomas M.
From Pyrrhonism to Post-Modernism. GLIDDEN, David K.
Hume and Pascal: Pyrrhonism versus Nature. MAIA NETO, José R.
Pyrrhonism's Arguments Against Value. MC PHERRAN, Mark L.
Rediscovering Scepticism. BAILEY, Alan.
Scepticism and Relativity. BARNES, Jonathan.

PYTHAGORAS
Pythagoras—The First Animal Rights Philosopher. VIOLIN, Mary Ann.

QUALIA
"Inverted Earth" in *Philosophical Perspectives, 4: Action Theory and Philosophy of Mind, 1990*, BLOCK, Ned.
Functionalism, the Absent Qualia Objection and Eliminativism. AVERILL, Edward Wilson.
Qualia and Theory Reduction: A Criticism of Paul Churchland. BACHRACH, Jay E.
Qualities and Qualia: What's in the Mind?. SHOEMAKER, Sydney.

QUALITY OF LIFE
Ethical Considerations Regarding Public Opinion Polling During Election Campaigns. MICHALOS, Alex C.
Is Happiness Relative?. VEENHOVEN, Ruut.
Measuring the Quality of Life: Why, How and What?. HÄYRY, Matti.
The Oregon Priority-Setting Exercise: Quality of Life and Public Policy. HADORN, David C.
The Significance of a Wish. ACKERMAN, Felicia.

QUALITY(-TIES)
"Are There Aesthetic Qualities?" in *XIth International Congress in Aesthetics, Nottingham 1988*, SOMERVILLE, James.
"Perception and Reality" in *Information, Semantics and Epistemology*, SOSA, Ernest.
"Phenomenal States" in *Philosophical Perspectives, 4: Action Theory and Philosophy of Mind, 1990*, LOAR, Brian.
Descartes on Colour. COTTINGHAM, John.
Dravya, Guna and *Paryāya* in Jaina Thought. SONI, Jayandra.
Mathematical Expressibility, Perceptual Relativity, and Secondary Qualities. PEREBOOM, Derk.
Phenomenal Qualities and the Nontransitivity of Matching. BURGESS, John A.
Qualities and Qualia: What's in the Mind?. SHOEMAKER, Sydney.
Sensory Qualities and 'Homunctionalism': A Review Essay of W G Lycan's *Consciousness*. KOBES, Bernard W.
La teoría de las cualidades sensibles en la *Summula Philosophiae Naturalis* atribuida a Guillermo de Ockham. LARRE, Olga L.

QUANTIFICATION
"Belief, Nominalism, and Quantification" in *Philosophical Perspectives, 4: Action Theory and Philosophy of Mind, 1990*, TOMBERLIN, James E.
"Is Existence What Existential Quantification Expresses?" in *Perspectives on Quine*, ORENSTEIN, Alex.
"The Problem of De Re Modality" in *Themes From Kaplan*, FINE, Kit.
"Quantification, Time, and Necessity" in *Philosophical Applications of Free Logic*, COCCHIARELLA, Nino B.
"Quine on Quantifying In" in *Propositional Attitudes: The Role of Content in Logic, Language, and Mind*, FINE, Kit.
Classes and Attributes in Extended Modal Systems: Proceedings of the Colloquium in Modal and Many Valued Logic. MARCUS, Ruth Barcan.
Conditionals, Quantification, and Strong Mathematical Induction. COHEN, Daniel H.
A Functional Calculus of First Order Based on Strict Implication. MARCUS, Ruth Barcan.
A Generalized Quantifier Logic for Naked Infinitives. VAN DER DOES, Jaap.
The Identity of Individuals in a Strict Functional Calculus of Second Order. MARCUS, Ruth Barcan.
Is Utilitarianism Useless?. HAUSMAN, Daniel M.
Modal Logic. MARCUS, Ruth Barcan.
A Notorious Affair Called Exportation. BURDICK, Howard.
Predication and Physical Law. SCHEIBE, Erhard.
Théories d'algébres de Boole munies d'idéaux distingués, II. TOURAILLE, Alain.

QUANTIFIER(S)
Actuality and Quantification. HAZEN, Allen.

QUANTIFIER(S)
Aristotelian Syllogisms and Generalized Quantifiers. WESTERSTAHL, Dag.
The Axiomatization of Randomness. VAN LAMBALGEN, Michiel.
A Basic Free Logic. WU, Kathleen Johnson.
Eine Bemerkung zu spektralen Darstellungen von ρ-stelligen Aufzählbaren. DEUTSCH, Michael.
Complexly Fractionated Syllogistic Quantifiers. PETERSON, Philip L.
Formatives. ENGLEBRETSEN, George.
Intermediate Quantifiers versus Percentages. CARNES, Robert D and PETERSON, Philip L.
The Last Word on Elimination of Quantifiers in Modules. GUTE, Hans B and REUTER, K K.
Noun Phrases, Quantifiers, and Generic Names. LOWE, E J.
On the Ontology of Branching Quantifiers. PATTON, Thomas.
Relative Elimination of Quantifiers for Henselian Valued Fields. BASARAB, Serban A.
A Truth-Functional Logic for Near-Universal Generalizations. CARLSTROM, Ian F.
Verification, Falsification, and the Logic of Enquiry. MILNE, Peter.
Weitere verschärfungen zu den Reduktionstypen.... DEUTSCH, Michael.

QUANTITY(-TIES)
"Real Quantities and Their Sensible Measures" in *Philosophical Perspectives on Newtonian Science*, SKLAR, Lawrence.
Cantidad o ex-tensión?. BOLZÁN, J E.
Discussione di alcune questioni di cosmologia neo-tomista. BLANDINO, Giovanni.

QUANTUM LOGIC
The Deduction Theorem for Quantum Logic—Some Negative Results. MALINOWSKI, Jacek.
The Philosophy of Quantum Mechanics. BUB, Jeffrey.
Quantum Logic, Copenhagen Interpretation and Instrumentalism. RAINA, Dhruv.

QUANTUM MECHANICS
"Projections Are a Law of Nature" in *Studies on Mario Bunge's "Treatise"*, BURGOS, María Esther.
"Realism and Classicism, or Something More? Some Comments on Mario Bunge's Philosophy of Quantum Mechanics" in *Studies on Mario Bunge's "Treatise"*, STÖCKLER, Manfred.
Causality, Determinism and Objective Reality in Modern Physics. NARAYAN, S Shankar.
Chaos and Indeterminism. HOBBS, Jesse.
Fine's "Shaky Game" (and Why Noa is No Ark for Science). SCHLAGEL, Richard H.
Heuristics and the Generalized Correspondence Principle. RADDER, Hans.
Hidden Locality, Conspiracy and Superluminal Signals. KRONZ, Frederick M.
Holism and Nonseparability. HEALEY, Richard A.
Interpreting State Reduction from the Practices-up. CORDERO, Alberto.
Kochen's Interpretation of Quantum Mechanics. ARNTZENIUS, Frank.
Laudan's Model of Axiological Change and the Bohr-Einstein Debate 77. FOLSE JR, Henry J.
Más allá de la presuposición newtoniana: propiedades genuinamente disposicionales en la mecánica cuántica. MARTINEZ, Sergio.
The Measurement Problem: Some "Solutions". ALBERT, David Z and LOEWER, Barry.
Nonlocal Influences and Possible Worlds—A Stapp in the Wrong Direction. CLIFTON, Robert K and BUTTERFIELD, Jeremy N and REDHEAD, Michael L G.
On Some Alleged Difficulties in the Interpretation of Quantum Mechanics. DIEKS, Dennis.
The Philosophy of Quantum Mechanics. BUB, Jeffrey.
Primary Qualities are Secondary Qualities Too. PRIEST, Graham.
The Problem of Properties in Quantum Mechanics. BUB, Jeffrey.
Prolegomenon to a Proper Interpretation of Quantum Field Theory. TELLER, Paul.
Quantum Gravity: Some Philosophical Reflections. ALTEKAR, E V.
Quantum Realism: A Reply to Professor Fenner. BENNETT, Barbara J.
Randomness and Probability in Dynamical Theories: On the Proposals of the Prigogine School. BATTERMAN, Robert.
Realism, Idealism and Quantum Mechanics. LIST, C J.
Relativité et quanta: leurs mutuelles exisgences et les corrélations d'Einstein-Podolsky-Rosen. COSTA DE BEAUREGARD, Olivier.
Some Comments Concerning Spin and Relativity. WEINGARD, Robert.
Theorie antireduktionistischer Argumente: Fallstudie Bohr. HOYNINGEN-HUENE, Paul.
Time-Travel and Topology. MAUDLIN, Tim.
Unbounded Operators and the Incompleteness of Quantum Mechanics. HEATHCOTE, Adrian.
What is the Logical Form of Probability Assignment in Quantum Mechanics?. HALPIN, John F.

QUANTUM PHYSICS
Autonomy and Quantum Physics: Nietzsche, Heidegger, and Heisenberg. SEIGFRIED, Hans.
Metaphysical Awakening in Philosophy of Quantum Physics. FOLSE, Henry J.
A Note on Schrödinger's Cat and the Unexpected Hanging Paradox. HOLTZMANN, Jack M.
Perspectives on Quantum Reality versus Classical Reality. HOME, Dipankar.
Quantum Physics and Logical Truth (in Italian). GIANNETTO, Enrico.
Quantum Physics and the Identity of Indiscernibles. FRENCH, Steven and REDHEAD, Michael.
Quantum Physics, Philosophy, and the Image of God: Insights from Wolfgang Pauli. LAURIKAINEN, K V.
Real Dispositions in the Physical World. THOMPSON, Ian J.

QUANTUM THEORY
Beyond the Big Bang: Quantum Cosmologies and God. DREES, Willem B.
Intelligibility in Science. DILWORTH, Craig (ed).
Bohr's Idea of Complementarity and Plato's Philosophy. MAHOOTIAN, Farzad.
Born's Probabilistic Interpretation: A Case Study of 'Concepts in Flux'. BELLER, Mara.
Causal Independence in EPR Arguments. BUTTERFIELD, Jeremy.
Comments on 'Nonlocal Influences and Possible Worlds'. STAPP, Henry P.
Conditionalisation and Quantum Probabilities. MILNE, Peter.
Heuristics and the Generalized Correspondence Principle. RADDER, Hans.
Independence from Future Theories: A Research Strategy in Quantum Theory. RUEGER, Alexander.
The Infinite Apparatus in the Quantum Theory of Measurement. ROBINSON, Don.
Jarrett Completeness and Superluminal Signals. KRONZ, Frederick M.
Logic, Contradiction and Quantum Theory. SMITH, Joseph Wayne.
The Nature of Physical Reality. POLKINGHORNE, John C.
A New Theory of the Relationship of Mind and Matter. BOHM, David.
La pertinence du concept d'horizon de réalité en physique théorique contemporaine. COHEN-TANNOUDJI, Gilles.
Prolegomenon to a Proper Interpretation of Quantum Field Theory. TELLER, Paul.
Quantum Cosmology and the Beginning of the Universe. SMITH, Gerrit.
Quantum Propensition Theory: A Testable Resolution of the Wave/Particle Dilemma. MAXWELL, Nicholas.
Realism and the Collapse of the Wave-Packet. KRIPS, Henry.
Wanted Dead or Alive: Two Attempts to Solve Schrödinger's Paradox. ALBERT, David and LOEWER, Barry.

QUESTION(S)
"Another Experience of the Question, or Experiencing the Question Other-Wise" in *Who Comes after the Subject?*, AGACINSKI, Sylviane.
Alternatives et questions dans la littérature romanesque. COMETTI, Jean-Pierre.
Épistémologie et questionnement: le modèle en tant que forme de l'interrogation scientifique. BORUTTI, Silvana.
Estetica e interrogazione. GARRONI, Emilio.
Explanation and the Theory of Questions. CROSS, Charles B.
Implied Questions. WISNIEWSKI, Andrzej.
Meyer's Theory of Problematology. GOLDEN, James L and JAMISON, David L.
Problématicité, rationalité et interrogativité. CARRILHO, Manuel Mari.
Le questionnement, comme synthèse de l'humain. LEMPEREUR, Alain.
Space and Its Questions (in Czechoslovakian). PATOCKA, Jan.

QUESTIONING
Nietzsche: The Body and Culture—Philosophy as a Philological Genealogy. BLONDEL, Eric.
The Question of Ethics. SCOTT, Charles E.
The Question of God in Heidegger's Phenomenology. KOVACS, George.
Changing the Subject: Heidegger, "the" National and Epochal. SCHMIDT, Dennis J.
How to Put Questions to Nature. SINTONEN, Matti.
Learning Disabilities: A Questionable Construct. KLATT, Heinz-Joachim.
Teaching by Questioning. WHALLEY, Michael.
The Questioning of Values in Theology (in French). WIDMER, Gabriel-Ph.
Vérité à Faire: Merleau-Ponty's Question Concerning Truth. WALDENFELS, Bernhard.

QUETELET, A
The Taming of Chance. HACKING, Ian.

QUINE
Classics of Analytic Philosophy. AMMERMAN, Robert R (ed).
Epistemology and Skepticism: An Enquiry into the Nature of Epistemology. CHATALIAN, George.
The Metaphysics of Meaning. KATZ, Jerrold J.
Perspectives on Quine. BARRETT, Robert (ed).
Pragmatism: From Peirce to Davidson. MURPHY, John P.
Properties as Processes: A Synoptic Study of Wilfried Sellars' Nominalism. SEIBT, Johanna.
"A Backward Look at Quine's Animadversions on Modalities" in *Perspectives on Quine*, MARCUS, Ruth Barcan.
"Carnap, Quine and the Rejection of Intuition" in *Perspectives on Quine*, CREATH, Richard.

QUINE
"A Central Problem for a Speech-Dispositional Account of Logic and Language" in *Perspectives on Quine*, BERGER, Alan.
"Doing Without Meaning" in *Perspectives on Quine*, QUINTON, Anthony.
"Genetic Explanation in *The Roots of Reference*" in *Perspectives on Quine*, PARSONS, Charles.
"Holism and Naturalized Epistemology Confronted with the Problem of Truth" in *Perspectives on Quine*, LAUENER, Henri.
"Immanent and Transcendent Approaches to the Theory of Meaning" in *Perspectives on Quine*, HARMAN, Gilbert.
"Indeterminacy and Mental States" in *Perspectives on Quine*, FOLLESDAL, Dagfinn.
"Is Existence What Existential Quantification Expresses?" in *Perspectives on Quine*, ORENSTEIN, Alex.
"Learning and Meaning" in *Perspectives on Quine*, ULLIAN, Joseph S.
"Let Me Accentuate the Positive" in *Reading Rorty*, QUINE, W V.
"Logic and the World" in *Themes From Kaplan*, ALMOG, Joseph.
"Meaning, Truth and Evidence" in *Perspectives on Quine*, DAVIDSON, Donald.
"Natural Kinds" in *Perspectives on Quine*, HACKING, Ian.
"Ontological Relativity in Quine and Davidson" in *The Mind of Donald Davidson*, MALPAS, J E.
"The Question of Translatability: Benjamin, Derrida, Quine" in *Hermeneutics and the Poetic Motion, Translation Perspectives V—1990*, TURK, Horst.
"Quine as a Member of the Tradition of the Universality of Language" in *Perspectives on Quine*, HINTIKKA, Jaakko.
"Quine on Quantifying In" in *Propositional Attitudes: The Role of Content in Logic, Language, and Mind*, FINE, Kit.
"Quine on Underdetermination" in *Perspectives on Quine*, BERGSTRÖM, Lars.
"Quine's Physicalism" in *Perspectives on Quine*, STROUD, Barry.
"Quine" in *Perspectives on Quine*, DREBEN, Burton.
"Rebuilding the Ship while Sailing on the Water" in *Perspectives on Quine*, HAACK, Susan.
"The Refutation of Indeterminacy" in *Perspectives on Quine*, KATZ, Jerrold.
"Testing Theories of Interpretation" in *Truth and Interpretation: Perspectives on the Philosophy of Donald Davidson*, VERMAZEN, Bruce.
"Theories as Mere Conventions" in *Scientific Theories*, KYBURG JR, Henry E.
"Translation Theories and the Decipherment of Linear B" in *Truth and Interpretation: Perspectives on the Philosophy of Donald Davidson*, WALLACE, John.
"Two Conceptions of Philosophy" in *Perspectives on Quine*, STRAWSON, P F.
"Understanding Our Actual Scheme" in *The Mind of Donald Davidson*, SIITONEN, Arto.
"Why and How to Naturalize Epistemology" in *Perspectives on Quine*, KOPPELBERG, Dirk.
Analiticidad, empirismo y verdad necesaria. HERNÁNDEZ IGLESIAS, Manuel Angel.
Behaviourism, Neuroscience and Translational Indeterminacy. WARMBRŌD, Ken.
Epistemologia e teoria politica. ZOLO, Danilo.
Equivalent Descriptions. BEN-MENAHEM, Yemima.
Extensionality, Underdetermination and Indeterminacy. SOLOMON, Miriam.
Finding Ourselves: Personal Identity and the Limits of Possible-World Arguments. BECK, Simon.
Física y Semántica en la filosofía de Quine. FUSTEGUERAS, Aurelio P.
From Russell to Quine: Basic Statements, Foundationalism, Truth, and Other Myths. LINDBERG, Jordan J.
Incommensurability and the Indeterminacy of Translation. SANKEY, Howard.
The Indeterminacy Thesis Reformulated. GEMES, Ken.
Interpretatie en filosofische methode. BUEKENS, Filip.
Logic and Empiricism. BOSTOCK, David.
More on Quine's Dilemma of Undetermination. GIBSON, Roger F.
A Notorious Affair Called Exportation. BURDICK, Howard.
On Defining Identity. SAVELLOS, Elias E.
On Naturalizing Epistemology. ALMEDER, Robert.
On the Ontology of Branching Quantifiers. PATTON, Thomas.
On the Propositional Attitudes. COLEMAN, Keith.
Onderbepaaldheid van theorie en onbepaaldheid van vertaling: Enige ontwikkelingen in Quine's filosofie. PERRICK, M.
The Paradox of Epistemology: A Defense of Naturalism. KETCHUM, Richard J.
Presentism and the Indeterminacy of Translation. HARDCASTLE, Gary L.
Quine on Theory and Language. TANJI, Nobuharu.
Quine's Relativism. HUGLY, Philip and SAYWARD, Charles.
Reflexiones en torno a la oración oblicua. MUÑOZ, Angel and CAROSIO, Alba.
Semantics without Reference. GAUKER, Christopher.
Systems of Combinatory Logic Related to Quine's 'New Foundations'. HOLMES, M R.
The Task of a Theory of Meaning. SAYRE, Patricia.
Truth. ULLIAN, Joseph S.
Two Dogmas of Neo-Empiricism: The "Theory-Informity" of Observation and the Quine-Duhem Thesis. GREENWOOD, John D.
Uno sguardo sulla filosofia americana contemporanea. CENTRONE, Marino.
Visual Perception and the Wages of Indeterminacy. MONTGOMERY, Richard.

RACE(S)
Vulgarity and Authenticity: Dimensions of Otherness in the World of Jean-Paul Sartre. CHARMÉ, Stuart Zane.
"Unspeakable Things Unspoken: The Afro-American Presence in American Literature" in *The Tanner Lectures on Human Values, Volume XI*, MORRISON, Toni.
"But Would That Still Be Me?" Notes on Gender, "Race," Ethnicity, as Sources of "Identity". APPIAH, Anthony.
La imagen del indígena en el pensamiento colombiano del siglo XIX: La perspectiva de J M Samper. GÓMEZ-MULLER, Alfredo.

RACISM
"Bernanosian Barbs and the Maritain's Marigny Lecture" in *From Twilight to Dawn: The Cultural Vision of Jacques Maritain*, BUSH, William.
Hegel and Kant—A Refutation of their Racism. NEUGEBAUER, Christian.
Just War Theory: The Case of South Africa. MILLER, S R.
On African Feminism: Two Reasons for the Rejection of Feminism. KWAME, Safro.
El pensamiento filosófico de Martin Luther King, Jr. STERLING, Marvin C.
Reflections on the Philosophy of Hitlerism. HAND, Seán (trans) and LEVINAS, Emmanuel.
Scientific Racism in the Philosophy of Science: Some Historical Examples. UEBEL, Thomas E.
Wittgenstein on Jews: Some Counter-Examples. WASSERMANN, Gerhard D.

RADHAKRISHNAN
The Nature and Significance of Intuition: A View Based on a Core Idea Held by S Radhakrishnan. FITZ, Hope K.

RADIATION
A Critical Look at Arguments for Food Irradiation. SMITH, Tony.

RADICAL TRANSLATION
Logical Form and Radical Interpretation. MC CARTHY, Tim.

RADICALISM
Socialism, Feminism and Philosophy: A Radical Philosophy Reader. SAYERS, Sean (ed).
"Conservative and Radical Critiques of Nuclear Policy" in *Issues in War and Peace: Philosophical Inquiries*, LITKE, Robert.
"Radical Politics in a New Key?" in *Critique and Construction: A Symposium on Roberto Unger's "Politics"*, JUDT, Tony.
The Feminist Revelation. SOMMERS, Christina.
Métaphysique radicale. MARGOLIS, Joseph.
The Neglected Background of Radical Liberalism: P E Dove's Theory of Property. CUNLIFFE, John.
On the Empirical Status of Radical Feminism: A Reply to Schedler. MUI, Constance L.
Radical Theology, Postmodernity and Christian Life in the Void. COWDELL, Scott.

RADICE, R
Ontologia e creazione in Filone Alessandrino: Dialogo con Giovanni Reale e Roberto Radice. MARTÍN, Josè Pablo.

RADIN, M
Radin on Personhood and Rent Control. GREENBERG, Dan.

RAHNER, K
Le paradoxe de la conscience erronáe d'Abálard à Karl Rahner. BELMANS, Théo G.

RAILTON, P
Azar y explicación: Algunas observaciones. PÉREZ RANSANZ, Ana Rosa.

RAMANA
Ramana Maharsi on the Theories of Creation in Advaita Vedānta. SHARMA, Arvind.

RAMANUJA
Rāmānuja's Hermeneutics of the *Upanisads* in Comparison with Sankara's Interpretation. SAWAI, Yoshitsugu.

RAMSEY, F
Philosophical Papers: F P Ramsey. MELLOR, D H (ed).
Weights or the Value of Knowledge. RAMSEY, F P.

RAMSEY, P
The Making of a Nuclear Peace: The Task of Today's Just War Theorists. SICHOL, Marcia W.
Principle Monism and Action Descriptions: Situationism and its Critics Revisited. PINCHES, Charles.

RAND, A
Atheism, Ayn Rand, and other Heresies. SMITH, George H.
The Ideas of Ayn Rand. MERRILL, Ronald E.

RANDOMNESS
"Determinism, Probability and Randomness in Classical Statistical Physics" in *Imre Lakatos and Theories of Scientific Change*, CLARK, Peter.

RANDOMNESS
The Axiomatization of Randomness. VAN LAMBALGEN, Michiel.
El azar objetivo como medida matemática de desorden. MARTÍNEZ, Sergio.
La objetividad del azar en un mundo determinista. MARTÍNEZ, S.
On the Necessity for Random Sampling. JOHNSTONE, D J.
Randomness and Probability in Dynamical Theories: On the Proposals of the Prigogine School. BATTERMAN, Robert.
Randomness by Design. DEMBSKI, William.

RANKE, L
Alle origini della riflessione di Leopold von Ranke sulla storia: K F Bachmann e J G Fichte. GHELARDI, Maurizio.

RANKING
A Conjecture Concerning the Ranking of the Sciences. HUMPHREYS, Paul.
Ordering Pairwise Comparison Structures. DELVER, R and MONSUUR, H and STORCKEN, A J A.
The Ranking of Preference. RAWLING, Piers.

RAPAPORT, A
Filosofía y teoría general de sistemas en el pensamiento de A Rapoport. SAXE FERNÁNDEZ, Eduardo E.

RAPE
Abortion in Rape Cases. BEABOUT, Greg.
Enforced Pregnancy, Rape, and the Image of Woman. CUDD, Ann E.
On the Nature of Rape. BOGART, J H.

RATIFIABILITY
Ratifiability, Game Theory, and the Principle of Independence of Irrelevant Alternatives. EELLS, Ellery and HARPER, William L.
A Reconstruction of Jeffrey's Notion of Ratifiability in Terms of Counterfactual Beliefs. SHIN, Hyung Song.

RATIO
The Driving Ratio in Plato's Divided Line. DREHER, John Paul.
Erasing and Redrawing the Number Line: An Exercise in Rationality. SPARROW, Edward G.
Eudoxos and Dedekind: On the Ancient Greek Theory of Ratios and its Relation to Modern Mathematics. STEIN, Howard.

RATIONAL
Baffling Phenomena: And Other Studies in the Philosophy of Knowledge and Valuation. RESCHER, Nicholas.
The Legal-Rational State: A Comparison of Hobbes, Bentham and Kelsen. LEE, Keekok.
"An Internalist Conception of Rational Action" in *Philosophical Perspectives, 4: Action Theory and Philosophy of Mind, 1990*, AUDI, Robert.
"Rational Egoism, Self, and Others" in *Identity, Character, and Morality: Essays in Moral Psychology*, BRINK, David O.
Arguing for Rational Suicide. HUMPHRY, Derek.
Eleatics Against Each Other (in Hungarian). KAMPIS, György.
Les enjeux égalitaires du consensus rationnel: Habermas et ses sources. MARCIL-LACOSTE, Louise.
Experiencia de lo sublime y principios racionales. ARTOLA, José María.
L'aspect rationnel et l'aspect religieux de la philosophie de Plotin. BRUNNER, Fernand.
The Philosophical Basis of Rational-Emotive Therapy (RET). ELLIS, Albert.
Plato and Davidson: Parts of the Soul and Weakness of Will. PENNER, Terrence M.
La teoria hegeliana dell'autocoscienza e della sua razionalità. VARNIER, Giuseppe.
The Initial Form of Empiristic and Aprioristic Conception of Knowledge on the World (in Polish). MORAWIEC, E.
Weakness of Will and Rational Action. AUDI, Robert.

RATIONAL CHOICE(S)
The Dynamics of Rational Deliberation. SKYRMS, Brian.
Foundations of Social Theory. COLEMAN, James S.
Varieties of Social Explanation: An Introduction to the Philosophy of Social Science. LITTLE, Daniel.
"'Why Be Moral?' and Reforming Selves". WILLIAMSON, A Mark.
Apriorisme et théorie du choix rationnel. KAUFMANN, J Nicolas.
Commensurability as a Prerequisite of Rational Choice: An Examination of Sidgwick's Position. RICHARDSON, Henry S.
The Mutual Investment Game: Peculiarities of Indifference. CUBITT, Robin P and HOLLIS, Martin.
Non-Dominance, Third Person and Non-Action Newcomb Problems, and Metatickles. SOBEL, Jordan Howard.
Rational Choice Theory Considered as Psychology and Moral Philosophy. MONGIN, Philippe.
A Rational Choice Theory of Punishment. STERBA, James P.

RATIONALISM
see also Reason
The Devil and Secular Humanism: The Children of the Enlightenment. RADEST, Howard B.
Explaining Religion: Criticism and Theory from Bodin to Freud. PREUS, J Samuel (ed).
The Political Philosophy of Michael Oakeshott. FRANCO, Paul.
Sacred Fragments: Recovering Theology for the Modern Jew. GILLMAN, Neil.
Between Rationalism and Relativism: On Larry Laudan's Model of Scientific Rationality. GROBLER, Adam.
Can There Be Justified Philosophical Beliefs?. NIELSEN, Kai.
Charles Hartshorne's Rationalism. GUTOWSKI, Piotr.
A Dilemma for Bartley's Pancritical Rationalism. HAUPTLI, Bruce W.
The Epistemology of J M Keynes. O'DONNELL, Rod.
Fisiormorfismo de la razón versus racionalismo. PACHO, Julián.
A intersubjectividade em Gabriel Marcel. MORUJÁO, Alexandre Fradique.
Logic and Language in the *Chuang Tzu*. ALT, Wayne E.
Metodi e immagini della scienza nel "Centro di studi metodologici" di Torino (1945-1952). QUARTA, Antonio.
Moral Dilemmas. MAC INTYRE, Alasdair.
Moral Epistemology and the Supervenience of Ethical Concepts. AUDI, Robert.
Nature, Self, and Gender: Feminism, Environmental Philosophy, and the Critique of Rationalism. PLUMWOOD, Val.
Ein neu gefundener Brief von Leibniz an Lambert van Velthuysen: Mit einer Einführung von Albert Heinekamp. HEIN, Isolde.
Popper on Induction. SWANN, Andrew J.
Rationalism, Expertise and the Dreyfuses' Critique of AI Research. ROBINSON, William S.
Rationalism, Supervenience, and Moral Epistemology. KLAGGE, James.
Rescuing Natural Law Theory from the Rationalists. DENNEHY, Raymond.
Su alcuni aspetti del neoilluminismo di L Geymonat. STOMEO, Anna.
The Problem of Infinity in Kant's Works (in German). RÖD, Wolfgang.

RATIONALITY
Aristotle's Psychology. ROBINSON, Daniel N.
Artificial Intelligence and Human Cognition. WAGMAN, Morton.
Between Freiburg and Frankfurt: Toward a Critical Ontology. DALLMAYR, Fred R.
The Communicative Ethics Controversy. BENHABIB, Seyla (ed).
The Concept of Objectivity: An Approximation. BUTLER, Kenneth G.
Do the Right Thing: Studies in Limited Rationality. RUSSELL, Stuart.
Foundations of Moral and Political Philosophy. PAUL, Ellen Frankel (ed).
The Fragmentation of Reason. STICH, Stephen.
How to Build a Person: A Prolegomenon. POLLOCK, John L.
Human Interests: Reflections on Philosophical Anthropology. RESCHER, Nicholas.
Identity, Character, and Morality: Essays in Moral Psychology. FLANAGAN, Owen (ed).
In Praise of the Cognitive Emotions. SCHEFFLER, Israel.
Inference and Understanding: A Philosophical and Psychological Perspective. MANKTELOW, K I.
Kant's Theory of Freedom. ALLISON, Henry E.
The Last Choice: Preemptive Suicide in Advanced Age. PRADO, C G.
Leibniz' Position der Rationalität. KAEHLER, Klaus Erich.
Logic in the Husserlian Context. TITO, Johanna Maria.
Markets, Managers and Theory in Education. HALLIDAY, John.
I Modelli l'Invenzione e la Conferma. PETRONI, Angelo Maria.
Moral und Politik aus der Sicht des Kritischen Rationalismus. SALAMUN, Kurt (ed).
L'ordine della certezza: Scientificità e persuasione in Descartes. BONICALZI, Francesca.
Il Paradigma del Sapere. LENTINI, Luigi.
Philosophy and Cognitive Science. FETZER, James H.
Rationality in Action: Contemporary Approaches. MOSER, Paul K (ed).
Razionalitá critica: nella filosofia moderna. LAMACCHIA, Ada (ed).
Suicide: Right or Wrong?. DONNELLY, John (ed).
Theories of Science in Society. COZZENS, Susan E (ed).
"Demystifying Underdetermination" in *Scientific Theories*, LAUDAN, Larry.
"Epistemic Universalizability: From Skepticism to Infallibilism" in *Doubting: Contemporary Perspectives on Skepticism*, ADLER, Jonathan E.
"Faith and Rationality" in *Key Themes in Philosophy*, BARRETT, D C.
"Is Akratic Action Always Irrational?" in *Identity, Character, and Morality: Essays in Moral Psychology*, MC INTYRE, Alison.
"Rationality and Objectivity in Science, *or* Tom Kuhn Meets Tom Bayes" in *Scientific Theories*, SALMON, Wesley C.
"Rationality and Social Norms" in *Logic, Methodology and Philosophy of Science, VIII*, ELSTER, Jon.
"Rationality between Modernity and Postmodernity" in *Life-World and Politics: Between Modernity and Postmodernity*, SCHRAG, Calvin O.
"Rationality Unbound" in *Acting and Reflecting: The Interdisciplinary Turn in Philosophy*, LEVI, Isaac.
"Rationality, Responsibility, and Pathological Indifference" in *Identity, Character, and Morality: Essays in Moral Psychology*, WHITE, Stephen L.
"Scientific Revolutions and Scientific Rationality: The Case of the Elderly Holdout" in *Scientific Theories*, WORRALL, John.
Achilles' Revenge. DAKO, Martin.
Arational Actions. HURSTHOUSE, Rosalind.
Bachelard and Scientific Realism. TIJIATTAS, Mary.
Bayes' Bayesianism. EARMAN, John.
Clever Bookies and Coherent Beliefs. CHRISTENSEN, David.

RATIONALITY
Co-ordination, Salience and Rationality. MILLER, Seumas.
Compassion. SNOW, Nancy E.
Conditional Probabilities, Conditionalization, and Dutch Books. SOBEL, Jordan Howard.
La crisi dei fondamenti della scienza: Un recupero dell'ilemorfismo?. DEL RE, Giuseppe.
Critical Thinking and Thinking Critically: Response to Siegel. FINOCCHIARO, Maurice A.
A Dilemma for Subjective Bayesians—and How to Resolve It. MILNE, Peter.
Divine Reason and Virtue in St Thomas's Natural Law Theory. KILLORAN, John B.
Doxastic Paradoxes Without Self-Reference. KOONS, Robert Charles.
Emotions and Rationality. BERENSON, F M.
Epistemology and Political Rationality. FUTERNICK, Ken.
Erasing and Redrawing the Number Line: An Exercise in Rationality. SPARROW, Edward G.
The Ethics of Inarticulacy. KYMLICKA, Will.
Explanation and Understanding in Social Science. SKORUPSKI, John.
Feminist Theory and Its Discontents. TRESS, Daryl Mc Gowan.
Fostering the Disposition to be Rational. SIEGEL, Harvey.
From Truth to 'Alhieia to Opening and Rapture. MALY, Kenneth.
Hidden Agendas. FRIEDMAN, Robert.
Ideal Rationality and Handwaving. RICHTER, Reed.
Island Biogeography, Species-Area Curves, and Statistical Errors: Applied Biology and Scientific Rationality. SHRADER-FRECHETTE, Kristin.
James, Rationality and Religious Belief. WAINWRIGHT, W J.
Judgment and Rationality in Lyotard's Discursive Archipelago. HENDLEY, Steven.
Kantian Freedom Naturalized. MELCHERT, Norman.
Kierkegaard irrazionalista? Filosofi e filosofie nella interpretazione del filosofo danese. FRANCHI, Alfredo.
Knowledge, Belief and Revelation: A Reply to Patrick Lee. HOITENGA JR, Dewey J.
The Logic of Rational Play in Games of Perfect Information. BONANNO, Giacomo.
Man, History, and Philosophy in Husserl's Crisis of European Sciences (in Czechoslovakian). MAJOR, L.
Modernity, the Individual and Rationality in Marxism (Surrealism and Revolution). CLOUDSLEY, Tim.
Moral Scepticism and Inductive Scepticism. BLACK, Robert.
Moral Theories, Impartiality, and the Status of Non-Rational, Sentient Beings. FILICE, Carlo.
Must Thinking Be Critical to Be Critical Thinking? Reply to Finocchiaro. SIEGEL, Harvey.
Mystical Experience, Hermeneutics, and Rationality. SHEAR, Jonathan.
Non-Rational Cognitive Processes as Changes of Distinctions. HEYLIGHEN, Francis.
On Bolzano's Conception of the Essentials of Ethics and its Coherences (in Czechoslovakian). HALA, Vlastimil.
On Marx's Conception of Rationality. MULLICK, Mohini.
Overloading Intentions for Efficient Practical Reasoning. POLLACK, Martha E.
Practical Reason or Metapreferences? An Undogmatic Defense of Kantian Morality. NIDA-RÜMELIN, Julian.
Pragmática del lenguaje y racionalidad comunicativa. DE ZAN, J.
Précis of "Whose Justice? Which Rationality?". MAC INTYRE, Alasdair.
Psychology and Controversy. AGASSI, Joseph.
Racionalidad y libertad. FERNÁNDEZ DEL VALLE, Agustín Basave.
Rational and Caring Teachers: How Dispositional Aims Shape Teacher Preparation. ARNSTINE, Barbara.
The Rational Law-Maker and the Pragmatics of Legal Interpretation. DASCAL, Marcelo and WRÓBLEWSKI, Jerzy.
Rational Trust and Deferential Belief. NORRIS, Stephen P.
La rationalité du théisme: la philosophie de la religion de Richard Swinburne. PADGETT, Alan G.
Rationality and Moral Status. BILOW, Scott H.
Rationality and Reasonableness. BURBULES, Nicholas C.
Rationality and Social Labor in Marx. KHALIL, Elias L.
The Rationality of Escapism and Self Deception. LONGEWAY, John L.
Rationality of *p*-Adic Poincaré Series: Uniformity in *p*. MACINTYRE, Angus.
Rationality, Consistency and Truth. FRENCH, Steven.
Rationality, Correlativity, and the Language of Process. HALL, David Lynn and AMES, Roger T.
Rationality, Culture and Values. CHATTOPADHYAYA, D P.
Rationality, Reasons, and the Sociology of Knowledge (in Serbo-Croatian). KAISER, Matthias.
Reason and Imagination (in Dutch). VAN PEURSEN, C A.
Reason, Rationality and the Irrational. NAYAK, G C.
La reivindicación de la racionalidad en K O Apel. SMILG VIDAL, Norberto.
Response to Diamond. MC NAUGHTON, David.
Response to McNaughton. DIAMOND, Cora.
Response to W J Norman's "Has Rational Economic Man a Heart". LA CASSE, Chantale and ROSS, Don.
Retaliation Rationalized: Gauthier's Solution to the Deterrence Dilemma. MAC INTOSH, Duncan.
Romanticism, Rationality and Alienation—the Triple-H-Theory Revisited. BRUNKHORST, Hauke.
Le satori dans le bouddhisme zen et la rationalité. HÉLAL, Georges.
Scepticism and Autonomy. HOOKWAY, Christopher.
Scientific Rationality—A Rethinking. CHAUDHURY, Mahasweta.
Self-Interest and the New Bashing of Economics. KIRZNER, Israel M.
Settled Objectives and Rational Constraints. MC CANN, Hugh J.
Solving the Problem of Induction Using a Values-Based Epistemology. ELLIS, Brian.
Some Remarks on the Rationality of Induction. INDURKHYA, Bipin.
Stephen P Stich, "The Fragmentation of Reason". COHEN, L Jonathan.
The Superfluity of the Original Position. DEN HARTOGH, G A.
Die Theorie des kommunikativen Handelns in Diskussion. KISSLING, Christian.
Time Preference. ZIFF, Paul.
Tra Kant e Hegel: per una riaffermazione dell'antico concetto di società civile. MARINI, Giuliano.
The Transcendental Method of Metaphysics of Coreth and Muck and Its Relation to Analytic Philosophy. RUNGGALDIER, Edmund.
When Do People Begin?. GRISEZ, Germain.
The World Reconsidered: A Brief *AggiornamentoF* for Leftist Intellectuals. SKIRBEKK, Gunnar.
Zum Wandel der Metaphysik nach ihrem Ende. BUCHHEIM, Thomas.

RATIONING
Market Mechanisms and Principles of Justice. LOEWY, Erich H.
Should Basic Care Get Priority? Doubts about Rationing the Oregon Way. VEATCH, Robert M.

RAWLS, J
An Audience for Moral Philosophy?. EDELMAN, John T.
Descent into Subjectivity: Studies of Rawls, Dworkin and Unger in the Context of Modern Thought. MURPHY JR, Cornelius F.
Moral Dealing: Contract, Ethics, and Reason. GAUTHIER, David.
Rawls: "A Theory of Justice" and Its Critics. KUKATHAS, Chandran.
Reading Rawls: Critical Studies on Rawls' 'A Theory of Justice'. DANIELS, Norman (ed).
What Is Justice? Classic and Contemporary Readings. SOLOMON, Robert C (ed).
"The Priority of Democracy to Philosophy" in *Reading Rorty*, RORTY, Richard.
"When the Owl of Minerva Takes Flight at Dawn: Radical Constructivism in Social Theory" in *Critique and Construction: A Symposium on Roberto Unger's "Politics"*, BURNS, Robert P.
Autonomy, Liberalism and State Neutrality. MASON, Andrew D.
Free Speech, Free Exchange, and Rawlsian Liberalism. SHAPIRO, Daniel.
Games, Fairness, and Rawls's *A Theory of Justice*. LADEN, Anthony.
Global Injustices. MC BRIDE, William L.
John Rawls: de l'autonomie morale à la fiction de contrat social. RICOEUR, Paul.
Justification et justice procédurale. DUHAMEL, André.
The Justification of Justice as Fairness: A Two Stage Process. VAGGALIS, Ted.
La pensée de Rawls face au défi communautarien. IROEGBU, Pantaleon.
Le projet de John Rawls. LAMBERT, Roger.
La ragione e i valori nella determinazione delle norme. CORTESE, Roberto.
Rawls's Difference Principle and a Problem of Sacrifice. VOICE, Paul.
Rawls, Sandel and the Self. CANEY, S.
Rawlsian Nash Solutions. FABELLA, Raul V.
Self, Society, and Kantian Impersonality. SORELL, Tom.
The Superfluity of the Original Position. DEN HARTOGH, G A.
Time Preference. ZIFF, Paul.
Toward a Reconciliation of Liberalism and Communitarianism. ELLIS, Ralph D.
Transition to Pragmatic Liberalism: Diversity, Contingency, and Social Solidarity. LINDGREN, Ralph.
Why Surfers Should Be Fed: The Liberal Case for an Unconditional Basic Income. VAN PARIJS, Philippe.

RAZ, J
Law and Exclusionary Reasons. ALEXANDER, Larry.

REACTION(S)
Nancy Cruzan in China. ANNAS, George J.

READING
The Anatomy of Philosophical Style. LANG, Berel.
Nine Talmudic Readings. ARONOWICZ, Annette (trans).
"The Face and Reading: Immediacy and Mediation" in *Re-Reading Levinas*, CRITCHLEY, Simon (trans) and GREISCH, Jean.
"They Read Novels, Don't They?" Using Novels in Teaching Philosophy. BOWLDEN, Larry S.
Basal Readers—'Dominant But Dead' versus Gadamer and Language for Understanding. WIRTH, Arthur G.
Essay on the Notion of Reading. ROSE, Rebecca Fine (trans) and WEIL, Simone and TESSIN, Timothy.
Reading Nietzsche. RISSER, James.
The Status of Fiction: Between Nostalgia and Nihilism (in French). IMHOOF, Stefan.

READING
Tipos de lectura, tipos de texto. PEREDA, Carlos.
Wittgenstein: Whose Philosopher?. ANSCOMBE, G E M.

REAGAN, T
The Difference-Deficit Debate: Theoretical Smokescreen for a Conservative Ambush. MC DADE, Laurie A.

REAL
On an Alleged Refutation of Hilbert's Program Using Gödel's First Incompleteness Theorem. DETLEFSEN, Michael.
Real Possibility. DEUTSCH, Harry.
Le relazioni divine secondo S Tommaso d'Aquino: Riproposizione di un problema e prospettive di indagine. VENTIMIGLIA, Giovanni.

REAL NUMBER(S)
Jumping with Random Reals. BARTOSZYNSKI, Tomek and JUDAH, Haim.
The Kunen-Miller Chart (Lebesgue Measure, the Baire Property, Laver Reals and Preservation Theorems for Forcing). JUDAH, Haim and SHELAH, Saharon.
Real Numbers, Continued Fractions and Complexity Classes. LABHALLA, Salah and LOMBARDI, Henri.

REALE, G
Ontologia e creazione in Filone Alessandrino: Dialogo con Giovanni Reale e Roberto Radice. MARTÍN, Josè Pablo.

REALISM
Anglo-American Philosophy of Law: An Introduction to Its Development and Outcome. LEVY, Beryl Harold.
Being True to the World: Moral Realism and Practical Wisdom. JACOBS, Jonathan A.
The Case for Dualism. SMYTHIES, John R (ed).
Donald Davidson. EVNINE, Simon.
Harré and His Critics. BHASKAR, Roy (ed).
The Idea of the Miraculous: The Challenge to Science and Religion. WILLIAMS, T C.
Instrumental Realism: The Interface between Philosophy of Science and Philosophy of Technology. IHDE, Don.
Knowledge, Fiction, and Imagination. NOVITZ, David.
The Logical Basis of Metaphysics. DUMMETT, Michael.
Metaphysics: A Contemporary Introduction. POST, John F.
Military Ethics: Looking Toward the Future. FOTION, Nicholas G.
Modernity, Aesthetics, and the Bounds of Art. MC CORMICK, Peter J.
Mystical Monotheism: A Study in Ancient Platonic Theology. KENNEY, John Peter.
The Philosopher's Joke. WATSON, Richard A.
The Philosophical Theology of John Duns Scotus. ADAMS, Marilyn McCord (ed).
Philosophie Juridique Européenne. TRIGEAUD, Jean-Marc.
Physicalism in Mathematics. IRVINE, Andrew D (ed).
Realism with a Human Face. PUTNAM, Hilary.
Science and Relativism: Some Key Controversies in the Philosophy of Science. LAUDAN, Larry.
The Secret Connexion: Causation, Realism, and David Hume. STRAWSON, Galen.
Swimming Against the Current in Contemporary Philosophy: Occasional Essays and Papers. VEATCH, Henry B.
Varieties of Moral Personality: Ethics and Psychological Realism. FLANAGAN, Owen.
"Against Instrumentalism" in *Studies on Mario Bunge's "Treatise"*, VOLLMER, Gerhard.
"Contrastive Empiricism" in *Scientific Theories*, SOBER, Elliott.
"Early Advocates of Lasting World Peace: Utopians or Realists?" in *Celebrating Peace*, BOK, Sissela.
"Experimental Realism" in *Harré and His Critics*, ARONSON, Jerry.
"Exploring the Human Umwelt" in *Harré and His Critics*, HARRÉ, Rom.
"Introduction: Realism and Human Being" in *Harré and His Critics*, BHASKAR, Roy.
"Inverted Earth" in *Philosophical Perspectives, 4: Action Theory and Philosophy of Mind, 1990*, BLOCK, Ned.
"Mario Bunge's Realist Semantics: An Antidote against Incommensurability?" in *Studies on Mario Bunge's "Treatise"*, BARTELS, Andreas.
"The Mind-Body Problem" in *The Case for Dualism*, SMYTHIES, John R.
"Modest Realism, Experience and Evolution" in *Harré and His Critics*, MANICAS, Peter.
"On Mario Bunge's Semantical Realism" in *Studies on Mario Bunge's "Treatise"*, FERRATER-MORA, José.
"Realism and the Global Topology of Space-Time" in *Harré and His Critics*, WEINGARD, Robert.
"The Realism of the Symbolic" in *Harré and His Critics*, SMITH, Charles W.
"Realism, Approximate Truth, and Philosophical Method" in *Scientific Theories*, BOYD, Richard.
"Realism, Conventionality, and 'Realism About'" in *Meaning and Method: Essays in Honor of Hilary Putnam*, BOYD, Richard.
"Realism, Reference and Theory" in *Key Themes in Philosophy*, HARRÉ, Rom.
"Realism" in *A Companion to Ethics*, SMITH, Michael.
"Rom Harré: Realism and the Turn to Social Constructionism" in *Harré and His Critics*, SHOTTER, John.
"Rorty, Realism and the Idea of Freedom" in *Reading Rorty*, BHASKAR, Roy.
"Non-Scientific Realism" about Propositional Attitudes as a Response to Eliminativist Arguments. HANNAN, Barbara.
"Threading-the-Needle: The Case For and Against Common-Sense Realism". TIBBETTS, Paul.
Aberrations of a Sledgehammer: Reply to Devitt. LUNTLEY, Michael.
Aberrations of the Realism Debate. DEVITT, Michael.
Acceptance Without Belief. MAHER, Patrick.
Aquinas versus Epistemological Criticism: A Case for Philosophy *in* Science. DEL RE, Giuseppe.
Being a Realist about Relativism (In Ethics). SAYRE-MC CORD, Geoffrey.
Believing What We Do Not See: The Case Against van Fraassen's Conception of Observation. DOBSON, Andrew.
Berkeley and Common Sense Realism. PAPPAS, George S.
Beyond Numerical and Causal Accuracy: Expanding the Set of Justificational Criteria. RAMSEY, Jeffry L.
Beyond Realism: Nietzsche's New Infinite. CONWAY, Daniel W.
Capital Punishment and Realism. COCKBURN, David.
Causation: Reductionism Versus Realism. TOOLEY, Michael.
Comment: Selective Anti-Realism. MC MULLIN, Ernan.
Commentary on Sayre-McCord's 'Being a Realist about Relativism'. WONG, David B.
Conclusion: Legal Institutions and Limitations to Cognition and Power. O'BRIEN, James.
Contents and Causes: A Reply to Blackburn. STURGEON, Nicholas L.
Contingentie als uitgangspunt: Het denken van Richard Rorty. GEERTSEMA, H G.
Could I Conceive Being a Brain in a Vat?. COLLIER, John D.
Di cose grammaticali: Un itinerario campanelliano. ALUNNI, Charles.
Empiricism versus Realism: High Points in the Debate During the Past 150 Years. DILWORTH, Craig.
Entwurf eines Klassifikationsschemas für philosophische Positionen. WIMMER, Franz.
Explanation and Scientific Realism. GASPER, Philip.
Fine's "Shaky Game" (and Why Noa is No Ark for Science). SCHLAGEL, Richard H.
Idéalisme ou réalisme?. LARGEAULT, Jean.
The Importance of Being Human. MC NAUGHTON, David.
In Defence of Unrepresentative Realism. TONGS, A R.
In Defense of Southern Fundamentalism. HORGAN, Terence and GRAHAM, George.
The Inference to the Best Explanation. BEN-MENAHEM, Y.
Intuitionism and Vagueness. SCHWARTZ, Stephen P and THROOP, William.
Is Aristotle an Internal Realist? Nussbaum and the Divine Perspective. EARLS, C Anthony.
Just Causes. BLACKBURN, Simon.
Laudan's Model of Axiological Change and the Bohr-Einstein Debate 77. FOLSE JR, Henry J.
The Logical Structure of the First Antinomy. LOPARIC, Zeljko.
Making Noises in Counterpoint or Chorus: Putnam's Rejection of Relativism. JOHNSON, Jeffery L.
Meaning and Value. SCHIFFER, Stephen.
Meaning in a Realist Perspective. THERON, Stephen.
Meaning, Truth and Realism in Bultmann and Lindbeck. FERGUSSON, David.
Metaphysical Realism and Psychologistic Semantics. HORGAN, Terence.
A Modal Argument for Narrow Content. FODOR, Jerry A.
Modal Realism Without Counterparts. HALE, Susan C.
Moral Planes and Intrinsic Values. ANDERSON, James C.
Moral Realism and the Meaning of Life. MARGOLIS, Joseph.
Moral Truth and Coherence: Comments on Goldman. STEUP, M.
Must We Return to Moral Realism?. ROSEN, Michael.
Nominalism and Abstract Reference. MORELAND, J P.
On Boyd. HACKING, Ian.
On the Epistemic Status of Considered Moral Judgments. TIMMONS, Mark.
On the Genuine Queerness of Moral Properties and Facts. GARNER, Richard T.
On the Nature of Einstein's Realism. POLIKAROV, Azaria.
The Participant Irrealist At Large in the Laboratory. HACKING, Ian.
Peirce's Logic of Discovery: Abduction and the Universal Categories. TURRISI, Patricia A.
Peirce's Realism, Intentionality and Final Causation. TURIANO, Mark.
The Persistence of Counterexample: Re-examining the Debate over Leibniz Law. LANDINI, Gregory and FOSTER, Thomas.
La philosophie ouverte de F Gonseth aboutit-elle à une conception réaliste ou relativiste. LAUENER, Henri.
Physicalist Theories of Color. BOGHOSSIAN, Paul A and VELLEMAN, J David.
Piecemeal Realism. FINE, Arthur.
The Poverty of Naturalistic Moral Realism: Comments on Timmons. HOLMGREN, Margaret.
Primary Qualities are Secondary Qualities Too. PRIEST, Graham.
The Problem of Who: Multiple Personality, Personal Identity and the Double Brain. APTER, Andrew.

REASON

Critique of Dialectical Reason, Volume 2: Jean-Paul Sartre. HOARE, Quintin (trans).
David Hume and the Problem of Reason. DANFORD, John W.
Fichte's Theory of Subjectivity. NEUHOUSER, Frederick.
For What May I Hope? Thinking with Kant and Kierkegaard. FENDT, Gene.
The Fragmentation of Reason. STICH, Stephen.
How to Play Theological Ping-Pong: And Other Essays on Faith and Reason. ABRAHAM, William J (ed).
Hume's Place in Moral Philosophy. CAPALDI, Nicholas.
Ideals and Illusions: On Reconstruction and Deconstruction in Contemporary Critical Theory. MC CARTHY, Thomas.
Ideas, Principios y Dialectica. LAFUENTE, Maria Isabel.
Kant's Model of the Mind: A New Interpretation of Transcendental Idealism. WAXMAN, Wayne.
Leibniz' Position der Rationalität. KAEHLER, Klaus Erich.
Mathematics and the Image of Reason. TILES, Mary E.
Metaphysical Delusion. COWLEY, Fraser.
Moral Dealing: Contract, Ethics, and Reason. GAUTHIER, David.
Die Moral der Vernunft Tanszendentale Handlungs-und Legitimationstheorie in der Philosophie Kants. SANDERMANN, Edmund.
The Persistence of Modernity: Essays on Aesthetics, Ethics, and Postmodernism. WELLMER, Albrecht.
Principles of Ethics. ROSMINI, Antonio.
A Progress of Sentiments: Reflections on Hume's "Treatise". BAIER, Annette C.
Published Essays, 1966-1985 (The Collected Works of Eric Voegelin, Volume 12). SANDOZ, Ellis (ed).
The Question of Ethics. SCOTT, Charles E.
Reasons and Experience. MILLAR, Alan.
Reflexion und Metareflexion bei Platon und Fichte. ZEHNPFENNIG, Barbara.
The Tragedy of Reason: Toward a Platonic Conception of Logos. ROOCHNIK, David.
Trois essais sur la pensée. THEAU, Jean.
Vernunft und Kontingenz: Rationalität und Ethos in der Phänomenologie. ORTH, Ernst Wolfgang (ed).
What is History? And Other Late Unpublished Writings (The Collected Works of Eric Voegelin, Vol 28). HOLLWECK, Thomas A (ed).
"Experience of the Other: Between Appropriation and Disappropriation" in *Life-World and Politics: Between Modernity and Postmodernity*, WALDENFELS, Bernhard.
"Life-World: Variations on a Theme" in *Life-World and Politics: Between Modernity and Postmodernity*, DALLMAYR, Fred R.
"Λογοσ ε Ομονοια: algumas considerações em torno da razão sofística" in *Dinâmica do Pensar: Homenagem a Oswaldo Market*, VAZ PINTO, Maria José.
"Maritain and the Future of Reason" in *From Twilight to Dawn: The Cultural Vision of Jacques Maritain*, BOYLE, William J.
"Reason and Experiment in Newton's *Opticks*: Comments on Peter Achinstein" in *Philosophical Perspectives on Newtonian Science*, HUGHES, R I G.
"Reason and Reality: A Prolegomenon to their Varieties" in *Harré and His Critics*, LUCAS, J R.
"Should the Ancient Masters Value Reason?" in *Chinese Texts and Philosophical Contexts*, HANSEN, Chad.
"The Fragmentation of Reason": Précis of Two Chapters. STICH, Stephen P.
The 'Artificial Reason' of the Law. BICKENBACH, Jerome E.
Alternativen und Irrtum in der Kritischen Philosophie Kants. LOH, Werne.
El arte y la urbanidad de la razón. CORDUA, Carla.
Comment on Colmo's "Reason and Revelation in the Thought of Leo Strauss". LOWENTHAL, David.
Da secularidade da Filosofia. COUTINHO, Jorge.
The De-Con-Struction of Reason. GLYNN, Simon.
Does Reason Command Itself for Its Own Sake?. KRAENZEL, Frederick.
Dretske on the Explanatory Role of Belief. BAKER, Lynne Rudder.
Du fondement de la loi morale, une éthique de la raison ou du sentiment?. DAVAL, R.
Due note: Ritorni Rosminiani—Il momento di Ugo Spirito. PAOLETTI, Laura.
The Enlightenment—a Stranded Project? Habermas on Nietzsche as a 'Turning Point' to Postmodernity. NAGL, Ludwig.
Epistemic Leaks and Epistemic Meltdowns: A Response to William Morris on Scepticism with Regard to Reason. KARLSSON, Mikael M.
Errors of an Ill-Reasoning Reason: The Disparagement of Emotions in the Moral Life. LAURITZEN, Paul.
Espoir et désespoir de la raison chez Kant. GRIMALDI, Nicolas.
Faith and Reason: Reflections on MacIntyre's 'Tradition-constituted Enquiry'. MARKHAM, Ian.
Feminism and Relativism. RUSSELL, Denise.
Filosofía latinoamericana: Posibilidad o realidad?. BETANCOURT, Raúl Fornet.
Flaw, Conformity of Critical Dialogue? (in French). BÜHLER, Pierre.
Gendered Reason: Sex Metaphor and Conceptions of Reason. ROONEY, Phyllis.
Goodbye and Farewell: Siegel versus Feyerabend. NORDMANN, Alfred.
Hamanns Metakritik im ersten Entwurf. BAYER, Oswald.
The Insufficiency of Descartes' Provisional Morality. COOLIDGE JR, Francis P.
Is There a Distinction Between Reason and Emotion in Mencius?. WONG, David B.
The Joy of Transgression: Bataille and Kristeva. MARCHAK, Catherine.
Kant's Doctrine of Heuristics: An Interpretation of the Ideas of Reason. GRACYK, Theodore A.
Kant's First Analogy Revisited. BUESSEM, George E.
Kant's Search for the Philosopher's Stone. AXIOTIS, Ares.
King Solomon and Everyman: A Problem in Coordinating Conflicting Moral Intuitions. RORTY, Amelie Oksenberg.
Knowledge, Reason and Human Autonomy: A Review Article. KRISHNA, Daya.
Law and Exclusionary Reasons. ALEXANDER, Larry.
Logique et métaphysique. POUBLANC, Franck.
Mythe et raison: Propos contemporains. FONTAINE-DE VISSCHER, Luce.
La naturaleza y la historia como fundamento para un concepto renovada de razón. PADILLA, Leonel Eduardo.
The Nietzsche Temptation in the Thought of Albert Camus. DUVALL, William E.
Nietzsche: The Divination Paradigm of Knowledge in Western Culture. BULHOF, Ilse N.
Ontological Reductionism and Faith Versus Reason: A Critique of Adams on Ockham. FREDDOSO, Alfred J.
Penny Pinching and Backward Induction. HOLLIS, Martin.
Principio de Razón o fundamento de Amor. MENDEZ, J R.
El problema del conocimiento en Pascal. CASTRO MÉNDEZ, Silvia.
Radical Critique, Scepticism and Commonsense. GAITA, Raimond.
La ragione e i valori nella determinazione delle norme. CORTESE, Roberto.
Reason and Imagination (in Dutch). VAN PEURSEN, C A.
Reason and Reasonableness in the Philosophy of Brand Branshard. RECK, Andrew J.
Reason and Revelation in the Thought of Leo Strauss. COLMO, Christopher A.
Reason and the Child. WEINSTEIN, Mark.
Reason in Criticism. MIRI, Mrinal.
Reason, Rationality and the Irrational. NAYAK, G C.
Reflections on Blanshard, Reason, and Religion. FERRÉ, Frederick.
As relações entre o Deus da Razão e o Deus da Fé. RENAUD, Michel.
The Rooting and Uprooting of Reason: On *Spacings* by John Sallis. MALY, Kenneth.
Sankara on Reason, Scriptural Authority and Self-Knowledge. UPADHYAYA, K N.
Socratic Reason and Socratic Revelation. MC PHERRAN, Mark L.
Sul controllo nel procedimento di determinazione dei principi dell'ordinamento. COSTANZO, Angelo.
The Contradiction of Belief and Reason in the Middle Ages: the Case of Boetius de Dacia (in Hungarian). JOÓS, Ernest.
The Oscillation of the Concept of Reason in Michel Foucault (in German). BENJOWSKI, Regina.
Verità di ragione e verità di fede. MESSINESE, Leonardo.
Wittgenstein's Lectures on Religious Belief. MARTIN, Michael.
Would Hegel Have Liked to Burn Down All the Churches and Replace Them with Philosophical Academies?. LUFT, Eric V D.
Zu Jürgen Habermas' Option für Fortschritt, Vernunft und Demokratie. BOGNER, Hagen.

REASONABLE DOUBT

Probability Out of Court: Notes on 'Guilt Beyond Reasonable Doubt'. COHEN, Stephen and BERSTEN, Michael.

REASONABLENESS

Atheism, Ayn Rand, and other Heresies. SMITH, George H.
Morally Untenable Beliefs. BURKE, Richard J.
Rationality and Reasonableness. BURBULES, Nicholas C.
Reason and Reasonableness in the Philosophy of Brand Branshard. RECK, Andrew J.
Reasonable Evidence of Reasonableness. KELMAN, Mark.

REASONING

see also Deduction, Induction, Moral Reasoning, Thinking
Clear Thinking: A Practical Introduction. RUCHLIS, Hy.
Do the Right Thing: Studies in Limited Rationality. RUSSELL, Stuart.
Inference and Understanding: A Philosophical and Psychological Perspective. MANKTELOW, K I.
Knowledge Representation and Defeasible Reasoning. KYBURG JR, Henry E (ed).
Morality and Modernity. POOLE, Ross.
The Origin of Thought. ROSMINI, Antonio.
An Outline of the Philosophy of Knowledge and Science. BLANDINO, Giovanni.
Reasoning and Revision in Hybrid Representation Systems. NEBEL, Bernhard.
Representing and Reasoning With Probabilistic Knowledge: A Logical Approach to Probabilities. BACCHUS, Fahiem.
Talking Philosophy: A Wordbook. SPARKES, A W.
What If...? Toward Excellence in Reasoning. HINTIKKA, Jaakko.

REASONING

Within Reason: A Guide to Non-Deductive Reasoning. BURBIDGE, John.

"Acting Human in Our Time" in *The Question of Humanism: Challenges and Possibilities*, ADAMCZEWSKI, Zygmunt.

"Belief Revision, Non-Monotonic Reasoning, and the Ramsey Test" in *Knowledge Representation and Defeasible Reasoning*, CROSS, Charles.

"Inexact and Inductive Reasoning" in *Logic, Methodology and Philosophy of Science, VIII*, PARIS, J and VENCOVSKÁ, A.

"Inheritance Theory and Path-Based Reasoning: An Introduction" in *Knowledge Representation and Defeasible Reasoning*, CARPENTER, Bob and THOMASON, Richmond.

"Non-Monotonic Reasoning by Axiomatic Extensions" in *Logic, Methodology and Philosophy of Science, VIII*, JÄGER, Gerhard.

An Alternative Logical Framework for Dialectical Reasoning in the Social and Policy Sciences. SABRE, Ru Michael.

Can An Argument Be Both Valid and Invalid Too?. NEBLETT, William R.

Critical Thinking and Thinking Critically: Response to Siegel. FINOCCHIARO, Maurice A.

The Emergence of Analogy: Analogical Reasoning as a Constraint Satisfaction Process. VAN DORMAEL, Jan.

The Ethical Decision-Making Processes of Information Systems Workers. PARADICE, David B and DEJOIE, Roy M.

How the Child Reasons. THAYER-BACON, Barbara.

The Logic of Impossible Quantities. SHERRY, David.

Must Thinking Be Critical to Be Critical Thinking? Reply to Finocchiaro. SIEGEL, Harvey.

On Axiomatization of Many-Valued Logics Associated with Formalization of Plausible Reasonings. ANSHAKOV, O M and FINN, V K and SKVORTSOV, D P.

Philosophy, Argument, and Narration. VERENE, Donald Phillip.

The Place of Argumentation in the Theory of Reasoning. JOHNSON, Ralph H.

Pragmatic Conditional Reasoning: Context and Content Effects on the Interpretation of Causal Assertions. HILTON, Denis J.

The Pragmatic Fallacy. SALMON, Nathan.

Reasoning and Computation in Leibniz. SPRUIT, Leen and TAMBURRINI, Guglielmo.

Remarks on Analogy. DA COSTA, Newton C A and SETTE, A M.

Residual Natural Evil and Anthropic Reasoning. MC LEAN, Murdith.

Structural Representation and Surrogative Reasoning. SWOYER, Chris.

REASONS

Natural Reasons: Personality and Polity. HURLEY, S L.

Rationality in Action: Contemporary Approaches. MOSER, Paul K (ed).

"Functional Explanations and Reasons as Causes" in *Philosophical Perspectives, 3: Philosophy of Mind and Action Theory, 1989*, SAYRE-MC CORD, Geoffrey.

"Metaepistemology and Skepticism" in *Doubting: Contemporary Perspectives on Skepticism*, FUMERTON, Richard.

"Practical Thinking, Reasons for Doing, and Intentional Action" in *Philosophical Perspectives, 4: Action Theory and Philosophy of Mind, 1990*, CASTAÑEDA, Héctor-Neri.

"Reasons and Causes" in *Philosophical Perspectives, 3: Philosophy of Mind and Action Theory, 1989*, DRETSKE, Fred.

"Reasons Explanation of Action: An Incompatibilist Account" in *Philosophical Perspectives, 3: Philosophy of Mind and Action Theory, 1989*, GINET, Carl.

Evidence and Reasons for Belief. FOLEY, Richard.

Rationality, Reasons, and the Sociology of Knowledge (in Serbo-Croatian). KAISER, Matthias.

Reason and Emotion. FRICKER, Miranda.

The Strong Programme for the Sociology of Science, Reflexivity and Relativism. NOLA, Robert.

REBELLION(S)

Discourses on Political Violence: The Problem of Coherence. DU TOIT, A B.

REBIRTH

Karma and Rebirth in *Alberuni's India*. SHARMA, Arvind.

Personal Identity and Rebirth. STOEBER, Michael.

RECEPTION

La estética de la recepción desde la teoría platónica del arte. ORTIZ DE URBINA, Ricardo Sánchez.

RECIPROCITY

Ontology and Alterity in Merleau-Ponty. JOHNSON, Galen A (ed).

Constructing Justice. GIBBARD, Allan.

RECKLESSNESS

Intention, Agency and Criminal Liability: Philosophy of Action and the Criminal Law. DUFF, R A.

RECOGNITION

Intentions in Communication. COHEN, Philip R (ed).

Nietzsches Scheitern am Werk. HELLER, Edmund.

Speech Acts and Literary Theory. PETREY, Sandy.

"Woman's Experience: Renaming the Dialectic of Desire and Recognition" in *Writing the Politics of Difference*, MILLS, Patricia J.

Anerkennung: Fichtes Grundlegungen des Rechtsgrundes. JANKE, Wolfgang.

RECOLLECTION

"Plato's Theory of Mind" in *Psychology (Companions to Ancient Thought: 2)*, LOVIBOND, Sabina.

A Middle Platonic Reading of Plato's Theory of Recollection. SCHRENK, Lawrence P.

Sense-Experience and the Argument for Recollection in Plato's *Phaedo*. BEDU-ADDO, J T.

RECONSTRUCTION

Ideals and Illusions: On Reconstruction and Deconstruction in Contemporary Critical Theory. MC CARTHY, Thomas.

"Why Must History Always Be Rewritten?" in *Perspectives on Ideas and Reality*, LAKATOS, László.

Has the History of Philosophy Ruined the Environment?. ATTFIELD, Robin.

Once Again Pure Exchange Economies: A Critical View Towards the Structuralistic Reconstructions by Balzer & Stegmüller. REQUATE, Till.

Reconstructing the Political. JANICAUD, Dominique.

The Reconstruction of Institutions. COLAPIETRO, Vincent M.

Reconstruction, Dialectic and Praxis. RIORDAN, Patrick.

Reflexiones en torno a la metodología de la historia de la filosofía. BENÍTEZ, Laura.

RECURSION THEORY

"Pathologies" in Two Syntactic Categories of Partial Maps. MONTAGNA, Franco.

A 1-Generic Degree Which Bounds a Minimal Degree. KUMABE, Masahiro.

Complexity for Type-2 Relations. TOWNSEND, Mike.

Constructions by Transfinitely Many Workers. KNIGHT, Julia F.

An Existence Theorem for Recursion Categories. HELLER, Alex.

Operative versus Combinatory Spaces. IVANOV, Lyubomir.

Some New Double Induction and Superinduction Principles. SMULLYAN, Raymond M.

Verification of Concurrent Programs: the Automata-Theoretic Framework. VARDI, Moshe Y.

RECURSIVE FUNCTION(S)

Arithmetizing Uniform NC. ALLEN, B.

Boundedness Theorems for Dilators and Ptykes. KECHRIS, Alexander S.

Bounds in Weak Truth-Table Reducibility. HABART, Karol.

Diagonalization and Fixed Points. TONELLA, Guido.

Fixed Points and Diagonal Method. NEGRI, Maurizio.

On a Complexity-Based Way of Constructivizing the Recursive Functions. KROON, F W and BURKHARD, W A.

On a Theorem of Günter Asser. CALUDE, Cristian and SÂNTEAN, Lila.

Relativized Gödel Speed-Up and the Degree of Succinctness of Representations. SOLOMON, Martin K.

Some Results on Bounded Truth-Table Degrees. DITCHEV, Angel V.

A Strong Boundedness Theorem for Dilators. KECHRIS, Alexander S and WOODIN, W H.

RECURSIVELY ENUMERABLE SETS

"Automorphisms of the Lattice of Recursively Enumerable Sets and Hyperhypersimple Sets" in *Logic, Methodology and Philosophy of Science, VIII*, HERRMANN, Eberhard.

Boolean Algebras and Orbits of the Lattice of R.E. Sets Modulo the Finite Sets. CHOLAK, Peter.

The Complexity of Intrinsically R.E. Subsets of Existentially Decidable Models. CHISHOLM, John.

Correction to "Undecidability of $L(F_\infty)$ and Other Lattices of R.E. Substructures" (Corrigendum). DOWNEY, Rod.

The Degree of a Σ_n Cut. CHONG, C T and MOURAD, K J.

Degrees of Orderings Not Isomorphic to Recursive Linear Orderings. JOCKUSCH JR, Carl G and SOARE, Robert I.

The Density of Infima in the Recursively Enumerable Degrees. SLAMAN, Theodore A.

Effective Extensions of Partial Orders. KUMAR ROY, Dev.

Fixed Points and Diagonal Method. NEGRI, Maurizio.

Jumps of Nontrivial Splittings of Recursively Enumerable Sets. INGRASSIA, Michael A and LEMPP, Steffen.

Lattice Nonembeddings and Initial Segments of the Recursively Enumerable Degrees. DOWNEY, Rod.

Maximal R.E. Equivalence Relations. CARROLL, Jeffrey S.

Non-Bounding Construction. SHOENFIELD, J R.

On a Complexity-Based Way of Constructivizing the Recursive Functions. KROON, F W and BURKHARD, W A.

The Ordertype of β-R.E. Sets. SUTNER, Klaus.

Some Remarks on the Algebraic Structure of the Medvedev Lattice. SORBI, Andrea.

Some Results on Bounded Truth-Table Degrees. DITCHEV, Angel V.

Undecidability and Initial Segments of the (R.E.) TT-Degrees. HAUGHT, Christine Ann and SHORE, Richard A.

Weakly Semirecursive Sets. JOCKUSCH JR, Carl G and OWINGS JR, James C.

RECURSIVENESS

Computability, Complexity, Logic. BÖRGER, E.

RECURSIVENESS
Effective Model Theory versus Recursive Model Theory. CHISHOLM, John.
Minimal Degrees Recursive in 1-Generic Degrees. CHONG, C T and DOWNEY, R G.
Recursive Surreal Numbers. HARKLEROAD, Leon.

REDISTRIBUTION
Justice, Redistribution, and the Family. POST, Stephen G.
Nozick on Social Justice. AGARWALA, Binod Kumar.

REDUCIBILITY
Bounds in Weak Truth-Table Reducibility. HABART, Karol.
On Restricted Forms of Enumeration Reducibility. WATSON, Phil.
On the Irreducibility of the Will. GARCIA, J L A.
Undecidability and Initial Segments of the (R.E.) TT-Degrees. HAUGHT, Christine Ann and SHORE, Richard A.

REDUCTION
The Chain of Change: A Study of Aristotle's "Physics" VII. WARDY, Robert.
"Counterfactual Reduction" in *Imre Lakatos and Theories of Scientific Change*, RANTALA, V.
Interpreting State Reduction from the Practices-up. CORDERO, Alberto.
Pluralistic Ontology and Theory Reduction in the Physical Sciences. ROHRLICH, Fritz.
Seven Types of Obloquy: Travesties of Marxism. GERAS, Norman.
A Unification-Theoretic Method for Investigating the *k*-Provability Problem. FARMER, William.
Weitere verschärfungen zu den Reduktionstypen.... DEUTSCH, Michael.

REDUCTIONISM
Explaining Human Action. LENNON, Kathleen.
Philosophical Foundations of Health Education. LAURA, Ronald S.
The Philosophy of Science. BOYD, Richard (ed).
"Physicalism, Reductionism and Hilbert" in *Physicalism in Mathematics*, HALLETT, Michael.
AIDS, Myth, and Ethics. SUNDSTRÖM, Per.
An Ambiguity in Parfit's Theory of Personal Identity. CURZER, Howard.
Can Marxism Help Biology?. KASSIOLA, Joel.
Causation: Reductionism Versus Realism. TOOLEY, Michael.
Contributi piagetiani ad una scienza della mente. BORELLA, Silvia.
Critical Marxism as an Historical Process of Society and Science (in German). SANDKÜHLER, Hans Jörg.
Emergenz Bausteine für eine Begriffsexplikation. STÖCKLER, Manfred.
A Historico-Philosophical Investigation of Anti-Science: The Phenomenological Encounter. RAINA, Dhruv.
Is the Central Upanishadic Teaching a Reductionist Thesis?. PULIGANDLA, Ramakrishna.
The Logical Status of Modal Reductionism. MOSER, Paul K and VANDER NAT, Arnold.
Mental Causation and Non-Reductive Monism. MACDONALD, Cynthia and MACDONALD, Graham.
Molecular Biology and the Unity of Science. KINCAID, Harold.
The Nature of Physical Reality. POLKINGHORNE, John C.
Personal Identity and Reductionism. GARRETT, Brian.
The Pincovian Persuasion: Six Problems in Virtue Ethics (A Free Response to Seung). BUDZISZEWSKI, J.
Reduction and the Part/Whole Relation. KRECZ, Charles A.
Reduction, Elimination, and the Mental. SCHWARTZ, Justin.
The Reductionist Ideal in Cognitive Psychology. MONTGOMERY, Richard.
Self-Organization, Emergent Properties and the Unity of the World. ROTH, Gerhard and SCHWEGLER, Helmut.
Theorie antireduktionistischer Argumente: Fallstudie Bohr. HOYNINGEN-HUENE, Paul.
Theory and Reality in the Work of Jean Henry Fabre. YAVETZ, Ido.
Wetten en verhalen. KWA, Chunglin.

REDUNDANCY
The Minimal and Semiminimal Notions of Truth. FOX, J.
Object-Dependent Thoughts and Psychological Redundancy. NOONAN, Harold W.

REEDER, H
Never say "Never": A Response to Reeder's "Wittgenstein Never Was a Phenomenologist". GIER, Nicholas F.

REFERENCE(S)
Frege and Other Philosophers. DUMMETT, Michael.
Has Semantics Rested on a Mistake?. WETTSTEIN, Howard.
Writers and Philosophers: A Sourcebook of Philosophical Influences on Literature. THOMAS, Edmund J.
"Direct Reference and Propositional Attitudes" in *Themes From Kaplan*, SOAMES, Scott.
"Direct Reference, the Semantics of Thinking, and Guise Theory" in *Themes From Kaplan*, CASTAÑEDA, Héctor-Neri.
"Mario Bunge on Semantics" in *Studies on Mario Bunge's "Treatise"*, BUNGE, Mario.
"The Mode-of-Presentation Problem" in *Propositional Attitudes: The Role of Content in Logic, Language, and Mind*, SCHIFFER, Stephen.
"On Direct Reference" in *Themes From Kaplan*, DEUTSCH, Harry.
"Personal References" in *Information, Semantics and Epistemology*, LOAR, Brian.
"Referência e valor cognitivo" in *Dinâmica do Pensar: Homenagem a Oswaldo Market*, BRANQUINHO, João.
Abstract Singular Reference: A Dilemma for Dummett. MILLER, Alexander.
Aspects of the Problem of Reference (1): Phenomenology, Hermeneutics and Deconstruction. RAJAN, R Sundara.
Aspects of the Problem of Reference (I). RAJAN, R Sundara.
Aspects of the Problem of Reference (II). RAJAN, R Sundara.
The Causal Theory of Reference and Religious Language. HARRIS, James F.
Descriptions and Group Reference. MUKHERJI, Nirmalangshu.
Direct Reference, Meaning, and Thought. RECANATI, François.
Disjoint Reference into NP. SELLS, Peter.
Essai sur le thème du réferentiel. ORY, André.
Filosofía desde la teoría causal de la referencia. NUBIOLA, Jaime.
Frege-Russell Semantics?. WETTSTEIN, Howard.
Future Individuals. TEICHMANN, Roger.
Gangesa and Transfer of Meaning. SAHA, Sukharanjan.
God and Man: Action and Reference in Hobbes. BERTMAN, Martin A.
Indexicality: The Transparent Subjective Mechanism for Encountering a World. CASTAÑEDA, Héctor-Neri.
John Scottus Eriugena: Recent Works of Consultation. MC EVOY, James J.
Making Sense of Words. MC CULLOCH, Gregory.
The Myth of the Essential Indexical. MILLIKAN, Ruth.
Nominalism and Abstract Reference. MORELAND, J P.
On Wishing there were Unicorns. CLARK, Stephen R L.
Opacidad y presuposición. ARANOVICH, Raúl.
Putting One's Foot in One's Head—Part I: Why. PERLIS, Donald.
References in Narrative Text. WIEBE, Janyce M.
Remnants of Schiffer's Principle [P]. SEYMOUR, Daniel.
Semantics without Reference. GAUKER, Christopher.
Sentidos, referencias y concepto en Frege. MARTINEZ FREIRE, P.
Thinking of Something. FITCH, Gregory.
Translation Failure Between Theories. SANKEY, Howard.
Transzendentale Argumente pragmatisch relativiert: Über fundamentale Optionen in der Philosophie. LAUENER, Henri.
What Goodman Leaves Out. ELGIN, Catherine Z.

REFERENT
Foucault and The Referent. LUNN, Forrest.
Self-Making and World-Making. BRUNER, Jerome.

REFERENTIAL OPACITY
Referential Opacity in Aristotle. SPELLMAN, Lynne.
You and She. WILLIAMS, C J F.

REFERENTIALISM
Proper Names, Cognitive Contents, and Beliefs. BRAUN, David M.

REFERRING
"Referring to Things That No Longer Exist" in *Philosophical Perspectives, 4: Action Theory and Philosophy of Mind, 1990*, CHISHOLM, Roderick M.

REFLECTION
"Between Being and Essence: Reflection's Logical Disguises" in *Essays on Hegel's Logic*, DAHLSTROM, Daniel O.
Alle origini della riflessione di Leopold von Ranke sulla storia: K F Bachmann e J G Fichte. GHELARDI, Maurizio.
È possibile un'esperienza di Dio?. CAVADI, Augusto.
Education and the Cultivation of Reflection. SCHNEIDER, Herbert W.
Humanizing the Humanities: Some Reflections on George Steiner's "Brutal Paradox". KARIER, Clarence J.
Ontología hermenéutica y reflexión filológica: el acceso a la filosofía de H G Gadamer. DOMINGO, Agustín.
Plato's Line Revisited: The Pedagogy of Complete Reflection. WOOD, Robert E.
Response to Merkle and Pritscher. SMITH, Phil.
Secondary Reflection and Marcelian Anthropology. MICHAUD, Thomas A.
Soggettività e autocoscienza: Prospettive e problemi in Dieter Henrich. CELANO, Bruno.
Some Fundamental Aspects of Socioecological Theory and Policy, Part I (in German). OPIELKA, Michael.
Todor Pavlov (1890-1977)—The Generalization of Reflection (in German). HOLZ, Hans Heinz.

REFLECTIVE EQUILIBRIUM
The Fragmentation of Reason. STICH, Stephen.
The Highest Moral Knowledge and the Truth Behind Internalism. DE PAUL, Michael R.
Utilitarianism and the Idea of Reflective Equilibrium. TERSMAN, Folke.

REFLEXIVITY
"Kant, Hegel and the Possibility of a Speculative Logic" in *Essays on Hegel's Logic*, DUQUETTE, David A.
Dicendum est eum non esse hominem: Ein mögliches frühes Zeugnis für die anthropologische Gewichtung.... KÖHLER, Theodor Wolfram.
Hope: Its Essence and Forms (in Polish). SYMOTIUK, Stefan.
More about Thoughts. DUMMETT, Michael.
The Problem of Theoretical Self-Reflexivity in Peirce and Santayana. DILWORTH, David A.

REFLEXIVITY
Sartre on Pre-Reflective Consciousness. AGRAWAL, M M.
The Strong Programme for the Sociology of Science, Reflexivity and Relativism. NOLA, Robert.
You and She. WILLIAMS, C J F.

REFORM(S)
"Can Responsibility Be Diminished?" in *Liability and Responsibility*, KENNY, Anthony.
"A Return to the Crossroads: A Maritainian View of the New Educational Reformers" in *From Twilight to Dawn: The Cultural Vision of Jacques Maritain*, HANCOCK, Curtis L.
"Scientific Atheism" in the Era of Perestrojka. MELNICK, A James.
Aufklärung und Reform. SCHNEIDERS, Werner.
Considerazioni in margine a un'interpretazione di Bruno. MANZONI, Claudio.
Deficiencies in Contemporary Theories of Justice. LÖTTER, H P P.
Discipline-Based Art Education: Conceptions and Misconceptions. EISNER, Elliot W.
Is There a New Teacher Unionism?. URBAN, Wayne J.
The On-Going Deconstruction of Marxism-Leninism. BUCHHOLZ, Arnold and SWIDERSKI, E M.
PES and School Reform. TOZER, Steven.
A Proposal for Health Care: Revolution Not Reform. BARNET, Robert J.
A Response to Beck, Giarelli/Chambliss, Leach, Tozer, and Macmillan. GREENE, Maxine.

REFORMATION
Zu Grundfragen des Toleranzproblems in Vergangenheit und Gegenwart. WOLLGAST, Siegfried.

REFUSAL OF TREATMENT
Justified Limits on Refusing Intervention. CHERVENAK, Frank A and MC CULLOUGH, Laurence B.

REFUTABILITY
Popper's Demarcation of Science Refuted. AGASSI, Joseph.

REFUTATION
On Pure Refutation Formulations of Sentential Logics. SKURA, Tomasz.

REGAN, T
Moral Theories, Impartiality, and the Status of Non-Rational, Sentient Beings. FILICE, Carlo.

REGRESSION
Corresponding Regressions, Procedural Evidence, and the Dialectics of Substantive Theory, Metaphysics, Methodology. CHAMBERS, William.
Inferring Formal Causation from Corresponding Regressions. CHAMBERS, William V.
Must Scientific Diagrams Be Eliminable? The Case of Path Analysis. GRIESEMER, James R.
Untangling Cause, Necessity, Temporality, and Method: Response to Chamber's Method of Corresponding Regressions. WILLIAMS, Richard N.

REGRETS
Moral Conflicts in Kantian Ethics. MC CARTY, Richard.

REGULARITY(-TIES)
The Secret Connexion: Causation, Realism, and David Hume. STRAWSON, Galen.
Miracles and Ghazali's First Theory of Causation. BAHLUL, Raja.
On Regular Modal Logics with Axiom.... SWIRYDOWICZ, Kazimierz.

REGULATION(S)
Are Physicians a "Delinquent Community"?: Issues in Professional Competence, Conduct, and Self-Regulation. SWAZEY, Judith P.
Are Physicians a "Delinquent Community"?: Issues in Professional Competence, Conduct, Self-Regulation: Comment. LAMMERS, Stephen E.
Beyond Bean Counting: Establishing High Ethical Standards in the Public Accounting Profession. COHEN, Jeffrey R and PANT, Laurie W.
Critical Synthesis on the Uses and Justifications for the Regulations of Intellectual Property. SNAPPER, John.
The Ethics of Rent Control. HANLY, Ken.
Necesidad y existencia del código de moral profesional. MUÑOZ BARQUERO, Elizabeth.
New Directions in Nursing Home Ethics. COLLOPY, Bart and BOYLE, Philip and JENNINGS, Bruce.
The Regulation of Virtue: Cross-Currents in Professional Ethics. JENNINGS, Bruce.
Some Problems of Legal Language. KNAPP, Viktor.

REGULATIVE IDEA(S)
"Winch and Schutz on the Regulative Idea of a Social Science" in *Life-World and Politics: Between Modernity and Postmodernity*, O'NEILL, John.
Mapping the Human Genome: Some Thoughts for Those Who Say "There Should Be A Law On It". SKENE, Loane.

REHABILITATION
Treatment and Rehabilitation as a Mode of Punishment. MARTIN, Rex.

REICH, H
Relating Science and Theology with Complementarity: A Caution. SHARPE, Kevin J.

REICHENBACH
Quantum Physics and Logical Truth (in Italian). GIANNETTO, Enrico.
A Short Vindication of Reichenbach's "Event-Splitting". PFEIFER, Karl.

REID
Bayle, Leibniz, Hume and Reid on Extension, Composites and Simples. CUMMINS, Phillip.
Chisholm, Reid and the Problem of the Epistemic Surd. LEHRER, Keith.
Coming To Be Without a Cause. SULLIVAN, T D.
Du fondement de la loi morale, une éthique de la raison ou du sentiment?. DAVAL, R.
Elements of Speech Act Theory in the Work of Thomas Reid. SCHUHMANN, Karl and SMITH, Barry.
Hume, Reid and Innate Ideas: A Response to John P Wright. GALLIE, Roger D.
Keith Lehrer and Thomas Reid. CHISHOLM, Roderick M.
The Scottish Influence on French Aesthetic Thought: Later Developments. MANNS, James W.

REIFICATION
"Thing and Thought" in *Knowledge Representation and Defeasible Reasoning*, PERLIS, Don.

REINCARNATION
The Evidence for Reincarnation. COCKBURN, David.
In Defence of Reincarnation. DANIELS, Charles B.
Karma and Reincarnation in Advaita Vedānta. SHARMA, Arvind.
Personal Identity, Reincarnation, and Resurrection. IALACCI, Michael.
The Possibility of Reincarnation. NOONAN, Harold W.
Punyadāna or Transference of Merit—A Fiction. KRISHAN, Y.

REINER, H
Duty and Inclination: The Phenomenological Value Ethics of Hans Reiner. GÖRTZEN, René.

REJECTION
The Method of Axiomatic Rejection for the Intuitionistic Propositional Logic. DUTKIEWICZ, Rafal.
Providence, Freedom and Human Destiny. TALBOTT, Thomas.

RELATION(S)
see also International Relation(s)
The Idea of a Social Science and its Relation to Philosophy (Second Edition). WINCH, Peter.
Wittgenstein and Contemporary Philosophy of Language. RUNDLE, Bede.
The 'Gay Science' of Nietzsche (in Dutch). ESTERHUYSE, Willie.
Cloture Intervallaire et Extension Logique d'une Relation. ILLE, Pierre.
Complexity for Type-2 Relations. TOWNSEND, Mike.
Cook Wilson as Critic of Bradley. TACELLI, Ronald K.
A Dialogue on Value, I: Values and Relations. LACHS, John.
Effective Extensions of Partial Orders. KUMAR ROY, Dev.
Essai sur le thème du réferentiel. ORY, André.
A Formal Representation of Declaration-Related Legal Relations. HANSSON, Sven Ove.
Indexicality: The Transparent Subjective Mechanism for Encountering a World. CASTAÑEDA, Héctor-Neri.
The Interpretability Logic of Peano Arithmetic. BERARDUCCI, Alessandro.
Interpretation of Relevant Logics in a Logic of Ternary Relations. ORLOWSKA, Ewa.
Many-Sorted Elementary Equivalence. DZIERZGOWSKI, Daniel.
Maximal R.E. Equivalence Relations. CARROLL, Jeffrey S.
The Metaphilosophy of Dialogue. KUCZYNSKI, Janusz.
Mr Keynes on Probability. RAMSEY, F P.
A New Interpretation of Russell's Multiple-Relation Theory of Judgment. LANDINI, Gregory.
Not Very Likely: A Reply to Ramsey. WATT, D E.
Notions of Relative Ubiquity for Invariant Sets of Relational Structures. BANKSTON, Paul and RUITENBURG, Wim.
Philosophie et mythologie dans la dernière philosophie de Schelling. MAESSCHALCK, Marc.
Problems Concerning the Presence of the Composer in His Music (in Polish). BUCZEK, Barbara.
Reduction and the Part/Whole Relation. KRECZ, Charles A.
Regressive Partition Relations, *n*-Subtle Cardinals, and Borel Diagonalization. KANAMORI, Akihiro.
Relations and Sixteenth-Century Mexican Logic. REDMOND, Walter.
Le relazioni divine secondo S Tommaso d'Aquino: Riproposizione di un problema e prospettive di indagine. VENTIMIGLIA, Giovanni.
Remarks about the Idea of the University (in Dutch). ROSSOUW, H W.
Rules and Relations: Some Connectionist Implications for Cognitive Science and Language. CILLIERS, F P.
Russell on Pastness. KENYON, Timothy A.
Stability for Pairs of Equivalence Relations. TOFFALORI, Carlo.
State-Spaces and Meaning Relations Among Predicates. ARNTZENIUS, Frank.
A Theorem on Labelled Trees and the Limits of Its Provability. PFEIFFER, Helmut.
What Philosophy for Judaism and Christianity? (in French). DUPONCHEELE, Joseph.

RELATION(S)
What was Leibniz's Problem about Relations?. BURDICK, Howard.
'The Darkness of This Time': Wittgenstein and the Modern World. BOUVERESSE, Jacques.

RELATIONISM
Absolutism and Relationism in Space and Time: A False Dichotomy. HINCKFUSS, Ian.
An Alleged Analogy Between Numbers and Propositions. CRANE, Tim.
Comments on Schiffer's *Remnants of Meaning*. RICHARD, Mark.
Embedding and Uniqueness in Relationist Theories. MUNDY, Brent.
The Relational Theory of Belief (A Reply to Richard). SCHIFFER, Stephen.
Relationism and Temporal Topology. LE POIDEVIN, Robin.
Substance, Relations, and Arguments About the Nature of Space-Time. TELLER, Paul.

RELATIONSHIP(S)
Descartes Among the Scholastics. GRENE, Marjorie.
Difference and Subjectivity: Dialogue and Personal Identity. JACQUES, Francis.
Nicholas of Cusa's de Pace Fidei and Cribratio Alkorani: Translation and Analysis. HOPKINS, Jasper.
Wittgenstein, Ethics and Aesthetics: The View from Eternity. TILGHMAN, B R.
"The Fiduciary Relationship and the Nature of Professions" in *Ethics, Trust, and the Professions: Philosophical and Cultural Aspects*, SOKOLOWSKI, Robert.
"Mind and Body" in *Key Themes in Philosophy*, WILKES, K V.
"A New Visualization of the Mind-Brain Relationship" in *The Case for Dualism*, HARRISON, Stephen.
"Reflections on Chinese Language and Philosophy" in *Hermeneutics and the Poetic Motion, Translation Perspectives V—1990*, SOO, Francis.
"Science and Religion" in *Science and Religion: One World-Changing Perspectives on Reality*, MELSEN, A G M van.
"Through the Looking Glass: Philosophy, Research Programmes and the Scientific Community" in *Imre Lakatos and Theories of Scientific Change*, NICOLACOPOULOS, Pantelis D.
The Aesthetic Relation of Musical Performer and Audience. PUTMAN, Daniel.
Art and Morality: On the Problem of Stating a Problem. HATTINGH, J P.
Democracy and the Church-State Relationship. KAINZ, Howard.
Friendship and Education. WHITE, Patricia.
The Lover-Beloved Relationship Reconsidered. HOLMES, Richard and DANIEL, Mano.

RELATIVE
Las proposiciones de relativo en Alberto de Sajonia. TALEGÓN, César.
Relative Identity and Locke's Principle of Individuation. UZGALIS, William L.

RELATIVISM
see also Cultural Relativism, Ethical Relativism
After the Demise of the Tradition: Rorty, Critical Theory, and the Fate of Philosophy. NIELSEN, Kai.
Objectivity, Relativism, and Truth: Philosophical Papers, Volume 1. RORTY, Richard.
Philosophie Juridique Européenne. TRIGEAUD, Jean-Marc.
Science and Relativism: Some Key Controversies in the Philosophy of Science. LAUDAN, Larry.
Varieties of Social Explanation: An Introduction to the Philosophy of Social Science. LITTLE, Daniel.
Vernunft und Kontingenz: Rationalität und Ethos in der Phänomenologie. ORTH, Ernst Wolfgang (ed).
"Beyond Objectivity and Relativism: Feyerabend's 'Two Argumentative Chains' and Sociology" in *The Social Horizon of Knowledge*, JARY, David.
"Mario Bunge on Epistemology" in *Studies on Mario Bunge's "Treatise"*, BUNGE, Mario.
"Moral Relativism and Strict Universalism" in *The Moral Domain: Essays in the Ongoing Discussion between Philosophy and the Social Sciences*, NUNNER-WINKLER, Gertrud.
"On Relativism" in *Studies on Mario Bunge's "Treatise"*, BOUDON, Raymond.
"Rationality, Relativism, Feminism" in *Writing the Politics of Difference*, WINANT, Terry.
"Relativism" in *A Companion to Ethics*, WONG, David B.
Agent-Action Judgements. TILLEY, John J.
Azande Logic *Verus* Western Logic?. TRIPLETT, Timm.
Being a Realist about Relativism (In Ethics). SAYRE-MC CORD, Geoffrey.
The Bellman's Map: Does Antifoundationalism Entail Incommensurability and Relativism?. CHURCHILL, John.
Between Rationalism and Relativism: On Larry Laudan's Model of Scientific Rationality. GROBLER, Adam.
Bradley and Lonergan's Relativist. TESKE, Roland.
Chalmers on Method. GOWER, Barry.
Commentary on Sayre-McCord's 'Being a Realist about Relativism'. WONG, David B.
Conventionalism in Physics. MORRIS, W T.
A Dialogue on Value, II: Why Is There Something Good, Not Simply Something?. KOHÁK, Erazim.
Feminism and Relativism. RUSSELL, Denise.
Gilbert Harman's Internalist Moral Relativism. POJMAN, Louis P.
Hayden White: "Historicism" as Linguistic Relativism in Historiography (in Polish). POMORSKI, Jan.
Historical Relativism as a Manifestation of the Cognitive Activity of a Historian According to Collingwood (in Polish). ZDYBEL, Jolanta.
How to Defend Science Against Scepticism: A Reply to Barry Gower. CHALMERS, Alan.
Is Knowledge Socially Determined? A Critique. CHAUDHURY, Mahasweta.
Legal Positivism and Democracy in the Twentieth Century. SQUELLA, Agustí.
Making Noises in Counterpoint or Chorus: Putnam's Rejection of Relativism. JOHNSON, Jeffery L.
Moral Planes and Intrinsic Values. ANDERSON, James C.
Moral Relativism and Deontic Logic. HUGLY, Philip and SAYWARD, Charles.
Nietzsche and the Cultural Resonance of the 'Death of God'. ROBERTS, Richard H.
A Note on Verisimilitude and Relativization to Problems. MONGIN, Philippe.
Philosophers as Professional Relativists: Canadian Philosophical Association Presidential Address 1990. BUTTS, Robert E.
Problemas lógicos en el relativismo ético. CAMACHO, Luis A.
Putnam's Realism and Relativity: An Uneasy Balance. THROOP, William and DORAN, Katheryn.
Quine's Relativism. HUGLY, Philip and SAYWARD, Charles.
Recent Work on Ethical Relativism. STEWART, Robert M and THOMAS, Lynn L.
Relativism, Ineffability, and the Appeal to Experience: A Reply to the Myth Makers. BARNES, L Philip.
Replies and Comments. PUTNAM, Hilary.
Rhetoric and Argumentation: Relativism and Beyond. KIENPOINTNER, Manfred.
Sartre, Aron et le relativisme historique. BAUGH, Bruce.
Stout on Relativism, Liberalism, and Communitarianism. QUIRK, Michael J.
The Strong Programme for the Sociology of Science, Reflexivity and Relativism. NOLA, Robert.
Transzendentale Argumente pragmatisch relativiert: Über fundamentale Optionen in der Philosophie. LAUENER, Henri.
What Putnam Should Have Said: An Alternative Reply to Rorty. HARTZ, Carolyn G.

RELATIVITY
"The Mind-Body Problem" in *The Case for Dualism*, SMYTHIES, John R.
"Phenomenalism, Relativity and Atoms: Rehabilitating Ernst Mach's Philosophy of Science" in *Logic, Methodology and Philosophy of Science, VIII*, WOLTERS, Gereon.
Der Begriff der Bewegung bei Kant: Über den Grundbegriff der Empirie und die empirischen Begriffe. HOFFMANN, Thomas Sören.
Cohen on Einstein's Simultaneity *Gedankenexperiment*. WHITE, V Alan.
The De-Con-Struction of Reason. GLYNN, Simon.
Ernst Mach Leaves "The Church of Physics". BLACKMORE, John.
God and Real Time. CRAIG, William Lane.
Is Happiness Relative?. VEENHOVEN, Ruut.
Kinship and Moral Relativity. PARGETTER, Robert.
On Relativity Theory and Openness of the Future. STEIN, Howard.
On the Nature of Einstein's Realism. POLIKAROV, Azaria.
On the Origin of Spin in Relativity. SACHS, Mendel.
Prolegomenon to a Proper Interpretation of Quantum Field Theory. TELLER, Paul.
Realismo e fenomenismo nella fisica moderna. BLANDINO, Giovanni.
The Role of Perceptual Relativity in Berkeley's Philosophy. MUEHLMANN, Robert.
Scepticism and Relativity. BARNES, Jonathan.
Two Kinds of Agent-Relativity. HUMBERSTONE, I L.

RELEVANCE
The Sweep of Probability. SCHLESINGER, George N.
Corroboration and Conditional Positive Relevance. WAGNER, Carl G.
Epistemic Paternalism: Communication Control in Law and Society. GOLDMAN, Alvin I.
Independent Evidence of Religion. D'SOUZA, Felix.
Nonrules and Plausibility: An Illustration in Pragmatic Theory. POWELL, Mava Jo.
Propositional Relevance. BOWLES, George.
Relevance and Paraconsistency—A New Approach. AVRON, A.
Relevance as an Explanation of Communication. ROBERTS, Lawrence D.
Some Syntactical Properties of Intermediate Predicate Logics. SUZUKI, Nobu-Yuki.

RELEVANCE LOGIC
The Justification for Relevance Logic. BAGHRAMIAN, Maria.

RELEVANT LOGICS
Cartesian Scepticism and Relevant Alternatives. SCHRECK, P A.
Corrections to Some Results for BCK Logics and Algebras. BUNDER, M W.
Gentzenization and Decidability of Some Contraction-Less Relevant Logics. BRADY, Ross T.
Interpretation of Relevant Logics in a Logic of Ternary Relations. ORLOWSKA, Ewa.

RELEVANT LOGICS
The Irrelevance of Classical Logic. KEENE, G B.
Models for Relevant Modal Logics. FUHRMANN, André.
Non-Commutative Intuitionistic Linear Logic. ABRUSCI, V Michele.
On the Logic of Contingent Relevant Implication: Conceptual Incoherence in the Intuitive Interpretation of *R*. LANCE, Mark.
On the Structure of De Morgan Monoids with Corollaries on Relevant Logic and Theories. SLANEY, John K.
Orlowska's Relevant Implications, Relevant Logics and Analytic Implication. GIAMBRONE, Steve.
Peirced Clean Through. MEYER, Robert K.
Relevance and Paraconsistency—A New Approach. AVRON, A.
Relevance and Paraconsistency—A New Approach, Part II: The Formal Systems. AVRON, Arnon.
Relevance and Paraconsistency—A New Approach, Part III: Cut-Free Gentzen-Type Systems. AVRON, Arnon.
Relevant Containment Logics and Certain Frame Problems of AI. SYLVAN, Richard.
Routley-Meyer Type Semantics for Urquhart's C. MÉNDEZ, José M.
Truth Table Logic with a Survey of Embeddability Results. TENNANT, Neil.

RELIABILISM
Knowledge in Perspective: Selected Essays in Epistemology. SOSA, Ernest.
The Trouble With Goldman's Reliabilism. GLEB, Gary.

RELIABILITY
Firth's Critique of Epistemological Rule-Utilitarianism. SHOPE, Robert K.
The Need for Charity in Semantics. WARMBRŌD, Ken.
Probability Out of Court: Notes on 'Guilt Beyond Reasonable Doubt'. COHEN, Stephen and BERSTEN, Michael.

RELIGION
see also Atheism, Buddhism, Christianity, Evil(s), Faith, God, Hinduism, Humanism, Immortality, Judaism, Metaphysics, Miracle(s), Mysticism, Theism
"Also sprach Herakleitos". WOHLFART, Günter.
'Religion' and the Religions in the English Enlightenment. HARRISON, Peter.
Archetypal Process: Self and Divine in Whitehead, Jung, and Hillman. GRIFFIN, David Ray (ed).
Atheism, Ayn Rand, and other Heresies. SMITH, George H.
Die Aufhebung der Begriffs-philosophie. KRONABEL, Christoph.
Behind the Masks of God: An Essay Toward Comparative Theology. NEVILLE, Robert Cummings.
Benjamin Constant and the Post-Revolutionary Mind. FONTANA, Biancamaria.
Blaise Pascals: "Pensées" (1656-1662) Systematische 'Gedanken' über. KIRSCH, Ulrich.
Celebrating Peace. ROUNER, Leroy S (ed).
Chinese Buddhist Apocrypha. BUSWELL JR, Robert E (ed).
Chinese Texts and Philosophical Contexts. ROSEMONT JR, Henry (ed).
Christian Faith and Historical Understanding (Second Edition). NASH, Ronald H.
The Co-Existence of God and Evil. TRAU, Jane Mary.
Core Questions in Philosophy: A Text With Readings. SOBER, Elliott.
A Cultivated Mind: Essays On J S Mill Presented to John M Robson. LAINE, Michael (ed).
David Hume and the Problem of Reason. DANFORD, John W.
David Hume: Historiker und Philosoph. LÜTHE, Rudolf.
The Devil and Secular Humanism: The Children of the Enlightenment. RADEST, Howard B.
Dialogue with the Other: The Inter-Religious Dialogue. TRACY, David.
Dictionary of Religion and Philosophy. MAC GREGOR, Geddes.
The Difference Between Truth and Opinion: How the Misuse of Language Can Lead to Disaster. COONEY, Timothy J.
Discussioni sul neo-Tomismo: Per il progresso della Filosofia Cristiana. BLANDINO, Giovanni.
Divine Nature and Human Language: Essays in Philosophical Theology. ALSTON, William P.
Escape from God. TURNER, Dean.
Essays on the Context, Nature, and Influence of Isaac Newton's Theology. FORCE, James E (ed).
Explaining Religion: Criticism and Theory from Bodin to Freud. PREUS, J Samuel (ed).
Franz Rosenzweig: Existentielles Denken und gelebte Bewährung. SCHMIED-KOWARZIK, Wolfdietrich.
From Unity to Pluralism: The Internal Evolution of Thomism. MC COOL, Gerald A.
Glück und Lebenssinn: Eine religionsphilosophische Untersuchung. DRESCHER, Johannes.
Grace, Politics and Desire: Essays on Augustine. MEYNELL, Hugo A (ed).
The Great Goddess and the Aistian Mythical World. VYCINAS, Vincent.
A Hindu Perspective on the Philosophy of Religion. SHARMA, Arvind.
A History of Women Philosophers, Volume II: Medieval, Renaissance and Enlightenment, A.D. 500-1600. WAITHE, Mary Ellen (ed).
Hobbes. TUCK, Richard.
Hope and Its Hieroglyph: A Critical Decipherment of Ernst Bloch's "Principle of Hope". ROBERTS, Richard H.
How to Play Theological Ping-Pong: And Other Essays on Faith and Reason. ABRAHAM, William J (ed).
The Idea of Christian Charity: A Critique of Some Contemporary Conceptions. GRAHAM, Gordon.
The Idea of the Miraculous: The Challenge to Science and Religion. WILLIAMS, T C.
Idea, mente, specie: Platonismo e scienza in Johannes Marcus Marci (1595-1667). MOCCHI, Giuliana.
In Defense of Mystical Ideas: Support for Mystical Beliefs from a Purely Theoretical Viewpoint. CHAPMAN, Tobias.
In Partnership with God: Contemporary Jewish Law and Ethics. SHERWIN, Byron L.
Inscriptions and Reflections: Essays in Philosophical Theology. SCHARLEMANN, Robert P.
Introduction to Philosophy: Classical and Contemporary Readings. POJMAN, Louis P.
John Craige's Mathematical Principles of Christian Theology. NASH, Richard.
John Dewey: Religious Faith and Democratic Humanism. ROCKEFELLER, Steven C.
Key Themes in Philosophy. GRIFFITHS, A Phillips (ed).
Kierkegaard in Golden Age Denmark. KIRMMSE, Bruce H.
Kierkegaards Phänomenologie der Freiheitserfahrung. DISSE, Jörg.
The Law of Karma: A Philosophical Study. REICHENBACH, Bruce R.
The Legacy of Hermann Cohen. KLUBACK, William.
The Making of a Nuclear Peace: The Task of Today's Just War Theorists. SICHOL, Marcia W.
The Metaphysics of Religious Belief. SHOOMAN, A P.
Metaphysik als Metahistorik oder Hermeneutik des unreinen Denkens Die Philosophie Max Müllers. RUIZ-PESCE, Ramón Eduardo.
Modern Faith and Thought. THIELICKE, Helmut.
The Moral Animus of David Hume. SIEBERT, Donald T.
Myth and Philosophy: A Contest of Truths. HATAB, Lawrence J.
New Harvest: Transplanting Body Parts and Reaping the Benefits. KEYES, C Don (ed).
Nicholas of Cusa's de Pace Fidei and Cribratio Alkorani: Translation and Analysis. HOPKINS, Jasper.
Nine Talmudic Readings. ARONOWICZ, Annette (trans).
The Noble Savage: Jean-Jacques Rousseau, 1754-1762. CRANSTON, Maurice.
Nonviolence in Theory and Practice. HOLMES, Robert L.
Phenomenology of the Truth Proper to Religion. GUERRIÈRE, Daniel (ed).
The Philosophy in Christianity. VESEY, Godfrey (ed).
Philosophy in World Perspective: A Comparative Hermeneutic of the Major Theories. DILWORTH, David A.
Philosophy of the "Gita". PATEL, Ramesh N.
The Place of the Hidden Moon: Erotic Mysticism in the Vaisnava-sahajiyā Cult of Bengal. DIMOCK JR, Edward C.
Platonic Piety. MORGAN, Michael L.
Sacred Fragments: Recovering Theology for the Modern Jew. GILLMAN, Neil.
Science and Religion: One World-Changing Perspectives on Reality. FENNEMA, Jan (ed).
Science versus Religion. CLEMENTS, Tad S.
Scienza, Filosofia e Religione tra '600 e '700 in Italia. PREDAVAL MAGRINI, Maria Vittoria (ed).
Self and Non-Self: The Drigdrisyaviveka Attributed to Samkara. RAPHAEL (trans).
Spirit and Existence: A Philosophy Inquiry into the Meaning of Spiritual Existence. GELVEN, Michael.
Thinking Philosophically: An Introduction to Philosophy with Readings. GUSMANO, Joseph J.
Thinking the Unthinkable: Meanings of the Holocaust. GOTTLIEB, Roger S (ed).
To Be at Home: Christianity, Civil Religion, and World Community. ROUNER, Leroy S.
To Die or Not to Die?. BERGER, Arthur S (ed).
The Transcendental Temptation: A Critique of Religion and the Paranormal. KURTZ, Paul.
Die Wiederkehr im Unterschied. PEETZ, Siegbert.
Yoga on War and Peace. TIGUNAIT, Pandit Rajmani.
"Arguments for the Existence of God" in *Key Themes in Philosophy*, SWINBURNE, R G.
"The Background to Augustine's Denial of Religious Plurality" in *Grace, Politics and Desire: Essays on Augustine*, VANDERSPOEL, John.
"The Breakdown of the Newtonian Synthesis of Science and Religion: Hume, Newton, and the Royal Society" in *Essays on the Context, Nature, and Influence of Isaac Newton's Theology*, FORCE, James E.
"The Chinese Case in a Philosophy of World Religions" in *Understanding the Chinese Mind: The Philosophical Roots*, NEVILLE, Robert C.
"Christianity, Humanism, and St Thomas Aquinas" in *The Question of Humanism: Challenges and Possibilities*, MC LAUGHLIN, R J.
"Il corpuscolarismo italiano nel 'Giornale de' Letterati' di Roma (1668-1681)" in *Scienza, Filosofia e Religione tra '600 e '700 in Italia*, LOPICCOLI, Fiorella.

RELIGION

"Creation and Big Bang: The Word as Space of Creation" in *Science and Religion: One World-Changing Perspectives on Reality*, VAHANIAN, G.
"Herrad of Hohenbourg" in *A History of Women Philosophers, Volume II: Medieval, Renaissance and Enlightenment, A.D. 500-1600*, GIBSON, Joan.
"Historical Interaction between Science and Religion" in *Science and Religion: One World-Changing Perspectives on Reality*, PEDERSEN, O.
"How Could Ethics Depend on Religion?" in *A Companion to Ethics*, BERG, Jonathan.
"Ideology and Religion: A Hermeneutic Conflict" in *Phenomenology of the Truth Proper to Religion*, KEARNEY, Richard.
"The Language of Ecstasy and the Ecstasy of Language" in *The Bible as Rhetoric: Studies in Biblical Persuasion and Credibility*, BARRETT, Cyril.
"Newton and Fundamentalism, II" in *Essays on the Context, Nature, and Influence of Isaac Newton's Theology*, POPKIN, Richard H.
"Newton as a Bible Scholar" in *Essays on the Context, Nature, and Influence of Isaac Newton's Theology*, POPKIN, Richard H.
"Phenomenologies and Religious Truth" in *Phenomenology of the Truth Proper to Religion*, WESTPHAL, Merold.
"Religion and *On Liberty*" in *A Cultivated Mind: Essays On J S Mill Presented to John M Robson*, HAMBURGER, Joseph.
"Religion and Society in the Age of Theodosius" in *Grace, Politics and Desire: Essays on Augustine*, BARNES, Timothy D.
"Religion and the Making of Society" in *Critique and Construction: A Symposium on Roberto Unger's "Politics"*, DAVIS, Charles.
"Religious Truth and Scientific Truth" in *Phenomenology of the Truth Proper to Religion*, CLAYTON, Philip.
"Science and Religion Coming Across" in *Science and Religion: One World-Changing Perspectives on Reality*, HÜBNER, J.
"Science and Religion" in *Science and Religion: One World-Changing Perspectives on Reality*, MELSEN, A G M van.
"Sir Isaac Newton, 'Gentleman of Wide Swallow'? Newton and the Latitudinarians" in *Essays on the Context, Nature, and Influence of Isaac Newton's Theology*, FORCE, James E.
"Truth in Religion and Truth of Religion" in *Phenomenology of the Truth Proper to Religion*, DUPRÉ, Louis.
"The Truth, the Nontruth, and the Untruth Proper to Religion" in *Phenomenology of the Truth Proper to Religion*, GUERRIÈRE, Daniel.
Der "Atheist" und der "Theologe": Schopenhauer als Hörer Schleiermachers. REGEHLY, Thomas.
"Et la religion le remplit de fureur...". BOULAD-AYOUB, Josiane.
"Extrinsic Cognoscibility": A Seventeenth Century Supertranscendental Notion. DOYLE, John P.
The "Kalam" Cosmological Argument and the Hypothesis of a Quiescent Universe. CRAIG, William Lane.
"Keine festbegrenzte und Wahrhaft anschauliche Vorstelling". SCHREURS, Nico.
"Kierkegaardian Faith: 'The Condition' and the 'Response'. FERREIRA, M Jamie.
"Lest Anyone Should Fall": A Middle Knowledge Perspective on Perseverance and Apostolic Warnings. CRAIG, William Lane.
"Scientific Atheism" in the Era of Perestrojka. MELNICK, A James.
La "Scuola di Padova" ed i problemi dell'ontologia italiana contemporanea. MANGIAGALLI, Maurizio.
"Sociátá" et "communion" chez saint Thomas d'Aquin. LA SOUJEOLE, Benoît-Dominique.
'Desire' in Yoga and Jung. COWARD, Harold.
The 'New' Nietzsche. COOPER, David E.
'The Appearing God' in Hegel's *Phenomenology of Spirit*. JAMROS, Daniel P.
'Why Did It Happen to Me?'. THOMAS, J L H.
1668 Appendix to Leviathan. WRIGHT, George (trans) and HOBBES, Thomas.
The A/Theology of Don Cupitt: A Theological Option in Our Post-Modern Age. TARBOX JR, Everett J.
Acerca de uma tese ricoeuriana. SUMARES, Manuel.
Advaita and Religious Language. GRIMES, John.
Algunos giros en torno a san Juan de la Cruz. VALDIVIA, Benjamín.
Alvin Plantinga and Natural Theology. BROWN, Hunter.
Analisi fenomenologica del concetto di religione. MONDIN, Battista.
The Antinomy of Divine Necessity. SCHRADER, David E.
Antropología del trabajo según la Encíclica "Laborem Excercens". QUESADA GUARDIA, Annabelle.
Apology, Speculation, and Philosophy's Fate. VAN NESS, Peter H.
Aquinas on Almsgiving, Justice and Charity: An Interpretation and Reassessment. POPE, Stephen J.
Aquinas on Resolution in Metaphysics. TAVUZZI, Michael.
The Argument from Religious Experience: A Narrowing of Alternatives. KETCHUM, Richard.
Aristotle and Aquinas on Indignation: From Nemesis to Theodicy. NERNEY, Gayne.
Aristotle in Dante's Paradise. BOURBEAU, Marguerite.
The Assurance of Faith. WOLTERSTORFF, Nicholas.
El ateísmo Freudeano. MARLASCA, Antonio.
An Atheological Argument from Evil Natural Laws. SMITH, Quentin.
Augustine's Theology of the Trinity: Its Relevance. CLARK, Mary T.
Auschwitz, Morality and the Suffering of God. SAROT, Marcel.
Authenticity as Virtue (in Dutch). STRUYKER BOUDIER, C E M.
The Authorship of Faith. SESSIONS, W L.
The Barth Legacy: New Athanasius or Origen Redivivus? A Response to T F Torrance. MULLER, Richard A.
The Bhakti Tradition in Hinduism—Bhakti Yoga an Overview. PILLAI, A S Narayana.
Biblical Hermeneutics and the Search for Religious Truth (in French). THEISSEN, Gerd.
Biblical Narrative and the Theology of Metonymy. WARD, Graham.
Eine bisher unbeachtete Quelle des "Streits der Fakultäten". SELBACH, Ralf.
Blanshard's Ethics of Belief and Metaphysical Postulates. PHILLIPS, Winfred George.
The Body as Understood in Contemporary Thought and Biblical Categories. VERGOTE, Antoine.
Boston University Studies in Philosophy and Religion, Volumes 1-10. SMART, Ninian.
Bowne and Peirce on the Logic of Religious Belief. ANDERSON, Douglas R.
The Buddha as an Owner of Property and Permanent Resident in Medieval Indian Monasteries. SCHOPEN, Gregory.
Buddhist Anthropology vis-à-vis Modern Philosophy and Contemporary Neurophysiology. BUGAULT, Guy.
A Case Against Theistic Morality. VARMA, Ved Prakash.
The Caterus Objection. FORGIE, J William.
The Causal Theory of Reference and Religious Language. HARRIS, James F.
A Certain 'Politics of Speech': 'Religious Pluralism' in the Age of the McDonald's Hamburger. SURIN, Kenneth.
Certain Hope. PHILLIPS GRIFFITHS, A.
Choiceless Awareness. SEN, Sanat Kumar.
Christ, Moral Absolutes, and the Good: Recent Moral Theology. PINCKAERS, Servais.
Christelijke filosofie. WYLLEMAN, A.
Comment on Colmo's "Reason and Revelation in the Thought of Leo Strauss". LOWENTHAL, David.
The Community as Sacrament. LIDERBACH, Daniel.
The Concept of Religion. HESTEVOLD, H Scott.
The Condemnation of 1277: Another Light on Scotist Ethics. INGHAM, Mary E.
Considerazioni in margine a un'interpretazione di Bruno. MANZONI, Claudio.
The Contents of the Daoist Religion and Its Cultural Function. CAI, Hou.
Contingentie als uitgangspunt: Het denken van Richard Rorty. GEERTSEMA, H G.
Could God Make a Contradiction True?. GOLDSTICK, D.
Craig, Mackie and the *Kalam* Cosmological Argument. OPPY, Graham.
La création *ex nihilo* en question. CERBELAUD, Dominique.
Creation, Creativity and Necessary Being. HUGHES, Martin.
The Creationist Theory of Abrupt Appearances: A Critique. STRAHLER, Arthur N.
Creative Insecurity and "Tiptoe Experiences". HOWIE, John.
Cristianesimo tragico, cristianesimo ludico: i due volti della fedeltà al Dio dialettico. GARGANO, Monica.
A Critique of Plantinga's Theological Foundationalism. ZEIS, John.
Crossed Fingers and Praying Hands: Remarks on Religious Belief and Superstition. RAY, R J.
Cuarenta años del "Instituto Filosófico de Balmesiana". FORMENT, Eudaldo.
Cuestiones actuales de epistemología teológica: Aportes de la teología de la liberación. SCANNONE, J C.
Culpabilidad, rito y ritualismo: Una aproprimación psicoanaliítica. RODRIGUEZ AMENABAR, S M.
Cusanus and Eriugena. BEIERWALTES, Werner.
Da secularidade da Filosofia. COUTINHO, Jorge.
David Hume and the Mysterious Shroud of Turin. SCHOEN, Edward L.
David Hume on Religion in England. ROTH, Robert J.
David Hume's *Dialogues Concerning Natural Religion*: Otherness in History and in Text. MANNING, Robert J S.
Democracy and the Church-State Relationship. KAINZ, Howard.
Desacralization and the Disenchantment of the World. WENNEMANN, Daryl.
A Dialogic Interpretation of Hume's *Dialogues*. SESSIONS, William Lad.
Il dibattito sulla verità tra Blondel e Garrigou-Lagrange. BERTOLDI, Francesco.
Dieu tout-puissant et souffrant. RICHARD, Jean.
Directions in Historicism: Language, Experience, and Pragmatic Adjudication. DAVANEY, Sheila Greeve.
Discovering God in Western Civilization. BRESLAUER, S Daniel.
The Distinction between *Res Significata* and *Modus Significandi* in Aquinas's Theological Epistemology. ROCCA, Gregory.
Divine Knowledge and Divine Control: A Response to Gordon and Sadowsky. BASINGER, David.
Divine Unity and Superfluous Synonymity. LEVINE, Michael P.

RELIGION

Does Faith Create Its Own Objects?. MAC KINNON, Donald M.
Il doppio volto dell'ineffabile in L Wittgenstein. TODISCO, Orlando.
Down to Earth and Up to Religion: Kantian Idealism in Light of Kierkegaard's Leap of Faith. PERL, Paul.
È possibile un'esperienza di Dio?. CAVADI, Augusto.
Educating Intelligent Believers and Unbelievers. NODDINGS, Nel.
La eleccion de un maestro. VAN STEENBERGHEN, Fernand.
The Emerging Tension Between Self and Society, As Exemplified in Augustine. THOMPSON JR, George B.
Empirical Theology: A Revisable Tradition. DEAN, William.
The Epistemological Significance of the Inner Witness of the Holy Spirit. ABRAHAM, William J.
The Epistemological Significance of Transformative Religious Experiences: A Kierkegaardian Exploration. EVANS, C Stephen.
Escaping from Reality or Coming to Terms with It—What is Religion? (in German). POLLACK, Detlef.
La esencia metafísica de Dios. DERISI, Octavio N.
Eternity and Simultaneity. LEFTOW, Brian.
Etica del desarrollo: algunos principios y orientaciones a la luz de la docrina social de la Iglesia Católica. BRENES, Víctor.
The Evidence for Reincarnation. COCKBURN, David.
Evil and the Proper Basicality of Belief in God. DRAPER, Paul.
An Examination of Marxist Doctrine in the Traditions of Russian Religious Philosophy. STEPANOVA, E A.
The Experience of Value and Theological Argumentation. DEVENISH, Philip E.
Faith and Reason: Reflections on MacIntyre's 'Tradition-constituted Enquiry'. MARKHAM, Ian.
Faith and the Possibility of Private Meaning. GURREY, Charles S.
The Faith Dimension of Humanism. EARLES, Beverley.
Faith in the Open Society: The Limits of Hermeneutics. AGASSI, Joseph.
Feminism and Pluralism in Contemporary Theology. STENGER, Mary Ann.
Feminist Spirituality as a Path to Humanism. FRANKEL, Lois.
Fideísmo y autoritarismo en Lutero. CAPPELLETTI, Angel.
Filosofía cristiana y apologética en Mons Audino Rodríguez y Olmos. CATURELLI, Alberto.
Filosofia e ascesi nel Seicento: Il caso francese. BOSCO, Domenico.
Filosofía y Cristianismo (En el Centenario de Heidegger). CARDONA, Carlos.
Filosofía y fe en Descartes. FERNANDEZ, Javier.
Flaw, Conformity of Critical Dialogue? (in French). BÜHLER, Pierre.
Foi et intelligence dans l'"unique arguments": Un plan pour "Proslogion II-IV". LABBÉ, Y.
Footprints in the Snow. SEERVELD, Calvin.
Foreknowledge, Middle Knowledge and "Nearby" Worlds. DAVISON, Scott A.
Forgiveness: A Christian Model. ADAMS, Marilyn McCord.
Fragmentation, Meditation and Transformation: The Teachings of J Krishnamurti. NARAYANA MOORTY, J S R L.
Freud's Warning to Potential Believers. EBISCH, Glen A.
From Immanentism to Atheism. LY, Gabriel.
G Marcel: a dimensão metafísica da esperança. DA COSTA FREITAS, Manuel Barbosa.
Gadamer over 'Vermittlung': de Hegeliaanse draad in zijn hermeneutiek. VAN DER HOEVEN, J.
God and Gratuitous Evil: A Reply to Yandell. CHRZAN, Keith.
God's Ability to Will Moral Evil. BROWN, Robert F.
Habermas and Theological Ethics (in French). BÜHLER, Pierre.
Habermas et la théologie: Notes pour une discussion entre la théologie et la "Théorie de l'agir communicationnel". KISSLING, Christian.
Hegel and the Gods of Greece (in Hungarian). KERENYI, Karoly.
A Heideggerian Analysis of Fundamentalism: A Brief Discussion. O'CONNELL, Colin.
Hell, This Isn't Necessary After All. WALTERS, Kerry S.
Hick and Saints: Is Saint-Production a Valid Test?. PENTZ, Rebecca.
Hindu Doubts About God: Towards a Mīmāmsā Deconstruction. BILIMORIA, Purusottama.
Historicism and the Understanding of Theology in Troeltsch's Times (in German). NOWAK, Kurt.
History as Argument for Revision in Moral Theology. GRISEZ, Germain.
The History of the Christian Philosophical Reflection on Peace. WASKIEWICZ, Hanna.
Homicide and Love. SMITH, Steven G.
How Can We Speak of God? How Can We Speak of Anything. FORREST, Peter.
Humanist Religion for the Troubled. RUSTERHOLTZ, Wallace P.
Hume and Pascal: Pyrrhonism versus Nature. MAIA NETO, José R.
Hume on Divine Amorality. WALLS, Jerry L.
Hume Revisited: A Problem With the Free Will Defense. MARKHAM, Ian.
Hume's "Of Miracles," Peirce, and the Balancing of Likelihoods. MERRILL, Kenneth R.
Hume's *Dialogues* and the Redefinition of the Philosophy of Religion. SCHNER, George.
Hume's Reproduction Parody of the Design Argument. DRAPER, Paul.
Hutcheson's Account of Beauty as a Response to Mandeville. MICHAEL, Emily and MICHAEL, Fred S.
Ibn 'Arabi o la renovación espiritual del sufismo. SERRANO RAMÍREZ, Jose M.
Die immerwährende Schöpfung als fundamentaler Seinsvorgang. KNAPPIK, G J.
In Defence of Theological Compatibilism. FLINT, Thomas P.
In Defense of Anselm. ASPENSON, Steven S.
Independent Evidence of Religion. D'SOUZA, Felix.
Indian Thought Is a Systematic Body of Thought. SHAH, K J.
The Ins and Outs of Mysticism. HART, Kevin.
A intersubjectividade em Gabriel Marcel. MORUJÁO, Alexandre Fradique.
Intimacy: A General Orientation in Japanese Religious Values. KASULIS, Thomas P.
Irony and Argument in *Dialogues*, XII. DAVIS, Scott.
Is Anything Sacred? Christian Humanism and Christian Nihilism. CUPITT, Don.
James and Bowne on the Philosophy of Religious Experience. DOTTERER, Donald W.
James, Rationality and Religious Belief. WAINWRIGHT, W J.
Jewish Faith and the Holocaust. COHN-SHERBOK, Dan.
John Wyclif's Metaphysics of Scriptural Integrity in the *De Veritate Sacrae Scripturae*. TRESKO, Michael.
K J Shah's 'Philosophy, Religion, Morality, Spirituality: Some Issues'. GHOSE, A M.
Karma and Reincarnation in Advaita Vedānta. SHARMA, Arvind.
Kierkegaard irrazionalista? Filosofi e filosofie nella interpretazione del filosofo danese. FRANCHI, Alfredo.
Kierkegaard on the Limits of Christian Epistemology. WISDO, David.
Kierkegaard on Theistic Proof. STERN, Kenneth.
Kierkegaard's Pragmatist Faith. EMMANUEL, Steven M.
Kierkegaard, Nietzsche, and the Death of God. NASH, Ronald H.
The Knight of Faith. ADAMS, Robert Merrihew.
Knowing Good and Evil. WILLIAMS, C J F.
Knowledge as Bondage: An Unconventional Approach. SEN, Sanat Kumar.
Knowledge, Belief and Revelation: A Reply to Patrick Lee. HOITENGA JR, Dewey J.
L'"irrisio fidei" chez Raymond Lulle et S Thomas D'Aquin. SERVERAT, Vincent.
L'aspect rationnel et l'aspect religieux de la philosophie de Plotin. BRUNNER, Fernand.
The Latin Avicenna as a Source of Thomas Aquinas's Metaphysics. WIPPEL, John F.
Liberation Theology and the Interpretation of Political Violence. SONTAG, Frederick.
The Literal Sense of Scripture. WILLIAMS, Rowan.
Logic and Logos—The Search for Unity in Hegel and Coleridge: II: The 'Otherness" of God. PERKINS, Mary Anne.
Il Logos come immagine di Dio in Filone di Alessandria. BELLETTI, Bruno.
Lonergan's Method in Ethics and the Meaning of Human Sexuality. FRISBY, Mark E.
Makin on the Ontological Argument. OPPY, Graham.
Mansel's Agnosticism. FITZGERALD, Timothy.
The Many-Gods Objection and Pascal's Wager. JORDAN, Jeff.
Marcel on the Problem of Freedom. SUGUMAR, Devaki.
Marranos (Pigs), or from Coexistence to Toleration. SHELL, Marc.
Marxisten und Christen für eine gerechte, friedliche Welt. NEHRING, Hartmut.
Masaryk's "Anthropism" (in Czechoslovakian). NOVY, Lubomir.
Masaryk's Religious Thinking (in Czechoslovakian). FUNDA, Otakar A.
Meaning, Truth and Realism in Bultmann and Lindbeck. FERGUSSON, David.
Meister Eckhart and the Neoplatonic Heritage: The Thinker's Way to God. WOODS, Richard.
Metaphor in the Language of Religion. PANDHARIPANDE, Rajeshwari.
Metaphysics, Religion and Yoruba Traditional Thought. OLADIPO, Olusegun.
Method Divorced from Content in Theology: An Assessment of Lonergan's *Method in Theology*. REYNOLDS, Terrence.
Methodological Alternatives in Process Theology. BROWN, Delwin and GREEVE DAVANEY, Sheila.
Methodological, Epistemological, and Ontological Motifs in the Thought of Reinhold Niebuhr. AYERS, Robert H.
Michel de Montaigne: La "nottola" dell'Umanesimo francese. LONGO, Margherita.
Middle Knowledge and the Damnation of the Heathen: A Response to William Craig. HASKER, William.
Misconceptions of the Social Sciences. SEGAL, Robert A.
Morality and Religion: Necessary Bedfellows in Education?. LOSITO, William F.
A Morality Based on Trust: Some Reflections on Japanese Morality. YAMAMOTO, Yutaka.
Myth and Morality: The Love Command. HEFNER, Philip.
Naturalistic Ethics and the Argument from Evil. NELSON, Mark T.
The Nature of Faith: Religious, Monotheistic, and Christian. YANDELL, Keith E.
Neuhaus and Murray on Natural Law and American Politics. LAWLER, Peter A.

RELIGION

Neutrality Between Religion and Irreligion. LINDSAY, Ronald A.

A New Humanism. CHURCH, F Forrester.

A New Humanism: A Response. COLLINS, Jacqueline A.

A New Humanism: A Response. DOERR, Edd.

A New Humanism: A Response. ERICSON, Edward L.

A New Humanism: A Response. HARRIS, W Edward.

A New Humanism: A Response. MAIN, William.

A New Humanism: A Response. PHIFER, Kenneth W.

A New Humanism: A Response. WILSON, Edwin H.

Una nuova questioni di Egidio Romano "De subjecto theologiae". LUNA, Concetta.

An Oath of Silence: Wittgenstein's Philosophy of Religion. JOHNSON, Charles W.

L'odissea dell'ateismo e del nichilismo. FABRO, Cornelio.

Omnipotence Need Not Entail Omniscience. SONTAG, Frederick.

On Franco-Ferraz, Theism and the Theatre of the Mind. BADÍA-CABRERA, Miguel A.

Ontological Reductionism and Faith Versus Reason: A Critique of Adams on Ockham. FREDDOSO, Alfred J.

Oratio Placabilis Deo Eriugena's Fragmentary Eucharistic Teaching. SMITH, R U.

Le origini dell'ateismo antico (quinta parte). ZEPPI, Stelio.

Orthodoxy or Atheism? Remarks on the New Edition of Hegel's Lectures on Religion (in Hungarian). MOLNÁR, László M.

Le paradoxe de la conscience erronée d'Abálard à Karl Rahner. BELMANS, Théo G.

Pascal critique des philosophes, Pascal philosophe. BOUCHILLOUX, Hélène.

Pascal on Self-Caused Belief. DAVIS, Stephen T.

Pascal, etica, politica, socialità. DEREGIBUS, Arturo.

Patripassianism, Theopaschitism and the Suffering of God. SAROT, Marcel.

Paul Tillich and Inter-religious Dialogue. FOERSTER, John.

Il pensiero di Aldo Capitini e la filosofia del neoidealismo. CESA, Claudio.

Personalist and Pragmatist Persons. STUHR, John J.

Philosophical and Religious Implications of Cognitive Social Learning Theories of Personality. ROTTSCHAEFER, William A.

Philosophie et mythologie dans la dernière philosophie de Schelling. MAESSCHALCK, Marc.

Philosophie et religion. TROISFONTAINES, Claude.

Philosophieren als Sein zum Tode: Zur Interpretation von Platons "Phaidon". FISCHER, Norbert.

Philosophy and Religion (in Dutch). DHONDT, U.

Philosophy, Religion, Morality, Spirituality: Some Issues. SHAH, K J.

Plantinga and Probabilistic Atheism. CHRZAN, Keith.

Plantinga, Pluralism and Justified Religious Belief. BASINGER, David.

Plato's *Parmenides* and St Thomas's Analysis of God as One and Trinity. KLEIN, Sherwin.

Porphyry's Criticism of Christianity and The Problem of Augustine's Platonism. EVANGELIOU, Christos.

Possibility of Dialogic Encounter of Religious and Philosophical Humanitas (in Serbo-Croatian). SKLEDAR, Nikola.

Post-Holocaust Theodicy: Images of Deity, History, and Humanity. FREY, Robert Seitz.

Postcritical Religion and the Latent Freud. KEISER, R Melvin.

Pour une interprétation féministe de l'idée chrétienne de Dieu. DION, Michel.

Le pouvoir, existential de l'être humain. SCHÜSSLER, Werner.

Prefacing Pluralism: John Hick and the Mastery of Religion. LOUGHLIN, Gerard.

Les présupposés métaphysiques de la "lisibilité" de l'être. KÜHN, Rolf.

La prétendue intuition de Dieu dans le De Coelo d'Aristote. BODÉÜS, Richard.

Principle Monism and Action Descriptions: Situationism and its Critics Revisited. PINCHES, Charles.

A Problem for Radical (Onto-Theos) Pluralism. BILIMORIA, Purusottama.

The Problem of Atheism in Recent Soviet Publications. DAHM, Helmut.

Problems of Understanding. MEHTA, J L.

Process Theology as Empirical, Rational, and Speculative: Some Reflections on Method. GRIFFIN, David Ray.

Prometheus or Cain? Albert Camus's Account of the Western Quest for Justice. WARD, Bruce K.

Protecting God: The Lexical Formation of Trinitarian Language. BARRIGAR, Christian J.

Providence and Political Responsibility: The Nature of Praxis in an Age of Apocalypse. LAKELAND, Paul.

Providence, Freedom and Human Destiny. TALBOTT, Thomas.

Psychiatry, Religious Conversion, and Medical Ethics. POST, Stephen G.

La puissance d'être selon Tillich. GOUNELLE, André.

Punyadāna or Transference of Merit—A Fiction. KRISHAN, Y.

Radical Enlightenment and Freethinkers (in German). POTT, Martin.

Radical Theology, Postmodernity and Christian Life in the Void. COWDELL, Scott.

Ramana Maharsi on the Theories of Creation in Advaita Vedānta. SHARMA, Arvind.

Rational Suicide and Christian Virtue. MAGUIRE, Daniel C.

La rationalité du théisme: la philosophie de la religion de Richard Swinburne. PADGETT, Alan G.

A Re-Examination of the Nature of Religion. BARUA, Archana.

A Reading of Aquinas's Five Ways. FOGELIN, Robert J.

The Recent Revival of Divine Command Ethics. QUINN, Philip L.

Reconstruction, Dialectic and Praxis. RIORDAN, Patrick.

Reflections on Blanshard, Reason, and Religion. FERRÉ, Frederick.

As relações entre o Deus da Razão e o Deus da Fé. RENAUD, Michel.

Relating Science and Theology with Complementarity: A Caution. SHARPE, Kevin J.

The Relation between Science and Theology: The Case for Complimentarity Revisited. REICH, K Helmut.

Relativism, Ineffability, and the Appeal to Experience: A Reply to the Myth Makers. BARNES, L Philip.

The Relevance of Historical Evidence for Christian Faith: A Critique of a Kierkegaardian View. EVANS, C Stephen.

Religion and Cultural Evolution. MASSIMINI, Fausto and FAVE, Antonella Delle.

La religión en la constitución de los Estados Unidos de América. PÉREZ ESTÉVEZ, Antonio.

Religion in Wittgenstein's Mirror. PHILLIPS, D Z.

Religion, Nothingness, and the Challenge of Post-Modern Thought: An Introduction to the Philosophy of K Nishitani. JAMES, George A.

Religions in the Balance. FENNER, Peter.

Religious Commitment and Secular Reason: A Reply to Professor Weithman. AUDI, Robert.

A Religious Theory of Religion: Critical Notice. BYRNE, Peter.

Renaissance Humanism and the Religious Culture of the First Jesuits. O'MALLEY, John W.

Republic: 2. BANAJI, V F.

Residual Natural Evil and Anthropic Reasoning. MC LEAN, Murdith.

Resources in Schelling for New Directions in Theology. BROWN, Robert F.

A Response to Gerard Loughlin's "Prefacing Pluralism: John Hick and the Mastery of Religion". HICK, John.

The Return of the Initiate: Hegel on Bread and Wine. AUXIER, Randall E.

Richard Rufus of Cornwall and the Authorship of the *Scriptum super Metaphysicam*. NOONE, Timothy B.

The Roles of Predictions in Science and Religion. SCHOEN, Edward L.

Die Rolle des Individuums und seine Beteiligung an gesellschaftlichen Prozessen. SCHLIWA, Harald and ZEDDIES, Helmut.

Die Rolle des unglücklichen Bewusstseins in Hegels *Phänomenologie des Geistes*. STEWARD, Jon.

Romano Guardini's Theological Critique of the Modern Age (in Dutch). VAN DER VLOET, J.

The Sacred, Secular, and Profane in Augustine's World of Shadows. SPENCER, Jon Michael.

San Ignacio de Loyola y el humanismo. GARCÍA-MATEO, Rogelio.

Sant'Agostino e Hegel a confronto. CALEO, Marcello.

Saving Faith from Kant's Remarkable Antinomy. QUINN, Philip L.

Het scheppende en herscheppende woord: zijn blijvende actualiteit. DENGERINK, J D.

Scientific Humanism and Religion. WILSON, Edward O.

Scientific Research and the Christian Faith. PETERS, Ted.

Scientism, Interpretation, and Criticism. GORSKI, Philip S.

The Search for an Ethical Sacrament: From Bonhoeffer to Critical Social Theory. FLOYD, Wayne Whitson.

Self and Suffering: Deconstruction and Reflexive Definition in Buddhism and Christianity. MELLOR, Philip A.

The Self in Medieval Japanese Buddhism: Focusing on Dōgen. KIMURA, Kiyotaka.

Some Observations on the Influence of Christian Scholastic Authors on Jewish Thinkers in the 13th and 14th Century. REEDIJK, Wim M.

Some Perspectives in Eriugenian Studies: Three Recent Studies. OTTEN, Willemien.

Sophia and the Devil: Kant in the Face of Russian Religious Metaphysics. AKHUTIN, A V.

Speech, Sin and the Word of God (in Dutch). GESTRICH, Christof.

Spinoza en de geopenbaarde godsdienst. DE DIJN, H.

Spiritual Traditions and Science and Technology. BAKAR, Osman.

St Augustine and the Second Way. KLUGE, Eike-Henner W.

Le statut de la philosophie chez Étienne Gilson. PROUVOST, Géry.

Stewardship: Whose Creation Is It Anyway?. BARAD-ANDRADE, Judith.

Structure and Meaning in St Augustine's *Confessions*. CROSSON, Frederick J.

The Structure of Philo's Commentary on the Pentateuch. THORNE, Gary W A.

Sur le concept de Révélation. GABORIAU, Florent.

Sur le concept de tradition. GABORIAU, Florent.

Swinburne on Credal Belief. MAITZEN, Stephen.

T G Masaryk—A Modern Thinker (in Czechoslovakian). OPAT, Jaroslav.

Technological Faith and Christian Doubt. FERRÉ, Frederick.

La tensione tra possibilità e necessità nell'argomento ontologico di Leibniz. NICOLOSI, Salvatore.

La teología de la historia en la Ciudad de Dios. OROZ RETA, José (trans) and BAGET-BOZZO, Giovanni.

RELIGION
A Teologia e a Filosofia perante os desafios da Cultura Contemporânea. POLICARPO, J.
The Questioning of Values in Theology (in French). WIDMER, Gabriel-Ph.
The Theosophic Discourse According to Jacob Boehme (in French). DEGHAYE, Pierre.
Theme and Commentary. GREEN, Thomas F.
La théologie de Heidegger. CRÉTELLA, Henri.
Theology and the Necessity of Natures. ANGLIN, W S.
Theology and the Social Sciences—Discipline and Antidiscipline. MURPHY, Nancey.
Theology as the Queen (Bee) of the Disciplines?. VAUX, Kenneth.
Die Theorie der moralischen Entwicklung von Lawrence Kohlberg und seiner Schule und die Moraltheologie. BUCHER, Anton.
Thomas Aquinas and the Renewal of Philosophy: Some Reflections on the Thomism of Mercier (in Dutch). STEEL, C.
La toute-puissance du Dieu du théisme dans le champ de la perversion. ANSALDI, Jean.
Toward a Pragmatic Conception of Religious Faith. GOLDING, Joshua L.
Toward One Santayana: Recent Scholarship. KERR-LAWSON, Angus.
Towards a Philosophy of Buddhist Religion. HOFFMAN, Frank J.
Tradition and Ethics: Prospects in a Liberal Society. GUROIAN, Vigen.
Tradition and Interpretation. VAN BEECK, Frans Jozef.
Two Designs of Universal History. KANTOR, K M.
Ultramontanisme et gallicanisme engagentils deux visions de la société. BRESSOLETTE, Claude.
Understanding the Question: Wittgenstein on Faith and Meaning. EISENSTEIN, Gabe.
Ungeklärte Fragen im Dialog zwischen Glaube und Naturwissenschaft. FISCHER, Johannes.
Universe Indexed Properties and the Fate of the Ontological Argument. SENNETT, James F.
The Value-Ought of Self-Realization: A Phenomenological Approach. VELASSERRY, Sebastian.
Das vergeistigte Glück: Gedanken zum christlichen Eudämonieverständnis. DEMMER, Klaus.
Verily, Nietzsche's Judgment of Jesus. ROTH, Robin A.
Verità di ragione e verità di fede. MESSINESE, Leonardo.
W T Harris' Philosophy as Personalism. LAUDER, Robert E.
Wainwright, Maritain and Aquinas on Transcendent Experiences. ROY, Louis.
Waiting for the Vanishing Shed. PHILLIPS, D Z.
Was Spinoza a Marrano of Reason?. POPKIN, Richard H.
What Philosophy for Judaism and Christianity? (in French). DUPONCHEELE, Joseph.
Whitehead and Genuine Evil. BARINEAU, R Maurice.
Why Didn't God Create the World Sooner?. LEFTOW, Brian.
Why Natural Theology, Still, Yet?. HUTCHINGS, Patrick.
Why Plantinga Must Move from Defense to Theodicy. WALLS, Jerry L.
Wittgenstein's Gift to Contemporary Analytic Philosophy of Religion. KELLENBERGER, J.
Wittgenstein's Lectures on Religious Belief. MARTIN, Michael.
Wittgenstein: On Seeing Problems from a Religious Point of View. HIGH, Dallas M.
The Word That Became the Absolute: Relevance of Sankara's Ontology of Language. GUPTA, Som Raj.
Would Hegel Have Liked to Burn Down All the Churches and Replace Them with Philosophical Academies?. LUFT, Eric V D.
Zu Grundfragen des Toleranzproblems in Vergangenheit und Gegenwart. WOLLGAST, Siegfried.
'Following Nature' in Butler's Sermons. BRINTON, Alan.
'Postmodern Critical Augustinianism': A Short *Summa* in Forty Two Responses to Unasked Questions. MILBANK, John.

RELIGIOUS
Enriching Business Ethics. WALTON, Clarence C (ed).
"God's World and Man Becoming: How Can Science Possibly Help Us Transcend Dogmatism?" in *Science and Religion: One World-Changing Perspectives on Reality*, VAN DER VEKEN, J.
Cosmology and Religion. JAKI, Stanley.
Il doppio volto dell'ineffabile in L Wittgenstein. TODISCO, Orlando.
L'emozione creatrice: Il significato della morale nella prospettiva di Bergson. PESSINA, Adriano.
Per una nuova edizione della *Epistola* lockiana sulla tolleranza. MONTUORI, Mario.
Peter Gardner on Religious Upbringing and the Liberal Ideal of Religious Autonomy. MC LAUGHLIN, T H.
Praxis and Ultimate Reality: Intellectual, Moral and Religious Conversion as Radical Political Conversion. MARSH, James L.
The Prophetic and the Priestly. CHILDRESS, James F.

RELIGIOUS BELIEF(S)
Explaining Religion: Criticism and Theory from Bodin to Freud. PREUS, J Samuel (ed).
In Partnership with God: Contemporary Jewish Law and Ethics. SHERWIN, Byron L.
The Metaphysics of Religious Belief. SHOOMAN, A P.
Science versus Religion. CLEMENTS, Tad S.
"Current Religious Perspectives on the New Reproductive Techniques" in *Beyond Baby M: Ethical Issues in New Reproductive Techniques*, BRODY, Baruch.
Bowne and Peirce on the Logic of Religious Belief. ANDERSON, Douglas R.
The Concept of Religion. HESTEVOLD, H Scott.
Conceptos religiosos y vida religiosa. BASSOLS, Alejandro Tomasini.
James, Rationality and Religious Belief. WAINWRIGHT, W J.
Plantinga, Pluralism and Justified Religious Belief. BASINGER, David.
Towards a Philosophy of Buddhist Religion. HOFFMAN, Frank J.
Wittgenstein's Gift to Contemporary Analytic Philosophy of Religion. KELLENBERGER, J.

RELIGIOUS EDUCATION
Justice Powell and the Parochial Schools Case: A Case for Judicial Statesmanship. WALTMAN, Jerold.

RELIGIOUS EXPERIENCE(S)
The Epistemological Significance of the Inner Witness of the Holy Spirit. ABRAHAM, William J.
If There Is a God, Any Experience Which Seems to Be of God, Will Be Genuine. LEVINE, Michael P.
James and Bowne on the Philosophy of Religious Experience. DOTTERER, Donald W.
Kenny and Religious Experiences. JORDAN, J.

RELIGIOUS FREEDOM
Religious Liberty, Religious Dissent and the Catholic Tradition. COWDIN, Daniel M.
The Separation of Church and State: Some Questions for Professor Audi. WEITHMAN, Paul J.

RELIGIOUS LANGUAGE
Science versus Religion. CLEMENTS, Tad S.
The Causal Theory of Reference and Religious Language. HARRIS, James F.
Choosing Religious Languages: A Note on Two 'Proofs' of God's Existence. SAPADIN, Eugene.

REMEDY(-DIES)
Economics, Ethics, and Tort Remedies: The Emerging Concept of Hedonic Value. KARNS, Jack E.

REMORSE
Good and Evil: An Absolute Conception. GAITA, Raimond.

RENAISSANCE
A History of Women Philosophers, Volume II: Medieval, Renaissance and Enlightenment, A.D. 500-1600. WAITHE, Mary Ellen (ed).
Moral Philosophy from Montaigne to Kant: An Anthology, Volume I & II. SCHNEEWIND, J B (ed).
The Noble Savage: Jean-Jacques Rousseau, 1754-1762. CRANSTON, Maurice.
Utopia: Sir Thomas More. LOGAN, George M (ed).
Vico: A Study of the 'New Science' (Second Edition). POMPA, Leon.
"Marie le Jars de Gournay" in *A History of Women Philosophers, Volume II: Medieval, Renaissance and Enlightenment, A.D. 500-1600*, ZEDLER, Beatrice H.
"Medieval and Renaissance Ethics" in *A Companion to Ethics*, HALDANE, John.
"Oliva Sabuco de Nantes Barrera" in *A History of Women Philosophers, Volume II: Medieval, Renaissance and Enlightenment, A.D. 500-1600*, WAITHE, Mary Ellen.
"Roswitha of Gandersheim, Christine Pisan, Margaret More Roper and Teresa of Avila" in *A History of Women Philosophers, Volume II: Medieval, Renaissance and Enlightenment, A.D. 500-1600*, WAITHE, Mary Ellen.
"What Is Renaissance Humanism?" in *The Question of Humanism: Challenges and Possibilities*, ANDIC, Martin.
Il "De imaginum, signorum et idearum compositione" di Giordano Bruno, ed il significato filosofico .... STURLESE, Rita.
Allocution Made to a Magistrate. PAREL, A J (ed & trans) and MACHIAVELLI, Niccolò.
Bruno e la matematica a lui contemporanea: In margine al "De Minimo". AQUILECCHIA, Giovanni.
Considerazioni in margine a un'interpretazione di Bruno. MANZONI, Claudio.
Di cose grammaticali: Un itinerario campanelliano. ALUNNI, Charles.
Filosofia e ascesi nel Seicento: Il caso francese. BOSCO, Domenico.
La filosofia: in soccorso de' governi. COLAPIETRA, Raffaele.
Giambattista Vico and the Quarrel between the Ancients and the Moderns. LEVINE, Joseph M.
Infiniti mondi e mondo nuovo: Conquista dell'America e critica della civilità europea in Giordano Bruno. RICCI, Saverio.
King Lear and Natural Law. YOUNG, R V.
Machiavelli's Notions of Justice: Text and Analysis. PAREL, A J.
Machiavelli's Sisters: Women and "the Conversation" of Political Theory. ZERILLI, Linda M G.
Marsilius on Rights. TIERNEY, Brian.
Philosophical and Normative Dimensions and Aspects of the Idea of Renaissance. GREGORIOS, Paulos Mar.

RENAISSANCE
Il rapporto Parmenide-Telesio dal Persio al Maranta. ARTESE, Luciano.
Relations and Sixteenth-Century Mexican Logic. REDMOND, Walter.
Renaissance Humanism and the Religious Culture of the First Jesuits. O'MALLEY, John W.
Renaissance Ideas and the Idea of the Renaissance. TRINKAUS, Charles.
Rilievi di struttura sul *De deo abscondito* di Nicola Cusano. DELCÒ, Alessandro.
Synderesis, the Spark of Conscience, in the English Renaissance. GREENE, Robert A.
The Concept of History in the Renaissance (in Hungarian). RASZLAI, Tibor.

RENOUVIER
Charles Renouvier e le scuole di morale in Francia nel XIX secolo. ROSSI, Fabio.

RENT
Radin on Personhood and Rent Control. GREENBERG, Dan.

RENUNCIATION
The Knight of Faith. ADAMS, Robert Merrihew.

RENYI, A
The Autonomy of Probability Theory (Notes on Kolmogorov, Rényi, and Popper). LEBLANC, Hugues.

REPETITION
"The Art of Forgetfulness, Schopenhauer and Contemporary Repetitive Music" in *XIth International Congress in Aesthetics, Nottingham 1988*, DE MUL, Jos.

REPLACEMENT
Utilitarian Killing, Replacement, and Rights. PLUHAR, Evelyn.

REPRESENTABILITY
Representing and Reasoning With Probabilistic Knowledge: A Logical Approach to Probabilities. BACCHUS, Fahiem.
Semantica della "Vorstellung" e valore della teoria in *Erkenntnis und Irrtum* di Ernst Mach. BELLOMO, Andrea.

REPRESENTATION(S)
About Time: Inventing the Fourth Dimension. FRIEDMAN, William J.
Artificial Intelligence and Human Cognition. WAGMAN, Morton.
Artificial Intelligence: Its Scope and Limits. FETZER, James H.
Hermeneutics and the Poetic Motion, Translation Perspectives V—1990. SCHMIDT, Dennis J (ed).
Lesbian Philosophies and Cultures. ALLEN, Jeffner (ed).
Meaning and Mental Representation. CUMMINS, Robert.
Mimesis as Make-Believe: On the Foundations of the Representational Arts. WALTON, Kendall L.
The Philosopher's Joke. WATSON, Richard A.
Philosophy and Cognitive Science. FETZER, James H.
Reasoning and Revision in Hybrid Representation Systems. NEBEL, Bernhard.
Understanding the Representational Mind. PERNER, Josef.
The Unity of Understanding: A Study in Kantian Problems. SCHWYZER, Hubert.
"Artificial Intelligence as Epistemology?" in *Information, Semantics and Epistemology*, DASCAL, Marcelo.
"Everyday Knowledge as Representation of Reality" in *The Social Horizon of Knowledge*, MARUSZEWSKI, Tomasz.
"Neural Representation and Neural Computation" in *Philosophical Perspectives, 4: Action Theory and Philosophy of Mind, 1990*, CHURCHLAND, Patricia Smith and SEJNOWSKI, Terrence J.
"Representation and the Self in Stoicism" in *Psychology (Companions to Ancient Thought: 2)*, LONG, A A.
"Translation as Transgression" in *Hermeneutics and the Poetic Motion, Translation Perspectives V—1990*, ROSS, Stephen David.
"...A Presence of Absence...". BATKIN, Norton.
Art, Life and Reality. NOVITZ, David.
Beyond the "Limits" of *Mundane Reason*. BOGEN, David.
Descartes on Sensory Representation: A Study of the *Dioptrics*. MAC KENZIE, Ann Wilbur.
Estructuras y representaciones. DE LA SIENRA, Adolfo García.
Fictional Objects in Literature and Mental Representations. BACHRACH, Jay E.
Der Gegenstand der Vorstellungen und die transzendentale Apperzeption. LÓPEZ-FERNÁNDEZ, Alvaro.
Individualism and Semantic Development. PATTERSON, Sarah.
Intentionality and Modern Philosophical Psychology—II: The Return to Representation. LYONS, Willia.
Kant e o problema da origem das representações elementares: apontamentos. MARQUES, U R de Azevedo.
Kripke Semantics for Knowledge Representation Logics. ORLOWSKA, Ewa.
Logic and Knowledge Representation. PETROV, V V and PEREVERZEV, V N.
Meinongian Theories of Generality. SANTAMBROGIO, Marco.
Natural Generativity and Imitation. SARTWELL, Crispin.
On Capturing Cities. GOODMAN, Nelson.
On Naturalizing the Semantics of Mental Representation. SILVERS, Stuart.
Philosophy as an Art. LEVINSON, Jerrold.
Pictorial Representation in Biology. TAYLOR, Peter J and BLUM, Ann S.
Pictures and Depictions: A Consideration of Peacocke's Views. KEMP, G N.
Reinterpreting Images. SLEZAK, Peter.
Relativized Gödel Speed-Up and the Degree of Succinctness of Representations. SOLOMON, Martin K.
Representation and the Freedom of the Will. STAMPE, Dennis W.
Représentation philosophique par réseau sémantique variable. BOSS, Gilbert and LONGEART, Maryvonne.
The Representational Content of Musical Experience. DE BELLIS, Mark.
Representations and Realism. APPIAH, Anthony.
Les représentations de l'action. SAINT SERNIN, Bertrand.
Response to Stampe's "Representation and the Freedom of the Will". GIBSON, Martha I.
The Role of Music in Nietzsche's *Birth of Tragedy*. HECKMAN, Peter.
Schematism and Schemata: Kant and the P.D.P.. VAN DE VIJVER, Gertrudis.
Science in the Age of Mechanical Reproduction: Moral and Epistemic Relations Between Diagrams and Photographs. LYNCH, Michael.
Semantica della "Vorstellung" e valore della teoria in *Erkenntnis und Irrtum* di Ernst Mach. BELLOMO, Andrea.
Structural Representation and Surrogative Reasoning. SWOYER, Chris.
Truth and Teleology. PAPINEAU, David.
What Good is Irony?. LEVINSON, Henry S.
Wittgenstein and Psychology. SHOTTER, John.
Wittgenstein: Representaciones y pensamientos. RABOSSI, Eduardo.
Wo lag der Fehler der kategorialen Repräsentation? Zu Sinn und Reichweite einer Selbstkritik Husserls. LOHMAR, Dieter.

REPRESENTATIONALISM
The Representational Theory of Mind: An Introduction. STERELNY, Kim.
The Antinomy of Perception: Merleau-Ponty and Causal Representation Theory. HASS, Lawrence.
Dialectical Perception: A Synthesis of Lenin and Bogdanov. WRIGHT, Edmond.
Malebranche versus Arnauld. COOK, Monte.

REPRESENTATIVE GOVERNMENT(S)
"Arendt and Representative Democracy" in *The Realm of Humanitas: Responses to the Writings of Hannah Arendt*, KATEB, George.

REPRESENTATIVE REALISM
Der sinnliche Gehalt der Wahrnehmung. SCHANTZ, Richard.
Representative Realism and Absolute Reality. ENGLISH, Parker.

REPRESENTATIVE(S)
The Virtue of a Representative. WOLGAST, Elizabeth.

REPRESSION
Freud Contra Sartre: Repression or Self-Deception?. MIRVISH, Adrian.
Repression of Sexuality in Philosophy and the Return of the Repressed in Freud's Psychoanalysis (in Serbo-Croatian). KORDIC, Radoman.
The Perversion of Emancipation into Repression (in German). SCHMIDT, Hartwig.

REPRODUCTION(S)
Beyond Baby M: Ethical Issues in New Reproductive Techniques. BARTELS, Dianne M (ed).
New Harvest: Transplanting Body Parts and Reaping the Benefits. KEYES, C Don (ed).
"Arguing with Success: Is In Vitro Fertilization Research or Therapy?" in *Beyond Baby M: Ethical Issues in New Reproductive Techniques*, CAPLAN, Arthur L.
"Current Religious Perspectives on the New Reproductive Techniques" in *Beyond Baby M: Ethical Issues in New Reproductive Techniques*, BRODY, Baruch.
"Essential Ethical Considerations for Public Policy on Assisted Reproduction" in *Beyond Baby M: Ethical Issues in New Reproductive Techniques*, TAUER, Carol.
"Medical Techniques for Assisted Reproduction" in *Beyond Baby M: Ethical Issues in New Reproductive Techniques*, TAGATZ, George.
"Science, Conscience, and Public Policy: Historical Reflections on Controversial Reproductive Issues" in *Beyond Baby M: Ethical Issues in New Reproductive Techniques*, EYLER, John.
"Sexuality and Assisted Reproduction: An Uneasy Embrace" in *Beyond Baby M: Ethical Issues in New Reproductive Techniques*, HAROWSKI, Kathy J.
Are Pregnant Women Fetal Containers?. PURDY, Laura.
Artificial Means of Reproduction and Our Understanding of the Family. MACKLIN, Ruth.
Copies, Reproducibility and Aesthetic Adequacy. CHANG, Briankle G.
Hume's Reproduction Parody of the Design Argument. DRAPER, Paul.
Monstrous Imagination: Progeny as Art in French Classicism. HUET, Marie-Hélène.
Morality in Flux: Medical Ethics in the People's Republic of China. QIU, Ren-Zong.
The Overdue Death of a Feminist Chameleon: Taking a Stand on Surrogacy Arrangements. TONG, Rosemarie.

REPRODUCTION(S)
Reproducibility as a Methodological Imperative in Experimental Research. HONES, Michael.
Species as Historical Individuals. KLUGE, Arnold G.
Spontaneity and the Generation of Rational Beings in Leibniz's Theory of Biological Reproduction. FOUKE, Daniel C.
The *Trés Riches Heures*: An Illuminated Manuscript in the Age of Mechanical Reproduction. CAMILLE, Michael.
Using Arendt and Heidegger to Consider Feminist Thinking on Women and Reproductive/Infertility Technologies. KLAWITER, Maren.
Why Have Children?. ANSCOMBE, G E M.

REPUBLIC(S)
"The Political Origins of Democracy" in *Writing the Politics of Difference*, HOWARD, Dick.

REPUBLICANISM
Cato's Letters, John Locke, and the Republican Paradigm. HAMOWY, Ronald.
J G A Pocock's Republicanism and Political Theory: A Critique and Reinterpretation. SHAPIRO, Ian.
Not So Virtuous Republics: Montesquieu, Venice, and the Theory of Aristocratic Republicanism. CARRITHERS, David W.

RESCHER, N
"'Ought' Does Imply 'Can'". SAPONTZIS, Steve F.
La verdad. ALVAREZ GÓMEZ, Mariano.

RESEARCH
Causality in Sociological Research. KARPINSKI, Jakub.
Library Research Guide to Philosophy: Illustrated Search Strategy and Sources. LIST, Charles J.
Structures in Mathematical Theories: Reports of the San Sebastian International Symposium, 1990. DÍEZ, Amparo (ed).
"'Subjects' versus 'Persons' in Social Psychological Research" in *Harré and His Critics*, SECORD, Paul F.
"I Don't Know Why I Did It" in *Harré and His Critics*, CROWLE, Tony.
"The Methodology of Scientific Research Programmes and Some Developments in High Energy Physics" in *Imre Lakatos and Theories of Scientific Change*, GAVROGLU, Kostas.
"Research Programmes and Paradigms as Dialogue Structures" in *Imre Lakatos and Theories of Scientific Change*, KOUTOUGOS, Aris.
"Through the Looking Glass: Philosophy, Research Programmes and the Scientific Community" in *Imre Lakatos and Theories of Scientific Change*, NICOLACOPOULOS, Pantelis D.
Accountability and Responsibility in Research. WOOLF, Patricia K.
Animals in Biomedical Research: The Undermining Effect of the Rhetoric of the Besieged. GLUCK, John P and KUBACKI, Steven R.
Captives of Controversy: The Myth of the Neutral Social Researcher in Contemporary Scientific Controversies. SCOTT, Pam and RICHARDS, Evelleen and MARTIN, Brian.
Child Development and Research Ethics: A Changing Calculus of Concerns. THOMPSON, Ross A.
Commentary: "Love Canal and the Ethics of Environmental Health". FESSENDEN-RADEN, June and BROWN JR, Stuart M.
Commentary: "The University and Industrial Research: Selling Out?". CAMPBELL, L Leon.
The Conceptual Bind in Defining the Volitional Component of Alcoholism. VATZ, Richard E and WEINBERG, Lee S.
Conceptual Issues in Nursing Ethics Research. PENTICUFF, Joy Hinson.
Educational Research and Bhaskar's Conception of Discovery. CORSON, David.
Educational Research in Mexico. SANCHEZ-PUENTES, Ricardo.
Embryo Research and Abortion—the Arguments that Swayed Parliament. SHORT, David S.
Epistemology, Practical Research, and Human Subjects. ROSS, Murray and SELMAN, Mark.
Ethical Dilemmas Posed By Recent and Prospective Developments with Respect to Agricultural Research. JOHNSON, Glenn L.
The Ethics of *Ex Utero* Research on Spare 'Non-Viable' IVF Human Embryos. BAYLIS, Françoise E.
From the Logic of Mathematical Discovery to the Methodology of Scientific Research Programmes. YUXIN, Zheng.
The Influence of Non-Anonymity Deriving from Feedback of Research Results on Marketing Professionals' Research Ethics. AKAAH, Ishmael P.
Is Collaborative Research Exploitative?. LADWIG, James G.
Love Canal and the Ethics of Environmental Health. BRUMMER, James.
Means and Ends in Wild Life Management. LEOPOLD, Aldo.
The Moral Status of Animals and Their Use in Research: A Philosophical Review. DEGRAZIA, David.
New Creations? Commentary. BALK, Roger A.
New Creations? Commentary. FREEDMAN, Benjamin and GOULET, Marie-Claude.
New Creations? Commentary. MACER, Darryl.
Noncompliance in AIDS Research. ARRAS, John D.
Nursing Responsibility for the Placebo Effect. CONNELLY, Robert J.
On the Dearth of Philosophical Contributions to Medicine. YARBOROUGH, Mark.
On the Uniqueness of Biological Research. PORTMANN, Adolph.
Pharaoh's Magicians: The Ethics and Efficacy of Human Fetal Tissue Transplants. BARRY, Robert and KESLER, Darrel.
Philosophiehistorische Forschung und historischer Materialismus. THOM, Martina.
The *Rezeptionsgeschichte* of the Paris Manuscripts. MAIDAN, Michael.
Toward A Value-Laden Theory: Feminism and Social Science. BERNICK, Susan E.
The University and Industrial Research: Selling Out?. HILL, Judith M.
When Scientists are Wrong: Admitting Inadvertent Error in Research. LEIBEL, Wayne.

RESEMBLANCE(S)
Copies, Reproducibility and Aesthetic Adequacy. CHANG, Briankle G.
Location and Range. SCHLESINGER, George N.
Machines as Persons?. HANFLING, Oswald.
Natural Generativity and Imitation. SARTWELL, Crispin.
Reinterpreting Images. SLEZAK, Peter.
The Very Idea of Perfect Realism. FISHER, John Andrew.

RESENTMENT
Benevolence and Resentment. STEPHENSON, Wendell.

RESISTANCE
Bertrand Russell. ALCARO, Mario.
The Tanner Lectures On Human Values, Volume XII. PETERSON, Grethe B (ed).
"Joining the Resistance: Psychology, Politics, Girls, and Women" in *The Tanner Lectures On Human Values, Volume XII*, GILLIGAN, Carol.
"Nonviolent Resistance as the Moral Equivalent of War" in *In the Interest of Peace: A Spectrum of Philosophical Views*, CHURCHILL, R Paul.
Genetically Engineered Herbicide Resistance, Part Two. COMSTOCK, Gary.
Le thème de la révolution dans la pensée de Sartre. CREMA, Cristina Diniz Mendonça.
Student Resistance in Philosophy for Children. LARDNER, A T.

RESOLUTION
Good Intentions Aside: A Manager's Guide to Resolving Ethical Problems. NASH, Laura L.
Aquinas on Resolution in Metaphysics. TAVUZZI, Michael.
Moral Dilemmas, Compromise and Compensation. DAY, J P.

RESOURCE(S)
Animal Experimentation and the Argument from Limited Resources. FINK, Charles K.
Equality of What: Welfare, Resources, or Capabilities?. DANIELS, Norman.
Resources, Capacities, and Ownership: The Workmanship Ideal and Distributive Justice. SHAPIRO, Ian.
When is Original Appropriation *Required*?. SCHMIDTZ, David.

RESPECT
"Rights" in *A Companion to Ethics*, ALMOND, Brenda.
Animal Liberators are Not Anti-Science. MAGEL, Charles.
On Respect. BLUM, Alex.
Respect for Persons and Self-Respect: Western and Indian. GHOSH-DASTIDAR, Koyeli.
Some Remarks on Respect and Human Rights. BARNES, Annette.

RESPONSE(S)
Contemplating Music—Source Readings in the Aesthetics of Music, Volume II: Import. KATZ, Ruth (ed).

RESPONSIBILITY(-TIES)
The Call to Personhood. MC FADYEN, Alistair I.
Intention, Agency and Criminal Liability: Philosophy of Action and the Criminal Law. DUFF, R A.
Interpreting Political Responsibility. DUNN, John.
Liability and Responsibility. FREY, R G (ed).
Moral Philosophy from Montaigne to Kant: An Anthology, Volume I & II. SCHNEEWIND, J B (ed).
The Non-Reality of Free Will. DOUBLE, Richard.
The Political Responsibility of Intellectuals. MACLEAN, Ian (ed).
Responsibility and Criminal Liability. SISTARE, C T.
Thinking the Unthinkable: Meanings of the Holocaust. GOTTLIEB, Roger S (ed).
Das Tier in der Moral. WOLF, Ursula.
Universalism versus Communitarianism: Contemporary Debates in Ethics. RASMUSSEN, David.
"Apperception and Epistemic Responsibility" in *Central Themes in Early Modern Philosophy*, KITCHER, Patricia.
"Heritage and Collective Responsibility" in *The Political Responsibility of Intellectuals*, JEDLICKI, Jerzy.
"Intellectuals and Responsibility" in *The Political Responsibility of Intellectuals*, SHILS, Edward.
"Is Free Will Incompatible with Something or Other?" in *Key Themes in Philosophy*, GRIFFITHS, A Phillips.
"The Legacy of Baby Doe: Nurses' Ethical and Legal Obligations to Severely Handicapped Newborns" in *Biomedical Ethics Reviews, 1987*, MARTIN, Darlene Aulds.
"Moral Responsibility, Values, and Making Decisions about Biotechnology" in *Agricultural Bioethics: Implications of Agricultural Biotechnology*, HOLLANDER, Rachelle D.

RESPONSIBILITY(-TIES)

"The Nurse's Role: Responsibilities and Rights" in *Biomedical Ethics Reviews, 1987*, FOWLER, Marsha D M.
"The Political Irresponsibility of Intellectuals" in *The Political Responsibility of Intellectuals*, TAMÁS, G M.
"The Political Responsibility of Intellectuals" in *The Political Responsibility of Intellectuals*, MONTEFIORE, Alan.
"Rationality, Responsibility, and Pathological Indifference" in *Identity, Character, and Morality: Essays in Moral Psychology*, WHITE, Stephen L.
"Responsibility and 'Free Will'" in *Key Themes in Philosophy*, VESEY, Godfrey.
"Responsibility and Future Generations: A Constructivist Model" in *Philosophy of Technology*, SMITH, Janet Farrell.
"Responsibility and the Act of Interpretation: The Case of Law" in *The Political Responsibility of Intellectuals*, MACLEAN, Ian.
"Textual Responsibility" in *The Political Responsibility of Intellectuals*, LECERCLE, J J.
Agency and Morality. BROOK, Richard.
Beggars and Kings: Cowardice and Courage in Shakespeare's *Richard II*. JENSEN, Pamela K.
Het belang van Husserls aanzet tot een fenomenologie van de bewustzijnsperspectieven. FREDERIX, Lode.
Business and Professional Ethics: An Oxymoron?. PORTER, Jack Nusan.
Community Responsibility and the Development of Oregon's Health Care Priorities. GARLAND, Michael J and HASNAIN, Romana.
Concerns of College Students Regarding Business Ethics: A Replication. PETERSON, Robert A and BELTRAMINI, Richard F and KOZMETSKY, George.
Conditional Intention. CARTWRIGHT, J P W.
Emotions and Responsibility. TURSKI, George.
Ethical Considerations and Ramifications of the 1989 Generic Drug Scandal. HEACOCK, Marian V and ORVIS, Gregory P.
Ethical Issues in Bankruptcy: A Jewish Perspective. TAMARI, Meir.
The Ethical Significance of Corporate Law. NESTERUK, Jeffrey.
Ethics and the Professional Responsibility of Lawyers (Commentary). LENNERTZ, James E.
The Ethics of Suspicion. BERNASCONI, Robert.
Ethik zwischen globaler Verantwortung und spekulativer Weltschematik. JOOS, Egbert.
Final Summary (in Czechoslovakian). KOLAKOWSKI, L.
Fingarette on the Disease Concept of Alcoholism. CORLETT, J Angelo.
Global Responsibility. AGASSI, Joseph.
History, Lying, and Moral Responsibility. PORK, Andrus.
Hume on Responsibility and Punishment. RUSSELL, Paul.
Lucien, Lévy-Bruhl: Una introduzione (di C Prandi). IANNOTTA, Daniella.
Metaphysics of the Person, Determinism and Responsibility. FAY, Thomas A.
Morally Untenable Beliefs. BURKE, Richard J.
Necesidad y existencia del código de moral profesional. MUÑOZ BARQUERO, Elizabeth.
No Moral Responsibility Without Alternative Possibilities. WEBBER, May A.
Nothingness and Responsibility (in Czechoslovakian). HEJDANEK, L.
Oppression and Victimization; Choice and Responsibility. WENDELL, Susan.
Origen y desembocadura de la acción: el sujeto inevitable. CRUZ, Manuel.
The Political Economy of Tardive Dyskinesia: Asymmetries in Power and Responsibility. COHEN, David and MC CUBBIN, Michael.
The Question of Responsibility in the Context of Instructional Technology. TAYLOR, William and KONSTANTELLOU, Eva.
Reactions to Ethical Dilemmas: A Study Pertaining to Certified Public Accounts. CLAYPOOL, G A and FETYKO, D F and PEARSON, M A.
Rehabilitating Responsibility. GADEN, Gerry.
Response: "The Rooting and Uprooting of Reason: On *Spacings* by John Sallis". SALLIS, John.
Responsibility As a Moral Principle? A Critical Reflection on Hans Jonas' Ethics of Responsibility? (in German). KETTNER, Matthias.
Responsibility in the Tradition of Czech Thought (in Czechoslovakian). ZUMR, J.
Responsibility, the Theory of Values, and the Theory of Knowledge (in Czechoslovakian). MERCIER, A.
Responsibility—A Challenge in Terms of Philosophy (in German). RÖSEBERG, Ulrich.
Responsibility: Repudiators Referring to the Divided Centre of Action in the Physical Agent (in Czechoslovakian). PEARS, D.
Roberts on Responsibility for Action and Character in the *Nicomachean Ethics*. BRICKHOUSE, Thomas C.
Romano Guardini's Theological Critique of the Modern Age (in Dutch). VAN DER VLOET, J.
Social Apriori of Responsibility in Scheler's Phenomenology (in Serbo-Croatian). VEAUTHIER, Frank W.
La tecnología desde un punto de vista ético. RAMÍREZ, E Roy.
The Philosophy of Responsibility (in German). SCHRÖDER, Richard.
Wovor und wodurch sind wir verantworlich? Die Instanzen der Verantwortung. MAIER, Maria.

RESTRAINT(S)

The Ethics of Mechanical Restraints. MOSS, Robert J and LA PUMA, John.

RESULT(S)

An Experimental Assessment of Alternative Teaching Approaches for Introductory Business Ethics. BURTON, Scot and JOHNSTON, Mark W and WILSON, Elizabeth J.
Whose Genome Project?. MACER, Darryl.

RESURRECTION

"Keine festbegrenzte und Wahrhaft anschauliche Vorstelling". SCHREURS, Nico.
Personal Identity, Reincarnation, and Resurrection. IALACCI, Michael.
Vida y Resurrección en el pensamiento de Erich Fromm. CHAVES, Flory.

RETALIATION

Retaliatory Punishment as a Categorical Imperative. HÖFFE, Ottfried.

RETARDATION

Response to Diamond. MC NAUGHTON, David.
Response to McNaughton. DIAMOND, Cora.

RETIREMENT

Is Mandatory Retirement Unfair Age Discrimination?. WEDEKING, Gary A.
De natuurlijke ouderdom: een grenzeloze geschiedenis. BIJSTERVELD, Karin.

RETRIBUTION

What Is Justice? Classic and Contemporary Readings. SOLOMON, Robert C (ed).
"A New Theory of Retribution" in *Liability and Responsibility*, HAMPTON, Jean.

RETRIBUTIVE JUSTICE

"Retributive Hatred: An Essay on Criminal Liability and the Emotions" in *Liability and Responsibility*, MURPHY, Jeffrie G.

RETRIBUTIVISM

Davis and the Unfair-Advantage Theory of Punishment: A Critique. SCHEID, Don E.

REVELATION

A Hindu Perspective on the Philosophy of Religion. SHARMA, Arvind.
The Transcendental Temptation: A Critique of Religion and the Paranormal. KURTZ, Paul.
Comment on Colmo's "Reason and Revelation in the Thought of Leo Strauss". LOWENTHAL, David.
Knowledge, Belief and Revelation: A Reply to Patrick Lee. HOITENGA JR, Dewey J.
Reason and Revelation in the Thought of Leo Strauss. COLMO, Christopher A.
Socratic Reason and Socratic Revelation. MC PHERRAN, Mark L.
Sur le concept de Révélation. GABORIAU, Florent.
Sur le concept de tradition. GABORIAU, Florent.

REVERSAL

A Dilemma of Late Life Memory. MC KEE, Patrick.

REVIEW(S)

Constitutional Democracy and the Legitimacy of Judicial Review. FREEMAN, Samuel.
Does Strict Judicial Scrutiny Involve the *Tu Quoque* Fallacy?. SCHEDLER, George.

REVISION(S)

Reasoning and Revision in Hybrid Representation Systems. NEBEL, Bernhard.
"Belief Revision, Non-Monotonic Reasoning, and the Ramsey Test" in *Knowledge Representation and Defeasible Reasoning*, CROSS, Charles.
The Gärdenfors Impossibility Theorem in Non-Monotonic Contexts. MAKINSON, David.
Quine on Theory and Language. TANJI, Nobuharu.
Theory Contraction through Base Contraction. FUHRMANN, André.
Theory Revision and Probability. SCHLECHTA, Karl.
Two Methods of Constructing Contractions and Revisions of Knowledge Systems. ROTT, Hans.

REVIVAL(S)

Music Performance and the Tools of the Trade. GODLOVITCH, Stan.

REVOLUTION(S)

see also Scientific Revolution
The Noble Savage: Jean-Jacques Rousseau, 1754-1762. CRANSTON, Maurice.
The Power of Ideology. MÉSZÁROS, István.
"Egalité ou fraternité" in *Égalité Uguaglianza*, OPPICI, Patrizia.
"L'égalité en 1789" in *Égalité Uguaglianza*, D'HONDT, Jacques.
"Pacifism and Revolution" in *In the Interest of Peace: A Spectrum of Philosophical Views*, DONAGHY, John.
"Routine and Revolution" in *Critique and Construction: A Symposium on Roberto Unger's "Politics"*, SUNSTEIN, Cass R.
"La 'grande illusion' du XVIIIe siècle" in *Égalité Uguaglianza*, ROSSO, Corrado.
"Construindo a 'ordem anárquica". PIOZZI, Patrícia.
Aufklärung und Reform. SCHNEIDERS, Werner.
Havel and Habermas on Identity and Revolution. MATUSTIK, Martin J.
The Ironist's Cage. ROTH, Michael S.

REVOLUTION(S)
Justus Möser: De Revolutie en de grondslagen van de moderne staat. WALRAVENS, Else.
Le thème de la révolution dans la pensée de Sartre. CREMA, Cristina Diniz Mendonça.
Il linguaggio ideologico della rivoluzione. MATHIEU, Vittorio.
Locke, Lockean Ideas, and the Glorious Revolution. SCHWOERER, Lois G.
Marx's Theory of Revolutionary Change. PANICHAS, George E and HOBART, Michael E.
The Modernity of St Thomas' Political Philosophy. WALTER, Edward.
Revolution, Civil Society and Democracy. ARATO, Andrew.
Rosmini interprete della Rivoluzione francese e di Rousseau. BOTTO, Evandro.
Ruminations of a Slow-witted Mind. PIKE, Burton (trans) and LUFT, David S and MUSIL, Robert.
The Skeptic's Burke: *Reflections on the Revolution in France,* 1790-1990. MOSHER, Michael A.
Two Views of the Revolution: Gramsci and Sorel, 1916-1920. SCHECTER, Darrow.
Unamuno y la Revolución de Octubre. ROBLES, Laureano.
Ways to See a Revolution and World Outlook: Alexander von Humboldt (in German). HERLITZIUS, Erwin.
Writing the Revolution—The Politics of Truth in Genet's *Prisoner of Love.* CRITCHLEY, Simon.

REWARD(S)
Religion and Cultural Evolution. MASSIMINI, Fausto and FAVE, Antonella Delle.
Reward, Punishment, and the Strategy of Evolution. SCHRADER, Malcolm E.

RHEES, R
Working with Wittgenstein's Builders. BIRSCH, Douglas and DORBOLO, Jon.

RHETORIC
The Bible as Rhetoric: Studies in Biblical Persuasion and Credibility. WARNER, Martin (ed).
Dialogue with the Other: The Inter-Religious Dialogue. TRACY, David.
Das Ethische in der Rhetorik des Aristoteles. WÖRNER, Markus Hilmar.
Kalkulierte Absurditäten. STRUB, Christian.
A Philosophical Daybook: Post-Critical Investigations. POTEAT, William H.
The Rhetoric of Berkeley's Philosophy. WALMSLEY, Peter.
Toward the Death of Man. KLUBACK, William.
"'In the Sermon Which I Have Just Completed, Wherever I Said Aristotle, I Meant Saint Paul'" in *The Bible as Rhetoric: Studies in Biblical Persuasion and Credibility*, JASPER, David.
"'Truth' and 'Rhetoric' in the Pauline Epistles" in *The Bible as Rhetoric: Studies in Biblical Persuasion and Credibility*, KENNEDY, George.
"History and Rhetoric in the Prophets" in *The Bible as Rhetoric: Studies in Biblical Persuasion and Credibility*, BARTON, John.
"Love as Rhetorical Principle: The Relationship Between Content and Style in the Rhetoric of St Augustine" in *Grace, Politics and Desire: Essays on Augustine*, SUTHERLAND, Christine Mason.
Affirmative Action Rhetoric. RADIN, Margaret Jane.
Against Common Sense: Avoiding Cartesian Anxiety. BINEHAM, Jeffery L.
Aristotele professore?. NATALI, Carlo.
Cartesian Syntax. ENGLEBRETSEN, George.
Community, Law, and the Idiom and Rhetoric of Rights. MAC INTYRE, Alasdair.
Did Plato Coin *Rhētorikē*?. SCHIAPPA, Edward.
Etica, retórica y política en la antropología aristotélica. MARTIN, Victor R.
Die Figuren des Menschlichen. MEYER, Michel.
History and Neo-Sophistic Criticism: A Reply to Poulakos. SCHIAPPA, Edward.
In Defense of Plato: A Short Polemic. ROOCHNIK, David.
Interpreting Sophistical Rhetoric: A Response to Schiappa. POULAKOS, John.
Irreducible Dualisms and the Residue of Commonsense: On the Inevitability of Cartesian Anxiety. HIKINS, James W and CHERWITZ, Richard A.
Neo-Sophistic Rhetorical Criticism or the Historical Reconstruction of Sophistic Doctrines?. SCHIAPPA, Edward.
On Behalf of Skeptical Rhetoric. FALZER, Paul R.
Parody and the Argument from Probability in the *Apology*. LEWIS, Thomas J.
Persuasion: Jane Austen's Philosophical Rhetoric. KASTELY, James L.
Philosophical Argument and the Rhetorical Wedge. JOHNSTONE JR, Henry W.
Philosophy, Argument, and Narration. VERENE, Donald Phillip.
Practical Intuition and Rhetorical Example. SCHOLLMEIER, Paul.
Practicing the Arts of Rhetoric: Tradition and Invention. FARRELL, Thomas B.
Response to Slezak: *Nein, Ich verstehe nicht*. KEITH, William.
Rhetoric and Argumentation: Relativism and Beyond. KIENPOINTNER, Manfred.
Rhetoric and Ethics: Adam Smith on Theorizing about the Moral Sentiments. GRISWOLD JR, Charles L.
Rhetoric as Praxis: An Alternative to the Epistemic Approach. ZHAO, Shanyang.
The Rhetoric of Martianus Capella and Anselm de Besate in the Tradition of Menippean Satire. BENNETT, Beth S.
The Rhetoric of Opposition in Thomas More's *Utopia*: Giving Form to Competing Philosophies. WEGEMER, Gerard.
Rights as Rhetoric: Nonsense on Stilts?. O'NEILL, William.
The Uses of Rhetoric: Indeterminacy in Legal Reasoning, Practical Thinking and Interpretation of Literary Figures. OLMSTED, Wendy Raudenbush.

RICHARD, M
The Relational Theory of Belief (A Reply to Richard). SCHIFFER, Stephen.

RICOEUR, P
The Cogito and Hermeneutics: The Question of the Subject in Ricoeur. JERVOLINO, Domenico.
Kalkulierte Absurditäten. STRUB, Christian.
"As Real As It Gets...": Ricoeur and Narrativity. KELLNER, Hans.
Acerca de uma tese ricoeuriana. SUMARES, Manuel.
Bibliographie de Paul Ricoeur: Compléments (jusqu'en 1990). VANSINA, Frans.
O discurso filosófico e a unidade da verdade nas primeiras obras de Paul Ricoeur. RENAUD, Michel.
Hermenêutica e Estruturalismo. ROCHA, Acílio Estanqueiro.
Limning the Liminal: Carr and Ricoeur on Time and Narrative. PELLAUER, David.
A lógica do sentido na filosofia hermenêutica. COSTA, Miguel Dias.
Paul Ricoeur e Gabriel Marcel. DE LOURDES SIRGADO GANHO, Maria.
Una reflexión sobre el pensamiento científico técnico. CORONA, N A.
A significação "crítica" de Le volontaire et l'involontaire. HENRIQUES, Fernanda.

RIDLEY, M
A Commentary on Ridley's Cladistic Solution to the Species Problem. WILKINSON, Mark.

RIEMANN
The Development of Modern Mathematics and Plato's Parable of the Cave. MAURIN, Krzysztof.

RIFKIN, J
"Maritain and Rifkin: Two Critiques" in *From Twilight to Dawn: The Cultural Vision of Jacques Maritain*, TRAPANI JR, John G.

RIGHT
see also Good, Virtue(s)
Moral Pluralism and Legal Neutrality. SADURSKI, Wojciech.
The Right to Self-Determination. BERG, Jonathan.

RIGHT TO DIE
To Die or Not to Die?. BERGER, Arthur S (ed).
Cruzan and Caring for Others. LYNN, Joanne and GLOVER, Jacqueline.
Cruzan: No Rights Violated. ROBERTSON, John A.
A Hostage to Technology. CRANFORD, Ronald E.
How Can They?. BUSALACCHI, Pete.
Missouri Stands Alone. COLBY, William H.
Nancy Cruzan in China. ANNAS, George J.
On Taking Substituted Judgment Seriously. BARON, Charles.

RIGHT TO LIFE
Response to 'Rescuing the Innocent'. GARDNER, G T G.
Response to 'Rescuing the Innocent'. MORROW, James.
The Sanctity of Life and Substituted Judgement: The Case of Baby J. HORNETT, Stuart I.
The Significance of a Wish. ACKERMAN, Felicia.

RIGHT(S)
see also Human Rights, Legal Right(s)
Contemporary Perspectives on Masculinity: Men, Women, and Politics in Modern Society. CLATTERBAUGH, Kenneth.
Égalité Uguaglianza. FERRARI, Jean (ed).
Fonti diritto e regole. DE GIACOMO, Claudio.
Interpreting Political Responsibility. DUNN, John.
Kant's System of Rights. MULHOLLAND, Leslie A.
Law, Culture, and Values: Essays in Honor of Gray L Dorsey. VOJCANIN, Sava Alexander (ed).
Philosophical Foundations of Health Education. LAURA, Ronald S.
Political Writings—Kant. REISS, Hans (ed).
The Realm of Rights. THOMSON, Judith Jarvis.
Robert Nozick: Property, Justice, and the Minimal State. WOLFF, Jonathan.
Science and Moral Values. VOLLRATH, John.
Theory and Practice in Medical Ethics. GRABER, Glenn C.
Thomas Hobbes' Theory of Obligation: A Modern Interpretation. FORSBERG, Ralph P.
"L'égalité des droits en 1789" in *Égalité Uguaglianza*, GOYARD-FABRE, Simone.
"L'idée d'égalité et la notion moderne du droit" in *Égalité Uguaglianza*, RENAUT, Alain.
"The Nurse's Role: Responsibilities and Rights" in *Biomedical Ethics Reviews, 1987*, FOWLER, Marsha D M.
"Rights" in *A Companion to Ethics*, ALMOND, Brenda.

RIGHT(S)
Les "droits naturels" et les "titres" selon Robert Nozick. SWEET, William.
A propósito del filósofo del derecho Giorgio del Vecchio. DI PIETRO, Alfredo.
An Alternative to Property Rights in Human Tissue. SWAIN, Margaret S and MARUSYK, Randy W.
Are Property Rights Problematic?. GAUS, Gerald F and LOMASKY, Loren E.
The Basic Right to Liberty. PANICHAS, George E.
Basic Rights and Constitutional Interpretation. LYONS, David.
Blanshard's Critique of Ethical Subjectivism. JOHNSON, Oliver A.
Brand Blanshard and Gewirth: Ethics and Rights. HOWIE, John.
Child Abuse: Parental Rights and the Interests of the Child. ARCHARD, David.
The Chinese Moral Ethos and the Concept of Individual Rights. TAO, Julia.
A Comment on the Argument Between Gewirth and his Critics. ROSS, Steven.
Community, Law, and the Idiom and Rhetoric of Rights. MAC INTYRE, Alasdair.
Los derechos de la mujer, legalidad y realidad. COMESAÑA, Santalices Gloria.
Doctors' Rights and Patients' Obligations. MARSHALL, Sandra E.
Domesticated and Then Some. DURAN, Jane.
Le droit de l'État et le devoir de l'individu. PFERSMANN, Otto.
Economic Rights: A Test Case for Catholic Social Teaching. MC CANN, Dennis P.
A Formal Representation of Declaration-Related Legal Relations. HANSSON, Sven Ove.
From Dialogue Rights to Property Rights. SHEARMUR, Jeremy.
Grammatica e diritto: Una normatività fragile?. VITALE, Vincenzo.
Human Rights and Freedom: Is Kant Relevant to the Current Discussion?. SCHWEIDLER, Walter.
Humble Rebel Henry David Thoreau (in Czechoslovakian). JANAT, B.
Informational Property: Logorights. SCHULMAN, J Neil.
The Integral Self: Systematic Illusion or Inescapable Task?. COLAPIETRO, Vincent M.
Intellectual Property and Copyright Ethics. ALFINO, Mark.
J S Mill's Concept of Maturity as the Criterion in Determining Children's Eligibility for Rights. KIM, Ki Su.
Just War Theory: The Case of South Africa. MILLER, S R.
Justified Limits on Refusing Intervention. CHERVENAK, Frank A and MC CULLOUGH, Laurence B.
Kant's visie op de Franse Revolutie en op de grondslagen van het recht. VAN DER WAL, G A.
Land Rights and Aboriginal Sovereignty. THOMPSON, Janna.
Marsilius on Rights. TIERNEY, Brian.
Maternal Rights, Fetal Harms: Commentary. KINLAW, Kathy.
Maternal Rights, Fetal Harms: Commentary. STRONG, Carson.
Mental Handicap and Citizenship. SPICKER, Paul.
The Moral Status of the Corporation. EWIN, R E.
Nozick on Rights and Minimal State. AGARWALA, Binod Kumar.
On Social Rights. SANDU, Gabriel and KUOKKANEN, Martti.
The Perils of Love: Why Women Need Rights. INGRAM, Attracta.
Prisoners' Rights and Correctional Privatization: A Legal and Ethical Analysis. THOMAS, Charles W.
Property Rights and Preservationist Duties. GOODIN, Robert E.
Reply to Shearmur's "From Dialogue Rights to Property Rights". MICHELMAN, Frank.
Response to Lyons' "Basic Rights and Constitutional Interpretations". LUCKHARDT, Grant.
Rights and Rights Violators: A New Approach to the Nature of Rights. GERT, Heather J.
Rights and Structure in Constitutional Theory. MILLER, Geoffrey P.
Rights and Utilitarianism. EWIN, R E.
Rights as Rhetoric: Nonsense on Stilts?. O'NEILL, William.
The Rights of Organizations. GORDLEY, James.
Rights, Systems of Rights, and Unger's System of Rights: Part I. EIDENMÜLLER, Horst.
The Rights-Interpretation of Desert. GARCÍA, Jorge.
Rights-Talk Will Not Sort Out Child-Abuse: Comment on Archard on Parental Rights. MIDGLEY, Mary.
Rileggendo Marx: "diritti" e "bisogni". BADALONI, Nicola.
Self-Ownership and the Right of Property. MACK, Eric.
The Significance of Rights Language. GOLDING, Martin P.
So Animal a Human..., or the Moral Relevance of Being An Omnivore. GEORGE, Kathryn Paxton.
Sobre la naturaleza de los "derechos". HERNÁNDEZ, Héctor H.
Soggetto e senso del diritto nell'esperienza giuridica moderna: appunti in tema di positività. FIASCHI, Giovanni.
Species, Individuals, and Domestication: A Commentary on Jane Duran's "Domesticated and Then Some". VARNER, Gary E.
Taking Rights Seriously in the Abortion Case. DWORKIN, Ronald.
Trade Secrets and the Justification of Intellectual Property: A Comment on Hettinger. PAINE, Lynn Sharp.
Utilitarian Killing, Replacement, and Rights. PLUHAR, Evelyn.
Why Democracy and Rights Do Not Mix. NELSON, John O.
Why Negative Rights Only?. JORDAN, Jeff.

RIGHTNESS
Skepticism About Goodness and Rightness. GOLDMAN, Alan H.
Soggetto e senso del diritto nell'esperienza giuridica moderna: appunti in tema di positività. FIASCHI, Giovanni.

RIGID DESIGNATOR(S)
"Dubbing and Redubbing: The Vulnerability of Rigid Destination" in *Scientific Theories*, KUHN, Thomas S.
All the Difference in the World. CRANE, Tim.
The Extent of Russell's Modal Views. MAGNELL, Thomas.
On Rigidity and Persistence. WILLIAMSON, Timothy.
Units of Measurement and Natural Kinds: Some Kripkean Considerations. VAN BRAKEL, J.

RING(S)
F-Multipliers and the Localization of Hilbert Algebras. BUSNEAG, Dumitru.
Schanuel's Conjecture and Free Exponential Rings. MACINTYRE, Angus.

RISK(S)
"Cybernetics, Culpability, and Risk" in *Philosophy of Technology*, ANDERSON, Lyle V.
"Risk, Causation, and Harm" in *Liability and Responsibility*, ROBINSON, Glen O.
Decisionmaking Competence and Risk—Comments on Wicclair. BROCK, Dan W.
L'essere mortale dei mortali: Un'analisi sul problema della morte nel pensiero del secondo Heidegger. CICCHESE, Gennaro.
The Ethics of Corporate Health Insurance. LIGHT, Donald W.
The Ethics of Mechanical Restraints. MOSS, Robert J and LA PUMA, John.
An Experimental Analysis of Risk Taking. DAHLBÄCK, Olof.
Implications of Behavioral Consistency in Dynamic Choice Under Uncertainty. DARDANONI, Valentino.
Is IVF Good Medicine?. CONNOR, Pauline.
Patient Decision-Making Capacity and Risk. WICCLAIR, Mark R.
Risk-Related Standard Inevitable in Assessing Competence—Comments on Wicclair. SKENE, Loane.

RITE(S)
Culpabilidad, rito y ritualismo: Una aproprimación psicoanaliítica. RODRIGUEZ AMENABAR, S M.

RITUAL
Platonic Piety. MORGAN, Michael L.
Sacred Fragments: Recovering Theology for the Modern Jew. GILLMAN, Neil.
The Concept of Religion. HESTEVOLD, H Scott.
Culpabilidad, rito y ritualismo: Una aproprimación psicoanaliítica. RODRIGUEZ AMENABAR, S M.
Yajna and the Doctrine of Karma: A Contradiction in Indian Thought about Action. KRISHNA, Daya.

ROBBINS, L
Common Sense and the Foundations of Economic Theory: Duhem versus Robbins. SHEARMUR, Jeremy.

ROBENSTINE, C
Response to Robenstine's "The Dead Horse Phenomenon in Educational Theory". BROSIO, Richard.

ROBERTS, J
Roberts on Responsibility for Action and Character in the *Nicomachean Ethics*. BRICKHOUSE, Thomas C.

ROBESPIERRE
Sartre's onuitgevoerde project: de Robespierre-biografie. DETHIER, Hubert.

RODRIGUEZ, A
Filosofía cristiana y apologética en Mons Audino Rodríguez y Olmos. CATURELLI, Alberto.

ROEMER, J
The Politics and Morality of Unequal Exchange: Emmanuel and Roemer, Analysis and Synthesis. SCHWEICKART, David.

ROHRLICH, F
Some Clarifications and Cautions Essential for Good Philosophy of Science Teaching. DAVSON-GALLE, Peter.

ROIG, A
The Master-Slave Dialectic in Latin America: The Social Criticism of Zea, Freire, and Roig. SCHUTTE, Ofelia M.

ROLE(S)
The Political Responsibility of Intellectuals. MACLEAN, Ian (ed).
"A Reply to John Burbidge's "Where is the Place of Understanding?"" in *Essays on Hegel's Logic*, HOULGATE, Stephen.
The 'Teacher as Midwife': New Wine in Old Skins?. SANCHEZ, Karen L.
The Clinical Ethicist at the Bedside. LA PUMA, John and SCHIEDERMAYER, David L.
Commentary: "The University and Industrial Research: Selling Out?". CAMPBELL, L Leon.
Handsome Lake's Teachings: The Shift from Female to Male Agriculture in Iroquois Agriculture. HOLLY, Marilyn.
Role Differentiation Problems in Professional Ethics. WANGERIN, Paul T.

ROLE(S)
Role Theory: A Reconstruction. VAN VONDEREN, Marijke L.
The Roles of Predictions in Science and Religion. SCHOEN, Edward L.
Rousseau's Political Defense of the Sex-Roled Family. WEISS, Penny.
Taking Role Moralities Seriously. WUESTE, Daniel E.

ROMAN
Jurisculture, Volume I: Greece and Rome. DORSEY, Gray L.
On Duties: Cicero. GRIFFIN, M T (ed).
"Edward Gibbon in History: Aspects of the Text in 'The History of the Decline and Fall of the Roman Empire'" in *The Tanner Lectures on Human Values, Volume XI*, POCOCK, J G A.
"Roman Humanism" in *The Question of Humanism: Challenges and Possibilities*, BOOTH, Allan.

ROMANCE
Why Do I Love Thee? A Response to Nozick's Account of Romantic Love. SMITH, Tara.

ROMANIAN
Romania's Revolution and its Prospects. BRUCAN, Silviu.

ROMANO, E
Una nuova questioni di Egidio Romano "De subjecto theologiae". LUNA, Concetta.

ROMANTICISM
American Philosophy and the Romantic Tradition. GOODMAN, Russell B.
Delicate Subjects: Romanticism, Gender, and the Ethics of Understanding. ELLISON, Julie.
Knowledge, Fiction, and Imagination. NOVITZ, David.
Philosophical Fragments. FIRCHOW, Peter (trans).
Romanticism and the Sciences. CUNNINGHAM, Andrew (ed).
Style and Music: Theory, History, and Ideology. MEYER, Leonard B.
"Genius in Romantic Natural Philosophy" in *Romanticism and the Sciences*, SCHAFFER, Simon.
"Poetry and Modernity" in *The Tanner Lectures On Human Values, Volume XII*, PAZ, Octavio.
"Romantic Philosophy and Organization of the Disciplines: the Founding of the Humboldt University of Berlin" in *Romanticism and the Sciences*, SHAFFER, Elinor S.
"Romanticism and the Sciences" in *Romanticism and the Sciences*, KNIGHT, David.
"Solidarity or Singularity? Richard Rorty between Romanticism and Technocracy" in *Reading Rorty*, FRASER, Nancy.
"William Blake and the Romantic Perception of Humanism" in *The Question of Humanism: Challenges and Possibilities*, ABRAHAMS, Cecil.
The Aesthetics of Imperfection. HAMILTON, Andy.
Cientificidad y Romanticismo: Acerca de las relaciones entre cientismo, gnosticismo y romanticismo. KOSLOWSKI, Peter.
East-West Philosophy in Nineteenth-Century America: Emerson and Hinduism. GOODMAN, Russell B.
Fault-Lines in Kierkegaard and Hawthorne: *The Sickness unto Death* and "Ethan Brand". BENOIT, Raymond.
Gelehrter zwischen Romantik und Hegelianismus in Finnland—Johan Vilhelm Snellman (1806-1881). HÄNTSCH, Carola.
Kants Logik der Synthesis und die Schliessung einer "unübersehbaren Kluft". FUNKE, Gerhard.
Paradojas del Romanticismo. KERKHOFF, Manfred.
Questioning "the Romantic Ideology": Wordsworth. WOLFSON, Susan J.
Romanticism and Modernity. LARMORE, Charles.
Romanticism, Rationality and Alienation—the Triple-H-Theory Revisited. BRUNKHORST, Hauke.

RORTY, R
After the Demise of the Tradition: Rorty, Critical Theory, and the Fate of Philosophy. NIELSEN, Kai.
The Anatomy of Philosophical Style. LANG, Berel.
Ideals and Illusions: On Reconstruction and Deconstruction in Contemporary Critical Theory. MC CARTHY, Thomas.
Reading Rorty. MALACHOWSKI, Alan (ed).
Rorty's Humanistic Pragmatism: Philosophy Democratized. KOLENDA, Konstantin.
"Auto-da-Fé: Consequences of Pragmatism" in *Reading Rorty*, WILLIAMS, Bernard.
"Biting the Bullet: Rorty on Private and Public Morality" in *Reading Rorty*, GUIGNON, Charles B and HILEY, David R.
"Conversational Politics: Rorty's Pragmatist Apology for Liberalism" in *Reading Rorty*, BURROWS, Jo.
"Deep Epistemology Without Foundations (in Language)" in *Reading Rorty*, MALACHOWSKI, Alan R.
"Descartes, Rorty and the Mind-Body Fiction" in *Reading Rorty*, HORNSBY, Jennifer.
"Fact and Fiction" in *Reading Rorty*, CLARK, Michael.
"Let Me Accentuate the Positive" in *Reading Rorty*, QUINE, W V.
"Mirrors and Veils, Thoughts and Things: The Epistemological Problematic" in *Reading Rorty*, YOLTON, John W.
"Philosophy and the Mirage of Hermeneutics" in *Reading Rorty*, HOLÓWKA, Jacek.
"The Poetics of Personhood" in *Reading Rorty*, HOLLIS, Martin.
"Redefining Philosophy as Literature: Richard Rorty's 'Defence' of Literary Culture" in *Reading Rorty*, FISCHER, Michael.
"Rorty in the Epistemological Tradition" in *Reading Rorty*, TAYLOR, Charles.
"Rorty's Talk-About" in *Reading Rorty*, HOUGHTON, David.
"Rorty, Realism and the Idea of Freedom" in *Reading Rorty*, BHASKAR, Roy.
"The World from its Own Point of View" in *Reading Rorty*, SORELL, Tom.
Contingentie als uitgangspunt: Het denken van Richard Rorty. GEERTSEMA, H G.
Interrupting Olivier's Socio-Political Conversation: Another Postmodern Proposal. ALLEN, J G.
The Irony of Richard Rorty and the Question of Political Judgment. WEISLOGEL, Eric L.
Liberalismo e democrazia: la giustificazione estetica di Rorty. MARRONE, Pierpaolo.
Misreading Rorty. KOLENDA, Konstantin.
Over de ambivalente rol van de theoriegeladenheidsthese in Rorty's 'overwinning' van de traditie. KRIBBE, Pamela.
Richard Rorty and the Image of Modernity. BRADLEY, James.
Richard Rorty: An Interview (in Hebrew). KULKA, Tomas.
Rorty, Davidson and Truth. BAGHRAMIAN, Maria.
Thus Spoke Rorty: The Perils of Narrative Self-Creation. CONWAY, Daniel W.
The Unbearable Seriousness of Irony. FERRARA, Alessandro.
What Putnam Should Have Said: An Alternative Reply to Rorty. HARTZ, Carolyn G.

ROSENZWEIG, F
Franz Rosenzweig: Existentielles Denken und gelebte Bewährung. SCHMIED-KOWARZIK, Wolfdietrich.
"The Face of Truth in Rosenzweig, Levinas, and Jewish Mysticism" in *Phenomenology of the Truth Proper to Religion*, COHEN, Richard A.
Franz Rosenzweig e Friedrich Meinecke. D'ANTUONO, Emilia.
Tempo ed eternità: La filosofia narrante di F Rosenzweig. DI MARCO, Chiara.
The Foundations of Franz Rosenzweig's Theory of Knowledge (in Hebrew). AMIR, Yehoyada.

ROSMINI
Due note: Ritorni Rosminiani—Il momento di Ugo Spirito. PAOLETTI, Laura.

ROSMINI, A
Rosmini interprete della Rivoluzione francese e di Rousseau. BOTTO, Evandro.

ROSS, A
Paradigms of Legal Science. JORI, Mario.

ROSS, D
On 'High-Mindedness'. GARCIA, Jorge.

ROSS, S
On Some Paradoxes of the Infinite. ALLIS, Victor and KOETSIER, Teunis.

ROSSI-LANDI, F
Il "parlare commune" come lume storico-naturale della "riproduzione sociale". MININNI, Giuseppe.
L'epoché di Husserl in Ferruccio Rossi-Landi. PONZIO, Augusto.
Sulla semiotizzazione dell' "a priori": Rossi-Landi e Hjelmslev. CAPUTO, Cosimo.

ROSSOUW, G
Continuing the Conversation—A Reply to My Interlocutors. OLIVIER, G.

ROSWITHA OF GANDERSHEIM
"Roswitha of Gandersheim, Christine Pisan, Margaret More Roper and Teresa of Avila" in *A History of Women Philosophers, Volume II: Medieval, Renaissance and Enlightenment, A.D. 500-1600*, WAITHE, Mary Ellen.

ROUSSEAU
Jean-Jacques: The Early Life and Work of Jean-Jacques, 1712-1754. CRANSTON, Maurice.
Nature and Politics: Liberalism in the Philosophies of Hobbes, Locke, and Rousseau. RAPACZYNSKI, Andrzej.
The Noble Savage: Jean-Jacques Rousseau, 1754-1762. CRANSTON, Maurice.
Différentielles et intégrales sociales chez Rousseau. BACHTA, Abdelkader.
Emile's Education. SHAVER, Robert.
La influencia de Rousseau en el pensamiento de Kant. DE LOS ANGELES GIRALT, María.
Jean-Jacques Rousseau and the Fusion of Democratic Sovereignty with Aristocratic Government. CRANSTON, Maurice.
Jean-Jacques Rousseau et Friedrich Schiller: le théâtre sous le feu des lumières. MATTE, Martin.
Jean-Jacques Rousseau on the Physiogonomy of the Modern City. ELLISON, Charles E.
Jean-Jacques Rousseau, Sexist?. THOMAS, Paul.
Kant, Pestalozzi and the Role of Ideology in Educational Thought. ADAMS, Ian.
Le promeneur solitaire: Rousseau and the Emergence of the Post-Social Self. GAUTHIER, David.
Nietzsche contra Rousseau: Goethe versus Catilina?. BLONDEL, Eric.
Rosmini interprete della Rivoluzione francese e di Rousseau. BOTTO, Evandro.

ROUSSEAU
Rousseau et Kant: A propos de la genèse de la théorie kantienne des idées. PICHÉ, Claude.
Rousseau intimiste et la fusion des cultures?. GRASSI, Marie-Claire.
Rousseau's Liberalism. SORENSEN, L R.
Rousseau's Political Defense of the Sex-Roled Family. WEISS, Penny.
Rousseau, the General Will, and Individual Liberty. KAIN, Philip J.
Le sens de la révolution méthodologique introduite par Rousseau dans la science politique. GOYARD-FABRE, Simone.

ROUSSELOT, P
From Unity to Pluralism: The Internal Evolution of Thomism. MC COOL, Gerald A.

ROUTLEY, R
In Defense of Human "Chauvinism": A Response to R Routley and V Routley. PASKE, Gerald H.

ROYCE
Toward the Death of Man. KLUBACK, William.
Josiah Royce: la metafisica della comunità. BUZZI GRASSI, Elisa.

ROZANOV
Vasilii Vasil'evich Rozanov: "My Soul Is Woven of Filth, Tenderness, and Grief". KUVAKIN, V A.

RUBEN
Ruben and the Metaphysics of the Social World. TUOMELA, Raimo.

RUETHER, R
Pour une interprétation féministe de l'idée chrétienne de Dieu. DION, Michel.

RULE UTILITARIANISM
Firth's Critique of Epistemological Rule-Utilitarianism. SHOPE, Robert K.
Hume's Ethics: Acts, Rules, Dispositions and Utility. SHIRLEY, Edward.

RULE(S)
Fonti diritto e regole. DE GIACOMO, Claudio.
Il Paradigma del Sapere. LENTINI, Luigi.
Practical Reason and Norms. RAZ, Joseph.
"On the Nature of a Social Order" in *Logic, Methodology and Philosophy of Science, VIII*, PÖRN, Ingmar.
'Rules' and 'Knowledge'. HARRISON III, Frank R.
Conventions, règles et nécessité. VOIZARD, Alain.
Czeslaw Znamierowski's Conception of Constitutive Rules. CZEPITA, Stanislaw.
The Epistemological Moral Relevance of Democracy. NINO, Carlos S.
Getting Rule-Following Straight. WONG, James.
The Inductive Support of Inductive Rules: Themes from Max Black. SANFORD, David H.
Interpretation and the Social Reality of Law. GOLDFORD, Dennis.
Later Wittgenstein on Objectivity of Rules. BEHERA, Sathrughna.
Malcolm on Wittgenstein on Rules. MOSER, Paul K.
Moore's Moral Rules. PERKINS JR, Ray.
No Rules without Virtues: No Virtues without Rules. BRAYBROOKE, David.
Non-Rational Cognitive Processes as Changes of Distinctions. HEYLIGHEN, Francis.
Nonrules and Plausibility: An Illustration in Pragmatic Theory. POWELL, Mava Jo.
A Note on Hooker's "Rule Consequentialism". CARSON, Tom.
Pragmatic Principles and Language. BHAT, P R.
Reglas, comunidades y juicios. ZALABARDO, José Luis.
Rule-Scepticism: Kripkean Understanding in Wittgenstein's Perspective. BEHERA, Satrughna.
Rules and Relations: Some Connectionist Implications for Cognitive Science and Language. CILLIERS, F P.
Self-Conscious Individual versus Social Soul: The Rationale of Wittgenstein's Discussion of Rule Following. SAVIGNY, Eike V.
Toward a Narrative Conception of Legal Discourse. PATTERSON, Dennis.
Virtues and Rules. ROBERTS, Robert C.
Why Narrative Is Not Enough. FULLER, Steve.
Wittgenstein sobre la noción de regla en Frege. PADILLA GÁLVEZ, Jesús.
Wittgenstein versus Hart: Two Models of Rules for Social and Legal Theory. HUND, John.
Wittgenstein's Account of Rule-Following. PEARS, David.
Zu einem "der tiefsten philosophischen Probleme". SIEGWART, Geo.

RULER(S)
Allocution Made to a Magistrate. PAREL, A J (ed & trans) and MACHIAVELLI, Niccolò.

RUSHDIE, S
The Empirical Author: Salman Rushdie's *The Satanic Verses*. CLOSE, Anthony.

RUSSELL
Bertrand Russell. ALCARO, Mario.
Bertrand Russell: The Psychobiography of a Moralist. BRINK, Andrew.
Classics of Analytic Philosophy. AMMERMAN, Robert R (ed).
Epistemology and Skepticism: An Enquiry into the Nature of Epistemology. CHATALIAN, George.
Mathematics and the Image of Reason. TILES, Mary E.
The Metaphysics of the "Tractatus". CARRUTHERS, Peter.
Pulling up the Ladder: The Metaphysical Roots of Wittgenstein's Tractatus. BROCKHAUS, Richard R.
"Human Order in the Natural Universe: Rediscovering Russell's Social Philosophy" in *Perspectives on Ideas and Reality*, MEZEI, György Iván.
"Logic in Russell's Logicism" in *The Analytic Tradition: Philosophical Quarterly Monographs, Volume 1*, HYLTON, Peter.
"The Russell-Hook Debates of 1958: Arguments from the Extremes on Nuclear War and the Soviet Union" in *In the Interest of Peace: A Spectrum of Philosophical Views*, GAY, William.
"Russellian Intensional Logic" in *Themes From Kaplan*, ANDERSON, C Anthony.
Una aproximación ontológica a la realidad fisica. HÜBNER, Adolf.
Bertrand Russell and Liberty: A Question Revisited. PADIA, Chandrakala.
Definite Descriptions. DANIELS, Charles B.
Descriptions and Group Reference. MUKHERJI, Nirmalangshu.
Descriptions: Contemporary Philosophy and the Nyāya. SHAW, J L.
Education and the Emotions: The Relevance of the Russellian Perspective. MATTAI, Bansraj.
The Extent of Russell's Modal Views. MAGNELL, Thomas.
La filosofía mística de Russell y lo indecible en el *Tractatus*. TOMASINI BASSOLS, Alejandro.
Frege-Russell Semantics?. WETTSTEIN, Howard.
From Russell to Quine: Basic Statements, Foundationalism, Truth, and Other Myths. LINDBERG, Jordan J.
Genuine Names and Knowledge by Acquaintance. DONNELLAN, Keith S.
A Global Point of View on Russell's Philosophy. RODRÍGUEZ-CONSUEGRA, Francisco.
How Not to Russell Carnap's *Aufbau*. RICHARDSON, Alan.
Indefinite Descriptions: In Defense of Russell. LUDLOW, Peter and NEALE, Stephen.
La interpretación russelliana de Leibniz y el atomismo metodológico de Moore. RODRÍGUEZ CONSUEGRA, Francisco.
El logicismo russelliano: su significado filosófico. RODRÍGUEZ CONSUEGRA, Francisco.
More on Russell's Hypothesis. HINDERLITER, Hilton.
A New Interpretation of Russell's Multiple-Relation Theory of Judgment. LANDINI, Gregory.
On Russell's Principle of Induction. DA COSTA, Newton C A and FRENCH, Steven.
Reflexiones en torno a la oración oblicua. MUÑOZ, Angel and CAROSIO, Alba.
Russell and the Ethical Concern of Wittgenstein's *Tractatus*. IGLESIAS, Teresa.
Russell on Ordinary Names and Synonymy. PINEAU, Lois.
Russell on Pastness. KENYON, Timothy A.
Russell's Theory of Definite Descriptions. LAMBERT, Karel.
Russell, Logicism, and the Choice of Logical Constants. BYRD, Michael.
Should Children Be Taught to Obey Their Conscience?. HUGHEN, Richard.
Tautology: How Not to Use a Word. DREBEN, Burton and FLOYD, Juliet.
The Influence of Roger Boskovic on Bertrand Russell's Early Philosophy of Physics (in Serbo-Croatian). LEWIS, Albert C.
A Tradition of Natural Kinds. HACKING, Ian.
Universal Sentences: Russell, Wittgenstein, Prior, and the Nyāya. SHAW, J L.
Unpublished Correspondence between Russell and Wittgenstein. MC GUINNESS, B F and VON WRIGHT, G H.
Vagueness, Natural Language and Logic. BERKELEY, Istvan S N.
Was the Axiom of Reducibility a Principle of Logic?. LINSKY, Bernard.

RUSSIAN
see also Soviet
La Logica Simbolica: nella produzione scientifica in lingua russa (1961-1983). PENNINO, Luciano.
Russische Philosophie. GOERDT, Wilhelm.
Statism and Anarchy. SHATZ, Marshall (ed).
An Examination of Marxist Doctrine in the Traditions of Russian Religious Philosophy. STEPANOVA, E A.
Kant in Russia: The Initial Phase (continued). NEMETH, Thomas.
The Last Utopia: Entropy and Revolution in the Poetics of Evgeny Zamjatin. SICHER, Efraim.
Marx and Russia. NAARDEN, Bruno.
MYSL' and the Intuitivist Debate in the Early 1920s. NETHERCOTT, Frances.
La prima edizione sovietica di Solov'ev. MASTROIANNI, Giovanni.
Sophia and the Devil: Kant in the Face of Russian Religious Metaphysics. AKHUTIN, A V.

RUSSMAN, T
"A Reply to Russman's 'A Faith of True Proportions'" in *Thomistic Papers, V*, SULLIVAN, Thomas D.

RYLE, G
Analysis as a Method in Philosophy with Special Reference to A J Ayer. SRINIVAS, K.
The Ontology of Mental Images. HOLBROOK, Daniel.
Seeing in the Mind's Eye. BORUAH, Bijoy H.

SABOTAGE
Ecosabotage and Civil Disobedience. MARTIN, Michael.
SABUCO, O
"Oliva Sabuco de Nantes Barrera" in *A History of Women Philosophers, Volume II: Medieval, Renaissance and Enlightenment, A.D. 500-1600*, WAITHE, Mary Ellen.
SACRAMENT(S)
The Community as Sacrament. LIDERBACH, Daniel.
Oratio Placabilis Deo Eriugena's Fragmentary Eucharistic Teaching. SMITH, R U.
SACRED
'Religion' and the Religions in the English Enlightenment. HARRISON, Peter.
Spirit and Existence: A Philosophy Inquiry into the Meaning of Spiritual Existence. GELVEN, Michael.
"The Civil and the Sacred" in *The Tanner Lectures On Human Values, Volume XII*, GELLNER, Ernest.
Analisi fenomenologica del concetto di religione. MONDIN, Battista.
Desacralization and the Disenchantment of the World. WENNEMANN, Daryl.
Is Anything Sacred? Christian Humanism and Christian Nihilism. CUPITT, Don.
The Sacred, Secular, and Profane in Augustine's World of Shadows. SPENCER, Jon Michael.
SACRIFICE(S)
Justice and the Good Life. DWORKIN, Ronald.
Pour une philosophie du sens et de la valeur. VASSILIE-LEMENY, Sorin-Titus.
Rawls's Difference Principle and a Problem of Sacrifice. VOICE, Paul.
SADOWSKY, J
Divine Knowledge and Divine Control: A Response to Gordon and Sadowsky. BASINGER, David.
SAINT(S)
Hick and Saints: Is Saint-Production a Valid Test?. PENTZ, Rebecca.
SALLIS, J
The Rooting and Uprooting of Reason: On *Spacings* by John Sallis. MALY, Kenneth.
SALMON, N
"Referência e valor cognitivo" in *Dinâmica do Pensar: Homenagem a Oswaldo Market*, BRANQUINHO, João.
On Rigidity and Persistence. WILLIAMSON, Timothy.
A Priority and Ways of Grasping a Proposition. WONG, Kai-Yee.
Salmon on the A Priori. BERTOLET, Rod.
SALMON, W
Azar y explicación: Algunas observaciones. PÉREZ RANSANZ, Ana Rosa.
Explanation, Causation and Laws. EDGINGTON, Dorothy.
Kitcher and Salmon's *Scientific Explanation*; and Salmon's *Four Decades of Scientific Explanation*. FETZER, James H.
Probabilistic Causality from a Dynamical Point of View. VON PLATO, Jan.
Sobre causación y unificación según Wesley Salmon. OLIVÉ, León.
SALVATION
"Lest Anyone Should Fall": A Middle Knowledge Perspective on Perseverance and Apostolic Warnings. CRAIG, William Lane.
Approaches to the Theory of Purusarthas. RAJAN, R Sundara.
Fragmentation, Meditation and Transformation: The Teachings of J Krishnamurti. NARAYANA MOORTY, J S R L.
Hell, This Isn't Necessary After All. WALTERS, Kerry S.
Hick and Saints: Is Saint-Production a Valid Test?. PENTZ, Rebecca.
K J Shah's 'Philosophy, Religion, Morality, Spirituality: Some Issues'. GHOSE, A M.
Nature et fonction de la Mémoire dans À la recherche du temps perdu. ZÉPHIR, Jacques J.
SAMENESS
"La 'grande illusion' du XVIIIe siècle" in *Égalité Uguaglianza*, ROSSO, Corrado.
Locke on Personal Identity. WINKLER, Kenneth P.
Mismidad y diferencia. COUTO-SOARES, Maria Luisa.
Narrative Identity. RICOEUR, Paul.
Sartre and Our Identity as Individuals. DILMAN, Ilham.
SAMPER, J
La imagen del indígena en el pensamiento colombiano del siglo XIX: La perspectiva de J M Samper. GÓMEZ-MULLER, Alfredo.
SAMPLING
On the Necessity for Random Sampling. JOHNSTONE, D J.
SANCTION(S)
Proof and Sanction in Mill's Utilitarianism. COHEN, Stephen.
Sanction and the Law According to St Thomas Aquinas. HENLE, R J.
SANCTITY OF LIFE
In Partnership with God: Contemporary Jewish Law and Ethics. SHERWIN, Byron L.
SANDEL, M
Rawls, Sandel and the Self. CANEY, S.
SANKARA
Quest for Certainty: A Comparative Study of Heidegger and Sankara. GRIMES, John A.
Causality: Sankara and Aristotle. DHAVAMONY, Mariasusai.
Rāmānuja's Hermeneutics of the *Upanisads* in Comparison with Sankara's Interpretation. SAWAI, Yoshitsugu.
Sankara and Derrida on Philosophy of Language. COWARD, Harold.
Sankara on Reason, Scriptural Authority and Self-Knowledge. UPADHYAYA, K N.
Some Self-Centric Tendencies in Sankara Advaita. JHINGRAN, Saral.
The Word That Became the Absolute: Relevance of Sankara's Ontology of Language. GUPTA, Som Raj.
SANSKRIT
Introduction to Dharmakirti's Theory of Inference as Presented in *Pramānavārttika Svopajñavrtti* 1-10. HAYES, Richard P and GILLON, Brendan S.
Lost Buddhist Texts: The Rationale of Their Reconstruction in Sanskrit. CHINCHORE, Mangala R.
SANTAYANA
George Santayana y la Ironia de la Materia. IZUZQUIZA, Ignacio.
Doubt and Faith: Santayana and Kierkegaard on Fundamental Belief. SARTWELL, Crispin.
Interpreting *Interpretations*. GROSSMAN, Morris.
Mozart and Santayana and the Interface Between Music and Philosophy. DILWORTH, David A.
Multiple Realities in Santayana's Last Puritan. VAITKUS, Steven.
The Problem of Theoretical Self-Reflexivity in Peirce and Santayana. DILWORTH, David A.
Santayana's Peirce. HOUSER, Nathan.
Substrative Materialism. KERR-LAWSON, Angus.
Toward One Santayana: Recent Scholarship. KERR-LAWSON, Angus.
What Good is Irony?. LEVINSON, Henry S.
Why the Problem of the External World is a Pseudo-Problem: Santayana and Danto. SHIRLEY, Edward S.
SARTRE
Being and Becoming: A Critique of Post-Modernism. CENTORE, F F.
Jean-Paul Sartre. HENGELBROCK, Jürgen.
Phänomenologische Philosophie. STRÖKER, Elisabeth.
The Power of Consciousness and the Force of Circumstances in Sartre's Philosophy. BUSCH, Thomas W.
Vulgarity and Authenticity: Dimensions of Otherness in the World of Jean-Paul Sartre. CHARMÉ, Stuart Zane.
"Authenticity, Conversion, and the City of Ends in Sartre's *Notebooks for an Ethics*" in *Writing the Politics of Difference*, ANDERSON, Thomas C.
"Existentialism, Humanism, and Positivism" in *The Question of Humanism: Challenges and Possibilities*, HAYES, Calvin.
"Love and Perfect Coincidence in a Sartrean Ethics" in *Writing the Politics of Difference*, BELL, Linda A.
"Sartre and the Humanism of Spontaneity" in *The Question of Humanism: Challenges and Possibilities*, HORNYANSKY, Monica C.
"'Making the Human' in Sartre's Unpublished Dialectical Ethics" in *Writing the Politics of Difference*, BOWMAN, Elizabeth A and STONE, Robert V.
"Two Concepts of Liberty" Thirty Years Later: A Sartre-Inspired Critique. MC BRIDE, William L.
An Abyss of Difference: Laing, Sartre and Jaspers. KIRSNER, Douglas.
Against Cartesian Dualism: Strawson and Sartre on the Unity of Person. MUI, Constance.
Authenticity: A Sartrean Perspective. CATALANO, Joseph.
La dialettica come "dépasser" in Sartre. TOGNONATO, Claudio.
El enigma de la libertad humana en Gabriel Marcel. O'CALLAGHAN, Paul.
Los escritos póstumos de J P Sartre (I). AMORÓS, Celia.
Freedom and Autonomy: The Kantian Analytic and a Sartrean Critique. BEAVERS, Anthony.
Freud Contra Sartre: Repression or Self-Deception?. MIRVISH, Adrian.
Das Individuum, die Politik und die Philosophie. GRUNWALD, Sabine.
Le thème de la révolution dans la pensée de Sartre. CREMA, Cristina Diniz Mendonça.
The Lover-Beloved Relationship Reconsidered. HOLMES, Richard and DANIEL, Mano.
Le problème politique chez Sartre et Foucault. KNEE, Phili.
The Role of Subjectivity in the Realism of Thomas Nagel and Jean-Paul Sartre. WIDER, Kathleen.
Sartre and his Successors: Existential Marxism and Postmodernism at Our *Fin de Siecle*. MC BRIDE, William L.
Sartre and James on the Role of the Body in Emotion. BAUGH, Bruce.
Sartre and Our Identity as Individuals. DILMAN, Ilham.
Sartre and Political Legitimacy. KNEE, Philip.
Sartre and Sexism. BARNES, Hazel E.
Sartre and the Objectivity of Values (in French). FRIEDLI, Serge.
Sartre on Anguish. JAMBOR, Mishka.
Sartre on Pre-Reflective Consciousness. AGRAWAL, M M.
Sartre on Surpassing the Given. BUSCH, Thomas W.
Sartre's Being-for-Heidegger, Heidegger's Being-for-Sartre. MARTINOT, Steve.

SARTRE
Sartre's onuitgevoerde project: de Robespierre-biografie. DETHIER, Hubert.
Sartre, Aron et le relativisme historique. BAUGH, Bruce.
Tenets of Freedom. BLUM, Alex.

SATIRE
The Rhetoric of Berkeley's Philosophy. WALMSLEY, Peter.
Lucian: The Sale of Lives (in Hebrew). SCOLNICOV, Samuel (trans).
The Rhetoric of Martianus Capella and Anselm de Besate in the Tradition of Menippean Satire. BENNETT, Beth S.

SATISFACTION
The Normal Rewards of Success. WHYTE, J T.
Validity and Satisfaction in Imperative Logic. SEGERBERG, Krister.

SAUSSURE, F
Language, Speech and Writing: Merleau-Ponty and Derrida on Saussure. FREE, George.
Saussure: Signs, System, and Arbitrariness. HOLDCROFT, David.

SAYING
"On Davidson's "Saying That"" in *Truth and Interpretation: Perspectives on the Philosophy of Donald Davidson*, BURGE, Tyler.

SAYRE-MCCORD, G
Commentary on Sayre-McCord's 'Being a Realist about Relativism'. WONG, David B.

SCAHILL, J
Stopping the Thought That Stops Thought: Response to John Scahill. ENGEL, David.

SCANDINAVIAN
Scandinavian Extraction Phenomena Revisited: Weak and Strong Generative Capacity. MILLER, Philip H.
Should Ethical Concerns Regulate Science? The European Experience with the Human Genome Project. RIX, Bo Andreassen.
Social Science as Moral Philosophy?: Reflections on Alan Wolfe's *Whose Keeper?*. MASON, John R.

SCARCITY
Ownership as Theft. GRUNEBAUM, James O.

SCEPTICISM
After the Demise of the Tradition: Rorty, Critical Theory, and the Fate of Philosophy. NIELSEN, Kai.
The Analytic Tradition: Philosophical Quarterly Monographs, Volume 1. BELL, David (ed).
Doubting: Contemporary Perspectives on Skepticism. ROTH, Michael D (ed).
Epistemology and Skepticism: An Enquiry into the Nature of Epistemology. CHATALIAN, George.
The Moral Animus of David Hume. SIEBERT, Donald T.
Natural Reasons: Personality and Polity. HURLEY, S L.
Other Human Beings. COCKBURN, David.
An Outline of the Philosophy of Knowledge and Science. BLANDINO, Giovanni.
Philosophy of the Ancients. RICKEN, Friedo.
Reasons and Experience. MILLAR, Alan.
The Secret Connexion: Causation, Realism, and David Hume. STRAWSON, Galen.
The Transcendental Temptation: A Critique of Religion and the Paranormal. KURTZ, Paul.
Zetetic Skepticism. UMPHREY, Stewart.
"Arbitrary Reasons" in *Doubting: Contemporary Perspectives on Skepticism*, LUPER-FOY, Steven.
"Brains Don't Lie: They Don't Even Make Many Mistakes" in *Doubting: Contemporary Perspectives on Skepticism*, TYMOCZKO, Thomas.
"Epistemic Compatibilism and Canonical Beliefs" in *Doubting: Contemporary Perspectives on Skepticism*, KLEIN, Peter D.
"Epistemic Universalizability: From Skepticism to Infallibilism" in *Doubting: Contemporary Perspectives on Skepticism*, ADLER, Jonathan E.
"The Intelligibility of Scepticism" in *The Analytic Tradition: Philosophical Quarterly Monographs, Volume 1*, SKORUPSKI, John.
"Justifying Beliefs: The Dream Hypothesis and Gratuitous Entities" in *Doubting: Contemporary Perspectives on Skepticism*, BAR-ON, Dorit.
"Klein on Certainty and Canonical Beliefs" in *Doubting: Contemporary Perspectives on Skepticism*, FELDMAN, Richard.
"Metaepistemology and Skepticism" in *Doubting: Contemporary Perspectives on Skepticism*, FUMERTON, Richard.
"Moore and Philosophical Skepticism" in *The Analytic Tradition: Philosophical Quarterly Monographs, Volume 1*, BALDWIN, Thomas.
"Postmodernism and Other Skepticisms" in *Feminist Ethics*, PIERCE, Christine.
"Radical Interpretation and Global Skepticism" in *Truth and Interpretation: Perspectives on the Philosophy of Donald Davidson*, KLEIN, Peter D.
"Skepticism and Everyday Knowledge Attributions" in *Doubting: Contemporary Perspectives on Skepticism*, COHEN, Stewart.
"Skepticism and Rationality" in *Doubting: Contemporary Perspectives on Skepticism*, FOLEY, Richard.
"Skepticism in the Face of Philosophy" in *Re-Reading Levinas*, BERNASCONI, Robert.
"Two Roads to Skepticism" in *Doubting: Contemporary Perspectives on Skepticism*, MOSER, Paul K.
Anscombian and Cartesian Scepticism. HAMILTON, Andy.
Anti-Realism and Skepticism in Ethics. SCHUELER, G F.
An Anti-Sceptical Fugue. GILLETT, Grant.
Burgeoning Skepticism. DE VRIES, Willem.
Cartesian Scepticism and Relevant Alternatives. SCHRECK, P A.
Cartesian Skepticism and Inference to the Best Explanation. VOGEL, Jonathan.
Chalmers on Method. GOWER, Barry.
The Classical Roots of Hume's Skepticism. OLSHEWSKY, Thomas M.
The Cogito and the Diallelus. ZELLNER, Harold.
Contagious Folly: *An Adventure* and Its Skeptics. CASTLE, Terry.
Davidson and the Sceptic: The Thumbnail Version. CRAIG, Edward.
Empirical Tests are Only Auxiliary Devices. LAI, Tyrone.
Epistemic Justification and Psychological Realism. TAYLOR, James E.
Epistemic Leaks and Epistemic Meltdowns: A Response to William Morris on Scepticism with Regard to Reason. KARLSSON, Mikael M.
Die erkenntniskritische Wendung Descartes' als Konsequenz geschichtlicher Entwicklung des Leib-Seele-Dualismus. POHLENZ, G.
El escepticismo crítico en el Diccionario de Bayle. ARROYO, Julián.
Fichte on Skepticism. BREAZEALE, Daniel.
From Pyrrhonism to Post-Modernism. GLIDDEN, David K.
From What Can't Be Said To What Isn't Known. MC KINNON, Christine.
Getting Rule-Following Straight. WONG, James.
Getting to the Truth Through Conceptual Revolutions. KELLY, Kevin and GLYMOUR, Clark.
Healthy Scepticism. FRANKLIN, James.
How to Defend Science Against Scepticism: A Reply to Barry Gower. CHALMERS, Alan.
Husserl and Hume: Overcrowding Scepticism?. MURPHY, Richard T.
Independent Evidence of Religion. D'SOUZA, Felix.
The Inductive Support of Inductive Rules: Themes from Max Black. SANFORD, David H.
Is the Skeptical Attitude the Attitude of a Skeptic?. PAPRZYCKA, Katarzyna.
Lonergan's Performative Transcendental Argument Against Scepticism. REHG, William R.
Max on Moore. STROLL, Avrum.
McGinn on Concept Scepticism and Kripke's Sceptical Argument. SARTORELLI, Joseph.
Meno, the Slave-Boy, and the *Elenchos*. BENSON, Hugh H.
Moral Scepticism and Inductive Scepticism. BLACK, Robert.
Moral Skepticism and Moral Education. BARCALOW, Emmett.
Moral Skepticism and the Dangerous Maybe: Reconsidering Mackie's *Ethics*. METCALFE, John F.
Moral Skepticism. COPP, David.
Moral Truth and Coherence: Comments on Goldman. STEUP, M.
Natural Law, Skepticism, and Methods of Ethics. SCHNEEWIND, J B.
La naturaleza y la historia como fundamento para un concepto renovada de razón. PADILLA, Leonel Eduardo.
Naturalism and Scepticism. BELL, Martin and MC GINN, Marie.
On Behalf of Skeptical Rhetoric. FALZER, Paul R.
On the Question of Nietzsche's "Scientism". GALLO, Beverly E.
Philosophical Scepticism: An Intelligible Challenge. GRUNDY, Jeremy.
The Possibilities of Scepticisms: Philosophy and Theology without Apology. JACKSON, Timothy P.
Radical Critique, Scepticism and Commonsense. GAITA, Raimond.
Rediscovering Scepticism. BAILEY, Alan.
A Refutation of Popperian Inductive Scepticism. GEMES, Ken.
A Restoration of Popperian Inductive Scepticism. MILLER, David.
The Role of Kant's Refutation of Idealism. HYMERS, Michael.
Rule-Scepticism: Kripkean Understanding in Wittgenstein's Perspective. BEHERA, Satrughna.
Scepticism and Autonomy. HOOKWAY, Christopher.
Scepticism and Dreaming: Imploding the Demon. WRIGHT, Crispin.
Scepticism and Relativity. BARNES, Jonathan.
Scepticism: the Current Debate. ODEGARD, Douglas.
Scepticism: The External World and Meaning. BAR-ON, Dorit.
Scepticism: Three Recently Presented Arguments Examined. DURRANT, Michael.
Self-Synthesis, Self-Knowledge, and Skepticism. MAZOUÉ, James G.
A Sellarsian Hume?. LIVINGSTON, Donald.
Skepticism About Goodness and Rightness. GOLDMAN, Alan H.
Skepticism and Legal Interpretation. NATHAN, Daniel O.
Skepticism, Enigma and Integrity: Horizons of Affirmation in Nietzsche's Philosophy. HULL, Robert.
Unfair to Nozick. BRUECKNER, Anthony.
Wittgenstein escéptico?. CABANCHIK, Samuel.

SCHAJOWICZ, L
Hierofanías: Una retrospectiva de la obra de Ludwig Schajowicz. KERKHOFF, Manfred.

SCHARFSTEIN
Scharfstein as a Metaphysician of Art (in Hebrew). LURIE, Yuval.

SCHEDLER, G
Abortion, Coercive Pregnancy, and Adoption. JAMES, David N.
On the Empirical Status of Radical Feminism: A Reply to Schedler. MUI, Constance L.

SCHELER
Max Scheler's Concept of the Person: An Ethics of Humanism. PERRIN, Ron.
Analisi fenomenologica del concetto di religione. MONDIN, Battista.
The Anomaly of World: From Scheler to Heidegger. SCHALOW, Frank.
Contemporary Ethics and Scheler's Phenomenology of Community. VACEK, Edward.
A Critical Examination of Scheler's Justification of the Existence of Values. MOOSA, Imtiaz.
The Life of Order and the Order of Life: Eric Voegelin on Modernity and the Problem of Philosophical Anthropology. LEVY, David J.
Max Scheler's Analysis of Illusions, Idols, and Ideologies. IBANA, Rainier R A.
Max Scheler: Theory of Forms of Knowledge and Perspective of Overcoming the Crisis of European Culture (in Polish). RUBA, Marek.
Social Apriori of Responsibility in Scheler's Phenomenology (in Serbo-Croatian). VEAUTHIER, Frank W.

SCHELLING
Moralische Verbindlichkeit oder Erziehung. LANGEWAND, Alfred.
Schellings Philosophie der Kunst: Göttliche Imagination und Ästhetische Einbildungskraft. BARTH, Bernhard.
Die Wiederkehr im Unterschied. PEETZ, Siegbert.
"Romantic Philosophy and Organization of the Disciplines: the Founding of the Humboldt University of Berlin" in *Romanticism and the Sciences*, SHAFFER, Elinor S.
"Schelling and the Origins of His *Naturphilosophie*" in *Romanticism and the Sciences*, MORGAN, S R.
Das "objektive Denken" in Schellings Naturphilosophie. BUCHHEIM, Thomas.
Art's Autonomy and Absolute Idealism: The Role of Aesthetics in Schelling's Philosophy (in Dutch). BRAECKMAN, A.
Ein Bedürfnis nach Schelling. BRAUN, Hermann.
Freedom Is Our Divinity (in German). EHRHARDT, Walter E.
Hölderlin über Urteil und Sein. GRAESER, Andreas.
El idealismo alemán como mitología de la razón. INNERARITY, Daniel.
The Later Schelling's Conception of Dialectical Method, in Contradistinction to Hegel's. BEACH, Edward A.
On the Source of the Eternal Truths. BEACH, Edward A (trans) and VON SCHELLING, F W J.
Philosophie et mythologie dans la dernière philosophie de Schelling. MAESSCHALCK, Marc.
Resources in Schelling for New Directions in Theology. BROWN, Robert F.
Schelling on Hegel: From his Lectures in Munich and Berlin (in Hungarian). FEHÉR, I.
Schelling's Treatise on the Essence of Human Freedom and Heidegger's Thought. FROMAN, Wayne J.
Het Schellingonderzoek op nieuwe wegen. BRAECKMAN, A.
Schellings metaphysikkritische Sprachphilosophie. ROSENAU, Hartmut.
The Concept of "Foundation" in Schelling (in Hungarian). VETO, Miklos.
The Evil Beyond Good and Evil (in German). BOLZ, Norbert.
Von der dreifachen Vollendung des Deutschen Idealismus und der unvollendeten metaphysischen Wahrheit. JANKE, Wolfgang.

SCHEMATA
Kants Schemata als Anwendungsbedingungen von Kategorien auf Anschauungen. LOHMAR, Dieter.
Der Übergang vom Bestimmt-Bestimmenden zum freien Schema in Kants Kritik der Urteilskraft. KAULBACH, Friedrich.

SCHEMATISM
Construction and the Role of Schematism in Kant's Philosophy of Mathematics (also in Portuguese). WINTERBOURNE, A T.
Las criticas de J Bennett a la doctrina kantiana del esquematismo. JÁUREGUI, Claudia.
Schematism and Schemata: Kant and the P.D.P.. VAN DE VIJVER, Gertrudis.

SCHEMATIZATION
Une version de l'épistémologie gonséthienne: le béton et les cailloux. BONSACK, François.

SCHIAPPA, E
Interpreting Sophistical Rhetoric: A Response to Schiappa. POULAKOS, John.

SCHIFFER, S
Comments on Schiffer's *Remnants of Meaning*. RICHARD, Mark.
A Dilemma for Sentential Dualism. MOSER, Paul K.
A Pieced Quilt: A Critical Discussion of Stephen Schiffer's *Remnants of Meaning*. ANTONY, Louise.
Remnants of Schiffer's Principle [P]. SEYMOUR, Daniel.

SCHILLEBEECKX, E
"Radical Hermeneutics and Religious Truth: The Case of Sheehan and Schillebeeckx" in *Phenomenology of the Truth Proper to Religion*, CAPUTO, John D.

SCHILLER
Experiencia de lo sublime y principios racionales. ARTOLA, José María.
Jean-Jacques Rousseau et Friedrich Schiller: le théâtre sous le feu des lumières. MATTE, Martin.

SCHIZOPHRENIA
Readings in Existential Psychology and Psychiatry. HOELLER, Keith (ed).
Dementia Praecox as a Failure of Neoteny. BEMPORAD, Jules R.
Toward the Obsolescence of the Schizophrenia Hypothesis. SARBIN, Theodore R.

SCHLEGEL
"The Place of Friedrich Schlegel in the Development of Historical-Comparative Linguistics" in *Leibniz, Humboldt, and the Origins of Comparativism*, KOERNER, Konrad.

SCHLEIDEN, M
Elementos dinámicos de la teoría celular. GONZÁLEZ RECIO, José Luis.

SCHLEIERMACHER
Delicate Subjects: Romanticism, Gender, and the Ethics of Understanding. ELLISON, Julie.
Modern Faith and Thought. THIELICKE, Helmut.
"Romantic Philosophy and Organization of the Disciplines: the Founding of the Humboldt University of Berlin" in *Romanticism and the Sciences*, SHAFFER, Elinor S.
Der "Atheist" und der "Theologe": Schopenhauer als Hörer Schleiermachers. REGEHLY, Thomas.
"Keine festbegrenzte und Wahrhaft anschauliche Vorstelling". SCHREURS, Nico.
The Development of Otto's Thought 1898-1917. MINNEY, Robin.
Friedrich Schleiermacher und die Praktische Philosophie. TROWITZSCH, Michael.
Struttura e finalità dei dialoghi platonici: Che cosa significa "venire in soccorso al discorso"?. SZLEZÁK, Thomas A.

SCHLESINGER, G
Corroboration and Conditional Positive Relevance. WAGNER, Carl G.
The Many-Gods Objection and Pascal's Wager. JORDAN, Jeff.
Twice Told Tales: A Reply to Schlesinger. COHEN, L Jonathan.

SCHLICK
Conditio sine qua non? Zuordnung in the Early Epistemologies of Cassirer and Schlick. RYCKMAN, Thomas.
The Problem of Protocol Statements and Schlick's Concept of 'Konstatierungen'. ZHAI, Zhenming.

SCHMITT, C
Rethinking Politics: Carl Schmitt vs Hegel. WINFIELD, Richard Dien.

SCHNEEWIND, J
Reply to Dahl, Baier and Schneewind. MAC INTYRE, Alasdair.

SCHNEIDER, M
French Philosophers in Conversation: Levinas, Schneider, Serres, Irigaray, Le Doeuff, Derrida. MORTLEY, Raoul.

SCHOLARSHIP
The Behavior of the NCAA: A Question of Ethics. STIEBER, John.
Erfurt, Ampl Q 70A: A Quaestiones-commentary on the Second Part of Alexander de Villa Dei's *Doctrinale*. KNEEPKENS, C H.

SCHOLASTICISM
see also Thomism
Descartes Among the Scholastics. GRENE, Marjorie.
A New Reading of Aristotle's *Hyle*. POLIS, Dennis F.
Once Again the Ockhamist Statutes of 1339 and 1340: Some New Perspectives. THIJSSEN, J M M H.
Some Observations on the Influence of Christian Scholastic Authors on Jewish Thinkers in the 13th and 14th Century. REEDIJK, Wim M.

SCHOOL(S)
Justice Powell and the Parochial Schools Case: A Case for Judicial Statesmanship. WALTMAN, Jerold.
Philosophy in the *"Gymnasium:"* European Observations and Recommendations. VAN DER LEEUW, Karel and MOSTERT, Pieter.
Pisces Economicus: The Fish as Econontic Man. BOULIER, Bryan L and GOLDFARB, Robert S.
State Education Service or Prisoner's Dilemma: The 'Hidden Hand' as Source of Education Policy. JONATHAN, R.

SCHOOLING
The School and the Home: Partners or Pariahs—A Response to Kennedy on Home Schools. ENGEL, David E.
Thinking About Home Schooling: Some Historical, Philosophical, and Cultural Reasons. KENNEDY, David.

SCHOPENHAUER
Ästhetik des Abschieds: Kritik der Moderne. EBELING, Hans.
Pulling up the Ladder: The Metaphysical Roots of Wittgenstein's Tractatus. BROCKHAUS, Richard R.
"The Art of Forgetfulness, Schopenhauer and Contemporary Repetitive Music" in *XIth International Congress in Aesthetics, Nottingham 1988*, DE MUL, Jos.

SCHOPENHAUER

Der "Atheist" und der "Theologe": Schopenhauer als Hörer Schleiermachers. REGEHLY, Thomas.
Arthur Schopenhauer als Staatsdenker. WÜRKNER, Joachim.
Die Bedeutung der Mathematik Für die Philosophie Schopenhauers. RADBRUCH, Knut.
Eléments pour une philosophie de l'expression. UCCIANI, Louis.
Ghost Story (in German). SAUTET, Marc.
Hegel and Schopenhauer as Partisans of Goethe's Theory of Color. LAUXTERMANN, P F H.
Heidegger und Schopenhauer. HECKER, Hellmuth.
Kants Theorie der Gegenstandserkenntnis und Schopenhauers Lehre vom Ding an sich. BAUMANN, Lutz.
Nihilism and the Impossibility of Political Philosophy. BASINSKI, Paul A.
Notes sur une référence fugitive: Schopenhauer lecteur de Plotin. UCCIANI, Louis.
Schopenhauer and Hegel (in Hebrew). SIGAD, Ran.
Schopenhauer en de kunst van het verzaken. DE MARTELAERE, Patricia.
Schopenhauer und Fichtes Schrift "Die Bestimmung des Menschen". DECHER, Friedhelm.
Schopenhauers "objektives Interesse". NEYMEYR, Barbara.
Schopenhauers Entwurf einer asketischen Tugendethik. WOLF, Jean-Claude.
Schopenhauers Idee einer rekonstruktiven Ethik (mit Anwendungen auf die moderne Medizin-Ethik). BIRNBACHER, Dieter.
Schopenhauers Straftheorie und die aktuelle Strafzweckdiskussion. KÜPPER, Georg.
Schopenhauers Wille und Platons Eros. VOIGTLÄNDER, Hanns-Dieter.
Schopenhauersche Weltsicht und totalitäre Humanität im Werke Thomas Manns. KRISTIANSEN, Borge.
The Transfigurations of Intoxication: Nietzsche, Schopenhauer, and Dionysus. NUSSBAUM, Martha C.
La vie, ou le point de rupture: Schopenhauer-Nietzsche. UCCIANI, Louis.
Wahnbildung und Wirklichkeit des Willens. GRÄTZEL, Stephan.
Zur Erkenntnistheorie des Ästhetischen: Schopenhauers Beziehung zu Kant. DÖRFLINGER, Bernd.

SCHRODINGER

Wanted Dead or Alive: Two Attempts to Solve Schrödinger's Paradox. ALBERT, David and LOEWER, Barry.

SCHUON, F

Comment on Huston Smith's Review of *The Essential Writings of Frithiof Schuon. ANDERSON, Tyson.*
Response to Tyler Anderson. SMITH, Huston.

SCHUTZ, A

"Paramount Reality" in Schutz and Gurwitsch. KASSAB, Elizabeth Suzanne.
Animal Faith, Puritanism, and the Schutz-Gurwitsch Debate: A Commentary. LYMAN, Stanford M.
The Ethics Behind the Absence of Ethics in Alfred Schutz's Thought. BARBER, Michael.
Finitude Rediscovered. BARBER, Michael.
Interpretación mundanel e identidad propia. GARCÍA-GÓMEZ, Jorge.
Multiple Realities in Santayana's Last Puritan. VAITKUS, Steven.
Notes on the Specification of "Meaning" in Schutz. EMBREE, Lester.
Reflections on the Schutz-Gurwitsch Correspondence. LANDGREBE, Ludwig.
The Worldly Self in Schutz: On Sighting, Citing, and Siting the Self. LANGSDORF, Lenore.

SCHWANN, T

Elementos dinámicos de la teoría celular. GONZÁLEZ RECIO, José Luis.

SCIENCE

see also Anthropology, Biology, Economics, Human Sciences, Matter, Medicine, Natural Sciences, Physics, Quantum Mechanics
Acting and Reflecting: The Interdisciplinary Turn in Philosophy. SIEG, Wilfried (ed).
African Philosophy: The Essential Readings. SEREQUEBERHAN, Tsenay.
Aspectos Metodológicos de la Investigación Científica. GONZÁLEZ, Wenceslao J (ed).
Berkeley's Revolution in Vision. ATHERTON, Margaret.
Beyond Ethnocentrism: A Reconstruction of Marx's Concept of Science. MC KELVEY, Charles.
Beyond Natural Selection. WESSON, Robert.
Beyond the Big Bang: Quantum Cosmologies and God. DREES, Willem B.
Causality in Sociological Research. KARPINSKI, Jakub.
Colour: A Philosophical Introduction (Second Edition). WESTPHAL, Jonathan.
Il compito della filosofia: Saggio su Windelband. OLIVA, Rossella Bonito.
Consciousness and the Computational Mind. JACKENDOFF, Ray.
Critical Traditions in Contemporary Archaeology. PINSKY, Valerie (ed).
Demystifying Mentalities. LLOYD, G E R.
Essays on the Context, Nature, and Influence of Isaac Newton's Theology. FORCE, James E (ed).
Études sur/Studies on Hélène Metzger. FREUDENTHAL, Gad.
Evolution als Höherentwicklung des Bewusstseins. KUMMER, Christian.
Evolution: Probleme und neue Aspekte ihrer Theorie. SCHEFFCZYK, Leo (ed).
Evolutionary Instability: Logical and Material Aspects of a Unified Theory of Biosocial Evolution. GEIGER, Gebhard.
Existence et Subjectivité: Études de Psychologie Phénoménologique. THINÈS, Georges.
Experiment: Right or Wrong. FRANKLIN, Allan.
Foundations of Cognitive Science: The Essential Readings. GARFIELD, Jay L.
Harré and His Critics. BHASKAR, Roy (ed).
Hobbes. TUCK, Richard.
How to Build a Conscious Machine. ANGEL, Leonard.
The Idea of a Social Science and its Relation to Philosophy (Second Edition). WINCH, Peter.
The Idea of the Miraculous: The Challenge to Science and Religion. WILLIAMS, T C.
Idea, mente, specie: Platonismo e scienza in Johannes Marcus Marci (1595-1667). MOCCHI, Giuliana.
Imre Lakatos and Theories of Scientific Change. GAVROGLU, Kostas (ed).
Inference and Understanding: A Philosophical and Psychological Perspective. MANKTELOW, K I.
Instrumental Realism: The Interface between Philosophy of Science and Philosophy of Technology. IHDE, Don.
Intelligibility in Science. DILWORTH, Craig (ed).
Interpreting Evolution: Darwin and Teilhard de Chardin. BIRX, H James.
An Invitation To Cognitive Science. LEIBER, Justin.
Kant's Transcendental Psychology. KITCHER, Patricia.
Key Themes in Philosophy. GRIFFITHS, A Phillips (ed).
L'inertie et l'espace-temps absolu de Newton à Einstein. GHINS, Michel.
Leibniz, Humboldt, and the Origins of Comparativism. DE MAURO, Tullio (ed).
The Limits of Influence: Psychokinesis and the Philosophy of Science. BRAUDE, Stephen E (ed).
Logic in the Husserlian Context. TITO, Johanna Maria.
Logic, Methodology and Philosophy of Science, VIII. FENSTAD, J E (ed).
Logic, Methodology and Philosophy of Science, VII. MARCUS, Ruth Barcan (ed).
Matter, Morals and Medicine: The Ancient Greek Origins of Science, Ethics and the Medical Profession. CARELLA, Michael Jerome.
Meaning and Mental Representation. CUMMINS, Robert.
Meaning and Method: Essays in Honor of Hilary Putnam. BOOLOS, George (ed).
Methods and Problems in Greek Science: Selected Papers. LLOYD, G E R.
I Modelli l'Invenzione e la Conferma. PETRONI, Angelo Maria.
Moral und Politik aus der Sicht des Kritischen Rationalismus. SALAMUN, Kurt (ed).
Narrative in Culture: The Uses of Storytelling in the Sciences, Philosophy, and Literature. NASH, Christopher (ed).
The Natural and the Normative: Theories of Spatial Perception from Kant to Helmholtz. HATFIELD, Gary.
Nomic Probability and the Foundations of Induction. POLLOCK, John L.
Objectivity, Relativism, and Truth: Philosophical Papers, Volume 1. RORTY, Richard.
L'ordine della certezza: Scientificità e persuasione in Descartes. BONICALZI, Francesca.
The Origins of Aristotelian Science. FEREJOHN, Michael.
An Outline of the Philosophy of Knowledge and Science. BLANDINO, Giovanni.
Il Paradigma del Sapere. LENTINI, Luigi.
Las paradojas del Infinito. BOLZANO, Bernard.
Particles and Waves: Historical Essays in the Philosophy of Science. ACHINSTEIN, Peter.
Perspectives on Ideas and Reality. NYÍRI, J C (ed).
Philosophical Perspectives on Newtonian Science. BRICKER, Phillip (ed).
Philosophische Hermeneutik. INEICHEN, Hans.
Philosophy and Cognitive Science. FETZER, James H.
Philosophy and the Spontaneous Philosophy of the Scientists and Other Essays. ELLIOTT, Gregory (ed).
The Philosophy of Action: An Introduction. MOYA, Carlos J.
The Philosophy of Science. BOYD, Richard (ed).
The Power of Ideology. MÉSZÁROS, István.
Psychoanalysis, Scientific Method, and Philosophy. HOOK, Sidney (ed).
Realism with a Human Face. PUTNAM, Hilary.
Reasoning and Revision in Hybrid Representation Systems. NEBEL, Bernhard.
Relating Humanities and Social Thought (Science, Ideology, and Value, Volume 4). EDEL, Abraham.
Romanticism and the Sciences. CUNNINGHAM, Andrew (ed).
Science and Moral Values. VOLLRATH, John.
Science and Reason. KYBURG JR, Henry E.
Science and Relativism: Some Key Controversies in the Philosophy of Science. LAUDAN, Larry.
Science and Religion: One World-Changing Perspectives on Reality. FENNEMA, Jan (ed).
Science versus Religion. CLEMENTS, Tad S.

SCIENCE

Scientific Theories. SAVAGE, C Wade (ed).
Scienza, Filosofia e Religione tra '600 e '700 in Italia. PREDAVAL MAGRINI, Maria Vittoria (ed).
Shaping Genes: Ethics, Law and Science of Using Genetic Technology in Medicine and Agriculture. MACER, Darryl.
Some Truer Method. DURHAM, Frank (ed).
Structures in Mathematical Theories: Reports of the San Sebastian International Symposium, 1990. DÍEZ, Amparo (ed).
Studies on Mario Bunge's "Treatise". WEINGARTNER, Paul (ed).
Teoria e interpretazione: Per un'epistemologia delle scienze umane. BORUTTI, Silvana.
Theories of Science in Society. COZZENS, Susan E (ed).
Three Great Traditions. PEDERSEN, Olaf.
The Transcendental Temptation: A Critique of Religion and the Paranormal. KURTZ, Paul.
Vernunft und Kontingenz: Rationalität und Ethos in der Phänomenologie. ORTH, Ernst Wolfgang (ed).
Vico: A Study of the 'New Science' (Second Edition). POMPA, Leon.
Whose Science? Whose Knowledge? Thinking from Women's Lives. HARDING, Sandra.
"Il 'Giornale de' Letterati' e le 'scienze della vita': dibattiti e interventi" in *Scienza, Filosofia e Religione tra '600 e '700 in Italia*, BOARETTI, Tiziano.
"L'Accademia delle scienze di Bologna: l'edizione del primo tomo dei 'Commentarii' (1731)" in *Scienza, Filosofia e Religione tra '600 e '700 in Italia*, DE ZAN, Mauro.
"Are There Alternatives?" in *Acting and Reflecting: The Interdisciplinary Turn in Philosophy*, NEWELL, Allen.
"Beginning" in *Essays on Hegel's Logic*, MAKER, William.
"The Breakdown of the Newtonian Synthesis of Science and Religion: Hume, Newton, and the Royal Society" in *Essays on the Context, Nature, and Influence of Isaac Newton's Theology*, FORCE, James E.
"A Comment on Three Topics in Volume 7 of the *Treatise*: Teleology, the Mind-Body Problem, and Health and Disease" in *Studies on Mario Bunge's "Treatise"*, DUBROVSKY, Bernardo.
"Conceptual Change and the Progress of Science" in *Logic, Methodology and Philosophy of Science, VIII*, PEARCE, David.
"Il corpuscolarismo italiano nel 'Giornale de' Letterati' di Roma (1668-1681)" in *Scienza, Filosofia e Religione tra '600 e '700 in Italia*, LOPICCOLI, Fiorella.
"Creation and Big Bang: The Word as Space of Creation" in *Science and Religion: One World-Changing Perspectives on Reality*, VAHANIAN, G.
"Development of Science as a Change of Types" in *Imre Lakatos and Theories of Scientific Change*, HÖRZ, Herbert.
"The Emergence of a Reseearch Programme in Classical Thermodynamics" in *Imre Lakatos and Theories of Scientific Change*, MOULINES, C Ulises.
"Ethical Implications of Newtonian Science" in *Philosophical Perspectives on Newtonian Science*, HARRIS, Errol.
"Ethics and Science" in *Logic, Methodology and Philosophy of Science, VIII*, AGAZZI, Evandro.
"The Ethics of Science as a Form of the Cognition of Science" in *Logic, Methodology and Philosophy of Science, VIII*, YUDIN, Boris G.
"Feminism, Science, and the Anti-Enlightenment Critiques" in *Feminism/Postmodernism*, HARDING, Sandra.
"Fundamental Issues in Theology and Science" in *Science and Religion: One World-Changing Perspectives on Reality*, TORRANCE, T F.
"Giovanni Gualberto (Alberto) De Soria e la 'Cosmologia'" in *Scienza, Filosofia e Religione tra '600 e '700 in Italia*, PONZELLINI, Ornella.
"God's World and Man Becoming: How Can Science Possibly Help Us Transcend Dogmatism?" in *Science and Religion: One World-Changing Perspectives on Reality*, VAN DER VEKEN, J.
"Historical Interaction between Science and Religion" in *Science and Religion: One World-Changing Perspectives on Reality*, PEDERSEN, O.
"Hume's Interest in Newton and Science" in *Essays on the Context, Nature, and Influence of Isaac Newton's Theology*, FORCE, James E.
"Impact of Global Modelling on Modern Methodology of Science" in *Logic, Methodology and Philosophy of Science, VIII*, GVISHIANI, J M.
"Impressions of Philosophy" in *Acting and Reflecting: The Interdisciplinary Turn in Philosophy*, SCHWARTZ, Thomas.
"Imre Lakatos in China" in *Imre Lakatos and Theories of Scientific Change*, DAINIAN, Fan.
"Information Theory and the *Treatise*: Towards a New Understanding" in *Studies on Mario Bunge's "Treatise"*, KARY, Michael.
"The Interface Between Statistics and the Philosophy of Science" in *Logic, Methodology and Philosophy of Science, VIII*, GOOD, I J.
"Is There a Role for Theology in an Age of Secular Science?" in *Science and Religion: One World-Changing Perspectives on Reality*, DURANT, J R.
"Leibniz and the Philosophical Analysis of Science" in *Logic, Methodology and Philosophy of Science, VIII*, DUCHESNEAU, François.
"Making a World of Precision: Newton and the Construction of a Quantitiative World View" in *Some Truer Method*, WESTFALL, Richard S.
"Mario Bunge on his *Treatise* as a Philosophy" in *Studies on Mario Bunge's "Treatise"*, BUNGE, Mario.
"Mario Bunge on Philosophy of Science and Technology" in *Studies on Mario Bunge's "Treatise"*, BUNGE, Mario.
"Mario Bunge's Philosophy of Logic and Mathematics" in *Studies on Mario Bunge's "Treatise"*, MIRÓ, Francisco.
"Maritain and Rifkin: Two Critiques" in *From Twilight to Dawn: The Cultural Vision of Jacques Maritain*, TRAPANI JR, John G.
"Maritain's Account of the Social Sciences" in *From Twilight to Dawn: The Cultural Vision of Jacques Maritain*, NELSON, Ralph.
"Method and the Authority of Science" in *Key Themes in Philosophy*, TILES, Mary.
"The Method of Hegel's *Science of Logic*" in *Essays on Hegel's Logic*, WINFIELD, Richard Dien.
"The Methodology of Scientific Research Programmes: A Retrospect" in *Imre Lakatos and Theories of Scientific Change*, WATKINS, John.
"Modern Ethical Theory and Newtonian Science: Comments on Errol Harris" in *Philosophical Perspectives on Newtonian Science*, GRIER, Philip T.
"Newton's Legacy" in *Some Truer Method*, PURRINGTON, Robert D and DURHAM, Frank.
"Newton's Method and Newton's Style" in *Some Truer Method*, COHEN, I Bernard.
"The Non-Statement View: A Dialogue between Socrates and Theaetetus" in *Studies on Mario Bunge's "Treatise"*, WEINGARTNER, Paul.
"Ontology and Its Discontent" in *Studies on Mario Bunge's "Treatise"*, AGASSI, Joseph.
"Phenomenalism, Relativity and Atoms: Rehabilitating Ernst Mach's Philosophy of Science" in *Logic, Methodology and Philosophy of Science, VIII*, WOLTERS, Gereon.
"Philosophy and the Academy" in *Acting and Reflecting: The Interdisciplinary Turn in Philosophy*, GLYMOUR, Clark.
"Philosophy and the Sciences" in *Acting and Reflecting: The Interdisciplinary Turn in Philosophy*, SUPPES, Patrick.
"Philosophy at Carnegie Mellon: Past, Present, Future" in *Acting and Reflecting: The Interdisciplinary Turn in Philosophy*, HAUGELAND, John.
"Philosophy of Science and Archaeology" in *Critical Traditions in Contemporary Archaeology*, DUNNELL, Robert C.
"Philosophy, Science and Man" in *Logic, Methodology and Philosophy of Science, VIII*, FEDOSEYEV, Pyotr.
"Pier Caterino Zeno le vicende culturali del 'Giornale de' Letterati d'Italia'" in *Scienza, Filosofia e Religione tra '600 e '700 in Italia*, GENERALI, Dario.
"Rationality Unbound" in *Acting and Reflecting: The Interdisciplinary Turn in Philosophy*, LEVI, Isaac.
"Realism, Reference and Theory" in *Key Themes in Philosophy*, HARRÉ, Rom.
"Religious Truth and Scientific Truth" in *Phenomenology of the Truth Proper to Religion*, CLAYTON, Philip.
"Science and Religion Coming Across" in *Science and Religion: One World-Changing Perspectives on Reality*, HÜBNER, J.
"Science and Religion—the Jewish Position" in *Science and Religion: One World-Changing Perspectives on Reality*, BLOEMENDAL, M.
"Science and Religion" in *Science and Religion: One World-Changing Perspectives on Reality*, MELSEN, A G M van.
"Scientific Philosophical and Sociopolitical Aspects of the Work of Mario Bunge" in *Studies on Mario Bunge's "Treatise"*, ROSENTHAL, Erwin.
"The Scientist as 'Homo Loquens'" in *Harré and His Critics*, HARRIS, Roy.
"The Significance of the *Treatise* in the Light of the Western Philosophical Tradition" in *Studies on Mario Bunge's "Treatise"*, CUPANI, Alberto.
"Strong and Weak Methods" in *Logic, Methodology and Philosophy of Science, VIII*, FILKORN, Vojtech.
"The Tetrad Project" in *Acting and Reflecting: The Interdisciplinary Turn in Philosophy*, SPIRTES, Peter and SCHEINES, Richard and GLYMOUR, Clark.
"Theology and the Sciences in the German Romantic Period" in *Romanticism and the Sciences*, GREGORY, Frederick.
"Transcending Newton's Legacy" in *Some Truer Method*, STAPP, Henry P.
"Two Conceptions of Philosophy" in *Perspectives on Quine*, STRAWSON, P F.
"What Are General Equilibrium Theories?" in *Acting and Reflecting: The Interdisciplinary Turn in Philosophy*, HAUSMAN, Dan.
"Eigen Elements" Emerging from the Interaction of Two Knowing and Acting Subjects. VALLÉE, Robert.
The "New" Scholars in Philosophy of Education, 1976-1986. QUANTZ, Richard A.
"Non-Scientific Realism" about Propositional Attitudes as a Response to Eliminativist Arguments. HANNAN, Barbara.
The "Tally Argument" and the Validation of Psychoanalysis. RICHARDSON, Robert C.
'Inference to the Best Explanation' of 'Inference to the Best Interpretation'? Een antwoord op Derksens ..... MOOIJ, A W M.
A Contribution to the Early History of Psychoanalysis (in Serbo-Croatian). MACHO, Thomas H.
A Note on the Nature of Mathematical Thinking (in Polish). LUBANSKI, M.
Absolutism and Relationism in Space and Time: A False Dichotomy. HINCKFUSS, Ian.
Acceptance Without Belief. MAHER, Patrick.
Accountability and Responsibility in Research. WOOLF, Patricia K.
Adequacy Criteria for a Theory of Fitness. ROSENBERG, Alexander.
Adventures of the Concept of Mass and Matter. HELLER, Michael.

SCIENCE

Aesthetic Constraints on Theory Selection: A Critique of Laudan. MARTIN, James E.

Against Logicist Cognitive Science. OAKSFORD, Mike and CHATER, Nick.

Agency and Probabilistic Causality. PRICE, Huw.

Aggregation of Preferences: The Fuzzy Case. BILLOT, Antoine.

Animal Liberators are Not Anti-Science. MAGEL, Charles.

Animals in Biomedical Research: The Undermining Effect of the Rhetoric of the Besieged. GLUCK, John P and KUBACKI, Steven R.

An Anomaly in the D-N Model of Explanation. BLUM, Alex.

Antropología y Agresión: notas para un análisis filosófico. FERNÁNDEZ TRESGUERRES, Alfonso.

Aquinas versus Epistemological Criticism: A Case for Philosophy in Science. DEL RE, Giuseppe.

Are All False Theories Equally False? A Remark on David Miller's Problem and Geometric Conventionalism. MORMANN, Thomas.

The Art of Philosophy. COOPER, Neil.

Assessing Functional Explanations in the Social Sciences. KINCAID, Harold.

Assessing Inductive Logics Empirically. SMOKLER, Howard.

Atheism, Theism and Big Bang Cosmology. SMITH, Quentin.

An Attempt at Interpretation of the Thomistic Hylomorphic Theory in View of Contemporary Physics. JANIK, J A.

Attraction and Repulsion in Comprehension of Boskovic, Hegel and Engels (in Serbo-Croatian). STOILJKOVIC, Dragoslav.

Autonomy and Quantum Physics: Nietzsche, Heidegger, and Heisenberg. SEIGFRIED, Hans.

The Axiomatic Method: Its Origin and Purpose. AGASHE, S D.

Azar y explicación: Algunas observaciones. PÉREZ RANSANZ, Ana Rosa.

Bachelard and Scientific Realism. TIJIATTAS, Mary.

Barrow and Tipler on the Anthropic Principle versus Divine Design. CRAIG, William Lane.

Bayes' Bayesianism. EARMAN, John.

Die Bedeutung der Mathematik Für die Philosophie Schopenhauers. RADBRUCH, Knut.

Behavior, Biology, and Information Theory. SENCHUK, Dennis M.

Behavioral Paradigm for a Psychological Resolution of the Free Will Issue. HARCUM, E Rae.

Belief Attribution in Science: Folk Psychology under Theoretical Stress. TROUT, J D.

Bentham, Science and the Construction of Jurisprudence. JACOBS, Struan.

Between Rationalism and Relativism: On Larry Laudan's Model of Scientific Rationality. GROBLER, Adam.

Beyond Numerical and Causal Accuracy: Expanding the Set of Justificational Criteria. RAMSEY, Jeffry L.

Biological Foundations of Prediction in an Unpredictable Environment. MARUSIC, M.

Biology and the Social Sciences. WILSON, Edward O.

Bohr's Idea of Complementarity and Plato's Philosophy. MAHOOTIAN, Farzad.

Born's Probabilistic Interpretation: A Case Study of 'Concepts in Flux'. BELLER, Mara.

Boskovic on His Own Theory of Forces: From a Sentence to the Theory of Natural Philosophy (in Serbo-Croatian). MARTINOVIC, Ivica.

Boskovic's Ideas on the Nature of Cognition Process (in Yugoslavian). DORDEVIC, Radomir.

Boskovic's Philosophical Understanding of Matter (in Serbo-Croatian). STOJKOVIC, Andrija B K.

Boskovic's Theory of Forces in His Treatise "De Continuitatis Lege" (in Serbo-Croatian). BRUNSKO, Zagorka.

Brentano e Fichte negli scritti "minori" di E Husserl. BELLO, A Ales.

Breve examen científico y filosófico de la teoría de la evolución. FALGUERAS, Ignacio.

Bruno e la matematica a lui contemporanea: In margine al "De Minimo". AQUILECCHIA, Giovanni.

Byerly and Michod on Fitness. SMITH, John Maynard.

Can a Theory-Laden Observation Test the Theory?. FRANKLIN, A (and others).

Can Marxism Help Biology?. KASSIOLA, Joel.

Causal Independence in EPR Arguments. BUTTERFIELD, Jeremy.

A Causal Interaction Constraint on the Initial Singularity?. STOEGER, W R and HELLER, Michael.

Causal Paradoxes in Special Relativity. ARNTZENIUS, Frank.

Causal Propensities: Statistical Causality versus Aleatory Causality. SALMON, Wesley C.

Causality Assessment in Epidemiology. VINEIS, Paolo.

Causality, Determinism and Objective Reality in Modern Physics. NARAYAN, S Shankar.

Causes and Laws: The Asymmetry Puzzle. BYERLY, Henry.

Causes, Proximate and Ultimate. FRANCIS, Richard C.

The Challenge to Lakatos Restated. AKEROYD, F Michael.

Chalmers on Method. GOWER, Barry.

Chance and Law in Irreversible Thermodynamics, Theoretical Biology and Theology. PEACOCKE, Arthur.

The Changing Nature of the Social Sciences. MASTERS, Roger D.

Chaos and Indeterminism. HOBBS, Jesse.

Cherniak on Scientific Realism. BROWN, Harold I.

China's Traditional Mode of Thought and Science. DISHENG, Yang.

The Chromosome Theory of Mendelian Inheritance: Explanation and Realism in Theory Construction. VICEDO, Marga.

Churchland and the Talking Brain. MUKHERJI, Nirmalangshu.

El cincuentenario de los Grundlagen der Mathematik de Hilbert y Bernays. RAGGIO, Andrés R.

The Classroom as a Model of the World. STURGEON, Kareen B.

Cognitivism and Cognitive Science (in Portuguese). OLIVEIRA, M B de.

Cohen on Einstein's Simultaneity Gedankenexperiment. WHITE, V Alan.

Les combinaisons de la vie, l'organisation du vivant, le réseau du soi. LIVET, Pierre.

The Comeuppance of Science and Technology. CLEVELAND, Harlan.

Coming To Be Without a Cause. SULLIVAN, T D.

A Comment on Maxwell's Resolution of the Wave/Particle Dilemma. SQUIRES, Euan J.

Commentary on Byerly and Michod. LENNOX, James G.

A Commentary on Ridley's Cladistic Solution to the Species Problem. WILKINSON, Mark.

Commentary on the Paper by H C Byerly and R E Michod's "Fitness and Evolutionary Explanation". BRITO DA CUNHA, A.

Comments on "Fitness and Evolutionary Explanation". KLEINER, Scott A.

Comments on Wilkinson's Commentary. RIDLEY, Mark.

Comments on 'Nonlocal Influences and Possible Worlds'. STAPP, Henry P.

Complexity and Evolution: What Everybody Knows. MC SHEA, Daniel W.

Compromiso Ontico y Teorías Científicas. MAYORGA, Alejandro and VARGAS, Celso.

Concepts of Process in Social Science Explanations. VAYDA, Andrew P and MC CAY, Bonnie J and EGHENTER, Cristina.

Conceptual Selection. HULL, David L.

The Concrete and the Abstract Science: Description versus Explanation. GUPTA, Amitabha.

Condiciones del surgimiento y desarrollo de la Psicología Humanista. CARPINTERO, Helio and MAYOR, Luis and ZALBIDEA, M A.

Conditional Probabilities, Conditionalization, and Dutch Books. SOBEL, Jordan Howard.

Conditionalisation and Quantum Probabilities. MILNE, Peter.

A Conjecture Concerning the Ranking of the Sciences. HUMPHREYS, Paul.

Connectionism, Competence, and Explanation. CLARK, Andy.

Conocimiento y determinismo. LAGUNILLA, Ana E Galán.

Consciousness and Commissurotomy: III—Toward the Improvement of Alternative Conceptions. NATSOULAS, Thomas.

Consciousness and the Practice of Science. CONRAD, Deborah.

Consciousness for the Twenty-First Century. CSIKSZENTMIHALYI, Mihaly.

Considerazioni sul problema della conoscenza. BACCARI, Luciano.

Constructing or Completing Physical Geometry?. CARRIER, Martin.

Construction and the Role of Schematism in Kant's Philosophy of Mathematics (also in Portuguese). WINTERBOURNE, A T.

Contemporary Shapes of Scientific Realism (in Czechoslovakian). PARUSNIKOVA, Zuzana.

Contrastive Explanations. LIPTON, Peter.

Contributi piagetiani ad una scienza della mente. BORELLA, Silvia.

Conventionalism in Physics. MORRIS, W T.

Corresponding Regressions, Procedural Evidence, and the Dialectics of Substantive Theory, Metaphysics, Methodology. CHAMBERS, William.

The Cosmological Constant: Einstein's Greatest Mistake?. RAY, Christopher.

Cosmology and Religion. JAKI, Stanley.

Counterfactuals and the Complexity of Causal Notions. PIZZI, Claudio.

The Creationist Theory of Abrupt Appearances: A Critique. STRAHLER, Arthur N.

A Critical Look at Arguments for Food Irradiation. SMITH, Tony.

A Critique of Mellor's Argument against 'Backwards' Causation. RIGGS, Peter J.

A Crucial Distinction: Initial Data and Law Application Instances. FLICHMAN, Eduardo.

Crypto-theologie: hoffentlich ein Ende: Reactie op Callebaut en Wachelder. SOONTIENS, Frans.

El cuádruple problema de la inducción: Crítica de la solución popperiana del problema de Hume. GARCÍA NORRO, Juan José.

The Curve Fitting Problem: A Solution. TURNEY, Peter.

Darwin's Long and Short Arguments. SINTONEN, Matti.

The Darwinian Synthesis: A Critique of the Rosenberg/Williams Argument. VAN BALEN, G.

David Hull's Evolutionary Model for the Progress and Process of Science. OLDROYD, David.

Davy Refuted Lavoisier Not Lakatos. ZUCKER, Arthur.

Dementia Praecox as a Failure of Neoteny. BEMPORAD, Jules R.

Desarrollos actuales de la epistemología dialéctica. MENDOZA, Celina A Lértora.

Describing the Emotions: A Review of The Cognitive Structure of Emotions by Ortony, Clore and Collins. BEN-ZEEV, Aaron.

The Development of Modern Mathematics and Plato's Parable of the Cave. MAURIN, Krzysztof.

SCIENCE

Diagnosis Without Doctors. MAZOUÉ, James G.
La dialéctica del deseo como realización de la identidad en Henri Bergson. ELÓSEGUI, María.
Dialogue on Science, Society, and the Generative Order. BOHM, D and KELLY, Sean.
Did Kuhn Kill Logical Empiricism?. REISCH, George A.
Dimensions of Observability. KOSSO, Peter.
Direct and Indirect Causes. SPOHN, Wolfgang.
The Discursive Formation of the Body in the History of Medicine. LEVIN, David Michael and SOLOMON, George F.
Distant Action in Classical Electromagnetic Theory. MUNDY, Brent.
Does Representational Content Arise from Biological Function?. HALL, Richard J.
The Drama of Galileo, The Past and the Present. VOISE, Waldemar.
An Economic Model of Scientific Activity and Truth Acquisition. GOLDMAN, Alvin I and SHAKED, Moshe.
Economie in de spiegel van de natuurwetenschappen. KUIPERS, Theo A F.
Ecosystems as Circuits: Diagrams and the Limits of Physical Analogies. TAYLOR, Peter J and BLUM, Ann S.
Editologie et Scientificite. BAUDET, Jean C.
Educational Research and Bhaskar's Conception of Discovery. CORSON, David.
Elementos dinámicos de la teoría celular. GONZÁLEZ RECIO, José Luis.
Elements of a Wittgensteinian Philosophy of the Human Sciences. SCHATZKI, Theodore R.
Embedding and Uniqueness in Relationist Theories. MUNDY, Brent.
Emergenz Bausteine für eine Begriffsexplikation. STÖCKLER, Manfred.
Empirical and Philosophical Reactions to Harcum's "Behavioral Paradigm for a Psychological Resolution of ...". POLLIO, Howard R and HENLEY, Tracy.
Empirical Equivalence and Undetermination. LAUDAN, Larry and LEPLIN, Jarrett.
Empirical Tests are Only Auxiliary Devices. LAI, Tyrone.
Empiricism versus Realism: High Points in the Debate During the Past 150 Years. DILWORTH, Craig.
Ends and Meaning in Machine-Like Systems. ATLAN, H.
Envy and Jealousy. BEN-ZEEV, Aaron.
Epigenetic Landscaping: Waddington's Use of Cell Fate Bifurcation Diagrams. GILBERT, Scott F.
L'epiglottide nell'antichità tra medicina e filosofia. REPICI, Luciana.
Epiphenomenalism and Machines: A Discussion of Van Rooijen's Critique of Popper. PECNJAK, Davor.
An Epistemic Analysis of Explanations and Causal Beliefs. GÄRDENFORS, Peter.
Epistemic Paternalism: Communication Control in Law and Society. GOLDMAN, Alvin I.
Epistemología contemporánea y filosofía cristiana. ZANOTTI, Gabriel J.
Epistemological Time Asymmetry. SAVITT, Steven F.
Épistémologie et questionnement: le modële en tant que forme de l'interrogation scientifique. BORUTTI, Silvana.
Equivalent Descriptions. BEN-MENAHEM, Yemima.
Erneuerung als Grundmechanismus der Evolution. EBELING, Werner.
Ernst Mach Leaves "The Church of Physics". BLACKMORE, John.
Estrategias metacientíficas: Parte II. HIDALGO TUÑÓN, Alberto.
Evolutionary Naturalistic Justifications of Morality: A Matter of Faith and Works. ROTTSCHAEFER, William A.
Expectation, Modelling and Assent in the History of Optics: Part I—Alhazen and the Medieval Tradition. CROMBIE, A C.
Expectation, Modelling and Assent in the History of Optics—II. Kelper and Descartes. CROMBIE, A C.
Expecting Nature's Best: Optimality Models and Perfect Adaptation. HOLCOMB, H R.
Explaining Science. KORB, Kevin B.
Explanation and Causality: Some Suggestions from Econometrics. GALAVOTTI, Maria Carla.
Explanation and Scientific Realism. GASPER, Philip.
Explanation and the Theory of Questions. CROSS, Charles B.
Explanation and Understanding in Social Science. SKORUPSKI, John.
Explanation in Biology. SMITH, John Maynard.
Explanation in Physical Theory. CLARK, Peter.
Explanation, Causation and Laws. EDGINGTON, Dorothy.
Explanation—Opening Address. SMART, J J C.
Explanation. REDHEAD, Michael.
The Explanatory Tools of Theoretical Population Biology. COOPER, Gregory.
Externalism and Marr's Theory of Vision. FRANCESCOTTI, Robert M.
Factor Analysis, Information-Transforming Instruments, and Objectivity: A Reply and Discussion. MULAIK, Stanley A.
Falsification and Disconfirmation in Cosmology. ZYCINSKI, Joseph.
Faustian Phenomena: Teleology in Goethe's Interpretation of Plants and Animals. CORNELL, John F.
Fear and Loathing (and Other Intentional States) in Searle's Chinese Room. JACQUETTE, Dale.
Feminism and Philosophy of Science. LONGINO, Helen E.
La filosofía de la ciencia en Platón: Una introducción. PEREZ DE LABORDA, Alfonso.
Filosofía y teoría general de sistemas en el pensamiento de A Rapoport. SAXE FERNÁNDEZ, Eduardo E.
Fine's "Shaky Game" (and Why Noa is No Ark for Science). SCHLAGEL, Richard H.
Física y Semántica en la filosofía de Quine. FUSTEGUERAS, Aurelio P.
Fitness and Evolutionary Explanation. BYERLY, Henry C and MICHOD, Richard E.
Fitness and Evolutionary Explanation: A Response. BYERLY, Henry C and MICHOD, Richard E.
Fix It and Be Damned: A Reply to Laudan. WORRALL, John.
Florilegi filosofici ed enciclopedie in Germania nella prima metà del Duecento. STURLESE, Loris.
Formalisme et intuitionnisme en philosophie des mathématiques. LARGEAULT, Jean.
Fragility and Deterministic Modelling in the Exact Sciences. TAVAKOL, R K.
Freiheit und Bindung menschlicher Entscheidungen. KLEMENT, H W and RADERMACHER, F J.
Freud and the Question of Truth (in Serbo-Croatian). GÖRLICH, Bernard.
From Boskovic's Supplements to the Poem of Benedikt Stay (in Serbo-Croatian). D'AGOSTINO, Salvo.
From Presentation to Representation in E B Wilson's *The Cell*. MAIENSCHEIN, Jane.
Functional Support for Anomalous Monism. EDWARDS, Jim.
Functionalism, the Absent Qualia Objection and Eliminativism. AVERILL, Edward Wilson.
Functions As Selected Effects: The Conceptual Analyst's Defense. NEANDER, Karen.
The Future of the Past: From the History of Historiography to Historiology. GRANDAZZI, Alexandre.
The Geometry of Legal Principles. CHUAQUI, Rolando and MALITZ, Jerome.
Getting to the Truth Through Conceptual Revolutions. KELLY, Kevin and GLYMOUR, Clark.
Giacomo Andrea Giacomini: un clinico padovano tra Metafisica e Scienza. FEDERSPIL, Giovanni.
Global Arguments for the Safety of Engineered Organisms. KLINE, David and GENDEL, Stephen M.
Glymour on Deoccamization and the Epistemology of Geometry. DURAN, Jane.
Gonseth et le discours théologique. MOREL, Bernard.
A Green Parrot is Just as Much a Red Herring as a White Shoe: A Note on Confirmation, Background Knowledge.... FRENCH, Steven.
Hacking's Experimental Argument for Realism. HOLCOMB III, Harmon R.
Hattiangadi's Theory of Scientific Problems and the Structure of Standard Epistemologies. GIUNTI, Marco.
Hegel and the Humean Problem of Induction. SUCHTING, W A.
Herbert Simon's Computational Models of Scientific Discovery. DOWNES, Stephen M.
The Hermetic Influence on the Rise of Modern Science. MITRA, Prabir.
Heuristics and the Generalized Correspondence Principle. RADDER, Hans.
Hidden Locality, Conspiracy and Superluminal Signals. KRONZ, Frederick M.
A Historico-Philosophical Investigation of Anti-Science: The Phenomenological Encounter. RAINA, Dhruv.
History, Indian Science and Policy-Making: A Philosophical Review. BHARGAVI, V and SUBRAMANIAM, K.
Hobbes' Science of Human Nature. SACKSTEDER, William.
The Hole Truth. BUTTERFIELD, Jeremy.
Holism and Measurement (in Serbo-Croatian). BALZER, Wolfgang.
Horwich, Hempel, and Hypothetico-Deductivism. GEMES, Ken.
How Did Morality Evolve?. IRONS, William.
How Do Scientific Explanations Explain?. KINOSHITA, Joyce.
How Nancy Cartwright Tells the Truth. FRANKLIN, Allan.
How the Models of Chemistry Vie. HOFMANN, James R.
How to Defend Science Against Scepticism: A Reply to Barry Gower. CHALMERS, Alan.
How to Put Questions to Nature. SINTONEN, Matti.
Husserl's Philosophy of Science and the Semantic Approach. MORMANN, Thomas.
Hypotheses, Probability, and Waves. ACHINSTEIN, Peter.
Hypothesis Tests and Confidence Intervals in the Single Case. JOHNSTONE, D J.
If It Aint's Broke, Don't Fix It. LAUDAN, Larry.
Ignoramus, Ignorabimus!. BUENO, Gustavo.
The Impact of Activist Pressures on Recombinant DNA Research. RABINO, Isaac.
The Impact of Science Studies on Political Philosophy. LATOUR, Bruno.
In Defence of Unrepresentative Realism. TONGS, A R.
Incommensurability and the Indeterminacy of Translation. SANKEY, Howard.
Independence from Future Theories: A Research Strategy in Quantum Theory. RUEGER, Alexander.
Inferring Formal Causation from Corresponding Regressions. CHAMBERS, William V.
The Infinite Apparatus in the Quantum Theory of Measurement. ROBINSON, Don.

SCIENCE

Intentionalistic Explanations in the Social Sciences. SEARLE, John R.
Interpretation and Theory in the Natural and the Human Sciences: Comments on Kuhn and Taylor. LACEY, Hugh.
Interpreting State Reduction from the Practices-up. CORDERO, Alberto.
La investigación y las metodologías en las Ciencias Humanas. DACAL ALONSO, José Antonio.
The Irrelevance of Bootstrapping. CHRISTENSEN, David.
Irreversibility and Statistical Mechanics: A New Approach?. BATTERMAN, Robert W.
Is Confirmation Differential?. ERWIN, Edward and SIEGEL, Harvey.
Is History and Philosophy of Science Withering on the Vine?. FULLER, Steve W.
Is Neuroscience Relevant to Philosophy?. CHURCHLAND, Patricia Smith.
Is Scientific Methodology Interestingly Atemporal?. CUSHING, James T.
Is the Skeptical Attitude the Attitude of a Skeptic?. PAPRZYCKA, Katarzyna.
Island Biogeography, Species-Area Curves, and Statistical Errors: Applied Biology and Scientific Rationality. SHRADER-FRECHETTE, Kristin.
Ist die Naturphilosophie eine abgelegte Gestalt des modernen Geistes?. WAHSNER, Renate.
Jarrett Completeness and Superluminal Signals. KRONZ, Frederick M.
Johan Jacob Ferguson, geb um 1630 im Haag(?), gest vor dem 24 November 1706, vermutlich am 6 Oktober 1691 in Amsterdam. VAN MAANEN, Jan A.
The Justification of Kepler's Ellipse. BAIGRIE, Brian S.
Kant on Concepts and Intuitions in the Mathematical Sciences. FRIEDMAN, Michael.
Kennen en kunnen: Een repliek op Wardekker. HARBERS, Hans.
Kitcher and Kant. BHAVE, S M.
Kitcher and Salmon's *Scientific Explanation*; and Salmon's *Four Decades of Scientific Explanation*. FETZER, James H.
Kochen's Interpretation of Quantum Mechanics. ARNTZENIUS, Frank.
Kritik der Soziobiologie des Menschen. KASPAR, Rudolf F.
Kuhn's Conception of Incommensurability. HOYNINGEN-HUENE, Paul.
A Kuhnian Model of Falsifiability. STONE, Mark A.
L'étude du vivant et la méthodologie ouverte. PILET, Paul-Emile.
The Lakatos Award Lecture: The Nature of Reality. REDHEAD, Michael.
The Last Word on Induction?. HOWSON, Colin.
The Laws of Physics as Nomic Universals. ZYCINSKI, Jozef.
Let's Razor Ockham's Razor. SOBER, Elliott.
Lewis's Functionalism and Reductive Materialism. KERNOHAN, Andrew.
Lezioni di filosofia della scienza di Guilio Preti. LECIS, Pier Luigi.
Light Problems: Reply to Chen. ACHINSTEIN, Peter.
Limited Explanations. CLARK, Stephen R L.
The Limits of Explanation. SWINBURNE, Richard.
Local Incommensurability and Communicability. CHEN, Xiang.
Location and Range. SCHLESINGER, George N.
Logicism, Pragmatism and Metascience: Towards a Pancritical-Pragmatic Meta-Level Discourse. AXTELL, G S.
Man Not a Subject of Science?. SLEZAK, Peter.
Man, History, and Philosophy in Husserl's Crisis of European Sciences (in Czechoslovakian). MAJOR, L.
The Many Faces of Irreversibility. DENBIGH, K G.
Marxism as the Foundation of Philosophies of Science: *The Case of G Lukács' Ontology of Social Being*. TUCHANSKA, Barbara.
Más allá de la presuposición newtoniana: propiedades genuinamente disposicionales en la mecánica cuántica. MARTÍNEZ, Sergio.
Masaryk's "Anthropism" (in Czechoslovakian). NOVY, Lubomir.
Massively Parallel Distributed Processing and a Computationalist Foundation for Cognitive Science. LYNGZEIDETSON, Albert E.
Materiali per una storia dell'epistemologia in Italia. CASTELLANA, Mario.
Mathematical Modelling and Constrastive Explanation. MORTON, Adam.
Mathematical Physics and Elementary Logic. MUNDY, Brent.
Mathématiques et ontologie: les symétries en physique. BOUTOT, Alain.
Les mathématiques, la biologie et le statut scientifique de la philosophie pour Bergson. SOULEZ, Philippe.
Die Mathematisierung als Konstruktion theoretischer Denkformen in der Abfolge naturwissenschaftlicher Weltbilder. GÖTTLICHER, Gerd.
The Meaning of Mathematical Expressions: Does Philosophy Shed Any Light on Psychology?. ERNEST, Paul.
Means and Ends in Wild Life Management. LEOPOLD, Aldo.
The Measurement Problem: Some "Solutions". ALBERT, David Z and LOEWER, Barry.
Measuring the Success of Science. NIINILUOTO, Ilkka.
Medical Critique [Krytyka Lekarska]: A Journal of Medicine and Philosophy—1897-1907. LÖWY, Ilana.
Medicine in John Locke's Philosophy. SANCHEZ-GONZALEZ, Miguel A.
Mental Misrepresentation. MALONEY, J Christopher.
Metaphysical Awakening in Philosophy of Quantum Physics. FOLSE, Henry J.
Metaphysics of the Person, Determinism and Responsibility. FAY, Thomas A.
Metaphysics, MSRP and Economics. GLASS, J C and JOHNSON, W.
Metaphysics, Pragmatic Truth and the Underdetermination of Theories. PEREIRA JR, Alfredo and FRENCH, Steven.
Metodi e immagini della scienza nel "Centro di studi metodologici" di Torino (1945-1952). QUARTA, Antonio.
A Middle Platonic Reading of Plato's Theory of Recollection. SCHRENK, Lawrence P.
Modelos de cambio científico en la filosofía actual de la ciencia. STRÖKER, Elisabeth.
Models of Memory: Wittgenstein and Cognitive Science. STERN, David G.
Modularity of Mind Revisited. BENNETT, Laura J.
Molecular Biology and the Unity of Science. KINCAID, Harold.
More on Russell's Hypothesis. HINDERLITER, Hilton.
Multiple Personality and Irrationality. GILLETT, Grant R.
Must Psychology Be Individualistic?. EGAN, Frances.
Must Scientific Diagrams Be Eliminable? The Case of Path Analysis. GRIESEMER, James R.
Na de sociale wending het roer nogmaals om. LATOUR, Bruno.
Natural Complex versus Natural System. KHALIL, Elias L.
Natural Problems and Artificial Intelligence. HENLEY, Tracy.
Natural Selection as Natural History. VAN DER STEEN, Wim J.
A Naturalistic Theory of Archaic Moral Order. CAMPBELL, Donald.
Naturalized Epistemology Sublimated: Rapprochement without the Ruts. FULLER, Steve.
The Nature of Physical Reality. POLKINGHORNE, John C.
De natuurlijke ouderdom: een grenzeloze geschiedenis. BIJSTERVELD, Karin.
Natuurlijke selectie, doelgerichtheid en een uitzonderlijke samenloop van omstandigheden: Een kritiek op F Soontiëns. SLURINK, Pouwel.
A New Theory of the Relationship of Mind and Matter. BOHM, David.
Nicola Abbagnano tra esistenzialismo e neoilluminismo. QUARTA, Antonio.
Nietzsche and the Philosophy of Scientific Power: Will to Power as Constructive Interpretation. BABICH, Babette E.
Nietzsche's "Will to Power" Nachlass. HELLER, Peter.
The No-Slip Condition of Fluid Dynamics. DAY, Michael A.
Non-Rational Cognitive Processes as Changes of Distinctions. HEYLIGHEN, Francis.
Nonlocal Influences and Possible Worlds—A Stapp in the Wrong Direction. CLIFTON, Robert K and BUTTERFIELD, Jeremy N and REDHEAD, Michael L G.
Nota sobre la causalidad apotética a la escala psicológica. FUENTES ORTEGA, Juan Bautista.
Note on Entropy, Disorder and Disorganization. DENBIGH, K G.
A Note on Popper's Equation of Simplicity with Falsifiability. TURNEY, Peter.
A Note on Van Fraassen's Explanatory Contrastiveness. PAPRZYCKA, Katarzyna.
Objectivity and Growth of Knowledge. CHAUDHURY, Mahasweta.
La objetividad del azar en un mundo determinista. MARTÍNEZ, S.
La objetividad y la distinción ciencia/ética. PUTNAM, Hilary and MURILLO, Lorena.
Observation: An Empirical Discussion. GILMAN, Daniel.
On Being an Aristotelian. MEYNELL, Hugo A.
On Bolzano's Conception of the Essentials of Ethics and its Coherences (in Czechoslovakian). HALA, Vlastimil.
On Bureaucracy and Science: A Response to Fuller. TWENEY, Ryan D.
On Cauchy's Notion of Infinitesimal. CUTLAND, Nigel J (and others).
On Causality, Heritability and Fitness. ETTINGER, Lia and JABLONKA, Eva and FALK, Raphael.
On Kant's Conception of Science and the Critique of Practical Reason. KÖRNER, Stephan.
On Naturalizing Epistemology. ALMEDER, Robert.
On Relativity Theory and Openness of the Future. STEIN, Howard.
On Saving the Phenomena and the Mice: A Reply to Bourgeois Concerning Van Fraassen's Image of Science. FOSS, Jeff.
On Some Alleged Difficulties in the Interpretation of Quantum Mechanics. DIEKS, Dennis.
On the Adaptations of Organisms and the Fitness of Types. ETTINGER, Lia and JABLONKA, Eva and MC LAUGHLIN, Peter.
On the Aim of Scientific Theories in Relating to the World: A Defence of the Semantic Account. BAUR, Michael.
On the Alleged Impossibility of a Science of Accidents in Aristotle. URBANAS, Alban.
On the Alleged Impossibility of Inductive Probability. EELLS, Ellery.
On the Dearth of Philosophical Contributions to Medicine. YARBOROUGH, Mark.
On the Nature and Norms of Theoretical Commitment. HORWICH, Paul.
On the Objectivity of the Laws of Physics. HAMAN, Krzysztof E.
On the Origin of Spin in Relativity. SACHS, Mendel.
On the Other Side of the Open Science (in Serbo-Croatian). POLSEK, Darko.
On the Phenomenon of Marginality in Epistemology: Gonseth and his Tradition. WITKOWSKI, Lech.
On the Possibility of Directed Mutations in Bacteria: Statistical Analyses and Reductionist Strategies. SARKAR, Sahotra.
On the Possibility of Lawful Explanation in Archaeology. SALMON, Merrilee H.
On the Problem of the Essence of Truth in the Natural Sciences (in Dutch). KOCKELMANS, J.
On the Uniqueness of Biological Research. PORTMANN, Adolph.
On Two Recent Accounts of Colour. MC GINN, Marie.
An Oscillatory Model of the Growth of Scientific Knowledge. AKEROYD, F Michael.

SCIENCE

The Other European Science of Nature?. UBEROI, J P S.
An Outline of My Main Contributions to Economic Science. ALLAIS, Maurice.
P W Bridgman's Operational Perspective on Physics: Part I—Origins and Development. MOYER, Albert E.
Para una teoría latinoamericana de las relaciones de la ciencia con la literatura: la cienciapoesía. CATALÁ, Rafael.
El paradigma computacional aplicado al estudio de la vida. GUTIÉRREZ, Claudio.
Paradigmas cartesianos. LOPARIC, Z.
Paradigms, Populations and Problem-Fields: Approaches to Disagreement. ALLCHIN, Douglas.
The Parallel Fallacy: On Comparing Art and Science. TOPPER, David.
Parity for the Theoretical Ghosts and Gremlins: Response to Pollio/Henley and Rychlak. HARCUM, E Rae.
The Participant Irrealist At Large in the Laboratory. HACKING, Ian.
Pascal critique des philosophes, Pascal philosophe. BOUCHILLOUX, Hélène.
Pavlov's View on the Inheritance of Acquired Characteristics .... WINDHOLZ, George and LAMAL, P A.
Peirce and Evolution: Comment on O'Hear. GOMILA, Antoni.
Perception and Neuroscience. GILLETT, Grant R.
Persistent Propensities: Portrait of a Familiar Controversy. NORDMANN, Alfred.
Perspectives on Quantum Reality versus Classical Reality. HOME, Dipankar.
La pertinence du concept d'horizon de réalité en physique théorique contemporaine. COHEN-TANNOUDJI, Gilles.
The Phenotype as the Level of Selection: Cave organisms as Model Systems. KANE, Thomas C and RICHARDSON, Robert C and FONG, Daniel W.
Philip Kitchers Soziobiologie-Kritik. VOLLMER, Gerhard.
The Philosophical Basis of Rational-Emotive Therapy (RET). ELLIS, Albert.
Philosophical Elements in Penrose's and Hawking's Research in Contemporary Cosmology. DREES, Wim.
Philosophical Objections to the Kinetic Theory. NYHOF, John.
La philosophie du chaos. BOUTOT, Alain.
La philosophie ouverte de F Gonseth aboutit-elle à une conception réaliste ou relativiste. LAUENER, Henri.
Philosophische Anstösse in der computerunterstützten Intelligenz-Forschung. HRACHOVEC, Herbert.
Philosophy and Cognitive Science (in Czechoslovakian). PSTRUZINA, Karel.
Philosophy and the Rise of Modern Science. SALMON, Wesley.
The Philosophy of Quantum Mechanics. BUB, Jeffrey.
Philosophy of Science and the Persistent Narratives of Modernity. ROUSE, Joseph.
Philosophy of Science: From Justification to Explanation. KANTOROVICH, Aharon.
Pictorial Representation in Biology. TAYLOR, Peter J and BLUM, Ann S.
Piecemeal Realism. FINE, Arthur.
Plato's Ontology and the Role of Mathematics in the Description of Nature. ZYCINSKI, Joseph.
Plato, the History of Science and Our Understanding of Nature (in German). GLOY, Karen.
Play of the Whole of Wholes (in Czechoslovakian). AXELOS, Kostas.
Plural World of Contemporary Science and Philosophy (in Serbo-Croatian). LELAS, Srdjan.
Pluralistic Ontology and Theory Reduction in the Physical Sciences. ROHRLICH, Fritz.
Politics in Hobbes' Mechanics: The Social as Enabling. LYNCH, William T.
Popper's Demarcation of Science Refuted. AGASSI, Joseph.
Por qué los estados mentales no son clases naturales?. HANSBERG, Olbeth.
Positivism and the Pragmatic Theory of Observation. OBERDAN, Thomas.
Praktijkontwikkeling en wetenschappelijke (onderwijs)kunde: Een reactie op Boon e.a.. WARDEKKER, Wim.
Preconditions of Predication: From Qualia to Quantum Mechanics. FORSTER, Malcolm.
Predication and Deduction in Aristotle: Aspirations to Completeness. SMITH, Robin.
Predication and Physical Law. SCHEIBE, Erhard.
Predication, Fiction, and Artificial Intelligence. RAPAPORT, William J.
Presentism and the Indeterminacy of Translation. HARDCASTLE, Gary L.
La prima edizione sovietica di Solov'ev. MASTROIANNI, Giovanni.
Primary Qualities are Secondary Qualities Too. PRIEST, Graham.
La primera antinomia kantiana: el origen y los límites del Universo. PUYAU, Hermes.
El principio antrópico. PEREZ DE LABORDA, A.
El principio de exclusión y sus aplicaciones. GARZÓN, León.
Probabilistic Causality from a Dynamical Point of View. VON PLATO, Jan.
Probabilistic Causality: A Rejoinder to Ellery Eells. DUPRÉ, John.
Probability and Epistemology. PIENKOWSKI, M.
The Problem of Causation and Time-Symmetry in Physics. BHARUCHA, Filita.
The Problem of Properties in Quantum Mechanics. BUB, Jeffrey.
El problema del conocimiento en Pascal. CASTRO MÉNDEZ, Silvia.
Problema psicofísico y realidad cuántica en la física heterodoxa de David Bohm. MONSERRAT, Javier.
Problemas conceptuales y políticas de desarrollo tecnológico. QUINTANILLA, Miguel Ángel.
Processes, Substances, and Leibniz's Epistemology: A Case for Essentialism in Contemporary Physics. PIRO, Francesco.
Progress in Mathematics and Other Arts. SEDZIWY, Stanislaw.
Prolegomenon to a Proper Interpretation of Quantum Field Theory. TELLER, Paul.
Property in Science and the Market. O'NEILL, John.
Psychoanalysis: Acceptance and Overcoming of the Philosophical Heritage (in Serbo-Croatian). JOVANOVIC, Gordana.
Psychology and Controversy. AGASSI, Joseph.
Putnam and Truth (in Serbo-Croatian). JAKIC, Mirko.
Quantum Cosmology and the Beginning of the Universe. SMITH, Gerrit.
Quantum Gravity: Some Philosophical Reflections. ALTEKAR, E V.
Quantum Logic, Copenhagen Interpretation and Instrumentalism. RAINA, Dhruv.
Quantum Physics and Logical Truth (in Italian). GIANNETTO, Enrico.
Quantum Physics and the Identity of Indiscernibles. FRENCH, Steven and REDHEAD, Michael.
Quantum Propensition Theory: A Testable Resolution of the Wave/Particle Dilemma. MAXWELL, Nicholas.
Quine on Theory and Language. TANJI, Nobuharu.
R J Boskovic's "Theoria" — A Sign Post to the Essence of the Modern Natural Science (in Serbo-Croatian). ZENKO, Franjo.
R J Boskovic's Philosophy of Space (in Serbo-Croatian). ROSSI, Arcangelo.
Randomness and Probability in Dynamical Theories: On the Proposals of the Prigogine School. BATTERMAN, Robert.
Rationalism, Expertise and the Dreyfuses' Critique of AI Research. ROBINSON, William S.
Real Dispositions in the Physical World. THOMPSON, Ian J.
The Real Meaning of 'Meaning'. CARTER, Alan.
Realism About What?. JONES, Roger.
Realism and Simplicity in the Castle-East Debate on the Stability of the Hereditary Units. VICEDO, Marga.
Realism and the Collapse of the Wave-Packet. KRIPS, Henry.
Realism, Idealism and Quantum Mechanics. LIST, C J.
Realismo e fenomenismo nella fisica moderna. BLANDINO, Giovanni.
Recent Work in the Philosophy of Biology. STERELNY, Kim.
Recent Work on Naturalized Epistemology. MAFFIE, James.
Reduction and the Part/Whole Relation. KRECZ, Charles A.
Reduction, Elimination, and the Mental. SCHWARTZ, Justin.
Reflections on Blanshard, Reason, and Religion. FERRÉ, Frederick.
A Refutation of Popperian Inductive Scepticism. GEMES, Ken.
Reinventing Certainty: The Significance of Ian Hacking's Realism. GROSS, Alan G.
Rejection Without Acceptance. MATHESON, Carl A and KLINE, A David.
The Relation between Science and Theology: The Case for Complimentarity Revisited. REICH, K Helmut.
Relativité et quanta: leurs mutuelles exisgences et les corrélations d'Einstein-Podolsky-Rosen. COSTA DE BEAUREGARD, Olivier.
Remarks on the Modularity of Mind. SHANNON, Benny.
A Reply to Mayo's Criticisms of Urbach's "Randomization and the Design of Experiments". URBACH, Peter.
Reply to Wilson's "Shadows on the Cave Wall: Philosophy and Visual Science". HARDIN, C L.
Représentation structurelle de la relation partie-tout. STAHL, Gérold.
Representations of the Natural System in the Nineteenth Century. O'HARA, Robert J.
Reproducibility as a Methodological Imperative in Experimental Research. HONES, Michael.
Research Programmes and Empirical Results. AKEROYD, F M.
A Response to A G A Bello's Methodological Preliminaries. ANYANWU, Kane C.
Response to Ehring's 'Papineau on Causal Asymmetry'. PAPINEAU, David.
The Role of Homunculi in Psychology. WARD, Andrew.
The Roles of Predictions in Science and Religion. SCHOEN, Edward L.
Ruben and the Metaphysics of the Social World. TUOMELA, Raimo.
Ruder Boskovic as a Humanist and Scientist (in Serbo-Croatian). SUPEK, Ivan.
Schematism and Schemata: Kant and the P.D.P.. VAN DE VIJVER, Gertrudis.
Science and Consciousness. WOJCIECHOWSKI, Jerzy A.
Science and Truthlikeness. PANDIT, G L.
Science in the Age of Mechanical Reproduction: Moral and Epistemic Relations Between Diagrams and Photographs. LYNCH, Michael.
Scientia e fide. BLANDINO, Giovanni.
Scientific Evidence: Creating and Evaluating Experimental Instruments and Research Techniques. BECHTEL, William.
Scientific Explanation: Causation *and* Unification. SALMON, Wesley C.
Scientific Humanism and Religion. WILSON, Edward O.
Scientific Instruments, Scientific Progress and the Cyclotron. BAIRD, Davis and FAUST, Thomas.

SCIENCE

Scientific Knowledge and Human Happiness. ROY, Krishna.

Scientific Pluralism and the Plurality of the Sciences: Comments on David Hull's *Science as a Process*. DUPRÉ, John.

Scientific Racism in the Philosophy of Science: Some Historical Examples. UEBEL, Thomas E.

Scientific Rationality—A Rethinking. CHAUDHURY, Mahasweta.

Scientific Realism and Experimental Practice in High-Energy Physics. HONES, Michael J.

Scientific Realism, Perceptual Beliefs, and Justification. OTTE, Richard.

Scientific Research and the Christian Faith. PETERS, Ted.

Search for Beliefs to Live by Consistent with Science. SPERRY, R W.

Self-Organization, Emergent Properties and the Unity of the World. ROTH, Gerhard and SCHWEGLER, Helmut.

The Semantic Approach to Evolutionary Theory. ERESHEFSKY, Marc.

A Semiotical Reflection on Biology, Living Signs and Artificial Life. EMMECHE, Claus.

Shadows on the Cave Wall: Philosophy and Visual Science. WILSON, Hugh R.

Simultaneity, Conventionality and Existence. PETKOV, Vesselin.

Singular Causation and Law. IRZIK, Gürol.

Singular Explanation and the Social Sciences. RUBEN, David-Hillel.

Sobre causación y unificación según Wesley Salmon. OLIVÉ, León.

Sobre la génesis de la conciencia de si mismo. BEJARANO, Teresa.

Social Epistemology and the Brave New World of Science and Technology Studies. FULLER, Steve.

Social Science-Based Understandings of Science: Reflections on Fuller. KRUGLANSKI, Arie W.

Sociology, Selection, and Success: A Critique of David Hull's Analysis of Science and Systematics. DONOGHUE, Michael J.

Sociology: An Infirm Science. BUSINO, Giovanni and FERGUSON, Jeanne.

Socrates, the Craft Analogy, and Science. GRAHAM, Daniel W.

Solving the Problem of Induction Using a Values-Based Epistemology. ELLIS, Brian.

Some Aspects of R G Collingwood's Doctrine of Absolute Presuppositions. SAARI, Heikki.

Some Characteristics of Boskovic's Scientific Methodology (in Serbo-Croatian). FESTINI, Heda.

Some Comments Concerning Spin and Relativity. WEINGARD, Robert.

Some Features of Hume's Conception of Space. FRASCA-SPADA, Marina.

Some Theoretical and Methodological Questions Concerning Harcum's Proposed Resolution of the Free Will Issue. RYCHLAK, Joseph F.

Species as Historical Individuals. KLUGE, Arnold G.

Species, Higher Taxa, and the Units of Evolution. ERESHEFSKY, Marc.

Spiritual Traditions and Science and Technology. BAKAR, Osman.

State-Spaces and Meaning Relations Among Predicates. ARNTZENIUS, Frank.

Statistical Explanation, Probability, and Counteracting Conditions. GRIMES, Thomas R.

Stich, Content, Prediction, and Explanation in Cognitive Science. WALLIS, Charles S.

Structural Analogies Between Physical Systems. KROES, Peter.

Substance, Relations, and Arguments About the Nature of Space-Time. TELLER, Paul.

Sulla semiotizzazione dell' "a priori": Rossi-Landi e Hjelmslev. CAPUTO, Cosimo.

Supervenience and Singular Causal Claims. WOODWARD, James.

A Suspicious Feature of the Popper/Miller Argument. GOOD, I J.

Swann versus Popper on Induction: An Arbitration. SETTLE, Tom.

Symptomatic Acts and the Value of Evidence in Causal Decision Theory. MAHER, Patrick.

Synthetic Mechanics Revisited. BURGESS, John P.

Taking Mathematics Seriously?. ZYCINSKI, Joseph.

Teleo-theologie und kein Ende: Reactie op Soontiens. CALLEBAUT, Werner and WACHELDER, J.

Teleological Underdetermination. OKRENT, Mark.

Teleology and the Concepts of Causation. VON GLASERSFELD, Ernst.

Ten Types of Scientific Progress. KUKLA, Andre.

Tendencias actuales en filosofía de la tecnología. CAMACHO, Luis.

Teorías físicas sobre el origen del Universo. GRATTON, Fausto T L.

Testing for Convergent Realism. ARONSON, Jerrold L.

The Fundamental Hypotheses of Mechanics in Lazare N M Carnot's Thought (in Italian). DRAGO, Antonino and MANNO, Salvatore D.

The Gnoseological Aspect of Boskovic's "Theory of Natural Philosophy" (in Serbo-Croatian). ACIMOVIC, Mirko.

The Influence of Roger Boskovic on Bertrand Russell's Early Philosophy of Physics (in Serbo-Croatian). LEWIS, Albert C.

The Object and the Concept: Spinoza's Theory with Regard to the Development of Modern Natural Science (in German). GOLDENBAUM, Ursula.

The Phenomenalism of Newton and Boskovic: A Comparative Study (in Serbo-Croatian). PRINCE, Augustus.

The Philosophical Invariables of Masaryk's Thinking (in Czechoslovakian). SROVNAL, Jindrich.

The Relationship Between the Humanities and the Natural and Technical Sciences (in German). PACHO, Julián.

Theorie antireduktionistischer Argumente: Fallstudie Bohr. HOYNINGEN-HUENE, Paul.

Theory and Reality in the Work of Jean Henry Fabre. YAVETZ, Ido.

A Theory of Probability. REEVES, T V.

Theory of the Apparatus and Theory of the Phenomena: The Case of Low Dose Electron Microscopy. SWIJTINK, Zeno G.

Theory Pursuit: Between Discovery and Acceptance. WHITT, Laurie Anne.

Theory Structure and Theory Change in Contemporary Molecular Biology. CULP, Sylvia and KITCHER, Philip.

There's More Than One Way to Recognize a Darwinian: Lyell's Darwinism. RECKER, Doren.

Thomas S Kuhn and L Fleck: Two Sociologists of Science. FLURI, Philippe H.

Thoughts and Theses on Causality. TILANDER, A.

Three Accounts of Paradigm Shift. MUKHERJEE, Nilratan.

Time-Travel and Topology. MAUDLIN, Tim.

Todos contra la Sociobiología. SÁNCHEZ, Manuel Esteban.

Toward the Obsolescence of the Schizophrenia Hypothesis. SARBIN, Theodore R.

Translation Failure Between Theories. SANKEY, Howard.

Truth and Teleology. PAPINEAU, David.

Truth in Interpretation: The Case of Psychoanalysis. ROTH, Paul A.

Truth, Content, and the Hypothetico-Deductive Method. GRIMES, Thomas R.

Two Brains, Two Minds? Wigan's Theory of Mental Duality. PUCCETTI, Roland.

Two Dogmas of Neo-Empiricism: The "Theory-Informity" of Observation and the Quine-Duhem Thesis. GREENWOOD, John D.

Two Kinds of Conceptual-Scheme Realism. CLAYTON, Philip.

Two Problems of Induction?. O'NEILL, John.

Two Qualms About Functionalist Marxism. DICKMAN, Joel.

Tycho's System and Galileo's *Dialogue*. MARGOLIS, Howard.

Ultimate Reality and Meaning in Africa: Some Methodological Preliminaries—A Test Case. BELLO, A G A.

Unbounded Operators and the Incompleteness of Quantum Mechanics. HEATHCOTE, Adrian.

Understanding Science: A Two-Level Reflection. DAS GUPTA, Amitabha.

Unification, Realism and Inference. MORRISON, Margaret.

The Unity of the Natural Sciences: Comment on Portmann. VON UEXKUELL, Thure.

Untangling Cause, Necessity, Temporality, and Method: Response to Chamber's Method of Corresponding Regressions. WILLIAMS, Richard N.

The Uses of Humanistic History. PORTER, Theodore M.

Van Rooijen and Mayr versus Popper: Is the Universe Causally Closed?. SETTLE, Tom.

Vectors and Change. BIGELOW, John and PARGETTER, Robert.

Wanted Dead or Alive: Two Attempts to Solve Schrödinger's Paradox. ALBERT, David and LOEWER, Barry.

Was Descartes a Liar? Diagonal Doubt Defended. SLEZAK, Peter.

Was heisst "sich in der Gesellschaft orientieren"?. BÖHME, Gernot.

Wetenschapsontwikkeling en kundes. BOON, Louis (and others).

Wetten en verhalen. KWA, Chunglin.

What are Discernible?. SCHLESINGER, George N.

What is a Law of Nature? A Humean Answer. URBACH, Peter.

What is the Explanandum of the Anthropic Principle?. WILSON, Patrick A.

What is the Logical Form of Probability Assignment in Quantum Mechanics?. HALPIN, John F.

What Is This Stuff Called Fitness?. OLLASON, J G.

What Is Wrong with the Miracle Argument?. CARRIER, Martin.

When Scientists are Wrong: Admitting Inadvertent Error in Research. LEIBEL, Wayne.

Whewell's Developmental Psychologism: A Victorian Account of Scientific Progress. METCALFE, John F.

Whither Social Epistemology? A Reply to Fuller. SCHMAUS, Warren.

Who or What is the Preembryo?. MC CORMICK, Richard A.

Whose Genome Project?. MACER, Darryl.

Why Are Graphs so Central in Science?. KROHN, Roger.

Why Natural Selection Leads to Complexity. BENZON, William L and HAYS, David G.

Why Scientists Gather Evidence. MAHER, Patrick.

Why the Anti-Reductionist Consensus Won't Survive: The Case of Classical Mendelian Genetics. WATERS, C Kenneth.

Why the Standard View Is Standard: People, Not Machines, Understand Patients' Problems. MILLER, Randolph A.

Wissenschaftsphilosophie in der DDR—Versuch einer kritischen Betrachtung. HÖRZ, Herbert.

Young and Lloyd on the Particle Theory of Light: A Response to Achinstein. CHEN, Xiang.

Zande Logic and Western Logic. JENNINGS, Richard C.

Zeeman-Göbel Topologies. HEATHCOTE, Adrian.

Zu einem "der tiefsten philosophischen Probleme". SIEGWART, Geo.

SCIENCE EDUCATION

The Goals of Science Education. MARTIN, Michael.

SCIENCE EDUCATION
Some Clarifications and Cautions Essential for Good Philosophy of Science Teaching. DAVSON-GALLE, Peter.
What is the Price of a Rich Life?. MEYER, Zofia Golab.

SCIENTIFIC
David Hume and the Problem of Reason. DANFORD, John W.
"Judgment and Policy: The Two-Step in Mandated Science and Technology" in *Philosophy of Technology*, LEVY, Edwin.
"My Poetic World Versus the Real, Scientific World" in *XIth International Congress in Aesthetics, Nottingham 1988*, PASKOW, Alan.
Una discussione di epistemologia. BLANDINO, Giovanni and FEDERSPIL, G.
È possibile un'esperienza di Dio?. CAVADI, Augusto.
Fix It and Be Damned: A Reply to Laudan. WORRALL, John.
From the Logic of Mathematical Discovery to the Methodology of Scientific Research Programmes. YUXIN, Zheng.
If It Aint's Broke, Don't Fix It. LAUDAN, Larry.
Must Scientific Diagrams Be Eliminable? The Case of Path Analysis. GRIESEMER, James R.
An Oscillatory Model of the Growth of Scientific Knowledge. AKEROYD, F Michael.
Scientific Explanation: Causation *and* Unification. SALMON, Wesley C.
Scientific Instruments, Scientific Progress and the Cyclotron. BAIRD, Davis and FAUST, Thomas.

SCIENTIFIC LANGUAGE
Science versus Religion. CLEMENTS, Tad S.
Materiali per una storia dell'epistemologia in Italia. CASTELLANA, Mario.

SCIENTIFIC METHOD
L'ordine della certezza: Scientificità e persuasione in Descartes. BONICALZI, Francesca.
Psychoanalysis, Scientific Method, and Philosophy. HOOK, Sidney (ed).
Science versus Religion. CLEMENTS, Tad S.
"Newtonianism Before and After the Einsteinian Revolution" in *Some Truer Method*, AGASSI, Joseph.
"Scientific Method and the Objectivity of Epistemic Value Judgments" in *Logic, Methodology and Philosophy of Science, VIII*, SHRADER-FRECHETTE, Kristin.
Aristotle's Causality Theory. ANDRIOPOULOS, D Z.
The Axiomatic Method: Its Origin and Purpose. AGASHE, S D.
Comment: Selective Anti-Realism. MC MULLIN, Ernan.
The Concrete and the Abstract Science: Description versus Explanation. GUPTA, Amitabha.
Consciousness and the Practice of Science. CONRAD, Deborah.
The Degeneration of Popper's Theory of Demarcation. GRÜNBAUM, Adolf.
Deride, Abide or Dissent: On the Ethics of Professional Conduct. HAUPTMAN, Robert and HILL, Fred.
Dewey and the Theory of Knowledge. THAYER, H S.
Epistemology as Hypothesis. PUTNAM, Hilary and PUTNAM, Ruth Anna.
Herbert Simon's Computational Models of Scientific Discovery. DOWNES, Stephen M.
A Historico-Philosophical Investigation of Anti-Science: The Phenomenological Encounter. RAINA, Dhruv.
Is Scientific Methodology Interestingly Atemporal?. CUSHING, James T.
The Justification of Kepler's Ellipse. BAIGRIE, Brian S.
Light Problems: Reply to Chen. ACHINSTEIN, Peter.
Metodi e immagini della scienza nel "Centro di studi metodologici" di Torino (1945-1952). QUARTA, Antonio.
Piecemeal Realism. FINE, Arthur.
Scientific Method and the Study of Society. NARASIMHAN, R.
Scientific Rationality—A Rethinking. CHAUDHURY, Mahasweta.
Some Characteristics of Boskovic's Scientific Methodology (in Serbo-Croatian). FESTINI, Heda.
The Concept of History in the Renaissance (in Hungarian). RASZLAI, Tibor.
Truth, Method, and Objectivity: *Husserl and Gadamer on Scientific Method*. NUYEN, A T.
Young and Lloyd on the Particle Theory of Light: A Response to Achinstein. CHEN, Xiang.

SCIENTIFIC PHILOSOPHY
Modelos de cambio científico en la filosofía actual de la ciencia. STRÖKER, Elisabeth.
Scientific Instruments, Scientific Progress and the Cyclotron. BAIRD, Davis and FAUST, Thomas.

SCIENTIFIC REALISM
Der sinnliche Gehalt der Wahrnehmung. SCHANTZ, Richard.
Bachelard and Scientific Realism. TIJIATTAS, Mary.
Cherniak on Scientific Realism. BROWN, Harold I.
Contemporary Shapes of Scientific Realism (in Czechoslovakian). PARUSNIKOVA, Zuzana.
Hacking's Experimental Argument for Realism. HOLCOMB III, Harmon R.
Phenomenology and Scientific Realism: Husserl's Critique of Galileo. SOFFER, Gail.
Reinventing Certainty: The Significance of Ian Hacking's Realism. GROSS, Alan G.
Scientific Realism and Experimental Practice in High-Energy Physics. HONES, Michael J.
Scientific Realism and Postmodern Philosophy. MURPHY, Nancey.
Scientific Realism, Perceptual Beliefs, and Justification. OTTE, Richard.

SCIENTIFIC REVOLUTION
I Modelli l'Invenzione e la Conferma. PETRONI, Angelo Maria.
Il Paradigma del Sapere. LENTINI, Luigi.
"Scientific Revolutions and Scientific Rationality: The Case of the Elderly Holdout" in *Scientific Theories*, WORRALL, John.
The Comeuppance of Science and Technology. CLEVELAND, Harlan.
King Lear and Natural Law. YOUNG, R V.
A Kuhnian Model of Falsifiability. STONE, Mark A.
Rejection Without Acceptance. MATHESON, Carl A and KLINE, A David.

SCIENTIFIC THEORY(-RIES)
Scientific Theories. SAVAGE, C Wade (ed).
Theories of Science in Society. COZZENS, Susan E (ed).
"Lakatos on the Evaluation of Scientific Theories" in *Imre Lakatos and Theories of Scientific Change*, AVGELIS, Nikolaos.
The Challenge to Lakatos Restated. AKEROYD, F Michael.
Embeddability, Syntax, and Semantics in Accounts of Scientific Theories. TURNEY, Peter.
Metaphysics, Pragmatic Truth and the Underdetermination of Theories. PEREIRA JR, Alfredo and FRENCH, Steven.
On Empirical Interpretation. MUNDY, Brent.
Rejection Without Acceptance. MATHESON, Carl A and KLINE, A David.
Science and Truthlikeness. PANDIT, G L.
Scientific Rationality—A Rethinking. CHAUDHURY, Mahasweta.
The Semantic Approach to Evolutionary Theory. ERESHEFSKY, Marc.
Semantica della "Vorstellung" e valore della teoria in *Erkenntnis und Irrtum* di Ernst Mach. BELLOMO, Andrea.
Some Clarifications and Cautions Essential for Good Philosophy of Science Teaching. DAVSON-GALLE, Peter.
La teoría de la ciencia de Guillermo de Ockham: una imagen prospectiva. LARRE, Olga and BOLZÁN, J E.
Theory and Reality in the Work of Jean Henry Fabre. YAVETZ, Ido.
Uno sguardo sulla filosofia americana contemporanea. CENTRONE, Marino.
Why Scientists Gather Evidence. MAHER, Patrick.

SCIENTISM
After the Demise of the Tradition: Rorty, Critical Theory, and the Fate of Philosophy. NIELSEN, Kai.
Philosophical Foundations of Health Education. LAURA, Ronald S.
"Physics, Life and Mind" in *Science and Religion: One World-Changing Perspectives on Reality*, GIERER, A.
"A Revived Natural Theology" in *Science and Religion: One World-Changing Perspectives on Reality*, POLKINGHORNE, J C.
Cientificidad y Romanticismo: Acerca de las relaciones entre cientismo, gnosticismo y romanticismo. KOSLOWSKI, Peter.
On the Question of Nietzsche's "Scientism". GALLO, Beverly E.
Scientism, Interpretation, and Criticism. GORSKI, Philip S.

SCIENTIST(S)
Animal Experimentation: The Consensus Changes. LANGLEY, Gill (ed).

SCOTTISH
The Scottish Influence on French Aesthetic Thought: Later Developments. MANNS, James W.

SCRIPT(S)
"Wilhelm von Humboldt und das Problem der Schrift" in *Leibniz, Humboldt, and the Origins of Comparativism*, STETTER, Christian.

SCRIPTURE(S)
Chinese Buddhist Apocrypha. BUSWELL JR, Robert E (ed).
Politics Drawn From the Very Words of Holy Scripture—Jacques-Benigne Bossuet. RILEY, Patrick (ed).
"Memory and Scripture in the Conversion of Augustine" in *Grace, Politics and Desire: Essays on Augustine*, COWARD, Harold G.
John Wyclif's Metaphysics of Scriptural Integrity in the *De Veritate Sacrae Scripturae*. TRESKO, Michael.
The Literal Sense of Scripture. WILLIAMS, Rowan.
Sankara on Reason, Scriptural Authority and Self-Knowledge. UPADHYAYA, K N.

SCRIVEN, M
Singular Explanation and the Social Sciences. RUBEN, David-Hillel.

SEARLE, J
"Meanings Just Ain't in the Head" in *Meaning and Method: Essays in Honor of Hilary Putnam*, DEVITT, Michael.
Another Look at the Derrida-Searle Debate. ALFINO, Mark.
Closing the Chinese Room. WEISS, Thomas.
Fear and Loathing (and Other Intentional States) in Searle's Chinese Room. JACQUETTE, Dale.
Linguistic Forms and Social Obligations: A Critique of the Doctrine of Literal Expression in Searle. BOGEN, David.
On Knowing and Naming. BEARDS, Andrew.
Searle on Natural Agency. BISHOP, John.

SEARLE, J
Searle's Oplossing voor het lichaam-geest probleem: ipse dixit—Een reactie op Anne Ruth Mackor. MEIJSING, Monica.
Sobre la semántica de los nombres propios. SCHIRN, Matthias.

SECHEVILLE, J
El averroísmo de Juan de Sècheville. RODRÍGUEZ, Juan Acosta.

SECONDARY QUALITY(-TIES)
Lockes Qualitäten: Erwiderung auf Casati. KIENZLE, Bertram.
Primary and Secondary Qualities: A Reply to Kienzle. CASATI, Roberto.
Qualities and Qualia: What's in the Mind?. SHOEMAKER, Sydney.

SECONDARY SCHOOL(S)
P4C as "Pre-Secondary" Philosophy. DUPUIS, Adrian M and THOMPSON, A Gray.
P4C: A Remedy for Education. MOSTERT, Pieter.

SECRET(S)
The Political Philosophy of Sissela Bok. FAREY, Caroline.

SECULAR
The Devil and Secular Humanism: The Children of the Enlightenment. RADEST, Howard B.
Ethics Without God (Revised Edition). NIELSEN, Kai.
"Secular Humanism and Eupraxophy" in *The Question of Humanism: Challenges and Possibilities*, KURTZ, Paul.
"Faith" in a Broad Sense as a Goal in Promoting Human Development. BECK, Clive.
Da secularidade da Filosofia. COUTINHO, Jorge.
Religious Commitment and Secular Reason: A Reply to Professor Weithman. AUDI, Robert.
The Sacred, Secular, and Profane in Augustine's World of Shadows. SPENCER, Jon Michael.
Silvio Spaventa e Antonio Labriola, gli 'aspetti-pedagogici'. DE CUMIS, Nicola Siciliani.

SECULARISM
"Human Suffering and Our Post-Civilized Cultural Mind: A Maritainian Analysis" in *From Twilight to Dawn: The Cultural Vision of Jacques Maritain*, CALIFANO, Joseph J.

SECULARIZATION
"The Secularization of Philosophy" in *Writing the Politics of Difference*, VATTIMO, Gianni.

SECURITY
"Common Security through Alternative Defense" in *In the Interest of Peace: A Spectrum of Philosophical Views*, HAMPSCH, George.

SEDUCTION
Explaining Without Blaming the Victim. ILLINGWORTH, Patricia M L.

SEEING
L'ordine della certezza: Scientificità e persuasione in Descartes. BONICALZI, Francesca.
Seeing in the Mind's Eye. BORUAH, Bijoy H.
Seeing the Original. BASS, Walter.

SEESKIN, K
Parody and the Argument from Probability in the *Apology*. LEWIS, Thomas J.

SEGAL, R
Theology and the Social Sciences—Discipline and Antidiscipline. MURPHY, Nancey.

SEGERBERG, K
Intentions, Actions, and Routines: A Problem in Krister Segerberg's Theory of Action. ELGESEM, Dag.
A Lemma in the Logic of Action. SURENDONK, Timothy J.

SEGUNDO, J
"The Humanistic Implications of Liberation Theology: Juan Luis Segundo and Karl Marx" in *The Question of Humanism: Challenges and Possibilities*, HEWITT, Marsha A.

SELECTION
The Phenotype as the Level of Selection: Cave organisms as Model Systems. KANE, Thomas C and RICHARDSON, Robert C and FONG, Daniel W.

SELF(-VES)
see also Ego, Personal Identity
The Authentic Self: Toward a Philosophy of Personality. LACENTRA, Walter.
Difference and Subjectivity: Dialogue and Personal Identity. JACQUES, Francis.
Evolution als Höherentwicklung des Bewusstseins. KUMMER, Christian.
Existentialism. COOPER, David E.
Das Ich im deutschen Idealismus und das Selbst im Zen-Buddhist Fichte und Dogen. NAGASAWA, Kunihiko.
The Looking-Glass Self: An Examination of Self-Awareness. CANFIELD, John.
The Many Dimensions of the Human Person. STEGER, E Ecker.
Mind Only: A Philosophical and Doctrinal Analysis of the Vijñānavāda. WOOD, Thomas E.
Mind-Body. MOULYN, Adrian C.
The Power of Consciousness and the Force of Circumstances in Sartre's Philosophy. BUSCH, Thomas W.
Rawls: "A Theory of Justice" and Its Critics. KUKATHAS, Chandran.
The Realizations of the Future: An Inquiry into the Authority of Praxis. ALLAN, George.
Reflexion und Metareflexion bei Platon und Fichte. ZEHNPFENNIG, Barbara.
Selbsttäuschung. LÖW-BEER, Martin.
Self, Society, and Personal Choice. MEYERS, Diana T.
Vulgarity and Authenticity: Dimensions of Otherness in the World of Jean-Paul Sartre. CHARMÉ, Stuart Zane.
Wittgenstein: Meaning and Mind, Volume 3 of an Analytical Commentary on Philosophical Investigations. HACKER, P M S.
"Are Selves Real?" in *Harré and His Critics*, JENSEN, Uffe J.
"Jung and Whitehead on Self and Divine: The Necessity for Symbol and Myth" in *Archetypal Process: Self and Divine in Whitehead, Jung, and Hillman*, SLUSSER, Gerald H.
"Philosophy Becomes Autobiography: The Development of the Self in the Writings of Simone de Beauvoir" in *Writing the Politics of Difference*, PILARDI, Jo-Ann.
"Representation and the Self in Stoicism" in *Psychology (Companions to Ancient Thought: 2)*, LONG, A A.
"The Self and the State" in *The Tanner Lectures On Human Values, Volume XII*, HOWE, Irving.
"The Social Self and the Partiality Debates" in *Feminist Ethics*, FRIEDMAN, Marilyn.
"To Illuminate Your Trace": Self in Late Modern Feminist Theology. KELLER, Catherine.
'Pride Produces the Idea of Self': Hume on Moral Agency. RORTY, Amélie.
Aphasia—The Worm's Eye View of a Philosophic Patient and the Medical Establishment. ALEXANDER, Edwin.
The Chinese Moral Ethos and the Concept of Individual Rights. TAO, Julia.
Les combinaisons de la vie, l'organisation du vivant, le réseau du soi. LIVET, Pierre.
Communitarianism and the Question of Tolerance. PASSERIN D'ENTRÈVES, Maurizio.
The Emerging Tension Between Self and Society, As Exemplified in Augustine. THOMPSON JR, George B.
Fragmented Selves and the Problem of Ownership. BRENNAN, Andrew.
From Brahma to a Blade of Grass. COLLINS, Alfred.
Heidegger on the Self, Authenticity and Inauthenticity. MANSBACH, Abraham.
Henri Bergson and Postmodernism. MULDOON, Mark S.
How Many Selves Make Me?. CLARK, Stephen R L.
How Many Selves Make Me?. WILKES, Kathleen V.
Individual and Social Morality in Japan and the United States: Rival Conceptions of the Self. MAC INTYRE, Alasdair.
The Integral Self: Systematic Illusion or Inescapable Task?. COLAPIETRO, Vincent M.
Le promeneur solitaire: Rousseau and the Emergence of the Post-Social Self. GAUTHIER, David.
Narrative Identity. RICOEUR, Paul.
Nietzsche on Authenticity. GOLOMB, Jacob.
Nursing Responsibility for the Placebo Effect. CONNELLY, Robert J.
A Picture of the Self Which Supports the Moral Responsibility. ANDERSON, Susan Leigh.
The Postmodern Flavor of Blondel's Method. LONG, Fiachra.
Rawls, Sandel and the Self. CANEY, S.
Response to Mendus's "Liberal Man". BINNS, Peter.
Revealing the Truth of Art. BOWIE, Andrew.
Role Taking, Corporeal Intersubjectivity, and Self: Mead and Merleau-Ponty. BOURGEOIS, Patrick L and ROSENTHAL, Sandra B.
Same Human Being, Same Person?. THORNTON, Mark.
The Self and Social Criticism. HARVEY, Charles W.
Self and Suffering: Deconstruction and Reflexive Definition in Buddhism and Christianity. MELLOR, Philip A.
The Self in Confucian Ethics. SHUN, Kwong-Loi.
The Self in Medieval Japanese Buddhism: Focusing on Dōgen. KIMURA, Kiyotaka.
Self-Notions. PERRY, John.
Self-Ownership and the Right of Property. MACK, Eric.
Self-Ownership, Equality, and the Structure of Property Rights. CHRISTMAN, John.
Self-Potential as a Yoruba Ultimate: A Further Contribution to URAM Yoruba Studies. LAWUYI, Olatunde B.
Some Philosophical Directions Towards a Simple Theory of the Self. MANN, David W.
Some Self-Centric Tendencies in Sankara Advaita. JHINGRAN, Saral.
A Thinker's Agency in Thinking. NAMBIAR, Sankaran.
Time, Self and Consciousness: Some Conceptual Patterns in the Context of Indian Thought. BALSLEV, Anindita.
True and False Pleasures. LOVIBOND, Sabina.
Wittgenstein, Strawson y la no-posesión. BARINGOLTZ, Eleonora.
The Word That Became the Absolute: Relevance of Sankara's Ontology of Language. GUPTA, Som Raj.

SELF-ACTUALIZATION
The Authentic Self: Toward a Philosophy of Personality. LACENTRA, Walter.
The Recovery of the Soul: An Aristotelian Essay on Self-fulfilment. RANKIN, Kenneth.

SELF-ASCRIPTION
Conceptual Necessity, Causality and Self-Ascriptions of Sensation. KAUFMAN, Frederik.
Myself. WILLIAMS, C J F.

SELF-AWARENESS
"First-Person Access" in *Philosophical Perspectives, 4: Action Theory and Philosophy of Mind, 1990*, SHOEMAKER, Sydney.
Attitudes Towards the Body: Philosophy and Common Sense. WILLIAMSON, Colwyn.
Conscience de soi et langage intérieur: quelques spéculations. MORIN, Alain and EVERETT, James.

SELF-CONSCIOUSNESS
Die Aufhebung der Begriffs-philosophie. KRONABEL, Christoph.
Fichte's Theory of Subjectivity. NEUHOUSER, Frederick.
How to Build a Person: A Prolegomenon. POLLOCK, John L.
The Looking-Glass Self: An Examination of Self-Awareness. CANFIELD, John.
"The Development of Self-Consciousness: Baldwin, Mead, and Vygotsky" in *Reconsidering Psychology: Perspectives from Continental Philosophy*, MARKOVA, Ivana.
Der Begriff des Selbstbewusstseins bei Kant. GLOY, Karen.
Etwas ist in mir da—Zu Ulrich Posthast: Philosophisches Buch. WOLF, Ursula.
Glasnost and Enlightenment. OLSON, Alan M.
Human Nature Technologically Revisited. ENGELHARDT JR, H Tristram.
Kant in Hegels begtipsleer. DE VOS, L.
Die Rolle des unglücklichen Bewusstseins in Hegels *Phänomenologie des Geistes*. STEWARD, Jon.

SELF-CONTROL
Fingarette on the Disease Concept of Alcoholism. CORLETT, J Angelo.

SELF-CRITICISM
Wo lag der Fehler der kategorialen Repräsentation? Zu Sinn und Reichweite einer Selbstkritik Husserls. LOHMAR, Dieter.

SELF-DECEPTION
Belief, Contradiction, and the Logic of Self-Deception. DA COSTA, Newton C A and FRENCH, Steven.
Freud Contra Sartre: Repression or Self-Deception?. MIRVISH, Adrian.
Hidden Agendas. FRIEDMAN, Robert.
The Rationality of Escapism and Self Deception. LONGEWAY, John L.

SELF-DEFENSE
Understanding War: A Philosophical Inquiry. MC MURTRY, John.
"Punishment and Self-Defense" in *Liability and Responsibility*, FLETCHER, George P.
Self-Defence and National Defence. DE ROOSE, Frank.

SELF-DETERMINATION
Fichte's Theory of Subjectivity. NEUHOUSER, Frederick.
Ethics Committees. COHEN, Cynthia B (ed).
Hegel's Legend of Self-Determination. KAMAL, Muhammad.
The Patient Self-Determination Act. MC CLOSKEY, Elizabeth Leibold.
The Right to Self-Determination. BERG, Jonathan.

SELF-DEVELOPMENT
On the Concept of Freedom in the *I Ching*: A Deconstructionist View of Self-Cultivation. SCHULZ, Larry J and CUNNINGHAM, Thomas J.
To Catch a Thief: Chu Hsi (1130-1200) and the Hermeneutic Art. BERTHRONG, John.

SELF-ESTEEM
The Community of Inquiry and the Development of Self-Esteem. LAGO, Juan Carlos.
Some More Ideas About the Relation Between Philosophy for Children and Self-Esteem. GAZZARD, Ann.

SELF-IDENTITY
New Harvest: Transplanting Body Parts and Reaping the Benefits. KEYES, C Don (ed).
Philosophy of the "Gita". PATEL, Ramesh N.
Impersonal Friends. WHITING, Jennifer E.

SELF-IMAGE
Attitudes Towards the Body: Philosophy and Common Sense. WILLIAMSON, Colwyn.

SELF-INSTRUCTION
Critics and Historical Continuity. CARTER, John.

SELF-INTEREST(S)
An Audience for Moral Philosophy?. EDELMAN, John T.
Ethics, Politics, and Human Nature. PAUL, Ellen Frankel (ed).
Aggregation of Preferences: The Fuzzy Case. BILLOT, Antoine.
Beyond Self-Interest and Altruism: A Reconstruction of Adam Smith's Theory of Human Conduct. KHALIL, Elias L.
The Ethical Roots of Business. VOGEL, David.
Self-Interest and the New Bashing of Economics. KIRZNER, Israel M.
Sidgwick and Self-Interest. CRISP, Roger.
The Varieties of Self-Interest. EPSTEIN, Richard A.

SELF-KNOWLEDGE
Epistemic Justification: Essays in the Theory of Knowledge. ALSTON, William P.
Human Goodness: Generosity and Courage. PYBUS, Elizabeth.
An Outline of the Philosophy of Knowledge and Science. BLANDINO, Giovanni.
El autoconocimiento del alma según Avicena latino. OYARZABAL, Manuel.
Choiceless Awareness. SEN, Sanat Kumar.
L'identité personnelle et la source des concepts. SHALOM, Albert.
Sankara on Reason, Scriptural Authority and Self-Knowledge. UPADHYAYA, K N.
Seeing Our Seeing and Knowing Our Knowing. BEN-ZEEV, Aaron.
Self-Synthesis, Self-Knowledge, and Skepticism. MAZOUÉ, James G.
Socrates in Dallas: Managing the Facilities. CASTRO, Barry.
Soggettività e autocoscienza: Prospettive e problemi in Dieter Henrich. CELANO, Bruno.
La teoria hegeliana dell'autocoscienza e della sua razionalità. VARNIER, Giuseppe.

SELF-LOVE
The Paradox of Aquinas's Altruism: From Self-Love to Love of Others. HAYDEN, R Mary.
Pride, Hypocrisy and Civility in Mandeville's Social and Historical Theory. DICKEY, Laurence.

SELF-MANAGEMENT
Self-Management in the Context of the Disintegration of "Reali-Existing" Socialism. STANOJEVIC, Miroslav.

SELF-PREDICATION
Does Wittgenstein's Concept of Language Game Patterns Come Up with a Solution to the Platonic Problem ... (in German). LÜTTERFELDS, Wilhelm.
The Recurring Problem of the Third Man. HALES, Steven D.
Self-Predication and Synonymy. SILVERMAN, Allan.
Two Kinds of Naming in the *Sophist*. STOUGH, Charlotte.

SELF-REALIZATION
"The Philosophy of Work and the Future of Civilization: Maritain, Weil and Simon" in *From Twilight to Dawn: The Cultural Vision of Jacques Maritain*, DOERING, Bernard.
The Value-Ought of Self-Realization: A Phenomenological Approach. VELASSERRY, Sebastian.

SELF-REFERENCE
Irony and the Discourse of Modernity. BEHLER, Ernst.
Wittgenstein: Meaning and Mind, Volume 3 of an Analytical Commentary on Philosophical Investigations. HACKER, P M S.
Definability in Self-Referential Systems. SOBRINHO, J Zimbarg.
Dicendum est eum non esse hominem: Ein mögliches frühes Zeugnis für die anthropologische Gewichtung.... KÖHLER, Theodor Wolfram.
Doxastic Paradoxes Without Self-Reference. KOONS, Robert Charles.
Intensional Paradoxes. PRIEST, Graham.
Myself. WILLIAMS, C J F.
On Metainductive Sentences. TRIVEDI, Saam.
Vom Sein zur Selbstreferentialität: Überlegungen zur Theorie autopoietischer Systeme Niklas Luhmanns. GRIPP-HAGELSTANGE, Helga.

SELF-REFUTATION
Where Does the Self-Refutation Objection Take Us?. RAMSEY, William.

SELF-RESPECT
Self, Society, and Personal Choice. MEYERS, Diana T.
"Kant and Fichte: An Ethics of Self-Respect in Individualism" in *Abeunt Studia in Mores: A Festschrift for Helga Doblin*, ECKBLAD, Joyce.

SELF-SACRIFICE
Suicide: Right or Wrong?. DONNELLY, John (ed).

SELF-TRANSCENDENCE
Experiential Method: Qualitative Research in the Humanities Using Metaphysics and Phenomenology. KIDD, James W.

SELF-VERIFICATION
Intorno all'autofondazione delle norme: Ragione formale e principio razionale tra logica e diritto. SCIACCA, Fabrizio.

SELFHOOD
How to Build a Conscious Machine. ANGEL, Leonard.
Substance and Selfhood. LOWE, E J.

SELLARS, W
Properties as Processes: A Synoptic Study of Wilfried Sellars' Nominalism. SEIBT, Johanna.
Sellar's Two Images of the World. AUNE, Bruce.
A Sellarsian Hume?. LIVINGSTON, Donald.

SEMANTICS
see also Linguistics, Meaning
Alltagssprachliche Metakommunikation im Englischen und Deutschen. WELTE, Werner.

SEMANTICS

Causality in Sociological Research. KARPINSKI, Jakub.
Events in the Semantics of English: A Study in Subatomic Semantics. PARSONS, Terence.
Has Semantics Rested on a Mistake?. WETTSTEIN, Howard.
Information, Semantics and Epistemology. VILLANUEVA, Enrique (ed).
Intentions in Communication. COHEN, Philip R (ed).
Kalkulierte Absurditäten. STRUB, Christian.
Meaning and Mental Representation. CUMMINS, Robert.
Meaning and Speech Acts: Volume I, Principles of Language Use. VANDERVEKEN, Daniel.
Meaning and Speech Acts: Volume II, Formal Semantics of Success and Satisfaction. VANDERVEKEN, Daniel.
Meaning and Truth: The Essential Readings in Modern Semantics. GARFIELD, Jay L (ed).
The Metaphysics of the "Tractatus". CARRUTHERS, Peter.
Mimesis as Make-Believe: On the Foundations of the Representational Arts. WALTON, Kendall L.
Properties as Processes: A Synoptic Study of Wilfried Sellars' Nominalism. SEIBT, Johanna.
Saggio di semantica. BRÉAL, Michel.
Semantic Structures. JACKENDOFF, Ray.
Sensations: A Defense of Type Materialism. HILL, Christopher S.
Studies on Mario Bunge's "Treatise". WEINGARTNER, Paul (ed).
Themes From Kaplan. ALMOG, Joseph (ed).
Truth and Interpretation: Perspectives on the Philosophy of Donald Davidson. LE PORE, Ernest (ed).
"Afterthoughts" in *Themes From Kaplan*, KAPLAN, David.
"Biosemantics and the Normative Properties of Thought" in *Philosophical Perspectives, 3: Philosophy of Mind and Action Theory, 1989*, FORBES, Graeme.
"Cognitive Access and Semantic Puzzle" in *Propositional Attitudes: The Role of Content in Logic, Language, and Mind*, OWENS, Joseph I.
"Cognitive Significance Without Cognitive Content" in *Themes From Kaplan*, WETTSTEIN, Howard.
"Content and Norms in a Natural World" in *Information, Semantics and Epistemology*, PEACOCKE, Christopher.
"Davidson's Semantics and Computational Understanding of Language" in *The Mind of Donald Davidson*, BOJADZIEV, Damjan.
"Direct Reference, the Semantics of Thinking, and Guise Theory" in *Themes From Kaplan*, CASTAÑEDA, Héctor-Neri.
"Informational Independence as a Semantical Phenomenon" in *Logic, Methodology and Philosophy of Science, VIII*, HINTIKKA, Jaakko and SANDU, Gabriel.
"Inheritance Theory and Path-Based Reasoning: An Introduction" in *Knowledge Representation and Defeasible Reasoning*, CARPENTER, Bob and THOMASON, Richmond.
"Learnability of Semantic Theory" in *Truth and Interpretation: Perspectives on the Philosophy of Donald Davidson*, MATTHEWS, Robert J.
"Linguistic Theory and Davidson's Program in Semantics" in *Truth and Interpretation: Perspectives on the Philosophy of Donald Davidson*, HIGGINBOTHAM, James.
"Mario Bunge on Semantics" in *Studies on Mario Bunge's "Treatise"*, BUNGE, Mario.
"Mario Bunge's Realist Semantics: An Antidote against Incommensurability?" in *Studies on Mario Bunge's "Treatise"*, BARTELS, Andreas.
"The Necessity for Cooperation between Philosophical and Empirical Research" in *The Moral Domain: Essays in the Ongoing Discussion between Philosophy and the Social Sciences*, TUGENDHAT, Ernst.
"On Mario Bunge's Semantical Realism" in *Studies on Mario Bunge's "Treatise"*, FERRATER-MORA, José.
"Semantic Innocence and Psychological Understanding" in *Philosophical Perspectives, 3: Philosophy of Mind and Action Theory, 1989*, HORNSBY, Jennifer.
"Semantics and Methodological Solipsism" in *Truth and Interpretation: Perspectives on the Philosophy of Donald Davidson*, LYCAN, William G.
"Semantics and Semantic Competence" in *Philosophical Perspectives, 3: Philosophy of Mind and Action Theory, 1989*, SOAMES, Scott.
"A Study in Comparative Semantics" in *Propositional Attitudes: The Role of Content in Logic, Language, and Mind*, LE PORE, Ernest and LOEWER, Barry.
"Tense and Singular Propositions" in *Themes From Kaplan*, SALMON, Nathan.
"What a Truth Theory Need Not Tell Us" in *Truth and Interpretation: Perspectives on the Philosophy of Donald Davidson*, GRANDY, Richard E.
"As Real As It Gets...": Ricoeur and Narrativity. KELLNER, Hans.
Aberrations of a Sledgehammer: Reply to Devitt. LUNTLEY, Michael.
Aberrations of the Realism Debate. DEVITT, Michael.
Actualism, Ontological Commitment, and Possible World Semantics. MENZEL, Ch.
Algebraization of Paraconsistent Logic P^1. LEWIN, R A and MIKENBERG, I F and SCHWARZE, M G.
An Almost General Splitting Theorem for Modal Logic. KRACHT, Marcus.
Author, Writer, Text: *The Will to Power*. MAGNUS, Bernd.
B-Varieties with Normal Free Algebras. TEMBROWSKI, Bronislaw.
A Case for a Heretical Deontic Semantics. EDELBERG, Walter.
The Causal Efficacy of Content. SEGAL, Gabriel and SOBER, Elliott.
A Complete Deductive-System for Since-Until Branching-Time Logic. ZANARDO, Alberto.
Complexly Fractionated Syllogistic Quantifiers. PETERSON, Philip L.
Concerted Instant-Interval Temporal Semantics I: Temporal Ontologies. BOCHMAN, Alexander.
Concerted Instant-Interval Temporal Semantics II: Temporal Valuations and Logics of Change. BOCHMAN, Alexander.
Conditionals and Monotonic Belief Revisions: the Success Postulate. ARLO COSTA, Horacio L.
Constructive Modal Logics I. WIJESEKERA, Duminda.
A Constructivism Based on Classical Truth. MIGLIOLI, P (and others).
Davidson's Paratactic Analysis of Mood. MILLER, Seumas.
Definite Descriptions and Definite Generics. OJEDA, Almerindo E.
Deontic Logic and Possible World Semantics: A Historical Sketch. WOLENSKI, Jan.
A Dilemma for Sentential Dualism. MOSER, Paul K.
Disjoint Reference into NP. SELLS, Peter.
Dynamic Predicate Logic. GROENENDIJK, Jeroen and STOKHOF, Martin.
Embeddability, Syntax, and Semantics in Accounts of Scientific Theories. TURNEY, Peter.
A essência da técnica segundo Heidegger. RENAUD, Michel.
Even and *Even If*. LYCAN, William G.
Every World Can See a Reflexive World. HUGHES, G E.
Extending Montague's System: A Three Valued Intensional Logic. ALVES, E H and GUERZONI, J A D.
An Extension of Ono's Completeness Result. SUZUKI, Nobu-Yuki.
Física y Semántica en la filosofía de Quine. FUSTEGUERAS, Aurelio P.
Frege-Russell Semantics?. WETTSTEIN, Howard.
From Russell to Quine: Basic Statements, Foundationalism, Truth, and Other Myths. LINDBERG, Jordan J.
General Canonical Models for Graded Normal Logics (Graded Modalities IV). CERRATO, C.
A General Possible Worlds Framework for Reasoning about Knowledge and Belief. WANSING, Heinrich.
A Generalization of the Adequacy Theorem for the Quasi-Senses. BONOTTO, Cinzia.
A Generalized Quantifier Logic for Naked Infinitives. VAN DER DOES, Jaap.
Grammar, Semantics and Conditionals. DUDMAN, V H.
How Ideas Became Meanings: Locke and the Foundations of Semantic Theory. HANNA, Robert.
Husserl's Philosophy of Science and the Semantic Approach. MORMANN, Thomas.
Indefinite Descriptions: In Defense of Russell. LUDLOW, Peter and NEALE, Stephen.
Indeterminate Identity, Contingent Identity and Abelardian Predicates. NOONAN, Harold W.
Indexicality: The Transparent Subjective Mechanism for Encountering a World. CASTAÑEDA, Héctor-Neri.
The Indispensability of *Sinn*. FORBES, Graeme.
Infinitary Combinatorics and Modal Logic. BLASS, A.
Intensionality and Boundedness. MORRILL, Glyn.
Intermediate Predicate Logics Determined by Ordinals. MINARI, Pierluigi and TAKANO, Mitio and ONO, Hiroakira.
L'interpretazione costruttiva dell'implicazione. MORICONI, Enrico.
Intuitionistic Sentential Calculus with Identity. LUKOWSKI, Piotr.
Intuitive Semantics for Some Three-Valued Logics Connected with Information, Contrariety and Subcontrariety. VAKARELOV, Dimitir.
Kant and Conceptual Semantics: A Sketch. POSY, Carl J.
Kant's Theory of Empirical Judgment and Modern Semantics. HANNA, Robert.
Kantian and Non-Kantian Logics. PUGA, Leila Z and DA COSTA, Newton C A and CARNIELLI, Walter A.
Knowing through the Body. JOHNSON, Mark.
Kripke Semantics for Knowledge Representation Logics. ORLOWSKA, Ewa.
L'Assertion dans les contextes épistémiques; garants objectaux et bases d'évaluation. MOULOUD, Noël.
The Language of Thought: No Syntax Without Semantics. CRANE, Tim.
A Lemma in the Logic of Action. SURENDONK, Timothy J.
Il linguaggio ideologico della rivoluzione. MATHIEU, Vittorio.
Logical Constants and the Glory of Truth-Conditional Semantics. LYCAN, William G.
Logical Form and Radical Interpretation. MC CARTHY, Tim.
Lukasiewicz Logic and Wajsberg Algebras. RODRIGUEZ, Antonio J and TORRENS, Antoni.
Making Sense of Words. MC CULLOCH, Gregory.
Mechanical Proof Procedures for Many-Valued Lattice-Based Logic Programming. SUBRAHMANIAN, V S.
Meinongian Theories of Generality. SANTAMBROGIO, Marco.
Metaphysical Realism and Psychologistic Semantics. HORGAN, Terence.
Models for Relevant Modal Logics. FUHRMANN, André.
The Myth of the Essential Indexical. MILLIKAN, Ruth.

SEMANTICS
The Need for Charity in Semantics. WARMBRŌD, Ken.
New Semantics for the Extensional but Hyper-Intensional Part..... BRESSAN, Aldo.
On Husserl's Theory of the Constitution of Objectiving Meaning (in Czechoslovakian). ZATKA, V.
On Naturalizing the Semantics of Mental Representation. SILVERS, Stuart.
On Negation. KOKTOVÁ, Eva.
On Respecting Puzzles About Belief Ascription (A Reply to Devitt). LYCAN, William G.
On Saying That Again. HAND, Michael.
On the Aim of Scientific Theories in Relating to the World: A Defence of the Semantic Account. BAUR, Michael.
On the Development of Paraconsistent Logic and Da Costa's Work. LOFFREDO D'OTTAVIANO, Itala M.
On the Methodology of Possible World Semantics, I: Correspondence Theory. PEARCE, David and WANSING, Heinrich.
On the Purported Pragmatico-Semantic Foundation of Linguistics and AI Through Wittgenstein's Late Philosophy. LEINFELLNER-RUPERTSBERGER, Elisabeth.
Opacidad y presuposición. ARANOVICH, Raúl.
Physicalism and Intentional Attitudes. MOSER, Paul K.
A Pragmatic Analysis of Tautological Utterances. WARD, Gregory L and HIRSCHBERG, Julia.
The Pragmatic Fallacy. SALMON, Nathan.
Pragmatics and Pragmatism. SULLIVAN, Patrick F.
The Progressive and the Imperfective Paradox. LASCARIDES, Alex.
Pronouns and Propositional Attitudes. SOAMES, Scott.
The Real Difficulty with Burley's Realistic Semantics. FITZGERALD, Michael J.
Realism Without Representation: A Response to Appiah. DEVITT, Michael.
Reductive and Nonreductive Simile Theories of Metaphor. TIRRELL, Lynne.
Reference and Pronominal Descriptions. WILSON, George M.
Related Semantics for All Lewis, Lemmon and Feys' Modal Logics. SYLVAN, Richard.
Relevant Containment Logics and Certain Frame Problems of AI. SYLVAN, Richard.
Représentation philosophique par réseau sémantique variable. BOSS, Gilbert and LONGEART, Maryvonne.
Representations and Realism. APPIAH, Anthony.
Routley-Meyer Type Semantics for Urquhart's C. MÉNDEZ, José M.
The Semantic Approach to Evolutionary Theory. ERESHEFSKY, Marc.
Semantic Holism is Seriously False. MASSEY, Gerald J.
Semantic Holism. BELNAP JR, Nuel D and MASSEY, Gerald J.
Semantica aristotelica e sillogistica modale. MARIANI, Mauro.
Semantics and Supervenience. BONEVAC, Daniel.
Semantics without Reference. GAUKER, Christopher.
Sobre la semántica de los nombres propios. SCHIRN, Matthias.
Some Descending Chains of Incomplete Model Logics. XU, Ming.
Staving Off Catastrophe: A Critical Notice of Jerry Fodor's *Psychosemantics*. JONES, Todd and MULAIRE, Edmond and STICH, Stephen.
Structural Representation and Surrogative Reasoning. SWOYER, Chris.
Teorías de verdad y teorías del significado. VARGAS, Celso.
Thoughts on the Taxonomy and Semantics of Value Terms. MARIETTA JR, Don E.
Topos Based Semantics for Constructive Logic with Strong Negation. KLUNDER, Barbara.
Toward a Formalization of Dialectical Logic. THOMASON, Steven K.
Truth and Understanding. HIGGINBOTHAM, James.
The Two Barbaras. THOM, Paul.
Two Kinds of Agent-Relativity. HUMBERSTONE, I L.
Variations on da Costa *C* Systems and Dual-Intuitionistic Logics (I). SYLVAN, Richard.
Visual Perception and the Wages of Indeterminacy. MONTGOMERY, Richard.
Vom "Wahr-Lachen" der Moderne: Karl Valentins Semantik paradoxer Lebenswelten. GÖNNER, Gerhard.
Wittgenstein and "Mad Pain". KELLY, Michael Lee.
The Word as Will and Idea: Semantics in the *Tractatus*. COHEN, Daniel H.
Wovor und wodurch sind wir verantworlich? Die Instanzen der Verantwortung. MAIER, Maria.

SEMIOLOGY
Saussure: Signs, System, and Arbitrariness. HOLDCROFT, David.
"Le signe en défaut". ROBIN, Régine.
Le corps et ses langages: quelques perspectives de travail historique. COURTINE, Jean-Jacques.
Glenn Gould: "archilecteur" *des Variations Goldberg*. GUERTIN, Ghyslaine.
Les objets de la sémiologie théâtrale: le texte et le spectacle. VIGEANT, Louise.
Sémiologie visuelle, peinture et intertextualité. PAQUET, Bernard.

SEMIOTICS
see also Sign(s)
Artificial Intelligence: Its Scope and Limits. FETZER, James H.
French Philosophers in Conversation: Levinas, Schneider, Serres, Irigaray, Le Doeuff, Derrida. MORTLEY, Raoul.
Kommunikations-Theoretische Schriften II: Symbolische Erkenntnis und Kommunikation. UNGEHEUER, Gerold (ed).
L'objet-peinture: Pour une théorie de la réception. PAQUIN, Nycole.
Language and "The Feminine" in Nietzsche and Heidegger. GRAYBEAL, Jean.
Musical Aesthetics: A Historical Reader, Volume III, The Twentieth Century. LIPPMAN, Edward A (ed).
The Potential of Modern Discourse: Musil, Peirce, and Perturbation. FINLAY, Marike.
Spuren der Macht. RÖTTGERS, Kurt.
"Beyond Signifiers" in *Writing the Politics of Difference*, DILLON, Martin C.
Analyse critique de quelques modèles sémiotiques de l'idéologie (deuxième partie). TREMBLAY, Robert.
Comme en un miroir: quelques remarques historiques sur l'arbitraire du signe. LATRAVERSE, François.
L'epoché di Husserl in Ferruccio Rossi-Landi. PONZIO, Augusto.
Il y a vingt-cinq ans la sémiotique.... KHOURI, Nadia.
The Joy of Transgression: Bataille and Kristeva. MARCHAK, Catherine.
L'écriture réparatrice. HAREL, Simon.
L'explicite et l'implicite dans la conception du signe chez Hobbes. POLIAKOV, Igor.
On Scholarly Developments in Legal Semiotics. JACKSON, Bernard S.
Rethinking the Dialectic: A Social Semiotic Perspective for Educators. HAMMER, Rhonda and MC LAREN, Peter.
A Semiotical Reflection on Biology, Living Signs and Artificial Life. EMMECHE, Claus.
Sémiotique des "genres": Une théorie de la réception. PAQUIN, Nycole.
La sémiotique, les objets singuliers et la complexité. THÉRIEN, Gilles.
Le statut sémiotique de la perspective dans l'oeuvre picturale. CARANI, Marie.
Sulla semiotizzazione dell' "a priori": Rossi-Landi e Hjelmslev. CAPUTO, Cosimo.
Le tournant cognitif en sémiotique. MEUNIER, Jean-Guy.
Vers une mise en signe de l'installation. RÉGIMBALD, Manon.

SEMLER, J
Modern Faith and Thought. THIELICKE, Helmut.

SEN, A
"The Flaws in Sen's Case Against Paretian Libertarianism" in *Acting and Reflecting: The Interdisciplinary Turn in Philosophy*, PRESSLER, Jonathan.

SENSATION(S)
see also Emotion(s), Feeling(s), Perception
Central Themes in Early Modern Philosophy. COVER, J A (ed).
Colour: A Philosophical Introduction (Second Edition). WESTPHAL, Jonathan.
Reasons and Experience. MILLAR, Alan.
Sensations: A Defense of Type Materialism. HILL, Christopher S.
"Descartes on the Representationality of Sensation" in *Central Themes in Early Modern Philosophy*, WILSON, Margaret D.
A proposito dell'interesse di Dilthey per l'antropologia cinquecentesca. ORSUCCI, Andrea.
Art and Neurology: A Discussion. HALPIN, David M G and SORRELL, Martin.
Conceptual Necessity, Causality and Self-Ascriptions of Sensation. KAUFMAN, Frederik.
Could Someone Else Have Had My Headache?. STONE, Jim.
Descartes on Sensations and 'Animal Minds'. SENCERZ, Stefan.
Disembodying 'Bodily' Sensations. COMBES, Richard.
Just Can't Find the Words: How Expression is Achieved. KING, Debra W.
On Excluding Something from Our Gathering: The Lack of Moral Standing of Non-Sentient Entities. LANDMAN, Willem A.
The Representational Content of Musical Experience. DE BELLIS, Mark.
Seeing in the Mind's Eye. BORUAH, Bijoy H.
Sensations and Judgments of Perception: Diagnosis and Rehabilitation of Some of Kant's Misleading Examples. KOTZIN, Rhoda and BAUMGÄRTNER, Järg.

SENSE DATA
Der sinnliche Gehalt der Wahrnehmung. SCHANTZ, Richard.
Die erkenntniskritische Wendung Descartes' als Konsequenz geschichtlicher Entwicklung des Leib-Seele-Dualismus. POHLENZ, G.
Why the Problem of the External World is a Pseudo-Problem: Santayana and Danto. SHIRLEY, Edward S.

SENSE IMPRESSION(S)
Cool Red. LEVINE, Joseph.
Reply to Levine's "Cool Red". HARDIN, C L.
Shadows on the Cave Wall: Philosophy and Visual Science. WILSON, Hugh R.

SENSE(S)
Has Semantics Rested on a Mistake?. WETTSTEIN, Howard.
"Frege on Sense and Linguistic Meaning" in *The Analytic Tradition: Philosophical Quarterly Monographs, Volume 1*, BURGE, Tyler.

SENSE(S)
Constituição do sentido e justificação da validade: Heidegger e o problema da filosofia transcendental. APEL, Karl-Otto.
A Generalization of the Adequacy Theorem for the Quasi-Senses. BONOTTO, Cinzia.
A lógica do sentido na filosofia hermenêutica. COSTA, Miguel Dias.
Making Sense of Words. MC CULLOCH, Gregory.
New Semantics for the Extensional but Hyper-Intensional Part..... BRESSAN, Aldo.
Plato and the Senses of Words. BLACKSON, Thomas A.
Reflexiones en torno a la sensibilidad externa. ALVAREZ-CASTELLANOS, Juan José Sánchez.
Sense, Passions and Morals in Hume and Kant. NUYEN, A T.
Sense-Experience and the Argument for Recollection in Plato's *Phaedo*. BEDU-ADDO, J T.
El ser y el sentido: Notas husserlianas. PEGUEROLES, Juan.
Some Thoughts on Common Scents. ALMAGOR, Uri.
The Concept of Sense in Merleau-Ponty (in Czechoslovakian). SIVAK, Jozef.
Why 'Art' Doesn't Have Two Senses. ROWE, M W.
'I Heard a Plaintive Melody'. HANFLING, Oswald.

SENSIBILITY
Kant's Transcendental Psychology. KITCHER, Patricia.
Le Philosophie et les Passions. MEYER, Michel.
An Argument for Utilitarianism: A Defence. NG, Yew-Kwang and SINGER, Peter.

SENSIBLES
La teoría de las cualidades sensibles en la *Summula Philosophiae Naturalis* atribuida a Guillermo de Ockham. LARRE, Olga L.

SENSUALITY
Giuseppe De Luca e la polemica sulla moralità di Péguy. FIORENTINO, Fernando.

SENTENCE(S)
see also Proposition(s)
Comentario a las "Sentencias" de Isidoro de Sevilla. ORTEGA MUÑOZ, Juan F.
Formatives. ENGLEBRETSEN, George.
Logical Constants and the Glory of Truth-Conditional Semantics. LYCAN, William G.
Universal Sentences: Russell, Wittgenstein, Prior, and the Nyāya. SHAW, J L.

SENTIENCE
From Sentience To Symbols. PICKERING, John (ed).
Machines as Persons?. CHERRY, Christopher.
On Excluding Something from Our Gathering: The Lack of Moral Standing of Non-Sentient Entities. LANDMAN, Willem A.
On Utilitarianism and Utilitarian Attitudes. MILLER, Harlan B.
Souls and Sentientism. RYDER, Richard D.

SENTIMENT(S)
A Progress of Sentiments: Reflections on Hume's "Treatise". BAIER, Annette C.
Du fondement de la loi morale, une éthique de la raison ou du sentiment?. DAVAL, R.
Human Nature Technologically Revisited. ENGELHARDT JR, H Tristram.
Le lezioni di Husserl sull'etica e sulla teoria del valore. DONNICI, Rocco.
Natural Virtues, Natural Vices. BAIER, Annette C.

SENTIMENTALISM
Morals, Motivation and Convention: Hume's Influential Doctrines. SNARE, Francis.
In Defense of Sentimentality. SOLOMON, Robert C.

SEPARATION
Alexander Hamilton: The Separation of Powers. PRATT, Ronald L.
Causal Independence in EPR Arguments. BUTTERFIELD, Jeremy.
Establishing of the Object of Metaphysics—Separation (in Polish). MARYNIARCZYK, A.

SEQUENCE(S)
About Prikry Generic Extensions. SURESON, Claude.
Recursive Surreal Numbers. HARKLEROAD, Leon.
Sequencing Rules and Coherence in Discourse. TSUI, Amy B M.
Some Extensions of Built-Upness on Systems of Fundamental Sequences. KADOTA, Noriya.
A Theory of Probability. REEVES, T V.
Weak Cylindric Set Algebras and Weak Subdirect Indecomposability. ANDRÉKA, H and NÉMETI, I and THOMPSON, R J.

SEQUENT CALCULUS
The Undecidability of k-Provability. BUSS, Samuel R.

SEQUENZ CALCULUS
Classification of Intermediate Predicate Logics Under the Type of Deductive Completeness. TAKANO, Mitio and YAMAKAMI, Tomoyuki.
Paraconsistency and the J-Systems of Arruda and da Costa. URBAS, Igor.
Relevance and Paraconsistency—A New Approach, Part III: Cut-Free Gentzen-Type Systems. AVRON, Arnon.
The t-Variable Method in Gentzen-Style Automatic Theorem Proving. EDWALD, Tryggvi.
Tait-Systems for Fragments of *Lm*. COLUMBUS, Joachim.
Uniform Proofs as a Foundation for Logic Programming. MILLER, Dale and NADATHUR, Gopalan and PFENNING, Frank and SCEDROV, Andre.

SERIES
Rationality of p-Adic Poincaré Series: Uniformity in p. MACINTYRE, Angus.

SERRES, M
French Philosophers in Conversation: Levinas, Schneider, Serres, Irigaray, Le Doeuff, Derrida. MORTLEY, Raoul.

SET THEORY
Logic, Methodology and Philosophy of Science, VII. MARCUS, Ruth Barcan (ed).
Parts of Classes. LEWIS, David.
The Borel Conjecture. JUDAH, Haim and SHELAH, Saharon and WOODIN, W H.
Double Extension Set Theory. KISIELEWICZ, Andrzej.
The Dual Cantor-Bernstein Theorem and the Partition Principle. BANASCHEWSKI, Bernhard and MOORE, Gregory H.
An Equivalent of the Axiom of Choice in Finite Models of the Powerset Axiom. ABIAN, Alexander and AMIN, Wael A.
Equivalent Versions of a Weak Form of the Axiom of Choice. SHANNON, G.
An Extension of Borel Determinacy. MARTIN, Donald A.
Iteration Again. BOOLOS, George.
The Kunen-Miller Chart (Lebesgue Measure, the Baire Property, Laver Reals and Preservation Theorems for Forcing). JUDAH, Haim and SHELAH, Saharon.
Mathematics Without Truth (A Reply to Maddy). FIELD, Hartry.
More Axioms for the Set-Theoretic Hierarchy. POLLARD, Stephen.
Multiset Theory. BLIZARD, Wayne D.
Negative Membership. BLIZARD, Wayne D.
On Omniscience and a 'Set of All Truths': A Reply to Bringsjord. GRIM, Patrick.
On the Lengths of Proofs of Set Theoretical Statements in Zermelo-Fraenkel Set Theory and Kelley-Morse Theory.... CORRADA, Manuel.
A Problem in the Foundations of Set Theory. MADDY, Penelope.
Provable Forms of Martin's Axiom. SHANNON, Gary P.
Shelah's pcf Theory and Its Applications. BURKE, Maxim R and MAGIDOR, Menachem.
Small Sets. HAZEN, A P.
Some Results on Higher Suslin Trees. DAVID, R.
The Strength of the Failure of the Singular Cardinal Hypothesis. GITIK, Moti.
A Strengthening of Scott's ZF-Minus-Extensionality Result. POLLARD, Stephen.
Successors of Singular Cardinals and Measurability Revisited. APTER, Arthur W.
Systems of Combinatory Logic Related to Quine's 'New Foundations'. HOLMES, M R.
Towards a Modal-Structural Interpretation of Set Theory. HELLMAN, Geoffrey.
The Union Axiom in Zermelo Set Theory. GONZÁLEZ, Carlos G.
Upward Directedness of the Rudin-Keisler Ordering of P-Points. LAFLAMME, Claude.
The Uses and Abuses of the History of Topos Theory. MC LARTY, Colin.
Weak Axioms of Determinacy and Subsystems of Analysis II. TANAKA, Kazuyuki.

SET(S)
see also Class(es)
"Free Sets for Commutative Families of Functions" in *Logic, Methodology and Philosophy of Science, VIII*, ABRAHAM, Uri.
"Sets Are Universals" in *Physicalism in Mathematics*, BIGELOW, John.
Absolutely Independent Sets of Generation of Filters in Boolean Algebras. GRYGIEL, Joanna.
Almost Hugeness and a Related Notion. BARBANEL, Julius.
Bolzano's Contribution to Cognition and/or the Creation of Theory of Sets (in Czechoslovakian). VECERKA, Kazimir.
Boolean Algebras and Orbits of the Lattice of R.E. Sets Modulo the Finite Sets. CHOLAK, Peter.
The Cardinality of Powersets in Finite Models of the Powerset Axiom. ABIAN, Alexander and AMIN, Wael A.
Finite Support Iteration and Strong Measure Zero Sets. PAWLIKOWSKI, Janusz.
Hereditarily Finite Finsler Sets. BOOTH, David.
Iteration Again. BOOLOS, George.
A Metatheorem for Constructions by Finitely Many Workers. KNIGHT, J F.
Minimal Degrees Recursive in 1-Generic Degrees. CHONG, C T and DOWNEY, R G.
Nonstandard Arithmetic of Hilbert Subsets. YASUMOTO, Masahiro.
On Restricted Forms of Enumeration Reducibility. WATSON, Phil.
On the Existence of Large p-Ideals. JUST, Winfried (and others).
On the Quasi-Ordering of Borel Linear Orders Under Embeddability. LOUVEAU, Alain and SAINT-RAYMOND, Jean.
Projective Subsets of Separable Metric Spaces. MILLER, Arnold W.

SET(S)
Propositional Functions and Families of Types. SMITH, Jan M.
A Question About Semilattices. WOLNIEWICZ, Boguslaw.
Ramsey Ultrafilters and the Reaping Number—Con(r < u). GOLDSTERN, M and SHELAH, S.
Reducts of (C,+,·) Which Contain +. MARKER, D and PILLAY, A.
Relativized Gödel Speed-Up and the Degree of Succinctness of Representations. SOLOMON, Martin K.
Set Theoretic Properties of Loeb Measure. MILLER, Arnold W.
Some New Double Induction and Superinduction Principles. SMULLYAN, Raymond M.
Some Remarks on ω-Powers of Enumerated Sets and Their Applications to ω-Operations. ORLICKI, Andrzej.
Some Results about Borel Sets in Descriptive Set Theory of Hyperfinite Sets. ZIVALJEVIC, Bosko.
Straight Talk about Sets. JUBIEN, Michael.
Weakly Minimal Groups of Unbounded Exponent. LOVEYS, James.

SEUNG, T
The Pincovian Persuasion: Six Problems in Virtue Ethics (A Free Response to Seung). BUDZISZEWSKI, J.

SEVENTEENTH CENTURY
see Modern

SEX
"Sex" in *A Companion to Ethics*, BELLIOTTI, Raymond A.
Dr Chipley's Warning. WHITE, Ronald.
Handsome Lake's Teachings: The Shift from Female to Male Agriculture in Iroquois Agriculture. HOLLY, Marilyn.
Rousseau's Political Defense of the Sex-Roled Family. WEISS, Penny.
Sex and Virtue. PUTMAN, D.

SEXES
Feminism and Philosophy of Science. LONGINO, Helen E.
On the Issue of Sex Differences. ALLEN, Elizabeth.

SEXISM
"Nuclearism and Sexism: Overcoming Their Shared Metaphysical Basis" in *Issues in War and Peace: Philosophical Inquiries*, SMITHKA, Paula.
Jean-Jacques Rousseau, Sexist?. THOMAS, Paul.
Sartre and Sexism. BARNES, Hazel E.

SEXTUS EMPIRICUS
Pyrrhonism's Arguments Against Value. MC PHERRAN, Mark L.

SEXUAL INTERCOURSE
San Agustín y la sexualidad conyugal. BURKE, Cormac.

SEXUALITY
The Authentic Self: Toward a Philosophy of Personality. LACENTRA, Walter.
Bertrand Russell: The Psychobiography of a Moralist. BRINK, Andrew.
Patterns of Dissonance. BRAIDOTTI, Rosi.
"Closing Up the Corpses: Diseases of Sexuality and the Emergence of the Psychiatric Style of Reasoning" in *Meaning and Method: Essays in Honor of Hilary Putnam*, DAVIDSON, Arnold I.
"Sexuality and Assisted Reproduction: An Uneasy Embrace" in *Beyond Baby M: Ethical Issues in New Reproductive Techniques*, HAROWSKI, Kathy J.
Le genre vernaculaire ou la nostalgie de la tradition: A propos d'Ivan Illich. KWASCHIN, Sylvie.
I Love Myself When I am Laughing: A New Paradigm for Sex. DAVIS, Karen Elizabeth.
Just Looking: Voyeurism and the Grounds of Privacy. NATHAN, Daniel O.
Kant, Teleology, and Sexual Ethics. COOKE, Vincent M.
Lonergan's Method in Ethics and the Meaning of Human Sexuality. FRISBY, Mark E.
Repression of Sexuality in Philosophy and the Return of the Repressed in Freud's Psychoanalysis (in Serbo-Croatian). KORDIC, Radoman.

SHAH, K
K J Shah's 'Philosophy, Religion, Morality, Spirituality: Some Issues'. GHOSE, A M.

SHAKESPEARE
Beggars and Kings: Cowardice and Courage in Shakespeare's *Richard II*. JENSEN, Pamela K.
King Lear and Natural Law. YOUNG, R V.

SHANON, B
Modularity of Mind Revisited. BENNETT, Laura J.

SHARING
Consciousness and Synchronic Identity. MATHESON, Carl.

SHEAF(-VES)
Boolean Powers of Abelian Groups. EDA, Katsuya.
Sheaves in Universal Algebra and Model Theory: Part I. IDZIAK, Pawel M.
Sheaves in Universal Algebra and Model Theory: Part II. IDZIAK, Pawel M.

SHEARMUR, J
Reply to Shearmur's "From Dialogue Rights to Property Rights". MICHELMAN, Frank.

SHEEHAN, T
"Radical Hermeneutics and Religious Truth: The Case of Sheehan and Schillebeeckx" in *Phenomenology of the Truth Proper to Religion*, CAPUTO, John D.

SHEFFER FUNCTIONS
There are Denumerably Many Ternary Intuitionistic Sheffer Functions. CUBRIC, Djordje.

SHER, G
Preferential Hiring and the Question of Competence. PHILIPS, Michael.

SHIKIBU, M
"Murasaki Shikibu" in *A History of Women Philosophers, Volume II: Medieval, Renaissance and Enlightenment, A.D. 500-1600*, WAITHE, Mary Ellen.

SHOEMAKER, S
Functionalism, the Absent Qualia Objection and Eliminativism. AVERILL, Edward Wilson.

SHRADER-FRECHETTE, K
Reply to Shrader-Frechette's "Biological Holism and the Evolution of Ethics". CALLICOTT, J Baird.

SIDDHASENA
The Biographies of Siddhasena (II). GRANOFF, Phyllis.

SIDGWICK
Commensurability as a Prerequisite of Rational Choice: An Examination of Sidgwick's Position. RICHARDSON, Henry S.
Sidgwick and Self-Interest. CRISP, Roger.
Time Preference. ZIFF, Paul.

SIEGEL, H
Goodbye and Farewell: Siegel versus Feyerabend. NORDMANN, Alfred.
Rationality and Reasonableness. BURBULES, Nicholas C.

SIEWERTH, G
El problema de la culpa y del "otro" en Heidegger y Siewerth. CABADA, Manuel.
Ser y Dios, entre filosofía y teología, en Heidegger y Siewerth. CABADA, Manuel.

SIGHT
Berkeley's Revolution in Vision. ATHERTON, Margaret.
An Oath of Silence: Wittgenstein's Philosophy of Religion. JOHNSON, Charles W.

SIGN(S)
see also Symbol(s)
Philosophical Hermeneutics and Literary Theory. WEINSHEIMER, Joel.
The Potential of Modern Discourse: Musil, Peirce, and Perturbation. FINLAY, Marike.
Saussure: Signs, System, and Arbitrariness. HOLDCROFT, David.
Works of Love? Reflections on "Works of Love". FENDT, Gene.
Il "De imaginum, signorum et idearum compositione" di Giordano Bruno, ed il significato filosofico .... STURLESE, Rita.
"Le signe en défaut". ROBIN, Régine.
Can Peirce Be a Pragmaticist and an Idealist?. PETERSON, John.
Comme en un miroir: quelques remarques historiques sur l'arbitraire du signe. LATRAVERSE, François.
La palabra interior: La filosofía del lenguaje en San Agustín. PEGUEROLES, Juan.
Sign, Symbol, and System. ELGIN, Catherine Z.
Vers une mise en signe de l'installation. RÉGIMBALD, Manon.

SIGNIFICANCE
The Appropriation of Significance: The Concept of *Kang-Tung*in the *I Ching*. TONG, Lik Kuen.
La dialettica come "dépasser" in Sartre. TOGNONATO, Claudio.

SIGNIFICATION
Pour une philosophie du sens et de la valeur. VASSILIE-LEMENY, Sorin-Titus.
"Beyond Signifiers" in *Writing the Politics of Difference*, DILLON, Martin C.
Arte y significación. ECHAURI, Raul.
Finitude Rediscovered. BARBER, Michael.
The Heterogeneity of Poetic Language in Kristeva (in Japanese). NARUSE, Katsuji.

SILENCE
The Other Side of Language: A Philosophy of Listening. FIUMARA, Gemma Corradi.
Proust: The Creative Silence. CARANFA, Angelo.

SILVER, C
Legal Positivism, Social Rules, and *Riggs* versus *Palmer*. BEEHLER, Rodger.

SIMILARITY
Meaning and Mental Representation. CUMMINS, Robert.
Choice Procedure Consistent with Similarity Relations. AIZPURUA, Jose Maria and NIETO, Jorge and URIARTE, Jose Ramon.
First-Order Logics for Comparative Similarity. WILLIAMSON, Timothy.
The Principle of Relevant Similarity. LEWIS, Gary W.
Similarity According to Jen-Jen. HSENG-HONG, Yeh.

SIMILE(S)
"Uguaglianza, riconoscimento del simile e principio d'autorità nell'ultimo Diderot" in *Égalité Uguaglianza*, GOGGI, Gianluigi.
Reductive and Nonreductive Simile Theories of Metaphor. TIRRELL, Lynne.
Some Observations About Plato's *Phaedo*. MASCHLER, Chaninah.

SIMMEL, G
"Difficoltà" con Simmel: Considerazioni in margine ad un convegno. LANDKAMMER, Joachim.
Deconstruction as Symbolic Play: Simmel/Derrida. WEINSTEIN, Deena and WEINSTEIN, Michael A.
Incommensurability and Recurrence: from Oresme to Simmel. SMALL, Robin.
A Theoretical Note on Simmel's Concept of Acquaintance. DOUBT, Keith.

SIMON
Simon and Socrates. BRUMBAUGH, Robert S.

SIMON, H
Herbert Simon's Computational Models of Scientific Discovery. DOWNES, Stephen M.

SIMON, Y
Freedom in the Modern World: Jacques Maritain, Yves R Simon, Mortimer J Adler. TORRE, Michael D (ed).
"Approaches to Democratic Equality: Maritain, Simon, and Kolnai" in *Freedom in the Modern World: Jacques Maritain, Yves R Simon, Mortimer J Adler*, HITTINGER, John P.
"Democracy and Philosophy: On Yves R Simon and Mortimer J Adler" in *Freedom in the Modern World: Jacques Maritain, Yves R Simon, Mortimer J Adler*, ANASTAPLO, George.
"Freedom and Determination: An Examination of Yves R Simon's Ontology of Freedom" in *Freedom in the Modern World: Jacques Maritain, Yves R Simon, Mortimer J Adler*, GREEN, Catherine.
"Freedom and Economic Organization in a Democracy" in *Freedom in the Modern World: Jacques Maritain, Yves R Simon, Mortimer J Adler*, NELSON, Ralph.
"Freedom and Practical Rationality in the Thought of Yves R Simon" in *Freedom in the Modern World: Jacques Maritain, Yves R Simon, Mortimer J Adler*, MULVANEY, Robert J.
"Maritain, Simon, and Vichy's Elite Schools" in *Freedom in the Modern World: Jacques Maritain, Yves R Simon, Mortimer J Adler*, HELLMAN, John.
"Metaphysical Foundations of Freedom in the Social and Political Thought of Yves R Simon" in *Freedom in the Modern World: Jacques Maritain, Yves R Simon, Mortimer J Adler*, UDOIDEM, S Iniobong.
"Modernization of the Law of the *Prise de Conscience*" in *Freedom in the Modern World: Jacques Maritain, Yves R Simon, Mortimer J Adler*, CALIFANO, Joseph J.
"Parallels on Work, Theory and Practice in Yves R Simon and John Paul II" in *Freedom in the Modern World: Jacques Maritain, Yves R Simon, Mortimer J Adler*, GUEGUEN, John A.
"Recollections of Three Thinkers: Adler, Simon, and Maritain" in *Freedom in the Modern World: Jacques Maritain, Yves R Simon, Mortimer J Adler*, GALLAGHER, Donald A.
"Yves R Simon's Contribution to a Structural Political Pluralism" in *Freedom in the Modern World: Jacques Maritain, Yves R Simon, Mortimer J Adler*, KOYZIS, David T.

SIMPLICITY
Colour: A Philosophical Introduction (Second Edition). WESTPHAL, Jonathan.
A Note on Popper's Equation of Simplicity with Falsifiability. TURNEY, Peter.
On Simplicity of Formulas. KRYNICKI, Michal and SZCZERBA, Leslaw.
Realism and Simplicity in the Castle-East Debate on the Stability of the Hereditary Units. VICEDO, Marga.

SIMPLIFICATION
Why is Conjunctive Simplification Invalid?. THOMPSON, Bruce R.

SIMULATION
Aristotle's Technical Simulation and its Logic of Causal Relations. LOECK, Gisela.
Ethics Committee Simulations. WINSTON, Morton.

SIMULTANEITY
Change, Cause and Contradiction: A Defence of the Tenseless Theory of Time. LE POIDEVIN, Robin.
Cohen on Einstein's Simultaneity *Gedankenexperiment*. WHITE, V Alan.
Simultaneity, Conventionality and Existence. PETKOV, Vesselin.

SIN(S)
Metaphysical Conundrums at the Root of Moral Disagreement. MC DERMOTT, John M.
Saving Faith from Kant's Remarkable Antinomy. QUINN, Philip L.
Speech, Sin and the Word of God (in Dutch). GESTRICH, Christof.

SINCERITY
Sincerity and Japanese Values. REASONER, Paul.

SINGER, P
The Morality of Killing and Causing Suffering: Reasons for Rejecting Peter Singer's Pluralistic Consequentialism. LANDMAN, Willem A.
Singer's Cookbook. JOHNSON, Edward.

SINGH, H
Productivity and X-Efficiency: A Reply to Singh and Frantz. SARAYDAR, Edward.

SINGULAR TERM(S)
Philosophical Logic. STRAWSON, P F (ed).

SINGULARITY
The Nature of Causation: A Singularist Account. TOOLEY, Michael.

SINGULARS
Abstract Singular Reference: A Dilemma for Dummett. MILLER, Alexander.

SITUATION ETHICS
Principle Monism and Action Descriptions: Situationism and its Critics Revisited. PINCHES, Charles.
Sustaining Non-Rationalized Practices: Body-Mind, Power and Situational Ethics—Interview with Hubert and Stuart Dreyfus. FLYVBJERG, Bent.

SITUATION(S)
The Nature of Irony: Toward a Computational Model of Irony. LITTMAN, David C and MEY, Jacob L.
Las situaciones objetivas en las *Investigaciones Lógicas* de Edmundo Husserl. MULLIGAN, Kevin.

SITUATIONAL LOGIC
"Monotonic Solution of The Frame Problem in The Situation Calculus" in *Knowledge Representation and Defeasible Reasoning*, SCHUBERT, Lenhart.

SKILL(S)
Ethical Expertise and Moral Maturity: Conflict or Complement?. MOSS, Lenny.
General Thinking Skills: Are There Such Things?. ANDREWS, John N.
The Higher Level Skills: Tomorrow's 'Basics'. EDUC COMMISSION OF STATES.
Perhaps by Skill Alone. MISSIMER, Connie.
Teaching Philosophy: Skills and Mentalities. RICHARD, Arsene.

SKILLEN, T
Community as Compulsion? A Reply to Skillen on Citizenship and the State. ELLIOT, Gregory and OSBORNE, Peter.

SLAVERY
Democratic Individuality. GILBERT, Alan.
American Slavery and the Holocaust: Their Ideologies Compared. THOMAS, Laurence.
Freedom Not to be Free: The Case of the Slavery Contract in J S Mill's *On Liberty*. ARCHARD, David.
The Master-Slave Dialectic in Latin America: The Social Criticism of Zea, Freire, and Roig. SCHUTTE, Ofelia M.

SLEEP
Aristotle on Sleep and Dreams. GALLOP, David (trans).

SLEIGH, R
Leibniz on Superessentialism and World-Bound Individuals. COVER, Jan A.

SLEZAK, P
Cognitive Science on a Wing and a Prayer. KEITH, William.
Response to Slezak: *Nein, Ich verstehe nicht*. KEITH, William.

SLIPPERY SLOPE
Identity and Discrimination. WILLIAMSON, Timothy.

SMART, J
Consequentialism and the Unforeseeable Future. NORCROSS, Alastair.

SMELL
Some Thoughts on Common Scents. ALMAGOR, Uri.
The Trouble with Fragrance. ELLIS, John.

SMITH
Criteria of Certainty: Truth and Judgment in the English Enlightenment. COPE, Kevin L.
The Authorship of the *Abstract* Revisited. NELSON, John O.
Beyond Self-Interest and Altruism: A Reconstruction of Adam Smith's Theory of Human Conduct. KHALIL, Elias L.
La ética de Adam Smith: un utilitarismo de la simpatía. TASSET, José L.
Hume on Responsibility and Punishment. RUSSELL, Paul.
Markets and Morals. SMITH, G W.
Rhetoric and Ethics: Adam Smith on Theorizing about the Moral Sentiments. GRISWOLD JR, Charles L.
Utility and Morality: Adam Smith's Critique of Hume. MARTIN, Marie A.
Adam Smith and Social Justice: The Ethical Basis of *The Wealth of Nations*. OSSAR, Jacob.
Freedom, Commodification, and the Alienation of Labor in Adam Smith's "Wealth of Nations". WERHANE, Patricia H.

SMITH, E
Note on the Integration of Prototype Theory and Fuzzy-Set Theory. FUHRMANN, G.

SMITH, G
"Response to Smith's 'Markets and Morals'" in *Philosophy and Politics*, LOCKE, Don.

SMITH, H
Comment on Huston Smith's Review of *The Essential Writings of Frithiof Schuon. ANDERSON, Tyson.*

SMITH, J
The Authorship of the *Abstract* Revisited. NELSON, John O.

SMITH, M
Smith Against the Ethicists. LUBAN, David.

SMITH, Q
A Defence of the New Tenseless Theory of Time. OAKLANDER, L Nathan.

SMOKING
Smoking in Public: A Moral Imperative for the Most Toxic of Environmental Wastes. LUDINGTON, David M.

SMOOK, R
Smook on Logical and Extralogical Constants. HITCHCOCK, David and GEORGE, Rolf.

SMORYNSKI, C
On an Alleged Refutation of Hilbert's Program Using Gödel's First Incompleteness Theorem. DETLEFSEN, Michael.

SNEED, J
"Louis Althusser and Joseph D Sneed: A Strange Encounter in Philosophy of Science?" in *Imre Lakatos and Theories of Scientific Change*, BALTAS, Aristides.

SNELLMAN, J
Gelehrter zwischen Romantik und Hegelianismus in Finnland—Johan Vilhelm Snellman (1806-1881). HÄNTSCH, Carola.

SOCIAL
Creativity in George Herbert Mead. GUNTER, Pete A Y (ed).
The Crisis in Health Care: Ethical Issues. MC KENZIE, Nancy F (ed).
Evolutionary Instability: Logical and Material Aspects of a Unified Theory of Biosocial Evolution. GEIGER, Gebhard.
Gerechtigkeit, Wohlfahrt und Rationalität. SCHMIDT, Johannes.
The Power of Ideology. MÉSZÁROS, István.
Speech Acts and Literary Theory. PETREY, Sandy.
"Aristotelian Social Democracy" in *Liberalism and the Good*, NUSSBAUM, Martha C.
"The Ethics of Social Commitment" in *Biomedical Ethics Reviews, 1990*, BAILLIE, Harold W and GARRETT, Thomas M.
"A Feminist Theory of Social Differentiation" in *Feminism/Postmodernism*, YEATMAN, Anna.
"Marx Against Morality" in *A Companion to Ethics*, WOOD, Allen.
"Work in Organizations as Social Activity" in *Harré and His Critics*, RODRIGUEZ LOPEZ, Jose Luis.
The "New" Scholars in Philosophy of Education, 1976-1986. QUANTZ, Richard A.
"Threading-the-Needle: The Case For and Against Common-Sense Realism". TIBBETTS, Paul.
A Comparison of John Dewey and Lawrence Kohlberg's Approach to Moral Education. SOCOSKI, Patrick M.
Legal Positivism, Social Rules, and *Riggs* versus *Palmer*. BEEHLER, Rodger.
El lugar de la doctrina social de la reflexión teológico moral cristiana. BRIANCESCO, E.
Marketing Ethics: Some Dimensions of the Challenge. CAMENISCH, Paul F.
Moral Realism and the Meaning of Life. MARGOLIS, Joseph.
On Social Rights. SANDU, Gabriel and KUOKKANEN, Martti.
Rationality and Social Labor in Marx. KHALIL, Elias L.
Rethinking the Dialectic: A Social Semiotic Perspective for Educators. HAMMER, Rhonda and MC LAREN, Peter.
Social Communication and Interest Relationships (in German). LUUTZ, Wolfgang.
Social Epistemics and Social Psychology. GOLDMAN, Alvin.
Social Epistemology and Social Cognition. CORLETT, J Angelo.
Social Epistemology and the Brave New World of Science and Technology Studies. FULLER, Steve.
What is Social about Social Epistemics?. MAFFIE, James.
Whither Social Epistemology? A Reply to Fuller. SCHMAUS, Warren.
Who's the Horse? A Response to Corlett. HEYES, Cecilia.
The World Reconsidered: A Brief *AggiornamentoF* for Leftist Intellectuals. SKIRBEKK, Gunnar.

SOCIAL CHANGE
"Between Dewey and Gramsci: Unger's Emancipatory Experimentalism" in *Critique and Construction: A Symposium on Roberto Unger's "Politics"*, WEST, Cornel.
"Commonsense Reasoning, Social Change, and the Law" in *Critique and Construction: A Symposium on Roberto Unger's "Politics"*, VAN ZANDT, David E.
"Cultural Tradition, Historical Experience, and Social Change: The Limits of Convergence" in *The Tanner Lectures on Human Values, Volume XI*, EISENSTADT, S N.
"Modern Democracy and Political Philosophy" in *Writing the Politics of Difference*, LEFORT, Claude.
"Social Theory and Political Practice: Unger's Brazilian Journalism" in *Critique and Construction: A Symposium on Roberto Unger's "Politics"*, SIMON, William H.
Antropología del trabajo según la Encíclica "Laborem Excercens". QUESADA GUARDIA, Annabelle.
The Changing Face of Civil Society in Eastern Europe. KOLARSKA-BOBINSKA, Lena.
Cuatro modelos de desarrollo costarricense: un análisis y evalución ética. CROCKER, David A.
Deficiencies in Contemporary Theories of Justice. LÖTTER, H P P.
From Patriarchal Socialism to Socialist Democracy: Thoughts on a New Theory of Society. MOCEK, Reinhard.
The Futility of Psychotherapy. ALBEE, George W.
Illusions and Visions: Models Of and In Modern Societies. MARZ, Lutz.
Marxism and Social Change: Some Theoretical Reflections. TRIPATHY, Laxman Kumar.
Olivier's Postmodern Proposal: A Few Comments. LÖTTER, H P P.
Philosophical and Normative Dimensions and Aspects of the Idea of Renaissance. GREGORIOS, Paulos Mar.
Reflections on the Eastern European Revolutions: The God that Failed. MAZLISH, Bruce.
O Saber, a Ética e a Ação Social. CARDOSO D EOLIVEIRA, Roberto.
What Happened in Eastern Europe in 1989?. CHIROT, Daniel.

SOCIAL CONDITION(S)
L'Utopia di Fourier. TUNDO, Laura.
Adam Smith and Social Justice: The Ethical Basis of *The Wealth of Nations*. OSSAR, Jacob.
Cartesian Feminists. LONGACRE, Judith.
La ética como conciencia en el subdesarrollo. RAMÍREZ, E Roy.
Philosophy of African Intellectuals. WAMBA-DIA-WAMBA, Ernest.

SOCIAL CONSCIOUSNESS
From Sentience To Symbols. PICKERING, John (ed).
The Social Horizon of Knowledge. BUCZKOWSKI, Piotr (ed).
"Remarks on the Structure of Social Consciousness" in *The Social Horizon of Knowledge*, BUCZKOWSKI, Piotr.
El factor prelógico en el desarrollo de América Latina: El teorema del preconsciente colectivo. MANSILLA, H C F.
Para una teoría latinoamericana de las relaciones de la ciencia con la literatura: la cienciapoesía. CATALÁ, Rafael.
Reply to Stephenson on Biomedical Research. GENDIN, Sidney.
Las Sociedades de Pensamiento y la Revolución Francesa. RHENÁN SEGURA, Jorge.
Why the Mind is Not in the Head But in the Society's Connectionist Network. FISCHER, Roland.

SOCIAL CONTRACT
Community: The Tie That Binds. ROUSSEAU, Mary F.
Leviathan: Hobbes. TUCK, Richard (ed).
"The Social Contract Tradition" in *A Companion to Ethics*, KYMLICKA, Will.
Business Ethics and Extant Social Contracts. DUNFEE, Thomas W.
Consensus, Contracts, and Committees. MORENO, Jonathan D.
Crime, Minorities, and the Social Contract. LAWSON, Bill.
Hobbes and the Philosophy of International Relations. RAMOSE, Mogobe B.
Jean-Jacques Rousseau and the Fusion of Democratic Sovereignty with Aristocratic Government. CRANSTON, Maurice.
John Rawls: de l'autonomie morale à la fiction de contrat social. RICOEUR, Paul.
Locke, Lockean Ideas, and the Glorious Revolution. SCHWOERER, Lois G.
Spinoza en het ontstaan van de staat. VERBEEK, Bruno.

SOCIAL CONTROL
"The Problem of Linguistic Empowerment" in *Abeunt Studia in Mores: A Festschrift for Helga Doblin*, MERRILL, Sarah A Bishop.
AIDS and the Psycho-Social Disciplines: The Social Control of 'Dangerous' Behavior. KAPLAN, Mark S.
Institutional Mental Health and Social Control: The Ravages of Epistemological Hubris. FARBER, Seth.

SOCIAL CRITICISM
Creative Characters. YOUNG-BRUEHL, Elisabeth.
Hermeneutics and Critical Theory in Ethics and Politics. KELLY, Michael (ed).
"Social Criticism without Philosophy: An Encounter between Feminism and Postmodernism" in *Feminism/Postmodernism*, FRASER, Nancy and NICHOLSON, Linda J.
The Self and Social Criticism. HARVEY, Charles W.
Social Criticism and Political Philosophy. BARRY, Brian.

SOCIAL DARWINISM
"Transmitting Theoretical Frames: The Case of Social Darwinism" in *Perspectives on Ideas and Reality*, ORTHMAYR, Imre.
Scientific Racism in the Philosophy of Science: Some Historical Examples. UEBEL, Thomas E.

SOCIAL DETERMINISM
Engels y Darwin en el origen del hombre: Elementos para una discusión. GALLARDO, Helio.
Is Knowledge Socially Determined? A Critique. CHAUDHURY, Mahasweta.
Libertad individual frente a determinación social. FRANCISCO PÉREZ, M.

SOCIAL ENGINEERING
Human Nature, Social Engineering, and the Reemergence of Civil Society. RAU, Zbigniew.

SOCIAL ETHICS
Can Utilitarianism Be Salvaged as a Theory for Social Choice?. VAN ASPEREN, G M.
Psychology and Standards of Reasonable Expectation. SCHOEMAN, Ferdinand.

SOCIAL HISTORY
Marx as a Social Historian. MAHON, Joseph.
The Methodologies of Social History: A Critical Survey and Defense of Structurism. LLOYD, Christopher.

SOCIAL INSTITUTION(S)
"The Flaws in Sen's Case Against Paretian Libertarianism" in *Acting and Reflecting: The Interdisciplinary Turn in Philosophy*, PRESSLER, Jonathan.
Capitalismo, Socialidad y participación. PASSANITI, Daniel.
Evans-Pritchard on Persons and Their Cattle-Clocks: A Note on the Anthropological Account of Man. CHANDRA, Suresh.
Libertarianism. BARRY, Norman.
The Varieties of Self-Interest. EPSTEIN, Richard A.

SOCIAL ORDER
The Savage Anomaly: The Power of Spinoza's Metaphysics and Politics. NEGRI, Antonio.
To Be at Home: Christianity, Civil Religion, and World Community. ROUNER, Leroy S.
"The Loss of Responsibility" in *The Political Responsibility of Intellectuals*, HANKISS, Elemer.
"On the Nature of a Social Order" in *Logic, Methodology and Philosophy of Science, VIII*, PÖRN, Ingmar.
The 'Artificial Reason' of the Law. BICKENBACH, Jerome E.
Protective Norms as a Basis for Cooperation between Non-Privileged Constituencies. HEDMAN, Carl.

SOCIAL PHIL
see also Authority(-ties), Communism, Conservatism, Equality, Ethics, Freedom, Political Phil, Progress, Punishment, Society(-ties), Utopia
A "Realizacção da Razão": Um Programa Hegeliano?. BARATA-MOURA, José.
After Principles. BARDEN, Garrett.
Against Architecture: The Writings of Georges Bataille. HOLLIER, Denis.
Agricultural Bioethics: Implications of Agricultural Biotechnology. GENDEL, Steven M (& other eds).
Alterity, Identity, Image: Contributions Towards a Theoretical Perspective. CORBEY, R (ed).
Amythia: Crisis in the Natural History of Western Culture. RUE, Loyal D.
The Anatomy of Judgment. REGAL, Philip J.
Atheism, Ayn Rand, and other Heresies. SMITH, George H.
The Call to Personhood. MC FADYEN, Alistair I.
Collected Works, Volume 26, Engels: 1882-1889. ENGELS, Frederick.
Community: The Tie That Binds. ROUSSEAU, Mary F.
Contemporary Perspectives on Masculinity: Men, Women, and Politics in Modern Society. CLATTERBAUGH, Kenneth.
Critical Theory and Philosophy. INGRAM, David.
Critique and Construction: A Symposium on Roberto Unger's "Politics". LOVIN, Robin W (ed).
Critique of Dialectical Reason, Volume 2: Jean-Paul Sartre. HOARE, Quintin (trans).
The Critique of Power: Reflective Stages in a Critical Social Theory. HONNETH, Axel.
Dämonie und Gesellschaft. CATTEPOEL, Jan.
De l'épistémologie à la politique: La philosophie de l'histoire de Karl R Popper. RUELLAND, Jacques G.
The Death of Industrial Civilization. KASSIOLA, Joel Jay.
Demystifying Mentalities. LLOYD, G E R.
Descent into Subjectivity: Studies of Rawls, Dworkin and Unger in the Context of Modern Thought. MURPHY JR, Cornelius F.
The Devil and Secular Humanism: The Children of the Enlightenment. RADEST, Howard B.
The Dynamics of Rational Deliberation. SKYRMS, Brian.
Essays on Heidegger and Others: Philosophical Papers, Volume 2. RORTY, Richard.
Essentially Speaking: Feminism, Nature and Difference. FUSS, Diana.
Euthanasia: Toward an Ethical Social Policy. THOMASMA, David C.
Feminism/Postmodernism. NICHOLSON, Linda J (ed).
Foundations of Social Theory. COLEMAN, James S.
From Twilight to Dawn: The Cultural Vision of Jacques Maritain. REDPATH, Peter A (ed).
Gerechtigkeit, Wohlfahrt und Rationalität. SCHMIDT, Johannes.
The Health Crisis. SZUMSKI, Bonnie (ed).
Historia del nombrar: Dos episodios de la subjetividad. THIEBAUT, Carlos.
History and Spirit: An Inquiry into the Philosophy of Liberation. KOVEL, Joel.
Integrity in Health Care Institutions: Humane Environments for Teaching, Inquiry, and Healing. BULGER, Ruth Ellen (ed).
Introduction Critique au Droit Naturel. HERVADA, Javier.
Irony and the Discourse of Modernity. BEHLER, Ernst.
Issues in War and Peace: Philosophical Inquiries. KUNKEL, Joseph (ed).
Jurisculture, Volume I: Greece and Rome. DORSEY, Gray L.
Justice and the Good Life. DWORKIN, Ronald.
The Last Choice: Preemptive Suicide in Advanced Age. PRADO, C G.
Liberalism and the Good. DOUGLASS, R Bruce (ed).
The Making of a Nuclear Peace: The Task of Today's Just War Theorists. SICHOL, Marcia W.
Mannheim and Hungarian Marxism. GABEL, Joseph.
Marxism and Philosophy in the Twentieth Century: A Defense of Vulgar Marxism. HUDELSON, Richard.
Medical Work in America: Essays on Health Care. FREIDSON, Eliot.
Medicine and Money: A Study of the Role of Beneficence in Health Care Cost Containment. MARSH, Frank H.
Michel Foucault's Force of Flight: Towards an Ethics for Thought. BERNAUER, James W.
Military Ethics: Looking Toward the Future. FOTION, Nicholas G.
Models and Concepts of Ideology. RITSERT, Jürgen.
The Moral Animus of David Hume. SIEBERT, Donald T.
The Moral Domain: Essays in the Ongoing Discussion between Philosophy and the Social Sciences. WREN, Thomas E (ed).
Moral Philosophy: Theories, Skills, and Applications. FALIKOWSKI, Anthony F.
Moral und Politik aus der Sicht des Kritischen Rationalismus. SALAMUN, Kurt (ed).
Morality and Modernity. POOLE, Ross.
Myth and Modern Philosophy. DANIEL, Stephen H.
Narrative in Culture: The Uses of Storytelling in the Sciences, Philosophy, and Literature. NASH, Christopher (ed).
Nation und Ethos: Die Moral des Patriotismus. KLUXEN-PYTA, Donate.
Natural Reasons: Personality and Polity. HURLEY, S L.
Negotation Games: Applying Game Theory to Bargaining and Arbitration. BRAMS, Steven J.
Objectivity, Relativism, and Truth: Philosophical Papers, Volume 1. RORTY, Richard.
On Durkheim's Rules of Sociological Method. GANE, Mike.
Ontology and Alterity in Merleau-Ponty. JOHNSON, Galen A (ed).
Overcoming Foundations: Studies in Systematic Philosophy. WINFIELD, Richard Dien.
Patterns of Dissonance. BRAIDOTTI, Rosi.
The Persistence of Modernity: Essays on Aesthetics, Ethics, and Postmodernism. WELLMER, Albrecht.
Philosophical Streets: New Approaches to Urbanism. CROW, Dennis (ed).
Le Philosophie et les Passions. MEYER, Michel.
Philosophy and the Spontaneous Philosophy of the Scientists and Other Essays. ELLIOTT, Gregory (ed).
The Philosophy of Money: Georg Simmel (Second Edition). FRISBY, David (ed & trans).
Philosophy of Sport. HYLAND, Drew A.
Philosophy of Technology. DURBIN, Paul T (ed).
Philosophy of the "Gita". PATEL, Ramesh N.
Postmodernism—Philosophy and the Arts (Continental Philosophy III). SILVERMAN, Hugh J (ed).
The Power of Ideology. MÉSZÁROS, István.
The Realizations of the Future: An Inquiry into the Authority of Praxis. ALLAN, George.
The Realm of Humanitas: Responses to the Writings of Hannah Arendt. GARNER, Reuben (ed).
Reflexões, 3: Filosofia Política Sociologia cultura Portuguesa Temas Literários. DE MELO, Romeu.
Relating Humanities and Social Thought (Science, Ideology, and Value, Volume 4). EDEL, Abraham.
Responsibility and Criminal Liability. SISTARE, C T.
Rorty's Humanistic Pragmatism: Philosophy Democratized. KOLENDA, Konstantin.
Shaping Genes: Ethics, Law and Science of Using Genetic Technology in Medicine and Agriculture. MACER, Darryl.
Social Theory of Modern Societies: Anthony Giddens and His Critics. HELD, David (ed).
La sociedad sin hombres: Niklas Luhmann o la teoría como escándalo. IZUZQUIZA, Ignacio.
Spuren der Macht. RÖTTGERS, Kurt.
Taking Sides: Clashing Views on Controversial Bioethical Issues (Fourth Edition). LEVINE, Carol (ed).
The Tanner Lectures on Human Values, Volume XI. PETERSON, Grethe B (ed).
Thinking the Unthinkable: Meanings of the Holocaust. GOTTLIEB, Roger S (ed).
Understanding War: A Philosophical Inquiry. MC MURTRY, John.
Varieties of Social Explanation: An Introduction to the Philosophy of Social Science. LITTLE, Daniel.
Who Comes after the Subject?. CADAVA, Eduardo (ed).
Work, Inc.: A Philosophical Inquiry. BYRNE, Edmund F.
Writing the Politics of Difference. SILVERMAN, Hugh J (ed).

SOCIAL PHIL

SOCIAL PHIL

The Consequences of Endorsing Sentimental Homicide. BARRY, Robert L.
Constrained Discourse and Public Life. MOON, J Donald.
Constructing Justice. GIBBARD, Allan.
El consumo como sistema ideológico. MÁRQUEZ FERNÁNDEZ, Alvaro B.
Contagious Folly: *An Adventure* and Its Skeptics. CASTLE, Terry.
Contemporary Ethics and Scheler's Phenomenology of Community. VACEK, Edward.
La contribución de la filosofía al cambio social en América Latina. FORNET-BETANCOURT, Raúl.
Controverses autour de l'ontologie du droit. DE MUNCK, Jean.
Crime, Minorities, and the Social Contract. LAWSON, Bill.
The Crisis in Psychoanalysis: Resolution Through Husserlian Phenomenology and Feminism. NISSIM-SABAT, Marilyn.
The Crisis of Authority. OLDS, Mason.
Critical Fanonism. GATES JR, Henry Louis.
Critical Interaction: Judgment, Decision, and the Social Testing of Moral Hypotheses. IANNONE, A P.
A Critical Look at Arguments for Food Irradiation. SMITH, Tony.
La critique du modèle industriel comme histoire de la rareté: Une introduction à la pensée d'Ivan Illich. ACHTERHUIS, Hans.
Cross-Cultural Philosophizing. RANLY, Ernest W.
Cruzan and Caring for Others. LYNN, Joanne and GLOVER, Jacqueline.
Cruzan: No Rights Violated. ROBERTSON, John A.
Cultural Theory Looks at Identity and Contradiction. COCKS, Joan.
Culture as an Open System. VAN PEURSEN, C A.
De la matérialité du discours saisi dans l'institution. KREMER-MARIETTI, Angèle.
De la problématique diltheyenne à l'intégralisme de Jean Granier. AJERAR, Hassane.
Deep Ecology versus Ecofeminism: Healthy Differences or Incompatible Philosophies?. SESSIONS, Robert.
A Defense of Equal Opportunity for Welfare. ARNESON, Richard J.
Deinstitutionalization: Cycles of Despair. SCULL, Andrew.
Democracy and Justice in Health Policy. JENNINGS, Bruce.
El desarrollo como proceso: una investigación filosófica. DOWER, Nigel.
Descartes et Corneille ou les démesures de l'*ego*. BEYSSADE, Jean-Marie.
Desire and Duty in Kant. GRIGG, Russell.
Desperately Seeking Science: The Creation of Knowledge in Family Practice. GOLDSTEIN, Jared.
Deugden en plichtsbesef. STEUTEL, J W.
Development of an Institutional Policy on Artificial Hydration and Nutrition. KOSHUTA, Monica A and SCHMITZ, Phyllis J and LYNN, Joanne.
The Development of Moral Reasoning and the Foundations of Geometry. MACNAMARA, John.
The Dialectic of National and Universal Commitments in Christian-Marxist Dialogue. WILL, James E.
Dialogo sobre humanismo y Marxismo (primera parte). SILVA CAMARENA, Juan Manuel.
Dialogue and Understanding (in German). FRITZSCHE, Helmut.
Dialogue as a Way of Being Human. YIN, Lu-jun.
Dialogue—A New Utopia?. GÓRNIAK-KOCIKOWSKA, Krystyna.
Did Freud Develop a Social Philosophy? (in Serbo-Croatian). FLEGO, Gvozden.
A Different Different Voice: On the Feminist Challenge in Moral Theory. ROONEY, Phyllis.
Difficulties with the Principle of Equal Opportunity for Welfare. CHRISTIANO, Thomas.
Disarming the Baby with the Gun: Reply to Audrey Thompson. GLASS, Ronald David.
The Disorder of Things. MAJOR-POETZL, Pamela.
Distributive Justice and Utility. GOLDSTICK, D.
Division and Difference in the "Discipline" of Economics. AMARIGLIO, Jack and RESNICK, Stephen and WOLFF, Richard.
Do Not Despair: There is Life after Constructivism. BIJKER, Wieke.
Do These Feminists Like Women?. SOMMERS, Christina.
The Doctrine of Double Effect and Affirmative Action. JORDAN, Jeff.
Does Sommers Like Women? More on Liberalism, Gender Hierarchy, and Scarlett O'Hara. FRIEDMAN, Marilyn.
Domination and Moral Struggle: the Philosophical Heritage of Marxism Reviewed. HONNETH, Axel.
Don Quijote: voluntad y representación. MURILLO, Roberto.
Las dos grandes paradojas?. SERRANO, Augusto.
Double Standards, Racial Equality and the Right Reference Class. ADLER, Jonathan E.
Duty to Treat or Right to Refuse?. DANIELS, Norman.
Ecofeminism and Androcentric Epistemology. DURAN, Jane.
Ecofeminism and the Eating of Animals. ADAMS, Carol J.
Ecofeminist Theory and Grassroots Politics. LAHAR, Stephanie.
Ecological Feminism and Ecosystem Ecology. WARREN, Karen J and CHENEY, Jim.
The Economic Analysis of Institutions. RICKETTS, Martin.
Economic Rights: A Test Case for Catholic Social Teaching. MC CANN, Dennis P.
The Economics of (Very) Primitive Societies. TULLOCK, Gordon.
Ecosocialism—Utopian and Scientific. HAYWARD, Tim.
The Effects of Patrol Officers' Defensiveness Toward the Outside World on Their Ethical Orientations. SHERNOCK, Stan K.
Les effets de la perestroïka dans les *Voprosy filosofii*. DENNES, Maryse.
The Elusiveness of Human Nature. SMITHURST, Michael.
Emile's Education. SHAVER, Robert.
Emotions and Rationality. BERENSON, F M.
Emotions and Responsibility. TURSKI, George.
Encountering Dallmayr. KIVISTO, Peter.
Enforced Pregnancy, Rape, and the Image of Woman. CUDD, Ann E.
Engels y Darwin en el origen del hombre: Elementos para una discusión. GALLARDO, Helio.
Les enjeux égalitaires du consensus rationnel: Habermas et ses sources. MARCIL-LACOSTE, Louise.
Enlightenment Psychology and Political Reaction in Plato's Social Philosophy: an Ideological Contradiction?. BRYANT, Joseph M.
Entre el duelo y la melancolia. SILVA CAMARENA, Juan Manuel.
Environmental Ethics and the Case for Hunting. KING, Roger J H.
Epistemology, Practical Research, and Human Subjects. ROSS, Murray and SELMAN, Mark.
Equal Educational Opportunity as a Public Policy. BUNTING, I A.
Equal Opportunity and the Family. VALLENTYNE, Peter and LIPSON, Morry.
Equality of What: Welfare, Resources, or Capabilities?. DANIELS, Norman.
Eradicating the Obvious. CLARK, Stephen R L.
Essai sur le thème du réferentiel. ORY, André.
Ethical Challenges of HIV Infection in the Workplace. LEONARD, Arthur S.
An Ethical Justification of Women's Studies, Or What's a Nice Girl Like You Doing in a Place like This?. MC GRATH, Lynette.
The Ethical Limitations of the Market. ANDERSON, Elizabeth.
The Ethico-Legal Meaning of Voluntary. BOURKE, Vernon J.
Ethics and Advocacy in Forecasting for Public Policy. WACHS, Martin.
Ethics and News. MACHAMER, Peter K and BOYLAN, Barbara.
Ethics Committees. COHEN, Cynthia B (ed).
Ethics Consultation as Moral Engagement. MORENO, Jonathan D.
The Ethics of Statistical Discrimination. MAITZEN, Stephen.
Ethics Without Free Will. SLOTE, Michael.
Ethics, Public Policy, and Human Fetal Tissue Transplantation. CHILDRESS, James F.
Ethik zwischen globaler Verantwortung und spekulativer Weltschematik. JOOS, Egbert.
Euthanasia in China: A Report. DA PU, Shi.
The Evidence of Experience. SCOTT, Joan W.
Evolution, "Typology" and "Population Thinking". GREENE, Marjorie.
The Exile of Literature: Poetry and the Politics of the Other(s). MURPHY, Bruce F.
Existen los universales culturales?. WIREDU, Kwasi and GARCÍA MONSIVÁIS, Blanca.
An Experimental Analysis of Risk Taking. DAHLBÄCK, Olof.
Explaining Without Blaming the Victim. ILLINGWORTH, Patricia M L.
Exploring Extreme Violence (Torture). MACHAN, Tibor R.
El factor prelógico en el desarrollo de América Latina: El teorema del preconsciente colectivo. MANSILLA, H C F.
Los Factores Originales de la Sociedad en Tomás de Aquino. BEUCHOT, Mauricio.
Failure of a Renaissance (Why It Is Impossible to Remain a Marxist in East Central Europe). VAJDA, Mihaly.
The Faith Dimension of Humanism. EARLES, Beverley.
The Fate of Independent Thought in Traditional China. WHITE, Harry.
Feminism and Ecology: On the Domination of Nature. MILLS, Patricia Jagentowicz.
Feminism and Relativism. RUSSELL, Denise.
Feminist Fears in Ethics. NODDINGS, Nel.
Feminist Philosophy and the Genetic Fallacy. CROUCH, Margaret A.
The Feminist Revelation. SOMMERS, Christina.
Feminist Theory and Its Discontents. TRESS, Daryl Mc Gowan.
Feminist Theory and the Politics of Inclusion. FISHER, Linda.
Feminist Theory, Plurality of Voices and Cultural Imperialism. HERNANDEZ, Adriana.
Filosofía de la liberación como nuevo pensamiento a partir de los oprimidos y como de-strucción (3a parte). ANIZAR, Humberto Encarnación.
Filosofía de la violencia. MAGGIOLO, Roberto Jiménez.
Final Summary (in Czechoslovakian). KOLAKOWSKI, L.
Fingarette on the Disease Concept of Alcoholism. CORLETT, J Angelo.
Foucault et la psychothérapie. DREYFUS, Hubert L.
Free Speech, Free Exchange, and Rawlsian Liberalism. SHAPIRO, Daniel.
Freedom and Realms of Living. CI, Jiwei.
Freedom Not to be Free: The Case of the Slavery Contract in J S Mill's *On Liberty*. ARCHARD, David.
Freedom, Commodification, and the Alienation of Labor in Adam Smith's "Wealth of Nations". WERHANE, Patricia H.
Freud devait-il choisir entre les deux conceptions du symbole que lui attribue Lévi-Strauss?. CHARRON, Ghyslain.
Freud on Civilization and Neurosis. FLUXMAN, Tony.
Freud, Marxism and the Frankfurt School (in Serbo-Croation). FLEGO, Gvozden.

SOCIAL PHIL

From Class Struggle to Struggle without Classes?. BALIBAR, Etienne.
From Hegel to Lukacs: The Problem of Ontology from the Point of View of Social and Natural Theory (in German). MOCEK, Reinhard.
From Historical Marxisms to Historical Materialism: Toward the Theory of Ideology. MOCNIK, Rastko.
From Nothingness to No-thing-ness: the Roots of Ferry and Renaut's Humanism. BARBIERO, Daniel.
Fundamental Question of Philosophy: Remarks on the Pending Philosophical Reappraisal of the Past in the GDR (in German). SCHRÖDER, Richard.
Fundamental Values in the Thought of Confucius and Mencius (in Polish). CYRANOWSKA, Maria.
The Futility of Psychotherapy. ALBEE, George W.
Future through Self-Organization (in German). ARTZT, M.
Games, Fairness, and Rawls's *A Theory of Justice*. LADEN, Anthony.
Een gedesoriënteerde veranderingswetenschap. GASTELAARS, M.
Gendered Reason: Sex Metaphor and Conceptions of Reason. ROONEY, Phyllis.
A Genetic Exploration of Women's Subjugation: The Adventures of a Gadfly. MITTRA, Aditya Barna.
Genetics, Neuroscience, and Biotechnology. LAPPÈ, Marc.
Le genre vernaculaire ou la nostalgie de la tradition: A propos d'Ivan Illich. KWASCHIN, Sylvie.
Geschiedenis als muurbloempje. PRINS, Ad.
Getting the Subject Back into the World: Heidegger's Version. KERR, Fergus.
Ghost Story (in German). SAUTET, Marc.
Les gisants et les pleureuses: Pour un tombeau de Michel Foucault. AUZIAS, Jean-Marie.
Giving Voice to the Pragmatic Majority in New Jersey. HILL, T Patrick.
Global Injustices. MC BRIDE, William L.
Global Responsibility. AGASSI, Joseph.
Goodbye and Farewell: Siegel versus Feyerabend. NORDMANN, Alfred.
Gorz on Work and Liberation. SAYERS, Sean.
Government and Character. PINCOFFS, Edmund L.
Grandeur et limites du *Marx* de Michel Henry. CANTIN, Serge.
A Great Intellectual Current Worthy of National Pride. CHANGLU, Qiao.
The Greatest Happiness Principle. SPRIGGE, T L S.
Ground, Pivot, Motion: Ecofeminist Theory, Dialogics, and Literary Practice. MURPHY, Patrick.
Grundlegende Aspekte zur Problematik von Erkenntnis und Praxis. FORSCHE, Joachim.
Habermas and Solidarity. FUNK, Nanette.
Habermas on Strategic and Communicative Action. JOHNSON, James.
Hacia el saber del hombre: Dialéctica, lógica y ontológica en Aristóteles. MARÍN, Victor R.
Hacia un desarrollo de la cultura y una cultura del desarrollo. ROSALES, Amán.
Handsome Lake's Teachings: The Shift from Female to Male Agriculture in Iroquois Agriculture. HOLLY, Marilyn.
Hayek's Theory of Cultural Evolution: An Evaluation in the Light of Vanberg's Critique. HODGSON, Geoffrey M.
Health Care in Common: Setting Priorities in Oregon. GARLAND, Michael J and HASNAIN, Romana.
Hegel's Critical Theory and Feminist Concerns. HAYIM, Gila J.
Hegel's Critique of Liberalism and Natural Law: Reconstructing Ethical Life. GARZA JR, Abel.
Hegel, Croce, Gentile: On the Idea of the "Ethical State". SANTORO, Liberato and CASALE, Giuseppe.
Hegel, Marx, Nietzsche, and the Future of Self-Alienation. SCHACHT, Richard.
Her Terrain is Outside His "Domain". PEEPLES, S Elise.
Hermeneutics: A Protreptic. JOHNSON, Gregory R.
Hidden Agendas. FRIEDMAN, Robert.
Historicisms New and Old: "Charles Dickens" Meets Marxism, Feminism, and West Coast Foucault. NEWTON, Judith.
History as Geneology: Wittgenstein and the Feminist Deconstruction of Objectivity. LAMPSHIRE, Wendy L.
Hobbes on Capital Punishment. HEYD, David.
A Hostage to Technology. CRANFORD, Ronald E.
How Can They?. BUSALACCHI, Pete.
How Individualistic Is Methodological Individualism?. MADISON, G B.
How Many Selves Make Me?. CLARK, Stephen R L.
How Many Selves Make Me?. WILKES, Kathleen V.
How to Get Rid of Your Expensive Philosopher of Science and Still Keep Control Over the Fuzzing Conversation of Mankind. VISKER, Rudi.
Human Nature, Social Engineering, and the Reemergence of Civil Society. RAU, Zbigniew.
Human Rights and Freedom: Is Kant Relevant to the Current Discussion?. SCHWEIDLER, Walter.
Humanity, Morality, and Liberty. DUBCEK, Alexander A.
A Hungarian Christian-Marxist Dialogue and Its Lessons. LUKÁCS, József.
I Love Myself When I am Laughing: A New Paradigm for Sex. DAVIS, Karen Elizabeth.
La imagen del indígena en el pensamiento colombiano del siglo XIX: La perspectiva de J M Samper. GÓMEZ-MULLER, Alfredo.
Imagination and the Sense of Identity. HERTZBERG, Lars.
The Impact of Activist Pressures on Recombinant DNA Research. RABINO, Isaac.
The Impact of the French Revolution on the Development of Philosophy. NETOPILIK, Jakub.
The Importance of Being Human. DIAMOND, Cora.
The Importance of Being Human. MC NAUGHTON, David.
In Defense of Sentimentality. SOLOMON, Robert C.
In Praise of Clutter as a Necessary Part of the Feminist Perspective. AYIM, Maryann.
The Inadequacy of a Deontological Analysis of Peer Relations in Organizations. MARTIN, Robert M.
Independence of Irrelevant Alternatives in the Theory of Voting. BORDES, Georges and TIDEMAN, Nicolaus.
India and the Theory of the Asiatic Mode of Production (in Hungarian). RENNER, Zsuzsanna.
Indigenous Ends and Alien Means: A Footnote on Indian Renaissance. CHAUDHURI, Minakshi Ray.
La influencia de Rousseau en el pensamiento de Kant. DE LOS ANGELES GIRALT, María.
Information Privacy and Performance Appraisal: An Examination of Employee Perceptions and Reactions. MOSSHOLDER, Kevin W and GILES, William F and WESOLOWSKI, Mark A.
Informational Property: Logorights. SCHULMAN, J Neil.
Informed Consent or Informed Rejection of Pesticide Use: A Concept for Environmental Action. ORTON, David.
Informing Clients About Limits to Confidentiality. PIZZIMENTI, Lee Ann.
The Intellectual Compatibility of Marx and Engels. HUNLEY, J D.
The Intellectual in the Post Modern Age: East/West Contrasts. BAYARD, Caroline.
Intentional Single and Joint Action. TUOMELA, Raimo.
Intentionality and the Ecological Approach. LOOREN DE JONG, H.
Intersubjectivity and Critical Consciousness: Remarks on Habermas's Theory of Communicative Action. WAGNER, Gerhard and ZIPPRIAN, Heinz.
Irigaray on Subjectivity. SCHUTTE, Ofelia.
Is Happiness Relative?. VEENHOVEN, Ruut.
Is Mandatory Retirement Unfair Age Discrimination?. WEDEKING, Gary A.
Is the Post- in Postmodernism the Post- in Postcolonial?. APPIAH, Kwame Anthony.
Is There a Natural Law?. WALDSTEIN, Wolfgang.
Izydora Dambska's Philosophy of Culture (in Polish). BOBER, Ireneusz.
J S Mill and Indian Education. ZASTOUPIL, Lynn.
J S Mill's Concept of Maturity as the Criterion in Determining Children's Eligibility for Rights. KIM, Ki Su.
Japan's Dilemma with the Definition of Death. KIMURA, Rihito.
The Jargon of Authenticity: Adorno and Feminist Essentialism. PHELAN, Shane.
Jean-Jacques Rousseau, Sexist?. THOMAS, Paul.
Jevons's Applications of Utilitarian Theory to Economic Policy. PEART, Sandra J.
Judaism, Justice, and Access to Health Care. MACKLER, Aaron L.
Judgment and Rationality in Lyotard's Discursive Archipelago. HENDLEY, Steven.
Jugement juridique et jugement pratique: de Kant à la philosophie du langage. LENOBLE, J and BERTEN, A.
Justice and Aristotelian Practical Reason. DAHL, Norman.
Justice, Redistribution, and the Family. POST, Stephen G.
The Justification of Justice as Fairness: A Two Stage Process. VAGGALIS, Ted.
Keynesian Uncertainty and the Weight of Arguments. RUNDE, Jochen.
Killing Machines. ANNAS, George J.
L'homme n'est pas l'humain. BOUCHARD, Guy.
L'institution juridique: imposition et interprétation. SÈVE, René.
Langage privé et communauté: Kripke et Wittgenstein. DUMOUCHEL, Paul.
The Last Utopia: Entropy and Revolution in the Poetics of Evgeny Zamjatin. SICHER, Efraim.
Law and Culture: The Conception of Legal Culture (in Polish). GRYKO, Czeslaw.
Law and Psychiatry: The Problems That Will Not Go Away. SZASZ, Thomas.
Le promeneur solitaire: Rousseau and the Emergence of the Post-Social Self. GAUTHIER, David.
Le thème de la révolution dans la pensée de Sartre. CREMA, Cristina Diniz Mendonça.
Leben als Passion: Elias Canettis "Masse und Macht" als Beitrag zum Begreifen der Moderne. DIETZSCH, Steffen.
The Lesbian, the Mother, the Heterosexual Lover: Irigaray's Recodings of Difference. HOLMLUND, Christine.
Liberalism, Aboriginal Rights, and Cultural Minorities. DANLEY, John R.
Libertad individual frente a determinación social. FRANCISCO PÉREZ, M.
Libre spéculation sur le rapport du vivant et du social. TOSEL, André.
Life and Cognition. FROLOV, Ivan T.
Limning the Liminal: Carr and Ricoeur on Time and Narrative. PELLAUER, David.

SOCIAL PHIL

Linguistic Forms and Social Obligations: A Critique of the Doctrine of Literal Expression in Searle. BOGEN, David.
Literacy as Disempowerment: The Role of Documentary Texts. DE CASTELL, Suzanne.
Le locutoire et l'illocutoire dans les énonciations relatives aux normes juridiques. AMSELEK, Paul.
The Logic of Causal Inference: Econometrics and the Conditional Analysis of Causation. HOOVER, Kevin D.
Lonergan's Recovery of the Notion of Natural Right: Introduction to a New Context for an Old Discussion. BRAIO, Frank Paul.
Loving Your Mother: On the Woman-Nature Relationship. ROACH, Catherine.
Loyalty: The Police. EWIN, R E.
Lukács on the Ontology of Social Existence and Marx's Understanding of Society (in German). LENDVAI, Ferenc L.
Lyotard's "Kantian Socialism". GEIMAN, Kevin Paul.
Machines as Persons?. CHERRY, Christopher.
Machines as Persons?. HANFLING, Oswald.
Maîtrise, marché et société industrielle. VAN PARIJS, Philippe.
The Making and Molding of Child Abuse. HACKING, Ian.
Making Interpersonal Comparisons Coherently. BARRETT, Martin and HAUSMAN, Daniel.
Making the Citizens Good: Aristotle's City and Its Contemporary Relevance. SIMPSON, Peter.
Malebranche and the Vision in God: A Note on *The Search After Truth*, III, 2, iii. NADLER, Steven.
Man and Hermeneutics. ROY, Krishna.
Mandatory AIDS Testing: The Legal, Ethical and Practical Issues. WERDEL, A Alyce.
The Market for Bodily Parts: A Response to Ruth Chadwick. TADD, G V.
Marriage is an Institution Created by God: A Philosophical Analysis. BOYLE, Joseph.
Marx and Perestroika. ROCKMORE, Tom.
Marx and Russia. NAARDEN, Bruno.
Marx as a Social Historian. MAHON, Joseph.
Marx's 'Critique of Hegel's *Philosophy of Right*'. JACKSON, M W.
Marx's Historical Understanding of the Proletariat and Class in 19th-Century England. MAZLISH, Bruce.
Marx, Engels and Max Weber on Eastern Societies—With a Special Respect to China (in Hungarian). DRUCKER, György.
Masaryk's "Anthropism" (in Czechoslovakian). NOVY, Lubomir.
Masaryk's Religious Thinking (in Czechoslovakian). FUNDA, Otakar A.
Matters of Conscience. SIMS, Pamela F.
Max Scheler: Theory of Forms of Knowledge and Perspective of Overcoming the Crisis of European Culture (in Polish). RUBA, Marek.
Medical Ethics in Ireland: A Decade of Change. DOOLEY, Dolores.
Medicine and Business: An Unhealthy Mix?. BROCK, Dan W.
The Message of Affirmative Action. HILL JR, Thomas E.
La metáfora como resolución de un problema comunicativo-lingüístico. FERNÁNDEZ, Teresa Bejaran.
The Metaphilosophy of Dialogue. KUCZYNSKI, Janusz.
The Metaphoric Structure of Sociological Explanation. CORRADI, Consuelo.
Methodological Individualism and Marx: Some Remarks on Jon Elster, Game Theory, and Other Things. WOLFF, Robert Paul.
The Micro-Macro Problem in Collective Behavior: Reconciling Agency and Structure. LEE, Raymond L M.
Misreading Rorty. KOLENDA, Konstantin.
Missouri Stands Alone. COLBY, William H.
Le modèle industriel comme modèle énergétique. BERTEN, André.
Modernité et postmodernité: un enjeu politique?. BERTEN, André.
Modernity, the Individual and Rationality in Marxism (Surrealism and Revolution). CLOUDSLEY, Tim.
Monadic Marxism: A Critique of Elster's Methodological Individualism. MOGGACH, Douglas.
Monstrous Imagination: Progeny as Art in French Classicism. HUET, Marie-Hélène.
Montesquieu and China. HONGXUN, Hou.
Moral Behavior at Public Performances. OLDS, Mason.
Moral Imagination, Freedom, and the Humanities. KEKES, John.
Moral Judgment. ROBERTSON, Emily.
The Moral Ontology of Charles Taylor: Contra Deconstructivism. HOY, Terry.
Moral Pluralism. WOLGAST, Elizabeth.
Moral Responsibility, Psychiatric Disorders and Duress. ELLIOTT, Carl.
Moraliteit en magie. LESAGE, Dieter.
Morality in Flux: Medical Ethics in the People's Republic of China. QIU, Ren-Zong.
The Morality of Feminism. SEVENHUIJSEN, Selma.
Morals by Appropriation. FREEMAN, Samuel.
Motherhood and the Possibility of a Contemporary Discourse for Women. GREY, Mary.
Must the State Justify Its Educational Policies?. HESLEP, Robert D.
Nancy Cruzan in China. ANNAS, George J.
Narrative Identity. RICOEUR, Paul.
La naturaleza y la historia como fundamento para un concepto renovada de razón. PADILLA, Leonel Eduardo.
Nature, Self, and Gender: Feminism, Environmental Philosophy, and the Critique of Rationalism. PLUMWOOD, Val.
Nietzsche and Fascism. WILLIAMS, Howard.
Nietzsche and the Cultural Resonance of the 'Death of God'. ROBERTS, Richard H.
Nietzsche contra Rousseau: Goethe versus Catilina?. BLONDEL, Eric.
Nietzsche in America: Fashion and Fascination. VAN DER WILL, Wilfried.
Nietzsche on Woman. THOMPSON, J L.
Nietzsche, Socrates and Pragmatism. RORTY, Richard.
No Time for an AIDS Backlash. MURPHY, Timothy F.
Noncompliance in AIDS Research. ARRAS, John D.
Der Normgeltungsbegriff als probabilistischer Begriff: Zur Logik des soziologischen Normbegriffs. LÜBBE, Weyma.
A Note on the Jural Relation. BUTLER, Ken.
Nothingness and Responsibility (in Czechoslovakian). HEJDANEK, L.
Nueva modernidad adveniente y cultura emergente en América Latina. SCANNONE, J C.
The Nurture of War: "Just War" Theory's Contribution. SANTONI, Ronald E.
The Occasion Fleeting: A Talk with Richard Selzer. JOSYPH, Peter.
On African Feminism: Two Reasons for the Rejection of Feminism. KWAME, Safro.
On J L Fischer's Reflections About Categories of Dialectic Materialism (in Czechoslovakian). TOSENOVSKY, Ludvik.
On Primoratz's Definition of Terrorism. SINNOTT-ARMSTRONG, Walter.
On Taking Socratic Irony Seriously (in Hebrew). SCOLNICOV, Samuel.
On Taking Substituted Judgment Seriously. BARON, Charles.
On the Empirical Status of Radical Feminism: A Reply to Schedler. MUI, Constance L.
On the Issue of Sex Differences. ALLEN, Elizabeth.
On the Morality of Waging War Against the State. MILLER, Seumas.
On the Philosophy of the Czech Avant-garde, Part II (in Czechoslovakian). STROHS, S.
The On-Going Deconstruction of Marxism-Leninism. BUCHHOLZ, Arnold and SWIDERSKI, E M.
Once Again Pure Exchange Economies: A Critical View Towards the Structuralistic Reconstructions by Balzer & Stegmüller. REQUATE, Till.
One Man's Reflection on a Masculine Role in Feminist Ethics: Epistemic versus Political Privilege. BOYD, Dwight.
Oppression and Victimization; Choice and Responsibility. WENDELL, Susan.
Our Inner Divinity: Humanism and the Spiritual Enterprise. ARISIAN, Khoren.
Outrageous Fortune: Selling Other People's Cells. ANNAS, George J.
Over Overdrijven. GRIFFIOEN, S.
El papel de la comunicación espontánea en los procesos de evolución social. RODRÍGUEZ HÖLKEMEYER, Patricia.
Para una teoría latinoamericana de las relaciones de la ciencia con la literatura: la cienciapoesía. CATALÁ, Rafael.
El paradigma de sistemas: posibilidades para una prácica social emancipadora. RODRÍGUEZ HÖLKEMEYER, Patricia.
Paradojas del Romanticismo. KERKHOFF, Manfred.
The Paradox of Aquinas's Altruism: From Self-Love to Love of Others. HAYDEN, R Mary.
The Paradox of Group Beneficence. OTSUKA, Michael.
Le partage des philosophes. SOULEZ, Philippe.
Pascal, etica, politica, socialità. DEREGIBUS, Arturo.
The Patient Self-Determination Act. MC CLOSKEY, Elizabeth Leibold.
A Peep into Man's History: The Lessons for Today. SINGH, Ajai R and SINGH, Shakuntala A.
El pensamiento de Heidegger y Marcuse en relación con la ecología. ARRIETA, Jeannette and HAYLING, Annie.
El pensamiento filosófico de Martin Luther King, Jr. STERLING, Marvin C.
Il pensiero dello "Stato" in Husserl: recenti problemi critici. FALCIONI, Daniela.
Per l'Europa dopo il crollo della Cortina di Ferro. GRYGIEL, Stanislaw.
The Perils of Love: Why Women Need Rights. INGRAM, Attracta.
Persona y sociedad según Jacques Maritain. WASHBURN, Jimmy.
Personal Identity and Brain Transplants. SNOWDON, P F.
Personal Identity and the Idea of a Human Being. MADELL, Geoffrey.
The Philosopher as Insider and Outsider: How to Advise, Compromise, and Criticize. KAMM, Frances M.
The Philosopher's Prism: Foucault, Feminism, and Critique. ALADJEM, Terry K.
Philosophers on Gender and Sexuality. VADAKKEMURIYIL, A.
Philosophical and Normative Dimensions and Aspects of the Idea of Renaissance. GREGORIOS, Paulos Mar.
Philosophie et société. BERTEN, André.
Philosophiehistorische Forschung und historischer Materialismus. THOM, Martina.
Philosophische Uberlegungen zu "Menschenwürde" und Fortpflanzungs-Medizin. SCHÖNE-SEIFERT, Bettina.
Philosophy and a Career in Counseling. ANGELETT, William.
Philosophy and Politics: On Fred Dallmayr's "Critical Encounters". MISGELD, Dieter.

SOCIAL PHIL

Philosophy and the Theory of Social Behaviour. HAMLYN, D W.
Philosophy of Culture and Its Place in the Scientific Achievement of Roman Ingarden (in Polish). MAJEWSKA, Zofia.
Philosophy of Culture in the Works of Szymon Starowolski (1588-1656) (in Polish). SZYDLOWSKI, Piotr.
Plato's Three Waves and the Question of Utopia. HYLAND, Drew A.
Play and the Theory of Basic Human Goods. CELANO, Anthony J.
Plural But Equal: Group Identity and Voluntary Integration. ROBACK, Jennifer.
Political Economy and Mimetic Desire: A Postmodernist Reading of "Babette's Feast". SHAPIRO, Michael J.
The Political Economy of Tardive Dyskinesia: Asymmetries in Power and Responsibility. COHEN, David and MC CUBBIN, Michael.
Possibility of Dialogic Encounter of Religious and Philosophical Humanitas (in Serbo-Croatian). SKLEDAR, Nikola.
Postmodernist Elitism and Postmodern Struggles. GROSSBERG, Lawrence.
The Pot at the End of the Rainbow: Political Myth and the Ecological Crisis. DOYLE, Timothy.
Le pouvoir de la différence. DELIVOYATSIS, Socratis.
La práctica tecnológica. HERRERA JIMÉNEZ, Rodolfo.
Practical Reason or Metapreferences? An Undogmatic Defense of Kantian Morality. NIDA-RÜMELIN, Julian.
Précis of "Whose Justice? Which Rationality?". MAC INTYRE, Alasdair.
Presidential Campaigns, Television News and Voter Turnout. WALTER, Edward.
Prichard, Davidson and Action. GUSTAFSON, Don.
Pride, Hypocrisy and Civility in Mandeville's Social and Historical Theory. DICKEY, Laurence.
The Principle of Unity of Theory and Practice in Marxism: A Critique. DIMITRAKOS, D.
The Problem of Other Cultures and Other Periods in Action Explanations. MARTIN, Rex.
The Problem of Unauthorized Welfare. VALLENTYNE, Peter.
Le problème politique chez Sartre et Foucault. KNEE, Phili.
El proceso de formación de la clase obrera de las minas en Asturias. MORADIELLOS, Enrique.
Process Metaphysics and Minimalism: Implications for Public Policy. KEFFER, Steven and KING, Sallie and KRAFT, Steven.
Productivity and X-Efficiency: A Reply to Singh and Frantz. SARAYDAR, Edward.
Professional Education of African Americans: A Challenge to Ethical Thinking. HARRIS, William M.
Prologomena to Jozef Tischner's Philosophy of Culture (in Polish). WIECZOREK, Krzysztof.
Property Rights and Preservationist Duties. GOODIN, Robert E.
Protective Norms as a Basis for Cooperation between Non-Privileged Constituencies. HEDMAN, Carl.
Prudence: Aristotelian Perspectives on Practical Reason. HASLAM, Nick.
La psychologie de 1850 à 1950. FOUCAULT, Michel.
Public Input Into Health Care Policy: Controversy and Contribution in California. COLBERT, Treacy.
Qu'est-ce qu'interpréter?. MERCIER, André.
Qu'est-ce que la Critique? (Critique et *Aufklärung*). FOUCAULT, M Michel.
La Querelle de la Moralité du Théâtre au XVIIe Siècle. FUMAROLI, M Marc.
Racial Bias, the Death Penalty, and Desert. MEYERS, Christopher.
Racionalidad y libertad. FERNÁNDEZ DEL VALLE, Agustín Basave.
Radical Hermeneutics, Critical Theory, and the Political. DOODY, John A.
The Ranking of Preference. RAWLING, Piers.
Rasgos de la communidad agustiniana según la 'Regula recepta'. ANOZ, José.
Ratifiability, Game Theory, and the Principle of Independence of Irrelevant Alternatives. EELLS, Ellery and HARPER, William L.
Rational Chocolate Addiction or How Chocolate Cures Irrationality. ELLIOTT, C S.
Rational Choice Theory Considered as Psychology and Moral Philosophy. MONGIN, Philippe.
Rationality and Social Labor in Marx. KHALIL, Elias L.
The Rationality of Escapism and Self Deception. LONGEWAY, John L.
Rationality, Culture and Values. CHATTOPADHYAYA, D P.
Rationality, Economic Action and Scarcity (in Hungarian). FEKETE, László.
Rawls, Sandel and the Self. CANEY, S.
Rawlsian Nash Solutions. FABELLA, Raul V.
Real Selves: Persons as a Substantial Kind. LOWE, E J.
Realism, Naturalism and Social Behaviour. OUTHWAITE, William.
Reason and Emotion. FRICKER, Miranda.
Reason, Rationality and the Irrational. NAYAK, G C.
Reassessing Autonomy in Long-Term Care. AGICH, George J.
Reconstructing the Subject: Feminism, Modernism, and Postmodernism. HEKMAN, Susan.
The Reconstruction of Institutions. COLAPIETRO, Vincent M.
Reflections on Ideas of Social Philosophy and Indian Code of Conduct. DASGUPTA, Manashi.
Reflections on the Nature of Ideology. VAN DOAN, Tran.
Reflections on the Philosophy of Hitlerism. HAND, Seán (trans) and LEVINAS, Emmanuel.
Réflexiones sur l'idéee de la guerre dans la philosophie présocratique. FREUND, Julien.
Reinvigorating the International Christian-Marxist Dialogue. MOJZES, Paul.
Remaking the She-Devil: A Critical Look at Feminist Approaches to Beauty. DAVIS, Kathy.
Renaissance of Democracy?. LEFORT, Claude and HARVEY, Robert.
Reply to Chmielewski: Cooperation by Definition. GORDON, David.
Reply to Gordon: Discourse at Work. CHMIELEWSKI, Philip J.
Reply to Marsh's "Reply to McKinney on Lonergan". MC KINNEY, Ronald H.
Reply to Maryann Ayim's "In Praise of Clutter as a Necessary Part of the Feminist Perspective". WENDELL, Susan.
Repression of Sexuality in Philosophy and the Return of the Repressed in Freud's Psychoanalysis (in Serbo-Croatian). KORDIC, Radoman.
Reproductive Gifts and Gift Giving: The Altruistic Woman. RAYMOND, Janice G.
Respect for Persons and Self-Respect: Western and Indian. GHOSH-DASTIDAR, Koyeli.
Respect for Privacy: Western and Indian. GHOSH-DASTIDAR, Koyeli.
Response to "Literacy as Disempowerment". RAITZ, Keith L.
Response to Berlin and McBride. RENICK, Timothy M.
Response to Diamond. MC NAUGHTON, David.
Response to Lyons' "Basic Rights and Constitutional Interpretations". LUCKHARDT, Grant.
Response to McNaughton. DIAMOND, Cora.
A Response to My Critics. DALLMAYR, Fred.
Response to Slote's "Ethics Without Free Will". VAN INWAGEN, Peter.
Response to W J Norman's "Has Rational Economic Man a Heart". LA CASSE, Chantale and ROSS, Don.
Response to Wilkie's "Habits of the Heart". RAITZ, Keith L.
Responsibility in the Tradition of Czech Thought (in Czechoslovakian). ZUMR, J.
Responsibility, the Theory of Values, and the Theory of Knowledge (in Czechoslovakian). MERCIER, A.
Responsibility—A Challenge in Terms of Philosophy (in German). RÖSEBERG, Ulrich.
Responsibility: Repudiators Referring to the Divided Centre of Action in the Physical Agent (in Czechoslovakian). PEARS, D.
Rethinking Feminist Humanism. STRAUS, Nina Pelikan.
Rethinking the Commons. HERRING, Ronald J.
Rethinking the Family. KYMLICKA, Will.
Reward, Punishment, and the Strategy of Evolution. SCHRADER, Malcolm E.
The *Rezeptionsgeschichte* of the Paris Manuscripts. MAIDAN, Michael.
Rights and Rights Violators: A New Approach to the Nature of Rights. GERT, Heather J.
Rights and Structure in Constitutional Theory. MILLER, Geoffrey P.
Rights as Rhetoric: Nonsense on Stilts?. O'NEILL, William.
The Rights of Organizations. GORDLEY, James.
Rights-Talk Will Not Sort Out Child-Abuse: Comment on Archard on Parental Rights. MIDGLEY, Mary.
Role Differentiation Problems in Professional Ethics. WANGERIN, Paul T.
Role Theory: A Reconstruction. VAN VONDEREN, Marijke L.
Die Rolle des Individuums und seine Beteiligung an gesellschaftlichen Prozessen. SCHLIWA, Harald and ZEDDIES, Helmut.
Rousseau intimiste et la fusion des cultures?. GRASSI, Marie-Claire.
Ruminations of a Slow-witted Mind. PIKE, Burton (trans) and LUFT, David S and MUSIL, Robert.
Sartre and Our Identity as Individuals. DILMAN, Ilham.
Sartre and Sexism. BARNES, Hazel E.
The Satanic Novel: A Philosophical Dialogue on Blasphemy and Censorship. SPRIGGE, T L S.
Schelling's Treatise on the Essence of Human Freedom and Heidegger's Thought. FROMAN, Wayne J.
The Science of Caring. PUKA, Bill.
Scientific Humanism and Religion. WILSON, Edward O.
Scientific Knowledge and Human Happiness. ROY, Krishna.
The Search for an Ethical Sacrament: From Bonhoeffer to Critical Social Theory. FLOYD, Wayne Whitson.
Selected Problems of Albert Caracciolo's Philosophy of Culture (in Polish). TECZA, Beata.
The Self and Social Criticism. HARVEY, Charles W.
Self-Conscious Individual versus Social Soul: The Rationale of Wittgenstein's Discussion of Rule Following. SAVIGNY, Eike V.
Self-Defence and National Defence. DE ROOSE, Frank.
Self-Interest and the New Bashing of Economics. KIRZNER, Israel M.
Self-Potential as a Yoruba Ultimate: A Further Contribution to URAM Yoruba Studies. LAWUYI, Olatunde B.
Le sens de la révolution méthodologique introduite par Rousseau dans la science politique. GOYARD-FABRE, Simone.
Seven Types of Obloquy: Travesties of Marxism. GERAS, Norman.
Siting, Justice, and Conceptions of Good. ENGLISH, Mary.
Social Apriori of Responsibility in Scheler's Phenomenology (in Serbo-Croatian). VEAUTHIER, Frank W.

SOCIAL PHIL

Social Communication and Interest Relationships (in German). LUUTZ, Wolfgang.
Social Criticism and Political Philosophy. BARRY, Brian.
Social Movements and Individual Identity: A Critique of Freud on the Psychology of Groups. WARTENBERG, Thomas E.
The Social Philosophy of Marxism: The Founders and the Present Day. SHEVCHENKO, V N.
Social Responsibility and Strategic Management: Toward an Enterprise Strategy Classification. MEZNAR, Martin B and CHRISMAN, James J and CARROLL, Archie B.
Social Science as Moral Philosophy?: Reflections on Alan Wolfe's *Whose Keeper*?. MASON, John R.
Sociedad informatizada y poder político. RICHARDS, Edgardo.
Sociologie in de Weimarrepubliek. HABERMAS, Jürgen.
Sociology: An Infirm Science. BUSINO, Giovanni and FERGUSON, Jeanne.
Solitude. KOCH, Philip J.
Some Aspects of the Relationship Between the Theory of Socialism and the Perception of an Era (in German). BRIE, André (and others).
Some Fundamental Aspects of Socioecological Theory and Policy, Part I (in German). OPIELKA, Michael.
Some Fundamental Aspects of Socioecological Theory and Policy, Part II (in German). OPIELKA, Michael.
Some Reflections on Post-Marxism and Post-Christianity: A Response to Professor Arthur Mc Govern. STOJANOVIC, Svetozar.
Some Remarks on a Historical Theory of Justice and its Application to Ireland. MC KIM, Robert.
Some Remarks on Respect and Human Rights. BARNES, Annette.
Some Thoughts About Heterosexualism. HOAGLAND, Sarah Lucia.
Some Thoughts on Common Scents. ALMAGOR, Uri.
Speaking About the Unspeakable: Genocide and Philosophy. FREEMAN, Michael.
Spiritual Values and "The Goddess". BRANDEN, Victoria.
Starting Thought From Women's Lives: Eight Resources for Maximizing Objectivity. HARDING, Sandra.
Stout on Relativism, Liberalism, and Communitarianism. QUIRK, Michael J.
Le stratège militaire. POIRIER, Lucien.
Study of Society and Polity: Scientific and Philosophical. CHATTOPADHYAYA, D P.
The Subject in Feminism. BRAIDOTTI, Rosi.
Subjective Boundaries and Combinations in Psychiatric Diagnoses. MIROWSKY, John.
Subjectivisation as Control or Resistance: An Examination of Reformation Theology and Marxism. PATTMAN, Rob.
La subversion de l'"elenchos" juridique dans l'"Apologie de Socrate". DORION, Louis-André.
Super-yo y vida moral: Una valoración tomista de la hipótesis psicoanalítica. PITHOD, Abelardo.
Superestructura ideológica de las relaciones sociales. MÁRQUEZ FERNÁNDEZ, Alvaro B.
Sur l'éthique et la rationalité de l'État social. MARION, Normand.
Surrogate Decisionmaking and Other Matters. GREENLAW, Jane.
Sustaining Non-Rationalized Practices: Body-Mind, Power and Situational Ethics—Interview with Hubert and Stuart Dreyfus. FLYVBJERG, Bent.
Synderesis, the Spark of Conscience, in the English Renaissance. GREENE, Robert A.
A Synthetic Formulation of Nietzsche's Aesthetic Model. JOVANOVSKI, Thomas.
System-Theoretical Bases of Social Theory (in German). LUHMANN, Niklas.
Systems of Interpretation and the Function of the Metaphor. CRIDER, Cathleen and CIRILLO, Leonard.
T G Masaryk—A Modern Thinker (in Czechoslovakian). OPAT, Jaroslav.
Tacit Consent. CARR, Craig L.
Tecnología y sociedad. HERRERA, Rodolfo.
The Temporality of Illness: Four Levels of Experience. TOOMBS, S Kay.
Le temps de l'action. BOYER, Alain.
Teología de la liberación y doctrina social de la Iglesia hoy. GALLI, C M.
The Aristotelian Debate in African Philosophy: Miscellaneous Remarks on a Denied Discourse (in German). NEUGEBAUER, Christian.
The Common European Home (in German). FEIEREIS, Konrad.
The Concept of Environment from the Point of View of Philosophy of Culture (in Polish). CHYMUK, Maria.
The Conception of Culture According to Jozef Chalasinski (1904-1979) (in Polish). GRYKO, Czeslaw.
The Differences Between the Capitalist and the Modern Society (in German). KRÜGER, Hans-Peter.
The Enticing Thing About Stalinism (in German). PÄTZOLT, Harald.
The Functional Conception of Culture and the Explanation of the Value-Shaping Process (in Polish). BROZI, Krzysztof J.
The Hopeless Realist (in Serbo-Croatian). WIGGERHAUS, Rolf.
The Meaning of Discussions on Democratic Socialism in Czechoslovakia (in Czechoslovakian). KAMARYT, Jan.
The Metacultural Hypothesis and the Foundations of Cultural Activity (in Polish). PORENA, Boris.
The Other Nietzsche: Criticism of Moral Utopia (in German). MAURER, Reinhart.
The Passing On of Values (in French). PIGUET, J-Claude.
The Perversion of Emancipation into Repression (in German). SCHMIDT, Hartwig.
The Philosophy of Responsibility (in German). SCHRÖDER, Richard.
The Process of Evolution in a Holistic World (in German). SOSCHINKA, Hans-Ulrich.
The World of Human Community in Hanna Arendt's Work (in Czechoslovakian). KOUBA, Pavel.
Theologie und Sozialvorstellungen bei Thomas Müuntzer (in Czechoslovakian). LAUBE, Adolf.
A Theoretical Note on Simmel's Concept of Acquaintance. DOUBT, Keith.
A Theory of Social Justice?. HORTON, John.
Theory of Social Movements: Theory *for* Social Movements?. ROOTES, C A.
Therapeutic Professions and the Diffusion of Deficit. GERGEN, Kenneth J.
Time Preference. ZIFF, Paul.
To the History of Glory and Fall of the Book "Civilization at the Crossroads" after August 1968 (in Czechoslovakian). SINDELAR, Jan.
Todor Pavlov (1890-1977)—The Generalization of Reflection (in German). HOLZ, Hans Heinz.
Toward a Reconciliation of Liberalism and Communitarianism. ELLIS, Ralph D.
Toward A Value-Laden Theory: Feminism and Social Science. BERNICK, Susan E.
Towards a Feminist Reassessment of Intellectual Virtue. BRAATEN, Jane.
Trade Secrets and the Justification of Intellectual Property: A Comment on Hettinger. PAINE, Lynn Sharp.
Travail et nature dans l'Antiquité. MULLER, Robert.
Treating the Troops. HOWE, Edmund G and MARTIN, Edward D.
Treating the Troops: A Commentary. ANNAS, George J and GRODIN, Michael A.
Treating the Troops: A Commentary. LEVINE, Robert J.
Troeltsch and Nietzsche: Critical Reflections on Ernst Troeltsch's Portrayal of Nietzsche (in German). SCHÜSSLER, Ingeborg.
Twenty Years Since *Women and Madness*: Toward a Feminist Institute of Mental Health and Healing. CHESLER, Phyllis.
Two Aspects of the Christian-Marxist Dialogue: A Protestant Response. FRITZSCHE, Helmut.
Two Cartesian Arguments for the Simplicity of the Soul. ZIMMERMAN, Dean W.
Two Conceptions of Civil Rights. EPSTEIN, Richard A.
Two Designs of Universal History. KANTOR, K M.
Two Souls in One Body. HACKING, Ian.
Uguaglianza e temporalità nella "Democrazia in America". BAGLIONI, Emma.
Umuntu Ngumuntu Ngabantu: An African Concept of Humanity. SHUTTE, Augustine.
The Unavoidability of Gender. SCHEMAN, Naomi.
Uninformed Consent. MARCUS, Ruth Barcan and KUCKLICK, B and BERCOVITCH, S.
The Unitarian Universalist Association: Humanism or Theism?. KURTZ, Paul and BULLOUGH, Vern L.
Using Arendt and Heidegger to Consider Feminist Thinking on Women and Reproductive/Infertility Technologies. KLAWITER, Maren.
Using the Market to Measure Deserved Punishment. DAVIS, Michael.
Utilitarianism and the 'Punishment' of the Innocent: The General Problem. SMILANSKY, Saul.
Varieties of Pluralism in a Polyphonic Society. RORTY, Amelie Oksenberg.
The Varieties of Self-Interest. EPSTEIN, Richard A.
Verlichtingsfilosofie twee eeuwen later; J F Lyotard als postmoderne Kant. VAN PEPERSTRATEN, Frans.
Vers une Pédagogie du Dialogue. TONOIU, Vasile.
Vida y Resurrección en el pensamiento de Erich Fromm. CHAVES, Flory.
Virtue Theory and Abortion. HURSTHOUSE, Rosalind.
A Vision of the Health Decisions Movement. CRAWSHAW, Ralph.
The Vita Femina and Truth. BURNEY-DAVIS, Terri and KREBBS, R Stephen.
Vom Sein zur Selbstreferentialität: Überlegungen zur Theorie autopoietischer Systeme Niklas Luhmanns. GRIPP-HAGELSTANGE, Helga.
War and Crime. HOLYST, Brunon.
Was heisst "sich in der Gesellschaft orientieren"?. BÖHME, Gernot.
Was Karl Marx a Social Scientist?. FLEW, Antony.
We Mortals. LINGIS, Alphonso.
Welchen Platz kann die Philosophie künftig in unserem Lande beanspruchen und vor welchen Aufgaben steht sie?. RÜDIGER, Wolfgang.
Well-Being and Time. VELLEMAN, J David.
Werkzeugproduktion im Tierreich und menschliche Werkzeugproduktion. BEURTON, Peter.
What Are *Civil* Rights?. WEINREB, Lloyd L.
What is Philosophy of Culture? (in Polish). NOWICKI, Andrzej.
What is Terrorism?. PRIMORATZ, Igor.
What is the Problem Concerning Social Entities?. THOMPSON, J L.
What Makes Us So Different from the Apes?. LAYNG, Tony.
Where Are All the Pragmatist Feminists?. SEIGFRIED, Charlene Haddock.
Where Does the Self-Refutation Objection Take Us?. RAMSEY, William.
Whose Life is it Anyway?. TRUSTED, Jennifer.
Why Have Children?. ANSCOMBE, G E M.

SOCIAL PHIL
Why is Kitsch Bad? (in Hebrew). KULKA, Tomas.
Why Markets Don't Stop Discrimination. SUNSTEIN, Cass R.
Why Negative Rights Only?. JORDAN, Jeff.
Why Surfers Should Be Fed: The Liberal Case for an Unconditional Basic Income. VAN PARIJS, Philippe.
Wie van de drie: Wil de ware wetenschapsonderzoeker opstaan?. BIJSTERVELD, Karin and MESMAN, Jessica.
Wittgenstein on Jews: Some Counter-Examples. WASSERMANN, Gerhard D.
Wittgenstein versus Hart: Two Models of Rules for Social and Legal Theory. HUND, John.
Wittgenstein, eskimo's en emoties. POTT, Heleen.
Work and Family: Should Parents Feel Guilty?. PAINE, Lynn Sharp.
Your Daughter or Your Dog? A Feminist Assessment of the Animal Research Issue. SLICER, Deborah.

SOCIAL POLICY(-CIES)
Euthanasia: Toward an Ethical Social Policy. THOMASMA, David C.
The Conceptual Bind in Defining the Volitional Component of Alcoholism. VATZ, Richard E and WEINBERG, Lee S.
New Directions in Nursing Home Ethics. COLLOPY, Bart and BOYLE, Philip and JENNINGS, Bruce.

SOCIAL PROBLEMS
"Human Suffering and Our Post-Civilized Cultural Mind: A Maritainian Analysis" in *From Twilight to Dawn: The Cultural Vision of Jacques Maritain*, CALIFANO, Joseph J.
"Jacques Maritain and the Future of Democratic Authority" in *From Twilight to Dawn: The Cultural Vision of Jacques Maritain*, O'DONNELL, Charles P.
"Pactos inicuos" y acuerdo racional. RABOTNIKOF, Nora.
Marx as a Social Historian. MAHON, Joseph.

SOCIAL PROGRESS
La práctica tecnológica. HERRERA JIMÉNEZ, Rodolfo.

SOCIAL PSYCHOLOGY
Spuren der Macht. RÖTTGERS, Kurt.
"'Subjects' versus 'Persons' in Social Psychological Research" in *Harré and His Critics*, SECORD, Paul F.
"An Empirical Interpretation of Ethogenics" in *Harré and His Critics*, ARGYLE, Michael.
"From National Character to the Mechanism of Stereotyping" in *Perspectives on Ideas and Reality*, HUNYADY, György.
AIDS and the Psycho-Social Disciplines: The Social Control of 'Dangerous' Behavior. KAPLAN, Mark S.
Attitudes, Leprechauns and Neutrinos: The Ontology of Behavioral Science. CHANDLER, Marthe.
Epistemology, Psychology, and Goldman. CORLETT, J Angelo.
El factor prelógico en el desarrollo de América Latina: El teorema del preconsciente colectivo. MANSILLA, H C F.
Social Epistemics and Social Psychology. GOLDMAN, Alvin.
Social Epistemology and Social Cognitive Psychology. SCHMITT, Frederick.

SOCIAL RELATIONS
The Call to Personhood. MC FADYEN, Alistair I.
"The Origin of Ethics" in *A Companion to Ethics*, MIDGLEY, Mary.
Anarchism and Feminism. MOODY, Thomas E.
Emile's Education. SHAVER, Robert.
The History of the Christian Philosophical Reflection on Peace. WASKIEWICZ, Hanna.
Superestructura ideológica de las relaciones sociales. MÁRQUEZ FERNÁNDEZ, Alvaro B.
War and Crime. HOLYST, Brunon.

SOCIAL RESPONSIBILITY
Essentials of Business Ethics. MADSEN, Peter (ed).
Work, Inc.: A Philosophical Inquiry. BYRNE, Edmund F.
"The Loss of Responsibility" in *The Political Responsibility of Intellectuals*, HANKISS, Elemer.
Business Ethics and Social Responsibility in Finance Instruction: An Abdication of Responsibility. HAWLEY, Delvin D.
Choosing Social Responsibility Over Law: The *Soldier of Fortune* Classified Advertising Cases. TOMLINSON, Don E.
Corporate Social Responsibility and the Marketplace. COTTRILL, Melville T.
Economic Efficiency and the Quality of Life. JACOBSEN, Rockney.
Etica del desarrollo: algunos principios y orientaciones a la luz de la docrina social de la Iglesia Católica. BRENES, Víctor.
An Issue in Corporate Social Responsibility: An Experiential Approach to Establish the Value of Human Life. DALTON, Dan R and COSIER, Richard A.
The Law of Business Ethics and Social Responsibility. BURKE III, William T.
Linguistic Forms and Social Obligations: A Critique of the Doctrine of Literal Expression in Searle. BOGEN, David.
A Proposal for Corporate Ethical Reform: The Ethical Dialogue Group. PAYNE, Stephen L.
The Relative Importance of Social Responsibility in Determining Organizational Effectiveness: Student Responses. KRAFT, Kenneth L.
The Relative Importance of Social Responsibility in Determining Organizational Effectiveness. KRAFT, Kenneth.
The Role of Ethics and Social Responsibility in Achieving Organizational Effectiveness: Students Versus Managers. KRAFT, Kenneth L and SINGHAPAKDI, Anusorn.
Social Responsibility and Strategic Management: Toward an Enterprise Strategy Classification. MEZNAR, Martin B and CHRISMAN, James J and CARROLL, Archie B.

SOCIAL ROLE(S)
"Nourishing Professionalism" in *Ethics, Trust, and the Professions: Philosophical and Cultural Aspects*, FREIDSON, Eliot.
Role Morality as a Complex Instance of Ordinary Morality. ANDRE, Judith.

SOCIAL SCIENCES
see also Economics, History, Law, Political Science
Demystifying Mentalities. LLOYD, G E R.
Harré and His Critics. BHASKAR, Roy (ed).
The Humanities in the Nineties: A View From the Netherlands. ZÜRCHER, Erik (ed).
The Idea of a Social Science and its Relation to Philosophy (Second Edition). WINCH, Peter.
Marxism and Philosophy in the Twentieth Century: A Defense of Vulgar Marxism. HUDELSON, Richard.
Models and Concepts of Ideology. RITSERT, Jürgen.
The Moral Domain: Essays in the Ongoing Discussion between Philosophy and the Social Sciences. WREN, Thomas E (ed).
Philosophische Hermeneutik. INEICHEN, Hans.
Reading Rawls: Critical Studies on Rawls' 'A Theory of Justice'. DANIELS, Norman (ed).
Social Theory of Modern Societies: Anthony Giddens and His Critics. HELD, David (ed).
The Taming of Chance. HACKING, Ian.
Varieties of Social Explanation: An Introduction to the Philosophy of Social Science. LITTLE, Daniel.
"Davidson and Social Science" in *Truth and Interpretation: Perspectives on the Philosophy of Donald Davidson*, ROOT, Michael.
"Exploring the Human Umwelt" in *Harré and His Critics*, HARRÉ, Rom.
"I Don't Know Why I Did It" in *Harré and His Critics*, CROWLE, Tony.
"Mario Bunge's Influence on the Administrative and Systems Sciences" in *Studies on Mario Bunge's "Treatise"*, MATTESSICH, Richard V.
"Maritain's Account of the Social Sciences" in *From Twilight to Dawn: The Cultural Vision of Jacques Maritain*, NELSON, Ralph.
"Rationality and Social Norms" in *Logic, Methodology and Philosophy of Science, VIII*, ELSTER, Jon.
"Rom Harré: Realism and the Turn to Social Constructionism" in *Harré and His Critics*, SHOTTER, John.
"Winch and Schutz on the Regulative Idea of a Social Science" in *Life-World and Politics: Between Modernity and Postmodernity*, O'NEILL, John.
An Alternative Logical Framework for Dialectical Reasoning in the Social and Policy Sciences. SABRE, Ru Michael.
Aportes para el debate en torno a la teología de la liberción. RUBIOLO, E.
Assessing Functional Explanations in the Social Sciences. KINCAID, Harold.
The Changing Nature of the Social Sciences. MASTERS, Roger D.
Concepts of Process in Social Science Explanations. VAYDA, Andrew P and MC CAY, Bonnie J and EGHENTER, Cristina.
The Conditions of Fruitfulness of Theorizing About Mechanisms in Social Science. STINCHCOMBE, Arthur L.
A Conjecture Concerning the Ranking of the Sciences. HUMPHREYS, Paul.
Deconstructing/Deconstructive Inquiry: The Politics of Knowing and Being Known. LATHER, Patti.
Do Not Despair: There is Life after Constructivism. BIJKER, Wieke.
Elements of a Wittgensteinian Philosophy of the Human Sciences. SCHATZKI, Theodore R.
Ethics in Educational Policy Analysis. WILLERS, Jack Conrad.
Explanation and Understanding in Social Science. SKORUPSKI, John.
Een gedesoriënteerde veranderingswetenschap. GASTELAARS, M.
Intentionalistic Explanations in the Social Sciences. SEARLE, John R.
Misconceptions of the Social Sciences. SEGAL, Robert A.
Na de sociale wending het roer nogmaals om. LATOUR, Bruno.
The Problem of Other Cultures and Other Periods in Action Explanations. MARTIN, Rex.
Response to the Presidential Address: Willer's "Ethics in Educational Policy Analysis". DRAKE, William E.
The *Rezeptionsgeschichte* of the Paris Manuscripts. MAIDAN, Michael.
The School and the Home: Partners or Pariahs—A Response to Kennedy on Home Schools. ENGEL, David E.
Scientism, Interpretation, and Criticism. GORSKI, Philip S.
Singular Explanation and the Social Sciences. RUBEN, David-Hillel.
Social Science Knowledge and Explanations in Educational Studies. DALE, Michael.
Social Science-Based Understandings of Science: Reflections on Fuller. KRUGLANSKI, Arie W.
A Structuralist Rousseau: On the Anthropology of Claude Lévi-Strauss. HONNETH, Axel.
Theology and the Social Sciences—Discipline and Antidiscipline. MURPHY, Nancey.
Theology as the Queen (Bee) of the Disciplines?. VAUX, Kenneth.

SOCIAL SCIENCES
Toward A Value-Laden Theory: Feminism and Social Science. BERNICK, Susan E.
Was Karl Marx a Social Scientist?. FLEW, Antony.
Wertfreiheit und Ethik in den Sozial-und Naturwissenschaften. ZIMMERMANN, Rolf.
Wittgenstein and Social Science. TRIGG, Roger.

SOCIAL SCIENTIST(S)
Captives of Controversy: The Myth of the Neutral Social Researcher in Contemporary Scientific Controversies. SCOTT, Pam and RICHARDS, Evelleen and MARTIN, Brian.
Marx as a Social Historian. MAHON, Joseph.

SOCIAL STRUCTURE(S)
Critique of Dialectical Reason, Volume 2: Jean-Paul Sartre. HOARE, Quintin (trans).
Rawls: "A Theory of Justice" and Its Critics. KUKATHAS, Chandran.
La sociedad sin hombres: Niklas Luhmann o la teoría como escándalo. IZUZQUIZA, Ignacio.
Whose Science? Whose Knowledge? Thinking from Women's Lives. HARDING, Sandra.
"The Theory of Structuration" in *Social Theory of Modern Societies: Anthony Giddens and His Critics*, THOMPSON, John B.
Animal Liberation as a Valid Response to Structural Violence. LISZT, Amy.
Response to Finsen's "Response to Lizst's Animal Liberation as a Valid Response to Structural Violence". LISZT, Amy.
Response to Lizst's "Animal Liberation as a Valid Response to Structural Violence". FINSEN, Susan.
Social Space as a Determinant of "Collective Thinking" (in Polish). SYMOTIUK, Stefan.

SOCIAL SYSTEM(S)
Community: The Tie That Binds. ROUSSEAU, Mary F.
La práctica tecnológica. HERRERA JIMÉNEZ, Rodolfo.
Search for Indian Traditional Paradigm of Society. SHARMA, K N.
Tecnología y sociedad. HERRERA, Rodolfo.

SOCIAL THEORY(-RIES)
Critique and Construction: A Symposium on Roberto Unger's "Politics". LOVIN, Robin W (ed).
The Critique of Power: Reflective Stages in a Critical Social Theory. HONNETH, Axel.
The Meaning of Socialism. LUNTLEY, Michael.
Social Theory of Modern Societies: Anthony Giddens and His Critics. HELD, David (ed).
"False Universality" in *Critique and Construction: A Symposium on Roberto Unger's "Politics"*, GALSTON, William A.
"Hermeneutics and Modern Social Theory" in *Social Theory of Modern Societies: Anthony Giddens and His Critics*, BAUMAN, Zygmunt.
"Presences and Absences: Time-Space Relations and Structuration Theory" in *Social Theory of Modern Societies: Anthony Giddens and His Critics*, GREGORY, Derek.
"Programmatic Thought and the Critique of the Social Disciplines" in *Critique and Construction: A Symposium on Roberto Unger's "Politics"*, TRUBEK, David M.
"A Reply to My Critics" in *Social Theory of Modern Societies: Anthony Giddens and His Critics*, GIDDENS, Anthony.
"Social Theory as Critique" in *Social Theory of Modern Societies: Anthony Giddens and His Critics*, BERNSTEIN, Richard J.
"War and the Nation-State in Social Theory" in *Social Theory of Modern Societies: Anthony Giddens and His Critics*, SHAW, Martin.
"When the Owl of Minerva Takes Flight at Dawn: Radical Constructivism in Social Theory" in *Critique and Construction: A Symposium on Roberto Unger's "Politics"*, BURNS, Robert P.
Conclusion: Legal Institutions and Limitations to Cognition and Power. O'BRIEN, James.
A Critique of Marx's Extension of the Principles of Dialectical Materialism into the Phenomena of Social Life. NYONG, Prince David.
The Impact of Science Studies on Political Philosophy. LATOUR, Bruno.
The Marxist Conception of Tradition. STEPANYANTS, Marietta.
Marxist Historians and the Question of Class in the French Revolution. AMARIGLIO, Jack and NORTON, Bruce.
Philosophical and Religious Implications of Cognitive Social Learning Theories of Personality. ROTTSCHAEFER, William A.
Philosophy and the Theory of Social Behaviour. HAMLYN, D W.
The Primacy of the Political: Towards a Theory of National Integration. RAJAN, R Sundara.
Scientific Method and the Study of Society. NARASIMHAN, R.
Theory of Social Movements: Theory *for* Social Movements?. ROOTES, C A.

SOCIAL WELFARE
Policraticus. NEDERMAN, Cary J (ed & trans).

SOCIALISM
Bertrand Russell. ALCARO, Mario.
Contemporary Perspectives on Masculinity: Men, Women, and Politics in Modern Society. CLATTERBAUGH, Kenneth.
Marx's Radical Critique of Capitalist Society: A Reconstruction and Critical Evaluation. ARNOLD, N Scott.
The Meaning of Socialism. LUNTLEY, Michael.
New Reflections on the Revolution of Our Time. LACLAU, Ernesto.
Resurrecting Marx: The Analytical Marxists on Freedom, Exploitation, and Justice. GORDON, David.
Socialism, Feminism and Philosophy: A Radical Philosophy Reader. SAYERS, Sean (ed).
L'Utopia di Fourier. TUNDO, Laura.
"The Origins of Some of Our Misconceptions" in *Perspectives on Ideas and Reality*, LUDASSY, Mária.
Art and Aesthetics and the Crisis of Culture. MORAWSKI, Stefan.
Beyond Mourning and Melancholia on the Left. DUBIEL, Helmut.
A Contribution to the Discussion of the Doctrinal Preconditions of the Deformation of Socialism. KOLODII, A F.
Democracy and Socialism: Philosophical *Aporiae*. CUNNINGHAM, Frank.
Ecosocialism—Utopian and Scientific. HAYWARD, Tim.
Elites and Systematic Change in Hungary. SZALAI, Erzsebet.
Friends and Enemies of Liberalism. ARCHARD, David.
From Propaganda to "Oeffentlichkeit" in Eastern Europe: Four Models of the Public Space Under State Socialism. SUKOSD, Miklos.
Future through Self-Organization (in German). ARTZT, M.
Gorbatschews "Erneurung des Sozialismus"—Ideologie in der Krise des Kommunismus. KUX, Ernst.
The Ideology of Intellectuals and the Chinese Student Protest Movement of 1989. CALHOUN, Craig.
The Intellectuals at the End of History. BRUNKHORST, Hauke.
Is Karl Marx to Blame for "Barracks Socialism"?. BUTENKO, A P.
Karl Marx and African Emancipatory Thought: A Critique of Marx's Euro-centric Metaphysics. SEREQUEBERHAN, Tsenay.
Kommunismus—Utopie und Wirklichkeit. HAVEMANN, Robert.
Le thème de la révolution dans la pensée de Sartre. CRÉMA, Cristina Diniz Mendonça.
Lyotard's "Kantian Socialism". GEIMAN, Kevin Paul.
Market Order or Commanded Chaos. FLEW, Antony.
The Meaning of Recent Changes in Eastern Europe. MARKOVIC, Mihailo.
Political Justice in Post-Communist Societies: The Case of Hungary. BENCE, György.
Recent Work in Political Philosophy. GRAHAM, Gordon.
Reflections on the Eastern European Revolutions: The God that Failed. MAZLISH, Bruce.
Responsibility—A Challenge in Terms of Philosophy (in German). RÖSEBERG, Ulrich.
Self-Management in the Context of the Disintegration of "Reali-Existing" Socialism. STANOJEVIC, Miroslav.
Social Communication and Interest Relationships (in German). LUUTZ, Wolfgang.
The Social Philosophy of Marxism: The Founders and the Present Day. SHEVCHENKO, V N.
Some Aspects of the Relationship Between the Theory of Socialism and the Perception of an Era (in German). BRIE, André (and others).
Some Basic Problems of a Political Theory of Modern Socialism (in German). SEGERT, Dieter.
The Sources of Stalinism. TSIPKO, A.
Swedish Model or Swedish Culture?. TRAGARDH, Lars.
The Development of a Concept of Modern Socialism: Theses under Discussion (in German). BRIE, Michael.
The Meaning of Discussions on Democratic Socialism in Czechoslovakia (in Czechoslovakian). KAMARYT, Jan.
The Party's Claim to Power: The Power of Knowledge in "Real Socialism" (in German). MARZ, Lutz.
Theologie und Sozialvorstellungen bei Thomas Müuntzer (in Czechoslovakian). LAUBE, Adolf.
The Theoretical Premises of Scientific Socialism and Its Mode of Thought. YUQUAN, Tao.
To the History of Glory and Fall of the Book "Civilization at the Crossroads" after August 1968 (in Czechoslovakian). SINDELAR, Jan.
The Unity of Human Rights in Western and Eastern Europe: Meditation about Human Rights. FÖLDESI, Tamás.
Was Marx a Socialist?. TSIPKO, A.
The Welfare State: What is Left?. PRYCHITKO, David L.

SOCIALITY
I, We and Body: First Joint Symposium of Philosophers from Africa and from the Netherlands. KIMMERLE, Heinz (ed).

SOCIALIZATION
Ethics, Politics, and Human Nature. PAUL, Ellen Frankel (ed).
Self, Society, and Personal Choice. MEYERS, Diana T.
"Heiligsprechung des Imaginären: Das Imaginäre in Cornelius Castoriadis' Gesellschaftstheorie" in *The Social Horizon of Knowledge*, LÖVENICH, Friedhelm.
El papel de la comunicación espontánea en los procesos de evolución social. RODRÍGUEZ HÖLKEMEYER, Patricia.

SOCIETY(-TIES)

Adorno's Aesthetic Theory: The Redemption of Illusion. ZUIDERVAART, Lambert.
Controlling Technology: Contemporary Issues. THOMPSON, William B.
Demystifying Mentalities. LLOYD, G E R.
The Dice-Playing God: Reflections on Life in a Post-Modern Age. KRIEGLSTEIN, Werner.
Fictions of Reality in the Age of Hume and Johnson. DAMROSCH, Leo.
Foundations of Social Theory. COLEMAN, James S.
Herrschaft und Versöhnung: Einführung in das Denken Theodor W Adornos. KAGER, Reinhard.
Hobbes. TUCK, Richard.
Jurisculture, Volume I: Greece and Rome. DORSEY, Gray L.
Law, Culture, and Values: Essays in Honor of Gray L Dorsey. VOJCANIN, Sava Alexander (ed).
Marx's Radical Critique of Capitalist Society: A Reconstruction and Critical Evaluation. ARNOLD, N Scott.
Metaphysics of Natural Complexes (Second Edition). WALLACE, Kathleen (ed).
New Reflections on the Revolution of Our Time. LACLAU, Ernesto.
Nietzsche: A Frenzied Look. ACKERMANN, Robert John.
The Place of the Hidden Moon: Erotic Mysticism in the Vaisnava-sahajiyā Cult of Bengal. DIMOCK JR, Edward C.
Self, Society, and Personal Choice. MEYERS, Diana T.
Theories of Science in Society. COZZENS, Susan E (ed).
"Ethics in Small-Scale Societies" in *A Companion to Ethics*, SILBERBAUER, George.
"Religion and Society in the Age of Theodosius" in *Grace, Politics and Desire: Essays on Augustine*, BARNES, Timothy D.
"Religion and the Making of Society" in *Critique and Construction: A Symposium on Roberto Unger's "Politics"*, DAVIS, Charles.
"A Reply to My Critics" in *Social Theory of Modern Societies: Anthony Giddens and His Critics*, GIDDENS, Anthony.
"Technology and Society: A View from Sociology" in *Studies on Mario Bunge's "Treatise"*, GINGRAS, Yves and NIOSI, Jorge.
"Sociátá" et "communion" chez saint Thomas d'Aquin. LA SOUJEOLE, Benoît-Dominique.
'Domina et Regina Virtutum': Justice and *Societas* in *De Officiis*. ATKINS, E M.
Communism: A Post-Mortem. BAUMAN, Zygmunt.
El desarrollo como proceso: una investigación filosófica. DOWER, Nigel.
Dialogue on Science, Society, and the Generative Order. BOHM, D and KELLY, Sean.
Las dos grandes paradojas?. SERRANO, Augusto.
The Emerging Tension Between Self and Society, As Exemplified in Augustine. THOMPSON JR, George B.
Los Factores Originales de la Sociedad en Tomás de Aquino. BEUCHOT, Mauricio.
The Foundations of Professionalism: Fifty Years of the Philosophy of Education Society in Retrospect. GIARELLI, James M and CHAMBLISS, J J.
Human Nature, Social Engineering, and the Reemergence of Civil Society. RAU, Zbigniew.
Humanist Religion for the Troubled. RUSTERHOLTZ, Wallace P.
La influencia de Rousseau en el pensamiento de Kant. DE LOS ANGELES GIRALT, María.
John Scottus Eriugena: Recent Works of Consultation. MC EVOY, James J.
Langage privé et communauté: Kripke et Wittgenstein. DUMOUCHEL, Paul.
Le promeneur solitaire: Rousseau and the Emergence of the Post-Social Self. GAUTHIER, David.
Libre spéculation sur le rapport du vivant et du social. TOSEL, André.
Lukács on the Ontology of Social Existence and Marx's Understanding of Society (in German). LENDVAI, Ferenc L.
Montaigne's 'Des Cannibales' and Natural Sources of Virtue. HOROWITZ, Maryanne Cline.
Paternalistic Laws. GOLDMAN, Alan H and GOLDMAN, Michael N.
Philosophie et société. BERTEN, André.
Problemas conceptuales y políticas de desarrollo tecnológico. QUINTANILLA, Miguel Ángel.
Propriété de soi et propriété du monde extérieur. COUTURE, Jocelyne.
Questioni di filosofia politica. VECA, Salvatore.
The Role of Aristotle's *Praxis* Today. GUY, Alfred.
Rosmini interprete della Rivoluzione francese e di Rousseau. BOTTO, Evandro.
Scientific Method and the Study of Society. NARASIMHAN, R.
Society as a Department Store. LEGUTKO, Ryszard.
Society as an "Accidental Product of Human Activities": Max Horkheimer's Social Theory and Critique. BALOG, Andreas.
Sur l'éthique et la rationalité de l'État social. MARION, Normand.
Tecnología y sociedad. HERRERA, Rodolfo.
Tully's Locke. DEN HARTOGH, Govert.
Varieties of Pluralism in a Polyphonic Society. RORTY, Amelie Oksenberg.
Was heisst "sich in der Gesellschaft orientieren"?. BÖHME, Gernot.
Wetenschapsontwikkeling en kundes. BOON, Louis (and others).

SOCIOBIOLOGY

Ethics, Politics, and Human Nature. PAUL, Ellen Frankel (ed).
Evolutionary Instability: Logical and Material Aspects of a Unified Theory of Biosocial Evolution. GEIGER, Gebhard.
Philosophy and Cognitive Science. FETZER, James H.
The Science of the Mind (Second Edition). FLANAGAN, Owen.
"On the Implications of Sociobiology for Nuclear Weapons Policy" in *Issues in War and Peace: Philosophical Inquiries*, SCHONSHECK, Jonathan.
The Biological Justification of Ethics: A Best-Case Scenario. ROSENBERG, Alexander.
Causes, Proximate and Ultimate. FRANCIS, Richard C.
Cultural Evolution, Biology and Language: Empirical and Rational Criteria of Selection (in German). DORSCHEL, Andreas.
The Elusiveness of Human Nature. SMITHURST, Michael.
How Did Morality Evolve?. IRONS, William.
Kritik der Soziobiologie des Menschen. KASPAR, Rudolf F.
Moral und Biologie. RICHTER, Klaus.
A Naturalistic Theory of Archaic Moral Order. CAMPBELL, Donald.
El paradigma de sistemas: posibilidades para una prácica social emancipadora. RODRÍGUEZ HÖLKEMEYER, Patricia.
Philip Kitchers Soziobiologie-Kritik. VOLLMER, Gerhard.
Recent Work in the Philosophy of Biology. STERELNY, Kim.
Sociology, Selection, and Success: A Critique of David Hull's Analysis of Science and Systematics. DONOGHUE, Michael J.
Taking Mathematics Seriously?. ZYCINSKI, Joseph.
Todos contra la Sociobiología. SÁNCHEZ, Manuel Esteban.
Warum lebt der Mensch moralisch?. BURKHARDT, Cornelia and FRANKENHÄUSER, Gerald.

SOCIOLOGY

Beyond Ethnocentrism: A Reconstruction of Marx's Concept of Science. MC KELVEY, Charles.
Causality in Sociological Research. KARPINSKI, Jakub.
Critical Traditions in Contemporary Archaeology. PINSKY, Valerie (ed).
Dämonie und Gesellschaft. CATTEPOEL, Jan.
Mannheim and Hungarian Marxism. GABEL, Joseph.
Die moderne Gesellschaft im Rechtsstaat. BAURMANN, Michael.
Nation und Ethos: Die Moral des Patriotismus. KLUXEN-PYTA, Donate.
On Durkheim's Rules of Sociological Method. GANE, Mike.
La sociedad sin hombres: Niklas Luhmann o la teoría como escándalo. IZUZQUIZA, Ignacio.
Structures in Mathematical Theories: Reports of the San Sebastian International Symposium, 1990. DÍEZ, Amparo (ed).
Unsere postmoderne Moderne (Second Edition). WELSCH, Wolfgang.
Das Verhängnis Erste Philosophie. EBELING, Hans.
"Seek and Ye Might Find" in *Scientific Theories*, CAPLAN, Arthur L.
"The Sociotechnology of Sociotechnical Systems: Elements of a Theory of Plans" in *Studies on Mario Bunge's "Treatise"*, SENI, Dan Alexander.
"Technology and Society: A View from Sociology" in *Studies on Mario Bunge's "Treatise"*, GINGRAS, Yves and NIOSI, Jorge.
"The Wittgenstein-Problem in Sociology or: the 'Linguistic Turn' as a Pirouette" in *The Social Horizon of Knowledge*, RITSERT, Jürgen.
Animal Faith, Puritanism, and the Schutz-Gurwitsch Debate: A Commentary. LYMAN, Stanford M.
Bestandserhaltung oder Kritik oder: Weder Bestandserhaltung noch Kritik—Die Intention der Systemtheorie Niklas Luhmanns. POLLACK, Detlef.
Biology and the Social Sciences. WILSON, Edward O.
Captives of Controversy: The Myth of the Neutral Social Researcher in Contemporary Scientific Controversies. SCOTT, Pam and RICHARDS, Evelleen and MARTIN, Brian.
The Concept of Jurisprudence. ALEXY, Robert and DREIER, Ralf.
Conception of Values in Polish Sociology (in Polish). STYK, Jozef.
Desacralization and the Disenchantment of the World. WENNEMANN, Daryl.
The Metaphoric Structure of Sociological Explanation. CORRADI, Consuelo.
Na de sociale wending het roer nogmaals om. LATOUR, Bruno.
Der Normgeltungsbegriff als probabilistischer Begriff: Zur Logik des soziologischen Normbegriffs. LÜBBE, Weyma.
On Bureaucracy and Science: A Response to Fuller. TWENEY, Ryan D.
Science in the Age of Mechanical Reproduction: Moral and Epistemic Relations Between Diagrams and Photographs. LYNCH, Michael.
Sociologie in de Weimarrepubliek. HABERMAS, Jürgen.
Sociology: An Infirm Science. BUSINO, Giovanni and FERGUSON, Jeanne.
Some Fundamental Aspects of Socioecological Theory and Policy, Part II (in German). OPIELKA, Michael.
Stereotypes and Group-Claims. HARVEY, J.
The Strong Programme for the Sociology of Science, Reflexivity and Relativism. NOLA, Robert.
System-Theoretical Bases of Social Theory (in German). LUHMANN, Niklas.
Technique of Painting and Sociology of Picture (in Czechoslovakian). HLAVACEK, Josef.
Theory of Social Movements: Theory *for* Social Movements?. ROOTES, C A.
Thomas S Kuhn and L Fleck: Two Sociologists of Science. FLURI, Philippe H.

SOCIOLOGY
Vom Sein zur Selbstreferentialität: Überlegungen zur Theorie autopoietischer Systeme Niklas Luhmanns. GRIPP-HAGELSTANGE, Helga.
Wie van de drie: Wil de ware wetenschapsonderzoeker opstaan?. BIJSTERVELD, Karin and MESMAN, Jessica.

SOCIOLOGY OF KNOWLEDGE
Vernunft und Kontingenz: Rationalität und Ethos in der Phänomenologie. ORTH, Ernst Wolfgang (ed).
"The Defence of a Social System Against Its Ideology: A Case Study" in *The Social Horizon of Knowledge*, NOWAK, Leszek.
"Remarks on the Structure of Social Consciousness" in *The Social Horizon of Knowledge*, BUCZKOWSKI, Piotr.
Philosophy and the Sociology of Knowledge: An Investigation into the Nature of Orthodoxy (Astikya) in Hindu Thought. SHARMA, Arvind.
Rationality, Reasons, and the Sociology of Knowledge (in Serbo-Croatian). KAISER, Matthias.
Social Space as a Determinant of "Collective Thinking" (in Polish). SYMOTIUK, Stefan.
Sociology of Knowledge with Special Reference to Karl Popper. MANDAL, Sunil Baran.
The Sociology of Knowledge: Toward an Existential View of Business Ethics. PHILLIPS, Nelson.
Study of Society and Polity: Scientific and Philosophical. CHATTOPADHYAYA, D P.
Transcultural Dialogue and the Problem of the Concept of Ultimate Reality and Meaning. SINGLETON, Michael.

SOCRATES
Socrates: An Annotated Bibliography. NAVIA, Luis E.
Zetetic Skepticism. UMPHREY, Stewart.
"The True Temper of a Teacher" in *Abeunt Studia in Mores: A Festschrift for Helga Doblin*, RUCKER, Darnell.
The 'Teacher as Midwife': New Wine in Old Skins?. SANCHEZ, Karen L.
The Book of Anaxagoras. BRUMBAUGH, Robert S.
Death Is One of Two Things. RUDEBUSCH, George.
Dire e ascoltare nella tipologia del "sofista", del "filosof-re" e del pensatore socratico. MARCHETTI, Giancarlo.
The Good in Plato's *Gorgias*. WHITE, F C.
Meno, the Slave-Boy, and the *Elenchos*. BENSON, Hugh H.
Nietzsche, Socrates and Pragmatism. RORTY, Richard.
Le origini dell'ateismo antico (quinta parte). ZEPPI, Stelio.
Parody and the Argument from Probability in the *Apology*. LEWIS, Thomas J.
The Serious Play of Plato's *Euthydemus*. ROOCHNIK, David.
Simon and Socrates. BRUMBAUGH, Robert S.
Socrates and Alcibiades: Eros, Piety, and Politics. HOWLAND, Jacob A.
Socrates and Asclepius: The Final Words. SANTILLI, Paul C.
Socrates' Critique of Cognitivism. MATSON, Wallace I and LEITE, Adam.
Socrates, the Craft Analogy, and Science. GRAHAM, Daniel W.
Socratic Pragmatics: Maieutic Dialogues. HANKE, Michael.
Socratic Reason and Socratic Revelation. MC PHERRAN, Mark L.
El trilema de Aristófanes y los presupuestos normativos del diálgo crítico. MALIANDI, Ricardo.
Two Varieties of Temperance in the *Gorgias*. CURZER, Howard J.
Vlastos on the Unity of Virtue: Why Pauline Predication Will Not Save the Biconditionality Thesis. WAKEFIELD, Jerome C.

SOCRATIC METHOD
On Taking Socratic Irony Seriously (in Hebrew). SCOLNICOV, Samuel.
Socrates in Dallas: Managing the Facilities. CASTRO, Barry.
La subversion de l'"elenchos" juridique dans l'"Apologie de Socrate". DORION, Louis-André.

SOLIDARITY
Objectivity, Relativism, and Truth: Philosophical Papers, Volume 1. RORTY, Richard.
Rorty's Humanistic Pragmatism: Philosophy Democratized. KOLENDA, Konstantin.
Habermas and Solidarity. FUNK, Nanette.

SOLIPSISM
Change, Cause and Contradiction: A Defence of the Tenseless Theory of Time. LE POIDEVIN, Robin.
Knowledge of the External World. AUNE, Bruce.
"Semantics and Methodological Solipsism" in *Truth and Interpretation: Perspectives on the Philosophy of Donald Davidson*, LYCAN, William G.
Altruism and the Avoidance of Solipsism. CHONG, Kim-Chong.
Saving Psychological Solipsism. MALONEY, J Christopher.
Solipsism in Kant's Practical Philosophy and the Discourse of Ethics. KUHLMANN, Wolfgang.
Towards a Reasonable Version of Methodological Solipsism. ROWLANDS, Mark.

SOLITUDE
Solitude. KOCH, Philip J.
Tiempo, soledad y muerte: La encrucijada del poeta. RADCHIK, Laura.

SOLON OF ATHENS
The Epic Hero as Politico. CAMPBELL, Blair.

SOLTIS, J
The Role of Moral Intuition in Applied Ethics: A Consideration of Positions of Peirce and Strike and Soltis. MC CARTHY, Christine.

SOLUTION(S)
Equivocation in The Surprise Exam Paradox. FERGUSON, Kenneth G.

SOMMERS, C
"They Lived Happily Ever After": Sommers on Women and Marriage. FRIEDMAN, Marilyn.
Does Sommers Like Women? More on Liberalism, Gender Hierarchy, and Scarlett O'Hara. FRIEDMAN, Marilyn.

SOMMERS, F
Predication and Logic of Language (I). GANGADEAN, Ashok.

SONG(S)
Nature' Song. SALLIS, John.

SOONTIENS, F
Natuurlijke selectie, doelgerichtheid en een uitzonderlijke samenloop van omstandigheden: Een kritiek op F Soontiëns. SLURINK, Pouwel.
Teleo-theologie und kein Ende: Reactie op Soontiens. CALLEBAUT, Werner and WACHELDER, J.

SOPHISM
A Case for a Heretical Deontic Semantics. EDELBERG, Walter.
Dire e ascoltare nella tipologia del "sofista", del "filosof-re" e del pensatore socratico. MARCHETTI, Giancarlo.
Eristic, Antilogic, Sophistic, Dialectic: Plato's Demarcation of Philosophy from Sophistry. NEHAMAS, Alexander.
Grammaire et Liturgie dans les "Sophismes" du XIIIe Siècle. ROSIER, Irène and ROY, Bruno.
The Serious Play of Plato's *Euthydemus*. ROOCHNIK, David.

SOPHISTS
Philosophy of the Ancients. RICKEN, Friedo.
History and Neo-Sophistic Criticism: A Reply to Poulakos. SCHIAPPA, Edward.
Interpreting Sophistical Rhetoric: A Response to Schiappa. POULAKOS, John.
Neo-Sophistic Rhetorical Criticism or the Historical Reconstruction of Sophistic Doctrines?. SCHIAPPA, Edward.

SOPHOCLES
Hermeneutical Studies: Dilthey, Sophocles, and Plato. WILSON, Barrie A.
"Antigone's Dilemma" in *Re-Reading Levinas*, CHANTER, Tina.
Autonomy, Empathy, and Transcendence in Sophocles' *Antigone*: A Phenomenological Perspective. NISSIM-SABAT, Marilyn.
M Heideggers Auslegung von Sophokles' "Oedipus Tyrannus" (in Japanese). SEKIGUCHI, Hiroshi.
Sophoclean Logic (*Antigone* 175-81). O'SULLIVAN, Neil.

SOREL, G
Two Views of the Revolution: Gramsci and Sorel, 1916-1920. SCHECTER, Darrow.

SORENSEN, R
Ideal Rationality and Handwaving. RICHTER, Reed.
On a Moorean Solution to Instability Puzzles. KROON, Frederick W.
Was Descartes a Liar? Diagonal Doubt Defended. SLEZAK, Peter.

SORIA, G
"Giovanni Gualberto (Alberto) De Soria e la 'Cosmologia'" in *Scienza, Filosofia e Religione tra '600 e '700 in Italia*, PONZELLINI, Ornella.

SORITES
Fictional Incompleteness as Vagueness. SORENSEN, Roy A.
The Sorites Paradox and Higher-Order Vagueness. BURGESS, John A.

SOTERIOLOGY
Middle Knowledge and the Soteriological Problem of Evil. HUNT, David P.

SOUL(S)
see also Mind
Aristotle's Psychology. ROBINSON, Daniel N.
Ethics with Aristotle. BROADIE, Sarah.
Locke and French Materialism. YOLTON, John W.
Love's Knowledge: Essays on Philosophy and Literature. NUSSBAUM, Martha C.
Psychology (Companions to Ancient Thought: 2). EVERSON, Stephen (ed).
The Recovery of the Soul: An Aristotelian Essay on Self-fulfilment. RANKIN, Kenneth.
Towards a Christian Philosophy. OWENS, Joseph I.
The Vatican, the Law and the Human Embryo. COUGHLAN, Michael J.
What is History? And Other Late Unpublished Writings (The Collected Works of Eric Voegelin, Vol 28). HOLLWECK, Thomas A (ed).
"Aristotle's Philosophy of Mind" in *Psychology (Companions to Ancient Thought: 2)*, IRWIN, T H.
"Greek Medical Models of Mind" in *Psychology (Companions to Ancient Thought: 2)*, HANKINSON, R J.
"Heraclitus' Theory of Soul and Its Antecedents" in *Psychology (Companions to Ancient Thought: 2)*, SCHOFIELD, Malcolm.

SOUL(S)

"Imaginal Soul and Ideational Spirit: A Response to James Heisig" in *Archetypal Process: Self and Divine in Whitehead, Jung, and Hillman*, WINQUIST, Charles E.
"In Defense of the Demon" in *The Case for Dualism*, HARRISON, Jonathan.
"Plato's Theory of Mind" in *Psychology (Companions to Ancient Thought: 2)*, LOVIBOND, Sabina.
"Plotinus and Soul-Body Dualism" in *Psychology (Companions to Ancient Thought: 2)*, EMILSSON, Eyjólfur K.
"Responses" in *Archetypal Process: Self and Divine in Whitehead, Jung, and Hillman*, HILLMAN, James.
"Skull's Darkroom: The *Camera Obscura* and Subjectivity" in *Philosophy of Technology*, BAILEY, Lee W.
Aristotle's Motionless Soul. TWEEDALE, Martin.
El autoconocimiento del alma según Avicena latino. OYARZABAL, Manuel.
Death Is One of Two Things. RUDEBUSCH, George.
Dehātmavāda or the Body as Soul: Exploration of a Possibility within Nyāya Thought. LATH, Mukund (trans) and SHUKLA, Pandit Badrinath.
Descartes und der reale Unterschied zwischen der Seele und dem Körper. IMLAY, Robert A.
Glose sur le prologue du traité "de l'âme" d'Aristote. VERNIER, Jean-Marie.
A Great Philosopher's Not So Great Account of Great Virtue: Aristotle's Treatment of 'Greatness of Soul'. CURZER, Howard J.
Some Observations About Plato's *Phaedo*. MASCHLER, Chaninah.
Souls Without Longing. PLATT, Michael.
Two Cartesian Arguments for the Simplicity of the Soul. ZIMMERMAN, Dean W.
Two Souls in One Body. HACKING, Ian.
Zygotes, Souls, Substances, and Persons. BOLE III, Thomas J.

SOUND(S)

Sound, Speech, and Music. BURROWS, David.
A Response to A G A Bello's Methodological Preliminaries. ANYANWU, Kane C.
Thought and Language. SAHA, Sukharanjan.
Ultimate Reality and Meaning in Africa: Some Methodological Preliminaries—A Test Case. BELLO, A G A.

SOUNDNESS

Complementary Sentential Logics. VARZI, Achille C.
Related Semantics for All Lewis, Lemmon and Feys' Modal Logics. SYLVAN, Richard.

SOURCE(S)

A Theory of Probability. REEVES, T V.

SOUTH AFRICAN

Continuing the Conversation—A Reply to My Interlocutors. OLIVIER, G.
Interrupting Olivier's Socio-Political Conversation: Another Postmodern Proposal. ALLEN, J G.
Just War Theory: The Case of South Africa. MILLER, S R.
Olivier's Postmodern Proposal: A Few Comments. LÖTTER, H P P.
A Response to Olivier's Postmodern, but Pre-South African Proposal. ROSSOUW, G.
Structural Violence and Fallible Plans: A Case Study in Philosophy and Educational Planning. MOULDER, J.

SOVEREIGNTY

The Legal-Rational State: A Comparison of Hobbes, Bentham and Kelsen. LEE, Keekok.
"Human Survival and the Limits of National Sovereignty" in *In the Interest of Peace: A Spectrum of Philosophical Views*, WINSTON, Morton.
Land Rights and Aboriginal Sovereignty. THOMPSON, Janna.
Some Thoughts About Heterosexualism. HOAGLAND, Sarah Lucia.
Sovranità e obbedienza. CATANIA, Alfonso.
The Truth about Lies in Plato's *Republic*. PAGE, Carl.

SOVIET

see also Russian
Russische Philosophie. GOERDT, Wilhelm.
"Soviet Ethics and New Thinking" in *In the Interest of Peace: A Spectrum of Philosophical Views*, GUSEYNOV, A A.
A Contribution to the Discussion of the Doctrinal Preconditions of the Deformation of Socialism. KOLODII, A F.
Dialogue or Mutual Accusations?. SAGATOVSKII, V N.
Les effets de la perestroïka dans les *Voprosy filosofii*. DENNES, Maryse.
History, Lying, and Moral Responsibility. PORK, Andrus.
Human Nature, Social Engineering, and the Reemergence of Civil Society. RAU, Zbigniew.
Lenin and Philosophy: Should We Not Pose This Problem Anew?. VOLODIN, A.
Life and Cognition. FROLOV, Ivan T.
Marxism in the USSR Today. FISK, Milton.
Perestrojka der Philosophie?. IGNATOW, Assen.
Die Perestrojka in der Sowjetischen Philosophie: Mythos oder Realität. BYKOVA, M.
The Problem of Atheism in Recent Soviet Publications. DAHM, Helmut.
Die Rolle der Philosophiegeschichte im "Neuen philosophischen Denken" in der UdSSR. VAN DER ZWEERDE, Evert.
Some Basic Problems of a Political Theory of Modern Socialism (in German). SEGERT, Dieter.
Unamuno y la Revolución de Octubre. ROBLES, Laureano.
Vasilii Vasil'evich Rozanov: "My Soul Is Woven of Filth, Tenderness, and Grief". KUVAKIN, V A.
The World of Man and Man in the World in Light of the New Philosophical Thinking. DZHAKHAIA, L G.

SPACE

Being-in-the-World: A Commentary on Heidegger's "Being and Time", Division 1. DREYFUS, Hubert L.
Kant's Model of the Mind: A New Interpretation of Transcendental Idealism. WAXMAN, Wayne.
L'inertie et l'espace-temps absolu de Newton à Einstein. GHINS, Michel.
Mind-Body. MOULYN, Adrian C.
"Catastrophic Possibilities of Space-Based Defense" in *Philosophy of Technology*, BELLA, David.
"First-Order Spacetime Geometry" in *Logic, Methodology and Philosophy of Science, VIII*, GOLDBLATT, Robert.
"Newton on Space and Time: Comments on J E McGuire" in *Philosophical Perspectives on Newtonian Science*, CARRIERO, John.
"Predicates of Pure Existence: Newton on God's Space and Time" in *Philosophical Perspectives on Newtonian Science*, MC GUIRE, J E.
"Presences and Absences: Time-Space Relations and Structuration Theory" in *Social Theory of Modern Societies: Anthony Giddens and His Critics*, GREGORY, Derek.
"Realism and the Global Topology of Space-Time" in *Harré and His Critics*, WEINGARD, Robert.
"A Reply to David Duquette's "Kant, Hegel and the Possibility of a Speculative Logic"" in *Essays on Hegel's Logic*, PINKARD, Terry.
Absolutism and Relationism in Space and Time: A False Dichotomy. HINCKFUSS, Ian.
Blackburn on Filling in Space. RICE, Hugh.
Constructing or Completing Physical Geometry?. CARRIER, Martin.
Constructions by Transfinitely Many Workers. KNIGHT, Julia F.
Constructive Compact Operators on a Hilbert Space. ISHIHARA, Hajime.
Definitions of Compact. HOWARD, Paul E.
Discussione di alcune questioni di cosmologia neo-tomista. BLANDINO, Giovanni.
Embedding and Uniqueness in Relationist Theories. MUNDY, Brent.
From Discrete to Continuous Time. KEISLER, H Jerome.
How Euclidean Geometry Has Misled Metaphysics. NERLICH, Graham.
Kants Theorie der geometrischen Erkenntnis und die nichteuklikische Geometrie. SCHIRN, Matthias.
A Metatheorem for Constructions by Finitely Many Workers. KNIGHT, J F.
Nelson Algebras Through Heyting Ones[1]:1. SENDLEWSKI, Andrzej.
An Omniscience Principle, the König Lemma and the Hahn-Banach Theorem. ISHIHARA, Hajime.
On the Existence of Large *p*-Ideals. JUST, Winfried (and others).
Operative versus Combinatory Spaces. IVANOV, Lyubomir.
Partition Properties and Prikry Forcing on Simple Spaces. HENLE, J M.
Projective Subsets of Separable Metric Spaces. MILLER, Arnold W.
R J Boskovic's Philosophy of Space (in Serbo-Croatian). ROSSI, Arcangelo.
Sheaves in Universal Algebra and Model Theory: Part I. IDZIAK, Pawel M.
Some Features of Hume's Conception of Space. FRASCA-SPADA, Marina.
Space and Its Questions (in Czechoslovakian). PATOCKA, Jan.
Substance, Relations, and Arguments About the Nature of Space-Time. TELLER, Paul.
Substances and Space-Time: What Aristotle Would Have Said to Einstein. MAUDLIN, Tim.
Taxonomies of Model-Theoretically Defined Topological Properties. BANKSTON, Paul.
Telesio e la cultura napoletana. STURLESE, Rita.
Weak Cylindric Set Algebras and Weak Subdirect Indecomposability. ANDRÉKA, H and NÉMETI, I and THOMPSON, R J.
Zeno's Paradox of Extension. MC KIE, John R.

SPADE, P

The Real Difficulty with Burley's Realistic Semantics. FITZGERALD, Michael J.
Tu scis regem sedere. D'ORS, Angel.

SPAEMANN, R

Utilitaristische Ethik als Antwort auf die ökologische Krise. WOLF, Jean-Claude.

SPANISH

Velázquez et Goya. PIERRE, Christian (trans).
La diffusione del pensiero spagnolo contemporaneo nell'Italia di oggi. SAVIGNANO, Armando.
Filósofo hispanista. FORMENT, Eudaldo.
Heidegger en la filosofia española: La eficacia de Heidegger en las filosofías de Ortega y Zubiri. RAMOS, Antonio Pintor.
Marranos (Pigs), or from Coexistence to Toleration. SHELL, Marc.

SPATIALITY

Against Architecture: The Writings of Georges Bataille. HOLLIER, Denis.
Being-in-the-World: A Commentary on Heidegger's "Being and Time", Division 1. DREYFUS, Hubert L.

SPATIALITY
The Natural and the Normative: Theories of Spatial Perception from Kant to Helmholtz. HATFIELD, Gary.
Philosophical Streets: New Approaches to Urbanism. CROW, Dennis (ed).
"*In Situ*: Beyond the Architectonics of the Modern" in *Postmodernism—Philosophy and the Arts (Continental Philosophy III)*, WATSON, Stephen H.

SPAVENTA, B
Venti lettere inedite di Angelo Camillo De Meis a Bertrando Spaventa. RASCAGLIA, Maria.

SPAVENTA, S
Silvio Spaventa e Antonio Labriola, gli 'aspetti-pedagogici'. DE CUMIS, Nicola Siciliani.

SPEAKING
A Philosophical Daybook: Post-Critical Investigations. POTEAT, William H.
Dire e ascoltare nella tipologia del "sofista", del "filosof-re" e del pensatore socratico. MARCHETTI, Giancarlo.
Libri da salvare. POLC, Jaroslav.
Music, Meaning, and the Art of Elocution. TROTT, Elizabeth Anne.

SPECIAL RELATIVITY
Causal Paradoxes in Special Relativity. ARNTZENIUS, Frank.
Some Comments Concerning Spin and Relativity. WEINGARD, Robert.

SPECIALIZATION
DBAE: Complaints, Reminiscences, and Response. BROUDY, Harry S.

SPECIES
Beyond Natural Selection. WESSON, Robert.
Brouwer's Intuitionism (Studies in the History and Philosophy of Mathematics, Vol 2). VAN STIGT, W P.
A Commentary on Ridley's Cladistic Solution to the Species Problem. WILKINSON, Mark.
Comments on Wilkinson's Commentary. RIDLEY, Mark.
Conceptual Selection. HULL, David L.
Conciencia de catástrofe, poder y libertad. DEI, H Daniel.
Domesticated and Then Some. DURAN, Jane.
Il polipo di Trembley (1740) e la "catena delle verità": Note di ricerca. TODESCO, Fabio.
The Servant Species: Humanity as Priesthood. LINZEY, Andrew.
Species as Historical Individuals. KLUGE, Arnold G.
Species, Higher Taxa, and the Units of Evolution. ERESHEFSKY, Marc.
Species, Individuals, and Domestication: A Commentary on Jane Duran's "Domesticated and Then Some". VARNER, Gary E.

SPECIESISM
Animal Experimentation: The Moral Issue. BAIRD, Robert M (ed).
Singer's Cookbook. JOHNSON, Edward.

SPECTATOR(S)
Wollheim's Theory of Artist as Spectator: A Complication. OLDS, Clifton.

SPECTRUM PROBLEM
Eine Bemerkung zu spektralen Darstellungen von ρ-stelligen Aufzählbaren. DEUTSCH, Michael.
What is Wrong in Inverting Spectra. CASATI, Roberto.

SPECULATION
Apology, Speculation, and Philosophy's Fate. VAN NESS, Peter H.
Divine Irony and the Natural Law: Speculation and Edification in Aquinas. HIBBS, Thomas S.
La logica di Hegel come testo filosofico (II). COSTA, Filippo.

SPECULATIVE
"Kant, Hegel and the Possibility of a Speculative Logic" in *Essays on Hegel's Logic*, DUQUETTE, David A.
How is Philosophy Possible?. SCHICK JR, Theodore W.

SPEECH
Saggio di semantica. BRÉAL, Michel.
Saussure: Signs, System, and Arbitrariness. HOLDCROFT, David.
Sound, Speech, and Music. BURROWS, David.
"A Nice Derangement of Epitaphs" in *Truth and Interpretation: Perspectives on the Philosophy of Donald Davidson*, DAVIDSON, Donald.
"Speech Versus Writing" in Derrida and Bhartrhari. COWARD, Harold G.
Aphasia—The Worm's Eye View of a Philosophic Patient and the Medical Establishment. ALEXANDER, Edwin.
Conscience de soi et langage intérieur: quelques spéculations. MORIN, Alain and EVERETT, James.
A Critique of Derrida's Hegel Deconstruction: Speech, Phonetic Writing, and Hieroglyphic Script in Logic, Law, Art. CUTROFELLO, Andrew.
Language, Speech and Writing: Merleau-Ponty and Derrida on Saussure. FREE, George.
Phrases nominales énonciatives et phrases verbales. STAHL, Gérold.
Speech, Sin and the Word of God (in Dutch). GESTRICH, Christof.
Thought and Language. SAHA, Sukharanjan.
Transzendentale Argumente pragmatisch relativiert: Über fundamentale Optionen in der Philosophie. LAUENER, Henri.

SPEECH ACT(S)
Intentions in Communication. COHEN, Philip R (ed).
Meaning and Speech Acts: Volume I, Principles of Language Use. VANDERVEKEN, Daniel.
Meaning and Speech Acts: Volume II, Formal Semantics of Success and Satisfaction. VANDERVEKEN, Daniel.
Speech Acts and Literary Theory. PETREY, Sandy.
Wahrheit—Diskurs—Demokratie: Studien zur "Konsensustheorie der Wahrheit". SCHEIT, Herbert.
Wittgenstein and Contemporary Philosophy of Language. RUNDLE, Bede.
"Speaker Plans, Linguistic Contexts, and Indirect Speech Acts" in *Knowledge Representation and Defeasible Reasoning*, MC CAFFERTY, Andrew.
Another Look at the Derrida-Searle Debate. ALFINO, Mark.
Elements of Speech Act Theory in the Work of Thomas Reid. SCHUHMANN, Karl and SMITH, Barry.
Everyday Argumentation from a Speech Act Perspective. GROOTENDORST, Rob.
Is There More to Speech Acts Than Illocutionary Force and Propositional Content?. HAJDIN, Mane.
Le locutoire et l'illocutoire dans les énonciations relatives aux normes juridiques. AMSELEK, Paul.
Sequencing Rules and Coherence in Discourse. TSUI, Amy B M.

SPENGLER
Hegel, Spengler, and the Enigma of World History: Progress or Decline?. FARRENKOPF, John.

SPERBER, D
Author's Position in Interpretation of a Work of Art (in Japanese). WATANABE, Hiroshi.

SPIEGELBERG, H
Herbert Spiegelberg 1904-1990. SCHUHMANN, Karl.

SPIN MATRICES
On the Origin of Spin in Relativity. SACHS, Mendel.

SPINOZA
The Anatomy of Philosophical Style. LANG, Berel.
Expressionism in Philosophy: Spinoza. DELEUZE, Gilles.
History and the Paradoxes of Metaphysics in "Dantons Tod". TAYLOR, Rodney.
The Savage Anomaly: The Power of Spinoza's Metaphysics and Politics. NEGRI, Antonio.
"Definition, Essence, and Understanding in Spinoza" in *Central Themes in Early Modern Philosophy*, PARKINSON, G H R.
"Ethics IP5: Shared Attributes and the Basis of Spinoza's Monism" in *Central Themes in Early Modern Philosophy*, GARRETT, Don.
"Hegel's Criticism of Spinoza's Concept of the Absolute" in *Essays on Hegel's Logic*, BYRNE, Laura.
"Notes on a Neglected Masterpiece, II: Theological-Political Treatise as a Prolegomenon to the Ethics" in *Central Themes in Early Modern Philosophy*, CURLEY, Edwin.
"Spinoza and Descartes and the Existence of Extended Substance" in *Central Themes in Early Modern Philosophy*, WOOLHOUSE, R S.
Amour de l'être et ambition de gloire: le spinozisme de Vauvenargues. BOVE, Laurent.
La création du Nouveau par le Hasard et par le temps: un vieux thème épicurien. LARGEAULT, Jean.
De las maravillas acerca de lo uno y lo múltiple o sobre los avatares del amor neoplatónico en Baruch de Espinosa. ALBIAC, Gabriel.
Deleuze und Spinozas "Ethik". OITTINEN, Vesa.
A Disproof of the Existence of God. WEEKS, Ian.
Hume Contra Spinoza?. KLEVER, Wim.
L'Habitude, activité fondatrice de l'existence actuelle dans la philosophie de Spinoza. BOVE, Lauren.
Least Parts and Greatest Wholes Variations on a Theme in Spinoza. SACKSTEDER, William.
Naturalism, Freedom and Ethics in Spinoza. DE DIJN, Herman.
Nietzsche e Spinoza. BIUSO, Alberto G.
La réception de Spinoza dans la littérature néerlandaise. HENRARD, Roger.
Spinoza en de geopenbaarde godsdienst. DE DIJN, H.
Spinoza en het ontstaan van de staat. VERBEEK, Bruno.
Spinoza on the Eternity of the Human Mind. LUCASH, Frank.
Spinoza's Materialist Ethics: The Education of Desire. RAVVEN, Heidi M.
Spinoza's Two Causal Chains. GILEAD, Amihud.
Spinoza's Two Theories of Morality. LUCASH, Frank.
Spinoza, Heidegger, and the Ontological Argument. SINGER, Brent A.
Spinoza—Beyond Hobbes and Rousseau. GEISMANN, Georg.
Sur quelques textes de Spinoza relatifs à la notion de loi. PREPOSIET, Jean.
The Object and the Concept: Spinoza's Theory with Regard to the Development of Modern Natural Science (in German). GOLDENBAUM, Ursula.
Was Spinoza a Marrano of Reason?. POPKIN, Richard H.

SPIRIT(S)
see also Minds, Soul(s)
Die Aufhebung der Begriffs-philosophie. KRONABEL, Christoph.
Encyclopedia of the Philosophical Sciences in Outline and Critical Writings—G W F Hegel. BEHLER, Ernst (ed).

SPIRIT(S)
Estetica: Come Scienza dell'Espressione e Linguistica Generale. CROCE, Benedetto.
From Hegel to Nietzsche: The Revolution in Nineteenth-Century Thought. LÖWITH, Karl.
Hegel In His Time—Jacques D'Hondt. BURBIDGE, John (trans).
Hegel: o la rebelión contra el límite. IZUZQUIZA, Ignacio.
History and Spirit: An Inquiry into the Philosophy of Liberation. KOVEL, Joel.
Reflexões, 3: Filosofia Política Sociologia cultura Portuguesa Temas Literários. DE MELO, Romeu.
Spirit and Existence: A Philosophy Inquiry into the Meaning of Spiritual Existence. GELVEN, Michael.
"Sobria ebrietas": Nietzsche y las perpleijidades del espíritu. CRUZ CRUZ, Jua.
Hegel: fenomenología del espíritu. MONTOYA, Rocío Basurto.
Ist die Naturphilosophie eine abgelegte Gestalt des modernen Geistes?. WAHSNER, Renate.
Philosophy and Religion (in Dutch). DHONDT, U.
The Beginning and Structure of the "Phaenomenology of Mind" (in Hungarian). PÖGGELER, Otto.
Time in Hegel's *Phenomenology of Spirit*. FLAY, Joseph C.
Toward One Santayana: Recent Scholarship. KERR-LAWSON, Angus.

SPIRITUAL
Nicolai Hartmann's New Ontology. WERKMEISTER, W H.
Our Inner Divinity: Humanism and the Spiritual Enterprise. ARISIAN, Khoren.

SPIRITUALISM
Spiritual Values and "The Goddess". BRANDEN, Victoria.

SPIRITUALITY
History and Spirit: An Inquiry into the Philosophy of Liberation. KOVEL, Joel.
On the Problem of Empathy (Third Revised Edition). STEIN, Edith.
Philosophy of the "Gita". PATEL, Ramesh N.
Spirit and Existence: A Philosophy Inquiry into the Meaning of Spiritual Existence. GELVEN, Michael.
The Yoga-Sūtra of Patañjali: A New Translation and Commentary. FEUERSTEIN, Georg.
"The Mystique of the Nonrational and a New Spirituality" in *Archetypal Process: Self and Divine in Whitehead, Jung, and Hillman*, HEISIG, James W.
Bondedness, *Moyo* and *Umunthu* as the Elements of aChewa Spirituality: Organizing Logic and Principle of Life. SINDIMA, Harvey.
Consciousness for the Twenty-First Century. CSIKSZENTMIHALYI, Mihaly.
Feminist Spirituality as a Path to Humanism. FRANKEL, Lois.
Philosophy, Religion, Morality, Spirituality: Some Issues. SHAH, K J.
Spiritual Traditions and Science and Technology. BAKAR, Osman.
Transcultural Dialogue and the Problem of the Concept of Ultimate Reality and Meaning. SINGLETON, Michael.

SPLITTING
Jumps of Nontrivial Splittings of Recursively Enumerable Sets. INGRASSIA, Michael A and LEMPP, Steffen.

SPONTANEITY
"Being Is Better than Freedom" in *Freedom in the Modern World: Jacques Maritain, Yves R Simon, Mortimer J Adler*, DENNEHY, Raymond.
"Sartre and the Humanism of Spontaneity" in *The Question of Humanism: Challenges and Possibilities*, HORNYANSKY, Monica C.
A Contribution of the Conception of "Discursivity" and "Spontaneiti" of Thinking (in Czechoslovakian). BENYOVSZKY, Ladislav.
Spontaneity and the Generation of Rational Beings in Leibniz's Theory of Biological Reproduction. FOUKE, Daniel C.

SPORT(S)
Philosophy of Sport. HYLAND, Drew A.

SPRING, J
Re-Viewing the Political Structure of Knowledge. LEACH, Mary S.

SQUADRITO, K
Response to Squadrito's "Commentary: Interests and Equal Moral Status". DE GRAZIA, David.

SRI LANKA
"Buddhism, Sri Lanka, and the Prospects for Peace" in *Celebrating Peace*, SMART, Ninian.

STABILITY
The Dynamics of Rational Deliberation. SKYRMS, Brian.
Evolutionary Instability: Logical and Material Aspects of a Unified Theory of Biosocial Evolution. GEIGER, Gebhard.
"Towards the Structural Stability Theory" in *Logic, Methodology and Philosophy of Science, VIII*, ZILBER, B I.
Constructing Strongly Equivalent Nonisomorphic Models for Unstable Theories. HYTTINEN, Tapani and TUURI, Heikki.
The Curve Fitting Problem: A Solution. TURNEY, Peter.
Differentially Algebraic Group Chunks. PILLAY, Anand.
Fragility and Deterministic Modelling in the Exact Sciences. TAVAKOL, R K.
Omitting Types for Stable CCC Theories. NEWELSKI, Ludomir.
On a Moorean Solution to Instability Puzzles. KROON, Frederick W.
On Type Definable Subgroups of a Stable Group. NEWELSKI, Ludomir.
Rich Models. ALBERT, Michael H and GROSSBERG, Rami P.
The Spectrum of Resplendency. BALDWIN, John T.
Stability for Pairs of Equivalence Relations. TOFFALORI, Carlo.
Truth and Stability in Descartes' *Meditations*. BENNETT, Jonathan.
Unidimensional Theories are Superstable. HRUSHOVSKI, Ehud.

STAGE(S)
"Kierkegaard's Stages on Life's Way: How Many Are There?" in *Writing the Politics of Difference*, MICHELSEN, John M.
A Conceptual Model of Corporate Moral Development. REIDENBACH, R Eric and ROBIN, Donald P.

STALIN
A Contribution to the Discussion of the Doctrinal Preconditions of the Deformation of Socialism. KOLODII, A F.

STALINISM
Georg Lukács and Stalinism (in German). TIETZ, Udo.
Is Karl Marx to Blame for "Barracks Socialism"?. BUTENKO, A P.
The Sources of Stalinism. TSIPKO, A.
The Enticing Thing About Stalinism (in German). PÄTZOLT, Harald.

STAMPE, D
Response to Stampe's "Representation and the Freedom of the Will". GIBSON, Martha I.

STANDARD OF LIVING
Economic Efficiency and the Quality of Life. JACOBSEN, Rockney.

STANDARD(S)
"Excellence, Equity, and Equality" Clarified. GREEN, Thomas F.
Defining the Ethical Standards of the High-Technology Industry. FIMBEL, Nancie and BURSTEIN, Jerome S.
The Priority of Excellence Reconsidered. BULL, Barry L.
Toward A Value-Laden Theory: Feminism and Social Science. BERNICK, Susan E.

STAPP, H
Nonlocal Influences and Possible Worlds—A Stapp in the Wrong Direction. CLIFTON, Robert K and BUTTERFIELD, Jeremy N and REDHEAD, Michael L G.

STAROWOLSKI, S
Philosophy of Culture in the Works of Szymon Starowolski (1588-1656) (in Polish). SZYDLOWSKI, Piotr.

STATE OF NATURE
From Precision to Peace: Hobbes and Political Language. MINOGUE, Kenneth.
The Symmetry Enigma in Hobbes. HAJI, Ishtiyaque.
Why (Legal) Rules Often Fail to Control Human Behavior. CROMBAG, H F M.

STATE RIGHTS
Kant: del derecho de libertad a la exigencia racional del Estado. PASTORE, Romano.

STATE(S)
see also Mental States
Atheism, Ayn Rand, and other Heresies. SMITH, George H.
Hegels Theorie des Gesetzes. BOGDANDY, Armin Von.
Interpreting Political Responsibility. DUNN, John.
Knowledge in Flux: Modeling the Dynamics of Epistemic States. GÄRDENFORS, Peter.
The Legal-Rational State: A Comparison of Hobbes, Bentham and Kelsen. LEE, Keekok.
The Limits of Government: An Essay on the Public Goods Arguments. SCHMIDTZ, David.
Nation und Ethos: Die Moral des Patriotismus. KLUXEN-PYTA, Donate.
The Nature of Politics. MASTERS, Roger D.
Patriarcha and Other Writings: Sir Robert Filmer. SOMMERVILLE, Johann P (ed).
Robert Nozick: Property, Justice, and the Minimal State. WOLFF, Jonathan.
Statism and Anarchy. SHATZ, Marshall (ed).
"Hobbes e as metáforas do Estado" in *Dinâmica do Pensar: Homenagem a Oswaldo Market*, DOS SANTOS, Leonel Ribeiro.
"The Origins of Some of Our Misconceptions" in *Perspectives on Ideas and Reality*, LUDASSY, Mária.
"The Self and the State" in *The Tanner Lectures On Human Values, Volume XII*, HOWE, Irving.
"The State and Legitimacy" in *Key Themes in Philosophy*, BARRY, Norman.
I "systemata subordinata" e il problema della partecipazione in Hobbes. SORGI, Giuseppe.
1668 Appendix to Leviathan. WRIGHT, George (trans) and HOBBES, Thomas.
A proposito di Stato e totaliarismo nel pensiero di Marx. SIENA, Robertomaria.
Arthur Schopenhauer als Staatsdenker. WÜRKNER, Joachim.
Autonomy, Liberalism and State Neutrality. MASON, Andrew D.
Community as Compulsion? A Reply to Skillen on Citizenship and the State. ELLIOT, Gregory and OSBORNE, Peter.
Conscious and Unconscious States. BEN-ZEEV, Aaron.
The Crisis of Authority. OLDS, Mason.

STATE(S)
Democracy and the Church-State Relationship. KAINZ, Howard.
Las dos grandes paradojas?. SERRANO, Augusto.
Le droit de l'État et le devoir de l'individu. PFERSMANN, Otto.
Fideísmo y autoritarismo en Lutero. CAPPELLETTI, Angel.
The Formation of the Modern State: A Reconstruction of Max Weber's Arguments. AXTMANN, Roland.
From Propaganda to "Oeffentlichkeit" in Eastern Europe: Four Models of the Public Space Under State Socialism. SUKOSD, Miklos.
Gramsci, Croce and the Italian Political Tradition. BELLAMY, Richard.
Hegel as Advocate of Machiavelli (in German). JAMME, Christoph.
Hegel, Croce, Gentile: On the Idea of the "Ethical State". SANTORO, Liberato and CASALE, Giuseppe.
Homer's Contest: Nietzsche on Politics and the State in Ancient Greece. SMITH, Bruce.
A Hostage to Technology. CRANFORD, Ronald E.
Justus Möser: De Revolutie en de grondslagen van de moderne staat. WALRAVENS, Else.
Lenin, Gorbachev, and 'National-Statehood': Can Leninism Countenance the New Soviet Federal Order?. GLEASON, Gregory.
Must the State Justify Its Educational Policies?. HESLEP, Robert D.
Norberto Bobbio ideologo del neoilluminismo: Per una rilettura di "Politica e cultura". QUARANTA, Mario.
Nozick on Rights and Minimal State. AGARWALA, Binod Kumar.
On the Morality of Waging War Against the State. MILLER, Seumas.
Over leesbaarheid en maakbaarheid van de geschiedenis. WEYEMBERGH, Maurice.
Il pensiero dello "Stato" in Husserl: recenti problemi critici. FALCIONI, Daniela.
Perestrojka der Philosophie?. IGNATOW, Assen.
The Philosophy of Quantum Mechanics. BUB, Jeffrey.
Political Justice in Post-Communist Societies: The Case of Hungary. BENCE, György.
Research Note On Equity and Ethics in State-Promotion of Agricultural Products. ADELAJA, Adesoji O and BRUMFIELD, Robin G.
Rethinking Politics: Carl Schmitt vs Hegel. WINFIELD, Richard Dien.
The Rule of Law in *The German Constitution*. HANCE, Allen S.
Spinoza en het ontstaan van de staat. VERBEEK, Bruno.
Staat als Konsens mündiger Bürger? Zur Staatsansicht deutscher Vormärzliberaler. LIEPERT, Anita.
State Education Service or Prisoner's Dilemma: The 'Hidden Hand' as Source of Education Policy. JONATHAN, R.

STATEMENT(S)
The Nature of Irony: Toward a Computational Model of Irony. LITTMAN, David C and MEY, Jacob L.

STATES OF AFFAIRS
Nursing Ethics: Current State of the Art. FRY, Sara T.

STATESMANSHIP
On Duties: Cicero. GRIFFIN, M T (ed).
Cicero's Focus: From the Best Regime to the Model Statesman. NICGORSKI, Walter.
Weaving and Practical Politics In Plato's *Statesman*. COLE, Eve Browning.

STATIONARY SETS
Full Reflection of Stationary Sets Below $\aleph_\omega$. JECH, Thomas and SHELAH, Saharon.
Partitioning Pairs of Countable Sets of Ordinals. VELLEMAN, Dan.

STATISTICAL MECHANICS
The Infinite Apparatus in the Quantum Theory of Measurement. ROBINSON, Don.
Irreversibility and Statistical Mechanics: A New Approach?. BATTERMAN, Robert W.

STATISTICAL THEORY
Within Reason: A Guide to Non-Deductive Reasoning. BURBIDGE, John.
Factor Analysis, Information-Transforming Instruments, and Objectivity: A Reply and Discussion. MULAIK, Stanley A.
Mathematical Statistics and Metastatistical Analysis. RIVADULLA, Andrés.

STATISTICS
Causality in Sociological Research. KARPINSKI, Jakub.
Representing and Reasoning With Probabilistic Knowledge: A Logical Approach to Probabilities. BACCHUS, Fahiem.
The Taming of Chance. HACKING, Ian.
"The Interface Between Statistics and the Philosophy of Science" in *Logic, Methodology and Philosophy of Science, VIII*, GOOD, I J.
The Ethics of Statistical Discrimination. MAITZEN, Stephen.
Explanation in Physical Theory. CLARK, Peter.
Hidden Locality, Conspiracy and Superluminal Signals. KRONZ, Frederick M.
Hypothesis Tests and Confidence Intervals in the Single Case. JOHNSTONE, D J.
Intermediate Quantifiers versus Percentages. CARNES, Robert D and PETERSON, Philip L.
The Misuse of Maternal Mortality Statistics in the Abortion Debate. BECKWITH, Francis J.
Statistical Explanation, Probability, and Counteracting Conditions. GRIMES, Thomas R.

STATUS
"Hegel and the Problem of the Differentia" in *Essays on Hegel's Logic*, HALPER, Edward.
"The Social Status of Art: Why the Institutional Approach is not Sufficient" in *XIth International Congress in Aesthetics, Nottingham 1988*, DZIEMIDOK, Bohdan.
The Case Against Art: Wunderlich on Joyce. MAHAFFEY, Vicki.
Commentary: Interests and Equal Moral Status. SQUADRITO, Kathy.
The Distinction Between Equality in Moral Status and Deserving Equal Consideration. DE GRAZIA, David.
The Status of Frozen Embryos. ANDERSON, Susan Leigh.
The Subjection of Children. AVIRAM, Aharon.

STAVENHAGEM, R
O Saber, a Ética e a Ação Social. CARDOSO D EOLIVEIRA, Roberto.

STEALING
Morality and Ethics in Organizational Administration. ADELMAN, Howard.

STEINER, G
Humanizing the Humanities: Some Reflections on George Steiner's "Brutal Paradox". KARIER, Clarence J.

STEINTHAL, H
"'Lautform, innere Sprachform, Form der Sprachen'" in *Leibniz, Humboldt, and the Origins of Comparativism*, BARBA, Mario.

STEREOTYPE(S)
"From National Character to the Mechanism of Stereotyping" in *Perspectives on Ideas and Reality*, HUNYADY, György.
Reasonable Evidence of Reasonableness. KELMAN, Mark.
Separating Care and Cure: An Analysis of Historical and Contemporary Images of Nursing and Medicine. JECKER, Nancy S and SELF, Donnie J.

STICH, S
Justification, Truth, Goals, and Pragmatism: Comments on Stich's "Fragmentation of Reason". HARMAN, Gilbert.
Stephen P Stich, "The Fragmentation of Reason". COHEN, L Jonathan.
Stephen P Stich, "The Fragmentation of Reason". GOLDMAN, Alvin I.
Stich, Content, Prediction, and Explanation in Cognitive Science. WALLIS, Charles S.
Why We Should Care Whether Our Beliefs Are True. LYCAN, William G.

STIRNER
The Self-Overcoming of Nihilism: Nishitani Keiji. PARKES, Graham (trans).

STOCHASTIC
Aggregation Theorems and Multidimensional Stochastic Choice Models. MARLEY, A A J.
Fragility and Deterministic Modelling in the Exact Sciences. TAVAKOL, R K.
Induction and Stochastic Independence. AGASSI, Joseph.

STOCKER, M
On 'High-Mindedness'. GARCIA, Jorge.

STOICISM
"Representation and the Self in Stoicism" in *Psychology (Companions to Ancient Thought: 2)*, LONG, A A.
A Christian Philosopher in a "Broken World". VERBEKE, Gerard.
Giustino Martire, il primo platonico cristiano. GIRGENTI, Giuseppe.
Sur une façon stoïcienne de ne pas être. BRUNSCHWIG, Jacques.

STOICS
Parental Nature and Stoic Οικειοσισ. BLUNDELL, Mary Whitlock.
Perceptual Content in the Stoics. SORABJI, Richard.

STOKES, G
The No-Slip Condition of Fluid Dynamics. DAY, Michael A.

STONE, C
Moral Planes and Intrinsic Values. ANDERSON, James C.

STORY(-RIES)
Narrative in Culture: The Uses of Storytelling in the Sciences, Philosophy, and Literature. NASH, Christopher (ed).
"Stories of Sublimely Good Character" in *XIth International Congress in Aesthetics, Nottingham 1988*, CALLEN, Donald.
The Design, Use and Evaluation of Philosophical Stories for Children. CHING-CHUNG, Chao.
The Role of Stories in a Community of Inquiry. HON-MING, Chen.

STOUD, B
"Two Roads to Skepticism" in *Doubting: Contemporary Perspectives on Skepticism*, MOSER, Paul K.

STOUPPE, J
Was Spinoza a Marrano of Reason?. POPKIN, Richard H.

STOUT, J
Stout on Relativism, Liberalism, and Communitarianism. QUIRK, Michael J.

STRATEGY
Essentially Speaking: Feminism, Nature and Difference. FUSS, Diana.
Military Ethics: Looking Toward the Future. FOTION, Nicholas G.
The Tanner Lectures On Human Values, Volume XII. PETERSON, Grethe B (ed).
"Legitimate Defense and Strategic Defense" in *Issues in War and Peace: Philosophical Inquiries*, STERBA, James P.

STRATEGY

"The Man in the Teflon Suit: A Flaw in the Argument for Strategic Defense" in *Issues in War and Peace: Philosophical Inquiries*, HOEKEMA, David.
"Strategy: A New Era?" in *The Tanner Lectures On Human Values, Volume XII*, LUTTWAK, Edward N.
Clever Bookies and Coherent Beliefs. CHRISTENSEN, David.
Development Aid: The Moral Obligation to Innovation. DUNDON, Stanislaus J.
Entrance Strategies for Philosophy. FOGG, Walter L.
Evaluating Cognitive Strategies: A Reply to Cohen, Goldman, Harman, and Lycan. STICH, Stephen P.
Extension of Gurevich-Harrington's Restricted Memory Determinacy Theorem. YAKHNIS, Alexander and YAKHNIS, Vladimir.
Habermas on Strategic and Communicative Action. JOHNSON, James.
The Progressive and the Imperfective Paradox. LASCARIDES, Alex.
Social Responsibility and Strategic Management: Toward an Enterprise Strategy Classification. MEZNAR, Martin B and CHRISMAN, James J and CARROLL, Archie B.
Le stratège militaire. POIRIER, Lucien.

STRATIFICATION

Musical Aesthetics: A Historical Reader, Volume III, The Twentieth Century. LIPPMAN, Edward A (ed).

STRAUSS, L

"Foundationalism and Foundation in Strauss and Maritain" in *From Twilight to Dawn: The Cultural Vision of Jacques Maritain*, ASSELIN, D T.
Reason and Revelation in the Thought of Leo Strauss. COLMO, Christopher A.
Strauss's Three Burkes: The Problem of Edmund Burke in *Natural Right and History*. LENZNER, Steven J.

STRAWSON

Kalkulierte Absurditäten. STRUB, Christian.
Leibniz and Strawson: A New Essay in Descriptive Metaphysics. BROWN, Clifford.
Against Cartesian Dualism: Strawson and Sartre on the Unity of Person. MUI, Constance.
A Determinist Dilemma. PERSSON, Ingmar.
Naturalism and Scepticism. BELL, Martin and MC GINN, Marie.
Strawson and the Refutation of Idealism. STEINHOFF, Gordon.
Wittgenstein, Strawson y la no-posesión. BARINGOLTZ, Eleonora.

STREAM OF CONSCIOUSNESS

Divided Minds. HIRSCH, Eli.

STRENGTH

Toughness as a Political Virtue. GALSTON, William.

STRESS(ES)

Welcome 'Ethical Stress': A Humean Analysis and A Practical Proposal. MERRILL, Sarah A.

STRICT IMPLICATION

The Deduction Theorem in a Strict Functional Calculus of First Order Based on Strict Implication. MARCUS, Ruth Barcan.

STRIKE, K

The Role of Moral Intuition in Applied Ethics: A Consideration of Positions of Peirce and Strike and Soltis. MC CARTHY, Christine.

STRING(S)

On a Theorem of Günter Asser. CALUDE, Cristian and SÂNTEAN, Lila.

STROUD, B

"Justifying Beliefs: The Dream Hypothesis and Gratuitous Entities" in *Doubting: Contemporary Perspectives on Skepticism*, BAR-ON, Dorit.

STRUCTURALISM

"Prolegomena to a Structural Theory of Belief and Other Attitudes" in *Propositional Attitudes: The Role of Content in Logic, Language, and Mind*, KAMP, Hans.
An Axiomatic Basis of Accounting: A Structuralist Reconstruction. BALZER, Wolfgang and MATTESSICH, Richard.
Deleuze und Spinozas "Ethik". OITTINEN, Vesa.
Hermenêutica e Estruturalismo. ROCHA, Acílio Estanqueiro.
History as Geneology: Wittgenstein and the Feminist Deconstruction of Objectivity. LAMPSHIRE, Wendy L.
Kitcher's Circumlocutionary Structuralism. HAND, Michael.
Metaphor, Literalism, and the Non-Verbal Arts. BREDIN, Hugh.
The Methodologies of Social History: A Critical Survey and Defense of Structurism. LLOYD, Christopher.
Philosophical Prolegomena of Structural Thinking (in Czechoslovakian). CHVATIK, Kvetoslav.
Représentation structurelle de la relation partie-tout. STAHL, Gérold.
A Structuralist Rousseau: On the Anthropology of Claude Lévi-Strauss. HONNETH, Axel.
The Structuralist View of Mathematical Objects. PARSONS, Charles.
Structure and Ontology. SHAPIRO, Stewart.
Theoretical Explanation and Errors of Measurement. FORGE, John.
Towards a Modal-Structural Interpretation of Set Theory. HELLMAN, Geoffrey.

STRUCTURE(S)

Evolutionary Instability: Logical and Material Aspects of a Unified Theory of Biosocial Evolution. GEIGER, Gebhard.
Foundations of Social Theory. COLEMAN, James S.
Linguistic Behaviour. BENNETT, Jonathan.
Meaning and Truth: The Essential Readings in Modern Semantics. GARFIELD, Jay L (ed).
Modernity, Aesthetics, and the Bounds of Art. MC CORMICK, Peter J.
Semantic Structures. JACKENDOFF, Ray.
Structures in Mathematical Theories: Reports of the San Sebastian International Symposium, 1990. DÍEZ, Amparo (ed).
"On the Deep Structure of Violence" in *In the Interest of Peace: A Spectrum of Philosophical Views*, LITKE, Robert.
"Seek and Ye Might Find" in *Scientific Theories*, CAPLAN, Arthur L.
"Towards the Structural Stability Theory" in *Logic, Methodology and Philosophy of Science, VIII*, ZILBER, B I.
"Threading-the-Needle: The Case For and Against Common-Sense Realism". TIBBETTS, Paul.
Beethoven's Ninth Symphony: The Sense of an Ending. SOLOMON, Maynard.
Concepts of "Action", "Structure" and "Power" in 'Critical Social Realism': A Positive and Reconstructive Critique. PATOMÄKI, Heikki.
Conductive $\aleph_0$-Categorical Theories. SCHMERL, James H.
Connection Structures. BIACINO, Loredana and GERLA, Giangiacomo.
Estructura lógica y ontología en el *Tractatus*. MARTÍNEZ, Sergio.
Estructuras y representaciones. DE LA SIENRA, Adolfo García.
The Formal Language L_t and Topological Products. BERTOSSI, L E.
Kernels in N-Normal Symmetric Heyting Algebras. GALLI, A and SAGASTUME, M.
Many-Sorted Elementary Equivalence. DZIERZGOWSKI, Daniel.
The Micro-Macro Problem in Collective Behavior: Reconciling Agency and Structure. LEE, Raymond L M.
Non-Commutative Intuitionistic Linear Logic. ABRUSCI, V Michele.
Notions of Relative Ubiquity for Invariant Sets of Relational Structures. BANKSTON, Paul and RUITENBURG, Wim.
Phrase Structure Parameters. FODOR, Janet Dean and CRAIN, Stephen.
The Reconstruction of Institutions. COLAPIETRO, Vincent M.
Reducts of (C,+,·) Which Contain +. MARKER, D and PILLAY, A.
Relevance and Paraconsistency—A New Approach. AVRON, A.
Rich Models. ALBERT, Michael H and GROSSBERG, Rami P.
Rights and Structure in Constitutional Theory. MILLER, Geoffrey P.
Some Remarks on the Algebraic Structure of the Medvedev Lattice. SORBI, Andrea.
The Special Model Axiom in Nonstandard Analysis. ROSS, David.
Structural Analogies Between Physical Systems. KROES, Peter.
Structural Representation and Surrogative Reasoning. SWOYER, Chris.
Structural Violence and Fallible Plans: A Case Study in Philosophy and Educational Planning. MOULDER, J.
Structure and Meaning in St Augustine's *Confessions*. CROSSON, Frederick J.
The Structure of the Models of Decidable Monadic Theories of Graphs. SEESE, D.
Structure/Antistructure and Agency under Oppression. LUGONES, Maria C.
Taxonomies of Model-Theoretically Defined Topological Properties. BANKSTON, Paul.
The Beginning and Structure of the "Phaenomenology of Mind" (in Hungarian). PÖGGELER, Otto.
Theory Structure and Theory Change in Contemporary Molecular Biology. CULP, Sylvia and KITCHER, Philip.
Thoughts and Feelings and Things: A New Psychiatric Epistemology. HUNDERT, Edward M.
Universal Structures in Power $\aleph_1$. MEKLER, Alan H.
Weakly Minimal Groups of Unbounded Exponent. LOVEYS, James.
When Is Arithmetic Possible?. MC COLM, Gregory L.
Wofür sind wir verantwortlich?. NEUMAIER, Otto.

STRUGGLE

Critique of Dialectical Reason, Volume 2: Jean-Paul Sartre. HOARE, Quintin (trans).
Heidegger's *Kampf*: The Difficulty of Life. CAPUTO, John D.
Postmodernist Elitism and Postmodern Struggles. GROSSBERG, Lawrence.

STUDENT(S)

Concerns of College Students Regarding Business Ethics: A Replication. PETERSON, Robert A and BELTRAMINI, Richard F and KOZMETSKY, George.
A Cross-Cultural Comparison of the Ethics of Business Students. LYSONSKI, Steven and GAIDIS, William.
An Inquiry into the Meaning of Teacher Clarity in Recent Research and into the Value of the Research for the Teacher. CRABTREE, Walden.
Principled Moral Reasoning: Is It a Viable Approach to Promote Ethical Integrity?. WEBER, James and GREEN, Sharon.
The Role of Ethics and Social Responsibility in Achieving Organizational Effectiveness: Students Versus Managers. KRAFT, Kenneth L and SINGHAPAKDI, Anusorn.

STURGEON, N
Just Causes. BLACKBURN, Simon.
Reply to Sturgeon's "Contents and Causes" A Reply to Blackburn. BLACKBURN, Simon.
Sturgeon's Defence of Moral Realism. JOBE, Evan K.

STYLE
The Chronology of Plato's Dialogues. BRANDWOOD, Leonard.
Style and Music: Theory, History, and Ideology. MEYER, Leonard B.
Blanshard on Philosophical Style. SMITH, John E.
Stephen Hilmy on Matters of Method and Style. COVEOS, Costis M.

SUAREZ
La analogía del ser en Suárez. ROIG GIRONELLA, J.
Essentialism Old and New: Suarez and Brody. KRONEN, John D.

SUBJECT(S)
Human Consciousness. HANNAY, Alastair.
Self and Non-Self: The Drigdrisyaviveka Attributed to Samkara. RAPHAEL (trans).
"'Subjects' versus 'Persons' in Social Psychological Research" in *Harré and His Critics*, SECORD, Paul F.
"Beautiful Things and the Aesthetic Subject" in *XIth International Congress in Aesthetics, Nottingham 1988*, VAN DER SCHOOT, Albert.
"Literature and Philosophy at the Crossroads: Proustian Subjects" in *Writing the Politics of Difference*, MC DONALD, Christie.
The 'Gay Science' of Nietzsche (in Dutch). ESTERHUYSE, Willie.
Aristotelian Syllogisms and Generalized Quantifiers. WESTERSTAHL, Dag.
Autopoesis—Subject—Reality (in German). ZIEMKE, Axel and STÖBER, Konrad.
The Core of Aesthetics. WOLLHEIM, Richard.
Cross-Cultural Philosophizing. RANLY, Ernest W.
Getting the Subject Back into the World: Heidegger's Version. KERR, Fergus.
Henri Bergson and Postmodernism. MULDOON, Mark S.
L'inquiétante étrangeté de Jules Amédée Barbey d'Aurevilly. ROMEYER DHERBEY, Gilbert.
Reconstructing the Subject: Feminism, Modernism, and Postmodernism. HEKMAN, Susan.
Reflection in Politics and the Question of a Political Subject (in Czechoslovakian). HEJDANEK, Ladislav.
Subject en zelfervaring. BERNET, R.
The Subject in Feminism. BRAIDOTTI, Rosi.
The Subject of Hermeneutics and the Hermeneutics of the Subject. RICHARDSON, William.
Subject-Object Theories. BAHM, Archie J.
Le sujet en dernier appel. MARION, Jean-Luc.
Sujeto, acto y operación. GAMARRA, Daniel.

SUBJECTIVE
Acceptance of Others and Concern for Oneself (in French). MULLER, Denis.
Challenge: Subjectivist Naturalism. FOLDVARY, Fred E.
La distinción entre intereses subjetivos y objetivos y su importancia para la Etica. PATZIG, Günther.
References in Narrative Text. WIEBE, Janyce M.
Response: Subjective Values and Objective Values. MACHAN, Tibor R.
Subjective Boundaries and Combinations in Psychiatric Diagnoses. MIROWSKY, John.
Tradition and Its Value: A Contribution to the History of Polish Marxist Philosophical Thought (in Polish). GRADKOWSKI, Waldemar.
What is it Like to be an Aardvark?. TIGHLMAN, B R.

SUBJECTIVISM
A "Realizacção da Razão": Um Programa Hegeliano?. BARATA-MOURA, José.
"On Subjective Appreciation of Objective Moral Points" in *Logic and Ethics*, SRZEDNICKI, J.
"Subjectivism" in *A Companion to Ethics*, RACHELS, James.
Blanshard's Critique of Ethical Subjectivism. JOHNSON, Oliver A.
Dewey and the Theory of Knowledge. THAYER, H S.
An Examination of Marxist Doctrine in the Traditions of Russian Religious Philosophy. STEPANOVA, E A.
Intersubjectivity without Subjectivism. SINGER, Beth J.
The Reformed Subjectivist Principle Revisited. FORD, Lewis S.
Substance and Selfhood. LOWE, E J.
Voix et Existence. DIAGNE, Oumar.

SUBJECTIVITY
The Cogito and Hermeneutics: The Question of the Subject in Ricoeur. JERVOLINO, Domenico.
Difference and Subjectivity: Dialogue and Personal Identity. JACQUES, Francis.
Empiricism and Subjectivity: An Essay on Hume's Theory of Human Nature. BOUNDAS, Constantin V (trans).
Existence et Subjectivité: Études de Psychologie Phénoménologique. THINÈS, Georges.
Fichte's Theory of Subjectivity. NEUHOUSER, Frederick.
God and Subjectivity. GALGAN, Gerald J.
Historia del nombrar: Dos episodios de la subjetividad. THIEBAUT, Carlos.
Historische Objektivitat. WEBERMAN, David.
L'objet-peinture: Pour une théorie de la réception. PAQUIN, Nycole.
Modernity, Aesthetics, and the Bounds of Art. MC CORMICK, Peter J.
Moralische Verbindlichkeit oder Erziehung. LANGEWAND, Alfred.
Nietzsches Scheitern am Werk. HELLER, Edmund.
An Outline of the Philosophy of Knowledge and Science. BLANDINO, Giovanni.
Patterns of Dissonance. BRAIDOTTI, Rosi.
Philosophical Essays. CARTWRIGHT, Richard.
The Question of Ethics. SCOTT, Charles E.
Das Verhängnis Erste Philosophie. EBELING, Hans.
Who Comes after the Subject?. CADAVA, Eduardo (ed).
"Another Experience of the Question, or Experiencing the Question Other-Wise" in *Who Comes after the Subject?*, AGACINSKI, Sylviane.
"The Objective Appearance of Pyrrhonism" in *Psychology (Companions to Ancient Thought: 2)*, EVERSON, Stephen.
"On Becoming a Subject: Lacan's Rereading of Freud" in *Reconsidering Psychology: Perspectives from Continental Philosophy*, BERGOFFEN, Debra B.
"Skull's Darkroom: The *Camera Obscura* and Subjectivity" in *Philosophy of Technology*, BAILEY, Lee W.
"What Is the 'Subjectivity' of the Mental?" in *Philosophical Perspectives, 4: Action Theory and Philosophy of Mind, 1990*, LYCAN, William G.
Ambiguity, Inductive Systems, and the Modeling of Subjective Probability Judgements. MONETA, Giovanni B.
Aphasia and Inner Language. LANTÉRI-LAURA, Georges and WALKER, R Scott.
Art, Truth and the Education of Subjectivity. HEPBURN, Ronald W.
Der Begriff des Selbstbewusstseins bei Kant. GLOY, Karen.
The Definition of 'Art'. ROWE, M W.
A Dilemma for Subjective Bayesians—and How to Resolve It. MILNE, Peter.
Ernst Mach and the Elimination of Subjectivity. HAMILTON, Andy.
Etwas ist in mir da—Zu Ulrich Posthast: Philosophisches Buch. WOLF, Ursula.
Fragmentos póstumos Friedrich Nietzsche. GIACOIA JUNIOR, Oswaldo.
From Nothingness to No-thing-ness: the Roots of Ferry and Renaut's Humanism. BARBIERO, Daniel.
From Philosophical Psychology to Philosophical Anthropology (in Dutch). VERGOTE, A.
Hume and Intrinsic Value. THOMAS, D A Lloyd.
Identity and Subjectivity (in Serbo-Croatian). FRANK, Manfred.
Irigaray on Subjectivity. SCHUTTE, Ofelia.
Kant, Mendelssohn, Lambert, and the Subjectivity of Time. FALKENSTEIN, Lorne.
Objective and Subjective Aspects of Pain. GRAHEK, Nikola.
On Appealing to the Evidence. PHILLIPS, Hollibert E.
On Two Recent Accounts of Colour. MC GINN, Marie.
Perception and Neuroscience. GILLETT, Grant R.
Psychanalyse et existentialisme: A propos de la théorie lacanienne de la subjectivité. VAN HAUTE, P.
Riproposta di una teoria della soggettività in un'epoca di decostruzione del soggetto. LATORA, Salvatore.
The Role of Subjectivity in the Realism of Thomas Nagel and Jean-Paul Sartre. WIDER, Kathleen.
Soggettività e autocoscienza: Prospettive e problemi in Dieter Henrich. CELANO, Bruno.
Subjektivität, Allgemeingültigkeit und Apriorität des Geschmacksurteils bei Kant. BAUM, Manfred.
Le supplément poétique. WATTEYNE, Nathalie.
La teoria hegeliana dell'autocoscienza e della sua razionalità. VARNIER, Giuseppe.
Three Notions of Judgement (in Czechoslovakian). KOTATKO, Petr.
A Unique Way of Existing: Merleau-Ponty and the Subject. SIEGEL, Jerrold.

SUBJUNCTIVE(S)
"Tenses, Temporal Quantifiers and Semantic Innocence" in *Truth and Interpretation: Perspectives on the Philosophy of Donald Davidson*, RICHARDS, Barry.
What is a Law of Nature? A Humean Answer. URBACH, Peter.

SUBLIME
"The Bible and the Rhetorical Sublime" in *The Bible as Rhetoric: Studies in Biblical Persuasion and Credibility*, POLAND, Lynn.
"The Existential Sublime: From Burke's Aesthetics to the Socio-Political" in *XIth International Congress in Aesthetics, Nottingham 1988*, CROWTHER, Paul.
"Stories of Sublimely Good Character" in *XIth International Congress in Aesthetics, Nottingham 1988*, CALLEN, Donald.
Análisis de la doctrina ética de las "observaciones sobre lo bello y sublime". GONZÁLEZ PORTA, Mario A.
Experiencia de lo sublime y principios racionales. ARTOLA, José María.
La réflexion dans l'esthétique kantienne. LYOTARD, Jean-François.
The Notion of Sublime in Kant and Hegel: A Psycho-Analytical Reading (in Serbo-Croatian). ZIZEK, Slavoj.

SUBSTANCE(S)
see also Attribute(s), Matter
Central Themes in Early Modern Philosophy. COVER, J A (ed).

SUBSTANCE(S)
David Hume's Theory of Mind. FLAGE, Daniel E.
Expressionism in Philosophy: Spinoza. DELEUZE, Gilles.
Leibniz and Strawson: A New Essay in Descriptive Metaphysics. BROWN, Clifford.
Locke and French Materialism. YOLTON, John W.
The Recovery of the Soul: An Aristotelian Essay on Self-fulfilment. RANKIN, Kenneth.
"Spinoza and Descartes and the Existence of Extended Substance" in *Central Themes in Early Modern Philosophy*, WOOLHOUSE, R S.
Algunas consideraciones sobre la substancia en la metafísica de Juan Duns Escoto. BEUCHOT, Mauricio.
Aquinas versus Epistemological Criticism: A Case for Philosophy *in* Science. DEL RE, Giuseppe.
El concepto de substancia sensible en Aristóteles: Génesis histórica de la cuestión. BLAQUIER, Carlos P.
Dravya, Guna and *Paryāya* in Jaina Thought. SONI, Jayandra.
Essentialism Old and New: Suarez and Brody. KRONEN, John D.
Haecceitas and the Bare Particular. PARK, Woosuk.
Locke on Personal Identity. WINKLER, Kenneth P.
Locke on Real Essence. OWEN, David W D.
Locke on the Ontology of Matter, Living Things and Persons. CHAPPELL, Vere.
Per una rilettura dei libri "M" e "N" della *Metafisica* di Aristotele alla luce delle "dottrine non scritte" di Platone. CATTANEI, Elisabetta.
Processes, Substances, and Leibniz's Epistemology: A Case for Essentialism in Contemporary Physics. PIRO, Francesco.
Real Selves: Persons as a Substantial Kind. LOWE, E J.
Relative Identity and Locke's Principle of Individuation. UZGALIS, William L.
El reloj de Dios (Glosas provisionales a un principio leibniziano). MUÑOZ, Jacobo.
Sachverhalt and *Gegenstand* are Dead. THOMPKINS, E F.
Spinoza on the Eternity of the Human Mind. LUCASH, Frank.
Substance and Selfhood. LOWE, E J.
La substance composée chez Leibniz. CHAZERANS, Jean-François.
Substance: Prolegomena to a Realist Theory of Identity. AYERS, Michael.
Substancia y sustantividad: Tomás de Aquino y X Zubiri. CERCÓS SOTO, José Luis.
Sulla matrice della teoria della sostanza nel *Discorso di metafisica* di Leibniz. DELCÓ, Alessandro.
Sur le vague en mathématiques. GRANGER, G G.

SUBSTANTIVALISM
The Hole Truth. BUTTERFIELD, Jeremy.
Substance, Relations, and Arguments About the Nature of Space-Time. TELLER, Paul.

SUBSTITUTION
"Problems of Admissibility and Substitution, Logical Equations and Restricted Theories of Free Algebras" in *Logic, Methodology and Philosophy of Science, VIII*, RYBAKOV, V V.
Cylindric Algebras with Terms. FELDMAN, Norman.
The Deduction Theorem in a Strict Functional Calculus of First Order Based on Strict Implication. MARCUS, Ruth Barcan.
Finite Logics and the Simple Substitution Property. HOSOI, Tsutomu and SASAKI, Katsumi.
The Minimal and Semiminimal Notions of Truth. FOX, J.
Problems of Substitution and Admissibility in the Modal System Grz and in Intuitionistic Propositional Calculus. RYBAKOV, V V.
The Simple Substitution Property of Gödel's Intermediate Propositional Logics S_n's. SASAKI, Katsumi.

SUBSTITUTIVITY
Leibniz's Philosophy of Logic and Language (Second Edition). ISHIGURO, Hide.
Referential Opacity in Aristotle. SPELLMAN, Lynne.

SUBSTRATUM(-TA)
Ousia, Substratum, and Matter. SFEKAS, Stanley.
Substrative Materialism. KERR-LAWSON, Angus.

SUBVERSION
"Essence and Subversion in Hegel and Heidegger" in *Writing the Politics of Difference*, MC CUMBER, John.
"Hegel and the Subversion of Systems: *Der Fall Adorno*" in *Writing the Politics of Difference*, DONOUGHO, Martin.
"Subversion of System/Systems of Subversion" in *Writing the Politics of Difference*, SHAPIRO, Gary.

SUCCESS
Measuring the Success of Science. NIINILUOTO, Ilkka.

SUCHODOLSKI, B
Bogdan Suchodolski's Philosophy of Culture (in Polish). TRUCHLINSKA, Bogumila.

SUFFERING
Animal Experimentation: The Consensus Changes. LANGLEY, Gill (ed).
Animal Experimentation: The Moral Issue. BAIRD, Robert M (ed).
Sacred Fragments: Recovering Theology for the Modern Jew. GILLMAN, Neil.
Spirit and Existence: A Philosophy Inquiry into the Meaning of Spiritual Existence. GELVEN, Michael.
"Kierkegaard's Phenomenology of Faith as Suffering" in *Writing the Politics of Difference*, WESTPHAL, Merold.
"What's Wrong with Bitterness?" in *Feminist Ethics*, MC FALL, Lynne.
'Why Did It Happen to Me?'. THOMAS, J L H.
Auschwitz, Morality and the Suffering of God. SAROT, Marcel.
Capital Punishment and Realism. COCKBURN, David.
Patripassianism, Theopaschitism and the Suffering of God. SAROT, Marcel.
Post-Holocaust Theodicy: Images of Deity, History, and Humanity. FREY, Robert Seitz.
Recognizing Suffering. CASSELL, Eric J.
Remaking the She-Devil: A Critical Look at Feminist Approaches to Beauty. DAVIS, Kathy.
Self and Suffering: Deconstruction and Reflexive Definition in Buddhism and Christianity. MELLOR, Philip A.
The Thought That Learning Is by Ordeal: An Original Essay. WOODRUFF, Paul B.

SUFFICIENT REASON(S)
Universalität des Prinzips vom zureichenden Grund. NICOLÁS, Juan A.

SUFFRAGE
Locke on Taxation and Suffrage. HUGHES, Martin.

SUFISM
Ibn 'Arabi o la renovación espiritual del sufismo. SERRANO RAMÍREZ, Jose M.

SUICIDE
The Last Choice: Preemptive Suicide in Advanced Age. PRADO, C G.
Suicide: Right or Wrong?. DONNELLY, John (ed).
Arguing for Rational Suicide. HUMPHRY, Derek.
Buddhist Views of Suicide and Euthanasia. BECKER, Carl B.
The Consequences of Endorsing Sentimental Homicide. BARRY, Robert L.
Killing Machines. ANNAS, George J.
On Lying and the Role of Content in Kant's Ethics. SEDGWICK, Sally.
Rational Suicide and Christian Virtue. MAGUIRE, Daniel C.

SULLIVAN, H
The Matrix of Personality: A Whiteheadian Corroboration of Harry Stack Sullivan's Interpersonal Theory of Psychiatry. REGAN, Thomas J.

SULLIVAN, T
"A Faith of True Proportions: Reply to Sullivan" in *Thomistic Papers, V*, RUSSMAN, Thomas A.

SUPEREGO
El factor prelógico en el desarrollo de América Latina: El teorema del preconsciente colectivo. MANSILLA, H C F.
Super-yo y vida moral: Una valoración tomista de la hipótesis psicoanalítica. PITHOD, Abelardo.

SUPEREROGATION
"Pacifism, Duty, and Supererogation" in *In the Interest of Peace: A Spectrum of Philosophical Views*, CADY, Duane L.
Charity and Moral Imperatives. ODEGARD, Douglas.
Moral Dilemmas, Disjunctive Obligations, and Kant's Principle that 'Ought' Implies 'Can'. JACQUETTE, Dale.
Supererogation and the Fulfillment of Duty. MELLEMA, Gregory.

SUPERMAN
Emerson and Nietzsche's 'Beyond-Man'. STACK, George J.
Troeltsch and Nietzsche: Critical Reflections on Ernst Troeltsch's Portrayal of Nietzsche (in German). SCHÜSSLER, Ingeborg.

SUPERSTITIONS
Crossed Fingers and Praying Hands: Remarks on Religious Belief and Superstition. RAY, R J.

SUPERSTRUCTURE(S)
El lugar de las superestructuras y los intelectuales en la filosofía política de Gramsci. RUIZ, Angel.
Problemas lógicos en el relativismo ético. CAMACHO, Luis A.

SUPERVENIENCE
Explaining Human Action. LENNON, Kathleen.
"Explanatory Exclusion and the Problem of Mental Causation" in *Information, Semantics and Epistemology*, KIM, Jaegwon.
Anomalism, Supervenience, and Davidson on Content-Individuation. ROWLANDS, Mark.
Causation in the Philosophy of Mind. JACKSON, Frank and PETTIT, Philip.
Causation: Reductionism Versus Realism. TOOLEY, Michael.
Consciousness Naturalized: Supervenience Without Physical Determinism. SENCHUK, Dennis M.
Davidson's Troubles with Supervenience. KLAGGE, James.
Disjunctive Laws and Supervenience. SEAGER, William.
A Modal Argument for Narrow Content. FODOR, Jerry A.
Moral Epistemology and the Supervenience of Ethical Concepts. AUDI, Robert.
Rationalism, Supervenience, and Moral Epistemology. KLAGGE, James.
The Reason Why: Response to Crane. PAPINEAU, David.
Semantics and Supervenience. BONEVAC, Daniel.

SUPERVENIENCE
Supervenience and Singular Causal Claims. WOODWARD, James.
Supervenience Is a Two-Way Street. MILLER, Richard B.
Supervenience, Determination, and Dependency. GRIMES, Thomas.
Supervenience, Goodness and Higher-Order Universals. ODDIE, Graham.
Why Indeed? Papineau on Supervenience. CRANE, Tim.

SUPPOSITION(S)
La teoría de la suposición y los idiomas modernos. KNABENSCHUCH DE PORTA, Sabine.

SUPREME COURT
Affirmative Action Revisited: Justice and Public Policy Considerations. VANTERPOOL, Rudolph V.
Does Strict Judicial Scrutiny Involve the *Tu Quoque* Fallacy?. SCHEDLER, George.
Justice Powell and the Parochial Schools Case: A Case for Judicial Statesmanship. WALTMAN, Jerold.
Neutrality Between Religion and Irreligion. LINDSAY, Ronald A.

SURBER, J
Commentary: "Individual and Corporate Responsibility". FRENCH, Peter A.

SURREAL NUMBERS
Recursive Surreal Numbers. HARKLEROAD, Leon.

SURROGACY
The Overdue Death of a Feminist Chameleon: Taking a Stand on Surrogacy Arrangements. TONG, Rosemarie.
Parental Obligations and the Ethics of Surrogacy: A Causal Perspective. NELSON, James Lindemann.

SURROGATE MOTHERHOOD
Beyond Baby M: Ethical Issues in New Reproductive Techniques. BARTELS, Dianne M (ed).
"The Case of Baby M" in *Beyond Baby M: Ethical Issues in New Reproductive Techniques*, MERRICK, Janna.
"Surrogacy and the Family: Social and Value Considerations" in *Beyond Baby M: Ethical Issues in New Reproductive Techniques*, ASCH, Adrienne.
"Surrogacy Arrangements: An Overview" in *Beyond Baby M: Ethical Issues in New Reproductive Techniques*, BARTELS, Dianne M.
"Surrogacy: A Question of Values" in *Beyond Baby M: Ethical Issues in New Reproductive Techniques*, ROTHMAN, Barbara Katz.
"Surrogate Motherhood Agreements: The Risks to Innocent Human Life" in *Beyond Baby M: Ethical Issues in New Reproductive Techniques*, BOPP JR, James.
"The Vatican 'Instruction' and Surrogate Motherhood" in *Beyond Baby M: Ethical Issues in New Reproductive Techniques*, BERQUIST, Richard.
On Surrogacy: Morality, Markets, and Motherhood. MOODY-ADAMS, Michele M.
Surrogate Motherhood. PROKOPIJEVIC, Miroslav.

SURROGATE(S)
Reproductive Gifts and Gift Giving: The Altruistic Woman. RAYMOND, Janice G.
Surrogate Decisionmaking and Other Matters. GREENLAW, Jane.

SURVEILLANCE
Ethics, Public Policy, and Managing Advanced Technologies: The Case of Electronic Surveillance. OTTENSMEYER, Edward J and HEROUX, Mark A.

SURVIVAL
"Human Survival and the Limits of National Sovereignty" in *In the Interest of Peace: A Spectrum of Philosophical Views*, WINSTON, Morton.
"Nuclear Space and Time" in *In the Interest of Peace: A Spectrum of Philosophical Views*, STAHL, Gary.
"Philosophy Is Not a Luxury" in *Feminist Ethics*, GINZBERG, Ruth.
"Which Values are Conducive to Human Survival? A Bunge-Test of Bunge-Ethics" in *Studies on Mario Bunge's "Treatise"*, ZECHA, Gerhard.
Cuestiones de sobrevivencia. MILLÁN, Gustavo Ortiz (trans) and SOSA, Ernest.
Global Responsibility. AGASSI, Joseph.
The Thought That Learning Is by Ordeal: An Original Essay. WOODRUFF, Paul B.

SUTHERLAND, S
Certain Hope. PHILLIPS GRIFFITHS, A.

SWANN, A
Swann versus Popper on Induction: An Arbitration. SETTLE, Tom.

SWEDISH
Swedish Model or Swedish Culture?. TRAGARDH, Lars.

SWINBURNE, R
If There Is a God, Any Experience Which Seems to Be of God, Will Be Genuine. LEVINE, Michael P.
Limited Explanations. CLARK, Stephen R L.
La rationalité du théisme: la philosophie de la religion de Richard Swinburne. PADGETT, Alan G.
Swinburne on Credal Belief. MAITZEN, Stephen.
Two Cartesian Arguments for the Simplicity of the Soul. ZIMMERMAN, Dean W.

SYLLOGISM(S)
Aristotelian Syllogisms and Generalized Quantifiers. WESTERSTAHL, Dag.
Aristotle's Apodeictic Syllogism. JOHNSTON, David.
Circularity of Thought in Hegel's Logic. BALABAN, Oded.
Complexly Fractionated Syllogistic Quantifiers. PETERSON, Philip L.
Intermediate Quantifiers versus Percentages. CARNES, Robert D and PETERSON, Philip L.
Liar Syllogisms and Related Paradoxes. SLATER, B H.
Semantica aristotelica e sillogistica modale. MARIANI, Mauro.

SYLLOGISTIC
La Logica Simbolica: nella produzione scientifica in lingua russa (1961-1983). PENNINO, Luciano.
The Origins of Aristotelian Science. FEREJOHN, Michael.
The Logic of the Liar from the Standpoint of the Aristotelian Syllogistic. KELLY, Charles J.
Tree Proofs for Syllogistic. SIMONS, Peter M.
The Two Barbaras. THOM, Paul.

SYMBOL(S)
see also Semiotics
Artificial Intelligence: Its Scope and Limits. FETZER, James H.
Claude Lévi-Strauss. LEACH, Edmund.
From Sentience To Symbols. PICKERING, John (ed).
How to Play Theological Ping-Pong: And Other Essays on Faith and Reason. ABRAHAM, William J (ed).
Inscriptions and Reflections: Essays in Philosophical Theology. SCHARLEMANN, Robert P.
Metaphysik als Metahistorik oder Hermeneutik des unreinen Denkens Die Philosophie Max Müllers. RUIZ-PESCE, Ramón Eduardo.
Relating Humanities and Social Thought (Science, Ideology, and Value, Volume 4). EDEL, Abraham.
"Heiligsprechung des Imaginären: Das Imaginäre in Cornelius Castoriadis' Gesellschaftstheorie" in *The Social Horizon of Knowledge*, LÖVENICH, Friedhelm.
"Human Symbols as Functioning Objects: A First Look at John William Miller's Contribution to Semiotics" in *The Philosophy of John William Miller*, COLAPIETRO, Vincent M.
"The Necessity for Symbol and Myth: A Literary Amplification" in *Archetypal Process: Self and Divine in Whitehead, Jung, and Hillman*, SELLERY, J'Nan Morse.
"The Realism of the Symbolic" in *Harré and His Critics*, SMITH, Charles W.
The Community as Sacrament. LIDERBACH, Daniel.
Deconstruction as Symbolic Play: Simmel/Derrida. WEINSTEIN, Deena and WEINSTEIN, Michael A.
Freud devait-il choisir entre les deux conceptions du symbole que lui attribue Lévi-Strauss?. CHARRON, Ghyslain.
The Joy of Transgression: Bataille and Kristeva. MARCHAK, Catherine.
Man as the Animal Symbolism in the Conception of S Langer (in Polish). BYTNIEWSKI, Pawel.
The *Nagaraja*: Symbol and Symbolism in Hindu Art and Iconography. DURAN, Jane.
Perennial Modernity: Forms as Aesthetic and Symbolic. MAQUET, Jacques.
Russell's Theory of Definite Descriptions. LAMBERT, Karel.
Sign, Symbol, and System. ELGIN, Catherine Z.

SYMBOLIC
Language and "The Feminine" in Nietzsche and Heidegger. GRAYBEAL, Jean.

SYMBOLIC LOGIC
Logic for an Overcast Tuesday. RAFALKO, Robert J.
La Logica Simbolica: nella produzione scientifica in lingua russa (1961-1983). PENNINO, Luciano.

SYMBOLISM
In Praise of the Cognitive Emotions. SCHEFFLER, Israel.
Kommunikations-Theoretische Schriften II: Symbolische Erkenntnis und Kommunikation. UNGEHEUER, Gerold (ed).
Musical Aesthetics: A Historical Reader, Volume III, The Twentieth Century. LIPPMAN, Edward A (ed).
The Philatelic Commemoration of American Education. WILLERS, Jack Conrad.
Simbolismo y metafísica. MUÑOZ TRIGUERO, Isidro.

SYMBOLIZATION
The Core of Aesthetics. WOLLHEIM, Richard.
On Capturing Cities. GOODMAN, Nelson.
Realism, Irrealism, and Ideology: A Critique of Nelson Goodman. MITCHELL, W J T.
Why Natural Theology, Still, Yet?. HUTCHINGS, Patrick.

SYMMETRY
N-Normal Factors in Finite Symmetric Heyting Algebras. GALLI, Adriana C and SAGASTUME, Marta.
The Problem of Causation and Time-Symmetry in Physics. BHARUCHA, Filita.
Rawlsian Nash Solutions. FABELLA, Raul V.
The Symmetry Enigma in Hobbes. HAJI, Ishtiyaque.

SYMPATHY
Hume's Place in Moral Philosophy. CAPALDI, Nicholas.
Beyond Self-Interest and Altruism: A Reconstruction of Adam Smith's Theory of Human Conduct. KHALIL, Elias L.
Conscience, Sympathy and the Foundation of Morality. CI, Jiwei.
La ética de Adam Smith: un utilitarismo de la simpatía. TASSET, José L.
Merleau-Ponty's Phenomenology of Sympathy. MATUSTIK, Martin J.

SYNCHRONICITY
Musical Time as a Practical Accomplishment: A Change in Tempo. WEEKS, P A D.

SYNCRETISM
"Who Compiled the *Chuang Tzu*?" in *Chinese Texts and Philosophical Contexts*, ROTH, Harold.

SYNDERESIS
Synderesis, the Spark of Conscience, in the English Renaissance. GREENE, Robert A.

SYNDICALISM
Two Views of the Revolution: Gramsci and Sorel, 1916-1920. SCHECTER, Darrow.

SYNONYMY
Divine Unity and Superfluous Synonymity. LEVINE, Michael P.
Russell on Ordinary Names and Synonymy. PINEAU, Lois.
Self-Predication and Synonymy. SILVERMAN, Allan.

SYNTACTIC MODEL(S)
The Meaning of Mathematical Expressions: Does Philosophy Shed Any Light on Psychology?. ERNEST, Paul.

SYNTACTICS
Semantic Structures. JACKENDOFF, Ray.
"Pathologies" in Two Syntactic Categories of Partial Maps. MONTAGNA, Franco.
Syntactic Form and Textual Rhetoric: The Cognitive Basis for Certain Pragmatic Principles. PRIDEAUX, Gary D.

SYNTAX
see also Grammar(s)
"Linguistic Theory and Davidson's Program in Semantics" in *Truth and Interpretation: Perspectives on the Philosophy of Donald Davidson*, HIGGINBOTHAM, James.
"Some Notes on Morphology and Syntax in Classical Chinese" in *Chinese Texts and Philosophical Contexts*, PULLEYBLANK, Edwin G.
Cartesian Syntax. ENGLEBRETSEN, George.
Connectionism, Modularity, and Tacit Knowledge. DAVIES, Martin.
Constructive Interpolation Theorems for $S2^0$ and S2. BARCA, Anne and MC ROBBIE, Michael.
Dynamic Predicate Logic. GROENENDIJK, Jeroen and STOKHOF, Martin.
Embeddability, Syntax, and Semantics in Accounts of Scientific Theories. TURNEY, Peter.
Intensionality and Boundedness. MORRILL, Glyn.
Is the Brain a Digital Computer?. SEARLE, John R.
The Language of Thought: No Syntax Without Semantics. CRANE, Tim.
The Meaning of Δυναμισ at *Timaeus* 31c. PRITCHARD, Paul.
On Negation. KOKTOVÁ, Eva.
Syntax and Pragmatics: Apartheid or Integration?. BOLKESTEIN, A Machtelt.

SYNTHESIS
Kants Logik der Synthesis und die Schliessung einer "unübersehbaren Kluft". FUNKE, Gerhard.
Philosophical Culture in the Warsaw-Lvov School (in Polish). GLUCHOWSKI, Gerard.
Self-Synthesis, Self-Knowledge, and Skepticism. MAZOUÉ, James G.

SYNTHETIC
De Kant-interpretatie van Evert Willem Beth. PEIJNENBURG, J.

SYNTHETIC A PRIORI
Kant en de mogelijkheid van de metafysica als wetenschap. PERRICK, M.
Kants Begriff der synthetischen Urteile a priori. ROS, Arno.

SYSTEM(S)
Artificial Intelligence: Its Scope and Limits. FETZER, James H.
Essays on Hegel's Logic. DI GIOVANNI, George (ed).
Ideas, Principios y Dialectica. LAFUENTE, Maria Isabel.
Nietzsches Scheitern am Werk. HELLER, Edmund.
Saussure: Signs, System, and Arbitrariness. HOLDCROFT, David.
Untersuchungen zur Theorie des hypothetischen Urteils. LINNEWEBER-LAMMERSKITTEN, Helmut.
"Beginning" in *Essays on Hegel's Logic*, MAKER, William.
"Mario Bunge on Ontology" in *Studies on Mario Bunge's "Treatise"*, BUNGE, Mario.
"Mario Bunge's Ontology as a Formal Foundation for Information Systems Concepts" in *Studies on Mario Bunge's "Treatise"*, WAND, Yair and WEBER, Ron.
"On the System" in *Studies on Mario Bunge's "Treatise"*, BOCHENSKI, Joseph M.
"Subversion of System/Systems of Subversion" in *Writing the Politics of Difference*, SHAPIRO, Gary.
CAHBI: Europe Needs a Universal Bioethical System. GUNNING, Karel.
Cicero's Focus: From the Best Regime to the Model Statesman. NICGORSKI, Walter.
Emergenz Bausteine für eine Begriffsexplikation. STÖCKLER, Manfred.
Ends and Meaning in Machine-Like Systems. ATLAN, H.
Equational Subsystems. WEAVER, George.
Hayek's Theory of Cultural Evolution: An Evaluation in the Light of Vanberg's Critique. HODGSON, Geoffrey M.
Note on Entropy, Disorder and Disorganization. DENBIGH, K G.
Prefacing Pluralism: John Hick and the Mastery of Religion. LOUGHLIN, Gerard.
Sign, Symbol, and System. ELGIN, Catherine Z.
Systematic Assumptions in Dilthey's Critique of Metaphysics. NENON, Thomas.
Theorizing about Morals. WALLACE, Jim.

SYSTEMS ANALYSIS
Evolutionary Instability: Logical and Material Aspects of a Unified Theory of Biosocial Evolution. GEIGER, Gebhard.
Current Trends in the Philosophy of Medicine. POTTER, Robert Lyman.

SYSTEMS THEORY
Ideals and Illusions: On Reconstruction and Deconstruction in Contemporary Critical Theory. MC CARTHY, Thomas.
Strukturanthropologie "Der menschliche Mensch". ROMBACH, Heinrich.
Das Verhängnis Erste Philosophie. EBELING, Hans.
Bestandserhaltung oder Kritik oder: Weder Bestandserhaltung noch Kritik—Die Intention der Systemtheorie Niklas Luhmanns. POLLACK, Detlef.
Filosofía y teoría general de sistemas en el pensamiento de A Rapoport. SAXE FERNÁNDEZ, Eduardo E.
System-Theoretical Bases of Social Theory (in German). LUHMANN, Niklas.
Understanding the System Construction in Logic. DAS, Ramesh Chandra.

TABLEAU SYSTEMS
Premiss Tree Proofs and Logic of Contradiction. SIKIC, Zvonimir.

TACHYONS
Causal Paradoxes in Special Relativity. ARNTZENIUS, Frank.

TACIT KNOWLEDGE
Connectionism, Modularity, and Tacit Knowledge. DAVIES, Martin.

TAKEOVER(S)
In Defense of Sharks: Moral Issues in Hostile Liquidating Takeovers. ALMEDER, Robert and CAREY, David.

TALKING
The Difference Between Truth and Opinion: How the Misuse of Language Can Lead to Disaster. COONEY, Timothy J.
Talking. VELASCO, Monica A.

TALMUD
Nine Talmudic Readings. ARONOWICZ, Annette (trans).

TANG, J
Tang Junyi's Philosophical View of History and His Explanation of the Philosophy of Wang Chuanshan. SHAFU, Xiao.

TAO
Can Knowledge Occur Unknowingly?. CHAUDHURI, Manjusree.
Heidegger and the Japanese Connection. BILIMORIA, Purusottama.

TAOISM
Bewusstsein und Natursein. CHO, Kah Kyung.
The Butterfly as Companion: Meditations on the First Three Chapters of the Chuang Tzu. WU, Kuang-Ming.
Chinese Buddhist Apocrypha. BUSWELL JR, Robert E (ed).
"Hsun Tzu and Chuang Tzu" in *Chinese Texts and Philosophical Contexts*, NIVISON, David S.
The Beautiful, the Ugly, and the Tao. COLEMAN, Earle J.
Beyond Naturalism: A Reconstruction of Daoist Environmental Ethics. PEERENBOOM, Randall P.
The Contents of the Daoist Religion and Its Cultural Function. CAI, Hou.
Hermeneutic Phenomenology and Taoism. KIDD, James W.
Taoist Visions of the Body. KOHN, Livia.

TARSKI
Meaning and Truth: The Essential Readings in Modern Semantics. GARFIELD, Jay L (ed).
The Implications of Error for Davidsonian Charity. LARSON, David.
Truths without Facts. SEN, Pranab Kumar.
La verdad. ALVAREZ GÓMEZ, Mariano.

TASTE
"Aesthetic Reasons" in *XIth International Congress in Aesthetics, Nottingham 1988*, CHARLTON, William.
Hume and the Paradox of Taste Again. WERTZ, S K.
Sobre el gusto y la verdad práctica. ARREGUI, Jorge Vicente.
Subjektivität, Allgemeingültigkeit und Apriorität des Geschmacksurteils bei Kant. BAUM, Manfred.
Über das Geschmacksurteil und die künstlerische Freiheit bei Kant (in Japanese). UE, Satoko.

TECHNOLOGY

"Politics, Technology and the Responsibility of the Intellectuals" in *The Political Responsibility of Intellectuals*, LEVY, David J.
"Pragmatism, *Praxis*, and the Technological" in *Philosophy of Technology*, MARGOLIS, Joseph.
"Recreating Motherhood: Ideology and Technology in American Society" in *Beyond Baby M: Ethical Issues in New Reproductive Techniques*, ROTHMAN, Barbara Katz.
"The Sociotechnology of Sociotechnical Systems: Elements of a Theory of Plans" in *Studies on Mario Bunge's "Treatise"*, SENI, Dan Alexander.
"Some Marxism Themes in the Age of Information" in *Perspectives on Ideas and Reality*, NYÍRI, J C.
"Surrogacy Arrangements: An Overview" in *Beyond Baby M: Ethical Issues in New Reproductive Techniques*, BARTELS, Dianne M.
"Technology and Society: A View from Sociology" in *Studies on Mario Bunge's "Treatise"*, GINGRAS, Yves and NIOSI, Jorge.
The Artificial Womb—Patriarchal Bone or Technological Blessing?. HEDMAN, Carl.
Beyond Malthusianism: Demography and Technology in John Stuart Mill's Stationary State. KURFIRST, Robert.
Biotechnology and Warfare. REINIKAINEN, Pekka.
The Comeuppance of Science and Technology. CLEVELAND, Harlan.
La critique du modèle industriel comme histoire de la rareté: Une introduction à la pensée d'Ivan Illich. ACHTERHUIS, Hans.
Defining the Ethical Standards of the High-Technology Industry. FIMBEL, Nancie and BURSTEIN, Jerome S.
Do Not Despair: There is Life after Constructivism. BIJKER, Wieke.
Ethics, Public Policy, and Managing Advanced Technologies: The Case of Electronic Surveillance. OTTENSMEYER, Edward J and HEROUX, Mark A.
Ethik zwischen globaler Verantwortung und spekulativer Weltschematik. JOOS, Egbert.
Éthique et technique: bioéthique. KEMP, Peter.
Killing Machines. ANNAS, George J.
Maîtrise, marché et société industrielle. VAN PARIJS, Philippe.
Le modèle industriel comme modèle énergétique. BERTEN, André.
Morality in Flux: Medical Ethics in the People's Republic of China. QIU, Ren-Zong.
La mort de Socrate et la vie des machines. BEAUNE, Jean-Claude.
Die Natur der Sprache: Von der Ontologie zur Technologie. HOTTOIS, Gilbert.
Nicola Abbagnano tra esistenzialismo e neoilluminismo. QUARTA, Antonio.
On the Dearth of Philosophical Contributions to Medicine. YARBOROUGH, Mark.
El pensamiento de Heidegger y Marcuse en relación con la ecología. ARRIETA, Jeannette and HAYLING, Annie.
La práctica tecnológica. HERRERA JIMÉNEZ, Rodolfo.
Problemas conceptuales y políticas de desarrollo tecnológico. QUINTANILLA, Miguel Ángel.
The Question of Responsibility in the Context of Instructional Technology. TAYLOR, William and KONSTANTELLOU, Eva.
Reclaiming Virtue: Philosophy in the Field of Educational Technology. BELLAND, John and SMITH, Phillip L.
Reconstructing the Political. JANICAUD, Dominique.
Una reflexión sobre el pensamiento científico técnico. CORONA, N A.
Sobre el conocimiento tecnológico. VILLORO, Luis.
Sociedad informatizada y poder político. RICHARDS, Edgardo.
Spiritual Traditions and Science and Technology. BAKAR, Osman.
Storicità tecnica e architettura. MAZZARELLA, Eugenio.
A Survey of Critical Theories of "Western Marxism". YUJIN, Zhao.
Technological Faith and Christian Doubt. FERRÉ, Frederick.
Technological Progress and Architectural Response. WINTERS, Edward.
Technology, Truth and Language: The Crisis of Theological Discourse. CROWLEY, Paul.
La tecnología desde un punto de vista ético. RAMÍREZ, E Roy.
Tecnología y sociedad. HERRERA, Rodolfo.
Tendencias actuales en filosofía de la tecnología. CAMACHO, Luis.
Text and Technology. CROWELL, Steven Galt.
The Relationship Between the Humanities and the Natural and Technical Sciences (in German). PACHO, Julián.
Using Arendt and Heidegger to Consider Feminist Thinking on Women and Reproductive/Infertility Technologies. KLAWITER, Maren.
Was heisst "sich in der Gesellschaft orientieren"?. BÖHME, Gernot.

TEICHMANN, J

Universals and Creativity. WESTPHAL, Jonathan.

TEILHARD

Evolution als Höherentwicklung des Bewusstseins. KUMMER, Christian.
Interpreting Evolution: Darwin and Teilhard de Chardin. BIRX, H James.
La tarea cósmica del hombre según Teilhard de Chardin. PATIÑO, Joel Rodríguez.

TELEOLOGICAL ETHICS

Wie kaatst moet de bal verwachten. MERTENS, T.

TELEOLOGICAL EXPLANATION

Explanation in Biology. SMITH, John Maynard.
Truth and Teleology. PAPINEAU, David.

TELEOLOGY

"Nietzsche's Thesis on Teleology" in *Looking After Nietzsche*, NANCY, Jean-Luc.
"Teleology and the Relationship Between Biology and the Physical Sciences in the Nineteenth and Twentieth Centuries" in *Some Truer Method*, BEATTY, John.
Anotaciones en torno al poder de la democracia. MOLINA, Carlos.
Barrow and Tipler on the Anthropic Principle versus Divine Design. CRAIG, William Lane.
Crypto-theologie: hoffentlich ein Ende: Reactie op Callebaut en Wachelder. SOONTIENS, Frans.
Cuestiones actuales de epistemología teológica: Aportes de la teología de la liberación. SCANNONE, J C.
Divenire, principio di causalità, affermazione teologica. SACCHI, Dario.
Etica e morale: mira teleogica e prospettiva deontologica. RICOEUR, Paul.
Faustian Phenomena: Teleology in Goethe's Interpretation of Plants and Animals. CORNELL, John F.
Kant, Teleology, and Sexual Ethics. COOKE, Vincent M.
Kants *Kritik der Urteilskraft*. RAYMAEKERS, Bart.
Maimonides: A Natural Law Theorist?. LEVINE, Michael.
Natuurlijke selectie, doelgerichtheid en een uitzonderlijke samenloop van omstandigheden: Een kritiek op F Soontiëns. SLURINK, Pouwel.
Objet et communauté transcendantale: autour d'un fragment du dernier Husserl. BENOIST, J.
Il problema teologico nel pensiero di Heidegger. PENATI, G.
Quelques remarques sur la composition de la *Dialectique de la faculté de juger téléologique*. KOPPER, Joachim.
Socrates, the Craft Analogy, and Science. GRAHAM, Daniel W.
Teleo-theologie und kein Ende: Reactie op Soontiens. CALLEBAUT, Werner and WACHELDER, J.
Teleological Underdetermination. OKRENT, Mark.
Teleologie: Chance oder Belastung für die Philosophie?. PLEINES, Jürgen-Eckardt.
Teleology and the Concepts of Causation. VON GLASERSFELD, Ernst.
War Demokrits Weltbild mechanistisch und antiteleologisch?. HIRSCH, Ulrike.

TELESIO

Telesio e la cultura napoletana. STURLESE, Rita.

TELEVISION

Television and the Crisis of Democracy. KELLNER, Douglas.
"The Televised and the Untelevised: Keeping an Eye On/Off the Tube" in *Postmodernism—Philosophy and the Arts (Continental Philosophy III)*, SEITZ, Brian.
"Television and the Aesthetics of Everyday Life" in *XIth International Congress in Aesthetics, Nottingham 1988*, LUKACS, Anthony.
Physical Environment Television Advertisement Themes: 1979 and 1989. PETERSON, Robin T.

TELLER, D

Reply to Teller's "Simpler Arguments Might Work Better". HARDIN, C L.

TEMPERAMENT(S)

"The True Temper of a Teacher" in *Abeunt Studia in Mores: A Festschrift for Helga Doblin*, RUCKER, Darnell.

TEMPERANCE

Two Varieties of Temperance in the *Gorgias*. CURZER, Howard J.

TEMPORAL LOGIC

"Tenses, Temporal Quantifiers and Semantic Innocence" in *Truth and Interpretation: Perspectives on the Philosophy of Donald Davidson*, RICHARDS, Barry.

TEMPORALITY

see also Time
About Time: Inventing the Fourth Dimension. FRIEDMAN, William J.
Probabilistic Causality. EELLS, Ellery.
Chronic Illness and the Temporal Structure of Human Life. DOUARD, John W.
Eternity and Simultaneity. LEFTOW, Brian.
Evans-Pritchard on Persons and Their Cattle-Clocks: A Note on the Anthropological Account of Man. CHANDRA, Suresh.
Musical Time as a Practical Accomplishment: A Change in Tempo. WEEKS, P A D.
The Nature of a Person-Stage. MC INERNEY, Peter K.
Nietzsche and Heidegger. LAWRENCE, Joseph P.
The Problem of Causation and Time-Symmetry in Physics. BHARUCHA, Filita.
Temporality and the Concept of Being. SHALOM, Albert.

TEMPTATION(S)

Nine Talmudic Readings. ARONOWICZ, Annette (trans).
The Nietzsche Temptation in the Thought of Albert Camus. DUVALL, William E.

TENSE LOGIC

Axiomatization of 'Peircean' Branching-Time Logic. ZANARDO, Alberto.
A Complete Deductive-System for Since-Until Branching-Time Logic. ZANARDO, Alberto.

TENSE LOGIC

Concerted Instant-Interval Temporal Semantics I: Temporal Ontologies. BOCHMAN, Alexander.
Concerted Instant-Interval Temporal Semantics II: Temporal Valuations and Logics of Change. BOCHMAN, Alexander.
Expressiveness and Completeness of an Interval Tense Logic. VENEMA, Yde.
Temporal Necessity and the Conditional. CROSS, Charles B.

TENSE(S)

Change, Cause and Contradiction: A Defence of the Tenseless Theory of Time. LE POIDEVIN, Robin.
"Referring to Things That No Longer Exist" in *Philosophical Perspectives, 4: Action Theory and Philosophy of Mind, 1990*, CHISHOLM, Roderick M.
"Tenses, Temporal Quantifiers and Semantic Innocence" in *Truth and Interpretation: Perspectives on the Philosophy of Donald Davidson*, RICHARDS, Barry.
Castañeda's Quasi-Indicators and the Tensed Theory of Time. SMITH, Quentin.
A Defence of the New Tenseless Theory of Time. OAKLANDER, L Nathan.
Future Individuals. TEICHMANN, Roger.
Historical Necessity and Conditionals. NUTE, Donald.
Not Over Yet: Prior's 'Thank Goodness' Argument'. KIERNAN-LEWIS, Delmas.

TERESA OF AVILA

"Roswitha of Gandersheim, Christine Pisan, Margaret More Roper and Teresa of Avila" in *A History of Women Philosophers, Volume II: Medieval, Renaissance and Enlightenment, A.D. 500-1600*, WAITHE, Mary Ellen.

TERM(S)

Cylindric Algebras with Terms. FELDMAN, Norman.
Formalization of Functionally Complete Propositional Calculus with the Functor of Implication.... LEJEWSKI, Czeslaw.
The Logic of the Liar from the Standpoint of the Aristotelian Syllogistic. KELLY, Charles J.
The Real Difficulty with Burley's Realistic Semantics. FITZGERALD, Michael J.
Reflections on the Usage of the Terms "Logic" and "Logical". PAUL, Gregor.

TERMINAL ILLNESS(ES)

Commentary— "Make Me Live": Autonomy and Terminal Illness. MISBIN, Robert I.
Toward An Expanded Vision of Clinical Ethics Education: From the Individual to the Institution. SOLOMON, Mildred Z (and others).

TERMINOLOGY

Talking Philosophy: A Wordbook. SPARKES, A W.

TERRORISM

"Terrorism and Violence: A Moral Perspective" in *Issues in War and Peace: Philosophical Inquiries*, HOLMES, Robert L.
"Why Terrorism Is Morally Problematic" in *Feminist Ethics*, BAR ON, Bat-Ami.
On Primoratz's Definition of Terrorism. SINNOTT-ARMSTRONG, Walter.
Terrorism and Argument from Analogy. WALLACE, G.
What is Terrorism?. PRIMORATZ, Igor.

TEST(S)

"Difficoltà" con Simmel: Considerazioni in margine ad un convegno. LANDKAMMER, Joachim.
Ambiguity, Generality, and Indeterminacy: Tests and Definitions. GILLON, Brendan S.
Thirty Great Ways to Mess Up a Critical Thinking Test. FACIONE, Peter A.
The Turing-Good Weight of Evidence Function and Popper's Measure of the Severity of a Test. GILLIES, Donald.

TESTABILITY

Logic and Empiricism. BOSTOCK, David.

TESTIMONY

The Argument from Religious Experience: A Narrowing of Alternatives. KETCHUM, Richard.
Ethical Considerations for the Forensic Engineer Serving as an Expert Witness. CARPER, Kenneth L.
Hume's Theorem on Testimony Sufficient to Establish a Miracle. SOBEL, Jordan Howard.
Knowledge, Belief and Revelation: A Reply to Patrick Lee. HOITENGA JR, Dewey J.

TESTING

Can a Theory-Laden Observation Test the Theory?. FRANKLIN, A (and others).
Empirical Tests are Only Auxiliary Devices. LAI, Tyrone.
Kinds of Truth and Psychoanalysis as a Myth: Some Epistemological Remarks on the Freudian Model (in Italian). BORUTTI, Silvana.
Mandatory AIDS Testing: The Legal, Ethical and Practical Issues. WERDEL, A Alyce.
Testing for Convergent Realism. ARONSON, Jerrold L.

TEXT(S)

Bakhtin and the Epistemology of Discourse. THOMSON, Clive (ed).
Fictions of Reality in the Age of Hume and Johnson. DAMROSCH, Leo.
Hermeneutical Studies: Dilthey, Sophocles, and Plato. WILSON, Barrie A.
Nietzsche: The Body and Culture—Philosophy as a Philological Genealogy. BLONDEL, Eric.
The Noble Savage: Jean-Jacques Rousseau, 1754-1762. CRANSTON, Maurice.
Spuren der Macht. RÖTTGERS, Kurt.
"The Devil in *Doktor Faustus*: Reflections on Untranslatability" in *Hermeneutics and the Poetic Motion, Translation Perspectives V—1990*, NENON, Monika and NENON, Thomas.
"History, Truth, and Narrative" in *The Bible as Rhetoric: Studies in Biblical Persuasion and Credibility*, SUTHERLAND, Stewart.
"Textual Responsibility" in *The Political Responsibility of Intellectuals*, LECERCLE, J J.
Frontières des études littéraires: science de la littérature, science des discours. ANGENOT, Marc.
The Interpretation of Texts, People and Other Artifacts. DENNETT, Daniel C.
Marxist Literary Aesthetics. MILLER, Seumas.
Les objets de la sémiologie théâtrale: le texte et le spectacle. VIGEANT, Louise.
Revealing Gendered Texts. FREELAND, Cynthia A.
Text and Technology. CROWELL, Steven Galt.
Textual Deference. SMITH, Barry.
Tipos de lectura, tipos de texto. PEREDA, Carlos.
Work and Text. CURRIE, Gregory.

TEXTBOOK(S)

Applying Ethics: A Text with Readings (Third Edition). OLEN, Jeffrey.
Aristotelian Logic. PARRY, William T.
The Big Questions: A Short Introduction to Philosophy (Third Edition). SOLOMON, Robert C.
Business Ethics. SHAW, William H.
Clear Thinking: A Practical Introduction. RUCHLIS, Hy.
Conduct and Character: Readings in Moral Theory. TIMMONS, Mark.
Critical Reasoning (Third Edition). CEDERBLOM, Jerry.
The Elements of Reasoning. CONWAY, David.
Essentials of Business Ethics. MADSEN, Peter (ed).
Ethics in Nursing: An Anthology. PENCE, Terry.
Fundamentals of Philosophy (Third Edition). STEWART, David.
A Guided Tour of Selections from Aristotle's Nicomachean Ethics. BIFFLE, Christopher.
How Should I Live? Philosophical Conversations About Moral Life. FEEZELL, Randolph M.
Une introduction à l'analyse du discours argumentatif. MENDENHALL, Vance.
Introduction to Philosophy: Classical and Contemporary Readings. POJMAN, Louis P.
Justice: Alternative Political Perspectives (Second Edition). STERBA, James P (ed).
Logic for an Overcast Tuesday. RAFALKO, Robert J.
Logical Forms: An Introduction to Philosophical Logic. SAINSBURY, Mark.
Moral Philosophy: Theories, Skills, and Applications. FALIKOWSKI, Anthony F.
Morality in Practice (Third Edition). STERBA, James P.
Nonviolence in Theory and Practice. HOLMES, Robert L.
Philosophical Writing: An Introduction. MARTINICH, A P.
Philosophy of Law (Fourth Edition). FEINBERG, Joel.
Philosophy of Law: An Introduction to Jurisprudence (Revised Edition). MURPHY, Jeffrie G.
Philosophy: An Introduction Through Literature. KLEIMAN, L (ed).
Philosophy: Theory and Practice. THIROUX, Jacques P.
Taking Sides: Clashing Views on Controversial Bioethical Issues (Fourth Edition). LEVINE, Carol (ed).
Understanding Arguments: An Introduction to Informal Logic (Fourth Edition). FOGELIN, Robert J.
Well and Good: Case Studies in Biomedical Ethics (Revised Edition). THOMAS, John E.
What If...? Toward Excellence in Reasoning. HINTIKKA, Jaakko.
The Bright Side of Textbook Controversies. SCAHILL, John.
Buchphilosophie und philosophische Praxis. RÖTTGERS, Kurt.
Textbook Controversies and Community. WATRAS, Joseph.

TEXTUAL CRITICISM

Lost Buddhist Texts: The Rationale of Their Reconstruction in Sanskrit. CHINCHORE, Mangala R.
Mozart and Santayana and the Interface Between Music and Philosophy. DILWORTH, David A.
Una nuova questioni di Egidio Romano "De subjecto theologiae". LUNA, Concetta.
The Text of the Nyāya-Sūtras: Some Problems. KRISHNA, Daya.
Work and Text. CURRIE, Gregory.
Zum Verbleib der Königsberger Kant-Handschriften: Funde und Desiderate. STARK, Werner.

TEXTUALITY

"321 CONTACT: Textuality, the Other, Death" in *Re-Reading Levinas*, BEREZDIVIN, Ruben.

THAYER, H

Contextualizing Knowledge: A Reply to "Dewey and the Theory of Knowledge". HICKMAN, Larry.

THEATER

"Postmodernism and Theater" in *Postmodernism—Philosophy and the Arts (Continental Philosophy III)*, MC GLYNN, Fred.

"Il teatro della memoria di Giulio Camillo Delminio: un tentativo di riorganizzare il sapere nel Cinquecento" in *Razionalitá critica: nella filosofia moderna*, NARDELLI, Domenica.

"La 'présence' de l'acteur au théâtre" in *XIth International Congress in Aesthetics, Nottingham 1988*, SAISON, Maryvonne.

Jean-Jacques Rousseau et Friedrich Schiller: le théâtre sous le feu des lumières. MATTE, Martin.

Les objets de la sémiologie théâtrale: le texte et le spectacle. VIGEANT, Louise.

La Querelle de la Moralité du Théâtre au XVIIe Siècle. FUMAROLI, M Marc.

THEISM

see also Atheism

Does God Exist? The Great Debate. MORELAND, J P.

Atheism, Theism and Big Bang Cosmology. SMITH, Quentin.

A Case Against Theistic Morality. VARMA, Ved Prakash.

Kierkegaard on Theistic Proof. STERN, Kenneth.

Limited Explanations. CLARK, Stephen R L.

The Limits of Explanation. SWINBURNE, Richard.

La rationalité du théisme: la philosophie de la religion de Richard Swinburne. PADGETT, Alan G.

THEME(S)

"La tematica della follia tra Umanesimo nordico e Umanesimo latino: l'*Encomium Moriae* di Erasmo da Rotterdam" in *Razionalitá critica: nella filosofia moderna*, CASTELLANO, Veneranda.

THEOCENTRISM

Prologomena to Jozef Tischner's Philosophy of Culture (in Polish). WIECZOREK, Krzysztof.

THEODICY

The Co-Existence of God and Evil. TRAU, Jane Mary.

A Hindu Perspective on the Philosophy of Religion. SHARMA, Arvind.

Aristotle and Aquinas on Indignation: From Nemesis to Theodicy. NERNEY, Gayne.

Auschwitz, Morality and the Suffering of God. SAROT, Marcel.

Philosophy of History is Heternomous Philosophy (in German). SCHULTE, Christoph.

Post-Holocaust Theodicy: Images of Deity, History, and Humanity. FREY, Robert Seitz.

Prefacing Pluralism: John Hick and the Mastery of Religion. LOUGHLIN, Gerard.

Prometheus or Cain? Albert Camus's Account of the Western Quest for Justice. WARD, Bruce K.

A Response to Gerard Loughlin's "Prefacing Pluralism: John Hick and the Mastery of Religion". HICK, John.

Why Plantinga Must Move from Defense to Theodicy. WALLS, Jerry L.

THEODOSIUS

"Religion and Society in the Age of Theodosius" in *Grace, Politics and Desire: Essays on Augustine*, BARNES, Timothy D.

THEOLOGY

see also God, Miracle(s)

Die Aufhebung der Begriffs-philosophie. KRONABEL, Christoph.

Beyond the Big Bang: Quantum Cosmologies and God. DREES, Willem B.

Divine Nature and Human Language: Essays in Philosophical Theology. ALSTON, William P.

Essays on the Context, Nature, and Influence of Isaac Newton's Theology. FORCE, James E (ed).

Evolution: Probleme und neue Aspekte ihrer Theorie. SCHEFFCZYK, Leo (ed).

Explaining Religion: Criticism and Theory from Bodin to Freud. PREUS, J Samuel (ed).

Fallen Freedom: Kant on Radical Evil and Moral Regeneration. MICHALSON JR, Gordon E.

For What May I Hope? Thinking with Kant and Kierkegaard. FENDT, Gene.

Franz Rosenzweig: Existentielles Denken und gelebte Bewährung. SCHMIED-KOWARZIK, Wolfdietrich.

God and Subjectivity. GALGAN, Gerald J.

Hellenic and Christian Studies. ARMSTRONG, A H.

How to Play Theological Ping-Pong: And Other Essays on Faith and Reason. ABRAHAM, William J (ed).

The Humanities in the Nineties: A View From the Netherlands. ZÜRCHER, Erik (ed).

The Idea of Christian Charity: A Critique of Some Contemporary Conceptions. GRAHAM, Gordon.

Inscriptions and Reflections: Essays in Philosophical Theology. SCHARLEMANN, Robert P.

Interpreting Evolution: Darwin and Teilhard de Chardin. BIRX, H James.

John Craige's Mathematical Principles of Christian Theology. NASH, Richard.

Kierkegaards Phänomenologie der Freiheitserfahrung. DISSE, Jörg.

Linguistic Behaviour. BENNETT, Jonathan.

Modern Faith and Thought. THIELICKE, Helmut.

Mystical Monotheism: A Study in Ancient Platonic Theology. KENNEY, John Peter.

Nicholas of Cusa's de Pace Fidei and Cribratio Alkorani: Translation and Analysis. HOPKINS, Jasper.

The Philosophical Theology of John Duns Scotus. ADAMS, Marilyn McCord (ed).

Philosophische Hermeneutik. INEICHEN, Hans.

The Philosophy in Christianity. VESEY, Godfrey (ed).

Russische Philosophie. GOERDT, Wilhelm.

Sacred Fragments: Recovering Theology for the Modern Jew. GILLMAN, Neil.

The World of the Imagination: Sum and Substance. BRANN, Eva T H.

"Does Gilson Theologize Thomistic Metaphysics?" in *Thomistic Papers, V*, KNASAS, John F X.

"Does Philosophy 'Leave Everything as it is'? Even Theology?" in *The Philosophy in Christianity*, BAMBROUGH, Renford.

"A Faith of True Proportions: Reply to Sullivan" in *Thomistic Papers, V*, RUSSMAN, Thomas A.

"Fundamental Issues in Theology and Science" in *Science and Religion: One World-Changing Perspectives on Reality*, TORRANCE, T F.

"The Humanistic Implications of Liberation Theology: Juan Luis Segundo and Karl Marx" in *The Question of Humanism: Challenges and Possibilities*, HEWITT, Marsha A.

"Hume's Interest in Newton and Science" in *Essays on the Context, Nature, and Influence of Isaac Newton's Theology*, FORCE, James E.

"Is There a Role for Theology in an Age of Secular Science?" in *Science and Religion: One World-Changing Perspectives on Reality*, DURANT, J R.

"Newton's God of Dominion: The Unity of Newton's Theological, Scientific, and Political Thought" in *Essays on the Context, Nature, and Influence of Isaac Newton's Theology*, FORCE, James E.

"Notes on a Neglected Masterpiece, II: Theological-Political Treatise as a Prolegomenon to the Ethics" in *Central Themes in Early Modern Philosophy*, CURLEY, Edwin.

"Political Theology and the Ethics of Peace" in *Celebrating Peace*, MOLTMANN, Jürgen.

"Reason in Mystery" in *The Philosophy in Christianity*, KRETZMANN, Norman.

"Reconciling Concepts between Natural Science and Theology" in *Science and Religion: One World-Changing Perspectives on Reality*, WEIDLICH, W.

"Sir Isaac Newton, 'Gentleman of Wide Swallow'? Newton and the Latitudinarians" in *Essays on the Context, Nature, and Influence of Isaac Newton's Theology*, FORCE, James E.

"Some Further Comments on Newton and Maimonides" in *Essays on the Context, Nature, and Influence of Isaac Newton's Theology*, POPKIN, Richard H.

"Theology and Cosmology Beyond the Big Bang Theory" in *Science and Religion: One World-Changing Perspectives on Reality*, DREES, W B.

"Theology and the Sciences in the German Romantic Period" in *Romanticism and the Sciences*, GREGORY, Frederick.

Der "Atheist" und der "Theologe": Schopenhauer als Hörer Schleiermachers. REGEHLY, Thomas.

"To Illuminate Your Trace": Self in Late Modern Feminist Theology. KELLER, Catherine.

The A/Theology of Don Cupitt: A Theological Option in Our Post-Modern Age. TARBOX JR, Everett J.

The Absolute in Morality and the Christian Conscience. FUCHS, Josef.

Apophasis and Metaphysics in the *Periphyseon* of John Scottus Eriugena. CARABINE, Deirdre.

The Barth Legacy: New Athanasius or Origen Redivivus? A Response to T F Torrance. MULLER, Richard A.

Eine bisher unbeachtete Quelle des "Streits der Fakultäten". SELBACH, Ralf.

The Cases *For* and *Against* Theological Approaches to Business Ethics. TRUNDLE JR, Robert C.

Chance and Law in Irreversible Thermodynamics, Theoretical Biology and Theology. PEACOCKE, Arthur.

Christ, Moral Absolutes, and the Good: Recent Moral Theology. PINCKAERS, Servais.

A Christian Response to Professor Zagorka Golubovic. ZADEMACH, Wieland.

Crypto-theologie: hoffentlich ein Ende: Reactie op Callebaut en Wachelder. SOONTIENS, Frans.

Cuestiones actuales de epistemología teológica: Aportes de la teología de la liberación. SCANNONE, J C.

David Hume's Theology of Liberation. BARRUS, Roger M.

Directions in Historicism: Language, Experience, and Pragmatic Adjudication. DAVANEY, Sheila Greeve.

The Distinction between *Res Significata* and *Modus Significandi* in Aquinas's Theological Epistemology. ROCCA, Gregory.

The Emerging Tension Between Self and Society, As Exemplified in Augustine. THOMPSON JR, George B.

THEOLOGY

Empirical Theology: A Revisable Tradition. DEAN, William.
Godsverduistering en Godsdienstfilosofie. DE BOER, Th.
Godsverduistering en Godsdienstfilosofie. VAN DER HOEVEN, J.
Gonseth et le discours théologique. MOREL, Bernard.
Habermas and Theological Ethics (in French). BÜHLER, Pierre.
Habermas et la théologie: Notes pour une discussion entre la théologie et la "Théorie de l'agir communicationnel". KISSLING, Christian.
Historicism and the Understanding of Theology in Troeltsch's Times (in German). NOWAK, Kurt.
History as Argument for Revision in Moral Theology. GRISEZ, Germain.
Liberation Theology and the Interpretation of Political Violence. SONTAG, Frederick.
La loi et ses législateurs ou les avatars du théologico-politique. TOSEL, André.
MacIntyre, Tradition, and the Christian Philosopher. HIBBS, Thomas S.
Meister Eckhart and the Neoplatonic Heritage: The Thinker's Way to God. WOODS, Richard.
Metaphysical Conundrums at the Root of Moral Disagreement. MC DERMOTT, John M.
Method Divorced from Content in Theology: An Assessment of Lonergan's *Method in Theology*. REYNOLDS, Terrence.
Moral Dreams and Practical Realities. LINZEY, Andrew.
Motherhood and the Possibility of a Contemporary Discourse for Women. GREY, Mary.
Una nuova questioni di Egidio Romano "De subjecto theologiae". LUNA, Concetta.
On Tolerance (in French). DÜRRENMATT, Friedrich and BÜHLER, Pierre.
Pannenberg's Doctrine of God. O'DONNELL, John.
Por um novo modelo de saber: Problemática do discurso Filosófico-Teológico. DINIS, Alfredo.
The Possibilities of Scepticisms: Philosophy and Theology without Apology. JACKSON, Timothy P.
Possibility of Philosophical-Theological Discourse (in Serbo-Croatian). BELIC, Miljenko.
La prétendue intuition de Dieu dans le De Coelo d'Aristote. BODÉÜS, Richard.
A Problem for Radical (Onto-Theos) Pluralism. BILIMORIA, Purusottama.
The Prophetic and the Priestly. CHILDRESS, James F.
Protecting God: The Lexical Formation of Trinitarian Language. BARRIGAR, Christian J.
La puissance d'être selon Tillich. GOUNELLE, André.
Radical Theology, Postmodernity and Christian Life in the Void. COWDELL, Scott.
A Re-Examination of the Nature of Religion. BARUA, Archana.
Relating Science and Theology with Complementarity: A Caution. SHARPE, Kevin J.
The Relation between Science and Theology: The Case for Complimentarity Revisited. REICH, K Helmut.
A Religious Theory of Religion: Critical Notice. BYRNE, Peter.
Resources in Schelling for New Directions in Theology. BROWN, Robert F.
Scientific Research and the Christian Faith. PETERS, Ted.
El significado de lo teológico en Walter Benjamin. BOSCÁN, Antonio S.
Some Perspectives in Eriugenian Studies: Three Recent Studies. OTTEN, Willemien.
Technology, Truth and Language: The Crisis of Theological Discourse. CROWLEY, Paul.
Teleo-theologie und kein Ende: Reactie op Soontiens. CALLEBAUT, Werner and WACHELDER, J.
La teología de la creación y el problema de los orígenes. PODESTA, Gustavo.
La teología de la historia en la "ciudad de Dios" (2). OROZ RETA, José (trans) and BAGET BOZZO, Giovanni.
La teología de la historia en la Ciudad de Dios. OROZ RETA, José (trans) and BAGET-BOZZO, Giovanni.
A Teologia e a Filosofia perante os desafios da Cultura Contemporânea. POLICARPO, J.
The Questioning of Values in Theology (in French). WIDMER, Gabriel-Ph.
The Theological Secret of Th W Adorno's Aesthetic Theory (in German). HOLZ, Hans Heinz.
La théologie de Heidegger. CRÉTELLA, Henri.
Theologie und Sozialvorstellungen bei Thomas Müuntzer (in Czechoslovakian). LAUBE, Adolf.
Theology as the Queen (Bee) of the Disciplines?. VAUX, Kenneth.
Die Theorie der moralischen Entwicklung von Lawrence Kohlberg und seiner Schule und die Moraltheologie. BUCHER, Anton.
Die Theorie des kommunikativen Handelns in Diskussion. KISSLING, Christian.
The Vatican's Dilemma: On the Morality of IVF and the Incarnation. DUCHARME, Howard.
Das vergeistigte Glück: Gedanken zum christlichen Eudämonieverständnis. DEMMER, Klaus.

THEOREM(S)

The Sweep of Probability. SCHLESINGER, George N.
"A Dilworth Decomposition Theorem" in *Logic, Methodology and Philosophy of Science, VIII*, FOREMAN, Matthew.
Aggregation Theorems and Multidimensional Stochastic Choice Models. MARLEY, A A J.
The Gärdenfors Impossibility Theorem in Non-Monotonic Contexts. MAKINSON, David.
The Relevance of Gödel's Theorem to Husserl's *Formal and Transcendental Logic*. BOULOS, Pierre J.

THEORETICAL CONCEPTS

"Transmitting Theoretical Frames: The Case of Social Darwinism" in *Perspectives on Ideas and Reality*, ORTHMAYR, Imre.
The Ethics Behind the Absence of Ethics in Alfred Schutz's Thought. BARBER, Michael.

THEORETICAL ENTITY(-TIES)

"The Relative Autonomy of Theoretical Science and the Role of Crucial Experiments" in *Imre Lakatos and Theories of Scientific Change*, CHRISTIDES, T M and MIKOU, M.
Aspetti di attualità teoretica del pensiero procliano negli studi di Werner Beierwaltes. SCOTTI, Nicoletta.

THEORETICAL REASON

The Place of Argumentation in the Theory of Reasoning. JOHNSON, Ralph H.
Validity and Practical Reasoning. MITCHELL, David.

THEORETICAL TERM(S)

Kripke on Theoretical Identifications: A Rejoinder to Perrick. BUXTON, James.

THEORY(-RIES)

see also Educational Theory(-ries), Ethical Theory(-ries), Political Theory, Recursion Theory, Set Theory
Bertrand Russell: The Psychobiography of a Moralist. BRINK, Andrew.
Causality in Sociological Research. KARPINSKI, Jakub.
A Companion to Ethics. SINGER, Peter (ed).
Epistemology and Skepticism: An Enquiry into the Nature of Epistemology. CHATALIAN, George.
Experiment: Right or Wrong. FRANKLIN, Allan.
Explaining Religion: Criticism and Theory from Bodin to Freud. PREUS, J Samuel (ed).
Fichte's Theory of Subjectivity. NEUHOUSER, Frederick.
Fonti diritto e regole. DE GIACOMO, Claudio.
Intentions in Communication. COHEN, Philip R (ed).
Introducing Persons: Theories and Arguments in the Philosophy of Mind. CARRUTHERS, Peter.
Introduction Critique au Droit Naturel. HERVADA, Javier.
Knowledge in Perspective: Selected Essays in Epistemology. SOSA, Ernest.
The Logical Basis of Metaphysics. DUMMETT, Michael.
Markets, Managers and Theory in Education. HALLIDAY, John.
Modernity, Aesthetics, and the Bounds of Art. MC CORMICK, Peter J.
Moral Dilemmas. GOWANS, Christopher W (ed).
Narrative in Culture: The Uses of Storytelling in the Sciences, Philosophy, and Literature. NASH, Christopher (ed).
Philosophy: Theory and Practice. THIROUX, Jacques P.
Razionalitá critica: nella filosofia moderna. LAMACCHIA, Ada (ed).
Reasons for Living: A Basic Ethics. PORTER, Burton F.
Science and Relativism: Some Key Controversies in the Philosophy of Science. LAUDAN, Larry.
Structures in Mathematical Theories: Reports of the San Sebastian International Symposium, 1990. DÍEZ, Amparo (ed).
Teoria e interpretazione: Per un'epistemologia delle scienze umane. BORUTTI, Silvana.
Theories of Criminal Justice: A Critical Reappraisal. ELLIS, Ralph D.
Untersuchungen zur Theorie des hypothetischen Urteils. LINNEWEBER-LAMMERSKITTEN, Helmut.
"'Lopp'd and Bound': How Liberal Theory Obscures the Goods of Liberal Practices" in *Liberalism and the Good*, SALKEVER, Stephen G.
"Development of Science as a Change of Types" in *Imre Lakatos and Theories of Scientific Change*, HÖRZ, Herbert.
"Distance, Disinterest, and Autonomy: Gardens as a Challenge to the Theory of Art" in *XIth International Congress in Aesthetics, Nottingham 1988*, MILLER, Mara.
"The Feistiness of Feminism" in *Feminist Ethics*, CARD, Claudia.
"Heraclitus' Theory of Soul and Its Antecedents" in *Psychology (Companions to Ancient Thought: 2)*, SCHOFIELD, Malcolm.
"Invidious Contrasts within Theory" in *Meaning and Method: Essays in Honor of Hilary Putnam*, SKLAR, Lawrence.
"The Methodology of Scientific Research Programmes: A Retrospect" in *Imre Lakatos and Theories of Scientific Change*, WATKINS, John.
"The Structure of American Theoretical Archaeology: A Preliminary Report" in *Critical Traditions in Contemporary Archaeology*, EMBREE, Lester.
"Theories of Compensation" in *Liability and Responsibility*, GOODIN, Robert E.
"Towards the Structural Stability Theory" in *Logic, Methodology and Philosophy of Science, VIII*, ZILBER, B I.
Can a Theory-Laden Observation Test the Theory?. FRANKLIN, A (and others).

THEORY(-RIES)
A Causal Interaction Constraint on the Initial Singularity?. STOEGER, W R and HELLER, Michael.
The Chromosome Theory of Mendelian Inheritance: Explanation and Realism in Theory Construction. VICEDO, Marga.
The Conditions of Fruitfulness of Theorizing About Mechanisms in Social Science. STINCHCOMBE, Arthur L.
Conductive $\aleph_0$-Categorical Theories. SCHMERL, James H.
Constructing or Completing Physical Geometry?. CARRIER, Martin.
A Decidable Ehrenfeucht Theory with Exactly Two Hyperarithmetic Models. REED, R C.
Decidable Fragments of Field Theories. TUNG, Shih-Ping.
Domination and Moral Struggle: the Philosophical Heritage of Marxism Reviewed. HONNETH, Axel.
The Drama of Galileo, The Past and the Present. VOISE, Waldemar.
Elementary Theory of Free Heyting Algebras. IDZIAK, Pawel M.
The Elementary Theory of the Natural Lattice is Finitely Axiomatizable. CEGIELSKI, Patrick.
Elementos dinámicos de la teoría celular. GONZÁLEZ RECIO, José Luis.
Equational Subsystems. WEAVER, George.
Ethics and the Limits of Consistency. BAMBROUGH, Renford.
The Explanatory Tools of Theoretical Population Biology. COOPER, Gregory.
Extended Bar Induction in Applicative Theories. RENARDEL DE LAVALETTE, Gerard R.
Hattiangadi's Theory of Scientific Problems and the Structure of Standard Epistemologies. GIUNTI, Marco.
The Institution of Law. BANKOWSKI, Zenon.
Interpretation and Theory in the Natural and the Human Sciences: Comments on Kuhn and Taylor. LACEY, Hugh.
Intuitionistic Categorial Grammar. RANTA, Aarne.
Kuhn's Conception of Incommensurability. HOYNINGEN-HUENE, Paul.
Local Incommensurability and Communicability. CHEN, Xiang.
Lucien, Lévy-Bruhl: Una introduzione (di C Prandi). IANNOTTA, Daniella.
The Many Faces of Irreversibility. DENBIGH, K G.
Marx's Theory of Revolutionary Change. PANICHAS, George E and HOBART, Michael E.
Marxism and Social Change: Some Theoretical Reflections. TRIPATHY, Laxman Kumar.
The Modal Logic of Pure Provability. BUSS, Samuel R.
Modal Logics with *n*-ary Connectives. GHILARDI, S and MELONI, C G.
Neo-Sophistic Rhetorical Criticism or the Historical Reconstruction of Sophistic Doctrines?. SCHIAPPA, Edward.
New Operators for Theory Change. HANSSON, Sven.
Omitting Types for Stable CCC Theories. NEWELSKI, Ludomir.
On Comparison of Theories by Their Contents. WOLENSKI, Jan.
On Generalizations of a Theorem of Vaught. BIRÓ, Balázs.
On the Methodology of Possible World Semantics, I: Correspondence Theory. PEARCE, David and WANSING, Heinrich.
On the Nature and Norms of Theoretical Commitment. HORWICH, Paul.
On the Nature of Einstein's Realism. POLIKAROV, Azaria.
On Theories of Non-Monotonic Consequence Operations II. FIJALKOWSKA, Dorota and FIJALKOWSKI, Jan.
Popular Art and Aesthetic Theory: Why the Muse Is Unembarrassed. ANDERSON, Richard L.
The Principle of Unity of Theory and Practice in Marxism: A Critique. DIMITRAKOS, D.
Research Programmes and Empirical Results. AKEROYD, F M.
Response to Powell's "Theory and Practice". SKIDELSKY, Robert.
Rich Models. ALBERT, Michael H and GROSSBERG, Rami P.
Rights and Structure in Constitutional Theory. MILLER, Geoffrey P.
Some Remarks on a Historical Theory of Justice and its Application to Ireland. MC KIM, Robert.
The Spectrum of Resplendency. BALDWIN, John T.
The Structure of the Models of Decidable Monadic Theories of Graphs. SEESE, D.
Synthetic Mechanics Revisited. BURGESS, John P.
The Task of a Theory of Meaning. SAYRE, Patricia.
Telling It Like It Was: Historical Narratives on Their Own Terms. NORMAN, Andrew P.
La Teoría del conocimiento en Santo Tomás de Aquino. BEUCHOT, Mauricio.
Teorías físicas sobre el origen del Universo. GRATTON, Fausto T L.
Théories d'algébres de Boole munies d'idéaux distingués, II. TOURAILLE, Alain.
Theorizing about Morals. WALLACE, Jim.
Theory and Practice. POWELL, J Enoch.
Theory Contraction through Base Contraction. FUHRMANN, André.
Theory of the Apparatus and Theory of the Phenomena: The Case of Low Dose Electron Microscopy. SWIJTINK, Zeno G.
Theory Pursuit: Between Discovery and Acceptance. WHITT, Laurie Anne.
Theory Revision and Probability. SCHLECHTA, Karl.
Theory Structure and Theory Change in Contemporary Molecular Biology. CULP, Sylvia and KITCHER, Philip.
There's More Than One Way to Recognize a Darwinian: Lyell's Darwinism. RECKER, Doren.
Thoughts on the Future of Marxism. LEVINE, Andrew.
Toward a Theory of Bribery. DANLEY, John R.
Towards a Potential-Pragmatic Account of Peirce's Theory of Truth. SFENDONI-MENTZOU, Demetra.
Translation Failure Between Theories. SANKEY, Howard.
Truth, Content, and the Hypothetico-Deductive Method. GRIMES, Thomas R.
Two Dogmas of Neo-Empiricism: The "Theory-Informity" of Observation and the Quine-Duhem Thesis. GREENWOOD, John D.
Unidimensional Theories are Superstable. HRUSHOVSKI, Ehud.
Varying Modal Theories. LUCAS, T and LAVENDHOMME, R.
Verisimilitude Based on Concept Analysis. ORLOWSKA, Ewa.
What is Empirical in Mathematics?. PETERSON, Philip L.
What Is Jurisprudence About? Theories, Definitions, Concepts, or Conceptions of Law?. BAYLES, Michael D.
What is so Practical about Theory? Lewin Revisited. SANDELANDS, Lloyd E.
What Is Wrong with the Miracle Argument?. CARRIER, Martin.
Why the Anti-Reductionist Consensus Won't Survive: The Case of Classical Mendelian Genetics. WATERS, C Kenneth.
Wollheim's Theory of Artist as Spectator: A Complication. OLDS, Clifton.

THEOSOPHY
The Theosophic Discourse According to Jacob Boehme (in French). DEGHAYE, Pierre.

THERAPY
see also Psychotherapy
The "Tally Argument" and the Validation of Psychoanalysis. RICHARDSON, Robert C.
The Ethics of Conversion Therapy. MURPHY, Timothy F.
The Philosophical Basis of Rational-Emotive Therapy (RET). ELLIS, Albert.
Philosophy and a Career in Counseling. ANGELETT, William.
The Political Economy of Tardive Dyskinesia: Asymmetries in Power and Responsibility. COHEN, David and MC CUBBIN, Michael.

THERMODYNAMICS
"Determinism, Probability and Randomness in Classical Statistical Physics" in *Imre Lakatos and Theories of Scientific Change*, CLARK, Peter.
"The Emergence of a Reseearch Programme in Classical Thermodynamics" in *Imre Lakatos and Theories of Scientific Change*, MOULINES, C Ulises.
"The Relative Autonomy of Theoretical Science and the Role of Crucial Experiments" in *Imre Lakatos and Theories of Scientific Change*, CHRISTIDES, T M and MIKOU, M.
Chance and Law in Irreversible Thermodynamics, Theoretical Biology and Theology. PEACOCKE, Arthur.
Note on Entropy, Disorder and Disorganization. DENBIGH, K G.
Philosophical Objections to the Kinetic Theory. NYHOF, John.
Randomness and Probability in Dynamical Theories: On the Proposals of the Prigogine School. BATTERMAN, Robert.

THING IN ITSELF
Kants Theorie der Gegenstandserkenntnis und Schopenhauers Lehre vom Ding an sich. BAUMANN, Lutz.

THING(S)
Algunas observaciones sobre la noción de *Pragma* en Aristóteles. FEMENÍAS, María Luisa.

THINKING
see also Cognition, Critical Thinking, Reasoning
Clear Thinking: A Practical Introduction. RUCHLIS, Hy.
Inference and Understanding: A Philosophical and Psychological Perspective. MANKTELOW, K I.
Inscriptions and Reflections: Essays in Philosophical Theology. SCHARLEMANN, Robert P.
Locke and French Materialism. YOLTON, John W.
Understanding the Representational Mind. PERNER, Josef.
"The Future of Continental Philosophy" in *Writing the Politics of Difference*, STAMBAUGH, Joan.
"Practical Thinking, Reasons for Doing, and Intentional Action" in *Philosophical Perspectives, 4: Action Theory and Philosophy of Mind, 1990*, CASTAÑEDA, Héctor-Neri.
A Contribution of the Conception of "Discursivity" and "Spontaneiti" of Thinking (in Czechoslovakian). BENYOVSZKY, Ladislav.
A Note on the Nature of Mathematical Thinking (in Polish). LUBANSKI, M.
Artificial Intelligence and Wittgenstein. CASEY, Gerard.
General Thinking Skills: Are There Such Things?. ANDREWS, John N.
Must Thinking Bats be Conscious?. HANNA, Patricia.
Nietzsche and the Critique of Oppositional Thinking. SCHRIFT, Alan D.
On the Duality of China's Traditional Mode of Thought and the Difficulty of Transforming It. ZIHLIN, Li.
Social Space as a Determinant of "Collective Thinking" (in Polish). SYMOTIUK, Stefan.
Teaching Johnny to Think. SANDERS, James and MC PECK, John.
The Legacy of Hamann—Thinking, Language and Economy (in Hungarian). RATHMANN, János.
A Thinker's Agency in Thinking. NAMBIAR, Sankaran.
Thinking (Beyond) Being. STENSTAD, Gail.

THINKING
Thinking of Something. FITCH, Gregory.
Thinking versus Thought. KRISHNA, Daya.
Thought and Language. SAHA, Sukharanjan.
William James and the Nature of Thinking: A Framework for Elfie. MELVILLE, Mary E.

THIRD MAN ARGUMENT
Human Consciousness. HANNAY, Alastair.
Plato's "Parmenides". MEINWALD, Constance C.
The Development of Wittgenstein's Views about the Other Minds Problem. TER HARK, M R M.

THIRD WORLD
Beyond Ethnocentrism: A Reconstruction of Marx's Concept of Science. MC KELVEY, Charles.
"Tradition and Convolution—Settings of Aesthetic Phenomena in the Third World" in *XIth International Congress in Aesthetics, Nottingham 1988*, ERZEN, Jale.
"Unger, Castoriadis, and the Romance of a National Future" in *Critique and Construction: A Symposium on Roberto Unger's "Politics"*, RORTY, Richard.

THOMAS, S
Quantifying Support. BLACK, John.

THOMISM
From Twilight to Dawn: The Cultural Vision of Jacques Maritain. REDPATH, Peter A (ed).
From Unity to Pluralism: The Internal Evolution of Thomism. MC COOL, Gerald A.
The Preface to Thomistic Metaphysics. KNASAS, John F X.
Thomistic Papers, V. RUSSMAN, Thomas A (ed).
"Creative Intuition in American Film: Maritain at the Movies" in *From Twilight to Dawn: The Cultural Vision of Jacques Maritain*, LAUDER, Robert E.
"Does Gilson Theologize Thomistic Metaphysics?" in *Thomistic Papers, V*, KNASAS, John F X.
"Exiles and Fugitives: The Maritain-Tate-Gordon Letters" in *From Twilight to Dawn: The Cultural Vision of Jacques Maritain*, DUNAWAY, John M.
"Maritain and Happiness in Modern Thomism" in *From Twilight to Dawn: The Cultural Vision of Jacques Maritain*, HUDSON, Deal W.
"Prudence as the Cornerstone of the Contemporary Thomistic Philosophy of Freedom" in *Freedom in the Modern World: Jacques Maritain, Yves R Simon, Mortimer J Adler*, MAHONEY, Marianne.
"Thomism and Divine Absolute Power" in *Thomistic Papers, V*, KENNEDY, Leonard A.
An Attempt at Interpretation of the Thomistic Hylomorphic Theory in View of Contemporary Physics. JANIK, J A.
Christelijke filosofie. WYLLEMAN, A.
Il dibattito sulla verità tra Blondel e Garrigou-Lagrange. BERTOLDI, Francesco.
The Doctrine of Double Effect: Its Philosophical Viability. BOLE, Thomas.
La eleccion de un maestro. VAN STEENBERGHEN, Fernand.
Establishing of the Object of Metaphysics—Separation (in Polish). MARYNIARCZYK, A.
L'unité-unicité de l'"esse" Thomiste. PASQUA, Hervé.
MacIntyre, Tradition, and the Christian Philosopher. HIBBS, Thomas S.
Moral Dilemmas. MAC INTYRE, Alasdair.
A New Reading of Aristotle's *Hyle*. POLIS, Dennis F.
Thomas Aquinas and the Renewal of Philosophy: Some Reflections on the Thomism of Mercier (in Dutch). STEEL, C.
The Transcendental Method of Metaphysics of Coreth and Muck and Its Relation to Analytic Philosophy. RUNGGALDIER, Edmund.

THOMPSON, B
Complexly Fractionated Syllogistic Quantifiers. PETERSON, Philip L.
Intermediate Quantifiers versus Percentages. CARNES, Robert D and PETERSON, Philip L.

THOREAU
Humble Rebel Henry David Thoreau (in Czechoslovakian). JANAT, B.

THOUGHT
The Analytic Tradition: Philosophical Quarterly Monographs, Volume 1. BELL, David (ed).
Frege and Other Philosophers. DUMMETT, Michael.
Frege in Perspective. WEINER, Joan.
Idea, mente, specie: Platonismo e scienza in Johannes Marcus Marci (1595-1667). MOCCHI, Giuliana.
Linguistic Behaviour. BENNETT, Jonathan.
Michel Foucault's Force of Flight: Towards an Ethics for Thought. BERNAUER, James W.
The Origin of Thought. ROSMINI, Antonio.
Sound, Speech, and Music. BURROWS, David.
Trois essais sur la pensée. THEAU, Jean.
"The Basis of Lawful Behavior: Rules or Connections" in *Acting and Reflecting: The Interdisciplinary Turn in Philosophy*, MC CLELLAND, Jay.
"Biosemantics and the Normative Properties of Thought" in *Philosophical Perspectives, 3: Philosophy of Mind and Action Theory, 1989*, FORBES, Graeme.
"The Fatality of Thought" in *The Philosophy of John William Miller*, JOHNSTONE JR, Henry W.
"Hannah Arendt: la memoria come spazio del pensiero" in *Razionalitá critica: nella filosofia moderna*, FISTETTI, Francesco.
"Neo-Fregean Thoughts" in *Philosophical Perspectives, 3: Philosophy of Mind and Action Theory, 1989*, BOËR, Steven E.
"Thing and Thought" in *Knowledge Representation and Defeasible Reasoning*, PERLIS, Don.
"Thought and Perception: The Views of Two Philosophical Innovators" in *The Analytic Tradition: Philosophical Quarterly Monographs, Volume 1*, DUMMETT, Michael.
Das "objektive Denken" in Schellings Naturphilosophie. BUCHHEIM, Thomas.
Croce e la storia della cultura. TESSITORE, Fulvio.
Dall'attualismo al tensionalismo. SIMONE, Aldo.
Decir lo mismo (Frege y Santo Tomás). SANGUINETI, Juan J.
Demonstrative Content: A Reply to John McDowell. PEACOCKE, Christopher.
Die Wissenschaft denkt nicht. SALANSKIS, Jean-Michel.
La diffusione del pensiero spagnolo contemporaneo nell'Italia di oggi. SAVIGNANO, Armando.
Direct Reference, Meaning, and Thought. RECANATI, François.
Dummett and the Origins of Analytical Philosophy, or the Philosophy of Thought vs Philosophy of Language (in German). DÖLLING, Evelyn and DÖLLING, Johannes.
The Fate of Independent Thought in Traditional China. WHITE, Harry.
Frege and the Analysis of Thoughts. GARAVASO, Pieranna.
From Truth to 'Alhieia to Opening and Rapture. MALY, Kenneth.
If Children thought Like Adults. GAUKER, Christopher.
De jonge Wittgenstein (1889-1921): Denken als ethos. DE DIJN, H.
Karl Marx and African Emancipatory Thought: A Critique of Marx's Euro-centric Metaphysics. SEREQUEBERHAN, Tsenay.
The Language of Thought: No Syntax Without Semantics. CRANE, Tim.
The Limits of Thought—and Beyond. PRIEST, Graham.
Malebranche and the Vision in God: A Note on *The Search After Truth*, III, 2, iii. NADLER, Steven.
Metamorphoses: On the Limits of Thought. ALEXAKOS, Panos D.
Il mondo Il soggetto Lo smarrimento. INCARDONA, Nunzio.
More about Thoughts. DUMMETT, Michael.
Object-Dependent Thoughts and Psychological Redundancy. NOONAN, Harold W.
Pensiero e trascendenza. SANCIPRIANO, Mario.
Philosophical Prolegomena of Structural Thinking (in Czechoslovakian). CHVATIK, Kvetoslav.
The Poetic Theory of the Stoic 'Aristo'. ASMIS, Elizabeth.
A Thinker's Agency in Thinking. NAMBIAR, Sankaran.
Thought and Being in Kant and Hegel. HOULGATE, Stephen.
Thoughts Which Only I Can Think. WILLIAMS, C J F.
Thoughts. SMITH, David Woodruff.
Wittgenstein: Representaciones y pensamientos. RABOSSI, Eduardo.

THREAT(S)
Negotation Games: Applying Game Theory to Bargaining and Arbitration. BRAMS, Steven J.
On Häyry and Airaksinen's 'Hard and Soft Offers as Constraints'. DAY, J P.
What is Terrorism?. PRIMORATZ, Igor.

TICHY, P
Offices and God. HUGLY, Philip and SAYWARD, Charles.

TILLICH
Paul Tillich and Inter-religious Dialogue. FOERSTER, John.
La puissance d'être selon Tillich. GOUNELLE, André.

TIME
About Time: Inventing the Fourth Dimension. FRIEDMAN, William J.
Being-in-the-World: A Commentary on Heidegger's "Being and Time", Division 1. DREYFUS, Hubert L.
Caminhos do Filosofar. MIRANDA, Maria do Carmo Tavares de.
Change, Cause and Contradiction: A Defence of the Tenseless Theory of Time. LE POIDEVIN, Robin.
The Immutability of God in the Theology of Hans Urs Von Balthasar. O'HANLON, G F.
Kant's Model of the Mind: A New Interpretation of Transcendental Idealism. WAXMAN, Wayne.
L'inertie et l'espace-temps absolu de Newton à Einstein. GHINS, Michel.
The Legacy of Hermann Cohen. KLUBACK, William.
Mind-Body. MOULYN, Adrian C.
The Ontology of Physical Objects: Four-Dimensional Hunks of Matter. HELLER, Mark.
Philosophical Perspectives on Newtonian Science. BRICKER, Phillip (ed).
Proust: The Creative Silence. CARANFA, Angelo.
"Absolute Time versus Absolute Motion: Comments on Lawrence Sklar" in *Philosophical Perspectives on Newtonian Science*, BRICKER, Phillip.
"Back to the Future" in *Postmodernism—Philosophy and the Arts (Continental Philosophy III)*, TAYLOR, Mark C.
"First-Order Spacetime Geometry" in *Logic, Methodology and Philosophy of Science, VIII*, GOLDBLATT, Robert.

TOPOLOGY
A Topological Interpretation of Diagonalizable Algebras. HAWRANEK, Jacek.
The Uses and Abuses of the History of Topos Theory. MC LARTY, Colin.
Zeeman-Göbel Topologies. HEATHCOTE, Adrian.

TORRANCE, T
The Barth Legacy: New Athanasius or Origen Redivivus? A Response to T F Torrance. MULLER, Richard A.

TORT(S)
Economics, Ethics, and Tort Remedies: The Emerging Concept of Hedonic Value. KARNS, Jack E.
Punitive Damages: New Twists in Torts. WALTON, Clarence C.
Torts of Necessity: A Moral Theory of Compensation. KLEPPER, Howard.

TORTURE
Exploring Extreme Violence (Torture). MACHAN, Tibor R.
The Juncture of Law and Morality in Prohibitions Against Torture. MARAN, Rita.

TOTALITARIANISM
The Realm of Humanitas: Responses to the Writings of Hannah Arendt. GARNER, Reuben (ed).
"Democracy and the Political" in *The Realm of Humanitas: Responses to the Writings of Hannah Arendt*, WOLIN, Sheldon S.
"Totalitarianism and Population Superfluity" in *The Realm of Humanitas: Responses to the Writings of Hannah Arendt*, RUBENSTEIN, Richard L.
A proposito di Stato e totaliarismo nel pensiero di Marx. SIENA, Robertomaria.
The Body Politic: Democratic Metaphors, Totalitarian Practices, Erotic Rebellions. BERGOFFEN, Debra B.
European Counterimages: Problems of Periodization and Historical Memory. DINER, Dan.
From Propaganda to "Oeffentlichkeit" in Eastern Europe: Four Models of the Public Space Under State Socialism. SUKOSD, Miklos.
Das Imperiale an der Identitätsphilosophie: Spuren des Totalitären in der abendländischen Philosophie. MANSILLA, Hugo C F.
Kant and the Origins of Totalitarianism. SIEBERS, Tobin.
Nietzsche and Ernst Jünger: From Nihilism to Totalitarianism. OHANA, David.
Rediscovering the Left. HOWARD, Dick.
Renaissance of Democracy?. LEFORT, Claude and HARVEY, Robert.
Schopenhauersche Weltsicht und totalitäre Humanität im Werke Thomas Manns. KRISTIANSEN, Borge.

TOTALIZATION
Critique of Dialectical Reason, Volume 2: Jean-Paul Sartre. HOARE, Quintin (trans).

TOULMIN, S
Modelos de cambio científico en la filosofía actual de la ciencia. STRÖKER, Elisabeth.
Towards a Research Agenda for Informal Logic and Critical Thinking. WEINSTEIN, Mark.

TOURNIER, M
Metamorphoses: On the Limits of Thought. ALEXAKOS, Panos D.

TRADITION
After Principles. BARDEN, Garrett.
A Companion to Ethics. SINGER, Peter (ed).
In Partnership with God: Contemporary Jewish Law and Ethics. SHERWIN, Byron L.
Three Great Traditions. PEDERSEN, Olaf.
"Buddhist Ethics" in *A Companion to Ethics*, DE SILVA, Padmasiri.
"Christian Ethics" in *A Companion to Ethics*, PRESTON, Ronald.
"Classical Chinese Ethics" in *A Companion to Ethics*, HANSEN, Chad.
"Cultural Tradition, Historical Experience, and Social Change: The Limits of Convergence" in *The Tanner Lectures on Human Values, Volume XI*, EISENSTADT, S N.
"Indian Ethics" in *A Companion to Ethics*, BILIMORIA, Purusottama.
"Innovation and Tradition in Post-Modernism" in *XIth International Congress in Aesthetics, Nottingham 1988*, ROSE, Margaret A.
"Is Liberalism Good Enough?" in *Liberalism and the Good*, SCHMITZ, Kenneth L.
"Islamic Ethics" in *A Companion to Ethics*, NANJI, Azim.
"Jewish Ethics" in *A Companion to Ethics*, KELLNER, Menachem.
"Tradition as Innovation" in *XIth International Congress in Aesthetics, Nottingham 1988*, KUCZYNSKA, Alicja.
"Tradition, Influence and Innovation" in *XIth International Congress in Aesthetics, Nottingham 1988*, HERMEREN, Goran.
"Tradition, Innovation, Kunstrezeption und Kuntswirkung—zu einigen Problemen" in *XIth International Congress in Aesthetics, Nottingham 1988*, ERHARD, John.
Eradicating the Obvious. CLARK, Stephen R L.
Farewell to the Tradition: Doing without Metaphysics and Epistemology. NIELSEN, Kai.
Feminist Philosophy and the Genetic Fallacy. CROUCH, Margaret A.
Footprints in the Snow. SEERVELD, Calvin.
Is There a Natural Law?. WALDSTEIN, Wolfgang.
The Marxist Conception of Tradition. STEPANYANTS, Marietta.
Practicing the Arts of Rhetoric: Tradition and Invention. FARRELL, Thomas B.
Responsibility in the Tradition of Czech Thought (in Czechoslovakian). ZUMR, J.
Spiritual Traditions and Science and Technology. BAKAR, Osman.
Sur le concept de tradition. GABORIAU, Florent.
Tradition and Ethics: Prospects in a Liberal Society. GUROIAN, Vigen.
Tradition and Interpretation. VAN BEECK, Frans Jozef.
Tradition and Its Value: A Contribution to the History of Polish Marxist Philosophical Thought (in Polish). GRADKOWSKI, Waldemar.
Wittgenstein and the Transmission of Traditions. O'HEAR, Anthony.

TRADITIONAL LOGIC
Aristotelian Logic. PARRY, William T.
Logic for an Overcast Tuesday. RAFALKO, Robert J.
The Irrelevance of Classical Logic. KEENE, G B.

TRADITIONALISM
MacIntyre and the Indispensability of Tradition. SCHNEEWIND, J B.
Progressive Traditionalism as the Spirit of Collingwood's Philosophy. KISSELL, Michael A.
The Skeptic's Burke: *Reflections on the Revolution in France*, 1790-1990. MOSHER, Michael A.

TRAGEDY
The Tragedy of Reason: Toward a Platonic Conception of Logos. ROOCHNIK, David.
"Tragic Action and Aesthetic Contempolation" in *XIth International Congress in Aesthetics, Nottingham 1988*, BOULLART, Karel.
Cristianesimo tragico, cristianesimo ludico: i due volti della fedeltà al Dio dialettico. GARGANO, Monica.
La figure d'Héraclite dans la pensée du jeune Nietzsche. VOELKE, André-Jea.
Freud: Uma Concepção Agónica da Educação. BARBOSA, Manuel.
Hegel, Antigone, and the Possibility of Ecstatic Dialogue. WILLETT, Cynthia.
M Heideggers Auslegung von Sophokles' "Oedipus Tyrannus" (in Japanese). SEKIGUCHI, Hiroshi.
Socrates and Alcibiades: Eros, Piety, and Politics. HOWLAND, Jacob A.
Socrates and Asclepius: The Final Words. SANTILLI, Paul C.
The Tragic World of John Dewey. JACQUES, Robert A.

TRAINING
Der Ursprung der Erziehungsziele in der Lehre von Plato, Aristoteles und Neill. EGGER, Paul.

TRANSCENDENCE
Caminhos do Filosofar. MIRANDA, Maria do Carmo Tavares de.
"The Principle of Transcendence and the Foundation of Axiology" in *Logic and Ethics*, GRZEGORCZYK, Andrzej.
"Faith" in a Broad Sense as a Goal in Promoting Human Development. BECK, Clive.
Autonomy, Empathy, and Transcendence in Sophocles' *Antigone*: A Phenomenological Perspective. NISSIM-SABAT, Marilyn.
La dialettica come "dépasser" in Sartre. TOGNONATO, Claudio.
The Idea of Transcendence. COBURN, Robert C.
Il pensiero di Aldo Capitini e la filosofia del neoidealismo. CESA, Claudio.
Pensiero e trascendenza. SANCIPRIANO, Mario.
Per una rilettura dei libri "M" e "N" della *Metafisica* di Aristotele alla luce delle "dottrine non scritte" di Platone. CATTANEI, Elisabetta.
Some Reflections on Husserl's Approach to the Problem of Transcendence. DHAR, Benulal.

TRANSCENDENTAL
Glück und Lebenssinn: Eine religionsphilosophische Untersuchung. DRESCHER, Johannes.
Kant's Model of the Mind: A New Interpretation of Transcendental Idealism. WAXMAN, Wayne.
Kant's Transcendental Psychology. KITCHER, Patricia.
Die Moral der Vernunft Tanszendentale Handlungs-und Legitimationstheorie in der Philosophie Kants. SANDERMANN, Edmund.
Spuren der Macht. RÖTTGERS, Kurt.
Das Verhängnis Erste Philosophie. EBELING, Hans.
"Übergang e antecipação em Kant" in *Dinâmica do Pensar: Homenagem a Oswaldo Market*, MARQUES, António.
"Extrinsic Cognoscibility": A Seventeenth Century Supertranscendental Notion. DOYLE, John P.
Constituição do sentido e justificação da validade: Heidegger e o problema da filosofia transcendental. APEL, Karl-Otto.
Davidson's Transcendental Arguments. MAKER, William.
Fichte on Skepticism. BREAZEALE, Daniel.
La filosofía transcendental: el destino de un proyecto ilustrado. FLAMARIQUE, Lourdes.
Der Gegenstand der Vorstellungen und die transzendentale Apperzeption. LÓPEZ-FERNÁNDEZ, Alvaro.
Husserl's Presuppositionless Philosophy. REED-DOWNING, Teresa.
The Incoherence of Kant's Transcendental Dialectic: Specifying the Minimal Conditions for Dialectical Error. HERMAN, David J.

TRANSCENDENTAL
Ingarden und Husserls transzendentaler Idealismus. HAEFLIGER, Gregor.
Is Transcendental Idealism Coherent?. BALDNER, Kent.
Kant on Justification in Transcendental Philosophy. PEREBOOM, Derk.
Metafisica todavia? (conclusión). SANABRIA, José Rubén.
Objet et communauté transcendantale: autour d'un fragment du dernier Husserl. BENOIST, J.
On the Paradoxical Inception and Motivation of Transcendental Philosophy in Plato and Husserl. HOPKINS, Burt C.
On Wittgenstein's Transcendental Ethics. PRASAD, Rajendra.
Sensations and Judgments of Perception: Diagnosis and Rehabilitation of Some of Kant's Misleading Examples. KOTZIN, Rhoda and BAUMGÄRTNER, Järg.
Transcendental Idealism: The Dialectical Dimension. GLOUBERMAN, M.
Transzendentale Argumente pragmatisch relativiert: Über fundamentale Optionen in der Philosophie. LAUENER, Henri.
Universalität des Prinzips vom zureichenden Grund. NICOLÁS, Juan A.

TRANSCENDENTAL ARGUMENT(S)
Lonergan's Performative Transcendental Argument Against Scepticism. REHG, William R.

TRANSCENDENTAL DEDUCTION
Una lettura idealistica della "Analitica Trascendentale". BELLINI, Ornella.
The Unity of Understanding: A Study in Kantian Problems. SCHWYZER, Hubert.
Community and Utopia: A Transcendental Deduction. POPOV, Stefan.
Kants Theorie der Gegenstandserkenntnis und Schopenhauers Lehre vom Ding an sich. BAUMANN, Lutz.
The Role of Kant's Refutation of Idealism. HYMERS, Michael.
Why Natural Theology, Still, Yet?. HUTCHINGS, Patrick.

TRANSCENDENTAL EGO
Logic in the Husserlian Context. TITO, Johanna Maria.

TRANSCENDENTALISM
Geschichte, Freiheit und Struktur. RUMPEL, Roland.
"'On How We are and How We Are not to Return to the Things Themselves'" in *Ontology and Alterity in Merleau-Ponty*, WATSON, Stephen.
Nuove ricerche sul 'Liber metaphysicus' *di Giambattista Vico*. CACCIATORE, Giuseppe.
La philosophie ouverte de F Gonseth aboutit-elle à une conception réaliste ou relativiste. LAUENER, Henri.
The Transcendental Method of Metaphysics of Coreth and Muck and Its Relation to Analytic Philosophy. RUNGGALDIER, Edmund.
Transcendentalism About Content. DEVITT, Michael.

TRANSCENDENTALS
Finitude Rediscovered. BARBER, Michael.
Potenzialità conoscitive del Trascendentale di Husserl. O'DWYER BELLINETTI, Luciana.
Thomas d'Aquin a-t-il tente d'exprimer le principe d'individuation à l'intérieur des proprietés.... CASPAR, Philippe.

TRANSFERENCE
Gangesa and Transfer of Meaning. SAHA, Sukharanjan.
The Metamathematics-Popperian Epistemology Connection and its Relation to the Logic of Turing's Programme. BEAUSOLEIL, Jean-Roch.
Who or What is the Preembryo?. MC CORMICK, Richard A.

TRANSFORMATION
The Death of Industrial Civilization. KASSIOLA, Joel Jay.
The Epistemological Significance of Transformative Religious Experiences: A Kierkegaardian Exploration. EVANS, C Stephen.
Fragmentation, Meditation and Transformation: The Teachings of J Krishnamurti. NARAYANA MOORTY, J S R L.
Identity, Transformation, and What Matters in Survival. MARTIN, Raymond.
The Relevance of Meditative Thinking. ERICKSON, Stephen A.
Sri Aurobindo and the Process of Physical Transformation. REDDY, V Ananda.

TRANSFORMATIONAL GRAMMAR(S)
"Linguistics: What's Wrong with 'The Right View'" in *Philosophical Perspectives, 3: Philosophy of Mind and Action Theory, 1989*, DEVITT, Michael and STERELNY, Kim.
Explanation-Explication Conflict in Transformational Grammar. DAS GUPTA, Amitabha.
Three Models of Competence: A Critical Evaluation of Chomsky. MUKHERJI, Arundhati.

TRANSGRESSION(S)
"Translation as Transgression" in *Hermeneutics and the Poetic Motion, Translation Perspectives V—1990*, ROSS, Stephen David.
La ética como conciencia en el subdesarrollo. RAMÍREZ, E Roy.
Genealogy and *Différance*. SCOTT, Charles E.
Ultimate Double Binds. SCHÜRMANN, Reiner.

TRANSITIVITY
Probabilistic Causality. EELLS, Ellery.
Copies, Reproducibility and Aesthetic Adequacy. CHANG, Briankle G.
Phenomenal Qualities and the Nontransitivity of Matching. BURGESS, John A.
The Ranking of Preference. RAWLING, Piers.
Truth Table Logic with a Survey of Embeddability Results. TENNANT, Neil.

TRANSLATABILITY
"The Devil in *Doktor Faustus*: Reflections on Untranslatability" in *Hermeneutics and the Poetic Motion, Translation Perspectives V—1990*, NENON, Monika and NENON, Thomas.
"The Question of Translatability: Benjamin, Derrida, Quine" in *Hermeneutics and the Poetic Motion, Translation Perspectives V—1990*, TURK, Horst.

TRANSLATION
Hermeneutics and the Poetic Motion, Translation Perspectives V—1990. SCHMIDT, Dennis J (ed).
"Bold Counsels and Carpenters: Pagan Translation" in *Hermeneutics and the Poetic Motion, Translation Perspectives V—1990*, LEAVEY JR, John P.
"The Exemplary Status of Translating" in *Hermeneutics and the Poetic Motion, Translation Perspectives V—1990*, SCHMIDT, Lawrence K.
"Facts That Don't Matter" in *Meaning and Method: Essays in Honor of Hilary Putnam*, ELGIN, Catherine Z.
"Immanent and Transcendent Approaches to the Theory of Meaning" in *Perspectives on Quine*, HARMAN, Gilbert.
"On Translation and M/others: Samuel Beckett's *The Unnamable*" in *Hermeneutics and the Poetic Motion, Translation Perspectives V—1990*, HANSON, Susan.
"Translation and Language Games" in *Hermeneutics and the Poetic Motion, Translation Perspectives V—1990*, ROSE, Marilyn Gaddis.
"Translation as Transgression" in *Hermeneutics and the Poetic Motion, Translation Perspectives V—1990*, ROSS, Stephen David.
"Wittgenstein's Philosophy of Language and the Question of Translation" in *Hermeneutics and the Poetic Motion, Translation Perspectives V—1990*, FLESCHE, David E.
The Application of Montague Translations in Universal Research and Typology. TENT, Katrin.
Behaviourism, Neuroscience and Translational Indeterminacy. WARMBRŌD, Ken.
The Dating of Rule IV-B in Descartes's *Regulae ad directionem ingenii*. VAN DE PITTE, Frederick P.
Destruktion und Übersetzung: Zu den Aufgaben von Philosophiegeschichte nach Martin Heidegger. OPILIK, Klaus.
Indeterminacy, Empirical Evidence, and Methodological Pluralism. ROUSE, Joseph.
Is Kripke's Puzzle Really a Puzzle. CORLETT, J Angelo.
Meaning, Understanding and Translation. STROUD, Barry.
Onderbepaaldheid van theorie en onbepaaldheid van vertaling: Enige ontwikkelingen in Quine's filosofie. PERRICK, M.
Presentism and the Indeterminacy of Translation. HARDCASTLE, Gary L.
Some Modifications of the Gödel Translation of Classical Intuitionistic Logic. BORICIC, Branislav.
Sophoclean Logic (*Antigone* 175-81). O'SULLIVAN, Neil.
Translation Failure Between Theories. SANKEY, Howard.
Il volgarizzamento del "De Rerum natura" di Bernardino Telesio a opera di Francesco Martelli. PIEROZZI, Letizia and SCAPPARONE, Elisabetta.

TRANSLATION RULE(S)
Meaning and Speech Acts: Volume II, Formal Semantics of Success and Satisfaction. VANDERVEKEN, Daniel.

TRANSMISSION
Argumentation and Values (in French). BOREL, Marie-Jeanne.

TRANSPLANTATION
Biomedical Ethics Reviews, 1987. HUMBER, James M (ed).
New Harvest: Transplanting Body Parts and Reaping the Benefits. KEYES, C Don (ed).
Ethics, Public Policy, and Human Fetal Tissue Transplantation. CHILDRESS, James F.
Fetal Neural Transplantation: Placing the Ethical Debate within the Context of Society's Use of Human Material. JONES, D Gareth.
Heads, Feds, and Beds: Ethical Dilemmas in the Delivery of Medical Care. WILLIAMS, Arthur R.
Personal Identity and Brain Transplants. SNOWDON, P F.
Pharaoh's Magicians: The Ethics and Efficacy of Human Fetal Tissue Transplants. BARRY, Robert and KESLER, Darrel.

TRAVEL
Time-Travel and Topology. MAUDLIN, Tim.

TREATMENT(S)
Integrity in Health Care Institutions: Humane Environments for Teaching, Inquiry, and Healing. BULGER, Ruth Ellen (ed).
"The Virtue of Feeling and the Feeling of Virtue" in *Feminist Ethics*, SPELMAN, Elizabeth V.
HIV and the Obligation to Treat. SHELDON, Mark.
The Noncompliant Substance Abuser: Commentary. CASSEL, Christine and LA PUMA, John.
The Noncompliant Substance Abuser: Commentary. STELL, Lance K.
Treating the Troops. HOWE, Edmund G and MARTIN, Edward D.
Treating the Troops: A Commentary. ANNAS, George J and GRODIN, Michael A.
Treating the Troops: A Commentary. LEVINE, Robert J.
Treatment and Rehabilitation as a Mode of Punishment. MARTIN, Rex.

TREE(S)
Boundedness Theorems for Dilators and Ptykes. KECHRIS, Alexander S.
An Extension of Borel Determinacy. MARTIN, Donald A.
Notions of Relative Ubiquity for Invariant Sets of Relational Structures. BANKSTON, Paul and RUITENBURG, Wim.
On Scott and Karp Trees of Uncountable Models. HYTTINEN, Tapani and VÄÄNÄNEN, Jouko.
Some Results on Higher Suslin Trees. DAVID, R.
A Theorem on Labelled Trees and the Limits of Its Provability. PFEIFFER, Helmut.
Tree Proofs for Syllogistic. SIMONS, Peter M.
Undecidability and Initial Segments of the (R.E.) TT-Degrees. HAUGHT, Christine Ann and SHORE, Richard A.
Verification of Concurrent Programs: the Automata-Theoretic Framework. VARDI, Moshe Y.

TREND(S)
Theories of Criminal Justice: A Critical Reappraisal. ELLIS, Ralph D.
Danger Signs of Unethical Behavior: How to Determine If Your Firm Is at Ethical Risk. COOKE, Robert Allan.

TRIAD(S)
The Potential of Modern Discourse: Musil, Peirce, and Perturbation. FINLAY, Marike.

TRIBALISM
To Be at Home: Christianity, Civil Religion, and World Community. ROUNER, Leroy S.

TRINITY
The Immutability of God in the Theology of Hans Urs Von Balthasar. O'HANLON, G F.
"Logos and Trinity: Patterns of Platonist Influence on Early Christianity" in *The Philosophy in Christianity*, DILLON, John.
Augustine's Theology of the Trinity: Its Relevance. CLARK, Mary T.
Locke on Personal Identity and the Trinity Controversy of the 1690s. WEDEKING, Gary.
Oratio Placabilis Deo Eriugena's Fragmentary Eucharistic Teaching. SMITH, R U.
Protecting God: The Lexical Formation of Trinitarian Language. BARRIGAR, Christian J.
Sant'Agostino e Hegel a confronto. CALEO, Marcello.
Trinidad y ontología trascendental: Ideas en torno al libro IX del "De Trinitate" de S Agustín. RODRÍGUEZ VALLS, Francisco.

TRIVIAL TRUTH(S)
Philosophy in the *Big Typescript*: Philosophy as Trivial. LUCKHARDT, C Grant.
This Article Should Not Be Rejected by *Mind*. LARAUDOGOITIA, Jon Perez.

TROELTSCH, E
Historicism and the Understanding of Theology in Troeltsch's Times (in German). NOWAK, Kurt.
Troeltsch and Nietzsche: Critical Reflections on Ernst Troeltsch's Portrayal of Nietzsche (in German). SCHÜSSLER, Ingeborg.

TROPE(S)
Tropes and Laws. FUHRMANN, André.

TROTSKY, L
The Blackmail of the Single Alternative: Bukharin, Trotsky and Perestrojka. DAY, Richard B.
The Pros and Cons of Trotsky's Marxism (in German). HEDELER, Wladislaw.
Trotsky's Dialectic. THATCHER, Ian D.

TRUE
True Contradictions. PARSONS, Terence.

TRUST
Ethics, Trust, and the Professions: Philosophical and Cultural Aspects. PELLEGRINO, Edmund D (ed).
"Is Trust of Professionals a Coherent Concept?" in *Ethics, Trust, and the Professions: Philosophical and Cultural Aspects*, VEATCH, Robert M.
"The Phenomenon of Trust and the Patient-Physician Relationship" in *Ethics, Trust, and the Professions: Philosophical and Cultural Aspects*, ZANER, Richard M.
"The Politics of Trust in American Health Care" in *Ethics, Trust, and the Professions: Philosophical and Cultural Aspects*, FOX, Daniel M.
"Professional Paradigms" in *Ethics, Trust, and the Professions: Philosophical and Cultural Aspects*, LANGAN, John.
"Trust and Distrust in Professional Ethics" in *Ethics, Trust, and the Professions: Philosophical and Cultural Aspects*, PELLEGRINO, Edmund D.
"Whom Can Women Trust?" in *Feminist Ethics*, BAIER, Annette C.
Can the Discussion Partners Trust Each Other?. FÖLDESI, Tamás.
G Marcel: a dimensão metafísica da esperança. DA COSTA FREITAS, Manuel Barbosa.
The Molested. MAY, William F.
A Morality Based on Trust: Some Reflections on Japanese Morality. YAMAMOTO, Yutaka.
Rational Trust and Deferential Belief. NORRIS, Stephen P.
Shrewd Bargaining on the Moral Frontier: Toward a Theory of Morality in Practice. DEES, J Gregory and CRAMPTON, Peter C.

TRUTH CONDITION(S)
"What Davidson Should Have Said" in *Information, Semantics and Epistemology*, LE PORE, Ernest and LOEWER, Barry.
Historical Necessity and Conditionals. NUTE, Donald.
Logical Constants and the Glory of Truth-Conditional Semantics. LYCAN, William G.
The Normal Rewards of Success. WHYTE, J T.
Truth and Teleology. PAPINEAU, David.

TRUTH FUNCTION(S)
Logical Forms: An Introduction to Philosophical Logic. SAINSBURY, Mark.
Indicative Conditionals Are Truth-Functional. HANSON, William H.
Post's Functional Completeness Theorem. PELLETIER, Francis Jeffry and MARTIN, Norman M.
A Truth-Functional Logic for Near-Universal Generalizations. CARLSTROM, Ian F.

TRUTH TABLE(S)
Bounds in Weak Truth-Table Reducibility. HABART, Karol.
Material Implication and Entailment. CENIZA, Claro R.
Some Results on Bounded Truth-Table Degrees. DITCHEV, Angel V.
Truth Table Logic with a Survey of Embeddability Results. TENNANT, Neil.

TRUTH VALUE(S)
The Implications of Error for Davidsonian Charity. LARSON, David.
Logic Without Truth. ALCHOURRÓN, Carlos E and MARTINO, Antonio A.
New Semantics for the Extensional but Hyper-Intensional Part..... BRESSAN, Aldo.
Universal Sentences: Russell, Wittgenstein, Prior, and the Nyāya. SHAW, J L.
Verisimilitude by Power Relations. ODDIE, Graham.

TRUTH(S)
Adorno's Aesthetic Theory: The Redemption of Illusion. ZUIDERVAART, Lambert.
Ästhetik des Abschieds: Kritik der Moderne. EBELING, Hans.
The Bible as Rhetoric: Studies in Biblical Persuasion and Credibility. WARNER, Martin (ed).
Cálculo y ser (Aproximación a Leibniz). MARZOA, Felipe Martínez.
Caminhos do Filosofar. MIRANDA, Maria do Carmo Tavares de.
The Concept of Objectivity: An Approximation. BUTLER, Kenneth G.
The Dice-Playing God: Reflections on Life in a Post-Modern Age. KRIEGLSTEIN, Werner.
The Difference Between Truth and Opinion: How the Misuse of Language Can Lead to Disaster. COONEY, Timothy J.
Donald Davidson. EVNINE, Simon.
Frege and Other Philosophers. DUMMETT, Michael.
Good and Evil: An Absolute Conception. GAITA, Raimond.
Ideas, Principios y Dialectica. LAFUENTE, Maria Isabel.
In Defense of Mystical Ideas: Support for Mystical Beliefs from a Purely Theoretical Viewpoint. CHAPMAN, Tobias.
The Kernel of Truth in Freud. LAWTON, Philip.
Leibniz's Philosophy of Logic and Language (Second Edition). ISHIGURO, Hide.
Logic and Ethics. GEACH, Peter (ed).
The Logical Basis of Metaphysics. DUMMETT, Michael.
Meaning and Truth: The Essential Readings in Modern Semantics. GARFIELD, Jay L (ed).
Metaphysics: A Contemporary Introduction. POST, John F.
Myth and Philosophy: A Contest of Truths. HATAB, Lawrence J.
Nietzsche and the Question of Interpretation. SCHRIFT, Alan D.
Nietzsche On Truth and Philosophy. CLARK, Maudemarie.
Nietzsches Scheitern am Werk. HELLER, Edmund.
Objectivity, Relativism, and Truth: Philosophical Papers, Volume 1. RORTY, Richard.
On True and False Ideas, New Objections to Descartes' Meditations and Descartes' Replies. ARNAULD, Antoine (trans).
Overcoming Foundations: Studies in Systematic Philosophy. WINFIELD, Richard Dien.
The Persistence of Modernity: Essays on Aesthetics, Ethics, and Postmodernism. WELLMER, Albrecht.
Phenomenology of the Truth Proper to Religion. GUERRIÈRE, Daniel (ed).
The Philosopher's Joke. WATSON, Richard A.
Philosophical Essays. CARTWRIGHT, Richard.
Philosophical Logic. STRAWSON, P F (ed).
Philosophical Papers: F P Ramsey. MELLOR, D H (ed).
Pour une philosophie du sens et de la valeur. VASSILIE-LEMENY, Sorin-Titus.
A Progress of Sentiments: Reflections on Hume's "Treatise". BAIER, Annette C.
Properties as Processes: A Synoptic Study of Wilfried Sellars' Nominalism. SEIBT, Johanna.
Quest for Certainty: A Comparative Study of Heidegger and Sankara. GRIMES, John A.
Towards a Christian Philosophy. OWENS, Joseph I.
Truth and Interpretation: Perspectives on the Philosophy of Donald Davidson. LE PORE, Ernest (ed).

TRUTH(S)

Wahrheit—Diskurs—Demokratie: Studien zur "Konsensustheorie der Wahrheit". SCHEIT, Herbert.
What is History? And Other Late Unpublished Writings (The Collected Works of Eric Voegelin, Vol 28). HOLLWECK, Thomas A (ed).
Wittgenstein and Contemporary Philosophy of Language. RUNDLE, Bede.
"'Truth' and 'Rhetoric' in the Pauline Epistles" in *The Bible as Rhetoric: Studies in Biblical Persuasion and Credibility*, KENNEDY, George.
"Approximation and the Two Ideas of Truth" in *Studies on Mario Bunge's "Treatise"*, NOWAKOWA, Izabella and NOWAK, Leszek.
"A Coherence Theory of Truth and Knowledge" in *Reading Rorty*, DAVIDSON, Donald.
"A Coherence Theory of Truth and Knowledge" in *Truth and Interpretation: Perspectives on the Philosophy of Donald Davidson*, DAVIDSON, Donald.
"Divine Truth in Husserl and Kant: Some Issues in Phenomenological Theology" in *Phenomenology of the Truth Proper to Religion*, HART, James G.
"Empirical Content" in *Truth and Interpretation: Perspectives on the Philosophy of Donald Davidson*, DAVIDSON, Donald.
"The Ethical Root of Language" in *Logic and Ethics*, GORMALLY, M C.
"History, Truth, and Narrative" in *The Bible as Rhetoric: Studies in Biblical Persuasion and Credibility*, SUTHERLAND, Stewart.
"How the Fable Becomes a World" in *Looking After Nietzsche*, CANNING, Peter.
"Logic and Pragmatic Truth" in *Logic, Methodology and Philosophy of Science, VIII*, DA COSTA, Newton C A.
"Marginalia Sino-logica" in *Understanding the Chinese Mind: The Philosophical Roots*, HARBSMEIER, Christoph.
"Meaning, Truth and Evidence" in *Perspectives on Quine*, DAVIDSON, Donald.
"Methodology and Ontology" in *Imre Lakatos and Theories of Scientific Change*, SMART, J J C.
"Nietzsche Medused" in *Looking After Nietzsche*, PAUTRAT, Bernard.
"Partial Truths about Partial Truth" in *Studies on Mario Bunge's "Treatise"*, MARQUIS, Jean-Pierre.
"Phenomenologies and Religious Truth" in *Phenomenology of the Truth Proper to Religion*, WESTPHAL, Merold.
"Pragmatism, Davidson and Truth" in *Truth and Interpretation: Perspectives on the Philosophy of Donald Davidson*, RORTY, Richard.
"Radical Hermeneutics and Religious Truth: The Case of Sheehan and Schillebeeckx" in *Phenomenology of the Truth Proper to Religion*, CAPUTO, John D.
"Realism, Approximate Truth, and Philosophical Method" in *Scientific Theories*, BOYD, Richard.
"Religious Truth and Scientific Truth" in *Phenomenology of the Truth Proper to Religion*, CLAYTON, Philip.
"Semantics and Methodological Solipsism" in *Truth and Interpretation: Perspectives on the Philosophy of Donald Davidson*, LYCAN, William G.
"Some Remarks on Davidson's Theory of Truth" in *The Mind of Donald Davidson*, VARGA VON KIBÉD, Matthias.
"The Source of the Concept of Truth" in *Meaning and Method: Essays in Honor of Hilary Putnam*, DUMMETT, Michael.
"La trahison de la trahison des clercs" in *The Political Responsibility of Intellectuals*, GELLNER, Ernest.
"Truth and the Wisdom of Enduring" in *Phenomenology of the Truth Proper to Religion*, FARLEY, Edward.
"Truth in Meaning" in *Truth and Interpretation: Perspectives on the Philosophy of Donald Davidson*, LE PORE, Ernest.
"Truth in Religion and Truth of Religion" in *Phenomenology of the Truth Proper to Religion*, DUPRÉ, Louis.
"The Truth, the Nontruth, and the Untruth Proper to Religion" in *Phenomenology of the Truth Proper to Religion*, GUERRIÈRE, Daniel.
"Truth, Understanding and the Artist's Vision" in *XIth International Congress in Aesthetics, Nottingham 1988*, SAVILE, Anthony.
"Truth-Value of Ethical Statements" in *Logic and Ethics*, PRZELECKI, Marian.
"Veritable Reflections" in *Reading Rorty*, VISION, Gerald.
"What a Truth Theory Need Not Tell Us" in *Truth and Interpretation: Perspectives on the Philosophy of Donald Davidson*, GRANDY, Richard E.
"When the Truth Is in the Telling" in *The Philosophy of John William Miller*, STROUT, Cushing.
L' "altro inizio" della filosofia: I *Beiträge zur Philosophie* di Heidegger. SAMONÀ, Leonardo.
"Amicus plato, sed magis amica veritas" (Notas sobre el conflicto amistad-verdad). CARRETERO, Joaquín M.
"The Fragmentation of Reason": Précis of Two Chapters. STICH, Stephen P.
"The Logic of Implication". BALZER, Noel.
Acceptance Is Not Enough: A Critique of Hamblin. JOHNSON, Ralph H.
Anti-Realism Untouched. MELIA, Joseph.
Aristotle on Dialectic. HAMLYN, D W.
Art Works, But How?—Kant and Aesthetics/Heidegger and Truth. SYNNING, Ralph.
Art, Truth and the Education of Subjectivity. HEPBURN, Ronald W.
Between Rationalism and Relativism: On Larry Laudan's Model of Scientific Rationality. GROBLER, Adam.
Biblical Hermeneutics and the Search for Religious Truth (in French). THEISSEN, Gerd.
Can Art Save Us? A Meditation on Gadamer. DEVEREAUX, Mary.
Can Fiction Be Stranger Than Truth? An Aristotelian Answer. GALLOP, David.
Ce que Ferdinand Gonseth a d'important à dire à l'épistémologie contemporaine. JORGE, Maria M A.
Coherence, Anti-realism, and the Vienna Circle. YOUNG, James O.
The Concept of Mathematical Truth. ROTA, Gian-Carlo.
El concepto de verdad en la física moderna. ROMERO BARÓ, José María.
El concepto tradicional de verdad en Santo Tomás. FORMENT, Eudaldo.
Congruenza, schematismo, sintesi: Prospettive leibniziane intorno al criterio di verità secondo Giambattista Vico. PINCHARD, Bruno.
Consideraciones en torno al concepto de verdad según el pragmatismo. GORDILLO, Lourdes.
A Constructivism Based on Classical Truth. MIGLIOLI, P (and others).
Context Principle, Fruitfulness of Logic and the Cognitive Value of Arithmetic in Frege. RUFFINO, Marco Antonio.
Correspondence, Consensus, and Coherence and the Rape of Democracy. PASK, Gordon.
La création du Nouveau par le Hasard et par le temps: un vieux thème épicurien. LARGEAULT, Jean.
A Defense of Ethical Noncognitivism. COBURN, Robert C.
O discurso filosófico e a unidade da verdade nas primeiras obras de Paul Ricoeur. RENAUD, Michel.
An Economic Model of Scientific Activity and Truth Acquisition. GOLDMAN, Alvin I and SHAKED, Moshe.
Eradicating the Obvious. CLARK, Stephen R L.
Ethics and Coherence. DE GEORGE, Richard T.
For Anil Gupta. HART, W D.
Freud and the Question of Truth (in Serbo-Croatian). GÖRLICH, Bernard.
From Russell to Quine: Basic Statements, Foundationalism, Truth, and Other Myths. LINDBERG, Jordan J.
From Truth to 'Alhieia to Opening and Rapture. MALY, Kenneth.
How Nancy Cartwright Tells the Truth. FRANKLIN, Allan.
How to Get Rid of Your Expensive Philosopher of Science and Still Keep Control Over the Fuzzing Conversation of Mankind. VISKER, Rudi.
The Identity Theory of Truth. BALDWIN, Thomas.
In Search of a Theory of Truth in Nyāya. SAHA, Sukharanjan.
Is Aristotle an Internal Realist? Nussbaum and the Divine Perspective. EARLS, C Anthony.
Justification, Truth, Goals, and Pragmatism: Comments on Stich's "Fragmentation of Reason". HARMAN, Gilbert.
Kant and the Origins of Totalitarianism. SIEBERS, Tobin.
Kinds of Truth and Psychoanalysis as a Myth: Some Epistemological Remarks on the Freudian Model (in Italian). BORUTTI, Silvana.
Kitcher's Circumlocutionary Structuralism. HAND, Michael.
L'universalisation de l'herméneutique chez Hans-Georg Gadamer. GRONDIN, Jean.
Lenguaje y verdad en Aristóteles. RODRIGUEZ, M L.
Let's Razor Ockham's Razor. SOBER, Elliott.
Liar Syllogisms and Related Paradoxes. SLATER, B H.
La libertad como búsqueda de la verdad en el joven Agustín. WEISMANN, F J.
Logics of Truth. TURNER, Raymond.
Logics Preserving Degrees of Truth. NOWAK, Marek.
La loi de vérité. POULAIN, Jacques.
Martin Heidegger and the Place of Language. VAN RODEN ALLEN, Robert.
La matemática: certeza y verdad. CAÑON LOYES, Camino.
Max on Moore. STROLL, Avrum.
Meaning, Truth and Realism in Bultmann and Lindbeck. FERGUSSON, David.
Meaning, Truth Conditions and the Internal Point of View: The Ethical Dilemma. GOOSSENS, Charles.
Metaphor and the Varieties of Lexical Meaning. HINTIKKA, Jaakko and SANDU, Gabriel.
Metaphysics, Pragmatic Truth and the Underdetermination of Theories. PEREIRA JR, Alfredo and FRENCH, Steven.
The Minimal and Semiminimal Notions of Truth. FOX, J.
Necessary A Posteriori Truth. SWINBURNE, Richard.
Nietzsche, Socrates and Pragmatism. RORTY, Richard.
On Making a Coherence Theory of Truth True. SYLVAN, Richard.
On Omniscience and a 'Set of All Truths': A Reply to Bringsjord. GRIM, Patrick.
On the Concept of Mímésis (in Czechoslovakian). VEJRAZKA, Michal.
On the Problem of the Essence of Truth in the Natural Sciences (in Dutch). KOCKELMANS, J.
On the Source of the Eternal Truths. BEACH, Edward A (trans) and VON SCHELLING, F W J.
Per l'Europa dopo il crollo della Cortina di Ferro. GRYGIEL, Stanislaw.
Philosophy in the *Big Typescript*: Philosophy as Trivial. LUCKHARDT, C Grant.
Il polipo di Trembley (1740) e la "catena delle verità": Note di ricerca. TODESCO, Fabio.
Pragmatic Truth and the Logic of Induction. DA COSTA, Newton C A and FRENCH, Steven.

TRUTH(S)
Putnam and Truth (in Serbo-Croatian). JAKIC, Mirko.
The Question of Ethics in Foucault's Thought. SCOTT, Charles E.
Quine's Relativism. HUGLY, Philip and SAYWARD, Charles.
Rationality, Consistency and Truth. FRENCH, Steven.
Rejoining *Alētheia* and Truth: or Truth Is a Five-Letter Word. HATAB, Lawrence J.
Replies and Comments. PUTNAM, Hilary.
Response to Donald Vandenberg's "Co-intentional Pedagogy". GREENE, Maxine.
Revealing the Truth of Art. BOWIE, Andrew.
Richard Rorty: An Interview (in Hebrew). KULKA, Tomas.
The Role of Music in Nietzsche's *Birth of Tragedy*. HECKMAN, Peter.
Rorty, Davidson and Truth. BAGHRAMIAN, Maria.
Saying Good-bye to Historical Truth. SPENCE, Donald P.
Science and Truthlikeness. PANDIT, G L.
Semantics and Supervenience. BONEVAC, Daniel.
Sinn-Wahrheit-Ort: Tres etapas en el pensamiento de Heidegger. BERCIANO V, Modesto.
Sobre el gusto y la verdad práctica. ARREGUI, Jorge Vicente.
Sobre justificación y verdad: respuesta a León Olivé. VILLORO, Luis.
The Stilling of the *Aufhebung: Streit* in "The Origin of the Work of Art". PROTEVI, John.
Technology, Truth and Language: The Crisis of Theological Discourse. CROWLEY, Paul.
A Teologia e a Filosofia perante os desafios da Cultura Contemporânea. POLICARPO, J.
La teoría consensual de la verdad de Jürgen Habermas. BELARDINELLI, Sergio.
The Problem of Cognition and Truth in Aesthetics (in Czechoslovakian). SINDELAR, Dusan.
Time and Propositions. SMITH, Quentin.
To Tell a Good Tale: Kierkegaardian Reflections on Moral Narrative and Moral Truth. TURNER, Jeffrey S.
Tomás de Aquino: la aprehensión del acto de ser (II). GONZÁLEZ, Orestes J.
Towards a Potential-Pragmatic Account of Peirce's Theory of Truth. SFENDONI-MENTZOU, Demetra.
Transcendentalism About Content. DEVITT, Michael.
Transzendentale Argumente pragmatisch relativiert: Über fundamentale Optionen in der Philosophie. LAUENER, Henri.
Truth and Language-World Connections. GROVER, Dorothy.
Truth and Stability in Descartes' *Meditations*. BENNETT, Jonathan.
Truth and Understanding. HIGGINBOTHAM, James.
Truth at a World is a Modality. LINSKY, Bernard.
Truth in Epistemology. STURGEON, Scott.
Truth in Interpretation: The Case of Psychoanalysis. ROTH, Paul A.
Truth, Content, and the Hypothetico-Deductive Method. GRIMES, Thomas R.
Truth, Justification and the Inescapability of Epistemology: Comments on Copp. RUSSELL, Bruce.
Truth, Method, and Objectivity: *Husserl and Gadamer on Scientific Method*. NUYEN, A T.
Truth. ULLIAN, Joseph S.
Truths without Facts. SEN, Pranab Kumar.
Unamuno: De la decepción de la verdad, a la apología de la veracidad. SILVA CAMARENA, Juan Manuel.
Understanding the System Construction in Logic. DAS, Ramesh Chandra.
Vacuous Truth. ALMEDER, Robert F.
Verdad e inteligibilidad: Los rasgos invariables de la teoría platónica de las ideas. LUIS DEL BARCO, José.
Verdad e inteligibilidad: Los rasgos invariantes de la doctrina platónica de las ideas. LUIS DEL BARCO, José.
Verdad e inteligibilidad: Los rasgos invariables de la doctrina platónica de las ideas. LUIS DEL BARCO, José.
La verdad. ALVAREZ GÓMEZ, Mariano.
Verità di ragione e verità di fede. MESSINESE, Leonardo.
Vérité à Faire: Merleau-Ponty's Question Concerning Truth. WALDENFELS, Bernhard.
The Vita Femina and Truth. BURNEY-DAVIS, Terri and KREBBS, R Stephen.
Von der dreifachen Vollendung des Deutschen Idealismus und der unvollendeten metaphysischen Wahrheit. JANKE, Wolfgang.
Wege der Seinsfrage: Aus Anlass der 100. GANDER, Hans-Helmuth.
The What and the How. ALMOG, Joseph.
Why We Should Care Whether Our Beliefs Are True. LYCAN, William G.
Writing the Revolution—The Politics of Truth in Genet's *Prisoner of Love*. CRITCHLEY, Simon.

TRUTHFULNESS
Ethical Practice in Clinical Medicine. ELLOS, William J.
Unamuno: De la decepción de la verdad, a la apología de la veracidad. SILVA CAMARENA, Juan Manuel.

TRYING
He Doesn't Really Want to Try. ADAMS, Frederick.
He Wants to Try. MELE, Alfred R.

TUGGLE, D
On the Possibility of Lawful Explanation in Archaeology. SALMON, Merrilee H.

TURING, A
The Metamathematics-Popperian Epistemology Connection and its Relation to the Logic of Turing's Programme. BEAUSOLEIL, Jean-Roch.
The Turing-Good Weight of Evidence Function and Popper's Measure of the Severity of a Test. GILLIES, Donald.

TURNER, D
Some Improvements to Turner's Algorithm for Bracket Abstraction. BUNDER, M W.

TWENTIETH
Bakhtin and the Epistemology of Discourse. THOMSON, Clive (ed).
Being and Becoming: A Critique of Post-Modernism. CENTORE, F F.
Bertrand Russell. ALCARO, Mario.
Bertrand Russell: The Psychobiography of a Moralist. BRINK, Andrew.
Classics of Analytic Philosophy. AMMERMAN, Robert R (ed).
Claude Lévi-Strauss. LEACH, Edmund.
Controlling Technology: Contemporary Issues. THOMPSON, William B.
Creativity in George Herbert Mead. GUNTER, Pete A Y (ed).
De l'épistémologie à la politique: La philosophie de l'histoire de Karl R Popper. RUELLAND, Jacques G.
Echoes: After Heidegger. SALLIS, John.
Encounter on the Narrow Ridge: A Life of Martin Buber. FRIEDMAN, Maurice.
Franz Rosenzweig: Existentielles Denken und gelebte Bewährung. SCHMIED-KOWARZIK, Wolfdietrich.
Freedom in the Modern World: Jacques Maritain, Yves R Simon, Mortimer J Adler. TORRE, Michael D (ed).
French Philosophers in Conversation: Levinas, Schneider, Serres, Irigaray, Le Doeuff, Derrida. MORTLEY, Raoul.
Herrschaft und Versöhnung: Einführung in das Denken Theodor W Adornos. KAGER, Reinhard.
The Ideas of Ayn Rand. MERRILL, Ronald E.
La intersubjectividad en Husserl, Volume I and II. IRIBARNE, Julia V.
Jean-Paul Sartre. HENGELBROCK, Jürgen.
Marxism and Philosophy in the Twentieth Century: A Defense of Vulgar Marxism. HUDELSON, Richard.
Michel Foucault's Force of Flight: Towards an Ethics for Thought. BERNAUER, James W.
The Mind of Donald Davidson. BRANDL, Johannes (ed).
On Walter Benjamin: Critical Essays and Recollections. SMITH, Gary (ed).
Perspectives on Quine. BARRETT, Robert (ed).
Philosophical Events: Essays of the '80s. RAJCHMAN, John.
The Philosophy of John William Miller. FELL, Joseph P (ed).
Philosophy's Journey: From the Presocratics to the Present (Second Edition). KOLENDA, Konstantin.
The Politics of Being: The Political Thought of Martin Heidegger. WOLIN, Richard.
The Power of Consciousness and the Force of Circumstances in Sartre's Philosophy. BUSCH, Thomas W.
Proust: The Creative Silence. CARANFA, Angelo.
Re-Reading Levinas. BERNASCONI, Robert (ed).
Reading Habermas. RASMUSSEN, David M.
Reading Rorty. MALACHOWSKI, Alan (ed).
Readings in Existential Psychology and Psychiatry. HOELLER, Keith (ed).
Studies on Mario Bunge's "Treatise". WEINGARTNER, Paul (ed).
Swimming Against the Current in Contemporary Philosophy: Occasional Essays and Papers. VEATCH, Henry B.
Vernunft und Kontingenz: Rationalität und Ethos in der Phänomenologie. ORTH, Ernst Wolfgang (ed).
Vulgarity and Authenticity: Dimensions of Otherness in the World of Jean-Paul Sartre. CHARMÉ, Stuart Zane.
Who Comes after the Subject?. CADAVA, Eduardo (ed).
Wittgenstein's Lectures on the Foundations of Mathematics, Cambridge 1939. DIAMOND, Cora (ed).
Wittgenstein: A Bibliographical Guide. FRONGIA, Guido.
Wittgenstein: Meaning and Mind, Volume 3 of an Analytical Commentary on Philosophical Investigations. HACKER, P M S.
"Impressions of Philosophy" in *Acting and Reflecting: The Interdisciplinary Turn in Philosophy*, SCHWARTZ, Thomas.
"L'idée d'égalité et la notion moderne du droit" in *Égalité Uguaglianza*, RENAUT, Alain.
"Philosophy and the Academy" in *Acting and Reflecting: The Interdisciplinary Turn in Philosophy*, GLYMOUR, Clark.
L' "altro inizio" della filosofia: I *Beiträge zur Philosophie* di Heidegger. SAMONÀ, Leonardo.
A "Con-versão" da Filosofia em Martin Heidegger. ESTÊVÁO, Carlos.
The "Middle Wittgenstein": From Logical Atomism to Practical Holism. STERN, David G.
Il "parlare commune" come lume storico-naturale della "riproduzione sociale". MININNI, Giuseppe.
La "riabilitazione" della δυναμιζ e dell'ενεργεια in Heidegger. VOLPI, Franco.
La "Scuola di Padova" ed i problemi dell'ontologia italiana contemporanea. MANGIAGALLI, Maurizio.
"Sigma": conoscenza e metodo. SAVA, Gabriella.
A proposito dell'interesse di Dilthey per l'antropologia cinquecentesca. ORSUCCI, Andrea.

TWENTIETH

Acerca de uma tese ricoeuriana. SUMARES, Manuel.
Action or/and Dwelling. BOEDER, Heribert.
The Ambivalent Unthought of the Overman and the Duality of Heidegger's Political Thinking. HAAR, Michel.
Announcement of the Endless in Horkheimer, Adorno and Habermas (in Serbo-Croatian). SIEBERT, Rudolf J.
But Suppose We Were to Take the Rectorial Address Seriously...Gérard Granel's *De l'université*. FYNSK, Christopher.
Can Genealogy Be Critical? A Somewhat Unromantic Look at Nietzsche and Foucault. VISKER, Rudi.
Il carteggio Xavier Léon: corrispondenti italiana. QUILICI, Leana and RAGGHIANTI, Renzo.
The Case for a New American Pragmatism. LAVINE, Thelma Z.
Changing the Subject: Heidegger, "the" National and Epochal. SCHMIDT, Dennis J.
Concepts of Culture: Lonergan and the Anthropologists. KLEIN, Dennis.
The Concert: Mao's Panopticon. TALMOR, Sascha.
Un confronto sempre attuale: Leggendo--A Lambertino, Psicoanalisi e morale in Freud. DOVOLICH, Claudia.
Consideraciones en torno al concepto de verdad según el pragmatismo. GORDILLO, Lourdes.
Constituição do sentido e justificação da validade: Heidegger e o problema da filosofia transcendental. APEL, Karl-Otto.
Continuità e discontinuità tra Husserl e Heidegger: genesi e sviluppo d una polemica filosofica. RIZZACASA, Aurelio.
Creative Insecurity and "Tiptoe Experiences". HOWIE, John.
Crisis of Modernity and Process Thought in Max Horkheimer's Early Work (in Serbo-Croatian). FILANDRA, Sacir.
Critical Fanonism. GATES JR, Henry Louis.
A Critique of Derrida's Hegel Deconstruction: Speech, Phonetic Writing, and Hieroglyphic Script in Logic, Law, Art. CUTROFELLO, Andrew.
Croce e la storia della cultura. TESSITORE, Fulvio.
Dasein and Gelassenheit in Heidegger (in Czechoslovakian). PAUZA, M.
Deconstruction or Dialectics? (in Serbo-Croation). BRUNKHORST, Hauke.
Derrida's Other Conversation. DAVIES, Paul.
A determinação heideggeriana de fenómeno em *Sein und Zeit* como superação do "cepticismo metódico". DAS NEVES, Jorge César.
The Development of Otto's Thought 1898-1917. MINNEY, Robin.
Dialectical Perception: A Synthesis of Lenin and Bogdanov. WRIGHT, Edmond.
La dialettica come "dépasser" in Sartre. TOGNONATO, Claudio.
Dialogue or Mutual Accusations?. SAGATOVSKII, V N.
La diffusione del pensiero spagnolo contemporaneo nell'Italia di oggi. SAVIGNANO, Armando.
O discurso filosófico e a unidade da verdade nas primeiras obras de Paul Ricoeur. RENAUD, Michel.
The Doubleness of the Unthought of the Overman: Ambiguities of Heideggerian Political Thought. HAAR, Michel.
Ein Husserlmanuskript über Ästhetik. SCARAMUZZA, Gabriele and SCHUHMANN, Karl.
Empiricism versus Realism: High Points in the Debate During the Past 150 Years. DILWORTH, Craig.
L'epocalità metafisica di Nietzsche: "Sentiero interrotto" della filosofia heideggeriana. TRAVERSO, Patrizia.
Los escritos póstumos de J P Sartre (I). AMORÓS, Celia.
A essência da técnica segundo Heidegger. RENAUD, Michel.
L'essere mortale dei mortali: Un'analisi sul problema della morte nel pensiero del secondo Heidegger. CICCHESE, Gennaro.
Filosofia dell'esistenza e cristologia: La Weltanschauung cristiana di R Guardini. DI MARCO, Chiar.
Filosofia e cultura ne "Il Politecnico" de E Vittorini. DE SIENA, Santa.
La filosofía mística de Russell y lo indecible en el *Tractatus*. TOMASINI BASSOLS, Alejandro.
Form of Life in Wittgenstein's Later Work. GARVER, Newton.
Franz Rosenzweig e Friedrich Meinecke. D'ANTUONO, Emilia.
Gabriel Marcel na correspondência com Gaston Fessard. CABRAL, Roque.
Genealogy and *Différance*. SCOTT, Charles E.
The Genesis of Wittgenstein's Later Philosophy in His Failure as a Phenomenologist. HALLETT, Garth.
Gentile e gli 'epigoni" dell'hegelismo napoletano: il carteggio con Sebastiano Maturi. SAVORELLI, Alessandro.
Getting Rule-Following Straight. WONG, James.
A Global Point of View on Russell's Philosophy. RODRÍGUEZ-CONSUEGRA, Francisco.
Gottlob Frege, lettere a Wittgenstein. PENCO, Carlo and PARODI, Alessandra.
Habermas and Arendt on the Philosopher's "Error": Tracking the Diabiological in Heidegger. BERNASCONI, Robert.
Heidegger After Farias. ROCKMORE, Tom.
Heidegger and Emancipation. OLIVIER, G.
Heidegger at 100, in America. KOLB, David.
Heidegger e la duplicità del presente. PENZO, Maurizio.
Heidegger e o Oriente ou da Extrema In-diferença Ocidental. DO CARMO SILVA, Carlos Henrique.
Heidegger on Nietzsche and Nihilism (in Czechoslovakian). MAJOR, L.
Heidegger's Apology: Biography as Philosophy and Ideology. KISIEL, Theodore.
Heidegger's *Kampf*: The Difficulty of Life. CAPUTO, John D.
Heidegger's Rector's Address: A Loss of the Question of Ethics. SCOTT, Charles.
Heidegger, pensador con biografía. RODRÍGUEZ, Ramón.
Heidegger: vita e distino—Sullo biografia heideggeriana di Hugo Ott. ESPOSITO, Costantino.
Heideggers Denken und die Ökologie. PADRUTT, Hanspeter.
Henry James and the Paradox of Literary Mastery. BLAIR, Sara.
Hermeneutic or Metaphysical Hegelianism? Kojève's Dilemma. REDDING, Paul.
Hermenêutica e Estruturalismo. ROCHA, Acílio Estanqueiro.
Hierofanías: Una retrospectiva de la obra de Ludwig Schajowicz. KERKHOFF, Manfred.
An Historical Sketch of Pluralism. RECK, Andrew J.
History, Historicism, Narratives: Identity in the Philosophy of History of Karl Popper. PARLEJ, Piotr.
How I Slugged It Out with Toril Moi and Stayed Awake. BEDIENT, Calvin.
El humanismo de Albert Camus. QUESADA, Anabelle.
An Impatient Man and his Papers. HINTIKKA, Jaakko.
In Defence of Heidegger. JANUSZ, Sharon and WEBSTER, Glenn.
Indigenous Ends and Alien Means: A Footnote on Indian Renaissance. CHAUDHURI, Minakshi Ray.
La inocencia y el mal en la obra de Albert Camus. JIMÉNEZ, Alexander.
Intenzione e azione in Wittgenstein. RAINONE, Antonio.
L'interpretazione del conflitto fra norme nell'ultimo Kelsen. CELANO, Brun.
Introducción a la filosofía de Gaos. SALMERÓN, Fernando.
Italian Marxism and Philosophy of Culture (in Polish). PAPULI, Giovanni.
L'esthétique de John Dewey et le contexte urbain. GAVIN, William J.
Lacan Between Freud and Heidegger (in Serbo-Croatian). VETTER, Helmut.
Learning from Lonergan at Eleven. DALY, T V.
Lenguaje y metafísica en Alfred J Ayer. BEUCHOT, Mauricio.
Lezioni di filosofia della scienza di Guilio Preti. LECIS, Pier Luigi.
Liberalismo e democrazia: la giustificazione estetica di Rorty. MARRONE, Pierpaolo.
Life and Cognition. FROLOV, Ivan T.
A lógica do sentido na filosofia hermenêutica. COSTA, Miguel Dias.
Logos and the Place of the Other. BIRMINGHAM, Peg E.
The Lover-Beloved Relationship Reconsidered. HOLMES, Richard and DANIEL, Mano.
Lucien, Lévy-Bruhl: Una introduzione (di C Prandi). IANNOTTA, Daniella.
Metodi e immagini della scienza nel "Centro di studi metodologici" di Torino (1945-1952). QUARTA, Antonio.
Need, Denial and Abandonment: Heidegger and the Turn. URPETH, James R.
Never say "Never": A Response to Reeder's "Wittgenstein Never Was a Phenomenologist". GIER, Nicholas F.
La obra de Humberto Giannini: Un modo diferente de filosofar. ECHEVERRÍA, José.
On Heidegger and National Socialism: A Triple Turn?. ROCKMORE, Tom.
On the Coherence of Historical Materialism. NIELSEN, Kai.
On the Philosophy of the Czech Avant-garde, Part II (in Czechoslovakian). STROHS, S.
The Other Comes to Teach Me: A Review of Recent Levinas Publications. GIBBS, Robert.
Over de ambivalente rol van de theoriegeladenheidsthese in Rorty's 'overwinning' van de traditie. KRIBBE, Pamela.
Pannenberg's Doctrine of God. O'DONNELL, John.
Paul Ricoeur e Gabriel Marcel. DE LOURDES SIRGADO GANHO, Maria.
El personalismo cristiano de Emmanuel Mounier. ARAYA, Eval A.
Peter Dews' Logics of Disintegration: Poststructuralism/Critical Theory. BUTLER, Judith.
Peter Winch, *Simone Weil: The Just Balance*. WILLIAMS, Rowan.
The Philosophical Achievement of Peter A Bertocci. RECK, Andrew J.
Philosophy in the *Big Typescript*: Philosophy as Trivial. LUCKHARDT, C Grant.
Political Openings. WOOD, David.
Politics and the Limits of Metaphysics: Heidegger, Ferry and Renaut, and Lyotard. FÓTI, Véronique M.
Porosity: Violence and the Question of Politics in Heidegger's *Introduction to Metaphysics*. MC NEILL, William.
Postilla. GALASSO, Giuseppe.
Potenzialità conoscitive del Trascendentale di Husserl. O'DWYER BELLINETTI; Luciana.
Pragmatic Naturalism: The Philosophy of Sidney Hook (1902-1989). KURTZ, Paul.
Il problema teologico nel pensiero di Heidegger. PENATI, G.
Prolegomena to an Understanding of Heidegger's Turn. GRONDIN, Jean.
Qu'est-ce que l'expressionnisme allemand?. RICHARD, Lionel.
Reading Kristeva: A Response to Calvin Bedient. MOI, Toril.
La realtà umana nel pensiero di Xavier Zubiri. QUINTÁS, Alfonso López and NICOLOSI, Mauro.
Recent Canadian Work on Wittgenstein: 1980-1989. WILLIAMSON, George.

TWENTIETH

Reconstructing the Political. JANICAUD, Dominique.
Reflections on the Schutz-Gurwitsch Correspondence. LANDGREBE, Ludwig.
Retreat from Radicality: Pöggeler on Heidegger's Politics. EDLER, Frank H W.
Richard Rorty: An Interview (in Hebrew). KULKA, Tomas.
Riproposta di una teoria della soggettività in un'epoca di decostruzione del soggetto. LATORA, Salvatore.
Roderick Firth: His Life and Work. RAWLS, John.
Sachverhalt and *Gegenstand* are Dead. THOMPKINS, E F.
Santayana's Peirce. HOUSER, Nathan.
Scepticism: Three Recently Presented Arguments Examined. DURRANT, Michael.
Scientia e fide. BLANDINO, Giovanni.
Seeing Metaphor as Seeing-as. TIRRELL, Lynne.
Sellar's Two Images of the World. AUNE, Bruce.
El sentido del Universo en José Vasconcelos (2a parte). PATIÑO, Joel Rodríguez.
Shattering: Toward a Politics of Daimonic Life. KRELL, David Farrell.
A significação "crítica" de Le volontaire et l'involontaire. HENRIQUES, Fernanda.
Society as an "Accidental Product of Human Activities": Max Horkheimer's Social Theory and Critique. BALOG, Andreas.
Some Remarks on the Linguistic Turn. PERUZZI, Alberto.
Souls Without Longing. PLATT, Michael.
Stephen Hilmy on Matters of Method and Style. COVEOS, Costis M.
Storicità tecnica e architettura. MAZZARELLA, Eugenio.
The Subject of Hermeneutics and the Hermeneutics of the Subject. RICHARDSON, William.
Systematic Assumptions in Dilthey's Critique of Metaphysics. NENON, Thomas.
Tang Junyi's Philosophical View of History and His Explanation of the Philosophy of Wang Chuanshan. SHAFU, Xiao.
Telling Tales: Notes on Heidegger's "Career," the "Heidegger Affair," and the Assumptions of Narrativity. DAVIES, Paul.
Tenets of Freedom. BLUM, Alex.
The Early and Later Deconstruction in Derrida's Writings (in Hebrew). LANDAU, Iddo.
The Foundations of Franz Rosenzweig's Theory of Knowledge (in Hebrew). AMIR, Yehoyada.
The Legacy of Hamann—Thinking, Language and Economy (in Hungarian). RATHMANN, János.
The Problem of the History-Making Role of Ideas in American Historical Thought (in Polish). CABAJ, Jerzy.
The Reception of Nietzsche in Hungary between the Two World Wars (in Hungarian). KISS, Endre.
The Time of the Political. BIRMINGHAM, Peg.
Toward One Santayana: Recent Scholarship. KERR-LAWSON, Angus.
Two Ways of Grounding Meaning. GERRARD, Steve.
Ultimate Double Binds. SCHÜRMANN, Reiner.
The Unbearable Seriousness of Irony. FERRARA, Alessandro.
A Unique Way of Existing: Merleau-Ponty and the Subject. SIEGEL, Jerrold.
A Very Short Guide to Understanding Wittgenstein. RESNICK, Larry.
Vico in Voegelin. CAPORALI, Riccardo.
Views on Nietzsche in the GDR (in Hungarian). BOGNAR, Laszlo.
Was Moore a Positivist?. O'CONNOR, David.
Why Pluralism Now?. GARVER, Eugene.
Wittgenstein and the Transmission of Traditions. O'HEAR, Anthony.
Wittgenstein on Names and Family Resemblances. HYMERS, Michael.
Wittgenstein's Influence: Meaning, Mind and Method. GRAYLING, A C.
Wittgenstein: Whose Philosopher?. ANSCOMBE, G E M.
Wo lag der Fehler der kategorialen Repräsentation? Zu Sinn und Reichweite einer Selbstkritik Husserls. LOHMAR, Dieter.
'The Darkness of This Time': Wittgenstein and the Modern World. BOUVERESSE, Jacques.

TWO-VALUED LOGIC

A Two-Valued Logic for Reasoning about Different Types of Consequence in Kleene's Three-Valued Logic. KONIKOWSKA, Beata.

TYCHO

Tycho's System and Galileo's *Dialogue*. MARGOLIS, Howard.

TYPE THEORY

Propositional Functions and Families of Types. SMITH, Jan M.

TYPE(S)

"Development of Science as a Change of Types" in *Imre Lakatos and Theories of Scientific Change*, HÖRZ, Herbert.
The Completeness of Provable Realizability. MINTS, G E.
Inductive Types and Type Constraints in the Second-Order Lambda Calculus. MENDLER, Nax Paul.
Kripke-Style Models for Typed Lambda Calculus. MITCHELL, John C and MOGGI, Eugenio.
λ-Definability on Free Algebras. ZAIONC, Marek.
Logical Constants Across Varying Types. VAN BENTHEM, Johan.
Omitting Types for Stable CCC Theories. NEWELSKI, Ludomir.
On Simplicity of Formulas. KRYNICKI, Michal and SZCZERBA, Leslaw.
On the Absoluteness of Types in Boolean Valued Lattices. NISHIMURA, Hirokazu.
On the Adaptations of Organisms and the Fitness of Types. ETTINGER, Lia and JABLONKA, Eva and MC LAUGHLIN, Peter.
On Type Definable Subgroups of a Stable Group. NEWELSKI, Ludomir.
The Ordertype of β-R.E. Sets. SUTNER, Klaus.
A Partial Functions Version of Church's Simple Theory of Types. FARMER, William M.
Weakly Minimal Groups of Unbounded Exponent. LOVEYS, James.
Weitere verschärfungen zu den Reduktionstypen.... DEUTSCH, Michael.

TYPOLOGY

Evolution, "Typology" and "Population Thinking". GREENE, Marjorie.

TYRANNY

Policraticus. NEDERMAN, Cary J (ed & trans).
Salisburian Stakes: The Uses of 'Tyranny' in John of Salisbury's *Policraticus*. FORHAN, Kate Langdon.

ULTIMATE REALITY

What is Ultimate in George Lukács's Ontology?. JOÓS, Ernest.
William Wadsworth: Nature, Imagination, Ultimate Reality and Meaning. MAHONEY, John L.

ULTRAFILTERS

Notes on Modal Definability. VAN BENTHEM, Johan.
Ramsey Ultrafilters and the Reaping Number—Con($\mathfrak{r} < \mathfrak{u}$). GOLDSTERN, M and SHELAH, S.
Shelah's pcf Theory and Its Applications. BURKE, Maxim R and MAGIDOR, Menachem.
Théories d'algébres de Boole munies d'idéaux distingués, II. TOURAILLE, Alain.

ULTRAPOWERS

Sub-Arithmetical Ultrapowers: A Survey. MC LAUGHLIN, Thomas G.

UNAMUNO

Unamuno y el problema de Dios. FORMENT, Eudaldo.
Unamuno y la Revolución de Octubre. ROBLES, Laureano.
Unamuno: De la decepción de la verdad, a la apología de la veracidad. SILVA CAMARENA, Juan Manuel.

UNBELIEF

Educating Intelligent Believers and Unbelievers. NODDINGS, Nel.

UNCERTAINTY

Implications of Behavioral Consistency in Dynamic Choice Under Uncertainty. DARDANONI, Valentino.
Keynesian Uncertainty and the Weight of Arguments. RUNDE, Jochen.
A Note on Schrödinger's Cat and the Unexpected Hanging Paradox. HOLTZMANN, Jack M.
Uncertainty and the Shaping of Medical Decisions. BERESFORD, Eric B.

UNCONSCIOUS

Readings in Existential Psychology and Psychiatry. HOELLER, Keith (ed).
Hegel, Nietzsche, and Freud on Madness and the Unconscious. BERTHOLD-BOND, Daniel.
A Philosophical Resistance to Freud. SACHS, David.

UNDECIDABILITY

Correction to "Undecidability of $L(F_\infty)$ and Other Lattices of R.E. Substructures" (Corrigendum). DOWNEY, Rod.
Elementary Theory of Free Heyting Algebras. IDZIAK, Pawel M.
Grammar Logics. FARIÑAS DEL CERRO, Luis and PENTTONEN, Martti.
Undecidability and Initial Segments of the (R.E.) TT-Degrees. HAUGHT, Christine Ann and SHORE, Richard A.

UNDERDETERMINATION

Science and Relativism: Some Key Controversies in the Philosophy of Science. LAUDAN, Larry.
"Demystifying Underdetermination" in *Scientific Theories*, LAUDAN, Larry.
"Quine on Underdetermination" in *Perspectives on Quine*, BERGSTRÖM, Lars.
Empirical Equivalence and Undetermination. LAUDAN, Larry and LEPLIN, Jarrett.
Equivalent Descriptions. BEN-MENAHEM, Yemima.
Extensionality, Underdetermination and Indeterminacy. SOLOMON, Miriam.
Metaphysics, Pragmatic Truth and the Underdetermination of Theories. PEREIRA JR, Alfredo and FRENCH, Steven.
More on Quine's Dilemma of Undetermination. GIBSON, Roger F.
Onderbepaaldheid van theorie en onbepaaldheid van vertaling: Enige ontwikkelingen in Quine's filosofie. PERRICK, M.
Teleological Underdetermination. OKRENT, Mark.

UNDERDEVELOPMENT

La ética como conciencia en el subdesarrollo. RAMÍREZ, E Roy.
Medio ambiente y derecho. ROMERO, Jorge Enrique.

UNDERSTANDING

Being-in-the-World: A Commentary on Heidegger's "Being and Time", Division 1. DREYFUS, Hubert L.
Inference and Understanding: A Philosophical and Psychological Perspective. MANKTELOW, K I.

UNDERSTANDING
Intelligibility in Science. DILWORTH, Craig (ed).
The Many Dimensions of the Human Person. STEGER, E Ecker.
Philosophical Hermeneutics and Literary Theory. WEINSHEIMER, Joel.
Speech Acts and Literary Theory. PETREY, Sandy.
Understanding the Representational Mind. PERNER, Josef.
The Unity of Understanding: A Study in Kantian Problems. SCHWYZER, Hubert.
"Explanation and Understanding in the Science of Human Behavior" in *Reconsidering Psychology: Perspectives from Continental Philosophy*, SCHRAG, Calvin O.
"Hegel's *Science of Logic*: Ironies of the Understanding" in *Essays on Hegel's Logic*, FLAY, Joseph C.
"A Reply to John Burbidge's "Where is the Place of Understanding?"" in *Essays on Hegel's Logic*, HOULGATE, Stephen.
"Semantic Innocence and Psychological Understanding" in *Philosophical Perspectives, 3: Philosophy of Mind and Action Theory, 1989*, HORNSBY, Jennifer.
"Truth, Understanding and the Artist's Vision" in *XIth International Congress in Aesthetics, Nottingham 1988*, SAVILE, Anthony.
"Understanding and the Principle of Compositionality" in *Philosophical Perspectives, 4: Action Theory and Philosophy of Mind, 1990*, GRANDY, Richard E.
"What Davidson Should Have Said" in *Information, Semantics and Epistemology*, LE PORE, Ernest and LOEWER, Barry.
"Where is the Place of Understanding?" in *Essays on Hegel's Logic*, BURBIDGE, John.
Blind Grasping and Fregean Senses. SCHWEIZER, Paul.
Dialogue and Understanding (in German). FRITZSCHE, Helmut.
Emotions and Rationality. BERENSON, F M.
Hegel and the Overcoming of the Understanding. BAUR, Michael.
The Last Word on *Philosophical Investigations* 43a. SAVIGNY, Eike V.
Meaning, Understanding and Translation. STROUD, Barry.
Notes on the Specification of "Meaning" in Schutz. EMBREE, Lester.
Psychoanalysis: A Form of Life?. BREARLEY, Michael.
Responsibility, the Theory of Values, and the Theory of Knowledge (in Czechoslovakian). MERCIER, A.
Truth and Understanding. HIGGINBOTHAM, James.
Understanding Science: A Two-Level Reflection. DAS GUPTA, Amitabha.
What is so Practical about Theory? Lewin Revisited. SANDELANDS, Lloyd E.
Wittgenstein: Whose Philosopher?. ANSCOMBE, G E M.

UNESCO
Lifelong Education: The Institutionalisation of an Illiberal and Regressive Ideology. BAGNALL, Richard G.

UNGER, R
Critique and Construction: A Symposium on Roberto Unger's "Politics". LOVIN, Robin W (ed).
Descent into Subjectivity: Studies of Rawls, Dworkin and Unger in the Context of Modern Thought. MURPHY JR, Cornelius F.
"False Universality" in *Critique and Construction: A Symposium on Roberto Unger's "Politics"*, GALSTON, William A.
"Practical Reason and Social Democracy" in *Critique and Construction: A Symposium on Roberto Unger's "Politics"*, HAWTHORN, Geoffrey.
"Programmatic Thought and the Critique of the Social Disciplines" in *Critique and Construction: A Symposium on Roberto Unger's "Politics"*, TRUBEK, David M.
"Psychiatry as Scientific Humanism: A Program Inspired by Roberto Unger's *Passion*" in *Critique and Construction: A Symposium on Roberto Unger's "Politics"*, HOBSON, J Allan.
"Religion and the Making of Society" in *Critique and Construction: A Symposium on Roberto Unger's "Politics"*, DAVIS, Charles.
"Routine and Revolution" in *Critique and Construction: A Symposium on Roberto Unger's "Politics"*, SUNSTEIN, Cass R.
"Unger's *Politics* and the Appraisal of Political Possibility" in *Critique and Construction: A Symposium on Roberto Unger's "Politics"*, DUNN, John.
"Unger, Castoriadis, and the Romance of a National Future" in *Critique and Construction: A Symposium on Roberto Unger's "Politics"*, RORTY, Richard.
"When the Owl of Minerva Takes Flight at Dawn: Radical Constructivism in Social Theory" in *Critique and Construction: A Symposium on Roberto Unger's "Politics"*, BURNS, Robert P.
Conflicting Views of Liberalism. SKOBLE, Aeon James.
Rights, Systems of Rights, and Unger's System of Rights: Part I. EIDENMÜLLER, Horst.

UNIFICATION
"Fundamental Issues in Theology and Science" in *Science and Religion: One World-Changing Perspectives on Reality*, TORRANCE, T F.
Categorical Grammars Determined from Linguistic Data by Unification. BUSZKOWSKI, Wojciech and PENN, Gerald.
Ellipsis and Higher-Order Unification. DALRYMPLE, Mary and SHIEBER, Stuart M and PEREIRA, Fernando C N.
Sobre causación y unificación según Wesley Salmon. OLIVÉ, León.
The Undecidability of k-Provability. BUSS, Samuel R.
Unification, Realism and Inference. MORRISON, Margaret.
A Unification-Theoretic Method for Investigating the k-Provability Problem. FARMER, William.

UNIFIED SCIENCE
The Philosophy of Science. BOYD, Richard (ed).
Explanation and Scientific Realism. GASPER, Philip.
Explanation. REDHEAD, Michael.
How Do Scientific Explanations Explain?. KINOSHITA, Joyce.

UNIFORMITY
Rationality of p-Adic Poincaré Series: Uniformity in p. MACINTYRE, Angus.
Thoughts and Theses on Causality. TILANDER, A.
Two Problems of Induction?. O'NEILL, John.

UNION(S)
Enriching Business Ethics. WALTON, Clarence C (ed).
Work, Inc.: A Philosophical Inquiry. BYRNE, Edmund F.
Better the Union Theory. HONDERICH, Ted.
Is There a New Teacher Unionism?. URBAN, Wayne J.
The Union Axiom in Zermelo Set Theory. GONZÁLEZ, Carlos G.

UNIQUENESS
"Demystifying Underdetermination" in *Scientific Theories*, LAUDAN, Larry.

UNIT(S)
Units of Measurement and Natural Kinds: Some Kripkean Considerations. VAN BRAKEL, J.

UNITARIANISM
The Unitarian Universalist Association: Humanism or Theism?. KURTZ, Paul and BULLOUGH, Vern L.

UNITED STATES
see also American
Enriching Business Ethics. WALTON, Clarence C (ed).
La religión en la constitución de los Estados Unidos de América. PÉREZ ESTÉVEZ, Antonio.

UNITY
Critique of Dialectical Reason, Volume 2: Jean-Paul Sartre. HOARE, Quintin (trans).
Fichte's Theory of Subjectivity. NEUHOUSER, Frederick.
For What May I Hope? Thinking with Kant and Kierkegaard. FENDT, Gene.
Hegel: o la rebelión contra el límite. IZUZQUIZA, Ignacio.
Material Beings. VAN INWAGEN, Peter.
L'Utopia di Fourier. TUNDO, Laura.
"Plurality and Unity in the Configuration of the Chinese People" in *The Tanner Lectures on Human Values, Volume XI*, XIAOTONG, Fei.
Divine Unity and Superfluous Synonymity. LEVINE, Michael P.
Evolution and Nostalgia in Hegel's Theory of Desire. BERTHOLD-BOND, Daniel.
How Many Selves Make Me?. WILKES, Kathleen V.
The Integral Self: Systematic Illusion or Inescapable Task?. COLAPIETRO, Vincent M.
Leibniz's "Analysis of Multitude and Phenomena into Unities and Reality". RUTHERFORD, Donald.
Logic and Logos—The Search for Unity in Hegel and Coleridge: I, Alienation and the Logocentric Response. PERKINS, Mary Anne.
Logic and Logos—The Search for Unity in Hegel and Coleridge: II: The 'Otherness" of God. PERKINS, Mary Anne.
Molecular Biology and the Unity of Science. KINCAID, Harold.
The Nature of a Person-Stage. MC INERNEY, Peter K.
The Principle of Unity of Theory and Practice in Marxism: A Critique. DIMITRAKOS, D.
Self-Organization, Emergent Properties and the Unity of the World. ROTH, Gerhard and SCHWEGLER, Helmut.
La teoria aristotelica dell'apodissi. SAINATI, Vittorio.
The Doubts about Post-Modernism (in Czechoslovakian). AJVAZ, Michal.
Thinking of Unity (in Dutch). AERTSEN, Jan A.
The Unity of Moral Virtues in Aristotle's *Nicomachean Ethics*. TELFER, Elizabeth.
The Unity of the Natural Sciences: Comment on Portmann. VON UEXKUELL, Thure.
The Unity of the Vices. JACOBS, Jonathan and ZEIS, John.
Vlastos on the Unity of Virtue: Why Pauline Predication Will Not Save the Biconditionality Thesis. WAKEFIELD, Jerome C.

UNIVERSAL GRAMMAR
The Application of Montague Translations in Universal Research and Typology. TENT, Katrin.

UNIVERSAL(S)
Aristotelian Logic and the Arabic Language in Alfarabi. ABED, Shukri B.
Introduction to Metaphysics: The Fundamental Questions. SCHOEDINGER, Andrew B (ed).
Kants Kategorischer Imperativ als Leitfaden humaner Praxis. NISTERS, Thomas.
Metaphysical Delusion. COWLEY, Fraser.
Philosophical Papers: F P Ramsey. MELLOR, D H (ed).
A Philosophy of Morals. HELLER, Agnes.
"Sets Are Universals" in *Physicalism in Mathematics*, BIGELOW, John.

UNIVERSAL(S)

"Universal Prescriptivism" in *A Companion to Ethics*, HARE, R M.
Are There Cultural Universals?. WIREDU, Kwasi.
Cultural Fundamentals in Philosophy. ORUKA, H Odera.
Cultural Fundamentals in Philosophy: Obstacles in Philosophical Dialogues. ORUKA, Henry Odera.
The Dating of Rule IV-B in Descartes's *Regulae ad directionem ingenii*. VAN DE PITTE, Frederick P.
The Ethics Behind the Absence of Ethics in Alfred Schutz's Thought. BARBER, Michael.
Existen los universales culturales?. WIREDU, Kwasi and GARCÍA MONSIVÁIS, Blanca.
Gadamer's Concrete Universal. KERBY, Anthony Paul.
Hegel and the Overcoming of the Understanding. BAUR, Michael.
El problema de los universales en Juan de Santo Tomás en Juan de Santo Tomás. BEUCHOT, Mauricio.
Sobre los universales. DÍAZ, Adolfo García.
La storia universale come storia comparata in Max Weber. DI MARCO, Giuseppe Antonio.
Supervenience, Goodness and Higher-Order Universals. ODDIE, Graham.
The Heraclitus' Lesson (in Portuguese). SANTOS, M C A dos.
The Passing On of Values (in French). PIGUET, J-Claude.
Two Anonymous 12th-Century Tracts on Universals. DIJS, Judith.
Two Designs of Universal History. KANTOR, K M.
Universals and Creativity. WESTPHAL, Jonathan.
Universals and Predication of Species. PETERSON, John.
Vectors and Change. BIGELOW, John and PARGETTER, Robert.

UNIVERSALISM

Leibniz' Position der Rationalität. KAEHLER, Klaus Erich.
Universalism versus Communitarianism: Contemporary Debates in Ethics. RASMUSSEN, David.
"Against the Neglect of "Content" in the Moral Theories of Kohlberg and Habermas" in *The Moral Domain: Essays in the Ongoing Discussion between Philosophy and the Social Sciences*, DöBERT, Rainer.
"Moral Relativism and Strict Universalism" in *The Moral Domain: Essays in the Ongoing Discussion between Philosophy and the Social Sciences*, NUNNER-WINKLER, Gertrud.
A Post-Metaphysical Moral: An Introduction to the Moral Theory of Jürgen Habermas (in French). HUNYADI, Mark.
How to Defend Science Against Scepticism: A Reply to Barry Gower. CHALMERS, Alan.
Universalistische Ethik und Urteilskraft: ein aristotelischer Blick auf Kant. HÖFFE, Otfried.

UNIVERSALITY

Philosophie Juridique Européenne. TRIGEAUD, Jean-Marc.
"Quine as a Member of the Tradition of the Universality of Language" in *Perspectives on Quine*, HINTIKKA, Jaakko.
L'universalisation de l'herméneutique chez Hans-Georg Gadamer. GRONDIN, Jean.
Subjektivität, Allgemeingültigkeit und Apriorität des Geschmacksurteils bei Kant. BAUM, Manfred.
Les trois sortes d'universalité dans l'herméneutique de H G Gadamer. MARGOLIS, Joseph.
Universal Sentences: Russell, Wittgenstein, Prior, and the Nyāya. SHAW, J L.
Universalismo o eurocentrismo. SPAEMANN, Robert.
Universalität des Prinzips vom zureichenden Grund. NICOLÁS, Juan A.
Universality Biases: *How Theories About Human Nature Succeed*. HORNSTEIN, Gail A and STAR, Susan Leigh.

UNIVERSALIZABILITY

Some Remarks about Ethical Universalism. MOSER, Shia.
Universalizability and the Summing of Desires. PERSSON, Ingmar.
Universalizability and the Summing of Desires: Reply to Ingmar Persson. HARE, R M.

UNIVERSALIZATION

Discourse and the Moral Point of View: Deriving a Dialogical Principle of Universalization. REHG, William.
Intersubjectivity and Critical Consciousness: Remarks on Habermas's Theory of Communicative Action. WAGNER, Gerhard and ZIPPRIAN, Heinz.

UNIVERSE

"Nation and Universe" in *The Tanner Lectures on Human Values, Volume XI*, WALZER, Michael.
The Drama of Galileo, The Past and the Present. VOISE, Waldemar.
La primera antinomia kantiana: el origen y los límites del Universo. PUYAU, Hermes.
Quantum Cosmology and the Beginning of the Universe. SMITH, Gerrit.
El sentido del Universo en José Vasconcelos (2a parte). PATIÑO, Joel Rodríguez.
El sentido del Universo en José Vasconcelos. PATIÑO, Joel Rodríguez.
La teología de la creación y el problema de los orígenes. PODESTA, Gustavo.
Teorías físicas sobre el origen del Universo. GRATTON, Fausto T L.

Towards a View of Time as Depth. ARGYROS, Alexander J.
What is the Explanandum of the Anthropic Principle?. WILSON, Patrick A.
Why Didn't God Create the World Sooner?. LEFTOW, Brian.
'What Place, then, for a creator?': Hawking on God and Creation. CRAIG, William Lane.

UNIVERSE OF DISCOURSE

L'epoché di Husserl in Ferruccio Rossi-Landi. PONZIO, Augusto.

UNIVERSITY(-TIES)

The Behavior of the NCAA: A Question of Ethics. STIEBER, John.
But Suppose We Were to Take the Rectorial Address Seriously...Gérard Granel's *De l'université*. FYNSK, Christopher.
Commentary: "The University and Industrial Research: Selling Out?". CAMPBELL, L Leon.
Heidegger's Rector's Address: A Loss of the Question of Ethics. SCOTT, Charles.
The Justification of "English". MEYNELL, Hugo A.
Philosophy within the Activity of the Nagyszombat (Trnava) University (in Hungarian). ORAVCOVÀ, Mariana.
Remarks about the Idea of the University (in Dutch). ROSSOUW, H W.
The University and Industrial Research: Selling Out?. HILL, Judith M.

UNIVOCITY

Univocità dell'essere e intenzionalià del conoscere. ANTONELLI, Mauro.

UNKNOWN

Can Knowledge Occur Unknowingly?. CHAUDHURI, Manjusree.

UNMOVED MOVER

The Chain of Change: A Study of Aristotle's "Physics" VII. WARDY, Robert.

UPANISHADS

Is the Central Upanishadic Teaching a Reductionist Thesis?. PULIGANDLA, Ramakrishna.
Rāmānuja's Hermeneutics of the *Upanisads* in Comparison with Sankara's Interpretation. SAWAI, Yoshitsugu.
The Word That Became the Absolute: Relevance of Sankara's Ontology of Language. GUPTA, Som Raj.

URBAN SYSTEM(S)

Philosophical Streets: New Approaches to Urbanism. CROW, Dennis (ed).

URQUHART, A

A Solution to a Problem of Urquhart. KRACHT, Marcus.

USE

Dream and Culture: An Anthropological Study of the Western Intellectual Tradition. PARMAN, Susan.
The River of the Mother of God, and Other Essays by Aldo Leopold. FLADER, Susan L (ed).
Pragmatic Principles and Language. BHAT, P R.

USEFUL

"Utility". BROOME, John.

USEFULNESS

The Conditions of Fruitfulness of Theorizing About Mechanisms in Social Science. STINCHCOMBE, Arthur L.
Usefulness in Literary History. SMALL, Ian and GUY, Josephine.

USURY

"Nominalism, Usury, and Bourgeois Man" in *Freedom in the Modern World: Jacques Maritain, Yves R Simon, Mortimer J Adler*, MANCINI, Matthew J.

UTILITARIANISM

see also Consequentialism
Animal Experimentation: The Moral Issue. BAIRD, Robert M (ed).
Gerechtigkeit, Wohlfahrt und Rationalität. SCHMIDT, Johannes.
Morality and Modernity. POOLE, Ross.
Morality—What's In It For Me?: A Historical Introduction to Ethics. NELSON, William N.
Science and Moral Values. VOLLRATH, John.
"Consequentialism" in *A Companion to Ethics*, PETTIT, Philip.
"Utilitarian Ethics and Superpower Negotiations: Lost Opportunities for Nuclear Peace" in *In the Interest of Peace: A Spectrum of Philosophical Views*, LACKEY, Douglas.
"Utility and the Good" in *A Companion to Ethics*, GOODIN, Robert E.
"Everyone's Doing It"—A Reply to Richard DeGeorge. GREEN, Ronald M.
"Hume and Hume's Connexions". KLEMME, Heiner.
Actual Preferences, Actual People. GOODIN, Robert E.
Amoralism—On the Limits of Moral Thinking. SANDOE, Peter.
Amoralism: Reply to Peter Sandoe. HARE, R M.
An Argument for Utilitarianism: A Defence. NG, Yew-Kwang and SINGER, Peter.
Can Utilitarianism Be Salvaged as a Theory for Social Choice?. VAN ASPEREN, G M.
La estructura consecuencialista del utilitarismo. GUTIÉRREZ, Gilberto.
Ethical Myopia: The Case of "Framing" by Framing. SINGER, Alan E and LYSONSKI, Steven and SINGER, Ming and HAYES, David.
Ethics Without Free Will. SLOTE, Michael.
External and Now-For-Then Preferences in Hare's Theory. HAJDIN, Mane.
Fanaticism: Reply to Thomas Wetterström. HARE, R M.
The Greatest Happiness Principle. SPRIGGE, T L S.

UTILITARIANISM
Indirect Utilisme. ROSIER, Theo.
Is Utilitarianism Useless?. HAUSMAN, Daniel M.
Jevons's Applications of Utilitarian Theory to Economic Policy. PEART, Sandra J.
A Note on the Death Penalty as the Best Bet. BAYLES, Michael D.
On Intuitions. WETTERSTRÖM, Thomas.
On Utilitarianism and Utilitarian Attitudes. MILLER, Harlan B.
The Problem of Unauthorized Welfare. VALLENTYNE, Peter.
Proof and Sanction in Mill's Utilitarianism. COHEN, Stephen.
Punishment and the Utilitarian Criterion of Right and Wrong. SCHALLER, Walter E.
Reading Hobbes in Other Words: Contractarian, Utilitarian, Game Theorist. HARDIN, Russell.
Response to Slote's "Ethics Without Free Will". VAN INWAGEN, Peter.
Rights and Utilitarianism. EWIN, R E.
Singer's Cookbook. JOHNSON, Edward.
Tooley and the Trolley. FISCHER, John Martin.
Utilitarian Killing, Replacement, and Rights. PLUHAR, Evelyn.
Utilitarian Strategies in Bentham and John Stuart Mill. KELLY, P J.
Utilitarianism and the 'Punishment' of the Innocent: The General Problem. SMILANSKY, Saul.
Utilitarianism and the Idea of Reflective Equilibrium. TERSMAN, Folke.
Utilitaristische Ethik als Antwort auf die ökologische Krise. WOLF, Jean-Claude.
Welfarism and Utilitarianism: A Rehabilitation. NG, Yew-Kwang.
Your Daughter or Your Dog? A Feminist Assessment of the Animal Research Issue. SLICER, Deborah.

UTILITY
"Utility". BROOME, John.
Apriorisme et théorie du choix rationnel. KAUFMANN, J Nicolas.
Discovering Right and Wrong: A Realist Response to Gauthier's Morals by Agreement. GENOVA, A C.
Distributive Justice and Utility. GOLDSTICK, D.
An Experimental Analysis of Risk Taking. DAHLBÄCK, Olof.
The Geometry of Legal Principles. CHUAQUI, Rolando and MALITZ, Jerome.
Making Interpersonal Comparisons Coherently. BARRETT, Martin and HAUSMAN, Daniel.
On Some Multiattribute Value Function Generalizations of the EQQ Model in the Context of Personal Inventory Decisions. TROUTT, Marvin D.
On the Descriptive Adequacy of Levi's Decision Theory. MAHER, Patrick and KASHIMA, Yoshihisa.
Ratifiability, Game Theory, and the Principle of Independence of Irrelevant Alternatives. EELLS, Ellery and HARPER, William L.
Utility and Morality: Adam Smith's Critique of Hume. MARTIN, Marie A.
The Value of Perfect Information in Non-linear Utility Theory. SCHLEE, Edward E.

UTOPIA
L'Utopia di Fourier. TUNDO, Laura.
Utopia: Sir Thomas More. LOGAN, George M (ed).
"Les utopies littéraires au XVIIIe siècle" in *Égalité Uguaglianza*, IMBROSCIO, Carmelina.
"Der geschlossne Handelsstaat"—Zur konservativen Kritik einer aufklärerischen Utopie. MARQUARDT, Jochen.
(Post-) Metaphysik und (Post-) Moderne: Zur Sache des "schwachen Denkens". FRÜCHTL, Josef.
Community and Utopia: A Transcendental Deduction. POPOV, Stefan.
Dialogue—A New Utopia?. GÓRNIAK-KOCIKOWSKA, Krystyna.
Kommunismus—Utopie und Wirklichkeit. HAVEMANN, Robert.
The Last Utopia: Entropy and Revolution in the Poetics of Evgeny Zamjatin. SICHER, Efraim.
Notes sur utopie et marxisme. ARANTES, Urias Corrêa.
Plato's Three Waves and the Question of Utopia. HYLAND, Drew A.
Political Errors (in Serbo-Croatian). NOERR, Gunzelin Schmid.
The Other Nietzsche: Criticism of Moral Utopia (in German). MAURER, Reinhart.

UTOPIANISM
"Early Advocates of Lasting World Peace: Utopians or Realists?" in *Celebrating Peace*, BOK, Sissela.
Campanella's "Civitas Solis" Is Ruled by Love Without Emotion (in German). ZÖHRER-ERNST, Ulla.

UTTERANCE(S)
The Foundations of Linguistic Theory: Selected Writings of Roy Harris. LOVE, Nigel (ed).
Demonstrative Utterances. BERCKMANS, Paul.

VACUOSITY
Vacuity. RAMER, Alexis Manaster.

VAGUENESS
The Metaphysics of the "Tractatus". CARRUTHERS, Peter.
"Through a Glass Darkly: Vagueness in the Metaphysics of the Analytic Tradition" in *The Analytic Tradition: Philosophical Quarterly Monographs, Volume 1*, SACKS, Mark.
"Vagueness, Logic and Interpretation" in *The Analytic Tradition: Philosophical Quarterly Monographs, Volume 1*, HOOKWAY, Christopher.
Fictional Incompleteness as Vagueness. SORENSEN, Roy A.
Intuitionism and Vagueness. SCHWARTZ, Stephen P and THROOP, William.
Is There Higher-Order Vagueness?. SAINSBURY, Mark.
Process Vagueness. SORENSEN, Roy A.
The Sorites Paradox and Higher-Order Vagueness. BURGESS, John A.
Vague Identity and Vague Objects. GARRETT, Brian.
Vague Objects. TYE, Michael.
Vague Objects. ZEMACH, Eddy M.
Vagueness, Natural Language and Logic. BERKELEY, Istvan S N.

VALENCY
Valency, Adicity, and Adity in Peirce's MS 482. BURCH, Robert W.

VALENTIN, K
Vom "Wahr-Lachen" der Moderne: Karl Valentins Semantik paradoxer Lebenswelten. GÖNNER, Gerhard.

VALIDATION
What Is Wrong with the Miracle Argument?. CARRIER, Martin.

VALIDITY
The Communicative Ethics Controversy. BENHABIB, Seyla (ed).
"Criticisms of the Usual Rationale for Validity in Mathematics" in *Physicalism in Mathematics*, DAVIS, Chandler.
Can An Argument Be Both Valid and Invalid Too?. NEBLETT, William R.
Constituição do sentido e justificação da validade: Heidegger e o problema da filosofia transcendental. APEL, Karl-Otto.
Logic and Artificial Intelligence: An Exposition. DE SWART, H C M.
On Scholarly Developments in Legal Semiotics. JACKSON, Bernard S.
Validity and Practical Reasoning. MITCHELL, David.
Validity and Satisfaction in Imperative Logic. SEGERBERG, Krister.

VALLABHA
The Celebration of Emotion: Vallabha's Ontology of Affective Experience. TIMM, Jeffrey R.

VALLICELLA, W
Reply to Vallicella: Heidegger and Idealism. SMITH, Quentin.

VALUATION
Baffling Phenomena: And Other Studies in the Philosophy of Knowledge and Valuation. RESCHER, Nicholas.
"The Individual's Horizon and Valuation" in *The Social Horizon of Knowledge*, FALKIEWICZ, Andrzej.
An Axiomatic Basis of Accounting: A Structuralist Reconstruction. BALZER, Wolfgang and MATTESSICH, Richard.
Concerted Instant-Interval Temporal Semantics II: Temporal Valuations and Logics of Change. BOCHMAN, Alexander.
The Quarrel Theorem: First Attempt to the Logic of Lie. MAJCHER, B.
Semantic Holism is Seriously False. MASSEY, Gerald J.
Semantic Holism. BELNAP JR, Nuel D and MASSEY, Gerald J.

VALUE FREE
Wertfreiheit und Ethik in den Sozial-und Naturwissenschaften. ZIMMERMANN, Rolf.

VALUE JUDGMENT(S)
Moral Theory and Medical Practice. FULFORD, K W M.
"Scientific Method and the Objectivity of Epistemic Value Judgments" in *Logic, Methodology and Philosophy of Science, VIII*, SHRADER-FRECHETTE, Kristin.
On Some Multiattribute Value Function Generalizations of the EQQ Model in the Context of Personal Inventory Decisions. TROUTT, Marvin D.

VALUE THEORY
Education as a Human Right: A Theory of Curriculum and Pedagogy. VANDENBERG, Donald.
How Wide Is the Gap Between Facts and Values?. RESCHER, Nicholas.
Pyrrhonism's Arguments Against Value. MC PHERRAN, Mark L.
Lo que no sabemos sobre los valores. INGARDEN, Roman.
Rational Chocolate Addiction or How Chocolate Cures Irrationality. ELLIOTT, C S.
A Returning to the Source: The Philosophy of Alain Locke. BIRT, Robert E.
A Study of the Foundations of Ethical Decision Making of Clinical Medical Ethicists. SELF, Donnie J and SKEEL, Joy D.
Thoughts on the Taxonomy and Semantics of Value Terms. MARIETTA JR, Don E.

VALUE(S)
After Principles. BARDEN, Garrett.
Beyond Natural Selection. WESSON, Robert.
The Co-Existence of God and Evil. TRAU, Jane Mary.
Community: The Tie That Binds. ROUSSEAU, Mary F.
Controlling Technology: Contemporary Issues. THOMPSON, William B.
Ethics with Aristotle. BROADIE, Sarah.
Euthanasia: Toward an Ethical Social Policy. THOMASMA, David C.
Key Themes in Philosophy. GRIFFITHS, A Phillips (ed).
Law, Culture, and Values: Essays in Honor of Gray L Dorsey. VOJCANIN, Sava Alexander (ed).
Logic and Ethics. GEACH, Peter (ed).

VALUE(S)

Max Scheler's Concept of the Person: An Ethics of Humanism. PERRIN, Ron.
Moral Dilemmas. GOWANS, Christopher W (ed).
Natural Reasons: Personality and Polity. HURLEY, S L.
The Philosophy of Money: Georg Simmel (Second Edition). FRISBY, David (ed & trans).
Philosophy of Sport. HYLAND, Drew A.
Pour une philosophie du sens et de la valeur. VASSILIE-LEMENY, Sorin-Titus.
The Question of Ethics. SCOTT, Charles E.
The Realizations of the Future: An Inquiry into the Authority of Praxis. ALLAN, George.
The Realm of Rights. THOMSON, Judith Jarvis.
Relating Humanities and Social Thought (Science, Ideology, and Value, Volume 4). EDEL, Abraham.
Saussure: Signs, System, and Arbitrariness. HOLDCROFT, David.
Science and Moral Values. VOLLRATH, John.
Theory and Practice in Medical Ethics. GRABER, Glenn C.
To Be at Home: Christianity, Civil Religion, and World Community. ROUNER, Leroy S.
The Vatican, the Law and the Human Embryo. COUGHLAN, Michael J.
"Anti-Art and Anti-Criticism—The Killers of Art or its Rescuers?" in *XIth International Congress in Aesthetics, Nottingham 1988*, SEPÄNMAA, Yrö.
"The Body and Human Values in Augustine of Hippo" in *Grace, Politics and Desire: Essays on Augustine*, MILES, Margaret R.
"Covenant, Leadership, and Value Formation in Academic Health Centers" in *Integrity in Health Care Institutions: Humane Environments for Teaching, Inquiry, and Healing*, BULGER, Roger J.
"Facts and Values in the Physician-Patient Relationship" in *Ethics, Trust, and the Professions: Philosophical and Cultural Aspects*, BROCK, Dan W.
"How to Reason About Value Judgments" in *Key Themes in Philosophy*, CLARK, Stephen R L.
"Le kitsch en tant que valeur communicative" in *XIth International Congress in Aesthetics, Nottingham 1988*, STÉPHANOV, Ivan.
"Needs and Values" in *Logic and Ethics*, WOLNIEWICZ, Boguslaw.
"Negative Values" in *Logic and Ethics*, ELZENBERG, H.
"Neutralities" in *Liberalism and the Good*, ACKERMAN, Bruce A.
"The Principle of Transcendence and the Foundation of Axiology" in *Logic and Ethics*, GRZEGORCZYK, Andrzej.
"Reason, Spontaneity, and the *Li*—A Confucian Critique of Graham's Solution to the Problem of Fact and Value" in *Chinese Texts and Philosophical Contexts*, FINGARETTE, Herbert.
"Surrogacy: A Question of Values" in *Beyond Baby M: Ethical Issues in New Reproductive Techniques*, ROTHMAN, Barbara Katz.
"La trahison des clercs" in *The Political Responsibility of Intellectuals*, GELLNER, Ernest.
"Value Judgments and Normative Claims" in *Key Themes in Philosophy*, SINGER, Marcus G.
"Values and Academic Health Centers: A Commentary and Recommendations" in *Integrity in Health Care Institutions: Humane Environments for Teaching, Inquiry, and Healing*, PELLEGRINO, Edmund D.
"Virtue, The Missing Link to the Last Volume of the *Treatise*" in *Studies on Mario Bunge's "Treatise"*, FORMAN, Frank.
"Which Values are Conducive to Human Survival? A Bunge-Test of Bunge-Ethics" in *Studies on Mario Bunge's "Treatise"*, ZECHA, Gerhard.
"Who Chooses?" in *Chinese Texts and Philosophical Contexts*, ROSEMONT JR, Henry.
"The Logic of Implication". BALZER, Noel.
'Queerness' and the Objectivity of Value: A Response to J L Mackie. SPOERL, Joseph.
A Phenomenologically and Psychologically Based Concept of Ethics (in Czechoslovakian). BAYEROVA, M.
Adapting Kohlberg to Enhance the Assessment of Manager's Moral Reasoning. WEBER, James.
Aesthetic Constraints on Theory Selection: A Critique of Laudan. MARTIN, James E.
Argumentation and Values (in French). BOREL, Marie-Jeanne.
A Comment on Fry's "The Role of Caring in a Theory of Nursing Ethics". BOYER, Jeannine Ross and NELSON, James Lindemann.
Community and Autonomy: Logically Incompatible Values?. MASON, Andrew.
Community Values in Vermont Health Planning. WALLACE-BRODEUR, Paul H.
Conception of Values in Polish Sociology (in Polish). STYK, Jozef.
Concerning the Interests of Insects. GROSSINGER, Robin.
Creative Value. ODDIE, Graham.
A Critical Examination of Scheler's Justification of the Existence of Values. MOOSA, Imtiaz.
A Dialogue on Value, I: Values and Relations. LACHS, John.
A Dialogue on Value, II: Why Is There Something Good, Not Simply Something?. KOHÁK, Erazim.
Differences in Moral Values Between Corporations. NYSTROM, Paul C.
La dignità dell'uomo da Kant a Hegel. PAOLINELLI, Marco.
Duty and Inclination: The Phenomenological Value Ethics of Hans Reiner. GÖRTZEN, René.
Dworkin and His Critics: The Relevance of Ethical Theory in Philosophy of Law. BALL, Stephen W.
Educação para valores e maturidade pessoal do educador. ROCHA, Filipe.
Ellis, Epistemic Values, and the Problem of Induction. VOLLRATH, John.
The Ethical Limitations of the Market. ANDERSON, Elizabeth.
Ethical Values of Individuals at Different Levels in the Organizational Hierarchy of a Single Firm. HARRIS, James R.
Feminist Reflections on Humans and Other Domestic Animals. ROMAIN, Dianne.
Fix It and Be Damned: A Reply to Laudan. WORRALL, John.
La fondazione dei valori nell'assiologia critica di Nicola Petruzzellis. TURCO, Giovanni.
Forgiveness: A Christian Model. ADAMS, Marilyn McCord.
Giving Voice to the Pragmatic Majority in New Jersey. HILL, T Patrick.
Health Care in Common: Setting Priorities in Oregon. GARLAND, Michael J and HASNAIN, Romana.
How Would an *Übermensch* Regard His Past and Future?. MC INERNEY, Peter K.
If It Aint's Broke, Don't Fix It. LAUDAN, Larry.
La inocencia y el mal en la obra de Albert Camus. JIMÉNEZ, Alexander.
Institutional Animal Care and Use Committees and the Moderate Position. STEPHENSON, Wendell.
Intimacy: A General Orientation in Japanese Religious Values. KASULIS, Thomas P.
Is Creativity Good?. HALPER, Edward.
An Issue in Corporate Social Responsibility: An Experiential Approach to Establish the Value of Human Life. DALTON, Dan R and COSIER, Richard A.
The Justification of "English". MEYNELL, Hugo A.
Knowing When to Stop: The Limits of Medicine. JECKER, Nancy S.
L'esthétique de John Dewey et le contexte urbain. GAVIN, William J.
Le lezioni di Husserl sull'etica e sulla teoria del valore. DONNICI, Rocco.
Medical Futility, Medical Necessity: The - Problem - Without - A - Name. CALLAHAN, Daniel.
Norms and Values. HANSSON, Sven Ove.
On the Historical Triviality of Art. STOLNITZ, Jerome.
The Ontological Status of the Principle of the Excluded Middle. STRAUSS, Daniël F M.
Organizational Value Contention and Managerial Mindsets. LIEDTKA, Jeanne.
Il pensiero di Aldo Capitini e la filosofia del neoidealismo. CESA, Claudio.
Persona y sociedad según Jacques Maritain. WASHBURN, Jimmy.
The Philosophical Achievement of Peter A Bertocci. RECK, Andrew J.
The Philosophy of the Welfare State. BARRY, Norman P.
Public Input Into Health Care Policy: Controversy and Contribution in California. COLBERT, Treacy.
Questioni di filosofia politica. VECA, Salvatore.
La ragione e i valori nella determinazione delle norme. CORTESE, Roberto.
Reply to Stephenson on Biomedical Research. GENDIN, Sidney.
Response: Subjective Values and Objective Values. MACHAN, Tibor R.
Responsibility As a Moral Principle? A Critical Reflection on Hans Jonas' Ethics of Responsibility? (in German). KETTNER, Matthias.
Responsibility, the Theory of Values, and the Theory of Knowledge (in Czechoslovakian). MERCIER, A.
Rights-Talk Will Not Sort Out Child-Abuse: Comment on Archard on Parental Rights. MIDGLEY, Mary.
Sartre and the Objectivity of Values (in French). FRIEDLI, Serge.
Sincerity and Japanese Values. REASONER, Paul.
Skepticism About Goodness and Rightness. GOLDMAN, Alan H.
Solving the Problem of Induction Using a Values-Based Epistemology. ELLIS, Brian.
The Freedom of Values and the Value of Freedom (in Czechoslovakian). SLEJSKA, D.
The Operation of Values: Knowledge in the Conception of G H Mead (in Polish). HETMANSKI, Marek.
The Passing On of Values (in French). PIGUET, J-Claude.
The Questioning of Values in Theology (in French). WIDMER, Gabriel-Ph.
Tradition and Its Value: A Contribution to the History of Polish Marxist Philosophical Thought (in Polish). GRADKOWSKI, Waldemar.
The Unity of Human Rights in Western and Eastern Europe: Meditation about Human Rights. FÖLDESI, Tamás.
Value Concepts and Preconventional, Conventional and Postconventional Morality (in Dutch). VOS, H M.
The Value of Perfect Information in Non-linear Utility Theory. SCHLEE, Edward E.
The Value-Ought of Self-Realization: A Phenomenological Approach. VELASSERRY, Sebastian.
Values, the Environment and the Creative Act. THOMAS, John C.
Verily, Nietzsche's Judgment of Jesus. ROTH, Robin A.
A Vision of the Health Decisions Movement. CRAWSHAW, Ralph.
Well-Being and Time. VELLEMAN, J David.
What is Philosophy of Culture? (in Polish). NOWICKI, Andrzej.
Wittgenstein and the Transmission of Traditions. O'HEAR, Anthony.

VALUING
A Case for Apathy. NEUMANN, Michael.
Knowing and Valuing Fairness. HINTON, J M.

VAN AKEN, J
More Axioms for the Set-Theoretic Hierarchy. POLLARD, Stephen.

VAN FRAASSEN, B
Believing What We Do Not See: The Case Against van Fraassen's Conception of Observation. DOBSON, Andrew.
Definite Descriptions. DANIELS, Charles B.
Embeddability, Syntax, and Semantics in Accounts of Scientific Theories. TURNEY, Peter.
Explanation and the Theory of Questions. CROSS, Charles B.
A Note on Van Fraassen's Explanatory Contrastiveness. PAPRZYCKA, Katarzyna.
On Saving the Phenomena and the Mice: A Reply to Bourgeois Concerning Van Fraassen's Image of Science. FOSS, Jeff.
State-Spaces and Meaning Relations Among Predicates. ARNTZENIUS, Frank.
Two Principles of Bayesian Epistemology. TALBOTT, W J.

VAN GELDER, T
Nuclear Stalemate: A Superior Escape from the Dilemmas of Deterrence. SCHONSHECK, Jonathan.

VAN HELMONT, J
"Visages de Van Helmont, depuis Hélène Metzger jusqu'aà Walter Pagel" in *Études sur/Studies on Hélène Metzger*, HALLEUX, Robert.

VAN INWAGEN, P
Could This Be Magic?. JUBIEN, Michael.
Response to van Inwagen's "Logic and the Free Will Problem". SLOTE, Michael.

VAN ROOIJEN, J
Epiphenomenalism and Machines: A Discussion of Van Rooijen's Critique of Popper. PECNJAK, Davor.
Van Rooijen and Mayr versus Popper: Is the Universe Causally Closed?. SETTLE, Tom.

VANBERG, V
Hayek's Theory of Cultural Evolution: An Evaluation in the Light of Vanberg's Critique. HODGSON, Geoffrey M.

VARIABLE(S)
Causality in Sociological Research. KARPINSKI, Jakub.
The Institutionalization of Organizational Ethics. SIMS, Ronald R.
The t-Variable Method in Gentzen-Style Automatic Theorem Proving. EDWALD, Tryggvi.

VARIETY
"What Now Little Man? Comedy, Tragedy, and the Politics of Antihumanism" in *The Question of Humanism: Challenges and Possibilities*, AJZENSTAT, Samuel.
The Answer to Dziobiak's Question. PALASINSKI, Marek.
Axiomatization of the De Morgan Type Rules. HERRMANN, B.
B-Varieties with Normal Free Algebras. TEMBROWSKI, Bronislaw.
On Some Operators on Pseudovarieties. GRACZYNSKA, Ewa.
The Pincovian Persuasion: Six Problems in Virtue Ethics (A Free Response to Seung). BUDZISZEWSKI, J.
Relatively Congruence-Distributive Subquasivarieties of Filtral Varieties. CZELAKOWSKI, Janusz.

VASCONCELOS, J
El sentido del Universo en José Vasconcelos (2a parte). PATIÑO, Joel Rodríguez.
El sentido del Universo en José Vasconcelos. PATIÑO, Joel Rodríguez.

VASILYEV, N
"The Logical Ideas of N A Vasiliev and Modern Logic" in *Logic, Methodology and Philosophy of Science, VIII*, SMIRNOV, V A.

VATICAN
"The Vatican 'Instruction' and Surrogate Motherhood" in *Beyond Baby M: Ethical Issues in New Reproductive Techniques*, BERQUIST, Richard.

VATTIMO, G
(Post-) Metaphysik und (Post-) Moderne: Zur Sache des "schwachen Denkens". FRÜCHTL, Josef.
Las aventuras de la differencia (G Vattimo). PEGUEROLES, Juan.

VAUVENARGUES, L
Amour de l'être et ambition de gloire: le spinozisme de Vauvenargues. BOVE, Laurent.

VECTOR(S)
Vectors and Change. BIGELOW, John and PARGETTER, Robert.

VEDANTA
Some Self-Centric Tendencies in Sankara Advaita. JHINGRAN, Saral.

VEGETARIANISM
Ecofeminism and the Eating of Animals. ADAMS, Carol J.
Reply to Weir: Unnecessary Fear, Nutrition, and Vegetarianism. SAPONTZIS, Steve F.
Response to Sapontzis's Reply. WEIR, Jack.
So Animal a Human..., or the Moral Relevance of Being An Omnivore. GEORGE, Kathryn Paxton.
Unnecessary Pain, Nutrition, and Vegetarianism. WEIR, Jack.
Vegetarianism and Virtue: On Gassendi's Epicurean Defense. MICHAEL, Emily.

VELAZQUEZ, D
Velázquez et Goya. PIERRE, Christian (trans).

VERB(S)
Phrases nominales énonciatives et phrases verbales. STAHL, Gérold.

VERIFICATION
Artificial Intelligence: Its Scope and Limits. FETZER, James H.
A Hindu Perspective on the Philosophy of Religion. SHARMA, Arvind.
Wittgenstein and Contemporary Philosophy of Language. RUNDLE, Bede.
"Sigma": conoscenza e metodo. SAVA, Gabriella.
Anti-Realism Untouched. MELIA, Joseph.
The Roles of Predictions in Science and Religion. SCHOEN, Edward L.
Verification of Concurrent Programs: the Automata-Theoretic Framework. VARDI, Moshe Y.
Verification, Falsification and Cancellation in KT. WILLIAMSON, Timothy.
Verification, Falsification, and the Logic of Enquiry. MILNE, Peter.

VERIFICATIONISM
"Quine on Underdetermination" in *Perspectives on Quine*, BERGSTRÖM, Lars.
Verificationism and Anti-Realism. ROGERSON, Kenneth.

VERISIMILITUDE
"Corroboration, Verisimilitude, and the Success of Science" in *Imre Lakatos and Theories of Scientific Change*, NIINILUOTO, Ilkka.
A Note on Verisimilitude and Relativization to Problems. MONGIN, Philippe.
On Comparison of Theories by Their Contents. WOLENSKI, Jan.
Verisimilitude Based on Concept Analysis. ORLOWSKA, Ewa.
Verisimilitude by Power Relations. ODDIE, Graham.
Verisimilitude by Power Relations: A Response to Oddie. BRINK, Chris and HEIDEMA, Johannes.

VERNANT, J
Mythe et raison: Propos contemporains. FONTAINE-DE VISSCHER, Luce.

VERNENGO, R
On Ideal Form, Empowering Norms, and "Normative Functions". PAULSON, Stanley L.

VIABILITY
The Ethics of *Ex Utero* Research on Spare 'Non-Viable' IVF Human Embryos. BAYLIS, Françoise E.

VICE(S)
Anger as a Vice: A Maimonidean Critique of Aristotle's Ethics. FRANK, Daniel H.
Boors and Bumpkins, Snobs and Snoots. GODLOVITCH, S.
Natural Virtues, Natural Vices. BAIER, Annette C.
The Unity of the Vices. JACOBS, Jonathan and ZEIS, John.

VICKERS, B
In Defense of Plato: A Short Polemic. ROOCHNIK, David.

VICO
Human Nature and Historical Knowledge: Hume, Hegel and Vico. POMPA, Leon.
Vico: A Study of the 'New Science' (Second Edition). POMPA, Leon.
Die Wiederkehr im Unterschied. PEETZ, Siegbert.
Congruenza, schematismo, sintesi: Prospettive leibniziane intorno al criterio di verità secondo Giambattista Vico. PINCHARD, Bruno.
La filosofia: in soccorso de' governi. COLAPIETRA, Raffaele.
Gestualità e mito: i due caratteri distintivi della lingua originaria secondo Vico. CANTELLI, Gianfranco.
Giambattista Vico and the Quarrel between the Ancients and the Moderns. LEVINE, Joseph M.
Heracles and the Passage from Nature to Culture in G Vico's *La Scienza Nuova*. MIUCCIO, Giuliana.
Nuove ricerche sul 'Liber metaphysicus' *di Giambattista Vico*. CACCIATORE, Giuseppe.
Vico in Voegelin. CAPORALI, Riccardo.
Vico, pensatore antimoderno: L'interpretazione di Eric Voegelin. ZANETTI, Gianfrancesco.
Vico: dalla collocazione storica all'efficiacia teoretica. FRANCHINI, Raffaello.

VICTIM(S)
Thinking the Unthinkable: Meanings of the Holocaust. GOTTLIEB, Roger S (ed).
Explaining Without Blaming the Victim. ILLINGWORTH, Patricia M L.
Free Will and Being a Victim. SMILANSKY, S.
In Praise of Clutter as a Necessary Part of the Feminist Perspective. AYIM, Maryann.
Oppression and Victimization; Choice and Responsibility. WENDELL, Susan.
Reasonable Evidence of Reasonableness. KELMAN, Mark.
Reply to Maryann Ayim's "In Praise of Clutter as a Necessary Part of the Feminist Perspective". WENDELL, Susan.

VIDONI
Ignoramus, Ignorabimus!. BUENO, Gustavo.

VIENNA CIRCLE
Coherence, Anti-realism, and the Vienna Circle. YOUNG, James O.

VILLARI, P
La filosofia civile di Pasquale Villari. URBINATI, Nadia.

VIOLATION(S)
Rights and Rights Violators: A New Approach to the Nature of Rights. GERT, Heather J.

VIOLENCE
In the Interest of Peace: A Spectrum of Philosophical Views. KLEIN, Kenneth H (ed).
"Absolute Violence and the Idea of War" in *In the Interest of Peace: A Spectrum of Philosophical Views*, HOLMES, Robert.
"Camus Revisited: Neither Victim nor Executioner" in *In the Interest of Peace: A Spectrum of Philosophical Views*, BOVE, Laurence.
"On the Deep Structure of Violence" in *In the Interest of Peace: A Spectrum of Philosophical Views*, LITKE, Robert.
"Terrorism and Violence: A Moral Perspective" in *Issues in War and Peace: Philosophical Inquiries*, HOLMES, Robert L.
Animal Liberation as a Valid Response to Structural Violence. LISZT, Amy.
Discourses on Political Violence: The Problem of Coherence. DU TOIT, A B.
Éthique et technique: bioéthique. KEMP, Peter.
Exploring Extreme Violence (Torture). MACHAN, Tibor R.
Filosofía de la violencia. MAGGIOLO, Roberto Jiménez.
Liberation Theology and the Interpretation of Political Violence. SONTAG, Frederick.
A lógica do sentido na filosofia hermenêutica. COSTA, Miguel Dias.
Porosity: Violence and the Question of Politics in Heidegger's *Introduction to Metaphysics*. MC NEILL, William.
Response to Finsen's "Response to Lizst's Animal Liberation as a Valid Response to Structural Violence". LISZT, Amy.
Response to Lizst's "Animal Liberation as a Valid Response to Structural Violence". FINSEN, Susan.
Structural Violence and Fallible Plans: A Case Study in Philosophy and Educational Planning. MOULDER, J.
Thinking the Other Without Violence? An Analysis of the Relation Between the Philosophy of Lévinas and Feminism. MANNING, Robert J S.
Violence: Can It Be Ethical?. FRINGS, Manfred.
What is Terrorism?. PRIMORATZ, Igor.
Whose Right? Ronald Dworkin, Women, and Pornographers. LANGTON, Rae.

VIRTUE(S)
Aristotelis Ethica Evdemia. WALZER, R R (ed).
The Early Essays and Ethics of Robert Boyle. HARWOOD, John T (ed).
Ethics with Aristotle. BROADIE, Sarah.
A Guided Tour of Selections from Aristotle's Nicomachean Ethics. BIFFLE, Christopher.
Kant's System of Rights. MULHOLLAND, Leslie A.
Kant's Theory of Freedom. ALLISON, Henry E.
Mind in Action: Essays in the Philosophy of Mind. RORTY, Amelie Oksenberg.
A Philosophy of Morals. HELLER, Agnes.
A Progress of Sentiments: Reflections on Hume's "Treatise". BAIER, Annette C.
Science and Moral Values. VOLLRATH, John.
Theory and Practice in Medical Ethics. GRABER, Glenn C.
"Are There Virtues Inherent in a Profession?" in *Ethics, Trust, and the Professions: Philosophical and Cultural Aspects*, MEILAENDER, Gilbert.
"Natural Affection and Responsibility for Character: A Critique of Kantian Views of the Virtues" in *Identity, Character, and Morality: Essays in Moral Psychology*, TRIANOSKY, Gregory.
"Some Advantages of Virtue Ethics" in *Identity, Character, and Morality: Essays in Moral Psychology*, SLOTE, Michael.
"The Virtue of Feeling and the Feeling of Virtue" in *Feminist Ethics*, SPELMAN, Elizabeth V.
"Virtue Theory" in *A Companion to Ethics*, PENCE, Greg.
"Virtue, The Missing Link to the Last Volume of the *Treatise*" in *Studies on Mario Bunge's "Treatise"*, FORMAN, Frank.
"Why Honesty Is a Hard Virtue" in *Identity, Character, and Morality: Essays in Moral Psychology*, BAIER, Annette C.
The Ambiguity of Political Virtue: A Response to Wolgast. LEVINSON, Sanford.
Antropología en la Q D "De virtutibus in communi" de Santo Tomás. CORSO, Laura E.
Aristotle's Much Maligned *Megalopsychos*. CURZER, Howard J.
Authenticity as Virtue (in Dutch). STRUYKER BOUDIER, C E M.
Benevolence and Resentment. STEPHENSON, Wendell.
Boors and Bumpkins, Snobs and Snoots. GODLOVITCH, S.
Comments: "A Moral Ideal for Everyone and No One". HUNT, Lester.
The Consequences of Endorsing Sentimental Homicide. BARRY, Robert L.
La crítica kantiana a la virtud como término medio. MAURI, Margarita.
Deugden en plichtsbesef. STEUTEL, J W.
Divine Reason and Virtue in St Thomas's Natural Law Theory. KILLORAN, John B.
Ethical Impressionism: A Response to Braybrooke. BONEVAC, Daniel.
The Ethical Theory of Peter A Bertocci. PADGETT, Jack F.
The Good in Plato's *Gorgias*. WHITE, F C.
A Great Philosopher's Not So Great Account of Great Virtue: Aristotle's Treatment of 'Greatness of Soul'. CURZER, Howard J.
Historical Perspectives on the Morality of Virtue. WHITE, Richard.
Ignatian Discernment: A Philosophical Analysis. HUGHES, Gerard J.
In a Crazy Time the Crazy Come Out Well: Machiavelli and the Cosmology of His Day. BASU, Sammy.
Loyalty: The Police. EWIN, R E.
Making the Citizens Good: Aristotle's City and Its Contemporary Relevance. SIMPSON, Peter.
Montaigne's 'Des Cannibales' and Natural Sources of Virtue. HOROWITZ, Maryanne Cline.
Murphy and Mercy. ADLER, Jacob.
Natural Virtues, Natural Vices. BAIER, Annette C.
No Rules without Virtues: No Virtues without Rules. BRAYBROOKE, David.
On the Teachability of ARETé in Plato (in Czechoslovakian). MOURAL, Josef.
The Pincovian Persuasion: Six Problems in Virtue Ethics (A Free Response to Seung). BUDZISZEWSKI, J.
La prudencia (II). DERISI, Octavio N.
Rational Suicide and Christian Virtue. MAGUIRE, Daniel C.
Reclaiming Virtue: Philosophy in the Field of Educational Technology. BELLAND, John and SMITH, Phillip L.
The Regulation of Virtue: Cross-Currents in Professional Ethics. JENNINGS, Bruce.
Salisburian Stakes: The Uses of 'Tyranny' in John of Salisbury's *Policraticus*. FORHAN, Kate Langdon.
The Scope of Deliberation: A Conflict in Aquinas. IRWIN, T H.
Sex and Virtue. PUTMAN, D.
The Significance of the Moral Concept of Virtue in St Augustine's Ethics. TORCHIA, N Joseph.
Solitude. KOCH, Philip J.
St Thomas on the Motives of Unjust Acts. WEITHMAN, Paul J.
Toughness as a Political Virtue. GALSTON, William.
The Unity of Moral Virtues in Aristotle's *Nicomachean Ethics*. TELFER, Elizabeth.
The Unity of the Vices. JACOBS, Jonathan and ZEIS, John.
Vegetarianism and Virtue: On Gassendi's Epicurean Defense. MICHAEL, Emily.
Virtue Ethics and Maori Ethics. PERRETT, Roy W and PATTERSON, John.
Virtue Ethics and the Appeal to Human Nature. WOODRUFF, Paul.
The Virtue of a Representative. WOLGAST, Elizabeth.
Virtue Theory and Abortion. HURSTHOUSE, Rosalind.
Virtues and Rules. ROBERTS, Robert C.
Virtues and Values: A Platonic Account. SEUNG, T K.
Vlastos on the Unity of Virtue: Why Pauline Predication Will Not Save the Biconditionality Thesis. WAKEFIELD, Jerome C.
What is Virtue Ethics All About?. TRIANOSKY, Gregory.
'Following Nature' in Butler's Sermons. BRINTON, Alan.

VISION
Berkeley's Revolution in Vision. ATHERTON, Margaret.
"Poetic Vision and the Hope for Peace" in *Celebrating Peace*, LEVERTOV, Denise.
Reply to Teller's "Simpler Arguments Might Work Better". HARDIN, C L.
Simpler Arguments Might Work Better. TELLER, Davida Y.
Die Sprachen und das Denken: Klein Bestandsaufnahme zum linguistischen Relativismus (Sapir-Whorf-Hypothese). FRANZEN, Winfried.
Visione in Dio e visione di Dio nella filosofia di Malebranche. NICOLOSI, Salvatore.

VISUAL
Insularity and the Persistence of Perceptual Illusion. CAM, Philip.
The Praxiology of Perception: Visual Orientations and Practical Action. COULTER, Jeff and PARSONS, E D.
Reply to Wilson's "Shadows on the Cave Wall: Philosophy and Visual Science". HARDIN, C L.
Shadows on the Cave Wall: Philosophy and Visual Science. WILSON, Hugh R.
Visual Fictions. CURRIE, Gregory.
Visual Perception and the Wages of Indeterminacy. MONTGOMERY, Richard.
Why Are Graphs so Central in Science?. KROHN, Roger.

VISUAL ART(S)
Unsere postmoderne Moderne (Second Edition). WELSCH, Wolfgang.
"Art of the Untruth? On Post Modern Visual Art" in *XIth International Congress in Aesthetics, Nottingham 1988*, KAULINGFREKS, Ruud.
Perceptual Aspects of Art for the Blind. ARNHEIM, Rudolf.
Perennial Modernity: Forms as Aesthetic and Symbolic. MAQUET, Jacques.
Le statut sémiotique de la perspective dans l'oeuvre picturale. CARANI, Marie.
The Very Idea of Perfect Realism. FISHER, John Andrew.

VITALISM
Bergsonism. DELEUZE, Gilles.
VITTORINI, E
Filosofia e cultura ne "Il Politecnico" de E Vittorini. DE SIENA, Santa.
VLASTOS, G
Forms and Causes In Plato's *Phaedo*. BYRNE, Christopher.
Vlastos on the Unity of Virtue: Why Pauline Predication Will Not Save the Biconditionality Thesis. WAKEFIELD, Jerome C.
VOCABULARY(-RIES)
The Philosopher's Dictionary. MARTIN, Robert M.
The Irony of Richard Rorty and the Question of Political Judgment. WEISLOGEL, Eric L.
VOCATION(S)
Markets, Managers and Theory in Education. HALLIDAY, John.
"John Stuart Mill and the East India Company" in *A Cultivated Mind: Essays On J S Mill Presented to John M Robson*, LLOYD, Trevor.
Metafísica de la vocación. AGUAYO CRUZ, Enrique Ignacio.
VOEGELIN, E
The Balance of Consciousness: Eric Voegelin's Political Theory. KEULMAN, Kenneth.
Eric Voegelin's View of History as a Drama of Transfiguration. HUGHES, Glenn.
The Life of Order and the Order of Life: Eric Voegelin on Modernity and the Problem of Philosophical Anthropology. LEVY, David J.
Vico in Voegelin. CAPORALI, Riccardo.
Vico, pensatore antimoderno: L'interpretazione di Eric Voegelin. ZANETTI, Gianfrancesco.
VOGEL, D
A Reaction to Vogel's "The Ethical Roots of Business". MC MAHON, Thomas F.
VOICE
"On Translation and M/others: Samuel Beckett's *The Unnamable*" in *Hermeneutics and the Poetic Motion, Translation Perspectives V—1990*, HANSON, Susan.
Exit, Voice, and Ethics. KEELEY, Michael and GRAHAM, Jill W.
VOID
Aristotle, the Direction Problem, and the Structure of the Sublunar Realm. KRONZ, Frederick.
VOLITION(S)
Aristotle's Psychology. ROBINSON, Daniel N.
The Conceptual Bind in Defining the Volitional Component of Alcoholism. VATZ, Richard E and WEINBERG, Lee S.
Intenzione e azione in Wittgenstein. RAINONE, Antonio.
Is Davidson a Volitionist In Spite of Himself?. CLEVELAND, Timothy.
VOLTAIRE
"Et la religion le remplit de fureur...". BOULAD-AYOUB, Josiane.
VOLUNTARINESS
Responsibility and Criminal Liability. SISTARE, C T.
A Case Against Dutch Euthanasia. FENIGSEN, Richard.
Volunteering Children. MC DONNELL, Kevin.
VOLUNTARISM
The Condemnation of 1277: Another Light on Scotist Ethics. INGHAM, Mary E.
Epistemic Obligations and Doxastic Voluntarism. GOGGANS, Phil.
L'affirmation de l'existence de Dieu selon Austin Farrer. HENDERSON, Edward H.
VOLUNTARY
Ethics with Aristotle. BROADIE, Sarah.
The Ethico-Legal Meaning of Voluntary. BOURKE, Vernon J.
VON BALTHASAR, H
The Immutability of God in the Theology of Hans Urs Von Balthasar. O'HANLON, G F.
VON MISES, L
Hermeneutics: A Protreptic. JOHNSON, Gregory R.
VON MISES, R
El azar objetivo como medida matemática de desorden. MARTÍNEZ, Sergio.
VON NEUMANN, J
En busca del contenido físico de la regla de Luders. MARTÍNEZ, Sergio and MURILLO, Lorena.
VON WRIGHT, G
Professor Von Wright on Action. DEWASHI, Mahadev.
Time, Change and Contradiction. SMITH, Joseph Wayne.
VOTING
Independence of Irrelevant Alternatives in the Theory of Voting. BORDES, Georges and TIDEMAN, Nicolaus.
The Pareto Rule and Strategic Voting. MAC INTYRE, Ian.
Presidential Campaigns, Television News and Voter Turnout. WALTER, Edward.
VOYEURISM
Just Looking: Voyeurism and the Grounds of Privacy. NATHAN, Daniel O.
VULGARITY
Vulgarity and Authenticity: Dimensions of Otherness in the World of Jean-Paul Sartre. CHARMÉ, Stuart Zane.
"Un essai de vulgarisation" in *Études sur/Studies on Hélène Metzger*, BENSAUDE-VINCENT, Bernadette.
VULNERABILITY
"Foreknowledge and the Vulnerability of God" in *The Philosophy in Christianity*, LUCAS, J R.
Response to Mendus's "Liberal Man". BINNS, Peter.
WADDINGTON, C
Epigenetic Landscaping: Waddington's Use of Cell Fate Bifurcation Diagrams. GILBERT, Scott F.
WAINWRIGHT, W
Wainwright, Maritain and Aquinas on Transcendent Experiences. ROY, Louis.
WAISMANN, F
H L A Hart and the "Open Texture" of Language. BIX, Brian.
WAKING
Aristotle on Sleep and Dreams. GALLOP, David (trans).
WALLON, H
Sobre la génesis de la conciencia de si mismo. BEJARANO, Teresa.
WALZER, M
The Making of a Nuclear Peace: The Task of Today's Just War Theorists. SICHOL, Marcia W.
Equality. MILLER, David.
Social Criticism and Political Philosophy. BARRY, Brian.
WANG, H
On a Complexity-Based Way of Constructivizing the Recursive Functions. KROON, F W and BURKHARD, W A.
WANTING
He Doesn't Really Want to Try. ADAMS, Frederick.
He Wants to Try. MELE, Alfred R.
Wanting, Getting, Having. HUMBERSTONE, I L.
WAR(S)
see also Nuclear War
Bertrand Russell. ALCARO, Mario.
In the Interest of Peace: A Spectrum of Philosophical Views. KLEIN, Kenneth H (ed).
Issues in War and Peace: Philosophical Inquiries. KUNKEL, Joseph (ed).
Understanding War: A Philosophical Inquiry. MC MURTRY, John.
Yoga on War and Peace. TIGUNAIT, Pandit Rajmani.
"Absolute Violence and the Idea of War" in *In the Interest of Peace: A Spectrum of Philosophical Views*, HOLMES, Robert.
"Christian Peacemakers in the Warmaking State" in *Celebrating Peace*, BERRIGAN, Daniel.
"The Credibility of Ecclesiastical Teaching on the Morality of War" in *Celebrating Peace*, YODER, John H.
"Exposing Warism" in *Issues in War and Peace: Philosophical Inquiries*, CADY, Duane L.
"Nonviolent Resistance as the Moral Equivalent of War" in *In the Interest of Peace: A Spectrum of Philosophical Views*, CHURCHILL, R Paul.
"Pragmatic Pacifism: A Methodology for Gaining the Ear of the Warist" in *In the Interest of Peace: A Spectrum of Philosophical Views*, SMITHKA, Paula.
"Strategy: A New Era?" in *The Tanner Lectures On Human Values, Volume XII*, LUTTWAK, Edward N.
"War and Peace" in *A Companion to Ethics*, MC MAHAN, Jeff.
"War and the Nation-State in Social Theory" in *Social Theory of Modern Societies: Anthony Giddens and His Critics*, SHAW, Martin.
"War, Omnicide, and Sanity: The Lesson of the Cuban Missile Crisis" in *Issues in War and Peace: Philosophical Inquiries*, SOMERVILLE, John.
The Anatomy of Aggression. LUPER-FOY, Steven.
Clausewitz ou l'oeuvre inachevée: l'esprit de la guerre. PHILONENKO, Alexis.
Ghost Story (in German). SAUTET, Marc.
Hobbes and the Myth of "Final War". PASQUALUCCI, Paolo.
Kant's Theory of Peace and the Main Aspects of the Recent Discussion Surrounding It (in German). ZAHN, Manfred.
Nietzsche: Moralist or Immoralist?—The Verdict of the European Protestant Theologians in the First World War. BAILEY, Charles E.
The Nurture of War: "Just War" Theory's Contribution. SANTONI, Ronald E.
The Occasion Fleeting: A Talk with Richard Selzer. JOSYPH, Peter.
On the Morality of Waging War Against the State. MILLER, Seumas.
Le partage des philosophes. SOULEZ, Philippe.
Réflexiones sur l'idéee de la guerre dans la philosophie présocratique. FREUND, Julien.
Self-Defence and National Defence. DE ROOSE, Frank.
Le stratège militaire. POIRIER, Lucien.
The Unjust Treatment of Polemarchus. PAGE, Carl.
La via della pace: in merito ad un recente libro. ZANUSO, Francesca.
War and Crime. HOLYST, Brunon.

WARDEKKER, K
Kennen en kunnen: Een repliek op Wardekker. HARBERS, Hans.

WARRANT(S)
Firth's Critique of Epistemological Rule-Utilitarianism. SHOPE, Robert K.

WATKINS, J
The Last Word on Induction?. HOWSON, Colin.

WATRAS, J
The Bright Side of Textbook Controversies. SCAHILL, John.

WAVE MECHANICS
A Comment on Maxwell's Resolution of the Wave/Particle Dilemma. SQUIRES, Euan J.
Distant Action in Classical Electromagnetic Theory. MUNDY, Brent.
Quantum Propension Theory: A Testable Resolution of the Wave/Particle Dilemma. MAXWELL, Nicholas.
Realism and the Collapse of the Wave-Packet. KRIPS, Henry.

WAVE(S)
Particles and Waves: Historical Essays in the Philosophy of Science. ACHINSTEIN, Peter.
Hypotheses, Probability, and Waves. ACHINSTEIN, Peter.

WEAKNESS(ES)
Weakness of the Will. GOSLING, Justin.
Weakness of Will and Rational Action. AUDI, Robert.
Weakness of Will as a Species of Executive Cowardice. SWANTON, Christine.

WEALTH
Approaches to the Theory of Purusarthas. RAJAN, R Sundara.

WEAPON(S)
Military Ethics: Looking Toward the Future. FOTION, Nicholas G.
Biotechnology and Warfare. REINIKAINEN, Pekka.

WEBER, M
The Formation of the Modern State: A Reconstruction of Max Weber's Arguments. AXTMANN, Roland.
Los fundamentos discursivos de la democracia y los conflictos de intereses. GUARIGLIA, Osvaldo.
Marx, Engels and Max Weber on Eastern Societies—With a Special Respect to China (in Hungarian). DRUCKER, György.
Sociologie in de Weimarrepubliek. HABERMAS, Jürgen.
La storia universale come storia comparata in Max Weber. DI MARCO, Giuseppe Antonio.
Wertfreiheit und Ethik in den Sozial-und Naturwissenschaften. ZIMMERMANN, Rolf.

WEBER, W
Models and Concepts of Ideology. RITSERT, Jürgen.

WEIGHT
Keynesian Uncertainty and the Weight of Arguments. RUNDE, Jochen.

WEIL, E
Après Weil, avec Weil: Une lecture de Gilbert Kirscher. LABARRIÈRE, Pierre-Jean.

WEIL, S
Peter Winch, *Simone Weil: The Just Balance*. WILLIAMS, Rowan.
Les présupposés métaphysiques de la "lisibilité" de l'être. KÜHN, Rolf.

WEINBERGER, O
The Institution of Law. BANKOWSKI, Zenon.

WEISBERG, R
Is the Creative Process in Art a Form of Puzzle Solving?. LEDDY, Thomas.

WEISS, P
"'Aufbruch oder Schwanengesang'?" in *XIth International Congress in Aesthetics, Nottingham 1988*, KRENZLIN, Norbert.

WEITHMAN, P
Religious Commitment and Secular Reason: A Reply to Professor Weithman. AUDI, Robert.

WEITZ, M
Why 'Art' Doesn't Have Two Senses. ROWE, M W.

WELFARE
Gerechtigkeit, Wohlfahrt und Rationalität. SCHMIDT, Johannes.
A Defense of Equal Opportunity for Welfare. ARNESON, Richard J.
Difficulties with the Principle of Equal Opportunity for Welfare. CHRISTIANO, Thomas.
Equality of What: Welfare, Resources, or Capabilities?. DANIELS, Norman.
Preferences and Politics. SUNSTEIN, Cass R.
The Problem of Unauthorized Welfare. VALLENTYNE, Peter.
Welfarism and Utilitarianism: A Rehabilitation. NG, Yew-Kwang.
Why Surfers Should Be Fed: The Liberal Case for an Unconditional Basic Income. VAN PARIJS, Philippe.

WELFARE STATE
Convictions. HOOK, Sidney.
Active Citizenship as Political Obligation. SKILLEN, Tony.
German Collectivism and the Welfare State. NEAMAN, Elliot Yale.
The New Consensus: II—The Democratic Welfare State. FRIEDMAN, Jeffrey.
The Philosophy of the Welfare State. BARRY, Norman P.
Swedish Model or Swedish Culture?. TRAGARDH, Lars.
The Welfare State: What is Left?. PRYCHITKO, David L.

WELL-BEING
Jurisculture, Volume I: Greece and Rome. DORSEY, Gray L.
Justice and the Good Life. DWORKIN, Ronald.
Brand Blanshard and Gewirth: Ethics and Rights. HOWIE, John.
A Comment on the Argument Between Gewirth and his Critics. ROSS, Steven.
Land, Well-Being and Compensation. PARGETTER, Robert and YOUNG, Robert and BIGELOW, John.
Well-Being and Time. VELLEMAN, J David.

WESTERN
see Occidental
Other Selves: Philosophers on Friendship. PAKALUK, Michael (ed).
"'Tradition' et 'Innovation' dans la musique" in *XIth International Congress in Aesthetics, Nottingham 1988*, TAMBA, Akira.
Boston University Studies in Philosophy and Religion, Volumes 1-10. SMART, Ninian.
Heidegger e o Oriente ou da Extrema In-diferença Ocidental. DO CARMO SILVA, Carlos Henrique.
A Survey of Critical Theories of "Western Marxism". YUJIN, Zhao.
Zande Logic and Western Logic. JENNINGS, Richard C.

WESTERN CIVILIZATION
Amythia: Crisis in the Natural History of Western Culture. RUE, Loyal D.
Convictions. HOOK, Sidney.
Dream and Culture: An Anthropological Study of the Western Intellectual Tradition. PARMAN, Susan.
Law, Culture, and Values: Essays in Honor of Gray L Dorsey. VOJCANIN, Sava Alexander (ed).
Discovering God in Western Civilization. BRESLAUER, S Daniel.

WESTERN PHILOSOPHY
Philosophy in World Perspective: A Comparative Hermeneutic of the Major Theories. DILWORTH, David A.
Weakness of the Will. GOSLING, Justin.
Has the History of Philosophy Ruined the Environment?. ATTFIELD, Robin.

WHEWELL, W
Hypotheses, Probability, and Waves. ACHINSTEIN, Peter.
Whewell's Developmental Psychologism: A Victorian Account of Scientific Progress. METCALFE, John F.

WHISTLEBLOWING
Can Whistleblowing Be FULLY Legitimated? A Theoretical Discussion. DANDEKAR, Natalie.
Commentary on Layton's "Engineering Needs a Loyal Opposition". ANDERSON, Robert M (and others).

WHITE, H
Hayden White: "Historicism" as Linguistic Relativism in Historiography (in Polish). POMORSKI, Jan.

WHITE, S
The Ethics of Postmodernism. GIBBONS, Michael T.

WHITEHEAD
Archetypal Process: Self and Divine in Whitehead, Jung, and Hillman. GRIFFIN, David Ray (ed).
"Eternal Objects and Archetypes, Past and Depth: Response to Hopper" in *Archetypal Process: Self and Divine in Whitehead, Jung, and Hillman*, COBB JR, John B.
"Imaginal Soul and Ideational Spirit: A Response to James Heisig" in *Archetypal Process: Self and Divine in Whitehead, Jung, and Hillman*, WINQUIST, Charles E.
"Jung and Whitehead on Self and Divine: The Necessity for Symbol and Myth" in *Archetypal Process: Self and Divine in Whitehead, Jung, and Hillman*, SLUSSER, Gerald H.
"Language as Metaphorical: A Reply to John Cobb" in *Archetypal Process: Self and Divine in Whitehead, Jung, and Hillman*, HOPPER, Stanley R.
"The Mystique of the Nonrational and a New Spirituality" in *Archetypal Process: Self and Divine in Whitehead, Jung, and Hillman*, HEISIG, James W.
"The Necessity for Symbol and Myth: A Literary Amplification" in *Archetypal Process: Self and Divine in Whitehead, Jung, and Hillman*, SELLERY, J'Nan Morse.
"Once More: The Cavern Beneath the Cave" in *Archetypal Process: Self and Divine in Whitehead, Jung, and Hillman*, HOPPER, Stanley R.
"Psychocosmetics and the Underworld Connection" in *Archetypal Process: Self and Divine in Whitehead, Jung, and Hillman*, KELLER, Catherine.
Aristotelian and Whiteheadian Conceptions of Actuality: I. FETZ, Reto Luzius and FELT, James W.
Aristotelian and Whiteheadian Conceptions of Actuality: II. FETZ, Reto Luzius and FELT, James W.
Blanshard on Philosophical Style. SMITH, John E.
Independent Evidence of Religion. D'SOUZA, Felix.
Knowledge as Active, Aesthetic, and Hypothetical: A Pragmatic Interpretation of Whitehead's Cosmology. FRISINA, Warren G.

WHITEHEAD
The Matrix of Personality: A Whiteheadian Corroboration of Harry Stack Sullivan's Interpersonal Theory of Psychiatry. REGAN, Thomas J.
The Modes of Actuality. FORD, Lewis S.
Process Thought and the Spaciness of Mind. EDWARDS, Rem B.
The Reformed Subjectivist Principle Revisited. FORD, Lewis S.
Whitehead and Genuine Evil. BARINEAU, R Maurice.
Whitehead and Leibniz: Conflict and Convergence. MOONEY, Tim.

WHITMAN
George Kateb's Ahistorical Emersonianism. MARX, Leo.
Strange Attractors: How Individualists Connect to Form Democratic Unity. ROSENBLUM, Nancy.
Walt Whitman and the Culture of Democracy. KATEB, George.
Walt Whitman: Jacobin Poet of American Democracy. MOSHER, Michael.
Whitman and Memory: A Response to Kateb. BROMWICH, David.

WHOLE(S)
Parts of Classes. LEWIS, David.
G E Moore on the Values of Whole and Parts: A Critique. PAL, Jagat.
Least Parts and Greatest Wholes Variations on a Theme in Spinoza. SACKSTEDER, William.
Matrix Representation of Husserl's Part-Whole-Foundation Theory. BLECKSMITH, Richard and NULL, Gilbert.
Partial Wholes. BARNES, Jonathan.

WHOLENESS
Holism and Nonseparability. HEALEY, Richard A.

WIGAN, A
Two Brains, Two Minds? Wigan's Theory of Mental Duality. PUCCETTI, Roland.

WILDERNESS
The River of the Mother of God, and Other Essays by Aldo Leopold. FLADER, Susan L (ed).
El eslabón entre la conservación y el desarrollo sostenible: Maribel Gómez Mata. JANZEN, Daniel H.

WILDLIFE
Leopold's "Means and Ends in Wild Life Management". HARGROVE, Eugene C and CALLICOTT, J Baird.
Means and Ends in Wild Life Management. LEOPOLD, Aldo.

WILKERSON, T
"T E Wilkerson on Originality in Art and Morals" in *XIth International Congress in Aesthetics, Nottingham 1988*, SPECTOR, Arnold.

WILKINSON, M
Comments on Wilkinson's Commentary. RIDLEY, Mark.

WILL
Hegel: o la rebelión contra el límite. IZUZQUIZA, Ignacio.
The Philosophical Theology of John Duns Scotus. ADAMS, Marilyn McCord (ed).
Plotin: Traité sur la liberté et la volonté de l'Un. LEROUX, Georges.
Readings in Existential Psychology and Psychiatry. HOELLER, Keith (ed).
Weakness of the Will. GOSLING, Justin.
Freedom and Human Nature. FLEW, Antony.
L'interpretazione del conflitto fra norme nell'ultimo Kelsen. CELANO, Brun.
Kierkegaardian Transitions: Paradox and Pathos. FERREIRA, M Jamie.
King Solomon and Everyman: A Problem in Coordinating Conflicting Moral Intuitions. RORTY, Amelie Oksenberg.
Libertad y necesidad en el 'Cur Deus Homo' de San Anselmo de Canterbury (segunda parte). CORTI, E C.
Nuestra voluntad es "de Dios". FERNÁNDEZ BURILLO, Santiago A.
Nuestra voluntad es "de Dios". FERNÁNDEZ BURILLO, Santiago A.
On the Irreducibility of the Will. GARCIA, J L A.
Προαιρεσις in Epictetus. DOBBIN, Robert.
Representation and the Freedom of the Will. STAMPE, Dennis W.
Response to Stampe's "Representation and the Freedom of the Will". GIBSON, Martha I.
Schopenhauer en de kunst van het verzaken. DE MARTELAERE, Patricia.
Schopenhauers "objektives Interesse". NEYMEYR, Barbara.
Schopenhauers Wille und Platons Eros. VOIGTLÄNDER, Hanns-Dieter.
Wahnbildung und Wirklichkeit des Willens. GRÄTZEL, Stephan.
Weakness of Will and Rational Action. AUDI, Robert.
Weakness of Will as a Species of Executive Cowardice. SWANTON, Christine.
Wille, Willkür, and the Imputability of Immoral Actions. HUDSON, Hud.
Willkür und Wille bei Kant. STEKELER-WEITHOFER, Pirmin.
The Word as Will and Idea: Semantics in the *Tractatus*. COHEN, Daniel H.

WILL TO POWER
Nietzsche (I and II): The Will to Power as Art, The Eternal Recurrence of the Same—Heidegger. KRELL, David Farrell (trans).
Nietzsche (III and IV): The Will to Power as Knowledge and as Metaphysics—Heidegger. KRELL, David Farrell (ed).
Nietzsche On Truth and Philosophy. CLARK, Maudemarie.
Nietzsche: A Frenzied Look. ACKERMANN, Robert John.
From Philosophy to Politics: On Nietzsche's Ironic Metaphysics of Will to Power. PARENS, Erik.
From Philosophy to Politics: On Nietzsche's Ironic Metaphysics of Will to Power. PARENS, Erik.
Nietzsche on Woman. THOMPSON, J L.

WILL, F
Concerning F L Will's *Beyond Deduction*. SINGER, Marcus G.

WILLIAM OF AUVERGNE
William of Auvergne and the Eternity of the World. TESKE, Roland J.

WILLIAMS, B
Ethics and the Limits of Consistency. BAMBROUGH, Renford.
The Possibility of Reincarnation. NOONAN, Harold W.

WILLING
Intentional Single and Joint Action. TUOMELA, Raimo.
Prichard, Davidson and Action. GUSTAFSON, Don.
Willing and Acting in Husserl's Lectures on Ethics and Value Theory. NENON, Thomas J.

WILSON, D
Author's Position in Interpretation of a Work of Art (in Japanese). WATANABE, Hiroshi.

WILSON, E
Evolutionary Naturalistic Justifications of Morality: A Matter of Faith and Works. ROTTSCHAEFER, William A.
Theology and the Social Sciences—Discipline and Antidiscipline. MURPHY, Nancey.

WILSON, H
Reply to Wilson's "Shadows on the Cave Wall: Philosophy and Visual Science". HARDIN, C L.

WILSON, J
Cook Wilson as Critic of Bradley. TACELLI, Ronald K.

WINCH, P
"Winch and Schutz on the Regulative Idea of a Social Science" in *Life-World and Politics: Between Modernity and Postmodernity*, O'NEILL, John.
Peter Winch, *Simone Weil: The Just Balance*. WILLIAMS, Rowan.

WINDELBAND, W
Il compito della filosofia: Saggio su Windelband. OLIVA, Rossella Bonito.

WINQUIST, C
"A Riposte" in *Archetypal Process: Self and Divine in Whitehead, Jung, and Hillman*, HEISIG, James W.

WISDO, D
"Kierkegaardian Faith: 'The Condition' and the 'Response'. FERREIRA, M Jamie.

WISDOM
Matter, Morals and Medicine: The Ancient Greek Origins of Science, Ethics and the Medical Profession. CARELLA, Michael Jerome.
Wisdom: Its Nature, Origins, and Development. STERNBERG, Robert J.
"Power and Wisdom: The Expert as Mediating Figure in Contemporary Polish History" in *The Political Responsibility of Intellectuals*, KURCZEWSKI, Jacek.
Gustavo Bontadini un metafisico per vocazione. LATORA, Salvatore.
Moral oder Klugheit? Überlegungen zur Gestalt der Autonomie des Politischen im Denken Kants. SCHMITZ, Heinz-Gerd.
Philosophy and Wisdom. MC KEE, Patrick.
The Thought That Learning Is by Ordeal: An Original Essay. WOODRUFF, Paul B.
Two Varieties of Temperance in the *Gorgias*. CURZER, Howard J.
The Wisdom of Plato's Aristophanes. SALMAN, Charles.

WISH(ES)
Aristotle and Protagoras: The Good Human Being as the Measure of Goods. GOTTLIEB, Paula.

WISHING
On Wishing there were Unicorns. CLARK, Stephen R L.

WIT
Kant über den Witz und Kants Witz. RITZEL, Wolfgang.

WITCHCRAFT
Tipos ideales en historia. TOZZI, María Verónica.

WITTGENSTEIN
After the Demise of the Tradition: Rorty, Critical Theory, and the Fate of Philosophy. NIELSEN, Kai.
Colour: A Philosophical Introduction (Second Edition). WESTPHAL, Jonathan.
Epistemology and Skepticism: An Enquiry into the Nature of Epistemology. CHATALIAN, George.
Gödel's Theorem in Focus. SHANKER, S G (ed).
In Defense of Mystical Ideas: Support for Mystical Beliefs from a Purely Theoretical Viewpoint. CHAPMAN, Tobias.
The Logical Basis of Metaphysics. DUMMETT, Michael.
The Looking-Glass Self: An Examination of Self-Awareness. CANFIELD, John.
The Metaphysics of Meaning. KATZ, Jerrold J.
The Metaphysics of the "Tractatus". CARRUTHERS, Peter.

WITTGENSTEIN

The Other Side of Language: A Philosophy of Listening. FIUMARA, Gemma Corradi.
Pulling up the Ladder: The Metaphysical Roots of Wittgenstein's Tractatus. BROCKHAUS, Richard R.
Reasons and Experience. MILLAR, Alan.
The Social Horizon of Knowledge. BUCZKOWSKI, Piotr (ed).
Wittgenstein and Contemporary Philosophy of Language. RUNDLE, Bede.
Wittgenstein's Lectures on the Foundations of Mathematics, Cambridge 1939. DIAMOND, Cora (ed).
Wittgenstein, Ethics and Aesthetics: The View from Eternity. TILGHMAN, B R.
Wittgenstein: A Bibliographical Guide. FRONGIA, Guido.
Wittgenstein: Meaning and Mind, Volume 3 of an Analytical Commentary on Philosophical Investigations. HACKER, P M S.
"How to Turn the *Tractatus* Wittgenstein into (Almost) Donald Davidson" in *Truth and Interpretation: Perspectives on the Philosophy of Donald Davidson*, SMART, J J C.
"Wittgenstein's Notion of Secondary Meaning and Davidson's Account of Metaphor—A Comparison" in *The Mind of Donald Davidson*, SCHULTE, Joachim.
"Wittgenstein's Philosophy of Language and the Question of Translation" in *Hermeneutics and the Poetic Motion, Translation Perspectives V—1990*, FLESCHE, David E.
"The Wittgenstein-Problem in Sociology or: the 'Linguistic Turn' as a Pirouette" in *The Social Horizon of Knowledge*, RITSERT, Jürgen.
Un "mapa de ontologías". PEREDA, Carlos.
The "Middle Wittgenstein": From Logical Atomism to Practical Holism. STERN, David G.
"Phénoménologie" de l'expression. CHAUVIRE, Christiane.
À propos d'arguments qui s'ignorent. VIGNAUX, Georges.
An Anti-Sceptical Fugue. GILLETT, Grant.
Una aproximación ontológica a la realidad fisica. HÜBNER, Adolf.
Artificial Intelligence and Wittgenstein. CASEY, Gerard.
Avoiding the Fly Bottle. KOLENDA, Konstantin.
Certainty and Authority. WINCH, Peter.
Comment on Huston Smith's Review of *The Essential Writings of Frithiof Schuon. ANDERSON, Tyson.*
Comments on Freud and Wittgenstein, and on Adolf Grünbaum's "Foundations of Psychoanalysis". FISCHER, Kurt Rudolf.
El concepto de Filosofia y conocimiento en Ludwig Wittgenstein. ESPARZA-BRACHO, Jesús.
Conceptos religiosos y vida religiosa. BASSOLS, Alejandro Tomasini.
La condición pública del lenguaje y la autoridad de la primera persona. ROLLINS, Mark.
Conventions, règles et nécessité. VOIZARD, Alain.
La démonstration mystifiante: Wittgenstein et Beuys. LA CHANCE, Michaël.
The Development of Wittgenstein's Views about the Other Minds Problem. TER HARK, M R M.
Does Wittgenstein's Concept of Language Game Patterns Come Up with a Solution to the Platonic Problem ... (in German). LÜTTERFELDS, Wilhelm.
Il doppio volto dell'ineffabile in L Wittgenstein. TODISCO, Orlando.
Elements of a Wittgensteinian Philosophy of the Human Sciences. SCHATZKI, Theodore R.
Eléments pour une "philosophie de la psychologie". PETIT, Jean-Luc.
Estructura lógica y ontología en el *Tractatus*. MARTÍNEZ, Sergio.
Ética sin raíces. VARGAS, Alberto.
La filosofía mística de Russell y lo indecible en el *Tractatus*. TOMASINI BASSOLS, Alejandro.
Fondamento e verità. CAMPANALE, Domenico.
Fools and Heretics. BAMBROUGH, Renford.
La force du nombre: remarques autour de la notion de communauté. FAUCHER, Luc.
Form of Life in Wittgenstein's Later Work. GARVER, Newton.
From What Can't Be Said To What Isn't Known. MC KINNON, Christine.
The Genesis of Wittgenstein's Later Philosophy in His Failure as a Phenomenologist. HALLETT, Garth.
Getting Rule-Following Straight. WONG, James.
Goethe and Wittgenstein. ROWE, M W.
Gottlob Frege, lettere a Wittgenstein. PENCO, Carlo and PARODI, Alessandra.
History as Geneology: Wittgenstein and the Feminist Deconstruction of Objectivity. LAMPSHIRE, Wendy L.
Ideas de mundo en el *Tractatus*. ROJO, Roberto.
An Impatient Man and his Papers. HINTIKKA, Jaakko.
Intenzione e azione in Wittgenstein. RAINONE, Antonio.
De jonge Wittgenstein (1889-1921): Denken als ethos. DE DIJN, H.
Kant und Wittgenstein. STETTER, Christian.
Language and Conversation. GAITA, Raimond.
The Last Word on *Philosophical Investigations* 43a. SAVIGNY, Eike V.
Later Wittgenstein on Objectivity of Rules. BEHERA, Sathrughna.
Los límites de mi lenguaje—los límites de mi mundo. KLOYBER, Christian.
Malcolm on Wittgenstein on Rules. MOSER, Paul K.
Models of Memory: Wittgenstein and Cognitive Science. STERN, David G.
Moore's Paradox Revisited. LINVILLE, Kent and RING, Merrill.
Never say "Never say 'Never'": A Reply to Nicholas Gier. REEDER, Harry P.
Never say "Never": A Response to Reeder's "Wittgenstein Never Was a Phenomenologist". GIER, Nicholas F.
Nombres y objetos en el *Tractatus*. VALDÉS, Margarita M.
An Oath of Silence: Wittgenstein's Philosophy of Religion. JOHNSON, Charles W.
Observar un aspecto. GIANOTTI, José Arthur.
On 'This is Red and This is Blue': *Tractatus* 6.3751. SAHU, Neelamani.
On the Purported Pragmatico-Semantic Foundation of Linguistics and AI Through Wittgenstein's Late Philosophy. LEINFELLNER-RUPERTSBERGER, Elisabeth.
On Wittgenstein's Transcendental Ethics. PRASAD, Rajendra.
Il paradosso del fondamento nella simbolica del gioco e sogno della libertà. MASULLO, Aldo.
Philosophical Scepticism: An Intelligible Challenge. GRUNDY, Jeremy.
La philosophie des sciences de Hertz et le Tractatus. LEROUX, Jean.
Philosophizing. PALMA, A B.
Philosophy in the *Big Typescript*: Philosophy as Trivial. LUCKHARDT, C Grant.
The Philosophy of Logical Wholism. MC CARTY, David Charles.
Problèmes de l'expression. ROSSET, Clément.
Psychoanalysis: A Form of Life?. BREARLEY, Michael.
Der psychophysische Materialismus in der Perspektive Kants und Wittgensteins. MENDONÇA, W P.
Qué miden los juegos de lenguaje?. LORENZ, Kuno.
Reading the Darkness: Wittgenstein and Indoctrination. MC CARTY, Luise Prior and MC CARTY, David Charles.
Recent Canadian Work on Wittgenstein: 1980-1989. WILLIAMSON, George.
Reglas, comunidades y juicios. ZALABARDO, José Luis.
Religion in Wittgenstein's Mirror. PHILLIPS, D Z.
Remarques sur l'analyse des termes mentaux chez Wittgenstein. BERNIER, Paul.
Rule-Scepticism: Kripkean Understanding in Wittgenstein's Perspective. BEHERA, Satrughna.
Russell and the Ethical Concern of Wittgenstein's *Tractatus*. IGLESIAS, Teresa.
Sachverhalt and *Gegenstand* are Dead. THOMPKINS, E F.
Self-Conscious Individual versus Social Soul: The Rationale of Wittgenstein's Discussion of Rule Following. SAVIGNY, Eike V.
La simplicidad en el *Tractatus*. ANSCOMBE, G E M.
Sobre la semántica de los nombres propios. SCHIRN, Matthias.
Sobre tópicos y términos primitivos de la intensión. SARABIA, Jaime.
Some Objections To Garavaso's Wittgenstein. HUMPHREY, John A.
Stephen Hilmy on Matters of Method and Style. COVEOS, Costis M.
La teoría del significado como uso en Wittgenstein. HERRERA, Alejandro.
Tractatus: Críticas al logicismo. NUÑO, Juan A.
Two Ways of Grounding Meaning. GERRARD, Steve.
Understanding the Question: Wittgenstein on Faith and Meaning. EISENSTEIN, Gabe.
Universal Sentences: Russell, Wittgenstein, Prior, and the Nyāya. SHAW, J L.
Unpublished Correspondence between Russell and Wittgenstein. MC GUINNESS, B F and VON WRIGHT, G H.
A Very Short Guide to Understanding Wittgenstein. RESNICK, Larry.
Wittgenstein and "Mad Pain". KELLY, Michael Lee.
Wittgenstein and Marx—Some Methodological Remarks (in German). RAATZSCH, Richard.
Wittgenstein and Psychology. SHOTTER, John.
Wittgenstein and Social Science. TRIGG, Roger.
Wittgenstein and the Color Incompatibility Problem. JACQUETTE, Dale.
Wittgenstein and the Transmission of Traditions. O'HEAR, Anthony.
Wittgenstein escéptico?. CABANCHIK, Samuel.
Wittgenstein et l'institution du langage. SEYMOUR, Michel.
Wittgenstein et le cognitivisme. OUELLET, Pierre.
Wittgenstein on 2, 2, 2...: The Opening of Remarks on the Foundations of Mathematics. FLOYD, Juliet.
Wittgenstein on Criteria and Other Minds. TEMKIN, Jack.
Wittgenstein on Emotion. PATEL, Kartikeya C.
Wittgenstein on Frazer's *Golden Bough*. COVEOS, Costis M.
Wittgenstein on Freud's 'Abominable Mess'. CIOFFI, Frank.
Wittgenstein on Jews: Some Counter-Examples. WASSERMANN, Gerhard D.
Wittgenstein on Logical Form and Kantian Geometry. SUMMERFIELD, Donna M.
Wittgenstein on Mathematical Proof. WRIGHT, Crispin.
Wittgenstein on Names and Family Resemblances. HYMERS, Michael.
Wittgenstein on Tolstoi's *What is Art*?. BEARDSMORE, R W.
Wittgenstein sobre la noción de regla en Frege. PADILLA GÁLVEZ, Jesús.
Wittgenstein versus Hart: Two Models of Rules for Social and Legal Theory. HUND, John.
Wittgenstein y el fisicalismo. HALLER, Rudolf.
Wittgenstein's "Remarks on Colour". ERICKSON, Glenn W.
Wittgenstein's Account of Rule-Following. PEARS, David.
Wittgenstein's Critique of Mechanistic Atomism. MC DONOUGH, Richard.

WITTGENSTEIN
Wittgenstein's Gift to Contemporary Analytic Philosophy of Religion. KELLENBERGER, J.
Wittgenstein's Holism. PEARS, David.
Wittgenstein's Indeterminism. SCHEER, Richard K.
Wittgenstein's Influence: Meaning, Mind and Method. GRAYLING, A C.
Wittgenstein's Lectures on Religious Belief. MARTIN, Michael.
Wittgenstein's Phenomenology Revisited. GIER, Nicholas F.
Wittgenstein's Philosophies of Mathematics. GERRARD, Steve.
Wittgenstein, eskimo's en emoties. POTT, Heleen.
Wittgenstein, Hans Lipps y los supuestos de la predicación. LÁZARO, Ramón Castilla.
Wittgenstein, Strawson y la no-posesión. BARINGOLTZ, Eleonora.
Wittgenstein: la tentación de lo místico. CABRERA, Isabel.
Wittgenstein: On Seeing Problems from a Religious Point of View. HIGH, Dallas M.
Wittgenstein: Representaciones y pensamientos. RABOSSI, Eduardo.
Wittgenstein: Whose Philosopher?. ANSCOMBE, G E M.
The Word as Will and Idea: Semantics in the *Tractatus*. COHEN, Daniel H.
Words like Faces (in Dutch). LESAGE, D.
Working with Wittgenstein's Builders. BIRSCH, Douglas and DORBOLO, Jon.
'I Heard a Plaintive Melody'. HANFLING, Oswald.
'The Darkness of This Time': Wittgenstein and the Modern World. BOUVERESSE, Jacques.

WITTIG, M
Essentially Speaking: Feminism, Nature and Difference. FUSS, Diana.

WOJTYLA, K
La persona humana: Síntesis de la concepción antropológica de K Wojtyla. JIMÉNEZ GUERRERO, A.

WOLFE, A
Social Science as Moral Philosophy?: Reflections on Alan Wolfe's *Whose Keeper?*. MASON, John R.

WOLFF
Kommunikations-Theoretische Schriften II: Symbolische Erkenntnis und Kommunikation. UNGEHEUER, Gerold (ed).
Eine bisher unbeachtete Quelle des "Streits der Fakultäten". SELBACH, Ralf.
From Philosophical Psychology to Philosophical Anthropology (in Dutch). VERGOTE, A.

WOLFF, R
Discourses on Political Violence: The Problem of Coherence. DU TOIT, A B.

WOLGAST, E
The Ambiguity of Political Virtue: A Response to Wolgast. LEVINSON, Sanford.

WOLLHEIM, R
Philosophy as an Art. LEVINSON, Jerrold.
Wollheim's Theory of Artist as Spectator: A Complication. OLDS, Clifton.

WOLNIEWICZ, B
Comments on a Question of Wolniewicz. HAWRANEK, Jacek.

WOMAN
see also Feminism
"Love between Us" in *Who Comes after the Subject?*, IRIGARAY, Luce.
A Genetic Exploration of Women's Subjugation: The Adventures of a Gadfly. MITTRA, Aditya Barna.
Nietzsche and the Woman Question. DIETHE, Carol.

WOMEN
see also Feminism
Bakhtin and the Epistemology of Discourse. THOMSON, Clive (ed).
Feminist Ethics. CARD, Claudia (ed).
A History of Women Philosophers, Volume II: Medieval, Renaissance and Enlightenment, A.D. 500-1600. WAITHE, Mary Ellen (ed).
The Place of the Hidden Moon: Erotic Mysticism in the Vaisnava-sahajiyā Cult of Bengal. DIMOCK JR, Edward C.
Whose Science? Whose Knowledge? Thinking from Women's Lives. HARDING, Sandra.
"Antigone's Daughters Reconsidered: Continuing Reflections on Women, Politics, and Power" in *Life-World and Politics: Between Modernity and Postmodernity*, ELSHTAIN, Jean Bethke.
"Feminism and Peace Theory: Women as Nurturers versus Women as Public Citizens" in *In the Interest of Peace: A Spectrum of Philosophical Views*, DUHAN, Laura.
"La femme intellectuelle au XVIIIe siècle ou l'inégalité des sexes" in *Égalité Uguaglianza*, GEFFRIAUD-ROSSO, Jeannette.
"Joining the Resistance: Psychology, Politics, Girls, and Women" in *The Tanner Lectures On Human Values, Volume XII*, GILLIGAN, Carol.
"Philosophy Is Not a Luxury" in *Feminist Ethics*, GINZBERG, Ruth.
"The Virtue of Feeling and the Feeling of Virtue" in *Feminist Ethics*, SPELMAN, Elizabeth V.
"Whom Can Women Trust?" in *Feminist Ethics*, BAIER, Annette C.
"Woman's Experience: Renaming the Dialectic of Desire and Recognition" in *Writing the Politics of Difference*, MILLS, Patricia J.
"They Lived Happily Ever After": Sommers on Women and Marriage. FRIEDMAN, Marilyn.
Los derechos de la mujer, legalidad y realidad. COMESAÑA, Santalices Gloria.
Does Sommers Like Women? More on Liberalism, Gender Hierarchy, and Scarlett O'Hara. FRIEDMAN, Marilyn.
Enforced Pregnancy, Rape, and the Image of Woman. CUDD, Ann E.
Explaining Without Blaming the Victim. ILLINGWORTH, Patricia M L.
The Expression of Experience: Code's Critique of Gilligan's Abortion Study. PITT, Alice.
Gendered Reason: Sex Metaphor and Conceptions of Reason. ROONEY, Phyllis.
In Praise of Clutter as a Necessary Part of the Feminist Perspective. AYIM, Maryann.
Loving Your Mother: On the Woman-Nature Relationship. ROACH, Catherine.
Machiavelli's Sisters: Women and "the Conversation" of Political Theory. ZERILLI, Linda M G.
Maternal Rights, Fetal Harms: Commentary. KINLAW, Kathy.
Maternal Rights, Fetal Harms: Commentary. STRONG, Carson.
Monstrous Imagination: Progeny as Art in French Classicism. HUET, Marie-Hélène.
Nietzsche on Woman. THOMPSON, J L.
The Overdue Death of a Feminist Chameleon: Taking a Stand on Surrogacy Arrangements. TONG, Rosemarie.
The Perils of Love: Why Women Need Rights. INGRAM, Attracta.
Reply to Maryann Ayim's "In Praise of Clutter as a Necessary Part of the Feminist Perspective". WENDELL, Susan.
Reproductive Gifts and Gift Giving: The Altruistic Woman. RAYMOND, Janice G.
Rethinking the Family. KYMLICKA, Will.
Starting Thought From Women's Lives: Eight Resources for Maximizing Objectivity. HARDING, Sandra.
The Subject in Feminism. BRAIDOTTI, Rosi.
Where Are All the Pragmatist Feminists?. SEIGFRIED, Charlene Haddock.
Whose Right? Ronald Dworkin, Women, and Pornographers. LANGTON, Rae.
Women, Madness, and Special Defences in the Law. BOETZKES, Elisabeth and TURNER, Susan (Guerin) and SOBSTYL, Edrie.

WOMEN'S STUDIES
The Humanities in the Nineties: A View From the Netherlands. ZÜRCHER, Erik (ed).
"Double Trouble": An Introduction. FRASER, Nancy.
An Ethical Justification of Women's Studies, Or What's a Nice Girl Like You Doing in a Place like This?. MC GRATH, Lynette.

WONG, D
David Wong on Emotions in Mencius. IHARA, Craig K.

WOOD, D
The Deconstruction of Time. LLEWELYN, John.

WOODWARD, J
More on Russell's Hypothesis. HINDERLITER, Hilton.

WORD PROBLEMS
La dialettica come "dépasser" in Sartre. TOGNONATO, Claudio.
Phrase Structure Parameters. FODOR, Janet Dean and CRAIN, Stephen.

WORD(S)
"Culture and the Word" in *Hermeneutics and the Poetic Motion, Translation Perspectives V—1990*, SCHMIDT, Dennis J and GADAMER, Hans-Georg.
Fondamento e verità. CAMPANALE, Domenico.
Making Sense of Words. MC CULLOCH, Gregory.
La palabra interior: La filosofía del lenguaje en San Agustín. PEGUEROLES, Juan.
Plato and the Senses of Words. BLACKSON, Thomas A.
Speech, Sin and the Word of God (in Dutch). GESTRICH, Christof.
Theoria, Aisthesis, Mimesis and Doxa. MÉCHOULAN, Éric.
Verbum-Signum: La définition du langage chez s Augustin et Nicolas de Cues. HENNIGFELD, Jochem.
Words like Faces (in Dutch). LESAGE, D.

WORDSWORTH
William Wadsworth: Nature, Imagination, Ultimate Reality and Meaning. MAHONEY, John L.

WORK
The Noble Savage: Jean-Jacques Rousseau, 1754-1762. CRANSTON, Maurice.
Work, Inc.: A Philosophical Inquiry. BYRNE, Edmund F.
"Workplace Democracy for Teachers: John Dewey's Contribution" in *Philosophy of Technology*, BYRNE, Edmund F.
"Working in America": A New Approach for the Humanities. SESSIONS, Robert.
A proposito di Stato e totaliarismo nel pensiero di Marx. SIENA, Robertomaria.
La comprensión aristotélica del trabajo. INNERARITY, Carmen.
Gorz on Work and Liberation. SAYERS, Sean.

WORK
Noia, acedia ed epochè. BOTTANI, Livio.
Reply to Gordon: Discourse at Work. CHMIELEWSKI, Philip J.
Travail et nature dans l'Antiquité. MULLER, Robert.
Words on Work. GRAY, C B.
Work and Family: Should Parents Feel Guilty?. PAINE, Lynn Sharp.

WORK ETHIC
"The Philosophy of Work and the Future of Civilization: Maritain, Weil and Simon" in *From Twilight to Dawn: The Cultural Vision of Jacques Maritain*, DOERING, Bernard.
Gorz on Work and Liberation. SAYERS, Sean.

WORK OF ART
Wittgenstein, Ethics and Aesthetics: The View from Eternity. TILGHMAN, B R.
"A Postmodern Language in Art" in *Postmodernism—Philosophy and the Arts (Continental Philosophy III)*, OLKOWSKI-LAETZ, Dorothea.
Art Works, But How?—Kant and Aesthetics/Heidegger and Truth. SYNNING, Ralph.
Identifying Musical Works of Art. JACOBS, Jo Ellen.
Persons as Natural Works of Art. ALDRICH, Virgil.
Pierre Menard's *Don Quixote*. BAILEY, George.

WORKER(S)
Work, Inc.: A Philosophical Inquiry. BYRNE, Edmund F.
"Freedom and Economic Organization in a Democracy" in *Freedom in the Modern World: Jacques Maritain, Yves R Simon, Mortimer J Adler*, NELSON, Ralph.
"Work in Organizations as Social Activity" in *Harré and His Critics*, RODRIGUEZ LOPEZ, Jose Luis.
Ethical Challenges of HIV Infection in the Workplace. LEONARD, Arthur S.
Two Models of Preferential Treatment for Working Mothers. BABER, H E.

WORKING CLASS
Political Self-Education of the English Working Class. PEPPERELL, Keith C.
El proceso de formación de la clase obrera de las minas en Asturias. MORADIELLOS, Enrique.

WORKS
"Gilson's Use of History In Philosophy" in *Thomistic Papers, V*, MAURER, Armand A.
Los escritos póstumos de J P Sartre (I). AMORÓS, Celia.
Introducción a la filosofía de Gaos. SALMERÓN, Fernando.
La polémica sobre el espinosismo de Lessing. FERNÁNDEZ LORENZO, Manuel.
Rhetoric and Ethics: Adam Smith on Theorizing about the Moral Sentiments. GRISWOLD JR, Charles L.
Richard Rufus of Cornwall and the Authorship of the *Scriptum super Metaphysicam*. NOONE, Timothy B.
Work and Text. CURRIE, Gregory.

WORLD VIEW(S)
Moral und Politik aus der Sicht des Kritischen Rationalismus. SALAMUN, Kurt (ed).
Philosophy in World Perspective: A Comparative Hermeneutic of the Major Theories. DILWORTH, David A.
"Rorty in the Epistemological Tradition" in *Reading Rorty*, TAYLOR, Charles.
"The World from its Own Point of View" in *Reading Rorty*, SORELL, Tom.
Beyond the Real/Apparent World: From Signs to Imaging in Nietzsche. WATSON, James R.
Filosofia dell'esistenza e cristologia: La Weltanschauung cristiana di R Guardini. DI MARCO, Chiar.
Law and Culture: The Conception of Legal Culture (in Polish). GRYKO, Czeslaw.
Die Mathematisierung als Konstruktion theoretischer Denkformen in der Abfolge naturwissenschaftlicher Weltbilder. GÖTTLICHER, Gerd.
The Concept of History in the Renaissance (in Hungarian). RASZLAI, Tibor.
Wie kaatst moet de bal verwachten. MERTENS, T.

WORLD(S)
see also Possible World(s)
The Concept of Objectivity: An Approximation. BUTLER, Kenneth G.
Evolution: Probleme und neue Aspekte ihrer Theorie. SCHEFFCZYK, Leo (ed).
A Philosophical Daybook: Post-Critical Investigations. POTEAT, William H.
The Power of Consciousness and the Force of Circumstances in Sartre's Philosophy. BUSCH, Thomas W.
"Heidegger and the Problem of World" in *Reconsidering Psychology: Perspectives from Continental Philosophy*, RICHARDSON, William J.
"Interpretation and Overinterpretation: World, History, Texts" in *The Tanner Lectures On Human Values, Volume XII*, ECO, Umberto.
"Logic and the World" in *Themes From Kaplan*, ALMOG, Joseph.
"My Poetic World Versus the Real, Scientific World" in *XIth International Congress in Aesthetics, Nottingham 1988*, PASKOW, Alan.
The Hole Truth. BUTTERFIELD, Jeremy.
Hume and Belief in the Existence of an External World. COSTA, Michael J.
Ideas de mundo en el *Tractatus*. ROJO, Roberto.
Kuhn's Conception of Incommensurability. HOYNINGEN-HUENE, Paul.
Meditation on the Two Consciousnesses and on the Three Worlds of Popper (in Hungarian). RADI, Peter.
Il mondo Il soggetto Lo smarrimento. INCARDONA, Nunzio.
Non-World Making in Chuang Tzu. WU, Kuang-Ming.
Per una filosofia del corpo. PELLECCHIA, Pasquale.
A Response to Kuang-Ming Wu's "Non-World-Making". FLEMING, Jesse.
Sellar's Two Images of the World. AUNE, Bruce.
The Scheme of the Game of Man and World (Towards the Formation of the Planetary Man) (in Hungarian). AXELOS, Kostas.
The World as a Whole and the World of Man (in Czechoslovakian). PATOCKA, Jan.
Truth and Language-World Connections. GROVER, Dorothy.
'The Darkness of This Time': Wittgenstein and the Modern World. BOUVERESSE, Jacques.

WORRAL, J
If It Aint's Broke, Don't Fix It. LAUDAN, Larry.

WORSHIP
Spirit and Existence: A Philosophy Inquiry into the Meaning of Spiritual Existence. GELVEN, Michael.
The Concept of Religion. HESTEVOLD, H Scott.

WORTH
"On the Primacy of Character" in *Identity, Character, and Morality: Essays in Moral Psychology*, WATSON, Gary.

WREEN, M
Hornsby's Puzzles: Rejoinder to Wreen and Hornsby. KOSROVANI, Emilio.

WRIGHT, L
On the Possibility of Lawful Explanation in Archaeology. SALMON, Merrilee H.

WRITING
Library Research Guide to Philosophy: Illustrated Search Strategy and Sources. LIST, Charles J.
A Philosophical Daybook: Post-Critical Investigations. POTEAT, William H.
Philosophical Fragments. FIRCHOW, Peter (trans).
Philosophical Writing: An Introduction. MARTINICH, A P.
Writing and the Moral Self. LANG, Berel.
"Merleau-Ponty and Derrida: Writing on Writing" in *Ontology and Alterity in Merleau-Ponty*, SILVERMAN, Hugh J.
"The Televised and the Untelevised: Keeping an Eye On/Off the Tube" in *Postmodernism—Philosophy and the Arts (Continental Philosophy III)*, SEITZ, Brian.
"Speech Versus Writing" in Derrida and Bhartrhari. COWARD, Harold G.
La apuesta literaria de Nietzsche. MONTORO, Marcial Moreno.
A Critique of Derrida's Hegel Deconstruction: Speech, Phonetic Writing, and Hieroglyphic Script in Logic, Law, Art. CUTROFELLO, Andrew.
Language, Speech and Writing: Merleau-Ponty and Derrida on Saussure. FREE, George.
Libri da salvare. POLC, Jaroslav.
Reading Nietzsche. RISSER, James.
Response: "The Rooting and Uprooting of Reason: On *Spacings* by John Sallis". SALLIS, John.
Writing the Revolution—The Politics of Truth in Genet's *Prisoner of Love*. CRITCHLEY, Simon.

WRONGNESS
"A New Theory of Retribution" in *Liability and Responsibility*, HAMPTON, Jean.

WYCLYF
John Wyclif's Metaphysics of Scriptural Integrity in the *De Veritate Sacrae Scripturae*. TRESKO, Michael.

YANDELL, K
God and Gratuitous Evil: A Reply to Yandell. CHRZAN, Keith.

YI CHIH
Mencius' Criticism of Mohism: An Analysis of *Meng Tzu* 3A:5. SHUN, Kwong-Loi.

YOGA
Yoga on War and Peace. TIGUNAIT, Pandit Rajmani.
The Yoga-Sūtra of Patañjali: A New Translation and Commentary. FEUERSTEIN, Georg.
'Desire' in Yoga and Jung. COWARD, Harold.
The Bhakti Tradition in Hinduism—Bhakti Yoga an Overview. PILLAI, A S Narayana.
The Notion of *Klesa* and Its Bearing on the Yoga Analysis of Mind. BALSLEV, Anindita N.
Sri Aurobindo and the Process of Physical Transformation. REDDY, V Ananda.

YOUNG, T
Light Problems: Reply to Chen. ACHINSTEIN, Peter.
Young and Lloyd on the Particle Theory of Light: A Response to Achinstein. CHEN, Xiang.

YOUTH
Sex, Drugs and Rock 'n Roll: Youth, Instruction and Experience in Contemporary American Film. ANGELO, Richard.

YOVEL, Y
Was Spinoza a Marrano of Reason?. POPKIN, Richard H.

YUGOSLAVIAN
Lacan in Slovenia—An Interview with Slavoj Zizek and Renata Salecl. DEWS, Peter and OSBORNE, Peter.

ZAGORIN, P
Reply to Professor Zagorin's "Historiography and Postmodernism: Reconsideration". ANKERSMIT, Frank R.

ZAMJATIN, E
The Last Utopia: Entropy and Revolution in the Poetics of Evgeny Zamjatin. SICHER, Efraim.

ZEA, L
The Master-Slave Dialectic in Latin America: The Social Criticism of Zea, Freire, and Roig. SCHUTTE, Ofelia M.

ZEEMAN, E
Zeeman-Göbel Topologies. HEATHCOTE, Adrian.

ZEN BUDDHISM
The Butterfly as Companion: Meditations on the First Three Chapters of the Chuang Tzu. WU, Kuang-Ming.
Das Ich im deutschen Idealismus und das Selbst im Zen-Buddhist Fichte und Dogen. NAGASAWA, Kunihiko.
Heidegger e o Oriente ou da Extrema In-diferença Ocidental. DO CARMO SILVA, Carlos Henrique.
Le satori dans le bouddhisme zen et la rationalité. HÉLAL, Georges.

ZENO
"Pier Caterino Zeno le vicende culturali del 'Giornale de' Letterati d'Italia'" in *Scienza, Filosofia e Religione tra '600 e '700 in Italia*, GENERALI, Dario.
Zeno's Paradox of Extension. MC KIE, John R.

ZENO'S PARADOX(ES)
Eleatics Against Each Other (in Hungarian). KAMPIS, György.
Zeno's Paradox of Extension. MC KIE, John R.

ZIMMERMAN, M
The Quest for Transformational Experience. BULKLEY, Kelly.

ZIONISM
Encounter on the Narrow Ridge: A Life of Martin Buber. FRIEDMAN, Maurice.
The Realm of Humanitas: Responses to the Writings of Hannah Arendt. GARNER, Reuben (ed).

ZNAMIEROWSKI, C
Czeslaw Znamierowski's Conception of Constitutive Rules. CZEPITA, Stanislaw.

ZOOLOGY
Critica della filosofia zoologica per Battista Grassi. MESCHIARI, Alberto.

ZUBIRI, X
La determinación de la esencia en X Zubiri y Tomás de Aquino. SOTO, José Cercós.
Heidegger en la filosofia española: La eficacia de Heidegger en las filosofías de Ortega y Zubiri. RAMOS, Antonio Pintor.
Una Metafísica estructural de la evolución. CONILL, Jesús.
La realtà umana nel pensiero di Xavier Zubiri. QUINTÁS, Alfonso López and NICOLOSI, Mauro.
Reflexiones en torno a la sensibilidad externa. ALVAREZ-CASTELLANOS, Juan José Sánchez.
Sobre le estructura dinámica de la realidad. MONSERRAT, Javier.
Substancia y sustantividad: Tomás de Aquino y X Zubiri. CERCÓS SOTO, José Luis.
X Zubiri in Roma: Natura, Storia, Dio. JAVIERRE ORTAS, A M.

Guidance on the Use of the Author Index With Abstracts

Each entry in this section begins with the author's name and contains the complete title of the article or book, other bibliographic information, and an abstract if available. The list is arranged in alphabetical order with the author's last name first. Articles by multiple authors are listed under each author's name. Names preceded by the articles De, La, Le, etc. or the prepositions Da, De, Van, Von, etc. are usually treated as if the article or preposition were a part of the last name.

Almost all of the abstracts are provided by the authors of the articles and books; where an abstract does not appear, it was not received from the author prior to the publication of this edition. The staff of the *Index* prepares some abstracts. These abstracts are followed by "(staff)".

In order to locate all the articles and books written by a given author, various spellings of the author's name should be checked. This publication uses the form of the author's name given in the article or book. Hence, variations of an author's name may appear in this index. Particular care should be given to names that have a space, a dash, or an apostrophe in them. Because the computer sorts on each character, the names of other authors may be filed between different spellings of a given author's name.

AACH, John. Psychologism Reconsidered. Synthese, 85(2), 315-338, N 90.

Frege's and Husserl's arguments against psychologism are criticized and found dependent on a conception of psychology that, though prevalent in their day, is no longer accepted. Psychology started moving out of reach of their arguments at least since 1913 with behaviorism, but being uninterested in psychology, they did not notice this. Their philosophical descendents continued the error by accepting the issue as closed. A psychologism based on B F Skinner's behaviorism is outlined that eludes their arguments, and an attack is launched against their contention that logic is entirely independent of psychology. Instead, a more reciprocal relation is proposed.

ABED, Shukri B. *Aristotelian Logic and the Arabic Language in Alfarabi*. Albany, SUNY Pr, 1991.

This book explores the reaction of tenth-century Arab philosopher Abu Nasr Alfarabi to the logical works of Aristotle. From numerous short treatises the author develops a systematic and comprehensive topical survey of Alfarabi's logical writings. The book is divided into two major parts: language as a tool of logic and logic as a tool with which to analyse language. The first five chapters deal with Alfarabi's analysis of the meaning of various terms as they are used in logic and philosophy. Alfarabi refutes the Arab grammarians who claimed that Arab logicians were building a language within a language and shows that the philosophical meaning of terms are in fact their most original and essential meanings. The final chapter deals with Alfarabi's analysis of certain aspects of the Arabic language (such as copula) and demonstrates that Arabic, like any natural language, conforms to universal logical structures of which natural languages are only a concrete expression.

ABIAN, Alexander and AMIN, Wael A. The Cardinality of Powersets in Finite Models of the Powerset Axiom. Notre Dame J Form Log, 32(2), 290-293, Spr 91.

It is shown that in a finite model of the set-theoretical Powerset axiom a set *s* and its powerset *P*(*s*) have the same number of elements. Additional results are also derived.

ABIAN, Alexander and AMIN, Wael A. An Equivalent of the Axiom of Choice in Finite Models of the Powerset Axiom. Notre Dame J Form Log, 31(3), 371-374, Sum 90.

It is shown that in a finite model for the set-theoretical Powerset axiom every set *s* has a Choice set iff every set *s* has a Meet set $\cap s$. Moreover, the Choice set of *s* is unique and is equal to $\cap s$, where $\cap s$ is a singleton and $\cap s \in s$.

ABRAHAM, Uri. "Free Sets for Commutative Families of Functions" in *Logic, Methodology and Philosophy of Science, VIII*, FENSTAD, J E (ed), 205-212. New York, Elsevier Science, 1989.

ABRAHAM, William J. The Epistemological Significance of the Inner Witness of the Holy Spirit. Faith Phil, 7(4), 434-450, O 90.

This paper seeks to explore the significance of a specific kind of religious experience for the rationality of religious belief. The context for this is a gap between what is often allowed as rational and what is embraced as certain in the life of faith. The claim to certainty at issue is related to the work and experience of the Holy Spirit; this experience has a structure which is explored phenomenologically. Thereafter various ways of cashing in the epistemic value of the purported claim to certainty are examined.

ABRAHAM, William J (ed) and PREVOST, Robert W (ed) and MITCHELL, Basil. *How to Play Theological Ping-Pong: And Other Essays on Faith and Reason*. Grand Rapids, Eerdmans, 1991.

ABRAHAMS, Cecil. "William Blake and the Romantic Perception of Humanism" in *The Question of Humanism: Challenges and Possibilities*, GOICOECHEA, David (ed), 99-104. Buffalo, Prometheus, 1991.

ABRAMS, Dominic and HOGG, Michael A. The Context of Discourse: Let's Not Throw the Baby Out with the Bathwater. Phil Psych, 3(2-3), 219-225, 1990.

An examination of Ian Parker's definitions of discourse reveals them to be nondistinctive and of limited utility. It is argued that discourse analysis should be integrated with, rather than set against, social psychology. Discourse analysts should attend to the issues of the representativeness and generality of their evidence, should be wary of attributing causality to discourse, and should consider the advantages of systematically investigating, rather than asserting, the social consequences of the use of different discourses.

ABRAMSKY, Samson. Domain Theory in Logical Form. Annals Pure Applied Log, 51(1-2), 1-77, Mr 91.

ABRUSCI, V Michele. Non-Commutative Intuitionistic Linear Logic. Z Math Log, 36(4), 297-318, 1990.

ACERO, Juan José. Platón, el lenguaje y el marciano. Rev Filosof (Spain), 3, 205-210, 1990.

This note is a review of "Language and the Problem of Knowledge," the first part of Noam Chomsky's *Managua Lectures*, Chomsky's favorite way of understanding language, i.e., through posing what he calls Plato's problem and trying to find a solution to it, is briefly described and its ingredients sorted out. It is held that Chomsky's approach searches for a commitment both to materialism and innatism. However, it is argued that Chomsky's way of conciliating both commitments is not free from strains. Finally, his arguments for innatism are briefly discussed.

ACHINSTEIN, Peter. Hypotheses, Probability, and Waves. Brit J Phil Sci, 41(1), 73-102, Mr 90.

ACHINSTEIN, Peter. Light Problems: Reply to Chen. Stud Hist Phil Sci, 21(4), 677-684, D 90.

ACHINSTEIN, Peter. "Newton's Corpuscular Query and Experimental Philosophy" in *Philosophical Perspectives on Newtonian Science*, BRICKER, Phillip (ed), 135-173. Cambridge, MIT Pr, 1990.

This paper discusses Newton's professed methodological position regarding induction and "hypotheses," and considers to what extent it is put into practice in defense of his own corpuscular theory of light.

ACHINSTEIN, Peter. *Particles and Waves: Historical Essays in the Philosophy of Science*. New York, Oxford Univ Pr, 1991.

The unifying theme of this volume is the nature of the philosophical problems surrounding the postulation of light waves, molecules, and electrons. How is it possible to defend theoretical claims about such "unobservables"? This issue is examined in the context of actual scientific practice in three 19th century episodes: the debate between particle and wave theories of light, Maxwell's kinetic theory of gases, and J. J. Thomson's discovery of the electron. The book contains three parts, each devoted to one of three topics, beginning with an essay presenting the historical background of the episode and an introduction to the philosophical issues.

ACHTERHUIS, Hans. La critique du modèle industriel comme histoire de la rareté: Une introduction à la pensée d'Ivan Illich. Rev Phil Louvain, 89(81), 47-62, F 91.

The philosophy of I Illich is expounded from the angle of the concept of scarcity. This concept only appears in Illich's latest works, but the author shows that it is already presupposed in early works like 'Deschooling Society' and 'Medical Nemesis' falling back on an earlier analysis (H. Achterhuis, 'Het Rijk van de schaarste', 1988), that was by the way influenced stongly by Illich, some implications of 'the reign of scarcity', that in philosophy started with the invidious individualism of Thomas Hobbes, are examined. This culminates in a critique of the industrial system in general and the 'development myth' in particular.

ACIMOVIC, Mirko. The Gnoseological Aspect of Boskovic's "Theory of Natural Philosophy" (in Serbo-Croatian). Filozof Istraz, 32-33(5-6), 1501-1510, 1989.

Das Problem dieses Exurses wurde thematisiert als Versuch der Betonung einiger Grundfragen im Bereich der gnoseologischen Gründe Boskovic's Naturphilosophie. Es handelt sich, zwar, um die relativistische Erkenntnistheorie, die Boskovic, mit seinem bedeutenden Werk *Theoria philosophiae naturalis*, gegründet hat. Im Grunde dieser gnoseologischen Konzeption, befindet sich die Lehre über die Relativität der sinnlichen, vernünftigen und reflexiven Erkenntnisse der Welt, die im Wesen auch relativ ist. (edited)

ACKERMAN, Bruce A. "Neutralities" in *Liberalism and the Good*, DOUGLASS, R Bruce (ed), 29-43. New York, Routledge, 1990.

ACKERMAN, Felicia. "Analysis, Language, and Concepts: The Second Paradox of Analysis" in *Philosophical Perspectives, 4: Action Theory and Philosophy of Mind, 1990*, TOMBERLIN, James E (ed), 535-543. Atascadero, Ridgeview, 1990.

This paper distinguishes two paradoxes of analysis: the standard one (which I call the first paradox) and another one (which I call the second paradox). Having offered a solution to the first elsewhere, I offer a solution to the second here.

ACKERMAN, Felicia. "Content, Character, and Nondescriptive Meaning" in *Themes From Kaplan*, ALMOG, Joseph (ed), 5-21. New York, Oxford Univ Pr, 1989.

ACKERMAN, Felicia. The Significance of a Wish. Hastings Center Rep, 21(4), 27-29, Jl-Ag 91.

ACKERMANN, Robert John. *Nietzsche: A Frenzied Look*. Amherst, Univ of Mass Pr, 1990.

ADAM, Michel. L'horizon philosophique de Pierre Charron. Rev Phil Fr, 181(3), 273-293, Jl-S 91.

ADAMCZEWSKI, Zygmunt. "Acting Human in Our Time" in *The Question of Humanism: Challenges and Possibilities*, GOICOECHEA, David (ed), 217-222. Buffalo, Prometheus, 1991.

ADAMS, Carol J. Ecofeminism and the Eating of Animals. Hypatia, 6(1), 125-145, Spr 91.

In this essay, I will argue the contemporary ecofeminist discourse, while potentially adequate to deal with the issue of animals, is now inadequate because it fails to give consistent conceptual place to the domination of animals as a significant aspect of the domination of nature. I will examine six answers ecofeminists could give for not including animal explicitly in ecofeminist analyses and show has a persistent patriarchal ideology regarding animals as instruments has kept the experience of animals from being fully incorporated within ecofeminism.

ADAMS, Fred and DREBUSHENKO, David and FULLER, Gary and STECKER, Robert. Narrow Content: Fodor's Folly. Mind Lang, 5(3), 213-229, Autumn 90.

For ten years Fodor and other cognitive scientists presumed that we need narrow content (content essentially independent of one's environment) to get around Twin-Earth examples and to do psychology. We show why broad content psychology (using content essentially dependent upon one's environment) is *not really challenged* by Twin-Earth examples, despite appearances. We explain (1) why narrow content is *not content*, and why (2) even if we concoct a notion of content* for narrow content, it still will be *unable to explain* intentional behavior. Thus, we herald the demise of narrow content: one cannot use it and does not need it.

ADAMS, Frederick. He Doesn't Really Want to Try. Analysis, 51(2), 109-112, Mr 91.

Some like to reject things that seem clearly true—such as that when one intentionally tries to do A, one wants to do A. This has been rejected by Alfred

Mele. My paper replies to Mele arguing that his grounds for rejection fail. Mele thinks that instead of wanting A (outright) one can merely want to try A. But what does this difference come to—between wanting to A and wanting to try to A? Not much. I say that if one tries something but does not want to A, it is not A-ing that one is trying.

ADAMS, Ian. Kant, Pestalozzi and the Role of Ideology in Educational Thought. J Phil Educ, 24(2), 257-269, Wint 90.

The article outlines a conception of political ideology and then explores the possibility of there being distinct moral and educational ideologies. Since all concern the ideal way of life, there are obvious questions about how they relate to each other. Several different kinds of relationship between the political and the educational are suggested. Kant is taken as a particularly interesting example, his political and educational ideas being relatively independent of each other, while both are separate extensions of his moral ideology. Pestalozzi's ideas are then analysed as a contrasting and unusual case of a purely educational ideology.

ADAMS, M E and CIGNOLI, R. A Note on the Axiomatization of Equational Classes of *n*-Valued Lukasiewicz Algebras. Notre Dame J Form Log, 31(2), 304-307, Spr 90.

It is shown that each nontrivial equational subclass of *n*-valued Lukasiewicz algebras is determined by a canonical equation that has the least possible number of variables.

ADAMS, Marilyn McCord. Forgiveness: A Christian Model. Faith Phil, 8(3), 277-304, Jl 91.

Recent literature on the topic of forgiveness explores the question whether, in the field of secular ethics, forgiveness is not a flower but a weed. After analyzing approaches by A Kolnai, P Twambley, J Murphy, and H Morris, I sketch a theological point of view and offer my own characterization of forgiveness, contending that the latter is "at home" within the former. My methodological moral is that, given the differential adaptability of forgiveness to (at least some) secular and religious value theories, Christian philosophers risk distortion when they fail to integrate their ethical reflections with their theological commitments.

ADAMS, Marilyn McCord (ed) and WOLTER, Allan B. *The Philosophical Theology of John Duns Scotus*. Ithaca, Cornell Univ Pr, 1990.

ADAMS, Robert M (ed) and LOGAN, George M (ed). *Utopia: Sir Thomas More*. New York, Cambridge Univ Pr, 1989.

ADAMS, Robert Merrihew. The Knight of Faith. Faith Phil, 7(4), 383-395, O 90.

The essay is about the "Preliminary Expectoration" of Kierkegaard's *Fear and Trembling*. It argues that "the absurd" there refers primarily to the practical paradox that in faith (so it is claimed) one must simultaneously renounce and gladly accept a loved object. In other words it is about a problem of detachment as a feature of religious life. The paper goes on to interpret, and discuss critically, the views expressed in the book about both renunciation (infinite resignation) and the nature of faith.

ADAMS, Robert Merrihew. "Time and Thisness" in *Themes From Kaplan*, ALMOG, Joseph (ed), 23-42. New York, Oxford Univ Pr, 1989.

ADELAJA, Adesoji O and BRUMFIELD, Robin G. Research Note On Equity and Ethics in State-Promotion of Agricultural Products. J Agr Ethics, 4(1), 82-88, 1991.

Many state governments in the United States promote locally-produced farm products. This paper discusses issues related to the ethics and equity of such promotional programs. The paper argues that generic promotion is generally easier to justify in terms of ethics and equity than brand promotion. It also argues that informative and factual brand promotions are easier to justify than deceptive and persuasive brand promotion. Additional equity issues arising when taxpayers finance state-promotional programs are also discussed.

ADELMAN, Howard. Morality and Ethics in Organizational Administration. J Bus Ethics, 10(9), 665-678, S 91.

The article is a detailed case study of theft and fraud by an employee in an organization. The analysis suggests that in the process of dealing with the employee, the issue was not *primarily* one of ethics, but of two moral principles in conflict, compassion and concern for a fellow human being and the morality governing responses to betrayal. The latter governed the results because that morality was congruent with the predominant ethics of the organization concerned with preserving the authority structure and integrity of the organization rather than the personal welfare of the individual in the organization. In sum, the paper argues that, based on this case, organizational behavior towards individual employees may be determined by individual morality that is reinforced by organizational "ethical" principles more concerned with the self-interest of the organization than ethics per se.

ADLER, Jacob. Murphy and Mercy. Analysis, 50(4), 262-268, O 90.

ADLER, Jonathan E. Conservatism and Tacit Confirmation. Mind, 99(396), 559-570, O 90.

Epistemic conservatism is the position that a statement's being believed provides reasons to continue to believe it. I argue that for many beliefs, conservatism can be justified through an extension of traditional grounds. These beliefs receive *tacit confirmation* over and above the confirmation justifying their acceptance. They are confirmed because they provide background information in testing, and so run the risk of falsification; and the confirmation is tacit because it is the unintended consequence of the normal testing procedure. Applications are made to questions of acceptance, the warrant for foundational beliefs, and underdetermination.

ADLER, Jonathan E. Double Standards, Racial Equality and the Right Reference Class. J Applied Phil, 8(1), 69-81, 1991.

There is a popular way of appealing to consistency of judgment or principle whose result is to rule out relevant information. To avoid the danger of judging similar cases differently, relevantly different cases are treated alike. So the information distinguishing them is lost. I try to formulate, defend and apply a requirement upon determining whether situations are similar with respect to a principle. Adherence to the requirement is a way to prevent the loss of information through illicit appeals to consistency. Part II examines a difficulty for the requirement proposed. The difficulty concerns determinateness: given the requirement's broad scope, it cannot yield judgments on specific cases without prejudging substantive issues. Without reaching any solution to the difficulty, I point out that parallel difficulties arise for similar requirements in diverse areas, and that the problem can be mitigated to varying degrees in actual applications of these requirements.

ADLER, Jonathan E. "Epistemic Universalizability: From Skepticism to Infallibilism" in *Doubting: Contemporary Perspectives on Skepticism*, ROTH, Michael D (ed), 83-98. Norwell, Kluwer, 1990.

Epistemic justification is universalizable. If someone is justified in a belief than anyone else, in relevantly similar circumstances, is also justified in that belief. Given universalizability, together with some assumptions, a skeptical argument is generated. In part I, I defend this skeptical argument against objections to an earlier version. Part II asks what happens when we do not assume that, in almost all cases, no matter how good one's epistemic position, there is someone in a position at least as good, whose justification was actually defeated. In that case the above skeptical argument becomes an argument for infallibilism.

ADLER, Max. Marx and Dialectics (in German). Deut Z Phil, 38(9), 849-858, 1990.

ADLER, Mortimer J. "Great Books, Democracy and Truth" in *Freedom in the Modern World: Jacques Maritain, Yves R Simon, Mortimer J Adler*, TORRE, Michael D (ed), 33-45. Notre Dame, Univ Notre Dame Pr, 1989.

ADLER, Pierre (trans) and BRAGUE, Rémi and D'URSEL, Laurent (trans). Aristotle's Definition of Motion and its Ontological Implications. Grad Fac Phil J, 13(2), 1-22, 1990.

ADLER, Pierre (trans) and REINER, Hans and PASKIN, David (trans). The Emergence and Original Meaning of the Name 'Metaphysics'. Grad Fac Phil J, 13(2), 23-53, 1990.

AERTSEN, Jan A. Thinking of Unity (in Dutch). Tijdschr Filosof, 52(3), 399-420, S 90.

Two fundamentally different conceptions of unity can be found in the philosophical tradition. My thesis is that both of them go back to one text, Plato's *Parmenides*. Plato argues that if the One is posed as *unity* (the first hypothesis), the one is unthinkable and unnamable. If the one is posed as *being* (the second hypothesis), we think a plurality. (edited)

AGACINSKI, Sylviane. "Another Experience of the Question, or Experiencing the Question Other-Wise" in *Who Comes after the Subject?*, CADAVA, Eduardo (ed), 9-23. New York, Routledge, 1991.

AGARWALA, Binod Kumar. Nozick on Rights and Minimal State. J Indian Counc Phil Res, 6(3), 1-12, My-Ag 89.

Nozick's view that rights are side-constraints on actions is examined and refuted on the ground that it presumes that the only rights we have are rights to liberties and it violates the Kantian principles that individuals are ends and not merely means. Nozick's conceptions of natural rights and state of nature and his derivation of a state with night watchman duties from the state of nature are examined and refuted, by showing the irrelevance of his counter example to the principle of fairness.

AGARWALA, Binod Kumar. Nozick on Social Justice. J Indian Counc Phil Res, 5(2), 1-14, Ja-Ap 88.

Nozick's arguments against social justice that we can't intervene in a situation which is not of our own making, that distribution of goods arise out of the voluntary exchanges, that principles advanced as principles of justice are unhistorical end result principles, that implementation of such principles will require continuous interference with people's lives, are considered and refuted. His entitlement theory of justice is also examined and found inadequate because it presupposes that free market will ensure full employment, and these principles allow differences in holdings arising due to unequal and arbitrary distribution of talent, accidents of birth, unequal needs, etc.

AGASHE, S D. The Axiomatic Method: Its Origin and Purpose. J Indian Counc Phil Res, 6(3), 109-118, My-Ag 89.

It is suggested that the axiomatic method was discovered while investigating a specific geometric problem, namely, that of the comparison of two figures. This problem must have motivated Proposition 14, "to construct a square equal to a given rectilinear figure," in Book 2 of Euclid's *Elements*. Books 1 and 2 read *backwards* indicate how the original problem led, through a series of subproblems, to definitions, postulates and common notions. This successful solution of a problem inspired the subsequent conception of the axiomatic method as a *forward-moving* process of open-ended deduction and as a way to organize knowledge logically.

AGASSI, Joseph. Faith in the Open Society: The Limits of Hermeneutics. Method Sci, 22(4), 183-200, 1989.

Religious claims are compatible with democracy, but the claims for certitude of religious claims do not agree with pluralist participatory democracy. Such claims rest on hermeneutic studies of sacred texts and by now hermeneutics is so explosive that it must allow for doubt to stay even if certitude in principle is somewhat upheld: the divine message is unknown.

AGASSI, Joseph. Global Responsibility. J Applied Phil, 7(2), 217-221, O 90.

Concern with global responsibility for survival as such invites the creation of a specific international organization. The new body should adjudicate as to which disputes are open (such as, for example, concerning the advisability of building nuclear plants) and which are not (for example, white supremacy); most significantly, the new body should carefully guard its credibility by sticking to veracity, by avoiding deceit even in extreme situations. In particular it behooves us all to confess that we have no solution to our most urgent problems.

AGASSI, Joseph. Induction and Stochastic Independence. Brit J Phil Sci, 41(1), 141-142, Mr 90.

Popper's refutation of the strange view that inductive learning from experience follows the calculus of probability was challenged by the proposal to judge the dependence of current events on past ones a matter of probability. Croupiers tossing dies to decide whether to spin their wheels or call the same results as past ones, follow this proposal. Whether nature follows this proposal, or when, is a matter for conjectures that can be empirically tested, and refuted or not.

AGASSI, Joseph. "Newtonianism Before and After the Einsteinian Revolution" in *Some Truer Method*, DURHAM, Frank (ed), 145-174. New York, Columbia Univ Pr, 1990.

AGASSI, Joseph. "Ontology and Its Discontent" in *Studies on Mario Bunge's "Treatise"*, WEINGARTNER, Paul (ed), 105-122. Amsterdam, Rodopi, 1990.

AGASSI, Joseph. Popper's Demarcation of Science Refuted. Method Sci, 24(1), 1-7, 1991.

AGASSI, Joseph. Psychology and Controversy. Method Sci, 23(1), 11-27, 1990.

Psychological schools of thought advance competing theories of learning as major items in their comprehensive views. Their controversies are supposed to help the advancement of learning but their theories do not recognize controversy as a means of learning—as they should. No learning theory is acceptable which fails to recognize the significance of controversy for the advancement of learning.

AGAZZI, Evandro. "Ethics and Science" in *Logic, Methodology and Philosophy of Science, VIII*, FENSTAD, J E (ed), 49-61. New York, Elsevier Science, 1989.

The aim of the paper is the harmonization of autonomy and moral responsibility of science. Autonomy means internal independence as to the evaluation of *cognitive* validity of scientific statements. This does not imply independence in the evaluation of scientific *activities*: goals, means, conditions and consequences of these activities actually imply moral evaluations, in the sense of a compatibility of different *values* involved. A mutual assumption of responsibility by the scientific community and the social environment is the proper tool for this harmonization.

AGICH, George J. Medicine as Business and Profession. Theor Med, 11(4), 311-324, D 90.

This paper analyzes one dimension of the frequently alleged contradiction between treating medicine as a business and as a profession, namely the incompatibility between viewing the physician patient relationship in economic and moral terms. The paper explores the utilitarian foundations of economics and the deontological foundations of professional medical ethics as one source for the business/medicine conflict that influences beliefs about the proper understanding of the therapeutic relationship. It, then, focuses on the contrast and distinction between medicine as business and profession by critically analyzing the classic economic view of the moral status of medicine articulated by Kenneth Arrow. The paper concludes with a discussion of some advantages associated with regarding medicine as a business.

AGICH, George J. Reassessing Autonomy in Long-Term Care. Hastings Center Rep, 20(6), 12-17, N-D 90.

The realities of long-term care call for a refurbished concrete concept of autonomy that systematically attends to the history and development of persons and takes account of the experiences of daily living. The concept of autonomy as independence and its corollary aversion to dependency of all sorts is criticized. It is argued that the concept of autonomy that should guide ethical thought is actual autonomy as it emerges in the concrete life world rather than autonomy regarded ideally. Identification with self is argued to be prior to the concept of autonomy as independence or autonomy predicated on free choice.

AGRAWAL, M M. Sartre on Pre-Reflective Consciousness. J Indian Counc Phil Res, 6(1), 121-127, S-D 88.

Sartre's claim that the 'pre-reflective' consciousness, though noncognitive, is nevertheless 'knowledge' is ambiguous. Consciousness' consciousness of itself cannot be knowledge *that* 'I am such and such consciousness'; since 'such and such' involves a conceptual recognition of ordinary 'reflective' consciousness, it would turn, contrary to Sartre's intention, the pre-reflective consciousness into a quasi-cognitive experience. The essence of pre-reflective consciousness, therefore, must be placed simply in the simultaneity of pure being-consciousness with the Sartrean reflective consciousness.

AGUAYO CRUZ, Enrique Ignacio. Metafísica de la vocación. Logos (Mexico), 18(53), 109-123, My-Ag 90.

La vocación es el llamado que nos invita a desarrollar una actividad determinada. Ese llamado dimana, a nuestro juicio, de dos fuentes: la misma persona, pues ella siente atracción hacia una forma precisa de labor; y de lascaracterísticas propias que presenta un trabajo, lo que hace que nos fijemosen él y no en otro. Para conocerla, hay que examinarla en su esencia, prescindiendo de sus manifestaciones singulares. De allí nuestro estudio: *metafísica de la vocación*. La investigación está estructurada así: definición de vocación; tipos de vocación; dimensiones de la vocación; maneras de descubrir la vocación; y comentario final.

AIHARA, Setsuko (trans) and PARKES, Graham (trans) and KEIJI, Nishitani. *The Self-Overcoming of Nihilism: Nishitani Keiji*. Albany, SUNY Pr, 1990.

In this work from 1949 the Japanese philosopher Nishitani Keiji (1900-1990) sketches the history of European nihilism as the context for a consideration of how the problem posed by nihilism might be resolved. In the course of three chapters on Nietzsche, and one each on Max Stirner, Russian nihilism, and Heidegger. Nishitani shows the way in which nihilism—as long as it is plumbed to its uttermost depths—will eventually "overcome itself." In the book's final two chapters, dealing with nihilism in the modern Japanese context and the problem of atheism, the background of Zen thought from which Nishitani approaches his topic comes to the fore.

AIRAKSINEN, Timo and HÄYRY, Matti. In Defence of "Hard" Offers: A Reply to J P Day. Philosophia (Israel), 20(3), 325-327, D 90.

In commenting on our earlier article in *Philosophia*, J P Day raises four issues: those concerning (1) the correct interpretation of the concept of "conditional offers," (2) the relationship of hard conditional offers to liberty, (3) the role of preferences in distinguishing offers from threats, and (4) the moral wrongness of some forms of offering. Two of these points, the second and the third, give rise to some further argument.

AIZPURUA, Jose Maria and NIETO, Jorge and URIARTE, Jose Ramon. Choice Procedure Consistent with Similarity Relations. Theor Decis, 29(3), 235-254, N 90.

We deal with the approach, initiated by Rubinstein, which assumes that people, when evaluating pairs of lotteries, use similarity relations. We interpret these relations as a way of modelling the imperfect powers of discrimination of the human mind and study the relationship between preferences and similarities. The class of both preferences and similarities that we deal with is larger than that considered by Rubinstein. The extension is made because we do not want to restrict ourselves to lottery spaces. Thus, under the above interpretation of a similarity, we find that some of the axioms imposed by Rubinstein are not justified if we want to consider other fields of choice theory. We show that any preference consistent with a pair of similarities is monotone on a subset of the choice space. We establish the implication upon the similarities of the requirement of making indifferent alternatives with a component which is zero. Furthermore, we show that Rubinstein's general results can also be obtained in this larger class of both preferences and similarity relations.

AJERAR, Hassane. De la problématique diltheyenne à l'intégralisme de Jean Granier. Rev Phil Fr, 180(4), 637-649, O-D 90.

AJVAZ, Michal. The Doubts about Post-Modernism (in Czechoslovakian). Filozof Cas, 38(6), 807-817, 1990.

This article reacts to Vaclav Belohradsky's paper "The Arrival of Gypsy Time or Just Strolling Round Europe" and to Umberto Eco's paper "The Originality in Repetition" which dealtwith postmodern thinking and were published in the journal *Svedectvi*, no. 88/1989. The author calls in question Belohradsky's duality of "spiritual process," characteristic for traditional European philosophy which asks for a unifying beginning and aim, and the aimless "strolling" of postmodern thinking which accepts the plurality of viewpoints. (edited)

AJZENSTAT, Samuel. "What Now Little Man? Comedy, Tragedy, and the Politics of Antihumanism" in *The Question of Humanism: Challenges and Possibilities*, GOICOECHEA, David (ed), 193-204. Buffalo, Prometheus, 1991.

AKAAH, Ishmael P. The Influence of Non-Anonymity Deriving from Feedback of Research Results on Marketing Professionals' Research Ethics. J Bus Ethics, 9(12), 949-959, D 90.

The study examines, in the context of Crawford's (1970) study items, the influence of non-anonymity deriving from feedback of research results on marketing professionals' research ethics judgments, particularly that of response patterns (social desirability of responses) and item omissions. The results indicate that such non-anonymity does not significantly influence the social desirability of responses or item omissions—thus suggesting the appropriateness of its use to stimulate research ethics responses.

AKEROYD, F M. Research Programmes and Empirical Results. Brit J Phil Sci, 39(1), 51-58, Mr 88.

According to Lakatos (1970) a theory within a research programme can only be eliminated by a better theory. This author claims that Hopkins's (1912) classic paper eliminated four theories within the 'Nutritional Chemistry' research programme of the 1900's and left a survivor a theory without excess empirical content: the Vitamin Theory. Other leading scientists were converted to the new theory and first isolated putative vitamins in 1915.

AKEROYD, F Michael. The Challenge to Lakatos Restated. Brit J Phil Sci, 41(3), 437-439, S 90.

This paper replies to the response of Zucker (1988) to Akeroyd (1986). The author presents evidence that by 1789 Lavoisier's original generalisation of the 'Oxygen Theory of Acids' had been refined by his follower de Fourcroy into a comprehensive and coherent segment of the 'hard core' of a research programme. The work of Davy on chlorine in 1815 not only destroyed a concept in the absence of a rival concept but also a key postulate in the 'hard core' of a Lakatosian style research programme.

AKEROYD, F Michael. An Oscillatory Model of the Growth of Scientific Knowledge. Brit J Phil Sci, 41(3), 407-414, S 90.

This paper proposes a new model of scientific progress which is based on an analogy with the well-known oscillatory reactions which occur in chemical systems. The reactants are analogous to 'protocol sentences,' the products equivalent to 'basic statements' (Popper, 1959) and the reactive intermediates equivalent to the plurality of competing scientific hypotheses alternately generated then refuted as proposed in Popper (1983).

AKHUTIN, A V. Sophia and the Devil: Kant in the Face of Russian Religious Metaphysics. Soviet Stud Phil, 29(4), 59-89, Spr 91.

ALADJEM, Terry K. The Philosopher's Prism: Foucault, Feminism, and Critique. Polit Theory, 19(2), 277-291, My 91.

There is a connection between Michel Foucault's extreme resistance to the perspectives of enlightenment reason and critique, and that of certain feminist theories. That resistance entails a certain humility before its objects of inquiry which, if applied beyond historical contexts, may be instructive for feminist critics of modernity interested in local, contextual struggles with power. It expands upon conceptions of the individual, equality, toleration and truth in liberalism, recalling their origins and revealing their elements much as the prism, with light.

ALARCÓN, Enrique. Naturaleza, espíritu, finalidad. Anu Filosof, 23(1), 125-131, 1990.

ALBEE, George W. The Futility of Psychotherapy. J Mind Behav, 11(3-4), 369-384, Sum-Autumn 90.

While psychotherapy is helpful to individual clients, the slim cadre of therapists and the vast number of disturbed people precludes any hope that more than a relative few will receive help. Nowhere is the futility of psychotherapy as obvious as among the poor and powerless whose suffering, crowding, and despair will yield only to social and political solutions. In the United States the expansion of the number of psychiatric diagnoses and the demographic changes in populations will only make larger the gap in numbers between therapists and clients. Psychotherapy is an expensive oddity to the poor, but their taxes will help the affluent obtain prepaid care. Psychotherapy does reveal some of the social and economic factors, like bad parenting, homelessness and unemployment, that cause emotional disturbances. But one-to-one treatment, medical or psychological, does not, and cannot, affect incidence. (edited)

ALBERT, David Z and LOEWER, Barry. The Measurement Problem: Some "Solutions". Synthese, 86(1), 87-98, Ja 91.

ALBERT, David and LOEWER, Barry. Wanted Dead or Alive: Two Attempts to Solve Schrödinger's Paradox. Proc Phil Sci Ass, 1, 277-285, 1990.

ALBERT, Michael H and GROSSBERG, Rami P. Rich Models. J Sym Log, 55(3), 1292-1298, S 90.

ALBIAC, Gabriel. De las maravillas acerca de lo uno y lo múltiple o sobre los avatares del amor neoplatónico en Baruch de Espinosa. El Basilisco, 2, 27-42, N-D 89.

ALBIZU, Edgardo. El desaparecer de lo eterno en sí mismo: Una clave del pensamiento de Hegel. Dialogos, 25(56), 81-85, Jl 90.

The work shows the importance of the idea of Verschwinden in the philosophy of Hegel. It has four parts: (1) dialectic and signs; (2) strict dialectic: to place, to knock, to disappear; (3) the transversal dialectic-semiological circle: logic, language, law; (4) disappearance of eternal in itself as speculative keystone. Dialectic's main operative aspects are presented as a play of logical and linguistical moments. Therein is very important the passage from *Dasein* to *Gesetztsein*, where the disappearance proves to have a fundamental function.

ALCARO, Mario. *Bertrand Russell*. Firenze, Ed Cultura Pace, 1990.

ALCHOURRÓN, Carlos E and MARTINO, Antonio A. Logic Without Truth. Ratio Juris, 3(1), 46-67, Mr 90.

Between the two horns of Jorgensen's dilemma, the authors opt for that according to which logic deals not only with truth and falsity but also with those concepts not possessing this semantic reference. Notwithstanding the "descriptive" prejudice, deontic logic has gained validity among modal logics. The technical foundation proposed consists in an abstract characterization of logical consequence. By identifying in the abstract notion of consequence the primitive from which to begin, it is possible to define the connectives—even those of obligation—by means of the rules of introduction or elimination in a context of derivation.

ALDRICH, Virgil. Persons as Natural Works of Art. Amer Phil Quart, 28(3), 245-249, Jl 91.

Works of art are not natural kinds. They are artifacts. This distinguishes them from aesthetic objects which may be natural, like a flower or a snowflake. Persons are not natural kinds. They are conventional, inventive, and artificial. Like works of art, they are artifacts. A person, making a work of art, is imitating the kind of activity that made him. So a person is a natural work of art—'Nature' with the capital N.

ALEGRÍA, Hernando Muciño. Viktor Emil Frankl médico y filósofo. Logos (Mexico), 18(52), 87-112, Ja-Ap 90.

La intención ha sido inquietar, motivar e invitar al lector a acercarse directamente a Frankl, para conocerlo o conocerlo mejor. Presento, pues, en este breve estudio, un panorama sobre la vida y obra de Frankl. Sobre su formación, sus escritos, su pensamiento, etc. La naturaleza del mismo estudio me ha obligado a dar sólo pistas sobre la filosofía frankliana. Soy consciente que son más las interrogantes que se abren que las respuestas que se dan.

ALELIUNAS, Romas. "A New Normative Theory of Probabilistic Logic" in *Knowledge Representation and Defeasible Reasoning*, KYBURG JR, Henry E (ed), 387-403. Norwell, Kluwer, 1990.

ALEXAKOS, Panos D. Metamorphoses: On the Limits of Thought. Thought, 66(260), 5-13, Mr 91.

ALEXANDER, Edwin. Aphasia—The Worm's Eye View of a Philosophic Patient and the Medical Establishment. Diogenes, 150, 1-23, Sum 90.

"Zeus suddenly zapped me with a thunderbolt." This is how I, a philosopher, experienced a stroke. Strokes make language (speaking, reading, writing) at first inaccessible, though concepts remain intact. This abstract reviews theories about left and right brain function, particularly the work of pioneers Broca and Wernecke. I am proposing that a new aspect be considered in stroke-related aphasia: *self-reflective language*, which acknowledges that concepts remain functional, thus enabling medical and other therapists to cooperate with the patients in a more positive and playful atmosphere, so that language recovery can occur earlier and with far greater success.

ALEXANDER, Larry. Law and Exclusionary Reasons. Phil Topics, 18(1), 5-22, Spr 90.

Joseph Raz argues that if certain conduct is demanded of me by those with legal authority, then, as a consequence of that demand, I have a second-order, preemptive reason to disregard all first-order reasons that bear on the justifiability of that conduct except for the first-order reason that the conduct is legally demanded. I argue, to the contrary, that the mandates of legal authorities-laws-affect first-order reasons for acting and their overall balance, but that they are not second-order, exclusionary reasons; however, they can (and perhaps should) *demand* a response as if they had overriding normative weight, and they perhaps should even claim to possess such weight.

ALEXY, Robert and DREIER, Ralf. The Concept of Jurisprudence. Ratio Juris, 3(1), 1-13, Mr 90.

The first part of this article contains (i) considerations as to the relationship between jurisprudence and legal dogmatics, legal philosophy, and sociology of law; (ii) considerations about the status of jurisprudence both as a meta- and an object-theory. These lead to the suggestion that jurisprudence should be defined as a general juristic theory of law and legal science. In the second part, the character and elements of this definition are explained systematically. The article's main thesis is that jurisprudence is not distinguished from legal philosophy and sociology of law by its subject or its method, but by the specifically juristic research aspect or perspective it is based upon.

ALFINO, Mark. Another Look at the Derrida-Searle Debate. Phil Rhet, 24(2), 143-152, 1991.

This paper discusses both the rhetoric and content of the exchange between John Searle and Jacques Derrida in the mid-1980's. I argue that Searle's initial understanding of Derrida's position was seriously deficient and I try to reconstruct the central dispute in the debate over the nature of intentionality and "iterability." In a more recent phase of the debate, Searle uses the Wittgensteinian notion of speech act theory. I argue that Searle's use of Wittgenstein is not cogent and does not address the central questions raised by the initial debate.

ALFINO, Mark. Intellectual Property and Copyright Ethics. Bus Prof Ethics J, 10(2), 85-109, Sum 91.

This article argues that current and future disputes over copyright law will not be solved by clarifying traditional conceptions of natural property of intellectual property. Only by looking at the historical and social context of the development of the notion of authorship and intellectual property markets can we understand the social values which rulings on copyright should promote. In light of a critical historical survey, I argue that the public policy goals of copyright law will only be realized by producers and consumers who obligate themselves to support new information technologies and pricing mechanisms.

ALIDAEE, Bahram. A Note on the Permutationally Convex Games. Theor Decis, 30(2), 109-111, Mr 91.

If marginal worth vector of a game for an ordering is in the core, the game does not have to be a p.c. game.

ALLAIS, Maurice. An Outline of My Main Contributions to Economic Science. Theor Decis, 30(1), 1-26, Ja 91.

ALLAN, George. *The Realizations of the Future: An Inquiry into the Authority of Praxis*. Albany, SUNY Pr, 1990.

A model of praxis is developed to account for various attempts in Western culture to determine the essential conditions for human fulfillment. Each attempt's inadequacy leads to a proposed bedder answer which also proves inadequate. Hedonistic goods can be sustained only by suppressing individual freedom; norms of selfhood can reconcile individual and communal goods but only if the latter is actually realized; progressivist beliefs about the realization of such a community, in or beyond history, prove implausible. Recent historicist alternatives are no better. Philosophers discussed include: Aristotle, Augustine, Ibn Khaldun, Kant, Hegel, Kierkegaard, Dewey, Royce, Sartre, Oakeshott, Whitehead, Arendt, Lyotard.

ALLCHIN, Douglas. Paradigms, Populations and Problem-Fields: Approaches to Disagreement. Proc Phil Sci Ass, 1, 53-66, 1990.

Kuhn's distinction of within- and between-paradigm thinking can be extended using his notion of a problem-field. Hull's notion of populational variation applies within paradigms; his type specimen approach allows one to analyze disagreement and identify the problem-field. Categories of questions or problem frames can also partition debate, establishing interparadigm variation. A case where multiple simultaneous paradigms compete highlights the role of empirical domains. The Ox-Phos Controversy in bioenergetics (1961-1977) serves as a case study. Conclusions are framed as strategies for scientists.

ALLEN, B. Arithmetizing Uniform *NC*. Annals Pure Applied Log, 53(1), 1-50, Jl 91.

ALLEN, Collin and HAUSER, Marc D. Concept Attribution in Nonhuman Animals. Phil Sci, 58(2), 221-240, Je 91.

The demise of behaviorism has made ethologists more willing to ascribe mental states to animals. However, a methodology that can avoid the charge of excessive anthropomorphism is needed. We describe a series of experiments that could help determine whether the behavior of nonhuman animals towards dead conspecifics is concept mediated. These experiments form the basis of a general point. The behavior of some animals is clearly guided by complex mental processes. The techniques developed by comparative psychologists and behavioral ecologists are able to provide us with the tools to critically evaluate hypotheses concerning the continuity between human minds and animal minds.

ALLEN, Elizabeth. On the Issue of Sex Differences. Dialogue (PST), 33(2-3), 61-63, Ap 91.

The objective of this article is to look at two opposing arguments relating to the origin of sex differences and to examine their strengths and weaknesses. Stemming from an apparent fear of feminist equality Michael Levin asserts the rightness of innate sex differences, an argument countered by Ruth Bleier. Mr. Levin's argument is riddled with stereotypes, evasions and fallacies, yet, both arguments lack strong scientific evidence. The conclusion points out the danger of such an argument as Levin's.

ALLEN, J G. Interrupting Olivier's Socio-Political Conversation: Another Postmodern Proposal. S Afr J Phil, 9(4), 224, N 90.

ALLEN, Jeffner (ed). *Lesbian Philosophies and Cultures*. Albany, SUNY Pr, 1990.

Essays and experimental writing by twenty-one lesbian philosophers who write from a variety of perspectives. Themes include 'living in the plural,' 'dis/connections,' and 'writing desire.' Areas of philosophy treated include ethics and social philosophy, epistemology and metaphysics, and aesthetics. The authors are from the USA and Canada. Key to the anthology is a focus on multiculturalism.

ALLEN, R E (trans) and PLATO,. *The Dialogues of Plato, Volume II*. New Haven, Yale Univ Pr, 1991.

ALLEN, R T. Governance by Emotion. J Brit Soc Phenomenol, 22(2), 15-29, My 91.

This article develops the scheme presented by S Strasser (*Phenomenology of Feeling*) to show how specific emotions are necessary to the governance of action. Acting without the capacity for emotion, e.g., by habit, is a secondary and derivative possibility, requiring previous guidance by emotion by oneself or others. Felt desires and aversions initiate action. Hope, fear and confidence in one's powers and means translate general aims into specific courses of action, while lack of confidence and resignation lead to abstention from action. Experiences of satisfaction terminate action, while those of dissatisfaction or disappointment either terminate it or initiate further attempts, hope or no hope of success at a second attempt.

ALLEN, W B. Black and White Together: A Reconsideration. Soc Phil Pol, 8(2), 172-195, Spr 91.

ALLESCH, Christian. "Kantian and Phenomenological Traditions in Psychological Aesthetics" in *XIth International Congress in Aesthetics, Nottingham 1988*, WOODFIELD, Richard (ed), 1-5. Nottingham, Nottingham Polytech, 1990.

ALLINSON, Robert E. "An Overview of the Chinese Mind" in *Understanding the Chinese Mind: The Philosophical Roots*, ALLINSON, Robert E (ed), 1-25. New York, Oxford Univ Pr, 1989.

ALLINSON, Robert E (ed). *Understanding the Chinese Mind: The Philosophical Roots*. New York, Oxford Univ Pr, 1989.

This book attempts to show that an understanding of the Chinese mind is enhanced by dialogues between nine philosophers with a reputation both in Western and Chinese philosophy. It formulates both classical and contemporary Chinese viewpoints in linguistics, epistemology, philosophy of religion, aesthetics, metaphysics, ethics, and comparative philosophy. The result is a unified volume which both engages in a hermeneutics of cross-cultural interpretation and provides a bridge between Chinese philosophy and topical issues in contemporary Western philosophy. A comprehensive bibliography of both Oriental and Western languages makes the book a valuable reference source for Chinese and comparative philosophy.

ALLIS, Victor and KOETSIER, Teunis. On Some Paradoxes of the Infinite. Brit J Phil Sci, 42(2), 187-194, Je 91.

In the paper below the authors describe three super-tasks. They show that although the abstract notion of a super-task may be, as Benecerraf suggested, a conceptual mismatch, the completion of the three super-tasks involved can be defined rather naturally, without leading to inconsistency, by means of a particular kinematical interpretation combined with a principle of continuity.

ALLISON, Henry E. *Kant's Theory of Freedom*. New York, Cambridge Univ Pr, 1990.

ALLMAN, John. Paul de Man, Deconstruction, and Discipleship. Phil Lit, 14(2), 324-339, O 90.

The article, by studying the relation between the work of Paul de Man and that of one of his influential students—Barbara Johnson—illustrates how the relation between the originators of deconstruction and their successors resembles that between master and disciple.

ALMAGOR, Uri. Some Thoughts on Common Scents. J Theor Soc Behav, 20(3), 181-195, S 90.

ALMEDER, Robert F (ed) and HUMBER, James M (ed). *Biomedical Ethics Reviews, 1987*. Clifton, Humana Pr, 1988.

ALMEDER, Robert F. Vacuous Truth. Synthese, 85(3), 507-524, D 90.

In this essay I argue that the correspondence theory of truth is meaningless because it violates a necessary condition for any expression being meaningful. Specifically, I argue that knowing what a term means implies being able to pick out those items to which it refers, assuming that there is something in the extensional domain of the expression. In the case of the correspondence theory of truth this principle is violated because we do not have any reliable decision procedure for picking out those sentences that satisfy the traditional correspondence definition of truth.

ALMEDER, Robert (ed) and HUMBER, James M (ed). *Biomedical Ethics Reviews, 1990*. Clifton, Humana Pr, 1991.

ALMEDER, Robert and CAREY, David. In Defense of Sharks: Moral Issues in Hostile Liquidating Takeovers. J Bus Ethics, 10(7), 471-484, Jl 91.

In this essay we defend the view that from a purely rule-utilitarian perspective there is no sound argument favoring the immorality of hostile liquidating buyouts. All arguments favoring such a view are seriously flawed. Moreover, there are some good argument favoring the view that such buyouts may be morally obligatory from the rule-utilitarian perspective. We also defend the view that most of the "shark repellents" in the market are immoral. If we are right in our arguments there is no justification, moral or otherwise, for any form of legislation that would constrain the practice of hostile liquidating buyouts.

ALMEDER, Robert. On Naturalizing Epistemology. Amer Phil Quart, 27(4), 263-279, O 90.

In this essay I examine the six major arguments in favor of the "replacement thesis" (Quine's thesis) to the effect that the only meaningful questions are those that admit of resolution by appeal to the methods of the natural sciences as we now know them. I show that not only are all the arguments proposed flawed in some crucial way, the project itself is essentially incoherent.

ALMOG, Joseph. "Logic and the World" in *Themes From Kaplan*, ALMOG, Joseph (ed), 43-65. New York, Oxford Univ Pr, 1989.

ALMOG, Joseph (ed) and PERRY, John (ed) and WETTSTEIN, Howard (ed). *Themes From Kaplan*. New York, Oxford Univ Pr, 1989.

ALMOG, Joseph. The What and the How. J Phil, 88(5), 225-244, My 91.

ALMOND, Brenda. "Rights" in *A Companion to Ethics*, SINGER, Peter (ed), 259-269. Cambridge, Blackwell, 1991.

Rights provide an internationally understood language for moral and political debate, and belong to a tradition of ethical reasoning that goes back to antiquity. Complex questions exist concerning the analysis of rights. They are, however, an essential part of our moral vocabulary and no more suspect than other moral terms. They also have a number of pragmatic justifications, including their potential influence on the practice of present-day governments. Rights belong to the tradition of liberal individualism and as such have been attacked by utilitarians, Marxists and conservatives. Nevertheless, they contribute to the public good and are themselves part of that good.

ALONSO, Luz García. La ética y los derechos humanos en la filosofía clásica. Logos (Mexico), 18(54), 33-46, S-D 90.

ALSTON, William P. *Divine Nature and Human Language: Essays in Philosophical Theology*. Ithaca, Cornell Univ Pr, 1990.

The book is divided into three parts. The first group of essays is devoted to the kind of meaning terms carry in application to God and to what is involved in referring to God. The second deals with issues concerning divine knowledge, divine eternity, and other aspects of the divine nature. The third part is concerned with divine activity in the world and with God as the foundation of ethics.

ALSTON, William P. *Epistemic Justification: Essays in the Theory of Knowledge*. Ithaca, Cornell Univ Pr, 1990.

These essays deal with basic issues concerning epistemic concepts, positions, and orientations, as well with the more specific topic of one's knowledge of one's own conscious states. Part I deals with foundationalism, defending a form of the view. Part II examines concepts of justification and considers the relation of justification and knowledge. Part III looks at internalist and externalist approaches to epistemology. Part IV is concerned with the epistemology of self-knowledge.

ALSTON, William P. Externalist Theories of Perception. Phil Phenomenol Res, 50 SUPP, 73-97, Fall 90.

The title refers to theories that require a certain sort of relation between X and an experience of S in order that S perceive X. The relation might be causal, counterfactual, doxastic, or otherwise. It is argued against such theories that there are possible cases in which X stands in the required relation to an experience of S and S does not perceive X and cases in which X is perceived though it does not stand in the required relation.

ALT, Wayne E. Logic and Language in the *Chuang Tzu*. Asian Phil, 1(1), 61-76, 1991.

ALTEKAR, E V. Quantum Gravity: Some Philosophical Reflections. Indian Phil Quart, SUPP 18(2), 27-45, Ap 91.

ALTHUSSER, Louis and ELLIOTT, Gregory (ed). *Philosophy and the Spontaneous Philosophy of the Scientists and Other Essays*. New York, Verso, 1990.

Collected here are Althusser's most significant philosophical writings from 1965 to 1978, intended to contribute to a left-wing critique of Stalinism. At the same time they chart his critique of the theoretical system in his own works. (staff)

ALUNNI, Charles. Di cose grammaticali: Un itinerario campanelliano. G Crit Filosof Ital, 69(2), 222-240, My-Ag 90.

ALVAREZ GÓMEZ, Mariano. La verdad. Dialogo Filosof, 6(3), 355-391, S-D 90.

ÁLVAREZ, Margarita Mauri. Breves notas acerca de la *Política* de Aristóteles. Sapientia, 45(177), 205-210, Jl-S 90.

ALVAREZ-CASTELLANOS, Juan José Sánchez. Reflexiones en torno a la sensibilidad externa. Anu Filosof, 24(1), 89-111, 1991.

This paper consists of a series of reflections of external sensitive knowledge: what does it mean to know a color, a sound, etc. Three different views are compared Zubiri, Leonardo Polo and Aquinas.

ALVARGONZÁLEZ, David. Problemas en torno al concepto de "ciencias humanas" como ciencias con doble plano operatorio. El Basilisco, 2, 51-56, N-D 89.

According to G Bueno's philosophy, human sciences could be characterized as possessing two different operation levels. In this work, the author, making use of some research carried out by himself and by some others (Bueno, Velarde, Fuentes) about the gnoseology of human sciences, realizes some of the problems concerning Bueno's idea of human sciences and suggests several future research prospects. Bueno replies in his article "Sobre el alcance da una ciencia meda..." (*El Basilisco*, Number 2, 1989: 57-73).

ALVES, E H and GUERZONI, J A D. Extending Montague's System: A Three Valued Intensional Logic. Stud Log, 49(1), 127-132, Mr 90.

In this note we present a three-valued intensional logic, which is an extension of both Montague's intensional logic and Lukasiewicz three-valued logic. Our system is obtained by adapting Gallin's version of intensional logic (see Gallin, D, *Intensional and Higher-order Modal Logic*). Here we give only the necessary modifications to the latter. An acquaintance with Gallin's work is presupposed.

AMARIGLIO, Jack and RESNICK, Stephen and WOLFF, Richard. Division and Difference in the "Discipline" of Economics. Crit Inquiry, 17(1), 108-137, Autumn 90.

The article argues that the "discipline" of economics is an agnostic field of fundamentally different and conflicting discourses. Neoclassical, Keynesian, and Marxian schools are distinguished by the ways they understand both unity and difference in economics; key means by which these schools define and mark differences are their different uses of "scientific" epistemological positions, differences in theoretical "entry points," and diverse concepts of causality. The paper criticizes foundationalist epistemologies and reductionist forms of causal explanation, especially humanism and structuralism, in neoclassical, Keynesian, and traditional Marxian economics and offers a nonessentialist conception of knowledge and causality as an alternative.

AMARIGLIO, Jack and NORTON, Bruce. Marxist Historians and the Question of Class in the French Revolution. Hist Theor, 30(1), 37-55, F 91.

This article evaluates the centrality of class in the "social interpretation" of the French Revolution. The social interpreters introduce an admirable complexity, which, however, stems from loose, multiple, contradictory notions of class influenced partly by Joseph Barnave's "stage theory" of pre-Revolutionary France and by "vulgar Marxism"; these notions contrast with the concept of class—surplus-labor extraction—developed in the three volumes of Marx's *Capital*. Using this alternative concept would preserve the social interpreters' class focus—contrary to revisionist historians' reformulations—yet also would convey the many class divisions in pre-Revolutionary France and the multiple class positions historical agents simultaneously occupied.

AMES, Roger T. "The Mencian Conception of *Ren xing*: Does it Mean 'Human Nature'?" in *Chinese Texts and Philosophical Contexts*, ROSEMONT JR, Henry (ed), 143-175. La Salle, Open Court, 1991.

AMES, Roger T and HALL, David Lynn. Rationality, Correlativity, and the Language of Process. J Speculative Phil, 5(2), 85-106, 1991.

AMIEL, H F. "Voir vivre, sans vivre": Extraits du *Journal Intime*. Philosophique (France), 1(89), 5-20, 1989.

AMIN, Wael A and ABIAN, Alexander. The Cardinality of Powersets in Finite Models of the Powerset Axiom. Notre Dame J Form Log, 32(2), 290-293, Spr 91.

It is shown that in a finite model of the set-theoretical Powerset axiom a set s and its powerset $P(s)$ have the same number of elements. Additional results are also derived.

AMIN, Wael A and ABIAN, Alexander. An Equivalent of the Axiom of Choice in Finite Models of the Powerset Axiom. Notre Dame J Form Log, 31(3), 371-374, Sum 90.

It is shown that in a finite model for the set-theoretical Powerset axiom every set s has a Choice set iff every set s has a Meet set $\cap s$. Moreover, the Choice set of s is unique and is equal to $\cap s$, where $\cap s$ is a singleton and $\cap s \in s$.

AMIR, Yehoyada. The Foundations of Franz Rosenzweig's Theory of Knowledge (in Hebrew). Iyyun, 39(4), 381-422, O 90.

AMMERMAN, Robert R (ed). *Classics of Analytic Philosophy*. Indianapolis, Hackett, 1990.

AMORÓS, Celia. Los escritos póstumos de J P Sartre (I). Rev Filosof (Spain), 4, 143-160, 1990.

AMSELEK, Paul. Le locutoire et l'illocutoire dans les énonciations relatives aux normes juridiques. Rev Metaph Morale, 95(3), 385-413, Jl-S 90.

L'acte de prescription de normes de conduite, et notamment de normes juridiques, est-il un acte "normatif", un simple acte de dire des normes, de prononcer des paroles ayant objectivement, de par elles-mêmes, valeur d'énoncés de normes, et notamment de normes juridiques? C'est ce que paraît suggérer l'expression même "dire—édicter—le droit", et c'est de fait le point de vue généralement développé par la théorie éthique et juridique. Cette étude montre qu'il y a là une aberration au sens propre du terme, c'est-à-dire un écart par rapport à la réalité.

ANAND, Mulk Raj. "Art Nonsense" or the Nine Flavours. Diotima, 18, 55-57, 1990.

ANAPOLITANOS, D A. The Continuous and the Discrete: Leibniz Versus Berkeley. Phil Inq, 13(1-2), 1-24, Wint-Spr 91.

The argument concerning the continuous and the discrete started long ago. The basic positions and issues have been quite clearly defined from the very start. The issue of the compactness of the mathematical continuum was not in the forum, of course, but the property of density or, more appropriately the property of infinite divisibility of finite magnitudes was a burning problem. My aim in this paper is not to trace the problem in the thoughts of the ancients, but to give a critical account of the argument concerning the continuous and the discrete by comparing Leibniz's continualist position with Berkeley's non-continualist one.

ANAPOLITANOS, D A. "Proofs and Refutations: A Reassessment" in *Imre Lakatos and Theories of Scientific Change*, GAVROGLU, Kostas (ed), 337-345. Norwell, Kluwer, 1989.

ANASTAPLO, George. "Democracy and Philosophy: On Yves R Simon and Mortimer J Adler" in *Freedom in the Modern World: Jacques Maritain, Yves R Simon, Mortimer J Adler*, TORRE, Michael D (ed), 79-85. Notre Dame, Univ Notre Dame Pr, 1989.

ANDEREGGEN, Ignacio E M. El conocimiento de Dios en la exposición de Tomás de Aquino sobre el "De divinis nominibus" de D Areopagita. Sapientia, 45(178), 269-276, O-D 90.

ANDEREGGEN, Ignacio E M. Conocimientos negativo y conocimiento afirmativo de Dios en Santo Tomás y en Hegel. Sapientia, 46(180), 91-98, Ap-Je 91.

ANDERSON, Allan W. The Seasonal Structure Underlying the Arrangement of the Hexagrams in the *Yijing*. J Chin Phil, 17(3), 275-299, S 90.

ANDERSON, C Anthony (ed) and OWENS, Joseph (ed). *Propositional Attitudes: The Role of Content in Logic, Language, and Mind*. Stanford, CSLI, 1990.

The papers treat problems about quantifying into modal contexts, discourse representation treatments of complex propositional attitudes, comparisons between the semantical ideas of Frege and Davidson, the sense in which language is social, the idea of "narrow content" mental states, Cartesian access to our mental states, Burge's and Putnam's thought experiments about mind and meaning, the new (or direct) theory of reference, Kripke's "Pierre Puzzle", problems with propositions as objects of the propositional attitudes, and the connection between consciousness and intentionality. Authors are Burge, Donnellan, K Fine, Gunderson, Kamp, LePore, Loewer, Mason, Owens, Stalnaker, N Salmon, Schiffer, Searle, and Wallace.

ANDERSON, C Anthony. "Russellian Intensional Logic" in *Themes From Kaplan*, ALMOG, Joseph (ed), 67-103. New York, Oxford Univ Pr, 1989.

Alonzo Church's formalization of the intensional logic implicit in Russell's *Principles of Mathematics* is shown to imply Axioms of Infinity in all types except the type of individuals. However, it is further shown that the theory has some paradoxical consequences for reasoning involving propositional attitudes. Modifications are suggested which better capture Russell's concept of a propositional function and models are constructed for the revised theory. Further changes are urged which, it is argued, accord better with the possibility of generalizing Russellian intensional logic. Criticism is offered of two other Russellian approaches to intentional logic by John Myhill and George Bealer.

ANDERSON, Douglas R. Bowne and Peirce on the Logic of Religious Belief. Personalist Forum, 6(2), 107-121, Fall 90.

In this paper I explore some similarities of thought between C S Peirce and Borden P Bowne, the originators of American pragmatism and personalism. In particular, I examine their approaches to the question of the origin of religious belief. I try to show that each argues that religious belief begins in nonrational ways but then grows into what we might call rational belief.

ANDERSON, Elizabeth. The Ethical Limitations of the Market. Econ Phil, 6(2), 179-205, O 90.

An alternative framework to welfare economics is offered for deciding whether something is properly treated as a commodity. It is argued that different kinds of goods are properly subject to different norms of production and exchange. Some values and ideals can be realized only by circulating goods according to nonmarket norms—for example, the exchange of gift values should be sensitive to the motives and personalities of the exchangers, and the provision of shared values should be nonexclusive. The analysis is applied to prostitution, marriage contracts, labor contracts, parks, schools, streets, blood, and in-kind welfare provisions.

ANDERSON, James C. Moral Planes and Intrinsic Values. Environ Ethics, 13(1), 49-58, Spr 91.

In his book *Earth and Other Ethics*, Christopher Stone attempts to account for the moral dimension of our lives insofar as it extends to nonhuman animals, plants, species, ecosystems, and even inanimate objects. In his effort to do this, he introduces a technical notion, the *moral plane*. Moral planes are defined both by the ontological commitments they make and by the governance rules (moral maxims) that pertain to the sorts of entities included in the plane. By introducing these plans, Stone is left with a set of problems. 1) Do the planes provide anything more objective than a set of alternative ways of looking at moral problems? 2) How can one resolve apparent conflicts between the recommendations forthcoming from distinct planes? 3) Why do certain entities constitute moral plans; and how do we decide which planes to "buy into?" Stone's answers to these questions endorse a series of concessions to moral relativism. In this paper I outline an alternative to Stone's moral planes which, while sympathetic to his ethical concern, comes down squarely on the side of moral realism.

ANDERSON, Kenneth S and BULLER, Paul F and KOHLS, John J. The Challenge of Global Ethics. J Bus Ethics, 10(10), 767-775, O 91.

The authors argue that the time is ripe for national and corporate leaders to move consciously towards the development of global ethics. This paper presents a model of global ethics, a rationale for the development of global ethics, and the implications of the model for research and practice.

ANDERSON, Lyle V. "Cybernetics, Culpability, and Risk" in *Philosophy of Technology*, DURBIN, Paul T (ed), 3-25. Norwell, Kluwer, 1989.

This essay argues two interrelated theses on morality and technology: 1) Amoral or cybernetic models of relations between technological and bureaucratic mechanisms, for analyzing such generalizations as "The arms race has taken on a life of its own," is insufficient for the case of automated missle-launch as the latest logico-historical phase of that race. 2) An Aristotelian/legal notion of culpable ignorance is sufficient; it both describes what is wrong with the technologically driven evolution of the arms race, and predicts requisite de-escalating arms policies whereby the techno-historical process could (and now has?) devolved from the precipice of automated launch.

ANDERSON, Richard L. Popular Art and Aesthetic Theory: Why the Muse Is Unembarrassed. J Aes Educ, 24(4), 33-46, Wint 90.

Other writers have shown that Western theories of art fall into four aesthetic traditions—mimesis theories that emphasize representation of subject matter, pragmatic theories that view art as socially or spiritually uplifting, emotionalist theories that focus on art's ability to evoke strong feelings, and theories that concentrate on formal utilization of the medium. This paper argues that although all four theories focus upon the fine arts, Western *popular* arts derive from, or are closely related to, the same theories: The proverbial man or woman on the street typically values and evaluates the arts in terms that relate closely to traditional academic aesthetics.

ANDERSON, Robert M (and others). Commentary on Layton's "Engineering Needs a Loyal Opposition". Bus Prof Ethics J, 2(3), 61-67, Spr 83.

ANDERSON, Susan Leigh. A Picture of the Self Which Supports the Moral Responsibility. Monist, 74(1), 43-54, Ja 91.

It is usually maintained that for a person to be held morally accountable for an action that action must 1) be done *freely* and 2) be, in a significant sense, the self's action. A contradiction would arise if these conditions are interpreted as claiming that: 1') no antecedent conditions, including the self's character, determine the action and 2') the action follows from the self's character being what it is. The author argues that while both 1) and 2) are necessary conditions for moral responsibility, neither 1') nor 2') give us the correct interpretations of those conditions.

ANDERSON, Susan Leigh. The Status of Frozen Embryos. Pub Affairs Quart, 4(4), 311-322, O 90.

In considering the recent Davis case in which a divorcing couple fought for the right to control the fate of seven frozen embryos created through IVF technology, it is argued that it is necessary to decide on the status of the embryos and that to do so will also shed light on the abortion controversy. The pros and cons of considering the embryos to be first material possessions, then persons, and finally as entities which fall somewhere in between are discussed before deciding that the last view is the most defensible.

ANDERSON, Thomas C. "Authenticity, Conversion, and the City of Ends in Sartre's *Notebooks for an Ethics*" in *Writing the Politics of Difference*, SILVERMAN, Hugh J (ed), 99-110. Albany, SUNY Pr, 1991.

Jean-Paul Sartre's posthumous *Cahiers pour une morale* contains the only extant portions of the ethics promised at the end of *Being and Nothingness*. This article shows that the *Cahiers*, in its treatment of authenticity and pure reflection (conversion), presents Sartre's alternative to his portrayal of bad faith and accomplice reflection in BN. The *Cahiers'* description of authentic love, generosity, and the city of ends also presents Sartre's alternative to the conflictual human relations emphasized in BN. Thus, the *Cahiers* shows that *Being and Nothingness* was never intended to depict the definitive human condition, but only its state before conversion.

ANDERSON, Tyson. Comment on Huston Smith's Review of *The Essential Writings of Frithiof Schuon. Phil East West, 41(3), 365-368, Jl 91.*

Smith is wrong to think that one must choose between Schuon's work and contemporary philosophy; dialogue between the two is what is needed. Smith is also wrong in suggesting that Heidegger and Wittgenstein are not independent thinkers; they in fact exhibit intellectual independence but not autonomy from the subject matter and questions being raised. Finally, Rorty's openness to dialogue is preferable to ahistorical philosophical dogmatism.

ANDERSON, Tyson. Reply to Huston Smith. Phil East West, 41(3), 370-371, Jl 91.

The major difference between traditional and contemporary philosophy is the nonessentialism of the latter. There are no fixed and timeless essences in Smith's sense. Locating meaning within the context of human lives and language games makes more sense out of the diverse and changing meanings of religious ideas ("Buddha," "Christ") in world history than does essentialism.

ANDERSON, Wilda. *Diderot's Dream*. Baltimore, Johns Hopkins U Pr, 1990.

This book focuses first on the natural-historical and technical writings of Denis Diderot, especially the *Encyclopedia, D'Alembert's Dream* and the *Interpretation of Nature* to explore Diderot's idiosyncratic materialism, which denied any separation between mind and body. This materialism grounded both his understanding and practice of literary writing, and the second half of the book explores the *Supplement to Bougainville's Voage*, the *Salon of 1767* and *Rameau's Nephew* in its light. A picture emerges of Diderot's unified intellectual project, which was to provide the context and medium for the French Enlightenment understood as a continuing material and mental dialogue that refused to accept any concept as unchanging truth.

ANDIC, Martin. "Were Plato and Aristotle Humanists?" in *The Question of Humanism: Challenges and Possibilities*, GOICOECHEA, David (ed), 27-40. Buffalo, Prometheus, 1991.

ANDIC, Martin. "What Is Renaissance Humanism?" in *The Question of Humanism: Challenges and Possibilities*, GOICOECHEA, David (ed), 83-98. Buffalo, Prometheus, 1991.

ANDRE, Judith. Role Morality as a Complex Instance of Ordinary Morality. Amer Phil Quart, 28(1), 73-84, Ja 91.

Role morality is not in conflict with "ordinary" morality but a complex instance of it. Role morality cannot be reduced to contractual obligation, nor to protection of the vulnerable; it exists even when the role itself is morally objectionable. A role obligates someone holding it because others expect, desire, and/or depend upon one's actions. The obligation increases if one has voluntarily assumed the role and when one makes implicit or explicit promises and contracts. Profiting from a role leads to the further obligations of gratitude and fair play. All of these obligations, however, are only *prima facie*.

ANDRÉKA, H and NÉMETI, I and THOMPSON, R J. Weak Cylindric Set Algebras and Weak Subdirect Indecomposability. J Sym Log, 55(2), 577-588, Je 90.

In this note we prove that the abstract property "weakly subdirectly indecomposable" does not characterize the class IWs_α of weak cylindric set algebras. However, we give another (similar) abstract property characterizing IWs_α. The original property does characterize the directed unions of members of IWs_α iff α is countable. Free algebras will be shown to satisfy the original property.

ANDREW, Edward. The Foxy Prophet: Machiavelli versus Machiavelli on Ferdinand the Catholic. Hist Polit Thought, 11(3), 409-422, Autumn 90.

ANDREWS, John N. General Thinking Skills: Are There Such Things? J Phil Educ, 24(1), 71-79, Sum 90.

ANDRIOPOULOS, D Z. Aristotle's Causality Theory. Phil Inq, 10(1-2), 23-36, Wint-Spr 88.

ANGEL, Leonard. *How to Build a Conscious Machine*. Boulder, Westview Pr, 1989.

Can a conscious machine be built? In part I, a pure agency attributive language learning device (PAI) is designed. In parts II and III insights gained therefrom are applied to the philosophical problems of consciousness attribution. The views of Searle and Dreyfus are analyzed and found wanting. The conclusion reached is that we have no reason at present to think that there are insuperable philosophical or practical obstacles to building conscious machines.

ANGELETT, William. Philosophy and a Career in Counseling. Int J Applied Phil, 5(2), 73-75, Fall 90.

ANGELO, Richard. Sex, Drugs and Rock 'n Roll: Youth, Instruction and Experience in Contemporary American Film. Phil Stud Educ, /, 1-18, 1987-88.

ANGENOT, Marc. Frontières des études littéraires: science de la littérature, science des discours. Horiz Phil, 1(1), 23-34, 1990.

ANGLIN, W S. Theology and the Necessity of Natures. Faith Phil, 8(2), 225-236, Ap 91.

In this paper we give a definition of a 'nature' which 1) captures the idea that a nature is a kind of constant in the midst of change; 2) does *not* sanction the inference of the conclusion 'Christ has to be human' from the premiss 'Christ has human nature'; 3) enables us to defend the logical coherence of certain theological claims; and 4) accords with many of our pre-analytic intuitions about 'natures.'

ANÍZAR, Humberto Encarnación. Filosofía de la liberación como nuevo pensamiento a partir de los oprimidos y como de-strucción (2a parte). Logos (Mexico), 18(52), 9-32, Ja-Ap 90.

ANÍZAR, Humberto Encarnación. Filosofía de la liberación como nuevo pensamiento a partir de los oprimidos y como de-strucción (3a parte). Logos (Mexico), 18(53), 47-82, My-Ag 90.

ANKERSMIT, Frank R. Reply to Professor Zagorin's "Historiography and Postmodernism: Reconsideration". Hist Theor, 29(3), 275-296, O 90.

Discussions between modernists and postmodernists are often hampered by the fact that the latter use an argumentative style unacceptable to the modernist. In this essay I attempt to give an exposition of the postmodernist conception of history that is in agreement with the modernist requirements for argumentative style. The central thesis is (1) that the modernist cannot deny the presence in historical writing of a logical entity I have called the 'narrative substance', and (2) that if the presence of this entity is admitted one can derive from its logical nature most of the postmodernist conceptions that the modernist ordinarily objects to.

ANNAS, George J. Crazy Making: Embryos and Gestational Mothers. Hastings Center Rep, 21(1), 35-38, Ja-F 91.

ANNAS, George J. Ethics Committees: From Ethical Comfort to Ethical Cover. Hastings Center Rep, 21(3), 18-21, My-Je 91.

ANNAS, George J. Killing Machines. Hastings Center Rep, 21(2), 33-35, Mr-Ap 91.

ANNAS, George J. Nancy Cruzan in China. Hastings Center Rep, 20(5), 39-41, S-O 90.

ANNAS, George J. Outrageous Fortune: Selling Other People's Cells. Hastings Center Rep, 20(6), 36-39, N-D 90.

ANNAS, George J and GRODIN, Michael A. Treating the Troops: A Commentary. Hastings Center Rep, 21(2), 24-27, Mr-Ap 91.

ANNAS, Julia. "Epicurus' Philosophy of Mind" in *Psychology (Companions to Ancient Thought: 2)*, EVERSON, Stephen (ed), 84-101. New York, Cambridge Univ Pr, 1991.

The article gives an account of Epicurus's philosophy of mind in terms of Epicurus's attempt to meet four constraints: atomism, empiricism, physicalism and finally a non-reductivist respect for our "folk psychology" conception of ourselves as agents. Drawing on passages from the book on agency in *On Nature*, the article argues that Epicurus's theory is more worthy of serious respect than sometimes assumed.

ANOZ, José. Rasgos de la communidad agustiniana según la 'Regula recepta'. Augustinus, 35(137-138), 81-98, Ja-Je 90.

ANSALDI, Jean. La toute-puissance du Dieu du théisme dans le champ de la perversion. Laval Theol Phil, 47(1), 3-11, F 91.

La théisme se caractérise par un savoir préalable sur Dieu, savoir antérieur à la lecture des Écritures. Il a déjà été mis en cause par Luther, et Freud l'a lui-même attaqué en lisant l'association "théisme—toute-puissance" dans le cadre de l'obsessionalité. Grâce à l'apport de la réflexion et de la clinique lacaniennes, il est maintenant possible d'affiner encore et de tester une lecture perverse de cette association. L'article qui suit applique cette démarche sur un texte théologique particulier, qui là-dessus en représente beaucoup d'autres, l'*Institution chrétienne* de Calvin.

ANSCOMBE, G E M. La simplicidad en el *Tractatus*. Dianoia, 35(35), 1-10, 1989.

ANSCOMBE, G E M. Why Have Children? Proc Cath Phil Ass, 63, 48-53, 1990.

I offer an analogue to the question, another question which we can imagine being asked given certain developments of fashion. The analogous question is: "Why digest food?" Technology would allow us to be nourished without doing what many don't want to do. The refined *pleasure* of eating, long denigrated by the Church, is its real point.

ANSCOMBE, G E M. Wittgenstein: Whose Philosopher? Philosophy, 28, 1-10, 90 Supp.

Wittgenstein is rather a "philosophers's philosopher" as was Plato, than an ordinary man's philosopher as was Aristotle. This is apparent in some of the questions that he asked about fairly regular philosophical topics, but also in his especial investigations of topics not usually investigated by philosophers: a good example is *reading*.

ANSHAKOV, O M and FINN, V K and SKVORTSOV, D P. On Axiomatization of Many-Valued Logics Associated with Formalization of Plausible Reasonings. Stud Log, 48(4), 423-447, D 89.

This paper studies a class of infinite-valued predicate logics. A sufficient condition for axiomatizability of logics from that class is given.

ANTISERI, Dario. Note ad un recente libro sull'incontro-scontro tra Croce e Gentile. Filosofia, 41(3), 365-380, S-D 90.

ANTONELLI, Mauro. Univocità dell'essere e intenzionalià del conoscere. G Crit Filosof Ital, 69(1), 101-123, Ja-Ap 90.

ANTONY, Louise. A Pieced Quilt: A Critical Discussion of Stephen Schiffer's *Remnants of Meaning*. Phil Psych, 4(1), 119-137, 1991.

Stephen Schiffer, in his recent book, *Remnants of Meaning*, argues against the possibility of any compositional theory of meaning for natural language. Because the argument depends on the premise that there is no possible naturalistic reduction of the intentional to the physical, Schiffer's attack on theories of meaning is of central importance for theorists of mind. I respond to Schiffer's argument by showing that there is at least one reductive account of the mental that he has neglected to consider—the computationalist account known as the Representation Theory of Mind. Not only is this view immune from the criticisms Schiffer mounts against other reductivist theories, but it solves problems that arise on Schiffer's own non-reductive account of the relativism between the intentional and the physical.

ANTONY, Louise. "Semantic Anorexia: On the Notion of 'Content' in Cognitive Science" in *Meaning and Method: Essays in Honor of Hilary Putnam*, BOOLOS, George (ed), 105-135. New York, Cambridge Univ Pr, 1990.

Hilary Putnam has recently argued against the possibility of a scientific "vindication" of folk psychology. I defend the Representation Theory of Mind against these arguments, by disputing Putnam's assumption that narrow contents are necessary for a computation construal of the attitudes. Putnam mistakenly presumes that the RTM is meant to provide psychological answers to a set of essentially *semantic* questions.

ANYANWU, Kane C. A Response to A G A Bello's Methodological Preliminaries. Ultim Real Mean, 14(1), 61-69, Mr 91.

African process philosophy cannot be adequately studied and understood with the static concepts and analytic logic developed in western philosophy. Dr. Bello's proposal that African philosophy should be "scientific" and "logical" confuses pre-Einsteinian science and the logic in *Principia Mathematica* with contemporary science and holistic logic or the logic of aesthetics. African process philosophy calls for a holistic logic, and Dr Bello further errs by improperly applying the meaning of words from a Western dictionary to reality as experienced in African process philosophy as if the identity of words in different philosophical systems necessarily implies the identity of meaning.

APEL, Karl-Otto. Constituição do sentido e justificação da validade: Heidegger e o problema da filosofia transcendental. Rev Port Filosof, 45(3), 413-461, Jl-S 89.

The author interprets Heidegger's thought in terms of a transformation of transcendental philosophy, leading to its radicalization and finally its destruction. In the place of this project, the author proposes a transcendental philosophy of a linguistic and pragmatic kind, which seeks to establish a compromise between the thematics of anti-predicative constitution of sense and the demand for intersubjective validity.

APPIAH, Anthony. "But Would That Still Be Me?" Notes on Gender, "Race," Ethnicity, as Sources of "Identity". J Phil, 87(10), 493-499, O 90.

This paper proposes that what I call the "ethical" identities associated with gender, "race" and ethnicity characteristically presuppose falsehoods about Kripkean metaphysical identity; that "race" and gender have interestingly different relations to metaphysical identity; that all three are central to the life plans of many in our culture; and that, as we defeat racism and sexism, these identities will assume new forms.

APPIAH, Anthony. Representations and Realism. Phil Stud, 61(1-2), 65-74, F 91.

This article seeks to show why Michael Devitt is wrong to say that realism is not a fundamentally semantical doctrine.

APPIAH, Kwame Anthony. Is the Post- in Postmodernism the Post- in Postcolonial? Crit Inquiry, 17(2), 336-357, Wint 91.

I start by discussing an exhibition of African art; I then propose that in each domain where the notion "postmodern" has been applied there is "an antecedent practice that laid claim to a certain exclusivity of insight and...postmodernism is a name for the rejection of that claim to exclusivity." I suggest this rejection reflects the increasing commodification of the arts, and then argue that postcoloniality does not always involve the same sort of opposition to an antecedent practice. Finally, I explore through Yambo Ouologuem's novel, *Le Devoir de Violence*, the very unpostmodern ethical humanism of the postcolonial African novel.

APTER, Andrew. The Problem of Who: Multiple Personality, Personal Identity and the Double Brain. Phil Psych, 4(2), 219-248, 1991.

The received view of multiple personality disorder (MPD) presupposes a form of realism, according to which the 'secondary personality' is an independent conscious entity joined to the psyche of the host. The received view of MPD is endorsed by the majority of psychologists, as are the major diagnostic criteria for MPD. Realism of this type, gives rise to a certain problem concerning the personal identity of the secondary personality, namely, who this individual is. It is argued that three broad answers to the Question of Who in the context of MPD have been proposed in the history of psychology and psychiatry: psychological realism (Janet and the Dissociationist School); psychological anti-realism (Freud and the Psychoanalytic School), and neural realism (Wigan, Sperry and Gazzaniga). These views are examined. In addition, the relationship of the Question of Who to the traditional problem of personal identity is examined. It is argued that philosophers such as Locke, Reid and Parfit have either overlooked or presupposed the Question of Who.

APTER, Arthur W. Successors of Singular Cardinals and Measurability Revisited. J Sym Log, 55(2), 492-501, Je 90.

AQUILECCHIA, Giovanni. Bruno e la matematica a lui contemporanea: In margine al "De Minimo". G Crit Filosof Ital, 69(2), 151-159, My-Ag 90.

ARAI, Toshiyasu. Derivability Conditions on Rosser's Provability Predicates. Notre Dame J Form Log, 31(4), 487-497, Fall 90.

ARANOVICH, Raúl. Opacidad y presuposición. Rev Filosof (Argentina), 5(1), 3-16, My 90.

Since the very beginning of semantics, the analysis of denotative phrases and of propositional attitudes have been taken for the two faces of a single problem: the problem of reference. In this paper, some accounts that support the binding of these problems are discussed, and an alternative account, where the subjects are treated independently, is suggested. This account, that goes along the lines of analysis of Frege, Strawson and Karttunen, is focused on the relationship between certain operators and the presupposition of the "embedded" sentence.

ARANTES, Urias Corrêa. Notes sur utopie et marxisme. Manuscrito, 13(2), 59-81, O 90.

The present paper examines the little-studied question of the relations between utopia and Marxism in the classical texts of Marx and Engels and in Marxist literature, particularly in French. It is maintained that such relations are characterized in Marx by a large ambiguity, but also that this character disappears later on, starting with the later text by Engels on this question. The suggestion that such disappearance reveals a dimension of the process of ossification of Marxism leads to a reflection on the possible meaning of a reassessment of modern utopia as a privileged form of political thought. Charles Fourier's elaborations are emphasized.

ARATO, Andrew. Revolution, Civil Society and Democracy. Praxis Int, 10(1-2), 24-38, Ap-Jl 90.

ARAÚJO, Alberto Filipe. Educação e democracia: Subsídios para uma consciência educacional pluralizante. Rev Port Filosof, 46(2), 269-282, Ap-Je 90.

On the bases of fundamental texts of international institutions (OCDE and UNESCO) and chiefly of the law which determines the Portuguese Educational System (LBSE), the author seeks to examine the guarantees of having plurality of thought in educational institutions. In other words, there is attempt to suggest ways by which—at least theoretically—the formation of the democratic educational consciousness can be maintained against positivist positions. It is also suggested that only a so-administered education can guarantee the rebirth and even the survival of the democratic educational spirit.

ARAYA, Eval A. El personalismo cristiano de Emmanuel Mounier. Rev Filosof (Costa Rica), 28(67-68), 135-140, D 90.

This work pretends to analyze the essential philosophical aspects of the personalism in Emmanuel Mounier. First of all, it is presented in an outline of the historical and social context of France at the time the author lived. Next the essay focuses the attention on the core principal that allows the building of this philosophy, specifically his concept of person and the characteristics that define it. Finally, the essay concludes with the examination of some Christian statements which make up the Mounerean personalism.

ARCHARD, David 362 AUTHOR INDEX WITH ABSTRACTS

ARCHARD, David. Child Abuse: Parental Rights and the Interests of the Child. J Applied Phil, 7(2), 183-194, O 90.

I criticise the 'liberal' view of the proper relationship between the family and State, namely that, although the interests of the child should be paramount, parents are entitled to rights of both privacy and autonomy which should be abrogated only when the child suffers a specifiable harm. I argue that the right to bear children is not absolute, and that it only grounds a right to rear upon an objectionable proprietarian picture of the child as owned by its producer. If natural parents have any rights to rear they derive from duties to bring their children into rational maturity where they can exercise rights for themselves. The presumption that natural parents are best suited to rear their own children should be discounted, as should the assumption that alternatives to natural parenting are unacceptably bad. I reject the suggestion that parents should be 'licensed' but argue for a much closer monitoring of the family. Familial privacy, which such monitoring breaches, is shown to have a culturally specific and, given the facts of abuse, dubious value. In conclusion, I briefly specify the forms of monitoring I approve.

ARCHARD, David. Freedom Not to be Free: The Case of the Slavery Contract in J S Mill's *On Liberty*. Phil Quart, 40(161), 453-465, O 90.

This article defends J S Mill's argument in Chapter V of his *On Liberty* that individuals should not be permitted to contract into slavery. Discounting reasoning from considerations of involuntariness or third party harms, it suggests that a slavery contract is a *self-abrogating* exercise of freedom whose interdiction is consistent with Mill's liberty principle. It also rebuts the charge that forbidding voluntary enslavement represents a significant concession to paternalism and distinguishes the case of slavery from that of suicide. Finally, it considers the possible reasoning to a broader principle that liberty may be limited for the sake of liberty.

ARCHARD, David. Friends and Enemies of Liberalism. Rad Phil, 57, 31-32, Spr 91.

This is a review article devoted to seven recently published books of moral and political theory. It notes the current intellectual dominance of the philosophical doctrine of liberalism, and reviews the options open to conservative and socialist critics of liberalism.

ARGYLE, Michael. "An Empirical Interpretation of Ethogenics" in *Harré and His Critics*, BHASKAR, Roy (ed), 131-153. Cambridge, Blackwell, 1990.

ARGYROS, Alexander J. Towards a View of Time as Depth. Diogenes, 151, 29-50, Fall 90.

ARISIAN, Khoren. Our Inner Divinity: Humanism and the Spiritual Enterprise. Relig Hum, 24(4), 185-191, Autumn 90.

ARISTOTLE and GALLOP, David (trans). *Aristotle on Sleep and Dreams*. Peterborough, Broadview Pr, 1990.

ARLO COSTA, Horacio L. Conditionals and Monotonic Belief Revisions: the Success Postulate. Stud Log, 49(4), 557-566, D 90.

One of the main applications of the logic of theory change is to the epistemic analysis of conditionals via the so-called *Ramsey test*. In the first part of the present note this test is studied in the "limiting case" where the theory being revised is inconsistent, and it is shown that this case manifests and intrinsic incompatibility between the Ramsey test and the AGM postulate of "success". The paper then analyses the use of the postulate of success, and a weakening of it, generating axioms of conditional logic via the test, and it is shown that for certain purposes both success and weak success are quite superfluous. This suggests the proposal of abandoning both success and weak success entirely, thus permitting retention of the postulate of "preservation" discarded by Gärdenfors.

ARMSTRONG, A H. *Hellenic and Christian Studies*. Brookfield, Gower, 1991.

A series of papers focusing on the thought of Plotinus as set into the Hellenistic world. The ancient struggle between Hellenistic and Christian forms of worship and religion are also considered. (staff)

ARMSTRONG, A H. "On Not Knowing too Much About God" in *The Philosophy in Christianity*, VESEY, Godfrey (ed), 129-145. New York, Cambridge Univ Pr, 1989.

ARMSTRONG, D M and HEATHCOTE, Adrian. Causes and Laws. Nous, 25(1), 63-73, Mr 91.

It is argued that there is no analytic or conceptual connection linking singular causation with a law of nature. Nevertheless, there are good a posteriori grounds for holding that, just as heat is nothing but motion of molecules, so singular causation is nothing but the instantiation of a law.

ARMSTRONG, Mary Beth. Professional Ethics and Accounting Education: A Critique of the 8-Step Method. Bus Prof Ethics J, 9(1-2), 181-191, Spr-Sum 90.

A model for teaching ethics, currently proposed in the accounting literature, is an "8-Step Method." The method is intended for use in existing accounting courses as an aid in analyzing case studies. This paper illustrates use of the model and lists five of its strengths. The paper also discusses five weaknesses of the model and concludes that integrating discussion of ethical cases in existing accounting courses is a necessary, but not a sufficient condition for growth in moral reasoning to take place. Accounting educators must also offer separate courses in accounting ethics to their students.

ARNAULD, Antoine (trans) and KREMER, Elmar J (trans). *On True and False Ideas, New Objections to Descartes' Meditations* and Descartes' Replies. Lewiston, Mellen Pr, 1990.

ARNDT, Andreas. Zwischen Enttäuschung und Versöhnung: Hegel, die deutsche Misere und die Französiche Revolution. Tijdschr Stud Verlich Denken, 17(3-4), 249-263, 1989.

Hegel's remarks on the French Revolution are shown as related to his view of the political and social developments in Germany. He became more and more a critic of the *results* of the French Revolution, because he saw a conjunction between the *terreur* and abstract morality on the one side and the civil society in the capitalism on the other. The outstanding political and social emancipation in Germany makes him a critic of capitalism before he was the dominating mode of production. The state had to subdue the "Leviathan" of the civil society, but this state should be a result of political emancipation from feudalism: the representation of the idea of right. So Hegel's so called "accommodation" on the state is a compromise between the critique of feudalism and the insight in the development of capitalism as a result of the French Revolution.

ARNESON, Richard J. A Defense of Equal Opportunity for Welfare. Phil Stud, 62(2), 187-195, My 91.

ARNHEIM, Rudolf. Perceptual Aspects of Art for the Blind. J Aes Educ, 24(3), 57-65, Fall 90.

Haptic aesthetic experience, available to the blind, comes about by touch, mostly in sculpture, and by kinesthesis, mostly in the dance. Together with the sense of hearing, the perceptual input of sightless people makes for entirely dynamic experiences. Their direct relation to the human body creates an intimate connection with the self, as distinguished from vision, which is a distance sense medium.

ARNOLD, N Scott. Economists and Philosophers as Critics of the Free Enterprise System. Monist, 73(4), 621-641, O 90.

This paper provides a taxonomy of criticisms of the free enterprise system by economists and philosophers. It argues that a common failing of these criticisms is the unwarranted assumption that state action restricting private property rights would solve the problems critics have identified. Both economists and philosophers need to articulate more fully alternative institutional arrangements and explain how the latter would solve the problems they have identified without creating difficulties that are equally serious or worse. Some positive suggestions about how this might be done are offered.

ARNOLD, N Scott. *Marx's Radical Critique of Capitalist Society: A Reconstruction and Critical Evaluation*. New York, Oxford Univ Pr, 1990.

For Marx, the ills of capitalist society (primarily exploitation and alienation) are not accidental or incidental; rather, they are embedded in the very structure of the capitalist economic system. This book explicates and critically evaluates these charges. It is further argued that Marx's radical critique of capitalist society presupposes a set of alternative institutional arrangements that do not have the defects attributed to capitalism. After articulating Marx's vision of the two phases or stages of post-capitalist society (later called 'socialism' and 'communism'), it is shown that both are "utopian" visions that could never exist in reality.

ARNOLD, Robert M and FORROW, Lachlan and FRADER, Joel. Teaching Clinical Ethics in the Residency Years: Preparing Competent Professionals. J Med Phil, 16(1), 93-112, F 91.

Formal training in clinical ethics must become a central part of residency curricula to prepare practitioners to manage the ethical dimensions of patient care. Residency educators must ground their teaching in an understanding of the conceptual, biomedical, and psychosocial aspects of the important ethical issues that arise in that field of practice. Four aspects of professional competence in clinical ethics provide a useful framework for curricular planning. The physician should learn to (1) recognize ethical issues as they arise in clinical care and identify hidden values and unacknowledged conflicts; (2) think clearly and critically about these issues in ways that lead to ethically justifiable courses of action; (3) apply those practical skills needed to implement an ethically justifiable course of action; and (4) judge when the management of a clinical situation requires consultation with individuals or institutional bodies with additional expertise or authority. We argue that these practical goals can be accomplished with a relatively modest emphasis on the theoretical aspects of medical ethics.

ARNSTINE, Barbara. Rational and Caring Teachers: How Dispositional Aims Shape Teacher Preparation. Proc Phil Educ, 46, 2-21, 1990.

ARNSTINE, Donald. Art, Aesthetics, and the Pitfalls of Discipline-Based Art Education. Educ Theor, 40(4), 415-422, Fall 90.

Discipline-based art education proposes to teach art history, art criticism, aesthetics, and art production. The program's breadth is admirable, but its academic approach and its cognitive claims have drawbacks. Because art education so academically conceived risks offering activities to students that will not be experienced aesthetically, students will fail to realize the point of art: the enhancement of the immediate quality of experience. And an exclusive emphasis on the traditional fine arts, to the exclusion of popular art, will have a socially conservative impact, since only contemporary art can be employed in the critical examination of one's own culture.

ARNTZENIUS, Frank. Causal Paradoxes in Special Relativity. Brit J Phil Sci, 41(2), 223-243, Je 90.

It has been argued that the existence of faster than light particles in the context of special relativity would imply the possibility to influence the past, and that this would lead to paradox. In this paper I argue that such conclusions cannot safely be drawn without consideration of the equations of motion of such particles. I show that such equations must be non-local, that they can be deterministic, and that they can avoid the suggested paradoxes. I also discuss conservation of energy-momentum, and how instantaneous action at a distance can avoid similar paradoxes.

ARNTZENIUS, Frank. Kochen's Interpretation of Quantum Mechanics. Proc Phil Sci Ass, 1, 241-249, 1990.

Kochen has suggested an interpretation of quantum mechanics in which he denies that wavepackets ever collapse, while affirming that measurements have definite results. In this paper I attempt to show that his interpretation is untenable. I then suggest ways in which to construct similar, but more satisfactory, hidden variable interpretations.

ARNTZENIUS, Frank. State-Spaces and Meaning Relations Among Predicates. Topoi, 10(1), 35-42, Mr 91.

It has often been suggested that the meaning of terms is theory dependent. Bas van Fraassen has proposed a particular way of inferring which sentences are true in virtue of meaning, given a theory in so-called "state-space format". I examine his claims by means of simple examples.

ARONOWICZ, Annette (trans) and LEVINAS, Emmanuel. *Nine Talmudic Readings*. Bloomington, Indiana Univ Pr, 1990.

ARONSON, Jerrold L. Testing for Convergent Realism. Brit J Phil Sci, 40(2), 255-259, Je 89.

The convergent realist maintains that as our theories lead to better predictions and greater accuracy, they depict nature more accurately while the anti-realist holds that it is a real possibility for a series of highly successful hypotheses to end up wandering further from the truth. This paper examines how this issue can be empirically settled by setting up a crucial experiment to decide between these rival hypotheses.

ARONSON, Jerry. "Experimental Realism" in *Harré and His Critics*, BHASKAR, Roy (ed), 48-63. Cambridge, Blackwell, 1990.

ARP, Kristana. Intentionality and the Public World: Husserl's Treatment of Objectivity in the Cartesian Meditations. Husserl Stud, 7(2), 89-101, 1990.

ARRAS, John D. Getting Down to Cases: The Revival of Casuistry in Bioethics. J Med Phil, 16(1), 29-51, F 91.

This article examines the emergence of casuistical case analysis as a methodological alternative to more theory-driven approaches in bioethics research and education. Focusing on *The Abuse of Casuistry* by A Jonsen and S Toulmin, the article articulates the most characteristic features of this modern-day casuistry and discusses some problems with casuistry as an 'anti-theoretical' method. It is argued that casuistry so defined is 'theory modest' rather than 'theory free' and that ethical theory can still play a significant role in casuistical analysis. It is concluded that casuistry represents a promising alternative to the regnant model of 'applied ethics'. (edited)

ARRAS, John D. Noncompliance in AIDS Research. Hastings Center Rep, 20(5), 24-32, S-O 90.

ARREGUI, Jorge Vicente. Sobre el gusto y la verdad práctica. Anu Filosof, 23(1), 163-176, 1990.

ARRIETA, Jeannette and HAYLING, Annie. El pensamiento de Heidegger y Marcuse en relación con la ecología. Rev Filosof (Costa Rica), 28(67-68), 141-147, D 90.

The study of the environment where the human being unfolds itself as an important aspect might be particulary important for any thinking person of our time. The development of the science and technology implicate too the environment could be affected by many forms. Therefore, it is necessary to rescue the intellectual's thought like Heidegger and Marcuse, which can trace the problem from a very contemporary perspective.

ARROYO, Julián. El escepticismo crítico en el Diccionario de Bayle. Pensamiento, 47(186), 239-246, Ap-Je 91.

The article is one chapter of the unpublished doctoral dissertation, "The Critical Skepticism as Method in Bayle's Work", (Complutense University, Madrid, 1989). The Dictionary is the literary platform to expose his ideas that will renew the mental situation of the age. Bayle reivindicates the historical facts and values them critically. The latter is the most personal part of Bayle's Dictionary and makes the difference between this work and other dictionaries. This informs and interprets at a more skeptical than doctrinal level, stimulates the reflection (positive skepticism). History was simple narration without punctual facts. These facts will now be the point of departure toward the truth (critical skepticism). The irrational elements of error from the historical manifestation will question his (in)sufficient critical model of rationality, which requires him to overcome fideism and skepticism.

ARTEMOV, Sergel and DZHAPARIDZE, Giorgie. Finite Kripke Models and Predicate Logics of Provability. J Sym Log, 55(3), 1090-1098, S 90.

ARTESE, Luciano. Il rapporto Parmenide-Telesio dal Persio al Maranta. G Crit Filosof Ital, 70(1), 15-34, Ja-Ap 91.

ARTHUR, Richard. "Foils for Newton: Comments on Howard Stein" in *Philosophical Perspectives on Newtonian Science*, BRICKER, Phillip (ed), 49-56. Cambridge, MIT Pr, 1990.

This paper is largely a gloss on Howard Stein's 'On Locke, "the Great Huygenius, and the incomparable Mr. Newton"', an examination of Newton's methodology and metaphysics. Using Huygens and Locke as foils, Stein argues that Newton's metaphysics and method are considerably more sophisticated by contrast, involving an inherent dialectic that allows for revision of his "tentatively first principles." Although sympathetic to Stein's argument as to the nondogmatism of Newton's metaphysics, I argue that Newton would no more acknowledge the revisability of his mathematical principles than Nagel, say, would acknowledge the susceptibility to theoretical criticism of an empirical law.

ARTOLA, José María. Experiencia de lo sublime y principios racionales. Rev Filosof (Spain), 3, 83-112, 1990.

ARTZT, M. Future through Self-Organization (in German). Deut Z Phil, 38(5), 422-435, 1990.

ASCH, Adrienne. "Surrogacy and the Family: Social and Value Considerations" in *Beyond Baby M: Ethical Issues in New Reproductive Techniques*, BARTELS, Dianne M (ed), 243-259. Clifton, Humana Pr, 1990.

ASMIS, Elizabeth. The Poetic Theory of the Stoic 'Aristo'. Apeiron, 23(3), 147-201, S 90.

This is an examination of the only Stoic poetic theory whose outlines have been

preserved. The author, whose name is only partially legible, may have been Aristo of Chios, and the text occupies about seven papyrus columns of Philodemus's *On Poems* 5. The Stoic analysed poems as having two components, thought (*dianoia*) and verbal composition (*synthesis*), and classified all poems as good, bad, and indifferent. It is argued that, in a revision of Plato's poetics, the Stoic required morally good thought, as judged by reason, and corresponding linguistic expression, as judged by experienced hearing.

ASPENSON, Steven S. In Defense of Anselm. Hist Phil Quart, 7(1), 33-45, Ja 90.

ASSELIN, D T. "Foundationalism and Foundation in Strauss and Maritain" in *From Twilight to Dawn: The Cultural Vision of Jacques Maritain*, REDPATH, Peter A (ed), 119-131. Notre Dame, Univ Notre Dame Pr, 1990.

ATHERTON, Margaret. *Berkeley's Revolution in Vision*. Ithaca, Cornell Univ Pr, 1990.

ATHERTON, Margaret. Corpuscles, Mechanism, and Essentialism in Berkeley and Locke. J Hist Phil, 29(1), 47-67, Ja 91.

While recently Locke and Berkeley have been understood to be involved with corpuscular mechanism, Locke is generally taken as a supporter while Berkeley is thought to be a critic. But there are many passages in which Locke is negative about corpuscles, while Berkeley endures talk of corpuscles. I argue corpuscular mechanism must be understood as a complex of positions. Berkeley and Locke reject the geometric or essentialist aspects of this position while endorsing a machine model. I suggest a reevaluation of the relationship of these philosophers to each other and to contemporary science.

ATKINS, E M. 'Domina et Regina Virtutum': Justice and *Societas* in *De Officiis*. Phronesis, 35(3), 258-289, 1990.

'This one virtue is the mistress and queen of all the virtues' (III.28). I want here to argue that in *De Officiis* justice is 'mistress and queen' in two ways: first, it is the most important of the four primary virtues; secondly, and consequently, it helps to define the other virtues, which must be limited by it. *De Officiis* contains the earliest theory of justice we possess that explicitly defines justice as that which builds up society; I hope then to show that the resulting conception of justice is very different from anything that we have seen before. Finally, I want to ask how Cicero came to articulate this view: is he merely transcribing a theory developed by someone else and appropriate to a different historical context? Or is he expounding views that his own life and thought have led him to adopt, to adapt, and to use?

ATLAN, H. Ends and Meaning in Machine-Like Systems. Commun Cog, 23(2-3), 143-156, 1990.

In this article the author is concerned with the most complex and the most central problem which the cyberneticians of the second order occupied themselves with: the problem of meaning. The emergence of meaning was tied up there already with the finality and functionality of systems. Still the author's interpretation of both these things is at the basis of a turnabout with regard to the cybernetics of the second order: meaning for him precedes finality. The relation between "ends and meaning" is illustrated through the formalism of the Boolean networks.

ATTFIELD, Robin. Has the History of Philosophy Ruined the Environment? Environ Ethics, 13(2), 127-137, Sum 91.

I review and appraise Eugene C Hargrove's account of the adverse impacts of Western philosophy on attitudes to the environment. Although significant qualifications have to be entered, for there are grounds to hold that philosophical traditions which have encouraged taking nature seriously are not always given their due by Hargrove, and that environmental thought can draw upon deeper roots than he allows, his verdict that the history of philosophy has discouraged preservationist attitudes is substantially correct. Environmental philosophy thus has a significant (if not quite an unrivalled) role to play in the reconstruction of many of the traditional branches of philosophy, as well as in the protection of the natural world.

AUBERT, Roger. Désiré Mercier et les débuts de l'Institut de Philosophie. Rev Phil Louvain, 88(78), 147-167, My 90.

AUDI, Robert. Intention, Cognitive Commitment, and Planning. Synthese, 86(3), 361-378, Mr 91.

This paper defends a cognitive-motivational account of intending against recent criticism by J Garcia, connects intending with a number of other concepts important in the theory of action — including decision, volition, and planning — and explores some principles of intention transfer construed as counterparts of epistemic principles governing closure for belief and justification. Several routes to intention formation are described; the role of intentions in planning is examined; and a holistic conception of intention formation and change is stressed. The proposed conception of intending as embodying at once a cognitive and a motivational commitment to action is thus shown to help in understanding both the explanation of action and the rationality of agents.

AUDI, Robert. "An Internalist Conception of Rational Action" in *Philosophical Perspectives, 4: Action Theory and Philosophy of Mind, 1990*, TOMBERLIN, James E (ed), 227-245. Atascadero, Ridgeview, 1990.

AUDI, Robert. Moral Epistemology and the Supervenience of Ethical Concepts. S J Phil, SUPP 29, 1-24, 1990.

AUDI, Robert. Religious Commitment and Secular Reason: A Reply to Professor Weithman. Phil Pub Affairs, 20(1), 66-76, Wint 91.

AUDI, Robert. Weakness of Will and Rational Action. Austl J Phil, 68(3), 270-281, S 90.

This paper first characterizes weakness of will in some detail and, in that light, appraises some plausible arguments intended to show that it implies irrationality. The second main part of the paper formulates and assesses a number of models of rational action that make the assumption of its irrationality plausible; proposes a wider, holistic conception of rational action; and extends that notion to rationality in general. On the basis of this holistic view of rationality, it is argued that incontinent action, like certain of its epistemic counterparts, need not be irrational.

AUNE, Bruce. "Action, Inference, Belief, and Intention" in *Philosophical Perspectives, 4: Action Theory and Philosophy of Mind, 1990*, TOMBERLIN, James E (ed), 247-271. Atascadero, Ridgeview, 1990.

AUNE, Bruce. *Knowledge of the External World*. New York, Routledge, 1991.

This book is concerned with our knowledge of the external world. The first half is devoted to the views of major historical figures—specifically, Descartes, Locke, Berkeley, Hume, Kant, and J S Mill. The second half has both a destructive and a constructive part. The destructive part is focused on the attempts of Wittgenstein and others to dispose of the problem as an illusion or nest of confusions; it is argued that these attempts fail. The constructive part provides a reconstruction of the problem and a solution based on probability theory and the aims of rational inquiry.

AUNE, Bruce. Sellar's Two Images of the World. J Phil, 87(10), 537-545, O 90.

This paper offers a critical commentary on the two images of the world that Sellars described in "Philosophy and the Scientific Image of Man." It is argued that Sellars's two images are significantly similar to the two "systems of ideas" that Hume discussed in his *Treatise of Human Nature* and *Enquiry Concerning the Human Understanding* and that Sellars's remarks about his two images provide a very helpful, demystifying approach to the widely discussed notion of alternative conceptual schemes.

AUROUX, Sylvain. "Representation and the Place of Linguistic Change before Comparative Grammar" in *Leibniz, Humboldt, and the Origins of Comparativism*, DE MAURO, Tullio (ed), 213-238. Philadelphia, John Benjamins, 1990.

Grammarians did not wait for the nineteenth century to notice that languages change. In order to understand the representation of linguistic change before comparative grammar, we propose to use the Aristotelian concept of mobility, which asserts that a subject *S* moves from one property *x* to a property *y*. The choice of real objects for the elements {*S, x, y,*} was a matter of theoretical discussion and maturation. The emergence of comparativism was not a matter of mere empirical knowledge but the effect of a theoretical mutation, which will reject the classical diffusionist model, the monogenetism, and replace the use of the concept of *figure* by the one of *phonetic law*.

AUXIER, Randall E. The Return of the Initiate: Hegel on Bread and Wine. Owl Minerva, 22(2), 191-208, Spr 91.

There has been much debate as to whether Hegel's ultimate loyalties lie with the purely Greek form of philosophizing, or with the Christianized version: "secularism" versus "religionism". The essay examines this question with regard to Hegel's use of images drawn from the Eleusianian Mysteries in *The Phenomenology of Spirit*. Special attention is given to the ancient, symbolic act of drinking wine and eating bread as practiced by both Christians and pagans. Hegel's cryptic allusions are followed out regarding their implications for understanding the Symposium and the Last Supper. Interpretations are given of how Hoelderlin and Heidegger differ from Hegel in viewpoint.

AUXIER, Randall. Concentric Circles: An Exploration of Three Concepts in Process Metaphysics. SW Phil Rev, 7(1), 151-172, Ja 91.

This paper examines the following: (1) the history of the concepts of potentiality, actuality and possibility, beginning with Aristotle; (2) the various ways process metaphysicians and reductive metaphysicians define and employ these concepts; (3) the effect of evolutionary thinking on the concept of necessity in metaphysical argumentation; and (4) how process metaphysicians explicitly embrace circular argumentation as a legitimate means of expounding metaphysical systems (due to their view of necessity). Peirce, Bergson, Dewey and Whitehead are discussed throughout, and a call is made for the development of a vocabulary which sorts out the differences among reductive and antireductive metaphysical schools.

AUZIAS, Jean-Marie. Les gisants et les pleureuses: Pour un tombeau de Michel Foucault. Rev Int Phil, 44(173), 262-276, 1990.

AVERILL, Edward Wilson. Functionalism, the Absent Qualia Objection and Eliminativism. S J Phil, 28(4), 449-467, Wint 90.

The absent qualia objection to a functionalist definition of 'pain' can be answered by showing that states that instantiate the definition must have a qualitative character. Earl Conee holds that Sydney Shoemaker's defense of functionalism along these lines will not work. In this essay Conee's criticism is shown to be faulty, but it is also shown that Shoemaker does not prove his case. Building on what Shoemaker does show, it is argued that a functionalist should supplement his definition of 'pain' with an eliminativist position on qualitative character. Of course this position undercuts the absent qualia objection to functionalism.

AVGELIS, Nikolaos. "Lakatos on the Evaluation of Scientific Theories" in *Imre Lakatos and Theories of Scientific Change*, GAVROGLU, Kostas (ed), 157-167. Norwell, Kluwer, 1989.

In this paper I consider the problem of evaluation of scientific theories focusing on the claims concerning theory acceptance posed by logical empiricism and critical rationalism (Popper and above all Lakatos). Also I try to point out to some difficulties arising from the criteria of acceptability of scientific theories formulated by Lakatos and trace some implications for the methodology of scientific research.

AVIRAM, Aharon. The Paternalistic Attitude Toward Children. Educ Theor, 41(2), 199-211, Spr 91.

The paper examines and refutes the argument concerning paternalism towards children within Mill's liberal view, an argument which justifies unqualified paternalism towards children in the present in order to "fit them to future admission to the priviledges of freedom." It is claimed that this argument is invalid in its unqualified legitimation of paternalism towards children. Its primary error consists of its contradicting Mill's own moderate paternalistic framework by asking the wrong question. Rather than asking the question: should paternalism towards children be allowed? it should ask: should paternalism towards children be considered under the same conditions guiding paternalistic actions towards adults? It is further argued that this faulty starting point makes it easier for Mill to commit two basic logical errors: first, making a leap from hypothetical assumptions to evident conclusions and, second, making a leap from evidence relevant to a section of the population under discussion to conclusions referring to the entire population.

AVIRAM, Aharon. The Subjection of Children. J Phil Educ, 24(2), 213-234, Wint 90.

The paper surveys representative examples of the four categories of arguments usually employed to justify the prevailing inferior legal status of children: paternalistic moral arguments, utilitarian moral arguments, moral arguments based on logical considerations and practical arguments referring to the (alleged) harm to society or to the development of children that would (allegedly) stem from the equalisation of children's status. It is shown that although some of the arguments refer to real problems, they are either unsound or not strong enough to justify the prevailing inferiority of children. The paper concludes with a discussion of the desired approach and strategies for the establishment of a more equal status for children.

AVRON, A. Relevance and Paraconsistency—A New Approach. J Sym Log, 55(2), 707-732, Je 90.

We describe a new approach to the notions of relevance and of paraconsistency. Our basic idea is that of "relevance domains". Inside each such domain classical logic is valid. Limitations on its use are imposed only with respect to inferences in which more than one domain is involved. There are two basic binary relations over the collections of domains. One is relevance. The other is grading. The corresponding language is purely intensional, and its primitve connectives are strictly relevant. A sound and complete axiomatization of the logic which corresponds to the resulting algebraic structures is provided.

AVRON, Arnon. Relevance and Paraconsistency—A New Approach, Part II: The Formal Systems. Notre Dame J Form Log, 31(2), 168-202, Spr 90.

In part I of this paper we introduced what we called "relevance structures." These algebraic structures are based on the idea of relevance domains which are graded according to "degrees of reality" and related (or not) by a certain relevance relation. In the present part we describe the logic RMI which corresponds to these structures, proving it to be sound and strongly complete relative to them. The language of RMI is similar to that of the systems of Anderson and Belnap, but unlike them it is purely intensional: no extensional connective is definable in it, and all its primitive binary connectives have the variable-sharing property. We show that the expressive power of RMI is nevertheless very strong and sufficient for all our needs. In addition, we investigate the main fragments of RMI, as well as its most important extensions. One of these extensions is the system RM (of Dunn and McCall), which is obtained from RMI by adding an axiom to the effect that any two sentences are relevant to each other.

AVRON, Arnon. Relevance and Paraconsistency—A New Approach, Part III: Cut-Free Gentzen-Type Systems. Notre Dame J Form Log, 32(1), 147-160, Wint 91.

The systems RMI is a purely relevance logic based on the intuitive ideas of relevance domains and degrees of significance. In this paper, we show that unlike the systems of Anderson and Belnap, RMI has a corresponding cut-free, Gentzen-type version. This version manipulates *hypersequents* (i.e., finite sequences of ordinary sequents), and no translation of those hypersequents into the language of RMI is possible. This shows that RMI is multiple-conclusioned in nature and hints on possible applications of it to the study of parallelism.

AWERBUCH-FRIEDLANDER, Tamara and KANAMORI, Akihiro. The Complete 0. Z Math Log, 36(2), 133-141, 1990.

AXELOS, Kostas. Play of the Whole of Wholes (in Czechoslovakian). Filozof Cas, 38(5), 605-611, 1990.

Ce petit texte tiré par l'auteur lui-même de son livre Horizons du monde (Paris, Éditions de Minuit, 1974) montre bien la préoccupation majeure du philosophe, à savoir de montrer que tout le système philosophique, toute l'histoire de la philosophie et de la science aussi bien que toute l'activité humaine en cache une autre. De se trouver en quête de l'être e veut dire rien d'autre que de se trouver en auête du jeu: du jeu du lanage, du jeu de la pensée, du jeu du travail, de l'amour, de la lutte, de la mort, en bref du jeu du monde. Axelos, à la suite de ses deux maêtres, Marx et Heidegger poursuit dans ce texte déjà vieux mais non vielli sa destruction de la métaphysique de l'étant au profit d'une construction du "Jeu", du *cela* qui tout en nous permettant de jouir en le jouant joueson jeu avec nous.

AXELOS, Kostas. The Scheme of the Game of Man and World (Towards the Formation of the Planetary Man) (in Hungarian). Magyar Filozof Szemle, 5-6, 626-629, 1990.

AXIOTIS, Ares. Kant's Search for the Philosopher's Stone. Int Stud Phil, 23(1), 3-21, 1991.

Kant's attempt to provide a rational foundation for ethics poses an insuperable stumbling-block for his general philosophical ambitions. For the unity of judgment, sentiment, and will in moral consciousness cannot be accommodated within his existing framework of distinctions. A pure practical reason, at once both cognitive and conative, must be a concrete or self-particularizing universal. The idea of a rational sentiment cuts across the concept/intuition distinction which underlies the division between reason and sensibility. Far from being just a topical issue in moral philosophy, the motivation problem is recognised by Kant as the key to transcendental idealism.

AXTELL, G S. Comparative Dialectics: Nishida Kitarō's Logic of Place and Western Dialectical Thought. Phil East West, 41(2), 163-184, Ap 91.

Buddhist logic is often misunderstood by Westerners who assume a representationalist conception of the relationship of language to the world, and who artificially distance the 'laws of thought' (non-contradiction and excluded-middle) from the problem of contrarity or opposition with which they are historically and logically connected. Kyoto school Zen scholar Nishida Kitaro (1870-1945) was actively engaged in comparing Buddhist logic with Aristotelian, Hegelian and Marxian logics. In this essay I attempt to further this pursuit by moving the discussion beyond these historical figures to the arena of contemporary dialectical philosophy. "Comparative dialectics" emerges as a viable comparative methodology.

AXTELL, G S. Logicism, Pragmatism and Metascience: Towards a Pancritical-Pragmatic Meta-Level Discourse. Proc Phil Sci Ass, 1, 39-49, 1990.

The faults of the logical empiricist account of metascientific discourse are examined through a study of the modifications Carnap makes to the program over four decades. As empiricists acquiesced on the distinction between theory and observation, Carnap attempted to retain his metascientific objectivism through reliance on an equally suspect sharp distinction between the theoretic and the pragmatic. Carnap understood his later philosophy as a modification of the program in the direction of pragmatism. But neither the key notion of 'external questions,' nor the particular version of instrumentalism Carnap employed are genuinely compatible with pragmatism. This underscores the need to clarify what is unique to pragmatist accounts of cognitive evaluation and norm governance.

AXTMANN, Roland. The Formation of the Modern State: A Reconstruction of Max Weber's Arguments. Hist Polit Thought, 11(2), 295-311, Sum 90.

To explain the rise of the modern state, Weber analyses the dynamic interplay, and the historically specific interlocking, of political, cultural, economic and geopolitical structures of social action. This argument is developed by analysing the structure of the feudal system of domination; the position of the Catholic church within the feudal polity and its transformative impact on it; the effect of the medieval cities and the developing urban economy on the feudal system; and, finally, the connection between military conflicts, bureaucratization of political structures and capitalist development.

AYERS, Michael. Substance: Prolegomena to a Realist Theory of Identity. J Phil, 88(2), 69-90, F 91.

Traditionally (to ignore heresies) substances are the ultimate subjects of predication, are real unities, are material, endure through time, are active principles of change, and fall into naturally bounded kinds. It is argued that these characterizations together mark logical differences from nonsubstances only explicable on the traditional assumption that substances are the real or natural individuals, given as such at the pretheoretical level of experience, while nonsubstances are abstractions sliced out of reality by the mind, or by language. This contrast implies the need for a realist theory of identity to replace orthodox conceptualism.

AYERS, Robert H. Methodological, Epistemological, and Ontological Motifs in the Thought of Reinhold Niebuhr. Mod Theol, 7(2), 153-173, Ja 91.

The argument in this article is that Reinhold Niebuhr's theology can be fully understood only if proper attention is given to certain motifs in his thought, namely, a dialectical methodology of polar opposites, a Jamesean epistemology and a Whiteheadean ontology. Niebuhr was not an opponent of rationality but of only those systems of thought which made reason ultimate. While a holistic view requires an ultimate frame of reference (a transcendent but historical revelation), this revelation must be made relevant to human culture and knowledge. In this task reason has a role to play in terms of the above motifs.

AYIM, Maryann. In Praise of Clutter as a Necessary Part of the Feminist Perspective. Hypatia, 6(2), 211-215, Sum 91.

A comment on Susan Wendell's paper "Oppression and Victimization; Choice and Responsibility" that appeared in *Hyatia*, 5(3).

BABER, H E. Two Models of Preferential Treatment for Working Mothers. Pub Affairs Quart, 4(4), 323-334, O 90.

I argue that programs for enabling working mothers to reorganize their work so that they may devote more time to childcare—especially extended "maternity leave"—are both unfair and detrimental to women's interests. Rather we should support the provision of cheap, adequate childcare so that working mothers, like working fathers, can minimize the amount of time they spend with their children. I suggest, heretically, that feminists' goal should not be to reorganize the workplace to accommodate characteristically female patterns of labor force participation but rather to make it feasible for women in the workforce to behave like traditional males.

BABICH, Babette E. Nietzsche and the Philosophy of Scientific Power: Will to Power as Constructive Interpretation. Int Stud Phil, 22(2), 79-92, 1990.

From a radically Kantian epistemic perspective, Nietzsche questions the very possibility of knowledge as such. Thus Nietzsche regards the achievements of scientific knowledge as constitutions of the effective, working, kind. By conceiving the world in its entirety as "will to power" and attending to the ambiguities and singularities of what is Real, Nietzsche's postmodern conception of science articulates the interpretative dynamic on both sides of the subject/object cut.

BACCARI, Luciano. Considerazioni sul problema della conoscenza. Aquinas, 34(1), 73-83, Ja-Ap 91.

BACCELLI, Luca. Il dibattito italiano sullo statuto della filosofia politica: Contributo ad una bibliographia. Teoria, 10(1), 93-101, 1990.

BACCELLI, Luca. Lo statuo della filosofia politica nel dibattito italiano. Teoria, 10(1), 63-91, 1990.

BACCHUS, Fahiem and KYBURG JR, Henry E and THALOS, Mariam. Against Conditionalization. Synthese, 85(3), 475-506, D 90.

This paper presents a challenge to the doctrines of Bayesian epistemology by a critical analysis of Bayesian principles. We first examine the Dutch Book principle, pointing out that an agent with logical capabilities can avoid a Dutch even if he does not possess a unique distribution over his beliefs. We then examine a dynamic Dutch Book argument, presented by Teller, that claims to support conditioning. We argue that it provides not much more than the static Dutch Book arguments. Finally we examine van Fraassen's principle of reflection, and conclude that rather than enforcing reasonable behavior, this principle can force an agent to do what is unreasonable.

BACCHUS, Fahiem. *Representing and Reasoning With Probabilistic Knowledge: A Logical Approach to Probabilities*. Cambridge, MIT Pr, 1990.

This book examines two different forms of probabilistic information: statistical information about relative frequencies, and information about an agent's probabilistically graded degrees of belief. Formal, logical, tools are developed for representing and reasoning with these two types of information. The logics developed are extensions of first-order logic; thus the languages contain quantifiers. The languages are also able to represent a wide range of qualitative probabilistic information; thus there is no reliance on exact point valued estimates. Finally, a formal system is developed for relating these two types of probabilities through a mechanism of direct inference, yielding statistically founded degrees of beliefs.

BACHMAN, James and HINTIKKA, Jaakko. *What If...? Toward Excellence in Reasoning*. Mountain View, Mayfield, 1991.

This introduction to reasoning uses Hintikka's interrogative model of inquiry. Logical and informal inferences are construed as steps in the same process of inquiry. All new information enters as answers to questions, as in the Socratic questioning method. Other innovations include 1) we distinguish definitory rules of reasoning (they merely tell what is permissible) from strategic principles (they tell how to reason well); 2) logical rules are formulated so that they apply directly to ordinary language reasoning; 3) the interrogative model is used to analyze and to construct arguments, 4) novel treatments are given of scientific reasoning and of several fallacies.

BACHRACH, Jay E. Fictional Objects in Literature and Mental Representations. Brit J Aes, 31(2), 134-139, Ap 91.

The notion of mental representation as it occurs in cognitive science helps us resolve certain problems about fictional objects as they occur in literature. Possible world analysis of such objects does not work. But we can advert to representations generated in reading a text and take such representations as criteria for what the work contains.

BACHRACH, Jay E. Qualia and Theory Reduction: A Criticism of Paul Churchland. Iyyun, 39(3), 281-294, Jl 90.

Two issues about Paul Churchland's approach to mental phenomena and their objects are discussed: first, the place qualia have when folk science is logically reduced to neuroscience and second, whether the move from folk psychology to neuroscience adequately accounts for perceptual experience and qualia. As to the first, qualia are shown to have nothing to do with his proposed theory reduction. As to the second, neuroscience is shown not able to replace all phenomenal accounts of sentience.

BACHRACH, Sarah and HOFFMASTER, Barry. "Ethical Issues in Prescribing Drugs for the Aged and the Dying" in *Biomedical Ethics Reviews, 1987*, HUMBER, James M (ed), 5-29. Clifton, Humana Pr, 1988.

BACHTA, Abdelkader. Différentielles et intégrales sociales chez Rousseau. Arch Phil, 53(4), 647-660, O-D 90.

The aim of this survey is to demonstrate the existence of differentials and social integrals in Rousseau's speech. In *Le discours sur l'inégalité parmi les hommes* (*The Speech on Inequality between Men*), which is a book on the philosophy of history, the social seems to be the image of the mathematical differential in the sense that the evolution of human things is achieved through successive differentiations. In *Le contrat social* (*The Social Contract*), the social is rather the image of the mathematical integral. This is easily perceived when we take into consideration the concepts of contract, of general will, and so on.

BACHTA, Abdelkader. Le Kantisme de la théorie cantorienne de l'infini. Arch Phil, 54(2), 269-279, Ap-Je 91.

This survey discusses the commonly accepted idea relative to the divorce between Kantian and Cantorian philosophies of mathematics. It shows that Kant and Cantor are opposite to each other at the level of the possibility as well as of the reality of the infinite. It specifies that these two thinkers meet each other when dealing with the definition of possibility and existence conditions. In a nutshell, Cantor inherited the two Kantian concepts of totality and reality, but he used them in a non-Kantian way.

BACKOF, Jeanne F and MARTIN JR, Charles L. Historical Perspectives: Development of the Codes of Ethics in the Legal, Medical and Accounting Professions. J Bus Ethics, 10(2), 99-110, F 91.

Members of the legal, medical and accounting professions are guided in their professional behavior by their respective codes of ethics. These codes of ethics are not static. They are ever evolving, responding to forces that are exogenous and endogenous to the professions. Specifically, changes in the ethical codes are often due to economic and social events, governmental influence, and growth and change within the professions. This paper presents a historical analysis of the major events leading to changes in the legal, medical and accounting codes of ethics.

BADALONI, Nicola. Rileggendo Marx: "diritti" e "bisogni". Teoria, 10(1), 5-16, 1990.

BADÍA-CABRERA, Miguel A. On Franco-Ferraz, Theism and the Theatre of the Mind. Hume Stud, 16(2), 131-139, N 90.

Although the theatrical structure of Hume's *Dialogues Concerning Natural Religion* may give a clue for an understanding of the existence and nature of God, it does not thence follow neither that Hume offers no final solutions to these problems nor that none of the characters present the victorious, i.e., Hume's own viewpoint, such as Maria Franco-Ferraz presumes in "Theatre and Religious Hypothesis" (Hume Studies, 15[1], 220-235, N 88). On the contrary, it is more probably that the *Dialogues* offer a definitive position on behalf of its author about the problems of theism as his main theoretical intention.

BAGET BOZZO, Giovanni and OROZ RETA, José (trans). La teología de la historia en la "ciudad de Dios" (2). Augustinus, 35(139-140), 321-367, Jl-D 90.

BAGET-BOZZO, Giovanni and OROZ RETA, José (trans). La teología de la historia en la Ciudad de Dios. Augustinus, 35(137-138), 31-80, Ja-Je 90.

BAGHRAMIAN, Maria. The Justification for Relevance Logic. Phil Stud (Ireland), 32, 32-43, 1988-90.

BAGHRAMIAN, Maria. Rorty, Davidson and Truth. Ratio, 3(2), 101-116, D 90.

In his various essays and books Richard Rorty has not only attacked realism and the correspondence theory of truth, but has also suggested that we should cease to think of truth as a topic of philosophical interest. Rorty has based many of his arguments on a pragmatist interpretation of Donald Davidson's philosophy of language. In this article I argue that (1) Davidson's causal and holistic theory of meaning leads to a sophisticated realism rather than pragmatism, and hence cannot be used to support Rorty's views on truth. (2) Rorty's position on truth, on its own, does not withstand close scrutiny.

BAGLIONI, Emma. Politica e diritto in Hobbes. Riv Int Filosof Diritto, 67(1), 115-119, Ja-Mr 90.

BAGLIONI, Emma. Uguaglianza e temporalità nella "Democrazia in America". Riv Int Filosof Diritto, 67(2), 192-218, Ap-Je 90.

BAGNALL, Richard G. Lifelong Education: The Institutionalisation of an Illiberal and Regressive Ideology. Educ Phil Theor, 22(1), 1-7, 1990.

This paper is a critique of Kenneth Wain's recent explication of the UNESCO concept of 'lifelong education'. In the 'maximalist' interpretation adopted by Wain, all of life's events are viewed as being educative, education is equated with learning, and is denied any normative properties. However, contrary to the United Nations charter, the interpretation is essentially illiberal, in that it denies the practical possibility of any rights to educational engagement in the more traditional sense. It is also, on its own criteria (coherence and practical fruitfulness), regressive, in that it is strictly impracticable according to its own principles.

BAHLUL, Raja. Miracles and Ghazali's First Theory of Causation. Phil Theol, 5(2), 137-150, Wint 90.

In the 17th Discussion of his Tahafut al-Falasifah ("Incoherence of the Philosophers"), Ghazali presents two theories of causation which, he claims, accommodate belief in the possibility of miracles. The first of these, which is usually taken to represent Ghazali's own position, is a form of occasionalism. In this paper I argue that Ghazali fails to prove that this theory is compatible with belief in the possibility of miracles.

BAHM, Archie J. Subject-Object Theories. J Indian Counc Phil Res, 6(1), 87-94, S-D 88.

A survey of twenty-three possible kinds of theories pertaining to relations between subjective and objects distinguishable in examining the nature of knowledge. Two diagrams depict possibilities for distinguishing between subjective and nonsubjective and between objective and nonobjective aspects, and between subjective and objective aspects. Printer's omission of vertical lines and underlining from the diagrams make the article somewhat unintelligible.

BAIER, Annette C. MacIntyre on Hume. Phil Phenomenol Res, 51(1), 159-163, Mr 91.

MacIntyre's treatment of Hume's ethics, in *Whose Justice, Which Rationality?* is praised for its rich textual basis, and criticised for its over-emphasis on Hume's endorsement of early capitalist forms of life, what MacIntyre calls his "anglicising subversion" of Scottish culture. Hume was cosmopolitan more than "anglophile," as were many other Scots in the eighteenth century.

BAIER, Annette C. Natural Virtues, Natural Vices. Soc Phil Pol, 8(1), 24-34, Autumn 90.

Hume's writings have been invoked both by sociobiologists who wish to draw normative conclusions from facts about human nature and its capacities for cooperation, and also by their critics, who point to Hume's warnings about the apparent impossibility of deducing an "ought" from an "is." He does make facts about what is normal in human populations highly relevant to what it is reasonable of us to take as moral standards, but the step from such facts to normative endorsement takes complicated footwork. Our nature has multiple potential, and ambivalence, especially concerning our proven sexist and racist tendencies, is part of that nature.

BAIER, Annette C. *A Progress of Sentiments: Reflections on Hume's "Treatise"*. Cambridge, Harvard Univ Pr, 1991.

Hume's *Treatise* explores a succession of versions of human reason, and in his third book endorses a social and "lively" reason. The anti-rationalist arguments are directed against a limited intellectualist version of reason, and prepare the ground for Hume's constructive account of reason and morality.

BAIER, Annette C. "What Emotions Are About" in *Philosophical Perspectives, 4: Action Theory and Philosophy of Mind, 1990*, TOMBERLIN, James E (ed), 1-29. Atascadero, Ridgeview, 1990.

Emotions have "deep" as well as surface objects, and refer to the life history of the person whose emotions they are, in particular to previous occurrances of the emotion in question. Their generality is historical and autobiographical.

BAIER, Annette C. "Whom Can Women Trust?" in *Feminist Ethics*, CARD, Claudia (ed), 233-245. Lawrence, Univ Pr of Kansas, 1991.

The main questions addressed are whether women can trust women more justifiably than they can trust men, and in particular whether and when daughters should trust their mothers. The work of Nancy Chodorow, on "the reproduction of mothering," and of Francine du Plessix Gray, on women-women and mother-daughter relations in the Soviet Union, are discussed. The conclusions drawn are guarded, but not pessimistic.

BAIER, Annette C. "Why Honesty Is a Hard Virtue" in *Identity, Character, and Morality: Essays in Moral Psychology*, FLANAGAN, Owen (ed), 259-282. Cambridge, MIT Pr, 1990.

Honesty in speech is related to candor in all sorts of expression, verbal and nonverbal, in the complex way that speech is related to non-verbal expression. It is best understood as an "artificial" virtue, in Hume's sense.

BAIER, Annette. "Real Humean Causes" in *Central Themes in Early Modern Philosophy*, COVER, J A (ed), 245-271. Indianapolis, Hackett, 1990.

Hume endorses rules for using experience to find out what "really" causes what, and it is argued that in Part III of *Treatise* Book One he has adhered to these rules in his own investigation into what causes our causal inferences. This makes his account of cause a subtle exercise in "reflexion."

BAIER, Kurt. "Egoism" in *A Companion to Ethics*, SINGER, Peter (ed), 197-204. Cambridge, Blackwell, 1991.

BAIGRIE, Brian S. The Justification of Kepler's Ellipse. Stud Hist Phil Sci, 21(4), 633-664, D 90.

This paper submits that the foundations of science are generated by a process of ossification whereby lively arguments are converted into unimaginative and rigid facts that serve for a time as the basis for cognitive authority of the well-founded theories in their respective domains. The mechanism advanced for this process is that the ossified facts are the by-product of a newly imposed theory which classifies theories, principles, laws, observations, etc., in a way which seems to be entirely natural. This account is developed exclusively in terms of the process whereby Kepler's laws of planetary motion came to be regarded by the scientific community as facts on which mathematicians had to found their mechanical theories.

BAILEY, Alan. Rediscovering Scepticism. Eidos, 8(2), 153-176, D 89.

Most present-day epistemologists assume that the protagonist of Descartes' "First Meditation" is a paradigm instance of someone who uses sceptical arguments to arrive at a sceptical conclusion about the extent of our knowledge of the world. This paper examines the differences between this so-called Cartesian scepticism and the Pyrrhonean scepticism described by Sextus Empiricus, and attempts to show that Pyrrhonean scepticism is by far the more philosophically interesting of the two positions.

BAILEY, Charles E. Nietzsche: Moralist or Immoralist?—The Verdict of the European Protestant Theologians in the First World War. Hist Euro Ideas, 11, 799-814, 1989.

During the First World War, aghast at reports of Teutonic ferocity and barbarism, Allied intellectuals blamed this departure from international morality on the teachings of an "unholy Trinity": Friedrich Nietzsche, Heinrich von Treitschke, and a Prussian cavalry general, Friedrich von Bernhardi. European Protestant theologians engaged in a vociferous propaganda war and, surprising, found Nietzsche the only member of the trio without blemish. The British scolded primarily Bernhardi, and the French pilloried especially Treitschke, while the German Protestants even rejoiced that, ironically, Nietzsche had reawakened an interest in the heroic side of Christianity.

BAILEY, George. Pierre Menard's *Don Quixote*. Iyyun, 39(3), 339-357, Jl 90.

Jorge Borges' *Pierre Menard, Author of Don Quixote* and Arthur Danto's discussion of this story are much cited as proof that notationally identical texts may not be the same work. I argue that neither Borges' story nor Danto's discussion justifies this thesis, and then argue that any literary work instantiated by a given text is instantiated by all notationally identical texts, regardless of their etiology.

BAILEY, Lee W. "Skull's Darkroom: The *Camera Obscura* and Subjectivity" in *Philosophy of Technology*, DURBIN, Paul T (ed), 63-79. Norwell, Kluwer, 1989.

The Western notion that soul must be restricted to the inner chambers of the skull serves the Newtonian view of the mechanistic world. This subjectivism is not self-evident, however. Its place in philosophy is nourished by an unacknowledged root metaphor, the *camera obscura*, a dark room allowing light to be projected onto a blank screen, revealing the outer scene. This paradigm was seen as a model for the eye by Leonardo, and evidence for the accuracy of perception by Locke, who explicitly used it to model mind itself. Renaissance individualism, perspective art and modern psychological theories of projection all disclose skull's darkroom hidden in the shadows of subjectivism. This technology, still modeling soul in cinema and television projection, aids in the repression of soul's flowing participation in world.

BAILLIE, Harold W and GARRETT, Thomas M. "The Ethics of Social Commitment" in *Biomedical Ethics Reviews, 1990*, HUMBER, James M (ed), 11-28. Clifton, Humana Pr, 1991.

This article presents an argument in favor of a national health care plan, claiming that health care is a social good serving human dignity, that sharing in social goods identifies one as a member of the society, and that membership in society is necessary and appropriate for human dignity. Further, the health care to be provided must be at minimum adequate to allow participation in society, and when such participation cannot be attained treatment is not required. Finally, we call for a combined social effort to define "adequate health care," led by the health care professions and the government.

BAIRD, Davis and FAUST, Thomas. Scientific Instruments, Scientific Progress and the Cyclotron. Brit J Phil Sci, 41(2), 147-175, Je 90.

Studying the development of the cyclotron between 1929 and 1940, we urge a conception of scientific knowledge which includes the production of new instruments and new instrumental techniques. We focus on three details in the development of the cyclotron: producing ions, focusing the ion beam, and creating and maintaining the vacuum. We describe eight components central to the success of the cyclotron: 1) experimental idea, 2) theoretical test, 3) empirical test, 4) functional design, 5) intuition, 6) tinkering, 7) adapting components from other sources, 8) knowing when the instrument is working. We argue that the process of instrument creation proceeds by emulation and adaptation of previously successful instruments and instrumental techniques. This explains why instrument creation proceeds from a relatively simple guiding idea through a plethora of engineering and scientific complexities; simple ideas can be emulated and adapted in many new contexts. The result is the accumulation of new scientific instruments and instrumental techniques—scientific progress.

BAIRD, Robert M (ed) and ROSENBAUM, Stuart E (ed). *Animal Experimentation: The Moral Issue*. Buffalo, Prometheus, 1991.

This collection of sixteen essays raises and discusses the moral question: is experimentation on animals morally justified, and, if so, under what conditions? Part one introduces the issues to those unfamiliar with moral philosophy. Part two contains position statements by Peter Singer and Tom Regan, two foremost animal advocates, along with critiques of their views. Part three introduces arguments of those who support animal experimentation. Part four contains a position statement adopted by the deans of thirteen medical schools, as well as proposals for addressing the conditions of animals in experimental facilities. Part five, a concluding essay, challenges assumptions of those on both sides of the issue.

BAKAR, Osman. Spiritual Traditions and Science and Technology. Asian J Phil, 2(1), 81-103, Sum 90.

In this essay the author seeks to highlight the important role spirituality has played throughout human history in the development and progress of science and technology. In many cultural traditions and civilizations, spirituality and science and technology were shown to possess common epistemological sources and to have been largely represented by the same individuals. The real credit, however, goes to philosophical spirituality or spiritual philosophy which the author clearly distinguishes from popular spirituality and modern secular philosophy. The essay specifically examines the role played by such "philosophical spiritualities" as Pythagoreanism, Hermeticism, Platonism and Aristotelianism in Jewish, Christian and Islamic science, and the roles played by Taoist, Hindu and Islamic spirituality in Chinese, Indian and Islamic civilizations respectively. The essay concludes with a discussion of the possibility of cultivating a new science based on the surviving spiritual traditions of humanity.

BAKER, Lynne Rudder. Dretske on the Explanatory Role of Belief. Phil Stud, 63(1), 99-111, Jl 91.

Fred Dretske's account of the explanatory role of belief is rightly regarded as ingenious. However, I believe that it ultimately falls to vicious circularity: A state has an explanatory role in virtue of having meaning; explanatory role is equated with causal role; and a state has meaning in virtue of having a causal role in behavior. The only way that I see for Dretske to get out of the circle is to give up his account of the explanatory role of belief.

BAKER, Lynne Rudder. "On a Causal Theory of Content" in *Philosophical Perspectives, 3: Philosophy of Mind and Action Theory, 1989*, TOMBERLIN, James E (ed), 165-186. Atascadero, Ridgeview, 1989.

This paper is a critique of Jerry A Fodor's naturalistic theory of meaning in *Psychosemantics*. Fodor proposes to give, in nonintentional and nonsemantic terms, a sufficient condition for a mental representation to express a certain property. "On a Causal Theory of Content" argues that the "only" clause of the sufficient condition fails, because the account of misrepresentation actually applies to nothing, and that the "all" clause fails, because Fodor's Causal Theory implicitly employs two criteria for identity of appearances.

BAKHTIN, M M and HOLQUIST, Michael (ed) and LIAPUNOV, Vadim (ed). *Art and Answerability: Early Philosophical Essays—M M Bakhtin*. Austin, Univ of Texas Pr, 1990.

BAKUNIN and SHATZ, Marshall (ed). *Statism and Anarchy*. New York, Cambridge Univ Pr, 1991.

BALABAN, Oded. Circularity of Thought in Hegel's Logic. Rev Metaph, 44(1), 95-109, S 90.

According to Hegel, concepts are the result of predication, whereas there must be a concept, attaching to the subject, that precedes predication. This circularity, and Hegel's answer to it, is the clue to understanding the limits of Hegelian idealism that ascribes superiority to the universal as against the individual. Hegel's circularity arises since his philosophy attributes primacy to thought over sensation.

BALDASSARRE, Mariarosa. Per una storia dell'idea di Europa: Riflessioni storiografiche. Sapienza, 43(3), 321-328, Jl-S 90.

BALDNER, Kent. Is Transcendental Idealism Coherent? Synthese, 85(1), 1-23, O 90.

I argue that transcendental idealism can be understood as a coherent and plausible account of experience. I begin by proposing an interpretation of the claim that we know only appearances that does not imply that the objects of experience are anything other than independently real objects. As I understand it, the claim here is about *how* objects appear to us, and not about *what* objects appear to us. After this, I offer a version of a correspondence account of veridical experience, in virtue of which these independent entities can satisfy the contents of our experiences. Specifically, I claim that veridical experience can be construed as a kind of map of reality in itself, and that these independent entities satisfy the contents of our experiences when they are, given the proper method of projection, the objects mapped by those experiences.

BALDWIN, John T. The Spectrum of Resplendency. J Sym Log, 55(2), 624-636, Je 90.

A model M of a finite language is resplendent if every sigma 1-1 formula satisfiable in an elementary extension of M is satisfiable in M. In this paper we show some of Shelah's techniques for counting models of first order theories extend to counting resplendent models. In particular, if T is not superstable T has the maximal number of resplendent models in every uncountable power. If T is strictly superstable T has both-2 models in all sufficiently large powers. If T is not unstable, strictly stable, or small and strictly superstable every homogeneous resplendent model of T is saturated.

BALDWIN, Thomas. The Identity Theory of Truth. Mind, 100(397), 35-52, Ja 91.

Surprisingly, both Bradley and his critics, Moore and Russell, at one time agreed in holding the truth of a judgment to consist in its identity with a fact. For Bradley, such an identity is unattainable; hence truth is impossible. But the introduction of propositions in the early philosophy of Moore and Russell makes the application of the identity theory straightforward. However, it also leads to unacceptable consequences concerning falsehood, and for this reason Moore and Russell abandoned the theory. But its influence on Russell's later work is readily discerned; and even today Lewis's theory of possible worlds approximates towards the position.

BALDWIN, Thomas. "Moore and Philosophical Skepticism" in *The Analytic Tradition: Philosophical Quarterly Monographs, Volume 1*, BELL, David (ed), 117-136. Cambridge, Blackwell, 1990.

It is often maintained that Moore attempted to refute scepticism by a direct appeal to common sense, to our conviction that we do have the kinds of knowledge which sceptics hold that we lack. It is shown that this interpretation of Moore is mistaken. Instead Moore argued that sceptical arguments require presumptions that we have good reason to reject because we are less certain of them than we are of the claims to knowledge which these arguments controvert. Moore's argument is not entirely convincing, but he should not be treated as a naive and dogmatic defender of common sense.

BALES, Eugene F. Memory, Forgetfulness and the Disclosure of Being in Heidegger and Plotinus. Phil Today, 34(2), 141-151, Sum 90.

This paper addresses the concepts of recollection or remembering in the writings of Heidegger and Plotinus. What is thereby brought out is (1) that Heidegger's hermeneutical project and Plotinus's metaphysics do have much in common; (2) that Heidegger's and Plotinus's notion of the "Origin" are in fact similar, if not the "same" (understood in Heidegger's sense); and (3) that Heidegger's insistence on the interconnection of historicity and Being is not at odds with Plotinus's apparent acceptance of the eternity of Being grounded in the transcendent One.

BALIBAR, Etienne. From Class Struggle to Struggle without Classes? Grad Fac Phil J, 14(1), 7-21, 1991.

BALIÑAS, Carlos. Filósofos naúfragos. El Basilisco, 2, 13-18, N-D 89.

BALK, Roger A. New Creations? Commentary. Hastings Center Rep, 21(1), 33-34, Ja-F 91.

Homologous gene targetting cannot be described as a benign process and the question of what ethical and social control should be placed on its development is very real. The appropriate response is to limit specific human designs strictly, rather than outlawing a very promising technology. But the speed at which developments are taking place in this one area of biotechnology poses a genuine challenge to keep up even for those who are active participants in this field. So for those concerned to evaluate its ethical impact, getting at the implications of these developments is a major problem.

BALL, Stephen W. Dworkin and His Critics: The Relevance of Ethical Theory in Philosophy of Law. Ratio Juris, 3(3), 340-384, D 90.

Two deficiencies characterize the vast critical literature that has accumulated around Dworkin's theory of law. On the one hand, the main lines of the debate tend to get lost in the crossfire of objections by critics and rejoinders by Dworkin—with little dialogue between the critics, or any systematic interrelation or resolution of these largely isolated disputes. On the other hand, such arguments on various points of Dworkin's jurisprudence tend to neglect or obscure underlying issues in philosophical ethics. The present essay is a critical analysis addressing each of these deficiencies in an attempt both to clarify and to advance the debate. The analysis hinges on three basic propositions: (1) that this debate in jurisprudence has overlooked relevant issues about the nature of moral values; (2) that theories of law, in general, are best assessed in terms of separate descriptive and normative issues, corresponding to a fact/value distinction in ethics; and (3) that the debate on Dworkinian rights has assumed a confused and historically superficial contrast with the utilitarian tradition, in ethical theory as well as in philosophy of law.

BALL, Stephen W. Linguistic Intuitions and Varieties of Ethical Naturalism. Phil Phenomenol Res, 51(1), 1-38, Mr 91.

The purpose of this essay is to develop, and defend, a linguistic argument against various forms of ethical naturalism. This type of argument - associated historically with G E Moore's "open question" test and its subsequent rendition by emotivists or noncognitivists—is now widely regarded as circular and/or logically invalid, at different stages. Contrary to both standard criticisms, the pre-philosophic linguistic intuitions of native speakers can provide helpful evidence against ethical naturalism. Variations on both objections are considered, with emphasis on the current emotivist use of the argument. The essay begins with the rejection of a new form of invalidity objection, waged by Harman as well as Putnam, in connection with naturalistic reductions of science and with Kripke's philosophy of language. Contrary to their objection, it is argued that linguistic intuitions are relevant to assessing not only the analyticity of naturalistic definitions in ethics, but also the prospect of synthetically identifying moral and physicalistic properties. The essay concludes with an analysis of the application and limitations of the open question argument, as related to other, nonsemantic forms of naturalism.

BALOG, Andreas. Society as an "Accidental Product of Human Activities": Max Horkheimer's Social Theory and Critique. Phil Soc Crit, 16(2), 127-141, 1990.

BALSLEV, Anindita N. The Notion of *Klesa* and Its Bearing on the Yoga Analysis of Mind. Phil East West, 41(1), 77-88, Ja 91.

This paper focuses on the possibility of framing a theory of mind on the basis of the insights obtained from the corpus of the Yoga literature. An examination of the notion of 'Klesa' shows how the cognitive and the volitional aspects of our mental life are intimately related to the affective. The Yoga analysis does not warrant any artificial splitting up of emotion and cognition in opposite camps. The paper deals with ideas that are particularly interesting for those who today in the West are involved with such polemical issues as whether emotions are rational or irrational, passive or active, intentional or not.

BALSLEV, Anindita. Time, Self and Consciousness: Some Conceptual Patterns in the Context of Indian Thought. J Indian Counc Phil Res, 5(1), 111-119, S-D 87.

This paper examines the inherent philosophical tensions between the Brahmanical and the Buddhist interpretations of time and consciousness, which are shown to have decisive impact on the formulations of a theory of self or no-self. Referring to various conceptual moves that reflect the internal differences that are present in each of these traditions, different configurations of ideas are disclosed, such as the diverse conceptual schemes where a notion of an identical self is seen operating along with a notion of an absolute time or a view of time as appearance. One also comes across a view of discrete time which leads to a total rejection of the idea of an identical self. The challenge and complexity of a philosophical account of time, self and consciousness is demonstrated with help of the polemical literature.

BALTAS, Aristides. "Louis Althusser and Joseph D Sneed: A Strange Encounter in Philosophy of Science?" in *Imre Lakatos and Theories of Scientific Change*, GAVROGLU, Kostas (ed), 269-286. Norwell, Kluwer, 1989.

It is argued that the analytic approach of J Sneed to the structure of theories of mathematical physics and the Marxist approach of L Althusser to the phenomenon of science in general share a common philosophical ground that legitimates an attempt at the corresponding synthesis. This may provide an interesting alternative to the views on the structure and on the history of science currently under discussion. A summary of the views of both Sneed and Althusser is presented and the common ground between the two is delimited. The points where the two approaches diverge are discussed. Finally, a first attempt at their synthesis is made.

BALZER, Noel. "The Logic of Implication". J Value Inq, 24(4), 253-268, O 90.

This paper demonstrates the necessary connection in material implication. The argument shows the necessary connection depends on (1) the principle that an instance of a class is the class; (2) truth and falsity occur as instances of themselves; (3) truth (T) is in falsity but falsity (F) is not in truth. From this, truth implies truth, truth does not imply falsity, falsity implies truth and falsity implies falsity.

BALZER, W. "On Incommensurability" in *Imre Lakatos and Theories of Scientific Change*, GAVROGLU, Kostas (ed), 287-304. Norwell, Kluwer, 1989.

A new "derivation" is given for the identity of incommensurability with inconsistency. Starting from the Kuhnian idea of incommensurability as a tension between a partial and a full match between concepts and meanings this result is obtained in several steps of clarification and derivation. Examples are briefly considered.

BALZER, Wolfgang and MATTESSICH, Richard. An Axiomatic Basis of Accounting: A Structuralist Reconstruction. Theor Decis, 30(3), 213-244, My 91.

Set-theoretic axiomatizations are given for a model of accounting with double classification, and a general core-model for accounting. The empirical status, and "representational" role of systems of accounts, as well as the problem of how to assign "correct" values to the good accounted, are analyzed in precise terms. A net of special laws based on the core-model is described.

BALZER, Wolfgang. Holism and Measurement (in Serbo-Croatian). Filozof Istraz, 34(1), 227-238, 1990.

Holism maintains that theories can be evaluated only in a global way, that there is no way to test or reject 'isolated hypotheses', and that all empirical theories form a large net such that changes at one point of the net necessitate changes at other places. This idea seems to conflict with the views of practising scientists concerning the functioning of measurement in their theories. This conflict, in the author's opinion, is the main reason why practising scientists either reject as false, or at least neglect, the utterances of the present day philosophy of science. The author's thesis is that the 'global' of holism becomes rather 'local' when looking at *specific* theories in some detail. (edited)

BAMBACH, Charles R. History and Ontology: A Reading of Nietzsche's Second "Untimely Meditation". Phil Today, 34(3), 259-272, Fall 90.

This essay offers a reading of Nietzsche's "On the Uses and Disadvantages of History for Life" (1874) which focuses on the problem of ontology. I argue that in this early piece Nietzsche's discussion of German historical consciousness is not simply a form of value-focused cultural criticism, but a way to grasp the historicity of human being. Here, the young Nietzsche redefines historical knowledge not as scientific truth, but as a form of interpretation. This hermeneutic account of history overturns the Cartesian notion of consciousness and offers insight into an understanding of history as lived temporality rather than as an epistemologically determined "field" of study. Such a reading forces us back to an ontological rather than merely axiological reading of Nietzsche's entire corpus.

BAMBROUGH, Renford. "Does Philosophy 'Leave Everything as it is'? Even Theology?" in *The Philosophy in Christianity*, VESEY, Godfrey (ed), 225-236. New York, Cambridge Univ Pr, 1989.

BAMBROUGH, Renford. "Ethics and the Limits of Consistency" in *Logic and Ethics*, GEACH, Peter (ed), 1-20. Norwell, Kluwer, 1991.

BAMBROUGH, Renford. Ethics and the Limits of Consistency. Proc Aris Soc, 90, 1-15, 1989-90.

BAMBROUGH, Renford. Fools and Heretics. Philosophy, 28, 239-250, 90 Supp.

BANAJI, V F. Republic: 2. Indian Phil Quart, 17(4), 429-487, O 90.

More than forty years have passed since India gained independence. What is it that has held back the development of the country? Eschewing conventional interpretations, the present study explores a variety of psychosocial impediments to India's economic progress and considers the role 'Indian' philosophy could have played in retarding the country's development. The differing viewpoints have been given form in a dialogue which has been patterned, somewhat irreverently, on Plato's great work.

BANASCHEWSKI, Bernhard and MOORE, Gregory H. The Dual Cantor-Bernstein Theorem and the Partition Principle. Notre Dame J Form Log, 31(3), 375-381, Sum 90.

This paper examines two propositions, the Dual Cantor-Bernstein Theorem and the Partition Principle, with respect to their logical interrelationship and their history. It is shown that the Refined Dual Cantor-Bernstein Theorem is equivalent to the Axiom of Choice.

BANERJEE, Hiranmoy. The Objectivity of Moral Values: The Search in a Wrong Place. J Indian Counc Phil Res, 5(3), 157-161, My-Ag 88.

Moral values consisting of a set of rules or virtues cannot be discovered empirically or logically ensuring their near-universal acceptance. They are held to be invented to counteract man's limited sympathies. Moral reasoning justifiably uses the universalizability principle because we must ignore distinction of persons in choosing preferences to be satisfied. But why do invented values or chosen preferences have objective validity? The value system reflects a way of life and values are the stuff of which man is made. Our justification for our value-system consists in seeing that our whole way of thinking or acting makes no sense without it. Values can be criticized and transformed only within a value-charged view of the universe.

BANKOWSKI, Zenon. The Institution of Law. Ratio Juris, 4(1), 79-85, Mr 91.

The aim of this work is to see how notions of exclusionary reason and formality can fit into both a philosophic and sociological account of law. I show how institutions are important to the notion of legality. My long term aim in this work is to develop a participatory theory of legality where formal and substantive views interact.

BANKSTON, Paul and RUITENBURG, Wim. Notions of Relative Ubiquity for Invariant Sets of Relational Structures. J Sym Log, 55(3), 948-986, S 90.

Given a finite lexicon L of relational symbols and equality, one may view the collection of all L-structures on the set of natural numbers ω as a space in several different ways. We consider it as (i) the space of outcomes of certain infinite two-person games; (ii) a compact metric space; and (iii) a probability measure space. For each of these viewpoints, we can give a notion of relative ubiquity, or largeness, for invariant sets of structures on ω. For example, in every sense of relative ubiquity considered here, the set of dense linear orderings on ω is ubiquitous in the set of linear orderings on ω.

BANKSTON, Paul. Taxonomies of Model-Theoretically Defined Topological Properties. J Sym Log, 55(2), 589-603, Je 90.

BAPAT, Jyotsna. A Candidate Paradigm for Human Ecology. Indian Phil Quart, 18(2), 335-359, Ap 91.

The sociological theories, have so far, failed to give environment its due credit; while the environmental theories, have ignored the social dimension. Therefore there is a need to develop a new paradigm that brings the two together in a new synthesis. Such a task demands a theoretical analysis and critique at the level of concepts, compatibility and the modes of synthesis accompanied by appropriate methodology. The article elaborates such a synthesis of the adaptive dynamics theory with the critical social theory.

BAPTIST, Gabriella. "Ways and Loci of Modality" in *Essays on Hegel's Logic*, DI GIOVANNI, George (ed), 127-143. Albany, SUNY Pr, 1990.

BAR ON, Bat-Ami. "Why Terrorism Is Morally Problematic" in *Feminist Ethics*, CARD, Claudia (ed), 107-125. Lawrence, Univ Pr of Kansas, 1991.

BAR-ON, A Zvie. Divine Foresight and Human Moral Responsibility (in Hebrew). Iyyun, 40(2), 151-158, Ap 91.

BAR-ON, Dorit. "Justifying Beliefs: The Dream Hypothesis and Gratuitous Entities" in *Doubting: Contemporary Perspectives on Skepticism*, ROTH, Michael D (ed), 141-146. Norwell, Kluwer, 1990.

Part I of the paper I clarify the dispute between Paul Moser, a defender of common-sense realism, and Barry Stroud, who develops a skeptical argument. In part II I argue that Moser's defense of the realist hypothesis as the best explanation of the contents of our experiences requires much more elaboration and explication before its superiority over its skeptical competitors can be established.

BAR-ON, Dorit. Scepticism: The External World and Meaning. Phil Stud, 60(3), 207-231, N 90.

In this paper, I compare and contrast two kinds of scepticism, Cartesian scepticism about the external world and Quinean scepticism about meaning. I expose Quine's metaphysical claim that there are no facts of the matter about meaning as a sceptical response to a sceptical problem regarding the possibility of our knowledge of meanings. I argue that this sceptical response is overkill; for the sceptical problem about our knowledge of meanings may receive a treatment similar to the naturalistic treatment Quine himself offered for the problem of our knowledge of the external world. Further, I suggest that a naturalistic treatment of Quinean meaning scepticism may fare better than Quine's own naturalistic treatment of external world scepticism.

BARAD-ANDRADE, Judith. Stewardship: Whose Creation Is It Anyway? Between Species, 7(2), 102-109, Spr 91.

BARATA-MOURA, José. *A "Realizacção da Razão": Um Programa Hegeliano?*. Lisbon, Caminho, 1990.

The book deals both systematically and historically with the theme: the realization of reason. Special chapters are dedicated to Hegel, Feuerbach, Cieszkowski, Köppen, Bauer, Ruge, Marx, and M Hess. More than as an abstract human faculty in competition for hegemony, rationality is viewed as structuring dimension of humanity itself.

BARATA-MOURA, José. "O inimigo da liberdade: sobre o sentido do materialismo para Fichte" in *Dinâmica do Pensar: Homenagem a Oswaldo Market*, FAC LETRAS UNIV LISBOA (ed), 1-45. Lisboa, Fac Letras U Lisboa, 1991.

Im Rahmen einer Erläuterung der praktischen Grundlage des Idealismus Fichtes werden die erkenntnistheoretischen, ontologischen, ethischen und politischen Zusammenhänge seines Materialismusbegriffes erforscht. Das fichteanische Bestreiten jeder ontischen Selbstbegründung der Materialität überhaupt funktioniert vorwiegend als Anruf an eine egoische sowie gemeinschaftliche vernünftige Ausübung der handelnden Freiheit und Selbständigkeit.

BARBA, Mario. "'Lautform, innere Sprachform, Form der Sprachen'" in *Leibniz, Humboldt, and the Origins of Comparativism*, DE MAURO, Tullio (ed), 263-280. Philadelphia, John Benjamins, 1990.

Heymann Steinthal's (1823-1899) typological studies bring together the history of languages and the general theory of language with a classification scheme which orders all the descriptive and historical data by means of general principles. This paper presents Steinthal's scheme and discusses the problem at its source, namely, Wilhelm von Humboldt's (1767-1835) conception of language as 'form' and formative organ of thought. For Steinthal, the different *Weltansichten* achieved by national languages are displayed not only in their semantic systems of single representations, but also in the structure of their grammars and in the way they construct syntagmatic and apperceptive relationships between one representation and another. According to Steinthal, the grammatical structure and the rules of syntax also depend on the diverse *innere Form* of languages as distinguished by means of the articulated sounds.

BARBANEL, Julius. Almost Hugeness and a Related Notion. Notre Dame J Form Log, 32(2), 255-265, Spr 91.

We consider a natural weakening of hugeness. In contrast to the supercompact situation, this notion fits into a nice hierarchy with almost hugeness, hugeness, and *n*-hugeness.

BARBER, Michael. The Ethics Behind the Absence of Ethics in Alfred Schutz's Thought. Human Stud, 14(2-3), 129-140, Jl 91.

Alfred Schutz seemed reluctant to discuss ethics, settling for a value-free Weberian descriptions. The author argues that this reluctance can be traced to his suspicion about in-groups's capacity to marginalize out-groups, often in the name of ethical beliefs. Schutz's evasion of ethics itself, though, depends on the ethical principle that the subjective viewpoint of the other ought to be taken seriously. Because of this principle, underlying even Schutz's epistemological innovations, Schutz's thought converges with the ethical theory of Emmanuel Levinas.

BARBER, Michael. Finitude Rediscovered. Phil Theol, 5(1), 73-80, Fall 90.

According to Alfred Schutz's theory of signification, based as it is on Husserl's theory of appresentation, through marks and indications we overcome the small transcendences of space and time, through signs the medium transcendences of the Other's difference from us, and through symbols the great transcendences of other finite provinces of meaning. This paper examines the implications of the correlations between these transcendences and significations, and argues that Schutz's order of significations reveals the profound irony that the more signifier-users seek to tame and subdue transcendences through significations, the more they discover how transcendences escape their dominion.

BARBIERO, Daniel. From Nothingness to No-thing-ness: the Roots of Ferry and Renaut's Humanism. Phil Soc Crit, 16(3), 179-191, 1990.

BARBOSA, Manuel. Freud: Uma Concepção Agónica da Educação. Rev Port Filosof, 46(2), 251-267, Ap-Je 90.

The author sketches what can be considered the key concepts of Freud's thought concerning education; this thought implies a certain anthropology. Freud's reflection on education is agonic and implies tragic aspects.

BARCA, Anne and MC ROBBIE, Michael. Constructive Interpolation Theorems for $S2^0$ and S2. Rep Math Log, 23, 3-15, 1989.

BARCALOW, Emmett. Moral Skepticism and Moral Education. J Thought, 24(3-4), 35-54, Fall-Wint 89.

BARCELÓ, Alfons. "Are There Economic Laws?" in *Studies on Mario Bunge's "Treatise"*, WEINGARTNER, Paul (ed), 379-396. Amsterdam, Rodopi, 1990.

The paper has two parts. The first is a brief outline of the current state of economic science. The second explains a simple theorem which aspires to the status of an "economic law." This "Theorem on Self-Reproducing Goods" has the peculiarity of relating a quotient of prices with biological and technical parameters perfectly knowable. The field of reference of this theorem is very restricted, but its historical domain is extremely wide. These qualities (trans-systemic validity and quantitative precision) tend to be unexpected features in the human sciences. Therefore this "statement of law" is of relevant epistemological interest.

BARD, Terry R. *Medical Ethics in Practice*. Bristol, Hemisphere, 1990.

The increase in medical capabilities to aid and sustain life, and the lack of specific guidelines to govern the use of these advances, pose unanticipated theoretical and practical dilemmas. This book provides a "real world" approach to medical ethics and reports on the clinical application of ethical concerns in an actual healthcare setting, presenting the process by which Boston's Beth Israel Hospital has begun to address ethical concerns. This text demonstrates and shares "an ethical vision," effecting a greater understanding of the ethical component of issues in daily life experience and within the context of the biotechnical world.

BARDEN, Garrett. *After Principles*. Notre Dame, Univ Notre Dame Pr, 1990.

There are mutually incompatible horizons; there are no given a priori moral principles in the form of propositions. But relativism is insufficiently radical as it retains the shadow of a deductive image of mind and a restricted image of the moral. This is simply the domain of deliberation and choice and a moral tradition is a set of values from which the moral actor must willy-nilly begin. Moral actors are alike in that they create themselves by their questions which arise within, but do not radically confine the questioner to, tradition. Discussion between moral actors is thus radically possible.

BARINEAU, R Maurice. Whitehead and Genuine Evil. Process Stud, 19(3), 181-188, Fall 90.

Ely, Madden, Hare and Schulweis have charged that Whitehead's solution to the problem of evil does not allow for the actuality of genuine evils. This charge is based upon a faulty understanding of Whitehead's theory of evil, an inappropriate understanding of what should constitute "apparent evil," and a failure to take sufficient notice of those passages in which Whitehead makes reference to what must be labeled "genuine evil."

BARINGOLTZ, Eleonora. Wittgenstein, Strawson y la no-posesión. Cuad Filosof, 21(34), 43-55, My 90.

This paper deals with an attempt to elucidate some aspects of the no-ownership theory as it is held by Wittgenstein at the beginning of the thirties. It analyses mainly the original version understood as a theory which intends to dissolve rather than eliminate the notion of subject (self or ego) by substituting a new one. This matter must be faced in connection with Wittgenstein's thoughts about privacy theories regarding primary experiences, and paying special attention to the serious problems arising from them in the field of grammar. Lastly, Strawson's version of the no-ownership theory is briefly exposed and evaluated.

BARKER, Stephen. *Even, Still* and Counterfactuals. Ling Phil, 14(1), 1-38, F 91.

The 'classical view' concerning the semantics of counterfactual conditionals is that a causal or logical connection between antecedent and consequent is not a necessary condition for a counterfactual's truth. The classical view is held by nearly all writers on counterfactuals, e.g., Lewis, Stalnaker, Jackson, Pollock, Kvart, amongst others. So-called *even-if*-conditionals (also known as *semifactuals*) are adduced as indisputable evidence for the classical view. I argue, to the contrary, that detailed examination of the function of the words *even* and *still* in and out of counterfactuals, shows that a connexive thesis is not only maintainable but likely to be correct.

BARKOVICH, Greg. A Reflection on Saint Augustine's *Confessions*. Gnosis, 3(3), 111-116, D 90.

BARLINGAY, S S. Ontology and History. J Indian Counc Phil Res, 8(1), 57-68, S-D 90.

History is a story of men interacting with one another and requires the background of cosmocantric, astro-geographical world, modified by historical beings and historians, as anthropocentric world. The world is a two-track world. Man modifies the world through doing, destiny, willing, thinking, experiencing. The experience is consigned to memory but recollected. The recollection is selective, interest-oriented, evaluative. The experiencing process requires a first-person, knower regarding himself as independent of his universe. Historical actions are author-oriented, responsible and presuppose temporality of different types vis-a-vis past-present-future. History is manifestation of man's term of life.

BARLINGAY, S S. Re-understanding Indian Philosophy. J Indian Counc Phil Res, 6(2), 109-125, Ja-Ap 89.

'Indian philosophy' is just philosophy; philosophers alone are Indian. So it should not be judged by some different standard. Indian philosophy emerged from Purva Mimamsa religious fabric. But Sankara, Vedanta, Buddhism-Jainism also enriched it. The basic assumptions of Indian philosophy are (1) world existing by itself, (2) knower (as separated from the world), and (3) having ability to know the world. Each system also had its assumptions, in addition. Using all these problems of philosophy would appear in different perspective. This is attempted in this paper.

BARLINGAY, S S. Social Reality and Moral Order. J Indian Counc Phil Res, 7(3), 75-91, My-Ag 90.

BARNES, Annette. Some Remarks on Respect and Human Rights. Phil Stud (Ireland), 32, 263-273, 1988-90.

Some have claimed that since each person is equally entitled to respect each person gets exactly the same human rights. I discuss whether the notion of "being capable of being viewed imaginatively from their own point of view" is, as one philosopher suggests, capable of rendering this attitude of respect intelligible and whether, if it is, anything would follow about people being entitled to respect. I show that if people's entitlement to respect could be made plausible, it would follow that they had at least one human right.

BARNES, Eric. The Causal History of Computational Activity: Maudlin and Olympia. J Phil, 88(6), 304-316, Je 91.

BARNES, Hazel E. Sartre and Sexism. Phil Lit, 14(2), 340-347, O 90.

Although Sartre's rhetoric reveals a personal sexism that he never wholly eradicated, his philosophy supports the claims of feminism both in early and later phases. It argues women's capacity for and right to self-determination as presented in Beauvoir's *The Second Sex*. It can be useful to those who call for a distinctively feminist perspective in ethics and epistemology and challenge the tenets of traditional philosophy as being one-sidedly male and therefore truncated.

BARNES, Jonathan. Partial Wholes. Soc Phil Pol, 8(1), 1-23, Autumn 90.

(i) An exposition of the moral philosophy of Alexander Pope with special reference to the importance of parts and wholes. (ii) An attempt to give a clear mereological formulation to Pope's theory. (iii) An attempt to show that the theory, however interpreted, is either trivially true or excitingly false.

BARNES, Jonathan. Scepticism and Relativity. Phil Stud (Ireland), 32, 1-31, 1988-90.

I discuss 1) the connections between scepticism and relativism in the works of Sextus Empiricus, arguing that these two very different notions are occasionally confounded; and 2) Sextus' criticisms of certain dogmatic theories about relatives, arguing that most of these criticisms hit their targets.

BARNES, L Philip. Relativism, Ineffability, and the Appeal to Experience: A Reply to the Myth Makers. Mod Theol, 7(1), 101-114, O 90.

In *The Myth of Christian Uniqueness*, edited by John Hick and Paul Knitter, it is argued that each religion reveals and initiates communion with the divine. The author of this article suggests that a strong case could be made for this position if it could be shown positively that different religious doctrines and experiences agree in a way analogous to the agreement between sense experiences of the same object, or negatively if the differences between religions could be explained away satisfactorily, and agreement produced in this way. The conclusion is reached that religions do not agree in either of the senses identified.

BARNES, Timothy D. "Religion and Society in the Age of Theodosius" in *Grace, Politics and Desire: Essays on Augustine*, MEYNELL, Hugo A (ed), 157-175. Calgary, Univ Calgary Pr, 1990.

BARNET, Robert J. A Proposal for Health Care: Revolution Not Reform. Bus Prof Ethics J, 9(3-4), 147-160, Fall-Wint 90.

BARNETT, Randy E. "Rights and Remedies in a Consent Theory of Contract" in *Liability and Responsibility*, FREY, R G (ed), 135-172. New York, Cambridge Univ Pr, 1991.

BARON, Charles. On Taking Substituted Judgment Seriously. Hastings Center Rep, 20(5), 7-8, S-O 90.

The author argues that *Cruzan* was rightly decided by the US Supreme Court. Though he believes the Missouri law involved was bad, it was not unconstitutional. To the extent that it required "clear and convincing" evidence of her wishes for "substituting judgment" from Nancy Cruzan, it did not burden the death decision process significantly more than requiring *some* evidence of her wishes or requiring that her family make the decision for her. Are *these* latter requirements unconstitutional?

BARRETT, Cyril. "The Language of Ecstasy and the Ecstasy of Language" in *The Bible as Rhetoric: Studies in Biblical Persuasion and Credibility*, WARNER, Martin (ed), 205-221. New York, Routledge, 1990.

The question I address myself to is whether mystical and prophetic writing is anything more than a skillful use of words. My conclusion is that it is more, just as good poetry is. As Sartre says: the poet captures reality in the web of language. So does the prophet and mystic. What he captures cannot be said in any language other than that in which he captured it. To be a prophet in ancient times one had to be a poet; likewise to be a mystic worth attention in our day.

BARRETT, D C. "Faith and Rationality" in *Key Themes in Philosophy*, GRIFFITHS, A Phillips (ed), 135-143. New York, Cambridge Univ Pr, 1989.

BARRETT, Martin and HAUSMAN, Daniel. Making Interpersonal Comparisons Coherently. Econ Phil, 6(2), 293-300, O 90.

BARRETT, Robert (ed) and GIBSON, Roger (ed). *Perspectives on Quine*. Cambridge, Blackwell, 1990.

BARRIE, John A. G H Bantock as Educational Philosopher. J Phil Educ, 24(1), 93-106, Sum 90.

This article places G H Bantock firmly within the English literary critical tradition—with important philosophic as well as literary roots in S T Coleridge. An exploratory case is made out for "seeing" Bantock's educational output as philosophic, provided that a more European conception rather than a strictly analytic conception of the nature of philosophy is entertained.

BARRIGAR, Christian J. Protecting God: The Lexical Formation of Trinitarian Language. Mod Theol, 7(4), 299-310, Jl 91.

BARROSO, Inmaculada Acosta. La naturaleza como vida en la interpretación hegeliana de Aristóteles. Themata, 6, 9-22, 1989.

This article is a study of Hegel's interpretation of Aristotle. The validity of this interpretation is confirmed through a commentary of the Hegelian texts which contain it, confronting them with the correspondent texts of Aristotle's commentators. The central point tries to demonstrate that idea of act—which is central to Aristotelian philosophy—can be applied to the concept of nature. According to the Hegelian interpretation, the result of it is a concept of nature much less static than in the scholastic interpretations, and which in a great measure can be assimilated to the idea of life.

BARRUS, Roger M. David Hume's Theology of Liberation. Interpretation, 18(2), 251-272, Wint 90-91.

This paper examines what might be called the theology of liberalism through an analysis of the arguments and the action of Hume's *Dialogues Concerning Natural Religion*. Liberalism presents itself as having no particular metaphysical or theological presuppositions. It appears as nonpartisan. This is the surface meaning of liberal toleration. Hume shows, however, principally through the drama of the *Dialogues*, that liberalism is inherently partisan. It has its own implicit teaching on religion. Liberal toleration is fundamentally hostile to traditional religious belief. Hume develops the theological or metaphysical presuppositions of liberalism in and through the dramatic confrontation between the characters of the *Dialogues*.

BARRY JR, James. The Physics of Modern Perception: Beyond Body and World. J Speculative Phil, 4(4), 287-297, 1990.

BARRY, Brian. "How Not to Defend Liberal Institutions" in *Liberalism and the Good*, DOUGLASS, R Bruce (ed), 44-58. New York, Routledge, 1990.

Traditional arguments for basic liberal rights addressed to religious believers depend on the existence of a balance of forces or presuppose an essentially liberal religious outlook. A recent argument derived liberal rights from an idea of state neutrality. It is claimed by some that this provides a principled case grounded in fairness that should lead anyone, however repressive his or her religious beliefs may be, to espouse liberal rights. This claim is unfounded in that to make headway it first requires the abandonment of religious dogmatism. It is also questionable that even liberals should embrace neutrality.

BARRY, Brian. Social Criticism and Political Philosophy. Phil Pub Affairs, 19(4), 360-373, Fall 90.

This is a critique of two books by Michael Walzer: *Interpretation and Social Criticism* (1987) and *The Company of Critics* (1988). The focus is on Walzer's proposed methodology of 'social criticism' and his hostility to the kind of political philosophy represented by John Rawls. The conclusion reached is that Walzer fails in his attempt to drive a wedge between a method of 'interpretation' (which he endorses) and that used by Rawls and others. Rather, they are offering an interpretation of prevailing Western political ideas, which are arguably inherently universalistic, that is a rival to Walzer's preferred appeal to parochial values.

BARRY, Norman P. "Libertarianism" in *Philosophy and Politics*, HUNT, G M K (ed), 109-127. New York, Cambridge Univ Pr, 1991.

BARRY, Norman P. The Philosophy of the Welfare State. Crit Rev, 4(4), 545-568, Fall 90.

This is a critique of the variety of ethical and economic justifications that have been produced for existing Western welfare states. It concentrates on the claims of needs, rights, citizenship, egalitarianism and communitarianism. All of these are ambiguous and, when translated into policies produce counter-intuitive results. It is argued that the welfare state does not produce the public good of relieving distress but a series of private goods, the consumption of which leads to inequalities and inefficiences. It is recommended that welfare theories should be placed in a framework of constitutionalism.

BARRY, Norman. Libertarianism. Philosophy, 26, 109-127, 90 Supp.

This is a critical examination of the conceptual problems associated with the moral and political doctrine of libertarianism. Its major concern is to explicate the meaning of subjectivism, in a methodological and normative sense, and to see whether it defeats all perfectionist arguments. The author concludes that it does not and that a libertarian political philosophy must be ultimately grounded in certain values and institutions that have intrinsic worth, despite the difficulty of demonstrating intrinsic value. This ultimately skeptical essay includes discussions of utilitarianism, public choice and natural rights as approaches to individualistic ethics and politics.

BARRY, Norman. "The State and Legitimacy" in *Key Themes in Philosophy*, GRIFFITHS, A Phillips (ed), 191-206. New York, Cambridge Univ Pr, 1989.

Two theories of the state are identified in this paper: the agency theory and the organic theory. The agency theory understands the state as an artifice constructed by rational individuals to solve public good problems of market society. The organic theory claims that this cannot explain legitimacy in a moral sense. Legitimacy requires the acceptance of traditional values irrespective of choice. The author proposes a third theory. It explains traditional values of legitimacy but uses the doctrine of constitutionalism to explain how the demand for public goods is transmitted through the state.

BARRY, Robert L. The Consequences of Endorsing Sentimental Homicide. Listening, 26(1), 66-86, Wint 91.

This article examines the impact of a social policy endorsing voluntary euthanasia. It suggests that such a policy would break down barriers, now already feeble, to suicide by incompetent persons. Both the healing and legal professions would become deeply involved in voluntary euthanasia to sustain these policies, to the detriment of their credibility with the general public. It points out that such a policy would be difficult to contain because of the lack of any clear distinctions between the kinds of suffering that would be invoked to justify voluntary euthanasia. Such a policy could not provide quick relief to pain or suffering and at the same time have sufficient safeguards to guarantee that those not desiring it would not be induced into it. And limiting voluntary euthanasia to the competent and rational would induce the incompetent and irrational to attempt it as a sign that they too are competent and rational.

BARRY, Robert and KESLER, Darrel. Pharaoh's Magicians: The Ethics and Efficacy of Human Fetal Tissue Transplants. Thomist, 54(4), 575-607, O 90.

This work first points the history of failures of human fetal tissue transplants. It then reviews all of the scientific problems and difficulties involved in claims that human fetal tissue transplants are successful. It argues that human fetal tissue transplants involve some very severe ethical problems which its proponents do not face up to, and it concludes by rejecting calls for federal funding of research on human fetal transplantation.

BARRY, Vincent and OLEN, Jeffrey. *Applying Ethics: A Text with Readings (Third Edition)*. Belmont, Wadsworth, 1989.

BARTELS, Andreas. "Mario Bunge's Realist Semantics: An Antidote against Incommensurability?" in *Studies on Mario Bunge's "Treatise"*, WEINGARTNER, Paul (ed), 39-58. Amsterdam, Rodopi, 1990.

The paper critically reconsiders Mario Bunge's attempt to develop a realist semantics for scientific theories as performed in his *Treatise on Basic Philosophy*, Vol. 1 & 2 (1974). Bunge is right to reject formal semantics as a tool to explain meaning formation in material scientific theories. But he is wrong to locate the failure of formal semantics in the Fregean tradition which treats reference and truth as interdependent concepts. It is argued that the attempt to keep the notion of reference for concepts in scientific theories totally apart from the truth of expense of accepting mysterious reference-fixing capacity of the scientist's mind.

BARTELS, Dianne M (ed). *Beyond Baby M: Ethical Issues in New Reproductive Techniques*. Clifton, Humana Pr, 1990.

BARTELS, Dianne M. "Surrogacy Arrangements: An Overview" in *Beyond Baby M: Ethical Issues in New Reproductive Techniques*, BARTELS, Dianne M (ed), 173-181. Clifton, Humana Pr, 1990.

BARTH, Bernhard. *Schellings Philosophie der Kunst: Göttliche Imagination und Ästhetische Einbildungskraft*. Freiburg, Alber, 1991.

This book proposes that the concept of imagination is the key to all understanding of Schelling's philosophy of art. Schelling's analysis of artistic production in terms of imaginative achievement shows that his philosophy of art is also a practical theory of art, which attempts to show that art can constitute a sufficient representation of the Absolute. Schelling's groundwork for a theory of art criticism verifies this claim by mediating it through philosophical reflection.

BARTH, E M. Argumentation—Distributed or Monological? Commun Cog, 24(1), 15-24, 1991.

BARTH, E M. In the Service of Human Society: Formal, Information, or Anti-Logical? Inform Log, 12(1), 1-10, Wint 90.

BARTKY, Sandra Lee. *Femininity and Domination: Studies in the Phenomenology of Oppression*. New York, Routledge, 1990.

An essay collection that tries to lay out those "moments" in the consciousness of self and world that characterize not an abstract and universal, but a socially and temporally situated feminine consciousness. Among the topics treated are the "lived experience" of female embodiment and female sexuality, sexual objectification and self-objectification, shame, the interiorization of cultural domination, peculiarly feminine modes of self-deception and of what are, arguably, repressive feminine satisfactions, and a variety of modes of both self-estrangement and self-recovery. The work includes a series of critiques of a number of widely received views in political philosophy, ethics and moral psychology.

BARTLETT, Robert (trans) and STRAUSS, Leo. Some Remarks on the Political Science of Maimonides and Farabi. Interpretation, 18(1), 3-30, Fall 90.

BARTON, John. "History and Rhetoric in the Prophets" in *The Bible as Rhetoric: Studies in Biblical Persuasion and Credibility*, WARNER, Martin (ed), 51-64. New York, Routledge, 1990.

BARTOSZYNSKI, Tomek and JUDAH, Haim. Jumping with Random Reals. Annals Pure Applied Log, 48(3), 197-213, Ag 90.

In the first part we study the relationship between basic properties of the ideal of measure zero sets and the properties of measure algebra. The second part is devoted to the structure of the set of random reals over models of ZFC.

BARUA, Archana. A Re-Examination of the Nature of Religion. J Dharma, 15(3), 212-222, Jl-S 90.

BASARAB, Serban A. Relative Elimination of Quantifiers for Henselian Valued Fields. Annals Pure Applied Log, 53(1), 51-74, Jl 91.

A general result on relative elimination of quantifiers for Henselian valued fields of characteristic zero is provided by algebraic and basic model-theoretic methods.

BASINGER, David. Divine Knowledge and Divine Control: A Response to Gordon and Sadowsky. Relig Stud, 26(2), 267-275, Je 90.

In an earlier article, I argued that unless theists grant God middle knowledge—a certain form of divine omniscience—they must acknowledge that the creation of this world was a significant gamble. Subsequently, David Gordon and James Sadowsky argued that I am mistaken. This essay is a response to their criticisms and a reaffirmation of my position.

BASINGER, David. Plantinga, Pluralism and Justified Religious Belief. Faith Phil, 8(1), 67-80, Ja 91.

Alvin Plantinga has argued that to defend their religious beliefs, theists need only engage in negative apologetics—defend their beliefs against potential defeaters. I argue that the undeniable existence of pervasive religious pluralism places knowledgeable theists under the *prime force* obligation to attempt to produce positive evidence for their religious beliefs.

BASINSKI, Paul A. Nihilism and the Impossibility of Political Philosophy. J Value Inq, 24(4), 269-284, O 90.

BASS, Walter. Seeing the Original. J Aes Educ, 24(2), 75-81, Sum 90.

BASSIRY, G R. Ethics, Education, and Corporate Leadership. J Bus Ethics, 9(10), 799-805, O 90.

The purpose of this study is to determine the relative frequency of course offerings on social issues and business ethics in American business schools. Specifically, a random sample of the curricula of 119 American business schools was analyzed in order to gauge the importance given to coursework on ethics and social issues. The findings indicated that the incidence of such courses was generally low in American business curricula, particularly at the graduate level. These findings are discussed in light of the current concern for more responsible corporate behavior.

BASSOLS, Alejandro Tomasini. Conceptos religiosos y vida religiosa. Dianoia, 35(35), 91-105, 1989.

The purpose of this paper is to examine, along Wittgensteinian lines, the grammar of three important religious concepts, viz., faith, God and prayer. Instead of asking about the meaning of the words, I describe their natural context, the questions that can be sensibly asked, the behaviors they give rise to, etc., that is, their place in our lives. The main contention is that once this task has been done, we no longer feel the need to ask about existence-proofs, introspective analysis or supernatural connections. Religion can be understood and enjoyed in a non-theistic way.

BASU, Sammy. In a Crazy Time the Crazy Come Out Well: Machiavelli and the Cosmology of His Day. Hist Polit Thought, 11(2), 213-239, Sum 90.

BASU, Sandhya. Gettier's Principle for Deducibility of Justification. J Indian Counc Phil Res, 5(2), 87-95, Ja-Ap 88.

BATKIN, Norton. "...A Presence of Absence...". J Aes Educ, 24(2), 14-24, Sum 90.

BATTERMAN, Robert W. Irreversibility and Statistical Mechanics: A New Approach? Phil Sci, 57(3), 395-419, S 90.

I discuss a broad critique of the classical approach to the foundations of statistical mechanics (SM) offered by N S Krylov. He claims that the classical approach is in principle incapable of providing the foundations for interpreting the "laws" of statistical physics. Most intriguing are his arguments against adopting a de facto attitude towards the problem of irreversibility. I argue that the best way to understand his critique is as setting the stage for a positive theory which treats SM as a theory in its own right, involving a completely different conception of a system's state. As the orthodox approach treats SM as an extension of the classical or quantum theories (one which deals with large systems), Krylov is advocating a major break with the traditional view of statistical physics.

BATTERMAN, Robert. Randomness and Probability in Dynamical Theories: On the Proposals of the Prigogine School. Phil Sci, 58(2), 241-263, Je 91.

I discuss recent work in ergodic theory and statistical mechanics, regarding the compatibility and origin of random chaotic behavior in deterministic dynamical systems. A detailed critique of some quite radical proposals of the Prigogine school is given. I argue that their conclusion regarding the conceptual bankruptcy of the classical conceptions of an exact microstate and unique phase space trajectory is not completely justified. The analogy they want to draw with quantum mechanics is not sufficiently close to support their most radical conclusion.

BAUDET, Jean C. Editologie et Scientificite. Commun Cog, 23(4), 323-329, 1990.

L'épistemologie, *étude du passage des états de moindre connaissance aux états de connaissance plus poussée*, se trouve dans la délicate position de devoir définir tous les termes qui constituent sa définition. Qu'est-ce qu'une *étude* (une science, une discipline?), qu'un *passage* (une histoire, un processus?), qu'un *état de connaissance* (un *statut questionis*, une bibliothèque, une université?)...Ce sont bien là des questions épistémologiques. La littérature spécialisée comporte d'interminables gloses sur ce problème que l'ont peut appeler "le cercle vicieux épistémologique". Nous n'échapperons à la circularité qu'en appliquant la bonne vieille méthode socratique: démontrer le mouvement en marchant—tenter de surmonter les difficultés fondationnelles de l'épistémologie en "faisant de l'épistémologie."

BAUGH, Bruce. Sartre and James on the Role of the Body in Emotion. Dialogue (Canada), 29(3), 357-373, 1990.

BAUGH, Bruce. Sartre, Aron et le relativisme historique. Dialogue (Canada), 29(4), 557-573, 1990.

BAUM, Manfred. Subjektivität, Allgemeingültigkeit und Apriorität des Geschmacksurteils bei Kant. Deut Z Phil, 39(3), 272-284, 1991.

In this article three Kantian doctrines concerning the judgment of taste are discussed and defended against criticisms raised by Ralf Meerbote, Paul Guyer, and Lewis White Beck: 1) that there is a free interplay of the cognitive powers which is distinct from the harmony of these powers as required for cognition, 2) that the claim to universal validity precedes the feeling of pleasure in making a judgment on the beautiful, and 3) that the pure aesthetic judgment is a synthetic *a priori* judgment.

BAUMAN, Zygmunt. Communism: A Post-Mortem. Praxis Int, 10(3-4), 185-192, O 90-Ja 91.

The collapse of communism was the last blow to modern projects of large-scale (total) social engineering; the administrative system could not survive the onslaught of postmodern values of choice and self-assembled identity and of postmodern politics of diffuse dissent and shifting allegiances.

BAUMAN, Zygmunt. "Hermeneutics and Modern Social Theory" in *Social Theory of Modern Societies: Anthony Giddens and His Critics*, HELD, David (ed), 34-55. New York, Cambridge Univ Pr, 1990.

BAUMANN, Lutz. Kants Theorie der Gegenstandserkenntnis und Schopenhauers Lehre vom Ding an sich. Schopenhauer Jahr, 71, 17-25, 1990.

According to Kant a synthetic proposition emerges a priori in the forthcoming cognition as the implementation of an indefinite thought from the object. In Schopenhauer's interpretation, however, Kant is said to have strictly separated representation and aspect thus—unsuccessfully—relating the two concepts capitalizing on the realistic-dogmatic thinking not yet solved. Schopenhauer's teachings concerning the dogmatic separation of positions do not, in spite of all perspicacity his critique displays, do justice to Kant's basic proposition. Rather, Schopenhauer's own teachings must be seen as the attempt to overcome the dogmatic elements in Kant's thinking by merely arguing dogmatically.

BAUMGARTNER, James E. "Polarized Partition Relations and Almost-Disjoint Functions" in *Logic, Methodology and Philosophy of Science, VIII*, FENSTAD, J E (ed), 213-222. New York, Elsevier Science, 1989.

BAUMGÄRTNER, Järg and KOTZIN, Rhoda. Sensations and Judgments of Perception: Diagnosis and Rehabilitation of Some of Kant's Misleading Examples. Kantstudien, 81(4), 401-412, 1990.

Commentators have pointed out that Kant's remarks about the 'subjectivity' of sensible qualities and of judgments of perception fail to conform to some central teachings of the *Critique of Pure Reason*. In our view Kant's remarks and examples (the color of a rose, "The room is warm"), as formulated, are indeed un-Critical. We discuss some strategies which have been advanced in order to deal with these examples but which we consider to be unsatisfactory. We propose a new strategy by which we can rehabilitate the examples and use them to help to illuminate Kant's Critical theory of empirical knowledge.

BAUR, Michael. Hegel and the Overcoming of the Understanding. Owl Minerva, 22(2), 141-158, Spr 91.

The aim of this essay is to articulate the movement which takes place in the chapter on "Force and the Understanding" in Hegel's *Phenomenology of Spirit*. This movement is crucial, since it represents the overcoming of what might be called "objectivism," the stance by which knowing consciousness seeks to maintain a separation between itself and the objects known. Although Hegel borrows much of his terminology from the Newtonian scientific paradigm, this essay attempts to show that Hegel's argument is not restricted to Newtonian science, but in fact applies to any "objectivistic" scientific paradigm.

BAUR, Michael. On the Aim of Scientific Theories in Relating to the World: A Defence of the Semantic Account. Dialogue (Canada), 29(3), 323-333, 1990.

According to the "received view," a scientific theory is an axiomatic-deductive linguistic structure which must include some kind of "correspondence rules." According to the "semantic view," a scientific theory need only specify models which are said to be "isomorphic" with phenomenal systems. In this paper, I consider both the received and the semantic views as they bear on the issue of how a theory relates to the phenomena. Then I offer a critique of some arguments frequently put forth in support of the semantic view. Finally, I suggest a more convincing argument in favour of the semantic view.

BAURMANN, Michael. *Die moderne Gesellschaft im Rechtsstaat*. Freiburg, Alber, 1991.

This book addresses fundamental problems of a legitimate legal order. Authors from different fields, including jurisprudence, sociology, philosophy, and political science, present their views on such central issues as civil disobedience, the legitimation of punishment, paternalism, or democratic procedures. All contributions are centrally concerned with the common basic issue of what collectivities can be permitted to do to individuals.

BAXTER, Donald L M. Berkeley, Perception, and Identity. Phil Phenomenol Res, 51(1), 85-98, Mr 91.

Berkeley says both that one *sometimes* immediately perceives the same thing by sight and touch, and that one *never* does. To solve the contradiction I recommend and explain a distinction Berkeley himself makes-between two uses of 'same'. This solution unifies two seemingly inconsistent parts of Berkeley's whole project: He argues both that what we see are bits of light and color organized into a language by which God speaks to us about tactile sensations, and yet that we directly see ordinary objects. My solution explains how these can come to the same thing.

BAYARD, Caroline. The Intellectual in the Post Modern Age: East/West Contrasts. Phil Today, 34(4), 291-302, Wint 90.

Both the philosopher Jean François Lyotard and the playwright turned dissident Vaclav Havel have concerned themselves with ethical issues and their treatment by intellectuals in the postmodern age. Both are simultaneously aware and weary of the intellectual as sublime master-figure handed down from Kant and kept alive by modernity's philosophers (Kant, Adorno, Habermas). Both are conscious of being reflections of the figure of the intellectual as opponent of dogma as well as representatives of an elite who may be tempted to bring the species to perfection. While their respective narratives are grounded within different cultures (Western European/East European) they do interpret for us to the complex ethics of postmodernity which simultaneously call for sharing silenced voices and also for exerting our constant suspiciousness over words. (edited)

BAYER, Oswald. Hamanns Metakritik im ersten Entwurf. Kantstudien, 81(4), 435-453, 1990.

Among the most important texts in our philosophical tradition are undisclosed first drafts of Hamann's "Metacritique of the Purism of Reason." Along with a first edition of one of the two draft texts, the author here provides a sample of the comprehensive commentary to Hamann's "Kantschriften," which he has been working on for the past 15 years. It is his intention to show that Johann Georg Hamann was not an irrationalist but a radical enlightener of a stature equal to that of Kant and also Hegel.

BAYEROVA, M. A Phenomenologically and Psychologically Based Concept of Ethics (in Czechoslovakian). Filozof Cas, 38(3), 302-325, 1990.

A phenomenological concept of ethics is based on the mode of revealing social values in analogy to the interpretation of "the subject," the limits of this theory being outlined by the term pertaining to the material within the formal. This involves the possibility of identifying what are called materially determined objects which constitute values and "practical objectivities," i.e., all the concrete cultural forms, in pure consciousness, based on the specific theory of acts which makes it possible to consider theoretical positionality in unity with practical one, which is realized in the sphere of emotions and will. The objective bounds of the phenomenological method are formed by its "psychological" foundation in spite of the introduction of a number of substantial differences from the idea intentionality and description as applied by Brentano. (edited)

BAYEROVA, Marie. Husserl—Bolzano II (in Czechoslovakian). Estetika, 27(3), 167-183, 1990.

BAYLES, Michael D. A Note on the Death Penalty as the Best Bet. Crim Just Ethics, 10(1), 7-10, Wint-Spr 91.

BAYLES, Michael D. What Is Jurisprudence About? Theories, Definitions, Concepts, or Conceptions of Law? Phil Topics, 18(1), 23-40, Spr 90.

BAYLIS, Françoise E. The Ethics of *Ex Utero* Research on Spare 'Non-Viable' IVF Human Embryos. Bioethics, 4(4), 311-329, O 90.

BAYNES, Kenneth (trans) and HONNETH, Axel. *The Critique of Power: Reflective Stages in a Critical Social Theory*. Cambridge, MIT Pr, 1991.

BEABOUT, Greg. Abortion in Rape Cases. Proc Cath Phil Ass, 63, 132-138, 1990.

BEACH, Edward A. The Later Schelling's Conception of Dialectical Method, in Contradistinction to Hegel's. Owl Minerva, 22(1), 35-54, Fall 90.

By means of engaging in a metatheoretical comparison of the two thinkers's approaches and analyzing their essential differences, it is possible to pinpoint the sources of their metaphysical as well as epistemological disagreements. I show that, whereas Hegel took his task to be the progressive sublation (*Aufhebung*) of the logical antinomies that his dialectic would encounter along its way, Schelling was concerned to find the path of conative reproduction (*Erzeugung*) by which certain universal forms of volition, which he called "potencies" (*Potenzen*), would sequentially emerge in poses of mutual reinforcement or conflict. Schelling's insistence on the primacy of individuality over universality, existence over essence, and volition over reason issued an important challenge to Hegelian philosophy. The paper concludes with a critical evaluation of the two thinkers's respective methods.

BEACH, Edward A (trans) and VON SCHELLING, F W J. On the Source of the Eternal Truths. Owl Minerva, 22(1), 55-67, Fall 90.

BEARDS, Andrew. On Knowing and Naming. Method, 8(2), 106-128, O 90.

The article attempts a critical examination of positions adopted in debates concerning naming and reference from the viewpoint of Bernard Lonergan's philosophy. Evaluations of the relative strengths and weakness of the arguments of Kripke, Putnam, and Searle are offered.

BEARDSMORE, R W. Wittgenstein on Tolstoi's *What is Art*? Phil Invest, 14(3), 187-204, Jl 91.

BEATTY, John. "Teleology and the Relationship Between Biology and the Physical Sciences in the Nineteenth and Twentieth Centuries" in *Some Truer Method*, DURHAM, Frank (ed), 113-144. New York, Columbia Univ Pr, 1990.

BEAUNE, Jean-Claude. La mort de Socrate et la vie des machines. Philosophique (France), 1(89), 21-38, 1989.

When one considers the ethical questions which are raised by biology and medical practice today, it seems an important change has occurred in the way death is represented. Our contemporaries have recaptured a philosophical image through which the body as machine can be evoked as well the ancient image of "remote and yet close" death dating back to the XVIIIth century. The death of Socrates the philosopher, who was completely devoted to the spirit and the truth is thus neutralized in Limbo, retaining but the shadow of its tragedy in the collective indifference of our contemporaries and present-day machines.

BEAUSOLEIL, Jean-Roch. The Metamathematics-Popperian Epistemology Connection and its Relation to the Logic of Turing's Programme. Brit J Phil Sci, 40(3), 307-322, S 89.

Turing's programme, the idea that intelligence can be modelled computationally, is set in the context of a parallel between certain elements from metamathematics and Popper's schema for the evolution of knowledge. The parallel is developed at both the formal level, where it hinges on the recursive structuring of Popper's schema, and at the formal level, where a few key issues common to both epistemology and metamathematics are briefly discussed. In light of this connection Popper's principle of transference, akin to Turing's belief in the relevance of the theory of computation for modelling psychological functions, is widened into the extended principle of transference. Thus Turing's programme gains a solid epistemological footing.

BEAVERS, Anthony. Freedom and Autonomy: The Kantian Analytic and a Sartrean Critique. Phil Theol, 5(2), 151-168, Wint 90.

I argue that, despite their extensive disagreements at the level of first-order ethics, there are equally extensive agreements between Sartre and Kant at the metaethical level. Following a brief exposition of the principal metaethical similarities, I offer a defense of Sartre's general moral theory against the more rigid first-order consequences which Kant claims to be able to assert.

BECHTEL, William. Scientific Evidence: Creating and Evaluating Experimental Instruments and Research Techniques. Proc Phil Sci Ass, 1, 559-572, 1990.

The production of evidence for scientific hypotheses and theories often depends upon complete instruments and techniques for employing them. An important epistemological question arises as to how the reliability of these instruments and techniques is assessed. To address that question, this paper examines the introduction of electron microscopy and cell fractionation in cell biology. One important claim is that scientists often arrive at their techniques for employing instruments like the electron microscope and the ultracentrifuge by tinkering and that they evaluate the resulting techniques in part by whether they produce plausible data given developing theories.

BECK, Clive. "Faith" in a Broad Sense as a Goal in Promoting Human Development. Proc Phil Educ, 46, 90-100, 1990.

BECK, Clive. North American, British and Australian Philosophy of Education from 1941 to 1991: Links, Trends, Prospects. Educ Theor, 41(3), 311-320, Sum 91.

BECK, Simon. Finding Ourselves: Personal Identity and the Limits of Possible-World Arguments. S Afr J Phil, 10(1), 1-6, F 91.

Quine has suggested that while the method of using science-fiction cases, or arguments from possible worlds, to establish conclusions about the nature of personal identity has its uses, it also has limits which are usually ignored. That the method has limits is agreed by writers in this general field, but there is by no means agreement as to precisely what the limits Quine gestures at are, or even what they concern. In this article, various limits which have been put forward are discussed and evaluated in the light of prominent examples in the literature.

BECKER, Carl B. Buddhist Views of Suicide and Euthanasia. Phil East West, 40(4), 543-556, O 90.

BECKWITH, Francis J. The Misuse of Maternal Mortality Statistics in the Abortion Debate. Ethics Med, 7(2), 18-19, Sum 91.

The purpose of this article is to show how the abortion-rights argument—that early abortion is safer than childbirth—is morally irrelevant. This abortion-rights argument, which played a large part in the U.S. Supreme Court's *Roe v. Wade* (1973) decision, makes the mistake of assuming that because something is safer than something else one is therefore not obligated to perform the latter. The author also points out that prolifers are not exempt from misusing statistics, such as when they argue that abortion is not justified since there are so many couples wanting to adopt children. This argument clearly begs the question.

BEDAU, Hugo Adam (ed). *Civil Disobedience in Focus*. New York, Routledge, 1991.

A collection of a dozen essays on civil disobedience, divided into two groups. The first set includes Plato's "Crito", the well-known essays by Thoreau and Martin Luther King, Jr, and two essays by recent critics. The second set begins with Rawls's position in "A Theory of Justice", and includes critical essays and alternative views by six contemporary philosophers. Introduction, bibliography, and index.

BEDIENT, Calvin. How I Slugged It Out with Toril Moi and Stayed Awake. Crit Inquiry, 17(3), 644-649, Spr 91.

BEDNARZ JR, John (trans) and LUHMANN, Niklas. *Political Theory in the Welfare State*. Hawthorne, de Gruyter, 1990.

BEDU-ADDO, J T. Sense-Experience and the Argument for Recollection in Plato's *Phaedo*. Phronesis, 36(1), 27-60, 1991.

BEEHLER, Rodger. For One Concept of Liberty. J Applied Phil, 8(1), 27-43, 1991.

The essay enquires whether a negative concept of liberty suffices for political and legal discourse. A contemporary argument alleging the inviability of a negative concept of liberty is examined and exposed as wanting, while street-smart claims on behalf of a 'positive' concept of liberty are shown to be deployments of the negative concept, misdescribed. The truth that lack of money is lack of freedom in societies with a money economy and coercively enforced property rights is established with supporting examines, and its implications for need satisfaction assessed. Judgment is concluded that the negative concept of liberty is both the only viable concept of liberty and demonstrably adequate for morally sensitive engagement with political life.

BEEHLER, Rodger. Legal Positivism, Social Rules, and *Riggs* versus *Palmer*. Law Phil, 9(3), 285-293, Ag 90.

BEETS, S Douglas. Personal Morals and Professional Ethics: A Review and Empirical Examination of Public Accounting. Bus Prof Ethics J, 10(2), 63-84, Sum 91.

BÉGIN, Luc. Nozick et la stabilité des principes de justice distributive. Lekton, 1(2), 55-80, 1991.

In *Anarchy, State and Utopia* Nozick maintains that Rawlsian principles of justice cannot be stable. He rather suggests that only libertarian principles can resolve the problem of stability. This proposal of Nozick is criticized on the ground of the incapability of his "entitlement theory" to avoid some criticals he addresses to non-libertarian theories. His appeal to rights in order to support his thesis is also analysed and criticized on the light of a moral motivation theory.

BEHE, B K and WESTRA, L S and BOWEN, K L. Agricultural Practices, Ecology, and Ethics in the Third World. J Agr Ethics, 4(1), 60-77, 1991.

The increasing demand for horticultural products for nutritional and economic purposes by lesser developed countries (LDC's) is well-documented. Technological demands of the LDC's producing horticultural products is also increasing. Pesticide use is an integral component of most agricultural production, yet chemicals are often supplied without supplemental information vital for their safe and efficient implementation. Illiteracy rates in developing countries are high, making pesticide education even more challenging. For women, who perform a significant share of agricultural tasks, illiteracy rates are even higher than for men. The dilemma exists of how a developing country can improve its nutritional and economic situation without giving consideration to social and environmental consequences.

BEHERA, Sathrughna. Later Wittgenstein on Objectivity of Rules. Indian Phil Quart, SUPP 18(2), 1-12, Ap 91.

The objective of this paper is to show the objectivity of rules that has been a matter of recent discussion on the understanding of language in Wittgenstein's game model grammar. The central them of Wittgenstein's game-model is that rules (regel) govern the language games and the possibility of language presupposes the possibility of rules. In other words, rules constitute a language system. I conclude with the note, so far as Wittgenstein's notion of rules is concerned, that rules that govern our language use are constitutive to that system and the very constitutive character of rules ascertains their objectivity in various language games. Grammar pertaining to rules displays their necessity, thus bringing rules back into the language-games.

BEHERA, Satrughna. Rule-Scepticism: Kripkean Understanding in Wittgenstein's Perspective. Indian Phil Quart, SUPP 18(1), 17-30, Ja 91.

This paper is an attempt to give a critical account of Saul Kripke's (1982) sceptical interpretation of 'following a rule' in the later philosophy of Wittgenstein. According to Kripke 'rule-scepticism' follows from the fact that in following a rule any rule could be followed since there is no objective ground of knowing which is the correct rule to be followed. He maintains that Wittgenstein gives a 'skeptical solution' to this sceptical problem by committing himself to a communitarian view of language and rules. This brings Wittgenstein closer to the Humean tradition which leads our concept of rules and rule-following to a virtual collapse. I come to the conclusion with the view that the foundation for language proposed by Kripke to get over the rule-scepticism is agreement in responses that is, the mere fact that we agree in our responses in following a rule is sufficient to make language possible.

BEHLER, Ernst (ed) and HEGEL, G W F. *Encyclopedia of the Philosophical Sciences in Outline and Critical Writings—G W F Hegel*. New York, Continuum, 1990.

BEHLER, Ernst. *Irony and the Discourse of Modernity*. Seattle, Univ Washington Pr, 1990.

BEIERWALTES, Werner. Cusanus and Eriugena. Dionysius, 13, 115-152, D 89.

BEIERWALTES, Werner. Der Harmonie-Gedanke im frühen Mittelalter. Z Phil Forsch, 45(1), 1-21, Ja-Mr 91.

BEJARANO, Teresa. Sobre la génesis de la conciencia de si mismo. Themata, 6, 23-44, 1989.

Human consciousness and predication are—it is proposed—based on the same capacity. I detect in someone—in P—a mental content—a conception of the thing T—that is different from my knowledge of T. Then, first, I separate what belongs to the mind of P from what is mine—from myself already. And, second, the predication appears (and the syntactic language, since syntax is necessary only for predicative-interrogative functions): the predication originally wants to complete/put right the *given* (*thematic*) piece, that is—we propose—the insufficient/erroneous mental content of the hearer, not the reference (*in pace* "the Building-Block").

BELARDINELLI, Sergio. La teoría consensual de la verdad de Jürgen Habermas. Anu Filosof, 24(1), 115-123, 1991.

This article is a critical presentation of Habermas's "Consensual Theory of Truth" as a theory without experience, with a careful analysis of the practical expectations linked by Habermas to this theory.

BELARMINO, Pedro. Los "Derechos Humanos". El Basilisco, 3, 67-88, Ja-F 90.

BELARMINO, Pedro. La "objeción de conciencia". El Basilisco, 2, 73-88, N-D 89.

BELDA PLANS, Pilar. La doctrina del don de San Agustín de Hipona. Espiritu, 38(99), 71-78, Ja-Je 89.

BELIC, Miljenko. Possibility of Philosophical-Theological Discourse (in Serbo-Croatian). Filozof Istraz, 34(1), 5-16, 1990.

Im vorliegenden Artikel werden jene Ähnlichkeiten und Unterschiede betrachtet, welche als solche einen fruchtbaren Boden für den beiderseitig nützlichen Dialog darstellen, u. z. zuerst auf dem vielschichtigen Bereich der Wahrheitssuche, dann aber auch in bezug auf den Ausgangspunkt der Philosophie (bzw. die Ausgangspunkte verschiedener Philosophien) wie auch bei der Anwendung der Philosophie auf Theologie, die sich der Philosophie bedient, um die Offenbarung gedanklich zu verarbeiten. Schliesslich wird der Einfluss des erkennenden

Subjekts selber auf eigenen Standpunkt zum erkannten Objekt hervorgestellt. Es gibt einen solchen Einfluss, der aber auch seine Begrenzug hat. Beides kann mann insbesondere beim Aufbauen eigener Weltanschauung und im Zusammenhang mit der Frage über das mögliche Bestehen oder Nichtbestehen einer sog. christlichen Philosophie feststellen.

BELL, David (ed) and COOPER, Neil (ed). *The Analytic Tradition: Philosophical Quarterly Monographs, Volume 1*. Cambridge, Blackwell, 1990.

Essays by David Bell, Thomas Baldwin, Tyler Burge, Michael Dummett, Bill Hart, Christopher Hookway, Peter Hylton, Wolfgang Künne, Mark Sacks, and John Skorupski, on the nature and origins of the analytic tradition in contemporary philosophy. There are papers on such figures as Frege, Russell, Moore, Peirce, Husserl, and Wittgenstein; and on such themes as the limits of scepticism, the nature of thought and its relation to language and perception, and changing attitudes within the analytic tradition to logic, analysis, clarity, and vagueness.

BELL, Linda A. "Love and Perfect Coincidence in a Sartrean Ethics" in *Writing the Politics of Difference*, SILVERMAN, Hugh J (ed), 89-97. Albany, SUNY Pr, 1991.

When critics consider Sartre's view of love, they typically concentrate on the circle of concrete relations with others in *Being and Nothingness*, where love is presented as a game of mirrors, a "perpetual hopeless struggle of each against the other." In relationships between characters in Sartre's plays as well as in other writings, two additional views of love emerge. One might be called "the common enemy" view. The other, the most important and least recognized, is a love that affirms human freedom, that is lucid yet nonetheless joyful, and that seeks perfect confidence and coincidence only as a regulative ideal.

BELL, Martin and MC GINN, Marie. Naturalism and Scepticism. Philosophy, 65(254), 399-418, O 90.

BELLA, David. "Catastrophic Possibilities of Space-Based Defense" in *Philosophy of Technology*, DURBIN, Paul T (ed), 27-40. Norwell, Kluwer, 1989.

The development of advanced spaced-based weaponry requires new ways of thinking. If deployed, the firing of these weapons would likely be highly automated in a time of crisis. This paper calls for a meta-system level of assessment that views opposing sides as components of a single global system. From this perspective, a catastrophic loss of control on a global scale becomes a serious threat that is not accommodated by current assessment approaches.

BELLAMY, Richard. Gramsci, Croce and the Italian Political Tradition. Hist Polit Thought, 11(2), 313-337, Sum 90.

Gramsci is frequently studied in an ahistorical manner, as the culmination and synthesis of a tradition composed of Hegel, Marx and Lenin. This paper implicitly suggests that an Italian reading of him would modify such a view. In the first section, the supposedly Hegelian Italian tradition is revealed as curiously Kantian, with Machiavelli being interpreted (in ways later adopted by Gramsci) as the 'moral politician'. Section two looks at the manner Croce employed this political language to defend the liberal regime. Section three examines Gramsci's critical revision of this defence. Section four concludes the paper by comparing their conceptions of the State and its relation to civil society, criticising the weaknesses of their views. Although no explicit comparison can be made in this paper, it is plain that neither version is straightforwardly Hegelian, Marxist or Leninist in character.

BELLAND, John and SMITH, Phillip L. Reclaiming Virtue: Philosophy in the Field of Educational Technology. J Thought, 25(1-2), 56-65, Spr-Sum 90.

BELLER, Mara. Born's Probabilistic Interpretation: A Case Study of 'Concepts in Flux'. Stud Hist Phil Sci, 21(4), 563-588, D 90.

BELLETTI, Bruno. Il Logos come immagine di Dio in Filone di Alessandria. Sapienza, 43(3), 311-320, Jl-S 90.

BELLINI, Ornella. *Una lettura idealistica della "Analitica Trascendentale"*. Milano, Giuffre, 1990.

The paper examines the development of the Kantian-Hegelian philosophy in England and its influence on the oxonian idealistic thought. It is concerned specially with the philosophical personality of Edward Caird, who together Green is one of the most important thinkers of the first generation of oxonian idealists. The reading of the "Transcendental Analytic" of the *Critique of Pure Reason* is new because the "Hegelian" Caird interprets Kant through Hegel and prefers the edition of 1781 instead of that of 1787.

BELLIOTTI, Raymond A. "Sex" in *A Companion to Ethics*, SINGER, Peter (ed), 315-326. Cambridge, Blackwell, 1991.

This essay applies and analyzes Greek dualist, Judeo-Christian, Love and Intimacy, Contractualist, Kantian, Marxist, and Feminist perspectives in the context of sexual ethics. The essay concludes that the most persuasive outlook on sexual ethics is a Contractualist model as modified by certain Kantian principles, but which pays special heed when defining "exploitation" to Marxisms, sensitivity to economic coercion and Feminism's concern with pervasive male oppression. Even this preferred outlook, however, needs clearer distinctions between "justified persuasion," "unjustified manipulation," and "implicit economic coercion."

BELLO, A Ales. Brentano e Fichte negli scritti "minori" di E Husserl. Aquinas, 33(2), 405-409, My-Ag 90.

BELLO, A G A. Ultimate Reality and Meaning in Africa: Some Methodological Preliminaries—A Test Case. Ultim Real Mean, 14(1), 53-61, Mr 91.

BELLOMO, Andrea. Semantica della "Vorstellung" e valore della teoria in *Erkenntnis und Irrtum* di Ernst Mach. Ann Fac Lett Filosof, 32, 455-486, 1989.

BELMANS, Théo G. Le paradoxe de la conscience erronée d'Abálard à Karl Rahner. Rev Thomiste, 90(4), 570-586, O-D 90.

BELNAP JR, Nuel D. Before Refraining: Concepts for Agency. Erkenntnis, 34(2), 137-169, Mr 91.

The paper offers a foundation for a semantics for "a sees to it that Q". Eleven simple postulates are motivated. "Tree" and x encode a picture of branching time consisting of "moments" gathered into maximal chains called "histories." "Instant" imposes a time-like ordering. "Agent" consists of agents, and "choice" assigns to each agent and each moment in "Tree" a set of "possible choices," where each possible choice is a set of histories. There are applications to infinite chains of choices, to the equivalence between doing and refraining to do, and to the inconsistency of contemplation and action.

BELNAP JR, Nuel D and PERLOFF, Michael. "Seeing To It That: A Canonical Form for Agentives" in *Knowledge Representation and Defeasible Reasoning*, KYBURG JR, Henry E (ed), 167-190. Norwell, Kluwer, 1990.

This paper introduces the stit (seeing to it that) theory of agency, which stresses the distinction between agentive and nonagentive sentences. The stit sentence, with an agent term as subject and any arbitrary declarative as complement, represents a canonical form for agentives. In its semantics, stit theory portrays agents as making choices against a background of branching time. There are demonstrations of the benefits of stit theory, including, for example, the agentiveness of refraining and the restricted complement thesis: that constructions concerned with agency—deontic, imperatival, intentional, could-have—restrict their complements to agentives.

BELNAP JR, Nuel D and MASSEY, Gerald J. Semantic Holism. Stud Log, 49(1), 67-82, Mr 90.

The conjecture we call *semantic holism* claims that if we start with a "sound and nontrivial" but indeterminate truth-table semantics, then to remove any "semantic indeterminacy" in any row in the table of any connective of propositional calculus, is to jump straight to classical semantics. We show 1) why semantic holism is plausible and 2) why it is nevertheless false. And 3) we pose a series of questions concerning the number of possible steps or jumps between "sound and nontrivial" indeterminate semantics and classical semantics.

BELOFF, John. "Dualism: A Parapsychological Perspective" in *The Case for Dualism*, SMYTHIES, John R (ed), 167-185. Charlottesville, Univ Pr of Virginia, 1989.

Whether all mental activity could, in principle, be explained in physicalist terms is, at present, undecidable. If, however, the existence of paranormal cognition and action (psi phenomena) is granted, the physicalist solution becomes insupportable and the interactionist view of the mind-brain relationship becomes almost irresistible. There we try to show that psi phenomena must be taken very seriously.

BELOFF, John (ed) and SMYTHIES, John R (ed). *The Case for Dualism*. Charlottesville, Univ Pr of Virginia, 1989.

BELSEY, Andrew. Boethius and the Consolation of Philosophy, or, How to Be a Good Philosopher. Ratio, 4(1), 1-15, Je 91.

At many times when the tradition of free enquiry has not been respected by rulers, philosophers have had to practice their profession under pressure, Socrates and Boethius being two early examples. Boethius wrote his *Consolation* to justify the worthwhileness of philosophy. But the consolation offered by this text is not obvious, because the dialogue form enables it to be artfully constucted, full of twists, ironies and paradoxes. An analysis of the textual convolutions leads to a debate about the nature of philosophy and whether its consolation should be other-worldly stoicism or political engagement with the evils of this world.

BELTRAMINI, Richard F and PETERSON, Robert A and KOZMETSKY, George. Concerns of College Students Regarding Business Ethics: A Replication. J Bus Ethics, 10(10), 733-738, O 91.

In 1984 we reported the results of surveying a nationwide sample of college students about selected business ethics issues. We concluded that (a) college students were in general concerned about the issues investigated and (b) female students were relatively more concerned than were male students. The present study replicated our earlier study and not only corroborated both of its conclusions, but also found a higher level of concern than had been observed previously.

BEMPORAD, Jules R. Dementia Praecox as a Failure of Neoteny. Theor Med, 12(1), 45-51, Mr 91.

The theology of neoteny assumes that adult animals that are higher on the phylogenetic scale retain juvenile characteristics, such as curiousity, ability to learn and playfulness, for greater periods of their lifetime. Failure of this process could result in the negative symptoms of dementia praecox, a chronic mental illness that strikes individuals in adolescence. A possible mechanism in the etiology of dementia praecox may be the failure of regulator genes to program structural genes to produce enzymes necessary for neoteny. Positive symptoms of the disorder may be conceptualized as the organisms aberrant response to this activation failure.

BEN-MENAHEM, Y. The Inference to the Best Explanation. Erkenntnis, 33(3), 319-344, N 90.

In a situation in which several explanations compete, is the one that is better qua explanation also the one we should regard as the more likely to be true? Realists usually answer in the affirmative. They then go on to argue that since realism provides the best explanation for the success of science, realism can be inferred to. Nonrealists, on the other hand, answer the above question in the negative, thereby renouncing the inference to realism. In this paper I separate the two issues. In the first section it is argued that a rationale can be provided for the inference to the best explanation; in the second, that this rationale cannot justify an inference to realism. The defence of the inference rests on the claim that our standards of explanatory power are subject to critical examination, which, in turn, should be informed by empirical considerations. By means of a comparison of the realist's explanation for the success of science with that of conventionalism and instrumentalism it is then shown that realism does not offer a superior explanation and should not, therefore, be inferred to.

BEN-MENAHEM, Yemima. Equivalent Descriptions. Brit J Phil Sci, 41(2), 261-279, Je 90.

The existence of empirically equivalent but seemingly incompatible descriptions of reality lies at the root of conventionalism. The conventionalist argues that if there are incompatible descriptions which are equally good candidates for being true, and if only one can be true, the decision as to which it is can only be taken on the basis of 'soft' subjective criteria. That truth could be a matter of choice is, however, repugnant to the realist. In this paper the conventionalist's claim that empirical equivalence engenders freedom at the level of theory construction is defended against three types of counter argument: a) a purported refutation of conventionalism by Hilary Putnam; b) a stategy of trivilizing the phenomenon of empirical equivalence due to Quine; c) the claim that conventionalism presupposes an untenable dichotomy between theory and observation, and is undermined once this dichotomy is no longer upheld.

BEN-ZEEV, Aaron. Conscious and Unconscious States. Phil Stud (Ireland), 32, 44-62, 1988-90.

Consciousness is a mental mode of discriminating certain information which also involves some degree of self-awareness. Postulating unconscious entities is natural in a substantive approach which conceives of the mind as consisting of entities and a storage place for them. The case is different in a relational approach where the mind is considered as consisting of dispositions (or capacities) and actualized states. Most postulated unconscious entities belong in the suggested relational view to one of the following categories: a) dispositions; b) theoretical entities; c) information which the agent can in principle discriminate but does not.

BEN-ZEEV, Aaron. Describing the Emotions: A Review of *The Cognitive Structure of Emotions* by Ortony, Clore and Collins. Phil Psych, 3(2-3), 305-317, 1990.

This paper critically examines Ortony, Clore and Collins's book *The Cognitive Structure of Emotions*. The book is found to present a very valuable, comprehensive and systematic account of emotions. Despite its obvious value the book has various flaws; these are discussed and an alternative is suggested.

BEN-ZEEV, Aaron. Envy and Jealousy. Can J Phil, 20(4), 487-516, D 90.

Envy involves the wish to have what someone else has and which is important for the subject's self-definition; jealousy involves the wish not to lose something, which is important for the subject's self-definition, to someone else. It is argued that this difference has significant implications. The paper begins with a brief explanation of the conceptual tools with which the two emotions are analyzed. It then compares the components of each emotion and draws some general implications from this comparison. The paper ends with a discussion of the moral value of the two emotions.

BEN-ZEEV, Aaron. Seeing Our Seeing and Knowing Our Knowing. Man World, 24(1), 89-92, Ja 91.

In *Charmides* Plato argues that knowing our knowing is impossible for the same reason that seeing our seeing is impossible: like seeing, knowing does not possess the essential properties of its objects. Contrary to Plato, there are mental capacities which are their own object, e.g., desiring our desires and thinking about our thinking. Without interpreting Plato's text, the paper discusses the problem suggested in the text: what is the difference between mental capacities that can refer to themselves and those that cannot; and to which of these knowing our knowing pertain?

BENCE, György. Political Justice in Post-Communist Societies: The Case of Hungary. Praxis Int, 10(1-2), 80-89, Ap-Jl 90.

BENCIVENGA, Ermanno. Incompleteness of a Free Arithmetic. Log Anal, 31(121-122), 79-84, Mr-Je 88.

An arithmetical theory *FQ* is defined whose logical basis is free quantification theory. A finitary consistency proof of *FQ* is given. It is then proved that all recursive functions are representable in *FQ*. There follows a proof of Gödel's first theorem for *FQ*.

BENHABIB, Seyla (ed) and DALLMAYR, Fred (ed). *The Communicative Ethics Controversy*. Cambridge, MIT Pr, 1990.

This collection of essays introduces readers to the communicative ethics controversy, generated by Karl Otto-Apel's and Jürgen Habermas's program of formulating a "communicative" or "discourse ethic." The introduction and afterword by Fred Dallmayr and Seyla Benhabib respectively situate this debate in the context of current controversies in Anglo-American thought.

BENÍTEZ, Laura. Reflexiones en torno a la metodología de la historia de la filosofía. Dianoia, 34(34), 181-194, 1988.

BENJOWSKI, Regina. The Oscillation of the Concept of Reason in Michel Foucault (in German). Deut Z Phil, 38(10), 913-920, 1990.

BENNETT, Barbara J. Quantum Realism: A Reply to Professor Fenner. J Speculative Phil, 4(3), 267-274, 1990.

I defend a "Newtonian" mathematical realism in the interpretation of QM. Developments in QM show that quantum microphysical reality may be different from experimental reality, so that the latter cannot always stand for the former. The mathematical representation of quantum entities may then be seen as a more faithful one than that of measurement-results. I argue that a "cut" needs to be made, not between unobservables and observables, but between the microphysical domain of QM and the macrophysical domain of CM. The question of observer-dependence is then clarified by means of the cut, which serves to separate autonomous microphysical systems from the cognitive, macrophysical aspects of measurement. Mathematical realism makes possible this essential ontological distinction.

BENNETT, Beth S. The Rhetoric of Martianus Capella and Anselm de Besate in the Tradition of Menippean Satire. Phil Rhet, 24(2), 128-142, 1991.

The purpose of this discussion of Martianus Capella's *De nuptiis* and Anselm's *Rhetorimachia* is to establish the indebtedness of both works to the tradition of Menippean satire. The use of prosimetric form and conventional satiric themes signify the authors' attempts to enhance the acceptability of their work with medieval audiences, while showcasing their knowledge and literary skills. Thus, when viewed together, the two works illustrate how intermingled literary tastes and rhetorical efforts were for the medieval mind. Furthermore, Anselm's work is evidence that the tradition of Menippean satire continued, beyond Martianus Capella and Boethius, into the late Middle Ages.

BENNETT, Colin J. Computers, Personal Data, and Theories of Technology: Comparative Approaches to Privacy Protection in the 1990s. Sci Tech Human Values, 16(1), 51-69, Wint 91.

Public policies designed to regulate the use of information technology to protect personal data have been based on different theoretical assumptions in different states, depending on whether the problem is defined in technological, civil libertarian, or bureaucratic terms. However, the rapid development, dispersal, and decentralization of information technology have facilitated a range of new surveillance practices that have in turn rendered the approaches of the 1960s and 1970s obsolete. The networking of the postindustrial state will require a reconceptualization of the dynamic relationship between organizational practices and information technology and a more comprehensive appreciation of the privacy problem. With the call for the development of a more coherent information policy in a number of countries, there is evidence that policymakers have been taking this more holistic view.

BENNETT, Jane. Deceptive Comfort: The Power of Kafka's Stories. Polit Theory, 19(1), 73-95, F 91.

Kafka's stories are relevant to political theory in two ways. They evoke experiences of frustration, exhaustion, and interference in a way that challenges the image of power derived from theoretical approaches; and, by calling attention to links between theories of power and certain ideals of self, they offer insight into what I call the "existential" function of theory. This essay seeks to articulate just how Kafka's fiction achieves political understanding that theory does not, and it fosters an engagement between the stories of Kafka and the theories of Steven Lukes and Michel Foucault—opposing theories that now appear to share some common ground.

BENNETT, Jonathan. *Linguistic Behaviour*. Indianapolis, Hackett, 1990.

BENNETT, Jonathan. Truth and Stability in Descartes' *Meditations*. Can J Phil, SUPP 16, 75-108, 1990.

This paper argues that the treatment of skepticism in Descartes's *Meditations* contains an important, usually overlooked, strand: a concern with beliefs that are stable, as distinct from true, certain, etc. This strand emphasizes causes of doubt rather than reasons for doubt.

BENNETT, Laura J. Modularity of Mind Revisited. Brit J Phil Sci, 41(3), 429-436, S 90.

BENOIST, J. Objet et communauté transcendantale: autour d'un fragment du dernier Husserl. Tijdschr Filosof, 53(2), 311-326, Je 91.

Sur la base de l'etude d'un fragment du dernier Husserl ("Teleologie Universelle"), l'auteur met en evidence comment la constitution originaire de l'ego dans le processus d'autotemporalisation est en fait tributaire du Rapport a Autrui, en fait premier. Il plaide pour la pensee de l'objet, qui, en thematisant la distance de l'objet a moi-meme, permet d'approcher la distance primordiale de moi a moi en tant qu 'expose a Autrui, alors que la pensee de l'etre resorbe cette alterite.

BENOIT, Raymond. Fault-Lines in Kierkegaard and Hawthorne: *The Sickness unto Death* and "Ethan Brand". Thought, 66(261), 196-205, Je 91.

BENSAUDE-VINCENT, Bernadette. "Un essai de vulgarisation" in *Études sur/Studies on Hélène Metzger*, FREUDENTHAL, Gad , 45-57. Leiden, Brill, 1990.

BENSON, Hugh H. Meno, the Slave-Boy, and the *Elenchos*. Phronesis, 35(2), 128-158, 1990.

I argue that the *Meno* provides a strong *prima facie* case against those who maintain that Socrates understood his *elenchos* as a method for acquiring knowledge. A careful examination of the structure of this dialogue suggests that in offering the theory of recollection Plato takes himself to be going beyond the Socratic method, not replacing or revising it. The theory of recollection, first introduced in the *Meno*, is presented as a substantive view about how knowledge is to be acquired once the Socratic *elenchos* has achieved its aim, i.e., once it has eliminated the interlocutor's false conceit.

BENSON, Paul. Feminist Second Thoughts About Free Agency. Hypatia, 5(3), 47-64, Fall 90.

This essay suggests that common themes in recent feminist ethical thought can dislodge the guiding assumptions of traditional theories of free agency and thereby foster an account of freedom which might be more fruitful for feminist discussion of moral and political agency. The essay proposes constructing that account around a condition of normative-competence. It argues that this view permits insight into why women's labor of reclaiming and augmenting their agency is both difficult and possible in a sexist society.

BENYOVSZKY, Ladislav. A Contribution of the Conception of "Discursivity" and "Spontaneiti" of Thinking (in Czechoslovakian). Filozof Cas, 38(6), 788-806, 1990.

For a long time, the question after thinking has been asked as a question after something that stands "beside" opinion or sensuality. Such questioning and thereby already a specific fixation of the problem is linked with certain significant characteristics of thinking among which the "discursivity" and "spontaneity" of thinking have undoubtedly played one of the most important roles. This paper follows the theme of spontaneity and discursivity in one of its most elaborated forms, in the form which it acquired in the German classical philosophy. The author tries to grasp and more fully analyse the internal structure of Kant's conception of discursivity and thus make its constitutive moments—"comparison," "reflection" and "abstraction"—appear in a more expressive way. (edited)

BENZON, William L and HAYS, David G. Why Natural Selection Leads to Complexity. J Soc Biol Struct, 13(1), 33-40, F 90.

While science has accepted biological evolution through natural selection, there is no generally agreed explanation for why evolution leads to ever more complex organisms. Evolution yields organismic complexity because the universe is, in its very fabric, inherently complex, as suggested by Ilya Prigogine's work on dissipative structures. Because the universe is complex, increments in organismic complexity yield survival benefits: (1) more efficient extraction of energy and matter, (2) more flexible response to vicissitudes, (3) more effective search. J J Gibson's ecological psychology provides a clue to the advantages of sophisticated information processing while the lore of computational theory suggests that a complex computer is needed efficiently to perform complex computations (i.e., sophisticated information processing).

BERARDUCCI, Alessandro. The Interpretability Logic of Peano Arithmetic. J Sym Log, 55(3), 1059-1089, S 90.

BERCIANO V, Modesto. El evento (ereignis) como concepto fundamental de la filosofía de Heidegger (1a parte). Logos (Mexico), 18(53), 29-45, My-Ag 90.

Event's concept is basic in Heidegger's philosophy. He takes it of Hölderlin and makes an ample exposition in *Beiträge zur Philosophie* (1936/38). The being isn't something ontical, but the four elements happening: earth, sky, gods, mortals. Later, in *Einblick in das, was ist*, event is considered destiny.

BERCIANO V, Modesto. El evento (Ereignis) como concepto fundamental de la filosofía de Heidegger (2a parte). Logos (Mexico), 18(54), 69-84, S-D 90.

Very much important in Heidegger's later philosophy is the relation man-being-event. In *Der Satz der Identität* he speaks about the joint participation of being and man. It isn't given one without the other. Both are given in the event (*es gibt*). This concept is more basic here that being and man. Finally in *Zeit und Sein* event is the one that gives being and time.

BERCIANO V, Modesto. Sinn-Wahrheit-Ort: Tres etapas en el pensamiento de Heidegger. Anu Filosof, 24(1), 9-48, 1991.

Three stages can be identified in Heidegger's thought. First, he searches fruitlessly for the meaning of being. In a second step truth emerges from general unveilment process, which includes man. In the third stage the truth of being is a time-space event and destiny.

BERCKMANS, Paul. Demonstrative Utterances. Phil Stud, 60(3), 281-295, N 90.

BERCOVITCH, S and MARCUS, Ruth Barcan and KUCKLICK, B. Uninformed Consent. Science, 205, 644-647, 1979.

A response to the editorial "Informed Consent May Be Hazardous to Health," *Science*, vol. 204. In particular what is cited is the failure to distinguish the subject of an experiment who volunteers and the special doctor-client relationship, also, the failure to distinguish rights and benefits. The subject has a right to know. That is not a benefit conferred.

BERENSON, F M. Emotions and Rationality. Int J Moral Soc Stud, 6(1), 33-46, Spr 91.

The deeply entrenched view that emotions necessarily interfere with reason is still with us in spite of recent work to the contrary. We are led to regard emotions as something that happens to a creature who would still be intelligible to us as a human agent quite independently of this crucial emotional dimension. The picture of a person which emerges is fraught with serious conceptual difficulties.

BERENSON, Frances. Comprensión intercultural y arte. Anu Filosof, 23(1), 9-23, 1990.

Two opposing views about the possibility of understanding the art of cultures other than one's own are examined: (1) the view that there are insurmountable difficulties about understanding in this context; (2) the view that art is a universal 'language' and therefore accessible to anyone's understanding. Two versions of the theory which gives rise to the above problem are discussed: Strong and weak relativism; the consequences of both versions are examined in detail. The main argument of the paper is designed to show that difficulties raised about intercultural understanding of art are based on a serious misconception embedded in the way that the problem is set up. Finally, an alternative approach is offered.

BERENSON, Frances. What is this Thing Called 'Love'? Philosophy, 66(255), 65-79, Ja 91.

In the course of examining whether and how love fits into theories of emotions based on various necessary conditions significant differences emerge between love and other emotions. These are of such importance that, clearly, a different treatment of 'love' is necessary. Any analysis of love needs to focus not so much on necessary conditions but on the variety of criteria arising from the meaning of the concept and, *imperatively*, from the contemplation of the lived experience of loving. Such an approach will exclude idealized conceptions of superhuman love and eliminate the possibility of accommodating conceptions of love to our preferences and our conveniences.

BERENSON, Robert A. Commentary: When Opportunity Knocks. Hastings Center Rep, 20(6), 33-34, N-D 90.

BERESFORD, Eric B. Uncertainty and the Shaping of Medical Decisions. Hastings Center Rep, 21(4), 6-11, Jl-Ag 91.

BEREZDIVIN, Ruben. "321 CONTACT: Textuality, the Other, Death" in *Re-Reading Levinas*, BERNASCONI, Robert (ed), 190-200. Bloomington, Indiana Univ Pr, 1991.

BEREZDIVIN, Ruben (trans) and DERRIDA, Jacques. "At This Very Moment in This Work Here I Am" in *Re-Reading Levinas*, BERNASCONI, Robert (ed), 11-48. Bloomington, Indiana Univ Pr, 1991.

BERG, Jonathan. "How Could Ethics Depend on Religion?" in *A Companion to Ethics*, SINGER, Peter (ed), 525-533. Cambridge, Blackwell, 1991.

BERG, Jonathan. The Right to Self-Determination. Pub Affairs Quart, 5(3), 211-225, Jl 91.

BERGER, Alan. "A Central Problem for a Speech-Dispositional Account of Logic and Language" in *Perspectives on Quine*, BARRETT, Robert (ed), 17-35. Cambridge, Blackwell, 1990.

BERGER, Arthur S (ed) and BERGER, Joyce (ed). *To Die or Not to Die?*. New York, Praeger, 1990.

Builds a foundation for thinking or rethinking about the issues associated with the subject of helping or allowing a person to die. Cross-disciplinary, cultural, and legal perspectives are considered side by side to provide a useful text for a variety of areas of interest: medicine, nursing, theology, law, public health; the disciplines of philosophy, ethics, psychology and sociology; and to seriously ill patients and their families. (staff)

BERGER, Joyce (ed) and BERGER, Arthur S (ed). *To Die or Not to Die?*. New York, Praeger, 1990.

Builds a foundation for thinking or rethinking about the issues associated with the subject of helping or allowing a person to die. Cross-disciplinary, cultural, and legal perspectives are considered side by side to provide a useful text for a variety of areas of interest: medicine, nursing, theology, law, public health; the disciplines of philosophy, ethics, psychology and sociology; and to seriously ill patients and their families. (staff)

BERGER, René. Science and Art: The New Golem From the Transdisciplinary to an Ultra-disciplinary Epistemology. Diogenes, 152, 124-146, Wint 90.

The purpose of the essay is first to state that after the "disciplinary" tradition, new ways of envisioning reality are taking place, often called: multi-, pluri-, inter-, trans-disciplinary. On his part, the author assumes that beyond these trends, a new Configuration is emerging, symbolized by the New Golem announced by Norbert Wiener. What counts for our future stems from the relationship between Man and Machine, which is no longer a matter of adjustment, but a true process of *co-evolution*. With the question: does not the *ultra-disciplinary* open up to the *ultra-human*?

BERGOFFEN, Debra B. The Body Politic: Democratic Metaphors, Totalitarian Practices, Erotic Rebellions. Phil Soc Crit, 16(2), 109-126, 1990.

Appealing to the writings of Hobbes, Lacan and Atwood, this paper explores the political and psychoanalytic potency of the body politic metaphor. It suggests that totalitarian practices and power are grounded in a logic that terrorizes our desire for totality; that this logic draws on and viciously distorts the psychology of legitimation of the social contract tradition; and that this desire for a body politic may be confronted another desire, the desire of the erotic body. This revolutionary/rebellious desire remembers what the desire for totality forgets: the desiring body's desire to be whole is not the whole of desire.

BERGOFFEN, Debra B. "On Becoming a Subject: Lacan's Rereading of Freud" in *Reconsidering Psychology: Perspectives from Continental Philosophy*, FAULCONER, James E (ed), 210-233. Pittsburgh, Duquesne Univ Pr, 1990.

An examination of Freud's and Lacan's accounts of human subjectivity which explores the ways in which Lacan reads Freud's analyses of (1) embodiment and desire, (2) the Oedipal drama, and (3) the dynamics of repression/repetition, to reassess the relationship between the ego and the subject. This reassessment moves the center of attention from sexuality to language. The subject's identity is envisioned as a function of the relationship between desire and its representations which in turn is envisioned as the drama of the imaginary and the symbolic. Here we discover that Lacan's rereading of Freud remains fundamentally indebted to Freud's account of the dual power of language.

BERGSON, Henri and PAUL, N M (trans) and PALMER, W S (trans). *Matter and Memory*. Cambridge, MIT Pr, 1991.

BERGSTRÖM, Lars. "Quine on Underdetermination" in *Perspectives on Quine*, BARRETT, Robert (ed), 38-52. Cambridge, Blackwell, 1990.

An interpretation of Quine's thesis of underdetermination is proposed. It is argued that the thesis may be completely trivial, and that the arguments for it are weak, but that it is compatible with Quine's verificationism. Quine's views on whether empirically equivalent theories have the same truth value is criticized.

BERKELEY, Istvan S N. Vagueness, Natural Language and Logic. Eidos, 9(1), 49-65, Je 90.

In section I of this paper, I briefly discuss natural language vagueness, indicating how it can be both useful and problematic. Section II deals with Frege's views on natural language vagueness. Russell's opinions are mentioned in this section also. The later Wittgenstein's position and his critique of Frege are discussed in section III. Finally, in section IV, I argue that the Fregean view on the applicability of logical rules of inference to natural language, with respect to vagueness, is fundamentally incorrect and that a suggestion in the spirit of the later Wittgenstein is to be preferred.

BERKOWITZ, Leonard J. Students: A Source-Spot for Arguments. Inform Log, 13(1), 41-44, Wint 91.

The most important part of an informal logic course is the opportunity for students to apply their newly developed skills to actual pieces of reasoning (as opposed to artificial textbook examples). It is only through such practice that the skills are really learned. In this paper, I examine the possible sources for such "real-life" arguments; the most commonly used sources are found inadequate. I then suggest how our students themselves can be the best source for such arguments. I describe in detail the assignment I use to generate arguments which students find interesting and important.

BERNARD-WEIL, E. A priori et a posteriori dans la pratique cognitive: le modele de la regulation des couples ago-antagonistes. Commun Cog, 23(2-3), 193-210, 1990.

Three couples have to be considered to advance in cognition researches: the couples formed by *praxis* and cognition, by model of the cognition and model of the known, by a priori and a posteriori, to which we can add the couple of realism and conceptualism (or relativism). A general model, so-called the model for the regulation of agonistic antagonistic couples (MRAAC) allows us to better accept and even to simulate the dynamics of these couples without having to establish a hierarchy between the two elements of the couple neither to search a middle way. Finally, a few examples are evoked, showing the fruitfulness of considering the circularity, the paradox, the ago-antagonistic couple as foundation (but evanescent!) of cognition and *praxis*. (edited)

BERNASCONI, Robert. The Ethics of Suspicion. Res Phenomenol, 20, 3-18, 1990.

The essay begins by contrasting Levinasian ethics with traditional conceptions of ethics, such as those of Aristotle and Kant. Levinas only rarely addresses directly the leading philosophical representatives of the Western ethical tradition or its critics like Nietzsche. In reconstructing Levinas's response to contemporary suspicion of ethics, it is found that certain passages in Levinas point to the possibility of developing an ethics that is suspicious of ethics. It would be an ethics that would seek less to answer the question of what I ought to do, than question the complacency that tends to accompany specifical ethical systems.

BERNASCONI, Robert. Habermas and Arendt on the Philosopher's "Error": Tracking the Diabiological in Heidegger. Grad Fac Phil J, 14(2)-15(1), 3-24, 1991.

The question of Heidegger's political error and the moral failure arising from his apparent lack of remorse is here posed within the wider context of the time-honored ideal of the philosophical life. It is this ideal which allows judgment of Heidegger the philosopher to reflect on one's assessment of his work. The approach provides the backdrop for a reexamination of the responses that the Heidegger affair elicited from Arent, Habermas, Rorty and Levinas. Heidegger's failures reflect not just on him and his work, but on the still deeply held ideal of philosophy as a way of life.

BERNASCONI, Robert. "One-Way Traffic: The Ontology of Decolonization and its Ethics" in *Ontology and Alterity in Merleau-Ponty*, JOHNSON, Galen A (ed), 67-80. Evanston, Northwestern Univ Pr, 1991.

"One-Way Traffic" presents Levinas's enigmatic essay "Meaning and Sense" as it relates to Merleau-Ponty. Levinas finds that Merleau-Ponty's politics of decolonization fits the latter's anti-Platonic insistence on fundamental historicity. Meanwhile, Levinas's return to Platonism in "a new way" maintains the irreducibility of ethics to culture. However, an argument is made, *pace* Levinas, for recognizing the possibility of an encounter between cultures at the level of radical alterity. This introduces the possibility of an ethical culture that does not act from moral superiority but that instead finds the origin of ethics in having its complacency challenged.

BERNASCONI, Robert (ed) and CRITCHLEY, Simon (ed). *Re-Reading Levinas*. Bloomington, Indiana Univ Pr, 1991.

The book responds to Levinasian ethics by juxtaposing it with the problematics of deconstruction, feminism, psychotherapy, and the ethical status of animals. Derrida's essay on Levinas, "At this very moment in this work here I am," Levinas's essay on Derrida, "Wholly Otherwise," and Irigaray's "questions to Emmanuel Levinas" appear in English translation for the first time. Essays by a number of the leading exponents of Levinas's thought explore the possibility of an ethical saying that is irreducible to the ontological said. Taken as a whole the volume attempts to open a new chapter in the critical assimilation of Levinas.

BERNASCONI, Robert. "Skepticism in the Face of Philosophy" in *Re-Reading Levinas*, BERNASCONI, Robert (ed), 149-161. Bloomington, Indiana Univ Pr, 1991.

When in *Otherwise than being* Levinas observes that the refutation of skepticism has failed to present skepticism's return, it is to suggest that skepticism's disdain for and reliance on the *logos* provides a model for Levinas's own thematizing of the unthematizable. "Skepticism in the Face of Philosophy" suggests that Levinas appeals to skepticism as part of his response to Derrida's objection in "Violence and Metaphysics." When Derrida subsequently returned to Levinas in "At this very moment" he seemed oblivious of Levinas's response. An analysis of that essay helps articulate what governs the similarities and difference between the two thinkers.

BERNAUER, James W. *Michel Foucault's Force of Flight: Towards an Ethics for Thought*. Atlantic Highlands, Humanities Pr, 1990.

This book offers a comprehensive, chronological reading of his published and unpublished writings and claims that Foucault's achievement was to have fashioned a series of inquiries that make it possible to question the activity of thought itself as an ethical practice. This ethic historicizes Kant's great questions. Not "What can I know?" but rather "How have my questions been produced?" In place of the questions on hope and obligation, one asks "How have exclusions operated in delineating the realms of obligation and aspiration for me?"

BERNET, R. Subject en zelfervaring. Tijdschr Filosof, 53(1), 23-43, Mr 91.

Eine phänomenologische Analyse des Selbstbewusstseins erbringt den Nachweis, dass die Selbsterfahrung stets eine Erfahrung des Selbstverlusts impliziert. Dieser Befund beruht auf der richtig verstandenen Intentionalität bzw. Transzendenz des Subjekts. Diese These wird im vorliegenden Artikel vor allem mit dem Hinweis auf die Phänomene des moralischen Gewissens, der synthetischen Funktion des Ich, der differenziellen Struktur von Selbstbezug und Selbstrepräsentation, sowie der leiblich bestimmten, affektiven Selbsterfahrung illustriert. (edited)

BERNICK, Susan E. Toward A Value-Laden Theory: Feminism and Social Science. Hypatia, 6(2), 118-136, Sum 91.

Marjorie Shostak's ethnography, *Nisa: The Life and Words of a !Kung Woman,* is analyzed as a case study of feminist social science. Three principles of feminist research are suggested as standards for evaluation. After discussion of the principles and analysis of the text, I raise a criticism of the principles as currently sketched. The entire project is framed by the question of how best to resolve conflict between researcher and participant accounts.

BERNIER, Paul. Remarques sur l'analyse des termes mentaux chez Wittgenstein. Lekton, 1(1), 121-134, 1990.

BERNIER, Réjane. L'ontogenèse de l'individu: ses aspects scientifiques et philosophiques. Arch Phil, 54(1), 3-42, Ja-Mr 91.

The scope of this study is to show that individuality does not belong either to inanimate bodies or to biological species but is an attribute of the "living being" as commonly understood. The ontogenesis of the individual is analyzed with reference to three aspects: (1) morphogenetic or formative, from the time a new living being becomes distinct from its progenitors, in both cases of vegetative and sexual reproduction; (2) immunological, from which an organism establishes its "self" and distinguishes between "self" and "non-self"; (3) psychological, in which the entire relational history of the living being with the outside world can be seen. (edited)

BERNS, Egidius. Derrida's huishouding. Alg Ned Tijdschr Wijs, 82(4), 269-281, O 90.

This article means to introduce to the heart of Jacques Derrida's philosophy. In the first part attention is paid to the problem of the delimitation and consequently of that of economy (as the law of the inside), closure and deconstruction. In the second part the problem of the delimitation is connected with the well-known issues of Derrida's thinking: writing and difference.

BERNSTEIN, David. A Problem Solving Interpretation of Argument Analysis. Inform Log, 12(2), 79-85, Spr 90.

BERNSTEIN, Richard J. "Judging—The Actor and the Spectator" in *The Realm of Humanitas: Responses to the Writings of Hannah Arendt*, GARNER, Reuben (ed), 235-254. New York, Lang, 1990.

BERNSTEIN, Richard J. "Social Theory as Critique" in *Social Theory of Modern Societies: Anthony Giddens and His Critics*, HELD, David (ed), 19-33. New York, Cambridge Univ Pr, 1990.

BERQUIST, Richard. "The Vatican 'Instruction' and Surrogate Motherhood" in *Beyond Baby M: Ethical Issues in New Reproductive Techniques*, BARTELS, Dianne M (ed), 221-234. Clifton, Humana Pr, 1990.

This paper distinguishes and clarifies three levels of ethical reflection based, respectively, on consequences, on autonomy, and on human dignity considered totally and integrally. The ethical force and the ethical limitations of arguments on the first two levels are shown to depend, ultimately, on the third level. Considered in the light of human dignity, the Vatican's concerns for safeguarding embryonic life and for protecting the link between marriage and procreation, as expressed in the 1987 "Instruction on Respect for Human Life and its Origin and on the Dignity of Procreation," become plausible and even compelling.

BERRIGAN, Daniel. "Christian Peacemakers in the Warmaking State" in *Celebrating Peace*, ROUNER, Leroy S (ed), 181-191. Notre Dame, Univ Notre Dame Pr, 1990.

BERSTEN, Michael and COHEN, Stephen. Probability Out of Court: Notes on 'Guilt Beyond Reasonable Doubt'. Austl J Phil, 68(2), 229-240, Je 90.

The essay is critical of an essay by Barbara Davidson and Robert Pargetter, "Guilt Beyond Reasonable Doubt," in which those authors offer a characterization of the requirements for a verdict of guilty. In particular, this essay criticizes the role they suggest for "probability" and their application of Keynes's notion of "evidential weight." The essay suggests that attempts to import a formal notion of probability or a Keynesian notion of evidential weight into an analysis of "beyond reasonable doubt" are misconceived both in terms of legal reality and in terms of a recommendation, or prescription, for rational behavior of a juror.

BERTEN, A and LENOBLE, J. Jugement juridique et jugement pratique: de Kant à la philosophie du langage. Rev Metaph Morale, 95(3), 339-365, Jl-S 90.

Philosophy of law is, at the moment, experiencing something of a revival in interest in the United States and in Germany in the wake of the criticisms of Dworkin and Habermas directed against analytical legal positivism. This movement of reappraisal, at a philosophical level, is linked to contemporary reinterpretations of practical reason. Above and beyond the differing and, at times, antinomical forms which this reappraisal can take, all of them aim to reinterpret practical judgment in the light of the Kantian theory of reflexive judgment. This article seeks to show both the possibilities and inadequacies of these contemporary reinterpretations of ethics, inadequacies which recent discoveries in the domain of the philosophy of language can help overcome. We ultimately wish to show how that may help advance beyond what are, for the moment, the initial stages of a renewed theory of juridical judgment.

BERTEN, André. Le modèle industriel comme modèle énergétique. Rev Phil Louvain, 89(81), 22-35, F 91.

BERTEN, André. Modernité et postmodernité: un enjeu politique? Rev Phil Louvain, 89(81), 84-112, F 91.

BERTEN, André. Philosophie et société. Rev Phil Louvain, 88(78), 272-291, My 90.

BERTHOLD-BOND, Daniel. Evolution and Nostalgia in Hegel's Theory of Desire. Clio, 19(4), 367-388, Sum 90.

My purpose is to indicate the importance of a second, often overlooked, dimension of desire in Hegel's philosophy, which contrasts with the primary character of desire as evolutionary. This second "face" of desire exerts an exactly opposite force, being straightforwardly retrogressive and nostalgic. I trace this nostalgic face of desire out through a variety of contexts in Hegel's writings, and in my conclusion I raise the question of whether Hegel does not himself finally succumb to the lures of nostalgia in his vision of Absolute Knowledge. I tentatively answer this question in the negative.

BERTHOLD-BOND, Daniel. Hegel, Nietzsche, and Freud on Madness and the Unconscious. J Speculative Phil, 5(3), 193-213, 1991.

The article seeks to clarify Hegel's theory of the role of the unconscious in madness by way of comparison to Nietzsche and Freud. I argue that Hegel, like Nietzsche and Freud, regards a theory of the unconscious as crucial to the development of a decisively new orientation for psychology, and emphasizes the need for an understanding of illness as essential for an appreciation of health. My comparison centers around the themes of the origin and value of madness, the idea of regression, the nature of the body and instincts, the theory of sublimation, and the diagnosis of the mental health of culture.

BERTHOLD-BOND, Daniel. A Kierkegaardian Critique of Heidegger's Concept of Authenticity. Man World, 24(2), 119-142, Ap 91.

The article has three purposes: 1) to analyze two common criticisms of Heidegger's account of authenticity that the distinction between authentic and inauthentic being is problematic, and that the portrait of authenticity is extraordinarily abstract and formal; 2) to make suggestions about the origin of these two problems within Heidegger's larger phenomenological project; and 3) to argue that Soren Kierkegaard's analysis of the aesthetic mode of existence promises a way of resolving these problems.

BERTHRONG, John. To Catch a Thief: Chu Hsi (1130-1200) and the Hermeneutic Art. J Chin Phil, 18(2), 195-212, Je 91.

BERTI, Enrico. Être et non-être chez Aristote: contraires ou contradictoires? Rev Theol Phil, 122(3), 365-373, 1990.

L'être et le non-être chez Aristote s'opposent, grâce à leurs multiples significations, de nombreuses façons: (1) considérés sans autre détermination, ils sont en contradiction; (2) pris en relation avec un sujet, ils se privent mutuellement; (3) convertibles avec l'Un et le Multiple respectivement, ils s'opposent en tant qu'antithèses. La seule opposition qui n'existe pas entre eux est celle de l'implication réciproque.

BERTMAN, Martin A. God and Man: Action and Reference in Hobbes. Hobbes Stud, 3, 18-34, 1990.

Provoked by the question, "Why does Hobbes use the concept of purpose for human actions but not in his general explanation of nature?," this paper shows how Hobbes's nominalist orientation provides for science on a perspectival basis and how difficult it is for him to reconcile these in terms of values.

BERTOLDI, Francesco. Il dibattito sulla verità tra Blondel e Garrigou-Lagrange. Sapienza, 43(3), 293-310, Jl-S 90.

BERTOLET, Rod. Salmon on the A Priori. Analysis, 51(1), 43-48, Ja 91.

Nathan Salmon claims that the theory of cognitive information content of simple declarative sentences he develops in Frege's Puzzle has the consequence that sentences such as 'Hesperus, if it exists, is Phosphorus' are a priori, and defends this counterintuitive result. I argue that one who accepts his theory need not agree that such sentences are a priori. The reason is that given the theoretical perspective Salmon adopts, a priority is best seen as sentence relative; hence while 'Hesperus, if it exists, is Hesperus' is a priori, 'Hesperus, if it exists, is Phosphorus' is not.

BERTOSSI, L E. The Formal Language L_t and Topological Products. Z Math Log, 36(2), 89-94, 1990.

In this paper a new topological product of algebraic-topological structures is introduced. This product includes the usual direct product with the Tychonov topology. Then some model-theoretic results are presented; in particular, a classification of the topological powers of the topological Boolean algebra with two elements. Some results on syntactical properties of those formulas of the formal language L_t which are preserved under the new product are obtained.

BESANÇON, Alain. El marxismo, ciencia, ideología, gnosis? Espiritu, 35(93), 55-62, Ja-Je 86.

BEST, Katherine (trans) and GÖSSMANN, Elisabeth. "Hildegard of Bingen" in *A History of Women Philosophers, Volume II: Medieval, Renaissance and Enlightenment, A.D. 500-1600*, WAITHE, Mary Ellen (ed), 27-65. Norwell, Kluwer, 1989.

It is problematic to refer to Hildegard of Bingen as a philosopher, even though she was familiar with the philosophical currents of her time and could animatedly and competently take a stand on them. More appropriately, one could call her a theologian, even though she would be loath to claim such authority for herself, in regard to her writing. Her works, including the letters, function to a large extent as a visionary literature, and it is not by chance that she, as a woman, chooses these stylistic means. Within her visionary experience, she comes to a philosophical-theological view of the world which displays original traits and sometimes emphasizes polemical aspects, but, in addition, raises many unanswered questions about the influences affecting a 12th-century Benedictine woman's view of the world and of mankind.

BEST, Steven. Marx and the Problem of Conflicting Models of History. Phil Forum, 22(2), 167-192, Wint 90-91.

Some critics argue that Marx has conflicting models of history: a "continuist" model that interprets history as a unified, evolutionary movement, and a "discontinuist" model that sees capitalist society as a break from all preceeding social formations. I argue that Marx in fact does have multiple models of history, but that these are not incompatible or contradictory. Rather, Marx adopts a "perspectival" or "contextualist" approach that employs different models to gain different perspectives on the historical process. I provide a close reading of the "discontinuity" model based on an analysis of Marx's *Grundrisse*.

BETANCOURT, Raúl Fornet. Filosofía latinoamericana: Posibilidad o realidad? Logos (Mexico), 18(54), 47-68, S-D 90.

BETZ, Hans-Georg. The Post-Modern Challenge: From Marx to Nietzsche in the West German Alternative and Green Movement. Hist Euro Ideas, 11, 815-830, 1989.

BEUCHOT, Mauricio. Algunas consideraciones sobre la substancia en la metafísica de Juan Duns Escoto. Dianoia, 36(36), 181-188, 1990.

BEUCHOT, Mauricio. Los Factores Originales de la Sociedad en Tomás de Aquino. Logos (Mexico), 18(52), 33-39, Ja-Ap 90.

BEUCHOT, Mauricio. Filosofía e historia de la filosofía. Dianoia, 34(34), 206-213, 1988.

BEUCHOT, Mauricio. Lenguaje y metafísica en Alfred J Ayer. Logos (Mexico), 19(56), 9-20, My-Ag 91.

BEUCHOT, Mauricio. El problema de los universales en Juan de Santo Tomás en Juan de Santo Tomás. Rev Filosof (Venezuela), 12, 33-42, 1989.

BEUCHOT, Mauricio. La Teoría del conocimiento en Santo Tomás de Aquino. Rev Filosof (Venezuela), 13, 9-23, 1989.

BEUCHOT, Mauricio. El tratado de las obligaciones dialógicas en la Edad Media: el caso de Robert Fland. Dianoia, 34(34), 169-179, 1988.

BEURTON, Peter. Werkzeugproduktion im Tierreich und menschliche Werkzeugproduktion. Deut Z Phil, 38(12), 1168-1182, 1990.

BEWAJI, J A I. Dr C Neugebauer's Critical Note on Ethnophilosophy in the Philosophical Discourse in Africa: Some Remarks. Quest, 5(1), 95-103, Je 91.

BEYER, Wilhelm Raimund. Schattenseiten der Hegelei: Fallsbeispiel—Lassalles Hegel-Rhapsodie. Deut Z Phil, 39(1), 22-35, 1991.

BEYSSADE, Jean-Marie. Descartes et Corneille ou les démesures de l'*ego*. Laval Theol Phil, 47(1), 63-82, F 91.

L'auteur examine la relation entre la philosophie cartésienne de la liberté et un événement majeur du XVII^{ue} siècle français: le théâtre de Pierre Corneille. Il souligne une coïncidence de dates et une rencontre de thèmes.

BHARGAVI, V and SUBRAMANIAM, K. History, Indian Science and Policy-Making: A Philosophical Review. J Indian Counc Phil Res, 8(1), 115-128, S-D 90.

BHARUCHA, Filita. The Problem of Causation and Time-Symmetry in Physics. J Indian Counc Phil Res, 7(3), 13-22, My-Ag 90.

BHASKAR, Roy (ed). *Harré and His Critics*. Cambridge, Blackwell, 1990.

BHASKAR, Roy. "Introduction: Realism and Human Being" in *Harré and His Critics*, BHASKAR, Roy (ed), 1-13. Cambridge, Blackwell, 1990.

BHASKAR, Roy. "Rorty, Realism and the Idea of Freedom" in *Reading Rorty*, MALACHOWSKI, Alan (ed), 198-232. Cambridge, Blackwell, 1991.

BHAT, P R. Pragmatic Principles and Language. Indian Phil Quart, 18(2), 285-313, Ap 91.

The following pragmatic principles are discussed in the paper: 1) The Principle of Regularity in Use. 2) The Principle of Economy of Vocabulary, which includes, a) economy of vocabulary and b) formulation of compound words. 3) The Principle of Elasticity of Rules which includes, a) operational definitions of words, b) extending the uses of terms, c) restricting the uses of terms, d) metaphorical uses. 4) Creative Uses of Words. 5) The Concept of Enabling Institution. When this principle is applied to a) emphasizing a name or a criterion, b) conceptualizing, one finds pragmatic principle at work.

BHATTACHARYYA, Kalidas. Indian Philosophy in the Context of World Philosophy. J Indian Counc Phil Res, 6(2), 1-16, Ja-Ap 89.

BHATTACHARYYA, Sibajiban. Professor Matilal on Some Topics of Indian Philosophy. J Indian Counc Phil Res, 5(1), 159-165, S-D 87.

This is a critical review of Professor Bimal Krishna Matilal's outstanding book *Logic, Language and Reality* (Delhi, Motilal Banarsidass, 1985). In this book Professor Matilal has discussed many problems, examined many alternative interpretations of topics of Nyaya. He convincingly refutes Vidyabhusana's theory that Indian logic of Gautama was greatly influenced by Aristotle's works. The Nyaya explanation of false cognition is not to postulate any subjective content, but to analyse what is cognised in terms of what is real. About the Nyaya theory of prejudgmental perception, he holds that the state is 'never *known* to us'.

BHAVE, S M. Kitcher and Kant. J Indian Counc Phil Res, 6(3), 145-152, My-Ag 89.

Kitcher's criticism of Kant on the grounds of subjectivity and circularity is shown to be based on convenient misconstruction of Kant's thesis. Kitcher states apriorism in terms of psychologistic epistemology; demands a process that warrants a priori knowledge and dismisses imposition of categorical framework as a dubious warrant. Apriorism being a self-sufficient thesis needs no extraneous epistemology to justify itself. The subject of knowledge is human reason and the warranting process for mathematical knowledge is the groping for it in primitive societies. Emergence of non-Euclidean geometry shows not that the categories are dubious but that they are incomplete.

BIACINO, Loredana and GERLA, Giangiacomo. Connection Structures. Notre Dame J Form Log, 32(2), 242-247, Spr 91.

B L Clarke, following a proposal of A N Whitehead, presents an axiomatized calculus of individuals based on a primitive predicate "*x* is connected with *y*". In this article we show that a proper subset of Clarke's system of axioms characterizes the complete orthocomplemented lattices, while the whole of Clarke's system characterizes the complete atomless Boolean algebras.

BICKENBACH, Jerome E. The 'Artificial Reason' of the Law. Inform Log, 12(1), 23-32, Wint 90.

BIEL, Joseph. Learning Anew from Old Arguments. Teach Phil, 13(3), 209-215, S 90.

The article attempts to draw some conclusions about the nature of philosophical inquiry based upon the way in which classical texts are generally used in the classroom. Philosophical texts are not presented as solutions to problems. Rather, they are used to create a sense of mystery about the self and the world.

BIFFLE, Christopher. *A Guided Tour of Selections from Aristotle's Nicomachean Ethics*. Mountain View, Mayfield, 1990.

BIGELOW, John and PARGETTER, Robert and YOUNG, Robert. Land, Well-Being and Compensation. Austl J Phil, 68(3), 330-346, S 90.

BIGELOW, John. "Sets Are Universals" in *Physicalism in Mathematics*, IRVINE, Andrew D (ed), 291-307. Norwell, Kluwer, 1990.

BIGELOW, John and PARGETTER, Robert. Vectors and Change. Brit J Phil Sci, 40(3), 289-306, S 89.

Vectors, we will argue, are not just mathematical abstractions. They are also physical properties—universals. What make them distinctive are the rich and varied essences of these universals, and the complex pattern of internal relations which hold amongst them.

BIGELOW, John. The World Essence. Dialogue (Canada), 29(2), 205-217, 1990.

BIGELOW, John. Worlds Enough for Time. Nous, 25(1), 1-19, Mr 91.

The fact that time passes (or so it seems) is expressed in sentences like this: What is present was once future, and will soon be past. Standard theories of time and tense make such assertions vacuous. I argue for a nonstandard theory, in which tenses are specialized modal operators. On this theory, what is actually present was future, because there is some nonactual world in which it is future, some possible world in which it has the property of futurity. Something which is present was once future, in part because it would have been future, if what is actually present were past. The passage of time is no less real than possible worlds.

BIJKER, Wieke. Do Not Despair: There is Life after Constructivism. Kennis Methode, 14(4), 324-345, 1990.

BIJSTERVELD, Karin. De natuurlijke ouderdom: een grenzeloze geschiedenis. Kennis Methode, 15(1), 62-86, 1991.

Bruno Latours program to reveal the production of 'nature' and 'society' by following scientists at work, is used to describe post-war discussions in The Netherlands about aging. Physicians initially interpreted certain phenomena as aspects of 'natural' aging, whereas they later tried to categorize these phenomena as the consequences of the treatment and environment of the elderly. Social scientists at first saw retirement as a highly traumatic event, but later proposed to see retirement as part of a natural mental development of elderly people. Although the article shows the utility of Latours program, it also mentions some methodological problems.

BIJSTERVELD, Karin and MESMAN, Jessica. Wie van de drie: Wil de ware wetenschapsonderzoeker opstaan? Kennis Methode, 14(4), 384-389, 1990.

Review of Malcolm Ashmore, Michael Mulkay and Trevor Pinch: *Health and Efficiency: A Sociology of Health Economics*, Open University Press, Milton Keynes, 1989.

BILGRAMI, Akeel. "Meaning, Holism and Use" in *Truth and Interpretation: Perspectives on the Philosophy of Donald Davidson*, LE PORE, Ernest (ed), 101-122. Cambridge, Blackwell, 1986.

This paper defends the idea of a truth-conditional semantic theory against Michael Dummett's criticisms. It situates the dispute in the connection between meaning and holism and defends Davidson's holism against Dummett's criticisms of it. It also criticizes John McDowell's and Christopher Peacocke's discussions of these subjects.

BILIMORIA, Purusottama. Heidegger and the Japanese Connection. J Brit Soc Phenomenol, 22(1), 3-20, Ja 91.

Against the current furor over Heidegger's alleged links with Nazis, the paper explores Heidegger's associations with the non-Western world. Heidegger was responsible for a small revolution among a group of Japanese philosophers who had been his students. He also had contacts with Chinese and Indian thinkers, and at a critical time in his life turned to a study of Taoism. Despite these contacts, and later conversations with J L Mehta and Raimundo Panikkar, Heidegger does not seem to have been deeply influenced by them. Post-Heideggerian philosophers have remained entrenched in the Eurocentric tradition, while it has been left to Asian scholars to pursue seriously the task of cross-cultural philosophizing which Heidegger had nevertheless thought a necessary anti-thesis to the 'Europeanisation of the world'.

BILIMORIA, Purusottama. Hindu Doubts About God: Towards a Mīmāmsā Deconstruction. Int Phil Quart, 30(4), 481-499, D 90.

The essay questions the prevailing view that Hindu philosophy either univocally and without recourse to reason accepts belief in the Transcendent (in one of its polymorphic forms) or forecloses doubt and disbelief in this matter. The Nyāya gave persuasive cosmological "proofs," basing their arguments on quasi-ontological, moral and authorial considerations (e.g., the magnificence of scripture, etc.) However, each such move was systematically criticised and refuted by the Mīmāmsā, ironically the most orthodox Indian school. Their critique echoes a kind of Humean, moral-*theodikē*, *onto-logos* and authorial scepticism, indicating a deconstructive tendency which Hinduism and Buddhism shared alike.

BILIMORIA, Purusottama. "Indian Ethics" in *A Companion to Ethics*, SINGER, Peter (ed), 43-57. Cambridge, Blackwell, 1991.

Ethics as the lived moral tradition has long been a prime Indian preoccupation, but ethics as a system of formal and abstract theorizing on moral issues appears to be absent. The article questions this supposition and shows by undertaking a historical survey of the growth of moral practices and ideas that the concern with ethics has been rich and varied in the Indian tradition. This is traced by examining the concept of dharma in ancient and classical thinking, virtue ethics of Jainism, and the modern extensions of key moral concepts such as satyagraha and ahimsa (nonviolent confrontation) in Gandhi's practical ethics.

BILIMORIA, Purusottama. A Problem for Radical (Onto-Theos) Pluralism. Sophia (Australia), 30(1), 21-33, Jl 91.

BILLOT, Antoine. Aggregation of Preferences: The Fuzzy Case. Theor Decis, 30(1), 51-93, Ja 91.

The basic purpose of this paper is to link both theorems of impossibility and existence by introducing fuzzy relations of preference and an exogeneous requirement, the planner's one, and then proving the fundamental part played by the extremist agents, leximin and leximax. In other words, to bring out the link between the planner's requirement and the difficulty of the transition from individual to collective, as well as the theoric relation between this requirement and the extremist agents, we define a fuzzy behavior of preference which allows us to build up two determinant fuzzy coalitions. These coalitions will be the base of the planner's requirement and the link between pessimistic results (Arrow's impossibility) and optimistic ones (May's theorem of majority choice).

BILOW, Scott H. Rationality and Moral Status. Proc Phil Educ, 46, 172-175, 1990.

Response to Mark Weinstein's "Reason and the Child." Questions the connection between "rationality" and children's moral status.

BINEHAM, Jeffery L. Against Common Sense: Avoiding Cartesian Anxiety. Phil Rhet, 24(2), 159-163, 1991.

BINNS, Peter. Response to Mendus's "Liberal Man". Philosophy, 26, 59-76, 90 Supp.

BINNS, Peter. "Response to Mendus's 'Liberal Man'" in *Philosophy and Politics*, HUNT, G M K (ed), 59-76. New York, Cambridge Univ Pr, 1991.

BIRD, Otto. "A Dialectical Version of Philosophical Discussion" in *Freedom in the Modern World: Jacques Maritain, Yves R Simon, Mortimer J Adler*, TORRE, Michael D (ed), 57-63. Notre Dame, Univ Notre Dame Pr, 1989.

BIRMINGHAM, Peg E. *Logos* and the Place of the Other. Res Phenomenol, 20, 34-54, 1990.

BIRMINGHAM, Peg. The Time of the Political. Grad Fac Phil J, 14(2)-15(1), 25-45, 1991.

In various essays, Lacoue-Labarthe argues that Keidegger's thinking contains an unacknowledged theory of mimesis understood as identification. This understanding of mimesis, Lacoue-Labarthe charges, permits Heidegger to identify with National Socialism. This essays suggests that Lacoue-Labarthe overlooks a crucial aspect of the discussion of destiny and historicity in Being and Time, namely, Geidegger's discussion of "Erwidert": Dasein's response to its repeatable historical possibilities. This notion of Erwidert, itself rooted in the temporality of the moment (Augenblick) allows for the possibility of thinking something like a "critical mimesis" in Being and Time, which, in turn, allows for a rethinking of Heidegger's understanding of a "people". The essay traces this notion in Heidegger's Nietzsche Lectures. The essay traces this notion in Heidegger's understanding of mimesis does not articulate a philosophy of history, but instead opens the way for rethinking political judgment.

BIRNBACHER, Dieter. "Natur" als Massstab menschlichen Handelns. Z Phil Forsch, 45(1), 60-76, Ja-Mr 91.

The essays examine the part that the concept of nature is made to play in recent ethics, especially in environmental ethics and the ethics of the new reproductive techniques. It argues against naturalistic tendencies in these fields and puts forward the thesis that naturalistic ways of thinking in ethics cannot, as is frequently done, be countered by naturalistic fallacy arguments, since the passage from is to ought in naturalistic ethical arguments is, generally, interpreted not as a deductive but as a normative step. Finally, normative arguments are given against taking nature as the model to guide our behavior with regard to it or to ourselves.

BIRNBACHER, Dieter. Schopenhauers Idee einer rekonstruktiven Ethik (mit Anwendungen auf die moderne Medizin-Ethik). Schopenhauer Jahr, 71, 26-44, 1990.

The contribution argues that Schopenhauer's ethics is the most up-to-date part of his philosophy. As against Kant's a priori moral philosophy it is resolutely anti-objectivist, concrete, and based on empirical anthropology. Moreover, it very closely anticipates modern reconstructivist ethics such as the "principles" approach in medical ethics adopted, among others, by Beauchamp and Childress. Some aspects of this approach are critically discussed and tentatively applied to some topics of current interest in medical ethics.

BIRÓ, Balázs. On Generalizations of a Theorem of Vaught. Notre Dame J Form Log, 31(2), 330-336, Spr 90.

This paper deals with the cylindric algebraic version of Vaught's theorem on the existence of prime models of atomic theories. It is proved that the algebraic version proved by Serény, which states that under certain conditions every isomorphism between two cylindric set algebras (*Cs*'s) is a lower base-isomorphism, extends to generalized cylindric algebras (*Gs*'s) although it does not extend to generalized weak cylindric set algebras (*Gws*'s); indeed, it is not true for weak cylindric set algebras (*Ws*'s).

BIRSCH, Douglas and DORBOLO, Jon. Working with Wittgenstein's Builders. Phil Invest, 13(4), 338-349, O 90.

BIRT, Robert E. A Returning to the Source: The Philosophy of Alain Locke. Quest, 4(2), 103-113, D 90.

BIRX, H James. *Interpreting Evolution: Darwin and Teilhard de Chardin*. Buffalo, Prometheus, 1991.

A critical examination of evolutionary ideas from Presocratic speculations to Carl Sagan and Stephen Jay Gould, emphasizing the crucial distinction between empirical facts and personal interpretations. Special attention focuses on the life, thought, and influence of both Charles Darwin the materialist and Pierre Teilhard de Chardin the spiritualist, pointing out their similarities and differences. Topics cover the origin of life, Henri Bergson, the ongoing conflict between biblical fundamentalism and scientific evolutionism, exobiology and mysticism. The author as naturalist and humanist views humankind from a cosmic perspective and within a holistic framework. Chapter endnotes and references, further readings, a bibliography and an index are included.

BISHOP, John D. The Moral Responsibility of Corporate Executives for Disasters. J Bus Ethics, 10(5), 377-383, My 91.

This paper examines whether or not senior corporate executives are morally responsible for disasters which result from corporate activities. The discussion is limited to the case in which the information needed to prevent the disaster is present within the corporation, but fails to reach senior executives. The failure of information to reach executives is usually a result of negative information blockage, a phenomenon caused by the differing roles of constraints and goals within corporations. Executives should be held professionally responsible not only for trying to prevent negative information blockage, but for succeeding. It is concluded that executives are professionaly responsible for fulfilling their moral obligation to prevent disasters.

BISHOP, John. Searle on Natural Agency. Austl J Phil, 68(3), 282-300, S 90.

It is argued that Searle's rejection of the possibility of free action in the natural causal order (in his *Minds, Brains, and Science*, Harvard University Press, 1984) is in serious tension with the causal account he has given of the satisfaction conditions for intentions (in his *Intentionality*, Cambridge University Press, 1983). The discussion emphasises the importance of defending a causal theory of action in order to resolve scepticism about the place of the agent in nature.

BISWAS, Goutam. Michael Polanyi's Aesthetics: A Phenomenological Study. J Indian Counc Phil Res, 5(1), 65-82, S-D 87.

BIUSO, Alberto G. Nietzsche e Spinoza. Arch Stor Cult, 4, 93-140, 1991.

BIX, Brian. H L A Hart and the "Open Texture" of Language. Law Phil, 10(1), 51-72, F 91.

H L A Hart and the "Open Texture" of Language tries to clarify the writings of both Hart and Friedrich Waismann on "open texture." In Waismann's work, "open texture" referred to the potential vagueness of words under extreme (hypothetical) circumstances. Hart's use of the term was quite different, and his work has been misunderstood because those differences were underestimated. Hart should not be read as basing his argument for judicial discretion on the nature of language; primarily, he was putting forward a policy argument for why rules should be applied in a way which would require that discretion.

BLACK, John. Quantifying Support. Inform Log, 13(1), 21-30, Wint 91.

I examine a quantitative scale for estimating argumentative support utilizing a version of the probability calculus. The degree of support an argument lends to its conclusion is measured by the amount of acceptability received by the conclusion from its premisses. Acceptability is assigned to the premisses and propagated through the support structure of the argument according to rules (for linked and convergent support) which echo the probabilistic rules for dealing with conjunction and disjunction respectively. Accommodation is made for such features as counter-considerations to premisses and inferences. The scheme is tested against Stephen Thomas's adjectival method of estimating support.

BLACK, Robert. Moral Scepticism and Inductive Scepticism. Proc Aris Soc, 90, 65-82, 1989-90.

Viewing moral scepticism as the rejection of objective desirabilities, inductive scepticism may be seen as the rejection of objective believabilities. Moral scepticism leads naturally to amoralism rather than subjectivism, and inductive scepticism undermines not our practices of induction but only a view about justification. The two scepticisms together amount to the adoption of a defensibly narrow, formal view of reason.

BLACKBURN, Simon. Hume and Thick Connexions. Phil Phenomenol Res, 50 SUPP, 237-250, Fall 90.

BLACKBURN, Simon. Just Causes. Phil Stud, 61(1-2), 3-17, F 91.

This paper considers the realist contention in ethics, that contrary to claims by some anti-realists, ethical properties are genuinely explanatory. From a 'projectivist' perspective I seek to explain why this is so, concluding that no argument against that point of view can derive from its phenomenon.

BLACKBURN, Simon. Reply to Sturgeon's "Contents and Causes" A Reply to Blackburn. Phil Stud, 61(1-2), 39-42, F 91.

BLACKMORE, John. Ernst Mach Leaves "The Church of Physics". Brit J Phil Sci, 40(4), 519-540, D 89.

A study of the published and unpublished parts of Ernst Mach's last notebook (1910-14) suggests that Max Planck's attack (1908-11) provoked Mach into opposing 'The Church of Physics' more strongly than previously realized. Shortly after Mach threatened to leave the discipline if belief in atoms were required. Albert Einstein tried to persuade him to accept atomism (September 1910). Mach declined to mention Einstein again in publications and increasingly criticized 'The Church of Physics'. (edited)

BLACKSON, Thomas A. Plato and the Senses of Words. J Hist Phil, 29(2), 169-182, Ap 91.

BLAIR, Sara. Henry James and the Paradox of Literary Mastery. Phil Lit, 15(1), 89-102, Ap 91.

In the writings of Henry James, the relation of freedom to literary mastery engenders a paradox of self-reference. His fictions essentialize their insights into the politics of legitimation, obscuring their dependence on forms of power James elsewhere exposes. The imaginative and ethical freedom they secure thus depends on a regulation that undermines the very possibility of freedom. This Jamesian circle proves hermeneutic, however, insofar as it figures the paradoxical interplay of freedom and regulation that informs the culture of modernity.

BLANDINO, Giovanni (ed) and MOLINARO, Aniceto. *The Critical Problem of Knowledge*. Vatican City, Pont U Lateranense, 1989.

The review *Aquinas*, of the Philosophical Faculty of the Pontifical University of Lateran in Rome, has promoted a discussion among the professors of the various Ecclesiastical Faculties of Philosophy in Rome about the solutions proposed by them to the Critical Problem of Knowledge. This book contains the papers written in English.

BLANDINO, Giovanni. La definizione di "retta" data da Euclide e le geometrie non-euclidee. Aquinas, 33(2), 257-270, My-Ag 90.

BLANDINO, Giovanni. Discussione di alcune questioni di cosmologia neo-tomista. Aquinas, 33(1), 29-38, Ja-Ap 90.

BLANDINO, Giovanni and FEDERSPIL, G. Una discussione di epistemologia. Aquinas, 33(3), 579-598, S-D 90.

The authors discuss about the following topics: 1) whether the induction has *an hypothetical-deductive-verificative structure*; 2) whether *all* the scientifical laws are *probabilistic*; 3) whether *all* the scientifical laws are not only probabilistic, but also *approximate*.

BLANDINO, Giovanni. *Discussioni sul neo-Tomismo: Per il progresso della Filosofia Cristiana*. Vatican City, Pont U Lateranense, 1990.

BLANDINO, Giovanni. *Le existentia de deo e le Immortalitate del Anima: Lineas de Philosophia del Esser*. Vatican City, Pont U Lateranense, 1990.

It is a short book on metaphysics and will be completed in the book *Questiones Ulterior de Philosophia del Esser*, (Texto in Interlingus con explicationes in Français, English, e Italiano), Pont. Univ. Urbaniana, U.M.I., Rome, 1991, 380 pages.

BLANDINO, Giovanni. *An Outline of the Philosophy of Knowledge and Science*. Rome, Coletti, 1989.

It is an outline for the students in the faculty of philosophy in the Pont. University of Lateran. Principal assertions: We have some (many) direct cognitions undeniably true (for example: "I see (subjectively) white"). We can prove the existence of a physical world and of other human subjects. Human knowledge cannot be reduced to images, nor to language. Classification of reasonings. Reply to the criticisms of D Hume and I Kant. Neo-empiricism. The principles of verification and falsification.

BLANDINO, Giovanni. Realismo e fenomenismo nella fisica moderna. Aquinas, 33(1), 149-156, Ja-Ap 90.

BLANDINO, Giovanni. Scientia e fide. Aquinas, 34(1), 127-133, Ja-Ap 91.

The author maintains that up to now, de facto, there is no contradiction among certainly revealed assertions "de fide Christians" and well proved scientific data; not only, but at present there is no opposition among theological sentences which are commonly accepted and well proved scientific data (for example, at the time of Galileo the sentence that the sun goes around the earth was not an assertion "de fide," but a commonly accepted theological sentence). The article is written in Interlingus, an artificial language which can be easily understood by any person who knows a Neo-Latin or an Anglo-Germanic language.

BLAQUIER, Carlos P. El concepto de substancia sensible en Aristóteles: Génesis histórica de la cuestión. Sapientia, 46(179), 51-58, Ja-Mr 91.

BLASI, Augusto. "How Should Psychologists Define Morality? or, The Negative Side Effects of Philosophy's Influence on Psychology" in *The Moral Domain: Essays in the Ongoing Discussion between Philosophy and the Social Sciences*, WREN, Thomas E (ed), 38-70. Cambridge, MIT Pr, 1990.

BLASS, A. Infinitary Combinatorics and Modal Logic. J Sym Log, 55(2), 761-778, Je 90.

We show that the propositional modal logic G, originally introduced to describe the modality "it is provable that," is also sound for various interpretations using filters on ordinal numbers, for example the end-segment filters, the closed-unbounded filters, or the ineffable filters. We also prove that G is complete for the end-segment filter interpretation. In the case of the club filter interpretation, we show that incompleteness of G is equiconsistent with the existence of Mahlo cardinals.

BLATZ, Charlie. Agricultura, desarrollo y autonomía. Rev Filosof (Costa Rica), 27(66), 339-348, D 89.

Approaching ethical autonomy first through a critique of Alisdair MacIntyre's discussion of selfhood and accountability in the context of practices, and then in a way departing from this view, I contrast economic and ethical autonomy and show the objectionable side of favoring the former at the expense of the latter. The contrast is carried out, in part, through contrasting product versus process approaches to agriculture and the disintegrated versus integrated lives that go with these approaches. I conclude with an explanation of some of what should be done in ag development policies to ensure both economic and ethical autonomy. (edited)

BLAY, Michel. "Léon Bloch et Hélène Metzger" in *Études sur/Studies on Hélène Metzger*, FREUDENTHAL, Gad , 67-84. Leiden, Brill, 1990.

Cet article a pour objet de présenter et de confronter deux approches françaises de la pensée newtonienne. D'une part, le travail de Léon Bloch, pénétré de philosophie positiviste, qui vise à saisir la pensée newtonienne à travers le système définitif, terminé, créé tel que le présentent les oeuvres officielles. Et, d'autre part, le travail de Hélène Metzger qui vise, en replaçant l'oeuvre de Newton dans le milieu intellectuel et spirituel accompagnant sa maturation et son développement, à saisir la pensée newtonienne dans son activité féconde et créatrice. Ces deux approches apparaissent finalement, pour une large part, complémentaires.

BLECKSMITH, Richard and NULL, Gilbert. Matrix Representation of Husserl's Part-Whole-Foundation Theory. Notre Dame J Form Log, 32(1), 87-111, Wint 91.

This paper pursues two aims, a general one and a more specific one. The general aim is to introduce and illustrate the use of Boolean matrices in representing the logical properties of one- and (mainly) two-place predicates over small finite universes, and hence of providing matrix characterizations of finite models for sets of axioms containing such predicates. This method is treated only to the extent required to pursue the more specific aim, which is to consider axiomatic systems involving the part-whole relation together with a relation of foundation employed by Husserl.

BLITZ, David. "Emergent Evolution and the Level Structure of Reality" in *Studies on Mario Bunge's "Treatise"*, WEINGARTNER, Paul (ed), 153-169. Amsterdam, Rodopi, 1990.

Emergent evolution is a philosophy which stresses the occurrence of qualitative novelty in the evolutionary process, in addition to mere quantitative increase or decrease. This article traces the background to emergence in late 19th and early 20th century philosophy and science. It then examines Mario Bunge's use of the concept of emergence in his ontology of "scientific materialism," and traces the evolution of Bunge's views on emergence, especially with respect to the emergence of distinct and irreducible levels of reality. The place of mind in Bunge's present schema is questioned, and an alternative proposal for the levels of reality is suggested: the physical, biological and social, followed by the mental and cultural.

BLIZARD, Wayne D. Multiset Theory. Notre Dame J Form Log, 30(1), 36-66, Wint 89.

The concept of multiset (a set in which elements may occur more than once) is introduced and the literature is surveyed. A first-order theory MST for multisets is defined using axioms similar to, but more general than, those of classical Zermelo-Fraenkel (ZF) set theory. MST contains an exact copy of ZF and is shown to be relatively consistent.

BLIZARD, Wayne D. Negative Membership. Notre Dame J Form Log, 31(3), 346-368, Sum 90.

Generalized sets whose characteristic functions may assume any integer value, positive or negative, are formalized in a first-order two-sorted theory MSTZ which contains an exact copy of ZFC and is relatively consistent.

BLOCK, Ned. "Can the Mind Change the World?" in *Meaning and Method: Essays in Honor of Hilary Putnam*, BOOLOS, George (ed), 137-170. New York, Cambridge Univ Pr, 1990.

If intentional content reduces to meaning of mental representations, and if internal information processors are sensitive to the "syntactic form" of the representations, not their meanings, then how can intentional content be causally relevant to behavior? So the computer model of the mind appears to have epiphenomenalist consequences. This paper shows that the reasoning just given is fallacious, and then goes on to discuss the issue of whether functionalism leads to epiphenomenalism.

BLOCK, Ned. "Inverted Earth" in *Philosophical Perspectives, 4: Action Theory and Philosophy of Mind, 1990*, TOMBERLIN, James E (ed), 53-79. Atascadero, Ridgeview, 1990.

The inverted spectrum argument challenges the computational approach to the mind with the possibility that things we both call red look to you the way things we both call green look to me even though we have the same computational makeup. This paper presents a different argument to the same conclusion based on the example of inverted earth, a place where colors and color language are both "inverted". It is argued that the inverted earth argument is superior to the inverted spectrum argument.

BLOCKER, H Gene and STEWART, David. *Fundamentals of Philosophy (Third Edition)*. New York, Macmillan, 1992.

This book contains all the resources needed for a first course in philosophy. Features are the usual topics in philosophy: metaphysics, epistemology, ethics, philosophy of religion, and social and political philosophy. In addition the third edition features a new section dealing with Eastern thought featuring philosophical themes found in such great Eastern thought systems as Hinduism, Buddhism, Confucianism, and Taoism. In addition to expository and analytical text material, the book also contains primary source readings from principal philosophers both classic and contemporary.

BLOCKER, H Gene. Interpreting Art. J Aes Educ, 24(3), 29-44, Fall 90.

The paper addresses the questions, do works *have* meaning? Can we *know* what they mean? And can we *say* what they mean? First, a "natural," i.e., nonconventional source of purposive, contextual and identity meaning is discussed; then the particular ways that source of natural meaning is developed in art works—*not*, it is argued, by conventional rules of the sort we find in the semantics of a natural language, but through very general conventions which govern how we are to treat meaning units in works of art, including an emphasis on contextual reinforcement.

BLOEMENDAL, M. "Science and Religion—the Jewish Position" in *Science and Religion: One World-Changing Perspectives on Reality*, FENNEMA, Jan (ed), 47-60. Norwell, Kluwer, 1990.

After an introduction about the fundamental principles of Judaism, the Jewish attitude towards the relation between science and religion is discussed in detail. Some examples are elaborated. The conclusion is, that there is no doubt in Jewish tradition about the absolute dominance of religion over secular sciences. Many warnings against science can be found, since it can take one away from God and Torah (Pentateuch) by mistaken rationalism. Nevertheless, from the very beginning of Judaism the importance of science (in particular natural science) was acknowledged for practical purposes and in order to strengthen our appreciation for the Creator of the world.

BLONDEL, Christine. "Hélène Metzger et la cristallographie" in *Études sur/Studies on Hélène Metzger*, FREUDENTHAL, Gad , 209-218. Leiden, Brill, 1990.

BLONDEL, Eric. "Ruminations": Notes de lecture sur quelques aphorismes de Nietzsche. Philosophique (France), 1(89), 107-114, 1989.

This paper is a translation and a careful philosophical commentary (sentence after sentence) and interpretation of four aphoristic sections of Nietzsche's *Beyond Good and Evil*, i.e., chapters 68, 65, 98, 94 (fourth part of the book: Maxims and Interludes). It takes up Nietzsche's challenge of interpretive "rumination" and tries to relate these short sections to Nietzsche's thought as a whole.

BLONDEL, Eric. Nietzsche contra Rousseau: Goethe versus Catilina? Hist Euro Ideas, 11, 675-683, 1989.

Nietzsche does not know Rousseau's philosophy, but he attacks him and his thought as images and doctrines of moral *ressentiment* and revolutionary spirit of anarchy—which is largely false. But what is the real issue in this case? A philosophy of reality.

BLONDEL, Eric and HAND, Seán (trans). *Nietzsche: The Body and Culture—Philosophy as a Philological Genealogy*. Stanford, Stanford Univ Pr, 1991.

The aim of the book, a translation from French (1986), is to re-center the whole thought of Nietzsche around the central question of culture (Kultur). But the method to be used has to be defined beforehand—it rests mainly on Nietzsche's text, which must be described not only as a discourse containing univocal statements, but as a polemic, equivocal, plural text where the variations and struggle of drives take place. But the main tension which determined Nietzsche's thought as such between a philological, i.e., linguistic reading of the text of culture and the genealogical, i.e., psychological and physiological ones. The book tries to define and locate the various ways of handling this problem and carefully studies the main three metaphors which the text of Nietzsche develops.

BLOSSER, Philip. The A Priori in Phenomenology and the Legacy of Logical Empiricism. Phil Today, 34(3), 195-205, Fall 90.

The legacy of logical empiricism poses major obstacles to an understanding of what phenomenologists mean by "the a priori." For Schlick and other logical empiricists, "a priori" propositions are "analytic" propositions. For phenomenologists such as Scheler and Husserl, "the a priori" applies, among other things, to the intuition of "essences." The views seem irreconcilable. Yet, when the concept of "analyticity" is examined in light of more recent discussions by Quine and others, a rapprochement in understanding, as well as a clarification of phenomenological usage, may be possible.

BLUM, Alex. An Anomaly in the D-N Model of Explanation. Brit J Phil Sci, 40(3), 365-367, S 89.

It is argued that the constraints placed on the non-law premisses of a D-N explanation are irrelevant to their function and will not salvage the deductive requirement from triviality.

BLUM, Alex. On a Mainstay of Incompatibilism. Iyyun, 39(3), 267-279, Jl 90.

It is argued that the incompatibilist's main modal principle, also known as the *Beta* principle, yields fatalism. The incompatibilist intuition is however vindicated by another principle which is shown to be sound.

BLUM, Alex. On Respect. Phil Inq, 10(1-2), 58-63, Wint-Spr 88.

The paper questions the nobility of respect.

BLUM, Alex. A Remark on Individual Constants. Iyyun, 40(1), 93-94, Ja 91.

A proof is presented of the semantic divergence between name and constant.

BLUM, Alex. Tenets of Freedom. Phil Inq, 12(1-2), 65-67, Wint-Spr 90.

The paper compares two conceptions of freedom with the agent's belief.

BLUM, Ann S and TAYLOR, Peter J. Ecosystems as Circuits: Diagrams and the Limits of Physical Analogies. Biol Phil, 6(2), 275-294, Ap 91.

Diagrams refer to the phenomena overtly represented, to analogous phenomena, and to previous pictures and their graphic conventions. The diagrams of ecologists Clarke, Hutchinson, and H. T. Odum reveal their search for physical analogies, building on the success of World War II science and the promise of cybernetics. H T Odum's energy circuit diagrams reveal also his aspirations for a universal and natural mean of reducing complexity to guide the management of diverse ecological and social systems. Graphic conventions concerning framing and translation of ecological processes onto the flat printed page facilitate Odum's ability to act as if ecological relations were decomposable into systems and could be managed by analysts external to the system.

BLUM, Ann S and TAYLOR, Peter J. Pictorial Representation in Biology. Biol Phil, 6(2), 125-134, Ap 91.

This introduction provides an overview of a special issue of *Biology and Philosophy* concerning the use of diagrams in biology. The introduction, as well as the articles, aims to stimulate philosophers, historians and sociologists of science to direct their attention to the role and special characteristics of pictorial and graphic representation in biology. We emphasize the heterogeneity of practice of representation in different circumstances, historical continuities in graphic conventions, and the cross-referential character of all images—perceptual, conceptual, verbal, and graphic.

BLUM, Lawrence A. "Vocation, Friendship, and Community: Limitations of the Personal-Impersonal Framework" in *Identity, Character, and Morality: Essays in Moral Psychology*, FLANAGAN, Owen (ed), 173-197. Cambridge, MIT Pr, 1990.

BLUNDELL, Mary Whitlock. Parental Nature and Stoic Οικειοσισ. Ancient Phil, 10(2), 221-242, Fall 90.

This paper attempts to reconcile the two forms of stoic *oikeiosis*, i.e., the natural impulses towards self-preservation and concern for others. It argues that *oikeiosis* towards our children depends on viewing them as an extension of the self, following the example of Nature's own attitude towards its products. Similarly the sage views all rational beings as extensions of his own reason, thus erasing the potential conflict between self-interest and altruism.

BOARETTI, Tiziano. "Il 'Giornale de' Letterati' e le 'scienze della vita': dibattiti e interventi" in *Scienza, Filosofia e Religione tra '600 e '700 in Italia*, PREDAVAL MAGRINI, Maria Vittoria (ed), 93-117. Milan, Angeli, 1990.

BOBER, Ireneusz. Izydora Dambska's Philosophy of Culture (in Polish). Ann Univ Mariae Curie-Phil, 10, 115-130, 1985.

The aim of the present paper is to justify the thesis that Izydora Dambska's dualism of personality is reflected in her philosophical works. Especially it is reflected in the philosophy of culture which is the scientific description of culture on the one hand, and the attempt to answer some questions of metaphysical and axiological nature on the other. This dualism occurs in her conception of culture, too. This is because Dambska's conception of culture derives from two opposite attitudes: the rationalistic (the origin of science) and the irrationalistic one (the origin of other domains of culture). The products of culture are axiologically oriented signitive creations which aim at actualization and communication of values at the expense of permanently breaking down conventions. In the works of culture man can also overcome his death by expressing his personality, the symbol of which is his own name.

BOCHENSKI, Joseph M. "On the System" in *Studies on Mario Bunge's "Treatise"*, WEINGARTNER, Paul (ed), 99-104. Amsterdam, Rodopi, 1990.

An ontology of the system, in some points different from that of Bunge, is sketched.

BOCHMAN, Alexander. Concerted Instant-Interval Temporal Semantics I: Temporal Ontologies. Notre Dame J Form Log, 31(3), 403-414, Sum 90.

The general problem of the relationship between instant-based and interval-based temporal semantics is studied. The paper is in two parts. In this first part we consider instant and interval temporal structures and specify conditions for their mutual definability.

BOCHMAN, Alexander. Concerted Instant-Interval Temporal Semantics II: Temporal Valuations and Logics of Change. Notre Dame J Form Log, 31(4), 580-601, Fall 90.

The general problem of the relationship between instant-based and interval-based temporal semantics is studied. The paper is in two parts. In the first part we specified conditions for the mutual definability of instant and interval temporal structures. In this second part we extend this 'area of agreement' for temporal semantics proper and consider some natural 'logics of change' generated by this correspondence.

BODEN, Margaret A. Interdisciplinary Epistemology. Synthese, 85(2), 185-197, N 90.

In commemorating Piaget we should not remember his psychology alone. He hoped for a biologically grounded epistemology, which would require interdisciplinary effort. This paper mentions some recent research in biology, embryology, and philosophy that is consonant with Piaget's epistemological aims. The authors do not cite Piaget as a prime intellectual influence, there being no distinctive Piagetian methodology outside psychology. But they each mention him as someone whose work is relevant to theirs and whose interdisciplinary aims will be achieved only if studies like these can be integrated in the future.

BODÉÜS, Richard. L'imagination au pouvoir. Dialogue (Canada), 29(1), 21-40, 1990.

Does Aristotle's theory of imagination provide some propositions we can use in order to grasp his concept of political science of "architectonic" practical wisdom (*phronesis*)? The answer is yes. Imagination, however, seems to be a necessary condition of intellectual virtue both in its task of finding out true political principles and, above all, of achieving deliberative processes according to such principles.

BODÉÜS, Richard. La prétendue intuition de Dieu dans le De Coelo d'Aristote. Phronesis, 35(3), 245-257, 1990.

Does Aristotle's *De Coelo* include some philosophical theology, as still recently sustained by A P Bos (1989)? A very crucial passage (i.e., II, 284 b3) seems to support this view. Once carefully examined, however, this passage only takes for granted the consistency of Aristotle's theory with the popular etymology of the word "theos," as advanced in Plato's *Cratylus* to point out the eternity of celestial bodies. And such a reply to Plato does not suggest, on Aristotle's side, any theological conviction at all.

BOEDER, Heribert. Action or/and Dwelling. Grad Fac Phil J, 14(2)-15(1), 47-59, 1991.

There is a thriving market for ethical "projects." Heidegger's thought cannot compete there. No theory of action, because the "epochal" character of truth itself, the resulting experience of a thinking that is expropriated of its proper topic and aethos, withdraws action into thinking itself. Concern with dwelling in the "house of speech." Here is our point of departure from Heidegger: approaching the spoken Word of the Sophiai, that philosophy has conceived in the corresponding types of logic. Recognise: sapientia sibi aedificavit domun.

BOEHNER, Philotheus (ed & trans). *Philosophical Writings: A Selection—William of Ockham*. Indianapolis, Hackett, 1990.

BOËR, Steven E. "Neo-Fregean Thoughts" in *Philosophical Perspectives, 3: Philosophy of Mind and Action Theory, 1989*, TOMBERLIN, James E (ed), 187-224. Atascadero, Ridgeview, 1989.

BOETZKES, Elisabeth and TURNER, Susan (Guerin) and SOBSTYL, Edrie. Women, Madness, and Special Defences in the Law. J Soc Phil, 21(2-3), 127-139, Fall-Wint 90.

In this article some legal/jurisprudential peculiarities of the Canadian Infanticide Statute are targeted. The Statute is unjust, since it cites mental imbalance (which ought to mitigate or excuse) as an element of the offence. This anomaly is attributed to prejudicial perceptions of women embedded in the law. Two such perceptions are traced—women as uniquely good (and thus particularly depraved in infanticide); and women as morally defective (and thus dangerous to society). Possible options for the reform of the law are considered, and a qualified recommendation made that post-partum depression serves as a special defence for homocide, pending a thorough legal reform addressing the perception of women in the law.

BOGART, J H. On the Nature of Rape. Pub Affairs Quart, 5(2), 117-136, Ap 91.

Four accounts of rape are delineated and analyzed. The preferred account is rape as any non-consensual sex, where consent is understood as informed, voluntary, effective consent. Some objections and implications are examined.

BOGDAN, Deanne. Toward a Rationale for Literary Literacy. J Phil Educ, 24(2), 199-212, Wint 90.

Arguments in Canada for the educational value of literature will shortly collide with arguments against censorship. Politically speaking, curriculum revisions have adopted an "affirmative action" policy towards literary content. Pedagogically speaking, the reader response, personal growth, or "engagement model" of literary education has influenced classroom methodology. The resulting bifurcation of enculturation and personal transformation is partly responsible for the increasing difficulty in adjudicating school text censorship disputes. This article examines justifications for teaching literature, then considers both the censorship of literary texts in the schools and the pedagogical implications of epistemological assumptions about the educational value of literature set out in official curriculum guidelines and implied in classroom practice. Its argument for a theory of *literary literacy* emphasizes the psycho-dynamics of literary experience as both engagement with and detached reflection upon the literary text.

BOGDANDY, Armin Von. *Hegels Theorie des Gesetzes*. Freiburg, Alber, 1991.

This book examines Hegel's concept of law in relation to continuing discussion on the State's instruments of order. Beginning from their basis in the logics of essence and of concepts, the author derives from them wholly new aspects of Hegel's philosophy of law. Civil laws are shown to be interpretations of society, and as such to comprise a systematic structure of freedom. The book concludes with a presentation of its historical field of reference.

BOGEN, David. Beyond the "Limits" of *Mundane Reason*. Human Stud, 13(4), 405-416, O 90.

This paper is a critical review of Melvin Pollner's book *Mundane Reason* (Cambridge University Press, 1987). The main argument of the paper is that Pollner's book is occupied with a series of paradoxes that arise from confusions within its own descriptive language. An attempt is made to 'unbind' the arguments of this otherwise extraordinary book through a Wittgensteinian analysis of its use of the concept of "world" and its understanding of the nature of "paradox."

BOGEN, David. Linguistic Forms and Social Obligations: A Critique of the Doctrine of Literal Expression in Searle. J Theor Soc Behav, 21(1), 31-62, Mr 91.

This paper argues that Searle's theory of speech acts is based ultimately upon a model of linguistic activity that cannot comprehend the local phenomena of speech. Drawing upon the work of Harvey Sacks, it is argued that the theory of speech acts comes to grief wherever it tries to provide formal remedies for the indexical properties of speech. Rather than construing indexical utterances as contingent, elliptical or variously incomplete versions of more complete and literal expressions, it is argued that the indexical properties of utterances are essential to their operation as cogent, coherent, linguistic and sociological objects.

BOGEN, James. Aristotelian Contraries. Topoi, 10(1), 53-66, Mr 91.

According to Aristotle's core notion of contrariety, contrariety is an incompatibility between properties and features, rather than concepts or bits of language. It is grounded in the powers and abilities of agents and the things they act upon, rather than in logic or conventions of language. This paper tries to explain the core notion, and how it bears on some logical and linguistic oppositions we think of as examples of contrariety.

BOGHOSSIAN, Paul A and VELLEMAN, J David. Physicalist Theories of Color. Phil Rev, 100(1), 67-106, Ja 91.

We argue that no known physicalist theory of color can adequately explain how colors are represented in visual experience, given certain reasonable epistemological and phenomenological constraints.

BOGHOSSIAN, Paul A. The Status of Content Revisited. Pac Phil Quart, 71(4), 264-278, D 90.

An extended reply to Michael Devitt's "Transcendentalism About Content" which is itself a critique of my paper "The Status of Content." I show that Devitt's central claims rest on a basic confusion about the argument they purport to criticize.

BOGNAR, Laszlo. Views on Nietzsche in the GDR (in Hungarian). Magyar Filozof Szemle, 6, 785-787, 1989.

BOGNER, Hagen. Zu Jürgen Habermas' Option für Fortschritt, Vernunft und Demokratie. Deut Z Phil, 39(3), 245-254, 1991.

New questions arising in view of the transformation processes evident in modern industrial societies and the radical processes of change occurring in Eastern Europe have prompted Habermas to seek new answers. Habermas's position on social evolution and on progress, reason and democracy are presented in this essay, and the inconsistencies in his argumentation, especially concerning the connection between progress and reason, are critically analyzed. Discussed are also the relationship between the market and democracy, and his links to Marx. The author considers Habermas's advocacy of radical democracy and a radical reformism aimed towards the "idea of a boundless society of communication" as contributing significantly to the restructuring and advancement of the project of modernity.

BOHM, D and KELLY, Sean. Dialogue on Science, Society, and the Generative Order. Zygon, 25(4), 449-467, D 90.

This article is an edited transcription of two conversations at Birkbeck College, London, in February 1987. Its primary concern is a transdisciplinary consciousness that refuses to comply with the tendency toward reductionism and simplification. Some of the problems the dialogue explores are (1) the notion of order (with particular reference to Bohm's recent reflections on the concept of the generative order), (2) the limits of knowledge and the concept of the Absolute, (3) the nature of perceptive or intuitive reason, (4) the relation between matter and mind, and (5) the contemporary global crisis and the possibility of creative evolution.

BOHM, David. A New Theory of the Relationship of Mind and Matter. Phil Psych, 3(2-3), 271-286, 1990.

The relationship of mind and matter is approached in a new way in this article. This approach is based on the causal interpretation of the quantum theory, in which an electron is regarded as an inseparable union of a particle and a field. This field has some new properties that can be seen to be the main sources of the differences between the quantum theory and the classical theory. These new properties suggest that the field may be regarded as containing objective and active information, and that the activity of this information is similar in certain key ways to the activity of information in our ordinary subjective experience. The analogy between mind and matter is thus fairly close. This analogy leads to the proposal of the general outlines of a new theory of mind, matter, and their relationship, in which the basic notion is participation rather than interaction. (edited)

BÖHME, Gernot. Was heisst "sich in der Gesellschaft orientieren"? Deut Z Phil, 39(3), 236-244, 1991.

This article deals with social theory as a means of social orientation. Orientative knowledge as a particular type of knowledge is discussed. The theses is that social theory does not cope with the request for social orientation any longer. Ways to answer the question "In what sort of society do we live?" are discussed: Capitalism, post-industrial society, knowledge or information society, risk society. Development of advanced societies seen as irreversible are put down. They concern: 1) work, 2) gender, 3) relation to nature, 4) technostructure, 5) obsolescence of culture.

BOJADZIEV, Damjan. "Davidson's Semantics and Computational Understanding of Language" in *The Mind of Donald Davidson*, BRANDL, Johannes (ed), 133-139. Amsterdam, Rodopi, 1989.

Evaluating the usefulness of Davidson's semantics to computational understanding of language requires an examination of the role of a theory of truth in characterizing sentence meaning and logical form, and in particular of the connection between meaning and belief. The suggested conclusion is that the relevance of Davidson's semantics for computational semantics lies not so much in its methods and particular proposals of logical form as in its general orientation towards "desubstantializing" meaning.

BOK, Sissela. "Early Advocates of Lasting World Peace: Utopians or Realists?" in *Celebrating Peace*, ROUNER, Leroy S (ed), 52-72. Notre Dame, Univ Notre Dame Pr, 1990.

BOKOR, Donald W and TERPSTRA, David E and REYES, Mario G C. Predictors of Ethical Decisions Regarding Insider Trading. J Bus Ethics, 10(9), 699-710, S 91.

This paper examines potential predictors of ethical decisions regarding insider trading. An interactionist perspective is taken, in which person variables, situational variables, and the interaction of these two sets of variables are viewed as influencing ethical decisions. The results of our study support such a perspective. Ethical decisions regarding insider trading appear to be a function of a complex set of interacting variables related to both the person and the situation. The implications of these findings are discussed.

BOLE III, Thomas J. Zygotes, Souls, Substances, and Persons. J Med Phil, 15(6), 637-652, D 90.

The thesis that the human zygote is essentially identical with the person into which it can develop is difficult to maintain, because the zygote can become several persons. In addition, the thesis depends upon ambiguities in the notions of human being, human individual, human body, and soul. A human being may be individual in the sense of either a biologically integrated unity or a psychologically integrated unity. A person is a psychologically integrated unity, because it must unify its experiences in morally imputable actions. To say that the zygote is a person requires one to assert that the zygote has the same principle of psychological integration, i.e., a rational soul, as one who can obviously manifest psychological integration. The assertion is incapable of being justified in empirical (e.g., nonreligious) terms.

BOLE, Thomas. The Doctrine of Double Effect: Its Philosophical Viability. SW Phil Rev, 7(1), 91-103, Ja 91.

I examine Boyle's thesis that the doctrine of double effect (DDE) has no underived moral significance apart from a context of exceptionless moral prohibitions against doing harms to innocents, and Donagan's counter that the Kantian notion that persons should not be treated as means merely renders DDE superfluous. I argue against both that no cogent argument can be given for exercising one's freedom in certain ways, e.g., by enlisting in the French Foreign Legion, which does not assume a standard of how one should exercise that freedom, from which standard one can reasonably dissent, and that DDE is necessary nonetheless.

BOLINGER, Dwight. Accent on *One*: Entity and Identity. J Prag, 15(3), 225-235, Mr 91.

The morphology of English long ago established a split between the indefinite article (*a, an*) and the numeral (*one*) from which it was derived by loss of accent. But accent continues to be lost under some conditions and strictly maintained under others. *One* as a nominalizer seems to be edging away from *one* as an individualizing pronoun, with accent playing the same role as before. On the other hand, a distinction that was thought to be quite clear - pronoun versus numeral - turns out to be rather blurry. In answer to *How many have you got?* the difference between *One* (quantity) and *Just this one* (identity) is mainly the point of view.

BOLKESTEIN, A Machtelt. Syntax and Pragmatics: Apartheid or Integration? J Prag, 16(2), 107-111, Ag 91.

BOLTON, Martha Brandt. "Leibniz and Locke on the Knowledge of Necessary Truths" in *Central Themes in Early Modern Philosophy*, COVER, J A (ed), 195-226. Indianapolis, Hackett, 1990.

BOLZ, Norbert. The Evil Beyond Good and Evil (in German). Deut Z Phil, 38(11), 1009-1018, 1990.

BOLZÁN, J E. Cantidad o ex-tensión? Sapientia, 45(176), 123-134, Ap-Je 90.

BOLZÁN, J E and LARRE, Olga. La teoría de la ciencia de Guillermo de Ockham: una imagen prospectiva. Sapientia, 45(177), 211-224, Jl-S 90.

BOLZÁN, J E and LARRE, Olga L. La teoría del tiempo en Ockham y la autenticidad de la *Summulae in Libros Physicorum*. Sapientia, 45(175), 39-48, Ja-Mr 90.

BOLZANO, Bernard. *Las paradojas del Infinito*. Mexico, Mathema, 1991.

BONANNO, Giacomo. The Logic of Rational Play in Games of Perfect Information. Econ Phil, 7(1), 37-66, Ap 91.

The language of propositional logic is used to analyze extensive games of perfect information. An explicit axiom of individual rationality is put forward and a strategy-profile is defined to be a rational solution of a given game if it can be deduced from the description of the game and the hypothesis that all players are rational. It is shown that non-recursive games (that is, games where no player moves more than once along any given play) always have a rational solution, but in general more than one. All the rational solutions, however, give rise to the same play, which coincides with the subgame-perfect equilibrium play. The approach is unconventional in that strategies are modelled as instances of material implication, rather than counterfactuals, and the analysis abstains from epistemic considerations.

BONEVAC, Daniel. Ethical Impressionism: A Response to Braybrooke. Soc Theor Pract, 17(2), 157-173, Sum 91.

BONEVAC, Daniel. Semantics and Supervenience. Synthese, 87(3), 331-361, Je 91.

BONICALZI, Francesca. *L'ordine della certezza: Scientificità e persuasione in Descartes*. Genova, Marietti, 1990.

BONOTTO, Cinzia. A Generalization of the Adequacy Theorem for the Quasi-Senses. Notre Dame J Form Log, 31(4), 560-575, Fall 90.

Bressan's sense language is considered in the paper and a version of the adequacy theorem for quasi-senses is proved. Furthermore, we consider a theory *T* based on that language, a definition system, and some strong [weak] extensions of *T* connected with a semantics for which the senses of the wfes are [are not] preserved by the principles of lambda-coversion. The designation rules for quasi-senses are given in a complete form also for strong theories. The synonymy relations are extended to strong and weak extensions of *T* and the adequacy theorem is generalized, e.g., by letting the wfes contain primitive and defined constants. By this result, it is possible to construct quasi senses for any choice of synonymy notion.

BONSACK, François. Une version de l'épistémologie gonséthienne: le béton et les cailloux. Dialectica, 44(3-4), 243-253, 1990.

An interpretation of Gonseth's epistemology that takes certain liberties as well as aiming at deeper understanding. On this interpretation, Gonseth suggests that there are two levels of knowledge: a) an intuitive and informal level close to everyday concerns and to action, which is expressed in natural language and involves concepts that retain a certain flexibility (in the metaphor of concrete, this is the cement); b) a level of theory or of simplifying schemes, which are more rigid and never entirely represent the lower level (this is the gravel of the concrete, which is not autonomous but is mixed in with the intuitive knowledge that it comes from and that gives it a meaning). In addition to these two levels, there is a further one which would be *reality*, for the intuitive level is already a schematization. *Schematic correspondence* is established between the three levels, and the schemes are judged according to their idoneity.

BOOLOS, George. Iteration Again. Phil Topics, 17(2), 5-21, Fall 89.

BOOLOS, George (ed). *Meaning and Method: Essays in Honor of Hilary Putnam*. New York, Cambridge Univ Pr, 1990.

The volume, a *Festschrift* for Hilary Putnam, is a collection of sixteen new essays on a variety of philosophical topics in which Putnam has taken an interest. The contributors are Louise Antony, Ned Block, George Boolos, Richard Boyd, Norman Daniels, Arnold Davidson, Michael Devitt, Michael Dummett, Catherine Elgin, Hartry Field, Jerry Fodor, Harold Hodes, Jerrold Katz, Martha Nussbaum, Ruth Anna Putnam, and Lawrence Sklar.

BOOLOS, George. "The Standard of Equality of Numbers" in *Meaning and Method: Essays in Honor of Hilary Putnam*, BOOLOS, George (ed), 261-277. New York, Cambridge Univ Pr, 1990.

BOON LEONG PHANG, Andrew. Jurisprudential Oaks from Mythical Acorns: The Hart-Dworkin Debate Revisited. Ratio Juris, 3(3), 385-398, D 90.

This article attempts to demonstrate, via the famous Hart-Dworkin debate on the nature and functions of judicial discretion, that substantial jurisprudential disputes as well as theories can, and do, arise from misconceived critiques, whether intended or otherwise. It also seeks to show that, whilst Dworkin's initial critique of Hart was misconceived, his theory of adjudication that arose as a result of responses to his initial views is a positive contribution to learning, although I argue that Dworkin's views are not, in the final analysis, sufficiently persuasive to constitute a radical departure from Hart's own views.

BOON, Louis (and others). Wetenschapsontwikkeling en kundes. Kennis Methode, 15(2), 150-163, 1991.

BOOTH, Allan. "Roman Humanism" in *The Question of Humanism: Challenges and Possibilities*, GOICOECHEA, David (ed), 41-57. Buffalo, Prometheus, 1991.

BOOTH, David. Hereditarily Finite Finsler Sets. J Sym Log, 55(2), 700-706, Je 90.

The set theory of Paul Finsler was Platonistic in its philosophical perspective and was unformalizable. The theory has been revived because of the discovery of new applications for non-well-founded sets. There are uncountably many hereditarily finite sets in the theory. Unusual combinatorial problems arise even in studying the structure of finite sets.

BOOTH, William James. Economies of Time: On the Idea of Time in Marx's Political Economy. Polit Theory, 19(1), 7-27, F 91.

BOPP JR, James. "Surrogate Motherhood Agreements: The Risks to Innocent Human Life" in *Beyond Baby M: Ethical Issues in New Reproductive Techniques*, BARTELS, Dianne M (ed), 201-220. Clifton, Humana Pr, 1990.

BORDES, Georges and TIDEMAN, Nicolaus. Independence of Irrelevant Alternatives in the Theory of Voting. Theor Decis, 30(2), 163-186, Mr 91.

In social choice theory there has been, and for some authors there still is, a confusion between Arrow's *Independence of Irrelevant Alternatives (IIA) and some choice consistency* conditions. In this paper we analyze this confusion. It is often thought that Arrow himself was confused, but we show that this is not so. What happened was that Arrow had in mind a condition we call *regularity*, which implies IIA, but which he could not state formally in his model because his model was not rich enough to permit certain distinctions that would have been necessary. It is the combination of regularity and IIA that he discusses, and the origin of the confusion lies in the fact that if one uses a model that does not permit a distinction between regularity and IIA, regularity looks like a consistency condition, which it is not. We also show that the famous example that 'proves' that Arrow was confused does not prove this at all if it is correctly interpreted.

BORDO, Susan. "Docile Bodies, Rebellious Bodies" in *Writing the Politics of Difference*, SILVERMAN, Hugh J (ed), 203-215. Albany, SUNY Pr, 1991.

BORDO, Susan. "Feminism, Postmodernism, and Gender-Scepticism" in *Feminism/Postmodernism*, NICHOLSON, Linda J (ed), 133-156. New York, Routledge, 1990.

BOREL, Marie-Jeanne. Argumentation and Values (in French). Rev Theol Phil, 123(2), 159-179, 1991.

The question "are values transmissible by discourse?"—similar to that which Meno put to Socrates concerning the teachability of virtue—might be answered in the negative. It is shown how such an answer is its own refutation. A possible affirmative answer requires a detour by which one distinguishes two sorts of transmission. Only the second one takes account of the idea of dialogue, an activity in which the speaker offers his speech to be heard and interpreted while implicitly indicating how it is to be "taken". This indication is made by way of the symbolic construction of an "ethos", a processus which is noted in Aristotle's rhetoric.

BORELLA, Silvia. Contributi piagetiani ad una scienza della mente. Aquinas, 33(1), 157-184, Ja-Ap 90.

BÖRGER, E. *Computability, Complexity, Logic*. New York, Elsevier No-Holland, 1989.

BORICIC, Branislav R. On Certain Normalizable Natural Deduction Formulations of Some Propositional Intermediate Logics. Notre Dame J Form Log, 29(4), 563-568, Fall 88.

We present several normalizable natural deduction formulations of certain propositional intermediate logics. The normal form theorem has been gotten as a consequence of the cut elimination theorem for corresponding sequent calculi.

BORICIC, Branislav. Some Modifications of the Gödel Translation of Classical Intuitionistic Logic. Bull Sect Log, 19(3), 84-86, O 90.

We consider some variants of the Gödel double-negation embeddings and describe some classes of superintuitionistic first-order predicate logics in which the classical first-order calculus is interpretable in such a way. Also, we find the minimal extensions of the Heyting logic in which the classical predicate logic can be embedded by means of these translations.

BOROVIK, Aleksandr Vasilievich and POIZAT, Bruno Petrovich. Tores et *p*-Groupes. J Sym Log, 55(2), 478-491, Je 90.

Dans un groupe de rang de Morley fini, les 2-sous-groupes maximaux sont localement finis et conjugués.

BORSCHE, Tilman. "Die Säkularisierung des 'Tertium comparationis'" in *Leibniz, Humboldt, and the Origins of Comparativism*, DE MAURO, Tullio (ed), 103-118. Philadelphia, John Benjamins, 1990.

It is well-known that both Leibniz and Humboldt compare languages. Similarities, which lie in the nature of the field, are obvious. What they do, however, is not quite the same type of thing. The underlying concept of language, the general epistemological foundation and, therefore, the purpose of studying languages is distinctly different between these two authors. The article presents and discusses these differences by first dealing with Leibniz's position on these questions, and subsequently with Humboldt's views. (edited)

BORUAH, Bijoy H. Emotion and Belief. J Indian Counc Phil Res, 5(1), 1-20, S-D 87.

Emotions are founded on beliefs, which are both reasons for and causes of emotions. The nature of belief-emotion causation is spelt out in terms of (a) evaluative and (b) existential beliefs. The appropriate combination of (a) and (b) explains the occurrence of emotions.

BORUAH, Bijoy H. Seeing in the Mind's Eye. J Indian Counc Phil Res, 6(3), 119-130, My-Ag 89.

Two theories of mental imagery—traditional empiricist and modern analytical—are shown to be biased towards two opposite ends, namely sentience-end and thought-end, respectively. Attempt is made to give an unbiased account of images by conceiving them as occupying an essentially indeterminate position which is akin both to sentience and thought.

BORUTTI, Silvana. Épistémologie et questionnement: le modële en tant que forme de l'interrogation scientifique. Rev Int Phil, 44(174), 370-393, 1990.

BORUTTI, Silvana. Kinds of Truth and Psychoanalysis as a Myth: Some Epistemological Remarks on the Freudian Model (in Italian). Epistemologia, 12(2), 213-234, Jl-D 89.

The main assumption of my paper is that the Freudian model is an interpretive model of a specific kind, and that the specific characters of this model refer to particular ways of reconstruction of the individual truth. The object the Freudian interpreter has to analyse (i.e., the unconscious) is an *inaccessible* text: that is, a full of blanks, distorted, ruined text. Freud distinguishes two ways of interpretation of the psychic text: the *interpretation*, meant as a translation from a surface meaning to a hidden meaning; and the *construction* of the patient's history. In this paper, I argue that, according to Freud, the construction is the basic way of interpretation. (edited)

BORUTTI, Silvana. *Teoria e interpretazione: Per un'epistemologia delle scienze umane*. Milan, Guerini, 1991.

This work's aim is to give a contribution to the contemporary discussion about the epistemological status of human sciences. Both in post-positivist and post-structuralist perspective, scholars share the epistemological thesis according to which objects in human sciences cannot be stated in formalized theories. But, if the construction of individual and social subjects escapes formalism, it nevertheless cannot be lacking in rigour. By means of a re-discussion of epistemological themes like scientific writing, theoretical models and metaphors, interpretation and translation, the author analyzes the patterns of reasoning of those sciences, like anthropology and psycho-analysis, where knowledge is a communicative exchange.

BOSCÁN, Antonio S. El significado de lo teológico en Walter Benjamin. Rev Filosof (Venezuela), 13, 123-134, 1989.

BOSCO, Domenico. Filosofia e ascesi nel Seicento: Il caso francese. Riv Filosof Neo-Scolas, 82(1), 3-45, Ja-Mr 90.

BOSS, Gilbert and LONGEART, Maryvonne. Représentation philosophique par réseau sémantique variable. Laval Theol Phil, 47(2), 185-192, Je 91.

La question du rapport entre l'intelligence artificielle et la philosophie est abordée ici dans la perspective de la représentation de la philosophie sur ordinateur. L'argument se développe en quatre points: 1) avantages de l'approche interdisciplinaire pour l'intelligence artificielle et la philosophie, 2) problèmes spécifiques de la représentation philosophique dus à son caractère réflexif, 3) conception d'une structure de réseaux sémantiques appropriée à la représentation philosophique et à la réflexion théorique sur ce mode même de représentation, 4) esquisse d'un tel réseau universel.

BOSSUET, Jacques-Benigne and RILEY, Patrick (ed). *Politics Drawn From the Very Words of Holy Scripture—Jacques-Benigne Bossuet*. New York, Cambridge Univ Pr, 1991.

BOSTOCK, David. Logic and Empiricism. Mind, 99(396), 571-582, O 90.

It is argued first that logic is empirical in the sense claimed by Quine in his 'Two

Dogmas of Empiricism', i.e., that it is open to revision in response to 'recalcitrant experience'. But it is observed second that there appears to remain another sense in which logic is not empirical. The discussion is confined to propositional logic, with quantum logic as the main example.

BOTTANI, Livio. Noia, acedia ed epochè. Sapienza, 44(2), 113-191, Ap-Je 91.

Acedia, ennui, boredom, melancholia, but also despair, distress have always represented and represent signs of negativity which are generically blamed from the official culture. On the contrary I have tried to show that those signs can be thought positive: as modalities of possibilities suspension of assent, of withdraw of consent; i.e., such as epoché as basis of a good ethics of dissidence.

BOTTO, Evandro. Rosmini interprete della Rivoluzione francese e di Rousseau. Riv Filosof Neo-Scolas, 81(4), 559-575, O-D 89.

L'articolo ricostruisce l'interpretazione della Rivoluzione francese e di Rousseau, elaborata da Antonio Rosmini. Mentre nei suoi scritti politici giovanili sono evidenti le influenze di pensatori "controrivoluzionari" come Carl Ludwig von Haller e Joseph de Maistre, nelle opera filosofico politiche della maturità Rosmini perviene ad una posizione più equilibrata e articolata: i principi affermati dalla Rivoluzione sono "veri e splendidi"; ma essa non ha sconfitto il dispotismo, ne ha soltanto cambiato la forma, perchè si è lasciata guidare da una concezione totalizzante della politica, di cui Rousseau è state uno dei principali ispiratori.

BOTTOMORE, Tom (trans) and FRISBY, David (ed & trans) and SIMMEL, Georg. *The Philosophy of Money: Georg Simmel (Second Edition)*. New York, Routledge, 1991.

BOUCHARD, Guy. L'homme n'est pas l'humain. Laval Theol Phil, 46(3), 307-315, O 90.

L'emploi générique du mot "homme" témoigne symboliquement de la subordination des femmes dans la société patriarcale, du sexisme du langage ordinaire et du caractère sexué de la conceptualité philosophique. Nous examinons les principales critiques féministes de ce vocable et les diverses suggestions de remplacement qui ont été proposées en insistant sur la dimension hétéropolitique du problème, c'est-à-dire sur la nécessité de le résoudre dans le cadre d'une redéfinition globale de la société.

BOUCHILLOUX, Hélène. Pascal critique des philosophes, Pascal philosophe. Rev Phil Fr, 181(3), 295-309, Jl-S 91.

BOUDON, Raymond. "On Relativism" in *Studies on Mario Bunge's "Treatise"*, WEINGARTNER, Paul (ed), 229-243. Amsterdam, Rodopi, 1990.

Relativism is defined here as the doctrine, advocated for instance by Hübner, according to which phenomena can always be explained by a number of incommensurable theories. Relativism rests upon a small number of typical arguments which can be detected beyond the variations in their presentation. Beyond this first thesis, the author suggests that these arguments appear as convincing because they mobilize *a priori* statements which can easily be conceived as going without saying and remain latent for this reason. Once the *a priori* are removed, the arguments appear as unconstraining.

BOULAD-AYOUB, Josiane. "Et la religion le remplit de fureur...". Philosophiques, 17(2), 3-22, Autumn 1990.

I intend to bring out the ideological determinations of Voltaire's *Mahomet ou le fanatisme* and of his attacks on religion. I will analyze his polemical stand against fanaticism and superstition in respect to the historical and societal context as well as the political consequences of this denunciation by the future author of the *Traité sur la Tolérance*. In conclusion the problem of the actuality of the Voltairian struggle will be examined in respect to the contemporary resurgences of religious fundamentalist views.

BOULIER, Bryan L and GOLDFARB, Robert S. Pisces Economicus: The Fish as Econontic Man. Econ Phil, 7(1), 83-86, Ap 91.

BOULLART, Karel. "Tragic Action and Aesthetic Contempolation" in *XIth International Congress in Aesthetics, Nottingham 1988*, WOODFIELD, Richard (ed), 10-12. Nottingham, Nottingham Polytech, 1990.

BOULOS, Pierre J. The Relevance of Gödel's Theorem to Husserl's *Formal and Transcendental Logic*. Gnosis, 3(3), 7-15, D 90.

BOULTING, Noel E. Edward Bullogh's Aesthetics and Aestheticism: Features of Reality to Be Experienced. Ultim Real Mean, 13(3), 201-221, S 90.

Bullough's view of aesthetic experience is related to his account of the beautiful and to our appreciation of a work of art, before the way his treatment of aesthetics slides into aestheticism is analysed. Three objections to this way of handling his writings are examined before it can be seen why Bullough's 'Psychical Distance' theory is indeterminate in relation to the origin and significance of aesthetic experience in our lives. Indeed, what he claims for aesthetic experience is compatible with either the demands of a substantive rationality or those of a qualitative sense.

BOUNDAS, Constantin V (trans) and DELEUZE, Gilles. *Empiricism and Subjectivity: An Essay on Hume's Theory of Human Nature*. New York, Columbia Univ Pr, 1991.

BOURBEAU, Marguerite. Aristotle in Dante's Paradise. Laval Theol Phil, 47(1), 53-61, F 91.

In Canto XI of the Inferno, Dante, through Virgil, explains the moral structure of Hell, which he basis explictly on Aristotle's Nicomachean Ethics, but nowhere does he state in the same way the principe of organization of the Paradiso. The aim of this paper, which was read at the "Villanova Conference on Medieval and Renaissance Studies" in Philadelphia, last September, is to propose the Aristotelian conception of philia, as understood by thirteenth-century interpreters, especially Thomas Aquinas, as a key to the understanding of Dante's Paradiso.

BOURDIEU, Pierre and COLLIER, Peter (trans). *The Political Ontology of Martin Heidegger*. Stanford, Stanford Univ Pr, 1991.

The book uses sociological and linguistic insights to challenge readings of Heidegger's philosophy which either ignore politics, or, alternatively, overinterpret the author's Nazi sympathies. It reconstructs the contemporary philosophical and social fields, situating his philosophy in relation to Cassirer's academic neo-Kantianism, and Junger's and Spengler's populist polemics on class and race. Heidegger's sublimation of the political discourse of the Weimar republic is shown to exemplify the process whereby all formally structured discourse arises from interaction between an expressive intent and the (largely internalised) censorship generated by the social field.

BOURGEOIS, Bernard and DERRIDA, Jacques. Réflexion sur l'état actuel et les perspectives de l'enseignement de la philosophie en France. Bull Soc Fr Phil, 85(1), 1-58, Ja-Mr 91.

BOURGEOIS, Patrick L and ROSENTHAL, Sandra B. Role Taking, Corporeal Intersubjectivity, and Self: Mead and Merleau-Ponty. Phil Today, 34(2), 117-128, Sum 90.

While at first there may seem to be no common ground between the interpretations of self as developed in the pragmatic philosophy of George Herbert Mead and in the existential phenomenology of Maurice Merleau-Ponty, on closer inspection their views can be found to house a fundamental and pervasive rapport between their respective positions. This paper attempts to explain the intersubjective nature of the self and the function of role taking in the development of the personal level of intersubjectivity out of a primordial, pre-personal sociality or corporeal intersubjectivity of the lived body. From such an analysis they can be seen to share a vision of the self that provides a contemporary understanding of a concrete, reflexive individual which undercuts the problematics of the various versions of a transcendental ego or of psychical contents paralleling or replacing an objective reality, and which inextricably interweaves the sense of one's self with the sense of one's existence in an intersubjective world.

BOURGEOIS, Patrick L and ROSENTHAL, Sandra B. Scientific Time and the Temporal Sense of Human Existence: Merleau-Ponty and Mead. Res Phenomenol, 20, 152-163, 1990.

This paper attempts to show that, though Merleau-Ponty and Mead develop philosophies representing differing contexts and traditions, they are led down converging pathways in their examination of the role of the present in temporal existence. For both, lived temporality entails the human praxis which gives rise to a perceived world, and incorporates a temporally extended present within which experience opens onto past and future and to which past and future adjust. Because of this, time, for both, moves as a whole and with depth. Both look at the priority of the present in a strict and in a broad sense, and explicate the sense of a depth of the present. In so doing, they each offer a view of time which is constitutive for the very sense of human existence.

BOURKE, Vernon J. The Ethico-Legal Meaning of Voluntary. Mod Sch, 67(3), 173-185, Mr 90.

Under discussion is the M'Naghten Rule (1842) that "disease of the mind" may excuse a person from legal responsibility. Aquinas's view of ethical voluntariness is helpful here, since it points up the possibility of defects both in knowing and willing moral actions. Various modifiers of voluntariness are described: ignorance of facts or laws, weakness of will, emotional factors (fear, anger), variations in circumstances. Greater precision in terminology on basic ethical concepts, such as voluntary, involuntary and nonvoluntary, would clarify use of the insanity plea.

BOUTOT, Alain. Mathématiques et ontologie: les symétries en physique. Rev Phil Fr, 180(3), 481-519, Jl-S 90.

BOUTOT, Alain. La philosophie du chaos. Rev Phil Fr, 181(2), 145-178, Ap-Je 91.

BOUVERESSE, Jacques. 'The Darkness of This Time': Wittgenstein and the Modern World. Philosophy, 28, 11-39, 90 Supp.

BOVE, Lauren. L'Habitude, activité fondatrice de l'existence actuelle dans la philosophie de Spinoza. Rev Phil Fr, 181(1), 33-46, 1991.

BOVE, Laurence. "Camus Revisited: Neither Victim nor Executioner" in *In the Interest of Peace: A Spectrum of Philosophical Views*, KLEIN, Kenneth H (ed), 197-206. Wolfeboro, Longwood, 1990.

BOVE, Laurence. "On Stories, Peacemaking, and Philosophical Method: Toward a Pluralistic Account of Non-Violence" in *Issues in War and Peace: Philosophical Inquiries*, KUNKEL, Joseph (ed), 267-278. Wolfeboro, Longwood, 1989.

BOVE, Laurent. Amour de l'être et ambition de gloire: le spinozisme de Vauvenargues. Phil Theol, 5(3), 187-220, Spr 91.

More than a parallelism or a simple relation of influence, I emphasize a genuine spiritual filiation between the author of the *Ethics* and Vauvenargues, the young French moralist of the eighteenth century, by following trains of thought in both thinkers from the common principle of *conatus* to their theory of glory. By isolating (in their mutual notion of time) a shared inspiration which has its roots in ancient philosophy, and particularly in Stoicism, a still better understanding of this affinity emerges.

BOVERO, Michelangelo. Hobbes y la apología moderna del artificio. Dianoia, 34(34), 215-230, 1988.

BOWEN, K L and WESTRA, L S and BEHE, B K. Agricultural Practices, Ecology, and Ethics in the Third World. J Agr Ethics, 4(1), 60-77, 1991.

The increasing demand for horticultural products for nutritional and economic purposes by lesser developed countries (LDC's) is well-documented. Technological demands of the LDC's producing horticultural products is also increasing. Pesticide use is an integral component of most agricultural production, yet chemicals are often supplied without supplemental information vital for their safe and efficient implementation. Illiteracy rates in developing countries are high, making pesticide education even more challenging. For women, who perform a significant share of agricultural tasks, illiteracy rates are even higher than for men. The dilemma exists of how a developing country can improve its nutritional and economic situation without giving consideration to social and environmental consequences.

BOWERS, C A. An Open Letter to Maxine Greene on "The Problem of Freedom in an Era of Ecological Interdependence". Educ Theor, 41(3), 325-330, Sum 91.

BOWIE, Andrew. Revealing the Truth of Art. Rad Phil, 58, 20-24, Sum 91.

BOWIE, Norman E. Challenging the Egoistic Paradigm. Bus Ethics Quart, 1(1), 1-21, Ja 91.

Most economists are committed to some version of egoism. After distinguishing among the various sorts of egoistic claims, I cite the empirical literature against psychological egoism and show that attempts to account for this data make these economists' previous empirical claims tautological. Moreover, the assumption of egoism has undesirable consequences, especially for students; if people believe that others behave egoistically, they are more likely to behave egoistically themselves. As an alternative to egoism I recommend the commitment model of Robert Frank. The equivalent of egoism at the organizational level is that business firms seek (should seek) to maximize profits. I present arguments to show that a conscious attempt by managers to maximize profits is likely to fail. A committed altruism is more likely to raise profits. I suggest that a firm should take as its primary purpose providing meaningful work for employees.

BOWLDEN, Larry S. "They Read Novels, Don't They?" Using Novels in Teaching Philosophy. Teach Phil, 13(4), 359-364, D 90.

BOWLES, George. Evaluating Arguments: The Premise-Conclusion Relation. Inform Log, 13(1), 1-20, Wint 91.

The purpose of this paper is to ascertain under what conditions an argument is good or bad with respect to the relation between its premises and its conclusion. In pursuance of this goal, it examines six competing theories. After considering arguments for or against these theories, the paper finds in favor of the sixth theory. It concludes that an argument is good, with respect to the relation between its premises and conclusion, when and only when attributed and actual degrees of favorable relevance of its premises to its conclusion agree.

BOWLES, George. Propositional Relevance. Inform Log, 12(2), 65-77, Spr 90.

The sense in which an argument's premises can be relevant or irrelevant to its conclusion is captured in the following definitions, which, in simpler versions, were mistakenly rejected over sixty-five years ago: "Proposition '*p*' is relevant to proposition '*q*' if and only if, considering only '*p*' and '*q*', the probability of '*q*' conditional on '*p*' is greater or less than 1/2; and '*p*' is irrelevant to '*q*' if and only if, considering only '*p*' and '*q*', the probability of '*q*' conditional on '*p*' is 1/2."

BOWMAN, Elizabeth A and STONE, Robert V. "'Making the Human' in Sartre's Unpublished Dialectical Ethics" in *Writing the Politics of Difference*, SILVERMAN, Hugh J (ed), 111-122. Albany, SUNY Pr, 1991.

BOXILL, Bernard R. "Equality, Discrimination and Preferential Treatment" in *A Companion to Ethics*, SINGER, Peter (ed), 333-342. Cambridge, Blackwell, 1991.

BOYD, Dwight R and KOHLBERG, Lawrence and LEVINE, Charles. "The Return of Stage 6: Its Principle and Moral Point of View" in *The Moral Domain: Essays in the Ongoing Discussion between Philosophy and the Social Sciences*, WREN, Thomas E (ed), 151-181. Cambridge, MIT Pr, 1990.

BOYD, Dwight R. "The Study of Moral Development: A Bridge over the "Is-Ought" Gap" in *The Moral Domain: Essays in the Ongoing Discussion between Philosophy and the Social Sciences*, WREN, Thomas E (ed), 129-150. Cambridge, MIT Pr, 1990.

BOYD, Dwight. One Man's Reflection on a Masculine Role in Feminist Ethics: Epistemic versus Political Privilege. Proc Phil Educ, 46, 286-299, 1990.

This paper addresses the question of a masculine role in the doing and teaching of feminist ethics. The problem is focused in terms of the identification of two minimal assumptions of feminist ethics and then explored in terms of what seems required of men in order to accommodate each of these assumptions in turn. Competing kinds of privilege integrate the analysis. It is argued first that men need to assume a relatively passive, supportive role in the face of women's "epistemic privilege" to interpret their gender-based oppression. Then, on the understanding of gender as a hierarchical relationship of power inequality between the sexes, an active masculine role is articulated in terms of the need for men to critique our gender-based political privilege. This is illustrated both in terms of how it is manifested in the failing to take up as our moral problem our complicity in crucial aspects of women's oppression, such as sexual violence, and in terms of how it is expressed more indirectly through the mapping of gender onto our place and way of doing and teaching ethics.

BOYD, Richard (ed) and GASPER, Philip (ed) and TROUT, J D (ed). *The Philosophy of Science*. Cambridge, MIT Pr, 1991.

BOYD, Richard. Realism, Anti-Foundationalism and the Enthusiasm for Natural Kinds. Phil Stud, 61(1-2), 127-148, F 91.

BOYD, Richard. "Realism, Approximate Truth, and Philosophical Method" in *Scientific Theories*, SAVAGE, C Wade (ed), 355-391. Minneapolis, Univ of Minn Pr, 1990.

BOYD, Richard. "Realism, Conventionality, and 'Realism About'" in *Meaning and Method: Essays in Honor of Hilary Putnam*, BOOLOS, George (ed), 171-195. New York, Cambridge Univ Pr, 1990.

BOYER, Alain. Le temps de l'action. Rev Phil Fr, 180(4), 651-663, O-D 90.

BOYER, Jeannine Ross and NELSON, James Lindemann. A Comment on Fry's "The Role of Caring in a Theory of Nursing Ethics". Hypatia, 5(3), 153-158, Fall 90.

Our response to Sara Fry's paper focuses on the difficulty of understanding her insistence on the *fundamental* character of caring in a theory of nursing ethics. We discuss a number of problems her text throws in the way of making sense of this idea, and outline our own proposal for how caring's role may be reasonably understood: not as an alternative *object of value*, competing with autonomy or patient good, but rather as an alternative *way of responding* toward that which is of value.

BOYLAN, Barbara and MACHAMER, Peter K. Ethics and News. Bus Prof Ethics J, 9(1-2), 53-64, Spr-Sum 90.

In this paper we consider a number of examples of ways in which ethical conflicts arise for professionals covering the news. The first part of the paper raises problems concerning the nature of news and the responsibilities of news professionals. The second part of the paper sketchily provides a way of thinking about professional ethics that can be applied to our problems about the news. We offer a few suggestions to resolve some of the conflicts that we have raised.

BOYLE, Joseph. Marriage is an Institution Created by God: A Philosophical Analysis. Proc Cath Phil Ass, 63, 2-15, 1990.

BOYLE, Philip and COLLOPY, Bart and JENNINGS, Bruce. New Directions in Nursing Home Ethics. Hastings Center Rep, 21(2), Supp 1-16, Mr-Ap 91.

In the face of critical changes now shaping nursing home care, this article examines a number of ethical problems: the cultural disparagement of nursing homes, the moral perplexities of access and placement, the constraints of the "total institution," the conflict between individiual autonomy and common good, the moral agency of nursing home residents, the use of restraints, the paradox of government regulation. The article calls on bioethics to direct explicit attention to long term care issues, particularly the issues of autonomy and regulation.

BOYLE, Robert and HARWOOD, John T (ed). *The Early Essays and Ethics of Robert Boyle*. Carbondale, So Illinois Univ Pr, 1991.

BOYLE, William J. "Maritain and the Future of Reason" in *From Twilight to Dawn: The Cultural Vision of Jacques Maritain*, REDPATH, Peter A (ed), 155-164. Notre Dame, Univ Notre Dame Pr, 1990.

BOZONIS, George. "Le Temps est-il un critere de l'Art" in *XIth International Congress in Aesthetics, Nottingham 1988*, WOODFIELD, Richard (ed), 13-14. Nottingham, Nottingham Polytech, 1990.

BRAATEN, Jane. Towards a Feminist Reassessment of Intellectual Virtue. Hypatia, 5(3), 1-14, Fall 90.

This paper presents an argument for reconceptualizing (human) intelligence as intellectual virtue, and makes some proposals as to how we would understand intellectual virtue if feminist values were taken into account. Several abilities are identified which are closely connected to one aim that is common to most feminists: the building of communities in which well-being is possible.

BRADFORD, Dennis E. *A Thinker's Guide to Living Well*. La Salle, Open Court, 1989.

This work is a plan for living more successfully. There is one best route: adopt a reasonable goal, postpone gratification, work hard, and learn from your mistakes. The plan involves understanding how to evaluate your health, how to eliminate bad habits, how to inculcate good habits, how to do your best in school, how to get and hold a job, how to become so wealthy that you don't need to work at a job anymore, and, most importantly, how to select a satisfying long-term project that will provide meaning, fulfillment, and tranquillity.

BRADLEY, James. Richard Rorty and the Image of Modernity. Heythrop J, 32(2), 249-253, Ap 91.

BRADY, Ross T. Gentzenization and Decidability of Some Contraction-Less Relevant Logics. J Phil Log, 20(1), 97-117, F 91.

The object is to provide Cut-free Gentzenizations for the contraction-less relevant logics DW, TW, and EW. Together with my earlier paper, "The Gentzenization and Decidability of RW", (JPL, 1990) this now establishes Gentzenizations for all the main contraction-less relevant logics. Dunn, in his Gentzenization of R_+, had introduced a second structural connective and use was made of this for RW. However, for DW, TW, and EW, a third structural connective is introduced, representing co-tenability. As a result, the decidability of DW and TW is proved using a method of Giambrone.

BRAECKMAN, A. Art's Autonomy and Absolute Idealism: The Role of Aesthetics in Schelling's Philosophy (in Dutch). Tijdschr Filosof, 53(2), 232-263, Je 91.

The transition from Schelling's *System des Transzendentalen Idealismus* (1800) marks the difference between romantic and idealistic aesthetics. Romantic aesthetics maintains that the Absolute cannot be recaptured. This idea is kept alife by the concept of irony. In idealistic aesthetics, this awareness is abandoned. The external character of the work of art is internalized, under the guise of "reason". Reason is not understood in an aesthetic way: as the ultimate principle of unison. Philosophy becomes an aesthetic construct. Art loses its exclusive epistemological significance; its transformation into an identity-theoretical paradigm of rationality as such, however, offers aesthetics an unparalleled philosophical strength. (edited)

BRAECKMAN, A. Het Schellingonderzoek op nieuwe wegen. Tijdschr Filosof, 53(1), 113-124, Mr 91.

The article provides a selective survey of major publications on Schelling. This survey includes both the volumes of the critical edition of Schelling's work (started in 1975) and other primary texts and documents that have been published recently, thanks to the political changes in Germany. Surveying the new scholarly work on Schelling, the author notices an important shift: in the wake of the new documentary material on Schelling, scholars tend to gradually pay more attention to the socio-historical context of Schelling's philosophy.

BRAGUE, Rémi and ADLER, Pierre (trans) and D'URSEL, Laurent (trans). Aristotle's Definition of Motion and its Ontological Implications. Grad Fac Phil J, 13(2), 1-22, 1990.

BRAIDOTTI, Rosi and GUILD, Elizabeth (trans). *Patterns of Dissonance*. New York, Routledge, 1991.

A critical evaluation of post-structuralist discussions about the death of the subject and the crisis of philosophical reason, in relation to feminist theorizations of an alternative female subjectivity and forms of knowledge. Emphasis on Foucault, Derrida, Deleuze and Irigaray as well as on English speaking feminist epistemologists like Harding and Haraway. The MAW conclusion points to an autonomous development of feminist philosophy of the subject, which is defined in an asymmetrical relationship to deconstructions of the classical subject of philosophy. The asymmetry is analysed in the light of Irigaray's notion of sexual difference and a position is put forth of feminist epistemological nomadism as the mode best suited to this new female feminist subjectivity.

BRAIDOTTI, Rosi. The Subject in Feminism. Hypatia, 6(2), 155-172, Sum 91.

Inaugural lecture as Professor of Women's Studies in the Arts Faculty of the University of Utrecht, May 16, 1990.

BRAIO, Frank Paul. Lonergan's Recovery of the Notion of Natural Right: Introduction to a New Context for an Old Discussion. Vera Lex, 10(2), 4-5,10, 1990.

BRAMS, Steven J. *Negotation Games: Applying Game Theory to Bargaining and Arbitration*. New York, Routledge, 1990.

Cooperative and noncooperative game theory are used to model the strategic choices of negotiators in both 2-person and n-person games. Exaggeration, posturing, threats, and even outright deception are shown to be rational responses in bargaining and arbitration situations. Different concepts of equilibrium and power are formalized, and their consequences are studied in cases ranging from the Bible to superpower conflict. The honesty-inducing properties of different bargaining procedures, and the convergence-inducing properties of different arbitration procedures, are derived and normatively evaluated.

BRAND, Myles. "Proximate Causation of Action" in *Philosophical Perspectives, 3: Philosophy of Mind and Action Theory, 1989*, TOMBERLIN, James E (ed), 423-442. Atascadero, Ridgeview, 1989.

A causal theory of action says, in essence, that any event involving a person is an action just in case that event has the requisite causal antecedents. In this paper, I argue that a successful causal theory requires that there is a single, unique type of event that proximately causes action. The argument is driven by the folk psychology of human action.

BRANDEN, Victoria. Spiritual Values and "The Goddess". Free Inq, 10(4), 36-37, Fall 90.

BRANDL, Johannes (ed) and GOMBOCZ, Wolfgang L (ed). *The Mind of Donald Davidson*. Amsterdam, Rodopi, 1989.

The fifteen papers in this volume present and discuss Davidson's views on truth, interpretation, and intentional action with special emphasis on their integration in a conception of mind based on the triangle of speaker, interpreter, and shared world. This conception is explained and defended in two original contributions by Donald Davidson. Other contributors deal with the token-identity theory, causal explanation, semantic paradoxes, indirect discourse, the building block theory of language, assertion and convention, metaphor, the third dogma of empiricism, ontological relativity, and externalism with respect to mental content.

BRANDL, Johannes. "What is Wrong with the Building Block Theory of Language?" in *The Mind of Donald Davidson*, BRANDL, Johannes (ed), 79-95. Amsterdam, Rodopi, 1989.

It is argued that Davidson's basic objection to the Building Block Method in semantics is neither that it gives the wrong explanation of how a first language is learned nor that it assigns a meaning to single words prior to interpreting a whole language. The arguments against Fregean concepts and truth-values as the references of predicates and sentences are found to be equally superficial as the arguments against a primitive notion reference defined in causal terms. Davidson's basic objection turns out to be that thoughts do not have a deep-structure which can be revealed by a correct analysis. His constraints on a theory of meaning do not allow for a distinction, as suggested by Dummett, between analysis and decomposition of thoughts. This forces us to a very general decision about how to do philosophy. As a nonreductivist I think it makes sense to assume a basic thought-structure. From this perspective the use of building blocks in semantics is vindicated.

BRANDT, R B. Roderick Firth's Contribution to Ethics. Phil Phenomenol Res, 51(1), 137-142, Mr 91.

Firth rejected both noncognitive and self-evidence theories of ethical statements. He offered an account of the actual meaning of ethical language, following his "radical empiricist" theory of meaning that the meaning of any statement can be expressed by a conjunction of statements which refer only to observable events, as Berkeley and Lewis held for "That daffodil if yellow." So he explained "That was morally wrong" as "If a person were factually omniscient, vividly imaginative, were devoid of interest and emotions concerned with particular persons/places, but were otherwise a normal human being, he would experience disapproval toward that act." People learn this meaning by correction of using "is wrong" to mean only "I disfavor/disapprove that." The article summarizes various criticisms made of this view.

BRANDT, Reinhard. "Das Wort sie sollen lassen stahn": Zur Edition und Interpretation philosophischer Texte, erläutert am B Kants. Z Phil Forsch, 44(3), 351-374, 1990.

The first section of the paper deals with the problems involved in the editing of philosophical writings and lectures taking Kant as an example; particular attention is paid to the *Anthropology* of 1798 which is of interest from an editorial point of view. Section 2 discusses the principles of interpreting philosophical works where this involves the authentic text and aims at objectivity, that is, is neither relativistic nor sceptical.

BRANDWOOD, Leonard. *The Chronology of Plato's Dialogues*. New York, Cambridge Univ Pr, 1991.

This work is a factual and critical account of the more important attempts made by scholars since 1867 to determine the order of composition of Plato's dialogues by examing the development of his prose style. For each investigation a check is made of the correctness of the methodology, the accuracy of the statistics and the appropriateness of the conclusions. Finally an assessment is carried out of what has been established so far, leading to a fairly definite view of the order of the dialogues of Plato's middle and late periods.

BRANN, Eva T H. *The World of the Imagination: Sum and Substance*. Savage, Rowman & Littlefield, 1991.

This book contains a fairly comprehensive critical review of work on the imagination in six fields: philosophy, psychology, logic, literature, visual arts and psychology. Under each of these headings it also presents a thesis, a defense of the imagination with respect to the acknowledgement of the faculty, the existence of mental images, the reality of the imaginary, the force of literary visualization, the establishment of an internal imaginative space, and the world-making power of the imagination. It concludes with an inquiry into the relation of the imagination to the intellect and into the imaginative life.

BRANQUINHO, João. "Referência e valor cognitivo" in *Dinâmica do Pensar: Homenagem a Oswaldo Market*, FAC LETRAS UNIV LISBOA (ed), 47-58. Lisboa, Fac Letras U Lisboa, 1991.

The aim of this paper is to assess the soundness of a Millian argument devised by Professor Nathan Salmon to show that the Fregean argument labelled by him *Frege's Puzzle* should be rejected as being (in a certain sense) fallacious. Salmon's counter argument consists sort of *reductio ab impossible*. The upshot of my discussion is to the effect that such a counter-argument should be rated as a *non sequitur*: it relies on wrong assumptions about the identity (and distinctness) of singular senses, and hence the conclusion is not forthcoming that the envisaged generalized strategy might be used to refute the Fregean account. (edited)

BRASH, Jorge (trans) and HARE, Richard N. La estructura de la ética y la moral. Dianoia, 34(34), 49-63, 1988.

(Spanish version of "The Structure of Ethics and Morals" from the author's *Essays in Ethical Theory* (Oxford, Oxford University Press, 1989). Contains a summary of the author's ethical theory, as set out in full in his *Moral Thinking* (Oxford, Oxford University Press, 1981).

BRATMAN, Michael E. "Intention and Personal Policies" in *Philosophical Perspectives, 3: Philosophy of Mind and Action Theory, 1989*, TOMBERLIN, James E (ed), 443-469. Atascadero, Ridgeview, 1989.

BRAUDE, Stephen E (ed). *The Limits of Influence: Psychokinesis and the Philosophy of Science*. New York, Routledge, 1991.

BRAUN, David M. Proper Names, Cognitive Contents, and Beliefs. Phil Stud, 62(3), 289-305, Je 91.

This paper argues that proper names do not have cognitive contents (or cognitive values), in the traditional sense. It attempts to explain, and criticize, traditional views about the connection between names's cognitive contents and speakers's beliefs. It argues that the traditional view of belief is implausible, and that no semantical feature of a name satisfies the traditional account of cognitive content. The article includes a critical examination of John Perry's recent theory of cognitive significance for proper names.

BRAUN, Hermann. Ein Bedürfnis nach Schelling. Phil Rundsch, 37(3), 161-196, 1990.

BRAYBROOKE, David. Natural Law Theory: The Link Between its Descriptive Strength and its Prescriptive Strength. Can J Phil, SUPP 16, 389-418, 1990.

Traditional natural law theory holds that genuine laws must accord with the universal set of moral rules. This position is much more robust than legal positivists allow, convenient as it often is to call "law" any rule that holds in a jurisdiction. Under democratic processes, laws will be stable only if they accord with people's endorsing M*, which they will be universally inclined to do insofar as they understand M* as optimally reconciling shared human purposes with typical human circumstances. If democratic processes do not prevail, the deviation of enactments from what they would otherwise be supplies a strong argument of long standing for democracy.

BRAYBROOKE, David. No Rules without Virtues: No Virtues without Rules. Soc Theor Pract, 17(2), 139-156, Sum 91.

BRÉAL, Michel and MARTONE, Arturo (trans). *Saggio di semantica*. Napoli, Liguori, 1990.

For the first time a complete edition of the Michel Bréal's *Essai de sémantique*, Paris, 1897, is presented to the public (edited by Arturo Martone, Ist Univ Orientale of Naples). The book presents many interesting problems that still can be revalued in a *pragmatic* point of view. A relevant interest consists, in particular, in the analysis of the human "intention" in the elaboration of linguistic facts. The edition includes the Italian translation, a long introduction and many notes of explanation to the book.

BREARLEY, Michael. Psychoanalysis: A Form of Life? Philosophy, 28, 151-167, 90 Supp.

BREAZEALE, Daniel. Fichte on Skepticism. J Hist Phil, 29(3), 427-453, Jl 91.

Though it is widely believed that Fichte was unconcerned with epistemological issues in general and with skeptical objections to philosophy in particular, his writings contain frequent discussions of skepticism. However, there is a manifest tension between what appears to be Fichte's *praise* of skepticism for its indispensable contribution to philosophy, his *criticism* of it as internally self-contradictory, and his *denouncement* of skepticism's allegedly harmful practical consequences. This essay shows how, for Fichte, "critical skepticism" represents a crucial step *beyond* the "ordinary standpoint" and *toward* an adequate philosophical standpoint. Finally, it is argued that the tenability of Fichte's critique of skepticism ultimately depends upon the tenability of his own version of transcendental idealism: the *Wissenschaftslehre*.

BREDIN, Hugh. Metaphor, Literalism, and the Non-Verbal Arts. Philosophia (Israel), 20(3), 263-277, D 90.

The literalist theory of metaphor holds that the meaning of a metaphorical expression is identical with its literal meaning. If this were true, the force of metaphor would seem to be unconnected with meaning, and this in turn suggests that metaphor could be found in nonverbal sign systems. Literalism is examined in Roman Jakobson and, in particular, Donald Davidson, and the conclusion is reached that literalism cannot be sustained. This conclusion favours the view that metaphor is primarily a verbal device.

BRELL JR, Carl D. Belief as a Condition of Knowledge: The Need for a Philosophical Perspective in Higher Education Reform. Proc Phil Educ, 46, 225-234, 1990.

BRENES, Víctor. Etica del desarrollo: algunos principios y orientaciones a la luz de la docrina social de la Iglesia Católica. Rev Filosof (Costa Rica), 27(66), 407-421, D 89.

This paper attempts at giving a synthetic view of the social doctrine of the Catholic Church, as well as some guiding principles as to its practice, from the perspective of the need for a moral approach to development. The task is specially important in Latin America, an underdeveloped and exploited part of the world. Emphasis is placed on personal and social responsibility as conceived of in the Catholic teachings.

BRENNAN, Andrew. Fragmented Selves and the Problem of Ownership. Proc Aris Soc, 90, 143-158, 1989-90.

The bundle theory of the self seems to conflict with the natural belief that a person is a single persisting subject of experience and action throughout life. The paper describes a certain kind of no-ownership possibility which confirms the bundle theory. Study of subjects with neurological deficits lends plausibility to the idea that personhood comes in degrees, and leaves open the possibility that some experiences are unowned altogether.

BRENNAN, Bernard F. Remarks on Marketing Ethics. J Bus Ethics, 10(4), 255-258, Ap 91.

BRESLAUER, S Daniel. Discovering God in Western Civilization. Bridges, 3(1-2), 69-89, Spr-Sum 91.

The Hebrew poet Hayyim Nahman Bialik anticipated the trauma of disbelief that accompanied the Jewish acceptance of modernity. Some thinkers, such as Harry Wolfson and Sherwin Wine, see the trauma as a clear choice between traditional Jewish belief on the one hand and secular atheism on the other. A study of medieval Jewish thought, however, shows a middle way, a way legitimated by such modern thinkers as John Wisdom. Statements of belief point to the preconceptions and assumptions about reality with which people encounter experience. The discovery of God in Western Civilization, on that account, means the discovery of a continuity between expectations about humanity and its world indicated in traditional beliefs associated with the word "God" and the operative expectations of contemporary men and women. (edited)

BRESSAN, Aldo. New Semantics for the Extensional but Hyper-Intensional Part..... Notre Dame J Form Log, 32(1), 47-86, Wint 91.

BRESSOLETTE, Claude. Ultramontanisme et gallicanisme engagentils deux visions de la société. Frei Z Phil Theol, 38(1-2), 3-26, 1991.

BRETON, Stanislas. Prague: le cimetière. Philosophique (France), 1(89), 87-89, 1989.

BRIANCESCO, E. El lugar de la doctrina social de la reflexión teológico moral cristiana. Stromata, 46(1-2), 83-103, Ja-Je 90.

BRICKER, Phillip. "Absolute Time versus Absolute Motion: Comments on Lawrence Sklar" in *Philosophical Perspectives on Newtonian Science*, BRICKER, Phillip (ed), 77-89. Cambridge, MIT Pr, 1990.

An attempt to clarify how the problem of absolute time and the problem of absolute motion relate to one another, especially with respect to causal attributions involving time and motion.

BRICKER, Phillip (ed) and HUGHES, R I G (ed). *Philosophical Perspectives on Newtonian Science*. Cambridge, MIT Pr, 1990.

A collection of papers delivered at a conference held at Yale University to honor the tercentenary of the publication of Isaac Newton's *Principia*. The six main papers are by Howard Stein, Peter Achinstein, Lawrence Sklar, Michael Friedman, J E McGuire, and Errol Harris. Topics include Newton's views on space and time, on God, on gravity, and on scientific methodology.

BRICKHOUSE, Thomas C. Roberts on Responsibility for Action and Character in the *Nicomachean Ethics*. Ancient Phil, 11(1), 137-148, Spr 91.

Contrary to the view recently defended by Professor Roberts, this paper argues that Aristotle develops a "recognizable theory of moral responsibility." But unlike other accounts of Aristotle's theory of responsibility, this paper attempts to show how an agent makes the morally relevant contribution to his character development even though the agent's early training precludes a meaningful choice between virtue and vice.

BRIE, André (and others). Some Aspects of the Relationship Between the Theory of Socialism and the Perception of an Era (in German). Deut Z Phil, 38(3), 193-201, 1990.

BRIE, Michael. The Development of a Concept of Modern Socialism: Theses under Discussion (in German). Deut Z Phil, 38(3), 218-229, 1990.

BRIGHAM, John and HARRINGTON, Christine. Realism in the Authority of Law. Soc Epistem, 5(1), 20-25, Ja-Mr 91.

BRINK, Andrew. *Bertrand Russell: The Psychobiography of a Moralist*. Atlantic Highlands, Humanities Pr, 1989.

By study of the earliest documents bearing on Russell's formative years, this book seeks to establish reasons for his attitude to sexual morality as stated, for example, in *Marriage and Morals* (1929). An intellectual prodigy, Russell was also the product of a pattern of attachment and loss which goes far to explaining his depressiveness, along with a proclivity for obsessively unhappy relations with the women in his life. The author is closely familiar with the primary biographical sources, having been an editor of *The Collected Papers of Bertrand Russell*.

BRINK, Chris and HEIDEMA, Johannes. Verisimilitude by Power Relations: A Response to Oddie. Brit J Phil Sci, 42(1), 101-104, Mr 91.

BRINK, David O. "Rational Egoism, Self, and Others" in *Identity, Character, and Morality: Essays in Moral Psychology*, FLANAGAN, Owen (ed), 339-378. Cambridge, MIT Pr, 1990.

I discuss two egoist replies to skepticism about the rational authority of morality. *Strategic egoism* argues that the cooperation and restraint that morality requires is the best strategy for promoting the agent's own independent good. However, there are limitations in strategic egoism. *Metaphysical egoism* claims that the good of others is part of the agent's own good so that benefiting others promotes the agent's own interests. My version of metaphysical egoism appeals to Aristotle's idea that the friend is "another-self" and understands friendship in terms of psychological continuity. Its account of the scope and weight of our reason to benefit others meshes well with our other-regarding duties.

BRINTON, Alan. 'Following Nature' in Butler's Sermons. Phil Quart, 41(164), 325-332, Jl 91.

BRISART, Robert. Nature et liberté dans l'ontologie fondamentale de Heidegger. Rev Phil Louvain, 88(80), 524-552, N 90.

It was Merleau-Ponty who stated that the whole of *Sein und Zeit* emerged from an indication given by Husserl and is nothing more than an explication of Husserl's *Natürlicher Weltbegriff* or *Lebenswelt*, which he held at the end of his life to be the foremost topic of phenomenology. This study is based essentially on the Marburg texts that surrounded the publication of *Sein und Zeit* and aims to show why it is very difficult to subscribe to Merleau-Ponty's allegations. In fact, as is shown by a major part of Heidegger's reading of Kant at the time, the existential analytic of the *Dasein*, the backbone of which is constituted by the distinction between the proper and the improper, proceeds from an extreme radicalisation of the typically modern conflict between nature and freedom. (edited)

BRITO DA CUNHA, A. Commentary on the Paper by H C Byerly and R E Michod's "Fitness and Evolutionary Explanation". Biol Phil, 6(1), 23-27, Ja 91.

Careless use of scientific terms leads to misunderstanding and imprecision. It becomes specially critical in the treatment of complex phenomena as adaptation, adaptedness and fitness. The value of the paper by Byerly and Michod is to try to clarify the situation giving precision in the treatment of fitness in evolutionary explanation. The author criticises their suggestion of terms as F-fitness, f-fitness, A-fitness, r-fitness, P-fitness and their concepts. Many other alphabetic fitnesses could be created in view of the complexity of problem. A critical analysis of the paper is presented. The author believes that the suggestion of the several alphabetic fitnesses will lead to unreadable papers and that what is necessary are explanations using precise wording.

BROADIE, Sarah. *Ethics with Aristotle*. New York, Oxford Univ Pr, 1991.

This is a close study (447 pages plus indexes) of Aristotle's conceptions of happiness, virtue, voluntary agency, practical wisdom, incontinence, pleasure and the ethical status of *theoria*. Recurrent themes are: the practical orientation of Aristotle's ethics, and his notion of action as value-judgement. The work explores his many-sided comparisons of practical reason with theoretical reason and *technē*; it ends by showing how commitment to his theoretic ideal may be understood as a fit expression of essentially practical excellence.

BROCK, Dan W and BUCHANAN, Allen E. *Deciding for Others: The Ethics of Surrogate Decision Making*. New York, Cambridge Univ Pr, 1989.

BROCK, Dan W. Decisionmaking Competence and Risk—Comments on Wicclair. Bioethics, 5(2), 105-112, Ap 91.

BROCK, Dan W. "Facts and Values in the Physician-Patient Relationship" in *Ethics, Trust, and the Professions: Philosophical and Cultural Aspects*, PELLEGRINO, Edmund D (ed), 113-138. Washington, Georgetown Univ Pr, 1991.

BROCK, Dan W. The Ideal of Shared Decision Making Between Physicians and Patients. Kennedy Inst Ethics J, 1(1), 28-47, Mr 91.

BROCK, Dan W. Medicine and Business: An Unhealthy Mix? Bus Prof Ethics J, 9(3-4), 21-37, Fall-Wint 90.

BROCK, Dan. Common-Sense Morality. Hastings Center Rep, 20(6), 19-21, N-D 90.

BROCKHAUS, Richard R. *Pulling up the Ladder: The Metaphysical Roots of Wittgenstein's Tractatus*. La Salle, Open Court, 1991.

Wittgenstein's early philosophy become widely known largely through the efforts of Russell and other empirically-minded British philosophers, and to a lesser extent, the scientifically-oriented German-speaking philosophers of the Vienna Circle. However, Wittgenstein's primary philosophical concerns arose in a far different context, and failure to grasp this has led to many misunderstandings of the *Tractatus*. From Brockhaus's detailed investigation of that context and its problem emerges this new and unified interpretation of Wittgenstein's early thought, which also affords fresh insights into the later Wittgenstein. (staff)

BROCKWAY, George P. "Miller on Economics" in *The Philosophy of John William Miller*, FELL, Joseph P (ed), 125-135. Lewisburg, Bucknell Univ Pr, 1990.

BRODY, Baruch. "Current Religious Perspectives on the New Reproductive Techniques" in *Beyond Baby M: Ethical Issues in New Reproductive Techniques*, BARTELS, Dianne M (ed), 45-63. Clifton, Humana Pr, 1990.

Various theological traditions have expressed a variety of concerns concerning aspects of the new reproductive techniques. This article traces and evaluates these concerns which involve reflections on the relation between procreation and conjugal intimacy, on the introduction of third parties into the reproductive process, on the confusion of lineage, on early abortions, on dehumanization of reproduction, and on commercialization and exploitation of human sexuality.

BRODY, Howard. The Chief of Medicine. Hastings Center Rep, 21(4), 17-22, Jl-Ag 91.

"The Chief of Medicine" is the first chapter from a forthcoming book, *The Healer's Power*. It is an imaginative revision of Dostoevsky's "The Grand Inquisitor" altered to depict a physician as the main character. It addresses themes of what sorts of power the physician must possess in order to be an effective healer.

BROGAN, Jacqueline Vaught. Language, Physics, and Geology (and a Few Words on Theology). Man World, 24(1), 1-12, Ja 91.

The purpose of this article is to explore the unexpected similarity among various recent developments in such disparate fields as language theory, nuclear physics, and geology, and to raise some interesting speculations regarding theological and philosophical considerations as a consequence. In particular, the essay examines the misunderstanding of deconstruction as a nihilistic abyss in relationship to the poetry of Wallace Stevens and demonstrates how a similar "gap" in language revealed in his poetry is discovered in different manifestations when pursuing the nutreno in nuclear physics or when studying plate tectonics is geology. The essay speculates that the continual crucifixion of the "word"—an inherent gap in the structure of the universe which makes all life possible—is the necessary condition for both language and life.

BROMILEY, Geoffrey W (trans) and THIELICKE, Helmut. *Modern Faith and Thought*. Grand Rapids, Eerdmans, 1990.

This book is a historical review of theological philosophy, written from the perspective of issues relevant to each time period. The issues examined include subjectivity, revelation, truth, faith, and the influence of several major thinkers. (staff)

BROMWICH, David. Whitman and Memory: A Response to Kateb. Polit Theory, 18(4), 572-576, N 90.

BROOK, Richard. Agency and Morality. J Phil, 88(4), 190-212, Ap 91.

BROOME, John. "Utility". Econ Phil, 7(1), 1-12, Ap 91.

This paper points out a prevalent ambiguity in the usage of the word "utility". It is sometimes used to mean good, and sometimes a representation of preferences. The paper argues that the ambiguity is very damaging, and that the word should be used in the second of these senses only.

BROSIO, Richard A. The Power of Hegemony vis-à-vis the Marketplace of Ideas: Response to Orton. Proc Phil Educ, 46, 156-158, 1990.

This work questions the validity of liberal assumptions concerning a "free market of opinion" and "public criteria for rationality." It was Dewey's accomplishment to see that commitment to free inquiry would have to be reconsidered because of monopoly capitalism's undermining of Smith's level playing field. Gramsci, et al., have explained that hegemony results in class definitions of reality, good, and even of common sense. With regard to the second liberal assumption, it too has been made problematic by the emergence of multiple discourses that characterize modernism and postmodernism.

BROSIO, Richard. Response to Robenstine's "The Dead Horse Phenomenon in Educational Theory". Phil Stud Educ, /, 164-172, 1987-88.

This essay defends two central components of Marxist thought: (1) the causal, dialectical relationships between the capitalist economy and superstructural institutions such as schools; (2) a commitment to dialectically arrived at, historically warranted, objectivity as opposed to ideology which seeks to obscure and misrepresent social reality. The defense has been mounted against "motivational" theorists, in education and elsewhere, who exaggerate human agency because of its alleged independence from the restrictions of economic causality. Relatedly, this defense focuses upon Marx's insistence that the dialectic method allows normative evaluation of the descriptive is, capitalist hegemony, and of fake ideological claims.

BROUDY, Harry S. DBAE: Complaints, Reminiscences, and Response. Educ Theor, 40(4), 431-435, Fall 90.

This article is a response to Donald Arnstine's criticism of discipline-based art education (*Educational Theory*, 40 (4), 415-422, Fall 90). He argues that DBAE may make art a form of escapism, hinder efforts to refine students' tastes, and by its academic orientation impair proper enjoyment of art. My exposition of DBAE as a full-fledged member of the general education curriculum argues that Arnstine's fears are groundless; that, on the contrary, DBAE has shown its ability to provide a foundation for genuine aesthetic literacy.

BROWN JR, Stuart M and FESSENDEN-RADEN, June. Commentary: "Love Canal and the Ethics of Environmental Health". Bus Prof Ethics J, 2(4), 23-25, Sum 83.

BROWN, Charles S. Problems with the Fregean Interpretation of Husserl. J Brit Soc Phenomenol, 22(1), 53-64, Ja 91.

BROWN, Clifford. *Leibniz and Strawson: A New Essay in Descriptive Metaphysics*. Munchen, Philosophia, 1990.

This work counters the picture of Leibniz's metaphysics drawn in Strawson's *Individuals* and also offers a substantive recasting of positions traditionally ascribed to Leibniz. The author identifies three ontological levels, critically distinguishes between full and complete concepts, and carefully discriminates among the varieties of the identity of indiscernibles principle. He argues that for Leibniz irreducible relations must necessarily obtain among individual substances, and that this claim does not violate the general framework of Leibniz's logic.

BROWN, David H. Dionysian and Apollonian Pathos of Distance: A New Image of World History. Dialogos, 26(57), 77-88, Ja 91.

BROWN, Delwin and GREEVE DAVANEY, Sheila. Methodological Alternatives in Process Theology. Process Stud, 19(2), 75-84, Sum 90.

This article served as the introductory public lecture at the "Conference on Methodological Alternatives in Process Theology," at Iliff School of Theology, Denver, Colorado, in January 1989, sponored by Iliff and the Center for Process Studies at Clarement, California. The paper presents a general understanding of process thought, and discusses three theological methodologies represented within this general perspective.

BROWN, Donald A and LEMONS, John and VARNER, Gary E. Congress, Consistency, and Environmental Law. Environ Ethics, 12(4), 311-327, Wint 90.

In passing the National Environmental Policy Act of 1969 (NEPA), Congress committed the nation to an ethical principle of living in "productive and enjoyable harmony" with the natural environment. Thus understood, NEPA can be given either (1) a technology-forcing interpretation or (2) an intelligent decision-making interpretation. We argue that in its subsequent decision to site a high-level nuclear waste repository at Yucca Mountain, Nevada, Congress acted inconsistently with this principle under either interpretation. We conclude that for the foreseeable future, the only way to handle the nation's nuclear wastes consistent with the environmental goal enunciated in NEPA is to leave them in temporary surface storage facilities, prohibit the licensing of any new nuclear power plants, and take all appropriate steps to reduce the nuclear weapons industry.

BROWN, Geoffrey. Is there an Ethics of Computing? J Applied Phil, 8(1), 19-26, 1991.

The article constitutes an attempt to answer the question contained in the title, by reference to three example topics: individual privacy, ownership of software, and computer 'hacking'. The ethical question is approached via the legal one of whether special, computer-specific legislation is appropriate. The conclusion is in the affirmative, and rests on the claim that computer technology has brought with it, not so much the potential for committing totally new kinds of crimes, as a distinctive set of linguistic and conceptual apparatus which makes it necessary to describe computer-related activity in special ways.

BROWN, Harold I. Cherniak on Scientific Realism. Brit J Phil Sci, 41(3), 415-427, S 90.

In the final chapter of *Minimal Rationality* Christopher Cherniak offers three arguments to show that an agent with finite cognitive resources is not capable of arriving at a true and complete theory of the universe. I discuss each of these arguments and show that Cherniak has not succeeded in making his antirealist case.

BROWN, Hunter. Alvin Plantinga and Natural Theology. Int J Phil Relig, 30(1), 1-19, Ag 91.

This article examines Alvin Plantinga's understanding of natural theology within the context of his reformed epistemology. It goes on to contrast that understanding with the presentation of natural theology by the Tübingen tradition as represented by Walter Kasper. The analysis suggests that Plantinga's contrast between the natural theology and reformed traditions is too sharp. Positively, some parallels between these traditions may be ecumenically significant.

BROWN, James Robert. "Π In the Sky" in *Physicalism in Mathematics*, IRVINE, Andrew D (ed), 95-120. Norwell, Kluwer, 1990.

This paper is an exposition and defence of Platonism in the philosophy of mathematics, in the spirit of Gödel. Among other things, it defends the perception of abstract entities, and offers a counterexample to the causal theory of knowledge.

BROWN, Montague. Natural Law and the Environment. Proc Cath Phil Ass, 63, 221-234, 1990.

The charge is often made that natural law ethics is based on a metaphysical analysis of the hierarchy of nature which places human beings at the top. This appears to grant us a *carte blanche* to treat fellow creatures as we please. But this interpretation of natural law is false. Its foundations are not metaphysical but practical. Our obligations stem from our recognition of fundamental, self-evident goods (such as life, knowledge, friendship, and beauty) and from the insight that to destroy these goods constitutes a contradiction of intentional valuation. Natural law does provide foundations for environmental responsibility.

BROWN, Richard S G. "Heidegger: What Is Called Humanism?" in *The Question of Humanism: Challenges and Possibilities*, GOICOECHEA, David (ed), 179-192. Buffalo, Prometheus, 1991.

BROWN, Robert F. God's Ability to Will Moral Evil. Faith Phil, 8(1), 3-20, Ja 91.

Pike, Reichenbach, and others, correctly hold that a God whose very nature prevents him from doing evil cannot properly be regarded as morally good. But they fail to show just *how* God's moral goodness can be effectively independent of his ontological goodness, how God can be "significantly free" and so be morally praiseworthy. I argue that their contention calls for a greater modification of classical theism than they realize, i.e., for abandoning the traditional subordination of God's will to God's (supposedly necessary) goodness. I explore a way of reconceiving the relation of God's will to his nature, so that he actually can be morally praiseworthy, free either to obey or to violate his own moral law.

BROWN, Robert F. Resources in Schelling for New Directions in Theology. Ideal Stud, 20(1), 1-17, Ja 90.

Schelling's philosophy is intrinsically significant for religious thought. His earliest, transcendental perspective depicts God as "nonexistent," totally free ground of the finite I, hence as not understandable by objectifying thought. His next essays portray God's life as a dynamic process undergirding both organic nature and spirit. His reflections on divine and human will, influenced by Boehme, embody a more consistent voluntarism and profound grasp of will as fallen than typically found in Christian theology. Finally, his lectures on mythology and revelation are a scarcely explored alternative to Hegelian and other philosophies of religion.

BROWN, Stuart. "Christian Averroism, Fideism and the 'Two-fold Truth'" in *The Philosophy in Christianity*, VESEY, Godfrey (ed), 207-223. New York, Cambridge Univ Pr, 1989.

BROWN, William and HARRIS, Claudia. Developmental Constraints on Ethical Behaviour in Business. J Bus Ethics, 9(11), 855-862, N 90.

Ethical behavior—the conscious attempt to act in accordance with an individually-owned morality—is the product of an advanced stage of the maturing process. Three models of ethical growth derived from research in human development are applied to issues of business ethics.

BROWNE, Derek. Ethics Without Morality. Austl J Phil, 68(4), 395-412, D 90.

Greek ethics used to be criticised for failing to respect some crucial principles of moral thinking. Now the idea of morality itself is under attack, and Greek ethics is said to be both more coherent and more attractive. This article defends the thesis that Greek ethics is different from modern morality. Ethics is the art of living well. It includes concerns that are a part of our 'morality', but the ancient concept organises those concerns differently. The article describes in some detail the special concerns and concepts that constitute the ancient ethical project.

BROWNING, Douglas. Logic and Ontology. SW Phil Rev, 7(1), 59-67, Ja 91.

Five interpretations of the common assumption that an appeal to logic is basic to proper ontological method are examined. Three of these, namely, those which assume a substantive input of appeal to logical form to the characteral content of ontology, are found to be unacceptable. The remaining two nonsubstantive theses, namely, that an appeal to logical form may serve as a means for designating the subject matter of ontology and for specifying certain necessary conditions on the acceptability of an ontological system, are seen to be more respectable.

BROYER, John Albin. "Comment on David L Miller's 'Consciousness, the Attitude of the Individual and Perspectives'" in *Creativity in George Herbert Mead*, GUNTER, Pete A Y (ed), 67-71. Lanham, Univ Pr of America, 1990.

BROZI, Krzysztof J. The Functional Conception of Culture and the Explanation of the Value-Shaping Process (in Polish). Ann Univ Mariae Curie-Phil, 11, 23-40, 1986.

The presentation of the most recent achievements of development psychology, especially advances in the field of moral development, has provided further arguments for functional analysis. The analysis is here presented from two perspectives, instrumental and institutional. With the instrumental approach, the dominant appears to be the needs indispensable for a given culture, determining its identity, that is, the cultural standard; with the institutional approach, in turn, it is a structure of human actions and cooperation transformed into a tradition. The principal thesis is a conviction that an examination of cultural organizations, that is, institutionalized human actions, constitutes the starting point of the analysis of culture and, hence, the analysis of values. (edited)

BRUCAN, Silviu. Romania's Revolution and its Prospects. Praxis Int, 10(3-4), 318-323, O 90-Ja 91.

BRUECKNER, Anthony. Unfair to Nozick. Analysis, 51(1), 61-64, Ja 91.

This is a defense of Nozick against the charge that his response to skepticism begs the question in virtue of its alleged assumption that the actual world is a normal, non-vat-world. It is argued that Nozick is not committed to that assumption.

BRUMBAUGH, Robert S. The Book of Anaxagoras. Ancient Phil, 11(1), 149-150, Spr 91.

In 1970, J Ferguson pointed out that "the book of Anaxagoras", which Socrates says in the *Apology* cost one drachma "in the Orchestra," had that price in a market far more likely to sell used or discarded books than new ones. This undercuts any length-from-price calculations and inferences which assume that the book in question would be a new, fresh copy.

BRUMBAUGH, Robert S. Simon and Socrates. Ancient Phil, 11(1), 151-152, Spr 91.

Diogenes Laertius has a brief account of a cobbler named Simon, whose shop Socrates frequented, and who noted down Socratic conversations. From Zeller (1885) through Guthrie (1969), historians have treated Simon as "fictitious." But the American School found and identified Simon's shop in the Agora (*Athenian Agora*, Second Edition, 1961). Thus a correction is in order, and Diogenes Laertius's account deserves a closer look.

BRUMFIELD, Robin G and ADELAJA, Adesoji O. Research Note On Equity and Ethics in State-Promotion of Agricultural Products. J Agr Ethics, 4(1), 82-88, 1991.

Many state governments in the United States promote locally-produced farm products. This paper discusses issues related to the ethics and equity of such promotional programs. The paper argues that generic promotion is generally easier to justify in terms of ethics and equity than brand promotion. It also argues that informative and factual brand promotions are easier to justify than deceptive and persuasive brand promotion. Additional equity issues arising when taxpayers finance state-promotional programs are also discussed.

BRUMMER, James. Love Canal and the Ethics of Environmental Health. Bus Prof Ethics J, 2(4), 1-22, Sum 83.

The purpose of the work is to show the interconnection between the scientific, political, moral and legal domains of choice upon the environmental health professionals who were involved in overseeing various health studies done at Love Canal. It suggests that environmental health is a unique area of study where various types of responsibilities apply and can come in conflict and that health professionals must address each of these arenas of responsibility in their investigation and administration of environmental health matters.

BRUNER, Jerome. *Acts of Meaning*. Cambridge, Harvard Univ Pr, 1990.

BRUNER, Jerome. Self-Making and World-Making. J Aes Educ, 25(1), 67-78, Spr 91.

BRUNKHORST, Hauke. Deconstruction or Dialectics? (in Serbo-Croation). Filozof Istraz, 34(1), 89-104, 1990.

The author considers three theses on the relationship between critical theory and postmodernism: theses about the separation between postmodernists and Heidegger, between postmodernists themselves, and between modernism and postmodernism.

BRUNKHORST, Hauke. The Intellectuals at the End of History. Praxis Int, 10(3-4), 250-260, O 90-Ja 91.

BRUNKHORST, Hauke. Romanticism, Rationality and Alienation—the Triple-H-Theory Revisited. Hist Euro Ideas, 11, 831-839, 1989.

BRUNNER, Fernand. L'aspect rationnel et l'aspect religieux de la philosophie de Plotin. Rev Theol Phil, 122(3), 417-430, 1990.

La doctrine de Plotin est traversée par une intention rationnelle, comme le montrent la recherche analytique du premier principe et la démarche synthétique d'explication du monde. Mais le moment rationnel, chez Plotin, ne se dissocie pas du moment religeux. Ce qui conduit l'auteur de l'article à exposer et à discuter l'opinion de Pierre Hadot (spirituels et philosophie antique, 2e éd., Paris, 1987, pp. 237-239), selon laquelle la sagesse antique est pruement et strictement rationnelle.

BRUNS, Gerald L. "The Otherness of Words: Joyce, Bakhtin, Heidegger" in *Postmodernism—Philosophy and the Arts (Continental Philosophy III)*, SILVERMAN, Hugh J (ed), 120-136. New York, Routledge, 1990.

BRUNS, Gerald L. Reply to Crewe and Conant. Crit Inquiry, 17(3), 635-638, Spr 91.

BRUNSCHWIG, Jacques. Sur une façon stoïcienne de ne pas être. Rev Theol Phil, 122(3), 389-403, 1990.

Essai d'explication de la théorie stoïcienne selon laquelle les "impulsions" sont dirigées vers des "prédicats", c'est-à-dire vers des items incorporels, qui ne sont pas des "étants". Les antécédents de cette théorie (chez Platon et les "dialecticiens") permettent d'y voir autre chose qu'un paradoxe artificiel ou gratuit. On examine son insertion dans divers contextes théoriques stoïciens, déterminés par les notions de fin, de bien, d'assentiment, de responsabilité morale et de destin.

BRUNSKO, Zagorka. Boskovic's Theory of Forces in His Treatise "De Continuitatis Lege" (in Serbo-Croatian). Filozof Istraz, 32-33(5-6), 1577-1584, 1989.

Boskovic's treatise *De continuitatis lege* contains an elaborated version of his theory of forces. Starting point of his research work in natural philosophy is two fundamental principles: the principle of simplicity and the analogy of nature. The first principle he took over from Newton, and the second from Leibniz. From the principles of continuity and inpenetrability of matter Boskovic derived the law of forces acting between fundamental points of matter. The force between the particles is repulsive or attractive depending on their mutual distance. It is repulsive at exiguous distances, and attractive at large distances in conformity with Newton's law. (edited)

BRUSHWOOD, David B and SCHULZ, Richard M. The Pharmacist's Role in Patient Care. Hastings Center Rep, 21(1), 12-17, Ja-F 91.

This article examines patient advocacy as a new role for pharmacists. As advocates, pharmacists would assist patients in drug use decisions while respecting patients' rights to make decisions. The role of patient advocate is contrasted with the existing distributive and clinical roles of pharmacists. The article discusses potential problems with pharmacists as patient advocates, such as interprofessional conflict and inadequate training. The authors conclude that the public would be well served by pharmacists who are patient advocates, and that legal scholars, ethicists, and health care analysts should seriously consider adopting policies that encourage such an expansion.

BRYANT, Joseph M. Enlightenment Psychology and Political Reaction in Plato's Social Philosophy: an Ideological Contradiction? Hist Polit Thought, 11(3), 377-395, Autumn 90.

BUB, Jeffrey. The Philosophy of Quantum Mechanics. Brit J Phil Sci, 40(2), 191-211, Je 89.

BUB, Jeffrey. The Problem of Properties in Quantum Mechanics. Topoi, 10(1), 27-34, Mr 91.

The properties of classical and quantum systems are characterized by different algebraic structures. We know that the properties of a quantum mechanical system form a partial Boolean algebra not embeddable into a Boolean algebra, and so cannot all be co-determinate. We also know that maximal Boolean subalgebras of properties can be (separately) co-determinate. A principled argument is developed justifying the selection of particular subsets of properties as co-determinate for a quantum system in particular physical contexts. These subsets are generated by sets of maximal Boolean subalgebras. If we are required to interpret quantum mechanics in this way, then predication for quantum systems is quite unlike the corresponding notion for classical systems. (edited)

BUBNER, Rüdiger. Metaphysik und Erfahrung. Neue Hefte Phil, 30-31, 1-14, 1991.

BUCAN, Daniel. Causalistico-Occasionalistic Dispute in Islam as Opposing of "Greek" and "Islamic" Spirit (in Serbo-Croatian). Filozof Istraz, 34(1), 41-56, 1990.

Die Auseinandersetzung zwischen den Anhängern des Kausalismus und des Okkasionalismus wird im Licht der These von der Entgegenstellung zweier unterschiedlicher Denkarten im Islam untersucht. Nach einem kurzen Überblick der okkasionalistischen und kausalistischen Grundansichten folgt am Beispiel der Erkenntnistheorien von al-Ghazali und Averroës eine eingehende Analyse ihrer gegensätzlichen Argumente. Das Wesentliche dieser Auseinandersetzung liegt in der unterschiedlichen Auffassung des ersten Ursprungs (d.h. Gottes), den Averroës als Vernunft, al-Ghazali dagegen als Willen begreift. (edited)

BUCHANAN, Allen E and BROCK, Dan W. *Deciding for Others: The Ethics of Surrogate Decision Making*. New York, Cambridge Univ Pr, 1989.

BUCHANAN, Allen E. "The Physician's Knowledge and the Patient's Best Interest" in *Ethics, Trust, and the Professions: Philosophical and Cultural Aspects*, PELLEGRINO, Edmund D (ed), 93-112. Washington, Georgetown Univ Pr, 1991.

BUCHER, Anton. Die Theorie der moralischen Entwicklung von Lawrence Kohlberg und seiner Schule und die Moraltheologie. Frei Z Phil Theol, 38(1-2), 57-82, 1991.

BUCHHEIM, Thomas. Das "objektive Denken" in Schellings Naturphilosophie. Kantstudien, 81(3), 321-338, 1990.

"Objective Thought" in Schelling's Philosophy of Identity does not mean thought directed at reality completely independent of the subject. Instead, it means the methodical reduction of the whole relation of objectivity and subjectivity to a basic level identifiable with the pure form of reason as such. The realisation of this reduction relies on the thinking I, in whose intellectual intuition the reduction begins, being a "Potenz," a more involved form, of the relation between subject and object as a whole. This I is not just one side of this relation. Schelling could later rightly call the procedure of his Philosophy of Identity "negative."

BUCHHEIM, Thomas. Zum Wandel der Metaphysik nach ihrem Ende. Phil Rundsch, 37(3), 197-226, 1990.

The crucial metaphysical issues are still ontological. Yet it is not enough to make the concept of a theoretical object into the fundament of all ontology. The status of both a radically singular thing and of the thinker himself elude clarification in terms of this concept. It is rather the elements of the whole situation that man finds himself in that determine the main features of his ontology. The article describes such a train of metaphysical reflection, starting from a Kantian form of metaphysics, then moving to a discussion of philosophers like Wolfgang Cramer, Josep König and Emmanuel Lévinas.

BUCHHOLZ, Arnold and SWIDERSKI, E M (trans). The On-Going Deconstruction of Marxism-Leninism. Stud Soviet Tho, 40(1-3), 231-240, 1990.

The changes in the political and cultural life of the Soviet Union had a considerable time lead over changes in the official ideology. The decisive breakthrough into the ideology was in the autumn of 1989. The traditional studies subject of "Marxist-Leninist philosophy" was reorganized into the general subject of "philosophy," the subject "History of the CPSU" into "Socio-Political History of the 20th Century." The most significant conceptual synopsis of the "perestroika ideology" is to be found in the new teaching handbook for high schools under the title "Introduction into Philosophy." The crucial innovation embodied in this work is that the chapter on the so-called "basic question of philosophy," the fundamental materialistic postulate for all hierarchical derivations of ideology and practical consequences, has been dropped. The work also reveals the unmistakable attempt to draw upon Kantian philosophy in the interpretation of fundamental philosophical questions.

BUCHLER, Justus and WALLACE, Kathleen (ed) and MARSOOBIAN, Armen (ed). *Metaphysics of Natural Complexes (Second Edition)*. Albany, SUNY Pr, 1990.

BUCHMANN, Margret and FLODEN, Robert E. Coherent Programs in Teacher Education: When Are They Educational? Proc Phil Educ, 46, 304-314, 1990.

Advocates of "program coherence" assume that tightly connected experiences are needed to give teacher education programs sufficient power. "Coherence" and "program" have positive associations with harmony and wholeness. Associations with behaviorism and efficiency suggest difficulties with these concepts. Teacher educators should consider the metaphor of a sparkling diamond, implying that teacher education can benefit from the incorporation of many facets—variegated ideas and practices—among which different patterns of connection may be drawn. Program coherence can be valuable if it helps students build interconnections while also inviting a reweaving of beliefs and ties to what is as yet unknown.

BUCHWALTER, Andrew. Hegel, Marx, and the Concept of Immanent Critique. J Hist Phil, 29(2), 253-279, Ap 91.

BUCKLE, Stephen. "Natural Law" in *A Companion to Ethics*, SINGER, Peter (ed), 161-174. Cambridge, Blackwell, 1991.

BUCZEK, Barbara. Problems Concerning the Presence of the Composer in His Music (in Polish). Ann Univ Mariae Curie-Phil, 10, 41-52, 1985.

The relation between the composer and his piece of music, significant for the evolution of music, can be analyzed from the initial outline of the piece to its inclusion in the universe of culture. Precomposition occurs in relation to a sphere of possibilities proper for a given epoch, but its range is perceived by the creator in an individual way. From among the means available to him the composer chooses those that best fit his aims. Only in the case of inner freedom of the creator and pure intention of creating a work of art may there appear in the piece, significantly emphasized, the composer's individual likes, deliberations and experiences, his own characteristic values and the originality of his talent. His experiences and his conception of time are impressed on the metric-rhythmical and formal configurations. Various domains of the composer's personality are therefore present and recognizable in his work. The reception of his work is a meeting with a man passing over the highest values he possesses. (edited)

BUCZKOWSKI, Piotr. "Remarks on the Structure of Social Consciousness" in *The Social Horizon of Knowledge*, BUCZKOWSKI, Piotr (ed), 87-109. Amsterdam, Rodopi, 1991.

BUCZKOWSKI, Piotr (ed). *The Social Horizon of Knowledge*. Amsterdam, Rodopi, 1991.

This book brings together seven critical essays in the sociology of knowledge. Concepts such as social consciousness and knowledge, as well as Wittgenstein's "Linguistic Turn" and Feyerabend's "Two Argumentative Chains" are subject to critical scrutiny. (staff)

BUDZISZEWSKI, J. The Pincovian Persuasion: Six Problems in Virtue Ethics (A Free Response to Seung). Soc Theor Pract, 17(2), 251-271, Sum 91.

This paper, part of a symposium entitled *The Future of Virtue Ethics: Its Political Relevance*, offers a sympathetic critique of Edmund Pincoff's book *Quandaries and Virtues: Against Reductivism in Ethics* and replies to another critique by Thomas K Seung. It addresses six problems in the Pincovian theory of virtue: 1) how to escape from a relativism of virtues; 2) how virtue is defined; 3) whether "reductionism" means what is seems to mean; 4) whether Pincoff is against all foundationalism, or only a certain kind; 5) how religion is or is not related to education in virtue; and 6) whether virtue can be taught at all.

BUEKENS, Filip. Interpretatie en filosofische methode. Alg Ned Tijdschr Wijs, 83(2), 89-102, Ap 91.

The paper links Davidson's claim that most of our beliefs are true with an examination of his philosophical method. Comparing Davidson's method of interpretation with Quine's method of translation, I try to show that, contrary to Quine, Davidson does not infer that we must look for something less than truth (or distal stimuli) from the fact that we sometimes may be mistaken about the world. This point is connected with Davidson's philosophical method: it's not because a reconstruction of a method that is sufficient to understand a person must leave room for local improvisations that the metaphysical conclusions based on the reconstruction are worthless.

BUENO SÁNCHEZ, Gustavo. El tratado de Ideología de Fray Zeferino Gonzalez. El Basilisco, 3, 3-16, Ja-F 90.

BUENO, Gustavo. Ignoramus, Ignorabimus!. El Basilisco, 4, 69-88, Mr-Ap 90.

BUENO, Gustavo. Libertad, Igualdad, Fraternidad. El Basilisco, 3, 29-34, Ja-F 90.

BUENO, Gustavo. Sobre el alcance de una "ciencia media" entre las ciencias humanas estrictas y los saberes prácticos positivos. El Basilisco, 2, 57-72, N-D 89.

BUESSEM, George E. Kant's First Analogy Revisited. Man World, 24(2), 143-153, Ap 91.

BUGAULT, Guy. Buddhist Anthropology vis-à-vis Modern Philosophy and Contemporary Neurophysiology. J Indian Counc Phil Res, 8(1), 69-76, S-D 90.

The author reminds us the outlines of Buddhist doctrine. Then he examines how a Buddhist reader could react to some examples of Modern Philosophy (Descartes) and also Analytical Philosophy (Wittgenstein). Besides he points out the new prospects of contemporary neurophysiology, such as they are depicted in Professor Changeux's book, *Neuronal Man* (New York, Pantheon Books, 1985). This provides us with a different idea of man. What a Buddhist monk will say, will he raise some objection of principle or not? Given that we usually think of religion and spiritualism as closely linked to each other, the answer to this question is both unexpected and enlightening.

BÜHLER, Pierre. Flaw, Conformity of Critical Dialogue? (in French). Rev Theol Phil, 123(1), 59-77, 1991.

This article reconsiders in a new way the old problem of the connection between faith and reason and tries to overcome the sterile alternatives of the two classic models of flaw or conformity. Drawing inspiration from the systemic approach, it describes a more dynamic interaction in which each partner intervenes at the critical point of the other: faith at the bifurcation into reason and unreasonableness, reason at the bifurcation into faith and disbelief. This double intersection proofs to be fructuous, as well as risky.

BÜHLER, Pierre. Habermas and Theological Ethics (in French). Rev Theol Phil, 123(2), 179-193, 1991.

The ethics of Jurgen Habermas are not yet well-known by Francophone theology. The article evaluates the promises and difficulties of a dialogue between theological ethics and the recent ethical works of Habermas. First, it attempts to honour his contribution to theological ethics; second, it formulates the critical points for debate with him.

BÜHLER, Pierre (trans) and DÜRRENMATT, Friedrich. On Tolerance (in French). Rev Theol Phil, 122(4), 449-465, 1990.

After a descriptive foreword about the philosophical and theological horizons of his approach, the author, inspired by the preamble of the Council from which he holds a medal, enlarges upon the problems of religious and political tolerance. In contrast to the model of Lessing, he defines an existential tolerance based on Kierkegaard, conceived of from the point of view of the individual who sets out to resist any englobing system, whether it be philosophical or theological, political or economic. He draws out the implications for the political realm.

BUKALA, C R. Consciousness: Creative and Self-Creating. Phil Today, 35(1), 14-25, Spr 91.

The greatest mystery of the human person is the mystery of human consciousness. A consideration of some aspects of the nature and meaning of consciousness leads to the thesis, "Human consciousness, in its freedom, directs itself towards specific objects, thus making itself to be a specific kind of consciousness." Each person decides what he/she will be by choosing the appropriate objects of consciousness. The conclusion that is reached is that we never really make ourselves to be exactly what we want to be, we merely "approximate" that which we intended in the act of self-creation.

BULGER, Roger J. "Covenant, Leadership, and Value Formation in Academic Health Centers" in *Integrity in Health Care Institutions: Humane Environments for Teaching, Inquiry, and Healing*, BULGER, Ruth Ellen (ed), 3-19. Iowa City, Univ of Iowa Pr, 1990.

BULGER, Ruth Ellen (ed) and REISER, Stanley Joel (ed). *Integrity in Health Care Institutions: Humane Environments for Teaching, Inquiry, and Healing*. Iowa City, Univ of Iowa Pr, 1990.

BULGER, Ruth Ellen and DUNN, Kim. "Values in Teaching and Learning: A Student-Teacher Dialogue" in *Integrity in Health Care Institutions: Humane Environments for Teaching, Inquiry, and Healing*, BULGER, Ruth Ellen (ed), 96-118. Iowa City, Univ of Iowa Pr, 1990.

BULHOF, Ilse N. Nietzsche: The Divination Paradigm of Knowledge in Western Culture. Hist Euro Ideas, 11, 937-954, 1989.

BULKLEY, Kelly. The Quest for Transformational Experience. Environ Ethics, 13(2), 151-163, Sum 91.

Michael E Zimmerman claims that the fundamental source of our society's destructive environmental practices is our "dualistic consciousness," our tendency to see ourselves as essentially *separate* from the rest of the world; he argues that only by means of the transformational experience of nondualistic consciousness can we develop a more life-enhancing environmental ethic. I suggest that dreams and dream interpretation may provide exactly this sort of experience. Dreams present us with powerful challenges to the ordinary categories and structures of our daily lives, and they reveal in numinous, *transformational* images how we are ultimately members of a web of being that includes all life. I offer Victor Turner's concept of *communitas* as a means of clarifying and unifying the issues Zimmerman and I are discussing. In conclusion I sketch out some of the practical applications of these ideas to the task of improving our society's treatment of the environment.

BULL, Barry L. The Priority of Excellence Reconsidered. Proc Phil Educ, 46, 208-219, 1990.

This paper reviews Thomas Green's recent argument that the pursuit of educational excellence is consistent with the ideal of equity and should take precedence over the pursuit of equality. It concludes that Green's ideal of excellence encompasses educational equality but excludes two important dimensions of educational justice—individual choice and participation—and that, therefore, these considerations should temper the legitimate pursuit of excellence.

BULLER, Paul F and KOHLS, John J and ANDERSON, Kenneth S. The Challenge of Global Ethics. J Bus Ethics, 10(10), 767-775, O 91.

The authors argue that the time is ripe for national and corporate leaders to move consciously towards the development of global ethics. This paper presents a model of global ethics, a rationale for the development of global ethics, and the implications of the model for research and practice.

BULLIS, Ronald K and HUNT, Eugene H. Applying the Principles of Gestalt Theory to Teaching Ethics. J Bus Ethics, 10(5), 341-347, My 91.

Teaching ethics poses a dilemma for professors of business. First, they have little or no formal training in ethics. Second, they have established ethical values that they may not want to impose upon their students. What is needed is a well-recognized, yet non-sectarian model to facilitate the clarification of ethical questions. Gestalt theory offers such a framework. Four Gestalt principles facilitate ethical clarification and another four Gestalt principles anesthetize ethical clarification. This article examines each principle, illustrates that principle through current business examples, and offers exercises for developing each principle.

BULLOUGH, Vern L and KURTZ, Paul. The Unitarian Universalist Association: Humanism or Theism? Free Inq, 11(2), 12-14, Spr 91.

BULYGIN, Eugenio. An Antinomy in Kelsen's Pure Theory of Law. Ratio Juris, 3(1), 29-45, Mr 90.

Some important ideas in Kelsen's Pure Theory of Law can be traced back to Kantian tradition, which has been very influential in Kelsen's thought, particularly in his early period. Among them we find the distinction between two radically different worlds (the world of facts and the world of norms), the normativity of legal science and the idea of validity as a binding force, based on the famous doctrine of the basic norm. These tenets and, especially, the use of a normative concept of validity prove to be incompatible with Kelsen's positivistic programme of a value-free legal science. The science of law cannot state that legal norms are obligatory or binding without trespassing the limits of Kelsen's ideal of a legal science; on the other hand, it is possible to define the concept of a legal system without resorting to the basic norm. So, if Kelsen is to be regarded as a consequent positivist, the Kantian ingredients of his theory must be rejected and the descriptive concept of validity as membership must be substituted for the normative notion of validity as a binding force.

BUNDER, M W. Corrections to Some Results for BCK Logics and Algebras. Log Anal, 31(121-122), 115-122, Mr-Je 88.

In Bunder, M W and Meyer, R K "A result for combinators, BCK-logics and BCK-algebras," *Logique et Analyse*, Volume 109, 1985 pages 33-40, we claimed that any two theorems of BCK logic have substitution instances so that either one can become a minor premise in a modus ponens step with the other as major premise. A Wronski pointed out the incorrectness of this. The present paper shows that the result is valid for condensed BCK logic (this was a conjecture of C A Meredith). The paper also gives a full proof of the fact that every BCK combinator has a principal type scheme. This fact is used to prove the condensed BCK logic result.

BUNDER, M W. Some Improvements to Turner's Algorithm for Bracket Abstraction. J Sym Log, 55(2), 656-669, Je 90.

The procedure for translating lambda terms into combinatory terms is called bracket abstraction. The efficiency of this procedure and the simplicity of the result are important to computing. Of the many forms of bracket that of D A Turner ["Another algorithm for bracket abstraction," *Journal of Symbolic Logic*, Vol. 44 (1979), pp. 267-270] was generally seen to be the best overall. The current paper shows how Turner's and other algorithms can be made even more efficient, while producing even simpler abstracts.

BUNGE, Mario. Game Theory is Not a Useful Tool for the Political Scientist. Epistemologia, 12(2), 195-212, Jl-D 89.

The applications of game theory to political processes are criticized for the following reasons. Firstly, the utility functions are not mathematically well defined. Secondly, their values are assigned arbitrarily. Consequently any thesis may be "proved" by arbitrarily filling the entries of the payoff matrices in question. Finally, political processes are far too complex to be modeled realistically on academic games. For these reasons game-theoretic politology is at best useless, at worst a rationalization of policies designed on totally different principles.

BUNGE, Mario. "Mario Bunge on Epistemology" in *Studies on Mario Bunge's "Treatise"*, WEINGARTNER, Paul (ed), 613-620. Amsterdam, Rodopi, 1990.

The author's replies to the comments on his views about epistemological relativism, instrumentalism, and information, made by R Boudon, G Vollmer, and M Kary. It is argued that relativism and instrumentalism fail to account for scientific and technological knowledge, and that the word 'information' designates so many different concepts that its use is misleading. These replies elucidate and supplement some of the points made in Volumes 5 and 6 of the author's *Treatise on Basic Philosophy* (1983).

BUNGE, Mario. "Mario Bunge on Ethics" in *Studies on Mario Bunge's "Treatise"*, WEINGARTNER, Paul (ed), 655-663. Amsterdam, Rodopi, 1990.

The author's replies to the comments on his views about values, morals and ethics made by E Garzón-Valdés, F Forman, and G Zecha. It is reaffirmed that basic needs and legitimate wants are the only solid foundations of moral norms, and that human survival depends upon the recognition of such needs and wants. These replies elucidate and supplement some of the points made in Volume 8 of the author's *Treatise on Basic Philosophy* (1989).

BUNGE, Mario. "Mario Bunge on his *Treatise* as a Philosophy" in *Studies on Mario Bunge's "Treatise"*, WEINGARTNER, Paul (ed), 667-671. Amsterdam, Rodopi, 1990.

The author's reaction to the evaluations of his philosophical system offered by A Cupani and E Rosenthal. The systematic (rather than historical) nature of his treatise, and its salient differences with Marxist philosophy, are stressed.

BUNGE, Mario. "Mario Bunge on Ontology" in *Studies on Mario Bunge's "Treatise"*, WEINGARTNER, Paul (ed), 587-609. Amsterdam, Rodopi, 1990.

The author's replies to the comments on his views about systems, emergence, levels, causality, teleology, and the mind-body problem, made by J M Bochenski, J Agassi, Y Wand and R Weber, D Blitz, M Espinoza, B Dubrovsky, W R Shea, and H Kurosaki. The relations between ontology on the one hand, and science and technology on the other, are examined, and the approaches to the mind-body problem that ignore the contributions of physiological psychology, are criticized. These replies elucidate and supplement some of the views expounded in Volumes 3 and 4 of the author's *Treatise on Basic Philosophy* (1977, 1979).

BUNGE, Mario. "Mario Bunge on Philosophy of Science and Technology" in *Studies on Mario Bunge's "Treatise"*, WEINGARTNER, Paul (ed), 623-651. Amsterdam, Rodopi, 1990.

The author's replies to the comments on his views about the nature of logic and mathematics and their relation to physics, the interpretations of probability, the philosophical constraints upon cosmological speculation, the realistic interpretation of quantum mechanics, the existence of economic laws, the philosophical underpinnings of management science, the sociology of science and technology, the nature of sociotechnical systems, and the nonstatement view of scientific theories, made by F Miró-Quesada, M Paty, M Garcia-Sucre, B Kanitscheider, M Stöckler, M E Burgos, A Barceló, R Mattessich, Y Gingras and J Niosi, D A Seni, and P Weingartner. These replies elucidate and supplement some of the points made in Volume 7 (Parts 1 and 2) of the author's *Treatise on Basic Philosophy* (1985).

BUNGE, Mario. "Mario Bunge on Semantics" in *Studies on Mario Bunge's "Treatise"*, WEINGARTNER, Paul (ed), 569-583. Amsterdam, Rodopi, 1990.

The author's replies to the comments on his views about language, meaning, and truth, made by M Dillinger, J Ferrater-Mora, A Bartels, J-P Marquis, and I and L Nowakow. The difference between reference and extension, the importance of the concept of partial truth of fact, the import of empty descriptions, and the need for a realistic semantics to account for science, are stressed. These replies elucidate and supplement some of the points made in the first two volumes of the author's *Treatise on Basic Philosophy* (1974).

BUNGE, Mario. "Mario Bunge's Life and Work" in *Studies on Mario Bunge's "Treatise"*, WEINGARTNER, Paul (ed), 677-708. Amsterdam, Rodopi, 1990.

BUNTING, I A. Equal Educational Opportunity as a Public Policy. S Afr J Phil, 10(2), 33-36, My 91.

In this article the author maintains that few writers in the field of education have a clear idea of what is involved in a government's commitment to equalize educational opportunities. The author argues that the phrase 'equal educational opportunity' must be understood within the context of a theory which attempts to justify the unequal distribution of educational goods in a society. This justification has to make use of the notion of 'fair competition' and has to be based on a 'principle of merit' and on a 'principle of equal life chances'. In conclusion a brief sketch of what a policy commitment to equality of educational opportunity must involve is given.

BURBIDGE, John (trans) and D'HONDT, Jacques. *Hegel In His Time—Jacques D'Hondt*. Peterborough, Broadview Pr, 1988.

Despite his reputation, Hegel was not a conservative defender of the Prussian regime. Documentary evidence from his letters and elsewhere shows that he was actively involved in the liberal and progressive movements of his day, was close to the liberal ministers in government, and at times was looked on suspiciously by the court. While he attacked the anti-semantic romanticism of the student movement many of its more responsible leaders were his friends and associates. An introduction analyses the Hegelian interpretation to be found in Jaques D'Hondt's writing.

BURBIDGE, John. "Where is the Place of Understanding?" in *Essays on Hegel's Logic*, DI GIOVANNI, George (ed), 171-182. Albany, SUNY Pr, 1990.

Hegel lists understanding, dialectic and speculative reason as the three aspects of logical reasoning, yet many interpret Hegel as opposing understanding to dialectical and speculative thought. The paper argues that Hegel discusses understanding in the third book of the *Science of Logic* on the Concept, while dialectic is covered in Book I on Being, and speculative reason in Book II on Essence. By identifying conceiving and understanding, we are better able to grasp Hegel's overall project: any speculative resolution will be subject to understanding's dissolution, just as understanding leads on to dialectical transitions and speculative resolutions.

BURBIDGE, John. *Within Reason: A Guide to Non-Deductive Reasoning*. Peterborough, Broadview Pr, 1990.

Working from the thesis that arguments from analogy are basic to all reasoning, this book proposes ways to analyze and assess nondeductive reasoning, including inductions, reasoning to explanations and reasoning to action. A final chapter suggests procedures for arguments that fit no standard pattern. All examples and most of the exercises are derived from central texts in the intellectual tradition, so that the development of reasoning skills is combined with reading and assessing short theoretical texts.

BURBULES, Nicholas C. Continuity and Diversity in Philosophy of Education: An Introduction. Educ Theor, 41(3), 257-263, Sum 91.

BURBULES, Nicholas C. Rationality and Reasonableness. Educ Theor, 41(2), 235-252, Spr 91.

BURBULES, Nicholas C. Varieties of Educational Dialogue. Proc Phil Educ, 46, 120-131, 1990.

BURCH, Robert W. Valency, Adicity, and Adity in Peirce's MS 482. Trans Peirce Soc, 27(2), 237-244, Spr 91.

BURDICK, Howard. A Notorious Affair Called Exportation. Synthese, 87(3), 363-377, Je 91.

In 'Quantifiers and Propositional Attitudes', Quine held a) that the rule of exportation is always admissible, and b) that there is a significant distinction between 'a believes-true (Ex)Fx' and '(Ex) a believes-true 'F' of x'. An argument of Hintikka's, also urged by Sleigh, persuaded him that these two intuitions are incompatible; and he consequently repudiated the rule of exportation. Hintikka and Kaplan propose to restrict exportation and quantifying in to favoured contexts - Hintikka to contexts where the believer knows who or what the person or thing in question is; Kaplan to contexts where the believer possesses a vivid name *of* the person or thing in question. The bulk of this paper is taken up with criticisms of these proposals. Its ultimate purpose, however, is to motivate an alternative approach, which imposes no restrictions on exportation or quantifying in, but repudiates Quine's other intuition: this is the approach taken in my 'A Logical Form for the Propositional Attitudes'.

BURDICK, Howard. What was Leibniz's Problem about Relations? Synthese, 88(1), 1-13, Jl 91.

Relations figure prominently in Leibniz's metaphysics. And yet Leibniz maintains that relations are "mere ideal things." The purpose of this paper is to establish that Leibniz tried to reduce relations because, like modern nominalist Nelson Goodman, he could not allow ordered pairs, etc., and so could not allow "Being a father of," for instance, as "an accident that is in two subjects at the same time." To establish this, I must argue against Ishiguro's and Hintikka's interpretations of Leibniz on relations, and show that what they say about the "windowlessness doctrine" is beside the point.

BURES, Radim. Ethical Dimensions of Human Attitudes to Nature. Rad Phil, 57, 10-13, Spr 91.

BURGE, Tyler. "Frege on Sense and Linguistic Meaning" in *The Analytic Tradition: Philosophical Quarterly Monographs, Volume 1*, BELL, David (ed), 30-60. Cambridge, Blackwell, 1990.

By consideration of a puzzle about Frege's views on vagueness I develop the claim that Frege's notion of sense is fundamentally different from modern notions of linguistic meaning. It is grounded not only in actual linguistic practice, use, and understanding, but in the potential for understanding the rational underpinnings of our practices and conceptions.

BURGE, Tyler. "On Davidson's "Saying That"" in *Truth and Interpretation: Perspectives on the Philosophy of Donald Davidson*, LE PORE, Ernest (ed), 190-208. Cambridge, Blackwell, 1986.

The article discusses Davidson's analysis of indirect discourse. It argues that the analysis is flawed by an inability to capture certain inferences. This inability is traced to treatment of "that" in that-clauses as a demonstrative and of the referent of "that" as a token rather than as some sort of abstract object.

BURGESS, John A. Phenomenal Qualities and the Nontransitivity of Matching. Austl J Phil, 68(2), 206-220, Je 90.

BURGESS, John A. The Sorites Paradox and Higher-Order Vagueness. Synthese, 85(3), 417-474, D 90.

BURGESS, John P. "Epistemology and Nominalism" in *Physicalism in Mathematics*, IRVINE, Andrew D (ed), 1-15. Norwell, Kluwer, 1990.

Since by ordinary commonsense and scientific criteria, mathematical physics provides us with a great deal of knowledge, nominalists who deny this must be invoking some suprascientific philosophico-theological criteria for "knowledge," rather as Bellarmine did against Galileo. The "causal theory of knowledge" as invoked by nominalists cannot be the same kind of "theory of knowledge" (a candidate analysis of the commonsense-scientific notion of "knowledge") as was Goldman's original causal theory of contingent knowledge, but rather must be a philosophico-theological dogma. This ought to seem obvious, but is argued at length in the paper.

BURGESS, John P. Synthetic Mechanics Revisited. J Phil Log, 20(2), 121-130, My 91.

Earlier results on eliminating numerical objects from physical theories are extended to results on eliminating geometrical objects.

BURGOS, María Esther. "Projections Are a Law of Nature" in *Studies on Mario Bunge's "Treatise"*, WEINGARTNER, Paul (ed), 365-376. Amsterdam, Rodopi, 1990.

In this article a critical analysis of Mario Bunge's interpretation of quantum mechanics is made. It is shown that this approach faces serious problems, in particular, those derived from the exclusion of the projection postulate. It is also concluded that every version of quantum mechanics referring to individual processes that does not include the concept of projection in its postulates, should confront the same kind of problems.

BURKARD, Kimberly and LANSING, Paul. Ethics and the Defense Procurement System. J Bus Ethics, 10(5), 357-364, My 91.

A large U.S. government investigation into arms procurement procedures with corporate contractors has recently led to guilty pleas to fraud and illegal use of classified documents. Operation Ill Wind has brought public attention to the criminal and unethical conduct of large defense contractors in their dealings with the government. This article will review how the defense contract bidding process operates and why illegal activity has been able to compromise the process. We will offer proposals to improve the process in light of the present inquiry.

BURKE III, William T. The Law of Business Ethics and Social Responsibility. Bridges, 2(3-4), 87-106, Fall-Wint 90.

Lawyers and those engaged in teaching the law find themselves generally considered somewhat of a cursed lot—in many cases, their coursework viewed as a "step-child" subject to the whim of a caring adoptive department or division. So it is alarming to many in the "more lofty fields of academe" to ever believe that ethics and the law mix. Their criticism of the two as synonymous in any way appears in virtually all business ethics texts as well as ironically a few business law and legal environment texts. Succumbing to this perception, usually masked as some "astute scholarly observation," will gradually knock out another strong basis for the expanded study of the law. This article is a most timely defense proving that the law does have, and has had for years, ethical "bottom-line, cost-saving" principles relevant to business.

BURKE, Cormac. San Agustín y la sexualidad conyugal. Augustinus, 35(139-140), 279-297, Jl-D 90.

BURKE, Maxim R and MAGIDOR, Menachem. Shelah's pcf Theory and Its Applications. Annals Pure Applied Log, 50(3), 207-254, D 90.

BURKE, Patrick. "Listening at the Abyss" in *Ontology and Alterity in Merleau-Ponty*, JOHNSON, Galen A (ed), 81-97. Evanston, Northwestern Univ Pr, 1991.

BURKE, Richard J. Morally Untenable Beliefs. Phil Rhet, 23(3), 168-183, 1990.

Beliefs tend to influence actions. If we want to prevent actions that are harmful to others, therefore, we cannot simply leave people free to believe whatever they choose. Philosophers must develop a concept of rational belief which serves to distinguish acceptable beliefs on social issues (including religious and political issues) from unacceptable ones. Epistemologies modelled on scientific method are too narrow for this purpose. I propose an epistemology based on the criteria for "plausible arguments" in Aristotle's *Rhetoric* to fill the bill.

BURKE, Richard. "Epistemological Pacifism" in *In the Interest of Peace: A Spectrum of Philosophical Views*, KLEIN, Kenneth H (ed), 259-267. Wolfeboro, Longwood, 1990.

Using Michael Walzer's formulation of the modern "just war" theory in *Just and Unjust Wars*, this paper argues that the average American citizen today cannot know whether a war policy pursued by his government is just. In particular, he cannot trust his government to be telling him enough of the relevant facts, for example whether serious diplomacy has been attempted first, since that government's record since 1945 has been one of repeated deceptions on military issues. To support killing, one's beliefs must be rational; and it would be irrational to believe our government until it reestablishes its moral authority.

BURKHARD, W A and KROON, F W. On a Complexity-Based Way of Constructivizing the Recursive Functions. Stud Log, 49(1), 133-149, Mr 90.

Hao Wang once wrote that the usual way of defining recursive functions involved constructively suspect quantification. He suggested in its stead a procedure that begins with obviously recursive functions, and allows other functions to count as constructively recursive if they can be evaluated within a number of steps given by functions already perceived as constructively recursive. The present paper presents a very general possibility result for constructive hierarchies of this type, using the resources of abstract complexity theory, and discusses some of the virtues and vices of the resulting approach to constructivizing the recursive functions.

BURKHARDT, Cornelia and FRANKENHÄUSER, Gerald. Warum lebt der Mensch moralisch? Deut Z Phil, 39(2), 141-146, 1991.

Morals mean more than a phenomenon of consciousness being controlled mentally and intellectually. For understanding morals in their entirety, you have to start out from the fundamental patterns of the order of living (standard patterns, interdependence, hierarchy, forming of traditions), and from the ethologic determination of the mutual relationship of what is congenital to people with what they have acquired. Morals are a (human) overshaping of biotically determined behaviour for controlling social relations of the individual, but at the same time, morals, embodied in conscience as an essential determination of what is allowed or what is not allowed, go beyond biotically determined behaviour.

BURNEY-DAVIS, Terri and KREBBS, R Stephen. The Vita Femina and Truth. Hist Euro Ideas, 11, 841-847, 1989.

BURNS, Robert P. "When the Owl of Minerva Takes Flight at Dawn: Radical Constructivism in Social Theory" in *Critique and Construction: A Symposium on Roberto Unger's "Politics"*, LOVIN, Robin W (ed), 130-158. New York, Cambridge Univ Pr, 1990.

This article first situates Unger in relation to Rawls, whom Unger criticizes. Most of the article criticizes Unger's attempt to create a radical and robust normative theory that may serve as the blueprint for the basic structure of a new post-Marxist society. Unger's "speculative-normative" theory is one-sided and dependent upon a flawed moral and religious vision. It does not truly transcend Kantian theories, such as Rawls's, or theories of the limit, such as Hannah Arendt's.

BURROW JR, Rufus. Moral Laws in Borden P Bowne's *Principles of Ethics*. Personalist Forum, 6(2), 161-181, Fall 90.

This essay is a study in the personalistic ethics of Borden P Bowne (1847-1910) and Edgar S Brightman (1884-1953). Though it was not Bowne's intention to develop a system of moral laws such as we find in Brightman's book, *Moral Laws*, we find in Bowne's work, albeit in germinal form, each of the laws Brightman develops. My conclusions are that Bowne's work serves as a basis for understanding Brightman's ethics, and that he not only anticipates Brightman's moral laws, but introduces two that Brightman does not, viz., the law of community, and the law of development.

BURROWS, David. *Sound, Speech, and Music*. Amherst, Univ of Mass Pr, 1990.

In this examination of the relation of thought to sound, the author offers the thesis that sound has played a liberating role in human evolution—indeed, has been fundamental in the development of what makes humans distinctive as a species. He proposes that the expansiveness of human thought stems primarily from the unique capacity of vocal sound to articulate meaning rapidly while simultaneously encouraging the listener to remain detached from the immediate physical world: thus the emphasis in speaking on the elsewhere and the otherwise, the former and the eventual.

BURROWS, Jo. "Conversational Politics: Rorty's Pragmatist Apology for Liberalism" in *Reading Rorty*, MALACHOWSKI, Alan (ed), 322-338. Cambridge, Blackwell, 1991.

BURSTEIN, Jerome S and FIMBEL, Nancie. Defining the Ethical Standards of the High-Technology Industry. J Bus Ethics, 9(12), 929-948, D 90.

At least five sets of ethical standards influence business people's decisions: general cultural, company, personal, situational, and industry standards. Each has an official or espoused form encoded in written documents such as policy statements and codes of ethics and an unofficial form that develops as people use the espoused standards. (We call these unofficial standards values in action.) To determine whether the high-technology industry deserves its reputation for moral laxness, a pilot questionnaire was designed. It asked employees to rate the acceptability in the workplace of ethical behaviors relating to safety, third parties, and cheating the company. The findings show that employees in high- and low-technology industries uphold espoused values of safety. Relations with third parties are influenced by the existence of company codes of ethics, especially in small companies. Actions involving cheating the company need to be investigated further.

BURTON, Gene E. Doctors and Their Advertising. Bus Prof Ethics J, 10(2), 31-48, Sum 91.

BURTON, Scot and JOHNSTON, Mark W and WILSON, Elizabeth J. An Experimental Assessment of Alternative Teaching Approaches for Introductory Business Ethics. J Bus Ethics, 10(7), 507-517, Jl 91.

This study employs a pretest-posttest experiment design to extend recent research pertaining to the effects of teaching business ethics material. Results on a variety of perceptual and attitudinal measures are compared across three groups of students—one which discussed the ethicality of brief business situations (the business scenario discussion approach), one which was given a more philosophically oriented lecture (the philosophical lecture approach), and a third group which received no specific lecture or discussion pertaining to business ethics. Results showed some significant differences across the three groups and demonstrated that for a single lecture, the method used to teach ethics can differentially impact ethical attitudes and perceptions. Various demographic and background variables did not moderate the relationship between the teaching method and the dependent variables, but the sex of the student was strongly associated with the ethical attitude and perception measures.

BUSALACCHI, Pete. How Can They? Hastings Center Rep, 20(5), 6-7, S-O 90.

BUSCH, Thomas W. *The Power of Consciousness and the Force of Circumstances in Sartre's Philosophy*. Bloomington, Indiana Univ Pr, 1990.

BUSCH, Thomas W. Sartre on Surpassing the Given. Phil Today, 35(1), 26-31, Spr 91.

BUSH, William. "Bernanosian Barbs and the Maritain's Marigny Lecture" in *From Twilight to Dawn: The Cultural Vision of Jacques Maritain*, REDPATH, Peter A (ed), 81-93. Notre Dame, Univ Notre Dame Pr, 1990.

Admiration for Maritain changed to caution as Bernanos realized the limitations of the philosopher's understanding of evil and sanctity, something demonstrated for the novelist in the Maritain-inspired censorship of his first novel, *Sous le soleil de Satan*. In the text of his 1938 Marigny lecture (*The Twilight of Civilization*) Maritain left himself particularly open to Bernanos's barbs by his remarks on progress, racism and Christian democracy. Bernanos's antipathy for Maritain's tendency towards a progressive Christianity espo using democracy and brotherhood is elucidated by her ferocious orthodoxy, which, he recalled, was the Christianity of Maritain's own godfather, Léon Bloy.

BUSINO, Giovanni and FERGUSON, Jeanne (trans). Sociology: An Infirm Science. Diogenes, 150, 37-63, Sum 90.

To understand the current crisis in sociology, we must examine its history. Sociology was founded on the mythic premise that a radically new society was emerging, a society endowed with universal characteristics. This led sociology to claim a total autonomy from classical knowledge. However, simultaneously, sociology proved incapable of clearly defining its boundaries, and borrowed heavily from the natural sciences to construct its analytical framework. To solve this crisis, we must accept that our society is not universal: its features testify to the permanence of the past, and only a thoroughly historical sociology can lead to a truly general knowledge about man.

BUSNEAG, Dumitru. *F*-Multipliers and the Localization of Hilbert Algebras. Z Math Log, 36(4), 331-338, 1990.

The aim of this work is to define the localization Hilbert algebra of a Hilbert algebra A with respect to topology *F* on A (in a similar way as for rings, monoids or distributive lattices). In the last part of the paper is proved that the maximal Hilbert algebra of fractions and the Hilbert algebra of fractions relative to a closed system (notions introduced by the author) are Hilbert algebra of localization.

BUSS, S R. Propositional Consistency Proofs. Annals Pure Applied Log, 52(1-2), 3-29, Ap 91.

Partial consistency statements can be expressed as polynomial-size propositional formulas. Frege proof systems have polynomial-size partial self-consistency proofs. Frege proof systems have polynomial-size proofs of partial consistency of extended Frege proof systems if and only if Frege proof systems polynomially simulate extended Frege proof systems. We give a new proof of Reckhow's theorem that any two Frege proof systems *p*-simulate each other. The proofs depend on polynomial size propositional formulas defining the truth of propositional formulas. These are already known to exist since the Boolean formula value problem is in alternating logarithmic time; this paper presents a proof of this fact based on construction which is somewhat simpler than the prior proofs of Buss and of Buss - Cook - Gupta - Ramachandran.

BUSS, Samuel R. The Modal Logic of Pure Provability. Notre Dame J Form Log, 31(2), 225-231, Spr 90.

We introduce a propositional modal logic PP of "pure" provability in arbitrary theories (propositional or first-order) where the □ operator means "*provable in all extensions*." This modal logic has been considered in another guise by Kripke. An axiomatization and a decision procedure are given and the □◇ subtheory is characterized.

BUSS, Samuel R. The Undecidability of *k*-Provability. Annals Pure Applied Log, 53(1), 75-102, Jl 91.

The *k*-provability problem is, given a first order formula θ and an integer *k*, to determine if θ has a proof consisting of *k* or fewer lines, i.e., formulas or sequents. This paper shows that the *k*-provability problem for the sequent calculus is undecidable.

BUSWELL JR, Robert E (ed). *Chinese Buddhist Apocrypha*. Honolulu, Univ of Hawaii Pr, 1990.

Modern scholarship has revealed that many of the most important Chinese Buddhist scriptures are not translations of Indian texts, as they purport to be, but actually composed in China by Chinese authors. Such indigenous, or "apocryphal," scriptures, are the subject of this volume. The studies compiled here address the role that apocryphal scriptures can play in documenting the social and political forces influencing Chinese religion and show the Buddhist canon to be not a fixed repository, but a fluctuating, tension-filled institution.

BUSZKOWSKI, Wojciech and PENN, Gerald. Categorical Grammars Determined from Linguistic Data by Unification. Stud Log, 49(4), 431-454, D 90.

We provide an algorithm for determining a categorial grammar form linguistic data that essentially uses unification of type-schemes assigned to atoms. The algorithm presented here extends an earlier one restricted to rigid categorial grammar by admitting non-rigid outputs. The key innovation is the notion of an optimal unifier, a natural generalization of that of a most general unifier.

BUTENKO, A P. Is Karl Marx to Blame for "Barracks Socialism"? Soviet Stud Phil, 29(2), 32-47, Fall 90.

BUTLER, Judith. "Gender Trouble, Feminist Theory, and Psychoanalytic Discourse" in *Feminism/Postmodernism*, NICHOLSON, Linda J (ed), 324-340. New York, Routledge, 1990.

BUTLER, Judith. Peter Dews' Logics of Disintegration: Poststructuralism/Critical Theory. Int Stud Phil, 22(3), 79-82, 1990.

BUTLER, Ken. A Note on the Jural Relation. Man World, 24(1), 93-96, Ja 91.

The article returns to a notion of justice which, so it is held, antecedes contemporary liberal notions of justice as fair process. Justice obtains when, it is argued, a kind of social interaction results in a specific outcome. If this process does not terminate in a prefigured outcome, under certain conditions then a state of injustice results.

BUTLER, Kenneth G. *The Concept of Objectivity: An Approximation*. New York, Lang, 1990.

The first chapter of this book situates the origins of the concept of objectivity in Presocratic thinking about appearance and causative reality. It situates emergence of the conception in the works of such Renaissance thinkers as Galileo. The second and third chapters situate the idea of objectivity between foundationalism and sceptical relativism. It argues that the structure of objectivity is composed of epistemic, metaphysical and psychological and methodological elements. These chapters argue that the concepts of truth and knowledge may be separated without a descent into scepticism. The fourth and final chapter argues the concept may be used fruitfully in a much wider range of decision contexts than is generally supposed.

BUTTERFIELD, Jeremy N and CLIFTON, Robert K and REDHEAD, Michael L G. Nonlocal Influences and Possible Worlds—A Stapp in the Wrong Direction. Brit J Phil Sci, 41(1), 5-58, Mr 90.

BUTTERFIELD, Jeremy. Causal Independence in EPR Arguments. Proc Phil Sci Ass, 1, 213-225, 1990.

I show that locality, as it occurs in EPR arguments for the incompleteness of quantum mechanics, can be construed as causal independence *à la* Lewis's analysis of causation. This construal has two benefits. It supplements recent analyses, which have not treated locality in detail. And it clarifies the relation between two EPR arguments that have recently been distinguished. It shows that the simpler of the two is more complex than has been thought; and that the other argument does not need 'counterfactual definiteness'.

BUTTERFIELD, Jeremy. The Hole Truth. Brit J Phil Sci, 40(1), 1-28, Mr 89.

Earman and Norton have recently revived Einstein's "hole argument." They argue that it shows spacetime substantivalists to be committed to a radical form of indeterminism. I reply to the argument both technically and philosophically. I give a technical definition of determinism that avoids the argument and is satisfied by general relativity. And philosophically, I argue that we can best avoid the argument by denying the transworld identity of spacetime points.

BUTTS, Robert E. Philosophers as Professional Relativists: Canadian Philosophical Association Presidential Address 1990. Can J Phil, 20(4), 617-624, D 90.

BUXTON, James. Kripke on Theoretical Identifications: A Rejoinder to Perrick. Log Anal, 31(121-122), 109-113, Mr-Je 88.

This paper examines an argument of Saul Kripke for the necessity of theoretical identification statements and defends it against a criticism of M Perrick ("Are Kripke's Theoretical Identifications Necessary Truths?", *Logique et Analyse*, Volume 115, September 1986, pages 381-384). It is argued that Perrick's criticism rests on a fallacy of ambiguity. Formal modal logic is used to examine a number of plausible interpretations of Kripke's argument, and Perrick's error is shown to arise from confusion concerning the scope of the modal necessity operator.

BUZZI GRASSI, Elisa. Josiah Royce: la metafisica della comunità. Riv Filosof Neo-Scolas, 81(4), 576-613, O-D 89.

In his *The Problem of Christianity* (1913), the American idealist J Royce (1855-1916) presented an original metaphysical theory grounded on the notion of "community of interpretation," which he developed from Peirce's semiotic. In this article the author analyses the metaphysic of community especially considering its logical and historical ties with the whole of Royce's philosophy; its relations with Peirce's theory; the epistemological theory of interpretation; the metaphysical implications of the concept of community. The metaphysic of community is the most accomplished result of Royce's effort to solve the problem of the one and the many, but the concept of interpretation alone cannot provide a sound philosophical foundation to the concept of community.

BYERLY, Henry C and MICHOD, Richard E. Fitness and Evolutionary Explanation. Biol Phil, 6(1), 1-22, Ja 91.

The aim is to clarify the roles of the concept "fitness" in evolutionary theory. Appealing to the structure of models of natural selection, we draw distinctions between how fitness is defined versus what fitness is a function of, between specific adaptive capacities versus overall adaptedness, and between fitness applied to organisms versus genotypes. We show how failure to distinguish these aspects of "fitness" confuses complex issues concerning evolutionary theory. A central result of the analysis is that overall adaptedness of organisms does not play a causal role in evolutionary explanations.

BYERLY, Henry C and MICHOD, Richard E. Fitness and Evolutionary Explanation: A Response. Biol Phil, 6(1), 45-53, Ja 91.

BYERLY, Henry. Causes and Laws: The Asymmetry Puzzle. Proc Phil Sci Ass, 1, 545-555, 1990.

Causal asymmetries in dependencies of variables in laws are commonly not reflected in the functional relations expressed in the law equation. For the case of the simple pendulum law, why can we cause the period to change by changing the length, but not change the length by changing the period? After surveying attempts to explain such asymmetries, I propose a new account based on an analysis of the relation between causes and laws. This analysis is used to criticize the very notion of causal laws and to clarify the role of ceteris paribus clauses in interpreting scientific laws.

BYKOVA, M. Die Perestrojka in der Sowjetischen Philosophie: Mythos oder Realität. Stud Soviet Tho, 40(1-3), 73-88, 1990.

The article analyzes the current development of philosophy in the USSR and its problems along with changes taking place in philosophy under the influence of perestroika. The present state of Soviet philosophy is seen as an awakening from dogmatism, as a determined conscious liberation from ideological fetters and state canon. From the viewpoint of global perestroika in the intellectual sphere, the philosophical development in the Soviet Union today may be treated as a period of critical reason and its further accumulation. It presents a kind of transitory state of social consciousness with new forms of thinking emerging as a result of the critical evaluation of the existing conceptual framework and its content. Hence the present state of philosophy may be termed perestroika-like only with regard to its dynamics, the search for true philosophic values, the desire to apply new criteria of creativity and originality, but not as a finished process, result or an achieved goal. What is implied is the process of change and its beginning, the movement towards the new which is still to be discovered, closely examined and put into practice.

BYRD, Michael. Russell, Logicism, and the Choice of Logical Constants. Notre Dame J Form Log, 30(3), 343-361, Sum 89.

It is here argued that Russell's *Principles of Mathematics* contains an intriguing idea about how to demarcate logical concepts from nonlogical ones. On this view, implication and generality emerge as the two fundamental logical concepts. Russell's 1903 proposals for defining other logical concepts from these basic ones are examined and extended. Despite its attractiveness, the proposal is ultimately unsatisfactory because of problems about defining negation and existential quantification.

BYRNE, Christopher. Forms and Causes In Plato's *Phaedo*. Dionysius, 13, 3-15, D 89.

Gregory Vlastos has argued that Aristotle and other commentators on the *Phaedo* have mistakenly interpreted Plato's Forms to be efficient causes. While Vlastos is correct that the Forms by themselves are not efficient causes, because of his neo-Kantianism he has misunderstood the close connection between the Forms and the explanation of change, including teleological change. This paper explores the connection in Plato's *Phaedo* between the Forms, the nature of change, and efficient causality, and argues that Aristotle's remarks are not as misplaced as Vlastos claims.

BYRNE, Edmund F. *Work, Inc.: A Philosophical Inquiry*. Philadelphia, Temple Univ Pr, 1990.

BYRNE, Edmund F. "Workplace Democracy for Teachers: John Dewey's Contribution" in *Philosophy of Technology*, DURBIN, Paul T (ed), 81-95. Norwell, Kluwer, 1989.

BYRNE, Laura. "Hegel's Criticism of Spinoza's Concept of the Absolute" in *Essays on Hegel's Logic*, DI GIOVANNI, George (ed), 113-126. Albany, SUNY Pr, 1990.

BYRNE, Peter. A Religious Theory of Religion: Critical Notice. Relig Stud, 27(1), 121-132, Mr 91.

The article reviews John Hick's theory of religion with a view to seeing whether it is a viable alternative to naturalism and confessionalism in the study of religion. It raises serious doubts about Hick's theory after reviewing its Kantian basis, its definitions of religion and its attempted realism.

BYTNIEWSKI, Pawel. Man as the Animal Symbolism in the Conception of S Langer (in Polish). Ann Univ Mariae Curie-Phil, 11, 203-219, 1986.

One of the significant dimensions of human subjectivity is the indirectness of the relation between man and his environment. In its cognitive respect, this indirectness is revealed in acts of symbolizing. This means that the use of signs is not only an expression act of intellect but also a mode of organizing experience, the knowledge of a subject. This idea, expressed in Cassirer's philosophy of symbolic forms, has found a specific version in the philosophy of S Langer. Cassirer's conception of the symbolic form as an a priori condition of experience is interpreted by Langer in terms of biologically given and also specific properties of the human species. Such an approach makes it possible to pose a question about the genesis of symbolic activity. The naturalism of Langer's conception largely restricts the domain of possible answers to this question, although even with these limitations the conception of man as "animal symbolicum" constitutes an original and inspiring proposition.

CABADA, Manuel. El problema de la culpa y del "otro" en Heidegger y Siewerth. Pensamiento, 47(186), 129-152, Ap-Je 91.

Se analizan en este artículo las implicaciones prácticas, de orden ético y antropológico, del pensamiento de Heidegger y Siewerth. La ontologización del problema de la conciencia, de la culpa y, en definitiva, de las relaciones intersubjetivas del hombre en Heidegger, que parece estar en la raíz de su comportamiento político, se enfrenta con la valoración filosófica de la vivencia humana del amor y del "otro" en las reflexiones sistemáticas de Siewerth, que le van a posibilitar además a éste un determinado acceso a la divinidad, vedado a Heidegger.

CABADA, Manuel. Ser y Dios, entre filosofía y teología, en Heidegger y Siewerth. Pensamiento, 47(185), 3-35, Ja-Mr 91.

Se analiza en este artículo la relación biográfica e ideológico-sistemática de Siewerth con Heidegger y de éste con aquél, con atención especial a su reflexión sobre el ser y la divinidad y a sus opuestas concepciones de la función de la teología en el ámbito de lo filosófico, con las consecuencias que de ello se derivan para la comprensión del pensamiento y del mismo talante vital de ambos pensadores.

CABAJ, Jerzy. The Problem of the History-Making Role of Ideas in American Historical Thought (in Polish). Ann Univ Mariae Curie-Phil, 11, 141-159, 1986.

The principal aim of the paper is the presentation of the views shaped by American historical thought about history-making role of ideas. The author concentrates especially on historiographic thought of the first half of the twentieth century, that is, on the period in which the role of ideas was perceived most fully. He also presents controversies and polemics which were taking place in this field between the leading proponents of presentism and the followers of the "anti-progressive" trend.

CABANCHIK, Samuel. Wittgenstein escéptico? Cuad Filosof, 21(34), 31-41, My 90.

The main object of this paper is to propose a skeptical interpretation of Wittgenstein's thought. In order to attain this end, I develop, in the first place, a criticism of Moore's notion of certainty. My point of view is, against Moore's, that 'certainty' and knowledge are, probably, incompatible notions, and that the possibility of a skeptical doubt about the assumed certainty is a necessary condition to distinguish between belief and knowledge, and to construe any kind of knowledge. On the other hand, I deal with what Kripke called "the skeptical paradox" in relation to the determination of linguistic meaning. Both the ideal of certainty and the presumption in favor of the objectivity of meaning are assumed in this paper as a symptom of the kind of philosophical thought which must be overcome.

CABRAL, Roque. Gabriel Marcel na correspondência com Gaston Fessard. Rev Port Filosof, 45(4), 549-559, O-D 89.

The recently published correspondence between Gabriel Marcel and Gaston Fessard gives some light on Marcel's personality and work.

CABRERA, Isabel. Wittgenstein: la tentación de lo místico. Dianoia, 35(35), 107-116, 1989.

In this paper I examine the notion of mystical which appears in the last part of the *Tractatus* (and in some remarks of the Notebook 1914-1916), trying to elucidate some of its epistemological and ethical implications. For this purpose I discuss the Villoro's and Zemach's thesis on mystical. Finally I reach the conclusion that the mystical remains for Wittgenstein as a temptation.

CACCIAPUOTI, Fabiana. Angelo Camillo De Meis nell'episolario di Francesco Fiorentino. G Crit Filosof Ital, 69(1), 75-100, Ja-Ap 90.

CACCIATORE, Giuseppe. Nuove ricerche sul 'Liber metaphysicus' *di Giambattista Vico*. Boll Centro Stud Vichiani, 20, 211-221, 1990.

CADAVA, Eduardo (ed) and CONNOR, Peter (ed) and NANCY, Jean-Luc (ed). *Who Comes after the Subject?*. New York, Routledge, 1991.

CADY, Duane L. "Exposing Warism" in *Issues in War and Peace: Philosophical Inquiries*, KUNKEL, Joseph (ed), 207-215. Wolfeboro, Longwood, 1989.

Warism is the view that war is both morally justified in principle and often morally justified in fact. Warism is a common presumption in our era. Like racism and sexism, this uncritical presumption that war is morally justifiable, even morally required, misguides our attitudes and institutions. One task of philosophers is to expose, examine and scrutinize such presumptions. Peace will not be taken seriously by academics or the general public until warism is made explicit, so that it may be examined alongside its alternatives in a less prejudicial climate.

CADY, Duane L. "Pacifism, Duty, and Supererogation" in *In the Interest of Peace: A Spectrum of Philosophical Views*, KLEIN, Kenneth H (ed), 125-132. Wolfeboro, Longwood, 1990.

Kant distinguishes between strict and broad duties. The former are obligatory (e.g., promise keeping); the latter are good to do but not necessarily wrong not to do (e.g., helping the needy). Popular moral judgment would seem to place pacifism in the latter group (at best). By exploring Kant's criteria for strict and broad duties and by comparing Kant's position with the "two moralities" of Lon Fuller, I examine a model of morality where obligation and supererogation are different only by degree. I close by considering the implications of this model for pacifism.

CAFFARRA, Carlos. Aspectos antropológicos de la fecundación in vitro. Sapientia, 46(179), 66-76, Ja-Mr 91.

CAHN, Steven M. Principled Divestiture and Moral Integrity. Analysis, 51(2), 112, Mr 91.

How is principled divestiture possible, for it passes the guilt of ownership from seller to buyer, thus exchanging one wrong for another? In response to this puzzle I posed (*Analysis* 47.3), Roger Shiner argues that since the seller does not cause the buyer to act, the seller maintains moral integrity. But your wish to sell your stock is logically equivalent to your wishing someone to buy it. By hypothesis you believe it wrong for anyone to buy it. So your wish to sell is the wish that someone else do wrong. And that desire is immoral. The puzzle thus remains unsolved.

CAI, Hou. The Contents of the Daoist Religion and Its Cultural Function. Chin Stud Phil, 22(2), 24-42, Wint 90-91.

The Daoist religion (*Daojiao*) is an ancient religion that took root and flourished in China's soil. It was created in the time of Emperor Shundi of the Eastern Han dynasty (126-164 AD) and today claims a history of over 1800 years. Its philosophical thought—which is a theory of moral and behavioral discipline whose core is a belief in immortals or supernatural beings (*shen-xian*)—derived its origins from what is called "the teachings of Huang [Huangdi, or the Yellow Emperor] and Lao [Lao Zi]." Consequently, it has always made its claim to being the "successor to the cultural influences of Huang and Lao" (*Huang-Lao ye feng*), and as such is considered to be one of the principle entities of China's traditional culture. In fact, Mr. Lu Xun went as far as to say: "All of China's roots are in the Daoist religion." What, however, are the real contents of the Daoist religion? And what are its cultural functions?

CALEO, Marcello. Sant'Agostino e Hegel a confronto. Sapienza, 44(1), 57-76, Ja-Mr 91.

CALHOUN, Craig. The Ideology of Intellectuals and the Chinese Student Protest Movement of 1989. Praxis Int, 10(1-2), 131-160, Ap-Jl 90.

Changes in the Chinese intellectual community shaped the student protest movement of 1989, though older intellectuals did not control it. The present paper examines key themes of democracy, cultural crisis, economic reform and treatment of intellectuals in the public statements of scientists, social scientists and humanists during the late 1980s. Special attention is focused on Fang Lizhe, Liu Binyan and others of widespread public influence.

CALIFANO, Joseph J. "Human Suffering and Our Post-Civilized Cultural Mind: A Maritainian Analysis" in *From Twilight to Dawn: The Cultural Vision of Jacques Maritain*, REDPATH, Peter A (ed), 201-214. Notre Dame, Univ Notre Dame Pr, 1990.

CALIFANO, Joseph J. "Modernization of the Law of the *Prise de Conscience*" in *Freedom in the Modern World: Jacques Maritain, Yves R Simon, Mortimer J Adler*, TORRE, Michael D (ed), 227-235. Notre Dame, Univ Notre Dame Pr, 1989.

CALLAHAN, Daniel. Medical Futility, Medical Necessity: The - Problem - Without - A - Name. Hastings Center Rep, 21(4), 30-35, Jl-Ag 91.

CALLEBAUT, Werner and WACHELDER, J. Teleo-theologie und kein Ende: Reactie op Soontiens. Kennis Methode, 15(2), 218-223, 1991.

CALLEN, Donald. "Stories of Sublimely Good Character" in *XIth International Congress in Aesthetics, Nottingham 1988*, WOODFIELD, Richard (ed), 15-17. Nottingham, Nottingham Polytech, 1990.

CALLICOTT, J Baird and HARGROVE, Eugene C. Leopold's "Means and Ends in Wild Life Management". Environ Ethics, 12(4), 333-337, Wint 90.

Leopold's lecture at Beloit College provides an important glimpse into his conversion from a philosophy of prudent scientific resource management to a land ethic and aesthetic. Leopold here advocates natural regulation not simply because of his growing concern that invasive management principles are limited, but also because of aesthetic considerations that were independent of his instrumental or "utilitarian" training at the Yale Forest School and in the US Forest Service. The lecture is helpful in correcting an unfortunate misreading of Leopold's famous essay, "The Land Ethic," according to which the land ethic is interpreted as being based primarily on human welfare and self-interest.

CALLICOTT, J Baird. Reply to Shrader-Frechette's "Biological Holism and the Evolution of Ethics". Between Species, 6(4), 193-195, Fall 90.

Contrary to Shrader-Frechette's allegations: the ecological concept of a biotic community is robust enough to support a holistic environmental ethic, though I do not claim that communities have interests or appeal to either a "balance of nature" or the discredited "diversity-stability" hypothesis; while I argue that ethics are naturally selected, my construction of ethics is not *analogous* to evolution; and an ecological-evolutionary land ethic is genuinely normative.

CALLICOTT, J Baird (ed) and FLADER, Susan L (ed). *The River of the Mother of God, and Other Essays by Aldo Leopold*. Madison, Univ Wisconsin Pr, 1991.

CALUDE, Cristian and SÂNTEAN, Lila. On a Theorem of Günter Asser. Z Math Log, 36(2), 143-147, 1990.

Our purpose is to present two natural characterizations of the class of unary primitive-recursive string-functions (over a fixed alphabet) as Robinson algebras.

CAM, Philip. Insularity and the Persistence of Perceptual Illusion. Analysis, 50(4), 231-235, O 90.

Many perceptual illusions persist in the face of conflicting knowledge or belief.

Why is that? I raise three possibilities, two of which depend upon limitations of access between perceptual and intellectual processing systems. The third depends upon the insularity or "narrow-mindedness" of perceptual systems. I argue that this third possibility has a number of virtues, and may illustrate a more general feature of mental organisation. Whichever way we go, however, the persistence of perceptual illusion raises deep questions about how our minds operate.

CAMACHO, Luis A. Problemas lógicos en el relativismo ético. Rev Filosof (Costa Rica), 27(66), 307-311, D 89.

The particular version of moral relativism which is probably most widespread in our country has its origins in Marxist thought: values are historically determined by economic factors and, ethics belong in the superstructure. This position fails precisely in the explanation of conflicts. Taking as a starting point some ideas developed by Hector-Neri Castañeda and David Crocker, this paper attempts to analyze a provisional systematization of this kind of relativism, with the purpose of showing its explanatory weakness. (edited)

CAMACHO, Luis. Tendencias actuales en filosofía de la tecnología. Rev Filosof (Costa Rica), 28(67-68), 21-25, D 90.

We are interested here in distinguishing two global trends in the philosophy of technology, which differ above all in their methods. One of the schools begins with the usual meaning of the terms, whereas the other begins by constructing a series of formalized definitions. Pirsig is a good example of the first approach; Bunge and his discipline Quintanilla gives us an example of the second trend. (edited)

CAMENISCH, Paul F. Marketing Ethics: Some Dimensions of the Challenge. J Bus Ethics, 10(4), 245-248, Ap 91.

We should seek an ethic internal to marketing arising from marketing's societal function, rather than imposing some "add-on" ethic. This suggests that marketing should enhance the information and the freedom the potential customer brings to the market transaction. Defining and achieving this information and freedom is difficult, but marketers suggest that the market itself drives our major violators, a suggestion less persuasive concerning increasingly complex goods and services. Marketing also is tempted to appeal to our baser, darker side. These problems are better addressed through self-regulation guided by a vision of advertising and business in the service of society, and by the marketer's own sense of integrity than through external regulation.

CAMILLE, Michael. The *Trés Riches Heures*: An Illuminated Manuscript in the Age of Mechanical Reproduction. Crit Inquiry, 17(1), 72-107, Autumn 90.

The history of this famous manuscript is told in terms of its rediscovery and mechanical reproduction in the nineteenth and twentieth centuries from the Gazette des Beaux Arts, through *Life* Magazine to the latest 16,000 dollar facsimile. The question of accessibility of the original and its disappearance behind these simulacra is related to the ways in which reproduction reinforces "high art" values and perpetuates the aristocratic associations of the original through various strategies never imagined by Walter Benjamin in his "the work of art in the Age of Mechanical Reproduction."

CAMPANALE, Domenico. Fondamento e verità. G Metaf, 12(1), 23-42, Ja-Ap 90.

CAMPBELL, Blair. The Epic Hero as Politico. Hist Polit Thought, 11(2), 189-211, Sum 90.

Traces the development of a variety of epic heroism (as epitomized in Homer's Achilles) into a political style within ancient Athens. This heroic style stipulates distinctive ideals regarding the objectives, techniques, and constituency proper for political participation.

CAMPBELL, Donald T and CZIKO, Gary A. Comprehensive Evolutionary Epistemology Bibliography. J Soc Biol Struct, 13(1), 41-82, F 90.

This is a comprehensive bibliography of books, articles, and book chapters dealing with evolutionary epistemology and selection theory. Over 1000 references are included; some are briefly annotated.

CAMPBELL, Donald. A Naturalistic Theory of Archaic Moral Order. Zygon, 26(1), 91-114, Mr 91.

Cultural evolution, producing group-level adaptations, is more problematic than the cultural evolution of individually confirmable skills, but it probably has occurred. The "conformist transmission," described by Boyd and Richerson (1985), leads local social units to become homogeneous in anadaptive, as well as adaptive, beliefs. The resulting intragroup homogeneity and intergroup heterogeneity makes possible a cultural selection of adaptive group ideologies. All archaic urban, division-of-labor social organizations had to overcome aspects of human nature produced by biological evolution, due to the predicament of genetic competition among the cooperators. The universal norms found in archaic moral systems are seen as curbs to this human nature, reinforced by beliefs in invisible sanction systems and rewarding and punishing afterlives (as in heaven or reincarnation). Perhaps the ubiquity of lavishly wasteful royal funerals is to be explained as contributing to this function.

CAMPBELL, L Leon. Commentary: "The University and Industrial Research: Selling Out?". Bus Prof Ethics J, 2(4), 37-39, Sum 83.

CANEY, S. Rawls, Sandel and the Self. Int J Moral Soc Stud, 6(2), 161-171, Sum 91.

Liberal political thought is often said to rest on an asocial conception of the self. This charge has, for example, been made against the liberal theorist Rawls. Rawls argues, in *A Theory of Justice* (1971), that individual liberty should be protected and that economic inequalities are legitimate only if they maximise the condition of the least advantaged. But Rawls's defence of these two principles of justice has been criticised by Sandel in *Liberalism and the Limits of Justice* (1982) on the grounds that it ignores the fact that we are social creatures. In particular, Sandel argues first that Rawls's device of the 'original position' presupposes an asocial conception of the self, and second that Rawls's texts reveal a commitment to an individualistic conception of the self. In my paper I argue that Sandel is mistaken and Rawls's theory of justice is not predicated upon an untenable conception of the self.

CANFIELD, John. *The Looking-Glass Self: An Examination of Self-Awareness*. New York, Praeger, 1990.

CANNING, Peter. "How the Fable Becomes a World" in *Looking After Nietzsche*, RICKELS, Laurence A (ed), 175-193. Albany, SUNY Pr, 1990.

CAÑÓN LOYES, Camino. La matemática: certeza y verdad. Dialogo Filosof, 6(3), 345-354, S-D 90.

CANTELLI, Gianfranco. Gestualità e mito: i due caratteri distintivi della lingua originaria secondo Vico. Boll Centro Stud Vichiani, 20, 77-116, 1990.

CANTIN, Serge. Grandeur et limites du *Marx* de Michel Henry. Dialogue (Canada), 29(3), 387-398, 1990.

The paper focuses on what its author makes out as the crux of the interpretation of Marx by Michel Henry, namely the ontological difference between Marx and Hegel. The purpose is to show that, however illuminating may be M Henry's approach to this fundamental issue, it fails to reach what is really at stake in the transition from Hegelianism to Marxism, in which ethics has become immanent in the historical process of making, in *praxis*.

CANTRALL, Janice and PENCE, Terry. *Ethics in Nursing: An Anthology*. New York, Natl League Nursing, 1990.

This collection of historical, seminal, classic and controversial articles begins with the assumption that ethical action in nursing is largely determined by philosophical views about the nature and function of nursing. The articles and excerpts from the nursing and other literature serve to explain, illustrate, advocate and/or critique various views about nursing and the moral implications of these views. Chapters include discussions of the concept of patient advocacy, nurses' rights, nurse-physician relationships, sexism, whistleblowing, nurse-nurse relationships, professional obligations, and institutional obligations. The chapters contain introductions and study questions.

CAPALDI, Nicholas. *Hume's Place in Moral Philosophy*. New York, Lang, 1989.

This is a systematic exposition of Hume's moral philosophy. Against the background of his predecessors, it outlines the argument in the *Treatise*, explains Hume's rejection of the moral "ought" by reference to his view on relations, exhibits the role of sympathy in developing the moral perspective, explains his account of moral judgment and its difference from moral sentiment, and examines the revisions in the *Enquiry*. The book concludes with an argument on behalf of Hume's Copernican Revolution in moral philosophy, where the perspective is that of an engaged agent. There is a thorough review of the secondary literature.

CAPEK, Milic. The Search for an Elusive *A Priori*. J Brit Soc Phenomenol, 22(1), 65-74, Ja 91.

CAPLAN, Arthur L. "Arguing with Success: Is In Vitro Fertilization Research or Therapy?" in *Beyond Baby M: Ethical Issues in New Reproductive Techniques*, BARTELS, Dianne M (ed), 149-170. Clifton, Humana Pr, 1990.

A great deal of the discussion of the ethics of in vitro fertilization presupposes that it is an established, efficacious form of therapy. This paper shows why IVF must still be viewed as experimental, innovative treatment and, thus, why the ethical framework for discussing this procedure ought to be seen as human experimentation rather than as the ethics of care or treatment.

CAPLAN, Arthur L. Bioethics on Trial. Hastings Center Rep, 21(2), 19-21, Mr-Ap 91.

CAPLAN, Arthur L. "Seek and Ye Might Find" in *Scientific Theories*, SAVAGE, C Wade (ed), 22-40. Minneapolis, Univ of Minn Pr, 1990.

Efforts to understand theory structure and dynamics have focused on the basic sciences for their paradigms. Such a focus distorts our understanding of the structure and dynamics of theories in the sciences. This paper uses the case of the evolution of thinking about renal dialysis in the field of nephrology to show how the examination of theories from applied science can inform the understanding of theory change.

CAPOBIANCO, Richard. Heidegger and the Critique of the Understanding of Evil as Privatio Boni. Phil Theol, 5(3), 175-185, Spr 91.

Despite the efforts of such notable thinkers as Sartre, Camus, and Ricoeur to affirm philosophically the being of evil, a systematic critique of the traditional metaphysical understanding of evil as *private of being* has not yet been fully worked out. The task of this paper is to sketch out just such a critique and to suggest a more adequate philosophical reflection on the being of evil by turning to the thought of Heidegger. Part I examines Heidegger's commentary on Aristotle's remarks on *steresis*. Aristotle is our teacher, Heidegger argues, in learning "to hold on to the wonder" of the *steresis*-"loss," "absence" — is. Part II considers Heidegger's recognition that the k-not at the very heart of our existence is yet much more complex. He turns to the fragments of Parmenides and Heraclitus to bring to light a dissembling-dimension of Being.

CAPORALI, Riccardo. Vico in Voegelin. Boll Centro Stud Vichiani, 20, 195-199, 1990.

CAPPELLETTI, Angel. Fideísmo y autoritarismo en Lutero. Rev Filosof (Costa Rica), 28(67-68), 197-207, D 90.

Nominalism had prepared in Luther the way to fideism, that came together with contempt of Aristotle and philosophy. Fideism, in turn, had facilitated affirmation of State's authority; strengthened the idea of absolute power of the sovereigns and justified as last genocide of German peasants.

CAPPELLETTI, Angel. Imitación y purificación en la estética de Aristóteles. Dialogos, 26(58), 15-31, Jl 91.

Se trata de mostrar la estrecha relación que hay entre los conceptos de *imitación* y de *purificación* en la *Poética* de Aristóteles. Puesto que imitar—conocer; y conocer—superar el temor y la compasion, se infiere que imitar—purificar.

CAPUTO, Cosimo. Sulla semiotizzazione dell' "a priori": Rossi-Landi e Hjelmslev. Il Protag, 6(13-16), 121-134, Ja 88-D 89.

CAPUTO, John D. Heidegger's *Kampf*: The Difficulty of Life. Grad Fac Phil J, 14(2)-15(1), 61-83, 1991.

This paper follows the thematics of "difficulty" from Heidegger's early Freiburg lectures through the 1930s. The paper also shows how the perspective on this notion shifts from that of Aristotle and Kierkegaard to that of Nietzsche and Jünger. It also presents implications for Heidegger's national socialist writings.

CAPUTO, John D. Incarnation and Essentialization: A Reading of Heidegger. Phil Today, 35(1), 32-42, Spr 91.

CAPUTO, John D. "Radical Hermeneutics and Religious Truth: The Case of Sheehan and Schillebeeckx" in *Phenomenology of the Truth Proper to Religion*, GUERRIÈRE, Daniel (ed), 146-172. Albany, SUNY Pr, 1990.

CARABINE, Deirdre. *Apophasis* and Metaphysics in the *Periphyseon* of John Scottus Eriugena. Phil Stud (Ireland), 32, 63-82, 1988-90.

CARANFA, Angelo. *Proust: The Creative Silence*. Lewisburg, Bucknell Univ Pr, 1990.

CARANI, Marie. Le statut sémiotique de la perspective dans l'oeuvre picturale. Horiz Phil, 1(2), 13-31, 1991.

Reviewed in semiotic terms, the working morphology—visual and plastic operators—and the methodology—pictorial perspectivism—favoured by post-Renaissance and XXth century artists clearly represents an effort to bypass a 'norm' or convention of art: the naturalistic paradigm. I borrow this normative valuation from the Tartu School of Semiotics. As a sequence of signs, any 'modern' work of art is thus not only conventional in Gombrich's sense, but can be evaluated precisely according to its level of conventionality. Putting these two concepts together we can say that a norm is a semiotic category wherein deviations expressed in terms of specific 'degrees of conventionality' constitute syntaxical relations of the artistic change.

CARBONE JR, Peter F. Thinking About Thinking: What Are We to Think? Proc Phil Educ, 46, 410-414, 1990.

CARD, Claudia. "The Feistiness of Feminism" in *Feminist Ethics*, CARD, Claudia (ed), 3-31. Lawrence, Univ Pr of Kansas, 1991.

This essay, introducing fourteen new essays, presents feminist ethics as a family of approaches to ethics at all levels of theory, rather than a set of positions, and as reflecting women's refusals to endure with grace the arrogance, indifference, hostility, and damage of oppressively sexist environments. It reviews the author's experience of this field over fifteen years, highlights the remaining essays, comments on heretical stylistic innovations in many of them, and supports the feistiness of feminist inquiry as part of the insubordination that has enabled feminist ethics to continue growing.

CARD, Claudia (ed). *Feminist Ethics*. Lawrence, Univ Pr of Kansas, 1991.

This book offers fifteen new essays in feminist ethics by Maria Lugones, Joyce Trebilcot, Marilyn Frye, Christian Pierce, Alison Jaggar, Bat-Ami Bar On, Ruth Ginzberg, Lynne McFall, Marilyn Friedman, Victoria Davion, Michele Moody-Adams, Elizabeth Spelman, Annette Baier, Sarah Hoagland, and the editor. Together they examine recent trends and developments in feminist ethics in the United States and explore specific topics in the area, often with a character ethics approach. Topics include cultural pluralism, postmodernism, terrorism, survival ethics, bitterness, integrity, partiality, trust, and care ethics.

CARD, Claudia. "Gender and Moral Luck" in *Identity, Character, and Morality: Essays in Moral Psychology*, FLANAGAN, Owen (ed), 199-218. Cambridge, MIT Pr, 1990.

As gendered beings in a society with a history of patriarchy, women and men inherit different pasts and consequently different social expectations, lines of communication, opportunities, and barriers, which become part of our "moral luck." In tracing the effect on ethical thinking, it is argued that Carol Gilligan's "different voice" is better understood as articulating an ethic of informal and personal relationships, by contrast with a dominant ethic of formal and impersonal ones, than as yielding care and justice ethics, and that both may be seriously flawed.

CARDONA, Carlos. Filosofía y Cristianismo (En el Centenario de Heidegger). Espiritu, 38(100), 101-114, Jl-D 89.

CARDOSO D EOLIVEIRA, Roberto. O Saber, a Ética e a Ação Social. Manuscrito, 13(2), 7-22, O 90.

The author uses Karl-Otto Apel's theory about the community of argumentation and its ethical components in order to examine the question of knowledge in the social sciences. The topic of relativism receives special attention, particularly in the field of anthropology. The problem of applied knowledge in social change programs, like development projects, is explored; that exploration relates to morality on the basis of an alternative development model, named ethno-development, as suggested by Rodolfo Stavenhagem. The article intends to make explicit both the ethical dimension of the model and the role of the democratic state in social transformation.

CARDY, Michael. "Pyrrhonism and the Concept of a Common Human Nature in Eighteenth-Century Aesthetic Thought" in *The Question of Humanism: Challenges and Possibilities*, GOICOECHEA, David (ed), 223-234. Buffalo, Prometheus, 1991.

The "Pyrrhonists of Antiquity" claimed that nothing could be known for sure, either through reason or intuition. Montaigne restated the position in a reflection on aesthetic ideas and challenged the bases of both aesthetic and moral philosophy. The thinkers studied in this paper attempted to defend a position threatened by the moral nihilism of pyrrhonist discourse.

CARELLA, Michael Jerome. *Matter, Morals and Medicine: The Ancient Greek Origins of Science, Ethics and the Medical Profession*. New York, Lang, 1991.

CAREY, David and ALMEDER, Robert. In Defense of Sharks: Moral Issues in Hostile Liquidating Takeovers. J Bus Ethics, 10(7), 471-484, Jl 91.

In this essay we defend the view that from a purely rule-utilitarian perspective there is no sound argument favoring the immorality of hostile liquidating buyouts. All arguments favoring such a view are seriously flawed. Moreover, there are some good argument favoring the view that such buyouts may be morally obligatory from the rule-utilitarian perspective. We also defend the view that most of the "shark repellents" in the market are immoral. If we are right in our arguments there is no justification, moral or otherwise, for any form of legislation that would constrain the practice of hostile liquidating buyouts.

CARINGELLA, Paul (ed) and HOLLWECK, Thomas A (ed) and VOEGELIN, Eric. *What is History? And Other Late Unpublished Writings (The Collected Works of Eric Voegelin, Vol 28)*. Baton Rouge, Louisiana St Univ Pr, 1990.

The volume contains five previously unpublished texts by Voegelin belonging in the context of Volumes IV and V of *Order and History* as well as other later published writings. The texts comprise an analysis of the transcendental structure of history in the title-piece, the discussion of constants in the search of order in "Anxiety and Reason," a critique of certain modern notions of 'self' in "The Eclipse of Reality," an attempt to reformulate the connections between physics and myth in "The Moving Soul," and a meditation on the question of *fides quaerens intellectum* in "The Beginning and the Beyond."

CARLOYE, Jack C. Consciousness and Introspective Knowledge. Method Sci, 24(1), 8-22, 1991.

CARLSON, Greg N (ed) and KYBURG JR, Henry E (ed) and LOUI, Ronald P (ed). *Knowledge Representation and Defeasible Reasoning*. Norwell, Kluwer, 1990.

This is a collection of essays on the interface between computer science, philosophy, and linguistics. The volume is divided into four parts. The first is Defeasible Reasoning and the Frame Problem, with papers by Donald Nute, Lenhart Schubert, Hector Geffner and Judea Pearl, and Michael Dunn. Second, Representation Problems and Ordinary Language, with papers by Don Perlis, Brendan Gillon, Nuel Belnap and Michael Perloff, and Andrew McCafferty. The third part concerns Inference Rules and Belief Revision, and has papers by Charles Cross, Judea Pearl, Teddy Seidenfeld, and by Hugues LeBlanc and Peter Roeper. Finally, there are papers on Logical Problems in Representing Knowledge by Bob Carpenter and Richmond Thomason, Ronald Loui, Robin Giles, and Romas Aleliunas.

CARLSTROM, Ian F. A Truth-Functional Logic for Near-Universal Generalizations. J Phil Log, 19(4), 379-405, N 90.

Empirical systems may not exactly satisfy universal laws such as transitivity. This paper studies possible effects of such errors on our logical systems. First-order logic is syntactically expanded by a closure quantifier for near-universal generalizations, with a probability measure providing a continuous-valued semantics. A limit concept of vanishing error recaptures a two-valued logic. An extension of first-order natural deduction to this new system is proved to be complete. Individual probability quantifiers are shown to be inadequate for capturing the concept of a near-universal law.

CARNES, Robert D and PETERSON, Philip L. Intermediate Quantifiers versus Percentages. Notre Dame J Form Log, 32(2), 294-306, Spr 91.

In his 1986 paper (*Notre Dame Journal of Formal Logic*) Thompson offers rules for determining validity and invalidity of so-called "statistical syllogisms" (syllogisms with percentages replacing the traditional quantities of universal and particular) which are both *un*sound and *in*complete. As a result, his claim that the genuine 5-quantity syllogistic (the traditional syllogistic with the three "intermediate" quantities added, expressible by "few", "many", and "most") is included in his system is trivial, *if* true at all. It turns out not to be even true, as revealed by detailed examination of distribution, Thompson's rules, and his claims for equivalences.

CARNIELLI, Walter A and PUGA, Leila Z and DA COSTA, Newton C A. Kantian and Non-Kantian Logics. Log Anal, 31(121-122), 3-9, Mr-Je 88.

CAROSIO, Alba and MUÑOZ, Angel. Reflexiones en torno a la oración oblicua. Rev Filosof (Venezuela), 11, 1-44, 1989.

Consideraciones desde el punto de vista de la semántica actual y medieval, en especial de Alberto de Sajonia, acerca de la influencia de la oración incrustada en el valor de verdad de la proposición.

CARPENTER, Bob and THOMASON, Richmond. "Inheritance Theory and Path-Based Reasoning: An Introduction" in *Knowledge Representation and Defeasible Reasoning*, KYBURG JR, Henry E (ed), 309-343. Norwell, Kluwer, 1990.

CARPER, Kenneth L. Ethical Considerations for the Forensic Engineer Serving as an Expert Witness. Bus Prof Ethics J, 9(1-2), 21-34, Spr-Sum 90.

The professional engineer serving as an expert witness plays an essential role in the resolution of disputes involving technical engineering matters. Objective, competent analyses of engineering failures can establish the most probable technical causes. Unbiased, articulate presentations of these findings can contribute to rational settlements. In order for the forensic engineer to perform the assignment with integrity, the expert must be ever mindful of tendencies toward bias and other aspects of the adversarial environment that may interfere with the search for truth. The engineering expert is in a position of great responsibility. Professional reputations and personal fortunes may easily be impacted unfairly by inaccurate statements. The tests of ethical commitment involved in forensic engineering may be more challenging than those encountered in any other field of engineering endeavor. Specific moral problems faced by the forensic engineering expert witness are discussed in this paper, along with guidelines recently established by professional engineering societies.

CARPINTERO, Helio and MAYOR, Luis and ZALBIDEA, M A. Condiciones del surgimiento y desarrollo de la Psicología Humanista. Rev Filosof (Spain), 3, 71-82, 1990.

American Humanistic Psychology grew in the 1950s and 1960s in the USA, in a situation of great insatisfaction and restlessness. The paper reviews the main principles of Humanistic Psychology conceived as a Third Force or a new path out of the mechanicism of behaviorism and the determinism and irrationalism of psychoanalysis. Its aims, as defined by Maslow, Bugental and Sutich and some of its American and European roots are here reviewed. Stress is also laid on the Zeitgeist and its influence upon the efforts to build a psychology based on the normal, free, creative man.

CARR, Craig L. Tacit Consent. Pub Affairs Quart, 4(4), 335-345, O 90.

This article discusses whether it is possible to express consent tacitly. It argues against the predominant contemporary belief that the concept of tacit consent is incoherent defends the view that tacit consent is an important factor in the way normative relations amongst persons are developed and transformed.

CARRACEDO, Jose Rubio. La razón ética. Themata, 6, 155-168, 1989.

The main purpose of this paper is to explain the peculiarity of moral justification (the ethic reason). The author begins by establishing the definite inadequateness of logic-empirical approach. After that, he examines Popper's and Albert's rational criticism as applied to moral justification to find it also unsatisfactory. Finally, the paper focuses on the dialogical-constructivist approach of ethics (mainly in Lorenzen's, Apel's and Habermas's terms) to find it a more adequate explanation of characteristic traits of moral justification, although too much influenced by the cognitivist turn of philosophy.

CARRETERO, Joaquín M. "Amicus plato, sed magis amica veritas" (Notas sobre el conflicto amistad-verdad). Dialogo Filosof, 6(3), 392-400, S-D 90.

CARRIER, David. Art History in the Mirror Stage: Interpreting *Un Bar aux Folies Bergères*. Hist Theor, 29(3), 297-320, O 90.

CARRIER, David. *"Pale Fire* Solved" in *Acting and Reflecting: The Interdisciplinary Turn in Philosophy*, SIEG, Wilfried (ed), 75-87. Norwell, Kluwer, 1990.

CARRIER, Martin. Constructing or Completing Physical Geometry? Phil Sci, 57(3), 369-394, S 90.

The aim of this paper is to discuss the relation between the observation basis and the theoretical principles of general relativity. More specifically, this relation is analyzed with respect to constructive axiomatizations of the observation basis of space-time theories, on the one hand, and in attempts to complete them, on the other. The two approaches exclude one another so that a choice between them is necessary. I argue that the completeness approach is preferable for methodological reasons.

CARRIER, Martin. "Some Aspects of Hélène Metzger's Philosophy of Science" in *Études sur/Studies on Hélène Metzger*, FREUDENTHAL, Gad , 135-150. Leiden, Brill, 1990.

Metzger conceived of science as a succession of ideas, rather than of factual discoveries, and stressed the difference between past theories and present-day science. It is the task of the historian of science to reconstruct (or to "revive") the original structure of now rejected theories. Regarding methodology Metzger holds that although theories cannot be derived from the facts, they can be evaluated by their ability to explain them. The central ingredient of this evaluation is a theory's simplicity. In particular, the following evolutionary pattern is advanced. A simple idea is expanded into a full-grown theory and thereby becomes increasingly complex. So, in the end the theory is replaced by some other simple idea and the whole process repeats itself.

CARRIER, Martin. What Is Wrong with the Miracle Argument? Stud Hist Phil Sci, 22(1), 23-36, Mr 91.

One of the arguments advanced in favor of Scientific Realism is the "Miracle Argument." It says that for the anti-realist the predictive success of science appears as an utter miracle. This argument indeed has some *prima facie* plausibility, provided that it is sharpened by construing "predictive success" as prediction of previously unknown laws and the occurrence of a consilience of inductions. Still, the history of science teaches us that it is possible to arrive at predictive success in this sense by employing radically non-referring theoretical mechanisms. The Miracle Argument is thus unsound. Rather, the capacity of a theory to generate predictive success can be traced back to its "classificatity correspondence."

CARRIERO, John. "Newton on Space and Time: Comments on J E McGuire" in *Philosophical Perspectives on Newtonian Science*, BRICKER, Phillip (ed), 109-133. Cambridge, MIT Pr, 1990.

J E McGuire, in "Existence, Actuality and Necessity: Newton on Space and Time," *Annals of Science* 35 (1978), pp. 463-508, and "Predicate of Pure Existence: Newton on God's Space and Time" (contained in the present volume), argues that Newton sees space and time as logical consequences of the divine existence. I criticize this understanding and offer an alternative account, according to which space and time are necessary (efficient) causal consequences emanating from God. I also provide an interpretation of certain comments penned by Newton in the so-called "Des Maizeaux" drafts (which were eventually incorporated into the preface to the French edition of the Leibniz-Clarke correspondence) concerning Clarke's claim in the correspondence that space and time are "properties" of God.

CARRILHO, Manuel Mari. Problématicité, rationalité et interrogativité. Rev Int Phil, 44(174), 309-328, 1990.

CARRITHERS, David W. Not So Virtuous Republics: Montesquieu, Venice, and the Theory of Aristocratic Republicanism. J Hist Ideas, 52(2), 245-268, Ap-Je 91.

CARROLL, Archie B and MEZNAR, Martin B and CHRISMAN, James J. Social Responsibility and Strategic Management: Toward an Enterprise Strategy Classification. Bus Prof Ethics J, 10(1), 47-66, Spr 91.

CARROLL, Jeffrey S. Maximal R.E. Equivalence Relations. J Sym Log, 55(3), 1048-1058, S 90.

The lattice of r.e. equivalence relations has not been carefully examined even though r.e. equivalence relations have proved useful in logic. A maximal r.e. equivalence relation has the expected lattice theoretic definition. It is proved that, in every pair of r.e. nonrecursive Turing degrees, there exist maximal r.e. equivalence relations which intersect trivially. This is, so far, unique among r.e. submodel lattices.

CARROLL, Noël. Beauty and the Genealogy of Art Theory. Phil Forum, 22(4), 307-334, Sum 91.

CARRUTHERS, Peter. *Introducing Persons: Theories and Arguments in the Philosophy of Mind*. New York, Routledge, 1989.

The book is a clear and succinct introduction to a range of issues in the philosophy of mind, with particular emphasis on arguments for and against the views considered. It also weaves together the topics into an original argument, including a vigorous defence of contemporary materialism, an original argument against private language and concepts, and a new defence of Parfitian views on personal identity. Topics covered include: other minds, the case for dualism, problems with dualism, behaviorism and functionalism, the case for materialism, 'private languages', personal identity, and boundaries of personhood.

CARRUTHERS, Peter. *The Metaphysics of the "Tractatus"*. New York, Cambridge Univ Pr, 1990.

This book aims to make sense of the early Wittgenstein's metaphysical doctrines, showing how powerful arguments may be deployed in their support. Considered at length are the doctrine of the priority of logic over metaphysics, the nature and purpose of Wittgenstein's programme of analysis for ordinary language, and the arguments supporting the existence of Simples. The book also locates the main conflict between Wittgenstein's early and late philosophies in his earlier commitment to the objectivity of logic, which is shown to be the true target of attack of his later discussion of rule-following.

CARSE, Alisa L. The 'Voice of Care': Implications for Bioethical Education. J Med Phil, 16(1), 5-28, F 91.

This paper examines the 'justice' and 'care' orientations in ethical theory as characterized in Carol Gilligan's research on moral development and the philosophical work it has inspired. Focus is placed on challenges to the justice orientation—in particular, to the construal of impartiality as the mark of the moral point of view, to the conception of moral judgment as essentially principle-driven and dispassionate, and to models of moral responsibility emphasizing norms of formal equality and reciprocity. Suggestions are made about the implications of these challenges, and of the care orientation in ethics, for the ethical theory taught, the issues addressed, and the skills and sensitivities encouraged through bioethical education.

CARSON, Anne. "Just for the Thrill": Sycophantizing Aristotle's *Poetics*. Arion, 1(1), 142-154, Wint 90.

CARSON, Tom. A Note on Hooker's "Rule Consequentialism". Mind, 100(397), 117-121, Ja 91.

Brad Hooker presents an argument to show that rule-consequentialism (RC) is considerably less demanding than act-consequentialism (AC). I offer criticisms of Hooker's argument. I also argue that, at most, Hooker's arguments work for certain formulations of RC and not others. Hooker needs to show that those formulations of RC which are not very demanding are more plausible than those formulations which are very demanding.

CARTER, Alan. The Real Meaning of 'Meaning'. Heythrop J, 32(3), 355-368, Jl 91.

CARTER, John. Critics and Historical Continuity. Phil Stud Educ, /, 128-131, 1987-88.

CARTER, Richard B. Ethics as Drawn from the Method. Philosophica, 46(2), 107-117, 1990.

This article argues that characteristically modern ethics comprises the replacement of questions concerning whether some act is good with questions concerning its feasibility, and that this replacement is itself a consequence of Descartes's collapsing of theoretical analysis with practical ("poristic") analysis. When this replacement defines the procedures of ethics, algebraic analysis concerning the search for the solution to some particular problem replaces all theoretical modes of thought concerning principles of correct action. It argues further that Descartes justified this replacement by postulating that no clearly and distinctly grasped solution was ever repugnant to Deity.

CARTER, William R. Why Personal Identity Is Animal Identity. Logos (USA), 11, 71-81, 1990.

I argue that a person is properly regarded as an animal, a physical organism, and that personal identity is therefore animal identity. We should reject psychological accounts of diachronic personal identity. Moreover, I argue that we should have reservations concerning the proposal that a person is a four-dimensional entity, something that is extended through time in the manner of a process or an event. Unlike an event, a person is 'all present' at any time when she exists.

CARTWRIGHT, J P W. Conditional Intention. Phil Stud, 60(3), 233-255, N 90.

CARTWRIGHT, Richard. *Philosophical Essays*. Cambridge, MIT Pr, 1987.

CASALE, Giuseppe and SANTORO, Liberato. Hegel, Croce, Gentile: On the Idea of the "Ethical State". Phil Stud (Ireland), 32, 113-125, 1988-90.

The essay outlines the central tenets of Hegel's conception of the "Ethical State" and rejects the naive interpretations of Hegel's philosophy as advocating a totalitarian State. The dispute between Gentile and Croce is, then, seen as resulting fundamentally from the respective reading of Hegel by the two Italian philosophers. Gentile is inclined to identify ethics and politics, while Croce sees ethics and politics as distinct. In the light of Hegel's philosophy, Gentile-logically more coherent-privileges the sphere of "Objective Spirit"; Croce-more pragmatic-favours individual freedom and hence, "Subjective Spirit."

CASARES, Angel J. Aristóteles desde Heidegger. Dialogos, 26(58), 7-14, Jl 91.

This paper discusses an interpretation of Aristotle's "Doctrine of Cause" according to Heidegger's thinking, namely in *Die Frage nach der Fechnik*.

CASATI, Roberto and DOKIC, Jérome. Brains in a Vat, Language and Metalanguage. Analysis, 51(2), 91-93, Mr 91.

Putnam's argument against the hypothesis that we are Brains in a Vat (BIV), as reconstructed by M Dell'Utri in *Mind*, 99, pages 79-90, has four major flaws: a) the lack of a precise distinction between the object language and metalanguage; b) the improper use of Convention T in one major premiss; c) the lack of a definition of the operator 'in-the-image'; d) the difficulty of specifying, under the hypothesis that we are BIV, the status of our utterances.

CASATI, Roberto. Primary and Secondary Qualities: A Reply to Kienzle. Stud Leibniz, 22(2), 194-198, 1990.

The paper criticizes Bertram Kienzle's *"Primäre und Sekundäre Qualitäten bei John Locke"*, *Studia Leibnitiana*, XXI, 1989, pages 22-41: the definition Kienzle gives cannot allow him to distinguish primary from secondary qualities. I offer a criterion for the distinction in terms of dissectivity: a property is secondary if it is possible that one of its monadic determinables (or a determinable such that no relation is built in the predicate expressing it) is dissective (down to a certain site). Otherwise a property is primary.

CASATI, Roberto. What is Wrong in Inverting Spectra. Teoria, 10(1), 183-186, 1990.

I argue that spectrum inversion cannot satisfy some strong constraints on colour brightness. We cannot make sense of bright shadows, neither do flashes of darkness appear possible. Evidence for this claim of impossibility is provided by the fact that some inversions are not likely to preserve transparency (e.g., the one mapping green onto white), and this is a consequence of a link between relative colour brightness and transparency.

CASAUBÓN, Juan A. Los tres estados de la esencia según Santo Tomás de Aquino. Sapientia, 45(176), 87-94, Ap-Je 90.

CASCARDI, Anthony J. Aesthetic Liberalism: Kant and the Ethics of Modernity. Rev Int Phil, 45(176), 10-23, 1991.

CASEY, Edward S. "Back of 'Back to Beyond' and Creeping Dichotomism" in *Archetypal Process: Self and Divine in Whitehead, Jung, and Hillman*, GRIFFIN, David Ray (ed), 233-237. Evanston, Northwestern Univ Pr, 1989.

CASEY, Gerard. Artificial Intelligence and Wittgenstein. Phil Stud (Ireland), 32, 156-175, 1988-90.

This article assesses the value of Wittgenstein's thought on *the* basic issue in Artificial Intelligence, whether machines can or cannot think. Because of the manifest and significant dissimilarities between machines and human beings Wittgenstein believes that it makes no sense to attribute psychological characteristics to machines. I conclude that Wittgenstein's argument is sound if directed against the *actuality* of artificial intelligence. However, if directed against the *possibility* of artificial intelligence it must either arbitrarily denounce emerging AI-compatible language games or suffer itself to be outflanked by the seemingly inevitable and ultimately arational change of one language game for another.

CASPAR, Philippe. Thomas d'Aquin a-t-il tente d'exprimer le principe d'individuation à l'intérieur des proprietés.... Aquinas, 34(1), 41-50, Ja-Ap 91.

CASPARY, William R. Ethical Deliberations as Dramatic Rehearsal. Educ Theor, 41(2), 175-188, Spr 91.

CASSEL, Christine and LA PUMA, John. The Noncompliant Substance Abuser: Commentary. Hastings Center Rep, 21(2), 30-31, Mr-Ap 91.

CASSELL, Eric J. Recognizing Suffering. Hastings Center Rep, 21(3), 24-31, My-Je 91.

CASSINI, A. La justificación práctica del principio de no contradicción en Aristóteles. Critica, 22(65), 57-72, Ag 90.

The paper considers an Aristotelian argument to justify the principle of noncontradiction given in *Metaphysics* 1008b 12-31. This is a practical argument, because it refers to human action and its explanation. First, the article outlines the argument, which is shown to be incomplete. Then, it analyses two fundamental assumptions of the argument: (a) the explanation of actions; (b) the rationality of actions. The first states that all actions can be explained by means of a desire and a relevant belief; the second, that all actions are rational. It affirms that there are Aristotelian grounds to support both assumptions, despite the existence of *akrasía* or incontinent action. Finally, it shows that the argument, with these two assumptions as additional premises, is complete and it has inductive plausibility.

CASTAÑEDA, Héctor-Neri. "Direct Reference, the Semantics of Thinking, and Guise Theory" in *Themes From Kaplan*, ALMOG, Joseph (ed), 105-144. New York, Oxford Univ Pr, 1989.

CASTAÑEDA, Héctor-Neri. Indexicality: The Transparent Subjective Mechanism for Encountering a World. Nous, 24(5), 735-749, D 90.

CASTAÑEDA, Héctor-Neri. "Practical Thinking, Reasons for Doing, and Intentional Action" in *Philosophical Perspectives, 4: Action Theory and Philosophy of Mind, 1990*, TOMBERLIN, James E (ed), 273-308. Atascadero, Ridgeview, 1990.

CASTELLANA, Mario. Materiali per una storia dell'epistemologia in Italia. Il Protag, 6(13-16), 151-180, Ja 88-D 89.

CASTELLANO, Veneranda. "La tematica della follia tra Umanesimo nordico e Umanesimo latino: l'*Encomium Moriae* di Erasmo da Rotterdam" in *Razionalitá critica: nella filosofia moderna*, LAMACCHIA, Ada (ed), 11-41. Bari, Lacaita, 1989.

CASTILLO, Roberto. La imaginación creadora en el pensamiento de Gastón Bachelard. Rev Filosof (Costa Rica), 28(67-68), 65-70, D 90.

The fundamental thesis is: imagination is not only the simple faculty of passive reproduction of perceptible images, as it has been conceived in traditional philosophy, but also the active production of images. (edited)

CASTLE, Terry. Contagious Folly: *An Adventure* and Its Skeptics. Crit Inquiry, 17(4), 741-772, Sum 91.

Psychology has so far been unable to provide an adequate explanation of the so-called "collective hallucination," or delusion shared by two or more persons. The skeptical response to *An Adventure* (1911)—in which two Oxford lady dons claimed to have seen the ghost of Marie Antoinette at Versailles and printed voluminous "proofs" for their claims—illustrates the problem well. No contemporary skeptical theory, including the psychological concept of the *folie à deux*, seems to explain properly the uncanny nature of their belief or the bizarre reactions it provoked.

CASTRO MÉNDEZ, Silvia. El problema del conocimiento en Pascal. Rev Filosof (Costa Rica), 27(66), 429-437, D 89.

This article is a chronological review of Pascal works following along the thread of the gnoseological and methodological problems therein encloses. The author proposes that the apparent escepticism of the thoughts is only a rhetorical resource to show how reason is not sufficient to arrive to certainly by itself, and how the possibility of knowledge stands for a cognitive instance different from reason to which it must be submitted. (edited)

CASTRO, Barry. Socrates in Dallas: Managing the Facilities. Bridges, 2(3-4), 143-153, Fall-Wint 90.

It is suggested that a commitment to knowing oneself, both personally and in terms of one's organizational role, can provide a valuable link between the Socratic tradition and business ethics. The author explores the barriers to such self-knowledge at a meeting of facilities managers, and through that exploration is led to a clearer understanding of analogous barriers at the universities in which he has studied and taught. He notes that the ways in which we are building the facilities that dominantly inform most of our lives may well both reflect and add to such barriers, and argues that while we are unlikely to be able to clear them from our path, neither should we allow ourselves to pretend that they do not exist.

CAT HO, Nguyen and RASIOWA, Helena. Plain Semi-Post Algebras as a Poset-Based Generalization of Post Algebras and their Representability. Stud Log, 48(4), 509-530, D 89.

CATALÁ, Rafael. Para una teoría latinoamericana de las relaciones de la ciencia con la literatura: la cienciapoesía. Rev Filosof (Costa Rica), 28(67-68), 215-223, D 90.

This article explores the possibilities of creating a Latin American theory of the relations of literature and science. It uses as examples the works of José Martí, Ernesto Cardenal and Jorge Luis Borges. It also briefly discusses that the Latin American writers should bring, through their literary practice, knowledge of science to the population.

CATALANO, Joseph. Authenticity: A Sartrean Perspective. Phil Forum, 22(2), 99-119, Wint 90-91.

Distinguishing good and bad faith from authenticity and inauthenticity, I attempt to rehabilitate the notion of authenticity. I see Sartre returning in his study of Genet and in his *Critique* to the fundamental insight of the earlier *Transcendence of the Ego* that the self is an "object" of consciousness. While I view that Sartre always had a "social" view of the self, the study of Genet returns to the fundamental insight of the *Transcendence* by showing how the other's bad faith can affect our own interior life. The *Critique* adds the historical dimension of the self.

CATANIA, Alfonso. Sovranità e obbedienza. Riv Int Filosof Diritto, 67(2), 219-229, Ap-Je 90.

The essay starts from the hard question about what is the role that the doctrine of sovereignity plays in contemporary legal philosophy. It criticizes Carl Schmitt's interpretation of the political thought of Thomas Hobbes in terms of "decisionism". The author emphasizes the idea of external obedience as the origin of the modern secularized concept of State. Hobbes is not possible to talk of constituted power or positive law without any reference to an historical obedience. So obedience becomes part of the definition of the law itself. More than sovereignity is "recognition" that legal philosophy uses to legitimate power.

CATES, Lynn. Sobre la individualidad. Rev Latin De Filosof, 16(2), 219-234, Jl 90.

CATTANEI, E. I metodi della metafisica platonico-accademica "generalizzante" ed "elementarizzante" nei libri "M" e "N".... Riv Filosof Neo-Scolas, 82(2-3), 183-213, Ap-S 90.

CATTANEI, Elisabetta. Per una rilettura dei libri "M" e "N" della *Metafisica* di Aristotele alla luce delle "dottrine non scritte" di Platone. Riv Filosof Neo-Scolas, 81(4), 543-558, O-D 89.

CATTEPOEL, Jan. *Dämonie und Gesellschaft.* Freiburg, Alber, 1991.

Soren Kierkegaard devotes a large part of his work to one psychological phenomenon which has a consistently destructive effect on his society: the demonic. In relation to personalities such as Don Juan and Nero, Caesar and Richard III, he shows that they project their own fear, unfreedom and despair onto their victims, and that they do this through a "broken" form of communication which serves chiefly to convey logical antimonies. Kierkegaard discovers the same communicative form in ideologies and in "worldly" Christianity. His analysis offers a percipient explanation for the collapse of ideologies today.

CATURELLI, Alberto. Filosofía cristiana y apologética en Mons Audino Rodríguez y Olmos. Sapientia, 45(175), 49-70, Ja-Mr 90.

CATURELLI, Alberto. La filosofía iberoamericana en la obra de Alain Guy. Sapientia, 45(178), 311-314, O-D 90.

CAUCHI, Francesca. Nietzsche and Pessimism: The Metaphysics Hypostatised. Hist Euro Ideas, 13(3), 253-267, 1991.

CAVADI, Augusto. È possibile un'esperienza di Dio? Sapienza, 44(1), 3-12, Ja-Mr 91.

CAVAILLÉ, Jean-Pierre. Les sens trompeurs: Usage cartésien d'un motif sceptique. Rev Phil Fr, 181(1), 3-31, 1991.

CAVELL, Marcia. "Metaphor, Dreamwork and Irrationality" in *Truth and Interpretation: Perspectives on the Philosophy of Donald Davidson*, LE PORE, Ernest (ed), 495-507. Cambridge, Blackwell, 1986.

CAWS, Peter. Committees and Consensus: How Many Heads Are Better Than One? J Med Phil, 16(4), 375-391, Ag 91.

The first section of this paper asks why the notion of consensus has recently come to the fore in the medical humanities, and suggests that the answer is a function of growing technological and professional complexity. The next two sections examine the concept of consensus analytically citing some of the recent philosophical literature. The fourth section looks at committee deliberations and their desirable outcomes, and questions the degree to which consensus serves those outcomes. In the fifth and last section it is suggested that if I am to subscribe to a consensual outcome responsibly I must be personally committed to it, and that this requires a form of knowledge I call 'fiduciary', in this case knowledge of the competence and trustworthiness of other participants in deliberation whose expertise may have influenced my agreement.

CEDERBLOM, Jerry and PAULSEN, David W. *Critical Reasoning (Third Edition).* Belmont, Wadsworth, 1991.

CEGIELSKI, Patrick. The Elementary Theory of the Natural Lattice is Finitely Axiomatizable. Notre Dame J Form Log, 30(1), 138-150, Wint 89.

The set of positive integers with the divisibility relation is a lattice. We give an explicit finite axiomatization of the first order theory of this natural lattice, and an elimination of quantifiers (this gives a new proof of its decidability) in the language with only a binary predicate (for divisibility relation). The fact seem prominent because relatively few theories of structures are finitely axiomatizable (the theory of addition and the theory of multiplication are not).

CELANO, Anthony J. Play and the Theory of Basic Human Goods. Amer Phil Quart, 28(2), 137-146, Ap 91.

The article concentrates upon the meaning of the concept of play and its relevance to the ethics of basic moral goods. A small, but growing, number of moralists have recently asserted that they can easily identify certain actions that are universally choiceworthy. These actions are said to be so inherently good that they provide the basis for the moral life. The central argument of the article examines the definition of play as self-contained activity, and criticizes its facile inclusion among the list of basic goods. The article concludes with some criticisms of the general theory of basic moral goods.

CELANO, Brun. L'interpretazione del conflitto fra norme nell'ultimo Kelsen. Riv Int Filosof Diritto, 67(1), 13-50, Ja-Mr 90.

CELANO, Bruno. Per un'analisi del discorso dichiarativo. Teoria, 10(1), 165-181, 1990.

CELANO, Bruno. Soggettività e autocoscienza: Prospettive e problemi in Dieter Henrich. G Metaf, 12(1), 113-160, Ja-Ap 90.

CENIZA, Claro R. Material Implication and Entailment. Notre Dame J Form Log, 29(4), 510-519, Fall 88.

The so-called paradoxes of material implication are usually summarized by the following formulas: (1) "q → (p → q)," and (2) "-p → (p → q)." If we export (1), we obtain "(q.p) → q," in which the consequent "q" is entailed by the antecedent "q.p," the consequent being entailed by itself as now part of the new antecedent. Similarly, if we export (2), we get "(-p.p) → q" in which the antecedent is self-contradictory. This new formula is equivalent to the statement, if "'-p.p' is true, then 'q' is true," which is not paradoxical again since if a false statement is true, then any statement would be true, and "-p.p," being self-contradictory, is false. However, since "-p.p" cannot be true, it follows that the truth of a material conditional with a false antecedent is degenerate. Furthermore, the following formulas are tautologies: (3) "(p → q) ↔ [p ↔ (p.q)]," and (4) "(p → q) ↔ [(p → q) ↔ [(p.q) → q]]," both of which show that in every true material conditional, the antecedent is *logically* equivalent to the conjunction of the antecedent and the consequent, and therefore entails, albeit contingently, the consequent.

CENTORE, F F. *Being and Becoming: A Critique of Post-Modernism.* Westport, Greenwood Pr, 1991.

The main focus of the work is on the metaphysical foundations of post-modernism, deconstructionism, etc. The work shows that to be credible hyper-modernism requires a dichotomy between being and becoming such that only becoming is real. If, however, being and becoming can be reconciled, then this *avant-garde* position collapses. The work opens with a discussion of the current orthodoxy in philosophy, continues with the roles of Nietzsche, James, Hegel, Küng, Heidegger, and Sartre, and closes with an emphasis on the need for a non-Greek notion of being. There is also an appendix on how Hume *deduced* his doctrine of skepticism.

CENTRONE, Marino. Uno sguardo sulla filosofia americana contemporanea. Ann Fac Lett Filosof, 32, 529-552, 1989.

CERBELAUD, Dominique. La création *ex nihilo* en question. Rev Thomiste, 90(3), 357-372, Jl-S 90.

CERCÓS SOTO, José Luis. Substancia y sustantividad: Tomás de Aquino y X Zubiri. Anu Filosof, 23(2), 9-27, 1990.

CERRATO, C. General Canonical Models for Graded Normal Logics (Graded Modalities IV). Stud Log, 49(2), 241-252, Je 90.

Graded modalities investigate combinatorial properties of Kripke models: graded possibility and necessity operators use natural numbers as grades so to capture models' features expressible with reference to finite cardinalities. The theory of graded modalities has been developed in a way closely resembling the classical one; canonical models was already introduced to prove completeness and compactness of Graded Normal Logics (GNLs). We prove such canonical models do not exist for GNLs with symmetric models, so that we introduce a new kind of canonical models, the general ones, that exist and work well in every case.

CESA, Claudio. Il pensiero di Aldo Capitini e la filosofia del neoidealismo. G Crit Filosof Ital, 68(3), 273-294, S-D 89.

CHADBOURNE, Richard M. "Two Converts: Augustine and Pascal" in *Grace, Politics and Desire: Essays on Augustine*, MEYNELL, Hugo A (ed), 33-51. Calgary, Univ Calgary Pr, 1990.

CHAFFIN, Deborah G. "A Reply to Gabriella Baptist's "Ways and Loci of Modality"" in *Essays on Hegel's Logic*, DI GIOVANNI, George (ed), 145-152. Albany, SUNY Pr, 1990.

I offer a brief reconstruction of the place and meaning of the modalities in Hegel's *Science of Logic*. Contra Baptist, I argue for a dialectical continuity between the form and content of the various modes in which the actual manifests itself in externality. Thus, the stages in reflection's real unity with immediacy (the modalities) are the internal differentiations of the absolute. Hegel allows us to understand why actuality is genetically presupposed by possibility and yet, ontologically, is more determinate. We can understand why necessity envelops contingency without undercutting or eliminating it. Hegel does not ignore the irreducibility of otherness, of alterity; yet neither does he confuse such otherness with negation.

CHAKRAVARTI, A. Two Concepts of Justice. J Indian Counc Phil Res, 6(1), 29-37, S-D 88.

My aim is to establish two things about the concept of justice. These are (i) that this concept is a *universal concept* when used as an ethical theory, a theory as a means to do 'good' and 'fairness' to each and every individual of a society in an impartial way, and (ii) that this concept is a *subjective concept* in the sense that there is personal justice, justice of one's own which specially belongs to a just person. Therefore, it will not be a contradiction to say that the concept of justice possesses both universal and subjective characteristics at the same time.

CHAKRAVARTI, Mihirvikash and HELEN, Mercy. Disagreement in Philosophy. J Indian Counc Phil Res, 5(1), 95-102, S-D 87.

This paper examines the basic presupposition of Lazerowitz's metaphilosophy, namely, the position that philosophers disagree. From Descartes downward the position has been treated as if it is an axiom, but we have shown that, in having denied truth-value to philosophical propositions, Lazerowitz has unconsciously committed himself to the position that there can never be any disagreement among them and thereby destroyed the very basis of his metaphilosophy. In this connection, we have also mentioned the difficulties Lazerowitz has to face in finding any particular logical value in terms of which the utterances which constitute his metaphilosophy can be characterized.

CHAKRAVARTI, Sitansu S. On Kaplan's Logic of Demonstratives. J Indian Counc Phil Res, 6(1), 83-86, S-D 88.

CHALIER, Catherine. "Ethics and the Feminine" in *Re-Reading Levinas*, BERNASCONI, Robert (ed), 119-129. Bloomington, Indiana Univ Pr, 1991.

CHALMERS, Alan. How to Defend Science Against Scepticism: A Reply to Barry Gower. Brit J Phil Sci, 40(2), 249-253, Je 89.

CHAMBERS, William V. Inferring Formal Causation from Corresponding Regressions. J Mind Behav, 12(1), 49-70, Wint 91.

A statistical method for inference of formal causes was introduced. The procedure, referred to as the method of corresponding regressions, was explained and illustrated using a variety of simulated causal models. The method reflects IV/DV relations among variables traditionally limited to correlational or structural equation analysis. The method was applied to additive, subtractive, multiplicative, recursive and reflected models, as well as models of unrelated and correlated dependent variables. Initial applications to data from physical science, biology, economics, marketing and psychology were developed, with generally supportive results.

CHAMBERS, William. Corresponding Regressions, Procedural Evidence, and the Dialectics of Substantive Theory, Metaphysics, Methodology. J Mind Behav, 12(1), 83-92, Wint 91.

A defense of the method of corresponding regressions was presented. The confounding of formal cause metaphysics with efficient cause methodology was discussed and a rationale for a formal cause methodology was presented. Time-series simulations were used to illustrate the primacy of structural tautologies over temporal transformations. Conclusions supported the use of corresponding regressions as a means of inferring formal causality.

CHAMBLISS, J J and GIARELLI, James M. The Foundations of Professionalism: Fifty Years of the Philosophy of Education Society in Retrospect. Educ Theor, 41(3), 265-274, Sum 91.

The Philosophy of Education Society is discussed as a case study in professionalization. Although those working in philosophy of education have discussed the nature of the discipline, the emphasis of the Society has been a professional one, which views philosophers of education as a distinct professional class of exclusive and selectively initiated members, whose interests are with other philosophers. This has resulted in the neglect of philosophy of education as a public enterprise, open to all citizens for the purpose of educational dialogue. An appeal is made for philosophy's increased participation in public life.

CHAMPAGNE, R A. Jacques Derrida's Response to the Call for Ethics. Int J Moral Soc Stud, 6(1), 3-18, Spr 91.

Until recently, there seemed to have been little at stake ethically in Derrida's explorations of the relationships among literature, philosophy, language, and meaning. The discoveries concerning the hidden complicities of both the philosopher Martin Heidegger and the literary critic Paul de Man with the National Socialist Party during the 1930s and 1940s have incited Derrida to become involved in ethical re-readings of their texts. Derrida's reflections on their writings suggest that what Heidegger and de Man did not say constitutes lying about the truth. Distinguishing between lies and truth is crucial for the roles of philosophy and literature and their communities of followers. Derrida's deconstructions of Heidegger and de Man posit the importance of an ultra-ethics, not subject to political or ideological motives, while reflecting the values of a community, for the survival of philosophy and literature.

CHANDLER, John. Feminism and Epistemology. Metaphilosophy, 21(4), 367-381, O 90.

Feminists charge dominant epistemologies with male bias. The critiques examined here see this bias as arising from reliance on male experience to the exclusion of that of women, and as resulting in defective theories of knowledge. This paper examines the claim that male experience is not merely partial, but is in general cognitively inferior to women's, so that its replacement, rather than supplementation, is required. Doubts are raised about the existence of male and female experiences, and the psychoanalytic and Marxist grounds for privileging the latter.

CHANDLER, John. Killing and Letting Die—Putting the Debate in Context. Austl J Phil, 68(4), 420-431, D 90.

This paper argues that (1) the distinction between killing and letting die is not an instance of that between acts and omissions; (2) that which deaths one counts as killings as opposed to lettings-die (or neither) is influenced by one's moral beliefs; (3) that the moral significance of such distinctions as between killing and letting die, acting and omitting, doing and allowing, and intending and foreseeing cannot be decided in isolation from deciding between wider ethical theories.

CHANDLER, Marthe. Attitudes, Leprechauns and Neutrinos: The Ontology of Behavioral Science. Phil Stud, 60(1-2), 5-17, S-O 90.

Social psychologists and survey researchers insist that attitudes, like neutrinos, are real theoretical entities, identified and measured by observations of their effects. Philosophers are skeptical of this claim for a number of reasons: the lack of predictive success in social sciences, and the "holistic" nature of our understanding of human actions. I argue that doubts about attitudes often depend on a failure to distinguish old-fashioned behaviorism from contemporary behavioral science. I provide reasons for thinking that attitudes are just as real as neutrinos and suggest an alternative explanation for the lack of progress in behavioral science.

CHANDRA, Suresh. Evans-Pritchard on Persons and Their Cattle-Clocks: A Note on the Anthropological Account of Man. J Indian Counc Phil Res, 6(2), 31-51, Ja-Ap 89.

CHANG, Briankle G. Copies, Reproducibility and Aesthetic Adequacy. Brit J Aes, 31(3), 265-267, Jl 91.

This paper argues that the notion of "non-transitivity," as proposed by Graham Oddie and David Ward, fails to refute the possibility of the *exact sameness of look* between a copy and its original. The original formulation of the non-transitivity thesis is modified by introducing the distinction between the succession condition and the non-transitivity condition. It is demonstrated that the non-transitivity condition alone does not preclude the possibility to reproduce an *aesthetically adequate* copy from the original.

CHANGLU, Qiao. A Great Intellectual Current Worthy of National Pride. Chin Stud Phil, 22(3), 3-19, Spr 91.

The treatise expounds that a thinking trend that man is considered the basis of government existed in the Spring and Autumn and the Warring States periods, which is a pride of Chinese people. The characteristics of the trend is the emphasis upon the improvement of the social positions for ordinary people, the objection against the persecution and massacre to people, and the advocation of the existence of the universal benevolence of human being. The main representatives of this trend were Guan Zhong, Confucius, Mo Di, Yang Zhu, Mencius, Lao Dan, Zhuang Zhou and Xun Qing.

CHANTER, Tina. "Antigone's Dilemma" in *Re-Reading Levinas*, BERNASCONI, Robert (ed), 130-146. Bloomington, Indiana Univ Pr, 1991.

CHAPMAN, Tobias. *In Defense of Mystical Ideas: Support for Mystical Beliefs from a Purely Theoretical Viewpoint*. Lewiston, Mellen Pr, 1989.

The purpose of this book is to defend a number of theses which are closely associated with the "mystical" tradition in philosophy, from the point of view of contemporary analytical philosophy. The early Wittgenstein's distinction between what can be said and what can only be "shown" is defended with particular emphasis on the idea that some very ordinary truths, even about logic, are necessarily ineffable; so that no particular objection to religious language can be made on this score. There are also defences of the ontological argument, the unreality of time and discussions of epistemology and the nature of the self.

CHAPPELL, Vere. Locke on the Ontology of Matter, Living Things and Persons. Phil Stud, 60(1-2), 19-32, S-O 90.

After some remarks about his ontology in general, I lay out Locke's conception of three of the kinds of things he holds there to be: material masses, organisms, and persons. These all belong to the more general category of *compounded substances*, but differ in the nature of their elements and in the manner of their compounding. In the case of organisms and persons, I argue, Locke is committed to a doctrine of double existence: two distinct things at the same place and time. Some of my account is speculative; but much of it is directly supported by textual evidence.

CHARLTON, William. "Aesthetic Reasons" in *XIth International Congress in Aesthetics, Nottingham 1988*, WOODFIELD, Richard (ed), 18-21. Nottingham, Nottingham Polytech, 1990.

The author was not given the chance to correct the proofs of this piece. The title should be 'Aesthetic Tastes'. It distinguishes taste, a discriminative ability, from tastes, acquired likings. Tastes in literature and representational arts are often extensions of or analogous to dispositions of character. Other tastes are skills of various kinds, such as skills in interpreting visual selection and seeing or hearing things are related; and some very the aesthetic aspect of skills which are primarily practical.

CHARMÉ, Stuart Zane. *Vulgarity and Authenticity: Dimensions of Otherness in the World of Jean-Paul Sartre*. Amherst, Univ of Mass Pr, 1991.

This book analyzes the idea of "vulgarity" as a key to Sartre's view of existential authenticity. Part I examines "vulgarity" as that which undermines the inauthenticity of civilized attitudes toward nature and the body. The ambivalent quality of vulgarity is presented in relation to phenomena such as obscenity, ugliness, scatology, laughter, illness, odor, and nausea. Part II reconstructs Sartre's implicit mythology of the vulgar Other. His views of Jews, women, homosexuals, and blacks represent elements in Sartre's quest for an authentic self. Throughout the book, reference is made to Sartre's use of religious metaphors to characterize both bad faith and authenticity.

CHARRON, Ghyslain. Freud devait-il choisir entre les deux conceptions du symbole que lui attribue Lévi-Strauss? Dialogue (Canada), 29(3), 375-386, 1990.

CHATALIAN, George. *Epistemology and Skepticism: An Enquiry into the Nature of Epistemology*. Carbondale, So Illinois Univ Pr, 1991.

The author seeks to restore the classical tradition in epistemology in part by assembling data about philosophical skepticism throughout the history of philosophy. He outlines the central theses in the epistemology of Quine, Russell and Wittgenstein, examining the implicit claims made by such theses about ancient skeptics, Sophists and Plato. The author argues against analytic epistemology and favors a classical approach. (staff)

CHATER, Nick and OAKSFORD, Mike. Against Logicist Cognitive Science. Mind Lang, 6(1), 1-38, Spr 91.

We argue that the plausibility of classical "logicist" cognitive science depends on its ability to provide a proof-theoretic account of the defeasible inferencing found in almost every area of cognitive activity. We assess attempts in Artificial Intelligence to carry out this proof-theoretic programme using non-monotonic logics. We note that such logics allow only unacceptably weak disjunctive conclusions and that the theorem proving algorithms over such logics are computationally intractable due to their reliance on th NP-hard problem of consistency checking. We suggest that the programme of classical cognitive science is infeasible and address a number of objections to this conclusion.

CHATTOPADHYAYA, D P. Rationality, Culture and Values. J Indian Counc Phil Res, 8(1), 1-15, S-D 90.

Here I defend the thesis of culture-relative rationality. Secondly, I examine three concepts of rationality as developed in economics, evolutionary biology and psychological behaviourism. I call these concepts REM (Rational Economic Man), REB (Rationality in Evolutionary Biology) and ROB (Rationality of Behaviour). Thirdly, I argue to show the limits of each one of these concepts of rationality. I particularly highlight their inability to capture the normative aspect of economic action, evolutionary adaptation and behavioural reinforcement. Fourthly, I indicate how normative considerations can be plausibly accommodated within the frameworks of REM, REB and ROB. Finally, I briefly and critically discuss some allied concepts of rationality defined in terms of 1) appropriateness of the end-means relationship, 2) universalisability and 3) enforceability.

CHATTOPADHYAYA, D P. Study of Society and Polity: Scientific and Philosophical. J Indian Counc Phil Res, 5(2), 97-126, Ja-Ap 88.

CHAUDHURI, Manjusree. Can Knowledge Occur Unknowingly? J Indian Counc Phil Res, 6(1), 39-45, S-D 88.

The problem is a misleading one. The central question: do I know that I know p when I do know p? actually conceals within it two different questions relating to two different approaches to the problem. The first question, one of epistemic psychology, is: when knowledge does occur, do we know its occurrence as such?—a question about knowledge *of* knowledge. The second one, a question of epistemic logic, is: when I have knowledge, how do I know that what I am having is knowledge, not belief or anything else?—a question about knowledge *upon* knowledge. Philosophers lose sight of this bilaterality of approaches and misread it as a single question inviting single answer.

CHAUDHURI, Minakshi Ray. Indigenous Ends and Alien Means: A Footnote on Indian Renaissance. J Indian Counc Phil Res, 5(2), 147-151, Ja-Ap 88.

CHAUDHURY, Mahasweta. Is Knowledge Socially Determined? A Critique. J Indian Counc Phil Res, 7(3), 67-74, My-Ag 90.

CHAUDHURY, Mahasweta. Objectivity and Growth of Knowledge. J Indian Counc Phil Res, 5(2), 59-85, Ja-Ap 88.

Popper's ascription of 'growth' as the most important feature to scientific knowledge is examined with reference to his pluralistic metaphysics of World 1, World 2 and World 3. I have defended Popper in his ascription of growth and objectivity to scientific knowledge but nevertheless argued that if knowledge in the objective sense is growing, then he cannot have an 'epistemology without a knowing subject'. And even if Popper admits knowing subject into his epistemology, that fact does not necessarily make his theory subjectivist.

CHAUDHURY, Mahasweta. Scientific Rationality—A Rethinking. J Indian Counc Phil Res, 7(1), 99-119, S-D 89.

CHAUMONT, Jean-Michel. L'être de l'humain: Notes sur la tradition communautarienne. Rev Phil Louvain, 89(81), 144-163, F 91.

CHAUVIRE, Christiane. "Phénoménologie" de l'expression. Philosophique (France), 1(90), 27-34, 1990.

CHAVES, Carmen. El proyecto crítico de Kant. Rev Filosof (Costa Rica), 28(67-68), 209-213, D 90.

Under the light of Kant's evolving thought and the later philosophical thought, Kant's philosophy is shown as a critical reasoning directed towards the creation of a new concept of philosophy. The action, instead of ontological or theological theory, as the foundation and origin of human reality. But in Kant, the action is restricted to a non-dialectic concept. His thought is only the beginning of a new philosophy that will surpass the philosophy of the "cogito" and in which faith, understood as an adhesion to reason, will occupy a central position.

CHAVES, Flory. Vida y Resurrección en el pensamiento de Erich Fromm. Rev Filosof (Costa Rica), 28(67-68), 99-105, D 90.

The main purpose of this piece of work is to investigate, in the Erich Fromm work, two main aspects fundamental for mankind: life and resurrection. Principal sections of the work are: brief biography, general philosophical thought, and a deep study of the indicated thesis. Finally, the conclusions are indicated.

CHAZERANS, Jean-François. La substance composée chez Leibniz. Rev Phil Fr, 181(1), 47-66, 1991.

CHEN, Xiang. Local Incommensurability and Communicability. Proc Phil Sci Ass, 1, 67-76, 1990.

Kuhn regards local incommensurability as an unavoidable result of changes in worldview, but his account fails to explain both historical cases in which rivals with different paradigms obtained consensus, and psychological experiments in which people with different cultural backgrounds accurately presented other points of view. Although the conditions required to generate local incommensurability were present in the dispute between Brewster and Herschel on light absorption, they succeeded in communicating. Ultimately Brewster understood his opponent's position, in the same way that subjects in Barsalou's recent psychological experiments proved able to comprehend alien conceptual structures. Building upon recent cognitive theories of graded conceptual structures, I offer a new account of incommensurability, which accommodates these historical cases and psychological results. By correcting and extending Kuhn's account I show that local incommensurability may be a matter of degree.

CHEN, Xiang. Young and Lloyd on the Particle Theory of Light: A Response to Achinstein. Stud Hist Phil Sci, 21(4), 665-676, D 90.

Achinstein claims that the method nineteenth-century wave theorists employed in theory appraisal is one that can be reconstructed probabilistically. By putting the examples Achinstein cites into their historical contexts, I argue that such nineteenth-century wave theorists as Thomas Young and Humphrey Lloyd in their theory appraisals actually employed a criterion that emphasizes a theory's conceptual completeness, including its coherence, consistency, and simplicity. These conceptual considerations cannot be incorporated into a Bayesian framework, nor be classified as a probabilistic reasoning, because we cannot simply assign a zero or a low prior probability to a conceptually incomplete theory.

CHENEY, Jim and WARREN, Karen J. Ecological Feminism and Ecosystem Ecology. Hypatia, 6(1), 179-197, Spr 91.

Ecological feminism is a feminism which attempts to unite the demands of the women's movement with those of the ecological movement. Ecofeminists often appeal to "ecology" in support of their claims, particulary claims about the importance of feminism to environmentalism. What is missing from the literature is any sustained attempt to show respects in which ecological feminism and the science of ecology are engaged in complementary, mutually supportive projects. In this paper we attempt to do that by showing ten important similarities which establish the need for and benefits of on-going dialogue between ecofeminists and ecosystem ecologists.

CHENG, Chung-ying. "Chinese Metaphysics as Non-Metaphysics: Confucian and Daoist Insights into the Nature of Reality" in *Understanding the Chinese Mind: The Philosophical Roots*, ALLINSON, Robert E (ed), 167-208. New York, Oxford Univ Pr, 1989.

This book is a collection of important essays on the Confucian/Neo-Confucian philosophy integrated in a theoretical framework of onto-hermeneutical thinking toward both analytical reconstruction of Confucian/Neo-Confucian philosophy and illumination of universal reality (*tao*) and human nature (*hsing*).

CHENG, Chung-ying. *New Dimensions of Confucian and Neo-Confucian Philosophy*. Albany, SUNY Pr, 1991.

CHERRY, Christopher. Machines as Persons? Philosophy, 29, 11-24, 91 Supp.

Many have argued that it is intelligible to ascribe sentience, and even personhood, to an artificially produced entity, not made of flesh and blood. Even were it conceded that such an artefact ('mobile system') were engineered to resemble the human form and to mimic the range human behavior, our knowledge that it was an *imitation* would, typically, inhibit or demolish any readiness to ascribe sentient states. In large part, this is function of primitive, but complex, attitudes and reactions to humankind. This complex is investigated in more and less problematic cases, including uncanny ones. It is tentatively concluded that the status of advanced machines may best be understood in terms of fictitious personnages.

CHERVENAK, Frank A and MC CULLOUGH, Laurence B. Justified Limits on Refusing Intervention. Hastings Center Rep, 21(2), 12-18, Mr-Ap 91.

CHERWITZ, Richard A and HIKINS, James W. Irreducible Dualisms and the Residue of Commonsense: On the Inevitability of Cartesian Anxiety. Phil Rhet, 23(3), 229-241, 1990.

CHESLER, Phyllis. Twenty Years Since *Women and Madness*: Toward a Feminist Institute of Mental Health and Healing. J Mind Behav, 11(3-4), 313-322, Sum-Autumn 90.

This article reviews the development of a feminist analysis of female and male psychology from 1970 to 1990; the acceptance, rejection or indifference to feminist theory and practice by women in general and by female patients and mental health practitioners in specific. The article describes what feminist therapy ideally is and discusses the need for a Feminist Institute of Mental Health.

CHIBAUDEL, Pierre. Sur le fragment des trois ordres de Blaise Pascal. Arch Phil, 53(4), 631-645, O-D 90.

Are those "orders" distinct levels of reality or incompatible forms of mind, or societies ignoring one another? It depends on the one according to which we speak. The notion of order is not perceived without experiencing the change of order, as any change of order implies a change of the notion of order. Pascal here proposes, together with this philosophical experience, one of his inventions, the "raison figurante," and thus proceeds towards a lay Christianity.

CHIESA, Curzio. Idées de négations. Rev Theol Phil, 122(3), 353-364, 1990.

Cet article examine le texte du *De Ideis* d'Aristote dans lequel on trouve l'argument tiré de l'"unité d'une multiplicité": le prédicat commun à plusieurs choses est considéré par les Platoniciens comme une Idée séparée. Aux yeux d'Aristote cet argument postule des Idées également pour les négations. Mais paradoxalement, la deuxième version de l'argument indique que les prédicats négatifs se réfèrent à une Idée positive, ce qui semble annuler la critique aristotélicienne.

CHILD, James W. The Moral Foundations of Intangible Property. Monist, 73(4), 578-600, O 90.

CHILDRESS, James F. Ethics, Public Policy, and Human Fetal Tissue Transplantation. Kennedy Inst Ethics J, 1(2), 93-121, Je 91.

This article focuses on the deliberations of the National Institutes of Health Human Fetal Tissue Transplanation Research Panel in 1988. It explores various arguments for and against the use of fetal tissue for transplantation research, following elective abortion, and for and against the use of federal funds for such research. After examining the relevance of various positions on the moral status of the fetus and the morality of abortion, the article critically examines charges that such research, especially with federal funds, would involve complicity in the moral evil of abortion, would legitimate abortion practices, and would provide incentives for abortions. Finally, it considers whether the donation model is appropriate for the transfer of human fetal tissue and whether the woman who chooses to have an abortion is the appropriate donor of the tissue.

CHILDRESS, James F. The Prophetic and the Priestly. Hastings Center Rep, 20(6), 18-19, N-D 90.

CHINCHORE, Mangala R. Krtapranasa and Akrtabhyagama: An Analysis, Defence and Rationale of the Buddhist Theory of Action. Indian Phil Quart, 18(2), 231-270, Ap 91.

This paper attempts to present a satisfactory analysis of the Buddhist theory of action in contrast to the non-Buddhist, and bring out the rationale and implications of the former. The paper has four sections. The first outlines the differences between the Buddhist and the non-Buddhist theory of action. The second and the third articulate respectively features of the non-Buddhist and the Buddhist perspectives and spell out their rationales. In the last, the richness and profundity of the Buddhist approach is brought out by highlighting prominent implications of it.

CHINCHORE, Mangala R. Lost Buddhist Texts: The Rationale of Their Reconstruction in Sanskrit. Indian Phil Quart, 17(3), 285-312, Jl 90.

This paper aims at spelling out the rationale of reconstructing in Sanskrit those philosophical and other Buddhist texts not available in it from their Tibetan or Chinese translations. The first section presents an outline of the aspects of the diversified culture which flourished in the Indian subcontinent within the framework of a broadly unifying civilization, while the second brings out importance of Sanskrit as a common medium of intellectual exchange contributing to widening and deepening of vistas of comprehension. The last section highlights the need and necessity of embarking upon such a project and shows the shortcomings of accomplishing it otherwise.

CHING-CHUNG, Chao. The Design, Use and Evaluation of Philosophical Stories for Children. Thinking, 9(2), 1-4, 1990.

CHIPPINDALE, Christopher. "Philosophical Lessons from the History of Stonehenge Studies" in *Critical Traditions in Contemporary Archaeology*, PINSKY, Valerie (ed), 68-79. New York, Cambridge Univ Pr, 1990.

CHIROT, Daniel. What Happened in Eastern Europe in 1989? Praxis Int, 10(3-4), 278-305, O 90-Ja 91.

The revolutions of 1989 in Eastern Europe were the result both of communism's economic and moral failures. The former had been well understood and studied for a long time, but the latter, because they were difficult to measure or even grasp, were not. For that reason, the revolutions of 1989 were quite unexpected. This suggests that most fashionable social science theories about revolution, which have been almost entirely based on materialistic theories and on class analysis, have been missing a key aspect of all revolutionary situations, moral outrage. Difficult as it may be, future students of revolution ought to learn to study morality.

CHISHOLM, John. The Complexity of Intrinsically R.E. Subsets of Existentially Decidable Models. J Sym Log, 55(3), 1213-1232, S 90.

CHISHOLM, John. Effective Model Theory versus Recursive Model Theory. J Sym Log, 55(3), 1168-1191, S 90.

CHISHOLM, Roderick M. Firth and the Ethics of Belief. Phil Phenomenol Res, 51(1), 119-128, Mr 91.

CHISHOLM, Roderick M. Keith Lehrer and Thomas Reid. Phil Stud, 60(1-2), 33-38, S-O 90.

CHISHOLM, Roderick M. "Referring to Things That No Longer Exist" in *Philosophical Perspectives, 4: Action Theory and Philosophy of Mind, 1990*, TOMBERLIN, James E (ed), 545-556. Atascadero, Ridgeview, 1990.

CHISHOLM, Roderick M. "Why Singular Propositions?" in *Themes From Kaplan*, ALMOG, Joseph (ed), 145-150. New York, Oxford Univ Pr, 1989.

CHISICK, Harvey. The Ambivalence of the Idea of Equality in the French Enlightenment. Hist Euro Ideas, 13(3), 215-223, 1991.

Based on entries in encyclopedias and 'philosophical dictionaries' published in France during the eighteenth century, this article examines prevailing attitudes toward equality. It finds that on the one hand virtually all writers adhered to the doctrine of natural equality, but that on the other, all regarded this primal equality as without direct application in contemporary society. Rather, the doctrine of natural equality was used primarily as an argument to encourage the upper classes to treat their social inferiors with more compassion and consideration, and so to enhance social harmony. This use of a potentially radical idea suggests that mainstream Enlightenment thought was characterized more by a humane conservatism than social or political radicalism.

CHMIELEWSKI, Philip J. Reply to Gordon: Discourse at Work. Int Phil Quart, 31(2), 227-229, Je 91.

CHO, Kah Kyung. *Bewusstsein und Natursein*. Freiburg, Alber, 1991.

Husserl's theory of intuition and Heidegger's inquiry into nature come under a new light in these highly revealing and critical studies. Professor Cho combines an exceptionally intimate knowledge of German philosophical tradition with a profound Eastern insight. It is a unique contribution to critical understanding of current Continental thought.

CHO, Kah Kyung. Phenomenology as Cooperative Task: Husserl-Farber Correspondence during 1936-37. Phil Phenomenol Res, 50 SUPP, 27-43, Fall 90.

Both Farber's straightforward questions and Husserl's unusually detailed answers documented in this article deserve their place in the annals of phenomenology. Husserl denies a critic's charge that he "borrowed" Brentano's ideas, and he gives a standard phenomenologist answer to the questions of historical materialism and "evolutionary" philosophy. We also learn why instead of a translation of *Logical Investigations*, as Husserl wished, its commentary version, *The Foundations of Phenomenology*, came into our hands. While Husserl exhorts his American followers to cooperate under the aspect of eternity, he also reveals his worries, as "a nationally ostracized man," and as a father.

CHOLAK, Peter. Boolean Algebras and Orbits of the Lattice of R.E. Sets Modulo the Finite Sets. J Sym Log, 55(2), 744-760, Je 90.

An important program in the study of the structure of the lattice of r.e. sets modulo finite sets is the classification of the orbits. We show: For every delta_3 Boolean Algebra there exist two hyperhypersimple sets *A* and *B* such that the principal filter formed by each of these two sets is isomorphic to the given Boolean Algebra, the sets are not delta_2 automorphic, but the sets are delta_3 automorphic. This theorem is a generalization of the result by Soare that maximal sets do not form a delta_2 orbit.

CHONG, C T and MOURAD, K J. The Degree of a Σ_n Cut. Annals Pure Applied Log, 48(3), 227-235, Ag 90.

CHONG, C T and DOWNEY, R G. Minimal Degrees Recursive in 1-Generic Degrees. Annals Pure Applied Log, 48(3), 215-225, Ag 90.

CHONG, Kim-Chong. Altruism and the Avoidance of Solipsism. Phil Inq, 11(3-4), 18-26, Sum-Fall 89.

I wish to discuss the claim made in Thomas Nagel's 'The Possibility of Altruism', that all personal judgments must be based on their impersonal correlates. Indeed, one is committed to holding an impersonal judgment about the same situation that one has, in personal terms, made a judgment about. The cost of denying this, in the practical case, is what Nagel calls, 'dissociation' from the impersonal standpoint. This means an inability to make judgments about others, that one makes about oneself—something which Nagel claims has its analogue in solipsism. Section I summarizes the main argument in chapter 11 of this book. Section II presents my objections.

CHRISMAN, James J and MEZNAR, Martin B and CARROLL, Archie B. Social Responsibility and Strategic Management: Toward an Enterprise Strategy Classification. Bus Prof Ethics J, 10(1), 47-66, Spr 91.

CHRISTENSEN, David. Clever Bookies and Coherent Beliefs. Phil Rev, 100(2), 229-247, Ap 91.

"Dutch Book" arguments are often used to show that beliefs should be probabilistically coherent. Apparently similar betting-loss-based arguments ("Dutch Strategies") have been advanced to support other requirements, including conditionalization and, most recently, van Fraassen's "Reflection." I argue that Reflection is absurd. However, this provides no *reductio ad absurdum* of betting-loss-based arguments in general. Understanding how and when betting losses indicate irrationality reveals that Dutch Strategies have none of the force Dutch books have. Thus we may reject Reflection while retaining the classic arguments for coherence. Unfortunately, we must also abandon Dutch Strategy justifications for Conditionalization.

CHRISTENSEN, David. The Irrelevance of Bootstrapping. Phil Sci, 57(4), 644-662, D 90.

The main appeal of the currently popular "bootstrap" account of confirmation developed by Clark Glymour is that it seems to provide an account of evidential relevance. This account has, however, had severe problems; and Glymour has revised his original account in an attempt to solve them. I argue that this attempt fails completely, and that any similar modifications must also fail. If the problems can be solved, it will only be by radical revisions which involve jettisoning bootstrapping's basic approach to theories. Finally, I argue that there is little reason to think that even such drastic modifications will lead to a satisfactory account of relevance.

CHRISTIANO, Thomas. Difficulties with the Principle of Equal Opportunity for Welfare. Phil Stud, 62(2), 179-185, My 91.

CHRISTIDES, T M and MIKOU, M. "The Relative Autonomy of Theoretical Science and the Role of Crucial Experiments" in *Imre Lakatos and Theories of Scientific Change*, GAVROGLU, Kostas (ed), 147-153. Norwell, Kluwer, 1989.

CHRISTIE, John R R. "Hélène Metzger et l'historiographie de la chimie du XVIIIe siècle" in *Études sur/Studies on Hélène Metzger*, FREUDENTHAL, Gad , 99-108. Leiden, Brill, 1990.

This essay provides a narratological analysis of Metzger's historiography, with the aim of revealing certain basic contradictions. These stem from Metzger's philosophical, conceptual approach to analysis in a field, history, which also makes basic narrative demands. Metzger contradictorily advocates fine-grained analysis of conceptual change, *and* recognition of unchanging conceptual foundations. The antitheses in which her work was caught have broader implications for her discipline, the history of science.

CHRISTMAN, John. Autonomy and Personal History. Can J Phil, 21(1), 1-24, Mr 91.

In this paper, I attempt to clarify the notion of individual autonomy. I critically appraise currently influential views of autonomy, particularly ones manifesting a hierarchial conception of the self. I conclude that these views focus too narrowly on a "time slice" of the person in that they center on attitudes a person has about the desires she has at a time. In the new model I develop I focus on the manner in which the agent *came to have* a set of desires. The key element of autonomy is, on my view, the agent's acceptance or rejection of the process of desire formation—the factors that give rise to the development of the desire—rather than the agent's identification with the desire itself.

CHRISTMAN, John. Self-Ownership, Equality, and the Structure of Property Rights. Polit Theory, 19(1), 28-46, F 91.

The principle of self-ownership is a difficult sticking point for egalitarianism. For allowing people with differential talents to exercise the prerogatives of ownership over their skills results in severe inequality of condition. I attempt to dissolve this conflict by introducing a general thesis about the structure of ownership. I argue that there are two importantly different aspects of ownership which must be considered separately in normative debates concerning property rights. Specifically, I claim that the rights associated with the "control" of the object are fundamentally different in structure and scope from the rights to the income flows from such assets. Utilizing this distinction, I try to show that the essence of self-ownership is indeed consistent with mechanisms instituted to achieve equality of condition.

CHRZAN, Keith. God and Gratuitous Evil: A Reply to Yandell. Relig Stud, 27(1), 99-103, Mr 91.

CHRZAN, Keith. Plantinga and Probabilistic Atheism. Int J Phil Relig, 30(1), 21-27, Ag 91.

In "The Probabilistic Problem of Evil" Alvin Plantinga uses Bayes's Theorem to reduce the atheistic argument to one involving only "a priori" probabilities whose meaningfulness he convincingly oppugns. Plantinga neglects to model the atheists's repudiation of theistic defenses, however, and he depicts a priori probabilities as essential components of the atheistic argument. A proper mathematical model of probabilistic atheism creates a prima facie case for atheism and foists the burden of proof upon the theist.

CHUAQUI, Rolando and MALITZ, Jerome. The Geometry of Legal Principles. Theor Decis, 30(1), 27-49, Ja 91.

We discuss several possible legal principles from the standpoint of Bayesian decision theory. In particular, we show that a compelling legal principle implies compatibility with decisions based on maximizing the expected utility.

CHUNG, Bongkil. The Relevance of Confucian Ethics. J Chin Phil, 18(2), 143-159, Je 91.

CHURCH, Alonzo. "Intensionality and the Paradox of the Name Relation" in *Themes From Kaplan*, ALMOG, Joseph (ed), 151-165. New York, Oxford Univ Pr, 1989.

CHURCH, F Forrester. A New Humanism. Relig Hum, 25(1), 3-13, Wint 91.

CHURCHILL, John. The Bellman's Map: Does Antifoundationalism Entail Incommensurability and Relativism? S J Phil, 28(4), 469-484, Wint 90.

Two conclusions are often drawn from the rejection of foundationalist epistemologies: the incommensurability of different conceptual schemes and radical relativism. The *fact* of relativism is distinguished from the conclusion that claims to truth are better or worse than any others, and the *prospect* of incommensurability is distinguished from *a priori* insistence on incomparability. Both distinctions clarify how antifoundationalism is consistent with integrity in philosophical argument.

CHURCHILL, Larry R. AIDS and 'Dirt': Reflections on the Ethics of Ritual Cleanliness. Theor Med, 11(3), 185-192, S 90.

AIDS and the responses and attitudes it evokes surpass the analytic abilities of standard bioethics. These responses and attitudes are explored in terms of literary and anthropological categories, such as dirt, disorder, pollution and ritual cleanliness. Implications for medical education are suggested.

CHURCHILL, Larry R and DANIS, Marion. Autonomy and the Common Weal. Hastings Center Rep, 21(1), 25-31, Ja-F 91.

Recent studies indicate that patients may choose more medical services than physicians think beneficial. As a result, the autonomy of patients conflicts with the potential for just distribution of finite medical resources. The patient-as-citizen and the physician-as-citizen are proposed as concepts to bring autonomy and social justice into a common frame of reference. The recent work of Daniel Callahan and Norman Daniels is discussed, as well as 'citizenship' in medical ethics codes. Possible objections are presented and rebutted.

CHURCHILL, R Paul. "Democracy and the Threat of Nuclear Weapons" in *Issues in War and Peace: Philosophical Inquiries*, KUNKEL, Joseph (ed), 255-266. Wolfeboro, Longwood, 1989.

Nuclear weapons policies are made in a manner inconsistent with fundamental principles of democratic and constitional government. Nuclear deterrence is "managed" by a nuclear elite who often act in a secretive, autocratic, and non-accountable manner. Arguments in support of the current policymaking process fail to show that the merits of weapons policies made autocratically outweight losses in democratic control over the process. The requirements for successful deterrence need not greatly restrict a more democratized process. Furthermore, at present, there is no case for the claim that policies made democratically would be inferior to those made by nuclear elites.

CHURCHILL, R Paul. "Nonviolent Resistance as the Moral Equivalent of War" in *In the Interest of Peace: A Spectrum of Philosophical Views*, KLEIN, Kenneth H (ed), 61-70. Wolfeboro, Longwood, 1990.

This paper challenges the widely held view that war is the only form of contest that can settle decisively and completely the ultimate differences which lead to international conflicts. It is argued that nonviolent resistance can supplant war as a social institution by supplying what only warfare has been thought capable of providing: the self-enforcement of the outcome of an ultimate contest. Moreover, nonviolent resistance can provide a decisive and complete resolution of ultimate contests at vastly lower costs in human life and suffering.

CHURCHLAND, Patricia Smith. Is Neuroscience Relevant to Philosophy? Can J Phil, SUPP 16, 323-341, 1990.

CHURCHLAND, Patricia Smith and SEJNOWSKI, Terrence J. "Neural Representation and Neural Computation" in *Philosophical Perspectives, 4: Action Theory and Philosophy of Mind, 1990*, TOMBERLIN, James E (ed), 343-382. Atascadero, Ridgeview, 1990.

CHURCHLAND, Paul M. "Folk Psychology and the Explanation of Human Behavior" in *Philosophical Perspectives, 3: Philosophy of Mind and Action Theory, 1989*, TOMBERLIN, James E (ed), 225-241. Atascadero, Ridgeview, 1989.

CHURCHLAND, Paul M. "On the Nature of Theories: A Neurocomputational Perspective" in *Scientific Theories*, SAVAGE, C Wade (ed), 59-101. Minneapolis, Univ of Minn Pr, 1990.

CHVATIK, Kvetoslav. Philosophical Prolegomena of Structural Thinking (in Czechoslovakian). Filozof Cas, 38(4), 450-462, 1990.

This text originated in the mid-seventies as a component of the three-part manuscript concerning the aesthetics of Prague structuralism: Part 1 contains the history of Prague School, Part 2 philosophical prolegomena, Part 3 systematic structural aesthetics. An abbreviated version of the manuscript was published in German under the inaccurate title "Tschechoslowakischer Strukturalismus" (Fink, Munich 1981): its centre of gravity lies in a systematic development of the *aesthetics* of Prague School. The present text is a core of the explanation of the philosophical starting points of structural aesthetics. (edited)

CHYMUK, Maria. The Concept of Environment from the Point of View of Philosophy of Culture (in Polish). Ann Univ Mariae Curie-Phil, 10, 53-63, 1985.

The author discusses various definitions of environment, among others, by Aristotle, Marx, and modern encyclopedias. She analyzes the concept of environment in a report of the General Secretary of UNESCO, entitled "Man and Environment" of 1969, and in the Bill of the Seym of the Polish People's Republic, "About the Protection and Shaping of the Environment" of January 1, 1980. She poses a series of questions about what is environment, for whom, for what, when, and what kind of environment it is. In her considerations about this problem, the noun "environment" should be accompanied by an appropriate modifier (biological, geographical, social, cultural, domestic, productive, cosmic). In the conclusion of her study the author declares her support for that definition according to which environment is a space of possible encounters. It depends on us if this space (air, water, soil, food, products of human labour) is optimal or polluted. What formerly was distant, has become close today. That is why in the modern world mutual contacts and cooperation between even the most distant nations have become as necessary as never before.

CI, Jiwei. Conscience, Sympathy and the Foundation of Morality. Amer Phil Quart, 28(1), 49-59, Ja 91.

CI, Jiwei. Freedom and Realms of Living. Phil East West, 41(3), 303-326, Jl 91.

CIARAMELLI, Fabio. "Levinas's Ethical Discourse between Individuation and Universality" in *Re-Reading Levinas*, BERNASCONI, Robert (ed), 83-105. Bloomington, Indiana Univ Pr, 1991.

For Levinas ethics is based on the radical asymmetry of a responsibility which is *mine* beyond any possible generalization. But in the very particularity of such an unmediated obligation which singularizes me, there also lies a dimension of universality transcending the *nic et nunc* of my individuality. This paper, first draft of a book in French (*Transcendence et ethique Essai sur Levinas*, Brussels, 1989) finds in Levinas's reflections on the *prophetic* and the *messianic* a possible issue to the dilemma of the universality of ethics and its irreducible origin in the asymmetry of my own individuation.

CIBULKA, J. Historicism and Phenomenology (in Czechoslovakian). Filozof Cas, 38(3), 282-301, 1990.

Der deutsche Historismus suchte den Standpunkt zu suggerieren, dass die einzeinen historischen Welten untereinander inkommensurabei sind, dass sie nur von der eigenen partiellen Vernunft beherrscht werden. Die phänomenologische Philosophie interpretiert im Gegenteil auch die Anschauung unter dem Aspekt universaler überhistorischer Strukturen. Die vorliegende Studie analysiert den gegensätzlichen Zugang Diltheys und Husserls zur Allgemeinheit und Singularität des Erlebens. Sie zeigt, wie die phänomenologische Philosophie eine Sensibilität für alles entwickelte, was sich in unserem Eleben einer rationalisierenden Universalitätsdeutung widersetzt, wie garde diese zur Wiege der Ontologie der Faktizität bei Heidegger und Merleaun-Ponty wurde. (edited)

CIBULKA, Josef. The Critical and the Dogmatic Tendency of Phenomenological Philosophy (in Czechoslovakian). Filozof Cas, 38(6), 736-745, 1990.

Ernst Tugendhat stellt fest, dass die phänomenologische Philosophie in sich auf der einen Seite eine kritische Tendenz enthält, nach welcher gegen alle vermeintliche Erkenntnis die regulative Idee einer letzten Ausweisung aufzustellen ist, auf der anderen Seite die dogmatische Tendenz einer absoluten Gegebenheit. Eine Dogmatisierung der Wesensschau wurde oft irrtümlicherweise als das Wertvollste im Husserl'schen Denken betrachtet. Eugen Fink, obwohl er vor allem die kritischen transzendentalen Husserlschen Motive entwickelte, drückte suggestiv auch die Position des Dogmatismus einer absoluten Selbsgtebung aus: Das phänomenologische Sehen legitimiert sich ausschliesslich durch seinen eigenen Vollzug. (edited)

CICCHESE, Gennaro. L'essere mortale dei mortali: Un'analisi sul problema della morte nel pensiero del secondo Heidegger. Aquinas, 34(1), 85-102, Ja-Ap 91.

CICERO and GRIFFIN, M T (ed). *On Duties: Cicero*. New York, Cambridge Univ Pr, 1991.

CICOVACKI, Predrag. Locke on Mathematical Knowledge. J Hist Phil, 28(4), 511-524, O 90.

Locke argues that mathematical knowledge is objective real knowledge, and his account of it is based on his theory of complex ideas of mixed modes and relations. Such ideas are originals and archetypes, not copies of existing things. Archetypes are framed in such a way that existing things necessarily conform to them. This is why mathematical knowledge is, in Kantian terms, a priori. Moreover, mathematical knowledge concerns the real, not the nominal, essence of complex ideas; for this reason mathematical knowledge is always instructive, not trifling, but synthetic. Locke's account is an anticipation of Kant's theory of mathematical knowledge.

CIGNOLI, R and ADAMS, M E. A Note on the Axiomatization of Equational Classes of *n*-Valued Lukasiewicz Algebras. Notre Dame J Form Log, 31(2), 304-307, Spr 90.

It is shown that each nontrivial equational subclass of *n*-valued Lukasiewicz algebras is determined by a canonical equation that has the least possible number of variables.

CILLIERS, F P. Rules and Relations: Some Connectionist Implications for Cognitive Science and Language. S Afr J Phil, 10(2), 49-55, My 91.

Connectionism is introduced as a new paradigm in cognitive science. After a discussion of the basic principles, connectionism is placed in a broader theoretical framework. The significance of the paradigm is investigated by examining an important critique of it by Fodor and Pylyshyn. Central issues concern the status of rules and of mental representations. Finally, the prospect of finding interest relationships between connectionism and post-structuralism is mentioned.

CINI, Marcello. "Continuity and Discontinuity in the Definition of a Disciplinary Field: The Case of XXth Century Physics" in *Imre Lakatos and Theories of Scientific Change*, GAVROGLU, Kostas (ed), 83-94. Norwell, Kluwer, 1989.

CIOFFI, Frank. Wittgenstein on Freud's 'Abominable Mess'. Philosophy, 28, 169-192, 90 Supp.

CIRILLO, Leonard and CRIDER, Cathleen. Systems of Interpretation and the Function of the Metaphor. J Theor Soc Behav, 21(2), 171-195, Je 91.

CLARK, Andy. Connectionism, Competence, and Explanation. Brit J Phil Sci, 41(2), 195-222, Je 90.

What kind of knowledge does a connectionist model embody in a set of heights? I consider the knowledge ascribed by a classical competence theory of a domain and find that such knowledge is not even tacitly represented in such models. Some methodological consequences of this are examined.

CLARK, Andy. Connectionist Minds. Proc Aris Soc, 90, 83-102, 1989-90.

Arguments from connectionist models of mind to eliminativist conclusions are shown to be marred by an unmotivated focus on the units and weights level of description of such systems. Well-motivated analyses of such systems may ascend to much higher levels, rendering the eliminativist conclusion at best uncertain.

CLARK, Mary T. Augustine's Theology of the Trinity: Its Relevance. Dionysius, 13, 71-84, D 89.

Scripture rather than the *Enneads* of Plotinus is the source of Augustine's understanding of the Trinity. Rather than underemphasizing the Persons of the Trinity in his defence of their unity (against Arians) he spoke from his earliest works of the actions of the "economic" Trinity: the triadic character of the metaphysics of creation and of the salvific work of Christ and of the soul's return to the Father. Then in considering the "immanent" Trinity he spoke of how Father, Son, and Holy Spirit are related to one another and are a paradigm for the Christian love of neighbor. It is therefore concluded that to be God is to be related as Father, Son, and Holy Spirit, and that the "visible and invisible missions" (creation and sanctification) are proper to the Persons sent, so that the missions reveal the processions with the Trinity. The doctrine of the Trinity is therefore relevant to the moral life and to the prayer life of the Christian, and to adequate understanding of God.

CLARK, Maudemarie. *Nietzsche On Truth and Philosophy*. New York, Cambridge Univ Pr, 1991.

CLARK, Michael. "Fact and Fiction" in *Reading Rorty*, MALACHOWSKI, Alan (ed), 171-183. Cambridge, Blackwell, 1991.

CLARK, Peter. "Determinism, Probability and Randomness in Classical Statistical Physics" in *Imre Lakatos and Theories of Scientific Change*, GAVROGLU, Kostas (ed), 95-110. Norwell, Kluwer, 1989.

CLARK, Peter. Explanation in Physical Theory. Philosophy, 27, 155-175, 90 Supp.

CLARK, Robin. "Incremental Acquisition and a Parametrized Model of Grammar" in *Acting and Reflecting: The Interdisciplinary Turn in Philosophy*, SIEG, Wilfried (ed), 89-105. Norwell, Kluwer, 1990.

CLARK, Stephen R L. Eradicating the Obvious. J Applied Phil, 8(1), 121-125, 1991.

Applied philosophy too often becomes an excuse to state the 'obvious', in the conviction that 'modern', educated Anglophones can tell what is right or wrong without the need to think of genuine alternatives, or talk to our neighbours. A better philosophical method begins with the realization that the present is impermanent, that things have changed enormously, and may change again with terrifying speed. It is by questioning what 'reasonable people' take for granted that we progress, and maybe rediscover ancient truths.

CLARK, Stephen R L. How Many Selves Make Me? Philosophy, 29, 213-233, 91 Supp.

Stories of 'multiple personalities', and the admitted multiplicity of human personality, do not count against pre-Cartesian conceptions of the mental. First, the stories too readily accepted by some commentators of Eve or Miss Beauchamp are very poorly attested. Second, insofar as they are believable, they only reflect the normal confusion and chargefulness of thought and motive, which can be transcended in a proper self-consciousness. Both narrative theory and Plotinian analysis are resources in the attempt to understand the self and its many personalities.

CLARK, Stephen R L. "How to Reason About Value Judgments" in *Key Themes in Philosophy*, GRIFFITHS, A Phillips (ed), 173-190. New York, Cambridge Univ Pr, 1989.

The need to be seen to 'have opinions' is an implication of democracy, and a grave danger to careful thought. One way of improving the level of argument is to practise the art of rhetoric, to learn to make 'the worse side better'. Another, and more philosophical, route is to accept the risk of being found wholly in the wrong. Both answers—the rhetorician's and the shaman's—make clear that we cannot rely on simple moral systems (utilitarian or libertarian) to solve all our crises. Philosophers can provide no magic calculations, but only the insight to be "fiercer with ourselves, gentler with others' opinions."

CLARK, Stephen R L. Limited Explanations. Philosophy, 27, 195-210, 90 Supp.

Responding to Swinburne's paper (*Philosophy* 27, 177-94, 90 Supp), I offer Philo's reply to Cleanthes, and Demea's reassertion of a more traditional theism. I suggest that Swinburne's argument only works if Platonism is assumed, and that we do not need a God like Swinburne's if Platonism is true. There are real epistemological advantages to a Platonic theism, and consequences can be drawn from it about the probability of finding alien intelligence.

CLARK, Stephen R L. On Wishing there were Unicorns. Proc Aris Soc, 90, 247-265, 1989-90.

Standard translations of claims about the existence of nonexistence of fabulous or fictional entities are unsatisfactory. 'Unicorns don't exist' cannot mean that nothing is called a unicorn (for some things are), nor that nothing has the properties traditionally associated with unicorns (for to wish that they did is not to wish that any presently existing thing be transformed). The real being of nonexistents rests in the Cauldron of Story. 'Particular existence' and 'fact' have no priority over nonparticular existence and fiction: on the contrary, the latter constitute the wider field within which 'fact' and 'particular existence' have their place.

CLARK, Stephen R L. Taylor's Waking Dream: No One's Reply. Inquiry, 34(2), 195-215, Je 91.

Taylor recognizes the problems posed by the ideals of disengaged reason and the affirmation of 'ordinary life' for unproblematic commitment to other ideals of universal justice and the like. His picture of 'the modern identity' neglects too much of present importance, and he is too disdainful of Platonic realism to offer a convincing solution. The romantic expressivism that he seeks to re-establish as an important moral resource can only avoid destructive effects if it is taken in his original and Platonic context.

CLARKE, Murray. Epistemic Norms and Evolutionary Success. Synthese, 85(2), 231-244, N 90.

Recent debates concerning the nature of epistemic justification primarily turn on two distinctions: the objective-subjective distinction and the internal-external distinction. Alvin Goldman has defended a reliable process account of epistemic justification that is externalist and objectivist in nature. John Pollock, in contrast, defends an account that is both internalist and subjectivist in nature. There are deep insights into the nature of epistemic justification contained in both views. Lately, Pollock has "scared up" more trouble in Tucson by attempting a novel, naturalized account of epistemic justification. Data from cognitive psychology and biology is, however, radically at odds with Pollock's project, as I shall attempt to show.

CLATTERBAUGH, Kenneth. *Contemporary Perspectives on Masculinity: Men, Women, and Politics in Modern Society*. Boulder, Westview Pr, 1990.

This book surveys the major perspectives on masculinity, perspectives that offer a definition of masculinity, an account of how it is created and maintained, and an evaluation of masculinity. The perspectives examined are biological and classical conservatism, radical and liberal profeminism, men's rights perspectives, mythopoetic perspectives, socialism, and black and gay perspectives. Each perspective's relationship to feminism is also explored. The book brings out the philosophical assumptions on which these perspectives depend and offers the criticisms with which each must contend. The conclusion of the book indicates some new directions for research and for philosophical inquiry.

CLAY, Diskin (ed & trans) and CLAY, Jenny Strauss (ed & trans) and HORWITZ, Robert (ed & trans). *Questions Concerning the Law of Nature: John Locke*. Ithaca, Cornell Univ Pr, 1990.

CLAY, Jenny Strauss (ed & trans) and HORWITZ, Robert (ed & trans) and CLAY, Diskin (ed & trans). *Questions Concerning the Law of Nature: John Locke*. Ithaca, Cornell Univ Pr, 1990.

CLAYPOOL, G A and FETYKO, D F and PEARSON, M A. Reactions to Ethical Dilemmas: A Study Pertaining to Certified Public Accounts. J Bus Ethics, 9(9), 699-706, S 90.

This study discusses how perceptions of ethics are formed by certified public accountants (CPAs). Theologians are used as a point of comparison. When considering CPA ethical dilemmas, both subject groups in this research project viewed 'confidentiality' and 'independence' as more important than 'recipient of responsibility' and 'seriousness of breach'. Neither group, however, was insensitive to any of the factors presented for its consideration. CPA reactions to ethical dilemmas were governed primarily by provisions of the CPA ethics code; conformity to that code may well be evidence of higher stage moral reasoning.

CLAYTON, Philip. "Religious Truth and Scientific Truth" in *Phenomenology of the Truth Proper to Religion*, GUERRIÈRE, Daniel (ed), 43-59. Albany, SUNY Pr, 1990.

The argument proceeds through three moments. First, it appears that science and religion are diametrically opposed, given the traditional descriptions of the two. But, second, contemporary developments on both sides suggest that we now construe them as identical: many philosophers argue the subjective nature of scientific knowledge and practice (e.g., paradigm "conversions"); and philosophers of religion defend a critical and doubting approach to religious truth and practice. After a detailed examination of the phenomena in question, I mediate the two views, linking scientific and religious truth more closely than the tradition while insisting on four essential contrasts.

CLAYTON, Philip. Two Kinds of Conceptual-Scheme Realism. S J Phil, 29(2), 167-179, Sum 91.

Hilary Putnam has provocatively questioned whether any kind of realism is compatible with acknowledging the pervasive role of conceptual schemes and, if so, what kind? As is well known, his answers are "yes" and "internal realism." In this essay I defend his response to the first question and attack his answer to the second. Let's assume that ontological conventionalism and causal realism fail. We still wouldn't be saddled with internal realism if a completely non-epistemic metaphysical realism can be designed. I thus propose a *regulative realism*, arguing that (non-internal) realism and truth express necessary postulates of our rational discourse.

CLEAR, Edeltraud Harzer. Isvarakrsna's Two-Level-Perception: Propositional and Non-Propositional. J Indian Phil, 18(4), 305-340, D 90.

CLEARY JR, Donald L. What's It All About? The Critical Method of Analysis as Applied to Drama. J Aes Educ, 25(2), 89-96, Sum 91.

CLEARY, Denis (trans) and ROSMINI, Antonio and WATSON, Terence (trans). *Principles of Ethics*. Durham, Rosmini, 1988.

CLEARY, Denis (ed & trans) and ROSMINI, Antonio and WATSON, Terence (ed & trans). *The Origin of Thought*. Durham, Rosmini, 1987.

CLEARY, J C and HIGONNET, Patrice. "Plasticity into Power: Two Crises in the History of France and China" in *Critique and Construction: A Symposium on Roberto Unger's "Politics"*, LOVIN, Robin W (ed), 267-295. New York, Cambridge Univ Pr, 1990.

CLELAND, Carol E. The Difference Between Real Change and *Mere* Cambridge Change. Phil Stud, 60(3), 257-280, N 90.

Following the lead of Bertrand Russell, most analytic philosophers have rejected the idea that change involves anything more than a mere difference in the properties or relations exemplified by an object at different times. A lake does not *become* warmer in the sense that there is an active process of transition whereby it goes from a lower temperature to a higher temperature; rather, a lake simply *has* a lower temperature at an earlier time and *has* a higher temperature at a later time. Peter Geach has disparagingly christened such changes "*mere* Cambridge changes." In the first part of this paper, I revisit Zeno's paradoxes of motion. I argue that the standard mathematical solutions fail to work, and conclude that the cinematographical theory of change is inadequate to account for motion (the paradigm of change). Subsequently, I develop a new account of change, an account which takes seriously the notion that changing (moving, warming, growing, shattering, etc.) objects actually *become* different. Finally, I return to Zeno's paradoxes, showing how they can be resolved using my newly developed theory of change.

CLELAND, Carol. On the Individuation of Events. Synthese, 86(2), 229-254, F 91.

This paper develops a new theory of events. As in Lombard's account, events are identified with changes. Changes are not, however, individuated in terms of physical objects but, rather, in terms of particularized properties (tropes). A distinction is drawn between states, which are determin*ate* properties, and phases, which are determin*able* properties. Subsequently, a concrete phase is defined as an *instance* of a phase. In opposition to Bennett, it is argued that instances of (determinable) properties (i.e., concrete phases) are basic particulars. Concrete change is then defined in terms of concrete phases: A concrete change is constituted by the time-ordered exemplification of differing states by the same concrete phase. Finally events are identified with concrete changes. Thus, identity conditions for events can be stated in terms of identities of concrete phases, time-ordered pairs of states, and times. I argue that this account is superior to the most widely discussed proposals (by Davidson, Kim, Quine/Lemmon, Lombard and Bennett) for identity conditions of events.

CLEMENTS, Tad S. *Science versus Religion*. Buffalo, Prometheus, 1990.

Are science and supernaturalism compatible? This book tries to demonstrate that scientific disciplines and supernatural religions have overlapping subject-matters, but seek to justify their knowledge claims by means of logically incompatible epistemologies, and therefore that they are fundamentally incompatible. It argues for the cognitive superiority of scientific cognition over all other alleged ways of knowing. And it recommends a humanism grounded in science and reason in dealing with human problems of every sort and at every level.

CLEVELAND, Harlan. The Comeuppance of Science and Technology. J Soc Biol Struct, 13(1), 1-9, F 90.

CLEVELAND, Timothy. Is Davidson a Volitionist In Spite of Himself? S J Phil, 29(2), 181-193, Sum 91.

CLIFTON, Robert K and BUTTERFIELD, Jeremy N and REDHEAD, Michael L G. Nonlocal Influences and Possible Worlds—A Stapp in the Wrong Direction. Brit J Phil Sci, 41(1), 5-58, Mr 90.

CLINES, David. "Deconstructing the Book of Job" in *The Bible as Rhetoric: Studies in Biblical Persuasion and Credibility*, WARNER, Martin (ed), 65-80. New York, Routledge, 1990.

CLOSE, Anthony. The Empirical Author: Salman Rushdie's *The Satanic Verses*. Phil Lit, 14(2), 248-267, O 90.

This essay argues that the furore over Salman Rushdie's *The Satanic Verses* highlights poignantly the futility of the tendency in modern poetics and criticism to banish reference to the empirical author from literary interpretation. The case against such banishment is argued theoretically with arguments drawn from speech-act theory and semantics, and concretely with a discussion of Rushdie's fiction, particularly *The Satanic Verses*.

CLOUDSLEY, Tim. Modernity, the Individual and Rationality in Marxism (Surrealism and Revolution). Hist Euro Ideas, 11, 849-856, 1989.

Permeating the conception of modernity in its contemporary usages is a tragic mood, rooted in a perception that the Marxist project has failed—that history has not seen an 'aufhebung' of alienation, fragmentation and bourgeois reason, and that the Marxist mode of critique as part of praxis has exhausted its possibilities. This article argues that Marx's project of overcoming the dichotomies of fact and value, knowledge and experience, in critical thought and concrete practice, should not however be rejected in favour of either scientism or a Nietzschean enthronement of taste over reason and ethics.

COADY, C A J. "Politics and the Problem of Dirty Hands" in *A Companion to Ethics*, SINGER, Peter (ed), 373-383. Cambridge, Blackwell, 1991.

COBB JR, John B. "Eternal Objects and Archetypes, Past and Depth: Response to Hopper" in *Archetypal Process: Self and Divine in Whitehead, Jung, and Hillman*, GRIFFIN, David Ray (ed), 125-128. Evanston, Northwestern Univ Pr, 1989.

Whitehead's eternal objects are unlike Jung's archetypes in that the latter are limited in number and have a normative role. But Jung's archetypes can be understood as types of past events whose frequent repetition gives them peculiar causal efficacy in the present. More generally Jung's "depth" corresponds to the actual (past) world that largely constitutes each Whiteheadian occasion.

COBB-STEVENS, Richard. Being and Categorial Intuition. Rev Metaph, 44(1), 43-66, S 90.

COBBEN, Paul. Over het morele en zedelijke handelen, toegelicht aan het instituut huwelijk. Tijdschr Filosof, 52(4), 667-696, D 90.

The article is a reaction to R Bubner's determination of practical reason, that aims to do justice to the finiteness and historicity of man. It is argued that Hegel's concept of the moral subject meets better the requirements made by Bubner upon the alternative determination of practical reason than his own proposal. Nevertheless also Hegel hasn't succeeded in getting Bubner's problem solved. This is illustrated by Hegel's conception of the institute of family. As a conclusion an alternative to this conception is developed.

COBURN, Robert C. A Defense of Ethical Noncognitivism. Phil Stud, 62(1), 67-80, Ap 91.

COBURN, Robert C. The Idea of Transcendence. Phil Invest, 13(4), 322-337, O 90.

COCCHIARELLA, Nino B. "Quantification, Time, and Necessity" in *Philosophical Applications of Free Logic*, LAMBERT, Karel (ed), 242-256. New York, Oxford Univ Pr, 1991.

A logic of actual and possible objects if formulated in which *existence* and *being*, as second-level concepts represented by first-order (objectual) quantifiers, are distinguished. A free logic of actual objects is then distinguished as a subsystem of the logic of actual and possible object. Several complete first-order tense logics are then formulated in which temporal versions of possibilism and actualism are characterized in terms of the free logic of actual objects and the wide logic of actual and possible objects. It is then shown how a number of different modal logics can be interpreted within quantified tense logic, with the latter providing a paradigmatic framework in which to distinguish the interplay between quantifiers, tenses and modal operators and within which we can formulate different temporal versions of actualism and possibilism.

COCKBURN, David. Capital Punishment and Realism. Philosophy, 66(256), 177-190, Ap 91.

Amnesty International's utilitarian argument against capital punishment cannot be defended. A different, and stronger, argument might treat the suffering of the condemned man as a perception of the horror of the execution. The utilitarian approach has close analogies with a general form of 'realism' which suggests that we should think of ourselves as 'measuring instruments' in order to overcome the colouring of our thought by our own nature. The attempt to overcome a 'merely human perspective' in morality often leads, paradoxically, to a strongly human morality, and may lead in the more general case to 'idealism'.

COCKBURN, David. The Evidence for Reincarnation. Relig Stud, 27(2), 199-207, Je 91.

The paper considers Ian Stevenson's evidence for reincarnation. The suggestion that we are *right* to speak of reincarnation since this would provide the best explanation of this data is rejected, as is Bernard Williams's defence of the claim that we would be *wrong* to speak of reincarnation in such cases. A different model of the form that argument about such matters might take is put forward. It is suggested that the question of whether we should ever speak of a live human being as the reincarnation of one who has died is, fundamentally, an ethical one.

COCKBURN, David. *Other Human Beings*. New York, St Martin's Pr, 1991.

A view of what a person is cannot be separated from a view of how another is to be treated. My thought about *myself* is not the model on which my thought about others must be based; and the 'objective', third person, world is not the world as described by physical science. The philosophical mind/body contrast seriously distorts discussions of the nature and value of people, and of their identity over time. We need to acknowledge the tangible, persisting human being—with its distinctive bodily form and having its own distinctive value—as a fundamental feature of our thought.

COCKS, Joan. Cultural Theory Looks at Identity and Contradiction. Quest, 4(2), 38-60, D 90.

This essay considers questions of identity and contradiction in the contexts of gender, sexuality, ethnicity and race. It moves from illustrating the fertility of fractures in identity in Frantz Fanon and George Lamming, to discussing the historical and cultural roots of the assertion and then disintegration of the fixed, coherent self. It explores the promise and the danger of collective self-certainty in 20th century anticolonial movements, ethnic nationalism, feminist politics, and sexual countercultures. In conclusion, it looks at theoretical contributions to the conceptualization of collective identity and contradiction in Marx, Gramsci, and Foucault.

COGNETTI, Giuseppe. La prima e seconda edizione della "Geschichte des Materialismus" di Friedrich Albert Lange. G Crit Filosof Ital, 70(1), 76-108, Ja-Ap 91.

COHEN, Cynthia B (ed). Ethics Committees. Hastings Center Rep, 20(5), 33-38, S-O 90.

COHEN, Daniel H. Conditionals, Quantification, and Strong Mathematical Induction. J Phil Log, 20(3), 315-326, Ag 91.

The complex internal logic of the principle of strong mathematical induction poses special problems for formalization. The principle involves no less than three (first-order) universal quantifiers and two separate implications. If conditionals are used for both roles, then five conditionals need to be deployed. The combined resources of the relevant logic R and the logic of conditional assertions CA are brought to bear on the problem, leading to the conclusion that the classical suppression of a separate base is unjustified.

COHEN, Daniel H. The Word as Will and Idea: Semantics in the *Tractatus*. Phil Stud (Ireland), 32, 126-140, 1988-90.

According to the semantics in Wittgenstein's *Tractatus*, a picture and what is pictured must have the same logical form. However necessary that may be, it cannot suffice to make one fact a picture of another. The grounds for the pictorial relation, it is argued, must be found in the transcendental will. Following a suggestion by Ramsey, the semantic resources of the *Tractatus* are used to construct a new interpretation of propositions as equivalence classes of facts. The nature of the involvement of the will helps explain why ethics and logic are alike ineffable.

COHEN, David and MC CUBBIN, Michael. The Political Economy of Tardive Dyskinesia: Asymmetries in Power and Responsibility. J Mind Behav, 11(3-4), 465-488, Sum-Autumn 90.

Tardive dyskinesia is a serious, well-publicized adverse effect resulting from long-term neuroleptic drug use. However, little progress has been made during the last two decades in ensuring that these drugs are prescribed with necessary caution. Incentives and constraints operating on the major participants (patients, families, physicians, institutions, drug companies, society) in the decision-making process leading to the prescription of neuroleptics increase the likelihood that the benefits of drugs will be exaggerated and their adverse effects minimized. When combined with imbalances of power, these factors ensure that persons having little power and information to make the decision to prescribe will bear most costs of that decision. This points to the operation of an inefficient system which can be expected to yield sub-optimal results. We suggest ways to make the decision process more efficient by more closely aligning responsibility with cost. If those who hold power in the decision process are held accountable for the unwanted risks they impose upon others, both the use of neuroleptics and its inevitable iatrogenesis would probably be reduced.

COHEN, G A. Marxism and Contemporary Political Philosophy. Can J Phil, SUPP 16, 363-387, 1990.

I ask why Nozick exercises some Marxists more than he does any egalitarian liberals. I reply that, by contrast with egalitarian liberals, Marxists are reluctant to reject the idea of self-ownership, since it plays a role both in their account of capitalist exploitation and in their conception of the good society. I argue that the stated reluctance disfigures the Marxian treatment of those two topics.

COHEN, I Bernard. "Newton's Method and Newton's Style" in *Some Truer Method*, DURHAM, Frank (ed), 15-57. New York, Columbia Univ Pr, 1990.

COHEN, Jeffrey R and PANT, Laurie W. Beyond Bean Counting: Establishing High Ethical Standards in the Public Accounting Profession. J Bus Ethics, 10(1), 45-56, Ja 91.

Business professions are increasingly faced with the question of how to best monitor the ethical behavior of their members. Conflicts could exist between a profession's desire to self-regulate and its accountability to the public at large. This study examines how members of one profession, public accounting, evaluate the relative effectiveness of various self-regulatory and externally imposed mechanisms for promoting a climate of high ethical behavior. Specifically, the roles of independent public accountants, regulatory and rule setting agencies, and undergraduate accounting education are investigated. (edited)

COHEN, L Jonathan. Stephen P Stich, "The Fragmentation of Reason". Phil Phenomenol Res, 51(1), 185-188, Mr 91.

Stich objects to founding any rule of inference on an appeal to reflective equilibrium. But Stich fails to see that, if we think that someone has a really absurd and unacceptable rule of inference, it cannot have properly passed his reflective equilibrium test, because we always suppose that he has principles by reference to which we can teach him his error. Nor can we accept Stich's own attempt to found rules of inference on considerations of utility it is possible for a cognitive principle to be an intellectual error even if a pragmatically useful one.

COHEN, L Jonathan. Twice Told Tales: A Reply to Schlesinger. Phil Stud, 62(2), 197-200, My 91.

The important problem about the analysis of testimonial corroboration in probabilistic terms is not, as G Schlesinger supposes, 'What are mathematically sufficient and necessary conditions for the truth of the statement that the probability of a specified conclusion on two specified pieces of testimony is greater than on one?' but rather 'What are the conditions (in probabilistic terms) that a conscientious juror would intuitively feel that he needed to assume if he were to think of himself as entitled to infer in a particular case (where there is no other evidence) that a concurring testimony or a converging piece of evidence, is corroborative'.

COHEN, Philip R (ed) and MORGAN, Jerry (ed) and POLLACK, Martha E (ed). *Intentions in Communication*. Cambridge, MIT Pr, 1990.

COHEN, Philip R and LEVESQUE, Hector J. Teamwork. Nous, 25(4), 487-512, S 91.

COHEN, Richard A. "The Face of Truth in Rosenzweig, Levinas, and Jewish Mysticism" in *Phenomenology of the Truth Proper to Religion*, GUERRIÈRE, Daniel (ed), 175-201. Albany, SUNY Pr, 1990.

COHEN, Stephen and BERSTEN, Michael. Probability Out of Court: Notes on 'Guilt Beyond Reasonable Doubt'. Austl J Phil, 68(2), 229-240, Je 90.

The essay is critical of an essay by Barbara Davidson and Robert Pargetter, "Guilt Beyond Reasonable Doubt," in which those authors offer a characterization of the requirements for a verdict of guilty. In particular, this essay criticizes the role they suggest for "probability" and their application of Keynes's notion of "evidential weight." The essay suggests that attempts to import a formal notion of probability or a Keynesian notion of evidential weight into an analysis of "beyond reasonable doubt" are misconceived both in terms of legal reality and in terms of a recommendation, or prescription, for rational behavior of a juror.

COHEN, Stephen. Proof and Sanction in Mill's Utilitarianism. Hist Phil Quart, 7(4), 475-487, O 90.

The essay examines Mill's proof of the utilitarian principle in *Utilitarianism* and attempts to articulate what Mill himself would have regarded as the proof. It is suggested that the easiest construction of the proof would involve Mill in conflating the proof with the sanction for the principle. Other possibilities—including, in the end, the possibility which this essay favors—require that important steps in the proof be regarded as immediate or intuitive, rather than supported by reasons. Questions are raised concerning what Mill is trying to prove, what "the utilitarian principle" is which functions in the proof, and what the relation is between duty and sanction.

COHEN, Stewart. "Skepticism and Everyday Knowledge Attributions" in *Doubting: Contemporary Perspectives on Skepticism*, ROTH, Michael D (ed), 161-169. Norwell, Kluwer, 1990.

COHEN-TANNOUDJI, Gilles. La pertinence du concept d'horizon de réalité en physique théorique contemporaine. Dialectica, 44(3-4), 323-332, 1990.

By means of examples from quantum theory, from the physics of basic interactions and from cosmology, Gonseth's concept of the horizon of reality is shown to be relevant and modern.

COHN-SHERBOK, Dan. Jewish Faith and the Holocaust. Relig Stud, 26(2), 277-293, Je 90.

This study explores the theological responses of a number of Jewish writers to the question: Where was God when six million died? The author formulates a traditional solution to this problem based on the doctrine of eternal reward in the afterlife.

COLAPIETRA, Raffaele. La filosofia: in soccorso de' governi. G Crit Filosof Ital, 69(2), 241-250, My-Ag 90.

COLAPIETRO, Vincent M. "Human Symbols as Functioning Objects: A First Look at John William Miller's Contribution to Semiotics" in *The Philosophy of John William Miller*, FELL, Joseph P (ed), 70-83. Lewisburg, Bucknell Univ Pr, 1990.

John William Miller transformed the absolute idealism of Hegel, Royce, etc. into a unique philosophical perspective he called "historical idealism." Central to this transformation was a serious and sustained examination of the role symbols play in human knowing and thinking. In particular, Miller's attempt to explain human symbols as "functioning objects" is an important but neglected contribution to semiotics. This paper concerns both the details of this explanation and its implications.

COLAPIETRO, Vincent M. The Integral Self: Systematic Illusion or Inescapable Task? Listening, 25(3), 192-210, Fall 90.

This paper explores one way of answering the following question: How can the multiplicity of thoughts, feelings, decisions, etc., constitutive of a human life be conceived in such a way as to do justice to both this multilevel heterogeneity and some overarching identity? It undertakes this exploration in light of a pronounced tendency in some contemporary discussions of human subjectivity to exalt multiplicity and to denigrate unity.

COLAPIETRO, Vincent M. The Reconstruction of Institutions. J Speculative Phil, 4(3), 237-248, 1990.

Drawing upon Anthony Giddens and John Dewey, this paper offers the beginning of a *general* theory of institutions. It argues that the tendency to see institutions as merely incidental provisions for human practices is mistaken. Stated positively, this paper contends that any adequate theory of human action must show how institutions are simultaneously empowering and constraining structures. It makes several specific suggestions about how to exhibit this aspect of institutions.

COLAPIETRO, Vincent M. The Vanishing Subject of Contemporary Discourse: A Pragmatic Response. J Phil, 87(11), 644-655, N 90.

The purpose of this paper is to offer a *pragmatic* response to the "decentering of the subject" (i.e., the attempt to displace the paradigm of consciousness conceived as a dynamic, intentional subject with the paradigm of language understood as a system of differences). More specifically, the objective is to show that the position of the classical American pragmatists (Peirce, James, Dewey, and Mead) effectively decenters the subject without denying the reality of our own enduring forms of personal agency.

COLBERT, Treacy. Public Input Into Health Care Policy: Controversy and Contribution in California. Hastings Center Rep, 20(5), 21, S-O 90.

COLBY, Kenneth M and COLBY, Peter M and STOLLER, Robert J. Dialogues in Natural Language with GURU, a Psychologic Inference Engine. Phil Psych, 3(2-3), 171-187, 1990.

The aim of this project was to explore the possibility of constructing a psychologic inference engine that might enhance introspective self-awareness by delivering inferences about a user based on what he said in interactive dialogues about his closest opposite-sex relation. To implement this aim, we developed a computer program (GURU) with the capacity to simulate human conversation in colloquial natural language. The psychologic inferences offered represent the authors' simulations of their commonsense psychology responses to expected user-input expressions. The heuristics of the natural language processor and its relation to output responses are described in enough detail for the operations of the implementation to be understood. Evaluation of this new cognitive agent presents, we hope, puzzles for artificial intelligence and cognitive science.

COLBY, Peter M and COLBY, Kenneth M and STOLLER, Robert J. Dialogues in Natural Language with GURU, a Psychologic Inference Engine. Phil Psych, 3(2-3), 171-187, 1990.

The aim of this project was to explore the possibility of constructing a psychologic inference engine that might enhance introspective self-awareness by delivering inferences about a user based on what he said in interactive dialogues about his closest opposite-sex relation. To implement this aim, we developed a computer program (GURU) with the capacity to simulate human conversation in colloquial natural language. The psychologic inferences offered represent the authors' simulations of their commonsense psychology responses to expected user-input expressions. The heuristics of the natural language processor and its relation to output responses are described in enough detail for the operations of the implementation to be understood. Evaluation of this new cognitive agent presents, we hope, puzzles for artificial intelligence and cognitive science.

COLBY, William H. Missouri Stands Alone. Hastings Center Rep, 20(5), 5-6, S-O 90.

COLE, Eve Browning. Weaving and Practical Politics In Plato's *Statesman*. S J Phil, 29(2), 195-208, Sum 91.

Plato's *Statesman* is typically read for its demonstration of the method of division, or as an exercise in definition, rather than as a contribution to political philosophy. Yet the dialogue does make a significant, if prima facie rather peculiar, contribution to political thought, which deserves consideration in its own right. Here, I draw out and discuss some of the political implications of two puzzling central features of *Statesman*: the myth of reversing cosmic cycles, and the comparison of statesmanship to weaving. The description of political "techne", and the corresponding vision of human social life, which the dialogue offers are both distinctive and appealing.

COLEMAN, Earle J. The Beautiful, the Ugly, and the Tao. J Chin Phil, 18(2), 213-226, Je 91.

Various suggestions are proposed in order for the penultimate status of beauty in Taoism, i.e., the fact that the concept of beauty, which has a central place in Greek aesthetics, plays a lesser, somewhat equivocal role in Taoist philosophy of art. A discussion of Tao as the cosmic source of all mundane beauties leads to the conclusion that nature cannot be ugly for the Taoist. Finally, it is argued that the Taoist view of beauty is superior to any contextualist theory, for cases of simple beauty, which cannot be accomodated by contextualism, are rendered intelligible by the Taoist perspective.

COLEMAN, James S. *Foundations of Social Theory*. Cambridge, Harvard Univ Pr, 1990.

This book provides a theory linking the behavior of individuals with organizational behavior and society as a whole. Part 1 deals with elementary actions and relations, covering actors and resources, interest and control, and rights to act. Part 2 considers systems of social exchange, authority systems, trust, norms, and social capital. Part 3 examines corporate action, including constitutions, social choice, rights and corporate actors, and revoking authority. Part 4 discusses modern society and the corporation. The last part develops a formal mathematical analysis of the theory.

COLEMAN, John and LOCAL, John. The "No Crossing Constraint" in Autosegmental Phonology. Ling Phil, 14(3), 295-338, Jl 91.

We examine a disquieting problem concerning the ability of the "No Crossing Constraint" (NCC) to constrain multiplanar Autosegmental Phonological Representations (APRs). Some "multiplanar" APRs are planar graphs, but some are necessarily nonplanar graphs. The NCC does not restrict the class of nonplanar graphs, so either we drop or modify the NCC, or we retain the NCC and cease to recognize nonplanar APRs as well-formed. We present examples of necessarily nonplanar APRs, and conclude that the first alternative must be selected. Thus the NCC is not a constraint, since it does not reduce or restrict the class of well-formed APRs.

COLEMAN, Jules L and HECKATHORN, Douglas D and MASER, Steven M. "A Bargaining Theory Approach to Default Provisions and Disclosure Rules in Contract Law" in *Liability and Responsibility*, FREY, R G (ed), 173-254. New York, Cambridge Univ Pr, 1991.

COLEMAN, Jules L and MURPHY, Jeffrie G. *Philosophy of Law: An Introduction to Jurisprudence (Revised Edition)*. Boulder, Westview Pr, 1989.

COLEMAN, Keith. On the Propositional Attitudes. Auslegung, 17(2), 137-155, Sum 91.

In this paper, the logical structure of sentences expressing the propositional attitudes is examined. After consideration is given to what a successful account of the logical nature of these sentences must satisfy, accounts by Kaplan, Quine, and Davidson are examined. The conclusion reached is that the propositional attitudes typically are relations between persons and sentences and that the rendering of the logical structure of complex sentences requires a higher order language that reflects the logical nature of the metalanguage.

COLES, Robert. "Institutions and the Shaping of Character" in *Integrity in Health Care Institutions: Humane Environments for Teaching, Inquiry, and Healing*, BULGER, Ruth Ellen (ed), 44-51. Iowa City, Univ of Iowa Pr, 1990.

COLLE, Reymond. Conceptos centrales de la filosofía política en Chile democrático. Logos (Mexico), 19(55), 73-82, Ja-Ap 91.

Presenta los resultados de una investigacion de las "Declaraciones de Principios" ideologicas de los partidos formados legalmente en Chile para las elecciones presidenciales Democraticas (1989). Se realizo el analisis de contenido con procedimientos computacionales, logrando power en evidencia que los conceptos centrales son: El hombre, la democracia, la economia, lo social, el estado, etc. Tambien se muestran las relaciones entre estos conceptos.

COLLIER, Andrew. The Inorganic Body and the Ambiguity of Freedom. Rad Phil, 57, 3-9, Spr 91.

COLLIER, John D. Could I Conceive Being a Brain in a Vat? Austl J Phil, 68(4), 413-419, D 90.

I assume Putnam's argument that we are not brains in vats is sound, in the sense that we cannot state a true theory that we are brains in vats, by granting him the premise that any distinctions we can make must ideally be knowable by us. Granting this premise, I argue that there is still a sense in which it is conceivable that the theory that we are brains in vats is true, even though we could not state this truth. I argue that the second sense is the one that is relevant for the issue of metaphysical realism.

COLLIER, Peter (trans) and BOURDIEU, Pierre. *The Political Ontology of Martin Heidegger*. Stanford, Stanford Univ Pr, 1991.

The book uses sociological and linguistic insights to challenge readings of Heidegger's philosophy which either ignore politics, or, alternatively, overinterpret the author's Nazi sympathies. It reconstructs the contemporary philosophical and social fields, situating his philosophy in relation to Cassirer's academic neo-Kantianism, and Junger's and Spengler's populist polemics on class and race. Heidegger's sublimation of the political discourse of the Weimar republic is shown to exemplify the process whereby all formally structured discourse arises from interaction between an expressive intent and the (largely internalised) censorship generated by the social field.

COLLINI, Stefan. "From Sectarian Radical to National Possession" in *A Cultivated Mind: Essays On J S Mill Presented to John M Robson*, LAINE, Michael (ed), 242-272. Buffalo, Univ of Toronto Pr, 1991.

COLLINI, Stefan. The Member for Westminster: Doctrinaire Philosopher, Party Hack, or Public Moralist? Utilitas, 2(2), 307-322, N 90.

COLLINS, Alfred. From Brahma to a Blade of Grass. J Indian Phil, 19(2), 143-189, Je 91.

COLLINS, Jacqueline A. A New Humanism: A Response. Relig Hum, 25(1), 14-15, Wint 91.

COLLOPY, Bart and BOYLE, Philip and JENNINGS, Bruce. New Directions in Nursing Home Ethics. Hastings Center Rep, 21(2), Supp 1-16, Mr-Ap 91.

In the face of critical changes now shaping nursing home care, this article examines a number of ethical problems: the cultural disparagement of nursing homes, the moral perplexities of access and placement, the constraints of the "total institution," the conflict between individiual autonomy and common good, the moral agency of nursing home residents, the use of restraints, the paradox of government regulation. The article calls on bioethics to direct explicit attention to long term care issues, particularly the issues of autonomy and regulation.

COLMO, Christopher A. Reason and Revelation in the Thought of Leo Strauss. Interpretation, 18(1), 145-160, Fall 90.

Reason and revelation each seem unable to refute the other. This fact looms large in Leo Strauss's understanding both of philosophy and of the relation between theory and practice. In a critique of three interpretations of Strauss, including that of Stanley Rosen, the article argues that Strauss neither concluded nor needed to conclude that philosophy is an act of the will.

COLMO, Christopher A. Reply to Lowenthal. Interpretation, 18(2), 313-315, Wint 90-91.

A brief response to Lowenthal, questioning whether a contradiction in a position is sufficient to refute even a profound position. For example, Socrates claims to know what he does not know. Would finding a contradiction in this claim suffice to refute it?

COLOMER, Eusebi. Entorn del libre de F canals i Vidal: "Sobre la esencia del conocimiento". Espiritu, 37(97), 73-88, Ja-Je 88.

COLUMBUS, Joachim. Tait-Systems for Fragments of *Lm*. J Non-Classical Log, 6(2), 47-70, N 89.

In our context we define Tait-calculi for the implication free fragment of the *m*-valued Lukasiewicz-logic and prove soundness and completeness for both the propositional and predicate logic. The calculus is used to answer two questions arising in the context of the hierarchy of Lukasiewicz-systems. The first one handles about the truth-values of true L_m formulas in L_n where (m-1) divides (n-1) and is used that there are no intermediate logics between classical logic and the three-respectively the four-valued system of Lukasiewicz. At last we prove cut-elimination for the systems under considerations.

COMBES, Richard. Disembodying 'Bodily' Sensations. J Speculative Phil, 5(2), 107-131, 1991.

Raw feels (e.g., pains) seem to present themselves to consciousness as being bodily fixtures and thereby appear recalcitrant to both the dualist view that these sensations are non-extended and the materialist view that, while extended, they are geographically confined to the contral nervous system. This paper supplies an account of localization that reconciles the habit of attributing bodily coordinates to somesthetic phenomena with either dualism or materialism. It is reasonable to suppose that these feelings, while originally given to consciousness as non-local, later become associated with their putative anatomical causes only as a result of experience.

COMESAÑA, Santalices Gloria. Análisis político-epistemológico de la obra de arte según Walter Benjamin. Rev Filosof (Venezuela), 12, 67-73, 1989.

Basándonos en el trabajo de Walter Benjamín "La Obra de Arte en la era de su reproductibilidad técnica", tratamos de analizar su concepción de la obra de arte como expresión de una nueva forma de la percepción y de una posibilidad política revolucionaria. Todo esto a partir de la irrupción histórica de modernas técnicas reproductivas del objeto artístico y de nuevas formas de arte derivadas de esas mismas técnicas. Con el objeto de justificar sus análisis sobre el arte que le era contemporáneo, Benjamín formula una serie de conceptos originales cuya significación afirmamos. Ponemos también de relieve el carácter avanzado y precursor de dichos conceptos. En fin, destacamos la originalidad de la estética benjaminiana y sus posibilidades de aplicación actual.

COMESAÑA, Santalices Gloria. Los derechos de la mujer, legalidad y realidad. Rev Filosof (Venezuela), 13, 135-143, 1989.

Pensamos que, a lo largo de la Historia, nunca han sido respetados ni mucho menos reconocidos plenamente los derechos de la mujer, pese a haber sido enunciados en algunas ocasiones con mayor o menor solemnidad por mujeres aisladas o instituciones. En ausencia de un verdadero enclave o "lugar" político en el que puedan sustentarse estos derechos, y en ausencia de un real acceso de la mujer a la condición *ciudadana*, los Derechos de la Mujer, pese a todas las proclamaciones y promesas oficiales, permanecen y permanecerán como letra muerta, hasta que las mujeres (junto con los hombres) logremos la creación de ese "lugar político" en el cual únicamente, los Derechos de todos los seres humanos, y especificamente los de la mujer, podrán concretarse.

COMESAÑN SANTALICES, Gloria M. "El segundo sexo", vigencia y proyección. Rev Filosof (Venezuela), 11, 45-72, 1989.

COMETTI, Jean-Pierre. Alternatives et questions dans la littérature romanesque. Rev Int Phil, 44(174), 419-428, 1990.

COMPAGNONI, Francesco. Quale statuto per l'embrione umano? Riv Int Filosof Diritto, 67(2), 302-304, Ap-Je 90.

COMSTOCK, Gary L. "The Case against bGH" in *Agricultural Bioethics: Implications of Agricultural Biotechnology*, GENDEL, Steven M (& other eds), 309-339. Ames, Iowa St Univ Pr, 1990.

Bovine growth hormone (bGH) is a protein that occurs naturally in cattle. Researchers can now produce it using techniques of genetic engineering. I examine two moral arguments that claim to show that dairy farmers should not adopt this technology. The first argument is based on considerations tied to humane treatment of animals. The second is based on grounds of distributive justice. I find that both arguments have merit.

COMSTOCK, Gary. Genetically Engineered Herbicide Resistance, Part Two. J Agr Ethics, 3(2), 114-146, 1990.

Should we continue to support publicly funded research on genetically engineered herbicide resistant crops? In Part One, I discussed the difference between science and ethics, presented a brief history of weed control, and explained three moral principles undergirding my environmentalist perspective. I then argued that unqualified endorsement (E) of the research is unjustified, as is unqualified opposition (O). In Part Two, I argue against qualified endorsement (QE), and for qualified opposition (QO).

CONANT, James. On Bruns, on Cavell. Crit Inquiry, 17(3), 616-634, Spr 91.

CONANT, James (ed) and PUTNAM, Hilary. *Realism with a Human Face*. Cambridge, Harvard Univ Pr, 1990.

CONILL, Jesús. Una Metafísica estructural de la evolución. Rev Filosof (Spain), 4, 265-276, 1990.

CONLON, James. Kansas, Oz, and the Function of Art. J Aes Educ, 24(3), 99-106, Fall 90.

The question of this paper is the role of art in human life. The question is approached by analyzing the 1939 film classic, *The Wizard of Oz*, which is an artistic—though nonmodernist—attempt to explore the same question. Using the phenomenology of imaginative experience that the film provides, I argue that a mimetic theory of art, in any form, is inadequate. The power of art in human life simply cannot be explained by its ability to reflect or reveal the world. Rather, art creates an alternative world, a new form of experience. I then argue that such a view of art is not escapist, but a key to understanding the human place in the world and the process of history.

CONNELLY, James. Was R G Collingwood the Author of "The Theory of History"? Hist Theor, 29(4), 14-20, D 90.

This article argues against the case presented by James Patrick in "Is the 'Theory of History' Collingwood's First Essay in the Philosophy of History?" (in the same issue of *History and Theory*) that Collingwood was the author of the typescript of this title found among the paper of J A Smith in Magdalen College Oxford. The article concludes by arguing that the typescript was definitely *not* written by Collingwood.

CONNELLY, Robert J. Nursing Responsibility for the Placebo Effect. J Med Phil, 16(3), 325-341, Je 91.

The placebo effect is a common phenomenon in therapy and research but has received very little attention as such in nursing research. This article reviews some of the literature which shows the placebo effect, which can be positive or negative, is a significant force. Then it is argued that, while all health professionals have a general obligation to benefit their patients, nursing has a special, specific obligation to enhance the placebo effect, to maximize a positive effect and minimize a negative effect. Nursing education, current polity statements, and circumstances of clinical practice explain this obligation. Nursing research is needed to clarify the multiple ways in which the social and physical environment can trigger a placebo effect. As nursing expands its knowledge of this effect, it can begin to educate patients to the self-care implications of this pervasive but misunderstood phenomenon.

CONNOLLY, William E. "Freedom and Contingency" in *Life-World and Politics: Between Modernity and Postmodernity*, WHITE, Stephen K (ed), 166-190. Notre Dame, Univ Notre Dame Pr, 1989.

CONNOLLY, William E. "Identity and Difference in Liberalism" in *Liberalism and the Good*, DOUGLASS, R Bruce (ed), 59-85. New York, Routledge, 1990.

Three variants of liberal theory conceal the paradoxical character of the relationship between identity and difference. The first, liberal individualism, does so by failing to contest the contingent character of established standards of normality; the second, liberal individuality, by seeking a private haven for individuality to be; the third, civil liberalism, by identifying an intrinsic purpose through which differences can be harmonized. This essay challenges the apolitical character of all three perspectives.

CONNOR, Pauline. Is IVF Good Medicine? Ethics Med, 7(1), 11-13, Spr 91.

CONNOR, Peter (ed) and CADAVA, Eduardo (ed) and NANCY, Jean-Luc (ed). *Who Comes after the Subject?*. New York, Routledge, 1991.

CONRAD, Deborah. Consciousness and the Practice of Science. J Indian Counc Phil Res, 6(3), 57-65, My-Ag 89.

CONWAY, Daniel W. Beyond Realism: Nietzsche's New Infinite. Int Stud Phil, 22(2), 93-109, 1990.

Despite his attack on metaphysical speculation, Nietzsche is generally received as a closet realist who identifies objective reality with a primordial chaos. By portraying Nietzsche as a metaphysical realist, this standard interpretation attributes to him the privileged "God's eye point of view" that his perspectivism discredits. Some readers attempt to salvage Nietzsche from the scrapheap of realism by presenting perspectivism as continuous with some strain of antirealism. But these attempts often ignore Nietzsche's apparent embrace of the categories and vocabulary of realism. I argue that Nietzsche is perhaps best described as an antirealist who appreciates the pragmatic advantages of realism.

CONWAY, Daniel W. A Moral Ideal for Everyone and No One. Int Stud Phil, 22(2), 17-29, 1990.

Dissatisfied with the reviews of *Thus Spoke Zarathustra*, Nietzsche occasionally composed his own. In addition to praising *Zarathustra*, Nietzsche's "reviews" celebrate the unprecedented problems of interpretations that *Zarathustra* presents. Nietzsche gives us a clue to his dual appreciation of *Zarathustra* in the subtitle: "A Book for Everyone and No One." Perhaps we should take Nietzsche's subtitle seriously by reading *Zarathustra* as simultaneously "a book for everyone and no one." Only by writing *Zarathustra* for everyone *and* no one can Nietzsche target his desired audience: those free spirits who will use and discard *Zarathustra* while creating themselves anew.

CONWAY, Daniel W. Thus Spoke Rorty: The Perils of Narrative Self-Creation. Phil Lit, 15(1), 103-110, Ap 91.

Richard Rorty claims to inherit from Nietzsche the model of narrative self-creation that he (Rorty) has recently defended. But the "Nietzchean" liberalism that Rorty recommends bears a strong resemblance to the advanced nihilism against which Nietzsche warns us. The narrative self-creation that Rorty recommends would oblige many of us to adopt the ascetic strategy of world-denial that is characteristic of slave morality.

CONWAY, David and MUNSON, Ronald. *The Elements of Reasoning*. Belmont, Wadsworth, 1990.

CONWAY, Stephen. Bentham, the Benthamites, and the Nineteenth-Century British Peace Movement. Utilitas, 2(2), 221-243, N 90.

COOK, Deborah. Nietzsche and Foucault on *Ursprung* and Genealogy. Clio, 19(4), 299-309, Sum 90.

This is a scholarly article which engages in a close reading of three pages of Foucault's "Nietzsche, Genealogy, History." The author shows that Foucault has misinterpreted Nietzsche's use of the term "*Ursprung*." Foucault claims that Nietzsche uses this term disparagingly to refer to "metaphysical" origins. The author demonstrates that in the texts Foucault has chosen to support his reading, Nietzsche used the word "*Ursprung*" to refer to historical origins. A brief account of the significance of this misreading appears at the end of the paper.

COOK, Monte. Malebranche versus Arnauld. J Hist Phil, 29(2), 183-199, Ap 91.

Recent interpreters of Arnauld's theory of ideas take Arnauld to be a direct realist of some sort. It might seem, then that they would find Arnauld's theory better than Malebranche's at least to the extent that only for Malebranche's representationalism do ideas form a veil preventing our having knowledge of the external world. Nevertheless, proponents of this interpretation of Arnauld's theory of ideas have denied that the theory fares any better against this objection than Malebranche's. This article seeks to strengthen and to some extent correct the case for this assessment.

COOKE, Robert Allan. Danger Signs of Unethical Behavior: How to Determine If Your Firm Is at Ethical Risk. J Bus Ethics, 10(4), 249-253, Ap 91.

This paper is designed to do three things. First, it discusses some of the key trends in business ethics in the academic and corporate communities. Initiatives like the Arthur Andersen Business Ethics Program are noted. Secondly, the paper examines certain basic misconceptions about the field and concludes that the adage that good ethics is good business is still true. Finally, the paper highlights fourteen business attitudes or practices that may put a firm at ethical risk. For example, the paper discusses the risk of using ethics as simply a public relations initiative.

COOKE, Vincent M. Kant, Teleology, and Sexual Ethics. Int Phil Quart, 31(1), 3-13, Mr 91.

This article is an analysis of the role of teleology in Kant's moral philosophy, and shows how a use of teleology enables him to avoid what otherwise might be, and is frequently thought to be, an empty formalism. It uses what he has to say about sexual morality as a case study. Texts from the Lectures of 1775-80, the *Groundwork*, the *Critique of Judgment*, and the *Metaphysics of Morals* are examined to support the main thesis.

COOKE, Vincent M. Moral Obligation and Metaphysics. Thought, 66(260), 65-74, Mr 91.

The article is an analysis of the kind of metaphysics required to ground moral obligation, i.e., the fact that there are certain things we ought or ought not to do whether we want to do them or not. It argues that many of those who have been associated with the Neo-Aristotelian trends in recent philosophy, e.g., Anscombe, Foot, Donagan, MacIntyre, Grisez, and Finnis, lack such a metaphysics and therefore fail to account adequately for moral obligation.

COOLIDGE JR, Francis P. The Insufficiency of Descartes' Provisional Morality. Int Phil Quart, 31(3), 275-293, S 91.

This paper offers a critique of Descartes' claim to have derived the provisional morality from his method and an evaluation of the morality according to the standards he formulated in his letter to the translator of the Principles. On the basis of an examination of the Rules and the Discourse a two-fold case is made. First, it is shown that the morality is insufficient according to the aforementioned standards because it is inadequate to regulate the actions of life and ensure that one lives well. Second, it is argued that Descartes cannot make his derivation of the morality completely clear and that the morality cannot be truly derived from his method.

COONEY, Timothy J. *The Difference Between Truth and Opinion: How the Misuse of Language Can Lead to Disaster*. Buffalo, Prometheus, 1991.

COOPER, David E. The 'New' Nietzsche. Hist Euro Ideas, 11, 857-863, 1989.

By 'the "new" Nietzsche' is meant Nietzsche as interpreted by a number of recent French philosophers—Deleuze, Derrida, Blanchot, etc.—and their followers. On this interpretation, Nietzsche is less a philosopher than a 'counterphilosopher', keen to 'subvert the philosophical tradition'. He himself does not offer new doctrines, but engages in rhetorical 'ruses'. This interpretation is criticized on several grounds. It misconstrues crucial passages on Nietzsche; it relies on a parody of the history of philosophy; and it illegitimately assumes that a 'perspectivist' can provide no nonperspectival criteria of truth.

COOPER, David E. *Existentialism*. Cambridge, Blackwell, 1990.

Existentialism is interpreted as an attempt to overcome various modes of alienation—from the world, from others, and from oneself. Having examined the existentialist critiques of Husserl's phenomenology, the author describes the dissolution of various alienating dualisms, such as mind versus body and reason versus passion. The later chapters discuss self-alienation, authenticity, bad faith, anxiety, and freedom. A final chapter examines the prospects for an existentialist ethics. Authors discussed include Kierkegaard, Heidegger, Jaspers, Ortega, Sartre and Merleau-Ponty.

COOPER, Gregory. The Explanatory Tools of Theoretical Population Biology. Proc Phil Sci Ass, 1, 165-178, 1990.

COOPER, Neil. The Art of Philosophy. Philosophy, 66(256), 169-175, Ap 91.

The paper aims to give reasons for regarding philosophy as an art. The philosopher uses his imagination to *create* structures of thought. Philosophy has four faces, qua empirical resembling science and history, qua conceptual resembling logic, qua normative resembling morality and qua picture-making resembling art. The metaphysicians pictures must never be capricious; they have to be earned and justified. Pure edification is not enough. He has to hold in balance himself both as artist and as "minute philosopher." He has, moreover, a special aesthetic responsibility to present his thought as literature while preserving clarity, vigour and cogency, wherever possible.

COOPER, Neil (ed) and BELL, David (ed). *The Analytic Tradition: Philosophical Quarterly Monographs, Volume 1*. Cambridge, Blackwell, 1990.

Essays by David Bell, Thomas Baldwin, Tyler Burge, Michael Dummett, Bill Hart, Christopher Hookway, Peter Hylton, Wolfgang Künne, Mark Sacks, and John Skorupski, on the nature and origins of the analytic tradition in contemporary philosophy. There are papers on such figures as Frege, Russell, Moore, Peirce, Husserl, and Wittgenstein; and on such themes as the limits of scepticism, the nature of thought and its relation to language and perception, and changing attitudes within the analytic tradition to logic, analysis, clarity, and vagueness.

COOPER, W E. William James's Theory of Mind. J Hist Phil, 28(4), 571-593, O 90.

Neutral monist, panpsychist, naturalist, and phenomenological interpretations of James's theory of mind are canvassed. Culling the true tenets from each, I make a case for a reconciling view on the basis of a distinction between mental and proto-mental properties. The resulting interpretation is compared to two forms of panpsychism identified by T Nagel in his essay of that name.

COPE, Kevin L. *Criteria of Certainty: Truth and Judgment in the English Enlightenment*. Lexington, Univ Pr Kentucky, 1990.

COPP, David. Moral Skepticism. Phil Stud, 62(3), 203-233, Je 91.

"Moral skepticism" is the thesis that no moral code or standard is or could be objectively justified. It constitutes as important a challenge to anti-skeptical moral theory as does skepticism about God to theistic philosophies. It expresses intuitive doubts, but it also entails the falsity of a variety of philosophical theories. It entails a denial of moral knowledge and truth, but one could reject it without holding that there is such knowledge or truth. An anti-skeptical theory could be a familiar "epistemic theory," but it could also be a "practical theory," according to which some moral code has an appropriate justification in practical reason.

COPP, David. Normativity and the Very Idea of Moral Epistemology. S J Phil, SUPP 29, 189-210, 1990.

This paper sketches a cognitivist theory of normative and moral judgment: A normative proposition is true only if a corresponding norm or standard is relevantly justified or has an appropriate standing. A moral proposition is true only if a corresponding moral standard is justified. A norm is not a proposition, and the relevant type of justification is not epistemic. Various 'practical' theories, such as Brandt's, Gauthier's, and Kant's, propose controversial accounts of the sense in which a moral norm can be justified or 'authoritative'. The existence of moral truth and knowledge turns on the existence of relevantly justified moral standards.

CORBEY, R (ed) and LEERSSEN, J T (ed). *Alterity, Identity, Image: Contributions Towards a Theoretical Perspective*. Amsterdam, Rodopi, 1991.

CORBIN, Michel. Du libre arbitre selon s Thomas d'Aquin. Arch Phil, 54(2), 177-212, Ap-Je 91.

In Aquinas there are two different notions of freedom: 1) according to Revelation and Patristic theology freedom means acquiescing to the will of God; 2) according to Aristotle's rationalism it is a faculty of yes and no.

CORDERO, Alberto. Interpreting State Reduction from the Practices-up. Proc Phil Sci Ass, 1, 263-275, 1990.

This paper examines some sources of the concept of objective state reduction in quantum physics. Using case studies from nuclear physics and quantum chemistry, the question of whether one can induce a collapse theory from the practices of scientists working on specific problems is considered. A specific proposal is explored, with emphasis on such features as coherence, testability, unifying power and fertility. It is shown that, contrary to recent suggestions by many scholars, collapse theories are promising developments worthy of further study. Some philosophical implications of the development of collapse theories are discussed.

CORDERO, Ronald A. Law, Morality, and *la Reconquista*. Pub Affairs Quart, 4(4), 347-363, O 90.

As a result of northward migration, both legal and illegal, Hispanic culture is "recapturing" large parts of North America. I argue that the breach of immigration laws involved is largely not of the sort that would merit moral condemnation and that it would be difficult to condemn the phenomenon from either an act-utilitarian or a most-rational-principle point of view.

CORDUA, Carla. El arte y la urbanidad de la razón. Dialogos, 26(58), 109-128, Jl 91.

The essay examines Kant's discussion of the fine arts in the *Critique of Judgement*, and concludes that this work does not contain a philosophy fo art. This position is taken for the following reasons: 1) Kant's neo-classical tastes and opinions on art and beauty go unexamined in the third *Critique*. 2) Art is discussed in the context of the demonstration of a third faculty of reason, viz. judgment, and its function, aesthetic judgment. 3) The main characteristics of artistic creation and skills are recognized when Kant considers the possibility of an "art of Nature", but not as part of human activity and ability. This excludes an adequate treatment of what we call 'art'. 4) Kant's book is mainly destined to help critical philosophy to become a system and to solve the problems of harmonizing the three sides of reason studied in Kant's *Critiques*.

CORLETT, J Angelo. Epistemology, Psychology, and Goldman. Soc Epistem, 5(2), 91-100, Ap-Je 91.

Alvin Goldman argues that there is a connection between primary individual epistemology (PIE) and experimental cognitive psychology (ECP). I challenge Goldman's implication that PIE, but not social epistemics, concerns the evaluation of the reliability of human cognition and that PIE, but not social epistemics, is related to ECP. I argue that social epistemics is concerned with the evaluation of the reliability of human cognition and is related to social cognitive psychology (SCP). Moreover, there are two areas of epistemics: individual and social. Individual epistemics concerns the analysis of individual human knowledge apart from a social context, while social epistemics concerns individual or group knowledge in a social context. Each field concerns primary epistemics in that each concerns the evaluation of the reliability of human cognition.

CORLETT, J Angelo. Fingarette on the Disease Concept of Alcoholism. Theor Med, 11(3), 243-249, S 90.

Herbert Fingarette argues that alcoholism is not a disease and that the alleged alcoholic under certain circumstances has the power to control his or her drinking disorders. I shall analyze Fingarette's argument and show that his position rests on some logical and conceptual confusions. (edited)

CORLETT, J Angelo. Is Kripke's Puzzle Really a Puzzle. Theoria, 55(2), 95-113, 1989.

In his famous essay, "A Puzzle About Belief," Saul Kripke poses a puzzle regarding belief. In this paper I shall first describe Kripke's puzzle. Second, I shall introduce and examine five positions one might take in attempting to solve Kripke's Puzzle. In so doing, I shall show why each of these attempts fails to solve Kripke's Puzzle. The significance of this analysis is that if Kripke's Puzzle remains unresolved, then (as Kripke himself claims) the normal apparatus for belief ascription needs rethinking.

CORLETT, J Angelo. Social Epistemology and Social Cognition. Soc Epistem, 5(2), 135-149, Ap-Je 91.

This paper constitutes a formal reply to my commentators on my paper, "Epistemology, Psychology, and Goldman," which appears in the same issue. Here I deal with Maffie's concerns about native and acquired methods, whether or not social cognitive processes are native, cognitive solipsism, Schmitt's concerns about whether or not social cognitive psychology is relevant to social knowledge or justified belief, and whether or not knowledge must be social, psychological individualism, Goldman's concern as to whether or not there are cognitive processes unique to social cognition, as well as Heyes's concern that I may have uncritically adopted the findings of social psychology. I also set forth an analysis of social knowledge called "social reliabilism."

CORNELL, John F. Faustian Phenomena: Teleology in Goethe's Interpretation of Plants and Animals. J Med Phil, 15(5), 481-492, O 90.

J W von Goethe was a daring and wide-ranging biologist as well as a great playwright. His work was a whole: for him, theory and theatre were both based on keen observation of life. Even 'Faustian' striving, the blind upward urge of life, can be found in significant details of organisms and their evolution, according to Goethe. Such observations cannot be dismissed as sheer poetry. On the contrary, his teleology provides a broad empirical background for the organismic approach in biomedical science, while exposing inconsistencies in strict reductionist doctrines.

CORONA, N A. Una reflexión sobre el pensamiento científico técnico. Stromata, 46(1-2), 139-151, Ja-Je 90.

CORRADA, Manuel. On the Lengths of Proofs of Set Theoretical Statements in Zermelo-Fraenkel Set Theory and Kelley-Morse Theory.... J Non-Classical Log, 7(1-2), 73-77, My-N 90.

This paper deals with the complexity of proofs in two set theories. One is Zermelo-Fraenkel's theory, ZF. The other one is the Kelley-Morse theory, KM, which allows the existence of sets but also of classes. The main result is, roughly stated, to prove the existence of a theorem referring only to sets, which is a theorem of both ZF and KM, whose shortest proof in ZF is enormously longer than its shortest proof in KM. As a consequence, finitistic results are studied, and it is exhibited an inconsistent theory which, however, has not feasible formal proof of contradiction.

CORRADI, Consuelo. The Metaphoric Structure of Sociological Explanation. Phil Soc Crit, 16(3), 161-178, 1990.

CORRINGTON, Robert S. "Finite Idealism: The Midworld and Its History" in *The Philosophy of John William Miller*, FELL, Joseph P (ed), 85-95. Lewisburg, Bucknell Univ Pr, 1990.

CORSO, Laura E. Antropología en la Q D "De virtutibus in communi" de Santo Tomás. Sapientia, 46(180), 99-110, Ap-Je 91.

CORSON, David. Educational Research and Bhaskar's Conception of Discovery. Educ Theor, 41(2), 189-198, Spr 91.

As a critical realist the British philosopher Roy Bhaskar is concerned with 'emancipatory social practice'. For him the world cannot be rationally changed unless it is adequately interpreted and this interpretation has as its prerequisite the philosophical idea of the independent existence of the natural *and* the social world; he extends his ideas from the sciences directly into the social sciences. His organizing theme is: *the nature of, and the prospects for, human emancipation*. This article is an attempt to give Bhaskar's ideas some exposure among those working in philosophy and in education. It sets Bhaskar's key ideas against those of other philosophers whose theories have had impact on educational thought and inquiry: John Dewey, Karl Popper and W V O Quine. The article concludes with an expository account of Bhaskar's conception of discovery, points to its strengths and relevance for education, and presents an interpretation of its stage.

CORTESE, Roberto. La ragione e i valori nella determinazione delle norme. Filosofia, 41(3), 381-408, S-D 90.

CORTI, E C. Libertad y necesidad en el 'Cur Deus Homo' de San Anselmo de Canterbury (segunda parte). Stromata, 46(3-4), 337-360, Jl-D 90.

COSIER, Richard A and DALTON, Dan R. An Issue in Corporate Social Responsibility: An Experiential Approach to Establish the Value of Human Life. J Bus Ethics, 10(4), 311-315, Ap 91.

While the notion of establishing a "value" for human life may be uncomfortable for some, we argue that it is a fundamental requirement for many aspects of public policy. We compare a number of approaches which have been traditionally relied on to make estimations. Also, we provide an exercise which provides an unusual, but we hope provocative, perspective on the evaluation of human life.

COSTA DE BEAUREGARD, Olivier. Relativité et quanta: leurs mutuelles exisgences et les corrélations d'Einstein-Podolsky-Rosen. Rev Metaph Morale, 95(4), 547-559, O-D 90.

Unlike various interpretations of quantum mechanics based upon the phenomenology of macroscopic experimentation, this one rests entirely upon the formalism of relativistic quantum mechanics per se. The concept of causality is likened to that of a conditional probability endowed with two specific features: "non-separability" of occurrences in the sense of the quantal calculus of probabilities (Jordan, 1926); invariance under rotations (Lorentz and Poincaré, 1905) and reversals of axes (Lüders, 1952) of the spatiotemporal Cartesian reference frame, entailing cause-effect reversibility.

COSTA, Filippo. La logica di Hegel come testo filosofico (II). Teoria, 10(1), 103-143, 1990.

COSTA, Michael J. Hume and Belief in the Existence of an External World. Phil Stud (Ireland), 32, 99-112, 1988-90.

The author addresses for Hume the question, What is the nature of the psychological state that *constitutes* belief in the existence of an external world? The interpretation developed describes this belief as a disposition to (1) produce vivid ideas of appropriate types filling in gaps between constant and coherent impressions and (2) use the resulting product as the base on which to develop and justify causal inferences. It is argued that this account best explains the various relevant things that Hume has to say, including especially Hume's claim that belief in body cannot be justified, yet is presupposed in all our reasonings.

COSTA, Miguel Dias. A lógica do sentido na filosofia hermenêutica. Rev Port Filosof, 46(1), 143-168, Ja-Mr 90.

This article presents Paul Ricoeur's most recent thought from the perspective of how sense is produced; in the process, possibilities and limits of the hermeneutical circle are discussed. Using as a point of departure the phenomenological and ontological presuppositions of his philosophy, questions concerning interpretations of texts, imagination, creativity, action, time, narrative, ideology and utopia are dealt with. After calling attention to a certain logocentrism, i.e., a mixture of Logos and a supposed reality, in the resolution of these questions, an attempt is made to rethink the relationship between sense and *consensus* between the positions defended by Ricoeur and the hypothesis of Rene Girard concerning mimetic desire and violence is established.

COSTANZO, Angelo. Sul controllo nel procedimento di determinazione dei principi dell'ordinamento. Riv Int Filosof Diritto, 66(4), 577-595, O-D 89.

CÔTÉ, Antoine. Aristote admet-il un infini en acte et en puissance en "Physique III, 4-8"? Rev Phil Louvain, 88(80), 487-503, N 90.

Aristotle's doctrine of the infinite, which he sets out in *Physics* III, 4-8, has given rise to two apparently irreconcilable interpretations. Some commentators hold that Aristotle admits only the existence of a potential infinite, whereas others hold that it was rather the hypothesis of an actual and a potential infinite that the Stagirite upheld. If it is true that the text of the *Physics* appears to lend justification to both interpretations, it is because Aristotle, while using only the language of act and potency, attempts to provide an answer to two different problems: (1) a classifying or metaphysical problem, and (2) a descriptive or physical problem. The Stagirite needs on the one hand, to situate the infinite in the ontological hierarchy by distinguishing it from actual beings and pure non-beings—and in this case the infinite is said to be "in potency"—but he also needs, on the other hand, to specify the intrinsic nature of the infinite as a physical entity. This investigation will show, then, that like all natural phenomena the *apeiron* exists both in actuality and in potency.

COTTINGHAM, John. Descartes on Colour. Proc Aris Soc, 90, 231-246, 1989-90.

The first half of the paper looks at various arguments which Descartes offers for the conclusion that colours do not inhere in objects, and attempts to uncover the fundamental rationale for his claim that colour properties do not belong to objects 'in themselves'. The second half raises some general critical questions about Descartes' account of colour perception; examines the Cartesian claim that there is a certain 'arbitrariness' about the qualitative aspects of our perceptions of colour; and defends the Cartesian idea that there is a certain 'opacity' in our perceptions of colour (as against, for example, our perceptions of shape).

COTTRILL, Melville T. Corporate Social Responsibility and the Marketplace. J Bus Ethics, 9(9), 723-729, S 90.

Most work to date seeking to link CSR level and performance has treated CSR as a strictly firm level variable. It is the argument of this author that any investigation of CSR that fails to incorporate industry level realities, particularly of an economic nature, will be fatally deficient. Hypotheses are proposed, building off the work of James Post, the gravamen of which is that CSR level depends significantly on industrial and economic status. The hypotheses are tested against a currently popular database and receive moderate support.

COUGHLAN, Michael J. *The Vatican, the Law and the Human Embryo*. Iowa City, Univ of Iowa Pr, 1990.

The book examines the bases for the Vatican's ethical teaching and, in particular, for its calls for civil legislation to protect the 'rights' of the human embryo. It is argued that the current position taken by the Church does not meet the demands of natural law ethics and therefore accords neither with the Chruch's traditional Thomistic perspective nor with what is required for insisting on legislation in a pluralistic democracy. The pivotal flaw in the Church's position lies in the inadequacy of the argument that the human embryo is a person, an inadequacy which is exacerbated if ensoulment is held to be an essential attribute of persons.

COULOUBARITSIS, Lambros. La logique du mythe et la question du non-être. Rev Theol Phil, 122(3), 323-340, 1990.

Le titre de mon exposé peut soulever quelques questions: peut-on parler de logique du mythe, alors même que l'interrogation sur le mythe n'a lieu que dans le sillage d'une mise en forme du logos, c'est-à-dire d'une rationalité ou d'une argumentativité? Mieux, quel sens y a-t-il de parler, d'autre part, du non-être à une époque comme la nôtre où la pratique du non-être dans la philosophie, se tient aux confins, voire au-delà de la rationalité, comme sa limite propre? Ces deux apories sont réelles et je ne chercherai pas à les dissimuler; au contraire, elles forment l'horizon de ma réflexion. Pour mieux les affronter je commencerai par la question du non-être qui, je crois, appartient plus directement à l'ordre philosophique, c'est-à-dire post-mythique, alors que la question du mythe est plus ambiguë et concerne aussi la pensée pré-philosophique.

COULTER, Jeff and PARSONS, E D. The Praxiology of Perception: Visual Orientations and Practical Action. Inquiry, 33(3), 251-272, S 90.

This paper is concerned with the development of the idea that most of what is glossed as "perception" turns out to consist in arrays of visual orientations, heterogeneous forms of *activities* and achievements, irreducible to physiological characterization. Some philosophical and sociological consequences of this point are explored.

COURCELLE, Bruno. The Monadic Second-Order Logic of Graphs IV: Definability Properties of Equational Graphs. Annals Pure Applied Log, 49(3), 193-255, O 90.

We establish that every equational graph can be characterized, up to isomorphism, by a formula of monadic second-order logic. It follows that the isomorphism of two equational graphs is decidable. We also establish that a graph specified in an equational graph by monadic second-order formulas is equational.

COURT, Raymond. "La réhabilitation de l'allégorie: baroque et modernité" in *XIth International Congress in Aesthetics, Nottingham 1988*, WOODFIELD, Richard (ed), 22-25. Nottingham, Nottingham Polytech, 1990.

COURTINE, Jean-Jacques. Le corps et ses langages: quelques perspectives de travail historique. Horiz Phil, 1(2), 1-11, 1991.

COUSE, G S. Collingwood's Detective Image of the Historian and the Study of Hadrian's Wall. Hist Theor, 29(4), 57-77, D 90.

This is essentially an examination of Collingwood's contention that "scientific history" could prove its point "as conclusively as a demonstration in mathematics." It did so through a detective-like gathering of circumstantial evidence (excluding the content of testimony) and educing conclusions purely by inference. Collingwood's commentaries on Wall findings elucidate and partially confirm that contention, and incidentally his theory of historical explanation. Archaeologists have attained decisive answers to questions about selected Wall sites, but lines of inference therefrom to conclusions about the whole Wall system have been too complex to permit more than a general consensus, changing as research proceeds.

COUTINHO, Jorge. Da secularidade da Filosofia. Rev Port Filosof, 46(3), 331-354, Jl-S 90.

The problem of the proper relation between the sacred and the profane was the object of Church teaching and of philosophy in particular. In the right attitude of secular the autonomy supposes that the philosophical reason doesn't lose its own dignity, its value and its function, letting itself absorb wholly by faith; in compensation however the relative character absorb wholly by faith; in compensation however the relative character of such an autonomy prevents this from being ignored by the other, losing sight of it in its philosophical horizon. The possibility of a philosophy qualified as Christian seems to derive from an approach of the problem from this point of view.

COUTO-SOARES, Maria Luisa. Mismidad y diferencia. Anu Filosof, 23(2), 131-137, 1990.

COUTTS, Mary Carrington. Teaching Ethics in the Health Care Setting, Part I. Kennedy Inst Ethics J, 1(2), 171-185, Je 91.

Prepared as part of the Scope Note Series from the National Reference Center for Bioethics Literature (NRC) at Georgetown University, this is an annotated bibliography on teaching ethics in health care education and in hospitals. Provides references to position statements by professional organizations on the importance of teaching health care ethics, background material, references to articles on teaching methods and evaluation of ethics education. Includes program descriptions for a number of ethics education programs. Reprints available from the NRC, call 800-MED-ETHX for information.

COUTURE, Jocelyne and LAMBEK, Joachim. Philosophical Reflections on the Foundations of Mathematics. Erkenntnis, 34(2), 187-209, Mr 91.

This article was written jointly by a philosopher and a mathematician. It has two aims: to acquaint mathematicians with some of the philosophical questions at the foundations of their subject and to familiarize philosophers with some of the answers to these questions which have recently been obtained by mathematicians. In particular, we argue that, if these recent findings are borne in mind, four different basic philosophical positions, logicism, formalism, platonism and intuitionism, if stated with some moderation, are in fact reconcilable although with some reservations in the case of logicism, provided one adops a nominalistic interpretation of Plato's ideal objects. This eclectic view has been asserted by Lambek and Scott (LS 1986) on fairly technical grounds, but the present argument is meant to be accessible to a wider audience and to provide some new insights.

COUTURE, Jocelyne. Propriété de soi et propriété du monde extérieur. Lekton, 1(2), 99-130, 1991.

COVEOS, Costis M. Stephen Hilmy on Matters of Method and Style. Phil Invest, 14(2), 131-142, Ap 91.

In his recent book *The Later Wittgenstein,* S. S. Hilmy puts forth the view that the non-linearity of Wittgenstein's style was a drawback he was all too eager to eliminate and as much unable to overcome to his dissatisfaction. In my paper I try to show that Wittgenstein's dissatisfaction did not stem from his inability "to write in a more stylistically conventional manner", as Hilmy puts it, but from his inability to achieve a novel method of projection of the linguistic territory, one that could exhibit the dazzling complexity of language and at the same time retain the linearity required in book-writing.

COVEOS, Costis M. Wittgenstein on Frazer's *Golden Bough*. Philosophy, 65(254), 518-521, O 90.

In his discussion of the notion of "depth" of a practice, in view of Frazer's explanation of it, Wittgenstein is mentioning the "strange relationship between Siegfried and Brunhilde in the *Nibelungenlied*." It is my opinion that he is making a wrong reference: there is nothing in the medieval poem that could possibly count as "relationship" between Siegfried and Brunhilde, whereas in the Wagnerian music-drama *Der Ring des Nibelungen* there is the incestuous relationship between Sieglinde and her brother Siegmund. I believe that this misplacement deprives Wittgenstein's remark of its full explanatory power.

COVER, J A (ed) and KULSTAD, Mark (ed). *Central Themes in Early Modern Philosophy*. Indianapolis, Hackett, 1990.

This collection of new essays provides a cross-sampling of the important current work in the history of seventeenth- and eighteenth-century philosophy, particularly in the areas of metaphysics and epistemology. Every major figure (by one reckoning) from Descartes to Kant is considered, some receiving attention in multiple essays (especially Spinoza, Descartes, Malebranche, Leibniz). A diverse range of themes is also addressed—from doctrines of substance, essence, and causality to sensation, epistemic responsibility, and knowledge of necessary truths. Contributors include M Wilson, R S Woolhouse, D Garrett, G H R Parkinson, E Curley, R Sleigh Jr, M Bolton, N Jolley, A Baier, and P Kitcher.

COVER, Jan A. Leibniz on Superessentialism and World-Bound Individuals. Stud Leibniz, 22(2), 175-183, 1990.

In this discussion we present an alternative to the standard reading of Leibniz's considered views on *de re* modality. In particular, we argue that although Leibniz regarded the intrinsic properties of an individual as being essential to it, he did not commit himself to the doctrine of world-bound individuals. We further argue that he did subscribe to a version of counterpart theory as a way of treating modal discourse, and that this does not conflict with Leibniz's views on transworld identity. After offering a critique of the standard account and a sketch of our alternative, we treat at length an important third reading of Leibnizian modality offered recently by Robert C Sleigh, Jr.

COVERDALE, John. A Response to 'Psychoactive Drug Prescribing in Japan'. J Med Phil, 16(2), 155-157, Ap 91.

The method of analysis for deciding whether or not to prescribe medications is not substantially different in psychiatry than in medicine as has been claimed. A biopsychosocial approach is used for framing cost-benefit considerations. When weights are attributed to potential outcomes that are not readily commensurable with each other, psychiatrists may be guided by established professional guidelines, peer review, continuing medical education, professional or public debate, as well as by ethics committees.

COVEY, Edward. Physical Possibility and Potentiality in Ethics. Amer Phil Quart, 28(3), 237-244, Jl 91.

COWARD, Harold G. "Speech Versus Writing" in Derrida and Bhartrhari. Phil East West, 41(2), 141-162, Ap 91.

This study identifies points of formal and substantive contact between Derrida and traditional Indian thought. Reading Bhartrhari with Derrida highlights the error of previous interpretations that have read the *Vākyapadiya* through Advaitic eyes. It also highlights Bhartrhari's accommodation of Buddhist stress on individual experience while retaining an orthodox grounding in Vedic *dharma*, now reinterpreted as *Sabdatattva*. Derrida, however, challenges Bhartrhari's notion of *pratibhā* or "pure" mystical perception. The study calls into question current suggestions that Derrida can be understood as a Mādhyamikan Buddhist—for this analysis shows him to agree with Bhartrhari on exactly those points which separate Bhartrhari and Nāgārjuna.

COWARD, Harold G. "Memory and Scripture in the Conversion of Augustine" in *Grace, Politics and Desire: Essays on Augustine*, MEYNELL, Hugo A (ed), 19-30. Calgary, Univ Calgary Pr, 1990.

Augustine's answer is best understood in terms of the dynamics of memory and scripture. Unlike our modern education with its reliance on printed books rather than memory, Augustine was immersed in a traditional education which stressed the memorization of texts. Throughout his life, with varying degrees of intensity, Augustine was exposed to the contents of the Christian Scriptures. That the Scriptures became firmly ingrained in his memory and consciousness is evidenced by the fact that throughout the *Confessions*, scriptural citations are woven into the fabric of Augustine's writing. The thesis of this essay is that the two processes of memory and scripture provide the essential dynamics for the understanding of Augustine's conversion experience. We examine the roles of memory and scripture first in Augustine's childhood experience of religion, second in his adolescent rebellion, and finally in his conversion and mature religious experience.

COWARD, Harold. 'Desire' in Yoga and Jung. J Indian Counc Phil Res, 5(1), 57-64, S-D 87.

Jung's encounter with Patañjali's *Yoga SlOutras* helped him to enlarge the awareness of his own consciousness, and provided him with clues as to how to better make present its contents. According to Patañjali desire is created by memory traces (*samsklOaras*) from this and previous lives. Similarly, for Jung desire is created by the record of past human actions and is recorded in the personal and collective unconscious. But whereas the goal for Patañjali is to purge out all desire, Jung thinks such a result to be psychologically impossible.

COWARD, Harold. Sankara and Derrida on Philosophy of Language. J Indian Counc Phil Res, 6(3), 13-21, My-Ag 89.

A comparison of Derrida and Sankara on language reveals sharp contrasts. Whereas difference is the *avidyOla* to be overcome for Sankara, difference manifested in the dynamic tension of language is basic to Derrida. This distinction carries over into their contrasting perceptions of the end-goal. For Derrida the goal is a call for moral action; for Sankara action associated with difference is *saguna* Brahman that must be negated for the ultimate *nirguna* Brahman to be experienced. Derrida's belief that perception free of language just does not occur challenges Sankara's claim of an ultimate "perception" free of the *avidyOla* of language.

COWDELL, Scott. Radical Theology, Postmodernity and Christian Life in the Void. Heythrop J, 32(1), 62-71, Ja 91.

Postmodern philosophy and literary theory have spawned sufficient theology that contours of a postmodern Christian life are becoming visible. The article considers features of the postmodern challenge to modernity and its liberal theological project. Radical versions of Christian spirituality and ecclesiology suitable for 'post-liberal' conditions are sought from Mark C Taylor, Thomas J J Altizer and Don Cupitt. The continuing possibility of a liberal approach is affirmed, supported in part by the identification of a 'hidden God' in the work of Taylor and Altizer.

COWDIN, Daniel M. Religious Liberty, Religious Dissent and the Catholic Tradition. Heythrop J, 32(1), 26-61, Ja 91.

This article asks whether the Catholic Church's ethical endorsement of civil religious liberty implies a corresponding endorsement of freedom within the Church, i.e., dissent. It concludes that there is a relevant connection between the two, based not on the endorsement of religious liberty per se, but rather on the particular social grounding of the endorsement in *Dignitatis Humanae*. A conditional right to dissent is defended.

COWEN, Robert H. Two Hypergraph Theorems Equivalent to BPI. Notre Dame J Form Log, 31(2), 232-240, Spr 90.

Techniques originally developed for establishing NP-Completeness are adapted to prove that two compactness theorems concerning hypergraphs are equivalent to the Prime Ideal Theorem for Boolean algebras (BPI). In addition, some possible connections between NP-Completeness and BPI are explored.

COWLEY, Fraser. *Metaphysical Delusion*. Buffalo, Prometheus, 1991.

Metaphysical doctrines differ from common knowledge and belief and from scientific theories in being matters of faith. Faith has motives and has to be induced by ritual activities, principally verbal. The objections to countless doctrines are commonplace truths. The principal instrument of delusion is linguistic disconnection. Linguistic transcendentalism has replaced the sophistries of scepticism as the justifying theory. A language on this view is a theory, truth is relative to a language, and from promises in one no conclusion follows in another. Thus we have a metaphysical justification for double-talk and may speak with a forked tongue and a clear conscience.

COWLING, Maurice. *Mill and Liberalism (Second Edition)*. New York, Cambridge Univ Pr, 1990.

COZZENS, Susan E (ed) and GIERYN, Thomas F (ed). *Theories of Science in Society*. Bloomington, Indiana Univ Pr, 1990.

CRABTREE, Walden. An Inquiry into the Meaning of Teacher Clarity in Recent Research and into the Value of the Research for the Teacher. Phil Stud Educ, /, 70-81, 1986.

An analysis of experimental research studies dealing with the concept of *teacher clarity*, done since 1978, led to the following conclusions: (1) the concept, *teacher clarity*, included the following uses, among others: "easily understood"; "answering questions well"; "using language at an 'appropriate' cognitive level"; "the use of structuring and of examples"; and "proper pacing." (2) A strong positive correlation was found between students' learning and *teacher clarity*; (3) conceptualization and research methods in the studies examined were judged to be meaningful and defensible; and (4) the research was thought to provide clear, useful knowledge for classroom teachers and teacher educators.

CRAIG, Edward. Davidson and the Sceptic: The Thumbnail Version. Analysis, 50(4), 213-214, O 90.

Davidson's device of the omniscient interpreter is ineffective against the sceptic; its sole effect is to transform a doubt about the truth of a belief into a doubt about its content.

CRAIG, Robert P. The Common Good, Human Rights and Education: A Need for Conceptual Reformulization. J Thought, 24(3-4), 55-67, Fall-Wint 89.

CRAIG, William Lane. The "Kalam" Cosmological Argument and the Hypothesis of a Quiescent Universe. Faith Phil, 8(1), 104-108, Ja 91.

Although Stewart Goetz is correct that the *kalam* cosmological argument does not rule out the possibility that the finite temporal series of past events was initiated by a distinct personal agent in an eternal, quiescent universe, this does not appreciably mitigate the force of the argument for theism. For the atheist will hardly be inclined to admit the existence of an eternal, changeless, personal Prime Mover rather than the fact that the universe began to exist. Moreover, since the existence of a quiescent universe is physically impossible, it could have existed only be means of a miracle so stupendous that it involved the suspension of all the laws of nature. The Prime Mover would thus have to be Lord over all the universe, a conclusion which even a successful *kalam* argument for the beginning of the universe does not attain.

CRAIG, William Lane. "Lest Anyone Should Fall": A Middle Knowledge Perspective on Perseverance and Apostolic Warnings. Int J Phil Relig, 29(2), 65-74, Ap 91.

The classical doctrine of perseverance of the saints sits ill with scriptual warnings against apostasy. The position that these warnings are God's *means* of preserving the elect seems to collapse to a Molinist Doctrine of perseverance according to which the elect *can* freely apostasize but *will* not due to God's extrinsically efficacious grace. This leads to some interesting results for the nature of human freedom.

CRAIG, William Lane. Barrow and Tipler on the Anthropic Principle versus Divine Design. Brit J Phil Sci, 39(3), 389-395, S 88.

Barrow and Tipler's contention that the Anthropic Principle is obviously true and removes the need for an explanation of fine-tuning fails because the Principle is trivially true, and only within the context of a World Ensemble, whose existence is not obvious, does a selection effect become significant. Their objections to divine design as an explanation of fine-tuning are seen to be misconceived.

CRAIG, William Lane. God and Real Time. Relig Stud, 26(3), 335-359, S 90.

The article extends the analysis of Alan Padgett of divine eternity. Divine timelessness implies a B-theory of time, which theory seems untenable. On the preferable A-theory, the key to understanding God's relationship to time is to distinguish between metaphysical and physical time. God exists in metaphysical time, as Padgett argues, but also, *pace* Padgett, in physical cosmic time as well.

CRAIG, William Lane. 'What Place, then, for a creator?': Hawking on God and Creation. Brit J Phil Sci, 41(4), 473-491, D 90.

Hawking's claim to have eliminated the need for a Creator does not affect the need for a Leibnizian Sufficient Reason for the universe, nor does it address the need of a Creator as a metaphysical First Cause. It is dubious with respect to a temporally First Cause, since Hawking's model rests on the use of 'imaginary' time, which is physically unintelligible and metaphysically illicit, as it converts time into space and denies temporal becoming.

CRAIN, Stephen and FODOR, Janet Dean. Phrase Structure Parameters. Ling Phil, 13(6), 619-659, D 90.

CRAMER, Konrad. Metaphysik und Erfahrung in Kants Grundlegung der Ethik. Neue Hefte Phil, 30-31, 15-68, 1991.

CRAMPTON, Peter C and DEES, J Gregory. Shrewd Bargaining on the Moral Frontier: Toward a Theory of Morality in Practice. Bus Ethics Quart, 1(2), 135-167, Ap 91.

From a traditional moral point of view, business practitioners often seem overly concerned about the behavior of their peers in deciding how they ought to act. We propose to account for this concern by introducing a mutual trust perspective, where moral obligations are grounded in a sense of trust that others will abide by the same rules. When grounds for trust are absent, the obligation is weakened. We illustrate this perspective by examining the widespread ambivalence with regard to deception about one's settlement preferences in negotiation. On an abstract level, such deception generally seems undesirable, though in many individual cases it is condoned, even admired as shrewd bargaining. Because of the difficulty in verifying someone's settlement preferences, it is hard to establish a basis for trusting the relevations of the other party, especially in competitive negotiations with relative strangers.

CRANDALL, Lee A. Advocacy of Just Health Policies as Professional Duty: Cultural Biases and Ethical Responsibilities. Bus Prof Ethics J, 9(3-4), 41-53, Fall-Wint 90.

This paper argues that American health professionals embrace an individualist ideology that leads to a reductionist approach to issues of social justice. The consequence is a failure to address concerns of equity in access to care that are inherent in the role of the healer and in the claim to professional status. Unless a professional culture that promotes justice is developed, there will be increasing regulation and deprofessionalization of health professions.

CRANE, Tim. All the Difference in the World. Phil Quart, 41(162), 1-25, Ja 91.

The 'twin earth' arguments of Putnam and Burge are generally supposed to establish that certain intentional states have 'broad contents', 'narrow contents', or some combination thereof. This paper disputes the distinction between broad and narrow content. The twin earth arguments only establish their conclusions if certain implausible assumptions are made about natural kinds and the relation between thought and language. Once these assumptions are discarded, it is clear that the contents of intentional states can be shared by 'twins' and yet have truth-conditions: so they are neither broad nor narrow.

CRANE, Tim. An Alleged Analogy Between Numbers and Propositions. Analysis, 50(4), 224-230, O 90.

Some philosophers have attempted to undermine the claim that propositional attitudes are relations—between thinkers and abstract propositions—by arguing that ascriptions of attitudes are analogous to ascriptions of physical magnitudes such as temperatures. These may be seen as relations to numbers, relative to a unit of measurement, even though they are really nonrelational properties. But there is no analogy of a unit of measurement in the case of the attitudes. Two different numbers may 'index' the same temperature, but two different propositions cannot 'index' the same belief. The analogy therefore fails.

CRANE, Tim. The Language of Thought: No Syntax Without Semantics. Mind Lang, 5(3), 187-212, Autumn 90.

In *From Folk Psychology to Cognitive Science*, Stephen Stich argues that semantic notions should have no place in mature cognitive psychology. His alternative, the 'Syntactic Theory of the Mind', is based on the idea that thinking is manipulating 'symbols' that belong to a purely syntactic language, governed only by syntactic rules. This paper disputes Stich's claim by showing that there is no way to individuate the mind's syntactic categories independently of any semantic notions. Stich's theory will collapse either into Fodor's Representational Theory of the Mind, or into eliminative materialism.

CRANE, Tim. Why Indeed? Papineau on Supervenience. Analysis, 51(1), 32-37, Ja 91.

David Papineau (*Analysis* 50 (2), pp. 66-71) attempts to derive the thesis of mental-physical supervenience from the thesis that physics is complete. I accept the argument's validity, but show that the crucial premise of the completeness of physics is either trivially true—by definition—or as controversial as supervenience itself.

CRANFORD, Ronald E. A Hostage to Technology. Hastings Center Rep, 20(5), 9-10, S-O 90.

CRANSTON, Maurice. Jean-Jacques Rousseau and the Fusion of Democratic Sovereignty with Aristocratic Government. Hist Euro Ideas, 11, 417-425, 1989.

The author argues that Rousseau's distinction between the concepts of 'government' and 'sovereignty' enables him to follow Calvin in combining the republican idea of a people ruling itself with an aristocratic system of elite control, and by eliminating Calvin's theological power, to transform the Genevan model of a constitution into one resembling Sparta.

CRANSTON, Maurice. *Jean-Jacques: The Early Life and Work of Jean-Jacques, 1712-1754*. Chicago, Univ of Chicago Pr, 1991.

An intellectual biography, concentrating on the personal experience which animated Rousseau's early writings, notably the two Discourses, the Political Economy and the Letter to M d'Alembert. It is argued that these writings form with the later work a coherent whole and that Rousseau was justified in claiming to have produced a "system". Rousseau's pamphlet controversy with Rameau in the 1750's on the subject of music is seen as a considered critique of rationalism and a plea for what afterwards became known as "romanticism". The book is based on manuscript sources, and aims to throw new light on Rousseau's debt to Pietist influences and on his complicated relationship with the sceptical philosophers of the Enlightenment.

CRANSTON, Maurice. *The Noble Savage: Jean-Jacques Rousseau, 1754-1762*. Chicago, Univ of Chicago Pr, 1991.

This book covers the most productive years of Rousseau's life. It traces the circumstances in which he wrote *The Social Contract, Emile* and *La nouvelle Heloise*. There were years spent in relative solitude in the French countryside, a period clouded by quarrels with nearly all the other philosophers of the French Enlightenment but enlived by friendships with aristocratic neighbours and an intense love affair with the Comtesse d'Houdetot. The book ends with Rousseau's escape to Switzerland after a warrant for the arrest of the author of *Emile* (on a charge of subverting religion) is issued by the Paris Parliament.

CRAVO, Maria R and MARTINS, João P. How to Change Your Mind. Nous, 25(4), 537-551, S 91.

In this paper, we investigate the rules that should underlie a computer program that is capable of revising its beliefs or opinions. Such a program maintains a model of its environment. All the inferences drawn are added to the knowledge base. Among the propositions in the knowledge base, there are some in which the program believes, and others in which the program does not believe. Inputs from the outside world or reasoning carried out by the program may lead to the detection of contradictions, in which case the program has to revise its beliefs in order to get rid of the contradiction and to accommodate the new information. (edited)

CRAWSHAW, Ralph. A Vision of the Health Decisions Movement. Hastings Center Rep, 20(5), 21-22, S-O 90.

CREATH, Richard. "Carnap, Quine and the Rejection of Intuition" in *Perspectives on Quine*, BARRETT, Robert (ed), 55-66. Cambridge, Blackwell, 1990.

CRELINSTEN, Gordon L. The Physician-Societal Relationship. Bus Prof Ethics J, 9(3-4), 79-82, Fall-Wint 90.

CREMA, Cristina Diniz Mendonça. Le thème de la révolution dans la pensée de Sartre. Trans/Form/Acao, 13, 21-40, 1990.

L'oeuvre de Sartre pourrait être lue comme l'incarnation de l'esprit "pathétique" et "héroïque" de l'époque de la guerre et de la Résistance. Sous le coup de feu des barricades de 44, une philosophie de la révolution commence à éclore—elle fut forgée à chaud durant cette époque de "haute température historique". C'est de la généralisation théorique de cette expérience politique cruciale, c'est-à-dire de la cristallisation du "mythe" de la Résistance, que vient, à mon avis, l'idée satrienne de révolution.

CRESSWELL, M J. Modality and Mellor's McTaggart. Stud Log, 49(2), 163-170, Je 90.

This paper explores amodal analogue of Hugh Mellor's version of McTaggart's argument against the reality of tense. I show that if Mellor's argument succeeds in showing that the present moment cannot be any more real than any other moment then it also shows that the actual world cannot be any more real than any other possible world.

CRÉTELLA, Henri. La théologie de Heidegger. Heidegger Stud, 6, 11-25, 1990.

Rather than a philosophy, Heidegger's thinking is the discovery of what has been left unthought in the whole history of philosophy. This unthought must be named theology in this Christian (but not clerical) sense in which theology is closely bound up with a peculiar anthropology. The Heideggerian analysis of Dasein is the preliminary condition of such an anthropology. It requires the resolution to exist authentically. That happens through the language thanks to which "the unknown god" can set us free. Thus Heidegger's theology is not an intellectual construction but the uncovering of the human *question*.

CREWE, Jonathan. Gerald Bruns's Cavell. Crit Inquiry, 17(3), 609-615, Spr 91.

CRIDER, Cathleen and CIRILLO, Leonard. Systems of Interpretation and the Function of the Metaphor. J Theor Soc Behav, 21(2), 171-195, Je 91.

CRISP, Roger. Sidgwick and Self-Interest. Utilitas, 2(2), 267-280, N 90.

The paper concerns Henry Sidgwick's conception of self-interest, or utility. It is argued, against D Parfit and J B Schneedwind, that Sidgwick's view consists in an informed desire theory constrained by an experience requirement. Sidgwick's view is then subjected to three objections: (a) the experience requirement is mistaken; (b) self-interest, if it does consist in the fulfillment of desire, does not consist only in the fulfillment of desire; (c) self-interest does not consist in the fulfillment of desire. A revised account of self-interest is offered, and a problem for this account solved in the light of a Sidgwickian distinction.

CRISTAUDO, Wayne. Theorising Ideas: *Idee* and *Vorstellung* from Kant to Hegel to Marx. Hist Euro Ideas, 12(6), 813-825, 1990.

The paper depicts the conceptual and normative shifts of the terms *Idee* and *Vorstellung* from Kant to Hegel to Marx. The paper also highlights the importance of the opposition between *Vorstellung* and *Idee* in Marx's thought. It is also argued that Marx's critique of German idealism is undermined by an oversimplification of the nature of ideas and a failure to appreciate the kinds of problems which led Kant and Hegel to their respective taxonomies of cognitive terms.

CRISTIN, Renato. Phänomenologie und Monadologie: Husserl und Leibniz. Stud Leibniz, 22(2), 163-174, 1990.

The essay purposes to show that Leibniz fills a central position in Husserl's thought, especially as regards the phenomonological determination of the intersubjectivity's problem. Husserl achieves an implicit revaluation of the thought of Leibniz, that according to this interpretation isn't dogmatic. The idea of a monadological phenomenology can consent to overcome the aporias of the intersubjectivity's theory, seen as cognitive's harmony among subjects and as intermonadic's community. This comparison with Leibniz will suggest a way of development of the posthusserlian phenomenology, pointing out at the same time a topical element of Leibniz's thought.

CRITCHLEY, Simon. ""Bois"—Derrida's Final Word on Levinas" in *Re-Reading Levinas*, BERNASCONI, Robert (ed), 162-189. Bloomington, Indiana Univ Pr, 1991.

This essay is an extended and detailed commentary on Jacques Derrida's second and hitherto largely undiscussed essay on Levinas's work 'At this very moment in this work here I am'; particular attention is paid to how Levinas's later work aticulates the saying within the said, and how the question of sexual difference arises in Levinas's conception of ethics.

CRITCHLEY, Simon (trans) and GREISCH, Jean. "The Face and Reading: Immediacy and Mediation" in *Re-Reading Levinas*, BERNASCONI, Robert (ed), 67-82. Bloomington, Indiana Univ Pr, 1991.

Greisch's essay offers a reading of Levinas's *Otherwise than Being or Beyond Essence* that traces the themes of the face and reading and immediacy and mediation. Particular attention is paid to the relation between the work of Levinas and that of Wittgenstein and Eric Weil.

CRITCHLEY, Simon (ed) and BERNASCONI, Robert (ed). *Re-Reading Levinas*. Bloomington, Indiana Univ Pr, 1991.

The book responds to Levinasian ethics by juxtaposing it with the problematics of deconstruction, feminism, psychotherapy, and the ethical status of animals. Derrida's essay on Levinas, "At this very moment in this work here I am," Levinas's essay on Derrida, "Wholly Otherwise," and Irigaray's "questions to Emmanuel Levinas" appear in English translation for the first time. Essays by a number of the leading exponents of Levinas's thought explore the possibility of an ethical saying that is irreducible to the ontological said. Taken as a whole the volume attempts to open a new chapter in the critical assimilation of Levinas.

CRITCHLEY, Simon (trans) and LEVINAS, Emmanuel. "Wholly Otherwise" in *Re-Reading Levinas*, BERNASCONI, Robert (ed), 3-10. Bloomington, Indiana Univ Pr, 1991.

This is the first English translation of an article by Levinas where he relates his own concerns to those of Derrida's work.

CRITCHLEY, Simon. Writing the Revolution—The Politics of Truth in Genet's *Prisoner of Love*. Rad Phil, 56, 25-34, Autumn 90.

As part of an ongoing commentary of Derrida's *Glas* (cf. 'A commentary on Derrida's Reading of Hegel in *Glas*', *Bulletin of the Hegel Society of Great Britain*, No. 18 (1988), pp. 6-32), this essay attempts to invert the Derridian and Sartrean interpretations of Genet's work through a reading of his posthumously published novel, *Prisoner of Love*. I argue that Genet's attempt to tell the truth of the Palestinian resistance leads him to embrace the Hegelian notion of *Sittlichkeit* that his work was thought, by Derrida, to undermine.

CROCE, Benedetto. *Estetica: Come Scienza dell'Espressione e Linguistica Generale*. Milan, Adelphi, 1990.

CROCKER, David A. Cuatro modelos de desarrollo costarricense: un análisis y evalución ética. Rev Filosof (Costa Rica), 27(66), 317-332, D 89.

One task of international development ethics is to assess the development options open to particular nations at particular times. The paper applies philosophical and ethical reflection to the national debate on development options for Costa Rica. (edited)

CROMBAG, H F M. Why (Legal) Rules Often Fail to Control Human Behavior. Method Sci, 22(3), 138-148, 1989.

CROMBIE, A C. Expectation, Modelling and Assent in the History of Optics—II. Kelper and Descartes. Stud Hist Phil Sci, 22(1), 89-115, Mr 91.

CROMBIE, A C. Expectation, Modelling and Assent in the History of Optics: Part I—Alhazen and the Medieval Tradition. Stud Hist Phil Sci, 21(4), 605-632, D 90.

CROPSEY, Joseph. On Ancients and Moderns. Interpretation, 18(1), 31-51, Fall 90.

CROSS, Charles B. Explanation and the Theory of Questions. Erkenntnis, 34(2), 237-260, Mr 91.

In *The Scientific Image* B. C. van Fraassen argues that a theory of explanation ought to take the form of a theory of *why*-questions, and a theory of this form is what he provides. Van Fraassen's account of explanation is good, as far as it goes. In particular, van Fraassen's theory of *why*-questions adds considerable illumination to the problem of alternative explanations in psychodynamics. But van Fraassen's theory is incomplete because it ignores those classes of explanations that are answers not to *why*-questions but to *how*-questions. In this article I provide a unified theory of explanatory questions that comprehends both *how*-questions and *why*-questions, and I show that a question-theoretic approach to explanation can be defended independently of van Fraassen's programme of Constructive Empiricism.

CROSS, Charles B. Temporal Necessity and the Conditional. Stud Log, 49(3), 345-363, S 90.

Temporal necessity and the subjunctive conditional appear to be related by the principle of Past Predominance, according to which past similarities and differences take priority over future similarities and differences in determining the comparative similarity of alternative possible histories with respect to the present moment. R H Thomason and Anil Gupta have formalized Past Predominance in a semantics that combines selection functions with branching time; in this paper I show that Past Predominance can be formalized and axiomatized using ordinary possible worlds semantics (without branching time).

CROSS, Charles. "Belief Revision, Non-Monotonic Reasoning, and the Ramsey Test" in *Knowledge Representation and Defeasible Reasoning*, KYBURG JR, Henry E (ed), 223-244. Norwell, Kluwer, 1990.

P Gärdenfors has proved (*Phil Rev*, 1986) that the Ramsey rule and the methodologically conservative Preservation principle are incompatible given innocuous-looking background assumptions about belief revision. Gärdenfors gives up the Ramsey rule; I argue for preserving the Ramsey rule and interpret Gärdenfors's theorem as showing that no rational belief-reviser can avoid reasoning nonmonotonically. I argue against the Preservation principle and show that counterexamples to it always involve nonmonotonic reasoning. I then construct a new formal model of belief revision that does accommodate nonmonotonic reasoning.

CROSSON, Frederick J. Structure and Meaning in St Augustine's *Confessions*. Proc Cath Phil Ass, 63, 84-97, 1990.

One of the reasons why the structure of the *Confessions* has been missed is that the conversion scene in the garden has been taken as the center or axis of the story. But if the center is properly identified, it can be seen why the last three books on scripture are added to the narrative books. At the most fundamental level, the *Confessions* is a reflection on two modes in which the divine is manifested, the metaphors for which are seeing and hearing.

CROUCH, Margaret A. Feminist Philosophy and the Genetic Fallacy. Hypatia, 6(2), 104-117, Sum 91.

Feminist philosophy seems to conflict with traditional philosophical methodology. For example, some uses of the concept of gender by feminist philosophers seem to commit the genetic fallacy. I argue that use of the concept of gender need not commit the genetic fallacy, but that the concept of gender is problematic on other grounds.

CROW, Dennis (ed). *Philosophical Streets: New Approaches to Urbanism*. Washington, Maisonneuve Pr, 1990.

The purpose of this book is to open discussion between city planning and the humanities. The links between architecture and aesthetics, space and time in both philosophy and urbanism, and theory and practice are discussed. (staff)

CROWE, Frederick. Thomas Aquinas and the Will: A Note on Interpretation. Method, 8(2), 129-134, O 90.

CROWELL, Steven Galt. Text and Technology. Man World, 23(4), 419-440, O 90.

Jacques Derrida has criticized Heidegger's philosophy as caught in the "metaphysics of presence." But how might Heidegger analyze and criticize the phenomenon of deconstruction? This paper interprets central Derridean notions such as text, trace, *differance*, and the avowed aims of deconstructive practice in terms of those concepts Heidegger worked out in his reflections on technology: enframing (*Gestell*) and standing reserve (*Bestand*). If technology in Heidegger's sense is the "truth of Being" in the present age, I argue that deconstruction shows itself to be a form of "technological" thinking concerned with cultural matters, "texts" as standing reserve.

CROWLE, Tony. "I Don't Know Why I Did It" in *Harré and His Critics*, BHASKAR, Roy (ed), 154-164. Cambridge, Blackwell, 1990.

CROWLEY, Paul. Technology, Truth and Language: The Crisis of Theological Discourse. Heythrop J, 32(3), 323-339, Jl 91.

The radical critique of language initiated by Heidegger, developed in Gadamer's philosophic hermeneutics, and completed by Derrida, has left open the very possibility of a truth-telling discourse in theology. Taking Heidegger's critique of technology and instrumentalist usages of language as the point of departure, the author traces the development of the crisis facing theological discourse. Gadamer and Derrida represent two different reactions to the Heideggerian project, and deconstruction poses the greatest threat to the possibility of theological discourse, as is evident in the work of Mark Taylor. The author concludes that only a full-circle return to the metaphysical terrain with which Heidegger began, and which Gadamer accepted, can rescue theology from its current crisis.

CROWTHER, Paul. "The Existential Sublime: From Burke's Aesthetics to the Socio-Political" in *XIth International Congress in Aesthetics, Nottingham 1988*, WOODFIELD, Richard (ed), 26-31. Nottingham, Nottingham Polytech, 1990.

CRUZ CRUZ, Jua. "Sobria ebrietas": Nietzsche y las perpleijidades del espíritu. Anu Filosof, 23(2), 29-50, 1990.

CRUZ, Manuel. Origen y desembocadura de la acción: el sujeto inevitable. Critica, 22(64), 97-119, Ap 90.

This paper formally deals with the unfolding of an answer to the question: to whom is an action to be ascribed? or, stated more precisely, it pretends to be an analysis of the principle that he action pertains to whom it is attributed to. In order to avoid falling into subjectivistic or individualistic positions, which might totally ascribe the meaning of an action solely to the agent, the matter is studied from the inter-subjective control of the action—taking special account of the proposals advanced by Hart, Feinberg and Gardiner. (edited)

CSIKSZENTMIHALYI, Mihaly. Consciousness for the Twenty-First Century. Zygon, 26(1), 7-25, Mr 91.

Human action and experience are the outcome of genes and memes. Not only are both of these represented in consciousness, but consciousness mediates their claims and thus governs our choices. Hence it is important how consciousness is ordered and where it is directed. Sorokin's typology of the sensate and the ideational ("spiritual"), and the dialectic between them, is relevant to this issue. In our period of history, the sensate factors of materialism and secularism need to be dialectically counterbalanced by the reinforcement of memes that value the spiritual intimations of the realm beyond the senses. As we approach the twenty-first century, the memes that will undergird our spirituality will be those that resacralize nature and emphasize our unity as humans with all of universal reality, in an idea of common "beinghood." Spiritual systems that accord with this trend in evolution will have to respect three conditions. They will integrate the sensate and the ideational; reflect the importance of the "flow" state of optimal experience, which matches ever-complexifying skills with comparable challenges; and move the fulcrum of their worldview from the human being to the network of beings and its evolution.

CUA, Antonio S. "The Concept of *Li* in Confucian Moral Theory" in *Understanding the Chinese Mind: The Philosophical Roots*, ALLINSON, Robert E (ed), 209-235. New York, Oxford Univ Pr, 1989.

This essay proposes a systematic account of the Confucian concept of *li* (ritual rules, propriety, rules of proper conduct) in terms of its extensive scope, functions, and justifications. The scope comprises any rule that admits of reasoned justification particularly in terms of the delimiting, supportive, and ennobling functions. The ultimate justifications appeal to the necessity of resolving human conflict and the Confucian ideal of human excellence. The essay concludes with some suggestions on the connection between ritual and moral rules in the development of a Confucian moral philosophy.

CUBITT, Robin P and HOLLIS, Martin. The Mutual Investment Game: Peculiarities of Indifference. Analysis, 51(3), 113-120, Je 91.

A game is presented in which there are no dominant strategies but which resembles the Prisoner's Dilemma in that 1) each player's optimal choices are independent of the other player's and 2) the Pareto optimal outcome is apparently not guaranteed by self-interested play. It is argued that an account of a rational requirement to cooperate in the game would require a reformulation of Game Theory to allow players *either* to choose for themselves to play as a team *or* to describe outcomes in terms of the actions leading up to them and, thereby, to recognize social or moral relationships.

CUBRIC, Djordje. There are Denumerably Many Ternary Intuitionistic Sheffer Functions. Notre Dame J Form Log, 29(4), 579-582, Fall 88.

The existence of denumerably many ternary intuitionistic Sheffer functions is shown. To prove that we use Nishimura lattice.

CUCULOVSKI, Ljubomir. Relationship Between Consciousness and Reality (in Serbo-Croatian). Filozof Istraz, 34(1), 173-180, 1990.

Gegenstand dieses Aufsatzes ist die Ermittlung möglicher Ursachen der Diskrepanz von Bewusstsein und Wirklichkeit, der Umstand, dass das Bewusstsein ausserstande ist, sich selbst zu verwirklichen, nach vorausgesetzter Verwirklichung einzig sich allein in der Wirklichkeit wiederzufinden. Die Ursache der Nichtübereinstimmung von Bewusstsein und Wirklichkeit liegt in der Unfähigkeit des Bewusstseins, sich selbst zu verwirklichen, Wirklichkeit zu werden, liegt im sog. Schein- bzw. ideologischen Bewusstsein, das nicht das Bewusstsein der Wirklichkeit selbst, der Gesamtheit historischen Geschehens ist, das als Pseudobewusstsein, als Ausdruck von Partialität ohnehin nicht in der Lage ist, die Gesamtheit menschlichen Geschehens zu umfassen; daher die Unfähigkeit des Bewusstseins zur Selbstverwirklichung. (edited)

CUDD, Ann E. Conventional Foundationalism and the Origins of the Norms. S J Phil, 28(4), 485-503, Wint 90.

Some current theories of morality and language rely on a rational choice account of convention to reduce that aspect of sociality to the nonsocial. The argument schema they use (I call *conventional foundationalism*) builds on Lewis's work on conventions. I criticize Lewis's theory of convention, showing it must make tacit appeals to preexisting normative structures in order for interacting agents to have the common knowledge required to solve coordination games. This shows that conventions do not have a nonsocial foundation. I apply this criticism to distinguish two competing accounts of the origins of the conventions of war.

CUDD, Ann E. Enforced Pregnancy, Rape, and the Image of Woman. Phil Stud, 60(1-2), 47-59, S-O 90.

Enforced pregnancy is any pregnancy a woman is forced to continue, or over which she has lost control of her care and maintenance to the state or another individual. This article argues that enforced pregnancy degrades the image of woman, thus harming all women, not only those who become pregnant against their will. I show that the argument is parallel to the argument that rape harms women as a group, by depicting them as weak, vulnerable, sexual beings. This harm is usually ignored in the abortion debate, but I argue that its recognition has important political and moral significance.

CUÉLLAR, Hortensia. Filosofía, hoy. Anu Filosof, 24(1), 125-137, 1991.

Contemporary philosophy, having grown inside the cultural background of modern times, also cherishes in a clearer, although less attractive way, the genuine metaphysical enterprise which proceeds from the *philosophia prima*. This sort of philosophy deserves to be called not only post-modern, but supra-modern, classical.

CULP, Sylvia and KITCHER, Philip. Theory Structure and Theory Change in Contemporary Molecular Biology. Brit J Phil Sci, 40(4), 459-483, D 89.

Traditional approaches to theory structure and theory change in science of not fare well when confronted with the practice of certain fields of science. We offer and account of contemporary practice in molecular biology designed to address two questions: Is theory change in this area of science gradual or saltatory? What is the relation between molecular biology and the fields of traditional biology? Our main focus is a recent episode in molecular biology, the discovery of enzymatic RNA. We argue that our reconstruction of this episode shows that traditional approaches to theory structure and theory change need considerable refinement if they are to be defended as generally applicable.

CUMMINS, Phillip D. Hume on the Idea of Existence. Hume Stud, 17(1), 61-82, Ap 91.

In the *Treatise* Hume claims one's idea of existence is not distinct from the idea of what one conceives to be existent. From clues in his extremely terse defence of his claim I construct an argument that is logically valid and founded on premises he is likely to have considered both cogent and consistent with his main philosophical principles. I also examine briefly and incompletely what his position on existence and the idea of existence does and does not include.

CUMMINS, Phillip. Bayle, Leibniz, Hume and Reid on Extension, Composites and Simples. Hist Phil Quart, 7(3), 299-314, Jl 90.

I examine in varying degrees of detail the views of Bayle, Leibniz, Hume and Reid on the composition of extension. Comparison of their positions ultimately concerns their selection from among the following inconsistent set of principles:

(1) Actual composites presuppose actual, not potential, parts. (2) Actual composites presuppose true unities, i.e., if some entity is a composite, then there are two or more individuals which are not composites. (3) Extension is by nature composite, i.e., if some entity is extended, then it is composite. (4) Extension presupposes extension, i.e., if something is a part of an extended thing, then it is an extended thing.

CUMMINS, Robert. *Meaning and Mental Representation*. Cambridge, MIT Pr, 1991.

Existing accounts of the nature of mental representation are examined for their compatibility with current computational theories of cognition. Accounts based on similarity, covariance (including causal theories) and adaptational role are all found to be incompatible with empirical assumptions of computationalism. Functional role accounts are found to be consistent with computationalism, but to need substantial reformulation to address the same issues as rival accounts. Computationalism seems to require an interpretationalist theory according to which *r* represents *d* when the system's program disciplines *r* as the laws of some domain discipline *d*.

CUNLIFFE, John. The Neglected Background of Radical Liberalism: P E Dove's Theory of Property. Hist Polit Thought, 11(3), 467-490, Autumn 90.

This paper examines the unduly neglected contribution of P. E. Dove to liberal theories of communal property in land. Those theories are normally associated with the (early) Herbert Spencer and with Henry George. Before them Dove acutely addressed similar issues and proposed similar solutions. His general theoretical ambition was to prescribe a regime which would realize both the natural right to natural resources and full individual property rights in produced assets. The first section explicates Dove's position on the central themes; the second pursues the affinities and contrasts between that position and those of other theorists; and the final section examines the theoretical coherence of Dove's position.

CUNNINGHAM, Andrew (ed) and JARDINE, Nicholas (ed). *Romanticism and the Sciences*. New York, Cambridge Univ Pr, 1990.

The work aims to provide a comprehensive treatment of the relationship between romanticism and the sciences. The 22 articles are divided into sections on the romantic movement, romanticism in the life sciences, romanticism in the physical sciences, and the sciences in romantic literature. The editorial preface and introduction oppose earlier accounts which portrayed romanticism in the sciences as an aberration, and argues that the romantic movement played major roles in the formation of the disciplines and ideologies of natural science.

CUNNINGHAM, Frank. Democracy and Socialism: Philosophical *Aporiae*. Phil Soc Crit, 16(4), 269-289, 1990.

Socialist theory after the fall of recent socialism confront the problem of showing how socialism can avoid authoritarianism. Liberal-democratic theory must show how its core values can take precedence over values embedded in the world's various traditions while still preserving pluralism. As part of a defence of the 'retrievalist' option defended, among others, by C B Macpherson, whereby socialist and liberal-democratic theory and practice should be integrated, solution to the first problem is sought in a solution to the second. The article concludes that "comprehensive" philosophy integrate democratic criteria into its pursuit, while liberal-democratic and socialist theory be entirely subsumed into extra-philosophic democratic projects.

CUNNINGHAM, Thomas J and SCHULZ, Larry J. On the Concept of Freedom in the *I Ching*: A Deconstructionist View of Self-Cultivation. J Chin Phil, 17(3), 301-313, S 90.

CUPANI, Alberto. "The Significance of the *Treatise* in the Light of the Western Philosophical Tradition" in *Studies on Mario Bunge's "Treatise"*, WEINGARTNER, Paul (ed), 533-545. Amsterdam, Rodopi, 1990.

The paper praises Bunge's *Treatise* for showing that most of the traditional philosophical problems are questions of permanent human interest, and for giving them an answer based on Science and open to progress. At the same time, the paper criticizes the ideal of a scientific philosophy as a system of ideas which would convince everybody, arguing that every philosophy (also Bunge's) is somehow personal and that a scientific reformulation of philosophical questions does not exclude aspects which cannot be handled scientifically, so that Philosophy cannot become completely scientific without somehow ceasing to be Philosophy.

CUPITT, Don. Is Anything Sacred? Christian Humanism and Christian Nihilism. Relig Hum, 24(4), 151-159, Autumn 90.

Cupitt uses examples from the history of art to illustrate two main tendencies of modern religious thought. In Christian humanism (e.g., Rembrandt) religious ideas are fulfilled as they disappear into universal human experience. In the more recent and stranger tradition of religious nihilism, the Divine becomes the sublime 'Abstract Sacred' of high Modernism and Abstract Expressionism. Perhaps future religious thought will encompass both the human image and the void, moving between the two.

CURLEY, Edwin. "Notes on a Neglected Masterpiece, II: Theological-Political Treatise as a Prolegomenon to the Ethics" in *Central Themes in Early Modern Philosophy*, COVER, J A (ed), 109-159. Indianapolis, Hackett, 1990.

This article asks the following question: suppose all of Spinoza's works had perished except the *Theological-Political Treatise* and the table of contents of the *Ethics*, how much of the teaching of the latter work on those topics could we reconstruct from the earlier one? I argue that we could work out quite a bit of Spinoza's teaching, particularly in relation to Parts I, III, and IV, and that the more popular (and sometimes more expansive) way Spinoza's ideas are presented in the earlier illuminates the later one.

CURREN, Randall R. Public Discourse in the Development of Educational Policy. Proc Phil Educ, 46, 185-188, 1990.

The topic of this paper is the government's proper role in facilitating public deliberation about education policy. An argument for the existence of a governmental duty to justify its current policies is examined and rejected, and arguments are made for (1) a broader conception of what responsible leadership in this domain entails, and (2) the importance of distributing the responsibility to bear the information costs of public deliberations in a way that is sensitive to the creation of incentives to misrepresent and to the possible detrimental impact of those costs on the delivery of (first-order) educational services.

CURRIE, G. "Frege and Popper: Two Critics of Psychologism" in *Imre Lakatos and Theories of Scientific Change*, GAVROGLU, Kostas (ed), 413-430. Norwell, Kluwer, 1989.

CURRIE, Gregory. Visual Fictions. Phil Quart, 41(163), 129-143, Ap 91.

The standard view of fictions in visual media, as I reconstruct it, is that the viewer imagines himself to be watching the action; and in the case of cinema, to be watching from the position of the camera. I argue that this is false, and that we can explain what is distinctively *visual* about visual fictions without this assumption.

CURRIE, Gregory. Work and Text. Mind, 100(399), 325-340, Jl 91.

CURTIN, Deane. Toward An Ecological Ethic of Care. Hypatia, 6(1), 60-74, Spr 91.

This paper argues that the language of rights cannot express distinctively ecofeminist insights into the treatment of nonhuman animals and the environment. An alternative is proposed in the form of a politicized ecological ethic of care which can express ecofeminist insights. The paper concludes with consideration of an ecofeminist moral issue: how we choose to understand ourselves morally in relation to what we are willing to count as food. "Contextual moral vegetarianism" represents a response to a politicized ecological ethic of care.

CURZER, Howard J. Aristotelian Form and End. Dialogos, 26(58), 33-46, Jl 91.

In several passages Aristotle speaks as if the formal and final causes of organisms are simply the same. Aristotle's interpreters have routinely accepted this interpretation. Yet I shall provide two reasons why Aristotle should distinguish between the form and end of organisms, two explanations of how someone might mistakenly come to identify the form and end of organisms, and two problems for Aristotle's ethical theory which follow from the identification of human form and end. I shall also provide an alternative interpretation of the passages in question.

CURZER, Howard J. Aristotle's Much Maligned *Megalopsychos*. Austl J Phil, 69(2), 131-151, Je 91.

Modern moral philosophers as well as Aristotle's commentators find Aristotle's *megalopsychos* rather repulsive. In this paper, I rebut the accusations that the *megalopsychos* is 1) conceited, 2) snobbish, 3) ungrateful and manipulative, 4) inactive and remote, 5) oblivious and immoral, 6) insufficiently concerned with honor, 7) self-absorbed, 8) unable to form perfect friendships, 9) unneighborly, untrustworthy, unsympathetic, inaccessible, and insufficiently benevolent, and 10) obsessed with and motivated by honor. Then I suggest several explanations for the contemporary prejudice against the *megalopsychos*.

CURZER, Howard J. A Great Philosopher's Not So Great Account of Great Virtue: Aristotle's Treatment of 'Greatness of Soul'. Can J Phil, 20(4), 517-537, D 90.

Some interpreters take *megalopsychia* (greatness of soul) to be fundamentally concerned with honor, but I argue that greatness and self-knowledge are the core components of *megalopsychia*. Not only is Aristotle's treatment of *megalopsychia* internally inconsistent, it also clashes with certain other parts of Aristotle's ethics. These problems arise because Aristotle defines *megalopsychia* as a combination of unrelated characteristics. After describing these problems I show how Aristotle could avoid them by modifying his treatment of *megalopsychia* and by fleshing out his doctrine of the mean in a way which allows for great virtue.

CURZER, Howard J. The Supremely Happy Life in Aristotle's *Nicomachean Ethics*. Apeiron, 24(1), 47-69, Mr 91.

Some interpreters (intellectualists) believe that the supremely happy life of X 7-8 ultimately aims at contemplation alone and excellently exercises theoretical reason but neglects practical reason. Other interpreters (inclusivists) believe that the supremely happy life of X 7-8 ultimately aims at both contemplation and virtuous action, and excellently exercises both theoretical and practical reason. I shall argue that the supremely happy life of X 7-8 ultimately aims at contemplation, but excellently exercises both theoretical and practical reason. Thus the intellectualists and the inclusivists are each half right.

CURZER, Howard J. Two Varieties of Temperance in the *Gorgias*. Int Phil Quart, 31(2), 153-159, Je 91.

It is generally thought that the *Gorgias* presents a simple choice between the life of virtue and the life of vice, while the *Republic* presents several different sorts and degrees of virtue and vice. In particular, the temperance of a ruler is integrated with wisdom while the temperence of an auxiliary is not. This paper offers an interpretation of *Gorgias* 506c-509c (Socrates' speech) which shows Plato implicitly distinguishing exactly these two varieties of temperence. Thus, Plato suggests in the *Gorgias* exactly the same two sorts of virtuous life that he presents in the *Republic*.

CURZER, Howard. An Ambiguity in Parfit's Theory of Personal Identity. Ratio, 4(1), 16-24, Je 91.

In *Reasons and Persons* Parfit vacillates between two views of personal identity. Both views have unpalatable consequences. According to one view, the question, "Is person A the same as person C?" is always empty. According to the other view, this question is empty only some of the time. The first view is elegant, but it has consequences which are counterintuitive and incompatible with Parfit's later claims. The second view is commonsensical, but its only coherent version is vulnerable to an argument made by Parfit, himself.

CUSHING, James T. Is Scientific Methodology Interestingly Atemporal? Brit J Phil Sci, 41(2), 177-194, Je 90.

CUTLAND, Nigel J (and others). On Cauchy's Notion of Infinitesimal. Brit J Phil Sci, 39(3), 375-378, S 88.

CUTROFELLO, Andrew. A Critique of Derrida's Hegel Deconstruction: Speech, Phonetic Writing, and Hieroglyphic Script in Logic, Law, Art. Clio, 20(2), 123-137, Wint 91.

This article begins by sketching a reading of Hegel that is suggested in Derrida's essay "The Pit and the Pyramid." According to this reading, Hegel's texts exhibit a kind of "phonocentrism." In response, an alternative reading is suggested, one which argues that Hegel can be read not as absolutely privileging speech over writing, but rather as recognizing complementary and mutually exclusive excellences of both speech and writing. To this end, Hegel's philosophy of art and philosophy of law are considered. In conclusion, however, it is explicitly acknowledged that the main argument of Derrida's essay had not been addressed.

CUTTER, Mary Ann Gardell. Negotiating Criteria and Setting Limits: The Case of AIDS. Theor Med, 11(3), 193-200, S 90.

The classification of clinical problems, such as AIDS, requires choices. Choices are made on epistemic (i.e., knowledge-based) and non-epistemic (i.e., action-based) grounds. That is, the ways in which we classify clinical problems, such as AIDS, involve a balancing of different understandings of clinical reality and of clinical values among participants of the clinical community. On this view, the interplay between epistemic and non-epistemic interests occurs within the embrace of particular clinical contexts. The ways in which we classify AIDS is the topic of this paper. We consider the extent to which we construct clinical reality; we examine a suggested classification of AIDS; and we conclude suggesting that the choice regarding how to classify AIDS is the result of negotiation among participants in the clinical community.

CYRANOWSKA, Maria. Fundamental Values in the Thought of Confucius and Mencius (in Polish). Ann Univ Mariae Curie-Phil, 11, 77-90, 1986.

The article is an attempt to consider the status and social role of the system of ethical values in classical Chinese philosophy. Indicating their universality and objective character, the author analyses the significance of two concepts crucial for this tradition—Tao and shen. She also makes a comparison of some trends in Kant's ethics with the ideas of Chinese thinkers on the functions of emotions, reason, and will in the moral behaviour of the individual.

CYZYK, Mar. Hamartia, Akrasia: Ignorance, and Blame in Aristotle's Philosophy. Kinesis, 18(1), 17-35, Wint 90.

CZELAKOWSKI, Janusz. Relatively Congruence-Distributive Subquasivarieties of Filtral Varieties. Bull Sect Log, 19(2), 66-70, Je 90.

CZEPITA, Stanislaw. Czeslaw Znamierowski's Conception of Constitutive Rules. Ratio Juris, 3(3), 399-406, D 90.

The article presents the conception of constitutive rules formulated in the twenties by a Polish philosopher of law: Czeslaw Znamierowski. The author of the article analyses characteristic features of Znamierowski's approach to constitutive rules as opposite to imperative rules and stresses a highly original character of this approach against the background of the ideas of A Reinach, H Kelsen and L Duguit. The article contains also a comparison of Znamierowski's conception with the contemporary ideas of J R Searle.

CZIKO, Gary A and CAMPBELL, Donald T. Comprehensive Evolutionary Epistemology Bibliography. J Soc Biol Struct, 13(1), 41-82, F 90.

This is a comprehensive bibliography of books, articles, and book chapters dealing with evolutionary epistemology and selection theory. Over 1000 references are included; some are briefly annotated.

D'AGOSTINO, Fred. Ethical Pluralism and the Role of Opposition in Democratic Politics. Monist, 73(3), 437-463, Jl 90.

Why should opposition to a democratically elected government be tolerated? Why should opposition parties be restrained in the criticism of government? Three standard answers to these questions are considered and rejected as inadequate—fallibilism, scepticism, and pragmatism. It is proposed that ethical pluralism provides a basis for adequately answering questions of these kinds, this being the view, in particular, that there are incompatible and (partially) incommensurable accounts of the good. The advantages of such an approach are considered and its applicability to Wollheim's well-known paradox is displayed.

D'AGOSTINO, Salvo. From Boskovic's Supplements to the Poem of Benedikt Stay (in Serbo-Croatian). Filozof Istraz, 32-33(5-6), 1605-1610, 1989.

Boskovic's 1755 criticism of Newton's two-sphere experiment as one of his alleged proofs of absolute motion is examined with some detail. Boskovic does not deny Newton's argument on the ground of its a priori character, but on its epistemological status. He also does not see it as convenient to introduce Newton's absolute space as an a priori principle into his own theory of forces. On the other hand, Boskovic has adopted the a priori principle of continuity in his theory. A priori principles are allowed, stated Boskovic in his important 1762 letter to Stefano Conti, in physical theory, as his examples of the principle of continuity and the principle of simplicity in nature demonstrate. In addition, the principle of inertia can neither be proved a posteriori (against Newton) nor a priori, as is the case for Boskovic's principle of continuity.

D'ANTUONO, Emilia. Franz Rosenzweig e Friedrich Meinecke. Arch Stor Cult, 4, 271-305, 1991.

D'HONDT, Jacques and BURBIDGE, John (trans). *Hegel In His Time—Jacques D'Hondt*. Peterborough, Broadview Pr, 1988.

Despite his reputation, Hegel was not a conservative defender of the Prussian regime. Documentary evidence from his letters and elsewhere shows that he was actively involved in the liberal and progressive movements of his day, was close to the liberal ministers in government, and at times was looked on suspiciously by the court. While he attacked the anti-semantic romanticism of the student movement many of its more responsible leaders were his friends and associates. An introduction analyses the Hegelian interpretation to be found in Jaques D'Hondt's writing.

D'HONDT, Jacques. "L'égalité en 1789" in *Égalité Uguaglianza*, FERRARI, Jean (ed), 47-58. Napoli, Liguori, 1990.

Analyse de l'emploi de la notion d'égalité pendant la révolution française: il se modifie selon les étapes du drame historique, selon le changement des situations relatives des acteurs, et selon la compréhension qu'ils out de celte situation. Certains historians prétendent que l'égalité n'avait été qu'un leurre pour une partie de la population. Un sens historique plus profond permet cependant d' y discerne le motif de grandes actions révolutionnaires á l'époque, et une annonce, certes confuse, d'un lointain avenir.

D'ORS, Angel. Tu scis regem sedere. Anu Filosof, 24(1), 49-74, 1991.

This work examines Richard Kilvington's Sophisma 47, in the context of the Doctrine of Obligations. Its aim is to revise the thesis of P V Spade, who attributes to Kilvington an intermediate position between Burley and Swyneshed, and interprets the Doctrine of Obligations in general as a Theory of Counterfactuals.

D'SOUZA, Felix. Independent Evidence of Religion. Bijdragen, 2, 122-138, 1991.

Religion has remained an undeniable phenomenon throughout the stretch of human history. However, to make itself permanently relevant, religion has to, from time to time, renew its significant role in the lives of men. The purpose of this article is to investigate and demonstrate some of the ways in which religion can provide an independent evidence to what it stands for. A failure in not providing this independent evidence would sound the death-knell of religion itself. Can religion point out "something" that is still meaningful and significant to very walk of life...? (edited)

D'URSEL, Laurent (trans) and BRAGUE, Rémi and ADLER, Pierre (trans). Aristotle's Definition of Motion and its Ontological Implications. Grad Fac Phil J, 13(2), 1-22, 1990.

DA COSTA FREITAS, Manuel Barbosa. G Marcel: a dimensão metafísica da esperança. Rev Port Filosof, 45(4), 531-548, O-D 89.

Human hope is actively experienced in terms of unlimited, absolute trust in a sustaining, ever-present transcendence. The verb "to hope" may be translated as "I hope in you for us", showing that true hope is unseparable from a more or less conscious experience of communion and recourse in a power that guarantees this very communion. This metaphysical root of hope is what causes mankind to face and overcome despair. Hope is the most adequate response of the finite "I" to an absolute "Thou", to whom one owes everything and to whom it would be unjust to impose limits.

DA COSTA, Newton C A and FRENCH, Steven. Belief, Contradiction, and the Logic of Self-Deception. Amer Phil Quart, 27(3), 179-197, Jl 90.

The apparently paradoxical nature of self-deception has attracted a great deal of controversy in recent years. Focussing on those aspects of the phenomenon which involve the holding of "contradictory" beliefs, it is our intention to argue that this presents no "paradox" if a non-classical, "paraconsistent", doxastic logic is adopted. (On such logics, see, for example, N C A da Costa, 'On the theory of inconsistent formal systems', Notre Dame J Formal Logic 11(1974), 497-510, and A I Arruda, 'A survey of paraconsistent logic', in A I Arruda, N C A da Costa and R Chuaqui, *Mathematical Logic in Latin America*, North-Holland, 1984, pp. 1-41.)

DA COSTA, Newton C A and PUGA, Leila Z and CARNIELLI, Walter A. Kantian and Non-Kantian Logics. Log Anal, 31(121-122), 3-9, Mr-Je 88.

DA COSTA, Newton C A. "Logic and Pragmatic Truth" in *Logic, Methodology and Philosophy of Science, VIII*, FENSTAD, J E (ed), 247-261. New York, Elsevier Science, 1989.

This is basically an expository paper, in which I report some aspects of the work done by I Mikenberg, R Chuaqui, S French and myself in the field of pragmatic truth (see, for example, I Mikenberg, N C A da Costa and R Chuaqui, "Pragmatic Truth and Approximation to Truth," *Journal for Symbolic Logic*, 51 (1986), 201-221). I try to show that the concept of pragmatic truth, at least in one of its possible interpretations, can be treated mathematically, and has important applications in the philosophy of science.

DA COSTA, Newton C A and FRENCH, Steven. On Russell's Principle of Induction. Synthese, 86(2), 285-295, F 91.

An improvement on Horwich's so-called "pseudo-proof" of Russell's principle of induction is offered, which, we believe, avoids certain objections to the former. Although strictly independent of our other work in this area, a connection can be made and in the final section we comment on this and certain questions regarding rationality, etc.

DA COSTA, Newton C A and FRENCH, Steven. Pragmatic Truth and the Logic of Induction. Brit J Phil Sci, 40(3), 333-356, S 89.

We apply the recently elabrated notions of 'pragmatic truth' and 'pragmatic probability' to the problem of the construction of a logic of inductive inference. It is argued that the system outlined here is able to overcome many of the objections usually levelled against such attempts. We claim, furthermore, that our view captures the essentially cumulative nature of science and allows us to explain why it is indeed reasonable to accept and believe in the conclusions reached by inductive inference.

DA COSTA, Newton C A and SETTE, A M. Remarks on Analogy. Teoria, 10(2), 49-58, 1990.

We study analogy as akind of inductive reasoning, that is, a kind of non-demonstrative inference. It is examined in connection with other forms of inductive inference, and we also delineate how it can be mathematized from the point of view of category theory.

DA GAMA CAEIRO, Francisco. "Nota acerca da recepção de Kant no pensamento filosófico português" in *Dinâmica do Pensar: Homenagem a Oswaldo Market*, FAC LETRAS UNIV LISBOA (ed), 59-89. Lisboa, Fac Letras U Lisboa, 1991.

This study calls attention to the brief dominance of Kant's doctrine in Portugal, throughout the nineteenth century. A comparison analysis with Spanish and Brasilian philosophical thought renders the specific nature of the Portuguese case more understandable, for which an adequate explanation must be found. (edited)

DA PU, Shi. Euthanasia in China: A Report. J Med Phil, 16(2), 131-138, Ap 91.

Euthanasia in China is gaining increasing acceptance among physicians, intellectuals, and even the people. This paper surveys current attitudes towards euthanasia and suggests why it should be legalized.

DACAL ALONSO, José Antonio. La investigación y las metodologías en las Ciencias Humanas. Logos (Mexico), 19(55), 17-53, Ja-Ap 91.

DAHL, Norman. Justice and Aristotelian Practical Reason. Phil Phenomenol Res, 51(1), 153-158, Mr 91.

DAHLBÄCK, Olof. An Experimental Analysis of Risk Taking. Theor Decis, 29(3), 183-202, N 90.

A descriptive model of risk taking is presented according to which the utility of a choice of a risk-filled course of action is a function of the utility values and the probabilities of the outcomes of this choice and of an individual parameter indicating an inclination to take risks of a certain magnitude. According to this model, favorable and unfavorable outcomes are weighed differently in decisions. The moments of the probability distribution over the utility values of outcomes are not explicitly considered. The model has been tested by asking 71 university-level students to design risk-filled action alternatives assumed to be equal in utility to alternatives having only one outcome. Outcomes were fictitious and monetary. The risk-taking model gives a better explanation of the utility of alternatives than a model according to which expected utility is maximized, but the improvement is rather small. (edited)

DAHLSTROM, Daniel O. "Between Being and Essence: Reflection's Logical Disguises" in *Essays on Hegel's Logic*, DI GIOVANNI, George (ed), 99-111. Albany, SUNY Pr, 1990.

This paper suggests (a) how the account of reflection in its immediacy (what Hegel calls '*Schein*' and is here translated 'disguise') provides the essential *Vorstruktur* to Hegel's science of logic, and (b) the successes and failures of Hegel's account.

DAHM, Helmut. The Problem of Atheism in Recent Soviet Publications. Stud Soviet Tho, 41(2), 85-126, Mr 91.

DAINIAN, Fan. "Imre Lakatos in China" in *Imre Lakatos and Theories of Scientific Change*, GAVROGLU, Kostas (ed), 59-67. Norwell, Kluwer, 1989.

DAKO, Martin. Achilles' Revenge. J Value Inq, 25(3), 271-277, Jl 91.

This paper presents a logical paradox as a dialogue, pertinent to Hector-Neri Castañeda's 'deliberation.' The deliberation's conclusion, expressed as "All things considered, I ought to...," leads to paradox when what follows is "do the opposite of what rational consideration dictates." A discussion of a distinction between "to not...," and "not to...," follows. Regarding the "conflict-solving ought" as linguistically of a higher type than ones entering into premises resolves the paradox. This in turn offers an explication for "higher order principles" in moral theory. The resulting linguistic stratification is generally useful, as in understanding the status of Kant's Categorical Imperative.

DALE, Michael. Social Science Knowledge and Explanations in Educational Studies. Educ Theor, 41(2), 135-152, Spr 91.

This paper argues that knowledge and explanations in the social sciences are not radically distinct from knowledge and explanation in the natural sciences. Three characteristics of social science inquiry alleged to have radical epistemological consequences are examined. These characteristics are: 1) social inquiry is value-laden; 2) social reality is complex and changing; and 3) study of social practices must take into account the meanings that these practices have for the human subjects who engage in them. These characteristics do not carry the radical epistemological consequences often attributed to them. Finally, it is shown that social scientific knowledge stands in the same relations to commonsense beliefs about social reality as natural scientific knowledge does to commonsense beliefs about the natural world.

DALHAUS, E and ISRAELI, A and MAKOWSKY, J A. On the Existence of Polynomial Time Algorithms for Interpolation Problems in Propositional Logic. Notre Dame J Form Log, 29(4), 497-509, Fall 88.

Let G and H be two (possibly quantified) propositional formulas with $x_1,...,x_n$ the only common variables such that $G \rightarrow H$ is valid. An interpolant $I(x_1,...x_n)$ is a quantifier-free propositional formula such that both $G \rightarrow I$ and $I \rightarrow H$ are valid. We study the complexity of finding such an interpolant and show that this problem is intimately related to the complexity hierarchy between logarithmic and polynomial space. Especially, we show that the interpolation problem for certain formula classes is of the same degree of difficulty as the corresponding satisfiability problem.

DALLMAYR, Fred R. *Between Freiburg and Frankfurt: Toward a Critical Ontology*. Amherst, Univ of Mass Pr, 1991.

The book deals with the rift or tension marking our age: the rift between traditional metaphysics and post-metaphysics, between Western modernity and post-modernity. The book highlights the tension by focusing on two Continental schools of thought. The "Freiburg School" represented chiefly by Heidegger, and the "Frankfurt School" of critical theory represented chiefly by Adorno and Habermas. Concentrating on a series of distinct issues, the study vindicates the intertwining of critique and (Heideggerian) ontology; in doing so, it steers a course between modernity and post-modernity, between critical autonomy and worldliness (or lifeworld).

DALLMAYR, Fred R. "Life-World: Variations on a Theme" in *Life-World and Politics: Between Modernity and Postmodernity*, WHITE, Stephen K (ed), 25-65. Notre Dame, Univ Notre Dame Pr, 1989.

DALLMAYR, Fred. A Response to My Critics. Human Stud, 14(1), 23-31, Ja 91.

DALLMAYR, Fred (ed) and BENHABIB, Seyla (ed). *The Communicative Ethics Controversy*. Cambridge, MIT Pr, 1990.

This collection of essays introduces readers to the communicative ethics controversy, generated by Karl Otto-Apel's and Jürgen Habermas's program of formulating a "communicative" or "discourse ethic." The introduction and afterword by Fred Dallmayr and Seyla Benhabib respectively situate this debate in the context of current controversies in Anglo-American thought.

DALRYMPLE, Mary and SHIEBER, Stuart M and PEREIRA, Fernando C N. Ellipsis and Higher-Order Unification. Ling Phil, 14(4), 399-452, Ag 91.

We present a new method for characterizing the interpretive possibilities generated by elliptical constructions in natural language. Unlike previous analyses, which postulate ambiguity of interpretation or derivation in the full clause source of the ellipsis, our analysis requires no such hidden ambiguity. Further, the analysis follows relatively directly form an abstract statement of the ellipsis interpretation problem. It predicts correctly a wide range of interactions between ellipsis and other semantic phenomena such as quantifier scope and bound anaphora. Finally, although the analysis itself is stated nonprocedurally, it admits of a direct computational method for generating interpretations.

DALTON, Dan R and COSIER, Richard A. An Issue in Corporate Social Responsibility: An Experiential Approach to Establish the Value of Human Life. J Bus Ethics, 10(4), 311-315, Ap 91.

While the notion of establishing a "value" for human life may be uncomfortable for some, we argue that it is a fundamental requirement for many aspects of public policy. We compare a number of approaches which have been traditionally relied on to make estimations. Also, we provide an exercise which provides an unusual, but we hope provocative, perspective on the evaluation of human life.

DALY, T V. Learning from Lonergan at Eleven. Method, 9(1), 44-62, Mr 91.

DAMROSCH, Leo. *Fictions of Reality in the Age of Hume and Johnson*. Madison, Univ Wisconsin Pr, 1989.

DANCY, Jonathan. "An Ethic of Prima Facie Duties" in *A Companion to Ethics*, SINGER, Peter (ed), 219-229. Cambridge, Blackwell, 1991.

A brief account of Ross' concept of a *prima facie* duty, with some criticisms.

DANCY, Jonathan. "Intuitionism" in *A Companion to Ethics*, SINGER, Peter (ed), 411-420. Cambridge, Blackwell, 1991.

A short introductory account of intuitionism, mainly concentrating on the works of Ross, McDowell and Nagel.

DANDEKAR, Natalie. Can Whistleblowing Be FULLY Legitimated? A Theoretical Discussion. Bus Prof Ethics J, 10(1), 89-108, Spr 91.

DANFORD, John W. *David Hume and the Problem of Reason*. New Haven, Yale Univ Pr, 1990.

Hume's reflections on the power and limits of reason led him to see a defect in the most widely accepted accounts of the epistemology of modern science itself. Science does not produce clear and certain knowledge, on a level quite distinct from "prudence" or judgments from experience, as has been claimed. Hume showed instead that except in mathematics we are always limited, in our search for knowledge, to what experience teaches. Genuine knowledge of the principles of morals, i.e., is not less accessible than is knowledge of the principles of physics. Indeed the abstract sciences, i.e., physics, because of their distance from what Hume called "common life," are more vulnerable to the distortions which commonly plague abstract systems of any kind. Hume's investigations led him to see that genuine political science consists in the careful and balanced study of history, where the principles of morals and indeed human nature can be explored in all their variety and complexity. Hume's *Essays*, the *History of England*, and the *Dialogues* should be viewed as the center of his philosophy; they constitute his attempt to discern the outlines of the moral universe, the human world as a whole.

DANIEL, Mano and HOLMES, Richard. The Lover-Beloved Relationship Reconsidered. Auslegung, 17(2), 101-108, Sum 91.

While Sartre claims all human relations share the same fundamental ontological structure, the dismal picture he paints in *Being and Nothingness* in which he describes the lover-beloved relation as two subjectivities in conflict is a far cry from the optimistic portrayal in *What is Literature* of the reader writer relation as the mutual collaboration of two freedoms. By reviewing and revising Sartre's account of the nature of consciousness as it stands before itself or another we enable the expansion of the realm of human relationships beyond the ostensible limits prescribed in *Being and Nothingness*.

DANIEL, Stephen H. *Myth and Modern Philosophy*. Philadelphia, Temple Univ Pr, 1990.

Current research in philosophic historiography and literary theory (e.g., by Foucault and Derrida) highlights mythic features identifiable in the modern philosophies of Bacon, Descartes, Berkeley, Mandeville, Vico, Diderot, Condillac, Herder, Hamann, and others. This book challenges the dominant contemporary view of modern philosophy as antithetical to myth and fable. By comparing poststructuralist, deconstructive, hermeneutic, and semiotic strategies, Daniel shows how a Romanticist approach discloses figurative concerns in modern rationalism and empiricism that cannot be dismissed as rhetorical embellishments but must be considered as central in reasoning.

DANIELS, Charles B. Definite Descriptions. Stud Log, 49(1), 87-104, Mr 90.

Three views on definite descriptions are summarized and discussed, including that of P F Strawson in which reference failure results in lack of truth value. When reference failure is allowed, a problem arises concerning Universal Instantiation. Van Fraassen solves the problem by the use of supervaluations, preserving as well such theorems as 'a=a' and 'Fa or not-Fa', even when the term 'a' fails to refer. In the present paper a form of relevant, quasi-analytic implication is set out which allows reference failure to infect even 'a=a' and 'Fa or not-Fa' with lack of truth-value. Reference failure causes lack of truth-value in a subwff to spread throughout any wff built up by the classical connectives. As a result *none* of the classical first-order axiom schemes remain as axiom schemes in the system presented.

DANIELS, Charles B. In Defence of Reincarnation. Relig Stud, 26(4), 501-504, D 90.

In response to J J MacIntosh's "Reincarnation and Relativized Identity" (*Relig Stud* XXV, 153-65), in which MacIntosh argues that reincarnation is impossible, this article defends the possibility of reincarnation by showing that MacIntosh makes an unjustified shift from epistemological concerns, e.g., whether and how things can be verified and evidence produced, to ontological concerns, e.g., whether or not reincarnation has actually taken place. But if such arguments like MacIntosh's are allowed, they can be also used to conclude that even bodily continuity itself cannot be relied upon as a criterion for personal identity.

DANIELS, Norman. Duty to Treat or Right to Refuse? Hastings Center Rep, 21(2), 36-46, Mr-Ap 91.

DANIELS, Norman. Equality of What: Welfare, Resources, or Capabilities? Phil Phenomenol Res, 50 SUPP, 273-296, Fall 90.

DANIELS, Norman. "Human Rights, Population Again, and Intergenerational Equity" in *Meaning and Method: Essays in Honor of Hilary Putnam*, BOOLOS, George (ed), 355-380. New York, Cambridge Univ Pr, 1990.

DANIELS, Norman. The Profit Motive and the Moral Assessment of Health Care Institutions. Bus Prof Ethics J, 10(2), 3-30, Sum 91.

DANIELS, Norman (ed). *Reading Rawls: Critical Studies on Rawls' 'A Theory of Justice'*. Stanford, Stanford Univ Pr, 1989.

DANIELS, Norman and SABIN, James E. When Is Home Care Medically Necessary? Commentary. Hastings Center Rep, 21(4), 37-38, Jl-Ag 91.

DANIS, Marion and CHURCHILL, Larry R. Autonomy and the Common Weal. Hastings Center Rep, 21(1), 25-31, Ja-F 91.

Recent studies indicate that patients may choose more medical services than physicians think beneficial. As a result, the autonomy of patients conflicts with the potential for just distribution of finite medical resources. The patient-as-citizen and the physician-as-citizen are proposed as concepts to bring autonomy and social justice into a common frame of reference. The recent work of Daniel Callahan and Norman Daniels is discussed, as well as 'citizenship' in medical ethics codes. Possible objections are presented and rebutted.

DANLEY, John R. Liberalism, Aboriginal Rights, and Cultural Minorities. Phil Pub Affairs, 20(2), 168-185, Spr 91.

In *Liberalism, Community, and Culture*, Will Kymlicka defends the claim that some minorities are members of cultures which are vulnerable and therefore sufficiently disadvantaged with respect to the members of other cultures that rectification requires the provision of special "unequal" minority rights. By resting the argument only upon cultural vulnerability, Kymlicka fails to take into consideration important moral differences between the rights of aboriginal peoples and other cultural minorities. Special "unequal" rights are grounded morally (at least in part) in the existence of treaties between autonomous or semi-autonomous aboriginal peoples and the nation within whose borders they now reside, regardless of the vulnerability of the culture.

DANLEY, John R. Toward a Theory of Bribery. Bus Prof Ethics J, 2(3), 19-39, Spr 83.

I defend the position that bribery is the offering or giving or promising to give something of value with the corrupt intent to induce another person to violate the positional duties of her role. I argue not only that this model captures the historical understandings in our culture, but will function better in cross cultural contexts than other definitions which identify "corrupt intent" with "violations of the public interest." Bribery in itself is neither moral or immoral. The moral significance of bribery rests entirely upon whether the violation of positional duties is morally wrong.

DANSHEN, Huang. A Critique of One Interpretation of Practical Materialism. Chin Stud Phil, 22(4), 3-27, Sum 91.

Practical materialism is another name of Marx's materialist conception of history, but some scholars interpret it in recent times into practical ontology or practical monism. They consider practice as the foundation of the whole universe and maintain there is nothing beyond practice. They distort Marxist dialectical materialism into intuitional or technical materialism. They expound and prove their doctrine by Marx's sayings, human practice and knowledge and natural sciences in twentieth century. But practical ontology is not materialism at all. It is a modern kind of idealism. It is not Marx's doctrine. All its grounds of argumentation are false.

DARDANONI, Valentino. Implications of Behavioral Consistency in Dynamic Choice Under Uncertainty. Theor Decis, 29(3), 223-234, N 90.

This paper considers two fundamental aspects of the analysis of dynamic choices under risk: the issue of the dynamic consistency of the strategies of a non EU maximizer, and the issue that an individual whose preferences are nonlinear in probabilities may choose a strategy which is in some appropriate sense dominated by other strategies. A proposed way of dealing with these problems, due to Karni and Safra and called 'behavioral consistency', is described. The implications of this notion of 'behavioral consistency' are explored, and it is shown that while the Karni and Safra approach obtains dynamically consistent behavior under nonlinear preferences, it may imply the choice of 'dominated' strategies even in very simple decision trees.

DAS GUPTA, Amitabha. Explanation-Explication Conflict in Transformational Grammar. J Indian Counc Phil Res, 6(2), 93-108, Ja-Ap 89.

DAS GUPTA, Amitabha. Understanding Science: A Two-Level Reflection. J Indian Counc Phil Res, 5(3), 55-70, My-Ag 88.

DAS NEVES, Jorge César. A determinação heideggeriana de fenómeno em *Sein und Zeit* como superação do "cepticismo metódico". Rev Port Filosof, 45(3), 379-402, Jl-S 89.

With Heidegger's text to determine the phenomenality of the phenomenon in *Sein und Zeit*, one recognizes that it is philosophy's most fundamental problem that is being rethought, but not in terms of "foundations of the science(s)", "certitude", "apodicti evidence" — as much of the philosophy in modern times has sought to do. Edmund Husserl's thought is paradigmatic of this attitude, attributing to philosophy the work of founding through "methodological scepticism". However Husserl approaches the matter of the phenomentality of the phenomenon within the context of phenomenological reduction. The 7th paragraph of *Dein und Zeit* determines the concept of phenomenon as that which "shows-itself-in-itself" and does so by establishing reciprocal relations between the phenomenon and other deficient forms of donation — "appearence" (Schein) and "manifestation" (Erscheinung)! In this way, the question of donation, i.e., the question of truth (*aletheia* / relevation) takes up again its first place in the context of phenomenological thought, relegating the methodological question concerning certitude to a derived status.

DAS, Bhupendra Chandra. The Advaita Theory of Liberation. Indian Phil Quart, SUPP 17(4), 1-22, O 90.

The paper explicates the Advaita concept of *Moksa* which is realisation of Brahman or the state of complete cessation of suffering. It is eternal and ultimate goal. All such information about *Moksa* is obtained from Scripture, etc. Conclusions: (1) Nothing much is gained by quoting *Sruti* for the support of this theory, rather, we should ascertain if this theory is rationally defensible. (2) Changelessness of liberation is not intelligible. (3) Liberation is illusory and impossible as an ideal. (4) There is little justification for the distinction between two types of *Mukti*: (1) *Jivanmukti; (2) Videhamukti* from the standpoint of the *Mukta*. (edited)

DAS, Paritosh Kumar. The 'Body': A Husserlian Phenomenological Analysis. J Indian Counc Phil Res, 7(1), 150-158, S-D 89.

DAS, Paritosh Kumar. The Concept of Ego in Husserl's Philosophy. Indian Phil Quart, SUPP 18(2), 13-26, Ap 91.

DAS, Ramesh Chandra. Understanding the System Construction in Logic. Indian Phil Quart, 17(3), 349-359, Jl 90.

DASCAL, Marcelo. "Artificial Intelligence as Epistemology?" in *Information, Semantics and Epistemology*, VILLANUEVA, Enrique (ed), 224-241. Cambridge, Blackwell, 1990.

The relationships between artificial intelligence (AI) and epistemology are critically examined. It is shown that many AI programs—including expert systems—rely on a traditional conception of knowledge as a set of accurate representations coupled with a set of formal procedures of justification. Such a conception has been the target of recent and persuasive philosophical criticism. Furthermore, it does not serve well the purposes of AI itself. An alternative, 'pragmatic' conception of knowledge, is suggested as a sounder basis, both for AI and epistemology.

DASCAL, Marcelo. "Leibniz on Particles: Linguistic Form and Comparatism" in *Leibniz, Humboldt, and the Origins of Comparativism*, DE MAURO, Tullio (ed), 31-60. Philadelphia, John Benjamins, 1990.

Different modes of analysis and classification of the particles proposed by Leibniz are surveyed and compared with those of his predecessors and contemporaries. It is agreed that, in his mature account, Leibniz assigns to particles the role of bearers of the form or structure of sentences and discourse. But he carefully distinguishes this kind of 'form' from sheer logical forms. He may thus be credited with the attempt to provide a non-reductionist account of 'linguistic form'. Though this level of form involves regularity and, therefore, universality, it can only be properly identified through the observation of variability across languages: an important role for comparatism is thus established within Leibniz's framework.

DASCAL, Marcelo and WRÓBLEWSKI, Jerzy. The Rational Law-Maker and the Pragmatics of Legal Interpretation. J Prag, 15(5), 421-444, My 91.

In so far as legal discourse in general, and legal interpretation in particular, is a communicative process, it is subject to rationality assumptions. In so far as it is a more regimented communicative process than ordinary communication, it should be expected that such assumptions play a more important and reliable role in the interpretation of legal discourse than in the interpretation of other forms of discourse. In an earlier installment of our interdisciplinary project of bringing together pragmatics and the theory of legal interpretation, we referred to the need to rely on rationality assumptions. We alluded briefly to the theoretical construct of a 'rational law-maker' as expressing this need. Given the importance of this notion, it deserves a more careful scrutiny - which we purport to provide in the present paper. We delineate a profile of the 'rational law-maker' (and of its counterpart, the 'rational law-interpreter'), and analyze their role in legal reasoning, in the determination of the meaning of legal texts, and in the ideologies of legal interpretation.

DASGUPTA, Manashi. Reflections on Ideas of Social Philosophy and Indian Code of Conduct. J Indian Counc Phil Res, 6(1), 149-158, S-D 88.

The article is a brief exposition of the *Bhagavadgita* as a text of Indian social philosophy. Indian categories of social thought, unlike the Western ones, permit a distinction between the perishable 'person' and the indestructible 'self' of the individual performing chosen roles on the structured stage of the society. The autonomous human actor (person) endowed with senses, reason, faculties of locomotion and choice performs his actions leaving an indelible mark on the stage. The indestructible self remains unmoved by the quality of the performance as long as the person acts in disinterested commitment to duty in consistency with his *personally chosen* role.

DASHENG, Gao and TSING, Zou. "Philosophy of Technology in China" in *Philosophy of Technology*, DURBIN, Paul T (ed), 133-151. Norwell, Kluwer, 1989.

DAVAL, R. Du fondement de la loi morale, une éthique de la raison ou du sentiment? Philosophique (France), 1(91), 31-42, 1991.

DAVANEY, Sheila Greeve. Directions in Historicism: Language, Experience, and Pragmatic Adjudication. Zygon, 26(2), 201-220, Je 91.

This article examines the current affirmation within theology of historicism, with its assumption that the historical realm, broadly construed, is the only arena of human activity and knowledge and its repudiation of traditional forms of foundationalism and correspondence theories of truth. The essay performs this task by analyzing the work of Gordon Kaufman and William Dean, setting forth their commonly shared historicism, pragmatism, and constructivist approaches to theology, as well as their differences concerning nonlinguistic dimensions of experience. The essay also focuses on the move by both thinkers to include nature in their understanding of history and to offer biocultural interpretations of human existence.

DAVEY, J R N. "Nietzsche: Art and Existence" in *XIth International Congress in Aesthetics, Nottingham 1988*, WOODFIELD, Richard (ed), 32-37. Nottingham, Nottingham Polytech, 1990.

The paper argues that Nietzsche's aesthetics is dominated by the *Leifmotif* of the nature of the relationship between art and existence. It is further argued that there are three attempts within his thought to resolve the question: 1) the *Attistenmetaphysik*, 2) the *Via Experimentavis* and 3) the artist's philosophy of creativity. The underlying of the argument is that changes in Nietzsche's view of art are forced by changes in his view of Beasming.

DAVID, R. Some Results on Higher Suslin Trees. J Sym Log, 55(2), 526-536, Je 90.

DAVIDSON, Arnold I. "Closing Up the Corpses: Diseases of Sexuality and the Emergence of the Psychiatric Style of Reasoning" in *Meaning and Method: Essays in Honor of Hilary Putnam*, BOOLOS, George (ed), 295-325. New York, Cambridge Univ Pr, 1990.

DAVIDSON, Donald. "A Coherence Theory of Truth and Knowledge" in *Reading Rorty*, MALACHOWSKI, Alan (ed), 120-138. Cambridge, Blackwell, 1991.

This is a reprint from *Kant oder Hegel*, ed D Henrich, Klett-Cotta, 1983, with "Afterthoughts 1987" added. The afterthoughts regret the use of the terms "coherence", "correspondence" and "theory". The original essay argued that all that counts as evidence or justification for a belief must come from the same totality of belief from which the belief comes. Therefore we must reject the idea that our knowledge of the world requires epistemic intermediaries like sense data, sensations, or sensory stimulations. A correct account of what gives our simplest empirical beliefs their content shows why there is a presumption that such beliefs are true.

DAVIDSON, Donald. "A Coherence Theory of Truth and Knowledge" in *Truth and Interpretation: Perspectives on the Philosophy of Donald Davidson*, LE PORE, Ernest (ed), 307-319. Cambridge, Blackwell, 1986.

It is argued that all that counts as evidence or justification for a belief must come from the same totality of belief from which the belief comes. Therefore we must reject the idea that our knowledge of the world requires epistemic intermediaries like sense data, sensations, or sensory stimulations. A correct account of what gives our simplest empirical beliefs their content also shows why there is a presumption that such beliefs are true.

DAVIDSON, Donald. "The Conditions of Thought" in *The Mind of Donald Davidson*, BRANDL, Johannes (ed), 193-200. Amsterdam, Rodopi, 1989.

This summary paper explains why we are not constrained to start from a solipsistic, or first person point of view in considering the nature of thought. My aim here is to suggest the nature of an acceptable externalism. According to this view, knowledge of other minds need not be a problem in addition to the problem of empirical knowledge. The essential step toward determining the content of someone else's thought is made by discovering what normally causes those thoughts. Hence I believe that there could not be thoughts in one mind if there were not other thoughtful creatures with which the first mind shared a natural world.

DAVIDSON, Donald. "Empirical Content" in *Truth and Interpretation: Perspectives on the Philosophy of Donald Davidson*, LE PORE, Ernest (ed), 320-332. Cambridge, Blackwell, 1986.

The dispute between Schlick and Neurath over the foundations of empirical knowledge illustrates the difficulties in trying to draw epistemological conclusions from a verificationist theory of meaning. It also shows how assuming the general correctness of science does not automatically avoid, or provide an easy answer to, skepticism. But while neither Schlick nor Neurath arrived at a satisfactory account of empirical knowledge, there are promising hints of a better theory in their writings. These hints, augmented by further ideas in Hempel, Carnap and particularly Quine, suggest the direction a naturalistic epistemology should take.

DAVIDSON, Donald. "Meaning, Truth and Evidence" in *Perspectives on Quine*, BARRETT, Robert (ed), 68-79. Cambridge, Blackwell, 1990.

Whether a theory of meaning and evidence is proximal or distal depends on whether the criterion for interpersonal sameness of meaning is given in terms of private events (experience, sensations, stimulations of the nerve endings) or in terms of the shared external objects and events that constitute the subject matter of our most basic thought and talk. Quine's official theory is proximal. Such a theory may easily conflict with the common sense, or distal, doctrine that in the plainest cases translation depends on external items of common interest. It is urged that a distal theory is clearly superior.

DAVIDSON, Donald. "A Nice Derangement of Epitaphs" in *Truth and Interpretation: Perspectives on the Philosophy of Donald Davidson*, LE PORE, Ernest (ed), 433-446. Cambridge, Blackwell, 1986.

It is generally assumed that linguistic communication requires a shared language governed by conventions. This essay argues that two speakers need not speak the same language in order to understand each other, and that much successful interpretation depends on imaginative improvisation rather than on the mastery of fixed rules and conventions.

DAVIDSON, Donald. "What is Present to the Mind?" in *The Mind of Donald Davidson*, BRANDL, Johannes (ed), 3-18. Amsterdam, Rodopi, 1989.

The propositional objects of the mind, and their constituents, are supposed to have the following two properties: they identify, or help to identify, a thought by giving its content; and they constitute an essential aspect of the psychology of the thought by being grasped or otherwise known by the person with the thought. The problem is to understand this psychological relation. Apparently we have to find objects about which error is impossible—objects that must be what they seem. But there simply are no such objects. This, however, need not prevent us from specifying the subjective state of the thinker by relating him to an object without assuming that this object itself has a subjective status, that it is "known" by the thinker, or is "before his mind." Once we grant this possibility, we are free to divorce the semantic need for content-specifying objects from the idea that there must be any objects at all with which someone who has an attitude is in psychic touch.

DAVIES, Martin. Connectionism, Modularity, and Tacit Knowledge. Brit J Phil Sci, 40(4), 541-555, D 89.

In this paper, I define tacit knowledge as a kind of causal-explanatory structure, mirroring the derivational structure in the theory that is tacitly known. On this definition, tacit knowledge does not have to be explicitly represented. I then take the notion of a modular theory, and project the idea of modularity to several different levels of description; in particular, to the processing level and the neurophysiological level. The fundamental description of a connectionist network lies at a level between the processing level and the physiological level. At this level, connectionism involves a characteristic departure from modularity, and a correlative absence of syntactic structure. This is linked to the fact that tacit knowledge descriptions of networks are only approximately true. A consequence is that strict causal systematicity in cognitive processes poses a problem for the connectionist program.

DAVIES, Paul. Derrida's Other Conversation. Res Phenomenol, 20, 67-84, 1990.

DAVIES, Paul. "A Fine Risk: Reading Blanchot Reading Levinas" in *Re-Reading Levinas*, BERNASCONI, Robert (ed), 201-226. Bloomington, Indiana Univ Pr, 1991.

DAVIES, Paul. Telling Tales: Notes on Heidegger's "Career," the "Heidegger Affair," and the Assumptions of Narrativity. Grad Fac Phil J, 14(2)-15(1), 267-293, 1991.

DAVIES, Stephen. Functional and Procedural Definitions of Art. J Aes Educ, 24(2), 99-106, Sum 90.

The two main approaches to art's definition, functionalism and proceduralism, are opposed because procedures of the relevant type often are employed without regard to the function of art (construed usually as its providing enjoyable aesthetic experience). The two approaches differ on whether an acceptable definition should (1) accept "hard cases" (such as readymades) as artworks, (2) be evaluative or descriptive, (3) account for the importance of art.

DAVIES, Stephen. The Ontology of Musical Works and the Authenticity of their Performances. Nous, 25(1), 21-41, Mr 91.

Philosophers disagree about the ontology of musical works, some authors characterizing them as timbreless, ahistorical sound structures and other writers characterizing them as indexed to the means of performance, the composer, and the time and place of composition. The recent move to authentic performance also is controversial in some respects. The connection between the two—what is required for authentic performance depends on what one takes to be constitutive of the work—is rarely remarked. I explore this connection. In practice it is agreed that authenticity involves the use of instruments and performance practices from the time of the work's composition. This favours the view that historically founded conventions determine the identity of musical works.

DAVION, Victoria M. "Integrity and Radical Change" in *Feminist Ethics*, CARD, Claudia (ed), 180-192. Lawrence, Univ Pr of Kansas, 1991.

DAVIS, Anne J and LIASCHENKO, Joan. Nurses and Physicians on Nutritional Support: A Comparison. J Med Phil, 16(3), 259-283, Je 91.

During the last decade, several court cases have focused attention on the moral and legal aspects of withholding or withdrawing food and fluids from certain

DAVIS, Chandler 422 AUTHOR INDEX WITH ABSTRACTS

patients. The courts have not been unanimous in their judgments on these matters. In attempting to explore this issue, this article reviews both the nursing and medical literature on the withdrawing and withholding of food and fluids with particular attention to empirical studies. Several themes which emerge from the literature are used to explore the similarities and differences between the practices of nursing and medicine where nutritional support is concerned.

DAVIS, Chandler. "Criticisms of the Usual Rationale for Validity in Mathematics" in *Physicalism in Mathematics*, IRVINE, Andrew D (ed), 343-356. Norwell, Kluwer, 1990.

It is argued that speaking of mathematical existence and truth as though they were independent of the speaker and irrelevant to description of the world of experience, leads to errors in the practise of mathematics. Several examples in 20th-century mathematics are analysed. It is proposed that mathematics for different purposes may properly be held to different criteria of validity.

DAVIS, Charles. "Religion and the Making of Society" in *Critique and Construction: A Symposium on Roberto Unger's "Politics"*, LOVIN, Robin W (ed), 242-255. New York, Cambridge Univ Pr, 1990.

DAVIS, Dena S. Rich Cases: The Ethics of Thick Description. Hastings Center Rep, 21(4), 12-17, Jl-Ag 91.

DAVIS, Karen Elizabeth. I Love Myself When I am Laughing: A New Paradigm for Sex. J Soc Phil, 21(2-3), 5-24, Fall-Wint 90.

This paper critically examines discourses of sexuality, subjectivity and desire from Freud and Lacan to Foucault and feminism. It argues that regardless of whether sexuality is seen to be instinctual or culturally constructed, the metaphor of desire as hunger has limited the range of inquiry and understanding by continually submerging the social situatedness and relatedness of sexuality. The paper offers a new metaphor that captures the nuances of sexual expression in a way that is neither naturalistic nor moralistic: sexuality is like laughter. Laughter is universal but culturally specific; always relational within a social meaning context; and can carry a range of expressions, from intimacy and pleasure to derision and hostility.

DAVIS, Kathy. Remaking the She-Devil: A Critical Look at Feminist Approaches to Beauty. Hypatia, 6(2), 21-43, Sum 91.

Cosmetic surgery provides a problematic case for feminist theorizing about femininity and women's relationship with their bodies. Feminist accounts of femininity and beauty are unable to explain cosmetic surgery without undermining the women who opt for it. I argue that cosmetic surgery may have less to do with beauty and more to do with being ordinary, taking one's life into one's own hands, and determining how much suffering is fair.

DAVIS, Michael. Gewirth and the Pain of Contradiction. Phil Forum, 22(3), 211-227, Spr 91.

The argument from contradiction is commonly thought to be decisive. If I cannot hold a certain position "except on pain of contradiction," I cannot (it is thought) rationally hold it. Though noncontradiction is certainly desirable in rational justification, it is not a necessary condition. We can find examples of positions that, though inconsistent, seem rationally defensible. Recent developments in nonstandard logics also permit us to provide a clear sense in which such positions are logical. This has important consequences for ethics, especially for theories like that of Gewirth's *Reason and Morality*.

DAVIS, Michael. Thinking Like an Engineer: The Place of a Code of Ethics in the Practice of a Profession. Phil Pub Affairs, 20(2), 150-167, Spr 91.

Most discussions of professional ethics dismiss the idea of a code of ethics from the outset. Codes are described as self-serving, unrealistic, inconsistent, mere guides for novices, and so on. I do not do that. Instead, focusing on the Challenger disaster, I argue that a code of professional ethics is central to advising individual professionals how to conduct themselves, to judging their conduct, and ultimately to understanding professions.

DAVIS, Michael. Using the Market to Measure Deserved Punishment. Iyyun, 39(3), 295-319, Jl 90.

This paper defends, against the charge of result-rigging, the market arguments I have used elsewhere to help assess criminal desert. The paper does that in part by showing that certain seemingly attractive alternatives are in fact unjust, implausible, or equivalent in effect to the market I used. But, by choosing alternatives carefully, the paper builds a positive case for thinking that my results should be stable over the whole range of just and plausible alternatives, that something real is being measured.

DAVIS, Nancy. "Contemporary Deontology" in *A Companion to Ethics*, SINGER, Peter (ed), 205-218. Cambridge, Blackwell, 1991.

Central to deontological moral views is the belief that acting morally involves the self-conscious acceptance of limitations on how we may act, constraints that place limits both on our pursuit of our own interests and our pursuit of the general good. This essay analyzes the nature and structure of deontological constraints, and identifies some problems with deontological moral views. It is suggested that—at least in the form propounded by contemporary deontologists (and sympathizers) like Alan Donagan, Charles Fried, and Thomas Nagel—deontological moral views are seriously flawed.

DAVIS, Scott. Irony and Argument in *Dialogues*, XII. Relig Stud, 27(2), 239-257, Je 91.

The paper argues that, despite Hume's seeming unwillingness to come down on one side or another at the close of the *Dialogues Concerning Natural Religion*, the dialogues present a single, cumulative argument, that the conclusion of the argument is in fact that pronounced by Philo in the concluding dialogue, but that there is a brutal irony in that conclusion, namely that the only successful claimant for "true Christianity" is the practice of the natural sciences, with the express exclusion of all the practices and beliefs that have traditionally been thought constitutive of the Christian faith. The paper concludes with some tentative remarks suggesting the place of such an interpretation in the context of contemporary philosophy of religion.

DAVIS, Stephen T. Pascal on Self-Caused Belief. Relig Stud, 27(1), 27-37, Mr 91.

DAVIS, Wayne A. The World-Shift Theory of Free Choice. Austl J Phil, 69(2), 206-211, Je 91.

Baxter proposed that a free choice determines which natural, deterministic world is to be actual until the next choice. This is supposed to resolve the apparent contradiction between free will and determinism without denying either and without incurring the defects of familiar compatibilisms. I show that the issue of incompatibilism versus compatibilism is, in world-shift terms, the issue of whether choices are essentially or only potentially transitions between natural worlds. The theory that choices are essentially world shifting denies determinism. The theory that choices are only potentially world shifting avoids none of the alleged defects of familiar compatibilisms.

DAVISON, Scott A. Foreknowledge, Middle Knowledge and "Nearby" Worlds. Int J Phil Relig, 30(1), 29-44, Ag 91.

In this paper, I develop one argument against the possibility of God's foreknowing free actions, and another against the possibility of God's possessing "middle knowledge" concerning free actions. The arguments articulate precisely the following idea: freedom requires a kind of contingency, but knowledge requires that no such contingency attach to the connection between a fact and the process which produces belief in a putative knower of that fact; hence no free actions can be foreknown or known through "middle knowledge." Although neither argument is completely successful, they highlight the importance of the question, How exactly *could* God know such things?

DAVSON-GALLE, Peter. Applied Ethics and Meta-Philosophy. Phil Context, 20, 37-52, 1990.

In response to Nesbitt (same volume) I consider applied ethics' metaphilosophical status. I judge: no particular methodology constitutes a sufficient condition for philosophising (thus its satisfaction doesn't make doing applied ethics philosophising); "generality" of content isn't a sufficient condition, nor necessary (thus failure to satisfy this doesn't rule out applied ethics); the thinkers' cognitive purpose type isn't a sufficient condition though it might be necessary (but applied ethics satisfies this as well as normative ethics); semantically necessary content and critical thinking methodology are individually necessary and jointly sufficient and applied ethics fails to satisfy these but so does normative ethics.

DAVSON-GALLE, Peter. Some Clarifications and Cautions Essential for Good Philosophy of Science Teaching. Educ Phil Theor, 22(1), 25-28, 1990.

This paper is a response to Fritz Rohrlich's "Four Philosophical Issues Essential for Good Science Teaching," *Educ Phil Theor* 20 (ii), 1-6, 1988. Among other things, it chides Rohrlich for a muddled discussion of the discovery/invention distinction and for a misleadingly optimistic view of theory justification.

DAY, J P. Moral Dilemmas, Compromise and Compensation. Philosophy, 66(257), 369-375, Jl 91.

Often, but not always, moral dilemmas, otherwise moral conflicts, can be resolved either by compromise or by compensation. Making good compromises and good compensations requires knowledge of all the relevant facts of the case. It also requires creation, otherwise invention, and Sartre is right in saying that 'there is this in common between art and morality'.

DAY, J P. On Häyry and Airaksinen's 'Hard and Soft Offers as Constraints'. Philosophia (Israel), 20(3), 321-323, D 90.

(1) Although *ordinary offers*, unlike threats, do not curtail liberty, it is arguable that there are *irresistible temptations* which, unlike alleged 'offers which one cannot refuse', do curtail liberty. (2) Whether a speech-act *is* a threat or an offer depends on the intention of the speech-agent and not on the desire of the speech-patient. But whether a speech-patient *feels* threatened or offered-to by a speech-act does depend on her desire.

DAY, Michael A. The No-Slip Condition of Fluid Dynamics. Erkenntnis, 33(3), 285-296, N 90.

In many applications of physics, boundary conditions have an essential role. The purpose of this paper is to examine from both a historical and philosophical perspective one such boundary condition, namely, the no-slip condition of fluid dynamics. The historical perspective is based on the works of George Stokes and serves as the foundation for the philosophical perspective. It is seen that historically the acceptance of the no-slip condition was problematic. Philosophically, the no-slip condition is interesting since the use of the no-slip condition illustrates nicely the use of scientific models. But more importantly, both the use and justification of the no-slip condition illustrate clearly how theories can holistically approach the world through model construction. Further, since much of the debate over scientific realism occurs in the realm of models, a case is made that an understanding of the role of the no-slip condition has something to offer to this debate.

DAY, Richard B. The Blackmail of the Single Alternative: Bukharin, Trotsky and Perestrojka. Stud Soviet Tho, 40(1-3), 159-188, 1990.

This essay investigates the origins of perestroika in terms of the Hegelian subject-object dialectic. Marx understood Reason as science; Stalin saw planners as subjects and citizens as objects. Bukharin believed citizen consciousness could be planned indirectly through rules and institutions. Bukharin is seen as a predecessor of Gorbachev, whose reforms are interpreted as "scientific Stalinism" and compared with the market theory of Milton Friedman and Friedrich Hayek. Leon Trotsky's project for democratic planning is considered as an alternative to perestroika and market theory, with citizens determining their own rules.

DAY, Richard B. Hegel, Marx, Lukács: The Dialectic of Freedom and Necessity. Hist Euro Ideas, 11, 907-934, 1989.

Lukacs argues that Hegel's *false ontology* identified the real present with "the actually attained realm of reason." Although Marx repudiated Hegel's ontology, he ended with the same problem: in the real present of communist society, universalization of technological culture would enable producers to reach mutual recognition of socially necessary labour in a scientific plan. For Lukacs, technology imposes the need to choose without indicating how we "ought" to choose. To avoid "superficially reductionist" conclusions, Marxism must reappropriate Hegel's *genuine ontology* and acknowledge the need for ethical choice in circumstances beyond choice—or the ontological contradiction between freedom and necessity.

DE BELLIS, Mark. The Representational Content of Musical Experience. Phil Phenomenol Res, 51(2), 303-324, Je 91.

In *Sense and Content*, Christopher Peacocke draws a distinction between sensational and representational properties of experience, illustrating it with ambiguous figures and their musical analogue, the tritone. The present paper, invoking music-theoretical accounts of musical listening, argues that musical experience has a representational content sufficiently rich to render Peacocke's postulation of sensational qualities unnecessary. (Content must be understood here on a fine grained conception, rather than, say as a set of possible worlds.)

DE BOER, Th. Godsverduistering en Godsdienstfilosofie. Phil Reform, 55(2), 170-176, 1990.

The article discusses the concept of transcendence in the philosophy of religion. Is it to be conceived in the terms of omnipotence and omnipresence or as an incidence in the course of events and a disturbance. The concept of Being cannot be the keystone of philosophical theology because Being has no sense in itself. Meaning is bestowed on it in the form of justification and forgiveness. Being cannot justify itself with the exception of the Being of God in the ontological argument. According to this there exists an internal relation between goodness and presence in the sense of assistance.

DE CASTELL, Suzanne. Literacy as Disempowerment: The Role of Documentary Texts. Proc Phil Educ, 46, 74-84, 1990.

DE CUMIS, Nicola Siciliani. Silvio Spaventa e Antonio Labriola, gli 'aspetti-pedagogici'. G Crit Filosof Ital, 69(1), 1-21, Ja-Ap 90.

DE DIJN, H. De jonge Wittgenstein (1889-1921): Denken als ethos. Tijdschr Filosof, 52(4), 697-703, D 90.

DE DIJN, H. Spinoza en de geopenbaarde godsdienst. Alg Ned Tijdschr Wijs, 82(4), 241-251, O 90.

DE DIJN, Herman. Naturalism, Freedom and Ethics in Spinoza. Stud Leibniz, 22(2), 138-150, 1990.

The naturalist conception of man as conatus is spinoza is not linked to a utilitarian or hedonist conception of ethics. On the contrary, it is accommodated to an ethics of virtue and to quasi-religious attitudes. This is possible because conatus is interpreted as a kind of free activity seen as emanating from an internal, quasi-automatic source of activity.

DE GARAY, Jesús. Plotino: la libertad como primer principio. Themata, 6, 51-76, 1989.

DE GEORGE, Richard T. Ethics and Coherence. Proc Amer Phil Ass, 64(3), 39-52, N 90.

As metaethical issues have receded in importance, ethics as coherence has emerged. Internal coherence gives precedence to theory; external coherence to moral experience. Conventional morality coheres with other practices and beliefs of a society. Critical morality demands broader coherence, as does any claim to a global morality. Although Anglo-American ethical theory claims to be universal, it is often parochial. The antidote is broad coherence, which on the international level requires compromise and negotiation, and which gives all the objectivity, realism and cognitive content of which morality is capable.

DE GEORGE, Richard T. Green and "Everybody's Doing It". Bus Ethics Quart, 1(1), 95-100, Ja 91.

Green's conditions for justifying "less-than-ideal actions" are equivalent to a truncated act utilitarian analysis. They do not look at the effects on all concerned or compare the harm done by alternative courses of action. The conditions justify bribery for inefficient and marginal businesses, and so yield counter-intuitive results. How and when the conditions apply depend on one's prior intuitions. Hence the conditions do not present a convincing and useful decision scheme for dealing with cases in which "everyone's doing it."

DE GIACOMO, Claudio. *Fonti diritto e regole*. Napoli, Ed Sci Ital, 1990.

The metaphor "sources of law" is often considered misleading as generic term. Nevertheless, the sources of law show a particular kind of meta-rule that is present in many forms in the various juridical traditions. But, above all, the "sources" show an interesting theoretic problem: they form part of the legal system (as norms) but also they originate the positive system (as normative facts). This work shows, according to constitutive rules, how the "sources" represent the inevitable conceptual connection between legal positive system (position) and hypothetical normative model (such as Kelsen's Grundnorm).

DE GRAZIA, David. The Distinction Between Equality in Moral Status and Deserving Equal Consideration. Between Species, 7(2), 73-77, Spr 91.

This essay concerns two normative concepts whose conflation in animal ethics debates leads to intellectual mischief: 1) equality in moral status, and 2) one's interests' having moral weight equal to the identical interests of others. After distinguishing and clarifying these concepts, I present a preliminary case for the thesis that animals are unequal in moral status—though their interests should be given equal consideration. In making my case, I note some general implications for the use of animals in research.

DE GRAZIA, David. Response to Squadrito's "Commentary: Interests and Equal Moral Status". Between Species, 7(2), 79-80, Spr 91.

DE JONG, B M. Inside World-Outside World: Epistemology on the Conscious Action of the Nervous System. Method Sci, 22(4), 230-236, 1989.

An epistemological analysis of the relation between conscious experience and brain activity leads to discerning the reality of both an "inside" and an "outside" world. This distinction implies a complementary description of natural phenomena, which indicates two valid lines of achieving knowledge. Phenomena described within one "world" do not need to be explained by arguments from the other "world". The position of the individual being in both the outside and the inside world, marks the relation between these two worlds. Two examples indicate that a clear discrimination of linguistic terms, which refer to either the inside or the outside world, clarifies discussion about behavior, consciousness and actions of the brain.

DE KIRCHNER, Beatriz Bossi. Contemplación y Dios en Aristóteles. Sapientia, 45(177), 189-204, Jl-S 90.

DE LA SIENRA, Adolfo García. Estructuras y representaciones. Critica, 22(64), 3-22, Ap 90.

The aim of the present paper is to set a philosophical basis in order to discuss the type of representation that holds between mathematical structures and those aspects of the real world which they represent. It is maintained that an actualized version of Aristotelian metaphysics is suited for this purpose. The connection between the abstract, rigid concepts of mathematics, and the concepts of metaphysics is attempted through the concept of a fundamental measurement. The existence and degree of uniqueness of a fundamental measurement is established as a representation theorem asserting the existence of a homomorphism from what I call an ontological structure into a numerical one. (edited)

DE LA SIENRA, Adolfo García. Teoría general de las decisiones. Critica, 23(67), 41-58, Ap 91.

Starting from Simon's (1976) opposition between procedural and substantive rationality, the paper addresses the question whether it is possible to characterize the former in general terms, and discusses the problem of overcoming the aforementioned opposition. It tries to show, by means of the concept of a general decision structure, that even though it is not possible to characterize procedural rationality in an exhaustive and fully general way, at least it is possible to introduce a scheme within which it is possible to pose problems of procedural rationality, or even to postulate some axiomatic restrictions for the same. It is not hard to see that substantive rationality is a particular case of this scheme, namely, the case in which it is possible to *measure* certain theoretical parameters and adopt as rules of decision certain classical principles grounded upon the concept of expected utility. The paper does not provide, however, the details that show how the special theory is obtainable out of the more general one.

DE LANEY, James S and DYCK, Arthur J. "National Health Insurance: An Ethical Assessment" in *Biomedical Ethics Reviews, 1990*, HUMBER, James M (ed), 87-129. Clifton, Humana Pr, 1991.

Four concrete proposals to enact National Health Insurance (NHI) in the US were assessed to evaluate arguments for and against NHI, and to account for its absence in the US. Sometimes implicitly, sometimes explicitly, each proposal claims to be more just, necessary, likely to succeed, and cognitively sound than other proposals. Politically, proponents of one plan have successfully blocked others. Conclusions drawn: 1) public debate over principles is needed; 2) to reduce discrimination, care should not be rationed, but rather waste, excessive profits, and inefficiencies; 3) there is a right to health care akin to communal protection of individual lives by military, police, and firefighting services.

DE LORENZO, Javier. De lógica y matemática o donde situar el mundo matemático. El Basilisco, 4, 19-30, Mr-Ap 90.

DE LOS ANGELES GIRALT, María. La influencia de Rousseau en el pensamiento de Kant. Rev Filosof (Costa Rica), 28(67-68), 119-127, D 90.

Where does the vinculum between Rousseau and Kant begin and where does it end? This work searches for an answer through an analysis of the state of nature and private property, of the social pact as society's basis, of their social ideas and the study of liberty and moral will of both authors. The reading about Rousseau cultivated the transformation of Kantian thought into humanism. (edited)

DE LOS ANGELES IMAZ LIRA, María. Conceptos filosóficos como sustrato del sentido de la muerte, desde la época prehispánica hasta la actual. Logos (Mexico), 19(55), 55-70, Ja-Ap 91.

DE LOURDES SIRGADO GANHO, Maria. Paul Ricoeur e Gabriel Marcel. Rev Port Filosof, 46(1), 169-179, Ja-Mr 90.

Gabriel Marcel is a philosopher with whom Paul Ricoeur maintained an interesting relationship for more than thirty years. This article seeks to present those aspects of Ricoeur's philosophy which have Marcel as their source. The work that serves as a base for understanding this relationship is *Entretiens Paul Ricoeur-Gabriel Marcel*, in essence a dialogue between a discipline and his mentor. At the same time, this dialogue reveals the fundamental future of Gabriel Marcel's philosophy.

DE MARTELAERE, Patricia. Schopenhauer en de kunst van het verzaken. Alg Ned Tijdschr Wijs, 83(2), 129-141, Ap 91.

Schopenhauer's is strictly hierarchical theory of art, in which the value of a particular art form is measured by its capability of, objectively, representing the most perfect manifestations of metaphysical Will and, subjectively, inducing in the spectator a state of will-lessness, resignation, hence bliss. This article tries to reformulate Schopenhauer's heavily laden metaphysical system thinking into more accessible terms of contemporary art appreciation. At the same time it is shown how system and Inspiration often collided in Schopenhauer's thoughts and produced interesting but inconsistent views on e.g., aesthetic pleasure and sublime discrepancy, conceptual and 'ideal' knowledge in philosophy versus literature, the intensification of Will in music, and tragedy as ultimate resignation.

DE MAURO, Tullio (ed) and FORMIGARI, Lia (ed). *Leibniz, Humboldt, and the Origins of Comparativism*. Philadelphia, John Benjamins, 1990.

DE MELO, Romeu. *Reflexões, 3: Filosofia Política Sociologia cultura Portuguesa Temas Literários*. Lisbon, Noticias, 1990.

DE MONTICELLI, Roberta. Philosophical Asceiticism (in French). Rev Theol Phil, 123(1), 35-48, 1991.

The writer speaks of the mental sphere as the totality of intentional experience which constitutes intelligent life; and of reality as all that which is given to us in a world proper to experience while transcending the experiences through which it is actually given. Arguments are presented to support the following hypotheses: a) that which is mental is not real; b) the mental sphere is the domain of philosophy; c) these two hypotheses make of philosophy a rational and non-positive research; d) in order to reach the domain of this research, a radical modification of the natural cognitive attitude is required, of which I attempt to describe the fundamental stages.

DE MUL, Jos. "The Art of Forgetfulness, Schopenhauer and Contemporary Repetitive Music" in *XIth International Congress in Aesthetics, Nottingham 1988*, WOODFIELD, Richard (ed), 143-146. Nottingham, Nottingham Polytech, 1990.

In this article the relevance of Schopenhauer's aesthetics of music for the understanding of the repetitive music of Steve Reich is discussed. In is not only argued that Schopenhauer's aesthetics provides us with an elucidating view on Reich's music, but also that it's experience of timelessness enables us to develop a more coherent interpretation of Schopenhauer. Although Schopenhauer claims that the musical experience leads us beyond the manifold in space and time, his examples—the temporal-teleological compositions of Mozart — contradict this claim. Reinterpreted from the context of Reich's music (prefigured by Nietzsche's composition "Das Fragment an sich") and Freud's theory of the unconsciousness, this contradiction vanishes.

DE MUNCK, Jean. Controverses autour de l'ontologie du droit. Rev Metaph Morale, 95(3), 415-423, Jl-S 90.

DE MURALT, André. L'être du non-être en perspective aristotélicienne. Rev Theol Phil, 122(3), 375-388, 1990.

Il s'agit dans cette étude de montrer que le non-être pour Aristote ne possède aucune entité univoque (contre Parménide), aucun être "objectif" (critique d'Occam à Duns Scot), malgré l'interprétation que donne Grégoire de Rimini de quelques textes des *Catégories*. Car le non-être est une négation et celle-ci est une opération d'opposition contradictoire, ce qui permet de dire que dans la proposition: 'le non-être n'est pas', l'intellect conçoit la notion d'être selon le mode d'exercice intelligible propre à la négation. C'est là la seule entité "objective" qui puisse convenir à la notion de non-être.

DE PAUL, Michael R. The Highest Moral Knowledge and the Truth Behind Internalism. S J Phil, SUPP 29, 137-160, 1990.

DE PIERRIS, Graciela. The Structure of Empirical Knowledge. Dialogos, 26(57), 187-199, Ja 91.

DE QUEIROZ, Ruy J G B. Meaning as Grammar plus *Consequences*. Dialectica, 45(1), 83-86, 1991.

In his notes on *Intuitionistic Type Theory*, Martin-Löf provides an account of meaning that lacks the force of a convincing new perspective on the term *constructive*. Following Gentzen ('the meaning of a proposition is determined by its *assertability conditions'), he claims that the introduction rule gives the meaning to the corresponding proposition. I should like to say that it covers one* and *only one* of its fundamental aspects, corresponding roughly to 'sentence formation' (cf., Wittgenstein's later account of propositions). The *normalisation* rule, i.e., the explanation of *consequences*, cover the other aspect: 'the use of the sign in the language-game'.

DE ROOSE, Frank. Self-Defence and National Defence. J Applied Phil, 7(2), 159-168, O 90.

The paper begins with the suggestion that the aura of respectability that surrounds the notion of self-defence may render that notion suitable as a rallying point for agreement on the ethical legitimacy of warfare. I first argue that self-defensive killing by a person X is morally justified if three conditions obtain: (1) X is together with at least one other person in a situation in which one of the persons will be killed through actions of the other person(s); (2) X is not responsible for bringing about that situation; (3) unless X kills another person, X him- or herself will be killed. Next, I show that on the basis of this principle military operations are morally justified only if there are no alternatives to executing them that would save more lives or prevent the total loss of freedom for people. The paper concludes with the observation that the morality of individual self-defensive killing is unable to justify most of current national defence policies.

DE S CAMERON, Nigel M. The Editor's Response to "The Embryo Debate: The Archbishop of York's Speech to the House of Lords". Ethics Med, 6(1), 2-4, Spr 90.

This article offers an analysis of and reply to the Archbishop of York's influential House of Lords speech on the Human Fertilisation and Embryology bill in the British Parliament. The focus is on embryo research. The Archbishop maintains that the case *against* embryo research rests on 'biological, theological and philosophical mistakes'. Yet, Cameron argues, it is not necessary to be convinced of the 'personhood' of the early embryo in order to oppose embryo research: the minorities on the Warnock Committee opposed it on other grounds. The Christian response will be based on the incarnation of Jesus Christ, who himself became a zygote.

DE S CAMERON, Nigel M. Human Fertilisation and Embryology. Ethics Med, 6(3), 37, Autumn 90.

The author briefly reviews the course of the debates in Britain on in vitro technology and embryo research, and offers comment on the failure of opponents to embryo research to secure Parliamentary support for their position. He notes the generally more conservative view taken, for example, by the Council of Europe's *ad hoc* committee (CAHBI).

DE SANTIS, Stefano. Distorted Tradition: Etymological Observations about the Misuse of Some Philosophical Terms in Modern Indian English. J Indian Counc Phil Res, 5(2), 15-26, Ja-Ap 88.

DE SIENA, Santa. Filosofia e cultura ne "Il Politecnico" de E Vittorini. Il Protag, 6(13-16), 205-223, Ja 88-D 89.

DE SILVA, Padmasiri. "Buddhist Ethics" in *A Companion to Ethics*, SINGER, Peter (ed), 58-68. Cambridge, Blackwell, 1991.

In Buddhist ethics, there is a close integration of *the ethical* as rational argument and analysis, as a normative recommendation for the good life, as a social expression of harmonious living, an intense personal quest and as a mode of character development. It is critical of the current theories of determinism and indeterminism and upholds a notion of free will and the distinction between good and bad, and all these are coloured by the Buddhist concept of moral causation. Buddhist ethics in its own way has a "consequentialist" focus, while rights and duties are respected. Upholds a sophisticated altruism and a way of dealing with the fact-value dichotomy.

DE SOUSA, Ronald. Emotions, Education and Time. Metaphilosophy, 21(4), 434-446, O 90.

This paper explores some aspects of the temporality of emotion. Emotions take shape in "paradigm scenarios": we cannot respond emotionally to present situations without being in a special relation to a certain privileged set of past experiences. By the same token the paradigm scenarios are liable to act as screens, ("transference"), concealing from us the reality of the particular present with the shadow of the past. A central problem for emotional education is to find a way in which we can achieve both flexibility and growth in our repertoire of paradigm scenarios.

DE SWART, H C M. Logic and Artificial Intelligence: An Exposition. Method Sci, 22(3), 125-137, 1989.

This paper gives an exposition of logic and artificial intelligence (AI) which can be understood by the nonspecialist. Logic studies patterns of reasoning rather than concrete arguments. These patterns are described in a suitable formal language. If a pattern of reasoning is valid, it can be applied to quite different domains resulting in correct concrete arguments. There is a small set of valid elementary patterns from which any valid pattern can be built up by composition. If we equip a computer with these elementary patterns, the computer is able to simulate reasoning and hence possesses AI. These ideas are incorporated in logic programming languages.

DE VALK, J M M. Edmund Burke en zijn "Reflections on the Revolution in France". Tijdschr Stud Verlich Denken, 17(3-4), 277-288, 1989.

DE VOS, L. Kant in Hegels begtipsleer. Tijdschr Filosof, 52(3), 443-468, S 90.

Hegels Lehre vom Begriff setzt Kants Lehre der transzendentalen Einheit der Apperzeption fort, sie führt deren nicht vorhandene Momente aus und legt eine spekulative Alternative zu ihr dar. Diese drei Seiten bilden in ihrer Einheit Hegels kritisches Verhältnis zu Kant. Auf der spekulativen Fassung des "ich denke"—Gedankens als des Begriffs stützen sich alle weiteren Kritiken in der *Wissenschaft der Logik*. Wenn Hegels Aufhebung aber nicht gelingt, bleibt das idealistische Problem, was Reinheit des Denken zu bedeuten hat.

DE VRIES, Willem. Burgeoning Skepticism. Erkenntnis, 33(2), 141-164, S 90.

This paper shows that the resources mobilized by recent arguments against individualism in the philosophy of mind also suffice to construct a good argument against a Humean-style skepticism about our knowledge of extra-mental reality. The argument constructed, however, will not suffice to lay to rest the attacks of a truly global skeptic who rejects the idea that we usually know what our occurrent mental states are.

DE VROEY, Michel. The Base Camp Paradox: A Reflection on the Place of Tâtonnement in General Equilibrium Theory. Econ Phil, 6(2), 235-253, O 90.

DE WAELE, Jean-Pierre. "A Concise Theory of Dialectics" in *Harré and His Critics*, BHASKAR, Roy (ed), 189-205. Cambridge, Blackwell, 1990.

In this paper an attempt is made to put an end to the stagnation of constructive ideas concerning this concept of dialectics interpreted in the Hegelian and Marxist sense as a general theory of "becoming". A formalized presentation and analysis of causal sequences of facts is used as a basis for the rigorous definition of "negation of the negation". This theory has already found applications in the author's "*Daders van Dodingen" (in Dutch), two volumes, (Kluwer, 1990).*

DE ZAN, J. Pragmática del lenguaje y racionalidad comunicativa. Stromata, 46(1-2), 105-137, Ja-Je 90.

DE ZAN, Mauro. "L'Accademia delle scienze di Bologna: l'edizione del primo tomo dei 'Commentarii' (1731)" in *Scienza, Filosofia e Religione tra '600 e '700 in Italia*, PREDAVAL MAGRINI, Maria Vittoria (ed), 203-259. Milan, Angeli, 1990.

DE-SHALIT, A. Bargaining with the Not-Yet-Born: Gauthier's Contractarian Theory of Inter-Generational Justice and Its Limitations. Int J Moral Soc Stud, 5(3), 221-234, Autumn 90.

It is nowadays acknowledged that we have obligations to future generations, to consider them when distributing resources, and to refrain from damaging the environment. But a question arises: on what moral grounds should we base our duties to future generations? In this paper I discuss Gauthier's theory of justice between generations. I argue that it cannot serve as the moral grounds for our obligations to our posterity, because there are a few general characteristics essential to Gauthier's model of justice as mutual benefit which are absent in the context of inter-generational relations. In the absence of these characteristics the generations are unlikely to be able to come to the sort of agreement described by Gauthier.

DEAN, William. Empirical Theology: A Revisable Tradition. Process Stud, 19(2), 85-102, Sum 90.

Empirical theology began at the University of Chicago, growing out of the classical American philosophies of W James, J Dewey, and A N Whitehead. In the face of postmodern trends, the essay argues, empirical theology must abandon empirical foundationalism without abandoning realism; it must acknowledge its own speculative character without becoming subjectivistic. The argument is advanced by (1) recognizing (through a study of W James) that empirical theology is based on "the particular" rather than on experience; (2) demonstrating that empirical theology's mind-body monism protects it from the indictment of religious experience in Wayne Proudfoot's *Religious Experience*.

DEBOWSKI, Jozef. Husserl's Phenomenology of Knowledge and Cognition (in Polish). Ann Univ Mariae Curie-Phil, 11, 233-251, 1986.

The present paper contains a reconstruction and discussion of the main ideas and conceptual distinctions of Edmund Husserl's phenomenological philosophy. Among others, this concerns explanations of such conceptual terms as: intentionality (Intentionalität), intention (Intention), fulfillment (Erfüllung), visible fullness (Fülle), and other, equally fundamental notions. In the concluding sections of the paper the author also juxtaposes E Husserl's conceptual apparatus, elaborated by him mainly in Logische Untersuchungen, with appropriate distinctions introduced into philosophy by K Twardowski several years earlier. Apart from that, the author also poses a thesis that, without considering E Husserl's theoretical propositions (especially the theory of intentionality developed on the basis of F Brentano's assertions), it is impossible to comprehend either the philosophical identity of the creator of phenomenology or the main ideas and developmental tendencies of the whole twentieth-century philosophy along with its decidedly antimetaphysical disposition.

DECHER, Friedhelm. Schopenhauer und Fichtes Schrift "Die Bestimmung des Menschen". Schopenhauer Jahr, 71, 45-67, 1990.

Schopenhauer's main work "Die Welt als Wille und Vorstellung" is interconnected with Fichte's "Die Bestimmung des Menschen" in a manifold way. This investigation is mainly concentrated on two ranges of problems. The first one comprises the interdependence of energy, physical inevitability and freedom. In this respect Fichte has expounded thoughts in his work recognizable in Schopenhauer not only in regard of their content but even down to the very formulation. Moreover, impressive parallels between the two thinkers exist in view of their insight into the abysmal quality of mere representation. Not only does Schopenhauer depend on Fichte's work for important stimulation; he has even borrowed from it certain ways of looking at and resolving problems.

DECLÈVE, Henri. L'histoire de la philosophie et son temps. Laval Theol Phil, 47(1), 95-111, F 91.

Qu'offre au lecteur philosophe le travail du philologue ou de l'historien? L'établissement d'un texte fiable et d'une chronologie des oeuvres sont-ils secondaires, là où il s'agit de saisir à nouveau le mouvement et la logique d'une pensée, dont les écrits ne seraient à tout prendre que des indices? Rassember de manière critique en un corpus les textes d'un auteur du passé, c'est restituer, par-delà une suite de faits datés, la temporalité qui est la condition de production et de communication du travail philosophique. Ainsi seulement peuvent apparaître et prendre sens aujourd'hui les fondements pratiques et éthiques des philosophies "antérieures".

DEES, J Gregory and CRAMPTON, Peter C. Shrewd Bargaining on the Moral Frontier: Toward a Theory of Morality in Practice. Bus Ethics Quart, 1(2), 135-167, Ap 91.

From a traditional moral point of view, business practitioners often seem overly concerned about the behavior of their peers in deciding how they ought to act. We propose to account for this concern by introducing a mutual trust perspective, where moral obligations are grounded in a sense of trust that others will abide by the same rules. When grounds for trust are absent, the obligation is weakened. We illustrate this perspective by examining the widespread ambivalence with regard to deception about one's settlement preferences in negotiation. On an abstract level, such deception generally seems undesirable, though in many individual cases it is condoned, even admired as shrewd bargaining. Because of the difficulty in verifying someone's settlement preferences, it is hard to establish a basis for trusting the relevations of the other party, especially in competitive negotiations with relative strangers.

DEGHAYE, Pierre. The Theosophic Discourse According to Jacob Boehme (in French). Rev Theol Phil, 122(4), 531-547, 1990.

Jacob Boehme (1575-1624) is the founder of a mystic theology known by the name of theosophy. Theosophic discourse is more than human discourse on divine manifestation: it is also and foremost the discourse of God through his acts. The discourse of God is expressed anew through the discourse of humankind in whom God is self-regenerative. In this way the spiritual body is formed which is the end of revelation.

DEGNAN, Michael. Does Aristotle Beg the Question in His Defense of the Principle of Non-Contradiction? Proc Cath Phil Ass, 63, 146-159, 1990.

Aristotle's defense of the principle of non-contradiction (PNC) appears to beg the question, for Dancy and Mavrodes both claim that he defends the principle by showing that acceptance of it is a necessary condition for believing that one's words have meaning. I argue that Dancy and Mavrodes misconstrue the defense, for Aristotle refutes the denial of PNC by showing its truth is necessary for meaningfully denying PNC. I show that even three and multi-valued logics require the truth of PNC. Since the defense aims at refutation and not belief modification it escapes the charge of question begging.

DEGRAZIA, David. The Moral Status of Animals and Their Use in Research: A Philosophical Review. Kennedy Inst Ethics J, 1(1), 48-70, Mr 91.

This article provides a philosophical review of 1) leading theories of the moral status of animals, 2) pivotal theoretical issues on which more progress needs to be made, and 3) applications to the setting of animal research. Such an examination demonstrates that the practical implications of leading theories converge far more than might be expected. It is hoped that this review also helps to clarify particularly troubling issues that remain so that they can be treated adequately.

DEHORNOY, Patrick. A Coding of the Countable Linear Orderings. Stud Log, 49(4), 585-590, D 90.

The paper discusses a coding of the linear orderings on the set of positive integers by means of functions, extending earlier work by A Denjoy. A combinatorial characterization of the codes of well orderings is established.

DEI, H Daniel. Conciencia de catástrofe, poder y libertad. Rev Filosof (Costa Rica), 27(66), 399-405, D 89.

There is an increasing catastrophe conscience to the actual threat of destruction of the species and its ecosystem. The proposal allows us to think on the character and existential dimension of that catastrophe conscience.

DEJOIE, Roy M and PARADICE, David B. The Ethical Decision-Making Processes of Information Systems Workers. J Bus Ethics, 10(1), 1-21, Ja 91.

An empirical investigation was conducted to determine whether management information systems (MIS) majors, on average, exhibit ethical decision-making processes that differ from students in other functional business areas. The research also examined whether the existence of a computer-based information system in an ethical dilemma influences ethical decision-making processes. Although student subjects were used, the research instrument has been highly correlated with educational levels attained by adult subjects in similar studies. Thus, we feel that our results have a high likelihood of generalization to the MIS professional community. The results indicate that MIS majors exhibit more socially-oriented ethical decision-making processes than non-MIS majors measured by the Defining Issues Test. The results also indicate that the existence of a computer-based information system in an ethical dilemma may influence ethical decision-making processes. The study makes no statement regarding MIS majors making "more (or less) ethical" decisions. The business ethics literature is reviewed, details of the study are presented, implications for management are considered, and directions for future research are suggested.

DEL CARMEN PAREDES MARTIN, M. La recepción de la "crítica de la razón pura" en el joven Hegel. Logos (Mexico), 18(52), 41-58, Ja-Ap 90.

The work wants to elucidate the degree of influence of Kant's *Critque of Pure Reason* in the philosophical development of Hegel at *Jena,* before he wrote the *Phenomenology of Spirit*. It contends that philosophical study of Hegel's development could only be successful if the basic concepts and positions of this author are not observed in isolation, because they grew in contact with other philosophies. The work deals with Hegel's discussion of Kant's idealism in *Glauben und Wissen* (*Faith and Knowledge*), Jena 1802. In this essay, Kant's theoretical philosophy is considered by Hegel as part of an implicit direction of speculative thought which, nonetheless, needs to be fully developed on more adequate grounds. The failure of Kantian transcendentalism to found objectivity through consciousness and thought claims a new programme for the task of philosophy, based on the constitutive character of the operations of speculative reason.

DEL RE, Giuseppe. Aquinas versus Epistemological Criticism: A Case for Philosophy *in* Science. Phil Sci (Tucson), 2, 15-28, 1986.

In philosophical comments on results of natural sciences basic concepts of traditional ontology are often criticized as meaningless. In this paper, some conclusions of the general theory of the systems as well as tenets of organismic biology are compared with conceptual schemes of Aristotle and Thomas Aquinas. Analogies between the scientific notion of the system and the metaphysical concept of substance are developed after accepting epistemological realism and introducing differentiations of various "levels of reality."

DEL RE, Giuseppe. La crisi dei fondamenti della scienza: Un recupero dell'ilemorfismo? Sapienza, 44(1), 51-55, Ja-Mr 91.

DELBOSCO, Héctor J. El problema de la "acción intencional" en el conocimiento sensible. Sapientia, 45(176), 105-122, Ap-Je 90.

The article sets the question if we must necessarily admit that in sensible knowledge the object exerts upon cognitive powers something else than a mere physical action, i.e., an "intentional" one. After analyzing St. Thomas's position, it studies other authors and commentators about the subject, and considers some of modern science's contributions concerning sensation. It comes to the conclusion that recognizing "intentional action" is the only way to give a coherent explanation of man's objective knowledge of reality. Finally the work explains the metaphysical backgrounds of the thesis, especially the body's participation in spiritual perfection as condition of their intentional activity.

DELCÒ, Alessandro. Rilievi di struttura sul *De deo abscondito* di Nicola Cusano. Filosofia, 41(3), 313-323, S-D 90.

DELCÓ, Alessandro. Sulla matrice della teoria della sostanza nel *Discorso di metafisica* di Leibniz. Filosofia, 42(1), 29-48, Ja-Ap 91.

DELEUZE, Gilles and TOMLINSON, Hugh (trans) and HABBERJAM, Barbara (trans). *Bergsonism*. Cambridge, MIT Pr, 1991.

DELEUZE, Gilles. The Conditions of the Question: What Is Philosophy? Crit Inquiry, 17(3), 471-478, Spr 91.

DELEUZE, Gilles and BOUNDAS, Constantin V (trans). *Empiricism and Subjectivity: An Essay on Hume's Theory of Human Nature*. New York, Columbia Univ Pr, 1991.

DELEUZE, Gilles and JOUGHIN, Martin (trans). *Expressionism in Philosophy: Spinoza*. Cambridge, Zone Books, 1990.

DELIVOYATSIS, Socratis. Le pouvoir de la différence. Rev Int Phil, 44(173), 179-197, 1990.

DELVER, R and MONSUUR, H and STORCKEN, A J A. Ordering Pairwise Comparison Structures. Theor Decis, 31(1), 75-94, Jl 91.

Following an introduction to the merits of pairwise comparison methods, we present various ordering algorithms for complete binary preferential structures. These procedures generalize the well-known numbering algorithm to the intransitive case. A new form of independence of irrelevant alternatives is presented. Moreover, various other criteria and characterizations for these algorithms are presented. Aside from solving ranking problems and making explicit value criteria and structures of human preference, our algorithms are applicable to subjects such as task-sequencing and artificial intelligence projects.

DEMBSKI, William. Randomness by Design. Nous, 25(1), 75-106, Mr 91.

DEMMER, Klaus. Das vergeistigte Glück: Gedanken zum christlichen Eudämonieverständnis. Gregorianum, 72(1), 99-115, 1991.

The article tries to shed light on the Christian understanding of eidaimonia as being a key notion of traditional catholic moral theology. It is based on biblical data and the thomistic tension between beatitude and felicity. It is up to the christian believer to transform the common desire for felicity in the light of his ultimate end, and this demands a whole life history. Examples are drawn from the life option for marriage and celibacy. The main idea is to develop an uncompleted Kantian issue using terms of contemporary transcendental philosophy.

DEMOPOULOS, William. The Homogeneous Form of Logic Programs with Equality. Notre Dame J Form Log, 31(2), 291-303, Spr 90.

DEN HARTOGH, G A. The Superfluity of the Original Position. Tijdschr Filosof, 53(2), 264-310, Je 91.

After 1971 John Rawls has modified his theory of justice in important ways. He now intends to adapt the arrangement of the "basic structure" to an explicit ideal of the person and of society; "primary goods" are therefore to be distributed in accordance with the "needs" of the exercise of the moral power of "rationality" (autonomy); and hence the amount of the equal basic liberties is no longer required to be maximal but only adequate. I make two points: (a) In the new argument the idea of the original position (o.p.) has no role to play, not even an illustrative or "dramatizing" one. When the argument has been made outside of the o.p. have to repeat the entire argument in order to reach the desired conclusions. (b) The argument does not support the "difference principle", but rather a principle of guaranteeing a social minimum. For the position of the least advantaged equally need not to be maximal but only adequate.

DEN HARTOGH, Govert. Tully's Locke. Polit Theory, 18(4), 656-672, N 90.

In the state of nature the world is the common property of all mankind. Appropriation by labour does not end this communal ownership; it does not give any rights of disposal beyond use. When the invention of money creates scarcity of land, even this limited natural right can no longer be acquired. People then transfer their natural rights *in toto* to a political community, receiving legal rights in exchange. This is James Tully's influential interpretation of Locke's *Second Treatise* (*A Discourse on Property*, 1980), which I criticise in detail. Appropriation of an object ends communal ownership; it gives a right of alienation. The invention of money does not undermine the legitimacy of this original acquisition. Entering into civil society people resign no rights but only the power to decide authoritatively any controversy concerning their (natural) rights.

DENBIGH, K G. The Many Faces of Irreversibility. Brit J Phil Sci, 40(4), 501-518, D 89.

Irreversibility, it is claimed, is a much broader concept than is entropy increase, as is shown by the occurrence of certain processes which are irreversible without seeming to involve any intrinsic entropy change. These processes include the spreading outwards into space of particles, or of radiation, and they also include certain biological and mental phenomena. For instance, the irreversible and treelike branching which is characteristic of natural evolution is not entropic when it is considered in itself—i.e., in abstraction from accompanying biochemical and physiological activity. What appears to be the common feature of all forms of irreversibility is the fanning out of trajectories, new entities or new states, in the temporal direction towards the future.

DENBIGH, K G. Note on Entropy, Disorder and Disorganization. Brit J Phil Sci, 40(3), 323-332, S 89.

In the effort to make the concept of entropy more readily understandable, it has often been said to be a measure of disorder, or of disorganization. However these contentions are by no means generally true, as is shown by means of counter-examples. The situation has been further confused by an assumption that the original entropy of thermodynamics and statistical mechanics is the same as Shannon's measure of 'uncertainty', as used in information theory. This too is untrue. The only fairly simple interpretation of entropy, other than its thermodynamic definition, is that it is a logarithmic measure of the number of system's accessible quantum states.

DENGERINK, J D. Het scheppende en herscheppende woord: zijn blijvende actualiteit. Phil Reform, 56(1), 62-80, 1991.

DENKEL, Arda. *Principia Individuationis*. Phil Quart, 41(163), 212-228, Ap 91.

This paper discusses individuation *at a point in time*. It argues that a principle of individuation that does not assume the Identity of Indiscernibles fails the Indiscernibility of Identicals. Consequently, principles such as matter, substratum or position are inadequate, for they allow inconsistent properties in the same object. Since distinct indiscernibles are possible, no version of the Identity of Indiscernibles can be sufficient. A satisfactory principle should conjoin qualities with position without creating commitment to absolute space. Hence objects are compresences of particular qualities. Individuators embodying less than all the qualities of the object can be adequate *through time* only.

DENNEHY, Raymond. "Being Is Better than Freedom" in *Freedom in the Modern World: Jacques Maritain, Yves R Simon, Mortimer J Adler*, TORRE, Michael D (ed), 253-262. Notre Dame, Univ Notre Dame Pr, 1989.

DENNEHY, Raymond. Rescuing Natural Law Theory from the Rationalists. Vera Lex, 10(1), 14-16, 1990.

The article's aim is to unfold Jacques Maritain's distinctive contribution to natural law theory, which contribution furnishes a vindication for natural morality and natural right. His application of connatural knowledge to the natural law theory enabled him to retrieve the latter from intellectual disrepute by answering the question that the rationalists' idealization of natural law could not answer: "If the natural law is truly natural, how come all peoples do not follow the same moral practices?"

DENNES, Maryse. Les effets de la perestroïka dans les *Voprosy filosofii*. Rev Phil Fr, 180(4), 665-678, O-D 90.

DENNETT, Daniel C. The Interpretation of Texts, People and Other Artifacts. Phil Phenomenol Res, 50 SUPP, 177-194, Fall 90.

The interpretation of texts (hermeneutics), people (intentional psychology), artifacts, and evolutionary design processes (adaptationism) are shown to be practices governed by the same principles, subject to the same problems and controversies, and limited by the same ultimate indeterminacies. In every exercise of interpretation, the intentions of the "author" (if any) are only defeasible indicators of meaning or function, and beyond an assessment of current or future functional prowess, there are no deeper facts to ground an original or fundamental attribution of meaning.

DENNETT, Daniel C. Real Patterns. J Phil, 88(1), 27-51, Ja 91.

DENNETT, Daniel C. "Ways of Establishing Harmony" in *Information, Semantics and Epistemology*, VILLANUEVA, Enrique (ed), 18-27. Cambridge, Blackwell, 1990.

DENTON, David E. Method and Message: Commentary on the Future of Philosophy of Education. Phil Stud Educ, /, 105-107, 1986.

The analytic work of Ayer, Ryle, and Scheffler was appropriate for their time, their methods having numerous "messages" on which to work at hand. The Vow of Rigor, Ricoeur's term, has so inhibited the proposing of powerful, philosophical images—messages, in short—analytic work has reached its sterile end. Rorty, by rediscovering Dewey and admitting that something important had been going on on the Continent, becomes the darling of the USA-philosophic establishment. Why? He has pointed to sources of messages, philosophic messages, which could not be generated by analytic philosophy. For philosophy of education to have a future, the Vow of Rigor must be balanced with the Vow of Obedience to compelling images.

DEREGIBUS, Arturo. Pascal, etica, politica, socialità. Filosofia, 41(3), 255-312, S-D 90.

DERISI, Octavio N. Capacidad de la mente humana para alcanzar el ser de las cosas, hasta el mismo *Esse subsistens* (II). Sapientia, 46(180), 83-90, Ap-Je 91.

DERISI, Octavio N. La esencia metafísica de Dios. Aquinas, 33(3), 471-486, S-D 90.

DERISI, Octavio N. Humanismo y humanismo cristiano. Sapientia, 46(179), 35-50, Ja-Mr 91.

DERISI, Octavio N. La prudencia (II). Sapientia, 45(176), 83-86, Ap-Je 90.

DERRIDA, Jacques and BEREZDIVIN, Ruben (trans). "At This Very Moment in This Work Here I Am" in *Re-Reading Levinas*, BERNASCONI, Robert (ed), 11-48. Bloomington, Indiana Univ Pr, 1991.

DERRIDA, Jacques and BOURGEOIS, Bernard. Réflexion sur l'état actuel et les perspectives de l'enseignement de la philosophie en France. Bull Soc Fr Phil, 85(1), 1-58, Ja-Mr 91.

DESCARTES, René and HEFFERNAN, George (trans). *Meditations on First Philosophy: A Bilingual Edition—René Descartes*. Notre Dame, Univ Notre Dame Pr, 1990.

DESLAURIERS, Marguerite. Character and Explanation in Aristotle's *Ethics* and *Poetics*. Dialogue (Canada), 29(1), 79-93, 1990.

DESLAURIERS, Marguerite. Plato and Aristotle on Division and Definition. Ancient Phil, 10(2), 203-219, Fall 90.

DETHIER, Hubert. Sartre's onuitgevoerde project: de Robespierre-biografie. Tijdschr Stud Verlich Denken, 17(3-4), 307-325, 1989.

DETLEFSEN, Michael. Brouwerian Intuitionism. Mind, 99(396), 501-534, O 90.

It is argued that Brouwer's critique of classical logic was not so much focused on particular principles (e.g., the law of excluded middle) as on the use of *any* kind of logical inference in mathematical proof. He believed that genuine mathematical reasoning requires genuine mathematical insight (or intuition), and thus cannot accommodate the use of topic-neutral forms of inference. Alternative views of knowledge and language which might underlie such a view are discussed, as are certain connections between the thought of Brouwer and Poincaré.

DETLEFSEN, Michael. On an Alleged Refutation of Hilbert's Program Using Gödel's First Incompleteness Theorem. J Phil Log, 19(4), 343-377, N 90.

It is argued that an instrumentalist notion of proof such as that represented in Hilbert's viewpoint is not obligated to satisfy the conservation condition that is generally regarded as a constraint on Hilbert's Program. A more reasonable soundness condition is then considered and shown not to be counter-exemplified by Gödel's First Theorem. Finally, attention is given to the question of what a theory is; whether it should be seen as a "list" or corpus of beliefs, or as a *method* for selecting beliefs. The significance of this question for assessing "intensional" results like Gödel's Second Theorem, and their bearing on Hilbert's Program are discussed.

DEUTSCH, Harry. Contingency and Modal Logic. Phil Stud, 60(1-2), 89-102, S-O 90.

One of the logical problems with which Arthur Prior struggled is the problem of finding, in Prior's phrase, a "logic for contingent beings." The difficulty is that from minimal modal principles and classical quantification theory, it appears to follow immediately that every possible object is a necessary existent. The historical development of quantified modal logic (QML) can be viewed as a series of attempts to solve this problem. I review the extant solutions, finding them all wanting. Then I suggest a new solution inspired by Kripke's theory of rigid designation and Kaplan's logic of demonstratives.

DEUTSCH, Harry. "On Direct Reference" in *Themes From Kaplan*, ALMOG, Joseph (ed), 167-195. New York, Oxford Univ Pr, 1989.

In this paper I try to point up certain persistent confusions and misunderstandings concerning the notion of direct reference. I argue that the notion is a relative one requiring a "double-indexed" semantics and the distinction between (in Kaplan's terminology) "context" and "circumstance". I then argue that quantified modal logic with varying domains and directly referential terms for contingent objects can be based on classical quantification theory, provided we give up the rule of necessiation. I argue that this rule fails for intuitive reasons when rigid or directly referential terms denoting contingent objects are allowed.

DEUTSCH, Harry. Real Possibility. Nous, 24(5), 751-755, D 90.

Suppose you are solicited for funds by the American Cancer Society, and you believe that the lines of research pursued by the Society could well lead to a cure. So you say to yourself "This could lead to a cure" and you send the money. But why? What beliefs prompt you to act in this way? Surely it is not just that you believe that there is some possible world in which the society's line of research leads to a cure. For that would not explain why you send money. Instead, you believe that there is a "real possibility," a possibility for the actual world, that a cure will be found along these lines. I sketch a semantics for real possibility which treats it as a future-oriented modal-temporal notion.

DEUTSCH, Michael. Eine Bemerkung zu spektralen Darstellungen von ρ-stelligen Aufzählbaren. Z Math Log, 36(2), 163-184, 1990.

For any sets "xEl*y" resp. "xEly" means: x is an element of y resp. x is an element of y or is equal y. Theorem: For any first order formula A one can find a closed prenex first order formula B with the prefix EAEA...A (without the equality sign and without function symbols) containing just one (binary) predicate variable P with A is satisfiable (resp. satisfiable in a finite model), ↔ B is satisfiable (resp. satisfiable in a finite model), ↔ B is satisfiable on a domain (resp. finite domain) of sets with interpretation of P by El, ↔ B is satisfiable on a domain (resp. finite domain) of sets with interpretation of P by El*. A similar result can be proved if we allow arbitrary many set variables in B and choose the prefix AEEA. A third theorem gives an analogous spectral representation of enumerable and coenumerable predicates.

DEUTSCH, Michael. Weitere verschärfungen zu den Reduktionstypen.... Z Math Log, 36(4), 339-355, 1990.

DEVANEY, Mike. Risk, Commitment, and Project Abandonment. J Bus Ethics, 10(2), 157-159, F 91.

This article deals briefly with the most loathsome of business topics—the admission of failure. Rather than actively encouraging project "Anti-champions," many organizations experiencing financial duress inadvertently stifle opposing opinion. In some cases recognition is delayed until it is too late. This is unfortunate since failure can be managed like any other business situation. Companies with CEOs that foster open communications between finance and operations are more likely to avoid escalating commitment to failed projects.

DEVARAJA, N K. Language, Logic and Reality. Indian Phil Quart, 17(3), 325-347, Jl 90.

The paper critically explores relationship between language and reality. The optimistic assumption inspiring realist thinkers (cf. Naiyāyikas) and proponents of ideal language (e.g., Russell) that our symbolic structures can mirror/represent the actual structural relationships in reality leads to emergence of paradoxes/dilemmas (Zeno, Nāgārjuna). Even exact mathematical symbolism fails to represent movement (e.g., Achilles') and relationships of physical forces—thus necessitating continuing revisions of laws, theories, even factual data. Conclusion: no strict correspondence exists between language and reality as studied by natural and cultural sciences. Symbolism directly refers to meanings characterized in terms or categories deriving from varied human interests.

DEVENISH, Philip E. The Experience of Value and Theological Argumentation. Process Stud, 19(2), 103-115, Sum 90.

Two types of argumentation regarding the experience of value are necessary to theistic philosophy. One describes the experience of value in order to identify the relevant evidence for theistic interpretation. Another analyzes the concepts utilized in such a description in order to specify and to clarify its ontic, as well as its noetic presuppositions. The work of Schubert Ogden is exemplary in both respects.

DEVEREAUX, Mary. Can Art Save Us? A Meditation on Gadamer. Phil Lit, 15(1), 59-73, Ap 91.

It is a commonplace that Western culture is in moral crisis. One response has been to turn to art to fill the vacuum created by the collapse of traditional morality. I analyze one version of this appealing but deeply paradoxical view of art: Hans-Georg Gadamer's proposal to find in art a source of moral instruction which neither reverts to foundationalism nor leads to relativism. I argue that Gadamer's romantic picture of art overlooks the possibility that the authority of tradition and our tranformation by it may be part of the problem instead of the solution.

DEVINE, Philip E. AIDS and the L-Word. Pub Affairs Quart, 5(2), 137-147, Ap 91.

I use the AIDS epidemic, and the controversies surrounding it, as a way of probing the weaknesses of the liberal tradition, at least in its most popular versions. The AIDS epidemic, I argue, creates serious problems for the following versions of liberalism: 1) the idea that the government, and our conception of political justice, should be neutral among "life styles," 2) the idea of a right to health care, when combined with the anti-paternalist preconceptions of many liberals, and 3) the "liberalism of fear" advocated by Judith Shklar.

DEVITT, Michael. Aberrations of the Realism Debate. Phil Stud, 61(1-2), 43-63, F 91.

The issue of realism about the physical world is distinct from the semantic issue of correspondence truth. So it is an aberration to identify the two issues (Dummett), to dismiss the realism issue out of hostility to correspondence truth (Rorty, Fine), to think that that issue is one of interpretation, or to argue against realism by criticizing various claims about truth and reference (Putnam, Laudan). It is also an aberration to identify realism with nonskepticism, truth-as-the-aim-of-science, or scientific convergence. Realism is an overarching metaphysical issue which should be settled before any of these epistemic and semantic issues.

DEVITT, Michael and STERELNY, Kim. "Linguistics: What's Wrong with 'The Right View'" in *Philosophical Perspectives, 3: Philosophy of Mind and Action Theory, 1989*, TOMBERLIN, James E (ed), 497-531. Atascadero, Ridgeview, 1989.

Fodor names the view that linguistics is about linguistic competence, "the Right View." On this view the grammar discovered by linguists is psychologically real. The paper finds difficulties for this idea of the grammar, particularly for the version of it that requires speakers to have propositional knowledge of the grammar. The paper urges a different view of linguistics: it is about the properties of linguistic symbols. This view is usually conflated with "the Right View." The paper offers a diagnosis of this conflation. In the course of the argument, the relevance of linguistic intuitions is examined.

DEVITT, Michael. "Meanings Just Ain't in the Head" in *Meaning and Method: Essays in Honor of Hilary Putnam*, BOOLOS, George (ed), 79-104. New York, Cambridge Univ Pr, 1990.

Searle rejects Putnam's claim that meanings just ain't in the head. The paper defends Putnam, arguing that Searle's rejection involves a magical theory of reference. This theory, which is also the basis of Searle's famous opposition to causal theories of names and computational theories of the mind, is magical in holding that the reference of a mental representation is determined by something internal and intrinsic to the mind. In particular, Searle thinks that a mental state has a phenomenological property that "reaches out" to its own cause. Finally, the paper demonstrates dualistic and vitalistic elements in Searle's thinking.

DEVITT, Michael. On Removing Puzzles About Belief Ascription. Pac Phil Quart, 71(3), 165-181, S 90.

Lycan is critical of the traditional semantics of belief sentences for ignoring the psychological reality that makes these sentences true. The paper is more critical, urging that we should put the metaphysics of the mind before semantics. When we do, well-known problems about beliefs sentences—discovered by Frege, Kripke, Richard, and Castaneda—seem much more tractable: they are not deep puzzles about us, but rather routine problems about semantics. Lycan tends to exaggerate these problems because of a lingering attachment to the traditional talk of propositions, possible worlds, and the like. This attachment is reflected also in his mistakenly embracing "direct reference."

DEVITT, Michael. Realism Without Representation: A Response to Appiah. Phil Stud, 61(1-2), 75-77, F 91.

Appiah agrees that the traditional argument about realism has been over a metaphysical thesis. Nevertheless, he claims that this thesis is implicitly semantic because the entities the thesis commits us to must be identified as the referents of our representations. This claim is false. We can identify the entities directly. And even if we do use reference to identify them, the notion in question need only be deflationary and hence not, in any interesting sense, semantic.

DEVITT, Michael. Transcendentalism About Content. Pac Phil Quart, 71(4), 247-263, D 90.

Transcendentalism about truth conditional content is the view that eliminativism about such content is not simply empirically false, but "incoherent." Arguments to this effect employ a question-begging strategy: they start by applying notions to the eliminativist that are laden with precisely the theory that she thinks should be abandoned; they overlook that she would think that notions from a replacement theory were the appropriate ones to apply. The paper starts with a naive example of the strategy and then gives close attention to a recent example, Boghossian's "The Status of Content."

DEWASHI, Mahadev. Professor Von Wright on Action. Indian Phil Quart, SUPP 17(3), 29-36, Jl 90.

DEWS, Peter and OSBORNE, Peter. Lacan in Slovenia—An Interview with Slavoj Zizek and Renata Salecl. Rad Phil, 58, 25-31, Sum 91.

DHAR, Benulal. Some Reflections on Husserl's Approach to the Problem of Transcendence. Indian Phil Quart, SUPP 18(1), 47-64, Ja 91.

Edmund Husserl's phenomenology makes a 'radical' attempt to solve a long-standing problem of epistemology, namely, the problem of transcendence. In the present paper, a modest attempt has been made to review some of the approaches to the problem of transcendence made in modern times particularly, by Descartes, Berkeley, Hume, and Kant with special emphasis on Husserl's radical approach to the problem. At what this paper finally aims is to show that perhaps Husserl does not quite succeed fully in solving the problem of transcendence in his phenomenological theory of knowledge.

DHAVAMONY, Mariasusai. Causality: Sankara and Aristotle. Int Phil Quart, 31(2), 173-187, Je 91.

Both Sankara and Aristotle start form the axiom that nothing can come out of nothing. Coming to be in the absolute sense is impossible. From the totally non-existent nothing can come into being. The article after analyzing the divergence and convergences between the two philosophies of causality, suggests a meeting-point. If pressed to its logical conclusion, the doctrine of the pre-existence of the effect in its cause as an appearance will lead us in the direction of a metaphysics of love and will show that the pure Act contains particular acts not merely as the exemplary model contains its image but also as the unique Act of love which only gives without receiving in return.

DHONDT, U. Philosophy and Religion (in Dutch). Tijdschr Filosof, 53(1), 3-22, Mr 91.

The article takes up the problematic of the opposition between metaphysical doctrines concerning the existence of God and an anthropological analysis of the religious life. Agnosticism is actually a theoretical stance. Philosophical thinking is, we can argue, necessarily based on an original theoretical understanding, which is prior to the bifurcation between theory and praxis. (edited)

DI CESARE, Donatella. "The Philosophical and Anthropological Place of Wilhelm von Humboldt's Linguistic Typology" in *Leibniz, Humboldt, and the Origins of Comparativism*, DE MAURO, Tullio (ed), 157-180. Philadelphia, John Benjamins, 1990.

Guided by his anthropological interests, Humboldt founds linguistic typology on the diversity of human nature. The diversity that language presents in the form of historical languages becomes the object of comparative linguistics, which through the comparison of different languages aims at finding the historically realized ways in which human thought has been proceeding. A concept such as "linguistic type" cannot serve as a theoretical basis for a classification of languages. In many passes of his work Humboldt directly opposes such a classification: inasmuch as they are individual, languages are not susceptible of classification. (edited)

DI GIOVANNI, George (ed). *Essays on Hegel's Logic*. Albany, SUNY Pr, 1990.

The volume deals with a range of topics all related to Hegelian logic—whether a speculative logic is possible, whether Hegelian logic requires a metalogic, or whether it can and ought to make an absolute beginning. It also examines, conceptually and historically, the *being-nothing* dialectic, the relation of *essence* to *show* (*Schein*), and Hegel's treatment of the modal categories. It proposes radically different views of the role of the *understanding* in Hegelian logic and a radically different view of the necessity underlying it. It concludes with an essay contrasting Hegel's logic with Aristotle's.

DI GIOVANNI, George. "A Reply to Cynthia Willett's "The Shadow of Hegel's *Science of Logic*" in *Essays on Hegel's Logic*, DI GIOVANNI, George (ed), 93-98. Albany, SUNY Pr, 1990.

The essay grants that Aristotle's metaphysics is totally governed by the concept of Being, and that it therefore ultimately fails to conceptualize the reality of Becoming. It denies, however, that the same applies to Hegel's logic (1) by distinguishing between the cosmological assumptions implicit in Aristotle's metaphysics and Hegel's concept of nature; (2) by arguing that Hegel's logic is *science of thought* in the first place and *science of being* only by implication; and (3) by showing how 'negativity' is just as present at every stage of the logic as it is in the original Being-Nothing dialectic.

DI LEO, Jeffrey R. Peirce's Haecceitism. Trans Peirce Soc, 27(1), 79-107, Wint 91.

DI MARCO, Chiar. Filosofia dell'esistenza e cristologia: La Weltanschauung cristiana di R Guardini. Aquinas, 33(1), 185-202, Ja-Ap 90.

DI MARCO, Chiara. Tempo ed eternità: La filosofia narrante di F Rosenzweig. Aquinas, 33(3), 627-638, S-D 90.

DI MARCO, Giuseppe Antonio. La storia universale come storia comparata in Max Weber. Arch Stor Cult, 4, 165-187, 1991.

DI PIETRO, Alfredo. A propósito del filósofo del derecho Giorgio del Vecchio. Sapientia, 45(176), 149-157, Ap-Je 90.

DI PRISCO, C A and FULLER, M and HENLE, J M. The Normal Depth of Filters on an Infinite Cardinal. Z Math Log, 36(4), 293-296, 1990.

DI SALLE, Robert. "The 'Essential Properties' of Matter, Space, and Time: Comments on Michael Friedman" in *Philosophical Perspectives on Newtonian Science*, BRICKER, Phillip (ed), 203-209. Cambridge, MIT Pr, 1990.

DIAGNE, Oumar. Voix et Existence. Quest, 5(1), 36-49, Je 91.

In our modern world we are used to generalized modes of communication, such as radio, television, and the press. In this context we have developed an objectivist conception of communication, as the one expressed in the model: sender / medium / receiver. The present article sets out to show that communication cannot be reduced to models which take communication to be objectifiable and quantifiable, as if human relations could be reduced to mechanical processes of interaction. The voice constitutes an irreplaceable factor in the communication between individuals. It is a form of subjective communication which is both more basic than other forms and harbours aspects of communication that cannot be reduced to other forms of communication.

DIAMOND, Cora. The Importance of Being Human. Philosophy, 29, 35-62, 91 Supp.

DIAMOND, Cora. Response to McNaughton. Philosophy, 29, 83-84, 91 Supp.

DIAMOND, Cora (ed). *Wittgenstein's Lectures on the Foundations of Mathematics, Cambridge 1939*. Chicago, Univ of Chicago Pr, 1990.

DÍAZ, Adolfo García. Fabricas o escuelas de Filosofia? Rev Filosof (Venezuela), 12, 11-14, 1989.

DÍAZ, Adolfo García. Sobre los universales. Rev Filosof (Venezuela), 12, 15-31, 1989.

DIBRELL, William. Persons and the Intentional Stance. J Crit Anal, 9(1), 13-25, 1988.

DICKER, Georges. The Moderns in an Introductory Analytic Course. Teach Phil, 13(3), 265-272, S 90.

DICKEY, Laurence. Pride, Hypocrisy and Civility in Mandeville's Social and Historical Theory. Crit Rev, 4(3), 387-431, Sum 90.

This paper seeks to show that Bernard Mandeville's primary purpose in *The Fable of the Bees* was to historicize the concept of self-love (*amour-propre*) articulated by seventeenth-century French Jansenists and *moralistes*; that in doing so Mandeville constructed a theory designed to explain the inter-subjective constraints and forces of social discipline which characterize commercial societies; and that a full understanding of Mandeville's achievement depends upon an appreciation of the way in which pride in his theory becomes socialized into hypocrisy at a decisive moment in the civilizing process, a moment after which, Mandeville argues, cultural institutions themselves can contain that unfettered self-interest which his contemporaries fearfully associated with the triumph of commerce.

DICKMAN, Joel. Two Qualms About Functionalist Marxism. Phil Sci, 57(4), 631-643, D 90.

In *Karl Marx's Theory of History: A Defence* (1978), G A Cohen has developed a distinctively functionalist interpretation of historical materialism. In this paper I outline Cohen's novel reconstruction of Marx and subject it to two independent internal criticisms. I first argue that explanations cannot conform to Cohen's functionalist model. I then suggest that even if there could be explanations having the structure he has proposed, they would fail to be helpful in illuminating the causal kernel of Marx's theory. Finally I sketch a neglected but more promising approach to clarifying historical materialism, due to Geoffrey Hellman.

DIEFENBECK, James A. "Acts and Necessity in the Philosophy of John William Miller" in *The Philosophy of John William Miller*, FELL, Joseph P (ed), 43-58. Lewisburg, Bucknell Univ Pr, 1990.

DIEFENBECK, James A. Bringing Things About. J Speculative Phil, 5(3), 180-192, 1991.

DIEKS, Dennis. On Some Alleged Difficulties in the Interpretation of Quantum Mechanics. Synthese, 86(1), 77-86, Ja 91.

The article opposes a recent claim by Albert and Loewer that certain mathematical features of the quantum mechanical formalism (namely, the superposition principle and linear evolution) necessitate an interpretation which is radically different from the way the formalisms of classical physics are usually interpreted. In particular, there is no need to introduce "minds" or "many worlds." Some recent attempts to give consistent interpretations of a more traditional kind are briefly sketched.

DIETHE, Carol. Nietzsche and the Woman Question. Hist Euro Ideas, 11, 865-875, 1989.

In contrast to conventional contemporary opinion on female sexuality, Nietzsche does not seek to deny women's sexual desire: in fact, he sees woman as little more than the embodiment of a sexual urge which is powered by the craving to become pregnant. Woman is therefore simultaneously a predator on man and dependent on him. Nietzsche pours scorn on female emancipation, because it deflects woman from what he sees as her biological destiny: motherhood. In his insistence on woman's maternal mission, Nietzsche is a typical Wilhelmine thinker. His views on woman are thus a curious amalgam of iconoclasm and conventionality.

DIETRICH, Eric. Replies to My Computational Commentators. Soc Epistem, 4(4), 369-375, O-D 90.

DIETZSCH, Steffen. Leben als Passion: Elias Canettis "Masse und Macht" als Beitrag zum Begreifen der Moderne. Deut Z Phil, 38(7), 677-683, 1990.

The idea of this article is Canetti's view of human existence in mass-era as fight (in a political sense); his paradoxical ethic means: how to survive without being victorious? Canetti's conclusion is: it will survive altogether or no one! Canetti explains this with his anthropological and etnographical experiences as message of enlightenment today.

DÍEZ, Amparo (ed) and ECHEVERRÍA, J (ed) and IBARRA, A (ed). *Structures in Mathematical Theories: Reports of the San Sebastian International Symposium, 1990*. Vizcaya, Univ Pais Vasco, 1990.

This book contains a selection of 76 contributed papers to the International Symposium on Structures in Mathematical Theories (San Sebastian, Spain, 25-29 September, 1990). They are distributed in five sections: Mathematical and Empirical Theories; Applications of Mathematical Theories; History and Sociology of Mathematical Theories; Methods of Research into Mathematics; Structures of Mathematical Theories. Philosophers of science, historians and mathematicians coming from 19 countries (Belgium, Brazil, Canada, China, England, Finland, France, Germany, Holland, Japan, India, Israel, Italy, Mexico, Poland, Spain, Switzerland, URSS and USA) present their research on mathematical theories: their structures, historical evolutions and interrelations with other sciences and technologies.

DIFFEY, T J. "Art and Meaning" in *XIth International Congress in Aesthetics, Nottingham 1988*, WOODFIELD, Richard (ed), 38-41. Nottingham, Nottingham Polytech, 1990.

For works of art to have meaning is for them necessarily to be objects of understanding. Such understanding is not propositional but grounded in the capacity to follow something done in a medium. A medium shows without saying. Reference in art, which is apparent, is suspended. Works of art are not truth-bearers.

DIJS, Judith. Two Anonymous 12th-Century Tracts on Universals. Vivarium, 28(2), 85-117, N 90.

The article consists of a critical edition of two tracts found in the manuscript Patis B N Lat 17813, with an introduction. The author of the first tract—probably Walter of Mortagne—elaborates on the ontological status of *genus* and *species*. The second tract concerns the properties of the corresponding terms. The introduction discusses possible authors, refuting Hauréau's attribution of the second tract to Roscellinus; it also disputes the use of the term 'status-doctrine', since the term 'status' in the 12th century is used by very different doctrines and consequently not to be associated with any one.

DILLINGER, Mike. "On the Concept of 'a Language'" in *Studies on Mario Bunge's "Treatise"*, WEINGARTNER, Paul (ed), 5-26. Amsterdam, Rodopi, 1990.

The concept of 'a language' is developed as a systems-theoretic construct, derived from Bunge's (1979) systems ontology and Palmer's (1978) analysis of representation as used in psychology, further constrained by Bunge's epistemology. 'A language' is a specific case of a representational system in a social/communicative context: a represent*ing* system (of linguistic forms) is systematically related to a represent*ed* system (of conceptual structures) by a 'yoking' relation, in which each is in the environment of the other and two-way many-to-many relations characterize their interactions. This view is seen as a way of developing Saussure's (1916) program for linguistics.

DILLON, John. "Logos and Trinity: Patterns of Platonist Influence on Early Christianity" in *The Philosophy in Christianity*, VESEY, Godfrey (ed), 1-13. New York, Cambridge Univ Pr, 1989.

A study of the influence of Platonism on two central areas of Early Christian doctrine, the relation of God the Son to the Father, and the mutual relations of the persons of the Trinity. In the former case, *logos*-theory and the figure of the demiurge are important; the the latter, particularly Porphyry's theory of the relation between Being, Life and Mind.

DILLON, Martin C. "Beyond Signifiers" in *Writing the Politics of Difference*, SILVERMAN, Hugh J (ed), 177-191. Albany, SUNY Pr, 1991.

In this paper, I present a series of arguments designed to demonstrate the fallacies inherent in a retreat to linguistic immanence which might be characterized as "post-hermeneutic" and "semeiological reductionism." These arguments attempt to show a) that the skeptical-reductionist position is self-referentially inconsistent (since, in conceiving language as effectively *causa sui*, it both deifies language and forecloses the possibility of accounting for its own genesis), and b) that the position entails a species of relativism that is tantamount to philosophical suicide (because it denies the possibility of even that open-ended kind of truth necessary to the rational adjudication of competing cognitive claims).

DILLON, Martin C. "Écart: Reply to Lefort's 'Flesh and Otherness'" in *Ontology and Alterity in Merleau-Ponty*, JOHNSON, Galen A (ed), 14-26. Evanston, Northwestern Univ Pr, 1991.

In his paper on "Flesh and Otherness," Lefort suggests that the limits of "a philosophy of Flesh" cannot adequately accommodate "the other, the third one, the representative of otherness." I argue that the idea which expresses itself through Merleau-Ponty's doctrine of the reversibility of Flesh articulates an ontology uniquely capable of disclosing the kind of transcendence known as alterity, but that Merleau-Ponty erred in the presentation of that doctrine.

DILMAN, Ilham. Sartre and Our Identity as Individuals. Philosophy, 29, 245-264, 91 Supp.

The purpose of this paper is a double one: 1) to understand better what is meant by 'self' when, for instance, someone has cause to ask 'Who am I?' or it is said of him that he has not been 'himself,' and 2) through criticism to appreciate Sartre's contribution to an understanding of this—to be clear about what he obscures and to appreciate what he illuminates. Accordingly the paper divides into the following sections: 1) Identity: 'Sameness of Person' and 'Authenticity of Self', 2) Sartre's Rejection of the Objectivist View, 3) Sartre's Ontology: Being and Nothingness, 4) The Falseness of our Positive Being: From the Ontological to the Contingent, 5) Between Non-being and False Identity: Untelling Sartre's Story, 6) Human Non-being and Genuine Identity, 7) Conclusion.

DILWORTH, Craig. Empiricism versus Realism: High Points in the Debate During the Past 150 Years. Stud Hist Phil Sci, 21(3), 431-462, S 90.

The paper presents some of the more conspicuous forms the empiricism vs. realism issue has taken in the philosophy of science since the time of Comte, Whewell and Mill. Other authors treated include Mach, Boltzmann, Poincaré, Duhem, Campbell, Hempel and Harré. It is argued that later authors, such as van Fraassen, Laudan, Cartwright, Hacking and Putnam, have misunderstood the issue. Realism is not the view that science aim to produce theories ever closer to the truth (an empiricist conception), but that it is an important task of science to investigate the *causes* of phenomena, conceived as emanating from the real world.

DILWORTH, Craig (ed). *Intelligibility in Science*. Amsterdam, Rodopi, 1991.

DILWORTH, David A. Mozart and Santayana and the Interface Between Music and Philosophy. Monist, 73(3), 464-478, Jl 90.

DILWORTH, David A. *Philosophy in World Perspective: A Comparative Hermeneutic of the Major Theories*. New Haven, Yale Univ Pr, 1991.

DILWORTH, David A. The Problem of Theoretical Self-Reflexivity in Peirce and Santayana. Bull Santayana Soc, 8, 1-9, Fall 90.

DIMITRAKOS, D. The Principle of Unity of Theory and Practice in Marxism: A Critique. Phil Inq, 12(3-4), 58-76, Sum-Fall 90.

DIMOCK JR, Edward C. *The Place of the Hidden Moon: Erotic Mysticism in the Vaisnava-sahajiyitaicā Cult of Bengal*. Chicago, Univ of Chicago Pr, 1989.

DINER, Dan. European Counterimages: Problems of Periodization and Historical Memory. Praxis Int, 10(1-2), 14-23, Ap-Jl 90.

DINIS, Alfredo. Por um novo modelo de saber: Problemática do discurso Filosófico-Teológico. Rev Port Filosof, 46(3), 355-378, Jl-S 90.

An analysis of structural causes in the conflicts that the heliocentric and evolutionary theories provoked reveals the persistent presence of some elements which hinder the understanding and the resolution of those conflicts. These elements can lead to errors of a methological nature affecting the analysis of the themes in question; they can also lead to acritical, dogmatic positions. It is necessary not only to have an awareness of the possibility of methological errors, but also to cultivate a new attitude towards new knowledge coming from the study of both physical and human nature. In this way, a new model of knowledge from a philosophical and theological perspective — especially necessary nowadays in the area of ethics—can confront the criticism and change of traditional conceptions, not defensively as a threat, but positively as something vital and necessary.

DION, Michel. Pour une interprétation féministe de l'idée chrétienne de Dieu. Laval Theol Phil, 47(2), 169-184, Je 91.

La théologie féministe américaine a entrepris, depuis deux décennies déjà, une réinterprétation féministe de l'idée chrétienne de Dieu. Deux de ses représentantes les plus importantes, Mary Daly et Rosemary R Ruether, ont fondé cette réinterprétation sur des concepts hérités tant de philosophies athées du 19e siècle (Nietzsche, Feuerbach, Marx) que de théologies du 20e siècle (Tillich, Whitehead, Théologie latino-américaine de la libération).

DISHENG, Yang. China's Traditional Mode of Thought and Science. Chin Stud Phil, 22(2), 43-62, Wint 90-91.

The idea that China's inability to produce its own modern science led to its falling behind in the last 300 years has become a major ingredient in today's critique of China's traditional culture. The problem of modes of thought has very broad connotations; the most significant of these is the question of dialectical thinking versus formal-logical thought. Ancient Chinese thought was extremely rich in the nature of dialectical thinking—it possessed those characteristics, and one should say that in this regard it was superior to the thought of ancient Greece; but in terms of formal-logical thinking, China did not attain the loftiness of ancient Greece. (edited)

DISSE, Jörg. *Kierkegaards Phänomenologie der Freiheitserfahrung*. Freiburg, Alber, 1991.

This book is concerned with the structure of the concrete *experience* of freedom, taking as examples Kierkegaard's existential analysis in his main pseudonymous works. In contrast to the views or prejudices of modernity, freedom can only be adequately understood as unimpeded autonomy. It is demonstrated with the aid of Kierkegaard's phenomenology of concrete existence that freedom is a dialectic between autonomy and dependence, reaching its peak in the relationship with God. The basis for this interpretation is formed by an account of Kierkegaard's "stages of experience". These are seen as forming a theory of different stages of freedom, starting from which the relationship between freedom and finitude, freedom and relation to God, freedom and objectivity are explicated. Here the analysis is continously oriented to the basic problematics of Kierkegaard's thought, and it is intended as a contribution both to the theory of freedom and to Kierkegaard studies themselves.

DITCHEV, Angel V. Some Results on Bounded Truth-Table Degrees. Z Math Log, 36(3), 263-271, 1990.

DIXON, Nicholas. History of Modern Philosophy as an Issues-Based Introductory Course. Teach Phil, 13(3), 253-263, S 90.

My paper describes a method of teaching history of modern philosophy in a way which is accessible to students with no background in philosophy. The main innovation of the course is that the readings are organized around three themes: (1) theory of knowledge; (2) philosophy of religion; (3) the free will problem. This provides continuity between the readings, a feature often missing in historical courses. Moreover, seeing how different philosophical methods—rationalism (Descartes), empiricism (Hume), pragmatism (James), and twentieth century analytic philosophy (Russell)—approach the same issues deepens students' understanding of these methods.

DO CARMO SILVA, Carlos Henrique. Heidegger e o Oriente ou da Extrema In-diferença Ocidental. Rev Port Filosof, 45(3), 301-348, Jl-S 89.

The present article attempts to establish a relationship between some of Heidegger's views on philosophy and its openness to Eastern thought. The conclusion is that the pretended orientalism of Heidegger's philosophy is nothing more than a paradoxical effect of hermeneutics viewed from Western thought. (edited)

DOBBIN, Robert. Προαιρεσις in Epictetus. Ancient Phil, 11(1), 111-135, Spr 91.

DÖBERT, Rainer. "Against the Neglect of "Content" in the Moral Theories of Kohlberg and Habermas" in *The Moral Domain: Essays in the Ongoing Discussion between Philosophy and the Social Sciences*, WREN, Thomas E (ed), 71-108. Cambridge, MIT Pr, 1990.

The article aims at clarifying the role of content in structural theories of moral development. It is shown that moral research deals exclusively with "structured content" where content has a double meaning of "givens of the moral conflict" (input of reasoning) and "moral decision" (output). It is demonstrated that moral research does not focus on justice but on the universal core domain of the morally right. The misidentification of 'content' has led to misleading procedural constructions, to ill-defined moral operations, to unnecessary and dangerous relativistic implications especially with respect to moral decisions. Not philosophical speculation but a careful examination of operationalizations might help.

DOBSON, Andrew. Believing What We Do Not See: The Case Against van Fraassen's Conception of Observation. Dialogue (PST), 33(2-3), 51-55, Ap 91.

DOEPKE, F. The Practical Importance of Personal Identity. Logos (USA), 11, 83-91, 1990.

By a generalization of Parfit's argument for the unimportance of personal identity in survival, it is argued that the practical significance that appears to attach to our identity belongs to the relation of direct control, which we exercise through will. What explains the special concern and moral responsibility that normally pertains only to ourselves is that it is ordinarily just ourselves whom we animate by our decisions. But thought experiments involving amnesia and replication seem to show that direct control only contingently coexists with personal identity. If so, the practically important question is whom we can control directly and the metaphysical question of our identity is either of theoretical or merely academic interest. The practical importance of the metaphysics of personal identity is defended by showing that our beliefs about which things we are determine what we can will. Such beliefs influence emotions of fear and the like and circumscribe our sense of responsibility.

DOERING, Bernard. "The Philosophy of Work and the Future of Civilization: Maritain, Weil and Simon" in *From Twilight to Dawn: The Cultural Vision of Jacques Maritain*, REDPATH, Peter A (ed), 49-67. Notre Dame, Univ Notre Dame Pr, 1990.

DOERR, Edd. A New Humanism: A Response. Relig Hum, 25(1), 21-22, Wint 91.

DOKIC, Jérome and CASATI, Roberto. Brains in a Vat, Language and Metalanguage. Analysis, 51(2), 91-93, Mr 91.

Putnam's argument against the hypothesis that we are Brains in a Vat (BIV), as reconstructed by M Dell'Utri in *Mind*, 99, pages 79-90, has four major flaws: a) the lack of a precise distinction between the object language and metalanguage; b) the improper use of Convention T in one major premiss; c) the lack of a definition of the operator 'in-the-image'; d) the difficulty of specifying, under the hypothesis that we are BIV, the status of our utterances.

DÖLLING, Evelyn and DÖLLING, Johannes. Dummett and the Origins of Analytical Philosophy, or the Philosophy of Thought vs Philosophy of Language (in German). Deut Z Phil, 38(8), 751-758, 1990.

DÖLLING, Johannes and DÖLLING, Evelyn. Dummett and the Origins of Analytical Philosophy, or the Philosophy of Thought vs Philosophy of Language (in German). Deut Z Phil, 38(8), 751-758, 1990.

DOMBROWSKI, Daniel A. Nature as Personal. Phil Theol, 5(1), 81-96, Fall 90.

I first examine Origen's notion of nature as personal, and secondly a modern presentation of the same theme by Erazim Kohak. I then consider possible scientific support given to both these authors' accounts by Lovejoy. I conclude that there are many strengths in viewing nature as a whole as both divine and personal.

DOMINGO, Agustín. Ontología hermenéutica y reflexión filológica: el acceso a la filosofía de H G Gadamer. Pensamiento, 47(186), 195-217, Ap-Je 91.

El autor analiza la relevancia que la reflexión filológica tiene en la ontología hermenéutica de Gadamer. Para ello se detiene en momentos significativos de su trayectoria académica y personal con el fin de acceder a datos importantes en la sensibilidad gadameriana que nos permitan valorar con mayor precisión la génesis de la recuperación ontológica de la hermenéutica que hace este singular discípulo de Heidegger. Cuál es la relación de Gadamer con las tradiciones filosóficas que articulan el primer tercio del siglo XX? Qué papel desempeña Platón en la trayectoria filosófica de estos primeros años? Cómo influye la pasión por la palabra poética en la articulación de la experiencia hermenéutica?

DONADÍO MAGGI, María C. Si la filosofía política es ciencia práctica. Logos (Mexico), 19(55), 95-108, Ja-Ap 91.

DONAGAN, Alan. Real Human Persons. Logos (USA), 11, 1-16, 1990.

The grounds for the commonsense view of human persons as individuals so constituted as, with normal nurture, to develop certain bodily, sensory, and rational capacities, which were endorsed by philosophers from Aristotle to Descartes, are shown to be strong. Yet that view has recently been dislodged by new reductionist views according to which the criteria of personal identity are matters of 'experience'. The reasons for these views are explored and found wanting.

DONAGHY, John. "Pacifism and Revolution" in *In the Interest of Peace: A Spectrum of Philosophical Views*, KLEIN, Kenneth H (ed), 207-216. Wolfeboro, Longwood, 1990.

Guenther Lewy's *Peace and Revolution* attacks organized American pacifism for abandoning pacifism to support revolution. His analysis caricatures pacifism as merely a moralistic opposition to killing. Yet a pacifism based on the principle of the inviolable dignity of the human person does create a tension between justice and non-killing, which is reducible neither to mere opposition to killing nor to unqualified support for violent revolutionary movements. Gandhi's remarks on courage and nonviolence point to an ethic for pacifism in the face of violent revolution. Suggestions toward a theory of revolutionary nonviolence conclude the paper.

DONN, Mike. Help in Finding Missing Premises. Teach Phil, 13(2), 159-164, Je 90.

An informal yet structured method for finding the missing premises of an argument is presented: Develop a scenario in which the premises of the argument are true while the conclusion is false. Negating this scenario will result in a missing premise (crucial assumption). This technique is explained, justified, and examples are provided using arguments.

DONNELLAN, Keith S. Genuine Names and Knowledge by Acquaintance. Dialectica, 44(1-2), 99-112, 1990.

I examine the connection Bertrand Russell makes between the possibility of genuinely naming something and being, in his special sense, acquainted with it. The most interesting and powerful argument he has for supposing that acquaintance is necessary for genuine naming is based on considerations about the ascription of existence and nonexistence. After some exploration of this, I try to show that acquaintance and genuine naming can be divorced: acquaintance is neither a sufficient condition (in a sense) nor a necessary condition for genuine naming. I attempt to show the latter using the special case of the first person pronoun. The argument makes interim use of the analysis of indexicals given by David Kaplan, but, in the end, I try to get the same result without direct appeal to any *analysis* of indexicals.

DONNELLY, John (ed). *Suicide: Right or Wrong?*. Buffalo, Prometheus, 1990.

A balanced collection of 18 essays that debate the pros and cons of suicide. Topics include attempts to define suicide, and various arguments about the rationality and morality of deliberately taking one's own life. The contributors are Aquinas, R Brandt, P Devine, J Donnelly, J Fletcher, R Frey, M Gonsalves, G Graber, Hume, Kant, J Oates, T O'Keeffe, Seneca, E Shneidman, S Stern-Gillet, T Szasz, and W Tolhurst.

DONNICI, Rocco. Le lezioni di Husserl sull'etica e sulla teoria del valore. G Crit Filosof Ital, 70(1), 109-129, Ja-Ap 91.

DONOGHUE, Michael J. Sociology, Selection, and Success: A Critique of David Hull's Analysis of Science and Systematics. Biol Phil, 5(4), 459-472, O 90.

DONOUGHO, Martin. "Hegel and the Subversion of Systems: *Der Fall Adorno*" in *Writing the Politics of Difference*, SILVERMAN, Hugh J (ed), 31-41. Albany, SUNY Pr, 1991.

DONOUGHO, Martin. "A Reply to Edward Halper's "Hegel and the Problem of the Differentia"" in *Essays on Hegel's Logic*, DI GIOVANNI, George (ed), 203-211. Albany, SUNY Pr, 1990.

This reply seeks to clarify what Halper might mean by some of his claims, in regard to Aristotle, Kant, then Hegel. The Aristotelian problem seems to be the ontological status of the differentia, or how the categories differentiate. Halper interprets Kant as ignoring this problem; but then it is hard to see what Kant is doing here. As for Hegel, although he links his own theory of conceptual self-differentiation with Aristotle, the link is obscure. I briefly examine how 'difference' enters at the beginning of the *Logic*, in the section on '*Etwas*'.

DOODY, John A. Radical Hermeneutics, Critical Theory, and the Political. Int Phil Quart, 31(3), 329-341, S 91.

This essay reviews the work of John D Caputo, "Radical Hermeneutics", raising the question of whether politics, in the sense intended by Jürgen Habermas, can be defended. It is argued that, contrary to Caputo's own claims for the deconstructive spirit of radical hermeneutics, this position is more likely to result in the illusions of abstract theory that Habermas' universalist approach to politics. A convergence of these two contemporary approaches to the political is then suggested, one which is more in keeping with Habermas' project.

DOOLEY, Dolores. Medical Ethics in Ireland: A Decade of Change. Hastings Center Rep, 21(1), 18-21, Ja-F 91.

This article explains the central issues in medical ethics which were publicly debated in Ireland during the 1980s. Debates concentrated on foetal rights, rights of access to abortion information, clinical trials legislation and increased medical litigation. The country's dominant ethical framework of the Catholic Church seemed unable to accommodate the moral disagreements that emerged during this decade. At the same time, medical litigation increased as one sign of a new challenge to the predominant paternalistic model of medical practice in Ireland. This article concludes that the 1980s started a search for a less denominational discourse to negotiate the cultural diversity in the Republic.

DORAN, Katheryn and THROOP, William. Putnam's Realism and Relativity: An Uneasy Balance. Erkenntnis, 34(3), 347-356, My 91.

Recently, Hilary Putnam has attempted to achieve a delicate balance between relativism and metaphysical realism. Many of Putnam's critics claim that he has

AUTHOR INDEX WITH ABSTRACTS 431 DOUBLE, Richard

either lost his balance or that he is left with an incoherent mixture of relativism and realism. We argue that there is a natural way of avoiding the apparent incoherences and sustaining the balancing act, if one acknowledges that the relativist claims are made from a detached perspective which serves very different purposes than the agent's perspective within which Putnam emphasizes his commonsense realism.

DORBOLO, Jon and BIRSCH, Douglas. Working with Wittgenstein's Builders. Phil Invest, 13(4), 338-349, O 90.

DORDEVIC, Radomir. Boskovic's Ideas on the Nature of Cognition Process (in Yugoslavian). Filozof Istraz, 32-33(5-6), 1495-1500, 1989.

The paper points out that Ruder Boskovic dealt with the problems of various sciences and at the same time tried to create a corresponding synthetic vision of the world in general; he tried to investigate "the last foundations of everything that exists" which has always been the characteristic of great thinkers, philosophers. The author, however, believes that there are numerous problems where the essence and sense of Boskovic's philosophical ideas attempt to be established. (edited)

DÖRFLINGER, Bernd. Zur Erkenntnistheorie des Ästhetischen: Schopenhauers Beziehung zu Kant. Schopenhauer Jahr, 71, 68-77, 1990.

DORION, Louis-André. Le statut de l'argument dialectiques d'après *Réf soph* 11, 172a9-15. Dialogue (Canada), 29(1), 95-110, 1990.

DORION, Louis-André. La subversion de l'"elenchos" juridique dans l'"Apologie de Socrate". Rev Phil Louvain, 88(79), 311-344, O 90.

It is generally accepted that the origin of dialectic refutation stems from the judicial practice of the *elenchus*. However, close examination of the corpus of Attic orators (Antiphon, Lysias, etc.) reveals that the *elenchus*, as practised before the courts, consisted of evidence which was primarily based on the testimony of witnesses or on probable causes. The judicial *elenchus* thus appears foreign to the *erotesis*, the legal procedure by which the accuser and the accused could cross-examine one another. In his *Apology of Socrates*, the account of a trial, Plato totally ignores traditional means of presenting evidence and the *erotesis* thus becomes the new basis for dialectic refutation (e.g., the cross-examination of Meletus by Socrates). Uniting the judicial procedures of the *elenchus* and the *erotesis* in this manner, Plato specifically inaugurates the dialectic practice of refutation.

DORN, Georg J W (ed) and WEINGARTNER, Paul (ed). *Studies on Mario Bunge's "Treatise"*. Amsterdam, Rodopi, 1990.

The studies in this volume discuss in detail Bunge's great attempt to combine specialised philosophical disciplines in a synthesis within the eight volumes of his *Treatise on Basic Philosophy*. The book contains 32 articles and Bunge's 32 replies to them, a short autobiography of Mario Bunge and a bibliography of his publications. The topics which have been dealt with mainly are Bunge's semantical realism, his systemic ontology, his concept of emergent evolution, his epistemological realism, his ethics, and—most prominently—his philosophy of science and technology. (edited)

DORN, Georg (ed) and MARCUS, Ruth Barcan (ed) and WEINGARTNER, Paul (ed). *Logic, Methodology and Philosophy of Science, VII*. Amsterdam, North-Holland, 1986.

Proceedings of the invited papers of the Seventh International Congress of Logic, Methodology and Philosophy of Science, held in Salzburg, Austria in 1983. Three papers in each of the following categories were delivered: Proof Theory and Foundations of Mathematics, Model Theory and its Applications, Recursion Theory and Theory of Computation, Axiomatic Set Theory, Philosophical Logic, Methodology of Science, Foundations of Probability and Induction, Foundations and Philosophy of the Physical Sciences, Foundations and Philosophy of Biology, Foundations and Philosophy of Psychology, Foundations and Philosophy of the Social Sciences, Foundations and Philosophy of Linguistics.

DORSCHEL, Andreas. Cultural Evolution, Biology and Language: Empirical and Rational Criteria of Selection (in German). Deut Z Phil, 38(10), 984-992, 1990.

Das Konzept einer darwinistisch ansetzenden funktiionalen Erklärung und das einer rationalen Nachkonstruktion der Kulturevolution werden miteinander konfrontiert. Dabei wird eine Antwort auf die Frage versucht, wie sich unter Bedingungen, die im Selektionskriterium der Gesamtfitness ("inclusive fitness") theoretisch adäquat erfasst werden können, rationale, auf fitness irreduzible Selektionskriterien für Handlungen und Aussagen, nämlich: Wahrheit und normative Richtigkeit, herausbilden können.

DORSEY, Gray L. *Jurisculture, Volume I: Greece and Rome*. New Brunswick, Transaction Books, 1989.

Jurisculture traces the influences of a prevailing view of reality upon the organization and regulation of society. This volume covers the ancient Greek view that gods control events and the organization of society under the authority of patriarchs believed to be influential with the gods, and the complete reorganization of Roman society and law under the influence of the ideas of the pre-Socratics, Plato, and the Stoics of a rational universe and rational human beings.

DORTER, Kenneth. Levels of Knowledge in the *Theaetetus*. Rev Metaph, 44(2), 343-373, D 90.

The *Theaetetus*'s examination of knowledge is not merely a series of false starts and failures, but a progression through different levels of knowledge, which reflects that of the Divided Line. It passes from perceptual to interpretive to mathematical knowledge, before foundering in a discussion which constantly evokes (but never invokes) the theory of forms and doctrine of recollection. This leads us toward the suggestions made indirectly by the opening drama, and directly by Socrates' digression, that the pursuit of wisdom is not ultimately satisfied even by adequate definitions, but eventually entails a change from one kind of life to another, like the "turning around of the soul" in the allegory of the Cave.

DORTER, Kenneth. "The Modern Spirit and the Paradox of Humanism" in *The Question of Humanism: Challenges and Possibilities*, GOICOECHEA, David (ed), 273-294. Buffalo, Prometheus, 1991.

The humanistic demand for certainty, with which Descartes ushered in the modern period, progressively "humanized" metaphysical thinking. In Plato, Aristotle, and Plotinus the ontological difference between Being and beings was independent of thinking. But after Descartes it became the difference between the world as perceived and as it is in itself (Spinoza, Leibniz): no longer is there an ontological difference outside consciousness. After Kant's rejection of knowledge of the in-itself, metaphysics was further humanized: not only the ontological difference, but Being itself was inseparable from thinking (Hegel, Heidegger). Today the question of Being is largely displaced by humanistic questions. The impetus for this progressive displacement of the ontological by the humanistic is explored in terms of technology, will, and individualism.

DOS SANTOS, Leonel Ribeiro. "Hobbes e as metáforas do Estado" in *Dinâmica do Pensar: Homenagem a Oswaldo Market*, FAC LETRAS UNIV LISBOA (ed), 217-242. Lisboa, Fac Letras U Lisboa, 1991.

Le propos de cet essai est d'analyser certains motifs métaphoriques et rhétoriques qui structurent et envellopent la pensée politique de Hobbes, à savoir, l'allégorie du Grand Corps artificiel et mécanique, les symboles thériomorphes et l'usage ironique de l'Écriture au service de la justification du pouvoir absolu. D'emblée, ce fonctionnement rhétorique et métaphorique du discours de Hobbes semble ne s'accorder point avec une philosophie qui, en toute conviction et sévérité, a instruit, au niveau de la théorie de la science et du langage, le procès de la rhétorique et de la métaphore. Néanmoins on essaie de surmonter cette contradiction et de comprendre une telle pratique discursive sur le fonds d'une réinterprétation des déclarations du philosophe anglais concernant la rhétorique et la métaphore et dans le cadre de l'anthropologie et psychologie hobbésiennes.

DOSEN, Kosta. Logical Constants as Punctuation Marks. Notre Dame J Form Log, 30(3), 362-381, Sum 89.

This paper presents a proof-theoretical approach to the question "What is a logical constant?" This approach starts with the assumption that logic is the science of formal deductions, and that basic formal deductions are structural deductions, i.e., deductions independent of any constant of the language to which the premises and conclusions belong. Logical constants, on which the remaining formal deductions are dependent, may be said to serve as "punctuation marks" for some structural features of deductions; this punctuation function, exhibited in equivalences which amount to analyses of logical constants, is taken as a criterion for being a logical constant. The paper presents an account of philosophical analysis which covers the proposed analyses of logical constants. Some related assumptions concerning logic are also considered. In particular, since a logical system is completely determined by its structural deductions, alternative logical systems arise by changing structural deductions while having constants with the same punctuation function. Some other approaches to the question "What is a logical constant?," grammatical, model-theoretical, and proof-theoretical, are briefly considered.

DOSSA, Shiraz. Hannah Arendt's Political Theory: Ethics and Enemies. Hist Euro Ideas, 13(4), 385-398, 1991.

DOTTERER, Donald W. James and Bowne on the Philosophy of Religious Experience. Personalist Forum, 6(2), 123-141, Fall 90.

DOUARD, John W. Chronic Illness and the Temporal Structure of Human Life. Bus Prof Ethics J, 9(3-4), 161-171, Fall-Wint 90.

DOUARD, John. Ethics, AIDS, and Community Responsibility. Theor Med, 11(3), 213-226, S 90.

In the discussion of the responsibilities of society to the HIV infected and uninfected, a serious question seems to have been left out of the picture: To what extent are people who are not infected, have no special relationship to the infected and have no *professional* responsibilities for the care of AIDS patients under an obligation to come to the aid of people with the HIV? In this paper, I shall examine our responsibilities, as members of society, for the welfare of others to whom we may or may not have a special relationship. I shall argue that those responsibilities flow from the conditions that structure our transactions with others; conditions that make such transactions possible.

DOUBLE, Richard. Determinism and the Experience of Freedom. Pac Phil Quart, 72(1), 1-8, Mr 91.

Determinism is often thought to be embarrassed by what is held to be our ineluctable, introspectively available, and behaviorally manifested belief that we enjoy libertarian-style, two-way free will. In this paper I argue that such a belief in libertarian freedom is not inescapable, either epistemically or psychologically. Our first-person feeling about freedom psychologically prompts a belief in libertarian freedom only if we make an error that determinists need not make. So, determinists should concede neither that we all believe in libertarian freedom, nor that we should. Along the way I provide a general formula for when our "experiential beliefs" should not be counted as actually held beliefs.

DOUBLE, Richard. *The Non-Reality of Free Will*. New York, Oxford Univ Pr, 1991.

This book has two parts. In the first, an attempt is made to construct the most reasonable compatibilistic account of *free will*, a development of the hierarchical view of Harry Frankfurt. In the second, that compatibilist view and libertarian theories in general are found to be unacceptable. The reason both types of theories fail is held to be because (1) *free will* and *moral responsibility* are conflicting paradigm concepts that logically cannot denote logically nonconflicting classes of entities, and (2) these terms are also irretrievably value-laden, and, on the moral nonrealism argument that is developed, cannot denote classes of entities outside the mind. Thus, in the deep sense in which philosophers and common sense care most about, we can be neither free nor unfree, nor do we enjoy responsibility nor are we debarred from it.

DOUBT, Keith. A Theoretical Note on Simmel's Concept of Acquaintance. J Theor Soc Behav, 20(3), 263-276, S 90.

This paper discusses the problem of knowing the other in social interaction and sociological inquiry, in particular in how this matter is depicted through Georg Simmel's concept of acquaintance. Acquaintance is a knowledge of that aspect of another that is turned toward others and to the world; it is not necessarily a knowledge of what is intrinsically essential to another. The epistemological nature of discretion, gossip, familiarity, and self-knowledge are formulated in light of this concept. The problems of hermeneutics are related directly to issues of social understanding in everyday life.

DOUGHERTY, Charles J. The Costs of Commercial Medicine. Theor Med, 11(4), 275-286, D 90.

The purpose of this paper is to review the rising influence of commercialism in American medicine and to examine some of the consequences of this trend. Increased competition subverts physician collegiality, draws hospitals into for-profit ownership and behavior, and leads clinical investigators into secrecy and possibly into bias and abuse. Medicine faces a deprofessionalization evidenced in loss of control over the clinical setting and over self-regulation. Health care becomes a commodity relying on cultivation of desires instead of satisfaction of needs, even as many basic needs go unmet. Patients become consumers empowered with lawsuits and the connection of medicine to the relief of suffering is attenuated. Medical encounters are increasingly impersonal, dominated by specialization, technology, and bureaucracy. Patients are losing their physician-advocates to new conflicts of interests, physicians are losing their impulse to charity, and trust in the doctor-patient relationship and in medicine generally is eroding.

DOUGHERTY, Charles J. "The Moral Case for National Health Insurance" in *Biomedical Ethics Reviews, 1990*, HUMBER, James M (ed), 29-60. Clifton, Humana Pr, 1991.

Utilitarian, contractarian, and egalitarian arguments are put forward on behalf of national health insurance (NHI), that is, an arrangement to provide universal coverage for basic health care operated at least in part by the federal government. NHI will maximize the number of lives lived well, make the least well-off lives better, and express our common human dignity. Libertarian and practical arguments against NHI are considered and rejected. NHI will not destroy the best features of American medicine nor is it a task beyond the ability of government. Concluding remarks about feelings, attitudes, and national character are offered.

DOUGLASS, R Bruce (ed) and MARA, Gerald M (ed) and RICHARDSON, Henry S (ed). *Liberalism and the Good*. New York, Routledge, 1990.

DOUGLASS, R Bruce and MARA, Gerald M. "The Search for a Defensible Good: The Emerging Dilemma of Liberalism" in *Liberalism and the Good*, DOUGLASS, R Bruce (ed), 253-280. New York, Routledge, 1990.

DOVOLICH, Claudia. Un confronto sempre attuale: Leggendo—A Lambertino, Psicoanalisi e morale in Freud. Aquinas, 34(1), 167-177, Ja-Ap 91.

DOWDEN, Bradley H. A Linear Continuum of Time. Phil Math, 6(1), 53-64, 1991.

In the basic theories of science, time is treated as a real-valued variable, which suggests that physical time has the topological structure of a linear continuum. The claim that time does have this structure is defended against a variety of objections. Typical objections are that black holes are rips in space-time, that a unification of quantum mechanics and relativity require discontinuity in time, that time is merely assumed continuous because no physical experiment has so far indicated otherwise, and that there are alternative systems of mathematics for science which do not treat time as a real-valued variable.

DOWER, Nigel. El desarrollo como proceso: una investigación filosófica. Rev Filosof (Costa Rica), 27(66), 281-292, D 89.

This paper explores the relationship between development as a present process and development as a future state of societies being developed, and the ways in which a conception of the latter enters into the justification of the former. Does it provide a *goal* to which the present process is directed, or rather a *criterion* for assessing present activity? Arguably both aspects are significant to justification, whatever particular conceptions of genuine development are adopted.

DOWER, Nigel. "World Poverty" in *A Companion to Ethics*, SINGER, Peter (ed), 273-283. Cambridge, Blackwell, 1991.

This chapter examines different responses to the question: Ought the rich in the North to help the very poor in the South? I argue for a moderate but significant duty of caring in response to the evils of extreme poverty; first by rejecting the claims that aid does not help, that we have only societal and not trans-national duties of caring, and that we have no duty of general caring; and second, by rejecting the claim at the other extreme that we have a duty to care as much as we can.

DOWLER, E W. Two Conservative Views of Nationality and Personality: A A Grigor'ev and K N Leont'ev. Stud Soviet Tho, 41(1), 19-32, Ja 91.

DOWNES, Stephen M. Herbert Simon's Computational Models of Scientific Discovery. Proc Phil Sci Ass, 1, 97-108, 1990.

This paper is a critical evaluation of Herbert Simon's work on scientific discovery. I argue that Simon's approach, while instructive to philosophers of science, is lacking in several respects. Simon fails to adequately support his claims that certain psychological mechanisms are responsible for scientific discovery, and he ignores crucial social, rather than purely psychological, aspects of the discovery process.

DOWNEY, R G and CHONG, C T. Minimal Degrees Recursive in 1-Generic Degrees. Annals Pure Applied Log, 48(3), 215-225, Ag 90.

DOWNEY, Rod. Correction to "Undecidability of $L(F_\infty)$ and Other Lattices of R.E. Substructures" (Corrigendum). Annals Pure Applied Log, 48(3), 299-301, Ag 90.

The proof of the main result is corrected.

DOWNEY, Rod. Lattice Nonembeddings and Initial Segments of the Recursively Enumerable Degrees. Annals Pure Applied Log, 49(2), 97-119, O 90.

It is shown that for any r.e. degree a there is a nonzero r.e. degree b below a such that no lattice with a "critical triple" can be embedded below a. This includes, for instance, the lattice 1-3-1, and says initial segments of the r.e. degrees "look rather distributive."

DOWNIE, R S. Professions and Professionalism. J Phil Educ, 24(2), 147-159, Wint 90.

In this paper I shall try to identify the essential nature of professions. Sociologists are interested in the characteristics which professions in fact display, but my philosophical concern, while it overlaps with and draws from sociological analyses, is directed more towards the evaluative question of what enables professions to perform a unique and socially valuable function, distinct from business or commerce. The examination will help to determine whether some occupations, such as accountancy or the civil service, do perform this socially important function. Finally I shall examine teaching in the light of the criteria.

DOYLE, John P. "Extrinsic Cognoscibility": A Seventeenth Century Supertranscendental Notion. Mod Sch, 68(1), 57-80, N 90.

This essay explores the area of intentionality in late scholasticism. For Suarez the subject of metaphysics is "real being" which is transcendental but exclusive of beings of reason. After Suarez, the Calvinist Clemens Timpler says that the subject of metaphysics is "the intelligible," which encompasses both real and unreal, even impossible, beings. Also for 17th century Jesuit logicians what seems common to real beings and beings of reason, including impossible objects, is "cognoscibility." More precisely, this is "extrinsic cognoscibility," which is labeled "supertranscendental." In Timpler and the Jesuits I see anticipations of Meinong's *Gegenstandstheorie*.

DOYLE, Timothy. The Pot at the End of the Rainbow: Political Myth and the Ecological Crisis. Phil Soc Act, 16(4), 47-61, O-D 90.

A constant theme of discussion which attempts to overcome the environmental crisis on this planet revolves around the necessity for both changes to the structure of political processes and individual or group attitudes. Both of these are important. Attitudes and politics will not change, however, if the bedrock of unassailable truths—myths—remains unquestioned. It is this bedrock of ideas which constantly legitimates both social and political structures and compatible attitudes, values and goals. In short, myth is the basis for ideology and political organisation.

DRAGO, Antonino and MANNO, Salvatore D. The Fundamental Hypotheses of Mechanics in Lazare N M Carnot's Thought (in Italian). Epistemologia, 12(2), 305-330, Jl-D 89.

Though Lazare Carnot's mechanics is universally recognized as the starting point of technical physics, it received rare attention in the past. Recent studies attributed to it more merits than in the past. It is the first formulation of mechanics which is entirely experimental, even in the principles. Moreover, it introduced many important novelties, among which the work concept and the mechanical energy conservation (which is widely employed in several theorems). Therefore today this theory has to be recognized as a formulation of a high theoretical value. The present paper examines its principles, which Carnot presented in the last book on mechanics and names "hypotheses." (edited)

DRAKE, William E. Response to the Presidential Address: Willer's "Ethics in Educational Policy Analysis". Phil Stud Educ, /, 12-17, 1986.

DRAPER, Paul. Evil and the Proper Basicality of Belief in God. Faith Phil, 8(2), 135-147, Ap 91.

Alvin Plantinga claims that certain beliefs entailing God's existence can be properly basic. He uses this claim to suggest two distinct replies to evidential arguments from evil against theism. In "Reason and Belief in God" he offers what he calls his "highroad" reply, and in a more recent article he suggests what I call his "modest" reply. First I show that Plantinga's highroad reply fails, because it relies on a faulty analysis of probability on total evidence. Then I reformulate his modest reply so that is applies specifically to David Hume's evidential argument from evil. And finally, I show that a certain "existential" problem of evil undermines Plantinga's modest reply to Hume's argument.

DRAPER, Paul. Hume's Reproduction Parody of the Design Argument. Hist Phil Quart, 8(2), 135-148, Ap 91.

In Part VII of David Hume's *Dialogues Concerning Natural Religion*, Philo presents an argument for the conclusion that, like plants and animals, the universe was brought into existence by reproduction. The purpose of this argument is to parody the design argument offered by Cleanthes. I begin by showing how Philo's analysis of this parody is based on Hume's inductive logic as explained in the *Treatise*. Then I argue that this analysis is flawed. And finally, I present my own analysis of the parody. I conclude that the parody successfully points to a serious defect in Cleanthes's design argument.

DRAVID, N S. Tolerance in Indian Culture and Its Philosophical Basis. J Indian Counc Phil Res, 5(2), 151-157, Ja-Ap 88.

DREBEN, Burton. "Quine" in *Perspectives on Quine*, BARRETT, Robert (ed), 81-95. Cambridge, Blackwell, 1990.

DREBEN, Burton and FLOYD, Juliet. Tautology: How Not to Use a Word. Synthese, 87(1), 23-49, Ap 91.

We discuss the character and philosophical significance of Wittgenstein's use of "tautology" in the *Tractatus*, a use which was not clear. Wittgenstein justified or shifted the term from rhetoric to logic, and hence shaped (misshaped?) debates concerning the nature and scope of logic from the time of the Vienna Circle onward. We discuss relevant historical uses of "tautology" in philosophy from Leibniz, Kant, Hegel, Bradley, Mauthner and the early Moore and Russell, and document Russell's later (1918) jump to the verbiage of "tautology", as well as C I Lewis's and Ramsey's attempts to wrest a philosophical lesson from the *Tractatus*'s new use.

DREBUSHENKO, David and ADAMS, Fred and FULLER, Gary and STECKER, Robert. Narrow Content: Fodor's Folly. Mind Lang, 5(3), 213-229, Autumn 90.

For ten years Fodor and other cognitive scientists presumed that we need narrow content (content essentially independent of one's environment) to get around Twin-Earth examples and to do psychology. We show why broad content psychology (using content essentially dependent upon one's environment) is *not really challenged* by Twin-Earth examples, despite appearances. We explain (1) why narrow content is *not content*, and why (2) even if we concoct a notion of content* for narrow content, it still will be *unable to explain* intentional behavior. Thus, we herald the demise of narrow content: one cannot use it and does not need it.

DREES, W B. "Theology and Cosmology Beyond the Big Bang Theory" in *Science and Religion: One World-Changing Perspectives on Reality*, FENNEMA, Jan (ed), 99-129. Norwell, Kluwer, 1990.

The author discusses various approaches to science-and-religion, opting for a constructive form of consonance. The bulk of the paper discusses theology in the context of the Big Bang theory and of various quantum cosmologies, with special emphasis on Hawking's approach. Religious arguments based upon the apparent beginning of the Universe, its contingency and its (anthropic) order are shown to fail, as do arguments based upon the apparent completeness of complete theories. The possibility of two descriptions, from within time and from a timeless perspective, offers interesting theological possibilities.

DREES, Willem B. *Beyond the Big Bang: Quantum Cosmologies and God*. La Salle, Open Court, 1990.

Religious use and abuse of contemporary cosmological theories, the Big Bang theory and recent quantum cosmologies like the one by Stephen Hawking, are discussed in detail. Among the topics considered are 'the beginning', design arguments (anthropic principles), complete theories, the nature of time and perspectives for the far future. The author is critical of dominant 'critical realist' perspectives in Anglo-Saxon science-and-religion, arguing for 'constructive consonance' instead; 'constructive' covering both epistemological and ethical aspects. The book thus combines a substantial discussion of cosmology and theology with fundamental reflections on the nature of theology in relation to science.

DREES, Wim. Philosophical Elements in Penrose's and Hawking's Research in Contemporary Cosmology. Phil Sci (Tucson), 4, 13-46, 1990.

This article aims at elucidating the philosophical elements in two contemporary (post 1975) research programs in theoretical cosmology. The programs of R Penrose and S W Hawking differ with respect to their view of the basic structures behind space and time, the interpretation of quantum physics, the arrow of time, and the specialness of our Universe. The differences show up both in the content of their work and in the arguments used to defend their programs. The present article shows that these differences are partly of a philosophical (mainly metaphysical) nature, probably the "dangerous but fascinating territory" mentioned by Penrose. A comparison of two different programs makes it easier to see some of the implicit or explicit decisions involved. (edited)

DREHER, John Paul. The Driving Ratio in Plato's Divided Line. Ancient Phil, 10(2), 159-172, Fall 90.

Plato's figure of the divided line zestfully taps into a main current of 5th and 4th century Greek geometry at the same time that it models his view that any cognitive success achieved by the mind intensifies the passion for further inquiry. Whenever we learn that what we have been looking at is a shadow, and come to identify the object which cast the shadow, we are driven to wonder whether that object itself could in its turn be the shadow of something yet more real.

DREIER, Ralf and ALEXY, Robert. The Concept of Jurisprudence. Ratio Juris, 3(1), 1-13, Mr 90.

The first part of this article contains (i) considerations as to the relationship between jurisprudence and legal dogmatics, legal philosophy, and sociology of law; (ii) considerations about the status of jurisprudence both as a meta- and an object-theory. These lead to the suggestion that jurisprudence should be defined as a general juristic theory of law and legal science. In the second part, the character and elements of this definition are explained systematically. The article's main thesis is that jurisprudence is not distinguished from legal philosophy and sociology of law by its subject or its method, but by the specifically juristic research aspect or perspective it is based upon.

DRESCHER, Johannes. *Glück und Lebenssinn: Eine religionsphilosophische Untersuchung*. Freiburg, Alber, 1991.

"What should I do for my life to have a meaning?" This basic existential question explored by the book in three respects. First, perfect happiness is expounded as the meaning-complex which guides action. Secondly, as far as the question is concerned, whether this happiness is attainable, hope is shown to be the path of access to the possibility of happiness, but all interpretations claiming to show that it is a state which can be produced are shown to be untenable. This demonstrates hope to be a religious concept. Lastly, the consequences for the actor are discussed, with the result that "morality" and "living in hope" are revealed as identical concepts. From this emerges the religious dimension of morality.

DRETSKE, Fred. *Explaining Behavior: Reasons in a World of Causes*. Cambridge, MIT Pr, 1988.

Commonsense psychology is committed to the idea that reasons held explain behavior. To vindicate this idea, it is not enough that reasons, internal states with content, cause behavior. Their content—*what* is believed and *what* is desired—must also figure in the explanation of why this behavior occurs. It is shown that this result can be achieved by analyzing representation in informational terms (what information a structure has acquired the function of carrying) and identifying behavior, not with the bodily movements that beliefs and desires cause, but with the process in which they cause them.

DRETSKE, Fred. How Beliefs Explain: Reply to Baker. Phil Stud, 63(1), 113-117, Jl 91.

Lynne Baker argues that my account of the way beliefs explain behavior is circular. It is circular, she says, because the behavior beliefs are called upon to explain precisely the behavior from which beliefs acquire their content. If beliefs acquire a content by being recruited to cause B, they cannot, later, be called upon to explain B by appeal to this content. I show, in reply, that the explanatory task involved in the content-acquisition process is not the explanatory task that beliefs are called upon to perform once they have acquired a content. The account is not, therefore, circular.

DRETSKE, Fred. "Reasons and Causes" in *Philosophical Perspectives, 3: Philosophy of Mind and Action Theory, 1989*, TOMBERLIN, James E (ed), 1-15. Atascadero, Ridgeview, 1989.

For the purposes of making reasons explanatorily relevant to behavior, it is not enough to think of them, following Davidson, as causes of behavior. Their content or meaning—what it is that is believed and desired—must be a causally relevant property. If it isn't, the mental, qua mental, is epiphenomenal. It is argued that the kind of relational, informational properties that might plausibly be taken to underlie content can acquire an explanatory role in learning. Internal indicators, carriers of information, are, during concept learning, recruited to play causal roles in the production of output. Thus does meaning become explanatorily relevant to behavior.

DRETSKE, Frederick. "Does Meaning Matter?" in *Information, Semantics and Epistemology*, VILLANUEVA, Enrique (ed), 1-4. Cambridge, Blackwell, 1990.

In order to avoid epiphenomenalism, modern materialists, at least those who are realists about the mind, must find an explanatory role for intentional properties, those that underlie the meaning or content of cognitive states. A way is sketched to do this, a way of making what we think and desire relevant to what we do. By thinking of behavior as a causal process culminating in bodily movement, the extrinsic properties determining content can be made causally relevant, not to the bodily movements, but to the processes (= behaviors) having such movements as their product.

DREYFUS, Hubert L. *Being-in-the-World: A Commentary on Heidegger's "Being and Time", Division 1*. Cambridge, MIT Pr, 1991.

This is a guide to one of the most influential philosophical works of this century: Division I of Part One of *Being and Time*, where Martin Heidegger works out an original and powerful account of being-in-the-world which he then uses to ground a profound critique of traditional ontology and epistemology. My commentary opens the way for a new appreciation of this difficult philosopher, revealing a rigorous and illuminating vocabulary that is indispensable for talking about the phenomenon of world.

DREYFUS, Hubert L. Foucault et la psychothérapie. Rev Int Phil, 44(173), 209-230, 1990.

DROIXHE, Daniel. "Le voyage de 'Schreiten': Leibniz et les débuts du comparatisme finno-ougrien" in *Leibniz, Humboldt, and the Origins of Comparativism*, DE MAURO, Tullio (ed), 3-29. Philadelphia, John Benjamins, 1990.

The Leibniz' correspondence extrait allows to see how he himself worked out the search for the Finno-Ugrian cradle in the South-Urals area. The constitution of the family is considered through the adjunction of Estonian (which seems to be, in the generic sense, a synonym for 'Finn') or Permian. What was, for Leibniz, the place of the Finno-Ugrian family in the reconstruction of a general proto-language? This is one of the questions broached in the last part, while the '*schreiten* topic' reappears to some extent in the long historical walk of the Scythian-Indo-Europeans. (edited)

DROST, Mark P. Aristotle and Nietzsche on Art as Imitation of Nature. Dialogos, 26(58), 47-62, Jl 91.

The classical concept of *art as imitation of nature* refers both to the aesthetic *representation* of a form of nature through an image (or some other artifactitious representation), and to the *process* of art which is an imitation of the creative process of nature. The concept is central to Aristotle's and Nietzsche's theories of art. These theories are worth comparing because each tells us that *art is the complement of nature*; since each theory is founded upon a different conception of nature, the theories of art are consequently different. Whereas Aristotle has a naturalistic conception of art, Nietzsche has an artistic conception of nature. I outline each theory and compare them with a view to understanding the complementary nature of artistic imitation in general.

DRUCKER, György. Marx, Engels and Max Weber on Eastern Societies—With a Special Respect to China (in Hungarian). Magyar Filozof Szemle, 5-6, 425-440, 1990.

One of the omissions committed by Marxism in the Stalin era was that they did not examine the special historical development of Eastern societies. Marx's ideas on the East can be detected in the methodological passages of his preparatory studies to the *Capital*, in the relevant passages of Volumes I and II and in his publicistic work. Weber's views on the subject can be found in his studies on the sociology of state, religion and economy. (edited)

DRYDEN, Richard. Birth Defects: Traditional Beliefs Challenged by Scientific Explanations. Bioethics, 4(4), 330-339, O 90.

In Papua New Guinea, traditional beliefs about health and sickness are being challenged by scientific medical explanations. In the context of birth defects, the traditional explanations include a substantial 'supernatural' component in addition to environmental and hereditary factors. Birth of an abnormal baby was commonly interpreted as a form of punishment for overstepping traditional constraints on social behaviour, particularly by the mother. It is proposed that traditional explanations form part of a harmonious world view that structures everyday community life, and that care should be taken by medical practitioners when introducing scientific explanations to avoid unnecessary erosion of social harmony.

DU TOIT, A B. Discourses on Political Violence: The Problem of Coherence. S Afr J Phil, 9(4), 191-213, N 90.

Taking Robert Paul Wolff's seminal article arguing for the fundamental incoherence of the concept of violence as a point of departure, the scope of the argument is broadened to that of the coherence of different discourses on political violence. It is shown how both the liberal discourse on political violence—in political contexts—as well as positivist discourses on political violence—in academic contexts—involve different construals of such basic categories as that of legitimacy, rationality and identity. A coherent discourse is defined as one that would enable us to apply generally well-founded criteria for distinguishing legitimate from illegitimate violence in internally consistent ways to a variety of relevant cases, and to do so in ways which provide appropriate justifications and allow critical questioning. (edited)

DU TOIT, André. Legitimate Anachronism as a Problem for Intellectual History and for Philosophy. S Afr J Phil, 10(3), 87-95, Ag 91.

The author investigates legitimate anachronism as a specific instance of the general problem of the relation of philosophy to the history of thought. Starting from Febvre's identification of anachronism, anachronism proper is distinguished from the 'untimely' nature of dissident, revolutionary or seminal thought. As a historiographical category it is next distinguished from ordinary historical errors, contextual errors, inferential errors as well as from projective errors. It is argued that when both the history of thought, as the object of study, as well as the disciplines of philosophy and intellectual history themselves are understood as discursive practices it becomes possible to see in what sense anachronism may be legitimate as well as necessary. (edited)

DUBCEK, Alexander A. Humanity, Morality, and Liberty. Free Inq, 11(1), 29, 60, Wint 90-91.

DUBIEL, Helmut. Beyond Mourning and Melancholia on the Left. Praxis Int, 10(3-4), 241-249, O 90-Ja 91.

DUBOSE, Derrick Albert. The Equivalence of Determinacy and Iterated Sharps. J Sym Log, 55(2), 502-525, Je 90.

DUBROVSKY, Bernardo. "A Comment on Three Topics in Volume 7 of the *Treatise*: Teleology, the Mind-Body Problem, and Health and Disease" in *Studies on Mario Bunge's "Treatise"*, WEINGARTNER, Paul (ed), 193-204. Amsterdam, Rodopi, 1990.

Reflexive commentaries on the ideas of Mario Bunge. Emphasis is made on the pitfalls of the use of teleological ideas in biology. Examples are discussed. The need for a consistent interdisciplinary approach for the mind-body problem is upheld. The monist materialist position is defended. The idea of discontinuity between health and disease is presented.

DUBSKY, Ivan. Clocks and Time (in Czechoslovakian). Filozof Cas, 38(3), 241-258, 1990.

This study aspires to be a contribution to phenomenological chronology rather than to its component, namely chronometry. Through measurement we strive to approach a given because that which is real is measurable (Max Planck). Of decisive importance for further contemplation was Aristotle's identification of "being in time" with "being in number": time is calculable and hence measurable. The problem of time has later been reduced in modern science to the issues of chronometry. The second part of this article, therefore, discusses the question of chronometry, ensuing from the "natural" clock of nature and the world and switching over to the change which occurred with the quantification of time and together with instrumentalization, the invention of the clock, its various shapes, their ingenuities and imperfections. (edited)

DUBUCS, J. Embedded Probabilities. Theor Decis, 30(3), 279-284, My 91.

The paper is a discussion review of John M. Vickers, *Chance and Structure*, Clarendon Press, Oxford (1988). The increasing interest for second and higher-order probabilities is explained by reference to the rise of cognitive psychology. The analogy between probability and quantification is discussed and opposed to the analogy between probability and modality.

DUCHARME, Howard. The Vatican's Dilemma: On the Morality of IVF and the Incarnation. Bioethics, 5(1), 57-66, Ja 91.

The Vatican's position on in vitro fertilization (IVG), found in the *Instruction on Bioethics* (1987), is that all IVF is immoral, for it violates the normative procreative act of married spouses. The dilemma created is, if all instances of IVF are immoral, then God's act in the Incarnation (granting the traditional doctrine) must also have been immoral. Conversely, if God's act in the Incarnation was not immoral, then at least some cases of human IVF are not immoral either. A resolution is offered. Two diagrams are employed.

DUCHESNEAU, François. "Leibniz and the Philosophical Analysis of Science" in *Logic, Methodology and Philosophy of Science, VIII*, FENSTAD, J E (ed), 609-624. New York, Elsevier Science, 1989.

Leibnizian analysis reflects the aim of a combinative expression for both phenomena and substances. Leibniz construed the analytical method as a tool for systematic hypothesis framing, as a means of achieving demonstrations whenever infiniteness prevails in the nexus of terms that would express the order of nature.

DUDMAN, V H. Grammar, Semantics and Conditionals. Analysis, 50(4), 214-224, O 90.

Any semantic theory is bound to presume some structure in the messages it analyses, and the success of the theory depends on getting this structure right. But discovering this structure is the business of grammar. Therefore grammar is a necessary preliminary to semantics. Semantic theories of conditionals vividly illustrate this. All presume a provably untenable ternary structure: antecedent, operator, consequent. And all can be shown committed as a result to a thoroughly unbelievable set of connections between sentences and their informational burdens. Actually, a conditional has five immediate factors, none of them an antecedent or a consequent.

DUDMAN, V H. Jackson Classifying Conditionals. Analysis, 51(3), 131-136, Je 91.

'If Sly Pete *calls* he *will win*' and 'If Sly Pete *had called* he *would have won*' differ only in tense *t*, respectively present and past. The underlying reasoning always involves lighting upon some state of affairs which (according to the thinker's then "stock of beliefs") is actual at *t*, and presuming that state of affairs to endure as events unfold from *t* until the later time that the judgment is intuitively about. The presuming is inevitably tacit. And the same "stock" can furnish different states of affairs for preservation, enabling different lines of underlying reasoning, with different presumptions and even different *reactions*, some but not all respondents assenting to the same judgment on the basis of the same "stock," in accordance with an observation published by Gibbard in 1981.

DUFF, Barry E. "Event" in Dewey's Philosophy. Educ Theor, 40(4), 463-470, Fall 90.

The paper demonstrates that a particular concept of 'event' is the logically fundamental concept in Dewey's "Experience and Nature" (arguably his central philosophical work) but that it has been overlooked by critics. Dewey's concept is explained and it is shown how his concept of 'object' is developed from it. However, Dewey's concept of event conflates two concepts. The two are distinguished and it is shown that this enables a consistent interpretation of all of the uses of 'event' in the book. It is concluded that any interpretation of this work which does not discuss Dewey's concept of 'event' is inadequate.

DUFF, R A. *Intention, Agency and Criminal Liability: Philosophy of Action and the Criminal Law*. Cambridge, Blackwell, 1990.

The book aims to introduce students of law and of philosophy to some central problems in the philosophy of action, by considering the way in which they are involved in issues concerning criminal liability—in particular in issues concerning *mens rea*. These problems are approached through an examination of various controversial cases in English and in Scots law, and of current controversies in the law. Topics discussed include: intention and intentional action, and the relevance of intention to responsibility; consequentialist and non-consequentialist conceptions of agency; dualism; recklessness; criminal attempts.

DUGRÉ, François. Le rôle de l'imagination dans le mouvement animal et l'action humaine chez Aristotle. Dialogue (Canada), 29(1), 65-78, 1990.

DUHAMEL, André. Justification et justice procédurale. Lekton, 1(2), 39-53, 1991.

Est-il possible de construire une procédure moralement neutre permettant de justifier des principes de justice sociale? J'examine sous cet angle deux tentatives: 1) le principle d'universalisation des jugements moraux (Kant), 2) la théorie de la justice comme équité (Rawls). Ni l'une ni l'autre ne s'affranchissent de tout présupposé moral, et la procédure proposée demeure circulaire. Je conclus que cette circularité est inévitable et constitue une caractéristique positive de la justification en philosophie morale.

DUHAN, Laura. "Feminism and Peace Theory: Women as Nurturers versus Women as Public Citizens" in *In the Interest of Peace: A Spectrum of Philosophical Views*, KLEIN, Kenneth H (ed), 247-257. Wolfeboro, Longwood, 1990.

Women can best contribute to the cause of peace by their role as active public citizens rather than through their role as nurturers. Women are citizens, one of whose roles requires them to nurture others, not nurturers seeking an opportunity to enter the public sphere. Teaching people traits needed for effective parenting will not create a generation of peace activists. Instead, feminists need to emphasize education for citizenship which constitutes both women and men as cooperative, active citizens. The argument draws support from the writings of Wollstonecraft, Arendt, Elshtain, Martin and Dewey and takes shape through philosophical critique of opposing views.

DUHAN, Laura. The Philosopher as Hero. Teach Phil, 13(2), 97-102, Je 90.

Joseph Campbell's analysis of the mythological motif of the hero's journey is applied to philosophy. The greatest philosophers present their ideas in the context of the story of an intellectual journey, using motifs typical of the hero's journey. They set out to meet what is not known and their stories give us suggestions on how to deal with the unknown. The journeys of Socrates, Descartes and Hume are analyzed as examples.

DUMMETT, Michael. "'A Nice Derangement of Epitaphs': Some Comments on Davidson and Hacking" in *Truth and Interpretation: Perspectives on the Philosophy of Donald Davidson*, LE PORE, Ernest (ed), 459-476. Cambridge, Blackwell, 1986.

DUMMETT, Michael. *Frege and Other Philosophers*. New York, Clarendon/Oxford Pr, 1991.

DUMMETT, Michael. *The Logical Basis of Metaphysics*. Cambridge, Harvard Univ Pr, 1991.

AUTHOR INDEX WITH ABSTRACTS 435 DURAN, Jane

DUMMETT, Michael. More about Thoughts. Notre Dame J Form Log, 30(1), 1-19, Wint 89.

DUMMETT, Michael. "The Source of the Concept of Truth" in *Meaning and Method: Essays in Honor of Hilary Putnam*, BOOLOS, George (ed), 1-15. New York, Cambridge Univ Pr, 1990.

DUMMETT, Michael. "Thought and Perception: The Views of Two Philosophical Innovators" in *The Analytic Tradition: Philosophical Quarterly Monographs, Volume 1*, BELL, David (ed), 83-103. Cambridge, Blackwell, 1990.

DUMOUCHEL, Paul. Langage privé et communauté: Kripke et Wittgenstein. Lekton, 1(1), 23-40, 1990.

This article criticizes Kripke's argument against following a rule privately. First by showing that the community acts just as blindly as the isolated individual when it thinks it agrees upon following a rule. Then by showing that the argument is self-referential in a way which makes it impossible to formulate the skeptical argument if the skeptical solution were true.

DUNAWAY, John M. "Exiles and Fugitives: The Maritain-Tate-Gordon Letters" in *From Twilight to Dawn: The Cultural Vision of Jacques Maritain*, REDPATH, Peter A (ed), 27-35. Notre Dame, Univ Notre Dame Pr, 1990.

A descriptive and evaluative survey of the letters between two literary couples, the Maritains and Tates, highlighting the role these writers played in the literary world, especially in the '50s and '60s. A revised version appears as introduction to *Exiles and Fugitives*, forthcoming under the auspices of Louisiana State University Press in 1992.

DUNCAN, Hugh D. "Comment on David L Miller's 'Consciousness, the Attitude of the Individual and Perspectives'" in *Creativity in George Herbert Mead*, GUNTER, Pete A Y (ed), 49-54. Lanham, Univ Pr of America, 1990.

DUNDON, Stanislaus J. Development Aid: The Moral Obligation to Innovation. J Agr Ethics, 4(1), 31-48, 1991.

The prominent role of basic needs strategies to attain ethically acceptable development goals raises the question of the ability of development agencies to find and employ basic need strategies. The obligation to prevent severe human suffering leads to the obligation to employ basic needs strategies to attain basic needs goals. The history of failure by development agencies in finding and employing basic needs tools leads to a further obligation to cultivate bureaucratic environments which foster profound innovation. (edited)

DUNFEE, Thomas W. Business Ethics and Extant Social Contracts. Bus Ethics Quart, 1(1), 23-51, Ja 91.

Extant social contracts, deriving from communities of individuals, constitute a significant source of ethical norms in business. When found consistent with general ethical theories through the application of a filtering test, these real social contracts generate prima facie duties of compliance on the part of those who expressly or impliedly consent to the terms of the social contract, and also on the part of those who take advantage of the instrumental value of the social contracts. Business people typically participate in multiple communities and, as a consequence, encounter conflicting ethical norms. Priority rules can be devised to resolve such conflicts. The framework of extant social contracts merges normative and theoretical research in business ethics and specifies a domain for empirical studies.

DUNN, J Michael. "The Frame Problem and Relevant Predication" in *Knowledge Representation and Defeasible Reasoning*, KYBURG JR, Henry E (ed), 89-95. Norwell, Kluwer, 1990.

DUNN, J Michael. Relevant Predication 2: Intrinsic Properties and Internal Relations. Phil Stud, 60(3), 177-206, N 90.

DUNN, John. *Interpreting Political Responsibility*. Princeton, Princeton Univ Pr, 1990.

The task of political theory is to show human beings how they have good reason to act in the historical situation in which they find themselves. Modern academic study of political theory has proved increasingly ineffectual in carrying out this task. Human dependence on political agency has deepened greatly and will certainly continue to increase unless the species itself is eventually exterminated. But human comprehension of the nature and implications of this dependency has made distressingly little progress. To do better, it is essential to restore a richly understood concept of prudence to the centre of political understanding.

DUNN, John. "Unger's *Politics* and the Appraisal of Political Possibility" in *Critique and Construction: A Symposium on Roberto Unger's "Politics"*, LOVIN, Robin W (ed), 71-89. New York, Cambridge Univ Pr, 1990.

Roberto Unger's *Politics* is the most ambitious attempt to capture the nature of modern politics to appear for many decades. It seeks to fuse a keen interest in institutional causality and an intense scepticism about claims to knowledge in human affairs with a vivid faith in human possibilities. The key term which links Unger's scepticism with his faith is the term 'plasticity'. But this term is less convincingly applied in the second of these contexts. *Politics* is an imaginatively invigorating work. But as an approach to political judgment it is also singularly unconvincing.

DUNN, Kim and BULGER, Ruth Ellen. "Values in Teaching and Learning: A Student-Teacher Dialogue" in *Integrity in Health Care Institutions: Humane Environments for Teaching, Inquiry, and Healing*, BULGER, Ruth Ellen (ed), 96-118. Iowa City, Univ of Iowa Pr, 1990.

DUNNELL, Robert C. "Philosophy of Science and Archaeology" in *Critical Traditions in Contemporary Archaeology*, PINSKY, Valerie (ed), 5-9. New York, Cambridge Univ Pr, 1990.

In the 1930s, archaeological interest in philosophy of science was slight, explanation being taken to be self-evident. In the 1960s, the New Archaeology saw philosophy of science as having prescriptive value in trying to make archaeology scientific. When this effort failed, most archaeologists discounted the value of philosophy of science altogether. Philosophers, on the other hand, have only recently taken an interest in archaeology. The results thus far have been of little value to archaeology because they (1) underestimate the diversity of archaeology; (2) are largely based on secondary, programmatic literature; and (3) address issues of little import to archaeology.

DUPONCHEELE, Joseph. What Philosophy for Judaism and Christianity? (in French). Bijdragen, 1, 37-57, 1991.

Is it an offense to human reason or a sin against the Holy Spirit to question the most fundamental postulate in philosophy, that is: the idea of perfect being is linked with that of "undivided unity" and every distinction in being or between beings, which implies a plurality of beings, is supposedly linked with their imperfect aspects or must be caused by a principle of imperfection? However such a postulate reduces the essential assertions of Judaism and Christianity to a mysterious turn of mind, and discards the great human questions of love and death as irrational concerns. Therefore, would it not be possible to construct a new form of philosophy on the following contradictory principle in every being: there is at least one distinctive relationship which expresses the perfection of the Real? This being would unveil its essence in "relationality". To be is "to make be" and to be absolutely is to let be absolutely. The thesis of the essential relationality of being allows us to start afresh with all the classical questions and to give a fresh answer. It provides us with a new understanding of Judaism and Christianity which shows their outstanding complementarity and leads us to indestructible hope.

DUPRÉ, John. Probabilistic Causality: A Rejoinder to Ellery Eells. Phil Sci, 57(4), 690-698, D 90.

In an earlier paper (Dupré 1984), I criticized a thesis sometimes defended by theorists of probabilistic causality, namely, that a probabilistic cause must raise the probability of its effect in every possible set of causally relevant background conditions (the "contextual unanimity thesis"). I also suggested that a more promising analysis of probabilistic causality might be sought in terms of statistical relevance in a fair sample. Ellery Eells (1987) has defended the contextual unanimity thesis against my objections, and also raised objections of his own to my positive claims. In this paper I defend and amplify both my objections to the contextual unanimity thesis and my constructive suggestion.

DUPRÉ, John. Scientific Pluralism and the Plurality of the Sciences: Comments on David Hull's *Science as a Process*. Phil Stud, 60(1-2), 61-76, S-O 90.

This paper provides a detailed critical discussion of David Hull's *Science as a Process*. In addition to discussion of Hull's application of the category 'historical individual' to both species and scientific research programs, it is argued that despite the considerable interest of Hull's account of scientific progress, profound differences between the methodologies of various areas of science make it unlikely to have uniform relevance to these.

DUPRÉ, Louis. "Truth in Religion and Truth of Religion" in *Phenomenology of the Truth Proper to Religion*, GUERRIÈRE, Daniel (ed), 19-42. Albany, SUNY Pr, 1990.

Is it possible to reflect on religious truth from a position outside faith without seriously distorting what faith itself understands by its truth? As long as philosophy and theology remained united—until the end of the middle ages—such a reflection was neither needed nor attempted. The standpoint which an independent philosophy in the modern age has taken with respect to the problem of truth, where the knowing subject becomes the source of truth, would appear to render such an effort suspect. Nevertheless, this essay argues, we are justified in approaching the truth of religion through the models available in present philosophy: correspondence, coherence, disclosure. In all three cases, however, the *application* of the models needs to be qualified if it is to account for truth as faith itself understands it.

DUPUIS, Adrian M and THOMPSON, A Gray. P4C as "Pre-Secondary" Philosophy. Thinking, 4(2), 33-35, 1982.

Since philosophy is taught in numerous secondary schools, it seems appropriate that it be started in elementary schools. Math, history, science, etc. are begun in elementary school and involve basic content of secondary education. The *Philosophy for Children* program provides the basis for secondary school philosophy, and in the language and "experience" of children.

DUQUETTE, David A. "Kant, Hegel and the Possibility of a Speculative Logic" in *Essays on Hegel's Logic*, DI GIOVANNI, George (ed), 1-16. Albany, SUNY Pr, 1990.

This essay is a comparative study of Kant's and Hegel's conceptions of philosophical logic. It examines the continuity between the two thinkers' views on the nature of transcendental thought, but also shows how Hegel departs from Kant, especially regarding the manner in which pure speculative thought can provide systematic unity for the fundamental concepts of thought. Central to my concern is to show how Kant's view of logic points the way to Hegel's and yet how Hegel's enterprise is possible despite Kant's critique of pure reason.

DURAN, Jane. Domesticated and Then Some. Between Species, 6(4), 176-180, Fall 90.

Two possible views with regard to the question of the moral status of domesticated species/breeds versus naturally occurring species of animals are examined and analyzed. One view contrasts domesticated breeds with naturally-occurring species, to the detriment of the former, focusing on weaknessess or defects. The second notes areas of similarity between naturally-occurring species and domesticated breeds. It is concluded that domesticated breeds (and individuals) are entitled to at least as much in the way of moral status as species occurring in nature. By way of development of the argument, the views of Singer, Rachels, Taylor and others are alluded to, and three sorts of positions on the larger question of animal rights contrasted.

DURAN, Jane. Ecofeminism and Androcentric Epistemology. Int J Applied Phil, 5(2), 9-14, Fall 90.

Three lines of argument support the notion that the ecofeminist critique of deep ecology is related to the feminist critique of science. The first recapitulates the ecofeminist critique, and indicates that this critique could be more thoroughly developed than it is. The second cites the development of the resource management and ecological sciences as disciplines. The third line develops the notion that recent advances in epistemology provide at least the bare beginnings of a new epistemology which might be useful in the development of a deeper ecology.

DURAN, Jane. *Epistemics*. Lanham, Univ Pr of America, 1989.

Drawing on recent work in cognitive science, philosophy of mind and standard normative epistemology, I develop a naturalized theory of epistemic justification with a descriptively-oriented, contextualized overview. The work examines normative theories both *qua* normative theories and from the standpoint of our intuitions about the project of epistemic justification.

DURAN, Jane. Glymour on Deoccamization and the Epistemology of Geometry. Brit J Phil Sci, 40(1), 127-134, Mr 89.

Three lines of argument are employed to show that Glymour's position on the epistemology of geometry is probably not as strong theoretically as the position of the underdeterminists whom he attempts to refute. The first argument center on Glymours' implicit use of a realist position on intertheoretic reference; the second line of argument refutes Glymour's contention that his criteria for choosing among theories are strongly based and not a priori; and a third line of argument rephrases Glymour's original position in a way which more clearly shows its implicit structure.

DURAN, Jane. I Know What I Know, If You Know What I Mean. Soc Epistem, 5(2), 151-159, Ap-Je 91.

The conclusion that part of the naturalization of epistemology involves attention to macrolevel phenomena is supported by three major lines of argument. The first line cites the work of Scribner and Luria and brings it to bear on the contextualization of reasoning processes. The second line asks us to recognize Kashev's work on a speech-act account of epistemic justification, and the third line develops a brief outline of what the heart of the process of epistemic justification looks like when modeled along the lines of sociolinguistic and/or speech-act theory.

DURAN, Jane. The *Nagaraja*: Symbol and Symbolism in Hindu Art and Iconography. J Aes Educ, 24(2), 37-47, Sum 90.

Employing three major lines of argument, I conclude that many of the traditional problems surrounding the use of symbols are best addressed by viewing non-Western pieces of art, and I specifically employ the art of India as exemplary. It is concluded that symbolism is reliant upon the conventional, as Dickie and others have argued, that "intentionalist criticism" makes even less sense in non-Western pieces than in our own tradition, and that, *contra* some critics of Langerian lines, some works are simultaneously symbols and rife with the symbolic.

DURAN, Jane. On Decadence. Philosophy, 65(254), 455-464, O 90.

Several lines of argument are employed to support the notion that decadence, as a concept applying to art work, has at least four key elements. Rowland's citation of the decadence of late Thai temple work is taken as exemplary, and Carroll's work on art-horror, as well as Meeson's on the use of symbol, are utilized. It is concluded that the decadent is contrived for effect, categorically interstitial, rife with the obviously symbolic, and sensual in its effects. The list of hallmarks is not taken to be a set of necessary and sufficient conditions, but rather a filling-out of what we mean by artistic decadence.

DURANT, J R. "Is There a Role for Theology in an Age of Secular Science?" in *Science and Religion: One World-Changing Perspectives on Reality*, FENNEMA, Jan (ed), 161-172. Norwell, Kluwer, 1990.

DURBIN, Paul T (ed). *Philosophy of Technology*. Norwell, Kluwer, 1989.

Discussions from a philosophical perspective of the complex social problems associated with technology. Problems are of three sorts, practical (e.g., nuclear war, policy for directed scientific or technological work); historical (e.g., the *camera obscura* and its influence on modern epistemology); and international/intergenerational (e.g., philosophy of technology in China and responsibility for future generations). Authors included: Friedrich Rapp, Lyle Anderson, David Bella, Edwin Levy, Lee Bailey, Edmund Byrne, Larry Hickman, Joseph Margolis, Gao Dasheng and Zou Tsing, Wojciech Gasparski, and Janet F Smith.

DURHAM, Frank and PURRINGTON, Robert D. "Newton's Legacy" in *Some Truer Method*, DURHAM, Frank (ed), 1-13. New York, Columbia Univ Pr, 1990.

DURHAM, Frank and PURRINGTON, Robert D. "Newton, Nonlinearity and Determinism" in *Some Truer Method*, DURHAM, Frank (ed), 175-226. New York, Columbia Univ Pr, 1990.

DURHAM, Frank (ed) and PURRINGTON, Robert D (ed). *Some Truer Method*. New York, Columbia Univ Pr, 1990.

DURRANT, Michael. Scepticism: Three Recently Presented Arguments Examined. Phil Invest, 14(3), 252-266, Jl 91.

I consider three sceptical arguments advanced by Jonathan Dancy, 1) You don't know that you are not a brain suspended in a vat of liquid in a laboratory and wired to a computer which is feeding you your current experiences under the control of some ingenious scientist; 2) the sceptical argument from the possibility of error; 3) the sceptical argument concerning the lack of justification of arguments from experience. In all three types of case it is argued that the sceptic of necessity has to presuppose what he implicitly denies in order for him to intelligibly advocate his own position. Such forms of scepticism are thus *radically* unjustified.

DÜRRENMATT, Friedrich and BÜHLER, Pierre (trans). On Tolerance (in French). Rev Theol Phil, 122(4), 449-465, 1990.

After a descriptive foreword about the philosophical and theological horizons of his approach, the author, inspired by the preamble of the Council from which he holds a medal, enlarges upon the problems of religious and political tolerance. In contrast to the model of Lessing, he defines an existential tolerance based on Kierkegaard, conceived of from the point of view of the individual who sets out to resist any englobing system, whether it be philosophical or theological, political or economic. He draws out the implications for the political realm.

DUTKIEWICZ, Rafal. The Method of Axiomatic Rejection for the Intuitionistic Propositional Logic. Stud Log, 48(4), 449-459, D 89.

We prove that the intuitionistic sentential calculus is *L*-decidable (decidable in the sense of Lukasiewicz), i.e., the sets of these of Int and of refected formulas are disjoint and their union is equal to all formulas. A formula is rejected if it is a sentential variable or is obtained from other formulas by means of three rejection rules. One of the rules is original, the remaining two are Lukasiewicz's rejection rules: by detachment and by substitution. We extensively use the method of Beth's semantic tableaux.

DUVALL, William E. The Nietzsche Temptation in the Thought of Albert Camus. Hist Euro Ideas, 11, 955-963, 1989.

Camus admired Nietzsche as a lucid diagnostician of the modern predicament who confronted the death of God, absurdity and nihilism yet sought to live joyously "believing in nothing." But in *L'Homme revolté*, Camus ends his essay on Nietzsche by condemning him, by blaming him for both Nazism and Stalinism. Camus, a moralist insisting on the value of human community and solidarity, had to fight free of Nietzsche. His predicament is symptomatic of many contemporary French thinkers who have felt the appeal of the Nietzsche temptation; Camus alone was able to free himself from Nietzsche and achieve a coherent moral position.

DUXBURY, Neil. Women's Law. Ratio Juris, 3(1), 81-83, Mr 90.

DWORKIN, Ronald. "Foundations of Liberal Equality" in *The Tanner Lectures on Human Values, Volume XI*, PETERSON, Grethe B (ed), 1-119. Salt Lake City, Univ of Utah Pr, 1990.

DWORKIN, Ronald. *Justice and the Good Life*. Lawrence, Univ of Kansas Pr, 1990.

DWORKIN, Ronald. Taking Rights Seriously in the Abortion Case. Ratio Juris, 3(1), 68-80, Mr 90.

DYCK, Arthur J and DE LANEY, James S. "National Health Insurance: An Ethical Assessment" in *Biomedical Ethics Reviews, 1990*, HUMBER, James M (ed), 87-129. Clifton, Humana Pr, 1991.

Four concrete proposals to enact National Health Insurance (NHI) in the US were assessed to evaluate arguments for and against NHI, and to account for its absence in the US. Sometimes implicitly, sometimes explicitly, each proposal claims to be more just, necessary, likely to succeed, and cognitively sound than other proposals. Politically, proponents of one plan have successfully blocked others. Conclusions drawn: 1) public debate over principles is needed; 2) to reduce discrimination, care should not be rationed, but rather waste, excessive profits, and inefficiencies; 3) there is a right to health care akin to communal protection of individual lives by military, police, and firefighting services.

DZELZAINIS, Martin (ed) and MILTON, John. *Political Writings—John Milton*. New York, Cambridge Univ Pr, 1991.

DZHAKHAIA, L G. The World of Man and Man in the World in Light of the New Philosophical Thinking. Soviet Stud Phil, 29(3), 28-37, Wint 90-91.

DZHAPARIDZE, Giorgie. Decidable and Enumerable Predicate Logics of Provability. Stud Log, 49(1), 7-21, Mr 90.

DZHAPARIDZE, Giorgie and ARTEMOV, Sergei. Finite Kripke Models and Predicate Logics of Provability. J Sym Log, 55(3), 1090-1098, S 90.

DZIEMIDOK, Bohdan. "The Social Status of Art: Why the Institutional Approach is not Sufficient" in *XIth International Congress in Aesthetics, Nottingham 1988*, WOODFIELD, Richard (ed), 42-44. Nottingham, Nottingham Polytech, 1990.

DZIENKOWSKI, John S. Taking Positional Conflicts of Interest Seriously. Bus Prof Ethics J, 9(1-2), 109-128, Spr-Sum 90.

DZIERZGOWSKI, Daniel. Many-Sorted Elementary Equivalence. Notre Dame J Form Log, 29(4), 530-542, Fall 88.

A theory T in a many-sorted language L can effectively be replaced by a L^*-theory T^*, L^* being the one-sorted language canonically associated to L. On the other hand, some many-sorted notions cannot be directly transposed to the corresponding one-sorted notions (see for example J L Hook, *Journal of Symbolic Logic* 50 (1985), p. 372-374). In this paper, we study how many-sorted elementary equivalence can be replaced by one-sorted elementary equivalence: if M, N are L-structures, we show when the elementary equivalence of M and N implies, or is implied by the elementary equivalence of M^* and N^* (M^* and N^* being the associated L^*-structures). As an example, L is taken to be the language of Simple Type Theory, and four different ways to define L^* are considered, depending on the presence of symbols ε^i, S^i ($x \varepsilon^i y$: x is of type i, y of type i+1 and $x \varepsilon y$; $S^i(x)$: x is of type i). Then we characterize the many-sorted languages for which these results can be generalized.

EARLES, Beverley. The Faith Dimension of Humanism. Relig Hum, 25(2), 55-65, Spr 91.

EARLS, Anthony. The Case of the Unmitigated Blackguard or Saving Kant's Moral Feelings. SW Phil Rev, 7(1), 119-128, Ja 91.

EARLS, C Anthony. Is Aristotle an Internal Realist? Nussbaum and the Divine Perspective. Kinesis, 18(1), 1-15, Wint 90.

EARMAN, John. Bayes' Bayesianism. Stud Hist Phil Sci, 21(3), 351-370, S 90.

EBELING, Hans. *Ästhetik des Abschieds: Kritik der Moderne*. Freiburg, Alber, 1991.

The "Aesthetics of Parting" is an invitation and encouragement to hold fast to the project of modern times. Philosophy cannot claim that it is either more or less important than art; rather, art is the only possible "other" which philosophy can have. It is only through the combination of these that modernity can develop to fruition. The first part of the book clarifies the status of aesthetic judgement as lying between theoretical truth and practical challenge and demand. The second part analyzes the stupendous truth which art conveys, its subversive rightness and its unprotected truthfulness.

EBELING, Hans. *Das Verhängnis Erste Philosophie*. Freiburg, Alber, 1991.

Ebeling intends to contain the contents of metaphysics and metaphysical critique against the new metaphysics of the later Heidegger and against the metabiological systems theory of Luhmann. This occurs through the transformation of First Philosophy, which according to Kant still remains with us, even if this type of philosophy is destroyed on the foundations of metaphysics.

EBELING, Werner. Erneuerung als Grundmechanismus der Evolution. Deut Z Phil, 38(7), 671-675, 1990.

EBERLE, Rolf. Classification by Comparison with Paradigms. Amer Phil Quart, 27(4), 295-304, O 90.

The article shows—by specifying truth-conditions for atomic sentences—that principled classifications with respect to all but universal or empty properties (and relations) can provably always be effected by simultaneous comparison and contrast with suitable exemplars that are designated by predicates either positively (if they exemplify possession of the quality) or negatively (if they exemplify its absence). Given that positive exemplars are paradigms, sentences such as "birds are feathered," in the sense of "typical birds are feathered," will be true of them; vague predicates apply to qualitative neighborhoods around them; and comparatives can be justified by typical exemplars.

EBISCH, Glen A. Freud's Warning to Potential Believers. Relig Hum, 24(4), 170-175, Autumn 90.

The question considered in this article is whether, in the absence of conclusive proof for or against the existence of God, it is justified to believe for the sake of the psychological comfort such faith provides. This issue is approached by considering arguments developed in Freud's *The Future of an Illusion*. The conclusion reached by Freud is that due to the lack of adequate evidence for religious belief, one is obligated by reason not to believe. This view is then briefly contrasted with the contrary position of William James. The conclusion reached is that the type of religious faith being accepted is relevant to its justification. One which leads to beneficial social results as well as psychological comfort to the believer may be justified, while one that gives comfort but encourages passivity, ignorance and superstition does not.

ECHAURI, Raúl. Arte y conocimiento. Sapientia, 45(177), 185-188, Jl-S 90.

ECHAURI, Raul. Arte y significación. Anu Filosof, 23(2), 139-146, 1990.

Si bien el arte tiene una enorme significación y relevancia para el espíritu humano, él no tiene como tarea propia significar el mundo, es decir, comunicar un mensaje, instruirnos sobre la realidad o brindarnos un conocimiento. Indudablemente, el arte imitativo o representativo, que recurre a la imagen, puede hacerlo, dado que la imagen es portadora natural de significación, pero si lo hace es por añadidura. Y el arte no "significa", porque las formas artísticas no son signos. Ellas, en todo caso, se autosignifican, dado que su dimensión artística se agota en ellas mismas, como señala pertinentemente Gilson.

ECHAURI, Raúl. La noción de ser en Tomás de Sutton. Sapientia, 45(176), 135-140, Ap-Je 90.

ECHEVERRÍA, J (ed) and DÍEZ, Amparo (ed) and IBARRA, A (ed). *Structures in Mathematical Theories: Reports of the San Sebastian International Symposium, 1990*. Vizcaya, Univ Pais Vasco, 1990.

This book contains a selection of 76 contributed papers to the International Symposium on Structures in Mathematical Theories (San Sebastian, Spain, 25-29 September, 1990). They are distributed in five sections: Mathematical and Empirical Theories; Applications of Mathematical Theories; History and Sociology of Mathematical Theories; Methods of Research into Mathematics; Structures of Mathematical Theories. Philosophers of science, historians and mathematicians coming from 19 countries (Belgium, Brazil, Canada, China, England, Finland, France, Germany, Holland, Japan, India, Israel, Italy, Mexico, Poland, Spain, Switzerland, URSS and USA) present their research on mathematical theories: their structures, historical evolutions and interrelations with other sciences and technologies.

ECHEVERRÍA, José. La obra de Humberto Giannini: Un modo diferente de filosofar. Dialogos, 26(57), 167-172, Ja 91.

ECKBLAD, Joyce. "Kant and Fichte: An Ethics of Self-Respect in Individualism" in *Abeunt Studia in Mores: A Festschrift for Helga Doblin*, MERRILL, Sarah A Bishop (ed), 266-273. New York, Lang, 1990.

ECKBLAD, Joyce. "Nietzsche and Merleau-Ponty: The Body as Attitude" in *Abeunt Studia in Mores: A Festschrift for Helga Doblin*, MERRILL, Sarah A Bishop (ed), 274-287. New York, Lang, 1990.

ECO, Umberto. "Interpretation and Overinterpretation: World, History, Texts" in *The Tanner Lectures On Human Values, Volume XII*, PETERSON, Grethe B (ed), 141-202. Salt Lake City, Univ of Utah Pr, 1991.

EDA, Katsuya. Boolean Powers of Abelian Groups. Annals Pure Applied Log, 50(2), 109-115, N 90.

Let *A*-super-*B* be a Boolean power of an abelian group *A* for a complete Boolean algebra *B*. Let *C*-sub-κ be the collapsing algebra which makes an infinite cardinal κ to be countable. A characterization of cotorsion-free groups is obtained by using the C-sub-κth Boolean power of the integer group *Z*. A relationship between algebraical compactness of Boolean powers and distributivity of Boolean algebras is also discussed.

EDEL, Abraham. *Relating Humanities and Social Thought (Science, Ideology, and Value, Volume 4)*. New Brunswick, Transaction Books, 1990.

Social thought and the humanities are examined as modes of inquiry, functioning disciplines in historical contexts, and expressions of basic human values. The 17 papers span diverse fields—anthropology, law, morality, education, history, art, biography—and consider problems of both social policy and social theory. Argument is directed against prevalent dichotomies, e.g., individual-social, theory-practice, elite-mass; their consequences are found particularly harmful in education. A long concluding paper attempts to formulate a philosophical perspective on humanities and public policy.

EDELBERG, Walter. A Case for a Heretical Deontic Semantics. J Phil Log, 20(1), 1-35, F 91.

I might owe you a particular horse. Or, I might owe you a horse without owing you any particular one. The received view is that quantifier/operator scope distinctions of standard deontic logics successfully account for the difference between these two kinds of cases. Yet certain logical data call the received view into serious question. Three attempts to save the view by deploying non-quantificational treatments of anaphora fail. An alternative proposal locates the difference in the interpretation of the relevant individual variables.

EDELBERG, Walter. The Fifth Meditation. Phil Rev, 99(4), 493-533, O 90.

Descartes advances his principal case for genuine, full-blown epistemological rationalism in the sciences only in Meditation Five, in the arguments that there are true and immutable geometrical natures and that our ideas of them are innate. Although recent commentators have charged Descartes with hopeless confusion and downright inconsistency here, a perfectly coherent reading of these arguments is possible. The new reading of the arguments suggests a larger interpretation of the Cartesian system, on which the three "principal attributes" of thought, extension, and supreme perfection play a far more extensive role in Descartes's metaphysics and epistemology than is typically assumed.

EDELMAN, John T. *An Audience for Moral Philosophy?*. New York, St Martin's Pr, 1991.

EDGINGTON, Dorothy. Explanation, Causation and Laws. Critica, 22(66), 55-73, D 90.

EDINGER, Walter. Respect for Donor Choice and the Uniform Anatomical Gift Act. J Med Human, 11(3), 135-142, Fall 90.

EDLER, Frank H W. Retreat from Radicality: Pöggeler on Heidegger's Politics. Grad Fac Phil J, 14(2)-15(1), 295-323, 1991.

EDUC COMMISSION OF STATES. The Higher Level Skills: Tomorrow's 'Basics'. Thinking, 4(2), 22-28, 1982.

EDWALD, Tryggvi. The t-Variable Method in Gentzen-Style Automatic Theorem Proving. Z Math Log, 36(3), 253-261, 1990.

The paper describes experiments in Automatic Theorem proving in the first-order predicate calculus (with equality). The approach is sequential non-resolution decomposition, based on Gentzen's logistic calculi. An actual implementation (in LISP) of the method is discussed in some detail, and its most important shortcomings mentioned.

EDWARDS, Jim. Functional Support for Anomalous Monism. Philosophy, 27, 45-64, 90 Supp.

EDWARDS, M J. Porphyry and the Intelligible Triad. J Hellen Stud, 110, 14-25, 1990.

The sequence being-life-intellect, which constitutes the intelligible triad of the later Neoplatonists, describes the procession of the self-conscious intellect from being. Pierre Hadot has argued that Augustine and Victorinus found it in Porphyry (232—c. 305 AD) and that Porphyry is the author of a commentary on Plato's Parmenides in which the triad occurs. This article maintains that he did not employ the terms in the required sense, and offers further reasons for doubting that the commentary is his.

EDWARDS, Michael. "The World Could Not Contain the Books" in *The Bible as Rhetoric: Studies in Biblical Persuasion and Credibility*, WARNER, Martin (ed), 178-194. New York, Routledge, 1990.

John's Gospel is a thoroughly literary as well as a thoroughly religious text. It searches for origin in a multiple re-writing of the opening of Genesis. It replies to the anxiety of Ecclesiastes about the making of many books by its open-ended celebration of all the books that could be written about Jesus, the Word and the ultimate origin of all writing. It becomes *the* book by relating its own words to the Word of creation and re-creation, and by gathering the whole of the Old Testament 'scriptures' into the single work which they prepare.

EDWARDS, Rem B. Process Thought and the Spaciness of Mind. Process Stud, 19(3), 156-166, Fall 90.

The process claim that matter is mentally infused and that mind or consciousness is spatially and temporally extended is explored. The views of Peirce, Whitehead, Hartshorne, Cobb, Ford and Griffin on the following questions are examined: If spacy, where are the occasions of human consciousness, how are they related to the brain, how large are they, and can they be externally perceived directly or with instruments? It is proposed that what is internally experienced as human consciousness is objectively identical with the synthetic unity of those brain waves known to be correlated with wakeful awareness. If so, modern scanning technology can literally find us in our brains. Possible objections are discussed.

EELLS, E. "Bayesian Problems of Old Evidence" in *Scientific Theories*, SAVAGE, C Wade (ed), 205-223. Minneapolis, Univ of Minn Pr, 1990.

According to standard Bayesian confirmation theory, a piece of evidence confirms a hypothesis (for a given individual) if and only if the evidence raises the (subjective) probability of the hypothesis. But if the evidence is already known—has (subjective) probability 1—then this cannot happen, according to standard probability theory. This seemingly paradoxical result is called the problem of old evidence, and was raised by Clark Glymour (*Theory and Evidence*, Princeton, 1980) against Bayesian confirmation theory. I clarify several versions of the problem, discuss several Bayesian responses, and offer my own solution to the problem.

EELLS, Ellery. On the Alleged Impossibility of Inductive Probability. Brit J Phil Sci, 39(1), 111-116, Mr 88.

Popper and Miller argued, in a 1983 paper, that there is no such thing as *probabilistic inductive support* of hypotheses. They show how to divide a hypothesis into two "parts," where evidence only *probabilistically supports* the "part" that the evidence *deductively* implies, and *probabilistically countersupports* the "*rest*" of the hypothesis. I argue that by distinguishing between *support that is purely deductive in nature* and *support of a deductively implied hypothesis*, we can see that their argument fails to establish (in any important way of interpreting it) their conclusion that "all probabilistic support is purely deductive." Their argument is *not* "completely devastating to the inductive interpretation of the calculus of probability," as claimed.

EELLS, Ellery. *Probabilistic Causality*. New York, Cambridge Univ Pr, 1991.

This book explores and refines current philosophical conceptions of probabilistic causality. In a probabilistic theory of causation, causes increase the probability of their effects rather than necessitate their effects in the way traditional theories have specified. Taking into account issues involving spurious correlation, probabilistic causal interaction, disjunctive causal factors, and temporal ideas, the book advances the idea of what it is for one factor to be a positive causal factor for another. But perhaps the most novel feature of the book is a new theory of token-level probabilistic causation, in which the evolution of the probability of an event from around the time of an earlier event is crucial.

EELLS, Ellery and HARPER, William L. Ratifiability, Game Theory, and the Principle of Independence of Irrelevant Alternatives. Austl J Phil, 69(1), 1-19, Mr 91.

The main result of this paper is that various natural developments of the recent decision criterion of *ratifiability* (based on Jeffrey 1981, 1983), as well as some natural implications of classical *game theory* (Nash 1951) for individual decision, are in conflict with Sen's (1970) seemingly plausible *alpha* and *beta* conditions, which are sometimes together called the *principle of independence of irrelevant alternatives*. Examples are given that the authors argue tell *against the alpha and beta criteria*, and *in favor of the ratifiability idea*; and it is explained how these examples and arguments about *individual decision making* derive *further support* from *Nash equilibrium ideas in classical game theory*.

EGAN, Frances. Must Psychology Be Individualistic? Phil Rev, 100(2), 179-203, Ap 91.

It has recently been argued (by Jerry Fodor and others) that explanatory psychological theories must employ individuative principles that take no account of the subject's environment or social context. These arguments are criticized as inconclusive. The article then examines Tyler Burge's claim that David Marr's theory of early vision supports the thesis that psychological individuation is context-sensitive, and argues that attention to the explanatory goals of psychology suggests that contextual factors will not play a role in individuation.

EGGER, Paul. *Der Ursprung der Erziehungsziele in der Lehre von Plato, Aristoteles und Neill*. Berne, Haupt, 1990.

This book examines the origins of training in the teaching of Plato, Aristotle, and A S Neill. It locates their teaching within their appropriate historical contexts. (staff)

EGHENTER, Cristina and VAYDA, Andrew P and MC CAY, Bonnie J. Concepts of Process in Social Science Explanations. Phil Soc Sci, 21(3), 318-331, S 91.

Social scientists using one or another concept of process have paid little attention to underlying issues of methodology and explanation. Commonly, the concept used is a loose one. When it is not, there often are other problems, such as errors of reification and of assuming that events sometimes connected in a sequence are invariably thus connected. While it may be useful to retain the term "process" for some sequences of intelligibly connected actions and events, causal explanation must be sought with respect to the *events* constituting processes rather than with respect to processes regarded as unitary entities.

EHRHARDT, Walter E. Freedom Is Our Divinity (in German). Deut Z Phil, 38(6), 521-527, 1990.

Die Einheit der Philosophie *Schellings* kann nur behauptet werden, wenn das Prinzip Freiheit auch die Spätschriften bestimmt. Freiheit ist dieser nachkantischen Philosophie nicht ein Seiendes, sondern das, was sein soll. Nicht was ist, sondern was sein soll, wird gewellt. Eine gewollte Gottheit, Freiheit, "das deontische Prinzip", ist es, die die positive Philosophie in den geschichtlichen Erfahrungen der Mythologie und Offenbarung nachweist. Das gleiche Prinzip, as Schellings Frühwerk zum A und O erklärte, leitet also auch hier, und es ist unnötig, Brüche oder unbegründete Schritte bei Schelling zu vermuten.

EHRING, Douglas. Motion, Causation, and the Causal Theory of Identity. Austl J Phil, 69(2), 180-194, Je 91.

Proponents of a causal theory of physical object identity argue that a causal account is demonstratively superior to a continuity theory. For example, Armstrong has claimed that whereas a continuity theory has trouble with motion, the casual theory has no such trouble. In this paper, I explore the causal theory of identity as applied to the problem of motion in the context of various leading theories of causation. I argue that the causal theory is in no better position to deal with motion that continuity theory once the concept of causation is spelled out within any of these traditional theories of causation.

EHRING, Douglas. Nonbranching and Nontransitivity. Analysis, 50(4), 268-271, O 90.

One strategy for avoiding violations of transitivity in a theory of physical object identity is to include a "nonbranching" restriction which excludes the possibility of multiple simultaneous stages being gen-identical to the same earlier stage. In this paper, I argue that although this way of understanding the nonbranching condition does in fact immunize a theory of identity against violations of identity in the standard duplication case, this condition does not guarantee against all such violations. I propose a way of formulating the nonbranching condition which avoids this difficulty.

EHRING, Douglas. Preemption, Direct Causation, and Identity. Synthese, 85(1), 55-70, O 90.

In this paper I argue that (a) if preemption is possible, then direct causation is not explanatorily basic, i.e., given preemption there must be some mechanism for the transmission of c's causal influence to its direct effects, and (b) if direct causation is not explanatorily basic, then the causal theory of identity thesis is false, i.e., that it is not the case that identity over time is in general partly a matter of causation. I conclude that direct causation is not explanatorily basic and that the causal theory of identity as a perfectly general thesis ought to be rejected.

EIDENMÜLLER, Horst. Rights, Systems of Rights, and Unger's System of Rights: Part I. Law Phil, 10(1), 1-28, F 91.

Critical legal scholarship has so far been concerned primarily with trashing or deconstructing the belief clusters of "liberalism." Negative posturing of this kind is not the only feature of the movement, though. Roberto Unger has dreamt up a sociopolitical vision that presents an "empowered democracy." An important element of his "empowered democracy" is a new system of rights. Part I of my essay contains an analysis of the notion of a *subjective right*. I argue that both Hohfeld's fundamental legal conceptions and Unger's various rights can by described by a simple deontic relation that I define as *right*. I then discuss a set of normative criteria that can help us evaluate systems of rights. Part II (to appear in the following issue) contains a detailed critique of Unger's system of rights based on these normative criteria. The tenet of this part is that Unger's system of rights is contradictory, opaque, impracticable, costly, and not fully backed by what Unger offers as a background justification for it.

EISENSTADT, S N. "Cultural Tradition, Historical Experience, and Social Change: The Limits of Convergence" in *The Tanner Lectures on Human Values, Volume XI*, PETERSON, Grethe B (ed), 441-505. Salt Lake City, Univ of Utah Pr, 1990.

EISENSTEIN, Gabe. Understanding the Question: Wittgenstein on Faith and Meaning. Relig Stud, 26(4), 463-470, D 90.

EISNER, Elliot W. Discipline-Based Art Education: Conceptions and Misconceptions. Educ Theor, 40(4), 423-430, Fall 90.

The general purpose of this article is to examine the major features of discipline-based art education and the conceptions that practitioners and scholars hold about it. In particular, this article examines the views of Professor Donald Arnstine as he discusses what he regards the strengths and weaknesses of discipline-based art education to be. Several of his conclusions, it is argued, rest upon misconceptions of discipline-based art education. The article tries to rectify these misconceptions and to respond to other concerns that he and others have about the structure and function of discipline-based art education.

ELAM, Diane. Ms en abyme: Deconstruction and Feminism. Soc Epistem, 4(3), 293-308, Jl-S 90.

Many have claimed that there is a necessary conflict between deconstruction and feminism. This article argues, on the contrary, that they share a rethinking of the political as undecidable or indeterminate. Instead of thinking of feminism and deconstruction as epistemological theories or political discourses, this article situates the disciplinary status of each as excluded from the law and displaced into the field of ethics.

ELDER, Crawford L. Antirealism and Realist Claims of Invariance. S J Phil, 29(1), 1-20, Spr 91.

Realists maintain that this or that aspect of the world would remain unaltered, if we were to adopt different attitudes or beliefs about it. Antirealists sometimes agree: the aspect is a projection of our minds, they say, but one projected so as to be thus invariant. But how can what is projected, and hence not really real, really be invariant? Blackburn replies that the assertions of invariance belong to expressive discourse, the assertion of projectedness to fact-stating discourse. Putnam replies that *no* discourse corresponds to the way the world is. I show that neither solution works.

ELGESEM, Dag. Intentions, Actions, and Routines: A Problem in Krister Segerberg's Theory of Action. Synthese, 85(1), 153-176, O 90.

The aim of this paper is to make a critical assessment of Krister Segerberg's theory of action. The first part gives a critical presentation of the key concepts in Segerberg's informal theory of action. These are the ideas that motivate the formal models he develops. In the second part it is argued that if one takes all of Segerberg's motivating ideas seriously, problems are forthcoming. The main problem is that on this theory the agents seem to be bound to realize all of their intentions, a problem that stems from Segerberg's attempt to individuate actions in terms of the agent's intentions. On the ground that this unfortunate result is forthcoming in both of Segerberg's approaches to the logic of action it is concluded that the conceptual basis of the theory is problematic.

ELGIN, Catherine Z. "Facts That Don't Matter" in *Meaning and Method:*

Essays in Honor of Hilary Putnam, BOOLOS, George (ed), 17-29. New York, Cambridge Univ Pr, 1990.

Responsibility for the indeterminacy of translation is usually assigned to Quine's behaviorist assumptions. I argue that Putnam's Twin Earth examples show that behaviorism is not to blame. Neither Fodor's 'language of thought' or Searle's introspectibly plain facts about one's own idiolect have the resources to determine whether my term 'beech' should be translated as 'beech' or as 'elm'. Translation manuals that answer to all identifiably relevant facts, behavioral or not, still conflict.

ELGIN, Catherine Z. Sign, Symbol, and System. J Aes Educ, 25(1), 11-21, Spr 91.

ELGIN, Catherine Z. What Goodman Leaves Out. J Aes Educ, 25(1), 89-96, Spr 91.

ELIAS, Robert H. "Literature, History, and What Men Learn" in *The Philosophy of John William Miller*, FELL, Joseph P (ed), 136-152. Lewisburg, Bucknell Univ Pr, 1990.

ELLIOT, Gregory and OSBORNE, Peter. Community as Compulsion? A Reply to Skillen on Citizenship and the State. Rad Phil, 58, 14-15, Sum 91.

ELLIOT, Robert. "Environmental Ethics" in *A Companion to Ethics*, SINGER, Peter (ed), 284-293. Cambridge, Blackwell, 1991.

This article describes a variety of environmental ethics from the anthropocentric to the holistic. It highlights relationships between them and reviews the arguments which might be used to justify them.

ELLIOT, Robert. Personal Identity and the Causal Continuity Requirement. Phil Quart, 41(162), 55-75, Ja 91.

It has been argued by many that causal continuity is necessary for personal identity. An argument against this view is presented and a number of counter-arguments rebutted. Some general conclusions are drawn concerning the nature of personal identity.

ELLIOTT, C S. Rational Chocolate Addiction or How Chocolate Cures Irrationality. Int J Moral Soc Stud, 6(2), 172-184, Sum 91.

Most people experience moments of lack of will power. When faced with a conflict between short-run desires and what they know is 'best in the long-run', they often choose to follow temptation - only to regret it later. However, individuals know this, and have learned how to precommit or bind themselves to long-run optimal behavior. One common method is to self-administer chocolate as a positive reinforcer. This paper provides an economic explanation of why a voluntary chocolate reward can be an effective means of countering short-run temptations. In addition, because the effectiveness of chocolate in this role may increase, the rationality of psychological addiction to chocolate is explored.

ELLIOTT, Car. Beliefs and Responsibility. J Value Inq, 25(3), 233-248, Jl 91.

ELLIOTT, Carl. Moral Responsibility, Psychiatric Disorders and Duress. J Applied Phil, 8(1), 45-56, 1991.

The paper is a discussion of moral responsibility and excuses in regard to psychiatric disorders involving abnormal desires (e.g., impulse control disorders such as kleptomania and pyromania, psychosexual disorders such as exhibitionism, obsessive-compulsive disorder and others). It points out problems with previous approaches to the question of whether or not to excuse persons with these disorders, and offers a new approach based on the concept of duress. There is a discussion of duress in regard to non-psychiatric cases based on the core notion of duress involving a choice between undesirables, and the paper concludes with an argument that moral blame for individuals with these sorts of disorders should often be lessened and in some cases removed entirely.

ELLIOTT, Gregory (ed) and ALTHUSSER, Louis. *Philosophy and the Spontaneous Philosophy of the Scientists and Other Essays*. New York, Verso, 1990.

Collected here are Althusser's most significant philosophical writings from 1965 to 1978, intended to contribute to a left-wing critique of Stalinism. At the same time they chart his critique of the theoretical system in his own works. (staff)

ELLIS, Albert. The Philosophical Basis of Rational-Emotive Therapy (RET). Int J Applied Phil, 5(2), 35-41, Fall 90.

ELLIS, Brian. Solving the Problem of Induction Using a Values-Based Epistemology. Brit J Phil Sci, 39(2), 141-160, Je 88.

In this paper it is argued that to show that our scientific inductive practices are rational, we need a theory of rationality in which rationality is defined in terms of optimal strategies for maximising epistemic value. The principal aim of this paper is to sketch such a theory, and to show how it can be used both to explain and to justify our practices. The theory required is one which takes certain epistemic values to be both natural and fundamental, and construes inductive rules as being just more or less useful strategies for promoting these values. What is required to solve the problem of induction is therefore a naturalistic, values-based epistemology which will account adequately for our scientific inductive practices.

ELLIS, Carol S and ELLIS, Ralph D. *Theories of Criminal Justice: A Critical Reappraisal*. Wolfeboro, Longwood, 1989.

Usable both as scholarly resource and as textbook, this book draws together empirical research and philosophical theory to spotlight the many weaknesses of the most popular approaches to criminal justice theory—deterrence, rehabilitation, and retribution. A firm grounding in empirical realities of criminology is essential for theorizing, and one ends up with a completely different philosophy depending on these facts. This book's thesis is that these facts lead to rejection of utilitarianism (because neither deterrence nor rehabilitation works under present social circumstances) and retribution (because of the degree of determinism in human nature). By contrast, a 'communitarian' approach *can* work, by emphasizing the society's responsibility to create opportunities so as to *produce* fewer criminals.

ELLIS, Gary. "Infertility and the Role of the Federal Government" in *Beyond Baby M: Ethical Issues in New Reproductive Techniques*, BARTELS, Dianne M (ed), 111-130. Clifton, Humana Pr, 1990.

ELLIS, John. The Trouble with Fragrance. Phronesis, 35(3), 290-302, 1990.

This paper investigates the ancient Greek commentators' interpretation of Aristotle's doctrine of inherence, as suggested by his remarks at *Categories* ch. 2. Specifically, the views of Ammonius, Simplicius, Philoponus, Olympiodorus and Elias are discussed with respect to their solution of the problem of fragrance, viz., how can an apple's fragrance be an accident of the apple and, contrary to Aristotle's doctrine of inherence, separate from it? The article shows that there is a development in the discussions of the commentators from solutions which imply a weak construal of inherence towards solutions which imply a strong construal. It also turns out that their solutions to the problem require a rethinking of Aristotle's psychology, in particular his theory of smell.

ELLIS, Ralph D and ELLIS, Carol S. *Theories of Criminal Justice: A Critical Reappraisal*. Wolfeboro, Longwood, 1989.

Usable both as scholarly resource and as textbook, this book draws together empirical research and philosophical theory to spotlight the many weaknesses of the most popular approaches to criminal justice theory—deterrence, rehabilitation, and retribution. A firm grounding in empirical realities of criminology is essential for theorizing, and one ends up with a completely different philosophy depending on these facts. This book's thesis is that these facts lead to rejection of utilitarianism (because neither deterrence nor rehabilitation works under present social circumstances) and retribution (because of the degree of determinism in human nature). By contrast, a 'communitarian' approach *can* work, by emphasizing the society's responsibility to create opportunities so as to *produce* fewer criminals.

ELLIS, Ralph D. Toward a Reconciliation of Liberalism and Communitarianism. J Value Inq, 25(1), 55-64, Ja 91.

Communitarianism has been criticized because it pays too little attention to the injustice resulting from 'community values,' whereas liberalism endorses an abstract concept of justice but either opposes or pays too little attention to the processes through which the community inculcates values in its members. This paper attempts to reconcile these opposing views by proposing that there are certain values (such as justice) which must be endorsed by any rational being to the extent that she is a rational being, and that communities of rational beings must give priority to these universal human values over those values which are specific to certain cultures, communities, or ways of life.

ELLISON, Charles E. Jean-Jacques Rousseau on the Physiogonomy of the Modern City. Hist Euro Ideas, 12(4), 479-502, 1990.

ELLISON, Julie. *Delicate Subjects: Romanticism, Gender, and the Ethics of Understanding*. Ithaca, Cornell Univ Pr, 1990.

ELLOS, William J. *Ethical Practice in Clinical Medicine*. New York, Routledge, 1990.

In this study, basic yet controversial issues such as death and dying, truth-telling, confidentiality, and physician-patient relationships are treated in great depth—issues whose principles and complexities it is vital for the practising medical ethicist to grasp. It first presents the theoretical sources of virtue ethics and then works through a number of medical ethics cases using the materials from the sources. In addition, it is the first book to address directly practical clinical problems from an historical perspective by using classic texts. (edited)

ELÓSEGUI, María. La dialéctica del deseo como realización de la identidad en Henri Bergson. Themata, 6, 45-50, 1989.

Bergson saw the reality of a vital self, made up of dialectic and contradiction, caused by the stress between desires. However he did not know how to justify this contradiction which is present in life, because he rejected the role of matter's negativity, whose origin placed in the positiveness of spirit; in this way he equates the two as identical. Though Bergson did not read Hegel, it is proposed that one should re-read Bergson's work from a dialectic perspective. Dialectically desires are creative. Human existence is a dialectical process in which each individual proposes the goal to the fulfillment of his personal identity.

ELOVAARA, Raili. "How to Recognise Metaphors in Literature" in *XIth International Congress in Aesthetics, Nottingham 1988*, WOODFIELD, Richard (ed), 45-49. Nottingham, Nottingham Polytech, 1990.

The article distinguishes five criteria for determining metaphors: 1) the falsity of an expression when taken literally; 2) the lack of a literal referent; 3) the lack of congruence with the context when a statement is read literally; 4) the speaker doesn't believe in the literal truth of his statement or is not interested in knowing whether it is literally true; 5) the pointlessness of the truth of a literal reading. Metaphors which can also be understood literally or which one might want to call symbols raise problems. Some solutions are suggested.

ELSHTAIN, Jean Bethke. "Antigone's Daughters Reconsidered: Continuing Reflections on Women, Politics, and Power" in *Life-World and Politics: Between Modernity and Postmodernity*, WHITE, Stephen K (ed), 222-235. Notre Dame, Univ Notre Dame Pr, 1989.

Building on a previous discussion of The Antigone, appropriated to a feminist analysis that eschews narrow utilitarian and contractarian construals, Elshtain here draws upon the Sophocles play to reissue a critique of liberal, radical, and Marxist feminisms insofar as each either privileges the state or a future perfect version of a feminized collective authority. She goes on to argue that Hegel's reading of The Antigone misses what is most powerful and poignant in the story of Antigone's resistance to Creon, namely, Antigone's transgressive words and deeds.

ELSTER, Jon. "Rationality and Social Norms" in *Logic, Methodology and Philosophy of Science, VIII*, FENSTAD, J E (ed), 531-552. New York, Elsevier Science, 1989.

ELZENBERG, H. "Negative Values" in *Logic and Ethics*, GEACH, Peter (ed), 21-31. Norwell, Kluwer, 1991.

EMBREE, Lester. Notes on the Specification of "Meaning" in Schutz. Human Stud, 14(2-3), 207-218, Jl 91.

Uses of "meaning" and "understanding" in Alfred Schutz's work are classified as scientific (philosophical and pure and applied social scientific) and everyday (non-practical, e.g., recreational, and practical, including observational and participational by actors and partners), linguistic and non-linguistic, individual and collective, deliberate and routine, etc., to show that there are at least fifty-six (56) multideterminate types in his philosophy.

EMBREE, Lester. "The Structure of American Theoretical Archaeology: A Preliminary Report" in *Critical Traditions in Contemporary Archaeology*, PINSKY, Valerie (ed), 28-37. New York, Cambridge Univ Pr, 1990.

Questionnaire responses are interpreted to show the components of the collective research effort that the fifty-year-old tradition of researchers here called "theoretical archaeologists" recognize. The "empirical archaeology" of data collection and analysis and the "theorizing of explanatory models" make up "substantive research," which is complemented by reflections upon it from within archaeology that are here called "metaarchaeology" and which are different from the reflections from without called "philosophy of archaeology." On this basis of this structure, closer historical analysis can be performed on archaeological research practice and philosophers of archaeology can have a better chance of knowing what they are talking about.

EMILSSON, Eyjólfur K. "Plotinus and Soul-Body Dualism" in *Psychology (Companions to Ancient Thought: 2)*, EVERSON, Stephen (ed), 148-165. New York, Cambridge Univ Pr, 1991.

EMMANUEL, Steven M. Kierkegaard's Pragmatist Faith. Phil Phenomenol Res, 51(2), 279-302, Je 91.

The aim of this paper is to show that the Kierkegaardian conception of faith can be defended along traditional pragmatist lines. I interpret the Absolute Paradox as a conceptual expression for the total incommensurability between an infinite God and a finite human intellect. As such, the paradox clears logical space for faith by showing that theoretical reason is incapable of deciding the question of whether Christianity is true. However, where theoretical reason cannot decide the option between belief and unbelief, and where the attainment of an eternal happiness is effectively precluded by the failure to believe, the venture to become Christian may be validated on practical grounds.

EMMECHE, Claus. A Semiotical Reflection on Biology, Living Signs and Artificial Life. Biol Phil, 6(3), 325-340, Jl 91.

It is argued, that theory of signs, especially in the tradition of the great philosopher Charles Sanders Peirce (1839-1914) can inspire the study of central problems in the philosophy of biology. Three such problems are considered: 1) The nature of biology as a science, where a semiotically informed pluralistic approach to the theory of science is introduced. 2) The peculiarity of the general object of biology, where a realistic interpretation of sign- and information-concepts is required to see sign-processes as immanent in nature. 3) The possibility of an artificial construction of life, hereby discussed as a conceptual problem in the present form of the artificial life project and its implied definition of life.

ENDICOTT, Ronald P. Macdonald on Type Reduction via Disjunction. S J Phil, 29(2), 209-214, Sum 91.

In her book *Mind-Body Identity Theories*, Cynthia Macdonald argues that reductive strategies that appeal to disjunctive properties are unsuccessful because physical state types can serve to realize virtually any mental type, so that the disjunctive properties ultimately have all disjuncts in common (making them indistinguishable). I argue that a) Macdonald wrongly presupposes "logical" vs. "metaphysical" possibility; b) she conflates the possibility of, e.g., "pain being something other than C-fibers" (true but irrelevant) with the possibility of "C-fibers being something other than pain" (false when rightly understood); and c) the falsity of the latter proposition is evident by paying close attention to the distinction between "core" and "total" realizations.

ENGEL, David E. The School and the Home: Partners or Pariahs—A Response to Kennedy on Home Schools. Phil Stud Educ, /, 45-49, 1986.

ENGEL, David. Stopping the Thought That Stops Thought: Response to John Scahill. Phil Stud Educ, /, 185-187, 1987-88.

ENGELHARDT JR, H Tristram. Human Nature Technologically Revisited. Soc Phil Pol, 8(1), 180-191, Autumn 90.

In the light of recent developments in genetic science, we can foresee a time in the not too far distant future when man can biologically redesign human nature. Arguments against genetic engineering often parallel arguments against contraception: they assume an intrinsic value to the results of natural processes. These arguments, however, involve theological premises that are not articulatable in secular moral terms. As long as the usual moral tests of beneficence and respect for autonomy are satisfied, genetic engineering should thus be viewed on par with other medical technologies, when we consider its secular moral significance.

ENGELHARDT JR, H Tristram. "Integrity, Humaneness, and Institutions in Secular Pluralist Societies" in *Integrity in Health Care Institutions: Humane Environments for Teaching, Inquiry, and Healing*, BULGER, Ruth Ellen (ed), 33-43. Iowa City, Univ of Iowa Pr, 1990.

In the post-modern context one must attend to values at two levels. At the secular level there will be no content-full understanding of the goals of social institutions that can be discovered by reason alone. The integrity of these institutions will depend upon peaceably acquiring the consent and authority of all individuals involved. Procedural means will be used to allow moral strangers to collaborate. A central role will be given to rights to privacy and toleration. At the private level, however, the integrity of institutions depends upon the articulation of their own particular understandings of morality and humaneness. These institutions will sustain the differences that make secular mediation important and interesting.

ENGELS, Frederick. *Collected Works, Volume 26, Engels: 1882-1889*. New York, Intl Publ, 1990.

ENGLEBRETSEN, George. Cartesian Syntax. Phil Inq, 12(1-2), 59-64, Wint-Spr 90.

The "Cartesian" theory of logical syntax was most fully formulated by the Port-Royal logicians. A brief survey of their work, especially the *Logique*, shows that they took a statement to have a deep structure analyzable as a predication. It is a joining or separating of two terms by a positive or negative copula. Complex terms were also viewed as (implicit) predication. The logical syntax of predication requires no recourse to semantic distinctions among terms, nor does it distinguish atomic from molecular statements.

ENGLEBRETSEN, George. Formatives. Notre Dame J Form Log, 30(3), 382-389, Sum 89.

An answer to the question of 'sentential unity' (What makes a sentence a single linguistic unit rather than just a string of words?) is one of the goals of any theory of logical syntax. A 'Fregean' theory claims that a sentence is a function (unsaturated expression, containing gaps) whose gaps are filled with either arguments (saturated, gap-less) or other functions which have already been saturated. A 'Leibnizian' theory construes a sentence as a syntactically complex subject (quantified term) plus a syntactically complex predicate (qualified term). Subjects and predicates just naturally fit one another to form sentences. An 'Aristotelian' theory takes a sentence to consist of a pair of terms connected by a binary formative expression (functor), whose only role is to connect terms to form more complex expressions (e.g., sentences). After an examination of the formal nature of such functors, it is argued that this third sort of theory not only answers better the question of sentential unity, but it also provides a better account of the nature of logical constants in general.

ENGLEMAN, K H and MARTIN, J E. The Mind's I Has Two Eyes. Philosophy, 65(254), 510-515, O 90.

ENGLER, Wolfgang. Power, Knowledge and Freedom: The Meaning of Foucault's Threefold Break with the History of Ideas (in German). Deut Z Phil, 38(9), 874-886, 1990.

ENGLISH, Mary. Siting, Justice, and Conceptions of Good. Pub Affairs Quart, 5(1), 1-17, Ja 91.

Hazardous waste treatment plants, radioactive waste burial grounds, garbage incinerators... Whether such "LULUs" (locally unwanted land uses) are needed and whether they can be made safe are important issues. This paper, however, explores a different issue: the strategies being used to site such facilities, and the distributive principles tacitly adopted to justify these strategies. The paper concludes with the argument that when, in order to attain some widely valued goods, an undesirable byproduct must be distributed, utilitarianism and libertarianism will prove inadequate, as will procedural justice. Nevertheless, procedural justice may be the only recourse, for it may be the only means to a fuller justice.

ENGLISH, Parker. Representative Realism and Absolute Reality. Int J Phil Relig, 28(3), 127-145, D 90.

This paper clarifies J L Mackie's idea that representative realism should treat material substances as groups of submicroscopic entities. In particular, it *distinguishes* perceived objects, as identical with the perceptions of them, from the material substances which cause our perceiving those objects. Under this form of representative realism, the experience of absolute reality does *not* prove that perceived objects are unreal. It does not do so even under the assumption that this experience does prove absolute reality to be more important than perceived objects are.

ENGMANN, Joyce. Cosmic Justice in Anaximander. Phronesis, 36(1), 1-25, 1991.

EPSTEIN, Richard A. "Beyond Foreseeability: Consequential Damages in the Law of Contract" in *Liability and Responsibility*, FREY, R G (ed), 89-134. New York, Cambridge Univ Pr, 1991.

EPSTEIN, Richard A. Two Conceptions of Civil Rights. Soc Phil Pol, 8(2), 38-59, Spr 91.

EPSTEIN, Richard A. The Varieties of Self-Interest. Soc Phil Pol, 8(1), 102-120, Autumn 90.

ERESHEFSKY, Marc. The Semantic Approach to Evolutionary Theory. Biol Phil, 6(1), 59-80, Ja 91.

Paul Thompson, John Beatty, and Elisabeth Lloyd argue that attempts to resolve certain conceptual issues within evolutionary biology have failed because of a general adherence to the received view of scientific theories. They maintain that such issues can be clarified and resolved when one adopts a semantic approach to theories. In this paper, I argue that such conceptual issues are just as problematic on a semantic approach. Such issues arise from the complexity involved in providing formal accounts of theoretical laws and scientific explanations. That complexity is due to empirical and pragmatic considerations, not one's adherence to a particular formal approach to theories. This analysis raises a broader question. How can any formal account properly represent the complex nature of empirical phenomena?

ERESHEFSKY, Marc. Species, Higher Taxa, and the Units of Evolution. Phil Sci, 58(1), 84-101, Mr 91.

A number of authors argue that while species are evolutionary units, individuals and real entities, higher taxa are not. I argue that drawing the divide between species and higher taxa along such lines has not been successful. Common conceptions of evolutionary units either include or exclude both types of taxa. Most species, like all higher taxa, are not individuals, but historical entities. Furthermore, higher taxa are neither more nor less real than species. None of this implies that there is no distinction between species and higher taxa; the point is that such a distinction is more subtle than many authors have claimed.

ERHARD, John. "Tradition, Innovation, Kunstrezeption und Kuntswirkung—zu einigen Problemen" in *XIth International Congress in Aesthetics, Nottingham 1988*, WOODFIELD, Richard (ed), 50-54. Nottingham, Nottingham Polytech, 1990.

ERICKSON, Glenn W. *Negative Dialectics and the End of Philosophy*. Wolfeboro, Longwood, 1990.

Part One is antiphilosophical; Part Two, postphilosophical. After formalizing the methodology of Merleau-Ponty's *Phenomenology* as a "negative dialectics" seeking to undermine traditional empiricist and intellectualist positions, Part One applies the methodology to the issues of time and space, ideality and reality, literal speech and metaphor, form and function, art and technology, logic and rhetoric. Part Two explores tree and wood imagery in a variety of philosophical contexts in order to disclose the horizon of philosophy in Indo-European lexicon and cult. A new theory of truth as steadfastness and an account of the structures of worldhood are proposed.

ERICKSON, Glenn W. Wittgenstein's "Remarks on Colour". Dialogos, 26(57), 113-136, Ja 91.

A detailed commentary on Wittgenstein's posthumous "Remarks on Colour" ("RC"), the article treats especially of Wittgenstein's distinction between the natural history and the geometry of color, his interpretation of Goethe's color theory, and his analysis of the distinction between seeing and observing. Certain infelicities of Wittgenstein's preliminary reflections on the concept of the purity of color, published as Part III of the "RC", are separated out from his genuine insights in a manner parallel to the revisions he made himself, published as Part I.

ERICKSON, Stephen A. Nietzsche and Post-Modernity. Phil Today, 34(2), 175-178, Sum 90.

ERICKSON, Stephen A. The Relevance of Meditative Thinking. J Speculative Phil, 5(1), 25-41, 1991.

ERICSON, Edward L. A New Humanism: A Response. Relig Hum, 25(1), 19-20, Wint 91.

ERJAVEC, Ales. "Postmodernism and Critical Theory" in *XIth International Congress in Aesthetics, Nottingham 1988*, WOODFIELD, Richard (ed), 55-58. Nottingham, Nottingham Polytech, 1990.

ERNEST, Paul. The Meaning of Mathematical Expressions: Does Philosophy Shed Any Light on Psychology? Brit J Phil Sci, 41(4), 443-460, D 90.

The paper reviews a number of approaches to meaning in the philosophical literature, including post-Fregean, syntactical, proof-theoretic, model-theoretic, and holistic approaches. They are evaluated with respect to their applicability to the psychology of learning mathematics. A theoretical model of the meaning of mathematical expressions is proposed, based on this synthetic review. It is elaborated elsewhere.

ERWIN, Edward and SIEGEL, Harvey. Is Confirmation Differential? Brit J Phil Sci, 40(1), 105-119, Mr 89.

ERZEN, Jale. "Tradition and Convolution—Settings of Aesthetic Phenomena in the Third World" in *XIth International Congress in Aesthetics, Nottingham 1988*, WOODFIELD, Richard (ed), 59-61. Nottingham, Nottingham Polytech, 1990.

ESPARZA-BRACHO, Jesús. El concepto de Filosofia y conocimiento en Ludwig Wittgenstein. Rev Filosof (Venezuela), 12, 55-65, 1989.

This work intends to analyze the nature of philosophy in Wittgenstein's thinking, through the logical analysis of formal language structure, going to logical and grammatical analysis of ordinary language. It concludes in a metaphysical agnosticism, expressed in a scepticistic view for philosophical knowledge, caused by a reduced use of the word "knowledge." This position entails an ontologization of a meaning theory, because language and words are expected to be used only for meaning. We conclude pointing out that there is another kind of language, the philosophical one; it has, as a scientific language, a translinguistic range.

ESPINOZA, Miguel. "The Four Causes" in *Studies on Mario Bunge's "Treatise"*, WEINGARTNER, Paul'(ed), 171-190. Amsterdam, Rodopi, 1990.

The realist metaphysics argued for in this essay can be stated in four propositions: (1) philosophy is the quest for intelligibility; (2) intelligibility and rationality are intrinsic properties of nature; (3) knowledge is the presence of the intelligibility of natural systems in the intellect; and (4) formal and final causes are as natural and as rationally conceivable as efficient causes. The main object is to restore the ontological value of formal and final causes which, according to Mario Bunge, were "killed" by modern science. Bunge's opinion is underlied by his scientific realism; thus the present article is also a criticism of some of the theses of that doctrine from the point of view of realist metaphysics.

ESPOSITO, Costantino. "Esserci e differenza ontologica in Heidegger" in *Razionalitá critica: nella filosofia moderna*, LAMACCHIA, Ada (ed), 127-169. Bari, Lacaita, 1989.

ESPOSITO, Costantino. Heidegger: vita e distino—Sullo biografia heideggeriana di Hugo Ott. G Metaf, 11(3), 477-491, S-D 89.

ESPOSITO, Joan (trans) and TURCHETTO, Maria. The Divided Machine: Capitalist Crisis and the Organization of Labor. Grad Fac Phil J, 14(1), 209-240, 1991.

ESSER, P H. F M Dostoievsky (1821-1881): Great Existentialist-Psychiatrist. Method Sci, 22(4), 201-217, 1989.

To live is wanting to be different, to be creative. Great writers are both individual and universal. They ask, looking for an answer or suck out the question's content. Reality is not what an individual is working at, but what goes on in his mind. *The Devils* reflects Dostoievsky's own life. Theocracy is needed, not democracy. Socialism is atheism. You are what you believe. God is directly involved in this world. Dostoievsky believed Christ will return to Russia, which has the task to unite all nations.

ESTERHUYSE, Willie. The 'Gay Science' of Nietzsche (in Dutch). S Afr J Phil, 10(3), 79-87, Ag 91.

In this article the author demonstrates that Nietzsche's philosophical texts thoroughly undermine the notion of the subject as a foundational concept. In this respect his texts can be termed anti-metaphysical. In arguing his point, Nietzsche develops a theory on text, interpretation and metaphor which enables him to do away with the subject as a privileged epistemological starting point. In doing so, he equally undermines traditional notions of truth and authority—introducing metaphors such as "play" and "dance" to articulate the view that the interpretative process displays an "infinite" character. His views, however, do not result in a form of anti-humanism. The "death of God" does not imply the "death of man". Nietzsche, on the contrary, situates man in a different context to metaphysics, describing man as a variable and function of a dynamic and complex network of relations.

ESTÊVÁO, Carlos. A "Con-versão" da Filosofia em Martin Heidegger. Rev Port Filosof, 45(3), 403-412, Jl-S 89.

The aim of this article is to set off the specificity of Heidegger's philosophy face to the apparent "linguistical privilege" that stands out from his work. In spite of the co-implication of ontological problematic and language, Heidegger places that one on a radically different level of perspective either metaphysical or scientific. A "con-versão" is then demanded, which leads us to a definition from other ways of truth concerning the Being, and to a "re-versão" of it as a place, a welling-place of Being. The philosophical thought must therefore take upon itself as permanently "required" , as privileged modality of the native saying, and become walker under the "suggestion" of the Language of Being, without ever submitting itself to methods, laws, subjects or rational systematization of the reality, but rather the reality itself as a region of free space, of glade of path, which entangle us and make us return to the intimacy of the Being.

ESTRADA, Olga C (ed). Las ideas en Centroamerica: De 1838 a 1970. Rev Filosof (Costa Rica), 27(65), 5-276, Je 89.

ETTINGER, Lia and JABLONKA, Eva and FALK, Raphael. On Causality, Heritability and Fitness. Biol Phil, 6(1), 27-29, Ja 91.

We comment on Byerly's and Michod's paper "Fitness and evolutionary explanation". We emphasize that fitness should be attributed to types only, and not to individuals. We define fitness as the measure of the causal and heritable contribution of a trait to the reproductive success of individuals (representing a type) which possess this trait, in a specific environment. The research program of evolutionary biologists studying the evolution of adaptations is realized when the fitness of a certain type is found.

ETTINGER, Lia and JABLONKA, Eva and MC LAUGHLIN, Peter. On the Adaptations of Organisms and the Fitness of Types. Phil Sci, 57(3), 499-513, S 90.

We claim that much of the confusion associated with the "tautology problem" about survival of the fittest is due to the mistake of attributing fitness to individuals instead of to types. We argue further that the problem itself cannot be solved merely by taking fitness as the aggregate cause of reproductive success. We suggest that a satisfying explanation must center not on logical analysis of the concept of general adaptedness but on the empirical analysis of single adapted traits and their causal relationship to changes in allele frequencies.

EVANGELIOU, Christos. Porphyry's Criticism of Christianity and The Problem of Augustine's Platonism. Dionysius, 13, 51-70, D 89.

Porphyry, as a representative of Platonism, presented Augustine with a serious problem because he had advanced a philosophical criticism of the Christian faith. This study shows that a response to Porphyry's challenge was part of Augustine's purpose in writing *The City of God*, especially Book X. In this sense, Augustine may be considered a belated apologist whose witness seems to confirm Harnack's hypothesis regarding the fragments of Porphyry's lost book. It also helps our understanding of the prolonged conflict between Christianity and Hellenism.

EVANS, C Stephen. The Epistemological Significance of Transformative Religious Experiences: A Kierkegaardian Exploration. Faith Phil, 8(2), 180-192, Ap 91.

This paper attempts to explore the notion that some religious experiences may have value in justifying or making religious belief rational without those experiences being considered as evidence. Rather, the epistemological value of the experiences is seen as transforming the individual to make it possible for the person to gain religious knowledge, either by giving the person skills or abilities needed properly to consider other evidence, or by activating some basic belief-forming disposition. The distinction Alvin Plantinga draws between evidence and ground provides an initial starting point for considering the significance of such experiences. Kierkegaard's analysis of the experience of encountering God in Christ is then explored as a concrete illustration of the possibilities of transformative religious experience.

EVANS, C Stephen. The Relevance of Historical Evidence for Christian Faith: A Critique of a Kierkegaardian View. Faith Phil, 7(4), 470-485, O 90.

If we assume that Christian faith involves a propositional component whose content is historical, then the question arises as to whether Christian faith must be based on historical evidence, at least in part. One of Kierkegaard's pseudonyms, Johannes Climacus, argues in *Philosophical Fragments* that though faith does indeed have such a historical component, it does not depend on evidence, but rather on a first-hand experience of Jesus for which historical records serve only as an occasion. I argue that Climacus's account is coherent, and that on such a view historical evidence is not sufficient for faith for anyone. However, in contrast to Climacus, I argue that evidence might still be valuable and even necessary for some people. The resulting danger that the decision about faith might become a question for scholarship is best met, not by insulating faith from historical scholarship, but by recognizing the ability of faith to supply a context in which the evidence available is sufficient.

EVANS, C Stephen. "Where There's a Will There's a Way: Kierkegaard's Theory of Action" in *Writing the Politics of Difference*, SILVERMAN, Hugh J (ed), 73-88. Albany, SUNY Pr, 1991.

This article articulates Kierkegaard's understanding of human action and the related concepts of choice and will. Contrary to MacIntyre's claim that Kierkegaard defends a concept of radical criterionless choice, Kierkegaard's position is a variation of the Aristotelian view that a choice is the resolution of a process of deliberation about a wish or desire, though Kierkegaard insists that there is a gap between intellectual judgment and action that must be filled by a leap. However, this only commits Kierkegaard to standard liberation views of free action, not to a doctrine of radical choice. Kierkegaard's view of action is essential to understanding his ethics and helps resolve both Davidsonian puzzles over weakness of will and Frankfurt-type counter-examples to libertarian freedom.

EVANS, Fred. Cognitive Psychology, Phenomenology, and the "Creative Tension of Voices". Phil Rhet, 24(2), 105-127, 1991.

EVANS, Fred. Language and Political Agency: Derrida, Marx, and Bakhtin. S J Phil, 28(4), 505-523, Wint 90.

EVANS, Fred. Marx, Nietzsche, and the "New Class". J Speculative Phil, 4(3), 249-266, 1990.

EVANS, J Claude. Two-Steps-in-One-Proof: The Structure of the Transcendental Deduction of the Categories. J Hist Phil, 28(4), 553-570, O 90.

EVASDAUGHTER, Elizabeth N. "Julian of Norwich" in *A History of Women Philosophers, Volume II: Medieval, Renaissance and Enlightenment, A.D. 500-1600*, WAITHE, Mary Ellen (ed), 191-222. Norwell, Kluwer, 1989.

Julian thought of knowledge as a set of propositions or understandings which described reality reliably, if at times dimly or partially. She was convinced that we could know with certainty that God loves us, wants to save our souls, and will do so. She offered, as a model to her readers, her intellectual behavior during her visions and after; she applied human reason to the solution of religious problems with the help of revealed truths. She held that images given in visions or in meditation, which moderns usually attribute to the unconscious, came from God and were a significant source of understanding. The optimism which inspired her epistemology as a whole also inspired her remarks on the value of the knowledge of God for human progress and happiness. In this regard as in others, her ultimate argument was that God wills us to know.

EVERETT, James and MORIN, Alain. Conscience de soi et langage intérieur: quelques spéculations. Philosophiques, 17(2), 168-188, Autumn 1990.

This text proposes a definition of self-awareness and explains its social origin. It is postulated that the social milieu permits a movement to a more objective perspective for self-perception, and that this movement is then reproduced in the brain by specific cognitive processes. It is suggested that inner speech represents one such cognitive process, which acts like a mirror to reflect subjective experience back upon itself; the self would be generated by this reflective activity. It is argued that inner speech has a preeminent position among the cognitive processes implicated in self-awareness. The problem of self-awareness in primates is discussed, and the article concludes with ideas concerning schizophrenia, prayer, meditation, and psychodysleptic drugs.

EVERSON, Stephen. "The Objective Appearance of Pyrrhonism" in *Psychology (Companions to Ancient Thought: 2)*, EVERSON, Stephen (ed), 121-147. New York, Cambridge Univ Pr, 1991.

EVERSON, Stephen (ed). *Psychology (Companions to Ancient Thought: 2)*. New York, Cambridge Univ Pr, 1991.

EVNINE, Simon. *Donald Davidson*. Stanford, Stanford Univ Pr, 1991.

The book provides an introduction to and a critical evaluation of the philosophy of Donald Davidson. There are chapters on the various components of his philosophies of mind and language, and on the metaphysical and epistemological ramifications of these views, such as Davidson's arguments against scepticism and conceptual schemes. My conclusion about Davidson's work is that it combines two antagonistic approaches to propositional content, one which goes with the causal explanatory view of the causal theory of action and anomalous monism, and one which goes with the more hermeneutic approach of the work on radical interpretation and the principle of charity.

EWALD, François. Ethics and Politics (in German). Deut Z Phil, 38(10), 897-902, 1990.

EWIN, R E. Loyalty: The Police. Crim Just Ethics, 9(2), 3-15, Sum-Fall 90.

This paper seeks to establish how satisfactory loyalty is as a motivation to duty among police. It takes the report of the Fitzgerald Commission on police corruption in Queensland as a focus for discussion, but also deals with argument about whether loyalty is itself a virtue. There are important faults with loyalty as moral motivation; the paper discusses the limitations that must be imposed on liberty if those faults are to be avoided.

EWIN, R E. The Moral Status of the Corporation. J Bus Ethics, 10(10), 749-756, O 91.

Corporations are moral persons to the extent that they have rights and duties, but their moral personality is severly limited. As artificial persons, they lack the emotional make-up that allows natural persons to show virtues and vices. That fact, taken with the representative function of management, places significant limitations on what constitutes ethical behavior by management. A common misunderstanding of those limitations can lead ethical managers to behave unethically and can lead the public to have improper expectations of corporations.

EWIN, R E. Rights and Utilitarianism. Phil Papers, 19(3), 213-224, N 90.

People disagree about what to do (often because they disagree about what is the case); because of that disagreement, social life requires a notion of a right that cannot be accommodated by utilitarianism. Hence, utilitarianism cannot be an adequate moral theory for any society.

EYLER, John. "Science, Conscience, and Public Policy: Historical Reflections on Controversial Reproductive Issues" in *Beyond Baby M: Ethical Issues in New Reproductive Techniques*, BARTELS, Dianne M (ed), 29-43. Clifton, Humana Pr, 1990.

EZCURRA, Alicia Villar (trans) and LEVINAS, E. Filosofía, justicia y amor. Dialogo Filosof, 6(3), 308-321, S-D 90.

FABELLA, Raul V. Rawlsian Nash Solutions. Theor Decis, 30(2), 113-126, Mr 91.

We investigate the conditions which guarantee the choice of Rawlsian solutions by players of unequal maximin positions bargaining under Nash rules. The conditions, viz., subsymmetry and the location of the Pareto set, relate to the structure of the utility set, *S*.

FABREGA JR, Horacio. An Ethnomedical Perspective of Medical Ethics. J Med Phil, 15(6), 593-625, D 90.

Ethnomedicine is the field that analyzes medical traditions comparatively. An ethnomedical approach is used in the essay to analyze the topic of medical ethics. General properties of medical ethics as realized in different societies are outlined. These pertain to the healer's relations with clients, with other healers, and with the group or society. The conditions of medical practice and the influence of social and political factors that affect them are discussed in relation to medical ethical questions. Unique developments of contemporary medical science that affect and condition practice and raise new ethical questions are examined in light of ethnomedical generalizations. The essay aims to clarify the cultural bases of medicine generally and ethical aspects of medical practice and care more specifically.

FABRO, Cornelio. L'odissea dell'ateismo e del nichilismo. Sapienza, 43(4), 401-410, O-D 90.

FAC LETRAS UNIV LISBOA (ed). *Dinâmica do Pensar: Homenagem a Oswaldo Market*. Lisboa, Fac Letras U Lisboa, 1991.

FACIONE, Peter A. Thirty Great Ways to Mess Up a Critical Thinking Test. Inform Log, 12(2), 106-112, Spr 90.

This humorous guide offers quick, practical advice on assessment, especially CT testing. Eleven rules, like "Set no instructional priorities," and "Emphasize the trivial," apply to all educational testing. Fourteen apply to multiple-choice strategies. "No stems should avoid stating things negatively," and "Tip off wrong answers by category mistakes," rival PDQ Bach. Five rules apply directly to CT assessment. To ruin your next CT test write questions which: target information recall about CT but don't require CT itself; ignore differences in gender interests, domain-specific knowledge, etc.; are boring, time-consuming and yet entirely uncomplicated; require official CT vocabulary; and presume students think like trained experts.

FALCIONI, Daniela. Il pensiero dello "Stato" in Husserl: recenti problemi critici. Riv Int Filosof Diritto, 67(2), 296-301, Ap-Je 90.

FALGUERAS, Ignacio. Breve examen científico y filosófico de la teoría de la evolución. Espiritu, 37(98), 111-118, Jl-D 88.

FALIKOWSKI, Anthony F. *Moral Philosophy: Theories, Skills, and Applications*. Englewood Cliffs, Prentice-Hall, 1990.

FALK, Raphael and ETTINGER, Lia and JABLONKA, Eva. On Causality, Heritability and Fitness. Biol Phil, 6(1), 27-29, Ja 91.

We comment on Byerly's and Michod's paper "Fitness and evolutionary explanation". We emphasize that fitness should be attributed to types only, and not to individuals. We define fitness as the measure of the causal and heritable contribution of a trait to the reproductive success of individuals (representing a type) which possess this trait, in a specific environment. The research program of evolutionary biologists studying the evolution of adaptations is realized when the fitness of a certain type is found.

FALKENSTEIN, Lorne. Berkeley's Arguments for Other Minds. Hist Phil Quart, 7(4), 431-440, O 90.

The literature on Berkeley is almost unanimous in taking this claim to know the existence of other finite spirits to rest on an argument from analogy. I show that this is not so and that Berkeley uses a causal argument to prove that there are other minds. Questions of the degree to which it is legitimate for Berkeley to appeal to causes, particularly occasional causes, are addressed in the process.

FALKENSTEIN, Lorne. Kant's Account of Intuition. Can J Phil, 21(2), 165-193, Je 91.

This paper outlines the history of the distinction between a higher and a lower cognitive function up to Kant. It is argued that Kant initially drew the distinction in Scholastic terms—as a distinction between a capacity to image particulars and a capacity to represent universals. However, features of his project in the *Critique* led him to reformulate the distinction in terms of immediacy and mediacy. Nonetheless, for certain purposes the older, Scholastic distinction retained its attractiveness, and this is the ground for much of the subsequent difficulty with his account of intuitions and concepts.

FALKENSTEIN, Lorne. Kant, Mendelssohn, Lambert, and the Subjectivity of Time. J Hist Phil, 29(2), 227-251, Ap 91.

On the basis of an examination of Kant's correspondence with Mendelssohn, 1766-1770, I argue that already in 1770 Kant had before him a decisive refutation of the view that time is imposed by the mind on its representations, and that Kant did not hold any such view of the subjectivity of time in his later work. Kant's mature view is that time is subjective only in the sense that it is the manner in which the empirically observable subject receives sensory matter, not in the sense that the subject actually produces this manner of receptivity.

FALKENSTEIN, Lorne. Was Kant a Nativist? J Hist Ideas, 51(4), 573-597, O-D 90.

Kant's claim that space and time are "forms of intuition" is contrasted with the nativist claim that space is an innate idea or construct of the mind and with the empiricist claim that space is given in or learned from experience. It is argued that the nativism/empiricism debate masks a more fundamental disagreement between sensationism and constructivism. Kant's account of space- and time-cognition is shown to be neither sensationist nor constructivist and as a consequence to be "nativistic" in a sense which commentators from Vaihinger and Kemp Smith to Patricia Kitcher have failed to capture.

FALKIEWICZ, Andrzej. "The Individual's Horizon and Valuation" in *The Social Horizon of Knowledge*, BUCZKOWSKI, Piotr (ed), 111-128. Amsterdam, Rodopi, 1991.

An individual has its own life and lifes of its broader existences, such as its family, its social group, its nation, the mankind, i.e., it lives in its own horizon and in horizons of its broader existences. Valuation means placement of oneself in the horizons of broader existences and adoption of their preferences as one's own. The individual's values are requirements of the existences of which it is... or better, it feels part. Every individual has its own hierarchy of values: certain existences seem to it more important, other less important. And in like manner, social groups, macrogroups, nations, cultural formations have also their own hierarchies of values. In order to understand this we call human culture we must imagine a place in which such hierarchies, group and individual, infinite in number, meet.

FALZER, Paul R. On Behalf of Skeptical Rhetoric. Phil Rhet, 24(3), 238-254, 1991.

The essay proposes that rhetoric should remain in the skeptical tradition. It suggests that the age of technology has altered rhetoric's mandate: instead of establishing a relationship between knowledge and praxis, rhetorical practice now broaches the relationship, renders it transparent, and thereby serves as the principle means of restraining human-kind's compulsion to act. The conception advanced in this essay maintains that rhetoric is an insufficiently justified practice occupying the region between individual and culture. Moreover, it is proposed that this conception brings rhetoric's dependence on philosophy to an end.

FANG-TONG, Liu. The State of Studies on Western Philosophy in China. Stud Soviet Tho, 40(4), 267-292, D 90.

The work purports to outline the state of studies on western philosophy in China and summarize their successes and failure. It is divided into three sections. The first section took the torturous course of the study of western philosophy from 1919 to 1979 as a 60-year samsara. The second one described the great strides of these studies since about 1979 while China returned to the road of reform and openness. In the third one the author proposed following ideas as necessary for further improving studies on western philosophy in China: (1) abandon the tendency to confuse politics and scholarship; (2) reinvestigate the relations between western philosophy and Marxism; (3) make the study of western philosophy Chinese; (4) promote pluralism in philosophy.

FARBER, Paul. The Politics of Professionalism. Proc Phil Educ, 46, 265-269, 1990.

FARBER, Seth. Institutional Mental Health and Social Control: The Ravages of Epistemological Hubris. J Mind Behav, 11(3-4), 285-299, Sum-Autumn 90.

I argue in this essay that the phenomena we classify as "mental illness" result largely from the refusal of socially authorized "experts" to recognize—and thus to constitute—the Other (the developing person, the social deviant) as a subject. I suggest that Institutional Mental Health refuses to do this not merely because it seeks to aggrandize its own power but also because it fears to acknowledge that we are all participants in a process of historical development. It denies this because it is historically conditioned by its own moment of origin in the project of the Enlightenment. It is consequently wed to an ethos of rationalized order that does not accommodate, much less support, the unpredictable creative power of the Other (the individual) and that sustains instead the project of mastery, of domination, of discovering eternal laws that will (supposedly) enable Reason to master history and to master the Other. For this reason Institutional Mental Health and its diverse ideologies, ranging from the psychoanalytic to genetic defect models, constitute a major obstacle to the evolution of humanity.

FAREY, Caroline. The Political Philosophy of Sissela Bok. J Applied Phil, 8(1), 87-93, 1991.

Sissela Bok's two main works, on lying and secrets, have not received all the attention they deserve. This is possibly because the underlying structure from which she is working is not, at least according to the critics, made sufficiently explicit. I believe that this structure is found in Sissela Bok's commitment to the fundamental tenets of democracy. This not only provides a framework that is clearly discernible but also gives her books an urgency, and supplies the solid basis necessary for taking up the challenges she puts forward. This is particularly important now that new democracies in Eastern Europe are looking to established democracies in the West for guidelines.

FARIÑAS DEL CERRO, Luis and PENTTONEN, Martti. Grammar Logics. Log Anal, 31(121-122), 123-134, Mr-Je 88.

In this paper we present a simple method to define modal logics for formal grammars. Given a formal grammar, we associate with each rule an axiom of a modal logic. By this construction, testing whether a word is generated by a formal grammar is equivalent with proving a theorem in the logic. First constructions produce multimodal logics possessing several agents [Ko], but the technique can be applied to construct also more classical logics with only one modal operator. Our approach is suggested by a method used in logic programming, where the analysis or generation of a sentence is transformed to theorem proving [Co, PW]. Other related work is done by Wolper [Wo], who defines an extension of the linear temporal logic of programs to include regular expressions.

FARLEY, Edward. "Truth and the Wisdom of Enduring" in *Phenomenology of the Truth Proper to Religion*, GUERRIÈRE, Daniel (ed), 60-74. Albany, SUNY Pr, 1990.

FARMER, William M. A Partial Functions Version of Church's Simple Theory of Types. J Sym Log, 55(3), 1269-1291, S 90.

Church's simple theory of types is a system of higher-order logic in which functions are assumed to be total. We present in this paper a version of Church's system called PF in which functions may be partial. The semantics of PF, which is based on Henkin's general-models semantics, allows terms to be nondenoting but requires formulas to always denote a standard truth value. We prove that PF is complete with respect to its semantics. The reasoning mechanism in PF for partial functions corresponds closely to mathematical practice, and the formulation of PF adheres tightly to the framework of Church's system.

FARMER, William. A Unification-Theoretic Method for Investigating the *k*-Provability Problem. Annals Pure Applied Log, 51(3), 173-214, Mr 91.

The *k*-provability problem for an axiomatic system *A* is to determine, given a positive integer *k* and a formula *F*, whether or not there is a proof of *F* in *A* containing at most *k* lines. We investigate the *k*-provability problem for first-order axiomatic systems that contain a finite number of axiom schemata and rules for inference. We show that the *k*-provability problem for such a system reduces to (essentially) the unification problem for second-order terms. By solving various subproblems of this unification problem (which is itself undecidable), we solve the *k*-provability problem for a variety of systems, including several formulations of Peano arithmetic.

FARRELL, Thomas B. Practicing the Arts of Rhetoric: Tradition and Invention. Phil Rhet, 24(3), 183-212, 1991.

FARRENKOPF, John. Hegel, Spengler, and the Enigma of World History: Progress or Decline? Clio, 19(4), 331-344, Sum 90.

FAUCHER, Luc. La force du nombre: remarques autour de la notion de communauté. Lekton, 1(1), 41-61, 1990.

FAULCONER, James E. "Heidegger and Psychological Explanation: Taking Account of Derrida" in *Reconsidering Psychology: Perspectives from Continental Philosophy*, FAULCONER, James E (ed), 116-135. Pittsburgh, Duquesne Univ Pr, 1990.

The author outlines Derrida's critique of Heidegger, arguing that though Derrida shows us an important rereading of Heidegger, his critique fails because it misunderstands Heidegger's notion of *Ereignis* and it fails to provide something to fill its theoretical function. The author discusses the relevance of Derrida's rereading of Heidegger to psychological theory, suggesting three things: (1) psychological phenomena are essentially temporal; (2) current psychological theories and methods must be rethought rather than discarded—psychological explanation is fictive (but not fictional), and it must be rethought as such; and (3) psychological explanation must explicitly question the relation of mental illness to social de-formation.

FAULCONER, James E and WILLIAMS, Richard N. "Reconsidering Psychology" in *Reconsidering Psychology: Perspectives from Continental Philosophy*, FAULCONER, James E (ed), 9-60. Pittsburgh, Duquesne Univ Pr, 1990.

The authors give a brief history of the concept of the self, beginning with Greek philosophy and carrying it through Kant. They discuss the work of Heidegger as a critique of as well as an alternative to the concepts of that history, and they suggest some implications for psychological theory of this alternative to and critique of the hypostatized, reified self, including the conclusion that psychological explanation must center on the temporal character of human beings rather than on a search for an atemporal principle of explanation.

FAULCONER, James E (ed) and WILLIAMS, Richard N (ed). *Reconsidering Psychology: Perspectives from Continental Philosophy*. Pittsburgh, Duquesne Univ Pr, 1990.

This collection of essays makes a case against mainstream psychology that is skeptical of the traditional metaphysics from which that psychology stems. The essays focus on problems in psychology to which the continental philosophical tradition contributes a useful aalternative. The essays take their lead from a variety of thinkers, including Hegel, Husserl, Heidegger, Sartre, Derrida, Habermas, Gadamer, and Lacan. They deal with methods and methodology as well as strictly philosophical issues and more specifically psychological questions. They are aimed at those who practice, teach, and study psychology more than they are at philosophers.

FAURSCHOU, Gail. "Obsolescence and Desire: Fashion and the Commodity Form" in *Postmodernism—Philosophy and the Arts (Continental Philosophy III)*, SILVERMAN, Hugh J (ed), 234-259. New York, Routledge, 1990.

In the first section of this article, the fashion system is theorized as a sociological and cultural logic of reproduction that arises with the forms of abstraction unique to consumer society. In the second section, "Fashion Landscapes" analyzes the marketing of Ralph Lauren's home furnishings while "Cosmetic Cybernetics" looks at the advertising of skin care "technologies." References are made to the work of Fredric Jameson, Walter Benjamin, and Jean Baudrillard.

FAUST, Thomas and BAIRD, Davis. Scientific Instruments, Scientific Progress and the Cyclotron. Brit J Phil Sci, 41(2), 147-175, Je 90.

Studying the development of the cyclotron between 1929 and 1940, we urge a conception of scientific knowledge which includes the production of new instruments and new instrumental techniques. We focus on three details in the development of the cyclotron: producing ions, focusing the ion beam, and creating and maintaining the vacuum. We describe eight components central to the success of the cyclotron: 1) experimental idea, 2) theoretical test, 3) empirical test, 4) functional design, 5) intuition, 6) tinkering, 7) adapting components from other sources, 8) knowing when the instrument is working. We argue that the process of instrument creation proceeds by emulation and adaptation of previously successful instruments and instrumental techniques. This explains why instrument creation proceeds from a relatively simple guiding idea through a plethora of engineering and scientific complexities; simple ideas can be emulated and adapted in many new contexts. The result is the accumulation of new scientific instruments and instrumental techniques—scientific progress.

FAVE, Antonella Delle and MASSIMINI, Fausto. Religion and Cultural Evolution. Zygon, 26(1), 27-47, Mr 91.

The end of the twentieth century marks the slow disintegration of both the Marxist and capitalist socioeconomic theories, inasmuch as both have proven inadequate to meet basic issues of human existence. Their inadequacy rests on the tendency to use the criteria of extrinsic rewards, quantification, production, and consumption to evaluate human personhood and human activity. What is needed is a third alternative to these two systems, one that is based on intrinsic rewards and cultivates internal values rather than production, consumption, and quantification. Religious communities have traditionally been such an alternative and seem to represent an ordered nucleus of information that can counter the inadequacies of Marxism and capitalism. To carry out this function, religions must (1) minimize the trivial differences that set belief systems against one another; (2) support bimodal cultural evolution that allows the old and the new to coexist; and (3) discover the unifying factors that cut across human groups.

FAY, Thomas A. Heidegger on Logic and Language: Some Aporiai. Tijdschr Filosof, 52(3), 421-442, S 90.

This article traces the development of Heidegger's thought on logic and language from his earliest writings in 1912 in *Literarische Rundschau fur das katolische Deutschland,* through the dissertation of 1914 and the *Habilitationschrift* of 1916 and on into the middle and late writings. It argues that a change or development takes place in Heidegger's thought and that while in the earliest writings he seemed to be both aware of, and sympathetic to the new developments in logic, that by the late period of his thought this had changed to outright hostility, and that in the end Heidegger's approach to philosophy is incompatible with logic as it has traditionally been understood. And finally, it is argued that the position of the late Heidegger drives him into *aporiai*, or insoluable difficulties.

FAY, Thomas A. Metaphysics of the Person, Determinism and Responsibility. Asian J Phil, 2(1), 43-55, Sum 90.

There is everywhere evident in our contemporary society a more or less complete denial of personal responsibility. That such a denial of responsibility should come to pass is not at all surprising since many philosophers, social scientists, and especially psychologists, regard man as a purely material being, and nothing else. If he is purely material, then he is as determined in his actions as the stone to fall or water to boil at 100 degrees centigrade. And further, if totally determined because he is a purely material being, then man is not free and certainly not responsible for his actions. But how did we arrive at the moral and metaphysical vision of man which robs him of his spiritual dimension, of the nobility of moral responsibility, and reduces him to a purely material stimulus-response mechanism.

FEAGIN, Susan. "Appreciation and Justification" in *XIth International Congress in Aesthetics, Nottingham 1988*, WOODFIELD, Richard (ed), 62-65. Nottingham, Nottingham Polytech, 1990.

In an effort to better understand what constitutes appreciation, I discuss how the concept of justification applies to having emotional responses to works of literary fiction. I distinguish between the relevance and appropriateness of a response, and between justifiably responding and having a justification for responding (in a given way). I conclude that such justifications do not merely enable one to appreciate a work of fiction, but are partly constitutive of appreciation.

FEDERSPIL, G and BLANDINO, Giovanni. Una discussione di epistemologia. Aquinas, 33(3), 579-598, S-D 90.

The authors discuss about the following topics: 1) whether the induction has *an hypothetical-deductive-verificative structure*; 2) whether *all* the scientifical laws are *probabilistic*; 3) whether *all* the scientifical laws are not only probabilistic, but also *approximate*.

FEDERSPIL, Giovanni. Giacomo Andrea Giacomini: un clinico padovano tra Metafisica e Scienza. Hist Phil Life Sci, 13(1), 73-95, 1991.

As Professor of Theoretical Medicine for Surgeons at Padua University between 1824 and 1849, Giacomini achieved a position of great academic professionalism and prestige, not only in Padau, but throughout Italy and Europe. His fundamental medical thesis became part of the established field of medical practise that existed into the first decades of the 19th century. This thesis, derived directly from a vitalistic concept of biological phenomena, was based on the existence of a 'life force' that is distinct from the forces of physical-chemistry, having its own specific laws, contrary to those of physical-chemistry. Using this concept Giacomini was able to distinguish two causes of death: mechanical illness and dynamic illness. The nosographic and therapeutic beliefs of Giacomini were based on his distinction between the 'mechanical' or 'dynamic' effects of drugs. Giacomini's medical philosophy is the result of an interweaving of scientific theories and metaphysical ideas. The merits and limits of this philosophy must be analysed in the light of modern epistemology to explain why Giacomini was unable to develop fully clinical anatomy.

FEDOSEYEV, Pyotr. "Philosophy, Science and Man" in *Logic, Methodology and Philosophy of Science, VIII*, FENSTAD, J E (ed), 3-25. New York, Elsevier Science, 1989.

FEENSTRA, Ronald J. Pre-existence and Personal Identity. Logos (USA), 11, 127-142, 1990.

Some recent critics of the doctrine of the pre-existence of Christ have argued that, if Jesus Christ pre-existed as the divine Son of God, then he must have been conscious of that pre-existent life even during his life on earth, and therefore either he was not truly human or his experience as a human person differed from that of other humans in theologically unacceptable ways. This essay addresses this criticism by identifying the theory of personal identity over time that seems to underlie it, arguing that this theory is inadequate, defending a more acceptable theory of personal identity over time, and applying the latter theory to the topic of the pre-existence of Christ.

FEEZELL, Randolph M and HANCOCK, Curtis L. *How Should I Live? Philosophical Conversations About Moral Life*. New York, Paragon House, 1991.

FEFERMAN, Solomon. Infinity in Mathematics: Is Cantor Necessary? Phil Topics, 17(2), 23-45, Fall 89.

FEHÉR, I. Schelling on Hegel: From his Lectures in Munich and Berlin (in Hungarian). Magyar Filozof Szemle, 1-2, 73-128, 1990.

FEHÉR, István M. "Heidegger's Way In, Through, and Out of Politics: The Story of His Rectorate" in *Perspectives on Ideas and Reality*, NYÍRI, J C (ed), 130-173. Budapest, Kiskonyvtara, 1990.

FEHER, Judit. A Brief Survey of Indian Buddhistic Logic (in Hungarian). Magyar Filozof Szemle, 5-6, 463-472, 1990.

The author's concern is to give a very short account of some fundamental issues of Indian Buddhist logic. The paper deals with the classical period of Buddhist logic beginning in India with the activity of Dignága (5th c. A.D.) and Dharmakírti (7th c.). Since Buddhist logic and epistemology are closely related, they are used as convertible terms, which results in a kind of epistemological logic. All through the paper the author draws parallels between Buddhist and Aristotelian reasoning. (edited)

FEIEREIS, Konrad. The Common European Home (in German). Deut Z Phil, 38(5), 411-421, 1990.

FEINBERG, Joel and GROSS, Hyman. *Philosophy of Law (Fourth Edition)*. Belmont, Wadsworth, 1991.

This revision of our textbook-anthology has many new features: more legal realism and the Critical Legal Studies movement, Dworkin's exchange with J L Markie and also his article on abortion, five new Supreme Court cases in the Liberty section, articles on privacy by Alan Ryan and Richard Posner, J J Thomson's "Self-Defense and Rights," a new subsection on "The Machinery of Justice," Tom Nagel on compensatory discrimination, Fuller's Speluncean Explores" and *US versus Holmes*, Curley's "Excusing Rape," a new subsection on attempts and completed crimes, and five new articles on punishment (Hart, Moore, Hampton, Murphy and Bedan).

FEINGLASS, Joe and SALMON, J Warren and WHITE, William. The Futures of Physicians: Agency and Autonomy Reconsidered. Theor Med, 11(4), 261-274, D 90.

The corporatization of US health care has directed cost containment efforts toward scrutinizing the clinical decisions of physicians. This stimulated a variety of new utilization management interventions, particularly in hospital and managed care settings. Recent changes in fee-for-service medicine and physicians' traditional agency relationships with patients, purchasers, and insurers are examined here. New information systems monitoring of physician ordering behavior has already begun to impact on physician autonomy and the relationship of physicians to provider organizations in both for-profit and 'not-for-profit' sectors. As managed care practice settings proliferate, serious ethical questions will be raised about agency relationships with patients. This article examines health system dynamics altering the historical agency relationship between the physician and patient and eroding the traditional autonomy of the medical profession in the United States. The corporatization of medicine and the accompanying information systems monitoring of physician productivity is seen to account of such change, now posing serious ethical dilemmas.

FEKETE, László. Rationality, Economic Action and Scarcity (in Hungarian). Magyar Filozof Szemle, 1-2, 1-29, 1990.

The philosophical tradition of the enlightenment concerning moral economy has begun to vanish since the turn of the eighteenth and nineteenth century. The problem comes from the very fact that moral cannot be defined on the basis of *a priori* economic rationality as well as economy on the basis of some eternal moral values. In spite of that, nineteenth-century political economy and moral philosophy made a lot of effort to do it. The reason of the failure of these theoretical attempts, at least from the analytic point of view, was caused by the well-established tautology of nineteenth-century economic as well as social thought, namely, scarcity. (edited)

FELDMAN, Fred. "A Simpler Solution to the Paradoxes of Deontic Logic" in *Philosophical Perspectives, 4: Action Theory and Philosophy of Mind, 1990*, TOMBERLIN, James E (ed), 309-341. Atascadero, Ridgeview, 1990.

I give an informal sketch of a system of deontic logic based upon the view presented in *Doing the Best We Can*. I show that this system provides solutions to some of the most interesting paradoxes of deontic logic. I discuss Castaneda's Paradox of the Second Best Plan; several versions of Aqvist's Good Samaritan Paradox including Tomberlin's Paradox of the Knower and Forrester's Paradox of Gentle Murder; and Chisholm's Paradox of Contrary to Duty Imperatives. I also briefly discuss Powers' Suzy Mae Paradox.

FELDMAN, Fred. Some Puzzles About the Evil of Death. Phil Rev, 100(2), 205-227, Ap 91.

This paper provides a new formulation of the deprivation thesis. According to this view, a person's death is bad for him if and only if his welfare level at the nearest world at which he does not then die is greater than his welfare level at the nearest world at which he does. This provides a basis from which to answer four Epicurean questions about the evil of death: (1) How can a person's death be bad for him if he doesn't exist when it takes place? (2) Does the deprivation thesis presuppose an illegitimate comparison between goods received in life and goods received while dead? (3) When is death bad for the one who dies? (4) Why isn't prenatal nonexistence just as bad as death?

FELDMAN, Norman. Cylindric Algebras with Terms. J Sym Log, 55(2), 854-866, Je 90.

Cylindric algebras with terms, like cylindric algebras, has its roots in first order predicate logic. The setting is two-sorted algebras—one sort for terms and one for Boolean elements. The term part behaves like a substitution algebra, and the Boolean part, like a cylindric algebra. The operation between the two represents substitution of terms in formulas. An axiomatization for cylindric algebras with terms is given and it is shown that, like cylindric algebras, the representation theorem also follows from local finiteness. Furthermore, it is shown that the existence of Skolem function in a cylindric algebra with terms also yields representation.

FELDMAN, Richard. "Klein on Certainty and Canonical Beliefs" in *Doubting: Contemporary Perspectives on Skepticism*, ROTH, Michael D (ed), 121-126. Norwell, Kluwer, 1990.

In "Epistemic Compatibilism and Canonical Beliefs" Peter Klein argues that we can know that the preponderance of our common-sense beliefs about the external world are true, although we cannot know with respect to any particular belief about the world that it is true. Klein argues that we fail to know each particular proposition because there is a doubt-maker for it, whereas there is no doubt-maker for the general proposition about the preponderance of our beliefs. I argue that, given Klein's account of what makes a proposition doubtful, the general proposition about our beliefs is doubtful and thus not known.

FELICE, Domenico. *Pour l'histoire de la fortune de Montesquieu en Italie (1789-1945)*. Bologna, Thema, 1990.

Le livre vise à éclairer quelques aspects significatifs de l'histoire de la fortune de Montesquieu en Italie. Il est divisé en quatre chapitres: le premier présente un sondage sur le rayonnement, en France et en Italie, des oeuvres du Président pendant la période révolutionnaire et napoléonienne (1789-1815); le second examine la présence de quelques thèmes fondamentaux de l'*Esprit des Lois* à l'intérieur de la culture démocratique du "Triennio Giacobino" italien (1796-1799); le troisième analyse l'attitude manifestée à l'égard de Montesquieu par V Cuoco (1770-1823) et G D Romagnosi (1761-1835); enfin, le quatrième chapitre évoque les étapes fondamentales de la fortune de Montesquieu en Italie au cours de la période comprise entre la Restauration et la IIe Guerre Mondiale.

FELL, Joseph P. "Miller: The Man and His Philosophy" in *The Philosophy of John William Miller*, FELL, Joseph P (ed), 21-31. Lewisburg, Bucknell Univ Pr, 1990.

FELL, Joseph P (ed). *The Philosophy of John William Miller*. Lewisburg, Bucknell Univ Pr, 1990.

FELLMANN, Ferdinand. *Phänomenologie als ästhetische Theorie*. Freiburg, Alber, 1991.

This book takes a new and systematic approach to the historical preconditions for and precursors of Husserl's phenomenology, in order to lay bare the aesthetic dimension of phenomenological thought. The author shows that important aspects of phenomenology become comprehensible only when they are related to the structures of narrative representation. Reconsidering the work of Hermann Lotze and Rudolf Eucken, two major representatives of the philosophy of mind under late idealism, the author brings to light the history of the constellation of problems from which phenomenology as an aesthetic theory arose.

FELT, James W (trans) and FETZ, Reto Luzius. Aristotelian and Whiteheadian Conceptions of Actuality: I. Process Stud, 19(1), 15-27, Spr 90.

A translation of section 3.1 of *Whitehead: Prozessdenken und Substanzmetaphysik* (Freiburg/München: 1981). Studies the relationship of Whitehead's metaphysics to the traditional philosophy of substance, especially Aristotle's, and concludes that Whitehead's own conception of an 'actual entity' can in decisive points be regarded as a retrieval and a radicalization of the genuinely Aristotelian concept of entity. Translations of sections 3.2 and 3.3 are to follow as a series.

FELT, James W (trans) and FETZ, Reto Luzius. Aristotelian and Whiteheadian Conceptions of Actuality: II. Process Stud, 19(3), 145-155, Fall 90.

A translation of section 3.2 of *Whitehead: Prozessdenken und Substanzmetaphysik* (Freiburg/Munchen, 1981). Studies the relationship of Whitehead's metaphyics to the traditional philosophy of substance, especially Aristotle's, and concludes that Whitehead's own conception of an 'actual entity' can in decisive points be regarded as a retrieval and a radicalization of the genuinely Aristotelian concept of entity. Translation of section 3.1 appeared in a previous issue; of 3.3 to follow.

FEMENÍAS, María Luisa. Algunas observaciones sobre la noción de *Pragma* en Aristóteles. Rev Latin De Filosof, 16(2), 213-217, Jl 90.

What is the meaning of the word *prâgma* when Aristotle says that nouns are symbols of *tà prágmata*? In order to give an answer three meanings of *prâgma* are analysed: (1) that of which something is said (the subject-matter); (2) sense; and (3) concept. We conclude the *prágmata* are no things in a strong ontological sense as the "outside world," but "things as signified."

FENDT, Gene. *For What May I Hope? Thinking with Kant and Kierkegaard*. New York, Lang, 1990.

This book is a dramatic exhibition of the place of hope in philosophy. It argues for a common starting point for Kant and Kierkegaard by analysing their use of the concepts self and task. It shows the centrality of hope in Kant's philosophy and dramatizes its final breakdown. It then shows how hope plays in various characters of Kierkegaard's authorship. The text dramatizes, as well, the hopes of writing—especially philosophical and scientific writing—and plays on the hopes of readers.

FENDT, Gene. *Works of Love? Reflections on "Works of Love"*. Potomac, Scripta Human, 1990.

In writing on Kierkegaard an author should consider—as Kierkegaard did—not only his purpose in writing, but the purposes of writing—which may contradict him. This book offers a poly-vocalic reading of *Works of Love*, grounded in a poststructuralist theory of signs, which leads—as a matter of literary and psychological, if not ontological, course—to *Fear and Trembling*.

FENG, Qi. A Hierarchy of Ramsey Cardinals. Annals Pure Applied Log, 49(3), 257-277, O 90.

Assuming the existence of a measurable cardinal, we define a hierarchy of Ramsey cardinals and a hierarchy of normal filters. We study some combinatorial properties of this hierarchy. We show that this hierarchy is absolute with respect to the Dodd-Jensen core model, extending a result of Mitchell which says that being Ramsey is absolute with respect to the core model.

FENIGSEN, Richard. A Case Against Dutch Euthanasia. Ethics Med, 6(1), 11-18, Spr 90.

FENNEMA, J G. "The Discussion on Identity Among African Philosophers" in *I, We and Body: First Joint Symposium of Philosophers from Africa and from the Netherlands*, KIMMERLE, Heinz (ed), 65-78. Atlantic Highlands, Gruner, 1989.

African identity as a problem—cultural and political on the one hand and philosophical on the other—is subject of discussion amongst philosophers ever since their countries gained independence. The article gives a brief survey of the various positions together with a description of their converging development over the last thirty years. One can roughly distinguish a traditionalist or ethnophilosophical approach and a "modern" philosophical one. There are a static, timeless notion of thinking and identity ("Roots-concept") and a more dynamic one based on the ability to deal with the variety of influences and problems Africa is facing today.

FENNEMA, Jan (ed) and PAUL, Iain (ed). *Science and Religion: One World-Changing Perspectives on Reality*. Norwell, Kluwer, 1990.

Scientific points of view and expectations need to be in dialogue with religious forms of understanding — and religious traditions need to take account of the new scientific perspectives on the world and the ethical problems generated by science, medicine and technology. "Science and Religion" presents its title theme from different angles, giving surveys of developments that are taking place in the natural sciences and in theology, followed by essays that consider in retrospect the traditional dichotomy between science and religion, and finally there are essays that enlarge upon expectations for the future.

FENNER, Peter. Religions in the Balance. Sophia (Australia), 30(1), 16-20, Jl 91.

FENSTAD, J E (ed) and FROLOV, I T (ed) and HILPINEN, R (ed). *Logic, Methodology and Philosophy of Science, VIII*. New York, Elsevier Science, 1989.

This volume contains all the invited papers to the eight international congress of logic, methodology and philosophy of science held in Moscow in 1987. In addition to sectional papers there were two symposia, one on new patterns of explanation in science, and one on science and ethics.

FERBER, Rafael. *Platos Idee des Guten*. St Augustin, Richarz, 1989.

The second, enlarged edition of *Platos Ideaa des Guten* ([1]1984) gives a new reconstruction of an "exasperatingly difficult but ever fascinating topic" (H Cherniss), i.e., of the platonic theory of the ideal numbers and the two principles which were contained in the so-called "unwritten doctrines" (Aristotle). In the outlook it gives new information on the reception of Plato's idea of the good in P Natorp and M Heidegger. Also includes an updated bibliography.

FEREJOHN, Michael. *The Origins of Aristotelian Science*. New Haven, Yale Univ Pr, 1991.

This book defends a comprehensive interpretation of Aristotle's theory of demonstrative knowledge as that theory is presented throughout most of the *Posterior Analytics* and parts of the *Prior Analytics*. The first part of the book is an investigation into the foundationalist character of Aristotle's theory, and a defense of a "two-stage" interpretation of Aristotelian demonstration according to which the construction of syllogistic demonstrations is preceded by a nonsyllogistic procedure descended from Platonic Division. The second part is a close study of the specific sorts of nonaccidental connections Aristotle permits between the terms of demonstrative premises.

FERGUSON, Jeanne (trans) and BUSINO, Giovanni. Sociology: An Infirm Science. Diogenes, 150, 37-63, Sum 90.

To understand the current crisis in sociology, we must examine its history. Sociology was founded on the mythic premise that a radically new society was emerging, a society endowed with universal characteristics. This led sociology to claim a total autonomy from classical knowledge. However, simultaneously, sociology proved incapable of clearly defining its boundaries, and borrowed heavily from the natural sciences to construct its analytical framework. To solve this crisis, we must accept that our society is not universal: its features testify to the permanence of the past, and only a thoroughly historical sociology can lead to a truly general knowledge about man.

FERGUSON, Kenneth G. Equivocation in The Surprise Exam Paradox. S J Phil, 29(3), 291-302, Fall 91.

FERGUSSON, David. Meaning, Truth and Realism in Bultmann and Lindbeck. Relig Stud, 26(2), 183-198, Je 90.

The theology of Rudolf Bultmann is dominated by a theory of meaning which suggests a non-realist account of religion. By contrast, the conception of theological truth which dominates his dialectical thought is clearly realist. It is argued that this fundamental collision between meaning and truth vitiates his theological program. In the more recent and subtle philosophical theology of George Lindbeck a similar collision between a functional concept of meaning and an ontological concept of truth can be detected. Theological realism, however, requires a theory of meaning which distinguishes between truth and use.

FERNÁNDEZ BURILLO, Santiago A. Nuestra voluntad es "de Dios". Espiritu, 37(98), 137-152, Jl-D 88.

FERNÁNDEZ BURILLO, Santiago A. Nuestra voluntad es "de Dios". Espiritu, 38(99), 17-44, Ja-Je 89.

FERNÁNDEZ DEL VALLE, Agustín Basave. Racionalidad y libertad. Logos (Mexico), 19(56), 103-117, My-Ag 91.

FERNÁNDEZ LORENZO, Manuel. La polémica sobre el espinosismo de Lessing. El Basilisco, 1, 65-74, S-O 89.

FERNANDEZ RODRIGUEZ, Jose Luis. El conocimiento de los cuerpos según Malebranche (I). Anu Filosof, 23(1), 25-59, 1990.

FERNÁNDEZ TRESGUERRES, Alfonso. Antropología y Agresión: notas para un análisis filosófico. El Basilisco, 3, 17-28, Ja-F 90.

Ni la respuesta aubientalista al problema de la agresión humana (caso de Montagu) ni la innatista (Lorenz, Eibesfeldt o Wilson) resultan satisfactorias. Desde ninguna de ellas se puede explicar ni comprender lo distintivo y peculiar del comportamiento agresivo del ser humano. Ello sólo es posible en el Marco de una antropología filosófica materialista, en la que biologia y cultura son vistas en relación dialéctica. Con ello se quiere senalar una posible línea explicativa al problema de la agresión humana, pero también defender la especificidad de la antropología filosófica frente a los intentos eto lógicos y sociobiológicos de hacerla desaparecer en el ambito de la biología o la zoología.

FERNÁNDEZ, Alvaro López. Juicios de percepción y de experiencia en Kant. Dialogos, 26(58), 75-107, Jl 91.

Neither Kant nor the Kantian literature deals with the problem of the relation between synthetical judgements, and judgements of perception and of experience. Different kinds of judgements of experience, i.e., of objective judgements, can be recognized. Kant's new division of judgements in the *Prolegomena* allows to distinguish between different sorts of synthetical a priori and synthetical a posteriori judgements. It is a valid distinction, that enriches the old one. Finally, its relation with the problem of the Transcendental Deduction is examined.

FERNANDEZ, Javier. Filosofía y fe en Descartes. Pensamiento, 47(187), 323-327, Jl-S 91.

The article tries to study in an analytical way, some of the main aspects which confront Descartes with the Catholic doctrine. The central questions analyzed are the concept of God, concretely the Carterian definition of God as "causa sui," and the subject of the end and the sense of the creation. In the second place it studies the concept of man and at last the continued creation. The conclusion of the article is that Descartes was a "fideista" who sustained during his life a deep credence in God, but his philosophy is very far from the Catholic orthodoxy.

FERNÁNDEZ, Teresa Bejaran. La metáfora como resolución de un problema comunicativo-lingüístico. Dialogos, 26(58), 129-162, Jl 91.

FERNÁNDEZ, Teresa Bejarano. Adquisición del lenguaje y antropología. Dialogo Filosof, 7(1), 32-45, Ja-Ap 91.

FERRARA, Alessandro. The Unbearable Seriousness of Irony. Phil Soc Crit, 16(2), 81-107, 1990.

A critical assessment of Rorty's "ironic philosophy" is attempted. Among the main conclusions: (1) Rorty's account of how "vocabularies" change is untenable; (2) because he fails to provide any view of what it means for a vocabulary to be better than another, Rorty cannot claim to have differentiated his position from "vulgar relativism"; (3) Rorty overlooks the contingency of the split between private autonomy and public justice; (4) Rorty's view of the self as centerless is inconsistent; (5) throughout Rorty's argument we can find quite unironic assumptions about the reality of the self and of the moral life, about progress and the good life.

FERRARI, Jean (ed) and POSTIGLIOLA, Alberto (ed). *Égalité Uguaglianza*. Napoli, Liguori, 1990.

FERRARIN, Alfredo. Metafisica e dialettica: quattro saggi sull'interpretazione hegeliana di Aristotele. Teoria, 10(1), 145-152, 1990.

FERRATER-MORA, José. "On Mario Bunge's Semantical Realism" in *Studies on Mario Bunge's "Treatise"*, WEINGARTNER, Paul (ed), 29-37. Amsterdam, Rodopi, 1990.

FERRÉ, Frederick. Reflections on Blanshard, Reason, and Religion. Ideal Stud, 20(2), 122-139, My 90.

Blanshard's confidence in the culture-free nature and accomplishments of science ignores recent criticisms by Kuhn, Hanson, Toulmin, Lakatos, and Feyerabend. Our theoretical expectations significantly filter what we perceive; the community of scientists is more "human" than Blanshard acknowledged. Religion, likewise, is a more complex phenomenon than Blanshard allowed. Neither simply a set of theoretical dogmas nor merely an ethical society, religion rightly shares with science the interplay of community value-commitments and universal theoretical claims. Blanshard's undoubted wisdom and systematic brilliance may be celebrated without accepting his magisterial view of reason.

FERRÉ, Frederick. Technological Faith and Christian Doubt. Faith Phil, 8(2), 214-224, Ap 91.

Technology, an object of little-considered but intense faith in our modern civilization, has long posed deep problems for Biblical thought. If technology is defined broadly enough, Christian attitudes toward it illuminate conflicting responses to culture itself. Should technology be regarded as liberating (Cox) or strictly in the domain of sin (Ellul)?

FERREIRA, M Jamie. "Kierkegaardian Faith: 'The Condition' and the 'Response'. Int J Phil Relig, 28(2), 63-79, O 90.

This essay addresses the much-debated question of 'volitionalist' vs. 'anti-volitionalist' interpretations of Climacus's 'leap of faith'. It argues that the latter kind of interpretation, appealing to 'miracle' or 'grace', obscures the role of human activity in the acquisition of faith. It proposes an alternative account in which faith is neither passive and ineffable nor the direct result of a deliberate decision, and it does so by developing the implications of Climacus's claim that in faith Socratic validity is renewed.

FERREIRA, M Jamie. Kierkegaardian Transitions: Paradox and Pathos. Int Phil Quart, 31(1), 65-80, Mr 91.

This article challenges the terms of the current debate concerning 'volitionalist' readings of the Kierkegaardian 'leap' of faith by initiating an exploration of the category of transition. It highlights the relevance of the activity of imagination in two ways: first, in the paradoxical transitions described in several Kierkegaardian accounts of selfhood, and second, in a variety of indications in the Climacus writings and the journals of a broadened concept of 'will' or 'decision'.

FERREIRA, Manuel Carmo. "Maimon, crítico de Kant" in *Dinâmica do Pensar: Homenagem a Oswaldo Market*, FAC LETRAS UNIV LISBOA (ed), 101-110. Lisboa, Fac Letras U Lisboa, 1991.

Maimons *Versuch über die Transzendentalphilosophie* enthält die wesentlichen Punkte der Kritik an Kant, dessen Denken er umstösst, eben wenn er dieses zu rechtfertigen scheint. Indem Maimon den Grund und die Legitimation der transzendentalen Synthesis als Enstehung einer wirklichen Objektivität und Notwendigkeit diskutiert, stellt er die Elemente der kantischen Antwort an *quid juris* der wissenschaftlichen Erkenntnis in Frage. Maimon "coligiert" Skeptizismus (Hume) mit Dogmatismus (Spinoza und Leibniz) in einem formal kantischen Kontext und radikalisiert den transzendentalen Standpunkt im Sinne des Idealismus.

FESSENDEN-RADEN, June and BROWN JR, Stuart M. Commentary: "Love Canal and the Ethics of Environmental Health". Bus Prof Ethics J, 2(4), 23-25, Sum 83.

FESTERVAND, Troy A and VITELL, Scott J and RAWWAS, Mohammed Y A. The Business Ethics of Pharmacists: Conflicts Practices and Beliefs. J Bus Ethics, 10(4), 295-301, Ap 91.

This paper represents the responses of 377 pharmacists to a mail survey examing their views concerning ethical conflicts and practices. Besides identifying the sources of ethical conflicts, pharmacists were asked how ethical standards have changed over the last 10 years as well as the factors influencing these changes. Conclusions and implications are outlined and future research needs are examined.

FESTINI, Heda. Some Characteristics of Boskovic's Scientific Methodology (in Serbo-Croatian). Filozof Istraz, 32-33(5-6), 1489-1494, 1989.

In discussion of Boskovic's scientific method, consideration is given to those facets that make Boskovic a successor, as well as a corrector (in the spirit of contemporary methodology and the philosophy of science) of the main points of Galileo's "method of new science." He and D Pulic (1865) from Dubrovnik were forerunners of C S Peirce's (1867) interpretations of scientific discovery as a retroductive procedure. Boskovic adopted but also corrected Galileo's general dynamic approach to science in terms of (a) interpreting the relationship between mathematics and experience (a correction in the direction of Popper, 1934/59 and Laudan, 1977); (b) introduction of a refutation in the process of accepting scientific theory (deepening in Popper's direction and expanding as does the J Cohen [1970] inductive confirmation); (c) the thesis that scientific theory is never outdated (later found in the work of Feyerabend, 1970; Lakatos, 1970; and Laudan, 1977, 1984).

FETYKO, D F and CLAYPOOL, G A and PEARSON, M A. Reactions to Ethical Dilemmas: A Study Pertaining to Certified Public Accounts. J Bus Ethics, 9(9), 699-706, S 90.

This study discusses how perceptions of ethics are formed by certified public accountants (CPAs). Theologians are used as a point of comparison. When considering CPA ethical dilemmas, both subject groups in this research project viewed 'confidentiality' and 'independence' as more important than 'recipient of responsibility' and 'seriousness of breach'. Neither group, however, was insensitive to any of the factors presented for its consideration. CPA reactions to ethical dilemmas were governed primarily by provisions of the CPA ethics code; conformity to that code may well be evidence of higher stage moral reasoning.

FETZ, Reto Luzius and FELT, James W (trans). Aristotelian and Whiteheadian Conceptions of Actuality: I. Process Stud, 19(1), 15-27, Spr 90.

A translation of section 3.1 of *Whitehead: Prozessdenken und Substanzmetaphysik* (Freiburg/München: 1981). Studies the relationship of Whitehead's metaphysics to the traditional philosophy of substance, especially Aristotle's, and concludes that Whitehead's own conception of an 'actual entity' can in decisive points be regarded as a retrieval and a radicalization of the genuinely Aristotelian concept of entity. Translations of sections 3.2 and 3.3 are to follow as a series.

FETZ, Reto Luzius and FELT, James W (trans). Aristotelian and Whiteheadian Conceptions of Actuality: II. Process Stud, 19(3), 145-155, Fall 90.

A translation of section 3.2 of *Whitehead: Prozessdenken und Substanzmetaphysik* (Freiburg/Munchen, 1981). Studies the relationship of Whitehead's metaphyics to the traditional philosophy of substance, especially Aristotle's, and concludes that Whitehead's own conception of an 'actual entity' can in decisive points be regarded as a retrieval and a radicalization of the genuinely Aristotelian concept of entity. Translation of section 3.1 appeared in a previous issue; of 3.3 to follow.

FETZER, James H. *Artificial Intelligence: Its Scope and Limits*. Norwell, Kluwer, 1990.

This book explores the foundations of AI from the perspective of the theory of knowledge. Drawing a distinction between signs that are significant for the users of a system and those that are significant for a system itself, the standard conception that the theory of computability defines the boundaries of thought is subjected to a thorough critique. The author contends that AI can succeed by utilizing artificial languages in lieu of natural languages and that its contributions to humankind do not depend upon the prospects for the design and construction of thinking machines.

FETZER, James H. Kitcher and Salmon's *Scientific Explanation*; and Salmon's *Four Decades of Scientific Explanation*. Phil Sci, 58(2), 288-306, Je 91.

The author suggests that Salmon's history of work on scientific explanation during the past four decades is not entirely successful, since he does not completely separate the history of his own understanding of the problem from the historical record of the problem itself. Nevertheless, his work provides a valuable framework for exploring other contributions by Railton, Sintonen, Humphreys, Papineau, Cartwright, Woodward, Merrilee Salmon, and Kitcher.

FETZER, James H. *Philosophy and Cognitive Science*. New York, Paragon House, 1991.

This book provides a clearly written and highly accessible philosophical introduction to cognitive science. It examines the principal problems that cognitive science addresses, the solutions it considers, and the intellectual landscape against which its importance may be measured. Current issues in cognitive science are related to classic issues in the philosophy of mind and in the philosophy of science. Its eight chapters are entitled "A Science of Cognition?," "Minds and Machines," "The Nature of Language," "What is Mentality?," "Connectionism and Cognition," "Mental Development," "Are Humans Rational?," and "Mentality, Causality, Morality." References, indices of names and of subjects, and suggestions for further reading are included.

FEUERSTEIN, Georg. *The Yoga-Sūtra of Patañjali: A New Translation and Commentary*. Rochester, Inner Traditions, 1989.

FIASCHI, Giovanni. Soggetto e senso del diritto nell'esperienza giuridica moderna: appunti in tema di positività. Riv Int Filosof Diritto, 66(4), 596-632, O-D 89.

FIELD, Hartry. "'Narrow' Aspects of Intentionality and the Information-Theoretic Approach to Content" in *Information, Semantics and Epistemology*, VILLANUEVA, Enrique (ed), 102-116. Cambridge, Blackwell, 1990.

The author opposes "narrow content" views, but also opposes a certain approach to the theory of normal ("wide") content or to the theory of truth conditions. The approach he rejects would have it that a theory of content or truth conditions could be given directly, without a prior account of any narrow intentional relations of any sort. The author argues, by contrast, that certain intentional relations require a narrow, indeed purely computational, account: only by presupposing such narrow relations can we hope to give any theory of content or truth conditions. The author concentrates on information-theoretic approaches to content or truth conditions in his argument.

FIELD, Hartry. "Mathematics and Modality" in *Meaning and Method: Essays in Honor of Hilary Putnam*, BOOLOS, George (ed), 213-233. New York, Cambridge Univ Pr, 1990.

The paper argues against two attempts to use modality to yield philosophical rewards in the philosophy of mathematics. The first attempt is an effort to use the "necessary truth" of mathematics to undercut the epistemological worries that people have had about mathematics; the second attempt is an effort to supply some sort of modal translation of mathematics and its applications which would make mathematics epistemologically less problematic. In both cases, both general philosophical considerations and specific technical difficulties are brought to bear against the proposal.

FIELD, Hartry. Mathematics Without Truth (A Reply to Maddy). Pac Phil Quart, 71(3), 206-222, S 90.

This paper elaborates on the fictionalist conception of mathematics, and on how it accommodates the obvious fact that mathematical claims are important in application to the physical world. It also replies to Maddy's argument that fictionalism does not have the epistemological advantage over Platonism that it appears to have; the reply involves a discussion of whether mathematics should be regarded as conservative over second order physical theories as well as first order ones.

FIELD, Hartry. Metalogic and Modality. Phil Stud, 62(1), 1-22, Ap 91.

A platonist should view metalogical notions like implications and consistency as primitive notions explained by their rules of use, rather than as defined in the usual (model-theoretic or proof-theoretic) ways. These rules of use in effect make implication and consistency modal notions, though very austere ones. A non-platonist can adopt a modified version of this "modal" view of metalogic; the principles governing the implication and consistency operators can be known without relying on knowledge of mathematical entities. The usual reasons for suspicion about the use of modality for philosophical ends do not apply to the "modal" view of metalogic.

FIELDS, L. Deciding to Act. Phil Inq, 11(3-4), 1-17, Sum-Fall 89.

FIGALLO, Aldo V. $I\Delta_3$-Algebras. Rep Math Log, 24, 3-16, 1990.

In the present paper we develop an algebraic study of that part of three-valued Lukasiewicz propositional calculus that includes the connectives implication and necessity. The algebraic version which we have introduced plays an analogous role to that played by Boolean algebras in the case of two-valued propositional calculus. We study this variety of algebras completely and we obtain a formula to compute the number of elements of the finitely generated Lindenbaum algebra associated to this calculus.

FIJALKOWSKA, Dorota and FIJALKOWSKI, Jan. On Theories of Non-Monotonic Consequence Operations II. Bull Sect Log, 19(3), 79-83, O 90.

FIJALKOWSKI, Jan and FIJALKOWSKA, Dorota. On Theories of Non-Monotonic Consequence Operations II. Bull Sect Log, 19(3), 79-83, O 90.

FILANDRA, Sacir. Crisis of Modernity and Process Thought in Max Horkheimer's Early Work (in Serbo-Croatian). Filozof Istraz, 34(1), 143-157, 1990.

FILICE, Carlo. Moral Theories, Impartiality, and the Status of Non-Rational, Sentient Beings. Between Species, 6(2), 41-52, Spr 90.

FILIPIUK, Marion (ed) and ROBSON, John M (ed) and LAINE, Michael (ed) and MILL, John Stuart. *Additional Letters (Collected Works of John Stuart Mill, Volume XXXII)*. Buffalo, Univ of Toronto Pr, 1991.

FILIPIUK, Marion. "John Stuart Mill and France" in *A Cultivated Mind: Essays On J S Mill Presented to John M Robson*, LAINE, Michael (ed), 80-120. Buffalo, Univ of Toronto Pr, 1991.

FILKORN, Vojtech. "Strong and Weak Methods" in *Logic, Methodology and Philosophy of Science, VIII*, FENSTAD, J E (ed), 319-331. New York, Elsevier Science, 1989.

An analysis of the method as a sequence of the operations from an initial point toward a predetermined or a wanted aim is given. Operations can be single- or multi-valued. Sequences can be single-ramified or multi-ramified, and single- or multi-valued. They can be linear or cyclic. According to this, methods can be divided into the following categories: strong, semistrong, weak, and semiweak. All these methods correspond with appropriate pictures of science. It seems that a real science corresponds with a semiweak method and that is why science as a whole is not algorithmizable. Science and its method is in principle historical.

FILMER, Sir Robert and SOMMERVILLE, Johann P (ed). *Patriarcha and Other Writings: Sir Robert Filmer*. New York, Cambridge Univ Pr, 1991.

FIMBEL, Nancie and BURSTEIN, Jerome S. Defining the Ethical Standards of the High-Technology Industry. J Bus Ethics, 9(12), 929-948, D 90.

At least five sets of ethical standards influence business people's decisions: general cultural, company, personal, situational, and industry standards. Each has an official or espoused form encoded in written documents such as policy statements and codes of ethics and an unofficial form that develops as people use the espoused standards. (We call these unofficial standards values in action.) To determine whether the high-technology industry deserves its reputation for moral laxness, a pilot questionnaire was designed. It asked employees to rate the acceptability in the workplace of ethical behaviors relating to safety, third parties, and cheating the company. The findings show that employees in high- and low-technology industries uphold espoused values of safety. Relations with third parties are influenced by the existence of company codes of ethics, especially in small companies. Actions involving cheating the company need to be investigated further.

FINE, Arthur. Piecemeal Realism. Phil Stud, 61(1-2), 79-96, F 91.

This paper sketches standard responses to the explanationist defense of scientific realism, then considers whether more recent realist fragments that emphasize the role of causal analysis (namely, entity realism and the related topic-specific realism of Richard Miller) fare any better. The paper argues that they do not and, moreover, that they engender special problems of their own. The paper contends that realism, like instrumentalism, is primarily concerned with the character of scientific acceptance, an interpretive issue that goes beyond the range of evidence, and good philosophical sense. It concludes by reminding the reader of NOA, which shows how to do better.

FINE, Kit. "The Justification of Negation as Failure" in *Logic, Methodology and Philosophy of Science, VIII*, FENSTAD, J E (ed), 263-301. New York, Elsevier Science, 1989.

A justification is given for the use of the rule of negation as failure in Prolog and is related to a self-referential form of closure. General methodological remarks on the nature of the problem are also made.

FINE, Kit. "The Problem of De Re Modality" in *Themes From Kaplan*, ALMOG, Joseph (ed), 197-272. New York, Oxford Univ Pr, 1989.

This paper attempts to evaluate Quine's arguments against quantifying into modal contexts and, as such, both complements and expands on my paper "Quine on Quantifying In". Special attention is given to the conditions for quantification to be intelligible and the question of whether quantification must be referential.

FINE, Kit. "Quine on Quantifying In" in *Propositional Attitudes: The Role of Content in Logic, Language, and Mind*, ANDERSON, C Anthony (ed), 1-25. Stanford, CSLI, 1990.

The paper attempts to evaluate Quine's argument against quantifying into modal contexts. Two versions of the argument are distinguished, one of a broadly logical sort and the other relating to the nature of necessity. The first version is seen to depend upon an assumption of linguistic uniformity, which may be reasonable for certain ideal formal languages but which is problematic for natural languages; and the second version is seen to have some force in application to a metaphysical conception of modality, but to have none in application to a logical or analytic conception of modality.

FINE, Kit. A Study of Ontology. Nous, 25(3), 263-294, Je 91.

A constructional ontology is one which serves to construct complexes from simples. The paper is concerned with the general nature of such ontologies and with their study. It attempts to say how they are constituted and by what principles they are governed; and it also attempts to see how their study may lead one to adopt certain positions and to give certain definitions. In the course of making the framework precise, a certain approach to modality, in terms of the concept of requirement, is developed.

FINGARETTE, Herbert. "Reason, Spontaneity, and the *Li*—A Confucian Critique of Graham's Solution to the Problem of Fact and Value" in *Chinese Texts and Philosophical Contexts*, ROSEMONT JR, Henry (ed), 209-225. La Salle, Open Court, 1991.

This essay criticizes A C Graham's ethical thesis that rational conduct will always ensue if one considers all relevant factors and then acts as one is spontaneously inclined to act. The criticism is based on a Confucian point of view, in particular that Graham had failed to appreciate the fundamental and necessary role of tradition, social convention, and in general what Confucius labelled the Li.

FINK, Charles K. Animal Experimentation and the Argument from Limited Resources. Between Species, 7(2), 90-96, Spr 91.

Animal Experimentation and The Argument from Limited Resources. In condemning the use of animals in medical research, animal rights advocates are sometimes accused of showing more compassion for animals than for human beings. In this essay, I respond to this objection by arguing that the medical establishment is actually quite selective in its compassion for humanity; the vital interests of most people would be better served if animal research were abolished and our limited resources devoted to other forms of humanitarian aid, such as providing food and basic medical care to the poor.

FINLAY, Marike. *The Potential of Modern Discourse: Musil, Peirce, and Perturbation*. Bloomington, Indiana Univ Pr, 1990.

FINN, V K and ANSHAKOV, O M and SKVORTSOV, D P. On Axiomatization of Many-Valued Logics Associated with Formalization of Plausible Reasonings. Stud Log, 48(4), 423-447, D 89.

This paper studies a class of infinite-valued predicate logics. A sufficient condition for axiomatizability of logics from that class is given.

FINNIS, John. "Intention and Side-Effects" in *Liability and Responsibility*, FREY, R G (ed), 32-64. New York, Cambridge Univ Pr, 1991.

I defend English judicial rulings that undesired results may be intended, and results foreseen as certain may yet be not intended. To do so, I distinguish systematically between free choice and spontaneity, between rational and subrational motivations, and between moral norms which bear on intent and moral norms which bear on foreseen side effects. I criticise various well-known arguments of Glanville Williams. Against Anscombe's critique of the "doctrine of double effect" I deploy thoughts she proposed in her book *Intention*. A final section seeks to identify the moral rationale for the difference between intention and side-effects.

FINNIS, John. Object and Intention in Moral Judgments According to Aquinas. Thomist, 55(1), 1-28, Ja 91.

A close analysis of Aquinas, providing many passages in Latin and English, shows that (i) a common neo-scholastic schema of his analysis of deliberation and choice profoundly obscures the reality that choice is always the adoption of one among two or more alternative proposals each adjudged in deliberation to be somehow appropriate for one to choose; (ii) this adoption, in and by choice, settles not only the chosen means (proximate end(s)) and the intended (further) end(s) of one's action but also what is a correct description of the action for purposes of evaluating the act morally (primarily in antecedent deliberation).

FINOCCHIARO, Maurice A. Critical Thinking and Thinking Critically: Response to Siegel. Phil Soc Sci, 20(4), 462-466, D 90.

FINSEN, Susan. Response to Lizst's "Animal Liberation as a Valid Response to Structural Violence". Between Species, 6(4), 170-173, Fall 90.

In this response I agree with Liszt that animal liberation is in many cases a morally defensible response to the structural violence perpetrated upon animals. However, I disagree with Liszt's characterization of structural violence, as well as her claims that animal liberation is necessary, apt or in some sense legal. I argue that liberating animals may be neither necessary nor sufficient to cancel an individual's complicity in structural violence, and that other means, such as civil disobedience or refusal to pay one's taxes, are at least equally viable.

FIORENTINO, Fernando. Giuseppe De Luca e la polemica sulla moralità di Péguy. Sapienza, 43(4), 427-434, O-D 90.

FIRCHOW, Peter (trans) and SCHLEGEL, Friedrich. *Philosophical Fragments*. Minneapolis, Univ of Minn Pr, 1991.

FISCHER, Johannes. Ungeklärte Fragen im Dialog zwischen Glaube und Naturwissenschaft. Frei Z Phil Theol, 37(3), 441-464, 1990.

FISCHER, John Martin. Tooley and the Trolley. Phil Stud, 62(1), 93-100, Ap 91.

I lay out a version of the Trolley Problem, and I argue that a solution endorsed by Michael Tooley (following early work by Judith Thomson) is unacceptable. This solution appeals to property rights (in a certain way).

FISCHER, Kurt Rudolf. Comments on Freud and Wittgenstein, and on Adolf Grünbaum's "Foundations of Psychoanalysis". Filozof Istraz, 32-33(5-6), 1691-1700, 1989.

Freud und Wittgenstein waren Schlüsselfiguren in der Kultur des Wiener fin-de-siècle. Beide sehen sich vor eine Aufgabe gestellt, die noch niemals bewältigt worden ist. Eine wichtige Änlichkeit zwischen Freud und Wittgenstein scheint darin zu bestehen, dass sie etwas ganz Neues schaffen, was Form, Stil und Methode anbelangt, etwas von der Tradition Abgelöstes, Ahistorisches, von der Vergangenheit Separiertes. Das Ziel beider ist Auflösung und nicht Lösung: entweder, wie bei Freud und in seiner Nachfolge, durch Psychoanalyse, oder, wie bei Wittgenstein und in seiner Nachfolge, durch Logische Analyse und durch Sprachanalyse. Grünbaums Angriff auf Psychoanalyse ist anspruchvoll und kann als Forderung für und Suche nach einer Grundlage für ein Unternehmen verstanden werden, in dem bisher alles gut gelaufen ist. So konnte er auch als Freud der Psychoanalyse betrachtet werden Der Autor schläagt vor, dass wir noch eine ganze Weile die Spannung ertragen und von ihr profitieren, die sich einerseits aus dem Wunsch ergibt, die Psychoanalyse wissenschaftstheoretisch zu legitimieren und anderseits den impuls zur Legitimierung zu entschärfen.

FISCHER, Michael. "Redefining Philosophy as Literature: Richard Rorty's 'Defence' of Literary Culture" in *Reading Rorty*, MALACHOWSKI, Alan (ed), 233-243. Cambridge, Blackwell, 1991.

This article examines Richard Rorty's defense of a post-philosophical culture in *Consequences of Pragmatism* and other writings. Rorty apparently promotes literature by making it, not philosophy, the center of this culture. According to Rorty, philosophy fails to make good on its traditional promise to ground values and social arrangements in objective truth. Instead of succeeding where philosophy fails, literature presumably abandons the futile quest for referential truth. While seeming to praise literature, this account demeans it and leaves unclear why literature should acquire the cultural prominence Rorty wants it to have.

FISCHER, Norbert. Philosophieren als Sein zum Tode: Zur Interpretation von Platons "Phaidon". Frei Z Phil Theol, 37(1-2), 3-30, 1990.

FISCHER, Roland. Why the Mind is Not in the Head But in the Society's Connectionist Network. Diogenes, 151, 1-28, Fall 90.

The "loosely compacted persons" (of Peirce) are regarded as neuron-like units in the connectionist network of society that develops by experiencing itself. Mind is a boundary condition between the infant and society: with "all mental functions as internalized social relationships" (Vigotsky). Children who are not raised within and by society, but by wolves, for example, do not develop a human mind (although they possess a human brain). Mind is an interactional process within a hermeneutic circle that prevails between the individual (creator of society) and society (creator of individuals). Mind, that tactical and syntactical artefact of the adjective 'mental', may be matter's spontaneous organization that recognizes itself as "order out of chaos" (but we perceive it as our own intentional behavior that is objectified in sensory-motor closure). Hence, the distinction between matter and mind is—as already recognized by Anaxagoras—a matter of mind.

FISHBURN, Peter C and KILGOUR, D Marc. Binary 2 x 2 Games. Theor Decis, 29(3), 165-182, N 90.

The 2 x 2 game is the simplest interactive decision model that portrays concerned decision makers with genuine choices. There are two players, each of whom must choose one of two strategies, so that there are four possible outcomes. *Binary 2 x 2 games* are 2 x 2 games with no restrictions on the players' preference relations over the outcomes. They therefore generalize the strict ordinal 2 x 2 games and the ordinal 2 x 2 games, classes which have already been studied extensively. This paper enumerates the strategically distinct binary 2 x 2 games. It also identifies important subsets defined by the number of pure Nash equilibria and the occurrence of dominant strategies.

FISHER, Alec. Testing Fairmindedness. Inform Log, 13(1), 31-35, Wint 91.

Richard Paul is the leading exponent of '*strong*' critical thinking. The key element which distinguishes 'strong' critical thinking from other conceptions of critical thinking is its commitment to 'fairmindedness'. The fairminded critical thinker gives equal weight to arguments from perspectives other than his or her own. This paper critiques a test of fairmindedness devised by Richard Paul.

FISHER, John Andrew. The Very Idea of Perfect Realism. Phil Forum, 22(1), 49-64, Fall 90.

I define "perfect realism" as a style of replicative sculpture: exact replicas of inanimate objects or humans. Differentiating perfect realism from "photo" or "super" realism, and from representation, I criticize various defenses of this type of art. I argue that to understand perfect realism we need a theory of replication, which I sketch. Part of the account involves X (a replica) causing the perceptual experience that it is a Y when it is not. Hence perfect realism turns on the generic identities of things; it involves a metaphysical exploration of the way we constitute everyday reality.

FISHER, John. "Aesthetic Experience: Where Did We Go Wrong?" in *XIth International Congress in Aesthetics, Nottingham 1988*, WOODFIELD, Richard (ed), 66-69. Nottingham, Nottingham Polytech, 1990.

FISHER, Linda. Feminist Theory and the Politics of Inclusion. J Soc Phil, 21(2-3), 174-183, Fall-Wint 90.

FISHKIN, James S. On Squeamishness: A Response to Galston. Soc Theor Pract, 17(2), 199-206, Sum 91.

FISK, Milton. Marxism in the USSR Today. Stud Soviet Tho, 41(1), 33-49, Ja 91.

FISTETTI, Francesco. "Hannah Arendt: la memoria come spazio del pensiero" in *Razionalitá critica: nella filosofia moderna*, LAMACCHIA, Ada (ed), 171-204. Bari, Lacaita, 1989.

La critica di H Arendt a Heidegger riguarda l'identità heideggeriana tra "pensare" e "filosofare". Per Heidegger la grammatica del pensiero à la verità (anonima) dell'Essere, dunque una grammatica filosofica. Oggetto del pensiero, per la Arendt, sono le azioni e le sofferenze degli uomini. La memoria à la facoltà che preserva le storie (*stories*) degli uomini, non la storia dell'Essere (*Seinsgeschichte*).

FITCH, Gregory. Thinking of Something. Nous, 24(5), 675-696, D 90.

FITZ, Hope K. The Nature and Significance of Intuition: A View Based on a Core Idea Held by S Radhakrishnan. J Indian Counc Phil Res, 6(3), 152-159, My-Ag 89.

In this article, I present a view of intuition as an integral process of the mind which culminates in an act of insight. (The core idea for this view is found in the writings of Sarvepalli Radhakrishnan.) The process itself is one in which present impressions and related memories are brought to bear on a focus of concern. This process is grounded in reason. However, the act of insight does not involve reason. Intuition, so viewed, is not taken to be a nondiscursive form or independent way of gaining knowledge. Rather, it is one means to knowledge, and, as such, it can be accepted as one criterion for justification of a belief.

FITZGERALD, Desmond J. "Adler's *The Idea of Freedom*" in *Freedom in the Modern World: Jacques Maritain, Yves R Simon, Mortimer J Adler*, TORRE, Michael D (ed), 47-55. Notre Dame, Univ Notre Dame Pr, 1989.

This is a study of Mortimer Adler's *The Idea of Freedom* and the cooperative research procedures which were a feature of the Institute for Philosophical Research. In the 1950s and into the early 1960s Adler organized a team of researchers who studied all that they could find in the Western intellectual tradition on freedom. After much analysis Adler distinguished in Volume I (1958) a number of different meanings of freedom, and in Volume II (1961) reconstructed the arguments about the issues of freedom taken from these philosophers.

FITZGERALD, Michael J. The Real Difficulty with Burley's Realistic Semantics. Vivarium, 28(1), 17-25, My 90.

FITZGERALD, Timothy. Mansel's Agnosticism. Relig Stud, 26(4), 525-541, D 90.

FIUMARA, Gemma Corradi. *The Other Side of Language: A Philosophy of Listening*. New York, Routledge, 1990.

FLADER, Susan L (ed) and CALLICOTT, J Baird (ed). *The River of the Mother of God, and Other Essays by Aldo Leopold*. Madison, Univ Wisconsin Pr, 1991.

FLAGE, Daniel E. *David Hume's Theory of Mind*. New York, Routledge, 1991.

The bundle theory of mind is a thread that ties together many of the seemingly unrelated issues discussed in the first book of Hume's *Treatise*. The book shows how Hume defended the bundle theory by showing that his theory of the association of ideas provides the best explanation of various anomalous beliefs such as the belief in material substance. It also explains why, on Hume's own principles, the project of the *Treatise* failed, and why, in his *Enquiry concerning Human Understanding*, he rejected his earlier attempts to construct a theory of mind.

FLAMARIQUE, Lourdes. La filosofía transcendental: el destino de un proyecto ilustrado. Anu Filosof, 23(1), 61-78, 1990.

FLANAGAN, Owen. "Identity and Strong and Weak Evaluation" in *Identity, Character, and Morality: Essays in Moral Psychology*, FLANAGAN, Owen (ed), 37-65. Cambridge, MIT Pr, 1990.

The essay explores the connection between identity and reflection. I argue against Charles Taylor that strong evaluation is not a necessary feature of person, nor is it a necessary condition for moral goodness. However, I argue that strong evaluation is a good and that it plays an important role in certain kinds of social settings. Strong evaluation provides one with tools for avoiding certain kinds of parochialism and conservatism. But it is by no means a moral panacea.

FLANAGAN, Owen (ed) and RORTY, Amélie Oksenberg (ed). *Identity, Character, and Morality: Essays in Moral Psychology*. Cambridge, MIT Pr, 1990.

Nineteen original essays explore the interconnections between psychology and moral theory. Topics include: Identity, Commitment and Agency; Character, Temperament, and Emotion; Moral Psychology and the Source Virtues; Rationality, Responsibility, and Morality; Virtue Theory.

FLANAGAN, Owen. *The Science of the Mind (Second Edition)*. Cambridge, MIT Pr, 1991.

FLANAGAN, Owen. *Varieties of Moral Personality: Ethics and Psychological Realism*. Cambridge, Harvard Univ Pr, 1991.

The aim of the book is to argue for more psychologistically realistic ethical reflection. I argue that neither utilitarianism nor deontological nor virtue theories provide credible pictures of moral motivation and agency. Empirical research is brought to bear on the debates about the personal point of view, moral sainthood, liberal versus communitarian self, gender and moral identity, and the situation sensitivity of moral tracts. The idea that there is a single ideal type of moral personality is rejected.

FLAY, Joseph C. "Hegel's *Science of Logic*: Ironies of the Understanding" in *Essays on Hegel's Logic*, DI GIOVANNI, George (ed), 153-169. Albany, SUNY Pr, 1990.

I argue that the logic of the arguments in Hegel's *Science of Logic* is really no different from the logic traditionally used by philosophers. This does not involve an attempt, however, to "formalize" his logic. I show that what given Hegel's arguments their "dialectical necessity," and thus their force, is the rhetorical form of irony which governs his discourse. I also show that reliance on rhetorical form is not an empty matter, but in fact does give philosophical force to the categorial critique carried out in Hegel's *Logic*.

FLAY, Joseph C. "Merleau-Ponty and Hegel: Radical Essentialism" in *Ontology and Alterity in Merleau-Ponty*, JOHNSON, Galen A (ed), 142-157. Evanston, Northwestern Univ Pr, 1991.

The argument of this essay is that Merleau-Ponty missed something important in Hegel's system, causing him to go along with a distinction between an "early" and a "late" Hegel. I maintain that at the heart of the "mature Hegel" there is a doctrine of essence that supports the view of being that Merleau-Ponty saw only in Hegel's *Phenomenology of Spirit*. I call this doctrine "radical essentialism" and maintain that it is not Merleau-Ponty against Hegel, but Merleau-Ponty as *un copain de* Hegel. My view, if correct, would have consequences for the general interpretation of Hegel.

FLAY, Joseph C. Time in Hegel's *Phenomenology of Spirit*. Int Phil Quart, 31(3), 259-273, S 91.

Interpretations of Hegel's conception of time have either assumed some conception of time and then imposed it on Hegel, or have taken Hegel's discussion of time from some one place in his works and maintained that this was his general view. I argue that Hegel's view is a "contextual" one, i.e., a view that time is intelligible only if considered in the context of how reality is being thematized. The view developed in the *Phenomenology of Spirit* is then discussed in the context of its thematic, namely, the question of the nature of knowledge and the possibility for metaphysics.

FLECK, Leonard M. "National Health Insurance: How Just Must We Be?" in *Biomedical Ethics Reviews, 1990*, HUMBER, James M (ed), 131-188. Clifton, Humana Pr, 1991.

In the real world there are no perfectly just policy options for financing health care in America. How then can we rationally choose among non-ideal options and yet be respectful of the demands of justice? This essay offers a model of how that can be done. In part one I offer a summary of a model of non-ideal justice. In part two I summarize the deficiencies of our current approaches to financing health from the perspective of widely agreed on considered judgments of health care justice. In part three I show the deficiencies of competitive, pluralistic approaches to health financing and the moral advantages of a single comprehensive system that covers everyone, as in Canada.

FLECK, Leonard M. The Oregon Medicaid Experiment: Is It Just Enough? Bus Prof Ethics J, 9(3-4), 201-217, Fall-Wint 90.

Oregon has recently expanded its Medicaid program to cover 100 percent of the poor while at the same time imposing a rationing scheme that would restrict access to only costworthy health care. Critics have charged that this program is unjust. In this paper I argue that the Oregon proposal is defensible from the perspective of a moderately egalitarian, non-ideal theory of justice. Most importantly, I argue that the poor themselves would see the Oregon proposal as a moral improvement over their current state, and hence, would impose this rationing scheme on themselves in exchange for expanded access.

FLEGO, Gvozden. Did Freud Develop a Social Philosophy? (in Serbo-Croatian). Filozof Istraz, 32-33(5-6), 1738-1748, 1989.

Trotz zahlreicher Distanzierungen des späten Freuds von der Philosophie argumentiert der Autor, dass das Freudsche Denken nicht nur mehrere gemeinsame Punkte mit der Philosophie hat, sondern dass es selbst eine Philosophie enthält. Diese These lässt sich am besten an einigen Freudschen "kulturalistischen Shriften" (*Totem und Tabu, Massenpsychologie und Ich-Analyse, Die Zukunft einer Illusion, Das Unbehagen in der Kultur*) demonstrieren, in denen eine spezifische Sozialphilosophie am Werk ist. Den Menschen definiert Freud zunächst als Wesen der Triebe, die er (und damit auch sich selbst) in eigener kultureller Existenz ändert und statt triebhaftes und unbewusstes ein vernünftiges, bewusstes und sich übersichtliches Wesen zu werden tendiert. (edited)

FLEGO, Gvozden. Freud, Marxism and the Frankfurt School (in Serbo-Croation). Filozof Istraz, 34(1), 105-112, 1990.

Der Autor behauptet, dass der Kern des Denkens der frühen Periode der Frankfurter Schule die Synthese zwischen Ideen von Marx und Freud war. Damit bekommt das frühe Werk Erich Fromms eine andere Bedeutung als das in den meisten Geschichten der 'Schule' der Fall war. Trotzdem wurde der Höhepunkt dieser Orientation bei Marcuse (seit *Triebstruktur und Gesellschaft*) erreicht, bei dem man von einem Freudo-Hegelo-Marxismus reden kann. Mittels dieser Position konstruiert Marcuse einen gewissen Optimismus gegenüber hoffnungsloser Stellung von Horkheimer und Adorno und bewährt das (implizierte) gesellschaftstheoretische Paradigma für die Analyse der Lage des gegenwärtigen Menschen. Der Autor ist überzeugt, dass nicht die unmittelbare Lektüre der freudschen Arbeiten sondern gerade diese Denkfigur—nämlich freudo-/hegelo-/marsistische Umarbeitung seiner Ideen—bei spätem Adorno, bei Habermas wie auch bei A Lorenzer und K Horn am Werk war.

FLEMING, Jesse. A Response to Kuang-Ming Wu's "Non-World-Making". J Chin Phil, 18(1), 51-52, Mr 91.

FLESCHE, David E. "Wittgenstein's Philosophy of Language and the Question of Translation" in *Hermeneutics and the Poetic Motion, Translation Perspectives V—1990*, SCHMIDT, Dennis J (ed), 93-110. Binghamton, CRIT, 1990.

FLETCHER, George P. "Punishment and Self-Defense" in *Liability and Responsibility*, FREY, R G (ed), 415-430. New York, Cambridge Univ Pr, 1991.

FLETCHER, John C and WERTZ, Dorothy C. Privacy and Disclosure in Medical Genetics Examined in an Ethics of Care. Bioethics, 5(3), 212-232, Jl 91.

This paper examines moral reasoning of 682 geneticists from 19 nations responding to an open-ended questionnaire concerning six cases involving disclosure of 1) non-paternity to husbands; 2) test results to patients' spouses; 3) a patient's diagnosis to relatives at genetic risk; 4) ambiguous results; 5) fetal sex to parents who would abort the sex not desired; 6) patients' test results to insurers and employers. An ethics of care, based on patients' needs and providers' reponsibilities, is closer to clinicians' thinking than a "principle" approach, recommends full disclosure but recognizes the need to protect weaker members of society, especially women, and regards patients as members of communities.

FLEURY, Chantal. Analyse d'un corpus iconographique rassemblé par Maxime Préaud ou Aristote et la mélancolie. Horiz Phil, 1(1), 101-109, 1990.

FLEW, Antony. Communism: The Philosophical Foundations. Philosophy, 66(257), 269-282, Jl 91.

The thesis is that the conceptual system guiding all the political and social thinking of Marx and Engels derived not from empirical studies but from what Marx himself was pleased to call a 'philosophical analysis' of concepts. This analysis was itself vitiated by the failure of so-called German classical philosophy to come to terms with the challenge of Locke and Hume. The historicist conviction that "Communism lies at the end of all roads in the world" ultimately derives from Christian belief in a future Kingdom of God on earth; but lacks its rational foundation in putative Divine promises.

FLEW, Antony. Fogelin on Hume on Miracles. Hume Stud, 16(2), 141-144, N 90.

This reply to Fogelin argues, simply but sharply, that my view of what Hume was doing in Section X of his first *Enquiry* and not Fogelin's is correct, and was also Hume's own view, as there stated.

FLEW, Antony. Freedom and Human Nature. Philosophy, 66(255), 53-63, Ja 91.

The aim is to show that Leszek Kolakowski was right to urge that freedom as the absence of external constraint has no future unless we are creatures who can and cannot but make physically unnecessitated choices. It is argued that no one could even understand a denial of this fundamental and distinguishing fact of human nature without being equipped with premises sufficient for a demonstration of its truth. A second part makes an object lesson of B F Skinner's insistence that anything truly deserving the description 'Psychological Science' must start from a denial of this truth.

FLEW, Antony. Hume and Physical Necessity. Iyyun, 39(3), 251-266, Jl 90.

This paper is divided into five parts. The first reviews those essential elements in the concept of causation which are omitted from Hume's account. The second seeks the sort of experience by reference to which the relevant notions can be legitimated. The third examines "The idea or, rather, the ideas of power." The fourth considers what Hume might have learnt here from Locke's contribution. The fifth and last part applies earlier findings to Hume's treatment "Of liberty and necessity."

FLEW, Antony. Market Order or Commanded Chaos. Pub Affairs Quart, 5(1), 19-32, Ja 91.

This is a study of the socialist project, as persuasively presented in the two most widely circulated Marxist scriptures, and of why it has so obviously failed. Although discussing what was supposed to be Marx's conception of justice became a major academic industry in the West, Lenin and Stalin were surely faithful to Marx in maintaining that it was not abstract justice but increasing productivity which was going to justify socialism. So there can be no doubt but that, even in preferred terms of its progenitors, that project has failed, and failed spectacularly; for all the world to see.

FLEW, Antony. Was Karl Marx a Social Scientist? Free Inq, 11(2), 37-41, 57, Spr 91.

It was because Engels was so right in his first obituary assertion about Marx—that he was always and above all the revolutionary—that his second—that Marx was a social scientist comparable with Darwin as a biologist—was so wrong. Its falsity is shown, for instance, by the suppression in *Capital* of evidence refuting its Immiseration Thesis and the deliberate development in *The Civil War in France* of an inspiring but unhistorical account of the origins and nature of the Paris Commune. Consider too employments of "a bit of dialectics" to conceal falsifications of cherished theses.

FLICHMAN, Eduardo. A Crucial Distinction: Initial Data and Law Application Instances. Critica, 22(66), 75-85, D 90.

FLINT, Thomas P. In Defence of Theological Compatibilism. Faith Phil, 8(2), 237-243, Ap 91.

William Hasker has recently attacked the thesis that divine foreknowledge and human freedom are compatible. Hasker sees only two ways his opponents could respond to his argument: claim that we have causal power over God's past beliefs, or claim that we have counterfactual power over them. Hasker employs two principles in an attempt to show that the latter of these compatibilist responses collapses into the first, which he then criticizes. I argue that Hasker fails to discredit the second response, for his principles would be rejected by his adversaries, and his defence of the second principle is tantamount to begging the question.

FLODEN, Robert E and BUCHMANN, Margret. Coherent Programs in Teacher Education: When Are They Educational? Proc Phil Educ, 46, 304-314, 1990.

Advocates of "program coherence" assume that tightly connected experiences are needed to give teacher education programs sufficient power. "Coherence" and "program" have positive associations with harmony and wholeness. Associations with behaviorism and efficiency suggest difficulties with these concepts. Teacher educators should consider the metaphor of a sparkling diamond, implying that teacher education can benefit from the incorporation of many facets—variegated ideas and practices—among which different patterns of connection may be drawn. Program coherence can be valuable if it helps students build interconnections while also inviting a reweaving of beliefs and ties to what is as yet unknown.

FLORIDA, R E. Buddhist Approaches to Abortion. Asian Phil, 1(1), 39-50, 1991.

FLOYD, Juliet and DREBEN, Burton. Tautology: How Not to Use a Word. Synthese, 87(1), 23-49, Ap 91.

We discuss the character and philosophical significance of Wittgenstein's use of "tautology" in the *Tractatus*, a use which was not clear. Wittgenstein justified or shifted the term from rhetoric to logic, and hence shaped (misshaped?) debates concerning the nature and scope of logic from the time of the Vienna Circle onward. We discuss relevant historical uses of "tautology" in philosophy from Leibniz, Kant, Hegel, Bradley, Mauthner and the early Moore and Russell, and document Russell's later (1918) jump to the verbiage of "tautology", as well as C I Lewis's and Ramsey's attempts to wrest a philosophical lesson from the *Tractatus*'s new use.

FLOYD, Juliet. Wittgenstein on 2, 2, 2...: The Opening of Remarks on the Foundations of Mathematics. Synthese, 87(1), 143-180, Ap 91.

I use a detailed, line by line reading of the first three sections of Wittgenstein's *Remarks on the Foundation of Mathematics* to illustrate the point and importance of his discussions of mathematics and logic. The manuscript basis of *Remarks on the Foundation of Mathematics* is set into historical context, and I emphasize the relation of Wittgenstein's dialectical style of writing to his aims and achievements in criticizing the traditional categories of a priori and necessary truth. I maintain that his remarks on the following of a rule for an elementary arithmetical series place our thinking about logical inference in a new and original light.

FLOYD, Wayne Whitson. The Search for an Ethical Sacrament: From Bonhoeffer to Critical Social Theory. Mod Theol, 7(2), 175-193, Ja 91.

Theology for Dietrich Bonhoeffer was initially *criticism*, an attempt to speak truthfully, i.e., as concretely as possible. If the truth of the Christian Gospel becomes concrete in the sacrament, what then is the concreteness embodying ethical responsibility, the "ethical sacrament"? First, Bonhoeffer is contrasted with the Nazi antirational ideology against which he argued. Second, the essay shows how Bonhoeffer countered Nazism using the social-critical implications of transcendental philosophy. Third, Bonhoeffer is placed into conversation with the work of the Frankfurt School of Critical Theory, whose work coincided with Bonhoeffer's as to time, setting and theme.

FLURI, Philippe H. Thomas S Kuhn and L Fleck: Two Sociologists of Science. Indian Phil Quart, 18(2), 271-284, Ap 91.

FLUXMAN, Tony. Freud on Civilization and Neurosis. S Afr J Phil, 10(2), 44-48, My 91.

Freud's claim that civilization and instinctual satisfaction are at odds is evaluated. According to Freud human instincts are such that they conflict with the requirements of civilization. It is argued that neither Freud's theoretical considerations nor his case studies support this claim. The case studies, it is maintained, do not provide evidence that instinctual factors are central to the etiology of a neurosis. Instead it is the environment which should rather be assigned the central role. This gives rise to the possibility that instinctual satisfaction and societal demands are, in contrast to Freud's view, compatible in principle.

FLYVBJERG, Bent. Sustaining Non-Rationalized Practices: Body-Mind, Power and Situational Ethics—Interview with Hubert and Stuart Dreyfus. Praxis Int, 11(1), 93-113, Ap 91.

The purpose of the article is to analyze and evaluate the relationship between, on the one hand power, ethics and phenomenology, and on the other learning processes, skills and expertise, in the work of Hubert and Stuart Dreyfus. The importance of body and intuition to human learning is explored together with the question of rationalization and marginalization of human skills and practices in modern society. Caring, teaching and friendship are used as examples drawing on work by Maurice Merleau-Ponty, Michel Foucault, Soren Kirkegaard, Martin Heidegger and Jürgen Habermas. The concept 'situational ethics' is developed and compared to Aristotle's ethics. The Scandinavian 'ombudsman-institution' is discussed as an exemplar overcoming the dualism of rule-based versus situational ethics.

FODOR, Janet Dean and CRAIN, Stephen. Phrase Structure Parameters. Ling Phil, 13(6), 619-659, D 90.

FODOR, Jerry A. A Modal Argument for Narrow Content. J Phil, 88(1), 5-26, Ja 91.

FODOR, Jerry A. "Reply to Dretske's 'Does Meaning Matter?'" in *Information, Semantics and Epistemology*, VILLANUEVA, Enrique (ed), 28-35. Cambridge, Blackwell, 1990.

FODOR, Jerry A. "Substitution Arguments and the Individuation of Beliefs" in *Meaning and Method: Essays in Honor of Hilary Putnam*, BOOLOS, George (ed), 63-78. New York, Cambridge Univ Pr, 1990.

FODOR, Jerry A. You Can Fool Some of the People All of the Time, Everything Else Being Equal; Hedged Laws and Psychological Explanation. Mind, 100(397), 19-34, Ja 91.

FOERSTER, John. Paul Tillich and Inter-religious Dialogue. Mod Theol, 7(1), 1-27, O 90.

The article is a comprehensive survey of Tillich's ideas on the subject. It focusses on his later writings, including numerous unpublished sources. In a first part the author examines Tillich's theoretical approaches to the problem, in particular the use of religious typologies. The second part includes a discussion of the normative aspects in inter-religious dialogue, as well as examples of dialogues between Tillich and a Buddhist scholar. According to the author, Tillich's most useful ideas for the subject are his demand for a meta-level of discussion, rudimentarily outlined by Tillich himself through typological comparisons and the link between inter- and "intra-religious" dialogue.

FOGELIN, Robert J. A Reading of Aquinas's Five Ways. Amer Phil Quart, 27(4), 305-313, O 90.

This essay offers an alternative reading of Aquinas's so-called Five Ways as they appear in the *Summa Theologica*, suggesting, contrary to the standard interpretation, that they are not intended as *a posteriori* demonstrations of God's existence. They are, instead, specific responses to one of the objections that precedes them in the text, namely, that nature can be accounted for fully without reference to a Deity. Thus, instead of being scientific proofs for the existence of God, they are responses to a challenge from the science of Aquinas's time.

FOGELIN, Robert J and SINNOTT-ARMSTRONG, Walter. *Understanding Arguments: An Introduction to Informal Logic (Fourth Edition)*. San Diego, Harcourt Brace Jov, 1991.

FOGELMAN, Brian D and HUTCHINSON, D S. 'Seventeen' Subtleties in Plato's *Theaetetus*. Phronesis, 35(3), 303-306, 1990.

This short paper draws attention to yet another example of Plato's concern for philosophical methodology in the *Theaetetus*. Specifically, it provides an interpretation of Plato's enumeration of the cases where false belief is possible (192a ff) in light of an earlier passage which is more apparently connected with the theme of philosophical methodology (147c-e). In both cases it is argued that Plato demonstrates his preference for an analysis that yields a classification over the bare enumeration of individual cases.

FOGG, Walter L. Entrance Strategies for Philosophy. Teach Phil, 13(4), 365-371, D 90.

A workshop report describing some techniques used to introduce students to the topic of philosophy. One strategy asks students for their own definitions of "philosophy" and examples of philosophical questions. A second major strategy focuses on the notion of wisdom. One variant elicits student proposals for "wise person" referents. Another variant draws out and refines the student's image of a "wise person." Detailed steps are presented on some of these techniques and the comments of conferees at the workshop on the usefulness and drawbacks of such techniques are given throughout the report.

FÖLDESI, Tamás. Can the Discussion Partners Trust Each Other? Dialec Hum, 16(3-4), 47-57, Sum-Autumn 89.

The significance of the Christian-Marxist dialogue has been determined by the fact, that in a world torn apart by different contradictions, where the conflicts already threaten the future and survival of mankind, all kinds of getting closer to each other, trust building and conflict solving aiming at constructive dialogues and common grounds for action without giving up principles but preserving the integrity of one's ideas are progressive and are to be greeted. In the course of the dialogue it became evident that important as the readiness for dialogue of the participants may be, more is needed to succeed: it has to be clarified in more detail how, with what means it can be ensured that the dialogue, as part of a long process, will have enduring positive consequences. In the following I want to deal with these questions, based on the lessons of the dialogue.

FÖLDESI, Tamás. The Unity of Human Rights in Western and Eastern Europe: Meditation about Human Rights. Riv Int Filosof Diritto, 67(1), 82-92, Ja-Mr 90.

FOLDVARY, Fred E. Challenge: Subjectivist Naturalism. Vera Lex, 10(2), 21-22, 1990.

FOLEY, Richard. Evidence and Reasons for Belief. Analysis, 51(2), 98-102, Mr 91.

It is natural to think that having evidence for the truth of a proposition gives you an epistemic reason to belief it. Unfortunately, there are counterexamples to this attractively simple thesis. Belief in accordance with the evidence can itself affect the evidence, and when it does, evidence and epistemic reasons for belief can come apart. There is nonetheless a general, albeit more complicated, way in which evidence and epistemic reasons for belief are linked. They are subjunctively linked. Having adequate evidence for a proposition gives you an epistemic reason to believe it, unless believing the proposition would itself undermine the evidence.

FOLEY, Richard. "Skepticism and Rationality" in *Doubting: Contemporary Perspectives on Skepticism*, ROTH, Michael D (ed), 69-81. Norwell, Kluwer, 1990.

Skeptical hypotheses convince no one, and yet they have an enormous influence in epistemology. They provoke some epistemologists into endorsing metaphysical and linguistic positions that antecedently would have seemed to have had little appeal, and they push others into an overly defensive posture from which it can seem that the test of an epistemology is how well it would fare in a hostile environment. There must be a third way. The author describes a different way of reacting to skeptical hypotheses—one that is neither dismissive of them nor submissive to them.

FOLLESDAL, Dagfinn. "Indeterminacy and Mental States" in *Perspectives on Quine*, BARRETT, Robert (ed), 98-109. Cambridge, Blackwell, 1990.

FOLLESDAL, Dagfinn. Noema and Meaning in Husserl. Phil Phenomenol Res, 50 SUPP, 263-271, Fall 90.

FOLLIERO-METZ, Grazia Dolores. *La Grecia "Tedesca" fra Nostalgia e Mito*. Rome, EUROMA, 1990.

This philosophical research aims at clarifying both in a genetic and systematic manner the significance of the rebirth of Greek studies in Germany between 1755 and 1870. It was not namely a generic classical erudition, but a precise analysis of the birth of a modern classical German culture which gave impulse to the movement. This program and this approach to the Greek world is both common to classicist as much as anticlassicist philosophers (Schiller, Hegel, Nietzsche), and is followed in the present work even in the akin fields of history of art and literature (Winckelmann, Moritz, Wieland, Goethe, Hölderlin, Wagner, Burckhardt), in the attempt of recreating an overall fresco of our latest European spiritual heritage.

FOLSE JR, Henry J. Laudan's Model of Axiological Change and the Bohr-Einstein Debate 77. Proc Phil Sci Ass, 1, 77-88, 1990.

According to the naturalistic normative axiology of Laudan's reticulated model of scientific change, empirical discoveries can provide a rational basis for axiological decisions concerning the epistemic goals scientific inquiry ought to pursue. The Bohr-Einstein debate over acceptance of quantum theory is analyzed as a case of axiological change. The participants' aims are incompatible due to different formulations of the goal of objective description, but neither doubts the realist commitment to the existence of microsystems or the intention of quantum mechanics to provide knowledge of them. Thus the general aim of realism is not at issue.

FOLSE, Henry J. Metaphysical Awakening in Philosophy of Quantum Physics. Int Stud Phil, 23(1), 89-98, 1991.

This article reviews John Bell, *Speakable and Unspeakable in Quantum Mechanics*; John Honner, *The Description of Nature: Niels Bohr and the Philosophy of Quantum Physics*; Henry Krips, *The Metaphysics of Quantum Theory*; Peter Gibbons, *Particles and Paradoxes*; and Harvey R Brown and Rom Harre, Eds., *Philosophical Foundations of Quantum Field Theory*. Two points of concensus emerge: the philosophical problems of quantum mechanics have not been solved, and their solution requires reconstructing classical ontological assumptions. The greatest philosophical embarassment of the quantum revolution is the lack of any developed alternative ontology on which to erect a world-view of quantum physics.

FONG, Daniel W and KANE, Thomas C and RICHARDSON, Robert C. The Phenotype as the Level of Selection: Cave organisms as Model Systems. Proc Phil Sci Ass, 1, 151-164, 1990.

FONTAINE-DE VISSCHER, Luce. Mythe et raison: Propos contemporains. Rev Phil Louvain, 88(80), 553-580, N 90.

The problem of the relationship of reason to myth offers a particularly remarkable example of the inevitable debate between the humane sciences and philosophy. The author has taken the risk of explicating the unexpressed philosophical a priori in the works of Walter Otto and Jean-Pierre Vernant, two Hellenists who were approximately contempories of Heidegger. In the former a remarkable parallel to Heidegger's "repetition" of the Presocratics is found. In the latter, however, in spite of his illuminating theory of a mutation in thought, which shook the famous "Greek miracle" (Burnet's theory), a degree of retentivity of Hegel's dialectic of the conquest of the spirit over the opaqueness of mythical imagination may still be found. However, a recent interpretation of Vernant's works by Jacques Derrida brings to light in them a notion of proto-rationality, which brings the Hellenist closer to Heidegger's views. It is seen how cultural phenomena as objects of scientific explanation are indissociable from the thought on the conditions that make them possible. All languages overlap and none enjoys a privileged position of absolute exteriority.

FONTANA, Biancamaria. *Benjamin Constant and the Post-Revolutionary Mind*. New Haven, Yale Univ Pr, 1991.

This book discusses Constant's political theories in the context of his historical setting. The unity of Constant's vision, encompassing not only politics, but also morality, aesthetics, and spirituality, is explored. (staff)

FORBES, Graeme. "Biosemantics and the Normative Properties of Thought" in *Philosophical Perspectives, 3: Philosophy of Mind and Action Theory, 1989*, TOMBERLIN, James E (ed), 533-547. Atascadero, Ridgeview, 1989.

This paper criticizes some naturalistic approaches to meaning based on the paradigm of biological explanations of functional facts.

FORBES, Graeme. The Indispensability of *Sinn*. Phil Rev, 99(4), 535-563, O 90.

In this paper I give a neo-Fregean semantics for propositional attitude ascriptions in which proper names are used in specifying the content of the attitude. The account exhibits substitution of such names as being like substitution within the scope of "so-called," and for this reason I call my theory the "logophoric" analysis. The paper ends with an application to Kripke's puzzle about belief.

FORCE, James E. "The Breakdown of the Newtonian Synthesis of Science and Religion: Hume, Newton, and the Royal Society" in *Essays on the Context, Nature, and Influence of Isaac Newton's Theology*, FORCE, James E (ed), 143-163. Norwell, Kluwer, 1990.

In the first part of this essay, the author examines the concepts of "general" and "special" providence in the context of some of the early members of the Royal Society such as Boyle and Newton. There is, in the thought of these scientist-theologians, a latent conflict between a purely mechanistic conception of the universe created by an all-powerful, generally provident God and a specially provident, miracle-working God who is still active in creation. This latent conflict is made explicit by David Hume.

FORCE, James E (ed). *Essays on the Context, Nature, and Influence of Isaac Newton's Theology*. Norwell, Kluwer, 1990.

This book is a series of collected essays, five by James E Force and five by Richard H Popkin. In their independent essays, the authors explore aspects of Newton's religious thought, e.g., the influence he had while alive on thinkers such as Whiston and Clarke, the influence he had on 18th-Century Millenarians such as Hartley and Priestley, the influence he had on David Hume, and the influence he had on 18th- and 19th-Century fundamentalism.

FORCE, James E. "Hume's Interest in Newton and Science" in *Essays on the Context, Nature, and Influence of Isaac Newton's Theology*, FORCE, James E (ed), 181-206. Norwell, Kluwer, 1990.

In this essay the author publishes all eleven of Hume's references to Newton. He uses these texts to controvert Peter Jones's revisionist contention that Hume lacked any interest whatsoever in science in general or in Newton in particular.

FORCE, James E. "Newton's God of Dominion: The Unity of Newton's Theological, Scientific, and Political Thought" in *Essays on the Context, Nature, and Influence of Isaac Newton's Theology*, FORCE, James E (ed), 75-102. Norwell, Kluwer, 1990.

The author argues in this essay that Newton's conception of a voluntaristic deity, a supremely powerful, absolute sovereign who is Lord God of and over creation, directly influences Newton's theology, natural philosophy, and politics and, moreover, provides the key to understanding the synthetic unity in his thought which constitutes his true incandescent genius.

FORCE, James E. "The Newtonians and Deism" in *Essays on the Context, Nature, and Influence of Isaac Newton's Theology*, FORCE, James E (ed), 43-73. Norwell, Kluwer, 1990.

The author argues, in contrast to recent modern interpreters, that Newton is *no* deist because Newton finally believes (unlike all other "deists") that the Bible is the record of the oldest human history and the source of all that is true in subsequent gentile (i.e., Egyptian and Greek) theology, even though the present text of scripture is much corrupted by idolotrous human accretions.

FORCE, James E. "Sir Isaac Newton, 'Gentleman of Wide Swallow'? Newton and the Latitudinarians" in *Essays on the Context, Nature, and Influence of Isaac Newton's Theology*, FORCE, James E (ed), 119-141. Norwell, Kluwer, 1990.

Newton has been widely recognized as the philosophical flower of the Latitudinarian movement. Force analyzes the arguments purporting to demonstrate Newton's "Latitudinarianism." He argues that Newton is *not* a Latitudinarian because his metaphysical voluntarism leads him to hold theological doctrines, e.g., his basically Puritan predestinarianism and his ardent millennialism, which are incompatible with the tolerant and liberal scepticism of the Latitudinarian divines.

FORD, Lewis S. Efficient Causation Within Concrescence. Process Stud, 19(3), 167-180, Fall 90.

Whitehead's early decision to treat the 'transition' between occasions in terms of efficient causation, and the 'conscrescence' within occasions in terms of final causation led to a very thin theory of efficient causation as 'concrescence' incorporated more and more of the functions of 'transition.' I propose we understand efficient causation in terms of the activity of physical prehension both between and within occasions. Robust interaction among physical prehensions within occasions is not really possible without concrescent elimination, but this becomes possible with the introduction of subjective aim. If so, Whitehead could revive the old term 'efficacity' to mean an active efficient causation within concrescence.

FORD, Lewis S. The Modes of Actuality. Mod Sch, 67(4), 275-283, My 90.

This essay questions the traditional thesis that there can be only one species of primary actualities. Any more runs the danger of incoherence. This Aristotelian principle may well be appropriate for enduring substances, which can inhabit both the past and the present, but poses difficulties if actualities are conceived of as events which are either present or past. Then is what is most fully actual (present) acting or (past) concrete determinateness? Is one to be denigrated in favor of the other? Moreover, no incoherence arises from the postulation of both as actual, though diversely, since concrete determinateness necessarily results from, and depends upon, present acting. God, transcending both present acting and past determinateness, constitutes the third mode of actuality as future creativity.

FORD, Lewis S. The Reformed Subjectivist Principle Revisited. Process Stud, 19(1), 28-48, Spr 90.

Whitehead's reformed subjectivist principle, that the primary togetherness of things is their togetherness in experience, is usually interpreted as a modification of the epistemological 'subjectivist principle' that Whitehead rejects. I argue that it comes from a later ontological reflection upon his major shift in PR, from the part II theory of concrescence (as starting from a single datum) to the theory of part III, and is only superficially attached to its present context. It articulates the deepening of Whitehead's panpsychism (that every actuality enjoys mentality) into pansubjectivity (there can be no actualization apart from subjectivity). The earlier theory of transition resulting in the datum for concrescence could affirm the former but not the latter.

FOREMAN, Matthew. "A Dilworth Decomposition Theorem" in *Logic, Methodology and Philosophy of Science, VIII*, FENSTAD, J E (ed), 223-244. New York, Elsevier Science, 1989.

FORGE, John. Theoretical Explanation and Errors of Measurement. Erkenntnis, 33(3), 371-390, N 90.

This paper discusses error of measurement in the framework of the instance view of explanation. As a point of departure the structuralist account of theories is adopted. Then errors of measurement are represented by means of uniformities.

FORGIE, J W. The Modal Ontological Argument and the Necessary A Posteriori. Int J Phil Relig, 29(3), 129-141, Je 91.

I consider modal ontological arguments of the form, 'God is possible; therefore, God actually exists', which conceive of God in terms of properties indexed to the actual world. The use of such α-indexed properties can ensure the validity of these arguments but it also transforms their possibility premisses into a posteriori claims. Because of this, a typical inquirer is not going to be able to get into some desired epistemic position toward the possibility premise (e.g., knowing it, or determining that it is rationally acceptable) without first having to get into that same position toward the conclusion of the argument. Thus it is not clear for whom these arguments could establish even the rationality of their conclusions.

FORGIE, J William. The Caterus Objection. Int J Phil Relig, 28(2), 81-104, O 90.

A successful ontological argument must meet Caterus's objection that the argument's conclusion lacks existential import. Caterus thought this was true of Descartes's argument because Descartes's conclusion was merely a hypothetical, or conditional, statement. However, it is easy—by a device I call "subjectizing" the argument—to produce an ontological argument with a categorical, not hypothetical, conclusion. Anselm's arguments, as well as certian contemporary modal arguments, are "subjectized" and so appear to avoid the Caterus objection. This paper examines the nature of the subjectizing process and argues that even though it yields ontological arguments with categorical conclusions it guarantees that those conclusions still lack existential import.

FORHAN, Kate Langdon. Salisburian Stakes: The Uses of 'Tyranny' in John of Salisbury's *Policraticus*. Hist Polit Thought, 11(3), 397-407, Autumn 90.

The best known aspect of John of Salisbury's thought is his theory of tyrannicide. Considered to be his most significant contribution to the history of ideas, the theory was essential to the defense of political violence in later political thought. Studies of his theory, focusing on the question of regicide, avoid the deeper significance of the *Policraticus* as a whole—the presentation of a "polycratic" society of mutual interdependence, rather than hierarchy and subordination. In it, the corporate metaphor becomes a metaphor for a politics of inclusion, and thus sets a foundation for institutional and legal developments in political theory.

FORMAN, Frank. "Virtue, The Missing Link to the Last Volume of the *Treatise*" in *Studies on Mario Bunge's "Treatise"*, WEINGARTNER, Paul (ed), 491-509. Amsterdam, Rodopi, 1990.

This chapter lays out some problems for Mario Bunge to tackle as he writes *The Good and the Right* to crown his life's achievement. How does ethics fit into his scientific metaphysics? What is the exact scope of a scientific ethics? Is it fixed for all mankind? The chapter begins with speculations on the evolution of morality and poses the puzzle that moral systems urged on humans usually go against self-interest. It concludes by stating the many virtues of virtue as a way around the puzzle and as a central basis for ethics.

FORMENT, Eudaldo. Amor y comunicación. Espiritu, 37(97), 5-34, Ja-Je 88.

FORMENT, Eudaldo. El concepto tradicional de verdad en Santo Tomás. Espiritu, 35(94), 111-126, Jl-D 86.

FORMENT, Eudaldo. Crítica de Heidegger al "intuicionalismo" cartesiano. Espiritu, 36(95), 49-67, Ja-Je 87.

FORMENT, Eudaldo. Cuarenta años del "Instituto Filosófico de Balmesiana". Espiritu, 38(100), 115-130, Jl-D 89.

FORMENT, Eudaldo. Filósofo hispanista. Espiritu, 38(100), 145-152, Jl-D 89.

FORMENT, Eudaldo. La interpretación de Santo Tomás en García Morente. Espiritu, 35(93), 13-34, Ja-Je 86.

FORMENT, Eudaldo. El personalismo de Santo Tomás. Sapientia, 45(178), 277-294, O-D 90.

FORMENT, Eudaldo. Unamuno y el problema de Dios. Espiritu, 36(96), 125-162, Jl-D 87.

FORMIGARI, Lia (ed) and DE MAURO, Tullio (ed). *Leibniz, Humboldt, and the Origins of Comparativism*. Philadelphia, John Benjamins, 1990.

FORNET-BETANCOURT, Raúl. La contribución de la filosofía al cambio social en América Latina. Logos (Mexico), 19(56), 119-130, My-Ag 91.

FORNET-BETANCOURT, Raúl. La cuestión de Dios en el pensar de Heidegger. Rev Filosof (Venezuela), 13, 43-56, 1989.

FORREST, Peter. The Compatability of Consequentialism with Deontological Convictions. Phil Inq, 12(1-2), 22-31, Wint-Spr 90.

The purpose of this paper is to explore the position which results from combining consequentialism with various deontological intuitions. There is no inconsistency in this position, although it results in various moral dilemmas.

FORREST, Peter. How Can We Speak of God? How Can We Speak of Anything. Int J Phil Relig, 29(1), 33-52, F 91.

The purpose of this paper is to show how we can speak of God even if God shares no properties with human beings, and even if God is simple. I stress the Lockean distinction between real and nominal essences. Although we have no knowledge of God's real essence we can know God's nominal essence.

FORROW, Lachlan and ARNOLD, Robert M and FRADER, Joel. Teaching Clinical Ethics in the Residency Years: Preparing Competent Professionals. J Med Phil, 16(1), 93-112, F 91.

Formal training in clinical ethics must become a central part of residency curricula to prepare practitioners to manage the ethical dimensions of patient care. Residency educators must ground their teaching in an understanding of the conceptual, biomedical, and psychosocial aspects of the important ethical issues that arise in that field of practice. Four aspects of professional competence in clinical ethics provide a useful framework for curricular planning. The physician should learn to (1) recognize ethical issues as they arise in clinical care and identify hidden values and unacknowledged conflicts; (2) think clearly and critically about these issues in ways that lead to ethically justifiable courses of action; (3) apply those practical skills needed to implement an ethically justifiable course of action; and (4) judge when the management of a clinical situation requires consultation with individuals or institutional bodies with additional expertise or authority. We argue that these practical goals can be accomplished with a relatively modest emphasis on the theoretical aspects of medical ethics.

FORROW, Lachlan. When Is Home Care Medically Necessary? Commentary. Hastings Center Rep, 21(4), 36-37, Jl-Ag 91.

FORSBERG, Ralph P. *Thomas Hobbes' Theory of Obligation: A Modern Interpretation*. Wolfeboro, Longwood, 1990.

The book is devoted to the problem of the correct interpretation of Hobbes's theory of political obligation, which states that citizens owe almost absolute obligation to their sovereign. The book tries to rectify the three most common interpretations, showing that Hobbes consistently defended the position that citizens are obliged to obey their sovereign, while using all three theories to justify that claim. Rather than choosing one as the correct interpretation, the book shows that Hobbes's interest in rhetoric and place in history led him to use all three theories in an attempt to pursuade diverse readers to accept his view.

FORSCHE, Joachim. Grundlegende Aspekte zur Problematik von Erkenntnis und Praxis. Deut Z Phil, 38(12), 1183-1186, 1990.

Es geht in dem Aufsatz um ein neues, ein humanes Rationalitätsverständnis: Es ist falsch, das Rationale auf das Empirische und Theoretische einzuschränken. Auch die nichtbegrifflichen Verhältnisse des Menschen zur Welt müssen in das Rationale einbezogen werden; so die geistig-emotionalen Formen der Erkenntnis (moralische, ästhetische, künstlerische Erkenntnis). Und auch dies: Die grundlegende philosophische These von der Erkennbarkeit der Welt und deren Veränderbarkeit muss ergänzt werden: A) Alles Seiende (Dinge, Prozesse, Erscheinungen) ist prinzipiell erkennbar—gleichwohl gibt es Grenzen der Begreifbarkeit. B) Alles Seiende ist veränderbar—gleichwohl gibt es Grenzen der Machbarkeit. (Unterscheide zwischen der prinzipiellen Erkennbarkeit des Wirklichen und dessen Begreifbarkeit, entsprechend zwischen Veränderbarkeit und Machbarkeit.)

FORSTER, Malcolm. Preconditions of Predication: From Qualia to Quantum Mechanics. Topoi, 10(1), 13-26, Mr 91.

FÓSCOLO, Norma. La comunicación en la vida cotidiana. Rev Filosof (Venezuela), 11, 83-94, 1989.

FOSS, Jeff. On Saving the Phenomena and the Mice: A Reply to Bourgeois Concerning Van Fraassen's Image of Science. Phil Sci, 58(2), 278-287, Je 91.

In the fusillade he lets fly against Foss (1984), Bourgeois (1987) sometimes hits a live target. I admit that I went beyond the letter of van Fraassen's *The Scientific Image* (1980), making inferences and drawing conclusions which are often absurd. I maintain, however, that the absurdities must be charged to van Fraassen's account. While I cannot redress every errant shot of Bourgeois, his essay reveals the need for further discussion of the concepts of *the phenomena* and *the observables* as used by van Fraassen.

FOSTER, John. "A Defense of Dualism" in *The Case for Dualism*, SMYTHIES, John R (ed), 1-23. Charlottesville, Univ Pr of Virginia, 1989.

FOSTER, Thomas and LANDINI, Gregory. The Persistence of Counterexample: Re-examining the Debate over Leibniz Law. Nous, 25(1), 43-61, Mr 91.

There has been much debate concerning the logical truth of Leibniz's principle that indiscernibility is sufficient for identity. Proposed refutations abound—from Kant's two water droplets and Black's symmetric spheres, to Ayer's universe in which all events eternally repeat. But just as frequent are defenses. For instance, drawing on considerations from relativistic physics, Hacking maintains that appeals to counterexamples based on imagined possible worlds can neither refute nor establish the principle. This paper challenges that opponents of the debate are guilty of equivocation. There is no "one" law of the Identity of Indiscernibles. New formulations are given and evaluated relative to the following theories of universals: Logical Realism, Attribute Realism, Phenomenalism, and Natural Realism.

FÓTI, Véronique M. Politics and the Limits of Metaphysics: Heidegger, Ferry and Renaut, and Lyotard. Grad Fac Phil J, 14(2)-15(1), 323-334, 1991.

FÓTI, Véronique. The Dimension of Color. Int Stud Phil, 22(3), 13-28, 1990.

FOTION, Nicholas G. *Military Ethics: Looking Toward the Future*. Stanford, Hoover Inst Pr, 1990.

Has modern military technology made certain versions of the pacifist (and realist) position more plausible? Mnay people say that such technology tends to destabilize peace because of its great destructive potential, its quick-strike capabilities, and its great "reach." Modern military technology also encourages permanent military-industrial complexes. However, this same technology makes "cleaner" wars possible (as became evident in the Gulf War). So, overall, it is not clear whether modern military technology has helped or hurt the pacifist argument.

FOUCAULT, M Michel. Qu'est-ce que la Critique? (Critique et *Aufklärung*). Bull Soc Fr Phil, 84(2), 35-63, Ap-Je 90.

FOUCAULT, Michel. La psychologie de 1850 à 1950. Rev Int Phil, 44(173), 159-176, 1990.

FOUKE, Daniel C. Spontaneity and the Generation of Rational Beings in Leibniz's Theory of Biological Reproduction. J Hist Phil, 29(1), 33-45, Ja 91.

This article explores tensions between Leibniz's mature theory of substances and his theory of biological reproduction. His theory of substances is that they "change continually according to a certain order which spontaneously leads it...through all its states" and emphasizes the freedom of creation from the necessity of divine intervention. However, when a preexisting human seed is raised to rationality in human reproduction, he claims that this occurs "not by the power of nature but by the power of God." This apparent inconsistency is explained as a consequence of conflicting Leibnizian views of God as both the exemplar of architectonic wisdom and ground of being. The former conception of God leads to a conception of nature as a closed and autonomous system, while the latter emphasizes creatural dependency.

FOULK, Gary. In Defense of Cahn's Scamps. Phil Stud Educ, /, 132-145, 1987-88.

While agreeing with some of the views in Steven Cahn's *Saints and Scamps: Ethics in Academia*, especially his objection to the use of student evaluations of teaching, this paper claims that teaching is an illocutionary, not a perlocutionary, act, that ideal academic requirements do not depend on the resources or priorities of a university, and that conflicts of interest cannot and should not be avoided, but rather be welcomed as a moral training ground.

FOWLER, D H. Yet More on *Meno* 82a-85d. Phronesis, 35(2), 175-181, 1990.

FOWLER, Mark C. Nietzsche as Instructor in Autonomy? Comments. Int Stud Phil, 22(2), 13-16, 1990.

FOWLER, Marsha D M. "The Nurse's Role: Responsibilities and Rights" in *Biomedical Ethics Reviews, 1987*, HUMBER, James M (ed), 145-155. Clifton, Humana Pr, 1988.

FOX, Daniel M. "The Politics of Trust in American Health Care" in *Ethics, Trust, and the Professions: Philosophical and Cultural Aspects*, PELLEGRINO, Edmund D (ed), 3-22. Washington, Georgetown Univ Pr, 1991.

FOX, J. The Minimal and Semiminimal Notions of Truth. Austl J Phil, 68(2), 157-167, Je 90.

FOX, Michael W. Prejudice and Progress in Animal and Environmental Protection. Between Species, 7(1), 47-49, Wint 91.

FOX, William. "The Classical Conception of Friendship" in *Abeunt Studia in Mores: A Festschrift for Helga Doblin*, MERRILL, Sarah A Bishop (ed), 185-205. New York, Lang, 1990.

FRACCHIA, Joseph. Marx's *Aufhebung* of Philosophy and the Foundations of Historical-Materialist Science. Hist Theor, 30(2), 153-179, My 91.

FRADER, Joel and FORROW, Lachlan and ARNOLD, Robert M. Teaching Clinical Ethics in the Residency Years: Preparing Competent Professionals. J Med Phil, 16(1), 93-112, F 91.

Formal training in clinical ethics must become a central part of residency curricula to prepare practitioners to manage the ethical dimensions of patient care. Residency educators must ground their teaching in an understanding of the conceptual, biomedical, and psychosocial aspects of the important ethical issues that arise in that field of practice. Four aspects of professional competence in clinical ethics provide a useful framework for curricular planning. The physician should learn to (1) recognize ethical issues as they arise in clinical care and identify hidden values and unacknowledged conflicts; (2) think clearly and critically about these issues in ways that lead to ethically justifiable courses of action; (3) apply those practical skills needed to implement an ethically justifiable course of action; and (4) judge when the management of a clinical situation requires consultation with individuals or institutional bodies with additional expertise or authority. We argue that these practical goals can be accomplished with a relatively modest emphasis on the theoretical aspects of medical ethics.

FRANCESCOTTI, Robert M. Externalism and Marr's Theory of Vision. Brit J Phil Sci, 42(2), 227-238, Je 91.

According to one brand of *externalism*, cognitive theories should individuate mental content *widely*—that is, partly in terms of environmental features. David Marr's theory of vision is often cited in support of this view. Many philosophers (most notably, Tyler Burge) regard it as a prime example of a fruitful cognitive theory that widely individuates the representations it posits. I argue that, contrary to popular belief, Marr's theory *does not* presuppose an externalist view of mental content.

FRANCHI, Alfredo. Kierkegaard irrazionalista? Filosofi e filosofie nella interpretazione del filosofo danese. Sapienza, 43(3), 271-291, Jl-S 90.

FRANCHI, Alfredo. Osservazioni sul bello naturale e sul bello artistico in filosofia. Sapienza, 44(1), 27-46, Ja-Mr 91.

FRANCHINI, Raffaello. Vico: dalla collocazione storica all'efficiacia teoretica. Boll Centro Stud Vichiani, 20, 117-130, 1990.

FRANCIS, Richard C. Causes, Proximate and Ultimate. Biol Phil, 5(4), 401-415, O 90.

Within evolutionary biology a distinction is frequently made between proximate and ultimate causes. One apparently plausible interpretation of this dichotomy is that proximate causes concern processes occurring during the life of an organism while ultimate causes refer to those processes (particularly natural selection) that shaped its genome. But "ultimate causes" are not sought through historical investigations of an organisms lineage. Rather, explanations referring to ultimate causes typically emerge from functional analyses. But these functional analyses do not identify causes of any kind, much less ultimate ones. So-called "ultimate explanations" are not about causes in any sense resembling those of proximate explanations. The attitude, implicit in the term "ultimate cause," that these functional analyses are somehow superordinate to those involving "proximate causes" is unfounded. "Ultimate causes" are neither ultimate nor causes.

FRANCIS, Richard P. "The Human Person in American Pragmatism" in *The Question of Humanism: Challenges and Possibilities*, GOICOECHEA, David (ed), 235-243. Buffalo, Prometheus, 1991.

FRANCISCO PÉREZ, M. Libertad individual frente a determinación social. Rev Filosof (Spain), 4, 161-197, 1990.

FRANCO, Paul. *The Political Philosophy of Michael Oakeshott*. New Haven, Yale Univ Pr, 1990.

FRANK, Daniel H. Anger as a Vice: A Maimonidean Critique of Aristotle's Ethics. Hist Phil Quart, 7(3), 269-281, Jl 90.

FRANK, Manfred. Identity and Subjectivity (in Serbo-Croatian). Filozof Istraz, 34(1), 239-254, 1990.

Der Autor versucht in diesem Artikel auf der Suche nach dem ursprünglichen Kompatriotismus des Menschen mit der Natur das Problem der Subjektivität und der Identität zu erläutern. Beginnend mit der irreführenden allgemeinen Überzeugung, dass die Subjektivität dh. die Gewissheit des Selbstbewusstseins eine der Grundcharakteristika der philosophischen Moderne sei, macht er darauf aufmerksam, dass das Problem der Subjektivität von dem der Identität fernzuhalten sei, wenn man die eigentliche Struktur des Identitätposlulats untersuchen will. So löst sich der Autor von der allgemeinen Vorstellung los, Schellings Philosophie sei eine Subjektphilosophie, und untersucht ihren eigentlichen Angelpunkt—die absolute identität. Dabei wird diese als "Identität von Identität und Differenz" erfasst dh. als Identität, die A zuerst als ein in und von der Selbstbejahung der absoluten Identität affirmiertes Objekt, dann als bejahendes Subjekt und schliesslich als Identität der beiden vorangehenden Momente ansieht.

FRANK, Manfred. Kants "Reflexionen zur Ästhetik": Zur Werkgeschichte der "Kritik der ästhetischen Urteilskraft". Rev Int Phil, 44(175), 552-580, 1990.

FRANKEL, Lois. Feminist Spirituality as a Path to Humanism. Free Inq, 10(4), 31,34-35, Fall 90.

FRANKEL, Lois. How's and Why's: Causation Un-Locked. Hist Phil Quart, 7(4), 409-429, O 90.

FRANKENHÄUSER, Gerald and BURKHARDT, Cornelia. Warum lebt der Mensch moralisch? Deut Z Phil, 39(2), 141-146, 1991.

Morals mean more than a phenomenon of consciousness being controlled mentally and intellectually. For understanding morals in their entirety, you have to start out from the fundamental patterns of the order of living (standard patterns, interdependence, hierarchy, forming of traditions), and from the ethologic determination of the mutual relationship of what is congenital to people with what they have acquired. Morals are a (human) overshaping of biotically determined behaviour for controlling social relations of the individual, but at the same time, morals, embodied in conscience as an essential determination of what is allowed or what is not allowed, go beyond biotically determined behaviour.

FRANKLIN, A (and others). Can a Theory-Laden Observation Test the Theory? Brit J Phil Sci, 40(2), 229-231, Je 89.

In this paper we examine the question of whether or not an experimental apparatus laden with the theory under test can be used to test the theory. The standard example arguing that it cannot is the use of a mercury thermometer to test whether or not objects expand as their temperature increases. The proper operation of the apparatus depends on the correctness of the theory. We argue, however, that if an independent calibration, one involving a standard that is independent of the theory, exists then one can, in fact, use the apparatus to test the theory.

FRANKLIN, Allan. *Experiment: Right or Wrong*. New York, Cambridge Univ Pr, 1990.

In this book I argue for an "evidence model" of science in which questions of theory choice, confirmation and refutation are decided on the basis of valid experimental evidence. I also present a Bayesian epistemology of experiment that provides reasonable belief in the validity of results. The fallibility and corrigibility of experimental results, of theoretical calculation, and of experiment—theory comparison are illustrated by two detailed case studies: experiment and the development of weak interaction theory from Fermi to V-A and the history of atomic parity violation experiments.

FRANKLIN, Allan. How Nancy Cartwright Tells the Truth. Brit J Phil Sci, 39(4), 527-529, D 88.

In this paper I argue that the attempt by Kline and Matheson (1986) to save the covering law model of explanation by substituting the approximate truth for the truth of the convering law is inadequate. I present examples, namely the deviation of planetary orbits form Kepler's Laws and the advance of the perihelion of Mercury to argue that Nancy Cartwright's insistence that causal factors must be included in any adequate model of explanation is correct.

FRANKLIN, Daniel Paul. Wishful Thinking and the Budget Deficit. Pub Affairs Quart, 3(4), 1-14, O 89.

The purpose of this article is to suggest that the application of the American "anti-political, political tradition" to the budget process produces deficit spending and stasis. The conclusion reached is that there are no apolitical solutions to what is, in its essence, a political problem (the distribution of goods through the budget process). A plan is presented to restructure the congressional committee system in order to make members more responsive to the will of their party and, thus, their political leaders. In addition, a corresponding case is made for the adoption of some form of a line-item veto for the president.

FRANKLIN, James. Healthy Scepticism. Philosophy, 66(257), 305-324, Jl 91.

The central argument for scepticism about the external world is the symmetry argument: that there is no reason to prefer the realist hypothesis to, say, the deceitful demon hypothesis. This argument is defended against the various standard objections, such as that the demon hypothesis is only a bare possibility, does not lead to pragmatic success, lacks coherence or simplicity, is ad hoc or parasitic, makes impossible demands for certainty, or contravenes some basic standards for a conceptual or linguistic scheme. Since the conclusion of the sceptical argument is not true, it is concluded that one can only escape the force of the argument through some large premise, such as an aptitude of the intellect for truth, if necessary divinely supported.

FRANKS, Joan M. Aristotle or Nietzsche? Listening, 26(2), 156-163, Spr 91.

It is argued that Alasdair MacIntyre has not dealt adequately with the problem of relativism in *After Virtue* and *Whose Justice? Which Rationality?* The success of Aristotle's moral theory does not justify its superiority. A case for objectivity may be found, however, in a development of Aristotle, noted by Aquinas, namely, that our grasp of law is a recognition of an order not of our making. The existence of God, then, remains central to the grounding of moral theory in terms of a tradition, but its terms of an objectivity which justifies the preference of one tradition over another.

FRANTZ, Roger and SINGH, Harinder. The Conflation of Productivity and Efficiency in Economics and Economic History. Econ Phil, 7(1), 87-90, Ap 91.

FRANZEN, Winfried. Die Sprachen und das Denken: Klein Bestandsaufnahme zum linguistischen Relativismus (Sapir-Whorf-Hypothese). Conceptus, 24(62), 3-31, 1990.

After some general remarks both on the problem of language and thought and on the linguistic relativity debate the present state of research and discussion shall be demonstrated by two examples. The first concerns the relation between colour vision and colour terms, the second some possible differences between China and the West with respect to the linguistic and cognitive use of counterfactuals. A concluding section will contain some systematic reflections.

FRASCA-SPADA, Marina. Some Features of Hume's Conception of Space. Stud Hist Phil Sci, 21(3), 371-411, S 90.

This article is an attempt to contribute both to the historical reconstruction of Hume's scientific background and to the interpretation of a much controversial aspect of his philosophy. The first part examines Barrow's *Mathematical Lectures* and Malezieu's *Elemens de Géométrie*, two mathematical textbooks quoted in Hume's *Treatise*. The treatment of the infinitely small is considered in detail, in order to clarify what exactly Hume might mean by "infinite divisibility." The second part focusses on Hume's conception of space in the *Treatise*, and is meant to show how it can contribute to a more refined interpretation of Hume's theory of knowledge.

FRASER, Nancy. "Double Trouble": An Introduction. Hypatia, 6(2), 152-154, Sum 91.

This piece sets the scene for the inaugural addresses by Rosi Braidotti and Selma Sevenhuijsen which follow and provides background information on the history of women's studies in the Netherlands.

FRASER, Nancy and NICHOLSON, Linda J. "Social Criticism without Philosophy: An Encounter between Feminism and Postmodernism" in *Feminism/Postmodernism*, NICHOLSON, Linda J (ed), 19-38. New York, Routledge, 1990.

We argue that, in their respective attempts to develop paradigms of "social criticism without philosophy," postmodernism and feminism have been prey to complementary shortcomings. The anti-essentialism and anti-foundationalism of postmodernism have been purchased at the cost of the robustness of social criticism, while the robustness of some feminist social criticism has been achieved at the cost of a continued appeal to essential natures. We propose a postmodern feminism that avoids both these problems. The result is social criticism without philosophy, but not without political bite.

FRASER, Nancy. "Solidarity or Singularity? Richard Rorty between Romanticism and Technocracy" in *Reading Rorty*, MALACHOWSKI, Alan (ed), 303-321. Cambridge, Blackwell, 1991.

I argue that Richard Rorty's recent writings manifest a stalemated sturggle between pragmatism and Romanticism. In his unsuccessful efforts to resolve this struggle, Rorty oscillates among three views of the relationship between Romanticism and pragmatism: first, an "invisible hand" view that casts them as "natural partners"; second, a "sublimity or decency?" view that casts them as antithetical to one another; and third, a "partition" position that allots each of them its own separate sphere of influence. But none of the three views is tenable. I propose a "recipe" for a "democratic-socialist-feminist pragmatism" that avoids some of Rorty's difficulties.

FREDDOSO, Alfred J. Ontological Reductionism and Faith Versus Reason: A Critique of Adams on Ockham. Faith Phil, 8(3), 317-339, Jl 91.

The purpose of this essay is to take issue with two aspects of Marilyn Adam's monumental work *William Ockham*. Part I deals with Ockham's ontology, arguing (i) that Adams does not sufficiently appreciate the use Ockham mades of the principle of ontological parsimony in his attempt to refute the thesis that there are extramental universals or common natures and (ii) that she sets an implausibly high standard of success for Ockham's project of showing that the only singular entities are substances and qualities. Part II argues that Adams fail to provide a convincing defense of Ockham's 'anti-secularist' answer to the question of how Christian thinkers should react to *prima facie* conflicts between the deliverances of faith and the deliverances of reason.

FREDERICK, William C. The Moral Authority of Transnational Corporate Codes. J Bus Ethics, 10(3), 165-177, Mr 91.

Ethical guidelines for multinational corporations are included in several international accords adopted during the past four decades. These guidelines attempt to influence the practices of multinational enterprises in such areas as employment relations, consumer protection, environmental pollution, political participation, and basic human rights. Their moral authority rests upon the competing principles of national sovereignty, social equity, market integrity, and human rights. Both deontological principles and experience-based value systems undergird and justify the primacy of human rights as the fundamental moral authority of these transnational and transcultural compacts. Although difficulties and obstacles abound in gaining operational acceptance of such codes of conduct, it is possible to argue that their guidelines betoken the emergence of a transcultural corporate ethic.

FREDERIX, Lode. Het belang van Husserls aanzet tot een fenomenologie van de bewustzijnsperspectieven. Tijdschr Filosof, 52(3), 468-494, S 90.

Husserls Versuch eine Phänomenologie als strenge Wissenschaft zu entwickeln, ist gegründet auf einem—phänomenologisch—nicht ganz richtigen, aber dennoch fundamentalen Gegensatz zwischen zwei "Einstellungen" (oder, wie wir sagen, "Bewusstseinsperspektiven"): der "natürlichen" und der "phänomenologischen". Dieser Gegensatz hat bei den Husserlinterpreten und -kommentatoren erstaunlich wenig Aufmerksamkeit und Interesse geregt. Das ist merkwürdig, nicht nur weil Husserl doch selbst wiederholt auf die Wichtigkeit dieses Gegensatzes hingewiesen hat, sondern auch wegen dessen philosophischen und praktischen Relevanz. Worin meinen wir diese Relevanz sehen zu können? (edited)

FREDRICKSON, Donald S. "Values and the Advance of Medical Science" in *Integrity in Health Care Institutions: Humane Environments for Teaching, Inquiry, and Healing*, BULGER, Ruth Ellen (ed), 68-95. Iowa City, Univ of Iowa Pr, 1990.

FREE, George. Language, Speech and Writing: Merleau-Ponty and Derrida on Saussure. Human Stud, 13(4), 293-307, O 90.

This paper examines the concept of language in Saussure and its place in the work of Merleau-Ponty and Derrida. Saussure criticized a positivist linguistics which analyzed the material properties of sound. Merleau-Ponty argues that this critique resulted in a new conception of linguistic form—one that provides the basis for a philosophy of speech that understands expression as the active articulation of a system of symbolic relations. Derrida, who focuses on the relation between speech and writing in Saussure, develops this idea with his notion of an originary writing and criticizes the phenomenological concept of speech as an internal, intentional unity.

FREEDMAN, Benjamin and GOULET, Marie-Claude. New Creations? Commentary. Hastings Center Rep, 21(1), 34-35, Ja-F 91.

This brief article deals with the appropriate attitude and approach to be taken to the ethics of transspecies research and manipulation. We argue that the quotidian approach of bioethics, using rights, autonomy, etc., is inadequate. Even the ethics of research is inapt: We are not, in the most relevant sense, talking of transspecies *research*. Research is a preliminary to a change in practice, and the ethics of research is the ethics of a means. But transspecies manipulation is, recursively, the change itself; research into doing it does it. Alternative approaches, including an ethics of change, are discussed.

FREELAND, Cynthia A. Revealing Gendered Texts. Phil Lit, 15(1), 40-58, Ap 91.

FREEMAN, Michael. Speaking About the Unspeakable: Genocide and Philosophy. J Applied Phil, 8(1), 3-17, 1991.

Genocide is a political catastrophe. Social-scientific approaches to genocide have been criticised because of their committment to logical empiricism. Ethical approaches based on liberal humanism have been criticised by post-Nietzchean philosophers for their attachment to allegedly outworn metaphysical assumptions. However, the deconstruction of social science and liberal ethics leads in the direction of relativism and nihilism, which are either useless or dangerous. The arguments against conventional social science and ethics are examined, and a counter-critique made of post-modern philosophy in order to clear the ground for constructive thinking about genocide. (edited)

FREEMAN, Samuel. Constitutional Democracy and the Legitimacy of Judicial Review. Law Phil, 9(4), 327-370, 1990-91.

It has long been argued that the institution of judicial review is incompatible with democratic institutions. I argue that if we see democracy not just as a form of government, but more basically as a form of sovereignty, then there is a way to conceive of judicial review as a legitimate democratic institution. I discuss the conditions under which judicial review is appropriate in a constitutional democracy. (edited)

FREEMAN, Samuel. Contractualism, Moral Motivation, and Practical Reason. J Phil, 88(6), 281-303, Je 91.

A discussion of T M Scanlon's contractualism as a foundational account of the nature of morality. The article discusses how contractualism provides an account of moral truth and objectivity that is based in an idealization of moral reasoning. It then develops contractualism's account of moral motivation to show how it provides a way to understand obscure but central aspects of Kantian views: the claims that moral reasons are of a special kind, and that moral motives have a basis in practical reason. This account is contrasted with human conceptions of moral motivation, which are argued to be incapable of accounting for the stringency of moral reasons and obligations.

FREEMAN, Samuel. Morals by Appropriation. Pac Phil Quart, 71(4), 279-309, D 90.

A critical assessment of the account of natural property and justice of market distributions argued for in David Gauthier's *Morals by Agreement*. Arguing that property is a cooperative institution that can be conventionally established in different ways, I contest his argument for the origins of property and markets in a state of nature. Then, working from Rawls's idea that property and markets are basic social institutions, I contest Gauthier's account of social cooperation, and the idea that each person is entitled to no more or less than his marginal contribution to productive output. His claims that freedom requires a market return to labor and capital are disputed. Finally I argue that Gauthier fails to establish the rationality of market distributions.

FREIDSON, Eliot. *Medical Work in America: Essays on Health Care*. New Haven, Yale Univ Pr, 1989.

FREIDSON, Eliot. "Nourishing Professionalism" in *Ethics, Trust, and the Professions: Philosophical and Cultural Aspects*, PELLEGRINO, Edmund D (ed), 193-220. Washington, Georgetown Univ Pr, 1991.

FREIRE, António. Paideia Helénica. Rev Port Filosof, 46(2), 227-250, Ap-Je 90.

Greek *paideia* demands in the perfect man *kalokagathía* (physical and moral beauty) and *areté*, which consists of harmony of the first, in addition to success. The Greek States, even the democratic ones, were so concerned with their hegemony that, if were not for *paideia* as culture to keep them together, they ran the risk of breaking apart through their intense rivalry. (edited)

FRENCH, Peter A. Commentary: "Individual and Corporate Responsibility". Bus Prof Ethics J, 2(4), 89-91, Sum 83.

FRENCH, Steven and DA COSTA, Newton C A. Belief, Contradiction, and the Logic of Self-Deception. Amer Phil Quart, 27(3), 179-197, Jl 90.

The apparently paradoxical nature of self-deception has attracted a great deal of controversy in recent years. Focussing on those aspects of the phenomenon which involve the holding of "contradictory" beliefs, it is our intention to argue that this presents no "paradox" if a non-classical, "paraconsistent", doxastic logic is adopted. (On such logics, see, for example, N C A da Costa, 'On the theory of inconsistent formal systems', Notre Dame J Formal Logic 11(1974), 497-510, and A I Arruda, 'A survey of paraconsistent logic', in A I Arruda, N C A da Costa and R Chuaqui, *Mathematical Logic in Latin America*, North-Holland, 1984, pp. 1-41.)

FRENCH, Steven. A Green Parrot is Just as Much a Red Herring as a White Shoe: A Note on Confirmation, Background Knowledge.... Brit J Phil Sci, 39(4), 531-535, D 88.

This paper criticizes a recent attempt to revive the Keynesian approach to confirmation through the explicit introduction of background knowledge. It is shown that rephrasing universal laws in terms of "specific fields of application" does not make them immune to Hempel's paradox. Furthermore, the Keynesian view remains open to many of the objections typically levelled against its Bayesian counterpart, while unable to avail itself of the most well known response of the latter.

FRENCH, Steven and PEREIRA JR, Alfredo. Metaphysics, Pragmatic Truth and the Underdetermination of Theories. Dialogos, 25(56), 37-67, Jl 90.

FRENCH, Steven and DA COSTA, Newton C A. On Russell's Principle of Induction. Synthese, 86(2), 285-295, F 91.

An improvement on Horwich's so-called "pseudo-proof" of Russell's principle of induction is offered, which, we believe, avoids certain objections to the former. Although strictly independent of our other work in this area, a connection can be made and in the final section we comment on this and certain questions regarding rationality, etc.

FRENCH, Steven and DA COSTA, Newton C A. Pragmatic Truth and the Logic of Induction. Brit J Phil Sci, 40(3), 333-356, S 89.

We apply the recently elabrated notions of 'pragmatic truth' and 'pragmatic probability' to the problem of the construction of a logic of inductive inference. It is argued that the system outlined here is able to overcome many of the objections usually levelled against such attempts. We claim, furthermore, that our view captures the essentially cumulative nature of science and allows us to explain why it is indeed reasonable to accept and believe in the conclusions reached by inductive inference.

FRENCH, Steven and REDHEAD, Michael. Quantum Physics and the Identity of Indiscernibles. Brit J Phil Sci, 39(2), 233-246, Je 88.

This paper is concerned with the question of whether atomic particles of the same species, i.e., with the same intrinsic state-independent properties of mass, spin, electric charge, etc, violate the Leibnizian Principle of the Identity of Indiscernibles, in the sense that, while there is more than one of them, their state-dependent properties may also all be the same. The answer depends on what exactly the state-dependent properties of atomic particles are taken to be. On the plausible interpretation that these should comprise all monadic and relational properties that can be expressed in terms of physical magnitudes associated with self-adjoint operators that can be defined for the individual particles, then the weakest form of the Principle is shown to be violated for bosons, fermions and higher-order paraparticles, treated in first quantization.

FRENCH, Steven. Rationality, Consistency and Truth. J Non-Classical Log, 7(1-2), 51-71, My-N 90.

The question of whether it can be rational to believe in a contradiction is discussed. By following a distinction between truth in the correspondence sense and a recent formulation of 'pragmatic' truth and noting an analogy with the distinction between 'factual' and 'representational' beliefs, it is argued that although it is irrational to hold a factual belief in a contradictory proposition, this may not be so for representational beliefs in structures which are pragmatically true only. The paper concludes with some brief considerations of scientific rationality in general.

FREUDENTHAL, Gad. "Epistémologie des sciences de la nature et herméneutique de l'histoire des sciences selon H Metzger" in *Études sur/Studies on Hélène Metzger*, FREUDENTHAL, Gad , 161-188. Leiden, Brill, 1990.

FREUDENTHAL, Gad. *Études sur/Studies on Hélène Metzger*. Leiden, Brill, 1990.

FREUDENTHAL, Gad. "Hélène Metzger: Eléments de biographie" in *Études sur/Studies on Hélène Metzger*, FREUDENTHAL, Gad , 197-208. Leiden, Brill, 1990.

FREUND, Julien. Réflexiones sur l'idéee de la guerre dans la philosophie présocratique. Rev Metaph Morale, 95(4), 513-535, O-D 90.

FREY, R G. "Animal Parts, Human Wholes: On the Use of Animals as a Source of Organs for Human Transplants" in *Biomedical Ethics Reviews, 1987*, HUMBER, James M (ed), 89-107. Clifton, Humana Pr, 1988.

This paper presents an argument designed to show that, if we are to continue to use animals as a source of organs for human transplants, we must be prepared to use some fellow humans as a source of organs for such transplants. The paper then attempts to specify which humans these are.

FREY, R G (ed) and MORRIS, Christopher W (ed). *Liability and Responsibility*. New York, Cambridge Univ Pr, 1991.

This book focuses on issues concerning liability in contract, tort, and criminal law. It is divided into four parts. The first is a conceptual overview of the issues at stake in a philosophical discussion of liability and responsibility. The second, third, and fourth sections present, in turn, more detailed explorations of the role of liability and responsibility in contracts, torts, and punishment. The book demonstrates the interdisciplinary character of the field of philosophy of law, with contributors taking into account recent developments in economics, political science, and rational choice theory.

FREY, Robert Seitz. Post-Holocaust Theodicy: Images of Deity, History, and Humanity. Bridges, 3(1-2), 9-32, Spr-Sum 91.

Auschwitz has yet to transform the divine dimension, historical paradigms, and images of woman and man to any functional extent on the level of the day-to-day. Historically and morally grounded characterization of Deity, temporal history, and humanity will be explored. History, faith, and morality as reflexive channels of connection between the human and the divine will be discussed. "Suffering God" will be examined closely, and attention will also focus on the Holocaust as a monumental problem in theodicy, anthropodicy, dysteleological human suffering, and eschatology. What kind of God is accessible to post-Holocaust humanity? is the recurrent question.

FREYDBERG, Bernard D. Nietzsche in Derrida's *Spurs*: Deconstruction as Deracination. Hist Euro Ideas, 11, 685-692, 1989.

Nietzsche's immersion in and fine grasp of the Western tradition informs his explorations of the darker impulses which undergird both this tradition and some major 20th century responses to it. The paper shows how Derrida's reading of Nietzsche in *Spurs* falls far short, wide and shallow of Nietzsche's measure in this crucial regard. Thus, Derrida is no heir of Nietzsche.

FRICKER, Miranda. Reason and Emotion. Rad Phil, 57, 14-19, Spr 91.

FRIEDLI, Serge. Sartre and the Objectivity of Values (in French). Rev Theol Phil, 123(1), 17-33, 1991.

Sartre's *Cahiers pour une morale* is a clear presentation of his ontological moral philosophy. This article attempts to analyze the basis of his ethic and to draw out its moral precepts.

FRIEDMAN, Jeffrey. The New Consensus: II—The Democratic Welfare State. Crit Rev, 4(4), 633-708, Fall 90.

FRIEDMAN, Marilyn. "They Lived Happily Ever After": Sommers on Women and Marriage. J Soc Phil, 21(2-3), 57-65, Fall-Wint 90.

This essay disusses numerous defects which appear in Christina Sommers's anti-feminist writings on traditional marriage and femininity. For example, citing no evidence whatsoever, Sommers makes often implausible claims about what "most women" want. In addition, Sommers disregards the deference to men which characterizes traditional femininity and which undermines her contention that traditional femininity can be nonoppressive. She, furthermore, defends traditional marriage and femininity with no substanstive moral analysis of the forms of life involved in them or in their feminist alternatives. Her final court of appeal is simply the alleged (and questionable) current popularity of those traditions.

FRIEDMAN, Marilyn. Does Sommers Like Women? More on Liberalism, Gender Hierarchy, and Scarlett O'Hara. J Soc Phil, 21(2-3), 75-90, Fall-Wint 90.

A rejoinder to Christina Sommer's commentary on may paper, "They Lived Happily Ever After...." Here, I identify further problems in Sommer's ongoing attempts to understand feminism. First, I point out numerous ways in which she distorts the feminist views which she discusses. Second, I argue that her portrait of a "gender feminist" is a fictional caricature which fails to illuminate contemporary feminist philosophy. Third, I analyze critically the impoverished liberal feminism which she offers as a substitute. Fourth, with supporting evidence from the novel, I contest Sommer's favorable reference to Rhett Butler's sexual domination of Scarlett O'Hara.

FRIEDMAN, Marilyn. Going Nowhere: Nagel on Normative Objectivity. Philosophy, 65(254), 501-509, O 90.

First, I sketch some obstacles to achieving the sort of normative objectivity defended by Thomas Nagel in *The View from Nowhere*. These obstacles include an inability to determine whether or not one's thinking is genuinely "detached," as Nagel would put it, from her "subjective particulars." Section II follows with the recommendation that we modify Nagel's conception of objectivity so as to take fuller account of the intersubjective social context in which so-called "objective" understanding occurs in practice. By reconstruing objectivity in terms of intersubjectivity, we can negotiate the obstacles to objectivity more wisely.

FRIEDMAN, Marilyn. "The Social Self and the Partiality Debates" in *Feminist Ethics*, CARD, Claudia (ed), 161-179. Lawrence, Univ Pr of Kansas, 1991.

The social conception of the self construes the self's interests, character, and identity as being constituted through relationships with others. This paper addresses two problems faced by the social conception of the self which have been highlighted by the current debates over moral impartiality and partiality. First, how can a self take a critical perspective on aspects of the social which, nevertheless, define her to be the self she is? Second, how is global moral concern, concern for distant strangers with whom a self as little or no relationship, possible? Throughout my discussion, I contrast feminist and nonfeminist approaches to these issues.

FRIEDMAN, Maurice. *Encounter on the Narrow Ridge: A Life of Martin Buber*. New York, Paragon House, 1991.

This book illuminates Buber's philosophy of dialogue, his philosophical anthropology, and his philosophy of religion by showing how they evolved as a response to the events and meetings of his long life, e.g., his Zionism, his mysticism and his discovery of Hasidism, his response to the First World War, his communal socialism, his translation of the Hebrew Bible, his opposition to Nazi Germany and his educational activities then and in the Weimar Republic and in Israel, his fight for Jewish-Arab rapprochement, his dialogue with Germans and Americans, his encounter with psychotherapy, and his replies to critics.

FRIEDMAN, Michael. "Kant and Newton: Why Gravity Is Essential to Matter" in *Philosophical Perspectives on Newtonian Science*, BRICKER, Phillip (ed), 185-202. Cambridge, MIT Pr, 1990.

FRIEDMAN, Michael. Kant on Concepts and Intuitions in the Mathematical Sciences. Synthese, 84(2), 213-257, Ag 90.

FRIEDMAN, Robert. Hidden Agendas. Int J Applied Phil, 5(2), 43-58, Fall 90.

By "hidden agendas" I mean unacknowledged criteria which are used in the process of hiring. There seems to be a widespread acceptance of this practice. I offer three kinds of reasons why the practice is morally inappropriate: it is disrespectful to candidates, it is unfair, and it is likely to lead to bad consequences (not only to candidates, but also to employers).

FRIEDMAN, William J. *About Time: Inventing the Fourth Dimension*. Cambridge, MIT Pr, 1990.

This book reviews and integrates psychological research since 1960 on the processes underlying the human experience of time. Temporal experience is divided into several component categories. Separate chapters consider perception, memory representation, orientation, development, and variations by culture, personality, and mental illnesses. The book shows that numerous distinct psychological processes contribute to temporal cognition and perception.

FRINGS, Manfred S. Heraclitus: Heidegger's 1943 Lecture Held at Freiburg University. J Brit Soc Phenomenol, 21(3), 250-264, O 90.

This is the second of three lectures on Pre-Socratic thought delivered from 1942 to 1944. Heidegger offers an entirely new grasp of Heraclitian fragments by suggesting fragment 16 (Diels) to be the clue for grasping the "Inception of Occidental Thought" as un-concealment from which no one can hide. This point joins up with the extensive discussion of A-letheia in the 1942/3 Parmenides Lecture. Fragment 16 is shown to be "center" while "surrounding" nine other fragments (123, 54, 8, 51, 64, 66, 30, 124, 93). Their sequence is not contrived. It emerges by itself in light of 16.

FRINGS, Manfred S. Heraclitus: Heidegger's 1944 Lecture Held at Freiburg University. J Brit Soc Phenomenol, 22(2), 64-82, My 91.

The 1944 lecture on Pre-Socratic thought does not link up directly with the 1943 and 1942 lectures. Its purpose is to investigate fragments containing the word "Logos." "Logos" is seen as "staying away," prompting a Heideggerian regress into its original region from which modern logic arose. "Logos" is explained in terms of the verb "legein" and "psyche." The latter offers novel insights into human logos as it is intertwined with hidden "Logos" through "homólogein," a word essential to grasp the complexity of logos and "Logos." As in the aforementioned lectures, the 1944 lecture offers highly interesting analyses of fragments concerned, which are sometimes stunning and almost mind-boggling.

FRINGS, Manfred. Violence: Can It Be Ethical? Phil Theol, 5(1), 65-72, Fall 90.

I offer an analysis of the notion of violence one of whose consequences may be that violence might be moral under some circumstances.

FRISBY, David (ed & trans) and BOTTOMORE, Tom (trans) and SIMMEL, Georg. *The Philosophy of Money: Georg Simmel (Second Edition)*. New York, Routledge, 1991.

FRISBY, Mark E. Lonergan's Method in Ethics and the Meaning of Human Sexuality. Proc Cath Phil Ass, 63, 235-256, 1990.

FRISINA, Warren G. Knowledge as Active, Aesthetic, and Hypothetical: A Pragmatic Interpretation of Whitehead's Cosmology. J Speculative Phil, 5(1), 42-64, 1991.

This paper examines some epistemological implications of Whitehead's cosmology. I argue that Whitehead's cosmological account of experience entails a definition of inquiry and knowledge similar to positions developed by American Pragmatists such as John Dewey. This is important for two reasons. First, it clarifies the commonalities that make the process-pragmatic dialogue so fruitful. Second, it reinforces the epistemological conclusions of each by showing how they can be supported from different directions.

FRITZSCHE, Helmut. Dialogue and Understanding (in German). Deut Z Phil, 38(5), 401-410, 1990.

FRITZSCHE, Helmut. Two Aspects of the Christian-Marxist Dialogue: A Protestant Response. Dialec Hum, 16(3-4), 113-121, Sum-Autumn 89.

FROLOV, I T (ed) and FENSTAD, J E (ed) and HILPINEN, R (ed). *Logic, Methodology and Philosophy of Science, VIII*. New York, Elsevier Science, 1989.

This volume contains all the invited papers to the eight international congress of logic, methodology and philosophy of science held in Moscow in 1987. In addition to sectional papers there were two symposia, one on new patterns of explanation in science, and one on science and ethics.

FROLOV, Ivan T. Life and Cognition. Soviet Stud Phil, 29(3), 6-27, Wint 90-91.

FROMAN, Wayne J. "Alterity and the Paradox of Being" in *Ontology and Alterity in Merleau-Ponty*, JOHNSON, Galen A (ed), 98-110. Evanston, Northwestern Univ Pr, 1991.

FROMAN, Wayne J. "Merleau-Ponty and *l'Écriture*" in *Writing the Politics of Difference*, SILVERMAN, Hugh J (ed), 193-202. Albany, SUNY Pr, 1991.

FROMAN, Wayne J. *Schelling's Treatise on the Essence of Human Freedom* and Heidegger's Thought. Int Phil Quart, 30(4), 465-480, D 90.

FRONGIA, Guido and MC GUINNESS, Brian. *Wittgenstein: A Bibliographical Guide*. Cambridge, Blackwell, 1990.

FRÜCHTL, Josef. (Post-) Metaphysik und (Post-) Moderne: Zur Sache des "schwachen Denkens". Phil Rundsch, 37(3), 242-250, 1990.

The term "weak thought" (*pensiero debole*) was coined by the Italian philosopher Gianni Vattimo. It draws its philosophical sense from Nietzsche's critique of domination and Heidegger's critique of metaphysics. The article tries to show that Vattimo's central problem lies in justifying the necessity of weak (non-foundational, non-subsumptive) thought. But both the ethics and the theory of truth in Vattimo lead into aporiae. With a rather adventurous combination of Nietzsche, Heidegger and Walter Benjamin, he ends up defending the concept of postmodernity.

FRY, Sara T. Nursing Ethics: Current State of the Art. J Med Phil, 16(3), 231-234, Je 91.

FRYE, Marilyn. "A Response to *Lesbian Ethics*: Why *Ethics*?" in *Feminist Ethics*, CARD, Claudia (ed), 52-59. Lawrence, Univ Pr of Kansas, 1991.

FUCHS, Josef. The Absolute in Morality and the Christian Conscience. Gregorianum, 71(4), 697-711, 1990.

FUCHS, Wolfgang. Retrieving Husserl from His Legacy. Teach Phil, 13(2), 103-109, Je 90.

This article describes the difficulties and rewards encountered in teaching Husserl's thought. Difficulties arise from the dryness of style, particularly when compared with thinkers he has influenced, as well as the inherent complexity of Husserl's work. Rewards occur by leading students to appreciate the importance of understanding the demanding, rigorous and fundamental nature of Husserl's thought. Concentrated upon doctrines were: "the principle of all principles," consciousness, and time.

FUENTES ORTEGA, Juan Bautista. Nota sobre la causalidad apotética a la escala psicológica. El Basilisco, 1, 57-64, S-O 89.

FUHRMANN, André. Models for Relevant Modal Logics. Stud Log, 49(4), 501-514, D 90.

We consider modal extensions of a wide class of relevant logics. A general method is given to obtain from a class FRM(L) of unreduced frames, characterising a (non-modal) logic L, a class FRM*(L.M) of frames characterising modal extensions L.M of L. For reduced frames an incompleteness phenomenon is displayed.

FUHRMANN, André. Theory Contraction through Base Contraction. J Phil Log, 20(2), 175-203, My 91.

An investigation of contraction and revision functions as applied to theories generated from a distinguished axiomatic base. The result is a logic of theory change from a foundationalist rather than coherentist point of view. Minimal assumptions about the underlying logic are being made and a paraconsistent closure operation is recommended for the purpose of changing inconsistent theories.

FUHRMANN, André. Tropes and Laws. Phil Stud, 63(1), 57-82, Jl 91.

The paper details a theory of how tropes (abstract particulars) compose to individuals. Natural laws are understood as facts about the distribution of tropes among possible individuals. The emerging theory of the laws of nature can explain why laws support the corresponding universal generalisations without succumbing to the many shortcomings of a regularity theory based on individuals.

FUHRMANN, G. Note on the Integration of Prototype Theory and Fuzzy-Set Theory. Synthese, 86(1), 1-27, Ja 91.

Many criticisms of prototype theory and/or fuzzy-set theory are based on the assumption that category representativeness (or typicality) is identical with fuzzy membership. These criticisms also assume that conceptual combination and logical rules (all in the Aristotelian sense) are the appropriate criteria for the adequacy of the above "fuzzy typicality." The present paper discusses these assumptions following the line of their most explicit and most influential expression by Osheron and Smith (1981). Several arguments are made against the above identification, the most important being that representativeness in prototype theory is exclusively based on element-to-element similarity while fuzzy membership is inherently an element-to-category relationship. Also the above criteria for adequacy are criticized from the viewpoint of both prototype theory and fuzzy-set theory as well as from that of both conceptual and logical combination, and also from that of integration.

FULFORD, K W M. *Moral Theory and Medical Practice*. New York, Cambridge Univ Pr, 1991.

This book aims to bring medicine and philosophy into closer partnership. An analysis is developed of the meanings of illness and disease considered as value terms. This shows the phenomena of illness to be highly significant for philosophy: pain, paralysis and compulsion for the philosophy of action; delusions for epistemology; hallucination for perception; addiction for volition; and psychosis for rationality. It also has practical implications - for disease classification and diagnosis (in primary care), for ethics (in psychiatry), and for the doctor-patient relationship. The groundwork is thus laid for a productive two-way trade between philosophical theory and medical practice.

FULFORD, K W M. The Potential of Medicine as a Resource for Philosophy. Theor Med, 12(1), 81-85, Mr 91.

In addition to the neglect of philosophy by medicine, emphasized in a recent editorial in this journal, there has been an equally important neglect of medicine by philosophy. Philosophy stands to gain from medicine in three respects: in materials, the conceptual difficulties arising in the practice of medicine being key data for philosophical enquiry; in methods, these data, through their problematic character, being ideally suited to the technique of linguistic analysis; and in results, the practical requirements of medicine placing a direct demand for progress on philosophical theory. The future of the relationship between philosophy and medicine depends on the development of a positive two-way trade between them.

FULLER, Gary and ADAMS, Fred and DREBUSHENKO, David and STECKER, Robert. Narrow Content: Fodor's Folly. Mind Lang, 5(3), 213-229, Autumn 90.

For ten years Fodor and other cognitive scientists presumed that we need narrow content (content essentially independent of one's environment) to get around Twin-Earth examples and to do psychology. We show why broad content psychology (using content essentially dependent upon one's environment) is *not really challenged* by Twin-Earth examples, despite appearances. We explain (1) why narrow content is *not content*, and why (2) even if we concoct a notion of content* for narrow content, it still will be *unable to explain* intentional behavior. Thus, we herald the demise of narrow content: one cannot use it and does not need it.

FULLER, M and DI PRISCO, C A and HENLE, J M. The Normal Depth of Filters on an Infinite Cardinal. Z Math Log, 36(4), 293-296, 1990.

FULLER, Steve W. Is History and Philosophy of Science Withering on the Vine? Phil Soc Sci, 21(2), 149-174, Je 91.

Nearly thirty years after the first stirrings of the Kuhnian revolution, history and philosophy of science continues to galvanize methodological discussions in all corners of the academy except its own. Evidence for this domestic stagnation appears in Warren Schmaus's thoughtful review of *Social Epistemology* in which Schmaus takes for granted that history of science is the ultimate court of appeal for disputes between philosophers and sociologists. As against this, this essay argues that such disputes may be better treated by experimental psychology. Humanistic methods typically (though not always) blind the historian to cognitive biases and limitations that make it difficult for philosophers and sociologists to mobilize historical research for settling their differences. It is also observed that the failure of philosophers to incorporate the methods and findings of experimental psychology is symptomatic of an artificially restrictive understanding of the normative dimension of their enterprise.

FULLER, Steve. Naturalized Epistemology Sublimated: Rapprochement without the Ruts. Stud Hist Phil Sci, 22(2), 277-293, Je 91.

Is epistemology legitimated on grounds quite apart from science, which can then be used to pass judgment on science? Or, is the epistemologist really only a scientist of science, whose own legitimacy is only as good as that of the scientists she studies? Despite this clear difference between, respectively, "classicists" and "naturalists," debate between the two sides always gets into a rut. This is because the naturalist does not sufficiently disentangle her position from that of the classicist. After showing this in the work of Alvin Goldman and Rom Harre, I propose a strategy whereby the naturalist tries to incorporate the classicist's criticisms of her position within her own framework without acquiescing to classicism. I argue that naturalists—especially historicist philosophers of science—need to take more seriously Dewey's point that knowledge is *in* the world that it is *about*.

FULLER, Steve. Social Epistemology and the Brave New World of Science and Technology Studies. Phil Soc Sci, 21(2), 232-244, Je 91.

In this article I respond to a variety of critics in history, philosophy, and psychology of my paper "Is History and Philosophy of Science Withering on the Vine?," which argued that the normative questions of "rationality" that have typically interested philosophers of science would be better served by conducting experiments in social psychology than by reconstructing the history of science. Here I elaborate this point in terms of the project of "social epistemology," which is sympathetic to the constructivism of both the positivists and recent sociologists of science. I express skepticism about a "tacit dimension" of scientific expertise that would allegedly escape experimental access, arguing that Polanyi and his followers are really making a political point about leaving scientists alone rather than an ontological point about the existential embeddedness of scientists in the world.

FULLER, Steve. Why Narrative Is Not Enough. Soc Epistem, 5(1), 70-74, Ja-Mr 91.

I argue that the narrative conception of legal discourse—the most recent outgrowth of the Wittgensteinian approach to rules—is insufficiently empirical to capture the sources of legal conflict and to provide useful strategies for resolving such conflict. According to the narrative conception, legal disputes arise from conflicting interpretations of the law. Clearly, the intent here is to keep debate open, but often closure is more important, especially when it is clear that the law is biased against certain social groups, in which case action is needed. However, this action-oriented perspective typically requires going beyond the "internal" conception of rules that the narrative conception still harbors.

FULLER, Timothy. Compatibilities on the Idea of Law in Thomas Aquinas and Thomas Hobbes. Hobbes Stud, 3, 112-134, 1990.

The central theme is that Aquinas and Hobbes have similar views of the relation between natural and civil law, and of the general purpose of civil law. Contrary to the opinion of many, Hobbes's discussion has many traditional elements of natural law theory, and Aquinas anticipates some "modern" conclusions about law. The distinction of classical and modern natural law ideas are not so sharp as is often thought. Some collateral issues about the nature of political authority are also considered.

FUMAROLI, M Marc. La Querelle de la Moralité du Théâtre au XVIIe Siècle. Bull Soc Fr Phil, 84(3), 65-97, Jl-S 90.

The conflict between the Renaissance's love for ancient drama and, both, the Reformation and Counter-Reformation, hostile as the primitive Church to drama, gave rise to a compromise in seventeenth century Roman Catholic countries. The opponents were concerned less with the morality of the written texts than with the ethical import of dramatic performance itself, suspecting it to be a parody of the Word incarnate. Can the language of truth and salvation coexist in the same Christian city with language filled with lies and leading to perdition? A kind of apologetics, aiming towards a "moralisation" of both the actors and the audience, gave a legitimate and even useful part to theater in the Catholic city. From a philosophical point of view, this quarrel is a chapter in the history of Christian Platonism (philosophy *versus* sophistry, distrust of *mimesis*). The move towards an Aristotelian and Ciceronian casuistry was crushed by the violent Port-Royal attack on theater, which paved the way for such a rigid stance as that of Rousseau.

FUMERTON, Richard. "Metaepistemology and Skepticism" in *Doubting: Contemporary Perspectives on Skepticism*, ROTH, Michael D (ed), 57-68. Norwell, Kluwer, 1990.

I explore the implications of the internalism/externalism controversy for the possibility of refuting traditional forms of skepticism. In particular I argue that philosophically interesting responses to skepticism may presuppose a version of internalism I call inferential internalism but that the possibility of refuting skepticism within that framework may depend on the plausibility of a highly controversial concept of probability as an internal relation between propositions.

FUNDA, Otakar A. Masaryk's Religious Thinking (in Czechoslovakian). Filozof Cas, 38(4), 441-449, 1990.

By religion Masaryk understands perception of life, man and world in the sense of transcendence of the dimension given to man, in the sense of moral appeal which enters human life in an unconditioned and absolute way. Masaryk speaks of a religion being "a life under the scope of eternity." He shares the doubts of modern man, i.e., of man at the turn of the 19th and 20th centuries, about the supernatural dogma and clerical church. Nevertheless, he does not solve this doubt by breaking with religion. He answers by an attempt at deeper command of religious question. He speaks of "a new religion without dogma, clergy and miracles, a religion of humanity." His religious thinking moves in coordinates of rational theism. Although he highly appreciates rational components, he steps beyond the border of the rational. To him religion is a question of life, an existentional one. (edited)

FUNK, Nanette. Habermas and Solidarity. Phil Inq, 12(3-4), 17-31, Sum-Fall 90.

FUNKE, Gerhard. Kants Logik der Synthesis und die Schliessung einer "unübersehbaren Kluft". Rev Int Phil, 45(176), 39-58, 1991.

FUSS, Diana. *Essentially Speaking: Feminism, Nature and Difference*. New York, Routledge, 1990.

FUSTEGUERAS, Aurelio P. Física y Semántica en la filosofía de Quine. Rev Filosof (Spain), 3, 49-70, 1990.

Physics and semantics are given a similar epistemological treatment in Quine's philosophy, insofar as Quine admits the evidential indeterminacy of both; however, Quine upholds a fundamental ontological distinction between physics and semantics: whereas the former deals with an objective reality, the latter lacks such an objective matter. The main goal of this paper is to discuss the assumptions leading Quine to uphold a distinction in ontological status between physics and semantics. Finally, I will take issue with Quine's assumptions and arguments.

FUTERNICK, Ken. Epistemology and Political Rationality. Proc Phil Educ, 46, 332-336, 1990.

FYNSK, Christopher. But Suppose We Were to Take the Rectorial Address Seriously...Gérard Granel's *De l'université*. Grad Fac Phil J, 14(2)-15(1), 335-362, 1991.

GABEL, Joseph and STEIN, William M (trans) and MC CRATE, James (trans). *Mannheim and Hungarian Marxism*. New Brunswick, Transaction Books, 1991.

This serves as a useful introduction to the force and character of Marxism in Central Europe. Mannheim was situated in the intellectual pitch of prewar Budapest, with its plethora of revisionist Marxists, anarchists, and intellectuals from a variety of areas who brought radical ideas into the mainstream of biological and social sciences, and which provided Budapest a special environment in which the cross-currents of Europe met. Gabel covers key figures and major concepts associated with Mannheim and the sociology of knowledge: ideology and false consciousness; the socially unattached intelligentsia; and the utopian conscience. (staff)

GABORIAU, Florent. Sur le concept de Révélation. Rev Thomiste, 90(4), 533-569, O-D 90.

GABORIAU, Florent. Sur le concept de tradition. Rev Thomiste, 90(3), 373-408, Jl-S 90.

GADAMER, Hans-Georg and SCHMIDT, Dennis J. "Culture and the Word" in *Hermeneutics and the Poetic Motion, Translation Perspectives V—1990*, SCHMIDT, Dennis J (ed), 11-23. Binghamton, CRIT, 1990.

GADAMER, Hans-Georg. Festrede zum 300: Geburstag von Gottfried Wilhelm Leibniz am 1 Juli 1946 in der Aula der Universitat Leipzig. Stud Leibniz, 22(1), 1-10, 1990.

Als derzeitiger Rektor der Universität Leipzig habe ich die Ehre, Sie im Namen der Universität als Gäste der Universität und Angehörige der Universität zu begrüssen. Uns führt das Gedenken an einen der grössten Söhne Leipzigs zusammen, und es ist mir eine besondere Freude, den Vertreter der Landesverwaltung und den Herrn Oberbürgermeister der Stadt Leipzig, Dr. Zeigner, bei uns zu begrüssen. Der Herr Oberbürgermeister wird uns die Ehre geben, selbst ein Wort an uns zu richten aus Anlass dieses Gedenktages eines der grössten Söhne dieser Stadt. Ich habe das Bewusstsein, dass die grosse Bereitwilligkeit, mit der Sie unserer Einladung gefolgt sind, einen Beitrag dazu bedeutet, dass die Universität im ganzen Leben unseres strebenden und arbeitenden Volkes ihren Platz befestige und stärke. Nichts kann dazu besser beitragen als das verbindende Gedächtnis an einen der grössten Gelehrten, die Leipzig hervorgebracht hat und die an der Universität Leipzig ausgebildet worden sind.

GADEN, Gerry. Rehabilitating Responsibility. J Phil Educ, 24(1), 27-38, Sum 90.

The idea of being and becoming a responsible person is investigated in order to secure a relevant developmental and educational perspective. Analyses of responsibility in terms of accountability (Haydon, 1978) and care and concern (Fingarette, 1969) are examined, and an independent position developed. The growth of responsibility is seen as that of a natural disposition to engage in the spirit of common activities, prompting and supported by the emergence of rational capacities. An appropriate education will stress this interdependence between rationality and sociability. Current forms of schooling inhibit the requisite engagement with the social and affective dimensions of learnable activities.

GÄHDE, Ulrich. "Bridge Structures and the Borderline Between the Internal and External History of Science" in *Imre Lakatos and Theories of Scientific Change*, GAVROGLU, Kostas (ed), 215-225. Norwell, Kluwer, 1989.

The paper deals with a recent refinement in the metatheoretical picture of empirical theories: the introduction of *bridge structures* (inner-theoretical constraints and inter-theoretical links) within the structuralist approach. It is argued that these concepts allow for a better and more detailed understanding of numerous developments in the history of science: they may help to regain terrain for what Lakatos called 'the internal history of science'. This thesis is illustrated by means of a (historical) case study. It refers to the elimination of anomalies which occurred in connection with the development of the so-called *cosmic distance scale*.

GAHRINGER, Robert E. "On Interpreting J W Miller" in *The Philosophy of John William Miller*, FELL, Joseph P (ed), 32-40. Lewisburg, Bucknell Univ Pr, 1990.

GAIDIS, William and LYSONSKI, Steven. A Cross-Cultural Comparison of the Ethics of Business Students. J Bus Ethics, 10(2), 141-150, F 91.

The ethical tendencies of university business students from the USA, Denmark, and New Zealand were examined by analyzing their reactions to ethical dilemmas presented in a set of ethical problem situations. These dilemmas dealt with coercion and control, conflict of interest, physical environment, paternalism and personal integrity. Findings indicate that students' reactions tended to be similar regardless of their country. A comparison of these findings to practicing managers indicated that students and practicing managers exhibit a similar degree of sensitivity to ethical dimensions of business decison making. Implications are drawn for business education and further research.

GAITA, Raimond. *Good and Evil: An Absolute Conception*. New York, St Martin's Pr, 1991.

GAITA, Raimond. Language and Conversation. Philosophy, 28, 101-115, 90 Supp.

GAITA, Raimond. Radical Critique, Scepticism and Commonsense. Philosophy, 29, 157-171, 91 Supp.

GALASSO, Giuseppe. Postilla. G Crit Filosof Ital, 69(2), 251-253, My-Ag 90.

GALASSO, Giuseppe. Storicità della poesia: estetica e storicismo in Francesco De Sanctis. Arch Stor Cult, 4, 141-163, 1991.

GALAVOTTI, Maria Carla. Explanation and Causality: Some Suggestions from Econometrics. Topoi, 9(2), 161-169, S 90.

GALE, Richard M. Freedom and the Free Will Defense. Soc Theor Pract, 16(3), 397-423, Fall 90.

Two versions of the free will defense are critically evaluated. The first is Plantinga's version according to which God has middle knowledge of how created free persons will act, the other Robert M Adams's which denies middle knowledge to God. The former fails because it gives God a freedom cancelling control over created "free" persons, the latter because it gives too watered-down a version of God's omniscience.

GALGAN, Gerald J. *God and Subjectivity*. New York, Lang, 1990.

The book is an essentially metaphysical monograph that is cast in a historical mode: it reports on first philosophy as a biography of the concept of being. Its thesis is that Anselm's notion of God provided a pivot on which philosophy turned from Aristotle's conception of substance as the object of "first philosophy" to Descartes' concept of the subject as the ground of "science." An effort is made to present Anselm's role as catalyst in this changeover with as much textual support as possible; and in this light, even Feuerbach appears as a kind of inversion of the Anselmian argument.

GALINDO, José Antonio. La libertad como autodeterminacíín en san Agustín. Augustinus, 35(139-140), 299-320, Jl-D 90.

GALLAGHER, Donald A. "The Philosophy of Culture in Jacques Maritain" in *From Twilight to Dawn: The Cultural Vision of Jacques Maritain*, REDPATH, Peter A (ed), 277-285. Notre Dame, Univ Notre Dame Pr, 1990.

The article or chapters in "The Philosophy of Culture in Jacques Maritain" aims to introduce a little-known topic of the great French philosopher to a wider audience. Culture is like a *leit-motiv* in Maritain. The theme is brought out in many works. "Culture" and "civilization" are basically the same for Maritain, unlike German usage. Culture is not an isolated phenomenon. It should be seen in its dynamic relation to religion and liberty. Modern culture is too dominated by demiurgic materialism. It should be opposed by theocentric humanism or culture.

GALLAGHER, Donald A. "Recollections of Three Thinkers: Adler, Simon, and Maritain" in *Freedom in the Modern World: Jacques Maritain, Yves R Simon, Mortimer J Adler*, TORRE, Michael D (ed), 13-30. Notre Dame, Univ Notre Dame Pr, 1989.

The purpose of the study is to draw portraits of three philosophers. As I put it, Adler is Demonstrator and Remonstrator, Simon the Distinguisher and Syllogizer, while Jacques Maritain is the Synthesizer and Prophetic Philosopher. These characteristics indicate the different approaches of our philosophers who have in view the same end. Their unity lies in their attempt to preserve and expand the great classical tradition in philosophy and in culture. Their originality consists in their fresh presentation of this idea.

GALLARDO, Helio. Engels y Darwin en el origen del hombre: Elementos para una discusión. Rev Filosof (Costa Rica), 27(66), 361-378, D 89.

The discussion of some of the production conditions in a study by F Engels: *The role of the work in the transition from monkey to man*, allows to establish its positive articulation with the theoretic Darwinism of XIX Century, and, at the same time, contributes to determine some strokes of its polemic with the social Darwinism during that term and its affirmation of a specific theoretic environment for the comprehension of the history and society: the historical materialism.

GALLI, A and SAGASTUME, M. Kernels in N-Normal Symmetric Heyting Algebras. J Non-Classical Log, 6(2), 5-17, N 89.

By adding a negation (satisfying double negation law) and contraposition rule to the Hilbert-Bernays positive propositional calculus, Moisil established the modal symmetric calculus. A symmetric Heyting algebra is the Lindembaum algebra of this calculus. A o-normal algebra is a symmetric Heyting algebra such that each x is greater or equal to v(x) (v(x) negation followed by pseudocomplement applied to x). We call n-normal algebra a symmetric Heyting algebra such that for each x, n+1 applications of v to x is greater or equal to n applications of v to x. We characterize simple and subdirectly irreducible n-normal algebras under certain conditions.

GALLI, Adriana C and SAGASTUME, Marta. N-Normal Factors in Finite Symmetric Heyting Algebras. J Non-Classical Log, 7(1-2), 43-50, My-N 90.

In a previous paper we defined n-normal algebras as a subvariety of the variety of symmetric Heyting algebras. We proved that every finite symmetric Heyting algebra is n-normal for some *n* greater than or less than 0 or it contains a "cyclic" element. In this communication we characterize the n-formal finite algebras by the property that every boolean element is strongly boolean. This characterization enables us to obtain a decomposition of a finite symmetric Heyting algebra as a product of two algebras: one n-normal and the other one cyclic without normal factors.

GALLI, C M. Teología de la liberación y doctrina social de la Iglesia hoy. Stromata, 46(1-2), 187-203, Ja-Je 90.

GALLIE, Roger D. Hume, Reid and Innate Ideas: A Response to John P Wright. Method Sci, 22(4), 218-229, 1989.

Reid's position in the inquiry is that the sensation of hardness suggests the conception of hardness to our mind by an original principle of our constitution. It seems to be Hume's view that this is innatism but it is hard to see how this view is justifiable. Wright's contentions that Reid attempts to found our ontological beliefs on the analysis of our ideas and that Reid believes that a belief implies a corresponding idea unlike Hume are considered, and it is argued that they are not made out.

GALLO, Beverly E. On the Question of Nietzsche's "Scientism". Int Stud Phil, 22(2), 111-119, 1990.

GALLOP, David (trans) and ARISTOTLE,. *Aristotle on Sleep and Dreams*. Peterborough, Broadview Pr, 1990.

GALLOP, David. Can Fiction Be Stranger Than Truth? An Aristotelian Answer. Phil Lit, 15(1), 1-18, Ap 91.

The acceptability of multiple endings in fiction is discussed, with reference to John Fowles's *The French Lieutenant's Woman* and other fictional works. Such endings are shown to violate Aristotelian requirements for plot-structure, and a rationale for those requirements is suggested. Fictional discourse owes a basic conformity to the fact-stating discourse it imitates, to sustain the illusion upon which its power depends. By disturbing that illusion, a multiple ending impairs the credibility of the story.

GALSTON, William A. "False Universality" in *Critique and Construction: A Symposium on Roberto Unger's "Politics"*, LOVIN, Robin W (ed), 14-28. New York, Cambridge Univ Pr, 1990.

GALSTON, William. Toughness as a Political Virtue. Soc Theor Pract, 17(2), 175-197, Sum 91.

GALVAN, Sergio. Underivability Results in Mixed Systems of Monadic Deontic Logic. Log Anal, 31(121-122), 45-68, Mr-Je 88.

The intention of this essay is to show that the general underivability result of normative propositions from descriptive ones (Hume's thesis formally formulated and derived in specific deontic systems), suitably weakened, can be extended to certain mixed systems that also include the bridge-principles 1) "If obligatory A, then necessary that obligatory A" and 2) "If obligatory A, then possible A". In particular, proof will be provided of the underivability, within these systems, of deontic formulae of obligation from any consistent set of alethic (and modal) formulae and of an even more restricted class of formulae of obligation (axiologically important obligation) within the alethic system KT5Q.

GAMARRA, Daniel. Sujeto, acto y operación. Sapientia, 45(175), 9-16, Ja-Mr 90.

GAMBRA, José Miguel. La metáfora en Aristóteles. Anu Filosof, 23(2), 51-68, 1990.

GAN, Barry. "Loving One's Enemies" in *In the Interest of Peace: A Spectrum of Philosophical Views*, KLEIN, Kenneth H (ed), 217-225. Wolfeboro, Longwood, 1990.

People committed to settling conflicts nonviolently often seek to convert their opponents. Gandhi and King both emphasized two characteristics of this conversion process. First, conversion is best attained without efforts to shame or embarrass opponents. Second, conversion usually occurs because opponents are shamed or embarrassed. These two observations suggest a predicament for nonviolent activists. How can one seek conversion of opponents that may entail their shame or embarrassment without seeking to shame or embarrass them? The answer lies first, with the nature of shame and embarrassment; second, with concepts of nonviolence and of loving one's enemies; third, with openness in nonviolent strategy.

GANDER, Hans-Helmuth. Wege der Seinsfrage: Aus Anlass der 100. Heidegger Stud, 6, 117-129, 1990.

The article discusses the basic thoughts of following works of Martin Heidegger, published in 1989: (1) "Beiträge zur Philosophie (Vom Ereignis)" is the second main publication. Heidegger articulates the perspective of the "Kehre" in his thinking. "Beiträge" constitutes the basis of his whole later philosophy. (2) "Vom Ursprung des Kunstwerkes" is the so-far unknown first conception of the famous "Holzwege" Treatise. (3) "Aufenthalte" is Heidegger's philosophical diary of his journey to Greece from 1962 with important thoughts to the Greek world in relation to the present. (4) The lecture "Der Begriff der Zeit" is an important prestep to "Sein und Zeit." (5) In the lecture "Überlieferte Sprache und technische Sprache" from 1962 Heidegger discusses the relation between language—technic—art.

GANE, Mike. *On Durkheim's Rules of Sociological Method*. New York, Routledge, 1989.

This work examines the theses of Durkheim's Rule of sociological method (in article form 1893, in book form 1894). It provides a detailed examination and critique of how the work has been read both in the anglo-saxion and the French tradition. It suggests a more adequate assessment of this work in the context of a deeper understanding of Durkheim's notion of historical transitions and the idea of complex rationalism.

GANERI, Jonardon. Dharmakirti on Inference and Properties. J Indian Phil, 18(3), 237-247, S 90.

GANGADEAN, Ashok. Predication and Logic of Language (I). Indian Phil Quart, 18(1), 1-51, Ja 91.

GANGADEAN, Ashok. Predication and Logic of Language (II). Indian Phil Quart, 18(2), 199-229, Ap 91.

GARAVASO, Pieranna. Frege and the Analysis of Thoughts. Hist Phil Log, 12(2), 195-210, 1991.

In both his earlier and later writings, Frege claims that distinct sentences can express the same thought, and that there is a correspondence between the parts of a thought and the parts of the sentence expressing it. The joint assertion of these claims gives rise to a problem: how can there be a correspondence between the parts of one thought and the parts of distinct sentences? This paper discusses Michael Dummett's and Gregory Currie's interpretations of Frege's views on the analysis of thoughts and proposes an alternative interpretation which answers the above problem and provides some insight into Frege's epistemology of thoughts and his theory of human communication.

GARCÍA GONZÁLEZ, Juan. El ser principial y Dios: Una observación a la teología de Maimónides. Espiritu, 37(97), 35-44, Ja-Je 88.

GARCÍA LÓPEZ, Tomás. La ética/moral en el Bachillerato español: Estado de la cuestión. El Basilisco, 2, 98-100, N-D 89.

GARCIA MARQUÉS, Alfonso. Potencia, finalidad y posibilidad en "Metafísica" IX, 3-4. Anu Filosof, 23(2), 147-159, 1990.

GARCÍA MÁYNEZ, Eduardo. Algunas reflexiones sobre la doctrina platónica de los preámbulos de las *Leyes*. Dianoia, 34(34), 1-6, 1988.

GARCÍA MONSIVÁIS, Blanca (trans) and WIREDU, Kwasi. Existen los universales culturales? Dianoia, 34(34), 35-48, 1988.

GARCÍA MONSIVÁIS, Blanca (trans) and PASSMORE, John. Los universales culturales. Dianoia, 34(34), 27-34, 1988.

What light can philosophers, as distinct from anthropologists, throw on the question whether there are cultural universals? First they can clarify the view that such universals exist by distinguishing between a loose, a tight and a rigid interpretation of the assertion that there are such universals. It then emerges that the rigid view is clearly false, the loose view not of any particular interest to philosophers but the tight view raises fundamental epistemological issues.

GARCÍA NORRO, Juan José. El cuádruple problema de la inducción: Crítica de la solución popperiana del problema de Hume. Rev Filosof (Spain), 3, 5-21, 1990.

The induction poses four different problems. The main one is the problem pointed out by Hume—the metaphysic problem of induction. It is argued that Popper misunderstands the nature of this question. Hence he has not been able to solve it as he claims. Hume's challenge perslsts.

GARCIA, J L A. The Intentional and the Intended. Erkenntnis, 33(2), 191-209, S 90.

The paper defends the thesis that for *S* to *V* intentionally is for *S* to *V* as (in the way) *S* intended to. For the normal agent the relevant sort of intention is an intention that one's intention to generate an instance of one's *V*-ing along some (usually dimly-conceived) productive path. Such an account allows us to say some actions are intentional to a greater or lesser extent (a desirable option for certain cases of 'wayward causal chains'), preserves the intuitive link between 'intention' and 'intentionally', and supports the common sense view that the concept of intending is more basic than those of acting with an intention and of acting intentionally. The remainder of the paper responds to certain apparent counterexamples offered by Audi, Harman, and Bratman. In the course of this, I discuss connections between intending to *V* and hoping to *V*, and I argue that one can intend to do what one doesn't expect to do, and that one always intends what one attempts.

GARCIA, J L A. On the Irreducibility of the Will. Synthese, 86(3), 349-360, Mr 91.

This paper criticizes the thesis that intending to do something is reducible to some combination of beliefs and desires. Against Audi's recent formulation of such a view I offer as counterexample a case wherein an agent who wants and expects to *V* has not yet decided whether to *V* and hence does not intend to. I try to show that whereas belief that one will *V* is not necessary for intending to *V*, as illustrated in cases of desperate attempts to *V*, one cannot intend to *V* without preferring to *V* (rather than not *V*) and thus one cannot intend to *V* without, in some sense, want to *V* (at least wanting it in preference to not *V*-ing). The connection of one's intentions with one's objectives, attempts, plans, and hopes is briefly treated, and some influential work by Davidson is criticized.

GARCIA, Jorge. On 'High-Mindedness'. Proc Cath Phil Ass, 63, 98-107, 1990.

I criticize Ross's and Stocker's arguments that *S*'s motives/intentions are always irrelevant to her moral duty. At least some duties cannot be fulfilled without having certain intentions. In hypothetical cases wherein *S* can do as she promised, but *not* with virtuous motives, I claim (a) she may have a *nonmoral obligation* to do the act even with her inadequate (or bad) motives, and (b) she may have a *comparative moral obligation* to do-the-act-viciously-rather-than-not-not-do-it-at-all, but deny (c) she has a *noncomparative moral obligation* to do it *even with the inadequate (or bad) motives*. Disposing of these objections permits a conception of duty that fits a virtue-based moral theory.

GARCÍA, Jorge. The Rights-Interpretation of Desert. Dialogos, 25(56), 143-156, Jl 90.

Desert-claims pose a difficulty for the thesis that justice can be understood entirely in terms of rights: (1) denying someone what she deserves seems as such to be an injustice, but (2) some philosophers (notably, Feinberg) have constructed situations in which a person deserves something to which she has no right, so (3) there seem to be cases in which there is injustice but no violation of a right. Distinguishing standard from deviant desert-claims, I show that the problematic cases are deviant and thus open the door to treating every standard desert-claim as a statement of rights. Distinguishing positive from negative desert-claims, I claim that whereas a standard positive desert-claim affirms that not conferring the good on the subject would violate her rights, a standard negative desert-claim affirms that imposing the bad thing on her would not violate her rights. I briefly sketch some normative implications and conclude by questioning the view of MacIntyre and others that the ancients' conception of justice in terms of desert places them at a great distance from us moderns who think of justice in terms of rights.

GARCIA, Romano. El ensimismamiento del poder: Maquiavelo y la ciencia política moderna. Pensamiento, 47(187), 257-295, Jl-S 91.

La intuición fundamental de Maquiavelo se refiere a la autonomía—*ensimismamiento*—del Poder. Autonomía frente a lo sobrenatural: *aseidad* en el terreno político, dentro de la corriente emancipadora del Renacimiento. Autonomía frente a la Revelación: el análisis político se diferencia, aisla y "define" respecto de los otros conocimientos. Autonomía frente a la moral, la cual no desaparece, sino que es reconvertida en moral del Poder. Autonomía frente a los grupos sociales, condición indispensable para la construcción de lo social como convivencia política. El Poder es un "dios mortal"—que dirá enseguida Hobbes—. La *virtù* refleja la capacidad demiúrgica del político, que puede someter a la *fortuna* y reducir a la necesidad. Supuesto fundamental de la reflexión maquiaveliana es la *verità effettuale*—inclinacón del hombre al mal—. Cierto determinismo en la naturaleza y en las pasiones humanes y la autonomía del Poder Llevan a Maquiavelo a unos planteamientos y enunciados, que permiten atribuir sentido científico a su pensamiento.

GARCÍA-GÓMEZ, Jorge. Interpretación mundanel e identidad propia. Rev Filosof (Spain), 4, 111-141, 1990.

GARCÍA-MATEO, Rogelio. San Ignacio de Loyola y el humanismo. Gregorianum, 72(2), 261-288, 1991.

GARCÍA-SUCRE, Máximo. "On the Relationship Between Mathematics and Physics" in *Studies on Mario Bunge's "Treatise"*, WEINGARTNER, Paul (ed), 323-334. Amsterdam, Rodopi, 1990.

We analyze the relationship between mathematics and physics starting from the definition of a family of research fields introduced by Bunge (1983) in his *Treatise on Basic Philosophy*. We propose that a special kind of generic properties of the collections of material objects are at the base of important connections between these two research fields. As a consequence we obtain the properties that mathematics is ontologically noncommittal, that its truths are not subject to experimental verification, and that its structure is of an atemporal character. Finally, we give a possible explanation of the fact that mathematical concepts and semantical rules adapt themselves so wonderfully to the statement of physical laws.

GÄRDENFORS, Peter. An Epistemic Analysis of Explanations and Causal Beliefs. Topoi, 9(2), 109-124, S 90.

The aim of the paper is to provide a unified analysis of explanations and causal beliefs based on the notion of a *contraction* of a belief state developed by the author in his book *Knowledge in Flux*. The main thesis about explanation is that the characteristic role of the *explanans* is to *convey some information* about the *explanandum*. Here the information conveyed is determined in relation to the *beliefs* of the explainer. Like for explanation, it is argued that causal claims are evaluated only in relation to a given state of belief. It is shown that J M Keynes was an early exponent of this idea.

GÄRDENFORS, Peter. "Is There Anything We Should Not Want to Know?" in *Logic, Methodology and Philosophy of Science, VIII*, FENSTAD, J E (ed), 63-78. New York, Elsevier Science, 1989.

The question in focus is: Could there be scientific knowledge, the possession of which would be inimical to ourselves or our welfare? Knowledge can be dangerous because it leads to *technology* that can be misused or because it is *counter-ideological* and threatens the established society. It is argued that for neither type there is no *scientific knowledge* that we should not have. As regards the first type it is not the scientific knowledge in itself that is dangerous, but the dangers depend on the knowledge being used for certain abominable applications. The conclusions are supported by an Aristotelian view on the goals of science.

GÄRDENFORS, Peter. *Knowledge in Flux: Modeling the Dynamics of Epistemic States*. Cambridge, MIT Pr, 1990.

In the first part of the book dynamic models of belief are presented. The models describe expansions, revisions and contractions of epistemic states. Propositional, probabilistic, and other types of models are considered. The models are described, firstly, via a set of rationality postulates and, secondly, via explicit constructions more or less amenable for computer implementations to handle updating knowledge-based systems. These two approaches are connected by a number of representation theorems. In the second part the models are applied to philosophical problem areas in cognitive science, resulting in epistemic analyses of propositional logic, conditionals, explanations and causal beliefs.

GARDINER, Robert W. Between Two Worlds: Humans in Nature and Culture. Environ Ethics, 12(4), 339-352, Wint 90.

In this essay, I set forth a view of humans as creatures living at once in two worlds: the world of nature and the world of culture. I explore some of the tensions and paradoxes entailed by this position, as well as the implications for ethics, both interhuman and environmental. I also critique the distortions entailed by ethical stances which draw too heavily on one polarity or the other without taking sufficient account of the discontinuities between them.

GARDNER, G T G. Response to 'Rescuing the Innocent'. Ethics Med, 7(2), 6-7, Sum 91.

GARDNER, Howard. The Tensions Between Education and Development. J Moral Educ, 20(2), 113-125, My 91.

Most scholars, including Lawrence Kohlberg, have maintained that the principles of human development can mesh readily with the goals of the educational system. However, children's intuitive theories and conceptions turn out to be so powerful that they often undermine the overt goals of education. Indeed, there is typically a disjunction between early forms of understanding, the forms that school attempts to inculcate, and the kinds of knowledge required for expert performance in a domain. Though the issue has not been investigated, such disjunctions may obtain in the moral domain as well. It should be possible to bridge the gap between developmental and educational concerns; but such connection can only take place if the robustness of early conceptions is fully acknowledged and appropriate interventions are designed.

GARFIELD, Jay L. *Foundations of Cognitive Science: The Essential Readings*. New York, Paragon House, 1990.

GARFIELD, Jay L (ed) and KITELEY, Murray (ed). *Meaning and Truth: The Essential Readings in Modern Semantics*. New York, Paragon House, 1991.

GARGANO, Monica. Cristianesimo tragico, cristianesimo ludico: i due volti della fedeltà al Dio dialettico. Filosofia, 42(1), 61-83, Ja-Ap 91.

GARLAND, Michael J and HASNAIN, Romana. Community Responsibility and the Development of Oregon's Health Care Priorities. Bus Prof Ethics J, 9(3-4), 183-200, Fall-Wint 90.

The paper describes Oregon's innovative use of community meetings to identify key values for health care priorities in public policy. The article describes the Oregon Health Decisions technique as a contribution to overcoming risks of unfairness, prejudice and impracticality critics have attributed to the process of rationing health care. A rich array of values were identified at community meetings leading to a balanced, multi-dimensioned basis for setting priorities. The article finally relates the Oregon process to the concept of social solidarity essential to the fair and prudent reform of third party financing in US health care.

GARLAND, Michael J and HASNAIN, Romana. Health Care in Common: Setting Priorities in Oregon. Hastings Center Rep, 20(5), 16-18, S-O 90.

The article reports on the theory, design and results of a state-wide community meetings program to identify values required for democratically guiding efforts in Oregon to budget for Medicaid and health insurance programs for "the uninsured" on the basis of explicit health care priorities. The meetings were organized for a government commission by Oregon Health Decisions, a private organization that promotes general citizen involvement in exploring the ethical aspects of health policy development. Values expressed by the general public are related to fundamental themes of justice and community solidarity.

GARNER, Reuben. "Authority, Authoritarianism, and Education" in *The Realm of Humanitas: Responses to the Writings of Hannah Arendt*, GARNER, Reuben (ed), 123-148. New York, Lang, 1990.

Hannah Arendt defined authority as an institution or person that compels obedience through its stature and its sense of responsibility. Maintenance of such authority is essential for schoolteachers. They acquire this authority through knowledge of subject matter and critical acceptance of the world. Arendt saw schools as passageways from the home privacy necessary for the well-being of children to the public participation of the mature citizen. She drew much criticism and finally reversed her position when she discussed problems of integration in this context. Adult education is training; true education is preparation for citizenship. Much scientific and technical training is alienating, but Arendt argues that appropriate humanistic study might overcome this estrangement.

GARNER, Reuben (ed). *The Realm of Humanitas: Responses to the Writings of Hannah Arendt*. New York, Lang, 1990.

This book has been developed and inspired by a conference on the work of Hannah Arendt held at New York University. It consists of essays on Jewish identity by Matti Megged and Leon Botstein; discussions of totalitarianism by Melvyn Hill, Reuben Garner, and Richard L Rubenstein; essays on education, philosophy, and political science by Reuben Garner, Paul Ricoeur, Shelden S Wolin, George Kateb, and Richard J Bernstein; and it includes a conclusion by Christopher Lasch.

GARNER, Richard T. On the Genuine Queerness of Moral Properties and Facts. Austl J Phil, 68(2), 137-146, Je 90.

John Mackie advanced two arguments in support of "moral skepticism," the argument from disagreement and the argument from queerness. The arguments have often been criticized, but I show that, properly understood, they remain troublesome for moral realists. David Brink argues that because "externalist" moral realism does not attribute built-in motivation to moral judgments it escapes the argument from queerness. I reply by showing how the genuine queerness of moral properties and facts lies not in their power to motivate, but in their alleged authority to bind—in what Mackie calls their objective prescriptivity. Naturalism is one way to evade the argument from queerness, and Brink thinks that queerness can be avoided by resorting to supervenience. I argue that Mackie anticipated this move, and that the genuine queerness of moral properties explains why they are different from other properties which can unproblematically supervene.

GARON, Joseph and RAMSEY, William and STICH, Stephen. "Connectionism, Eliminativism and the Future of Folk Psychology" in *Philosophical Perspectives, 4: Action Theory and Philosophy of Mind, 1990*, TOMBERLIN, James E (ed), 499-533. Atascadero, Ridgeview, 1990.

GARRETT, Brian. Personal Identity and Reductionism. Phil Phenomenol Res, 51(2), 361-373, Je 91.

GARRETT, Brian. Persons and Human Beings. Logos (USA), 11, 47-56, 1990.

What is it to be a person? What is the relation between a person and the animal (human being) he shares his matter with? Throughout, I shall assume a non-Cartesian conception of persons: persons are not immaterial (that is, non-spatial) substances, and have no immaterial parts. Hence, I take it as axiomatic that each person *shares his matter with* a human being. But are we entitled to assert, in addition, that the relation between a person and the animal he shares his matter with is that of *strict numerical identity*? In order to answer this question, it is important to be clear about what it is to be a person. I shall therefore begin by attempting to clarify some fundamental aspects of our concept of a person. (It is assumed throughout that the conditions of individuation and identity over time of human beings are relatively unproblematic.)

GARRETT, Brian. Vague Identity and Vague Objects. Nous, 25(3), 341-351, Je 91.

GARRETT, Don. "Ethics IP5: Shared Attributes and the Basis of Spinoza's Monism" in *Central Themes in Early Modern Philosophy*, COVER, J A (ed), 69-107. Indianapolis, Hackett, 1990.

Ethics IP5 states that substances cannot share attributes, and it plays an essential role in Spinoza's argument for substance monism. His demonstration of IP5, however, seems subject to two serious objections, both of which are raised in Jonathan Bennett's landmark book, *A Study of Spinoza's Ethics*. I consider a number of recent responses to these two objections, arguing both that none can fully overcome the objections, and that none provides a likely interpretation of Spinoza's intentions in offering the demonstration. I offer an interpretation of the demonstration that, I argue, does overcome the objections and provides a likely account of Spinoza's intentions. Central to this interpretation is what Bennett calls Spinoza's "explanatory rationalism."

GARRETT, Richard. Putnam on Kripke's Puzzle. Erkenntnis, 34(3), 271-286, My 91.

GARRETT, Richard and GRAHAM, George. Why not Naturalistic Psychology? Philosophia (Israel), 20(4), 377-385, F 91.

GARRETT, Thomas M and BAILLIE, Harold W. "The Ethics of Social Commitment" in *Biomedical Ethics Reviews, 1990*, HUMBER, James M (ed), 11-28. Clifton, Humana Pr, 1991.

This article presents an argument in favor of a national health care plan, claiming that health care is a social good serving human dignity, that sharing in social goods identifies one as a member of the society, and that membership in society is necessary and appropriate for human dignity. Further, the health care to be provided must be at minimum adequate to allow participation in society, and when such participation cannot be attained treatment is not required. Finally, we call for a combined social effort to define "adequate health care," led by the health care professions and the government.

GARRISON, James W. "Does Metaphysics Really Matter for Practice?" It Depends on the Practitioner. Educ Theor, 41(2), 221-226, Spr 91.

GARRISON, James W. The Paradox of Indoctrination: A Hermeneutical Solution. Proc Phil Educ, 46, 396-402, 1990.

GARRONI, Emilio. Estetica e interrogazione. Rev Int Phil, 44(174), 394-418, 1990.

It is argued the common idea of esthetics as "philosophy or science of art" is a typical "prejudice" that can be imputed to a metaphysical conception of philosophy (still peculiar even to the current antimetaphysical neopragmatism and deconstructivism) as knowledge of the experience "from outside" of the very experience. Philosophy, at least from Kant onwards, is rather a questioning, and a questioning about its possibility of self-questioning, i.e., an effort of comprehension "in the inside" of experience, something as a *durchschauen* in the sense of Wittgenstein. Then it is shown that esthetics, from its origins in the XVIII century and in the most significant authors (Dubos, Baumgarten, Batteux, Hume, Burke, Alembert, Diderot), is an analogous *durchschauen* on the exemplary occasion of what was said "fine arts," and "art" *tout court* at last, i.e., a precedent, a vehicle and even a fulfillment, in the *Kritik der Urteilskraft*, of a critical philosophy.

GARVER, Eugene. Essentially Contested Concepts: The Ethics and Tactics of Argument. Phil Rhet, 23(4), 251-270, 1990.

One of the appeals of the idea of essentially contested concepts is that it seems to promise conversation and discussion instead of alternating monologues with no mutual understanding. I claim, though, there is no universal duty to treat disputes as involving essentially contested concepts whenever possible. Whether essentially contested concepts are involved or not is not a question for theoretical determination, nor is there a universal duty to treat disputes as involving essentially contested concepts whenever possible. Instead, whether or not to regard others as participating in such a context is a tactical decision, not a moral one. Reflecting on the tactical considerations shows how one can aim at keeping a conversation going without being committed to listening or speaking to everyone and being forced to think that all voices are somehow equal. The absence of extra-discursive, whether ontological or moral, constraints on discourse does not entail that anything goes.

GARVER, Eugene. Why Pluralism Now? Monist, 73(3), 388-410, Jl 90.

It is no flaw in philosophic heroes of the past that they were not pluralists, that they saw no need to try to do justice to competing views but instead expressed conviction that they were about to put an end to controversy by putting philosophy on a firm scientific basis. But, while such behavior is no flaw for them, it would be for contemporary philosophy which seems to feel an obligation at least to appear more modest. Modern pluralism is a response to what Hume noticed as a novel phenomenon in his time, what he calls "parties from principle," factions based on ideas rather than interest. While conventional liberalism was designed to deal with parties from interest, parties from principle require more complicated, and more philosophical, practical responses.

GARVER, Newton. Form of Life in Wittgenstein's Later Work. Dialectica, 44(1-2), 175-201, 1990.

Malcolm wrote that the importance of *form of life* in Wittgenstein's later work could hardly be stressed too much. But that is just what has happened. Wittgenstein makes nothing of cultural differences, and so connotes no relativism when he speaks of forms of life. In the natural world, "this complicated form of life" of ours is distinguished from those of lions and dogs. Since no essence is involved (our form of life can be defined only by describing the whole hurly-burly of human activity), neither philosophical principles nor solutions to philosophical problems can be derived from Wittgenstein's concept.

GARVER, Newton. "The Pursuit of Ideals and the Legitimation of Means" in *Perspectives on Ideas and Reality*, NYÍRI, J C (ed), 7-27. Budapest, Kiskonyvtara, 1990.

The first part of this essay reviews Hannah Arendt's account of how violence, when used as a means, tends to attain greater reality—even into the future—than the professed end. The second part extends the theme of Isaiah Berlin's Agnelli Lecture, "On the Pursuit of the Ideal," that insisting on ideal goals regularly fails, and would be misguided in any case, by considering the ideal of a "just society." The ideal proves not only illusive but even indefinable, and pursuing it obscures the regulative function that the concept of justice has in a dynamic, healthy society.

GARZA JR, Abel. Hegel's Critique of Liberalism and Natural Law: Reconstructing Ethical Life. Law Phil, 9(4), 371-398, 1990-91.

This essay considers the evolution of Hegel's political and legal theory with respect to the emergence of a classical liberal society and modern natural law. I argue that Hegel abandoned his early concerns which focused on a revival of the Greek polis and ethics over legality and refocused his efforts at reaching a modern form of ethical life predicted on the acceptance of classical liberal society and modern natural law. I try to argue that Hegel wanted to achieve a present-day communal ethics without abolishing the modern individual subject endowed with "rights." However, I seek to draw attention to Hegel's criticism of empirical individualism nd social atomism.

GARZÓN, León. El principio de exclusión y sus aplicaciones. El Basilisco, 2, 3-12, N-D 89.

In this work the exclusion principle is applied to several items: atomic estructure, electronic gas, white dwarfs, etc. It is remarked how an evident fact, the indiscernibility of identical objects, formulated in a suitable way, allows us to explain such a variety of phenomena.

GARZÓN-VALDÉS, Ernesto. "Basic Needs, Legitimate Wants and Political Legitimacy in Mario Bunge's Conception of Ethics" in *Studies on Mario Bunge's "Treatise"*, WEINGARTNER, Paul (ed), 471-487. Amsterdam, Rodopi, 1990.

GASKINS, Richard H. The Structure of Self-Commentary in Hegel's Dialectical Logic. Int Phil Quart, 30(4), 403-417, D 90.

GASPARSKI, Wojciech. "Design Methodology: A Personal Statement" in *Philosophy of Technology*, DURBIN, Paul T (ed), 153-167. Norwell, Kluwer, 1989.

The methodology of design, as I understand it and develop for a quarter of the century, is the philosophy of science applied either to all practical sciences or to applied science or to the sciences of the artificial. It covers theoretical reflection on the design process and logic of change design serves as a conceptual preparation. It is divided into two parts: *pragmatic m* which deals with the analysis of the purpose of design, defines its essence, and analyzes the procedures applied in the process of designing; *apragmatic m* which focuses on the object of design and particularly on the language of design problems and solutions. Design methodology is a chapter of praxeological inquiry.

GASPER, Philip. Explanation and Scientific Realism. Philosophy, 27, 285-295, 90 Supp.

GASPER, Philip (ed) and BOYD, Richard (ed) and TROUT, J D (ed). *The Philosophy of Science*. Cambridge, MIT Pr, 1991.

GASTELAARS, M. Een gedesoriënteerde veranderingswetenschap. Kennis Methode, 14(4), 346-366, 1990.

GATES JR, Henry Louis. Critical Fanonism. Crit Inquiry, 17(3), 457-470, Spr 91.

GATHERCOLE, Peter. "Childe's Early Marxism" in *Critical Traditions in Contemporary Archaeology*, PINSKY, Valerie (ed), 80-87. New York, Cambridge Univ Pr, 1990.

V Gordon Childe (1892-1957) was Australian by birth and upbringing, but eventually became the leading European prehistorian of his time. Shortly before his death he described his involvement in Australian Labour politics between 1917 and 1922 as 'a sentimental excursion'. This article challenges that description, and the way it has been interpreted by many writers on Childe, by exploring the relationship between his philosophical position after 1914 and his political activities and writings up to the mid-1920s, when prehistoric archaeology became his professional interest.

GAUKER, Christopher. If Children thought Like Adults. Phil Psych, 4(1), 139-146, 1991.

This article is a critical review of two recent books on cognitive development: Ellen Markman's *Categorization and Naming in Children* and Frank Keil's *Concepts, Kinds and Cognitive Development*. Markman is criticized for presupposing that children have a grasp of the very sorts of concepts the acquisition of which she aims to explain. Keil is criticized for belaboring the obvious and for incoherent theorizing.

GAUKER, Christopher. Semantics without Reference. Notre Dame J Form Log, 31(3), 437-461, Sum 90.

A theory of reference may be either an *analysis* of reference or merely an account of the correct use of the verb "to refer." If we define the validity of arguments in the standard way, in terms of assignments of individuals and sets to the nonlogical vocabulary of the language, then, it is argued, we will be committed to seeking an *analysis* of reference. Those who prefer a metalinguistic account, therefore, will desire an alternative to standard semantics. One alternative is the Quinean conception of validity as essentially a matter of logical form. Another alternative is Leblanc's truth-value semantics. But these prove to be either inadequate for purposes of metatheory or philosophically unsatisfactory. This paper shows how validity (i.e., semantic consequence) may be defined in a way that avoids the problems facing these other alternatives to standard semantics and also permits a metalinguistic account of reference. The validity of arguments is treated as a matter of logical form, but validity for forms is defined on analogy with the definition of semantic consequence in truth-value semantics.

GAULD, Alan. "Cognitive Psychology, Entrapment, and the Philosophy of Mind" in *The Case for Dualism*, SMYTHIES, John R (ed), 187-253. Charlottesville, Univ Pr of Virginia, 1989.

Functionalism in the philosophy of mind is an attempt to get round problems that render the mind-brain identity theory untenable. But functionalism leans heavily on current cognitive psychology and "artificial intelligence", and cognitive psychology fails to give a tenable account even of so central a phenomen as human memory. In particular, doctrines which attempt to explain memory and thinking in terms of the generation and manipulation of "inner representations" (images, propositional representations, inner models) are incoherent. Functionalism thus leans upon a broken reed and must collapse. To make progress we must re-examine certain empirical assumptions commonly held by neuroscientists.

GAUS, Gerald F and LOMASKY, Loren E. Are Property Rights Problematic? Monist, 73(4), 483-503, O 90.

Alan Gibbard, along with a number of other philosophers, seems to believe that property rights are somehow especially problematic as they conflict with freedom. The arguments of the first three sections of this paper contend that property rights are no more problematic within the context of liberal theory than are other quintessentially liberal rights such as freedom of speech. Many theorists have, however, believed that the justification of title to private property diverges significantly from other strands of liberal justificatory theory. In the fourth section, we trace this belief back to special features of original acquisition theories.

GAUTHIER, David. *Le promeneur solitaire*: Rousseau and the Emergence of the Post-Social Self. Soc Phil Pol, 8(1), 35-58, Autumn 90.

Rousseau introduces his autobiographical writing with the claim that it "may be used as the first comparative work in the study of man." I argue that his endeavor to think the conditions of man's social existence determines his own need to live in a consciousness that is post-social; his "first comparative work" is to paint the portrait of the man who, rebuffed by society, has become the solitary that nature made him. But the actual portrait is more complex, unfinished and unfinishable, revealing a self that is separate, but incomplete.

GAUTHIER, David. *Moral Dealing: Contract, Ethics, and Reason*. Ithaca, Cornell Univ Pr, 1990.

GAUTHIER, David. Thomas Hobbes and the Contractarian Theory of Law. Can J Phil, SUPP 16, 5-34, 1990.

The revival of interest in contractarian theories of morals and politics may encourage us to enquire into the prospects for a contractarian theory of law, aiming at a rational reconstruction of legal practices and institutions from the perspective of agreement. I examine what is perhaps *the* historical attempt to understand law in contractarian terms—that of Thomas Hobbes—and urge the plausibility of building a theory of law on a generalized Hobbism.

GAUTHIER, Yvon. "Logical and Philosophical Foundations for Arithmetical Logic" in *Physicalism in Mathematics*, IRVINE, Andrew D (ed), 331-342. Norwell, Kluwer, 1990.

The author presents his views on the logical foundations and the philosophical motivations of an arithmetical logic, that is a logic based on arithmetic. He contends that Fermat's method of infinite descent is the main tool of a constructive arithmetical logic added with a quantifier which he defines as "effinite." The goal here is a defence of constructivism in logic and mathematics.

GAVIN, William J. L'esthétique de John Dewey et le contexte urbain. Arch Phil, 54(2), 241-254, Ap-Je 91.

This article revolves around the importance of "context" and it is divided into three sections. First, Dewey's personal biography is sketched, with emphasis placed upon his own transition from a pastoral context (Burlington, Vermont) to an urban one (New York City). Second, Dewey's view of philosopher proper is presented as one in which philosophy is not a self subsistent study, but rather reflects and perfects via critical analysis the concerns and values of a specific community. Finally, Dewey's approach is applied to "the city as context" and it is argued that the concepts of "space" and "time" function differently there than they do in other domains.

GAVROGLU, Kostas (ed) and GOUDAROULIS, Yorgos (ed) and NICOLACOPOULOS, Pantelis (ed). *Imre Lakatos and Theories of Scientific Change*. Norwell, Kluwer, 1989.

This volume includes texts of the talks given during a conference in 1986 titled "Criticism and the Growth of Knowledge: Twenty Years Later." The articles assess the developments in philosophy of science during the twenty years from the 1965 London Conference.

GAVROGLU, Kostas. "The Methodology of Scientific Research Programmes and Some Developments in High Energy Physics" in *Imre Lakatos and Theories of Scientific Change*, GAVROGLU, Kostas (ed), 123-133. Norwell, Kluwer, 1989.

The recent developments in elementary particle physics and gravitation are "read" within the context of Lakatos's methodology. Though it is possible to articulate the specific character of (positive and negative) heuristics, the notion of the hard core turns out to be highly problematic.

GAY, William. "From Nuclear Winter to Hiroshima: Nuclear Weapons and the Environment" in *Issues in War and Peace: Philosophical Inquiries*, KUNKEL, Joseph (ed), 189-205. Wolfeboro, Longwood, 1989.

Analyzes arguments that present the prospect for nuclear winter as the most recent and catastrophic view of the consequences of nuclear war. Then, contrasts the possibility of nuclear winter with the fact of Hiroshima and argues the difference is more one of degree than kind. Finally, on the basis of reflection on the Chernobyl and Challenger disasters, contends environmental philosophy needs to show that the unacceptability of the use of nuclear weapons should be insisted upon at levels well below the threshold for nuclear winter.

GAY, William. "The Russell-Hook Debates of 1958: Arguments from the Extremes on Nuclear War and the Soviet Union" in *In the Interest of Peace: A Spectrum of Philosophical Views*, KLEIN, Kenneth H (ed), 79-95. Wolfeboro, Longwood, 1990.

Draws contemporary lessons from the 'debates' between Bertrand Russell and Sidney Hook in the late 50s. Shows how Russell argued from the extreme thesis that everyone would be killed in nuclear war and how Hook argued from the extreme thesis that there would be no freedom under communism. Contends that even if their arguments are emotionally persuasive, they are factually suspect. Notes current parallels in arguments that nuclear war risks "omnicide" and that the Soviet Union is the "Evil Empire." Concludes that now the more serious pitfall in the public debate is residual extreme anti-Sovietism.

GAZZARD, Ann. Some More Ideas About the Relation Between Philosophy for Children and Self-Esteem. Thinking, 9(1), 17-20, 1990.

GEACH, Peter (ed). *Logic and Ethics*. Norwell, Kluwer, 1991.

GEACH, Peter. "Whatever Happened to Deontic Logic" in *Logic and Ethics*, GEACH, Peter (ed), 33-48. Norwell, Kluwer, 1991.

GEERTSEMA, H G. Contingentie als uitgangspunt: Het denken van Richard Rorty. Phil Reform, 56(1), 35-61, 1991.

This article gives a critical appraisal of the philosophy of R Rorty, especially in his book *Contingency, Irony, and Solidarity*. It shows the overall importance of the idea of contingency as Rorty's startingpoint, discusses his ideas about truth, language, world, self, irony and solidarity and points out several tensions and Inconsistencies. It concludes that Rorty does not succeed in his attempt to break with the philosophical tradition of the claim of reason over against common sense and the subject/object split.

GEFFNER, Hector and PEARL, Judea. "A Framework for Reasoning with Defaults" in *Knowledge Representation and Defeasible Reasoning*, KYBURG JR, Henry E (ed), 69-87. Norwell, Kluwer, 1990.

A new system of defeasible inference is presented. The system is made up of a body of six rules which allow proofs to be constructed very much like in natural deduction systems. Five of the rules possess a sound and clear probabilistic semantics that guarantees the high probability of the conclusion given the high probability of the premises. The sixth rule appeals to a notion of irrelevance; we explain both its motivation and use.

GEFFRIAUD-ROSSO, Jeannette. "La femme intellectuelle au XVIIIe siècle ou l'inégalité des sexes" in *Égalité Uguaglianza*, FERRARI, Jean (ed), 93-101. Napoli, Liguori, 1990.

GEHRKE, Mai and INSALL, Matt and KAISER, Klaus. Some Nonstandard Methods Applied to Distributive Lattices. Z Math Log, 36(2), 123-131, 1990.

It follows from the concurrency principle and local finiteness, that any distributive lattice D is contained in a hyperfinite lattice extension H. The paper investigates Stone duality, in particular completeness and Sikorski's lemma, in this setting. The familiar characterization of open and compact sets, due to A Robinson, led us to a class of lattices, the "R-lattices," which is broader than Boolean algebras and finite lattice theory, but strictly contained in the class of lattices subject to the TD-axiom for the underlying Stone space.

GEIGER, Gebhard. *Evolutionary Instability: Logical and Material Aspects of a Unified Theory of Biosocial Evolution*. New York, Springer-Verlag NY, 1990.

The recent sociobiology debate has raised fundamental and previously unresolved conceptual problems. This book offers approaches for their solution. The scientific applications comprise the dynamics and evolutionary instability of hierarchically organized systems, especially systems of interacting behavioural phenotypes in animals and man. The technical apparatus is thoroughly explained in intuitive terms within the text, and illustrated by numerous familiar examples and graphical representations, supplemented by an informal summary and discussion. The analyses offers new theoretical perspectives to such diverse fields as philosophy of science, evolutionary biology, general system theory and sociology.

GEIMAN, Kevin Paul. Lyotard's "Kantian Socialism". Phil Soc Crit, 16(1), 23-37, 1990.

The article provides a reading of Lyotard's différend in light of Kantian ethical socialism. I try to show that, despite objections to the contrary, there is a moral-political perspective that supports Lyotard's emphasis on heterogeneity and dissensus.

GEIRSSON, Heimir. The Contingent *A Priori*: Kripke's Two Types of Examples. Austl J Phil, 69(2), 195-205, Je 91.

In *Naming and Necessity* Kripke gives us two types of examples of contingent a priori truths. In the first type (Neptune Type) the reference fixer is "en rapport" with the object being named, while in the second type (Meter Type) he merely stipulates that whatever objects satisfies a given definite description will bear a given name. Instances of these examples and further modifications of them are discussed. While the Neptune Type examples faith, it is argued that the Meter Type examples can provide us with genuine contingent a priori truths.

GEISMANN, Georg. Spinoza—Beyond Hobbes and Rousseau. J Hist Ideas, 52(1), 35-53, Ja-Mr 91.

Spinoza's political thought can be taken as fitting only minimally into the philosophical line of Hobbes, Rousseau, and Kant; but it seems eminently suited to another, just as valuable, line of empirical analysts and theorists of politics, namely, that of Aristotle, Machiavelli, Montesquieu, Tocqueville, and Max Weber. In his political thinking Spinoza is a social scientist, interested in causal analyses. His "social theory" is part of his general theory of nature. He is interested in certain social technologies. Even more important and valuable than the contents of his work are the high standards of method he has achieved.

GELLNER, Ernest. "The Civil and the Sacred" in *The Tanner Lectures On Human Values, Volume XII*, PETERSON, Grethe B (ed), 301-349. Salt Lake City, Univ of Utah Pr, 1991.

The text is concerned with the emergence of the notion of civil society, and attempts to place this notice, which has recently had a great vogue in Eastern Europe, in historical context. It is normally equated with a plural society in which there are institutions which can defy the central state. However, there have been no societies which satisfy this criteria, but which would not satisfy the *modern* yearning for civil society, because the rival institutions in question were too heavily sacralized, and made excessive demands on their members, demands which would not be acceptable to modern man. A modern kind of *civil society* has to contain such institutions and associations, but at the same time there must be optional and not themselves be a burden on the individual. The article discusses the preconditions and historical development of such a social condition.

GELLNER, Ernest. "La trahison de la trahison des clercs" in *The Political Responsibility of Intellectuals*, MACLEAN, Ian (ed), 17-27. New York, Cambridge Univ Pr, 1990.

The article is concerned with Julien Benda's celebrated book, *'La Trahison des Clercs'*. The article points out that the book in fact sins against the very principles which it purports to defend. It commends the attachment of intellectuals to universal permanent values, rather than to specific and local interests, but it does so on pragmatic grounds, which would seem to contradict its only basic position. The main point of the article is that this paradox is inherent in the contemporary condition, where people may be led to enter universalist, and to rational conclusions precisely through their commitment to truth and reason. This paradox must be faced, which Benda did not do.

GELVEN, Michael. *Spirit and Existence: A Philosophy Inquiry into the Meaning of Spiritual Existence*. Notre Dame, Univ Notre Dame Pr, 1990.

Rather than asking whether an entity, spirit, exists; or what kind it is, this inquiry asks what it means to be spirit. Focusing on various ways we exist, such as to suffer, to worship, and to matter, it is shown that such modes constitute an approach to understanding what spirit means, and thus provides a philosophical basis for thinking about who we are. If it is meaningful to worship or to sacrifice, certain metaphysical accounts relying solely on nature are denied. A system of pronominal metaphysics is developed in which pronouns and infinitives are shown to be fundamental.

GEMELLI, Giuliana. "Le Centre international de synthèse dans les années trente" in *Études sur/Studies on Hélène Metzger*, FREUDENTHAL, Gad , 237-243. Leiden, Brill, 1990.

GEMES, Ken. Horwich, Hempel, and Hypothetico-Deductivism. Phil Sci, 57(4), 699-702, D 90.

In his paper, "Explanations of Irrelevance" (1983), Paul Horwich proposes an amended version of hypothetico-deductivism, (H-D*). In this discussion note it is shown that (H-D*) has the consequence that "*A* is a non-black raven" confirms "All ravens are black" relative to any tautology! It is noted that Horwich's (H-D*) bears a strong resemblance to Hempel's prediction criterion of confirmation and that the prediction criterion faces the same obstacle. A related problem for hypothetico-deductivism in its simplest form—that is, *E* confirms *H* iff *E* is an (observational) consequence of *H*—is displayed. The discussion concludes with a suggestion about how (H-D*) and simple hypothetico-deductivism might be amended in order to avoid these results.

GEMES, Ken. The Indeterminacy Thesis Reformulated. J Phil, 88(2), 91-108, F 91.

Quine's indeterminacy of translation thesis presumes certain notions (e.g., that of rival, empirically equivalent translation manuals) which cannot be accommodated within a Quinean framework. Quine's own notion of the identity of theories is incompatible with the claim that there can be rival manuals fitting an individual's speech. By Quinean lights there is no fact of the matter as to whether such purported rival manuals are genuine rival manuals or merely different versions of the same manual. An alternative indeterminacy thesis is presented. This alternative does some justice to the considerations that motivated Quine's original indeterminacy thesis.

GEMES, Ken. A Refutation of Popperian Inductive Scepticism. Brit J Phil Sci, 40(2), 183-184, Je 89.

GENDEL, Stephen M and KLINE, David. Global Arguments for the Safety of Engineered Organisms. Int J Applied Phil, 5(2), 59-64, Fall 90.

In numerous papers Winston Brill has argued for the safety of agricultural biotechnology. If his arguments are sound, the current regulatory maze is at best an avoidable nuisance and at worst a serious obstruction to scientific and economic development. We show that what appears in Brill's writings as a diverse set of arguments really, when pressed, relies on a single underlying argument. After making the central argument perspicuous we raise a number of conceptual and factual difficulties with it. Several counterexamples from evolutionary theory are discussed.

GENDEL, Steven M (& other eds). *Agricultural Bioethics: Implications of Agricultural Biotechnology*. Ames, Iowa St Univ Pr, 1990.

GENDEL, Steven M. "Biotechnology and Bioethics" in *Agricultural Bioethics: Implications of Agricultural Biotechnology*, GENDEL, Steven M (& other eds), 340-343. Ames, Iowa St Univ Pr, 1990.

GENDIN, Sidney. Reply to Stephenson on Biomedical Research. Between Species, 7(1), 9-11, Wint 91.

I dispute the claim that institutional animal care and use committees are doing honest jobs of monitoring the care of animals used in research. I deny that most experimenters are either competent or well-intentioned. I maintain that the people on the side of animal research are uncontroversially immoral and that they themselves know that.

GENERALI, Dario. "Pier Caterino Zeno le vicende culturali del 'Giornale de' Letterati d'Italia'" in *Scienza, Filosofia e Religione tra '600 e '700 in Italia*, PREDAVAL MAGRINI, Maria Vittoria (ed), 119-202. Milan, Angeli, 1990.

GENÍS, Octavi Fullat. La Fenomenología aplicada a la Educación. Rev Port Filosof, 46(2), 193-212, Ap-Je 90.

The author of this text seeks the answer to the following question: "What kind of method can strengthen or weaken the thesis that the act of educating is at its core a violent confrontation between two consciences?" The author decides in favor of phenomenological method. This approach also permits a view of the phenomenon's intersubjective character. The argument wants to demonstrate the efficacious qualities of the method when applied to education. Only this method can show the universal and necessary nature of education: a violent relation between two consciences. (edited)

GENOVA, A C. Discovering Right and Wrong: A Realist Response to Gauthier's Morals by Agreement. S J Phil, 29(1), 21-50, Spr 91.

I examine the adequacy of Gauthier's maximizing conception of practical rationality to provide a rational foundation and justification for morality. I argue that (1) his defense of moral subjectivism is both misdirected and implausible, and (2) his game-theoretic derivation of moral behavior construed as a system of impartial constraints on the pursuit of individual utility maximization can at best provide a necessary but not a sufficient condition for an adequate account of morality, whereas only an objective account offers a promise of adequacy. I conclude that we must dispense with Gauthier's maximizing conception of practical rationality.

GENSINI, Stefano. "'Vulgaris opinio babelica': Sui fondamenti storico-teorici della pluralità delle lingue nel pensiero di Leibniz" in *Leibniz, Humboldt, and the Origins of Comparativism*, DE MAURO, Tullio (ed), 61-83. Philadelphia, John Benjamins, 1990.

This paper tries to shed light on a neglected aspect of Leibniz's linguistic thought, namely, his ideas about linguistic varieties, seen as a consequence of ethnic, cultural and social differences, but also as a specific character of human language. It is argued that theoretical reason for the Leibnizian interest in languages and dialects can be drawn from his view about the origin of language. In the last part of the paper the author tries to add a re-interpretation of Leibniz's theory of language variety on the philosophical view of knowledge. The conclusion is, that ordinary language in Leibniz's theory becomes the basis even of the formalized languages and that the inner reason of this may be seen in his belief in the semantic omniformativity of historical languages. (edited)

GEORGE, Kathryn Paxton. So Animal a Human..., or the Moral Relevance of Being An Omnivore. J Agr Ethics, 3(2), 172-186, 1990.

It is argued that the question of whether or not one is required to be or become a strict vegetarian depends, not upon a rule or ideal that endorses vegetarianism on moral grounds, but rather upon whether one's own physical, biological nature is adapted to maintaining health and well-being on a vegetarian diet. Even if we accept the view that animals have rights, we still have no duty to make ourselves substantially worse off for the sake of other rights-holders. Moreover, duties to others, such as fetuses and infants, may require one to consume meat or animal products. Seven classes of individuals who are not required to be or become vegetarians are identified and their exemption is related to nutritional facts; these classes comprise most of the earth's population. (edited)

GEORGE, Rolf and HITCHCOCK, David. Smook on Logical and Extralogical Constants. Inform Log, 13(1), 37-40, Wint 91.

We maintain that Roger Smook has failed to produce a counter-example to our assumption that logical consequence can be defined on the basis of a distinction between logical and extralogical constants. Further, Smook's proposal to define this distinction in terms of a primitive notion of logical consequence is idiosyncratic and an unnecessary confession of failure by logical theory. We discuss the basis for distinguishing logical from extralogical constants in artificial and natural languages.

GEORGIEFF, Andrey. Modernism's Two Eternities. Hist Euro Ideas, 11, 693-699, 1989.

Time changes, destroys, annihilates. Time causes everything to be transient. Modern age sensed this profane attribute of time very quickly, whereby it reacted promptly with two different strategies of eternity, realizing the danger of its own extinction. The first strategy is accomplished by the principle of universal history, which functions paradoxically as a time dimension of eternity. The universal secures the fiction of timelessness, of infinity, while history ensures the continuity of eternity. Modern age bases its second strategy of eternity upon the principle of catastrophe. This form cultivated by modern age is of an aggressive, explosive kind. In it lies the vision of one bomb powerful enough to reduce the surface of the earth to rubble, disrupting the flow of life, forcefully extinguishing and exterminating time. It is the symbol for the end of time that must be brought to a standstill, so that modern age can preserve the illusion of its own survival. This essay poses the problem of the actual fruitless attempt on the part of modern age to secure its own eternity.

GERAS, Norman. Seven Types of Obloquy: Travesties of Marxism. Grad Fac Phil J, 14(1), 81-115, 1991.

The purpose of the essay is to illustrate some standard current caricatures of Marxism, to be found in the work even of serious scholars. That Marxist thought is *unavoidably* reductionist; that Marxists believe in the possibility of a world without any conflict or problems at all; that they believe in "absolute" knowledge; and in the prospect of an "end of politics"—these are examples of the sort of criticism the author contests.

GERGELY, András. "Liberal Ideas and Reality: Central Europe 1848-49" in *Perspectives on Ideas and Reality*, NYÍRI, J C (ed), 98-115. Budapest, Kiskonyvtara, 1990.

GERGEN, Kenneth J. Therapeutic Professions and the Diffusion of Deficit. J Mind Behav, 11(3-4), 353-367, Sum-Autumn 90.

The mental health professions operate largely so as to objectify a language of mental deficit. In spite of their human intentions, by constructing a reality of mental deficit the professions contribute to hierarchies of privilege, reduce natural interdependencies within the culture, and lend themselves to self-enfeeblement. This infirming of the culture is progressive, such that when common actions are translated into a professionalized language of mental deficit, and this language is disseminated, the culture comes to construct itself in these terms. This leads to an enhanced dependency on the professions and these are forced, in turn, to invent additional terms of mental deficit. Thus, concepts of infirmity have spiraled across the century, and virtually all remaining patterns of action stand vulnerable to deficit translation. Required within the professions are new linguistic formulations that create a reality of relationships without evaluative fulcrum.

GERLA, Giangiacomo and BIACINO, Loredana. Connection Structures. Notre Dame J Form Log, 32(2), 242-247, Spr 91.

B L Clarke, following a proposal of A N Whitehead, presents an axiomatized calculus of individuals based on a primitive predicate "*x* is connected with *y*". In this article we show that a proper subset of Clarke's system of axioms characterizes the complete orthocomplemented lattices, while the whole of Clarke's system characterizes the complete atomless Boolean algebras.

GERRARD, Steve. Two Ways of Grounding Meaning. Phil Invest, 14(2), 95-114, Ap 91.

GERRARD, Steve. Wittgenstein's Philosophies of Mathematics. Synthese, 87(1), 125-142, Ap 91.

Wittgenstein's philosophy of mathematics has long been notorious. Part of the problem is that it has not been recognized that Wittgenstein, in fact, had two chief post-*Tractatus* conceptions of mathematics. I have labelled these the *calculus* conception and the *language-game* conception. The calculus conception forms a distinct middle period. The goal of my article is to provide a new framework for examining Wittgenstein's philosophies of mathematics and the evolution of his career as a whole. (edited)

GERT, Heather J. Rights and Rights Violators: A New Approach to the Nature of Rights. J Phil, 87(12), 688-694, D 90.

Some philosophers have sought to clarify the notion of a right by considering the question: In virtue of what characteristics does a being have a right? This article asserts that if this is an important question, then it is equally important to ask: In virtue of what characteristics is a being capable of *violating* (*or respecting*) a right?

GESTRICH, Christof. Speech, Sin and the Word of God (in Dutch). Bijdragen, 2, 185-200, 1991.

As a being that—different from all other beings—is gifted with speech, man uses this very speech for sinning. Again, in this situation of sin, man is also approached by speech, approached by the word of God. Human freedom is closely connected with the human capacity of speech. Man can exist as "human" man only through encouraging and confirming bestowal. The first origin of such creative bestowal theology calls God. But such creative words are not available without limit. Only by a truly good word, the word of God, can the permanent process of self-justification be interrupted. From here, the author endeavours a new approach to Heidegger's thinking about speech: not man is the subject of speech, but vice versa, certain words form man. (edited)

GHELARDI, Maurizio. Alle origini della riflessione di Leopold von Ranke sulla storia: K F Bachmann e J G Fichte. G Crit Filosof Ital, 69(1), 22-38, Ja-Ap 90.

GHILARDI, S and MELONI, C G. Modal Logics with *n*-ary Connectives. Z Math Log, 36(3), 193-215, 1990.

GHINS, Michel. *L'inertie et l'espace-temps absolu de Newton à Einstein*. Brussells, Acad Royale Belgique, 1990.

The logical empiricists (Carnap, Reichenbach) attempted to reduce space-time theories to the behavior of rigid rods and isochronous clocks. This book offers an alternative to that approach (followed the actual position of Newton, Leibniz, Mach, Einstein and Weyl) according to which the structure of space-time must be such that it explains inertial effects, which are not apparent but real. The behavior of metrical devices do not have a foundational role but are rather the manifestation of a real inobservable metaphysical entity, absolute space-time, with an appropriate mathematical structure (different for classical mechanics, special relativity and general relativity).

GHOSE, A M. K J Shah's 'Philosophy, Religion, Morality, Spirituality: Some Issues'. J Indian Counc Phil Res, 7(3), 141-146, My-Ag 90.

The observations contain response to Professor K J Shah's paper [JICPR 7(3), Jan-April 1990]. The conclusion seeks a clarification on whether Shah is explicating a historical truth or offering an interpretation, or, finally, enunciating his own views. In this connection the history and meaning of terms like purusārthas (the principal objects of human life), viveka (discrimination) anubhava (spiritual experience), sāstra (sacred treatise or texts) dharma (law, order duty) and moksa (liberation) have been examined.

GHOSE, A M. Philosophical Anthropology in Greek Antiquity. J Indian Counc Phil Res, 7(2), 139-144, Ja-Ap 90.

Philosophical anthropology is traced back to *Apology* 38 a. The purpose is to highlight the place of ethical relativism in the thoughts of Socrates, Plato and Aristotle. The notions of function, degeneration, telos, choice, nature, excellence (relative to constitution), inequality (among men) are examined along with the notions of education and reciprocity. They point to the fact that 'ethical relativism' remains as an inalienable feature in the thoughts of those Greek philosophers.

GHOSH-DASTIDAR, Koyeli. Respect for Persons and Self-Respect: Western and Indian. J Indian Counc Phil Res, 5(1), 83-93, S-D 87.

In the first section of this paper I analyse the concept of respect for persons as found in contemporary Western thought, and show that it is bound up with a characteristically modern liberal version of the concept of person. I then proceed to analyse the concept of self-respect and explain how it is related to the concept of respect for persons. In the second section I try to understand the problem of respect for persons and self-respect from the traditional Indian perspective, and attempt to draw out the differences between the two approaches, Western and Indian.

GHOSH-DASTIDAR, Koyeli. Respect for Privacy: Western and Indian. J Indian Counc Phil Res, 6(1), 101-109, S-D 88.

GIACOIA JUNIOR, Oswaldo. Fragmentos póstumos Friedrich Nietzsche. Trans/Form/Acao, 13, 139-145, 1990.

GIACOTTO, Paolo. "Filosofia e politica in Giammaria Ortes" in *Scienza, Filosofia e Religione tra '600 e '700 in Italia*, PREDAVAL MAGRINI, Maria Vittoria (ed), 327-362. Milan, Angeli, 1990.

GIAMBRONE, Steve. Orlowska's Relevant Implications, Relevant Logics and Analytic Implication. Rep Math Log, 24, 37-47, 1990.

Some systems of relevant implication based on semantic relevance criteria as proposed by Orlowska and some modified versions thereof are examined. (One of theses turns out to be equivalent to a relatedness logic proposed by Epstein.) Major differences between these and traditional relevant logics are brought out, and a significant relationship between Orlowska's original systems and Parry's and Dunn's systems of Analytic Implication is proven. Some questions are raised about the fruitfulness of defining a relevant implication on a classical base. The paper ends with a very brief philosophical discussion of the general project of Weingartner and Schurz, Epstein et al.'s work on relatedness logic and the program of Relevant Logics.

GIANNETTO, Enrico. Quantum Physics and Logical Truth (in Italian). Epistemologia, 12(2), 261-276, Jl-D 89.

Since quantum physics has been developed, we must deal with the problem of a physical, empirical logic, just as relativity has given us the problem of a physical, empirical geometry. As stressed by Finkelstein, logic is indeed empirical and it constitutes a dynamical element of a physical theory, itself evolving conditionally to processes. Following such a perspective of a "physics of logic," in this paper, we analyse a problem concerning the definition itself of a quantum logic, that is if a truth value can be assigned or it does not to the microphysical enunciates. (edited)

GIANOTTI, José Arthur. Observar un aspecto. Dianoia, 35(35), 43-56, 1989.

GIARELLI, James M and CHAMBLISS, J J. The Foundations of Professionalism: Fifty Years of the Philosophy of Education Society in Retrospect. Educ Theor, 41(3), 265-274, Sum 91.

The Philosophy of Education Society is discussed as a case study in professionalization. Although those working in philosophy of education have discussed the nature of the discipline, the emphasis of the Society has been a professional one, which views philosophers of education as a distinct professional class of exclusive and selectively initiated members, whose interests are with other philosophers. This has resulted in the neglect of philosophy of education as a public enterprise, open to all citizens for the purpose of educational dialogue. An appeal is made for philosophy's increased participation in public life.

GIARELLI, James M. Philosophy, Education, and Public Practice. Proc Phil Educ, 46, 34-44, 1990.

GIBBARD, Allan. Constructing Justice. Phil Pub Affairs, 20(3), 264-279, Sum 91.

GIBBONS, Michael T. The Ethics of Postmodernism. Polit Theory, 19(1), 96-102, F 91.

GIBBS, Robert. The Other Comes to Teach Me: A Review of Recent Levinas Publications. Man World, 24(2), 219-233, Ap 91.

A handful of books by and about Levinas have recently appeared in English. This review examines the six philosophical books, focusing on the relation with the other person. The review introduces several of the main ethical concepts of Levinas' thought in two anthologies. It also examines the wide-ranging interest that he has stimulated, as presented in two collections of secondary writings. Thinkers as diverse as the post-modern Lyotard, Liberation Theologians and Philosophers, deconstructionist Derrida, radical and other feminists (including Irigaray), psychoanalysts, and Levinas' close friend Maurice Blanchot each draw on Levinas account of the other.

GIBSON, Annetta M and RANDALL, Donna M. Ethical Decision Making in the Medical Profession: An Application of the Theory of Planned Behavior. J Bus Ethics, 10(2), 111-122, F 91.

The present study applied Ajzen's (1985) theory of planned behavior to the explanation of ethical decision making. Nurses in three hospitals were provided with scenarios that depicted inadequate patient care and asked if they would report health professionals responsible for the situation. Study results suggest that the theory of planned behavior can explain a significant amount of variation in the intent to report a colleague. Attitude toward performing the behavior explained a large portion of the variance; subjective norms explained a moderate amount of the variance; and perceived behavioral control added little to the explanation of variance. Implications for research and practice are discussed.

GIBSON, Joan. "Herrad of Hohenbourg" in *A History of Women Philosophers, Volume II: Medieval, Renaissance and Enlightenment, A.D. 500-1600*, WAITHE, Mary Ellen (ed), 85-98. Norwell, Kluwer, 1989.

Herrad's most original contribution may be as an educator and spiritual director whose frequent focus on women is not yet fully explored. Among her contemporaries, Herrad may perhaps most usefully be compared to Alain de Lille, for her artistic presentation of philosophy, her didacticism and eclecticism, and her moral fervour. Among medieval women, Christine Pisan seems her nearest kin in artistry and breadth of interest and in dedication to instructing women. In the beauty, the grand sweep and cosmic scope of her project, Herrad can be compared with Dante. God's little bee has shown an artistic, moral and philosophical journey to God.

GIBSON, Joan. "Mechtild of Magdeburg" in *A History of Women Philosophers, Volume II: Medieval, Renaissance and Enlightenment, A.D. 500-1600*, WAITHE, Mary Ellen (ed), 115-140. Norwell, Kluwer, 1989.

Mechtild presents above all a metaphysics, an epistemology and an ethical psychology of love. Her emphasis on the union of human and divine, on the role of experience in knowledge, on concern for others, are all subordinated to a perception of love as the ruling principle of God and creation. Lacking an essentialist or causal analysis, except in terms of love, bearing little relation to scholastic forms of reasoning, her work nevertheless announces themes that have been fruitful in later medieval mysticism, both speculative and affective, and for attempts to integrate experience and commitment with philosophical reflection.

GIBSON, Martha I. Response to Stampe's "Representation and the Freedom of the Will". Soc Theor Pract, 16(3), 467-475, Fall 90.

Stampe argues that it is the distinctive representational capacity of the will which explains actions' being created by and originating *in* the will rather than in desires or external influences. It is argued that his account of how the representational capacity of the will creates the possibility of doing the action is incomplete, and that his model of this—promising—is importantly disanalogous. Questions are raised about whether what is required to complete the account will be consistent with the actions originating in the will rather than *in* desires or external influences.

GIBSON, Roger F. More on Quine's Dilemma of Undetermination. Dialectica, 45(1), 59-66, 1991.

Quine's doctrine of underdetermination of physical theory presents him with a dilemma: should he say of two global theory formulations that are empirically equivalent, logically compatible, equally simple, but which cannot be rendered logically equivalent by any known reconstrual of predicates, that they are both true (the ecumenical view) or that only one of them is true (the sectarian view)? If the former, then Quine's commitment to naturalism is at risk; if the latter, then his commitment to empiricism is at risk. When confronted with the dilemma Quine *initially* opted for the sectarian view. A C Genova finds Quine's sectarian resolution of the dilemma unsatisfactory. He advocates, instead, an ecumenical resolution of the dilemma which, he maintains, is compatible with Quine's (and Davidson's) most prominent views. I disagree; I argue that Genova's way out involves a relativistic notion of true that is incompatible with Quine's (and Davidson's) absolutist view of truth. I then present Quine's *latest* thoughts on the dilemma of underdetermination.

GIBSON, Roger (ed) and BARRETT, Robert (ed). *Perspectives on Quine*. Cambridge, Blackwell, 1990.

GIDDENS, Anthony. "A Reply to My Critics" in *Social Theory of Modern Societies: Anthony Giddens and His Critics*, HELD, David (ed), 249-301. New York, Cambridge Univ Pr, 1990.

GIEDYMIN, Jerzy. Geometrical and Physical Conventionalism of Henri Poincaré in Epistemological Formulation. Stud Hist Phil Sci, 22(1), 1-22, Mr 91.

An epistemological formulation of conventionalism is given in terms of the concept of poly-theory implicit in the writings of Hamilton, Hertz and Poincare. A poly-theory is a family of theories (in the usual sense) which share the same mathematical structure (e.g., Maxwell's equations of the electromagnetic field) and which differ with respect to experimentally indistinguishable ontologies of the unobservable world (e.g., either undulations versus action-at-a-distance). According to physical conventionalism every physical theory is a poly-theory. Geometrical conventionalism is a special case for systems of geometry-plus-physics as physical theories.

GIER, Nicholas F. Never say "Never": A Response to Reeder's "Wittgenstein Never Was a Phenomenologist". J Brit Soc Phenomenol, 22(1), 80-83, Ja 91.

GIER, Nicholas F. Wittgenstein's Phenomenology Revisited. Phil Today, 34(3), 273-288, Fall 90.

In this article I examine two recent attempts to relate Wittgenstein to the phenomenological tradition. First, I assess Merrill and Jaakko Hintikka's thesis that the *Tractatus* should be read as phenomenology. I contend that this view has one major flaw: Tractarian objects are not phenomena of immediate experience. Second, I respond to Harry P Reeder's proposal that Wittgenstein cannot be seen as a phenomenologist at all. In the rest of the essay, I attempt to answer Reeder's claims, among them: (1) Wittgenstein has a reductionist, not descriptivist, method; (2) he does not have any notion of the phenomenological reductions; and (3) he does not have a doctrine of intentionality or constitution.

GIERER, A. "Physics, Life and Mind" in *Science and Religion: One World-Changing Perspectives on Reality*, FENNEMA, Jan (ed), 61-71. Norwell, Kluwer, 1990.

The laws of physics from the basis for scientific explanations of events in space and time, including basic features of life. However, the application of scientific thought to its own foundations also reveals essential limitations of science: indeterminacy in quantum physics, the limits of decidability in mathematics, and, most likely, limitations of an algorithmic theory of the brain-mind relationship. These limits, in turn, are closely related to fundamental philosophical questions on the relationship between human knowledge and reality. Modern science is consistent with different philosophical, cultural and religious interpretations of man and the universe.

GIERYN, Thomas F (ed) and COZZENS, Susan E (ed). *Theories of Science in Society*. Bloomington, Indiana Univ Pr, 1990.

GIGLIOLI, Giovanna. La revolución teórica del Príncipe de Maquiavelo. Rev Filosof (Costa Rica), 28(67-68), 41-45, D 90.

The article focuses on the contents of *The Prince* of Machiavelli, regarding their historical insertion and militant scope, as an expression of political realism which comprises not only the means but also the ends. In that moment, Italian unity, in effect, appeared as the historically most progressive solution, purposefully requiring absolute autonomy of politics for its realization. Critically disengaged from the historical circumstances which allow it, this assertion of autonomy constitutes the theoretical and polemical legacy of Machiavelli.

GILBERT, Alan. *Democratic Individuality*. New York, Cambridge Univ Pr, 1990.

GILBERT, Paul. Collectives and Collections. J Applied Phil, 7(2), 229-230, O 90.

A brief review of some recent literature on the nature of collective action and decision, considering in particular whether these reflect attachment to communal moral norms or calculations by individual economic agents.

GILBERT, Scott F. Epigenetic Landscaping: Waddington's Use of Cell Fate Bifurcation Diagrams. Biol Phil, 6(2), 135-154, Ap 91.

From the 1930s through the 1970s, C H Waddington attempted to reunite genetics, embryology, and evolution. One of the means to effect this synthesis was his model of the epigenetic landscape. This image originally recast genetic data in terms of embryological diagrams and was used to show the identity of genes and inducers and to suggest the similarities between embryological and genetic approaches to development. Later, the image became more complex and integrated gene activity and mutations. These revised epigenetic landscapes presented an image of how mutations could alter developmental pathways to yield larger phenotypic changes. These diagrams became less important as the operon became used to model differential gene regulation.

GILBERTSON, Diana and NELSON, George. Machiavellianism Revisited. J Bus Ethics, 10(8), 633-639, Ag 91.

The field of management has had difficulty embracing the concept of Machiavellianism despite the myriad of studies produced by other fields of social science. It appears that Machiavellianism as a unitary personality construct has limited efficacy in the complex world of organizations. The authors suggest a multidimensional approach to understanding the impact of an individual's threat to organizational functioning. Viewing the construct as discontinuous with two manifestations, predatory and benign, suggestions are made as to the location within organizations where such individuals may be found. A research approach is also suggested.

GILEAD, Amihud. Spinoza's Two Causal Chains. Kantstudien, 81(4), 454-475, 1990.

The immanent chain of ideas, which is knowledge *sub specie aeternitatis* without qualification, is a precondition of the ideas of the common properties of all things, which as general are conceived *quadam sub specie aeternitatis* only. Whereas the transient chain is an inadequate, *sub specie durationis sive temporis* perception of reality, a cognition which requires correction by the method and rules of *ratio*, which constitute the bridge between the two chains, since the regulative goal of that correction can be achieved by *scientia intuitiva* alone, which displays the immanent chain. In any case, it is clear now why the transient chain alone without aids has no connection with the eternal essences of singular, changeable things, the essences that are the links composing the immanent chain.

GILES, James. Bodily Theory and Theory of the Body. Philosophy, 66(257), 339-347, Jl 91.

GILES, Robin. "Introduction to A Logic of Assertions" in *Knowledge Representation and Defeasible Reasoning*, KYBURG JR, Henry E (ed), 361-385. Norwell, Kluwer, 1990.

An assertion is regarded as an *act*, which has a *utility* for each state of the world. It can therefore be characterized by a real-valued *payoff function*, the analogue of the *truth function* of classical logic. A *connective* is determined by its action on the payoff values and is thus a (unary or binary) real-valued function. Practical examples are given to illustrate the significance of the principal connectives. The relation of *logical consequence* is discussed. In the particular case where only *linear* connectives are used, a generalization of Robinson's method of *resolution* gives a sound and complete deductive system.

GILES, William F and MOSSHOLDER, Kevin W and WESOLOWSKI, Mark A. Information Privacy and Performance Appraisal: An Examination of Employee Perceptions and Reactions. J Bus Ethics, 10(2), 151-156, F 91.

Role-failure acts (Waters and Bird, 1989) have been described as a form of morally questionable activity involving a failure to perform the managerial role. The present study examined employee perceptions and reactions with regard to one form of role-failure act, failure to maintain adequate privacy of performance appraisal information. The study assessed employees' attitudes toward various performance appraisal facets as an invasion of privacy and determined the relationships between these privacy-related attitudes and employees' satisfaction with components of their appraisal system, the system as a whole, and their jobs. Responses that organizations might take to counteract appraisal privacy concerns were also discussed.

GILL, Christopher. "Is There a Concept of Person in Greek Philosophy?" in *Psychology (Companions to Ancient Thought: 2)*, EVERSON, Stephen (ed), 166-193. New York, Cambridge Univ Pr, 1991.

This essay considers how far contemporary attempts to distinguish persons from non-persons by psychological criteria can be paralleled in Greek philosophy. It focusses on certain suggestive similarities between Aristotle's ways of distinguishing human from non-human psychological capacities and Daniel Dennett's functionalist criteria for personhood, and between the Stoic conception of the rational animal as a language-using animal and that of Donald Davidson. Although significant differences emerge between the ancient and modern theories considered, the philosophical projects are found to be sufficiently congruent to enable fine-grained comparisons between the types of criteria adduced.

GILL, Jerry H and SORRI, Mari. *A Post-Modern Epistemology*. Lewiston, Mellen Pr, 1989.

The theme of this book concerns the essentially disembodied character of human knowledge in Western philosophy. This mentalistic bias has not only characterized, but in addition distorted Western epistemological endeavor. The authors have the positive purpose of using human embodiment as crucial to knowledge in relation to experience, meaning, and knowing. (staff)

GILLETT, G R. The Neurophilosophy of Pain. Philosophy, 66(256), 191-206, Ap 91.

Pain is a complex neurological and psychological function which does not fit the traditional model of a self-evident (Cartesian) mental state. If we accept a more concept-based approach to the nature of mental ascriptions, we find that we get an analysis which is far more congenial to neurophysiology and psychology. This view suggests that a pain is a characteristic set of reactions by creatures like us to certain kinds of events.

GILLETT, Grant R. Multiple Personality and Irrationality. Phil Psych, 4(1), 103-118, 1991.

The phenomenology of Multiple Personality (MP) syndrome is used to derive an Aristotelian explanation of the failure to achieve rational integration of mental content. An MP subject is best understood as having failed to master the techniques of integrating conative and cognitive aspects of her mental life. This suggests that in irrationality the subject may lack similar skills basic to the proper articulation and use of mental content in belief formation and control of action. The view that emerges centres mind on the activity of a subject rather than a structured causal nexus.

GILLETT, Grant R. Perception and Neuroscience. Brit J Phil Sci, 40(1), 83-103, Mr 89.

Perception is often analysed as a process in which causal events from the environment act on a subject to produce states in the mind or brain. The role of the subject is an increasing feature of neuroscientific and cognitive literature. This feature is linked to the need for an account of the normative aspects of perceptual competence. A holographic model is offered in which objects are presented to the subject classified according to rules governing concepts and encoded in brain function in that form. This implies that the analysis of perception must consider not only the fact that there is an interaction between the perceiving subject and the perceived object but also that the interaction is shaped by a system of concepts which the subject uses in thought and action.

GILLETT, Grant. An Anti-Sceptical Fugue. Phil Invest, 13(4), 304-321, O 90.

Five main themes emerge from Wittgenstein's treatment of scepticism. They concern the legitimate use of 'know'; the internal relation between truth and meaning; the importance of action in thought; the need for points of reference in any system of communication; and the need for coherence of mental content. These combine to form a powerful anti-sceptical fugue of argumentation which has clear pragmatist leanings.

GILLETT, Grant. The Subject of Experience. Logos (USA), 11, 93-109, 1990.

A neo-Kantian analysis of personal identity begins with the subject of experience as rational concept-user and takes this as the metaphysical basis of thought life. Sartre adds an understanding of the subject as both an item for his own reflective self-knowledge and an item known by and in interaction with others. This converges with an extension of Kant's views based on the social nature of concepts and the communicability of mental content. Together the arguments provide a strong rebuttal of the neo-Humean analysis.

GILLIES, Donald. A Bayesian Proof of a Humean Principle. Brit J Phil Sci, 42(2), 255-256, Je 91.

Hume bases his argument against miracles on an informal principle. This paper gives a formal explication of this principle of Hume's, and then shows that this explication can be rigorously proved in a Bayesian framework.

GILLIES, Donald. The Turing-Good Weight of Evidence Function and Popper's Measure of the Severity of a Test. Brit J Phil Sci, 41(1), 143-146, Mr 90.

The "Turing-Good Weight of Evidence Function" was originally developed for code cracking purposes during the Second World War. Both Turing and Good gave a Bayesian justification of the function. This paper shows that it can also be interpreted and justified using Popper's ideas on corroboration.

GILLIGAN, Carol. "Joining the Resistance: Psychology, Politics, Girls, and Women" in *The Tanner Lectures On Human Values, Volume XII*, PETERSON, Grethe B (ed), 253-299. Salt Lake City, Univ of Utah Pr, 1991.

This paper examines three concepts of resistance: healthy resistance to psychological illness, political resistance, and psychological resistance (i.e., a reluctance to know what one knows). In addition, it traces a process whereby a healthy resistance turns into a political resistance or struggle which then comes under pressure to become a psychological resistance. This process is observed in women's psychological development at the time of adolescence and in men's psychological development in early childhood. The question is raised: what if women join girls's healthy resistance to not knowing and not speaking, and the psychological implications of this joining for girls, for women and for men are explored.

GILLIGAN, John J. "Teaching Peace in a Christian Context" in *Celebrating Peace*, ROUNER, Leroy S (ed), 15-32. Notre Dame, Univ Notre Dame Pr, 1990.

GILLMAN, Neil. *Sacred Fragments: Recovering Theology for the Modern Jew*. Philadelphia, Jewish Pub Soc, 1990.

Addresses many of the perplexing issues for Jewish theology today: How to we know that God exists? To whom do we pray? Where was God during the Holocaust? What is the point of ritual? How is it possible to believe that God revealed the Torah? Retaining the sacred fragments of the traditional system of belief, Gillman shows that there are viable answers to these questions, and explains how they can be rethought and reformulated despite the strains and tensions of modernity. (staff)

GILLON, Brendan S. Ambiguity, Generality, and Indeterminacy: Tests and Definitions. Synthese, 85(3), 391-416, D 90.

The problem addressed is that of finding a sound characterization of ambiguity. Two kinds of characterizations are distinguished: tests and definitions. Various definitions of ambiguity are critically examined and contrasted with definitions of generality and indeterminacy, concepts with which ambiguity is sometimes confused. One definition of ambiguity is defended as being more theoretically adequate than others which have been suggested by both philosophers and linguists. It is also shown how this definition of ambiguity obviates a problem thought to be posed by ambiguity for truth theoretical semantics. In addition, the best-known test for ambiguity, namely the test by contradiction, is set out, its limitations discussed, and its connection with ambiguity's definition explained. The text is contrasted with a test for vagueness first proposed by Peirce and a test for generality propounded by Margalit.

GILLON, Brendan S and HAYES, Richard P. Introduction to Dharmakirti's Theory of Inference as Presented in *Pramānavārttika Svopajñavrtti* 1-10. J Indian Phil, 19(1), 1-73, Mr 91.

GILLON, Brendan. "Bare Plurals as Plural Indefinite Noun Phrases" in *Knowledge Representation and Defeasible Reasoning*, KYBURG JR, Henry E (ed), 119-166. Norwell, Kluwer, 1990.

Bare plurals in English (e.g., "dogs") are liable to a range of construals, ranging from existential-like ones, as in "Dogs are on the lawn," to universal-like ones, as in "Dogs are mammals." It is argued that these noun phrases are the plural counterparts of singular indefinite noun phrases (i.e., noun phrases whose determiner is the indefinite article). The literal interpretation of such phrases results from the semantics of the indefinite article and the semantics of grammatical number, both of which are presented in the paper. The universal-like construal, it is maintained, is to be accounted for by pragmatic principles.

GILMAN, Daniel. Observation: An Empirical Discussion. Proc Phil Sci Ass, 1, 355-364, 1990.

Various claims for theory-laden perception have involved empirical as well as conceptual considerations. Thomas Kuhn cites New Look psychological research in discussing the role of a paradigm in perception (1970) and Paul Churchland (1988) appeals to biological evidence, as well as New Look sources similar to Kuhn's. This paper offers a critical examination of the empirical evidence cited by Kuhn and Churchland, including a look at the underlying experimental work. It also offers a comment on the application of such evidence in a naturalized epistemology.

GILSON, Etienne. "Remarks on Experience in Metaphysics" in *Thomistic Papers, V*, RUSSMAN, Thomas A (ed), 40-48. Notre Dame, Univ Notre Dame Pr, 1990.

GINET, Carl. "Reasons Explanation of Action: An Incompatibilist Account" in *Philosophical Perspectives, 3: Philosophy of Mind and Action Theory, 1989*, TOMBERLIN, James E (ed), 17-46. Atascadero, Ridgeview, 1989.

This rebuts two arguments against incompatibilism. The first, that one cannot determine (choose) an undetermined action, is rebutted by claiming that to determine an event is to act in a way that makes it the case that the event occurs and, therefore, determining one's own action requires only one's performing it. The second, that an undetermined action can have no explanation in terms of the agent's reasons, is rebutted by giving, for each of several sorts of reasons explanation, a sufficient condition for the explanation that is obviously compatible with the action's not being nomically necessitated by its antecedents.

GINGRAS, Yves and NIOSI, Jorge. "Technology and Society: A View from Sociology" in *Studies on Mario Bunge's "Treatise"*, WEINGARTNER, Paul (ed), 421-430. Amsterdam, Rodopi, 1990.

In his work on the philosophy of technology, Mario Bunge presents a view on the nature of science and technology and on their relations. Bunge also addresses the question of the relations between technology, economics and society. The aim of our paper is to compare his views with those coming out of recent research in sociology of science and technology and the economics of R-D. We conclude that Bunge's approach is too static and not sensitive enough to the historically changing relationships between science and technology as well as to the changing conceptions of science itself between the 16th and 20th century.

GINSBERG, Robert. "Experiencing the Death of Humanity" in *Issues in War and Peace: Philosophical Inquiries*, KUNKEL, Joseph (ed), 179-187. Wolfeboro, Longwood, 1989.

Intellectually we may grasp the complete destruction of humanity by nuclear war means, but we may also blunt the force of that meaning by rationalizations. Evasion and denial function in our addiction to weapons of mass destruction just as they do when individuals are addicted to life-threatening substances. We have strategies for intervention that shock addicts into experiencing their own threatened life. So too we need to bring humanity everywhere to experience its total extinction before it happens. Hope and despair are analyzed as consequences of the experience.

GINZBERG, Ruth. "Philosophy Is Not a Luxury" in *Feminist Ethics*, CARD, Claudia (ed), 126-145. Lawrence, Univ Pr of Kansas, 1991.

Survival can serve as a foundation for non-Eurocentric, non-androcentric moral theory, but only after abandoning radically individualistic, radically androcentric, Enlightenment concepts of the self. Feminist conceptions of the erotic, such as those articulated by Audre Lorde, define a new set of boundaries between self and community for an emerging feminist ethical paradigm in which such foundationalism is possible. What becomes clear is that philosophy can be no mere leisure pastime, intended only for those whose survival already is assured. Important philosophical insights emerge only when all, including those whose survival is not yet assured, are able to theorize the future.

GIRGENTI, Giuseppe. Giustino Martire, il primo platonico cristiano. Riv Filosof Neo-Scolas, 82(2-3), 214-255, Ap-S 90.

GITIK, Moti. The Strength of the Failure of the Singular Cardinal Hypothesis. Annals Pure Applied Log, 51(3), 215-240, Mr 91.

GIUNTI, Marco. Hattiangadi's Theory of Scientific Problems and the Structure of Standard Epistemologies. Brit J Phil Sci, 39(4), 421-439, D 88.

GJELSVIK, Olav. Dretske on Knowledge and Content. Synthese, 86(3), 425-441, Mr 91.

In this paper I discuss Fred Dretske's account of knowledge critically, and try to bring out how his account of informational content leads to cases of extreme epistemic good luck in his treatment of knowledge. My main interest, however, is to establish that the cases of epistemic luck arise because Dretske's account of knowledge in a fundamental way fails to take into account the role our actual recognitional capacities and powers of discrimination play in perceptually based knowledge. This result is, I believe, new. The paper has three sections. In Section 1 I give a short exposition of Dretske's theory and make some necessary qualifications about how it is to be understood. In Section 2 I discuss in greater detail how the theory actually works and provide some examples I think are very troublesome for Dretske. In Section 3 I argue that these cases establish my main claim. I also show that there are cases of epistemic bad luck due to Dretske's account of how information causes belief.

GLASS, J C and JOHNSON, W. Metaphysics, MSRP and Economics. Brit J Phil Sci, 39(3), 313-329, S 88.

Lakatos's MSRP is utilized to provide a response to Koertge's claim (in her 'Does Social Science Really Need Metaphysics?') that the heuristic significance of metaphysics has been vastly overrated. By outlining the hard cores and positive heuristics of the two major research programs in economics (the 'orthodox' and 'Marxist'), the respective metaphysics are shown to be non-vague and to exert an important regulative influence on theories and economy policy recommendations. The paper also shows how the adoption of the MSRP method of appraisal in economics would help to protect against the danger of entrenched metaphysical dogmatism with its implications both for economic policy recommendations and for moral and political recommendations.

GLASS, Ronald David. Disarming the Baby with the Gun: Reply to Audrey Thompson. Proc Phil Educ, 46, 250-253, 1990.

The paper argues that Audrey Thompson (in "The Baby with a Gun: A Feminist Inquiry into Plausibility, Certainty, and Context in Moral Education") misconstrues the issue of plausibility in moral dilemma examples, overlooks critical considerations concerning certainty in moral decision procedures, and falls short with her call for moral education to attend to the complex contextual features of moral situations. The paper argues that the concept of plausibility simply fails to capture morally salient features of situations, that we must have sufficient certainty in moral deliberations to resolve decisions in order to act, and that a moral education which fails to prepare people to take courageous moral action fails as moral education.

GLEASON, Gregory. Lenin, Gorbachev, and 'National-Statehood': Can Leninism Countenance the New Soviet Federal Order? Stud Soviet Tho, 40(1-3), 137-158, 1990.

One of the most intractable contemporary problems in the USSR is the Soviet federal dilemma. The late 1980s witnessed competing claims among the national minority groups of the USSR to rights of voice, representation, and cultural, economic, and even political sovereignty. Since the onset of *perestrojka*, the principle of 'national-statehood' has acquired a new legitimacy. Nationality is one of the pillars of the federal reform. The drive to create a 'new Soviet federalism' has become an important component of *perestrojka*. But, according to Leninist doctrine, the 'nation' is a transitional formation. Unless there is a significant departure from Leninist theory, the new acknowledgement of the 'rights of nations' in the USSR can only be a political—and thus temporary—concession. (edited)

GLEB, Gary. The Trouble With Goldman's Reliabilism. Austl J Phil, 68(4), 382-394, D 90.

GLEZER, Vadim D. "Vision and Mind" in *Logic, Methodology and Philosophy of Science, VIII*, FENSTAD, J E (ed), 517-527. New York, Elsevier Science, 1989.

GLIDDEN, David K. From Pyrrhonism to Post-Modernism. Ancient Phil, 10(2), 263-267, Fall 90.

GLOUBERMAN, M. Transcendental Idealism: The Dialectical Dimension. Dialectica, 45(1), 31-45, 1991.

Left wing interpreters of Kant's transcendental idealism argue that the doctrine must be exercised in order to disclose the viable philosophical content of the first *Critique*. For right wing interpreters, this leaves a Hamlet without the prince. I chart and defend a middle path. Transcendental idealism, while essential to Kant's position, renders that position philosophically indefensible. Constant misinterpretations of the doctrine results from a failure to appreciate the inter-theoretic (i.e., dialectical) relations between Kant's conceptualisation of sense-involving experience and the output of (what I call) 'Cartesian theory of error'.

GLOUBERMAN, Mark. Berkeley's Anti-Abstractionism: Reply to Moked. Iyyun, 40(3), 315-318, Jl 91.

In 'Berkeley's Anti-Abstractionism' (*Iyyun*, 40 (1), 1991) I reconstructed Berkeley's denial of abstract ideas as an attempt to repair an instability in Descartes's treatment of cognitive error: Berkeley denies that categorially erroneous representations of things have a status in cognition on a par with categorially correct ones. Gabriel Moked objects that *any* distinction having cognitive status is, for Berkeley, real. But this is ambiguous. To say that some distinction is real can be to say either that we make it, or that the items distinguished are really distinct. Again, then, Berkeley denies, what Descartes allows, that distinctions real in the first but not the second sense have a cognitive—'ideational'—status.

GLOUBERMAN, Mark. Berkeley's Cartesian Anti-Abstractionism. Iyyun, 40(1), 51-64, Ja 91.

In one central strand, Berkeley's anti-abstractionism is the denial that the metaphysically impossible can be cognitively represented: there are no abstract *ideas*. While the thesis is often interpreted by reference to empiricist assumptions, I reconstruct it as an attempt to overcome a structural problem which affects a Cartesian like Descartes for admitting the cognitive reality of *distinctiones rationis*. By assigning a purely verbal reality to the metaphysically impossible, Berkeley overcomes a severe Cartesian difficulty of distinguishing the clear and distinct from the unclear and indistinct. But the "solution", though internally consistent, is implausible relative to the data.

GLOUBERMAN, Mark. Certainty, the Cogito, and Cartesian Dualism. Stud Leibniz, 22(2), 123-137, 1990.

Arguably, Descartes accepted the mind/body split because of the resistance, at that time, of psychological phenomena to mechanistic-materialistic treatment. But what of the reasoning for dualism? Relative to a theoretical problem with the *cogito*-argument, I show that the case for dualism in the *Meditations* is flawed. *'Sum'* is deduced from *'cogito'*. Why then is the former said to be the first certainty? While, as I explain, *'cogito'* is clear but indistinct, *'sum'* is both clear and distinct—and for that reason qualifies. But the distinction of *'sum'* is of a special variety, and Descartes's subsequent case for the subject's immateriality fails because of an ambiguity. Cartesianism without dualism is not therefore a circle without a center.

GLOUBERMAN, Mark. Kant's Diversity Theory: A Dissenting View. Hist Phil Quart, 7(4), 461-474, O 90.

Contrary to the prevailing view that Kant, in sharply distinguishing sense from intellect, is the first to get the structure of experiential cognition aright, I show that Kant is reverting to a position deliberately rejected by his (Cartesian) predecessors. The sense/intellect issue reprises an older issue about matter and form. The issue is not dead yet—and certainly has not been decided in Kant's favour. Recent developments in fractal mathematics enable the question of reduction to be re-raised in a fashion that identifies a possibility that all the historical principals overlooked, viz., that of irrational form.

GLOVER, Jacqueline and LYNN, Joanne. Cruzan and Caring for Others. Hastings Center Rep, 20(5), 10-11, S-O 90.

This response to the policy issues decided by the U S Supreme Court's opinion in *Cruzan* aims to illuminate the folly of creating barriers to good decision-making about whether or not to use life-sustaining medical treatment and to encourage health care providers to care for their patients by advocating changes in such legal restrictions. Cruzan's positive contributions are noted, but the practical problems of excluding family views and allowing the states to insist upon a high standard of proof before relying on the patient's prior decisions are serious shortcomings of the ruling.

GLOY, Karen. Der Begriff des Selbstbewusstseins bei Kant. Deut Z Phil, 39(3), 255-261, 1991.

The essay is concerned with Kant's theory of selfconsciousness under three aspects: 1) The problem of self-reference, i.e. the aporetic structure of identifying someone as oneself. 2) The problem of self-knowledge. The point in question is whether the knowledge which the *Critique of Pure Reason* is claiming to be is possible. 3) The problem of the egological structures of consciousness at all. This is the main topic of the essay. After discussing Kant's arguments three alternative models are mentioned, the behaviouristical one (Strawson, Tugendhat), the transcendental-pragmatic one (Apel) and the quantum theoretical one (Ey).

GLOY, Karen. Hegels Geschichtsphilosophie im Vergleich mit anderen Geschichtskonzeptionen. Deut Z Phil, 39(1), 1-11, 1991.

GLOY, Karen. Plato, the History of Science and Our Understanding of Nature (in German). Deut Z Phil, 38(7), 651-659, 1990.

The contemporary discussion on nature between the ecological point of view and the opposite position, which insists on the scientific-technical progress, is based on two contrary conceptual frameworks, the holistic and the mathematical one. The essay points out that both of them, the last one subordinated to the first one, are included in Plato's concept of nature, set forth in his *Timaeus*. In reconstructing his concept of nature as a system it becomes obvious that it involves many difficulties, which are reappearing in contemporary controversies: whereas the holistic component includes inclusiveness, the mathematical one tends to endlessness.

GLUCHOWSKI, Gerard. Philosophical Culture in the Warsaw-Lvov School (in Polish). Ann Univ Mariae Curie-Phil, 10, 65-79, 1985.

In Polish philosophical literature there has not so far appeared a study developing a conception of philosophical culture which persisted among Polish philosophers in the interwar period. This conception was connected with the concept of logical culture and had the same origin. It therefore derived from the Warsaw-Lvov school and was propagated by its continuators. Similarly to logical culture, the conception of philosophical culture can be characterized by distinguishing in it theoretical and practical aspects. The concept of philosophical culture indicates certain features which should characterize a propagator of secular culture. These features include a rationalistic attitude to various opinions and an ability to perform a general synthesis combined with the principle of tolerance. (edited)

GLUCK, John P and KUBACKI, Steven R. Animals in Biomedical Research: The Undermining Effect of the Rhetoric of the Besieged. Ethics Behavior, 1(3), 157-173, 1991.

It is correctly asserted that the intensity of the current debate over the use of animals in biomedical research is unprecedented. The extent of expressed animosity and distrust has stunned many researchers. In response, researchers have tended to take a strategic defensive posture, which involves the assertion of several abstract positions that serve to obstruct resolution of the debate. Those abstractions include the notions that the animal protection movement is trivial and purely anti-intellectual in scope, that all science is good (and some especially so), and the belief that an ethical consensus can never really be reached between the parties.

GLYMOUR, Clark and KELLY, Kevin. Getting to the Truth Through Conceptual Revolutions. Proc Phil Sci Ass, 1, 89-96, 1990.

There is a popular view that the alleged meaning shifts resulting from scientific revolutions are somehow incompatible with the formulation of general norms for scientific inquiry. We construct methods that can be shown to be maximally reliable at getting to the truth when the truth changes in response to the state of the scientist or his society.

GLYMOUR, Clark. "Philosophy and the Academy" in *Acting and Reflecting: The Interdisciplinary Turn in Philosophy*, SIEG, Wilfried (ed), 63-71. Norwell, Kluwer, 1990.

GLYMOUR, Clark and SPIRTES, Peter and SCHEINES, Richard. "The Tetrad Project" in *Acting and Reflecting: The Interdisciplinary Turn in Philosophy*, SIEG, Wilfried (ed), 183-207. Norwell, Kluwer, 1990.

GLYNN, Simon. The De-Con-Struction of Reason. Man World, 24(3), 311-320, Jl 91.

If it is to avoid regress, reason cannot be self justifying, while in light of the breakdown of the synthetic/analytic distinction, and concomitantly of a thoroughgoing separation between experience and reason, or perception and conception, experience cannot provide an independent source of justification. Consequently, reason, and the laws of logic, are arguably simply conventional, pragmatic utility being the justification of such conventions. This thesis is underlined by the fact that, as Bohr's Complimentarity/Wavicle and Einstein's Time Dilation/Twin's Paradox demonstrate, the laws of logic can be, and regularly are, suspended when it is pragmatic to do so.

GLYNN, Simon. "The Dynamics of Alternative Realities" in *Reconsidering Psychology: Perspectives from Continental Philosophy*, FAULCONER, James E (ed), 175-197. Pittsburgh, Duquesne Univ Pr, 1990.

Detailed empirical evidence and analysis is deployed to argue that both our perceptual experience and conceptual understanding of reality is structured by and thus dependent upon socio-culturally normative preconceptions. The paper proceeds to examine the *ways* in which alternative constructions of reality, and those who hold them, are marginalized as stupid, bad, or most significantly for psychology, mad, and to point out the role played by the socio-political-economic power elite of the culture in controlling "reality construction." Consequently it is argued that pragmatic constructions, empowering as they do those who uphold them, stand the greatest chance of long-term survival.

GODLOVITCH, A. Artists, Computer Programs and Performance. Austl J Phil, 68(3), 301-312, S 90.

GODLOVITCH, S. Boors and Bumpkins, Snobs and Snoots. J Aes Educ, 24(2), 65-73, Sum 90.

GODLOVITCH, Stan. Music Performance and the Tools of the Trade. Iyyun, 39(3), 321-338, Jl 90.

Are the instruments of music the tools of the musician? If so, they are subject to the constraints attached to any functional items. But truly functional items are replaced if improvements exist. Traditional instruments are not the best means to achieve musical ends. Synthesizers are functionally superior. Musicians do not flock en bloc to synthesizers. Why not? Because the essence of musicianship involves victory over deliberate adversity.

GOERDT, Wilhelm. *Russische Philosophie*. Freiburg, Alber, 1991.

This book uses texts to document the history and current state of Russian philosophy and theology, as well as Soviet philosophy from about 1750 up to the present time. These texts are augmented by extensive notes and commentaries which provide further biographical and bibliographical material on individual philosophers and traditions. The book's detailed subject index is at the same time a prelude to a dictionary of Russian philosophical terminology. Goerdt's introduction outlines and analyses the most recent developments in Soviet philosophy, in the period since Gorbachev's coming to office. Together with the reference and descriptive work on "Russian Philosophy: Approaches and Perspectives" (1984), this volume forms a uniquely comprehensive international compendium which makes possible the reader's own independent introduction to Russian thought and its critical examination.

GOERNER, E A. Response to Hall's "Goerner on Thomistic Natural Law". Polit Theory, 18(4), 650-655, N 90.

GOETHALS, Susanne C. Nietzsche's Case for Inequality. Dialogue (PST), 33(1), 32-40, O 90.

My discussion in this paper is aimed at laying out the main tenets of Nietzsche's thought in a clear, coherent structure. Among the various categories discussed are epistemology, the will to power as a first principle, his moral genealogy and critique of Christianity, and the ramifications of these for the idea of human equality. Included also is a discussion of Nietzsche's method of inquiry and writing style, and how these themselves are revelatory of his thought.

GOGGANS, Phil. Epistemic Obligations and Doxastic Voluntarism. Analysis, 51(2), 102-105, Mr 91.

Deontologists about epistemic justification believe we have obligations to believe, disbelieve, and withhold belief. Such epistemic obligations seem to presuppose that we have voluntary control over our beliefs, which seems unlikely. In response to this objection, Richard Feldman and Paul Moser have argued separately that *epistemic* obligations do not presuppose doxastic voluntariness. This response fails, since the only plausible way of distinguishing obligations from purely valuative norms involves taking the former to imply the accountability of those subject to them, which in turn implies the subject's ability to control whether he fulfills or violates the obligation.

GOGGI, Gianluigi. "Uguaglianza, riconoscimento del simile e principio d'autorità nell'ultimo Diderot" in *Égalité Uguaglianza*, FERRARI, Jean (ed), 35-46. Napoli, Liguori, 1990.

GÖHLER, Gerhard. New Studies on Hegel's Philosophy of Law, versus on the Dialectics of Hegel and Marx (in Hungarian). Magyar Filozof Szemle, 1-2, 140-175, 1990.

GOICOECHEA, David (ed) and LUIK, John (ed) and MADIGAN, Tim (ed). *The Question of Humanism: Challenges and Possibilities*. Buffalo, Prometheus, 1991.

This volume of twenty-three papers on the ironies and ambiguities of humanism raises questions about: *The Varieties of Humanism, The Challenges to Humanism* and *The Enigmas of Humanism*. It is intended to be an introductory text for first-year philosophy students that they might not get oversimplified notions of humanism. Its conclusions form themselves in each reader as new beginnings for thinking, as such thinkers as: Plato, Aulus Gellius, Augustine, Pico, Kant, Heidegger, Foucault and Kurtz are allowed to dialogue.

GOICOECHEA, David. "Zarathustra and Enlightenment Humanism" in *The Question of Humanism: Challenges and Possibilities*, GOICOECHEA, David (ed), 170-178. Buffalo, Prometheus, 1991.

This paper examines the reasons for Zarathustra's transformation from enlightenment humanism to romanticism to postmodernism. As Zarathustra moves from lion to lioness to child the enlightenment arguments against the camel of Christian Platonism are alluded to and then it is seen why the no saying freedom of the humanist is deluded. Only the yes saying of the child is a creativity credible prelude in this age of the ethics of joy.

GOLAB-MEYER, Zofia. The Foundation of the Ability to Reach Conclusions—The Empirical Basis of Logic. Thinking, 9(3), 43-45, 1990.

GOLASZEWSKA, Maria. "The New Anti-Aestheticism" in *XIth International Congress in Aesthetics, Nottingham 1988*, WOODFIELD, Richard (ed), 70-73. Nottingham, Nottingham Polytech, 1990.

Art underwent such a great shock in the middle of the century that it caused the rift between Art and Anti-Art. The most extreme artistic antiaesthetism is Conceptual Art. In place of value categories such as beauty etc. Kossuth promoted the value of the relationship between a real object, its representation and its definition. Great Avant-Garde led up to the origin of a new aesthetic situation: artists organize "actions" instead of producing works of art, the works of art cease to be important (e.g., objects to be thrown away), the border-line between the maker and the recipient disappears, aesthetic values are not imparted directly by the work, but are to be looked for by perceivers, co-created by them.

GOLDBLATT, Robert. "First-Order Spacetime Geometry" in *Logic, Methodology and Philosophy of Science, VIII*, FENSTAD, J E (ed), 303-316. New York, Elsevier Science, 1989.

GOLDEN, James L and JAMISON, David L. Meyer's Theory of Problematology. Rev Int Phil, 44(174), 329-351, 1990.

GOLDENBAUM, Ursula. The Object and the Concept: Spinoza's Theory with Regard to the Development of Modern Natural Science (in German). Deut Z Phil, 38(8), 724-732, 1990.

GOLDFARB, Robert S and BOULIER, Bryan L. Pisces Economicus: The Fish as Econontic Man. Econ Phil, 7(1), 83-86, Ap 91.

GOLDFORD, Dennis. Interpretation and the Social Reality of Law. Soc Epistem, 5(1), 6-15, Ja-Mr 91.

Behavioral approaches to law fail to account for its character as an essentially argumentative practice which is simultaneously text and action both, for they presuppose a distinction between the empirical and objective, which pertain to action, and the normative and the subjective, which pertain to language and texts. Jurisprudence thereby becomes purely normative and remains external to empirical description and explanation of legal practice. In contrast, the interpretive approach conceives law as a social "synthetic-apriori" which undercuts the conventional normative-empirical dichotomy. Jurisprudence thus becomes fundamental to the description and explanation of ordinary political phenomena because law and constitutional forms comprise the synthetic-apriori structure of such phenomena.

GOLDING, Joshua L. Toward a Pragmatic Conception of Religious Faith. Faith Phil, 7(4), 486-503, O 90.

One issue in the debate about faith concerns the stance a religious person is committed to take on "God exists." I argue that this stance is best understood as an assumption that God exists for the purpose of pursuing a good relationship with God. The notion of an "assumption for practical purpose" is distinguished from notions such as "belief" and "hope." This stance is contrasted with others found in discussions of faith, and its ramifications for the problem of whether it is rational to have faith are discussed.

GOLDING, Martin P. The Significance of Rights Language. Phil Topics, 18(1), 53-64, Spr 90.

Using examples from legal and philosophical tests, this paper (historically and analytical) examines whether the introduction of the terminology of "rights" makes a distinctive contribution to moral discourse and what its limitations are. Part of the discussion considers A I Melden's book, *Rights in Human Lives* (1988), which argues that the introduction of rights language into popular moral discourse is an indication of moral progress. Some difficulties are raised for Melden's position by an examination of various forms of dispute settlement and the sorts of normative language appropriate to these forms.

GOLDMAN, Alan H and GOLDMAN, Michael N. Paternalistic Laws. Phil Topics, 18(1), 65-78, Spr 90.

Our dual thesis is that while only soft paternalism (overriding choices only if not truly voluntary) can be justified for private individuals interfering with actions of other individuals, society may need to exceed this limit when applying its laws to minorities with eccentric preferences. In these cases paternalistic laws can be justified if they remain soft to the majority and do not prove to be a major imposition on the minority, although restraining their voluntary choices.

GOLDMAN, Alan H. Skepticism About Goodness and Rightness. S J Phil, SUPP 29, 167-183, 1990.

GOLDMAN, Alvin I and SHAKED, Moshe. An Economic Model of Scientific Activity and Truth Acquisition. Phil Stud, 63(1), 31-55, Jl 91.

GOLDMAN, Alvin I. Epistemic Paternalism: Communication Control in Law and Society. J Phil, 88(3), 113-131, Mr 91.

Epistemic paternalism is the withholding of evidence from cognitive agents with an eye to their epistemic good, in particular, their acquisition of truth. Judges exclude items of evidence from juries; educational personnel neglect certain viewpoints in the classroom; and government agencies impose constraints on commercial speech. When do paternalistic practices promote true belief? Some relevant variables are discussed, such as the controller's expertise and the cognitive shortcomings of the audience. Other topics include expert identifiability, the role of extra-epistemic factors, and the institutional layering of regulation and deregulation in science and scholarship.

GOLDMAN, Alvin I. Stephen P Stich, "The Fragmentation of Reason". Phil Phenomenol Res, 51(1), 189-193, Mr 91.

GOLDMAN, Alvin. Social Epistemics and Social Psychology. Soc Epistem, 5(2), 121-125, Ap-Je 91.

GOLDMAN, Michael N and GOLDMAN, Alan H. Paternalistic Laws. Phil Topics, 18(1), 65-78, Spr 90.

Our dual thesis is that while only soft paternalism (overriding choices only if not truly voluntary) can be justified for private individuals interfering with actions of other individuals, society may need to exceed this limit when applying its laws to minorities with eccentric preferences. In these cases paternalistic laws can be justified if they remain soft to the majority and do not prove to be a major imposition on the minority, although restraining their voluntary choices.

GOLDSTEIN, Jared. Desperately Seeking Science: The Creation of Knowledge in Family Practice. Hastings Center Rep, 20(6), 26-32, N-D 90.

Physicians long for the comfort of a predictable structure in the clinical encounter, and are taught to seek it in a model of the scientific method that has elsewhere been discarded. But the course of a typical medical office visit is actually dependent upon a nondeterministic process of negotiation between patient and physician. A poststructuralist interpretive model is provided to highlight the difficulties inherent in a positivistic approach to patient evaluation. The clinical encounter may be considered to have had a successful outcome when the diagnostic process is in itself a therapeutic intervention.

GOLDSTEIN, Leon J. The Idea of History as a Scale of Forms. Hist Theor, 29(4), 42-50, D 90.

In Collingwood's *Essay on Philosophical Method* he offers what purports to be an account of philosophical concepts which he takes to be scales of forms of overlapping classes. The concept has a generic essence which is subject to change in degree, each such change resulting in a change in kind. Collingwood is mistaken in thinking he has offered an account of philosophical concepts, for what he says is true of open concepts—not sharply defined—philosophical or otherwise. The paper attempts to show that Collingwood's conception of history-as-inquiry is such an open concept and that his account of it in *The Idea of History* satisfies the characterization of "philosophical" concept in the earlier book.

GOLDSTERN, M and SHELAH, S. Ramsey Ultrafilters and the Reaping Number—Con($r < u$). Annals Pure Applied Log, 49(2), 121-142, O 90.

We show that it is consistent that the reaping number r is less than u, the size of the smallest base for an ultrafilter. To show that our forcing preserves certain ultrafilters, we prove a general partition theorem involving Ramsey ideals.

GOLDSTICK, D. Could God Make a Contradiction True? Relig Stud, 26(3), 377-387, S 90.

Descartes (rightly) insisted omnipotence entailed a capability even for the logically impossible—though its nonrealization was certain. An empiricist objection calls talk of such feats senseless (truthvalueless) because inconsistent, but aren't logically necessary truths often establishable inductively also, suggesting "truth"'s univocity? The translinguistic intelligibility of both logical rules and their infractions suggests it also. "Impossibility" is ambiguous, as what is perfectly achievable may yet have zero probability of realization because unwilled (like divine misbehaviour). If a divine wish existed for something logically impossible to occur, it would; not even (arguable) inconsistency of the protasis could invalidate/trivialize this subjective conditional.

GOLDSTICK, D. Distributive Justice and Utility. J Value Inq, 25(1), 65-71, Ja 91.

There is an "intuitive" case against utilitarianism deriving from the deontological requirements of *equality*. A not uncommon countermove, even for act-utilitarianism, seeks to neutralize that objection by citing the utility-maximizing character of those very "intuitions" in view of the known facts of sociology and psychology. Under scrutiny, such distributive-justice "intuitions" tend to lose their independent appeal. Just what should we be motivated to *equalize*—people's welfare, their share of resources, the marginal utility of their resources, or what? Utility maximization provides the only plausible criterion for deciding.

GOLDSTICK, Danny. "The 'Humanism' and the Humanism of Karl Marx" in *The Question of Humanism: Challenges and Possibilities*, GOICOECHEA, David (ed), 150-161. Buffalo, Prometheus, 1991.

Marx always regarded capitalism as inhumane. But in some early writings, under the influence of Feuerbach and of "true socialism", he used the very word "humanism" to favour a "moral" over a "communistic" class approach. "Alienation" under capitalism was especially people's estrangement from their human nature, he considered. In 1845, however, he changed his mind and viewed human nature as historically variable, and he even deprecated the idea of basing the normative upon the (currently) normal as being objectionably conservative.

GOLINSKI, Jan. "Hélène Metzger et l'interprétation de la chimie du XVIIe siècle" in *Études sur/Studies on Hélène Metzger*, FREUDENTHAL, Gad , 85-98. Leiden, Brill, 1990.

GOLOMB, Jacob. Nietzsche on Authenticity. Phil Today, 34(3), 243-258, Fall 90.

This article discusses Nietzsche's notion of authenticity (*Wahrhaftigkeit*) as opposed to *Wahrheit* and also its relation to the "Death of God". The primary model for authenticity is that of artistic creation rather than of biology. The object: an allurement (*Versuchung*) to authentic pathos = the positive 'Power' of the *Ubermensch* as opposed to negative (inauthentic) 'Power' of the 'Slave'. The freezing tactics, the geneaological and 'unmasking' methods and the theory of perspectives for enticing the reader to attain authenticity. How is it at all possible within the social context? One of the conclusions: authenticity is a regulative and corrective ideal rather than a viable norm.

GOLUBOVIC, Zagorka. A Marxist Approach to the Concept of Being/Becoming Human. Dialec Hum, 16(3-4), 65-84, Sum-Autumn 89.

A reassessment of Marx's key concepts on being/becoming human is offered in light of new philosophical/anthropological thinking. Instead of avoiding philosophical questions it is shown why it is necessary to reconsider "human nature" in terms of a continuity of human existence/experiences, of a universal expression of community life and specific human needs and their satisfaction within varieties of cultures. And also to reaffirm the concept of "history" in terms of a unique human sense of temporality and continuous/cumulative creation, i.e., as a continuation of "historical praxis," adding to this a new elaboration of the dialectics of praxis and alienation in terms of reaffirmation of critical theory of society.

GOMBOCZ, Wolfgang L (ed) and BRANDL, Johannes (ed). *The Mind of Donald Davidson*. Amsterdam, Rodopi, 1989.

The fifteen papers in this volume present and discuss Davidson's views on truth, interpretation, and intentional action with special emphasis on their integration in a conception of mind based on the triangle of speaker, interpreter, and shared world. This conception is explained and defended in two original contributions by Donald Davidson. Other contributors deal with the token-identity theory, causal explanation, semantic paradoxes, indirect discourse, the building block theory of language, assertion and convention, metaphor, the third dogma of empiricism, ontological relativity, and externalism with respect to mental content.

GÓMEZ ROBLEDO, Antonio. La democracia ateniense. Dianoia, 36(36), 61-71, 1990.

GÓMEZ-MORIANA, Antonio. Pragmatique du discours et réciprocité de perspectives (A propos de Don Quichotte et Don Juan). Horiz Phil, 1(1), 143-162, 1990.

GÓMEZ-MULLER, Alfredo. La imagen del indígena en el pensamiento colombiano del siglo XIX: La perspectiva de J M Samper. Logos (Mexico), 19(56), 21-49, My-Ag 91.

The ruling elite who undertook construction of the Columbia nation in the 19th century were the heirs of an ideological discourse on race that traced its roots to the symbolico-cultural representations of the Spanish colonial world. These representations, articulated around the myth of white superiority, founded a logic of exclusion which profoundly distorted the meaning of the first republican project. J M Samper elaborated a "theory" of race which established the principle of a conception of government as a "tutorship" of whites over non-whites.

GOMILA, Antoni. Peirce and Evolution: Comment on O'Hear. Inquiry, 33(4), 447-452, D 90.

After stressing the shortcomings of Darwinian accounts of self-consciousness and knowledge—i.e., in terms of their survival value—Anthony O'Hear presents Peirce's metaphysical hypotheses on cosmic evolution as an alternative approach that avoids those shortcomings. Although O'Hear does not straightforwardly defend Peirce's views, his argument suggests that only some teleological account of self-consciousness and knowledge is reasonable. The argument, though correct, is not enough to establish the metaphysical point O'Hear defends. Before developing his metaphysical ideas, Peirce's rejection of natural selection as an explanation for every phenomenon brought him to consider the more appropriate question of how natural selection could give rise to a different kind of evolution. This involved outlining an evolutionary account of the origin of self-consciousness and of the mechanisms of belief fixation. The point is not one about Peirce, of course, but about the relationship between, on the one hand, biological and, on the other, psychological and cultural phenomena.

GONÇALVES, Joaquim Cerqueira. "Filosofia e hermenêutica" in *Dinâmica do Pensar: Homenagem a Oswaldo Market*, FAC LETRAS UNIV LISBOA (ed), 127-131. Lisboa, Fac Letras U Lisboa, 1991.

La philosophie a un contenu, elle n'est pas seulement attitude critique. On doit cette exigence de contenu surtout a une certaine phénoménologie que l'herméneutique moderne a poursuivi. Dans ce sens, on peut dire que la philosophie est une herméneutique. C'est pour celà que la philosophie n'est pas seulement une méthode de rectification, pour dissiper les incompatibilités entre la pensée et le langage. La philosophie herméneutique est, par contre, construction, poiétique.

GÖNNER, Gerhard. Vom "Wahr-Lachen" der Moderne: Karl Valentins Semantik paradoxer Lebenswelten. Deut Z Phil, 38(12), 1202-1210, 1990.

The above article analyses texts from the literary works of Karl Valentin. It brings into focus his manipulation of everyday language by which he annuls the working of all forms of cognition. Valentin's handling of the 'categories' of space, time and numbers show a characteristic development of modern age. Questioning the reliability of these 'categories' and their workings eventually atomizes the world around us. By making use of Valentin's puns and his playing with language philosophy has the chance to control and criticize the decay of all we took for granted from a cognitive point of view.

GONZÁLEZ CARLOMÁN, Antonio. Grupo de Piaget y estructuras afines. El Basilisco, 4, 12-18, Mr-Ap 90.

Piaget's group INRC is widened to the group that we shall denominate INRCR1C1R2C2 and it will be seen that these two groups form a part of a set of groups which we shall denominate, "involutional groups", whose order is a power of two. Afterwards, relations of equivalence having a number of classes equal to a power of two are studied and it will be shown that a dual step exists between the involutional groups (Piaget's group being one of them), and these relations of equivalence (one of them is Wallon's pairs).

GONZÁLEZ PORTA, Mario A. Análisis de la doctrina ética de las "observaciones sobre lo bello y sublime". Themata, 6, 77-94, 1989.

GONZÁLEZ RECIO, José Luis. Elementos dinámicos de la teoría celular. Rev Filosof (Spain), 4, 83-109, 1990.

In this paper I discuss the applicability of Popper's and Kuhn's methodologies to the gestation and development of the Cell Theory. It is not difficult to verify that external history would result insufficient to explain the conformation of cytology as a science. However, it is easy to prove, at the same time, that Popper could not present himself as a good "biographer" of Schleiden's and Schwann's theory. Finally I conclude that Lakatos's scheme on research processes simulates, much better than those of Kuhn or Popper the genesis and the progressive consolidation of this branch of biology.

GONZÁLEZ, Carlos G. The Union Axiom in Zermelo Set Theory. Z Math Log, 36(4), 281-284, 1990.

GONZÁLEZ, José Emilio. La "Moral Social" de Eugenio María de Hostos. Dialogos, 26(57), 7-33, Ja 91.

GONZÁLEZ, Orestes J. Tomás de Aquino: la aprehensión del acto de ser (II). Anu Filosof, 24(1), 139-151, 1991.

From explicit pronouncements in the writings of Aquinas, this article elaborates on how the apprehension of the act of being is accomplished in the human intellect trough its natural habit, the *intellectus principiorum*. The basic conclusion states that direct (non discursive) reception of truth is implied in the apprehension of the actuality of extramental things.

GONZÁLEZ, Wenceslao J (ed). *Aspectos Metodológicos de la Investigación Científica*. Murcia, Univ de Murcia, 1990.

GONZALEZ, Wenceslao J. Intuitionistic Mathematics and Wittgenstein. Hist Phil Log, 12(2), 167-183, 1991.

The relation between Wittgenstein's philosophy of mathematics and mathematical intuitionism has raised a considerable debate. My attempt is to analyze if there is a commitment in Wittgenstein to themes characteristic of the intuitionist movement in mathematics and if that commitment is one important strain that runs through his *Remarks on the Foundations of Mathematics*. The intuitionistic themes to analyze in his philosophy of mathematics are: firstly, his attacks on the unrestricted use of the Law of Excluded Middle; secondly, his distrust of non-constructive *proofs*; and thirdly, his impatience with the idea that mathematics stands in need of a *foundation*. These elements are Fogelin's starting point for the systematic reconstruction of Wittgenstein's conception of mathematics.

GOOD, I J. "The Interface Between Statistics and the Philosophy of Science" in *Logic, Methodology and Philosophy of Science, VIII*, FENSTAD, J E (ed), 393-411. New York, Elsevier Science, 1989.

Many points of contact and mutual influences between statistics and philosophy of science are reviewed. Some of the topics mentioned are kinds of probability, weight of evidence (corroboration) and 'Bayes factors', tail-probabilities (P-values) possibly 'standardized', combination of P-values by a harmonic mean, Bayes/non-Bayes compromises, 'explicativity', induction, probabilistic causality, hierarchical Bayes, and penalized likelihood. A longer version of the work has been published, with discussion, in *Statistical Science*.

GOOD, I J. A Suspicious Feature of the Popper/Miller Argument. Phil Sci, 57(3), 535-536, S 90.

The *form* of argument used by Popper and Miller to attack the concept of probabilistic induction is applied to the slightly different situation in which some evidence *undermines* a hypothesis. The result is seemingly absurd, thus bringing the form of argument under suspicion.

GOODIN, Robert E. Actual Preferences, Actual People. Utilitas, 3(1), 113-119, My 91.

GOODIN, Robert E. Property Rights and Preservationist Duties. Inquiry, 33(4), 401-432, D 90.

The preservationist duties that conservationists would lay upon landowners to protect the natural environment obviously interfere with what those people do with their land. That is often taken to be an equally obvious—albeit possibly justifiable—violation of their rights in that property. But to say that, as landowners often do, would be to imply that property rights somehow embrace a 'right to destroy'. Closer inspection suggests that they do not. That would be a further right, additional to and independent of all the component rights standardly associated with the right to private property. A right to destroy is implicit neither in the concept nor in the justifications of property rights, as they are standardly conceived. Conservationist policies cannot, therefore, properly be opposed on the grounds that they would necessarily violate people's property rights.

GOODIN, Robert E. "Theories of Compensation" in *Liability and Responsibility*, FREY, R G (ed), 257-289. New York, Cambridge Univ Pr, 1991.

GOODIN, Robert E. "Utility and the Good" in *A Companion to Ethics*, SINGER, Peter (ed), 241-248. Cambridge, Blackwell, 1991.

GOODMAN, Nelson. On Capturing Cities. J Aes Educ, 25(1), 5-9, Spr 91.

GOODMAN, Nelson. Retrospections. J Aes Educ, 25(1), 97-98, Spr 91.

GOODMAN, Russell B. *American Philosophy and the Romantic Tradition*. New York, Cambridge Univ Pr, 1991.

I argue that the most substantial and interesting strain of American thought proceeds neither from Puritan theology nor from science, but from a peculiarly American form of Romanticism, with its origins in Europe and its first American instantiation in Ralph Waldo Emerson. The book examines Emerson's epistemology and metaphysics, William James's basic "mode of feeling the whole push," John Dewey's reconstructive poetics, and the development of Stanley Cavell's philosophy. It considers such Romantic issues as the naturalization of the divine, the cognitive role of feeling, and "the marriage of self and world."

GOODMAN, Russell B. East-West Philosophy in Nineteenth-Century America: Emerson and Hinduism. J Hist Ideas, 51(4), 625-645, O-D 90.

Emerson was a philosophical original, transforming everything he touched. Yet, he lived during the first great period of European Sanskrit scholarship, and this paper charts the course of Emerson's confrontation with and use of the ideas made accessible to him in the translations of Jones, Colebrooke, Burnouf, and others. The paper includes discussions of Emerson's undergraduate Prize essay on "Indian Superstition," of his 1938 lecture "Religion," and of such essays as "The Over-Soul," "Experience," and "Culture." It culminates in a discussion of the influence of the *Visnu Purana* on Emerson's "Plato" essay in *Representative Men*.

GOODPASTER, Kenneth E. Business Ethics and Stakeholder Analysis. Bus Ethics Quart, 1(1), 53-73, Ja 91.

Much has been written about stakeholder analysis as a process by which to introduce ethical values into management decision making. This paper takes a critical look at the assumptions behind this idea, in an effort to understand better the meaning of ethical management decisions. A distinction is made between stakeholder analysis and stakeholder synthesis. The two most natural kinds of stakeholder synthesis are then defined and discussed: strategic and multi-fiduciary. Paradoxically, the former appears to yield business without ethics and the latter appears to yield ethics without business. The paper concludes by suggesting that a third approach to stakeholder thinking needs to be developed, one that avoids the paradox just mentioned and that clarifies for managers (and directors) the legitimate role of ethical considerations in decision making.

GOOSEN, D P. Heidegger and Nietzsche—Thinkers of the 'Between'? (in Dutch). S Afr J Phil, 9(3), 140-148, Ag 90.

In this conversation it is argued that a logic of opposition often characterizes the conversation between Heideggerians and Nietzscheans—in spite of the fact that both Heidegger and Nietzsche criticized exclusive oppositions severely. The second part of this conversation consists of a brief discussion of the word 'between' as used by Nietzsche and Heidegger. Instead of dividing reality into opposing oppositions, they ponder the 'between'—the enigmatic space where exclusive oppositions are paralysed and self-assured identity is surrendered to the unrest of nonidentity. With reference to Nietzsche David Krell writes: 'It is Nietzsche's fatality to be both neutral (neither-or) and doubling (both-and), to be *between* the dead and the living, between (père) mort and *la (mère) vivante*, to be both death, *la mort*, and life, *la vie*, during that stretch of time that he himself, Nietzsche, Friedrich, is (was) alive, *le vivant*'. As far as I am concerned the same argument applies to Heidegger. The conclusion is simple: Neither Heidegger nor Nietzsche provides us with grounds in terms of which the one can be protected and the other be cast out oppositionally.

GOOSSENS, Charles. Meaning, Truth Conditions and the Internal Point of View: The Ethical Dilemma. Phil Inq, 11(3-4), 27-45, Sum-Fall 89.

This paper proposes a *via media* between intellectualism and voluntarism in moral philosophy. Central points in this paper are carefully proposed as a hypothesis. The meaning of a normative statement may be identified by giving its truth conditions. Necessary and sufficient truth conditions of normative statements may be found in certain dynamic social phenomena, 'commitments' for short. True normative propositions are true from the internal point of view of such 'commitments'. While these dynamic social phenomena are not or need not be speech acts, they may be universal, so that moral propositions may be both relative to 'commitments' and universal.

GORDILLO, Lourdes. Consideraciones en torno al concepto de verdad según el pragmatismo. Sapientia, 45(176), 141-148, Ap-Je 90.

GORDLEY, James. The Rights of Organizations. Listening, 26(2), 134-144, Spr 91.

GORDON, David. Reply to Chmielewski: Cooperation by Definition. Int Phil Quart, 31(1), 105-108, Mr 91.

GORDON, David. *Resurrecting Marx: The Analytical Marxists on Freedom, Exploitation, and Justice*. New Brunswick, Transaction Books, 1990.

The work of the analytical Marxists—a group of philosophers and economists who seek to reconstruct Marxist theory with the aid of modern developments in analytical philosophy and economics—is given a sustained examination and critique. The charge of the analytical Marxists that capitalism is inherently exploitative and unjust is evaluated and found wanting. The author argues that the analytical Marxists' dismissal of classical Marxism is appropriate, but that they have not constructed a superior theoretical structure to replace it. The analytical Marxists' reformulations of exploitation, theories of value, persons' rights, and market socialism are also considered.

GÖRLICH, Bernard. Freud and the Question of Truth (in Serbo-Croatian). Filozof Istraz, 32-33(5-6), 1663-1676, 1989.

Im Artikel ist von Freuds allgemeiner Auffassung der Funktion wissenschaftlicher Erkenntnis die Rede, aber auch von der Besonderheit, der Eigentümlichkeit des psychoanalytischen Untersuchungs- und Erkenntnisgegenstandes. Die Psychoanalyse steht im Dienste der Veränderung, ein frei schwebendes Erkenntnisinteresse ist ihr völlig fremd. Es werden bestimmte Übereinstimmungen mit Grundzügen einer geschichtsmaterialistischen Erkenntnisstheorie aufgewiesen. Trotzdem bleibt bei der psychoanalytischen Untersuchung eine gewisse Eigentümlichkeit beibehalten. Die Psychoanalyse ist ein therapeutischer Eingriff, sie will nämlich nichts beweisen, sondern nur etwas ändern. Sie beabsichtigt und leistet nichts anderes als die Aufdeckung des Unbewussten im Seelenleben, jenes Unbewussten, dass die Modelle noch nicht realisierter lebenspraktischer Entwürfe enthält.

GORMALLY, M C. "The Ethical Root of Language" in *Logic and Ethics*, GEACH, Peter (ed), 49-70. Norwell, Kluwer, 1991.

GÓRNIAK-KOCIKOWSKA, Krystyna. Dialogue—A New Utopia? Dialec Hum, 16(3-4), 133-146, Sum-Autumn 89.

Human activity is goal-oriented. People tend to realize their goals in communities. Common goal creates the need for its appealing vision. Most of the visions so far were utopian. One of the most important problems today is the danger of humans' self-annihilation either in the result of nuclear war or an ecological disaster. Endangered is the whole humanity, since we already *are* global society. To avoid the danger, cooperation between people is necessary. There are, however, serious differences between cultures, religions, nations, races, individuals, etc. One of the possibilities to abolish them is dialogue. Is it another utopia?

GOROVITZ, Samuel. "Professions, Professors, and Competing Obligations" in *Ethics, Trust, and the Professions: Philosophical and Cultural Aspects*, PELLEGRINO, Edmund D (ed), 177-192. Washington, Georgetown Univ Pr, 1991.

This chapter considers conflict between "the professional's fiduciary responsibility and obligations in respect to the common good," understood as specific to the context of each profession. Various professions are considered, with emphasis on academic settings. Professors must represent fairly, advocate, and advance the academic enterprise for the good of their classes, college or university, or even the nation; individual students trust the professor's knowledge and fairness in conveying it and in assessing performance. Defending a profession's basic values may require limiting its fiduciary responsibility; the evolution of a professional ethos required continuing moral judgment in determining the common good.

GORR, Michael. The Actus Reus Requirement: A Qualified Defense. Crim Just Ethics, 10(1), 11-17, Wint-Spr 91.

I argue that although the Actus Reus requirement is neither universal nor fundamental, it is still of considerable importance in a descriptively adequate account of the criminal law.

GORR, Michael. Private Defense. Law Phil, 9(3), 241-268, Ag 90.

GORR, Michael. Reply to Murphy and Husak. Crim Just Ethics, 10(1), 24-26, Wint-Spr 91.

GORSKI, Philip S. Scientism, Interpretation, and Criticism. Zygon, 25(3), 279-307, S 90.

What is the relationship between natural science, social science, and religion? Natural scientific understanding emerges from an instrumental and objectifying relation to the world; it is oriented toward control and manipulation of the physical world. Social-scientific understanding, by contrast, must begin with a practical and meaningful relation to the world: it is oriented toward the mediation of values and objective possibilities in the social world. Religion, by contrast, is a form of speculative reason about ultimate values, based on subjective claims of religious experience. Social science nevertheless shares with religion an orientation toward values and concern with the "good life." (edited)

GÖRTZEN, René. Duty and Inclination: The Phenomenological Value Ethics of Hans Reiner. J Value Inq, 25(2), 119-145, Ap 91.

After a brief introduction and general evaluation of Hans Reiner's ethics, I deal with the structure of his ethics system as related to passages on eudemonism and the criticism of Kant and Scheler. Then I examine Reiner's classification of values and the apriority of values, his principle of good and evil, the principle of moral right and wrong and the rules of priority, and final his reformulation of the categorical imperative. In the final section I give my criticism of Reiner. So I tackle the problem of the lack of any kind of social analysis and social criticism in his ethics. I also present a number of arguments to substantiate my thesis that in Reiner's ethics—contrary to what he himself suggests—situation does not play an essential role.

GOSLING, Justin. *Weakness of the Will*. New York, Routledge, 1990.

The author first surveys the treatment of "weakness of the will" in historical philosophic texts. He then discusses the problem in terms of irrationality, the passions, and varieties of weaknesses. (staff)

GÖSSMANN, Elisabeth and BEST, Katherine (trans). "Hildegard of Bingen" in *A History of Women Philosophers, Volume II: Medieval, Renaissance and Enlightenment, A.D. 500-1600*, WAITHE, Mary Ellen (ed), 27-65. Norwell, Kluwer, 1989.

It is problematic to refer to Hildegard of Bingen as a philosopher, even though she was familiar with the philosophical currents of her time and could animatedly and competently take a stand on them. More appropriately, one could call her a theologian, even though she would be loath to claim such authority for herself, in regard to her writing. Her works, including the letters, function to a large extent as a visionary literature, and it is not by chance that she, as a woman, chooses these stylistic means. Within her visionary experience, she comes to a philosophical-theological view of the world which displays original traits and sometimes emphasizes polemical aspects, but, in addition, raises many unanswered questions about the influences affecting a 12th-century Benedictine woman's view of the world and of mankind.

GÖTTLICHER, Gerd. Die Mathematisierung als Konstruktion theoretischer Denkformen in der Abfolge naturwissenschaftlicher Weltbilder. Deut Z Phil, 38(7), 691-695, 1990.

Mathematisation as development of theoretical forms in the process of reasoning is directly connected with succession of the view of nature in science. The change of mathematical means results for a big part from the change of subject-object relationship, which is a consequence of the increasing complexity of objects especially in physics. Mathematisation makes not only a contribution to the formation of a unified view of nature by constructing means for the reflection of the unity of phenomena in nature, but also by synthesizing different fashions of theoretical view.

GOTTLIEB, Paula. Aristotle and Protagoras: The Good Human Being as the Measure of Goods. Apeiron, 24(1), 25-45, Mr 91.

GOTTLIEB, Roger S (ed). *Thinking the Unthinkable: Meanings of the Holocaust*. Mahwah, Paulist Pr, 1990.

Thinking the Unthinkable is an anthology of twenty-six essays by such leading Holocaust commentators as Elie Wiesel, Emile Fackenheim, Jean-Paul Sartre, Hannah Arendt, Bruno Bettelheim, and Abraham Heschel. The purpose of this book is to serve our need to make meanings out of the Holocaust: to determine its impact on our personal lives, our society, and our future as human beings. The guiding thread of these essays is a shared belief that the Holocaust possesses terribly important meaning for us, meanings which may shape or alter our beliefs about human nature, morality, politics, and spiritual life.

GOUDAROULIS, Yorgos (ed) and GAVROGLU, Kostas (ed) and NICOLACOPOULOS, Pantelis (ed). *Imre Lakatos and Theories of Scientific Change*. Norwell, Kluwer, 1989.

This volume includes texts of the talks given during a conference in 1986 titled "Criticism and the Growth of Knowledge: Twenty Years Later." The articles assess the developments in philosophy of science during the twenty years from the 1965 London Conference.

GOUDAROULIS, Yorgos. "Many-Particle Physics: Calculational Complications That Become a Blessing for Methodology" in *Imre Lakatos and Theories of Scientific Change*, GAVROGLU, Kostas (ed), 135-145. Norwell, Kluwer, 1989.

The quantum mechanical behavior of the atomic structure induces all kinds of computational complications in understanding the behavior of many-particle systems. It is claimed that the task of handling the complexity of the many-particle problem is primarily conceptual rather than computational. By a reconstruction of the story of supercooled helium it is shown that the gap between atomic "simplicity" and "complex" macroscopic behavior is bridged through a continuous process of reinterpretation whereby the resulting "intermediaries" facilitate the creation of a theoretical framework with a relatively autonomous status with respect to the framework within which the two "extremes" are accommodated.

GOULA-MITACOU, Xéni. L'art comme pénétration d'un mystère. Diotima, 18, 34-40, 1990.

GOULD, Carol C. "On the Conception of the Common Interest: Between Procedure and Substance" in *Hermeneutics and Critical Theory in Ethics and Politics*, KELLY, Michael (ed), 253-273. Cambridge, MIT Pr, 1991.

GOULD, James. Abortion: Privacy versus Liberty. J Soc Phil, 21(1), 98-106, Spr 90.

Justices opposed to the 1973 abortion decision said there is no right to privacy in the Constitution. "Liberty" is there in the 5th Amendment, so why not use it. Justice Stewart did, stating it is a simple matter of negative liberty to grant this right. Justice White gives three easily refutable reasons not to use liberty as a basis. Justice Black fears the return of the famous Lockner doctrine if rights are judicially expanded, but neither he nor Rehnquist have any grounds for such a fear.

GOULET, Denis. Tareas y métodos en la ética del desarrollo. Rev Filosof (Costa Rica), 27(66), 293-305, D 89.

A broad survey of the facts concerning development, pseudo-development and anti-development, convinces us of the need for an ethics of development. None of the theoretical approaches not extant (Marxism, Positivism, Existentialism, traditional ethics) have proven capable of doing that. This is why it is urgent to analyze the tasks and methods of this new discipline.

GOULET, Marie-Claude and FREEDMAN, Benjamin. New Creations? Commentary. Hastings Center Rep, 21(1), 34-35, Ja-F 91.

This brief article deals with the appropriate attitude and approach to be taken to the ethics of transspecies research and manipulation. We argue that the quotidian approach of bioethics, using rights, autonomy, etc., is inadequate. Even the ethics of research is inapt: We are not, in the most relevant sense, talking of transspecies *research*. Research is a preliminary to a change in practice, and the ethics of research is the ethics of a means. But transspecies manipulation is, recursively, the change itself; research into doing it does it. Alternative approaches, including an ethics of change, are discussed.

GOUNELLE, André. La puissance d'être selon Tillich. Laval Theol Phil, 47(1), 13-21, F 91.

Que signifie la notion de "puissance d'être" qui joue un grand rôle dans la théologie de Tillich? Elle est, d'abord, puissance de résister au non-être, et de le dominer. Ensuite, elle rend compte du fait que Dieu est vivant, non pas identité statique et figée, mais dynamisme. Enfin, elle est puissance, à la fois transcendante et immanente, qui agit dans les êtres, et non pas sur eux, du dehors.

GOUREVITCH, Aron I. History and Historical Anthropology. Diogenes, 151, 75-89, Fall 90.

The experience of the modern humanities testifies to the shaping of a new trend—historical anthropology the meaning of which lies in revealing the human content of the historical process. For this purpose historical anthropology considers social man from the maximally great number of observation points, in all his manifestations. Working out new methods of studying social man, historical anthropology tends toward the attainment of new historical synthesis overcoming the disconnection of the history of socio-economic relations and the history of culture and mentalities. To implement such a program a polydiscipline approach is needed to pool the efforts of several disciplines. Historical anthropology faces complex theoretical problems associated with the new type of explaining the social behaviour of people.

GOUWS, A S. Account of a Philosophical Expedition in Search of the Elusive Paradigm (in Dutch). S Afr J Phil, 9(4), 214-221, N 90.

In this article the author discusses a cluster of related notions such as 'paradigm', 'conceptual scheme', 'frame of reference', etc. The neologism 'digm' is introduced as an umbrella term substituting for this whole cluster. Areas of convergence as well as divergence with this cluster are explored. As an example, the difference between Kuhn's use of the term 'paradigm' and its popular use is discussed. The article is a polemic against simplistic, foundationalist and substantialistic accounts of digms. In conclusion, two possibilities are considered: digms may be systematic in hitherto undreamed of ways, or they may be even less systematic than the way they are portrayed here. (edited)

GOWANS, Christopher W (ed). *Moral Dilemmas*. New York, Oxford Univ Pr, 1987.

This anthology brings together the principal contributions in the recent debate about whether or not there are moral dilemmas, that is, situations in which an agent morally ought to do one thing and morally ought to do another thing, even though the agent cannot do both. The volume begins with a detailed introduction by the editor, with the next four selections by Kant, Mill, Bradley and Ross providing historical background. The diverse perspectives in the contemporary discussion are set forth in the remaining essays by Lemmon, Williams, van Fraassen, Mc Connell, Nagel, Marcus, Hare, Conee, Foot, and Donagan.

GOWER, Barry. Chalmers on Method. Brit J Phil Sci, 39(1), 59-65, Mr 88.

GOWER, Barry. Hume on Probability. Brit J Phil Sci, 42(1), 1-19, Mr 91.

GOYARD-FABRE, Simone. "L'égalité des droits en 1789" in *Égalité Uguaglianza*, FERRARI, Jean (ed), 113-126. Napoli, Liguori, 1990.

L'originalité du XVIIIème siècle a été de transporter le concept d'égalité sur le terrain du droit. Certes, dans la philosophie de Hobbes ou de Locke, le postulat individualiste était déjà net, qui effaçait les différences entre les hommes: le droit naturel de chacun à la vie était reconnu égal au droit de tout autre. Mais il appartint à Rousseau d'opérer théoriquement la mutation qui arrache le concept d'égalité à ses racines jusnaturalistes pour lui donner un ancrage légaliste. Les Constituants de 1789, sans être hostiles à l'ordre naturel, insistèrent sur la nécessaire juridicisation de l'égalité, condition, selon eux, de la valorisation de l'homme et de la reconnaissance de sa dignité. Un problème redoutable se pose néanmoins car l'égalité des droits, en sa forme juridique, est toujours catégorielle, donc différentielle et l'on peut se demander si l'égalité n'enveloppe pas toujours, comme par essence, des inégalités.

GOYARD-FABRE, Simone. Le sens de la révolution méthodologique introduite par Rousseau dans la science politique. Laval Theol Phil, 47(2), 147-160, Je 91.

Dans la pensée de Rousseau, l'interrogation politique est tributaire de la révolution méthodologique qui le conduit au seuil d'une philosophie transcendantale. C'est en effet de manière inédite qu'il traite les maîtres-concepts autour desquels s'élabore, depuis le XVIIe siècle, la philosophie politique moderne. En retournant la logique hypothético-déductive des ouvrages classiques de son temps, il pénètre, sans le savoir, sur les terres et dans les voies de la philosophie critique: les conditions de possibilité et de légitimité de l'État résident, selon lui, dans une exigence philosophique *pure* qui est tout près de définir la volonté générale comme Idée *a priori* de la raison. Rousseau, par sa démarche radicalisante et critique, a fait d'une question de méthode un problème de fond dont l'enjeu est des plus graves puisque c'est à la faveur de la plus haute problématique que se déchiffrent les conditions de la liberté des hommes.

GRABER, Glenn C. "Should Abnormal Fetuses Be Brought to Term for the Sole Purpose of Providing Infant Transplant Organs?" in *Biomedical Ethics Reviews, 1989*, HUMBER, James M (ed), 5-24. Clifton, Humana Pr, 1990.

GRABER, Glenn C and THOMASMA, David C. *Theory and Practice in Medical Ethics*. New York, Continuum, 1989.

GRACYK, Theodore A. Kant's Doctrine of Heuristics: An Interpretation of the Ideas of Reason. Mod Sch, 68(3), 191-210, Mr 91.

The maxims of reason which Kant calls "heuristic principles" fit current criteria for heuristics of scientific inquiry. Because the categories of the understanding are insufficient to secure empirical knowledge, the Appendix to the Transcendental Dialectic provides a set of unrevisable, a priori heuristics to guide empirical inquiry; these are supplemented by revisable heuristics which arise in distinct sciences.

GRACZYNSKA, Ewa. On Some Operators on Pseudovarieties. Bull Sect Log, 19(4), 122-127, D 90.

GRADKOWSKI, Waldemar. Tradition and Its Value: A Contribution to the History of Polish Marxist Philosophical Thought (in Polish). Ann Univ Mariae Curie-Phil, 11, 7-22, 1986.

The present study is a discussion of the category of tradition. Tradition is understood as specific 'objectified thinking', that is a set of phenomena that are conveyed in time and social space in the shape of material and verbal symbols. Conveyance of tradition so understood has two aspects: subjective and objective. For every tradition is a carrier of defined values and although these values are practically conceptualized in the sphere conventionally referred to as objective, yet it is the subject creating those values that is of fundamental importance. Thus the questions about who is the tradition-making subject and who chooses values residing in it dominate the question about the contents, its inner substance and coherence. The paper therefore attempts to signal interrelations occurring between the two spheres that determine tradition: subjective and objective, pointing at the same time at the axiological importance of both.

GRAEFRATH, Bernd. Hume's Metaethical Cognitivism and the Natural Law Theory. J Value Inq, 25(1), 73-79, Ja 91.

GRAESER, Andreas. Hölderlin über Urteil und Sein. Frei Z Phil Theol, 38(1-2), 111-128, 1991.

The article provides an analysis of part of the fragment on 'Being and Judgment'. It argues to the effect that Hoelderlin is not attacking Fichte (as had been claimed by T Heurich) but Schelling. In fact, the argument employed by Hoelderlin is ad hominem and meant to establish that Schelling cannot be right on his own assumptions. Also, the article shows that Hoelderlin's argument is both lucid and relevant.

GRAHAM, Angus C. "Reflections and Replies" in *Chinese Texts and Philosophical Contexts*, ROSEMONT JR, Henry (ed), 267-322. La Salle, Open Court, 1991.

GRAHAM, Daniel W. Socrates, the Craft Analogy, and Science. Apeiron, 24(1), 1-24, Mr 91.

Plato's demand for teleological explanations in science has not been adequately explained. The demand has its roots in Socratic moral theory. Socrates finds in the crafts teleological practices which serve as paradigms of knowledge. In the *Gorgias* Plato regards Socrates as practicing a political art which is the first social science and hence a potential model for natural science. In the *Timaeus* Plato uses the craft analogy to structure his account of the natural world.

GRAHAM, George and HORGAN, Terence. In Defense of Southern Fundamentalism. Phil Stud, 62(2), 107-134, My 91.

Southern Fundamentalism, a form of realism about folk psychology, asserts that there is only a minimal conceptual gap between 1) satisfying ordinary, behavior-based, standards for the attribution of propositional attitudes, and 2) being a true believer; hence it is overwhelmingly likely that there are true believers. Under Southern Fundamentalism, the integrity of folk psychology is not threatened by debates about whether folk psychology is destined to become part of mature science, whether there is a language of thought, or whether any other of the strong empirical commitments sometimes attributed to folk psychology are satisfied.

GRAHAM, George and GARRETT, Richard. Why not Naturalistic Psychology? Philosophia (Israel), 20(4), 377-385, F 91.

GRAHAM, Gordon. *The Idea of Christian Charity: A Critique of Some Contemporary Conceptions*. Notre Dame, Univ Notre Dame Pr, 1990.

This book argues that the ethics and theology of Christianity cannot be isolated from one another and are crucially linked in the New Testament by the notions of "the Kingdom of God" and "repentence". Pursuing this line of argument further, the book proceeds to evaluate two prominent ideas of Christian charity. The first of these is psychological healing as that idea is to be found in pastoral counselling and the second that of social justice as this has been elaborated in liberation, theology and elsewhere. Both accounts of charity are rejected and in a final chapter a positive account of Christian charity as a virtue rather than a principal action is defended.

GRAHAM, Gordon. *Living the Good Life: An Introduction to Moral Philosophy*. New York, Paragon House, 1990.

This book introduces undergraduate students to the moral arguments of Plato, Aristotle, Kant, Kierkegaard, Nietzsche, Mill and Sartre in a dialectical manner that combines the introduction to historical thought with discussion of the concerns of modern philosophers. The topics critically examined include egoism, hedonism, existentialism, Kantianism and utilitarianism. The concluding chapter is on religion and the meaning of life.

GRAHAM, Gordon. Recent Work in Political Philosophy. Phil Quart, 40(161), 515-522, O 90.

This essay reviews eight recently published books in political philosophy. It finds the central theme of recent political philosophy to be an attack on liberalism. Some of this attack is from a traditional socialist perspective and some of it from other versions of communitarianism. The review concludes that by and large the attack on liberalism remains largely negative, and that however deep the flaws in liberalism no satisfactory positive alternative has yet emerged.

GRAHAM, Jill W and KEELEY, Michael. Exit, Voice, and Ethics. J Bus Ethics, 10(5), 349-355, My 91.

Hirschman's (1970) exit, voice, and loyalty framework draws attention to both economic and political behavior as instruments for organizational change. The framework is simple but powerful; it has stimulated much cross-disciplinary analysis and debate. This paper extends this analysis by examining normative implications of Hirschman's basic premise: that exit and voice are primarily mechanisms for enhancing organizational (versus individual) well-being.

GRAHAM, Keith. "Liberalism and Liberty: The Fragility of a Tradition" in *Key Themes in Philosophy*, GRIFFITHS, A Phillips (ed), 207-223. New York, Cambridge Univ Pr, 1989.

A connexion between liberalism and philosophical enquiry is noted, and two challenges to liberalism are considered: that its underlying ideal of individual autonomy, first, threatens to undermine its negative conception of liberty and, second, vitiates its justification of obedience to state authority. The first challenge is endorsed, the second characterized as problematic. The suggestion is made that the ontological individualism of the liberal tradition is in need of modification. The reality of collectives must be recognized, both for conceptual reasons and because of their importance in the modern world. The need for a postliberal political philosophy is stressed.

GRAHEK, Nikola. Objective and Subjective Aspects of Pain. Phil Psych, 4(2), 249-266, 1991.

The aim of this paper is to show that the empirical and conceptual constraints arising from the scientific research on pain phenomena should be taken into account in philosophical discussions concerning the nature and function of pain; otherwise, there is a good chance that philosophers will advocate too simplistic, confused or even outrightly mistaken theories or conceptions of pain. In order to prove this point, one of the most influential philosophical theories of pain—the so-called perceptual view of pain—is put to scrutiny in the light of the psychological, clinical and neurophysiological data coming from the field of pain research. More specifically, these data are presented in such a way as to show that the sensory quality or sensory aspect of pain is, contrary to objectivistic claims of the perceptual view of pain, a necessary component of our total pain experience.

GRANDAZZI, Alexandre. The Future of the Past: From the History of Historiography to Historiology. Diogenes, 151, 51-74, Fall 90.

GRANDY, Richard E. "Concepts, Prototypes and Information" in *Information, Semantics and Epistemology*, VILLANUEVA, Enrique (ed), 200-208. Cambridge, Blackwell, 1990.

The discovery of the psychological phenomenon of prototypes has been claimed to alter our understanding of how concepts are organized. This paper attempts to clarify some foundational questions about prototype theory. Specifically, it is argued that the reality of prototypes does not necessarily lead to the recognition of degrees of membership nor to the use of fuzzy logic. The relation between the organization of concepts and information about the world is explored and it is argued that information is one, but not the only one, force driving concept organization.

GRANDY, Richard E. "Understanding and the Principle of Compositionality" in *Philosophical Perspectives, 4: Action Theory and Philosophy of Mind, 1990*, TOMBERLIN, James E (ed), 557-572. Atascadero, Ridgeview, 1990.

A widely accepted principle about natural language is that meaning is compositional, but recently Cohen, Kittay and Schiffer have questioned this. Justification for the principle can be based on our exponentially large performance potential without depending on our alleged infinite semantic competence. I distinguish the claim that there must be compositional mechanisms from the claim that there must be an accessible theory of the mechanisms. The attacks on the principle do not refute it, but reveal non-trivial issues about formulation. A defensible version for natural languages with their ambiguities and context dependencies will not be easy to formulate.

GRANDY, Richard E. "What a Truth Theory Need Not Tell Us" in *Truth and Interpretation: Perspectives on the Philosophy of Donald Davidson*, LE PORE, Ernest (ed), 179-189. Cambridge, Blackwell, 1986.

To establish what information truth theories themselves provide about languages it is useful to focus on homophonic homomorphic theories. Minimalist truth theories, based on very weak logics, need only utilize substitution principles relating object language syntax to metalinguistic semantics. Such theories commit themselves to very little about logical truth. Apparent failures of substitutivity put constraints on the theory but imputing additional argument places apparently can always provide formal, if not ontological, solutions.

GRANGER, G G. Sur le vague en mathématiques. Dialectica, 44(1-2), 9-22, 1990.

Vagueness plays an important role in mathematics, even if it is negatively, as bringing out problems to be solved. We examine the meaning of three aspects of vagueness and their treatment: approximation, the notion of indetermined object ("l'objet quelconque"), and the process of axiomatization considered as an attempt to completely eliminate vagueness. The dialectic of vagueness and determination, which is doomed never to come to an end, is finally analysed as a tentative explanation and formulation of the formal operations correlative to the introduction of mathematical objects always more explicitly defined.

GRANOFF, Phyllis. The Biographies of Siddhasena (II). J Indian Phil, 18(4), 261-304, D 90.

GRASSI, Marie-Claire. Rousseau intimiste et la fusion des cultures? Hist Euro Ideas, 11, 559-563, 1989.

GRATTAN-GUINNESS, I. The Correspondence between George Boole and Stanley Jevons, 1863-1864. Hist Phil Log, 12(1), 15-35, 1990.

Although the existence of correspondence between George Boole (1815-1864) and William Stanley Jevons (1835-1882) has been known for a long time and part was even published in 1913, it has never been fully noted; in particular, it is not in the recent edition of Jevons's letters and papers. The texts are transcribed here, with indication of their significance. Jevons proposed certain quite radical changes to Boole's system, which Boole did not accept; nevertheless, they were to become well established.

GRATTON, Fausto T L. Teorías físicas sobre el origen del Universo. Stromata, 46(3-4), 241-258, Jl-D 90.

GRÄTZEL, Stephan. Wahnbildung und Wirklichkeit des Willens. Schopenhauer Jahr, 71, 79-84, 1990.

GRAY, C B. Words on Work. Gnosis, 3(3), 119-121, D 90.

This is a brief set of suggestions on what is the usefulness of studies in philosophy for occupational employment.

GRAY, V J. The Moral Interpretation of the 'Second Preface' to Arrian's *Anabasis*. J Hellen Stud, 110, 180-186, 1990.

GRAYBEAL, Jean. *Language and "The Feminine" in Nietzsche and Heidegger*. Bloomington, Indiana Univ Pr, 1990.

Nietzsche and Heidegger were both lovers of language, and their styles of writing demonstrate a relationship with a "feminine" dimension of language. Drawing on the theories of French psychoanalyst Julia Kristeva concerning the "symbolic" and "semiotic" dispositions in language, this book reads Nietzsche and Heidegger as writers whose experimentation with language is relevant both to their quests for nonmetaphysical ways of thinking and to the feminist project of moving beyond male dominance. It thus argues that the writings of Nietzsche and Heidegger are important for contemporary discussions about what it means to be women and men.

GRAYLING, A C. Wittgenstein's Influence: Meaning, Mind and Method. Philosophy, 28, 61-78, 90 Supp.

GRAZIANI, Andrea. Riflessioni sulla fondazione dell'assioma parmenideo. Sapienza, 43(4), 435-439, O-D 90.

GRECO, John. Internalism and Epistemically Responsible Belief. Synthese, 85(2), 245-277, N 90.

In this article the deontological (or responsibilist) conception of justification is discussed and explained. Arguments are put forward in order to derive the most plausible version of perspectival internalism, or the position that epistemic justification is a function of factors internal to the believer's cognitive perspective. The two most common considerations put forward in favor of perspectival internalism are the responsibilist conception of justification, and the intuition that two believers with like beliefs and experiences are equally justified in their like beliefs. It is argued that perspectival internalism is false, and that in fact the position is not supported by a responsibilist conception of justification. Two other forms of internalism are rejected. An internalist theory of justification is defended which is supported by a responsibilist conception of justification. (edited)

GREEN, Catherine. "Freedom and Determination: An Examination of Yves R Simon's Ontology of Freedom" in *Freedom in the Modern World: Jacques Maritain, Yves R Simon, Mortimer J Adler*, TORRE, Michael D (ed), 89-99. Notre Dame, Univ Notre Dame Pr, 1989.

GREEN, David E (trans) and LÖWITH, Karl. *From Hegel to Nietzsche: The Revolution in Nineteenth-Century Thought*. New York, Columbia Univ Pr, 1991.

GREEN, Joe L. Of *Praxis* and *Techne* and Cabbages and Kings. Proc Phil Educ, 46, 346-349, 1990.

This article responds to an argument by Professor Karl Hostetler which seeks to connect *techne* and *praxis* in teaching. Finding Hostetler's position to be fundamentally correct, it is criticized for introducing vague connections with the vocabularies of phenomenology, hermeneutics, and critical theory. It is argued, moreover, that the connections sought can be achieved only under a more restricted sense of "teaching." It is held (a) that teaching must serve *praxis*; (b) that *techne* is secondary to praxis; and that *phronesis*, or practical wisdom, must necessarily connect the two, yet is only meaningful as a contingent within specific teaching contexts.

GREEN, Karen. Dummett's Ought from Is. Dialectica, 45(1), 67-82, 1991.

Dummett has offered an argument which begins with certain criteria of adequacy for any account of the way in which communication functions and which ends with normative and revisionary conclusions concerning our logical practice. This argument, which hinges on Dummett's criticisms of holism, is inadequate as it stands, for the holist can give an adequate description of the functioning of communication. There is a plausible defence of intuitionism to be extracted from Dummett's writing, but it should be recognized that it has a normative starting point and does not follow from the criteria of adequacy with which Dummett apparently begins.

GREEN, Lawrence W. "The Revival of Community and the Public Obligation of Academic Health Centers" in *Integrity in Health Care Institutions: Humane Environments for Teaching, Inquiry, and Healing*, BULGER, Ruth Ellen (ed), 148-164. Iowa City, Univ of Iowa Pr, 1990.

GREEN, Ronald M. "Everyone's Doing It"—A Reply to Richard DeGeorge. Bus Ethics Quart, 1(2), 201-209, Ap 91.

In a previous article I laid out five criteria/conditions for determining when the claim that "Everyone's Doing It" is a legitimate moral justification for conduct. DeGeorge's accompanying response criticized this position for being a truncated form of act utilitarianism, for its heavy reliance on intuition, and for its susceptibility to misapplication. Here I maintain that DeGeorge has misinterpreted my view, and missed its central concern with publicity. Properly applied, I contend, this view actually elucidates some of the counter-intuitions DeGeorge arrays against it.

GREEN, Ronald M. The First Formulation of the Categorical Imperative as Literally a "Legislative" Metaphor. Hist Phil Quart, 8(2), 163-179, Ap 91.

GREEN, Ronald M. Physicians, Entrepreneurism and the Problem of Conflict of Interest. Theor Med, 11(4), 287-300, D 90.

This paper examines the ethical issues of conflict of interest raised by the burgeoning development of physician involvement in for-profit entrepreneurial activities outside their practice. After documenting the nature and extent of these activities, and their potential for conflicts of interest, the paper assesses the major arguments for and against physicians' referral of patients to facilities they own or in which they invest. The paper concludes that an outright ban on such activity seems ethically warranted.

GREEN, Ronald M. When is "Everyone's Doing It" a Moral Justification? Bus Ethics Quart, 1(1), 75-93, Ja 91.

The claim that "Everyone's doing it" is frequently offered as a reason for engaging in behavior that is widespread but less-than-ideal. This is particularly true in business, where competitors' conduct often forces hard choices on managers. When is the claim "Everyone's doing it" a morally valid reason for following others' lead? This discussion proposes and develops five *prima facie* conditions to identify when the existence of prevalent but otherwise undesirable behavior provides a moral justification for our engaging in such behavior ourselves. The balance of the discussion focuses on testing these conditions by applying them to a series of representative cases in business ethics.

GREEN, Sharon and WEBER, James. Principled Moral Reasoning: Is It a Viable Approach to Promote Ethical Integrity? J Bus Ethics, 10(5), 325-333, My 91.

In response to recent recommendations for the teaching of principled moral reasoning in business school curricula, this paper assesses the viability of such an approach. The results indicate that, while business students' level of moral reasoning in this sample are like most 18- to 21-year-olds, they may be incapable of grasping the concepts embodied in principled moral reasoning. Implications of these findings are discussed.

GREEN, Thomas F. "Excellence, Equity, and Equality" Clarified. Proc Phil Educ, 46, 220-224, 1990.

Remarks clarifying "Excellence, Equity and Equality," in *Handbook of Teaching and Policy*, Shulman and Sykes (New York: Longman, 1983), *q.v.* We know *in*justice better than justice. Arguments of educational *in*justice assume the same form. To show that a distribution is unjust show that it is based on irrelevant variables like race, class or gender. To rebut, show that it is based upon relevant variables like choice, tenacity, or some virtue. These are sufficient but not necessary grounds to advance and rebut claims of educational injustice. They are not parts of a principle of justice. Equity does not imply equality, but its achievement would advance excellence.

GREEN, Thomas F. Theme and Commentary. Proc Phil Educ, 46, 111-117, 1990.

William Losito urges that moral education need not be religious and Clive Beck that schools should teach about "faith in the broad sense." Anyone with strong, especially biblical, sensibilities will reject both. Better to ask how religious-like sentiments enter into moral development and what vocabularies distinguish the banal and mundane from the sacred. "In a world where nothing is sacred, moral education is impossible." Exploring this claim will explain why it seems that moral education is inescapably religious and why, religiously seen, nothing as indefinite as "faith in the broad sense" can have much educational worth.

GREENBERG, Dan. Radin on Personhood and Rent Control. Monist, 73(4), 642-659, O 90.

Professor Radin defends rent control by arguing that housing should not be treated as a market commodity because people depend for their personhood upon certain stable forms of property—a problematic claim. Why should landlords bear the burden of rent control laws, rather than all of society? Should all kinds of personhood be fostered, or just the kinds Radin favors? Finally, how much interference in others' lives should we permit for the sake of personhood? That is, are there other important goods, and to what extent should we pass over them in favor of personhood? Radin's answers are found unsatisfactory.

GREENE, G Robert and IBRAHIM, Nabil A and RUE, Leslie W and MC DOUGALL, Patricia P. Characteristics and Practices of "Christian-Based" Companies. J Bus Ethics, 10(2), 123-132, F 91.

There is a sizeable group of self-described "Christian" companies which have declared their belief in the successful merging of biblical principles with business activities. As these companies have become more visible, an increasing number of anecdotal newspaper and magazine articles about these companies have appeared. Surprisingly, no rigorous research had been conducted prior to our recent study. This article provides national estimates of the size and predominant characteristics of self-identified "Christian" companies. In addition, the study investigated the types of relationships these companies maintained with their employees, customers, communities, and suppliers.

GREENE, Marjorie. Evolution, "Typology" and "Population Thinking". Amer Phil Quart, 27(3), 237-244, Jl 90.

GREENE, Maxine. Cultural Literacy: Posing Queer Questions. Phil Stud Educ, /, 18-33, 1986.

GREENE, Maxine. A Response to Beck, Giarelli/Chambliss, Leach, Tozer, and Macmillan. Educ Theor, 41(3), 321-324, Sum 91.

GREENE, Maxine. Response to Donald Vandenberg's "Co-intentional Pedagogy". Proc Phil Educ, 46, 203-207, 1990.

GREENE, Robert A. Synderesis, the Spark of Conscience, in the English Renaissance. J Hist Ideas, 52(2), 195-219, Ap-Je 91.

Although the term itself is laughed off the Elizabethan stages and fades away in decadent Protestant scholasticism, the medieval idea of synderesis, Jerome's fourth and superintendent part of the soul, the "apex of the mind," the "pure part of conscience," survives under new designations during the Renaissance. The terms spark and natural instinct and the biblical expressions "the spirit of man" and "the candle of the Lord" are substituted by Calvin, St. German, Bacon, Culverwell, Herbert and Locke, to reiterate the humanistic conviction that man retains a vestige of his prelapsarian moral and intellectual integrity.

GREENLAW, Jane. Surrogate Decisionmaking and Other Matters. Hastings Center Rep, 20(6), 24-25, N-D 90.

GREENWOOD, John D. Two Dogmas of Neo-Empiricism: The "Theory-Informity" of Observation and the Quine-Duhem Thesis. Phil Sci, 57(4), 553-574, D 90.

It is argued that neither the "theory-informity" of observations nor the Quine-Duhem thesis pose any in principle threat to the objectivity of theory evaluation. The employment of *exploratory* theories does not generate incommensurability, but on the contrary is responsible for the mensurability and commensurability of *explanatory theories*, since exploratory theories enable scientists to make observations which are critical in the evaluation of explanatory theories. The employment of exploratory theories and other auxiliary hypotheses does not enable a theory to always accommodate recalcitrant observations to preserve evidential equivalence with a rival theory. Explanatory theories become rapidly degenerating if exploratory theories or other auxiliary hypotheses which inform the original confirmation base are modified to accommodate recalcitrant observations.

GREEVE DAVANEY, Sheila and BROWN, Delwin. Methodological Alternatives in Process Theology. Process Stud, 19(2), 75-84, Sum 90.

This article served as the introductory public lecture at the "Conference on Methodological Alternatives in Process Theology," at Iliff School of Theology, Denver, Colorado, in January 1989, sponored by Iliff and the Center for Process Studies at Clarement, California. The paper presents a general understanding of process thought, and discusses three theological methodologies represented within this general perspective.

GREGORIOS, Paulos Mar. Philosophical and Normative Dimensions and Aspects of the Idea of Renaissance. J Indian Counc Phil Res, 6(2), 75-91, Ja-Ap 89.

GREGORY, Derek. "Presences and Absences: Time-Space Relations and Structuration Theory" in *Social Theory of Modern Societies: Anthony Giddens and His Critics*, HELD, David (ed), 185-214. New York, Cambridge Univ Pr, 1990.

GREGORY, Frederick. "Theology and the Sciences in the German Romantic Period" in *Romanticism and the Sciences*, CUNNINGHAM, Andrew (ed), 69-81. New York, Cambridge Univ Pr, 1990.

Among the frameworks in which science and religion were discussed in the German Romantic period were the perspectives of Kant and of the romantic *Naturphilosophen*. By following representative thinkers of these two philosophical approaches, the author explores what each held for the relationship between natural science and religion. The neo-Kantian tradition is investigated through the work of Jakob Friedrich Fries, while the theological implications of romantic *Naturphilosophie* are followed in the work of Friedrich Schleiermacher.

GREISCH, Jean and CRITCHLEY, Simon (trans). "The Face and Reading: Immediacy and Mediation" in *Re-Reading Levinas*, BERNASCONI, Robert (ed), 67-82. Bloomington, Indiana Univ Pr, 1991.

Greisch's essay offers a reading of Levinas's *Otherwise than Being or Beyond Essence* that traces the themes of the face and reading and immediacy and mediation. Particular attention is paid to the relation between the work of Levinas and that of Wittgenstein and Eric Weil.

GREISCH, Jean. L'herméneutique dans la "phènoménologie comme telle". Rev Metaph Morale, 96(1), 43-63, Ja-Mr 91.

GRENE, Marjorie. *Descartes Among the Scholastics*. Milwaukee, Marquette Univ Pr, 1991.

GRENE, Marjorie. "Perception and Human Reality" in *Harré and His Critics*, BHASKAR, Roy (ed), 17-22. Cambridge, Blackwell, 1990.

GREY, Mary. Motherhood and the Possibility of a Contemporary Discourse for Women. Bijdragen, 1, 58-69, 1991.

Motherhood has been experienced by women both as a means of social control, as an experience of great suffering, as well as a meaningful source of self-identity. The article attempts a two-pronged approach: it investigates the links between motherhood, the motherhood of Mary and motherhood as permitted role for women in patriarchal monotheism through interpretations of 1 Tim. 2.16, as well as through the psychoanalytic theory of Julia Kristeva. Although Kristeva is criticized on theological grounds the article takes seriously her case that motherhood in monotheism involves a sacrifice of much that is authentically female. An attempt is made to construct a new Christian feminist discourse for motherhood—not confined to biological processes—but as a metaphor for the self-in-relation, for transformed human relations and a new God-language. Thus the beauty and power of what has been excluded from official ecclesial metaphor can be re-awakened and women can be acknowledged as active 'bearers of tradition'.

GREY, Thomas. Civil Rights versus Civil Liberties: The Case of Discriminatory Verbal Harassment. Soc Phil Pol, 8(2), 81-107, Spr 91.

GRIER, Philip T. "Abstract and Concrete in Hegel's Logic" in *Essays on Hegel's Logic*, DI GIOVANNI, George (ed), 59-75. Albany, SUNY Pr, 1990.

GRIER, Philip T. "Modern Ethical Theory and Newtonian Science: Comments on Errol Harris" in *Philosophical Perspectives on Newtonian Science*, BRICKER, Phillip (ed), 227-239. Cambridge, MIT Pr, 1990.

Responding to a paper by Errol Harris concerning the impact of Newtonian science on ethical theory, this essay focuses on subjectivism, voluntarism and relativism as tendencies promoted by the new mechanist cosmology. Changing attitudes toward theoretical and practical reason are examined, as well as related changes in modern philosophical anthropology. It is argued that, somewhat independently of the impact of Newtonian science, the rise of the expressivist anthropology in German Idealism and Romanticism, and the emergence of conceptions of reason connecting it to specific natural languages rather than to universal, objective structures of thought, have further undermined the claim of practical reason to deliver objective and universal moral judgments.

GRIESEMER, James R. Must Scientific Diagrams Be Eliminable? The Case of Path Analysis. Biol Phil, 6(2), 155-180, Ap 91.

Scientists use a variety of modes of representation in their work, but philosophers have studied mainly sentences expressing propositions. I ask whether diagrams are mere conveniences in expressing propositions or whether they are a distinct, ineliminable mode of representation in scientific texts. The case of path analysis, a statistical method for quantitatively assessing the relative degree of causal determination of variation as expressed in a causal path diagram, is discussed. Path analysis presents a worst case for arguments eliminability since path diagrams are usually presumed to be mathematically or logically "equivalent" in an important sense to sets of linear path equations. I argue that path diagrams are strongly generative, i.e., that they add analytical power to path analysis beyond what is supplied by linear equations, and therefore, that they are ineliminable in a strong scientific sense.

GRIFFIN, David Ray (ed). *Archetypal Process: Self and Divine in Whitehead, Jung, and Hillman*. Evanston, Northwestern Univ Pr, 1989.

GRIFFIN, David Ray. "Introduction: Archetypal Psychology and Process Philosophy" in *Archetypal Process: Self and Divine in Whitehead, Jung, and Hillman*, GRIFFIN, David Ray (ed), 1-76. Evanston, Northwestern Univ Pr, 1989.

GRIFFIN, David Ray. "A Metaphysical Psychology to Un-Locke Our Ailing World" in *Archetypal Process: Self and Divine in Whitehead, Jung, and Hillman*, GRIFFIN, David Ray (ed), 239-249. Evanston, Northwestern Univ Pr, 1989.

GRIFFIN, David Ray. Process Theology as Empirical, Rational, and Speculative: Some Reflections on Method. Process Stud, 19(2), 116-135, Sum 90.

Written for a conference bringing together advocates of the so-called empirical, rationalistic, and speculative forms of process theology, this essay defends the "s" word. Christian theology today, now that the method of authority is impossible, must seek to be both fully empirical and fully rational, making its claim to truth in terms of the normal criteria of self-consistency and adequacy to the facts (the latter criterion is defended against current detractors). Seeking to realize this idea of rational empiricism requires speculation, meaning the formation of hypotheses about what things are in themselves.

GRIFFIN, M T (ed) and CICERO,. *On Duties: Cicero*. New York, Cambridge Univ Pr, 1991.

GRIFFIOEN, S. Over Overdrijven. Phil Reform, 55(2), 140-151, 1990.

GRIFFITHS, A Phillips. "Conclusion" in *Philosophy and Politics*, HUNT, G M K (ed), 129-139. New York, Cambridge Univ Pr, 1991.

GRIFFITHS, A Phillips. Conclusion. Philosophy, 26, 129-139, 90 Supp.

GRIFFITHS, A Phillips. "Is Free Will Incompatible with Something or Other?" in *Key Themes in Philosophy*, GRIFFITHS, A Phillips (ed), 101-119. New York, Cambridge Univ Pr, 1989.

GRIFFITHS, A Phillips. Kant's Psychological Hedonism. Philosophy, 66(256), 207-216, Ap 91.

GRIFFITHS, A Phillips (ed). *Key Themes in Philosophy*. New York, Cambridge Univ Pr, 1989.

GRIGG, Richard. The Crucial Disanalogies Between Properly Basic Belief and Belief in God. Relig Stud, 26(3), 389-401, S 90.

GRIGG, Russell. Desire and Duty in Kant. Sophia (Australia), 30(1), 34-38, Jl 91.

GRIM, Patrick. On Omniscience and a 'Set of All Truths': A Reply to Bringsjord. Analysis, 50(4), 271-276, O 90.

In 'Grim on Logic and Omniscience' (*Analysis* 49 (1989), 186-9), Selmer Bringsjord suggests two escape routes from Grim's Cantorian arguments against omniscience and a 'set of all truths': one involving abandonment of the power set axiom, the other involving a new definition of omniscience. In this article Grim argues that neither escape succeeds.

GRIMALDI, Nicolas. Espoir et désespoir de la raison chez Kant. Kantstudien, 82(2), 129-145, 1991.

Why a criticism of aesthetical judgement precedes, in Kant's, the criticism of teleological judgement? The author displays how the analysis of the work of art prepares for the understanding how mechanical causality concurs for the final causality, how necessity is propitious to the works of liberty, and how, in Kant as in Leibniz, the order of Nature conspires to the order of Grace.

GRIMES, John A. *Quest for Certainty: A Comparative Study of Heidegger and Sankara*. New York, Lang, 1989.

This work examines the metaphysics of experience in the work of Heidegger and Sankara. The author compares the 'quest for Being' of both thinkers, especially considering their similarities in light of their widely divergent cultures. (staff)

GRIMES, John. Advaita and Religious Language. J Indian Counc Phil Res, 6(1), 67-82, S-D 88.

The status of religious discourse has been critiqued in various ways. A plethora of distinctions can be discerned along various lines. The sum result of this scholarship is that the very possibility of a philosophical understanding of religious discourse has been called into question. The purpose of this book is to show, because of its radically unique standpoint, Advaita's use and understanding of religious statements are not subject to these common criticisms. The work makes two contributions: (1) religious discourse is not only cognitive, but also valid; (2) contrary to common belief, it is more logically consistent to speak of the unqualified Absolute than of a theistic deity.

GRIMES, John. Some Problems in the Epistemology of Advaita. Phil East West, 41(3), 291-301, Jl 91.

N K Devaraja's *An Introduction to Sankara's Theory of Knowledge*, poses the question: How can direct knowledge be distinguished from indirect knowledge according to Advaita? This question, concerning Advaita's analysis of knowledge, involves the following problems: 1) What is the object of indirect knowledge? 2) Given that object, in what sense may it be said to be illuminated in indirect knowledge? 3) If a modification of the mind (vrtti) can be directly known, why cannot an object of inference also be directly known? 4)Why doesn't consciousness have direct access to the objects of mediate and immediate knowledge instead of being dependent upon a vrtti? 5) How can ignorance reside in consciousness?

GRIMES, Thomas R. Statistical Explanation, Probability, and Counteracting Conditions. Brit J Phil Sci, 39(4), 495-503, D 88.

GRIMES, Thomas R. Truth, Content, and the Hypothetico-Deductive Method. Phil Sci, 57(3), 514-522, S 90.

After presenting the major objections raised against standard formulations of the H-D method of theory testing, I identify what seems to be an important element of truth underlying the method. I then draw upon this element in an effort to develop a plausible formulation of the H-D method which avoids the various objections.

GRIMES, Thomas. Supervenience, Determination, and Dependency. Phil Stud, 62(1), 81-92, Ap 91.

I argue that determination and dependency are distinct relations and that standard formulations of supervenience express (at best) a form of determination but not dependency. I then develop a new type of supervenience that captures a form of dependency.

GRIMSHAW, Jean. "The Idea of a Female Ethic" in *A Companion to Ethics*, SINGER, Peter (ed), 491-499. Cambridge, Blackwell, 1991.

GRIPP-HAGELSTANGE, Helga. Vom Sein zur Selbstreferentialität: Überlegungen zur Theorie autopoietischer Systeme Niklas Luhmanns. Deut Z Phil, 39(1), 80-94, 1991.

Niklas Luhmann develops a new paradigm for the analysis of society—and even more: reality. Sociology is no longer conceptualized as action theory but as theory of "autopietische systeme". The article wants to explain the heuristical implicants of this change of paradigm: based on assumptions of modern physics and the cognitive sciences Luhmann declares all assumptions of identity as mere illusions. Instead of this he declares that there is no way to escape the self-reference of our mind—and the world. The article discusses if the theorem of self-reference and the way it is presented by Luhmann should be called meta-physical or not.

GRISEZ, Germain. History as Argument for Revision in Moral Theology. Thomist, 55(1), 103-116, Ja 91.

This article evaluates the appropriateness of using *The Making of Moral Theology*, by John Mahoney, S.J., as a historical introduction to Catholic moral theology. In my judgment it should not be used for the specified purpose, because Mahoney (1) holds dissenting positions, (2) does not accept Vatican II's teaching concerning the methodological requirements of moral theology, (3) takes positions which appear to deny infallibly proposed teachings, (4) commends views at odds with the Holy Office's 1956 Instruction on Situation Ethics, and (5) uses history to support one side of the current debate among Catholic moral theologians.

GRISEZ, Germain. When Do People Begin? Proc Cath Phil Ass, 63, 27-47, 1990.

The thesis of this paper is that most human individuals begin at fertilization and that both morality and law should consider all living human individuals to be persons. Five sorts of counterpositions are criticized: (i) that personhood is a status bestowed by others; (ii) that it is an attribute which some human individuals achieve through development; (iii) that only nonbodily entities are persons; (iv) that only human bodies having an adequate basis for intellectual acts are persons; and (v) that human individuality, and with it personhood, begins only at the primitive streak stage.

GRISWOLD JR, Charles L. Rhetoric and Ethics: Adam Smith on Theorizing about the Moral Sentiments. Phil Rhet, 24(3), 213-237, 1991.

In this paper I argue that Smith's *Theory of Moral Sentiments* possesses an intricate rhetorical form, and that Smith's choice of rhetorical form was a deliberate reflection of his substantive conception of how ethics ought to be done. In the course of spelling out his neo-Aristotelian conception of how ethics ought to be done, I argue that there is also a sophisticated Sceptical strategy underlying Smith's view as to how ethics ought to be done. The paper goes on to explore this unusual blend of strategies and assumptions. I conclude by pointing to some questions that any defender of Smith's take on ethics would have to address

GRISWOLD JR, Charles L. Unifying Plato: Charles Kahn on Platonic *Prolepsis*. Ancient Phil, 10(2), 243-262, Fall 90.

Do Plato's dialogues form a proper *corpus*, or are they more like pieces to unrelated puzzles? This is a difficult and fascinating question that has been discussed since antiquity, and is connected to important questions about the sense in which Plato had "a philosophy," a system of thought, etc. Charles Kahn has argued in a series of influential papers that at least some groups of dialogues are linked to each other "proleptically." Kahn combines this claim with an insistence on hermeneutic relevance of the dialogue form. In this paper I argue that his attempt fails, and indeed fails in ways that help us understand how best to resolve the famous "corpus" problem.

GROARKE, Leo. "Skepticism and International Affairs: Toward a New Realism" in *Issues in War and Peace: Philosophical Inquiries*, KUNKEL, Joseph (ed), 103-113. Wolfeboro, Longwood, 1989.

Contrary to the views of most philosophical commentators, I argue that skepticism and the political realism it entails provide a positive and illuminating outlook on international affairs.

GROBLER, Adam. Between Rationalism and Relativism: On Larry Laudan's Model of Scientific Rationality. Brit J Phil Sci, 41(4), 493-507, D 90.

GRODIN, Michael A and ANNAS, George J. Treating the Troops: A Commentary. Hastings Center Rep, 21(2), 24-27, Mr-Ap 91.

GROENENDIJK, Jeroen and STOKHOF, Martin. Dynamic Predicate Logic. Ling Phil, 14(1), 39-100, F 91.

GRONDIN, Jean. L'universalisation de l'herméneutique chez Hans-Georg Gadamer. Arch Phil, 53(4), 531-545, O-D 90.

The purpose of this article is to sort out the meaning of the universality claim specific to Gadamer's hermeneutics. The universalization of hermeneutics signals a departure from the methodological horizon of a hermeneutics of human sciences. In the first two sections of *Truth and Method*, Gadamer attempts to free the human sciences from the idea of method, by drawing on the reflections of Helmholtz. If hermeneutics raises a claim to universality, that is an ontological and philosophical claim, in the third part of the book, it is because the belonging to tradition and to a community of interrogation, which is inseparable from the truth claim in human sciences, is originally embedded in language itself. Language however should not be understood following the propositional logic of pure enunciation, but following the logic of question and answer. Every utterance stems from a dialogue outside of which it can have no sense. Understanding therefore strives to go back from what is said to this context of dialogue, in classical or Augustinian terms, to trace the external word back to the inner word, i.e., to the dialogue with oneself that is constitutive of our finitude.

GRONDIN, Jean. Prolegomena to an Understanding of Heidegger's Turn. Grad Fac Phil J, 14(2)-15(1), 85-108, 1991.

By examining the original intent of the third, unpublished part of "Being and Time," this article seeks to establish that the seeds of Heidegger's *Kehre* were sown well before 1933. It is therefore incorrect to interpret Heidegger's turn as a consequence of the philosopher's involvement with the Nazis. The paper also aims to set forth a philosophical basis for any interpretation of the *Kehre*.

GROOTENDORST, Rob. Everyday Argumentation from a Speech Act Perspective. Commun Cog, 24(1), 111-134, 1991.

GROSS, Alan G. Reinventing Certainty: The Significance of Ian Hacking's Realism. Proc Phil Sci Ass, 1, 421-431, 1990.

This paper examines Ian Hacking's arguments in favor of entity realism. It shows that his examples from science do not support his realism. Furthermore, his proposed criterion of experimental use is neither sufficient nor necessary for conferring a privileged status on his preferred unobservables. Nonetheless his insight is genuine; it may be most profitably seen as part of a more general effort to create a space for a new form of scientific and philosophical certainty, one that does not require foundations.

GROSS, Hyman and FEINBERG, Joel. *Philosophy of Law (Fourth Edition)*. Belmont, Wadsworth, 1991.

This revision of our textbook-anthology has many new features: more legal realism and the Critical Legal Studies movement, Dworkin's exchange with J L Markie and also his article on abortion, five new Supreme Court cases in the Liberty section, articles on privacy by Alan Ryan and Richard Posner, J J Thomson's "Self-Defense and Rights," a new subsection on "The Machinery of Justice," Tom Nagel on compensatory discrimination, Fuller's Speluncean Explores" and *US versus Holmes*, Curley's "Excusing Rape," a new subsection on attempts and completed crimes, and five new articles on punishment (Hart, Moore, Hampton, Murphy and Bedan).

GROSSBERG, Lawrence. Postmodernist Elitism and Postmodern Struggles. Grad Fac Phil J, 13(2), 215-240, 1990.

This article surveys the different discursive domains of the concept of postmodernism: culture, history, politics and theory. After critiquing the assumptions of the first three, it offers a theoretically grounded elucidation of the claim of historical postmodernity and of the importance of popular culture and everyday life in these configurations.

GROSSBERG, Rami P and ALBERT, Michael H. Rich Models. J Sym Log, 55(3), 1292-1298, S 90.

GROSSINGER, Robin. Concerning the Interests of Insects. Between Species, 7(1), 44-46, Wint 91.

GROSSMAN, Morris. Interpreting *Interpretations*. Bull Santayana Soc, 8, 18-28, Fall 90.

This paper is at once a review of the new MIT Press edition of *Interpretations of Poetry and Religion* as well as an overview of a central problem of Santayana criticism. The argument (pushed to hyperbolic or ironic extremes) is that there are no arguments, or univocal "positions," in Santayana and that he is best seen as a literary dramatist and ironist. Through the device of a "double moral grid," various instances of these dramatic ironies are presented. A preliminary discussion justifies this approach by reference to increased tendencies, in Richard Rorty and others, to equate philosophy and literature.

GROSSMANN, Andreas. Hegel, Heidegger, and the Question of Art Today. Res Phenomenol, 20, 112-135, 1990.

GROVER, Dorothy. Truth and Language-World Connections. J Phil, 87(12), 671-687, D 90.

Some difficulties of incorporating language-world connections in an analysis of truth are addressed. Hartry Field's suggestion ("Tarski's Theory of Truth," *The Journal of Philosophy*, 69, pages 347-75) that something like the causal-historical theories of reference be used to eliminate 'denotes' and 'applies' from base clauses, in a version of Tarski's truth definition, is shown to have true and false sentences connected by the same causal connections to reality. This poses a problem if we assume, as Field does, that truth has an explanatory role. For if truth itself has an explanatory role, one would expect true and false sentences to be connected in different ways to the world. Either different language-world connections must be found for truth and falsity; or, if truth itself does not have an explanatory role, we should abandon the idea of incorporating language-world connections in our analysis of truth.

GROVER, Robinson A. Individualism, Absolutism, and Contract in Hobbes' Political Theory. Hobbes Stud, 3, 89-111, 1990.

Philosophers tend to over-emphasize Hobbes's ties to continental sources and neglect his English background. English sources for Hobbes's thought include late Humanism, especially Raleigh's Essay on War; Stuart royal absolutism, especially James I's Speech to Parliament in 1609; and Common Law, especially Christopher Saint German's discussion of Law of Nature and of Contract in Doctor and Student. Hobbes's originality lies in his ability to synthesize a coherent theory out of disparate doctrines of individualism and absolutism. The Common Law concept of contract is the bridge that allows him to do this.

GRUEN, Lori. "Animals" in *A Companion to Ethics*, SINGER, Peter (ed), 343-353. Cambridge, Blackwell, 1991.

This work provides an easily accessible review of the current philosophical debate over the moral status of non-human animals. I suggest that the burden of proof falls on those who do not consider non-human animals appropriate targets of moral concern. Peter Singer's utilitarian view and Tom Regan's rights-based theory are discussed and the strengths and weaknesses of each examined. I conclude by suggesting a third approach, grounded on empathy, is worthy of further exploration.

GRÜNBAUM, Adolf. The Degeneration of Popper's Theory of Demarcation. Epistemologia, 12(2), 235-260, Jl-D 89.

In a 1983 book, Popper indicted inductivism anew, claiming that inductive confirmations can easily be found for bad theories. Popper's centerpiece, psychoanalytic theory, turns out to spell precisely the opposite moral, because its major postulates lack cogent inductive support, although they are falsifiable, which Popper denies. It is shown in the paper that, by 1983, Popper's theory of demarcation between science and nonscience has become a degenerative research program, unable to do justice to actual science. Finally, Popper misconstrues Einsteinian space-time as a conceptual outgrowth of the Parmenidean myth of a timeless world.

GRÜNBAUM, Adolf. "The Psychoanalytic Enterprise in Scientific Perspective" in *Scientific Theories*, SAVAGE, C Wade (ed), 41-58. Minneapolis, Univ of Minn Pr, 1990.

This paper examines critically Freud's own principal arguments for his theories of psychopathology, dream-formation and generation of slips. Besides, it offers (i) an unfavorable appraisal of the psychoanalytic method of free association qua method of *causal* inquiry; (ii) a negative verdict on the merits of the current neo-revisionist versions of psychoanalysis. The extant experimental evidence does not alter these critical conclusions.

GRUNDSTEIN-AMADO, Rivka. An Integrative Model of Clinical-Ethical Decision Making. Theor Med, 12(2), 157-170, Je 91.

The purpose of this paper is to propose a model of clinical-ethical decision making which will assist the health care professional to arrive at an ethically defensible judgment. The model highlights the integration between ethics and decision making. The model is composed of three major elements. The ethical component, the decision making component and the contextual component. The model suggests that in order to arrive at an ethically, justifiable sound decision one make reference to those three elements. (edited)

GRUNDY, Jeremy. Philosophical Scepticism: An Intelligible Challenge. Eidos, 8(2), 139-151, D 89.

GRUNEBAUM, James O. Ownership as Theft. Monist, 73(4), 544-563, O 90.

David Gauthier's *Morals by Agreement*, state of nature justification of a form of ownership which resembles private ownership fails. It fails, as do all other state of nature justifications, because it is grounded upon unrealistic conditions which make any form of ownership unnecessary and because it is question begging. Further, because Gauthier's form of ownership legitimates taking what another owns without his consent, Gauthier's form of ownership is like theft. And this resemblance to theft makes Gauthier's ownership impossible to put into practice.

GRUNWALD, Sabine. Das Individuum, die Politik und die Philosophie. Deut Z Phil, 38(5), 480-487, 1990.

The 40th and 50th can be characterized as a period of accumulation of political as well as philosophical, social and cultural patterns of thought which had a strong influence on the further directions of development of the work of J P Sartre. This article points out the contradictory networks especially the political and philosophical moments of this process and gives critical view on simplificating interpretations, which are trying to separate both sides from each other. Some inner-theoretical assumptions for the development of the Sartrean individual are investigated. The aim of our work is to stimulate a more differentiated discussion. Analyzing the theoretical background of the natural dialectics, the necessarity of a complex investigation of Sartre's philosophical positions is demonstrated.

GRYGIEL, Joanna. Absolutely Independent Sets of Generation of Filters in Boolean Algebras. Rep Math Log, 24, 25-35, 1990.

In this paper we consider the notion of absolute independence in Boolean algebras and its counterpart in classical logic. We prove that any countable generated filter in any Boolean algebra which contains finitely many coatoms has an absolutely independent set of generators. By use of this theorem we get some results on algebra and logic.

GRYGIEL, Stanislaw. Per l'Europa dopo il crollo della Cortina di Ferro. Aquinas, 34(1), 15-24, Ja-Ap 91.

GRYKO, Czeslaw. Law and Culture: The Conception of Legal Culture (in Polish). Ann Univ Mariae Curie-Phil, 10, 81-98, 1985.

The paper presents an analysis of the conception of "legal culture," indicating the incorrectness of the definitions proposed so far. For legal culture the analysis by the formal-dogmatic method of positive law in operation alone is found insufficient. Apart from the question about what is in agreement with the law, one should also ask if this is just. The positivistic approach does not facilitate legal culture, since it does not enable an evaluation of the legal system. According to the author, the need of natural law as a factor evaluating positive law is obvious. There also exists a real possibility of reconciling the conception of natural law with Marxist worldview. Legal culture is described as "...the wholeness of norms, values, opinions and behaviour expressing the ideas which determine the legal system, known to and obeyed by the authorities and the society, as well as enabling an evaluation of a given legal order and historical and spatial comparison with other legal systems." The paper also contains a narrower term, "the juristic culture," which characterizes legal culture of career people professionally dealing with the law. The necessary supplement of juristic culture is found in ethical culture.

GRYKO, Czeslaw. The Conception of Culture According to Jozef Chalasinski (1904-1979) (in Polish). Ann Univ Mariae Curie-Phil, 10, 131-148, 1985.

The paper indicates the place and role of the writings of J Chalasinski in Polish sociology of culture among whose representatives, such as Bronislaw Malinowski, Florian W Znaniecki, Ludwik Krzywicki, Stefan Czarnowski, and Stanislaw Ossowski, J Chalasinski should also be included, according to the author. The article emphasizes the cultural aspect of J Chalasinski's thought which constituted the main trend in his writings. Its "foundations" should be sought in sociology of education, whose co-creator was J Chalasinski together with F Znaniecki, in a period when this branch assumed a leading position in the science in the world. It constituted a basis for Chalasinski's considerations about the sociology of the village as an environment and of peasants as a social class as well as the problems of the intelligentsia. His theoretical construction is crowned with a theory of culture treated together with the problems of personality and nation. (edited)

GRZEGORCZYK, Andrzej. "The Principle of Transcendence and the Foundation of Axiology" in *Logic and Ethics*, GEACH, Peter (ed), 71-78. Norwell, Kluwer, 1991.

GUARIGLIA, Osvaldo. Los fundamentos discursivos de la democracia y los conflictos de intereses. Dianoia, 36(36), 83-95, 1990.

GUARIGLIA, Osvaldo. Para una metahistoria del narrativisimo. Dialogos, 26(57), 59-75, Ja 91.

GUEGUEN, John A. "Parallels on Work, Theory and Practice in Yves R Simon and John Paul II" in *Freedom in the Modern World: Jacques Maritain, Yves R Simon, Mortimer J Adler*, TORRE, Michael D (ed), 153-161. Notre Dame, Univ Notre Dame Pr, 1989.

The article focuses on representatives of two ancient traditions of discourse, one secular and academic, the other ecclesial and pastoral. It sets side by side the lectures of Yves Simon and the encyclical of John Paul II in order to observe their common insights into human work as reached through diverse but compatible methods (Aristotelian philosophy and Sacred Scripture), in the context of challenges both face from contrary forces at work in the modern world.

GUERRIÈRE, Daniel (ed). *Phenomenology of the Truth Proper to Religion*. Albany, SUNY Pr, 1990.

Beneath truth as "coherence of discourse" and truth as "adequation of mind and thing" lies truth as *alètheia* (manifestness, disclosure), rediscovered by phenomenological philosophy. This book collects articles by Anglophonic scholar-philosophers on the issue of the kind of *alètheia* that is peculiar to religion. The whole spectrum of phenomenology is represented: transcendental (Laycock and Hart), existential (Dupré, Clayton, Farley, and Guerrière), hermeneutic (Westphal, Caputo, and Kearney), ethical (Cohen), and deconstructive (Lowe). An introduction by the editor shows how the question of the truth proper to religion arises.

GUERRIÈRE, Daniel. "The Truth, the Nontruth, and the Untruth Proper to Religion" in *Phenomenology of the Truth Proper to Religion*, GUERRIÈRE, Daniel (ed), 75-101. Albany, SUNY Pr, 1990.

For phenomenology, truth is manifestness. The truth fundamental to religion would therefore be the manifestness of the salvational Power. The derivative truths proper to religion are the manifestive power of the original announcement of salvational experience, the manifestive power of tradition, and that of theological reflection. The criterion of all religious truth can only be fruitfulness. The non-truth proper to religion is that as opposed to which the truth appears as finite: the profane, the overt, and the *lēthe* (concealment). The untruth or falsity proper to religion is also explicated (including a critical study of anti-theism).

GUERTIN, Ghyslaine. Glenn Gould: "archilecteur" *des Variations Goldberg*. Horiz Phil, 1(2), 81-101, 1991.

GUERTIN, Ghyslaine. "Glenn Gould: La technologie au service d'une nouvelle définition de la musique" in *XIth International Congress in Aesthetics, Nottingham 1988*, WOODFIELD, Richard (ed), 74-77. Nottingham, Nottingham Polytech, 1990.

GUERZONI, J A D and ALVES, E H. Extending Montague's System: A Three Valued Intensional Logic. Stud Log, 49(1), 127-132, Mr 90.

In this note we present a three-valued intensional logic, which is an extension of both Montague's intensional logic and Lukasiewicz three-valued logic. Our system is obtained by adapting Gallin's version of intensional logic (see Gallin, D, *Intensional and Higher-order Modal Logic*). Here we give only the necessary modifications to the latter. An acquaintance with Gallin's work is presupposed.

GUIGNON, Charles B and HILEY, David R. "Biting the Bullet: Rorty on Private and Public Morality" in *Reading Rorty*, MALACHOWSKI, Alan (ed), 339-364. Cambridge, Blackwell, 1991.

Rorty's anti-foundationalism is motivated by his ideal of a liberal society which supports both private fulfillment and public justice. Such an "aesthetized culture" will allow for unconstrained "abnormal discourse" while simultaneously encouraging solidarity and tolerance. Rorty's "apologia" for this society builds on a minimalist, "existentialist" picture of a self whose highest goal is self-enlargement, and a "communitarian" dream of allegiance built solely on a shared sense of the contingency of all our beliefs and practices. We argue that Rorty's ideal society turns out to be self-defeating, and that the kind of hermeneutic approach Rorty rejects has more to offer for envisioning an ideal society.

GUILD, Elizabeth (trans) and BRAIDOTTI, Rosi. *Patterns of Dissonance*. New York, Routledge, 1991.

A critical evaluation of post-structuralist discussions about the death of the subject and the crisis of philosophical reason, in relation to feminist theorizations of an alternative female subjectivity and forms of knowledge. Emphasis on Foucault, Derrida, Deleuze and Irigaray as well as on English speaking feminist epistemologists like Harding and Haraway. The MAW conclusion points to an autonomous development of feminist philosophy of the subject, which is defined in an asymmetrical relationship to deconstructions of the classical subject of philosophy. The asymmetry is analysed in the light of Irigaray's notion of sexual difference and a position is put forth of feminist epistemological nomadism as the mode best suited to this new female feminist subjectivity.

GUIN, Philip. Coaching: Who Needs It and What is It? Thinking, 9(3), 36-39, 1990.

GUNNING, Karel. CAHBI: Europe Needs a Universal Bioethical System. Ethics Med, 6(3), 38-41, Autumn 90.

Bioethics is part of the ethics for the whole (pluralistic) society. Europe needs an *objective* ethical system, that is a system which is valid and acceptable for the whole community (Europe), but also a *universal* system, that is a system which is valid for all mankind. The article makes a plea for *humanitarian* bioethics, based on the same principles (recognition of the inherent dignity and equal and inalienable rights of every member of the human family) and aimed at the same ideals (freedom, justice and peace) as the Universal Declaration and the European Convention on Human Rights.

GUNTER, Pete A Y (ed). *Creativity in George Herbert Mead*. Lanham, Univ Pr of America, 1990.

This book presents a symposium on the role which the concept of creativity plays in the thought of George Herbert Mead. Among the concepts dealt with are: perspectives, the act, relativity, cosmology, system, the present, experience, temporality, novelty, ethical objectivity. The main speaker in the symposium is David Lewis Miller a student of Mead's and an editor of his works. Other symposiasts include Charles W Morris, H D Duncan, A J Reck, J A Reck, and H N Lee.

GUNZ, Sally and MC CUTCHEON, John. Some Unresolved Ethical Issues in Auditing. J Bus Ethics, 10(10), 777-785, O 91.

Independence is a fundamental concept to the audit. There is a clear relationship between independence and conflict of interest in all professions. This paper examines this relationship in the auditing profession and in the context of three specific practices. The paper analyses these practices by using the Davis model of conflict of interest. The results of this analysis give rise to some interesting questions for the ethical practices of the auditing profession.

GUOBAO, Jiang. Traditional Chinese Culture: Contemporary Developments —Profound Selections from the Works of Fang Dongmei. Chin Stud Phil, 22(2), 63-85, Wint 90-91.

Fang Dongmei was a native of Tongcheng, Anhui Province. He taught for over fifty years, and produced over ten major works. He devoted his entire life to the study of comparative cultures and comparative philosophy, developing a unique philosophy of Eastern and Western cultures. This article is limited to an objective appraisal of Fang Dongmei's discussions of the modernization of traditional Chinese culture.

GUPTA, Amitabha. The Concrete and the Abstract Science: Description versus Explanation. J Indian Counc Phil Res, 6(3), 67-87, My-Ag 89.

The philosophers and historians of science often debate as to whether the 'kernel' of science is either only description or only explanation, or both. Since this issue is directly linked with the nature and goal of science, it assumes great importance. The author looks at this debate by putting it in the context of a historically sensitive analysis of the growth of scientific knowledge and concludes that too restrictive a use of the word 'science' would leave out a wide range of activities that legitimately could come under it as their practitioners pursue them with various objectives, practical or otherwise. However, within that the author goes on to make a broad typological distinction between "concrete" and "abstract" science and identifies their main features.

GUPTA, Som Raj. The Word That Became the Absolute: Relevance of Sankara's Ontology of Language. J Indian Counc Phil Res, 7(1), 27-41, S-D 89.

The paper presents the view that language as the interpretative principle cannot encompass reality and ever remains adventitious to it. The interpreted world is a self-negating and tragic world, but the way out of this tragic ignorance does not lie in rejection of language but through participation in it. Man has to cease to be a user and manipulator of language; he has to become a passive and anonymous hearer of the word till he and the word come to coalesce. That will be the moment when the three primordial interconstitutive *others*—man, world and language—will get transformed into truth itself.

GUREVIC, R. Equational Theory of Positive Numbers with Exponentiation is Not Finitely Axiomatizable. Annals Pure Applied Log, 49(1), 1-30, S 90.

GUROIAN, Vigen. Tradition and Ethics: Prospects in a Liberal Society. Mod Theol, 7(3), 205-224, Ap 91.

GURREY, Charles S. Faith and the Possibility of Private Meaning. Relig Stud, 26(2), 199-205, Je 90.

GUSEYNOV, A A. "Soviet Ethics and New Thinking" in *In the Interest of Peace: A Spectrum of Philosophical Views*, KLEIN, Kenneth H (ed), 117-123. Wolfeboro, Longwood, 1990.

GUSMANO, Joseph J. *Thinking Philosophically: An Introduction to Philosophy with Readings*. Lanham, Univ Pr of America, 1990.

GUSTAFSON, Don. Prichard, Davidson and Action. Phil Invest, 14(3), 205-230, Jl 91.

This essay examines the structural similarities of Prichard's and Davidson's theories of action. Each is a view with a central role for the notion of primitive action. Differences of view are due to metaphysical presuppositions, one a dualist, the other physicalist. The structurally similar view is then assessed in light of a large set of linguistic data concerning 'action', 'causation', 'doing' and 'cause' and 'effect'; the collected data are inspired by the work of Z Vendler and others.

GUTE, Hans B and REUTER, K K. The Last Word on Elimination of Quantifiers in Modules. J Sym Log, 55(2), 670-673, Je 90.

Consider the structure with universe A group G, in the language where a relation symbol is introduced for every coset modulo A subgroup of a power of G; then this structure eliminates quantifiers. This result generalizes the well-known elimination by PP-formulae for Abelian groups and modules.

GUTIÉRREZ, Claudio. El paradigma computacional aplicado al estudio de la vida. Rev Filosof (Costa Rica), 28(67-68), 183-189, D 90.

The computational paradigm has given birth to a new discipline, parallel to artificial intelligence, under the name of artificial life. Both are interdisciplinary and make essential use of electronic computation. In both cases computing is a methodological tool. More importantly, both disciplines constitute a scientific effort to promote generalization of two contemporary empirical sciences: pscyhology and biology. Finally, some philosophical consequences of AI are examined. (edited)

GUTIÉRREZ, Gilberto. La estructura consecuencialista del utilitarismo. Rev Filosof (Spain), 3, 141-174, 1990.

Despite the possibility and actual existence of non-utilitarian versions of consequentialism, utilitarianism in its diverse formulations is conceived of as the paradigm of consequentialist theory. The latter is in turn construed as an essentially monist theory of the good which aims at developing an all-embracing theory of practical rationality. These features account for its denial of an ultimately independent status to moral or otherwise restrictions upon the rational obligation of agents to maximize the good. Paradoxes and counterintuitive results render doubtful its claims to performing as a sound and consistent moral theory.

GUTMANN, Amy and THOMPSON, Dennis. "Moral Conflict and Political Consensus" in *Liberalism and the Good*, DOUGLASS, R Bruce (ed), 125-147. New York, Routledge, 1990.

GUTOWSKI, Piotr. Charles Hartshorne's Rationalism. Process Stud, 19(1), 1-9, Spr 90.

The purpose of this article is to define Hartshorne's rationalism, to show its genesis and its limits. Hartshorne is a rationalist in the methodological sense, i.e., he believes that we can reach philosophically valuable knowledge (true, universal, necessary) only if it fulfills rationalistic criteria. He thinks, moreover, that differences between various metaphysical positions lie only in their logical structure, and that using exclusively objective logical criteria (e.g., consistency, coherence), we can select the best one. It is argued in the article that the criteria suggested by Hartshorne are neither purely logical (formal) nor objective, and that his metaphilosophy needs genuine empirical criteria for evaluating different metaphysical solutions as well as his own.

GUY, Alfred. The Role of Aristotle's *Praxis* Today. J Value Inq, 25(3), 287-289, Jl 91.

GUY, Josephine and SMALL, Ian. Usefulness in Literary History. Brit J Aes, 31(3), 259-264, Jl 91.

This essay examines and critiques various uses of the term 'literary history' in English Studies. It identifies two basic, but opposing kinds of literary history, the 'political' and the 'aesthetic'. It then examines their relative utility (where utility is defined in terms of the specificity of the explanations which a literary history provides) and demonstrates their deficiencies on these grounds. It suggests an outline for a literary history which might combine elements of the aesthetic and the political, and yet be specific in the accounts of literary works which it provides.

GVISHIANI, J M. "Impact of Global Modelling on Modern Methodology of Science" in *Logic, Methodology and Philosophy of Science, VIII*, FENSTAD, J E (ed), 333-350. New York, Elsevier Science, 1989.

GYEKYE, Kwame. "Person and Community in African Thought" in *I, We and Body: First Joint Symposium of Philosophers from Africa and from the Netherlands*, KIMMERLE, Heinz (ed), 47-63. Atlantic Highlands, Gruner, 1989.

HAACK, Susan. "Rebuilding the Ship while Sailing on the Water" in *Perspectives on Quine*, BARRETT, Robert (ed), 111-127. Cambridge, Blackwell, 1990.

This paper is intended as a modestly naturalistic contribution to the epistemology of empirical knowledge. Acknowledging the legitimacy of the traditional tasks of epistemology, but repudiating the traditional, *a priori* approach to those tasks. It has two basic themes: (1) that the explication of the concept of justification should be focussed on human subjects and the relation between their beliefs and their experiences; the explication offered is "Foundherentist." (2) That the ratification of criteria of empirical justification relies on one's presumed knowledge of human cognitive capacities; the ratification offered is conditional: if any criteria of justification are appropriately related to the goal of inquiry, the Foundherentist criteria are.

HAACK, Susan. Recent Obituaries of Epistemology. Amer Phil Quart, 27(3), 199-212, Jl 90.

This paper is a critique of two revolutionary trends in recent epistemological (or anti-epistemological) work: revolutionary nihilism, as represented by Rorty, according to which the traditional projects of epistemology are misconceived and should be abandoned; and revolutionary naturalism, as represented by Stich and the Churchlands, according to which the traditional projects of epistemolgy are misconceived and should be replaced by new, natural-scientific projects. In each case the revolutionaries' arguments are shown to be quite inconclusive, and their conclusions are shown to be self-defeating.

HAAFTEN, Wouter Van. The Justification of Conceptual Development Claims. J Phil Educ, 24(1), 51-69, Sum 90.

Developmental theories often claim that later stages are better than earlier stages. The question is, how such claims could be justified. I argue that the notion of inconsistency reduction cannot be of any help for moral, aesthetic, or religious development. Rather, it needs to be shown that the later stage uses better judgment criteria. I make some suggestions about conditions which stages must satisfy for such justification of conceptual development claims to be possible, and about the structure of the requisite argumentation which would involve a kind of natural bridge from is to ought.

HAAR, Michel. The Ambivalent Unthought of the Overman and the Duality of Heidegger's Political Thinking. Grad Fac Phil J, 14(2)-15(1), 109-136, 1991.

HAAR, Michel. The Doubleness of the Unthought of the Overman: Ambiguities of Heideggerian Political Thought. Res Phenomenol, 20, 87-111, 1990.

HAAR, Michel. Vie et totalité chez Nietzsche. Philosophique (France), 1(89), 115-134, 1989.

HAAS, Leonard J. Hide-and-Seek or Show-and-Tell? Emerging Issues of Informed Consent. Ethics Behavior, 1(3), 175-189, 1991.

This article reviews key philosophical and legal underpinnings of mental health professionals's obligation to obtain informed consent from consumers of their services. The basic components of informed consent are described, and strategies for clinically and ethically appropriate methods of obtaining informed consent are discussed. Emerging issues in informed consent involving duty to assess and protect against client dangerousness, obligations to third parties, and issues of deception are considered as well. The article proposes that part of the process of obtaining informed consent is the cultivation of a treatment environment that emphasizes beneficence and client autonomy.

HABART, Karol. Bounds in Weak Truth-Table Reducibility. Notre Dame J Form Log, 32(2), 233-241, Spr 91.

A necessary and sufficient condition on a recursive function is given so that arbitrary sets can be truth-table reduced via this function as the bound. A corresponding hierarchy of recursive functions is introduced and some partial results and an open problem are formulated.

HABBERJAM, Barbara (trans) and DELEUZE, Gilles and TOMLINSON, Hugh (trans). *Bergsonism*. Cambridge, MIT Pr, 1991.

HABERMAS, Jürgen. An Intersubjective Concept of Individuality. J Chin Phil, 18(2), 133-141, Je 91.

HABERMAS, Jürgen. "Justice and Solidarity: On the Discussion Concerning Stage 6" in *The Moral Domain: Essays in the Ongoing Discussion between Philosophy and the Social Sciences*, WREN, Thomas E (ed), 224-251. Cambridge, MIT Pr, 1990.

HABERMAS, Jürgen. Sociologie in de Weimarrepubliek. Kennis Methode, 14(4), 367-383, 1990.

HABIB, M A R. Horace's *Ars Poetica* and the Deconstructive Leech. Brit J Aes, 31(1), 13-25, Ja 91.

This paper considers Horace's literary-critical views in the light of deconstructive attitudes towards language and literature, examining the *Ars Poetica*, Horace's poetry and his political context, marked as it was by Augustus's programs of reform and the prevalence of philosophies of indifference toward the world. Using insights of Hegel and Marx on Roman religion, it is concluded that Horace's withdrawal into a private apolitical poetic sphere parallels the subversive gestures of deconstruction. For Horace, poetry itself is a deconstructive vehicle. But, as with deconstruction, Horace's gestures of noncommitment are merely commonplaces of his day and are politically impotent.

HACKER, Edward A and PARRY, William T. *Aristotelian Logic*. Albany, SUNY Pr, 1991.

HACKER, P M S. Experimental Methods and Conceptual Confusion: An Investigation into R L Gregory's Theory of Perception. Iyyun, 40(3), 289-314, Jl 91.

R L Gregory's empirical theory of perception is subjected to philosophical scrutiny. The key idea in his theory is that perceptions are hypotheses. The grammar of 'perceive' and 'perception' is examined and contrasted with that of 'hypothesize' and 'hypthesis' to the detriment of Gregory's account. One source of confusion is located in the homunculus fallacy, in particular in predicating of the brain or nervous system predicates (e.g., 'infer', 'decode', 'interpret') which it only makes sense to attribute to the whole organism.

HACKER, P M S. *Wittgenstein: Meaning and Mind, Volume 3 of an Analytical Commentary on Philosophical Investigations*. Cambridge, Blackwell, 1990.

HACKING, Ian. "Astronomical Improbability" in *Logic, Methodology and Philosophy of Science, VIII*, FENSTAD, J E (ed), 413-426. New York, Elsevier Science, 1989.

The paper analyses arguments based on very small probabilities, especially as they occur in tests of significance of observed astronomical events, such as the distribution of twin stars in the sky. It then proceeds to other uses of probability in cosmology, and concludes by criticising some but only some uses of the anthropic principle.

HACKING, Ian. The Making and Molding of Child Abuse. Crit Inquiry, 17(2), 253-288, Wint 91.

A detailed study of concept formation with striking moral consequences. Child abuse as a distinct notion came into being as battered baby syndrome in 1962. From then on it underwent rapid development, quickly covering any type of physical harm or neglect, and then, about 1975, becoming joined with sexual abuse and incest. Conflicts between medical, social and feminist models are discussed. There has been unending research and creation of agencies, but little agreed knowledge. After 30 years, in 1990, a US Presidential Panel declared that abuse was a "national emergency." What went wrong? Is child abuse a real category at all? Do we have an incorrect model for the type of human knowledge that is relevant?

HACKING, Ian. "Natural Kinds" in *Perspectives on Quine*, BARRETT, Robert (ed), 129-141. Cambridge, Blackwell, 1990.

An admiring examination of Quine's masterful paper, "Natural Kinds." Some points of difference. Quine thinks of the undefinable idea of "kind" as a useful primitive in concept formation which then becomes dispensable with the development of science. This may be a poor theory of concept formation, and "kind" may have quite other roles in our intellectual economy. Dispositional terms form a case in point. Quine argued that they could be explained only in terms of the concept "kind," but that expressions such as "soluble in water" could now be replaced by theoretical understanding. This is simply not true of "soluble in water," which remains a complex of unsolved theoretical and practical problems. An excessive idealistic optimism about the progress of physics, combined with too simple a psychology of learning, leads to a too early abandoning of the idea of "kind."

HACKING, Ian. On Boyd. Phil Stud, 61(1-2), 149-154, F 91.

A brief response to Boyd's criticisms of my paper "A Tradition of Natural Kinds." It discusses Boyd's contribution to the theory of cluster terms, and its connection with the idea of family resemblances. It argues that the "Tradition" is much more recent than is asserted by Boyd. It concludes by resisting the idea that human kinds should succumb to Boyd's essentialist treatment, not because my paper favoured some sort of constructionalism, but because detailed investigation of human kinds prompts a very different analysis from Boyd's lumping all kinds together, without discriminating fundamental differences.

HACKING, Ian. "The Parody of Conversation" in *Truth and Interpretation: Perspectives on the Philosophy of Donald Davidson*, LE PORE, Ernest (ed), 447-458. Cambridge, Blackwell, 1986.

Donald Davidson's "malapropism" paper ("A Nice Derangement of Epitaphs") makes radical interpretation a continuing exchange between a speaker and a hearer. "Truth in a Language," once the centrepiece of Davidson's theory of interpretation, almost drops out because a language is in flux from moment to moment. The present paper examines what this does to Davidson's theory. It welcomes the new attention to the many different ways in which we can make mistakes in speech and understanding. It regrets, however, that interpretation has been reduced to a semi-private language, two people on a desert island, rather than speakers in a community.

HACKING, Ian. The Participant Irrealist At Large in the Laboratory. Brit J Phil Sci, 39(3), 277-294, S 88.

HACKING, Ian. *The Taming of Chance*. New York, Cambridge Univ Pr, 1990.

A study of probability, determinism, information and control during the nineteenth century. It describes two radical and connected transformations in ideas. (1) Determinism was eroded, so that by the end of the century, indeterminism was thinkable. (2) The Enlightenment idea of human nature was displaced by the idea of normal people. These events are placed in a wide range of activities, ranging from medicine to mineralogy, and of enumerations, from the census to suicide. The geographical focus is chiefly on Britain and France but begins and ends with Prussia as an example. The concluding chapter is a detailed analysis of Peirce's conception of chance. Chance begins the book in a disorderly way, as the "superstition of the vulgar" and ends it as the carrier of a new kind of law, statistical law, that underwrites every kind of order.

HACKING, Ian. A Tradition of Natural Kinds. Phil Stud, 61(1-2), 109-126, F 91.

This paper argues that there is relatively noncontentious—neither "constructionalist" nor "essentialist"—tradition of natural kinds, represented by Mill, Whewell, Venn, Peirce, Russell, Quine and many more. Independence thesis: it is a fact about nature, independent of human judgment, that there are various kinds. Definability thesis: "natural kind" might be definable in only a rough-and-ready way, and there might be distinct types of kinds, defined in different ways. Utility thesis: the recognition of kinds plays a central role in practical daily affairs. Uniqueness thesis: there is a unique best taxonomy. The paper favours the first three theses and rejects the fourth one. It also urges that most kinds of people and their behaviour—"human kinds"—are not natural kinds in the sense of the tradition.

HACKING, Ian. Two Souls in One Body. Crit Inquiry, 17(4), 838-867, Sum 91.

Two questions are addressed: Is Multiple Personality Disorder "real," and in what senses? Does it matter whether a patient's post-theory memories of her past are true or not? Both questions are tackled by re-examining a case from the 1920s. She does conform to contemporary standards of MPD. Her treatment then yielded a set of "memories" quite different from what one would expect now, the actual practitioner discouraging half-remembered incest while a modern MPD therapist would abreact such material. This does matter; on the other hand the fact that the modern worker would uncover a great many alters does not show that the patient had them in fact, without their being elicited. It is also documented that the practitioner was not fully candid about his patient, and his success.

HADORN, David C. The Oregon Priority-Setting Exercise: Quality of Life and Public Policy. Hastings Center Rep, 21(3), Supp 11-16, My-Je 91.

The recent Oregon effort to set explicit priorities within its Medicaid program marked the first systematic application of the quality-adjusted life year concept to American social policy. Medical and surgical treatments were ranked in priority roughly in accordance with their expected net impacts on patients's quality of life and (to a lesser extent) length of life. Oregon eluded the ethical dangers inherent in the use of quality-of-life judgments by focusing on the *change* in quality of life afforded by *treatments*, rather than on *point-in-time* quality of life assessments of individual *patients*.

HAEFLIGER, Gregor. Ingarden und Husserls transzendentaler Idealismus. Husserl Stud, 7(2), 103-121, 1990.

In einer in dieser Zeitschrift erschienenen neueren Studie hat Ingrid M Wallner Roman Ingardens Interpretation des Husserlschen Idealismus sowie die damit zusammenhängende Ingardensche Husserl-Kritik einer neuen Beurteilung unterzogen. Wir greifen diese Diskussion auf und möchten im folgenden unter bezug auf Ingardens Sichtweise der sogenannten konstitutiven Probleme einige Gesichtspunkte zur Geltung bringen, die für eine (Neu-)Beurteilung von Ingardens Husserl-Lektüre wichtig sind.

HAIGHT, Mary R. Conditional Essences. Brit J Aes, 31(1), 48-57, Ja 91.

HAIGHT, Mary. Hypnosis and the Philosophy of Mind. Proc Aris Soc, 90, 171-189, 1989-90.

HAILPERIN, Theodore. Probability Logic in the Twentieth Century. Hist Phil Log, 12(1), 71-110, 1990.

This essay describes a variety of contributions which relate to the connection of probability with logic. Some are grand attempts at providing a logical foundation for probability and inductive inference. Others are concerned with probabilistic inference or, more generally, with the transmittance of probability through the structure (logical syntax) of language. In this latter context probability is considered as a semantic notion playing the same role as does truth value in conventional logic. At the conclusion of the essay two fully elaborated semantically based constructions of probability logic are presented.

HAJDIN, Mane. External and Now-For-Then Preferences in Hare's Theory. Dialogue (Canada), 29(2), 305-310, 1990.

HAJDIN, Mane. Is There More to Speech Acts Than Illocutionary Force and Propositional Content? Nous, 25(3), 353-357, Je 91.

The paper criticizes the view that knowing the illocutionary force and the propositional content of a speech act is *sufficient* for understanding it. It does so by showing that knowing who the promisor is and who the promisee is, which is essential for understanding the meaning of a promise, is not a part of knowing its illocutionary force and propositional content. Similarily, knowing who the 'requestor' is and who the 'requestee' it is not packed into our understanding of the illocutionary force and the propositional content of a request. Towards the end of the paper, the argument is applied to prescriptivist analysis of moral claims (which serve as the basis for most languages of deontic logic) and it is shown as that, for similar reasons, it does not fully capture the meaning of everyday ascriptions of duties.

HAJI, Ishtiyaque. The Symmetry Enigma in Hobbes. Dialogue (Canada), 29(2), 189-204, 1990.

HALA, Vlastimil. On Bolzano's Conception of the Essentials of Ethics and its Coherences (in Czechoslovakian). Filozof Cas, 38(4), 507-521, 1990.

The paper studies the essential ethic conception of Bolzano's in two main lines: first its place in the whole of Bolzano's work, i.e., first of all its relation to famous conceptions of Science Systemology, his fundamental work ("objects in themselves," relation of entailment, structure of science), and second its critical confrontation with opinions of Bolzano's predecessors and contemporaries, especially with practical philosophy of I Kant's. The author finds the fundamental issue between Bolzano and Kant in Bolzano's declining attitude towards Kant's "Copernican revolution" which also projected in his practical philosophy. Nevertheless, Bolzano shrewdly discovers some weaknesses of Kant's solution, e.g., his conception of "postulates." The author believes Bolzano's place in history of ethic theories is important not only from historical point of view (e.g., in relation to Brentano and Husserl) but Bolzano's requirement of coherent rational interpretation of ethic problems is important for systematic philosophy as well.

HALDANE, John. Incarnational Anthropology. Philosophy, 29, 191-211, 91 Supp.

The essay sets out difficulties facing currently favoured approaches in the philosophy of mind and then argues that reflection on the Christian Doctrine that, in the person of Jesus Christ, God became a man may reveal new ways of thinking about what *we* are. If sense is to be made of this doctrine we must think of a *single* subject possessed of divine and human attributes. Applying this idea in the philosophy of mind suggests a view which avoids both Cartesian dualism and physicalism.

HALDANE, John. "Medieval and Renaissance Ethics" in *A Companion to Ethics*, SINGER, Peter (ed), 133-146. Cambridge, Blackwell, 1991.

This essay provides a guide to moral philosophy from the eleventh to the sixteenth centuries. It sketches the background of western ethical theory in the writings of the church fathers and traces the development of the idea of natural law (*ius naturale*) through Aquinas up to Francisco Suarez. Various other issues are discussed, including voluntarism and the rise of humanism.

HALE, Bob. "Nominalism" in *Physicalism in Mathematics*, IRVINE, Andrew D (ed), 121-144. Norwell, Kluwer, 1990.

HALE, Susan C. Modal Realism Without Counterparts. SW Phil Rev, 7(1), 81-90, Ja 91.

In *On the Plurality of Worlds*, David Lewis argues that modal realism needs counterpart theory to make sense of our modal claims about ordinary individuals, e.g., claims like 'I could have been a better basketball player than I am'. Lewis argues against accepting trans-world individuals as the theoretical tool for this task in both of two senses: (1) individuals which exist at different worlds by being wholly present at different worlds, and (2) mereological sums which exist at different worlds by having parts at different worlds. I argue that trans-world individuals taken as mereological sums in this second sense can play the roles of ordinary individuals, so that modal realism does not need counterparts to make sense of our modal claims about ordinary individuals. There may be reasons for preferring counterparts to trans-world individuals taken as mereological sums for this purpose; I leave it to Lewis to offer such reasons.

HALES, Steven D. The Recurring Problem of the Third Man. Auslegung, 17(1), 67-80, Wint 91.

This paper is a discussion of the "third man" argument in Plato's *Parmenides*. Pretty much everyone agrees that Plato must have relied on three assumptions in his regress, which have become known as the One Over Many, Self-Predication, and Nonidentity assumptions. Most writers take Nonidentity to be a largely uncontroversial matter of stipulation. The main virtue of this paper is that it argues that nonidentity is consistent with Plato's explicit premises only if Plato accepted a view in the theory of reference which I believe he would have denied. It is also argued that TMA is purely an exercise in ontology and is little concerned with reference or language.

HALKOWSKA, Katarzyna. A Note on Matrices for Systems of Nonsense-Logics. Stud Log, 48(4), 461-464, D 89.

Some systems of nonsense-logic have arisen from investigations of mathematical theories containing conditional definitions of functions (partial functions). It is obvious that expressions containing such defined terms may be meaningless for some values of their variables. This shows that we encounter some difficulties in theories containing conditional definitions. For such theories neither the classical sentental calculus nor the classical algebra of sets is suitable. In the paper we consider a class of algebras which bears upon the logic of nonsense as the Boolean algebras bears upon the classical sentential calculus.

HALL, David Lynn and AMES, Roger T. Rationality, Correlativity, and the Language of Process. J Speculative Phil, 5(2), 85-106, 1991.

HALL, Pamela. Goerner on Thomistic Natural Law. Polit Theory, 18(4), 638-649, N 90.

This essay criticizes the interpretation of Thomistic natural law given by E A Goerner. It is argued that Goerner, discussing the two standards of right action in Aquinas's ethics (natural law and prudence), improperly relegates natural law to the minimal role of government of so-called "bad men." But his view fails to recognize the way in which natural law and prudence are interdependent for Thomas: the core sense of natural law is that of directedness to our connatural goods, and as such the natural law must guide prudence. Thus the natural law is not transcended even by the virtuous.

HALL, Richard J. Does Representational Content Arise from Biological Function? Proc Phil Sci Ass, 1, 193-199, 1990.

HALL, Robert W. Art and Morality in Plato: A Reappraisal. J Aes Educ, 24(3), 5-13, Fall 90.

HALLER, Rudolf. Wittgenstein y el fisicalismo. Dianoia, 35(35), 163-173, 1989.

HALLETT, Garth. The Genesis of Wittgenstein's Later Philosophy in His Failure as a Phenomenologist. Phil Theol, 5(4), 297-311, Sum 91.

The history of Wittgenstein's failed attempt at pure phenomenology illumines his later thought, both globally and in detail, as well as its relation to Husserlian phenomenology.

HALLETT, Michael. "Physicalism, Reductionism and Hilbert" in *Physicalism in Mathematics*, IRVINE, Andrew D (ed), 183-257. Norwell, Kluwer, 1990.

This paper starts from an anlysis of the difficulties facing Field's attempt, based on conservativeness results, to rid classical physics of any but instrumentalist uses of abstract mathematics. It is based on a detailed comparison with Hilbert, instructive because Hilbert too is often viewed as a reductionist wanting to reduce the notion of mathematical truth to the syntactic notions of conservativeness and consistency in order to avoid reference to abstract mathematical objects. An alternative view of Hilbert is argued for, based on an examination of his approach to geometry, and the "reference free" view that emerges from it, and a close analysis of his views on ideal elements. According to this, classical mathematics is not just a formal extension of "real" mathematics, but has content and meaning in itself.

HALLEUX, Robert. "Visages de Van Helmont, depuis Hélène Metzger jusqu'aà Walter Pagel" in *Études sur/Studies on Hélène Metzger*, FREUDENTHAL, Gad , 35-43. Leiden, Brill, 1990.

HALLIDAY, John. *Markets, Managers and Theory in Education.* Philadelphia, Falmer Pr, 1990.

This book is concerned with the logic of the relationship between educational theory and practice. However, it is not just an academic monograph located within the general area of the philosophy of education it is also a fundamental examination of three currently popular ideas: vocationalism, managerialism and consumerism. Halliday argues that the promoters of these ideas may share a mistaken belief in the value of pursuing a supposed ideal of objective precision in education. He traces the theoretical origins of this ideal and its practical consequences. He concludes by outlining the practical consequences of an alternative view.

HALLIWELL, Stephen. Aristotelian Mimesis Reevaluated. J Hist Phil, 28(4), 487-510, O 90.

A reappraisal of the philosophical credentials of Aristotle's view of artistic representation, in music, visual art and poetry. The article contends that this view offers a conception of representational signification which grows from a notion of 'likeness' (iconicity) but develops, in the *Poetics*, into a more complex, 'dual-aspect' mimeticism, which is neither formalist nor moralistic, and is designed to cope with works of art both as material artefacts and as imaginative conveyors of possible realities.

HALLMAN, Max O. Nietzsche's Environmental Ethics. Environ Ethics, 13(2), 99-125, Sum 91.

I argue that Nietzsche's thinking, contrary to the interpretation of Martin Heidegger, is compatible with an ecologically oriented, environmentally concerned philosophizing. In support of this contention, I show that Nietzsche's critique of traditional Western thinking closely parallels the critique of this tradition by environmentalist writers such as Lynn White, Jr. I also show that one of the principle thrusts of Nietzsche's own philosophizing consists of the attempt to overcome the kind of thinking that has provided a theoretical foundation for the technological control and exploitation of the natural world. Finally, I show that Nietzsche's notion of the will to power, at least in several of its formulations, has certain affinities to the ecosystem approach of modern ecologists.

HALPER, Edward. "Hegel and the Problem of the Differentia" in *Essays on Hegel's Logic*, DI GIOVANNI, George (ed), 191-202. Albany, SUNY Pr, 1990.

The problem of the differentia is whether or not the differentia belongs to the genus it differentiates. There are plausible arguments for both including it in and excluding it from the genus. This paper shows how the problem arises for Aristotle, and it argues that it is part of a more general problem inherent in drawing philosophical distinctions. The chief contention of this paper is that Hegel solves this problem by using a category to differentiate itself. The process of self-differentiation transforms a category into a new, richer category and, thus, drives the dynamic development of Hegel's categories.

HALPER, Edward. Is Creativity Good? Phil Inq, 10(1-2), 72-84, Wint-Spr 88.

This paper criticizes Nietzsche's *Thus Spoke Zarathustra* by examining the consequences it would have. Nietzsche is interpreted to advance the two-fold thesis that whatever is new is valuable for its own sake and that rationality is an obstacle to creativity that must be overcome. Such a position is implicit in much artistic experimentalism of this century and, especially, in works that aim to depict the primitive and nonrational. This paper argues that because these experimental works must rely on some conceptual scheme, their denial of the importance of reason is self-contradictory. It concludes that Nietzsche's mistake is to separate reason from creativity.

HALPIN, David M G and SORRELL, Martin. Art and Neurology: A Discussion. Brit J Aes, 31(3), 241-250, Jl 91.

HALPIN, John F. What is the Logical Form of Probability Assignment in Quantum Mechanics? Phil Sci, 58(1), 36-60, Mr 91.

The nature of quantum mechanical probability has often seemed mysterious. To shed some light on this topic, the present paper analyzes the logical form of probability assignment in quantum mechanics. To begin the paper, I set out and criticize several attempts to analyze the form. I go on to propose a new form which utilizes a novel, probabilistic conditional and argue that this proposal is, overall, the best rendering of the quantum mechanical probability assignments. Finally, quantum mechanics aside, the discussion here has consequences for counterfactual logic, conditional probability, and epistemic probability.

HAMAN, Ales. To Umberto Eco's Criticism of Icon (in Czechoslovakian). Estetika, 27(4), 251-256, 1990.

HAMAN, Krzysztof E. On the Objectivity of the Laws of Physics. Phil Sci (Tucson), 2, 77-80, 1986.

The peculiar character of geophysical research throws a new light on the nature of the laws of physics. A geophysicist constructs a map of a domain which reflects only some features of reality on certain scales. These maps strongly depend on the researcher himself. A certain indeterminism seems to be inseparably connected with this method: the better the resolution of the maps, the more unstable modes of evolution appear and the faster the errors grow.

HAMBURGER, Joseph. "Religion and *On Liberty*" in *A Cultivated Mind: Essays On J S Mill Presented to John M Robson*, LAINE, Michael (ed), 139-181. Buffalo, Univ of Toronto Pr, 1991.

HAMILTON, Andy. The Aesthetics of Imperfection. Philosophy, 65(253), 323-340, Jl 90.

The article is an evaluation of post-Romantic musical aesthetics, which has idealised, in opposed ways, both composition and improvisation. There arose in jazz and other improvised forms a "Romantic ideal" stressing (i) pure transmission of the musical idea; (ii) free and individual self-expression of the performer; (iii) spontaneity and "improvised feel." (I) is largely chimerical and (ii) is overrated, it is argued. But (iii) is important and expresses an "aesthetics of imperfection," in which unpredictability and immediacy counteract formal imperfection, and where structure and preparation play a distinctive role.

HAMILTON, Andy. Anscombian and Cartesian Scepticism. Phil Quart, 41(162), 39-54, Ja 91.

Anscombe's 'Sensory Deprivation Argument' (in 'The First Person') presents a subject in a tank, totally sensorily deprived and amnesiac, yet still apparently guaranteed to self-refer using 'I'. Since the subject has no conception of itself as embodied, she argued, 'I' must here refer to a Cartesian Ego or (Anscombe's conclusion) to nothing at all. However, this argument depends on an empty phenomenon of 'no unnoticed substitution' of the referent of 'I' or (a sceptical variant of the argument) a modal fallacy. One can reconstruct Anscombe's argument avoiding these fallacies, but paradoxically a Cartesian conclusion results. The way 'I' continues to refer in the absence of a Fregean conception, together with Anscombe's important claims about the circularity of the self-reference principle, does however suggest that the concept of a person is irrelevant to self-reference—a claim not easy to counter.

HAMILTON, Andy. Ernst Mach and the Elimination of Subjectivity. Ratio, 3(2), 117-135, D 90.

Elimination of the subject is a constant aim of positivism. The neutral monism of Mach's influential *Analysis of Sensations*, on which this article focusses, aspired to a pretheoretical subjectless 'given'. His rejection of the subject anticipates the nonsceptical solipsism of the Vienna Circle (and Wittgenstein); his opposition to objects as genuinely persisting entities anticipates the complementary phenomenalism. Mach's phenomenalism differs from Mill's because it is meant to be 'neutral', not mentalistic. But Mach offers both objective and subjective interpretations of his 'sensations'. Examination of his account of others', and of merely possible, sensations, shows that he lacks the resources to defend a neutralist middle way. Neutral monism nonetheless remained a strangely potent doctrine for the Vienna Circle, inspiring Carnap's conventionalist, neutralist constructionalism in the *Aufbau*, to be treated in a later article.

HAMILTON, Gordon J. "Augustine's Methods of Biblical Interpretation" in *Grace, Politics and Desire: Essays on Augustine*, MEYNELL, Hugo A (ed), 103-119. Calgary, Univ Calgary Pr, 1990.

HAMLYN, D W. Aristotle on Dialectic. Philosophy, 65(254), 465-476, O 90.

The paper criticizes the attempts by Martha Nussbaum and Terence Irwin to explain Aristotle's conception of dialectic as involving an appeal to *phainomena*, where these, as claimed by G E L Owen, involve opinions not just experience. These attempts fail to explain how that appeal provides a *method* for arriving at truth. A better account is offered, which sees Aristotle as concerned, not just with the attainment of truth, but with the acceptance of the conclusion of the dialectical argument by those involved. In this respect Aristotle's conception of dialectic is on a continuum with that of the Platonic Socrates.

HAMLYN, D W. Philosophy and the Theory of Social Behaviour. J Theor Soc Behav, 20(4), 297-304, D 90.

The paper celebrates the twentieth anniversary of the *Journal for the Theory of Social Behaviour*. It applauds the policy of the journal not to confine itself to social behaviour construed in a narrow sense, while offering both a philosophical justification of that policy and an illustration of the role of philosophy in the area. Social behaviour is, in a wider sense, all that follows from the fact that those concerned are social beings. Aspects of perception reflect that, in that only a social being could have the knowledge and concepts which are intrinsic to perception if that is properly construed.

HAMLYN, D W. "The Problem of the External World" in *Key Themes in Philosophy*, GRIFFITHS, A Phillips (ed), 1-13. New York, Cambridge Univ Pr, 1989.

The paper investigates the senses in which the world may be thought external, and argues that none of them supports doubt about the possibility of knowledge of the world. Scepticism sometimes depends on certain erroneous conceptions of perception, especially those which lead to belief in 'inner, representational states'. How we perceive things depends on the satisfaction of certain general conditions—on what concepts we have, on the kind of senses we have, and so on a kind of anthropocentricity; but this does not prevent objectivity, even in the case of secondary qualities.

HAMMER, Rhonda and MC LAREN, Peter. Rethinking the Dialectic: A Social Semiotic Perspective for Educators. Educ Theor, 41(1), 23-46, Wint 91.

HAMOWY, Ronald. Cato's Letters, John Locke, and the Republican Paradigm. Hist Polit Thought, 11(2), 273-294, Sum 90.

A number of scholars have recently argued that eighteenth-century Anglo-American political theory can best be understood as a product of Renaissance civic humanism, marked by an aversion to the marketplace and a propensity to couch political debate in the language of the ancient constitution rather than in terms of abstract rights. John Trenchard and Thomas Gordon's *Cato's Letters*, published during the 1720s, has been singled out as a particularly apt instance of a work written in the language of classical republicanism. A careful examination of this work, however, shows it to be clearly influenced by the sentiments expressed by the radical whigs and particularly by John Locke. The approval with which *Cato's Letters* was received during the eighteenth century supports the view that the Lockean paradigm played a substantial role in shaping political rhetoric and constituted a major force in eighteenth-century politics.

HAMPSCH, George H. "Marxism and Nuclear Deterrence" in *Issues in War and Peace: Philosophical Inquiries*, KUNKEL, Joseph (ed), 49-54. Wolfeboro, Longwood, 1989.

HAMPSCH, George. "Common Security through Alternative Defense" in *In the Interest of Peace: A Spectrum of Philosophical Views*, KLEIN, Kenneth H (ed), 299-302. Wolfeboro, Longwood, 1990.

HAMPTON, Jean. "A New Theory of Retribution" in *Liability and Responsibility*, FREY, R G (ed), 377-414. New York, Cambridge Univ Pr, 1991.

HAMRICK, William. Phenomenology and the Philosophy for Children Program. Thinking, 9(2), 9-12, 1990.

HANCE, Allen S. Prudence and Providence: On Hobbes's Theory of Practical Reason. Man World, 24(2), 155-167, Ap 91.

Focusing on the relationship between the traditional Aristotelian concept of *phronesis* and the Hobbesian concept of prudence, this paper argues that Hobbes's naturalistic and mechanistic understanding of phenomena in general has a decisive and ultimately deleterious effect on his understanding of political and ethical action. I contend that Hobbes's interpretation of prudence as an unreliable form of associative knowledge is mistaken and that Aristotle provides a more adequate account of our experience of practical reasoning.

HANCE, Allen S. The Rule of Law in *The German Constitution*. Owl Minerva, 22(2), 159-174, Spr 91.

Through an investigation of the concept of the rule of law in Hegel's essay, *The German Constitution* (1799-1802), this paper charts the development of Hegel's philosophy of right and assesses his evolving relationship to both older theories of politics (classical and feudal) and the modern natural right tradition. I conclude that while Hegel's early theory of legal relations is significantly influenced by modern theories of state-sovereignty and public law, his as yet weakly articulated concepts of abstract right and political freedom yield an excessively formal and non-democratic definition of law.

HANCOCK, Curtis L and FEEZELL, Randolph M. *How Should I Live? Philosophical Conversations About Moral Life*. New York, Paragon House, 1991.

HANCOCK, Curtis L. "A Return to the Crossroads: A Maritainian View of the New Educational Reformers" in *From Twilight to Dawn: The Cultural Vision of Jacques Maritain*, REDPATH, Peter A (ed), 241-260. Notre Dame, Univ Notre Dame Pr, 1990.

HAND, Michael. Kitcher's Circumlocutionary Structuralism. Can J Phil, 21(1), 81-89, Mr 91.

HAND, Michael. On Saying That Again. Ling Phil, 14(4), 349-365, Ag 91.

HAND, Seán (trans) and BLONDEL, Eric. *Nietzsche: The Body and Culture—Philosophy as a Philological Genealogy*. Stanford, Stanford Univ Pr, 1991.

The aim of the book, a translation from French (1986), is to re-center the whole thought of Nietzsche around the central question of culture (Kultur). But the method to be used has to be defined beforehand—it rests mainly on Nietzsche's text, which must be described not only as a discourse containing univocal statements, but as a polemic, equivocal, plural text where the variations and struggle of drives take place. But the main tension which determined Nietzsche's thought as such between a philological, i.e., linguistic reading of the text of culture and the genealogical, i.e., psychological and physiological ones. The book tries to define and locate the various ways of handling this problem and carefully studies the main three metaphors which the text of Nietzsche develops.

HAND, Seán (trans) and LEVINAS, Emmanuel. Reflections on the Philosophy of Hitlerism. Crit Inquiry, 17(1), 62-71, Autumn 90.

HANEN, Marsha and KELLEY, Jane. "Inference to the Best Explanation in Archaeology" in *Critical Traditions in Contemporary Archaeology*, PINSKY, Valerie (ed), 14-17. New York, Cambridge Univ Pr, 1990.

HANFLING, Oswald. Machines as Persons? Philosophy, 29, 25-34, 91 Supp.

Could there be artificial persons, made from artificial materials? It is thought that such beings ('a-people'), might *behave* like natural ('n-people'), but would lack an 'inner life'; and this would prevent us from treating them as real people. But this position is untenable. Scepticism about the feelings of a-people would be no better than that about the feelings of n-people. An a-person subjected to discrimination would be entitled to accuse us of 'artifactism'. In a practical situation, which I sketch in dialogue form, it would be impossible for us to avoid entering into an obligation of promising with an a-person.

HANFLING, Oswald. 'I Heard a Plaintive Melody'. Philosophy, 28, 117-133, 90 Supp.

Having introduced this remark, Wittgenstein asks 'Does he hear the complaint?' The 'expressive qualities' of music cannot be accounted for by the 'expressive theory', or any other. They belong in the context of a wider phenomenon of language which cannot be explained even to the extent of 'family resemblance'. Examples are Wittgenstein's 'What do light blue and dark blue have in common?', 'high' applied to sounds, 'a deep well, a deep sorrow', etc. Wittgenstein's discussions of 'secondary sense' are also relevant. Such uses of language are not merely accidental (like the two uses of 'bank'); and they are connected with what Wittgenstein called 'experiencing the meaning' of a word.

HANINK, James. Childhood Betrayed: A Personalist Analysis. Proc Cath Phil Ass, 63, 54-71, 1990.

This essay argues that children, born or preborn, are persons. As such, children deserve respect. Contemporary culture, however, often fails to meet their basic needs. Suggestions are made—from a personalist and communitarian perspective—on how we can move from the abandonment of children to a commitment to their flourishing. In part this means developing an economics of the common good, a deeper exploration of the strategies of nonviolence, and the nurturing of primary communities, beginning with the family.

HANKE, Michael. Socratic Pragmatics: Maieutic Dialogues. J Prag, 14(3), 459-465, Je 90.

Dialogue theory, as a part of pragmatics (from Greek pragmata 'acts', 'affairs', 'business'), can be traced back to Plato's theory of ideal philosophic communication, which again is reconstructable by means of interpretative conversation analysis of his dialogues. The process of dialegesthai presents philosophy not as a formal and compact system, but as a communicative activity, where philosophic issues are discussed and validity is established in consensus on the basis of evidence and logical reasoning. One approach to the analysis of Platonic communication theory is based on the metaphoric description of Socrates's method of midwifery (maieutic). The dyad of the pregnant one and the midwife corresponds to the production of philosophic knowledge by argumentative dialogue, in and by which a thought is 'brought out'. Being an exchange and interpretation of signs, Platonic dialectic can be regarded as a semiotic process. Furthermore, being dyadic and mutual, dialectic is a joint activity and (philosophic) communication.

HANKINS, Thomas L. "Newton's 'Mathematical Way' a Century After the *Principia*" in *Some Truer Method*, DURHAM, Frank (ed), 89-112. New York, Columbia Univ Pr, 1990.

Both the mathematical and experimental sciences a century after Newton's *Principia* were dominated by the enthusiasm for "analysis." The word "analysis" was bandied around by all and sundry, but there was little agreement as to what it meant. This article discusses the meaning of "analysis" at the end of the 18th century.

HANKINSON, R J. "Greek Medical Models of Mind" in *Psychology (Companions to Ancient Thought: 2)*, EVERSON, Stephen (ed), 194-217. New York, Cambridge Univ Pr, 1991.

HANKINSON, R J. Perception and Evaluation: Aristotle on the Moral Imagination. Dialogue (Canada), 29(1), 41-63, 1990.

HANKISS, Elemer. "The Loss of Responsibility" in *The Political Responsibility of Intellectuals*, MACLEAN, Ian (ed), 29-52. New York, Cambridge Univ Pr, 1990.

HANLY, Ken. The Ethics of Rent Control. J Bus Ethics, 10(3), 189-200, Mr 91.

Residential rent control is a contentious issue in many jurisdictions throughout the world. While tenant groups have often argued vociferously in defence of control, landlord groups and the vast majority of economists have been equally vehement in their criticisms. This paper examines some key normative issues involved in rent control. In particular I examine arguments in favor of control based on the alleged unfairness of 'windfall' profits, upon affordability, and finally on the creation of rights to security of tenure. Various objections by libertarian and 'free market' philosophers and economists are examined. I conclude with a somewhat limited defence of rent control as used in specific situations as part of a more comprehensive policy to satisfy the normative demands at the root of tenant pressure for rent control.

HANNA, Patricia. Must Thinking Bats be Conscious? Phil Invest, 13(4), 350-355, O 90.

HANNA, Robert. How Ideas Became Meanings: Locke and the Foundations of Semantic Theory. Rev Metaph, 44(4), 775-805, Je 91.

In book III of the *Essay* Locke takes the view that the meaning of a word is an idea in the mind of its utterer; this "semantic solipsism" has often been criticized and even derided. This paper presents a thorough explication of Locke's theory of meaning and suggests that a better understanding of it will expose important features of, and difficulties in, mainstream 20th century semantic theory.

HANNA, Robert. Kant's Theory of Empirical Judgment and Modern Semantics. Hist Phil Quart, 7(3), 335-351, Jl 90.

The central doctrines of the first *Critique* can be interpreted not only from an epistemological or a metaphysical point of view, but also from a *semantic* point of view. This is particularly true in the case of Kant's doctrine of empirical judgment. A semantic analysis of "atomic" (singular) empirical judgments reveals a deep puzzle in Kant's thinking about the precise role of concepts as logical subjects in empirical propositions—a puzzle which anticipates (and perhaps even originates) the "problem of singular reference" in Frege/Russell semantic theory.

HANNAN, Barbara. "Non-Scientific Realism" about Propositional Attitudes as a Response to Eliminativist Arguments. Behavior Phil, 18(2), 21-31, Fall-Wint 90.

Two arguments are discussed which have been advanced in support of eliminative materialism: the argument from reductionism and the argument from functionalism. It is contended that neither of these arguments is effective if "non-scientific realism" is adopted with regard to commonsense propositional attitude psychology and its embedded notions. "Non-scientific realism," the position that commonsense propositional attitude psychology is an independently legitimate descriptive/explanatory framework, neither in competition with science nor vulnerable to being shown false by science, is defended.

HANNAY, Alastair. *Human Consciousness*. New York, Routledge, 1990.

The book contests the theoretical redundancy of the first-person point of view in accounts of conscious intelligence. An historical sketch of the ways in which philosophers have approached human consciousness in the past is followed by discussions of the role of conscious phenomena in respect of the subject/object polarity in the analysis of experience, and of the concepts of action, behavioural control, and finally of interpersonal relationship. There is a concluding 'agenda' for future work on human consciousness which admits the theoretical significance of the first-person point of view.

HANSBERG, Olbeth. Por qué los estados mentales no son clases naturales? Dianoia, 36(36), 213-229, 1990.

HANSEN, Chad. "Classical Chinese Ethics" in *A Companion to Ethics*, SINGER, Peter (ed), 69-81. Cambridge, Blackwell, 1991.

HANSEN, Chad. "Language in the Heart-mind" in *Understanding the Chinese Mind: The Philosophical Roots*, ALLINSON, Robert E (ed), 75-124. New York, Oxford Univ Pr, 1989.

HANSEN, Chad. "Should the Ancient Masters Value Reason?" in *Chinese Texts and Philosophical Contexts*, ROSEMONT JR, Henry (ed), 179-207. La Salle, Open Court, 1991.

HANSEN, Karen. Growing Up on Screen—Images of Instruction. Phil Stud Educ, /, 19-25, 1987-88.

HANSON, Susan. "On Translation and M/others: Samuel Beckett's *The Unnamable*" in *Hermeneutics and the Poetic Motion, Translation Perspectives V—1990*, SCHMIDT, Dennis J (ed), 131-146. Binghamton, CRIT, 1990.

HANSON, William H. Indicative Conditionals Are Truth-Functional. Mind, 100(397), 53-72, Ja 91.

It is well known that one cannot consistently deny the truth-functionality of a class of conditionals while maintaining the joint correctness of *modus ponens* (mp) and conditional proof (cp) for the conditionals in that class. Yet often logicians who deny that many (or any) English conditionals are truth-functional tacitly endorse, or at least fail to question, the correctness of both mp and cp for (at least some nontrivial class of) English conditionals. This article argues that mp and cp are correct for many perfectly ordinary English indicative conditionals and that these conditionals are therefore truth-functional. It also considers alternative versions of cp for indicative conditionals proposed by Stalnaker and by Anderson and Belnap and argues that they are deficient. Finally, it gives examples of English indicative conditionals that are truth-functional if the arguments presented are correct.

HANSSON, Sven Ove. A Formal Representation of Declaration-Related Legal Relations. Law Phil, 9(4), 399-416, 1990-91.

A formal language is introduced that contains expressions for the dependency of a legal relation on the claims that the concerned individuals make and on the permissions that they grant. It is used for a classification of legal relations into six major categories: categorical obligation, categorical permission, claimable obligation, grantable permission, claim-dependent obligation and grant-dependent permission. Legal rights may belong to any of these six categories, but the characteristics of a right-holder are shown to be different in each of the six types.

HANSSON, Sven Ove. Norms and Values. Critica, 23(67), 3-13, Ap 91.

Although a norm predicate and a moral value predicate cannot be identical in meaning, they can be extensionally equivalent. It is proposed that in an idealized moral language, all norm predicates can be extensionally equivalent with a value expression. However, this interrelationship cannot be achieved through the conventional identification of a positive value predicate (such as "good" or "best") with a prescriptive norm predicate (such as "ought" or "duty"). Instead, a negative value predicate (such as "bad") can be equated with a prohibitive predicate (such as "wrong"). Prescriptive and permissive norm predicates can, in turn, be defined in terms of prohibitive predicates.

HANSSON, Sven Ove. The Revenger's Paradox. Phil Stud, 61(3), 301-305, Mr 91.

If John ought not to kill his wife's murderer, then he ought to kill either other persons than his wife's murderer, or no one at all. This is the revenger's paradox. Unlike the more commonly discussed deontic paradoxes, this new paradox is present not only in strong logics such as standard deontic logic (SDL), but also in much weaker logics that have been constructed to avoid the paradoxes of SDL. The revenger's paradox shows that any deontic logic with intersubstitutivity of logically equivalent expressions makes counterintuitive truth assignments to some deontic expressions.

HANSSON, Sven. New Operators for Theory Change. Theoria, 55(2), 114-132, 1989.

Two generalizations are performed on the model of theory contraction that was proposed by Alchourrón, Gärdenfors and Makinson. (1) Changes consisting of the simultaneous contraction by more than one proposition are introduced. Two extensions of partial meet contraction that cover this case are introduced. (2) Contractions are performed on sets that are not closed under logical consequence. The new operation of "minimal contraction" is introduced for such contractions. In conclusion, the author maintains that a diversity of change operators will be needed to represent the many types of theory change that take place in epistemic, normative and other contexts.

HÄNTSCH, Carola. Gelehrter zwischen Romantik und Hegelianismus in Finnland—Johan Vilhelm Snellman (1806-1881). Deut Z Phil, 39(1), 43-49, 1991.

HARA, Masayuki. Ji Kang's "Sheng-wu-aile-lun": Concerning Its Logical Development (in Japanese). Bigaku, 41(4), 11-21, Spr 91.

"Shēng-qú-āilè-lùn" is one of the most important musical writings in the history of Chinese music aesthetics. It overcame the difficulties of the Confucian view of music and established a new perspective, through an elaborated logical development. This is based on the six following theses: 1) "mind and sound are two different things"; 2) "music has no constant correspondence with specific emotions"; 3) "music imitates nothing"; 4) "music has its own intrinsic *harmonia* (hé)"; 5) "the essence of music is to be found in a balance of emotions, or rather, the *absence of emotional bias* (pínghé)"; 6) but at the level of its interaction with society, "it is mind, as not bound to specific emotions, that is essential to music". Finally, the text prescribes the ideal way of music as a means to suggest the ideal state of mind for the purpose of *cultivating life* (yangsheng).

HARBERS, Hans. Kennen en kunnen: Een repliek op Wardekker. Kennis Methode, 15(2), 174-181, 1991.

This reply to Wardekker's *Praxis development and practical (educational) science* makes two points. First, it argues, contra Wardekker, for the coherence of the so-called Agora-model of science - a model which, compared to its theoretical contrast: the Olympus-model of science, implies a change in perspective on science and society from differentiation towards integration of both. Wardekker'a ambiguous reading of the model is argued to rest on his overly normative way of analysing practical sciences. Second, after this change, it argues, more in line now with Wardekker, for the need of a reformulation of the problem of demarcation. This problem should not be stated any longer in epistemological terms of the truth of scientific knowledge, but in sociological and political terms of the power of science and scientists on the Agora.

HARBERS, Hans and VAN DER WINDT, Henny J. Welke natuur is het beschermen waard? Kennis Methode, 15(1), 38-61, 1991.

The development of the Dutch nature conservation movement is described. It is shown that "nature" is a controversial and variable concept. However, not all concepts of nature could be accepted. Both the material history and the social history of nature constrain the interpretative flexibility of 'nature'. Practices of the nature conservationists pin down nature materially and on the other hand, nature is socially negotiated. Because of the unity of the conceptual, the material and the social history of nature, a constructivistic analysis of 'nature' has to be extended with other, more sociological and political approaches.

HARBSMEIER, Christoph. "Marginalia Sino-logica" in *Understanding the Chinese Mind: The Philosophical Roots*, ALLINSON, Robert E (ed), 125-166. New York, Oxford Univ Pr, 1989.

HARBSMEIER, Christoph. "The Mass Noun Hypothesis and the Part-Whole Analysis of the White Horse Dialogue" in *Chinese Texts and Philosophical Contexts*, ROSEMONT JR, Henry (ed), 49-66. La Salle, Open Court, 1991.

HARCUM, E Rae. Behavioral Paradigm for a Psychological Resolution of the Free Will Issue. J Mind Behav, 12(1), 93-114, Wint 91.

This study provides data for a behavioral paradigm to resolve the free will issue in psychological terms. As predicted, college students selecting among many alternative responses consistently selected according to experimental set, environmental conditions, past experiences and other unknown factors. These explained and unexplained causal factors supplement one another and make varying relative contributions to different behaviors-the Principle of Behavioral Supplementarity. The more psychologically remote the causal factors, the greater proportion of unexplained ones relative to explained ones-the Principle of Remote Antecedence. Both the causal categories can be conceptualized in the incompatible terms of reductionism or intentionality, depending upon the dissociated belief state of the observer-the Principle of Behavioral Complementarity. Ordinarily, on utilitarian grounds, behaviors with psychologically contiguous antecedents are best conceptualized in a reductionistic belief state, and behaviors with remote antecedents are best conceptualized in an intentional belief state.

HARCUM, E Rae. Parity for the Theoretical Ghosts and Gremlins: Response to Pollio/Henley and Rychlak. J Mind Behav, 12(1), 151-162, Wint 91.

Pollio and Henley and Rychlak support the author's efforts to provide empirical evidence from different methodological perspectives for a role of agency in the science of human behavior. The hypothesized agent initiates behaviors independently of heredity and environment, but it also is responsive to those causal factors. In addition to certain labelling problems, a major difference between our views is that the commentors attempt to use a monistic voluntaristic mode of thinking to conceptualize the causal mechanisms, whereas the author advocates in addition, on utilitarian grounds, a second incompatible, mechanistic mode of thinking. The microprocess in the metaphysical view of voluntarism versus determinism are not empirically falsifiable, but hypotheses which propose different predictive values of the resultant theories under different conditions can be falsified. Neither theory is intrinsically more scientific, nor are methods associated with either theory intrinsically superior in the absence of context.

HARDCASTLE, Gary L. Presentism and the Indeterminacy of Translation. Stud Hist Phil Sci, 22(2), 321-345, Je 91.

I argue that the "anti-presentist" stance towards understanding past science, though well-motivated within naturalism, is comprised in light of the indeterminacy of translation. Anti-presentist structures are first motivated and evaluated on a naturalistic model of belief change. I then argue that the understanding of past science involves translation and that translation is indeterminate, and conclude that our understanding of past science is indeterminate. Charity and humanity make translation appear determinate, but these principles succeed only by employing the translator's present knowledge.

HARDCASTLE, Valerie Gray. Partitions, Probabilistic Causal Laws, and Simpson's Paradox. Synthese, 86(2), 209-228, F 91.

In "Causal Laws and Effective Strategies" (Cartwright 1979), Nancy Cartwright formalized an intuitive notion of probabilistic causality. Since that time, her formalization—and the viability of the project itself—has come under attack (most recently by Cartwright herself). In this paper I defend Cartwright's original project against the various counterexamples proposed by Germund Hesslow (1976) and Richard Otte (1985) and argue that the counterexamples do not actually present problems for the account of probabilistic causality itself, but rather point to difficulties in *describing* events prior to causal analysis. I shall proceed by first sketching Cartwright's (1979) account and then modifying it slightly according to Otte's prescriptions in order to allow for necessary and sufficient causes in Section 1. Next in Section 2, I shall outline the counterexamples and arguments directed against intuitive probabilistic causality models. And finally, in Section 3, I shall explicate why the counterexamples are not really counterexamples at all.

HARDIN, C L. Reply to Levine's "Cool Red". Phil Psych, 4(1), 41-50, 1991.

In may be doubted that a functional model of color vision that captures all of the phenomenologically important details is capable of plausible alternative realizations. Inverted qualia objections to functionalism or reductive materialism are therefore suspect. However, this line of argument does not dispose of absent qualia objections, and as long as materialists view qualia as local rather than global characteristics of matter, they may continue to be vulnerable to absent qualia arguments.

HARDIN, C L. Reply to Teller's "Simpler Arguments Might Work Better". Phil Psych, 4(1), 61-64, 1991.

The phenomenon of metamerism does have important lessons to teach philosophers, but attention to opponency has virtues of its own, particularly in putting the phenomenal structure of colors into the foreground, and in making the relations of colors to each other much clearer. The physiological basis of opponency is admittedly less secure than the basis for metamerism, but the concordance between psychophysical opponency models and early stage visual physiology is rather better than Teller suggests.

HARDIN, C L. Reply to Wilson's "Shadows on the Cave Wall: Philosophy and Visual Science". Phil Psych, 4(1), 79-81, 1991.

Visual shapes typically have their counterparts in structural features of physical objects, but colors do not. So Locke's oft-reviled resemblance criterion for distinguishing between primary and secondary qualities is not without merit.

HARDIN, Russell. Reading Hobbes in Other Words: Contractarian, Utilitarian, Game Theorist. Polit Theory, 19(2), 156-180, My 91.

Hobbes was among the first to discover that ordinary exchange is a Prisoner's Dilemma unless backed by coercive power. He is sometimes read to say the state of nature itself is a Prisoner's Dilemma that can be resolved only by contracting out. His best arguments imply that creating a sovereign to resolve quotidian Prisoner's Dilemma is merely a problem of coordinating on one of many possible governments, not a contractual problem. This view together with his great fear of disorder explains his conservative committment to extant government and opposition to revolution, which sit uncomfortably with his supposed contractarianism.

HARDING, Sandra. "Feminism, Science, and the Anti-Enlightenment Critiques" in *Feminism/Postmodernism*, NICHOLSON, Linda J (ed), 83-106. New York, Routledge, 1990.

HARDING, Sandra. Starting Thought From Women's Lives: Eight Resources for Maximizing Objectivity. J Soc Phil, 21(2-3), 140-149, Fall-Wint 90.

HARDING, Sandra. *Whose Science? Whose Knowledge? Thinking from Women's Lives*. Ithaca, Cornell Univ Pr, 1991.

This study continues the projects in the author's *The Science Question in Feminism* of showing how and why the philosophy and social studies of the natural sciences should treat the natural sciences as if they were special cases of social sciences. The first two sections develop and examine further the challenges feminism has raised to conventional views of the natural sciences and epistemology. The third section looks at the insights that post-colonial and other "other" scholarship can bring to both the feminist and pre-feminist controversies in epistemology and the philosophy and social studies of the sciences.

HARDT, Michael (trans) and NEGRI, Antonio. *The Savage Anomaly: The Power of Spinoza's Metaphysics and Politics*. Minneapolis, Univ of Minn Pr, 1991.

HARE, R M. Amoralism: Reply to Peter Sandoe. Theoria, 55(3), 205-210, 1989.

In response to an article by Peter Sandoe this article deals with the question of whether the author's moral theory is naturalistic or antinaturalistic, his use of the prescriptivity of 'I' and amoralism. These topics are examined in light of their relation to utilitarianism and the universalizability of moral judgments. (staff)

HARE, R M. Un enfoque Kantiano sobre el aborto. Dianoia, 36(36), 39-50, 1990.

This is a spanish translation of "A Kantian Approach to Abortion" in *Social Theory and Practice*, Volume 15, which was reprinted from *Right Conduct: Theories and Application*, edited by M D Bayles and K Henley, Second Edition, Random House, New York, 1989.

HARE, R M. Fanaticism: Reply to Thomas Wetterström. Theoria, 55(3), 186-190, 1989.

The author responds to criticisms of his moral theory leveled by Thomas Wetterstrom. Clarifications are made regarding the terms "suffering-utilitarianism" and "preference-utilitarianism." Also questions about preferences and moral convictions are discussed. (staff)

HARE, R M. Prudence and Past Preferences; Reply to Wlodizimierz Rabinowicz. Theoria, 55(3), 152-158, 1989.

This article is a response to an article by Wlodizimierz Rabinowicz in which Dr. Rabinowicz criticizes the author's theory of prudence and preferences. The author addresses issues including the universalizability of prudential judgments, actions and past, present and future preferences. (staff)

HARE, R M. "Universal Prescriptivism" in *A Companion to Ethics*, SINGER, Peter (ed), 451-463. Cambridge, Blackwell, 1991.

Ethical theories are classified, the main division being between descriptivism and non-descriptivism. Both varieties of descriptivism, viz. naturalism and intuitionism, are shown to lead to relativism. The earliest kind of non-descriptivism, emotivism, leads to irrationalism. By contrast, universal prescriptivism is a rationalist kind of non-descriptivism, relying for the rules of moral reasoning on the logic properties of moral judgements, viz. prescriptivity and universalizability; these properties are explained and confusions about them forestalled. It leads to a Kantian-utilitarian theory of moral reasoning, which acknowledges the two levels of moral thinking, intuitive and critical.

HARE, R M. Universalizability and the Summing of Desires: Reply to Ingmar Persson. Theoria, 55(3), 171-177, 1989.

In this article the author responds to an article by Ingmar Persson. It deals with the satisfying of self-interested desires and the universalizability of moral prescriptions over any possible situation having the same universal properties. (staff)

HARE, Richard N and BRASH, Jorge (trans). La estructura de la ética y la moral. Dianoia, 34(34), 49-63, 1988.

Spanish version of "The Structure of Ethics and Morals" from the author's *Essays in Ethical Theory* (Oxford, Oxford University Press, 1989). Contains a summary of the author's ethical theory, as set out in full in his *Moral Thinking* (Oxford, Oxford University Press, 1981).

HAREL, Simon. L'écriture réparatrice. Horiz Phil, 1(1), 81-100, 1990.

HARGROVE, Eugene C and CALLICOTT, J Baird. Leopold's "Means and Ends in Wild Life Management". Environ Ethics, 12(4), 333-337, Wint 90.

Leopold's lecture at Beloit College provides an important glimpse into his conversion from a philosophy of prudent scientific resource management to a land ethic and aesthetic. Leopold here advocates natural regulation not simply because of his growing concern that invasive management principles are limited, but also because of aesthetic considerations that were independent of his instrumental or "utilitarian" training at the Yale Forest School and in the US Forest Service. The lecture is helpful in correcting an unfortunate misreading of Leopold's famous essay, "The Land Ethic," according to which the land ethic is interpreted as being based primarily on human welfare and self-interest.

HARKLEROAD, Leon. Recursive Surreal Numbers. Notre Dame J Form Log, 31(3), 337-345, Sum 90.

This paper considers effectivizations of the two standard developments of the surreal number system, viz. via cuts and via sign sequences. Properties of both versions of "computable surreals" are investigated, and it is shown that the two effectivizations in fact yield different sets of surreals.

HARMAN, Gilbert. "Benefits to Moral Philosophy of the Computational Model of the Mind" in *Acting and Reflecting: The Interdisciplinary Turn in Philosophy*, SIEG, Wilfried (ed), 40-43. Norwell, Kluwer, 1990.

The computational model of mind suggests ways to explain certain aspects of our thinking about morality. A computationally feasible agent may have to distinguish intended from unintended consequences, as in the doctrine of double effect. And the need to be able to treat the world as a set of distinct objects and processes may help to explain the distinction we make between positive and negative duties.

HARMAN, Gilbert. "Immanent and Transcendent Approaches to the Theory of Meaning" in *Perspectives on Quine*, BARRETT, Robert (ed), 144-157. Cambridge, Blackwell, 1990.

An immanent approach to the theory of meaning takes translation to be the paradigm way to explain meaning. A transcendent approach offers an account of meaning apart from translation, for instance via truth conditions. Quine takes an immanent approach where Davidson takes a transcendent approach. The issue between these approaches is part of the larger issue separating the "Verstehen" tradition from Dilthey to Thomas Nagel on the one hand from the positivistic tradition (Hempel, Davidson, et al.) on the other hand.

HARMAN, Gilbert. "The Intrinsic Quality of Experience" in *Philosophical Perspectives, 4: Action Theory and Philosophy of Mind, 1990*, TOMBERLIN, James E (ed), 31-52. Atascadero, Ridgeview, 1990.

There are three familiar and related arguments against psychophysical functionalism and the computer model of the mind. The first is that we are directly aware of intrinsic features of our experience and argues that there is no way to account for this awareness in a functional view. The second claims that a person blind from birth can known all about the functional role of visual experience without knowing what it is like to see something red. The third claims that functionalism cannot account for the possibility of an inverted spectrum. All three arguments can be defused by distinguishing properties of the object of experience from properties of the experience of an object.

HARMAN, Gilbert. Justification, Truth, Goals, and Pragmatism: Comments on Stich's "Fragmentation of Reason". Phil Phenomenol Res, 51(1), 195-199, Mr 91.

If we distinguish advocating the method of reflective equilibrium from trying to define "justified" in terms of that method, we see that Stich's objections to any such definition are not objections to using the method. Stich's worries about truth are really worries about indeterminacy of translation or interpretation and can be avoided either by appealing to an immanent rather than a transcendent notion of truth ("P" is true if and only if P) or by fixing on the same interpretative scheme for beliefs and desires (I want my beliefs to be true$_I$ so that my desires will be more likely to come true$_I$.)

HARMAN, Gilbert. "The Meanings of Logical Constants" in *Truth and Interpretation: Perspectives on the Philosophy of Donald Davidson*, LE PORE, Ernest (ed), 125-134. Cambridge, Blackwell, 1986.

HAROWSKI, Kathy J. "Sexuality and Assisted Reproduction: An Uneasy Embrace" in *Beyond Baby M: Ethical Issues in New Reproductive Techniques*, BARTELS, Dianne M (ed), 131-147. Clifton, Humana Pr, 1990.

HARPER, A W J. Time and Identity. J Indian Counc Phil Res, 5(2), 127-131, Ja-Ap 88.

HARPER, William L and EELLS, Ellery. Ratifiability, Game Theory, and the Principle of Independence of Irrelevant Alternatives. Austl J Phil, 69(1), 1-19, Mr 91.

The main result of this paper is that various natural developments of the recent decision criterion of *ratifiability* (based on Jeffrey 1981, 1983), as well as some natural implications of classical *game theory* (Nash 1951) for individual decision, are in conflict with Sen's (1970) seemingly plausible *alpha* and *beta* conditions, which are sometimes together called the *principle of independence of irrelevant alternatives*. Examples are given that the authors argue tell *against the alpha and beta criteria*, and *in favor of the ratifiability idea*; and it is explained how these examples and arguments about *individual decision making* derive *further support* from *Nash equilibrium ideas in classical game theory*.

HARRÉ, Rom. "Exploring the Human Umwelt" in *Harré and His Critics*, BHASKAR, Roy (ed), 297-364. Cambridge, Blackwell, 1990.

The bulk of the article is a reply to criticisms. For physics defence is built around the idea of the human unwelt, the world as it is available to people through manipulations. This leads to a new defence of a realist reading of physical theory, and to a restatement of the ontology of powers and dispositions. For human sciences the defence is built around the idea of discursivity which leads to a defence of linguistic studies as the proper core of a scientific psychology.

HARRÉ, Rom. "Realism, Reference and Theory" in *Key Themes in Philosophy*, GRIFFITHS, A Phillips (ed), 53-68. New York, Cambridge Univ Pr, 1989.

The claim of this paper is that only by adopting an approach to the analysis of theorizing based on the highlighting of analogy relations, that is on an analysis of the content of theories, can a defensible form of realism be found.

HARRINGTON, Christine and BRIGHAM, John. Realism in the Authority of Law. Soc Epistem, 5(1), 20-25, Ja-Mr 91.

HARRIS, C E. Aborting Abnormal Fetuses: The Parental Perspective. J Applied Phil, 8(1), 57-68, 1991.

This paper focuses on the issue of aborting abnormal fetuses from the standpoint of the prerogatives and obligations of parents. First, two intuitively-based models of parenthood are developed. Five principles are developed for determining how the two models should be applied in making moral decisions. The conclusion is that abortions are justified in the first three categories (involving severe abnormalties), but not in the fifth category (involving only slight deformities). Finally, a check on these conclusions is provided by comparing them with a parental action that would generally be considered impermissible. (edited)

HARRIS, Claudia and BROWN, William. Developmental Constraints on Ethical Behaviour in Business. J Bus Ethics, 9(11), 855-862, N 90.

Ethical behavior—the conscious attempt to act in accordance with an individually-owned morality—is the product of an advanced stage of the maturing process. Three models of ethical growth derived from research in human development are applied to issues of business ethics.

HARRIS, Errol E. *Cosmos and Anthropos: A Philosophical Interpretation of the Anthropic Cosmological Principle*. Atlantic Highlands, Humanities Pr, 1991.

HARRIS, Errol E. "A Reply to Philip Grier's "Abstract and Concrete in Hegel's Logic"" in *Essays on Hegel's Logic*, DI GIOVANNI, George (ed), 77-84. Albany, SUNY Pr, 1990.

HARRIS, Errol. "Ethical Implications of Newtonian Science" in *Philosophical Perspectives on Newtonian Science*, BRICKER, Phillip (ed), 211-225. Cambridge, MIT Pr, 1990.

HARRIS, James F. The Causal Theory of Reference and Religious Language. Int J Phil Relig, 29(2), 75-86, Ap 91.

I examine the Causal Theory of Reference and some of its recent applications within religious language. I develop the consequences of applying the causal theory within religious language, and I argue that the attempts to use this theory ignore significant disadvantageous consequences for the religious person. I further argue that some minimalist descriptivist theory is preferable for the religious person within the context of religious language.

HARRIS, James R. Ethical Values of Individuals at Different Levels in the Organizational Hierarchy of a Single Firm. J Bus Ethics, 9(9), 741-750, S 90.

This study examines the ethical values of respondents by level in the organizational hierarchy of a single firm. It also explores the possible impacts of gender, education and years of experience on respondents' values as well as their perceptions of how the organization and professional associations influence their personal values. Results showed that, although there were differences in individuals' ethical values by hierarchical level, significantly more differences were observed by the length of tenure with the organization. While respondents, as a whole, were rather ambivalent in their perception of the organization's and professional associations' influence on their values, sales/service persons frequently felt pressured to modify their values in order to achieve company goals.

HARRIS, Kevin. Empowering Teachers: Towards a Justification for Intervention. J Phil Educ, 24(2), 171-183, Wint 90.

Although policy statements and documents tend to indicate the opposite, there is a common tendency today for teachers to experience a loss of control over central matters of schooling, and especially curriculum. This situation is supported by certain philosophers who argue, variously, for nonintervention by teachers, and for centralised curriculum determination, such as National Curricula. This paper argues for the legitimacy of ideologically based politically committed discourse and enquiry; and, given certain conditions, for the legitimacy and desirability of empowering teachers to control curricula, and offer substantive proposals for social change, towards the end of empowering their pupils to engage in rational social reconstruction.

HARRIS, Roy. "The Scientist as 'Homo Loquens'" in *Harré and His Critics*, BHASKAR, Roy (ed), 64-86. Cambridge, Blackwell, 1990.

The semantics of modern science is an inheritance from the seventeenth century, when Locke, as epistemologist to the Royal Society, instituted an account of language as part of the theoretical foundations of systematic inquiry into Nature. The account nowadays accepted in the natural science is a form of

surrogationalism. Its two basic tenets are 1) that words have meanings by 'standing for' entities, properties, relations, etc., and 2) that the entities, properties, relations, etc. are given independently of the words standing for them. From a linguistic point of view, such an account is open to fundamental objections, which this paper examines.

HARRIS, W Edward. A New Humanism: A Response. Relig Hum, 25(1), 15-16, Wint 91.

HARRIS, William M. Professional Education of African Americans: A Challenge to Ethical Thinking. Bus Prof Ethics J, 9(1-2), 159-170, Spr-Sum 90.

Race in America affects relations among faculty and students in the academy. The presence of African Americans in higher education has influenced and often challenged the teaching and research roles of white (and African American) faculty members. This paper suggests opportunities exist for improved college teaching through ethical considerations as a consequence to the context of conflict.

HARRISON III, Frank R. 'Rules' and 'Knowledge'. J Indian Counc Phil Res, 5(1), 29-55, S-D 87.

HARRISON, Janet K and ROTH, Patricia A. Orchestrating Social Change: An Imperative in Care of the Chronically Ill. J Med Phil, 16(3), 343-359, Je 91.

The ethical challenges of caring for the chronically ill are of increasing concern to nurses as they attempt to create humanitarian environments for long-term care. This article suggests two ethical perspectives to guide the agenda of the nursing profession to achieve social change in the care of the chronically ill and aging. First, a reemphasis on the public duties of the professions is recommended which extends beyond serving the interests of the nursing profession to recognizing the need to serve the common good. Second, the limitations of the autonomy paradigm are explored and the foundation for the development of a new moral paradigm is analyzed in terms of its' potential usefulness in addressing ethical problems of chronic illness. Several initiatives that nursing must undertake to facilitate the emergence of this paradigm are proposed.

HARRISON, Jonathan. "Deontic Logic and Imperative Logic" in *Logic and Ethics*, GEACH, Peter (ed), 79-129. Norwell, Kluwer, 1991.

The author attempts a refutation of the view that it is the function of moral sentences to express imperatives. He does this by means of a detailed comparison of the two things, viz., 1) the logical relations between moral judgements and factual judgements and moral judgements and one another, and 2) the logical relations between imperatives and factual judgements and imperatives and one another. He lists 29 differences between moral judgements and imperatives ('twenty-nine distinct damnations'). Since the 'logic' of imperatives and the 'logic of moral judgements is so different, they cannot be imperatives; they cannot even imply them.

HARRISON, Jonathan. "In Defense of the Demon" in *The Case for Dualism*, SMYTHIES, John R (ed), 59-80. Charlottesville, Univ Pr of Virginia, 1989.

In *Meditations* Descartes argues that mind is a different substance from matter (sometimes) on the grounds that it would be possible for a malicious demon to cause our belief that mind existed to be true while our belief that matter existed was false. The author contends that this argument is *valid*. He also uses, among other things, two pieces of science fiction—a story about a disembodied brain that could perceive from a place where it did not exist, and a story about a magic mouse—in an attempt to persuade his readers that its premises could be *true*.

HARRISON, Jonathan. *Time-Travel for Beginners and Other Stories*. Nottingham, Univ Nottingham, 1990.

This unconventional piece of work is best described by listing its contents, viz: A Model for Administrators; Journey to the Centre of the Atom; Carrollian Spaces; A Tale of Two Citizens; Desert Island Deontology; The Magic Looking Glass; Jocasta's Crime; The Inescapable I; The Island of the Unborn; The Ideal Marriage; War Between the Hemispheres; Utopias Unlimited; and Dr. Who and the Philosophers or Time-Travel for Beginners.

HARRISON, Peter. *'Religion' and the Religions in the English Enlightenment*. New York, Cambridge Univ Pr, 1991.

This study shows how, during the Enlightenment in England, the ideas 'religion' and 'religions' took on their modern meaning. In the wake of the crisis of religious authority caused by the Reformation, appeals to reason lead to an objectification of religious faith. 'Religion' thus arose as a means of categorising the religious life, now seen to be a matter of subscribing to certain beliefs and engaging in specific rituals. The concept 'religion', moreover, linked together the disparate beliefs and practices of those in 'other religions'. The birth of these two ideas made possible the discipline of comparative religion.

HARRISON, Peter. Do Animals Feel Pain? Philosophy, 66(255), 25-40, Ja 91.

Most assessments of the moral status of animals are founded on the premise that animals feel pain. This premise is generally supported by three arguments. (1) We know that animals feel pain because they behave much the same as we do when we feel pain. (2) Many animals have nervous systems which resemble our own in structure and function. (3) Evolutionary theory provides for no radical discontinuity between human and other species, and it is therefore unlikely that only humans feel pain. These arguments are examined in turn and are shown to be defective or, at best, inconclusive. It is suggested that the experience of pain is essential only in agents capable of free choice—people. Accordingly, some views about how animals ought to be treated need to be revised.

HARRISON, Stephen. "A New Visualization of the Mind-Brain Relationship" in *The Case for Dualism*, SMYTHIES, John R (ed), 113-165. Charlottesville, Univ Pr of Virginia, 1989.

HART, James G. Axiology as the Form of Purity of Heart: A Reading Husserliana XXVIII. Phil Today, 34(3), 206-221, Fall 90.

HART, James G. "Divine Truth in Husserl and Kant: Some Issues in Phenomenological Theology" in *Phenomenology of the Truth Proper to Religion*, GUERRIÈRE, Daniel (ed), 221-246. Albany, SUNY Pr, 1990.

HART, Kevin. The Ins and Outs of Mysticism. Sophia (Australia), 30(1), 8-15, Jl 91.

Through a brief reading of *The Ascent of Mount Carmel* by St John of the Cross, I examine certain relations between mystical texts and literary practice. I argue that mystical experience is structured rhetorically, and that it is impossible to tell for sure if mystical texts report particular experiences.

HART, W D. "Clarity" in *The Analytic Tradition: Philosophical Quarterly Monographs, Volume 1*, BELL, David (ed), 197-222. Cambridge, Blackwell, 1990.

Clarity is a cardinal virtue in the analytic canon, but has not been much treated for its own sake. Frege, the early Wittgenstein, Carnap and the later Wittgenstein had more or less explicit accounts of the nature and value of clarity. This essay is an attempt to lay out and examine those accounts.

HART, W D. For Anil Gupta. Proc Aris Soc, 90, 161-165, 1989-90.

The paradox of the liar is derivable in a plausible extension of the system Anil Gupta describes in "Remarks on Definitions and the Concept of Truth," *Proceedings of the Aristotelian Society*, LXXXIX (1988-89), pp. 227-246.

HARTMANN, Klaus. Metaphysik und Metaphysikkritik. Neue Hefte Phil, 30-31, 109-138, 1991.

HARTSHORNE, Charles. Hegel, Logic, and Metaphysics. Clio, 19(4), 345-352, Sum 90.

I try to show how my "ultimate contrasts" and standard logic, including modal logic, can do what Hegel's logic is supposed to do, and do it better. Ultimate contrasts or polarities, including cause-effect, independent-dependent, absolute-relative, and other similarly abstract and general contraries have their intrinsic logic. In each case one term is the including, the other the included, by the Aristotelian or ontological principle that the abstract is real only in the concrete; also the earlier is in the later, and not vice versa. In both memory and perception, the data are temporally prior, the independent is in the dependent.

HARTSHORNE, Charles. Response to Piotr Gutowski's "Charles Hartshorne's Rationalism". Process Stud, 19(1), 10-14, Spr 90.

This is a defense of my philosophy against various criticisms by a visiting philosopher from Poland. I find some gaps between views I hold and views that the criticisms seem directed against. Extreme rationalism and intuitionism, extreme materialism and idealism, also extreme dualism, extreme trust or extreme distrust in great philosophers, extreme holism (the truth is the whole), extreme trust in concrete experience and in mathematico-logical abstractions, by contrast to all these I present my views as moderate. In various other ways I argue that my thought is more subtle and justifiably complex than the critic realizes.

HARTZ, Carolyn G. What Putnam Should Have Said: An Alternative Reply to Rorty. Erkenntnis, 34(3), 287-295, My 91.

HARVEY, Charles W. The Self and Social Criticism. S J Phil, 29(2), 215-226, Sum 91.

This essay attempts to show how the human self can and does engage in social criticism. Appealing to sociological and phenomenological descriptions, the essay shows that there are elements of social-psychological connection and disconnection in all social criticism. Developing insights from George Herbert Mead and Edmund Husserl, the essay comments on the metaphysics of self in relation to social criticism, and on the legitimacy of social criticism from the standpoint of a reflective, but socially and historically situated self.

HARVEY, J. Stereotypes and Group-Claims. J Phil Educ, 24(1), 39-50, Sum 90.

The basic epistemological root extracted from the various concepts of a stereotype is a "group-claim"—a claim about one or a few attributes of some group of people. Conditions for epistemological adequacy for such claims are set out, which in turn allows for an examination of the morality of using such claims. The findings have implications for multiculturalism in education.

HARVEY, Robert (trans) and LEFORT, Claude. Renaissance of Democracy? Praxis Int, 10(1-2), 1-13, Ap-Jl 90.

HARWOOD, John T (ed) and BOYLE, Robert. *The Early Essays and Ethics of Robert Boyle*. Carbondale, So Illinois Univ Pr, 1991.

HASKER, William. Middle Knowledge and the Damnation of the Heathen: A Response to William Craig. Faith Phil, 8(3), 380-389, Jl 91.

William Craig has proposed the view that all those persons who are in fact lost suffer from "transworld damnation"—the property of being such that, in every world actualizable by God in which one exists, one "freely does not respond to God's grace and so is lost." I show that Craig's proposal implies a conclusion he cannot possibly accept—namely, that no one is every saved as a result of the preaching of the Gospel who would not have been saved otherwise.

HASLAM, Nick. Prudence: Aristotelian Perspectives on Practical Reason. J Theor Soc Behav, 21(2), 151-169, Je 91.

This paper presents an Aristotelian approach to the psychology of prudence, and examines the pertinence of this approach to contemporary psychological work on rationality, choice, and self-control. Aristotle's account of action is first introduced, followed by its implications for the study of behavioral myopia, concern for the personal future, self-continuity, practical intelligence, and social and ethical behavior.

HASNAIN, Romana and GARLAND, Michael J. Community Responsibility and the Development of Oregon's Health Care Priorities. Bus Prof Ethics J, 9(3-4), 183-200, Fall-Wint 90.

The paper describes Oregon's innovative use of community meetings to identify key values for health care priorities in public policy. The article describes the Oregon Health Decisions technique as a contribution to overcoming risks of unfairness, prejudice and impracticality critics have attributed to the process of rationing health care. A rich array of values were identified at community meetings leading to a balanced, multi-dimensioned basis for setting priorities. The article finally relates the Oregon process to the concept of social solidarity essential to the fair and prudent reform of third party financing in US health care.

HASNAIN, Romana and GARLAND, Michael J. Health Care in Common: Setting Priorities in Oregon. Hastings Center Rep, 20(5), 16-18, S-O 90.

The article reports on the theory, design and results of a state-wide community meetings program to identify values required for democratically guiding efforts in Oregon to budget for Medicaid and health insurance programs for "the uninsured" on the basis of explicit health care priorities. The meetings were organized for a government commission by Oregon Health Decisions, a private organization that promotes general citizen involvement in exploring the ethical aspects of health policy development. Values expressed by the general public are related to fundamental themes of justice and community solidarity.

HASS, Lawrence. The Antinomy of Perception: Merleau-Ponty and Causal Representation Theory. Man World, 24(1), 13-25, Ja 91.

HASTE, Helen. "Moral Responsibility and Moral Commitment: The Integration of Affect and Cognition" in *The Moral Domain: Essays in the Ongoing Discussion between Philosophy and the Social Sciences*, WREN, Thomas E (ed), 315-359. Cambridge, MIT Pr, 1990.

The problem of "extraordinary moral responsibility" lies in what motivates people to act beyond the call of duty, and for causes not directly related to their personal lives. This chapter explores data from varying degrees of "commitment" to causes perceived as moral, ranging from a teenage vegetarian to Gandhi, and traces the paths towards such commitment. A model is presented to account for the psychological processes involved, drawing on the work of Lazarus. Conceptual problems in defining and evaluating moral responsibility and commitment are discussed.

HATAB, Lawrence J. Heidegger and Myth: A Loop in the History of Being. J Brit Soc Phenomenol, 22(2), 45-64, My 91.

The essay examines how Greek myth was a prefiguration of Heidegger's alternative to the philosophical tradition, and how Heidegger's later thought can be called mythical. Part One analyzes four Heideggerian themes (being-in-the-world, finitude, unconcealment, granting) and their expression in prephilosophical Greek myth. Part Two stresses Heidegger's early references to mythical thinking as a portent of the later turn to poetical thinking. The history of Being then becomes a loop because of prephilosophical echoes in Heidegger's postphilosophical thought.

HATAB, Lawrence J. *Myth and Philosophy: A Contest of Truths*. La Salle, Open Court, 1990.

An interpretive study of the historical relationship between myth and philosophy in ancient Greece, from Homer to Aristotle. In this context, the book argues for a pluralistic notion of truth, so that the intelligibility of myth can be defended against an exclusively rational or objective view of the world. The study offers (1) a general analysis of myth; (2) a specific analysis of Greek myth, poetry, and the emergence of philosophy; (3) an analysis of both the incommensurability of myth and rationality, and the ways in which they overlap; (4) a critique of Plato's and Aristotle's demotion of traditional myth.

HATAB, Lawrence J. Rejoining *Alētheia* and Truth: or Truth Is a Five-Letter Word. Int Phil Quart, 30(4), 431-447, D 90.

HATFIELD, Gary. *The Natural and the Normative: Theories of Spatial Perception from Kant to Helmholtz*. Cambridge, MIT Pr, 1991.

HATTINGH, J P. Art and Morality: On the Problem of Stating a Problem. S Afr J Phil, 9(3), 125-132, Ag 90.

The central argument of this article is that the problem of the relationship between art and morality cannot be posed or argued in a philosophically, comprehensive or enlightening way within the cadres that are offered by the two opposing standard points of view which in the course of time have crystallized in the widely held schools of thought on art and morality and which have been institutionalized in the socio-political praxis. The standard points of view referred to are, on the one hand, moralism of which Plato and Tolstoy are the classical exponents, and on the other hand, aestheticism, in which the figure of Don Juan in the work of Kierkegaard, and the nineteenth century ideal of *l'art pour l'art*, are but two of the many examples. This state of affairs was not altered by the emergence of the art theory and praxis of the historical avant-garde in the early twentieth century or by Sartre's popularization of the ideal of a *littérature engagée*. The reasons for this can be traced back to the instrumentalistic view of art and morality which is presupposed by all of these four positions. (edited)

HAUGELAND, John. "The Intentionality All-Stars" in *Philosophical Perspectives, 4: Action Theory and Philosophy of Mind, 1990*, TOMBERLIN, James E (ed), 383-427. Atascadero, Ridgeview, 1990.

HAUGELAND, John. "Philosophy at Carnegie Mellon: Past, Present, Future" in *Acting and Reflecting: The Interdisciplinary Turn in Philosophy*, SIEG, Wilfried (ed), 44-47. Norwell, Kluwer, 1990.

HAUGHT, Christine Ann and SHORE, Richard A. Undecidability and Initial Segments of the (R.E.) TT-Degrees. J Sym Log, 55(3), 987-1006, S 90.

HAUGHTON, James G. "Determinants of the Culture and Personality of Institutions" in *Integrity in Health Care Institutions: Humane Environments for Teaching, Inquiry, and Healing*, BULGER, Ruth Ellen (ed), 141-147. Iowa City, Univ of Iowa Pr, 1990.

HAUPTLI, Bruce W. A Dilemma for Bartley's Pancritical Rationalism. Phil Soc Sci, 21(1), 86-89, Mr 91.

W W Bartley's pancritical rationalists face a dilemma: they must accept that not all criticism is tentative; claim that pancritical rationalism is only tentatively criticizable. They cannot allow for nontentative criticisms without compromising their rationalism. They cannot claim pancritical rationalism is only tentatively criticizable without showing an irrational commitment to criticism. Finally, they limit criticism and sacrifice integrity if they allow that their commitment to rationalism is not criticizable. None of these alternatives appears acceptable and, thus, pancritical rationalism (at least in its present guise) should be abandoned.

HAUPTMAN, Robert and HILL, Fred. Deride, Abide or Dissent: On the Ethics of Professional Conduct. J Bus Ethics, 10(1), 37-44, Ja 91.

In the professions of today are ethical concerns of no overwhelming importance? Are these concerns less important in certain professions rather than others? Do some practitioners carry a blasé attitude regarding ethics within their profession? This study, sometimes asking "life-blood," "career-jeopardizing" questions is less interested in electronic data results and more interested in actual respondent replies on dissent and competence. There is strong evidence that the ethical ethos that has given American society its direction has been damaged; further, it has been the professed professionals who have been the major contributors to the ethical decline.

HAUSER, Marc D and ALLEN, Collin. Concept Attribution in Nonhuman Animals. Phil Sci, 58(2), 221-240, Je 91.

The demise of behaviorism has made ethologists more willing to ascribe mental states to animals. However, a methodology that can avoid the charge of excessive anthropomorphism is needed. We describe a series of experiments that could help determine whether the behavior of nonhuman animals towards dead conspecifics is concept mediated. These experiments form the basis of a general point. The behavior of some animals is clearly guided by complex mental processes. The techniques developed by comparative psychologists and behavioral ecologists are able to provide us with the tools to critically evaluate hypotheses concerning the continuity between human minds and animal minds.

HAUSMAN, Carl R. Language and Metaphysics: The Ontology of Metaphor. Phil Rhet, 24(1), 25-42, 1991.

This article is a revision and development of the last chapter of the author's book, *Metaphor and Art* (1989). It proposes a way of understanding actual and possible experiences and the objects of these experiences in terms of an evolutionary realism based on Charles Peirce's semiotic conception of dynamical and immediate objects. It suggests that some of these objects are metaphorical in structure and that these objects make evolution possible.

HAUSMAN, Dan. "What Are General Equilibrium Theories?" in *Acting and Reflecting: The Interdisciplinary Turn in Philosophy*, SIEG, Wilfried (ed), 107-114. Norwell, Kluwer, 1990.

HAUSMAN, Daniel M. Is Utilitarianism Useless? Theor Decis, 30(3), 273-278, My 91.

This review of *Morality within the Limits of Reason* draws out the main theme of Russell Hardin's book, that the limits of human knowledge, the complexities of strategic circumstances, and the problems of value theory deprive utilitarianism of any simple and direct moral consequences. But the review questions whether these difficulties might not deprive utilitarianism of any substantive consequences at all.

HAUSMAN, Daniel and BARRETT, Martin. Making Interpersonal Comparisons Coherently. Econ Phil, 6(2), 293-300, O 90.

HAVEMANN, Robert. Kommunismus—Utopie und Wirklichkeit. Deut Z Phil, 39(2), 136-140, 1991.

HAWLEY, Delvin D. Business Ethics and Social Responsibility in Finance Instruction: An Abdication of Responsibility. J Bus Ethics, 10(9), 711-721, S 91.

The shareholder wealth maximization objective for corporate management can be a very effective tool for decision making. However, it can also be used to rationalize the commission of unethical or socially irresponsible actions. Overemphasis on the SWM objective by some companies can lead to dangerous or disastrous consequences for consumers, employees, or the general population. Even so, issues of business ethics and social responsibility (BE-SR) are almost totally ignored in corporate finance textbooks. If the typical coverage of corporate finance courses is represented by these textbooks, then financial educators are abdicating their responsibility to help prepare future corporate managers to recognize and deal with BE-SR issues effectively.

HAWRANEK, Jacek. Comments on a Question of Wolniewicz. Bull Sect Log, 19(4), 128-132, D 90.

HAWRANEK, Jacek. A Topological Interpretation of Diagonalizable Algebras. Bull Sect Log, 19(4), 117-121, D 90.

HAWTHORN, Geoffrey. "Practical Reason and Social Democracy" in *Critique and Construction: A Symposium on Roberto Unger's "Politics"*, LOVIN, Robin W (ed), 90-114. New York, Cambridge Univ Pr, 1990.

HAWTHORN, John. Natural Deduction in Normal Modal Logic. Notre Dame J Form Log, 31(2), 263-273, Spr 90.

A natural deduction system for a wide range of normal modal logics is presented, which is based on Segerberg's idea that classical validity should be preserved "in any modal context." The resulting system has greater flexibility than the common Fitch-style systems.

HAYDEN, R Mary. The Paradox of Aquinas's Altruism: From Self-Love to Love of Others. Proc Cath Phil Ass, 63, 72-83, 1990.

It is commonly held that altruism, especially within ethics, requires selflessness or disinterestedness. Aquinas, on the other hand, argues that altruism as well as objectivity and universality is rooted in self-love. This paradox is dispelled through his differentiations of the various types of self-love and through his characterization of the nature of love.

HAYES, Calvin. "Existentialism, Humanism, and Positivism" in *The Question of Humanism: Challenges and Possibilities*, GOICOECHEA, David (ed), 105-114. Buffalo, Prometheus, 1991.

This article attempts to relate Sartre's argument in "Existentialism is a Humanism" to metaethical theories in analytical philosophy and to offer a negative solution to the is-ought problem. I draw unexpected parallels between Sartre's existential ethics and positivist arguments for moral scepticism. I suggest a solution to the is-ought problem strictly, parallel to Popper's negative solution to the problem of induction. This entails that moral judgements can be refuted/criticized but not verified/justified and that they are subject to the same type of criticism (logical, factual, theoretical) that Popper argues is available for scientific theories.

HAYES, David and SINGER, Alan E and LYSONSKI, Steven and SINGER, Ming. Ethical Myopia: The Case of "Framing" by Framing. J Bus Ethics, 10(1), 29-36, Ja 91.

The behavioural decision-theoretic concepts of mental accounting, framing and transaction utility have now been employed in marketing models and techniques. To date, however, there has not been any discussion of the ethical issues surrounding these significant developments. In this paper, an ethical evaluation is structured around three themes: (i) utilitarian justification, (ii) the strategic exploitation of cognitive habits, and (iii) the claim of scientific status for the techniques. Some recommendations are made for ethical practices.

HAYES, Richard P and GILLON, Brendan S. Introduction to Dharmakīrti's Theory of Inference as Presented in *Pramāṇavārttika Svopajñavṛtti* 1-10. J Indian Phil, 19(1), 1-73, Mr 91.

HAYIM, Gila J. Hegel's Critical Theory and Feminist Concerns. Phil Soc Crit, 16(1), 1-21, 1990.

The paper contrasts "needs" with "desires"—both of which are based on types of cognition that are dialectically interlocked in Hegel's thought. Consciousness is associated with need and the ethics of dependency while self-consciousness constitutes the basis of desire and the ethics of engagement. The dialectic of need and desire is different for men and women, being situated along different laboring relationship with the world. For men, labor and desire have produced the structures and institutions of modern industrial society. Must the labor and desire of women produce a similar world? Or, is there an alternative feminist self-consciousness with a different cognition of engagement?

HAYLING, Annie and ARRIETA, Jeannette. El pensamiento de Heidegger y Marcuse en relación con la ecología. Rev Filosof (Costa Rica), 28(67-68), 141-147, D 90.

The study of the environment where the human being unfolds itself as an important aspect might be particulary important for any thinking person of our time. The development of the science and technology implicate too the environment could be affected by many forms. Therefore, it is necessary to rescue the intellectual's thought like Heidegger and Marcuse, which can trace the problem from a very contemporary perspective.

HÄYRY, Matti and AIRAKSINEN, Timo. In Defence of "Hard" Offers: A Reply to J P Day. Philosophia (Israel), 20(3), 325-327, D 90.

In commenting on our earlier article in *Philosophia*, J P Day raises four issues: those concerning (1) the correct interpretation of the concept of "conditional offers," (2) the relationship of hard conditional offers to liberty, (3) the role of preferences in distinguishing offers from threats, and (4) the moral wrongness of some forms of offering. Two of these points, the second and the third, give rise to some further argument.

HÄYRY, Matti. Measuring the Quality of Life: Why, How and What? Theor Med, 12(2), 97-116, Je 91.

In this paper three questions concerning quality of life in medicine and health care are analyzed and discussed: the motives for measuring the quality of life, the methods used in assessing it, and the definition of the concept. The purposes of the study are to find an ethically acceptable motive for measuring the quality of life; to identify the methodological advantages and disadvantages of the most prevalent current methods of measurement; and to present an approach towards measuring and defining the quality of life which evades the difficulties encountered and discussed. The analysis comprises measurements both in the clinical situation concerning individual patients and in research concerning whole populations.

HAYS, David G and BENZON, William L. Why Natural Selection Leads to Complexity. J Soc Biol Struct, 13(1), 33-40, F 90.

While science has accepted biological evolution through natural selection, there is no generally agreed explanation for why evolution leads to ever more complex organisms. Evolution yields organismic complexity because the universe is, in its very fabric, inherently complex, as suggested by Ilya Prigogine's work on dissipative structures. Because the universe is complex, increments in organismic complexity yield survival benefits: (1) more efficient extraction of energy and matter, (2) more flexible response to vicissitudes, (3) more effective search. J J Gibson's ecological psychology provides a clue to the advantages of sophisticated information processing while the lore of computational theory suggests that a complex computer is needed efficiently to perform complex computations (i.e., sophisticated information processing).

HAYWARD, Tim. Ecosocialism—Utopian and Scientific. Rad Phil, 56, 2-14, Autumn 90.

HAZEN, A P. Small Sets. Phil Stud, 63(1), 119-123, Jl 91.

Annoyed by philosophers who make heavy weather of null and unit sets, I explain how they can be treated as *facons de parler* in versions of set theory recognizing only multi-membered sets.

HAZEN, Allen. Actuality and Quantification. Notre Dame J Form Log, 31(4), 498-508, Fall 90.

A natural deduction system of quantified modal logic (S5) with an actuality operator and "rigid" quantifiers (ranging, at every world, over the domain of the actual world) is described and proved to be complete. Its motivation and relation to other systems are discussed.

HEACOCK, Marian V and ORVIS, Gregory P. Ethical Considerations and Ramifications of the 1989 Generic Drug Scandal. Bridges, 2(3-4), 113-125, Fall-Wint 90.

Generic drugs presently account for one in three prescriptions and their use is predicted to increase as many name-brand drug patents expire in the next decade. The bribery and fraud perpetrated in 1989 by several drug companies in order to obtain early FDA approval of their generic drug applications created an ethical and legal dilemma from which the drug industry has yet to recover. This article provides a historical background of the generic drug scandal. The philosophical purposes of generic drug approval and of the FDA's role in the approval process are also explored. The moral responsibilities of generic drug firms to the public as well as the fiscal responsibility due their owners are discussed. Generic drug firms are defined as being either socially responsible or socially responsive. The discussion of the scandal closes with a discourse on its possible ramifications in the form of remedies to prevent similar problems in the generic drug industry.

HEAL, Jane. "Pragmatism and Choosing to Believe" in *Reading Rorty*, MALACHOWSKI, Alan (ed), 101-115. Cambridge, Blackwell, 1991.

Rorty advocates pragmatism—assessing beliefs by their ability to enhance human life. I argue that this is incoherent because it wrongly assumes that we could choose all our beliefs. We should distinguish two pairs of questions: What is the case?/What should I believe? and What should I do?/What should I intend? The last three questions are practical. But practical questions presuppose the intelligibility of non-practical questions of their first form, in answering which pragmatic considerations cannot be relevant.

HEALEY, Richard A. Holism and Nonseparability. J Phil, 88(8), 393-421, Ag 91.

Some have claimed that quantum phenomena exhibit holism or nonseparability. Assessing such claims requires analysis of relevant concepts of holism and nonseparability. The article formulates concepts of holism and nonseparability and explores their relations. Holism is understood as the thesis that the properties of a whole fail to supervene on those of its parts. Nonseparability is the thesis that what happens at each point where a process occurs does not wholly determine the properties of the process. Although holism entails nonseparability on quite weak assumptions, nonseparability does not entail holism. Quantum theory, plausibly interpreted, instantiates nonseparability and perhaps also holism.

HEANEY, Sandra and LAURA, Ronald S. *Philosophical Foundations of Health Education*. New York, Routledge, 1990.

The purpose of this work was to elucidate the reasons which explain the crisis in health care, that it arises not from a failure of medicine but rather from the failure of the philosophical assumptions on which it rests. Exposing the limitations of this philosophical framework leads to the suggestion of an alternative approach to health care derived from a profoundly ecological and holistic philosophy of nature. It is concluded that advancement of community health depends on incorporating the best aims of conventional medicine into a comprehensive programme of education for health in which the responsibility for health is inextricably knit with a new consciousness of ecological stewardship.

HEATHCOTE, Adrian and ARMSTRONG, D M. Causes and Laws. Nous, 25(1), 63-73, Mr 91.

It is argued that there is no analytic or conceptual connection linking singular causation with a law of nature. Nevertheless, there are good a posteriori grounds for holding that, just as heat is nothing but motion of molecules, so singular causation is nothing but the instantiation of a law.

HEATHCOTE, Adrian. Unbounded Operators and the Incompleteness of Quantum Mechanics. Phil Sci, 57(3), 523-534, S 90.

A proof is presented that a form of incompleteness in quantum mechanics follows directly from the use of unbounded operators. It is then shown that the problems that arise for such operators are not connected to the *non-commutativity* of many pairs of operators in quantum mechanics and hence are an additional source of incompleteness to that which allegedly flows from the EPR paradox. Finally, it will be argued that the problem is not amenable to some simple solutions that will be considered.

HEATHCOTE, Adrian. Zeeman-Göbel Topologies. Brit J Phil Sci, 39(2), 247-261, Je 88.

In 1967 E C Zeeman argued that the Euclidean, i.e., manifold, topology of Minkowski space-time should be replaced by a strictly finer topology that was to have a closer connection with the indefinite metric. This proposal was extended in 1976 by Rudiger Gobel and Hawking, King and McCarthy to the space-times of General Relativity. It is the purpose of this paper to argue that these suggestions for replacement misrepresent the significance of the manifold topology and overstate the necessity for a finer topology. The motivation behind such arguments is a realist view of space-time topology as against (what can be construed to be) the instrumentalist position underlying some of the suggestions for replacement.

HECKATHORN, Douglas D and COLEMAN, Jules L and MASER, Steven M. "A Bargaining Theory Approach to Default Provisions and Disclosure Rules in Contract Law" in *Liability and Responsibility*, FREY, R G (ed), 173-254. New York, Cambridge Univ Pr, 1991.

HECKER, Hellmuth. Heidegger und Schopenhauer. Schopenhauer Jahr, 71, 86-96, 1990.

HECKMAN, Peter. The Role of Music in Nietzsche's *Birth of Tragedy*. Brit J Aes, 30(4), 351-360, O 90.

Disagreement exists as to whether Nietzsche values art for allowing us unique insight into the nature of reality, or whether he values art as a source of pleasant illusions which mask a painful reality. The argument of this paper is that this disagreement can be traced to the equivocal character of music as presented in *The Birth of Tragedy*. This essay shows that the unstable distinction between music and "musical mood," the assertion of a creative capacity inherent in music, and the systematic equivocation as to whether or not music should be construed as symbolic, all serve to frustrate anyone who would derive a straightforward message from the work regarding the function of art.

HEDELER, Wladislaw. The Pros and Cons of Trotsky's Marxism (in German). Deut Z Phil, 38(8), 771-774, 1990.

HEDMAN, Carl. The Artificial Womb—Patriarchal Bone or Technological Blessing? Rad Phil, 56, 15-24, Autumn 90.

HEDMAN, Carl. Protective Norms as a Basis for Cooperation between Non-Privileged Constituencies. Soc Theor Pract, 17(1), 69-84, Spr 91.

How should we view those norms that serve to protect the interests of individuals? Should we see them as indispensable, as Steven Lukes suggests? Or should we see them as deeply problematic, as Michael Sandel suggests? It is argued that while we should be agnostics with regard to the ultimate fate of such norms, we should not rule out the possibility of a progressive transitional role for a certain sort of protective norm. Specifically, we should take seriously the possibility that the various contemporary movements for equality will see the need to band together in a difference-respecting coalition if any of them are to succeed. In this way, norms that serve to protect each group's historically-conditioned central interests might play a deeply progressive transitional role.

HEFFERNAN, George (trans) and DESCARTES, René. *Meditations on First Philosophy: A Bilingual Edition—René Descartes*. Notre Dame, Univ Notre Dame Pr, 1990.

HEFNER, Philip. Myth and Morality: The Love Command. Zygon, 26(1), 115-136, Mr 91.

Following in general a history of religions analysis, the paper argues that myth lays a basis for morality in that it sets forth a picture of "how things really are" (the *is*), to which humans seek to conform their actions (morality, the *ought*). A parallel argument locates the capacity for morality and values orientation in the process of evolution itself. A hypothesis is formulated concerning the function of myth in the emergence of *Homo sapiens*, namely, to motivate the action required if creatures so culturally formed as humans were to survive. The Christian love command (understood as altruism) is interpreted as an example of the general hypothesis.

HEGEL, G W F and BEHLER, Ernst (ed). *Encyclopedia of the Philosophical Sciences in Outline and Critical Writings—G W F Hegel*. New York, Continuum, 1990.

HEIDELBERGER, Michael. "History of Science and Criticism of Positivism" in *Études sur/Studies on Hélène Metzger*, FREUDENTHAL, Gad, 151-160. Leiden, Brill, 1990.

HEIDEMA, Johannes and BRINK, Chris. Verisimilitude by Power Relations: A Response to Oddie. Brit J Phil Sci, 42(1), 101-104, Mr 91.

HEIL, John and MELE, Alfred. Mental Causes. Amer Phil Quart, 28(1), 61-71, Ja 91.

Garden-variety explanations of human behavior feature agents' reasons, states of mind with particular mental contents. Such states are commonly taken to contribute to the etiology of the behavior. Worries about this picture abound, however. One difficulty is to see how mental content could function causally. We advance an account of mental causation that squares with a standard conception of agency and with the notion that the content of mental states is often fixed in part by relational, non-intrinsic characteristics of agents.

HEIN, Isolde. Ein neu gefundener Brief von Leibniz an Lambert van Velthuysen: Mit einer Einführung von Albert Heinekamp. Stud Leibniz, 22(2), 151-162, 1990.

This work has an introduction by Albert Heinekamp (+20. Nov. 1991). Leibniz's correspondence with Velthuysen is an important one, because it is one of the few preserved of an early period. The introductory letter is made accessible here by a transcription. It gives an account of his works, of the ideas he is interested in and of his opinions, which partly only this letter gives proof of. The main subjects of the letter are Leibniz's praise of the intellectual freedom and the standard of science enjoyed in the Netherlands, in spite of the expulsion of the Labadists; Hobbes's philosophy of the state and finally decorum, Velthuysen's subject of various publications. Similarly decisive comments by Leibniz concerning decorum are hardly to be found elsewhere.

HEINEKAMP, A and SCHUPP, F. Lógica y metafísica de Leibniz: Principales líneas de interpretación durante el siglo XX. Dialogo Filosof, 7(1), 4-31, Ja-Ap 91.

HEINZMANN, Gerhard. L'épistémologie mathématique de Gonseth dans la perspective du pragmatisme de Peirce. Dialectica, 44(3-4), 279-286, 1990.

According to a pragmatist, philosophical thought bears on the link between the construction and the description of mathematical objects. Thanks to his development of "theorematic reasoning", Peirce succeeded in bringing forward a pragmatic interpretation of a mathematical structure, exhibiting however an inherent vagueness with regard to the categoricalness of the structure. In this matter, Gonseth's model of reconstruction of an axiomatic system can be resorted to: the logical genesis of a structure considered in his *Idoneism* corresponds to Peirce's program of explaining the meaning of a concept by means of a cumulative sequence of interpretants.

HEISER, John H. Plotinus and the *Apeiron* of Plato's *Parmenides*. Thomist, 55(1), 53-81, Ja 91.

HEISIG, James W. "The Mystique of the Nonrational and a New Spirituality" in *Archetypal Process: Self and Divine in Whitehead, Jung, and Hillman*, GRIFFIN, David Ray (ed), 167-201. Evanston, Northwestern Univ Pr, 1989.

HEISIG, James W. "A Riposte" in *Archetypal Process: Self and Divine in Whitehead, Jung, and Hillman*, GRIFFIN, David Ray (ed), 209-211. Evanston, Northwestern Univ Pr, 1989.

HEJDANEK, L. Nothingness and Responsibility (in Czechoslovakian). Filozof Cas, 39(1), 32-37, 1991.

HEJDANEK, Ladislav. Reflection in Politics and the Question of a Political Subject (in Czechoslovakian). Filozof Cas, 38(6), 746-761, 1990.

The paper analyses the meaning of "reflection" for a constitution of a "subject" on a general level and the results are applied to and verified on a political one. Philosophy that is conceived as a principal and systematic reflection on human activities, i.e., reflections which on one hand study hidden preconditions and bases for these activities and on the other their multiple connections with other activities and their incident circumstances as well as their position in the world, such philosophy will inevitably turn to the activities and practice which are, like philosophy itself, oriented to the wholeness. Philosophy finds this field in a political practice which, first of all, is related to a community as a whole and also to greater units, that is to the state, the superstate and ultimately to the wholeness of the world. (edited)

HEKMAN, Susan. Reconstructing the Subject: Feminism, Modernism, and Postmodernism. Hypatia, 6(2), 44-63, Sum 91.

Political agency is vital to the formulation of a feminist politics so feminists have attempted to create a subject that eschews the sexism of the Cartesian subject while at the same time retaining agency. This paper examines some of the principle feminist attempts to reconstitute the subject along these lines. It assesses the success of these attempts in light of the question of whether the subject is a necessary component of feminist theory and practice.

HÉLAL, Georges. Le satori dans le bouddhisme zen et la rationalité. Laval Theol Phil, 47(2), 203-213, Je 91.

L'auteur présente le concept de satori (compréhension) dans le bouddhisme Zen, en détermine le sens et la portée et tente de montrer en quoi il se rapproche et diffère de la connaissance rationnelle telle que nous l'entendons ordinairement dans la tradition philosophique occidentale.

HELD, David. "Citizenship and Autonomy" in *Social Theory of Modern Societies: Anthony Giddens and His Critics*, HELD, David (ed), 162-184. New York, Cambridge Univ Pr, 1990.

HELD, David (ed) and THOMPSON, John B (ed). *Social Theory of Modern Societies: Anthony Giddens and His Critics*. New York, Cambridge Univ Pr, 1990.

HELD, Virginia. Feminist Transformations of Moral Theory. Phil Phenomenol Res, 50 SUPP, 321-344, Fall 90.

This article examines how feminist critiques and reconceptualizations are transforming moral theory. The history of ethics can be shown to be gender biased. Such currently dominant moral theories as Kantian ethics and utilitarianism are especially unsatisfactory when considered from the points of view of women's experience. The article focuses on three positions in ethics which feminists are rethinking: the split between reason and emotion and the denigration of emotion; the conceptions of the public and the private and the assumption that the public is more relevant to moral theory; and the concept of the self as autonomous individual. Feminist work in ethics often values the caring emotions and the sensitivity and responsiveness involved in nurturance; it often claims that the household is as relevant to morality and to moral theory as is the polis; and it is developing concepts of the self as relational rather than as either atomistic or communal.

HELEN, Mercy and CHAKRAVARTI, Mihirvikash. Disagreement in Philosophy. J Indian Counc Phil Res, 5(1), 95-102, S-D 87.

This paper examines the basic presupposition of Lazerowitz's metaphilosophy, namely, the position that philosophers disagree. From Descartes downward the position has been treated as if it is an axiom, but we have shown that, in having denied truth-value to philosophical propositions, Lazerowitz has unconsciously committed himself to the position that there can never be any disagreement among them and thereby destroyed the very basis of his metaphilosophy. In this connection, we have also mentioned the difficulties Lazerowitz has to face in finding any particular logical value in terms of which the utterances which constitute his metaphilosophy can be characterized.

HELLER, Agnes. Freedom and Happiness in Kant's Political Philosophy. Grad Fac Phil J, 13(2), 115-131, 1990.

HELLER, Agnes. *A Philosophy of Morals*. Cambridge, Blackwell, 1990.

HELLER, Alex. An Existence Theorem for Recursion Categories. J Sym Log, 55(3), 1252-1268, S 90.

HELLER, Edmund. *Nietzsches Scheitern am Werk*. Freiburg, Alber, 1991.

This book starts by analysing Nietzsche's reasons for using the method of aphorisms and shows that this work has the character of fragments inherited on someone's death. This form expresses what is in a sense a catastrophe. Then the concrete reasons for this catastrophe are examined; it must not be mistaken for failure. This shows Nietzsche—in contrast to common prejudice—to be a strictly systematic thinker, who intended that a new start should be made for scientific philosophy, but who did not believe himself able to contribute more than fragments to this task.

HELLER, Mark. *The Ontology of Physical Objects: Four-Dimensional Hunks of Matter*. New York, Cambridge Univ Pr, 1991.

HELLER, Michael. Adventures of the Concept of Mass and Matter. Phil Sci (Tucson), 3, 15-35, 1988.

Commonplace statements say that physics is a science of matter, or of what can be measured. These statements are incompatible. "Matter" cannot be measured. It seems that the physical term closest to that of "matter" is "mass." The paper begins with an analysis of the prescientific evolution of the concepts of matter and mass. Afterwards, it is shown how the systematization of the mass concept, mainly in the work of Newton, has eliminated the notion of matter from modern physics. It turns out that modern materialism was not a consequence of classical physics but rather of the fact that the most influential minds overlooked the elimination of the notion of matter by physics from among its conceptual tools. The philosophical and cultural implications of this fact are briefly discussed.

HELLER, Michael and STOEGER, W R. A Causal Interaction Constraint on the Initial Singularity? Phil Sci (Tucson), 2, 61-75, 1986.

Modern cosmology presents us with a fundamental problem, that of characterizing the "Big Bang," or "initial singularity" (IS) in a causally adequate and understandable way. The problem itself is described rigorously in terms of the causal geometry used in the theory of relativity. From the apparent isotropy and homogeneity of the observable universe it seems clear that, despite other inherent difficulties, causality demands that either the IS or a three-dimensional Cauchy surface very near it be causally self-connected, and therefore non-spacelike. Recent attractive proposals, e.g., the inflationary scenario, automatically fulfil this requirement. The indirectly related problem of synchronization by observers *within* a spacetime is also discussed.

HELLER, Michael. The Meaning of Meaning. Phil Sci (Tucson), 2, 10-14, 1986.

Propositions every domain of which constitutes a semantic model for them are tautologies. Propositions which do not have semantic models are called contradictions. Propositions not every domain of which is their model are said to be empirical propositions. If one agrees to define the meaning of a proposition by referring to its models, it becomes evident that tautologies (every domain of a model) are contradictions (no models) are but limiting cases; between these two limits there stretches an infinitive region of propositions with different numbers of models. It follows that these are empirical propositions of different "degrees of empiricity." Examples are given.

HELLER, Peter. Nietzsche's "Will to Power" Nachlass. Int Stud Phil, 22(2), 35-44, 1990.

HELLMAN, Geoffrey. "Modal-Structural Mathematics" in *Physicalism in Mathematics*, IRVINE, Andrew D (ed), 307-330. Norwell, Kluwer, 1990.

This presents an overview of the author's *Mathematics without Numbers: Towards a Modal-Structural Interpretation* (Oxford University Press: 1989). A realist alternative to traditional "objects-platonism" is developed, respecting classical mathematical truth while bypassing certain problems of reference and epistemic access associated with the latter (posed, e.g., by Benacerraf). The interpretation synthesizes *structuralist* insights going back to Dedekind with suggestions of Putnam (1967) treating mathematics as *modal logic*. Precise translations of core mathematical theories (Peano arithmetic, real analysis) into modal second-order logic are provided, and accuracy and adequacy are established. Roots of the *axiom of infinity* are explored, and the cogency of second-order logic upheld. The approach is extended generically to cover scientific applications of mathematics. (Extensions to set theory are presented in the above-mentioned book.)

HELLMAN, Geoffrey. Never Say "Never"! On the Communication Problem between Intuitionism and Classicism. Phil Topics, 17(2), 47-67, Fall 89.

HELLMAN, Geoffrey. Towards a Modal-Structural Interpretation of Set Theory. Synthese, 84(3), 409-443, S 90.

HELLMAN, John. "Maritain, Simon, and Vichy's Elite Schools" in *Freedom in the Modern World: Jacques Maritain, Yves R Simon, Mortimer J Adler*, TORRE, Michael D (ed), 165-180. Notre Dame, Univ Notre Dame Pr, 1989.

The wartime correspondence of Jacques Maritain and Yves Simon reveals them as questioning the value of the pre-war French Catholic philosophical critique of fascism. The Uriage school, "spiritual university" of Petain's National Revolution, highlighted the tension between Maritain and Simon in the United States and certain enterprises in Vichy France. As Uriage drew the elite of young Catholic philosophers, the two friends became alarmed at Catholic crypto-fascism. When Uriage's influence surfaced in post-war "progressive" Catholic thinking, Maritain and Simon fought for new Christian Democratic political theory.

HELLMAN, John. "World War II and the Anti-Democratic Impulse in Catholicism" in *From Twilight to Dawn: The Cultural Vision of Jacques Maritain*, REDPATH, Peter A (ed), 95-116. Notre Dame, Univ Notre Dame Pr, 1990.

HEMMING, James. The Physiology of Moral Maturity. J Moral Educ, 20(2), 127-137, My 91.

One way of looking at moral maturity is as the outcome of growth, which has its roots in genetical sources—that is to say in an inherited propensity for social behaviour—and the existence within the brain of centres that have evolved to mediate such growth. A further, and related, factor in this evolution was the emergence of language, which both extended the range of perception and intensified the experiences of inter-personal life. In this paper, the evidence for an evolutionary approach to human morality is set out, and some conclusions drawn about how social/moral potentialities may best be nourished through brain development between birth and maturity, supplemented by the process of education.

HENDERSON, Edward H. L'affirmation de l'existence de Dieu selon Austin Farrer. Arch Phil, 54(1), 65-90, Ja-Mr 91.

This essay explains and tries to make cogent Austin Farrer's account of the affirmation of God's existence as it develops in his main philosophical works. *Faith and Speculation* argues that the affirmation of God is a practical response to felt unconditional demand or value and that such valuing response is not peculiar to affirming the existence of the divine person but is necessary also to affirming the existence of human persons, the most undeniably real individuals. If this is true, the affirmation of God extends rather than violates our most trustworthy kind of knowing. (edited)

HENDLEY, Steven. Judgment and Rationality in Lyotard's Discursive Archipelago. S J Phil, 29(2), 227-244, Sum 91.

There is a tension in Lyotard's recent work between his emphasis on the absence of a transcendent perspective on language as a whole and our need for a critical sense of judgement capable of evaluating the justice or legitimacy of incommensurable discursive regimes. This paper defends the consistency of these two aspects of Lyotard's work in terms of his treatment of the question of justice and his interpretation of Kant's understanding of judgement and concludes by arguing for the presence of a sense of rationality in Lyotard's retrieval of a critical sense of judgement consistent with our "postmodern condition".

HENGELBROCK, Jürgen. *Jean-Paul Sartre*. Freiburg, Alber, 1991.

This book supplies an introductory presentation of the basic philosophical thought of Jean-Paul Sartre, as it is developed within the field of problems whose poles are the concepts of freedom and necessity. Henglebrock's analysis is structured in terms of three works central to an understanding of Sartre: the early "Transcendence of the Ego", "Being and Nothingness", and the "Critique of Dialectical Reason". In particular the author examines the fatalistic tendencies of Sartre's notion of freedom, at the same time showing its emancipatory strength. He outlines existential pessimism and what is in a sense its optimistic reverse side in the praxis of living, as well as the contingency of existence in Sartre's view and the possibility of tolerating it through the ethos of authenticity. Moreover Hengelbrock examines the illumination which Sartre's works and his life cast on each other, and the reflection of Sartre's philosophical theories in his plays and literary work.

HENLE, J M and DI PRISCO, C A and FULLER, M. The Normal Depth of Filters on an Infinite Cardinal. Z Math Log, 36(4), 293-296, 1990.

HENLE, J M. Partition Properties and Prikry Forcing on Simple Spaces. J Sym Log, 55(3), 938-947, S 90.

HENLE, R J. Sanction and the Law According to St Thomas Aquinas. Vera Lex, 10(1), 5-6,18, 1990.

HENLEY, Kenneth. Protestant Hermeneutics and the Rule of Law: Gadamer and Dworkin. Ratio Juris, 3(1), 14-27, Mr 90.

The rule of law demands that the state's coercive power be used only according to settled general laws, applied impersonally. But an individualist theory of legal interpretation cannot provide the shared understanding required. Gadamer appeals to the practical wisdom of judges and lawyers, who will agree on how to apply law to new cases. But this account is adequate only for very cohesive societies. Dworkin's account rests on propositional knowledge of a supposed best interpretation of an entire legal system. But even if such a best interpretation is possible in theory, this possibility does not provide shared understandings in the social world.

HENLEY, Tracy and POLLIO, Howard R. Empirical and Philosophical Reactions to Harcum's "Behavioral Paradigm for a Psychological Resolution of ...". J Mind Behav, 12(1), 115-134, Wint 91.

This paper begins with a brief description and analysis of Harcum's "Behavioral Paradigm for a Psychological Resolution of the Free Will Issue" focusing on issues concerning first-person and third-person perspectives in psychological research and theory. This consideration is expanded to cover a variety of related issues including "unconscious processes" and philosophical discussions of free will. Two studies, similar to Harcum's original study, but analyzed from a first-person perspective, are reported and contrasted with Harcum's work. Results of these studies reveal that different individuals provide meanings for the same actions, e.g., sitting in one or another seat in a college classroom. The significance of these findings for psychological research concerning the experience and concept of free will are discussed in light of an alternative, existential-phenomenological approach to psychology.

HENLEY, Tracy. Natural Problems and Artificial Intelligence. Behavior Phil, 18(2), 43-55, Fall-Wint 90.

Artificial Intelligence has become big business in the military and in many industries. In spite of this growth there still remains no consensus about what AI really is. The major factor which seems to be responsible for this is the lack of agreement about the relationship between behavior and intelligence. In part certain ethical concerns generated from saying who, what and how intelligence is determined may be facilitating this lack of agreement.

HENNIGFELD, Jochem. Verbum-Signum: La définition du langage chez s Augustin et Nicolas de Cues. Arch Phil, 54(2), 255-268, Ap-Je 91.

Is the relationship between word and thing natural or arbitrary (*physeithesei*)? The conflict between these two alternatives is already present in the Greek world and determines in different variations the following history of philosophy of language. The canonic form of this contrast in the Middle Ages can be found in Augustinus. On the one hand the human word is a mere sign, that does not contribute anything towards the knowledge of the object. On the other hand, in the execution of the internal language lies the highest image of the divine Trinity and of the Verbum Dei. In *Idiota de mente* a synthesis between these opposite conceptions of language is found by Nikolaus of Cues.

HENRARD, Roger. La réception de Spinoza dans la littérature néerlandaise. Rev Phil Louvain, 88(80), 504-523, N 90.

In spite of his radical rationalism and his slight esteem for art, Spinoza has been studied by poets and writers. It was the German Romantics who found a source of inspiration—in fact in a highly subjective manner—in the thought of Spinoza. The reception of Spinoza in Dutch literature of the 19th and 20th centuries was very different. Van Vloten, the famous editor of the complete works of the philosopher, reduces Spinoza's thought to a kind of vitalism that dispenses with the Christian God. This naturalist interpretation strongly influenced authors at the turn of the century such as Brouwer, Multatuli, Gorter (who was to turn from Spinoza to Marx). At the start of the 20th century a "spiritualist" trend came into being as a reaction against positivism, and Spinoza was interpreted this time in an idealist manner, notably by Bierens de Haan, Van Schendel, Verwey, Van Eyck. These authors introduce progress into Spinoza's substance with the risk, however, of sliding into a kin dof national-socialism, as witnesssed by the example of Carp. It is noteworthy that Spinoza has exercised no influence on Dutch literature since the 1940-45 war, doubtless because of existentialism.

HENRICH, Dieter. Die Philosophie im einen Deutschland. Deut Z Phil, 39(3), 225-235, 1991.

HENRIQUES, Fernanda. A significação "crítica" de Le volontaire et l'involontaire. Rev Port Filosof, 46(1), 49-86, Ja-Mr 90.

This text seeks to find a hermeneutical principle which permits a reading of Ricoeur's work as a whole. In this context, it is proposed that Ricoeur's philosophy may be interpreted with the Kantian tradition of the critical thought as a *philosophy of limits* for reason; this is not to be taken in the original sense of the conditions of possibility for objective knowledge but rather as systematic investigation to discover the conditions which make possible thought and discourse concerning existence. It is thus that the "criticism" of *Le volontaire et l'involontaire*, the first work of his *Philosophy of the Will*, can be seen as determining these conditions of possibility by proposing fundamental theoretical principles of the constitution of unitary discourse in relation to the human experience, understood as historical and free existence.

HENRY, Michel. Quatre principes de la phénoménologie. Rev Metaph Morale, 96(1), 3-26, Ja-Mr 91.

HENRY-HERMANN, Grete. Conquering Chance. Phil Invest, 14(1), 1-80, Ja 91.

HEPBURN, Ronald W. Art, Truth and the Education of Subjectivity. J Phil Educ, 24(2), 185-198, Wint 90.

The arts do not instruct us about objective reality as do the natural sciences, but they have their own several ways of mediating truth. Their particularity does not frustrate their power to reveal. They can vividly present sustainable perspectives on the world—the human life-world, and they can intensify our awareness and grasp of it. Art even partly constitutes that world. But surely to move towards truth about the real must be to move *away* from appearances, human perspectives and subjectivity? This view is examined and rejected: educational implications are drawn from the discussion.

HERBENICK, Raymond M. Natural Fetal Dependency States and Fetal Dependency Principles. Proc Cath Phil Ass, 63, 173-181, 1990.

Redefining an elective abortion as withdrawal of total care and support of a human fetus has relied upon uncritical notions of fetal dependency states and principles for parental discharge of duties of care and support. Recent attempts at moral justification of elective abortion (e.g., M Bolton and S Ross) also indicate reliance on such unanalyzed notions. *Burns v Alcala* is used to show some moral oddities arising from these unanalyzed notions. Four types of possible natural fetal dependency states are then outlined. Four types of possible fetal dependency principles are thereafter developed. It appears some redefinitions of and moral justifications for elective abortion are inadequate if based on unanalyzed notions of fetal dependency.

HERBERT, R T. Is Coming to Believe in God Reasonable or Unreasonable? Faith Phil, 8(1), 36-50, Ja 91.

In this paper I contend that coming to believe that God exists is neither reasonable nor unreasonable, since coming to believe it is to be seen rather as "coming down" with the conviction that God exists (as one comes down with an ailment) than as an instance of being persuaded of or accepting something. I set forth what I take to be scriptural support for the ailment view and attempt to show that a key scriptural passage seeming to support the persuasion view does not really do so.

HERDER-DORNEICH, Philipp. Entrepreneurial Philosophy (in German). Deut Z Phil, 38(10), 944-952, 1990.

HERKERT, Joseph R. Management's Hat Trick: Misuse of "Engineering Judgment" in the Challenger Incident. J Bus Ethics, 10(8), 617-620, Ag 91.

HERLITZIUS, Erwin. Ways to See a Revolution and World Outlook: Alexander von Humboldt (in German). Deut Z Phil, 38(5), 448-460, 1990.

The literary work of Alexander von Humboldt, the German geologist, geographer, pioneer of ecology, and explorer of South America, emerged under growing conflicts in missions as a Prussian statesman. Humboldt's political philosophy reflects the Rights of Man, especially his opposition to colonial practice and ethnic discrimination. Prematurely he confided his sentiments to his intimate diary during the American experiences 1800-04—scarcely known until 1982. All his life he cherished ideals of the American and French revolutions, congenial to Jefferson's principles. Speculative philosophical systems were condemned. But some of Hegel's historicity focused attention on account to scientific revolutions. In "Kosmos" (1845-59) Humboldt explicitly confessed himself to the open-ended nature of intellectual power, of human goals and values.

HERMAN, A L. Jivacide, Zombies and *Jivanmuktas*. Asian Phil, 1(1), 5-13, 1991.

In discussing the meaning of life in the *Bhagavad Gītā* two obvious questions arise: first, what is the meaning of 'the meaning of life'?, and second, how does that meaning apply to the *Bhagavad Gītā*? In Part I of this brief paper I will attempt to answer the first question by focusing on one of the common meanings of that phrase; in Part II, I will apply that very common meaning to the *Bhagavad Gītā*; and in the third and final part, I will point to a puzzle, the paradox of the *jīvanmukta*, that would seem to follow from the discussion in the first two parts of this paper. My own feeling is that the concept of 'the meaning of life' is a Western invention [1]. This being so, perhaps it would be wise to probe for that concept and its meaning among Western authors. We turn first, then, to one ancient writer, Aristotle of Stagira, and conclude Part I with a modern writer also concerned with the meaning of life, Albert Camus.

HERMAN, Barbara. "Obligation and Performance: A Kantian Account of Moral Conflict" in *Identity, Character, and Morality: Essays in Moral Psychology*, FLANAGAN, Owen (ed), 311-337. Cambridge, MIT Pr, 1990.

HERMAN, David J. The Incoherence of Kant's Transcendental Dialectic: Specifying the Minimal Conditions for Dialectical Error. Dialectica, 45(1), 3-29, 1991.

Subjecting to a detailed analysis Kant's diagnosis of dialectical error in the Transcendental Dialectic of the first *Critique*, the author posits that Kant's understanding of such error is, to the extent that it conflates the subjective-objective, phenomenal-noumenal, and regulative-constitutive distinctions, fundamentally incoherent. The author argues not only that these three distinctions cannot on Kant's own terms be conflated, but also that Kant's treatment of dialectical error is further vitiated by circularity of argument: Kant proposes to explain the three distinctions by means of the notion of transcendental error, which however the distinctions themselves were supposed to explain in the first place. After showing that Kant's diagnosis of dialectical error cannot be salvaged even by resorting to the Kantian concept of "transcendental subreption", the author concludes that unless Kant could in some other way spell out the minimal conditions for dialectical error, Kant's very distinction between understanding and reason becomes difficult to justify.

HERMEREN, Goran. "Tradition, Influence and Innovation" in *XIth International Congress in Aesthetics, Nottingham 1988*, WOODFIELD, Richard (ed), 78-82. Nottingham, Nottingham Polytech, 1990.

HERNÁNDEZ IGLESIAS, Manuel Angel. Analiticidad, empirismo y verdad necesaria. El Basilisco, 6, 13-18, Jl-Ag 90.

This article is a historical review and an analysis of the outcome of the most important discussions on analyticity in contemporary empiricism. It is argued that analytic truths cannot be reduced to metalinguistic synthetic statements or linguistic rules, that analyticity must be defined in linguistic terms, without appeal to epistemic or metaphysical modalities and that, even if a sharp distinction between analytic and synthetic sentences is accepted, analytic truths are not necessary in a non trivial sense. It is concluded that the concept of analyticity has not the epistemological import that logical empiricist conventionalism attributed to it.

HERNANDEZ, Adriana. Feminist Theory, Plurality of Voices and Cultural Imperialism. Phil Stud Educ, /, 59-71, 1989.

This paper, written in the traditions of critical pedagogy, feminist pedagogy, and a Bakhtinian cultural perspective, has the purpose of analyzing important aspects developed by feminist theorist Maria Lugones around the ideas of plurality, difference, and voice in feminist theory development within the context of cultural imperialism. The main conceptual underpinnings of the transformative feminist pedagogy of difference I propose through this analysis are: dialogue as talking together in multiple voices; the subject as compound identities; an idea of community building theory disarticulating the hierarchy between theorists and theorized; a concept of "world"-travelling as lived experience; and a political project defined in terms of radical democracy.

HERNÁNDEZ, Héctor H. Sobre la naturaleza de los "derechos". Sapientia, 45(175), 17-30, Ja-Mr 90.

HEROUX, Mark A and OTTENSMEYER, Edward J. Ethics, Public Policy, and Managing Advanced Technologies: The Case of Electronic Surveillance. J Bus Ethics, 10(7), 519-526, Jl 91.

A vigorous debate has developed surrounding electronic surveillance in the workplace. This controversial practice is one element of the more general issues of employee dignity and management control, revolving around the use of polygraph and drug testing, "integrity" exams, and the like. Managers, under pressure from competitors, are making greater use of technologically advanced employee monitoring methods because they are available, and hold the promise of productivity improvement. In this paper, the context of electronic surveillance is described and analyzed from the perspectives of ethics, public policy, and managerial behavior.

HERRERA JIMÉNEZ, Rodolfo. La práctica tecnológica. Rev Filosof (Costa Rica), 27(66), 349-359, D 89.

The technological practice is characterized as a superior form of social practice, as a process of rational and conscious transformation and appropriation, and as an organized activity of concrete social systems. In this way, its differences from scientific and cultural practices and is productive dialectical unity are revealed.

HERRERA, Alejandro. El innatismo de Leibniz. Dianoia, 36(36), 111-120, 1990.

Leibniz's theory of monads demanded that all ideas were innate. However, in the *new essays* he holds a different kind of innatism, in which 1) there are not only innate ideas, but also innate propositions, 2) only certain sets of propositions and ideas are innate. I offer an explanation of this innatism, apparently in conflict with the first one. I also point out Leibniz's use of the notion of *disposition* to characterize his theory, which gets thus very close to contemporary Chomskyan innatism.

HERRERA, Alejandro. La teoría del significado como uso en Wittgenstein. Dianoia, 35(35), 203-210, 1989.

HERRERA, J Jesús. Existencia de Dios y libertad humana. Logos (Mexico), 18(53), 9-27, My-Ag 90.

HERRERA, Rodolfo. Tecnología y sociedad. Rev Filosof (Costa Rica), 28(67-68), 77-84, D 90.

The purpose of this paper is to elucidate the epistemological problems generated by the so-called "technological phenomenon" of contemporary society in relation to the concept of technology. The formulation of the problem, based on a philosophical materialistic concept and on a social systemic approach and analysis, dialectically explained, reveals and surpasses some ideological confusions, common in the discussion of the theme.

HERRING, Ronald J. Rethinking the Commons. Agr Human Values, 7(2), 88-104, Spr 90.

Common property has been theoretically linked to environmental degradation through the metaphor of "the tragedy of the commons," which discounts local solutions to commons dilemmas and typically posits the need for strong states or privatization. Though neither solution is theoretically or empirically adequate—because of the nature of states and nature in the real world—local arrangements for averting the tragedy suffer certain *lacunae* as well, including stringent boundary conditions and overlapping/overarching commons situations that necessitate larger scale cooperation than is possible in the face-to-face communities that are conducive to cooperation. Second-order or meta-commons issues expand the scope of inquiry necessarily beyond *conservation* to *preservation*. The Sundarbans illustrates the contradictory implications of the Leviathan solution to commons dilemmas, as well as the centrality of alternative perceptual framings of natural systems.

HERRMANN, B. Axiomatization of the De Morgan Type Rules. Stud Log, 49(3), 333-343, S 90.

We provide a finite base of the De Morgan type rules (= sequential rules of the propositional calculus which remain correct under dualization). A similar result is obtained for the implicational fragment of the propositional calculus. These results are essentially based on a special property concerning replacement of some equational theories.

HERRMANN, Eberhard. "Automorphisms of the Lattice of Recursively Enumerable Sets and Hyperhypersimple Sets" in *Logic, Methodology and Philosophy of Science, VIII*, FENSTAD, J E (ed), 179-190. New York, Elsevier Science, 1989.

The central question considered in the paper is when two hh-simple sets with isomorphic r.e. supersets structure are automorphic and when not. With every hh-simple set there is connected a family of ideals of r.e. supersets from which in particularly follows that, if the Boolean algebra of the r.e. supersets of a hh-simple set (modulo finite) is infinite, then the class of all hh-simple sets with this Boolean algebra decomposes into infinitely many nonempty one-types.

HERTZBERG, Lars. Imagination and the Sense of Identity. Philosophy, 29, 143-155, 91 Supp.

The assumption that we can establish philosophical conclusions about personal identity by asking what things about a person could have been imagined different from what they are is criticized. The question 'Can this be imagined?' cannot be addressed in the abstract; the answer to it depends on the context in which it is raised. Attempts to explore the concept of identity by appealing to thought experiments, though distinct from appeals to the imagination, are also confused, since they presuppose a definite answer to the question what would constitute using words with the same meaning in radically different circumstances.

HERVADA, Javier. *Introduction Critique au Droit Naturel*. Bordeaux, Biere, 1991.

HERZOG, Don. Puzzling Through Burke. Polit Theory, 19(3), 336-363, Ag 91.

HESLEP, Robert D. Must the State Justify Its Educational Policies? Proc Phil Educ, 46, 176-184, 1990.

The purpose here is to determine if a state, or political society, logically has to justify its educational policies. The conclusion is that a state must defend its educational policies under certain conditions for the reason that it is bound to explain any of its policies under the same conditions. The conditions are that members of a state ask it to justify its educational or other policies and that its justification of the policies does not threaten its interests. The claim of these conditions rests on the contention that both the state and its members are voluntary, and thus rational, agents.

HESTER, Marcus. Aristotle on the Function of Man in Relation to Eudaimonia. Hist Phil Quart, 8(1), 3-14, Ja 91.

In the *Nicomachean Ethics* Book I, chapter 7, Aristotle gives the uniqueness argument—each species has a unique essence, expressing its function, and the good for each species is just doing well its function. I argue that Aristotle's concept of eudaimonia is not dependent on the uniqueness argument. In fact, his concept of eudaimonia is derived from endoxa—the opinion of the many and the wise. Despite this independence, his concept of the fourteen moral virtues is somewhat dependent on the uniqueness argument. Even if the fourteen moral virtues all essentially involve reasoning, they *alone* are not unique to the human species.

HESTER, Marcus. Foundationalism and Peter's Confession. Relig Stud, 26(3), 403-413, S 90.

I argue that typical analyses of foundational beliefs, such as Aristotle on the law of noncontradiction or Hume on causation, are not really arguments; instead they are critical or transcendental clarifications. I derive from such examples six characteristics of dialectical or transcendental clarifications. Then I try to show that even if belief in the category of a particular personal God can be clarified in such ways, belief in a particular personal God, as expressed in say, Peter's confession, cannot be so clarified. Thus belief in a particular personal God is not a properly basic belief—a conclusion perhaps inconsistent with Plantinga.

HESTEVOLD, H Scott. The Concept of Religion. Pub Affairs Quart, 5(2), 149-162, Ap 91.

Offered is an analysis of what it is to be religious that is both narrow enough to exclude mere social-club rituals from the class of religious activities and broad enough to count as religious certain atheistic Buddhists. In short, to be religious is either to engage in nonverbal ritualistic behavior expressing commitment to a moral principal or to act worshipfully toward a supernatural being. The concept of religion is then analyzed in terms of what it is to be religious.

HETHERINGTON, Stephen Cade. Epistemic Internalism's Dilemma. Amer Phil Quart, 27(3), 245-251, Jl 90.

The paper's first part proposes a simple account of epistemic internalism, and then proceeds to describe a serious dilemma facing internalism. The result is that, necessarily, internalism is an empty concept. It is surprising how easily this result can be obtained: the paper's second part shows how Russell, Wittgenstein, Wilfrid Sellars, and A J Ayer were all aware of what is effectively the dilemma.

HETMANSKI, Marek. The Operation of Values: Knowledge in the Conception of G H Mead (in Polish). Ann Univ Mariae Curie-Phil, 11, 41-58, 1986.

The aim of the study is a presentation of the conception of G H Mead in which he stresses the genetic and functional relation of knowledge and cognition with activity. Contrary to traditional, rationalistic-aprioristic theories, it poses the problem of a cognitive and utilitarian (extra-cognitive) character of knowledge, and it also considers a possibility of the existence of an over-cognitive (aesthetic, moral) value of knowledge. The identity of cause and aim in activity and cognition, a similarity of the structure of both acts and the equivalence of their objects ("meaningful objects") are the properties of human activity which, according to Mead's conception, constitute an example of cancelling the traditional antinomy: "Pure" knowledge—practical knowledge. The universal and general character of knowledge is expressed not only in the form of "theoretical" cognition but mainly in forms of genetic practical-cognitive activity of man.

HETZLER, Florence M. Art and Philosophy: The Person in the Cybernetic Age. Phil Sci (Tucson), 4, 211-239, 1990.

HETZLER, Florence M. *Introduction to the Philosophy of Nature*. New York, Lang, 1990.

A study of Aquinas's commentary on the first book of the *Physics of Aristotle*, which summarizes the thought of the pre-Socratics and of Aristotle's approach to cosmology. A unit with all cross-reference in English, it clarifies the thought of the ancients and of the medieval Aquinas with regard to the philosophy of nature; it presents all of this as a basis for subsequent philosophy of nature.

HEWITT, Marsha A. "The Humanistic Implications of Liberation Theology: Juan Luis Segundo and Karl Marx" in *The Question of Humanism: Challenges and Possibilities*, GOICOECHEA, David (ed), 253-272. Buffalo, Prometheus, 1991.

The author looks at the influence of social theory on the thought of J L Segundo, especially that of Marx, and the implications of that influence. The author argues that liberation theology is more of a socialist humanism than a theology, in the classic sense of theology, by virtue of its movement into social analysis and socialist political thought and practice. The social theory of Marx is what constitutes the primary mediation of liberation theology's implicit humanism. Questions of personal salvation, for example, become absorbed into more fundamental questions of social and political liberation in liberation theology.

HEYD, David. Hobbes on Capital Punishment. Hist Phil Quart, 8(2), 119-134, Ap 91.

The article argues that for the consistently naturalistic theory of Hobbes the justification of capital punishment—unlike other punishments—is particularly problematic. Rational contractor cannot agree on punishments which they know they would be forced by their nature to resist. Furthermore, the contractarian justification is for Hobbes always utilitarian, but capital punishment is unique in its being a pure and total loss to the individual. Hobbes's awareness of this tension and his attempt to deal with it is critically analyzed, using notions of game theory and a comparison with non-naturalistic theories on this matter.

HEYD, Thomas. Understanding Performance Art: Art beyond Art. Brit J Aes, 31(1), 68-73, Ja 91.

While twentieth century art often unwittingly leaves the public wondering what qualifies a piece as art, performance artists have intentionally sought to question the relation between their pieces and the institution of art. In order to facilitate the interpretation of performance art pieces, this paper focusses on the claim that they are meant to be art that goes beyond art. To make any sense, practically speaking, such an undertaking has to face two difficulties, one historical and one logical, however. I conclude that the purported difficulties are only apparent, and introduce evidence to show that performance art pieces indeed may have succeeded in being art that goes beyond art.

HEYES, Cecilia. Who's the Horse? A Response to Corlett. Soc Epistem, 5(2), 127-134, Ap-Je 91.

HEYLIGHEN, Francis. Non-Rational Cognitive Processes as Changes of Distinctions. Commun Cog, 23(2-3), 165-181, 1990.

Rational cognitive processes are defined as processes constrained by an external system of rules. This constraint is represented by the conservation of distinctions, where a distinction is conceived as an element of cognitive structuration. Four classes of distinctions (patterns, states, rules, and values) and four classes of distinction processes (conservation, destruction, creation, and creation-and-destruction of distinctions) are defined. The resulting 4 x 4 grid is used to classify cognitive processes. This allows the modelling of "nonrational" phenomena, such as creativity, emotions, mystical experiences, in a relatively simply way, as incompletely distinction conserving processes.

HIBBS, Thomas S. Divine Irony and the Natural Law: Speculation and Edification in Aquinas. Int Phil Quart, 30(4), 419-429, D 90.

Readers of Aquinas often suppose that his doctrine of natural law provides an autonomous and complete moral theory. Yet Aquinas sees the natural law as but part of a more comprehensive moral pedagogy. He highlights the dialectical and instrumental status of law. The law fosters self-knowledge and intensifies the sense of the need for divine assistance. The engagement of the natural by the supernatural operates through dialectic and irony, through strategies that demand and allow for the reappropriation and perfection of the self.

HIBBS, Thomas S. MacIntyre, Tradition, and the Christian Philosopher. Mod Sch, 68(3), 211-223, Mr 91.

HICK, John. A Response to Gerard Loughlin's "Prefacing Pluralism: John Hick and the Mastery of Religion". Mod Theol, 7(1), 57-66, O 90.

This response claims that Loughlin has at a number of points seriously, and sometimes willfully, misrepresented Hick's work, thereby creating unreal problems. This is argued in detail and Loughlin's attack comprehensively rejected.

HICKMAN, Larry. Contextualizing Knowledge: A Reply to "Dewey and the Theory of Knowledge". Trans Peirce Soc, 26(4), 459-463, Fall 90.

HICKMAN, Larry. Dead Souls and Living Instruments. SW Phil Rev, 7(1), 1-18, Ja 91.

1990 Presidential Address of the Southwestern Philosophical Society. Philosophers who wish to defend absolute essences and existential necessity are compared to P Chichikov, the protagonist of N Gogol's novel *Dead Souls*. Both cases, it is argued, exhibit attempts to barter, buy, or sell entities that are no longer living, but that for various reasons still have vestigial effects. An appeal is made to regard classificatory schemes and categories as contextual and provisional, and to view necessity and cause and effect as features of judgment, not as having existence prior to or apart from human inquiry.

HICKMAN, Larry. "Doing and Making in a Democracy: Dewey's Experience of Technology" in *Philosophy of Technology*, DURBIN, Paul T (ed), 97-111. Norwell, Kluwer, 1989.

I offer a sketch for a reinterpretation of John Dewey as a philosopher of technology. Elements of his critique of technology include his characterization of the relation of theory to practice, of science to what is normally called "technology" and of the fine to the practical arts. Dewey's social and political philosophy is, I argue, best understood as a critique of technology. It is also as a critique of technology that his definition of truth as "warranted assertibility" becomes intelligible.

HIDALGO TUÑÓN, Alberto. Estrategias metacientíficas: Parte II. El Basilisco, 6, 26-48, Jl-Ag 90.

This paper (taken all at once part I and II) furnishes an operative classification of the current alternatives in philosophy of science. After critizing other classifications (Bunge's, Stegmuller's, Bachelard's and Piaget's), one needs a more mature approach. Three criterions together (Theory and experience conjugations; scientific truth varieties; and inmanence one) will makes possible separate four great metascientific strategies: 1) descriptionism; 2) theoreticism; 3) adequationism; and 4) circularism. A profound breakdown of the new philosophy of science (from Carnap and Popper to Sneed, Feyerabend, Hubner or Bueno) show that is possible to fit in a unique "spectrogramme" and to confront between them all varieties of metascientific analysis.

HIGGINBOTHAM, James. "Frege, Concepts and the Design of Language" in *Information, Semantics and Epistemology*, VILLANUEVA, Enrique (ed), 153-171. Cambridge, Blackwell, 1990.

HIGGINBOTHAM, James. "Linguistic Theory and Davidson's Program in Semantics" in *Truth and Interpretation: Perspectives on the Philosophy of Donald Davidson*, LE PORE, Ernest (ed), 29-48. Cambridge, Blackwell, 1986.

HIGGINBOTHAM, James. Truth and Understanding. Iyyun, 40(3), 271-288, Jl 91.

HIGH, Dallas M. Wittgenstein: On Seeing Problems from a Religious Point of View. Int J Phil Relig, 28(2), 105-117, O 90.

Discussed is the issue of how Wittgenstein's life and thought were intertwined, especially regarding his perspective on the nature of philosophy and his attitude toward religious belief. Drawing on new evidence about Wittgenstein's life, the essay explores the influence of Tolstoy and argues that Wittgenstein was religious, although unconventional. Discussed is his contention that he sees philosophical problems from a religious point of view. The radical implications for philosophy of religion are drawn from an analysis of Wittgenstein's contrast of wisdom as cold and faith as passion and the argument that religious faith is integral to all human activity.

HIGONNET, Patrice and CLEARY, J C. "Plasticity into Power: Two Crises in the History of France and China" in *Critique and Construction: A Symposium on Roberto Unger's "Politics"*, LOVIN, Robin W (ed), 267-295. New York, Cambridge Univ Pr, 1990.

HIKINS, James W and CHERWITZ, Richard A. Irreducible Dualisms and the Residue of Commonsense: On the Inevitability of Cartesian Anxiety. Phil Rhet, 23(3), 229-241, 1990.

HILEY, David R and GUIGNON, Charles B. "Biting the Bullet: Rorty on Private and Public Morality" in *Reading Rorty*, MALACHOWSKI, Alan (ed), 339-364. Cambridge, Blackwell, 1991.

Rorty's anti-foundationalism is motivated by his ideal of a liberal society which supports both private fulfillment and public justice. Such an "aesthetized culture" will allow for unconstrained "abnormal discourse" while simultaneously encouraging solidarity and tolerance. Rorty's "apologia" for this society builds on a minimalist, "existentialist" picture of a self whose highest goal is self-enlargement, and a "communitarian" dream of allegiance built solely on a shared sense of the contingency of all our beliefs and practices. We argue that Rorty's ideal society turns out to be self-defeating, and that the kind of hermeneutic approach Rorty rejects has more to offer for envisioning an ideal society.

HILL JR, Thomas E. The Message of Affirmative Action. Soc Phil Pol, 8(2), 108-129, Spr 91.

The message Affirmative Action programs convey depends, in part, upon the reasons presented for the program. They should convey respect and concern for fair opportunity for all, though this if often not the message received. Both forward-looking (consequentialist) and backward-looking (reparation) justifications, taken alone, tend to express the wrong message. An alternative rationale is suggested, drawing from recent ideas about how we value relationships across time, as organic wholes, in historical context, and conceived in terms more familiar from narrative literature than from accounting.

HILL, Christopher S. *Sensations: A Defense of Type Materialism*. New York, Cambridge Univ Pr, 1991.

This work confronts a number of the main metaphysical and epistemological questions about sensory states and their qualitative characteristics. The author is concerned to show that Type Materialism provides an adequate account of the ultimate metaphysical nature of sensations. (According to Type Materialism, sensations are possessed only by human beings and members of related biological species; for example, if Type Materialism is true, then silicon-based androids cannot have sensations. Type Materialism also claims that sensory states are *identical* with the neural states with which they are correlated.) Other topics include: the forms and limits of introspective awareness of sensations, the semantic properties of sensory concepts, knowledge of other minds, and unity of consciousness.

HILL, Fred and HAUPTMAN, Robert. Deride, Abide or Dissent: On the Ethics of Professional Conduct. J Bus Ethics, 10(1), 37-44, Ja 91.

In the professions of today are ethical concerns of no overwhelming importance? Are these concerns less important in certain professions rather than others? Do some practitioners carry a blasé attitude regarding ethics within their profession? This study, sometimes asking "life-blood," "career-jeopardizing" questions is less interested in electronic data results and more interested in actual respondent replies on dissent and competence. There is strong evidence that the ethical ethos that has given American society its direction has been damaged; further, it has been the professed professionals who have been the major contributors to the ethical decline.

HILL, Judith M. The University and Industrial Research: Selling Out? Bus Prof Ethics J, 2(4), 27-35, Sum 83.

HILL, R Kevin. Foucault's Critique of Heidegger. Phil Today, 34(4), 334-341, Wint 90.

Michel Foucault's "archaeological" works reveal an unsuspected unity of purpose if they are interpreted as a systematic effort to critique Martin Heidegger. Consequently, this phase of Foucault's work could be more aptly characterized as "post-hermeneutic" rather than "post-structuralist." Representative passages in Foucault concerning hermeneutic and phenomenological methodology, the nature of death, historicity and the attempt to ground philosophical inquiry in an analysis of human nature are discussed, and their relationship to Heideggerian texts clarified.

HILL, T Patrick. Giving Voice to the Pragmatic Majority in New Jersey. Hastings Center Rep, 20(5), 20, S-O 90.

In 1983, the New Jersey Citizens' Committee on Biomedical Ethics established an educational forum within which New Jerseyans could become better informed about and wrestle with the complex interplay of medicine, ethics, economics and public policy in a representative, pluralistic democracy. The committee assumed that citizens could establish a consensus on questions like who should decide to stop medical treatment and when? Three hundred public meeting and two surveys showed the assumption to be correct. Citizens emerged as pragmatists, gravitating towards centrist positions, as if complying with an unwritten social contract in which one person's autonomy is conditional on another's.

HILLMAN, James. "Back to Beyond: On Cosmology" in *Archetypal Process: Self and Divine in Whitehead, Jung, and Hillman*, GRIFFIN, David Ray (ed), 213-231. Evanston, Northwestern Univ Pr, 1989.

HILLMAN, James. "Responses" in *Archetypal Process: Self and Divine in Whitehead, Jung, and Hillman*, GRIFFIN, David Ray (ed), 251-265. Evanston, Northwestern Univ Pr, 1989.

HILPINEN, R (ed) and FENSTAD, J E (ed) and FROLOV, I T (ed). *Logic, Methodology and Philosophy of Science, VIII*. New York, Elsevier Science, 1989.

This volume contains all the invited papers to the eight international congress of logic, methodology and philosophy of science held in Moscow in 1987. In addition to sectional papers there were two symposia, one on new patterns of explanation in science, and one on science and ethics.

HILPINEN, Risto. Occasions for Argumentation. Commun Cog, 24(1), 55-58, 1991.

Different occasions for argumentation (argumentation situations) are defined on the basis of the possible relationships between two belief systems (the systems of the persons who engage in argumentation). Twelve different argumentation situations are distinguished in this way; these involve justificatory arguments, refutations, and criticisms of a person's presuppositions.

HILPINEN, Risto. "On the Characterization of Cognitive Progress" in *Imre Lakatos and Theories of Scientific Change*, GAVROGLU, Kostas (ed), 69-80. Norwell, Kluwer, 1989.

Cognitive progress is characterized in terms of the possible *changes* of a person's belief system. Sixteen possible belief change types are distinguished from each other; some of these changes, e.g., the increase of the informativeness or trustworthiness of the belief system with respect to some question, are regarded as intrinsically progressive, whereas others are regarded as intrinsically regressive changes.

HILTON, Denis J. Pragmatic Conditional Reasoning: Context and Content Effects on the Interpretation of Causal Assertions. J Prag, 14(5), 791-812, O 90.

The present study investigates two kinds of background knowledge which affect interpretations of 'If-then' conditionals that assert a causal relation between an antecedent and a consequent. The first factor was the presence of contextual assertions which affirmed or denied the existence of alternative plausible causes in the backgrounded 'causal field' in which the target conditional was evaluated. It was predicted that subjects would be more likely to treat the target antecedent as *sufficient* and *not necessary* when the presence of an alternative plausible cause was affirmed, and less likely to do so if its existence were denied. The second factor was the extremity or rarity of the consequent event. It was hypothesised that more extreme or rare consequents would be more likely to be judged to have antecedents that are *necessary* and *not sufficient*. Both major hypotheses received substantial support in a conditional reasoning task. (edited)

HINCKFUSS, Ian. Absolutism and Relationism in Space and Time: A False Dichotomy. Brit J Phil Sci, 39(2), 183-192, Je 88.

The traditional absolutist-relationist controversy about space and time conflates four distinct issues: existence, abstraction, relationality, and relativity. Terms which are relational, relative or abstract may denote items which possess contingent properties. Possession of such properties, including topological and geometrical properties, is therefore no indication of logical type. To fail to recognize the possibility of spaces, times and space-times of various logical types is to risk conflating two distinct ontological issues: a metaphysical issue concerning the existence of abstract objects and a question of physics concerning the existence of causally efficacious sub-strata which may or may not be needed to explain the contingent properties of the abstract objects.

HINDERLITER, Hilton. More on Russell's Hypothesis. Phil Sci, 57(4), 703-711, D 90.

Previous articles on Russell's hypothesis and on criteria for scientific explanations are used as a springboard for analyzing some modern trends in science. Specifically, recent suggestions of the concept of "creation from nothing" in Big-Bang cosmology are compared to Russell's hypothesis, in light of James Woodward's criteria for an explanation purporting to be scientific. The discussion is then extended to the broader question of the direction of scientific theorizing, through examples showing that one generation's science may not build conformably upon the mindset of the previous generation.

HINTIKKA, Jaakko. An Impatient Man and his Papers. Synthese, 87(2), 183-202, My 91.

Because of Wittgenstein's impatience as expositor, the problem background of his philosophical ideas is virtually impossible to gather from his so far published writings. Easy access to Wittgenstein's unpublished writings, especially to his notebooks, is therefore badly needed. The Cornell microfilm edition does not adequately serve this purpose, either, even though its availability means that the legal status of the bulk of Wittgenstein's *Nachlass* is that of published material. The two successive complete works editing projects (the first by a group led by Heringer and Nedo, the second by Nedo) have been abject failures. A change of the editor is therefore recommended.

HINTIKKA, Jaakko and SANDU, Gabriel. "Informational Independence as a Semantical Phenomenon" in *Logic, Methodology and Philosophy of Science, VIII*, FENSTAD, J E (ed), 571-589. New York, Elsevier Science, 1989.

Insofar as a formal or natural language can be treated game-theoretically, the notion of informational independence (II), in the sense of game theory, applies to its different ingredients. A notation is proposed for II and the most salient facts about it are noted. Even though II is not indicated syntactically in English, it is the gist of such varied phenomena as the *de dicto* vs. *de re* distinction, complex questions, negation-raising, branching quantifiers, actuality operators, etc. It is therefore an extremely important component of the overall semantics of natural languages, both for philosophical and for linguistic purposes.

HINTIKKA, Jaakko. Is There Completeness in Mathematics after Gödel? Phil Topics, 17(2), 69-90, Fall 89.

HINTIKKA, Jaakko and SANDU, Gabriel. Metaphor and the Varieties of Lexical Meaning. Dialectica, 44(1-2), 55-77, 1990.

The "meaning lines" connecting the references of an expression in different situations or scenarios ("worlds") are usually "drawn" with the help of both similarity and continuity. In metaphoric use, emphasis shifts predominantly on suitable similarity considerations; in metonymic use, it shifts on continuity considerations. Even though metaphoric meaning lines are nonstandard, they have to be "anchored" to a literal reference of the expression in some situation or world (not necessarily in the actual one). Hence metaphor is not a matter of truth or of a special kind of language act (use of sentences).

HINTIKKA, Jaakko. "Quine as a Member of the Tradition of the Universality of Language" in *Perspectives on Quine*, BARRETT, Robert (ed), 159-175. Cambridge, Blackwell, 1990.

Quine is considered here as a member of a largely tacit tradition of believers in the universality of (one's home) language and in the ineffability of semantics. This unacknowledged membership is consistent *inter alia* with Quine's disinterest in model theory, his criticism of modal logic and his belief in the indeterminacy of radical translation. It leaves Quine with the behavior of native speakers as the sole guide to the semantics of their jargon. In this direction, Quine is seriously handicapped by his disregard of strategic behavior as a clue to meaning.

HINTIKKA, Jaakko and BACHMAN, James. *What If...? Toward Excellence in Reasoning*. Mountain View, Mayfield, 1991.

This introduction to reasoning uses Hintikka's interrogative model of inquiry. Logical and informal inferences are construed as steps in the same process of inquiry. All new information enters as answers to questions, as in the Socratic questioning method. Other innovations include 1) we distinguish definitory rules of reasoning (they merely tell what is permissible) from strategic principles (they tell how to reason well); 2) logical rules are formulated so that they apply directly to ordinary language reasoning; 3) the interrogative model is used to analyze and to construct arguments, 4) novel treatments are given of scientific reasoning and of several fallacies.

HINTON, J M. Knowing and Valuing Fairness. Philosophy, 65(253), 271-296, Jl 90.

The first part of the article is concerned with what it is to value fairness. The second part sets forth, and in the upshot rejects, two arguments for the view that not valuing fairness is a cognitive failure—a view the author usually cannot help believing to be true. There are references to Philippa Foot, R M Hare, Sabina Lovibond, and others.

HIRSCH, Eli. Divided Minds. Phil Rev, 100(1), 3-30, Ja 91.

The author distinguishes between the "unity of consciousness" and the "unity of self-reflexiveness." The former is lost in cases of split brains but the author argues that the latter is not lost. Because Parfit tacitly assumes that the latter is lost, he erroneously supposes that split brain patients can exercise selective knowledge and control in each of their streams of consciousness.

HIRSCH, Ulrike. War Demokrits Weltbild mechanistisch und antiteleologisch? Phronesis, 35(3), 225-244, 1990.

Democritus is usually classified as a mechanistic and anti-teleological thinker. The article argues that this is an anachronistic classification and doesn't meet the intention of his philosophy. Evidence of this is given as follows: (1) The meaning of *tyche* and *physis* in Democritus's thought is developed in detail. (2) Pursuing traces in the first book of Lucretius a better understanding is established of the motivation of Democritus's theory of atoms and of his discussion with predecessors. (3) The claim that Democritus cannot distinguish between *causae efficientes* and *causae finales* is illustrated by analysing his embryology and his theory of milk-teeth.

HIRSCHBEIN, Ron. "Understanding the Cuban Missile Crisis: A Dialectical Approach" in *Issues in War and Peace: Philosophical Inquiries*, KUNKEL, Joseph (ed), 35-48. Wolfeboro, Longwood, 1989.

HIRSCHBEIN, Ron. "What If They Gave a Crisis and Nobody Came: A Hermeneutical Analysis" in *In the Interest of Peace: A Spectrum of Philosophical Views*, KLEIN, Kenneth H (ed), 45-59. Wolfeboro, Longwood, 1990.

I claim that an international crisis is a crisis of meaning—a struggle to interpret dangerous uncertainty. Hermeneutic anthropologists have more to contribute to our understanding of these wars of words than political realists; a crisis is a metaphor, not a thing. I argue that in order to conceptualize an ambiguous threat, decision makers liken it to a crisis inscribed in their memory. Once an episode is conceptualized as a crisis, it is managed in accord with dramaturgical and medical narratives that—according to thinkers as diverse as Thucydides and Habermas—are perennial crisis archetypes. I conclude that JFK and Kissinger managed comparable Soviet threats differently because JFK likened the threat to an heroic drama; Kissinger likened it to a routine medical problem.

HIRSCHBERG, Julia and WARD, Gregory L. A Pragmatic Analysis of Tautological Utterances. J Prag, 15(6), 507-520, Je 91.

The interpretation of tautological utterances of the form, e.g., if it rains, it rains has generally been characterized in the literature as a case of Gricean conversational implicature (Grice 1975). However, in recent years, this analysis, and indeed the entire Gricean program, has come under attack. Wirzbicka (1987) contends that tautology must be seen as a language-specific, attitudinal phenomenon, thus, in her view, vitiating Grice's universalist approach. In this paper, we take issue with this claim, pointing out certain flaws in Wierzbicka's 'radical semantics' approach to tautology. We then propose a new Gricean account of tautological utterances based upon a large corpus of naturally occurring data.

HISSETTE, Roland. Un nouveau début à l'édition léonine des oeuvres de saint Thomas d'Aquin. Rev Phil Louvain, 88(79), 395-403, O 90.

The first volume of the new edition of the *Opera Omnia* of Thomas Aquinas, requested by Leo XIII, appeared 108 years ago. This first volume of the "Leonine Edition" contains the commentaries on the *Peri Hermeneias* and the *Posterior Analytics*. But a systematic listing of the whole tradition of textual evidence, which is now seen as a condition *sine qua non* of a critical edition, was not attempted; it was not then possible to classify the evidence scientifically, because it was not known that they were all dependent on a basic model or *exemplar* divided into *peciae* ("pieces": the consecutive folded quarto sheets from which the text was to be copied). Consequently the handing on of the text has, in principle, to be studied *pecia* by *pecia*. As this prerequisite was not supplied, the two first volumes of the Leonine Edition are not critical, and this has made necessary a complete overhauling of the work of the first editors. Gratitude is due to Père Gauthier for having done this. This note attempts to set out his method. It will be noticed that not only the texts of Thomas come within the compass of his work, but also the texts of Aristotle on which he commented.

HITCHCOCK, David and GEORGE, Rolf. Smook on Logical and Extralogical Constants. Inform Log, 13(1), 37-40, Wint 91.

We maintain that Roger Smook has failed to produce a counter-example to our assumption that logical consequence can be defined on the basis of a distinction between logical and extralogical constants. Further, Smook's proposal to define this distinction in terms of a primitive notion of logical consequence is idiosyncratic and an unnecessary confession of failure by logical theory. We discuss the basis for distinguishing logical from extralogical constants in artificial and natural languages.

HITTINGER, John P. "Approaches to Democratic Equality: Maritain, Simon, and Kolnai" in *Freedom in the Modern World: Jacques Maritain, Yves R Simon, Mortimer J Adler*, TORRE, Michael D (ed), 237-252. Notre Dame, Univ Notre Dame Pr, 1989.

We examine three Catholic political philosophers on the problem of equality. They opposed racist claims about the inequality of races. They base natural law on the equality of human nature. Yet they criticize utopian demands for equality as totalitarian. They differed on aristocracy and the role of wealth and privilege in the social political order. On "equal opportunity," they sought to balance the rectification of great factual inequalities with the principle of subsidiarity and the positive role of the apparent "irrational" factors of wealth and social standing. Kolnai criticizes Maritain and Simon for ignoring the leveling features of democratic ideology.

HLAVACEK, Josef. Technique of Painting and Sociology of Picture (in Czechoslovakian). Estetika, 28(1), 51-64, 1991.

HLAVACEK, Lubos. Aesthetics of T G Masaryk (in Czechoslovakian). Estetika, 27(3), 129-166, 1990.

HLAVACEK, Lubos. Aesthetics of T G Masaryk II (in Czechoslovakian). Estetika, 27(4), 207-228, 1990.

HOAGLAND, Sarah Lucia. Some Thoughts About Heterosexualism. J Soc Phil, 21(2-3), 98-107, Fall-Wint 90.

HOAGLAND, Sarah Lucia. "Some Thoughts about 'Caring'" in *Feminist Ethics*, CARD, Claudia (ed), 246-263. Lawrence, Univ Pr of Kansas, 1991.

HOARE, Quintin (trans) and SARTRE, Jean-Paul. *Critique of Dialectical Reason, Volume 2: Jean-Paul Sartre*. New York, Verso, 1990.

HOBART, Michael E and PANICHAS, George E. Marx's Theory of Revolutionary Change. Can J Phil, 20(3), 383-401, S 90.

Recent scholarship, most notably that of G A Cohen, offers sympathetic and highly plausible interpretations of Marx's theory of history, his historical materialism. Such interpretations hold that the same set of factors explaining changes societies undergo within the course of a given historical epoch explain as well changes between historical epochs, i.e., social revolutions. This paper argues that even the most plausible reconstruction of the theory of history, that which employs functional explanations, cannot account for changes between historical epochs. Historical materialism, therefore, fails as a theory of revolutionary change.

HOBBES, Thomas and WRIGHT, George (trans). 1668 Appendix to Leviathan. Interpretation, 18(3), 323-413, Spr 91.

This article includes the first English translation of the Appendix which Thomas Hobbes wrote for the 1668 Latin edition of *Leviathan*, as well as an introduction and extensive notes on the text. Divided into three chapters, the Appendix contains a commentary on the Nicene Creed, legal and historical discussion of heresy, arguments as to the immortality of the soul and a response to critics of the English *Leviathan* of 1651. Hobbes also restates and develops his theory of the proposition and predication, his view of the justification of punishment and his theory of sovereignty.

HOBBES, Thomas and TUCK, Richard (ed). *Leviathan: Hobbes*. New York, Cambridge Univ Pr, 1991.

HOBBS, Jesse. Chaos and Indeterminism. Can J Phil, 21(2), 141-164, Je 91.

It is generally accepted that chaos theory severs the link between Laplacean determinism and predictability. To this epistemological conclusion I append the metaphysical thesis that, despite its deterministic mathematics, chaos theory actually undercuts Laplacean world-views by providing for the reliable magnification of miniscule perturbations, such as the quantum-level supplies in abundance. Normally the correspondence principle assures us that quantum-level indeterminism is not transmitted to higher levels. When higher levels are chaotic, however, there often appears to be no level at which quantum perturbations become stabilized. A pervasive indeterminism then seems to be the greatest likelihood, sprinkled with occasional deterministic pockets.

HOBSON, J Allan. "Psychiatry as Scientific Humanism: A Program Inspired by Roberto Unger's *Passion*" in *Critique and Construction: A Symposium on Roberto Unger's "Politics"*, LOVIN, Robin W (ed), 206-231. New York, Cambridge Univ Pr, 1990.

Unger's critique of psychiatry is inspiring but inadequate. While I agree with Unger's rejection of psychoanalysis and welcome his alternative emphasis upon passion as the felt tension between our longing for one another and our vulnerability to rejection, I propose that Unger's view of man, and of psychiatry, is biologically uninformed. Unger ignores scientific evidence that ultimately both supports and challenges the fundamental tenets of his social theory. I have attempted to redress this imbalance by proposing that the reconstruction of psychiatry proceed as scientific humanism. I call my alternative view of man "scientific humanism" to emphasize what I take to be robust biological evidence for both the evolutionary capability of the human brain-mind—which Unger recongizes—and for the physical basis and constraints on that system—which Unger ignores.

HODAPP, Paul. 'Fetal Rights'? An Attempt to Render Plausible a Conservative Response. Iyyun, 40(1), 19-36, Ja 91.

My aim in this paper was to discover if there are liberal assumptions in the conservative argument that fetuses have human rights. I claim there are two such assumptions: first, that it is unfair for adults to use themselves as the model for the proper subject of human rights, and second, that a human being as a bearer of moral rights is one who is developing entity who needs such rights to develop. I conclude that there is common ground on which a liberal moralist can find much that is plausible in the conservative argument.

HODES, Harold T. "Ontological Commitment: Thick and Thin" in *Meaning and Method: Essays in Honor of Hilary Putnam*, BOOLOS, George (ed), 235-260. New York, Cambridge Univ Pr, 1990.

Discourse carries thin commitment to objects of a certain sort iff it says or implies that there are such objects. It carries a thick commitment to such objects iff an account of what determines truth-values for its sentences say or implies that there are such objects. This paper presents two model-theoretic semantics for mathematical discourse, one reflecting thick commitment to mathematical objects, the other reflecting only a thin commitment to them. According to the latter view, for example, the semantic role of number-words is not designation but rather the encoding of cardinality-quantifiers. I also present some reasons for preferring this view.

HODES, Harold T. Where Do Natural Numbers Come From? Synthese, 84(3), 347-407, S 90.

This paper presents two model-theoretic semantics for languages with arithmetic notions ('is a natural number', 'less-than', 'the number of xs such that'); one reflects the Platonist theory about the underpinnings of truth for such languages; the other reflects an alternative view: that the semantic role of number-terms is not designation but is rather the encoding of cardinality-quantifiers. The discussion is then transposed to languages which also express modal notions. I prove a number of technical results about these semantics. The project was motivated by considerations that I presented in my 1984 paper in the *Journal of Philosophy* ("Logicism and the Ontological Commitments of Arithmetic").

HODGE, Joanna. Nietzsche, Heidegger, and the Critique of Humanism. J Brit Soc Phenomenol, 22(1), 75-79, Ja 91.

HODGSON, Geoffrey M. Hayek's Theory of Cultural Evolution: An Evaluation in the Light of Vanberg's Critique. Econ Phil, 7(1), 67-82, Ap 91.

In this paper it is argued that Hayek's theory of group selection has some support for modern biology, despite some recent critiques. However, group selection is inconsistent with methodological individualism, and does not support the free-market policies with which Hayek is associated.

HOEKEMA, David. "The Man in the Teflon Suit: A Flaw in the Argument for Strategic Defense" in *Issues in War and Peace: Philosophical Inquiries*, KUNKEL, Joseph (ed), 159-169. Wolfeboro, Longwood, 1989.

In this discussion I assume that a reliable and cost-effective defense against nuclear attack can be built and examine whether, given this assumption, it should be built. The argument commonly advanced in favor of strategic defense assumes that defense is morally preferable to offense. I argue that the truth of this moral premise depends crucially on whether defensive measures replace or supplement offensive means, illustrating the point with the analogy of a bulletproof suit. The argument for strategic defense, I conclude, would have application in the absence of deterrent threats but does not support supplementing deterrence with defense.

HOELLER, Keith (ed). *Readings in Existential Psychology and Psychiatry*. Seattle, REPP, 1990.

Arranged into topics from Anxiety to Will, this book will serve as an introduction to the field of existential psychology and psychiatry. Included are articles by Viktor Frankl, R D Laing, Rollo May, Carl Rogers, Paul Tillich, and many others. In addition, the book includes the first English translation of Medard Boss's "The Unconscious—What is It?" as well as a "Selected Bibliography of Existential Psychology and Psychiatry."

HOENIGSWALD, Henry M. "Descent, Perfection and the Comparative Method Since Leibniz" in *Leibniz, Humboldt, and the Origins of Comparativism*, DE MAURO, Tullio (ed), 119-132. Philadelphia, John Benjamins, 1990.

Change, comparability, and descent, applied to language, are ancient terms. The present article traces some aspects of the gradual yet profound transformation, over the last few centuries, of their content. Comparison for (typological) comparison's sake came to be distinct from the matching of contrast with homonymy which is sometimes called the *Comparative Method*. This procedure and its corollaries were used to establish and correlate lines of *descent* along which replacements, or 'changes' occur. These concepts became more and more uniformitarian (in the geological sense): there was no room left for typological ideals of primordial *perfection* or primordial simplicity to serve as criteria for the ancestral role. Special attention is paid to Leibniz, to the eighteenth century, to Wilhelm von Humboldt, and to later linguistics.

HÖFFE, Otfried. Universalistische Ethik und Urteilskraft: ein aristotelischer Blick auf Kant. Z Phil Forsch, 44(4), 537-563, 1990.

HÖFFE, Ottfried. Retaliatory Punishment as a Categorical Imperative. Riv Int Filosof Diritto, 66(4), 633-658, O-D 89.

HOFFMAN, Frank J. Towards a Philosophy of Buddhist Religion. Asian Phil, 1(1), 21-28, 1991.

HOFFMAN, Paul. Cartesian Passions and Cartesian Dualism. Pac Phil Quart, 71(4), 310-333, D 90.

Descartes retains the Aristotelian doctrine that when an agent acts on a patient, the action of the agent is one and the same as the passion in the patient. However, unlike his Aristotelian predecessors who located the agent's action in the patient, Descartes locates the agent's action in the agent. I examine briefly his motives for modifying, but not abandoning this doctrine. My central claim is that his use of this doctrine implies that he thinks there are modes straddling mind and body, but that such straddling modes do not conflict with his dualism, understood properly.

HOFFMAN, W Michael. Business and Environmental Ethics. Bus Ethics Quart, 1(2), 169-184, Ap 91.

This paper explores some interconnections between the business and environmental ethics movements. The first section argues that business has obligations to protect the environment over and above what is required by environmental law and that it should cooperate and interact with government in establishing environmental regulation. Business must develop and demonstrate environmental moral leadership. The second section exposes the danger of using the rationale of "good ethics is good business" as a basis for such business moral leadership in both the business and environmental ethics movements. The third section cautions against the moral shallowness inherent in the position or in the promotional strategy of ecological homocentrism which claims that society, including business, ought to protect the environment solely because of harm done to human beings and human interests. This paper urges business and environmental ethicists to promote broader and deeper moral perspectives than ones based on mere self-interest or human interest. Otherwise both movements will come up ethically short.

HOFFMANN, Thomas Sören. Der Begriff der Bewegung bei Kant: Über den Grundbegriff der Empirie und die empirischen Begriffe. Z Phil Forsch, 45(1), 38-59, Ja-Mr 91.

Kants Bewegungsbegriff wird durch das Gesamtwerk von der "Wahren Schaetzung" bis zum "Opus postumum" verfolgt, in den Zusammenhang der neuzeitlichen Kinematik gestellt und sodann in seiner *kritischen* Gestalt als "Praedikabile der Erfahrung ueberhaupt" von den "Metaphysischen Anfangsgruenden der Naturwissenschaft" aus bestimmt und untersucht. *Erfahrungslogisch* ergibt sich ein Begriff, der zugleich die Logik des Gebrauchs empirischer Begriffe, durch den erfahrene Bewegung intelligibel gemacht wird, erschliesst, als auch die Bewegung der Erfahrung selbst als ideellerEinheit der Formierung aeusserer Objektivitaet vermittelt. Dieser letzte, erfahrungsdynamische Aspekt wird vom "Opus postumum" her als Selbstdifferenzierung des einen Kontexts der Erfahrung zu verstehen versucht.

HOFFMASTER, Barry and BACHRACH, Sarah. "Ethical Issues in Prescribing Drugs for the Aged and the Dying" in *Biomedical Ethics Reviews, 1987*, HUMBER, James M (ed), 5-29. Clifton, Humana Pr, 1988.

HOFMANN, James R. How the Models of Chemistry Vie. Proc Phil Sci Ass, 1, 405-419, 1990.

Building upon Nancy Cartwright's discussion of models in *How the Laws of Physics Lie*, this paper addresses solid state research in transition metal oxides. Historical analysis reveals that in this domain models function both as the culmination of phenomenology and the commencement of theoretical explanation. Those solid state chemists who concentrate on the description of phenomena pertinent to specific elements or compounds assess models according to different standards than those who seek explanation grounded in approximate applications of the Schroedinger equation. Accurate accounts of scientific debate in this field must include both perspectives.

HOGAN, Pádraig. What Makes Practice Educational? J Phil Educ, 24(1), 15-26, Sum 90.

HOGG, Michael A and ABRAMS, Dominic. The Context of Discourse: Let's Not Throw the Baby Out with the Bathwater. Phil Psych, 3(2-3), 219-225, 1990.

An examination of Ian Parker's definitions of discourse reveals them to be nondistinctive and of limited utility. It is argued that discourse analysis should be integrated with, rather than set against, social psychology. Discourse analysts should attend to the issues of the representativeness and generality of their evidence, should be wary of attributing causality to discourse, and should consider the advantages of systematically investigating, rather than asserting, the social consequences of the use of different discourses.

HOITENGA JR, Dewey J. Knowledge, Belief and Revelation: A Reply to Patrick Lee. Faith Phil, 8(2), 244-251, Ap 91.

In a recent issue of *Faith and Philosophy*, Patrick Lee argues that religious belief in the fact of revelation, identified as the fact *that God reveals*, is based neither on knowledge nor on belief in testimony. He develops an alternative account of religious belief as "reasonable conviction." In response, I argue that his arguments on the first point fail, and I also raise objections to his alternative account. I show that the rationality of religious belief can be based on knowledge in a way which Lee overlooks, and that it is analogous to the rationality of non-religious belief in an important way which Lee is forced to give up.

HOLBROOK, Daniel. Consequentialism: The Philosophical Dog That Does Not Bark? Utilitas, 3(1), 107-112, My 91.

There is an incongruity in the current debate on consequentialism. Objections have been raised against consequentialism and there have been replies, but lacking is an initial statement of the arguments and other considerations that support consequentialism. In order to fill this gap in the debate, four lines of argument are examined: 1) the Semantical Argument, 2) Mill's Argument, 3) the

Responsibility Argument, and 4) the Main Argument. The Semantical Argument is found to be valid, but unsound. The other three arguments are found to support consequentialism.

HOLBROOK, Daniel. The Ontology of Mental Images. Indian Phil Quart, 18(1), 87-109, Ja 91.

Primarily this essay is a critique of Gilbert Ryle's theory of mind—especially the imagination—as presented in *The Concept of Mind*. I discuss, amongst other things, the idea of the location of the mind and mental events, Ryle's analysis of imagination as a species of pretending and play acting, the analogy of copies to mental images, and Sartre's account of mental images. I conclude that both Ryle's and Sartre's accounts of mental images ought to be replaced by a more positive ontological account of mental images.

HOLCOMB III, Harmon R. Hacking's Experimental Argument for Realism. J Crit Anal, 9(1), 1-12, 1988.

Ian Hacking has proposed that scientific realism is supported by arguments from experimental practice, not by arguments from theoretical success. I show that his argument from experiment cannot perform its intended function of both supporting realism about theoretical entities and bypassing the argument from theoretical success. That is, it may do either but it cannot do both.

HOLCOMB, H R. Expecting Nature's Best: Optimality Models and Perfect Adaptation. Phil Sci (Tucson), 4, 181-210, 1990.

An important issue in evolutionary ecology is to decide whether optimality models provide a sound theoretical basis for the field. Proper evaluation of optimality models requires a correct account of their structure. This article aims to elucidate the structure of optimality models so as to clarify the way in which the relation between models, methods, and theories contours the ontology of science. The analysis shows that a) the basic structure of optimality models is given by their origin as products of theory-laden optimization methods; b) the distinctive modality of the models is normative: they predict, not what organisms actually do, but what strategies organisms should use in various circumstances; c) despite appearances, optimality models have no necessary relation to the so-called "Panglossian" adaptationist program of viewing all organismic traits as optimally (perfectly) designed adaptations.

HOLDCROFT, David. *Saussure: Signs, System, and Arbitrariness*. New York, Cambridge Univ Pr, 1991.

HOLLANDER, Rachelle D. "Moral Responsibility, Values, and Making Decisions about Biotechnology" in *Agricultural Bioethics: Implications of Agricultural Biotechnology*, GENDEL, Steven M (& other eds), 279-291. Ames, Iowa St Univ Pr, 1990.

This chapter uses an illustration from nineteenth-century literature and some conceptual distinctions made by a contemporary philosopher to clarify important aspects of moral responsibility: foresight and nonexclusivity. Examples from current scientific literature demonstrate how value presumptions and differences often underlie uses of evidence in policy disputes. Current position statements from federal agencies and scientific organizations continue in this tradition. When these value assumptions go unnoticed, disputants cannot address issues of grave importance. Exercising only limited foresight, these individuals and institutions cannot behave responsibly. Incorporating views and addressing concerns outside of this mainstream is required for morally responsible behavior.

HOLLIER, Denis and WING, Betsy (trans). *Against Architecture: The Writings of Georges Bataille*. Cambridge, MIT Pr, 1989.

HOLLINGDALE, R G. Montinari and Nietzsche's Biography. Int Stud Phil, 22(2), 45-48, 1990.

HOLLIS, Martin and CUBITT, Robin P. The Mutual Investment Game: Peculiarities of Indifference. Analysis, 51(3), 113-120, Je 91.

A game is presented in which there are no dominant strategies but which resembles the Prisoner's Dilemma in that 1) each player's optimal choices are independent of the other player's and 2) the Pareto optimal outcome is apparently not guaranteed by self-interested play. It is argued that an account of a rational requirement to cooperate in the game would require a reformulation of Game Theory to allow players *either* to choose for themselves to play as a team *or* to describe outcomes in terms of the actions leading up to them and, thereby, to recognize social or moral relationships.

HOLLIS, Martin. Penny Pinching and Backward Induction. J Phil, 88(9), 473-488, S 91.

HOLLIS, Martin. "The Poetics of Personhood" in *Reading Rorty*, MALACHOWSKI, Alan (ed), 244-256. Cambridge, Blackwell, 1991.

Rorty sides with 'poets' against 'philosophers' in viewing a person as 'a network which is constantly reweaving itself' without an agent who is 'a master weaver, so to speak'. He thinks of communities as historical fellowships united by a shared discourse without any exterior goal. Yet he holds that some communities are better than others and that the better ones offer ways to 'achieve self-creation by the recognition of contingency'. If this is poetry, I prefer philosophy.

HOLLWECK, Thomas A (ed) and CARINGELLA, Paul (ed) and VOEGELIN, Eric. *What is History? And Other Late Unpublished Writings (The Collected Works of Eric Voegelin, Vol 28)*. Baton Rouge, Louisiana St Univ Pr, 1990.

The volume contains five previously unpublished texts by Voegelin belonging in the context of Volumes IV and V of *Order and History* as well as other later published writings. The texts comprise an analysis of the transcendental structure of history in the title-piece, the discussion of constants in the search of order in "Anxiety and Reason," a critique of certain modern notions of 'self' in "The Eclipse of Reality," an attempt to reformulate the connections between physics and myth in "The Moving Soul," and a meditation on the question of *fides quaerens intellectum* in "The Beginning and the Beyond."

HOLLY, Marilyn. Handsome Lake's Teachings: The Shift from Female to Male Agriculture in Iroquois Agriculture. Agr Human Values, 7(3-4), 80-94, Sum-Fall 90.

The shift from a traditional indigenous female agriculture to a new male agriculture in Iroquois culture was facilitated by the teachings of the early 19th century Seneca prophet and chief, Handsome Lake. This shift resulted in the disempowerment of women and occurred during a period of crises for the Iroquois; it was heavily influenced by exogenous pressures that, mediated by Handsome Lake's Code, led not only to a change of sex roles in agriculture but also to a shift in family structure toward the patriarchal family and to a change of ideology toward a patriarchal monotheism. Previously, Iroquois life and ideology had stressed a complementarity or balance of powers between the sexes. Handsome Lake's Code also retained certain aspects of the older Iroquois lifestyle and ideology. The crises undergone by the Iroquois might have been met differently, without the disempowerment of women, had it not been for exogenous influences.

HOLMES, Arthur F. *Shaping Character: Moral Education in the Christian College*. Grand Rapids, Eerdmans, 1991.

HOLMES, M R. Systems of Combinatory Logic Related to Quine's 'New Foundations'. Annals Pure Applied Log, 53(2), 103-133, Jl 91.

Systems TRC and TRCU of illative combinatory logic are introduced and shown to be equivalent in consistency strength and expressive power to Quine's set theory 'New Foundations' (NF) and the fragment NFU + Infinity of NF described by Jensen, respectively. Jensen demonstrated the consistency of NFU + Infinity relative to ZFC; the question of the consistency of NF remains open. TRC and TRCU are presented here as classical first-order theories, although they can be presented as equational theories; they are not constructive.

HOLMES, Richard and DANIEL, Mano. The Lover-Beloved Relationship Reconsidered. Auslegung, 17(2), 101-108, Sum 91.

While Sartre claims all human relations share the same fundamental ontological structure, the dismal picture he paints in *Being and Nothingness* in which he describes the lover-beloved relation as two subjectivities in conflict is a far cry from the optimistic portrayal in *What is Literature* of the reader writer relation as the mutual collaboration of two freedoms. By reviewing and revising Sartre's account of the nature of consciousness as it stands before itself or another we enable the expansion of the realm of human relationships beyond the ostensible limits prescribed in *Being and Nothingness*.

HOLMES, Robert L. *Nonviolence in Theory and Practice*. Belmont, Wadsworth, 1990.

HOLMES, Robert L. "Terrorism and Violence: A Moral Perspective" in *Issues in War and Peace: Philosophical Inquiries*, KUNKEL, Joseph (ed), 115-127. Wolfeboro, Longwood, 1989.

The argument is that terrorism is no worse than many widely approved forms of violence. The conclusion, however, is not that terrorism is not abhorrent. It is that many of the general accepted modes of violence, particularly in warfare, are equally as abhorrent.

HOLMES, Robert. "Absolute Violence and the Idea of War" in *In the Interest of Peace: A Spectrum of Philosophical Views*, KLEIN, Kenneth H (ed), 25-31. Wolfeboro, Longwood, 1990.

HOLMGREN, Margaret. The Poverty of Naturalistic Moral Realism: Comments on Timmons. S J Phil, SUPP 29, 131-135, 1990.

In this paper I offer a critique of the recent attempt to combine a coherentist moral epistemology with a naturalistic version of moral realism. I start from Timmons's Moral Twin Earth thought experiment and argue that this "new wave" moral realism requires us to reinterpret the terms "right" and "good" in such a way that they are stripped of any action-guiding force and rendered superfluous to the questions that are of real concern to us in our moral discourse. Because moral facts are natural facts for the new wave realist, and because there is no prescriptivity built into the physical world, this position entails that moral theories tell us nothing about what we ought to do.

HOLMLUND, Christine. The Lesbian, the Mother, the Heterosexual Lover: Irigaray's Recodings of Difference. Fem Stud, 17(2), 283-308, Sum 91.

This article surveys Irigaray's recodings of identity, equality, sameness and difference, concentrating on the three female figures who served as organizing tropes in the 1970s and 1980s. Irigaray's dialogues with male philosophers, the lesbian, the mother, and the heterosexual female lover provide multiple and overlapping alternatives to phallocentric models. The conclusion assesses the strategic value implicit in each, and in all, first with respect to metaphor, language and experience, then with respect to history, ideology and politics. Finally, I signal the need for further study of a fourth, more androgynous figure who haunts Irigaray's more recent writings: the angel.

HOLÓWKA, Jacek. "Philosophy and the Mirage of Hermeneutics" in *Reading Rorty*, MALACHOWSKI, Alan (ed), 187-197. Cambridge, Blackwell, 1991.

HOLOWKA, Jacek. "Winning Against and With the Opponent" in *Logic and Ethics*, GEACH, Peter (ed), 145-165. Norwell, Kluwer, 1991.

HOLQUIST, Michael (ed) and LIAPUNOV, Vadim (ed) and BAKHTIN, M M. *Art and Answerability: Early Philosophical Essays—M M Bakhtin*. Austin, Univ of Texas Pr, 1990.

HOLT JR, David K. Criticism: Foundation and Recommendation for Teaching. J Aes Educ, 25(2), 81-87, Sum 91.

HOLTZMANN, Jack M. A Note on Schrödinger's Cat and the Unexpected Hanging Paradox. Brit J Phil Sci, 39(3), 397-401, S 88.

HOLYST, Brunon. War and Crime. Dialec Hum, 16(3-4), 163-171, Sum-Autumn 89.

War's impact on crime is obvious. An increasing crime rate during wars and immediately afterwards is a well-known phenomenon. The state of war in a country results in immediate economic disorders. The war creates the climate of terror. The war teaches the manners of destruction and of overcoming the obstacles by means of organized aggression. The war is the first school of an individual terrorism during peace. Aggression is often a basis of both traditional crime and the armed offensive conflict.

HOLZ, Hans Heinz. The Theological Secret of Th W Adorno's Aesthetic Theory (in German). Deut Z Phil, 38(9), 866-873, 1990.

HOLZ, Hans Heinz. Todor Pavlov (1890-1977)—The Generalization of Reflection (in German). Deut Z Phil, 38(3), 245-254, 1990.

HOMANN, Frederick A. Boskovic's Philosophy of Mathematics (in Serbo-Croatian). Filozof Istraz, 32-33(5-6), 1511-1524, 1989.

Since Boskovic did not write an explicit philosophy of mathematics, it is necessary to locate him in the Roman College tradition of mathematics and philosophy deriving from Christopher and the Ratio Studiorum, and then to review his work in Newtonian natural philosophy and mathematics and their mutual relations. In this context, key texts in his dissertations and letters are examined to determine what Boskovic held about the experiential origin of mathematics, how mathematics grounded and developed his astronomy, geodesy, and speculative atomic theory, and what relation it had to physical reality on the microscopic and macroscopic levels. (edited)

HOME, Dipankar. Perspectives on Quantum Reality versus Classical Reality. J Indian Counc Phil Res, 6(2), 17-24, Ja-Ap 89.

HON, Giora. A Critical Note on J S Mill's Classification of Fallacies. Brit J Phil Sci, 42(2), 263-268, Je 91.

The objective of this paper is to expose the different strata that underlie Mill's classification of fallacies. Against the views on error of Aristotle, Bacon, Descartes and Spinoza, Mill seems to introduce new elements into the analysis of the notion of error. These elements originate in his professed empiricism. However, the paper concludes that Mill's empiricism bears layers of a different metaphysical outlook, namely, rationalism. His attempt to tackle the 'whole process' of argumentation in science: 'whether the ratiocinative or the experimental portion', proved imbalanced and predisposed towards the ratiocinative element. The underlying criterion of Mill's classification is in the final analysis logical and not empirical.

HON-MING, Chen. The Role of Stories in a Community of Inquiry. Thinking, 9(2), 5-8, 1990.

HONDERICH, Ted. Better the Union Theory. Analysis, 51(3), 166-173, Je 91.

An Identity Theory of the mind related to Davidson's Anomalous Monism faces the objection that it is epiphenomenalist. Gregory McCulloch (*Analysis*, 1990) tries to defend the theory against the objection but is unsuccessful. Cynthia and Graham Macdonald (*Philosophical Quarterly*, 1986, *Analysis*, 1991) also seek to resist the objection. They also fail. What is needed is the Union Theory, which has the supposed strengths of the Identity Theory and not its weaknesses.

HONES, Michael J. Scientific Realism and Experimental Practice in High-Energy Physics. Synthese, 86(1), 29-76, Ja 91.

The issue of scientific realism is discussed in terms of the specific details of the practice of experimental meson and baryon spectroscopy in the field of high-energy physics (HEP), during the period from 1966 to 1970. The philosophical positions of I Hacking, A Fine, J Leplin, and N Rescher that concern scientific realism are presented in such a manner as to allow for the evaluation of their appropriateness in the description of this experimental research field. This philosophical analysis focuses on the empirical adequacy of these four philosophical models that purport to describe the process of acquiring knowledge of the physical world. In this specific case, an experiment performed by the HEP research group at the University of Notre Dame to study a certain scattering interaction at 18.5 GeV/c is discussed. The specific details of the research practices employed in this experiment are analyzed in light of the philosophical models presented herein. A summary of the relevant aspects of this successful description is presented. (edited)

HONES, Michael. Reproducibility as a Methodological Imperative in Experimental Research. Proc Phil Sci Ass, 1, 585-599, 1990.

A methodological imperative, reproducibility, is proposed for experimental research. This is motivated by recent discussions of normative naturalism as well as the recent philosophical interest in experimental research. The importance of reproducing experimental results is examined in the specific context of the routine analysis of resonance production in high-energy pion-nucleon scattering at an incident beam momentum of 18.5 GeV/c. In this context, a more complex meaning of reproducibility emerges. It is suggested that this empirical evaluation of hypothetical imperatives should be at the core of the normative naturalist's program.

HONG, Edna H (ed & trans) and HONG, Howard V (ed & trans) and KIERKEGAARD, Soren. *For Self-Examination: Judge for Yourself*. Princeton, Princeton Univ Pr, 1990.

HONG, Howard V (ed & trans) and HONG, Edna H (ed & trans) and KIERKEGAARD, Soren. *For Self-Examination: Judge for Yourself*. Princeton, Princeton Univ Pr, 1990.

HONGXUN, Hou. Montesquieu and China. Chin Stud Phil, 22(1), 11-31, Fall 90.

HONNETH, Axel and BAYNES, Kenneth (trans). *The Critique of Power: Reflective Stages in a Critical Social Theory*. Cambridge, MIT Pr, 1991.

HONNETH, Axel. Domination and Moral Struggle: the Philosophical Heritage of Marxism Reviewed. Grad Fac Phil J, 14(1), 35-48, 1991.

HONNETH, Axel. A Structuralist Rousseau: On the Anthropology of Claude Lévi-Strauss. Phil Soc Crit, 16(2), 143-158, 1990.

Did positivistic confidence in the sciences move Lévi-Strauss to introduce structural linguistics into ethnographic research? The author perceives a more romantic impulse behind the ethnologist's work: the conviction that modern humans are painfully estranged from nature. To provide access to the cosmological worldview of archaic peoples and to demonstrate how humans could be bound up in solidarity with the cycle of nature, a contemporary science had to be introduced, since unmediated return was no longer possible: structuralism. Thus, we find in his work the birth of social scientific structuralism emerging from the spirit of Rousseauian romanticism.

HONOHAN, Iseult. Arendt and Benjamin on the Promise of History: A Network of Possibilities or One Apocalyptic Moment? Clio, 19(4), 311-330, Sum 90.

Two similar theories of history, those of Hannah Arendt and Walter Benjamin, are contrasted with a special focus on the political role of the historian. Both propose a critical monumental history. Benjamin sees a predominantly negative pattern in history, disrupted only by rare messianic events. Thus his account of history writing oscillates between radical separation from, and identity with, political action. Because the course of history is more open for Arendt and because her political action is less rare and less definitive, the historian's activity is not, from her perspective, a substitute for, but complementary to political action.

HOOK, Sidney. *Convictions*. Buffalo, Prometheus, 1990.

In this book the late Sidney Hook discusses the topic of suicide, voluntary euthanasia, liberal education, and academic freedom. He also puts forth a defense of Western culture. He argues that American educators must resist the shift to relax the academic standards at colleges and universities. (staff)

HOOK, Sidney (ed). *Psychoanalysis, Scientific Method, and Philosophy*. New Brunswick, Transaction Books, 1990.

HOOKWAY, Christopher. Scepticism and Autonomy. Proc Aris Soc, 90, 103-118, 1989-90.

HOOKWAY, Christopher. "Vagueness, Logic and Interpretation" in *The Analytic Tradition: Philosophical Quarterly Monographs, Volume 1*, BELL, David (ed), 61-82. Cambridge, Blackwell, 1990.

HOOVER, Kevin D. The Logic of Causal Inference: Econometrics and the Conditional Analysis of Causation. Econ Phil, 6(2), 207-234, O 90.

HOPKINS, Burt C. On the Paradoxical Inception and Motivation of Transcendental Philosophy in Plato and Husserl. Man World, 24(1), 27-47, Ja 91.

This paper illuminates common philosophical themes in the eidetic thought of Plato and Husserl. The author focuses primarily on Plato's account of the movement from doxa to arche, from out of which striking parallels with Husserl emerge. The status of philosophical access to the Eidos is investigated and it is shown that the initially paradoxical status of the Eidos is only resolved in the repetition of the methodological procedure, where that which is uncovered in reflection/recollection is found to be something previously "hidden" or "concealed." It is also shown that Plato's path to transcendental experience is best situated within Husserl's eidetic psychology, and not transcendental phenomenology.

HOPKINS, Jasper. *Nicholas of Cusa's de Pace Fidei and Cribratio Alkorani: Translation and Analysis*. Minneapolis, Banning Pr, 1990.

The book contains fundamental elements of Nicholas of Cusa's philosophy of religion and interpretation of the Koran.

HOPPER, Stanley R. "Language as Metaphorical: A Reply to John Cobb" in *Archetypal Process: Self and Divine in Whitehead, Jung, and Hillman*, GRIFFIN, David Ray (ed), 129-132. Evanston, Northwestern Univ Pr, 1989.

HOPPER, Stanley R. "Once More: The Cavern Beneath the Cave" in *Archetypal Process: Self and Divine in Whitehead, Jung, and Hillman*, GRIFFIN, David Ray (ed), 129-132. Evanston, Northwestern Univ Pr, 1989.

HORGAN, Terence and GRAHAM, George. In Defense of Southern Fundamentalism. Phil Stud, 62(2), 107-134, My 91.

Southern Fundamentalism, a form of realism about folk psychology, asserts that there is only a minimal conceptual gap between 1) satisfying ordinary, behavior-based, standards for the attribution of propositional attitudes, and 2) being a true believer; hence it is overwhelmingly likely that there are true believers. Under Southern Fundamentalism, the integrity of folk psychology is not threatened by debates about whether folk psychology is destined to become part of mature science, whether there is a language of thought, or whether any other of the strong empirical commitments sometimes attributed to folk psychology are satisfied.

HORGAN, Terence. "Mental Quausation" in *Philosophical Perspectives, 3: Philosophy of Mind and Action Theory, 1989*, TOMBERLIN, James E (ed), 47-76. Atascadero, Ridgeview, 1989.

First I argue that our common-sense belief in the efficacy of the mental presupposes that mental events are efficacious *qua* mental. Next I consider and reject several possible accounts of the relation I call "quausation." Third, I propose a positive account of quausation, in which patterns of conterfactual dependence figure centrally. Fourth, I argue that this account makes it very plausible that there is indeed mental quausation in the world, just as common sense supposes.

HORGAN, Terence. Metaphysical Realism and Psychologistic Semantics. Erkenntnis, 34(3), 297-322, My 91.

I propose a metaphysical position I call *limited metaphysical realism*, and I link it to a position in the philosophy of language I call *psychologistic semantics*. Limited metaphysical realism asserts that there is a mind-independent, discourse-independent world, but posits a sparse ontology. Psychologistic semantics construes truth not as direct word/world correspondence, and not as warranted assertibility (or Putnam's "ideal" warranted assertibility), but rather as *correct assertibility*. I argue that virtues of this package deal over each of the two broad positions that have recently dominated metaphysics and philosophy of language—positions I call package deal metaphysical realism, and package deal anti-realism.

HORNETT, Stuart I. The Sanctity of Life and Substituted Judgement: The Case of Baby J. Ethics Med, 7(2), 2-5, Sum 91.

In the recent case of Re J (a minor), the English Court of Appeal allowed life-saving treatment to be withdrawn from a handicapped neonate. In doing so, the Court not only had regard to the effect of the treatment on the patient, but also the patient's current and future 'quality of life'. Moreover, they applied a substituted judgement test and asked: "What would the child decide to do if he were capable of making a decision?" This test is surely inappropriate for neonates because the child's actual or assumed wishes or feelings can never be deduced.

HORNSBY, Jennifer. "Descartes, Rorty and the Mind-Body Fiction" in *Reading Rorty*, MALACHOWSKI, Alan (ed), 41-57. Cambridge, Blackwell, 1991.

HORNSBY, Jennifer. "Semantic Innocence and Psychological Understanding" in *Philosophical Perspectives, 3: Philosophy of Mind and Action Theory, 1989*, TOMBERLIN, James E (ed), 549-574. Atascadero, Ridgeview, 1989.

The paper attempts to dislodge the idea that accounts of propositional attitude explanation can be separated from accounts of sentential content (or meaning). The claim is that by seeing how a theory of truth can serve as a theory of sense, one sees the errors of methodological solipsism, and can provide an alternative philosophical understanding of psychological understanding.

HORNSTEIN, Gail A and STAR, Susan Leigh. Universality Biases: *How Theories About Human Nature Succeed*. Phil Soc Sci, 20(4), 421-436, D 90.

HORNYANSKY, Monica C. "Sartre and the Humanism of Spontaneity" in *The Question of Humanism: Challenges and Possibilities*, GOICOECHEA, David (ed), 244-252. Buffalo, Prometheus, 1991.

The article defends Sartre's humanism against Heidegger's criticism that as an example of "the modern metaphysics of subjectivity" it neglects being-in-the-world. It is true that Sartre cannot situate his thought in a grandiose concept of Being, or less grandly, of nature. Nevertheless, drawing on the etymology of *spondere*, it can be shown that in the relation between the spontaneity of pre-reflective consciousness and the responsibility of reflective consciousness, Sartre fully recaptures the social context of human existence. His descriptions of existential psychoanalysis, and of a society theory that would do justice to the complexities of human agency, are an ample answer to Heidegger's criticism.

HOROWITZ, Amir. Dretske on Perception. Ratio, 3(2), 136-141, D 90.

Dretske, in *Knowledge and the Flow of Information*, offers a comprehensive naturalistic account of knowledge, based on the concept of *information*. In the case of *perceptual* knowledge Dretske endorses the idea that the perceptual process consists of two distinct stages, a sensorial one and a cognitive one. The article tries to show that due to this distinction Dretske's model of perception cannot account for our acquiring perceptual beliefs about *objects* as unities of properties, and then argues that *every* model of perception which endorses that distinction will be subject to the same difficulty. Therefore the distinction must be rejected altogether.

HOROWITZ, Maryanne Cline. Montaigne's 'Des Cannibales' and Natural Sources of Virtue. Hist Euro Ideas, 11, 427-434, 1989.

Montaigne in his description of the Topinamba tribes of Brazil appears to assert a natural law as a basis for human virtue. Writing at the crossroads of natural law theory, Montaigne both gives a theoretical rejection of the human capacity to find natural law, and bold insights against torture and against unnecessary violence to humans or animals that place him at the beginning of the field of natural and human rights. Montaigne's statements that these nations live in accord with natural law belongs to a long rhetorical tradition, common to Cicero and Peter Martyr. Montaigne's matter-of-fact acceptance of cannibalism indicates the influence of the law common to humans and animals, the law of personal survival, proclaimed by the Epicureans and by Ulpian.

HORTON, John. A Theory of Social Justice? Utilitas, 3(1), 121-138, My 91.

A critical review of Brian Barry's *Theories of Justice* and *Democracy, Power and Justice: Essays in Political Theory*. Much of Barry's work is commended but it is argued that his account of 'justice as impartiality' suffers from several difficulties. These arise particularly from the problems that confront any attempt to develop a conception of impartiality which applies across generations and cultures but which also issue in genuinely substantive principles of justice.

HORWICH, Paul. On the Nature and Norms of Theoretical Commitment. Phil Sci, 58(1), 1-14, Mr 91.

It is not uncommon for philosophers to maintain that one is obliged to believe nothing beyond the *observable* consequences of a successful scientific theory. This doctrine is variously known as instrumentalism, fictionalism, constructive empiricism, theoretical skepticism and the philosophy of "as if." The purpose of the present paper is to subject such forms of scientific antirealism to a two-pronged critique. In the first place it is argued that there is no genuine difference between *believing* a theory and being disposed to *use* it to make predictions, design experiments, and so on; so traditional instrumentalism is incoherent. In the second place, a retrenched position is considered in which theoretical belief would be tolerated but said to be justified on merely *pragmatic*, and not *epistemic*, grounds. In criticizing this point of view it is shown that the onus of proof rests on anyone who maintains it; furthermore, the only possible rationale for it (which is based on underdetermination of theory by data) is described, and various deficiencies in this argument are exposed.

HORWITZ, Robert (ed & trans) and CLAY, Jenny Strauss (ed & trans) and CLAY, Diskin (ed & trans). *Questions Concerning the Law of Nature: John Locke*. Ithaca, Cornell Univ Pr, 1990.

HÖRZ, Herbert. "Development of Science as a Change of Types" in *Imre Lakatos and Theories of Scientific Change*, GAVROGLU, Kostas (ed), 33-46. Norwell, Kluwer, 1989.

HÖRZ, Herbert. Wissenschaftsphilosophie in der DDR—Versuch einer kritischen Betrachtung. Deut Z Phil, 39(1), 59-70, 1991.

Die Wissenschaftsphilosophen der DDR anerkannten als Rahmentheorie den dialektischen Materialismus. Mit der Akzeptanz-, Realisierungs- und Theoriekrise des Marxismus ist eine kritische Revision ihrer Ergebnisse erforderlich. Der Beitrag versucht, aus der Sicht eines Mitgestalters dieser Entwicklung, Ursachen für geistige Restriktionen und für kreative Leistungen aufzudecken. Er behandelt die prägenden Traditionen, die Krise des Diamat und den Rückzug in die Theorie, Philosophie in der DDR stand zwischen Apologie und Aufklärung. Als Heuristik genutzt, gerichtet gegen das Wahrheitsmonopol, brachte sie interessante Einsichten in Entwicklungs- und Erkenntnistheorie.

HÖSLE, Vittorio. The Greatness and Limits of Kant's Practical Philosophy. Grad Fac Phil J, 13(2), 133-157, 1990.

HÖSLE, Vittorio. Platonism and Anti-Platonism in Nicholas of Cusa's Philosophy of Mathematics. Grad Fac Phil J, 13(2), 79-112, 1990.

HOSOI, Tsutomu and SASAKI, Katsumi. Finite Logics and the Simple Substitution Property. Bull Sect Log, 19(3), 74-78, O 90.

A notion called the simple substitution property is defined and it is proved that all the intermediate logics defined by finite models enjoy the property. The property is useful and important for the mechanical theorem prover because it provides a mechanical strategy about substituting the variables in the axioms.

HOSTETLER, Karl. Community and Neutrality in Critical Thought. Educ Theor, 41(1), 1-12, Wint 91.

This paper challenges objectivism in critical thought. It contends that objectivism takes foundationalist and contextualist forms, the presumption common to these being that objectivity in the critique of social norms requires access to some neutral perspective. The paper offers a nonobjectivist alternative in which objectivity is secured through the clash of "prejudiced" views. Implications for the skills, content, and moral context of critical thinking are considered, particularly with reference to the status of community in critical thought, and how these differ from what is offered by objectivist and traditional liberal views.

HOSTETLER, Karl. Connecting *Techne* and *Praxis* in Teaching. Proc Phil Educ, 46, 337-345, 1990.

There is an uneasy but vital connection between techne and praxis. Praxis without techne is empty. Yet the exercise of techne has the potential to degrade praxis. This paper aims to explore the connection between techne and praxis in teaching and suggest a conception of teachers' techne compatible with the pursuit of praxis as a goal of schooling.

HOTTOIS, Gilbert. Die Natur der Sprache: Von der Ontologie zur Technologie. Stud Leibniz, 22(2), 184-193, 1990.

HOTTOIS, Guy. Le progrès: De la temporalité historico-anthropothéologique et symbolique. Laval Theol Phil, 46(3), 337-351, O 90.

Cette étude commence par l'analyse des présupposés philosophiques de l'idée de progrès qui sont l'anthropologocentrisme et la conception de la temporalité comme historique. Formellement, la notion de progrès est à comprendre comme le procès d'accomplissement de l'espèce humaine en tant que telle, c'est-à-dire conformément à la différence anthropologique qui la projette sur sa trajectoire d'évolution spécifique qui est symbolique (culturelle, historique). Ce devenir de l'anthropologos es conçu comme incommensurable (ontologiquement distinct) avec la temporalité de l'évolution biophysique. (edited)

HOUGHTON, David. "Rorty's Talk-About" in *Reading Rorty*, MALACHOWSKI, Alan (ed), 156-170. Cambridge, Blackwell, 1991.

HOULGATE, Stephen. "A Reply to John Burbidge's "Where is the Place of Understanding?"" in *Essays on Hegel's Logic*, DI GIOVANNI, George (ed), 183-189. Albany, SUNY Pr, 1990.

In this article I respond to John Burbidge's claim that understanding is the "motor" of Hegel's logic. The article strongly endorses Burbidge's claim, but argues that he is mistaken in holding that Hegel's dialectical analyses *always* end with an act of understanding which generates further dialectical development. In my view, the one-sided abstractions of understanding (or "either/or thinking") are indeed the source of dialectic, however dialectical analysis is not endlessly regenerated, but reaches a point of rest—for example, at the end of the *Science of Logic*—when the rhythm of dialectical development itself becomes explicitly thematised.

HOULGATE, Stephen. Thought and Being in Kant and Hegel. Owl Minerva, 22(2), 131-140, Spr 91.

HOULGATE, Stephen. World History as the Progress of Consciousness: An Interpretation of Hegel's Philosophy of History. Owl Minerva, 22(1), 69-80, Fall 90.

The purpose of this paper is to consider why Hegel claims that world history is the necessary progress of the consciousness of freedom, and to show that, contrary to what many of his critics (such as Marx and Nietzsche) assert, Hegel's view does not lead him to ignore the material, economic side of human life or to downplay the importance of human agency in history. To conclude, I suggest that Hegel's understanding of history as the development of the *consciousness* of freedom helps us understand what his conception of the so-called "end of history" entails.

HOURANI, Albert. "Islam in European Thought" in *The Tanner Lectures on Human Values, Volume XI*, PETERSON, Grethe B (ed), 223-287. Salt Lake City, Univ of Utah Pr, 1990.

HOUSE, Ian. Harrison on Animal Pain. Philosophy, 66(257), 376-379, Jl 91.

Peter Harrison ('Do Animals Feel Pain?', *Philosophy*, Volume 66, Number 255, January 1991, 25-40) is wrong to argue that animals do not feel pain. Because they behave as though they feel pain, have the equipment for feeling pain and are evolutionarily related to creatures which do feel pain (namely, human beings), we may conclude that animals feel pain. Harrison is, therefore, wrong to claim that we should treat animals well only for our own sakes and not at all for theirs.

HOUSER, Nathan. Santayana's Peirce. Bull Santayana Soc, 8, 10-13, Fall 90.

The question considered is how and to what extent was George Santayana influenced by his fellow Harvard alumnus, Charles S Peirce. After exploring some possible points of contact or influence, it is concluded that Peirce was not a central figure for Santayana. Nevertheless, at a crucial point in Santayana's development Peirce contributed an idea which grew to become of central importance for Santayana.

HOWARD, Dick. "The Political Origins of Democracy" in *Writing the Politics of Difference*, SILVERMAN, Hugh J (ed), 253-263. Albany, SUNY Pr, 1991.

Once one can no longer define politics in terms of "the" Revolution, what values can be taken as specifically political? From this contemporary question, the paper returns to the lessons of the U S Revolution as it took form between 1763 and 1800. It then returns once again to the present.

HOWARD, Dick. Rediscovering the Left. Praxis Int, 10(3-4), 193-204, O 90-Ja 91.

How can/should Western leftist or Marxist thought react to recent events in Eastern Europe? The author tries to show that the left, historically, is defined by its *democratic* component rather than by its social or state-centered orientation. More specifically, following his arguments in *From Marx to Kant*, the author claims that the problem of *democracy* emerged at the end of the 18th century but that the capitalist economy and socialist political dreams covered over the properly political dimension of the democratic project. The Eastern European revolutions force us to rethink the political philosophy of democracy.

HOWARD, Paul E. Definitions of Compact. J Sym Log, 55(2), 645-655, Je 90.

There are several formulations of the notion of compactness for topological spaces which are equivalent under the assumption of the axiom of choice. The logical relations between these formulations are investigated if the assumption of the axiom of choice is dropped.

HOWE, Edmund G and MARTIN, Edward D. Treating the Troops. Hastings Center Rep, 21(2), 21-24, Mr-Ap 91.

HOWE, Irving. "The Self and the State" in *The Tanner Lectures On Human Values, Volume XII*, PETERSON, Grethe B (ed), 203-251. Salt Lake City, Univ of Utah Pr, 1991.

HOWIE, John. Brand Blanshard and Gewirth: Ethics and Rights. Ideal Stud, 20(2), 155-168, My 90.

Gewirth's view that ethics is based on human rights is contrasted to Blanshard's view that human rights derive their support from ethics. For Blanshard intrinsic good is comprised of whatever both satisfies and fulfills human nature. Human rights and correlated duties depend entirely upon whether or not they foster this intrinsic good. For Gewirth, by contrast, human claim-rights, such as freedom and well-being, are the foundation of human agency required for moral action of any sort. Such rights, properly conceived, are the foundation and basis of ethics.

HOWIE, John. Creative Insecurity and "Tiptoe Experiences". Personalist Forum, 7(1), 37-50, Spr 91.

Peter A Bertocci uses "creative insecurity" in three different but overlapping ways. It characterizes the relationship of God to humankind, describes somewhat literally and somewhat metaphorically the life of God, and designates the "peak" or "tiptoe experiences." It is the key to Bertocci's view of creativity.

HOWLAND, Jacob A. Socrates and Alcibiades: Eros, Piety, and Politics. Interpretation, 18(1), 63-90, Fall 90.

Alcibiades II, a neglected dialogue included in the traditional Platonic canon, engages both Platonic and non-Platonic portraits of Socrates and Alcibiades in attempting to elucidate the philosophical and political implications of Socratic and Alcibiadian eros and the nature of Socratic piety.

HOWSON, C. Some Further Reflections on the Popper-Miller 'Disproof' of Probabilistic Induction. Austl J Phil, 68(2), 221-228, Je 90.

HOWSON, Colin. "Fitting Your Theory to the Facts: Probably Not Such a Bad Thing After All" in *Scientific Theories*, SAVAGE, C Wade (ed), 224-244. Minneapolis, Univ of Minn Pr, 1990.

HOWSON, Colin. The Last Word on Induction? Erkenntnis, 34(1), 73-82, Ja 91.

Recent arguments of Watkins, one purporting to show the impossibility of probabilistic induction, and the other to be a solution of the practical problem of induction, are examined and two are shown to generate inconsistencies in his system. The paper ends with some reflections on the Bayesian theory of inductive inference.

HOY, Terry. The Moral Ontology of Charles Taylor: Contra Deconstructivism. Phil Soc Crit, 16(3), 207-225, 1990.

HOYNINGEN-HUENE, Paul. Kuhn's Conception of Incommensurability. Stud Hist Phil Sci, 21(3), 481-492, S 90.

In this paper, I try to reconstruct Kuhn's conception of incommensurability and its development. First, Kuhn's presentation of incommensurability in his *Structure of Scientific Revolutions* of 1962 is analyzed. The problems involved in this conception lead to further developments of Kuhn's theory, mainly a theory of world constitution. By means of this theory, Kuhn is able to reformulate his incommensurability concept in his publications from the seventies and the eighties, and to answer some of the objections raised against it. In particular, some of the criticisms of Kuhnian incommensurability seem to rest on misunderstanding. Finally, I discuss a serious problem that Kuhn's incommensurability conception is faced with.

HOYNINGEN-HUENE, Paul. Theorie antireduktionistischer Argumente: Fallstudie Bohr. Deut Z Phil, 39(2), 194-204, 1991.

HRACHOVEC, Herbert. Philosophische Anstösse in der computerunterstützten Intelligenz-Forschung. Phil Rundsch, 37(4), 278-297, 1990.

HRUSHOVSKI, Ehud. Unidimensional Theories are Superstable. Annals Pure Applied Log, 50(2), 117-138, N 90.

A first order theory T of power λ is called unidimensional if any two λ^+-saturated models of T of the same (sufficiently large) cardinality are isomorphic. We prove here that such theories are superstable, solving a problem of Shelah. The proof involves an existence theorem and a definability theorem for definable groups in stable theories, and an analysis of their relation to regular types.

HSENG-HONG, Yeh. Similarity According to Jen-Jen. Thinking, 9(1), 35, 1990.

HUBERT, Bernard. Devenir et génération chez Platon. Rev Thomiste, 91(2), 281-289, Ap-Je 91.

HUBIN, Donald C. Irrational Desires. Phil Stud, 62(1), 23-44, Ap 91.

Many believe that the rational evaluation of actions depends on the rational evaluation of even basic desires. Hume, though, viewed desires as "original existences" which cannot be contrary to either truth or reason. Contemporary critics of Hume, including Norman, Brandt and Parfit, have sought a basis for the rational evaluation of desires that would deny some basic desires reason-giving force. I side with Hume against these modern critics. Hume's concept of rational evaluation is admittedly too narrow; even basic desires are, despite their nonrepresentational nature, subject to rational evaluation. But this evaluation is not relevant to their tendency to generate reasons for action, and does not undermine the spirit of the Humean view of rational action.

HÜBNER, Adolf. Una aproximación ontológica a la realidad fisica. Dianoia, 35(35), 57-79, 1989.

HÜBNER, J. "Science and Religion Coming Across" in *Science and Religion: One World-Changing Perspectives on Reality*, FENNEMA, Jan (ed), 173-181. Norwell, Kluwer, 1990.

If scientifical arguments and their employment and theological reflections likewise are isolated, the ones can lead to destructional events and the others remain inconsiderable and unimportant. But both arise from the same base: the common life and its questions. For serving to this life-context, which if the life-context of their own, science and theology have to meet each other. They need the dialogue mutually in confrontation, critique, assistance and arrangements. Results of systematical thinking will enter the actual discussion and promote it. But they must open the discussion and not lead into close systems, for close systems can stop living mutual communication.

HUDAC, Michael C. Merleau-Ponty on the Cartesian "Dubito": A Critical Analysis. Hist Phil Quart, 8(2), 207-219, Ap 91.

HUDELSON, Richard. *Marxism and Philosophy in the Twentieth Century: A Defense of Vulgar Marxism*. New York, Praeger, 1990.

HUDSON, Deal W. "Maritain and Happiness in Modern Thomism" in *From Twilight to Dawn: The Cultural Vision of Jacques Maritain*, REDPATH, Peter A (ed), 263-276. Notre Dame, Univ Notre Dame Pr, 1990.

The idea of happiness in modern Thomism is explored through the thought of Etienne Gilson, Yves R Simon, Josef Pieper, and Jacques Maritain. Each figure is shown to stress a different aspect of Aristotle's eudamonism in providing an account of happiness or beatitude consonant with a *finis ultimus* external to the human subject. Simon and Maritain are seen as surpassing Gilson's and Pieper's intellectualism for their richer accounts of imperfect or earthly happiness.

HUDSON, Hud. *Wille, Willkür,* and the Imputability of Immoral Actions. Kantstudien, 82(2), 179-196, 1991.

In this paper I investigate a popular objection to Kant's ethics which maintains that he has no (consistent) way to impute immoral actions to an agent. By way of defending Kant against this objection, I focus on some recent work on the *Wille/Willkür* distinction, and I identify and analyze the relations between four types of freedom which emerge in accordance with this distinction. Finally, I utilize these results in providing a reading of Kant's Reciprocity Thesis of freedom and moral law which, while being faithful to and making sense out of the texts, avoids the imputability problem altogether.

HUÉSCAR, Antonio R. Examen del "ahora". Rev Filosof (Spain), 4, 69-81, 1990.

HUET, Marie-Hélène. Monstrous Imagination: Progeny as Art in French Classicism. Crit Inquiry, 17(4), 718-737, Sum 91.

HUGHEN, Richard. Should Children Be Taught to Obey Their Conscience? J Thought, 24(3-4), 68-78, Fall-Wint 89.

If we seriously care about the moral education of young people, should we teach them to obey the dictates of conscience? Bertrand Russell said that the conscience is nothing but a source of irrational guilt and that it should be ignored. But Joseph Butler claimed that the conscience is the voice of rationality and morality and that it must be heeded. In this paper I briefly explore the views of Russell and Butler and then note that Aristotle's description of human nature and the human psyche when combined with Lawrence Kohlberg's stages of moral development throw some interesting light on the issue. There is a rational and an irrational conscience and children should be taught to heed the former and ignore the latter, and the task of moral education must be to help children recognize the difference.

HUGHES, G E. Every World Can See a Reflexive World. Stud Log, 49(2), 175-181, Je 90.

Let C be the class of frames in which every point is related to some irreflexive point. An axiomatic modal system, KMT, is defined. It is proved that KMT is characterized by C, has the finite model property, is decidable, and is not finitely axiomatizable; that C contains all the *finite* frames for KMT, but not all the infinite ones; and that the class of all frames for KMT is not definable by any first-order formula, but consists of those in which all the points accessible from any given point form a sub-frame which is not finitely colourable.

HUGHES, Gerard J. Ignatian Discernment: A Philosophical Analysis. Heythrop J, 31(4), 419-438, O 90.

An interpretation of Aristotle's views on the relationship between moral virtue and practical wisdom is advanced. It is suggested that Ignatius of Loyola's views on Christian decision making owe much to Aristotle, a fact not surprising given the climate in the University of Paris while Ignatius was studying there. This interpretation is contrasted with other less rationalist accounts of moral decision making.

HUGHES, Glenn. Eric Voegelin's View of History as a Drama of Transfiguration. Int Phil Quart, 30(4), 449-464, D 90.

Voegelin's view of what constitutes history is examined here. The essence of history is, he argues, the relationship between the significant constants and variables in human self-interpretation over time. The central constant of self-interpretation is the quest for meaning; the most important variable is the discovery of transcendent reality, and of the human relation to transcendence. The participation of humans in a transcendent reality means that history is a process in which spatiotemporal reality is transfigured through human participation in transcendent meaning; and means also that myth is a requisite form of expression for articulating the meaning of history.

HUGHES, Martin. Creation, Creativity and Necessary Being. Relig Stud, 26(3), 349-361, S 90.

To explore Kant's remarks about connections between ontological and cosmological arguments; to support Feuerbach's contention that some of the interest of these arguments lies in their implied view of the human mind; to suggest that the sum of these arguments may prove something important without proving the existence of God.

HUGHES, Martin. Locke on Taxation and Suffrage. Hist Polit Thought, 11(3), 423-442, Autumn 90.

The purpose is to investigate Locke's commitment to democracy. He evidently wants Parliament to represent all taxpayers. But most poor people were taxpayers. So Locke was a democrat because he wanted Parliament to represent the poor.

HUGHES, R I G. "Philosophical Perspectives on Newtonian Science" in *Philosophical Perspectives on Newtonian Science*, BRICKER, Phillip (ed), 1-16. Cambridge, MIT Pr, 1990.

This introductory essay paints a general picture of the philosophical issues raised by Newton's scientific work, and locates the topics discussed elsewhere in the volume within that picture.

HUGHES, R I G (ed) and BRICKER, Phillip (ed). *Philosophical Perspectives on Newtonian Science*. Cambridge, MIT Pr, 1990.

A collection of papers delivered at a conference held at Yale University to honor the tercentenary of the publication of Isaac Newton's *Principia*. The six main papers are by Howard Stein, Peter Achinstein, Lawrence Sklar, Michael Friedman, J E McGuire, and Errol Harris. Topics include Newton's views on space and time, on God, on gravity, and on scientific methodology.

HUGHES, R I G. "Reason and Experiment in Newton's *Opticks*: Comments on Peter Achinstein" in *Philosophical Perspectives on Newtonian Science*, BRICKER, Phillip (ed), 175-184. Cambridge, MIT Pr, 1990.

HUGLY, Philip and SAYWARD, Charles. Moral Relativism and Deontic Logic. Synthese, 85(1), 139-152, O 90.

If a native of India asserts "Killing cattle is wrong" and a Nebraskan asserts "Killing cattle is not wrong," and both judgments agree with their respective moralities and both moralities are internally consistent, then the moral relativist says both judgments are fully correct. At this point relativism bifurcates. One branch which we call content relativism denies that the two people are contradicting each other. The second branch which we call truth value relativism affirms that the two judgments are contradictory. Truth value relativism appears to be logically incoherent. We defend truth value relativism against this sort of charge of logical incoherence by showing it can be accommodated by the existing semantical metatheories of deontic logic. Having done this we go on to argue that truth value relativism is the best version of relativism. (edited)

HUGLY, Philip and SAYWARD, Charles. Offices and God. Sophia (Australia), 29(3), 29-34, O 90.

In "Existence and God" (*Journal of Philosophy*, Vol. 76, 403-420) Pavel Tichy presents an interpretation of Anselm's *Prosologian III* argument and raises doubts about one of the premises. It is argued here that the argument Tichy raises doubts about is not Anselm's.

HUGLY, Philip and SAYWARD, Charles. Quine's Relativism. Ratio, 3(2), 142-149, D 90.

A doctrine that occurs intermittently in Quine's work is that there is no extra-theoretic truth. It is argued that on its best interpretation the doctrine is inconsistent with three other doctrines accepted by Quine: bivalence, mathematical Platonism, and the disquotational account of truth.

HULL, David L. Conceptual Selection. Phil Stud, 60(1-2), 77-87, S-O 90.

John Dupré argues for pluralism with respect to both species and science. He insists that we need to recognize at least genealogical and ecological species and that science is a "loose and heterogeneous collection of more or less successful investigative practices." In response, I argue that a single species concept can and must include reference to the alternation of two processes, replication and interaction. A similar mechanism has characterized science since its inception.

HULL, Robert. Skepticism, Enigma and Integrity: Horizons of Affirmation in Nietzsche's Philosophy. Man World, 23(4), 375-391, O 90.

HUMBER, James M (ed) and ALMEDER, Robert F (ed). *Biomedical Ethics Reviews, 1987*. Clifton, Humana Pr, 1988.

HUMBER, James M (ed). *Biomedical Ethics Reviews, 1989*. Clifton, Humana Pr, 1990.

Biomedical Ethics Reviews (*BER*) is an annual publication designed to review and update the literature on issues of central importance in bioethics today. *BER: 1989* contains essays which address three topics: (1) Should abnormal fetuses be brought to term for the sole purpose of providing infant transplant organs? (2) Should physicians dispense drugs for profit? And (3) Should human death be taken to occur when persons permanently lose consciousness?

HUMBER, James M (ed) and ALMEDER, Robert (ed). *Biomedical Ethics Reviews, 1990*. Clifton, Humana Pr, 1991.

HUMBER, James M. "On Human Death" in *Biomedical Ethics Reviews, 1989*, HUMBER, James M (ed), 127-163. Clifton, Humana Pr, 1990.

In this paper I argue against both the neocortical and brain-death criteria for declaring human death. After rejecting these criteria, I analyze the concept of human death and use this analysis to argue for "a new approach to the problem of declaring human death—an approach in which acceptance of the traditional, heart-lung criteria for declaring human death is linked to legislation that allows for euthanasia whenever patients are brain-dead or permanently unconscious."

HUMBER, James M. Response to Gale's "Freedom and the Free Will Defense". Soc Theor Pract, 16(3), 425-433, Fall 90.

In "Freedom and the Free Will Defense," Richard Gale attempts to prove that the free will defense (FWD) fails to counter the problem of moral evil. In this essay, I argue that Gale's attack upon the FWD is unsuccessful. More specifically, I argue that (1) if compatibilism is true, Gale is correct and the FWD fails as a theodicy; however (2) if libertarianism is true, the FWD succeeds in its purpose; and (3) Gale never proves that libertarianism is false.

HUMBERSTONE, I L. Expressive Power and Semantic Completeness: Boolean Connectives in Modal Logic. Stud Log, 49(2), 197-214, Je 90.

HUMBERSTONE, I L. Two Kinds of Agent-Relativity. Phil Quart, 41(163), 144-166, Ap 91.

It is possible to relativize obligation-statements to specific agents in order to register the dependence of what an agent should do upon the circumstances of the agent in question (the options available to one agent not guaranteed to be the same as those available to any other agent). It is also possible to relativize obligation-statements to specific agents in order to impute the onus of obligation to one rather than another agent in a situation in which several agents are involved. The present paper advertises the distinction between these two kinds of agent-relativization.

HUMBERSTONE, I L. Wanting, Getting, Having. Phil Papers, 19(2), 99-118, Ag 90.

Motivational efficacy is not the only measure of strength for desires. An independent measure is given by how happy one would be to see a desire satisfied. A more precise spelling-out of this latter idea requires us to attend to the distinction between being happy—which is to say—being in a certain affective state, and being happy that such-and-such is the case: this is a propositional attitude whose relation to the affective state of happiness deserves to be thought about.

HUME, David and MEYER, Michel (ed). *Réflexions sur les passions*. Paris, Lib Gen Francaise, 1990.

HUMPHREY, John A. Some Objections To Garavaso's Wittgenstein. S J Phil, 29(3), 303-327, Fall 91.

HUMPHREYS, Paul. A Conjecture Concerning the Ranking of the Sciences. Topoi, 9(2), 157-160, S 90.

The notion of a causal invariant is used to establish a ranking of the sciences which closely corresponds to traditional rankings. The work of William Withering on digitalis and of John Snow on cholera is used to illustrate the argument.

HUMPHRY, Derek. Arguing for Rational Suicide. Listening, 26(1), 15-19, Wint 91.

The paper argues that nowadays there are two forms of suicide: (1) emotional suicide of people who are depressed or disturbed; and (2) rational or justifiable suicide—when a dying person chooses accelerated death rather than lingering suffering. Rational suicide is more appropriately called 'self-deliverance' or 'autoeuthanasia'. The paper sets out the criteria by which the average member of the Hemlock Society could ethically justify his or her self-destruction.

HUND, John. Wittgenstein versus Hart: Two Models of Rules for Social and Legal Theory. Phil Soc Sci, 21(1), 72-85, Mr 91.

In this essay, I contend that Wittgenstein's attempt to reduce abstract social rules to externally observable patterns of behavior emasculated his conception of a rule to the point of nonexistence. In traversing this ground, I liken Wittgenstein's theory to that of the jurist John Austin and the rule skepticism of the American legal realists, and I use Hart's critique of both of these approaches to substantiate the claim that, for Wittgenstein, *There is no such thing as a rule*. In passing, I draw into question a view that has been widely taken for granted lately, namely, that Wittgenstein was someone who merely "rediscovered" Durkheim and that he was writing in what is an essentially Durkheimian sociological tradition.

HUNDERT, Edward M. Thoughts and Feelings and Things: A New Psychiatric Epistemology. Theor Med, 12(1), 7-23, Mr 91.

HUNLEY, J D. The Intellectual Compatibility of Marx and Engels. Soc Theor Pract, 17(1), 1-22, Spr 91.

For the last thirty years, scholars have stressed differences between the ideas of Marx and Engels and have blamed the failures of twentieth-century communism on Engels alone. Drawing on Marx's and Engels' works and correspondence, Hunley shows in this article that Engels did not disagree with Marx about important issues and did not distort Marx's views after the latter's death. Contrary to the view that Marx was a humanist and Engels a positivist, for example, Hunley demonstrates that the writings of both men present an extreme tension between humanism and positivism. Furthermore, Marx himself called Engels his alter ego.

HUNT, David P. Middle Knowledge and the Soteriological Problem of Evil. Relig Stud, 27(1), 3-26, Mr 91.

Anyone accepting the traditional Christian doctrines of soteriological exclusivism and post-mortem punishment, under which suffering is a never-ending constituent of the universe, appears to face a particularly virulent form of the problem of evil. William Craig, however, has recently argued that this problem can be alleviated by appeal to the theory of divine middle knowledge. I argue that Craig's use of this theory has two undesirable consequences: it entails evangelical fatalism, and it renders the theodicist vulnerable to the 'simulacrum strategy'. Both these defects reflect deeper weaknesses in the theory of middle knowledge.

HUNT, Eugene H and BULLIS, Ronald K. Applying the Principles of Gestalt Theory to Teaching Ethics. J Bus Ethics, 10(5), 341-347, My 91.

Teaching ethics poses a dilemma for professors of business. First, they have little or no formal training in ethics. Second, they have established ethical values that they may not want to impose upon their students. What is needed is a well-recognized, yet non-sectarian model to facilitate the clarification of ethical questions. Gestalt theory offers such a framework. Four Gestalt principles facilitate ethical clarification and another four Gestalt principles anesthetize ethical clarification. This article examines each principle, illustrates that principle through current business examples, and offers exercises for developing each principle.

HUNT, G M K (ed). *Philosophy and Politics*. New York, Cambridge Univ Pr, 1991.

This varied collection explores a recurrent theme connecting philosophy and politics: the relation between the nature of man and the structure of society. This is by no means the only intersection of interests between politics and philosophy—the contemporary collaboration on methodological issues has led political science to rival political theory—but it is above all the common concern of philosophy and politics with the nature of man as an essentially social being. This current collection approaches this absorbing problem by concentrating on the topical issue of the market economy, viewed as an attempt to resolve the clash between individual autonomy and collective action. Contributors include Norman Berry, Peter Binns, Don Locke, Susan Mendus, David Miller, Kenneth Minogue, A Phillips Griffiths, J Enoch Powell, Robert Skidelsky, and G W Smith.

HUNT, Lester. Comments: "A Moral Ideal for Everyone and No One". Int Stud Phil, 22(2), 31-34, 1990.

HUNT, Morton. The Natural History of Altruism. Free Inq, 11(1), 48-49, Wint 90-91.

HUNYADI, Mark. A Post-Metaphysical Moral: An Introduction to the Moral Theory of Jürgen Habermas (in French). Rev Theol Phil, 122(4), 467-483, 1990.

After reviewing the historical-systematic framework in which Habermas elaborates his philosophy (notably the differentiation between Max Weber's spheres of value and the consequent "war of the gods"), it is shown what strategy Habermas employs against an apparent scepticism of values. To reason traditionally considered as instrumental only, he opposes communicative reason, which is the only guarantee of universalism (particularly in the realm of morals) and founded upon the "pretentions of validity" which we uphold in every act of speech.

HUNYADY, György. "From National Character to the Mechanism of Stereotyping" in *Perspectives on Ideas and Reality*, NYÍRI, J C (ed), 174-200. Budapest, Kiskonyvtara, 1990.

HURLEY, Paul. The Many Appetites of Thomas Hobbes. Hist Phil Quart, 7(4), 391-407, O 90.

In this essay I turn to the source of the modern formulation of the desire-based account of practical reason, the works of Thomas Hobbes, and explore the account of desires/appetites that he employs, particularly in his discussion of self-preservation. I show that Hobbes appeals to not one, but several importantly distinct kinds of appetites, and that his recurrent arguments regarding the importance of self-preservation depend for their apparent plausibility upon subtle equivocations among these various kinds of appetites.

HURLEY, S L. *Natural Reasons: Personality and Polity*. New York, Oxford Univ Pr, 1989.

HURLEY, S L. Newcomb's Problem, Prisoners' Dilemma, and Collective Action. Synthese, 86(2), 173-196, F 91.

Among various cases that equally admit of evidentialist reasoning, the supposedly evidentialist solution has varying degrees of intuitive attractiveness. I suggest that cooperative reasoning may account for the appeal of apparently evidentialist behavior in the cases in which it is intuitively attractive, while the inapplicability of cooperative reasoning may account for the unattractiveness of evidentialist behaviour in other cases. A collective causal power with respect to agreed outcomes, not evidentialist reasoning, makes cooperation attractive in the Prisoners' Dilemma. And a natural though unwarranted assumption of such a power may account for the intuitive appeal of the one-box response in Newcomb's Problem.

HURST III, G Cameron. Death, Honor, and Loyalty: The Bushidō Ideal. Phil East West, 40(4), 511-527, O 90.

HURSTHOUSE, Rosalind. Arational Actions. J Phil, 88(2), 57-68, F 91.

According to the standard account of action-explanation, intentional actions are actions done because the agent has a certain desire/belief pair which explains the action by rationalising it. But *arational actions*—a subset of intentional actions explained by occurrent emotion—resist the ascription of any suitable belief to the agent. These actions challenge the standard account by forming a recalcitrant set of counterexamples to it. They also justify our questioning the semantic theory which holds that account in place; finally, they provide many examples where the judgements of reason cannot endorse the promptings of passion.

HURSTHOUSE, Rosalind. Virtue Theory and Abortion. Phil Pub Affairs, 20(3), 223-246, Sum 91.

Virtue theory is laid out in a framework that reveals the essential similarities and differences between it and deontological and utilitarian theories, revealing that many criticisms standardly made of it are misplaced. A major criticism - that it cannot get us anywhere - is rejected on the grounds that a normative theory which reaches practical conclusions that are not determined by premises about what is truly worthwhile or serious is guaranteed to be inadequate. This issue, concerning what sorts of concepts an adequate normative theory must contain, is highlighted by illustrating how virtue theory directs one to think about the problem of abortion.

HUSAK, Douglas N. Already Punished Enough. Phil Topics, 18(1), 79-99, Spr 90.

I argue that the suffering some convicted criminals have endured prior to the imposition of their formal sentence can be a good reason to reduce the severity of their punishments. I criticize reasons often given to reject the criminal's plea that he already suffered enough for his offense.

HUSAK, Douglas N. The Orthodox Model of the Criminal Offense. Crim Just Ethics, 10(1), 20-23, Wint-Spr 91.

I defend my view, argued in *Philosophy of Criminal Law*, that the distinction between actus reus and mens rea is not as useful as orthodox criminal theorists have tended to suppose. The objective of the actus reus principle is better served by the requirement that persons should not be punished for states of affairs over which they lack control.

HUTCHINGS, Patrick. Why Natural Theology, Still, Yet? Sophia (Australia), 30(1), 3-7, Jl 91.

The article is an ironical farewell to the founding editor of *Sophia*, Professor M J Charlesworth. When Charlesworth founded the journal thirty years ago, to discuss the epistemological status of God was, in a post-Kantian post-critical climate, Quixotic. In the present structuralist, post-structuralist, post-modern climate, the epistemological status of almost every branch of discourse is as problematic as Kant left 'God-talk'. We need an indefinite number of *Sophias*?

HUTCHINSON, D S and FOGELMAN, Brian D. 'Seventeen' Subtleties in Plato's *Theaetetus*. Phronesis, 35(3), 303-306, 1990.

This short paper draws attention to yet another example of Plato's concern for philosophical methodology in the *Theaetetus*. Specifically, it provides an interpretation of Plato's enumeration of the cases where false belief is possible (192a ff) in light of an earlier passage which is more apparently connected with the theme of philosophical methodology (147c-e). In both cases it is argued that Plato demonstrates his preference for an analysis that yields a classification over the bare enumeration of individual cases.

HUTCHINSON, D S. Aristotle and the Spheres of Motivation: *De Anima* III. Dialogue (Canada), 29(1), 7-20, 1990.

HUTTON, Patrick H. The Role of Memory in the Historiography of the French Revolution. Hist Theor, 30(1), 56-69, F 91.

Using the work of Maurice Halbwachs on collective memory as a theoretical guide, this essay considers the implications of the waning of the revolutionary tradition for historical writing about the French Revolution. The essay focuses on three renowned historians for whom the problem of memory was an issue: Jules Michelet, who wanted to resurrect the living memory of the Revolution; Alphonse Aulard, who wished only to commemorate it; and François Furet, who deconstructs the discourse through which its memory was sustained. The essay concludes with remarks about Pierre Nora's study of the French national memory, which situates history at a crossroads between tradition and historiography.

HYLAND, Drew A. *Philosophy of Sport*. New York, Paragon House, 1990.

HYLAND, Drew A. Plato's Three Waves and the Question of Utopia. Interpretation, 18(1), 91-109, Fall 90.

HYLTON, Peter. "Logic in Russell's Logicism" in *The Analytic Tradition: Philosophical Quarterly Monographs, Volume 1*, BELL, David (ed), 137-172. Cambridge, Blackwell, 1990.

HYMAN, David A. Commentary: When Opportunity Knocks. Hastings Center Rep, 20(6), 34-35, N-D 90.

HYMERS, Michael. The Role of Kant's Refutation of Idealism. S J Phil, 29(1), 51-68, Spr 91.

To interpret Kant's Refutation we must agree on its intended purpose. I argue that the Refutation develops a line of thought from the Transcendental Deduction and the 4th Paralogism of the 1781-*Critique*, where Kant hints that illusion presupposes a background of veridical perception. I draw on the 2-step structure of the 1787-Deduction, the addition of the Transcendental Expositions of Space and Time, and the rewriting of the Paralogisms to show that the Refutation supports the second premise of a strongly antiskeptical argument, thus extending the weakly antiskeptical conclusion of the Deduction.

HYMERS, Michael. Wittgenstein on Names and Family Resemblances. Eidos, 9(1), 11-30, Je 90.

The claim of the *Philosophical Investigations* that Augustine treats all words as names is, in part, a criticism of the view that some set of necessary and sufficient conditions delimits language. This, in turn, is an instance of Wittgenstein's broader complaint against delimiting concepts by necessary and sufficient conditions. Realism about universals not only treats concepts this way, but contributes to the view that all words are names. Bambrough's claim that Wittgenstein dissolves the dichotomy of realism and nominalism is defended. On this view, realism and nominalism are avoided by recognizing that objectivity must be understood in terms of *communicability*.

HYTTINEN, Tapani and TUURI, Heikki. Constructing Strongly Equivalent Nonisomorphic Models for Unstable Theories. Annals Pure Applied Log, 52(3), 203-248, Je 91.

HYTTINEN, Tapani and VÄÄNÄNEN, Jouko. On Scott and Karp Trees of Uncountable Models. J Sym Log, 55(3), 897-908, S 90.

Let A and B be countable relational models. If the models are nonisomorphic, there is a unique countable ordinal x with the property that A and B are equivalent in the finite quantifier infinitary language up to quantifier-rank x but not to x + 1. Let z be the first uncountable cardinal. In the paper we consider models A and B of cardinality z and construct trees which have a similar relation to A and B as x above. It turns out that the above ordinal x has two qualities which coincide in countable models but will differ in uncountable models. Respectively, two kinds of trees emerge from x, Scott and Karp trees. We construct two models with many mutually noncomparable Scott trees.

HYTTINEN, Tapani. Preservation by Homomorphisms and Infinitary Languages. Notre Dame J Form Log, 32(2), 167-172, Spr 91.

In this paper we study when sentences of infinitary languages are preserved by homomorphisms. This is done by using generalized Henkin construction. By the same technique we can also study when a sentence has an equivalent sentence which is in normal form.

IALACCI, Michael. Personal Identity, Reincarnation, and Resurrection. Logos (USA), 11, 143-157, 1990.

Contemporary philosophy presents two plausible solutions to the problem of personal identity: the psychological continuity view and the physical continuity view. Unfortunately, our intuitions support one view some of the time and the other view other times. We propose a third view, a view we call the inductive view, that requires both psychological and physical continuity. The inductive view not only prevents confusion in Williams-like scenarios, it also presents a better explanation to the problem of fission. The inductive view, moreover, requires that we distinguish identity from survival and recognize that the latter does not imply the former. We define reincarnation as the survival of a mind without its body. Resurrection is nothing but the divergence and reconvergence of mental and bodily continuity. We conclude that resurrection is possible.

IANNONE, A P. Critical Interaction: Judgment, Decision, and the Social Testing of Moral Hypotheses. Int J Moral Soc Stud, 6(2), 135-148, Sum 91.

This paper argues that both judgment and decision are central to moral and political life. It also argues that moral hypotheses, from particular rules to entire theories, and political hypotheses, from proposed policies and decisions to entire programs, are testable through, and only through, the joint activities of critical scrutiny and political practice. That is, both judgment and decision are crucial for testing them in what, as the paper explains, constitutes the social testing of moral and political hypotheses. In arguing for these theses, the paper critically examines some fashionable positions that undermine - and less fashionable ones that exaggerate - the role of judgment in this process.

IANNONE, A Pablo. Informing the Public: Ethics, Policy Making, and Objectivity in News Reporting. Phil Context, 20, 1-21, 1990.

This paper asks: Is objectivity possible in news reporting? How? Is it a good thing? Should it serve as a ground for policy making about news reporting? The paper distinguishes between the personal, institutional, and social testing senses of objectivity and defends four theses. First, all these senses of objectivity are relevant to news reporting, but inadequate as a sufficient ground for policy and decision making about it. Second, more significant are the political context in which discussions concerning objectivity take place and how these discussions affect not just news reporting but the public. Third, there is currently no good reason for accepting the hypothesis that, in such discussions, conflicting coexistent points of view are irreducible. Fourth, even if true, this hypothesis does not entail that objectivity in the social testing sense is impossible or a bad thing. In fact, the possibility of establishing its truth is grounded in objectivity as social testing.

IANNOTTA, Daniella. Lucien, Lévy-Bruhl: Una introduzione (di C Prandi). Aquinas, 33(2), 419-425, My-Ag 90.

IANNOTTA, Daniella. La passione dell'essere: Viaggio lungo i sentieri del nulla. Aquinas, 33(3), 487-509, S-D 90.

IBANA, Rainier R A. Max Scheler's Analysis of Illusions, Idols, and Ideologies. Phil Today, 34(4), 312-320, Wint 90.

A discussion of Scheler's critique of illusions, idols, and ideologies from the perspective of the contemporary debate between modernism and postmodernism. The author argues that Scheler has a postmodernist angle to his theory of values, but such a profile is situated within the context of the objective order of values. Hence, Scheler's postmodernism also pays due respect to the modernist's demand for a holistic and coherent vision of reality.

IBÁÑEZ, Alejandro Herrera. La distinción entre esencia y existencia en Avicena. Rev Latin De Filosof, 16(2), 183-195, Jl 90.

In this paper I examine (I) Avicenna's view that existence is an accident, (II) the status of the problem of the real distinction between essence and existence, and (III) the nature of Avicenna's essentialism. I conclude that Avicenna anticipated Frege and Russell in holding that existence is an accident of accidents. I also defend the view that Avicenna held that there is a real distinction between essence and existence. Finally, I hold that Avicenna's essentialism anticipates Meinong's view about nonexistent objects.

IBARRA, A (ed) and DÍEZ, Amparo (ed) and ECHEVERRÍA, J (ed). *Structures in Mathematical Theories: Reports of the San Sebastian International Symposium, 1990*. Vizcaya, Univ Pais Vasco, 1990.

This book contains a selection of 76 contributed papers to the International Symposium on Structures in Mathematical Theories (San Sebastian, Spain, 25-29 September, 1990). They are distributed in five sections: Mathematical and Empirical Theories; Applications of Mathematical Theories; History and Sociology of Mathematical Theories; Methods of Research into Mathematics; Structures of Mathematical Theories. Philosophers of science, historians and mathematicians coming from 19 countries (Belgium, Brazil, Canada, China, England, Finland, France, Germany, Holland, Japan, India, Israel, Italy, Mexico, Poland, Spain, Switzerland, URSS and USA) present their research on mathematical theories: their structures, historical evolutions and interrelations with other sciences and technologies.

IBRAHIM, Nabil A and RUE, Leslie W and MC DOUGALL, Patricia P and GREENE, G Robert. Characteristics and Practices of "Christian-Based" Companies. J Bus Ethics, 10(2), 123-132, F 91.

There is a sizeable group of self-described "Christian" companies which have declared their belief in the successful merging of biblical principles with business activities. As these companies have become more visible, an increasing number of anecdotal newspaper and magazine articles about these companies have appeared. Surprisingly, no rigorous research had been conducted prior to our recent study. This article provides national estimates of the size and predominant characteristics of self-identified "Christian" companies. In addition, the study investigated the types of relationships these companies maintained with their employees, customers, communities, and suppliers.

IDZIAK, Pawel M. Elementary Theory of Free Heyting Algebras. Rep Math Log, 23, 71-73, 1989.

IDZIAK, Pawel M. Sheaves in Universal Algebra and Model Theory: Part I. Rep Math Log, 23, 39-65, 1989.

IDZIAK, Pawel M. Sheaves in Universal Algebra and Model Theory: Part II. Rep Math Log, 24, 61-86, 1990.

IGLESIAS, Teresa. Death and the Beginning of Life. Ethics Med, 7(2), 8-17, Sum 91.

IGLESIAS, Teresa. Russell and the Ethical Concern of Wittgenstein's *Tractatus*. Phil Stud (Ireland), 32, 141-155, 1988-90.

IGNATOW, Assen. Perestrojka der Philosophie? Stud Soviet Tho, 40(1-3), 7-53, 1990.

The topic of this paper is the situation of the Soviet philosophy in the age of perestrojka. In the author's opinion is recent official Soviet philosophy an eclectic mixture of old and new. There are three kinds of theses in the contemporary version of Diamat: (1) old dogmatic Leninist theses; (2) new theses which are nevertheless compatible with the old; (3) genuine theses which are incompatible with the old dogmas. This heterogeneity is the beginning of the destruction of Diamat as a whole.

IHARA, Craig K. David Wong on Emotions in Mencius. Phil East West, 41(1), 45-53, Ja 91.

IHDE, Don. *Instrumental Realism: The Interface between Philosophy of Science and Philosophy of Technology*. Bloomington, Indiana Univ Pr, 1991.

Instrumental Realism is a comparative study of some recent developments in the philosophy of science as related to science's technologies. It opens by re-situating Kuhn in relation to earlier traditions in European philosophies (Husserl, Merleau-Ponty, and Foucault, and in technology, Heidegger) which stress a praxis and perception thesis. Then, turning to more recent developments, a 'school' of instrumental realists and near relations are analyzed (R Ackermann, H Dreyfus, I Hacking, P Heelan, and D Ihde, with P Galison and B Latour on experiment). A consensus is claimed concerning the necessity of a technological embodiment of science in instruments and with respect to the growth of scientific knowledge in and through such technologies.

ILLE, Pierre. Cloture Intervallaire et Extension Logique d'une Relation. Z Math Log, 36(3), 217-227, 1990.

ILLINGWORTH, Patricia M L. Explaining Without Blaming the Victim. J Soc Phil, 21(2-3), 117-126, Fall-Wint 90.

IMBROSCIO, Carmelina. "Les utopies littéraires au XVIIIe siècle" in *Égalité Uguaglianza*, FERRARI, Jean (ed), 75-80. Napoli, Liguori, 1990.

IMHOOF, Stefan. The Status of Fiction: Between Nostalgia and Nihilism (in French). Rev Theol Phil, 123(1), 99-106, 1991.

The work of Thomas Pavel entitled *Univers de la fiction* synthesizes the most recent research of literary theory. It incorporates the contributions of analytical philosophy, notably those of modal logic. According to Pavel, the reader of a work of fiction "lives" in a certain way in the world it describes. Yet one could object that a great pleasure of reading is derived, on the contrary, from the realization at each instant that one is *not* living in the fictional universe described in the text.

IMLAY, Robert A. Descartes und der reale Unterschied zwischen der Seele und dem Körper. Stud Leibniz, 22(1), 69-75, 1990.

This article is divided into four parts. Firstly, I try to show the Cartesian distinction between the mind and the body is an objective one. Secondly, I try to show that the transparence of mind and the non-transparence of body is the key. In the third part I reject the transparency of mind. In the fourth part I have some favourable things to say about Aristotelian dualism.

IMMERWAHR, John. The Anatomist and the Painter: The Continuity of Hume's *Treatise* and *Essays*. Hume Stud, 17(1), 1-14, Ap 91.

Commentators have tended to regard Hume's two early works (the *Treatise* and the *Essays, Moral and Political*) as unrelated projects. In this article, I argue that the *Essays* are the logical continuation of a chain of thought that is begun in the *Treatise* but not completed there. The logic of Hume's thought suggests that he can only continue his argument by shifting from the role of technical philosopher (anatomist) to that of a popular essayist (painter). The analysis centers primarily on a detailed reading of Hume's *Advertisements* and on the first Essay, "Of the Delicacy of Taste and Passion."

IMMERWAHR, John. Incorporating Gender Issues in Modern Philosophy. Teach Phil, 13(3), 241-252, S 90.

The following recommendations are explained and discussed: (1) focus on gender issues in writing both as they occur in classic texts and in students' own writing; (2) include discussions of those passages where major philosophers (Locke and Hume, for example) discuss gender issues; (3) discuss contemporary feminist perspectives on the classical philosophers of this period; (4) include texts of important women writers such as Anne Conway and Mary Wollstonecraft.

INCARDONA, Nunzio. Il mondo Il soggetto Lo smarrimento. G Metaf, 12(1), 3-8, Ja-Ap 90.

INCARDONA, Nunzio. Télos y arché: La physis del logos. Anu Filosof, 23(1), 133-138, 1990.

INDURKHYA, Bipin. Some Remarks on the Rationality of Induction. Synthese, 85(1), 95-114, O 90.

This paper begins with a rigorous critique of David Stove's recent book *The Rationality of Induction*. In it, Stove produced four different proofs to refute Hume's sceptical thesis about induction. I show that Stove's attempts to vindicate induction are unsuccessful. Three of his proofs refute theses that are not the sceptical thesis about induction at all. Stove's fourth proof, which uses the sampling principle to justify one particular inductive inference, makes crucial use of an unstated assumption regarding randomness. Once this assumption is made explicit, Hume's thesis once more survives. (edited)

INEICHEN, Hans. *Philosophische Hermeneutik*. Freiburg, Alber, 1991.

This book describes contemporary philosophical hermeneutics, developing its systematic approach and describing its historical development from Schleiermacher to Dilthey, Heidegger and Gadamer, and from them to Habermas, Apel and Ricoeur. Ineichen especially stresses a conception of language which preserves a relationship to the analytical philosophy of language and the theory of science. He demonstrates the complexity of the manner in which philosophical hermeneutics, as teaching about understanding an explication, brings one to the cultural and social sciences, and shows to what extent it can contribute to their better understanding.

INGARDEN, Roman. Lo que no sabemos sobre los valores. Rev Filosof (Spain), 4, 199-237, 1990.

INGHAM, Mary E. The Condemnation of 1277: Another Light on Scotist Ethics. Frei Z Phil Theol, 37(1-2), 91-103, 1990.

The purpose of this article is to highlight the importance of the Condemnation of 1277 on the development of Duns Scotus's understanding of causal freedom for moral choice and on the importance of the divine will in Scotist texts. The early distinction of nature from will in Scotus is not a dismissal of the intellect from moral life, but the difference between two distinct orders of causality. I argue that a better knowledge of historical context (1277) enhances our interpretation of Scotist ethics: his emphasis on human dignity, the prominence of the divine will, and the radical dependence of the created order. It also provides better insight into the rise of divine freedom as an important element of 14th century philosophy.

INGRAM, Attracta. The Perils of Love: Why Women Need Rights. Phil Stud (Ireland), 32, 245-262, 1988-90.

This paper offers a feminist perspective on the communitarian ethics of love as an alternative to rights-based moral theory. I argue that the contingency of love and the liability of women to exclude themselves from the web of care call for an ethic that makes room for rights as well as love. First, I describe how women may perceive and respond to the ethical options prominent in our society. Second, I argue that women need rights to secure a number of important though gender-neutral interests. Finally, I sketch a defence of rights against the charge that they destroy a politics of care.

INGRAM, David. *Critical Theory and Philosophy*. New York, Paragon House, 1990.

The book provides a nontechnical introduction to the figures, themes, and history of the Frankfurt School. The table of contents includes: The Philosophical Roots of Critical Theory (Kant, Hegel, and Marx); From Theory to Practice (Freud, Ideology, and the Frankfurt School from 1923-41); Weber and the Dialectic of Enlightenment (Lukacs, Adorno and Horkheimer); Marcuse and the New Politics of Liberation (*The Authoritarian Personality*, gative Dialectics, and *One-Dimensional Man*); Marcuse and Freud: The Instinctual Basis of Critique; Horkheimer and Habermas on Critical Methodology and its Rationale ("Traditional and Critical Theory" and *Knowledge and Human Interests*); Communication and Social Crisis: Habermas and Recent Critical Theory; The Critique of Ideology and the Dialectic of Reason Reconsidered; Critical Theory Confronts Postmodernism, Poststructuralism, and Feminism.

INGRAM, David. Dworkin, Habermas, and the CLS Movement on Moral Criticism in Law. Phil Soc Crit, 16(4), 237-268, 1990.

CLS advocates renew Marx's critique of liberalism by impugning the rationality of formal rights. Habermas and Dworkin argue against this view, while showing how liberal polity might permit reasonable conflicts between competing principles of right. Their models of legitimate legislation and adjudication, however, presuppose criteria of rationality whose appeal to truth ignores the manner in which law is—and sometimes ought to be—compromised. Hence a weaker version of the CLS critique may be applicable after all. I begin by discussing Weber's exclusion of morality from law. After criticizing economic and functionalist legal theory I show that the inconsistencies CLS scholars find in liberal doctrine are exaggerated. I conclude with a discussion of Dworkin and Habermas.

INGRASSIA, Michael A and LEMPP, Steffen. Jumps of Nontrivial Splittings of Recursively Enumerable Sets. Z Math Log, 36(4), 285-292, 1990.

INNERARITY, Carmen. La comprensión aristotélica del trabajo. Anu Filosof, 23(2), 69-108, 1990.

INNERARITY, Daniel. Las disonancias de la libertad (I). Anu Filosof, 23(1), 79-98, 1990.

INNERARITY, Daniel. Filosofía y rebeldía. Dialogo Filosof, 7(1), 95-108, Ja-Ap 91.

INNERARITY, Daniel. El idealismo alemán como mitología de la razón. Pensamiento, 47(185), 37-78, Ja-Mr 91.

Se trata de analizar el contenido de un documento que ha sido considerado como el acta fundacional del idealismo alemán. La controvertida cuestión de su autoría no se salda con una respuesta definitiva, aunque se rechaza como escasamente plausible la hipótesis de que Schelling fuera su autor. Pero lo decisivo no es tanto esta discusión técnica como el programa idealista que en este texto se contiene para los campos de la ética, la estética y la filosofía política y de la religión. En el trasfondo se encuentra la primera gran revisión de la idea moderna de libertad.

INNESS, Julie. Information, Access, or Intimate Decisions About One's Action? The Content of Privacy. Pub Affairs Quart, 5(3), 227-242, Jl 91.

An agent possesses privacy to the extent that she has control over aspects of her life. But which aspects? Three lines of response emerge from the legal and philosophical literature: privacy concerns information about oneself; privacy concerns access to oneself; privacy concerns intimate decisions about one's action. This paper contends that privacy involves all three areas. These apparently disparate areas of privacy are linked together by the common denominator of intimacy: privacy is the state of the agent having control over a realm of intimacy, a realm which contains an agent's decisions about intimate physical and informational access to herself and her decisions about her intimate actions.

INSALL, Matt and GEHRKE, Mai and KAISER, Klaus. Some Nonstandard Methods Applied to Distributive Lattices. Z Math Log, 36(2), 123-131, 1990.

It follows from the concurrency principle and local finiteness, that any distributive lattice D is contained in a hyperfinite lattice extension H. The paper investigates Stone duality, in particular completeness and Sikorski's lemma, in this setting. The familiar characterization of open and compact sets, due to A Robinson, led us to a class of lattices, the "R-lattices," which is broader than Boolean algebras and finite lattice theory, but strictly contained in the class of lattices subject to the TD-axiom for the underlying Stone space.

IRIBARNE, Julia V. *La intersubjectividad en Husserl, Volume I and II*. Buenos Aires, Ed Carlos Lohle, 1988.

This work offers an interpretation of Husserl's phenomenological philosophy as a new monadology. It emerges from a complementary study of the philosopher's early published statements or empathy and intersubjectivity and of his deep analysis of these issues in his manuscripts edited as *Zur Phänomenologie der Intersubjectivtät, I, II and III*. The phenomenological reduction being applied either to the meditating ego or to the world, it is by means of the statical approach—and even more fruitfully through the genetical approach—that appears the radical intersubjective intertwining. This is shown from the most original pre-reflective stratum, up to the highest constituted stratum, i.e. society and the interweaving of person.

IRIBARNE, Julia V. La problemática ética en el pensamiento de Husserl. Dianoia, 36(36), 51-60, 1990.

IRIGARAY, Luce. "Love between Us" in *Who Comes after the Subject?*, CADAVA, Eduardo (ed), 167-177. New York, Routledge, 1991.

IRIGARAY, Luce and WHITFORD, Margaret (trans). "Questions to Emmanuel Levinas: On the Divinity of Love" in *Re-Reading Levinas*, BERNASCONI, Robert (ed), 109-118. Bloomington, Indiana Univ Pr, 1991.

In this paper, Irigaray discusses alterity, and specifically the alterity of sexual difference, which she finds absent in Levinas's account of otherness. She argues that without sexual difference, society and religion are ethically at fault. The divinity of love, the spiritual dimension of the carnal relationship, and the recognition of women's subjectivity, are essential for the renewal of ethics, religion and society.

IRMSCHER, Johannes. Friedrich Nietzsche and Classical Philology Today. Hist Euro Ideas, 11, 963-966, 1989.

Nietzsche had achieved full mastery of philology as it was practised in his day, including the use of Latin as the language of the academic community. So there were good reasons for his extraordinary career in Basel. But early on Nietzsche began to feel uneasy about the stereotyped patterns that marked the groves of academe, which had become increasingly divorced from practical life and failed to make any impact on society. So he approached the study of Greek and Roman antiquity with new questions derived from adjacent disciplines and from the intellectual battles of his time. He found himself aligned with his Basel colleague Jacob Burckhardt, whom he looked upon as a teacher; his superior in Basel, Wilhelm-Vischer-Bilfinger, who was the same age as himself; and Johann Jacob Bachofen, a professor in Basel (the place where he died in 1887) from 1841 to 1843. The answers which Nietzsche came up with to these questions are a matter of controversy everywhere. But this cannot erase the fact that he explored uncharted territory, preserving the study of antiquity from lapsing into sterility.

IROEGBU, Pantaleon. La pensée de Rawls face au défi communautarien. Rev Phil Louvain, 89(81), 113-128, F 91.

IRONS, William. How Did Morality Evolve? Zygon, 26(1), 49-89, Mr 91.

This paper presents and criticizes Alexander's evolutionary theory of morality (1987). Earlier research, on which Alexander's theory is based, is also reviewed. The propensity to create moral systems evolved because it allowed ancestral humans to limit conflict within cooperating groups and thus form larger groups, which were advantageous because of intense between-group competition. Alexander sees moral codes as contractual, and the primary criticism of his theory is that moral codes are not completely contractual but also coercive. Ways of evaluating Alexander's theory as well as modified versions of it are discussed.

IRVINE, Andrew D (ed). *Physicalism in Mathematics*. Norwell, Kluwer, 1990.

This collection of all new papers on recent issues in the philosophy of mathematics includes contributions by John Bigelow, James Brown, John Burgess, Chandler Davis, Yvon Gauthier, Bob Hale, Michael Hallett, Geoffrey Hellman, Penelope Maddy, David Papineau, Michael Resnik, Peter Simons, Alasdair Urquhart, and Crispin Wright. Topics discussed include nominalism and realism in mathematics, Hilbert's programme, Hellman's modal-structural account of mathematics, and the possibility of developing a general semantics for mathematics which is physicalistically acceptable. Philosophers and mathematicians discussed include Benacerraf, Cantor, Dedekind, Dummett, Field, Frege, Gödel, Hilbert, Kitcher, Kronecker, Poincaré, Putnam and Quine. The book will be of primary interest to researchers in the philosophy of mathematics and to others interested in traditional philosophical problems concerning realism, nominalism, and the epistemology of abstract entities.

IRVINE, William B. "Can National Health Insurance Solve the Crisis in Health Care?" in *Biomedical Ethics Reviews, 1990*, HUMBER, James M (ed), 61-86. Clifton, Humana Pr, 1991.

Some form of national health insurance may soon be enacted in America. Many supporters of national health insurance have argued that such a plan would make American health care more affordable. In my paper, I first describe some of the causes of the high cost of health care in America. I go on to argue that these costs are not likely to be reduced by the enactment of national health insurance. I conclude by suggesting that a better way to deal with America's health care crisis is by weakening the monopoly status of health care professions in America.

IRVINE, William B. "The Case for Physician-Dispensed Drugs" in *Biomedical Ethics Reviews, 1989*, HUMBER, James M (ed), 59-73. Clifton, Humana Pr, 1990.

IRWIN, T H. Aristippus Against Happiness. Monist, 74(1), 55-82, Ja 91.

IRWIN, T H. "Aristotle's Philosophy of Mind" in *Psychology (Companions to Ancient Thought: 2)*, EVERSON, Stephen (ed), 56-83. New York, Cambridge Univ Pr, 1991.

IRWIN, T H. The Scope of Deliberation: A Conflict in Aquinas. Rev Metaph, 44(1), 21-42, S 90.

IRZIK, Gürol. Singular Causation and Law. Proc Phil Sci Ass, 1, 537-543, 1990.

Humean accounts of law are at the same time accounts of causation. Accordingly, since laws are nothing but contingent cosmic regularities, to be a cause is just to be an instance of such a law. Every particular cause-effect pair, according to these accounts, instantiates some law of nature. I argue that this claim is false. Singular causation without being governed by any law is logically and physically possible. Separating causes from laws enables us to see the distinct role each plays in science, especially in matters related to prediction and explanation.

ISHIGURO, Hide. *Leibniz's Philosophy of Logic and Language (Second Edition)*. New York, Cambridge Univ Pr, 1990.

ISHIHARA, Hajime. Constructive Compact Operators on a Hilbert Space. Annals Pure Applied Log, 52(1-2), 31-37, Ap 91.

ISHIHARA, Hajime. An Omniscience Principle, the König Lemma and the Hahn-Banach Theorem. Z Math Log, 36(3), 237-240, 1990.

ISRAELI, A and DALHAUS, E and MAKOWSKY, J A. On the Existence of Polynomial Time Algorithms for Interpolation Problems in Propositional Logic. Notre Dame J Form Log, 29(4), 497-509, Fall 88.

Let G and H be two (possibly quantified) propositional formulas with $x_1,...,x_n$ the only common variables such that $G \rightarrow H$ is valid. An interpolant $I(x_1,...x_n)$ is a quantifier-free propositional formula such that both $G \rightarrow I$ and $I \rightarrow H$ are valid. We study the complexity of finding such an interpolant and show that this problem is intimately related to the complexity hierarchy between logarithmic and polynomial space. Especially, we show that the interpolation problem for certain formula classes is of the same degree of difficulty as the corresponding satisfiability problem.

IVANOV, Lyubomir. Operative versus Combinatory Spaces. J Sym Log, 55(2), 561-572, Je 90.

IZUZQUIZA, Ignacio. *George Santayana y la Ironia de la Materia*. Barcelona, Anthropos, 1989.

This essay proposes an analysis of George Santayana's paradoxical materialism as a way of studying the whole architecture of Santayana's philosophy. In the book, the main philosophical issues of Santayana's ontology and epistemology are criticized. The conceptual relevance of concepts as "nature" and "matter" are put in relationship with the concepts of "spirit" and "essence". A special significance is given to concept of "essence" as an original way of combining ontology and epistemology. Also studies is Santayana's anthropological and sociological proposals in connection with his ontology. The point is marked on the tragical character of Santayana's whole philosophy.

IZUZQUIZA, Ignacio. *Hegel: o la rebelión contra el límite*. Zaragoza, Univ Zaragoza, 1990.

In this study an intent to reconstruct Hegel's thought is proposed. The concept of "limit" is a central perspective for establishing a coherent lecture of Hegelian philosophy. The war against dualism and scission is a first point of Hegelian thought present in young and mature Hegel's philosophy. The analysis of essential concepts in Hegel's philosophy (spirit, concept, freedom, good, will) shows them as steps in the destruction of limit inherited in the Kantian tradition. The reivindication of the unity between ontology, logic and ethical proposals, throughout the whole Hegelian production is claimed in the essay.

IZUZQUIZA, Ignacio. *La sociedad sin hombres: Niklas Luhmann o la teoría como escándalo*. Barcelona, Anthropos, 1990.

This essay presents Niklas Luhmann's sociological theory and its philosophical implications. Luhmann provides a new theory for sociological analysis of contemporary society, with aid of recent methodological instruments, such as paradox theory, communication theory, observation theory, autopietic systems theory, etc. For Luhmann, society is an autopoietic and self-referent system of communications which develops towards a progressive complexity. Each of social system—economy, law, politics, education, etc.—has its own way of reducing complexity. Luhmann reivindicates the necessity of a new method of analysis in social sciences distant from the traditional humanism of sociological tradition.

JABLONKA, Eva and ETTINGER, Lia and FALK, Raphael. On Causality, Heritability and Fitness. Biol Phil, 6(1), 27-29, Ja 91.

We comment on Byerly's and Michod's paper "Fitness and evolutionary explanation". We emphasize that fitness should be attributed to types only, and not to individuals. We define fitness as the measure of the causal and heritable contribution of a trait to the reproductive success of individuals (representing a type) which possess this trait, in a specific environment. The research program of evolutionary biologists studying the evolution of adaptations is realized when the fitness of a certain type is found.

JABLONKA, Eva and ETTINGER, Lia and MC LAUGHLIN, Peter. On the Adaptations of Organisms and the Fitness of Types. Phil Sci, 57(3), 499-513, S 90.

We claim that much of the confusion associated with the "tautology problem" about survival of the fittest is due to the mistake of attributing fitness to individuals instead of to types. We argue further that the problem itself cannot be solved merely by taking fitness as the aggregate cause of reproductive success. We suggest that a satisfying explanation must center not on logical analysis of the concept of general adaptedness but on the empirical analysis of single adapted traits and their causal relationship to changes in allele frequencies.

JACK, Julie. "Meaning—Norms and Objectivity" in *Logic and Ethics*, GEACH, Peter (ed), 167-197. Norwell, Kluwer, 1991.

JACKENDOFF, Ray. *Consciousness and the Computational Mind*. Cambridge, MIT Pr, 1989.

JACKENDOFF, Ray. The Problem of Reality. Nous, 25(4), 411-434, S 91.

Two alternative views of the fundamental question of a theory of mind are compared. The "philosophical" view asks how we can have knowledge of reality-beliefs and desires about things in the world; the "psychological" view asks how the brain functions such that the world seems to us the way it does. Examining representative problems in the areas of vision, language, music, social cognition, and body representation, it is shown that the "philosophical" view leads to intractable problems, while the "psychological" view leads to productive questions for research. A number of reasons are explored as to why the "philosophical" view of our relation to reality seems so compelling, despite its inadequacy in the face of empirical problems.

JACKENDOFF, Ray. *Semantic Structures*. Cambridge, MIT Pr, 1990.

This study is a large-scale exploration of the mental representation of concepts and their lexical and syntactic expression in English, building on the author's earlier books *Semantics and Cognition* and *Consciousness and the Computational Mind*. Besides discussing the conceptual structures of hundreds of words and constructions, the book deals with such crucial issues as Fodor's Language of Thought Hypothesis; 0-roles and 0-marking; arguments, modifiers, and adjuncts; binding and control; and the thematic linking hierarchy.

JACKSON, Bernard S. On Scholarly Developments in Legal Semiotics. Ratio Juris, 3(3), 415-424, D 90.

This article suggests that legal semiotics may mediate between the normativism of legal positivism and the scepticism of legal realism as to the concept of legal "validity." Equally, legal semiotics offers new tools for the study of the alleged unity of the legal system. It may also contribute to the enterprise of legal sociology, to the discursive readings of legal texts, and to the analysis of legal language. The literature on these various methods is briefly surveyed. The article concludes by documenting the activities of the International Association for the Semiotics of Law (conferences and publications), the Centre for Semiotic Research in Law, Government and Economics at Penn State University, and other colloquia in Europe and elsewhere.

JACKSON, Frank and PETTIT, Philip. Causation in the Philosophy of Mind. Phil Phenomenol Res, 50 SUPP, 195-214, Fall 90.

AUTHOR INDEX WITH ABSTRACTS 505 JACQUETTE, Dale

Causation has come to play an increasingly important role in the philosophy of mind, reaching its apotheosis in the doctrine that to be a mental state of kind K is to fill the causal role definitive of that kind of mental state. Ironically, there is, from this very functionalist perspective, a problem about how to understand the causal role of mental properties. This problem surfaces in the debates over the language of thought, over broad content, and over the eliminativist implications of connectionism. We offer a solution to the problem, and then apply it to the debate over connectionism and eliminativism.

JACKSON, Frank. Classifying Conditionals II. Analysis, 51(3), 137-143, Je 91.

Consider (1) If Booth had not killed Lincoln, someone else would have; (2) If Booth does not kill Lincoln, someone else will; and (3) If Booth did not kill Lincoln, someone else did. Many writers agree that (1) is importantly different from (3). The issue this paper is concerned with is where to place (2). In "Classifying Conditionals", *Analysis*, Volume 50, Number 2, March 1990, I argue that semantically speaking (2) should go with (1). I defend this contention against criticisms by V H Dudman and E J Lowe in *Analysis*, Volume 51, Number 3, June 1991.

JACKSON, Jennifer. "Against Tolerating the Intolerable" in *Logic and Ethics*, GEACH, Peter (ed), 131-144. Norwell, Kluwer, 1991.

The purpose of this article is to point up an asymmetry between opposing parties on controversial moral issues such as abortion. This asymmetry makes a nonsense of appeals for mutual tolerance. While everyone understands that practices which are uncontroversially wicked ought not to be tolerated, in respect of practices which are controversial, it may be said, we must respect each other's views—agree to disagree. But while toleration is comprehensible from those on one side: those who view a practice as innocent, it makes no sense from those on the other side: those who view a practice as wicked.

JACKSON, M W. Marx's 'Critique of Hegel's *Philosophy of Right*'. Hist Euro Ideas, 12(6), 799-811, 1990.

Karl Marx's unpublished critique of Georg Hegel's *Philosophy of Right* reads subsequent Prussian history back into Hegel's text. The context in which Hegel wrote the *Philosophy of Right* was one of nascent liberalism. The text of *Philosophy of Right* offers a picture of limited constitutional monarchy. The reactionary period that shed Marx's experience of Prussia came after Hegel and was partly aimed at suppressing Hegel's teaching for its perceived liberalism. To attribute the evils of the reaction to Hegel's political theory is like attributing the evils of Stalinism to Marx's economic theory.

JACKSON, Timothy P. The Possibilities of Scepticisms: Philosophy and Theology without Apology. Metaphilosophy, 21(4), 303-321, O 90.

Some philosophers judge scepticism to be meaningful but demonstrably false; others judge it to be meaningful and probably true; still others judge it to be meaningless and thus neither true nor false. How are we to clarify and/or adjudicate such disputes? I address this question by providing a taxonomy of scepticisms. This allows me to point out the strengths and weaknesses of several modern epistemological projects, as well as to locate them in a larger philosophical and theological context. I argue that rationality in any area of inquiry can be distinguished from both foundationalism and nihilism, and I support this by defending a form of metascepticism.

JACOB, Pierre. Externalism Revisited: Is There Such a Thing as Narrow Content? Phil Stud, 60(3), 143-176, N 90.

This paper offers an interpretation of Tyler Burge's famous thought experiment consistent with individualism. I offer pragmatic reasons to reject Burge's analysis of belief-ascriptions. Then I criticize the view that the contribution made by the proposition expressed by the 'that'-clause to the truth-conditions of the whole belief-ascription is identical to the content of the believer's thought. On my view the proposition expressed by the 'that'-clause in a belief-ascription is an *interpretation* of the believer's thought.

JACOBS, Jo Ellen. Identifying Musical Works of Art. J Aes Educ, 24(4), 75-85, Wint 90.

I propose that we should abandon the views of musical work as an ideal, a type, a megatype, or a compliance-class and simply acknowledge a musical work and a performance are synonymous. In much of the great Western music, the composer creates a score that is a blueprint for creating music that is heard as it is performed. However, locating the musical work in a performance corresponds closely to our aesthetic experience of *all* types of music (including ragas, jazz, aleatoric and other types of music not usually considered) and to the judgments critics and listeners make of music.

JACOBS, Jonathan A. *Being True to the World: Moral Realism and Practical Wisdom*. New York, Lang, 1990.

A realist account of practical wisdom is developed, chiefly in response to relativism. It is argued that there are objective moral facts and that they can be action-guiding. The role of moral imagination is explored and it is shown how realism can also enable us to better understand immorality, revealing it to involve error, ignorance or falsification. The role of social relations in the formation of self-conceptions and the development of moral knowledge and moral imagination is also examined.

JACOBS, Jonathan. Moral Imagination, Objectivity, and Practical Wisdom. Int Phil Quart, 31(1), 23-37, Mr 91.

Neither formal considerations of practical reason nor considerations of sensibility are adequate to account for the moral appreciation of other persons (and even ourselves). This appreciation, and the recognition of the moral significance of circumstances, actions and characters is an activity and product of moral imagination. It is explained how conception, affect and volition are joined in moral imagination and how the latter figures in deliberation and action.

JACOBS, Jonathan and ZEIS, John. The Unity of the Vices. Thomist, 54(4), 641-653, O 90.

The doctrine of the unity of the virtues is defended via a consideration of the unity of the vices.

JACOBS, Struan. Bentham, Science and the Construction of Jurisprudence. Hist Euro Ideas, 12(5), 583-594, 1990.

Bentham's jurisprudence, particularly as it appears in *An Introduction to the Principles of Morals and Legislation,* is examined in relation to science. The widely accepted view of Elie Halevy (in *The Growth of Philosophical Radicalism*) than Bentham conceives the principle of utility as the ethical counterpart to Newton's law of gravitation is criticized and rejected, as is the contention that David Hartley's association psychology shapes Bentham's outlook. My main positive argument is that Bentham's scientific model for jurisprudence is the botanical system in Carl Linnaeus's *Systema Naturae*.

JACOBS, Struan. John Stuart Mill on Induction and Hypothesis. J Hist Phil, 29(1), 69-83, Ja 91.

A study of the development of Mill's thought through successive editions of *A System of Logic*. His view of the genesis of most scientific laws, it is argued, progressively shifted from inductivism to hypothetico-deductivism. Mill's analysis of hypotheses and of methods for their assessment is considered in detail. New light is shed on relations between Mill's metascience and that of William Whewell.

JACOBS, Struan. Post-Liberalism versus Temperate Liberalism. Crit Rev, 4(3), 365-375, Sum 90.

John Gray's recent critique of liberalism, and his case for an apparently relativistic "post-Pyrrhonian" political philosophy, are shown to be wanting. Weaknesses in Gray's critique are identified and discussed: the characterization of liberalism as universally prescriptive, confusion about whether liberalism is a genuine tradition, and misunderstanding of the relation between conduct and the value of freedom. A formulation of liberalism that is not universalist ("temperate" liberalism) is offered, and it is shown that one of liberalism's vital concerns—controlling political power in order to protect freedom—is a hiatus in Gray's theory.

JACOBS, Wilhelm G. Ideal and Morality (in German). Deut Z Phil, 38(9), 801-808, 1990.

With "ideal" is intended an idea, which never can be real, but which let appear the reality always as insufficient. But morality demands its realization and maintains it as possible. Also isn't and hasn't morality an ideal.

JACOBSEN, Rockney. Economic Efficiency and the Quality of Life. J Bus Ethics, 10(3), 201-209, Mr 91.

A classical moral defense of profit seeking as the social responsibility of business in a competitive market is examined. That defense rests on claims about the directness of relationships between (a) profit seeking activity and standards of living and (b) standards of living and the quality of life. Responses to the classical argument tend to raise doubts about the directness of the first relationship. This essay challenges the directness of the second relationship, argues that the classical argument is invalid, and claims that an alternative description of the social responsibility of business is entailed by the classical premisses.

JACQUES, Francis and ROTHWELL, Andrew (trans). *Difference and Subjectivity: Dialogue and Personal Identity*. New Haven, Yale Univ Pr, 1991.

JACQUES, Robert A. The Tragic World of John Dewey. J Value Inq, 25(3), 249-261, Jl 91.

Traditionally and uncritically Dewey has been considered an optimist. But even a casual reading of any of his major works, not to mention his own dictionary definitions of optimism, belie the claim. Man stands immersed in an overwhelmingly indifferent, intermittently hostile, and ultimately obliterating nature. But Dewey is not accordingly a pessimist. For he is an advocate of social scientific action, the increase of man's estate even against the backdrop of its tenuousness and ultimate futility. In contrast to Nietzsche's often hyperbolical celebrations of tragedy and danger, Dewey presents us with a manifest and tragic attitude toward life.

JACQUETTE, Dale. Aesthetics and Natural Law in Newton's Methodology. J Hist Ideas, 51(4), 659-666, O-D 90.

The universality of natural law, as universal gravitation and the Three Laws of Motion of the *Principia Mathematica Philosophiae Naturalis* paradigmatically exemplify, is not discovered according to Newton, but made an aesthetic precondition for any generalization about natural phenomena correctly to be identified as law. Newton's concept of natural law is examined in light of its aesthetic virtues of simplicity, generality, universality, fecundity of explanation, and reference to idealized nonexistent objects and conditions extrapolated from local experimental progressions, as they appear in his occasional methodological remarks and *scholia* of the *Principia* and *Opticks*.

JACQUETTE, Dale. Fear and Loathing (and Other Intentional States) in Searle's Chinese Room. Phil Psych, 3(2-3), 287-304, 1990.

John R Searle's problem of the Chinese Room poses an important philosophical challenge to the foundations of strong artificial intelligence, and functionalist, cognitivist, and computationalist theories of mind. Searle has recently responded to three categories of criticisms of the Chinese Room and the consequences he attempts to conclude from it, redescribing the essential features of the problem, and offering new arguments about the syntax-semantics gap it is intended to demonstrate. Despite Searle's defense, the Chinese Room remains ineffective as a counterexample, and poses no real threat to artificial intelligence or mechanist philosophy of mind. The thesis that intentionality is a primitive irreducible relation exemplified by biological phenomena is preferred in opposition to Searle's contrary claim that intentionality is a biological phenomenon exhibiting abstract properties.

JACQUETTE, Dale. Moral Dilemmas, Disjunctive Obligations, and Kant's Principle that 'Ought' Implies 'Can'. Synthese, 88(1), 43-55, Jl 91.

In moral dilemmas, where circumstances prevent two or more equally justified *prima facie* ethical requirements from being fulfilled, it is often maintained that, since the agent cannot do both, conjoint obligation is overridden by Kant's principle that 'ought' implies 'can', but that the agent nevertheless has a disjunctive obligation to perform one of the otherwise obligatory actions or the other. Against this commonly received view, it is demonstrated that although Kant's ought-can principle may avoid logical inconsistency, the principle is incompatible with disjunctive obligation in standard deontic logic, and that it entails paradoxically that none of the conflicting dilemma actions will in fact occur. The principle appears to provide the only plausible safeguard against deontic antinomy, but cannot be admitted because of its collision with considered moral judgements.

JACQUETTE, Dale (trans) and PRESBURGER, Mojzesz. On the Completeness of a Certain System of Arithmetic of Whole Numbers in Which Addition Occurs as the Only Operation. Hist Phil Log, 12(2), 225-233, 1991.

Presburger's essay on the completeness and decidability of arithmetic with integer addition but without multiplication is a milestone in the history of mathematical logic and formal metatheory. The proof is constructive, using Tarski-style quantifier elimination and a four-part recursive comprehension principle for axiomatic consequence characterization. Presburger's proof for the completeness of first order arithmetic with identity and addition but without multiplication, in light of the restrictive formal metatheorems of Gödel, Church, and Rosser, takes the foundations of arithmetic in mathematical logic to the limits of completeness and decidability.

JACQUETTE, Dale. Wittgenstein and the Color Incompatibility Problem. Hist Phil Quart, 7(3), 353-365, Jl 90.

The transition in Wittgenstein's thought from the early to the later period, his rejection of logical atomism and the picture theory of meaning, is explained as a consequence of his dissatisfaction with the *Tractatus* solution to the color incompatibility problem. The argument is supported by historical evidence from F P Ramsey's critical review of Wittgenstein's logic, and a close examination of Wittgenstein's essay "Some Remarks on Logical Form," and the posthumous writings in which he sketches a philosophical grammar of color.

JÄGER, Gerhard. "Non-Monotonic Reasoning by Axiomatic Extensions" in *Logic, Methodology and Philosophy of Science, VIII*, FENSTAD, J E (ed), 93-110. New York, Elsevier Science, 1989.

JAGGAR, Alison M. "Feminist Ethics: Projects, Problems, Prospects" in *Feminist Ethics*, CARD, Claudia (ed), 78-104. Lawrence, Univ Pr of Kansas, 1991.

JAKI, Stanley. Cosmology and Religion. Phil Sci (Tucson), 4, 47-81, 1990.

The mutual coexistence between the natural sciences and religious thought results in many philosophically inspiring controversies. After approaching their background from the standpoint of the history of science, the author focuses upon ontological comments found in scientific theories belonging to modern cosmology. When defending the specific cognitive status of ontological questions, he determines an epistemological stance opposite to the one accepted by Stephen Hawking in his philosophy of creation.

JAKIC, Mirko. Putnam and Truth (in Serbo-Croatian). Filozof Istraz, 34(1), 181-194, 1990.

The paper presents an analysis and critique of Putnam's opinions about A Tarski's correspondence theory. The first part of the paper identifies and analyzes Putnam's positions from the first, externalist period of his philosophy of science. The second part analyzes the positions characterizing the second, internalist period of Putnam's philosophical thinking. The text indicates which are the basic causes of the changes in Putnam's approach to this theory of truth, which has a dominant position in the contemporary philosophy of science. The third part of the paper is a critique of all the individual notions held by Putnam in respect of the correspondence theory. The three parts of the paper are entitled as follows: (I) "Truth in the Extensionalist Period of Putnam's Philosophical Thinking," (II) "Truth in the Internalist Period of Putnam's Philosophical Thinking," and (III) "A Critique of Putnam's Notions of Truth."

JAKOVLJEVIC, Dragan. Questions of "Analytical" and "Non-Analytical" Philosophy (in Serbo Croatian). Filozof Istraz, 34(1), 31-40, 1990.

Im Aufsatz wird eine ganz allgemeine Auslegung der Differenz zwischen den sog. "analytischen" und den restlichen, "nichtanalytischen" Philosophien versucht, und anschliessend die Folgen, die sich aus jener Differenz für die Verständigungsprozesse zwischen den beiden Ausrichtungen gehörigen Philosophen ergeben kurz erörtert. Die angesprochene Differenz wird *auf der meta*-theoretischen Ebene loziert: sie ist *nicht* in den unterschiedlichen *Theorien* zu Fragen der Philosophie, sondern in den unterschiedlichen *me-thodologischen* und heuristischen *Auffassungen zu Fragen der philosophischen* Theorien*bildung* zu sehen. (edited)

JAKUSZKO, Honorata. The Academic Lehrjahre of Novalis—A Period of Search for His Own View of History (in Polish). Ann Univ Mariae Curie-Phil, 11, 161-176, 1986.

The aim of the article is a presentation of the development and transformations of the philosophical conceptions of Novalis which took place during his studies in Jena (1790-94). The author defends a thesis that the essense of these changes—which occurred under the influence of the thought of F Shlegel and F Schiller—consisted in Novalis discarding the Enlightenment vision of history for the sake of a conception which he called *Bildungsgeschichte*.

JAMBOR, Mishka. Sartre on Anguish. Phil Today, 34(2), 111-116, Sum 90.

JAMES, David N. Abortion, Coercive Pregnancy, and Adoption. Phil Context, 20, 53-64, 1990.

This paper responds to George Schedler's articles in the 1989 issue of *Philosophy in Context*. Schedler argues that restricting access to late abortions is justified on the basis of the instrumental value of fetuses to childless couples seeking to adopt newborns. Even if we leave aside worries about Schedler's view of justice, his utilitarian case for this proposal is defective because he underestimates the burdens of coercive pregnancy and overestimates the burdens of childless couples. I agree with Schedler that the interests of childless couples deserve moral consideration and increased social support, and suggest some non-coercive ways to do this.

JAMES, George A. Religion, Nothingness, and the Challenge of Post-Modern Thought: An Introduction to the Philosophy of K Nishitani. Int Phil Quart, 31(3), 295-308, S 91.

JAMES, William. Education for Judgment. Thinking, 9(3), 5-7, 1990.

JAMIESON, Dale. "Method and Moral Theory" in *A Companion to Ethics*, SINGER, Peter (ed), 476-487. Cambridge, Blackwell, 1991.

This paper is a survey of contemporary views of method and moral theory. It discusses the nature of moral theories, the methods of theorizing, and the role of examples.

JAMISON, David L and GOLDEN, James L. Meyer's Theory of Problematology. Rev Int Phil, 44(174), 329-351, 1990.

JAMME, Christoph. Hegel as Advocate of Machiavelli (in German). Deut Z Phil, 38(7), 629-638, 1990.

The article deals with the reception of Machiavelli by Hegel under the question: is Hegel a prerunner of modern totalitarianism? In the center of the interpretation stands the writing "Die Verfassung "Deutschlands," but also other texts like the "Philosophie des Rechts."

JAMROS, Daniel P. 'The Appearing God' in Hegel's *Phenomenology of Spirit*. Clio, 19(4), 353-365, Sum 90.

This article examines the phrase "der erscheinende Gott" from the conclusion of "Evil and its Pardon" in Hegel's *Phenomenology of Spirit*. When evil is pardoned, God appears. This appearance emerges from the discovery that an evil selfish consciousness is also a good universal consciousness, and therefore should be pardoned by the latter. Although it is difficult to identify the precise historical or literary situation Hegel had in mind, the section can still be appreciated as the incarnational basis for the *Phenomenology*'s chapter on religion: God appears because universal essence appears as the universal thinking of individual human consciousness.

JANAT, B. Humble Rebel Henry David Thoreau (in Czechoslovakian). Filozof Cas, 38(3), 273-281, 1990.

This study contemplates the life and work of this distinguished 19th century philosopher, particularly as seen from the viewpoint of the course and final stage of the 20th century. If the 19th century represents a spiritual prelude to the 20th century, then it is possible to name three thinkers whose ideas are fatefully projected in or still lie in wait as a source of inspiration of possible future in the last decade of the second millennium. Revolutions, wars and totalitarian states constitute a historical and political equivalent of Marx's and Nietzsche's ideas. Henry David Thoreau, a lesser-known and lesser epoch-making thinker, opens up and embodies a completely new path. (edited)

JANAWAY, Christopher. Plato's Analogy between Painter and Poet. Brit J Aes, 31(1), 1-12, Ja 91.

The paper offers a new interpretation of *Republic* Book 10 (598b-601b). Plato's example of the painter who paints images of a succession of craftsmen is argued to provide a sensible analogy with Homeric or tragic poets who produce 'images of excellence and all the other things they write about'. These poets are Plato's main target in Book 10. Plato supports the analogy with an argument directed against the assumption that to write poetry about a subject, one requires knowledge of it. The overall claim Plato makes is that poets who make convincing representations do not do so from knowledge.

JANICAUD, Dominique. Reconstructing the Political. Grad Fac Phil J, 14(2)-15(1), 137-151, 1991.

JANIK, J A. An Attempt at Interpretation of the Thomistic Hylomorphic Theory in View of Contemporary Physics. Phil Sci (Tucson), 2, 47-51, 1986.

Vibrations in a crystal lattice as excited states of this lattice, are quasi-particles (phonons) in the crystal, which is their "physical environment." It is suggested that physical objects known generally as particles, e.g., photons or electrons, are also quasi-particles of other physical environments. Thus we have a physical space, which fills the entire universe and which is the sum of various physical environments, and its excited states - particles, or rather quasi-particles. Phonons in a crystal are now interpreted, in view of hylomorphic theory, by suggesting that vibrational waves (acts of motion) are forms (formae), which actualize phonons; the crystal lattice is in this case the prime matter (materia prima). It is suggested that the term prime matter should be relativized, i.e., it should be introduced for a given class of material beings. It is possible that absolute prime matter should be identified with the above-mentioned physical space, whose excited states are forms actualizing material beings.

JANKE, Wolfgang. Anerkennung: Fichtes Grundlegungen des Rechtsgrundes. Kantstudien, 82(2), 197-218, 1991.

JANKE, Wolfgang. Von der dreifachen Vollendung des Deutschen Idealismus und der unvollendeten metaphysischen Wahrheit. Deut Z Phil, 39(3), 304-320, 1991.

JANSSEN, M C W and TAN, Y H. Why Friedman's Non-Monotonic Reasoning Defies Hempel's Covering Law Model. Synthese, 86(2), 255-284, F 91.

In this paper we will show that Hempel's covering law model can't deal very well with explanations that are based on incomplete knowledge. In particular the symmetry thesis, which is an important aspect of the covering law model, turns out to be problematic for these explanations. We will discuss an example of an electric circuit, which clearly indicates that the symmetry of explanation and prediction does not always hold. It will be argued that an alternative logic for causal explanation is needed. And we will investigate to what extent non-monotonic epistemic logic can provide such an alternative logical framework. Finally we will show that our non-monotonic logical analysis of explanation is not only suitable for simple cases such as the electric circuit, but that it also sheds new light on more controversial causal explanations such as Milton Friedman's explanation of the business cycle.

JANSSEN, Paul and STRÖKER, Elisabeth. *Phänomenologische Philosophie*. Freiburg, Alber, 1991.

This presentation of phenomenological philosophy focusses on the fundamental impulse which is at its core a philosophical method. It presents the most important themes dealt with by significant representatives of phenomenology — especially by Brentano, Husserl, Reinach, Gurwitsch, Schütz, Scheler, Heidegger, Sartre, Merleau-Ponty, Levinas—and their schools or the general approaches to which they belonged. Here it emphasizes the phenomenological method which constitutes the unity of phenomenological philosophy.

JANTZEN, Grace M. "'Where Two Are to Become One': Mysticism and Monism" in *The Philosophy in Christianity*, VESEY, Godfrey (ed), 147-166. New York, Cambridge Univ Pr, 1989.

JANUSZ, Sharon and WEBSTER, Glenn. In Defence of Heidegger. Philosophy, 66(257), 380-385, Jl 91.

In his essay "Heidegger's Quest for Being", *Philosophy*, October 1989, Volume 64, Paul Edwards unfairly attacks Martin Heidegger's philosophy. Among Edward's contentions: Heidegger "was looking for the referent of 'exists'" (467). Such is not the case; although, Heidegger is most interested in existence, judging existence as marvelously mysterious. Heidegger's view of existence is not a problem. Edward's view of Heidegger's view is a problem, as the questions about being are not simple questions about a constant in symbolic logic. Symbolic logic is irrelevant to Heidegger's philosophy: symbolic logic cannot detect most of Heidegger's meanings because it is a formal language dependent on natural language.

JANZEN, Daniel H. El eslabón entre la conservación y el desarrollo sostenible: Maribel Gómez Mata. Rev Filosof (Costa Rica), 27(66), 333-337, D 89.

Conserved wildlands are essential components in a society based on sustainable development. While conserved wildlands offer material goods of many kinds, they are equally as important as the living classrooms in which biocultural understanding learned. By understanding the complexity and processes of the natural world, the members of a sustainably developed society are better able to understand themselves and the kinds of decisions that are needed for them to be peaceful participants in sustained development.

JARDINE, Nicholas (ed) and CUNNINGHAM, Andrew (ed). *Romanticism and the Sciences*. New York, Cambridge Univ Pr, 1990.

The work aims to provide a comprehensive treatment of the relationship between romanticism and the sciences. The 22 articles are divided into sections on the romantic movement, romanticism in the life sciences, romanticism in the physical sciences, and the sciences in romantic literature. The editorial preface and introduction oppose earlier accounts which portrayed romanticism in the sciences as an aberration, and argues that the romantic movement played major roles in the formation of the disciplines and ideologies of natural science.

JARY, David. "Beyond Objectivity and Relativism: Feyerabend's 'Two Argumentative Chains' and Sociology" in *The Social Horizon of Knowledge*, BUCZKOWSKI, Piotr (ed), 39-57. Amsterdam, Rodopi, 1991.

Paul Feyerabend's philosophy is usually seen as 'irrationalist'. It is argued in this paper that the correct reading of Feyerabend's position supports neither objectivism or irrationalism; rather his work can be seen as moving the philosophical debate beyond objectivism or relativism. This interpretation is upheld by his own summary of his philosophical ideas in terms of two argumentative chains: one relativist, but the other an 'open' and 'realist' chain. Similarities are noted between Feyerabend's presentation of his own view as 'Millian' and Habermas's model of open discourse or Richard Bernstein's conception of practical discourse. This argument is developed in the paper with particular reference to sociology.

JASPER, David. "'In the Sermon Which I Have Just Completed, Wherever I Said Aristotle, I Meant Saint Paul'" in *The Bible as Rhetoric: Studies in Biblical Persuasion and Credibility*, WARNER, Martin (ed), 133-152. New York, Routledge, 1990.

Rhetoric, as understood by Plato, is at the heart of St Mark's Gospel as a disturbing art of persuasion. The Gospel is an example of a religious community 'entextualising' itself (following the departure of St Peter), maintaining its identity by an authoritative document which holds a 'secret', which is a threat and a drive to power. The rhetoric of power in Mark leads to a terrible Nietzschean vision of a church whose 'conscious misery is set up as the perfection of the world's misery'.

JAUMANN, Herbert. Was ist ein Polyhistor? Gehversuche auf einem verlassenen Terrain. Stud Leibniz, 22(1), 76-89, 1990.

Far from being part only of early modern learning, polyhistory as a way of gathering and shaping knowledge can be traced through the Middle Ages back to grammar and rhetoric (copia rerum) of Roman antiquity. Practical use and wise limitation (vs. scientia supervacua) have always been the regulations to polyhistorical libido sciendi. During the sixteenth and seventeenth centuries polyhistory assumed the very high standard of universitatis rerum historia (Mylaeus), before it was losing its value by the rise of the new Cartesian paradigm of subject-centered epistemology. It is indispensable to survey the whole of its tradition, however incompletely and tentatively, in order to come to due distance to a term with polemical connotations dating from early enlightenment when polyhistory lost its credit.

JÁUREGUI, Claudia. Las criticas de J Bennett a la doctrina kantiana del esquematismo. Rev Filosof (Argentina), 5(1), 37-48, My 90.

This paper deals with Bennett's objections to Kantian doctrine of schematism. It exhibits and analyses each one of Bennett's arguments to show that the difficulties that this author discovers in the theory of transcendental schemas have their origin in his own inadequate interpretation of the doctrine and not in the doctrine itself.

JAVIERRE ORTAS, A M. X Zubiri in Roma: Natura, Storia, Dio. Aquinas, 33(2), 225-241, My-Ag 90.

JECH, Thomas and SHELAH, Saharon. Full Reflection of Stationary Sets Below $\aleph_\omega$. J Sym Log, 55(2), 822-830, Je 90.

JECKER, Nancy S. Anencephalic Infants and Special Relationships. Theor Med, 11(4), 333-342, D 90.

This paper investigates the scope and limits of parents' and physicians' obligations to anencephalic newborns. Special attention is paid to the permissibility of harvesting anencephalic organs for transplant. My starting point is to identify the general justification for treating patients in order to benefit third parties. This analysis reveals that the presence of a close relationship between patients and beneficiaries is often crucial to justifying treating in these cases. In particular, the proper interpretation of the Kantian injunction against treating persons as means only takes on a different light in the context of special relationships. The implications of this analysis for our responsibilities to anencephalic infants is clarified.

JECKER, Nancy S. Knowing When to Stop: The Limits of Medicine. Hastings Center Rep, 21(3), 5-8, My-Je 91.

This paper considers the possibility that, under special circumstances, physicians who stand in a close personal relationship with a patient are ethically permitted to assist their patient in dying. The paper distinguishes between impersonal, quasi-personal, and personal relationships between physician and patient. The author argues that care for another may make it morally impossible to simply step aside and watch a protracted illness run a painful course, and that new tasks are added to the physician's role when the physician's relationship with a particular patient becomes personal, not just quasi-personal or impersonal.

JECKER, Nancy S and SELF, Donnie J. Separating Care and Cure: An Analysis of Historical and Contemporary Images of Nursing and Medicine. J Med Phil, 16(3), 285-306, Je 91.

This paper provides a philosophical critique of professional stereotypes in medicine. In the course of this critique, we also offer a detailed analysis of the concept of care in health care. The paper first considers possible explanations for the traditional stereotype that caring is a province of nurses and women, while curing is an arena suited for physicians and men. It then dispels this stereotype and fine tunes the concept of care. A distinction between 'caring for' and 'caring about' is made, and concomitant notions of parentalism are elaborated. Finally, the paper illustrates, through the use of cases, diverse models of caring. Our discussion reveals the complexity of care and the alternative modes of caring in health care.

JEDLICKI, Jerzy. "Heritage and Collective Responsibility" in *The Political Responsibility of Intellectuals*, MACLEAN, Ian (ed), 53-76. New York, Cambridge Univ Pr, 1990.

The author discusses the reasons why various human communities—such as the family, nation, church or a political party—can feel a burden of responsibility for their historical past, that is, for the deeds of ancestors. One may also ask how legitimized are claims that a society or an institution should confess to crimes committed by its past generations against its neighbors or rivals. The author defends the notion of inherited responsibility and stresses a moral value of 'symbolic compensation' in history.

JENNINGS, Bruce. Democracy and Justice in Health Policy. Hastings Center Rep, 20(5), 22-23, S-O 90.

Discussions of justice and equity in health policy have moved from the principle of equitable access to debates over rationing and specifications of the "basic" level of care. This question cannot be answered by medical criteria alone, nor is a calculus of cost effectiveness adequate. Grass roots community health decisions groups are placing the broad spectrum of values involved in allocation of health resources on the public agenda. There is a danger that these nonpartisan civic groups will be politicized by this issue more than ever before. There is also the possibility that they can play a constructive role in producing a social consensus on the health priorities public policy ought to reflect.

JENNINGS, Bruce and COLLOPY, Bart and BOYLE, Philip. New Directions in Nursing Home Ethics. Hastings Center Rep, 21(2), Supp 1-16, Mr-Ap 91.

In the face of critical changes now shaping nursing home care, this article examines a number of ethical problems: the cultural disparagement of nursing homes, the moral perplexities of access and placement, the constraints of the "total institution," the conflict between individiual autonomy and common good, the moral agency of nursing home residents, the use of restraints, the paradox of government regulation. The article calls on bioethics to direct explicit attention to long term care issues, particularly the issues of autonomy and regulation.

JENNINGS, Bruce. Possibilities of Consensus: Toward Democratic Moral Discourse. J Med Phil, 16(4), 447-463, Ag 91.

The concept of consensus is often appealed to in discussions of biomedical ethics and applied ethics, and it plays an important role in many influential ethical theories. Consensus is an especially influential notion among theorists who reject ethical realism and who frame ethics as a practice of discourse rather than a body of objective knowledge. It is also a practically important notion when moral decision making is subject to bureaucratic organization and oversight, as is increasingly becoming the case in medicine. Two models of consensus are examined and criticized: pluralistic consensus and overlapping consensus. As an alternative to these models, the paper argues that consensus refers to the dialogic aspects of a broader normative conception of democratic moral agency. When the preconditions for that dialogic democratic practice are met, consensus has a justificatory role in ethics; when they are not, consensus, as distinct from mere agreement, does not emerge and can have no moral authority.

JENNINGS, Bruce. The Regulation of Virtue: Cross-Currents in Professional Ethics. J Bus Ethics, 10(8), 561-568, Ag 91.

This paper argues that more attention should be paid to the civic functions of ethical discourse about the professions and to the moral virtues inherent in their practice and traditions. The ability of professional ethics to articulate civic ideals and virtues is discussed in relation to three issues. First, should professional ethics aim to enlighten ethical understanding or to motivate ethical conduct? Second, how should professional ethics define the professional's moral responsibilities in the face of ethical dilemma - should the professional attempt to resolve the dilemma ethically or to change the social conditions that create the dilemma in the first place? The third issue discussed in the paper is whether professional ethics should be based on the model of regulation and rational self-interest or on the model of virtue and a fundamental personal commitment to the idea of a certain form of life? In order for work in professional ethics to attain intellectual credibility among a non-philosophical audience, it must develop a coherent and convincing position on each of these issues.

JENNINGS, Richard C. Zande Logic and Western Logic. Brit J Phil Sci, 40(2), 275-285, Je 89.

In this paper I discuss logic from a naturalist point of view, characterizing it as those shared patterns of thought which are socially selected from among the various patterns of thought to which we are naturally inclined. Drawing on Evans-Pritchard's anthropology, I discuss a particular example of Zande thought. I argue that Evans-Pritchard's and Timm Triplett's analyses of this example make the mistake of applying Western logic to Zande Beliefs and thus find a contradiction. I argue that from the naturalistic point of view, Zande logic is different form Western logic and that there is no contradiction in Zande thought.

JENSEN, Pamela K. Beggars and Kings: Cowardice and Courage in Shakespeare's *Richard II*. Interpretation, 18(1), 111-143, Fall 90.

JENSEN, Uffe J. "Are Selves Real?" in *Harré and His Critics*, BHASKAR, Roy (ed), 256-271. Cambridge, Blackwell, 1990.

JERVOLINO, Domenico. *The Cogito and Hermeneutics: The Question of the Subject in Ricoeur*. Norwell, Kluwer, 1990.

In this study Jervolino furnishes a comprehensive review of the development of Ricoeur's thought. He sees a coherence in Ricoeur's work, centered on the critique of subjectivity, especially of the illusion of a self-posing subject. Ricoeur's subject, instead, asserts its meaningful presence in the convergence of acts of reflexion and of interpretation. In Jervolino's reading, Ricoeur's itinerary culminates in a stimulating assertion of the potentiality of the questing self to pose the problem of liberation in terms of a hermeneutics of human praxis.

JHINGRAN, Saral. Some Self-Centric Tendencies in Sankara Advaita. J Indian Counc Phil Res, 7(2), 97-104, Ja-Ap 90.

The article affirms the theocentric character of the Vedantic monism of Upanisads and contrasts it with the more self-centric stance of post-Sankara Advaita Vedanta. It argues that the transition from the first to the second was facilitated by certain self-centric tendencies in Sankara's thought which suggest the influence of Sankhyan dualism, such as Sankara's distinction between the self and the not-self, his preference to present the Vedantic Absolute in terms of the (Universal) Self and liberation in terms of self-realisation. His creed of renunciation also could best be justified on the basis of a relatively self-centric metaphysics and valuational approach.

JIMÉNEZ GUERRERO, A. La persona humana: Síntesis de la concepción antropológica de K Wojtyla. Espiritu, 35(93), 35-53, Ja-Je 86.

JIMÉNEZ GUERRERO, A. El ser perfectible de la persona humana. Espiritu, 36(95), 69-78, Ja-Je 87.

JIMÉNEZ, Alexander. La inocencia y el mal en la obra de Albert Camus. Rev Filosof (Costa Rica), 28(67-68), 113-118, D 90.

Albert Camus bases his moral and political concerns on presumptions that imply a "metaphysical" judgment of the world. His work ranks in two levels of reflection, the metaphysical and the political-moral, that are interlocked one with each other. The article seeks to point out this bond using as a pretext the theme of the evil and the human innocence.

JIMENEZ, Jose. "Try the Image—Temporality and Fullness in Aesthetic Experience" in *XIth International Congress in Aesthetics, Nottingham 1988*, WOODFIELD, Richard (ed), 83-86. Nottingham, Nottingham Polytech, 1990.

JINFU, Wang. Is It Practical Ontology or Is It the Dialectical Materialist Theory of Material Monism? Chin Stud Phil, 22(4), 56-75, Sum 91.

JIRIK, Vlastimil. The Picture in Movement and in Response (in Czechoslovakian). Estetika, 27(4), 229-242, 1990.

JIYUAN, Yu. On Plato's Theory of the *Metheksis* of Ideas. Phil Inq, 13(1-2), 25-37, Wint-Spr 91.

In Plato's philosophy, the concept "Metheksis" has two meanings. The first is "the participation of a particular thing in a Form"; the second is "the participation of a Form in another Form," viz., *metheksis* of ideas. Generally speaking, people are familiar with the first meaning of "metheksis"; but the second meaning is always overlooked. However, according to my view, the theory of the *metheksis* of ideas is one of the essential parts in Plato's dialogues. I'm going to interpret and analyse this doctrine in this article. This work, I think, will be helpful in disclosing the intent of the theory of ideas and understanding the development of Plato's metaphysics. (edited)

JOBE, Evan K. Sturgeon's Defence of Moral Realism. Dialogue (Canada), 29(2), 267-275, 1990.

In his "Moral Realism" Nicholas Sturgeon argues for the following theses: (1) moral principles can be tested and confirmed empirically; (2) the moral quality of an event is relevant to an explanation of why a person may perceive it as having that quality; (3) moral qualities of persons can play an essential role in scientific explanations of human conduct; and (4) moral realism is plausibly compatible with physicalism. The present paper presents a critique of Sturgeon's arguments and attempts to show that on each of these points Sturgeon fails to make a good case.

JOCKUSCH JR, Carl G. "Degrees of Functions with No Fixed Points" in *Logic, Methodology and Philosophy of Science, VIII*, FENSTAD, J E (ed), 191-201. New York, Elsevier Science, 1989.

JOCKUSCH JR, Carl G and SOARE, Robert I. Degrees of Orderings Not Isomorphic to Recursive Linear Orderings. Annals Pure Applied Log, 52(1-2), 39-64, Ap 91.

It is shown that for every nonzero r.e. degree c there is a linear ordering of degree c which is not isomorphic to any recursive linear ordering. It follows that there is a linear ordering of low degree which is not isomorphic to any recursive linear ordering. It is shown further that there is a linear ordering L such that L is not isomorphic to any recursive linear ordering, and L together with its 'infinitely far apart' relation is of low degree. Finally, an analogue of the recursion theorem for recursive linear orderings is refuted.

JOCKUSCH JR, Carl G and OWINGS JR, James C. Weakly Semirecursive Sets. J Sym Log, 55(2), 637-644, Je 90.

JOHN OF SALISBURY and NEDERMAN, Cary J (ed & trans). *Policraticus*. New York, Cambridge Univ Pr, 1991.

JOHNSON, Carla Ann Hage. Entitled to Clemency: Mercy in the Criminal Law. Law Phil, 10(1), 109-118, F 91.

JOHNSON, Charles W. An Oath of Silence: Wittgenstein's Philosophy of Religion. Phil Theol, 5(4), 283-295, Sum 91.

Following a clarification of the nature of the "sightedness" and "blindness" which Wittgenstein associated with religious and mystical apprehension, I argue that his account fails in both its visual and its religious senses. I close with an assessment of the extent to which descriptive language can be used to introduce a religious perspective in someone who presently lacks it.

JOHNSON, David. Induction and Modality. Phil Rev, 100(3), 399-430, Jl 91.

JOHNSON, Edward. Singer's Cookbook. Between Species, 7(1), 36-39, Wint 91.

JOHNSON, Galen A (ed) and SMITH, Michael B (ed). *Ontology and Alterity in Merleau-Ponty*. Evanston, Northwestern Univ Pr, 1991.

JOHNSON, Glenn L. Ethical Dilemmas Posed By Recent and Prospective Developments with Respect to Agricultural Research. Agr Human Values, 7(3-4), 23-35, Sum-Fall 90.

The US agricultural research establishment has been severely criticized by biological and physical scientists, humanists, and various activist groups. This paper demonstrates that logical positivism mitigates against the objective research of intrinsic (as opposed to exchange) values needed to satisfy such criticisms. Attention is given to the advantages of placing greater reliance on pragmatism and various forms of normativism. These philosophies have distinct advantages as guides for structuring and understanding the problem-solving and issue-oriented research that the land-grant colleges of agriculture are uniquely qualified to conduct. Such practical problems and issues will be numerous as we expand land use 50 to 100 million acres, double yields, and intensive land use in the next 50 years.

JOHNSON, Gregory R. Hermeneutics: A Protreptic. Crit Rev, 4(1-2), 173-211, Wint-Spr 90.

A contribution to recent debates on the applicability of phenomenological hermeneutics to the Austrian school economics of Ludwig von Mises and F A Hayek, this essay treats four questions: (1) What is hermeneutics? Answer: The phenomenological account of human Being-in-the-world, theoretical and practical. (2) What does hermeneutics offer to economics? Answer: Phenomenological accounts of both economic phenomena and economic science. (3 & 4) Is hermeneutics relativistic? Is it historicist? Answer: Yes, but so what? All knowing is relative to interpretive horizons. But horizons should not be seen as impediments to non-horizonal knowing, for there is no such thing. Rather, horizons should be interpreted as our *means of* knowing.

JOHNSON, James. Habermas on Strategic and Communicative Action. Polit Theory, 19(2), 181-201, My 91.

Habermas's analysis of rational action is the fulcrum for his broader theoretical project. If that analysis is faulty his larger project is jeopardized. I explore the role Habermas assigns to strategic action in order to scrutinize his central concept of communicative action. Using basic game theoretic concepts as a counterpoint I argue that he both misconstrues stategic action and fails to adequately explain the mechanism underlying communicative action. I conclude by sketching several ways that Habermas might seek to rectify deficiencies in his analysis of rational action.

JOHNSON, Jeffery L. Making Noises in Counterpoint or Chorus: Putnam's Rejection of Relativism. Erkenntnis, 34(3), 323-345, My 91.

Putnam's internal realism entails the simultaneous rejection of metaphysical realism and ("anything goes" or "total" or "cultural") relativism. Putnam argues, in some places, that relativism is self-contradictory, and in others, that it is self-refuting. This paper attempts the exegetical task of explicating these challenging arguments, and the critical task of suggesting that a full-blown epistemological relativism may be capable of surviving the Putman attack.

JOHNSON, Julian. Music in Hegel's *Aesthetics*: A Re-Evaluation. Brit J Aes, 31(2), 152-162, Ap 91.

Hegel's philosophy of music is fairly conservative. He argues that music should reflect clear, identifiable emotional states-the Baroque musical doctrine of unity of *Affekt*. But his discussion suggests the possibility of a more radical theory. The structuring of musical time by discrete events and the preservation of an identity through the negation inherent in temporal progression is seen to be the same process by which the subject develops its identity through time. Different styles of music (different ways of structuring time) may thus be seen as mediums for the creation and articulation of different models of subjectivity.

JOHNSON, Laurie M. Rethinking the Diodotean Argument. Interpretation, 18(1), 53-62, Fall 90.

Diodotus's speech in the Mytilenaean Debate of Thucydides' *History of the Peloponnesian War* serves two purposes. The first is to win a moderate sentence for the Mytilenaeans through an argument from expediency. The second is to show where the Athenian thesis (that men are compelled to pursue ever more power and thus cannot be blamed or deterred from their aggression) leads. The only way for Athens to control inferiors is through constant vigilance and repression. Diodotus's speech serves a dual purpose for Thucydides: to demonstrate statesmanship, and expose the logical consequences of the Athenian thesis.

JOHNSON, Lawrence E. *A Morally Deep World: An Essay on Moral Significance and Environmental Ethics*. New York, Cambridge Univ Pr, 1991.

JOHNSON, Mark F. Immateriality and the Domain of Thomistic Natural Philosophy. Mod Sch, 67(4), 285-304, My 90.

This article investigates certain interpretations given to the teaching of Thomas Aquinas by John F X Knasas, an interpreter of Thomas given to very metaphysical, existential interpretations of Aquinas. Knasas maintains that Aquinas denies that what he calls natural philosophy, or physics, can attain to an immaterial reality in the course of its proper investigation. The article shows that Knasas's reading is fundamentally unsound, and offers a vision of Thomas's understanding of metaphysics and natural philosophy that makes room for each, within its proper sphere.

JOHNSON, Mark. Knowing through the Body. Phil Psych, 4(1), 3-19, 1991.

Recent empirical studies of categorization, concept development, semantic structure, and reasoning reveal the inadequacies of all theories that regard knowledge as static, propositional, and sentential. These studies show that conceptual structure and reason are grounded in patterns of bodily experience. Structures of our spatial/temporal orientations, perceptual interactions, and motor programs provide an imaginative basis for our knowledge of, and reasoning about, more abstract domains. Such a view transcends both foundationalism and extreme relativism or scepticism.

JOHNSON, Oliver A. "Is" and "Ought": A Different Connection. J Value Inq, 25(2), 147-160, Ap 91.

The paper argues that at least one "ought" can be derived from an "is"; namely, one's duty to do whatever act he believes he ought to do. But such a view, because it offers a moral sanction for fanaticism, cannot provide a complete account of our duties, so must be supplemented by a second obligation; namely, that one has a duty to strive to do what is right. The paper concludes that a moral agent has fulfilled his full duty if, when he acts, he has met the requirements that both lay down.

JOHNSON, Oliver A. Blanshard's Critique of Ethical Subjectivism. Ideal Stud, 20(2), 140-154, My 90.

In his *Reason and Goodness* Brand Blanshard analyzes and criticizes three forms of ethical subjectivism—the moderate subjectivism of Hume, the individualistic subjectivism of Westermarck, and the extreme or radical subjectivism of the logical positivists. Although he is sympathetic to certain aspects of these theories, he concludes them to be fundamentally deficient. In my paper I review Blanshard's arguments, offer some defenses of the subjectivists, and enlarge on the general case against them. My conclusion, like that of Blanshard, is that objectivism is the only viable type of ethical theory.

JOHNSON, Ralph H. Acceptance Is Not Enough: A Critique of Hamblin. Phil Rhet, 23(4), 271-287, 1990.

Many informal logicians and critical thinking theorists have been persuaded by Hamblin's proposal that dialectical criteria (viz., acceptability) rather than alethic or epistemic criteria ought to be adopted in the assessment of arguments. In this article, I review Hamblin's arguments against alethic and epistemic criteria and find them flawed. I also argue that his proposal that dialectical criteria be adopted faces some serious problems.

JOHNSON, Ralph H. Hamblin on the Standard Treatment. Phil Rhet, 23(3), 153-167, 1990.

The purpose of this article is to examine the position developed by Hamblin in Chapter 7 of *Fallacies* (1970) in which he discusses three different types of criteria for the evaluation of arguments: alethic, epistemic and dialectical. In spite of persuasiveness of Hamblin's reasoning for acceptance as a dialectical standard, I shall argue here that there are severe problems with his position.

JOHNSON, Ralph H. The Place of Argumentation in the Theory of Reasoning. Commun Cog, 24(1), 5-14, 1991.

In this paper, I develop the thesis that argumentation plays a pivotal role in the theory of reasoning. Hence without an adequate account of argumentation, it will not be possible to develop a complete theory of reasoning. To defend this thesis, I begin with a brief account of the nature of argumentation, followed by a brief account of what a theory of reasoning comprises. Finally, I shall state the reasons that support my thesis, the most important of which is that argumentation is at or near the apex of the ladder of reasoning.

JOHNSON, W and GLASS, J C. Metaphysics, MSRP and Economics. Brit J Phil Sci, 39(3), 313-329, S 88.

Lakatos's MSRP is utilized to provide a response to Koertge's claim (in her 'Does Social Science Really Need Metaphysics?') that the heuristic significance of metaphysics has been vastly overrated. By outlining the hard cores and positive heuristics of the two major research programs in economics (the 'orthodox' and 'Marxist'), the respective metaphysics are shown to be non-vague and to exert an important regulative influence on theories and economy policy recommendations. The paper also shows how the adoption of the MSRP method of appraisal in economics would help to protect against the danger of entrenched metaphysical dogmatism with its implications both for economic policy recommendations and for moral and political recommendations.

JOHNSTON, David. Aristotle's Apodeictic Syllogism. Dialogue (Canada), 29(1), 111-121, 1990.

JOHNSTON, Mark W and BURTON, Scot and WILSON, Elizabeth J. An Experimental Assessment of Alternative Teaching Approaches for Introductory Business Ethics. J Bus Ethics, 10(7), 507-517, Jl 91.

This study employs a pretest-posttest experiment design to extend recent research pertaining to the effects of teaching business ethics material. Results on a variety of perceptual and attitudinal measures are compared across three groups of students—one which discussed the ethicality of brief business situations (the business scenario discussion approach), one which was given a more philosophically oriented lecture (the philosophical lecture approach), and a third group which received no specific lecture or discussion pertaining to business ethics. Results showed some significant differences across the three groups and demonstrated that for a single lecture, the method used to teach ethics can differentially impact ethical attitudes and perceptions. Various demographic and background variables did not moderate the relationship between the teaching method and the dependent variables, but the sex of the student was strongly associated with the ethical attitude and perception measures.

JOHNSTON, Mark. "Fission and the Facts" in *Philosophical Perspectives, 3: Philosophy of Mind and Action Theory, 1989*, TOMBERLIN, James E (ed), 369-397. Atascadero, Ridgeview, 1989.

JOHNSTONE JR, Henry W. "The Fatality of Thought" in *The Philosophy of John William Miller*, FELL, Joseph P (ed), 59-69. Lewisburg, Bucknell Univ Pr, 1990.

Miller taught that types of philosophy often arise from the effort to maintain and carry through their predecessors. Thus mechanistic materialism is the articulation of spiritualism, the protophilosophy according to which every event is the act of an agent. But materialism is itself "fated" to give rise to subjective idealism, according to which the alleged laws of nature have a purely mental status. Miller's view of the relations among types owes much to Hegel, but derives dialectic from more explicitly activistic presuppositions.

JOHNSTONE JR, Henry W. "A Miller Bibliography with a Brief Description of The Williams College Miller Archives" in *The Philosophy of John William Miller*, FELL, Joseph P (ed), 167-172. Lewisburg, Bucknell Univ Pr, 1990.

JOHNSTONE JR, Henry W. Philosophical Argument and the Rhetorical Wedge. Commun Cog, 24(1), 77-91, 1991.

It has long been held that philosophy, unlike the empirical sciences, is a purely rational activity. As such, particular data make no difference to conclusions. While this seems to associate philosophy with mathematics, the philosopher, unlike the mathematician, intends to persuade an audience rhetorically. To do so, the philosopher attempts to drive a wedge between the subject and the object, which both separates and simultaneously brings into existence both of them. Rhetorical success requires a collaboration betweeen arguer and audience. This audience, however, cannot be a universal audience as Perelman and Olbrechts-Tyteca claim, but must be a particular audience.

JOHNSTONE, D J. Hypothesis Tests and Confidence Intervals in the Single Case. Brit J Phil Sci, 39(3), 353-360, S 88.

JOHNSTONE, D J. On the Necessity for Random Sampling. Brit J Phil Sci, 40(4), 443-457, D 89.

JOLLEY, Nicholas. "Berkeley and Malebranche on Causality and Volition" in *Central Themes in Early Modern Philosophy*, COVER, J A (ed), 227-244. Indianapolis, Hackett, 1990.

As his *Commentaries* show, the young Berkeley, like Malebranche, accepted a form of occasionalism. In his mature philosophy, however, Berkeley departed from strict occasionalism by insisting that finite spirits are causally active in willing. This essay argues that the development of Berkeley's thought about causality is philosophically puzzling, for occasionalist teaching is more consistent with his immaterialism. It is suggested that two factors which help to explain Berkeley's mature position are his empiricist account of concepts and his commitment to the theological doctrine that the human mind is made in the image of God.

JONATHAN, R. State Education Service or Prisoner's Dilemma: The 'Hidden Hand' as Source of Education Policy. Educ Phil Theor, 22(1), 16-24, 1990.

JONES, D Gareth. Fetal Neural Transplantation: Placing the Ethical Debate within the Context of Society's Use of Human Material. Bioethics, 5(1), 23-43, Ja 91.

JONES, John D. Assessing Human Needs. Phil Theol, 5(1), 55-64, Fall 90.

This paper investigates the meaning of needs claims to determine conditions under which they can be falsified. Interpreting needs as necessary requirements, I consider two distinct versions of the statement "A needs X." One is hypothetical: "If A is to do or obtain Y, then A needs X." The other is categorical—"A needs X at hand"—and is derived from the hypothetical statement when A is in some manner to do Y. I argue that, despite some cases in which needs claims cannot be falsified, formal criteria can be adduced to falsify or, at least, challenge both versions of needs claims.

JONES, Roger. Realism About What? Phil Sci, 58(2), 185-202, Je 91.

Preanalytically, we are all scientific realists. But both philosophers and scientists become uncomfortable when forced into analysis. In the case of scientists, this discomfort often arises from practical difficulties in setting out a carefully described set of objects which adequately account for the phenomena with which they are concerned. This paper offers a set of representative examples of these difficulties for contemporary physicists. These examples challenge the traditional realist vision of mature scientific activity as struggling toward an ontologically well-defined world picture. They challenge antirealist alternatives as well.

JONES, Todd and MULAIRE, Edmond and STICH, Stephen. Staving Off Catastrophe: A Critical Notice of Jerry Fodor's *Psychosemantics*. Mind Lang, 6(1), 58-82, Spr 91.

Jerry Fodor's *Psychosemantics* is a sophisticated, spackling, and innovative attempt to defend commonsense psychology from its recent detractors. The arguments that Fodor sets forth in this volume will likely begin debates that will fill the literature for years to come. In this review we give an overview of Fodor's attempt to rescue commonsense psychology from the three challenges to it that have loomed largest in the literature. We also sketch what we see as the most obvious *prima facie* problems with the course that Fodor recommends.

JONSEN, Albert R. American Moralism and the Origin of Bioethics in the United States. J Med Phil, 16(1), 113-130, F 91.

The theology of John Calvin has deeply affected the American mentality through two streams of thought, Puritanism and Jansenism. These traditions formulate moral problems in terms of absolute, clear principles and avoid casuistic analysis of moral problems. This approach is designated American moralism. This article suggests that the bioethics movement in the United States was stimulated by the moralistic mentality but that the work of the bioethics has departed from this viewpoint.

JOOS, Egbert. Ethik zwischen globaler Verantwortung und spekulativer Weltschematik. Deut Z Phil, 38(7), 683-690, 1990.

JOÓS, Ernest. The Contradiction of Belief and Reason in the Middle Ages: the Case of Boetius de Dacia (in Hungarian). Magyar Filozof Szemle, 5-6, 485-498, 1990.

Der Aufsatz behandelt das erst 1954 in der Budapester Széchényi-Bibliothek neu entdeckte Werk "De aeternitate mundi" des Boetius von Dacia, das zuerst der ungarische Forscher Géza Sajó veröffentlicht hat. Der Verfasser der vorliegenden Studie stellt die Analyse der aus dem 13. Jahrhundert stammenden Abhandlung in den umfassenden Zusammenhang des Gegensatzes von Glauben und Wissen, wie er sich in den verschiedenen Epochen der christlichen Tradition und namentlich im Zeitalter der Hochscholastik ausprägte. Vor allem sucht er zu zeigen, wie Boetius von Dacia durch eine prinzipielle Grenzbestimmung naturwissenschaftlicher und philosophischer Vernunft einerseits den Ansprüchen des Wissens innerhalb der dem Verstand gesetzten Schranken volle Gerechtigkeit widerfahren zu lassen, zugleich aber für die Theologie eine eigengesetzliche Geltungssphäre zu sichern trachtete. (edited)

JOÓS, Ernest. What is Ultimate in George Lukács's Ontology? Ultim Real Mean, 13(4), 268-282, D 90.

George Lukács, the Marxist philosopher, was forced into successive autocriticisms because of his revisionist views. The last of his deviation was his *Ontology* which I labelled as his last autocriticism (see my book, *Lukács's Last Autocriticism—the Ontology*, Humanities Press, 1983). But the shortcomings of his *Ontology* soon appeared. Matter as first principle could not explain the emergence of thought or social genesis. Thus, his Marxist ideology was the victim of an ultimate reality which surfaced in his doctrine as an indispensable element not only in ontology proper, but in ethics and also in any theory of meaning.

JORDAN, J. Kenny and Religious Experiences. Sophia (Australia), 29(3), 10-20, O 90.

Anthony Kenny argues in *Faith and Reason* that religious experiences cannot provide epistemic justification for a belief in God. In this article I first examine Kenny's arguments for this claim; and second, I argue that Kenny's arguments fail because of a neglected distinction between propositional revelation and nonpropositional revelation.

JORDAN, Jeff. The Doctrine of Double Effect and Affirmative Action. J Applied Phil, 7(2), 213-216, O 90.

William Cooney has recently argued (*The Journal of Applied Philosophy*, Vol. 6, pp. 201-204) that the social programme of affirmative action, though controversial, can be supported by the doctrine of double effect in that, according to the doctrine, responsibility falls on the side of intended consequences and not on that of unintended consequences. The point of affirmative action is to include certain disadvantaged groups; it is not to exclude other groups, though this is an inevitable and foreseeable by-product. In this article I contend that Cooney's argument ignores two important conditions of the doctrine of double effect; namely, that the good which results from the intended effect must be at least commensurate with the harm that results from the unintended effect; and, that the intended good effect is causally separate from the unintended harmful effect. Any use of the doctrine which neglects these conditions leads to morally problematic cases. Further, once we take the conditions into account, we have good reason to think that the doctrine of double effect has no relevance to the affirmative action debate.

JORDAN, Jeff. Duff and the Wager. Analysis, 51(3), 174-176, Je 91.

Antony Duff has argued that Pascal's Wager fails because of an embarrassment of riches: given that any and every possible act could result in theistic belief and that an infinite utility attaches to theistic belief if God exists, then every possible act that one might do has an infinite expected utility. I argue that there is good reason to think Duff's objection fails. A Pascalian can accept all that Duff claims and still hold that the Wager recommends theistic belief—it just does not recommend how one should go about inculcating that belief.

JORDAN, Jeff. The Many-Gods Objection and Pascal's Wager. Int Phil Quart, 31(3), 309-317, S 91.

The many-gods objection to Pascal's Wager is one of the earliest critiques offered of the Wager and its most serious challenge. The objection arises because Pascal's betting partition (God exists, God does not exist) is not, despite appearances, exhaustive. Various critics have argued that a Pascalian wager can be constructed for any number of incompatible religions. In this paper I argue that the many-gods objection fails. First, because one of the objection's premises, that logical possibility entails positive probability, is false. Secondly, because there are plausible decision-theoretic ways that a Pascalian can pare her partition down to manageable proportions.

JORDAN, Jeff. Why Negative Rights Only? S J Phil, 29(2), 245-255, Sum 91.

Libertarians typically deny that there are any positive rights found in the foundations of the hierarchy of rights. Only negative rights are properly basic and so negative rights, especially the right to liberty, take moral precedence over positive rights, like the right to a minimum welfare. This sort of claim, though typical of libertarians, is also typically asserted without much argumentation. In this paper I examine and criticize two recent attempts—one by Jan Narveson in his *The Libertarian Idea*; the other by Tibor Machan in *Individuals and Their Rights*—to supply the reasons why basic rights are exclusively negative in nature.

JORDAN, William. "Augustine on Music" in *Grace, Politics and Desire: Essays on Augustine*, MEYNELL, Hugo A (ed), 123-135. Calgary, Univ Calgary Pr, 1990.

JORGE, Maria M A. Ce que Ferdinand Gonseth a d'important à dire à l'épistémologie contemporaine. Dialectica, 44(3-4), 295-311, 1990.

The author begins with a consideration of well-known trends of contemporary epistemology which finds in functionalist operationalism a 'response' to the paradox of knowledge achieved by transformation of the object (which leads to too much emphasis on the subject as a focus for epistemological investigation and, as a result, a lack of interest in the role of the *a posteriori*, of the object in cognitive construction). The author goes on to note the 'therapeutic' indications already available in the epistemology of Gonseth, which make it possible to reintegrate the idea of objectivity and of truth into knowledge. (edited)

JORI, Mario. Paradigms of Legal Science. Riv Int Filosof Diritto, 67(2), 230-254, Ap-Je 90.

JOSYPH, Peter. The Occasion Fleeting: A Talk with Richard Selzer. Med Human Rev, 5(1), 24-34, Ja 91.

JOUGHIN, Martin (trans) and DELEUZE, Gilles. *Expressionism in Philosophy: Spinoza*. Cambridge, Zone Books, 1990.

JOVANOVIC, Gordana. Psychoanalysis: Acceptance and Overcoming of the Philosophical Heritage (in Serbo-Croatian). Filozof Istraz, 32-33(5-6), 1653-1662, 1989.

Freud macht einen paradoxen Gebrauch vom philosophischen Erbe. Ausgehend vom cartesischen Postulat der Gewissheit des Bewusstseins, kommt Freud zu dem Schluss, der diesem Postulat widerspricht (Legitimierung des Unbewussten). Oder, obwohl in vielen Hinsichten rationalistischer Auffassung, betrachtet er doch Wahrnehmung als einen paradigmatischen bewussten psychischen Prozess. Weiter wird Brentanos immanente Objekbezogenheit psychischer Phänomene zu einer auch real-sozialen. Grundprinzipien und Modelle zer Freudschen Psychoanalyse sind unterschiedlich sowohl von ihrer geschichtlichen, theoretischen und methodologischen Herkunft als auch in ihrer Reichweite. (edited)

JOVANOVSKI, Thomas. A Synthetic Formulation of Nietzsche's Aesthetic Model. Dialogue (Canada), 29(3), 399-414, 1990.

JOWETT, Benjamin (trans). *On Homosexuality: Lysis, Phaedrus, and Symposium*. Buffalo, Prometheus, 1991.

JOZEFCZUK, Grzegorz. The Idea of Common Sense in the Philosophy of L Chwistek (in Polish). Ann Univ Mariae Curie-Phil, 11, 221-232, 1986.

As one of few representatives of modern Polish philosophy Leon Chwistek pays attention to the epistemological usefulness of the concept of common sense, and he proposes a special understanding of this concept, especially in Granice nauki (The Limits of Science). A characteristic feature of this conception is a distinction between common sense and the so-called popular worldview with which the notion of common sense has traditionally been associated. The study discusses this distinction as well as Chwistek's history of common sense, theoretical and practical aspects of the functioning of common sense, cognitive illusions created by everyday language and obstructing the identification of common sense, rules of common sense (mainly the principle of contradiction). For Chwistek common sense is an ability derived from man's practical and theoretical experience of many centuries, a specific form of theoretical-cognitive self-consciousness, manifesting itself in an acknowledgement of the obligatoriness of a certain minimum of logicality as a condition of the rationality of cognition.

JUÁREZ, Agustín Uña. Platonismo vivo: (Debate actual sobre Platón, la Academia y las Ideas). Rev Filosof (Mexico), 23(68), 211-219, My-Ag 90.

JUBIEN, Michael. Could This Be Magic? Phil Rev, 100(2), 249-267, Ap 91.

"Possible worlds" are sometimes held to be abstract entities (like maximal consistent propositions) that *represent* ways the concrete world might have been. David Lewis has charged that many proponents of this view—the "magical ersatzers"—cannot give a satisfactory account of the vital representation relation. In this paper Lewis's argument against magical ersatzism is analyzed and rejected (without endorsing ersatzism). The question whether the argument nevertheless applies to other entities, like sets, is also considered. Finally, some remarks about different conceptions of propositions are offered, with special attention to the kind of conception that fits best with ersatzism.

JUBIEN, Michael. Straight Talk about Sets. Phil Topics, 17(2), 91-107, Fall 89.

I argue that the nature of Platonist commitments to abstract entities is not well understood. In particular, a Platonist commitment to *sets* is very suspicious when properly understood. I argue that intensional entities like properties are actually more acceptable.

JUDAH, Haim and SHELAH, Saharon and WOODIN, W H. The Borel Conjecture. Annals Pure Applied Log, 50(3), 255-269, D 90.

JUDAH, Haim and BARTOSZYNSKI, Tomek. Jumping with Random Reals. Annals Pure Applied Log, 48(3), 197-213, Ag 90.

In the first part we study the relationship between basic properties of the ideal of measure zero sets and the properties of measure algebra. The second part is devoted to the structure of the set of random reals over models of ZFC.

JUDAH, Haim and SHELAH, Saharon. The Kunen-Miller Chart (Lebesgue Measure, the Baire Property, Laver Reals and Preservation Theorems for Forcing). J Sym Log, 55(3), 909-927, S 90.

JUDT, Tony. "Radical Politics in a New Key?" in *Critique and Construction: A Symposium on Roberto Unger's "Politics"*, LOVIN, Robin W (ed), 115-129. New York, Cambridge Univ Pr, 1990.

A discussion, with reference to some ideas of R Unger, of new forms of political philosophy which emerged in east-Central Europe during the 1970s and 1980s. The emphasis upon the relative unconcern with goal-oriented moral and political stances, their replacement with a renewed interest in rights-theory and, especially, the recreation of the category of civil society. The essay ends with some speculation on the paradox that, if successful in their project to delegitimise totalitarian politics, such theories risk undermining their own claims when faced with a return to the necessary compromises and state-referential concerns of a pluralist polis.

JUENGST, Eric T. Bioethics Inside the Beltway: The Human Genome Project. Kennedy Inst Ethics J, 1(1), 71-74, Mr 91.

JUST, Winfried (and others). On the Existence of Large *p*-Ideals. J Sym Log, 55(2), 457-465, Je 90.

We prove the existence of *p*-ideals that are nonmeagre subsets of $P(\omega)$ under various set-theoretic assumptions.

JUTRONIC-TIHOMIROVIC, Dunja. "Davidson on Convention" in *The Mind of Donald Davidson*, BRANDL, Johannes (ed), 121-132. Amsterdam, Rodopi, 1989.

The attempt is made to demonstrate that Davidson's claim that communication does not proceed along the lines of convention is controversial and finally misguided. It is claimed that the *framework* theory has 'key ingredients' and thus is necessary for communication. At its abstract level it is the same for every speaker and it is not acquired in different ways. The *prior* theory, having been learned in advance, has to be shared too. There is no clearly defined point when the *passing* theory will start converging in communication. It is shown that there is no qualitative difference among the three theories and that the passing theory, as defined, is not a theory but an *ad hoc* type of procedure.

KADANE, J B and SEIDENFELD, Teddy and SCHERVISH, M J. When Fair Betting Odds are Not Degrees of Belief. Proc Phil Sci Ass, 1, 517-524, 1990.

The "Dutch Book" argument, tracing back to Ramsey and to deFinetti, offers prudential grounds for action in conformity with personal probability. Under several structural assumptions about combinations of stakes (that is, assumptions about the combination of wagers), your betting policy is *coherent* only if your *fair odds* are probabilities. The central question posed here is the following one: Besides providing an operational test of coherent betting, does the "Book" argument also provide for adequate measurement (*elicitation*) of the agents degrees of beliefs? That is, are an agent's fair odds also his/her personal probabilities for those events? We argue the answer is "No!" The problem is caused by the possibility of state dependent utilities.

KADOTA, Noriya. Some Extensions of Built-Upness on Systems of Fundamental Sequences. Z Math Log, 36(4), 357-364, 1990.

We extend the concept of built-upness on systems of fundamental sequences introduced by Schmidt to study hierarchies defined by the systems, for classifying number-theoretic functions, such as the fast-growing, Hardy, the slow-growing, etc. We find conditions that such hierarchies do not collapse, and show theorems on existence of them for the whole of the second number class.

KADVANY, John. Dialectic and Diagonalization. Inquiry, 34(1), 3-25, Mr 91.

This essay is about mathematics as a written or literature language. Through historical and anthropological observations drawn from the history of Greek mathematics and the oral tradition preceding the rise of literacy in Greece, as well as considerations on the nature of alphabetic writing, it is argued that three essential linguistic features of mathematical discourse are jointly possible only through written, alphabetic language. The essay concludes with a discussion of how both alphabetic principles and issues related to literacy faced by the Greeks in the axiomatization of geometry play a central role in some specific metamathematical theories. Drawing extensively on the work of Árpád Szabó, Eric Havelock, and Albert Lord, the implications developed between Szabó's history of Greek mathematics and Havelock and Lord's theories of writing and oral traditions. (Homer's in particular) are the author's own, as are the applications to modern logic.

KADYRZHANOV, R K and NYSANBAYEV, A N. The Categorical Nature of Mathematical Cognition. Phil Math, 6(1), 39-52, 1991.

KAEHLER, Klaus Erich. *Leibniz' Position der Rationalität*. Freiburg, Alber, 1991.

This book reconstructs the foundational structure of rationality strictly under the universal presuppositions of Leibniz's "two great principles" of reason and of contradiction: quality and quantity of propositions, their relations and modalities, the whole doctrine of syllogistics and proof, and basically to all this the combinatoric syntax of terms. This is what the finite mind, but his "natural light of reason", comes to know about the formal structure of reality created by an originally perfect mind as "ultimate reason of things". It is only within this comprehensive range of metaphysical thought that Leibniz's genuine position of rationality—and especially its formal branch of logic—is to be constituted; on the other hand it is only this universally presupposed range of rationality, which allows for ground and theoretical coherence in Leibniz's admired intellectual versatility.

KAGER, Reinhard. *Herrschaft und Versöhnung: Einführung in das Denken Theodor W Adornos*. Frankfurt, Campus, 1988.

This text provides an introduction to the thought of Adorno, including discussion of his social theory, negative dialectic, and use of aesthetic theory as a model of communication. (staff)

KAIN, Philip J. Rousseau, the General Will, and Individual Liberty. Hist Phil Quart, 7(3), 315-334, Jl 90.

Within Rousseau scholarship there is serious disagreement concerning the correct way to understand Rousseau's social and political thought. For many, Rousseau does not allow for individual liberty, and also, for many, he is a muddled, confused, and inconsistent thinker. I argue that Rousseau does allow for individual liberty and that his major social and political doctrines are much more consistent than is usually thought to be the case. In my view, Rousseau is a very careful thinker, but his thought is difficult to understand and it is often misunderstood.

KAINZ, Howard. Democracy and the Church-State Relationship. Phil Theol, 5(3), 251-258, Spr 91.

There are good historical reasons for emphasis on separation of church and state in a democracy, but the separation can be carried too far. Concerning the relationship of church and state, various Christian denominations divide up into separatists and unificationists, and each tendency can lead into extremes which could under certain conditions be inimical to democracy. Going beyond questions of constitutional separation, one may argue for a mutual utility and complementarity of church and democratic polity. Whether a strictly necessary relationship is entailed is a more complex problem.

KAISER, Klaus and GEHRKE, Mai and INSALL, Matt. Some Nonstandard Methods Applied to Distributive Lattices. Z Math Log, 36(2), 123-131, 1990.

It follows from the concurrency principle and local finiteness, that any distributive lattice D is contained in a hyperfinite lattice extension H. The paper investigates Stone duality, in particular completeness and Sikorski's lemma, in this setting. The familiar characterization of open and compact sets, due to A Robinson, led us to a class of lattices, the "R-lattices," which is broader than Boolean algebras and finite lattice theory, but strictly contained in the class of lattices subject to the TD-axiom for the underlying Stone space.

KAISER, Matthias. Rationality, Reasons, and the Sociology of Knowledge (in Serbo-Croatian). Filozof Istraz, 34(1), 195-208, 1990.

The paper deals with some of the central tenets of the so-called 'Strong Programme in the Sociology of Knowledge'. It is argued that an interpretation of this school of thought which yields an original approach to the study of science is untenable on philosophical grounds. In this connection, the paper focusses on the causality- and symmetry-requirement of the Strong Programme. Arguments stemming from Donald Davidson are used to show that an epistemological interpretation of the causality-requirement seems impossible. The last two sections of the paper outline an alternative to the symmetry-requirement for the study of action and science. This alternative is claimed to form some middle-ground between the relativist conception of the Strong Programme and the strongly rational account dominant in traditional philosophy of science.

KAMAL, Muhammad. Hegel's Legend of Self-Determination. Indian Phil Quart, 17(3), 277-283, Jl 90.

Freedom is defined by Hegel in three different ways: freedom as self-determination which is the main feature of Being-for-self, as an activity to transcend Being and as social justice. The first definition is given in his logic and has become a ground for the dialectic of Master-Slave. Whereas the conceptions of mutual recognition and social justice which are described in the *Philosophy of Right* are distinct and contradict his previous definition of freedom. But still, the deduction of mutual recognition as a necessary condition for social justice is logically possible even from the conflicting relation between Master and Slave, and it can be proved that all three definitions supplement each other.

KAMARYT, Jan. The Meaning of Discussions on Democratic Socialism in Czechoslovakia (in Czechoslovakian). Filozof Cas, 38(5), 637-646, 1990.

The term democratic socialism was designed to separate a certain ideal or model of socialism from discredited reality of socialist development in Czechoslovakia. A new content of this particular term originated in the late 1960s in the economic, political and philosophical sphere, involving primarily a critique of Stalinism, tying on the democratic traditions as instruments aimed at superseding the political and spiritual crisis rise in the country. Out of Czechoslovakia's leading philosophers it was Karel Kosik, Robert Kalivoda and Radovan Richta who made the greatest contribution to the clarification of this term. These authors succeeded in profoundly analyzing the causes of the political and spiritual crisis as well as outlining a way out of it, the need of transforming the Stalinist bureaucratic system of political power into a democratic one. (edited)

KAMM, Frances M. The Philosopher as Insider and Outsider: How to Advise, Compromise, and Criticize. Bus Prof Ethics J, 9(1-2), 7-20, Spr-Sum 90.

KAMP, Hans. "Prolegomena to a Structural Theory of Belief and Other Attitudes" in *Propositional Attitudes: The Role of Content in Logic, Language, and Mind*, ANDERSON, C Anthony (ed), 27-90. Stanford, CSLI, 1990.

KAMPIS, György. Eleatics Against Each Other (in Hungarian). Magyar Filozof Szemle, 5-6, 473-484, 1990.

This paper examines Zeno's paradoxes. It is a general assumption that the reasoning of the paradoxes is wrong. The author points out that the logico-mathematical operations used in the treatment of the problem do not refute, but justify Zeno's reasoning. The author's analysis forwards the identification of the limits of natural science set by Eleatic doctrines and puts forward a suggestion for how they could be transcended. (edited)

KANAMORI, Akihiro and AWERBUCH-FRIEDLANDER, Tamara. The Complete 0. Z Math Log, 36(2), 133-141, 1990.

KANAMORI, Akihiro. Regressive Partition Relations, *n*-Subtle Cardinals, and Borel Diagonalization. Annals Pure Applied Log, 52(1-2), 65-77, Ap 91.

We consider natural strengthenings of H Friedman's Borel diagonalization propositions and characterize their consistency strengths in terms of the *n*-subtle cardinals. After providing a systematic survey of regressive partition relations and their use in recent independence results, we characterize *n*-subtletly in terms of such relations requiring only a finite homogeneous set, and then apply this characterization to extend previous arguments to handle the new Borel diagonalization propositions.

KANE, Thomas C and RICHARDSON, Robert C and FONG, Daniel W. The Phenotype as the Level of Selection: Cave organisms as Model Systems. Proc Phil Sci Ass, 1, 151-164, 1990.

KANEV, Krassimir. Bulgaria: The Romantic Period of the Opposition Continues. Praxis Int, 10(3-4), 306-317, O 90-Ja 91.

The article is an attempt to summarize the developments in Bulgaria after first multi-party elections since the Communist administration was dismissed in November 1989. An explanation is proposed in an attempt to answer the question why the Communist Party won these elections on the background of the post-war Bulgarian history. The characteristics of the modern political culture as well as the prospects for the development of the democratic process is outlined.

KANIOWSKI, Andrzej M. Critical Activity and Ethics: The Problem of Generalization. Praxis Int, 10(1-2), 117-130, Ap-Jl 90.

Critical social theorists who defend the rationalistic and cognitive approach of Kant against various widespread relativistic and contextualistic approaches in ethics at the same time are critical of some dualistic and subjectivistic constituents of Kantian ethics. Most characteristic for critical social theorists, despite all differences between their positions, is a more or less explicit intention to "dissolve" ethics in critical attitude of a social theorist and the moral standpoint of an individual. This intention is exemplified by arguments of Horkheimer, Benhabib and Habermas. The author attempts to defend the differentiation into two perspectives by introducing a discrimination between two points of reference, both of them having a constitutive function for a moral subject: the one of generality and the other of universality.

KANITSCHEIDER, Bernulf. "Does Physical Cosmology Transcend the Limits of Naturalistic Reasoning?" in *Studies on Mario Bunge's "Treatise"*, WEINGARTNER, Paul (ed), 337-350. Amsterdam, Rodopi, 1990.

Any type of ontology in the analytic tradition that may be called scientific must be subjected to critical examination and has to be fallible in some way. Metaphysical hypotheses cannot be subjected directly to empirical tests but are only vicariously testable, via the success of pertinent scientific theories. With a view on Mario Bunge's philosophy it is asked how naturalistic ontology, normally a presupposition of every scientific approach, can be put on the test bench.

KANTHAMANI, A. Does Prescriptivism Imply Naturalism? J Indian Counc Phil Res, 5(2), 41-46, Ja-Ap 88.

This paper is an attempt to briefly and sympathetically reconstruct the crucial line of argument against naturalism advanced recently by Hare in his three-layered theory of moral thinking. Focusing on the linguistic side of Hare's argument (a version of prescriptivism) that explores the relation between ethical universalizability and the verbal basis of moral conflict, it highlights how Hare opens ethics into an area where interpersonal conflicts are resolved without falling prey to the pure logic of preference.

KANTOR, Jay E. *Medical Ethics for Physicians-in-Training*. New York, Plenum Pr, 1989.

KANTOR, K M. Two Designs of Universal History. Soviet Stud Phil, 29(4), 35-58, Spr 91.

KANTOROVICH, Aharon. Philosophy of Science: From Justification to Explanation. Brit J Phil Sci, 39(4), 469-494, D 88.

The paper investigates the implications of a nonaprioristic philosophy of science. It starts by developing a sxheme of justification which draws its norms form the prevailing paradigm of rationality, which need not be universal or eternal. If the requirement for normativity is then abandoned we do not end up with a descriptive philosophy of science. The alternative to a prescriptive philosophy of science is a theoretical explanation of scientific decisions and acts. Explanation, rather than mere description, replaces justification; and the paradigm of rationality becomes a scientific paradigm. The implications of these results for the discovery-justification distinction are investigated. An explanatory philosophy of science deals with the generation, as well as with the selection of scientific conjectures; both contexts have an epistemic dimension.

KAPITAN, Tomis. Agency and Omniscience. Relig Stud, 27(1), 105-120, Mr 91.

One exercises agency only through intentional action, and an action is intentional only if among its causal antecedents is an intending of the agent's. But what could motivate someone to undertake an action unless he or she sensed both a need for the required effort and a chance that it might succeed, and how could this happen if the agent already knew what will happen? If it is going to occur, no need, and if slated not to occur, no chance. Hence, future-directed uncertainty is essential to intending, and an omniscient being cannot act at all.

KAPITAN, Tomis. In What Way is Abductive Inference Creative? Trans Peirce Soc, 26(4), 499-512, Fall 90.

Peirce's account of abduction has excited many who seek an explanation of scientific discovery in terms of rational processes. But Peirce was often unclear about the precise locus of novelty within abductive thought. Not only did he include the novel hypothesis within the premises of the standard forms for abductive inference, he cited "observation" and "instinct" as the proper sources of novelty. Here it is argued that while the hypothesis does indeed emerge in the course of reasoning about a problem, often through the application of heuristic rules, it does not do so as the conclusion of an inference.

KAPLAN, David. "Afterthoughts" in *Themes From Kaplan*, ALMOG, Joseph (ed), 565-614. New York, Oxford Univ Pr, 1989.

KAPLAN, David. "Demonstratives: An Essay on the Semantics, Logic, Metaphysics, and Epistemology of Demonstratives" in *Themes From Kaplan*, ALMOG, Joseph (ed), 481-563. New York, Oxford Univ Pr, 1989.

KAPLAN, Mark S. AIDS and the Psycho-Social Disciplines: The Social Control of 'Dangerous' Behavior. J Mind Behav, 11(3-4), 337-351, Sum-Autumn 90.

AIDS provides society an opportunity to expand and rationalize control over a broad range of psychological phenomena. Social control today is panoptical, involving dispersed centers and agents of surveillance and discipline throughout the whole community (as exemplified by workplace drug testing). The control of persons perceived as "dangerous" is effected partly through public psycho-social discourse on AIDS. This reproduces earlier encounters with frightening diseases, most notably the nineteenth-century cholera epidemic, and reveals a morally laden ideology behind modern efforts at public hygiene.

KAPLAN, Mark. Epistemology on Holiday. J Phil, 88(3), 132-154, Mr 91.

KARIER, Clarence J. Humanizing the Humanities: Some Reflections on George Steiner's "Brutal Paradox". J Aes Educ, 24(2), 49-63, Sum 90.

KARLSSON, Mikael M. Epistemic Leaks and Epistemic Meltdowns: A Response to William Morris on Scepticism with Regard to Reason. Hume Stud, 16(2), 121-130, N 90.

In *Hume Studies* 15 (April 1989), William E Morris attempts to defend the two pivotal arguments in Hume's chapter "Of scepticism with regard to reason" (*Treatise of Human Nature*, Book I, Part IV, Section I) and to show their importance for the overall argument of the *Treatise*. The present article, although a response to Morris, is primarily a discussion of Hume's two arguments—the "epistemic leak" and "epistemic meltdown" arguments. It is argued that Morris's attempted defense of these arguments fails, which is especially unfortunate, since his account of their significance for the *Treatise* as a whole is convincing.

KARNI, Reuven and SANCHEZ, Pedro and TUMMALA, V M Rao. A Comparative Study of Multiattribute Decision Making Methodologies. Theor Decis, 29(3), 203-222, N 90.

Three "real life" cases are considered in this paper to apply and compare the ranking obtained by the Analytic Hierarchy Process (AHP) and other Multicriteria Decision Making (MCDM) techniques such as Simple Additive Weighting (SAW), ELECTRE and Weighted Linear Assignment Method (WLAM). The results indicated that the AHP, SAW, and ELECTRE rankings do not differ significantly, however, the WLAM tends to exhibit more disagreement. However, because of the limited nature of this study, we do not suggest this as a general conclusion.

KARNS, Jack E. Economics, Ethics, and Tort Remedies: The Emerging Concept of Hedonic Value. J Bus Ethics, 9(9), 707-713, S 90.

This article reviews the development of hedonic value of life as a remedy in wrongful death and personal injury tort cases. Hedonic value estimates the worth of lost pleasures of living in an effort to compensate for intangible enjoyments, such as quality of education and environmental standards. This remedy goes well beyond the traditional approach which has compensated primarily for lost earnings and other expenses directly related to the tortious conduct. Most of the attention regarding hedonic value as a relatively new tort remedy has focused on its application in nonbusiness litigation. However, given the significant damage awards in recent cases, it is likely that this economic theory will arise in commercial litigation, especially products liability cases. The business community must be conversant with the ethical issues raised by this novel tort remedy in order to fashion a reasoned and socially acceptable contra-position.

KARPENKO, Alexander S. Characterization of Prime Numbers in Lukasiewicz's Logical Matrix. Stud Log, 48(4), 465-478, D 89.

KARPINSKI, Jakub. *Causality in Sociological Research*. Norwell, Kluwer, 1990.

Presents a comparative analysis of proposals of a causal interpretation of data of various types obtained in sociological research, including data from synchronic, diachronic and experimental studies, the essential point being the indication of those assumptions which one makes when suggesting and applying the various methods of analysis the semantic (conceptual) problems related to the proposals for the study of causes are also discussed. Finally, the author reflects on how we can speak about theories and models with reference to causal analysis. (staff)

KARY, Michael. "Information Theory and the *Treatise*: Towards a New Understanding" in *Studies on Mario Bunge's "Treatise"*, WEINGARTNER, Paul (ed), 263-280. Amsterdam, Rodopi, 1990.

The aim of this work is twofold: to show that information-theoretic interpretations of Shannon's theory of coding are adventitious; and to propose an alternative theory of information, quantitative and relevant to its essential standard usage in philosophy, science and technology. Among other objections, it is argued that using Shannon's theory as an information theory requires an invalid subjective interpretation of the theory of probability. The idea of a single multipurpose unit of information is also rejected. Instead information is related to accuracy of representation, quantified by an appropriate distance function.

KASHIMA, Yoshihisa and MAHER, Patrick. On the Descriptive Adequacy of Levi's Decision Theory. Econ Phil, 7(1), 93-100, Ap 91.

Isaac Levi has claimed that his modification of Bayesian decision theory can accommodate the choices many subjects make in the Allais and Ellsberg problems. In a test of this claim, Maher showed that subjects who make the Allais and Ellsberg choices violate Levi's theory. In response, Levi suggested that subjects were making a mistake, and that if their attention were drawn to the relevant considerations, they might adhere to his (Levi's) theory. In this paper, we report an experiment which shows that even when subjects's attention is drawn to the considerations Levi deems relevant, subjects persist in violating his theory.

KASPAR, Rudolf F. Kritik der Soziobiologie des Menschen. Conceptus, 24(63), 81-92, 1990.

In this paper I try to present some fundamental patterns of argumentation of sociobiology as well as some relevant examples of their application to human social behaviour. I then try to show which coneption of a human being underlies these assumptions. Sociobiology assumes genetical determinism even in highly complex human modes of behaviour, but it does not provide sufficient evidence for this claim. Although they *seem* plausible in many cases analogical inferences from animal to human confuct are very often arbitrary. I analyse the patterns of "explanation" in order to show the typical category mistakes and some of their consequences. I will argue that this leads to a *petitio principii*. I finally content that this vicious circle could only be avoided, if the conception of a human being (as a "gen-machine" underlying sociobiology would *really* become the basis of our pragmatic world and its anthropological interpretation. But this step seems highly improbable and ethically dubious.

KASSAB, Elizabeth Suzanne. "Paramount Reality" in Schutz and Gurwitsch. Human Stud, 14(2-3), 181-198, Jl 91.

Both Aron Gurwitsch and Alfred Schutz conceive of experienced reality as being manifold: Gurwitsch speaks of several "orders of existence" and Schutz develops a theory of "multiple realities". Furthermore, both thinkers consider the world of daily life to be among the several other realms of reality, so to say, the "most real", the most fundamental for experience and borrowing from William James to be the "paramount reality". The article aims at determining why and in what sense is the world of daily life the paramount reality for each Gurwitsch and Schutz respectively. The answer to these questions is sought in the writings of the two men pertinent to this issue as well as in their correspondence which extends between 1939 and 1959. Indeed, at first both scholars seem to characterize the world of daily life as being intersubjective and cultural, constituted by the social actions of the people living in it. However, whereas Gurwitsch calls this world the "perceptual world" and concerns himself with the analysis of the perceptual phenomena in it, Schutz calls it the "social world" and devotes his attention to the structure of the social actions in it.

KASSIOLA, Joel Jay. *The Death of Industrial Civilization*. Albany, SUNY Pr, 1990.

This book discusses the limits to economic growth and the problems facing contemporary society. It explores many urgent problems we must confront today: pollution of the environment, depletion of natural resources, and growing discontent with competition and materialism. The argument challenges the dominance of economic growth as our primary social goal, and looks at some alternatives suggested by political philosophers and environmentalists. The author hopes to awaken public consciousness to the "quiet" crisis of our industrial values, and recommends re-evaluation of these values, and the social institutions and public policies derived from them. The book should be of interest to philosophers, natural and social scientists as well.

KASSIOLA, Joel. Can Marxism Help Biology? Phil Soc Sci, 20(4), 467-482, D 90.

This review essay assesses the strengths and deficiencies of the volume, *The Dialectical Biologist*, by biologists Richard Levins and Richard Lewontin. This work is important for both natural and social scientists because it attempts the rare aim of arguing for the methodological significance to natural science of politics and political thought instead of the commonplace vice versa argument. The article's main conclusion is that the book is creative and richly suggestive but ultimately perplexing and dissatisfying because of the authors' flawed presentation, mostly the lack of discussion and supporting evidence for their bold and controversial claims about the political/ideological nature of science.

KASTELY, James L. *Persuasion*: Jane Austen's Philosophical Rhetoric. Phil Lit, 15(1), 74-88, Ap 91.

This essay explores Jane Austen's *Persuasion* as an inquiry into ethical nihilism. The essay argues that *Persuasion* conceives of nothingness as Anne Elliot's fate if she cannot create a community that can allow her to realize her excellence through an appropriate discourse. *Persuasion* conceives of skepticism as an ethical rather than as an epitemological problem, and it addresses this problem by arguing that rhetoric is an art of community. And *Persuasion* recommends a generous passion, such as Anne's, as the best hope for achieving a community through rhetoric.

KASULIS, Thomas P. Intimacy: A General Orientation in Japanese Religious Values. Phil East West, 40(4), 433-449, O 90.

KATEB, George. "Arendt and Representative Democracy" in *The Realm of Humanitas: Responses to the Writings of Hannah Arendt*, GARNER, Reuben (ed), 187-233. New York, Lang, 1990.

KATEB, George. Walt Whitman and the Culture of Democracy. Polit Theory, 18(4), 545-571, N 90.

KATZ, Ellen L and NAVIA, Luis E. *Socrates: An Annotated Bibliography*. Hamden, Garland, 1988.

This annotated bibliography of Socratic scholarship provides detailed descriptive information of over 1900 works on Socrates, from ancient times to the present. It includes chapters on the following categories of works: bibliographies and indexes, primary sources (Aristophanes, Xenophon, Plato), collections of primary source materials, the Socratic problem, the Aristophanic Socrates, the Xenophontean Socrates, the Platonic Socrates, the Aristotelian testimony, specific biographic literature, philosophical studies, Socrates' trial, studies on Plato's early dialogues, Socrates and Christ, the influence of Socrates, and Socrates in literature and fiction. It provides an index of authors, and a listing of the periodicals represented.

KATZ, Jerrold J. "Has the Description Theory of Names Been Refuted?" in *Meaning and Method: Essays in Honor of Hilary Putnam*, BOOLOS, George (ed), 31-61. New York, Cambridge Univ Pr, 1990.

KATZ, Jerrold J. *The Metaphysics of Meaning*. Cambridge, MIT Pr, 1990.

This book offers a radical reappraisal of the "linguistic turn" in twentieth-century philosophy. It shows that the naturalism which emerged to become the dominant philosophical position was never adequately established. The book critiques the major arguments for contemporary naturalism in both the Wittgensteinian and Quinean forms, and it presents a Platonist alternative to nonnaturalism. It argues for this alternative as the best explanation of the autonomy, objectivity, and normativity of disciplines like logic and linguistics.

KATZ, Jerrold J. "Why Intensionalists Ought Not Be Fregeans" in *Truth and Interpretation: Perspectives on the Philosophy of Donald Davidson*, LE PORE, Ernest (ed), 59-91. Cambridge, Blackwell, 1986.

KATZ, Jerrold. "The Refutation of Indeterminacy" in *Perspectives on Quine*, BARRETT, Robert (ed), 177-197. Cambridge, Blackwell, 1990.

KATZ, Michael S. The Teacher as Judge: A Brief Sketch of Two Fairness Principles. Proc Phil Educ, 46, 350-359, 1990.

KATZ, Ruth (ed). *Contemplating Music—Source Readings in the Aesthetics of Music, Volume II: Import*. Stuyvesant, Pendragon Pr, 1989.

The expression of affections or emotions is the essence and aim of music. This volume discusses the theory of emotional response to music as expressed from Augustine through the Baroque era. It is an attempt to formulate a theory which would do equal justice to the possibility of subjective distance as well as the appearance of objective fact, one which takes into account psychological aspects as well as historical conventions. (staff)

KAUFMAN, Frederik. Conceptual Necessity, Causality and Self-Ascriptions of Sensation. Int Stud Phil, 22(3), 3-11, 1990.

I argue that it is a necessary truth that sincere self-ascriptions of sensation are mostly true. Putnam and Davidson claim that it is a necessary truth that our beliefs in general are mostly the case; this suggests that the mostly true nature of sensation beliefs can be explained by reference to some such larger view having nothing in particular to do with sensations. I show, however, that the special status of sensation beliefs is not captured by general views about the relation between belief and truth. Though it is a necessary truth that sensation beliefs are mostly the case, this fact is best explained by considering the causal connections involved.

KAUFMANN, J Nicolas. Apriorisme et théorie du choix rationnel. Dialogue (Canada), 29(2), 219-246, 1990.

The objective of the paper is to examine the cogency of "Austrian apriorism" for the epistemological status of the axioms of rational choice theory on the following three grounds: (1) controversial status of the R-postulates in decision theory; (2) parallelism established by "Austrians" (Menger, von Mises) between the axioms of rational choice and the axioms of geometry, seen in the light of the Erlagen program; (3) Davidsonian view of the R-postulates as constitutive (a priori) principles for rational action.

KAUFMANN, Walter. *Goethe, Kant, and Hegel: Volume I, Discovering the Mind*. New Brunswick, Transaction Books, 1991.

KAULBACH, Friedrich. Der Übergang vom Bestimmt-Bestimmenden zum freien Schema in Kants Kritik der Urteilskraft. Rev Int Phil, 45(176), 76-91, 1991.

KAULINGFREKS, Ruud. "Art of the Untruth? On Post Modern Visual Art" in *XIth International Congress in Aesthetics, Nottingham 1988*, WOODFIELD, Richard (ed), 87-89. Nottingham, Nottingham Polytech, 1990.

KAVATHATZOPOULOS, Iordanis. Kohlberg and Piaget: Differences and Similarities. J Moral Educ, 20(1), 47-54, F 91.

Kohlberg's cognitive-stage-developmental theory is often described as a further development of Piaget's moral theory. In discussing the two theories, it is shown that Kohlberg attempts to describe the features of moral thought and not the formation of the independent moral function. Nevertheless, Kohlberg's later research, as well as research done by his disciples, approaches Piaget. In trying to study the issue of moral education in 'just communities', they reintroduce the Piagetian concept of cooperation in equality among the members of the group, and they use a collaborator or leader. However, their main interest remains in the description of the characteristics of the stages of individual moral reasoning and valuing of norms and community, and not the study of the process of acceleration towards the autonomous moral phase.

KAWAKAMI, Akitaka. Die Wahrheit des literarischen Kunstwerks: R Ingardens Begriff des Quasi-Urteils (in Japanese). Bigaku, 41(4), 22-33, Spr 91.

Im ersten Kapitel skizziere ich Ingardens Theorie des Quasi-Urteils. Im zweiten korrigiere ich sie vom pragmatischen Gesichtspunkt aus. Im dritten demonstriere ich, wie die fiktionalen sätze die Wahrheit in der Weise sagen können, dass sie die wahre Gestalt des dargestellten Gegentandes sehen lassen. Im vierten und fünften Kapitel prüfe ich den Wahrheitswert allgemeiner Sätze, die sich oft im literarischen Kunstwerk finden, im Vergleich mit wissenschaftlichen Sätzen. (edited)

KAZMI, Ali Akhtar. Parthood and Persistence. Can J Phil, SUPP 16, 227-250, 1990.

KEARNEY, Richard. "Ideology and Religion: A Hermeneutic Conflict" in *Phenomenology of the Truth Proper to Religion*, GUERRIÈRE, Daniel (ed), 126-145. Albany, SUNY Pr, 1990.

This article explores the relationship between the critiques of ideology and religion in Marx, Freud and Nietzsche. Developing Paul Ricoeur's distinction between a hermeneutics of suspicion and of affirmation, the analysis concludes with a defence of the possibility of religious truth within the context of a critical hermeneutics.

KECHRIS, Alexander S. Boundedness Theorems for Dilators and Ptykes. Annals Pure Applied Log, 52(1-2), 79-92, Ap 91.

KECHRIS, Alexander S and WOODIN, W H. A Strong Boundedness Theorem for Dilators. Annals Pure Applied Log, 52(1-2), 93-97, Ap 91.

KEELEY, Michael and GRAHAM, Jill W. Exit, Voice, and Ethics. J Bus Ethics, 10(5), 349-355, My 91.

Hirschman's (1970) exit, voice, and loyalty framework draws attention to both economic and political behavior as instruments for organizational change. The framework is simple but powerful; it has stimulated much cross-disciplinary analysis and debate. This paper extends this analysis by examining normative implications of Hirschman's basic premise: that exit and voice are primarily mechanisms for enhancing organizational (versus individual) well-being.

KEENE, G B. The Agnostic Fallacy. Philosophy, 65(253), 366-370, Jl 90.

KEENE, G B. The Irrelevance of Classical Logic. Phil Quart, 41(162), 76-82, Ja 91.

KEFFER, Steven and KING, Sallie and KRAFT, Steven. Process Metaphysics and Minimalism: Implications for Public Policy. Environ Ethics, 13(1), 23-47, Spr 91.

Using process philosophy, especially its view of nature and its ethic, we develop a process-based environmental ethic embodying minimalism and beneficience. From this perspective, we criticize the philosophy currently underlying public policy and examine some alternative approaches based on phenomenology and ethnomethodology. We conclude that process philosophy, minus its value hierarchy, is a powerful tool capable of supporting both radical and moderate changes in environmental policy.

KEIJI, Nishitani and PARKES, Graham (trans) and AIHARA, Setsuko (trans). *The Self-Overcoming of Nihilism: Nishitani Keiji*. Albany, SUNY Pr, 1990.

In this work from 1949 the Japanese philosopher Nishitani Keiji (1900-1990) sketches the history of European nihilism as the context for a consideration of how the problem posed by nihilism might be resolved. In the course of three chapters on Nietzsche, and one each on Max Stirner, Russian nihilism, and Heidegger. Nishitani shows the way in which nihilism—as long as it is plumbed to its uttermost depths—will eventually "overcome itself." In the book's final two chapters, dealing with nihilism in the modern Japanese context and the problem of atheism, the background of Zen thought from which Nishitani approaches his topic comes to the fore.

KEILKOPF, Charles F. Abortion as the Illicit Method of Birth Control. Proc Cath Phil Ass, 63, 193-203, 1990.

An ambiguity is detected in the natural law command not to act against the good of human sexual intercourse. It can mean: Do not inhibit the process of conception, or it can mean: Do not inhibit the product of intercourse—a conceptus. A case is made that a so-called minimal natural law theory forbids only frustrating conception as a product—as a conceptus.

KEISER, R Melvin. Postcritical Religion and the Latent Freud. Zygon, 25(4), 433-447, D 90.

Although Freud launches a devastating critique of religion, he makes significant contributions to religious maturity. On the "manifest" level, he attacks religion as illusion; on the "latent" level, however, he is preoccupied with religion as mystery deep in the psyche. This difference is between religion as "critical" or as "postcritical" (Polanyi)—as dualistically split from, or emergent within, the psyche. Postcritical religion appears in Freud as mystery, unity, feeling, meaning, and creative agency. We see why, for Freud, the mother as matrix keeps disappearing and what religious maturity is for "honest smallholders on this earth" who live within matrix as mystery.

KEISLER, H Jerome. From Discrete to Continuous Time. Annals Pure Applied Log, 52(1-2), 99-141, Ap 91.

A general metatheorem is proved which reduces a wide class of statements about continuous time stochastic processes to statements about discrete time processes. We introduce a strong language for stochastic processes, and a concept of forcing for sequences of discrete time processes. The main theorem states that a sentence in the language is true if and only if it is forced. Although the stochastic process case is emphasized in order to motivate the results, they apply to a wider class of random variables. At the end of the paper we illustrate how the theorem can be used with three applications involving submartingales.

KEITH, William. Cognitive Science on a Wing and a Prayer. Soc Epistem, 4(4), 343-355, O-D 90.

This paper argues that Peter Slezak's defense of cognitive science as a "hard" or natural science is untenable, due to his inadequate conceptualization of cognitive science and his rhetorical confusion about the exigencies of defending a new discipline.

KEITH, William. Response to Slezak: *Nein, Ich verstehe nicht*. Soc Epistem, 4(4), 361-367, O-D 90.

This article answers Peter Slezak's criticisms of an earlier piece. It argues (again) that cognitive science has no positivist/empiricist foundation in Chomskian syntactic theory, and outlines and evaluates Slezak's set of rhetorical strategies for defending a new discipline.

KEKES, John. Moral Depth. Philosophy, 65(254), 439-453, O 90.

Moral depth involves understanding the significance of contingency for human life in general and for our own lives in particular. The achievement of this understanding tends to be subversive because it is likely to elicit in us inappropriate emotional reactions and undermine our wholehearted engagement in making our lives good. Moral depth corrects the tendency of our emotions to get out of hand when we realize the unavoidable risks we face and it motivates us in the absence of any guarantees that our efforts will succeed. Thus moral depth provides a perspective on individual lives as manifestations of the general condition of humanity. The analysis proceeds by reflecting on Oedipus's growth in depth as shown by Sophocles in *Oedipus the King* and *Oedipus at Colonus*.

KEKES, John. Moral Imagination, Freedom, and the Humanities. Amer Phil Quart, 28(2), 101-111, Ap 91.

This paper develops a conception of moral imagination. The function of moral imagination is to enlarge the field of our possibilities and correct the mistakes we tend to make in judging what our possibilities are. Thus through moral imagination we acquire moral breadth and depth. But moral imagination also increases our freedom by increasing both our possibilities and our realism about what they are. Since one traditional task of the humanities is the cultivation of moral imagination, the humanities have an indispensable moral and educational role.

KELLENBERGER, J. Wittgenstein's Gift to Contemporary Analytic Philosophy of Religion. Int J Phil Relig, 28(3), 147-172, D 90.

What may be called "contemporary analytic philosophy of religion" is a style of philosophy that is at once carefully analytic and sympathetic toward religious belief. It is also, particularly in its reflections on the rationality of religion, rigorously theoretical. To this style of philosophical reflection Wittgenstein might send a gift: his advice to "look, not think." What this gift comes to regarding several issues is discussed. And, regarding religious rationality, it is argued that, while there may be various fruitful approaches to the issue, Wittgenstein's gift has a point for at least some of the new analytic treatments.

KELLER, Catherine. "To Illuminate Your Trace": Self in Late Modern Feminist Theology. Listening, 25(3), 211-224, Fall 90.

KELLER, Catherine. "Psychocosmetics and the Underworld Connection" in *Archetypal Process: Self and Divine in Whitehead, Jung, and Hillman*, GRIFFIN, David Ray (ed), 133-155. Evanston, Northwestern Univ Pr, 1989.

KELLER, Catherine. "Reconnecting: A Reply to Robert Moore" in *Archetypal Process: Self and Divine in Whitehead, Jung, and Hillman*, GRIFFIN, David Ray (ed), 163-165. Evanston, Northwestern Univ Pr, 1989.

KELLER, Monika. "The Emergence of Morality in Personal Relationships" in *The Moral Domain: Essays in the Ongoing Discussion between Philosophy and the Social Sciences*, WREN, Thomas E (ed), 255-282. Cambridge, MIT Pr, 1990.

The study reconstructs the development of interpersonal and moral sensitivity in close relationships. Friendship is chosen as a prototypical relationship of symmetry which fosters development of moral reciprocity and emotional intimacy. In a longitudinal study of 120 subjects at ages 7, 9, 12, 15 and 19 years descriptive social and prescriptive moral reasoning was assessed in an interview about a morally relevant conflict involving promise-keeping between best friends. Four developmental levels of reasoning about friendship and promise-keeping were described. In contra-distinction to Kohlberg's conception of preconventional morality the results document that early moral reasoning is empathic and genuinely normative.

KELLEY, Jane and HANEN, Marsha. "Inference to the Best Explanation in Archaeology" in *Critical Traditions in Contemporary Archaeology*, PINSKY, Valerie (ed), 14-17. New York, Cambridge Univ Pr, 1990.

KELLNER, Douglas. *Television and the Crisis of Democracy*. Boulder, Westview Pr, 1990.

The book presents a systematic, critically informed political and institutional study of television in the United States. Focusing on the relationships among television, the state, and business, the book traces the history of television broadcasting, emphasizing its socio-economic impact and its growing political power. Acknowledging that television has long served the interests of the powerful, the author points out that it has dramatized conflicts within society and has on occasion led to significant social criticism. Yet examination of the role of television in the 1980s suggests that television has worked in recent years to further the conservative hegemony of Reagan and Bush. Contrasting network television coverage with coverage by the alternative press, the author exposes a variety of issues that television ignored or played down which could put in question the conservative politics of the past decade.

KELLNER, Hans. "As Real As It Gets...": Ricoeur and Narrativity. Phil Today, 34(3), 229-242, Fall 90.

Paul Ricoeur's *Time and Narrative*, like the Christian Bible, has a tragi-comic form which reduces the pain and fragmentation of human temporal experience into the larger form of meaning which is narrative emplotment. Ricoeur accomplishes his redemption by creating a series of "quasi" concepts (i.e., quasi-events, quasi-characters, quasi-plots, etc.) which mediate the apparent gaps in life. Death, however, is a limit to this bridging process, both in human life and in historical discourse. Death plays a special role in Ricoeur's work, and illuminates his view of narrative.

KELLNER, Menachem. "Jewish Ethics" in *A Companion to Ethics*, SINGER, Peter (ed), 82-90. Cambridge, Blackwell, 1991.

KELLY, Charles J. The Logic of the Liar from the Standpoint of the Aristotelian Syllogistic. Notre Dame J Form Log, 32(1), 129-146, Wint 91.

By developing the syntactical insights implicit in the Aristotelian syllogistic, we can show that two strengthened versions of the Megarian Liar paradoxes are sophisms committing the old fashioned *in dictione* fallacies of amphiboly and equivocation.

KELLY, Charles J. On Some Logically Equivalent Propositions. Log Anal, 31(121-122), 135-142, Mr-Je 88.

KELLY, Charles J. On the Logic of Eternal Knowledge. Mod Sch, 68(2), 163-169, Ja 91.

KELLY, Eugene. Aquinas and the Deconstruction of History. Vera Lex, 10(2), 6-8, 1990.

This paper is a discussion of the means of interpreting pre-modern political theories with special reference to Aquinas. The claim that such historical texts can be read in limitless and incommensurable ways is discussed in connection with *ST*, Q. 94 Art 4-5. An effort is made to reconstruct a narration of Aquinas's moral vision as integrated within his social and political theory, and demonstrate that his concept of teleology plays a critical and limiting role in our contemporary understanding of that vision.

KELLY, Kevin. "Effective Epistemology, Psychology, and Artificial Intelligence" in *Acting and Reflecting: The Interdisciplinary Turn in Philosophy*, SIEG, Wilfried (ed), 115-126. Norwell, Kluwer, 1990.

KELLY, Kevin and GLYMOUR, Clark. Getting to the Truth Through Conceptual Revolutions. Proc Phil Sci Ass, 1, 89-96, 1990.

There is a popular view that the alleged meaning shifts resulting from scientific revolutions are somehow incompatible with the formulation of general norms for scientific inquiry. We construct methods that can be shown to be maximally reliable at getting to the truth when the truth changes in response to the state of the scientist or his society.

KELLY, Michael Lee. Wittgenstein and "Mad Pain". Synthese, 87(2), 285-294, My 91.

KELLY, Michael (ed). *Hermeneutics and Critical Theory in Ethics and Politics*. Cambridge, MIT Pr, 1991.

Twelve essays by philosophers (J Habermas, M Walzer, A Heller, T McCarthy, S Benhabib, A Wellmer, G Warnke, K Baynes, A Ophir, M Kelly, R Makkreel, C Gould) whose work in philosophical ethics or politics has been affected by the debates over the last 25 years in and between hermeneutics and critical theory. Hermeneutics and critical theory provide two distinct but related paradigms of critique, which are important for 3 reasons: each has developed a history of critique offering valuable insights; each represents a mode of philosophical reflection which demonstrates that historicity is necessary for critique; and each already inspires ethical and political critique.

KELLY, P J. Utilitarian Strategies in Bentham and John Stuart Mill. Utilitas, 2(2), 245-266, N 90.

KELLY, Sean and BOHM, D. Dialogue on Science, Society, and the Generative Order. Zygon, 25(4), 449-467, D 90.

This article is an edited transcription of two conversations at Birkbeck College, London, in February 1987. Its primary concern is a transdisciplinary consciousness that refuses to comply with the tendency toward reductionism and simplification. Some of the problems the dialogue explores are (1) the notion of order (with particular reference to Bohm's recent reflections on the concept of the generative order), (2) the limits of knowledge and the concept of the Absolute, (3) the nature of perceptive or intuitive reason, (4) the relation between matter and mind, and (5) the contemporary global crisis and the possibility of creative evolution.

KELMAN, Mark. Reasonable Evidence of Reasonableness. Crit Inquiry, 17(4), 798-817, Sum 91.

KELZ, Carlos R. El tránsito de la existencia al ser. Sapientia, 45(177), 167-184, Jl-S 90.

KEMAL, S. Community and the Evil Poem. Rev Int Phil, 45(176), 24-38, 1991.

This paper examines the social parameters that structure aesthetic judgements in Kant's conception, developing his claim that these judgements seek confirmation from other subjects rather than from the state of objects. It then shows the implications of this concept of confirmation for the relation of aesthetic to moral value.

KEMAL, S. Nietzsche's Genealogy: Of Beauty and Community. J Brit Soc Phenomenol, 21(3), 234-249, O 90.

KEMP, G N. Pictures and Depictions: A Consideration of Peacocke's Views. Brit J Aes, 30(4), 332-341, O 90.

Christopher Peacocke has recently presented a theory of pictorial representation which retains the commonsense appeal of a straightforwardly perceptual view, but which avoids some primary objections which motivate conventionalist accounts. The theory fails to accommodate an important distinction amongst types of pictures—one analogous to the distinction between names and definite descriptions—and therefore wrongly identifies the subjects of certain pictures. I recommend a revision which solves the difficulty.

KEMP, G Neville. Metaphor and Aspect-Perception. Analysis, 51(2), 84-90, Mr 91.

It is frequently suggested that metaphor involves expression or transmission of some sort of non-propositional content which is incapable of liberal expression, and that this can somehow be understood or explained, and that this can somehow be understood or explained in light of the phenomenon of seeing-as, or even regarded as an instance of it. I argue that few metaphors admit any direct inclusion under the notion of seeing-as (or, more broadly, 'aspect-perception'), and for those which seem to, much less explanation is in the offing that might initially be supposed.

KEMP, Peter. Éthique et technique: bioéthique. Aquinas, 34(1), 25-40, Ja-Ap 91.

KENNEDY, David. Thinking About Home Schooling: Some Historical, Philosophical, and Cultural Reasons. Phil Stud Educ, /, 34-44, 1986.

Home schooling challenges several creedal assumptions of universal, compulsory, state-provided schooling: that nationalized schooling is necessary to national unity, and that only certified "professionals" can teach children well. Home schooling is prophetic in relation to American culture and education. It prophesies the decentralization of educational settings and the de-institutionalization of children, leading to a dialectical return to local forms of community in which the lives of adults and children are integrated.

KENNEDY, George. "'Truth' and 'Rhetoric' in the Pauline Epistles" in *The Bible as Rhetoric: Studies in Biblical Persuasion and Credibility*, WARNER, Martin (ed), 195-203. New York, Routledge, 1990.

KENNEDY, Leonard A. "Thomism and Divine Absolute Power" in *Thomistic Papers, V*, RUSSMAN, Thomas A (ed), 49-62. Notre Dame, Univ Notre Dame Pr, 1990.

Perhaps the most common doctrine in late medieval philosophy was that God could, by His absolute power, do many things opposed to His wisdom and goodness. This article traces this doctrine from its beginning in Duns Scotus through three streams to its end in the early sixteenth century. It lists the things which God was alleged to be able to do by His absolute power and shows that this doctrine was opposed only by Thomists.

KENNEDY, Rick. The Alliance between Puritanism and Cartesian Logic at Harvard, 1687-1735. J Hist Ideas, 51(4), 549-572, O-D 90.

William Brittle used logic textbooks by Antoine LeGrand and Antoine Arnauld to compose two manuscript textbooks used at Harvard. The new logic's epistemology and method helped to strengthen Puritanism's declining intellectual dominance in New England.

KENNELLY, Laura B. Tory History Incognito: Hume's *History of England* in Goldsmith's *History of England*. Clio, 20(2), 169-183, Wint 91.

Oliver Goldsmith so carefully plagiarized Hume's *History* that it has been more influential than commonly recognized. Using the politically important material about the Tudors and the Stuarts as a point of comparison, this paper examines the following: changes Goldsmith made in the *History's* prose style and philosophical emphasis (he condensed and simplified, added drama, supported executing Charles I, and saw change as progress). Why? To support the status quo and Whig interpretations. In addition, consequences of Hume's work being doubly (partly in disguise as that of Goldsmith) transmitted to eighteenth- and nineteenth- century thought are explored.

KENNEY, John Peter. *Mystical Monotheism: A Study in Ancient Platonic Theology*. Hanover, Univ Pr New England, 1991.

An examination of the emergence of philosophical monotheism in Greco-Roman theology from Plato through Plotinus. Concentrates on the development of ancient Platonic theology, with particular attention to the relation of intelligibles to divinity. Argues that the theology of Plotinus constitutes a type of monotheism.

KENNY, Anthony. "Can Responsibility Be Diminished?" in *Liability and Responsibility*, FREY, R G (ed), 13-31. New York, Cambridge Univ Pr, 1991.

KENYON, Timothy A. Russell on Pastness. Dialogue (PST), 33(2-3), 57-59, Ap 91.

In "On the Experience of Time", Russell claims that a knowledge of an objective earlier/later relation cannot establish our original awareness of "pastness". He proposes a special knowledge of pastness derived from introspection upon memory. My paper summarizes both accounts, examining Russell's rejection of the former. I conclude that the objective relation could indeed form the epistemic basis of pastness. Thus, for Russell's purposes, the psychological account is unnecessary.

KERBER, Harald. Ist die Kantische Theorie eine Theorie entfremdeter Erkenntnis? Deut Z Phil, 39(3), 262-271, 1991.

In this contribution it shall be shown that Kant's idea of reason is not to be criticized in the sense of the other side of reason, as it is handled by the Böhmes'. But the retranscendentalisation of the social theory by Apel and Habermas is just as problematic. Kant's theory is to be seen in connection with the bourgeois society. Kant's 'I think' is corresponding unconsciously with a type of society in which the persons are objects of their own social structures. Therein is to be found the cause for the problem of alienation in the structure of Kant's theory.

KERBY, Anthony Paul. Gadamer's Concrete Universal. Man World, 24(1), 49-61, Ja 91.

An examination of the use of universality in Hans-Georg Gadamer's philosophical hermeneutics. Emphasis is on Gadamer's appropriation of the notion of concrete universality from Hegelian philosophy and the central importance of this type of universality for Gadamer's hermeneutics.

KERENYI, Karoly. Hegel and the Gods of Greece (in Hungarian). Magyar Filozof Szemle, 5-6, 596-606, 1990.

KERKHOFF, Manfred. Hierofanías: Una retrospectiva de la obra de Ludwig Schajowicz. Dialogos, 26(57), 35-57, Ja 91.

This is a seven part article on four books by the Austrian philosopher Ludwig Schajowicz: *Nito y existencia; Los nueuos sofistas; De Winckelmann a Heidegger; Elmundo trágico de los griegos y de Shakespeare*. This review tried to show the development of Schajowicz's ideas between 1961 and 1991.

KERKHOFF, Manfred. Paradojas del Romanticismo. Dialogos, 26(57), 149-165, Ja 91.

This is an article/review of Esleban Tollinchi's book "Romanticism y modernidad. Ideas fund amen tales de las culture del siglo XIX." (2 volumes, Editorial de la Universidad de Puerto Rico, 1989). The review follows closely the seventeen chapters of the book (ordered in terms of complexes of ideas).

KERNOHAN, Andrew. Lewis's Functionalism and Reductive Materialism. Phil Psych, 3(2-3), 235-246, 1990.

KERR, Fergus. Getting the Subject Back into the World: Heidegger's Version. Philosophy, 29, 173-190, 91 Supp.

KERR-LAWSON, Angus. Substrative Materialism. Bull Santayana Soc, 8, 14-17, Fall 90.

KERR-LAWSON, Angus. Toward One Santayana: Recent Scholarship. Trans Peirce Soc, 27(1), 1-25, Wint 91.

This survey of recent writings on Santayana, with emphasis on religion, politics, and aesthetics, focuses especially on three books, by John McCormick, Anthony Woodward, and John Lachs.

KESLER, Darrel and BARRY, Robert. Pharaoh's Magicians: The Ethics and Efficacy of Human Fetal Tissue Transplants. Thomist, 54(4), 575-607, O 90.

This work first points the history of failures of human fetal tissue transplants. It then reviews all of the scientific problems and difficulties involved in claims that human fetal tissue transplants are successful. It argues that human fetal tissue transplants involve some very severe ethical problems which its proponents do not face up to, and it concludes by rejecting calls for federal funding of research on human fetal transplantation.

KESSEL, Ros. Reforming Britain's National Health Service. Bus Prof Ethics J, 9(3-4), 121-132, Fall-Wint 90.

KETCHUM, Richard J. The Paradox of Epistemology: A Defense of Naturalism. Phil Stud, 62(1), 45-66, Ap 91.

The first part of the paper argues that there is no analysis of (or statement of sufficient conditions for) "justification." The problem is that as an analysis it would have to be lawlike. But if it were lawlike it could be used to support a counterfactual conditional to the effect that if I were justified in believing it I would satisfy its analysans. I argue that since no analysis can be so used there is no such analysis. In part II I show how the conclusion of part I supports naturalism and clarify one version of naturalism.

KETCHUM, Richard. The Argument from Religious Experience: A Narrowing of Alternatives. Faith Phil, 8(3), 354-367, Jl 91.

One position on the epistemic status of religious experiences is what I call the liberal position: those who have had a religious experience are justified on its basis in believing in God but the testimony of those who have had religious experiences does not justify others in believing in God. I argue that, though the liberal position is popular, it is unreasonable. The principle I use to support this view seems also to support an argument which appeals to religious experience as evidence that God exists. I argue that onus of proof considerations block the inference, however.

KETTNER, Matthias. A New Approach in Moral Theory (in Dutch). Bijdragen, 2, 201-206, 1991.

Discourse ethics as developed by Karl-Otto Apel and Jürgen Habermas transform the Kantian idea that normative justification requires consistent universalizability into a dialogical procedure between participants of practical discourse. In practical discourse we put normative proposals to the test of normative validity. However, discourse ethics has to account for the difference between the idea of practical discourse on the one hand and the brute fact that the world as it is often does not allow for conflicts to be resolved via discursive procedures. An account of guiding principles for the morally responsible *application* of practical discourse thus becomes part and parcel of the normative *theory* of practical communicative rationality. (edited)

KETTNER, Matthias. Responsibility As a Moral Principle? A Critical Reflection on Hans Jonas' Ethics of Responsibility? (in German). Bijdragen, 4, 418-439, 1990.

Hans Jonas's important work "The Imperative of Responsibility" develops new conceptual resources for ethics in the age of all-pervasive technology. Jonas's notion of collective moral responsibility with regard to the unforeseen and unintended consequences of collective action has been especially well received, at least in Germany, both in public debates about the demands for a New Ethics in the face of the environmental crisis as well as in political discourse about eco-ethical concerns. I discuss the key innovative features of Jonas's ethical framework against the background of currently predominant universalistic approaches in philosophical moral theory. I clarify the links between Jonas's concept of moral responsibility and a general theory of (moral) and nonmoral value. I then examine Jonas's argumentative strategy of founding moral responsibility in a (Neo-Aristotelian) concept of nature that countenances objective teleology in nature. (edited)

KEULMAN, Kenneth. *The Balance of Consciousness: Eric Voegelin's Political Theory*. University Park, Penn St Univ Pr, 1990.

This volume revives a classical notion of mind in a contemporary framework in response to attempts to deconstruct the image of the mind as a mirror reflecting 'reality,' challenging the conception of knowledge as accurate representation. Consciousness is considered as a product of cultural evolution, with an emphasis on mind embodied in personal, social, and historical life. The culture in which mind develops is a specific history embedded in the memories and archives of those who transmit it as "local knowledge." Any notion of consciousness has a complex relationship with the activities of explanation that organize society. Arguments are made in the context of contemporary philosophy of mind and political theory.

KEYES, C Don (ed). *New Harvest: Transplanting Body Parts and Reaping the Benefits*. Clifton, Humana Pr, 1991.

Physicians, as well as legal and ethical writers, address four ethical concerns: 1) the exceptional degree of conflict transplantation causes in basic biomedical principles, 2) the larger society's role in establishing policies, 3) legitimacy of organ (or tissue) source in relation to when human life begins and ends, and 4) self-identity issues, especially brain death and brain tissue grafting. As principal author, Keyes attempts to reconstruct respect for life in the light of conflicts caused by transplantation, beginning with a monistic interpretation of the mind-brain relation. He also argues that deontology and consequentialism are complementary, not mutually exclusive.

KHALIFA, A K. A Constructive Version of Sperner's Lemma and Brouwer's Fixed Point Theorem. Z Math Log, 36(3), 247-251, 1990.

KHALIL, Elias L. Beyond Self-Interest and Altruism: A Reconstruction of Adam Smith's Theory of Human Conduct. Econ Phil, 6(2), 255-273, O 90.

I attempt a reconstruction of Adam Smith's view of human nature as explicated in *The Theory of Moral Sentiments*. Smith's view of human conduct is neither functionalist nor reductionist, but interactionist. Conscience is neither made by Smith a function of public approval nor reduced to disguised self-interest, nor for that matter reduced to the self-contained impulse of altruism. For Smith, conscience maintains its moral autonomy through the switching of stations among spectators, actors, and people acted upon. I distinguish two types of station-switching, which places Smith's theory apart from the micro-functionalism of George Herbert Mead.

KHALIL, Elias L. Natural Complex versus Natural System. J Soc Biol Struct, 13(1), 11-31, F 90.

I draw an ontological distinction between two types of natural forms which are isomorphic across physics, biology, and human sciences. The first type, "natural complex," depicts purposeful forms involved in organic interaction. Examples include atoms, cells, organs, organisms, populations of organisms, households, firms, tribes, and nations. The second type, "natural system," depicts chaotic forms involved in topographic interaction. Examples include climates, water turbulence, geodynamics, ecosystems, and stock markets. I examine six dimensions which juxtapose the two natural forms. With respect to canons, natural complex is governed by "rules," while natural system by "principles." In regards to interaction, the former is "organic," while the latter "topographic." In relation to arrangement, the former is exemplified by "configuration," while the latter by "pattern." With respect to spatial arrangement, the former is typified by "organization," while the latter by "structure." In regards to temporal arrangement, the former is characterized by "process," while the latter by "dynamics." In relation to hierarchy, the former is distinguished by "complexity," while the latter by "complicatedness."

KHALIL, Elias L. Rationality and Social Labor in Marx. Crit Rev, 4(1-2), 239-265, Wint-Spr 90.

Textual exegesis is used to show that Marx's concept of social labor is transhistorical, referring to a collective activity of humans as a species. The collective nature of labor is suspended in capitalist production because of the anarchic character of market relations. But the suspension is skin deep: the sociality of labor asserts itself in a mediated manner through the alienated empowerment of goods with value. This is commodity fetishism, which vanishes when relations of production become actually collective—matching the transhistorical essence of labor. Marx's concept of social labor is adjudged inadequate. It amounts to asserting that the actions of agents could be *ex ante* calculated according to a global rationality. In this respect, Marx's concept of social labor is reminiscent of the equally deficient notion of perfect competition in mainstream neoclassical economics.

KHANIN, Dmitry. The Postmodern Posture. Phil Lit, 14(2), 239-247, O 90.

The thrust of the article is a critique of some aspects of the postmodernist theory and worldview as promoted by such authors as Baudrillard, Danto, Jameson. "The Postmodern Scene" by Croker and Cook is scrutinized to demonstrate ensuing absurdities of "postmodern posture." The main point is that the postmodern attempt to arrest history's forward motion, though understandable in our age, still leaves mankind "on the playground with the warped, old toys—like retarded children with no prospect of maturity."

KHANIN, Dmitry. "Structure of Methodology of an Aesthetic Theorem" in *XIth International Congress in Aesthetics, Nottingham 1988*, WOODFIELD, Richard (ed), 90-93. Nottingham, Nottingham Polytech, 1990.

KHOURI, Nadia. Il y a vingt-cinq ans la sémiotique.... Horiz Phil, 1(2), 161-174, 1991.

KIDD, James W and KIDD, Sunnie D. *Experiential Method: Qualitative Research in the Humanities Using Metaphysics and Phenomenology*. New York, Lang, 1990.

KIDD, James W. Hermeneutic Phenomenology and Taoism. Asian J Phil, 2(1), 71-80, Sum 90.

This presentation will utilize the thought of Martin Heidegger and Chuang Tzu as representative of Hermeneutic Phenomenology and Taoism. The themes will specifically be: 1) identity and variation; 2) discovering - describing - disclosing. Implications for society and research will both be presented.

KIDD, Sunnie D and KIDD, James W. *Experiential Method: Qualitative Research in the Humanities Using Metaphysics and Phenomenology*. New York, Lang, 1990.

KIENPOINTNER, Manfred. Rhetoric and Argumentation: Relativism and Beyond. Phil Rhet, 24(1), 43-53, 1991.

I want to refute the claim that forms of argumentation inspired and shaped by rhetorical devices ('rhetorical argumentation') can be distinguished clearly from rational, sound and scientific argumentation ('proper argumentation'). To do this, I try to refute anti-rhetorical reproaches like the following ones: rhetoric doesn't use neutral/impartial language; rhetoric doesn't (always) use valid inference schemes; rhetoric doesn't provide objective truth criteria. Furthermore, I try to show that the resulting 'rhetorical relativism' has several positive consequences.

KIENZLE, Bertram. Lockes Qualitäten: Erwiderung auf Casati. Stud Leibniz, 22(2), 199-202, 1990.

In this paper I reply to objections raised by Roberto Casati (in *Studia Leibnitiana*, 194-198) against my interpretation of Locke's famous distinction between primary and secondary qualities (cf. *Studia Leibnitiana* 21, 21-41, 1989). The thesis that secondary qualities can be read off observable bodies is defended against Casati's alleged counterexample. His defence of Peter Alexander's identification of (some) secondary qualities with corpuscular textures is shown to be unconvincing. The proposal that Locke's theory be interpreted by means of the distinction between determinate and determinable qualities is discussed, and it is suggested that the Lockean distinction be reinterpreted in terms of determinate qualities.

KIERKEGAARD, Soren and HONG, Howard V (ed & trans) and HONG, Edna H (ed & trans). *For Self-Examination: Judge for Yourself*. Princeton, Princeton Univ Pr, 1990.

KIERNAN-LEWIS, Delmas. Not Over Yet: Prior's 'Thank Goodness' Argument'. Philosophy, 66(256), 241-243, Ap 91.

KIGONGO, J K. Human Rights in the Context of Uganda's Political Experience. Quest, 5(1), 74-79, Je 91.

The work was intended to show that Uganda is on the threshold of political transformation. This development is an outcome of establishment of a government in 1986 which set out to emancipate the society from almost a century of state coercion to ensure political participation of individuals in the society's political process. The anticipated political freedom would presumably help to bring about harmony between the state and its citizens. The work, however, concludes that the society has yet to evolve a system of ethical values to support the political change. A solution is conceived to be in formal education.

KILGOUR, D Marc and FISHBURN, Peter C. Binary 2 x 2 Games. Theor Decis, 29(3), 165-182, N 90.

The 2 x 2 game is the simplest interactive decision model that portrays concerned decision makers with genuine choices. There are two players, each of whom must choose one of two strategies, so that there are four possible outcomes. *Binary 2 x 2 games* are 2 x 2 games with no restrictions on the players' preference relations over the outcomes. They therefore generalize the strict ordinal 2 x 2 games and the ordinal 2 x 2 games, classes which have already been studied extensively. This paper enumerates the strategically distinct binary 2 x 2 games. It also identifies important subsets defined by the number of pure Nash equilibria and the occurrence of dominant strategies.

KILLORAN, John B. Divine Reason and Virtue in St Thomas's Natural Law Theory. Vera Lex, 10(1), 17-18, 1990.

KIM, Chin-Tai. A Critique of Genealogies. Metaphilosophy, 21(4), 391-404, O 90.

Varieties of genetic argument are described and evaluted. A causal argument to the effect that a belief is true or false because of the nature of its cause is incomplete, requiring controversial premises concerning, notably, the conditions of reference. Nietzchean genealogy that explains how a false belief has resulted from a suppression of an originally apprehended truth presupposes the truth, hence is an ineffectual argument to establish it. Hegelian dialectic alone, among the varieties of genetic argument, has the structural advantage of grounding a truth. But the adequacy, even the possibility, of dialectic is left an unresolved issue.

KIM, Jaegwon. "Explanatory Exclusion and the Problem of Mental Causation" in *Information, Semantics and Epistemology*, VILLANUEVA, Enrique (ed), 36-56. Cambridge, Blackwell, 1990.

The paper begins with a description of the three main problems of mental causation currently in debate, and then focuses on one of these problems, i.e., "the exclusion problem". This problem arises as follows: if each mental event is in principle explainable in terms of neurophysiological antecedents and conditions, as many believe, then what explanatory job can there be for its (supposed) mental causes? Although token physicalism solves this problem for individual mental events, the problem is very much alive for mental properties, especially those who believe in the causal efficacy of mental properties while rejecting their physical reducibility. The paper discusses various putative solutions to this problem, and make certain proposals.

KIM, Jaegwon. "Mechanism, Purpose, and Explanatory Exclusion" in *Philosophical Perspectives, 3: Philosophy of Mind and Action Theory, 1989*, TOMBERLIN, James E (ed), 77-108. Atascadero, Ridgeview, 1989.

The question whether an action can be given both a "mechanistic" explanation in terms of its physiological antecedents and a "rationalizing" explanation in terms of beliefs and desires (especially, when the latter, too, is construed as a causal explanation) is raised again, and discussed in a more general setting. The paper argues for the following "exclusion principle": no event can have more than one *complete* and *independent* causal explanation. Some implications and applications of this principle are discussed.

KIM, Ki Su. J S Mill's Concept of Maturity as the Criterion in Determining Children's Eligibility for Rights. J Phil Educ, 24(2), 235-244, Wint 90.

The most commonly advanced justification for treating children differently from adults is that they are not mature and thus incapable of taking any form of independent action. In J S Mill's utilitarian philosophy, immaturity is used as the ground for not according rights to children and placing them under adult protection. In this paper, some philosophical and educational problems entailed by such an approach are analyzed. The conclusions suggest that in order to properly consider the question of children's rights it is necessary that we go beyond Mill's limited horizon of utilitarianism.

KIM, Kihyeon and LEHRER, Keith. The Fallibility Paradox. Phil Phenomenol Res, 50 SUPP, 99-107, Fall 90.

One doctrine of fallibilism, which is widely accepted, affirms that even the best justification we can have for most of what we believe leaves open the possibility of error. This doctrine and refinements thereof lead to paradox and inconsistency when combined with two plausible conditions of a criterion of justification. The first says that satisfaction of the criterion is a necessary condition of justification, and the second says that determination that the criterion is satisfied is a sufficient condition for justification. Solutions to the paradox suggest that we must give up either externalism, internalism or the doctrine of fallibilism.

KIMMERLE, Heinz (ed). *I, We and Body: First Joint Symposium of Philosophers from Africa and from the Netherlands*. Atlantic Highlands, Gruner, 1989.

The idea of a joint symposium of philosophers from Africa and from the Netherlands departs from the conviction that there are problems which they have in common. A group of these problems is about I (individual), We (community), and Body (the natural aspect of I and We). Although African thought traditionally concentrates on the We and European thought on the I there are opposite streams also in both traditions. Therefore, a differentiated view is necessary. The Body is the bearer of signs which are inscribed by the different ways of thought and of life.

KIMMERLE, Heinz. "The Position of Culture within Development" in *I, We and Body: First Joint Symposium of Philosophers from Africa and from the Netherlands*, KIMMERLE, Heinz (ed), 103-107. Atlantic Highlands, Gruner, 1989.

The dialogue between philosophers from Africa and from Western countries on common issues is only beginning. It is part of a cultural exchange. But it is not dependent on the imperatives of development politics. Art and philosophy are already on the highest level in the very beginning as can be seen, e.g., from the cave paintings of Lascaux or Lao Tse's Tao te king. Therefore, these core areas of culture can play a specific role with regard to development. Artists and philosophers from both cultures can meet on the level of complete equality.

KIMURA, Kiyotaka. The Self in Medieval Japanese Buddhism: Focusing on Dōgen. Phil East West, 41(3), 327-340, Jl 91.

I examined the revelation of the self in Dogen in this paper. As a result, it may have become clear that Dogen grappled with the problem of the self with the whole of his being, and that not only did he present a logical picture of the world as the self and the self as the world, but in his actual everyday life he was also aware of his inadequacies and sought to return to this true mode of being of the self, a mode of being which manifests itself as compassion or action for the welfare of others.

KIMURA, Rihito. "Fiduciary Relationships and the Medical Profession: A Japanese Point of View" in *Ethics, Trust, and the Professions: Philosophical and Cultural Aspects*, PELLEGRINO, Edmund D (ed), 235-245. Washington, Georgetown Univ Pr, 1991.

KIMURA, Rihito. Japan's Dilemma with the Definition of Death. Kennedy Inst Ethics J, 1(2), 123-131, Je 91.

Japan is unusual among industrialized countries in its reluctance to use brain criteria to determine death and harvest transplant organs. This results from public distrust of the medical profession due to an earlier incident, and from concern that technological interventions will threaten religious and cultural traditions surrounding death and dying. Public acceptance is growing, however, as medical professional groups and universities develop brain criteria, and as pressure from patients who could benefit from a transplant, as well as from foreign countries, increases.

KINCAID, Harold. Assessing Functional Explanations in the Social Sciences. Proc Phil Sci Ass, 1, 341-354, 1990.

Functionalism is a dominant but widely criticized perspective in social theory; this paper clarifies what functionalists claim, identifies what would count as evidence for those claims and evaluates some standard criticisms. Functionalism relies essentially on functional explanations of the form "A exists in order to B." I point out problems with previous accounts of such explanations, offer an improved account, and discuss in detail evidence that might confirm such explanations and its difficulties. I argue that some functionalist accounts can be confirmed and that, contra the critics, functionalism's problems are not inherent errors, "only" (avoidable) practical ones.

KINCAID, Harold. Molecular Biology and the Unity of Science. Phil Sci, 57(4), 575-593, D 90.

Advances in molecular biology have generally been taken to support the claim that biology is reducible to chemistry. I argue against that claim by looking in detail at a number of central results from molecular biology and showing that none of them supports reduction because (1) their basic predicates have multiple realizations, (2) their chemical realization is context-sensitive, and (3) their explanations often presuppose biological facts rather than eliminate them. I then consider the heuristic and confirmational implications of irreducibility and argue that purely biochemical approaches are likely to be unsound and to be unable to confirm an important range of statements. I conclude by sketching criteria for scientific unity that do not entail reducibility and yet leave an important place for identifying underlying mechanisms. Molecular biology, properly understood, provides an excellent paradigm of nonreductive unity between different explanatory levels.

KING, Debra W. Just Can't Find the Words: How Expression is Achieved. Phil Rhet, 24(1), 54-72, 1991.

This study identifies, defines, and examines expression through the use of phenomenological and linguistic distinctions. After a process of probing and testing through example, the value of these distinctions in communicating human experience is determined. Then, the text explores how metaphor affects the ability of language to communicate emotion and sensation. Finally, the author teases and tests Derrida's play of supplementarity and *differance* in hopes of revealing something unspeakable. This essay ultimately answers the question of language's ability to express human emotion and sensation. It thoroughly examines the relationship between philosophy and writing, and clearly explains how expression is achieved.

KING, Jeffrey C. Instantial Terms, Anaphora and Arbitrary Objects. Phil Stud, 61(3), 239-265, Mr 91.

In a number of recent works, Kit Fine has argued that instantial terms in applications of UG and EI, some uses of variables in mathematics, and some anaphoric pronouns refer to arbitrary objects. The author contrasts Fine's view with his own view according to which such expressions are *context dependent quantifiers*: quantifiers some of whose semantics features are determined by their linguistic contexts.

KING, Roger J H. Caring About Nature: Feminist Ethics and the Environment. Hypatia, 6(1), 75-89, Spr 91.

In this essay I examine the relevance of the vocabulary of an ethics of care to ecofeminism. While this vocabulary appears to offer a promising alternative to moral extensionism and deep ecology, there are problems with the use of this vocabulary by both essentialists and conceptualists. I argue that too great a reliance is placed on personal lived experience as a basis for ecofeminist ethics and that the concept of care is insufficiently determinate to explicate the meaning of care for nature.

KING, Roger J H. Environmental Ethics and the Case for Hunting. Environ Ethics, 13(1), 59-85, Spr 91.

Hunting is a complex phenomenon. I examine it from four different perspectives — animal liberation, the land ethic, primitivism, and ecofeminism — and find no moral justification for sport hunting in any of them. At the same time, however, I argue that there are theoretical flaws in each of these approaches. Hunting should be investigated within the broader context of patriarchal social relations between men and women. As an act of violence it constitutes one element of a cultural matrix which is destructive to both women and nature. (edited)

KING, Roger J H. How to Construe Nature: Environmental Ethics and the Interpretation of Nature. Between Species, 6(3), 101-108, Sum 90.

KING, Sallie and KEFFER, Steven and KRAFT, Steven. Process Metaphysics and Minimalism: Implications for Public Policy. Environ Ethics, 13(1), 23-47, Spr 91.

Using process philosophy, especially its view of nature and its ethic, we develop a process-based environmental ethic embodying minimalism and beneficience. From this perspective, we criticize the philosophy currently underlying public policy and examine some alternative approaches based on phenomenology and ethnomethodology. We conclude that process philosophy, minus its value hierarchy, is a powerful tool capable of supporting both radical and moderate changes in environmental policy.

KING-FARLOW, John. Emanating Causes: New Battle Lines for Natural Theology? Sophia (Australia), 29(3), 2-9, O 90.

KINLAW, Kathy. Maternal Rights, Fetal Harms: Commentary. Hastings Center Rep, 21(3), 22-23, My-Je 91.

KINOSHITA, Joyce. How Do Scientific Explanations Explain? Philosophy, 27, 297-311, 90 Supp.

KINZER, Bruce L. "John Stuart Mill and the Experience of Political Engagement" in *A Cultivated Mind: Essays On J S Mill Presented to John M Robson*, LAINE, Michael (ed), 182-214. Buffalo, Univ of Toronto Pr, 1991.

This article traces the course of J S Mill's engagement with the Victorian political system from the second half of the 1830s through his parliamentary career (1865-1868). Noting that within Mill's make-up there existed both a prodigious capacity for analysis and a striking impulse towards political activism, this essay examines the primary factors, political and personal, that shaped the ways in which these somewhat divergent characteristics were expressed during these decades. The conclusion is that the form and substance of that expression was markedly affected by the relative strength of these internal attributes at any particular time.

KIPNIS, Kenneth. Ethics and the Professional Responsibility of Lawyers. J Bus Ethics, 10(8), 569-576, Ag 91.

"Applied ethics" is sometimes understood on the engineering model: As engineers "apply" physics to human problems, so philosophers apply ethics to dilemmas of professional practice. It is argued that there is nothing in ethics comparable to physics. Using legal ethics as an example, it is suggested that political philosophy provides a better approach to understanding professional ethics. If, for example, the adversary system is a legitimate social institution, and if attorneys must adhere to certain principles in order for that institution to fulfill its purposes, then attorneys may be said to be subject to those ethical principles.

KIRK, Robert. Why Shouldn't We Be Able to Solve the Mind-Body Problem? Analysis, 51(1), 17-23, Ja 91.

McGinn has argued that there is a solution to the mind-body problem but is is in principle inaccessible to human beings. This article exposes a crucial flaw in his reasoning. He illegitimately assumes that a successful theory of the mind-body relation must confer a grasp of the concepts needed to describe, for example, the experiences of bats.

KIRMMSE, Bruce H. *Kierkegaard in Golden Age Denmark*. Bloomington, Indiana Univ Pr, 1990.

"Kierkegaard in Golden Age Denmark" is the only comprehensive intellectual biography of Soren Kierkegaard in English or any other language. The book describes and explains the development of Kierkegaard's thinking about religion and society in the context of Denmark's "Golden Age" of the first half of the 19th century. The Danish socio-economic, political, intellectual, and ecclesiastical milieu is analyzed in detail and serves as the basis for a careful treatment of Kierkegaard's later (1846 and after) authorship, particularly his notorious "attack on Christendom."

KIRSCH, Ulrich. *Blaise Pascals: "Pensées" (1656-1662) Systematische 'Gedanken' über*. Freiburg, Alber, 1991.

The internal logic of Pascal's chief work is explicated on the basis of the most recent developments in its editing and is shown to form a systematic argument about the incompatibility of man's mortality and impermanence with happiness. The logical order of this eudaimonistic ethics involves three steps: the critique of reason, the theory of human nature, and an apology for the Christian religion. The "géometrie du hasard" demonstrates the limits of and the possibilities for a reasonable proof of the existence of God and eternal life. Pascal's "doctrine of man" establishes that there are "vicious circles" of human misery and ascribes them to the transcience of existence. The philosophy of happiness proffers the ideals of universality, completeness and imperishability as essential criteria for ethics.

KIRSNER, Douglas. An Abyss of Difference: Laing, Sartre and Jaspers. J Brit Soc Phenomenol, 21(3), 209-215, O 90.

R D Laing assumed that human beings were always agents, no matter how apparently different or unintelligible their behavior might seem. This view contrasts with that of psychiatry, epitomised by Karl Jaspers who saw 'an abyss of difference' existing between normal and neurotic people on the one hand and psychotics on the other. Laing's challenge to Jaspers's view is very Sartrean. Sartre always maintained that no matter how alienated we are, we are fundamentally free. For both Sartre and Laing, the for-itself is irreducible to the in-itself. Laing's debt to Sartre is underscored and the paper examines Jaspers's view that the psychotic is 'ununderstandable' from a Laingian-Sartrean perspective. The denial of freedom or agent on the other of the abyss is not just a given; it demands that it ought to be crossed.

KIRZNER, Israel M. Self-Interest and the New Bashing of Economics. Crit Rev, 4(1-2), 27-40, Wint-Spr 90.

A spate of recent attacks on the rationality assumption in economic theory is noticed. Some of these attacks are fresh and, in many ways, original, but the central ideas underlying them are not new. They appear to have been provoked by the direction in which much of mainstream economics has been moving in recent years. On the other hand, it is suggested here, certain developments in contemporary economics, associated particularly with the revival of interest in the Austrian paradigm, offer a fresh understanding of the way in which the rationality assumption, its role in economics properly understood, is able to meet these old-new attacks.

KISIEL, Theodore. Heidegger's Apology: Biography as Philosophy and Ideology. Grad Fac Phil J, 14(2)-15(1), 363-404, 1991.

KISIELEWICZ, Andrzej. Double Extension Set Theory. Rep Math Log, 23, 81-89, 1989.

A new system of axioms for set theory is presented in this paper. By allowing the possibility of having two different extensions for some "irregular" sets, an extremely simple axiomatization is achieved.

KISS, Endre. The Reception of Nietzsche in Hungary between the Two World Wars (in Hungarian). Magyar Filozof Szemle, 6, 685-706, 1989.

Die Nietzsche-Rezeption der Jahr-hundertwende erwies sich als einer der wichtigsten intellektuellen Prozesse Ungarns, die das intellektuelle Leben des Landes für eine Zeit in zwei grosse Lager gespalten hat und im Zeichen einer allseitigen Relativisierung von absolut gesetzten (und offiziell auch als absolut geltenden) Werten eine selbst im europäischen Vergleich einmalige kritische und emanzipatorische Bewegung inaugurierte. Den Rezeptionslinien Nietzsches in der Zwischenkriegszeit gelang es nicht mehr, die Anregungen, die aus Nietzsches Denken kamen, nochmals so stark in den Mittelpunkt des intellektuellen Interesses zu stellen. Die Nietzsche-Rezeption der Vorkriegszeit hat sich insofern doch Dauer gezeigt, dass Nietzsches Name und die führenden Gehalte seiner philosophischen Relativierung zum bleibenden identitätsbildenden Teil der ungarischen geistigen Kultur geworden sind, die in der Geistigkeit der Zwischenkriegszeit etwa als "objektiver Geist" bis zuletzt nicht nur gegenwärtig, sondern in vielem auch qualifizierend, sogar bestimmend weiter wirkten. (edited)

KISSELL, Michael A. Progressive Traditionalism as the Spirit of Collingwood's Philosophy. Hist Theor, 29(4), 51-56, D 90.

"Progressive traditionalism" is the best way to define R G Collingwood's fundamental philosophical position in its theoretical and practical aspects. It is the logical consequence of his programme of "the rapprochement" between philosophy and history with dialectical rationalism as the theoretical instrument. The doctrine of "living past" is the vindication of the fusion of past heritage with creative elan of the present human thought, "absolute presuppositions" of civilization with everlasting change in human life. Certain practical inferences are made with regards to the present political situation.

KISSLING, Christian. Habermas et la théologie: Notes pour une discussion entre la théologie et la "Théorie de l'agir communicationnel". Frei Z Phil Theol, 38(1-2), 235-244, 1991.

Theology can show some limits of communicative action which are important for (social) ethics. In communicative action there is a category of acts directed neither by success nor by consensus: acts such as reconciliation, love, and forgiveness. These acts are often necessary for a consensus. Social ethics should not forget two insights: 1) Social ethics only deals with duties towards others without excluding the possibility of duties towards oneself. 2) Social ethics can only be useful for modern society as a synthesis of ethical theory and theory of society. In this way, Habermas's claim of the priority of the lifeworld gets moral significance. And theology, now, can found the expression of "structures of sin".

KISSLING, Christian. Die Theorie des kommunikativen Handelns in Diskussion. Frei Z Phil Theol, 37(1-2), 233-252, 1990.

The theory of communicative action has caused a variety of discussions in philosophy, and now in theology too: Communitarianism criticizes formalism in ethics that is a result of the unfounded claim of western rationality to be conception without presuppositions. Habermas's theory of the modern society as (political and economic) system and lifeworld could be of interest for various problems of social ethics. Moral theology should begin to deal with discursive ethics and to show that discursive ethics can only treat a part of practical problems. Finally, fundamental theology could show that the goal of communicative action is not attainable solely inside rationality.

KITCHENER, Richard F. Do Children Think Philosophically? Metaphilosophy, 21(4), 416-431, O 90.

Several philosophers (e.g., Lipman, Matthews) have argued that the received view—children cannot do philosophy—is mistaken and that the work of Jean Piaget, which supports the received view, is wrong both on empirical and conceptual grounds. Against these philosophers I argue that the conceptual basis of this "philosophy for children" movement is questionable: they have no clearly delineated notion of 'doing philosophy'; doing philosophy is often confused with thinking critically; behavioral criteria for doing philosophy are questionable on philosophical grounds; and the empirical claims made by these philosophers are false. Finally, I provide a Piagetian interpretation of this issue, distinguishing concrete philosophy from abstract philosophy, thus arguing for the basic correctness of Piaget's claims.

KITCHER, Patricia. "Apperception and Epistemic Responsibility" in *Central Themes in Early Modern Philosophy*, COVER, J A (ed), 273-304. Indianapolis, Hackett, 1990.

Previously I have argued that Kant's doctrine of apperception is best understood, not in terms of a special kind of nonsensory awareness, but merely as indicating that different mental states all belong to a contentually interconnected system of states. In this paper I try to do more justice to the "self-knowledge" side of apperception. To be epistemically responsible agents, we need to be able to monitor and so correct our beliefs. I argue that these considerations are not any kind of direct Cartesian awareness stand behind Kant's many claims about the necessity of being aware of our mental states.

KITCHER, Patricia. *Kant's Transcendental Psychology*. New York, Oxford Univ Pr, 1990.

For the last 100 years, historians have denigrated the psychology of the *Critique*. In opposition to both the Anglo-American and Continental approaches to Kant, I argue that we can only understand the deduction of the categories in terms of his attempt to fathom the psychological prerequisites of knowledge. In particular, I consider Kant's claims about the unity of the thinking self; the spatial form of perception; the relations among mental states necessary for content; the relation between perceptions and judgments; the structure of empirical concepts; and the limits of philosophical insight into psychological processes.

KITCHER, Philip and CULP, Sylvia. Theory Structure and Theory Change in Contemporary Molecular Biology. Brit J Phil Sci, 40(4), 459-483, D 89.

Traditional approaches to theory structure and theory change in science of not fare well when confronted with the practice of certain fields of science. We offer and account of contemporary practice in molecular biology designed to address two questions: Is theory change in this area of science gradual or saltatory? What is the relation between molecular biology and the fields of traditional biology? Our main focus is a recent episode in molecular biology, the discovery of enzymatic RNA. We argue that our reconstruction of this episode shows that traditional approaches to theory structure and theory change need considerable refinement if they are to be defended as generally applicable.

KITELEY, Murray (ed) and GARFIELD, Jay L (ed). *Meaning and Truth: The Essential Readings in Modern Semantics*. New York, Paragon House, 1991.

KITTLER, Friedrich. "The Mechanized Philosopher" in *Looking After Nietzsche*, RICKELS, Laurence A (ed), 195-207. Albany, SUNY Pr, 1990.

KIVISTO, Peter. Encountering Dallmayr. Human Stud, 14(1), 7-13, Ja 91.

This article assesses Fred Dallmayr's dialogue with various intellectual figures who have shaped modernist and postmodernist thought. Operating with "exegetical generosity," his essays in *Critical Encounters* (and elsewhere) are viewed as valuable models of what it means to engage in careful and judicious reading. A question is posed concerning the relationship of the intellectuals surveyed to Dallmayr's own project to develop a practical ontology.

KIVY, Peter. "The Profundity of Music" in *XIth International Congress in Aesthetics, Nottingham 1988*, WOODFIELD, Richard (ed), 94-98. Nottingham, Nottingham Polytech, 1990.

KLAGGE, James. Davidson's Troubles with Supervenience. Synthese, 85(2), 339-352, N 90.

KLAGGE, James. Rationalism, Supervenience, and Moral Epistemology. S J Phil, SUPP 29, 25-28, 1990.

KLAMI, Hannua Tapani (and others). Evidence and Legal Reasoning: On the Intertwinement of the Probable and the Reasonable. Law Phil, 10(1), 73-107, F 91.

The facts to be proven in a lawsuit can be more or less probable. But the recognition of the relevant facts may require discretion or evaluative operations; moreover, a just and equitable interpretation of a contract may depend on what the contracting parties knew about the intentions of each other. Can, e.g., negligence be more or less probable? Can Ought be proven? There is, however, a structural similarity between legal interpretation and the evaluation of evidence and not only an intertwinement between the so-called questions of fact and the questions of law. A number of situations is briefly analysed: the interpretation of contracts, the interest of the child, the basic concepts of the law of torts and the criminal intent.

KLATT, Heinz-Joachim. Learning Disabilities: A Questionable Construct. Educ Theor, 41(1), 47-60, Wint 91.

The field of special education insistently makes the claims that "learning disabilities" are the result of brain dysfunction, that they are properly categorized under the psychiatric label of "cognitive disorders," and that they are characterized by adequate rather than limited cognition, i.e., by normal or superior intelligence. All these claims are shown to be without foundation. It is argued that "LD" is a social construct that is readily and comprehensively explained as a result of bad schooling, low intelligence, and social pressures. The generally accepted and legislated definitions of LD are shown to serve political purposes rather than scientific imperatives.

KLAWITER, Maren. Using Arendt and Heidegger to Consider Feminist Thinking on Women and Reproductive/Infertility Technologies. Hypatia, 5(3), 65-89, Fall 90.

Modern technology and gender relations are deeply intertwined. There has yet to emerge, however, a feminist analysis of modern technology as a phenomenon and this has inhibited the development of a consistent feminist response and theory regarding infertility/reproductive technologies. After taking a look at the character of the ongoing debate surrounding reproductive/infertility technologies, this paper considers how the contributions of Hannah Arendt and Martin Heidegger might add some further insight to the debate and aid in the effort to develop such a feminist framework.

KLEIMAN, L (ed) and LEWIS, Stephen. *Philosophy: An Introduction Through Literature*. New York, Paragon House, 1990.

KLEIN, Dennis. Concepts of Culture: Lonergan and the Anthropologists. Method, 9(1), 23-43, Mr 91.

There are two major differences between Lonergan's concept of culture and the one modern-day anthropologists generally use. In terms of *description*, anthropologists employ a broader notion that includes the technical and social as well as the ideational, while Lonergan takes a narrower view that distinguishes the cultural from the technical and social and identifies it with the ideational (shared meanings and values). In terms of *explanation*, while anthropologists approach cultural phenomena either by way of diachronic or synchronic relations or by way of origins within the unconscious, Lonergan grounds such phenomena within the dynamic operational structure of conscious human intentionality.

KLEIN, Kenneth H (ed) and KUNKEL, Joseph C (ed). *In the Interest of Peace: A Spectrum of Philosophical Views*. Wolfeboro, Longwood, 1990.

KLEIN, Kenneth H (ed) and KUNKEL, Joseph (ed). *Issues in War and Peace: Philosophical Inquiries*. Wolfeboro, Longwood, 1989.

This volume consists of twenty original essays by philosophers, divided into three sections. The first section examines the ideologies of the two superpowers. Beginning with lessons of the Cuban Missile Crisis it includes essays on Marxism, libertarianism, realpolitik, and on how to know peace claims. The second section evaluates justifications for nuclear war. Essays are on moral skepticism, nuclear war as terrorism, strategic defense, and coming to grips with moral pluralism. The third section moves in the direction of promoting peace with essays on existential death, nuclear winter, warism, peacemaking, sexism, and the role of democracy.

KLEIN, Kenneth and KUNKEL, Joseph. "What Does Philosophy Add to Nuclear Discussions? An Introductory Essay" in *Issues in War and Peace: Philosophical Inquiries*, KUNKEL, Joseph (ed), 1-10. Wolfeboro, Longwood, 1989.

Philosophy has three major functions: the critical, the synthetic, and the moral. Critical thinking introduces clarification of terms and evaluation of arguments. Of particular concern is the cultural prevalence of warism, the rejection of peacemaking, and the sexism and lack of democracy in nuclear politics. The synthetic function is found in system building, and in particular in the ideological contrast of Western capitalistic libertarianism and Hobbesian realism with Soviet Marxism. The moral function is found in applying various ethical systems, such as just-war, deontology, and consequentialism, to war and peace issues.

KLEIN, Peter D. "Epistemic Compatibilism and Canonical Beliefs" in *Doubting: Contemporary Perspectives on Skepticism*, ROTH, Michael D (ed), 99-117. Norwell, Kluwer, 1990.

The paper argues for two points: (1) Absolute indubitability is a plausible rendering of what skeptics have required and (2) a very important belief can be absolutely indubitable. That belief is a meta-proposition, namely, that the preponderance of my canonical beliefs (those that I typically take for granted) is true. That meta-proposition can be certain although no canonical belief is certain. I formulate a very strict account of absolute indubitability and argue against Descartes' claim that if there are grounds for doubting each proposition in a set of propositions, there are grounds for doubting them all.

KLEIN, Peter D. "Radical Interpretation and Global Skepticism" in *Truth and Interpretation: Perspectives on the Philosophy of Donald Davidson*, LE PORE, Ernest (ed), 369-386. Cambridge, Blackwell, 1986.

The purpose of the paper is to assess Davidson's argument against global skepticism based upon his account of radical interpretation. After discussing global skepticism and contrasting it with other forms of skepticism, I argue that Davidson's account of belief contained in his theory of radical interpretation presupposes the very knowledge of causal relations that is questioned by the global skeptic and, moreover, whereas a Cartesian can justifiably assert that there are beliefs and wonder whether the beliefs are true, Davidson cannot even assert that there are "methodologically basic beliefs" (mental states which are typically caused by their objects) without begging the question against the global skeptic.

KLEIN, Sherwin. Plato's *Parmenides* and St Thomas's Analysis of God as One and Trinity. Thomist, 55(2), 229-244, Ap 91.

I show that Plato's analysis of the absolutely one (*Parmenides* 137b-142a) provides a basis for determining what God, as an absolutely simple unity, is not. Plato's analysis is seen to accord with St. Thomas's position. In the second part of the article, I use arguments at *Parmenides* 157b-159b and 159b-160b to determine what can be predicted of God, if St. Thomas's analysis of the Trinity is to accord with the articles of faith (God as an absolutely simple unity as well as a Trinity).

KLEINER, Scott A. Comments on "Fitness and Evolutionary Explanation". Biol Phil, 6(1), 29-32, Ja 91.

KLEINGELD, Paulien. Moral und Verwirklichung. Z Phil Forsch, 44(3), 425-441, 1990.

The main thesis of the article is that, despite claims to the contrary, Kant's *Critique of Practical Reason* can be connected with his philosophy of history. The author analyzes Kant's discussion of the possibility of the highest good, concentrating on (1) his concept of happiness, and (2) on the role of the postulate of God, who, as creator of the world, has brought the realm of morals and the realm of nature into harmony. Kant's philosophy of history is a possible interpretation of this 'harmony', in that it asserts that nature makes possible the realization of a moral world through human action.

KLEMENT, H W and RADERMACHER, F J. Freiheit und Bindung menschlicher Entscheidungen. Conceptus, 24(63), 25-42, 1990.

This essay is concerned with the question of human freedom of choice. Its conclusion is that whereas human beings, in contrast to lifeless things, have the formal freedom to make decisions, these are determined in their content by the state of all levels of what constitute human beings, in particular the currently available and stored (mainly linguistic) information at their disposal. This does not mean that decisions are simply determined by physical laws, since these are multifariously modified in their effects by the emergence of higher-order laws, in particular those at the level of language and society. It is also considered whether non-determination of human decision can be justified by appeal to quantum indeterminacy. At present no such effect has been demonstrated in the domain of neorophysiological processes, which is where it would have to be sought. However, it is not excluded in principle. A more plausible place to look for the possible influence of quantum indeterminacy is in the important, perhaps decisive role they might play in the emergence of regularities at the higher levels of evolution, thus exercising a considerable indirect influence on actual behaviour.

KLEMME, Heiner F. A Supplement to "David Hume to Alexander Dick: A New Letter". Hume Stud, 17(1), 87, Ap 91.

The two persons referred to by Hume in his letter to Sir Alexander Dick (18 March 1771) are likely to be the Reverands George Panton and William Smith. Smith played an important role in the development of American higher education. The letter is published in *Hume Studies*, 16(2), 87-88, 1991.

KLEMME, Heiner. "Hume and Hume's Connexions". Z Phil Forsch, 44(3), 474-478, 1990.

In August 1989, the Hume Society in conjunction with the British Society for the History of Philosophy held a conference at the University of Lancaster, England, on 'Hume and Hume's Connexions'. This conference report gives details on the papers held and stresses the need for scholarly researches into the historical setting of Hume's philosophy.

KLEPPER, Howard. Torts of Necessity: A Moral Theory of Compensation. Law Phil, 9(3), 223-239, Ag 90.

Tort cases in which an actor justifiably takes or damages the property of another have resisted analysis in terms of fault or economic efficiency. I argue that writers such as Jules Coleman and Judith Thomson, who locate the wrongfulness of the necessity torts in the infringement of a property right, have not illuminated the issue of why compensation is owed in these cases. My positive argument locates the wrongfulness of an uncompensated taking in these cases in the actor's interference with the autonomy of the property owner, and justifies compensation as a matter of corrective justice.

KLEVER, Wim. Hume Contra Spinoza? Hume Stud, 16(2), 89-105, N 90.

In a famous passage of his *Treatise of Human Nature* Hume sharply opposes Spinoza's 'hideous hypothesis'. However, by means of a careful comparison of the first book *Of the Understanding* with the second part of Spinoza's *Ethics* (*On the Nature and Origin of the Mind*) it is shown that Hume is rather close to some fundamentals of Spinoza's epistemology. It is suggested that Spinoza's text (instead of Bayle's article on Spinoza) has most probably been Hume's direct source and that his defamation of Spinoza's system was disingenuous.

KLINE, A David and MATHESON, Carl A. Rejection Without Acceptance. Austl J Phil, 69(2), 167-179, Je 91.

The claim that theory choice should always be comparative, i.e., that one theory cannot be rejected until a superior one is accepted, is an article of faith among writers in the history and philosophy of science. In this paper we attempt to show that 1) there are no good conceptual reasons for this claim, 2) the historical record does not support the thesis that the acceptance or rejection of a theory is always comparative, and 3) a straightforward reading of the historical record is complicated by sociological factors and a possible ambiguity in the words "accept" and "reject".

KLINE, David and GENDEL, Stephen M. Global Arguments for the Safety of Engineered Organisms. Int J Applied Phil, 5(2), 59-64, Fall 90.

In numerous papers Winston Brill has argued for the safety of agricultural biotechnology. If his arguments are sound, the current regulatory maze is at best an avoidable nuisance and at worst a serious obstruction to scientific and economic development. We show that what appears in Brill's writings as a diverse set of arguments really, when pressed, relies on a single underlying argument. After making the central argument perspicuous we raise a number of conceptual and factual difficulties with it. Several counterexamples from evolutionary theory are discussed.

KLINEFELTER, Donald S. How Is Applied Philosophy to Be Applied? J Soc Phil, 21(1), 16-26, Spr 90.

This essay addresses the genuine perplexity expressed by several moral philosophers about the nature and legitimacy of "applied ethics." I locate that perplexity in the larger context of what applied ethicists in several fields attempt to do, and I explore a modified classical casuist approach to *applied* ethics as particularly fruitful because it identifies the crux of the theory/practice problematic in paradigm or analogous cases rather than in contested normative theories or metaethical conceptual confusions. Whether this casuist approach qualifies as applied "moral philosophy" will depend on our response to several metaethical issues exposed throughout the essay.

KLONOSKI, Richard J. A Clue for a Classical Realist Contribution to the Debate Over the Value of Animals. Between Species, 7(2), 97-101, Spr 91.

The author analyzes and evaluates J Baird Callicott's environmental ethic (which Callicott defines as an "ethical holism") as Callicott presents this ethic in, "Animal Liberation: A Triangular Affair." The author argues that Callicott's outline of his holistic environmental ethic provides those interested in classical realist philosophy (e.g., like the philosophy of Plato) to contribute a metaphysical, foundational perspective to the debate in environmental ethics over the value of animals.

KLOSKO, George. Four Arguments Against Political Obligations from Gratitude. Pub Affairs Quart, 5(1), 33-48, Ja 91.

A D M Walker has recently attempted to develop a theory of political obligation based on the argument from gratitude ["Political Obligation and the Argument from Gratitude, *Philosophy and Public Affairs*, 17 (1988)]. I present four lines of criticism, focusing on the vagueness, lack of stringency, inappropriateness, and inapplicability of gratitude obligations as bases for political obligations. This article extends the controversy between Walker and myself begun in the 1989 *Philosophy and Public Affairs*.

KLOSTERMAIER, Klaus. The Nature of Buddhism. Asian Phil, 1(1), 29-37, 1991.

The paper forms part of a comprehensive study entitled "The Nature of Nature" which critically explores Western and Eastern views of nature. "The Nature of Buddhism" examines Theravāda, Vijñānavāda and Mādhyamika views of nature. Doing so it attempts to prove that notions of "nature" were not only an important part of the teaching of these Buddhist schools, but that they, in turn, determined to some extent "the nature of Buddhism," i.e., the self-understanding of Buddhism. Nature, if seen with Buddhist eyes, is a vehicle of Buddha's revelation.

KLOYBER, Christian. Los límites de mi lenguaje—los límites de mi mundo. Dianoia, 35(35), 123-132, 1989.

KLUBACK, William. *The Legacy of Hermann Cohen*. Atlanta, Scholars Pr, 1989.

KLUBACK, William. *Toward the Death of Man*. New York, Lang, 1991.

KLUGE, Arnold G. Species as Historical Individuals. Biol Phil, 5(4), 417-431, O 90.

The species category is defined as the *smallest historical individual* within which there is a parental pattern of ancestry and descent. The use of historical individual in this definition is consistent with the prevailing notion that species *per se* are not involved in processes—they are effects, not effectors. Reproductive isolation distinguishes biparental historical species from their parts, and it provides a basis for understanding the nature of the evidence used to discover historical individuals.

KLUGE, Eike-Henner W. St Augustine and the Second Way. Fran Stud, 49(27), 34-54, 1989.

The so-called second way of St Thomas Aquinas has usually been seen as having its historical roots in arguments for the existence of God originally raised by Avicenna. This paper demonstrates the untenability of such a claim, and shows that its actual roots are to be found in an argument first introduced by St Augustine in his *De Libero Arbitrio Voluntatis*.

KLUNDER, Barbara. Topos Based Semantics for Constructive Logic with Strong Negation. Bull Sect Log, 19(4), 133-138, D 90.

The aim of the paper is to show usefulness of topoi in the categorical analysis of the constructive logic with strong negation. In any topos we distinguish an object N and its truth-arrows that sets of morphisms from any object A to N have a Nelson algebra structure. The object N is defined as result of an application, to the classifying object, the topos counterpart of the well-known algebraic construction of Nelson algebras for a given Heyting algebra.

KLUXEN-PYTA, Donate. *Nation und Ethos: Die Moral des Patriotismus*. Freiburg, Alber, 1991.

Morality becomes real within the concrete ethos of a given society. The national identity of any such society will have evolved historically, like its collective morality. This identity, therefore, has a role to play insofar as the nation instantiates this ethos and insofar as the ethos preserves in the actualised idea of the nation that historical giveness which gave it its form. This involves the conjunction of destiny and perspective of meaning which makes it morally possible to accept one's own identity *together* with that of the collectivity. This constitutes the legitimacy of patriotism, which can thus be distinguished from nationalism. This thesis can be supported by comparing it with questions in history, philosophy and political science as well as with the history of the Federal Republic of Germany.

KNABENSCHUCH DE PORTA, Sabine. La teoría de la suposición y los idiomas modernos. Rev Filosof (Venezuela), 12, 75-99, 1989.

KNAPP, Viktor. Some Problems of Legal Language. Ratio Juris, 4(1), 1-17, Mr 91.

The author moves from the consideration of law as a set of rules serving as a means of socially regulating human conduct. He focuses on the fact that in order to fulfill its function, the law must be seen as a type of information. In this perspective law is a particular language and therefore gives rise to linguistic problems, linked to the technical character of juristic discourse. The author deals with some of the linguistic and sociological aspects of legal language and attempts to pinpoint some trends of interlingual development.

KNAPPIK, G J. Die immerwährende Schöpfung als fundamentaler Seinsvorgang. Stud Phil Christ, 27(1), 47-53, 1991.

KNASAS, John F X. "Does Gilson Theologize Thomistic Metaphysics?" in *Thomistic Papers, V*, RUSSMAN, Thomas A (ed), 3-24. Notre Dame, Univ Notre Dame Pr, 1990.

My article begins by defending Gilson from the complaints of T C O'Brien, John Wippel and John Quinn that he rest metaphysics upon revelation. I then turn to a genuinely troubling remark from Gilson's *The Elements of Christian Philosophy*: to grasp the Thomistic meaning of existence as *actus essendi* we must forsake the philosophical way—from creatures to God—for the theological way—from God to creatures. I show that this remark fails to contradict Gilson's longstanding thesis that the intellectual grasps *actus essendi* by judgment. I conclude with some emendations on Gilson's understanding of judgment as the philosophical approach to Thomistic metaphysics.

KNASAS, John F X. Materiality and Aquinas' Natural Philosophy: A Reply to Johnson. Mod Sch, 68(3), 245-257, Mr 91.

Against Mark Johnson, I defend my thesis that for Aquinas Natural philosophy cannot demonstrate the immaterial. *S.T.* I, 44, 2c unambiguously presents Aristotelian natural philosophy as going only to a celestial body. *In de Trin.* V, 4c likewise presents metaphysics as the only philosophical knowledge of immaterials. Moreover, Johnson provides nothing decisive to resolve in his favor *In de Trim.* V, 2, ad3m and *In VIII Phys*, lect. 23, n. 1172. The *primus motor alterius naturae a rebus naturalibus* of the first could still stand for a celestial body. The *primum principium* of the second could still stand for a metaphysical conclusion.

KNASAS, John F X. *The Preface to Thomistic Metaphysics*. New York, Lang, 1990.

The book intends to break the current impasse in neo-Thomist debate on how to begin metaphysics. The debate assumes that metaphysics starts with attaining concepts appreciated as spanning both the material and immaterial orders of reality. Taking inspiration from Joseph Owens's work in Aquinas, the author questions this assumption and shows that no philosophical nor textual exigency for the assumption exists. For the entry into metaphysics, he substitutes simply a judgmental grasp of the *esse* of sensible things. The book evaluates the *separatio*, natural philosophy, transcendental method, and judgment approaches to Thomistic metaphysics. It includes a discussion of the "Five Ways" and an appendix on the disagreement between Maritain and Gilson.

KNEE, Phili. Le problème politique chez Sartre et Foucault. Laval Theol Phil, 47(1), 83-93, F 91.

Ce texte cherche à mettre en évidence certains enjeux de la culture politique contemporaine par l'étude des échos entre les pensées de Sartre et Foucault: d'abord à travers un rappel de leur démarche philosophique fondamentale par laquelle ils semblent s'opposer radicalement; puis par l'analyse de leur approche respective du problème de la légitimité politique; enfin par l'évocation de leur posture commune dans l'action politique.

KNEE, Philip. Sartre and Political Legitimacy. Int Phil Quart, 31(2), 141-152, Je 91.

KNEEPKENS, C H. Erfurt, Ampl Q 70A: A Quaestiones-commentary on the Second Part of Alexander de Villa Dei's *Doctrinale*. Vivarium, 28(1), 26-54, My 90.

In this paper it is argued that the quaestiones-commentary on Alexander de Villa Dei's *Doctrinale* in the manuscript Erfurt, Ampl. Q.70A is part of the conceptualist grammatical tradition of the late 14th century. A characteristic feature of this theory is the absolute primacy of mental language to spoken or written language. An edition of the first question has been appended.

KNIGHT, David. "Romanticism and the Sciences" in *Romanticism and the Sciences*, CUNNINGHAM, Andrew (ed), 13-24. New York, Cambridge Univ Pr, 1990.

The world-views of "Romantics" and those engaged in the sciences around 1800 were not polar opposites. Neither group had a definite membership; but we can say that those influenced by romanticism disliked mechanical analogies, supported a dynamical science in which forces seemed more real than material particles, were fascinated by physiology, and saw science as personal knowledge. Davy saw himself as poet, philosopher and sage: and these categories allow us to sample the science of his day. Goethe the poet; Schelling and then Hegel the philosophers; and Davy as the sage, allow us to explore both tensions and rewards.

KNIGHT, J F. A Metatheorem for Constructions by Finitely Many Workers. J Sym Log, 55(2), 787-804, Je 90.

KNIGHT, Julia F. Constructions by Transfinitely Many Workers. Annals Pure Applied Log, 48(3), 237-259, Ag 90.

KNOWLTON, Calvin H. "The Ethics of Physicians Dispensing Drugs for Profit" in *Biomedical Ethics Reviews, 1989*, HUMBER, James M (ed), 75-93. Clifton, Humana Pr, 1990.

KOBES, Bernard W. "Individualism and Artificial Intelligence" in *Philosophical Perspectives, 4: Action Theory and Philosophy of Mind, 1990*, TOMBERLIN, James E (ed), 429-459. Atascadero, Ridgeview, 1990.

The explanatorily relevant properties of artificial intelligence programs such as T Winograd's SHRDLU depend (in ways relevant to the Burge-Fodor debate over individualism in cognitive science) on the AI machine's embedding in the actual world of speakers and physical objects. The result holds even if we assume that the machine has genuine propositional attitudes about an environment that does not exist.

KOBES, Bernard W. Sensory Qualities and 'Homunctionalism': A Review Essay of W G Lycan's *Consciousness*. Phil Psych, 4(1), 147-158, 1991.

Arguments are presented against W G Lycan's view that certain puzzles about sensory qualia can be solved by way of a "teleological" version of functionalism. Also, two thought-experiments are presented to show that, in 'Leopold has a homogeneously green after-image', 'homogeneously green' marks a property actually instantiated for exactly as long as the relevant sensuous experience lasts.

KOCH, Philip J. Solitude. J Speculative Phil, 4(3), 181-210, 1990.

The author of this phenomenologico-analytic celebration concentrates on the experiential world of solitude, exploring its perceptual, emotional, cognitive and volitional elements. Here emerge the differences between solitude and its opposite, engaged encounter, as well as its differences from loneliness, isolation, privacy and alienation. Suprisingly, solitude and encounter, though opposites, are found to form and interpenetrate each other. Turning to the evaluation of solitude, arguments for the epistemic, metaphysical and experiential primacy of solitude over encounter are collected, scrutinized and rejected. Five core virtues of solitude are then identified: Freedom, Attunement to Self, Attunement to Nature, Reflective Perspective, Creativity. Solitude and encounter emerge as coequal interpenetrating mutually enriching primary human experiences.

KOCKELMANS, J. On the Problem of the Essence of Truth in the Natural Sciences (in Dutch). Tijdschr Filosof, 53(1), 90-112, Mr 91.

In this essay some contemporary positions concerning the nature of truth in the natural sciences are examined briefly. It is argued that it will be necessary to rethink the essence of truth, not in terms of the classical correspondence theory, but rather in terms of the hermeneutic theory of truth as unconcealment. (edited)

KOCKELMANS, Joseph J. "Some Reflections on Empirical Psychology: Toward an Interpretive Psychology" in *Reconsidering Psychology: Perspectives from Continental Philosophy*, FAULCONER, James E (ed), 75-91. Pittsburgh, Duquesne Univ Pr, 1990.

The essay presents reasons why psychologists must make use of interpretive and critical methods in addition to the common empirical and descriptive ones. Hermeneutics is indispensable in both the theoretical part of psychology as well as its application to concrete, individual human beings.

KOERNER, Konrad. "The Place of Friedrich Schlegel in the Development of Historical-Comparative Linguistics" in *Leibniz, Humboldt, and the Origins of Comparativism*, DE MAURO, Tullio (ed), 239-261. Philadelphia, John Benjamins, 1990.

This paper demonstrates that Friedrich Schlegel's (1772-1829) Ueber die Sprache und Weisheit der Indier (1808) constitutes an important document in the development of linguistics as an autonomous field of study. The paper goes beyond Sebastiano Timpanaro's (1972) appraisal of Schlegel (in "Critica Storica") by showing that Schlegel's ideas about language and its study anticipated the three linds of nineteenth century linguistics that are usually associated with Bopp and Rask (comparative), Grimm (historical), and Humboldt (typological-philosophical), respectively. It is argued that the traditional view according to which Bopp's *Conjugationssystem* of 1816 marks the beginning of linguistics as a science is too facile and requires revision, and that F Schlegel's role in this development would have to be recognized, and not simply as that of a forerunner to historical-comparative grammar of Indo-European.

KOETSIER, Teunis and ALLIS, Victor. On Some Paradoxes of the Infinite. Brit J Phil Sci, 42(2), 187-194, Je 91.

In the paper below the authors describe three super-tasks. They show that although the abstract notion of a super-task may be, as Benecerraf suggested, a conceptual mismatch, the completion of the three super-tasks involved can be defined rather naturally, without leading to inconsistency, by means of a particular kinematical interpretation combined with a principle of continuity.

KOFMAN, Sarah. "Metaphoric Architectures" in *Looking After Nietzsche*, RICKELS, Laurence A (ed), 89-112. Albany, SUNY Pr, 1990.

'Metaphoric Architectures' examines architecture as Nietzschean metaphor for the scientific/philosophical construction of reality from concepts. The architectural metaphor emerges as metaphor of metaphor - of the totalizing project of the conceptual reduction of life/construction of reality. It further considers the overdetermination of this metaphor - via the will to power, conceptual edifices appear symptomatic of *weak* instincts, and its Nietzschean deconstruction in the juxtaposition of a plurality of architectural metaphors. A second part contrasts conceptualizing abstractions of philosopher-architect with the "Saturnalia" of "irrational man" who affirms a *multiplicity* of metaphors—the chaotic, non-hierarchical realms of appearance, lie, dream, art, myth.

KOHÁK, Erazim. A Dialogue on Value, II: Why Is There Something Good, Not Simply Something? J Speculative Phil, 5(1), 10-20, 1991.

The author argues that relation of two intrinsically value-less relata would not constitute value. Humans experience relations such as utility or relative perfection as value constituting to the extent to which they experience being as intrinsically good.

KOHL, Marvin. "Toward Understanding the Pragmatics of Absolute Pacifism" in *In the Interest of Peace: A Spectrum of Philosophical Views*, KLEIN, Kenneth H (ed), 227-236. Wolfeboro, Longwood, 1990.

Drawing principally upon arguments for and against Gandhian pacifism, the following are briefly examined: (1) the claim that nonviolence cannot be effective against resolute and brutal aggressors; (2) H J N Horsburgh's argument that, since we can never know with certainty how intractably brutal (or resolute) an adversary really is, we never have sufficient grounds for supposing that we are dealing with a situation in which violence would be justified; and (3) some variants of the claim that the ideal of pacifism "works" even though particular acts may not, because it serves to set a direction in which we can strive.

KOHLBERG, Lawrence and BOYD, Dwight R and LEVINE, Charles. "The Return of Stage 6: Its Principle and Moral Point of View" in *The Moral Domain: Essays in the Ongoing Discussion between Philosophy and the Social Sciences*, WREN, Thomas E (ed), 151-181. Cambridge, MIT Pr, 1990.

KÖHLER, Theodor Wolfram. *Dicendum est eum non esse hominem*: Ein mögliches frühes Zeugnis für die anthropologische Gewichtung.... Frei Z Phil Theol, 37(1-2), 31-50, 1990.

The phenomenon of self-consciousness ("reflexives Selbstverhältnis") seems to be basic for a systematic foundation and development of philosophical anthropology. Generally Descartes is considered to be the first in the later history of ideas who explicitly brought into relationship this phenomenon and the anthropological key question of how we should understand ourselves philosophically as human beings. In the present essay I tried to show that John Duns Scotus expressed quite similar ideas as Descartes in an interesting text of his commentary on the *Sentences*.

KOHLS, John J and BULLER, Paul F and ANDERSON, Kenneth S. The Challenge of Global Ethics. J Bus Ethics, 10(10), 767-775, O 91.

The authors argue that the time is ripe for national and corporate leaders to move consciously towards the development of global ethics. This paper presents a model of global ethics, a rationale for the development of global ethics, and the implications of the model for research and practice.

KOHN, Livia. Taoist Visions of the Body. J Chin Phil, 18(2), 227-252, Je 91.

KOKTOVÁ, Eva. On Negation. J Prag, 14(5), 761-790, O 90.

In this paper I present a description of the scoping properties of negation based on the topic-focus articulation of the sentence, within the framework of the Prague Functional Generative Description. In the primary case, negation has in its scope the focus, or the new information, of the sentence. The secondary cases are connected with the topicalization of negation and/or of the material in its scope. The material in the scope of negation may be syntactically structured in very diverse ways and it need not correspond to a constituent, which is an argument for the adequacy of the choice of the dependency model. The scoping properties of negation exhibit striking similarities to those of focusing particles and sentence adverbials, and therefore I propose to treat these expressions jointly.

KOLAKOWSKI, L. Final Summary (in Czechoslovakian). Filozof Cas, 39(1), 67-75, 1991.

KOLARSKA-BOBINSKA, Lena. The Changing Face of Civil Society in Eastern Europe. Praxis Int, 10(3-4), 324-336, O 90-Ja 91.

The transition to a market economy and democracy requires different organizational principles for the entire social order. The question arises: will a civil society, once repressed and restricted, fully develop and avail itself of new opportunities provided by the market and democracy? The article analyzes general factors contributing to passivity, slow emergence of civil society and deficiencies in grass-root activity. The heritage of the past is one of them. The anomy which is a by-product of ongoing changes is another. Anomy is caused by changing values and norms, changing social structure, decreasing material standard of living and several other factors.

KOLB, David. Heidegger at 100, in America. J Hist Ideas, 52(1), 140-151, Ja-Mr 91.

This essay charts the main trends and some representative works in Heidegger studies in America. Out of the indexed items mentioning Heidegger, 27 percent have been published in the last five years. These works show that Heidegger's texts no longer sustain a single unified agenda. The essay reviews trends and authors that stay close to Heidegger's vocabulary, and also those that put him into contact with other problematics than his own. In particular, the essay discusses attempts to re-do Heidegger's "fundamental ontology" as a contribution to current debates in the philosophy of mind, and also the reappropriation of Heidegger by the deconstructive movements that he helped create.

KOLENDA, Konstantin. Avoiding the Fly Bottle. SW Phil Rev, 7(1), 19-26, Ja 91.

Wittgenstein's writings are seen by many of his readers as therapies, akin to the treatment of an illness, but it is also the case that he shows how not to get into the fly-bottle to begin with. Closer attention to some early hints dropped early in the *Philosophical Investigations* will enable us to see how even small, carefully chosen steps can keep us from getting on a wrong track. Use of language brings to expression not just concepts in their logical, intellectual aspects but also puts into play our attitudes and responses.

KOLENDA, Konstantin. Misreading Rorty. Phil Lit, 15(1), 111-117, Ap 91.

Readers of Rorty's writings tend to fall into following misunderstandings. 1) Our moral beliefs have no justification; 2) Change in vocabularies is always arbitrary; 3) Pragmatic objectivity is incompatible with realism; 4) "Conversation" is irresponsible adlibbing; 5) Acceptance of the private/public distinction leads to narcissism. All of these misunderstandings can be removed by paying close attention to Richard Rorty's actual texts.

KOLENDA, Konstantin. *Philosophy's Journey: From the Presocratics to the Present (Second Edition)*. Prospect Heights, Waveland Pr, 1990.

KOLENDA, Konstantin. *Rorty's Humanistic Pragmatism: Philosophy Democratized*. Gainesville, Univ S Florida Pr, 1990.

This book defends Rorty's recommendation to redescribe our commerce with reality in terms of an activist conception of coping. That conception integrates knowledge, action, and hope. Rorty's position is positive and constructive, combining the best impulses of our humanistic and religious traditions. It liberates us from the oppressively narrow conception of philosophy as it is being practiced in dominant professional circles. It also has an application to cultural and political matters.

KOLESNYK, Alexander. Jan Hus und Thomas Müntzer—ein philosophiehistorischer Vergleich (in Czechoslovakian). Filozof Cas, 38(5), 612-623, 1990.

KOLODII, A F. A Contribution to the Discussion of the Doctrinal Preconditions of the Deformation of Socialism. Soviet Stud Phil, 29(3), 69-83, Wint 90-91.

KONIKOWSKA, Beata. A Two-Valued Logic for Reasoning about Different Types of Consequence in Kleene's Three-Valued Logic. Stud Log, 49(4), 541-555, D 90.

A formal language of two-valued logic is developed, whose terms are formulas of the language of Kleene's three-valued logic. The atomic formulas of the former language are pairs of formulas of the latter language joined by "consequence" operators. These operators correspond to the three "sensible" types of consequence (strong-strong, strong-weak and weak-weak) in Kleene's logic in analogous way as the implication connective in the classical logic corresponds to the classical consequence relation. The composed formulas of the considered language are built from the atomic ones by means of the classical connectives and quantifiers. A deduction system for the developed language is given, consisting of a set of decomposition rules for sequences of formulas. It is shown that the deduction system is sound and complete.

KONSTANTELLOU, Eva and TAYLOR, William. The Question of Responsibility in the Context of Instructional Technology. J Thought, 25(1-2), 113-125, Spr-Sum 90.

KOONS, Robert Charles. Doxastic Paradoxes Without Self-Reference. Austl J Phil, 68(2), 168-177, Je 90.

Both Richard Montague and Richmond Thomason have taken their discoveries of Liar-like paradoxes in epistemic (knowledge) and doxastic (belief) logics as compelling reasons for representing such notions only in languages in which no *self-reference* is possible, i.e., by representing such notions as *knowledge* or *belief* by means of sentential *operators* rather than by means of predicates which apply to sentences or to propositions with sentence-like structure. By constructing antinomies of belief and of rational probability in a modal operator logic, I show that paradoxes exist which do not depend in any way upon self-reference, thereby undermining the Montague-Thomason argument.

KOPPELBERG, Dirk. "Why and How to Naturalize Epistemology" in *Perspectives on Quine*, BARRETT, Robert (ed), 200-211. Cambridge, Blackwell, 1990.

A new picture of the connection between Quine's theory of knowledge and the reasoning of his forerunners in the Vienna Circle is delineated. The kinship in the thinking of Neurath and Quine is set forth. Quine's motives and reasons for naturalizing epistemology are explained and it is shown that some influential arguments of his more traditionally minded critics are inconclusive. The paper closes with some tentative remarks about the relationship between naturalistic epistemology and epistemological skepticism.

KOPPER, Joachim. Quelques remarques sur la composition de la *Dialectique de la faculté de juger téléologique*. Rev Int Phil, 44(175), 604-620, 1990.

The consideration in Chapter 76 of the *Critique of Judgement* is significant not only for afore said work but for the doctrine of knowledge stated in all three critiques, a doctrine which fails in the attempt of reconciling the autonomy of thinking with the reality of things. The reflection in Chapter 76 which is a reflection on transcendental philosophy itself does not revoke the doctrine but shows its limits, by realizing its distinction as inadequate for a real transcendental understanding of reality.

KORB, Kevin B. Explaining Science. Brit J Phil Sci, 42(2), 239-253, Je 91.

Ronald Giere's program to naturalize philosophy of science has two major components: the rejection of normative philosophies of science, especially Bayesianism, and the advocacy of a satisficing model of scientific judgment. Both halves of the program rest heavily upon studies in cognitive psychology of the difficulties people have reasoning to normative standards. I show that Giere's application of these results to scientific methodology is at best premature. Furthermore, I demonstrate that Giere's satisficing model itself is immodestly prone to committing a probabilistic fallacy.

KORDIC, Radoman. Repression of Sexuality in Philosophy and the Return of the Repressed in Freud's Psychoanalysis (in Serbo-Croatian). Filozof Istraz, 32-33(5-6), 1721-1730, 1989.

KÖRNER, Stephan. On Kant's Conception of Science and the Critique of Practical Reason. Kantstudien, 82(2), 173-178, 1991.

KÖRNER, Stephan. "On the Logic of Practical Evaluation" in *Logic and Ethics*, GEACH, Peter (ed), 199-224. Norwell, Kluwer, 1991.

KOSHUTA, Monica A and SCHMITZ, Phyllis J and LYNN, Joanne. Development of an Institutional Policy on Artificial Hydration and Nutrition. Kennedy Inst Ethics J, 1(2), 133-139, Je 91.

The issues involved in deciding whether to use artificial methods of delivering hydration and nutrition are often very difficult for patients, families, and health care providers. Once private and personal matters, these decisions now frequently involve the judicial system. Five years ago, Hospice of Washington recognized the need for a written policy and wrote the one published here. Its goal is to respect individual preferences and family concerns while addressing the nutrition and hydration needs of dying patients. The policy sets parameters on the issue, provides basic information, and encourages crafting the most fitting resolution to each situation.

KOSLOWSKI, Peter. Cientificidad y Romanticismo: Acerca de las relaciones entre cientismo, gnosticismo y romanticismo. Anu Filosof, 24(1), 75-88, 1991.

Scientism shares with gnosticism and romanticism faith in the absolute creative and cognitive power of man; faith in the fact that human knowledge imposes to the world the way of its 'uncovering' and 'apparition'. It likewise shares the belief in the autonomy and fictional character of knowledge.

KOSROVANI, Emilio. Hornsby's Puzzles: Rejoinder to Wreen and Hornsby. Analysis, 51(1), 55-61, Ja 91.

KOSSO, Peter. Dimensions of Observability. Brit J Phil Sci, 39(4), 449-467, D 88.

The concept of observability of entities in physical science is typically analysed in terms of the nature and significance of a dichotomy between observables and unobservables. In the present work, however, this categorization is resisted and observability is analysed in a descriptive way in terms of the information which one can receive through interaction with objects in the world. The account of interaction and the transfer of information is done using applicable scientific theories. In this way, the question of observability of scientific entities is put to science itself. The result is a demonstration that observability has many dimensions, some more epistemically significant than others.

KOSTER, Jan. "How Natural Is Natural Language?" in *Logic, Methodology and Philosophy of Science, VIII*, FENSTAD, J E (ed), 591-606. New York, Elsevier Science, 1989.

KOTATKO, Petr. Three Notions of Judgement (in Czechoslovakian). Filozof Cas, 38(5), 577-590, 1990.

The main aim of the paper is to identify the thought formation which should be taken as the primary object of intentional analysis under the title "judgement." Three demands which, although incompatible, are standardly connected with the notion of judgement, are characterized, namely: (1) being identified by the intentional content; (2) being the ultimate truth-value bearer; (3) being intersubjective (or ideally objective). This serves as a means for differentiation of three formations competing for the title "judgement," each satisfying a couple of those demands. As is shown in the paper, they (or corresponding levels of analysis) have been often confused. (edited)

KOTZIN, Rhoda and BAUMGÄRTNER, Järg. Sensations and Judgments of Perception: Diagnosis and Rehabilitation of Some of Kant's Misleading Examples. Kantstudien, 81(4), 401-412, 1990.

Commentators have pointed out that Kant's remarks about the 'subjectivity' of sensible qualities and of judgments of perception fail to conform to some central teachings of the *Critique of Pure Reason*. In our view Kant's remarks and examples (the color of a rose, "The room is warm"), as formulated, are indeed un-Critical. We discuss some strategies which have been advanced in order to deal with these examples but which we consider to be unsatisfactory. We propose a new strategy by which we can rehabilitate the examples and use them to help to illuminate Kant's Critical theory of empirical knowledge.

KOUBA, Pavel. The World of Human Community in Hanna Arendt's Work (in Czechoslovakian). Filozof Cas, 38(4), 547-557, 1990.

KOUTOUGOS, Aris. "Research Programmes and Paradigms as Dialogue Structures" in *Imre Lakatos and Theories of Scientific Change*, GAVROGLU, Kostas (ed), 361-374. Norwell, Kluwer, 1989.

After Kuhn's celebrated book the authority of normative metascience over actual scientific practice was seriously questioned. The critical question which I consider eventually emerging from this is the following: is it possible to have norms and values as internal parameters of an overall descriptive model for science? Research programmes and paradigms, interpreted from a systemic point of view, represent approximations of it. The possibility to improve upon this model requires an investigation of the presuppositions for rational communication in relation to concepts such as internality and comparability. Such improvement is attempted through exposing the preconceptions of the classical views on meaning and reference, an approach which dissolves the basic difficulties with comparability (incommensurability).

KOVACS, George. *The Question of God in Heidegger's Phenomenology*. Evanston, Northwestern Univ Pr, 1990.

This comprehensive investigation unearths and submits to a process of questioning Heidegger's insights and claims regarding the idea of God in the light of, and as ineluctable for, his rethinking the question of Being. It discerns three phases (dimensions) of the question of God in Heidegger's phenomenology. The first phase, as demonstrated in *Being and Time*, implies but leaves undeveloped the problem of God (critical reexamination of the metaphysical approach). In the second phase, as the writings that followed the first major work show, the question of God is separated from the question of Being; it becomes an explicit question. In the third phase, as the later and latest writings indicated, there is a new way of thinking about God; the postmetaphysical thinking about Being leads to a "truly divine notion of God." In the final analysis, the recapturing of the sense of wonder about Being does not extinguish but rather reawakens the question, as well as the sense of mystery, of God.

KOVEL, Joel. *History and Spirit: An Inquiry into the Philosophy of Liberation*. Boston, Beacon Pr, 1991.

KOWALCZYK, Stanislaw. Christians and Marxist Theory of Human Liberation. Dialec Hum, 16(3-4), 123-131, Sum-Autumn 89.

The purpose of the paper was the problem: what doctrinal, existential and social attitudes should be adopted by Christians towards the Marxist theory of human liberation? We distinguished two aspects: positive and negative. The first is an enumeration of possible cooperations between Christians and Marxists (for example the realization of the ideas of social justice, the defense of worker rights, etc.). The second part of the paper speaks about controversial elements of the Marxist concept of liberation. Doubts concern the diagnosis of the sources of alienation (economism and collectivism) and the method by which it should be overcome (proletarian dictatorship).

KOYZIS, David T. "Yves R Simon's Contribution to a Structural Political Pluralism" in *Freedom in the Modern World: Jacques Maritain, Yves R Simon, Mortimer J Adler*, TORRE, Michael D (ed), 131-139. Notre Dame, Univ Notre Dame Pr, 1989.

KOZMETSKY, George and PETERSON, Robert A and BELTRAMINI, Richard F. Concerns of College Students Regarding Business Ethics: A Replication. J Bus Ethics, 10(10), 733-738, O 91.

In 1984 we reported the results of surveying a nationwide sample of college students about selected business ethics issues. We concluded that (a) college students were in general concerned about the issues investigated and (b) female students were relatively more concerned than were male students. The present study replicated our earlier study and not only corroborated both of its conclusions, but also found a higher level of concern than had been observed previously.

KRABBE, Erik C W. Inconsistent Commitment and Commitment to Inconsistencies. Inform Log, 12(1), 33-42, Wint 90.

The paper surveys several instances of *horror contradictionis* (Aristotle, Rescher and Brandom). The perspective is then shifted from inconsistent *beliefs* to inconsistencies in *argumentation* and *dialogue*. What should happen if (apparent) contradictions arise in dialogue? It is argued that inconsistency is not a fallacy. Neither is inconsistency a foolproof indication of some weakness or blunder. Inconsistent positions may lead to a quandary. Good rules of dialogue should rule this out. There are several senses in which inconsistent statements can be said to be isolated one from the other. Thus many (apparent) inconsistencies are quite harmless. But some problems remain.

KRACHT, Marcus. An Almost General Splitting Theorem for Modal Logic. Stud Log, 49(4), 455-470, D 90.

Standard splitting theorems in modal logic characterize those modal algebras which split a given variety of weakly transitive algebras on the condition that the algebras are finite. In this paper, a complete characterization of splitting algebras is given without any assumption on the variety; it is only assumed that the algebra in question is finitely presentable.

KRACHT, Marcus. A Solution to a Problem of Urquhart. J Phil Log, 20(3), 285-286, Ag 91.

The problem of Urquhart, stated in 'Decidability and the finite model property', *Journal of Philosophical Logic*, 10, 1981, is to find an extension of S4 that is recursively axiomatizable, has the finite model property but is undecidable. This problem is solved by constructing a logic that in addition extends S4.Grz and defines a locally finite variety.

KRAENZEL, Frederick. Does Reason Command Itself for Its Own Sake? J Value Inq, 25(3), 263-270, Jl 91.

This paper criticizes the Kantian principle that reason legislates nothing except itself. It also argues that reason legislates itself for the welfare of the whole person or community, not for its own sake. Finally, this paper examines six modern viewpoints that owe something to Kant, and concludes that they either are unconvincing or derive their moral force from interest.

KRAFT, Kenneth L. The Relative Importance of Social Responsibility in Determining Organizational Effectiveness: Student Responses. J Bus Ethics, 10(3), 179-188, Mr 91.

This paper investigates the *relative* importance of social responsibility criteria in determining organizational effectiveness. The organizational effectiveness menu was used as a questionnaire with a sample of 151 senior undergraduates. Each respondent was asked to rate the importance of the criteria from three constituent perspectives within a service organization: (1) as a manager, (2) as an investor, (3) as an employee. Later, a subsample of students (n - 61) responded to the same questionnaire acting as a manager in an assigned case study. The results indicated that students acting as managers, investors, or employees rate social responsibility criteria among the least important of the determinants of organizational effectiveness. Moreover, while specific situations may call for changes in the relative importance of these criteria, social responsibility criteria were not viewed, generally, as the most important determinants of organizational effectiveness.

KRAFT, Kenneth L and SINGHAPAKDI, Anusorn. The Role of Ethics and Social Responsibility in Achieving Organizational Effectiveness: Students Versus Managers. J Bus Ethics, 10(9), 679-686, S 91.

This paper investigates the differences in perceptions between business students and service-sector managers regarding the role that ethics and social responsibility serve in determining organizational effectiveness. An organizational effectiveness instrument containing business ethics and social responsibility items served as a questionnaire for a sample of 151 senior business undergraduates and 53 service-sector managers. The results indicated that while students acting as managers rate some social responsibility issues as more important than do managers, they also rate ethical conduct and a few dimensions of social responsibility lower than do managers. The findings have direct implications for both business practitioners and educators.

KRAFT, Kenneth. The Relative Importance of Social Responsibility in Determining Organizational Effectiveness. J Bus Ethics, 10(7), 485-491, Jl 91.

This paper investigates the *relative* importance of social responsibility criteria in determining organizational effectiveness as seen by managers of two service industries. The Organizational Effectiveness Menu (Kraft and Jauch, 1988) was used as a questionnaire with a sample of 53 firms. The conclusion is that while managers view ethical conduct as among the most important determinants of organizational effectiveness, numerous other social responsibility criteria are assigned relatively low priority. A question remains as to what managers will actually do when faced with limited resources.

KRAFT, Steven and KEFFER, Steven and KING, Sallie. Process Metaphysics and Minimalism: Implications for Public Policy. Environ Ethics, 13(1), 23-47, Spr 91.

Using process philosophy, especially its view of nature and its ethic, we develop a process-based environmental ethic embodying minimalism and beneficience. From this perspective, we criticize the philosophy currently underlying public policy and examine some alternative approaches based on phenomenology and ethnomethodology. We conclude that process philosophy, minus its value hierarchy, is a powerful tool capable of supporting both radical and moderate changes in environmental policy.

KRAJICEK, Jan and PUDLÁK, Pavel and TAKEUTI, Gaisi. Bounded Arithmetic and the Polynomial Hierarchy. Annals Pure Applied Log, 52(1-2), 143-153, Ap 91.

Bounded arithmetic is a fragment of Peano arithmetic with induction axioms restricted to bounded formulas only. The main problem is to show that bounded arithmetic is not finitely axiomatizable. We have proved this using the assumption that the polynomial-time hierarchy does not collapse. This assumption is a famous unproved conjecture in complexity theory.

KRAJICEK, Jan. Exponentiation and Second-Order Bounded Arithmetic. Annals Pure Applied Log, 48(3), 261-276, Ag 90.

KRANCBERG, Sigmund. The Unity of Theory and Practice in Historical Perspective. Stud Soviet Tho, 41(3), 173-205, My 91.

KRAUT, Robert. "The Third Dogma" in *Truth and Interpretation: Perspectives on the Philosophy of Donald Davidson*, LE PORE, Ernest (ed), 398-416. Cambridge, Blackwell, 1986.

The idea of a *conceptual scheme*, and the correlative distinction between *scheme* and *content*, withstands Davidson's objections. I argue that the ontology of a discourse is partially determined by the expressive resources available in that discourse. This relation between ontology and the individuative/discriminative resources of a language grounds the idea that distinct languages might well "carve reality in different ways." Yet this idea presupposes (I argue) no outmoded dogmas about interpretation, truth, reference, the epistemologically given, or untranslatable languages. Despite Davidson's criticisms, the scheme-content idea is both intelligible and exciting.

KREBBS JR, R Stephen. Is Friedrich Nietzsche a Precursor to the Holistic Movement? Hist Euro Ideas, 11, 701-709, 1989.

KREBBS, R Stephen and BURNEY-DAVIS, Terri. The Vita Femina and Truth. Hist Euro Ideas, 11, 841-847, 1989.

KRECZ, Charles A. Reduction and the Part/Whole Relation. Phil Sci (Tucson), 3, 71-87, 1988.

This paper argues that a proper understanding of the part/whole relation will allow opponents of the reduction of a particular science to secure the status of the objects of that science, even if such reduction takes place. The science in question is biology. Thus, even if the laws of biology were to be implied by some other set of laws from physics and chemistry, the objects of biology are secure by the very fact that it part/whole relations not specified in the more fundamental theories. The claim is that the part/whole relation is nowhere dense, so that any part/whole relation will either be or imply a primitive relation which designates an ultimate intervenor. Biology designates such intervenors, and its status is secured thereby. Its reduction in no way threatens the integrity of its objects, and thus there should by no special controversy between the anti- and pro-reductionists concerning so-called "emergent" properties of wholes greater than the sum of their parts.

KRELL, David Farrell. Foreign Bodies in Strange Places: A Note on Maurice Merleau-Ponty, Georges Bataille, and Architecture. Phil Today, 35(1), 43-50, Spr 91.

The article examines the writings of Merleau-Ponty and Bataille with a view to architecture—an architecture of the flesh.

KRELL, David Farrell (trans). *Nietzsche (I and II): The Will to Power as Art, The Eternal Recurrence of the Same—Heidegger*. San Francisco, HarperCollins, 1990.

KRELL, David Farrell (ed). *Nietzsche (III and IV): The Will to Power as Knowledge and as Metaphysics—Heidegger*. San Francisco, HarperCollins, 1990.

KRELL, David Farrell. *Of Memory, Reminiscence, and Writing: On the Verge*. Bloomington, Indiana Univ Pr, 1990.

The book examines the models for memory that prevail in Western thought from Plato and Aristotle through Freud, Heidegger, and Derrida. It examines especially the models of memory as (1) inscription or incision of what is present for purposes of storage and retrieval and (2) containment of the past in an enclosed space that promises to restore the past to full presence. Such models have failed, and we are on the verge of more modest assessments of the powers of memory, reminiscence, and writing.

KRELL, David Farrell. Shattering: Toward a Politics of Daimonic Life. Grad Fac Phil J, 14(2)-15(1), 153-182, 1991.

The article poses the question of Heidegger's political debacle—his association with National Socialism—in terms of his failure to pose or resolve the question of *multiple* life-forms. Here, politics and theoretical biology mix.

KREMER, Elmar J (trans) and ARNAULD, Antoine (trans). *On True and False Ideas, New Objections to Descartes' Meditations* and Descartes' Replies. Lewiston, Mellen Pr, 1990.

KREMER-MARIETTI, Angèle. De la matérialité du discours saisi dans l'institution. Rev Int Phil, 44(173), 241-261, 1990.

KRENZLIN, Norbert. "'Aufbruch oder Schwanengesang'?" in *XIth International Congress in Aesthetics, Nottingham 1988*, WOODFIELD, Richard (ed), 99-101. Nottingham, Nottingham Polytech, 1990.

KRETZMANN, Norman. "Reason in Mystery" in *The Philosophy in Christianity*, VESEY, Godfrey (ed), 15-39. New York, Cambridge Univ Pr, 1989.

Philosophical theology, which employs analysis and argument in attempting to find rationally defensible legitimate interpretations of doctrines that seem *prima facie* irrational and to explore the implications of such interpretations, may seem to be necessarily curtailed by the inclusion of "mysteries" in Christian doctrine. Drawing on the work of medieval philosopher - theologians, especially Bonaventure, I try to show how this only apparent limitation on rational investigation was traditionally and should still be dealt with by philosophers concerned with the rationality of religion.

KRIBBE, Pamela. Over de ambivalente rol van de theoriegeladenheidsthese in Rorty's 'overwinning' van de traditie. Alg Ned Tijdschr Wijs, 83(3), 206-223, Jl 91.

In *Philosophy and the Mirror of Nature* (1980) Richard Rorty purports to demonstrate the impossibility of conceiving philosophy as motivated by epistemological questions. Rorty arrives at this conclusion via the three tenets of holism, pragmatism and materialism, which are all based upon the thesis of the radical theory-ladenness of observation. In the course of the book, however, Rorty weakens this thesis considerably. In my view the shifts in Rorty's standpoint regarding theory-ladenness undermine his position in two ways: they render his materialism doubtful and they confront his holism and pragmatism with the objection of Kantian idealism.

KRIEGLSTEIN, Werner. *The Dice-Playing God: Reflections on Life in a Post-Modern Age*. Lanham, Univ Pr of America, 1991.

In *The Dice-Playing God* the author relates Hegelian dialectics, as practiced by the Frankfurt School, to mysticism, Quantum Theory, and New Age spirituality. In the center of the debate is the possibility of *mimesis* and presence (Benjamin's Nowtime) as aesthetic experience of truth. The book deals with aesthetics of fascism, community creation, and dialectical wholeness. It critiques Habermas's rational communication model and proposes instead a creative model of dialectical communication. The book culminates in a proposal for *a materia*-based spirituality to overcome the shallowness of materialistic consumerism. The work is interspersed with narrations from the author's life, which provides a structural background for the discursive parts.

KRIFKA, Manfred. Four Thousand Ships Passed Through the Lock: Object-Induced Measure Functions on Events. Ling Phil, 13(5), 487-520, O 90.

KRIPS, Henry. Realism and the Collapse of the Wave-Packet. Brit J Phil Sci, 39(2), 225-232, Je 88.

Cartwright's argument for the collapse of the wave-packet is criticised. This enables us to rescue realism from the pressure put on it by Cartwright in the context of Quantum Theory.

KRISHAN, Y. Is Karma Evolutionary? J Indian Counc Phil Res, 6(1), 21-27, S-D 88.

Aurobindo and Radhakrishnan put forward the thesis that *Karmas* are evolutionary through the mechanism of rebirth of a soul. According to Aurobindo *Karmas* are not retributory, that rebirth of a soul is not just transmigration to any form of existence; rebirth is an ascension, a ladder for rising higher through various grades of life forms—plants, animal and humans. According to Radhakrishnan there is an inherent bond between a body and the soul, that rebirth cannot be in a body completely different from the present and that retrogression of a soul to lower forms of existence will be an extravaganza. Brahmanical, Buddhist and Jaina tests do not at all support the above thesis. They aver that there is no inherent bond between *Nirquna atma* and the body and that it is the *Karmas* which form the nexus between the two, that the process of rebirth is circular and not an evolutionary progression, that rebirths in the higher and lower life forms are retributory in accordance with the nature of accumulated *Karmas*.

KRISHAN, Y. Punyadāna or Transference of Merit—A Fiction. J Indian Counc Phil Res, 7(2), 125-137, Ja-Ap 90.

Punya means spiritual merit a person earns in future by doing a good *Karma* or moral act; *dāna* means a gift or donation. *Dāna* is a source of merit. *Punyadāna* therefore means beneficial transference or relinquishment of the merit of a moral act, that is likely to accrue, to another person of one's choice for his benefit either to multiply the transferor's merit potential or in fulfillment of one's commitment to total renunciation. This concept is quite popular in Hinduism and Buddhism. But this concept seriously compromises the doctrine of *Karma* according to which a person is personally and inescapably responsible for the acts done by him. It is a fictional concept as according to the doctrine of *Karma*, the time and form of maturation of *Karmas* (*Karma Vipāka*) is unknown, *adrsta*: no one knows when and how the *Karmas* fructify. Hence *punydāna* is like a transfer transaction in futures of uncertain time of maturity as well as of yield.

KRISHNA, Daya. Knowledge, Reason and Human Autonomy: A Review Article. J Indian Counc Phil Res, 7(1), 121-138, S-D 89.

The article presents Bannerjee's contentions in *Knowledge, Reasons and Human Autonomy*. How to overcome the 'otherness' of the 'other' is the central question for Bannerjee. The diverse forms of practical Reason in art, religion and morality, are basically escaped from the problem rather than attempts to solve it. The solution is found in the following two principles for the guidance of action: 1) 'So behave that your behaviour is in no circumstances governed either directly or remotely by dread of death and the desire for personal immortality.' 2) 'So behave that your behaviour is on no occasion governed either directly or remotely by aversion to bear the Cross.'

KRISHNA, Daya. The Text of the Nyāya-Sūtras: Some Problems. J Indian Counc Phil Res, 7(2), 13-40, Ja-Ap 90.

The article discusses the various problems raised by the fact that both Vācaspati Misra I (AD 960) and Vācaspati Misra II (AD 1450) tried to fix the text of the *Nyāya-sūtra* in classical times. It also discusses the discrepancies in the text as found in the works of Viswanātha Kesava Misra, Bhatta Vāgisvara and Rādhāmohan Gosvāmi Bhattācaryya. In the end it spells out the basic issues which will have to be settled before any attempt to fix the text of the *Nyāya-sūtra* can be undertaken.

KRISHNA, Daya. Thinking versus Thought. J Indian Counc Phil Res, 5(2), 47-57, Ja-Ap 88.

The article seeks to emphasize that every text is primarily a product of someone's thinking—an attempt at an answer to the questions that troubled him or to offer a tentative solution to the problems he encountered. Thus, the proper attitude to a text is not to try to decipher its meaning, but to ask what questions was it seeking to answer or what problems it was trying to solve. The prevalent attitude to texts, it is suggested, is primarily a hangover from the attitude to revelatory texts in the past, which needs to be given up.

KRISHNA, Daya. Yajna and the Doctrine of Karma: A Contradiction in Indian Thought about Action. J Indian Counc Phil Res, 6(2), 61-73, Ja-Ap 89.

The article draws attention to the contradiction involved in the theory of *Yajña* and the theory of *Karma* in the Indian tradition. The former requires that the fruits of the Yajña performed by the *rtviks* should accrue to the *Yajamāna* who has hired them for the purpose, while the latter requires that the fruits of action should accrue only to the person who has performed it. The article gives an interpretation of the theory of *Karma* in terms of the requirement of "moral intelligibility" of the universe and suggests possible ways of meeting the problem posed by it.

KRISTIANSEN, Borge. Schopenhauersche Weltsicht und totalitäre Humanität im Werke Thomas Manns. Schopenhauer Jahr, 71, 97-123, 1990.

KRIZAN, Mojmir. The Ideological Impasse of Gorbachev's Perestrojka. Stud Soviet Tho, 40(1-3), 113-135, 1990.

The principal argument of the article is that Gorbachev's project of *perestrojka* is incompatible with the ideology of Marxism-Leninism. The argument is based on the contraposition of two normative-political paradigms of rationalization of society: the utopian and the contractarian paradigm. Whereas Marxism-Leninism unequivocally pertains to the utopian paradigm, *perestrojka* can be understood as an attempt to introduce numerous elements of the contractarian paradigm into the Soviet economic and political system. In other words: the intention of *perestrojka* is to replace the project of monist modernization by pluralist modernization. Gorbachev's hesitation to give up Marxism-Leninism in favor of pluralism is caused both by his ideological conservatism and the requirements of political tactics.

KROES, Peter. "Philosophy of Science and the Technological Dimension of Science" in *Imre Lakatos and Theories of Scientific Change*, GAVROGLU, Kostas (ed), 375-382. Norwell, Kluwer, 1989.

The paper argues that philosophers of science have paid almost no attention to the technological dimension of science. Technological knowledge is considered to be nothing more than applied scientific knowledge, that is, scientific knowledge adapted to the realisation of an artefact. This view is criticized, on the grounds that it does not recognize the specific nature of technological knowledge.

KROES, Peter. Structural Analogies Between Physical Systems. Brit J Phil Sci, 40(2), 145-154, Je 89.

Structural analogies between physical *laws* have received considerable attention from philosophers of science. This paper, however, focusses on structural analogies between physical *systems*; this type of analogy plays and important role in the physical and technological sciences. A formal, set-theoretic description of structural analogies between physical systems is presented, and it is shown that a structural analogy between systems does not require a structural analogy with regard to the laws involved, nor conversely.

KROHN, Roger. Why Are Graphs so Central in Science? Biol Phil, 6(2), 181-203, Ap 91.

This paper raises the question of the prominence and use of statistical graphs in science, and argues that their use in problem solving analysis can best be understood in an 'interactionist' frame of analysis, including bio-emotion, culture, social organization, and environment as elements. We posit basic differences between visual, verbal, and numerical media of perception and communication. Graphs are thus seen as key interactive sites where different media are transformed into more interpretable forms. (edited)

KRONABEL, Christoph. *Die Aufhebung der Begriffs-philosophie*. Freiburg, Alber, 1991.

This book is a systematic examination of the stances taken by the Viennese thinker Anton Günther (1783-1863) vis-a-vis the philosophical thought of his times, especially German Idealism and post-Hegelian philosophy. Günther's profound speculative contributions influenced the theology of the first half of the nineteenth century as no other was able to do, but for various external reasons they were prevented from achieving full and lasting prominence. At the core of Günther's philosophy is the relationship between God and the world, whose conceivability appears to rule out the theological solution proposed in the idea of creatio ex nihilo. With this book, the author bestows appropriate recognition on an insufficiently heard voice in contemporary criticism of Idealism and in particular of Hegel. Furthermore, he presents the first systematic survey of Günther's philosophy and of his original theory of subjectivity.

KRONEN, John D. Essentialism Old and New: Suarez and Brody. Mod Sch, 68(2), 123-151, Ja 91.

A revived interest in essentialism characterizes much recent Anglo-American philosophy. In this article I compare and contrast one of the most articulate and well-argued recent versions of essentialism, that of Baruch Brody, with that of the last great system builder of the Schoolmen, Francis Suarez. I argue that Suarez's account of essentialism has advantages over Brody's because in positing a form that is entitative or thing-like as the chief constituent of the essences of substances Suarez's account is better able to explain the substantial unity of substances.

KRONZ, Frederick M. Hidden Locality, Conspiracy and Superluminal Signals. Phil Sci, 57(3), 420-444, S 90.

This paper involves one crucial assumption: namely, that the statistical predictions of quantum mechanics for Bell's variant of the EPR experiment will continue to be verified as detector efficiencies are improved and the need for coincidence counters is eliminated. This assumption entails that any hidden-variables theory for quantum mechanics must violate Bell's inequality—the inequality derived in Bell (1964). It is shown here that four locality conditions are involved in the derivation of Bell's inequality; and that a violation of any of the four locality conditions will either entail the existence of superluminal influences or the existence of superluminal signals (superluminal influences that can be used to transmit information), if conspiratorial theories can be ruled out. (edited)

KRONZ, Frederick M. Jarrett Completeness and Superluminal Signals. Proc Phil Sci Ass, 1, 227-239, 1990.

KRONZ, Frederick. Aristotle, the Direction Problem, and the Structure of the Sublunar Realm. Mod Sch, 67(4), 247-257, My 90.

KROON, F W and BURKHARD, W A. On a Complexity-Based Way of Constructivizing the Recursive Functions. Stud Log, 49(1), 133-149, Mr 90.

Hao Wang once wrote that the usual way of defining recursive functions involved constructively suspect quantification. He suggested in its stead a procedure that begins with obviously recursive functions, and allows other functions to count as constructively recursive if they can be evaluated within a number of steps given by functions already perceived as constructively recursive. The present paper presents a very general possibility result for constructive hierarchies of this type, using the resources of abstract complexity theory, and discusses some of the virtues and vices of the resulting approach to constructivizing the recursive functions.

KROON, Frederick W. On a Moorean Solution to Instability Puzzles. Austl J Phil, 68(4), 455-461, D 90.

According to Roy Sorensen (*Blindspots*, 1988), no rational agent could ever find herself believing [Ap]: p iff I don't believe p, since believing [Ap] would commit the agent both to *not* believing p and (consequently) to believing p. Sorensen thinks that [Ap] is as rationally incredible to an agent as the Moorean statement 'it is raining but I don't believe it'. The present paper disputes Sorensen's account by arguing that an agent's refusal to believe [Ap] may well create intolerable problems for her image of herself as extended over time. In addition, it argues that some [Ap]'s have the status of logical truisms whose acceptance is mandatory.

KRÜGER, Hans-Peter. Post-Modernism as the Lesser Evil: Criticism and Agreement in Lyotard's "Widerstreit" ("Conflict") (in German). Deut Z Phil, 38(7), 609-628, 1990.

In difference to "modern times" (Neuzeit), modernity is a structural potential of the sociocultural evolution. Modernity consists in a plurality of heterogenous competitions (economic, political, expert cultural and everyday cultural) which are permanently endangered by monopolization. The question for postmodernity is the question of changing the interdependence between these competitions on a global scale: the cultural competitions became evolutionarily leading by certain communication processes. This problem is discussed with J F Lyotard.

KRÜGER, Hans-Peter. The Differences Between the Capitalist and the Modern Society (in German). Deut Z Phil, 38(3), 202-217, 1990.

The east European state socialism died by its lack of modernisation. According to Habermas modern times have been split into class and modern structures. Rereading Marx in this way (against his philosophy of history including the proletarian mission) he thought the substitution of work and labor (as the substance of capitalism) by science technology and by modern forms of communication/intercourse. The question of socialism should be asked only under the condition of safeguarding the modern evolutionary advantages. These consist in economic, political and cultural forms of free competition.

KRUGLANSKI, Arie W. Social Science-Based Understandings of Science: Reflections on Fuller. Phil Soc Sci, 21(2), 223-231, Je 91.

What type of social science is ideally suited for ellucidating the nature of science? Some levels of social scientific analysis may be capable of illuminating aspects of science that are *nonunique* compared to other intellectual activities, other levels of analysis may elucidate aspects that render science *unique*. In regard to nonunique aspects, science is, first and foremost, a cognitive activity carried out in social contexts. Hence, a theory of how persons draw inferences and negotiate them with others should apply to the activities of scientists as well. Beyond the commonality it shares with cognitive activity as such science is a unique societal institution devoted to unique values, possessed of a unique structure and committed to unique assumptions. The implications of this analysis for metatheories of science and for science policy are considered.

KRYNICKI, Michal and SZCZERBA, Leslaw. On Simplicity of Formulas. Stud Log, 49(3), 401-419, S 90.

Simple formula should contain only few quantifiers. In the paper the methods to estimate quantity and quality of quantifiers needed to express a sentence equivalent to given one.

KUBACKI, Steven R and GLUCK, John P. Animals in Biomedical Research: The Undermining Effect of the Rhetoric of the Besieged. Ethics Behavior, 1(3), 157-173, 1991.

It is correctly asserted that the intensity of the current debate over the use of animals in biomedical research is unprecedented. The extent of expressed animosity and distrust has stunned many researchers. In response, researchers have tended to take a strategic defensive posture, which involves the assertation of several abstract positions that serve to obstruct resolution of the debate. Those abstractions include the notions that the animal protection movement is trivial and purely anti-intellectual in scope, that all science is good (and some especially so), and the belief that an ethical consensus can never really be reached between the parties.

KUBBINGA, Henk H. "Hélène Metzger et la théorie corpusculaire des stahliens au XVIIIe siècle" in *Études sur/Studies on Hélène Metzger*, FREUDENTHAL, Gad , 59-66. Leiden, Brill, 1990.

KUCKLICK, B and MARCUS, Ruth Barcan and BERCOVITCH, S. Uninformed Consent. Science, 205, 644-647, 1979.

A response to the editorial "Informed Consent May Be Hazardous to Health," *Science*, vol. 204. In particular what is cited is the failure to distinguish the subject of an experiment who volunteers and the special doctor-client relationship, also, the failure to distinguish rights and benefits. The subject has a right to know. That is not a benefit conferred.

KUCZYNSKA, Alicja. "Tradition as Innovation" in *XIth International Congress in Aesthetics, Nottingham 1988*, WOODFIELD, Richard (ed), 102-105. Nottingham, Nottingham Polytech, 1990.

KUCZYNSKI, Janusz. The Metaphilosophy of Dialogue. Dialec Hum, 16(3-4), 147-162, Sum-Autumn 89.

KUHLMANN, Wolfgang. Solipsism in Kant's Practical Philosophy and the Discourse of Ethics. Grad Fac Phil J, 13(2), 159-179, 1990.

KÜHN, Rolf. Les présupposés métaphysiques de la "lisibilité" de l'être. Arch Phil, 54(1), 43-64, Ja-Mr 91.

According to S Weil reading ("lecture") means interpreting reality without taking into account the exigency of a pure ontological manifestation, which the subject obtains only through a de-creation, a non-reading without any name or form. This aim is at once spiritual, ethical and religious, has implicit metaphysical ideas about God and His creation which do not allow any idea of a finite alterity really intended. Reflexive difficulties of S Weil are discussed concerning mainly the divine gift of human freedom necessarily rooted in a concrete bodily energy, which is more than a mere instrument, in order to reach a judgment free from passions and imaginations. The very idea of a free judgment—even considered as a de-creation or as void—does not indeed solve the difficulty of all the philosophies of consciousness which take indeed the place of God and assume His attributes. However, in such a discussion with S Weil we find a way to think more precisely the link between religion and thought and to see more clearly what a genuine philosophy of religion may be.

KUHN, Thomas S. "Dubbing and Redubbing: The Vulnerability of Rigid Destination" in *Scientific Theories*, SAVAGE, C Wade (ed), 298-318. Minneapolis, Univ of Minn Pr, 1990.

KUHSE, Helga. "Euthanasia" in *A Companion to Ethics*, SINGER, Peter (ed), 294-302. Cambridge, Blackwell, 1991.

The article provides an overview of the euthanasia debate. It draws distinctions between active and passive euthanasia, actions and omissions, killing and letting die, ordinary and extraordinary means, and the role of intention in treatment decisions. Questions are raised about the conceptual adequacy of these distinctions and their moral significance. Finally, there is a brief discussion of 'slippery slope' arguments and mention is made of the situation in *The Netherlands*, where doctors are practicing voluntary euthanasia in full view of the law.

KUIPERS, Theo A F. Economie in de spiegel van de natuurwetenschappen. Kennis Methode, 15(2), 182-197, 1991.

In order to evaluate the dilemma for economics of either trying to be as much like the natural sciences or striving for a unique, autonomous discipline a survey is presented of correspondences and plausible differences between economics and the natural sciences. Moreover, a number of specific inconsequences in economics are presented. Instead of accepting the dilemma, a path between is advocated. There are evident fundamental differences, all related to the presence of intentional subjects in real economies. However, this does not preclude that economics can make didactic and heuristic use of several cognitive patterns in the natural sciences. And the latter have their own inconsequences.

KUKATHAS, Chandran. *Rawls: "A Theory of Justice" and Its Critics*. Stanford, Stanford Univ Pr, 1990.

This book is designed to provide some sense of Rawl's theory and of its significance in contemporary political philosophy. Themes discussed include a historical interpretation of Rawl's *A Theory of Justice*, moral individualism, contractarian theory, as well as libertarian and commutarian critiques of Rawl's theory. (staff)

KUKLA, Andre. Ten Types of Scientific Progress. Proc Phil Sci Ass, 1, 457-466, 1990.

Laudan's taxonomy of scientific problems is not exhaustive. For one thing, it does not take into account projects which produce an increase of theoretical virtue in a theory that does not suffer from conceptual problems. A new taxonomy is proposed that distinguishes scientific projects on the basis of which theoretical virtue is altered, whether the alteration produces an increase or a decrease in virtue, and whether the alteration is due to a logical invention, a logical discovery, or an empirical discovery.

KULKA, Tomas. Richard Rorty: An Interview (in Hebrew). Iyyun, 39(4), 371-380, O 90.

KULKA, Tomas. Why is Kitsch Bad? (in Hebrew). Iyyun, 40(2), 173-186, Ap 91.

KULP, Christopher B. Dewey, Indetermincy, and the Spectator Theory of Knowledge. Mod Sch, 67(3), 207-221, Mr 90.

John Dewey offered a number of arguments to show that traditional epistemology is bankrupt because it is committed to the spectator theory of knowledge. This paper critically examines his argument against the spectator theory that is based on Heisenberg's principle of indeterminacy. After explicating Dewey's argument, I argue that he had failed to provide persuasive reason to reject one version of the spectator theory, and has provided no reason whatever to reject another version of the spectator theory.

KULSTAD, Mark (ed) and COVER, J A (ed). *Central Themes in Early Modern Philosophy*. Indianapolis, Hackett, 1990.

This collection of new essays provides a cross-sampling of the important current work in the history of seventeenth- and eighteenth-century philosophy, particularly in the areas of metaphysics and epistemology. Every major figure (by one reckoning) from Descartes to Kant is considered, some receiving attention in multiple essays (especially Spinoza, Descartes, Malebranche, Leibniz). A diverse range of themes is also addressed—from doctrines of substance, essence, and causality to sensation, epistemic responsibility, and knowledge of necessary truths. Contributors include M Wilson, R S Woolhouse, D Garrett, G H R Parkinson, E Curley, R Sleigh Jr, M Bolton, N Jolley, A Baier, and P Kitcher.

KULTGEN, John. Nuclear Deterrence and the Morality of Intentions. SW Phil Rev, 7(1), 105-117, Ja 91.

Finnis, Boyle, and Grisez argue that nuclear deterrence involves contingent intentions to do what is wrong (use nuclear weapons in war should the need arise) and they maintain that it is wrong to intend to do what it is wrong to do. I explore why bad intentions are wrong—they not only lead to bad actions but have bad consequences in themselves—and explain how this makes nuclear deterrence wrong.

KUMABE, Masahiro. A 1-Generic Degree Which Bounds a Minimal Degree. J Sym Log, 55(2), 733-743, Je 90.

KUMAR ROY, Dev. Effective Extensions of Partial Orders. Z Math Log, 36(3), 233-236, 1990.

The well-known result that every partial order has a linear extension has a nonconstructive proof. This paper looks at extensions of countable partial orders which are recursive or recursively enumerable, and shows that recursive partial orders have recursive extensions but r.e. partial orders may fail to have r.e. extensions. A coding argument shows that there are r.e. partial orders not isomorphic to recursive ones. This is in contrast with the situation for r.e. linear orders.

KUMMER, Christian. *Evolution als Höherentwicklung des Bewusstseins*. Freiburg, Alber, 1991.

This book tries to give a synthesis of two models explaining evolutionary progress: the "law of complexity and consciousness" by Teilhard de Chardin, and the theory of "hypercyclic" generation of biological information by Manfred Eigen. It is shown that the concept of self-organization of matter can only be accepted as far as this "self" is correlated to evolving consciousness.

KUNKEL, Joseph C (ed) and KLEIN, Kenneth H (ed). *In the Interest of Peace: A Spectrum of Philosophical Views*. Wolfeboro, Longwood, 1990.

KUNKEL, Joseph. "The Arms-Race Implications of Libertarian Capitalism" in *Issues in War and Peace: Philosophical Inquiries*, KUNKEL, Joseph (ed), 69-82. Wolfeboro, Longwood, 1989.

This essay examines the views of three theoreticians of libertarian capitalism: Nozick, Rand, and Friedman. While disagreeing on details each advocates strict government separation from the economy and concentration solely on negative duties of preventing harm to citizens. In drawing out the arms-race implications of this theory three issues are addressed: world hunger, world governance, and war. Regarding hunger, the rich cannot be taxed to feed the poor. Regarding world government, authority can only protect communities from interference by others. As three principles are violated by socialism capitalistic states may defend their nations against such violations.

KUNKEL, Joseph. "Deterrence or Disarmament: An Appraisal of Consequentialist Arguments" in *In the Interest of Peace: A Spectrum of Philosophical Views*, KLEIN, Kenneth H (ed), 141-153. Wolfeboro, Longwood, 1990.

This essay evaluates three national nuclear policies from an ethical perspective. The three policies are war-winning deterrence, minimum deterrence, and nuclear disarmament. War-winning deterrence of the Hobbesian persuasion is rejected as morally nihilistic in regard to war. Minimum deterrence and nuclear disarmament are examined within a consequentialist orientation. More specifically these postures are contrasted and appraised as viewed by two major ethical proponents, Gregory Kavka and Douglas Lackey. The implications of nuclear blackmail and the viability of nuclear disarmament figure prominently in this appraisal.

KUNKEL, Joseph (ed) and KLEIN, Kenneth H (ed). *Issues in War and Peace: Philosophical Inquiries*. Wolfeboro, Longwood, 1989.

This volume consists of twenty original essays by philosophers, divided into three sections. The first section examines the ideologies of the two superpowers. Beginning with lessons of the Cuban Missile Crisis it includes essays on Marxism, libertarianism, realpolitik, and on how to know peace claims. The second section evaluates justifications for nuclear war. Essays are on moral skepticism, nuclear war as terrorism, strategic defense, and coming to grips with moral pluralism. The third section moves in the direction of promoting peace with essays on existential death, nuclear winter, warism, peacemaking, sexism, and the role of democracy.

KUNKEL, Joseph and KLEIN, Kenneth. "What Does Philosophy Add to Nuclear Discussions? An Introductory Essay" in *Issues in War and Peace: Philosophical Inquiries*, KUNKEL, Joseph (ed), 1-10. Wolfeboro, Longwood, 1989.

Philosophy has three major functions: the critical, the synthetic, and the moral. Critical thinking introduces clarification of terms and evaluation of arguments. Of particular concern is the cultural prevalence of warism, the rejection of peacemaking, and the sexism and lack of democracy in nuclear politics. The synthetic function is found in system building, and in particular in the ideological contrast of Western capitalistic libertarianism and Hobbesian realism with Soviet Marxism. The moral function is found in applying various ethical systems, such as just-war, deontology, and consequentialism, to war and peace issues.

KÜNNE, Wolfgang. "The Nature of Acts: Moore on Husserl" in *The Analytic Tradition: Philosophical Quarterly Monographs, Volume 1*, BELL, David (ed), 104-116. Cambridge, Blackwell, 1990.

KUOKKANEN, Martti and SANDU, Gabriel. On Social Rights. Ratio Juris, 3(1), 89-94, Mr 90.

In this paper we analyze the concept of social right which denotes rights such as: right to adequate nutrition, right to an education, etc. This type of right has not been analyzed in the traditional theory, nor does it find a place in the Hohfeldean typology. Our main claim is that social rights are strong protective permissions. The notion of protected permission is analyzed with the help of two other notions: absence of prohibition and forbearance of interference.

KÜPPER, Georg. Schopenhauers Straftheorie und die aktuelle Strafzweckdiskussion. Schopenhauer Jahr, 71, 207-216, 1990.

KURCZEWSKI, Jacek. "Power and Wisdom: The Expert as Mediating Figure in Contemporary Polish History" in *The Political Responsibility of Intellectuals*, MACLEAN, Ian (ed), 77-99. New York, Cambridge Univ Pr, 1990.

KURFIRST, Robert. Beyond Malthusianism: Demography and Technology in John Stuart Mill's Stationary State. Utilitas, 3(1), 53-67, My 91.

KURLAND, Nancy B. The Ethical Implications of the Straight-Commission Compensation System—An Agency Perspective. J Bus Ethics, 10(10), 757-766, O 91.

This paper examines the role of the straight-commissioned salesperson in the context of agency theory and asserts that because the agent acts to benefit two principles, potential conflicts of interest arise. Temporal differences in receipt of rewards create a major conflict, while the firm's exhibition of both espoused and actual behaviors and information asymmetries intensify this conflict. Finally, in light of these inconsistencies, the ethical implications of the straight-commission compensation system are examined.

KUROSAKI, Hiroshi. "Mario Bunge on the Mind-Body Problem and Ontology: Critical Examinations" in *Studies on Mario Bunge's "Treatise"*, WEINGARTNER, Paul (ed), 215-223. Amsterdam, Rodopi, 1990.

Mario Bunge has discussed the so-called mind-body problem in many books and articles which I cite in the *References*. Probably there are others in which he discussed the problem, but I hope that the books and articles cited in the *References* are sufficient for us to understand his philosophy of the mind-body problem. First, I will sketch his philosophy of the mind-body problem—emergentist materialism—and second, I will ask questions about it.

KURTHEN, Martin (and others). The Locked-In Syndrome and the Behaviorist Epistemology of Other Minds. Theor Med, 12(1), 69-79, Mr 91.

In this paper, the problem of correct ascriptions of consciousness to patients in neurological intensive care medicine is explored as a special case of the general philosophical 'other minds problem'. It is argued that although clinical ascriptions of consciousness and coma are mostly based on behavioral evidence, a behaviorist epistemology of other minds is not likely to succeed. To illustrate this, the so-called 'total locked-in syndrome', in which preserved consciousness is combined with a total loss of motor abilities due to a lower ventral brain stem lesion, is presented as a touchstone for behaviorism. It is argued that this example of consciousness without behavioral expression does not disprove behaviorism specifically, but rather illustrates the need for a non-verificationist theory of other minds. It is further argued that a folk version of such a theory alread underlies our factual ascriptions of consciousness in clinical contexts. Finally, a non-behaviorist theory of other minds for patients with total locked-in syndrome is outlined.

KURTZ, Paul. Pragmatic Naturalism: The Philosophy of Sidney Hook (1902-1989). J Phil, 87(10), 526-534, O 90.

KURTZ, Paul. "Secular Humanism and Eupraxophy" in *The Question of Humanism: Challenges and Possibilities*, GOICOECHEA, David (ed), 308-325. Buffalo, Prometheus, 1991.

KURTZ, Paul. *The Transcendental Temptation: A Critique of Religion and the Paranormal*. Buffalo, Prometheus, 1991.

KURTZ, Paul and BULLOUGH, Vern L. The Unitarian Universalist Association: Humanism or Theism? Free Inq, 11(2), 12-14, Spr 91.

KUSCH, Martin. *On* "Why is There Something Rather Than Nothing?". Amer Phil Quart, 27(3), 253-257, Jl 90.

KUSPIT, Donald. "The Contradictory Character of Postmodernism" in *Postmodernism—Philosophy and the Arts (Continental Philosophy III)*, SILVERMAN, Hugh J (ed), 53-68. New York, Routledge, 1990.

KUTLESA, Stipe. Boskovic's Philosophy in the Evaluation of Franjo Markovic (1887): Origins and Results (in Serbo-Croatian). Filozof Istraz, 32-33(5-6), 1621-1638, 1989.

The aim of the study is to present the horizon of Markovic's evaluation of the philosophical work of Boskovic, emphasizing the deduction and justification of his atomic system: in Markovic's opinion, it was inspired primarily by philosophical reason, but took into account stimuli deriving from physical phenomena and their laws. Boskovic grounds his atomism on the theory of knowledge. The paper discussed Markovic's views expounded by Boskovic on the major issues of the theory of knowledge, i.e., the question of (non)innateness of ideas in the human mind, the certainty and range of our knowledge and the cognition of the being of outer objects. (edited)

KUVAKIN, V A. Vasilii Vasil'evich Rozanov: "My Soul Is Woven of Filth, Tenderness, and Grief". Soviet Stud Phil, 29(3), 38-61, Wint 90-91.

KUX, Ernst. Gorbatschews "Erneurung des Sozialismus"—Ideologie in der Krise des Kommunismus. Stud Soviet Tho, 40(1-3), 89-111, 1990.

KUYKENDALL, Eleanor H. "Sex, Gender, and the Politics of Difference" in *Writing the Politics of Difference*, SILVERMAN, Hugh J (ed), 217-223. Albany, SUNY Pr, 1991.

KVART, Igal and STELLINO, Ana Isabel (trans). Contrafácticos. Dianoia, 34(34), 93-140, 1988.

KWA, Chunglin. Wetten en verhalen. Kennis Methode, 15(1), 105-120, 1991.

A philosophical-anthropological interpretation of Nancy Cartwright's concept "causal story" and her critique of laws of nature is offered. It is argued that laws of nature "explain" phenomena by invoking a deeper reality, whereas causal stories (similar to myths) don't. Laws of nature turn (local) phenomena into instances of something global. Likewise they turn technical interventions in nature into local realizations of global control. Causal stories only represent particular instances of human interaction with nature. "Laws" may figure as more or less stable story elements, or "mythemes." They refer to other stories in which they also occur.

KWAME, Safro. On African Feminism: Two Reasons for the Rejection of Feminism. Int J Applied Phil, 5(2), 1-7, Fall 90.

There are at least two reasons for taking African feminism seriously. The first reason is that feminism as theorized or practised in the West ignores the interests of people of African descent. The second is that, as theorized and practised in the West, feminism ignores the history of African societies. In my view, these reasons do not provide a sufficient reason for the separation or rejection of the feminist movement. Any form of feminism that discriminates against women on the basis of color or sex is unworthy of its name.

KWASCHIN, Sylvie. Le genre vernaculaire ou la nostalgie de la tradition: A propos d'Ivan Illich. Rev Phil Louvain, 89(81), 63-83, F 91.

KYBURG JR, Henry E and BACCHUS, Fahiem and THALOS, Mariam. Against Conditionalization. Synthese, 85(3), 475-506, D 90.

This paper presents a challenge to the doctrines of Bayesian epistemology by a critical analysis of Bayesian principles. We first examine the Dutch Book principle, pointing out that an agent with logical capabilities can avoid a Dutch even if he does not possess a unique distribution over his beliefs. We then examine a dynamic Dutch Book argument, presented by Teller, that claims to support conditioning. We argue that it provides not much more than the static Dutch Book arguments. Finally we examine van Fraassen's principle of reflection, and conclude that rather than enforcing reasonable behavior, this principle can force an agent to do what is unreasonable.

KYBURG JR, Henry E (ed) and LOUI, Ronald P (ed) and CARLSON, Greg N (ed). *Knowledge Representation and Defeasible Reasoning*. Norwell, Kluwer, 1990.

This is a collection of essays on the interface between computer science, philosophy, and linguistics. The volume is divided into four parts. The first is Defeasible Reasoning and the Frame Problem, with papers by Donald Nute, Lenhart Schubert, Hector Geffner and Judea Pearl, and Michael Dunn. Second, Representation Problems and Ordinary Language, with papers by Don Perlis, Brendan Gillon, Nuel Belnap and Michael Perloff, and Andrew McCafferty. The third part concerns Inference Rules and Belief Revision, and has papers by Charles Cross, Judea Pearl, Teddy Seidenfeld, and by Hugues LeBlanc and Peter Roeper. Finally, there are papers on Logical Problems in Representing Knowledge by Bob Carpenter and Richmond Thomason, Ronald Loui, Robin Giles, and Romas Aleliunas.

KYBURG JR, Henry E. *Science and Reason*. New York, Oxford Univ Pr, 1990.

This is a general book about the relation between philosophy and science, as well as a gentle essay on the philosophy of science. The topics include Logic and Mathematics, Probability and Induction, a discussion of Measurement and Conventionalism. Idealization, Causality, and Modality are discussed—the general thesis being that while idealization is a useful practical device, metaphysical notions of causality and necessity are superstitious relics. Finally, there are chapters on Decision Theory, Epistemology, the role of Speculation, and the Limits of Science (none).

KYBURG JR, Henry E. "Theories as Mere Conventions" in *Scientific Theories*, SAVAGE, C Wade (ed), 158-174. Minneapolis, Univ of Minn Pr, 1990.

The thesis of this paper is that theories can be regarded as 'mere' linguistic conventions. To call something a convention is not to say that there are not good reasons for deciding among conventions. It is argued that there are, in fact, good *epistemic* reasons for deciding among conventions. These reasons are to be cashed out in terms of predictive factual content. But predictive factual content is not merely (or even often) a matter of deduction from theories and boundary conditions, but (usually) a matter of probabilistic inference. What counts in assessing the relative value of conventions are the sets of statements that each yields as having high probability.

KYJ, M J and REILLY, B J. Economics and Ethics. J Bus Ethics, 9(9), 691-698, S 90.

Business theory and management practices are outgrowths of basic economic principles. To evaluate the proper place of *ethics* in business, the meaning of ethics as defined by economic theory must be assessed. This paper contends that classical economic thought advocates a nonethical decision-making context and is not functional for a modern complex, interdependent environment.

KYMLICKA, Will. The Ethics of Inarticulacy. Inquiry, 34(2), 155-182, Je 91.

In his impressive and wide-ranging new book, *Sources of the Self*, Charles Taylor argues that modern moral philosophy, at least within the Anglo-American tradition, offers a 'cramped' view of morality. I argue that Taylor has misunderstood the basic structure of most modern moral theory, which seeks to relocate, rather than suppress, these important questions. In particular, he fails to note the difference between general and specific conceptions of the good, between procedures for assessing the good and specific outcomes of that procedure, and between society's enforcement of morality and an individual's voluntary compliance with morality. (edited)

KYMLICKA, Will. Rethinking the Family. Phil Pub Affairs, 20(1), 77-97, Wint 91.

KYMLICKA, Will. "The Social Contract Tradition" in *A Companion to Ethics*, SINGER, Peter (ed), 186-196. Cambridge, Blackwell, 1991.

Contractarians believe that we can identify principles of morality by asking what regulative standards the members of a community could freely and reasonably agree to. However, there have been many different interpretations of the content and normative force of the supposed "agreement". I discuss three versions of contractarian morality, grounded in natural law, mutual advantage, and impartiality respectively. I argue that these underlying approaches are so different that it is misleading to speak of "a social contract tradition". Rather, there is a social contract device that three distinct moral traditions have used for their own distinct reasons.

LA BRECQUE, Richard. Liberal Education in an Unfree World. Educ Theor, 40(4), 483-494, Fall 90.

An ongoing challenge in higher education is to integrate liberal education with specialized, occupationally oriented studies. A form of liberal education should be implemented, even in research-oriented institutions of higher education, for the purpose of developing occupational specialists who will be better equipped and hopefully disposed to examine critically the intended and unintended consequences of institutional activities in society, especially those in the economic sector. If such is successfully implemented, higher education may play a less subservient and more transformative role vis-à-vis the predominant priorities of the other institutions of society.

LA CASSE, Chantale and ROSS, Don. Response to W J Norman's "Has Rational Economic Man a Heart". Eidos, 8(2), 235-246, D 89.

LA CHANCE, Michaël. La démonstration mystifiante: Wittgenstein et Beuys. Lekton, 1(1), 199-219, 1990.

LA FLEUR, William R. Contestation and Consensus: The Morality of Abortion in Japan. Phil East West, 40(4), 529-542, O 90.

LA FOLLETTE, Hugh. "Personal Relationships" in *A Companion to Ethics*, SINGER, Peter (ed), 327-333. Cambridge, Blackwell, 1991.

Morality and personal relationships appear to conflict. Morality, as typically conceived, requires impartiality while personal relationships are partial to the core. Philosophers have responded to this conflict in two ways. Some, like Rachels, argue that obligations to friend and family are derivative from impartial moral principles. Others, like Williams argue that demands of personal relationships sometimes trump the demands of morality. I find both options distateful. I focus instead on ways impartial moral concern and personal relationships are mutually supportive. Doing so does not eliminate the tensions but does make it more amenable to resolution.

LA PUMA, John and SCHIEDERMAYER, David L. The Clinical Ethicist at the Bedside. Theor Med, 12(2), 141-149, Je 91.

In this paper we attempt to show how the goal of resolving moral problems in a patient's care can best be achieved by working at the bedside. The skills of the clinical ethics consultant include the ability to delineate and resolve ethical problems in a particular patient's case and to teach other health professionals to build their own frameworks for clinical ethical decision making. When the clinical situation requires it, clinical ethics consultants can and should assist primary physicians with case management. (edited)

LA PUMA, John and MOSS, Robert J. The Ethics of Mechanical Restraints. Hastings Center Rep, 21(1), 22-25, Ja-F 91.

LA PUMA, John and CASSEL, Christine. The Noncompliant Substance Abuser: Commentary. Hastings Center Rep, 21(2), 30-31, Mr-Ap 91.

LA SOUJEOLE, Benoît-Dominique. "Sociátá" et "communion" chez saint Thomas d'Aquin. Rev Thomiste, 90(4), 587-622, O-D 90.

LA TORRE, Massimo. "Degenerate Law": Jurists and Nazism. Ratio Juris, 3(1), 95-99, Mr 90.

The author mainly discusses a recent book (*Entartetes Recht*) by Bernd Rüthers. Some features of Nazi legal doctrine, in particular its decisionism, are dealt with. Special attention is devoted to Carl Schmitt. Finally Rüthers's criticism against legal institutionalism as a source of totalitarian conceptions of law is shown to be unjustified.

LABARRIÈRE, Pierre-Jean. Après Weil, avec Weil: Une lecture de Gilbert Kirscher. Arch Phil, 53(4), 661-675, O-D 90.

G Kirscher considers the masterwork of Erich Weil, "La logique de la philosophie," the aporia at the beginning, the eighteen categories. A difference from Hegel is that E Weil leaves room for the irreducible finiteness of the philosophising subject.

LABBÉ, Y. Foi et intelligence dans l'"unique arguments": Un plan pour "Proslogion II-IV". Rev Phil Louvain, 88(79), 345-368, O 90.

In the text of St. Anselm's proof a twofold request for faith is laid circularly around the two proofs of existence, based on a single argument. The outcome is an extremely firm procedural unity, the search for faith reversing itself into discovery at the point where intelligence passes from that which is thought also to be in reality to that which cannot be thought not to be.

LABHALLA, Salah and LOMBARDI, Henri. Real Numbers, Continued Fractions and Complexity Classes. Annals Pure Applied Log, 50(1), 1-28, N 90.

We compare some representations of real numbers from the viewpoint of recursive functionals and of complexity (via Cauchy sequences, Dedekind cuts and continued fraction). The impossibility of obtaining some functions as recursive functionals may be explicited in terms of complexity: 1) existence of sequence of low complexity whose image is not a recursive sequence, 2) existence of objects of low complexity whose images have high time-complexity. We also obtain quite high results of nonstability under addition for some representations. This work confirms that the unique representation of real numbers suitable for the ordinary calculs is via explicit Cauchy sequences of rationals.

LABRADA, Antonia. "L'image de l'homme dans la théorie kantienne du génie" in *XIth International Congress in Aesthetics, Nottingham 1988*, WOODFIELD, Richard (ed), 106-108. Nottingham, Nottingham Polytech, 1990.

The purpose of the work is to study the faculties which constitute genius. The conclusion is that the infinite of subjectivity is not expressed in creativity. This fact limits the Kantian theory of genius to the familiar bounds of critical philosophy. Thus, it is possible to assert that Kantian philosophy, including that which refers to the theory of genius and artistic creation, is a philosophy of nature and a philosophy of the finite spirit.

LACENTRA, Walter. *The Authentic Self: Toward a Philosophy of Personality*. New York, Lang, 1991.

This study contends that an adequate theory of personal growth should be based upon a human striving for authenticity, a striving revealed as a dynamic process of self-transcendence operating on three different levels: intellectual, moral, and religious. Just as the act of questioning propels man toward ever newer horizons of wisdom, so also does human and divine love explain the fullness of authentic moral and religious development. Bernard Lonergan's insights into personal development are used to critically evaluate specific aspects of the psychologies of personality developed by Freud, Adler, and Maslow.

LACEY, Hugh. Interpretation and Theory in the Natural and the Human Sciences: Comments on Kuhn and Taylor. J Theor Soc Behav, 20(3), 197-212, S 90.

Commenting on views of Kuhn and Taylor, I argue that the kind of theory sought in the natural sciences, and the interpretation of the epistemic values associated with it, are unintelligible if separated from commitment to the primacy of (technological) control as the stance towards nature. This suggests (1) that the quest for theory in the human sciences is problematic; (2) that natural sciences might take a different form if the epistemic values come to be interpreted in the light of a value other than control, e.g., social justice; and thence (3) there may be a complex reciprocity between the natural and human sciences.

LACHS, John. A Dialogue on Value, I: Values and Relations. J Speculative Phil, 5(1), 1-10, 1991.

LACHS, John. A Dialogue on Value, III: Is Everything Intrinsically Good? J Speculative Phil, 5(1), 20-24, 1991.

LACHS, John. The Philosophical Significance of Psychological Differences Among Humans. S J Phil, 29(3), 329-339, Fall 91.

LACHTERMAN, David. The Faculty of Desire. Grad Fac Phil J, 13(2), 181-213, 1990.

LACKEY, Douglas. "Utilitarian Ethics and Superpower Negotiations: Lost Opportunities for Nuclear Peace" in *In the Interest of Peace: A Spectrum of Philosophical Views*, KLEIN, Kenneth H (ed), 97-115. Wolfeboro, Longwood, 1990.

LACLAU, Ernesto. *New Reflections on the Revolution of Our Time*. New York, Verso, 1990.

LACOUE-LABARTHE, Philippe. "History and Mimesis" in *Looking After Nietzsche*, RICKELS, Laurence A (ed), 209-231. Albany, SUNY Pr, 1990.

LACZNIAK, Gene R and MURPHY, Patrick E. Fostering Ethical Marketing Decisions. J Bus Ethics, 10(4), 259-271, Ap 91.

This paper begins by examining several potentially unethical recent marketing practices. Since most marketing managers face ethical dilemmas during their careers, it is essential to study the moral consequences of these decisions. A typology of ways that managers might confront ethical issues is proposed. The significant organizational, personal and societal costs emanting from unethical behavior are also discussed. Both relatively simple frameworks and more comprehensive models for evaluating ethical decisions in marketing are summarized. Finally, the fact that organizational commitment to fostering ethical marketing decisions can be accomplished by top management leadership, codes of ethics, ethics seminars/programs and ethical audits is examined.

LACZNIAK, Gene R and MURPHY, Patrick E. International Marketing Ethics. Bridges, 2(3-4), 155-177, Fall-Wint 90.

This paper examines the ethical issues surrounding global marketing. Among the causes of ethical problems in the international arena are cultural relativism with its concomitant concerns of bribery and selling unsafe products, and strategic planning which often includes ethnocentric and deterministic ethical assumptions about managerial choice. Possible techniques to ensure ethical marketing practices include a worldwide code of ethics that incorporates the Sullivan principles and using stakeholder analysis to examine the marketing process. Specific ideas for ethical action pertaining to marketing are proposed including always providing high-quality, safe, and culturally appropriate products, and suspension of activities in markets where the ethical problems are too great. On a more general level, ethics should be treated as a significant input to international marketing strategy by top management and the regular development of "ethical impact statements" should be considered.

LADEN, Anthony. Games, Fairness, and Rawls's *A Theory of Justice*. Phil Pub Affairs, 20(3), 189-222, Sum 91.

The article has two sections, the first game-theoretic, the second primarily exegetical. In the first, a game-theoretic theorem linking fairness to the least cores of cooperative games is presented, argued for, and related to other conceptions of fairness, most significantly Thomas Scanlon's philosophical contractualism. In the second part, the fairness theorem from the first part motivates a sympathetic game theoretic account of justice as fairness. The original position is described as two games, in order to emphasize the role of stability in Rawls's arguments.

LADRIÈRE, Jean. Cent ans de philosophie à l'Institut Supérieur de Philosophie. Rev Phil Louvain, 88(78), 168-213, My 90.

LADRIÈRE, Jean. Metaphysics and Culture. Asian J Phil, 2(1), 1-24, Sum 90.

LADWIG, James G. Is Collaborative Research Exploitative? Educ Theor, 41(2), 111-120, Spr 91.

This article examines current forms of "Collaborative Research" in education as exploitation. Using Analytical Marxism's theoretical outline of exploitation in an analysis of what Pierre Bourdieu calls cultural capital, it is argued that four types of capitals are produced and exchanged in Collaborative Research: knowledge of teaching methods, knowledge of research methodologies, authorship of papers, and the form of the research itself. The social relations between teachers and educational reseachers are seen to be exploitative, to the benefit of researchers at the expense of teachers. Potentially less exploitative constructions of collaborative research are also explored.

LAFLAMME, Claude. Upward Directedness of the Rudin-Keisler Ordering of *P*-Points. J Sym Log, 55(2), 449-456, Je 90.

We prove that the upward directedness of the Rudin-Keisler ordering of P-points is independent of ZFC.

LAFLEUR, Claude. Logique et théorie de l'argumentation dans le "Guide de l'étudiant". Dialogue (Canada), 29(3), 335-355, 1990.

In the thirteenth-century "Student's Guide" of the Ripoll 109—discovered in 1927 by M Grabmann but still unedited—the section on logic occupies sixty of the ninety-nine columns. First attempt of this kind, the present study provides a general survey of the "Student's Guide's" treatment of logic, which is characterized by an insistance on *Topics* and *Sophistici Elenchi*. The privileged place attributed to these two Aristotle's treatises can probably be explained by the relevance of the argumentation theory found therein to the various oral disputations in which the Parisian arts masters and their bachelors were frequently required to take part.

LAFUENTE, Maria Isabel. *Ideas, Principios y Dialectica*. Leon, Univ de Leon, 1990.

The book analyzes dialectics and methodology of the *Critique of Pure Reason* under the light of Kant's works, in order to show that one system of rules aiming to attain the transformations of reality may not be construed either as a provisional, nor as a conjectural, or a ficticious one. It is also shown that doing doing what "must be" cannot be made to depend neither on the search for identities, nor on the fixation of differences, but only on accomplishing a system which renders possible the applications of reason to experience with only one end: *to search order in nature*.

LAGO, Juan Carlos. The Community of Inquiry and the Development of Self-Esteem. Thinking, 9(1), 12-16, 1990.

LAGUNILLA, Ana E Galán. Conocimiento y determinismo. Rev Filosof (Mexico), 23(68), 187-194, My-Ag 90.

LAHAR, Stephanie. Ecofeminist Theory and Grassroots Politics. Hypatia, 6(1), 28-45, Spr 91.

This essay proposes several guilding parameters for ecofeminisms, development as a moral theory. I argue that these provide necessary directives and contexts for ecofeminist analyses and social/ecological projects. In the past these have been very diverse and occasionally contradictory. Most important to the core of ecofeminism's vitality are close links between theory and political activism. I show how these originated in ecofeminism's history and advocate a continued participatory and activist focus in the future.

LAI, Tyrone. Empirical Tests are Only Auxiliary Devices. Brit J Phil Sci, 39(2), 211-223, Je 88.

We test a theory empirically by deducing from it a 'prediction' and comparing it with observation. In this paper, I argue tests are but auxiliary devices. Though definitely useful, they are dispensable. The reason for this is, there is a more important method of evaluating hypotheses, the method of progressive evaluation (MPE). To explain this point, I use a simple example in cryptanalysis. This example provides us with a model of an empirical investigation in compact form, making it much easier to see the rationality of the method used.

LAI, Whalen. In Defence of Graded Love. Asian Phil, 1(1), 51-60, 1991.

Mencius argued that all men would commiserate with a child in peril, i.e., we all love our own kind. Yet he opposed Mo-tzu who taught universal love for the human species. Defending his theory of greater love shown kin, Mencius cited the case of a son who was concerned with a proper burial for his parents. It seems that whereas the love of the child was based on empathy with its real suffering, the concern for the parents—whose corpses could not really suffer the pain of being mauled by wild dogs—was acquired through familial ties and lived intimacy.

LAI, Whalen. Of One Mind or Two? Query on the Innate Good in Mencius. Relig Stud, 26(2), 247-255, Je 90.

Mencius considers the good to be rooted in the mind. Yet in the case of a drowning sister-in-law, the natural instinct to save her is momentarily checked by the fear of breaking an incest taboo. Does that mean the mind of compassion is being contradicted by the mind of propriety? The essay examines and suggests ways to resolving this seeming "two-minded-ness" of the one good mind. It raises the issue of the "inner" nature of *jen* (humaneness) and the "outer" nature of *i* (rightness) anew.

LAINE, Michael (ed) and ROBSON, John M (ed) and FILIPIUK, Marion (ed) and MILL, John Stuart. *Additional Letters (Collected Works of John Stuart Mill, Volume XXXII)*. Buffalo, Univ of Toronto Pr, 1991.

LAINE, Michael (ed). *A Cultivated Mind: Essays On J S Mill Presented to John M Robson*. Buffalo, Univ of Toronto Pr, 1991.

The volume celebrates the completion, under the direction of John M Robson, of *The Collected Works of John Stuart Mill*. The papers that make up the volume are connected by a central unifying theme: the effect of various environments—domestic, political, administrative, religious, and cultural—on the thought and work of J S Mill. The contributors, Jean O'Grady, Jack Stillinger, Trevor Lloyd, Marion Filipiuk, Alan Ryan, Joseph Hamburger, Bruce Kinzer, Ann Robson, and Stefan Collini, have each developed at length his or her area of responsibility in keeping with the central theme.

LAKATOS, László. "Why Must History Always Be Rewritten?" in *Perspectives on Ideas and Reality*, NYÍRI, J C (ed), 116-129. Budapest, Kiskonyvtara, 1990.

LAKELAND, Paul. Providence and Political Responsibility: The Nature of Praxis in an Age of Apocalypse. Mod Theol, 7(4), 351-362, Jl 91.

The article seeks to further the rethinking of the Christian Doctrine of Providence for the "Postmodern" age. While both Hegel and Habermas provide some assistance in the task, Habermas's attention to the fragility of discourse leaves room for hope and renders his insights the more valuable. Using the category of discourse, the praxis of political responsibility is identified as the worldly locus of divine providence.

LAMACCHIA, Ada (ed). *Razionalitá critica: nella filosofia moderna*. Bari, Lacaita, 1989.

The purpose of this book is to collect some essays that demonstrate a critical trend taking place in some philosophical works, previously the Kant's *Critic*, differently from the ordinary way of thinking. Indeed, starting from 15th century in the history of philosophy some philosophers are to be met who were working and inquiring into the effective critical potentiality of the human mind. Therefore a critical philosophizing way is to be considered as an aware device, already in the origin of the modern time. The contributions of this book examine closely in this direction: the "madness" by Erasmus, the "theatre of the memory" by G Camillo, the notion of "being" by T Campanella, "the ontological difference" by M Heidegger, the "memory of the thought" by H Arendt, the "critical question" by J Habermas.

LAMACCHIA, Ada. "Tommaso Campanella: L'ente e l'analogia nella *Universalis Philosophia*" in *Razionalitá critica: nella filosofia moderna*, LAMACCHIA, Ada (ed), 65-124. Bari, Lacaita, 1989.

In the metaphysical work T Campanella devises the transcendental origin of the notion of the *being*, his primary structure, the logic-empirical and especially metaphysical predicability, in order to characterize the modern and critical task of the philosophy in comparison with that of the empirical sciences. The purpose of this essay is to examine in which way Campanella attains his task and to give remark to the identification of the difference between the Aristotelian *univoc* notion of the *universal* and the Platonic *analogical* notion of the *universal*. The last one authorizes the contact with the thing-itself and with the Primary One Being.

LAMAL, P A and WINDHOLZ, George. Pavlov's View on the Inheritance of Acquired Characteristics .... Synthese, 88(1), 97-111, Jl 91.

Pavlov's position on the inheritance of acquired characteristics we used to test selected theses of Laudan et al. (1986) concerning scientific change. It was determined that, despite negative experimental findings, Pavlov continued to accept the possibility of the inheritance of acquired habits. This confirms the main thesis I that, once accepted, theories persist despite negative experimental evidence. Pavlov's adherence to the concept of inheritance of acquired characteristics might possibly be explained by his early experiences. Adolescent readings of a popularized version of Darwin's theory, which included the concept of inheritance of acquired characteristics, profoundly influenced Pavlov's subsequent intellectual life. Overwhelmed by the theory, as originally presented, Pavlov was unable to alter his views in light of contrary findings.

LAMARQUE, Peter. The Death of the Author: An Analytical Autopsy. Brit J Aes, 30(4), 319-331, O 90.

An analytical critique of Roland Barthes's "The Death of the Author" and Michel Foucault's "What is an Author?" identifying and evaluating four principal theses: the Historicist Thesis, the Death Thesis, the Author Function Thesis and the *Ecriture* Thesis, all fundamental to poststructuralism. The analysis shows that in demoting "the author" and promoting the "text" over the "work" the theses threaten basic assumptions about literature and meaning. However, it also reveals that many of the premises are ill-supported and many of the arguments unsound. The case against literature is unproven.

LAMARQUE, Peter. "Make-Believe, Ontology and Point of View" in *XIth International Congress in Aesthetics, Nottingham 1988*, WOODFIELD, Richard (ed), 109-111. Nottingham, Nottingham Polytech, 1990.

The paper offers a brief defence of ten inter-related propositions concerning the nature and logic of fiction. It offers arguments for each proposition but its aim is principally to commend and consolidate a certain picture of the subject, based on the idea of fictive utterance defined within a practice of storytelling. It identifies distinctive features in make believe storytelling and argues for an "aspectival" view of fictional content and fictional ontology.

LAMBEK, Joachim and COUTURE, Jocelyne. Philosophical Reflections on the Foundations of Mathematics. Erkenntnis, 34(2), 187-209, Mr 91.

This article was written jointly by a philosopher and a mathematician. It has two aims: to acquaint mathematicians with some of the philosophical questions at the foundations of their subject and to familiarize philosophers with some of the answers to these questions which have recently been obtained by mathematicians. In particular, we argue that, if these recent findings are borne in mind, four different basic philosophical positions, logicism, formalism, platonism and intuitionism, if stated with some moderation, are in fact reconcilable although with some reservations in the case of logicism, provided one adops a nominalistic interpretation of Plato's ideal objects. This eclectic view has been asserted by Lambek and Scott (LS 1986) on fairly technical grounds, but the present argument is meant to be accessible to a wider audience and to provide some new insights.

LAMBERT, Karel (ed). *Philosophical Applications of Free Logic*. New York, Oxford Univ Pr, 1991.

This is a collection of essays or applications of free logic ranging from the philosophy of mathematics to the philosophy of religion. Some of the essays are by well-known philosophical logicians, and some are by younger persons. Three of the essays are new.

LAMBERT, Karel. Russell's Theory of Definite Descriptions. Dialectica, 44(1-2), 137-152, 1990.

This paper argues that Russell had two theories of definite descriptions—or at least two versions of his theory of definite descriptions. One of them is contained in *Principia Mathematica* and the other is contained in his famous essay "On Denoting." The two enterprises differ with respect to ultimate goals, formal character, and philosophical power. Though Russell himself appears to have run the two approaches together, it is important to distinguish between them for the reasons just stipulated.

LAMBERT, Karel. "A Theory of Definite Descriptions" in *Philosophical Applications of Free Logic*, LAMBERT, Karel (ed), 17-27. New York, Oxford Univ Pr, 1991.

This is an updated version of a pair of papers written in the early 1960s. It presents the first consistent and complete free description theory known in the literature of free logic as FD2.

LAMBERT, Roger. Le projet de John Rawls. Lekton, 1(2), 17-37, 1991.

LAMBETH, Edmund B. Waiting for a New St Benedict: Alasdair MacIntyre and the Theory and Practice of Journalism. Bus Prof Ethics J, 9(1-2), 97-108, Spr-Sum 90.

This article explores the goodness of fit of Alasdair MacIntyre's definition of a social practice to the development of journalism in the late 20th century. MacIntyre's model is found to frame well certain central questions about ethics and standards of excellence in journalism. However, MacIntyre's virtue-based approach to moral philosophy poses problems that need to be resolved before it can be "applied" to ethics in journalism and mass communication.

LAMENTOWICZ, Wojtek. Political Culture and Institution Building: Democratic Evolution at Work and the Case of Poland. Praxis Int, 10(1-2), 64-73, Ap-Jl 90.

The purpose of the study is to justify the explanatory power of conceptual distinctions between modes (i.e., revolution, reform and democratic evolution) and stages of changes (i.e., humanization, rationalisation, liberalisation and democratisation) which has led to the collapse of the communist political system in Central and Eastern Europe. Polish experience suggests that the transition to liberal democracy and market economy can be accomplished in three distinctive steps: (1) dismantling of authoritarian structures; (2) institution building such as party competition, independent judiciary, liberal constitutions; (3) growth of cultural roots which provide for consolidation of the democratic institutions. At present democratic institution building is still threatened by many challenging developments such as elitist corporatism, charismatic authoritarianism, political indifference and alienation among citizens, revolution of rising expectations which are frustrated by the hardships of economic transition, populist and nationalist cleavages.

LAMMERS, Stephen E. Are Physicians a "Delinquent Community"?: Issues in Professional Competence, Conduct, Self-Regulation: Comment. J Bus Ethics, 10(8), 591-594, Ag 91.

LAMPSHIRE, Wendy L. History as Geneology: Wittgenstein and the Feminist Deconstruction of Objectivity. Phil Theol, 5(4), 313-331, Sum 91.

The aim of the following paper is, firstly, to provide the reader with a brief exposition of the critical response offered by some current French feminists of the largely American, compensatory approach to feminist historiography. Secondly, I wish to show why the French feminist alternative itself provids an inadequate methodology for the resolution of the problems that it raises in its critique. Lastly, I shall suggest that the Wittgensteinian concept of 'family resemblance' contains the seeds of a plausible alternative to either the compensatory or the French structuralist approach to feminist historiography. The upshot of this latter claim is that the historical subject may be most fruitfully conceived genealogically, that is, as the dynamic product of an inexhaustible complex of historical and contextual resemblances constructed on the behalf of a specific interpretational task.

LANCE, Mark. On the Logic of Contingent Relevant Implication: Conceptual Incoherence in the Intuitive Interpretation of *R*. Notre Dame J Form Log, 29(4), 520-529, Fall 88.

The entailment system E of Anderson and Belnap was intended to codify the inferential role of a conditional which implied both necessity and relevance of antecedent to consequent, while their related system R implied only relevance. But the necessitation of a contingent relevant conditional should be a necessary relevant one; so if both R and E were correct, the system R□ should have been equivalent to E under the natural translation. The common response to the fact that it is not has been to reject E in favor of R□. It is argued in this paper, however, that considerations central to the project of relevance logic provide independent grounds for the rejection of R as a system of contingent relevant implication. A weaker system RI is defined by a set of natural deduction rules that *do* meet these intuitive considerations and it is shown that the addition of modal natural deduction rules to RI, yields a system RI□ which *is* equivalent to E. This fact is taken as evidence in favor of both RI and E and against R□.

LANCE, Mark. Probabilistic Dependence Among Conditionals. Phil Rev, 100(2), 269-276, Ap 91.

In a recent article in *The Philosophical Review*, Vann McGee attempts to extend Adams's account of the assertibility conditions of indicative conditionals to certain compounds containing these conditionals. I demonstrate, by way of two counterexamples, that McGee's account is not correct. His argument fails in that it does not take into account relations of probabilistic dependence among conditionals and, for this reason, no such approach which attempts to determine the probability of a conjunction of conditionals purely on the basis of the probability of the conjuncts (and their components) can work.

LANDAU, Iddo. The Early and Later Deconstruction in Derrida's Writings (in Hebrew). Iyyun, 40(2), 159-172, Ap 91.

LANDGREBE, Ludwig. Reflections on the Schutz-Gurwitsch Correspondence. Human Stud, 14(2-3), 107-127, Jl 91.

LANDINI, Gregory. A New Interpretation of Russell's Multiple-Relation Theory of Judgment. Hist Phil Log, 12(1), 37-69, 1990.

This paper offers an interpretation of Russell's multiple-relation theory of judgment which characterizes it as direct application of the 1905 theory of definite descriptions. The paper maintains that it was by regarding propositional symbols (when occurring as subordinate clauses) as disguised descriptions of complexes, that Russell generated the philosophical explanation of the hierarchy of orders and the ramified theory of types of *Principia mathematica* (1910). The interpretation provides a new understanding of Russell's abandoned book *Theory of Knowledge* (1913), the 'direction problems' and Wittgenstein's criticisms.

LANDINI, Gregory and FOSTER, Thomas. The Persistence of Counterexample: Re-examining the Debate over Leibniz Law. Nous, 25(1), 43-61, Mr 91.

There has been much debate concerning the logical truth of Leibniz's principle that indiscernibility is sufficient for identity. Proposed refutations abound—from Kant's two water droplets and Black's symmetric spheres, to Ayer's universe in which all events eternally repeat. But just as frequent are defenses. For instance, drawing on considerations from relativistic physics, Hacking maintains that appeals to counterexamples based on imagined possible worlds can neither refute nor establish the principle. This paper challenges that opponents of the debate are guilty of equivocation. There is no "one" law of the Identity of Indiscernibles. New formulations are given and evaluated relative to the following theories of universals: Logical Realism, Attribute Realism, Phenomenalism, and Natural Realism.

LANDKAMMER, Joachim. "Difficoltà" con Simmel: Considerazioni in margine ad un convegno. Riv Int Filosof Diritto, 67(1), 127-139, Ja-Mr 90.

LANDMAN, Willem A. The Morality of Killing and Causing Suffering: Reasons for Rejecting Peter Singer's Pluralistic Consequentialism. S Afr J Phil, 9(4), 159-171, N 90.

In this article the normative moral theory of the prolific Australian philosopher, Peter Singer, is analysed critically, specifically in respect of the way in which it bears upon actions of killing and causing suffering. First, an exposition and exegesis of Singer's theory is given, a theory that is a combination of classical and preference utilitarianism and which adds up to a kind of pluralistic consequentialism. It is shown how this theory addresses issues in applied or practical ethics, such as abortion, infanticide and the treatment of animals. Second, Singer's theory is then analysed critically in respect of the following: an internal criticism which introduces the notion of long-term desires; the counterintuitive consequences of this theory for the killing of persons, abortion and infanticide, and the killing of nonpersonal sentient animals; and the predistributive nature of the principle of equality which Singer proposes to operate as a second basic moral principle prior to the utility principle in his utilitarian calculation. (edited)

LANDMAN, Willem A. On Excluding Something from Our Gathering: The Lack of Moral Standing of Non-Sentient Entities. S Afr J Phil, 10(1), 7-19, F 91.

In this article I argue that the moral domain ought to be demarcated by sentience; entities which lack the capacity for enjoyment or suffering have no moral standing. First, I state the problem of moral standing and do the conceptual clarification that this requires. Second, I discuss the competing criteria of moral standing which have emerged in the history of moral philosophy, and I defend a sentience criterion by first rejecting more inclusive criteria and then presenting a positive argument. Third, I take a closer look at different kinds of nonsentient entities in order to establish whether they all enjoy an equal moral status: nonsentient living entities (certain categories of humans; lower animals; trees and plants; and aggregates or wholes) and inanimate or nonliving entities (natural objects; and artifacts). Fourth, in concusion I make some summary remarks and indicate how our answer to this seemingly obscure theoretical problem substantively informs the way in which we address moral dilemmas presented by experimentation on foetuses, abortion, the treatment of animals, and our actions in respect of the environment.

LANG, Berel. *The Anatomy of Philosophical Style*. Cambridge, Blackwell, 1990.

This book considers how literary theory and criticism can be applied to philosophical texts, and, from the other direction, how philosophical analysis can elucidate the central features of "literariness." In the literary study of philosophical writing, such issues are addressed as the identity and function of philosophical genres, the roles of implied author and reader in philosophical texts, and the use of figuration and tropes in philosophical discourse. The claim is defended that these stylistic features bear directly on the substantive philosophical issues addressed in the texts.

LANG, Berel. *Writing and the Moral Self*. New York, Routledge, 1991.

The book examines—and argues for—the relation between writing and ethics, beginning with grammar and extending to writing as it affects such social practices as affirmative action, the professionalization of academic discourse, totalitarianism and the phenomenon of genocide. Specific attention is paid to the writing and theories of Thoreau, Orwell, and Arendt, and to the conceptualization of theories of human nature in relation to ethical discourse.

LANGAN, John P (ed) and PELLEGRINO, Edmund D (ed) and VEATCH, Robert M (ed). *Ethics, Trust, and the Professions: Philosophical and Cultural Aspects*. Washington, Georgetown Univ Pr, 1991.

Does the fiduciary paradigm characteristic of the traditional learned professions continue to serve as an appropriate ethical model for the professions of today? Or does the fact that professional relationships are often because strangers mitigate against the feasibility of trust and trustworthiness? The fourteen essays in the volume take their positions on each side of the question. In addition to offering an array of philosophical points of view on the ethics of professions, these essays also provide insight into the sociology of the professions and the professional role in Asian and European contexts.

LANGAN, John. "Catholicism and Liberalism—200 Years of Contest and Consensus" in *Liberalism and the Good*, DOUGLASS, R Bruce (ed), 105-124. New York, Routledge, 1990.

Catholicism rejected liberalism and its revolutionary implications in the nineteenth century; then in the mid-twentieth century it accepted liberal views on democratic constitutional government and human rights; not it criticizes economic liberalism because of its failure to meet the basic needs of the poor and its encouragement of excessive consumption. Catholicism will continue to endorse the legal and political framework of liberal democracy and to resist the application of liberal ideas to its own structure and teaching; at the same time it enjoys the protections and opportunities that a liberal polity offers.

LANGAN, John. "Professional Paradigms" in *Ethics, Trust, and the Professions: Philosophical and Cultural Aspects*, PELLEGRINO, Edmund D (ed), 221-232. Washington, Georgetown Univ Pr, 1991.

The paradigm of single-professional, single-client interaction, while important, was never helpful for understanding some professions (ministry, teaching, accountancy); reliance on it can lead to misunderstanding contemporary changes in law and medicine as well. The common good needs to be understood as a broad term not confined within a single profession or institution. Professions, in contrast to crafts or techniques, are interactive.

LANGENDORFF, T and ZÜRCHER, Erik (ed). *The Humanities in the Nineties: A View From the Netherlands*. Bristol, SWETS, 1990.

LANGER, Monika. "Merleau-Ponty and Deep Ecology" in *Ontology and Alterity in Merleau-Ponty*, JOHNSON, Galen A (ed), 115-129. Evanston, Northwestern Univ Pr, 1991.

This essay argues that Merleau-Ponty's philosophy effectively anticipates deep ecology's concerns and responds to them in a way that can help resolve contemporary ecological crises. Merleau-Ponty offers a thorough critique of the Cartesian ontology which underpins our Western conception of alterity. That ontology dichotomizes reality, denies reciprocity and declares the nonhuman realm devoid of meaning. Merleau-Ponty embarks on a radically holistic philosophical interrogation and shows that traditional notions of "consciousness" and "nature" must be rejected. He outlines the main features of a new ontology in which self and nonself, human and nonhuman, intertwine in a mutual enfolding.

LANGEWAND, Alfred. *Moralische Verbindlichkeit oder Erziehung*. Freiburg, Alber, 1991.

For Kant, morality and education become correlative concepts. According to Herbart, though, Kant has not made the "paedogogical position" geniunely comprehensible. This book analyzes for the first time the dependence of the paedogogic critique of subjectivity on Herbart's disputes with Fichte and Schelling between 1795 and 1800. These concerned the three theoretical levels of the self, the theory of moral action, and the theory of religion. This historical/genetic interpretation shows that Kant's and Herbart's works, which defend the ethical/educational correlation, are able actually to treat it only as an ethical/educational dilemma.

LANGLEY, Gill (ed). *Animal Experimentation: The Consensus Changes*. New York, Routledge, 1989.

This collection of essays is a wide-ranging overview, addressing questions of practice and philosophy, policy and politics. It brings thoughtful, new insight to the fast-changing debate about animal use in biomedical research, testing and teaching. The contributors are internationally recognized authorities in fields which range from the subject of pain in animals to animal rights philosophy, and from human-animal relations to the refinement of experimental methods. (edited)

LANGLOIS, Monique. "Le Retour À La Figuration En Art Actuel: Tradition Et Innovation" in *XIth International Congress in Aesthetics, Nottingham 1988*, WOODFIELD, Richard (ed), 112-115. Nottingham, Nottingham Polytech, 1990.

LANGSDORF, Lenore. The Worldly Self in Schutz: On Sighting, Citing, and Siting the Self. Human Stud, 14(2-3), 141-157, Jl 91.

This essay is an appreciation of Alfred Schutz's understanding of human being as situated in the social world of mundane practical activity, rather than (as for the Cartesian tradition) in what may be seen or (as for the Whorfean tradition) in what may be said. The relative importance of doing, seeing, and saying as the site of the self is considered in the context of contemporary ("postmodernist") dismissal of traditional notions of the self, which endangers our understanding of ourselves as capable of discerning and carrying out moral, political, and intellectual activity.

LANGTON, Rae. Whose Right? Ronald Dworkin, Women, and Pornographers. Phil Pub Affairs, 19(4), 311-359, Fall 90.

According to a leading interpretation of liberal theory, that of Ronald Dworkin, the correct starting point for sound political thinking is to be found in a principle of equality. And according to Dworkin, when we apply that principle to the question of legislation about pornography, we can derive a traditional liberal conclusion: pornography ought to be permitted. I argue that, on the contrary, Dworkinian liberal theory justifies an "illiberal" conclusion about pornography: namely, that women have rights against a policy of permitting pornography, and so pornography ought to be prohibited. Moreover, the consumers of pornography would have no rights against a prohibitive government policy. This result may be viewed as a liberal vindication of a certain radical feminist argument; or, alternatively, as a sign that there are some problems with Dworkin's theory, as an interpretation of liberalism.

LANKFORD, E Louis. Artistic Freedom: An Art World Paradox. J Aes Educ, 24(3), 15-28, Fall 90.

LANNOY, Jean-Luc. "Il y a" et phénoménologie dans la pensée du jeune Lévinas. Rev Phil Louvain, 88(79), 369-394, O 90.

This article intends to show that, through his first important concept, " y a" (*there is*), the thought of Levinas comprises a historical and political dimension which is at the root of his critique of phenomenology. The first part of the article interrogates the historical and political significance of the concept *il y a*. The second shows that it is this concept thus understood which appears implicitly in the young Levinas's reading of Husserl and which motivates his critique. It follows from this analysis that from his early texts, the thought of Levinas is oriented under the impact of history towards a double conflictual determination of the subject which will influence his subsequent philosophical works. Through the recurrent metaphors of transparence and opacity in his early texts, the final part of this article endeavors to determine in what sense the concept *il y a*, also understood as that which cannot be assumed in our time, is in its extreme resistant to the phenomenological approach.

LANSING, Paul and BURKARD, Kimberly. Ethics and the Defense Procurement System. J Bus Ethics, 10(5), 357-364, My 91.

A large U.S. government investigation into arms procurement procedures with corporate contractors has recently led to guilty pleas to fraud and illegal use of classified documents. Operation Ill Wind has brought public attention to the criminal and unethical conduct of large defense contractors in their dealings with the government. This article will review how the defense contract bidding process operates and why illegal activity has been able to compromise the process. We will offer proposals to improve the process in light of the present inquiry.

LANTÉRI-LAURA, Georges and WALKER, R Scott (trans). Aphasia and Inner Language. Diogenes, 150, 24-36, Sum 90.

LANZ, Peter. "Davidson on Explaining Intentional Actions" in *The Mind of Donald Davidson*, BRANDL, Johannes (ed), 33-45. Amsterdam, Rodopi, 1989.

The empirist tradition has it that the genuine explanation of the occurrence of an event requires citing its cause and citing its real cause requires specifying a law that subsumes the explanandum-event and the explanans-event. Davidson denies that the mentalistically described antecedents of intentional actions can be subsumed under strict laws, but nonetheless affirms, that beliefs and desires are causes of actions. Some critics pointed out that this position is not a consistent one and levelled the charge of epiphenomenalism against it. It is shown that there are reasons for thinking that Davidson's position is sound.

LAPPÈ, Marc. Genetics, Neuroscience, and Biotechnology. Hastings Center Rep, 20(6), 21-22, N-D 90.

LARAUDOGOITIA, Jon Perez. This Article Should Not Be Rejected by *Mind*. Mind, 99(396), 599-600, O 90.

This article contains a demonstration not based on previous assumptions that the article itself should not be rejected by a journal like *Mind*. It is based on the plausibility, shown succinctly, of expressing in a language a notion of trivial truth relative to it without contradiction (although many other pragmatic notions could play the same role).

LARDNER, A T. Student Resistance in Philosophy for Children. Thinking, 9(2), 13-15, 1990.

LARGEAULT, Jean. La création du Nouveau par le Hasard et par le temps: un vieux thème épicurien. Arch Phil, 53(4), 589-602, O-D 90.

Does the future of a physical system with a deterministic course preexist in the initial conditions? In the affirmative, it can be compared with an intemporal design. Ch. Renouvier and H Bergson allude to the unfolding of the Spinozian substance and the fusion of the efficient and formal causes, which implies the erasing of time. The author claims that such traits are intrinsic to determinism. Determinism presupposes indeed a metaphysical choice: change is dependent on permanence and on eternal truths. Only two types of conceptions are possible. One is that existence derives from essence (Spinoza, Leibniz), the other that existence precedes and produces essence (Bergson, Popper, Prigogine).

LARGEAULT, Jean. Formalisme et intuitionnisme en philosophie des mathématiques. Rev Phil Fr, 180(3), 521-546, Jl-S 90.

LARGEAULT, Jean. Idéalisme ou réalisme? Arch Phil, 54(3), 409-429, Jl-S 91.

Both Greeks and Orientals were fascinated by change and diversity, and, from the point of view of the living, by all kinds of evil. Greeks privileged the immuable and permanent and so made room for rational science. Orientals want to retain all aspects of being in order to make diversity bearable and intelligible. They see it as a manifestation of unity, and are therefore idealists. Idealism implies ethical consequences, is a doctrine of action. It has also consequences for science in so far as science gives up rationality, is action or experimentation.

LARIVÉ, Marc. La question de l'être. Rev Thomiste, 91(2), 259-280, Ap-Je 91.

LARMORE, Charles. Romanticism and Modernity. Inquiry, 34(1), 77-89, Mr 91.

The leading strands of modern thought are not so easily harmonizable as thinkers such as Kant and Habermas have believed. Influential aspects of Romantic aesthetics involve a challenge to the hegemony of the forms of scientific and moral thought (prediction and control of nature, moral progress) that have established themselves in modern times.

LARRE, Olga L. La teoría de las cualidades sensibles en la *Summula Philosophiae Naturalis* atribuida a Guillermo de Ockham. Sapientia, 45(178), 295-310, O-D 90.

LARRE, Olga L and BOLZÁN, J E. La teoría del tiempo en Ockham y la autenticidad de la *Summulae in Libros Physicorum*. Sapientia, 45(175), 39-48, Ja-Mr 90.

LARRE, Olga and BOLZÁN, J E. La teoría de la ciencia de Guillermo de Ockham: una imagen prospectiva. Sapientia, 45(177), 211-224, Jl-S 90.

LARSON, David. The Implications of Error for Davidsonian Charity. Philosophia (Israel), 20(3), 311-320, D 90.

Complications are forced into Davidson's account of charitable interpretation by the need to correct for speaker error, since error tends to mislead charitable interpreters. I contend that the necessary complications are more fundamental and more damaging than Davidson recognizes. Specifically, I argue that Davidson cannot consistently require interpreters to judge whether their theories have true consequences.

LARSON, Gerald J. "The Rope of Violence and the Snake of Peace" in *Celebrating Peace*, ROUNER, Leroy S (ed), 135-146. Notre Dame, Univ Notre Dame Pr, 1990.

LARUE, Gerald A. "Ancient Ethics" in *A Companion to Ethics*, SINGER, Peter (ed), 29-40. Cambridge, Blackwell, 1991.

LARUELLE, François. L'Appel et le Phénomène. Rev Metaph Morale, 96(1), 27-41, Ja-Mr 91.

LASCARIDES, Alex. The Progressive and the Imperfective Paradox. Synthese, 87(3), 401-447, Je 91.

LATH, Mukund (trans) and SHUKLA, Pandit Badrinath. Dehātmavāda or the Body as Soul: Exploration of a Possibility within Nyāya Thought. J Indian Counc Phil Res, 5(3), 1-17, My-Ag 88.

LATHER, Patti. Deconstructing/Deconstructive Inquiry: The Politics of Knowing and Being Known. Educ Theor, 41(2), 153-173, Spr 91.

LATORA, Salvatore. Gustavo Bontadini un metafisico per vocazione. Sapienza, 43(4), 441-443, O-D 90.

LATORA, Salvatore. Riproposta di una teoria della soggettività in un'epoca di decostruzione del soggetto. Sapienza, 44(2), 217-223, Ap-Je 91.

LATOUR, Bruno. The Impact of Science Studies on Political Philosophy. Sci Tech Human Values, 16(1), 3-19, Wint 91.

The development of science studies has an important message for political theory. This message has not yet been fully articulated. It seems that the science studies field is often considered as the extension of politics to science. In reality, case studies show that it is a redefinition of politics that we are witnessing in the laboratories. To the political representatives (elected by humans) should be added the scientific representatives (spokespersons of nonhumans). Thanks to a book by Steven Shapin and Simon Schaffer, it is possible to reconstruct the origin of this divide between the two sets of representatives. A definition of modernism is offered. Then the article explains how to interpret the shift to "nonmodernism," that is, a historical period when the two branches of politics get together again.

LATOUR, Bruno. Na de sociale wending het roer nogmaals om. Kennis Methode, 15(1), 11-37, 1991.

LATRAVERSE, François. Comme en un miroir: quelques remarques historiques sur l'arbitraire du signe. Horiz Phil, 1(1), 1-22, 1990.

LAU, D C. "On the Expression *Zai You*" in *Chinese Texts and Philosophical Contexts*, ROSEMONT JR, Henry (ed), 5-20. La Salle, Open Court, 1991.

LAUBE, Adolf. Theologie und Sozialvorstellungen bei Thomas Müuntzer (in Czechoslovakian). Filozof Cas, 38(5), 624-636, 1990.

LAUDAN, Larry. "Demystifying Underdetermination" in *Scientific Theories*, SAVAGE, C Wade (ed), 267-297. Minneapolis, Univ of Minn Pr, 1990.

This paper examines the arguments of Quine, Goodman and others who have claimed that the thesis of underdetermination has dire epistemological consequences. It shows that underdetermination is a thesis about theory *semantics*, which has no interesting implications for the *epistemic* appraisal of theories.

LAUDAN, Larry and LEPLIN, Jarrett. Empirical Equivalence and Undetermination. J Phil, 88(9), 449-472, S 91.

Empirical equivalence—the thesis that there are empirically equivalent alternatives to any successful theory—and underdetermination—the thesis that theory acceptance is underdetermined by, and thus never epistemically warranted by, any conceivable body of evidence—are presuppositions of much twentieth century epistemology. This paper rejects both theses, and refutes the inference from the former to the latter. The key to these results is the dissociation of the class of empirical consequences of a theory from the class of its supporting instances. The wrongful assimilation of these classes is traced to a mistaken reduction of epistemic to semantic issues.

LAUDAN, Larry. If It Aint's Broke, Don't Fix It. Brit J Phil Sci, 40(3), 369-375, S 89.

LAUDAN, Larry. *Science and Relativism: Some Key Controversies in the Philosophy of Science*. Chicago, Univ of Chicago Pr, 1990.

This book is an examination and refutation of various forms of epistemic relativism.

LAUDER, Robert E. "Creative Intuition in American Film: Maritain at the Movies" in *From Twilight to Dawn: The Cultural Vision of Jacques Maritain*, REDPATH, Peter A (ed), 133-141. Notre Dame, Univ Notre Dame Pr, 1990.

This article applies Maritain's theory of art to film. Maritain claimed that a work of fine art was made up of two components: matter and form. Matter was the particular material that an artist used such as stone for a sculptor, oil and canvas for the painter, and the form was a creative intuition. The article suggests that if a film is to be attributed to one artist that artist is the director. It is the director's creative intuition that informs the work of art. The art is a masterpiece when there is a wedding between matter that is used properly and a creative intuition that is profound.

LAUDER, Robert E. W T Harris' Philosophy as Personalism. Ideal Stud, 20(1), 43-60, Ja 90.

The purpose of this article is to explore William Torrey Harris's philosophy as a personal idealism. Harris (1835-1909) was one of the most influential men in American education from 1879 to 1906 and his *Journal of Speculative Philosophy*, which appeared quarterly from 1867 until 1893, was the most influential publication on philosophy at that time. Harris's philosophy modelled on Hegel's has a deep pervading unity. Using an Hegelian dialectic to explain knowing Harris's also applies the dialectic to the Trinity. Actually Harris's doctrine of the Trinity is more Hegelian than orthodox Christian. A problem with Harris's personalism is that within it the freedom of the absolute and the freedom of human persons seem to be lost.

LAUENER, Henri. "Holism and Naturalized Epistemology Confronted with the Problem of Truth" in *Perspectives on Quine*, BARRETT, Robert (ed), 213-228. Cambridge, Blackwell, 1990.

To Quine's naturalism, resting on realistic behavioristic and holistic convictions, I oppose a pragmatically relativized form of transcendental philosophy. In order to avoid his thoroughgoing gradualism blurring important distinctions, I introduce a method which consists in a systematic relativization to contexts with fixed ontology and ideology. Meaning, reference, truth and factuality become purely internal notions determined by explicitly stated semantical rules. This method permits to reinstate clear boundaries between language and theory, between analytic and synthetic existence claims and truths. By imposing linguistic structures on our views about the world we create the segments of reality treated by our theories. My dissent with Quine is mainly due to deviating views on the proper function of conventional practices: analytical truths including the logical ones do not follow from but are created by accepting conventions. These generate truth without functioning as antecdotes of a logically true conditional.

LAUENER, Henri. La philosophie ouverte de F Gonseth aboutit-elle à une conception réaliste ou relativiste. Dialectica, 44(3-4), 287-293, 1990.

The author first proposes a more restrictive conception of scientific realism than the usually accepted one. He then shows that his own relativized version of transcendentalism and F Gonseth's open philosophy are not to be classified as realistic but belong to a brand of pragmatism incompatible with scientific realism in the strict sense described.

LAUENER, Henri. Transzendentale Argumente pragmatisch relativiert: Über fundamentale Optionen in der Philosophie. Erkenntnis, 33(2), 223-249, S 90.

Transcendental arguments do not issue in descriptive conclusions stating necessary truths (synthetic judgments *a priori*), but in normative conclusions concerning methodological choices. A method relativizing to contexts (i.e., practical situations) is advocated, thus opposing a piecemeal approach to the extreme holism of certain natualists. Realism and correspondence theory of truth are rejected and replaced by an imposition view resulting in a pluralistic worldview. According to the conception of language developed in the sequel questions concerning reference, truth, factuality and reality become strictly *internal*: they are settled in a context by choosing adequate syntactical, semantical and pragmatical rules. The notion of *external* truth once eliminated scientific theories can no longer be accepted on ground of their (illusory) truth content, but only for pragmatic reasons. Conceptually different theories have no common deductive consequences and are, therefore, semantically incommensurable.

LAURA, Ronald S and HEANEY, Sandra. *Philosophical Foundations of Health Education*. New York, Routledge, 1990.

The purpose of this work was to elucidate the reasons which explain the crisis in health care, that it arises not from a failure of medicine but rather from the failure of the philosophical assumptions on which it rests. Exposing the limitations of this philosophical framework leads to the suggestion of an alternative approach to health care derived from a profoundly ecological and holistic philosophy of nature. It is concluded that advancement of community health depends on incorporating the best aims of conventional medicine into a comprehensive programme of education for health in which the responsibility for health is inextricably knit with a new consciousness of ecological stewardship.

LAURIKAINEN, K V. Quantum Physics, Philosophy, and the Image of God: Insights from Wolfgang Pauli. Zygon, 25(4), 391-404, D 90.

Nobel Laureate in physics Wolfgang Pauli studied philosophy and the history of ideas intensively, especially in his later years, to form an accurate ontology vis-á-vis quantum theory. Pauli's close contacts with the Swiss psychiatrist C G Jung gave him special qualifications for also understanding the basic problems of empirical knowledge. After Pauli's sudden death in 1958, this work was maintained mainly in his posthumously published correspondence, which so far extends only to 1939. Because Pauli's view differs essentially from the direction physics research took after the deaths of the founding fathers of quantum theory, this article attempts to describe the main features in Pauli's revolutionary thought, which is based on nature's "epistemological lesson" as revealed by Pauli's atomic research. Pauli's conclusions have important implications for various issues in Western culture, not least with the limits of science and the relation of science to religion.

LAURITZEN, Paul. Errors of an Ill-Reasoning Reason: The Disparagement of Emotions in the Moral Life. J Value Inq, 25(1), 5-21, Ja 91.

Following R F Holland, I suggest that moral theories are usefully sorted according to whether they seek to make the moral agent invulnerable to the vicissitudes of life. I argue that those theorists that seek self-sufficiency typically disparage human emotions and have little room for emotions in the moral life. I show why these writers wish to discount emotions and highlight the unfortunate consequences of not taking emotions seriously.

LAUTER, H A. Cognitive Art. Phil Inq, 10(1-2), 85-95, Wint-Spr 88.

Marxist aestheticians (e.g., Theodor Adorno and Ernst Fischer) and Nelson Goodman are surprisingly similar in their views of art. They argue against emphasizing sensory and emotional aspects of art and stress its cognitive aspects instead. For Goodman art creation and appreciation are "ways of worldmaking." Marxists emphasize the "content" of art works and its power to change the world. Of course, there are important differences too. Goodman's "worldmaking" seemingly can take place in one's study (or in a museum or concert hall). Full-fledged Marxist experiencing of art eventually requires some action outside of the usual aesthetic environments.

LAUXTERMANN, P F H. Hegel and Schopenhauer as Partisans of Goethe's Theory of Color. J Hist Ideas, 51(4), 599-624, O-D 90.

LAVENDHOMME, R and LUCAS, T. Varying Modal Theories. Notre Dame J Form Log, 31(3), 389-402, Sum 90.

The notion of modal theory is extended by accepting the idea that axioms and language itself vary over a plurality of possible worlds. Inference rules involving different worlds are introduced and completeness is proved by using a notion of 'ugly diagram', which is a graphical means of detecting when a family of modal theories has no model.

LAVINE, Thelma Z. The Case for a New American Pragmatism. Free Inq, 11(3), 45-48, Sum 91.

LAWLER, James and ORUDJEV, Zaid. "Marxism, Humanism, and Ecology" in *The Question of Humanism: Challenges and Possibilities*, GOICOECHEA, David (ed), 162-169. Buffalo, Prometheus, 1991.

LAWLER, Peter A. Neuhaus and Murray on Natural Law and American Politics. Vera Lex, 10(1), 19-20, 1990.

According to Murray, only if natural law exists and is experienced as such by human beings can the liberal limitations of politics be affirmed as goods worthy of human beings. Despite his acknowledgment of the strength of this conclusion, Neuhaus is not quite ready to accept it as his own. He cannot quite abandon the "Augustinian" or "Protestant" suspicion that every attempt to root human morality or purpose in nature is elitist, reductionistic, and ultimately incredible.

LAWLOR, Leonard. A Little Daylight: A Reading of Derrida's "White Mythology". Man World, 24(3), 285-300, Jl 91.

LAWRENCE, Fred. Baur's "Conversation with Gadamer" and "Contribution to the Gadamer-Lonergan Discussion": A Reaction. Method, 8(2), 135-151, O 90.

LAWRENCE, Joseph P. Nietzsche and Heidegger. Hist Euro Ideas, 11, 711-717, 1989.

LAWSON, Bill. Crime, Minorities, and the Social Contract. Crim Just Ethics, 9(2), 16-24, Sum-Fall 90.

Certain passages in Locke's *The Second Treatise of Government* lead to the unsettling conclusion that the reality of being a possible victim of crime for many urban residents releases them from an obligation to obey governmental dictates and consequently from any moral or legal obligation to obey the law. If my reading of Locke is correct, the actions taken by urban residents to protect themselves can be viewed as neither civil disobedience nor vigilantism. Urban crime forces us to reassess our understanding of governmental protection.

LAWTON, Philip. *The Kernel of Truth in Freud*. Lanham, Univ Pr of America, 1991.

This monograph examines Freud's conceptions of scientific, artistic, historical, and clinical truth, and evaluates the veracity of Freudian psychoanalysis itself. The interpretation of Freud's works is guided by Ricoeur, Lacan, De Waelhens, and Vergote. The first part develops a Freudian philosophical anthropology, presenting the two systematic topographies but focusing on desire and the discovery of self. The paper then assesses the scientific status of psychoanalytic theory and explores the psychological sources of creativity. It closes with a treatment of universal and personal history and narrative truth.

LAWUYI, Olatunde B. Self-Potential as a Yoruba Ultimate: A Further Contribution to URAM Yoruba Studies. Ultim Real Mean, 14(1), 21-29, Mr 91.

LAYCOCK, Steven W. "God as the Ideal: The All-of-Monads and the All-Consciousness" in *Phenomenology of the Truth Proper to Religion*, GUERRIÈRE, Daniel (ed), 247-272. Albany, SUNY Pr, 1990.

Nothing could be more inimical to the eidetic project of an Husserlian phenomenological theology than the supposal the Deity is "formally" inaccessible to human consciousness in the phenomenological reflection. The "formal" presence of God must be congruent with the *eidos* of human mentality. This essay both clarifies the foundational desideratum and demonstrates the required congruence. It also shows that God, as infinite "Ideal," is incompletely constituted and "intentionally inexistent," since God, as the ongoing process of intending and realizing the Ideal is an incompletable activity.

LAYNG, Tony. What Makes Us So Different from the Apes? Between Species, 7(1), 40-43, Wint 91.

As we learn more about apes, we gain additional understanding about ourselves. We now know that physically we are very similar, and even the abilities we used to claim as uniquely human (rationality, abstract thought, complex communication, inventiveness, etc.) are not lacking in apes. We need to shift from self-flattering claims to having unique mental abilities to realizing that our mental superiority is merely a matter of degree. Humans must discuss past events and future activities, coordinate economic behavior, maintain a moral code, reckon their kin, and recount their myths. So the most fundamental difference between apes and ourselves is not our capacity to invent such things as tools, language, and a division of labor; it is in fact that the apes can get along quite well without these things while humans cannot.

LAZARI-PAWLOWSKA, Ija. "The Deductive Model in Ethics" in *Logic and Ethics*, GEACH, Peter (ed), 225-240. Norwell, Kluwer, 1991.

LÁZARO, Ramón Castilla. Wittgenstein, Hans Lipps y los supuestos de la predicación. Dialogos, 25(56), 123-133, Jl 90.

LE LANNOU, Jean-Michel. La loi du Styx, Leibniz et la politique du bonheur. Philosophique (France), 1(91), 11-29, 1991.

LE POIDEVIN, Robin. *Change, Cause and Contradiction: A Defence of the Tenseless Theory of Time*. New York, St Martin's Pr, 1991.

It is widely believed that there is such a thing as the passage of time and that only such passage could make possible genuine change in the world. The thesis of this book is that these widespread beliefs are fundamentally mistaken. The idea that time passes is incoherent, and we can account for genuine change by appealing to the links between change and causality. In the course of developing an original theory of change, the book discusses such controversial issues as temporal solipsism, simultaneous and backwards causation, closed time and time without change.

LE POIDEVIN, Robin. Creation in a Closed Universe, *Or* Have Physicists Disproved the Existence of God? Relig Stud, 27(1), 39-48, Mr 91.

Stephen Hawking has recently argued that if the universe is both finite and unbounded (and so has no beginning) then there is no place for a creator, for creation entails a first event. In this paper I argue that Hawking's 'no creation' argument rests upon assumptions about the linearity of time which are unjustifed if it is genuinely possible for the universe to be both unbounded and *finite*. I go on to consider a strengthened version of Hawking's argument based on principles concerning causality, but conclude that this version also fails.

LE POIDEVIN, Robin. Relationism and Temporal Topology. Phil Quart, 40(161), 419-432, O 90.

Questions concerning the topological structure of time are regarded by many contemporary philosophers as empirical in nature. In contrast, the debate between relationism and absolutism is considered to be *a priori*. This paper argues that the relationist is committed to ascribing certain topological properties to time, and that, therefore, either temporal topology is an a priori matter, or relationism makes unwarranted empirical assumptions.

LE PORE, Ernest and LOEWER, Barry. "A Study in Comparative Semantics" in *Propositional Attitudes: The Role of Content in Logic, Language, and Mind*, ANDERSON, C Anthony (ed), 91-111. Stanford, CSLI, 1990.

Two of the most influential philosophers of language, Gottlob Frege and Donald Davidson, share a conception of the goals of a theory of meaning for a natural language. Both think 1) that such a theory should encapsulate knowledge centrally involved in understanding a language, 2) that knowledge of the *truth conditions* of indicative sentences is central to that understanding, 3) that for an adequate account of understanding, a theory of meaning must be compositional in order to explain how complex expressions can be understood in terms of an understanding of their components, 4) that an account of compositional structure will systematize logical relations among sentences and both 5) emphasize the importance of paraphrase into quantificational languages for constructing semantic theories which systemize the truth conditions and logical relations of sentences. They differ as to how these goals can best be accomplished and in particular as to the ontology and ideology required to achieve them. Given these differences the question naturally arises of how to evaluate the two accounts. We address this question in our paper.

LE PORE, Ernest (ed). *Truth and Interpretation: Perspectives on the Philosophy of Donald Davidson*. Cambridge, Blackwell, 1986.

There are twenty-eight critical essays, including a substantial introduction to Davidson's philosophy of language, and three essays by Davidson himself, which make up this volume. The volume's six sections correspond to the major sections of Davidson's *Inquiries into Truth and Interpretation*. Each contains critical essays addressing, interpreting and further developing his views. The first section, written by the editor, gives an overview of the whole volume; the second section focuses on truth and meaning; the third, applications of Davidson's semantic theory; the fourth, radical interpretation; the fifth, language and reality; and the sixth, limits of the literal.

LE PORE, Ernest. "Truth in Meaning" in *Truth and Interpretation: Perspectives on the Philosophy of Donald Davidson*, LE PORE, Ernest (ed), 3-26. Cambridge, Blackwell, 1986.

The corpus of Donald Davidson's work is broad and resists terse summarization. In this introduction, I do not offer an exhaustive overview. Nothing substitutes for a careful reading of his papers on truth, meaning, interpretation, and their connections. In summarizing important aspects of his views, I hope only to give the reader a frame of reference for the essays that follow in the volume of which this is an introduction. Although I do, where appropriate, discuss briefly the ideas expressed in these essays, I offer neither synopses nor evaluations of these contributions.

LE PORE, Ernest and LOEWER, Barry. "What Davidson Should Have Said" in *Information, Semantics and Epistemology*, VILLANUEVA, Enrique (ed), 190-199. Cambridge, Blackwell, 1990.

In this paper, we articulate a way out of a difficulty harassing Donald Davidson's view that a theory of understanding for a language L is best understood in terms of a theory of truth for L. We argue that a theory of truth should be augmented with a *samesaying* relation between utterances in order to bridge the gap between what a speaker utters and what he says. We also argue that there is no need for empirical or formal constraints on the theory. Nor is there a need to modify or abandon Davidson's extensionalist framework.

LE PORE, Ernest and LOEWER, Barry. "What Davidson Should Have Said" in *The Mind of Donald Davidson*, BRANDL, Johannes (ed), 65-78. Amsterdam, Rodopi, 1989.

According to Davidson, a theory of meaning for a language L should specify information such that if someone had this information he would be in a position to understand L. He claims that a theory of truth for L fits this description. Many critics have argued that a truth theory is too weak to be a theory of meaning. We argue that these critics and Davidson's response to them have been misguided. Many critics have been misguided because they have not been clear about what a theory of meaning is supposed to do. These critics and Davidson himself, though, have also been misguided because they thought that by adding further conditions on a truth theory we can come up with an adequate theory of meaning. We will show that Davidson has available to him, though he apparently failed to see so, a reply to his critics in his own paratactic account of the semantics for indirect discourse reports.

LEACH, Edmund. *Claude Lévi-Strauss*. Chicago, Univ of Chicago Pr, 1989.

LEACH, Mary S. Mothers of In(ter)vention: Women's Writing in Philosophy of Education. Educ Theor, 41(3), 287-300, Sum 91.

This essay focuses on the emergence of women as both subjects and objects of study in philosophy of education and specifically within the Philosophy of Education Society. Correspondingly it discusses the impact of feminist theory on both the specific issues pursued in philosophy of education and its conception of "philosophy" as a mode of investigation.

LEACH, Mary S. Re-Viewing the Political Structure of Knowledge. Phil Stud Educ, /, 204-210, 1987-88.

LEAL, Fernando A. "Historia" de la naturaleza *versus* "Naturaleza" de la historia. Rev Filosof (Costa Rica), 28(67-68), 37-39, D 90.

According to the predominant manner of thinking for millenniums, the notion of the "history of nature" is contradictory because people talk about "nature" or character of history as purely human event, making the union of the natural process and impossible human development. I consider that "versus" has no place, by different reasons of the predominant manner of thinking, if the human versus nature opposition's concept yields, it will think in the Universe process as a natural history type less anthropomorfic and a history character less anthropocentric. (edited)

LEAVEY JR, John P. "Bold Counsels and Carpenters: Pagan Translation" in *Hermeneutics and the Poetic Motion, Translation Perspectives V—1990*, SCHMIDT, Dennis J (ed), 69-82. Binghamton, CRIT, 1990.

LEBLANC, Hugues. The Autonomy of Probability Theory (Notes on Kolmogorov, Rényi, and Popper). Brit J Phil Sci, 40(2), 167-181, Je 89.

Kolmogorov's account in his (1933) of an *absolute probability space* presupposes given a Boolean algebra, and so does Renyi's account in his [1955] and [1964] of a *relative probability space*. Anxious to prove probability theory 'autonomous', Popper supplied in his [1955] and [1957] accounts of probability spaces of which Boolean algebras are not and [1957] accounts of probability spaces of which fields are not prerequisites but byproducts instead. I review the accounts in question, showing how Popper's issue from and how they differ from Kolmogorov's and Renyi's, and I examine on closing Popper's notion of 'autonomous independence'. So as not to interrupt the exposition, I allow myself in the main text but a few proofs, relegating others to the *Appendix* and indicating as I go along where in the literature the rest can be found.

LEBLANC, Hugues and ROEPER, Peter. "Conditionals and Conditional Probabilities: Three Triviality Theorems" in *Knowledge Representation and Defeasible Reasoning*, KYBURG JR, Henry E (ed), 287-306. Norwell, Kluwer, 1990.

LEBLANC, Hugues and ROEPER, Peter and THAU, Michael and WEAVER, George. Henkin's Completeness Proof: Forty Years Later. Notre Dame J Form Log, 32(2), 212-232, Spr 91.

Provided here are two new completeness proofs for a first-order logic with denumerably many terms. The first proof, unlike Menkin's 1949 proof, does not call for the addition of extra terms; the second, especially suited for truth-value semantics, calls for the addition of denumerably many. Shown in the process is that a set of statements has a Henkin model, i.e., a model in which every member of the domain has a name, iff the set is what we call *instantially consistent* (i.e., iff *consistent in omega-logic*).

LEBLANC, Hugues and ROEPER, Peter. Indiscernibility and Identity in Probability Theory. Notre Dame J Form Log, 32(1), 1-46, Wint 91.

Specified in the paper are the circumstances under which two elements (sets, statements, etc.) are counted indiscernible under a conditional probability function or under an absolute one. The resulting notions and that of identity are then used to characterize and classify various families (some of them new) of Popper probability functions.

LECERCLE, J J. "Textual Responsibility" in *The Political Responsibility of Intellectuals*, MACLEAN, Ian (ed), 101-122. New York, Cambridge Univ Pr, 1990.

LECHTE, John. Kristeva and Holbein, Artist of Melancholy. Brit J Aes, 30(4), 342-350, O 90.

The article examines Julia Kristeva's psychoanalytic interpretation of Hans Holbein the Younger's *The Corpse of Christ in the Tomb* (1521), to be found in her book, *Soleil noir* (English translation: *Black Sun*). Of particular concern is the way that Kristeva, in pointing out that melancholia is equivalent to the collapse of the subject's psychic and imaginary capacities, links the truly startling, minimalist realism of Holbein's painting to the overcoming of melancholia: in effect, the representation of death, is a way of keeping (psychic) death at bay. The key aspects of Kristeva's psychoanalytic framework are explained, as is the relevance of Holbein's painting for a reevaluation of realism in art.

LECIS, Pier Luigi. Lezioni di filosofia della scienza di Guilio Preti. G Crit Filosof Ital, 69(3), 393-399, S-D 90.

LEDDY, Thomas. Is the Creative Process in Art a Form of Puzzle Solving? J Aes Educ, 24(3), 83-97, Fall 90.

Psychologists David Perkins and Robert Weisberg attempt to understand the creative process in art and science in terms of puzzle solving. Their model for creativity is intended to replace earlier theories which draw on such notions as inspiration, the unconscious, creative leap, and bisociation. Favoring the earlier theories, I argue that (1) creativity should not be understood in terms of puzzle solving, (2) problem solving should not be understood solely in terms of puzzle solving, and (3) creativity should not be understood solely in terms of problem solving. I look at specific examples, such as Karl Duncker's "candle problem."

LEE, Harold N. "Comment on David L Miller's 'Consciousness, the

Attitude of the Individual and Perspectives'" in *Creativity in George Herbert Mead*, GUNTER, Pete A Y (ed), 54-58. Lanham, Univ Pr of America, 1990.

LEE, Keekok. *The Legal-Rational State: A Comparison of Hobbes, Bentham and Kelsen*. Aldershot, Avebury, 1990.

This book explores the development of the notion of the legal-rational state through the legal theorising of Hobbes, Bentham and Kelsen and their respective accounts of legal positivism. An essential ingredient of modernity, its emergence is traced to Hobbes in the seventeenth century. Its further development is carried on by Bentham but its impoverishment may be attributed to Kelsen this century. This comparative study is undertaken within the framework of the positivist science of law and in the context of the political and economic preoccupations of their times.

LEE, Keekok. *The Positivist Science of Law*. Aldershot, Avebury, 1989.

This book attempts to (a) give a satisfactory identification of legal positivism, which to date does not exist; (b) remove a puzzle, there being no positivist science of law, notwithstanding that positivism as a general philosophy has a distinctive philosophy and methodology of science which have given rise to a whole range of positivist sciences in both the natural and social sciences such as physics, economics. By appreciating the application of that methodology and philosophy of science to the study of legal phenomena it solves the identity crisis about legal positivism and argues it is that missing positivist science of law.

LEE, Kwang-Sae. Two Ways of Morality: Confucian and Kantian. J Chin Phil, 18(1), 89-121, Mr 91.

LEE, Raymond L M. The Micro-Macro Problem in Collective Behavior: Reconciling Agency and Structure. J Theor Soc Behav, 20(3), 213-233, S 90.

The micro-macro problem in collective behavior is linked to the question of individualism-versus-collectivism in general sociological theory. The current literature in collective behavior is generally biased toward a methodological individualism. The role of structure occupies an ambiguous position in collective behavior theory. By applying Giddens's structuration theory to collective behavior, I argue that it is possible to conceptualize the notion of the collective in terms of a complex relationship between absent structure, antistructure, and consciousness of human agents.

LEE, Richard N. What Berkeley's Notions Are. Ideal Stud, 20(1), 19-41, Ja 90.

LEE, Steven. "Moral Counterforce" in *In the Interest of Peace: A Spectrum of Philosophical Views*, KLEIN, Kenneth H (ed), 155-166. Wolfeboro, Longwood, 1990.

Proponents of counterforce strategy claim that it is the only form of nuclear deterrence that is morally acceptable. But the case for moral counterforce faces a dilemma. Either a counterforce strategy includes no threats against cities, in which case it is not effective as a deterrent, or it includes threats against cities, in which case it is not morally acceptable. Arguments for both horns of this dilemma depend on the notion of intra-war deterrence. Due to the situation of mutual assured destruction, neither superpower can militarily suppress the capacity of the other to destroy its society. As a result, a nuclear weapons policy must be designed to deter an opponent from further attacks in the midst of war.

LEERSSEN, J T (ed) and CORBEY, R (ed). *Alterity, Identity, Image: Contributions Towards a Theoretical Perspective*. Amsterdam, Rodopi, 1991.

LEFORT, Claude. "Flesh and Otherness" in *Ontology and Alterity in Merleau-Ponty*, JOHNSON, Galen A (ed), 3-13. Evanston, Northwestern Univ Pr, 1991.

LEFORT, Claude. "Modern Democracy and Political Philosophy" in *Writing the Politics of Difference*, SILVERMAN, Hugh J (ed), 241-252. Albany, SUNY Pr, 1991.

LEFORT, Claude and HARVEY, Robert (trans). Renaissance of Democracy? Praxis Int, 10(1-2), 1-13, Ap-Jl 90.

LEFTOW, Brian. Eternity and Simultaneity. Faith Phil, 8(2), 148-179, Ap 91.

Boethius and later medieval writers assert that God is timeless. Yet in the course of modelling God's knowledge on human observation, they assert that God sees temporal events which are really present for Him to see. This entails that though God's acts of knowledge are not temporally simultaneous with temporal events, they are in some other sense simultaneous with them. I explore the attempt of Eleonore Stump and Norman Kretzmann to explain this other sort of simultaneity between eternal and temporal entities, then develop an alternate account of the relations of time and eternity.

LEFTOW, Brian. Time, Actuality and Omniscience. Relig Stud, 26(3), 303-321, S 90.

Can a timeless God know what is happening now? Many say "no," inferring that God cannot be both timeless and omniscient. But just what is it that God supposedly cannot know? To some, it is a truth essentially involving indexicals, e.g., "it is noon now." To others, it is an essentially tensed fact, e.g., that it is noon now. I show that this distinction matters. For a timeless God *can* know essentially tensed facts, and an inability to know essentially indexical truths should and would not count against what theists traditionally assert by saying that God is omniscient.

LEFTOW, Brian. Why Didn't God Create the World Sooner? Relig Stud, 27(2), 157-171, Je 91.

An old argument that the universe had no beginning runs this way: God is perfectly rational. There could be no reason to prefer one instant to any other as a time for the world to begin. So God would not select any one instant for this. Instead, He must always have been making the world. So the world must always have existed. This paper first displays this argument's surprising strength, then develops two ways to block it.

LEGUTKO, Ryszard. Society as a Department Store. Crit Rev, 4(3), 327-343, Sum 90.

In a departure from traditional Western political theory that is reminiscent of left-wing anarchism, contemporary libertarianism rejects the necessity of making political choices based on a value hierarchy, instead claiming that it is possible for all individuals to pursue their divergent values simultaneously—as long as each respects the equal rights of others to do the same. The caveat, however, hides a conflict of loyalties that would plague a libertarian society: on the one hand are the particular loyalties of one's preferred utopian community; on the other hand, loyalty to the larger "framework for utopias" within which one's utopia exists. The second loyalty implies a value relativism incompatible with the first one, meaning either that loyalty to the libertarian framework will undermine the utopias within it, or that the particular values of the utopias will destabilize the libertarian framework. (edited)

LEHMAN, Hugh and NEEDHAM, E A. Farming Salmon Ethically. J Agr Ethics, 4(1), 78-81, 1991.

Salmon farming is a rapidly expanding industry. In order for it to develop in an ethical manner, many ethical issues must be confronted. Among these are questions regarding the quality of life of salmon on farms. To develop reasonable answers to these questions considerable thought must be devoted to developing appropriate standards of care for salmon. If these questions are not addressed the results could be bad both for salmon and for salmon farmers.

LEHRER, Keith. Chisholm, Reid and the Problem of the Epistemic Surd. Phil Stud, 60(1-2), 39-45, S-O 90.

Chisholm asks whether Thomas Reid is a *methodist* or a *particularist* in epistemology. The problem of the epistemic surd arises for a particularist who affirms that some particular belief is evident without appealing as a methodist might to a general method for justification. Reid's solution to the problem is to insist that some beliefs are such that their evidence is itself evident. This feature of evidence is articulated by Reid in terms of a general principle of the trustworthiness of our faculties. Problems concerning Reid's views concerning subjects of predication, individual essences and the indivisibility of the self, which Chisholm raises, are also addressed.

LEHRER, Keith and KIM, Kihyeon. The Fallibility Paradox. Phil Phenomenol Res, 50 SUPP, 99-107, Fall 90.

One doctrine of fallibilism, which is widely accepted, affirms that even the best justification we can have for most of what we believe leaves open the possibility of error. This doctrine and refinements thereof lead to paradox and inconsistency when combined with two plausible conditions of a criterion of justification. The first says that satisfaction of the criterion is a necessary condition of justification, and the second says that determination that the criterion is satisfied is a sufficient condition for justification. Solutions to the paradox suggest that we must give up either externalism, internalism or the doctrine of fallibilism.

LEIBEL, Wayne. When Scientists are Wrong: Admitting Inadvertent Error in Research. J Bus Ethics, 10(8), 601-604, Ag 91.

LEIBER, Justin. *An Invitation To Cognitive Science*. Cambridge, Blackwell, 1991.

This account takes the later Wittgenstein as a Kuhnian collector of the anomalies in consciousness and folk psychology that call for a subpersonal and computational models of the mind/brain, models that Alan Turing definitely proposed in his work on programming, nativism, connectionism, and chaos-theoretical biology. Daniel Dennett writes, "Cognitive science, like every other field, has developed its own set of official myths about how it grew and what it is about: the well-beaten paths from Plato and Aristotle through Descartes to Turing, and on to today and tomorrow. Quick, before those ruts harden into concrete, read Leiber's book! With vigorously independent scholarship and many original observations, Leiber cuts back and forth across the familiar scenes, proving new perspectives that illuminate where we are and suggest where we might go next."

LEINFELLNER-RUPERTSBERGER, Elisabeth. On the Purported Pragmatico-Semantic Foundation of Linguistics and AI Through Wittgenstein's Late Philosophy. J Prag, 14(6), 853-881, D 90.

It has become customary to think of Wittgenstein's late philosophy as a pragmatico-semantic underpinning for research in linguistics and AI. However, this view is erroneous since Wittgenstein's rejection of empirical reference and nonlinguistic mentalism and his paradigmatic view of language games as games of chess and of meaning as language-intrinsic use effectively block such applications.

LEITE, Adam and MATSON, Wallace I. Socrates' Critique of Cognitivism. Philosophy, 66(256), 145-167, Ap 91.

Hubert Dreyfus has accused Socrates and Plato of being forerunners of modern-day Cognitivist philosophy of mind. However, a careful reading of the early dialogues reveals Socrates' aims to have been *anti*-Cognitivist; he showed that explicit definitions stating necessary and sufficient conditions for the applicability of moral terms are *impossible*, therefore rules are not sufficient to generate moral expertise. The theory of Forms results from Plato's attempt to develop a conception of knowledge consistent with this claim.

LEJEWSKI, Czeslaw. Formalization of Functionally Complete Propositional Calculus with the Functor of Implication.... Stud Log, 48(4), 479-494, D 89.

The most difficult problem that Lesniewski came across in constructing his system of the foundations of mathematics was the problem of 'defining definitions', as he used to put it. He solved it to his satisfaction only when he had completed the formalization of his *protothetic* and *ontology*. By formalization of a deductive system one ought to understand in this context the statement, as precise and unambiguous as possible, of the conditions as expression has to satisfy if it is added to the system as a new thesis. Now, some *protothetical* theses, and some *ontological* ones, included in the respective systems, happen to be definitions. In the present essay I employ Lesniewski's method of *terminological explanations* for the purpose of formalizing Lukasiewicz's system of implicational calculus of propositions, which system, without having recourse to quantification, I first extended some time ago into a functionally complete system. This I achieved by allowing for a rule of 'implicational definitions', which enabled me to define any proposition-forming functor for any finite number of propositional arguments.

LELAS, Srdjan. Plural World of Contemporary Science and Philosophy (in Serbo-Croatian). Filozof Istraz, 34(1), 17-30, 1990.

Nowadays we bear witness to three changes concerning science. First our image of science has changed from algorithmic text producing enterprise in direct relation to its objects in the world to imaginative contextual praxis which is the part of human culture. Second, we recognize not only that the way of thinking in science is more complex than has been thought, but also that it itself changes from sequential and deterministic into parallel and probabilistic. Third, the way science depicts the world of nature has been radically changed. Predictive, determined, dynamically stable, rigid world has been replaced with uncertain, risky, structurally chaotic, only partly predictable world. All these changes make the framework for a dialogue between science and philosophy new and potentially more fruitful if only illusions and vanity were overcome on both sides.

LEMKE, Dwight K and SCHMINKE, Marshall. Ethics in Declining Organizations. Bus Ethics Quart, 1(3), 235-248, Jl 91.

This paper explores the relationship between declining organizations and unethical behavior. Data form a four month long management simulation indicate that declining organizations demonstrate a greater propensity for unethical activities than do more successful companies. The results indicate that: 1) organizations in decline are more likely to be involved in unethical activities; 2) the more severe the decline is, the more unethical the behavior is likely to be; and 3) it is organizational decline and not initial propensities toward unethical conduct that explains the unethical behavior. The paper also discusses the implications of these findings and outlines future streams of research.

LEMONS, John and BROWN, Donald A and VARNER, Gary E. Congress, Consistency, and Environmental Law. Environ Ethics, 12(4), 311-327, Wint 90.

In passing the National Environmental Policy Act of 1969 (NEPA), Congress committed the nation to an ethical principle of living in "productive and enjoyable harmony" with the natural environment. Thus understood, NEPA can be given either (1) a technology-forcing interpretation or (2) an intelligent decision-making interpretation. We argue that in its subsequent decision to site a high-level nuclear waste repository at Yucca Mountain, Nevada, Congress acted inconsistently with this principle under either interpretation. We conclude that for the foreseeable future, the only way to handle the nation's nuclear wastes consistent with the environmental goal enunciated in NEPA is to leave them in temporary surface storage facilities, prohibit the licensing of any new nuclear power plants, and take all appropriate steps to reduce the nuclear weapons industry.

LEMOS, Noah M. Moral Goodness, Esteem, and Acting from Duty. J Value Inq, 25(2), 103-117, Ap 91.

LEMOS, Noah. The Highest Moral Knowledge and Internalism: Some Comments. S J Phil, SUPP 29, 161-165, 1990.

LEMPEREUR, Alain. Law: From Foundation to Argumentation. Commun Cog, 24(1), 97-110, 1991.

LEMPEREUR, Alain. Le questionnement, comme synthèse de l'humain. Rev Int Phil, 44(174), 471-495, 1990.

All the human activities can be founded on questioning. Now, in philosophy or in everyday life, it is hard to believe in absolute and definitive solutions, whatever problem concerned. Rejecting dogmatism, analyzing Heidegger's and Valéry's intuitions and resting upon Deleuze's and Meyer's criticism of ontology, a new rationality of questioning can emerge. It studies the interaction of questions and answers in each field of human intervention: from the use of rhetoric as problem solving to the possibility of an interrogative ethics, from "wild interrogation" to the idea of legal solutions to social conflictuality, from scientific inquiry to philosophical investigations.

LEMPP, Steffen and INGRASSIA, Michael A. Jumps of Nontrivial Splittings of Recursively Enumerable Sets. Z Math Log, 36(4), 285-292, 1990.

LENDVAI, Ferenc L. Lukács on the Ontology of Social Existence and Marx's Understanding of Society (in German). Deut Z Phil, 38(6), 528-540, 1990.

This study was first written and published in Hungarian on the occasion of Lukács's centenary (*Társadalmi Szemle* 40 (3), 41-54, 1985). Its concern is to expose the view that in the "Ontology," the main work of the later period, Lukács attempts to develop 'a great theory' of the 20th century based on Marx's fundamental views. "History and Class Consciousness," however, is closer to Marx's views and the late attempt to bring about a 'Renaissance of Marxism' is only a partial success: a gigantic torso, though it can serve as a fertile basis in rethinking the problem.

LENKA, Laxminarayan. Formulation of Grice's Three Intentions. Indian Phil Quart, SUPP 17(4), 23-32, O 90.

This paper is an exposition of the three conditions of communicative meaning advocated by H P Grice. Introducing the necessity of certain intentional constraint(s) it accounts the three necessary and sufficient constraints of 'communicative meaning'.

LENNERTZ, James E. Ethics and the Professional Responsibility of Lawyers (Commentary). J Bus Ethics, 10(8), 577-579, Ag 91.

LENNON, Kathleen. *Explaining Human Action*. La Salle, Open Court, 1991.

In this work, Kathleen Lennon shows how 'reasons' fit into the causal framework of the world, while defending their autonomy. This picture of human action respects materialism but rejects current attempts to reduce rationalizing explanations to functional or physical equivalents. A consequence of Dr Lennon's anti-reductionist view is that we cannot abandon our 'psychological' mode of describing human action without losing a unique way to capture some real structural features of the world.

LENNOX, James G. Commentary on Byerly and Michod. Biol Phil, 6(1), 33-37, Ja 91.

LENOBLE, J and BERTEN, A. Jugement juridique et jugement pratique: de Kant à la philosophie du langage. Rev Metaph Morale, 95(3), 339-365, Jl-S 90.

Philosophy of law is, at the moment, experiencing something of a revival in interest in the United States and in Germany in the wake of the criticisms of Dworkin and Habermas directed against analytical legal positivism. This movement of reappraisal, at a philosophical level, is linked to contemporary reinterpretations of practical reason. Above and beyond the differing and, at times, antinomical forms which this reappraisal can take, all of them aim to reinterpret practical judgment in the light of the Kantian theory of reflexive judgment. This article seeks to show both the possibilities and inadequacies of these contemporary reinterpretations of ethics, inadequacies which recent discoveries in the domain of the philosophy of language can help overcome. We ultimately wish to show how that may help advance beyond what are, for the moment, the initial stages of a renewed theory of juridical judgment.

LENTINI, Luigi. *Il Paradigma del Sapere*. Milan, Angeli, 1990.

LENZNER, Steven J. Strauss's Three Burkes: The Problem of Edmund Burke in *Natural Right and History*. Polit Theory, 19(3), 364-390, Ag 91.

LEONARD, Arthur S. Ethical Challenges of HIV Infection in the Workplace. Notre Dame J Law Ethics, 5(1), 53-73, Spr 90.

LEOPOLD, Aldo. Means and Ends in Wild Life Management. Environ Ethics, 12(4), 329-332, Wint 90.

Although research in wildlife management is repeating the history of agriculture, unlike agricultural research, which employs scientific means for economic ends, the ends of wildlife research are judged in terms of aesthetic satisfactions as governed by "good taste." Wild animals and plants are economically valuable only in the sense that human performers and works of art are: the means are of the brain, but the ends are of the heart. Wildlife management has forged ahead of agriculture in recognizing the invisible interdependencies in the biotic community. Moreover, it has admitted its inability to replace natural equilibria and its unwillingness to do so even if it could. Because many animals do not exhibit their natural behavior under laboratory conditions, researchers are dependent on observation in the wild. The difficulties involved in isolating variables are especially clear in the study of the natural cycle. It is a problem which seems to defy the experimental method.

LEPLIN, Jarrett and LAUDAN, Larry. Empirical Equivalence and Undetermination. J Phil, 88(9), 449-472, S 91.

Empirical equivalence—the thesis that there are empirically equivalent alternatives to any successful theory—and underdetermination—the thesis that theory acceptance is underdetermined by, and thus never epistemically warranted by, any conceivable body of evidence—are presuppositions of much twentieth century epistemology. This paper rejects both theses, and refutes the inference from the former to the latter. The key to these results is the dissociation of the class of empirical consequences of a theory from the class of its supporting instances. The wrongful assimilation of these classes is traced to a mistaken reduction of epistemic to semantic issues.

LEROUX, Georges. *Plotin: Traité sur la liberté et la volonté de l'Un*. Paris, Vrin, 1990.

LEROUX, Jean. La philosophie des sciences de Hertz et le Tractatus. Lekton, 1(1), 187-198, 1990.

This article provides a short discussion of Wittgenstein's theory of science in the *Tractatus*. Special attention is given to the fact that Wittgenstein's picture theory was borrowed from Hertz (*Prinzipien der Mechanik*). More generally, other epistemological topics touched upon in the *Tractatus* reveal that Wittgenstein's views on Mechanics and science were closely related to those of the German scientific tradition of his time.

LESAGE, D. Words like Faces (in Dutch). Tijdschr Filosof, 53(2), 205-231, Je 91.

There is a strong mentalistic tendency in the tradition of philosophy toward a depreciation of the exteriority of linguistic tokens. The point of Wittgenstein's critique is that there is an internal relation between the meaning of a linguistic token and its exteriority. This explains why we can be attached to our own language. This form of attachment may be called *linguistic particularism*. Linguistic particularism is not an unhappy aberration or an inconvenience that should be remedied; rather it is a fact that is intimately related to the structure of meaning. (edited)

LESAGE, Dieter. Moraliteit en magie. Alg Ned Tijdschr Wijs, 83(3), 161-173, Jl 91.

In the distribution of our efforts for other persons, we generally give a priority to persons who are near to us. From an impartial point of view, one may object against this attitude that it is egocentric and arbitrary. The question whether it is morally acceptable or not to give a moral significance to the proximity of persons who appeal to us is at the heart of the debate between universalist and particularist positions in the so-called anglo-saxon philosophy. By way of an analysis of the use of the pronoun "my" in the context of symbolic attitudes, this article develops an argument for the idea that, contrary to what has been suggested by William Godwin, the pronoun "my" can very well have a magic significance and that, moreover, this significance has unmistakably a moral bearing.

LESLIE, John. Ensuring Two Bird Deaths with One Throw. Mind, 100(397), 73-86, Ja 91.

In a symmetrical universe, killing a bird guarantees that your double kills another. He opens boxes just when you open boxes. This suggests morals when folk are significantly like you, morals affecting Newcomb's Problem, Prisoner's Dilemma and Voting Paradox. Do not open a box if this would mean that a scientist, watching your speeded-up computer replica, had ensured that you would be the poorer for it. Show kindness to your fellow prisoner if his similarity to yourself then makes him significantly likely to show kindness to you. Vote, fearing that if you do not then neither will your fellow Democrats.

LÉTOUBLON, Françoise. La notion de non-être dans l'histoire de la langue grecque archaïque. Rev Theol Phil, 122(3), 313-322, 1990.

L'étude de la langue grecque aux origines—Homère et Hésiode—confirme celle de la mythologie et montre que la notion même de non-être n'existe pas en Grèce à l'époque archaïque. La poétique homérique est une poétique de l'être, même quand il s'agit des Sirènes, montrées en pleine activité de mensonge. La poétique du mensonge (ou de la fiction?) apparaît, timidement d'ailleurs, avec Hésiode; mais il n'est jamais question du non-être à cette époque, même avec le terme χαος "vide". Personne ne s'étonneara de ce que la spéculation grecque sur le nonêtre commence, dans le vocabulaire aussi bien qu'en tant qu'objet philosophique, avec les Présocratiques, Xénophane et surtout Parménide. (edited)

LETTERI, Mark. The Theme of Health in Nietzsche's Thought. Man World, 23(4), 405-417, O 90.

This essay aims to demonstrate the deep-rootedness of the theme of health in Nietzsche's thought by relating it to much better known and studied motifs, namely, his naturalistic emphasis on the body, his anti-otherworldliness, and, perhaps most importantly, his ubiquitous emphasis on power, especially in the form of the theory of the will to power. It is suggested that the "moral" vocabulary of Nietzsche the "immoralist" is to a significant extent comprised of terms like "healthy" and "sick."

LEUNG, Edwin Sing Choe. Can There Be a Possible World in Which Memory Is Unreliable? Phil Inq, 11(3-4), 46-47, Sum-Fall 89.

This paper argues that there is at least a possible world in which memory is unreliable and that the actual world can be an such a world. In addition, the Wittgensteinian approach and the Hume-Strawson approach to memory are examined and refuted. The former approach is wrong because a necessary assumption might not be a right assumption; the latter is wrong because it is missing the whole point of the skeptics.

LEVERTOV, Denise. "Poetic Vision and the Hope for Peace" in *Celebrating Peace*, ROUNER, Leroy S (ed), 192-212. Notre Dame, Univ Notre Dame Pr, 1990.

LEVESQUE, Hector J and COHEN, Philip R. Teamwork. Nous, 25(4), 487-512, S 91.

LEVI, Isaac. "Rationality Unbound" in *Acting and Reflecting: The Interdisciplinary Turn in Philosophy*, SIEG, Wilfried (ed), 211-221. Norwell, Kluwer, 1990.

A critical discussion of the view of rationality taken by those who, like H A Simon, emphasize that rationality is bounded.

LEVI, Isaac. Reply to Maher and Kashima: "On the Descriptive Adequacy of Levi's Decision Theory". Econ Phil, 7(1), 101-103, Ap 91.

LEVIN, David Michael and SOLOMON, George F. The Discursive Formation of the Body in the History of Medicine. J Med Phil, 15(5), 515-537, O 90.

The principal argument of the present paper is that the human body is as much a reflective formation of multiple discourses as it is an effect of natural and environmental processes. This paper examines the implications of this argument, and suggests that recognizing the body in this light can be illuminating, not only for our conception of the body, but also for our understanding of medicine. Since medicine is itself a discursive formation, a science with both a history, and a future, it is argued that much can be learned by reflecting on the progression of models, or "paradigm-shifts," in terms of which modern medicine has articulated the human body that figures at the heart of its discourse. Four historical periods of medicine will be considered, each one governed by its own distinctive paradigm. (edited)

LEVIN, David Michael. "Justice in the Flesh" in *Ontology and Alterity in Merleau-Ponty*, JOHNSON, Galen A (ed), 35-44. Evanston, Northwestern Univ Pr, 1991.

In *The Visible and the Invisible*, Merleau-Ponty suggested a radically new interpretation of the nature of human embodiment, bringing it to articulation as "the flesh". This chapter argues that this interpretation brings to light, beneath the structure of subject and object, the functioning of a corporeal schema that already schematizes the fulfillment of the body's capacities in a body politic governed by justice. The argument hinges on showing that the reversibilities constitutive of the flesh form the roots of the reversibilities that later become essential for the achievement of social justice.

LEVIN, David Michael. "Postmodernism in Dance: Dance, Discourse, Democracy" in *Postmodernism—Philosophy and the Arts (Continental Philosophy III)*, SILVERMAN, Hugh J (ed), 207-233. New York, Routledge, 1990.

The main question in this chapter concerns the social and political significance of the postmodernist movement in dance. The discussion of this question is framed by an interpretation of the discourses of dance criticism and dance aesthetics, in terms of which the author proposes clear definitions of the avant garde, the modern, the modernist (modernism), and the postmodernist (postmodernism), drawing on the critical discourse about painting and sculpture that defined modernism in the sixties.

LEVIN, Janet. Analytic Functionalism and the Reduction of Phenomenal States. Phil Stud, 61(3), 211-238, Mr 91.

LEVIN, Michael. Realisms. Synthese, 85(1), 115-138, O 90.

It is argued that the general thesis of realism is ill-defined, as are various versions of its denial. Only specific theses of the form 'There are *K*'s' make clear sense. It is also argued that various efforts to deny realism always turn out to deny specific existential theses. Thus, it is argued, van Fraassen and Schwartz deny the existence of electrons.

LEVINAS, E and EZCURRA, Alicia Villar (trans). Filosofía, justicia y amor. Dialogo Filosof, 6(3), 308-321, S-D 90.

LEVINAS, Emmanuel and ARONOWICZ, Annette (trans). *Nine Talmudic Readings*. Bloomington, Indiana Univ Pr, 1990.

LEVINAS, Emmanuel and HAND, Seán (trans). Reflections on the Philosophy of Hitlerism. Crit Inquiry, 17(1), 62-71, Autumn 90.

LEVINAS, Emmanuel and CRITCHLEY, Simon (trans). "Wholly Otherwise" in *Re-Reading Levinas*, BERNASCONI, Robert (ed), 3-10. Bloomington, Indiana Univ Pr, 1991.

This is the first English translation of an article by Levinas where he relates his own concerns to those of Derrida's work.

LEVINE, Andrew. Thoughts on the Future of Marxism. Grad Fac Phil J, 14(1), 61-79, 1991.

This article reflects the demise of "Western Marxism" and the rise of "analytic Marxism." It is argued that Marxism today cannot be distinguished by its method or even by its substantive theoretical commitments, but by the kinds of explanatory and practical political projects to which it is committed.

LEVINE, Carol (ed). *Taking Sides: Clashing Views on Controversial Bioethical Issues (Fourth Edition)*. Guilford, Dushkin, 1991.

LEVINE, Charles and BOYD, Dwight R and KOHLBERG, Lawrence. "The Return of Stage 6: Its Principle and Moral Point of View" in *The Moral Domain: Essays in the Ongoing Discussion between Philosophy and the Social Sciences*, WREN, Thomas E (ed), 151-181. Cambridge, MIT Pr, 1990.

LEVINE, Elliott M. A Dionysian Songbook: the Mysterious Singing. Hist Euro Ideas, 11, 719-732, 1989.

Dionysius is known multivocally, Dionysius calls forth three actors—two are seen as irrational warring subjects, one is tyrant, the other is enslaved to blind passion. Both are *dialectic* opponents bound to Lord Apollo. Nietzsche names a favorite third person known only to dialogue. From the standpoint of each kaleidescope, accounts emerge to populate our landscape with ab extra inauthentic versions of the others. For Nietzsche the perspectives of the first two are but world views to be overcome, the third alone invites us to present celebration. Since Nietzsche this *dialogic* Dionysius has been heard by others, Albert Camus and Martin Buber especially.

LEVINE, Joseph M. Giambattista Vico and the Quarrel between the Ancients and the Moderns. J Hist Ideas, 52(1), 55-79, Ja-Mr 91.

LEVINE, Joseph. Cool Red. Phil Psych, 4(1), 27-40, 1991.

I argue that C L Hardin fails in his attempt to show that the qualitative character of color vision can be explained by reference to the underlying neurophysiological processes. I also elaborate on the claim that an "explanatory gap" separates physical and phenomenal descriptions of experience.

LEVINE, Michael P. Divine Unity and Superfluous Synonymity. J Speculative Phil, 4(3), 211-236, 1990.

The central claim of pantheism concerning the existence of a divine unity has a history of being misunderstood. In Part I of this paper I argue that some of the more prominent and influential interpretations of pantheistic unity, including Schopenhauer's, are blatant misunderstandings. In Part II, I offer a typology of models for the explanation of pantheistic unity. I do not attempt to specify fully just what is meant by pantheistic unity—that task is too large. Instead, as a way of beginning that analysis, I show that an adequate criterion of unity interestingly rules out some of the most historically prominent accounts.

LEVINE, Michael P. If There Is a God, Any Experience Which Seems to Be of God, Will Be Genuine. Relig Stud, 26(2), 207-217, Je 90.

LEVINE, Michael P. Madden's Account of Necessity in Causation. Phil Inq, 10(1-2), 1-22, Wint-Spr 88.

LEVINE, Michael. Maimonides: A Natural Law Theorist? Vera Lex, 10(2), 11-15,26, 1990.

After presenting a paradigm of natural law taken from Cicero and Aquinas, I discuss aspects of Maimonides' ethical theory that appear to conflict with doctrines of natural law. My conclusion will be that Maimonides' adaptation of the Aristotelian metaphysic and doctrine of the "Golden Mean" produced a teleological ethic that is reconcilable with his view that certain moral and legal injunctions are revealed. A doctrine of natural law is compatible with the ethical doctrines that Maimonides held. The thesis I pursue is antithetical to Marvin Fox's contention that "in Judaism there is no natural law doctrine, and in principle there cannot be."

LEVINE, Robert J. Treating the Troops: A Commentary. Hastings Center Rep, 21(2), 27-29, Mr-Ap 91.

LEVINSON, Henry S. What Good is Irony? Bull Santayana Soc, 8, 29-34, Fall 90.

LEVINSON, Jerrold. Philosophy as an Art. J Aes Educ, 24(2), 5-14, Sum 90.

This is a critical discussion of Richard Wollheim's *Painting as an Art*.

LEVINSON, Sanford. The Ambiguity of Political Virtue: A Response to Wolgast. Soc Theor Pract, 17(2), 295-305, Sum 91.

LEVITT, Tom. Love in *Thus Spoke Zarathustra*. Gnosis, 3(3), 101-109, D 90.

LEVVIS, Gary W. The Principle of Relevant Similarity. J Value Inq, 25(1), 81-87, Ja 91.

It is argued (1) that Michael Lavin's counterexamples to the principle of relevant similarity ("Why We Do Not Have to Treat Like Cases Alike," *J Value Inq*, 22(4), 313-318, Dec 88) are inadequate, and (2) that the principle is incapable of being disproven by way of counterexample.

LEVY, Beryl Harold. *Anglo-American Philosophy of Law: An Introduction to Its Development and Outcome*. New Brunswick, Transaction Books, 1991.

LEVY, David J. The Life of Order and the Order of Life: Eric Voegelin on Modernity and the Problem of Philosophical Anthropology. Man World, 24(3), 241-265, Jl 91.

The article sets the work of Voegelin in the context of twentieth century philosophy and political history. It focusses particularly on Voegelin's place in the development of philosophical and political anthropology.

LEVY, David J. "Politics, Technology and the Responsibility of the Intellectuals" in *The Political Responsibility of Intellectuals*, MACLEAN, Ian (ed), 123-142. New York, Cambridge Univ Pr, 1990.

The article develops an anthropological perspective on the responsibility of intellectuals in the face of political and technological change.

LEVY, Edwin. "Judgment and Policy: The Two-Step in Mandated Science and Technology" in *Philosophy of Technology*, DURBIN, Paul T (ed), 41-59. Norwell, Kluwer, 1989.

Mandated science is the work of scientists and technologists in the context of bodies mandated to make recommendations or decisions of a policy or legal nature. Examples include regulatory agencies, expert commissions, standard setting organizations, and the courts. The 'two step' is the attempt to make a sharp conceptual and procedural distinction between, on the one hand, scientific and, on the other hand, political/ethical considerations in public policy making. The paper shows that the 'two step' is often misguided and obfuscating especially in Mandated Science. While there may be practical reasons to subdivide policy deliberations involving science and technology, it is usually a mistake to think that scientific factors can thereby be isolated from value considerations. This is not simply another claim about the impossibility of value-free inquiry. I show just where and why there are significant philosophical questions in the mandated area.

LEVY, Stephen H. Charles S Peirce's Theory of Infinitesimals. Int Phil Quart, 31(2), 127-140, Je 91.

LEWIN, R A and MIKENBERG, I F and SCHWARZE, M G. Algebraization of Paraconsistent Logic P^1. J Non-Classical Log, 7(1-2), 79-88, My-N 90.

Using techniques developed by Blok and Pigozzi, we prove that paraconsistent logic P1, introduced by Sette, is algebraizable.

LEWIS, A D E. The Background to Bentham on Evidence. Utilitas, 2(2), 195-219, N 90.

LEWIS, Albert C. The Influence of Roger Boskovic on Bertrand Russell's Early Philosophy of Physics (in Serbo-Croatian). Filozof Istraz, 32-33(5-6), 1611-1620, 1989.

Bertrand Russell's first reference to Boscovichian "centres of force" was in a paper of 1894 written while a student at Cambridge University. By 1896 Russell thought the notion of a point mass as a centre of force was the best solution to the problems of the relativistic view of space which he held at the time. His ideas were expressed in response to Arthur Hannequin's *Essai critique sur l'hypothèse des atomes dans la science contemporaine* (1895). In 1897, however, Russell moved towards a plenal view of space more in keeping with current field theories. Nevertheless, as his correspondence with L L Whyte in the 1950s shows, he continued to have an admiration for Boscovich's ideas as the only theory true to Leibniz's philosophy and Newtonianism.

LEWIS, Bernard. "Europe and Islam" in *The Tanner Lectures On Human Values, Volume XII*, PETERSON, Grethe B (ed), 77-139. Salt Lake City, Univ of Utah Pr, 1991.

LEWIS, David. *Parts of Classes*. Cambridge, Blackwell, 1991.

The notion of part and whole applies to classes. The parts of a class (disregarding the null set) are exactly its subclasses, and so the smallest parts of a class are its one-membered singleton subclasses. A class is a fusion of singletons; the distinctively set-theoretical primitive operation is the relation of singletons to their members. Unfortunately, this primitive operation is ill-understood. However it is possible, using ideas of John P Burgess and A P Hazen, to bypass the primitive singleton operation: we can say that set theory is the general theory of all operations having the formal character of a singleton operation.

LEWIS, Stephen and KLEIMAN, L (ed). *Philosophy: An Introduction Through Literature*. New York, Paragon House, 1990.

LEWIS, Thomas J. Parody and the Argument from Probability in the *Apology*. Phil Lit, 14(2), 359-366, O 90.

Socrates' rhetoric in the *Apology* is now generally understood to be a parody of deceptive rhetoric in general, or of Gorgias's *Palamedes* in particular. But how can such masterful rhetoric be identified as a parody? Kenneth Seeskin argues that the test of the *Apology* as a parody is Socrates' refusal to use the powerfully deceptive argument from probability. This paper argues that the parody interpretation is undercut by Socrates' expert and virtually undetectable use of the argument from probability.

LEYDESDORFF, Loet and VAN DER MEULEN, Barend. Has the Study of Philosophy at Dutch Universities Changed under Economic and Political Pressures? Sci Tech Human Values, 16(3), 288-321, Sum 91.

From 1980 until 1985, the Dutch Faculties of Philosophy went through a period of transition. First, in 1982 the national government introduced a new system of financing research at the universities. This was essentially based on the natural sciences and did not match philosophers's work organization. In 1983 a drastic reduction in the budget for philosophy was proposed within the framework of a policy of introducing savings by distributing tasks among the universities. Recently, a visiting committee reported on the weak and strong areas of Dutch philosophy and proposed a policy to strenghten Dutch philosophy. This study explores the effects of the institutional reorganizations on the study of philosophy at the faculties, using scientometric methods. In addition to presenting empirical results, some methodological questions concerning the application of scientometric methods to a field of the humanities will be discussed. The number of publications went up as funding was cut back, and different subfields made different kinds of changes in orientation. The results show the relevance of publication-based data in research evaluation.

LIAPUNOV, Vadim (ed) and HOLQUIST, Michael (ed) and BAKHTIN, M M. *Art and Answerability: Early Philosophical Essays—M M Bakhtin*. Austin, Univ of Texas Pr, 1990.

LIASCHENKO, Joan and DAVIS, Anne J. Nurses and Physicians on Nutritional Support: A Comparison. J Med Phil, 16(3), 259-283, Je 91.

During the last decade, several court cases have focused attention on the moral and legal aspects of withholding or withdrawing food and fluids from certain patients. The courts have not been unanimous in their judgments on these matters. In attempting to explore this issue, this article reviews both the nursing and medical literature on the withdrawing and withholding of food and fluids with particular attention to empirical studies. Several themes which emerge from the literature are used to explore the similarities and differences between the practices of nursing and medicine where nutritional support is concerned.

LICHTENBERG, Judith. Truth, Neutrality, and Conflict of Interest. Bus Prof Ethics J, 9(1-2), 65-78, Spr-Sum 90.

I discuss two recent conflict-of-interest cases in journalism. In one, journalists who participated in an abortion-rights march were censured for violating their news organizations' conflict-of-interest policies. The second case raises the question whether journalists ought to disclose outside sources of income. I argue for the prohibition on political involvements, not because journalists can or ought to remain opinionless, but because such commitments create a *misleading* appearance of impropriety. I argue for disclosure of income, not because I think journalists are easily bought in a crude way, but because financial connections create a relationship between donor and beneficiary that can jeopardize the journalist's capacity to report news truthfully and fairly.

LIDERBACH, Daniel. The Community as Sacrament. Phil Theol, 5(3), 221-236, Spr 91.

I argue that the late twentieth century relies more upon the symbolic that upon the causal power of events acknowledged as sacraments. Since this is the case with the Eucharist no less than with other sacraments, the symbolic meaning of the Eucharist must be refocused. This may be accomplished through the concept of the numinous dimension of the Lord's Supper.

LIEDTKA, Jeanne. Organizational Value Contention and Managerial Mindsets. J Bus Ethics, 10(7), 543-557, Jl 91.

This paper focuses on the differing ways in which organizations send conflicting signals, in the form of contending organizational values, to their managers regarding the appropriate behavior in a given situation, and the impact that this has on the manager's decision-making process. It posits the existence of three different types of organizational value contention and examines their influence on the resulting patterns of sense-making and behavior evident in the manager's responses, based upon interview data from a cross-section of managers in two organizations.

LIEPERT, Anita. Staat als Konsens mündiger Bürger? Zur Staatsansicht deutscher Vormärzliberaler. Deut Z Phil, 39(2), 156-167, 1991.

LIGHT, Donald W. The Ethics of Corporate Health Insurance. Bus Prof Ethics J, 10(2), 49-62, Sum 91.

LILLY, Reginald. Foucault: Making a Difference. Man World, 24(3), 267-284, Jl 91.

LIND, Marcia. "Hume and Moral Emotions" in *Identity, Character, and Morality: Essays in Moral Psychology*, FLANAGAN, Owen (ed), 133-147. Cambridge, MIT Pr, 1990.

LINDBERG, Jordan J. From Russell to Quine: Basic Statements, Foundationalism, Truth, and Other Myths. Dialogue (PST), 33(1), 27-31, O 90.

In this paper I explicate the major features of both Russell's foundationalism and Quine's naturalized epistemology. I focus specifically on both philosophers' conception of a basic statement and on their notion of truth (i.e., correspondence and coherence). I conclude with some general criticisms of Russellian foundationalism and discuss how Quine's epistemology is more in keeping with Russell's own standards of epistemology.

LINDGREN, Ralph. Transition to Pragmatic Liberalism: Diversity, Contingency, and Social Solidarity. Mod Sch, 68(2), 111-122, Ja 91.

This paper presents two main arguments. First, Rawls's preference for an "overlapping consensus" is not serviceable as a justifying procedure in a modern democracy because the pluralism of belief systems impacts the interpretations given even jointly held convictions. Debates over interpretations of the Establishment Clause of the First Amendment illustrate this. Second, recent studies of the practice of negotiation show that zero-sum strategies are not as pervasive as Rawls assumes and that pragmatic bargaining does not invariably result in the instability that gives him pause about endorsing the pragmatic version of liberalism.

LINDOP, Clive. "Critical Thinking and Philosophy for Children: The Educational Value of Philosophy". Thinking, 9(3), 32-35, 1990.

Argues that characteristics of critical thinking: use of criteria in forming judgments sensitive to the context and a disposition for self-correction, are built-in features of philosophy and Philosophy for Children. Since Philosophy for Children programs offer pupils the philosophic perspective in the context of inquiry by (fictional) children like themselves, it encourages them to bring their own perspectives into the classroom dialogue for scrutiny and self-correction. This process exercises both reasoning skills and the disposition to be reasonable. Since education and philosophy share reasonableness as their goal, it is permissable to conclude the Philosophy for Children is a truly educational program.

LINDSAY, Ronald A. Neutrality Between Religion and Irreligion. Free Inq, 10(4), 17-20, Fall 90.

This article discusses the historical and philosophical foundations for the separation between Church and State. It concludes that the government should maintain a strict neutrality between the religious and the nonreligious. The article also refutes the argument that such neutrality results in hostility toward religion.

LINGIS, Alphonso. We Mortals. Phil Today, 35(2), 119-126, Sum 91.

LINGNER, Michael. "Methodische Aspekte des Kunstwissenschaftlichen Umgangs mit moderner Kunst" in *XIth International Congress in Aesthetics, Nottingham 1988*, WOODFIELD, Richard (ed), 116-119. Nottingham, Nottingham Polytech, 1990.

LINNEWEBER-LAMMERSKITTEN, Helmut. *Untersuchungen zur Theorie des hypothetischen Urteils*. Munster, Nodus, 1988.

Das Buch gibt einen Überblick über die wichtigsten Theorien zum hypothetischen Urteil resp. über die verschiedenen bedeutenden Implikationsbegriffe. Am Leitfaden einer Reihe signifikanter aussagen—und modallogischer Formeln werden die Systeme von C I Lewis, Ackermann, Anderson/Belnap, Sugihara, Parry, McCall, Stalnaker u.a. untersucht und ein eigenes leistungsfähiges System vorgeschlagen, in dem Simplifikationsformeln wie etwa p&q → p nicht ableitbar sind.

LINSKY, Bernard. Truth at a World is a Modality. Philosophia (Israel), 20(4), 387-394, F 91.

The Leibnizian notion that necessarily a is P if and only if a is P at all worlds does not succeed in reducing a modality to a relation between objects, properties and worlds. Nor does the analysis of 'truth at a world' as a metalinguistic relation allow one to avoid primitive modalities. David Lewis can analyze 'a is P at W' (as 'a is P and a is in w') but only at the cost of abandoning trans-world individuals. I argue that only by treating 'at w' as a modality like 'necessarily' is it possible to have transworld individuals and give an account of the Leibnizian notion.

LINSKY, Bernard. Was the Axiom of Reducibility a Principle of Logic? Russell, 10(2), 125-140, Wint 90-91.

It is often said that logicism was a failure because when it avoided the inconsistency of Frege's system, it succumbed to the adoption of clearly nonlogical principles, including the axiom of reducibility. I discuss both Russell's own qualms about the axiom as well as the objections of others and trace the history of the axiom and its central role in *Principia Mathematica*. In context, as part of an intensional logic, based on a particular metaphysical scheme, the axiom of reducibility can be seen to be in keeping with the rest of Russell's logic.

LINVILLE, Kent. Dialogue and Doubt in Descartes' First Meditation. Phil Invest, 14(2), 115-130, Ap 91.

Given the genre of Descartes's "First Meditation," its author should also be its sole actor. But this study shows those two roles are there played by distinct identities: Descartes the author, and a companion literary creation, Descartes the meditator. Unmasking these two separate identities reveals an implicit dialogic structure disguising a pervasive equivocation on the meaning of "believes" (and derivatively, "doubt") at the heart of the "Meditation." That ambiguity, once remarked, enables us to show that although Hume is correct in opposing Descartes's voluntarism, he is wrong in claiming that the passivity of belief results from our nature.

LINVILLE, Kent and RING, Merrill. Moore's Paradox Revisited. Synthese, 87(2), 295-309, My 91.

Moore's remarking the oddness of the sentences "*p*, but I don't believe that *p*" deserves Wittgenstein's praise as the "only discovery of Moore's that greatly impressed him." For as this study shows, Moore's sentences provide a metaphysically neutral datum with which to oppose *both* Cartesian dualism and, what many contemporary philosophers take to be its corrective, physicalism. Despite all manner of philosophical temptation to think otherwise, Moore's sentences make it to see that "I believe" statements neither arise from nor advert to a state of the (mind or brain or mind/brain of the) speaker.

LINZEY, Andrew. Moral Dreams and Practical Realities. Between Species, 7(2), 81-89, Spr 91.

LINZEY, Andrew. The Servant Species: Humanity as Priesthood. Between Species, 6(3), 109-121, Sum 90.

LIPMAN, Matthew. Philosophy is Also for the Young—At Least Possibly. Thinking, 9(3), 27, 1990.

This is a reprint of an Op-Ed editorial in the New York Times, October 20, 1974. Its aim was to announce the emergence of elementary school philosophy.

LIPMAN, Matthew. Response to Professor Kitchener's "Do Children Think Philosophically?". Metaphilosophy, 21(4), 432-433, O 90.

This is a reply to a paper in which Professor Kitchener maintains that children lack the meta-level cognitive skills essential for doing philosophy. The response asserts that it has not been shown that these skills are essential, or that all true philosophers use them. It proceeds to argue that, while many children may manifest mediocrity when they do philosophy, so do many adults. If one plays a game by the rules, one is considered a player, even if one is not a good player.

LIPPMAN, Edward A (ed). *Musical Aesthetics: A Historical Reader, Volume III, The Twentieth Century*. Stuyvesant, Pendragon Pr, 1990.

LIPSON, Morry and VALLENTYNE, Peter. Equal Opportunity and the Family. Pub Affairs Quart, 3(4), 27-45, O 89.

We build upon some work of James Fishkin concerning the incompatibility of liberal principles of equal opportunity and the principle of family autonomy (which says that the state should not interfere with how parents raise their children except in extreme cases). We formulate a principle that requires that children of the equivalent capacities have the same expectations concerning the development of skills that are generally useful (no matter what one's life plans are). This principle is incompatible with the principle of family of autonomy. We argue that liberals are deeply committed to this new principle, and that therefore they must reject the traditional family autonomy principle.

LIPTON, Peter. Contrastive Explanations. Philosophy, 27, 247-266, 90 Supp.

LISMAN, C David. A Critical Review of *The Moral Dimensions of Teaching*. Educ Theor, 41(2), 227-234, Spr 91.

LIST, C J. Realism, Idealism and Quantum Mechanics. Phil Sci (Tucson), 3, 57-69, 1988.

This paper is a critical evaluation of an argument (given by Eugene Wigner, for example) which purports to draw conclusions about the philosophical debate between subjective idealists and realists from some results in quantum mechanics. I first offer some background on the dispute between idealists and realists. Then I illustrate the kinds of considerations which might seem to lead from quantum mechanics to subjective idealism. To do this, I describe a device, the existenc of which purportedly demonstrates the ontological dependence upon observation of certain physical properties. Finally I take up the question of whether one may move from these quantum mechanical results to the subjective idealist's conclusion.

LIST, Charles J and PLUM, Stephen H. *Library Research Guide to Philosophy: Illustrated Search Strategy and Sources*. Ann Arbor, Pierian Pr, 1990.

This book is a guide for undergraduates and beginning graduate students writing papers on philosophy. It guides the student through the use of bibliographies, encyclopedias, the card catalog, interlibrary loan, indexes, and computer searching. It includes a selective bibliography to basic reference sources in philosophy and a summary of various forms philosophy papers might take. Throughout the book a single topic is developed (Nietzsche's thoughts on war) to illustrate research strategies. Numerous figures and illustrations are used to aid the student's understanding of research tools.

LISZT, Amy. Animal Liberation as a Valid Response to Structural Violence. Between Species, 6(4), 163-169, Fall 90.

LISZT, Amy. Response to Finsen's "Response to Lizst's Animal Liberation as a Valid Response to Structural Violence". Between Species, 6(4), 174-175, Fall 90.

LITKE, Robert. "Conservative and Radical Critiques of Nuclear Policy" in *Issues in War and Peace: Philosophical Inquiries*, KUNKEL, Joseph (ed), 139-145. Wolfeboro, Longwood, 1989.

I argue that ethical reasoning can prescribe two quite different kinds of change in nuclear policy. Conservative ethical reasoning prescribes change *within* the framework of the war system. An example would be 'just war' discussions of the ethical use of nuclear weapons. Radical ethical discussions argue that the war framework itself must be changed, because nuclear weapons make every war in which their use is a possibility immoral. Since nuclear weapons pose both short-term and long-range problems, I suggest that both moral perspectives are valuable.

LITKE, Robert. "On the Deep Structure of Violence" in *In the Interest of Peace: A Spectrum of Philosophical Views*, KLEIN, Kenneth H (ed), 33-43. Wolfeboro, Longwood, 1990.

Garver argues that violence is the violation of a person's right to their body or to their autonomy. I extend this account by showing that such violence is the disempowerment of a person with respect to their bodily capacities or decision-making abilities. I suggest that such violence is often self-defeating. Both Hobbes and Hegel offer accounts of why we seek to disempower or violate others in such ways, even though such behaviour may defeat our interests. The underlying mistake is to assume that one has nothing to learn from the person who is subsequently violated.

LITTLE, Daniel. *Varieties of Social Explanation: An Introduction to the Philosophy of Social Science*. Boulder, Westview Pr, 1991.

This book is an introduction to the philosophy of social science. It contains chapters on three central forms of explanation: causal explanation, rational choice theory, and interpretation theory. It then considers variants of these: functional and structural explanation, materialist explanation, statistical explanation, and public choice explanation. The final three chapters discuss more general problems: methodological individualism, various forms of relativism, and naturalism as a basis for social science methodology. The book is organized around a large number of examples of social explanations, in order to ensure that the abstract philosophical analysis bears a close relation to actual social science practice.

LITTMAN, David C and MEY, Jacob L. The Nature of Irony: Toward a Computational Model of Irony. J Prag, 15(2), 131-151, F 91.

LIU, Shu-Hsien. On the Functional Unity of the Four Dimensions of Thought in the *Book of Changes*. J Chin Phil, 17(3), 359-385, S 90.

Four layers of meaning can be identified in the *Book of Changes*; they are (1) a system of mystical symbolism, (2) a system of rational/natural symbolism, (3) a system of cosmological symbolism, and (4) a system of ethical/metaphysical symbolism. After studying the characteristics of each of them I find that each is succeeding the other and yet each is also interpenetrating into the other, and that a functional unity can be found among these four dimensions.

LIVET, Pierre. Les combinaisons de la vie, l'organisation du vivant, le réseau du soi. Philosophique (France), 1(89), 39-53, 1989.

LIVINGSTON, Donald. A Sellarsian Hume? J Hist Phil, 29(2), 281-290, Ap 91.

LLANO, Carlos. El conocimiento del singular en José Gaos. Dianoia, 36(36), 17-37, 1990.

This article points out the context of the discussion on the knowledge of the singular in the philosophy of José Gaos, who takes up the subject under the influence of Ortega y Gasset. The knowledge of the singular interests Gaos not so much in itself, but rather because of its relationship with the ideas of desinterested "detachment" and "meaning". Gaos produces an analysis of the types of concepts and of the struggle of the intelligence to capture the singular in all its wealth. One aspect of this purpose is his conviction that a strictly speculative thought (or way of thinking) is impossible, one in which all personal instances of the individual who thinks have been completely eliminated. It concludes with some critical remarks about the ontological and noetical aspects in the way of thinking of Gaos.

LLEWELYN, John. "Am I Obsessed by Bobby? (Humanism of the Other Animal)" in *Re-Reading Levinas*, BERNASCONI, Robert (ed), 234-245. Bloomington, Indiana Univ Pr, 1991.

Against Levinas and Kant, Llewelyn argues that our responsibility towards animals is not merely derivative.

LLEWELYN, John. The Deconstruction of Time. J Brit Soc Phenomenol, 21(3), 284-289, O 90.

LLOYD, Christopher. The Methodologies of Social History: A Critical Survey and Defense of Structurism. Hist Theor, 30(2), 180-219, My 91.

LLOYD, G E R. *Demystifying Mentalities*. New York, Cambridge Univ Pr, 1990.

The notion of distinct mentalities has often been invoked by anthropologists, historians and philosophers to describe and explain cultural diversity. This book rejects this psychologising talk and proposes an alternative approach which takes as its starting point the social contexts of communication. Discussing apparently irrational beliefs and behaviour (such as magic) and also classic instances of the emergence of science in Greece and in China, the study shows how different forms of thought coexist in a single culture but within conventionally defined social contexts.

LLOYD, G E R. *Methods and Problems in Greek Science: Selected Papers*. New York, Cambridge Univ Pr, 1991.

This collection of articles on Greek science contains fifteen of the most important papers published by G E R Lloyd in this area since 1961, together with three unpublished articles. The topics range over all areas and periods of Greek science, including astronomy, cosmology, biology and medicine from the earliest Presocratic philosophers to Ptolemy and Galen. Several focus on important methodological problems: others on the social background to Greek science, on the motivations of ancient Greek scientists, their aims and the implicit assumptions that influenced their work. Each article is preceded by an introduction that assesses scholarly debate on the topic since the original publication.

LLOYD, G E R. Plato and Archytas in the Seventh Letter. Phronesis, 35(2), 159-174, 1990.

A close analysis of the information given about Archytas in the Seventh Letter ascribed to Plato suggests that the author of that letter, while acknowledging Archytas's role in rescuing Plato from the tyrant Dionysius II of Syracuse, is nevertheless keen to dissociate Plato from Archytas and to underline his independence from Pythagoreanism. It is as if that author is conscious of the charges that were eventually to be made that Plato plagiarised his ideas from the Pythagoreans—or that (as Aristotle claimed in *Metaphysics* A chapter 6) his theory of Forms is a modification of Pythagoreanism.

LLOYD, Trevor. "John Stuart Mill and the East India Company" in *A Cultivated Mind: Essays On J S Mill Presented to John M Robson*, LAINE, Michael (ed), 44-79. Buffalo, Univ of Toronto Pr, 1991.

LOAR, Brian. "Personal References" in *Information, Semantics and Epistemology*, VILLANUEVA, Enrique (ed), 117-133. Cambridge, Blackwell, 1990.

LOAR, Brian. "Phenomenal States" in *Philosophical Perspectives, 4: Action Theory and Philosophy of Mind, 1990*, TOMBERLIN, James E (ed), 81-108. Atascadero, Ridgeview, 1990.

LOCAL, John and COLEMAN, John. The "No Crossing Constraint" in Autosegmental Phonology. Ling Phil, 14(3), 295-338, Jl 91.

We examine a disquieting problem concerning the ability of the "No Crossing Constraint" (NCC) to constrain multiplanar Autosegmental Phonological Representations (APRs). Some "multiplanar" APRs are planar graphs, but some are necessarily nonplanar graphs. The NCC does not restrict the class of nonplanar graphs, so either we drop or modify the NCC, or we retain the NCC and cease to recognize nonplanar APRs as well-formed. We present examples of necessarily nonplanar APRs, and conclude that the first alternative must be selected. Thus the NCC is not a constraint, since it does not reduce or restrict the class of well-formed APRs.

LOCK, Grahame. "The Intellectuals and the Imitation of the Masses" in *The Political Responsibility of Intellectuals*, MACLEAN, Ian (ed), 143-160. New York, Cambridge Univ Pr, 1990.

A distinction is drawn between Plato's ultra-minimal and his minimal state. In the former no provision has been made for any principle of justice legitimating the division of labour. In the latter this principle becomes clear: workmen must stick to their workbench. They must not try to become philosophers. But nor must philosophers attempt to become workmen or even representatives of the common people. Representation is imitation, and imitation corrupts. A comparison may be made with certain theories of lying (Oscar Wilde, Nietzsche) and Karl Kraus' account of the "true mask".

LOCKE, Don. Response to Smith's "Markets and Morals". Philosophy, 26, 33-44, 90 Supp.

LOCKE, Don. "Response to Smith's 'Markets and Morals'" in *Philosophy and Politics*, HUNT, G M K (ed), 33-44. New York, Cambridge Univ Pr, 1991.

LOCKE, John and MELLIZO, Carlos (trans). *John Locke: Segundo Tratado sobre el Gobierno Civil*. Madrid, Alianza, 1990.

LOCKE, Lawrence A. On Leo Katz, Double Jeopardy, and the Blockburger Test. Law Phil, 9(3), 295-309, Ag 90.

LOCKHART, Ted. A Decision-Theoretic Reconstruction of *Roe v Wade*. Pub Affairs Quart, 5(3), 243-258, Jl 91.

In this essay, I propose a probabilistic model for normative reasoning and apply it to Justice Blackmun's argument for the majority opinion in *Roe v. Wade*. Probabilities are associated with premises in the argument for which uncertainty was intimated, including those pertaining to the personhood of fetuses and the right of privacy. The probabilities are measured ordinally and a maximize-expected-justice decision principle is employed. I conclude that for certain plausible assessments of the pertinent probabilities the opposite decision would be the more reasonable outcome.

LOEB, Stephen E. The Evaluation of "Outcomes" of Accounting Ethics Education. J Bus Ethics, 10(2), 77-84, F 91.

This article explores five important issues relating to the evaluation of ethics education in accounting. The issues that are considered include (a) reasons for evaluating accounting ethics education (see Caplan, 1980, pp. 133-35); (b) goal setting as a prerequisite to evaluating the outcomes of accounting ethics education (see Caplan, 1980, pp. 135-37); (c) possible broad levels of outcomes of accounting ethics education that can be evaluated; (d) matters relating to accounting ethics education that are in need of evaluation (see Caplan, 1980, p. 136); and (e) possible techniques for measuring outcomes of accounting ethics education (see Caplan, 1980, pp. 144-49). The paper concludes with a discussion of the issues under consideration.

LOECK, Gisela. Aristotle's Technical Simulation and its Logic of Causal Relations. Hist Phil Life Sci, 13(1), 3-32, 1991.

The paper investigates Aristotle's simulation of the embryo (zygote) by a gear wheel mechanism. The paper aims to show that Aristotle, to achieve the verification of efficient cause, tackles a calculus of relations with a semantics of causal content, providing logico-causal deductions, an ancient casual analogue of the truth-preserving calculus of relations. The elements of this Aristotelian causal calculus are those relations among the components of composite things that Aristotle holds to be causal. To these causal relations he applies various operations, set extension and set restriction, substitution, generalization and particularization, in such a way that the causal content of the relations transformed is preserved, thus affording deductions of relations from relations that are valid in respect to their causal content. The paper finally aims to show that causal calculus, working well when applied to the gear wheel mechanism and the embryo, is not sound in every application. (edited)

LOEWER, Barry and ALBERT, David Z. The Measurement Problem: Some "Solutions". Synthese, 86(1), 87-98, Ja 91.

LOEWER, Barry and LE PORE, Ernest. "A Study in Comparative Semantics" in *Propositional Attitudes: The Role of Content in Logic, Language, and Mind*, ANDERSON, C Anthony (ed), 91-111. Stanford, CSLI, 1990.

Two of the most influential philosophers of language, Gottlob Frege and Donald Davidson, share a conception of the goals of a theory of meaning for a natural language. Both think 1) that such a theory should encapsulate knowledge centrally involved in understanding a language, 2) that knowledge of the *truth conditions* of indicative sentences is central to that understanding, 3) that for an adequate account of understanding, a theory of meaning must be compositional in order to explain how complex expressions can be understood in terms of an understanding of their components, 4) that an account of compositional structure will systematize logical relations among sentences and both 5) emphasize the importance of paraphrase into quantificational languages for constructing semantic theories which systemize the truth conditions and logical relations of sentences. They differ as to how these goals can best be accomplished and in particular as to the ontology and ideology required to achieve them. Given these differences the question naturally arises of how to evaluate the two accounts. We address this question in our paper.

LOEWER, Barry and ALBERT, David. Wanted Dead or Alive: Two Attempts to Solve Schrödinger's Paradox. Proc Phil Sci Ass, 1, 277-285, 1990.

LOEWER, Barry and LE PORE, Ernest. "What Davidson Should Have Said" in *Information, Semantics and Epistemology*, VILLANUEVA, Enrique (ed), 190-199. Cambridge, Blackwell, 1990.

In this paper, we articulate a way out of a difficulty harassing Donald Davidson's view that a theory of understanding for a language L is best understood in terms of a theory of truth for L. We argue that a theory of truth should be augmented with a *samesaying* relation between utterances in order to bridge the gap between what a speaker utters and what he says. We also argue that there is no need for empirical or formal constraints on the theory. Nor is there a need to modify or abandon Davidson's extensionalist framework.

LOEWER, Barry and LE PORE, Ernest. "What Davidson Should Have Said" in *The Mind of Donald Davidson*, BRANDL, Johannes (ed), 65-78. Amsterdam, Rodopi, 1989.

According to Davidson, a theory of meaning for a language L should specify information such that if someone had this information he would be in a position to understand L. He claims that a theory of truth for L fits this description. Many critics have argued that a truth theory is too weak to be a theory of meaning. We argue that these critics and Davidson's response to them have been misguided. Many critics have been misguided because they have not been clear about what a theory of meaning is supposed to do. These critics and Davidson himself, though, have also been misguided because they thought that by adding further conditions on a truth theory we can come up with an adequate theory of meaning. We will show that Davidson has available to him, though he apparently failed to see so, a reply to his critics in his own paratactic account of the semantics for indirect discourse reports.

LOEWY, Erich H. Market Mechanisms and Principles of Justice. Bus Prof Ethics J, 9(3-4), 103-119, Fall-Wint 90.

The history of health-care rationing is briefly reviewed and various philosophies of justice underwriting allocation are discussed. A "poor law" approach is contrasted with a "welfare" philosophy. When justice is seen from a minimalist perspective, a rationing system in which the market serves as the instrument of rationing results; a "poor law" approach permits a multi-tiered system while a "welfare" philosophy will see to it that all have equal access to essential services as health-care and education. It is concluded that no civilized country can afford to allow a pure market to control access to essential services, that a multi-tiered system tends to solidify existing class structure and that single-tiered systems of health-care and education are most apt to reduce class differences.

LOFFREDO D'OTTAVIANO, Itala M. On the Development of Paraconsistent Logic and Da Costa's Work. J Non-Classical Log, 7(1-2), 89-152, My-N 90.

LOGAN, George M (ed) and ADAMS, Robert M (ed). *Utopia: Sir Thomas More*. New York, Cambridge Univ Pr, 1989.

LOH, Werne. Alternativen und Irrtum in der Kritischen Philosophie Kants. Kantstudien, 82(1), 81-95, 1991.

LOHMAR, Dieter. Kants Schemata als Anwendungsbedingungen von Kategorien auf Anschauungen. Z Phil Forsch, 45(1), 77-92, Ja-Mr 91.

LOHMAR, Dieter. Wo lag der Fehler der kategorialen Repräsentation? Zu Sinn und Reichweite einer Selbstkritik Husserls. Husserl Stud, 7(3), 179-197, 1990.

LOJACONO, Ettore. Descartes e le "culture" barocche: Appunti su alcune recenti interpretazioni. G Crit Filosof Ital, 70(1), 1-14, Ja-Ap 91.

LOMASKY, Loren E and GAUS, Gerald F. Are Property Rights Problematic? Monist, 73(4), 483-503, O 90.

Alan Gibbard, along with a number of other philosophers, seems to believe that property rights are somehow especially problematic as they conflict with freedom. The arguments of the first three sections of this paper contend that property rights are no more problematic within the context of liberal theory than are other quintessentially liberal rights such as freedom of speech. Many theorists have, however, believed that the justification of title to private property diverges significantly from other strands of liberal justificatory theory. In the fourth section, we trace this belief back to special features of original acquisition theories.

LOMBARDI, Henri and LABHALLA, Salah. Real Numbers, Continued Fractions and Complexity Classes. Annals Pure Applied Log, 50(1), 1-28, N 90.

We compare some representations of real numbers from the viewpoint of recursive functionals and of complexity (via Cauchy sequences, Dedekind cuts and continued fraction). The impossibility of obtaining some functions as recursive functionals may be explicited in terms of complexity: 1) existence of sequence of low complexity whose image is not a recursive sequence, 2) existence of objects of low complexity whose images have high time-complexity. We also obtain quite high results of nonstability under addition for some representations. This work confirms that the unique representation of real numbers suitable for the ordinary calculs is via explicit Cauchy sequences of rationals.

LONG, A A. "Representation and the Self in Stoicism" in *Psychology (Companions to Ancient Thought: 2)*, EVERSON, Stephen (ed), 102-120. New York, Cambridge Univ Pr, 1991.

LONG, Fiachra. Maurice Blondel's Moral Logic. Phil Stud (Ireland), 32, 213-223, 1988-90.

LONG, Fiachra. The Postmodern Flavor of Blondel's Method. Int Phil Quart, 31(1), 15-22, Mr 91.

LONGACRE, Judith. Cartesian Feminists. Gnosis, 3(3), 49-72, D 90.

LONGEART, Maryvonne and BOSS, Gilbert. Représentation philosophique par réseau sémantique variable. Laval Theol Phil, 47(2), 185-192, Je 91.

La question du rapport entre l'intelligence artificielle et la philosophie est abordée ici dans la perspective de la représentation de la philosophie sur ordinateur. L'argument se développe en quatre points: 1) avantages de l'approche interdisciplinaire pour l'intelligence artificielle et la philosophie, 2) problèmes spécifiques de la représentation philosophique dus à son caractère réflexif, 3) conception d'une structure de réseaux sémantiques appropriée à la représentation philosophique et à la réflexion théorique sur ce mode même de représentation, 4) esquisse d'un tel réseau universel.

LONGENECKER, Clinton and LUDWIG, Dean. Ethical Dilemmas in Performance Appraisal Revisited. J Bus Ethics, 9(12), 961-969, D 90.

In managers' dynamic, real-world environments, they often feel it is necessary to exercise some creative discretion over employee ratings. They justify the inaccuracy by citing, among other things, the need to avoid confrontation with subordinates, damaging working relationships, and creating permanent written documents which may later harm a subordinate's career. This paper examines the ethics of this sort of deliberate manipulation of performance appraisal systems, and suggests some duties and obligations for both the organization and the manager engaged in performance appraisal. (edited)

LONGEWAY, John L. The Rationality of Escapism and Self Deception. Behavior Phil, 18(2), 1-20, Fall-Wint 90.

Escapism is defined as the attempt to avoid awareness of aversive beliefs. Strategies, and a few examples, of escapism are discussed. It is argued that self-deception is one species of escapism and that entrenched escapism is theoretically irrational except in the special case where it compensates for irrationality elsewhere. The results for entrenched escapism would apply to self-deception as well. The function of escapism, then, is to compensate for irrational patterns of belief formation, and to maintain effectiveness (for the sake of continuance of the species), insofar as that is possible, in situations in which a rational person would succumb to despair and suicide. (edited)

LONGINO, Helen E. Feminism and Philosophy of Science. J Soc Phil, 21(2-3), 150-159, Fall-Wint 90.

LONGO, Margherita. Michel de Montaigne: La "nottola" dell'Umanesimo francese. Ann Fac Lett Filosof, 32, 327-351, 1989.

LOOREN DE JONG, H. Intentionality and the Ecological Approach. J Theor Soc Behav, 21(1), 91-109, Mr 91.

In this paper it is attempted to sketch a non-mentalist, broadly ecological concept of intentionality. Whereas Gibson's ecological psychology emphasises direct coupling between organism nd environment, it is argued here that intentionality can be considered an organism-environment relation, characterised by the possibility of distancing the organism from the immediately present visual field. Borrowing Gibson's notion of indirect perception as the use of tools to sharpen perception, and supplementing it with Vygotskij's and Mead's theory of internalisation of psychological tools, it is suggested that intentionality is a graded phenomenon with different degrees of tightness of coupling between organism and environment.

LOPARIC, Z. Paradigmas cartesianos. Cad Hist Filosof Cie, 1(2), 185-212, Jl-D 89.

O presente artigo começa mostrando que existe um conflito entre a historiografia da ciência representada pela obra de Kuhn e a filosofia da ciência, em particular, a do neopositivismo lógico e a do intelectualismo racionalista do tipo fichteano. Em seguida, oferece uma crítica da abordagem gueroultiana de Descartes, tomada como aplicação exemplar do intelectualismo racionalista. O artigo tenta, ainda, propor uma leitura kuhniana de certos aspectos da ciência cartesiana, em particular, da teoria causal da percepção. Finalmente, toma distância do naturalismo kuhniano devido a sua incapacidade de dar conta de vários aspectos essenciais da revolução cartesiana da história do pensamento.

LOPARIC, Zeljko. Habermas e o Terror Prático. Manuscrito, 13(2), 111-116, O 90.

LOPARIC, Zeljko. The Logical Structure of the First Antinomy. Kantstudien, 81(3), 280-303, 1990.

LÓPEZ-FERNÁNDEZ, Alvaro. Der Gegenstand der Vorstellungen und die transzendentale Apperzeption. Kantstudien, 81(3), 265-279, 1990.

The object of representations (something in general = X), which Walker characterizes as "one of the most unfortunate casualities of Kantian scholarship," is examined. It is neither a thing-in-itself, in the usual sense, nor an empirical object. Phenomenical space and phenomenical time have an immediate reference to the object of representations. They are related to, but not identical with, space and time as such. The object of representations, on which, according to Kant, the unity of consciousness depends, is time as such.

LOPICCOLI, Fiorella. "Il corpuscolarismo italiano nel 'Giornale de' Letterati' di Roma (1668-1681)" in *Scienza, Filosofia e Religione tra '600 e '700 in Italia*, PREDAVAL MAGRINI, Maria Vittoria (ed), 19-92. Milan, Angeli, 1990.

LORAND, Ruth. Aesthetic Order. Manuscrito, 13(2), 39-57, O 90.

The concept of order is usually understood as the one presented by information theory. This theory distinguishes (as most of traditional philosophy and everyday thinking) between the states of maximal order and maximal disorder as two extremes by which every state is defined. I offer a theory of two types of order, a logical order and an intuitive order which are both essential and irreducible. Logical order, which I refer to as formal order, follows the philosophical tradition and information theory. Intuitive or integrative order defines aesthetic order: a very beautiful object exhibits a very high degree of order, yet not of logical order. Integrative order consists of the ordered elements without any ordering principle. It is sensitive to and affected by changes in its elements or background. Missing elements carry high information value and their redundancy and predictability is low in a high order set (which is the opposite of what happens in a high ordered formal set).

LORD, C. "The Concept of Fine Art: A Critique" in *XIth International Congress in Aesthetics, Nottingham 1988*, WOODFIELD, Richard (ed), 120-122. Nottingham, Nottingham Polytech, 1990.

LORD, Catherine. A Note on Ruth Lorand's 'Free and Dependent Beauty: A Puzzling Issue'. Brit J Aes, 31(2), 167-168, Ap 91.

LORENZ, Kuno. Qué miden los juegos de lenguaje? Dianoia, 35(35), 151-161, 1989.

It is argued that the metaphor 'Bild' (picture) in Wittgenstein to signal like functioning of propositions in the *Tractatus (T)* and in the *Philosophical Investigations (PU)*, i.e., the function of measuring rod vis à vis reality, hide an important change on the way from *T* to *PU*. In *T* a picture being a matter of fact represents a state of affairs, in *PU* it can, in a language game, be used to represent. In fact, the invention of language games in *PU* serves to *show* (active mode) what *is shown* (passive mode) in *T*; hence language games are icons of reality (display object-competence), whereas *T*-style propositions are symbols (display meta-competence).

LOSITO, William F. Morality and Religion: Necessary Bedfellows in Education? Proc Phil Educ, 46, 101-110, 1990.

One potentially subversive criticism of moral education is the claim that moral education necessarily entails a religious worldview and therefore is not appropriate for publicly supported schools in democratic, religiously pluralistic societies. The paper critiques the premise of this argument that moral values presuppose a religious ontology (referred to as the "religious ontology argument" throughout the paper). It is argued that there is a plausible model which includes definitions and standards friendly to the religious ontology argument yet discounts clearly the necessity of moral education presupposing a religious worldview.

LÖTHER, Rolf. "Evolution—Matter of Fact or Metaphysical Idea?" in *Logic, Methodology and Philosophy of Science, VIII*, FENSTAD, J E (ed), 481-493. New York, Elsevier Science, 1989.

LÖTTER, H P P. Deficiencies in Contemporary Theories of Justice. S Afr J Phil, 9(4), 172-185, N 90.

It is argued that contemporary theories of justice focus exclusively on nearly just societies and ignore the issues in radically unjust societies. As a result of this focus, these theories have four important shortcomings when they are viewed from the perspective of someone living in a radically unjust society. The first deficiency is that contemporary theories of justice do not provide sufficient guidance on the way in which injustice should be identified. The second deficiency of these theories is that they have a lack of clarity on the issue whether theories of justice are universally applicable to all societies. The third deficiency is the relative neglect of clear guidelines on an appropriate method that could be used for designing, constructing and justifying a theory of justice. The fourth deficiency of contemporary theories of justice is an absence of thorough evaluation of forms of political action that could be considered to be acceptable strategies for the transformation of a radically unjust society into a nearly just society. These shortcomings imply that these theories of justice cannot be applied to the problems of radically unjust societies in a simplistic fashion. (edited)

LÖTTER, H P P. Olivier's Postmodern Proposal: A Few Comments. S Afr J Phil, 9(4), 222, N 90.

LOUGHLIN, Gerard. Prefacing Pluralism: John Hick and the Mastery of Religion. Mod Theol, 7(1), 29-55, O 90.

John Hick is the name of the authorial force that seeks to press upon the plurality of his writings a coherent reading, a single system or pluralism. This essay shows that the mastery of authorial force is also at work in Hick's *An Interpretation of Religion* (1989), bringing religious diversity under the control of an all-embracing conceptuality. Pluralism is the name of this system, the name of a force that would master the religions, bringing them, like the texts, under the power of a single coherence and continuity; the reduction of plurality to pluralism. But text and religion are unmasterable!

LOUI, Ronald P (ed) and KYBURG JR, Henry E (ed) and CARLSON, Greg N (ed). *Knowledge Representation and Defeasible Reasoning*. Norwell, Kluwer, 1990.

This is a collection of essays on the interface between computer science, philosophy, and linguistics. The volume is divided into four parts. The first is Defeasible Reasoning and the Frame Problem, with papers by Donald Nute, Lenhart Schubert, Hector Geffner and Judea Pearl, and Michael Dunn. Second, Representation Problems and Ordinary Language, with papers by Don Perlis, Brendan Gillon, Nuel Belnap and Michael Perloff, and Andrew McCafferty. The third part concerns Inference Rules and Belief Revision, and has papers by Charles Cross, Judea Pearl, Teddy Seidenfeld, and by Hugues LeBlanc and Peter Roeper. Finally, there are papers on Logical Problems in Representing Knowledge by Bob Carpenter and Richmond Thomason, Ronald Loui, Robin Giles, and Romas Aleliunas.

LOUI, Ronald. "Defeasible Specification of Utilities" in *Knowledge Representation and Defeasible Reasoning*, KYBURG JR, Henry E (ed), 345-359. Norwell, Kluwer, 1990.

Introduces the idea that decision analysis can be given a basis in defeasible reasoning. An analysis is an argument, for which there can be counterarguments and defeating arguments. Utilities calculated for states depend on the level of detail with which states are described. Further computation can increase the amount of detail as well as deepen decision trees.

LOUVEAU, Alain and SAINT-RAYMOND, Jean. On the Quasi-Ordering of Borel Linear Orders Under Embeddability. J Sym Log, 55(2), 537-560, Je 90.

We provide partial answers to the following problem: Is the class of Borel linear orders well-quasi-ordered under embeddability? We show that it is indeed the case for those Borel orders which are embeddable in R^{ω}, with the lexicographic ordering. For Borel orders embeddable in R^2, our proof works in ZFC, but it uses projective determinacy for Borel orders embeddable in some R^n, $n < \omega$, and hyperprojective determinacy for the general case.

LOVE, Nigel (ed). *The Foundations of Linguistic Theory: Selected Writings of Roy Harris*. New York, Routledge, 1990.

Roy Harris, Professor Emeritus of General Linguistics at Oxford, believes that modern linguistic theory has been led astray by the fact that we are capable intellectually of decontextualising our own verbal behaviour. An interlocking system of fallacious doctrines about forms, meanings and communication has arisen to support the idea that one particular kind of decontextualising analysis is a prerequisite for, rather than a retrospective reflection on, that behaviour. The thirteen essays in this volume collectively illuminate Harris's case for adopting this position, and point towards an alternative linguistics based on the assumption that language and languages cannot usefully be studied in abstraction from the lives, behaviour and beliefs of human beings.

LÖVENICH, F. Kompensierte Moderne. Tijdschr Filosof, 52(4), 637-666, D 90.

As a critic of modernity Nietzsche seems to be some kind of postmodernist avant la lettre. But his 'position' to modernity is far from simple and unambiguous: in his enlightenment of modernity radical modernism as well as extreme antimodernism are mingled dialectically. This can be shown in the development of his notion of genius (*Genie*). In the first place accepted by Nietzsche as an appropriate notion to characterize the critique of modernity as it has been uttered first in romanticism (*Romantik*), Nietzsche soon comes to realize that the Genie as an ideal of decadence also turns into an integrative concept of modernity. Therefore it has to be replaced in his philosophy by his notion of superman (*übermensch*) that in his opinion is able to avoid the 'estheticization of reality', i.e., the strategy of social and cultural integration by modern culture-industry, which seems to be the result of the ideology of the Genie.

LÖVENICH, Friedhelm. "Heiligsprechung des Imaginären: Das Imaginäre in Cornelius Castoriadis' Gesellschaftstheorie" in *The Social Horizon of Knowledge*, BUCZKOWSKI, Piotr (ed), 129-172. Amsterdam, Rodopi, 1991.

LOVEYS, James. Weakly Minimal Groups of Unbounded Exponent. J Sym Log, 55(3), 928-937, S 90.

LOVIBOND, Sabina. "Plato's Theory of Mind" in *Psychology (Companions to Ancient Thought: 2)*, EVERSON, Stephen (ed), 35-55. New York, Cambridge Univ Pr, 1991.

LOVIBOND, Sabina. True and False Pleasures. Proc Aris Soc, 90, 213-230, 1989-90.

LOVIN, Robin W (ed). *Critique and Construction: A Symposium on Roberto Unger's "Politics"*. New York, Cambridge Univ Pr, 1990.

Essays by legal scholars, social theorists, historians and philosophers assess the implications of Robert Unger's *Politics* for several fields of thought. The essays are not intended as reviews of *Politics* but take it as a starting point for reflection on the authors' own viewpoints and disciplines.

LÖW-BEER, Martin. Living a Life and the Problem of Existential Impossibility. Inquiry, 34(2), 217-236, Je 91.

Taylor's book *Sources of the Self* faces the tasks of showing how persons are situated in moral traditions and how these can be used in moral arguments. It is argued that a minimal version of the principle of equal respect is built into the structure of communication, so that we have no choice but to ask for the normative justification of relationships. (edited)

LÖW-BEER, Martin. *Selbsttäuschung*. Freiburg, Alber, 1991.

This book gives an analysis of self-deception. Löw-Beer argues for the thesis that the self-deceiver tries to solve problems by breaking basic rules of reasoning. The book includes discussions of Freud's theory of defense, Habermas' theory of distorted communication, Fingarette's theory of disavowal and Sartre's theory of mauvaise foi.

LOWE, E J. Jackson on Classifying Conditionals. Analysis, 51(3), 126-130, Je 91.

A criticism is presented of Frank Jackson's recent attempt to draw a semantic distinction between 'indicative' and 'subjunctive' conditionals in terms of their allegedly different relationships to two principles, dubbed 'Support' and 'Conditional non-contradiction'. It is argued that when due allowance is made for context-sensitivity, both kinds of conditional can be seen to relate in the same way to those principles.

LOWE, E J. Noun Phrases, Quantifiers, and Generic Names. Phil Quart, 41(164), 287-300, Jl 91.

Frege and Russell have taught us that indefinite and plural noun phrases in natural language often function as quantifier expressions rather than as referring expressions, despite possessing many syntactical similarities with names. But it can be shown that in some of their most important uses such noun phrases are indeed genuinely namelike in their logical behaviour and that on such occasions they can plausibly be taken to name *sorts* or *kinds*, conceived as universals rather than particulars. Orthodox quantificational logic cannot adequately represent such usage.

LOWE, E J. Real Selves: Persons as a Substantial Kind. Philosophy, 29, 87-107, 91 Supp.

Following a defence of a broadly Aristotelian conception of substance, three different views of the ontological status of persons are explored: persons as biological substances (Aristotle, David Wiggins), persons as psychological modes (Hume, Derek Parfit), and persons as psychological substances. Difficulties for the first and second views are presented and a non-Cartesian version of the third view is developed and defended which has some affinities to the position of P F Strawson.

LOWE, E J. Substance and Selfhood. Philosophy, 66(255), 81-99, Ja 91.

A self is defined to be a being which can identify itself as the necessarily unique subject of certain thoughts and experiences. Various traditional theories of the ontological status of the self, both substantival and nonsubstantival, are criticized and rejected. A substantival theory is proposed and defended according to which the self is a simple substance distinct but not necessarily separable from the body. This theory is shown to be consistent with a naturalistic, evolutionary view of the emergence of mind.

LOWE, Walter. "Freud, Husserl, Derrida: An Experiement" in *Phenomenology of the Truth Proper to Religion*, GUERRIÈRE, Daniel (ed), 205-218. Albany, SUNY Pr, 1990.

LOWENTHAL, David. Comment on Colmo's "Reason and Revelation in the Thought of Leo Strauss". Interpretation, 18(1), 161-162, Fall 90.

LÖWITH, Karl and GREEN, David E (trans). *From Hegel to Nietzsche: The Revolution in Nineteenth-Century Thought*. New York, Columbia Univ Pr, 1991.

LOWRY, Atherton C. Condemned to Time: The Limits of Merleau-Ponty's Quest for Being. Int Phil Quart, 31(3), 319-327, S 91.

LÖWY, Ilana. Medical Critique [Krytyka Lekarska]: A Journal of Medicine and Philosophy—1897-1907. J Med Phil, 15(6), 653-673, D 90.

Medico-philosophical reflections were developed in the 19th and the 20th centuries by three consecutive generations of Polish physicians, active in what was later named the Polish School of Philosophy of Medicine. The second generation of this school published its own journal, *Medical Critique* [*Krytika Lekarska*], from 1897 to 1907. *Medical Critique* included numerous articles on the nature of medical knowledge, the reductionism versus holism debate in biology and medicine, the importance of teleologically-oriented approaches in medicine, the influence of theories and of *a priori* ideas on clinical observations and on 'clinical facts', the problem of classification of diseases, the normative and ethical dimension of medicine, and the ion relationships between philosophy, history and medicine. The existence of a journal dealing specifically with theoretical reflections on medicine undoubtedly contributed to the propagation of original work in the philosophy of medicine in Poland.

LÖWY, Ilana. "The Scientific Roots of Constructivist Epistemologies" in *Études sur/Studies on Hélène Metzger*, FREUDENTHAL, Gad , 219-235. Leiden, Brill, 1990.

LUBAN, David. Smith Against the Ethicists. Law Phil, 9(4), 417-433, 1990-91.

LUBANSKI, M. A Note on the Nature of Mathematical Thinking (in Polish). Stud Phil Christ, 27(1), 55-69, 1991.

In this paper we study the character of mathematical thinking. We analyze some examples of mathematical thinking which come from diverse branches of mathematics. We opt for the thesis mentioned that thinking is content in character. Modern mathematics is a very complicated science: it contains many multidirectional domains, its conceptions like on diverse abstraction levels and it connects with the real world. Mathematics today is an "open" science, developed continually. Therefore, we propose that the classical philosophical problems of mathematics ought to be studied "from below", i.e., through the *a posteriori* way.

LÜBBE, Weyma. Der Normgeltungsbegriff als probabilistischer Begriff: Zur Logik des soziologischen Normbegriffs. Z Phil Forsch, 44(4), 583-602, 1990.

LUCAS JR, George R. African Famine: New Economic and Ethical Perspectives. J Phil, 87(11), 629-641, N 90.

Recurrent episodes of famine in Ethiopia, the Sudan, etc. are widely thought to be caused by severe drought, by resulting destruction of agricultural capability, by "desertification," or by war. I argue, on the basis of recent population and food production statistics, that these conventional causal hypotheses regarding famine are false, and that the data instead support an alternative "entitlement exchange" theory developed by Amartya Sen (1981; 1988). I then suggest some of the alternative conceptions of moral obligation and public policies that follow from this analysis.

LUCAS, J R. "Foreknowledge and the Vulnerability of God" in *The Philosophy in Christianity*, VESEY, Godfrey (ed), 119-128. New York, Cambridge Univ Pr, 1989.

LUCAS, J R. "Reason and Reality: A Prolegomenon to their Varieties" in *Harré and His Critics*, BHASKAR, Roy (ed), 41-47. Cambridge, Blackwell, 1990.

LUCAS, T and LAVENDHOMME, R. Varying Modal Theories. Notre Dame J Form Log, 31(3), 389-402, Sum 90.

The notion of modal theory is extended by accepting the idea that axioms and language itself vary over a plurality of possible worlds. Inference rules involving different worlds are introduced and completeness is proved by using a notion of 'ugly diagram', which is a graphical means of detecting when a family of modal theories has no model.

LUCASH, Frank. Spinoza on the Eternity of the Human Mind. Phil Theol, 5(2), 103-113, Wint 90.

Spinoza's ideas on the eternity of the human mind have sparked much controversy. As opposed to most commentators, I argue that since substance is eternal, and the human mind can only be conceived in substance, the human mind must also be eternal. Only from a finite and partial view can the human mind be conceived of as having duration.

LUCASH, Frank. Spinoza's Two Theories of Morality. Iyyun, 40(1), 37-50, Ja 91.

Spinoza proposes two views of good, a subjective one and an objective one. According to the subjective view good varies from person to person; according to the objective view there is only one good which is common to all human beings. These views do not contradict each other because of Spinoza's distinction between adequate and inadequate ideas, the infinite and the finite, and essence and existence. I raise the question whether Spinoza views the chief good from the standpoint of his own finite contingency.

LUCE, Lila. Platonism from an Empiricist Point of View. Phil Topics, 17(2), 109-128, Fall 89.

LUCKHARDT, C Grant. Philosophy in the *Big Typescript*: Philosophy as Trivial. Synthese, 87(2), 255-272, My 91.

LUCKHARDT, Grant. Response to Lyons' "Basic Rights and Constitutional Interpretations". Soc Theor Pract, 16(3), 359-368, Fall 90.

LUCY, W N R. Nozick's Identity Crisis. J Applied Phil, 7(2), 203-212, O 90.

Both the general structure of Nozick's entitlement theory of justice and the particular arguments he directs against Rawls presuppose a conception of the person. The essay argues that this initial conception of the person is flawed and that Nozick must amend it. However, those amendments lead either to an equally flawed conception or to a conception which is substantially similar to that which Rawls invokes. On either possibility the entitlement theory is weakened. The argument has two steps. First, the initial conception of the person which emerges from *Anarchy, State and Utopia* is stated. Second, the problems with that initial conception lead to the elucidation of subsequent conceptions, only the last of which is capable of avoiding those problems. The cost of avoidance is, however, a high one for Nozick's arguments against Rawls, in particular, and the entitlement theory in general.

LUDASSY, Mária. "The Origins of Some of Our Misconceptions" in *Perspectives on Ideas and Reality*, NYÍRI, J C (ed), 28-40. Budapest, Kiskonyvtara, 1990.

LUDEKING, K. "Does Analytic Aesthetics Rest on a Mistake?" in *XIth International Congress in Aesthetics, Nottingham 1988*, WOODFIELD, Richard (ed), 123-127. Nottingham, Nottingham Polytech, 1990.

LUDINGTON, David M. Smoking in Public: A Moral Imperative for the Most Toxic of Environmental Wastes. J Bus Ethics, 10(1), 23-27, Ja 91.

Cigarette smoke is the most dangerous of the toxic elements in our environment. Smoking is responsible for almost 500,000 deaths each year in the United States—more than any other environmental toxin. The medical evidence is clear, mainstream and sidestream smoke kills people, and anyone who participates in the spreading of this smoke is acting unethically. Yet, when there are no governmental laws that ban smoking in public, most businesspeople allow smoking in their places of business. These businesspeople are acting in an unethical manner, a manner which endangers customers and employees. This paper examines the impact on the environment of smoking in public and concludes that businesses must move quickly to ban smoking, or we will need nationwide, uniform legal restrictions to force ethical action in this critical area.

LUDLOW, Peter and NEALE, Stephen. Indefinite Descriptions: In Defense of Russell. Ling Phil, 14(2), 171-202, Ap 91.

LUDWIG, Dean and LONGENECKER, Clinton. Ethical Dilemmas in Performance Appraisal Revisited. J Bus Ethics, 9(12), 961-969, D 90.

In managers' dynamic, real-world environments, they often feel it is necessary to exercise some creative discretion over employee ratings. They justify the inaccuracy by citing, among other things, the need to avoid confrontation with subordinates, damaging working relationships, and creating permanent written documents which may later harm a subordinate's career. This paper examines the ethics of this sort of deliberate manipulation of performance appraisal systems, and suggests some duties and obligations for both the organization and the manager engaged in performance appraisal. (edited)

LUDWIG, G. "An Axiomatic Basis as a Desired Form of a Physical Theory" in *Logic, Methodology and Philosophy of Science, VIII*, FENSTAD, J E (ed), 447-457. New York, Elsevier Science, 1989.

LUEGENBIEHL, Heinz C. Codes of Ethics and the Moral Education of Engineers. Bus Prof Ethics J, 2(4), 41-61, Sum 83.

Codes of engineering ethics, while having received significant academic attention, have been little used by practicing engineers. I show that their neglect is based on specific weaknesses in the codes, including conflicts between different codes and ethical perplexities within codes. More fundamentally, the codes fail to account for a required professional autonomy of the individual engineer. I propose an alternative model for codes of ethics, based on a function of providing assistance in decision-making in novel situations. The nature of a noncoercive "guides for ethical engineering decision-making" is justified and outlined.

LUFT, David S (trans) and PIKE, Burton (trans) and MUSIL, Robert. Ruminations of a Slow-witted Mind. Crit Inquiry, 17(1), 46-61, Autumn 90.

Abridgement of drafts of an incisive essay Musil wrote in 1933 in reaction to the

Nazis coming to power in Germany. (Complete text in Musil, *Precision and Soul*, University of Chicago Press.) A penetrating contemporary analysis of the cultural sources and prospects of Naxism's effects on German politics, culture and society, and on the role of Jews and anti-semitism in Nazi iconography. Written from Musil's own experience and intellectual conscience as writer, editor, and analytical social thinker.

LUFT, Eric V D. Would Hegel Have Liked to Burn Down All the Churches and Replace Them with Philosophical Academies? Mod Sch, 68(1), 41-56, N 90.

LUGONES, Maria C. "On the Logic of Pluralist Feminism" in *Feminist Ethics*, CARD, Claudia (ed), 35-44. Lawrence, Univ Pr of Kansas, 1991.

LUGONES, Maria C. Structure/Antistructure and Agency under Oppression. J Phil, 87(10), 500-507, O 90.

LUHMANN, Niklas and BEDNARZ JR, John (trans). *Political Theory in the Welfare State*. Hawthorne, de Gruyter, 1990.

LUHMANN, Niklas. System-Theoretical Bases of Social Theory (in German). Deut Z Phil, 38(3), 277-284, 1990.

LUIK, John. "An Old Question Raised Yet Again: Is Kant an Enlightenment Humanist?" in *The Question of Humanism: Challenges and Possibilities*, GOICOECHEA, David (ed), 117-137. Buffalo, Prometheus, 1991.

LUIK, John (ed) and GOICOECHEA, David (ed) and MADIGAN, Tim (ed). *The Question of Humanism: Challenges and Possibilities*. Buffalo, Prometheus, 1991.

This volume of twenty-three papers on the ironies and ambiguities of humanism raises questions about: *The Varieties of Humanism, The Challenges to Humanism* and *The Enigmas of Humanism*. It is intended to be an introductory text for first-year philosophy students that they might not get oversimplified notions of humanism. Its conclusions form themselves in each reader as new beginnings for thinking, as such thinkers as: Plato, Aulus Gellius, Augustine, Pico, Kant, Heidegger, Foucault and Kurtz are allowed to dialogue.

LUIS DEL BARCO, José. Verdad e inteligibilidad: Los rasgos invariables de la teoría platónica de las ideas. Espiritu, 37(97), 45-72, Ja-Je 88.

LUIS DEL BARCO, José. Verdad e inteligibilidad: Los rasgos invariables de la doctrina platónica de las ideas. Espiritu, 38(100), 131-144, Jl-D 89.

LUIS DEL BARCO, José. Verdad e inteligibilidad: Los rasgos invariantes de la doctrina platónica de las ideas. Espiritu, 37(98), 119-135, Jl-D 88.

LUKAC DE STIER, María Liliana. Qué conocemos de dios? Hobbes versus Tomas. Logos (Mexico), 18(52), 59-71, Ja-Ap 90.

LUKACS, Anthony. "Television and the Aesthetics of Everyday Life" in *XIth International Congress in Aesthetics, Nottingham 1988*, WOODFIELD, Richard (ed), 128-130. Nottingham, Nottingham Polytech, 1990.

LUKÁCS, József. A Hungarian Christian-Marxist Dialogue and Its Lessons. Dialec Hum, 16(3-4), 33-46, Sum-Autumn 89.

LUKOWSKI, Piotr. Intuitionistic Sentential Calculus with Classical Identity. Bull Sect Log, 19(4), 147-151, D 90.

Sentential calculus with identity /SCI/ has been created by Professor R Suszko. The discussion on SCI was a subject of many works. The intuitionalistic weaking of this calculus /ISCI/ is presented in Pslukowski's "Intuitionistic sentential calculus with identity", *Bull Sect Log*, 19, 3. In fact SCI is a classical propositional calculus with classical identity, while ISCI intuitionistic propositional calculus with intuitionistic identity. Thus in the present paper two strengthenings of ISCI, i.e., intuitionistic propositional calculus with classical identity /ISCI CI/ and classical propositional calculus with intuitionistic identity /SCI II/ are considered. There are also presented adequate semantics for both calculi.

LUKOWSKI, Piotr. Intuitionistic Sentential Calculus with Identity. Bull Sect Log, 19(3), 92-99, O 90.

The paper concerns the intuitionistic sentential calculus with identity *ISCI*, mentioned by professor R Suszko in his several papers. The work presents a semantics for ISCI, which combines the ideas of the matrix semantics for sentential calculi with the well-known Kripke-Grzegorczyk for the intuitionistic logic. Besides sketching a proof of the *strong* completeness theorem for ISCI, there are some straightforward connections between the new semantical construction and the modeling of SCI, i.e., the ordinary calculus with identity. The end of the work deals with a simplified version of the frame-matrix semantics for the intuitionistic logic without sentential identity.

LUMPKIN, James R and VITELL, Scott J and RAWWAS, Mohammed Y A. Consumer Ethics: An Investigation of the Ethical Beliefs of Eldery Consumers. J Bus Ethics, 10(5), 365-375, My 91.

Business and especially marketing ethics have come to the forefront in recent years. While consumers have been surveyed regarding their perceptions of ethical business and marketing practices, research has been minimal with regard to their perceptions of ethical *consumer* practices. In addition, few studies have examined the ethical beliefs of elderly consumers even though they are an important and rapidly growing segment. This research investigates the relationship between Machiavellianism, ethical ideology and ethical beliefs for elderly consumers. The results indicate that elderly consumers, while generally being more ethical than young consumers, are diverse in their ethical beliefs.

LUNA, Concetta. Una nuova questioni di Egidio Romano "De subjecto theologiae". Frei Z Phil Theol, 37(3), 397-439, 1990.

A new question by Giles of Rome about the subject of theology has been recently discovered in ms. Padova, BU 844, a collection of Giles' sermons. The new question can be considered as a first draft of Giles' *Quodl*.III,2 and was probably written before his *Tractatus de subiecto theologiae*. The article analyses also the chronological relationship of Giles' *Quodl*.III,2 with Henry of Ghent *Quodl*.XII,1 and Godrey of Fontaines' *Quodl*.I,5 and furnishes a first critical edition of the following texts: 1) Giles' new question *De subiecto theologiae*, 2) Giles' *Tractatus de subiecto theologiae*, 3) an anonymous question *De subiecto theologiae* (ms. Toulouse, BM 739).

LUNN, Forrest. Foucault and The Referent. Gnosis, 3(3), 73-88, D 90.

LUNTLEY, Michael. Aberrations of a Sledgehammer: Reply to Devitt. Phil Stud, 62(3), 315-323, Je 91.

LUNTLEY, Michael. *The Meaning of Socialism*. La Salle, Open Court, 1991.

Socialism is a philosophical practice devoted to the description of what is good for society. The good of society—which grows out of the ethical traditions of the community—provides the authority for collective action and interference in free market economics. It provides also the basis for our reflections on freedom, justice, democracy and citizenship. This book defends the priority of the Good over the Right, and the authority of the Good as the basis of legitimation for political action without threatening totalitarianism. This book argues that it is on such broadly communitarian lines that the development of socialism should be based.

LUPER-FOY, Steven. The Anatomy of Aggression. Amer Phil Quart, 27(3), 213-224, Jl 90.

I offer an analysis of competition, aggression, and related phenomena, and describe certain values whose pursuit leads to aggression and war. I then argue that we ought to abandon those values, and close with the suggestion that an interest in equality might be one of the values we ought to give up.

LUPER-FOY, Steven. "Arbitrary Reasons" in *Doubting: Contemporary Perspectives on Skepticism*, ROTH, Michael D (ed), 39-55. Norwell, Kluwer, 1990.

Practical skepticism says that because we ultimately have no reason to do one thing rather than another, we should do nothing. Theoretical skepticism says that since ultimately we have no reason to believe anything about the way things are, our views should all be dropped. Foundationalism and coherentism are both ways of trying to show that since our beliefs need not be arbitrary, the skeptic has no grounds for saying we should abandon them. Neither questions the skeptic's fundamental assumption that we ought to avoid all arbitrary beliefs and acts. Precisely this assumption is my target. Once it is rejected, we can say that even *if* our beliefs and acts ultimately are arbitrary, the skeptic cannot conclude that we should stop believing and acting. The skeptic's position no longer will be a threat to knowledge claims.

LURIE, Yuval. Scharfstein as a Metaphysician of Art (in Hebrew). Iyyun, 39(4), 441-460, O 90.

In his *Of Birds, Beasts, and Other Artists: An Essay on the Universality of Art*, Scharfstein constructs a metaphysical structure for artistic activities. I argue that the concept of singing and dancing apply to birds only in a poetic way; that the contrast between genius and talent is insightful for artistic activities and modernity; that the mystic element in art can be experienced in different ways: by creation and by observation.

LÜTHE, Rudolf. *David Hume: Historiker und Philosoph*. Freiburg, Alber, 1991.

This book describes David Hume's philosophy in terms of the groundwork for an empirical study of human beings and takes as a main theme the systematic relationship throughout Hume's works between philosophical reflection and historical experience. The first part of the book presents and explicates central portions of text taken from areas concerned with the theory of knowledge, the theory of the emotions, ethics, and the critique of religion. On the basis of these extracts, the second part of the work develops important results relating to Hume's historical works. Thus Hume's teachings on the theory of the state and the sociology of religion are dealt with in as much detail as his methodology of historical research. The key to understanding Hume's corpus is shown to be his anthropological thesis to the effect that human beings are governed more by emotions than by reason.

LÜTTERFELDS, Wilhelm. Does Wittgenstein's Concept of Language Game Patterns Come Up with a Solution to the Platonic Problem ... (in German). Deut Z Phil, 38(10), 940-943, 1990.

Der Begriff des Sprachspielparadigmas hat bei Wittgenstein die paradoxe Funktion eines Musters: Einerseits ist es ein Instrument der sprachlichen Darstellung, mit dem aller Ausdrucksgebrauch verglichen werden muss, soll er korrekt sein, was jedoch voraussetzt, dass das Paradigma die Muster-Eigenschaft selber besitzt; andererseits hat es die Funktion, die Referenz eines Ausdrucks allerest festzulegen, so dass das Paradigma die Muster-Eigenschaft selber nicht haben kann. Damit gerät Wittgenstein's Paradigmen-Begriff in den platonischen Selbstwiderspruch der Selbstprädikation, nach dem ideelle Paradigmen die Muster-Eigenschaft selber haben müssen und zugleich selber nicht haben können ("Die Grösse ist selber gross und nicht gross"). Diese Paradoxie kennzeichnet auch Kripkes Theorie des "Urmeters".

LUTTWAK, Edward N. "Strategy: A New Era?" in *The Tanner Lectures On Human Values, Volume XII*, PETERSON, Grethe B (ed), 1-53. Salt Lake City, Univ of Utah Pr, 1991.

LUUTZ, Wolfgang. Social Communication and Interest Relationships (in German). Deut Z Phil, 38(5), 443-447, 1990.

In this article the function of the social communication is examined by the struggle between contradictive interests. The author starts with a criticism of the conception of the "objective nature of the interests" in Marxist philosophy. In this connection he explains a dialogical interpretation of the interest constitution and examines the role of communicative needs by the intervention between contradictive moments of personal interests. The model of interest intervention in real socialism was characterized by a neglect of motivational role of social communication.

LUZZATTO, Stefano. Is Philosophy Detrimental to Mathematics Education? Phil Math, 6(1), 65-72, 1991.

LY, Gabriel. From Immanentism to Atheism. Asian J Phil, 2(1), 25-41, Sum 90.

LYCAN, William G. *Even* and *Even If*. Ling Phil, 14(2), 115-150, Ap 91.

It is argued that the English word "even" contributes to the truth-conditions of sentences in which it appears; specifically, "even" is a quantifier, a near-contrary of "only." Once this theory is in place, one can see why the conditional construction "even if" has the features it does.

LYCAN, William G. Logical Constants and the Glory of Truth-Conditional Semantics. Notre Dame J Form Log, 30(3), 390-400, Sum 89.

This paper endorses and defends M J Cresswell's view that the distinction drawn in linguistic semantics between strictly "logical" implication and merely lexical implication is bogus, and then explores the bad consequences that concession has for the Davidsonian semantic program. A pattern of semantic explanation made famous by Davidson's "The logical form of action sentences" is shown to be far less interesting than has been thought.

LYCAN, William G (ed). *Mind and Cognition: A Reader*. Cambridge, Blackwell, 1989.

A collection of contemporary readings in the philosophy of mind and cognitive science. Sections on Ontology from Behaviorism to Functionalism; Homuncular Functionalism and Other Teleological Theories; Instrumentalism; Eliminativism and Neurophilosophy; The "Language of Thought" Hypothesis; The Status of "Folk Psychology"; Consciousness, "Qualia" and Subjectivity; and Special Topics.

LYCAN, William G. On Respecting Puzzles About Belief Ascription (A Reply to Devitt). Pac Phil Quart, 71(3), 182-188, S 90.

This paper defends the author's "Two-Scheme" theory of belief content against some objections raised by Michael Devitt, and then applies the theory to some new puzzle cases. An interesting Sellarsian feature of the theory emerges, that gives it a noteworthy advantage over pure "Direct Reference" views of belief sentences.

LYCAN, William G. Pot Bites Kettle: A Reply to Miller. Austl J Phil, 69(2), 212-213, Je 91.

LYCAN, William G. "Semantics and Methodological Solipsism" in *Truth and Interpretation: Perspectives on the Philosophy of Donald Davidson*, LE PORE, Ernest (ed), 245-261. Cambridge, Blackwell, 1986.

LYCAN, William G. "What Is the 'Subjectivity' of the Mental?" in *Philosophical Perspectives, 4: Action Theory and Philosophy of Mind, 1990*, TOMBERLIN, James E (ed), 109-130. Atascadero, Ridgeview, 1990.

LYCAN, William G. Why We Should Care Whether Our Beliefs Are True. Phil Phenomenol Res, 51(1), 201-205, Mr 91.

LYMAN, Stanford M. Animal Faith, Puritanism, and the Schutz-Gurwitsch Debate: A Commentary. Human Stud, 14(2-3), 199-206, Jl 91.

It might be the case that a resolution of the Schutz-Gurwitsch debate on perspective can be obtained by treating the matter in terms of the fundamental changes in the bases of morality in the civil societies of the twentieth century. Santayana's outlook in *The Last Puritan* marks a fundamental break in the modern world; we can treat the Schutz-Gurwitsch debate as emblematic of the shift after that break—the movement from a society marked by an essentially intersubjective faith in the value of truth of both self and other to one that is characterized by the delegitimation of faith altogether. In the latter society, there is an agonizing quest for trust, but it is accompanied by a deep and widespread mistrust of everyone and everything.

LYNCH, Dennis A. Ernst Cassirer and Martin Heidegger: The Davos Debate. Kantstudien, 81(3), 360-370, 1990.

LYNCH, Michael. Science in the Age of Mechanical Reproduction: Moral and Epistemic Relations Between Diagrams and Photographs. Biol Phil, 6(2), 205-226, Ap 91.

Sociologists, philosophers and historians of science are gradually recognizing the importance of visual representation. This paper focuses on diagrams in biology, and tries to demonstrate how diagrams are an integral part of the production of scientific knowledge. In order to disclose some of the distinctive practical and analytical uses of diagrams, the paper contrasts the way diagrams and photographs are used in biological texts. (edited)

LYNCH, William T. Politics in Hobbes' Mechanics: The Social as Enabling. Stud Hist Phil Sci, 22(2), 295-320, Je 91.

This study traces the effect of a preexisting political agenda, concerned with threats to civil authority, upon Hobbes's approach to mechanical philosophy. In contrast to Shapin and Schaffer's more holistic approach, a multitude of intervening causes, having some degree of logical independence from Hobbes's political agenda, increasingly constrain the form of mechanical philosophy produced. Hobbes's political agenda is shown to provide the context for his critique of Descartes's *Meditations* and of Thomas White's *De Mundo*. Attention to the counterfactual import of historical claims suggests that the social nature of knowledge be seen as simultaneously constraining and enabling.

LYNGZEIDETSON, Albert E. Massively Parallel Distributed Processing and a Computationalist Foundation for Cognitive Science. Brit J Phil Sci, 41(1), 121-127, Mr 90.

My purpose in this brief paper is to consider the implications of a radically different computer architecture to some fundamental problems in the foundations of Cognitive Science. More exactly, I wish to consider the ramifications of the 'Godel-Minds-Machines' controversy of the late 1960s on a dynamically changing computer architecture which, I venture to suggest, is going to revolutionize which 'functions' of the human mind can and cannot be modelled by (non-human) computational automata. I will proceed on the presupposition that the reader is familiar with some of the fundamentals of computational theory and mathematical logic.

LYNN, Joanne and GLOVER, Jacqueline. Cruzan and Caring for Others. Hastings Center Rep, 20(5), 10-11, S-O 90.

This response to the policy issues decided by the U S Supreme Court's opinion in *Cruzan* aims to illuminate the folly of creating barriers to good decision-making about whether or not to use life-sustaining medical treatment and to encourage health care providers to care for their patients by advocating changes in such legal restrictions. Cruzan's positive contributions are noted, but the practical problems of excluding family views and allowing the states to insist upon a high standard of proof before relying on the patient's prior decisions are serious shortcomings of the ruling.

LYNN, Joanne and KOSHUTA, Monica A and SCHMITZ, Phyllis J. Development of an Institutional Policy on Artificial Hydration and Nutrition. Kennedy Inst Ethics J, 1(2), 133-139, Je 91.

The issues involved in deciding whether to use artificial methods of delivering hydration and nutrition are often very difficult for patients, families, and health care providers. Once private and personal matters, these decisions now frequently involve the judicial system. Five years ago, Hospice of Washington recognized the need for a written policy and wrote the one published here. Its goal is to respect individual preferences and family concerns while addressing the nutrition and hydration needs of dying patients. The policy sets parameters on the issue, provides basic information, and encourages crafting the most fitting resolution to each situation.

LYONS, David. Basic Rights and Constitutional Interpretation. Soc Theor Pract, 16(3), 337-357, Fall 90.

Chief Justice Taney invoked "original intent" to argue in the Dred Scott case that free African-Americans could not be US citizens. But "original intent" arguments are ambiguous, and original intent theory generally ignores their presupposition of an intentional consensus. "Original intent" arguments not making value-free purely historical claims do not presuppose such a consensus because they identify a justifying rationale that accords with the legal text and its historical context. This reconstruction of original intent reasoning is illustrated in connection with Oliver North's separation of powers challenge to the legislative authorization for independent prosecutors.

LYONS, Willia. Intentionality and Modern Philosophical Psychology—II: The Return to Representation. Phil Psych, 4(1), 83-102, 1991.

In rounded terms and modern dress a theory of intentionality is a theory about how humans take in information via the senses and in the very process of taking it in understand it and, most often, make subsequent use of it in guiding human behaviour. The problem of intentionality in this century has been the problem of providing an adequate explanation of how a purely physical causal system, the brain, can both receive information and at the same time understand it, that is, to put it even more briefly, how a brain can have semantic content. In two articles, on in the previous number of the journal and this present one, I engage in a critical examination of the two most thoroughly canvassed approaches to the theory and problem of intentionality in philosophical psychology over the last 100 years. In the first article, subtitled 'The modern reduction of intentionality', I examined the reductive approach pioneered by Carnap and reaching its apotheosis in the work of Daniel Dennett. In this second article, subtitled 'The return to representation', I examine the approach which can be traced back to the work of Noam Chomsky but which has been given its canonical treatment in the work of Jerry Fodor.

LYONS, William. Intentionality and Modern Philosophical Psychology, I: The Modern Reduction of Intentionality. Phil Psych, 3(2-3), 247-269, 1990.

In rounded terms and modern dress a theory of intentionality is a theory about how humans take in information via the senses and in the very process of taking it in understand it and, most often, make subsequent use of it in guiding human behaviour. The problem of intentionality in this century has been the problem of providing an adequate explanation of how a purely physical causal system, the brain, can both receive information and at the same time understand it, that is, to put it even more briefly, how a brain can have semantic content. In these two articles, one in this issue of the journal and one in the next, I engage in a critical examination of the two most thoroughly canvassed approaches to the theory and problem of intentionality in philosophical psychology over the last hundred years. In the first article, entitled "The Modern Reduction of Intentionality," I examine the approach pioneered by Carnap and reaching its apotheosis in the work of Daniel Dennett. In the second article, entitled "The Return to Representation," I examine the approach which can be traced back to the work of Noam Chomsky but which has been given its canonical treatment in the work of Jerry Fodor.

LYOTARD, Jean-François. La réflexion dans l'esthétique kantienne. Rev Int Phil, 44(175), 507-551, 1990.

LYSONSKI, Steven and GAIDIS, William. A Cross-Cultural Comparison of the Ethics of Business Students. J Bus Ethics, 10(2), 141-150, F 91.

The ethical tendencies of university business students from the USA, Denmark, and New Zealand were examined by analyzing their reactions to ethical dilemmas presented in a set of ethical problem situations. These dilemmas dealt with coercion and control, conflict of interest, physical environment, paternalism and personal integrity. Findings indicate that students' reactions tended to be similar regardless of their country. A comparison of these findings to practicing managers indicated that students and practicing managers exhibit a similar degree of sensitivity to ethical dimensions of business decison making. Implications are drawn for business education and further research.

LYSONSKI, Steven and SINGER, Alan E and SINGER, Ming and HAYES, David. Ethical Myopia: The Case of "Framing" by Framing. J Bus Ethics, 10(1), 29-36, Ja 91.

The behavioural decision-theoretic concepts of mental accounting, framing and transaction utility have now been employed in marketing models and techniques. To date, however, there has not been any discussion of the ethical issues surrounding these significant developments. In this paper, an ethical evaluation is structured around three themes: (i) utilitarian justification, (ii) the strategic exploitation of cognitive habits, and (iii) the claim of scientific status for the techniques. Some recommendations are made for ethical practices.

MAC CORMAC, Earl R. Metaphor and Pluralism. Monist, 73(3), 411-420, Jl 90.

MAC DONALD, Scott. Ultimate Ends in Practical Reasoning. Phil Rev, 100(1), 31-66, Ja 91.

This paper defends Aquinas's Aristotelian argument for the claim that there is a single ultimate end of human life against the charge that it involves an illicit transition from 'all chains must stop somewhere' to 'there is somewhere where all chains must stop'. Aquinas argues, successively and separately, that (A) each human action is for the sake of some end, (B) each human action is for the sake of some ultimate end, (C) there is some single ultimate end for the sake of which all the human actions of an individual human being are done, and (D) there is some single ultimate end for the sake of which all human actions are done. The paper claims that his arguments for (A)-(D) are cogent and suggest a powerful account of practical rationality that both clarifies the nature of teleological theories of practical rationality and provides resources for replying to common objections to theories of that sort.

MAC GREGOR, Geddes. *Dictionary of Religion and Philosophy*. New York, Paragon House, 1989.

This monograph (696 pages, 1392 columns) is designed as a practical tool for students. Since serious study of religion entails understanding of its philosophical implicates, the 3000+ entries include thinkers such as Kant and Peirce, and topics such as meaning/truth, logical fallacies, Vienna Circle, mind-body, and contemporary bioethical questions. Despite an especially detailed exploration of the Judeo-Christian tradition, not only is a wide spectrum of the world's religions represented (e.g., Hinduism, Islam, Zoroastrianism); so are many modern religious movements (e.g., Eckankar, Rastafarians). The classified bibliographies (36 columns) represent 24 areas (e.g., afterlife, biblical studies, bioethics, and Zen).

MAC INTOSH, Duncan. McClennen's Early Cooperative Solution to the Prisoner's Dilemma. S J Phil, 29(3), 341-358, Fall 91.

MAC INTOSH, Duncan. Retaliation Rationalized: Gauthier's Solution to the Deterrence Dilemma. Pac Phil Quart, 72(1), 9-32, Mr 91.

Gauthier claims: *1) a non-maximizing action is rational if it maximized to intend it.* If one intended to retaliate in order to deter an attack, *2) retaliation is rational*, for it maximized to intend it. I argue that even on sympathetic theories of intentions, actions and choices, *1)* is incoherent. But I defend *2)* by arguing that an action is rational if it maximizes on preferences it maximized to adopt given one's antecedent preferences. *2)* is true because it maximized to adopt preferences on which it maximizes to retaliate. I thus save the theory that rational actions must maximize, and extend it into the rational criticism of preferences.

MAC INTYRE, Alasdair. Community, Law, and the Idiom and Rhetoric of Rights. Listening, 26(2), 96-110, Spr 91.

A distinctively modern idiom and rhetoric of rights has generated rationally unresolvable conflicts. The genesis of this idiom and rhetoric can only be understood by specifying the necessary conditions for rational debate about shared moral norms within a society. These conditions can be satisfied only in a type of community structured in terms of a particular conception of law, one which requires a very different account of rights.

MAC INTYRE, Alasdair. Individual and Social Morality in Japan and the United States: Rival Conceptions of the Self. Phil East West, 40(4), 489-497, O 90.

Comparisons of Japanese and American ways of life in terms of contrasting emphases upon the individual and the social are challenged by the suggestion that Japanese conceptions of the individual and the social differ from American suggestions. Distinguishing features of Japanese conceptions include those which explain why Aristotelian views of the self are alien to Japanese thought and why Japanese modes of self-understanding afford no conceptual space for the other minds problem.

MAC INTYRE, Alasdair. Moral Dilemmas. Phil Phenomenol Res, 50 SUPP, 367-382, Fall 90.

Against theses of Bernard Williams and Bas C van Fraassen, it is argued that there are no facts about moral dilemmas, characterizable independently of any moral theory. It is further argued that any adequate theory which denies that there are genuine moral dilemmas must provide a convincing account of how and why moral agents take themselves to be in dilemmatic situations. The ability of rationalist theories, which deny that genuine moral dilemmas occur, to provide such account is examined. Aquinas's contribution receives particular attention.

MAC INTYRE, Alasdair. Précis of "Whose Justice? Which Rationality?". Phil Phenomenol Res, 51(1), 149-152, Mr 91.

Central to *Whose Justice? Which Rationality?* is the project of distinguishing between the standards appropriate to judging the rival claims about justice of philosophers working within the same socially embodied tradition of rational enquiry and those appropriate to judging the rival claims about justice of philosophers working within very different such traditions. When these are distinguished, it becomes clear that there is no such thing as tradition-independent rational enquiry, but that this does not afford support to relativist conclusions.

MAC INTYRE, Alasdair. Reply to Dahl, Baier and Schneewind. Phil Phenomenol Res, 51(1), 169-178, Mr 91.

The differences between Baier and myself arise from different conceptions of how social agreement is related to practices involving moral judgment and from incompatible understandings of the narrative of eighteenth century Scottish philosophy. Against Dahl I suggest that his arguments about Aristotelian practical rationality deprive *phronesis* of its place in that rationality and that those concerning relativism involve a misconstrual of my position. Against Schneewind I elucidate my conception of traditional further and argue that his claims about tradition-independent enquiry encounter serious difficulties.

MAC INTYRE, Ian. The Pareto Rule and Strategic Voting. Theor Decis, 31(1), 1-19, Jl 91.

This paper uses a particular choice rule over *sets* of alternatives under the Pareto rule. Starting from the sincere situation every strategic misrevelation of preference is shown to be an improvement for all voters. The existence of an equilibrium under successive misrepresentations by sincere voters is demonstrated.

MAC KENZIE, Ann Wilbur. Descartes on Sensory Representation: A Study of the *Dioptrics*. Can J Phil, SUPP 16, 109-147, 1990.

MAC KINNON, Donald M. Does Faith Create Its Own Objects? Relig Stud, 26(4), 439-451, D 90.

MACDONALD, Bradley J. Political Theory and Cultural Criticism: Towards a Theory of Cultural Politics. Hist Polit Thought, 11(3), 509-528, Autumn 90.

MACDONALD, Cynthia and MACDONALD, Graham. Mental Causation and Non-Reductive Monism. Analysis, 51(1), 23-32, Ja 91.

Non-reductive monism has been repeatedly subjected to the objection that it leads either to inconsistency or to epiphenomenalism. The authors respond to a recent charge that an earlier attempt of theirs to deal with this objection fails. They argue that the charge assumes a view of events as tropes, whereas non-reductive monism assumes a view of events as property exemplifications, and that the argument for non-reductive monism only leads to inconsistency or to epiphenomenalism on the assumption that events are tropes. However, non-reductive monists will reject this assumption for reasons which the authors outline.

MACDONALD, Graham and MACDONALD, Cynthia. Mental Causation and Non-Reductive Monism. Analysis, 51(1), 23-32, Ja 91.

Non-reductive monism has been repeatedly subjected to the objection that it leads either to inconsistency or to epiphenomenalism. The authors respond to a recent charge that an earlier attempt of theirs to deal with this objection fails. They argue that the charge assumes a view of events as tropes, whereas non-reductive monism assumes a view of events as property exemplifications, and that the argument for non-reductive monism only leads to inconsistency or to epiphenomenalism on the assumption that events are tropes. However, non-reductive monists will reject this assumption for reasons which the authors outline.

MACER, Darryl. New Creations? Commentary. Hastings Center Rep, 21(1), 32-33, Ja-F 91.

Ethical issues arising from the use of animal and human embryonic stem cell lines are discussed. Research in genetics is aided by some animal research, but the production of random mutations in transgenic animals has little ethical support from the principle of beneficence. The ethical guidelines, standards and limits of transgenic animal research need to be reexamined. The use of human embryonic stem cells makes us ask what the limits of human experimentation will be. If regulations are developed and enforced then society may not need to be so afraid of the slippery slope.

MACER, Darryl. *Shaping Genes: Ethics, Law and Science of Using Genetic Technology in Medicine and Agriculture*. Christchurch, Eubios Ethics Inst, 1990.

The ethics, law and science of genetic and reproductive technology in agriculture and medicine, and the associated literature, is reviewed and discussed. Bioethical approaches are suggested, together with identification of key questions that need resolving to solve such issues. Genetic engineering makes us think about questions that have existed long before the technology was developed, but in new ways and with a greater sense of urgency. International regulations are contrasted, and suggestions made on key points for the introduction and upgrading of regulations safeguarding the environment, animals and human autonomy and justice.

MACER, Darryl. Whose Genome Project? Bioethics, 5(3), 183-211, Jl 91.

The human genome project is an international effort to map and sequence the human genome, and originates with the work of numerous scientists during the twentieth century. The DNA sequence is shared by all human beings and thus could be said to be common property, and thus in accord with the United Nations Declaration of Human Rights, Article 27, all humanity should share in the scientific advancement and benefits. The decisions taken should include representatives of all people of the world, not just the funders of the scientific project. An international committee should be convened to consider the long range and universal ethical, social, and legal issues associated with this project.

MACHAMER, Peter K and BOYLAN, Barbara. Ethics and News. Bus Prof Ethics J, 9(1-2), 53-64, Spr-Sum 90.

In this paper we consider a number of examples of ways in which ethical conflicts arise for professionals covering the news. The first part of the paper raises problems concerning the nature of news and the responsibilities of news professionals. The second part of the paper sketchily provides a way of thinking about professional ethics that can be applied to our problems about the news. We offer a few suggestions to resolve some of the conflicts that we have raised.

MACHAN, Tibor R. Do Animals Have Rights? Pub Affairs Quart, 5(2), 163-173, Ap 91.

This paper argues that the conditions for possessing rights, namely, (metaphysical) free choice and moral responsibility, are not found in those animals considered by animal rights advocates to possess rights (e.g., Tom Reagan). It is also argued that contemporary evolutionary theory does not invalidate basic differences between species of animals. As M Adler shows, "modern theorists [of evolution] treat distinct species as natural kinds, not as man-made class distinctions." Thus it is not just a matter of degree but of kind that human beings are distinct from other animals and that what distinguishes them gives rise to distinct moral and political categories.

MACHAN, Tibor R. Exploring Extreme Violence (Torture). J Soc Phil, 21(1), 92-97, Spr 90.

In this paper I argue that while it may on occasion be morally proper to use extreme violence (e.g., torture) against someone, that is not to say that it is ever legally proper, in a just social order, to do the same. I explain why this is so and defend the position against what I take to be reasonable doubts.

MACHAN, Tibor R. Response: Subjective Values and Objective Values. Vera Lex, 10(2), 22, 1990.

This note is a brief clarification of the distinction between intrinsic or innate and objective (yet person relative) values. It contributes to the discussion in my *Capitalism and Individualism* (St. Martin Press, 1990) of the prominent classical liberal view of *unique* individuals and their supposedly subjective values versus the more plausible view of *human* individuals and their objective (yet diverse and individual-relative) values.

MACHIAVELLI, Niccolò and PAREL, A J (ed & trans). Allocution Made to a Magistrate. Polit Theory, 18(4), 525-527, N 90.

This is the first English translation of Machiavelli's oration on justice. He wrote this oration in the *protestatio de justitia* style of Florentine humanism, but probably did not deliver it himself. The value of this oration lies in the fact that it shows that Machiavelli had a sound grasp of the classical and the Christian conceptions of justice. It adds to our knowledge of Machiavelli's thought on an important issue.

MACHO, Thomas H. A Contribution to the Early History of Psychoanalysis (in Serbo-Croatian). Filozof Istraz, 32-33(5-6), 1641-1652, 1989.

In diesem Beitrag wird die in der Zeitschrift *Psyche* zwischen 1983 und 1987 entfachte Diskussion um die begriffsgeschichtliche Herkunft des Es, einer bekanntlich zentralen Kategorie Sigmund Freuds, fortgesetzt. Bemerkenswert erscheint an dieser Debatte in erster Linie ein impliziter Konsens der streitenden Experten: cum grano salis wird die philosophische Vorgeschichte der Psychoanalyse auf die 2. Hälfte des 19. Jahrhunderts datiert, wogegen sich zahlreiche wissenschaftliche Indizien geltend machen lassen. Es eröffnen sich die Fragen, die erst auf dem Boden einer neuen Allianz zwischen transzendentaler Anthropologie und Psychoanalyse gestellt, geschweige denn beantwortet werden können.

MACINTYRE, Angus. Rationality of *p*-Adic Poincaré Series: Uniformity in *p*. Annals Pure Applied Log, 49(1), 31-74, S 90.

MACINTYRE, Angus. Schanuel's Conjecture and Free Exponential Rings. Annals Pure Applied Log, 51(3), 241-246, Mr 91.

MACK, Eric. Self-Ownership and the Right of Property. Monist, 73(4), 519-543, O 90.

Classical liberal attempts to ground particular property rights entirely in particular exercises of "internal" self-ownership rights which expand the territory encompassed by that internal right are criticized. Limiting natural rights to such "internal" rights fails to give due recognition to the essential role of interaction with the external world in human life. Due recognition requires an "external" right to the practice of private property, i.e., to others' compliance with a set of rules which specify a system of entitlement-conferring actions which is coherent, functional and comprehensive and itself respects self-ownership.

MACKENZIE, Jim. Four Dialogue Systems. Stud Log, 49(4), 567-583, D 90.

The paper describes four dialogue systems, developed in the tradition of Charles Hamblin. The first system provides and answer for Achilles in Lewis Carroll's parable, the second and analysis of the fallacy of begging the question, the third a non-psychologistic account of conversational implicature, and the fourth and analysis of equivocation and of objections to it. Each avoids combinatorial explosions, and is intended for real-time operation.

MACKIE, Penelope. Causing, Enabling, and Counterfactual Dependence. Phil Stud, 62(3), 325-330, Je 91.

MACKLER, Aaron L. Judaism, Justice, and Access to Health Care. Kennedy Inst Ethics J, 1(2), 143-161, Je 91.

This paper develops the traditional Jewish understanding of justice (*tzedakah*) and support for the needy, especially as related to the provision of medical care. After an examination of justice in the Hebrew Bible, the values and institutions of *tzedakah* in Rabbinic Judaism are explored, with a focus on legal codes and enforceable obligations. A standard of societal responsibility to provide for the basic needs of all, with a special obligation to save lives, emerges. A Jewish view of justice in access to health care is developed on the basis of this general standard, as well as explicit discussion in legal sources. Society is responsible for the securing of access to all health care needed by any individual. Elucidation of this standard of need and corresponding societal obligations, and the significance of the Jewish model for the contemporary United States, are considered.

MACKLIN, Ruth. Artificial Means of Reproduction and Our Understanding of the Family. Hastings Center Rep, 21(1), 5-11, Ja-F 91.

MACKOR, Anne Ruth. Functionalisme versus dubbelaspecttheorie: tertium datur. Alg Ned Tijdschr Wijs, 83(1), 38-60, Ja 91.

This article is a critical reaction to a position recently defended by Meysing in an article in the *ANTW* and in her book *Mens of machine?* Meysing argues that physicalism does not offer an adequate 'foundation' for cognitive science nor a solution for the mind-body problem. She argues that the 'double aspect-theory' does a better job in both respects. Meysing claims to have refuted all forms on noneliminative physicalism, but she in fact only analyzes those physicalist theories that regard mental states as formal, computational states. In consequence she does not take into account one important noneliminative physicalist theory: the theory of John Searle. I argue that, although Searle's theory does not offer a foundation for cognitive science, it does solve the mind-body problem. I further show that Meysing's own answer to the mind-body problem is inadequate. (edited)

MACLEAN, Ian (trans) and MOLNAR, Miklós. "The Hungarian Intellectual and the Choice of Commitment or Neutrality" in *The Political Responsibility of Intellectuals*, MACLEAN, Ian (ed), 189-200. New York, Cambridge Univ Pr, 1990.

The author sets out to answer the question: how should intellectuals behave when faced with unpalable oral or political choices? He takes three examples from nineteenth-century Hungary—Ferenc Kazinczy, István Széchenyi and Károly Eötvös—to show the practical problems involved in choosing a course of action in difficult circumstances.

MACLEAN, Ian (ed) and MONTEFIORE, Alan (ed) and WINCH, Peter (ed). *The Political Responsibility of Intellectuals*. New York, Cambridge Univ Pr, 1990.

The many problems encountered in defining the relationship of intellectuals to the society in which they live are addressed in this book. Specialists in various disciplines from the United States, Great Britain, France, Holland, Poland and Hungary set out to explore the following issues: in what respects are intellectuals responsible for and to their societies? Should they seek to act as an independent arbiters of the values of those societies? Should they seek to give advice in the public domain, or should they withdraw from all involvement with politics? How should their preoccupation with truth and language find practical expression?

MACLEAN, Ian. "Responsibility and the Act of Interpretation: The Case of Law" in *The Political Responsibility of Intellectuals*, MACLEAN, Ian (ed), 161-187. New York, Cambridge Univ Pr, 1990.

This paper explores the relationship between truth-telling, good faith and meaning as arises in the drafting, interpretation and appreciation of the written text of the law. It is argued that no satisfactory notation for good faith in language exists, but that this is paradoxically a feature of democratic societies espoused to such values as virtue, truthfulness, justice and reason. The distinction between responsible and irresponsible uses of language, even in the domain of the law, can only be made contingently, and needs continual monitoring.

MACMILLAN, C J B. PES and the APA—An Impressionistic History. Educ Theor, 41(3), 275-286, Sum 91.

MACMILLAN, C J B. Telling Stories About Teaching. Proc Phil Educ, 46, 198-201, 1990.

MACNAMARA, John. The Development of Moral Reasoning and the Foundations of Geometry. J Theor Soc Behav, 21(2), 125-150, Je 91.

The paper criticizes the Piaget/Kohlberg theory of the development of moral reasoning in children. The main grounds for criticism are the theory's inability to illuminate the learning of the set of primitive expressions for moral discourse. In this it is contrasted with Hilbert's introduction of the set of primitives for geometry. Some analogies with Hilbert's use of ideal elements are suggested. This line of thought leads to the Brentano/Aquinas/Aristotle tradition, which appeals to basic unlearned principles of moral reasoning that generate basic moral intuitions.

MACNAMARA, John. Understanding Induction. Brit J Phil Sci, 42(1), 21-48, Mr 91.

The paper assimilates induction in empirical science to induction in geometry rather than in statistical inference. The special connection is that in geometry one typically examines individuals in the kind under study. The logic of count nouns restricted to natural kinds guides the definitions of *arbitrary object* and *particular property*, which play key roles. The affinity between deduction and induction is emphasized, yet two problems peculiar to induction are singled out. The paper does not set out to solve the problem of induction.

MACPHERSON, Dugald. Finite Axiomatizability and Theories with Trivial Algebraic Closure. Notre Dame J Form Log, 32(2), 188-192, Spr 91.

It is shown that every quasi-finitely axiomatized complete theory with trivial algebraic closure has the strict order property or is the theory of and indiscernible set, and conjectured that every finitely axiomatized ω-categorical theory with infinite models has the strict order property. It is also shown that complete theories with trivial algebraic closure and (for example) no quantifier-free unstable formulas are rather limited.

MADDY, Penelope. Mathematics and Oliver Twist. Pac Phil Quart, 71(3), 189-205, S 90.

Hartry Field's nominalistic project in the philosophy of mathematics comes in two versions depending on whether it is expressed in first or second order logic. In an earlier paper, 'Physicalistic Platonism' (in hysicalism in Mathematics, edited by Andrew Irvine), I argued that the second order version enjoys no epistemological advantage over the nontraditional version of Platonism I advocate. In this paper, I argue that the first order version involves an anemic view of our best scientific theory of space-time, a view of the sort a scientific realist like Field should reject.

MADDY, Penelope. "Physicalistic Platonism" in *Physicalism in Mathematics*, IRVINE, Andrew D (ed), 259-289. Norwell, Kluwer, 1990.

One motivation for nominalism in the philosophy of mathematics is physicalism, the belief that legitimate entities must be spatio-temporally located and causally efficacious. I outline a naturalized version of Platonism that should be just as physicalistically acceptable as the best version of Hartry Field's nominalism.

MADDY, Penelope. A Problem in the Foundations of Set Theory. J Phil, 87(11), 619-628, N 90.

This paper introduces a set theoretic problem independent of the current axioms, a problem more concrete than the familiar continuum hypothesis, and raises the question of whether or not it is a pseudo-problem. Many contemporary positions in the philosophy of mathematics, not all of them Platonistic, can be seen to answer this question in the negative, but these views are based on a version of scientific realism that has been called into question. Assuming a naturalistic perspective, I suggest that the legitimacy of this set theoretic problem may hang on a scientific question: is space continuous?

MADELL, Geoffrey. Personal Identity and the Idea of a Human Being. Philosophy, 29, 127-142, 91 Supp.

MADELL, Geoffrey. "Personal Identity and the Mind-Body Problem" in *The Case for Dualism*, SMYTHIES, John R (ed), 25-41. Charlottesville, Univ Pr of Virginia, 1989.

MADIGAN, Tim. "Afterword: The Answer of Humanism" in *The Question of Humanism: Challenges and Possibilities*, GOICOECHEA, David (ed), 326-339. Buffalo, Prometheus, 1991.

An examination of the historical evolution of humanism, with special emphasis on the anti-humanistic challenges presented to this worldview by Nietzsche, Marx and Heidegger and possible responses.

MADIGAN, Tim (ed) and GOICOECHEA, David (ed) and LUIK, John (ed). *The Question of Humanism: Challenges and Possibilities*. Buffalo, Prometheus, 1991.

This volume of twenty-three papers on the ironies and ambiguities of humanism raises questions about: *The Varieties of Humanism, The Challenges to Humanism* and *The Enigmas of Humanism*. It is intended to be an introductory text for first-year philosophy students that they might not get oversimplified notions of humanism. Its conclusions form themselves in each reader as new beginnings for thinking, as such thinkers as: Plato, Aulus Gellius, Augustine, Pico, Kant, Heidegger, Foucault and Kurtz are allowed to dialogue.

MADISON, G B. How Individualistic Is Methodological Individualism? Crit Rev, 4(1-2), 41-60, Wint-Spr 90.

MADISON, Gary Brent. "Flesh as Otherness" in *Ontology and Alterity in Merleau-Ponty*, JOHNSON, Galen A (ed), 27-34. Evanston, Northwestern Univ Pr, 1991.

MADSEN, Peter (ed) and SHAFRITZ, Jay M (ed). *Essentials of Business Ethics*. New York, Penguin Books, 1990.

This is a collection of essays and articles that address the most essential issues, problems and dilemmas in business ethics. It includes work from Peter Druker, Ralph Nader, Milton Friedman, Laura Nash, Patricia Werhane, Norman Bowie, Manuel Velasquez and other leading ethicists. It treats such essential issues as: defining business ethics, employee rights, management ethics, corporate social responsibility, environmental ethics and multinational ethics.

MAESSCHALCK, Marc. Essai sur le développement historique de la voie phénoménologique. Rev Phil Louvain, 89(82), 185-210, My 91.

Husserl's undertaking was essentially that of laying foundations: laying down the epistemological conditions for a new philosophical method making it possible to reestablish on non-metaphysical basis our intentional and intersubjective relationship to the world. The further development of the phenomenological path thus traced out was to bring about this aim. However, with Husserl's successors a general slide is to be observed from the foundation to the basis, which exacerbates the procedure of epoquality of the world in order to oppose, by means of a decidedly regressive philosophy, the pretentions of the constructivist philosophies, striving to accompany the self-production of concrete structures. This destiny of phenomenology is illustrated particularly by the return of Merleau-Ponty towards a metaphysical interpretation of conscience, which considers the world from the point of view of the superior destiny of the spirit which additionally determines the apparent contingency of the visible.

MAESSCHALCK, Marc. Philosophie et mythologie dans la dernière philosophie de Schelling. Rev Phil Fr, 181(2), 179-193, Ap-Je 91.

MAFFIE, James. Recent Work on Naturalized Epistemology. Amer Phil Quart, 27(4), 281-293, O 90.

Continuity lies at the heart of the recent naturalistic turn in epistemology. Naturalists are united by a shared commitment to the continuity of science and epistemology, and tend to advocate one or more species of continuity: contextual, semantic, epistemological methodological, metaphysical, and axiological. Naturalists divide, however, over the interpretation and scope of this continuity. The naturalism of Goldman, Kim and Sosa is criticised for leaving meta-epistemology methodologically and epistemologically autonomous from science. A more plausible approach naturalizes epistemology 'all the way up', i.e., including meta-epistemology itself.

MAFFIE, James. What is Social about Social Epistemics? Soc Epistem, 5(2), 101-110, Ap-Je 91.

J Angelo Corlett argues social cognition employs basic cognitive processes and Alvin Goldman is thus mistaken in excluding social epistemics from the domain of primary epistemics. Corlett's conclusion is correct but his argument inconclusive. His criticism is also too weak since it fails to question the foundations of Goldman's project. I argue Goldman's distinction between native process and acquired method lacks epistemic significance and conceptual precision. Moreover, if we grant the distinction, it cuts against Goldman's claim that native processes are nonsocial. I reject Goldman's distinction between social and nonsocial cognitive as imprecise, empirically ill-motivated, and without epistemic significance.

MAGEL, Charles. Animal Liberators are Not Anti-Science. Between Species, 6(4), 204-212, Fall 90.

Susan Sperling's claim, in her *Animal Liberators: Research and Morality*, that animal rightists constitute an antiscientific cult, that they fear experiments on animals because they regard such experiments as symbols for the scientific technological manipulation and corruption of nature, that the modern animal rights movement is not essentially different from the British nineteenth century antivivisection movement, are refuted. Animal rightists are concerned about the harming of animals. Protection of animals from physical, psychological, social harm during experiments is no more antiscientific than protection of humans from harming during experiments—a principle already well accepted by scientists.

MAGGIOLO, Roberto Jiménez. Filosofía de la violencia. Rev Filosof (Venezuela), 13, 57-78, 1989.

MAGIDOR, Menachem and BURKE, Maxim R. Shelah's pcf Theory and Its Applications. Annals Pure Applied Log, 50(3), 207-254, D 90.

MAGNAVACCA, Silvia. El "De Ente et Uno": una ontología agustiniana. Pat Med, 11, 3-26, 1990.

This paper deals with the Augustinian influence on Pico della Mirandola's *De ente et Uno*. The article starts with an account of that essay and points to Pico's doctrine on *transcendentales*. So, it proceeds to analyze his points of view about *unum, verum*, and *bonum*. Then it compares those points of view to Augustinian lectures about *modus, species*, and *ordo*. Finally, it closes up stating the similitudes between both doctrines and the ethical sense of Pico and Saint Augustine's ontology.

MAGNELL, Thomas. The Extent of Russell's Modal Views. Erkenntnis, 34(2), 171-185, Mr 91.

Russell has recently been held to have a modal logic, a full modal theory and a view of naming that anticipates Kripke's intuitions on rigid designation. It is argued here that no such claims are warranted. While Russell was not altogether silent on matters modal, he did not advance an identifiable modal logic or anything more than a modest modal theory. His view of naming involves a notion of guaranteed reference. But what Kripke's intuitions about rigidity primarily pertain to is fixed reference, something demonstrably different.

MAGNUS, Bernd. Author, Writer, Text: *The Will to Power*. Int Stud Phil, 22(2), 49-57, 1990.

MAGUIRE, Daniel C. Rational Suicide and Christian Virtue. Listening, 26(1), 41-50, Wint 91.

Death consciousness is so intense in our time that is has been dubbed "the age of death." In this climate, our moral dominion over dying is being reassessed in all contexts. This article offers a wholistic definition of "reason" and discusses the cognitive role of religious traditions such as Christianity, leading to a moral openness to suicide as a potentially reasonable option.

MAHAFFEY, Vicki. The Case Against Art: Wunderlich on Joyce. Crit Inquiry, 17(4), 667-692, Sum 91.

MAHER, Patrick. Acceptance Without Belief. Proc Phil Sci Ass, 1, 381-392, 1990.

Van Fraassen has maintained that acceptance of a scientific theory does not involve the belief that the theory is true. Blackburn, Mitchell and Horwich have claimed that this is incoherent. But van Fraassen identifies belief with subjective probability, and it is perfectly coherent to say that acceptance of a theory does not involve giving the theory a high subjective probability. Indeed, this claim is correct. However, van Fraassen is wrong to think that acceptance requires a high subjective probability that the theory is empirically adequate.

MAHER, Patrick and KASHIMA, Yoshihisa. On the Descriptive Adequacy of Levi's Decision Theory. Econ Phil, 7(1), 93-100, Ap 91.

Isaac Levi has claimed that his modification of Bayesian decision theory can accommodate the choices many subjects make in the Allais and Ellsberg problems. In a test of this claim, Maher showed that subjects who make the Allais and Ellsberg choices violate Levi's theory. In response, Levi suggested that subjects were making a mistake, and that if their attention were drawn to the relevant considerations, they might adhere to his (Levi's) theory. In this paper, we report an experiment which shows that even when subjects's attention is drawn to the considerations Levi deems relevant, subjects persist in violating his theory.

MAHER, Patrick. Symptomatic Acts and the Value of Evidence in Causal Decision Theory. Phil Sci, 57(3), 479-498, S 90.

A "symptomatic act" is an act that is evidence for a state that it has no tendency to cause. In this paper I show that when the evidential value of a symptomatic act might influence subsequent choices, causal decision theory may initially recommend against its own use for those subsequent choices. And if one knows that one will nevertheless use causal decision theory to make those subsequent choices, causal decision theory may favor the one-box solution in Newcomb's problem, and may recommend against making cost-free observations. But if one can control one's future choices, then causal decision theory never recommends against cost-free observation.

MAHER, Patrick. Why Scientists Gather Evidence. Brit J Phil Sci, 41(1), 103-119, Mr 90.

Evidence gathering is a central feature of scientific activity, and a desideratum for any philosophy of science is that it be able to explain this fact by identifying the function which evidence gathering serves. The philosophies of science developed by Popper and Kuhn cannot give such an explanation, whereas Bayesian philosophy of science can. Furthermore, the most satisfactory Bayesian explanation is obtained when we introduce a notion of acceptance in addition to that of probability. These facts provide an argument in favor of a Bayesian philosophy of science which incorporates a notion of acceptance.

MAHON, Joseph. Marx as a Social Historian. Hist Euro Ideas, 12(6), 749-766, 1990.

The Marx I present is a man obsessed with money and the state of his health, a man who has left an extensive record of the means by which a basically jobless revolutionary intellectual in exile manages to keep his family afloat, who chronicled the healing practices of many members of the medical profession, and of the German spas, as he wandered Europe and North Africa pursued by death. This Marx is the father of three daughters with whom he had a voluminous correspondence, with whose personal histories he has the closest familiarity; yet he fails in the end to understand the wider possibilities of the female experience. But I begin with Marx's writing on crime and punishment, moving thence to his sociological-cum-ethical review essay on suicide.

MAHONEY, John L. William Wadsworth: Nature, Imagination, Ultimate Reality and Meaning. Ultim Real Mean, 13(3), 177-200, S 90.

Wordsworth's is essentially a philosophy, a theology of nature. To the extent that human beings achieve a rapport with the life-giving forces of nature, they achieve a sense of the Divinity and a religious peace. To the extent that the imagination is nourished, it can create and recreate moments of vision that sustain and comfort in times of doubt and struggle, that generate a deeper, a spiritual love. This spiritual love, described in the closing lines of *The Prelude,* cannot act without 'Imagination' or 'Reason in her most exalted mood', drawing us to a 'Faith in life endless, the sustaining thought/ Of human Being, Eternity, and God' (14, 189-205).

MAHONEY, Marianne. "Prudence as the Cornerstone of the Contemporary Thomistic Philosophy of Freedom" in *Freedom in the Modern World: Jacques Maritain, Yves R Simon, Mortimer J Adler*, TORRE, Michael D (ed), 117-129. Notre Dame, Univ Notre Dame Pr, 1989.

MAHOOTIAN, Farzad. Bohr's Idea of Complementarity and Plato's Philosophy. Phil Sci (Tucson), 4, 111-144, 1990.

Bohr's idea of complementarity, Heisenberg's uncertainty principle (in the context of quantum theory), and Plato's diagram of the modes of cognition (the "divided line" of the *Republic*, Book 6) are examined to elucidate their reflections on the nature of scientific inquiry. The notion of complementarity and the principle of uncertainty imply restrictions on the proper use of scientific theories, by virtue of *the mutual limitation of fundamental concepts*. The epistemological lesson of this development is the *self-limitation of science*. (edited)

MAIA NETO, José R. Hume and Pascal: Pyrrhonism versus Nature. Hume Stud, 17(1), 41-49, Ap 91.

For both Hume and Pascal, philosophical reasoning would lead to destructive pyrrhonism were not for the intervention of nature, which sets constraints on philosophical doubt. The philosopher thus faces what Hume calls "the dangerous dilemma": either a dangerous life of reasoning, philosophy, and doubt, or a safer, but open to "errors, absurdities, and obscurities," non-philosophical life. Because Hume was aware that the dilemma could favor a transition to religious faith, he, contrary to Pascal, attempted to mitigate the dilemma by depriving it of normative content. But that such content cannot be avoided follows from Hume's own philosophy.

MAIDAN, Michael. The *Rezeptionsgeschichte* of the Paris Manuscripts. Hist Euro Ideas, 12(6), 767-781, 1990.

This article explores the ways in which texts written by Marx in 1844 (known later as *Economic-Philosophical Manuscripts*) become available to the public and the presuppositions which contributed to the actual discovery and to the shaping of those texts into their present form. Furthermore, it is argued that the seeds of the controversy about the relative merits of the *young* versus the *old* Marx were already present at the editorial process which gave birth to the versions of the *Paris Manuscripts* available to the public.

MAIENSCHEIN, Jane. From Presentation to Representation in E B Wilson's *The Cell*. Biol Phil, 6(2), 227-254, Ap 91.

Diagrams make it possible to present scientific facts in more abstract and generalized form. While some detail is lost, simplified and accessible knowledge is gained. E B Wilson's work in cytology provides a case study of changing uses of diagrams and accompanying abstraction. In his early work, Wilson presented his data in photographs, which he saw as coming closest to "fact." As he gained confidence in his interpretations, and as he sought to provide a generalized textbook account of cell development, he relied on increasingly abstract diagrams. In addition, he came to see that highly abstract and even schematic drawings could provide more than pictures directly from life.

MAIER, Maria. Wovor und wodurch sind wir verantworlich? Die Instanzen der Verantwortung. Conceptus, 24(63), 55-66, 1990.

Assuming that we must distinguish three basic kinds of related normative uses of the term 'responsibility', it is shown 1) that the common use of the term '*Instanz der Verantwortung*' (the German expression '*Instanz*' as opposed to '*Autorität*' is not translatable into English) is very limited (the term is used in this way when we have information only about that *before which* one is responsible, 2) that the term '*Instanz der Verantwortung*' is ambiguous in many respects (the specification of the *Instanz der Verantworung* also provides us with information *by virtue of which*one is responsible); and 3) what connections hold between the various *Instanzen der Verantworung*.

MAIER, Robert. Logics of Dialogue: A Necessary Multiplicity. Commun Cog, 23(4), 295-303, 1990.

If one can speak of a logic of dialogue, then there are necessarily multiple logics and not one; that is the main thesis of this article. This conclusion is established with the help of the following arguments: local and global properties, such as for example negation and stability, of dialogues are not—and cannot be—determined in single way.

MAIN, William. A New Humanism: A Response. Relig Hum, 25(1), 22-23, Wint 91.

MAITZEN, Stephen. The Ethics of Statistical Discrimination. Soc Theor Pract, 17(1), 23-45, Spr 91.

Many sorts of social policies rely on statistical discrimination (SD). By SD, I mean discrimination based on identifiable characteristics of persons as a means of screening for characteristics that are harder to identify (e.g., discrimination by race as a means of screening for socioeconomic disadvantage). Among many examples of such policies are (certain forms of) affirmative action and the practice of charging differential insurance premia based on age and gender. I suggest a general method for assessing the moral justification of policies that employ SD.

MAITZEN, Stephen. Swinburne on Credal Belief. Int J Phil Relig, 29(3), 143-157, Je 91.

Richard Swinburne devotes much of his book *Faith and Reason* to determining the standard of propositional belief required for belief in a religious creed. I challenge several of Swinburne's claims about credal belief. I argue that his concept of "belief relative to alternatives" and the weak credal belief it endorses have highly counterintuitive features. I show that Swinburne confuses weak belief with a distinct (and independent) standard of belief and that the confusion undermines the argument for his preferred standard. Finally, I defend a more satisfactory standard of credal belief against Swinburne's charge that it demands too much of religious adherents.

MAJCHER, B. The Quarrel Theorem: First Attempt to the Logic of Lie. Bull Sect Log, 19(4), 139-146, D 90.

The aim of this paper is to describe a language which is suitable for studying concepts similar to the "Liar's Paradox". In fact, the "Liar's Paradox" is expressed by a formula elementary for the logic of lie. The main theorem provides the combination condition for consistency of the set of formulas elementary in the same sense.

MAJEWSKA, Zofia. Philosophy of Culture and Its Place in the Scientific Achievement of Roman Ingarden (in Polish). Ann Univ Mariae Curie-Phil, 10, 157-175, 1985.

The study poses the problem of the place of philosophy of culture in the whole of the scientific achievement of Roman Ingarden. In spite of the extensive state of research in Ingarden's writings, these problems have remained almost unnoticed by scholars. Philosophy of culture was not constructed by Ingarden in a systematic way, nevertheless the great variety of aspects discussed in his writings made him touch the problems of this domain on many occasions. Philosophy of culture was not practised by Ingarden as a separate domain but it is implicitly present in the problems undertaken by the philosopher in the domains of various branches of philosophy. The fact of its neglect in Ingarden's thought results from a strong tendency to create separate classifications of philosopher's scholarly achievements. (edited)

MAJOR, John S. "Substance, Process, Phase: *Wuxing* in the *Huainanzi*" in *Chinese Texts and Philosophical Contexts*, ROSEMONT JR, Henry (ed), 67-78. La Salle, Open Court, 1991.

MAJOR, L. Heidegger on Nietzsche and Nihilism (in Czechoslovakian). Filozof Cas, 39(1), 91-106, 1991.

The paper deals with Heidegger's interpretation of Nietzche's philosophy from the point of view of the problem of nihilism. Nietzche is, according to Heidegger, an inspiration which is to be overcome. To overcome the nihilism is, according to Heidegger, not in the power of man, but only of being. The paper ends with a question whether Heidegger does not emphasize the powerlessness of man too much. (edited)

MAJOR, L. Man, History, and Philosophy in Husserl's Crisis of European Sciences (in Czechoslovakian). Filozof Cas, 38(3), 326-332, 1990.

This study is devoted to Husserl's late philosophy, claiming that a novel motive emerged in transcendental phenomenology, notably the demand for practicality, for involvement. Husserl made it imperative that philosophy should be an efficient instrument for man's humanization. The root causes of today's crisis of European humanity are to be found in the fact that European science had been led astray by false rationalism which in turn provoked a reaction in the shape of an upsurge of irrationalism. The cause of the crisis of European science inheres in that in modern times science parted with philosophy with which it had been originally associated and aligned. This finding led Husserl to the conclusion that there exists, and has ever existed, an intrinsic connection between European man, European history and European philosophy. (edited)

MAJOR-POETZL, Pamela. The Disorder of Things. Rev Int Phil, 44(173), 198-208, 1990.

MAJUMDAR, Aruna. Action and Explanation. J Indian Counc Phil Res, 7(3), 93-102, My-Ag 90.

MAKEHAM, John. Names, Actualities, and the Emergence of Essentialist Theories of Naming in Classical Chinese Thought. Phil East West, 41(3), 341-363, Jl 91.

In this paper the author advances the thesis that by the late third century B.C., discussions of the name and actuality/object, *ming-shi*, relationship by classical Chinese thinkers evidence a shift from nominalist theories of naming to essentialist theories of naming. According to the former, it is man who arbitrarily or conventionally determines which *ming* should be applied to which *shi*. According to the latter, there is a proper or correct correspondence between a given *ming* and a given *shi*, determined, variously, by what is ordained by 'Heaven' or by what is 'naturally so'/'so of itself' (*ziran*).

MAKER, William. "Beginning" in *Essays on Hegel's Logic*, DI GIOVANNI, George (ed), 27-43. Albany, SUNY Pr, 1990.

Hegel claims that his system is scientific as self-constitutive and that it originates as self-constitutive in the *Logic* which begins without presuppositions. He also holds that logic presupposed the *Phenomenology of Spirit*. I show how these two claims can be reconciled when we see that the *Phenomenology* is a presupposition, in the sense that it comes before the system and clears the path for it, and is not a presupposition in the sense of something which externally determines the character of logical discourse in a positive fashion. This reading refutes Dieter Henrich's famous critique of the *Logic*.

MAKER, William. Davidson's Transcendental Arguments. Phil Phenomenol Res, 51(2), 345-360, Je 91.

MAKINSON, David. The Gärdenfors Impossibility Theorem in Non-Monotonic Contexts. Stud Log, 49(1), 1-6, Mr 90.

Gärdenfors' impossibility theorem draws attention to certain formal difficulties in defining a conditional connective from a notion of theory revision, via the Ramsey test. We show that these difficulties are not avoided by taking the background inference operation to be non-monotonic.

MAKOWSKY, J A and DALHAUS, E and ISRAELI, A. On the Existence of Polynomial Time Algorithms for Interpolation Problems in Propositional Logic. Notre Dame J Form Log, 29(4), 497-509, Fall 88.

Let G and H be two (possibly quantified) propositional formulas with $x_1,...,x_n$ the only common variables such that $G \rightarrow H$ is valid. An interpolant $I(x_1,...x_n)$ is a quantifier-free propositional formula such that both $G \rightarrow I$ and $I \rightarrow H$ are valid. We study the complexity of finding such an interpolant and show that this problem is intimately related to the complexity hierarchy between logarithmic and polynomial space. Especially, we show that the interpolation problem for certain formula classes is of the same degree of difficulty as the corresponding satisfiability problem.

MAKSIMOVA, Larisa L. Definability Theorems in Normal Extensions of the Provability Logic. Stud Log, 48(4), 495-507, D 89.

MALACHOWSKI, Alan R. "Deep Epistemology Without Foundations (in Language)" in *Reading Rorty*, MALACHOWSKI, Alan (ed), 139-155. Cambridge, Blackwell, 1991.

MALACHOWSKI, Alan (ed). *Reading Rorty*. Cambridge, Blackwell, 1991.

MALBREIL, Germain. Descartes censuré par Huet. Rev Phil Fr, 181(3), 311-328, Jl-S 91.

MALHERBE, Jeanette. Some Dependence Relations of Empirical Belief. Auslegung, 17(1), 27-40, Wint 91.

Psychological states are not a *prima facie* natural kind, nor are they susceptible to straightforward empirical observation in the way that material objects are. It is plain though that mental states in general, and empirical beliefs in particular, are complexly related to their physical medium, causes and context, observation of which provides a means of access to them. These facts suggest that empirical beliefs may in some sense be dependent on their physical relata. This paper attempts to set out some of the relations that hold between empirical belief and its determining conditions. First, the idea of a dependence relation is presented. This is followed by the discussion of four such relations of empirical belief. Finally, some consequences are drawn about the nature of empirical belief and justification. A brief statement of seven assumptions about empirical belief which cannot be argued for here, but which make clear the paper's background, is appended.

MALIANDI, Ricardo. El trilema de Aristófanes y los presupuestos normativos del diálgo crítico. Critica, 22(65), 43-55, Ag 90.

Critical dialogue excludes both dogmatical and skeptical positions. The former, because they get stuck with monological proceedings. The latter, because they face a trilemma: they must 1) abstain from judging, or 2) commit performative selfcontradiction, or 3) try to make fun of the opponent (as Aristophanes does to Socrates in *The Clouds*). Critical dialogue presupposes not only the validity of the basic norm, which requires that consensus be reached through dialogue, but also of another norm, according to which *the dialogue must go on*.

MALINOWSKI, Grzegorz. Q-Consequence Operation. Rep Math Log, 24, 49-59, 1990.

A formal framework for reasoning by using rules of inference which lead from non-rejected assumptions to accepted conclusions is described.

MALINOWSKI, Jacek. The Deduction Theorem for Quantum Logic—Some Negative Results. J Sym Log, 55(2), 615-625, Je 90.

We prove that no logic treated as a consequence operation determined by any class of orthomodular lattices admits the deduction theorem. We extend those results to some broader class of logics determined by ortholattices. Conclusion: no orthomodular quantum logic admits the deduction theorem with respect to any binary connective.

MALITZ, Jerome and CHUAQUI, Rolando. The Geometry of Legal Principles. Theor Decis, 30(1), 27-49, Ja 91.

We discuss several possible legal principles from the standpoint of Bayesian decision theory. In particular, we show that a compelling legal principle implies compatibility with decisions based on maximizing the expected utility.

MALM, H M. Between the Horns of the Negative-Positive Duty Debate. Phil Stud, 61(3), 187-210, Mr 91.

This paper offers a resolution to the debate about the moral significance of the difference between duties not to cause harm and duties to prevent it. I develop an account of the moral significance of the difference between the duties which captures the strong points of each of the currently rival views, yet escapes their counterintuitive implications. The account focuses on the reasons that can justify or excuse violations of the duties in relevantly similar situations, includes a new definition of "stricter," and a set of principles explaining the sense in which duties not to cause harm are stricter than duties to prevent it.

MALM, H M. Directions of Justification in the Negative-Positive Duty Debate. Amer Phil Quart, 27(4), 315-324, O 90.

I argue that the traditional way in which we account for our evidence in favor of a morally significant difference between duties not to cause harm and duties to prevent harm is fundamentally flawed (with one flaw being the creation of a false dichotomy). I present an alternative method which requires a 180 degree change in our perspective. I argue that this method holds promise for a resolution to the debate about the duties. Also discussed are the relationships between this method and the values of autonomy and human welfare, as well as the notion of "morally significant in itself."

MALONEY, J Christopher. Mental Misrepresentation. Phil Sci, 57(3), 445-458, S 90.

An account of the contents of the propositional attitudes is fundamental to the success of the cognitive sciences if, as seems correct, the cognitive sciences do presuppose propositional attitudes. Fodor has recently pointed the way towards a naturalistic explication of mental content in his *Psychosemantics* (1987). Fodor's theory is a version of the causal theory of meaning and thus inherits many of its virtues, including its intrinsic plausibility. Nevertheless, the proposal may suffer from two deficiencies: (1) It seems not to provide an adequate explanation of misrepresentation. (2) It may also fail, as a species of empiricism, to provide a correct explication of the content of observational concepts and those nonobservational concepts whose meaning is to be traced to their causal connections with observational concepts.

MALONEY, J Christopher. Saving Psychological Solipsism. Phil Stud, 61(3), 267-283, Mr 91.

This paper defends naturalistic reduction of mental content and the notion of narrow content against the anti-individualist arguments of Lynne Rudder Baker.

MALPAS, J E. "Ontological Relativity in Quine and Davidson" in *The Mind of Donald Davidson*, BRANDL, Johannes (ed), 157-178. Amsterdam, Rodopi, 1989.

According to Quine the inscrutability of reference leads to ontological relativity, or, as Donald Davidson calls it, relativity of reference. Davidson accepts both inscrutability and the indeterminacy of translation which it grounds, but rejects any explicit relativity of reference or ontology. The reasons behind this rejection are set out and explained. Explicit relativization is shown to be at odds with indeterminacy. Some notion of the relativity of reference (or, more generally, interpretation) is nevertheless shown to be both possible and necessary. It is, however, a relativity which is compatible with commensurability—the idea of absolute incommensurability is ruled out along with the realist ideal of universal commensuration—as well as with indeterminacy. The indeterminacy thesis itself undergoes some slight elaboration, particularly in respect of the notion of empirical equivalence. In general the resulting account is one which retains both the absolute character of truth and some sense of the relativity of ontology against the background of Davidsonian holism.

MALPAS, Jeff. Holism and Indeterminacy. Dialectica, 45(1), 47-58, 1991.

Donald Davidson's account of the interrelation between attitudes, and linguistic and nonlinguistic behaviour is a thoroughly holistic one. The project of radical interpretation itself embodies a holistic approach to the interpretative task. Yet Davidson also accepts a degree of indeterminacy in interpretation. Davidson's commitment to both holism and indeterminacy can give rise to a problem in the Davidsonian position. That problem is explained and a solution proposed. The indeterminacy thesis is thereby clarified, as is the nature of Davidsonian holism.

MALY, Kenneth. From Truth to 'Alhieia to Opening and Rapture. Heidegger Stud, 6, 27-42, 1990.

MALY, Kenneth. The Rooting and Uprooting of Reason: On *Spacings* by John Sallis. Phil Today, 35(2), 195-208, Sum 91.

MANCARELLA, Angelo. Bobbio e la scienza politica in Italia. Il Protag, 6(13-16), 57-78, Ja 88-D 89.

MANCINI, Matthew J. "Maritain's American Illusions" in *From Twilight to Dawn: The Cultural Vision of Jacques Maritain*, REDPATH, Peter A (ed), 39-47. Notre Dame, Univ Notre Dame Pr, 1990.

MANCINI, Matthew J. "Nominalism, Usury, and Bourgeois Man" in *Freedom in the Modern World: Jacques Maritain, Yves R Simon, Mortimer J Adler*, TORRE, Michael D (ed), 217-225. Notre Dame, Univ Notre Dame Pr, 1989.

MANCOSU, Paolo. Generalizing Classical and Effective Model Theory in Theories of Operations and Classes. Annals Pure Applied Log, 52(3), 249-308, Je 91.

A family of theories of operations and classes, related to those used in Feferman's "explicit mathematics", is proposed for developing abstract versions of model theoretic results. These theories have a classical set-theoretical interpretation as well as various interpretations in which every object is explicitly presented. Thus, FMT_0 generalizes portions of countable and recursive mode theory; FMT further generalizes portions of countable and hyperarithmetical model theory and finally FMT_ω provides a generalization of the classical L(Q)-completeness theorem and of an admissible version of L(Q)-completeness due to Bruce and Keisler.

MANCOSU, Paolo. On the Status of Proofs by Contradiction in the XVIIth Century. Synthese, 88(1), 15-41, Jl 91.

In this paper I show that proofs by contradiction were a serious problem in seventeenth century mathematics and philosophy. Their status was put into question and positive mathematical developments emerged from such reflections. I analyse how mathematics, logic, and epistemology are intertwined in the issue at hand. The mathematical part describes Cavalieri's and Guldin's mathematical programmes of providing a development of parts of geometry free of proofs by contradiction. The main protagonist of this part is Wallis. Finally, I analyse some epistemological developments arising from the Cartesian tradition. In particular, I look at Arnauld's programme of providing an epistemologically motivated reformulation of Geometry free of proofs by contradiction. The conclusion explains in which sense these epistemological reflections can be compared with those informing contemporary intuitionism.

MANDAL, Sunil Baran. Sociology of Knowledge with Special Reference to Karl Popper. Indian Phil Quart, SUPP 17(4), 49-60, O 90.

MAÑERO, Salvador. La moral existencial de G Marcel. Pensamiento, 47(186), 153-178, Ap-Je 91.

En el l.er Centenario de Marcel sique sin der suficientemente atendido su pensamiento ético. La riqueza de materia moral en sus obras hace que aquí hayamos de conformarnos con una visión global. Elegimos para ella la perspectiva que nos proporciona la reflexión sobre la naturaleza de la moral que proyecta y la defensa por él mismo de su posibilidad. Desde ella apreciamos además apuntes al posible aprovechamiento moral de su teatro y a cierta evolución en sus apelaciones, ya a *valores* encarnados en *presencias*, ya a las exigencias de un *humanismo* auténtico, concretadas en lo que Marcel Llama "seguridades existenciales".

MANGIAGALLI, Maurizio. La "Scuola di Padova" ed i problemi dell'ontologia italiana contemporanea. Aquinas, 33(3), 639-668, S-D 90.

MANGIAGALLI, Maurizio. Lo sviluppo degli studi logici nel pensiero tedesco della seconda metà dell'800. Aquinas, 33(2), 271-296, My-Ag 90.

MANGIAGALLI, Maurizio. Lo sviluppo degli studi logici nel pensiero tedesco della seconda metà dell' '800. Aquinas, 34(1), 51-71, Ja-Ap 91.

MANICAS, Peter. "Modest Realism, Experience and Evolution" in *Harré and His Critics*, BHASKAR, Roy (ed), 23-40. Cambridge, Blackwell, 1990.

Both William James and Herbert Spencer struggled against a tide to recover for psychology problems which had been appropriated by the inquiry we call 'epistemology.' An examination of James's criticism of Spencer's 'transfigured realism' helps us in a reconsideration of Rom Harre's appropriation of J J Gibson, an appropriation designed to solve some of the same problems which bothered Spencer and James.

MANKTELOW, K I and OVER, D E. *Inference and Understanding: A Philosophical and Psychological Perspective*. New York, Routledge, 1990.

This book reviews work on linguistic inference, inductive thinking, and deductive reasoning, and links research in these areas with wider theoretical concerns, such as the question of rationality, evolutionary arguments, and artificial intelligence. It includes philosophical and psychological perspectives on these problems; a continuing theme is the comparison between normative and descriptive accounts of human thought.

MANN, David W. Some Philosophical Directions Towards a Simple Theory of the Self. Theor Med, 12(1), 53-68, Mr 91.

In the art of self-observation, an individual becomes simultaneously observer and observed, subject and object. While some philosophical psychologists have dismissed this *reflexivity*, the present author proposes that it is *the essential feature of the self*, making it the basis of a new, conceptually simple, structural and dynamic theory of the self. Drawing from psychopathology, poetry and literature, the author portrays normal and disordered psychological states as disturbances in reflexivity. Qualitative and quantitative variations in this core function are proposed to define discreet spectra of psychological situations. The author briefly examines the theory and practices of psychoanalytic and existential psychology, and proposes clinical applications of the new views here depicted. He attempts to show that inherent limits to our simultaneous knowledge of both aspects of the reflexive duality limit the precision and validity of all psychological theorization.

MANN, William E. "Definite Descriptions and the Ontological Argument" in *Philosophical Applications of Free Logic*, LAMBERT, Karel (ed), 257-272. New York, Oxford Univ Pr, 1991.

The article investigates some of the difficulties involved in casting St Anselm's Ontological Argument in the first-order predicate calculus with identity. It argues that Russell's Theory of Descriptions is particularly unsuited for giving a formal version of Anselm's argument, because of Anselm's distinction between modes of being and his consequent position that a term need not refer to a being *in re* in order to have meaning. Some alternative description theories which satisfy the general demands of a "free logic" are discussed, and it is suggested that Anselm's argument is more propitiously framed in one of these theories.

MANNING, Robert J S. David Hume's *Dialogues Concerning Natural Religion*: Otherness in History and in Text. Relig Stud, 26(3), 415-426, S 90.

MANNING, Robert J S. Thinking the Other Without Violence? An Analysis of the Relation Between the Philosophy of Lévinas and Feminism. J Speculative Phil, 5(2), 132-143, 1991.

MANNO, Salvatore D and DRAGO, Antonino. The Fundamental Hypotheses of Mechanics in Lazare N M Carnot's Thought (in Italian). Epistemologia, 12(2), 305-330, Jl-D 89.

Though Lazare Carnot's mechanics is universally recognized as the starting point of technical physics, it received rare attention in the past. Recent studies attributed to it more merits than in the past. It is the first formulation of mechanics which is entirely experimental, even in the principles. Moreover, it introduced many important novelties, among which the work concept and the mechanical energy conservation (which is widely employed in several theorems). Therefore today this theory has to be recognized as a formulation of a high theoretical value. The present paper examines its principles, which Carnot presented in the last book on mechanics and names "hypotheses." (edited)

MANNS, James W. The Scottish Influence on French Aesthetic Thought: Later Developments. J Hist Ideas, 52(1), 103-119, Ja-Mr 91.

The philosophy of Thomas Reid, and with it his expressionist aesthetic doctrine, was disseminated throughout France during the first half of the nineteenth century by Victor Cousin and Théodore Jouffroy, each of whom developed a following of his own. This paper traces the expansion, development, and ultimately the metamorphosis of expressionism in the hands of these followers. Closest attention is given to two works: Charles Leveque's *La Science du beau*, and Sully-Prudhomme's *L'Expression dans les beaux-arts*, the work which truly modernized expressionism.

MANSBACH, Abraham. Heidegger on the Self, Authenticity and Inauthenticity. Iyyun, 40(1), 65-91, Ja 91.

My aim of this paper is to show how the question of the Self permeates Heidegger's *Being and Time* and give an accurate picture of authentic and inauthentic modes of existence is possible only if they are analysed in relation to the problem of the Self. The conclusions are: 1) human existence in either mode-authentic or inauthentic—means the constant making of the Self; 2) examination of the apparatus of individuation—facing death, anxiety and the voice of conscience. I support the view that totally authentic existence is impossible for the authentic Self always involves a residue of inauthenticity; 3) the distinction Heidegger makes in *Metaphysical Foundations of Logic* between "neutral" and "tactical" Dasein, provides the metaphysical basis for authentic and inauthentic Self.

MANSILLA, H C F. El factor prelógico en el desarrollo de América Latina: El teorema del preconsciente colectivo. Rev Filosof (Costa Rica), 28(67-68), 191-196, D 90.

Sigmund Freud considered the instance called by him super-ego, stores aspects and historical knowledge of collective character too, and equally ideals of a basis and/or of a nation. It is important, for understanding of mass psychology, the analysis of these normative ideals because, like in individual psyche's case, they are internalized as prerational. (edited)

MANSILLA, Hugo C F. Das Imperiale an der Identitätsphilosophie: Spuren des Totalitären in der abendländischen Philosophie. Deut Z Phil, 39(1), 36-42, 1991.

MANZONI, Claudio. Considerazioni in margine a un'interpretazione di Bruno. Filosofia, 41(3), 325-343, S-D 90.

MAQUET, Jacques. Perennial Modernity: Forms as Aesthetic and Symbolic. J Aes Educ, 24(4), 47-58, Wint 90.

For Postmodernists, modernity in the visual arts began around 1900, ended in the 70s, and is to be deconstructed. In this article, it is argued that by liberating art from representation modern nonfigurative works made it possible for beholders to experience a composition of nonionic forms as a perceptual and symbolic Gestalt or cosmos. By doing so, 20th century modernity has made explicit a perennial and intercultural basis for aesthetic quality and symbolic meaning: formal composition. Postmodernist processes and products are intended to be "anti-form;" they repudiate composition and thus stand for chaos.

MARA, Gerald M (ed) and DOUGLASS, R Bruce (ed) and RICHARDSON, Henry S (ed). *Liberalism and the Good*. New York, Routledge, 1990.

MARA, Gerald M and DOUGLASS, R Bruce. "The Search for a Defensible Good: The Emerging Dilemma of Liberalism" in *Liberalism and the Good*, DOUGLASS, R Bruce (ed), 253-280. New York, Routledge, 1990.

MARAN, Rita. The Juncture of Law and Morality in Prohibitions Against Torture. J Value Inq, 24(4), 285-300, O 90.

International human rights law constitutes an evolving link between humankind's moral precepts on the one hand and bodies of law on the other. The place of moral considerations is not specifically addressed in other bodies of law. Moral precepts are integral to international human rights law. Religious and philosophical treatises have long questioned whether moral standards might ever formally become embodied in legal codes. This body of law takes significant steps towards an affirmative answer. Furthermore, it offers a practical tool towards eliminating torture from states' instruments for governing, and brings universally declared moral aspirations and legal authority into closer alignment.

MARCHAK, Catherine. The Joy of Transgression: Bataille and Kristeva. Phil Today, 34(4), 354-363, Wint 90.

MARCHETTI, Giancarlo. Dire e ascoltare nella tipologia del "sofista", del "filosof-re" e del pensatore socratico. Filosofia, 42(1), 17-28, Ja-Ap 91.

MARCIL-LACOSTE, Louise. Les enjeux égalitaires du consensus rationnel: Habermas et ses sources. Laval Theol Phil, 46(3), 317-335, O 90.

La reformulation critique du projet des Lumières que représente la théorie habermassienne de "raison décidée" et de "consensus rationnel" appelle un nouvel examen du point de vue du diagnostic et de la prospective. Suivant les pistes d'une telle ré-évaluation à même les indications fournies par Habermas en ce qui concerne la répression historique de la variante plébéienne de l'espace public, l'étude met en lumière la contribution des philosophies du sens commun esquissées au cours du XVIIIe siècle, ainsi que leurs rapports avec la question politique de l'égalité pour marquer les conditions critiques d'un recours émancipatoire au modèle du consensus rationnel.

MARCIL-LACOSTE, Louise. Perelman et la philosophie anglo-saxonne. Dialogue (Canada), 29(2), 247-266, 1990.

Analysant la manière dont la philosophie de C Perelman fut étudiée dans la pensée anglo-saxonne, une double contribution est ici mise en évidence, la contribution de la "Nouvelle Rhétorique" à une conception du raisonnable au sein de l'argumentation et surtout l'apport de Perelman à la philosophie politique, en particulier sa théorie de la justice et de son rapport à la notion d'égalité. Le diagnostic effectué permet de situer le modèle d'argumentation éthique de Perelman à mi-chemin entre le modèle de J Rawls et de R Nozick.

MARCONDES CÉSAR, Constança. Interprétation et philosophie de l'art. Diotima, 18, 23-24, 1990.

MARCONI, Diego. Dictionaries and Proper Names. Hist Phil Quart, 7(1), 77-92, Ja 90.

Until early XVIII century, monolingual dictionaries used to include proper names of persons and places. They disappeared from most dictionaries during the XVIII century. I examine the explicit motivations given by some among the few lexicographers who were against including proper names, as well as contemporary grammatical treatment of proper names as a separate category. Evidence of both kinds turns out to be inconclusive. An alternative explanation can be based on the influence of the "way of ideas" on dictionary making. Proper names may have disappeared from the dictionaries because the *analysis* of the *ideas* they were taken to stand for was no easy business.

MARCUS, Ruth Barcan. "A Backward Look at Quine's Animadversions on Modalities" in *Perspectives on Quine*, BARRETT, Robert (ed), 230-243. Cambridge, Blackwell, 1990.

Quine's grounds for the rejection of modal logic are traced. He sees C I Lewis's original work as an outcome of use-mention confusions. Additional grounds for rejection are (1) supposed problems of quantifying into modal contexts in modal predicate logic as initiated by Barcan (later Marcus); (2) substitution and identity puzzles in modal contexts; (3) apparent commitment of modal logic to "intensional" entities; (4) an invidious commitment to "essentialism." It is shown that none of the criticisms has been sustained. However it is not supposed by the author that essentialism is an untenable metaphysical view.

MARCUS, Ruth Barcan. Classes and Attributes in Extended Modal Systems: Proceedings of the Colloquium in Modal and Many Valued Logic. Acta Phil Fennica, 16, 123-135, 1963.

In Barcan's second order modal quantification theory, n'adic abstracts may be interpreted as designating attributes. Strict and material inclusion and equality are defined for attributes. Substitution for strict equality is unrestricted but proscribed for material equality in the scope of modal operators. The intuitive notion of a class in the sense of an aggregate or collection may be designated by a species of abstract; one in which the abstract specifies its referent by an inventory of proper names (not singular descriptions). Anything which is a member of an aggregate so described is necessarily a member of it by whatever name that thing is designated. More generally aggregates so described by inventory are necessarily equal, an extension of the necessity of identity for individuals.

MARCUS, Ruth Barcan. The Deduction Theorem in a Strict Functional Calculus of First Order Based on Strict Implication. J Sym Log, 11, 115-118, 1946.

It is shown that the Barcan quantificational extensions (S21, S41) of Lewis's S2 and S4 do not support an unrestricted substitution theorem for the strict conditional. Nor is it provable for the material conditional in S21. It is provable for the material conditional in S41 but for the strict conditional it is only provable in S41 where the premises are necessary.

MARCUS, Ruth Barcan. A Functional Calculus of First Order Based on Strict Implication. J Sym Log, 11, 1-16, 1946.

C I Lewis's modal propositional systems S2 and S4 are presented replacing the independent axioms with axiom schemata. They are then extended to first order quantification theory in a standard way (S21 and S41) with the addition of a permutation principle between the operator for possibility and the existential quantifier (the Barcan formula). Among results of interest are (1) provability of the converse of the Barcan formula; (2) a restricted substitution theorem for strict equivalents in S21; (3) an unrestricted substitution theorem for strict equivalence in S41; (4) substitution of material equivalences is proscribed in modal contexts. The latter yields a generalized solution to putative puzzles about substitution of extensional equivalences in the scope of modal operators. Results for S41 are extendable to S51.

MARCUS, Ruth Barcan. The Identity of Individuals in a Strict Functional Calculus of Second Order. J Sym Log, 12, 12-15, 1947.

The Barcan systems of first order quantified modal logic are extended to include functional and propositional variables, an abstraction operator and abstract formation along with axiom schemata for second order quantification theory and abstract elimination. Identity is introduced (I or =) and theorems proved about that relation including the proof that identity and necessary identity are strictly equivalent, i.e., the necessity of identity.

MARCUS, Ruth Barcan. "Introduction" in *Themes From Kaplan*, ALMOG, Joseph (ed), 3-4. New York, Oxford Univ Pr, 1989.

Some biographical remarks about David Kaplan.

MARCUS, Ruth Barcan (ed) and DORN, Georg (ed) and WEINGARTNER, Paul (ed). *Logic, Methodology and Philosophy of Science, VII*. Amsterdam, North-Holland, 1986.

Proceedings of the invited papers of the Seventh International Congress of Logic, Methodology and Philosophy of Science, held in Salzburg, Austria in 1983. Three papers in each of the following categories were delivered: Proof Theory and Foundations of Mathematics, Model Theory and its Applications, Recursion Theory and Theory of Computation, Axiomatic Set Theory, Philosophical Logic, Methodology of Science, Foundations of Probability and Induction, Foundations and Philosophy of the Physical Sciences, Foundations and Philosophy of Biology, Foundations and Philosophy of Psychology, Foundations and Philosophy of the Social Sciences, Foundations and Philosophy of Linguistics.

MARCUS, Ruth Barcan. Modal Logic. Cont Phil, 1, 87-101, 1968.

A survey of modal logic through 1967. Topics touched on are (1) the original motivations for the development of propositional modal logic; (2) modal quantification theory and associated problems of interpretation; (3) puzzles about identity and substitutivity in modal contexts; (4) essentialism and modalities; (5) semantical accounts of modalities; (6) syntactical accounts of modalities.

MARCUS, Ruth Barcan. Some Revisionary Proposals About Belief and Believing. Phil Phenomenol Res, 50 SUPP, 133-153, Fall 90.

A departure is proposed from those language oriented accounts of "x believes that P" where P is taken as a sentence (e.g., Davidson, J Fodor) or a quasi-linguistic proposition (e.g., Frege et al.). Believing is here viewed as relating an agent and an actual or non-actual state-of-affairs, P, where under local internal and external circumstances an agent is disposed to act as if P obtains. Although speech acts such as first person belief reports are often markers of believing, they are shown to be neither necessary nor sufficient conditions. The position therefore accommodates beliefs of non-language users. A further revisionary proposal recommends that belief avowals should be retroactively revised where P is impossible, analogous to retroactive revising of knowledge avowals where P does not obtain.

MARCUS, Ruth Barcan and KUCKLICK, B and BERCOVITCH, S. Uninformed Consent. Science, 205, 644-647, 1979.

A response to the editorial "Informed Consent May Be Hazardous to Health," *Science*, vol. 204. In particular what is cited is the failure to distinguish the subject of an experiment who volunteers and the special doctor-client relationship, also, the failure to distinguish rights and benefits. The subject has a right to know. That is not a benefit conferred.

MARGOLIS, Howard. Tycho's System and Galileo's *Dialogue*. Stud Hist Phil Sci, 22(2), 259-275, Je 91.

This paper shows that the familiar comment that Galileo ignored Tycho's system is mistaken. Actually, in emphatic and repeated language, Galileo dismisses the Ptolemaic possibility as soon as the question of planetary motions arises, narrowing the choice to Tycho and Copernicus. Galileo's tactics are put in the context of his need to satisfy the Church's censors, and of the Pope's subsequent angry complaint to the Florentine ambassador that he had been tricked by Galileo.

MARGOLIS, Joseph. Métaphysique radicale. Arch Phil, 54(3), 379-406, Jl-S 91.

"Métaphysique Radicale" demonstrates that an alternative to the classical tradition spanning Parmenides, Plato, and Aristotle (archism) may be replaced, without contradiction or incoherence, by another (an-archism) that may be traced principally from Protagoras (whom the archists repudiate) and (in a sense) Anaximander. The archist claim, which affirms the changelessness of the real and the identity of the real and the thinkable, is developed most fully in Aristotle (Book Gamma, *Metaphysics*) and depends on a metaphysical interpretation of the principles of non-contradiction and excluded middle. The an-archist alternative rests on demonstrating that the rejection of this interpretation is not self-contradictory or self-defeating. The theories of three American philosophers—W V Quine, Nelson Goodman, and Charles Sanders Peirce—are shown to incorporate the an-archist thesis (though with lapses in the direction of archism that are inessential to the an-archist project). Parallels in the European tradition are very briefly noted. The an-archist program is judged to be favored at present and in the near future.

MARGOLIS, Joseph. Moral Realism and the Meaning of Life. Phil Forum, 22(1), 19-48, Fall 90.

The untenability of the moral realist thesis is demonstrated through a close examination of the views of David Wiggins, Mark Platts, and Sabina Lovibond particularly. The discussion centers on the recent use of Hegel's notion of *Sittlichkeit* and fashionable allusions to Wittgenstein and Donald Davidson. Reference is also made, in passing, to the views of John Mackie, Richard Taylor, and others.

MARGOLIS, Joseph. "Pragmatism, *Praxis*, and the Technological" in *Philosophy of Technology*, DURBIN, Paul T (ed), 113-130. Norwell, Kluwer, 1989.

The general topic centers on the question of the sense in which a theory of technology is a theory of knowledge or inquiry. The argument considers what we might mean by possibility: both in the sense of compossibility and possibility relative to the actual world. The second option is favored and brought to bear on the views of Plantinga, Goodman, Quine, Heidegger, and Dewey.

MARGOLIS, Joseph. Les trois sortes d'universalité dans l'herméneutique de H G Gadamer. Arch Phil, 53(4), 559-571, O-D 90.

All theories concerned with knowledge, rationality, legitimation, universally valid norms and the like, etc., must confront, if they are committed to a strongly historicized sense of the very context of inquiry in which they pursue such questions, the puzzle of how to recover universal values or universal truths under the condition of radical history. There is a well-known quarrel, centered on this matter, that engaged Hans-Georg Gadamer and Jürgen Habermas. Three sorts of universality are implicated in the effort (the hermeneutic effort of Gadamer or the emancipatory effort of Habermas) to resolve the puzzle: (1) that of the hermeneutic problem; (2) that of any critical process by which to recover valid human norms; and (3) that of any successfully validated human norms. A review of the Gadamer/Habermas dispute confirms that the advantage lies with Gadamer, that there can be no rational procedure for recovering universal values (Habermas), but also that the conviction (Gadamer) that there are such values cannot be more than an undefended hope.

MARIANI, Mauro. Semantica aristotelica e sillogistica modale. Teoria, 10(2), 59-83, 1990.

MARIETTA JR, Don E. Thoughts on the Taxonomy and Semantics of Value Terms. J Value Inq, 25(1), 43-53, Ja 91.

The terms used to talk about value, especially "intrinsic" and "inherent," are muddled. The aspect of being valued as an end in itself and the aspect of having value independently of human ascription of value should be distinguished, as should different senses of being valued as a means and being valued as a functioning part of a whole. A semantic treatment of value terms can interpret most ascriptions of value as shorthand references to the act of valuing, but value which is independent of human valuing poses more complicated problems, especially when it is employed in ethical theory.

MARÍN CASANOVA, Jose A. La conceptión tolstoiana de la historia. Themata, 6, 95-105, 1989.

The article consists of a critical exposition of Tolstoy's *War and Peace* contents from the point of view of the philosophy of history. Providential fatalism, decadent nihilism and anti-individual totalitarism (sociological reductionism). These are in outline the reached conclusions on the historical understanding of an author who not only was an unquestionable writer but also must be going considered as an original thinker and therefore questionable.

MARÍN, Victor R. Hacia el saber del hombre: Dialéctica, lógica y ontológica en Aristóteles. Rev Filosof (Venezuela), 11, 95-120, 1989.

MARINI, Giuliano. Tra Kant e Hegel: per una riaffermazione dell'antico concetto di società civile. Teoria, 10(1), 17-28, 1990.

MARINOFF, Louis. The Inapplicability of Evolutionary Stable Strategy to the Prisoner's Dilemma. Brit J Phil Sci, 41(4), 461-472, D 90.

The Axelrod-Hamilton games-theoretic conflict model, which applies Maynard Smith's concept of evolutionarily stable strategy to the Prisoner's Dilemma, gives rise to an inconsistency between theoretical prescription and empirical results. Proposed resolutions of this problem are incongruent with the tenets of the models involved. The independent consistency of each model is restored, and the anomaly thereby circumvented, by a proof that no evolutionarily stable strategy exists in the Prisoner's Dilemma.

MARION, Jean-Luc. Réponses à quelques questions. Rev Metaph Morale, 96(1), 65-76, Ja-Mr 91.

MARION, Jean-Luc. Le sujet en dernier appel. Rev Metaph Morale, 96(1), 77-95, Ja-Mr 91.

MARION, Normand. Sur l'éthique et la rationalité de l'État social. Lekton, 1(2), 131-154, 1991.

MARKER, D and PILLAY, A. Reducts of (C,+,·) Which Contain +. J Sym Log, 55(3), 1243-1251, S 90.

MARKER, David. Enumerations of Turing Ideals with Applications. Notre Dame J Form Log, 31(4), 509-514, Fall 90.

We examine enumerations of ideals in the Turing degrees and give several applications to the model theory of first- and second-order arithmetic.

MARKHAM, Ian. Faith and Reason: Reflections on MacIntyre's 'Tradition-constituted Enquiry'. Relig Stud, 27(2), 259-267, Je 91.

MacIntyre's "Whose Justice? Which Rationality?" has certain implications for the faith and reason relationship. For MacIntyre commitment is not incompatible with reason. This is mistaken because commitment involves a closed account for disagreement. A closed account explains all those who disagree with a world-view in terms of factors internal to that world-view. It is for this reason that faith and reason are incompatible.

MARKHAM, Ian. Hume Revisited: A Problem With the Free Will Defense. Mod Theol, 7(3), 281-290, Ap 91.

The Free Will Defence is considered the strongest theodicy for evil. Platinga has shown that Mackie is wrong to suggest that God could have created creatures free and perfect. However, in part II of Hume's *Dialogues Concerning Religion*, Philo argues that God could have created a world with creatures free but tending to moderate evil rather than extreme forms of evil we see in this world. For example, we could imagine a world more like Luxembourg rather than Ceaucescu's Romania. I develop and sustain this objection to the Free Will Defence.

MARKIE, Peter and PATRICK, Timothy. *De Re* Desire. Austl J Phil, 68(4), 432-447, D 90.

MARKOVA, Ivana. "The Development of Self-Consciousness: Baldwin, Mead, and Vygotsky" in *Reconsidering Psychology: Perspectives from Continental Philosophy*, FAULCONER, James E (ed), 151-174. Pittsburgh, Duquesne Univ Pr, 1990.

MARKOVIC, Mihailo. The Meaning of Recent Changes in Eastern Europe. Praxis Int, 10(3-4), 213-223, O 90-Ja 91.

MARKS, Joel. Emotion East and West: Introduction to a Comparative Philosophy. Phil East West, 41(1), 1-30, Ja 91.

In recent years emotion has become the focus of intensive theoretical work among philosophers of the West, including philosophers of mind, moral psychologists, feminists, aestheticians, religious ethicists, and others. What is striking to a comparative philosopher is the almost total absence of references to Asian thought. This essay provides some background on the contemporary debate in the West and then goes on to consider issues for an expanded exchange among philosophers East and West. An extensive bibliography of contemporary work is included.

MARLASCA, Antonio. El ateísmo Freudeano. Rev Filosof (Costa Rica), 28(67-68), 159-169, D 90.

This essay is divided into two parts. In the first part, I make a study about the indisputable and clear theoretical-practical atheism of the founder of psychoanalysis. In the second part, I submit to criticism the Freudian thesis about religion, distinguishing his psychological theories. (edited)

MARLEY, A A J. Aggregation Theorems and Multidimensional Stochastic Choice Models. Theor Decis, 30(3), 245-272, My 91.

In many choice situations, the options are multidimensional. Numerous probabilistic models have been developed for such choices between multidimensional options and for the parallel choices determined by one or more components of such options. In this paper, it is assumed that a functional relation exists between the choice probabilities over the multidimensional options and the choice probabilities over the associated component unidimensional options. It is shown that if that function satisfies a *marginalization property* then it is essentially an arithmetic mean, and if the function satisfies a *likelihood independence property* then it is a weighted geometric mean. The results are related to those on the *combination of expert opinion*, and various probabilistic models in the choice literature are shown to have the geometric mean form.

MARQUARDT, Jochen. "Der geschlossne Handelsstaat"—Zur konservativen Kritik einer aufklärerischen Utopie. Deut Z Phil, 39(3), 294-303, 1991.

This essay treats, in the context of the collapse of the socialist states, the dialectic relationship between Enlightenment and conservative philosophies of history and their traditional modes of thinking. Taking the example of Fichte's "Handelsstaat" (1800) and the critique thereof by the conservative theorist Adam Heinrich Müller (1779-1829), we develop both positions from their origins and in their overlapping historical context. This conflict we take as paradigmatic of transformation in intellectual values understood as a process. This gains new interest in light of the contemporary social and institutional transformations in eastern Europe, especially in eastern Germany.

MARQUES, António and MOLDER, Filomena and NABAIS, Nuno. "Entrevista com o Professor Oswaldo Market Conduzida por" in *Dinâmica do Pensar: Homenagem a Oswaldo Market*, FAC LETRAS UNIV LISBOA (ed), 283-305. Lisboa, Fac Letras U Lisboa, 1991.

MARQUES, António. "Übergang e antecipação em Kant" in *Dinâmica do Pensar: Homenagem a Oswaldo Market*, FAC LETRAS UNIV LISBOA (ed), 133-142. Lisboa, Fac Letras U Lisboa, 1991.

Der vorliegende Text versucht die systematische Bedeutung des Begriffes *Übergang* im Kontext der kantischen Philosophie darzustellen. Im Zusammenhang des Programmes einer tranzendentalen Philosophie gehört der *Übergang* zu einer Konstellation anderer Begriffen oder Handlungen wie *antizipieren, schematisieren, anwenden* oder *Selbstaffizierung*. Solche Begriffe wirken nicht nur in den letzten Schriften Kants, sondern auch durch die gesamte transzendentale Deduktion der Kategorien und bei der Anwendungslehre oder der Schematismuslehre der ersten Kritik. *Übergang* bedeutet eigentlich ein Verfahren des transzendentalen Philosophes, dessen Ziel lautet: immer mehr apriorische Erkentnisse zu bestimmen, immer mehr Form im Gebiet des Empirisches zu antizipieren. Ohne dieses Verfahren zu erklären kann man nicht verstehen, warum bei der Philosophie Kants noch die Devise "forma dat esse rei" gilt.

MARQUES, U R de Azevedo. Kant e o problema da origem das representações elementares: apontamentos. Trans/Form/Acao, 13, 41-72, 1990.

Trata-se de considerar a origem das representações fundamentais (formas de receptividade e formas intelectuais), face à crítica de Kant às idéias inatas e abstratas.

MÁRQUEZ FERNÁNDEZ, Alvaro B. El consumo como sistema ideológico. Rev Filosof (Venezuela), 11, 73-82, 1989.

MÁRQUEZ FERNÁNDEZ, Alvaro B. Superestructura ideológica de las relaciones sociales. Rev Filosof (Venezuela), 13, 79-94, 1989.

MARQUIS, Jean-Pierre. "Partial Truths about Partial Truth" in *Studies on Mario Bunge's "Treatise"*, WEINGARTNER, Paul (ed), 61-78. Amsterdam, Rodopi, 1990.

MARRATI, Paola. Note sulle recenti traduzioni di *Essere e tempo* in Francia. Teoria, 10(1), 153-164, 1990.

MARRONE, Pierpaolo. Liberalismo e democrazia: la giustificazione estetica di Rorty. Aquinas, 33(2), 427-436, My-Ag 90.

MARSH, Frank H and YARBOROUGH, Mark. *Medicine and Money: A Study of the Role of Beneficence in Health Care Cost Containment*. Westport, Greenwood Pr, 1990.

MARSH, James L. Praxis and Ultimate Reality: Intellectual, Moral and Religious Conversion as Radical Political Conversion. Ultim Real Mean, 13(3), 222-240, S 90.

This essay is divided into three parts devoted respectively to intellectual, moral, and religious conversion. In each part I describe, first, Lonergan's conception of these three conversions and, second, I argue, drawing on the work of Marx and critical theory, that these three conversions imply radical political conversion. Capitalism is an essentially absurd, unjust, and fetishistic social system at odds with the full flowering of intellectual, moral, and religious conversion. Democratic socialism (not state socialism) more adequately expresses and realizes these three kinds of conversion.

MARSH, James L. Reply to McKinney on Lonergan: A Deconstruction. Int Phil Quart, 31(1), 95-104, Mr 91.

I argue that McKinney's deconstruction of Lonergan does not work and needs to be deconstructed itself on four different levels: the primacy of theory, the dialectic of language and thought, the self-correcting process of knowing, and the nature of dialectic. On all of these issues Lonergan is preferable because he is self-referentially consistent, descriptively adequate, and hermeneutically more nuanced and comprehensive. Lonergan is the true friend of difference.

MARSHALL, Sandra E. Doctors' Rights and Patients' Obligations. Bioethics, 4(4), 292-310, O 90.

HIV/AIDS has raised questions about the scope and limits of a right to confidentiality in doctor/patient relations. This paper argues that those whose job requires them to risk their lives have a right to information about those risks and that doctors are required to take such risks. Doctors, then, have a right to information about a patient's condition when that condition exposes the doctor to risk. Patients have an obligation to give such information but what if the patient refuses? The paper offers an argument that others may then have an obligation to reveal the information without the patient's consent.

MARSOOBIAN, Armen (ed) and WALLACE, Kathleen (ed) and BUCHLER, Justus. *Metaphysics of Natural Complexes (Second Edition)*. Albany, SUNY Pr, 1990.

MARTENS, Ekkehard. Philosophy for Children and Continental Philosophy. Thinking, 9(1), 2-7, 1990.

After pointing out the most commonly understood difference between Anglo-American philosophy and Continental philosophy, namely, logico-linguistic analysis versus personal reflection, the author shows how, from the standpoint of Continental philosophy, this distinction is unwarranted. By showing us how each of these aspects of philosophy is recommended for the philosophic education of the young by various writers from the Continental tradition, the author reveals how the practice of Philosophy for Children has long been proposed by Continental philosophers, albeit, not the whole methodology by any one particular philosopher at any one time. The paper reveals the sympathy that Continental philosophy therefore has for Philosophy for Children and concludes by questioning the place of the Eastern tradition in the ongoing dialogue about what philosophic inquiry with children should entail.

MARTIN JR, Charles L and BACKOF, Jeanne F. Historical Perspectives: Development of the Codes of Ethics in the Legal, Medical and Accounting Professions. J Bus Ethics, 10(2), 99-110, F 91.

Members of the legal, medical and accounting professions are guided in their professional behavior by their respective codes of ethics. These codes of ethics are not static. They are ever evolving, responding to forces that are exogenous and endogenous to the professions. Specifically, changes in the ethical codes are often due to economic and social events, governmental influence, and growth and change within the professions. This paper presents a historical analysis of the major events leading to changes in the legal, medical and accounting codes of ethics.

MARTIN, Brian and SCOTT, Pam and RICHARDS, Evelleen. Captives of Controversy: The Myth of the Neutral Social Researcher in Contemporary Scientific Controversies. Sci Tech Human Values, 15(4), 474-494, Autumn 90.

According to both traditional positivist approaches and also to the sociology of scientific knowledge, social analysts should not themselves become involved in the controversies they are investigating. But the experiences of the authors in studying contemporary scientific controversies—specifically, over the Australian Animal Health Laboratory, fluoridation, and vitamin C and cancer—show that analysts, whatever their intentions, cannot avoid being drawn into the fray. The field of controversy studies needs to address the implications of this process for both theory and practice.

MARTIN, C F J. On an Alleged Inconsistency in the Nicomachean Ethics (IX,4). J Hellen Stud, 110, 188-191, 1990.

MARTIN, Darlene Aulds. "The Legacy of Baby Doe: Nurses' Ethical and Legal Obligations to Severely Handicapped Newborns" in *Biomedical Ethics Reviews, 1987*, HUMBER, James M (ed), 157-178. Clifton, Humana Pr, 1988.

MARTIN, Deryl W and PETERSON, Jeffrey H. Insider Trading Revisited. J Bus Ethics, 10(1), 57-61, Ja 91.

A recent article in this journal argued that insider trading is an unethical practice leading to an inefficiently functioning market. The debate on this topic has primarily pitted ethical defenses of prohibition against economic arguments extolling its allowance. In addition to being incomplete, this approach ignores other unwanted economic effects of prohibition itself and unethical implications of its existence. This article shows that Adam Smith's free market concept, when properly interpreted, provides all the incentive structure necessary for an efficient and ethical marketplace even when insider trading is permitted.

MARTIN, Donald A. An Extension of Borel Determinacy. Annals Pure Applied Log, 49(3), 279-293, O 90.

We prove the determinacy of all Δ^1_1 games on arbitrary trees, and we use this result and the assumption that a measurable cardinal exists to demonstrate the determinacy of all games on ${}^{\omega}\omega$ that belong both to $(\omega^2 + 1)\,\Pi^1_1$ and to its dual.

MARTIN, Edward D and HOWE, Edmund G. Treating the Troops. Hastings Center Rep, 21(2), 21-24, Mr-Ap 91.

MARTIN, J E and ENGLEMAN, K H. The Mind's I Has Two Eyes. Philosophy, 65(254), 510-515, O 90.

MARTIN, James E. Aesthetic Constraints on Theory Selection: A Critique of Laudan. Brit J Phil Sci, 40(3), 357-363, S 89.

MARTÍN, Josè Pablo. Ontologia e creazione in Filone Alessandrino: Dialogo con Giovanni Reale e Roberto Radice. Riv Filosof Neo-Scolas, 82(1), 146-165, Ja-Mr 90.

MARTIN, Marie A. Utility and Morality: Adam Smith's Critique of Hume. Hume Stud, 16(2), 107-120, N 90.

This paper examines both Smith's specific criticisms of Hume's claim that utility is the "foundation of the chief part of morals" and Smith's more general objections to any theory that makes an appeal to utility an essential component of morality. I show that, while Smith does raise a number of genuine difficulties for Hume, he does not succeed in his most serious criticism, that is, that Hume's theory does not adequately capture the essentially social nature of morality.

MARTIN, Michael. Ecosabotage and Civil Disobedience. Environ Ethics, 12(4), 291-310, Wint 90.

I define ecosabotage and relate this definition to several well-known analyses of civil disobedience. I show that ecosabotage cannot be reduced to a form of civil disobedience unless the definition of civil disobedience is expanded. I suggest that ecosabotage and civil disobedience are special cases of the more general concept of conscientious wrongdoing. Although ecosabotage cannot be considered a form of civil disobedience on the basis of the standard analysis of this concept, the civil disobedience literature can provide important insights into the justification of ecosabotage. First, traditional appeals to a higher law in justifying ecosabotage are no more successful than they are in justifying civil disobedience. Second, utilitarian justifications of ecosabotage are promising. At present there is no a priori reason to suppose that some acts of ecosabotage could not be justified on utilitarian grounds, although such ecosaboteurs as Dave Foreman have not provided a full justification of its use in concrete cases.

MARTIN, Michael. The Goals of Science Education. Thinking, 4(2), 20-21, 1982.

MARTIN, Michael. Wittgenstein's Lectures on Religious Belief. Heythrop J, 32(3), 369-382, Jl 91.

In 1938 Wittgenstein gave a series of three lectures on religious belief at Cambridge. I argue first that the scope of Wittgenstein's claims in concerning the nature of religious belief is unclear. Second, I argue that he provides no clear case for the incommensurability of the language of believers and nonbelievers. Third, I argue that Wittgenstein gives no good reason to suppose that religious belief based on flimsy evidence should not be subject to rebuke.

MARTIN, Norman M and PELLETIER, Francis Jeffry. Post's Functional Completeness Theorem. Notre Dame J Form Log, 31(3), 462-475, Sum 90.

The paper provides a new proof, in a style accessible to modern logicians and teachers of elementary logic, of Post's Functional Completeness Theorem. Post's Theorem states the necessary and sufficient conditions for an arbitrary set of(2-valued) truth functional connectives to be expressively complete, that is, to be able to express every (2-valued) truth function or truth table. The theorem is stated in terms of five properties that an arbitrary connective may have, and claims that a set of connectives is expressively complete iff for each of the five properties there is a connective that lacks that property.

MARTIN, Raymond. Identity, Transformation, and What Matters in Survival. Logos (USA), 11, 57-70, 1990.

The situation considered is one in which we are given a choice among at least as good a set of alternatives as those we are typically given in our lives, and we choose just to promote selfish ends. The question is whether, under such circumstances, we might nevertheless choose cessation over continued existence. It is argued—without appeal to fission examples—that under such circumstances many of us would rather cease to exist than to continue, provided that in ceasing to exist we could transform into the persons we most want to be.

MARTIN, Rex. The Problem of Other Cultures and Other Periods in Action Explanations. Phil Soc Sci, 21(3), 345-366, S 91.

This essay develops a general account of one type of explanation found in history in particular: that an individual action is conceived as an exemplification of a rather complex schema of practical inference, under the provision that the facts which instantiate the various terms of the schema have an intelligible connection to one another. The essay then raises the question whether historians, anthropologists, and their contemporaneous audience can have an internal understanding of the actions of others, where those others come from radically different cultures or times form the historians or anthropologists. An account is offered that, arguably, can resolve this problem and do justice to both the claim of internal understanding and the presumed cultural differentness between the agents studied and the historians and anthropologist who do the study.

MARTIN, Rex. Treatment and Rehabilitation as a Mode of Punishment. Phil Topics, 18(1), 101-122, Spr 90.

The paper argues that treatment and rehabilitation can be a mode of punishment. This mode is distinguished from other modes (penalty, compensation) insofar as given punitive measures to exhibit, as a principal object, concern for the well-being of conficted offenders (and ultimately, also, for the well-being of society). Thus, prison inmates would be liable to sanctions under this particular mode of punishment where, in a system of rights, the peculiar status of being such an adjudged violator required the receipt of certain services or benefits that the violator (along with other citizens) has a right to. The argument is developed by reference to the example of work in prisons, where such work is conceived both as a requirement or general expectation attached to prisoner status and as a putative right (or, better, as one feature of a rights-tending policy of full employment).

MARTIN, Robert M. The Inadequacy of a Deontological Analysis of Peer Relations in Organizations. J Bus Ethics, 10(2), 133-139, F 91.

I argue for the inadequacy of the Kantian approach to the analysis of personal relations in business presented by Moberg and Meyer, in "A Deontological Analysis of Peer Relations in Organizations" (*Journal of Business Ethics*). It is unclear or implausible that the (mostly reasonable) principles of business relations they advocate really do follow from Kant's theory. Kant's theory, and deontological theories in general, do not yield reasonable principles of personal relations, particularly in the business context.

MARTIN, Robert M. *The Philosopher's Dictionary*. Peterborough, Broadview Pr, 1991.

A brief dictionary of philosophical terms, including entries for the best-known philosophers.

MARTIN, Victor R. Etica, retórica y política en la antropología aristotélica. Rev Filosof (Venezuela), 13, 25-42, 1989.

MARTINEZ FREIRE, P. Sentidos, referencias y concepto en Frege. Pensamiento, 46(184), 403-418, O-D 90.

La distinción de Frege entre sentido y referencia tiene un alcance mayor y matices más numerosos de los advertidos habitualmente. En términos muy sucintos y claros se explican las diversas acepciones de sentido y referencia, llevando el análisis más allá de los términos singulares hasta los enunciados asertivos completos y hasta los enunciados subordinados. Se discute la teoría fregeana de los valores veritativos como referencia y se señalan los casos de enunciados cuya referencia no es un valor veritativo. Asimismo se analiza la rígida contraposición de Frege entre objeto y concepto, aclarando por pasos sucesivos la naturaleza del concepto.

MARTÍNEZ, N G. The Priestley Duality for Wajsberg Algebras. Stud Log, 49(1), 31-46, Mr 90.

The Priestley duality for Wajsberg algebras is developed. The Wajsberg space is a De Morgan space endowed with a family of functions that are obtained in rather natural way. As a first application of this duality, a theorem about unicity of the structure is given.

MARTÍNEZ, S. La objetividad del azar en un mundo determinista. Critica, 22(65), 3-21, Ag 90.

The paper examines major attempts to characterize a notion of objective randomness in classical physics. It is shown that those attempts confuse a strict (metaphysical) thesis of determinism with the presence of irreducible probabilities. Moreover, it is argued that the problematic sense in which probabilities are irreducible in a deterministic world can be clarified once a distinction is made between a thesis of determinism and the 'separability thesis'. According to the latter the state of a physical system can be characterized completely in terms of the occurrent properties of the system.

MARTÍNEZ, Sergio. El azar objetivo como medida matemática de desorden. Dianoia, 36(36), 201-211, 1990.

MARTÍNEZ, Sergio and MURILLO, Lorena (trans). En busca del contenido físico de la regla de Luders. Dianoia, 34(34), 141-168, 1988.

MARTÍNEZ, Sergio. Estructura lógica y ontología en el *Tractatus*. Dianoia, 35(35), 23-28, 1989.

The aim of the paper is to establish the incompatibility of the ontology of the Tractatus, more precisely, of the logical structure of the simple objects, the structure of the logical space, *with the logical* structure of the world as this is implicit (in the relevant sense) in some of the most highly confirmed findings of modern physics. My argument starts by deducing some consequences from the semantic postulates in the Tractatus that assert the logical independence and the bivalence of "states of affairs." Next I show that these consequences are contradicted by the existence of physical systems of the Kochen-Specker type.

MARTÍNEZ, Sergio. Más allá de la presuposición newtoniana: propiedades genuinamente disposicionales en la mecánica cuántica. Critica, 22(66), 25-37, D 90.

MARTINICH, A P. Meaning and Intention: Black Versus Grice. Dialectica, 44(1-2), 79-98, 1990.

Grice's theory of meaning depends upon a distinction between what he calls "natural" and "nonnatural meaning." I show that this is not a proper distinction, and I replace it with two others. The first is cognitive and noncognitive meaning. The second is a subdivision of the first simple and communicative meaning. Grice's nonnatural meaning approximates most closely with communicative meaning. Another problem with Grice's theory is that he wrongly assumes that the function of the indicative mood is to express belief. When this assumption is eliminated, Grice's analysis can be revised in such a way that the major objections raised against it are eliminated.

MARTINICH, A P. *Philosophical Writing: An Introduction*. Englewood Cliffs, Prentice-Hall, 1989.

This book explains to undergraduates how to write a philosophical essay. One simple model for an essay is described in detail. The virtues of clarity, precision, and orderliness are emphasized. Various methods for writing drafts and making notes are presented. The book focuses on correct ways of writing an essay more than on mistakes to be avoided. For students who have little background in philosophy, there are chapters on basic logical concepts, such as validity and soundness, and explanations of such philosophical forms of argumentation as counterexamples, dialectical reasoning, and *reductio ad absurdum*.

MARTINO, Antonio A and ALCHOURRÓN, Carlos E. Logic Without Truth. Ratio Juris, 3(1), 46-67, Mr 90.

Between the two horns of Jorgensen's dilemma, the authors opt for that according to which logic deals not only with truth and falsity but also with those concepts not possessing this semantic reference. Notwithstanding the "descriptive" prejudice, deontic logic has gained validity among modal logics. The technical foundation proposed consists in an abstract characterization of logical consequence. By identifying in the abstract notion of consequence the primitive from which to begin, it is possible to define the connectives—even those of obligation—by means of the rules of introduction or elimination in a context of derivation.

MARTINOT, Steve. Sartre's Being-for-Heidegger, Heidegger's Being-for-Sartre. Man World, 24(1), 63-74, Ja 91.

MARTINOVIC, Ivica. Boskovic on His Own Theory of Forces: From a Sentence to the Theory of Natural Philosophy (in Serbo-Croatian). Filozof Istraz, 32-33(5-6), 1479-1488, 1989.

Boskovic constructed his theory of forces from his first idea expressed in *De viribus vivis* (1745) to the final synthesis in his masterpiece *Theoria philosophiae naturalis* (1758). In *De viribus vivis* Boskovic did not take a definite attitude toward whether his idea about forces in nature is a hypothesis, a theory, or just a sentence. On the contrary, from the very beginning of *Dissertationis de limine pars secunda* (1748) he used the term *theoria* with no exceptions. It testifies to Boskovic's scholarly self-awareness. (edited)

MARTINS, João P and CRAVO, Maria R. How to Change Your Mind. Nous, 25(4), 537-551, S 91.

In this paper, we investigate the rules that should underlie a computer program that is capable of revising its beliefs or opinions. Such a program maintains a model of its environment. All the inferences drawn are added to the knowledge base. Among the propositions in the knowledge base, there are some in which the program believes, and others in which the program does not believe. Inputs from the outside world or reasoning carried out by the program may lead to the detection of contradictions, in which case the program has to revise its beliefs in order to get rid of the contradiction and to accommodate the new information. (edited)

MARTONE, Arturo (trans) and BRÉAL, Michel. *Saggio di semantica*. Napoli, Liguori, 1990.

For the first time a complete edition of the Michel Bréal's *Essai de sémantique*, Paris, 1897, is presented to the public (edited by Arturo Martone, Ist Univ Orientale of Naples). The book presents many interesting problems that still can be revalued in a *pragmatic* point of view. A relevant interest consists, in particular, in the analysis of the human "intention" in the elaboration of linguistic facts. The edition includes the Italian translation, a long introduction and many notes of explanation to the book.

MARUSIC, M. Biological Foundations of Prediction in an Unpredictable Environment. Brit J Phil Sci, 40(4), 485-499, D 89.

This paper is an attempt to identify and define a common denominator for all receptor systems, a principle that underlies every type of recognition. The idea is explained through an analysis of the immune recognition system. It is argued that the challenges from the environment cannot be foreseen, in principle, and thus the specificity of recognition in an adult organism cannot be coded in the germ-line genes. The organism is thus forced that general readiness, the living world is able to react to the challenges that did not specifically exist at the same time the relevant receptors were constructed or even over a time covering the whole evolutionary history of the species. In other words, it is able to 'predict the unpredictable'. (edited)

MARUSYK, Randy W and SWAIN, Margaret S. An Alternative to Property Rights in Human Tissue. Hastings Center Rep, 20(5), 12-15, S-O 90.

This article proposes a three-tiered legal structure to resolve the ethical dilemma surrounding human tissue: the need to keep it free of property rights, yet accommodate the creation of such rights in biotechnological products. The first level continues to recognize a *persona* or the *rights of publicity* in humans. The second level classifies all tissue temporarily removed from the body as *res nullius*. The third level classifies tissue that is permanently removed from the body as *res communes*, but allows property rights to be created in products developed with the use of human tissue through the investment of labor.

MARUSZEWSKI, Tomasz. "Everyday Knowledge as Representation of Reality" in *The Social Horizon of Knowledge*, BUCZKOWSKI, Piotr (ed), 173-195. Amsterdam, Rodopi, 1991.

Everyday knowledge is analysed both from psychological and philosophical point of view. It was often contrasted with scientific knowledge becoming a victim of such comparison. Because notion of everyday knowledge is the natural concept it is more important to analyse its core than its fuzzy borders. Everyday knowledge is considered as homomorphic representation including an ordered set of information about the world and about oneself which results from physical or social practice. The following dimensions of everyday knowledge are discussed: pragmatic, "veracity", interpersonal and ethical dimension.

MARX, Leo. George Kateb's Ahistorical Emersonianism. Polit Theory, 18(4), 595-600, N 90.

MARYNIARCZYK, A. Establishing of the Object of Metaphysics—Separation (in Polish). Stud Phil Christ, 26(2), 55-87, 1990.

In the area of the philosophy of being, we can characterize the separation as a scientifically articulated method or as a cognitive and yet complex process. In this article we have endeavoured to present separation inasmuch as it is a cognitive process. Our aim has been to bring to light the specific character of separation as the process by which the object of metaphysics is singled out. Thus we have reconstructed the stages or moments of this process.

MARZ, Lutz. Illusions and Visions: Models Of and In Modern Societies. Praxis Int, 11(1), 37-50, Ap 91.

MARZ, Lutz. The Party's Claim to Power: The Power of Knowledge in "Real Socialism" (in German). Deut Z Phil, 38(10), 971-974, 1990.

Constitutive of the power of the Communist Party in the so-called "real socialism" was the power over knowledge of the society and of the individuals. The Party got to this knowledge in three ways: (1) The Party produced an illusionary knowledge with two functions. (2) The Party monopolized the real knowledge with two strategies. (3) The Party controlled the everyday behavior of the people with four methods. This special type of power over knowledge became a Gordian knot of the socialist society.

MARZOA, Felipe Martínez. *Cálculo y ser (Aproximación a Leibniz)*. Madrid, Visor, 1991.

El *esse* como la constitución de la *notio* o de la *idea* (*possibilitas, realitas*) y el *esse* como la verdad del enunciado resultan ser uno y lo mismo, y esto único es un *calculus* autosuficiente (por lo tanto no referente a algo, sino mero juego), que no poseemos, pero del cual podemos decir cómo sería en ciertos aspectos. De este "decir cómo sería" forman parte cosas como la redefinición de "substancia" y "existencia", la reconsideración de lo extenso, etc.

MAS, Oscar. Algunos márgenes de la condición humana. Rev Filosof (Costa Rica), 28(67-68), 107-111, D 90.

The human condition is characterized by the narrowness of its limits. Spacial and time limits, health and intellectual limits, and above all, the obysmal limits of the human origin and destiny. But life also presents certain margins of action: the quest for a stable social order, pace and happiness are as ingrained in the human condition as pain and death; and this deserves to be the object of philosophical reflection.

MASCHLER, Chaninah. Some Observations About Plato's *Phaedo*. Interpretation, 18(2), 177-210, Wint 90-91.

MASER, Steven M and COLEMAN, Jules L and HECKATHORN, Douglas D. "A Bargaining Theory Approach to Default Provisions and Disclosure Rules in Contract Law" in *Liability and Responsibility*, FREY, R G (ed), 173-254. New York, Cambridge Univ Pr, 1991.

MASI, Giuseppe. Osservazioni sul *Filebo*. G Metaf, 12(1), 9-19, Ja-Ap 90.

MASON, Andrew D. Autonomy, Liberalism and State Neutrality. Phil Quart, 40(161), 433-452, O 90.

The idea that respect for each person's autonomy requires the state to be neutral between different life-plans is considered. A number of different conceptions of autonomy are distinguished, each of which gives specific content to the underlying idea of self-direction, and so too are several different ways of regarding the requirement imposed on the state by respect for autonomy. It is argued that none of these ways of regarding respect for autonomy justifies state neutrality on any of the conceptions of autonomy distinguished.

MASON, Andrew. Community and Autonomy: Logically Incompatible Values? Analysis, 51(3), 160-166, Je 91.

A number of arguments which might be thought to show that community and autonomy are logically incompatible values are considered, but it is maintained that none of them is successful.

MASON, H E and WALLACE, John. "On Some Thought Experiments about Mind and Meaning" in *Propositional Attitudes: The Role of Content in Logic, Language, and Mind*, ANDERSON, C Anthony (ed), 175-199. Stanford, CSLI, 1990.

MASON, John R. Social Science as Moral Philosophy?: Reflections on Alan Wolfe's *Whose Keeper*? Bridges, 3(1-2), 91-114, Spr-Sum 91.

Alan Wolfe has studied recent changes in American and Scandinavian societies and related these changes to three approaches to moral obligation. In brief, he compares economic, political, and sociological approaches to moral obligation—then argues that the sociological approach enables us to be both "modern" and "moral." This paper attempts three tasks. First, it outlines Wolfe's substantive argument. Second, it highlights some relationships between that argument and various other critiques of contemporary culture. Finally, it evaluates Wolfe's contribution to a Christian critique of culture and argues that Wolfe should pay more attention to the religious concerns that animate the sociological tradition. (edited)

MASON, Richard V. Explaining Necessity. Metaphilosophy, 21(4), 382-390, O 90.

The aim is to show that The Problem of the Explanation of Necessary Truth arises from a particular context, or set of assumptions. We can make a *prima facie* distinction between necessary truth and necessity. The explanation of necessary truth poses further questions about truth and meaning. In a rationalist framework, to be necessary *is* to be explicable. Non-necessity may be seen as aberrant. The conclusion is not that we should become rationalists. It is that a logical notion uprooted from one context may not survive when transplanted to another.

MASSEY, Gerald J. Semantic Holism is Seriously False. Stud Log, 49(1), 83-86, Mr 90.

Semantic Holism is the claim that any semantic path from inferential semantics (the indeterminate semantics forced by the classical inference rules of PC) reaches all the way to classical semantics if it is even one step long. In our joint paper "Semantic Holism", Belnap and I showed that some such semantic paths are two steps long, but we left open a number of questions about the lengths of semantic paths. Here I answer the most important of these questions about the lengths of semantic paths that begin at inferential semantics but that do not even reach classical semantics. I do this by showing how to construct such an infinite semantic path from the members of the family of (n—1)-out-of-n-disjunction connectives.

MASSEY, Gerald J and BELNAP JR, Nuel D. Semantic Holism. Stud Log, 49(1), 67-82, Mr 90.

The conjecture we call *semantic holism* claims that if we start with a "sound and nontrivial" but indeterminate truth-table semantics, then to remove any "semantic indeterminacy" in any row in the table of any connective of propositional calculus, is to jump straight to classical semantics. We show 1) why semantic holism is plausible and 2) why it is nevertheless false. And 3) we pose a series of questions concerning the number of possible steps or jumps between "sound and nontrivial" indeterminate semantics and classical semantics.

MASSIMINI, Fausto and FAVE, Antonella Delle. Religion and Cultural Evolution. Zygon, 26(1), 27-47, Mr 91.

The end of the twentieth century marks the slow disintegration of both the Marxist and capitalist socioeconomic theories, inasmuch as both have proven inadequate to meet basic issues of human existence. Their inadequacy rests on the tendency to use the criteria of extrinsic rewards, quantification, production, and consumption to evaluate human personhood and human activity. What is needed is a third alternative to these two systems, one that is based on intrinsic rewards and cultivates internal values rather than production, consumption, and quantification. Religious communities have traditionally been such an alternative and seem to represent an ordered nucleus of information that can counter the inadequacies of Marxism and capitalism. To carry out this function, religions must (1) minimize the trivial differences that set belief systems against one another; (2) support bimodal cultural evolution that allows the old and the new to coexist; and (3) discover the unifying factors that cut across human groups.

MASSINI CORREAS, Carlos Ignacio. Santo Tomás y el desafío de la ética analítica contemporánea. Anu Filosof, 23(2), 161-172, 1990.

MASTERS, Roger D. The Changing Nature of the Social Sciences. Biol Phil, 6(3), 377-393, Jl 91.

Across a number of disciplines in the social sciences new research shows the implications of biological approaches to the understanding of human behavior. A collective review of nine recent books in fields ranging from economics, law, and political science to social psychology, anthropology, and sociology suggests the importance of the return to "naturalistic" approaches in each field. Differences in the quality of individual work show, however, the need for care and precision—and the danger of ignoring the unique characteristics of Homo sapiens.

MASTERS, Roger D. *The Nature of Politics*. New Haven, Yale Univ Pr, 1991.

The "nature of politics" needs to be examined by linking major issues in Western political philosophy to contemporary research in the life sciences. By relating evolutionary biology, social psychology, linguistics, and game theory to human politics, it is possible to restore the traditional emphasis on human nature in the exploration of philosophy and political theory. The "new naturalism" helps us to formulate decent and human standards of social life while providing a more scientific foundation for the study of human behavior.

MASTROIANNI, Giovanni. La prima edizione sovietica di Solov'ev. G Crit Filosof Ital, 69(1), 130-139, Ja-Ap 90.

MASULLO, Aldo. Il paradosso del fondamento nella simbolica del gioco e sogno della libertà. G Metaf, 12(1), 43-66, Ja-Ap 90.

MATERNA, P. Transparent Approach to Logical Necessity and Possibility. Filozof Cas, 39(1), 76-90, 1991.

Plurality of formal modal systems is a formal plurality only. From the viewpoint of transparent intensional logic (TIL) these systems are not able to semantically clarify the logical modalities ("box", "diamond"). TIL shows that, e.g., the problem of interpreting iteration of modalities is solvable if we distinguish between *de re* and *de dicto* supposition of modalities. Furthermore, there are some possibilities of a more fine classification of modalities if the temporal factor is taken into account.

MATHAUSER, Zdenek. Aesthetic Education and Aesthetic Atmosphere (in Czechoslovakian). Estetika, 27(4), 243-247, 1990.

MATHESON, Carl A and KLINE, A David. Rejection Without Acceptance. Austl J Phil, 69(2), 167-179, Je 91.

The claim that theory choice should always be comparative, i.e., that one theory cannot be rejected until a superior one is accepted, is an article of faith among writers in the history and philosophy of science. In this paper we attempt to show that 1) there are no good conceptual reasons for this claim, 2) the historical record does not support the thesis that the acceptance or rejection of a theory is always comparative, and 3) a straightforward reading of the historical record is complicated by sociological factors and a possible ambiguity in the words "accept" and "reject".

MATHESON, Carl. Consciousness and Synchronic Identity. Dialogue (Canada), 29(4), 523-530, 1990.

The fission problem for psychological-connection accounts of diachronic personal identity is well-known. Recently it has been argued that awareness accounts of synchronic identity face that same problem. In this paper, it is argued that 1) fission cannot be a problem for the awareness account, due to the nature of synchronic identity, and 2) the most counterintuitive result that the so-called branching cases entail is the possibility of two people sharing some of the same mental events at the same time.

MATHIEN, Thomas. The History of Philosophy, Inside and Out. Metaphilosophy, 21(4), 322-347, O 90.

This paper assesses R G Collingwood's claim that one can study the thought of the past from the inside. The limitations of this claim are pointed out, as are the limitations of approaching the history of philosophy externally as patterned communication among individuals in prescribed communicative relations with a preidentified population. Such a study cannot be begun without making interpretative decisions which specify what counts as "philosophic" communication. Distinct philosophical positions and periods produce different accounts of the philosophic past. Nevertheless external history can control these accounts.

MATHIEU, Vittorio. Il linguaggio ideologico della rivoluzione. Filosofia, 42(1), 3-15, Ja-Ap 91.

MATRAVERS, Derek. Who's Afraid of Virginia Woolf? Ratio, 4(1), 25-37, Je 91.

This paper attempts to resolve the apparent clash between our emotional responses to fictional characters and the cognitive theory of the emotions. It argues that we *do* experience emotions, we *do* have beliefs and desires concerning fictions, but that we do not act on them because we know we cannot; we know interaction between our worlds and fictional worlds to be impossible. It further argues that the problem is usually posed in a misleading manner; our emotional reaction to representations is largely determined by their intrinsic properties, not by whether or not what they report is actual.

MATSON, Wallace I and LEITE, Adam. Socrates' Critique of Cognitivism. Philosophy, 66(256), 145-167, Ap 91.

Hubert Dreyfus has accused Socrates and Plato of being forerunners of modern-day Cognitivist philosophy of mind. However, a careful reading of the early dialogues reveals Socrates' aims to have been *anti*-Cognitivist; he showed that explicit definitions stating necessary and sufficient conditions for the applicability of moral terms are *impossible*, therefore rules are not sufficient to generate moral expertise. The theory of Forms results from Plato's attempt to develop a conception of knowledge consistent with this claim.

MATSUO, Hiroshi. Nachahmung und Gestaltung—Baumgarten, *Meditationes* 73 (in Japanese). Bigaku, 41(2), 1-11, Autumn 90.

Die Entwicklung der ästhetischen Gedanken im. 18. Jahrhundert lässt sich als der Übergangsprozess vom Nachahmungsprinzip zum Gestaltungsprinzip auffassen. Es ist die Absicht vorliegender Arbeit, nachzuweisen, dass ein Gleichgewichtspunkt zwischen beiden Prinzipien im 73 der Baumgartenschen *Meditationes* liegt, wo drei Arten von den Verknüpfungen poetischer Vorstellungen den poetischen Regeln entgegengesetzt sind. Das erste Kapitel beschäftigt sich mit dem 71, wo die poetischen Regeln durch das Gestaltungsprinzip begründet sind, wonach der Künstler ein organisch gebildetes Ganzes hervorbringen müsse. (edited)

MATTAI, Bansraj. Education and the Emotions: The Relevance of the Russellian Perspective. Russell, 10(2), 141-157, Wint 90-91.

This paper investigates Bertrand Russell's globally oriented attitude to education as emanating from a pressing necessity to unequivocably demonstrate the linkage between moral understanding and moral obligation, i.e., between the mere intellectualization of virtues and the move to action by the truly virtuous. It is argued that Russell's primary interest in education was in advancing a theory of affective education as the most effective means to meet the social and moral challenges of the modern world, and that Russell's method, as educational theorist and teacher, on the one hand, and as philosopher (since his retreat from Hegelianism), on the other, is one and the same.

MATTE, Martin. Jean-Jacques Rousseau et Friedrich Schiller: le théâtre sous le feu des lumières. Philosophiques, 17(2), 101-145, Autumn 1990.

Does a kind of art hold in itself the criterion of its acceptance or of its rejection by the society in which it takes shape? Is the public to whom a work of art is aimed enabled to make the exploration it suggests to him? The *Lettre à d'Alembert sur les spectacles* by Rousseau and the lecture of Schiller, *"Was kann eine gute stehende Schaubübne eigentlich wirken?,"* give each one answer to both questions by the caracterisation of a way of feeling and working proper to aesthetic protagonists. I suggest to examine if the principles on which lay the reproof of the theatrical representation by Rousseau and the justification of the stage's efficacious by Schiller stem from and are worth according to the experience of theatrical enjoyment.

MATTESSICH, Richard V. "Mario Bunge's Influence on the Administrative and Systems Sciences" in *Studies on Mario Bunge's "Treatise"*, WEINGARTNER, Paul (ed), 397-420. Amsterdam, Rodopi, 1990.

This paper reviews vols. 3 and 4 of Bunge's *Treatise on Basic Philosophy* from the point of view of the administrative and systems sciences, and concludes that even where one feels compelled to disagree with the author's view, one is impressed by his forceful and clear presentation as well as the breadth of his philosophical panorama. The paper also discusses Bunge's systems philosophy (with illustrations of his major systems definitions postulates and theorems) in relation to the discussant's book *Instrumental Reasoning and Systems Methodology* (1978/80).

MATTESSICH, Richard and BALZER, Wolfgang. An Axiomatic Basis of Accounting: A Structuralist Reconstruction. Theor Decis, 30(3), 213-244, My 91.

Set-theoretic axiomatizations are given for a model of accounting with double classification, and a general core-model for accounting. The empirical status, and "representational" role of systems of accounts, as well as the problem of how to assign "correct" values to the good accounted, are analyzed in precise terms. A net of special laws based on the core-model is described.

MATTHEWS, Gareth B. Aristotelian Essentialism. Phil Phenomenol Res, 50 SUPP, 251-262, Fall 90.

This article reviews most of the recent efforts to characterize Aristotle's essentialism. Almost all founder on (1) a failure to appreciate that Aristotle does not have our idea of a thing "quite independently of the language in which the thing is referred to, if at all" and on (2) an inadequate appreciation of the fact that we couldn't determine whether having *p* belongs to the Aristotelian essence of an F without having at hand a satisfactory Aristotelian science of F's.

MATTHEWS, Robert J. "Learnability of Semantic Theory" in *Truth and Interpretation: Perspectives on the Philosophy of Donald Davidson*, LE PORE, Ernest (ed), 49-58. Cambridge, Blackwell, 1986.

MATUSTIK, Martin J. Havel and Habermas on Identity and Revolution. Praxis Int, 10(3-4), 261-277, O 90-Ja 91.

This is a shortened chapter from the manuscript "Post-Traditional Identity: A Reading of Habermas and Kierkegaard." It was presented in Habermas's Colloquium (October 1990) in the context of the 1989 events, the wave of nationalism, and the articulation of post-nationalist identity as a lifeworld compliment to constitutional patriotism in deliberative democracy. Habermas's permanent democratic revolution envisions procedurally integrated republic where post-traditional identity supervenes nation-state mentality; Havel's existential revolution dramatizes the 'how' requirement of autonomy, communication, and the community ideal. Havel's Levinasian-Kierkegaardian reading of 1989 embodies the vertical axis ommitted from Habermas's six interpretations of 1989 commented on in his *Nachholende Revolution*.

MATUSTIK, Martin J. Merleau-Ponty on Taking the Attitude of the Other. J Brit Soc Phenomenol, 22(1), 44-52, Ja 91.

Hegel's analysis of the struggle for recognition between two consciousnesses is reconciled by him only in the higher-level subjectivity of absolute consciousness. Merleau-Ponty argues for a paradigm shift from the constitutive model of consciousness and intersubjectivity to a dialogical model that bypasses the aporias of objectification. Dialogue avoids the consequence of mutual annihilation between two consciousnesses fighting for recognition in the objectifying paradigm. But in passing from the natural to the social level of intersubjective selfhood Merleau-Ponty falls short of articulating the linguisticality of the preconscious body-subject. The argument of the paper is that Merleau-Ponty's phenomenology of intersubjective selfhood, when further developed through a linguistic theory of communication, can account for Lacan's discourse of the other in the unconscious, on the one hand, and strengthen Habermas's linguistic theory of communicative ethics, on the other hand. (edited)

MATUSTIK, Martin J. Merleau-Ponty's Phenomenology of Sympathy. Auslegung, 17(1), 41-65, Wint 91.

Habermas's communicative ethics need not disregard existential ethics. Sympathy exercises primacy over jealosy in ontogenesis, figures as a counterfactual category in pathologies and adult crises, and grounds descriptively mature love and dialogue. A phenomenology of sympathy does not prove that we love and communicate, but, like Mead, shows the implications of individualization through socialization for normative discourse. The dialectic of alienating gazes is not normative but derivative notion. A phenomenology of adult sympathy does not desire an actual victory of lifeworld over system. The argument describes sympathy as both the operative and counterfactual condition of the possibility of communicative ethics.

MAUDLIN, Tim. Substances and Space-Time: What Aristotle Would Have Said to Einstein. Stud Hist Phil Sci, 21(4), 531-561, D 90.

This essay consists of two parts. The first is an exegetical analysis of the "stripping" argument of *Metaphysics* Z.3. I contend that the passage is not in *propria persona* and that the resolution of the aporia depends upon a careful consideration of the metaphysical relationship between essential properties and the subjects of which they are predicated. The second part applies this conclusion to a problem recently raised by John Earman and John Norton about whether the general theory of relativity is compatible with both determinism and a substantivalist interpretation of space-time. I argue that their difficulty can be avoided by an Aristotelian account of the essential properties of space-time.

MAUDLIN, Tim. Time-Travel and Topology. Proc Phil Sci Ass, 1, 303-315, 1990.

MAURER, Armand A. "Gilson's Use of History In Philosophy" in *Thomistic Papers, V*, RUSSMAN, Thomas A (ed), 25-40. Notre Dame, Univ Notre Dame Pr, 1990.

This article contains a translation and analysis of Gilson's "Remarques sur l'expérience en métaphysique," an address given in Brussels in 1953. Gilson proposes an auxiliary method of philosophizing on the basis of the history of philosophy. Using this method, he observes the principles laid down by philosophers and sees how they, or their successors, draw from their possible conclusions. If he cannot accept the conclusions, he must abandon the principles. Gilson uses this method fruitfully in his philosophical works, notably *Being and Some Philosophers* and *The Unity of Philosophical Experience*.

MAURER, Reinhart. The Other Nietzsche: Criticism of Moral Utopia (in German). Deut Z Phil, 38(11), 1019-1026, 1990.

MAURI, Margarita. La crítica kantiana a la virtud como término medio. Espiritu, 36(96), 163-168, Jl-D 87.

MAURIN, Krzysztof. The Development of Modern Mathematics and Plato's Parable of the Cave. Phil Sci (Tucson), 3, 111-146, 1988.

The evolution of modern mathematics illustrates Plato's parable of the Cave in the Seventh Book of his *Republic*. Examples concerning Riemann surfaces, the theory of function fields and imbedding theorems are provided to characterize the development of modern mathematics as an ongoing process of ascent from the empirical world of Plato's Cave to the realm of mathematical ideas. The abstract objects of mathematics, through projection and imbedding, become intimately related to the objects of our physical world. Our intellectual ascent is accomplished in several stages. As a result, the cave of empirical phenomena becomes brighter and brighter.

MAXWELL, Nicholas. Quantum Propensition Theory: A Testable Resolution of the Wave/Particle Dilemma. Brit J Phil Sci, 39(1), 1-50, Mr 88.

This paper develops a fully realistic version of quantum theory (QT), which solves the wave/particle problem. Quantum objects, such as electrons and atoms, are neither waves nor particles but *propensitions*, a new kind of fundamentally probabilistic entity, with probabilistic properties or propensities. It is suggested that probabilistic events occur whenever new particles or new stationary states are created. An experimental test is proposed: the new version of QT predicts that the exponential law of decay for decaying systems holds precisely for long times, whereas orthodox QT predicts departures from this law for long times.

MAY, Thomas (ed). *Philosophy Books, 1982-1986*. Bowling Green, Philosophy Doc Ctr, 1991.

MAY, Todd G. Kant the Liberal, Kant the Anarchist: Rawls and Lyotard on Kantian Justice. S J Phil, 28(4), 525-538, Wint 90.

This paper looks at two distinct interpretations of Kant's work that offer conflicting views of justice as derived from that work. It is argued that although Rawls got the Kantian intention right—to give a unified account of justice—Lyotard got the Kantian achievement right—a multiple and irreducible account of different spheres of justice. It is Lyotard's focus on the third Critique that allowed him to recognize both the impossibility of offering a unified account of justice and the possibilities for a more decentered account that are available. It is in the decenteredness of the account that it becomes anarchistic.

MAY, William F. The Molested. Hastings Center Rep, 21(3), 9-17, My-Je 91.

MAYOR, Luis and CARPINTERO, Helio and ZALBIDEA, M A. Condiciones del surgimiento y desarrollo de la Psicología Humanista. Rev Filosof (Spain), 3, 71-82, 1990.

American Humanistic Psychology grew in the 1950s and 1960s in the USA, in a situation of great insatisfaction and restlessness. The paper reviews the main principles of Humanistic Psychology conceived as a Third Force or a new path out of the mechanicism of behaviorism and the determinism and irrationalism of psychoanalysis. Its aims, as defined by Maslow, Bugental and Sutich and some of its American and European roots are here reviewed. Stress is also laid on the Zeitgeist and its influence upon the efforts to build a psychology based on the normal, free, creative man.

MAYORGA, Alejandro and VARGAS, Celso. Compromiso Ontico y Teorías Científicas. Rev Filosof (Costa Rica), 28(67-68), 231-236, D 90.

Popper was the first philosopher who introduced a criterion of demarcation between science and pseudo-science in which metaphysical ideas play a central role. MSRP developed by Lakatos and associates provides us with a new perspective within Popperian's epistemology for evaluating the influence of metaphysical ideas in science. In this report we present some criteria for characterizing the metaphysical component of scientific theories and determining when a theory is more profound than others. We use strongly the procedure presented by Ramsey. (edited)

MAZLISH, Bruce. Marx's Historical Understanding of the Proletariat and Class in 19th-Century England. Hist Euro Ideas, 12(6), 731-747, 1990.

Karl Marx saw himself as a historian as well as, or perhaps more than, a philosopher. Starting as a theoretician, he claimed to be an empirical historian. This claim is examined in regard to class and the proletariat. Upon examination, it turns out that Marx's empirical knowledge is based mainly on Engels's *Condition of the Working Class*. An examination of the relationship of the two men is first undertaken, and then of the *Condition* itself, emphasizing the latter's effort to comprehend the early stages of the Industrial Revolution. Especial note is given to the view of the proletariat, derived from Engels's experiences in Manchester, as intelligent and effectively without country or religion. The validity of these "empirical" observations concerning the proletariat, and their consequences for the Marxist conception of class are then further examined. A paradoxical conclusion is reached: Marx and Engels were better historians of the bourgeoisie than they were of the proletarians.

MAZLISH, Bruce. Reflections on the Eastern European Revolutions: The God that Failed. Praxis Int, 10(3-4), 236-240, O 90-Ja 91.

The author begins with the observation that in his recent book, *The Meaning of Karl Marx*, he was obviously off the mark in not foreseeing the failure of Marxism and the revolutions of 1989 in Eastern Europe. He was not alone in this regard; and the question becomes why. The answer lies in reviewing the nature of Marxism as a secular religion; as such is suffered from one fatal flaw: its millennial claims had to be measured by its earthly success, and not in a supranatural world. Unable either to deliver the material goods or to avoid the corruption of power, Marxism became a discredited creed. The second focus of the article is on the nature of the Soviet empire, and its collapse. This is seen as part of the general demise of empire after World War II, though the Soviet experience comes later and on the same continent (Eastern Europe). What is also different is that the Soviet empire is additionally an internal one, whose dissolution poses special problems and whose outcome is as yet unpredictable.

MAZOUÉ, James G. Diagnosis Without Doctors. J Med Phil, 15(6), 559-579, D 90.

Computer-based diagnostic systems are widely regarded as having only a supportive role in assisting physicians make diagnostic decisions. Continuing progress in the design of diagnostic software, however, may not only produce systems which have heuristic and consultative value, but which may render the traditional role of the physician as a 'polyfunctional practitioner' obsolete should it become feasible to replace practitioner-dependent diagnostic skill with more accurate, reliable and cost-effective computer-based programs. Should the implementation of such programs prove to be both a more practical and beneficial alternative than continuing to rely upon the exercise of practitioner-specific diagnostic skill, it would be unethical if the traditional role of the physician *qua diagnostician* were not phased out and supplanted by a more modular approach to medical decision making.

MAZOUÉ, James G. Self-Synthesis, Self-Knowledge, and Skepticism. Logos (USA), 11, 111-125, 1990.

In *Philosophical Explanations* Robert Nozick proposes an explanation of reflexive self-knowledge in terms of a self synthesizing itself through time in accordance with what he calls the "closest continuer schema." Skeptical possibilities remain, however, that undermine his proposal unless his account is supplemented with an Insulation Condition (IC): For any given act of reflexive self-reference *r*, no act of reflexive self-reference synthesizes itself around *r* other than the closest reflexive continuer of *r*'s closest reflexive predecessor. Although the addition of IC provides a partial vindication of Nozick's account, other skeptical questions about the referent of "I" would remain unanswered.

MAZZARELLA, Eugenio. Storicità tecnica e architettura. Arch Stor Cult, 4, 189-217, 1991.

The author places the modern functionalistic project of architecture in the philosophical perspective of Heideggerian reflections on technics. He analyzes the failure of this project in its rationalistic as well as in its organicist issue, connected to the abstractedness in the conceptions of function, disregarding its historical nature. Modern architecture is following the destiny of modern techne, which disavows its bond to physis, and for the human being physic is always historical, failing to solve the question "dwelling". "Dwelling" in the uneasiness of modern and post-modern experience of a simultaneous time, is the task to be faced by the "building" of archi-technon of our time.

MC BRIDE, William L. "Two Concepts of Liberty" Thirty Years Later: A Sartre-Inspired Critique. Soc Theor Pract, 16(3), 297-322, Fall 90.

After a brief initial reference to the historical circumstances of its origin, Berlin's famous distinction is first re-analyzed in light especially of his own later modifications and clarifications. To remedy some of the disadvantages of Berlin's preferred concept of "negative" liberty, the evolution of Sartre's concept of freedom from one of sheer negation in *Being and Nothingness* to his more nuanced later views is recalled. Finally, three situations in which the "negative liberty" concept yields inadequate understanding—those of formerly colonized African states, of the exclusion of women from clubs, and of the so-called "free market"—are explored.

MC BRIDE, William L. Global Injustices. Phil Inq, 12(3-4), 1-16, Sum-Fall 90.

Account is taken, first, of the diffusion of post-Marxist thought, and then of recent discussions of Marxism and justice. It is urged that analytic tools from the Marxian tradition be utilized in dealing with the phenomena of global injustices—increasingly exacerbated relationships of dominance and subordination between "First-" and "Third-World" countries—that are among the most salient in our world but that remain virtually unexamined by most North American philosophers. As an example of one outcome of this shift of attention, it is suggested that Third World countries' alleged obligations to repay international debts may be seen to lose their apparent validity when viewed from a global communitarian, non-nation-state-oriented perspective.

MC BRIDE, William L. Sartre and his Successors: Existential Marxism and Postmodernism at Our *Fin de Siecle*. Praxis Int, 11(1), 78-92, Ap 91.

MC BRIDE, William Thomas. Bakhtin's Marxist Formalism. Int Stud Phil, 23(1), 23-30, 1991.

MC CAFFERTY, Andrew. "Speaker Plans, Linguistic Contexts, and Indirect Speech Acts" in *Knowledge Representation and Defeasible Reasoning*, KYBURG JR, Henry E (ed), 191-220. Norwell, Kluwer, 1990.

This paper is a first step towards a detailed theory of indirect speech acts. From the philosophical literature, it argues for a contextual change theory of meaning—as proposed by David Lewis among others. It also makes use of work in computational linguistics on reconstructing a speaker's plan or intentions—especially the work of James Allen. It considers some very simple conversations about plans to see a movie, develops some default rules for reasoning about a speaker's plan given a context, and shows how these can begin to predict or explain what the indirect speech act will be.

MC CANN, Dennis P. Economic Rights: A Test Case for Catholic Social Teaching. Listening, 26(2), 145-155, Spr 91.

MC CANN, Hugh J. Settled Objectives and Rational Constraints. Amer Phil Quart, 28(1), 25-36, Ja 91.

This is a defense of the so-called "Simple View" of intentional action: the principle that anyone who A's intentionally intends to A. Rejecting this principle, it is argued, forces us to assign to other mental states the functional role of intention: that of providing settled objectives to guide deliberation and action. This is likely either to multiply entities, or to invite a revival of reductionist theories of intention. It also drives a wedge between intention and practical rationality, by forbidding agents to intend goals it is rational to seek. Finally, the states that are "substituted" for intention turn out to be subject to the same rational constraints as intention itself, and hence indistinguishable from it after all. Thus there is no basis for such supposed distinctions, and the simple view is to be preferred.

MC CARTHY, Christine. The Role of Moral Intuition in Applied Ethics: A Consideration of Positions of Peirce and Strike and Soltis. Phil Stud Educ, /, 117-127, 1989.

Peirce's view of moral intuition in applied ethics is examined, and compared with a contemporary view; conceptual questions about moral intuition are raised. Peirce rejects ethical reasoning, holding that conservative sentimentalism grounds morality. The instinctive mind and community maxims are the arbiters of ethical truth, giving insight into general laws. Peirce rejects relativism, hoping for convergence toward some limit in an infinite ethical inquiry. Strike and Soltis accept both moral intuition and moral reasoning; a reflective equilibrium is to be reached. Like Peirce, they reject ethical relativism, but do not adopt an ethical realism.

MC CARTHY, Thomas. *Ideals and Illusions: On Reconstruction and Deconstruction in Contemporary Critical Theory*. Cambridge, MIT Pr, 1991.

These eight studies of the thought of Jacques Derrida, Michel Foucault, Jürgen Habermas, Martin Heidegger, and Richard Rorty examine the critique of "impure reason" from the viewpoints of attackers and defenders of the Enlightenment tradition. They defend a position analogous to Kant's: ideas of reason are both unavoidable presuppositions of thought which have to be carefully reconstructed and persistent sources of illusions which have to be repeatedly deconstructed.

MC CARTHY, Tim. Logical Form and Radical Interpretation. Notre Dame J Form Log, 30(3), 401-419, Sum 89.

This paper concerns the empirical constraints on a characterization of logical relations in a natural language. Syntactic characterizations are distinguished from model-theoretic ones. It is shown that the structure of syntactic characterizations is largely underdetermined by the empirical constraints that naturally suggest themselves. However, an explanation of the notion of a logical constant is suggested that renders the model-theoretic characterization of logical relations in an extensional language determinate, relative to an idealized intentional psychology for its speakers.

MC CARTY, David Charles. The Philosophy of Logical Wholism. Synthese, 87(1), 51-123, Ap 91.

The present paper is on the replacement of atomistic interpretations of Wittgenstein's *Tractatus* by a wholistic interpretation on which the world-in-logical-space is not constructed out of objects but objects are abstracted from out of that space. Here, general arguments against atomism are directed toward a specific target, the four aspects of the atomistic reading of *Tractatus* given in the Hintikkas' *Investigating Wittgenstein* (Hintikka & Hintikka 1986). The aspects in question are called the semantical, metaphysical, epistemological and formal. (edited)

MC CARTY, David Charles and MC CARTY, Luise Prior. Reading the Darkness: Wittgenstein and Indoctrination. Proc Phil Educ, 46, 383-395, 1990.

MC CARTY, Luise Prior and MC CARTY, David Charles. Reading the Darkness: Wittgenstein and Indoctrination. Proc Phil Educ, 46, 383-395, 1990.

MC CARTY, Richard. Moral Conflicts in Kantian Ethics. Hist Phil Quart, 8(1), 65-79, Ja 91.

After distinguishing three criteria of adequacy for any acceptable moral theory's treatment of moral conflict, or conflicts of duties, I explain how Kant's ethics can satisfy all three. Although Kant denies the possibility of conflicting duties, he does allow conflicting "grounds of obligation." I develop a new interpretation of such conflicts, rejecting one proposed earlier by Onora O'Neill.

MC CAY, Bonnie J and VAYDA, Andrew P and EGHENTER, Cristina. Concepts of Process in Social Science Explanations. Phil Soc Sci, 21(3), 318-331, S 91.

Social scientists using one or another concept of process have paid little attention to underlying issues of methodology and explanation. Commonly, the concept used is a loose one. When it is not, there often are other problems, such as errors of reification and of assuming that events sometimes connected in a sequence are invariably thus connected. While it may be useful to retain the term "process" for some sequences of intelligibly connected actions and events, causal explanation must be sought with respect to the *events* constituting processes rather than with respect to processes regarded as unitary entities.

MC CLELLAND, Jay. "The Basis of Lawful Behavior: Rules or Connections" in *Acting and Reflecting: The Interdisciplinary Turn in Philosophy*, SIEG, Wilfried (ed), 48-52. Norwell, Kluwer, 1990.

MC CLOSKEY, Donald N. History, Differential Equations, and the Problem of Narration. Hist Theor, 30(1), 21-36, F 91.

MC CLOSKEY, Elizabeth Leibold. The Patient Self-Determination Act. Kennedy Inst Ethics J, 1(2), 163-169, Je 91.

MC CLUSKY, Frank and TESCHNER, George. Computer Alternatives in the History of Philosophy Classroom. Teach Phil, 13(3), 273-280, S 90.

The article describes the pedagogical and cognitive theory behind, and implementation of software that is used for teaching the history of philosophy. The software replaces traditional classroom teaching by presenting the reading assignments in a hypertext format that allows the student to receive exegetical comments on the text. Computerized questions allow for an individualized teaching and testing environment by branching the questions and providing hints and explanations. The program records student work in a database which is used for automated advising and diagnosis. The paper discusses the advantages of computer based instruction, the theory behind the design of exegetical hypertext, and the future development of such technology.

MC COLM, Gregory L. When Is Arithmetic Possible? Annals Pure Applied Log, 50(1), 29-51, N 90.

When a structure or class of structures admits an unbounded induction, we can do arithmetic on the stages of that induction: if only bounded inductions are admitted, then clearly each inductively definable relation can be defined using a finite explicit expression. Is the converse true? We examine evidence that the converse is true, in positive elementary induction (where explicit = elementary). We present a stronger conjecture involving the language L consisting of all $L_{\infty\omega}$ formulas with a finite number of variables, and examine a combinatorial property equivalent to "all L-definable relations are elementary."

MC COOL, Gerald A. *From Unity to Pluralism: The Internal Evolution of Thomism*. Bronx, Fordham Univ Pr, 1989.

MC CORMICK, Peter J. *Modernity, Aesthetics, and the Bounds of Art*. Ithaca, Cornell Univ Pr, 1990.

MC CORMICK, Richard A. Who or What is the Preembryo? Kennedy Inst Ethics J, 1(1), 1-15, Mr 91.

MC CRATE, James (trans) and GABEL, Joseph and STEIN, William M (trans). *Mannheim and Hungarian Marxism*. New Brunswick, Transaction Books, 1991.

This serves as a useful introduction to the force and character of Marxism in Central Europe. Mannheim was situated in the intellectual pitch of prewar Budapest, with its plethora of revisionist Marxists, anarchists, and intellectuals from a variety of areas who brought radical ideas into the mainstream of biological and social sciences, and which provided Budapest a special environment in which the cross-currents of Europe met. Gabel covers key figures and major concepts associated with Mannheim and the sociology of knowledge: ideology and false consciousness; the socially unattached intelligentsia; and the utopian conscience. (staff)

MC CUBBIN, Michael and COHEN, David. The Political Economy of Tardive Dyskinesia: Asymmetries in Power and Responsibility. J Mind Behav, 11(3-4), 465-488, Sum-Autumn 90.

Tardive dyskinesia is a serious, well-publicized adverse effect resulting from long-term neuroleptic drug use. However, little progress has been made during the last two decades in ensuring that these drugs are prescribed with necessary caution. Incentives and constraints operating on the major participants (patients, families, physicians, institutions, drug companies, society) in the decision-making process leading to the prescription of neuroleptics increase the likelihood that the benefits of drugs will be exaggerated and their adverse effects minimized. When combined with imbalances of power, these factors ensure that persons having little power and information to make the decision to prescribe will bear most costs of that decision. This points to the operation of an inefficient system which can be expected to yield sub-optimal results. We suggest ways to make the decision process more efficient by more closely aligning responsibility with cost. If those who hold power in the decision process are held accountable for the unwanted risks they impose upon others, both the use of neuroleptics and its inevitable iatrogenesis would probably be reduced.

MC CULLOCH, Gregory. Externalism and Experience. Analysis, 50(4), 244-250, O 90.

MC CULLOCH, Gregory. Making Sense of Words. Analysis, 51(2), 73-79, Mr 91.

MC CULLOUGH, Laurence B and CHERVENAK, Frank A. Justified Limits on Refusing Intervention. Hastings Center Rep, 21(2), 12-18, Mr-Ap 91.

MC CUMBER, John. "Essence and Subversion in Hegel and Heidegger" in *Writing the Politics of Difference*, SILVERMAN, Hugh J (ed), 13-29. Albany, SUNY Pr, 1991.

MC CUTCHEON, John and GUNZ, Sally. Some Unresolved Ethical Issues in Auditing. J Bus Ethics, 10(10), 777-785, O 91.

Independence is a fundamental concept to the audit. There is a clear relationship between independence and conflict of interest in all professions. This paper examines this relationship in the auditing profession and in the context of three specific practices. The paper analyses these practices by using the Davis model of conflict of interest. The results of this analysis give rise to some interesting questions for the ethical practices of the auditing profession.

MC DADE, Laurie A. The Difference-Deficit Debate: Theoretical Smokescreen for a Conservative Ambush. Phil Stud Educ, /, 65-79, 1987-88.

MC DERMOTT, John J. The Importance of Cultural Pedagogy. Thinking, 9(3), 2-4, 1990.

MC DERMOTT, John M. Metaphysical Conundrums at the Root of Moral Disagreement. Gregorianum, 71(4), 713-742, 1990.

Catholic morality presupposes natural law and metaphysics. The fundamental option theory involves, Rahner held, a "real absolute contradiction," because every choice, even one rejecting God, implicitly chooses God as its condition of possibility. Sin is irrational, as Pontifex and Maritain also witness. Individual free choices are intelligible only to God. Lest nominalism result, one must transcend a metaphysics based on the necessities of nature to a metaphysics of freedom. The Church's sacramental vision, preserving divine omnipotence and human freedom, structures reality and provides the *locus* for natural law, common good, and the significance of human symbols of love.

MC DONALD, Christie. "Literature and Philosophy at the Crossroads: Proustian Subjects" in *Writing the Politics of Difference*, SILVERMAN, Hugh J (ed), 135-144. Albany, SUNY Pr, 1991.

MC DONALD, David C. The Exclusion of Evidence Obtained by Constitutionally Impermissible Means in Canada. Crim Just Ethics, 9(2), 43-50, Sum-Fall 90.

MC DONALD, Don M and SCHOENFELDT, Lyle F and YOUNGBLOOD, Stuart A. The Teaching of Business Ethics: A Survey of AACSB Member Schools. J Bus Ethics, 10(3), 237-241, Mr 91.

This report presents the findings of a survey of business ethics education undertaken in the Fall of 1988. The respondents were the deans of colleges and universities associated with the AACSB. Ethics, as a curriculum topic, received significant coverage at over 90 percent of the institutions, with 53 percent indicating interest in increasing coverage of the subject. The tabulations of this survey may prove useful to schools seeking to compare or develop their emphases in business ethics.

MC DONNELL, Kevin. Volunteering Children. Proc Cath Phil Ass, 63, 182-192, 1990.

May infants or young children be subjects of medical experiments from which they as individuals cannot profit? Some have justified participation when and if the risks are minimal; others have claimed the studies are unjustifiable. This paper argues for understanding a young child's participation as expressing a family's projects and interests. Rather than create fictions of the individual child's informed consent, the family's moral agency is recognized as competent to involve and consent for its members.

MC DONOUGH, Richard. Wittgenstein's Critique of Mechanistic Atomism. Phil Invest, 14(3), 231-250, Jl 91.

MC DOUGALL, Patricia P and IBRAHIM, Nabil A and RUE, Leslie W and GREENE, G Robert. Characteristics and Practices of "Christian-Based" Companies. J Bus Ethics, 10(2), 123-132, F 91.

There is a sizeable group of self-described "Christian" companies which have declared their belief in the successful merging of biblical principles with business activities. As these companies have become more visible, an increasing number of anecdotal newspaper and magazine articles about these companies have appeared. Surprisingly, no rigorous research had been conducted prior to our recent study. This article provides national estimates of the size and predominant characteristics of self-identified "Christian" companies. In addition, the study investigated the types of relationships these companies maintained with their employees, customers, communities, and suppliers.

MC DOWELL, Banks. The Professional's Dilemma: Choosing Between Service and Success. Bus Prof Ethics J, 9(1-2), 35-52, Spr-Sum 90.

A conflict of interest faces professionals asked by a client about whether he needs services when that professional will furnish the service. Unnecessary services may be provided. Most professionals are committed to the ethical obligation to promote a client's welfare and at the same time are subject to financial and social pressure to succeed. This is a preliminary exploration whether that dilemma can be minimized by (a) redefining the ethical obligation, (b) expanding informed consent to require information about the dilemma, (c) dividing counselling and providing roles, (d) compelling ethical compliance by law, or (e) requiring professional education to more strongly motivate professionals to act ethically.

MC EVOY, James J. John Scottus Eriugena: Recent Works of Consultation. Phil Stud (Ireland), 32, 83-98, 1988-90.

Originally a lecture delivered at the Irish National Academy, this article aims to give complete and up-to-date information on the scholarly activities of the Society for the Promotion of Eriugenian Studies, on editions of Eriugena's writings and translations from Greek, on existing translations of individual works of his, and on published word-lists. It concludes with a reflection on the principle factors which have given rise to the current flourishing state of Eriugenian studies.

MC EVOY, James. Philosophie ancienne et médiévale. Rev Phil Louvain, 88(78), 243-254, My 90.

This publication contains the text of a public lecture delivered on 8 Nov. 1989 at the centenary celebrations of the foundation of the *Institut Supérieur de Philosophie*, by l'abbé Désiré Mercier, at Louvain (Belgium). Mercier's first appointment of a professor of the history of philosophy (1893) was Maurice de Wulf. His work and that of his successors in ancient and medieval philosophy is reviewed, together with the origin of the *Centre De Wulf—Mansion* and that of the *Centre de philosophie arabe* at the *Institut Supérieur*. The present and future policy of the CDWM are described.

MC EWAN, Hunter. Teaching Acts: An Unfinished Story. Proc Phil Educ, 46, 189-197, 1990.

This article looks at the analytic literature in the philosophy of teaching and considers the question of the nature of teaching acts. It criticizes the essentialism of this project—the desire to find criteria that will distinguish teaching from other acts and to describe the formal character of thinking in teaching. It proposes that teaching acts can only be understood historically and that narrative understanding is essential to an understanding of what it is to teach.

MC FADYEN, Alistair I. *The Call to Personhood*. New York, Cambridge Univ Pr, 1991.

The purpose of the book is to advance a Christian understanding of the person in social terms. This is achieved by weaving together Christian trinitarian theology and contemporary social thought. The basic position taken is that people call each other into autonomy and responsibility (and therefore personhood) before and in partnership with one another; we thus become the people we are as our identities are shaped through the patterns of relation, communication and exchange which surround and incorporate us. Personal identity is the way one is for others. The work explores the ethical and political implications of the view that one is called into personhood through relationships of a particular form and structure.

MC FALL, Lynne. "What's Wrong with Bitterness?" in *Feminist Ethics*, CARD, Claudia (ed), 146-160. Lawrence, Univ Pr of Kansas, 1991.

MC FEE, Graham. "Dance is a Performing Art" in *XIth International Congress in Aesthetics, Nottingham 1988*, WOODFIELD, Richard (ed), 131-135. Nottingham, Nottingham Polytech, 1990.

MC GHEE, Michael. A Fat Worm of Error? Brit J Aes, 31(3), 222-229, Jl 91.

Do the critics of Kant's disinterestedness claim really understand it? No, they fail to see that it is just the pleasure we take in the activity in which we are engaged by aesthetic ideas. This pleasure is to some degree articulable because it has a content. The 'much thought' by which aesthetic experience is constituted. This partially articulable content is a ground of aesthetic value, and generates reasons for communicable judgments.

MC GINN, Colin. "Radical Interpretation and Epistemology" in *Truth and Interpretation: Perspectives on the Philosophy of Donald Davidson*, LE PORE, Ernest (ed), 356-368. Cambridge, Blackwell, 1986.

MC GINN, Marie and BELL, Martin. Naturalism and Scepticism. Philosophy, 65(254), 399-418, O 90.

MC GINN, Marie. On Two Recent Accounts of Colour. Phil Quart, 41(164), 316-324, Jl 91.

The primary/secondary quality distinction gives rise to the following dilemma. *Either* colour is identified with some complex physical property, and the connection with phenomenology is lost. *Or* colour is understood in terms of the effect of primary qualities on perceiving subjects, but the resulting phenomenal qualities are beyond the scope of science. This paper argues that accounts of colour by McGinn and Westphal are unsuccessful in resolving this dilemma. It is argued, first, that McGinn's subjectivism does entail that colour is 'in the mind', and second, that Westphal does not avoid a reductive account that breaks the connection with phenomenal colour.

MC GLYNN, Fred. "Postmodernism and Theater" in *Postmodernism—Philosophy and the Arts (Continental Philosophy III)*, SILVERMAN, Hugh J (ed), 137-154. New York, Routledge, 1990.

MC GOVERN, Arthur F. Catholic and Marxist Views on Human Development. Dialec Hum, 16(3-4), 97-106, Sum-Autumn 89.

MC GOWAN, Richard. Justice: The Root of American Business Ideology and Ethics. J Bus Ethics, 9(11), 891-901, N 90.

Although there are many conceptions of "Justice," these different perceptions can provide many interesting insights into a business person's ethical standards as well as that person's decision-making processes. Using the Bishops' Pastoral Letter on the US Economy as the basis for asking questions about "justice," twenty-four business executives were interviewed about their conception of justice. An analysis of these interviews reveals that this group of business people operated under very different conceptions of "Justice" at the macroenvironmental and microenvironmental levels. This result has some interesting implications not only for those scholars concerned with business ethics but for everyone who has a stake in business education.

MC GRATH, Lynette. An Ethical Justification of Women's Studies, Or What's a Nice Girl Like You Doing in a Place like This? Hypatia, 6(2), 137-151, Sum 91.

The feminist in academe, says Paula Bennett, is like Procne married to Tereus, "inextricably wedded to the sources of her harm." An ethical justification of academic feminism can be found, not in cooperation and affiliation, but in the strategies currently necessary to ensure curricular and cultural diversity. Historically contextualized and strategically politicized, this ethic is founded on the claim that universities are places where we may all learn to know what is other than ourselves.

MC GREAL, Ian Philip. The New Dimensions of Chinese Medical Ethics. J Chin Phil, 18(2), 161-168, Je 91.

MC GUINNESS, B F and VON WRIGHT, G H. Unpublished Correspondence between Russell and Wittgenstein. Russell, 10(2), 101-124, Wint 90-91.

MC GUINNESS, Brian and FRONGIA, Guido. *Wittgenstein: A Bibliographical Guide*. Cambridge, Blackwell, 1990.

MC GUIRE, J E. "Predicates of Pure Existence: Newton on God's Space and Time" in *Philosophical Perspectives on Newtonian Science*, BRICKER, Phillip (ed), 91-108. Cambridge, MIT Pr, 1990.

MC INERNEY, Peter K. How Would an *Übermensch* Regard His Past and Future? Int Stud Phil, 22(2), 121-128, 1990.

Nietzsche conceived the self to be a bodily-based psychological system involving a relatively permanent hierarchy of instincts. This paper examines the positions that Nietzsche's overman would take on some basic questions about the relevance of his own past and future in light of his understanding of the natural status of the self and values. It considers whether an overman would consider himself to be equally responsible for all parts of his past, how an overman could have any legitimate basis for believing that he could form his future self through sublimation, and why an overman would remain one psychological system despite his cultivation of conflicting instincts in himself.

MC INERNEY, Peter K. The Nature of a Person-Stage. Amer Phil Quart, 28(3), 227-235, Jl 91.

Some notion of "a person at a time" is needed, because at any given time the current person-stage is available for dialogue, interaction, and observation in a way that earlier and later stages are not. The article explores three central features of the notion of a person-stage: the temporal extention of a person-stage, the nature of the "psychological connectedness" between the person-stages, and the types of unity in a person-stage. In light of the fact that the experienced and displayed characteristics of a person may fluctuate over relatively short periods of time, the paper considers whether and how psychological features that are constitutive of personal identity over time can exist inoperatively in a person-stage.

MC INERNY, Ralph. "Adler on Freedom" in *Freedom in the Modern World: Jacques Maritain, Yves R Simon, Mortimer J Adler*, TORRE, Michael D (ed), 65-72. Notre Dame, Univ Notre Dame Pr, 1989.

MC INERNY, Ralph. "Reflections on Maritain's *Le Crépuscule de la Civilisation*" in *From Twilight to Dawn: The Cultural Vision of Jacques Maritain*, REDPATH, Peter A (ed), 287-292. Notre Dame, Univ Notre Dame Pr, 1990.

MC INTYRE, Alison. "Is Akratic Action Always Irrational?" in *Identity, Character, and Morality: Essays in Moral Psychology*, FLANAGAN, Owen (ed), 379-400. Cambridge, MIT Pr, 1990.

Akratic action is generally thought to be essentially irrational. Three different lines of argument are developed which undermine this common conviction about *akrasia* (or "weakness of will" or "incontinence"). 1) The judgment that is violated in akratic action is not necessarily one that took more into account than the judgment that prompted the akratic alternative. 2) It need not be an uncontrolled appetite or some other nonrational source that prompts or motivates an akratic action. 3) The principle of continence is a *prima facie* rational requirement, and it may conflict with other higher order principles which characterize rationality in action.

MC KEE, Patrick. A Dilemma of Late Life Memory. J Applied Phil, 8(1), 83-86, 1991.

Unexpected but vivid and compelling memories are a wide-spread experience in late life. The experience has often been described in literature, and in recent years has been the object of extensive gerontological research under the label 'life review'. Such memories often include a reversal of judgment about a past act, relationship, event, etc. What earlier was judged to be so is, in the retrospect of late life, judged not to have been so after all. This presents a question: which judgment—the earlier or the later—has better epistemological credentials in such cases? Some obvious possible answers are considered and rejected. It would seem that the issue is not resolvable on epistemological grounds. A parallel dilemma seems to appear in other dimensions of experience. An example from aesthetic experience is briefly considered.

MC KEE, Patrick. Philosophy and Wisdom. Teach Phil, 13(4), 325-330, D 90.

MC KELVEY, Charles. *Beyond Ethnocentrism: A Reconstruction of Marx's Concept of Science*. Westport, Greenwood Pr, 1991.

MC KENZIE, Nancy F (ed). *The Crisis in Health Care: Ethical Issues*. New York, Penguin Books, 1990.

MC KERLIE, Dennis. Friendship, Self-Love, and Concern for Others in Aristotle's Ethics. Ancient Phil, 11(1), 85-101, Spr 91.

Aristotle calls a friend "another self." He does not mean that self-concern, properly understood, includes a concern for the friend. He thinks that we should have a concern for the friend's good that is independent and fundamental in the way that self-concern itself is. Aristotle defends this view by finding a common basis for both friendship and self-concern in the recognition of goodness in thoughts and perceptions. His ethical theory has the structure of self-referential eudaimonism, not egoistic eudaimonism.

MC KIE, John R. Zeno's Paradox of Extension. S J Phil, 29(1), 69-86, Spr 91.

MC KIM, Robert. Some Remarks on a Historical Theory of Justice and its Application to Ireland. Phil Stud (Ireland), 32, 224-244, 1988-90.

MC KINNEY, Ronald H. Deconstructing Lonergan. Int Phil Quart, 31(1), 81-93, Mr 91.

In this article, Bernard Lonergan's thought is "deconstructed" in accordance with Derridean techniques in order to foster dialogue between Lonerganian foundationalists and deconstructionists. Lonergan's own notion of "dialectic" is shown to be compatible with Derrida's thought and the warring logic at work in Lonergan's dialectical treatment of the self-correcting process of learning, language and thought, and common sense and theory is also examined. The result is the identification of some fundamental hierarchical oppositions within Lonergan's thought which contain the seeds for their own reversal.

MC KINNEY, Ronald H. An Entropic Analysis of Postmodernism. Phil Today, 34(2), 163-174, Sum 90.

In this article, I trace the fundamental differences between David Ray Griffin's "Constructive" or "Holistic" postmodernism and Jacques Derrida's "Deconstructive" postmodernism. A contemporary analysis of the notion of "entropy" provides the basis for comparison. Some key thinkers examined are Linda Hutcheon, Erich Jantsch, Jeremy Rifkin, Ilya Prigogine, David Bohm, and Orrin Klapp.

MC KINNEY, Ronald H. Reply to Marsh's "Reply to McKinney on Lonergan". Int Phil Quart, 31(3), 349-351, S 91.

A defense is made of the relative merits of deconstruction vis-a-vis Lonergan's foundational theory regarding their handling of the Problem of the One and the Many. The author's preference for paradox over clarity is made manifest.

MC KINNON, Christine. From What Can't Be Said To What Isn't Known. S J Phil, 29(1), 87-108, Spr 91.

This paper argues that there are important methodological and stylistic similarities between Wittgenstein's *Tractatus* and his *On Certainty* which can best be brought out by comparing the logical and metaphysical propositions of the former with the grammatical and framework propositions of the latter. Both these works are shown to be characterised by an antifoundationalist sentiment, and both works are shown to be investigations into limits: on the one hand into the limits of sensible discourse as circumscribed by metaphysical constraints, on the other into the limits of explanation and of legitimate knowledge claims as determined by epistemological considerations.

MC KINSEY, Michael. Anti-Individualism and Privileged Access. Analysis, 51(1), 9-16, Ja 91.

Burge and Davidson have both recently claimed that a given thought's being a wide psychological state is perfectly compatible with the thinker's having privileged access to that thought. Against this, I argue that Davidson's claim is based on a philosophically uninteresting conception of first person authority and that Burge's claim is based on an irrelevant conception of a "wide" psychological state. I propose a more adequate conception of wideness and give a simple argument that it is impossible to have privileged access to thoughts that are wide in this sense.

MC LAREN, Peter and HAMMER, Rhonda. Rethinking the Dialectic: A Social Semiotic Perspective for Educators. Educ Theor, 41(1), 23-46, Wint 91.

MC LARTY, Colin. The Uses and Abuses of the History of Topos Theory. Brit J Phil Sci, 41(3), 351-375, S 90.

The view that toposes originated as generalized set theory is a figment of set theoretically educated common sense. This false history obstructs understanding of category theory and especially of categorical foundations for mathematics. Problems in geometry, topology, and related algebra led to categories and toposes. Elementary toposes arose when Lawvere's interest in the foundations of physics and Tierney's in the foundations of topology led both to study Grothendieck's foundations for algebraic geometry. I end with remarks on a categorical view of the history of set theory, including a false history plausible form that point of view that would make it helpful to introduce toposes as a generalization from set theory.

MC LAUGHLIN, Brian P. "Type Epiphenomenalism, Type Dualism, and the Causal Priority of the Physical" in *Philosophical Perspectives, 3: Philosophy of Mind and Action Theory, 1989*, TOMBERLIN, James E (ed), 109-135. Atascadero, Ridgeview, 1989.

MC LAUGHLIN, Peter and ETTINGER, Lia and JABLONKA, Eva. On the Adaptations of Organisms and the Fitness of Types. Phil Sci, 57(3), 499-513, S 90.

We claim that much of the confusion associated with the "tautology problem" about survival of the fittest is due to the mistake of attributing fitness to individuals instead of to types. We argue further that the problem itself cannot be solved merely by taking fitness as the aggregate cause of reproductive success. We suggest that a satisfying explanation must center not on logical analysis of the concept of general adaptedness but on the empirical analysis of single adapted traits and their causal relationship to changes in allele frequencies.

MC LAUGHLIN, R J. "Christianity, Humanism, and St Thomas Aquinas" in *The Question of Humanism: Challenges and Possibilities*, GOICOECHEA, David (ed), 70-82. Buffalo, Prometheus, 1991.

Following St Thomas Aquinas, this paper argues that we should try intelligently, freely, and responsibly to achieve the highest human goods. If our intelligence leads us, as it leads Thomas, to affirm our creaturely status, then even without the aid faith it tells us that we should be religious. That God has spoken to us in a way requiring faith in Him, though not provable, is something that the philosopher can see as fitting, even necessary if we have in fact a supernatural destiny, knowledge of which is important for living well.

MC LAUGHLIN, T H. Peter Gardner on Religious Upbringing and the Liberal Ideal of Religious Autonomy. J Phil Educ, 24(1), 107-125, Sum 90.

Gardner has argued (*J Phil Educ*, 22(1), 89-105) against my view (*Phil Educ,* 18(1), 75-83; 19(1), 119-127) that it is possible to reconcile a commitment to the development of the autonomy of children with the right of parents to provide a form of substantial religious upbringing. Gardner's view is that parents concerned with autonomy should not provide such an upbringing, but favour an agnostic or atheistic one. This article examines and rejects the various arguments which Gardner uses to establish his conclusion, and restates my position.

MC LAUGHLIN, Thomas G. Sub-Arithmetical Ultrapowers: A Survey. Annals Pure Applied Log, 49(2), 143-191, O 90.

The paper aims to provide an up-to-the-minute survey of the structural properties of, and relationships between, ultrapowers (in the classical sense) obtained from ultrafilters in certain *countable* Boolean algebras, namely, the various algebras B_n = the algebra of subsets of the integers that are of n-th jump level of computability in the turing degrees (starting with n = 0, the case of the recursive sets). A large number of results known in the n = 0 case are extended to all n; and some distinctions are established between the cases n = 0 and n greater than 0.

MC LEAN, Murdith. Residual Natural Evil and Anthropic Reasoning. Relig Stud, 27(2), 173-188, Je 91.

MC LEOD, John. Change and Development. J Aes Educ, 25(2), 97-107, Sum 91.

MC MAHAN, Jeff. "War and Peace" in *A Companion to Ethics*, SINGER, Peter (ed), 384-395. Cambridge, Blackwell, 1991.

MC MAHON, Christopher. Authority and the Diffusion of Moral Expertise. Pub Affairs Quart, 5(3), 259-268, Jl 91.

MC MAHON, Thomas F. A Reaction to Vogel's "The Ethical Roots of Business". Bus Ethics Quart, 1(2), 211-222, Ap 91.

In this article, "The Ethical Roots of Business," (*Business Ethics Quarterly*, Volume 1, Number 1, January, 1991), David Vogel claims that Thomas Aquinas and other Catholic theologians considered profit as "inherently morally suspect." Furthermore, according to Jesus Christ a "moral business was a contradiction in terms." In this article McMahon challenges Vogel's position with citations from scripture scholars, moral theologians, legal experts, social ethicists, Vatican II documents and recent papal encyclicals. None of these sources condemn any respectable avocation, such as business. Rather than disapproval, they stress the dignity of the person, whether employer or employee. McMahon also demonstrates that the just price and money lending as conceptualized by Thomas Aquinas are not profiteering, as Vogel claims.

MC MULLIN, Ernan. Comment: Selective Anti-Realism. Phil Stud, 61(1-2), 97-108, F 91.

Comment on A Fine: "Piecemeal Realism." Fine's critique of scientific realism derives its force from a selective focus on mechanics. But what does the antirealist have to say about evolutionary theory or astrophysics? Furthermore, the circularity objection to the "explanationist" defence of realism can be countered. Fine's own position (NOA) reduces either to instrumentalism or to an unargued-for realism, depending on where the stress is laid.

MC MURTRY, John. *Understanding War: A Philosophical Inquiry*. Buffalo, Univ of Toronto Pr, 1989.

This study penetrates beneath the voluminously expanding literature on weapon systems developments, game-theoretical strategies of deterrence and attack, just war theory and the ethics of nuclear threat to a deep-structural analysis of the military paradigm of war as such. Beginning from its covert metaphysical assumptions and working upwards to the patterns of mass-homicide it justifies, the analysis lays bare the overall system of false premises, inferences and self-contradictions undergirding accepted military thought, explaining the hold of its unreason by larger, coercive patterns of economic exploitation and political rule. Complementing the monograph's critique of the military system of thought and action, is the development of an original theory of nonmilitary patterns of war which are not homicidal but emancipatory in nature.

MC NAMARA, Paul. Leibniz on Creation, Contingency and Per-Se Modality. Stud Leibniz, 22(1), 48-68, 1990.

Leibniz's first problem with contingency stems from his doctrine of divine creation (not his later doctrine of truth) and is solved via his concepts of necessity per se, etc. (not via his later concept of infinite analysis). I scrutinize some of the earliest texts in which the first problem and its solution occur. I compare his "per se modal concepts" with his concept of analysis and with the traditional concept of metaphysical necessity. I then identify and remove the main obstacle to Leibniz's employment of these concepts by reflecting on his concept of a world and comparing it with contemporary conceptions. Finally I sketch the place that this early problem and its solutions had in the context of his mature philosophy. A disagreement between Sleigh and Adams which hinges on the assumption that there is just one problem with competing solutions is seen to dissolve in this light.

MC NAUGHTON, David. The Importance of Being Human. Philosophy, 29, 63-81, 91 Supp.

Is the fact that someone is a human being morally significant *in itself*? Those who deny that it is hold that any differences in our response to a severely mentally handicapped human and to a chimpanzee cannot be justified. In opposing this view, Cora Diamond argues that we do not need a ground for such differential treatment. The moral particularist, whose position I defend, holds that 'being human' is sometimes, but not always, a morally relevant property. I differ from Diamond in maintaining that a justification for any differential treatment can and must be provided.

MC NAUGHTON, David. Response to Diamond. Philosophy, 29, 85-86, 91 Supp.

A Kantian cannot see severely mentally retarded human beings as objects of moral concern. In reply to the Kantian, Diamond suggests that we should see the retarded as sharing with us a human life, one in which they have been deprived of distinctive human capacities. In offering that reply she is not, she insists, trying to *justify* treating them as objects of special moral concern. The dispute between Diamond and the Kantian, I suggest, does not seem to be one about the application of a concept to a hard case within a mutually agreed practice. Rather, their conceptions of our moral practice differ sharply. But Diamond's reply is, I argue, still best understood as (part of) an attempted justification, not just part of her view of this particular case, but of the whole practice of which that view forms a part.

MC NEILL, William. Porosity: Violence and the Question of Politics in Heidegger's *Introduction to Metaphysics*. Grad Fac Phil J, 14(2)-15(1), 183-212, 1991.

To examine Heidegger's understanding of politics in 1935 via an interpretation of the nexus of violence, the *Polis* and uncanniness or 'unhomeliness' (*unheimlechkeit*) in Heidegger's reading of the *Antigone* chorus as presented in *Introduction to Metaphysics*. The paper argues that the *Polis* is to be understood in terms of a kind of "Porosity" (from the Greek *'Poros'*) as the site of finitude.

MC NULTY, T Michael. Economic Theory and Human Behavior. J Value Inq, 24(4), 325-333, O 90.

An examination of some impossibility results in microeconomic theory shows that recommendations that human beings act rationally as envisioned by that theory cannot be justified. Since it is clear that human beings do not in fact act rationally in this way, and Alexander Rosenberg has argued convincingly that they could not be rational in this way, we are left with the conclusion that microeconomic theory is not about human behavior at all.

MC PECK, John and SANDERS, James. Teaching Johnny to Think. Proc Phil Educ, 46, 403-409, 1990.

MC PHERRAN, Mark L. Pyrrhonism's Arguments Against Value. Phil Stud, 60(1-2), 127-142, S-O 90.

The article examines Pyrrhonism's primary arguments for suspending judgment on the objective goodness and badness of things and actions; especially Sextus Empiricus's 'Tenth Mode' (*PH* 1.145-163) and others found at the ends of his *Outlines of Pyrrhonism* and *Adversus Mathematicos*. The paper next offers a defense against J Annas's and J Barnes's charge that in some of his arguments Sextus conflates skepticism with relativism (and is thus an unwitting dogmatist). The paper concludes with a comment on the modern skeptical assumption *contra* the ancients that our first order normative judgments are unaffected by—are 'insulated from'—our second-order metaethical doubts.

MC PHERRAN, Mark L. Socratic Reason and Socratic Revelation. J Hist Phil, 29(3), 345-373, Jl 91.

On some accounts, Socrates is a consummate intellectualist who holds that discursive rationality is our only truthworthy guide in life (see *Crito* 46b). But this portrait seems very much at odds with Socrates's reliance on extrarational sources of information, such as his *daimonion*. This paper provides a resolution of this difficulty (especially as it is raised by *Euthyphro* 15c-d), offers a detailed account of the *daimonion* and its relation to 'secular' Socratic reason, and then replies to Gregory Vlastos's recent objections to accounts such as this that credit the extrarational with a genuine epistemic role in Socratic thought.

MC PHERRAN, Mark. Plato's Reply to the 'Worst Difficulty' Argument of the *Parmenides*: *Sophist* 248a-249d. Arch Gesch Phil, 68(3), 233-252, 1986.

This paper offers an interpretation of the 'Worst Difficulty' Argument of the *Parmenides* (133a-135a) that allows it—contrary to other popular accounts—to live up to Plato's suggestion that it constitutes a significant challenge to the early theory of Forms (concluding, as it does, that knowledge of the Forms is impossible). In light of Plato's hint that the argument is nonetheless flawed (133b), the paper surveys various plausible rebuttals, and then contends that Plato recognizes the best one available to him in the *Sophist* (248a-249d). Finally, the author examines the problem of actually attributing that solution to him.

MC ROBBIE, Michael and BARCA, Anne. Constructive Interpolation Theorems for $S2^0$ and S2. Rep Math Log, 23, 3-15, 1989.

MC SHEA, Daniel W. Complexity and Evolution: What Everybody Knows. Biol Phil, 6(3), 303-324, Jl 91.

The consensus among evolutionists seems to be (and has been for at least a century) that the morphological complexity of organisms increases in evolution, although almost no empirical evidence for such a trend exists. Most studies of complexity have been theoretical, and the few empirical studies have not, with the exception of certain recent ones, been especially rigorous; reviews are presented of both the theoretical and empirical literature. The paucity of evidence raises the question of what sustains the consensus, and a number of suggestions are offered, including the possibility that certain cultural and/or perceptual biases are at work. In addition, a shift in emphasis from theoretical to empirical inquiry is recommended for the study of complexity, and guidelines for future empirical studies are proposed.

MÉCHOULAN, Éric. Theoria, Aisthesis, Mimesis and Doxa. Diogenes, 151, 131-148, Fall 90.

Aesthetic theories and conceptions of memesis are often paradoxical, or even aporetical. With a historical analysis of the terms involved, it is maybe possible to circumvent such aporias. Before Parmenides the *theoria* is nothing but a collectively legitimated *aisthesis*. After him, and with Plato, *theoria* and *aisthesis* become ontologically opposed. Hence *mimesis* possessed no more social standing. And the same for *doxa*. In Greek, *doxa* means not only opinion, but glory, looking or seeming as well. Aesthetics deals with all these meanings. We must then link the epistemological question of mimesis to the aesthetical one of value and judgment.

MEESON, Philip. The Influence of Modernism on Art Education. Brit J Aes, 31(2), 103-110, Ap 91.

In contrast to the present move towards a rational curriculum in art education in Britain the previous influence of Modernism on art education is seen as directing classroom practices through the projection of certain stylistic beliefs. These beliefs are defined as: an attitude to history, the importance of the unconscious mind, the idea of progress and the notion of an avant garde. The occasion of Modernist influence is now seen as the high point of achievement in art education. An effective art education must rest on an idea of style not merely on the rational organization of practices.

MEGIVERN, James J. The Birth of the Death-Machine. Crim Just Ethics, 10(1), 2,45-48, Wint-Spr 91.

The article notes the irony in the way the guillotine emerged as a product of the French Revolution despite Enlightenment idealism. The physician who first proposed it had noble intentions, but ended up wanting nothing to do with it. Robespierre played a fascinating dual role, opposing the death penalty absolutely during the "first" revolution (1789), then himself leading the charge to guillotine the King and everyone else with anti-revolutionary ideas in the "second" revolution (1792). An odd sequence of events led to these machines being installed all over France on the very eve of its most tumultuous period, with the bloodiest of consequences.

MEHTA, J L. Problems of Understanding. J Indian Counc Phil Res, 7(2), 85-96, Ja-Ap 90.

MEIJSING, Monica. Searle's Oplossing voor het lichaam-geest probleem: ipse dixit—Een reactie op Anne Ruth Mackor. Alg Ned Tijdschr Wijs, 83(1), 61-68, Ja 91.

In my reaction to Mackor's "Functionalism versus Double-Aspect Theory" I argue that Searle, contrary to Mackor's claim, has no solution for the mind-body problem. His strategy to call the distinction between mind and body a "macro-micro distinction" can only seem to offer a solution, because Searle *says* it does. Furthermore, I defend the double-aspect theory against Mackor's charges.

MEILAENDER, Gilbert. "Are There Virtues Inherent in a Profession?" in *Ethics, Trust, and the Professions: Philosophical and Cultural Aspects*, PELLEGRINO, Edmund D (ed), 139-158. Washington, Georgetown Univ Pr, 1991.

MEINWALD, Constance C. *Plato's "Parmenides"*. New York, Oxford Univ Pr, 1991.

MEKLER, Alan H. Universal Structures in Power $\aleph_1$. J Sym Log, 55(2), 466-477, Je 90.

MELCHERT, Norman. Kantian Freedom Naturalized. Hist Phil Quart, 7(1), 67-75, Ja 90.

A naturalized account of Kant's views on human freedom will combine the most attractive features of both Hume-style compatibilism and extra-causal libertarianism. The key idea is that freedom is freedom from rationally undisciplined nature. The measure of our freedom is the degree to which we can transform the reasons there are for an action into reasons we have to perform that action. I explain the sense in which a kind of spontaneity in action is possible even in a causally determinate world.

MELE, Alfred R. Akratic Action and the Practical Role of Better Judgment. Pac Phil Quart, 72(1), 33-47, Mr 91.

Akratic action, traditionally conceived, is uncompelled, intentional action that conflicts with what the agent judges best at the time. This paper attacks the idea—advanced in different forms by Aristotle (on one reading), Davidson, and Hare—that there is a (non-artificial) species of evaluative judgment whose function or conceptual connection to intentional behavior is such as to preclude there being akratic intentions and actions against its instances. Rejecting the idea leaves it open that our evaluative judgments bear importantly on what we intend and do. An account of that bearing is developed and defended.

MELE, Alfred R. He Wants to Try. Analysis, 50(4), 251-253, O 90.

Is it a conceptual requirement on wanting to *try* to do something, *A*—or on an agent's acting on such a want—that the agent want to *A*? Certain alleged grounds for a negative answer are criticized and alternative grounds are offered. A case is constructed in which an agent who has no desire or want to *A* nevertheless wants to *try* to *A*, and acts on that want.

MELE, Alfred and HEIL, John. Mental Causes. Amer Phil Quart, 28(1), 61-71, Ja 91.

Garden-variety explanations of human behavior feature agents' reasons, states of mind with particular mental contents. Such states are commonly taken to contribute to the etiology of the behavior. Worries about this picture abound, however. One difficulty is to see how mental content could function causally. We advance an account of mental causation that squares with a standard conception of agency and with the notion that the content of mental states is often fixed in part by relational, non-intrinsic characteristics of agents.

MELENDO, Tomás. Sobre la "Metafísica del bien y del mal". Espiritu, 38(99), 45-60, Ja-Je 89.

MELHADO, Evan M. "Metzger, Kuhn, and Eighteenth-Century Disciplinary History" in *Études sur/Studies on Hélène Metzger*, FREUDENTHAL, Gad , 111-134. Leiden, Brill, 1990.

MELIA, Joseph. Anti-Realism Untouched. Mind, 100(399), 341-342, Jl 91.

There is an argument which purports to show that verificationism, and its modern successor, anti-realism, collapse into an absurd form of idealism. However, the argument assumes that these positions entail that every true proposition is knowable. I argue that the verificationists and anti-realists are not committed to this principle.

MELLEMA, Gregory. Supererogation and the Fulfillment of Duty. J Value Inq, 25(2), 167-175, Ap 91.

An act of supererogation is standardly characterized (in addition to satisfying other conditions) as one which the agent performing it has no duty or obligation to perform, or equivalently, as one which is not obligatory for the agent to perform. I argue that this standard characterization leads to serious difficulties, and I describe what I believe is a more satisfactory alternative.

MELLIZO, Carlos (trans) and LOCKE, John. *John Locke: Segundo Tratado sobre el Gobierno Civil*. Madrid, Alianza, 1990.

MELLOR, D H (ed). *Philosophical Papers: F P Ramsey*. New York, Cambridge Univ Pr, 1990.

This is a new edition of the previously published philosophical papers of F P Ramsey, with a full bibliography of Ramsey's published works and a new introduction by D H Mellor relating Ramsey's work to subsequent developments in philosophy.

MELLOR, Philip A. Self and Suffering: Deconstruction and Reflexive Definition in Buddhism and Christianity. Relig Stud, 27(1), 49-63, Mr 91.

MELNICK, A James. "Scientific Atheism" in the Era of Perestrojka. Stud Soviet Tho, 40(1-3), 223-229, 1990.

This article discusses how the Soviet atheistic establishment has been forced to adapt itself under Gorbachev's perestroika program. It examines the divergence between that establishment and the Council of Religious Affairs, "Gorbachevism" in the sphere of religion, the greater tolerance for religion based on economic reform needs, as well as the old and new characteristics of "scientific atheism" under Gorbachev. It concludes that the atheistic establishment has had to "re-think" its strategy and that this reappraisal all but challenges Leninist orthodoxy. Nevertheless, while the reformers have encouraged a "tactical and more humane detente toward religion," they have not yet moved to entirely eliminate the basis for ideological hostility toward it.

MELONI, C G and GHILARDI, S. Modal Logics with *n*-ary Connectives. Z Math Log, 36(3), 193-215, 1990.

MELSEN, A G M van. "Science and Religion" in *Science and Religion: One World-Changing Perspectives on Reality*, FENNEMA, Jan (ed), 27-34. Norwell, Kluwer, 1990.

MELVILLE, Mary E. William James and the Nature of Thinking: A Framework for Elfie. Thinking, 9(1), 32-34, 1990.

MENDENHALL, Vance. *Une introduction à l'analyse du discours argumentatif*. Ottawa, Univ of Ottawa Pr, 1990.

MENDEZ, J R. Principio de Razón o fundamento de Amor. Stromata, 46(1-2), 153-162, Ja-Je 90.

MÉNDEZ, José M. Routley-Meyer Type Semantics for Urquhart's C. J Non-Classical Log, 6(2), 41-46, N 89.

MENDLER, Nax Paul. Inductive Types and Type Constraints in the Second-Order Lambda Calculus. Annals Pure Applied Log, 51(1-2), 159-172, Mr 91.

MENDONÇA, W P. Der psychophysische Materialismus in der Perspektive Kants und Wittgensteins. Kantstudien, 81(3), 339-359, 1990.

MENDOZA, Celina A Lértora. Desarrollos actuales de la epistemología dialéctica. Logos (Mexico), 18(54), 85-113, S-D 90.

MENDUS, Susan. "Liberal Man" in *Philosophy and Politics*, HUNT, G M K (ed), 45-58. New York, Cambridge Univ Pr, 1991.

This paper draws attention to two features of human nature emphasised in modern liberal writing: firstly, human beings are private selves, not the occupiers of roles. Secondly, human beings are free and independent choosers. It is argued that emphasis on these features causes liberals to misrepresent the real nature of human existence, and also to present an impoverished picture of moral life. Specifically, the denial of our status as the occupiers of roles threatens to neglect the tragic nature of some moral dilemmas, while the insistence that we are free choosers threatens to deny the interdependence which often invests our lives with meaning.

MENDUS, Susan. Liberal Man. Philosophy, 26, 45-57, 90 Supp.

This paper discusses the conception of human nature implicit in modern liberal political theory. Through the use of two literary examples, it aims to show that liberal emphasis on man as an autonomous and independent agent is either an unwarranted idealisation or an unacceptable abstraction. The relationship between George and Lenny in John Steinbeck's novella *Of Mice and Men* suggests that we are dependent rather than independent. The example of Sophocles' *Antigone* suggests that liberalism cannot make sense of the tragic. Taken together, the two examples indicate ways in which liberalism both distorts and omits important aspects of life.

MENÉNDEZ UREÑA, Enrique. Algunas consecuencias del panenteismo krausista: ecología y mujer. El Basilisco, 4, 51-58, Mr-Ap 90.

MENZEL, Ch. Actualism, Ontological Commitment, and Possible World Semantics. Synthese, 85(3), 355-389, D 90.

Actualism is the doctrine that the only things there are, that have being in any sense, are the things that actually exist. In particular, actualism eschews *possibilism*, the doctrine that there are merely possible objects. It is widely held that one cannot both be an actualist and at the same time take possible world semantics seriously—that is, take it as the basis for a genuine theory of truth for modal languages, or look to it for insight into the modal structure of reality. For possible world semantics, it is supposed, commits one to possibilism. In this paper I take issue with this view. To the contrary, I argue that one can take possible world semantics seriously and yet remain in full compliance with actualist scruples.

MERCER, Mark and TALMAGE, Catherine J L. Meaning Holism and Interpretability. Phil Quart, 41(164), 301-315, Jl 91.

The authors argue that while meaning holism makes massive error possible, it does not, as Donald Davidson fears, threaten interpretability. Thus they hold, in opposition to Davidson, that meaning holism need not be constrained by an account of meaning according to which in the methodologically most basic cases the content of a belief is given by the cause of that belief. What ensures interpretability, they maintain, is not that speakers's beliefs are in the main true, but rather that beliefs have the contents they do because of events others can in principle identify and describe.

MERCIER, A. Responsibility, the Theory of Values, and the Theory of Knowledge (in Czechoslovakian). Filozof Cas, 39(1), 38-53, 1991.

Since knowledge is always cognition of values, the accepted theory of knowledge must be applicable to the elaborated theory of values like a glove on a hand. Then responsibility necessarily implying two partners as *sponsors* which cannot be but the tenants of cognition undertakings that do the job of uncovering values, e.g., a science and a moral discipline (promoting truth, resp. the good in some combination)—is assumed when, and only when these two undertakings agree in an equilibrium by which, e.g., in the example above, that which "can" be according to science agrees with that which "must" be according to morals[1]; this is precisely the authentic nature of technics[2]. It follows from this, that responsibility is not a problem for morals as such "in its splendid isolation" much rather it is only present there, where there is "generalized technics". On the material level, architecture is found to be the most general technics, because it implies at a time recourse to science (statics etc.), to art (beauty of buildings...), to morals (togetherness of people...) and to mystics[3] (mystery of the divine "presence"). On the spiritual level, philosophy is found to be the most general technics. (edited)

MERCIER, André. Qu'est-ce qu'interpréter? Diotima, 18, 7-22, 1990.

An introduction to the meeting of the International Academy of Philosophy of Art 1989 on *The Interpretation of the Art Work*, consisting in an account of what the Academy's oldest members (all beyond 80 years of age) might have said if attending the meeting: H Gouhier (Paris, b. 1898), H-G Gadamer (Heidelberg, b. 1900), R Schaerer (Geneva, b. 1901), P Weiss (Washington, b. 1901), E Grassi (Munich, b. 1902). L Senghor (Dakar and Paris, b. 1906), M Bill (Zurich, b. 1908), H Erni (Lucerne, b. 1909), G Argan (Rome, b. 1909), and a conclusion as to the extraordinary richness of views, which the author calls by Greek words as: synoratics, hermeneutics, maieutics, apodictics, euretics, aedetics, apeirotics, dorematics, and epicratetics.

MERKLE, Patricia. Problem Solving, Decision Making and Reflective Thinking. Phil Stud Educ, /, 38-49, 1987-88.

MERRICK, Janna. "The Case of Baby M" in *Beyond Baby M: Ethical Issues in New Reproductive Techniques*, BARTELS, Dianne M (ed), 183-200. Clifton, Humana Pr, 1990.

MERRILL, Kenneth R. Hume's "Of Miracles," Peirce, and the Balancing of Likelihoods. J Hist Phil, 29(1), 85-113, Ja 91.

The most important thesis of "Of Miracles" has no special connection with miracles: I mean the perfectly general thesis that testimonial evidence should be evaluated by the method of balancing likelihoods, which is a relatively informal version of the calculus of changes (or of probabilities). C S Peirce argues that the method is radically unsuited to the assessment of historical testimony. In this paper, I do essentially two things: (1) set out both an informal and a formal account of Hume's method; and (2) collect, systematize, and discuss Peirce's somewhat scattered animadversions upon Hume's use of this method. As part of (2), I explore some lines of thought that Peirce suggests but does not develop.

MERRILL, Ronald E. *The Ideas of Ayn Rand*. La Salle, Open Court, 1991.

A comprehensive survey of Rand's wide-ranging contributions: her literary techniques; her espousal and then rejection of a Nietzschean outlook; her contradictory attitude to feminism; her forays into ethics, epistemology, and metaphysics; the development of her political creed; her influence on—and hostility to—both conservatism and libertarianism. (staff)

MERRILL, Sarah A Bishop (ed). *Abeunt Studia in Mores: A Festschrift for Helga Doblin*. New York, Lang, 1990.

This four-hundred page volume includes work by colleagues and students of Helga Doblin, who taught Classics, including Greek and Latin, German, and Linguistics at Skidmore College before "retiring" to teach offers in New York State prisons and gifted children in Rudolph Steiner schools. An educator of the first rank has inspired essays on themes of education, liberation, and love, with considerable attention given to the role of women in the lives of the poets, writers, educators, linguists, philosophers, politicians, and psychologists whose were is discussed.

MERRILL, Sarah A Bishop. "Linguistics as a Borderline Case" in *Abeunt Studia in Mores: A Festschrift for Helga Doblin*, MERRILL, Sarah A Bishop (ed), 327-350. New York, Lang, 1990.

The purpose of this paper is to critically discuss Karl-Otto Apel's classification of modern linguistics, represented by Noam Chomsky's theory of generative grammar, as a borderline discipline between hermeneutical social science and "natural" empirical-analytic science. Apel's difficulties point as much to possible deficiencies in the metatheoretical Apelian standpoint or frame of reference as to something that distinguishes Chomskean linguistics *per se*. Apel ignores important distinctions and collapses others, namely science and metascience, or what I will here call Chomsky's metatheory and his linguistic theory; he conflates *langue* with competence, and (also mistakenly), *parole* with performance. Linguistics is an emancipatory science.

MERRILL, Sarah A Bishop. "The Problem of Linguistic Empowerment" in *Abeunt Studia in Mores: A Festschrift for Helga Doblin*, MERRILL, Sarah A Bishop (ed), 65-100. New York, Lang, 1990.

Naming is the language game most closely related to social control. This is true for both of the linguistic subjects of this paper: naming as uses of 1) proper names, and 2) common noun phrases. The philosophical and social psychological subject of this paper is the morality of linguistic power. Primarily descriptive, this article uses data obtained from years of study and care of children. A theory of "festal" and "command or control" strategies based on work by Suzanne Langer is offered, with programmatic suggestions for future research design in socio-linguistics and ethics.

MERRILL, Sarah A. Welcome 'Ethical Stress': A Humean Analysis and A Practical Proposal. J Soc Phil, 21(1), 27-45, Spr 90.

This paper describes the important phenomenon of ethical stress, taking the root metaphor back from the executive health management experts who would reduce the ethical to the psychological or physiological. Baptising a new concept is useful in understanding the common contemporary view that ethical matters and disagreements are to be avoided in ordinary discourse, or as Robert Bellah has shown, that they are "private." Hume's moral psychology and the objective foundation for his nonnaturalist ethics are used to highlight prior attention to this phenomenon in philosophy.

MERRITT, Sharyne. Marketing Ethics and Education: Some Empirical Findings. J Bus Ethics, 10(8), 625-632, Ag 91.

This study explores possible links between educational background and ethics among marketing professionals. Data from two surveys of members of the American Marketing Association suggest that marketing professionals with master's degrees and higher are similar to their less educated counterparts in both their ethical standards and their intended ethical behaviors. Marketers with business degrees, however, have lower ethical standards than do graduates of non-business programs, though they report behavior as ethical as that of their non-business educated peers. Business schools may be producing cynics likely to accept marginal behaviors of colleagues though not likely to engage in such behaviors themselves.

MERTENS, T. Wie kaatst moet de bal verwachten. Alg Ned Tijdschr Wijs, 83(2), 146-147, Ap 91.

The author reacts on a review of his dissertation "Critical Philosophy and Politics. Immanuel Kant on War and Peace." He emphasizes the priority of the concept of right over the concept of nature in Kant's political philosophy.

MESCHIARI, Alberto. Critica della filosofia zoologica per Battista Grassi. G Crit Filosof Ital, 69(3), 366-383, S-D 90.

MESMAN, Jessica and BIJSTERVELD, Karin. Wie van de drie: Wil de ware wetenschapsonderzoeker opstaan? Kennis Methode, 14(4), 384-389, 1990.

Review of Malcolm Ashmore, Michael Mulkay and Trevor Pinch: *Health and Efficiency: A Sociology of Health Economics*, Open University Press, Milton Keynes, 1989.

MESSINESE, Leonardo. Verità di ragione e verità di fede. Aquinas, 33(2), 297-312, My-Ag 90.

MÉSZÁROS, István. *The Power of Ideology*. New York, New York Univ Pr, 1990.

METAXOPOULOS, Emilio. "A Critical Consideration of the Lakatosian Concepts: 'Mature' and 'Immature' Science" in *Imre Lakatos and Theories of Scientific Change*, GAVROGLU, Kostas (ed), 203-214. Norwell, Kluwer, 1989.

METCALFE, John F. Moral Skepticism and the Dangerous Maybe: Reconsidering Mackie's *Ethics*. Eidos, 8(2), 217- 233, D 89.

Nothing new here: I rehearse the main arguments for moral skepticism and point out their weaknesses. I conclude that the garden-variety skepticism rooted in British Empiricism is neither as compelling nor as radical as that inspired by Nietzsche.

METCALFE, John F. Whewell's Developmental Psychologism: A Victorian Account of Scientific Progress. Stud Hist Phil Sci, 22(1), 117-139, Mr 91.

I attempt to reconstruct a Whewellian concept of evidence. This concept forces an interpretation of Whewell's philosophy that has the following features: 1) laws of nature are necessary but our knowledge of necessity has a purely psychological foundation; 2) neither a colligation of facts nor a consilience among colligations is evidence for the truth; 3) the inferences of discovery bring the human mind to a point where it cannot but see the world in a certain way—and that necessity justifies the laws so discovered.

MEUNIER, Jean-Guy. Le tournant cognitif en sémiotique. Horiz Phil, 1(2), 51-80, 1991.

MEY, Jacob L and LITTMAN, David C. The Nature of Irony: Toward a Computational Model of Irony. J Prag, 15(2), 131-151, F 91.

MEYER, Leonard B. *Style and Music: Theory, History, and Ideology*. Philadelphia, Univ of Penn Pr, 1989.

MEYER, Michael J and MOBERG, Dennis J. A Deontological Analysis of Peer Relations in Organizations. J Bus Ethics, 9(11), 863-877, N 90.

Using practical formalism a deontological ethical analysis of peer relations in organizations is developed. This analysis is composed of two types of duties derived from Kant's Categorical Imperative: negative duties to refrain from the use of peers and positive duties to provide help and assistance. The conditions under which these duties pertain are specified through the development of examples and conceptual distinctions. A number of implications are then discussed.

MEYER, Michel. Die Figuren des Menschlichen. Rev Int Phil, 44(174), 448-470, 1990.

MEYER, Michel. *Le Philosophie et les Passions*. Paris, Lib Gen Francaise, 1991.

This is the first history of the various theories of emotions. It goes from Plato to problemonology, after Kant, Hegel and existentialism. The author provides a theory of his own. Political theory, epidemonology, theory of consciousness, religion, are called upon all along.

MEYER, Michel (ed) and HUME, David. *Réflexions sur les passions*. Paris, Lib Gen Francaise, 1990.

MEYER, Robert K. Peirced Clean Through. Bull Sect Log, 19(3), 100-101, O 90.

It is well known that adding Peirce's Law $((p \rightarrow q) \rightarrow p) \rightarrow p$ to a formulation of *intuitionist* pure implication produces full classical implication. But what happens if we add this principle to (Church's) *relevant* implication? Answer: against the odds, as it were, the *same thing*!

MEYER, Zofia Golab. What is the Price of a Rich Life? Thinking, 9(1), 8-11, 1990.

The aim of this article is to draw the attention of science teachers to the problem of ecology. We have tested several hundred pupils from the big industrial city of Cracow and from the small villages and we have found quite a high ecological consciousness. This optimistic fact should not be wasted: it should be rationally used for the founding of a scientific base for the proper ecological behavior of societies.

MEYERS, Christopher. Racial Bias, the Death Penalty, and Desert. Phil Forum, 22(2), 139-148, Wint 90-91.

In the controversial 1987 ruling of *McCleskey v. Kemp*, the Supreme Court held that evidence of a racially biased application of the death penalty does not provide sufficient grounds for overturning a sentence of death. I argue in this paper that although the Court displayed a disturbingly inadequate understanding of prejudice and discrimination, its decision in *McCleskey* was nonetheless just, *assuming that only application, and not retribution, was at issue*. That is, if one starts with a presupposition that retribution provides a legitimate basis for punishment, then concerns over equitable application are relevant only when a defendant receives *more* than she or he deserves.

MEYERS, Diana T. *Self, Society, and Personal Choice*. New York, Columbia Univ Pr, 1989.

This book gives a procedural explication of the phenomenon of personal autonomy in terms of autonomy competency—a repertory of skills involving memory, imagination, communication, reason, and volition. It has often been claimed that women are less autonomous than men. Since this procedural view of personal autonomy makes sense of degrees of autonomy and episodes of autonomy, it enables us to see both why feminine socialization is less conducive to autonomy than masculine socialization and also how women have been more autonomous than has generally been recognized. Nevertheless, childhood socialization practices should be modified to promote autonomy, for autonomy is necessary for self-respect and equal opportunity is empty unless the competitors are autonomous.

MEYERSON, Denise. *False Consciousness*. New York, Clarendon/Oxford Pr, 1991.

MEYNELL, Hugo A. "Augustine and the Norms of Authentic Conversion" in *Grace, Politics and Desire: Essays on Augustine*, MEYNELL, Hugo A (ed), 3-15. Calgary, Univ Calgary Pr, 1990.

It is argued that there are norms for authentic conversion—for applying oneself in a thoroughgoing way to knowing what is true and doing what is good—and that these were set out with remarkable clarity and force by Augustine in some of the writings which followed soon after his conversion. The author tries to show that denial of the existence of such norms, for example by empiricists and relativists, is self-destructive.

MEYNELL, Hugo A (ed). *Grace, Politics and Desire: Essays on Augustine*. Calgary, Univ Calgary Pr, 1990.

This collection, which celebrates the sixteenth centenary of Augustine's conversion to Christianity, discusses the saint's account of the nature of his conversion, and his attitude to the politics, the poetry, and the rhetoric of his time. There were also essays on his analysis of 'concupiscence' or inordinate desire, his method of Scriptural interpretation, his theory of music, and his progressively hardening stance on the question of religious pluralism.

MEYNELL, Hugo A. The Justification of "English". J Aes Educ, 24(4), 5-15, Wint 90.

What is the point of teaching English literature? How is the existence of university departments specializing in the subject to be justified? Given that such a subject ought to have teaching and research devoted to it, of what should such teaching and research consist? Which authors and works are indispensable as objects of study, which better dispensed with, and why? It is deplored that the conventional academic wisdom can apparently produce no clear and cogent answers to such questions; and answers are provided and justified.

MEYNELL, Hugo A. On Being an Aristotelian. Heythrop J, 32(2), 233-248, Ap 91.

For all its incidental errors, Aristotle's philosophy is correct in its fundamentals; for example, its blend of rationalism and empiricism, its account of reality as what is to be known by asking 'What?' and 'Why?' and the conception of causality deriving from this, its view of reality as characterised by a hierarchy of 'forms', its conviction that the universe is intelligible and of the need of a transcendent intelligence to account for this, and the snug mesh of its theory of reality (science and 'metaphysics'—what Aristotle calls 'first philosophy') with its theory of value (ethics, aesthetics, politics).

MEZEI, György Iván. "Human Order in the Natural Universe: Rediscovering Russell's Social Philosophy" in *Perspectives on Ideas and Reality*, NYÍRI, J C (ed), 201-209. Budapest, Kiskonyvtara, 1990.

B Russell's social philosophy is much neglected compared to his achievement in logic or epistemology. The present article is written as a challenge to this bias. Russell's conceptions on man and society were based on common sense—this is the clue to its synthetic character—and their system could be referred to as liberal socialism which on the level of concrete institutional arrangements needs, however, further elaboration.

MEZNAR, Martin B and CHRISMAN, James J and CARROLL, Archie B. Social Responsibility and Strategic Management: Toward an Enterprise Strategy Classification. Bus Prof Ethics J, 10(1), 47-66, Spr 91.

MICCOLI, Paolo. Mnêmê, anámnêsis, mnêmosynê: Sull'identità dell'uomo storico. G Metaf, 11(3), 465-476, S-D 89.

MICHAEL, Emily and MICHAEL, Fred S. Hutcheson's Account of Beauty as a Response to Mandeville. Hist Euro Ideas, 12(5), 655-668, 1990.

MICHAEL, Emily. Vegetarianism and Virtue: On Gassendi's Epicurean Defense. Between Species, 7(2), 61-72, Spr 91.

Gassendi, who was influenced in the development of his moral theory by Epicurus, was, as was Epicurus, a vegetarian. Gassendi argues, in his *Philosophiae Epicuri Syntagma*, his reconstruction of Epicurus' theory, and in his *Syntagma Philosophicum*, presenting his own ethics, that abstaining from flesh is a moral requirement. Gassendi represents, as an Epicurean position, the view that obligations attendant upon rights pertain only to those bound together by a social contract, and, agreements with animals being infeasible, no obligations follow from their rights. This paper explores a Gassendist response to the question of why vegetarianism is a moral requirement.

MICHAEL, Fred S and MICHAEL, Emily. Hutcheson's Account of Beauty as a Response to Mandeville. Hist Euro Ideas, 12(5), 655-668, 1990.

MICHALOS, Alex C. Ethical Considerations Regarding Public Opinion Polling During Election Campaigns. J Bus Ethics, 10(6), 403-422, Je 91.

Commercial public opinion polling is an increasingly important element in practically all elections in democratic countries around the world. Poll results and pollsters are relatively new and autonomous voices in our human communities. Here I try to connect such polling directly to morality and democratic processes. Several arguments have been and might be used for and against banning such polling during elections, i.e., for and against effectively silencing these voices. I present the arguments on both sides of this issue, and try to show that there are reasonable responses to all the arguments in favour of banning polls. Then I review some proposed Canadian legislation concerning banning polls and, alternatively, requiring disclosure of methodological features of polls. Finally, I offer a model set of disclosure standards for the publication of poll results during election campaigns.

MICHALSON JR, Gordon E. *Fallen Freedom: Kant on Radical Evil and Moral Regeneration*. New York, Cambridge Univ Pr, 1991.

MICHAUD, Thomas A. Secondary Reflection and Marcelian Anthropology. Phil Today, 34(3), 222-228, Fall 90.

One of the most elusive though significant notions in Marcel's thought is secondary reflection. Various interpretations range from describing it as the consciousness within a religious faith-experience to a pre-reflective consciousness within the motility of the body. After reviewing some of these interpretations, this article develops the view that secondary reflection is a thinking, philosophical reflection which is capable of providing rational expression for inarticulate intuitive experiences of the mysteries of being. Exemplifications of this capability are offered through Marcelian looks at the anthropological *cum* metaphysical mysteries of human freedom and the person as incarnate being.

MICHELMAN, Frank. Reply to Shearmur's "From Dialogue Rights to Property Rights". Crit Rev, 4(1-2), 133-143, Wint-Spr 90.

In arguing instrumentally in defense of attributing negative-liberty rights to every individual, does it help to notice that whoever is denied negative liberties is thereby impeded from contributing to social dialogue about the arts and ethics of human wellbeing? Perhaps, but only on the conditions that (i) we understand individual identities as intersubjectively constituted, and (ii) we pursue universality in the distribution of social requisites of dialogic competence beyond negative liberties.

MICHELSEN, John M. "Kierkegaard's Stages on Life's Way: How Many Are There?" in *Writing the Politics of Difference*, SILVERMAN, Hugh J (ed), 43-53. Albany, SUNY Pr, 1991.

Efforts to relate the philosophy of the three stages to the basic dichotomies of passion and reflection, the subjective and the objective, suggest that the aesthetic has to be contrasted with the ethico-religious. The article shows that although this linking of the ethical to the religious is supported by a phenomenological analysis of parallel faith-structures, this analysis fails to appreciate fully the interdependence of the *noetic* and the *noematic* poles of experience. When this is taken into account, the dichotomy that emerges is between the aesthetic-religious and the ethical, between the solitary and the social individual.

MICHOD, Richard E and BYERLY, Henry C. Fitness and Evolutionary Explanation. Biol Phil, 6(1), 1-22, Ja 91.

The aim is to clarify the roles of the concept "fitness" in evolutionary theory. Appealing to the structure of models of natural selection, we draw distinctions between how fitness is defined versus what fitness is a function of, between specific adaptive capacities versus overall adaptedness, and between fitness applied to organisms versus genotypes. We show how failure to distinguish these aspects of "fitness" confuses complex issues concerning evolutionary theory. A central result of the analysis is that overall adaptedness of organisms does not play a causal role in evolutionary explanations.

MICHOD, Richard E and BYERLY, Henry C. Fitness and Evolutionary Explanation: A Response. Biol Phil, 6(1), 45-53, Ja 91.

MICKUNAS, Algis and STEWART, David. *Exploring Phenomenology (Second Edition)*. Athens, Ohio Univ Pr, 1990.

The purpose of this book is to introduce in concise, uncluttered and straightforward terms the history, development, and contemporary status of phenomenology. The book is organized so that extensive bibliographical entries (annotated) follow each major section. The second edition updates developments in phenomenological philosophy by discussing recent trends and noting significant works that have appeared in the last fifteen years.

MIDGLEY, Mary. Homunculus Trouble, or, What Is Applied Philosophy? J Soc Phil, 21(1), 5-15, Spr 90.

MIDGLEY, Mary. "The Origin of Ethics" in *A Companion to Ethics*, SINGER, Peter (ed), 3-13. Cambridge, Blackwell, 1991.

MIDGLEY, Mary. Rights-Talk Will Not Sort Out Child-Abuse: Comment on Archard on Parental Rights. J Applied Phil, 8(1), 103-114, 1991.

Argument about Rights can be either purely formal or substantial-meant to affect conduct. These two functions, which need different kinds of support, often become confused. Among 'moral theories', however, the language of rights is specially ill-suited for all-purpose use. Rights-language is of particularly limited use because it is simply the most competitive and litigious of such thought-systems. Its win-or-lose formula allows no more scope for doing justice to defeated claims than a lawcourt does. For the serious conflicts of value that underlie large moral problems, this is disastrous. (edited)

MIELKE, Dietmar. Zur inhaltlichen Bedeutung des Hegelschen "Schemas der Naturphilosophie" in den Epikurstudien des jungen Marx. Deut Z Phil, 39(3), 321-326, 1991.

Im vorliegenden Aufsatz wird beabsichtigt, die in der philosophischen Forschung als sehr befremdlich empfundene Anwesenheit des Hegelschen "Schemas der Naturphilosophie" im fünften Heft der Epikurstudien des jungen Marx aufzuklären, indem dessen theoretische Entwicklung von 1838 bis 1840, die um die Begründung einer wissenschaftlichen Wirklichkeitsauffassung kreist, in der Einheit von sachimmanenter und begriffsanalytischer Untersuchung rekonstruiert wird. Unter Zugrundelegung der diese theoretische Entwicklung wesentlich tragenden differenzierten Beziehung von Marx zu Epikur und insonderheit zu Aristoteles kann das erarbeitete Schema inhaltlich uno zeitlich bestimmt und gewertet werden.

MIGLIOLI, P (and others). A Constructivism Based on Classical Truth. Notre Dame J Form Log, 30(1), 67-90, Wint 89.

The paper is concerned with the study of the relationships between classical and constructive truth. An attempt is made of representing classical truth as a notion different from intuitionistic double negation even at the propositional level. To do so, a constructible negation and an operator T representing classical truth are introduced in the frame of constructive systems. Various of such systems are proposed for which suitable semantics are given. Furthermore, the problem of maximality of such systems is investigated.

MIKENBERG, I F and LEWIN, R A and SCHWARZE, M G. Algebraization of Paraconsistent Logic P^1. J Non-Classical Log, 7(1-2), 79-88, My-N 90.

Using techniques developed by Blok and Pigozzi, we prove that paraconsistent logic P1, introduced by Sette, is algebraizable.

MIKOU, M and CHRISTIDES, T M. "The Relative Autonomy of Theoretical Science and the Role of Crucial Experiments" in *Imre Lakatos and Theories of Scientific Change*, GAVROGLU, Kostas (ed), 147-153. Norwell, Kluwer, 1989.

MILBANK, John. 'Postmodern Critical Augustinianism': A Short *Summa* in Forty Two Responses to Unasked Questions. Mod Theol, 7(3), 225-237, Ap 91.

MILES, Margaret R. "The Body and Human Values in Augustine of Hippo" in *Grace, Politics and Desire: Essays on Augustine*, MEYNELL, Hugo A (ed), 55-67. Calgary, Univ Calgary Pr, 1990.

MILES, Murray. Some Recent Research on the Mind-Body Problem in Descartes. Manuscrito, 13(2), 85-109, O 90.

MILL, John Stuart and ROBSON, John M (ed) and FILIPIUK, Marion (ed) and LAINE, Michael (ed). *Additional Letters (Collected Works of John Stuart Mill, Volume XXXII)*. Buffalo, Univ of Toronto Pr, 1991.

MILL, John Stuart and ROBSON, John M (ed) and O'GRADY, Jean (ed). *Indexes to the Collected Works (Collected Works of John Stuart Mill, Vol XXXIII)*. Buffalo, Univ of Toronto Pr, 1991.

MILLÁN, Gustavo Ortiz (trans) and SOSA, Ernest. Cuestiones de sobrevivencia. Critica, 22(64), 55-93, Ap 90.

MILLAR, Alan. *Reasons and Experience*. New York, Clarendon/Oxford Pr, 1991.

The book provides an exploration of problems on the borderlands between philosophy of mind and epistemology, focusing on the role of sensory experiences in knowledge-acquisition. A key issue is whether, and if so how, such experiences contribute to the justification of beliefs. It is argued that they do with the help of the notion that justified belief is better which is competently acquired or retained. Competence here is conceptual competence. In line with this there is much discussion of the nature of concepts and their mastery. Other topics include reasons and evidence, groundless beliefs and scepticism.

MILLER JR, Fred D (ed) and PAUL, Ellen Frankel (ed) and PAUL, Jeffrey (ed). *Ethics, Politics, and Human Nature*. Cambridge, Blackwell, 1991.

Human nature, whether it is fixed by genetic endowment or malleable under the influence of social forces, is one of the most hotly debated questions in recent social thought. The contributors to this volume examine the concept of human nature and its role both in philosophical exploration and political prescription. The essays deal with such questions as the relation of self-interest to the proper design of government, whether there is something about human nature which creates a normative prohibition to genetic engineering, what the emerging discipline of sociobiology has to tell us about morality, and how different conceptions of human nature affect Aristotle, Hume, Kant, Rousseau, and current feminist theory.

MILLER JR, Fred D (ed) and PAUL, Ellen Frankel (ed) and PAUL, Jeffrey (ed). *Foundations of Moral and Political Philosophy*. Cambridge, Blackwell, 1990.

Questions regarding the foundations of ethics and politics have intrigued philosophers ever since Socrates first pointed out their importance. Many philosophers have agreed with the ancient Greeks that we cannot obtain the knowledge we need to lead the best lives as individuals or to pursue the wisest public policies unless we are guided by a correct normative theory providing basic definitions, analyses, or explications of concepts such as "good" and "bad," and "right" and "wrong," and basic judgments or principles regarding good things and right actions. However, the task of providing a correct account of the foundations of moral and political philosophy is both difficult and perplexing. There has recently been an enthusiastic revival of interest on the part of moral and political philosophers concerning such foundations. It is a field of great ferment and diversity, as reflected by the nine internationally-regarded philosophers who have written essays for this volume.

MILLER, Alexander. Abstract Singular Reference: A Dilemma for Dummett. S J Phil, 29(2), 257-269, Sum 91.

Michael Dummett has attempted to give an account of the semantics of abstract singular terms which steers a middle course between reductionism and full-blown platonism concerning their references: according to this middle position, reference, in the case of abstract singular terms, becomes "a matter wholly internal to the language." My main aim in this paper is to show that Dummett's arguments are in some considerable tension with more general features of his interpretation of Frege's philosophical semantics, so that given a reiteration of his arguments against the reductionist, the platonist position seems to be the only available alternative.

MILLER, Arnold W. Projective Subsets of Separable Metric Spaces. Annals Pure Applied Log, 50(1), 53-69, N 90.

In this paper two possible definitions of projective subsets of a separable metric space X are studied. A set C contained in X is relatively analytic in X iff there exists a complete separable metric space Y and Borel set B in X x Y such that C is the projection of B. A subset C of X is abstract projective iff there exists a Borel set B contained in a finite product of X with itself such that C is the projection of B onto the first coordinate. The main technique used is forcing.

MILLER, Arnold W. Set Theoretic Properties of Loeb Measure. J Sym Log, 55(3), 1022-1036, S 90.

In this paper we ask the question: to what extent do basic set theoretic properties of Loeb measure depend on the nonstandard universe and on properties of the model of set theory in which it lies? We show that assuming Martin's axiom and κ-saturation the smallest cover by Loeb measure zero sets must have cardinality less than κ. In contrast to this we show that the additivity of Loeb measure cannot be greater than ω_1. Define *cof(H)* as the smallest cardinality of a family of Loeb measure zero sets which cover every other Loeb measure zero set. We show that $card(\lfloor \log_2(H) \rfloor) \leq cof(H) \leq card(2^H)$ where *card* is the external cardinality. We answer a question of Paris and Mills concerning cuts in nonstandard models of number theory. (edited)

MILLER, Barry. Whether Any Individual at all Could Have a Guise Structure. Phil Stud, 61(3), 285-293, Mr 91.

At the heart of Castañeda's Guise Theory is his notion of guises, entities that are said to be the basic individuals constituting ordinary individuals like people, trees, and stones. This paper argues that the structure proposed for guises cannot be inferred from the evidence that is offered for it. Much more seriously, nothing with the kind of structure ascribed to guises could possibly be an individual. The reason is simply that no individual can be instantiated, whereas anything with a guise structure certainly can be instantiated. No individual, therefore, could have a guise structure.

MILLER, Dale and NADATHUR, Gopalan and PFENNING, Frank and SCEDROV, Andre. Uniform Proofs as a Foundation for Logic Programming. Annals Pure Applied Log, 51(1-2), 125-157, Mr 91.

MILLER, David H. Commentary—"Make Me Live": Autonomy and Terminal Illness. Hastings Center Rep, 20(5), 43-44, S-O 90.

MILLER, David L. "Consciousness, the Attitude of the Individual and Perspectives" in *Creativity in George Herbert Mead*, GUNTER, Pete A Y (ed), 3-44. Lanham, Univ Pr of America, 1990.

MILLER, David L. "Response to Comments on 'Consciousness, the Attitude of the Individual and Perspectives'" in *Creativity in George Herbert Mead*, GUNTER, Pete A Y (ed), 59-63. Lanham, Univ Pr of America, 1990.

MILLER, David. "Equality" in *Philosophy and Politics*, HUNT, G M K (ed), 77-98. New York, Cambridge Univ Pr, 1991.

The ideal of equality is integral to modern societies, mainly by virtue of their character as market economies. Analysis of the ideal in recent political philosophy has attempted to identify the most persuasive conception of simple equality—'equality of X'. However, scrutiny of the two most popular versions of simple equality—equality of welfare and equality of resources—suggests that no such conception will satisfy us. Instead, following Michael Walzer, we should regard equality as a complex artefact arising from many separate distributions of distinct types of goods. Under suitable constraints, this may create an equality of status among all members of society which appropriately meets the egalitarian aspirations of our contemporaries.

MILLER, David. Equality. Philosophy, 26, 77-98, 90 Supp.

The ideal of equality is integral to modern societies, mainly by virtue of their character as market economies. Analysis of the ideal in recent political philosophy has attempted to identify the most persuasive conception of simple equality—'equality of X'. However scrutiny of the two most popular versions of simple equality—equality of welfare and equality of resources—suggests that no such conception will satisfy us. Instead, following Michael Walzer, we should regard equality as a complex artefact arising from many separate distributions of distinct types of goods. Under suitable constraints, this may create an equality of status among all members of society which appropriately meets the egalitarian aspirations of our contemporaries.

MILLER, David. A Restoration of Popperian Inductive Scepticism. Brit J Phil Sci, 41(1), 137-139, Mr 90.

It is shown that the argument of Ken Gemes, 'A Refutation of Popperian Inductive Scepticism', *Brit J Phil Sci*, 40(2), 1989, pp 183f, involves division by zero; and that the principles that Gemes claims to be inconsistent are mutually consistent.

MILLER, Eugene G and THOMAS, Edmund J. *Writers and Philosophers: A Sourcebook of Philosophical Influences on Literature*. Westport, Greenwood Pr, 1990.

The intent of *Writers and Philosophers* is to provide philosophical resource for teachers and students of literature to help them acquire a greater understanding of the philosophical influences on more than a hundred major literary figures most commonly included in college literature textbooks. The text describes philosophical influences reflected in major literary works and includes as well references to philosophical works that have played a part in the authors' intellectual and aesthetic development. The entries are supplemented by brief bio-bibliographical profiles of major philosophers and a glossary of philosophical terms, concepts, and movements.

MILLER, Geoffrey P. Rights and Structure in Constitutional Theory. Soc Phil Pol, 8(2), 196-223, Spr 91.

This article proposes a model that unifies the analysis of constitutional rights (embodied in the bill of rights) and constitutional structure (embodied in separation of powers and federalism). It demonstrates that structural issues should be considered with reference to rights—the principle of liberty—and shows, conversely, that the analysis of rights should consider structual elements (e.g., that the expansion of rights increases the powers of the Supreme Court vis-a-vis the other branches). Drawing on the Federalist Papers, the article proposes a unified theory of rights and structure based on concepts of liberty, checks-and-balances, governmental energy, and faction-avoidance.

MILLER, Harlan B. On Utilitarianism and Utilitarian Attitudes. Between Species, 6(3), 128-129, Sum 90.

MILLER, Irwin. Health Policy Analysis as Ideology and as Utopian Rhetoric. Bus Prof Ethics J, 9(3-4), 173-182, Fall-Wint 90.

MILLER, Mara. "Distance, Disinterest, and Autonomy: Gardens as a

Challenge to the Theory of Art" in *XIth International Congress in Aesthetics, Nottingham 1988*, WOODFIELD, Richard (ed), 136-142. Nottingham, Nottingham Polytech, 1990.

MILLER, Philip H. Scandinavian Extraction Phenomena Revisited: Weak and Strong Generative Capacity. Ling Phil, 14(1), 101-113, F 91.

This article discusses the relevance of certain complex crossing extraction data from Norwegian and Swedish for the weak and strong adequacy of various formal grammars. It is first shown that the data allow to demonstrate that context free grammars are inadequate in weak generative capacity for generating Swedish. This is done by showing that the intersection of Swedish with a certain regular set is non-context free. Second, the relevance of the Swedish and Norwegian data for strong generative capacity is discussed, showing that it is impossible to generate them with either indexed grammars or tree adjoining grammars, while assigning them their usually assumed syntactic structures.

MILLER, Randolph A. Why the Standard View Is Standard: People, Not Machines, Understand Patients' Problems. J Med Phil, 15(6), 581-591, D 90.

The 'Standard View' regarding computer-based medical diagnostic decision support programs is that, while such systems may be useful adjuncts to human decision making, they cannot replace human diagnosticians. Mazoué (1990) disputes this viewpoint. He notes that human diagnosis is prone to a variety of errors, and claims that the processes of data collection for diagnosis and the intellectual task of making a diagnosis are independent. Mazoué believes that recent progress in computer-based diagnosis has been encouraging enough to consider the concept of "human-assisted computer diagnosis." This commentary explains why the Standard View would remain standard. Diagnosis is a complex process more involved than producing a nosological label for a set of patient descriptors. Efficient and ethical diagnostic evaluation requires a broad knowledge of people and of disease states. The state of the art in computer-based medical diagnosis does not support the optimistic claim that people can now be replaced by more reliable diagnostic programs.

MILLER, Richard B. Reply of a Mad Dog. Analysis, 51(1), 50-54, Ja 91.

In this paper I seek to defend "Mad Dog Modal Realism" from an objection by Devitt and Sterelny. Devitt and Sterelny allege that explanations invoking possible worlds are not explanations because they are not causal explanations. Strange to say, Lewis agrees that possibilia cannot figure in any "explanations." He accepts this restriction on the use of "explanation" and prefers to call the benefits of possibilia "analyses." I then go on to show how Lewis's answer to the epistemological objections of Lycan, Richards, et al. can be reformulated to answer Devitt and Sterelny.

MILLER, Richard B. Supervenience Is a Two-Way Street. J Phil, 87(12), 695-701, D 90.

It has been widely argued of late that the alleged supervenience of the nonphysical on the physical is all that the physicalist could want or need. With skepticism about reductive and eliminativist strategies on the rise, a supervenience argument for physicalism becomes increasingly attractive. However, the considerations offered in support of the supervenience of the nonphysical on the physical equally support the supervenience of the physical on the nonphysical. Thus the arguments do not establish ontological primacy. Supervenience may be useful in explaining physicalism, but it does not justify physicalism.

MILLER, S R. Just War Theory and the ANC's Armed Struggle. Quest, 4(2), 80-102, D 90.

It is plausible that some wars—including wars against governments waged by their own citizens—are just and others unjust. The ANC's armed struggle is morally justified, or at least is given a set of principles derivative from traditional just war theory. There may now be reason for suspending the armed struggle, though not at this stage abandoning it.

MILLER, S R. Just War Theory: The Case of South Africa. Phil Papers, 19(2), 143-161, Ag 90.

Can the ANC's armed struggle against the South African government be morally justified? Subject to certain qualification, yes. The armed struggle, however, ought to be suspended given the current willingness of the white government to negotiate. Abandonment would depend on the outcome of those negotiations.

MILLER, Seumas. Co-ordination, Salience and Rationality. S J Phil, 29(3), 359-370, Fall 91.

MILLER, Seumas. Davidson's Paratactic Analysis of Mood. J Prag, 15(1), 1-10, Ja 91.

According to Davidson's paratactic analysis of mood an uttered sentence in a nonindicative mood should be thought of as two utterances: an utterance of the corresponding indicative sentence, and an utterance of what he terms the moodsetter. The moodsetter of, for example, an imperative, is expressible by the sentence 'That utterance is a command'. There are a number of problems with this analysis. Firstly, the fact that it derives two speech acts from the utterance of every sentence makes the matter of determining the force of any given uttered sentence an unworkably complex affair. Secondly, in giving mood a purely semantic characterisation it unacceptably weakens the connection between mood and force.

MILLER, Seumas. Marxist Literary Aesthetics. Phil Soc Crit, 16(4), 303-319, 1990.

A central strain of Marxist literary aesthetics claims that the writing and reading of literary texts is of the same order as the production and consumption of commodities. On this kind of view a literary text is not simply (possibly) impregnated by ideology, but is constitutively ideological. I argue against this conception of literary texts.

MILLER, Seumas. On the Morality of Waging War Against the State. S Afr J Phil, 10(1), 20-27, F 91.

In this article the author provides an account of the conditions for justifying an internal war against the state. It makes use of principles derived from just war theory, and takes an essentially rights-based approach. Two specific areas of focus are the problem of knowledge of the outcome of waging war, and the problem of directing violence at noncombatants who are rights violators.

MILLIKAN, Ruth. The Myth of the Essential Indexical. Nous, 24(5), 723-734, D 90.

So-called "essential indexicals" in thought are indeed essential, but they are not indexical. It is *not* their semantics that distinguishes them, but their function, their psychological role.

MILLS, Eugene. Forbes's Branching Conception of Possible Worlds. Analysis, 51(1), 48-50, Ja 91.

Graeme Forbes argues that his "branching conception" of possible worlds meets an alleged counterexample to the thesis that identity across worlds must be "grounded" by nontrivial intrinsic properties. I argue that it does not. Forbes say that one world may branch from another by overlapping a separable course of events in the latter world; causal isolability is one criterion of separability. But since it is contingent that a course of events *C* is causally isolable, neither *C*'s causal isolability nor its separability can ground its identification across two appropriately chosen worlds. This defeats Forbes's thesis.

MILLS, Patricia J. "Woman's Experience: Renaming the Dialectic of Desire and Recognition" in *Writing the Politics of Difference*, SILVERMAN, Hugh J (ed), 123-133. Albany, SUNY Pr, 1991.

The article is a consideration of female identity formation illuminated through an analysis of the appropriation of Hegel and Freud by the first generation of the Frankfurt School (Horkheimer, Adorno, and Marcuse). I argue that a feminist critique of the civilizing myths used to explicate the dialectic of desire and recognition (Odysseus and Oedipus) must entail a reconsideration of motherhood and sisterhood that goes beyond contemporary feminist arguments which ignore heterosexual desire or see it only as woman's desire for domination. Central to this argument is an analysis of the relationship between heterosexual and homosexual desire as it relates to the formation of the social group.

MILLS, Patricia Jagentowicz. Feminism and Ecology: On the Domination of Nature. Hypatia, 6(1), 162-178, Spr 91.

This paper examines the attempt to bring together feminist and ecological concerns in the work of Isaac Balbus and Ynestra King, two thinkers who place the problem of the domination of nature at the center of contemporary liberation struggles. Through a consideration of the abortion issue (which foregrounds the relation between nature and history, and the problem of their "reconcilation") I argue against what I call their abstract pro-nature stance.

MILNE, Peter. Annabel and the Bookmaker: An Everyday Tale of Bayesian Folk. Austl J Phil, 69(1), 98-102, Mr 91.

MILNE, Peter. Conditionalisation and Quantum Probabilities. Austl J Phil, 69(2), 214-218, Je 91.

MILNE, Peter. A Dilemma for Subjective Bayesians—and How to Resolve It. Phil Stud, 62(3), 307-314, Je 91.

A Dutch book argument shows that rational individuals have something akin to perfect self-knowledge regarding their own degrees of belief. I explain why this conclusion fits ill with David Lewis's "Principal Principle" and suggest how the latter should be restricted.

MILNE, Peter. Frege, Informative Identities, and Logicism. Brit J Phil Sci, 40(2), 155-166, Je 89.

Frege's belief that arithmetic identities are informative is, I contend, incompatible with his conception of laws of logic. The latter are known to be true in virtue of sense alone.

MILNE, Peter. Verification, Falsification, and the Logic of Enquiry. Erkenntnis, 34(1), 23-54, Ja 91.

Our starting point is Michael Luntley's falsificationist semantics for the logical connectives and quantifiers: the details of his account are criticised but we provide an alternative falsificationist semantics that yields intuitionist logic, as Luntley surmises such a semantics ought. Next an account of the logical connectives and quantifiers that combines verificationist and falsificationist perspectives is proposed and evaluated. While the logic is again intuitionist there is, somewhat surprisingly, an unavoidable asymmetry between the verification and falsification conditions for negation, the conditional, and the universal quantifier. Lastly we are lead to a novel characterization of realism.

MILTON, John and DZELZAINIS, Martin (ed). *Political Writings—John Milton*. New York, Cambridge Univ Pr, 1991.

MINARI, Pierluigi and TAKANO, Mitio and ONO, Hiroakira. Intermediate Predicate Logics Determined by Ordinals. J Sym Log, 55(3), 1099-1124, S 90.

The paper deals with intermediate predicate logics which are semantically determined by classes of well-ordered Kripke frames with constant domain. The aim—loosely speaking—is to see whether and to what extent ordinals can be defined modulo Kripke-type semantics by sets of first-order formulas. The various results presented in the paper give partial answers to this question, both for countable and uncountable ordinals.

MINEAR, Paul S. "The Peace of God" in *Celebrating Peace*, ROUNER, Leroy S (ed), 118-131. Notre Dame, Univ Notre Dame Pr, 1990.

MINEAU, André. Human Rights and Nietzsche. Hist Euro Ideas, 11, 877-882, 1989.

Human rights have a double origin in ethics and politics, which confers meaning and historical impact upon them, and influences their development in theory as well as in practice. And since ethical thought and politics have conjugated, at a particular time in history, to produce positive basic rights, we are dealing, therefore, with a three-dimension issue uniting ethics, politics and law, and in which the first two dimensions represent the foundation and the justification of the third one. In this paper, we shall examine firstly the issue of justification as it can be viewed along 'traditional' lines. Secondly, we shall confront this approach with Nietzsche's critique.

MINGAY, J M and WALZER, R R (ed). *Aristotelis Ethica Evdemia*. New York, Oxford Univ Pr, 1991.

MININNI, Giuseppe. Il "parlare commune" come lume storico-naturale della "riproduzione sociale". Il Protag, 6(13-16), 135-147, Ja 88-D 89.

MINNEY, Robin. The Development of Otto's Thought 1898-1917. Relig Stud, 26(4), 505-524, D 90.

MINOGUE, K. Response to Miller's "Equality". Philosophy, 26, 99-108, 90 Supp.

Opposing egalitarianism does not entail supporting anti-egalitarianism: what it does involve is rejecting any determination of outcomes along the dimension of equality. Much support for egalitarianism trades on confusion with the problem of poverty. The two things are merely contingently related. Any attempt to construe inequality as a problem must look to a peculiarly oppressive despotism. Egalitarian doctrines construe human beings as organisms characterised by needs. Such rather dehumanising doctrines result from taking the principle of equality, which has an important but circumscribed place in Western law, politics, and manners, as if it described the only desirable relation between human beings.

MINOGUE, Kenneth. From Precision to Peace: Hobbes and Political Language. Hobbes Stud, 3, 75-88, 1990.

MINOGUE, Kenneth. "Response to Miller's 'Equality'" in *Philosophy and Politics*, HUNT, G M K (ed), 99-108. New York, Cambridge Univ Pr, 1991.

MINTS, G E. The Completeness of Provable Realizability. Notre Dame J Form Log, 30(3), 420-441, Sum 89.

Let A be a propositional formula and $rA[X]$ express in the predicate logic the statement "x realizes A." We prove that the classical derivability of $rA[t]$ for a lambda term t implies the intuitionistic derivability of A for the formulas A in the languages {implies, and, not} and {implies, and} where "and" is the so-called strong conjunction. (edited)

MIRANDA, Maria do Carmo Tavares de. *Caminhos do Filosofar*. Recife, Fund Cult Cid Recife, 1991.

The different ways of the Philosophy are the different paths of approach to the Being in metaphysical sense. This argument is developed in five views: 1) the fundamental and intrinsical relations of the Being itself and with the Thought and the Time. 2) Ontological and historical analysis about human nature. 3) The creative world of arts. 4) The character of human transcendence. 5) God in the Metaphysics. Finally the work presents the professional experience of the author in Recife, Brazil.

MIRHADY, David. Non-Technical *Pisteis* in Aristotle and Anaximenes. Amer J Philo, 112(1), 5-28, Spr 91.

MIRI, Mrinal. Reason in Criticism. J Indian Counc Phil Res, 6(2), 137-145, Ja-Ap 89.

MIRÓ, Francisco. "Mario Bunge's Philosophy of Logic and Mathematics" in *Studies on Mario Bunge's "Treatise"*, WEINGARTNER, Paul (ed), 285-299. Amsterdam, Rodopi, 1990.

MIROWSKY, John. Subjective Boundaries and Combinations in Psychiatric Diagnoses. J Mind Behav, 11(3-4), 407-423, Sum-Autumn 90.

The distinctions embodied in official psychiatric diagnoses represent arbitrary and subjective views of patients' problems. Historically, individual psychiatrists were free to superimpose their own distinctions and categories. In recent decades, a uniform set of concepts has been negotiated, promoted, and enforced. The uniform diagnoses improve descriptive communication and meet administrative needs. However, they remain arbitrary. This essay argues that a descriptive theory of psychiatric problems should distinguish the objective pattern of correlation among the thoughts, feelings, and behaviors in question from the subjective view of them embodied in diagnoses. A map of correlations among psychiatric symptoms reveals a graded circular spectrum, analogous to a color wheel. The psychiatric types are *not* empirical islands in correlationsal space. They are subjective points of reference on a circular continuum. (edited)

MIRVISH, Adrian. Freud Contra Sartre: Repression or Self-Deception? J Brit Soc Phenomenol, 21(3), 216-233, O 90.

The relation between the Sartre of *Being and Nothingness* and Freud is a highly complex one. For Sartre's criticism of the latter can be faulted in that it deals with superegological repression only. However, when one examines the classic notion of egological repression, this in turn can be severely faulted on the basis of a Sartrean type of approach. Combining and modifying both insights, however, Freud's great contributions concerning repression and the reality principle can be kept, while Sartre's extended critique frees up egological consciousness to play a more deliberate and active role in repression.

MISBIN, Robert I. Commentary— "Make Me Live": Autonomy and Terminal Illness. Hastings Center Rep, 20(5), 42-43, S-O 90.

I presented a patient with advanced cancer who would not discuss her terminal care. Should her physician write a Do Not Resuscitate Order without prior approval by the patient? Resuscitation of patients dying of cancer rarely brings any genuine benefit and is more likely to prolong suffering. Although a physician has a duty to tell the truth, he should not force this information on an unwilling patient. If a patient can only deal with her terminal illness by denying it, it is wrong for a physician to strip her of this defense by insisting that she exercise her "autonomy."

MISGELD, Dieter. Philosophy and Politics: On Fred Dallmayr's "Critical Encounters". Human Stud, 14(1), 15-22, Ja 91.

Fred Dallmayr's work is discussed in the article, with special reference to his book *Critical Encounters* (1987). His discussions of major philosophers of our times are examined and some conclusions drawn re the relation between philosophy and politics. Dallmayr's implicit hankering after the Greek polis and a community-supporting and community-building role for philosophy is challenged, especially with reference to a more pragmatist view of the relation between politics, philosophy, social science and social policy.

MISHRA, Aruna Ranjan. On the Causality of Sky. J Indian Phil, 19(2), 133-142, Je 91.

If eternality and all-pervasiveness is granted to space, time, soul and sky, then why only space and time be accepted as cause of anything non-eternal (i.e., an effect) anywhere on the ground that a cause is invariable precedent to effect? The article analyzes the Indian logical tradition and discovers how, finally, the sky was given a status of an inherent cause (of sound only) and argues for it a status of 'efficient cause of all products'.

MISSIMER, Connie. Perhaps by Skill Alone. Inform Log, 12(3), 145-153, Fall 90.

MITCHELL, Basil and ABRAHAM, William J (ed) and PREVOST, Robert W (ed). *How to Play Theological Ping-Pong: And Other Essays on Faith and Reason*. Grand Rapids, Eerdmans, 1991.

MITCHELL, David. Validity and Practical Reasoning. Philosophy, 65(254), 477-500, O 90.

Are steps in practical reasoning capable of a kind of validity distinct from the deductive validity which steps in theoretical reasoning can have? The answer partly depends on what, in general, validity is. The article expounds one attractive conception of validity-in-general which favours the answer 'yes', and which delivers appealing identifications of valid 'practical inferences'. This conception of validity is then shown to be revealingly defective as applied to theoretical reasoning. It is concluded that there is no distinctive practical validity, but that this does not jeopardise the possibility of people's arriving by intelligent practical reasoning at reasonable decisions.

MITCHELL, John C and MOGGI, Eugenio. Kripke-Style Models for Typed Lambda Calculus. Annals Pure Applied Log, 51(1-2), 99-124, Mr 91.

MITCHELL, W J T. Realism, Irrealism, and Ideology: A Critique of Nelson Goodman. J Aes Educ, 25(1), 21-35, Spr 91.

"Realism, Irrealism, and Ideology" explores the limitations of Nelson Goodman's account of representational realism, and suggests some problems for the relation of his overall thought (labelled "irrealism") to epistemological realism. The essay argues that Goodman's project is fundamentally equivocal about what lies inside and outside its domain, what subjects, that is, are amenable to an ahistorical, value-free description of referential chains. As long as Goodman remains inside his neutral, synchronic system, his claims hold good. When he takes on representational realism, however, he is compelled to enter the realms of history, value, and belief and transgress the proper limits of his own system. The result is an account of realism that is either vacuous (realism as the "habitual and familiar" mode of representation) or arbitrary (realism as the familiar at some times, the novel and strange at other times). The essay offers a corrective account of realism that seems more compatible with the core of Goodman's philosophy, and that resists the temptation to turn irrealism into a substitute for realist epistemology.

MITRA, Prabir. The Hermetic Influence on the Rise of Modern Science. Phil Sci (Tucson), 3, 89-110, 1988.

This paper examines the role of philosophical assumptions in historical reconstructions of the impact of the hermetic tradition on the rise of modern science. After pointing out the essential differences which exist in historiographic assessments of the intellectual legacy of Giordano Bruno, the negative consequences of using the positivist methodology in the history of science are discussed. The contextualist- structuralist approach is proposed to free historical reconstructions from unsubstantiated metascientific presuppositions.

MITSCHERLING, Jeff. The Historical Consciousness of Man. Hist Euro Ideas, 11, 733-741, 1989.

The twofold purpose of this paper is (i) to demonstrate the extent to which Gadamer's notion of 'effective-historical consciousness' is anticipated by Nietzsche's view of 'monumental history' and (ii) thereby to clarify a fundamental insight of Gadamer's hermeneutics that has often been misunderstood—namely, that effective-historical consciousness is always at work in any critique of morality, ideology or social policy. I argue that the critical dimension inherent in all hermeneutical reflection becomes obvious once we recognize that this reflection operates with a monumentalist, not an antiquarian, conception of history.

MITTAL, Kewal Krisha. 'Ontological Commitment' in the Context of the Buddhist Thought. J Indian Counc Phil Res, 5(1), 103-109, S-D 87.

MITTRA, Aditya Barna. A Genetic Exploration of Women's Subjugation: The Adventures of a Gadfly. J Indian Counc Phil Res, 8(1), 93-113, S-D 90.

MIUCCIO, Giuliana. Heracles and the Passage from Nature to Culture in G Vico's *La Scienza Nuova*. Diogenes, 151, 90-103, Fall 90.

How did an unsocial animal in the forest become the social animal without which civil history would have been impossible? How was it possible for the "bestione" to enter on the "corso" at whose term civil institutions had come to be? The paper explains how Giambattista Vico uses Heracles and his labours, understood not as fable but as elements of "vera narratio" or real history, to show that the nations and civil institutions generally "could not have been founded without religion or grow without valor."

MOBERG, Dennis J and MEYER, Michael J. A Deontological Analysis of Peer Relations in Organizations. J Bus Ethics, 9(11), 863-877, N 90.

Using practical formalism a deontological ethical analysis of peer relations in organizations is developed. This analysis is composed of two types of duties derived from Kant's Categorical Imperative: negative duties to refrain from the use of peers and positive duties to provide help and assistance. The conditions under which these duties pertain are specified through the development of examples and conceptual distinctions. A number of implications are then discussed.

MOCCHI, Giuliana. *Idea, mente, specie: Platonismo e scienza in Johannes Marcus Marci (1595-1667)*. Soveria Mannelli, Rubbettino, 1990.

This study is intended to illuminate another less noted aspect about the effect produced in Boemia through the movement of the new scientific and philosophic developments during the first decade of the sixteen hundreds. (staff)

MOCEK, Reinhard. From Hegel to Lukacs: The Problem of Ontology from the Point of View of Social and Natural Theory (in German). Deut Z Phil, 38(6), 541-550, 1990.

MOCEK, Reinhard. From Patriarchal Socialism to Socialist Democracy: Thoughts on a New Theory of Society. Praxis Int, 11(1), 51-64, Ap 91.

MÖCKEL, Christian. The Specific Features of Cognition Progress in Philosophy: Demonstrated by the Example of Max Adler (in German). Deut Z Phil, 38(9), 838-848, 1990.

The article discusses how a socialist, Max Adler (1873-1937), in the cultural and scientific atmosphere of the Viennese "fin de siècle" (Austria) in 1904, a philosophical synthesis drafted by Kant and Marx, clarified the discussion method of knowledge theorie for the question raised on knowledge theorie since 1883 between national economists (Menger, Schmoller), lawyers (Stammler) and philosophers (Windelband, Rickert, Cohen). In comparison to his time orthodox Marxism (Kautsky, Mehring) he obtained a depth, a productivity problem consciousners for the theorie of knowledge and scientific methods (social a priori).

MOCNIK, Rastko. From Historical Marxisms to Historical Materialism: Toward the Theory of Ideology. Grad Fac Phil J, 14(1), 117-137, 1991.

A theory of ideology is proposed on the assumption that only utterances have meaning. The vitious circle "meaning as the key to the communicative situation as the key to the meaning" is broken by the concept of "the subject supposed to believe" with whom communicating parties identify. This identification is conditional, beliefs ascribed to the subject supposed to believe are only possible. This explains why it is possible to understand utterances without necessarily sharing their ideological background. The scheme of ideological interpellation is an inversion of Lacan's scheme of psychoanalytic process. Common points and divergencies with Althusser and Habermas are shortly discussed.

MODRAK, Deborah K W. The *Nous*-Body Problem in Aristotle. Rev Metaph, 44(4), 755-774, Je 91.

Aristotle, pundits often say, has a *nous*-body problem. The psychophysical account that succeeds in the case of other psychological faculties and activities, they charge, breaks down in the case of the intellect. One formulation of this difficulty claims that the definition of the soul given in *de Anima*II.1 is incompatible with the account of *nous* in *de Anima*III and elsewhere in the corpus. Indeed there are four psychological concepts that raise the *nous*-body problem: the faculty for thought as described in *de Anima*III.4, the intellection of indivisible objects of thought in *de Anima*III.6, the active intellect of *de Anima*III.5 and the type of thinking likened to the activity of the divine mind in *Metaphysics*XII.6-8 and *Nicomachean Ethics*X.6-8. I consider each in turn and argue that Aristotle is on firmer ground here than is often believed.

MOGGACH, Douglas. Monadic Marxism: A Critique of Elster's Methodological Individualism. Phil Soc Sci, 21(1), 38-63, Mr 91.

Elster's work unstably combines Leibnizian and utilitarian conceptions of action and offers various deconstructions of rationality and individuality. His methodological individualism gives an inadequate account of its privileged object, individual teleologies, and a distorted account of the relational framework of social reproduction and transformation. Elster has not properly conceptualized the relation of the teleological act to patterns of material and social causality, and his rational choice theory proves unable to accommodate the interactions of his postulated monadic individuals. His most recent work clearly illustrates the limits of an individualist approach, while remaining committed to its principles.

MOGGI, Eugenio and MITCHELL, John C. Kripke-Style Models for Typed Lambda Calculus. Annals Pure Applied Log, 51(1-2), 99-124, Mr 91.

MOHANTA, D K. A Critique of Jayarasi's Critique of Perception. Indian Phil Quart, 17(4), 489-509, O 90.

In this paper we propose to discuss Jayarāsi's critique of the Nyāya view of perception only. And in fact, while criticising the Nyāya definition of perception, Jayarāsi criticises the possibility of valid knowledge in general. The paper is divided into two parts. The first part contains a straightforward exposition of Jayarasi's arguments against the possibility of perception and the second contains an assessment of the strength and weakness of Jayarasi's arguments.

MOI, Toril. Reading Kristeva: A Response to Calvin Bedient. Crit Inquiry, 17(3), 639-643, Spr 91.

The essay argues that Professor Bedient's account of Julia Kristeva's work is one-sided in that it emphasizes only the semiotic and takes no account of the symbolic process.

MOJZES, Paul. Reinvigorating the International Christian-Marxist Dialogue. Dialec Hum, 16(3-4), 7-15, Sum-Autumn 89.

A survey of the oscillations in the Christian-Marxist dialogue from the commencement of the dialogue in the middle 1950s to the end of the 1980s. The author summarizes themes of some of the major Christian-Marxist meetings in the 1980s and presents some of the tasks for such dialogue. The article contains an introduction and context for the other articles collected and edited by the author for this special issue of *Dialectics and Humanism*, all of which deal with various aspects of the dialogue.

MOKASHI, Ashwini A. Reflections on Aristotle's Criticism of Forms. Indian Phil Quart, SUPP 17(3), 1-16, Jl 90.

Aristotle considers his "Third-Man Argument" as fatal for Plato's "Theory of Ideas." Plato also considers the argument, but not as fatal. How could there be such great variance? How do we account for this difference? Plato and Aristotle are both concerned with how to understand reality. But (1) Plato's approach is anthropocentric, whereas that of Aristotle cosmocentric. (2) For Plato, the order of being is modelled on the order of soul. For Aristotle, between order of being and order of knowing, the first in itself should be the first for us. (3) Their temperamental difference. Platonic utopian approach clashes with Aristotle's realistic approach.

MOKED, Gabriel. A Note on Berkeley's Anti-Abstractionism. Iyyun, 40(1), 95-99, Ja 91.

MOKREJS, Antonin. Interpretation of Art as a Philosophical Problem (in Czechoslovakian). Estetika, 28(1), 38-50, 1991.

MOLDER, Filomena and MARQUES, António and NABAIS, Nuno. "Entrevista com o Professor Oswaldo Market Conduzida por" in *Dinâmica do Pensar: Homenagem a Oswaldo Market*, FAC LETRAS UNIV LISBOA (ed), 283-305. Lisboa, Fac Letras U Lisboa, 1991.

MOLDER, Maria Filomena. "A voz prometida: Sobre a imaginação na *Kritik der Urteilskraft*" in *Dinâmica do Pensar: Homenagem a Oswaldo Market*, FAC LETRAS UNIV LISBOA (ed), 143-152. Lisboa, Fac Letras U Lisboa, 1991.

Il s'agit de présenter le travail de l'imagination dans le cadre du rapport entre langage et concéptualisation, tel qu'il se déploie dans la troisième *Critique*. D'une part, à travers l'atmosphère nourrie par la constelation des concepts qui proviennent de la *voix* (*Stimme*), on cherche les effets mêmes de ce rapport dans l'effort philosophique de saisir l'expérience de la beauté. D'autre part, à partir de l'analyse du 59, on montre la façon dont Kant a conçu ce rapport-là, selon la détermination du concept comme forme symbolique. Par le rayonnement des passages entre mot et concept sur les passages entre image et idée, qu le procédé symbolique met en mouvement, il est possible, donc, d'établir les conditions d'un langage philosophique.

MOLINA, Carlos. Anotaciones en torno al poder de la democracia. Rev Filosof (Costa Rica), 28(67-68), 27-30, D 90.

This paper considers democracy both as a procedure and as a goal in terms of vertical and horizontal loyalties. The purpose is to define the actual limits of this type of regime in relation to the fulfillment of its own political teleology.

MOLINA, Mario A. El hombre agustiniamo: Itinerario tras el ser de la existencia. Augustinus, 35(139-140), 369-382, Jl-D 90.

MOLINARO, Aniceto and BLANDINO, Giovanni (ed). *The Critical Problem of Knowledge*. Vatican City, Pont U Lateranense, 1989.

The review *Aquinas*, of the Philosophical Faculty of the Pontifical University of Lateran in Rome, has promoted a discussion among the professors of the various Ecclesiastical Faculties of Philosophy in Rome about the solutions proposed by them to the Critical Problem of Knowledge. This book contains the papers written in English.

MÖLLER, Wolfgang. Emergent Psychoneural Monism: Mario Bunge and the Body and Soul Problem (in German). Deut Z Phil, 38(8), 733-738, 1990.

MOLNÁR, László M. Orthodoxy or Atheism? Remarks on the New Edition of Hegel's Lectures on Religion (in Hungarian). Magyar Filozof Szemle, 1-2, 176-183, 1990.

MOLNAR, Miklós and MACLEAN, Ian (trans). "The Hungarian Intellectual and the Choice of Commitment or Neutrality" in *The Political Responsibility of Intellectuals*, MACLEAN, Ian (ed), 189-200. New York, Cambridge Univ Pr, 1990.

The author sets out to answer the question: how should intellectuals behave when faced with unpalable oral or political choices? He takes three examples from nineteenth-century Hungary—Ferenc Kazinczy, István Széchenyi and Károly Eötvös—to show the practical problems involved in choosing a course of action in difficult circumstances.

MOLTMANN, Jürgen. "Political Theology and the Ethics of Peace" in *Celebrating Peace*, ROUNER, Leroy S (ed), 102-117. Notre Dame, Univ Notre Dame Pr, 1990.

MONDIN, Battista. Analisi fenomenologica del concetto di religione. Sapienza, 43(3), 241-269, Jl-S 90.

MONETA, Giovanni B. Ambiguity, Inductive Systems, and the Modeling of Subjective Probability Judgements. Phil Psych, 4(2), 267-285, 1991.

Gambles which induce the decision-maker to experience ambiguity about the relative likelihood of events often give rise to ambiguity-seeking and ambiguity-avoidance, which imply violation of additivity and Savage's axioms. The inability of the subjective Bayesian theory to account for these empirical regularities has determined a dichotomy between normative and descriptive views of subjective probability. This paper proposes a framework within which the two perspectives can be reconciled. First, a formal definition of ambiguity is given over a continuum ranging from ignorance to risk, and including ambiguous contexts as subsets. Second, it is shown that the system of inductive logic account for the effects of ambiguity. Then, Carnap's λ-system is applied as a psychological model and compared to Einhorn and Hogarth's non-normative psychological model. Finally, the implications of this research to the modeling of subjective judgements are discussed.

MONGIN, Philippe. A Note on Verisimilitude and Relativization to Problems. Erkenntnis, 33(3), 391-396, N 90.

This note aims at critically assessing a little-noticed proposal made by Popper in the second edition of *Objective Knowledge* to the effect that verisimilitude of scientific theories should be made relative to the problems they deal with. Using a simple propositional calculus formalism, it is shown that the "relativized" definition fails for the very same reason why Popper's original concept of verisimilitude collapsed—only if one of two theories is true can they be compared in terms of the suggested definition of verisimilitude.

MONGIN, Philippe. Rational Choice Theory Considered as Psychology and Moral Philosophy. Phil Soc Sci, 21(1), 5-37, Mr 91.

This article attempts to assess Jon Elster's contribution to rational choice in *Ulysses and the Sirens* and *Sour Grapes*. After reviewing Elster's analysis of functional versus intentional explanations, the essay moves on to the crucial distinction between the *thin* and *broad* theories of rationality. The former elaborates on the traditional economist's preference/feasible set apparatus; the latter is the more demanding theory which inquires into the rationality of beliefs and preferences. Elster's approach to the broad theory normally consists in using the thin theory as a reference point and in making purposefully limited departures from it. The essay illustrates the method while commenting on Elster's discussion of autonomous preferences in *Sour Grapes*. It goes on to stress some important analogies between Elster's use of the thin and broad theories, on one hand, and Weber's ideal-typical method, on the other. The final assessment is phrased in terms of these analogies; it is suggested that Elster is at his best when the ideal-typical method and his own separate from each other, that is, when he comes to grips with the broad theory in its own terms.

MONSERRAT, Javier. Problema psicofísico y realidad cuántica en la física heterodoxa de David Bohm. Pensamiento, 47(187), 297-312, Jl-S 91.

MONSERRAT, Javier. Sobre le estructura dinámica de la realidad. Pensamiento, 47(185), 79-90, Ja-Mr 91.

MONSUUR, H and DELVER, R and STORCKEN, A J A. Ordering Pairwise Comparison Structures. Theor Decis, 31(1), 75-94, Jl 91.

Following an introduction to the merits of pairwise comparison methods, we present various ordering algorithms for complete binary preferential structures. These procedures generalize the well-known numbering algorithm to the intransitive case. A new form of independence of irrelevant alternatives is presented. Moreover, various other criteria and characterizations for these algorithms are presented. Aside from solving ranking problems and making explicit value criteria and structures of human preference, our algorithms are applicable to subjects such as task-sequencing and artificial intelligence projects.

MONTAGNA, Franco. "Pathologies" in Two Syntactic Categories of Partial Maps. Notre Dame J Form Log, 30(1), 105-116, Wint 89.

MONTAGNA, Franco and SOMMARUGA, Giovanni. A Note on Some Extension Results. Stud Log, 49(4), 591-600, D 90.

In this note, a fully modal proof is given of some conservation results proved in a previous paper by arithmetic means. The proof is based on the extendability of Kripke models.

MONTANARI, Marcello. "Jürgen Habermas fra 'teoria critica' e 'neo-illuminismo'" in *Razionalitá critica: nella filosofia moderna*, LAMACCHIA, Ada (ed), 205-234. Bari, Lacaita, 1989.

The essay discusses the theory by Jurgen Habermas, according to which the *"Dialektik der Aufklärung"* by M Horkheimer and T W Adorno belongs to an irrationalistic current. By the interpretation of Ulysses's myth, reproposed by the authors, it is shown that instead the principal purpose of the *"Dialektik der Aufklärung"* is the definition of a new and more elevated form of rationality such that is doesn't exclude, but comprise in itself the "Lebenswelt".

MONTEFIORE, Alan. "The Political Responsibility of Intellectuals" in *The Political Responsibility of Intellectuals*, MACLEAN, Ian (ed), 201-228. New York, Cambridge Univ Pr, 1990.

This book addresses some of the many problems encountered in defining the relationship of intellectuals to the societies in which they live. In what respects, and why, are they responsible for or to those societies? In what ways should—or perhaps inevitably do—their own preoccupations with language, truth, interpretation and expression impinge upon their societies's politics? The contributors to this volume, whose papers result from much critical discussion between themselves, come from a wide variety of disciplines ranging from economics to linguistics, from sociology to philosophy, and are drawn from both America and Eastern and Western Europe.

MONTEFIORE, Alan (ed) and MACLEAN, Ian (ed) and WINCH, Peter (ed). *The Political Responsibility of Intellectuals*. New York, Cambridge Univ Pr, 1990.

The many problems encountered in defining the relationship of intellectuals to the society in which they live are addressed in this book. Specialists in various disciplines from the United States, Great Britain, France, Holland, Poland and Hungary set out to explore the following issues: in what respects are intellectuals responsible for and to their societies? Should they seek to act as an independent arbiters of the values of those societies? Should they seek to give advice in the public domain, or should they withdraw from all involvement with politics? How should their preoccupation with truth and language find practical expression?

MONTGOMERY, Richard. The Reductionist Ideal in Cognitive Psychology. Synthese, 85(2), 279-314, N 90.

I offer support for the view that physicalist theories of cognition don't reduce to neurophysiological theories. On my view, the mind-brain relationship is to be explained in terms of evolutionary forces, some of which tug in the direction of a reductionistic mind-brain relationship, and some of which tug in the opposite direction. This theory of forces makes possible an anti-reductionist account of the cognitive mind-brain relationship which avoids psychophysical anomalism. This theory thus also responds to the complaint which arguably lies behind the Churchlands' strongest criticisms of anti-reductionism—namely the complaint that anti-reductionists fail to supply principled explanations for the character of the mind-brain relationship. While lending support to anti-reductionism, the view defended here also insures a permanent place for mind-brain reduction as an explanatory ideal analogous to Newtonian inertial motion or Aristotelian natural motion.

MONTGOMERY, Richard. Visual Perception and the Wages of Indeterminacy. Proc Phil Sci Ass, 1, 365-378, 1990.

Three case studies offered here will support the conclusion that a successful scientific theory of visual cognition still makes room for some rather systematic and rather striking semantic indeterminacies—W V Quine's well-known pessimism about the wages of such indeterminacy not withstanding. The first case concerns the perception of shape, the second concerns color vision, and the third concerns the rules of inference involved in "unconscious inference" within the visual system.

MONTORO, Marcial Moreno. La apuesta literaria de Nietzsche. Dialogos, 26(57), 89-100, Ja 91.

MONTOYA, Rocío Basurto. Hegel: fenomenología del espíritu. Logos (Mexico), 18(52), 73-85, Ja-Ap 90.

MONTUORI, Mario. Per una nuova edizione della *Epistola* lockiana sulla tolleranza. Filosofia, 42(1), 85-107, Ja-Ap 91.

MOODY, Thomas E. Anarchism and Feminism. J Soc Phil, 21(2-3), 160-173, Fall-Wint 90.

MOODY-ADAMS, Michele M. "Gender and the Complexity of Moral Voices" in *Feminist Ethics*, CARD, Claudia (ed), 195-212. Lawrence, Univ Pr of Kansas, 1991.

Attempts to define a 'women's moral perspective' are shown 1) to mask the diversity of women's moral voices, and 2) to ignore the complexity of the moral domain. Particular attention is paid to Carol Gilligan's research: it is shown to mask diversity by putting the biology of sex at the core of a woman's moral identity. Finally, the complexity of women's and men's moral reasoning is shown to be rooted in the fact that the moral domain could be reduced to one, or even two, measures of significance.

MOODY-ADAMS, Michele M. On Surrogacy: Morality, Markets, and Motherhood. Pub Affairs Quart, 5(2), 175-190, Ap 91.

This paper attacks standard and non-standard defenses of paid surrogacy. In response to the standard views it is shown that: 1) motherhood—as a *sui-generis* activity—is not a proper subject of personal service contracts, and 2) parties to paid surrogate agreements accept legal and moral principles condemning the commodification of babies. Non-standard defenses reject barriers to the commodification of motherhood and babies. Needs-based arguments of this sort are unconvincing. Primacy-of-desires arguments, though somewhat stronger, undermine social practices that protect and enable complex commodity exchange—and hence undermine the market-centered aims of their defenders.

MOODY-ADAMS, Michele M. On the Alleged Methodological Infirmity of Ethics. Amer Phil Quart, 27(3), 225-235, Jl 90.

This article rejects two influential claims: Quine's claim that ethics is methodologically infirm, and the emotivist's claim that ethical disagreement is ultimately nonrational. The empirical foothold of ethics is shown to be the self-understandings of those addressed by ethical theory or debate, and the rationality of ethical disagreement is traced to its tendency to stimulate self-scrutiny. Ethical claims are not "testable" in the manner of scientific claims; the relation between ethics and experience is fundmentally different from that between science and experience. Though the methods of science and ethics differ, it is argued, ethics is nonetheless epistemologically respectable.

MOODY-ADAMS, Michele. "On the Old Saw That Character Is Destiny" in *Identity, Character, and Morality: Essays in Moral Psychology*, FLANAGAN, Owen (ed), 111-131. Cambridge, MIT Pr, 1990.

Sceptical claims that character undermines responsibility embody serious misconceptions about moral assessment and its justification. First, the sceptic fails to recognize that character assessments are parasitic upon ascriptions of responsibility. Second, the sceptic fails to see that persons have the capacity to act out of character, in spite of their initial constitutive luck. We understand this fact only when we view human action "from the inside" and discover that we cannot see ourselves as persons and yet deny that we are responsible for our actions.

MOOIJ, A W M. 'Inference to the Best Explanation' of 'Inference to the Best Interpretation'? Een antwoord op Derksens ..... Alg Ned Tijdschr Wijs, 83(1), 33-37, Ja 91.

This article is a reply to Derksen's article "Freud, Mooij en de empiristische boeman" (*ANTW* 82 (1990), 232-236), and it concentrates on the Tally Argument and the underlying Transference Argument and Success Argument. Here the hermeneutic conception of psychoanalysis is further defended.

MOON, J Donald. Constrained Discourse and Public Life. Polit Theory, 19(2), 202-229, My 91.

"Discourse-based" models of politics base the validity of political arrangements on their being acceptable to those who are subject to them, when acceptance is tested by a process of free discussion. Constrained discourse models specify the conditions of acceptable agreement, but in a circular way that can silence certain voices. However, "unconstrained discourse" is problematic, because the effort to make particular voices heard will threaten others. The hope for a fully consensual political life will be disappointed. Nonetheless, a modified version of a model of constrained discourse is attractive, for it offers the hope of achieving the highest possible degree of uncoerced agreement.

MOONEY, Tim. Whitehead and Leibniz: Conflict and Convergence. Phil Stud (Ireland), 32, 197-212, 1988-90.

The purpose of this paper is twofold. On the one hand it attempts to outline the major similarities and differences between the metaphysical doctrines of Whitehead and Leibniz. On the other it attempts to show that Whitehead's critique of Leibniz's system as one which necessitates an appeal to a '*deus ex machina*' can also be applied to his own 'process philosophy'. It is argued that Whitehead's alternative is not sustainable when considered in the light of his concept of the primordial nature of God.

MOORE, A W. A Kantian View of Moral Luck. Philosophy, 65(253), 297-321, Jl 90.

Although Kant's moral philosophy is closer to Aristotle's than is often supposed, there is, in Kant, non-Aristotelian hostility to the possibility of good moral luck. That is the author's starting point. He argues that it is nevertheless in the spirit of Kantianism to accept the possibility of bad moral luck, and he traces out the implications of this partly with respect to related Pauline doctrines in Christianity.

MOORE, A W. A Problem for Intuitionism: The Apparent Possibility of Performing Infinitely Many Tasks in a Finite Time. Proc Aris Soc, 90, 17-34, 1989-90.

The author explores an apparent problem for intuitionists deriving from Zeno's paradoxes, namely that it seems possible, in principle, to survey (construct, inspect) all of the natural numbers in a finite time. He argues that the intuitionists' best response to this problem is via a Wittgensteinian critique of the grammar of "infinity."

MOORE, F C T. Rome Inferences and Structural Opacity. Mind, 99(396), 601-608, O 90.

'Compulsion Theories' (in which choice or action is logically or causally compelled by antecedents) are refuted using an argument of Buridan. 'Rome inferences' have the form "I want to go to Rome if Socrates is there; Socrates is there; therefore I want to go to Rome." But such inferences are invalid. This provides a solution to 'Buridan's ass' (reviewed in Aristotle, Al-Ghazali, Ibn Rushd [Averroes], St. Augustine, Montaigne, and Spinoza). Rome inferences illustrate 'structural opacity' (cousin to referential opacity): logical terms too become opaque in oblique contexts. The notion of structural opacity also solves Wollheim's paradox of democracy.

MOORE, Gregory H and BANASCHEWSKI, Bernhard. The Dual Cantor-Bernstein Theorem and the Partition Principle. Notre Dame J Form Log, 31(3), 375-381, Sum 90.

This paper examines two propositions, the Dual Cantor-Bernstein Theorem and the Partition Principle, with respect to their logical interrelationship and their history. It is shown that the Refined Dual Cantor-Bernstein Theorem is equivalent to the Axiom of Choice.

MOORE, Robert L. "Psychocosmetics: A Jungian Response" in *Archetypal Process: Self and Divine in Whitehead, Jung, and Hillman*, GRIFFIN, David Ray (ed), 157-161. Evanston, Northwestern Univ Pr, 1989.

MOORE, Robin J. John Stuart Mill and Royal India. Utilitas, 3(1), 85-106, My 91.

The article concerns J S Mill's role in the conduct of relations between the East India Company and the Indian princely states, c. 1825-58. It attempts through archival analysis to evaluate Mill's contributions to the Company's policies for the states and to define his own policy preferences. In gereral, Mill was cautious about annexing princedoms and sought to balance western principles and traditional forms in their governance. Whereas he favoured western innovations and improvements in directly ruled British India, for security reasons he was more circumspect towards princely India.

MOOSA, Imtiaz. A Critical Examination of Scheler's Justification of the Existence of Values. J Value Inq, 25(1), 23-41, Ja 91.

Scheler's startling proclamation that values actually exist is scrutinized in this paper. Firstly his position is made clear on two issues: one, what is meant by "existence" of values; two, what are his reasons for concluding this. Secondly, his reasons are critically examined and refuted. It is shown that values exist for Scheler the way "ideal objects" exist for Husserl. And it is because Scheler believes that "feeling acts" (as opposed to "feeling states") are intentional, and that values are genuine objects of these acts, that he declares the independent existence of values. My paper attempts to show that the object of an intentional act need not be *existent* object.

MORADIELLOS, Enrique. El proceso de formación de la clase obrera de las minas en Asturias. El Basilisco, 2, 43-50, N-D 89.

MORAN, Thomas J and WALKER, Lawrence J. Moral Reasoning in a Communist Chinese Society. J Moral Educ, 20(2), 139-155, My 91.

This study examined the cross-cultural universality of Kohlberg's theory of moral reasoning development in the People's Republic of China—a culture quite different from the one out of which the theory arose. In particular, the applicability of the theory was evaluated in terms of its comprehensiveness and the validity of the moral stage model. An analysis of moral orientations provided an additional perspective on individuals' moral reasoning, in particular, in revealing group differences. Although, in general, the universal applicability of Kohlberg's approach was supported by these data, a subjective analysis of responses revealed some indigenous concepts, fundamental to Communist Chinese morality, that are not well tapped by the approach.

MORAVCSIK, Julius. "Meaning and Explanation" in *Themes From Kaplan*, ALMOG, Joseph (ed), 273-295. New York, Oxford Univ Pr, 1989.

This paper presents a theory of lexical meaning that differs both from standard Fregean accounts and from the Kripke-Putnam "rigid designator" approach. It posites a meaning structure that yields only necessary, not sufficient conditions of application. It is made up of a fourfold structure, indicating about the members of the extension what their constituency must be, what structured they hand, what agency is conceptually linked to them, and what functional specifications they fulfill. The essay shows how this theory solves more problems in semantics than either of the two key approaches mentioned above.

MORAWIEC, E. The Initial Form of Empiristic and Aprioristic Conception of Knowledge on the World (in Polish). Stud Phil Christ, 26(2), 7-22, 1990.

It is known that the rational knowledge on the world has emerged at the turn of VII to VI century.... It took first the form of an empirical and then the apriorist knowledge. The empirical knowledge on the world was initiated by thinkers founding the early Ionian school while the apriorist one was initiated by Parmenides of Elea. In the paper entitled as above the author has raised the problem of a theory of exercising these kinds of knowledge on the world. He is of the opinion that the origins of the theory of a rational knowledge have to be set earlier than it used to be. According to the author an analysis of both sensory and mental cognition, from the point of view of their value, was made as soon as in the early Ionian school and the Eleatic school. The author points out that in both schools two different conceptions of rational knowledge were established: an empiristic in the early Ionian school and an aprioristic in the Eleatic school. The paper contains a brief characteristic of both conceptions of rational knowledge.

MORAWSKI, Stefan. Art and Aesthetics and the Crisis of Culture. Praxis Int, 10(1-2), 104-116, Ap-Jl 90.

This paper deals with the main issues of interwar and afterwar thought on the crisis of culture, treating it as the background of the artistic and aesthetic ideas, focussing either on their peculiar mission resisting the cultural catastrophism or surrendering to it. It is emphasized that starting with the 50s, art and aesthetics reflect more and more on their own possible decline. On the other hand, postmodernism, which recently appeared to deny the crisis of art and culture in general, seems to be the very symptom of their degradation.

MOREL, Bernard. Gonseth et le discours théologique. Dialectica, 44(3-4), 353-361, 1990.

The effects of Gonseth's methodological and epistemological principles on theological reflection are as extensive as they are evocative. In this field, in which the frequent use of metaphors precludes unambiguous discourse, the full importance of the principle of idoneity is revealed. Uncritical dogmatism is prevented by the principle of revisability. The opposition between the ways of otherness and of innerness underscores the differences observed between scientific procedures (otherness) and spiritual ones (innerness); theology seeks to treat canonical facts objectively (by way of otherness) by means that are confirmed by actual experience (by way of innerness).

MORELAND, J P and NIELSEN, Kai. *Does God Exist? The Great Debate*. Nashville, Nelson, 1990.

The work contains the transcript of a debate between J. P. Moreland and Kai Nielsen on the existence of God followed by the responses of four philosophers (2 theists, 2 atheists) and final statements by Moreland and Nielsen. Peter Kreeft writes and introduction and conclusion to the volume. Among the issues covered are these: the Kalam cosmological argument, God and morality, problems in religious language and epistemology, miracles, Free will and theism, and design. Anthony Flew, Dallas Willard, William Lane Craig, and Keith Parsons contribute chapters to the book.

MORELAND, J P. Nominalism and Abstract Reference. Amer Phil Quart, 27(4), 325-334, O 90.

I focus on the debate about the nature of qualities between nominalists (qualities are abstract particulars) and realists (qualities are universals) by examining abstract reference. Realists claim that sentences like (1) "red resembles orange more than it does blue" and (2) "red is a color" incorporate abstract singular terms, e.g., "red," that refer to universals. Nominalists try to account for (1) and (2) by employing two basic strategies: abstract singular terms refer to sets of abstract particulars or reductive paraphrase. Both strategies are examined and rejected. Sentences like (1) and (2) provide evidence for a realist assay of qualities.

MORENO, Jonathan D and VEATCH, Robert M. Consensus in Panels and Committees: Conceptual and Ethical Issues. J Med Phil, 16(4), 371-373, Ag 91.

MORENO, Jonathan D. Consensus, Contracts, and Committees. J Med Phil, 16(4), 393-408, Ag 91.

Following a brief account of the puzzle that ethics committees present for the Western Philosophical tradition, I will examine the possibility that social contract theory can contribute to a philosophical account of these committees. Passing through classical as well as contemporary theories, particularly Rawls' recent constructivist approach, I will argue that social contract theory places severe contraints on the authority that may legitimately be granted to ethics committees. This, I conclude, speaks more about the suitability of the theory to this level of analysis than about the ethics committee phenomenon itself.

MORENO, Jonathan D. Ethics Consultation as Moral Engagement. Bioethics, 5(1), 44-56, Ja 91.

MORGAN, Jerry (ed) and COHEN, Philip R (ed) and POLLACK, Martha E (ed). *Intentions in Communication*. Cambridge, MIT Pr, 1990.

MORGAN, Michael L. *Platonic Piety*. New Haven, Yale Univ Pr, 1990.

MORGAN, S R. "Schelling and the Origins of His *Naturphilosophie*" in *Romanticism and the Sciences*, CUNNINGHAM, Andrew (ed), 25-37. New York, Cambridge Univ Pr, 1990.

MORGAN, Vance G. Common Ground: Aristotle on Human and Divine Noetic Activity. Dialogue (PST), 33(1), 11-25, O 90.

This article investigates whether the noetic activity of divine Nous in Aristotle might somehow be properly described as thinking in any way familiar to us, thus forming the basis of commonality between the mortal and the divine. The article concludes that Aristotle means to include human and divine nous under a common notion, connected by the immateriality of their activities. Due to the necessary attributes of the divine being's existence, however, the content of divine noetic activity differs significantly from anything we recognize as thought.

MORICONI, Enrico. L'interpretazione costruttiva dell'implicazione. Teoria, 10(2), 85-97, 1990.

MORIKAWA, Osamu. Some Modal Logics Based on a Three-Valued Logic. Notre Dame J Form Log, 30(1), 130-137, Wint 89.

Our purpose is formulating the modal systems K, M, S4 and S5 based on a three-valued logic (true, undefined, false). First we represent the systems by using a modified Gentzen-style formalism. Then we define suitable Kripke models and prove the completeness theorems for these systems.

MORIN, Alain and EVERETT, James. Conscience de soi et langage intérieur: quelques spéculations. Philosophiques, 17(2), 168-188, Autumn 1990.

This text proposes a definition of self-awareness and explains its social origin. It is postulated that the social milieu permits a movement to a more objective perspective for self-perception, and that this movement is then reproduced in the brain by specific cognitive processes. It is suggested that inner speech represents one such cognitive process, which acts like a mirror to reflect subjective experience back upon itself; the self would be generated by this reflective activity. It is argued that inner speech has a preeminent position among the cognitive processes implicated in self-awareness. The problem of self-awareness in primates is discussed, and the article concludes with ideas concerning schizophrenia, prayer, meditation, and psychodysleptic drugs.

MORMANN, Thomas. Are All False Theories Equally False? A Remark on David Miller's Problem and Geometric Conventionalism. Brit J Phil Sci, 39(4), 505-519, D 88.

David Miller has argued that we cannot make much sense of the idea that one false quantitative theory is a better approximation to the true state of affairs than is another false theory. In this note it is shown that Miller's scepticism concerning the possibility of ranking of false quantitative theories can be reformulated as a radical conventionalist thesis asserting that all metrical structures on a manifold of possible experimental outcomes are on an equal footing. This conventionalism can be criticised in a similar manner as traditional geometric conventionalism.

MORMANN, Thomas. Husserl's Philosophy of Science and the Semantic Approach. Phil Sci, 58(1), 61-83, Mr 91.

Husserl's mathematical philosophy of science can be considered an anticipation of the contemporary postpositivistic semantic approach, which regards mathematics and not logic as the appropriate tool for the exact philosophical reconstruction of scientific theories. According to Husserl, an essential part of a theory's reconstruction is the mathematical description of its domain, that is, the world (or the part of the world) the theory intends to talk about. Contrary to the traditional micrological approach favored by the members of the Vienna Circle, Husserl, inspired by modern geometry and set theory, aims at a *macrological* analysis of scientific theories that takes into account the global structures of theories as structured wholes. This is set in the complementary theories of manifolds and theory forms considered by Husserl himself as the culmination of his formal theory of science.

MOROS, Daniel A (and others). Chronic Illness and the Physician-Patient Relationship. J Med Phil, 16(2), 161-181, Ap 91.

The following article is a response to the position paper of the Hastings Center, "Ethical Challenges of Chronic Illness", a product of their three year project on Ethics and Chronic Care. The authors of this paper, three prominent bioethicists, Daniel Callahan, Arthur Caplan, and Bruce Jennings, argue that there should be a different ethic for acute and chronic care. In pressing this distinction they provide philosophical grounds for limiting medical care for the elderly and chronically ill. We give a critical survey of their position and reject it as well as any attempt to characterize the physician-patient relationship as a commercial contract. We emphasize, as central features of good medical practice, a commitment to be the patient's agent and a determination to acquire and be guided by knowledge. These commitments may sometimes conflict with efforts to have the physician serve as an instrument of social and economic policies limiting medical care.

MORPHIS, Maxine and RIESBECK, Christopher K. Feminist Ethics and Case-Based Reasoning: A Marriage of Purpose. Int J Applied Phil, 5(2), 15-28, Fall 90.

By rejecting abstract, rule-based reasoning in favor of contextually sensitive reasoning, feminist ethics has been accused of retreating to intuitions. Critics maintain that rule-oriented ethical systems achieve more desirable results. Feminist ethics can strengthen its proposals by understanding their relationship to case-based reasoning (CBR), an AI model of reasoning applicable to moral decision making. While CBR is a valuable tool in rule-based arenas, it is central in case-determined fields, i.e., fields dependent on the use of precedents to define concepts and their conditions of application. Aspects of the ethics of care considered intuitive are actually case-determined.

MORREALL, John. Cuteness. Brit J Aes, 31(1), 39-47, Ja 91.

I examine cuteness as a biological and an aesthetic category. First, I analyze our emotional and behavioral responses to cute things. Secondly, I show how these responses have had survival value for the human race. Thirdly, I discuss how our sensitivity to cuteness extends beyond its primary object—human infants—to animals, adult human beings, and inanimate objects. And lastly, I try to explain why cuteness is a second-class aesthetic property: because it elicits a simple, automatic response.

MORRILL, Glyn. Intensionality and Boundedness. Ling Phil, 13(6), 699-726, D 90.

The paper has a technical side, the formalisation of intensionality in categorial grammar, and an empirical side, the possible characterisation of boundedness in terms of intensional domains. Categorial grammar is presented as an implicational logic of extensional types. A proposal for intensional categorial grammar is made which incorporates a modal logic of intensional types. It is noted that the extensional system does not capture boundedness properties in phenomena such as relativisation and reflexivisation, but that the intensional system adds appropriate sensitivity. The paper thus introduces the idea of using modal extensions of categorial grammar to capture linguistic constraints.

MORRIS, Charles. "Comment on David L Miller's 'Consciousness, the Attitude of the Individual and Perspectives'" in *Creativity in George Herbert Mead*, GUNTER, Pete A Y (ed), 45-48. Lanham, Univ Pr of America, 1990.

MORRIS, Christopher W (ed) and FREY, R G (ed). *Liability and Responsibility*. New York, Cambridge Univ Pr, 1991.

This book focuses on issues concerning liability in contract, tort, and criminal law. It is divided into four parts. The first is a conceptual overview of the issues at stake in a philosophical discussion of liability and responsibility. The second, third, and fourth sections present, in turn, more detailed explorations of the role of liability and responsibility in contracts, torts, and punishment. The book demonstrates the interdisciplinary character of the field of philosophy of law, with contributors taking into account recent developments in economics, political science, and rational choice theory.

MORRIS, Christopher W. Punishment and Loss of Moral Standing. Can J Phil, 21(1), 53-79, Mr 91.

By what authority do we punish? What permits us to deprive people of their liberty or possessions for some wrong that they have committed? Deterrence, retribution, education may be some of the ends of our punitive practices, but they do not by themselves settle the matter of the moral rights of wrongdoers. What then to say about the moral status of wrongdoers? I argue that criminal acts alter their moral rights and lead to their forfeiture. I provide a contractarian account of the relationship between action and intention and the moral status of agents.

MORRIS, W T. Conventionalism in Physics. Brit J Phil Sci, 40(1), 135-136, Mr 89.

MORRISON, Margaret. Unification, Realism and Inference. Brit J Phil Sci, 41(3), 305-332, S 90.

This paper argues against the view that theory unification can provide a foundation for scientific realism. I begin with a critique of Michael Friedman's account of unification as formulated in his *Foundations of Space-Time Theories* and its relationship to arguments about theory conjunction given by Putnam and Boyd in the 1970s. Using historical and contemporary examples I argue that the reductionist aspects of Friedman's account and the model-theoretic framework that he uses is unable to capture basic aspects of the structure of scientific theories. I conclude by outlining independent reasons for thinking that unification cannot support realism, regardless of the shortcomings of Friedman's approach.

MORRISON, Toni. "Unspeakable Things Unspoken: The Afro-American Presence in American Literature" in *The Tanner Lectures on Human Values, Volume XI*, PETERSON, Grethe B (ed), 121-163. Salt Lake City, Univ of Utah Pr, 1990.

MORROW, James. Response to 'Rescuing the Innocent'. Ethics Med, 7(2), 7, Sum 91.

MORTENSEN, Chris. Models for Inconsistent and Incomplete Differential Calculus. Notre Dame J Form Log, 31(2), 274-285, Spr 90.

In Section 2, a nilpotent ring is defined. In section 3, nonclassical model theory is sketched and an incomplete model is defined. In Section 4, it is shown that the elements of equational differential calculus hold in this model, and a comparison with synthetic differential geometry is made. In Section 5, an inconsistent theory is defined with many, though not all, of the same properties.

MORTLEY, Raoul. *French Philosophers in Conversation: Levinas, Schneider, Serres, Irigaray, Le Doeuff, Derrida*. New York, Routledge, 1991.

Conversations with a number of Parisian philosophers, aimed at brining out the broad lines of their thinking, expressed in a clear and easily digested form. They are Emmanuel Levinas, Michèle le Doeuff, Luce Irigaray, Jacques Derrida, Michel Serres, and Monique Schneider.

MORTON, Adam. Mathematical Modelling and Constrastive Explanation. Can J Phil, SUPP 16, 251-270, 1990.

I discuss mathematical models which mediate between an established theory and observational data. Explanations which rely on such models are weak but often worth having. I try to assess their strength in terms of the Dretske-Garfinkel idea of contrastive explanation.

MORUJÁO, Alexandre Fradique. A intersubjectividade em Gabriel Marcel. Rev Port Filosof, 45(4), 513-529, O-D 89.

The meaning of intersubjectivity in Marcel is related to his intention of "restoring to human experience its ontological weight". He thus refuses contemporary rationalism and its epistemological pluralism which transforms the universal into collectivity and necessity into repetiveness. Fidelity and hope converge in that experience by which we become aware of our participation in an all-encompassing absolute reality. Intersubjectivity is an act of ontological communication: it is the fact of being together in the light that carries with itself, as if it were transfigured, the concrete experience which reveals the world to us. (edited)

MOS, Urszula. Sawa Frydman: A Polish Legal Realist. Ratio Juris, 4(1), 72-78, Mr 91.

Sawa Frydman is the representative of Polish legal theory, mostly active in the 1930s and 1940s. The purpose of the work is a presentation of his contribution to the history of legal realism in Europe. According to Frydman the meaning /sense/ of a normative act /statute/ cannot be said to inhere in it. Hence, legal interpretation is a construction, not a cognition. A notion of objectivity of legal interpretation should refer only to justification, not to the premises or result. These are the consequences of an objective state of affairs. Hence the importance of "is" as opposed to "ought to".

MOSER, Paul K. Consequentialism and Self-Defeat. Phil Quart, 41(162), 82-85, Ja 91.

In *Reasons and Persons* (1984) Derek Parfit argues that consequentialism is indirectly self-defeating. This paper shows that Parfit's argument needs some crucial refinement, owing to an overlooked ambiguity in the talk of the "aim" of consequentialism. This ambiguity enables an explanation of why consequentialism is not logically self-defeating.

MOSER, Paul K. A Dilemma for Sentential Dualism. Ling Phil, 13(6), 687-698, D 90.

In *Remnants of Meaning* (Cambridge, Mass., 1987), Stephen Schiffer opposes H P Grice's program of intention-based semantics, and presents a novel approach to truths affirming the existence of propositional attitudes. This paper shows that Schiffer's approach, called sentential dualism, faces a fatal dilemma. It shows that if we are going to eliminate belief-facts, we should eliminate belief-ascribing truths too.

MOSER, Paul K and VANDER NAT, Arnold. The Logical Status of Modal Reductionism. Log Anal, 31(121-122), 69-78, Mr-Je 88.

Represented by Carnap, Quine, Rescher, Kripke and others, modal reductionism aims to reduce all modal entities to nonmodal entities. This paper shows that the prominent versions of modal reductionism cannot provide a logical analysis of modal terms. It shows that those versions state *contingent* hypotheses concerning modal terms. The paper thus refutes an assumption common to many proponents of modal reductionism.

MOSER, Paul K. Malcolm on Wittgenstein on Rules. Philosophy, 66(255), 101-105, Ja 91.

In "Wittgenstein on Language and Rules," *Philosophy* 64 (1989), Norman Malcolm argues that following a rule must be, and according to Wittgenstein is, a *social* practice. This paper argues against both of these points. But its main aim is to cast doubt on the view that rule-following requires a social community.

MOSER, Paul K. Physicalism and Intentional Attitudes. Behavior Phil, 18(2), 33-41, Fall-Wint 90.

In *Saving Belief*, Princeton University Press, 1987, Lynne Rudder Baker argues against physicalist accounts of psychological states with intentional content. This paper shows that Baker's argument rests on a highly questionable inference, and thus that physicalism can escape unscathed. It sketches an approach to physicalism that is untouched by Baker's argument.

MOSER, Paul K (ed). *Rationality in Action: Contemporary Approaches*. New York, Cambridge Univ Pr, 1990.

The twenty-one selections in this collection fall under three main categories: individual decision theory; game theory and group decision making; reasons, desires, and irrationality. Including essays by Savage, Allais, Arrow, Simon, Sen and others, the collection has a general introduction on decision theory and a topical bibliography.

MOSER, Paul K. Some Recent Work in Epistemology. Phil Papers, 19(2), 75-98, Ag 90.

This is a review article on *Philosophical Perspectives, 2: Epistemology*, ed. J Tomberlin (Ridgeview, 1988). It focuses on three main questions: (i) what does it mean to say that a belief is justified; (ii) what are the necessary and sufficient conditions for epistemic justification; and (iii) what constitutes a correct answer to such questions?

MOSER, Paul K. "Two Roads to Skepticism" in *Doubting: Contemporary Perspectives on Skepticism*, ROTH, Michael D (ed), 127-139. Norwell, Kluwer, 1990.

MOSER, Shia. Some Remarks about Ethical Universalism. J Indian Counc Phil Res, 5(2), 27-40, Ja-Ap 88.

In both Isaiah's prophesy and in stoicism we find the idea of mankind united morally and politically. In the paper several formulations of *moral unity* and political unity are offered, but unlike in Isaiah and in stoicism, only an empirical connection is assumed. It is contended that this connection does not depend on the acceptance of a universally valid moral code. Finally, it is argued that internationalism, like other moral principles, has to appeal only to compassion, a sense of fairness, and prudence. (edited)

MOSHER, Michael A. The Skeptic's Burke: *Reflections on the Revolution in France,* 1790-1990. Polit Theory, 19(3), 391-418, Ag 91.

MOSHER, Michael. Walt Whitman: Jacobin Poet of American Democracy. Polit Theory, 18(4), 587-595, N 90.

MOSS, Lenny. Ethical Expertise and Moral Maturity: Conflict or Complement? Phil Soc Crit, 16(3), 227-235, 1990.

Hubert and Stuart Dreyfus have developed a five-stage model of skill acquisition drawing upon chess and driving as principal exemplars. Their hallmark of skill is not the attainment of general rules and principles but the movement away from rules toward a holistic and intuitive grasp of situations based upon a wealth of prior experience. Attempting to use this model to criticize Habermas's cognitivist moral philosophy, they have projected their own monological conception of ethical behavior. Rather than valorizing rule book toting moralism, *Discourse Ethics* draws upon those universalistic intuitions which only emerge with the pragmatic presuppositions of dialogical encounter.

MOSS, Robert J and LA PUMA, John. The Ethics of Mechanical Restraints. Hastings Center Rep, 21(1), 22-25, Ja-F 91.

MOSSHOLDER, Kevin W and GILES, William F and WESOLOWSKI, Mark A. Information Privacy and Performance Appraisal: An Examination of Employee Perceptions and Reactions. J Bus Ethics, 10(2), 151-156, F 91.

Role-failure acts (Waters and Bird, 1989) have been described as a form of morally questionable activity involving a failure to perform the managerial role. The present study examined employee perceptions and reactions with regard to one form of role-failure act, failure to maintain adequate privacy of performance appraisal information. The study assessed employees' attitudes toward various performance appraisal facets as an invasion of privacy and determined the relationships between these privacy-related attitudes and employees' satisfaction with components of their appraisal system, the system as a whole, and their jobs. Responses that organizations might take to counteract appraisal privacy concerns were also discussed.

MOSTERT, Pieter. P4C: A Remedy for Education. Thinking, 4(2), 37-38, 1982.

Philosophy for Children (P4C) is not a remedy for problems in education. To expect that philosophy for children will give children a meaning for going to school is an idle notion. But it is meaningful to integrate philosophical issues, in origin so familiar to children and so directly related to their prime interests, into the elementary school system. This should not be initially introduced in the form of a new discipline, but as a part of the already existing curriculum.

MOSTERT, Pieter and VAN DER LEEUW, Karel. Philosophy in the *"Gymnasium:"* European Observations and Recommendations. Teach Phil, 13(2), 141-157, Je 90.

MOULAKIS, Athanasios. Pride and the Meaning of *Utopia*. Hist Polit Thought, 11(2), 241-256, Sum 90.

The dramatic structure of *Utopia* is not mere frivolity (C S Lewis), but essential in conveying More's meaning in nonpropositional form. None of the voices of the dialogue speaks for More himself (pace Hexter). *Utopia* is neither a *regnum Christi* nor an ideal republic. It is a thought experiment in which institutions designed to combat avarice and sloth are seen to work in the absence *per impossible* of pride. In this light, *Utopia* agrees with the bulk of More's writings and the convictions he died for and need not be seen as an exceptional visionary moment prefiguring ideologies of centuries to come.

MOULDER, J. Structural Violence and Fallible Plans: A Case Study in Philosophy and Educational Planning. S Afr J Phil, 10(3), 75-79, Ag 91.

Johan Galtung defines structural violence as "the cause of the difference between what could have been and what is". He identifies six "mechanisms" that maintain the unequal distributions that feed structural violence. Although I accept his mechanisms, I use a case study to highlight the fact that plans to eliminate structural violence sometimes maintain it because they ride on false beliefs, insufficient information, or contestable concepts. Because these are epistemological issues, there is an indivisible link between philosophy and planning.

MOULINES, C Ulises. "The Emergence of a Research Programme in Classical Thermodynamics" in *Imre Lakatos and Theories of Scientific Change*, GAVROGLU, Kostas (ed), 111-121. Norwell, Kluwer, 1989.

MOULOUD, Noël. L'Assertion dans les contextes épistémiques; garants objectaux et bases d'évaluation. Rev Metaph Morale, 96(2), 197-206, Ap-Je 91.

MOULYN, Adrian C. *Mind-Body*. Westport, Greenwood Pr, 1991.

MOUNCE, H O. Art and Craft. Brit J Aes, 31(3), 230-240, Jl 91.

MOURAD, K J and CHONG, C T. The Degree of a Σ_n Cut. Annals Pure Applied Log, 48(3), 227-235, Ag 90.

MOURAL, Josef. On the Teachability of ARETE in Plato (in Czechoslovakian). Filozof Cas, 38(4), 463-480, 1990.

ARETE is one of the central concepts of so-called early Plato, but the well-known question whether it is teachable is often rather oversimplified. In the first part of the paper a survey of Platonic texts with explicit mentions of the problem of the teachability of ARETE is given. One finds a delicate equilibrium: in *Protagoras* first against, then for, in *Meno* first for, then against, and in *Euthydemus* neutrally; in *Clitophon* for, in *On Virtue* against, and in *Eryxias* neutrally. Thus a need to study the relevant texts more precisely arises; during this study several useful distinctions are introduced, always motivated by certain discovered shifts in usage. In the second part we use these distinctions in order to offer a more complex and a more adequate solution of the problem of teachability of ARETE. (edited)

MOUTSOPOULOS, E. De quelques interprétations philosophiques de l'idée artisique d'interprétation. Diotima, 18, 81-96, 1990.

This work concerns a synthetical view of papers on Interpretation, presented at the 1989 annual Session of the International Academy of Philosophy of Art. Contents: I. Methodological Preliminaries; II. The Mediative Presence of the Work of Art (Mystery and Mysterious; Communion with Transcendence; A Universe within the Universe; A Prolongation of Man); III. Semantics and Reality: the Mediation of the Interpreter (Artistic Hermeneutics; More or better Coming into Sight; Creating and Recreating; Creative Dialectics); IV. An Axiology in Motion. The main idea contained in the article is that artistic interpretation is an artistic axiology, and that being itself an interpretation of multiple data, the work of art needs its own interpretation either at the level of its actualization in the Aristotelian meaning of the term or at the level of its accomplishment in the structuralistic meaning that such a perspective may acquire.

MOUTSOPOULOS, Evanghélos A. Finalidad y dimensiones "kaíricas" de la estructura del ser. Anu Filosof, 23(2), 109-127, 1990.

1) Structure of beings is of *kairic* nature (from kairos): it is the reduction of their

MOYA, Carlos J 574 AUTHOR INDEX WITH ABSTRACTS

intentionality, i.e., of their ontic dynamism. 2) Structure operates in various yet homologous ways which are resumed into the same model of ontic behavior concerning simultaneous creation and overtaking of a series of discontinuities within the continuity of being; a model which favors the constitution of the programming and realization of beings. 3) Far from being a mere relation between substance and form, structure is the reminiscence of the prereality of beings and anticipates their final accomplishment. Kairic dimensions of the structure are general aspects of all its other functions and make possible the totalizing activity of beings under both preventive and irrevocable conditions favoring their ontic integration.

MOYA, Carlos J. *The Philosophy of Action: An Introduction*. Oxford, Polity Pr, 1990.

This book is an introductory inquiry into central issues in the philosophy of action. These include, among others, the distinction between actions and happenings, volitional theories, intention and intentional action, intentionality and science, laws and action explanation, causal theories of action, deviant causal chains. Special attention is devoted to Davidson's work. As the discussion of these topics develops, it is also argued, against causal approaches, that the scientific concept of cause is inappropriate to characterize intentional action and an alternative, antiscientistic account of human agency is tentatively put forward.

MOYER, Albert E. P W Bridgman's Operational Perspective on Physics: Part I—Origins and Development. Stud Hist Phil Sci, 22(2), 237-258, Je 91.

This article examines the intellectual milieu in which Harvard physicist Bridgman (1882-1961) fashioned his operational outlook and the particular path he followed as his thinking developed. An introductory section suggests that Bridgman served as an interpreter of modern physics who used operationalism for rhetorical ends. Specific topics in the main texts are: Bridgman's student years at Harvard; his later grappling with special relativity and dimensional analysis; and the emergence of operationalism in the context of his appraisal of general relativity. This article is the first portion of a two-part analysis; Part II will cover refinements in Bridgman's operational thinking and the publication and reception of his ideas.

MUEHLMANN, Robert. The Role of Perceptual Relativity in Berkeley's Philosophy. J Hist Phil, 29(3), 397-425, Jl 91.

My purpose herein is to demonstrate that Berkeley's only use of the argument from perceptual relativity (APR), in both of his major works, is *ad hominem*, that he uses it to undermine what he calls materialism. Specifically, I show that Berkeley does not use APR to conclude that sensible qualities are mind-dependent; rather he uses APR only to conclude that they are not in material substances; and that his real argument for the former is a quite different one: the heat-pain identification argument.

MUI, Constance L. On the Empirical Status of Radical Feminism: A Reply to Schedler. Int J Applied Phil, 5(2), 29-34, Fall 90.

This article addresses George Schedler's claim that, based on Popper's criteria, radical feminism is a nonempirical theory. I argue that Schedler's argument encounters serious conceptual and methodological problems. Besides operating under a misconception of radical feminism, he has misapplied Popper's criteria when he insisted that the radical feminist entertain an actual, as opposed to logical, counter*possibility* rather than a counterexample. I also criticize the positivist model underlying Schedler's analysis by distinguishing an empiricist from an empirical claim. Radical feminism is not an empiricist theory because it incorporates a moral imperative which is not itself empirical but is based on the empirical—i.e., on women's shared experiences in the real world. I then conclude my paper with a discussion concerning what I take to be the central problems of radical feminism.

MUI, Constance. Against Cartesian Dualism: Strawson and Sartre on the Unity of Person. SW Phil Rev, 7(1), 35-45, Ja 91.

Focusing on the unity of person, this paper finds a common place of dialogue between the analyst Strawson and the phenomenologist Sartre. It argues that both Strawson and Sartre have broken away from traditional dualism in their attempt to come up with an adequate account of the unity of operations which the person experiences. It begins with a critical analysis of Strawson's position, and then an analysis of Sartre's after giving two arguments against the orthodox interpretation of Sartrean ontology as a fancy version of Cartesian dualism. It demonstrates that both Strawson and Sartre have done more than refute Descartes. In their refutation they have constructed a new—and, I shall argue, better—paradigm in which to pose the proper question. It is a new paradigm which at least opens up the possibility for an intelligible dialogue concerning the unity of person.

MUKHERJEE, Niiratan. Three Accounts of Paradigm Shift. J Indian Counc Phil Res, 7(2), 41-69, Ja-Ap 90.

MUKHERJI, Arundhati. Three Models of Competence: A Critical Evaluation of Chomsky. Indian Phil Quart, SUPP 18(1), 1-15, Ja 91.

The paper deals with the critical assessment of some of the interpretations of Chomsky regarding the relation between competence and performance. Chomsky's competence as an idealized model of linguistic performance failed to accommodate the "appropriateness to the situation" as a crucial factor of our normal use of language. Next model taking competence as a central component of an idealized performance model becomes a matter of *knowing that* which is unconscious. Chomsky says intuition is the evidence for the unconscious knowledge. Intuition as evidence fails. Next shift stands—competence is completely remote from linguistic performance, which is totally abstract.

MUKHERJI, Nirmalangshu. Churchland and the Talking Brain. J Indian Counc Phil Res, 7(3), 133-140, My-Ag 90.

MUKHERJI, Nirmalangshu. Descriptions and Group Reference. J Indian Counc Phil Res, 6(3), 89-107, My-Ag 89.

MUKHOPADHYAY, Asok Kumar. Consciousness—From Behavioural Neurologist's Horizon. J Indian Counc Phil Res, 6(3), 49-55, My-Ag 89.

MULAIK, Stanley A. Factor Analysis, Information-Transforming Instruments, and Objectivity: A Reply and Discussion. Brit J Phil Sci, 42(1), 87-100, Mr 91.

MULAIRE, Edmond and JONES, Todd and STICH, Stephen. Staving Off Catastrophe: A Critical Notice of Jerry Fodor's *Psychosemantics*. Mind Lang, 6(1), 58-82, Spr 91.

Jerry Fodor's *Psychosemantics* is a sophisticated, spackling, and innovative attempt to defend commonsense psychology from its recent detractors. The arguments that Fodor sets forth in this volume will likely begin debates that will fill the literature for years to come. In this review we give an overview of Fodor's attempt to rescue commonsense psychology from the three challenges to it that have loomed largest in the literature. We also sketch what we see as the most obvious *prima facie* problems with the course that Fodor recommends.

MULAY, Sharmila R. Problems of the Notions of 'Entailment' and 'Material Implication'. Indian Phil Quart, SUPP 17(3), 17-27, Jl 90.

MULDOON, Mark S. Henri Bergson and Postmodernism. Phil Today, 34(2), 179-190, Sum 90.

One aspect that philosophically characterizes the postmodern moment is the radical critique of what modern philosophers understand as the "knowing subject." Paul Ricoeur's discussion of the "narrative self," in *Time and Narrative*, is a particular example of a postmodern alternative to the older Cartesian notion of the Cogito. Remarkably, Henri Bergson (1859-1941), a philosopher often dismissed in contemporary circles, holds to a similar notion of the self understood narratively. This is especially true in his last work, *The Two Sources of Morality and Religion*. Only prematurely, therefore, would one exclude Bergson from the present plethora of postmodern conversations.

MULHOLLAND, Leslie A. *Kant's System of Rights*. New York, Columbia Univ Pr, 1990.

The book provides a systematic treatment of Kant's theory of rights and its relation to freedom: the ethical foundations, the universal principle of rights, the innate right, propety, the general will, constitutional Rights, and the rights of nations. I show that there is a tension in Kant's thought between the principle of rational Consistency (natural Law) and the principle of consent. Kant is forced to resolve the tension by demonstrating that rational principle is prior to and limits consent. The discussion demonstrates that Kant's system of rights contains a theory of law with a basis in natural law.

MULLER, Denis. Acceptance of Others and Concern for Oneself (in French). Rev Theol Phil, 123(2), 195-212, 1991.

Since at present ethics is a popular subject, its status must be clarified. Taking as a starting point the recent works of Ricoeur, notably his distinction between ethical aims and moral norms, the author considers the articulation of common moral and theological ethics. The themes of subjectivity and alterity serve as leads. The ethics of Foucault are tested by this model, which permits us to take up again theologically the dialectic between the self and the other (in the twofold meaning of the face of the other and the transcendance of God).

MULLER, Richard A. The Barth Legacy: New Athanasius or Origen Redivivus? A Response to T F Torrance. Thomist, 54(4), 673-704, O 90.

MULLER, Robert. Travail et nature dans l'Antiquité. Rev Phil Fr, 180(4), 609-624, O-D 90.

MULLICK, Mohini. On Marx's Conception of Rationality. J Indian Counc Phil Res, 6(2), 127-135, Ja-Ap 89.

This paper explores the nature of the Marxian philosophical revolution through an analysis of Marx's conception of rationality. It argues that there is no room in this philosophy for instrumental reason and the fact-value dichotomy. The rational is necessarily the just. Further it argues that the revolutionary value of Marx's thought lies in his effort not merely to criticize 'irrational' theories of political economy and capitalist society, but to demonstrate their phenomenological rationality and their historical rationale as well. Marx's thought is thus at once theory and metatheory.

MULLIGAN, Kevin. Las situaciones objetivas en las *Investigaciones Lógicas* de Edmundo Husserl. Rev Filosof (Spain), 3, 23-48, 1990.

MULVANEY, Robert J. "Freedom and Practical Rationality in the Thought of Yves R Simon" in *Freedom in the Modern World: Jacques Maritain, Yves R Simon, Mortimer J Adler*, TORRE, Michael D (ed), 109-116. Notre Dame, Univ Notre Dame Pr, 1989.

MUNDY, Brent. Distant Action in Classical Electromagnetic Theory. Brit J Phil Sci, 40(1), 39-68, Mr 89.

The standard mathematical apparatus of classical electromagnetic theory in Minkowski space-time allows an interpretation in terms of retarded distant action, as well as the standard field interpretation. This interpretation is here presented and defended as a scientifically significant alternative to the field theory, casting doubt upon the common view that classical electromagnetic theory provides scientific support for the physical existence of fields as fundamental entites. The various types of consideration normally thought to provide evidence for the existence of the electromagnetic field are surveyed and analyzed in retarded distant action terms, from both a contemporary viewpoint and with regard to the late 19th century context, and that the customary historical explanation of the triumph of field theory as due to its empirical superiority is inadequate. An alternative explanation is suggested but not developed, appealing to non-empirical factors associated with the research program based on the conservation of energy.

MUNDY, Brent. Embedding and Uniqueness in Relationist Theories. Phil Sci, 58(1), 102-124, Mr 91.

Relationist theories of space or space-time based on embedding of a physical relational system A into a corresponding geometrical system B raise problems associated with the degree of *uniqueness* of the embedding. Such uniqueness problems are familiar in the *representational theory of measurement* (RTM), and are dealt with by imposing a condition of uniqueness of embedding up to composition with an "admissible transformation" of the space B. Friedman (1983) presents an alternative treatment of the uniqueness problem for embedding relationist theories. This method of solving the uniqueness problem is here argued to be substantially inferior to the RTM method. (edited)

MUNDY, Brent. Mathematical Physics and Elementary Logic. Proc Phil Sci Ass, 1, 289-301, 1990.

I outline an intrinsic (coordinate-free) formulation of classical particle mechanics, making no use of set theory or second-order logic. Physical quantities are accepted as real, but are constrained only by elementary axioms. This contrasts with the formulations of Field and Burgess, in which space-time regions are accepted as real and are assumed to satisfy second-order comprehension axioms. The present formulation is both logically simpler and physically more realistic. The theory is finitely axiomatizable, elementary, and even quantifier-free, but is provably empirically equivalent to the standard coordinate formulations.

MUNDY, Brent. On Empirical Interpretation. Erkenntnis, 33(3), 345-369, N 90.

The view that scientific theories are partially interpreted deductive systems (*theoretical deductivism*) is defended against recent criticisms by Hempel. Hempel argues that the reliance of theoretical inferences (both from observation to theory and also from theory to theory) upon *ceteris paribus* conditions or *provisos* must prevent theories from establishing deductive connections among observations. In reply I argue, first, that theoretical deductivism does not in fact require the establishing of such deductive connections: I offer alternative H-D analyses of these inferences. Second, I argue that when the refined character of scientific observation is taken into account, we find that a theory *may* after all establish such deductive connections among scientific observations, without reliance on provisos. (edited)

MUÑOZ BARQUERO, Elizabeth. Necesidad y existencia del código de moral profesional. Rev Filosof (Costa Rica), 27(66), 379-386, D 89.

Human survival needs regulations and the latter depends on the existence of codes. The professional moral code—part of the wider social moral code—originates as the most important expectation, that of an optimal and responsible professional exercise for the benefit of the community, which would favour survival in the best possible conditions. The accomplishment of such an ideal may depend on the response capacity of professional groups.

MUÑOZ TRIGUERO, Isidro. Simbolismo y metafísica. Dialogo Filosof, 7(1), 58-94, Ja-Ap 91.

MUÑOZ, Angel and CAROSIO, Alba. Reflexiones en torno a la oración oblicua. Rev Filosof (Venezuela), 11, 1-44, 1989.

Consideraciones desde el punto de vista de la semántica actual y medieval, en especial de Alberto de Sajonia, acerca de la influencia de la oración incrustada en el valor de verdad de la proposición.

MUÑOZ, Jacobo. El reloj de Dios (Glosas provisionales a un principio leibniziano). Rev Filosof (Spain), 3, 113-122, 1990.

MUNSON, Ronald and CONWAY, David. *The Elements of Reasoning*. Belmont, Wadsworth, 1990.

MURILLO, Lorena (trans) and MARTÍNEZ, Sergio. En busca del contenido físico de la regla de Luders. Dianoia, 34(34), 141-168, 1988.

MURILLO, Lorena (trans) and PUTNAM, Hilary. La objetividad y la distinción ciencia/ética. Dianoia, 34(34), 7-25, 1988.

MURILLO, Roberto. Don Quijote: voluntad y representación. Rev Filosof (Costa Rica), 28(67-68), 31-35, D 90.

We consider here the relationship between the free *autonomous* will of Don Quijote and the illusory representation of the cavalry, of which is both author and actor. We place (Quijote) as the last great platonic book in which the absolute does not exist the *nous* in front of the Supreme Idea of Good. Aesthetics and ethics converge in this way in a theatre that, even being illusory, defines any less authentic existence. (edited)

MURPHY JR, Cornelius F. *Descent into Subjectivity: Studies of Rawls, Dworkin and Unger in the Context of Modern Thought*. Wolfeboro, Longwood, 1990.

Rawls, Dworkin, and Unger struggle to make the world hospitable to human freedom. Working in different disciplines, the three share a disposition towards distancing the self from experience and attempting to transform that experience in thought. In political democracy, adjudication, and social association external realities are replaced with subjective purposes. Expressed in terms of contractarianism, constructive interpretation, and transformative praxis, these efforts are challenged on the grounds of their incompatibility with the general and enduring features of human existence. The loss of transcendence is countered with an understanding of the capacity of reason to discern a level of existence which surpasses, and enlightens, self-consciousness.

MURPHY, Bruce F. The Exile of Literature: Poetry and the Politics of the Other(s). Crit Inquiry, 17(1), 162-173, Autumn 90.

MURPHY, Jeffrie G. Gorr on Actus Reus. Crim Just Ethics, 10(1), 18-19, Wint-Spr 91.

MURPHY, Jeffrie G and COLEMAN, Jules L. *Philosophy of Law: An Introduction to Jurisprudence (Revised Edition)*. Boulder, Westview Pr, 1989.

MURPHY, Jeffrie G. "Retributive Hatred: An Essay on Criminal Liability and the Emotions" in *Liability and Responsibility*, FREY, R G (ed), 351-376. New York, Cambridge Univ Pr, 1991.

MURPHY, John P. *Pragmatism: From Peirce to Davidson*. Boulder, Westview Pr, 1990.

A comprehensive discussion of American pragmatism, this book follows the theme of anti-representationalism in pragmatism. The author traces the development of pragmatism from Peirce through post-Quinean pragmatism. (staff)

MURPHY, Mark C (ed) and SOLOMON, Robert C (ed). *What Is Justice? Classic and Contemporary Readings*. New York, Oxford Univ Pr, 1990.

An anthology of readings from a wide variety of sources on the origins of justice, social contract theory, theories of property and punishment and current theories. Authors include Plato, Aristotle, Locke, Rawls, Nozick, Jefferson, Hume, Smith, Kant, Hegel, Hayek, Camus, Walzer, Wolgast, and many others. Introductions and bibliography.

MURPHY, Nancey. Scientific Realism and Postmodern Philosophy. Brit J Phil Sci, 41(3), 291-303, S 90.

The debate over scientific or critical realism is characterized by confusion, which I claim is a result of approaching the issue from both modern and 'postmodern' perspectives. Modern thought is characterized by foundationalism in epistemology and representationalism in philosophy of language, while holism in epistemology and the theory of meaning as use in philosophy of language are postmodern. Typical forms of scientific realism (which seek referents for theoretical terms or correspondence accounts of the truth of scientific theories) are positions at home only in a modern framework. Postmodern presuppositions of other participants in the debate account for the ability of opponents to talk past one another.

MURPHY, Nancey. Theology and the Social Sciences—Discipline and Antidiscipline. Zygon, 25(3), 309-316, S 90.

In this review of papers by E O Wilson, Philip Gorski, and Robert Segal, I apply Wilson's description of the relations between a discipline and its antidiscipline (the science just below it in the hierarchy of sciences) to the relations between theology and the social sciences. I claim (*contra* Gorski) that a common methodology is applicable to natural science, social science, and theology. However, despite the fact that a discipline cannot ordinarily be reduced to its antidiscipline, I claim (with Segal) that it remains to be shown that a theistic interpretation of religious phenomena is superior to a social-scientific explanation. I see this as work to be done rather than an impossibility. Insofar as it is shown that theology cannot be reduced to social-scientific explanations, support is provided for the hypothesis of the existence of God.

MURPHY, Patrick E and LACZNIAK, Gene R. Fostering Ethical Marketing Decisions. J Bus Ethics, 10(4), 259-271, Ap 91.

This paper begins by examining several potentially unethical recent marketing practices. Since most marketing managers face ethical dilemmas during their careers, it is essential to study the moral consequences of these decisions. A typology of ways that managers might confront ethical issues is proposed. The significant organizational, personal and societal costs emanting from unethical behavior are also discussed. Both relatively simple frameworks and more comprehensive models for evaluating ethical decisions in marketing are summarized. Finally, the fact that organizational commitment to fostering ethical marketing decisions can be accomplished by top management leadership, codes of ethics, ethics seminars/programs and ethical audits is examined.

MURPHY, Patrick E and LACZNIAK, Gene R. International Marketing Ethics. Bridges, 2(3-4), 155-177, Fall-Wint 90.

This paper examines the ethical issues surrounding global marketing. Among the causes of ethical problems in the international arena are cultural relativism with its concomitant concerns of bribery and selling unsafe products, and strategic planning which often includes ethnocentric and deterministic ethical assumptions about managerial choice. Possible techniques to ensure ethical marketing practices include a worldwide code of ethics that incorporates the Sullivan principles and using stakeholder analysis to examine the marketing process. Specific ideas for ethical action pertaining to marketing are proposed including always providing high-quality, safe, and culturally appropriate products, and suspension of activities in markets where the ethical problems are too great. On a more general level, ethics should be treated as a significant input to international marketing strategy by top management and the regular development of "ethical impact statements" should be considered.

MURPHY, Patrick. Ground, Pivot, Motion: Ecofeminist Theory, Dialogics, and Literary Practice. Hypatia, 6(1), 146-161, Spr 91.

Ecofeminist philosophy and literary theory need mutually to enhance each other's critical praxis. Ecofeminism provides the grounding necessary to turn the Bakhtinian dialogic method into a critical theory applicable to all of one's lived experience, while dialogics provides a method for advancing the application of ecofeminist thought in terms of literature, the other as speaking subject, and the interanimation of human and nonhuman aspects of nature. In the first part of this paper the benefits of dialogics to feminism and ecofeminism are explored; in the second part dialogics as method is detailed; in the third part literary examples are discussed from a dialogical ecofeminist perspective.

MURPHY, Richard T. Husserl and Hume: Overcrowding Scepticism? J Brit Soc Phenomenol, 22(2), 30-44, My 91.

This article explores how Husserl utilized Hume's insight into the difference between reasoning concerning "relations of ideas" and that concerning "matters of fact" to overcome Hume's psychologism and scepticism and thereby to establish philosophy as rigorous science. It remains within the context of Husserl's own interpretation of Hume and relies on some of Husserl's explicit allusions to Hume. These admittedly sketchy investigations do show that Husserl rejected Kantianism to embrace Hume's radically subjectivist approach. That Husserl has overcome logical and transcendental psychologism more successfully than Hume is problematic.

MURPHY, Timothy F. The Ethics of Conversion Therapy. Bioethics, 5(2), 123-138, Ap 91.

MURPHY, Timothy F. No Time for an AIDS Backlash. Hastings Center Rep, 21(2), 7-11, Mr-Ap 91.

Increasingly evident in public discussions of AIDS is the sentiment that enough has been done on behalf of the disease, that other diseases are neglected given the privileges accorded to AIDS. Against this view it is argued that there have been no changes in the nature of the epidemic to warrant any lessening of biomedical or goverment efforts. On the contrary, given the way in which prejudicial social circumstances are implicated in the origins and perpetuation of the epidemic, circumstances prejudicial to gay men and drug users, it is argued that there remains a morally significant social obligation to fight AIDS.

MURRAY, Tim. "The History, Philosophy of Sociology of Archaeology: The Case of the Ancient Monuments Protection Act (1882)" in *Critical Traditions in Contemporary Archaeology*, PINSKY, Valerie (ed), 55-67. New York, Cambridge Univ Pr, 1990.

Controversy surrounding the passage of the first Ancient Monuments Protection Act in the UK is used to explore the social and cultural contexts of plausible archaeological knowledge claims during the nineteenth century. The paper develops an account of archaeological epistemology which stresses the significance of disciplinary history and sociology.

MUSGRAVE, Alan. "Deductive Heuristics" in *Imre Lakatos and Theories of Scientific Change*, GAVROGLU, Kostas (ed), 15-32. Norwell, Kluwer, 1989.

Is there a scientific discovery? Imre Lakatos said 'Yes', the logical positivists and Popperians said 'No'. Almost all agree that *if* there is a logic of discovery, *then* (discovery meaning coming up with something *new*) it must be a nondeductive or ampliative or inductive logic. This paper argues that there is a logic of discovery and it is deductive logic. It is shown that earlier attempts to describe logic of discovery only succeed in displaying patterns of argument from the context of justification or appraisal. Examples of deductive arguments to new hypotheses are presented and objections considered.

MUSIL, Robert and PIKE, Burton (trans) and LUFT, David S (trans). Ruminations of a Slow-witted Mind. Crit Inquiry, 17(1), 46-61, Autumn 90.

Abridgement of drafts of an incisive essay Musil wrote in 1933 in reaction to the Nazis coming to power in Germany. (Complete text in Musil, *Precision and Soul*, University of Chicago Press.) A penetrating contemporary analysis of the cultural sources and prospects of Naxism's effects on German politics, culture and society, and on the role of Jews and anti-semitism in Nazi iconography. Written from Musil's own experience and intellectual conscience as writer, editor, and analytical social thinker.

MYERS, Gerald E. James and Freud. J Phil, 87(11), 593-599, N 90.

William James and S Freud agreed that unconscious mental states occur, but James believed them to be personal, belonging to subjects or personalities, while Freud believed them to belong to no one; for Freud, unconscious mental states are impersonal dynamic systems. This historical issue is examined here by G F Myers who, relying on introspective evidence, proposes a view that mediates the James-Freud disagreement.

NAARDEN, Bruno. Marx and Russia. Hist Euro Ideas, 12(6), 783-797, 1990.

NABAIS, Nuno and MARQUES, António and MOLDER, Filomena. "Entrevista com o Professor Oswaldo Market Conduzida por" in *Dinâmica do Pensar: Homenagem a Oswaldo Market*, FAC LETRAS UNIV LISBOA (ed), 283-305. Lisboa, Fac Letras U Lisboa, 1991.

NABAIS, Nuno. "Necessidade e contingência nos primeiros escritos de Nietzsche" in *Dinâmica do Pensar: Homenagem a Oswaldo Market*, FAC LETRAS UNIV LISBOA (ed), 153-165. Lisboa, Fac Letras U Lisboa, 1991.

Nietzsche's determinism is usually related to the idea of repetition, which arises only in his work in 1881. However, the concept of *necessity* was already the object of his two first philosophical writings (from 1862) and also the main problem in his dialogue with Kant and Schopenhauer during the Basel period. The aim of this paper is to analyze this former theory of modality. We believe it can be helpful in order to understand some formulations of the *amor fati* which are found in the late works.

NADATHUR, Gopalan and MILLER, Dale and PFENNING, Frank and SCEDROV, Andre. Uniform Proofs as a Foundation for Logic Programming. Annals Pure Applied Log, 51(1-2), 125-157, Mr 91.

NADLER, Steven. Malebranche and the Vision in God: A Note on *The Search After Truth*, III, 2, iii. J Hist Ideas, 52(2), 309-314, Ap-Je 91.

There has been much debate on the identity of the theory of the origin of ideas Malebranche attacks in III.2.iii of the *Search After Truth*. I argue that it is a Cartesian theory, and show why the suggestions of other scholars fail.

NAGASAWA, Kunihiko. *Das Ich im deutschen Idealismus und das Selbst im Zen-Buddhist Fichte und Dogen*. Freiburg, Alber, 1991.

Fichte in the West and the Japanese Zen-master Dogen (1200-1253) in the Far East have both thought thoroughly about the problem of the "I" and "Self". In the former we find the "I" in terms of "Will" and voluntarism; in the latter we find the "I" in terms of "Practice" *hic et nunc*. The author gives us a detailed analysis of Fichte's transcendental rationale for the constitution of the "I" and of Dogen's immediate religious experience in Zen-meditation as a perspective for a new approach in philosophic thought between Asia and the West.

NAGL, Ludwig. The Enlightenment—a Stranded Project? Habermas on Nietzsche as a 'Turning Point' to Postmodernity. Hist Euro Ideas, 11, 743-750, 1989.

The essay deals with Habermas's critique (in *The Philosophical Discourse of Modernity*) of Nietzsche's endeavor to enthrone taste, "the Yes and No of the palate": some connections of Nietzsche's "aesthetic turn"—which inspires postmodern philosophies (like Derrida's)—with his theory of power and the concept of the "Dionysian" are analyzed. Habermas's reading of Nietzsche is contrasted with Alexander Nehamas's interpretation of this author; as a result, Nietzsche's aesthetically motivated attack on "moral vocabularies," his insistence that the "free spirit" has to invent individuality rather than to follow customary rules, is understood as an excessively radicalized, post-Kantian version of autonomy.

NAGL, Ludwig. Is Grünbaum's Critique of Habermas' Understanding Freud Definite? (in Serbo-Croatian). Filozof Istraz, 32-33(5-6), 1677-1690, 1989.

The author of this article discusses Grünbaum's interpretation of Freud and his thesis on the inconsistency of a hermeneutical (i.e., Habermas's and Ricoeur's) understanding of Freud. He mentions some motives which prompt him not to agree with this interpretation.

NAGL, Ludwig. Das neue (post-analytische) Interesse an der Präanalytischen Philosophie. Phil Rundsch, 37(4), 257-270, 1990.

Over the last decade not only a "post-analytic" way of doing philosophy but also a new interest in pre-analytic thought became apparent. Hilary Putnam's paper "William James's Ideas" (1989) documents the fusion of these two trends: themes which were long repressed in analytic discourse (practical philosophy beyond the fact/value dichotomy, a neo-pragmatic theory of truth) reappear with the help of "American Pragmatism." This anti-dogmatic stance is visible also in some recent studies on Peirce (Ch. Hookway) and James (G E Meyers). It may help to reestablish connections with contemporary "Continental" discourse (K O Apel and J Habermas f.i.).

NAMBIAR, Sankaran. A Thinker's Agency in Thinking. Indian Phil Quart, 17(4), 511-519, O 90.

The role of the thinker in the process of thinking is usually taken for granted. This article seeks to use Wittgensteinian insights in order to expose the actual status of the thinker. It is argued that we are misled by the grammar of language into believing that the ego, a psychological entity, is the sole agent of thinking when, on closer examination, it becomes clear that the 'I' which thinks is beyond thought, experience and attributes. A distinction is then made between thinking as a metaphysical activity involving the transcendental 'I' and thinking as a psychological, egocentric activity.

NANCY, Jean-Luc. "Nietzsche's Thesis on Teleology" in *Looking After Nietzsche*, RICKELS, Laurence A (ed), 49-65. Albany, SUNY Pr, 1990.

Young Nietzsche planned to write a dissertation on teleology, which means against metaphysical teleological. At the same time, he studied *democrit* and claimed for a "fictitious philology". The article shows the relationship between both themes and with the topic of *the art of truth*, or of truth itself as an art.

NANCY, Jean-Luc (ed) and CADAVA, Eduardo (ed) and CONNOR, Peter (ed). *Who Comes after the Subject?*. New York, Routledge, 1991.

NANJI, Azim. "Islamic Ethics" in *A Companion to Ethics*, SINGER, Peter (ed), 106-118. Cambridge, Blackwell, 1991.

The chapter aims to survey the spectrum of ethical thought in the Islamic Tradition from its beginnings to modern times. It suggests that a core of foundational values has throughout the intellectual history of Islam found ethical expression in a variety of writings, philosophical, legal, ethical, mystical and sectarian, to create a very diverse heritage of Muslim ethics. This heritage continues to influence Muslims today in decisions and choices about present and future ethical concerns in both the private and public realms affecting the individual and society.

NARASIMHAN, R. Scientific Method and the Study of Society. J Indian Counc Phil Res, 5(3), 101-116, My-Ag 88.

NARAYAN, S Shankar. Causality, Determinism and Objective Reality in Modern Physics. Indian Phil Quart, SUPP 17(4), 33-48, O 90.

The development of quantum mechanics has undermined the classical concepts of causality, determinism and the nature of reality in physics. The article traces the changes in these concepts from classical physics to the present day as the paradigm of physics has changed. (edited)

NARAYANA MOORTY, J S R L. Fragmentation, Meditation and Transformation: The Teachings of J Krishnamurti. J Indian Counc Phil Res, 5(2), 133-145, Ja-Ap 88.

Krishnamurti's teaching is unique in its analysis of human thinking in that he reveals how thought creates problems of conflict through fragmented self-identity. Krishnamurti shows that the means (meditation or 'choiceless awareness') to attain the end of freedom from the self (transformation) cannot be different from that end. I mention some difficulties in applying Krishnamurti's teaching to one's living: in particular, I show that there is a logical tension between Krishnamurti's teaching, on the one hand, and the enterprise of listening to his teaching, on the other. Since whatever a person hears from Krishnamurti is automatically translated by him into a goal-seeking and self-changing process, the listening necessarily creates conflict instead of ending it, which is the presumed aim of Krishnamurti's teaching. I also point out the difficulties of conceiving an existence which merely uses thought without becoming a prey to it through the notion of identity. I conclude the paper by saying that there is nothing one can hope to gain from hearing Krishnamurti's teachings except to learn of a different possibility for human nature, and to see that there is nothing one can deliberately do to realize it.

NARDELLI, Domenica. "Il teatro della memoria di Giulio Camillo Delminio: un tentativo di riorganizzare il sapere nel Cinquecento" in *Razionalitá critica: nella filosofia moderna*, LAMACCHIA, Ada (ed), 43-63. Bari, Lacaita, 1989.

NARUSE, Katsuji. The Heterogeneity of Poetic Language in Kristeva (in Japanese). Bigaku, 41(2), 39-49, Autumn 90.

The aim of the article is to elucidate the conceptual frameworks in Kristeva's theory of poetic language. Kristeva, based on Hegel's concept of judgment and Freudian theory of drive, emphasizes the dimension of production: the "process" of "rejection" ("negativity") as a dividing process that generates those separation and articulations themselves. For Kristeva, poetic language as a signifying process "represents" the heterogeneous movement constituting language and subject, through the dialectical interplay of "symbolic" which characterizes its static, systematizing phase and "semiotic" which characterizes its dynamic, transgressive phase. (edited)

NASH, Christopher (ed). *Narrative in Culture: The Uses of Storytelling in the Sciences, Philosophy, and Literature*. New York, Routledge, 1990.

NASH, Laura L. *Good Intentions Aside: A Manager's Guide to Resolving Ethical Problems*. Boston, Harvard Bus Schl Pr, 1991.

NASH, Richard. *John Craige's Mathematical Principles of Christian Theology*. Carbondale, So Illinois Univ Pr, 1991.

This work situates in historical context a rare early attempt to introduce mathematical reasoning into moral and theological dispute. An appendix makes the complete *Mathematical Principles of Christian Theology* available in English for the first time. After charting the wide range of responses elicited by the work and presenting a more complete biography of the author than previously existed, introducing new material and correcting several widely reproduced errors of fact, this book locates Craige's work and its responses within a context of profound intellectual change at the end of the seventeenth century, paying particular attention to mathematical and philosophical contexts.

NASH, Roger. Adam's Place in Nature: Respect or Domination? J Agr Ethics, 3(2), 102-113, 1990.

The creation story in Genesis speaks of humankind being given dominion over nature. Does this support the view that nature has solely instrumental value, and is of worth only insofar as it serves the necessities and conveniences of the human species? Does dominion amount to unfettered domination here? An interpretation of the story is advanced employing procedures of practical criticism. Three central images are focussed on: Adam's being given dominion over the other creatures, his naming of them, and his being made in God's likeness. It is argued that these images, in their qualification and enrichment of each other, develop the idea that animals are of worth independently of their usefulness to us. Other key parts of the Bible, that at first may seem to promote unfettered domination, are shown to be more properly read as supporting an animal-benign religious ethics.

NASH, Ronald H. *Christian Faith and Historical Understanding (Second Edition)*. Richardson, Probe Books, 1990.

NASH, Ronald H. Kierkegaard, Nietzsche, and the Death of God. Bridges, 3(1-2), 1-8, Spr-Sum 91.

Perhaps the earliest claim that Western Christendom is functionally godless appears in Friedrich Nietzsche's claim that God is dead. Nash's essay examines the context of Nietzsche's claim with a view to unpacking its meaning. In Nash's view, Nietzsche's famous claim was not an expression of his well-known atheism. It was instead a piece of cultural analysis. If God is dead, it can only be because people who used to believe in God no longer do so. Nash then traces Nietzsche's alternative to the cultural nihilism that he believed would follow a genuine recognition of the death of God, namely, his famous transvaluation of values. But Nietzsche was not the only nineteenth-century thinker who recognized the functional godlessness of Western Christendom. Soren Kierkegaard did much the same thing in his own way and in his own language several decades before Nietzsche. But unlike Nietzsche, Kierkegaard saw different implications of this calamity and offered a different agenda for concerned and informed citizens of the West. Nash spells out the important differences between the approaches of Nietzsche and Kierkegaard and offers his own view as to which approach is more adequate.

NATALI, Carlo. Aristotele professore? Phronesis, 36(1), 61-72, 1991.

NATHAN, Daniel O. Just Looking: Voyeurism and the Grounds of Privacy. Pub Affairs Quart, 4(4), 365-386, O 90.

After examining and rejecting standard utilitarian accounts of the wrongness of voyeurism, the paper identifies certain fundamental interests that are endangered by such invasions of privacy. Using hints drawn from nonconsequentialist analyses of the wrongness of lying, the upshot is an argument that victims of voyeurism are harmed in special ways that have been ignored by typical utilitarian accounts. The second half of the article develops the framework that the new account provides for the moral and legal consideration of privacy.

NATHAN, Daniel O. Skepticism and Legal Interpretation. Erkenntnis, 33(2), 165-189, S 90.

This is a critical examination of Ronald Dworkin's arguments against what he calls the "external" skeptic. The author argues that Dworkin's position underestimates the significance of this skeptical challenge, and in dismissing the challenge Dworkin indirectly undermines his own hopes of preserving the possibility of rational resolution of interpretive disagreements.

NATHAN, Elia. Relevancia de la historia de la filosofía para la filosofía. Dianoia, 34(34), 201-206, 1988.

Philosophy appeals in an essential way to its historic tradition, which acts as an authority relative to which problems and methodology can count as philosophical. In this case, the history of philosophy is reinterpreted creatively. But there is another way of doing history of philosophy, which is purely historiographic, and whose purpose is to explain "objectively" the past. Reasons are given why these two ways of doing history of philosophy should not be confused, as it is frequently done.

NATHANSON, Stephen. "Patriotism and the Pursuit of Peace" in *In the Interest of Peace: A Spectrum of Philosophical Views*, KLEIN, Kenneth H (ed), 315-323. Wolfeboro, Longwood, 1990.

NATSOULAS, Thomas. "Why Do Things Look as They Do?" Some Gibsonian Answers to Koffka's Question. Phil Psych, 4(2), 183-202, 1991.

NATSOULAS, Thomas. Consciousness and Commissurotomy: III—Toward the Improvement of Alternative Conceptions. J Mind Behav, 12(1), 1-32, Wint 91.

This is the third in a series of articles that address what is known or knowledgeably held about the consciousness of fully commissurotomized people. This installment discusses three alternative conceptions with which the present author does not agree. They are Eccles's dualist-interactionist conception, Gillett's linguistic conception, and Rey's eliminative conception. With regard to the first two of these, issues are raised with the intention of helping the respective proponent to improve his conception. In the case of the third, it is urged that the view not be promoted, for moral reasons, unless very strong evidence sometime becomes available in its favor.

NAVARRO, Pablo Eugenio. Normas, sistemas jurídicos y eficacia. Critica, 22(64), 41-53, Ap 90.

In this paper, I analyze the relation between efficacy and legal systems. The legal theory, generally, emphasizes the importance of the efficacy as an existence criterion of legal systems, though the jurists do not much to clarify the precise meaning of this concept. Nevertheless, we can relate the efficacy with the performance of legal systems. In this way, first, I criticize the concept of efficacy as the mere correspondence between state of affairs and norm contents; and, secondly, I analyze the concept of efficacy as the relation between motives, norm subjects, and actions.

NAVIA, Luis E and KATZ, Ellen L. *Socrates: An Annotated Bibliography*. Hamden, Garland, 1988.

This annotated bibliography of Socratic scholarship provides detailed descriptive information of over 1900 works on Socrates, from ancient times to the present. It includes chapters on the following categories of works: bibliographies and indexes, primary sources (Aristophanes, Xenophon, Plato), collections of primary source materials, the Socratic problem, the Aristophanic Socrates, the Xenophontean Socrates, the Platonic Socrates, the Aristotelian testimony, specific biographic literature, philosophical studies, Socrates' trial, studies on Plato's early dialogues, Socrates and Christ, the influence of Socrates, and Socrates in literature and fiction. It provides an index of authors, and a listing of the periodicals represented.

NAYAK, G C. Reason, Rationality and the Irrational. J Indian Counc Phil Res, 6(1), 94-100, S-D 88.

NEALE, Stephen and LUDLOW, Peter. Indefinite Descriptions: In Defense of Russell. Ling Phil, 14(2), 171-202, Ap 91.

NEAMAN, Elliot Yale. German Collectivism and the Welfare State. Crit Rev, 4(4), 591-618, Fall 90.

By studying the growth and development of the welfare state in Germany, one can detect a positive attitude towards collectivist solutions to societal problems which is at variance with the political and economic tenets of other Western liberal nations. The most characteristic form of this type of collectivism is the search for societal consensus based on the cooperation between government and private bodies in civil society, even if that means blurring the distinction between the economic and political spheres of public and private property. This "German model" has not only an economic and political structure, but is also determined by a number of concrete cultural factors, including a general consensus about the role of the state in redressing societal inequality. This means that the German model is not readily exportable, for example, to Eastern Europe.

NEANDER, Karen. Functions As Selected Effects: The Conceptual Analyst's Defense. Phil Sci, 58(2), 168-184, Je 91.

In this paper I defend an etiological theory of biological functions (according to which the proper function of a trait is the effect for which it was selected by natural selection) against three objections which have been influential. I argue, contrary to Millikan, that it is wrong to base our defense of the theory on a rejection of conceptual analysis, for conceptual analysis does not have an important role in philosophy of science. I also argue that biology requires a normative notion of a "proper function," and that a normative notion is not ahistorical.

NEBEL, Bernhard. *Reasoning and Revision in Hybrid Representation Systems*. New York, Springer-Verlag NY, 1990.

The dynamic aspects of knowledge representation systems—reasoning and revision—are the most important aspects of such systems. These aspects are investigated in the context of hybrid representation systems based on KL-ONE. A typical member of the family of such representation systems is analyzed from a semantic and algorithmic point of view, leading to a number of new computational complexity results for reasoning in such systems and a better understanding of the meaning of so-called terminological cycles. Finally, the revision problem is approached by extending the "logic of theory change"—developed by Gardenfors and others—to sets of propositions that are not deductively closed.

NEBLETT, William R. Can An Argument Be Both Valid and Invalid Too? Commun Cog, 24(1), 59-75, 1991.

The thesis of this paper, advanced in the spirit of the later Wittgenstein, is that an argument is best conceived as a linguistic entity employed as an instrument to achieve a certain goal, and thus, that one and the same argument may be employed to achieve different goals. The aim of the paper is to sketch a typology of different kinds of arguments based upon a typology of different kinds of argument goals, and to employ this typology to elucidate the nature of both rationally acceptable (successful) and rationally unacceptable (unsuccessful) arguments, and the difference between the two.

NEDERMAN, Cary J. Aristotelianism and the Origins of "Political Science" in the Twelfth Century. J Hist Ideas, 52(2), 179-194, Ap-Je 91.

In spite of a growing appreciation of the gradual and subtle processes according to which Aristotle's political and moral ideas were disseminated during the Latin Middle Ages, one still often encounters the claim that the Aristotelian conception of "political science" as an independent branch of inquiry was not available to medieval thinkers until after the reintroduction of his *Politics* into the West c. 1260. But examination of a range of twelfth-century texts in fact reveals that the status of "political science" distinct from other disciplines was already available.

NEDERMAN, Cary J. Nature, Justice, and Duty in the *Defensor Pacis*: Marsiglio of Padua's Ciceronian Impulse. Polit Theory, 18(4), 615-637, N 90.

This paper argues for a Ciceronian component in the political thought of Marsiglio of Padua. It is demonstrated that doctrines derived from Cicero's officiis form the basis for this claim that a universal, secular obligation exists on the part of all human beings to provide aid and to prevent injury to their fellows. Marsiglio posits this duty in order to justify a concerted program of trans-European opposition to the papacy's interference with the affairs of the Italian cities. Thus, Marsiglio's Ciceronianism is fundamental to grasping his whole theoretical framework.

NEDERMAN, Cary J (ed & trans) and JOHN OF SALISBURY,. *Policraticus*. New York, Cambridge Univ Pr, 1991.

NEEDHAM, E A and LEHMAN, Hugh. Farming Salmon Ethically. J Agr Ethics, 4(1), 78-81, 1991.

Salmon farming is a rapidly expanding industry. In order for it to develop in an ethical manner, many ethical issues must be confronted. Among these are questions regarding the quality of life of salmon on farms. To develop reasonable answers to these questions considerable thought must be devoted to developing appropriate standards of care for salmon. If these questions are not addressed the results could be bad both for salmon and for salmon farmers.

NEGRI, Antonio and HARDT, Michael (trans). *The Savage Anomaly: The Power of Spinoza's Metaphysics and Politics*. Minneapolis, Univ of Minn Pr, 1991.

NEGRI, Maurizio. Fixed Points and Diagonal Method. Z Math Log, 36(4), 319-329, 1990.

An abstract and generalized form of fixed point theorem is proved, from which particular fixed point theorems of recursion theory and number theory follow. The set of fixed point reveals a group structure induced from the recursive permutation group.

NEHAMAS, Alexander. Eristic, Antilogic, Sophistic, Dialectic: Plato's Demarcation of Philosophy from Sophistry. Hist Phil Quart, 7(1), 3-16, Ja 90.

Socrates cannot be distinguished from "the Sophists" on neutral, methodological grounds, but only through his denial, in contrast to them, that he is a teacher of anything, especially virtue. Plato, however, believes that *he* can teach what virtue is. In the *Republic* he tries to distinguish philosophy from sophistry on methodological grounds. In the process he appeals to specific philosophical views, and his distinction is no longer neutral.

NEHRING, Hartmut. Marxisten und Christen für eine gerechte, friedliche Welt. Deut Z Phil, 39(3), 331-333, 1991.

NEILL, Alex and RIDLEY, Aaron. Burning Passions. Analysis, 51(2), 106-108, Mr 91.

In this article we argue (against the view defended by Jerome Neu and O. H. Green, for example) that if a particular evaluative belief is held to be a conceptually necessary constituent of a given emotion, it cannot also be held to be causally efficacious in the production of that emotion.

NEIMAN, Alven M. Comments of Garrison on Greene: Does Metaphysics Really Matter for Practice? Educ Theor, 41(2), 213-219, Spr 91.

In a recent article Professor Jim Garrison argues that Dewey's metaphysics, as understood in recent books such as R W Sleeper's *The Necessity of Pragmatism*, provides an extremely useful framework for grounding, understanding and extending the education theory of Maxine Greene's *The Dialectic of Freedom*. In my paper I attack Garrison's conclusion, arguing that such a metaphysics is of little or no value for educational theory or practice.

NEIMAN, Alven M. Irony and Method: Comments on Burbules on Dialogue. Proc Phil Educ, 46, 132-146, 1990.

My remarks are meant as a commentary on the work of N Burbules on the pedagogical and philosophical methods of Socrates. I agree with Burbules that it is a mistake to take too seriously the idea of *a* Socratic method. However, I criticize him for failing to reject the Platonic dichotomy dialogue and dialectic. I argue that once we better understand Socrates' use of irony we will see that such a dichotomy cannot be taken too seriously in either philosophical or pedagogical terms.

NELSON, Alan. "Are Economic Kinds Natural?" in *Scientific Theories*, SAVAGE, C Wade (ed), 102-135. Minneapolis, Univ of Minn Pr, 1990.

This article compares kind terms in economics to those in folk psychology and Newtonian mechanics. It draws conclusions about kind terms generally and about economic science.

NELSON, D R and OBREMSKI, T E. Promoting Moral Growth Through Intra-Group Participation. J Bus Ethics, 9(9), 731-739, S 90.

Currently, an emphasis is being placed on the integration of ethical issues into the business curriculum. This paper investigates the viability of using student group interaction to induce an upward movement in the stages of moral development as advanced by Kohlberg. The results of a classroom experiment using graduate business law students suggest that formulating groups that mix stages of moral development can provide a robust environment for upward movement. In addition, the results suggest strategies for formulating effective groups, based upon entry levels as measured by the Defining Issues Test.

NELSON, George and GILBERTSON, Diana. Machiavellianism Revisited. J Bus Ethics, 10(8), 633-639, Ag 91.

The field of management has had difficulty embracing the concept of Machiavellianism despite the myriad of studies produced by other fields of social science. It appears that Machiavellianism as a unitary personality construct has limited efficacy in the complex world of organizations. The authors suggest a multidimensional approach to understanding the impact of an individual's threat to organizational functioning. Viewing the construct as discontinuous with two manifestations, predatory and benign, suggestions are made as to the location within organizations where such individuals may be found. A research approach is also suggested.

NELSON, James L. "Animals as a Source of Human Transplant Organs" in *Biomedical Ethics Reviews, 1987*, HUMBER, James M (ed), 109-139. Clifton, Humana Pr, 1988.

Xenograft represents an attempt to solve moral and social problems occasioned by organ transplantation—issues of donor consent, fairness in allocation, and sufficient supply—by replacing them with technical problems—getting non-human organs to function reliably in humans. But the practice raises more problems than it (even potentially) resolves; chief among them are the wrongs done to non-human "donors." The essay concludes that we are not justified in continuing efforts to transform xenograft into a standard therapy. However, it distinguishes between the moral perspective of society and research medicine, on the one hand, and patients and their proxies on the other, and argues that what would be immoral to offer (e.g., the heart of a chimp) may not be immoral to accept.

NELSON, James Lindemann and BOYER, Jeannine Ross. A Comment on Fry's "The Role of Caring in a Theory of Nursing Ethics". Hypatia, 5(3), 153-158, Fall 90.

Our response to Sara Fry's paper focuses on the difficulty of understanding her insistence on the *fundamental* character of caring in a theory of nursing ethics. We discuss a number of problems her text throws in the way of making sense of this idea, and outline our own proposal for how caring's role may be reasonably understood: not as an alternative *object of value*, competing with autonomy or patient good, but rather as an alternative *way of responding* toward that which is of value.

NELSON, James Lindemann. Parental Obligations and the Ethics of Surrogacy: A Causal Perspective. Pub Affairs Quart, 5(1), 49-61, Ja 91.

Parental obligations are often seen as proceeding from a kind of consent implied in not ending a pregnancy, in taking a child home, etc. Such obligations are better seen as among those which arise out of causal, rather than intentional, relationships. Being a biological parent involves, willy-nilly, placing a morally significant being at considerable risk of harm—there is accordingly a prima facie obligation to help the child avoid those harms. Surrogacy assigns that duty to others. While sometimes justifiable, this is much more complex than commonly recognized in discussions of either surrogate motherhood, or its male analogue, artificial insemination by donor.

NELSON, James Lindemann. Partialism and Parenthood. J Soc Phil, 21(1), 107-118, Spr 90.

A contribution to the development of a more adequate account of the proper relationship between impartiality and partiality that is available in mainstream ethical theories, this paper focuses on the moral character of parental affection. A recent essay by James Rachels, which shows what being a good parent would mean from an impartialist perspective, provides the stalking horse. But the heart of the critique, which stresses the inherently preferential character of parental love, undermines any fully impartialist view of the moral character of special affections. A discussion of the limitations of moral partialism in parental and other contexts concludes the paper.

NELSON, John O. Against Human Rights. Philosophy, 65(253), 341-348, Jl 90.

NELSON, John O. The Authorship of the *Abstract* Revisited. Hume Stud, 17(1), 83-86, Ap 91.

NELSON, John O. Why Democracy and Rights Do Not Mix. Pub Affairs Quart, 5(3), 269-277, Jl 91.

It is generally assumed without question by American and English officialdom that democracy and subjective rights are not only the Holy Grails of all political endeavor and wishful thinking but that one complements the other. "Why Democracy and Rights Do Not Mix" attempts to show that these assumptions are false: the subjective rights are not unmitigated goods and that democracy is not their proper habitat (if they have any).

NELSON, Mark T. Eliminative Materialism and Substantive Commitments. Int Phil Quart, 31(1), 39-49, Mr 91.

This paper is an attempt to bring some order to a recent debate over the mind/body problem. I formulate carefully the dualist, identity, and eliminativist positions and then examine the disagreement between eliminativists and their critics. I show how the apparent impasse between eliminativists and non-eliminativists can be helpfully interpreted in the context of the higher-order debate over methodological versus substantive commitments in philosophy. I argue that the non-eliminativist positions can be defended using Chisholm's defense of what he calls "particularism."

NELSON, Mark T. The Morality of a Free Market for Transplant Organs. Pub Affairs Quart, 5(1), 63-79, Ja 91.

In response to the growing shortage of organs for transplants, some have suggested a legalized free market for transplant organs. While such a market would probably increase the public supply of organs, it has been criticized on practical and moral grounds. I examine several moral objections to such a market, especially the "commodification" objection, that there is something intrinsically morally wrong with buying and selling organs. I conclude that it is difficult to identify any plausible moral principle which would rule out the sale of organs but not the donation of organs, or the sale of many other ordinary things.

NELSON, Mark T. Naturalistic Ethics and the Argument from Evil. Faith Phil, 8(3), 368-379, Jl 91.

Philosophical naturalism is the world view which tries to describe and explain all aspects of reality in purely natural, i.e., non-supernatural terms. Such a world view is a cluster of views usually including atheism, physicalism, radical empiricism or naturalized epistemology, and some sort of moral relativism, subjectivism or nihilism. In this paper I examine a problem which arises when the naturalist offers the argument from evil for atheism. Since the argument from evil is a moral argument it cannot be effectively employed by anyone who holds the denatured ethical theories which the naturalist typically holds. In the context of these naturalist ethical theories, the argument from evil fails to provide good reasons for either the naturalist or the theist to disbelieve in the God of theism. Obviously, this does not provide that naturalism is false, or that the argument from evil is unsound, but rather that certain naturalists' use of the argument has been misguided.

NELSON, Ralph. "Freedom and Economic Organization in a Democracy" in *Freedom in the Modern World: Jacques Maritain, Yves R Simon, Mortimer J Adler*, TORRE, Michael D (ed), 141-152. Notre Dame, Univ Notre Dame Pr, 1989.

Yves Simon tried to develop the socioeconomic as well as the political side of democracy. Seeking a middle way between liberalism and state socialism, he was particularly concerned with the integration of the working class in modern society. How to combine freedom and authority (direction) in industrial organizations? He examines the prospect of the worker acquiring a greater technical culture, and also the prospect for greater worker self-management, anticipating recent developments in the European workers' movement. He explored as well the need to apply the principles of freedom and authority to the changed conditions of agriculture.

NELSON, Ralph. "Maritain's Account of the Social Sciences" in *From Twilight to Dawn: The Cultural Vision of Jacques Maritain*, REDPATH, Peter A (ed), 143-153. Notre Dame, Univ Notre Dame Pr, 1990.

In a number of works, published mainly in the 30s and 40s, Maritain endeavored to define the social sciences, indicate their subdivisions, and show their relations to philosophy. What resulted from his inquiry, however, was not a single, consistent account of the social sciences, but two different accounts not easily reconcilable. Sociology, as the core social science, is viewed in some instances as an autonomous, theoretical discipline, yet in others as non-autonomous, practical, subordinated to moral philosophy. The conclusion, then, is that Maritain offers two inconsistent and incompatible accounts, leaving us in an in-escapable dilemma.

NELSON, William N. *Morality—What's In It For Me?: A Historical Introduction to Ethics*. Boulder, Westview Pr, 1990.

NEMETH, Thomas. Kant in Russia: The Initial Phase (continued). Stud Soviet Tho, 40(4), 293-338, D 90.

NÉMETI, I and ANDRÉKA, H and THOMPSON, R J. Weak Cylindric Set Algebras and Weak Subdirect Indecomposability. J Sym Log, 55(2), 577-588, Je 90.

In this note we prove that the abstract property "weakly subdirectly indecomposable" does not characterize the class IWs_α of weak cylindric set algebras. However, we give another (similar) abstract property characterizing IWs_α. The original property does characterize the directed unions of members of IWs_α iff α is countable. Free algebras will be shown to satisfy the original property.

NENON, Monika and NENON, Thomas. "The Devil in *Doktor Faustus*: Reflections on Untranslatability" in *Hermeneutics and the Poetic Motion, Translation Perspectives V—1990*, SCHMIDT, Dennis J (ed), 147-159. Binghamton, CRIT, 1990.

NENON, Thomas J. Willing and Acting in Husserl's Lectures on Ethics and Value Theory. Man World, 24(3), 301-309, Jl 91.

NENON, Thomas and NENON, Monika. "The Devil in *Doktor Faustus*: Reflections on Untranslatability" in *Hermeneutics and the Poetic Motion, Translation Perspectives V—1990*, SCHMIDT, Dennis J (ed), 147-159. Binghamton, CRIT, 1990.

NENON, Thomas. Systematic Assumptions in Dilthey's Critique of Metaphysics. Int Stud Phil, 22(3), 41-57, 1990.

NERI, Luigi. Il caso "Siris", ovvero la "seconda filosofia" di George Berkeley vescovo di Cloyne. G Crit Filosof Ital, 69(3), 320-341, S-D 90.

NERLICH, Graham. How Euclidean Geometry Has Misled Metaphysics. J Phil, 88(4), 169-189, Ap 91.

This paper aims to show that Leibniz's famous arguments for the ideality of space are invalid. The arguments have been taken to show that spatial relations of things to space are otiose and that only spatial relations of things to things can possibly matter. But Leibniz presupposes the symmetrics of Euclidean space throughout. Thus each of Leibniz's arguments requires an embedding in a well-defined space of just the kind he misled to repudiate.

NERLICH, Graham. "On Learning from the Mistakes of Positivists" in *Logic, Methodology and Philosophy of Science, VIII*, FENSTAD, J E (ed), 459-477. New York, Elsevier Science, 1989.

Two positivist mistakes are examined: that simultaneity is a special relativity convention and that general relativity endorses a total relativity of motion. Blindness to all else but parsimony and observationality let these persist. Newton's world is possible but *unsatisfactory*: it admits uncaused changes—uniform motions—into a deeply causal theory. Foundations for theories should contain not only a restrictive (parsimonious) core of theory but also a permissive core, which allows radical speculation on how theory may develop.

NERNEY, Gayne. Aristotle and Aquinas on Indignation: From Nemesis to Theodicy. Faith Phil, 8(1), 81-95, Ja 91.

The intention of this essay is to examine the accounts of indignation in the philosophical psychologies of Aristotle and Aquinas, and, in particular, Aquinas's criticism of Aristotle's evaluation of the ethical significance of this emotion. It is argued that Aquinas holds the truth concerning the nature of indignation not to be obtainable on the grounds of theological neutrality. The reason for this is that the philosophical account of indignation calls for a forthrightly theistic reflection on the ultimate meaning of this emotion. Thus, the account of *nemesis* within philosophical psychology finds its completion only in *theodicy*. The paper concludes with a reflection on the criticism that Aquinas's devaluation of indignation could undercut the emotional basis of the virtue of justice.

NERSESSIAN, Nancy J. "Scientific Discovery and Commensurability of Meaning" in *Imre Lakatos and Theories of Scientific Change*, GAVROGLU, Kostas (ed), 323-334. Norwell, Kluwer, 1989.

NESBITT, Winston. Should Philosophy be Applied? Phil Context, 20, 22-36, 1990.

Doubts are sometimes expressed about the appropriateness of philosophers devoting their professional attention to so-called 'applied philosophy'. In this paper, two attempts at dispelling these doubts, one by Tom L Beauchamp and one by Alisdair MacIntyre, are examined. These attempts have in common the rejection of the distinction between philosophy and applied philosophy. It is argued that neither makes an adequate case for this rejection, and that both, consequently, fail.

NESTERUK, Jeffrey. The Ethical Significance of Corporate Law. J Bus Ethics, 10(9), 723-727, S 91.

Corporate legal scholarship has failed in fundamental ways to grasp the ethical significance of corporate law and policy. While the broader economic and social consequences of particular legal developments are routinely debated, too little reflection is given to how such developments affect the moral quality of individual lives within the corporate hierarchy. What is needed is a framework for illuminating the interaction between developments in corporate legal doctrine and the ethical choices of corporate managers. The ethical significance of corporate law derives from two key factors. First, the corporation as an organization mediates between individuals in the corporate hierarchy and their ethical responsibiities. Second, the organizational choices and decision-making structure of the corporation are to a significant degree the product of corporate law.

NETHERCOTT, Frances. *MYSL'* and the Intuitivist Debate in the Early 1920s. Stud Soviet Tho, 41(3), 207-224, My 91.

NETOPILIK, Jakub. The Impact of the French Revolution on the Development of Philosophy. Hist Euro Ideas, 11, 35-41, 1989.

NETSCHKE-HENTSCHKE, Ada Babette. La transformation de la philosophie de Platon dans le "Prologos" d'Albinus. Rev Phil Louvain, 89(82), 165-184, My 91.

The introduction ("Prologos") to the dialogues of Plato by Albinus is a text which has received little attention. It is considered to be of no philosophical interest. Contrary to this widely-held view, we attempt to show that this text not merely displays an interpretation of Plato's dialogues with a systematic basis, but also indicates a turning-point in the interpretation of philosophy itself. With this is mind we hold that Albinus, with the support of the *Phaedrus* and the Republic, attributes to Plato a didactic program according to which the dialogues constitute a complete cycle of philosophical lectures. The ultimate aim (*telos*) of these lectures, according to Albinus, is the contemplation of the supreme God (the "*nous*"). As regards this religious aim, the concept of philosophy held by Albinus approaches that of Plotinus, while abandoning the interpretation of philosophy as a science.

NEUBERG, Marc. La contrainte. Dialogue (Canada), 29(4), 491-522, 1990.

Did Aristotle misinterpret the nature of coercion and of acting against one's own free will? If so and given the pervasive influence of Aristotle's account on subsequent philosophical thought, a fresh start has to be made on these matters. The author gives an analysis of threats, warnings, offers, acting under duress and acting out of one's own free will that differs considerably from the classic account and avoids the difficulties the latter encounters on the questions of responsibility and freedom.

NEUGEBAUER, Christian. Hegel and Kant—A Refutation of their Racism. Quest, 5(1), 50-73, Je 91.

The racism of Hegel and Kant is part and parcel of the European colonial ideology. Both racistic attitudes are not warranted and sustainable within the etifice of both Hegel and Kant. Their racistic attitudes are refuting their own prepositions (Hegel's philosophy of history and Kant's categorical imperative). Hegel is regarding Africa as part of the geographical world without history, law, reason and .... Kant is holding the same view, adding "methods" how to beat up the African in a proper way. Further, Kant adds, the African has now produced something of worth for the world. In the article, the empirical counter-evidences are given to refute Hegel and Kant.

NEUGEBAUER, Christian. The Aristotelian Debate in African Philosophy: Miscellaneous Remarks on a Denied Discourse (in German). Deut Z Phil, 38(11), 1091-1099, 1990.

There are two tendencies in the Aristotelian debate in African philosophy. First, the debate on 'substance' seeks to ease the incoherences in the Aristotelian concept of substance. The debate gains momentum with the raising of the African

Socialism: the point is to postulate an homo africanus as an homo philosophicus. The second tendency may be classified as the philosophico-historical current made up by three approaches: (1) the ethno-philosophical intention, (2) Aristotle as an African philosopher, and (3) the previous philosophico-historical current. The main thesis of the second tendency is that Aristotle has to be regarded as an African as well as a European philosopher and that the classical Egyptian philosophy has to be understood as part and parcel of the general history of philosophy.

NEUHOUSER, Frederick. *Fichte's Theory of Subjectivity*. New York, Cambridge Univ Pr, 1990.

NEUMAIER, Otto. Wofür sind wir verantworlich? Conceptus, 24(63), 43-54, 1990.

On the assumption that moral responsibility is a relation of the form "Person x is responsible for domain y to authority z", the following are investigated: 1) what it means to say that someone is responsible *for* something, 2) how the domain of moral responsibility is structured, and 3) what the connections are between the elements (object and content) of the domain of moral responsibility.

NEUMANN, Michael. A Case for Apathy. J Applied Phil, 7(2), 195-201, O 90.

Apathy may be a Bad Thing, but it is not always bad in the cases and ways it is alleged to be. The charge that the apathetic are irrational often stems from an oversimplification of political decision-making techniques. The apathetic need not, for example, simply deny the possibility of getting one's goals, or simply ignore the benefits of action. They may, instead, have learned from experience that an avidly desired and pursued goal is always more valued before than after its attainment, and that setting a low initial value on a goal may actually increase its final value. If the values of various alternatives are adjusted in the light of such knowledge, apathy looks much more rational. But that is not the end of the story. The adjustments may be either (i) a conventional and involuntary discounting and surcharging of existing alternatives in the light of known preference patterns, or (ii) a 'voluntary decision' to value or devalue a goal in order to obtain a certain result. The latter sort of adjustment requires the introduction of new alternatives into the decision problem, and revisions to our notion of when inaction is irrational.

NEUSNER, Jacob. The Historical Event as a Cultural Indicator: The Case of Judaism. Hist Theor, 30(2), 136-152, My 91.

NEVILLE, Robert C. "The Chinese Case in a Philosophy of World Religions" in *Understanding the Chinese Mind: The Philosophical Roots*, ALLINSON, Robert E (ed), 48-74. New York, Oxford Univ Pr, 1989.

After a brief review of the history of philosophy of religion, the essay develops certain comparative categories for identifying philosophic issues in Chinese and Western cultures. Basic Confucian and Taoist texts are analysed as test cases.

NEVILLE, Robert Cummings. *Behind the Masks of God: An Essay Toward Comparative Theology*. Albany, SUNY Pr, 1991.

The development of a theory of theological comparison of widely different religious traditions based on the diverse specification of abstract comparative categories. Test cases compare issues relating Buddhism, Christianity, and Confucianism.

NEWELL, Allen. "Are There Alternatives?" in *Acting and Reflecting: The Interdisciplinary Turn in Philosophy*, SIEG, Wilfried (ed), 54-56. Norwell, Kluwer, 1990.

NEWELSKI, Ludomir. Omitting Types for Stable CCC Theories. J Sym Log, 55(3), 1037-1047, S 90.

A countable complete theory T is ccc if for every A, S(A) is locally ccc as a topological space. Hence every superstable T is ccc. Assuming T is stable and ccc we construct sometimes models of power $\aleph_2$ omitting given types. We discuss variants of the notion of ccc theory. We give some independence results regarding existence of models of power continuum omitting certain families of types.

NEWELSKI, Ludomir. On Type Definable Subgroups of a Stable Group. Notre Dame J Form Log, 32(2), 173-187, Spr 91.

We investigate the way in which the minimal type-definable subgroup of a stable group *G* containing a set *A* originates. We give a series of applications on type-definable subgroups of a stable group *G*.

NEWTON, Judith. Historicisms New and Old: "Charles Dickens" Meets Marxism, Feminism, and West Coast Foucault. Fem Stud, 16(3), 449-470, Fall 90.

NEYMEYR, Barbara. Schopenhauers "objektives Interesse". Schopenhauer Jahr, 71, 136-147, 1990.

NG, Yew-Kwang and SINGER, Peter. An Argument for Utilitarianism: A Defence. Austl J Phil, 68(4), 448-454, D 90.

Our argument in favour of utilitarianism based on WMP (weak majority preference) and finite sensibility was queried by Kilpi. WMP states: For a society of n individuals choosing between two possibilities, x and y, if no individual prefers y to x, and at least n/2 individuals prefer x to y, then x increases social welfare and is socially preferable. Kilpi accepts WMP and finite sensibility but rejects the transitivity of social indifferences in the presence of imperfect individual sensibility. We defend our position by arguing that the ground for social indifference/preference is compelling and exact and hence social indifferences should be transitive. Issues of time duration and other complications are also addressed.

NG, Yew-Kwang. Welfarism and Utilitarianism: A Rehabilitation. Utilitas, 2(2), 171-193, N 90.

Welfarism and utilitarianism follow from some reasonable axioms. Welfare utilitarianism is preferable to preference utilitarianism when individual preferences differ from individual welfares due to imperfect knowledge, concern for the welfare of others, and irrational preferences. Nonutilitarian principles including rights-based ethics, knowledge as intrinsically good, and Rawls's principles are criticized. Most objections to welfarism are based on the confusion of nonultimate considerations with basic values which abounds in recent writings in moral philosophy. The dilemma of average versus total utility in optimal population theory can be resolved by distinguishing between ideal morality and self-interest.

NIARCHOS, Constantine G. Aesthetic Appreciation and Human Katharsis. Diotima, 18, 58-67, 1990.

NICGORSKI, Walter. Cicero's Focus: From the Best Regime to the Model Statesman. Polit Theory, 19(2), 230-251, My 91.

Cicero's *De Re Publica*, interpreted with the assistance of his other works, especially certain rhetorical writings, exposes an apparent but deferential dissent from Plato's magisterial treatment of the best political order. Learning the essential nature of politics from Plato, Ciocero postulates a best practicable regime in the form of the mixed regime. Though influenced by Roman experience, Cicero's is a universal response rather than a patriotic affirmation. His response reveals a critical role for the statesman. The model statesman/orator and his education commands his attention as a more useful focus than a concern with the details of a hypothetical best political order.

NICHOLSON, Graeme. "The Inevitability of Humanism" in *The Question of Humanism: Challenges and Possibilities*, GOICOECHEA, David (ed), 295-307. Buffalo, Prometheus, 1991.

NICHOLSON, Linda J (ed). *Feminism/Postmodernism*. New York, Routledge, 1990.

This book analyses the benefits and dangers of postmodernism for feminist theory. The contributors to this anthology examine the meaning of postmodernism both as a position on method and a diagnosis of the times. They consider issues such as the nature of personal and social identity today, the relevance of location in constituting theory, the political implications of recent aesthetic trends, and the consequences of changing work and family relations on women's lives.

NICHOLSON, Linda J and FRASER, Nancy. "Social Criticism without Philosophy: An Encounter between Feminism and Postmodernism" in *Feminism/Postmodernism*, NICHOLSON, Linda J (ed), 19-38. New York, Routledge, 1990.

We argue that, in their respective attempts to develop paradigms of "social criticism without philosophy," postmodernism and feminism have been prey to complementary shortcomings. The anti-essentialism and anti-foundationalism of postmodernism have been purchased at the cost of the robustness of social criticism, while the robustness of some feminist social criticism has been achieved at the cost of a continued appeal to essential natures. We propose a postmodern feminism that avoids both these problems. The result is social criticism without philosophy, but not without political bite.

NICOLACOPOULOS, Pantelis D. "Through the Looking Glass: Philosophy, Research Programmes and the Scientific Community" in *Imre Lakatos and Theories of Scientific Change*, GAVROGLU, Kostas (ed), 189-202. Norwell, Kluwer, 1989.

Can philosophy be organized along the lines of research programmes of the type described by Lakatos? Or are there different types of research programmes in philosophy that cannot be described as scientific? After discussing some relationships between philosophy of science and the natural sciences, some problems in teaching philosophy to science and technology students, and the major trends and turns of philosophy in our century, I answer "no" to the first and "yes" to the second question, mainly on the basis of certain important differences between science and philosophy. In philosophy there are no "stunning novel facts," "content increase," "problem shifts."

NICOLACOPOULOS, Pantelis (ed) and GAVROGLU, Kostas (ed) and GOUDAROULIS, Yorgos (ed). *Imre Lakatos and Theories of Scientific Change*. Norwell, Kluwer, 1989.

This volume includes texts of the talks given during a conference in 1986 titled "Criticism and the Growth of Knowledge: Twenty Years Later." The articles assess the developments in philosophy of science during the twenty years from the 1965 London Conference.

NICOLAS, Jean-Hervé. L'origine première des choses. Rev Thomiste, 91(2), 181-218, Ap-Je 91.

NICOLÁS, Juan A. Universalität des Prinzips vom zureichenden Grund. Stud Leibniz, 22(1), 90-105, 1990.

NICOLOSI, Mauro (trans) and QUINTÁS, Alfonso López. La realtà umana nel pensiero di Xavier Zubiri. G Metaf, 11(3), 339-362, S-D 89.

NICOLOSI, Salvatore. La dimostrazione "a posteriori" dell'esistenza di Dio nella filosofia di Leibniz. Aquinas, 33(3), 511-539, S-D 90.

NICOLOSI, Salvatore. La tensione tra possibilità e necessità nell'argomento ontologico di Leibniz. Sapienza, 43(4), 361-389, O-D 90.

NICOLOSI, Salvatore. Visione in Dio e visione di Dio nella filosofia di Malebranche. Aquinas, 33(1), 39-59, Ja-Ap 90.

NIDA-RÜMELIN, Julian. Practical Reason or Metapreferences? An Undogmatic Defense of Kantian Morality. Theor Decis, 30(2), 133-162, Mr 91.

This article presents the thesis that a critique of decisions is not necessarily (except in the trivial sense) a critique of preferences. This thesis runs contrary to the fundamental assumption in economic theory that a critique of decisions will always simultaneously be a critique of (subjective) preferences, since decision behavior is after all a 'manifestation' of preferences. If this thesis is right, then the paradigm of so-called 'instrumental rationality' is in serious trouble, not for external reasons but because of imminent inconsistencies. The thesis is developed in five parts: 1) A preliminary remark to the economic theory of rationality in general. 2) The cooperation problem as a challenge to the economic theory of rationality. 3) an account of the most interesting attempt to save the theory. 4) A critique of that attempt. 5) And the conclusion: practical reason is concerned with actions and not with preferences.

NIELSEN, Kai. *After the Demise of the Tradition: Rorty, Critical Theory, and the Fate of Philosophy*. Boulder, Westview Pr, 1991.

NIELSEN, Kai. Can There Be Justified Philosophical Beliefs? Iyyun, 40(3), 235-270, Jl 91.

NIELSEN, Kai. Defending the Tradition. J Indian Counc Phil Res, 6(2), 53-60, Ja-Ap 89.

NIELSEN, Kai and MORELAND, J P. *Does God Exist? The Great Debate*. Nashville, Nelson, 1990.

The work contains the transcript of a debate between J. P. Moreland and Kai Nielsen on the existence of God followed by the responses of four philosophers (2 theists, 2 atheists) and final statements by Moreland and Nielsen. Peter Kreeft writes and introduction and conclusion to the volume. Among the issues covered are these: the Kalam cosmological argument, God and morality, problems in religious language and epistemology, miracles, Free will and theism, and design. Anthony Flew, Dallas Willard, William Lane Craig, and Keith Parsons contribute chapters to the book.

NIELSEN, Kai. *Ethics Without God (Revised Edition)*. Buffalo, Prometheus, 1990.

NIELSEN, Kai. Farewell to the Tradition: Doing without Metaphysics and Epistemology. Philosophia (Israel), 20(4), 363-376, F 91.

NIELSEN, Kai. On Being Committed to Morality. Dialogos, 25(56), 135-141, Jl 90.

NIELSEN, Kai. On the Coherence of Historical Materialism. Phil Inq, 12(3-4), 48-57, Sum-Fall 90.

NIELSEN, Richard P. "'I Am We' Consciousness and Dialog as Organizational Ethics Method". J Bus Ethics, 10(9), 649-663, S 91.

There is a practical five-step method of ethics dialog developed by John Woolman, that was used by Robert K Greenleaf, a 20th century AT&T Corporate Vice-President, that includes: a) Friendly, emotive affect; b) discussion of mutual commonalities; c) discussion of issue entanglements; d) discussion of potential experimental solutions; and, e) trial and feedback discussion. This method of dialog appears to proceed with a type of consciousness considered by John Woolman and Bernard Lonergan as one where the "I" is conscious that "I" and "Others" are part of a more foundational, larger and prior "We." The corresponding type of consciousness is different. Woolman dialog as seen in four cases appears to be a concrete method that has some value both as an end in itself and as instrumental means that can: be issue effective, help build ethical organization/community culture, and help facilitate peaceful, evolutionary change and development. (edited)

NIELSEN, Richard P. Dialogic Leadership as Ethics Action (Praxis) Method. J Bus Ethics, 9(10), 765-783, O 90.

Dialogic leadership as ethics method respects, values, and works toward organizational objectives. However, in those situations where there may be conflicts and/or contradictions between what is ethical and what is in the material interest of individuals and/or the organization, the dialogic leader initiates discussion with others (peers, subordinates, superiors) about what is ethical with at least something of a prior ethics truth intention and not singularly a value neutral, constrained optimization of organizational objectives. Cases are considered where dialogic leadership (1) helped build ethical organizational culture; (2) was effective; and (3) as a by-product, produced integrative win-win results. Philosophical foundations for the method as well as differences between dialogic leadership and Theory *X* forcing leadership, Theory *Y* win-win integrative leadership, industrial democracy, participative management, action inquiry, and double-loop learning action science are explored. Limitations of the method are also explored.

NIETO, Jorge and AIZPURUA, Jose Maria and URIARTE, Jose Ramon. Choice Procedure Consistent with Similarity Relations. Theor Decis, 29(3), 235-254, N 90.

We deal with the approach, initiated by Rubinstein, which assumes that people, when evaluating pairs of lotteries, use similarity relations. We interpret these relations as a way of modelling the imperfect powers of discrimination of the human mind and study the relationship between preferences and similarities. The class of both preferences and similarities that we deal with is larger than that considered by Rubinstein. The extension is made because we do not want to restrict ourselves to lottery spaces. Thus, under the above interpretation of a similarity, we find that some of the axioms imposed by Rubinstein are not justified if we want to consider other fields of choice theory. We show that any preference consistent with a pair of similarities is monotone on a subset of the choice space. We establish the implication upon the similarities of the requirement of making indifferent alternatives with a component which is zero. Furthermore, we show that Rubinstein's general results can also be obtained in this larger class of both preferences and similarity relations.

NIINILUOTO, Ilkka. "Corroboration, Verisimilitude, and the Success of Science" in *Imre Lakatos and Theories of Scientific Change*, GAVROGLU, Kostas (ed), 229-243. Norwell, Kluwer, 1989.

NIINILUOTO, Ilkka. Measuring the Success of Science. Proc Phil Sci Ass, 1, 435-445, 1990.

The paper discusses alternative ways of defining and measuring institutional, pragmatic, empirical, and cognitive success in science. Four realist measures of epistemic credit are compared: posterior probability, confirmation (corroboration), expected verisimilitude, and probable verisimilitude. Laudan's nonrealist concept of the empirical problem-solving effectiveness of a theory is found to be similar to Hempel's notion of systematic power. It is argued that such truth-independent concepts alone are insufficient and inadequate to characterize cognitive success. But if they are used as truth-dependent epistemic utilities, they serve as fallible indicators of the truth or truthlikeness of a theory.

NINO, Carlos S. The Epistemological Moral Relevance of Democracy. Ratio Juris, 4(1), 36-51, Mr 91.

The author deals with one aspect of the justification of governmental action and its product (the law). He focuses on the authoritative character of legal rule, analyzing the apparent capacity of governments to produce reasons for action not grounded on substantive moral considerations. The assumption of that capacity seems necessary in order to establish a general moral obligation to obey a government irrespective of the actions required. This question is faced in connection with the thesis that only a particular form of government, democracy, is morally justified insofar as it rests on legal rules issued by a legitimate source.

NIOSI, Jorge and GINGRAS, Yves. "Technology and Society: A View from Sociology" in *Studies on Mario Bunge's "Treatise"*, WEINGARTNER, Paul (ed), 421-430. Amsterdam, Rodopi, 1990.

In his work on the philosophy of technology, Mario Bunge presents a view on the nature of science and technology and on their relations. Bunge also addresses the question of the relations between technology, economics and society. The aim of our paper is to compare his views with those coming out of recent research in sociology of science and technology and the economics of R-D. We conclude that Bunge's approach is too static and not sensitive enough to the historically changing relationships between science and technology as well as to the changing conceptions of science itself between the 16th and 20th century.

NISAN, Mordecai. "Moral Balance: A Model of How People Arrive at Moral Decisions" in *The Moral Domain: Essays in the Ongoing Discussion between Philosophy and the Social Sciences*, WREN, Thomas E (ed), 283-314. Cambridge, MIT Pr, 1990.

A model is presented for moral choice as distinguished from moral judgment. According to it, moral choices are aimed at maintaining a perceived acceptable balance between identity components, among which morality is central. People perceive it as desirable to affirm their identities, they calculate a balance for morality and other values according to their recent behavior, and a threshold below which they do not wish to fall. They allow themselves deviations from morality within the bounds of this threshold and with the aim of keeping a balanced identity. The model is supported by introspective and controlled studies.

NISHIMURA, Hirokazu. On the Absoluteness of Types in Boolean Valued Lattices. Z Math Log, 36(3), 241-246, 1990.

As G Takeuti ("Von Neumann algebras and Boolean valued analysis," *J Math Soc Japan*, 35, 1983, 1-21), von Neumann algebras with nontrivial centers can be regarded as Boolean valued factors, in which the type-correspondence theorem holds. This paper generalizes the theorem to general lattice-theoretic contexts such as seen in F Maeda ("Decomposition of general lattices into direct summands of type I, II, and III," *J Sci Hiroshima Univ*, A23, 1959, 151-170).

NISSIM-SABAT, Marilyn. Autonomy, Empathy, and Transcendence in Sophocles' *Antigone*: A Phenomenological Perspective. Listening, 25(3), 225-250, Fall 90.

George Steiner's view, in *Antigone*, that Antigone is autonomous and, concomitantly, lacks empathy, is critiqued. This view reflects Kantian ethics that emphasizes autonomy and respect for persons, but ignores that these are inseparable from empathy. Thus, despite Kant's honorific use of autonomy, his ethics cannot prevent pejorative conceptions of it, like Steiner's. Explication of Husserl's concept of transcendental intersubjectivity shows that phenomenology motivates a more adequate grasp of the relation between autonomy and empathy: they cannot be conceived adequately if conceived as mutually independent. Antigone is seen as exemplar of the unity of autonomy and empathy: the mundane correlate of transcendental intersubjectivity.

NISSIM-SABAT, Marilyn. The Crisis in Psychoanalysis: Resolution Through Husserlian Phenomenology and Feminism. Human Stud, 14(1), 33-66, Ja 91.

Psychoanalytic theory is bifurcated by two models. The work of two psychoanalysts, Schafer (hermeneutics) and Wallace (natural science), is examined. Freud's positivism and misogyny are shown to be inseparably linked. Husserl's *Crisis* shows that Galileo mistakenly construed natural science as the only possible science. Incipient motives towards a phenomenological reconceptualization of psychoanalysis as a science of the lifeworld exist in Wallace's perspective, but are neutralized by an erroneous theoretical direction. Husserl's exegesis of Galileo's motives for believing that there can be no science of human experiencing must be augmented by feminist philosophy of science. Psychoanalysis will overcome positivism only when it eliminates the misogyny built into it.

NISTERS, Thomas. *Kants Kategorischer Imperativ als Leitfaden humaner Praxis*. Freiburg, Alber, 1991.

Kant's moral philosophy is for a variety of reasons often accused of a fundamental incapacity to help people to act in better ways. The author demonstrates by means of a precise analytical commentary on central Kantian texts that these negative evaluations arise from misunderstandings. His result shows that Kant's ethics, particularly at their core, the categorical imperative, are still valid today as a guideline to prevent us from losing sight of the goal of moral conduct in life; his moral philosophy offers us a meaningful orientation for our actions.

NIVISON, David S. "Hsun Tzu and Chuang Tzu" in *Chinese Texts and Philosophical Contexts*, ROSEMONT JR, Henry (ed), 129-142. La Salle, Open Court, 1991.

L H Yearley (*Journal of Asian Studies*, Volume 39, Number 3, 1980) has argued that an apparent tension in Hsun Tzu—his ecstatic paeans on the "rites" in the context of an apparently uncommitted and disengaged utilitarian analysis of mind and civilization—points to an "exoteric-esoteric" split in his thinking, the "disengaged" stance being his real position. "Hsun Tzu and Chuang Tzu" holds on the contrary that Hsun Tzu takes Chuang Tzu's ideal of saving detachment in the midst of the artificial trammels of life, and pushes it to its limit: the creation, given the human situation, of the "rites" (forms of civilized order) and full emotional engagement in them are what is most natural to man. Therefore "rites and norms" are both utilitarian and man-made, and at the same time deserve an almost religious awe.

NOAM, Gil G. "Beyond Freud and Piaget: Biographical Worlds—Interpersonal Self" in *The Moral Domain: Essays in the Ongoing Discussion between Philosophy and the Social Sciences*, WREN, Thomas E (ed), 360-399. Cambridge, MIT Pr, 1990.

NODDINGS, Nel. Educating Intelligent Believers and Unbelievers. Bridges, 3(1-2), 57-67, Spr-Sum 91.

Intelligent belief and unbelief resemble each other in their emphasis on doubt, reflection, and a search for a soul-satisfying position. Because such a position is central to a fully human life, schools should provide opportunities to discuss and analyze religious issues. Examples of questions and issues are offered in five areas: metaphysics and meta-mathematics; political and social life; literature, art, and music; psychology and ethics; and current trends.

NODDINGS, Nel. Feminist Fears in Ethics. J Soc Phil, 21(2-3), 25-33, Fall-Wint 90.

An ethic of care has received considerable attention in the past few years. Some see the ethic as an important "female ethic." But others argue that the emphasis on gender in the ethics of care may impede progress toward an adequate moral theory. This objection is more a political concern than a theoretical one, although one could argue that a genderized ethic is necessarily inadequate theoretically. However feminists have long argued that political and theoretical concerns cannot be easily separated. Thus both concerns must be considered. In this paper I discuss several fears feminists have raised about the ethics of care and attempt to respond to them.

NOEL, Jana. Aristotle's Account of Practical Reasoning as a Theoretical Base for Research on Teaching. Proc Phil Educ, 46, 270-280, 1990.

NOERR, Gunzelin Schmid. Political Errors (in Serbo-Croatian). Filozof Istraz, 34(1), 113-132, 1990.

In diesem Artikel werden die Hauptpunkte des Verhältnisses von Marcuse und Freud betrachtet. Anhand der Begriffe von Eros und Thanatos stellt der Verfasser die Intention dar, die Marcuses Freud-Interpretatin leitet und die ihn von diesem unterscheidet. Weiter versucht er zu zeigen, inwiefern Eros und Thanatos in Marcuses Ansatz die Funktion einer Restituierung von Moral angesichts einer Gesellschaft, deren Zentrum die Destruktion zu sein scheint, erhalten. Abschliessend versucht er darzulegen, das der zentrale Widerspruch bei Marcuse seine aporetische Gestalt verliert, wenn man den Begriff der Triebstruktur, konsequenter als Marcuse es tut, aus einer naturalistichen Entgegensetzung zur Kultur herauslöst.

NOLA, Robert. The Strong Programme for the Sociology of Science, Reflexivity and Relativism. Inquiry, 33(3), 273-296, S 90.

David Bloor has advocated a bold hypothesis about the form any sociology of science should take in setting out the four central tenets of his 'strong programme' (SP). The first section of this paper discusses how three of these tenets are best formulated and how they relate to one another. The second section discusses how reasons can be causes of belief and how such reasons raise a serious difficulty for SP. The third section discusses how SP is committed to a form of relativism about truth. The fourth section discusses how one might deal with the problem of SP applying both to itself and to other sociological theories. In addition there is, throughout, a discussion of how rules of inference, methodologies, and philosophical doctrines either apply to SP or are exempt from applying. It is argued that SP must be a severely limited doctrine impotent to make evaluative claims about the worth of any theory, including itself.

NOLT, John. A Fully Logical Inductive Logic. Notre Dame J Form Log, 31(3), 415-436, Sum 90.

Carnap and his successors have explored various *a priori* probability assignments to possible worlds (state descriptions) in an effort to generate plausible inductive probabilities. Such assignments typically incorporate an a priori bias in favor of more orderly worlds. This paper presents an alternative approach that abjures such *a priori* favoritism. Instead, inductive probabilities are derived from explicit assumptions about the structure of the actual world. It is shown that even very simple empirical assumptions (such as the hypothesis that there is a specific upper bound on the number of kinds of things) can yield plausible inductive probabilities for a wide range of inferences. The results for these simple assumptions are not, however, satisfactory in all cases; further work may produce better assumptions.

NOONAN, Harold W. Indeterminate Identity, Contingent Identity and Abelardian Predicates. Phil Quart, 41(163), 183-193, Ap 91.

The paper discusses Evan's argument against vague identity. It argues that the argument is a good one but that an apparently parallel argument against contingent identity is not. The difference is argued to be due to the fact that modal predicates are inconstant in denotation—such predicates are dubbed Abelardian.

NOONAN, Harold W. Object-Dependent Thoughts and Psychological Redundancy. Analysis, 51(1), 1-9, Ja 91.

The paper argues against the thesis of Evans and McDowell that object dependent thoughts have a role in psychological explanation. It is argued that such thoughts are, in a sense explained, psychologically redundant. It is also argued that singular thoughts can be nondescriptive without being object-dependent. Counter-arguments are responded to.

NOONAN, Harold W. The Possibility of Reincarnation. Relig Stud, 26(4), 483-491, D 90.

The aim of the paper is to defend the logical possibility of reincarnation in the face of an apparent proof of impossibility deriving from Bernard Williams's "reduplication argument." Recent work on personal identity is referred to and assessed.

NOONE, Timothy B. Richard Rufus of Cornwall and the Authorship of the *Scriptum super Metaphysicam*. Fran Stud, 49(27), 55-91, 1989.

NORCROSS, Alastair. Consequentialism and the Unforeseeable Future. Analysis, 50(4), 253-256, O 90.

NORDMANN, Alfred. Goodbye and Farewell: Siegel versus Feyerabend. Inquiry, 33(3), 317-331, S 90.

The paper takes issue with Harvey Siegel's criticisms of Paul Feyerabend's *Farewell to Reason*. Against Siegel's rationalist misreading of Feyerabend's claims, it maintains that *Farewell to Reason* poses a simple, but deeply troubling question: do the success and the benefits of science and technology warrant or require a social arrangement which privileges the highly specialized development of certain human faculties at the expense of others? The response to Siegel concludes with a survey of more creative ways in which philosophy can and should take up Feyerabend's challenge.

NORDMANN, Alfred. Persistent Propensities: Portrait of a Familiar Controversy. Biol Phil, 5(4), 379-399, O 90.

Susan Mills and John Beatty's propensity interpretation of 'fitness' encountered very different philosophical criticisms by Alexander Rosenberg and Kenneth Waters. These criticisms and the rejoinders to them are both predictable and important. They are predictable as raising *kinds* of issues typically associated with disposition concepts (this is established through a systematic review of the problems generated by Carnap's dispositional interpretation of all scientific terms). They are important as referring the resolution of these issues to the development of evolutionary biology. This historical approach to the propensity interpretation of 'fitness' draws attention to the precarious relation between philosophical clarification of scientific concepts and any given state of the empirical arts.

NORMAN, Andrew P. Telling It Like It Was: Historical Narratives on Their Own Terms. Hist Theor, 30(2), 119-135, My 91.

The paper lays out the basic structure of the realism/anti-realism debate in the philosophy of history, and shows why each of the major portions in it are to be avoided. Sweeping denials of the story's capacity to accurately reflect the past are as misguided as the global affirmations they catalyze: the epistemic status of narrative historians must be assessed on a case-by-case basis. The scepticism of H White and Descartes, the realism of MacIntyre and Carr, and the anti-realism of Lyotard, Bartles and Mink are each examined in detail and found inadequate. Historical narratives *purport* to be true (contra the antirealists), sometimes *achieve* truth (contra the sceptics), without corresponding to plot structures in the lived part (contra the realists).

NORMORE, Calvin G. Doxology and the History of Philosophy. Can J Phil, SUPP 16, 203-226, 1990.

NORRIS, Stephen P. Rational Trust and Deferential Belief. Proc Phil Educ, 46, 235-238, 1990.

NORTON, Bruce and AMARIGLIO, Jack. Marxist Historians and the Question of Class in the French Revolution. Hist Theor, 30(1), 37-55, F 91.

This article evaluates the centrality of class in the "social interpretation" of the French Revolution. The social interpreters introduce an admirable complexity, which, however, stems from loose, multiple, contradictory notions of class influenced partly by Joseph Barnave's "stage theory" of pre-Revolutionary France and by "vulgar Marxism"; these notions contrast with the concept of class—surplus-labor extraction—developed in the three volumes of Marx's *Capital*. Using this alternative concept would preserve the social interpreters' class focus—contrary to revisionist historians' reformulations—yet also would convey the many class divisions in pre-Revolutionary France and the multiple class positions historical agents simultaneously occupied.

NORTON, Thomas W. Understanding Professional Misconduct: The Moral Responsibilities of Professionals. J Bus Ethics, 10(8), 621-623, Ag 91.

NORTON-SMITH, Thomas M. A Mathematical A Priorist Answers Philip Kitcher. Auslegung, 17(2), 109-118, Sum 91.

Philip Kitcher employs a naturalistic analysis of a priori knowledge in a negative critique of mathematical apriorism. I argue that the analysis is unsatisfactory because its necessary condition is too strong. Moreover, a revision of Kitcher's analysis which circumvents my objection is still unsatisfactory. I then develop an analysis of a priori knowledge that is sympathetic to the mathematical apriorist. Finally, I argue that my analysis is preferable because Kitcher's analysis yields a conclusion to which even he would object when it is coupled with his view of the importance of social challenges.

NOVAK, Michael. "The Philosophical Meaning of American Civilization in World History" in *Freedom in the Modern World: Jacques Maritain, Yves R Simon, Mortimer J Adler*, TORRE, Michael D (ed), 197-216. Notre Dame, Univ Notre Dame Pr, 1989.

NOVITZ, David. Art, Life and Reality. Brit J Aes, 30(4), 301-310, O 90.

NOVITZ, David. *Knowledge, Fiction, and Imagination*. Philadelphia, Temple Univ Pr, 1987.

The central purpose of this work is to explain how we can acquire knowledge from sources other than empirical science: in this case, literary fiction. It does so by resuscitating a romantic theory of knowledge, but avoids the excesses of eighteenth and nineteenth century romanticism by developing what the author calls a romantic realism. The topics covered include the problem of interpretation, emotional responses to fiction, metaphor, and the role played by literature in developing a sense of national identity.

NOVITZ, David. Love, Friendship, and the Aesthetics of Character. Amer Phil Quart, 28(3), 207-216, Jl 91.

People are often regarded as beautiful or ugly even when their physical appearances do not warrant such attributions. My concern is with the grounds on which we evaluate others aesthetically. In order to explain this, I explore the ways in which we attribute aesthetic concepts to character in the context of the personal relationships of love and friendship, emphasizing the deep needs that enter into these attributions. There is a tendency, I argue, for such attributions to be self-deceptive, but this, I show, is not confined to aesthetic attributions of character, but enters as well into our critical assessment of works of art.

NOVY, Lubomir. Masaryk's "Anthropism" (in Czechoslovakian). Filozof Cas, 38(4), 435-440, 1990.

There is some tension in Masaryk's philosophy: scepticism against faith, science against myth, philosophy against theology, Titanism against God, anthropocentrism against theocentrism, subjectivism against objectivism. In his "Russia and Europe" (1913) Masaryk tries to bridge over this tension by articulating scientific and philosophical "anthropism": man is the ultimate criterion as well as the actual object of science and philosophy. Anthropism is the basis of democracy (anthropocracy) which is the opposite to theocracy (based on the myth, on making a fetish of the outer world, God, society, the state, the sovereign, the church, the nation). Should democracy not turn into Titanism, i.e., a sort of "theocracy inside out," it must make a new living religion, it must become "a life sub specie aeternitatis." (edited)

NOWAK, Kurt. Historicism and the Understanding of Theology in Troeltsch's Times (in German). Deut Z Phil, 38(11), 1047-1063, 1990.

NOWAK, Leszek and NOWAKOWA, Izabella. "Approximation and the Two Ideas of Truth" in *Studies on Mario Bunge's "Treatise"*, WEINGARTNER, Paul (ed), 79-93. Amsterdam, Rodopi, 1990.

NOWAK, Leszek. "The Defence of a Social System Against Its Ideology: A Case Study" in *The Social Horizon of Knowledge*, BUCZKOWSKI, Piotr (ed), 59-85. Amsterdam, Rodopi, 1991.

The paper attempts to reconstruct the "logical history" of Marxist social theory in real socialism as being dependent on the history of real socialism itself. The main stages of Marxism are: people's utopia, ideology of political power, more and more disfunctional for the political power counter-ideology. The foundation for such an assessment is a theory presented in the author's *Power and Civil Society: Toward a Dynamic Theory of Real Socialism*, New York, Greenwood Press.

NOWAK, Marek. Logics Preserving Degrees of Truth. Stud Log, 49(4), 483-499, D 90.

NOWAKOWA, Izabella and NOWAK, Leszek. "Approximation and the Two Ideas of Truth" in *Studies on Mario Bunge's "Treatise"*, WEINGARTNER, Paul (ed), 79-93. Amsterdam, Rodopi, 1990.

NOWICKI, Andrzej. What is Philosophy of Culture? (in Polish). Ann Univ Mariae Curie-Phil, 10, 1-11, 1985.

The best way of characterizing philosophy of culture is to present ontological, epistemological and axiological problems which it takes into consideration. The main ontological problem of philosophy of culture is the question: in what way can people be present in the material objects created by them? What role do encounters play in our culture? There is no contradiction between the statements "we are the culture" and "culture is a totality of objects created by men," because the world of people exists first of all in a world of objects which are the exteriorization of their inner world. Among different ways of getting to know culture the best one is to get inside it and learn to know culture through the participation in a process of its self-creation. We can grasp the essence of culture while becoming a subject who creates it. The most important axiological problem is a problem of supreme values: are objects created by men (like masterpieces of music, painting, poetry, philosophy, scientific discoveries and findings) those goods which give sense and dignity to a human life?

NUBIOLA, Jaime. Filosofía desde la teoría causal de la referencia. Anu Filosof, 24(1), 153-163, 1991.

Through a 'fuzzy' grammar of identity it is possible to link the causal theory of reference with bioethics. Some arguments on abortion derived from the theory of natural kind terms point to a post-modernism in analytical philosophy.

NULL, Gilbert and BLECKSMITH, Richard. Matrix Representation of Husserl's Part-Whole-Foundation Theory. Notre Dame J Form Log, 32(1), 87-111, Wint 91.

This paper pursues two aims, a general one and a more specific one. The general aim is to introduce and illustrate the use of Boolean matrices in representing the logical properties of one- and (mainly) two-place predicates over small finite universes, and hence of providing matrix characterizations of finite models for sets of axioms containing such predicates. This method is treated only to the extent required to pursue the more specific aim, which is to consider axiomatic systems involving the part-whole relation together with a relation of foundation employed by Husserl.

NUNES CORREIA, Carlos João. "O mito de Narciso" in *Dinâmica do Pensar: Homenagem a Oswaldo Market*, FAC LETRAS UNIV LISBOA (ed), 91-99. Lisboa, Fac Letras U Lisboa, 1991.

By means of an analysis of the classical texts of the myth of Narcissus, especially the Homeric Hymn to Demeter and the third book of Ovid's *Metamorphoses*, we suggest an interpretation of the figures on this myth that doesn't match with the gnostic vision of a concentric love, centred on his own image, nor with the neoplatonic exegesis, for whom "Narcissus error" consisted in not having assumed the constitutive principle of his identity. In our opinion these two interpretations forget the importance of Narcissus' act of recognition which is build on the basis of the distinction between "self image" and "the self". Were this distinction not to be made, the effective enclosure of a subject caught in an image whose origin he could never discover, would occur. So, the perception of the difference between model and images becomes a central category of this myth of the *alterity*.

NUNNER-WINKLER, Gertrud. "Moral Relativism and Strict Universalism" in *The Moral Domain: Essays in the Ongoing Discussion between Philosophy and the Social Sciences*, WREN, Thomas E (ed), 109-128. Cambridge, MIT Pr, 1990.

A continuum of positions is sketched: Moral scepticism denying the independent existence of values (Marxist criticism of bourgeois morality; Skinner); cultural relativism assuming equivalent values (M Weber); two moralities (Gilligan); strict universalism assuming a rational procedure for justifying moral norms and consensual solutions to dilemmas (Kant; Habermas; Kohlberg); and 'qualified universalism' is advanced assuming a rational procedure for justifying norms yet allowing dissent in solving dilemmas (Gert) that is due to lack of empirical foresight and legitimate differences in value orientations. Empirical data questioning Gilligan's claim of sex specific moralities and illustrating the positions analyzed are presented.

NUÑO, Juan A. *Tractatus*: Críticas al logicismo. Dianoia, 35(35), 11-21, 1989.

NUSSBAUM, Martha C. "Aristotelian Social Democracy" in *Liberalism and the Good*, DOUGLASS, R Bruce (ed), 203-252. New York, Routledge, 1990.

NUSSBAUM, Martha C. *Love's Knowledge: Essays on Philosophy and Literature*. New York, Oxford Univ Pr, 1990.

NUSSBAUM, Martha C. "Perception and Revolution: 'The Princess Casamassima' and the Political Imagination" in *Meaning and Method: Essays in Honor of Hilary Putnam*, BOOLOS, George (ed), 327-353. New York, Cambridge Univ Pr, 1990.

NUSSBAUM, Martha C. The Transfigurations of Intoxication: Nietzsche, Schopenhauer, and Dionysus. Arion, 1(2), 75-111, Spr 91.

NUTE, Donald. "Defeasible Logic and The Frame Problem" in *Knowledge Representation and Defeasible Reasoning*, KYBURG JR, Henry E (ed), 3-21. Norwell, Kluwer, 1990.

We want to be able to infer what changes and what does not as a result of an event having occurred. An enormous number of axiom is required in classical logic to specify what does not change. McDermott suggests using one nonmonotonic frame axiom which says everything tends to remain unchanged, but Hanks and McDermott show that familiar nonmonotonic systems with multiple extensions cannot easily solve the frame problem using this approach. An alternative approach called *defeasible logic* handles the Hanks and McDermott example and other examples of nonmonotonic reasoning.

NUTE, Donald. Historical Necessity and Conditionals. Nous, 25(2), 161-175, Ap 91.

A possible world semantics is developed for a formal language containing tense operators, a historical necessity operator, and a conditional operator. An indeterministic stance is assumed and the notion of an actual world is replaced by the notion of an actual manifold, a set of worlds that has not yet been ruled out by either history or physics. It is argued that in general English conditional sentences cannot be represented by combinations of conditional operators and standards tense operators, and that all true intensional conditionals are historically necessary and all false intensional conditionals are historically impossible.

NUYEN, A T. Adorno and the French Post-Structuralists on the Other of Reason. J Speculative Phil, 4(4), 310-322, 1990.

French post-structuralist thought is largely a reaction to Hegel's metaphysics, seeing the Hegelian circle as one that encloses everything within it, leaving no residues, no remainders. It is largely the French post-structuralists who have called attention to the fragility of the Hegelian system. However, what is often overlooked is the fact that the post-structuralist motif appears in the works of Adorno, most notably in *Negative Dialectics*. This paper draws out the parallel between Adorno and the French writers and examines the adequacy of Adorno's program of negative dialectics.

NUYEN, A T. The Punishment of Attempts. Int J Applied Phil, 5(2), 65-71, Fall 90.

It has been argued that the practice of punishing criminal attempts that failed more leniently, particularly when the failure is due to luck or chance, is irrational. This paper argues that there are good reasons to think that differential punishment is justified. The argument relies on the fact that punishment is a *social* practice. It is therefore not irrational to take account of the social dimension of crime, viz., the effects on the victims. Since failed attempts affect victims differently, that gives a reason for treating them differently.

NUYEN, A T. Sense, Passions and Morals in Hume and Kant. Kantstudien, 82(1), 29-41, 1991.

The perceived gap between Hume and Kant on morality can be narrowed. Hume can be pushed closer to Kant by interpreting him as assigning a significant role to reason in the making of moral judgments. On the other hand, Kant can be shown to be closer to Hume than previously thought. Various stategies for showing this are canvassed, and it is argued that the most promising is the interpretation of Kant's feeling of respect for the moral law as the necessary non-cognitive element in the moral motive.

NUYEN, A T. Truth, Method, and Objectivity: *Husserl and Gadamer on Scientific Method*. Phil Soc Sci, 20(4), 437-452, D 90.

NUZZO, Angelica. Ancora una discussione su Hegel: logica, storia, fenomenologia. G Crit Filosof Ital, 69(3), 384-392, S-D 90.

NWACHUKWU, Osita and TSALIKIS, John. A Comparison of Nigerian to American Views of Bribery and Extortion in International Commerce. J Bus Ethics, 10(2), 85-98, F 91.

This study investigates the differences in the way bribery and extortion is perceived by two different cultures—American and Nigerian. Two hundred and forty American business students and one hundred and eighty Nigerian business students were presented with three scenarious describing a businessman offering a bribe to a government official and three scenarios describing a businessman being forced by pay a bribe to an official in order to do business. The Reidenbach-Robin instrument was used to measure the ethical reactions of the two samples to these scenarios. Results indicate that ethical reactions to bribery and extortion vary by (a) the nationality of the person offering the bribe, and (b) the country where the bribe is offered. In addition, Nigerians perceived some of the scenarios as being less unethical than did Americans.

NYASANI, Joseph M. "The Ontological Significance of 'I' and 'We' in African Philosophy" in *I, We and Body: First Joint Symposium of Philosophers from Africa and from the Netherlands*, KIMMERLE, Heinz (ed), 13-25. Atlantic Highlands, Gruner, 1989.

NYHOF, John. Philosophical Objections to the Kinetic Theory. Brit J Phil Sci, 39(1), 81-109, Mr 88.

Towards the end of the 19th century there were those who wished to see the kinetic theory abandoned. This paper attempts to show that this reaction was primarily due to philosophical objections rather than the result of scientific difficulties encountered by the kinetic theory. First the relevant philosophical background is examined as well as the relation between the kinetic theory and thermodynamics. Next the scientific difficulty known as the specific heats ratio anomaly is discussed and finally Boltzmann's philosophy of science is examined.

NYÍRI, J C (ed). *Perspectives on Ideas and Reality*. Budapest, Kiskonyvtara, 1990.

NYÍRI, J C. "Some Marxism Themes in the Age of Information" in *Perspectives on Ideas and Reality*, NYÍRI, J C (ed), 55-65. Budapest, Kiskonyvtara, 1990.

NYMAN, Heikki (ed) and WITTGENSTEIN, Ludwig. Philosophy: Sections 86-93 (pp 405-35) of the So-Called "Big Typescript" (Catalog Number 213)—Ludwig Wittgenstein. Synthese, 87(1), 3-22, Ap 91.

NYONG, Prince David. A Critique of Marx's Extension of the Principles of Dialectical Materialism into the Phenomena of Social Life. Indian Phil Quart, 17(3), 361-371, Jl 90.

The paper argues that dialectical materialism is unscientific and utopian. Marx's claim that social being determines thought is insufficient. Evaluating socialism as the ultimate ideology lacks a scientific gauge and brings in moral judgments, rejected by Marx, into social affairs. The system does not provide a new thesis to account for the new classed society in Communist countries. Events that condition social dynamics are not merely explained by the principles of economics. Capitalism solves inherent problems in itself, and its worker is, generally, happier. However, Marxism provides theoretical tools for studying social life and ideological weapons for sociopolitical emancipation.

NYSANBAYEV, A N and KADYRZHANOV, R K. The Categorical Nature of Mathematical Cognition. Phil Math, 6(1), 39-52, 1991.

NYSTROM, Paul C. Differences in Moral Values Between Corporations. J Bus Ethics, 9(12), 971-979, D 90.

This research compares the importance of moral values for corporations' managements, as reported by 97 knowledgeable employees in eight corporations. Does an employee consensus emerge within corporations and does it differ between corporations? To answer this question, an analysis of covariance technique was used to compare the importance of moral values between corporations versus within corporations. Results corroborate the hypothesis that closely matched corporations do differ significantly from one another in the importance of prevailing moral values. Evidence also suggests that the importance of prevailing moral values may be inversely related with company size. Implications for future research and for the practice of management are delineated.

O'BRIEN, Gerard J. Is Connectionism Commonsense? Phil Psych, 4(2), 165-178, 1991.

In this paper I critically examine the line of reasoning that has recently appeared in the literature that connects connectionism with eliminativism. This line of reasoning has it that if connectionist models turn out accurately to characterize our cognition, then beliefs, desires and the other intentional entities of commonsense psychology will be eliminated from our theoretical ontology. In complete contrast I argue (1) that not only is this line of reasoning mistaken about the eliminativist tendencies of connectionist models, but (2) that these models have the potential to provide a more robust vindication of commonsense psychology than classical computational models.

O'BRIEN, James. Conclusion: Legal Institutions and Limitations to Cognition and Power. Soc Epistem, 5(1), 44-60, Ja-Mr 91.

O'BRIEN, Wendell. Butler and the Authority of Conscience. Hist Phil Quart, 8(1), 43-57, Ja 91.

Butler's main answer to the question why one should be moral is that conscience has natural authority, and he takes the authority of conscience to be a "mere fact" of human nature. My concern is what he meant by that answer. I first review and criticize the major lines of interpretation of Butler's answer that have emerged in this century. I then offer my own interpretation (which I support by appeal to Butler's procedure in the bulk of his writings), which is that the authority of conscience is its natural *tendency* to govern and direct all other "principles of action."

O'CALLAGHAN, Paul. El enigma de la libertad humana en Gabriel Marcel. Anu Filosof, 23(1), 139-152, 1990.

The article attempts to show that for Gabriel Marcel, the existence and relevance of the free human act is not something obvious: it has very little to do with either 'doing what you want' or with distancing oneself intentionally from a series of indifferent options. Rather the free act is always exercised in a context of intersubjectivity, above all as the acceptance of a gift coming from another, for example, an act of hope. Only looking back on past actions can one really affirm that one has acted freely, and has become free.

O'CONNELL, Colin. A Heideggerian Analysis of Fundamentalism: A Brief Discussion. J Dharma, 15(2), 114-124, Ap-Je 90.

O'CONNOR, David. Was Moore a Positivist? Philosophia (Israel), 20(3), 247-262, D 90.

I present a revisionary reading of G E Moore. My claim is that from about 1910 onwards Moore was a positivist of a certain sort, what I describe as a commonsense positivist. I develop a case for this claim by means of a comparison between Moore's work before and after 1910.

O'CONNOR, Noreen. "Who Suffers?" in *Re-Reading Levinas*, BERNASCONI, Robert (ed), 229-233. Bloomington, Indiana Univ Pr, 1991.

O'CONNOR, Terence. Humor, Schooling, and Cultural Intelligence: A Response to Pritscher. Phil Stud Educ, /, 44-48, 1989.

Responding to Conrad Pritscher, this essay argues that a complete understanding of humor in schools requires understanding its cultural dimensions. Humor as a strategy of cultural resistance is used as an example. The essay calls for a serious use of humor in education.

O'DALY, Gerard. "Predestination and Freedom in Augustine's Ethics" in *The Philosophy in Christianity*, VESEY, Godfrey (ed), 85-97. New York, Cambridge Univ Pr, 1989.

O'DONNELL, Charles P. "Jacques Maritain and the Future of Democratic Authority" in *From Twilight to Dawn: The Cultural Vision of Jacques Maritain*, REDPATH, Peter A (ed), 71-79. Notre Dame, Univ Notre Dame Pr, 1990.

O'DONNELL, John. Pannenberg's Doctrine of God. Gregorianum, 72(1), 73-98, 1991.

O'DONNELL, Rod. The Epistemology of J M Keynes. Brit J Phil Sci, 41(3), 333-350, S 90.

This paper has two objectives, neither previously attempted in the published literature—first, to outline J M Keynes's theory of knowledge in some detail, and, secondly, to justify the contention that his epistemology is a variety of rationalism, and not, as many have asserted, a form of empiricism. Keynes's attitude to empirical data is also analysed as well as his views on prediction and theory choice.

O'DWYER BELLINETTI, Luciana. Potenzialità conoscitive del Trascendentale di Husserl. Aquinas, 33(2), 411-418, My-Ag 90.

O'GRADY, Jean (ed) and ROBSON, John M (ed) and MILL, John Stuart. *Indexes to the Collected Works (Collected Works of John Stuart Mill, Vol XXXIII)*. Buffalo, Univ of Toronto Pr, 1991.

O'GRADY, Jean. "'Congenial Vocation': J M Robson and the Mill Project" in *A Cultivated Mind: Essays On J S Mill Presented to John M Robson*, LAINE, Michael (ed), 3-18. Buffalo, Univ of Toronto Pr, 1991.

O'HANLON, G F. *The Immutability of God in the Theology of Hans Urs Von Balthasar*. New York, Cambridge Univ Pr, 1990.

This study shows how the trihitarian theology of Hans Urs von Balthasar opens up an approach to the contcoverted question of God's immutability and impassibility which succeeds in respecting both the transcendence and immanence of God. Von Balthasar attempts to reconcile two seemingly opposed perspectives: the elevation of God in classical Thomism, and his redeeming involvement with creation and its history in process thought.

O'HARA, Robert J. Representations of the Natural System in the Nineteenth Century. Biol Phil, 6(2), 255-274, Ap 91.

The 'Natural System' is the abstract notion of the order in living diversity. The richness and complexity of this notion is revealed by the diversity of representations of the Natural System drawn by ornithologists in the Nineteenth Century. These representations varied in overall form. Many of the systematics controversies of the last thirty years have their roots in the conceptual problems which surrounded the Natural System in the late 1800s, problems which were left unresolved when interest in higher-level systematics declined at the turn of this century. (edited)

O'HEAR, Anthony. Wittgenstein and the Transmission of Traditions. Philosophy, 28, 41-60, 90 Supp.

The Private Language Argument does not in itself show that an individual might not construct a language for himself, so long as that language refers to publicly accessible objects. Wittgenstein's remarks on rule-following, by contrast, do support a communitarian and conservative view of language and of epistemology. This conservatism need not be either relativistic or static; it did not prevent Wittgenstein from criticizing beliefs deeply embedded in his own culture, nor should it have done. The relation of Wittgenstein to more traditional forms of philosophical conservatism is touched on briefly.

O'MALLEY, John W. Renaissance Humanism and the Religious Culture of the First Jesuits. Heythrop J, 31(4), 471-487, O 90.

O'MEARA, Dominic. La question de l'être et du non-être des objets mathématiques chez Plotin et Jamblique. Rev Theol Phil, 122(3), 405-416, 1990.

Cet article traite du statut ontologique des objets mathématiques dans l'interprétation qu'en ont donné les néoplatoniciens Plotin et Jamblique. Tous deux réalistes, ils témoignent de l'influence d'Aristote et du stoïcisme. Plotin manifeste ainsi une tendance nominaliste dans le cadre de son réalisme, tendance critiquée par Jamblique qui, tout en décelant la présence des nombres à chaque niveau de la réalité, semble concevoir les objets mathématiques comme la projection par l'esprit humain de principes supérieurs.

O'NEIL, Rick. "Definition and Death" in *Biomedical Ethics Reviews, 1989*, HUMBER, James M (ed), 117-125. Clifton, Humana Pr, 1990.

Debate over the definition of death has involved a misunderstanding of the type of definition required. *Lexical* definitions beg the issue because many wish to redefine death. Choice among *theoretical* definitions is impossible because of lack of meta-criteria. We must settle for a *contextual* definition. Thus the paper evaluates the whole-brain and higher-brain formulations of death according to criteria established by the medical/legal context.

O'NEILL, J. "Postmodernism and (Post)Marxism" in *Postmodernism—Philosophy and the Arts (Continental Philosophy III)*, SILVERMAN, Hugh J (ed), 69-79. New York, Routledge, 1990.

Ten theses on postmodernism are advanced to show that it is a species of neotony (youth, novelty) that cannot possibly *épater la bourgeoisie* because capitalism has always devoured rational/ethical values.

O'NEILL, John. Property in Science and the Market. Monist, 73(4), 601-620, O 90.

O'NEILL, John. Two Problems of Induction? Brit J Phil Sci, 40(1), 121-125, Mr 89.

In this paper I distinguish two problems of induction: a problem of the uniformity of nature and a problem of the variety of nature. I argue that the traditional problem of induction that Popper poses—the problem of uniformity—is not that which is relevant to science. The problem relevant to science is that of the variety of nature.

O'NEILL, John. "Winch and Schutz on the Regulative Idea of a Social Science" in *Life-World and Politics: Between Modernity and Postmodernity*, WHITE, Stephen K (ed), 107-136. Notre Dame, Univ Notre Dame Pr, 1989.

Winch and Schutz are shown to have formulated a regulative principle of the lay translation of social science discourse. This principle of translation is essential to democratic institutions.

O'NEILL, Onora. "Kantian Ethics" in *A Companion to Ethics*, SINGER, Peter (ed), 175-185. Cambridge, Blackwell, 1991.

The main differences between Kant's ethics, contemporary Kantian ethics and the composite caricature of Kantian ethics often criticized by virtue ethicists should not be overlooked. These differences reflect distinct conceptions of freedom, action and practical reason. They explain why Kant, unlike contemporary theorists of justice has no difficulty in providing an account of the virtues.

O'NEILL, William. Rights as Rhetoric: Nonsense on Stilts? Listening, 26(2), 111-120, Spr 91.

In the essay entitled "Rights as Rhetoric: Nonsense on Stilts?" I consider 1) the justification of "natural rights" in John Rawl's contractarian theory, 2) the tacit role of "prejudice" in its elaboration, and 3) the implication of a theory of human rights which forsakes its "prejudice against prejudice." I argue, pace Alasdair MacIntyre, that human rights are best regarded rhetorically, i.e., as considerations of special suasive force in the practice of differing moral communities.

O'SHAUGHNESSY, Brian. "The Appearance of a Material Object" in *Philosophical Perspectives, 4: Action Theory and Philosophy of Mind, 1990*, TOMBERLIN, James E (ed), 131-151. Atascadero, Ridgeview, 1990.

O'SULLIVAN, Neil. Sophoclean Logic (*Antigone* 175-81). J Hellen Stud, 110, 191-192, 1990.

The aim of this note is to explain the direct logical connection of *Antigone* 178 ff. with what precedes. The particle *gar* in 178 introduces the justification of the claim just made, as it normally does, and there is no need to appeal to rarer usages or confusion on the speaker's part. A new interpretation of 181 is offered as a consequence of this argument.

OAKLANDER, L Nathan. A Defence of the New Tenseless Theory of Time. Phil Quart, 41(162), 26-38, Ja 91.

According to the new tenseless theory of time, our need to think and talk in tenses terms is perfectly consistent with time being tenseless. In an article by Quentin Smith (*Philosophical Studies*, 1987), both the token-reflexive and the date-version of the new tenseless theory are criticized. In this article the author shows how a careful attention to the type-token distinction and to the views of Kaplan on indexicals can overcome Smith's objections to the token-reflexive account. The article also responds to Smith's objections to the date-analysis.

OAKLEY, Justin. A Critique of Kantian Arguments Against Emotions as Moral Motives. Hist Phil Quart, 7(4), 441-459, O 90.

A central claim of Kant's ethics is that only acts done from duty have moral worth. In arguing for this claim, Kant maintains that motivation by emotion cannot be morally good. In this paper I show the falsity of the arguments advanced by Kant and his followers against emotions as moral motives. My strategy is to look at what Kantians themselves take to be necessary for a motive to have moral worth, and, focusing on the notion of *reliability*, I argue that duty has no more claim to be a morally worthy motive than do certain emotions, such as sympathy and compassion.

OAKSFORD, Mike and CHATER, Nick. Against Logicist Cognitive Science. Mind Lang, 6(1), 1-38, Spr 91.

We argue that the plausibility of classical "logicist" cognitive science depends on its ability to provide a proof-theoretic account of the defeasible inferencing found in almost every area of cognitive activity. We assess attempts in Artificial Intelligence to carry out this proof-theoretic programme using non-monotonic logics. We note that such logics allow only unacceptably weak disjunctive conclusions and that the theorem proving algorithms over such logics are computationally intractable due to their reliance on th NP-hard problem of consistency checking. We suggest that the programme of classical cognitive science is infeasible and address a number of objections to this conclusion.

OBERDAN, Thomas. Positivism and the Pragmatic Theory of Observation. Proc Phil Sci Ass, 1, 25-37, 1990.

This paper attempts to undermine Paul Feyerabend's claim, which is crucial to his critique of positivism, that the pragmatic theory of observation was first developed by Rudolf Carnap in his early discussions of protocol sentences. It is argued instead that Carnap's conception of protocols was founded on his analysis of language, so that his reasons for endorsing certain aspects of the pragmatic theory are nothing like Feyerabend's epistemological ones. These historical conclusions provide the basis for arguing that, despite Feyerabend's critique, Carnap's later views (in "The Methodological Character of Theoretical Concepts") clearly countenance theoretical influences on observational statements.

OBREMSKI, T E and NELSON, D R. Promoting Moral Growth Through Intra-Group Participation. J Bus Ethics, 9(9), 731-739, S 90.

Currently, an emphasis is being placed on the integration of ethical issues into the business curriculum. This paper investigates the viability of using student group interaction to induce an upward movement in the stages of moral development as advanced by Kohlberg. The results of a classroom experiment using graduate business law students suggest that formulating groups that mix stages of moral development can provide a robust environment for upward movement. In addition, the results suggest strategies for formulating effective groups, based upon entry levels as measured by the Defining Issues Test.

ODDIE, Graham. Backwards Causation and the Permanence of the Past. Synthese, 85(1), 71-93, O 90.

Can a present or future event bring about a past event? An answer to this question is demanded by many other interesting questions. Recent articles on the problem of backwards causation have drawn attention to the importance of the principle of the fixity of the past: that the past is now fixed. It can be shown that the standard argument against backwards causation (the bilking experiment) simply builds in the assumption of past fixity. A fixed past deprives future events of past efficacy. This has naturally led to the speculation that by abandoning past fixity real power over the past may be possible. In this paper I show that in order to have an interesting thesis of backwards causation it is not enough simply to drop past fixity. More must go. In particular, to ensure what could be called future-to-past efficacy we must abandon two entrenched principles of permanence: the principle of permanent fixity, and the principle of permanent truth. (edited)

ODDIE, Graham. Creative Value. Inquiry, 33(3), 297-316, S 90.

Free agents can create and destroy value, for how much value is realized may well depend on what such agents choose to do. Not only may such agents create and destroy value, but such creation and destruction seem to involve a dimension of value: I call it *creative value*. An explication of the twin concepts of *creating value* and *creative value* is given, motivated by two desiderata. It is then shown that creative value turns out to be equivalent to what Nozick has dubbed *originative value*, when his suggestive remarks are given a rigorous, although very natural, interpretation. Thus two highly plausible, but quite different, ways of characterizing creative value converge on a single concept. Furthermore, the account throws considerable light on two further areas of moral theory (namely, moral satisficing and the comparison principle) which turn out, rather unexpectedly, to be linked.

ODDIE, Graham. "Partial Interpretation, Meaning Variance, and Incommensurability" in *Imre Lakatos and Theories of Scientific Change*, GAVROGLU, Kostas (ed), 305-322. Norwell, Kluwer, 1989.

It is widely believed that the thesis that theories partially define their own theoretical terms entails the thesis of meaning-variance. Meaning-variance in turn is supposed to lead to the thesis of incommensurability, or at least pose severe problems for commensurability. And the incommensurability thesis goes hand-in-glove with some versions of antirealism, or idealism. This paper aims to show that none of these purported links exist.

ODDIE, Graham. Supervenience, Goodness and Higher-Order Universals. Austl J Phil, 69(1), 20-47, Mr 91.

Supervenience theses promise ontological economy without reducibility. The problem is that they face a dilemma: either the relation of supervenience entails reducibility or it is mysterious. Recently higher-order universals have been invoked to avoid the dilemma. This article develops a higher-order framework in which this claim can be assessed. It is shown that reducibility can be avoided, but only at the cost of a rather radical metaphysical proposal.

ODDIE, Graham. Verisimilitude by Power Relations. Brit J Phil Sci, 41(1), 129-135, Mr 90.

A number of different theories of truthlikeness have been proposed, but most can be classified into one of two different programme: the probability-content programme and the likeness programme. In Brink and Heidema [1987] we are offered a further proposal, with the attraction of some novelty. I argue that while the heuristic path taken by the authors is rather remote from what they call 'the well-worn paths', in fact their point of arrival is rather closer to existing proposals within the likeness approach than might at first appear. It is the purpose of this note to outline the logical connections and to assess which have been offered in favour of the new proposal.

ODEGARD, Douglas. Charity and Moral Imperatives. Theoria, 55(2), 81-94, 1989.

Questions of whether moral agents should help the destitute can be seen as practical questions, not as questions of moral duty. Deciding that something is charitable then does not establish that it should not be done. And to say that it should be done is not to sit in moral judgment on those who do not do it. It is to assess their actions critically in the light of their own priorities.

ODEGARD, Douglas. Scepticism: the Current Debate. Eidos, 8(2), 177-208, D 89.

Some recent positions on sceptical issues are considered by seeing how well a briefly sketched conception of justified certainty can survive the debate. According to the conception, we are sometimes justified in believing something without having any ground for doubt, although we do have a ground for thinking that there may be a ground for doubt. The conception is defended against three kinds of opponents: 1) those who, like Moore and Wittgenstein, think that some common-sense propositions are bedrock; 2) those who, like Dretske and Nozick, think that we can know ordinary things with certainty even though the things we know have doubtful implications; and 3) those who, like Stroud, Unger, Klein, Moser, and BonJour, think that very few matters, or at any rate very few empirical matters, are certain.

ODERBERG, David S. A Paradox About Authority. Analysis, 51(3), 153-160, Je 91.

This paper discusses the case of a sovereign elected by the people of a mythical state in order to safeguard and faithfully to transmit to his successors the people's sacred religious beliefs. After his election he enacts a law invalidating the election of heretics; but it turns out that he too fails under it. Is he validly elected? The question is left unanswered, but the source of the problem is discussed, various proposals are rejected, and both similarities to and differences from the Liar Paradox are noted.

OFFENBERGER, Niels. La oposición de los enunciados "estrictamente" particulares en perspectiva trivalente. Rev Filosof (Venezuela), 12, 113-124, 1989.

OGAZ, Charla Phyllis and SASSOWER, Raphael. Philosophical Hierarchies and Lyotard's Dichotomies. Phil Today, 35(2), 153-160, Sum 91.

This essay illustrates through Lyotard's work that dichotomies may be unavoidable. However, the consequence of their use turns them into ordered hierarchies, regardless of the intentions of those using them. And hierarchies are to be avoided, because their establishment is never perceived as a mere heuristic; instead, they influence public behavior.

OHANA, David. Nietzsche and Ernst Jünger: From Nihilism to Totalitarianism. Hist Euro Ideas, 11, 751-758, 1989.

The aesthetic-nihilistic revolution in western culture initiated by Nietzsche in the nineteenth century was transformed by Ernst Jünger into a modern vision of technology and a new political pattern of totalitarian nihilism. Over and above 'nihilism' and 'totalitarianism' as such, there is an additional dialectical phenomenon, namely a synthesis of both concepts: the nihilist mentality, whether from inner compulsion or immanent logic, is driven to acceptance of totalitarian behaviour which is characterised by its extreme dynamism. The structure of the essay reflects the emergence and crystallization of what I call 'nihilistic-totalitarian syndrome' from its philosophical basis to a fully-developed intellectual current in the form of a new and total consciousness expressed in Jünger's early writings.

OITTINEN, Vesa. Deleuze und Spinozas "Ethik". Deut Z Phil, 38(5), 470-473, 1990.

OJEDA, Almerindo E. Definite Descriptions and Definite Generics. Ling Phil, 14(4), 367-397, Ag 91.

OKRENT, Mark. Teleological Underdetermination. Amer Phil Quart, 28(2), 147-155, Ap 91.

OLADIPO, Olusegun. Metaphysics, Religion and Yoruba Traditional Thought. J Indian Counc Phil Res, 7(2), 71-83, Ja-Ap 90.

In this paper, I examine the issue of the extent to which it is tenable to assert, as many experts on African traditional thought have done, that Africans are religious in all things. I do this by considering the status of the belief in some nonhuman agencies and powers, for example, divinities, spirits, magic, witchcraft, etc., in the belief-system of an African people, the Yoruba. I argue that this assertion is mistaken because it is based on inadequate definition of religion which does not allow for a proper delimination between the religious and the realm of the metaphysical. In the second part of this paper, I attempt an analysis of 'metaphysics' and 'religion'. (edited)

OLDENQUIST, Andrew. The Origins of Morality: An Essay in Philosophical Anthropology. Soc Phil Pol, 8(1), 121-140, Autumn 90.

Scientific and philosophical explanations of morality are integrated by means of, first, a philosophical anthropology: the idea, following Aristotle, that basic morals and values depend on human nature; a theory of innate human sociality is defended along with universal requirements of cooperative living. Second, a "bridge theory" explains how wants and aversions turn into moral beliefs. The theory is "naturalistic," but it preserves Hume's Law because what is identical with an aversion under scientifically describable conditions is not, e.g., "Robbery is immoral," but "So-and-so believes robbery is immoral." Implications are discussed for utilitarianism, moral realism, and views of a number of philosophers and scientists on the relation of morality to evolved human nature.

OLDROYD, David. David Hull's Evolutionary Model for the Progress and Process of Science. Biol Phil, 5(4), 473-487, O 90.

Hull's *Science as a Process* (1988) is represented diagramatically. Transmission of scientific concepts is like the transmission of genes, via scientists (vehicles/interactors) and organisms (vehicles/interactors) respectively. There are demic lineages of ideas (in research programmes) and in organisms. However, Oldroyd argues that scientists try to improve their own ideas. They revive old and formulate new ideas. 'Acquired ideas' are transmitted. Hull's analogy works better for religions that for sciences. Religions try to conserve their ideas; scientific ideas are exposed to test and criticism. But Hull's 'struggle' model for science has merit. Competition and collaboration operate in science, as in the organic world.

OLDS, Clifton. Wollheim's Theory of Artist as Spectator: A Complication. J Aes Educ, 24(2), 25-30, Sum 90.

OLDS, Mason. The Crisis of Authority. Relig Hum, 24(4), 160-169, Autumn 90.

According to Nietzsche, the traditional sources of authority were predicated on the existence of God, and now that God was dead, the linchpin of authority was removed from society creating a crisis. So one of the ways to interpret intellectual history from the Middle Ages to the present is to view it as the disintegration and diminution of the monopolistic control the church had over a person's life. In both the secular and religious realms, the starting point and the conclusion are the same. Authority moves from the Christian monarch who ruled over all of life to the solitary individual who is the ultimate source of authority in his own life.

OLDS, Mason. Moral Behavior at Public Performances. Relig Hum, 25(1), 41-46, Wint 91.

The actions of people at public performances that unnecessarily hinder the audience's enjoyment of the performance can be demonstrated to be immoral in one of three ways: such actions violate 1) a rational maxim governing behavior that can be consistently and universally applied; 2) the greatest happiness for the greatest number of people; and 3) a person's right to an opportunity to enjoy the performance. Disruptive behavior cannot be justified because 1) it violates the principle of rational consistency; 2) it cannot put the happiness of one above the happiness of many; and 3) violation of the rights of others implies irresponsibility rather than responsibility. In other words, one has a moral obligation not to interfere with the enjoyment of others.

OLEN, Jeffrey and BARRY, Vincent. *Applying Ethics: A Text with Readings (Third Edition)*. Belmont, Wadsworth, 1989.

OLIVA, Rossella Bonito. *Il compito della filosofia: Saggio su Windelband*. Bologna, Morano, 1990.

OLIVÉ, León. Sobre causación y unificación según Wesley Salmon. Critica, 22(66), 115-129, D 90.

Salmon's idea that it is possible to consider as compatible and complementary what he calls the unification view and the causal view of scientific explanation is discussed. (Cf. his "Scientific Explanation, causation *and* unification," *Critica*, Number 66, December 1990). It is argued that, since the causal conception of scientific explanation presupposes a realist viewpoint, Salmon's suggestion to see both conceptions as compatible must assume also a realist conception of science, which in turn requires independent groundings. This idea runs against those of people like Railton and Kitcher, who pretend to avoid metaphysical implications of their viewpoint.

OLIVEIRA, M B de. Cognitivism and Cognitive Science (in Portuguese). Trans/Form/Acao, 13, 85-93, 1990.

The aim of the paper is to characterize a school of thought—cognitivism—and the discipline to which it gave rise. After a brief summary of the origins of cognitivism, the ontological and methodological principles which define it are described. The relationship that exists between computers and the functionalist idea of considering the mind as a system whose elements are characterized by their functions, and not by their material make-up is then presented. The paper concludes with a discussion about the nature and the name of the discipline generated by cognitivism, the suggestion being that it is a proto-science, to which the name "cognitive studies" is preferable to "cognitive science".

OLIVIER, G. Continuing the Conversation—A Reply to My Interlocutors. S Afr J Phil, 9(4), 225-226, N 90.

This is a reply to the responses by other philosophers to my earlier article, "Philosophy and Socio-Political Conversation: A Postmodern Proposal" (*S Afr J Phil*, 9(2)). It is shown that these responses, although critical of my argument, validate it by entering into a conversation with me. In reply to criticism that I failed to distinguish between conversation, dialogue, negotiation, etc., I remind my critics that conversation was used in a paradigmatic sense to govern all linguistic exchanges between people. The reply further deals with charges that my earlier article was not sufficiently sensitive to cultural and linguistic differences.

OLIVIER, G. Heidegger and Emancipation. S Afr J Phil, 9(3), 117-124, Ag 90.

In this article the possibility that contemporary 'counter-Enlightenment thinking' may have some roots in Heidegger's work by focusing on the place and status of emancipation (as Enlightenment-motif) in his philosophy as a whole, from *Being and Time* through to the later works, is examined. It is found that, whereas in the earlier phase of his thinking Heidegger still employed a concept of interactional liberation—termed 'emancipatory solicitude' by Dallmayr—the later Heidegger despairs of any possibility of human emancipation. Instead, it appears that he believes the heritage of the Enlightenment (or modernity) to consist in the rule (and self-enslavement) of man as subject, and in the hegemony of the world as 'picture', of science and especially of technology. The essay concludes with a consideration of *Gelassenheit* (letting-be) as a mode of being (proposed by Heidegger) which amounts to an alternative kind of emancipation.

OLKOWSKI-LAETZ, Dorothea. "A Postmodern Language in Art" in *Postmodernism—Philosophy and the Arts (Continental Philosophy III)*, SILVERMAN, Hugh J (ed), 101-120. New York, Routledge, 1990.

This essay explores the question of what would constitute a postmodern theory of language. Insofar as no single theory of language imposes itself upon us with an immediacy and insistence that forces recognition, we inventory the past, trying on historical forms like clothing. We either insist on a return to that form or parody it, treating the present as if it were framed by a past and future in order to preserve the identity of content by representing it. Are we constrained to this, or is there a postmodern theory of language waiting to emerge out of the conventional symbols and the dizzying shifts of meaning?

OLLASON, J G. What Is This Stuff Called Fitness? Biol Phil, 6(1), 81-92, Ja 91.

This paper considers a variety of attempts to define fitness in such a way as to defend the theory of evolution by natural selection from the criticism that it is a circular argument. Each of the definitions is shown to be inconsistent with the others. The paper argues that the environment in which an animal evolves can be defined only with respect to the properties of the phenotype of the animal and that it is therefore not illuminating to try to explain the phenotypic properties of the animal in terms of adaptation to an environment that is defined by those very properties. Furthermore, since there is no way that the environment can be defined independently of the presence of the animal there is no way that the quality of an animal can be assessed; and there can be no objective criteria by which *any* form of selection can be carried out, therefore there can be no criteria by which *natural* selection can be carried out. (edited)

OLMSTED, Wendy Raudenbush. The Uses of Rhetoric: Indeterminacy in Legal Reasoning, Practical Thinking and Interpretation of Literary Figures. Phil Rhet, 24(1), 1-24, 1991.

When interpretive theory aspires to a system of rules for legal reasoning and textual criticism, and skepticism arises that such rules are possible, the art of rhetoric offers an alternative, a reasoning that adapts rules to the particularities of situation and action. Rhetoric does not presuppose that rules or meanings of terms must be determinate in order to be used intelligently. Examples from mechanics, law, and literature suggest that the degree and kind of indeterminacy of rules and terms depend upon how formulations are used to direct observation and reasoning. Rhetoric allows us to discern degrees and kinds of indeterminacy, freeing us from the polarities of absolutely determinate rules that control reasoning and a destructive, radical indeterminacy of language.

OLSHEWSKY, Thomas M. The Classical Roots of Hume's Skepticism. J Hist Ideas, 52(2), 269-287, Ap-Je 91.

The contrast made by Sextus and Hume between Academicean and Pyrronean skepticism are notoriously incommensurate. Hume does not attribute to the former, as Sextus does, that doubting involves denial; Hume attributes to neither the probability claims Sextus attributes to the former; they come closest to a match in attributing inclination to credence to the Academiceans; the contrast of principle and nature so basic to Hume is absent from Sextus; and Hume's notion of mitigation finds no place in Sextus's account at all. There are good grounds for supposing that Hume modeled his account of Academic skepticism on Cicero's in the *Academica*, for whom no contrast such as those of Hume and Sextus existed. Hume's model for Pyrrhonism is his own *Treatise*, from which he tried to make rhetorical distancing in varying ways, settling on the contrast of the Enquiries as one kind of engagement rather than difference in doctrine.

OLSON, Alan M. Glasnost and Enlightenment. Phil Today, 34(2), 99-110, Sum 90.

This article provides a critical reassessment of Karl Jaspers's post-World War II social and political philosophy *vis-à-vis* recent developments in Eastern Europe as the basis for a critique of Francis Fukuyama's much-publicized quasi-Hegelian comments on the "end of history" and the alleged *fin de siècle* victory of liberal democracy. After contrasting the Western (Kantian) and Eastern (Marxist) versions of Enlightenment, the author concludes, by way of Jaspers and Berdyaev, that *Freiheits-Philosophie* and the notion of "rational autonomy" is fundamentally alien to the "Spirit of Byzantium" which has traditionally dominated Eastern European consciousness and probably will continue to do so.

ONO, Hiroakira and MINARI, Pierluigi and TAKANO, Mitio. Intermediate Predicate Logics Determined by Ordinals. J Sym Log, 55(3), 1099-1124, S 90.

The paper deals with intermediate predicate logics which are semantically determined by classes of well-ordered Kripke frames with constant domain. The aim—loosely speaking—is to see whether and to what extent ordinals can be defined modulo Kripke-type semantics by sets of first-order formulas. The various results presented in the paper give partial answers to this question, both for countable and uncountable ordinals.

OOSTERLING, Henk A F. "Oedipus and the Dogon: The Myth of Modernity Interrogated" in *I, We and Body: First Joint Symposium of Philosophers from Africa and from the Netherlands*, KIMMERLE, Heinz (ed), 27-45. Atlantic Highlands, Gruner, 1989.

OPAT, Jaroslav. T G Masaryk—A Modern Thinker (in Czechoslovakian). Filozof Cas, 38(4), 417-422, 1990.

The term "modern" is the antithesis to opportunist fashionability. The modernness of T G Masaryk's thinking is based on his concept of crisis of the industrial society. He tried to render the roots of this crisis as fully as possible starting from their social-economic and cultural-political causes up to the causes in morality and religion. The latter seem to be of utmost importance to him. Trying to find the way out of the crisis, Masaryk emphasized the methods of reforms. Whenever there were failures and failings of democracy he advocated their rectification but at the same time warned against their violent vanquishing putting stress on the positive and creative human work. As a democrat and humanist he was essentially against war. Before 1914 as a politician he endeavoured at preventing the outbreak of the war. During WWI as a revolutionary he concentrated on the elimination of the causes leading to war as well as on the democratic ways out of the war. It determined his relation to Austria-Hungary and to both Russian revolutions of 1917, too.

OPIELKA, Michael. Some Fundamental Aspects of Socioecological Theory and Policy, Part I (in German). Deut Z Phil, 38(9), 824-837, 1990.

The paper discusses the idea of a social-ecological theory as an integrative approach in the debate about a holistic social theory. In the introducing section the unsatisfactory answers by the current and leading social (and general) theories are presented (Behaviorism, Human Ecology, Systems Theory, Sociobiology). They are criticized because of their reductionist, "two-valued" logic: right/wrong, yes/no. As an alternative approach it is argued for social-ecological approach to action and (social) systems, which grounds in the tradition of a "theory of reflection" (G W F Hegel, G Günther, J Heinrichs). This perspective is based on: 1) a reconstructive epistemology; 2) on the distinction between four levels of reflection (i. subject - object, ii. reflexive subject, iii. subject - subject, iv. medial reflection); 3) therefore on a distinction between four levels of action (i. adaptive behaviour, ii. strategic action, iii. communicative action, iv. meta-communicative action) based on the building of systems through action. With respect to society this means the differentiation between: i. the economical-ecological system, ii. the political system, iii. the social-cultural system and, iv. the religious.

OPIELKA, Michael. Some Fundamental Aspects of Socioecological Theory and Policy, Part II (in German). Deut Z Phil, 38(10), 993-999, 1990.

OPILIK, Klaus. Destruktion und Übersetzung: Zu den Aufgaben von Philosophiegeschichte nach Martin Heidegger. Z Phil Forsch, 44(3), 479-484, 1990.

The article is a conference report of a German-Japanese symposium, which was organized by the chair of philosophy of the University of Munich (R Spaemann), 1989 in Munich; the conference articles were published with the title "Destruktion und Uebersetzung," edited by T Buchheim, Wienheim 1989. The central task of the conference was the elaboration of the terms 'Destruktion' und 'Uebersetzung' in their unity being fundamental for a characterization of Heidegger's thinking. By doing so a basis should be achieved for the explanation of a possible or even necessary ability to translate this thinking, which was partially done by the example of the meeting between Japan and Heidegger. Heidegger's understanding of history was a central point, and thus in connection with this his interpretation of modern technology.

OPPICI, Patrizia. "Egalité ou fraternité" in *Égalité Uguaglianza*, FERRARI, Jean (ed), 105-112. Napoli, Liguori, 1990.

OPPY, Graham. Craig, Mackie and the *Kalam* Cosmological Argument. Relig Stud, 27(2), 189-197, Je 91.

In "Professor Mackie and the Kalam Cosmological Argument," Professor William Lane Craig defends the kalam cosmological argument against some criticisms raised by J L Mackie (in his book *The Miracle of Theism*). In my article, I argue that Craig's defence is inadequate—Mackie's original objections *do* defeat the kalam cosmological argument.

OPPY, Graham. Makin on the Ontological Argument. Philosophy, 66(255), 106-114, Ja 91.

This article is a critique of Stephen Makin's "The Ontological Argument" (*Philosophy* 63, 1988, pp. 83-91). The principal claim of the article is that Makin's version of the ontological argument involves an equivocal use of expressions of the form "the concept of c." Moreover, it is argued that all non-modal ontological arguments are vitiated by different versions of the same fallacy.

OPPY, Graham. On Davies' Institutional Definition of Art. S J Phil, 29(3), 371-382, Fall 91.

ORAVCOVÀ, Mariana. Philosophy within the Activity of the Nagyszombat (Trnava) University (in Hungarian). Magyar Filozof Szemle, 3-4, 401-407, 1990.

ORENSTEIN, Alex. "Is Existence What Existential Quantification Expresses?" in *Perspectives on Quine*, BARRETT, Robert (ed), 245-270. Cambridge, Blackwell, 1990.

Quine's quip, the apparent tautology, "existence is what existential quantification expresses" nicely sums up the current entrenched view of existence claims. This paper attempts to refute that view. Proponents who refer to the "some" quantifier as "existential" foster the illusion that Quine's remark has the status of being a tautology. The argument of the paper is that there is a clash between a logical constraint on "all" and "some" (viz. that they are analogous to "and" and "or") and a philosophical explication of "some" in terms of the notion of existence. This conflict is exhibited in three areas: (1) sentences such as Moore's 'Some tame tigers don't exist'; (2) inclusive logic; and (3) free logic.

ORLICKI, Andrzej. Some Remarks on ω-Powers of Enumerated Sets and Their Applications to ω-Operations. Z Math Log, 36(2), 149-161, 1990.

The concept of co-power of an enumerated set has been introduced by Ersov in 1977. In the paper some applications of this concept to study of so-called ω-operators are given. In a sense, the paper is a continuation of the author's paper "On lifting of co-operations from the category of sets to the category of enumerated sets." AMS classification: 03D45.

ORLOWSKA, Ewa. Interpretation of Relevant Logics in a Logic of Ternary Relations. Bull Sect Log, 19(2), 39-48, Je 90.

ORLOWSKA, Ewa. Kripke Semantics for Knowledge Representation Logics. Stud Log, 49(2), 255-272, Je 90.

This article provides an overview of development of Kripke semantics for logics determined by information systems. The proposals are made to extend the standard Kripke structures to the structures based on information systems. The underlying logics are defined and problems of their axiomatization are discussed. Several open problems connected with the logics are formulated. Logical aspects of incompleteness of information provided by information systems are considered.

ORLOWSKA, Ewa. Verisimilitude Based on Concept Analysis. Stud Log, 49(3), 307-320, S 90.

In the paper ordering relations for comparison of verisimilitude of theories are introduced and discussed. The relations refer to semantic analysis of the results of theories, in particular to analysis of concepts the theories deal with.

OROZ RETA, José (trans) and BAGET BOZZO, Giovanni. La teología de la historia en la "ciudad de Dios" (2). Augustinus, 35(139-140), 321-367, Jl-D 90.

OROZ RETA, José (trans) and BAGET-BOZZO, Giovanni. La teología de la historia en la Ciudad de Dios. Augustinus, 35(137-138), 31-80, Ja-Je 90.

OROZ RETA, José. Tres grandes testigos de la luz interior: San Agustín, san Buenaventura y J Henry Newman. Augustinus, 35(139-140), 233-277, Jl-D 90.

ORSOLIC, Marko. Theology of Liberation and Marxism (in Serbo-Croation). Filozof Istraz, 34(1), 57-64, 1990.

In this paper the author discusses some problems concerning the relationship between contemporary tendencies in Marxism and theology of liberation.

ORSUCCI, Andrea. A proposito dell'interesse di Dilthey per l'antropologia cinquecentesca. G Crit Filosof Ital, 69(2), 254-261, My-Ag 90.

ORTEGA MUÑOZ, Juan F. Comentario a las "Sentencias" de Isidoro de Sevilla. Themata, 6, 107-123, 1989.

This article concerns the doctrinal synthesis of St. Isidore of Seville from a philosophical standpoint. After analyzing the Biblical antecedent the study concentrates on the form and contents of the three books of the *Sentences*. Special attention is given to those elements which influenced posterior philosophical thought the problems of God and the world, man and knowledge and the origin of evil. The work, which immediately precedes the 12th century Summas, is approached following the Augustine/Zubiri paradigm considering in particular the Divine character of reality created from nothing and which leads to God. Isidore's sentences have contributed to the systematization of philosophical Christian thought and has therefore been essential to the evolution of Latin scholastic philosophy both in content and structure.

ORTEGA Y GASSET, José and PIERRE, Christian (trans). *Velázquez et Goya*. Paris, Klincksieck, 1990.

ORTH, Ernst Wolfgang (ed). *Vernunft und Kontingenz: Rationalität und Ethos in der Phänomenologie*. Freiburg, Alber, 1991.

Internationally well-known philosophers entertain the questions as to a phenomenological rationality; also, the possibilities of a phenomenological theory of science, the relativity problem, the sociology of knowledge, as well as a rational, non-metaphysical ethics, are explored.

ORTHMAYR, Imre. "Transmitting Theoretical Frames: The Case of Social Darwinism" in *Perspectives on Ideas and Reality*, NYÍRI, J C (ed), 222-231. Budapest, Kiskonyvtara, 1990.

ORTIZ DE URBINA, Ricardo Sánchez. La estética de la recepción desde la teoría platónica del arte. El Basilisco, 1, 33-40, S-O 89.

ORTIZ DE URBINA, Ricardo Sánchez. El lugar de la crítica de arte. El Basilisco, 4, 3-11, Mr-Ap 90.

ORTON, David. Informed Consent or Informed Rejection of Pesticide Use: A Concept for Environmental Action. Phil Soc Act, 16(4), 31-46, O-D 90.

This paper describes a concept which arose from the experiences of environmentalists in Nova Scotia, Canada, who were organizing against forces spraying using the herbicide Roundup (active ingredient glyphosate) and the insecticide Bt (*Bacillus thuringtensis* variety kurstaki). The type of forestry which uses pesticides has been characterized as "pulpwood forestry" and has certain features such as clearcutting; the reduction of biodiversity through replacing the existing natural forest with a few selected softwood pulp species like balsam fir, black, white and red spruce; the elimination of hardwoods; even-aged management; use of pesticides to "protect" the pulpwood tree plantations; and use of industrial machinery for harvesting. Every year extensive forest spraying takes place in Nova Scotia and every year environmentalists and the public living close to forest spray sites engage in battle to try to stop or seriously impede the spraying.

ORTON, Robert E. Knowledge Growth and Teaching: Towards a Genetic Foundation for Teachers' Knowledge. Proc Phil Educ, 46, 147-155, 1990.

ORUDJEV, Zaid and LAWLER, James. "Marxism, Humanism, and Ecology" in *The Question of Humanism: Challenges and Possibilities*, GOICOECHEA, David (ed), 162-169. Buffalo, Prometheus, 1991.

ORUKA, H Odera. Cultural Fundamentals in Philosophy. Phil Theol, 5(1), 19-37, Fall 90.

This paper examines the notion of cultural universals and then seeks to identify what the author wishes to identify as "cultural fundamentals" in philosophy and philosophical debate. The paper then assays the extent to which such fundamentals are obstacles to the "birth" of potential philosophers. Lastly I suggest a solution to this problem.

ORUKA, Henry Odera. Cultural Fundamentals in Philosophy: Obstacles in Philosophical Dialogues. Quest, 4(2), 20-37, D 90.

L'auteur démontre en s'appuyant sur l'expérience d'une étudiante noire et sa propre expérience dans l'étude de la philosophie que la différence de 'background' (milieu) culturel est un facteur signcatif en philósophie. Il commente l'analyse des universaux culturels faite par Kwasi Wiredu et propose d'inclure l'intuition parmi les universaux culturels. Il traite de rôle de l'intuition dans les manifestations culturelles, spécialement en philosophie comme forme de culture cognitive. En outre, le rôle des fondements culturels en philosophie est démontré à l'aide de quelque positions typicques provenant de participants à un dialogue philosophique. Celle qui, par example, en tant que réministe, ou noire, ne paartage pas les hypothèses culturelles de la discussion, ne peut prendre part au dialogue de façon satisfaisante. Comme example d'étude philosophique à base d'autres fondements culturels, on traite de la philosophie de sages africaines.

ORVIS, Gregory P and HEACOCK, Marian V. Ethical Considerations and Ramifications of the 1989 Generic Drug Scandal. Bridges, 2(3-4), 113-125, Fall-Wint 90.

Generic drugs presently account for one in three prescriptions and their use is predicted to increase as many name-brand drug patents expire in the next decade. The bribery and fraud perpetrated in 1989 by several drug companies in order to obtain early FDA approval of their generic drug applications created an ethical and legal dilemma from which the drug industry has yet to recover. This article provides a historical background of the generic drug scandal. The philosophical purposes of generic drug approval and of the FDA's role in the approval process are also explored. The moral responsibilities of generic drug firms to the public as well as the fiscal responsibility due their owners are discussed. Generic drug firms are defined as being either socially responsible or socially responsive. The discussion of the scandal closes with a discourse on its possible ramifications in the form of remedies to prevent similar problems in the generic drug industry.

ORY, André. Essai sur le thème du réferentiel. Dialectica, 44(3-4), 229-242, 1990.

This article presents and analyses the notion of reference frame, to which Gonseth devoted his last book. A personal reference frame involving two aspects (natural and cognitive reference frames) is distinguished from a group reference frame which also takes various forms (linguistic, social, ideological and religious reference frames, the reference frames of a scientific community). Personal and group reference frames are in an existential symbiosis fostering interactions. This notion of reference frame may be used to advantage in describing and interpreting the relations between man and his fellow man, his organizations, and his natural environment.

OSBORNE, Peter and ELLIOT, Gregory. Community as Compulsion? A Reply to Skillen on Citizenship and the State. Rad Phil, 58, 14-15, Sum 91.

OSBORNE, Peter and DEWS, Peter. Lacan in Slovenia—An Interview with Slavoj Zizek and Renata Salecl. Rad Phil, 58, 25-31, Sum 91.

OSBORNE, Peter (ed) and SAYERS, Sean (ed). *Socialism, Feminism and Philosophy: A Radical Philosophy Reader*. New York, Routledge, 1990.

This is an anthology of articles from *Radical Philosophy*, 1985-1990. It covers topics which are central to current controversies on the left. The first section contains articles on philosophical issues of feminism with a particular focus on moral questions (contributors: C J Arthur, J Grimshaw, P Johnson, S Parsons, R Poole). The second section deals with controversies in socialist and Marxist philosophy, including analytical Marxism (R Harris, J McCarney, J Ree, S Sayers). The final section contains articles discussing concepts of nature and human nature, particularly in relation to environmental issues (T Benton, R Keat, V Plumwood).

OSSAR, Jacob. Adam Smith and Social Justice: The Ethical Basis of *The Wealth of Nations*. Auslegung, 17(2), 125-136, Sum 91.

OSTERMANN, Pascal. Many-Valued Modal Logics: Uses and Predicate Calculus. Z Math Log, 36(4), 367-376, 1990.

In any state of knowledge, there are some questions that cannot be answered, because we have too few informations. Many-valued modal logics are proposed to deal with them. The "many-valued" part allows to assign to a fact an arbitrary value-not exactly a probability, but a possibility measure—while the "modal" part allows to express metalogical concepts relevant to incomplete information (e.g., Chrétien de Troyes is a possible author of "Lancelot"). A modal predicate calculus with n values, called nS4*, is defined and proved to be (weakly) complete.

OTERO, Margarita. On Diophantine Equations Solvable in Models of Open Induction. J Sym Log, 55(2), 779-786, Je 90.

OTSUKA, Michael. The Paradox of Group Beneficence. Phil Pub Affairs, 20(2), 131-149, Spr 91.

OTTE, Richard. Scientific Realism, Perceptual Beliefs, and Justification. Proc Phil Sci Ass, 1, 393-404, 1990.

This paper investigates the justification of certain beliefs central to scientific realism. Some have claimed that the underdetermination of a theory by empirical evidence implies that belief in the truth of the theory and in the existence of the corresponding unobservable entities is unjustified. It is argued that the justification of certain realist beliefs is similar to the justification of our perceptual beliefs. Neither are justified by argument from more basic beliefs, and their underdetermination by the evidence does not affect their justification.

OTTEN, Willemien. The Interplay of Nature and Man in the *Periphyseon* of Johannes Scottus Eriugena. Vivarium, 28(1), 1-16, My 90.

This article analyzes the close relationship between the roles of man and nature in John Scottus Eriugena's *Periphyseon*. Its central argument is that one can only understand the position of man in nature through focusing on the structure of the work as a whole. The theologico-philosophical structure of "procession" and "return" provides the hermeneutical key in explaining the differences between man's epistemological function at the beginning of the work (the human mind investigates nature) and his eschatological role at the end (man lends creation back to God and restores nature to its former unity).

OTTEN, Willemien. Some Perspectives in Eriugenian Studies: Three Recent Studies. Frei Z Phil Theol, 37(3), 515-526, 1990.

This review article discusses three recent publications in the field of Eriugenian studies. In doing so it describes the history of Eriugenian studies in the twentieth century. The study of Johns Scottus Eriugena (810-877) is seen as divided into three major categories: historical, philosophical and literary. The author discusses the advances made in each category and analyzes the works under review according to these categories. Though incredible progression has been made, the author feels there is more need for interpretive studies which take the results of the three categories into account.

OTTENSMEYER, Edward J and HEROUX, Mark A. Ethics, Public Policy, and Managing Advanced Technologies: The Case of Electronic Surveillance. J Bus Ethics, 10(7), 519-526, Jl 91.

A vigorous debate has developed surrounding electronic surveillance in the workplace. This controversial practice is one element of the more general issues of employee dignity and management control, revolving around the use of polygraph and drug testing, "integrity" exams, and the like. Managers, under pressure from competitors, are making greater use of technologically advanced employee monitoring methods because they are available, and hold the promise of productivity improvement. In this paper, the context of electronic surveillance is described and analyzed from the perspectives of ethics, public policy, and managerial behavior.

OUDEMANS, Th C W. Heideggers "logische Untersuchungen". Heidegger Stud, 6, 85-105, 1990.

OUELLET, Pierre. Wittgenstein et le cognitivisme. Lekton, 1(1), 135-157, 1990.

OUTHWAITE, William. Realism, Naturalism and Social Behaviour. J Theor Soc Behav, 20(4), 365-377, D 90.

OUWENDORP, C. Het Dialectisch Humanistisch Grondmotief van Natuur en Vrijheid in de Pedagogiek als Wetenschap. Phil Reform, 55(2), 101-139, 1990.

This article considers the effect of the dialectical humanistic ground-motive of nature and freedom on education as a science. To guarantee freedom, Kant made a distinction between the realm of natural causality, which affords no leeway for human freedom, and a supertemporal realm of moral freedom. The great struggle in education after Kant was how these separate realms of nature and freedom, of 'Sein' and 'Sollen', could be given their place in a harmonic manner. Some of the main streams since Kant and Herbart are discussed in German and Dutch education and briefly confronted with what is termed 'Reformational Philosophy'.

OVER, D E and MANKTELOW, K I. *Inference and Understanding: A Philosophical and Psychological Perspective*. New York, Routledge, 1990.

This book reviews work on linguistic inference, inductive thinking, and deductive reasoning, and links research in these areas with wider theoretical concerns, such as the question of rationality, evolutionary arguments, and artificial intelligence. It includes philosophical and psychological perspectives on these problems; a continuing theme is the comparison between normative and descriptive accounts of human thought.

OWEN, David W D. Locke on Real Essence. Hist Phil Quart, 8(2), 105-118, Ap 91.

Locke's views on real essence, and its relationship to nominal essence, are notoriously difficult. His rejection of natural kinds, constituted by a unique real essence, makes the role of real essence problematic. But a careful look at what I call the real essence of unsorted particulars which, when combined with nominal essence, can be refined into the real essence of sorted particulars helps us understand the complex role real essence plays in Locke's thought.

OWENS, David. Causes and Coincidences. Proc Aris Soc, 90, 49-64, 1989-90.

The aim is to produce an analysis of causation which will enable us to distinguish causal relations from certain logical relations. It is argued that such an analysis should be based on the thesis that coincidences have no causes. There is also discussion of the difference between causal and constitutive relations.

OWENS, Joseph I. "Cognitive Access and Semantic Puzzle" in *Propositional Attitudes: The Role of Content in Logic, Language, and Mind*, ANDERSON, C Anthony (ed), 147-173. Stanford, CSLI, 1990.

In this paper I focus attention on an important but seldom noted supposition — the supposition that a subject's capacity to determine sameness and difference in her beliefs is independent of her knowledge of the external world. I argue that this principle is false, and that abandoning it enables one to resolve a number of semantic puzzles, e.g., Kripke's Pierce Puzzle.

OWENS, Joseph I. *Towards a Christian Philosophy*. Washington, Cath Univ Amer Pr, 1990.

OWENS, Joseph (ed) and ANDERSON, C Anthony (ed). *Propositional Attitudes: The Role of Content in Logic, Language, and Mind*. Stanford, CSLI, 1990.

The papers treat problems about quantifying into modal contexts, discourse representation treatments of complex propositional attitudes, comparisons between the semantical ideas of Frege and Davidson, the sense in which language is social, the idea of "narrow content" mental states, Cartesian access to our mental states, Burge's and Putnam's thought experiments about mind and meaning, the new (or direct) theory of reference, Kripke's "Pierre Puzzle", problems with propositions as objects of the propositional attitudes, and the connection between consciousness and intentionality. Authors are Burge, Donnellan, K Fine, Gunderson, Kamp, LePore, Loewer, Mason, Owens, Stalnaker, N Salmon, Schiffer, Searle, and Wallace.

OWINGS JR, James C and JOCKUSCH JR, Carl G. Weakly Semirecursive Sets. J Sym Log, 55(2), 637-644, Je 90.

OYARZABAL, Manuel. El autoconocimiento del alma según Avicena latino. Pensamiento, 47(186), 179-193, Ap-Je 91.

El tema del conocimiento de sía ocupa en el *De anima* de Avicena una relevancia inesperada para un pensador medieval. Su estudio nos permite, por una parte, detectar los esfuerzos de Avicena con vistas a sintetizar el neoplatonismo y el aristotelismo en la construcción de su psicología y antropología, al propugnar el autoconocimiento existencial inmediato del alma, su autoconocimiento esencial inmediato y mediato, y negarlo a nivel de la percepción sensible. Y, por otra parte, advertimos que Avicena funda sus principales tesis, como la espiritualidad y unidad del alma, en el hecho de la autointelección del yo.

PAALMAN-DE MIRANDA, Aïda B. Note on a Paper of D P Ellerman. Erkenntnis, 33(3), 397-398, N 90.

PACHO, Julián. Fisiormorfismo de la razón versus racionalismo. Pensamiento, 47(186), 219-238, Ap-Je 91.

Pese a la gran polémica que desde su reciente nacimiento acompaña a la "teoría evolucionista del conocimiento" (EE), aún falta un estudio de sus supuestos y, a fortiori, de su incidencia en los de la(s) filosofía(s) establecida(s). Para suplir esta carencia se ofrece en primer lugar una reconstrucción sistemática de la EE. En segundo lugar se analizan las consecuencias ontoepistémicas de un concepto de "razón" que, pensado por la EE como producto de la historia natural, no renuncia a determinar las condiciones de posibilidad de la verdad en general. Una de esas consecuencias sería tener que afirmar la estructura "fisiomorfa" de la razón.

PACHO, Julián. The Relationship Between the Humanities and the Natural and Technical Sciences (in German). Deut Z Phil, 38(9), 818-823, 1990.

Untersucht wird die Verantwortung der Geisteswissenschaften im Umgang mit Natur und Technik. Hierzu werden die in geisteswissenschaftlichen Kreisen tradierten Begriffen von Mensch, Natur und Technik berücksichtigt und folgende Thesen vertreten. Die allerseits bedauerte Trennung von *Natur*- und *Geistes*wissenschaften fördern die letzten durch ihren naturfremden Menschenbegriff, menschenfeindlichen Technikbegriff und selbstgefällige Ignoranz um die Natur. Darum gibt es keinen, der heutigen Naturwissenschaf gerechten Humanismus. Schliesslich wird die geläufige These bestritten, die dringende Wende im Umgang mit der Natur könne durch Rückbesinnung auf die "humanistische" Kultur erfolgen, sofern diese das Wissen um die Natur weiterhin nicht als ihre Sache betrachtet.

PADEN, Roger. Moral Metaphysics, Moral Revolution, and Environmental Ethics. Agr Human Values, 7(3-4), 70-79, Sum-Fall 90.

Many philosophers and environmentalists have advocated the development of a revolutionary new moral paradigm that treats natural objects as "morally considerable" in-themselves, independently of their relation to human beings. Often it is claimed that we need to develop a radically new theory of value to underpin this new paradigm. In this paper, I argue against this position and in favor of a more critical approach to environmental ethics. Such a critical approach, I believe, is not only more politically sound, but it is not open to the kinds of objections that afflict "biocentric moral theories" that depend on a conception of the intrinsic worth of nature. In the first sections of the paper, I develop a set of these criticisms. In the last part of the paper, I turn to examine the advantages of a critical approach to environmental ethics.

PADGETT, Alan G. La rationalité du théisme: la philosophie de la religion de Richard Swinburne. Arch Phil, 53(4), 603-629, O-D 90.

Richard Swinburne is one of England's most important philosophers of religion. His work in the philosophy of science and probability lays a foundation for his philosophy of religion. Swinburne's basic position is that, according to the standards of reason used in science and history, God probably exists. His rationalism in religious matters can be seen in his dealing with the problems of religious language, and the relationship between faith and reason. He defines "God" in a way that differs slightly from classical theism, insisting that theistic belief be coherent. He then argues that this God, more likely than not, exists, given our standards of argument in science and history. The argument that God exists is inductive in nature. It is a "cumulative case," not a deductive argument. Swinburne presents the traditional arguments for the existence of God in a modern, rigorous format which is fully aware of contemporary analytic philosophy and natural science.

PADGETT, Jack F. The Ethical Theory of Peter A Bertocci. Personalist Forum, 7(1), 51-72, Spr 91.

Peter Bertocci's ethical theory, rooted in the Personalism of Brightman and Bowne, emphasizes the worth and dignity of human beings. Bertocci's ethics combines a particular variant of rule-utilitarianism with his own version of virtue ethics, long before virtue ethics became a popular view. His ethical theory and its application to sex, love, and marriage offer a systematic attempt to clarify the meaning and relevance of ethics for daily life. By combining universal moral principles and a virtuous character, both held to be essential for the good life, Bertocci proposes a distinctive if not definitive systematic ethical theory.

PADIA, Chandrakala. Bertrand Russell and Liberty: A Question Revisited. J Indian Counc Phil Res, 5(3), 35-41, My-Ag 88.

PADILLA GÁLVEZ, Jesús. Wittgenstein sobre la noción de regla en Frege. Dialogos, 26(57), 101-111, Ja 91.

This paper analyzes the concept of rules presented in Frege's work. To do so, the criticism of his formal theory is discussed in detail from an informal viewpoint, elaborating at the same time the semantic argument proposed within it. Subsequently, we turn our attention to the connection between Frege's theory and the criticism made by Wittgenstein with respect to the concept of "Following a Rule". Wittgenstein's arguments against Frege's theory are represented extensively, while exposing in detail the corroboration of the language of thought mentioned. In this manner, this article attempts to underscore the bond between Frege and Wittgenstein.

PADILLA, Leonel Eduardo. La naturaleza y la historia como fundamento para un concepto renovada de razón. Rev Filosof (Costa Rica), 28(67-68), 149-152, D 90.

It is frequent to find sceptic and nihilistic attitudes in opposition to ideas of rationality as elements of discourse, modes of production, cultures and styles of life. Moreover, it is possible to affirm of the nature the proper rationality of vital teleconomic process, and the growing knowledge of their mechanisms, permit us to catch a glimpse of relational human being—nature, exempt of ecological damage and grounded in the guide idea of a liberating reason. (edited)

PADRUTT, Hanspeter. Heideggers Denken und die Ökologie. Heidegger Stud, 6, 43-66, 1990.

Heidegger's thinking as a 'saga about human living' and ecology (in the broad, not biological sense; oikein: living, dwelling) can be said to be neighbors. Three of Heidegger's fundamental thoughts prove themselves to be particularly important in this context: phenomenology's 'reserved forwardness', the 'shift of position' from the objectivizing subject to Da-sein (being there), and the possibility of a 'turning' out of the forgottenness of being. Since however the leading ideas of the ecological movement are partly captive to modern (Cartesian) objectivizing subjectivism and are generally rooted in occidental metaphysics, they are subjected and exposed to Heidegger's thinking. Some critical objections against Heidegger's thinking are also considered. Further references: Hanspeter Padrutt, *Der epochale Winter*, Diogenes, Zurich 1984, paperback 1990.

PAETZOLD, Heinz. "The Cultural Dynamics of Philosophical Aesthetics" in *XIth International Congress in Aesthetics, Nottingham 1988*, WOODFIELD, Richard (ed), 147-150. Nottingham, Nottingham Polytech, 1990.

The article outlines the development of philosophical aesthetics from German idealism to the aesthetics of postmodernity. The accent lies on the cultural impact of aesthetics. The article argues that we have three paradigms of aesthetic rationality today: the autonomous art, the problems of avantgardism and the architecture. Architecture, however, is closely related to the urban way of life. We have to avoid aesthetic absolutism, but we also must take into account the impact of aesthetics for our everyday-life.

PAGE, Carl. Philosophical Hermeneutics and its Meaning for Philosophy. Phil Today, 35(2), 127-136, Sum 91.

Gadamer's philosophical hermeneutics points to two basic questions: 1) what is philosophical about hermeneutics and 2) should philosophy be hermeneutical? Philosophical hermeneutics is philosophical because it is a metaphysically committed doctrine of human understanding. As such it concerns the metaphysical constitution of the act of understanding. It is therefore prior to all questions about understanding's procedures or activities. This is also its universality. Philosophical hermeneutics does not, however, prove that philosophy must be hermeneutical. It rests on an undefended presupposition of understanding's finitude that yields no reason why some but not all prejudices are capable of being transcended.

PAGE, Carl. The Truth about Lies in Plato's *Republic*. Ancient Phil, 11(1), 1-33, Spr 91.

Lies figure most thematically in the *Republic* than is commonly appreciated. Potential deceit is written into the foundations of the "city in speech." Conspicuously tied to the question of rule, lies subsequently emerge as necessary for the development of political responsibility (paedeutic lies) and the prevention of political pathology (pharmacological lies). The latter class includes the infamous "noble lie." Lying is commonly held to be always immoral because it compromises autonomy. Socrates's account reveals neither tyranny nor paternalism but a deep appreciation of the human soul's natural infirmities for the higher goods of political life. On this basis the morality of Socrates's lies are in each case defended in detail.

PAGE, Carl. The Unjust Treatment of Polemarchus. Hist Phil Quart, 7(3), 243-267, Jl 90.

In Plato's *Republic*, Polemarchus is often taken as the mouthpiece for a conventional and untenable notion of justice. A closer reading reveals Polemarchus has a much deeper symbolic role to play in the *Republic* as a whole. Polemarchus is animated by a view of friendship that is at the heart of all political association, a view that entails the gentlemanly and loyal defense of what is near and therefore dear. In order to defend his own claim to political responsibility, Socrates shows that philosophy is consistent with the spirit of Polemarchian friendship, but without capitulating to its major weakness, viz. being disposed to deal unjustly with what is outside of the circle of attachment.

PAGLIANI, Piero. Remarks on Special Lattices and Related Constructive Logics with Strong Negation. Notre Dame J Form Log, 31(4), 515-528, Fall 90.

The main purposes of this paper are to provide an algebraic analysis of a certain class of constructive logics with strong negation, and to investigate algebraically the relations between strong and nonconstructible negations definable in these logics. The tools used in this analysis are varieties of algebraic structures of ordered pairs called *special N-lattices* which were first introduced as algebraic models for Nelson's *constructive logic with strong negation* (CLSN). Via suitable restrictions of the domains, algebras of this type are shown to be algebraic models for the propositional fragments of E^0, CLSN, Intuitionistic Logic, and $E^0{}_+$. The differences between E^0 and CLSN are then studied, via the interrelations that the related algebras exhibit among strong and nonconstructible negations, properties of filters, and their behavior with respect to classically valid formulas.

PAINE, Lynn Sharp. Corporate Policy and the Ethics of Competitor Intelligence Gathering. J Bus Ethics, 10(6), 423-436, Je 91.

Competitor intelligence, information that helps managers understand their competitors, is highly valued in today's marketplace. Firms, large and small, are taking a more systematic approach to competitor intelligence collection. At the same time, information crimes and litigation over information disputes appear to be on the rise and survey data show widespread approval of unethical and questionable intelligence-gathering methods. Despite these developments, few corporations address the ethics of intelligence gathering in their corporate codes of conduct. Neither managers nor management educators have paid sufficient attention to this topic. From a review of questionable intelligence-gathering practices reported in various literatures, the author identifies some important ethical principles to help managers draw the line between legitimate and illegitimate methods of information acquisition. The paper also discusses the costs of failure to heed these principles and suggests steps managers can take to provide ethical leadership in this area.

PAINE, Lynn Sharp. Trade Secrets and the Justification of Intellectual Property: A Comment on Hettinger. Phil Pub Affairs, 20(3), 247-263, Sum 91.

This paper examines the rationale for trade secret principles. The author argues that trade secret protection is rooted in respect for individual liberty, confidential relationships, common morality, and fair competition. While trade secret protection may tend to promote the dissemination and use of ideas, this tendency alone does not fully explain or justify it. More generally, the paper argues for an approach to intellectual property that acknowledges the importance of ideas as dimensions of personality and shared ideas as foundations for cooperative relationships. Natural resources and tangible property models are inappropriate analogies for understanding rights in ideas. The paper argues that the burden of justification rests on those who favor disclosure obligations and general rights of access to ideas rather than, as Hettinger asserts, on those who support private rights to ideas.

PAINE, Lynn Sharp. Work and Family: Should Parents Feel Guilty? Pub Affairs Quart, 5(1), 81-99, Ja 91.

Many career-oriented parents feel guilty about the time they spend away from their children. This article examines the conventional view that these feelings are irrational, a remnant of a former era or a vestige of a mistaken psychology. The author argues that the conventional view is based on mistaken assumptions about the nature and origins of parents' guilt of feelings. She develops and defends an ideal of parenthood that explains why many parents continue to feel guilty about entrusting their children to the care of others, despite the reassurances of many child care experts. The author concludes that the absence-related guilt felt by many parents will be resolved only through radical changes in the patterns of work and career development associated with success in business and the professions.

PAKALUK, Michael (ed). *Other Selves: Philosophers on Friendship*. Indianapolis, Hackett, 1991.

The central philosophical works on friendship in the Western tradition are brought together in a single volume, to provide the background necessary for contemporary reflection on the subject. Included in the collection are: Plato's *Lysis*; Aristotle's *Ethics* VIII and IX; Cicero's *De Amicitia* (in its entirety); selections from Aelred of Rievaulx, Aquinas, Kant and Kierkegaard; and essays by Montaigne, Bacon, Emerson, and Telfer. The editor's introduction discusses the importance of friendship for contemporary moral philosophy, and headnotes highlight important themes in, and interconnections among, the selections.

PAL, Jagat. G E Moore on the Values of Whole and Parts: A Critique. Indian Phil Quart, 18(1), 73-86, Ja 91.

Moore claims that the value of whole differs in degree from the sum of the values of its parts. This paper is an attempt to show that this claim of Moore cannot be maintained consistently within his framework of ethics.

PAL, Jagat. The Open Question Argument. J Indian Counc Phil Res, 7(1), 145-150, S-D 89.

In this paper an attempt is made to show that Moore's open question argument, though a useful device for testing definition of good, does not logically establish his thesis that good is simple and indefinable within his framework of ethics. Because his argument rests on his notion of meaning and his notion of meaning is logically independent of simplicity and indefinability. Indefinability of good is based on simplicity; and that simplicity of good cannot be established on the basis of the intelligibility of the open question, since they are logically unconnected.

PALASINSKI, Marek. The Answer to Dziobiak's Question. Bull Sect Log, 19(2), 56-57, Je 90.

PALMA, A B. Philosophizing. Philosophy, 66(255), 41-51, Ja 91.

PALMER, W S (trans) and BERGSON, Henri and PAUL, N M (trans). *Matter and Memory*. Cambridge, MIT Pr, 1991.

PALMQUIST, Stephen R. Four Perspectives on Moral Judgement: The Rational Principles of Jesus and Kant. Heythrop J, 32(2), 216-232, Ap 91.

This article argues that Kant's conception of the Moral Law, far from contradicting Christian morality, complements three of Jesus' most important moral principles. Jesus' "Judge not..." can be viewed as a transcendental principle, thus corresponding to Kant's idea of practical freedom. Kant's "Do your duty" is basically a logical principle, not unlike Jesus' "Be perfect...". Jesus' "Do unto others..." is best regarded as an empirical principle. And Jesus' "Love God and man..." can be interpreted as proposing a hypothetical principle. Hence, the rational principles of Jesus and Kant can be recognized to be interrelated perspectives in a single moral system.

PANCERA, Carlo. "Una uguale educazione?" in *Égalité Uguaglianza*, FERRARI, Jean (ed), 81-92. Napoli, Liguori, 1990.

PANDHARIPANDE, Rajeshwari. Metaphor in the Language of Religion. J Dharma, 15(3), 185-203, Jl-S 90.

PANDIT, G L. Science and Truthlikeness. J Indian Counc Phil Res, 5(3), 125-138, My-Ag 88.

The paper explores *new priorities* for scientific realism as a dynamic framework to explain *how* scientific progress is possible or what makes it rational. In doing so it dispenses with the traditional priorities for the assumption that science aims at truth and that the progress which a science can make from an earlier to a later theory is a matter of their comparative degrees of *truthlikeness*. Thus, a version of scientific realism, alternative to Popperian/neo-Popperian versions, is identified for investigation within the framework of the methodology of theory-problem interactive systems the author has proposed elsewhere (1983, BSPS 73).

PANICHAS, George E. The Basic Right to Liberty. J Soc Phil, 21(1), 55-76, Spr 90.

This paper concerns the questions of how the right to liberty is best understood and in what sense this right is a basic human right. Arguments are offered to show that this right cannot be a general right to license, nor can the right comprise sets of either unilateral or bilateral liberty-rights correlating with prima facie duties of noninterference. A new model of the right to liberty, which views the right as a moral power-right, is offered and defended as the model for securing the right to liberty as a basic human right which is pre-theoretically compatible with different theories of such rights.

PANICHAS, George E and HOBART, Michael E. Marx's Theory of Revolutionary Change. Can J Phil, 20(3), 383-401, S 90.

Recent scholarship, most notably that of G A Cohen, offers sympathetic and highly plausible interpretations of Marx's theory of history, his historical materialism. Such interpretations hold that the same set of factors explaining changes societies undergo within the course of a given historical epoch explain as well changes between historical epochs, i.e., social revolutions. This paper argues that even the most plausible reconstruction of the theory of history, that which employs functional explanations, cannot account for changes between historical epochs. Historical materialism, therefore, fails as a theory of revolutionary change.

PANT, Laurie W and COHEN, Jeffrey R. Beyond Bean Counting: Establishing High Ethical Standards in the Public Accounting Profession. J Bus Ethics, 10(1), 45-56, Ja 91.

Business professions are increasingly faced with the question of how to best monitor the ethical behavior of their members. Conflicts could exist between a profession's desire to self-regulate and its accountability to the public at large. This study examines how members of one profession, public accounting, evaluate the relative effectiveness of various self-regulatory and externally imposed mechanisms for promoting a climate of high ethical behavior. Specifically, the roles of independent public accountants, regulatory and rule setting agencies, and undergraduate accounting education are investigated. (edited)

PANTIN, I and PLIMAK, E. The Ideas of Karl Marx at a Turning Point in Human Civilization. Soviet Stud Phil, 30(1), 42-69, Sum 91.

PAOLETTI, Laura. Due note: Ritorni Rosminiani—Il momento di Ugo Spirito. Filosofia, 41(3), 409-426, S-D 90.

PAOLINELLI, Marco. La dignità dell'uomo da Kant a Hegel. Riv Filosof Neo-Scolas, 82(2-3), 256-286, Ap-S 90.

PAPE, Helmut. Not Every Object of a Sign has Being. Trans Peirce Soc, 27(2), 141-177, Spr 91.

Peirce has a theory of proper names which likens proper names to common nouns and assigns to them the function of picking out the internal objects of our thought. The univocity of reference is not explained by the semantical role of organising thought contents but is achieved by their *use*. Peirce's view of proper names is compared with H N Castaneda's restricted variable/retrieval theory of proper names. A Sameness Principle for objects of thought and signs is introduced. The Meinongian thesis that there are objects which have neither existence nor being is a mere consequence of the functional meaning of all expressions which are purely referential.

PAPINEAU, David. "Has Popper Been a Good Thing?" in *Imre Lakatos and Theories of Scientific Change*, GAVROGLU, Kostas (ed), 431-440. Norwell, Kluwer, 1989.

This paper argues that certain aspects of Popper's thought have exerted a bad influence on subsequent philosophy of science. In particular, his focus on "acceptance" rather than belief has stopped philosophers of science making the obvious responses to Kuhn's and Feyerabend's relativistic arguments. And his scepticism about scientific truth has encouraged antirealist ideas about the evaluation of methodologies.

PAPINEAU, David. "Knowledge of Mathematical Objects" in *Physicalism in Mathematics*, IRVINE, Andrew D (ed), 155-182. Norwell, Kluwer, 1990.

Even if Hartry Field's fictionalist programme is technically adequate, and so shows how we *can* avoid beliefs about mathematical objects, there remains the question of why, if at all, we *ought* to. Papineau argues that the best defence of mathematical fictionalism lies in the impotence of mathematical proofs to establish categorical mathematical theorems, and defends this argument against Crispin Wright's neo-Fregeanism and Harold Hodes's neo-Russellianism.

PAPINEAU, David. The Reason Why: Response to Crane. Analysis, 51(1), 37-40, Ja 91.

In "Why Supervenience?" (*Analysis* 50, 1990, 66-71) Papineau argued that the supervenience of the mental on the physical followed from the completeness of physics. In "Why Indeed?" (*Analysis* 51, 1991, 32-37) Tim Crane retorted that the completeness of physics is either trivial or false. In this paper Papineau responds that, even if the completeness of physics *per se* is understood so as to become definitionally trivial, it is nontrivial whether mental categories thereby become defined as physical; moreover, if they don't, as seems likely, then their supervenience is nontrivial too, and follows from the completeness of physics as before.

PAPINEAU, David. Response to Ehring's 'Papineau on Causal Asymmetry'. Brit J Phil Sci, 39(4), 521-525, D 88.

PAPINEAU, David. Truth and Teleology. Philosophy, 27, 21-43, 90 Supp.

This paper defends both the teleological theory of mental representation and the rather old idea that the truth condition of a belief is that condition which guarantees that actions based on that belief will succeed. It turns out that these two ideas complement each other: the teleological theory is inadequate unless it incorporates the success-guaranteeing account; conversely, the success-guaranteeing account is incomplete until it is placed in a teleological context.

PAPPAS, George S. Berkeley and Common Sense Realism. Hist Phil Quart, 8(1), 27-42, Ja 91.

PAPPAS, George S. A Second Copy Thesis in Hume? Hume Stud, 17(1), 51-59, Ap 91.

PAPRZYCKA, Katarzyna. Is the Skeptical Attitude the Attitude of a Skeptic? Auslegung, 17(2), 119-123, Sum 91.

A genuine skeptic opens our minds to the possibility of deception. From this one ought not to draw the conclusion that we cannot know anything, as does the dogmatic skeptic (in effect identifying our actual world with the possible world of complete deception). Rather, one should take this claim as an invitation to consider the whole range of possibilities—worlds where we are deceived in various degrees. It is argued that the same strategy is exhibited by some scientific procedures (reduction, for instance). Thus, if the skeptic succeeds at all he merely effects a switch in the level of inquiry.

PAPRZYCKA, Katarzyna. A Note on Van Fraassen's Explanatory Contrastiveness. Method Sci, 24(1), 51-53, 1991.

PAPULI, Giovanni. Italian Marxism and Philosophy of Culture (in Polish). Ann Univ Mariae Curie-Phil, 10, 13-21, 1985.

In this paper, the author describes the situation of Italian philosophy beginning with the first half of the 20th century, and against this background he presents the evolution of Marxism in Italy and the process of the emergence of philosophy of culture. However, the main line of argument concerns the relations between Marxism and philosophy of culture and the tasks of philosophy of culture resulting from them. The connections of Marxism and philosophy of culture are here evident, since for Papuli the moment of the creation of the foundations of objective philosophy of culture is connected with the name of Labriola; it is then continued and developed in the writings of Gramsci and Banfi. In recent decades Italian Marxism has been directed towards the perspectives of the relations of culture with politics, authority, society, etc., that is, far from the apparent neutrality of knowledge. (edited)

PAQUET, Bernard. Sémiologie visuelle, peinture et intertextualité. Horiz Phil, 1(1), 35-55, 1990.

PAQUIN, Nycole. *L'objet-peinture: Pour une théorie de la réception*. Lasalle, Hurtubise, 1991.

PAQUIN, Nycole. Sémiotique des "genres": Une théorie de la réception. Horiz Phil, 1(2), 125-135, 1991.

PARADICE, David B and DEJOIE, Roy M. The Ethical Decision-Making Processes of Information Systems Workers. J Bus Ethics, 10(1), 1-21, Ja 91.

An empirical investigation was conducted to determine whether management information systems (MIS) majors, on average, exhibit ethical decision-making processes that differ from students in other functional business areas. The research also examined whether the existence of a computer-based information system in an ethical dilemma influences ethical decision-making processes. Although student subjects were used, the research instrument has been highly correlated with educational levels attained by adult subjects in similar studies. Thus, we feel that our results have a high likelihood of generalization to the MIS professional community. The results indicate that MIS majors exhibit more socially-oriented ethical decision-making processes than non-MIS majors measured by the Defining Issues Test. The results also indicate that the existence of a computer-based information system in an ethical dilemma may influence ethical decision-making processes. The study makes no statement regarding MIS majors making "more (or less) ethical" decisions. The business ethics literature is reviewed, details of the study are presented, implications for management are considered, and directions for future research are suggested.

PARAIN-VIAL, Jeanne. Transcendance ou présence? Diotima, 18, 41-45, 1990.

Les oeuvres d'art sont-elles les fruits d'une inspiration venue d'un monde transcendant ou la manifestation de la puissance créatrice humaine? Pour soutenir la thèse de l'inspiration qui correspond à l'expérience de beaucoup de grands artistes (de Platon à Proust en passant par Haydn, Mozart, Rilke, etc.). L'auteur montre que sousjacentes aux données sensibles (par ex. les sons en musique) l'attention humaine découvre des formes invisibles (par ex. la mélodie) qui elles-mêmes manifestent un sens; Celui-ci nous comble de joie quand précisément les formes sont belles. L'artiste met donc toutes ses forces physiques et intellectuelles à la disposition de la présence invisible d'une essence qu'il révèle aux autres par l'intermédiaire de l'oeuvre d'art.

PAREKH, Bhikhu. "Gandhi's Quest for a Nonviolent Political Philosophy" in *Celebrating Peace*, ROUNER, Leroy S (ed), 162-178. Notre Dame, Univ Notre Dame Pr, 1990.

Mahatme Gandhi felt that much of traditional political philosophy was statist and more or less accepted violence as a legitimate mode of political action. He set out to construct a new political philosophy based on a quasi-absolutist commitment to non-violence. In this article, the author outlines Gandhi's new political philosophy, especially his conceptions of freedom, equality and non-violent revolution. He compares these with their traditional western counterparts and examines their coherence and validity.

PAREL, A J (ed & trans) and MACHIAVELLI, Niccolò. Allocution Made to a Magistrate. Polit Theory, 18(4), 525-527, N 90.

This is the first English translation of Machiavelli's oration on justice. He wrote this oration in the *protestatio de justitia* style of Florentine humanism, but probably did not deliver it himself. The value of this oration lies in the fact that it shows that Machiavelli had a sound grasp of the classical and the Christian conceptions of justice. It adds to our knowledge of Machiavelli's thought on an important issue.

PAREL, A J. Machiavelli's Notions of Justice: Text and Analysis. Polit Theory, 18(4), 528-544, N 90.

This article surveys Machiavelli's thoughts on justice. Though he had a thorough grasp of the classical and the Christian conceptions of justice, the position he adopts is that of positivism: humans do not have a notion of natural justice, they arrive at the notion of justice only after law and state are established on the basis of force. But positive justice is an essential requirement of good government. Jus gentium and bellum justum are understood by Machiavelli in a positivistic fashion. They are for him instruments of reason of state.

PAREL, Anthony J. "Justice and Love in the Political Thought of St Augustine" in *Grace, Politics and Desire: Essays on Augustine*, MEYNELL, Hugo A (ed), 71-84. Calgary, Univ Calgary Pr, 1990.

This article examines how Augustine arrives at the idea that love is a more coherent principle of the political community than is civic justice. The latter conceals a good deal of injustice, especially when seen against the standard of 'true' justice. The division of regimes into just and unjust ones becomes unsatisfactory. On the other hand the division of regimes on the basis of the object of their love gives a better understanding of the true nature of the political community.

PARENS, Erik. From Philosophy to Politics: On Nietzsche's Ironic Metaphysics of Will to Power. Man World, 23(4), 393-404, O 90.

PARENS, Erik. From Philosophy to Politics: On Nietzsche's Ironic Metaphysics of Will to Power. Man World, 24(2), 169-180, Ap 91.

PARENT, David. Nietzsche's Arctic Zone of Cognition and Post-Structuralism. Hist Euro Ideas, 11, 759-767, 1989.

In *The Will to Power*, Nietzsche carries the sceptical philosophising of Descartes, Hume, Kant, and Schopenhauer to their logical culminations, whereas they themselves had stopped short of this. Although he is not a phenomenologist before the fact since his perspectivism and phenomenalism do not bracket out or deny all reality, his harsh intellectual asceticism leaves little of the world standing. The question thus arises whether his nihilism—and the poststructuralists—may not contain a distorting bias: a one-sided application of Occham's razor prohibiting affirmative statements, while giving free rein to epistemological scepticism and negative ones.

PARGETTER, Robert. Kinship and Moral Relativity. Philosophia (Israel), 20(4), 345-361, F 91.

PARGETTER, Robert and YOUNG, Robert and BIGELOW, John. Land, Well-Being and Compensation. Austl J Phil, 68(3), 330-346, S 90.

PARGETTER, Robert and BIGELOW, John. Vectors and Change. Brit J Phil Sci, 40(3), 289-306, S 89.

Vectors, we will argue, are not just mathematical abstractions. They are also physical properties—universals. What make them distinctive are the rich and varied essences of these universals, and the complex pattern of internal relations which hold amongst them.

PARIS, J and VENCOVSKÁ, A. "Inexact and Inductive Reasoning" in *Logic, Methodology and Philosophy of Science, VIII*, FENSTAD, J E (ed), 111-120. New York, Elsevier Science, 1989.

PARK, Woosuk. *Haecceitas* and the Bare Particular. Rev Metaph, 44(2), 375-397, D 90.

The major thesis of this paper is that at least from Scotus's point of view *haecceitas* cannot be understood as an individual essence or a coordinate quality. Once the misinterpretation of *haecceitas* as an individual essence or a coordinate quality is corrected, the view which directs our attention to the similarities between *haecceitas* and the bare particular can be appreciated much better. But there are also some apparent differences between *haecceitas* and the bare particular. The identification of some such differences is the secondary object of this paper.

PARK, Woosuk. Scotus, Frege, and Bergmann. Mod Sch, 67(4), 259-273, My 90.

Scotus's *haecceitas* and Bergmann's bare particular share many interesting characteristics. But they have also some crucial differences. This paper discusses some structural roots of such differences between *haecceitas* and the bare particular by using Frege as a medium. Cocchiarella's recent discussion of Frege's function-correlate enables us to assimilate Frege's ontology to the Avicennian-Scotistic tripartite ontology of individuals, universals, and common natures in themselves. Since Bergmann himself discussed Frege's ontology extensively, to the extent that Scotus's ontology is similar to Frege's ontology, we may have indirect evidence concerning how Bergmann would think about this interpretation of Scotus's *haecceitas* ontology.

PARKER, Ian. Discourse: Definitions and Contradictions. Phil Psych, 3(2-3), 189-204, 1990.

With the question "What is 'discourse'?" as the starting point, this paper addresses ways of identifying particular *discourses*, and attends to how these discourses should be distinguished from texts. The emergence of discourse analysis within psychology, and the continuing influence of linguistic and poststructuralist ideas on practitioners, provide the basis on which discourse-analytic research can be developed fruitfully. This paper discusses the descriptive, analytic and educative functions of discourse analysis, and addresses the cultural and political questions which arise when discourse analysts reflect on their activity. Suggestions for an adequate definition of discourse are proposed and supported by seven criteria which should be adopted to identify discourses, and which attend to contradictions between and within them. Three additional criteria are then suggested to relate discourse analysis to wider political issues.

PARKER, Ian. Real Things: Discourse, Context and Practice. Phil Psych, 3(2-3), 227-233, 1990.

The paper defends a realist approach to discourse, and outlines different varieties of 'object status' that may be accorded to items marked by nouns in discourse. Three realms are described: ontological object status; epistemological object status; and moral/political object status. A realist approach here also functions as a reply to criticisms of an earlier paper in the same issue of *Philosophical Psychology*, a paper which offers definitions of discourse and ten criteria for the identification of discourses.

PARKER, Kelly. The Values of a Habitat. Environ Ethics, 12(4), 353-368, Wint 90.

Recent severe environmental crises have brought us to recognize the need for a broad reevaluation of the relation of humans to their environments. I suggest that we consider the human-nature relation from two overlapping perspectives, each informed by the pragmatic philosophy of experience. The first is an anthropology, according to which humans are viewed as being radically continuous with their environments. The second is a comprehensive ecology, according to which both "natural" and "nonnatural" environments are studied as artificial habitats of the human organism (i.e., as artifacts). The pragmatic approach has two features which make it promising as a way to ground environmental thinking. First, it allows us to avoid a human-nature dichotomy and the many problems which that dichotomy has traditionally engendered. Second, it ties environmental questions to a common cultural experience and a philosophical position from which environmentalists can effectively engage mainstream educational and political discussions.

PARKES, Graham (trans) and KEIJI, Nishitani and AIHARA, Setsuko (trans). *The Self-Overcoming of Nihilism: Nishitani Keiji*. Albany, SUNY Pr, 1990.

In this work from 1949 the Japanese philosopher Nishitani Keiji (1900-1990) sketches the history of European nihilism as the context for a consideration of how the problem posed by nihilism might be resolved. In the course of three chapters on Nietzsche, and one each on Max Stirner, Russian nihilism, and Heidegger. Nishitani shows the way in which nihilism—as long as it is plumbed to its uttermost depths—will eventually "overcome itself." In the book's final two chapters, dealing with nihilism in the modern Japanese context and the problem of atheism, the background of Zen thought from which Nishitani approaches his topic comes to the fore.

PARKINSON, G H R. "Definition, Essence, and Understanding in Spinoza" in *Central Themes in Early Modern Philosophy*, COVER, J A (ed), 49-67. Indianapolis, Hackett, 1990.

The paper discusses Spinoza's reasons for using a geometrical mode of presentation in his *Ethics*. It argues that he is concerned, not just to demonstrate truths, but also to provide explanations. This view is defended by a consideration of Spinoza's use of definitions. Although these definitions are stipulative in form, Spinoza claims that they are true and that they state the essence of the thing defined. In discussing this claim, a distinction is drawn between the nuclear sense of the term 'essence' and the formal definition offered in Part II of the *Ethics*.

PARLEJ, Piotr. History, Historicism, Narratives: Identity in the Philosophy of History of Karl Popper. Int Stud Phil, 23(1), 31-46, 1991.

The Covering Laws Model doubly distorts the individual's uniqueness in historical accounts. First, narrative distortion of the singular phenomenon is due to the "narrative use of the sentence" (F R Ankersmitt). The individual can be conceived as unique (un-iterable) only in narrative accounts (stories), but narrative concatenation preserves only common, generalizable properties. Second, while narratives normally follow the protocol of *identification*, they abstract, due to their CLM-structure, only the repeatable features of entities, and arbitrarily shift into the mode of *explanation* (by deduction): description becomes prediction (PTO).

PARMAN, Susan. *Dream and Culture: An Anthropological Study of the Western Intellectual Tradition*. New York, Praeger, 1990.

PARODI, Alessandra (trans) and PENCO, Carlo. Gottlob Frege, lettere a Wittgenstein. Epistemologia, 12(2), 331-351, Jl-D 89.

PARRET, Herman. Le problématologique devant la faculté de juger. Rev Int Phil, 44(174), 352-369, 1990.

PARRY, Richard D. The Intelligible World-Animal in Plato's *Timaeus*. J Hist Phil, 29(1), 13-32, Ja 91.

Expanding on a previous article, I extend my analysis of the intelligible animal which contains all other intelligible animals to give a deeper insight into Plato's account of cosmology and of his theory of Forms. Analyzing the notion of containment which is at the heart of this peculiar Form, I show that this relation of containing is not that of genus to species, of entailment, or of class inclusion. Rather an important clue is taken from Plato's example of the sphere—"the shape which contains all the other shapes"—in order to explicate this peculiar notion of containment among Forms.

PARRY, William T and HACKER, Edward A. *Aristotelian Logic*. Albany, SUNY Pr, 1991.

PARSONS, Charles. "Genetic Explanation in *The Roots of Reference*" in *Perspectives on Quine*, BARRETT, Robert (ed), 273-290. Cambridge, Blackwell, 1990.

PARSONS, Charles. The Structuralist View of Mathematical Objects. Synthese, 84(3), 303-346, S 90.

PARSONS, E D and COULTER, Jeff. The Praxiology of Perception: Visual Orientations and Practical Action. Inquiry, 33(3), 251-272, S 90.

This paper is concerned with the development of the idea that most of what is glossed as "perception" turns out to consist in arrays of visual orientations, heterogeneous forms of *activities* and achievements, irreducible to physiological characterization. Some philosophical and sociological consequences of this point are explored.

PARSONS, Terence. *Events in the Semantics of English: A Study in Subatomic Semantics*. Cambridge, MIT Pr, 1991.

PARSONS, Terence. True Contradictions. Can J Phil, 20(3), 335-353, S 90.

This is a critical evaluation of views put forth by Graham Priest in his book *In Contradiction*. Priest holds that some sentences are both true and false, and, as a result, some contradictions are true. I argue that Priest's view is as coherent as its major competitor (which he rejects), the view that some sentences lack truth-value. But Priest's own arguments against truth-value gap views are uncompelling. Each view apparently cannot be stated without the statement violating the view itself; in both cases this difficulty can be got round by distinguishing denial of S from assertion of the negation of S.

PARTRIDGE, Ernest. "If Peace Were at Hand, How Would We Know It?" in *Issues in War and Peace: Philosophical Inquiries*, KUNKEL, Joseph (ed), 83-94. Wolfeboro, Longwood, 1989.

Despite radical reform in the Soviet Union, the Reagan Administration proposes no reduction in the Defense budget. This leads one to wonder just what behavior on the part of President Gorbachev is required to cause the US administration to change its opinions and policies regarding the Soviet Union. I argue that there is virtually no imaginable evidence, consistent with Mr. Gorbachev remaining in power, that might convince the determined conservative that the Soviet Union is no longer a threat to our security. Given certain assumptions, discussed here, the doctrine of "the Evil Empire" is practically (though not logically) non-falsifiable.

PARUSNIKOVA, Zuzana. Contemporary Shapes of Scientific Realism (in Czechoslovakian). Filozof Cas, 38(5), 591-604, 1990.

This article singles out new, frequently contradictory tendencies in the development of scientific realism which constitutes an influential trend in the contemporary Anglo-Saxon philosophy of science. In the first part the author discusses two basic principles of scientific realism: the term of truth as correspondence between thinking and the outside world and the term of objective progress in science. In this context, the author points to the problematic nature of these requirements, consisting in their metaphysical character. In the second part of her article the author explains how scientific realism comes to grips with the problem of truth in the light of the discontinuity of knowledge. (edited)

PAS, Johan. On the Angular Component Map Modulo *P*. J Sym Log, 55(3), 1125-1129, S 90.

For application in number theory, we introduced in [J Pas, "Uniform p-adic cell decomposition and local zeta functions," *J Reine Angew Math* 339 (1989) 137-172] a first order language for valued fields. This language contains a symbol for an angular component map modulo P. In this paper we give some partial results on the existence of such a map on an arbitrary valued field. We also prove that the language is essentially stronger than the natural language for p-adic fields in the sense that the angular component map modulo P cannot be defined, uniformly for almost all primes p, in terms of the natural language for p-adic fields.

PASK, Gordon. Correspondence, Consensus, and Coherence and the Rape of Democracy. Commun Cog, 23(2-3), 235-244, 1990.

The main intention of this paper is to compare and contrast the notions of coherence, correspondence and consensual truth valuation, especially insofar as they are given varied dynamic interpretation. In the context of society, culture, inter and intra personal interaction the prevailing confusion of these forms has counterproductive and occasionally, destructive consesquences. Many of these could be eliminated by a proper consideration of the fundamental matters involved and some appropriate methods for doing so are proposed.

PASKE, Gerald H. Genuine Moral Dilemmas and the Containment of Incoherence. J Value Inq, 24(4), 315-323, O 90.

It is sometimes argued that genuine moral dilemmas lead to the radical incoherence of ethics. I consider one such argument, that of Terrance McConnell, and show that such dilemmas do not necessarily lead to incoherence. The containment of incoherence requires that there be two independent, fundamental moral principles. I then show why it is at least plausible to suppose that there are two such principles.

PASKE, Gerald H. In Defense of Human "Chauvinism": A Response to R Routley and V Routley. J Value Inq, 25(3), 279-286, Jl 91.

R Routley and V Routley deplore the "invariable allocation of greater value or preference, on the basis of species, to humans." Contrary to their view, I argue that most human beings have moral priority over animals and, when a human being does not have moral priority over some animal there is still no moral obligation to give moral preference to the animal. Such purportedly chauvinistic treatment is justifiable because 1) most human beings possess morally relevant properties which give them priority over any animals, and 2) no animals possess properties which require that they be given priority over any humans.

PASKIN, David (trans) and REINER, Hans and ADLER, Pierre (trans). The Emergence and Original Meaning of the Name 'Metaphysics'. Grad Fac Phil J, 13(2), 23-53, 1990.

PASKOW, Alan. "My Poetic World Versus the Real, Scientific World" in *XIth International Congress in Aesthetics, Nottingham 1988*, WOODFIELD, Richard (ed), 151-155. Nottingham, Nottingham Polytech, 1990.

Once I sat on the rim of a large canyon and stared at the giant wall opposite me. An indefinable silence pervaded this scene. I perceived everything as in a way alive. I felt what I can only name...awe. My article outlines one possible answer to this vexatious question: Since I often experience the physical world as filled with poetic significance, how can my experience be reconciled with a scientific perspective that affirms its poetic *in*significance? How can I superimpose two images (for example, of the canyon)—the one of an awesom and purposive spectacle, the other of so much material shaped by geological forces—in order that I may see stereoscopically and thus live in one, unified world?

PASQUA, Hervé. L'unité-unicité de l'"esse" Thomiste. Rev Thomiste, 91(2), 302-308, Ap-Je 91.

PASQUALUCCI, Paolo. Hobbes and the Myth of "Final War". J Hist Ideas, 51(4), 647-657, O-D 90.

In chapter III of *Leviathan*, Hobbes's sentence "And when all the world is overcharged with inhabitants, then the last remedy of all is war; which provideth for every man, by victory, or death," does not express an isolated thought but a specific philosophy of history, according to which the development of the human race faces in overpopulation a problem which can be periodically solved by war only, until a final war of extermination decides for the definite destiny of a completely overpopulated world.

PASSANITI, Daniel. Capitalismo, Socialidad y participación. Sapientia, 45(178), 314-315, O-D 90.

PASSELL, Dan. Duties to Friends. J Value Inq, 25(2), 161-165, Ap 91.

PASSERIN D'ENTRÈVES, Maurizio. Communitarianism and the Question of Tolerance. J Soc Phil, 21(1), 77-91, Spr 90.

PASSERON, René. Art et cosmos. Diotima, 18, 46-50, 1990.

PASSMORE, John and GARCÍA MONSIVÁIS, Blanca (trans). Los universales culturales. Dianoia, 34(34), 27-34, 1988.

What light can philosophers, as distinct from anthropologists, throw on the question whether there are cultural universals? First they can clarify the view that such universals exist by distinguishing between a loose, a tight and a rigid interpretation of the assertion that there are such universals. It then emerges that the rigid view is clearly false, the loose view not of any particular interest to philosophers but the tight view raises fundamental epistemological issues.

PASTORE, Romano. Kant: del derecho de libertad a la exigencia racional del Estado. Rev Filosof (Venezuela), 13, 107-121, 1989.

PATEL, Kartikeya C. Wittgenstein on Emotion. Indian Phil Quart, 17(4), 407-427, O 90.

This essay critically evaluates Wittgenstein's analysis of emotion and compares it with James's theory of emotion. The essay focuses on Wittgenstein's claim that an emotion has a characteristic expression-behavior and argues that it is marred by the problems of circularity, individuation, and differentiation. I argue that these problems obtain due to Wittgenstein's failure to take into account the role of beliefs in general, those of phenomenological beliefs and subjective beliefs in particular. But despite these problems, Wittgenstein's analysis provides an important insight by bringing into light the contextual importance.

PATEL, Ramesh N. *Philosophy of the "Gita"*. New York, Lang, 1991.

This book argues that both Eastern and Western interpretations of the *Bhagavad-Gita* are methodologically inadequate and excessively speculative. It develops and applies a new hermeneutic called archaic coherentism, concluding that the Gita is best approached as coherent philosophical text rather than as religious scripture or literary work. Its careful exegesis unearths an innovative philosophy with complex but cogent concept structure exhibiting novel insights in philosophy of action and metaphysical theory. The work features a bridging of substance and process, with energy as ontic evanescence and individuation as *sui generis*. It also includes a new translation of the *Bhagavad-Gita*.

PATIÑO, Joel Rodríguez. El sentido del Universo en José Vasconcelos (2a parte). Logos (Mexico), 19(56), 51-100, My-Ag 91.

PATIÑO, Joel Rodríguez. El sentido del Universo en José Vasconcelos. Logos (Mexico), 19(55), 9-16, Ja-Ap 91.

El trabajo presenta el Universo entero en un proceso de transformación cósmica en el que va buscando su sentido final en su Creador. Inicia con la arquitectura del Universo desde los quanta y el átomo hasta la molécula y la célula viviente y de aquí al hombre. Continúa conla construcción y el acontecer histórico del Universo que, gracias a las revulsiones de la energía y a la Conciencia humana, se eleva desde elorden físico hasta el espíritu. Concluye con Dios sentido final del Universo en su totalidad, Mundo, Hombre e Historia.

PATIÑO, Joel Rodríguez. La tarea cósmica del hombre según Teilhard de Chardin. Logos (Mexico), 18(53), 83-95, My-Ag 90.

El trabajo, que continúa El Sentido del Universo, contiene la tarea que el hombre necesita realizar acerca del Universo en su totalided si quiere conservar su ser, su identidad y su valor en su hacer. La tarea cósmica comprende: El dominio del mundo, al que ha de servir el hombre si quiere servirse de èl. La Vida, de la cual se originó el hombre quien conlleva la responsabilidad de la Vida misma. El hacer del hombre para el hombre, en el que se fundamenta la trascendencia del Universo entero. Finalmente, el hacer del hombre para Dios como fin último de la—actividad humana en el Universo y sentido de su trascendencia.

PATOCKA, Jan. Space and Its Questions (in Czechoslovakian). Estetika, 28(1), 1-37, 1991.

PATOCKA, Jan. The World as a Whole and the World of Man (in Czechoslovakian). Filozof Cas, 38(6), 729-735, 1990.

Von der Auffassung des Raumes bei Kant ausgehend, entwickelt der Autor einige Motive der Erwägungen Finks über die Welt. Das Raumganze geht notwendig allen konkreten Beschränkungen voraus, die Beschränkung als solche gehört jedoch zum Ganzen mit derselben Notwendigkeit. Dieses Ganze bildet gemeinsam mit der Zeitdimension eine Fuge, die allem Einzelnen die Stelle und Weile seines Aufenthalts gewährt. Das Seiende erscheint auf dem Hintergrund dieser Fuge, die selbst keine Gestalt, welche in Erscheinung treten könnte, sondern herrschendes Gesetz des Erscheinens und Wiedersinkens des Seienden in die Verborgenheit ist. In dieser "Phänomenologie des Weltganzen" nimmt der Mensch eine Sonderstellung ein: er ist eins der zufälligen Seienden und zugleich ein Zentrum, dem alles, einschliesslich des Notwendigen, erscheint. Im Rahmen des gesamten Erscheinens gibt es also noch einen anderen Typ des Erscheinens, der in der Bewegung der menschlichen Existenz gründet; das Weltganze wird einerseits für diese Existenzbewegung zur Heimat, andererseits gewinnt es in ihr Transparenz und Verständlichkeit.

PATOMÄKI, Heikki. Concepts of "Action", "Structure" and "Power" in 'Critical Social Realism': A Positive and Reconstructive Critique. J Theor Soc Behav, 21(2), 221-250, Je 91.

The main objects of criticsm are Bhaskar's naturalist metaphors and his vacillating notion of social structure, which together are responsible for the structuralism of the TMSA. Furthermore, a re-interpreted and modified version of Habermas's theory of social action, and particularly of the idea of communicative action, is used to fill the logical gaps in 'critical realism'. Giddens's theory is criticized for three reasons. First, he has introduced an implausible definition of "structure," which is corrected along relationalist lines. Second, the critique of Gidden's conceptualisation of power and domination is the reason for attempts to disengage domination from power and power from the intended results of action. An attempt is also made to make the conception of power more general by incorporating into it an important insight of Foucault, namely the idea that there can be unintended ontical "effects of power." Third, it is argued that Giddens has undermined the openness of 'critical realism' with his successive theoretical moves, which have made his theory (of modern nation-states in particular) more precise in an unfortunate way. The notion of an iconic model is offered as a suggestive solution. (edited)

PATRICK, James. Is "The Theory of History" (1914) Collingwood's First Essay on the Philosophy of History? Hist Theor, 29(4), 1-13, D 90.

PATRICK, Timothy and MARKIE, Peter. *De Re* Desire. Austl J Phil, 68(4), 432-447, D 90.

PATTERSON, Dennis. The Importance of Asking the Right Questions. Soc Epistem, 5(1), 75-77, Ja-Mr 91.

This is a response to a critique of Patterson, "Toward a Narrative Conception of Legal Discourse" by the editor of *Social Epistemology*, Steve Fuller. The article contests the realist assumptions that underwrite Fuller's perspective.

PATTERSON, Dennis. Toward a Narrative Conception of Legal Discourse. Soc Epistem, 5(1), 61-69, Ja-Mr 91.

This article argues that law is best understood as a narrative practice. The article gives an account of the concepts of narrative, practice, and legal discourse. There is an extensive discussion of a legal illustration in support of the argument.

PATTERSON, John and PERRETT, Roy W. Virtue Ethics and Maori Ethics. Phil East West, 41(2), 185-202, Ap 91.

We present a three-stranded argument for the thesis that traditional New Zealand Maori ethics is a virtue ethics. *Descriptively* we argue that a virtue ethics model is a fruitful one for understanding the nature of Maori ethics. *Comparatively* we argue that Maori ethics displays important similarities (and dissimilarities) with other examples of virtue ethics, such as the Aristotelian tradition. *Metaethically* we argue that qua instance of a virtue ethics, Maori ethics implies certain conceptions of the self as a moral agent, of the nature and forms of moral education, and of the appropriate patterns of sociopolitical organization.

PATTERSON, Sarah. Individualism and Semantic Development. Phil Sci, 58(1), 15-35, Mr 91.

This paper takes issue with Tyler Burge's claim that intentional states are nonindividualistically individuated in cognitive psychology. A discussion of current models of children's acquisition of semantic knowledge is used to motivate a thought-experiment which shows that psychologists working in this area are not committed to describing the concepts children attach to words in terms of the concepts standardly attached to those words in the child's community. The content of the child's representational states are thus not individuated with reference to linguistic environment in the manner that Burge's nonindividualistic view requires. The paper concludes that the explanatory states of cognitive psychology are sometimes individualistically individuated.

PATTISON, George. Kierkegaard: Aesthetics and 'The Aesthetic'. Brit J Aes, 31(2), 140-151, Ap 91.

The work aims to show how Kierkegaard's use of the term 'the aesthetic' is rooted in an understanding of aesthetic categories derived from Romantic idealism. This is developed in relation to the ideality of art, the synthetic character of aesthetic experience and its timelessness. Kierkegaard's separation of art from the existential life-world is questioned, but the value of his critique of the 'outsider' syndrome affirmed.

PATTMAN, Rob. Subjectivisation as Control or Resistance: An Examination of Reformation Theology and Marxism. Hist Euro Ideas, 11, 967-978, 1989.

PATTON, Thomas E. On Begging the Question 'Who is N?'. Notre Dame J Form Log, 29(4), 553-562, Fall 88.

The Principle of Identifying Descriptions (PID), a view which Donnellan, in "Proper Names and Identifying Descriptions," seeks to refute by counterexample, ties the referent of a name N to the content of its user's answer to the question quoted in my title. As a preliminary to his counterexamples, Donnellan proposes to rule out as *question-begging* certain forms of answer to that question. His ground for this is that such answers would trivialize the PID's claim about proper name reference, so that even its proponents, once this is seen, would not wish to rely on them. This last, and the propriety of his epithet "question-begging," are obvious enough for two forms of answer that Donellan lists, but not at all obvious, in my view, for his third form. Nor can I find in his paper a coherent argument for ruling out this third form. But I am finally able to supply an argument of my own which vindicates Donnellan's rejection of these answers if not his epithet for them. My argument turns on a conceptual link between reference and belief.

PATTON, Thomas. On the Ontology of Branching Quantifiers. J Phil Log, 20(2), 205-223, My 91.

Hintikka, Barwise and others herald a logic of *branching quantifiers* as apt for certain English sentences which defy standard first-order symbolization. Quine opposes this logic on global theoretical grounds, but grants its first-order status: supporters and critic alike see the quantifiers in its novel arrays as ranging over ordinary objects. Here it contrasts with a logic universally agreed to be isomorphic with it, whose existential quantifiers range over *functions*. But I argue that no *autonomous* logic of branching quantifiers is in sight, and indeed that what look like first-order quantifiers in its arrays have no legitimate claim to that status.

PATY, Michel. "Reality and Probability in Mario Bunge's *Treatise*" in *Studies on Mario Bunge's "Treatise"*, WEINGARTNER, Paul (ed), 301-322. Amsterdam, Rodopi, 1990.

Bunge's objective conception of probability in physics is discussed, taking into consideration the historical background of the use of probability in physics and the peculiarity of each domain up to quantum physics. It is suggested that quantum probability might have a specificity which makes its relation to physics somewhat analogous to the problem of geometry with general relativity. If probabilities are a part of the mathematical formalism of physical theory, i.e., inherent to it and not just superimposed, the problem must be thought not only in terms of *interpretation*, but of *construction* of the physical theory, as any other mathematization of physics. It is a general feature of physical theories that their meaning (interpretation) has to be considered from inside the formalized structure of the theory.

PATZIG, Günther. La distinción entre intereses subjetivos y objetivos y su importancia para la Etica. Rev Filosof (Spain), 3, 175-193, 1990.

Starting from ideas of L Nelson, some guidelines are given for distinguishing merely subjective interests of individuals and groups of people from their objective ("real") interests. The burden of proof rests with those who want to discount subjective interests or to vindicate objective interests where subjective interests are lacking. There are clear cases of divergence of objective and merely subjective interests. In spite of recurring attempts to do this, it is argued that we cannot rightly identify subjective with individual and objective with collective interests, as e.g., Plato and some Marxist thinkers have done. This article appeared in its original German version as number 35 of the "Veröffentlichungen der Jungius-Gesellschaft der Wissenschaften" Göttingen 1978. An English translation appeared in "Contemporary German Philosophy" vol. 4, 1984, pp.126-144.

PÄTZOLT, Harald. The Enticing Thing About Stalinism (in German). Deut Z Phil, 38(10), 964-970, 1990.

PAUL, Ellen Frankel (ed) and MILLER JR, Fred D (ed) and PAUL, Jeffrey (ed). *Ethics, Politics, and Human Nature*. Cambridge, Blackwell, 1991.

Human nature, whether it is fixed by genetic endowment or malleable under the influence of social forces, is one of the most hotly debated questions in recent social thought. The contributors to this volume examine the concept of human nature and its role both in philosophical exploration and political prescription. The essays deal with such questions as the relation of self-interest to the proper design of government, whether there is something about human nature which creates a normative prohibition to genetic engineering, what the emerging discipline of sociobiology has to tell us about morality, and how different conceptions of human nature affect Aristotle, Hume, Kant, Rousseau, and current feminist theory.

PAUL, Ellen Frankel (ed) and MILLER JR, Fred D (ed) and PAUL, Jeffrey (ed). *Foundations of Moral and Political Philosophy*. Cambridge, Blackwell, 1990.

Questions regarding the foundations of ethics and politics have intrigued philosophers ever since Socrates first pointed out their importance. Many philosophers have agreed with the ancient Greeks that we cannot obtain the knowledge we need to lead the best lives as individuals or to pursue the wisest public policies unless we are guided by a correct normative theory providing basic definitions, analyses, or explications of concepts such as "good" and "bad," and "right" and "wrong," and basic judgments or principles regarding good things and right actions. However, the task of providing a correct account of the foundations of moral and political philosophy is both difficult and perplexing. There has recently been an enthusiastic revival of interest on the part of moral and political philosophers concerning such foundations. It is a field of great ferment and diversity, as reflected by the nine internationally-regarded philosophers who have written essays for this volume.

PAUL, Gregor. Reflections on the Usage of the Terms "Logic" and "Logical". J Chin Phil, 18(1), 73-87, Mr 91.

PAUL, Iain (ed) and FENNEMA, Jan (ed). *Science and Religion: One World-Changing Perspectives on Reality*. Norwell, Kluwer, 1990.

Scientific points of view and expectations need to be in dialogue with religious forms of understanding — and religious traditions need to take account of the new scientific perspectives on the world and the ethical problems generated by science, medicine and technology. "Science and Religion" presents its title theme from different angles, giving surveys of developments that are taking place in the natural sciences and in theology, followed by essays that consider in retrospect the traditional dichotomy between science and religion, and finally there are essays that enlarge upon expectations for the future.

PAUL, Jeffrey (ed) and PAUL, Ellen Frankel (ed) and MILLER JR, Fred D (ed). *Ethics, Politics, and Human Nature*. Cambridge, Blackwell, 1991.

Human nature, whether it is fixed by genetic endowment or malleable under the influence of social forces, is one of the most hotly debated questions in recent social thought. The contributors to this volume examine the concept of human nature and its role both in philosophical exploration and political prescription. The essays deal with such questions as the relation of self-interest to the proper design of government, whether there is something about human nature which creates a normative prohibition to genetic engineering, what the emerging discipline of sociobiology has to tell us about morality, and how different conceptions of human nature affect Aristotle, Hume, Kant, Rousseau, and current feminist theory.

PAUL, Jeffrey (ed) and PAUL, Ellen Frankel (ed) and MILLER JR, Fred D (ed). *Foundations of Moral and Political Philosophy*. Cambridge, Blackwell, 1990.

Questions regarding the foundations of ethics and politics have intrigued philosophers ever since Socrates first pointed out their importance. Many philosophers have agreed with the ancient Greeks that we cannot obtain the knowledge we need to lead the best lives as individuals or to pursue the wisest public policies unless we are guided by a correct normative theory providing basic definitions, analyses, or explications of concepts such as "good" and "bad," and "right" and "wrong," and basic judgments or principles regarding good things and right actions. However, the task of providing a correct account of the foundations of moral and political philosophy is both difficult and perplexing. There has recently been an enthusiastic revival of interest on the part of moral and political philosophers concerning such foundations. It is a field of great ferment and diversity, as reflected by the nine internationally-regarded philosophers who have written essays for this volume.

PAUL, Jeffrey. Property, Entitlement, and Remedy. Monist, 73(4), 564-577, O 90.

PAUL, N M (trans) and BERGSON, Henri and PALMER, W S (trans). *Matter and Memory*. Cambridge, MIT Pr, 1991.

PAULSEN, David W and CEDERBLOM, Jerry. *Critical Reasoning (Third Edition)*. Belmont, Wadsworth, 1991.

PAULSON, Stanley L. On Ideal Form, Empowering Norms, and "Normative Functions". Ratio Juris, 3(1), 84-88, Mr 90.

PAUTRAT, Bernard. "Nietzsche Medused" in *Looking After Nietzsche*, RICKELS, Laurence A (ed), 159-173. Albany, SUNY Pr, 1990.

PAUZA, M. Dasein and Gelassenheit in Heidegger (in Czechoslovakian). Filozof Cas, 39(1), 107-128, 1991.

The two key issues are as follows: how can the term Being (Sein) in Heidegger be characterized and how is the philosophy of Being possible? Being is an ontologically preceding process of becoming; grounded in this foundation, the philosophy of Being is possible. The thinking of Being is a patient, noble subjugation to being, waiting for man's appropriation. The essence of the thinking of Being (Sein), the philosophy of Being is allowed to flow into ladtingness (Gelassenheit). Gelassenheit constitutes a bolt in the bond of the intrinsically thinking ones, i.e., philosophers of Being. (edited)

PAVUR, Claude N. Restoring Cultural History: Beyond Gombrich. Clio, 20(2), 157-167, Wint 91.

E H Gombrich's "In Search of Cultural History" is deeply flawed by currently influential self-contradicting presuppositions (Lonergan's "counterpositions"). The self-discovery of our own subjectivity can reveal to what extent we are irrevocably bound to holistic and narrative modes of understanding. Gombrich's partial truth about the "Hegelian" excesses of such dynamics of consciousness does not justify his particularist conclusions, which would radically undermine this critically important integrative and foundational academic enterprise of cultural history.

PAWLIKOWSKI, Janusz. Finite Support Iteration and Strong Measure Zero Sets. J Sym Log, 55(2), 674-677, Je 90.

Any finite support iteration of posets with precalibre $\aleph_1$ which has the length of cofinality greater than ω_1 yields a model for the dual Borel conjecture in which the real line is covered by $\aleph_1$ strong measure zero sets.

PAYNE, Dinah and RAIBORN, Cecily A. Corporate Codes of Conduct: A Collective Conscience and Continuum. J Bus Ethics, 9(11), 879-889, N 90.

This paper discusses the vast continuum between the letter of the law (legality) and the spirit of the law (ethics or morality). Further, the authors review the fiduciary duties owed by the firm to its various publics. These aspects must be considered in developing a corporate code of ethics. The underlying qualitative characteristics of a code include clarity, comprehensiveness and enforceability. While ethics is indigenous to a society, every code of ethics will necessarily reflect the corporate culture from which that code stems and be responsive to the innumerable situations for which it was created. Several examples have been provided to illustrate the ease of applicability of these concepts.

PAYNE, Stephen L. A Proposal for Corporate Ethical Reform: The Ethical Dialogue Group. Bus Prof Ethics J, 10(1), 67-88, Spr 91.

PAZ, Octavio. "Poetry and Modernity" in *The Tanner Lectures On Human Values, Volume XII*, PETERSON, Grethe B (ed), 55-76. Salt Lake City, Univ of Utah Pr, 1991.

PEACOCKE, Arthur. Chance and Law in Irreversible Thermodynamics, Theoretical Biology and Theology. Phil Sci (Tucson), 4, 145-180, 1990.

There is an element of "necessity" in the universe, the giveness, from our point of view, of certain of its basic features: the fundamental constants, the nature of the fundamental particles (and so of atoms, and so of molecules, and so of complex organizations of molecules), the physical laws of the interrelation of matter, energy, space, and time. We are in the position, as it were, of the audience before the pianist begins his extemporisations—there is the instrument, there is the range of available notes, but what tune is to be played and on what principle and in what forms is it to be developed?

PEACOCKE, Christopher. "Content and Norms in a Natural World" in *Information, Semantics and Epistemology*, VILLANUEVA, Enrique (ed), 57-76. Cambridge, Blackwell, 1990.

PEACOCKE, Christopher. Demonstrative Content: A Reply to John McDowell. Mind, 100(397), 123-133, Ja 91.

PEACOCKE, Christopher. "Perceptual Content" in *Themes From Kaplan*, ALMOG, Joseph (ed), 297-329. New York, Oxford Univ Pr, 1989.

PEARCE, David. "Conceptual Change and the Progress of Science" in *Logic, Methodology and Philosophy of Science, VIII*, FENSTAD, J E (ed), 351-371. New York, Elsevier Science, 1989.

PEARCE, David and WANSING, Heinrich. On the Methodology of Possible World Semantics, I: Correspondence Theory. Notre Dame J Form Log, 29(4), 482-496, Fall 88.

This paper discusses the constraints on possible worlds semantic modelling that have been proposed by J Van Benthem ('Logical Semantics as an Empirical Science', *Studia Logica* 42, 1983, pp. 299-313). The structure of the possible worlds programme in logical semantics is compared with that of other scientific research traditions, and some logical and methodological aspects of semantic explanation are examined in the context of the 'correspondence theory'.

PEARL, Judea and GEFFNER, Hector. "A Framework for Reasoning with Defaults" in *Knowledge Representation and Defeasible Reasoning*, KYBURG JR, Henry E (ed), 69-87. Norwell, Kluwer, 1990.

A new system of defeasible inference is presented. The system is made up of a body of six rules which allow proofs to be constructed very much like in natural deduction systems. Five of the rules possess a sound and clear probabilistic semantics that guarantees the high probability of the conclusion given the high probability of the premises. The sixth rule appeals to a notion of irrelevance; we explain both its motivation and use.

PEARL, Judea. "Jeffrey's Rule, Passage of Experience, and *Neo*-Bayesianism" in *Knowledge Representation and Defeasible Reasoning*, KYBURG JR, Henry E (ed), 245-265. Norwell, Kluwer, 1990.

The main objective of this paper is to demonstrate, using familiar issues in probability kinematics, that to give an adequate account of belief revision we must postulate that belief states contain structural information which cannot be captured by purely algebraic descriptions of coherent probability functions. The movement which I call Neo-Bayesisanism acknowledges the insufficiency of coherence, explores concrete methods of representing and utilizing the structural information needed, and attempts to establish a theoretical characterization of this information.

PEARS, D. Responsibility: Repudiators Referring to the Divided Centre of Action in the Physical Agent (in Czechoslovakian). Filozof Cas, 39(1), 54-61, 1991.

PEARS, David. Wittgenstein's Account of Rule-Following. Synthese, 87(2), 273-283, My 91.

PEARS, David. Wittgenstein's Holism. Dialectica, 44(1-2), 165-173, 1990.

PEARSON, M A and CLAYPOOL, G A and FETYKO, D F. Reactions to Ethical Dilemmas: A Study Pertaining to Certified Public Accounts. J Bus Ethics, 9(9), 699-706, S 90.

This study discusses how perceptions of ethics are formed by certified public accountants (CPAs). Theologians are used as a point of comparison. When considering CPA ethical dilemmas, both subject groups in this research project viewed 'confidentiality' and 'independence' as more important than 'recipient of responsibility' and 'seriousness of breach'. Neither group, however, was insensitive to any of the factors presented for its consideration. CPA reactions to ethical dilemmas were governed primarily by provisions of the CPA ethics code; conformity to that code may well be evidence of higher stage moral reasoning.

PEART, Sandra J. Jevons's Applications of Utilitarian Theory to Economic Policy. Utilitas, 2(2), 281-306, N 90.

This paper demonstrates first that W S Jevons's analysis of economic policy is thoroughly utilitarian. Secondly, the striking similarity between Jevons and J S Mill on issues of economic policy is demonstrated and then accounted for in terms of a common goal, a wide-ranging programme for social reform. Jevons and Mill shared the intense desire to correct perceived social and economic injustices, as well as a methodological relativism—the method of weighing predicted benefits and costs in the light of their overall goal of social reform.

PECNJAK, Davor. Epiphenomenalism and Machines: A Discussion of Van Rooijen's Critique of Popper. Brit J Phil Sci, 40(3), 404-408, S 89.

One can observe only one's own subjective sphere. If the objective approach to science is taken, then epiphenomenal qualities cannot be scientifically proven. On the basis that other people are physically similar to Van Rooijen, he cannot conclude that others are epiphenomenally similar also. We cannot use the notion of configuration of matter in deciding whether or not humans are machines as Van Rooijen does. He also tacitly assumes that he is not a machine and according to similarity of configuration of matter, it is extrapolated to every other human being. This is not a valid argument.

PEDERSEN, O. "Historical Interaction between Science and Religion" in *Science and Religion: One World-Changing Perspectives on Reality*, FENNEMA, Jan (ed), 139-160. Norwell, Kluwer, 1990.

The paper is a purely historical survey written from the point of view of intellectual history. It argues that below the surface of well-known incidents between scientists and ecclesiastical authorities there has been an ongoing and largely beneficial interplay between the three great scientific traditions (Aristotelian, Platonic, Archimedean) and certain fundamental theological notions, such as God, creation, and in particular the *logos*-theology as an expression of the belief in the rationality of the world.

PEDERSEN, Olaf. *Three Great Traditions*. Aarhus, Aarhus Univ, 1990.

PEEPLES, S Elise. Her Terrain is Outside His "Domain". Hypatia, 6(2), 192-199, Sum 91.

A response to Puka's "The Liberation of Caring: A Different Voice for Gulligan's 'Different Voice.'"

PEERENBOOM, Randall P. Beyond Naturalism: A Reconstruction of Daoist Environmental Ethics. Environ Ethics, 13(1), 3-22, Spr 91.

In this paper I challenge the traditional reading of Daoism as naturalism and the interpretation of *wu wei* as "acting naturally." I argue that such an interpretation is problematic and unhelpful to the would-be Daoist environmental ethicist. I then lay the groundwork for a philosophically viable environmental ethic by elucidating the pragmatic aspects of Daoist thought. While Daoism so interpreted is no panacea for all of our environmental ills, it does provide a methodology that may prove effective in alleviating some of our discomfort.

PEETERS, L. Thought Rhythym and Experience in *Der Satz vom Grund* (in Dutch). S Afr J Phil, 9(3), 149-157, Ag 90.

In this article the author aims at understanding Heidegger's thought rhythm: the rhythm of his *Satz vom Grund* (rhythm in the sense of 'configuration of movement') would allow his audience and his readers to participate in his thinking which is not a mere concatenation of concepts but the experience of the sense of Being. The progress of Heidegger's thinking displays two basic forms: first of all a gyrational movement around words or sentences or the turning around of sentences by permutating subject and predicate. This whirl combines at strategic points on his path to Being with leaps into the unexplored. Vortex and leaps are the forms of Heidegger's thinking, movement which manifests wonder and anguish since in his experience there is no God to catch him during his fall into the abysmal void of Being.

PEETZ, Siegbert. *Die Wiederkehr im Unterschied*. Freiburg, Alber, 1991.

This book deals with the philosopher Ernst von Lasaulx (1805-1861) whose relevance to 19th century philosophy and history has to date been almost entirely overlooked. The analogy between Antiquity ('Paganism') and Christianity is shown to underlie Lasaulx thinking—a methodological principle which he shared with other prominent 19th century historians. The question arises whether such an approach might give new impulses to current issues in the philosophy of history.

PEGUEROLES, Juan. La "memoria Dei" en el libro X de Las confesiones. Espiritu, 35(93), 5-12, Ja-Je 86.

PEGUEROLES, Juan. Las aventuras de la differencia (G Vattimo). Espiritu, 36(95), 91-94, Ja-Je 87.

PEGUEROLES, Juan. El deseo infinito. Espiritu, 37(98), 157-161, Jl-D 88.

PEGUEROLES, Juan. El deseo y el amor en San Agustín. Espiritu, 38(99), 5-15, Ja-Je 89.

Intento de respuesta a A Nygren: el amor Dei en San Agustín es amor sui? 1) Amor sui o deseo; 2) Amor Dei o amor; 3) Amor Dei es amor o deseo? 4) Amor Dei es amor; 5) Del deseo al amor; 6) Deseo natural o amor natural? 7) Los grados del amor y de la libertad; 8) El amor Dei y la voluntad de poder.

PEGUEROLES, Juan. Dios y el hombre en San Agustin. Rev Filosof (Mexico), 23(68), 195-200, My-Ag 90.

PEGUEROLES, Juan. Libertad como posibilidad, libertad como necesidad: Juliano y San Agustín. Espiritu, 36(96), 109-124, Jl-D 87.

1) La imposibilidad del bien o la voluntad necesaria del mal; 2) El origen de la mala voluntad; 3) Se puede perder la libertad? 4) Los grados de la libertad: libertas in malis, libertas in bonis et in malis, libertas in bonis; 5) Dos conceptos de la libertad: libertad absoluta, libertad para el bien.

PEGUEROLES, Juan. La palabra interior: La filosofía del lenguaje en San Agustín. Espiritu, 35(94), 93-110, Jl-D 86.

1) Utilidad e inutilidad de los signos: De magistro, de doctrina christiana; 2) La voz y la palabra: los tres elementos del signo (signo, cosa, pensamiento), los tres problemas del signo (origen, interpretación, verdad); 3) La palabra interiory la palabra exterior; 4) Los presupuestos de la filosofía agustiniana del lenguaje.

PEGUEROLES, Juan. Postcriptum: La libertad como necesidad del bien, en San Agustín. Espiritu, 37(98), 153-156, Jl-D 88.

PEGUEROLES, Juan. El ser y el sentido: Notas husserlianas. Espiritu, 35(93), 63-70, Ja-Je 86.

PEGUIRON, Nicolas. La pensée gonséthienne et le mouvement systémique. Dialectica, 44(3-4), 343-351, 1990.

The problem of the beginning is important in Gonseth's thought. The solution that he gives, and on which his entire epistemology is based, is paradoxical in that it denies that knowledge may be built up ex nihilio; but, historically, knowledge did indeed at some time have to begin. The resolution of this paradox makes use of concepts adopted by the recent systemics movement.

PEHRSON, C W P. Plato's Gods. Polis, 9(2), 122-169, 1990.

Plato's philosophical revolution neither abandons nor marginalizes the gods of the tradition. His work is part of a continuous process of adapting and transforming orthodoxy to new values and new ideas of gods and humans. His arguments concern truth and falsity, but replies can be constructed which treat them as indices of conceptual changes. Traditional ideas of justice, of power and of agency are all radically different on this view, and this gives an unorthodox perspective and emphasis to Plato's own work. This 'incommensurable tradition' is elusive, but, like Plato's 'false tradition', it is the outcome of a particular interpretation.

PEIJNENBURG, J. De Kant-interpretatie van Evert Willem Beth. Alg Ned Tijdschr Wijs, 83(2), 114-128, Ap 91.

From 1942 until his death in 1964, the Dutch philosopher and logician E.W. Beth repeatedly criticized Frege's reading of Kant. According to Frege, Kant meant by 'analytic' ('synthetic') those statements that can(not) be proved exclusively by definitions and/or the laws of logic. According to Beth it is the other way round. J. Hintikka claimed to have elaborated these ideas of Beth's. The present article aims to show that this is only partly true: although Hintikka did extend Beth's interpretation of Kant's 'synthetic', he missed the point of Beth's reconstruction of 'analytic'.

PEKARSKY, Daniel. Burglars, Robber Barons, and the Good Life. Educ Theor, 41(1), 61-74, Wint 91.

Like Plato, John Dewey seems to believe that human flourishing is incompatible with a way of life that entails deliberately doing violence to others. In examining why Dewey believes this, and entertaining counter-arguments to his position, this article tries to illuminate Dewey's understanding of human flourishing, of the problem of evil, and of the costs to everyone of an oppressive socio-economic order.

PELLAUER, David. Limning the Liminal: Carr and Ricoeur on Time and Narrative. Phil Today, 35(1), 51-62, Spr 91.

This essay is a discussion of the differences between Carr and Ricoeur concerning whether experience is inherently ordered in a narrative fashion or if narrative is something added to what might be considered a fundamentally non-narrative experience. I try to show that the differences between these authors is due as much to their basic understandings of the limits of phenomenology, particularly when applied to the temporality of lived experience and to the question of cosmic time, as it is to the particular argument each makes in favor of his position.

PELLECCHIA, Pasquale. La cosmologia tra filosofia ed empirologia. Aquinas, 33(1), 61-99, Ja-Ap 90.

PELLECCHIA, Pasquale. Per una filosofia del corpo. Aquinas, 33(2), 313-341, My-Ag 90.

PELLECCHIA, Pasquale. La valenza della carità nelle forme della vita politica. Aquinas, 33(3), 601-626, S-D 90.

PELLEGRINO, Edmund D (ed) and VEATCH, Robert M (ed) and LANGAN, John P (ed). *Ethics, Trust, and the Professions: Philosophical and Cultural Aspects*. Washington, Georgetown Univ Pr, 1991.

Does the fiduciary paradigm characteristic of the traditional learned professions continue to serve as an appropriate ethical model for the professions of today? Or does the fact that professional relationships are often because strangers mitigate against the feasibility of trust and trustworthiness? The fourteen essays in the volume take their positions on each side of the question. In addition to offering an array of philosophical points of view on the ethics of professions, these essays also provide insight into the sociology of the professions and the professional role in Asian and European contexts.

PELLEGRINO, Edmund D. "Trust and Distrust in Professional Ethics" in *Ethics, Trust, and the Professions: Philosophical and Cultural Aspects*, PELLEGRINO, Edmund D (ed), 69-89. Washington, Georgetown Univ Pr, 1991.

The notion that trust is the basis of professional-client relationships has come to be greeted with increasing skepticism. There is both a general wariness of professional authority and a philosophical trend that regards trust between relative strangers as epistemically unsound. A phenomenological analysis, however, reveals that trust necessarily remains as ineradicable feature of professional relationships. It is in the nature of these relationships that we depend on the professional to use discretionary latitude for our benefit where the contingencies of our care cannot be anticipated. In addition, the establishment of a contract itself depends on a context of trust.

PELLEGRINO, Edmund D. "Values and Academic Health Centers: A Commentary and Recommendations" in *Integrity in Health Care Institutions: Humane Environments for Teaching, Inquiry, and Healing*, BULGER, Ruth Ellen (ed), 167-178. Iowa City, Univ of Iowa Pr, 1990.

PELLETIER, Francis Jeffry and MARTIN, Norman M. Post's Functional Completeness Theorem. Notre Dame J Form Log, 31(3), 462-475, Sum 90.

The paper provides a new proof, in a style accessible to modern logicians and teachers of elementary logic, of Post's Functional Completeness Theorem. Post's Theorem states the necessary and sufficient conditions for an arbitrary set of(2-valued) truth functional connectives to be expressively complete, that is, to be able to express every (2-valued) truth function or truth table. The theorem is stated in terms of five properties that an arbitrary connective may have, and claims that a set of connectives is expressively complete iff for each of the five properties there is a connective that lacks that property.

PEÑA, Lorenzo. Las reglas del juego: consideraciones críticas sobre "Radical Hermeneutics" de John Caputo. Pensamiento, 47(187), 313-322, Jl-S 91.

John Caputo has claimed that in limit situations playfulness breaks through as the abyssal ground of our being, thus showing reason to be what freely enacts any rules. As against such a view I argue that there are bound to be some rules any rational thought stands by. Now, we need ceaselessly to sift the entrenched beliefs about what is to count as a rational rule, since established standards and institutions quite often are nothing else but unduly stiff, narrow-minded constraints which, to that extent, depart from what alone is entitled to hold sway over rational thought in general.

PEÑA, Lorenzo. Sobre cuatro obras de Mauricio Beuchot. Espiritu, 38(99), 61-69, Ja-Je 89.

The paper examines Beuchot's approach and agrees that there are many coincidences between medieval Aristotelianism and analytical philosophy. Both pursue philosophical inquiry in an argumentative manner. Nowadays analytical philosophy also tends to recognize as genuine such traditional metaphysical problems as were debated by the Scholastics. The paper's only criticism at Beuchot's views concerns analogy and reduplicative *as*-clauses. It argues that on that issue the cleavage between medieval and analytical philosophy lies in the latter's tending to favor complete equivocality of the word "being." However, an alternative is possible, namely univocism, as implemented in combinatory logics, which while also rejecting reduplicative clauses is free from the ineffableness attendant upon equivocism.

PENATI, G. Il problema teologico nel pensiero di Heidegger. Riv Filosof Neo-Scolas, 81(4), 635-638, O-D 89.

PENCE, Greg. "Virtue Theory" in *A Companion to Ethics*, SINGER, Peter (ed), 249-258. Cambridge, Blackwell, 1991.

Virtue theory concerns analysis of virtue (moral character) and specific virtues (traits). The historical background of modern virtue theory is discussed, from ancient Greeks to MacIntyre. Criticims from Virtue Theory of other theories are discussed, especially the idea that utilitarianism is an impersonal, "Faceless" theory. Courage is used as a counterexample to the thesis of Eliminatism, the idea that Virtue Theory alone can be a complete moral theory without principles. Other questions are also discussed, such as relations between character and society; essentialism and virtues, feelings and virtues; and determinism.

PENCE, Terry and CANTRALL, Janice. *Ethics in Nursing: An Anthology*. New York, Natl League Nursing, 1990.

This collection of historical, seminal, classic and controversial articles begins with the assumption that ethical action in nursing is largely determined by philosophical views about the nature and function of nursing. The articles and excerpts from the nursing and other literature serve to explain, illustrate, advocate and/or critique various views about nursing and the moral implications of these views. Chapters include discussions of the concept of patient advocacy, nurses' rights, nurse-physician relationships, sexism, whistleblowing, nurse-nurse relationships, professional obligations, and institutional obligations. The chapters contain introductions and study questions.

PENCO, Carlo and PARODI, Alessandra (trans). Gottlob Frege, lettere a Wittgenstein. Epistemologia, 12(2), 331-351, Jl-D 89.

PENDLEBURY, Shirley. Practical Reasoning in Teaching: A Response to Jana Noel. Proc Phil Educ, 46, 281-285, 1990.

This brief critical response to Jana Noel's paper "Aristotle's Account of Practical Reasoning as a Theoretical Base for Research on Teaching" challenges her work on three counts: first, for misconstruing the relationship between practical reasoning and the practical syllogism; second, for assuming that a means-end account excludes intentionality; and, third, for implying that prior deliberation is a necessary condition for reasonable action in teaching. In elaborating these criticisms, the paper indicates some of the ways in which an Aristotelian account of practical reasoning illuminates the practice of teaching.

PENN, Gerald and BUSZKOWSKI, Wojciech. Categorical Grammars Determined from Linguistic Data by Unification. Stud Log, 49(4), 431-454, D 90.

We provide an algorithm for determining a categorial grammar form linguistic data that essentially uses unification of type-schemes assigned to atoms. The algorithm presented here extends an earlier one restricted to rigid categorial grammar by admitting non-rigid outputs. The key innovation is the notion of an optimal unifier, a natural generalization of that of a most general unifier.

PENNER, Terrence M. Plato and Davidson: Parts of the Soul and Weakness of Will. Can J Phil, SUPP 16, 35-74, 1990.

Akrasia is sometimes represented as a conflict of a rational desire with a desire from a different part or partition of the soul—either an irrational desire (Plato) or a less rational desire based upon a merely partial view of the evidence (Davidson). Against Plato, I argue that irrational desires cannot be converted into desires to do *particular* actions; against Davidson, that it's not clear how the 'partitioning' is to take place. I argue instead for a Socratic conception of *diachronic* belief-akrasia, in terms of temporary mind-changes, which, while not unlike Davidson's account, nevertheless makes no appeal to partitions.

PENNINO, Luciano. *La Logica Simbolica: nella produzione scientifica in lingua russa (1961-1983)*. Napoli, LER, 1990.

PENTICUFF, Joy Hinson. Conceptual Issues in Nursing Ethics Research. J Med Phil, 16(3), 235-258, Je 91.

Empirical studies that have attempted to describe nurses' ethical practice have used conceptual frameworks derived primarily from the disciplines of bioethics and psychology. These frameworks have not incorporated important concepts developed by nursing theorists over the past two decades. This article points out flaws in the past research frameworks and proposes a synthesis of ethical theory, nursing practice contexts, and empirical research methods to enrich theoretical development in nursing ethics.

PENTTONEN, Martti and FARIÑAS DEL CERRO, Luis. Grammar Logics. Log Anal, 31(121-122), 123-134, Mr-Je 88.

In this paper we present a simple method to define modal logics for formal grammars. Given a formal grammar, we associate with each rule an axiom of a modal logic. By this construction, testing whether a word is generated by a formal grammar is equivalent with proving a theorem in the logic. First constructions produce multimodal logics possessing several agents [Ko], but the technique can be applied to construct also more classical logics with only one modal operator. Our approach is suggested by a method used in logic programming, where the analysis or generation of a sentence is transformed to theorem proving [Co, PW]. Other related work is done by Wolper [Wo], who defines an extension of the linear temporal logic of programs to include regular expressions.

PENTZ, Rebecca. Hick and Saints: Is Saint-Production a Valid Test? Faith Phil, 8(1), 96-103, Ja 91.

John Hick proposes that we test the salvific power of the world religions by testing their saint-production. I shall argue that Hick's test is not simple, not necessarily fair and not strictly empirical. I shall argue that it is not simple by exposing the assumptions it relies on and various cases it must treat. I shall argue that it is not necessarily fair by explaining the condition it must meet in order to be fair. I shall argue that it is not strictly empirical by exposing the doctrinal question it must answer.

PENTZOPOULOU-VALALAS, Teresa. Experience and Causal Explanation in Medical Empiricism. Phil Inq, 10(1-2), 37-57, Wint-Spr 88.

The purpose of the work is (a) to show that the empiricists of the empirical medical school in antiquity laid down the foundations of a theory of knowledge centered on key concepts such as experience and observation, and (b) to bring to attention the significance of the eight etiological modes of ancient scepticism, which has been rather overlooked by modern scholars. Aenesidemus's criticism of causal explanation and the etiological modes provide evidence in support of the distinction between science and ideology. In this respect scepticists and empiricists defend science against ideology. It should be pointed out that the empiricists did not apply a methodology that had been laid down already, pretending to present us with a theory of knowledge, but that by stressing the importance of the steps to be taken in the field of medicine (observation, history, metabasis by way of the similar) offered the key steps to an empirical theory of knowledge.

PENZO, Maurizio. Heidegger e la duplicità del presente. Aquinas, 33(2), 343-363, My-Ag 90.

PEPERZAK, Adriaan. "Presentation" in *Re-Reading Levinas*, BERNASCONI, Robert (ed), 51-66. Bloomington, Indiana Univ Pr, 1991.

Discussion of Levinas' analysis of temporality and scepticism in his book entitled: *Otherwise Than Being or Beyond Essence*.

PEPPERELL, Keith C. Political Self-Education of the English Working Class. Phil Stud Educ, /, 103-114, 1987-88.

PERA, Marcello. "Methodological Sophisticationism: A Degenerating Project" in *Imre Lakatos and Theories of Scientific Change*, GAVROGLU, Kostas (ed), 169-187. Norwell, Kluwer, 1989.

Lakatos's project is taken as an attempt at looking for a universal methodology which fits scientific practice. Two main presuppositions of this project are examined, namely, that methodology offers a theory of scientific rationality, and that the aim of a theory of rationality is that of eliminating the personal factors which may enter into scientific decisions. It is argued that Lakatos was affected by a "Cartesian syndrome," according to which if there were no universal, sharp and impersonal criteria of demarcation and validation, or a precise logic of discovery, then science would degenerate into "mob psychology." Not differently from Feyerabend, Lakatos could not conceive of any middle ground between these two extremes. It is shown that, in spite of many subtleties and refinements, Lakatos's methodology does not require fewer conventional elements than Popper's, and, contrary to Lakatos's view, this does not imply that science is irrational.

PERCIVAL, Philip. Knowability, Actuality, and the Metaphysics of Context-Dependence. Austl J Phil, 69(1), 82-97, Mr 91.

PEREBOOM, Derk. Kant on Justification in Transcendental Philosophy. Synthese, 85(1), 25-54, O 90.

Kant's claim that the justification of transcendental philosophy is a priori is puzzling because it should be consistent with (1) his general restriction on the justification of knowledge, that intuitions must play a role in the justification of all nondegenerate knowledge, with (2) the implausibility of a priori intuitions being the only ones on which transcendental philosophy is founded, and with (3) his professed view that transcendental philosophy is not analytic. I argue that this puzzle can be solved, that according to Kant transcendental philosophy is justified a priori in the sense that the only empirical information required for its justification can be derived from any possible human experience. Transcendental justification does not rely on any more particular or special observations or experiments. Philip Kitcher's general account of apriority in Kant captures this aspect of a priori knowledge. Nevertheless, I argue that Kitcher's account goes wrong in the link it specifies between apriority and certainty.

PEREBOOM, Derk. Mathematical Expressibility, Perceptual Relativity, and Secondary Qualities. Stud Hist Phil Sci, 22(1), 63-88, Mr 91.

PEREDA, Carlos. Un "mapa de ontologías". Dianoia, 35(35), 81-89, 1989.

PEREDA, Carlos. Tipos de lectura, tipos de texto. Dianoia, 36(36), 181-188, 1990.

PEREIRA JR, Alfredo and FRENCH, Steven. Metaphysics, Pragmatic Truth and the Underdetermination of Theories. Dialogos, 25(56), 37-67, Jl 90.

PEREIRA JÚNIOR, A. Husserl's Time Perception (in Portuguese). Trans/Form/Acao, 13, 73-83, 1990.

A brief reconstruction of the first two sections of Edmund Husserl's *Vorlesungen zur Phanomenologie des inneren Zeitbewusstseins* is done, showing how, making use of the phenomenological method, the author develops his transcendental theory of time. A revaluation of the meaning of "perception of time" allows him to establish the basis which are, in our perspective, able to give an account of one of the most debatable questions about time, its asymmetry or unidirectionality. We furthermore discuss the main difficulties that affect Husserl in this project.

PEREIRA, Fernando C N and DALRYMPLE, Mary and SHIEBER, Stuart M. Ellipsis and Higher-Order Unification. Ling Phil, 14(4), 399-452, Ag 91.

We present a new method for characterizing the interpretive possibilities generated by elliptical constructions in natural language. Unlike previous analyses, which postulate ambiguity of interpretation or derivation in the full clause source of the ellipsis, our analysis requires no such hidden ambiguity. Further, the analysis follows relatively directly form an abstract statement of the ellipsis interpretation problem. It predicts correctly a wide range of interactions between ellipsis and other semantic phenomena such as quantifier scope and bound anaphora. Finally, although the analysis itself is stated nonprocedurally, it admits of a direct computational method for generating interpretations.

PEREVERZEV, V N and PETROV, V V. Logic and Knowledge Representation. Commun Cog, 23(4), 267-276, 1990.

PEREZ DE LABORDA, A. El principio antrópico. Dialogo Filosof, 7(1), 46-57, Ja-Ap 91.

PEREZ DE LABORDA, Alfonso. La filosofía de la ciencia en Platón: Una introducción. Aquinas, 33(1), 101-145, Ja-Ap 90.

PÉREZ ESTÉVEZ, Antonio. Kant y la Revolución Francesa. Rev Filosof (Venezuela), 12, 101-112, 1989.

PÉREZ ESTÉVEZ, Antonio. Moral y política en Kant. Rev Filosof (Venezuela), 13, 145-159, 1989.

PÉREZ ESTÉVEZ, Antonio. La religión en la constitución de los Estados Unidos de América. Rev Filosof (Venezuela), 11, 121-160, 1989.

PÉREZ RANSANZ, Ana Rosa. Azar y explicación: Algunas observaciones. Critica, 22(66), 39-54, D 90.

I examine some difficulties in the explanation of random events. In the first part, I discuss the Hempelian model for the probabilistic explanation of particular events, stressing its basic presuppositions and showing the problems these generate. In the second part, I analyze Salmon's and Railton's models making some criticisms to them. I propose to distinguish between explaining *why* and explaining *how possibly* and I claim that this distinction is useful to establish the scope and limits of probabilistic explanations of genuinely random events.

PERKINS JR, Ray. Moore's Moral Rules. J Hist Phil, 28(4), 595-599, O 90.

Chapter 5 of G E Moore's *Principia Ethica* is examined in the context of Tom Regan's thesis that Moore was Bloomsbury's prophet and moral liberator. Regan's claim is defended (in part) against Avrum Stroll and Thomas Baldwin. Moore seems to leave room for individual moral autonomy in the realm of actions falling under society's rules governing sexual conduct.

PERKINS JR, Raymond. "Nuclear Abolition and the Fear of Cheating" in *In the Interest of Peace: A Spectrum of Philosophical Views*, KLEIN, Kenneth H (ed), 167-174. Wolfeboro, Longwood, 1990.

PERKINS, Mary Anne. Logic and Logos—The Search for Unity in Hegel and Coleridge: I, Alienation and the Logocentric Response. Heythrop J, 32(1), 1-25, Ja 91.

This article, the first of three which compare the work of Hegel and Coleridge on the theme of Logos, sets out the importance of this theme to both against the background of their common experience and philosophical inheritance. It aims to show that Coleridge's work deserves comparison with that of Hegel despite its comparative obscurity and to demonstrate their common interests and concerns; notably the alienation which they believed was increasing within philosophical thought and human experience. The article concludes with a summary of the Logos as unifying principle in their work.

PERKINS, Mary Anne. Logic and Logos—The Search for Unity in Hegel and Coleridge: II: The 'Otherness" of God. Heythrop J, 32(2), 192-215, Ap 91.

PERKINS, Mary Anne. Logic and Logos—The Search for Unity in Hegel and Coleridge, III: A Different Logos. Heythrop J, 32(3), 340-354, Jl 91.

PERKINS, Robert L. "Kierkegaard's Teleological Humanism" in *The Question of Humanism: Challenges and Possibilities*, GOICOECHEA, David (ed), 138-149. Buffalo, Prometheus, 1991.

Kierkegaard belongs squarely within the broad category of Platonic-Christian humanism, his critique of Plato (and idealism generally) not withstanding. The scope and limit of Kierkegaard's own humanism and his views of other forms of humanism is indicated by his treatment of Socrates, who is Kierkegaard's code word for the highest and most profound achievements in morality and inwardness. Characterized by Kierkegaard as "the only philosopher in the realm of the purely human," Socrates is the criterion for measuring the successes and failures of humanism. Kierkegaard also uses Socrates polemically against his own age to criticize its elitism, aestheticism, romanticism, ethics, religious expression, and politics.

PERL, Paul. Down to Earth and Up to Religion: Kantian Idealism in Light of Kierkegaard's Leap of Faith. Dialogue (PST), 33(1), 1-9, O 90.

By exploring the implications of a Kantian ethic reshaped by Kierkegaard's "leap of faith," the article examines the supposition that the leap grew out of Kant's moral idealism. It concludes that the leap allows one to transcend ethical guilt produced when motives for moral conduct exceed duty alone. It also concludes that the leap relativizes Kant's law of the universal realm by introducing the principle that Christian faith elevates the individual above the ideal universals of philosophy.

PERLER, Dominik. Wilhelm von Ockham: Das Risiko, mittelalterlich zu denken. Frei Z Phil Theol, 37(1-2), 209-231, 1990.

PERLIS, Don. "Thing and Thought" in *Knowledge Representation and Defeasible Reasoning*, KYBURG JR, Henry E (ed), 99-117. Norwell, Kluwer, 1990.

Self-reference or self-applicability is an important theme throughout Computer Science, from recursive programs to undecidability results, from bootstrapping to program semantics. A relative latecomer to this list is Artificial Intelligence, for only recently has self-reference been seen as an important attribute of intelligent systems. This paper will give a bird's-eye (and personal) overview of some of the issues surrounding self-reference in AI, especially those related to non-monotonicity, reification, and intentionality.

PERLIS, Donald. Putting One's Foot in One's Head—Part I: Why. Nous, 25(4), 435-455, S 91.

What is meaning, what is it good for, and what is a naturalist (non-intentional) account of how it works? In this paper (part I of a two-part work), I will argue that the first two of these questions should be answered primarily in terms of processes inside the mind/brain, contrary to most recent thinking on this. In the sequel part (part II) I will argue that a key aspect of this is the physical body of the meaning agent, and propose a way in which this might work, and how an external notion of reference can be recaptured from internal processes.

PERLOFF, Michael and BELNAP JR, Nuel D. "Seeing To It That: A Canonical Form for Agentives" in *Knowledge Representation and Defeasible Reasoning*, KYBURG JR, Henry E (ed), 167-190. Norwell, Kluwer, 1990.

This paper introduces the stit (seeing to it that) theory of agency, which stresses the distinction between agentive and nonagentive sentences. The stit sentence, with an agent term as subject and any arbitrary declarative as complement, represents a canonical form for agentives. In its semantics, stit theory portrays agents as making choices against a background of branching time. There are demonstrations of the benefits of stit theory, including, for example, the agentiveness of refraining and the restricted complement thesis: that constructions concerned with agency—deontic, imperatival, intentional, could-have—restrict their complements to agentives.

PERLOFF, Michael. *Stit* and the Language of Agency. Synthese, 86(3), 379-408, Mr 91.

Stit, a sentence form first introduced in Belnap and Perloff (1988), encourages a modal approach to agency. Von Wright, Chisholm, Kenny, and Castañeda have all attempted modal treatments of agency, while Davidson has rejected such treatments. After a brief explanation of the syntax and semantics of *stit* and a restatement of several of the important claims of the earlier paper, I discuss the virtues of *stit* against the background of proposals made by these philosophers.

PERNER, Josef. *Understanding the Representational Mind*. Cambridge, MIT Pr, 1991.

The work traces children's growing understanding of the mind from birth to about 6 years. It focuses on the important changes taking place around 4 years which are interpreted as reflecting a change from representing mental states as relations to situations to representing them as holding representations of situations (metarepresentation). Experimental data documenting this change include the emerging understanding of the appearance-reality distinction, false beliefs, deception, the importance of informational access in knowledge formation, and insights into volitional processes.

PEROVICH JR, Anthony. A Comprehensive and Comprehensible Survey of Modern Philosophy. Teach Phil, 13(3), 227-231, S 90.

A semester course covering the history of philosophy from Descartes to the present must deal with intrinsically difficult texts that are hard to fit into a single, coherent story. However, a representative selection of modern texts may be read chronologically and divided into groupings that handle these problems: the texts for each episode are unified by related concerns, offer sufficient contrast to highlight the issues at stake, and complement one another so as to make each more comprehensible; the different topics of the various episodes, while not telling a single story, introduce students to a broad range of the concerns of modern philosophy.

PERRETT, Roy W and PATTERSON, John. Virtue Ethics and Maori Ethics. Phil East West, 41(2), 185-202, Ap 91.

We present a three-stranded argument for the thesis that traditional New Zealand Maori ethics is a virtue ethics. *Descriptively* we argue that a virtue ethics model is a fruitful one for understanding the nature of Maori ethics. *Comparatively* we argue that Maori ethics displays important similarities (and dissimilarities) with other examples of virtue ethics, such as the Aristotelian tradition. *Metaethically* we argue that qua instance of a virtue ethics, Maori ethics implies certain conceptions of the self as a moral agent, of the nature and forms of moral education, and of the appropriate patterns of sociopolitical organization.

PERRICK, M. Kant en de mogelijkheid van de metafysica als wetenschap. Alg Ned Tijdschr Wijs, 83(1), 24-32, Ja 91.

In Kant's philosophy there exists a close link between the question concerning the possibility of metaphysics as a science and the question concerning the possibility of the synthetic a priori. According to Kant metaphysics is primarily concerned with pure concepts of reason whose objective reality cannot be established. Thus conceived it cannot be a science. Metaphysics as a science is only possible if we consider metaphysics to be metaphysics of nature. As such it differs fundamentally from transcendent metaphysics and is more properly called epistemology. Metaphysics, whether we conceive of it as transcendent metaphysics or as metaphysics of nature, consists of synthetic a priori statements which hold 'by or through (bare) concepts'. We argue that one should distinguish three different meanings of this latter notion.

PERRICK, M. Onderbepaaldheid van theorie en onbepaaldheid van vertaling: Enige ontwikkelingen in Quine's filosofie. Alg Ned Tijdschr Wijs, 82(4), 282-299, O 90.

PERRIN, Ron. *Max Scheler's Concept of the Person: An Ethics of Humanism*. New York, St Martin's Pr, 1991.

A critical study of Max Scheler's personalist ethics grounded in Scheler's attempt to overcome the limitations of Kant's formalism. Scheler's phenomenological elaboration of normative experience explicates a "material ethic of values" that would achieve all the philosophical rigor Kant sought to establish in his critique of the transcendental conditions of practical reason. In his insistence that the Person be understood as the agency within all acts of human valuation Scheler's ethics constitute a unique and important contribution in the history of moral philosophy and to the study of moral development as both an individual and an historical phenomenon.

PERRY, John. "Individuals in Informational and Intentional Content" in *Information, Semantics and Epistemology*, VILLANUEVA, Enrique (ed), 172-189. Cambridge, Blackwell, 1990.

PERRY, John. Self-Notions. Logos (USA), 11, 17-31, 1990.

"Self-beliefs" are beliefs of the sort one ordinarily has about oneself and expresses with the first person. These contrast with the beliefs one has in "Casteñeda cases," in which one has a belief about oneself without knowing it. This paper advances an account of the nature of self-belief. According to this account, self-belief is a special case of interacting with things via notions that serve as repositories for information about objects with certain important relations to the knower, and as motivators for actions the success of which is dependent on the object in that relation to the agent. Identity is such a relation, and "self-notions" play this special role: they are the repositories for information gained in normally self-informative ways and the motivators of types of action whose success normally depends on facts about the agent. Self-beliefs involve such self-notions, while the beliefs that one has about oneself in Castañeda cases do not.

PERRY, John (ed) and ALMOG, Joseph (ed) and WETTSTEIN, Howard (ed). *Themes From Kaplan*. New York, Oxford Univ Pr, 1989.

PERSSON, Ingmar. A Determinist Dilemma. Ratio, 4(1), 38-58, Je 91.

It is argued that there are emotions the propositional bases of which are incompatible with determinism (as well as indeterminism): e.g., anger, gratitude, pride and contempt. In this respect, they are contrasted with dislike, liking and love. The emotions jeopardized by determinism are, however, deeply ingrained in us and uprooting them will cost us much effort and strain. This creates a dilemma: either we aspire to achieve attitudinal compliance with truth, including (in)determinism, which necessitates neglecting a majority of our other strivings, or we opt for leading a well-rounded, maximally fulfilling life, accepting our recalcitrant, irrational emotions.

PERSSON, Ingmar. Universalizability and the Summing of Desires. Theoria, 55(3), 159-170, 1989.

In *Moral Thinking* R M Hare maintains that imaginatively putting oneself into the place of another generates a preference that the preferences one would then have be fulfilled according to strength. It is here argued that, even given the correctness of this, there is a problem about deriving a utilitarian conclusion for *multi*lateral cases in which the agent acquires at least two preferences that its preferences in two possible situations be fulfilled: why add them together when they are concerned with two different possible worlds and so are not co-satisfiable? Principles, not acknowledged by Hare, which would legitimize this addition, are suggested.

PERUZZI, Alberto. Some Remarks on the Linguistic Turn. Teoria, 10(2), 117-130, 1990.

Some basic assumptions of analytic philosophy are discussed with reference to *The Origins of Analytic Philosophy* by Dummett, and in relation to the phenomenological tradition and the primary role of perception. The autonomy of language from other cognitive abilities is criticized, while denying the loss of objectivity for semantics. Antirealism is faced with the necessity of *distributive transcendence* (of truth over assertibility) linked to the author's notion of local *epoche*. The main conclusion is that a systematic theory of meaning has to take into account the structure of the cognitive genesis, meaning being traced back to non-linguistic constraints on concept formation.

PERUZZI, Alberto. The Theory of Descriptions Revisited. Notre Dame J Form Log, 30(1), 91-104, Wint 89.

The principal theories of descriptions from Russell until now are examined. The most important disadvantages of each theory are sketched. Descriptions are conceived in the context of model theory, taking preservation and classification theorems into account. Finally, the categorical formulation in topos theory is presented with reference to sheaves. Referential variation of descriptions leads to a general dynamical scheme of philosophical interest.

PESSINA, Adriano. L'emozione creatrice: Il significato della morale nella prospettiva di Bergson. Riv Filosof Neo-Scolas, 82(1), 87-119, Ja-Mr 90.

Il contributo di Bergson consiste nel superamento dell'impostazione positivistica ma la sua impostazione non riesce a raggiungere quell'evidenza a cui aspira- il presunto "empirismo" Bergsoniano e' in realta un'ermeneutica che Kantiene sullo sfondo una metafisica ma che, nel rifiuto del procedimento deduttivo, si condanna a manzenere in se ampi strati di aporeticita.

PETERS, Ted. Scientific Research and the Christian Faith. Thought, 66(260), 75-94, Mr 91.

PETERSON, Grethe B (ed). *The Tanner Lectures on Human Values, Volume XI*. Salt Lake City, Univ of Utah Pr, 1990.

PETERSON, Grethe B (ed). *The Tanner Lectures On Human Values, Volume XII*. Salt Lake City, Univ of Utah Pr, 1991.

PETERSON, Jeffrey H and MARTIN, Deryl W. Insider Trading Revisited. J Bus Ethics, 10(1), 57-61, Ja 91.

A recent article in this journal argued that insider trading is an unethical practice leading to an inefficiently functioning market. The debate on this topic has primarily pitted ethical defenses of prohibition against economic arguments extolling its allowance. In addition to being incomplete, this approach ignores other unwanted economic effects of prohibition itself and unethical implications of its existence. This article shows that Adam Smith's free market concept, when properly interpreted, provides all the incentive structure necessary for an efficient and ethical marketplace even when insider trading is permitted.

PETERSON, John. Can Peirce Be a Pragmaticist and an Idealist? Trans Peirce Soc, 27(2), 221-235, Spr 91.

This paper argues that depending on whether thirdness is equivalent to signs or the genus of signs, Peirce must sacrifice his pragmatism or his idealism respectively. This is so because 1), the former is inconsistent with Peirce's pragmatic view of meaning and in particular with his view that the meaning of a word comes down to a habit and 2), the latter precludes the identification of reality with Mind.

PETERSON, John. Universals and Predication of Species. Mod Sch, 68(2), 153-162, Ja 91.

It is argued that Aristotelian realism is the only view of universals under which predication by species is possible. Platonists construe 'a is F' as 'a exemplifies F'. Besides inviting an infinite regress of exemplifications as Ryle pointed out, this account of 'a is F' excludes our saying what a is in and of itself. Nominalist accounts of 'a is F' are no more successful. They generally end up reintroducing universals in attempting to eliminate them, as D M Armstrong has argued. And since they deny common features, they exclude species altogether and hence by species.

PETERSON, Philip L. Complexly Fractionated Syllogistic Quantifiers. J Phil Log, 20(3), 287-313, Ag 91.

PETERSON, Philip L and CARNES, Robert D. Intermediate Quantifiers versus Percentages. Notre Dame J Form Log, 32(2), 294-306, Spr 91.

In his 1986 paper (*Notre Dame Journal of Formal Logic*) Thompson offers rules for determining validity and invalidity of so-called "statistical syllogisms" (syllogisms with percentages replacing the traditional quantities of universal and particular) which are both *un*sound and *in*complete. As a result, his claim that the genuine 5-quantity syllogistic (the traditional syllogistic with the three "intermediate" quantities added, expressible by "few", "many", and "most") is included in his system is trivial, *if* true at all. It turns out not to be even true, as revealed by detailed examination of distribution, Thompson's rules, and his claims for equivalences.

PETERSON, Philip L. What is Empirical in Mathematics? Phil Math, 6(1), 91-109, 1991.

PETERSON, Robert A and BELTRAMINI, Richard F and KOZMETSKY, George. Concerns of College Students Regarding Business Ethics: A Replication. J Bus Ethics, 10(10), 733-738, O 91.

In 1984 we reported the results of surveying a nationwide sample of college students about selected business ethics issues. We concluded that (a) college students were in general concerned about the issues investigated and (b) female students were relatively more concerned than were male students. The present study replicated our earlier study and not only corroborated both of its conclusions, but also found a higher level of concern than had been observed previously.

PETERSON, Robin T. Physical Environment Television Advertisement Themes: 1979 and 1989. J Bus Ethics, 10(3), 221-228, Mr 91.

The study which this manuscript describes involved a content analysis of television advertisements appearing in 1979 and 1989. Advertisements appearing during each of the two years were classified as to whether they embraced ecology (physical environment) themes, by subject area, by size of firm, and by industry. Several important conclusions relating to the subject matter of the study were drawn. These were that television advertisers sponsor only a moderate number of ecologically responsible commercials, some of the advertisers' sponsorship may be traced to altruistic goals, the percentage of commercials with ecology themes has increased slightly from 1979 to 1989, and some changes in the topical areas that the advertisements feature have taken place. Also larger enterprises and firms in the manufacturing, retailing, and financial institution sectors sponsored relatively large numbers of ecologically responsible advertisements.

PETIT, Jean-Luc. Eléments pour une "philosophie de la psychologie". Rev Metaph Morale, 96(2), 181-195, Ap-Je 91.

In psychology, Wittgenstein declared himself to be "obscurantist": and when one seeks in his work elements for the renewal of the philosophy of psychology that is called for by the development of cognitive sciences? One finds that, not only does his grammatical analysis break up the unity of the basic concepts that are required in a model of the workings of the human mind (such as the new computational model), it casts out both the phenomenology of our intentional experience and the speculation about the mental or cerebral mechanisms that we need to postulate to take the former into account. Does not such an attitude nowadays run the risk of prevent us from seeing the philosophical relevance of the psychological theories of language and cognition?

PETKOV, Vesselin. Simultaneity, Conventionality and Existence. Brit J Phil Sci, 40(1), 69-76, Mr 89.

The present paper pursues two aims. First to show that the experiment proposed by Stolakis [1986] does not lead to absolute synchronization in a single frame of reference and therefore also to the measurement of one-way velocity of light. Second, by consecutively considering the problems of the conventionality of simultaneity and of existence to show that the simultaneity of distant events can be a matter of convention only in a four-dimensional world.

PETREY, Sandy. *Speech Acts and Literary Theory*. New York, Routledge, 1990.

PETRIE, Bradford. Nonautonomous Psychology. S J Phil, 28(4), 539-559, Wint 90.

PETRONI, Angelo Maria. *I Modelli l'Invenzione e la Conferma*. Milan, Angeli, 1990.

This volume considers the relevance of the 'New Philosophy of Science' beginning with an analysis of the effects of the Copernican revolution. The means and methods of scientific revolutions are analysed. (staff)

PETROV, V V and PEREVERZEV, V N. Logic and Knowledge Representation. Commun Cog, 23(4), 267-276, 1990.

PETTIT, Philip and SMITH, Michael. Backgrounding Desire. Phil Rev, 99(4), 565-592, O 90.

Assume that desire is always involved in the genesis of intentional action. Does this mean that in practical deliberation, the intentional agent takes the state of his desires into account? We argue that it does not: that while desire is always present in the background of intentioanl action, it need not figure in the foreground of deliberation. We then go on to show that this view of things—we call it 'the strict background view'—impacts on a number of current debates in moral philosophy. It undermines two well-known arguments, one in defence of cognitivism, the other in defence of utilitarianism, and it has an important significance for our understanding of autonomy, integrity and prudence.

PETTIT, Philip and JACKSON, Frank. Causation in the Philosophy of Mind. Phil Phenomenol Res, 50 SUPP, 195-214, Fall 90.

Causation has come to play an increasingly important role in the philosophy of mind, reaching its apotheosis in the doctrine that to be a mental state of kind K is to fill the causal role definitive of that kind of mental state. Ironically, there is, from this very functionalist perspective, a problem about how to understand the causal role of mental properties. This problem surfaces in the debates over the language of thought, over broad content, and over the eliminativist implications of connectionism. We offer a solution to the problem, and then apply it to the debate over connectionism and eliminativism.

PETTIT, Philip. "Consequentialism" in *A Companion to Ethics*, SINGER, Peter (ed), 230-240. Cambridge, Blackwell, 1991.

Consequentialists and their opponents both acknowledge universal values, or so it is argued in this paper. They differ on how the right option in any decision is supposed to respond to the relevant value. Intuitively, consequentialists look for the promotion of value, their opponents for the honouring of value. This distinction may be made precise in a number of ways. Plausibly, for example, to promote a value is to maximise its expected realisation; to honour the value is to act in a way that would promote its expected realisation if there were no other influences present. The distinction applies with all values and so the divide between consequentialists and their opponents is relevant in all areas of ethics.

PFEIFER, Karl. A Short Vindication of Reichenbach's "Event-Splitting". Log Anal, 31(121-122), 143-152, Mr-Je 88.

In "The Logical Form of Action Sentences" Donald Davidson argues that Hans Reichenbach's analysis of action and event sentences is "radically defective." I show that Reichenbach can easily deflect Davidson's objections, thus leaving their respective accounts largely comparable.

PFEIFFER, Helmut. A Theorem on Labelled Trees and the Limits of Its Provability. Z Math Log, 36(2), 107-122, 1990.

The set of all finite trees which are labelled by certain ordinals is provided with a binary relation such that it becomes a well-quasi-ordering. By mapping a subset of this set onto a certain system of ordinal notations, which W Buchholz introduced, it can be shown that the set being well-quasi-ordered cannot be proven in a system with iterated inductive definition. This continues the generization S Simpson gave for a result of H Friedman, who showed that Kruskal's Theorem cannot be proven in a certain system of arithmetic.

PFENNING, Frank and MILLER, Dale and NADATHUR, Gopalan and SCEDROV, Andre. Uniform Proofs as a Foundation for Logic Programming. Annals Pure Applied Log, 51(1-2), 125-157, Mr 91.

PFERSMANN, Otto. Le droit de l'État et le devoir de l'individu. Rev Metaph Morale, 95(4), 457-470, O-D 90.

PHELAN, James. Is *King Lear* Like the Pacific Ocean or the Washington Monument? Critical Pluralism and Literary Interpretation. Monist, 73(3), 421-436, Jl 90.

The essay examines the ontological status of the literary text as viewed by the critical pluralist. Are texts already constructed prior to interpretation or are they always constructed in the act of interpretation? Because pluralism is itself based on the principle of reciprocal priority, i.e., the idea that different valid systems can account for each other, the thorough-going pluralist will accept both views of the text's status. That conclusion means that pluralism is itself plural, that the different views give rise to different, reciprocally prior pluralisms.

PHELAN, Shane. The Jargon of Authenticity: Adorno and Feminist Essentialism. Phil Soc Crit, 16(1), 39-54, 1990.

This paper reviews Adorno's critique of the "jargon of authenticity" and turns it to an analysis of the problems facing contemporary American feminist theory. I argue that Audre Lorde manages to retain the idea of authenticity without falling into jargon while many white feminists have failed because she consistently returns us to material, social reality. Authenticity for her is not an abstraction from or transcendence of the historical, but is located within it. Finally, I argue that the problem of authenticity provides a useful approach to the current feminist debates about essentialism.

PHIFER, Kenneth W. A New Humanism: A Response. Relig Hum, 25(1), 17-18, Wint 91.

PHILIPS, Michael. Preferential Hiring and the Question of Competence. J Bus Ethics, 10(2), 161-163, F 91.

It is widely believed that preferential hiring practices inevitably result in hiring less qualified candidates for jobs. Indeed, this follows analytically from some definitions of "preferential hiring" (e.g., George Sher's). This paper describes several preferential hiring strategies that do not have this consequence. Sher's definition is thus shown to be inadequate and an alternative definition is proposed.

PHILLIPS GRIFFITHS, A. Certain Hope. Relig Stud, 26(4), 453-461, D 90.

PHILLIPS, D Z. Religion in Wittgenstein's Mirror. Philosophy, 28, 135-150, 90 Supp.

The is an examination of the sense in which Wittgenstein's Philosophy of Religion leaves everything where it is. Wittgenstein examines the relation of philosophy to religion in five contexts which are explored: a) the view that all religious beliefs are confused; b) confused accounts of religious beliefs; c) religion and superstition; d) reaction to religious beliefs where each person has to speak for himself; e) a pragmatic view of examples.

PHILLIPS, D Z. Waiting for the Vanishing Shed. Phil Theol, 5(4), 333-353, Sum 91.

An examination is offered of the claim that the possibility of religious belief is related to the possibility of "lucus naturae," in the special sense of the phrase which many philosophers have adopted, in terms of its implications for the notion of the limits of intelligibility. The exposition includes a critical assessment of arguments offered by Peter Winch, R. F. Holland, Norman Malcolm, and H. O. Mounce.

PHILLIPS, Hollibert E. On Appealing to the Evidence. Phil Forum, 22(3), 228-242, Spr 91.

This paper views evidence as an epistemic function. It examines and rejects the traditional trinitarian view of evidence which understands evidence as discovery. It argues that evidence, in contradistinction to states of affairs, is never "out there" to be found. The status of evidence is one of conferral or stipulation in the service of some narrative, not one of discovery, hence the world does not abound in evidence by virtue of its abounding states of affairs. There are no free-standing bits of evidence. No narrative, no evidence. This view favours knowledge as justified belief.

PHILLIPS, Hollibert. Special Problems in Teaching Modern Philosophy. Teach Phil, 13(3), 217-226, S 90.

This paper addresses the question of how to achieve enduring student interest and excitement in courses in the history of philosophy taught at the undergraduate level. Based on what I found successful in my own teaching, I addressed it in terms of six problem areas, the discussion of which hinted at crucial considerations of manner and matter. Urging against instructional drift, I emphasized the importance of students acquiring a sense of philosophical geography.

PHILLIPS, Nelson. The Sociology of Knowledge: Toward an Existential View of Business Ethics. J Bus Ethics, 10(10), 787-795, O 91.

Business ethics is the study of ethics as it applies to a particular sphere of human activity. As such, business ethics presupposes a difference between an individual's experience within a business organization and his or her experience outside the organization. But how do we examine this difference? How do we discuss an individual's experience of "everyday reality"? What processes create and sustain this reality, and how does one's version of "reality" affect what is, and what is not, ethical? This paper outlines an approach to these questions based on theory from the sociology of knowledge, an approach which makes some progress towards making business ethics more existential. (edited)

PHILLIPS, Winfred George. Blanshard's Ethics of Belief and Metaphysical Postulates. Relig Stud, 27(2), 139-156, Je 91.

PHILONENKO, Alexis. Clausewitz ou l'oeuvre inachevée: l'esprit de la guerre. Rev Metaph Morale, 95(4), 471-512, O-D 90.

PICARDI, Eva. "Davidson on Assertion, Convention and Belief" in *The Mind of Donald Davidson*, BRANDL, Johannes (ed), 97-107. Amsterdam, Rodopi, 1989.

The attitude of believing or "holding true" fulfills a twofold role in Davidson's theory of meaning: it provides the basic evidence for a theory of radical interpretation and it also constitutes the key notion in terms of which the linguistic act of assertion is to be characterized. It is, however, doubtful whether the notion of "holding true" can fulfill either of these two roles without presupposing an implicit grasp of the public significance of the practice of making assertions. The lack of specific conventions governing assertoric force and linking assertion to what is believed true is no ground for supposing that a theory of meaning can dispense with an account of the act of assertion: on the contrary, such an account is indispensable if we are to understand the bearing of the notion of truth on that of linguistic meaning.

PICHÉ, Claude. "Art and Democracy in Habermas" in *Writing the Politics of Difference*, SILVERMAN, Hugh J (ed), 265-274. Albany, SUNY Pr, 1991.

In the early sketch of the theory of communicative reason, Habermas had mentioned the feasibility of a philosophical aesthetics inspired by Piaget's conception of learning processes. With the publication of *The Philosophical Discourse of Modernity* however, Habermas seems to abandon aesthetics, and to confine the reflection on art to art criticism. His subjectivist view of art (truthfulness, expressivity) might be responsible for this giving up of philosophical aesthetics.

PICHÉ, Claude. Rousseau et Kant: A propos de la genèse de la théorie kantienne des idées. Rev Phil Fr, 180(4), 625-635, O-D 90.

PICKERING, John (ed) and SKINNER, Martin (ed). *From Sentience To Symbols*. Buffalo, Univ of Toronto Pr, 1990.

Consciousness has returned as a central issue to contemporary psychology and is providing a meeting ground for all who study the mind. This collection of writings on consciousness has been selected in the expectation that readers from one discipline will be able to find bridges to others. The book covers physical, biological, cognitive, philosophical, and social aspects of consciousness which are arranged in eleven sections, each preceded by editorial introduction and discussion. Its emphasis is on tracing all stages in the emergence of consciousness. The capacity for symbolic thought, for language, and for self-awareness is so much more highly developed in human beings than in other species that it amounts to a qualitative break in the evolutionary progression of mental powers. The authors are concerned with how it is that the direct awareness of the world which human beings share with other sentient organisms has been transcended to yield the unique human mode of being in the world. A key theme is the reflextive capacity of the human mind which brings into being and is brought into being by the human social and cultural context.

PIENKOWSKI, M. Probability and Epistemology. Phil Sci (Tucson), 2, 81-104, 1986.

Different interpretations of the concepts of chance and probability are briefly reviewed. They strongly depend on epistemological assumptions accepted at the beginning. In the interpretation of probability, as it operates within the empirical sciences, one of the major problems is to reconcile its "subjectivity" and "objectivity." The notion of a subjective representation of the world enables one to view the subjectivity and objectivity as complementary rather than opposing features of probability. "Randomness" turns out to be an epistemological category, and with the help of it one may explain the subjective representation of reality but not the real world itself. The "probability" description, like other epistemological constructions, cannot reach beyond the level of phenomena, especially as probabilistic laws can only be verified in a probabilistic manner. This lack of "equal rights" between deterministic and probabilistic laws suggests the existence of causality in the real world, although the concept of causality itself may need an essential broadening.

PIERCE, Christine. "Postmodernism and Other Skepticisms" in *Feminist Ethics*, CARD, Claudia (ed), 60-77. Lawrence, Univ Pr of Kansas, 1991.

PIEROZZI, Letizia and SCAPPARONE, Elisabetta. Il volgarizzamento del "De Rerum natura" di Bernardino Telesio a opera di Francesco Martelli. G Crit Filosof Ital, 69(2), 160-181, My-Ag 90.

PIERRE, Christian (trans) and ORTEGA Y GASSET, José. *Velázquez et Goya*. Paris, Klincksieck, 1990.

PIERSON, Dominique. Sur l'habitation poétique de l'homme. Heidegger Stud, 6, 107-113, 1990.

PIGDEN, Charles R. "Naturalism" in *A Companion to Ethics*, SINGER, Peter (ed), 421-431. Cambridge, Blackwell, 1991.

Naturalists proclaim that moral judgments are cognitive and sometimes true, but that no peculiarly moral facts or properties are needed to make them true. Hume's No-Ought-From-Is claim can be defended against Prior but poses no threat to naturalism. (It is just that in logic you don't get out what you haven't put in.) Moore's 'naturalistic fallacy' arguments would not disprove naturalism even if they were sound. But they rely on dubious premises particularly a 'publicity condition'. Thus the usual anti-naturalist arguments fail. However, the leading boards of naturalism all suffer from serious defects.

PIGUET, J-Claude. The Passing On of Values (in French). Rev Theol Phil, 123(2), 147-158, 1991.

The value is not passed on; only goods are passed on, and the value is not a good. Spiritual goods are often confused with values. But values can either be absolute or relative: when they are relative, they are added to goods, but when they are absolute, they are not relational. Between an absolute value and a good, there is not a relation but a linkage: the presence of the universal in the individual. This linkage calls on the freedom of the receiver, a freedom which is not however freedom of choice.

PIKE, Burton (trans) and LUFT, David S (trans) and MUSIL, Robert. Ruminations of a Slow-witted Mind. Crit Inquiry, 17(1), 46-61, Autumn 90.

Abridgement of drafts of an incisive essay Musil wrote in 1933 in reaction to the Nazis coming to power in Germany. (Complete text in Musil, *Precision and Soul*, University of Chicago Press.) A penetrating contemporary analysis of the cultural sources and prospects of Naxism's effects on German politics, culture and society, and on the role of Jews and anti-semitism in Nazi iconography. Written from Musil's own experience and intellectual conscience as writer, editor, and analytical social thinker.

PILARDI, Jo-Ann. "Philosophy Becomes Autobiography: The Development of the Self in the Writings of Simone de Beauvoir" in *Writing the Politics of Difference*, SILVERMAN, Hugh J (ed), 145-162. Albany, SUNY Pr, 1991.

This essay compares Beauvoir's notion of the self in her directly philosophical writings with her presentation of a self in her autobiographical writings. It begins by showing that Beauvoir's analysis in *The Second Sex* problematized her earlier existential-phenomenological notion of the self: the for-itself; consequently her existentialism gave way to determinism. The article proceeds to show that in the autobiographies both conceptions of the self are evident and that Beauvoir's autobiographical writings bear the mark of a thinker who wanted to preserve the tension between freedom and determinism inherent in *The Second Sex*.

PILET, Paul-Emile. L'étude du vivant et la méthodologie ouverte. Dialectica, 44(3-4), 333-341, 1990.

This study—dedicated to Ferdinand Gonseth—is divided into three parts. The first one is devoted to a critical analysis of some of the essential properties of the biological material. In the second the main difficulties of its experimental analysis are discussed. The final part summarises a few epistemological problems raised by research on the living objects; references being made to the thoughts of Th S Kuhn and in particular to those of F Gonseth.

PILLAI, A S Narayana. The Bhakti Tradition in Hinduism—Bhakti Yoga an Overview. J Dharma, 15(3), 223-231, Jl-S 90.

PILLAY, A and MARKER, D. Reducts of (C,+,·) Which Contain +. J Sym Log, 55(3), 1243-1251, S 90.

PILLAY, Anand. Differentially Algebraic Group Chunks. J Sym Log, 55(3), 1138-1142, S 90.

It is shown that a group interpretable in a differentially closed field K can be definably equipped with the structure of a differential algebraic group over K (in the sense of Kolchin). The proof depends on the theory of stable groups.

PINCHARD, Bruno. Congruenza, schematismo, sintesi: Prospettive leibniziane intorno al criterio di verità secondo Giambattista Vico. Boll Centro Stud Vichiani, 20, 141-156, 1990.

PINCHES, Charles. Principle Monism and Action Descriptions: Situationism and its Critics Revisited. Mod Theol, 7(3), 249-268, Ap 91.

Briefly reconstructing the situation ethics debate, I suggest a key but unresolved issue was the status of action descriptions, particularly moral ones. Situationalism, as its critic rightly saw, ignored the moral force of these descriptions by reforming them in terms of its moral theory. Yet, I argue that this strategy connects with a more widespread theoretical and ultimately reductive impulse I call "principle monism." Kantianism and utilitarianism both reveal this impulse as does situationisms strongest critic, Paul Ramsey. After arguing that principle monism disregards the complex texture of action descriptions, I offer suggestions for constructing a non-monist Christian ethics.

PINCKAERS, Servais. Christ, Moral Absolutes, and the Good: Recent Moral Theology. Thomist, 55(1), 117-140, Ja 91.

PINCOFFS, Edmund L. Government and Character. Soc Theor Pract, 17(2), 337-344, Sum 91.

PINEAU, Lois. Russell on Ordinary Names and Synonymy. Hist Phil Quart, 7(1), 93-108, Ja 90.

I argue against the view that Russell held a sense theory of names according to which each ordinary proper name is synonymous with some one definite description, and against Kripke's claim that this is the only charitable interpretation of Russell. I show that for Russell the definition of a proper name has nothing to do with synonymy, and indeed amounts to nothing more than a true description. This view is much closer to Kripke's own 'fix the reference' thesis than the one which he attributes to Russell.

PINK, T L M. Purposive Intending. Mind, 100(399), 343-359, Jl 91.

Aristotle's model of the practical deliberation that leads us to intend to do act A is that it is deliberation just about whether to do A. The model is defended by such as Anscombe, Davidson and Bratman, and entails an 'Identity thesis' that our reasons for intending to do A are just our reasons for doing A. The paper argues that this model of practical reason is false, as is the Identity thesis it entails. Intending is something we do for action coordinatory purposes. In being purposive intention resembles action and differs from desire.

PINKARD, Terry. "A Reply to David Duquette's "Kant, Hegel and the Possibility of a Speculative Logic"" in *Essays on Hegel's Logic*, DI GIOVANNI, George (ed), 17-25. Albany, SUNY Pr, 1990.

PINSKY, Valerie. "Commentary: A Critical Role for the History of Archaeology" in *Critical Traditions in Contemporary Archaeology*, PINSKY, Valerie (ed), 88-92. New York, Cambridge Univ Pr, 1990.

PINSKY, Valerie (ed). *Critical Traditions in Contemporary Archaeology*. New York, Cambridge Univ Pr, 1990.

PIOZZI, Patrícia. "Construindo a 'ordem anárquica". Trans/Form/Acao, 13, 11-20, 1990.

Este artigo pretende examinar alguns aspectos da doutrina social de Proudhon e de Bakunin, procurando relacionà-los com suas propostas de transformação social.

PIPER, Adrian M S. "Seeing Things". S J Phil, SUPP 29, 29-60, 1990.

PIPER, Adrian M S. "Higher-Order Discrimination" in *Identity, Character, and Morality: Essays in Moral Psychology*, FLANAGAN, Owen (ed), 285-309. Cambridge, MIT Pr, 1990.

PIPPIN, Robert B. *Modernism as a Philosophical Problem: On the Dissatisfactions of European High Culture*. Cambridge, Blackwell, 1991.

PIRO, Francesco. Processes, Substances, and Leibniz's Epistemology: A Case for Essentialism in Contemporary Physics. Phil Sci (Tucson), 2, 29-46, 1986.

Scientific interpretation of nature in terms of processes and events poses the question whether the metaphysical notion of substance can be still maintained in philosophical reflections, physical and biological phenomena. The ideas of Leibniz's essentialism are examined in order to establish a correspondence between conceptual schemes of classical metaphysics and new scientific theories. Modern interpretation of the theory of systems, in its version proposed by Prigogine, are analyzed in order to substantiate the validity of the traditional essentialist approach.

PITHOD, Abelardo. Super-yo y vida moral: Una valoración tomista de la hipótesis psicoanalítica. Sapientia, 46(180), 111-118, Ap-Je 91.

PITT, Alice. The Expression of Experience: Code's Critique of Gilligan's Abortion Study. J Moral Educ, 20(2), 177-190, My 91.

It is not clear how women's experiences and theories based on them can best be used to redress social inequality on the basis of sex difference. Appropriations of Gilligan's attempt to define women's process of moral reasoning in terms of difference risk being interpreted as accounts of female deficiency. However, Code's critique of an important aspects of Gilligan's research, the abortion study, on the grounds that abortion is only experienced by women, fails to fully recognise how abortion can be read as a socially constructed experience. Using a post-structuralist theory of language, I locate the experience of abortion as a site of contested meaning that plays itself out historically and socially in an attempt to find ways to think and theorise about experiences that do not collapse into essentialism.

PITTS, Robert E and WHALEN, Joel and WONG, John K. Exploring the Structure of Ethical Attributions as a Component of the Consumer Decision Model. J Bus Ethics, 10(4), 285-293, Ap 91.

The managerial ethics literature is used as a base for the inclusion of Ethical Attribution, as an element in the consumer's decision process. A situational model of ethical consideration is consumer behavior is proposed and examined for Personal versis Vicarious effects. Using a path analytic approach, unique structures are reported for Personal and Vicarious situations in the evaluation of a seller's unethical behavior. An attributional paradigm is suggested to explain the results.

PIZZI, Claudio. Counterfactuals and the Complexity of Causal Notions. Topoi, 9(2), 147-155, S 90.

In order to give a logical systematization to the plurality of causal notions with different degrees of complexity, two hierarchies are built moving from the minimal notion of causal relevance, based on non-nested counterfactuals. The first hierarchy is obtained by adding suitable conjuncts to any given causal notion, while the second is obtained by iterating counterfactual antecedents. The second hierarchy allows to give a proper place to the notions of overdetermining and preempting cause, which are a source of well-known difficulties for the standard counterfactual theory of causality.

PIZZIMENTI, Lee Ann. Informing Clients About Limits to Confidentiality. Bus Prof Ethics J, 9(1-2), 207-222, Spr-Sum 90.

PLACE, Ullin T. "Thirty Five Years On—Is Consciousness Still a Brain Process?" in *The Mind of Donald Davidson*, BRANDL, Johannes (ed), 19-31. Amsterdam, Rodopi, 1989.

The writer's 1956 contention that "the thesis that consciousness is a process in the brain is...a reasonable scientific hypothesis" is contrasted with Davidson's *a priori* argument in 'Mental Events' for the identity of propositional attitude tokens with some unspecified and unspecifiable brain state tokens. Davidson's argument is rejected primarily on the grounds that he has failed to establish his claim that there are and can be no psycho-physical bridge laws. The case for the empirical nature of the issue between the identity thesis and interactionism is restated in the light of an analysis of the causal relations involved. The same analysis is also used to demonstrate the incoherence of parallelism and epiphenomenalism as alternatives to interactionism.

PLANTINGA, Alvin. Justification in the 20th Century. Phil Phenomenol Res, 50 SUPP, 45-71, Fall 90.

Noting the enormous importance of justification in 20th century epistemology, I point to the bewildering variety of contemporary accounts of its nature (in Alston, Chisholm, Firth, Lehrer, Pollock, Goldman, BonJour and others). I then show how this blooming, buzzing confusion can be reduced to order and understood by tracing all of these conceptions back to their deontological roots in Descartes and Locke.

PLATO and ALLEN, R E (trans). *The Dialogues of Plato, Volume II*. New Haven, Yale Univ Pr, 1991.

PLATT, Michael. Souls Without Longing. Interpretation, 18(3), 415-465, Spr 91.

PLEINES, Jürgen-Eckardt. Teleologie: Chance oder Belastung für die Philosophie? Z Phil Forsch, 44(3), 375-398, 1990.

Within the Aristotelian tradition teleology has become a well-known concept in philosophy of nature and also in ethics, and it was in force without any doubt. Drawing the conclusions of the ideas which had been persuasive to the philosophy in the middle ages the teleological argument was nearly unacceptable to the position of enlightenment. In the meantime the situation has changed. The reason why the teleological argument became convinced, primary, was that Kant published his "critic of judgment," and in regard to his regulative position that the concept of objective idealism should gain gradually a common philosophical conviction.

PLIMAK, E and PANTIN, I. The Ideas of Karl Marx at a Turning Point in Human Civilization. Soviet Stud Phil, 30(1), 42-69, Sum 91.

PLUHAR, Evelyn. Reason and Reality Revisited. Between Species, 6(2), 63-70, Spr 90.

PLUHAR, Evelyn. Utilitarian Killing, Replacement, and Rights. J Agr Ethics, 3(2), 147-171, 1990.

The ethical theory underlying much of our treatment of animals in agriculture and research is the moral agency view. It is assumed that only moral agents, or persons, are worthy of maximal moral significance, and that farm and laboratory animals are not moral agents. However, this view also excludes human nonpersons from the moral community. Utilitarianism, which bids us maximize the amount of good (utility) in the world, is an alternative ethical theory. Although it has many merits, including impartiality and the extension of moral concern to all sentient beings, it also appears to have many morally unacceptable implications. In particular, it appears to sanction the killing of innocents when utility would be maximized. (edited)

PLUM, Stephen H and LIST, Charles J. *Library Research Guide to Philosophy: Illustrated Search Strategy and Sources*. Ann Arbor, Pierian Pr, 1990.

This book is a guide for undergraduates and beginning graduate students writing papers on philosophy. It guides the student through the use of bibliographies, encyclopedias, the card catalog, interlibrary loan, indexes, and computer searching. It includes a selective bibliography to basic reference sources in philosophy and a summary of various forms philosophy papers might take. Throughout the book a single topic is developed (Nietzsche's thoughts on war) to illustrate research strategies. Numerous figures and illustrations are used to aid the student's understanding of research tools.

PLUMWOOD, Val. Ethics and Instrumentalism: A Response to Janna Thompson. Environ Ethics, 13(2), 139-149, Sum 91.

I argue that Janna Thompson's critique of environmental ethics misrepresents the work of certain proponents of non-instrumental value theory and overlooks the ways in which intrinsic values have been related to valuers and their preferences. Some of the difficulties raised for environmental ethics (e.g., individuation) are real but would only be fatal if environmental ethics could not be supplemented by a wider environmental philosophy and practice. The proper context and motivation for the development of non-instrumental theories is not that of an objectivist value theory but rejection of the human domination and chauvinism involved in even the broadest instrumental accounts of nature as spiritual resource.

PLUMWOOD, Val. Nature, Self, and Gender: Feminism, Environmental Philosophy, and the Critique of Rationalism. Hypatia, 6(1), 3-27, Spr 91.

Rationalism is the key to the connected oppressions of women and nature in the West. Deep ecology has failed to provide an adequate historical perspective or an adequate challenge to human/nature dualism. A relational account of self enables us to reject an instrumental view of nature and develop an alternative based on respect without denying that nature is distinct from the self. This shift of focus links feminist, environmentalist, and certain forms of socialist critiques. The critique of anthropocentrisms is not sacrificed, as deep ecologists argue, but enriched.

POCOCK, J G A. "Edward Gibbon in History: Aspects of the Text in 'The History of the Decline and Fall of the Roman Empire'" in *The Tanner Lectures on Human Values, Volume XI*, PETERSON, Grethe B (ed), 289-384. Salt Lake City, Univ of Utah Pr, 1990.

PODESTA, Gustavo. La teología de la creación y el problema de los orígenes. Stromata, 46(3-4), 259-273, Jl-D 90.

POGGE, Thomas W. Die Folgen vorherrschender Moralkonzeptionen. Z Phil Forsch, 45(1), 22-37, Ja-Mr 91.

What if one's morality has effects that are, from its own point of view, counterproductive? What if the task of morality, as our own morality conceives it, would be better fulfilled by a revised version of this morality? Five answers to this problem are discussed. I argue against the two dominant answers: rigidity (no reason to make any revision) and elitism (we have reason to rethink which morality ought to be believed, but not which morality is true). I defend the plausibility of the pragmatic answer (we may have reason to revise our morality "all the way down"). For an early, briefer version in English, see *Social Research* 57/3 (1990).

PÖGGELER, Otto. The Beginning and Structure of the "Phaenomenology of Mind" (in Hungarian). Magyar Filozof Szemle, 1-2, 40-71, 1990.

Die *Phänomenologie des Geistes* ist dem Denken Hegels zum Schicksal geworden: sie legte die Krisis der Systementwicklung offen, indem sie der geschichtlichen Erfahrung Raum gab; zugleich suchte sie diese Krisis zu überwinden durch eine Logik, die "Leben" und "Geist" in ihre Grundbestimmungen aufnahm. Das Schicksal der Hegelschen Logik führt sienerseits zu der Frage, ob diese logische Gründung des Systems nicht unzulänglich blieb. Diese Frage steht auch hinter der Wirkungsgeschichte von Hegels Denken. (edited)

POHLENZ, G. Die erkenntniskritische Wendung Descartes' als Konsequenz geschichtlicher Entwicklung des Leib-Seele-Dualismus. Conceptus, 24(62), 73-97, 1990.

The radical sceptical and epistemological turn in the philosophy of modern times (Descartes) is based on the microphysiological reformulation of mind-body dualism and—perhaps more important—on an explicit sensibility for the peculiar nature of *qualia*, which appears 'revolutionary'. This context (including a special relation to Kant's theory) is analysed and reconstructed both systematically and historically. The sceptical reformulation of dualism in the *Meditations* does not at all presuppose any dualistic concept of the mental. The sceptical argumentation (as it is reconstructed in this paper) indeed has, in contrast to its modern epistemological reformulations, consequences for our fundamental concept of ourselves and of nature. Critical remarks are meant to offer some possible means for coming to grips with the so-far analysed problem situation (e.g., method of philosophical mind-body differentiation; reductio ad absurdum of the dream argument; repudiation of sense-data theory). (edited)

POIRIER, Lucien. Le stratège militaire. Rev Metaph Morale, 95(4), 437-456, O-D 90.

POIZAT, Bruno Petrovich and BOROVIK, Aleksandr Vasilievich. Tores et *p*-Groupes. J Sym Log, 55(2), 478-491, Je 90.

Dans un groupe de rang de Morley fini, les 2-sous-groupes maximaux sont localement finis et conjugués.

POJMAN, Louis P. Gilbert Harman's Internalist Moral Relativism. Mod Sch, 68(1), 19-39, N 90.

In a series of recent articles Gilbert Harman combines internalism with contractualism, producing an ingenious version of moral relativism which seems to avoid some of the standard objections to relativism. After a brief exposition of Harman's position in Part I, I offer an extended critique of his theory of internalist relativism. In Part II, I argue that Harman's arguments for the superiority of his theory over forms of ethical objectivism do not demonstrate such superiority. In Part III, I point out four additional problems with Harman's theory, and in Part IV, I argue that the internalist scheme of tying duty to motivation is problematic.

POJMAN, Louis P. *Introduction to Philosophy: Classical and Contemporary Readings*. Belmont, Wadsworth, 1991.

An introductory anthology made up of six parts: 1) What is Philosophy; 2) Theory of Knowledge; 3) Philosophy and Religion; 4) Philosophy of Mind; 5) Freedom of the Will, Responsibility and Punishment; and 6) Ethics. Two appendices follow on "How to Read and Write a Philosophy Paper" and "A Little Bit of Logic."

POLAND, Lynn. "The Bible and the Rhetorical Sublime" in *The Bible as Rhetoric: Studies in Biblical Persuasion and Credibility*, WARNER, Martin (ed), 29-49. New York, Routledge, 1990.

POLANSKY, Ronald and TORELL, Kurt. Power, Liberty, and Counterfactual Conditionals in Hobbes' Thought. Hobbes Stud, 3, 3-17, 1990.

Power and liberty in Hobbes are difficult to understand in themselves and in their relationships. He identifies power with cause, and cause is said always to be actual. It seems then that power can only be actual rather than potential. But if so, how can there be dispositional properties and counterfactual conditions? Without these liberty seems impossible. To explain how Hobbes may account for potentialities, the paper distinguishes two levels of motion, observable and unobservable. In addition, it shows that liberty only applies on the level of the observable motions and therefore has a status somewhat like a secondary quality.

POLC, Jaroslav. Libri da salvare. Aquinas, 33(2), 437-440, My-Ag 90.

POLIAKOV, Igor. L'explicite et l'implicite dans la conception du signe chez Hobbes. Philosophiques, 17(2), 23-51, Autumn 1990.

The author extricates and exposes at first the explicit model proposed by Hobbes to analyse semiotical phenomena, and the context in which this model is developed, showing by the way how this model, in many respects, might still be interesting for contemporary philosophers of language. Then, he reconstructs the approaches adopted by Hobbes, formulates the basic principles on which they rest, and identifies some problems of coherence resulting from the whole approach. He proposes, at last, an interpretation which enables us to solve some apparent contradictions met in the analysis of the model proposed by Hobbes by exploring anew the initial context of this model and the basic ontological categories which are implicated in Hobbes's semiotical analysis.

POLICARPO, J. A Teologia e a Filosofia perante os desafios da Cultura Contemporânea. Rev Port Filosof, 46(3), 297-308, Jl-S 90.

In the search for an answer to the problems of contemporary man, theology and philosophy find themselves in a common mission not only within the university context, but also in larger one involving the science and culture. Truth should be the main concern of the contemporary university, resisting at all costs that both itself and the worldview be reduced to a limited horizon; it should assure the harmonious unity of knowledge through an interdisciplinary convergence when truth occupies the first place. To the degree that a scholar — whatever his speciality may be — opens himself spontaneously towards interdisciplinary collaboration, he reveals his concern with the truth. Theology and Philosophy have here a special role given their peculiar vocation of synthesis, as well as being necessary in the search for man's most profound meaning.

POLIKAROV, Azaria. On the Nature of Einstein's Realism. Epistemologia, 12(2), 277-304, Jl-D 89.

It is argued (against A Fine's and D Howard's recent publications) that Einstein's philosophical conception is a realistic one. The features of the latter are specified (in an order of subordination), viz.,: philosophic-materialistic and scientific, essentialist, deterministic, critical, prorationalist, and convergent.

POLIS, Dennis F. A New Reading of Aristotle's *Hyle*. Mod Sch, 68(3), 225-244, Mr 91.

Hyle, often mis-translated 'matter,' is pivotal to continuing controversies on 'prime matter.' The literature is reviewed and found to involve fundamental misunderstandings of *Hyle* as an indeterminate 'stuff' or as a principle of passive potency. These arise from a conflation of Aristotle's *Hyle* with the 'mother of all becoming' of Plato's *Timaeus*. The conflation can be resolved by examining Aristotle's concepts of potency, substance and efficient cause. The confusion of *Hyle* and matter results from a failure to distinguish natural and artificial productions. *Hyle* actually is a concept of determinate dynamics similar to our 'law of nature.'

POLKINGHORNE, Donald. "Psychology after Philosophy" in *Reconsidering Psychology: Perspectives from Continental Philosophy*, FAULCONER, James E (ed), 92-115. Pittsburgh, Duquesne Univ Pr, 1990.

POLKINGHORNE, J C. "A Revived Natural Theology" in *Science and Religion: One World-Changing Perspectives on Reality*, FENNEMA, Jan (ed), 87-97. Norwell, Kluwer, 1990.

It is argued that the scientific perception of the universe's deep intelligibility and anthropic fruitfulness encourages the revival of natural theology in a modest insightful mode.

POLKINGHORNE, John C. The Nature of Physical Reality. Zygon, 26(2), 221-236, Je 91.

This account of the dynamical theory of chaos leads to a metaphysical picture of a world with an open future, in which the laws of physics are emergent-downward approximations to a more subtle and supple reality and in which there is downward causation through information input as well as upward causation through energy input. Such a metaphysical picture can accommodate both human and divine agency.

POLLACK, Detlef. Bestandserhaltung oder Kritik oder: Weder Bestandserhaltung noch Kritik—Die Intention der Systemtheorie Niklas Luhmanns. Deut Z Phil, 39(1), 95-99, 1991.

The reception of Niklas Luhmann's system theory up to this day strong influenced by the Frankfurter Schule has very often drawed in his theory in the opposition between apologetic and criticism of modern society. In order to destinate the intention of the system theory it is usefully to find out the opposite, to which Luhmann himself puts his theory. This opposite is the so called "old european" tradition of thinking, in which the "human synthesis of the whole" (liberty, equality, verity) is the highest. The approach of the system theory constitutes by the rejection of unity projects. Instead of synthesis difference is the highest term in Luhmann's theory.

POLLACK, Detlef. Escaping from Reality or Coming to Terms with It—What is Religion? (in German). Deut Z Phil, 38(7), 660-668, 1990.

POLLACK, Martha E (ed) and COHEN, Philip R (ed) and MORGAN, Jerry (ed). *Intentions in Communication*. Cambridge, MIT Pr, 1990.

POLLACK, Martha E. Overloading Intentions for Efficient Practical Reasoning. Nous, 25(4), 513-536, S 91.

POLLARD, Stephen. More Axioms for the Set-Theoretic Hierarchy. Log Anal, 31(121-122), 85-88, Mr-Je 88.

This paper offers a reformulation of Van Aken's axioms for set theory. A rank operator is taken as primitive rather than a binary relation of rank order. This allows for an easy transition to standard set theory. The paper concludes with a general discussion of structuralist justifications of set theoretic axioms.

POLLARD, Stephen. A Strengthening of Scott's ZF-Minus-Extensionality Result. Notre Dame J Form Log, 31(3), 369-370, Sum 90.

Scott's proof that ZF is not interpretable in ZF-minus-extensionality can be transformed into a proof that a theory much weaker than ZF is not interpretable in ZF-minus-extensionality.

POLLIO, Howard R and HENLEY, Tracy. Empirical and Philosophical Reactions to Harcum's "Behavioral Paradigm for a Psychological Resolution of ...". J Mind Behav, 12(1), 115-134, Wint 91.

This paper begins with a brief description and analysis of Harcum's "Behavioral Paradigm for a Psychological Resolution of the Free Will Issue" focusing on issues concerning first-person and third-person perspectives in psychological research and theory. This consideration is expanded to cover a variety of related issues including "unconscious processes" and philosophical discussions of free will. Two studies, similar to Harcum's original study, but analyzed from a first-person perspective, are reported and contrasted with Harcum's work. Results of these studies reveal that different individuals provide meanings for the same actions, e.g., sitting in one or another seat in a college classroom. The significance of these findings for psychological research concerning the experience and concept of free will are discussed in light of an alternative, existential-phenomenological approach to psychology.

POLLOCK, John L. *How to Build a Person: A Prolegomenon*. Cambridge, MIT Pr, 1989.

The book is a defense of token physicalism (mental state tokens are also physical state tokens), agent materialism (persons are physical objects), and strong AI. The particular version of strong AI defended is rational functionalism, according to which any system that appropriately mimics human rational architecture will possess thoughts, desires, and other mental states. The enterprise of constructing such an artificial person is underway in the OSCAR project, and the present state of the OSCAR project described. This includes a general theory of the sturcture of a rational agent, and some details about the structure of interest-driven defeasible reasoning.

POLLOCK, John L. *Nomic Probability and the Foundations of Induction*. New York, Oxford Univ Pr, 1990.

The objective of this book is to make sense of objective probability and probabilistic reasoning. It is urged that what is required is to couple state-of-the-art epistemology regarding defeasible reasoning with fairly standard mathematics. The theory begins by assuming a defeasible version of the statistical syllogism, and a slightly strengthened probability calculus, and then it is shown that theories of direct inference and statistical and enumerative induction can be derived as theorems. The induction principles are non-Bayesian, taking the form of the Nicod principle instead.

POLLOCK, John L. "Philosophy and Artificial Intelligence" in *Philosophical Perspectives, 4: Action Theory and Philosophy of Mind, 1990*, TOMBERLIN, James E (ed), 461-498. Atascadero, Ridgeview, 1990.

POLSEK, Darko. On the Other Side of the Open Science (in Serbo-Croatian). Filozof Istraz, 34(1), 255-257, 1990.

In this paper the author critically considers some theses from A Vujic's paper "Troubles with Popper," which is published in *Filozofska istrazivanja* 29 (2/1989), p. 671-674.

PÖLTNER, Günter. El concepto de "conformidad a fines" en la Crítica del Juicio Estético. Anu Filosof, 23(1), 99-112, 1990.

POMBO, Olga. "Hegel e a linguagem: estudo em forma de prefácio ou introdução" in *Dinâmica do Pensar: Homenagem a Oswaldo Market*, FAC LETRAS UNIV LISBOA (ed), 189-215. Lisboa, Fac Letras U Lisboa, 1991.

The aim of this paper is to understand Hegel's position concerning language in the *Enzyklopädie der philosophischen Wissenschaften im Grundrisse* calling attention to the points of continuity and rupture between Hegel and Leibniz, namely in what regards the praise of the German language and the nature of the linguistic signs.

POMERANTZ, Alfred. The Existence of Non-Existence of Things which are Not in the Mind. Philosophia (Israel), 20(4), 395-403, F 91.

POMORSKI, Jan. Hayden White: "Historicism" as Linguistic Relativism in Historiography (in Polish). Ann Univ Mariae Curie-Phil, 11, 189-202, 1986.

The study discusses the views of Hayden White, American historian and philosopher of culture, one of the leading modern representatives of the analytical tendency in philosophy of history, about the problem of relativism in historical sciences. White stands on the position that the subjective conditioning of historical cognition should be sought primarily in the specific way of using the narrative technique of imaging the past, typical of historians and philosophers of history: hence, studies on historical narration acquire fundamental significance for him. The author presents White's conception of narration, emphasizing those of its elements which are connected with the problem of relativism in its ontological, epistemological and linguistic aspects. Commenting on White's position, the author pays attention to the subjective manner of his viewing cultural phenomena which constitutes a considerable achievement in comparison with the so-far existing practice of the "analysts," and he also stresses the methodological individualism of White's own research practice.

POMPA, Leon. *Human Nature and Historical Knowledge: Hume, Hegel and Vico*. New York, Cambridge Univ Pr, 1990.

The purpose is to dispute the widely held view that historical knowledge rests upon inference from evidence supported ultimately by theories of human nature. Through substantial discussions of the works of Hume, Hegel and Vico, it is shown that such a view renders the distinction between historical fact and fiction unsustainable, because the historian must occupy a viewpoint external to historical reality itself. An alternative is developed in which it is argued that historical investigation can lead to knowledge of fact only where it is supported by a framework of inherited rather than inferential knowledge, which is constitutive within, rather than external to, historical consciousness.

POMPA, Leon. *Vico: A Study of the 'New Science' (Second Edition)*. New York, Cambridge Univ Pr, 1990.

PONCE ALBERCA, Carmen. Consideraciones en torno a la polémica Leibniz-Clarke. Espiritu, 36(95), 79-90, Ja-Je 87.

PONFERRADA, Gustavo E. El nombre propio de Dios. Sapientia, 45(178), 249-268, O-D 90.

PONFERRADA, Gustavo E. Santo Tomás y la prostitución. Sapientia, 45(177), 225-230, Jl-S 90.

PONZELLINI, Ornella. "Giovanni Gualberto (Alberto) De Soria e la 'Cosmologia'" in *Scienza, Filosofia e Religione tra '600 e '700 in Italia*, PREDAVAL MAGRINI, Maria Vittoria (ed), 261-325. Milan, Angeli, 1990.

PONZIO, Augusto. L'epoché di Husserl in Ferruccio Rossi-Landi. Il Protag, 6(13-16), 107-119, Ja 88-D 89.

POOLE, Ross. *Morality and Modernity*. New York, Routledge, 1991.

This book argues that the modern world calls into existence certain conceptions of morality but also creates ideals of rationality and agency which destroy the grounds for taking morality seriously. It argues that utilitarianism and Kantianism are moralities appropriate to the modern public world, and that a quasi-Aristotelian ethic of virtue is characteristic of private life. It presents a critique of some significant responses to modernity: neo-Kantian liberalism (Gewirth, Rawls and Habermas); nationalism; Nietzsche's 'positive' nihilism; and the evocation of past communities (MacIntyre). Finally, it argues that while 'we moderns' may lack sufficient reason to act as morality requires, we do have reason to hope for the kind of society which would make a rational practice of morality possible.

POPE, Stephen J. Aquinas on Almsgiving, Justice and Charity: An Interpretation and Reassessment. Heythrop J, 32(2), 167-191, Ap 91.

This article attempts to correct the current view of charity as opposed by justice by examining the treatment of this subject in the writings of Aquinas. It argues that the Thomistic notions of charity and almsgiving are much richer and more complex than what finds in modern uses of the same terms, that the harmony between justice and charity is superior to the opposition between these terms, tht charity in Thomas' view is more stringent than charity in classical liberalism and that these must not be confused or identified, and that at the same time charity in Thomas' view may be "ordered," i.e., intelligently and wisely submitted to the priorities established by practical wisdom. Finally, it argues that the strength of Thomas' view lies in the balance of universalism with an incorporation of the moral centrality of natural priorities.

POPKIN, Richard H. "The Crisis of Polytheism and the Answers of Vossius, Cudworth, and Newton" in *Essays on the Context, Nature, and Influence of Isaac Newton's Theology*, FORCE, James E (ed), 9-25. Norwell, Kluwer, 1990.

POPKIN, Richard H. "Newton and Fundamentalism, II" in *Essays on the Context, Nature, and Influence of Isaac Newton's Theology*, FORCE, James E (ed), 165-180. Norwell, Kluwer, 1990.

POPKIN, Richard H. "Newton as a Bible Scholar" in *Essays on the Context, Nature, and Influence of Isaac Newton's Theology*, FORCE, James E (ed), 103-118. Norwell, Kluwer, 1990.

POPKIN, Richard H. "Polytheism, Deism, and Newton" in *Essays on the Context, Nature, and Influence of Isaac Newton's Theology*, FORCE, James E (ed), 27-42. Norwell, Kluwer, 1990.

POPKIN, Richard H. "Some Further Comments on Newton and Maimonides" in *Essays on the Context, Nature, and Influence of Isaac Newton's Theology*, FORCE, James E (ed), 1-7. Norwell, Kluwer, 1990.

POPKIN, Richard H. Was Spinoza a Marrano of Reason? Philosophia (Israel), 20(3), 243-246, D 90.

POPOV, Stefan. Community and Utopia: A Transcendental Deduction. Phil Soc Crit, 16(4), 291-302, 1990.

POPP, Jerome. A Normative Theory of Teaching. Phil Stud Educ, /, 1-15, 1989.

PORÉE, Jérôme. Le temps du souffrir: Remarques critiques sur la phénoménologie de M Henry. Arch Phil, 54(2), 213-240, Ap-Je 91.

According to M Henry, and against Heidegger, transcendence is not the last secret of phenomenality; his own philosophy is one of immanence (but both philosophers may not be so wide apart as it seems); both deny the ethical dimension of the question about the meaning of being. We should link together time's ecstasy and self-intimacy of feeling and search in suffering for a presupposition both ethical and ontological of possible experience.

PORENA, Boris. The Metacultural Hypothesis and the Foundations of Cultural Activity (in Polish). Ann Univ Mariae Curie-Phil, 10, 23-40, 1985.

The Centre of Metacultural Studies and Experiments was founded in 1974 in Cantalupo in Sabina on the initiative of a small team of musicians interested in looking for new means to include musical practice in social life. The Centre at once appeared as a partner in the dialogue, both cultural and political, interested not only in music but also in the whole of the cultural development of the province and in the increase in its ability to undertake initiative in all domains, also economical. Those activities gave birth to two new theoretical-practical hypotheses, one connected with the concept of a self-generating circuit and the other with the professional model of a cultural worker on the basic level activity. The paper also presents experiments connected with composing, listening to, and analyzing music. (edited)

PORK, Andrus. History, Lying, and Moral Responsibility. Hist Theor, 29(3), 321-330, O 90.

Scholars's moral responsibility for the objective content of their investigations is an important, but neglected problem both in the English-speaking and Soviet philosophies of history. The re-writing of the Soviet history in the light of *glasnost* offers a good material for philosophical analysis of the moral issues. Identifying "lie" as a conscious distortion of truth, and assuming that the moral approach offers some support for the idea that more or less true (or at least more or less untrue) history can in many cases be objectively distinguished, the article pinpoints two main methods of lying in history: "direct lie" and "blank pages".

PÖRN, Ingmar. "On the Nature of a Social Order" in *Logic, Methodology and Philosophy of Science, VIII*, FENSTAD, J E (ed), 553-567. New York, Elsevier Science, 1989.

Three aspects of social orders are distinguished: control, influence and normative regulation. These are explored by means drawn from the modal logic of action and deontic logic. It is shown how a social order narrative may be constructed from positions of control, influence and normative regulation in a group of agents. The normative elements in the form of position rules constitute the kernel of a social order. The methodological approach of the paper is applied modal logic.

PORTER, Burton F. *Reasons for Living: A Basic Ethics*. New York, Macmillan, 1988.

A textbook in ethics which combines selections from primary sources with extensive expositions of the basic ethical problems and ideals. The problems include the relativism of knowledge and values, psychological and ethical egoism, and cosmic and scientific determinism. The ethical ideals include Cyrenaic and Epicurean hedonism, Bentham and Mill's utilitarianism, self-realization (both psychological and Aristotelian), naturalism and evolutionism, Stoic and Platonic rationalism, Kantian and Christian formalism, and scientific and existential humanism. The endnote deals with decision theory as it applies to choosing between life purposes.

PORTER, Jack Nusan. Business and Professional Ethics: An Oxymoron? Bridges, 2(3-4), 107-112, Fall-Wint 90.

Coming out of my personal background in Milwaukee and both as an academic and a businessman, I question whether anyone is really listening to the study of ethics. Isn't it all really situational anyway? Are we all too cynical or naive? I spent a few years at Harvard as a research associate and I question whether even Harvard is serious about business ethics, and it must be since it is the preeminent university in the world and others will follow if Harvard will lead. In the end, it will not be intellectual chatter that will spread the word about business ethics, an oxymoron anyway, but "honest business networks" set up in every neighborhood, every association, every profession, and every business. That is the only way to have a revolution in consciousness regarding the application of ethical standards in our lives and in our schools and businesses, including the biggest "business" of all—government.

PORTER, Theodore M. The Uses of Humanistic History. Phil Soc Sci, 21(2), 214-222, Je 91.

Written as a response to a paper by Steve Fuller in the same journal issue, this comment questions the importance of psychological studies of creativity for Fuller's project of "social epistemology." It identifies the transmutation of the private skills of the laboratory into public knowledge as perhaps the central problem now for history and philosophy of science. It proposes, finally, to investigate this process using a generalized concept of standardization, applied to instruments, measuring units, forms of publication, and the researchers themselves.

PORTMANN, Adolph. On the Uniqueness of Biological Research. J Med Phil, 15(5), 457-472, O 90.

The significance of the behavior of biological entities cannot be fully explained in terms of the physical and chemical processes upon which contemporary biological and medical research depends. The characteristic proper of biological entitites is that they are systems marked by 'inwardness', that is, a capacity to interpret meanings in order to reach goals. The significance of this characteristic is given in examples from the author's morphological research.

POST, John F. *Metaphysics: A Contemporary Introduction*. New York, Paragon House, 1991.

Topics include defining metaphysics, whether metaphysics is committed to essentialism or totalizing privileged vocabularies, what challenges it faces. Varieties of antimetaphysics come next, including deconstruction, followed by realism/antirealism and theories of reference and truth (especially Millikan's).

Subsequent chapters take up why there is anything at all; principles of sufficient reason; what is a thing; whether time and the universe have a beginning, possibly uncaused; nonreductive ways of unifying and explaining the phenomena, including intentionality, consciousness, value; conflicting ideas about God; relations between faith and reason; arguments for and against the existence of God; and whether metaphysicians can present an objectively correct vision of meaningful existence.

POST, Stephen G. Justice, Redistribution, and the Family. J Soc Phil, 21(2-3), 91-97, Fall-Wint 90.

This article is critical of all theories of distributive justice that fail to take into account familial duties and special relations. It deals with the so-called partiality-impartiality debate that has emerged as a serious topic in discussions of competing obligations.

POST, Stephen G. Nutrition, Hydration, and the Demented Elderly. J Med Human, 11(4), 185-192, Wint 90.

This article contends that removal of medical technologies used for providing nutrition and hydration to the severely demented elderly is morally acceptable. Nutrition and hydration are placed in the same category as other life extending medical technologies.

POST, Stephen G. Psychiatry, Religious Conversion, and Medical Ethics. Kennedy Inst Ethics J, 1(3), 207-223, S 91.

The interface between religion, psychiatry, and ethics is often a locus for considerable controversy. This article focuses on the response of American psychiatry to religious non conformism, and to religious conversion generally. At issue is the societal pressure against unpopular religious movements. The author argues for and ethic that conserves the freedom of religious conscience, and that guards against inquisitions in the guise of medical expertise and nosology.

POSTIGLIOLA, Alberto (ed) and FERRARI, Jean (ed). *Égalité Uguaglianza*. Napoli, Liguori, 1990.

POSTOW, B C. Piper's Criteria of Theory Selection. S J Phil, SUPP 29, 61-65, 1990.

Against Piper's criteria (1)-(4), I argue that (1) every normative moral theory regards as distorted some moral perceptions informed by rival theories, (2) a moral theory can hold that not everyone's pains are worth alleviating, (3) the victim of wrong may be ill-equipped to judge the victimizer or the wrong, and (4) only be appealing to moral reality can one say that bully systems pervert the meanings of 'innocent' and 'guilty'. To show that one moral theory enables us to understand the data of moral experience better than another theory, we need a criterion of the goodness of explanations of such data.

POSY, Carl J. Kant and Conceptual Semantics: A Sketch. Topoi, 10(1), 67-78, Mr 91.

POTEAT, William H. *A Philosophical Daybook: Post-Critical Investigations*. Columbia, Univ of Missouri Pr, 1990.

POTRC, Matjaz. "Externalizing Content" in *The Mind of Donald Davidson*, BRANDL, Johannes (ed), 179-191. Amsterdam, Rodopi, 1989.

Crude externalist theory of content is realistic and teleologically minded. On its basis, predicate notation can render the content's structure. Davidson's views concerning content are able to refine this theory. They are sophisticated externalist by being based on the implicit rejection of the two claims: the plausibility of the organism-environment dualism and the utility of epistemic intermediaries. It might be well impossible to defend a plausible version of externalism without such a kind of refinement.

POTT, Heleen. Wittgenstein, eskimo's en emoties. Kennis Methode, 15(1), 87-104, 1991.

POTT, Martin. Radical Enlightenment and Freethinkers (in German). Deut Z Phil, 38(7), 639-650, 1990.

POTTER, Jonathan (and others). Discourse: Noun, Verb or Social Practice? Phil Psych, 3(2-3), 205-217, 1990.

This paper comments on some of the different senses of the notion of discourse in the various relevant literatures and then overviews the basic features of a coherent discourse analytic programme in psychology. Parker's approach is criticised for (a) its tendency to reify discourses as objects; (b) its undeveloped notion of analytic practice; (c) its vulnerability to common sense assumptions. It ends by exploring the virtues of 'interpretative repertoires' over 'discourses' as an analytic/theoretical notion.

POTTER, Robert Lyman. Current Trends in the Philosophy of Medicine. Zygon, 26(2), 259-276, Je 91.

The philosophy of medicine, a developing discipline, is defined as critical reflection on the activity of medicine. The clinical encounter is both its central aspect and the focus for philosophical analysis. The most systematic example of this discipline employs a mixture of empiricism and phenomenology. Systems thought presents an organizing schema by which the philosophy of medicine can move toward a more comprehensive and fundamental analysis of its own agenda, which includes four main topics: understanding the patient-physician interaction, concepts of health and disease, foundations of medical ethics, and the dialogue between medicine and the larger culture.

POUBLANC, Franck. Logique et métaphysique. Rev Metaph Morale, 96(2), 147-180, Ap-Je 91.

En croyant déceler la contradiction au fond de toutes choses, la dialectique hégélienne prétend subvertir la rationalité classique au nom d'une Raison et d'une Logique supérieures. En réalité, rares sont les doctrines qui, avec autant de détermination et de systématicité, trahissent la vocation démystificatrice de la philosophie et se font mystificatrices à leur tour. Le présent article se propose de mettre en évidence les aspects les plus importants et les conséquences les plus graves d'une telle mystification.

POULAIN, Jacques. La loi de vérité. Philosophique (France), 1(91), 61-82, 1991.

POULAKOS, John. Interpreting Sophistical Rhetoric: A Response to Schiappa. Phil Rhet, 23(3), 218-228, 1990.

This article responds to a critique of the author's work on the Sophists. It argues against the possibility of objective historical reconstruction and for the inevitability of perspective and bias. It concludes that sophistical rhetoric is a construct that must be read not as inferior to but as opposing the rhetories of Plato and Aristotle.

POWELL, J Enoch. "Theory and Practice" in *Philosophy and Politics*, HUNT, G M K (ed), 1-10. New York, Cambridge Univ Pr, 1991.

POWELL, J Enoch. Theory and Practice. Philosophy, 26, 1-9, 90 Supp.

POWELL, Mava Jo. Nonrules and Plausibility: An Illustration in Pragmatic Theory. J Prag, 14(4), 589-627, Ag 90.

This study explores the consequences of positing a difference in illocutionary force and epistemic status between linguistic rules and nonrules. The former, guaranteeing warrants, decisively legislate the behaviour they predict; the latter, authorizing warrants, sanction decisions through discretionary qualification and impart presumptive assurance. An explication motivates the choice of 'plausibility' (which encodes a discretionary sense, a seemingness which may be used normatively) as epistemic criterion of nonrules. Rescher's (1976) system of plausible reasoning shows how Sperber and Wilson's (1986) conception of pragmatic relevance, a nonrule, may act as authorizing warrant to sanction plausibility values.

PRADO, C G. *The Last Choice: Preemptive Suicide in Advanced Age*. Westport, Greenwood Pr, 1990.

The central issue is whether suicide can be rational. The argument is that "preemptive" suicide, committed prior to conditions calling for surcease suicide, can be a rational alternative to a demeaning and personally destructive old age. Preemptive suicide is distinguished from suicide forced by pathological conditions, confusion, desperation, and the like. It is further argued that preemptive suicide can be a fitting and hence actually life-enhancing deliberate termination of life, and that, as such, it is the final act of affirmation of values.

PRASAD, Kamata. The Problem of Moral Freedom and Nicolai Hartmann. Indian Phil Quart, SUPP 18(1), 31-46, Ja 91.

The purpose of the work is to explain and evaluate Nicolai Hartmann's views over the problem of moral freedom mainly contained in the third volume of his *Ethik* published in 1926 in Germany. In fact, his most original contribution to the issue lies in his attempt to trace out the ontological possibility of moral freedom. The limits of his work extend only up to the demonstration of ethical necessity and ontological possibility of moral freedom. The author of the abstract has arrived at the conclusion that if we agree with the realism of Hartmann, he appears to be irrefutable even today.

PRASAD, Rajendra. On Wittgenstein's Transcendental Ethics. J Indian Counc Phil Res, 7(1), 1-26, S-D 89.

PRATT, Cornelius B. Multinational Corporate Social Policy Process for Ethical Responsibility in Sub-Saharan Africa. J Bus Ethics, 10(7), 527-541, Jl 91.

This article identifies the challenges that multinational corporations (MNCs) from the developed world face in sub-Saharan Africa and examines the direct foreign-investment and development interests of the region. In light of these challenges and interests, it also explores answers to the question "What is to be done?" (edited)

PRATT, Cornelius B. Public Relations: The Empiricial Research on Practitioner Ethics. J Bus Ethics, 10(3), 229-236, Mr 91.

An examination of the empirical literature on public relations ethics indicates serious doubts and concerns about the ethics of the public relations practice. Practitioners tend to perceive the ethics of their top management as higher than their own ethics, suggesting that top management (of which practitioners are a part) should be in the forefront of improving organizational and practitioner ethics. This article also discusses public relations practitioners' suggestions on how ethics in public relations can be improved. Sample members of the Public Relations Society of America most frequently suggest having ethics education, taking disciplinary action against violators of codes of ethics, and emphasizing professionalism of practitioners as strategies for improving practitioner ethics. This article also concludes that, because ethics education leads the list of suggestions, professional-development seminars and college-level courses might explore in further detail those ethics issues most common in the practice and might examine in group settings how the ethics of such issues are perceived by practitioners.

PRATT, Ronald L. Alexander Hamilton: The Separation of Powers. Pub Affairs Quart, 5(1), 101-115, Ja 91.

Hamilton's understanding of the separation of powers' principle marks his view of power as both discretionary and plenary. His view of government as "energetic" required a latitude in its use of power. It was his contention that government cannot foresee all the circumstances in which power must be used and, thus, the need for a latitude in judging when power is to be used. One factor that Hamilton did not consider, until late in his thinking, was the abuse of power. It is this factor which contemporary government faces, given that the Hamiltonian principle is still operative.

PRATTE, Richard. Philosophically Useful Kibitzing. Proc Phil Educ, 46, 45-50, 1990.

PREDAVAL MAGRINI, Maria Vittoria (ed). *Scienza, Filosofia e Religione tra '600 e '700 in Italia*. Milan, Angeli, 1990.

PREPOSIET, Jean. Sur quelques textes de Spinoza relatifs à la notion de loi. Philosophique (France), 1(91), 5-10, 1991.

PRESBURGER, Mojzesz and JACQUETTE, Dale (trans). On the Completeness of a Certain System of Arithmetic of Whole Numbers in Which Addition Occurs as the Only Operation. Hist Phil Log, 12(2), 225-233, 1991.

Presburger's essay on the completeness and decidability of arithmetic with integer addition but without multiplication is a milestone in the history of mathematical logic and formal metatheory. The proof is constructive, using Tarski-style quantifier elimination and a four-part recursive comprehension principle for axiomatic consequence characterization. Presburger's proof for the completeness of first order arithmetic with identity and addition but without multiplication, in light of the restrictive formal metatheorems of Gödel, Church, and Rosser, takes the foundations of arithmetic in mathematical logic to the limits of completeness and decidability.

PRESSLER, Jonathan. "The Flaws in Sen's Case Against Paretian Libertarianism" in *Acting and Reflecting: The Interdisciplinary Turn in Philosophy*, SIEG, Wilfried (ed), 129-141. Norwell, Kluwer, 1990.

PRESTON, Ronald. "Christian Ethics" in *A Companion to Ethics*, SINGER, Peter (ed), 91-105. Cambridge, Blackwell, 1991.

This chapter takes its place in a large international symposium of 47 chapters covering every aspect of ethics, religious and secular, past and present. The chapter discusses the protean nature of Christianity as an historical phenomenon, examines the roots of its ethics in its faith, commenting on the teachings of Jesus and St Paul, and refers to the main contemporary criticisms made of Christian ethics.

PREUS, J Samuel (ed). *Explaining Religion: Criticism and Theory from Bodin to Freud*. New Haven, Yale Univ Pr, 1991.

This book traces the historical emergence of the study of religion as a scientific, humanistic, secular enterprise independent of theology. The book also argues that the distinction between the two ultimately lies in their ways of explaining (accounting for) the existence of religion. Committed to transcendental accounts, theologians tend to resist attempts to provide naturalistic explanations—a strategy that retards progress in the understanding of religion as a creation of culture. For the study of religion, the author argues, theology is part of the data, not the explanation, of religion; part of its practice, not its theory.

PREVOST, Robert W (ed) and ABRAHAM, William J (ed) and MITCHELL, Basil. *How to Play Theological Ping-Pong: And Other Essays on Faith and Reason*. Grand Rapids, Eerdmans, 1991.

PRICE, David W. Hegel's Intertextual Dialectic: Diderot's *Le Neveu de Rameau* in the *Phenomenology of Spirit*. Clio, 20(3), 223-233, Spr 91.

PRICE, Huw. Agency and Probabilistic Causality. Brit J Phil Sci, 42(2), 157-176, Je 91.

Probabilistic accounts of causality have long had trouble with 'spurious' evidential correlations. Such correlations are also central to the case for causal decision theory—the argument that evidential decision theory is inadequate to cope with certain sorts of decision problem. However, there are now several strong defences of the evidential theory. Here I present what I regard as the best defence, and apply it to the probabilistic approach to causality. I argue that provided a probabilistic theory appeals to the notions of agency and effective strategy, it can avoid the problem of spurious causes. I show that such an appeal has other advantages; and argue that it is not illegitimate, even for a causal realist.

PRIDEAUX, Gary D. Syntactic Form and Textual Rhetoric: The Cognitive Basis for Certain Pragmatic Principles. J Prag, 16(2), 113-129, Ag 91.

That pragmatic principles are based on social factors is perhaps best illustrated by Grice's (1975) "Cooperative Principle". In this paper, however, it is argued that those pragmatic principles which have been proposed for dealing with syntactic form and information distribution within narratives are different in kind from those having a social and conventional basis. On the basis of both experimental and text data, it is argued that the former principles are a function of cognitive factors rather than purely social conventions, thereby requiring that a clear distinction be drawn between two different types of pragmatic principles.

PRIEST, Graham. Intensional Paradoxes. Notre Dame J Form Log, 32(2), 193-211, Spr 91.

The topic of this paper is that class of paradoxes of self-reference whose members involved intensional notions such as *knowing that, saying that,* etc. The paper discusses a number of solutions that have been proposed by, e.g., Prior and several AI workers, and argues that they are inadequate. It argues, instead, for a dialethic/paraconsistent resolution. A formal theory of propositions is given; this is based on arithmetic, and treats propositions as sentences. In the theory the paradoxes are accommodated in a satisfactory manner. An Appendix establishes that the contradictions in the theory do not spread to the underlying arithmetic machinery.

PRIEST, Graham. The Limits of Thought—and Beyond. Mind, 100(399), 361-370, Jl 91.

The paper argues that there are certain limits of thought that are dialetheic: whose very notion generates true contradictions. It does this by examining a family of related arguments including Berkeley's "master argument" for idealism, Kant's antinomies and the paradoxes of modern set-theory, using each to highlight aspects of the others. All the arguments can be seen to produce instances of Hegel's true infinite.

PRIEST, Graham. Primary Qualities are Secondary Qualities Too. Brit J Phil Sci, 40(1), 29-37, Mr 89.

The paper argues for realism in quantum mechanics. Specifically, the formalism of quantum mechanics should be understood as giving a complete description of quantum situations. When it is understood in this way, traditional primary properties of matter can be seen as similar to traditional secondary properties, though at a different level.

PRIGOGINE, Ilya. "The Rediscovery of Time" in *Logic, Methodology and Philosophy of Science, VIII*, FENSTAD, J E (ed), 29-46. New York, Elsevier Science, 1989.

PRIMEAUX, Patrick and STIEBER, John. Economic Efficiency: A Paradigm for Business Ethics. J Bus Ethics, 10(5), 335-339, My 91.

Current teaching, writing and thinking in business ethics reflects (more than) a tendency to subsume business into the theoretical, idealistic and impractical objectives of philosophical ethics. Professors Primeaux and Stieber argue against this tendency. They propose the basic business model of *economic efficiency* as a practical and appropriate paradigm for business ethics. Understood from a behavioral perspective, economic efficiency reflects all of the ethical considerations of the academic study of philosophical ethics, but in a much more concrete and applicable manner. In effect, they are proposing that any study of business ethics defines its starting point and focus of reference in terms of economic efficiency.

PRIMORATZ, Igor. What is Terrorism? J Applied Phil, 7(2), 129-138, O 90.

My aim in this paper is not to try to formulate the meaning the word 'terrorism' has in ordinary use; the word is used in so many different, even incompatible ways, that such an enterprise would quickly prove futile. My aim is rather to try for a definition that captures the trait, or traits, of terrorism which cause most of us to view it with moral repugnance. (edited)

PRINCE, Augustus. The Phenomenalism of Newton and Boskovic: A Comparative Study (in Serbo-Croatian). Filozof Istraz, 32-33(5-6), 1541-1565, 1989.

An attempt has been made to analyze the phenomenalistic reductions used by Newton and Boscovich and how these ideas influenced their philosophical concepts and scientific theories. Emphasis has been placed on (a) Newton's ideas of absolute space and time as compared to Boscovich's relative spatial and temporal concepts; (b) Newton's dynamic three-dimensional aspect (mass, length and time) and Boscovich's kinematical notion (length and time); (c) Newton's mass and naive atomism and Boscovich's point centers of force and their pattern distribution; (d) action at a distance; (e) other abstract ideas regarding continuity, force, inertia, etc., are also discussed. Boscovich's and Newton's (to a certain extent) ideas on kinematics have been interpreted in terms of the Merton College concept; in particular, that of Oresme. A method is suggested whereby Boscovich's curve of forces may be analyzed via Oresme's "configuration Doctrine" thereby affording the opportunity to possibly describe various phenomena.

PRINCIPE, Michael A. Hegel's *Logic* and Marx's Early Development. Int Stud Phil, 23(1), 47-60, 1991.

This paper reviews the relevant parts of Marx's intellectual development leading up to the famous remark: "Philosophy cannot be made a reality without the abolition of the proletariat, and the proletariat cannot be abolished without philosophy being made a reality." Crucial remarks from his preliminary notes for his dissertation send us back to Hegel's *Logic*. This provides the key for understanding a crucial footnote to his dissertation along with other pre-1843 writings. This story of Marx's struggle with Hegelian categories also allows us to see the fundamentally Young Hegelian nature of the above remark.

PRINS, Ad. Geschiedenis als muurbloempje. Kennis Methode, 14(4), 390-396, 1990.

Book review of R Vos (1989), *Drugs Looking for Diseases*. A descriptive model for the process of innovative drug research with special reference to the development of the beta blockers and the calcium antagonists. PhD Thesis, Groningen State University 1989. In the philosophy of science and history of science only little has been written on development of drugs. This book offers one of the first attempts to do so, on the basis of beta blockers and calcium antagonists for heart diseases such as angina pectoris and heart failure. While the historical chapters offer a very detailed description of research of various pharmaceutical firms, its analytical part lacks however a clear connection to the historical part. In this review it is furthermore argued that the analytical model for development, a "logic of profiles" which is a rational reconstructivist analysis, is not capable to describe properly the type of development as sketched in the historical part.

PRITCHARD, Michael S. On Becoming A Moral Agent: From Aristotle to Harry Stottlemeier. Thinking, 9(2), 16-24, 1990.

PRITCHARD, Paul. The Meaning of Δυναμισ at *Timaeus* 31c. Phronesis, 35(2), 182-193, 1990.

Giving a mathematical meaning to the term *dynamis* which appears at *Timaeus* 31c makes the passage as a whole nonsensical. It turns out that a more satisfactory, nonmathematical sense is available for the term *dynamis* in this place, and, furthermore, that the passage has been understood in this way both by the Neoplatonists and by medieval scholars—in fact the mistaken interpretation is the result of late nineteenth century scholarship, the newly discovered mathematical sense of *dynamis* being imported into contexts where it does not belong.

PRITSCHER, Conrad. Educating-Increasing Intelligence Levels by Developing a Sense of Humor. Phil Stud Educ, /, 31-43, 1989.

One usually "gets" a joke shortly after the punch line is told. One "gets" the joke without having the joke explained. The "getting it" is an act of intelligence. The "getting it" brings some additional and often higher level of order to what was previously seen as chaos. A major purpose of the paper is to help the reader better know that an excessive need to know in advance what will happen before it happens (highly exact definitions, great specification, an overly precise meaning, etc.), can prevent one from developing his or her own intelligence. The paper elaborates on these matters.

PRITSCHER, Conrad. Reflections on Reflecting. Phil Stud Educ, /, 26-37, 1987-88.

This paper attempts to explicate a view that focuses on balance between excessive thought and action unenlightened by thought; between the usefulness of differentiating and the function of making connections between what has been separated; between the need to know and the excessive need to be overly certain of what will happen before it happens. Some evidence to indicate that we have not balanced the above can be seen in Karp's report in which he writes that 58 percent of our nation's thirteen-year-olds believe it is against the law to form a third political party in our country. Karp goes on to elaborate that when such is the case for our nation's thirteen-year-olds, we are not dealing with an educational failure, but rather, with a subtle success. The success being that, in an unaware way, school administrators and teachers desire to develop docile, obedient students who can and will be easily controlled. Too much as well as too little reflection can lead to excessive control.

PROBYN, Elspeth. "Travels in the Postmodern: Making Sense of the Logical" in *Feminism/Postmodernism*, NICHOLSON, Linda J (ed), 176-189. New York, Routledge, 1990.

PROKOPIJEVIC, Miroslav. Surrogate Motherhood. J Applied Phil, 7(2), 169-181, O 90.

In the first part of this article I discuss some objections which assert that surrogacy is primarily—but not exclusively—harmful in a moral sense. After examination of mainly but not exclusively morality-dependent harms (objections from similarity with prostitution, exploitation, etc.) and after the discussion of possible non-morality-dependent harms (baby, couple, surrogate mother, agency, etc.), I argue, in the second part, that no one reason supports the possible prohibition of surrogacy. In the last part I try to show why moral reasons alone could not be sufficient to criminalize any kind of activity—including surrogacy—in a liberal order.

PROTEVI, John. The *Sinnsfrage* and the *Seinsfrage*. Phil Today, 34(4), 321-333, Wint 90.

Heidegger needs a purely temporal status for fundamental ontology, opened in *Being and Time* by the *Seinsfrage*, the "question of Being." The key term in *die Frage nach dem Sinn von Sein überhaupt* is *Sinn*. The article articulates the economy (range of possible interpretation) of *Sinn*—sensory sense, meaning sense, and directional sense—the *Sinnsfrage*—and shows how the last sense installs an irreducible spatiality in the descriptions of temporality, thereby disrupting the unity of fundamental ontology. This spatial disruption cannot be controlled by determining a proper "meaning sense" for *Sinn*, because the former is only one moment of the *Sinnsfrage*.

PROTEVI, John. The Stilling of the *Aufhebung: Streit* in "The Origin of the Work of Art". Heidegger Stud, 6, 67-83, 1990.

Hegel's notion of truth in the *Phenomenology* and the *logic* was compared to Heidegger's notion of truth in the "Origin of the Work of Art." The two notions of truth both involve an originary strife. For Hegel, truth is the certainty of the movement of spirit that occurs as the healing of an originary strife. For Heidegger, truth is the setting into work of the strife of world and earth. This strife is instigated by the originary strife of the clearing, that is, revealing and (double) concealing, in such a way that the strife in unhealable.

PROUVOST, Géry. Le statut de la philosophie chez Étienne Gilson. Rev Thomiste, 91(1), 112-118, Ja-Mr 91.

PRUCNAL, Tadeuss. A Note on Some Property of Purely Implicational Proportional Calculi. Bull Sect Log, 19(2), 49-50, Je 90.

Let F be a set of propositional formulae based on C /implication/. We consider those subsets of F for which: /P/ The formula CAB belongs to X if and only if every substitution that puts A in X also puts B in X. Let K be the family of all subsets of F which have the property /P/ and which are closed with respect to the substitution rule. Theorem: The set H is the smallest set in the family K, where H is the set of all implicational theses of the intuitionistic propositional calculus.

PRUFER, Thomas. Glosses on Heidegger's Architectonic Word-Play. Rev Metaph, 44(3), 607-612, Mr 91.

This article analyzes the shifts and ambiguities in Heidegger's use of four words: *Lichtung, Ereignis, Bergung, Wahrnis*.

PRYCHITKO, David L. The Welfare State: What is Left? Crit Rev, 4(4), 619-632, Fall 90.

The Left has turned to the welfare state after the collapse of socialism. They seem to avoid Claus Offe's analysis of the contradictions of the welfare state and the ever-present crises of crisis management. The author contends that Offe's neo-Schumpetarian argument helps explain, indeed, the instability of the welfare state, and contradictions of state intervention in general (including the socialist-interventionist State). However, Offe does not realize that his analysis leads one to doubt that the welfare state is a viable corrective to either unhampered markets or state socialism.

PRZELECKI, Marian. "Truth-Value of Ethical Statements" in *Logic and Ethics*, GEACH, Peter (ed), 241-253. Norwell, Kluwer, 1991.

According to a widely held view, all descriptive statements are assumed to be true or false, all value statements are denied any truth-value. The paper shows that this qualification is untenable: the model-theoretic definition of truth places both kinds of sentences in the same category. On the one hand, there are descriptive statements which are neither true nor false; on the other hand, there are true or false value statements. This conclusion follows from certain characteristic features of the language in which the definition of truth is couched.

PSTRUZINA, Karel. Philosophy and Cognitive Science (in Czechoslovakian). Filozof Cas, 38(6), 762-771, 1990.

The advancement of cognitive science represents a challenge to philosophy in terms of the orientation of future research. Cognitive science draws primarily on the findings of the theory of artificial intelligence which poses the threat of the loss of self-respect over our own intellectual abilities. Yet another stimulus comes in the shape of findings of neurosciences which make it possible for some of the existing hypotheses to be experimentally confirmed for the first time in the history of philosophy. For my part, I do not discern the role of philosophy in any generalizing function but rather in appropriating the historical wealth of philosophical thinking for a basic orientation of the research into cognitive processes on a new footing. Furthermore, findings of cognitive science make it possible to supersede that distorted theory of reflection and elaborate a theory of thinking. (edited)

PUCCETTI, Roland. "The Heart of the Mind: Intentionality versus Intelligence" in *The Case for Dualism*, SMYTHIES, John R (ed), 255-264. Charlottesville, Univ Pr of Virginia, 1989.

Brentano's thesis that mental acts always have directedness upon objects, whereas physical entities have none, is unchallenged in its first part but rejected in its second part by those who believe physical intentionality is or will be realized. I follow John Searle in denying that there is genuine understanding without intentionality. In particular, I argue that a psychological statement about, say, a subject seeing a flash of light in the right upper quadrant of his visual field is not reducible to a statement correctly describing the neurophysiological correlate of this.

PUCCETTI, Roland. Two Brains, Two Minds? Wigan's Theory of Mental Duality. Brit J Phil Sci, 40(2), 137-144, Je 89.

The London physician A L Wigan (Duality of the Mind 1844, 1985), having discovered at autopsy that a formerly cultivated man had gone through life with but one brain, concluded that we with two brains must have two minds. But if a single person had two minds, then single objects would be perceived doubly. I propose instead that each of the two brains is the biological substrate of a person having a single mind and lacking introspective access to the other person's mind: thus without double perception.

PUDLÁK, Pavel and KRAJICEK, Jan and TAKEUTI, Gaisi. Bounded Arithmetic and the Polynomial Hierarchy. Annals Pure Applied Log, 52(1-2), 143-153, Ap 91.

Bounded arithmetic is a fragment of Peano arithmetic with induction axioms restricted to bounded formulas only. The main problem is to show that bounded arithmetic is not finitely axiomatizable. We have proved this using the assumption that the polynomial-time hierarchy does not collapse. This assumption is a famous unproved conjecture in complexity theory.

PUGA, Leila Z and DA COSTA, Newton C A and CARNIELLI, Walter A. Kantian and Non-Kantian Logics. Log Anal, 31(121-122), 3-9, Mr-Je 88.

PUKA, Bill. Commentary: "Codes of Ethics and the Moral Education of Engineers". Bus Prof Ethics J, 2(4), 63-66, Sum 83.

PUKA, Bill. "The Majesty and Mystery of Kohlberg's Stage 6" in *The Moral Domain: Essays in the Ongoing Discussion between Philosophy and the Social Sciences*, WREN, Thomas E (ed), 182-223. Cambridge, MIT Pr, 1990.

A critique of attempts by Kohlberg and Habermas to install egalitarian justice as the standard of moral development. The empirical, methodological, and philosophical grounds for these attempts are faulted in turn. Criticisms of ideological bias in Kohlberg's stages are redirected at the core logic of justice principles. Justice is shown incapable of defining or solving key types of moral problems adequately. At the same time, Kohlberg's empirical stages of development (stages 1-5) are cleared of reputed associations with a stage 6 standard and recast as the progressive integration of individual respect and group benevolence rationales. Kohlberg's data are saved from Kohlberg's meta-theory.

PUKA, Bill. The Science of Caring. Hypatia, 6(2), 200-210, Sum 91.

A response to S Elise Peeple's comment "Her Terrain is Outside His 'Domain.'"

PULIGANDLA, Ramakrishna. Is the Central Upanishadic Teaching a Reductionist Thesis? Asian Phil, 1(1), 15-20, 1991.

The purpose of this paper is to examine the topic of reductionism from the standpoint of the Upanishadic teaching and show that, according to the Upanishads, both physicalistic and mentalistic reductionisms cannot, in principle, succeed; the reason for this is that both these reductionisms absolutize and ultimatize particular kinds of phenomena, the physical and the mental, respectively. The Upanishadic point is that no phenomenon can be ultimatized insofar as every phenomenon lacks self-existence, that is, composite and exists dependently and conditionally. In contrast, the Upanishadic reductionism does not absolutize any phenomena; all phenomena are reducible to Brahman but Brahman is not a phenomenon, whether physical or mental.

PULLEYBLANK, Edwin G. "Some Notes on Morphology and Syntax in Classical Chinese" in *Chinese Texts and Philosophical Contexts*, ROSEMONT JR, Henry (ed), 21-45. La Salle, Open Court, 1991.

PURDY, Laura. Are Pregnant Women Fetal Containers? Bioethics, 4(4), 273-291, O 90.

I explore the implications of fetuses being inside women and suggest that we can ignore neither women's right to control their bodies nor the welfare of the child the fetus may well become. Many contemporary social practices, however, see women's interests as less compelling than they are and so compromise them far too often in favor of fetus's alleged or real interests. I conclude that a more welfare-oriented society would remove many sources of conflict between woman and fetus and raise the question of what ought to be done about the remaining ones.

PURRINGTON, Robert D and DURHAM, Frank. "Newton's Legacy" in *Some Truer Method*, DURHAM, Frank (ed), 1-13. New York, Columbia Univ Pr, 1990.

PURRINGTON, Robert D and DURHAM, Frank. "Newton, Nonlinearity and Determinism" in *Some Truer Method*, DURHAM, Frank (ed), 175-226. New York, Columbia Univ Pr, 1990.

PURRINGTON, Robert D (ed) and DURHAM, Frank (ed). *Some Truer Method*. New York, Columbia Univ Pr, 1990.

PUSCH, James. Art, Stance and Education. Phil Stud Educ, /, 80-90, 1987-88.

PUTMAN, D. Sex and Virtue. Int J Moral Soc Stud, 6(1), 47-56, Spr 91.

This paper analyzes the role of character in sexual ethics. I first discuss three paradigm cases—sexual abuse of children, voyeurism, and adultery—and point out how an analysis of character complements utilitarian and rights considerations. The paper then discusses how certain virtues relate directly to the joy of sexual experience and how virtue theory can provide a useful framework for understanding the role of sex in human life. Virtue as the development of moral maturity provides a basis for analyzing character and is a valuable way to reflect on the role of sexuality in one's own life.

PUTMAN, Daniel. The Aesthetic Relation of Musical Performer and Audience. Brit J Aes, 30(4), 361-366, O 90.

I argue against the view held by Laszlo that sharing feelings is the primary function of the musician in relation to his or her audience. The emotions of the performer are clues for the audience to the power of the piece rather than being ends in themselves. The musical artifact is the primary source of the aesthetic experience. Several other conclusions in the aesthetics of performance follow from this argument.

PUTMAN, Daniel. The Compatibility of Justice and Kindness. Philosophy, 65(254), 516-517, O 90.

A D M Walker has claimed that kindness and justice are incompatible at times and that a person can possess one virtue without the other. I argue that, if an individual does not consider the other virtue, acts of "kindness" or "justice" are mimicry or luck. Walker claims one criterion of virtue is that it not block the minimal requirements of other virtues. But, without reflection on the parameters of each virtue, whether this happens or not is an accident. A person's acts become virtuous or not virtuous by coincidence. Justice and kindness need each other.

PUTNAM, Hilary and PUTNAM, Ruth Anna. Epistemology as Hypothesis. Trans Peirce Soc, 26(4), 407-433, Fall 90.

PUTNAM, Hilary. "Information and the Mental" in *Truth and Interpretation: Perspectives on the Philosophy of Donald Davidson*, LE PORE, Ernest (ed), 262-271. Cambridge, Blackwell, 1986.

PUTNAM, Hilary and MURILLO, Lorena (trans). La objetividad y la distinción ciencia/ética. Dianoia, 34(34), 7-25, 1988.

PUTNAM, Hilary. Philosophical Reminiscences with Reflections on Firth's Work. Phil Phenomenol Res, 51(1), 143-147, Mr 91.

PUTNAM, Hilary and CONANT, James (ed). *Realism with a Human Face*. Cambridge, Harvard Univ Pr, 1990.

PUTNAM, Hilary. Replies and Comments. Erkenntnis, 34(3), 401-423, My 91.

PUTNAM, Ruth Anna. "Doing What One Ought to Do" in *Meaning and Method: Essays in Honor of Hilary Putnam*, BOOLOS, George (ed), 279-293. New York, Cambridge Univ Pr, 1990.

I ask how one moves from knowing what one ought to do to doing it. In particular, I explore the role of what Hilary Putnam calls one's moral image of the world. Our moral images shape how we see the world and what we think about it because they reflect what we care about. Because we care our deliberations issue in practical oughts that are conclusive reasons for us. The whole process is charged with the moral energy that will ultimately carry us from knowledge to action.

PUTNAM, Ruth Anna and PUTNAM, Hilary. Epistemology as Hypothesis. Trans Peirce Soc, 26(4), 407-433, Fall 90.

PUTNAM, Ruth Anna. "The Moral Life of a Pragmatist" in *Identity, Character, and Morality: Essays in Moral Psychology*, FLANAGAN, Owen (ed), 67-89. Cambridge, MIT Pr, 1990.

An exploration of some of William James' writings in moral philosophy. Moral life consists of normal stretches shaped by one's character and directed by one's ideals, and of critical moments when one chooses new ideals or reaffirms old ones. These choices are limited by but modify one's character. The standard of moral objectivity is provided by a community of thinkers who care for one another, hence seek a most inclusive ideal. This notion is explored. James' moral philosophy calls for a sympathetic interpreter but has more to offer than most contemporary critics recognize.

PUYAU, Hermes. La primera antinomia kantiana: el origen y los límites del Universo. Stromata, 46(3-4), 235-239, Jl-D 90.

PYBUS, Elizabeth. *Human Goodness: Generosity and Courage*. Buffalo, Univ of Toronto Pr, 1991.

The book sets out to identity and establish the actual nature of human goodness. The account of goodness is intended to be neutral with regard to disputed theories within meta-ethics and philosophical psychology. The argument dissolves unnecessary distinctions, and shows that philosophers as apparently diverse as Aristotle and Kant can converge on the nature of goodness. Generosity and courage apparently provide different models for goodness, but really good people need both. Direct concern is identified as the first-order moral motive, while conscientiousness emerges on the condition for moral agency, which crucially involves both feeling and reason.

PYTOWSKA, Ewa. "Individuality and Collectivity: False Antonyms" in *Abeunt Studia in Mores: A Festschrift for Helga Doblin*, MERRILL, Sarah A Bishop (ed), 17-64. New York, Lang, 1990.

QI, Feng. The Liberal Teachings of the Young Liang Qichao. Chin Stud Phil, 22(1), 32-57, Fall 90.

QIU, Ren-Zong. Morality in Flux: Medical Ethics in the People's Republic of China. Kennedy Inst Ethics J, 1(1), 16-27, Mr 91.

In this paper the author gives a review of the developmemt of medical ethics since the new policy of reform and openness, and the value conflicts in medical care which contemporary China is faced with, especially the dilemmas surrounding reproductive technology, and attitudes and policies about euthanasia. The author concludes that in the changing context of modernization, in which different and even incompatible value systems must co-exist, it is best ot approach ethical dilemmas facing us with mutual respect and understanding.

QUANTZ, Richard A. The "New" Scholars in Philosophy of Education, 1976-1986. Phil Stud Educ, /, 108-138, 1986.

QUARANTA, Mario. Norberto Bobbio ideologo del neoilluminismo: Per una rilettura di "Politica e cultura". Il Protag, 6(13-16), 31-56, Ja 88-D 89.

QUARTA, Antonio. Metodi e immagini della scienza nel "Centro di studi metodologici" di Torino (1945-1952). Il Protag, 6(13-16), 225-242, Ja 88-D 89.

QUARTA, Antonio. Nicola Abbagnano tra esistenzialismo e neoilluminismo. Il Protag, 6(13-16), 3-30, Ja 88-D 89.

QUESADA GUARDIA, Annabelle. Antropología del trabajo según la Encíclica "Laborem Excercens". Rev Filosof (Costa Rica), 27(66), 423-427, D 89.

The purpose of this paper is to point out the anthropological foundations of labor as exposed in John Paul II's encyclical *Laborem Exercens*. Such foundations provide it with an ethical character, which becomes the instrument for individual and social development.

QUESADA, Anabelle. El humanismo de Albert Camus. Rev Filosof (Costa Rica), 28(67-68), 129-133, D 90.

With the *Fourth Letter to a German Friend*, begins the humanistic period. Also in *The Rebel*, Camus denies the absurd by affirming something of value in the universe: the human being, with his own nature and his longing for meaning. Of the absurd he keeps what is more valuable: rebellion; but now he does not aim it at the gods, but against humans who murder their fellowmen in the name of absolutist ideologies. (edited)

QUEVEDO, Amalia. Posibilidad e indeterminación: Aristóteles frente a Diodoro Crono. Themata, 6, 125-136, 1989.

In this article I expose the criticism made by Aristotle to megarian doctrine about possibility, and I impugn Hintikka's and others' arguments in favor of attributing the "Plenitude Principle" to Aristotle. I compare the different meaning acquired by the premises of Diodorus Cronus's "Master Argument," according to the way they appear: separately, in Aristotle's writings, or linked syllogistically in Diodoro's argument. In each case, they give a different and even antithetical notion of what is possible. Finally I examine the need which is characteristic of the past "qua talis" which allows to establish a certain comparison between history and poetry.

QUI, Ren-zong. "The Fiduciary Relationship between Professionals and Clients: A Chinese Perspective" in *Ethics, Trust, and the Professions: Philosophical and Cultural Aspects*, PELLEGRINO, Edmund D (ed), 247-262. Washington, Georgetown Univ Pr, 1991.

QUILICI, Leana and RAGGHIANTI, Renzo. Il carteggio Xavier Léon: corrispondenti italiana. G Crit Filosof Ital, 68(3), 295-368, S-D 89.

QUINE, W V. "Let Me Accentuate the Positive" in *Reading Rorty*, MALACHOWSKI, Alan (ed), 117-119. Cambridge, Blackwell, 1991.

QUINE, W V. "Three Indeterminacies" in *Perspectives on Quine*, BARRETT, Robert (ed), 1-16. Cambridge, Blackwell, 1990.

QUINN, Michael. Aristotle on Justice, Equality and the Rule of Law. Polis, 9(2), 170-186, 1990.

The aims of this work are: (1) To distinguish between formal and substantive justice, and to argue that while formal justice implies formal equality, nothing follows from this relation in terms of substantive principles of justice. (2) To show that Aristotle was aware of this relation, and of its lack of substantive import. (3) To argue that Aristotle's conception of justice is substantively inegalitarian in nature; and that finally, Aristotle tolerates a limited range of substantive principles, the prime indication of the acceptability of a constitution being that it possesses some substantive conception of justice, enshrined in law, which offers a basic security to the good and virtuous man.

QUINN, Philip L. The Recent Revival of Divine Command Ethics. Phil Phenomenol Res, 50 SUPP, 345-365, Fall 90.

This paper begins with a review of recent philosophical work on divine command ethics. Its central sections set forth two arguments for the divine command conception of morality. Following a tradition of medieval commentary, I try to show that a divine command theory best explains the scriptural cases of the immoralities of the patriarchs. I go on to argue that such a theory is a consequence of a strong version of the doctrine of divine sovereignty.

QUINN, Philip L. Saving Faith from Kant's Remarkable Antinomy. Faith Phil, 7(4), 418-433, O 90.

This paper is a critical study of Kant's antinomy of saving faith. In the first section, I sketch aspects of Kant's philosophical account of sin and atonement that help explain why he finds saving faith problematic from the moral point of view. I proceed in the next section to give a detailed exposition of Kant's remarkable antinomy and of his proposal for resolving it theoretically. In the third and final section, I argue that alternative ways of resolving the antinomy both respond to the deepest of Kant's moral concerns and comport better with the traditional Christian conviction that saving faith can have for its object the historical individual Jesus Christ.

QUINN, Timothy Sean. Kant's Apotheosis of Genius. Int Phil Quart, 31(2), 161-172, Je 91.

QUINTANILLA, Miguel Ángel. Problemas conceptuales y políticas de desarrollo tecnológico. Critica, 22(64), 23-39, Ap 90.

There are two kinds of conceptual problems in technological development: problems of understanding and problems of assessment. Using the conceptual frame of his recent book on the philosophy of technology, and looking to the specific problems posed by the design of technology policies in the developing countries, the author elucidates the basic concepts needed to understand the structure and dynamics of technological systems and the criteria for what he calls internal and external technology assessment.

QUINTÁS, Alfonso López and NICOLOSI, Mauro (trans). La realtà umana nel pensiero di Xavier Zubiri. G Metaf, 11(3), 339-362, S-D 89.

QUINTON, Anthony. "Doing Without Meaning" in *Perspectives on Quine*, BARRETT, Robert (ed), 294-308. Cambridge, Blackwell, 1990.

QUIRK, Michael J. Stout on Relativism, Liberalism, and Communitarianism. Auslegung, 17(1), 1-14, Wint 91.

In *Ethics After Babel*, Jeffrey Stout maintained that communitarian fears about the intractability of moral disputes in modern, liberal political orders are misplaced. Donald Davidson's refutation of "radically incommensurable conceptual schemes" demonstrated that any belief-systems must share a vast number of beliefs in common: thus beneath all moral disagreement there must be enough moral consensus to sustain rational moral discourse. I argue that Stout fails to analyze the need for agreement on relatively specific norms and propositions to make rational moral argument possible, and the extent to which skills of moral judgment have been eroded by liberal modernity.

RAATZSCH, Richard. Wittgenstein and Marx—Some Methodological Remarks (in German). Deut Z Phil, 38(10), 931-939, 1990.

The purpose of the article is to show that there are more resemblances between Wittgenstein's and Marx's philosophical and methodological positions than are commonly assumed by Marxist and analytical philosophers. The object of the demonstration are especially the "Poverty of Philosophy", the "German Ideology" and the remarks on philosophy and philosophical methods in the "Philosophical Investigations". It is shown that especially in characterizing the aim and the methods of a selfstanding philosophy Marx's and Wittgenstein's positions resemble one another.

RABINO, Isaac. The Impact of Activist Pressures on Recombinant DNA Research. Sci Tech Human Values, 16(1), 70-87, Wint 91.

The survey of 430 recombinant DNA scientists currently engaged in research assesses the impact of public attention, political advocacy, and litigation on their work. The findings show that most researchers feel they have benefitted from public attention to the field, but 34 percent feel they have been negatively affected. Sixty-one percent agree that as a result of litigation by activists, greater social responsibility on the part of scientists working in the field is required. Considerable concern is expressed regarding public ignorance, uninformed controversy, and the future impact of activist-inspired litigation, especially on the possible loss of the US competitive edge. Recommendations are made for a public education campaign focused on priority-target audiences (i.e., regulatory decision makers, other scientists, members of the media, and environmentalists).

RABINOWICZ, Wlodzimierz. Act-Utilitarian Prisoner's Dilemmas. Theoria, 55(1), 1-44, 1989.

Donald Regan and Derek Parfit have argued that act-utilitarianism (AU), unlike many other moral theories, is never self-defeating: the utilitarian goal—the best possible outcome—presupposes that everyone acts in accordance with the act-utilitarian principle. Their claim, however, can be shown to be violated by *future-oriented* versions of AU. Since only future is supposed to count, agents who act at different times are assigned different goals. Also, in some such versions of AU, the goals assigned to the agents are evaluated by time-sensitive criteria. These features make it possible to generate act-utilitarian prisoner's dilemmas and thereby to establish the "self-defeatingness" of a future-oriented AU.

RABINOWICZ, Wlodzimierz. Hare on Prudence. Theoria, 55(3), 145-151, 1989.

In *Moral Thinking*, Richard Hare defends, as a "requirement of prudence," the following demand: Adjust your present preferences for other times to your expected preferences at those times! He also puts forward a supposedly analytical principle of conditional self-endorsement: My full knowledge of a preference I would entertain under certain conditions entails my acquiring a corresponding conditional preference. I argue that this principle, if valid, creates unexpected obstacles for the requirement of prudence: my present knowledge of what I earlier preferred for now hinders me from satisfying my now-for-now preferences.

RABKIN, Mitchell T. "The Hospital-Academic Health Center Interface: The Community of Practice and the Community of Learning" in *Integrity in Health Care Institutions: Humane Environments for Teaching, Inquiry, and Healing*, BULGER, Ruth Ellen (ed), 130-140. Iowa City, Univ of Iowa Pr, 1990.

RABOSSI, Eduardo. Wittgenstein: Representaciones y pensamientos. Cuad Filosof, 21(34), 9-19, My 90.

Wittgenstein's picture theory is better viewed as a cognitive philosophical model than as a linguistic/referential/correspondentist proposal. Main points: (1) in the *Tractatus*, Wittgenstein advances a general theory of representations, and two special theories, i.e., of propositions *qua* representation (TPR), and of *Gedanken qua* representations (TGR); (2) TGR has precedence over TPR; (3) *Gedanken* are full mental events featuring syntactic structures of symbolic elements; (4) Wittgenstein's views are an alternative to Frege's antimentalistic approach, and to Russell's relational theory of propositional attitudes; (5) Wittgenstein's views are a counterexample to Cummins's suggestion that representative similarity implies images or forms as representations.

RABOTNIKOF, Nora. "Pactos inicuos" y acuerdo racional. Dianoia, 36(36), 97-110, 1990.

RACEVSKIS, Karlis. The Conative Function of the Other in *Les Mots et les Choses*. Rev Int Phil, 44(173), 231-240, 1990.

RACHELS, James. "Subjectivism" in *A Companion to Ethics*, SINGER, Peter (ed), 432-441. Cambridge, Blackwell, 1991.

RADBRUCH, Knut. Die Bedeutung der Mathematik Für die Philosophie Schopenhauers. Schopenhauer Jahr, 71, 148-153, 1990.

RADCHIK, Laura. Tiempo, soledad y muerte: La encrucijada del poeta. Logos (Mexico), 19(55), 109-117, Ja-Ap 91.

RADDER, Hans. Heuristics and the Generalized Correspondence Principle. Brit J Phil Sci, 42(2), 195-226, Je 91.

RADERMACHER, F J and KLEMENT, H W. Freiheit und Bindung menschlicher Entscheidungen. Conceptus, 24(63), 25-42, 1990.

This essay is concerned with the question of human freedom of choice. Its conclusion is that whereas human beings, in contrast to lifeless things, have the formal freedom to make decisions, these are determined in their content by the state of all levels of what constitute human beings, in particular the currently available and stored (mainly linguistic) information at their disposal. This does not mean that decisions are simply determined by physical laws, since these are multifariously modified in their effects by the emergence of higher-order laws, in particular those at the level of language and society. It is also considered whether non-determination of human decision can be justified by appeal to quantum indeterminacy. At present no such effect has been demonstrated in the domain of neorophysiological processes, which is where it would have to be sought. However, it is not excluded in principle. A more plausible place to look for the possible influence of quantum indeterminacy is in the important, perhaps decisive role they might play in the emergence of regularities at the higher levels of evolution, thus exercising a considerable indirect influence on actual behaviour.

RADEST, Howard B. *The Devil and Secular Humanism: The Children of the Enlightenment*. New York, Praeger, 1990.

RADEY, Charles. Telling Stories: Creative Literature and Ethics. Hastings Center Rep, 20(6), 25, N-D 90.

RADFORD, Colin. Belief, Acceptance, and Knowledge. Mind, 99(396), 609-617, O 90.

RADFORD, Colin. The Incoherence and Irrationality of Philosophers. Philosophy, 65(253), 349-354, Jl 90.

RADI, Peter. Meditation on the Two Consciousnesses and on the Three Worlds of Popper (in Hungarian). Magyar Filozof Szemle, 5-6, 512-530, 1990.

Die Einleitung des Aufsatzes behandelt die Unsicherheit um den Begriff des Bewusstseins und die damit zusammenhängende Termini auf Grund von Definitionen verschiedener Wörterbücher der Philosophie. Im Hauptteil behauptet der Author, dass hinter den verschiedenen Formulierungen grundsätzlich zwei verschiedene Bewusstseinsbegriffe verborgen sind. (edited)

RADIN, Margaret Jane. Affirmative Action Rhetoric. Soc Phil Pol, 8(2), 130-149, Spr 91.

RADNITZKY, Gerard. "Falsificationism Looked at from an 'Economic' Point of View" in *Imre Lakatos and Theories of Scientific Change*, GAVROGLU, Kostas (ed), 383-395. Norwell, Kluwer, 1989.

RAFALKO, Robert J. *Logic for an Overcast Tuesday*. Belmont, Wadsworth, 1990.

RAGGHIANTI, Renzo and QUILICI, Leana. Il carteggio Xavier Léon: corrispondenti italiana. G Crit Filosof Ital, 68(3), 295-368, S-D 89.

RAGGIO, Andrés R. El cincuentenario de los *Grundlagen der Mathematik* de Hilbert y Bernays. Rev Latin De Filosof, 16(2), 197-212, Jl 90.

The *Grundlagen der Mathematik* by David Hilbert and Paul Bernays is a classical work both in mathematical logic and in the philosophy of mathematics. Starting with Frege and in a double front, the technical analysis and the philosophical reflection, they reach up to Gödel's theorems. Every detail has been analyzed; every philosophical implication has been considered. People usually label the *Grundlagen* as formalism or finitism or instrumentalism. In reality they develop a theory of theoretical complexity which goes beyond the classical Kantian distinction of analytic and synthetic.

RAIBORN, Cecily A and PAYNE, Dinah. Corporate Codes of Conduct: A Collective Conscience and Continuum. J Bus Ethics, 9(11), 879-889, N 90.

This paper discusses the vast continuum between the letter of the law (legality) and the spirit of the law (ethics or morality). Further, the authors review the fiduciary duties owed by the firm to its various publics. These aspects must be considered in developing a corporate code of ethics. The underlying qualitative characteristics of a code include clarity, comprehensiveness and enforceability. While ethics is indigenous to a society, every code of ethics will necessarily reflect the corporate culture from which that code stems and be responsive to the innumerable situations for which it was created. Several examples have been provided to illustrate the ease of applicability of these concepts.

RAINA, Dhruv. A Historico-Philosophical Investigation of Anti-Science: The Phenomenological Encounter. J Indian Counc Phil Res, 6(1), 47-59, S-D 88.

RAINA, Dhruv. Quantum Logic, Copenhagen Interpretation and Instrumentalism. J Indian Counc Phil Res, 5(3), 79-89, My-Ag 88.

RAINONE, Antonio. Intenzione e azione in Wittgenstein. G Crit Filosof Ital, 70(1), 130-137, Ja-Ap 91.

RAITZ, Keith L. Response to "Literacy as Disempowerment". Proc Phil Educ, 46, 85-88, 1990.

RAITZ, Keith L. Response to Wilkie's "Habits of the Heart". Phil Stud Educ, /, 64-69, 1986.

RAJAN, R Sundara. Approaches to the Theory of Purusarthas. J Indian Counc Phil Res, 6(1), 129-147, S-D 88.

RAJAN, R Sundara. Aspects of the Problem of Reference (1): Phenomenology, Hermeneutics and Deconstruction. Indian Phil Quart, 17(4), 379-406, O 90.

RAJAN, R Sundara. Aspects of the Problem of Reference (I). Indian Phil Quart, 18(2), 153-197, Ap 91.

RAJAN, R Sundara. Aspects of the Problem of Reference (II). Indian Phil Quart, 18(1), 53-72, Ja 91.

RAJAN, R Sundara. Phenomenology and Psychoanalysis: The Hermeneutical Mediation. J Brit Soc Phenomenol, 22(2), 1-14, My 91.

RAJAN, R Sundara. The Primacy of the Political: Towards a Theory of National Integration. J Indian Counc Phil Res, 5(1), 133-152, S-D 87.

RAJCHMAN, John. *Philosophical Events: Essays of the '80s*. New York, Columbia Univ Pr, 1991.

RAMAT, Paolo. "Da Humboldt ai neogrammatici: Continuità e fratture" in *Leibniz, Humboldt, and the Origins of Comparativism*, DE MAURO, Tullio (ed), 199-210. Philadelphia, John Benjamins, 1990.

This paper examines the evolution of the concept of cross-linguistic comparison, from Humboldt to the Neogrammarians, and shows how the focus of comparison progressively shifted from an achronic, general ('philosophic') point of view to a diachronic, historically oriented one, quite in line with the developments of the comparative and reconstructive method in linguistics. The change in viewpoint is connected with the cultural evolution from Enlightenment thinking to Romanticism and, subsequently, to the Positivism of the neogrammarian period. It is shown that these changes must also be seen in the light of the socio-political evolution of Germany during the nineteenth century.

RAMER, Alexis Manaster. Vacuity. Ling Phil, 14(3), 339-348, Jl 91.

The purpose of this article is to dispute a recent claim of Pelletier's (1988) about the conditions under which it is formally possible to show that a language is noncontext-free. While the issue arises in Pelletier's follow-up on Pullum's (1985) and Higginbotham's (1985) arguments about the status of Higginbotham's (1984) proposal that the conditions on *such that* relative constructions in English make the language noncontext-free, I will only be interested in the mathematical question of what would need to be the case for such an argument to go through. I will take no position here on whether *such that* relatives, or any other construction, in English is noncontext-free, though I will suggest some reasons for thinking that the conditions on well-formedness for *such that* relatives in English are nontrivial and could quite possibly involve noncontext-freeness.

RAMÍREZ, E Roy. La ética como conciencia en el subdesarrollo. Rev Filosof (Costa Rica), 27(66), 313-315, D 89.

Underdevelopment may be judged in the light of the impoverished of human possibilities. To this impoverishment transnational transgressions contribute greatly. It is in this context that ethics could stand up to the state of siege human beings and entire groups are subjected to.

RAMÍREZ, E Roy. La tecnología desde un punto de vista ético. Rev Filosof (Costa Rica), 28(67-68), 17-20, D 90.

This paper deals with some of the ethical problems brought about by the possibilities opened by some technological developments, as well as with the ethical principles in the light of which those problems may be coped with.

RAMÓN, Rafael. Al-Fârâbî lógico: su exposicón de la "Isagogé" de Porfirio. Rev Filosof (Spain), 4, 45-67, 1990.

There are still many texts of al-Farabi which are unknown to the Spanish reader. To continue with a task which I formerly undertook, publishing: "Al-Farabi logico: Su Epistola de introduccion al arte de la logica", *Homenaje al Prof Dario Cabanelas*, Universidad de Granada, 1987, Vol I, pg 445-454, and "Los Articulos de necesario conocimiento para quien se inicie en el arte de la logica de Abu Nasr al-Farabi", *Anales del Seminario de Historia de la Filosofia*, 6 (1986-87) 143-153, I now present a short study and the Spanish translation on the *Kitab Isaguyi ay al-madjal* of al-Farabi: a short commentary and exposition on Porphyry's *Isagoge*.

RAMOS, Antonio Pintor. Heidegger en la filosofia española: La eficacia de Heidegger en las filosofías de Ortega y Zubiri. Rev Filosof (Mexico), 23(68), 150-186, My-Ag 90.

This study analyzes the influence of Heidegger's *Sein und Zeit* on Spanish Thought. It focuses on the two greatest thinkers of the XX Century Spain: Ortega y Gasset and Zubiri. While Ortega maintains a critical attitude towards Heidegger, Zubiri accepts entirely Heidegger's program and tries to transcend it. This divergent response is a reflection of two radically different philosophical projects.

RAMOS, Francisco José. Apuntes para un nuevo ámbito de la filosofía. Dialogos, 25(56), 69-80, Jl 90.

The first part of this paper is an analysis of the following verses of Hesiod's *Theogony*: ídmen pseuda pollá legein etymoisin ómoia / ídmen d' eut' ethélomen, alethéa gerysasthai. The saying (legin) of the poet's Muses is the simulation of truth. Simultaneously, the words of the Muses provide the dissimulation of the poet's thinking. Next there is a brief pointualization on Parmenides' mythological discourse. Parmenides' Being (eon) is an appropriation of the poet's verisimilitude. Finally, Plato's criticism of the poets and the written word are metaphysical requests that point to the truthfulness of philosophical discourse. (edited)

RAMOSE, Mogobe B. Hobbes and the Philosophy of International Relations. Quest, 5(1), 18-35, Je 91.

RAMSEY, F P. Mr Keynes on Probability. Brit J Phil Sci, 40(2), 219-222, Je 89.

RAMSEY, F P. Weights or the Value of Knowledge. Brit J Phil Sci, 41(1), 1-4, Mr 90.

RAMSEY, Jeffry L. Beyond Numerical and Causal Accuracy: Expanding the Set of Justificational Criteria. Proc Phil Sci Ass, 1, 485-499, 1990.

I argue that numerical and causal accuracy arguments can be successful only if (1) the theories in use are known to be true, (2) computational difficulties do not exist, and (3) the experimental data are stable and resolved. When any one or more of these assumptions are not satisfied, additional justificational considerations must be invoked. I illustrate the need for range of validity and intelligibility claims with examples drawn from chemical kinetics. My arguments suggest that the realist and antirealist accounts of justification are incomplete. Finally, I sketch some reasons why additional justificatory criteria are needed.

RAMSEY, William and STICH, Stephen and GARON, Joseph. "Connectionism, Eliminativism and the Future of Folk Psychology" in *Philosophical Perspectives, 4: Action Theory and Philosophy of Mind, 1990*, TOMBERLIN, James E (ed), 499-533. Atascadero, Ridgeview, 1990.

RAMSEY, William. Where Does the Self-Refutation Objection Take Us? Inquiry, 33(4), 453-465, D 90.

Eliminative materialism is the position that commonsense psychology is false and that beliefs and desires, like witches and demons, do not exist. One of the most popular criticisms of this view is that it is self-refuting or, in some sense, incoherent. Hence, it is often claimed that eliminativism is not only implausible, but necessarily false. Below, I assess the merits of this objection and find it seriously wanting. I argue that the self-refutation objection is (at best) a misleading reformulation of much more mundane objections to eliminativism and that, contrary to its advocates' endorsements, it adds nothing of genuine interest to the debate over the existence of propositional attitudes.

RANDALL, Donna M and GIBSON, Annetta M. Ethical Decision Making in the Medical Profession: An Application of the Theory of Planned Behavior. J Bus Ethics, 10(2), 111-122, F 91.

The present study applied Ajzen's (1985) theory of planned behavior to the explanation of ethical decision making. Nurses in three hospitals were provided with scenarios that depicted inadequate patient care and asked if they would report health professionals responsible for the situation. Study results suggest that the theory of planned behavior can explain a significant amount of variation in the intent to report a colleague. Attitude toward performing the behavior explained a large portion of the variance; subjective norms explained a moderate amount of the variance; and perceived behavioral control added little to the explanation of variance. Implications for research and practice are discussed.

RANKIN, Kenneth. *The Recovery of the Soul: An Aristotelian Essay on Self-fulfilment*. Toronto, McGill-Queens U Pr, 1991.

The current stalemate between philosophical theories results from blindness to how major problems bear on each other. Thus a libertarian theory of free will, an A-theory of time, a corporealist theory of personal identity, and a non-relativist interpretation of the foundation of ethics find mutual enlightenment in contributing conjointly to a psychocentric form of physicalism. The latter identifies what ensouls the body with the power to act intentionally in any one of several mutually exclusive ways. Besides being strictly physical this power is the primary causal power, all other powers deriving their status as powers by being constitutive of it.

RANLY, Ernest W. Cross-Cultural Philosophizing. Phil Today, 35(1), 63-72, Spr 91.

From the fact that cross-cultural communication does occur, cross-cultural philosophizing is possible. It is not applying deductively some universal definitions; it is not simply sharing common emotions; it is not simply translations of a text. Cross-cultural philosophizing occurs only when we are conscious of our enculturation and try to enter into the inner network of signs, language and rites of another culture. One must begin with the human community, with subject-as-subject, active subject. One must re-do embodiment, natural attitude, time, language and especially orality. Heidegger, Ricoeur and Dussel are helpful. One needs a hermeneutic and a philosophy of history. Let the project begin.

RANTA, Aarne. Intuitionistic Categorial Grammar. Ling Phil, 14(2), 203-239, Ap 91.

The paper presents an intuitionistic categorial grammar based on Martin-Löf's higher level type theory, which is richer than simple type theory in virtue of having families of types in addition to constant types. Classical categorial grammar, such as employed by Montague, is based on simple type theory. Intuitionistic grammar is shown to provide a compositional treatment of quantification and anapora. The paper contains, moreover, methodological discussion of formal grammars.

RANTALA, V. "Counterfactual Reduction" in *Imre Lakatos and Theories of Scientific Change*, GAVROGLU, Kostas (ed), 347-360. Norwell, Kluwer, 1989.

RAPACZYNSKI, Andrzej. *Nature and Politics: Liberalism in the Philosophies of Hobbes, Locke, and Rousseau*. Ithaca, Cornell Univ Pr, 1990.

RAPAPORT, William J. Predication, Fiction, and Artificial Intelligence. Topoi, 10(1), 79-111, Mr 91.

RAPHAEL (trans). *Self and Non-Self: The Drigdrisyaviveka Attributed to Samkara*. London, Kegan Paul Intl, 1990.

This work is a translated Sanskrit text that is an introduction to the basic principles of Sankara's Advaita Vedanta. It discusses Indian religious principles, various types of karma, the distinction between subject and object, and the four Vedic mantras. (staff)

RAPOPORT, Amnon. *Experimental Studies of Interactive Decisions*. Norwell, Kluwer, 1990.

The book includes 17 articles written by the author and his colleagues between 1967 and 1990. They all concern the interplay of theory and experimentation in the general area of group decision making. The models subjected to experimental testing mostly come from the mathematical theory of games. The decisions investigated in the book mostly concern strict competition, two-person bargaining under complete information, and coalition formation in small and large groups. The articles should appeal to social psychologists, experimental economists, decision theorists, and other scientists interested in the experimental study of interactive behavior.

RASCAGLIA, Maria. Venti lettere inedite di Angelo Camillo De Meis a Bertrando Spaventa. G Crit Filosof Ital, 69(1), 39-74, Ja-Ap 90.

RASIOWA, Helena and CAT HO, Nguyen. Plain Semi-Post Algebras as a Poset-Based Generalization of Post Algebras and their Representability. Stud Log, 48(4), 509-530, D 89.

RASMUSSEN, David M. *Reading Habermas*. Cambridge, Blackwell, 1990.

Reading Habermas argues that Habermas's concept of modernity provides the context for the theory of language as well as his approaches to law and ethics. The chapters are entitled: The Dilemmas of Modernity, The Strategy of the Theory of Communicative Action, Discourse Ethics, Communication and the Law, Reading Habermas: Modernity versus Postmodernity, Jürgen Habermas: A Bibliography by René Görtzen.

RASMUSSEN, David. *Universalism versus Communitarianism: Contemporary Debates in Ethics*. Cambridge, MIT Pr, 1990.

Universalism versus Communitarianism focuses on the question raised by recent work in normative philosophy, of whether ethical norms are best derived and justified on the basis of universal or communitarian standards. It is unique in representing both continental and American points of view as well as several generations of scholars. The essays are grouped in four parts that introduce the key issues involved in the debate and then take up ethics in historical perspective; practical reason and ethical responsibility; justification, application, and history; and communitarian alternatives.

RASZLAI, Tibor. The Concept of History in the Renaissance (in Hungarian). Magyar Filozof Szemle, 5-6, 499-511, 1990.

It is man's relation to the evaluation of his life that takes a fundamental turn with the Renaissance way of thinking. This study examines Renaissance historiography as *ars* in light of the new criteria Renaissance man judged his life by, i.e., historical fact, scientific method and historical view as such. The author's approach to the rise of historical view is twofold. The author also takes into consideration the rhetorical function of *historia* as a humanistic discipline. (edited)

RATHMANN, János. The Legacy of Hamann—Thinking, Language and Economy (in Hungarian). Magyar Filozof Szemle, 1-2, 30-39, 1990.

Hamann und Herder waren Gegner des Kantschen Kritizismus auf dem Gebiet der Sprachauffassung—darin besteht ihre Meinungsähnlichkeit. 1) Beide kritisierten den "absurden" Purismus Kants in der Sprachauffassung. 2) Die neue Herder—Hamannsche Sprachauffassung hatte ihren anthropologischen Hintergrund: das historische Herangehen an den Menschen und an die Menschheit. DIe den Durchbruch bildende Hamannsche Konzeption, dass sich die Sprache in einer Einheit mit dem Denken befindet, brachte den Verfasser zur Überzeugung, dass ein Durchbruch von solcher Tragweite nicht isoliert erreicht werden konnte, dass er sich also auf Hamanns ganze Denkweise auswirken musste, dass es z.b. auch bei Hamann starke ontologische Bestrebungen geben mussten, genau wie bei Herder. (edited)

RAU, Zbigniew. Human Nature, Social Engineering, and the Reemergence of Civil Society. Soc Phil Pol, 8(1), 159-179, Autumn 90.

RAUCHE, G A. Heidegger's Attempt at Rehousing Man Through the *Kehre des Denkens*. S Afr J Phil, 9(3), 133-139, Ag 90.

In this article the author's aim is to demonstrate the meaning and significance of Heidegger's *Kehre des Denkens* (the reversal of thinking). The latter is seen as an attempt to get unhoused man rehoused, thus leading him from an unauthentic to an authentic way of existence. It is shown that the hre des Denkens is not a change in Heidegger's overall position, but is already inherent in *Sein und Zeit*, which Heidegger himself declared a preparatory work for the shift in man's thinking to *Zeit und Sein*, from *Existenz* to *Ek-sistenz*, as it appeared in his later writings. If the *Kehre des Denkens* were seen as instrumental in getting unhoused man rehoused, a great deal of the criticism levied against this concept could be dismissed as irrelevant. Although the controversial nature of Heidegger's philosophy in general and concept of Being in particular is readily admitted, it is pointed out that all philosophical perspectives are controversial and that this does not detract from the merit of Heidegger's attempt to show man a way out of his present existential dilemma.

RAULET, Gérard. The Strategy of Forced Reconciliation (in Serbo-Croatian). Filozof Istraz, 34(1), 159-172, 1990.

The author discusses the aesthetic and historical-philosophical ideas of postmodernism. He begins by offering a general opinion about postmodernism: he sees it as a term which has been used up, and could today only be used to connect more recent tendencies in the arts with developments in philosophy and sociology. A forced reconciliation between the pluralist ideology of postmodern architecture and its appeal to satisfy everybody, its historicism and neo-populism is sought by the modern educated spirit. Whenever it becomes dualistic postmodernism can be attacked (with its own weapons): its awareness of new forces of production, as well as its "positive barbarism."

RAUTENBERG, Joseph and VEATCH, Henry. Does the Grisez-Finnis-Boyle Moral Philosophy Rest on a Mistake? Rev Metaph, 44(4), 807-830, Je 91.

This paper has three objectives. First, it seeks to point up the contrast between two major types of ethics in the present-day: on the one hand, an ethics of what might be called a natural law; on the other hand, an ethics in which our moral obligations would seem to be derived largely from logico-linguistic considerations as to the meaning of moral words. Second, as to the moral philosophy of the "Grifinnboyle," the paper seeks to show that their ethics is to be classified as being of the second type. Finally, it having been shown that this second type of a duty-ethic, or a linguistically based ethic, is to be found wanting philosophically, the conclusion is drawn that the Grifinnboyle moral philosophy rests on a mistake. (edited)

RAUTENBERG, Wolfgan. A Calculus for the Common Rules of.... Stud Log, 48(4), 531-537, D 89.

A Hilbert-style rule base for the common rules of (inverted) v and v in the language with one (not written) binary connective is presented, consisting of a binary and several unary rules. The (inverted) v-logic and the v-logic are the only proper nontrivial strengthenings of their common logic.

RAUTENBERG, Wolfgang. Common Logic of Binary Connectives Has Finite Maximality Degree (Preliminary Report). Bull Sect Log, 19(2), 36-38, Je 90.

RAVVEN, Heidi M. Spinoza's Materialist Ethics: The Education of Desire. Int Stud Phil, 22(3), 59-78, 1990.

I argue that Spinoza's focus in his account of ethics is on desire and its (re)education and only secondarily on reason as a *means* to the end of desire's (re)education. I argue that fully active reason is precisely a phase—albeit the final and consummate phase—of desire. The ethical life, according to Spinoza, is informed by this highest state of activity or desire, which also entails desire's universalization. I conclude that the conatus is the link between the divine and the human self-caused activity. Consequently, ethics, as the rational self-development of the conatus or desire, not knowledge, *per se*, is the ultimate form of the human-divine relation.

RAWLING, Piers. The Ranking of Preference. Phil Quart, 40(161), 495-501, O 90.

RAWLS, John. Roderick Firth: His Life and Work. Phil Phenomenol Res, 51(1), 109-118, Mr 91.

RAWWAS, Mohammed Y A and VITELL, Scott J and FESTERVAND, Troy A. The Business Ethics of Pharmacists: Conflicts Practices and Beliefs. J Bus Ethics, 10(4), 295-301, Ap 91.

This paper represents the responses of 377 pharmacists to a mail survey examing their views concerning ethical conflicts and practices. Besides identifying the sources of ethical conflicts, pharmacists were asked how ethical standards have changed over the last 10 years as well as the factors influencing these changes. Conclusions and implications are outlined and future research needs are examined.

RAWWAS, Mohammed Y A and VITELL, Scott J and LUMPKIN, James R. Consumer Ethics: An Investigation of the Ethical Beliefs of Eldery Consumers. J Bus Ethics, 10(5), 365-375, My 91.

Business and especially marketing ethics have come to the forefront in recent years. While consumers have been surveyed regarding their perceptions of ethical business and marketing practices, research has been minimal with regard to their perceptions of ethical *consumer* practices. In addition, few studies have examined the ethical beliefs of elderly consumers even though they are an important and rapidly growing segment. This research investigates the relationship between Machiavellianism, ethical ideology and ethical beliefs for elderly consumers. The results indicate that elderly consumers, while generally being more ethical than young consumers, are diverse in their ethical beliefs.

RAY, Christopher. The Cosmological Constant: Einstein's Greatest Mistake? Stud Hist Phil Sci, 21(4), 589-604, D 90.

The cosmological constant is frequently regarded as an *ad hoc* addition to the field equations of general relativity. Many writers also agree with Einstein's own verdict that it may have been his greatest mistake. However, the addition is neither *ad hoc* nor a mistake, but is the basis of a positive and fruitful development of the theoretical context of relativity.

RAY, R J. Crossed Fingers and Praying Hands: Remarks on Religious Belief and Superstition. Relig Stud, 26(4), 471-482, D 90.

After noting several remarks by Dewi Phillips, attention is paid to Ludwig Wittgenstein's reminders concerning the distinction between religious belief and superstition. It emerges that superstition and religious belief are not opposites but represent two separate realities altogether. Superstitions are seen to be manifestations of fear. In superstition fantastic claims are made concerning quasi-causal connections. Superstitions, unlike religious beliefs, are hypothetical in nature and are tenuously held. To see how the differences between the two realities might manifest themselves, examples from Andrei Konckalovsky's film *Shy People* are examined.

RAYMAEKERS, Bart. Kants *Kritik der Urteilskraft*. Tijdschr Filosof, 52(3), 495-512, S 90.

In this text is given a survey of the literature published on Kant's *Critique of Judgment* during the last two decades. First is focused on the publications on the third Critique as a whole, especially as far as they account for the systematic aspect. For the Critique of Aesthetic Judgment are indicated two main tendencies

RAYMOND, Janice G 612 AUTHOR INDEX WITH ABSTRACTS

in interpretation: authors who seek to integrate the aesthetics in the third Critique as a global concept and those who concentrate on a philosophy of art as such. Although the books on the Critique of Teleological Judgment are few, there is an increasing interest.

RAYMOND, Janice G. Reproductive Gifts and Gift Giving: The Altruistic Woman. Hastings Center Rep, 20(6), 7-11, N-D 90.

Reproductive gift relationships, such as altruistic surrogacy or egg donation, must be seen in the context of political gender inequality, not just as helping someone to have a child. Noncommercial surrogacy cannot be treated as a mere act of altruism—any valorizing of altruistic surrogacy and reproductive gift-giving must be assessed within the history, values, and the structures of women's reproductive inequality. Altruistic reproductive exchanges leave intact the status of women as a breeder class and create a new version of relinquishing motherhood and mothers for others.

RAYWID, Mary Ann. The Environmental Dependence of Dispositional Aims: Response to the Presidential Address. Proc Phil Educ, 46, 22-26, 1990.

RAZ, Joseph. The Politics of the Rule of Law. Ratio Juris, 3(3), 331-339, D 90.

The rule of law should be understood as part of the culture of democracy which requires a distribution of power between a periodically elected legislature and executive and an independent, but publicly accountable, judiciary in charge of a more slowly changing legal doctrine. The rule of law is also essential for the protection of individuals in fast changing pluralistic societies. In both its aspects the doctrine is a product of a particular historical culture, and requires a culture of legality, and not merely the introduction of a few legal rules, for its proper functioning.

RAZ, Joseph. *Practical Reason and Norms*. Princeton, Princeton Univ Pr, 1990.

REAGAN, Timothy. Difference as Deficit. Phil Stud Educ, /, 55-64, 1987-88.

This paper addresses the way in which minority language students in the public schools can best be identified conceptually. It is suggested that language differences in students can, and in some instances do, actually constitute language deficits in pragmatic (though not in cognitive or linguistic) terms as a consequence of social stratification and discrimination.

REASONER, Paul. Sincerity and Japanese Values. Phil East West, 40(4), 471-488, O 90.

Noting the conflation of religion, ethics and aesthetics in the Japanese arts tradition, this essay analyzes the coherence and content of the "ethical-aesthetic" complex by focusing on *makoto* (sincerity). After a brief look at sincerity in the West, the discussion centers on the place of *makoto* in ethics and aesthetics in Japan with attention to the haiku poets Bashō and Onitsura. The conclusion argues for the coherence of the unity of the "ethical-aesthetic" at a deep level when grounded in *internal sincerity*, given the assumption in the Japanese tradition that sincerity is a metaphysical principle.

RECANATI, François. Direct Reference, Meaning, and Thought. Nous, 24(5), 697-722, D 90.

It is argued that there are two distinct notions of "character" or "mode of presentation" at play in the work of David Kaplan and other theorists of direct reference: the "character" which constitutes the linguistic meaning of an indexical expression (i.e., the way in which the reference is linguistically presented) and the "character" which is crucially involved in the individuation of propositional attitudes (i.e., the way in which the reference is thought of). The relations between these two sorts of mode of presentation and their respective properties are investigated.

RECIO GARCÍA, Tomás. Presencia de Grecia y de Roma clásicas en la Revolución francesa de 1789. El Basilisco, 3, 41-48, Ja-F 90.

Apartados del artículo: 1) Los filósofos de la Ilustración. Se educaron en los Colegios religiosos de Jesuitas y padres del Oratorio. 2) La cultivada clase media, jóvenes revolucionarios, se educaron en los mismos Colegios, donde se empaparon de la cultura clásica (más en la romana). 3) Falsearon la interpretación de aquella Historia y la idealizaron. 4) Me limito a los oradores de la Convención: Robespierre, Saint Just, Desmoulins y Marat. Analizo sus citas de personajes clásicos y las contrasto con su verdadero significado dentro de su época. Mi juicio personal de la Revolución: Los ideales de Libertad, Igualdad y Fraternidad fueron traicionades entonces y sólo se abren paso en los siglos XIX y XX.

RECK, Andrew J. "Comment on David L Miller's 'Consciousness, the Attitude of the Individual and Perspectives'" in *Creativity in George Herbert Mead*, GUNTER, Pete A Y (ed), 65-67. Lanham, Univ Pr of America, 1990.

The author accepts the main lines of David L Miller's interpretation of Mead. He criticizes instead Mead's theory of time—past, present, and future.

RECK, Andrew J. The Enlightenment in American Law I: The Declaration of Independence. Rev Metaph, 44(3), 549-573, Mr 91.

This article is devoted to an examination of the Declaration of Independence as an expression of the Enlightenment ideas of such philosophers as John Locke, Jean Jacques Burlamaqui, and Francis Hutcheson. It explores both the explicit general theory of government, including the theory of rights, and the implicit particular theory of the British Empire, represented in the Declaration.

RECK, Andrew J. The Enlightenment in American Law II: The Constitution. Rev Metaph, 44(4), 729-754, Je 91.

The subject of the paper is the influence of the ideas of Enlightenment philosophers on the framing of the US Constitution. Philosophers discussed are Locke, Hume, Harrington, Montesquieu, and others. Among the founding fathers whose writings are examined are James Madison, John Adams, and Alexander Hamilton. The contention of this second paper in the series—the first on the Declaration of Independence, the third on the Bill of Rights—is that the Constitution, along with the documents focussed on in the other papers, is a consummate expression of Enlightenment thought.

RECK, Andrew J. An Historical Sketch of Pluralism. Monist, 73(3), 367-387, Jl 90.

The article aims to explore the meanings of pluralism in philosophy by offering an historical sketch. It also provides a glimpse of the philosophical background of critical pluralism. Part I discusses Aristotle, Leibniz, and William James, and distinguishes metaphysical and methodological pluralism. Part II examines Mortimer Adler's early theory of dialectic, Stephen Pepper's conception of metaphysics as world hypothesis, Kenneth Burke's dramatism, and Richard McKeon's metaphilosophy and in criticism is indispensable if dogmatism and skepticism are to be avoided.

RECK, Andrew J. The Philosophical Achievement of Peter A Bertocci. Personalist Forum, 7(1), 73-89, Spr 91.

This paper examines Bertocci's conceptions of the person, of the emotions, of value, and of God. It attempts to show that Bertocci, carrying on the tradition of personalism he inherited from Bowne and Brightman, nonetheless added to it in confrontation with the trends of positivism, Freudianism, behaviorism, and process metaphysics in contemporary thought.

RECK, Andrew J. Reason and Reasonableness in the Philosophy of Brand Branshard. Ideal Stud, 20(2), 112-121, My 90.

The author examines Blanshard's theories of reason and reasonableness. Tracing Blanshard's conception of reason in theory of knowledge, metaphysics, moral philosophy, religion, and his defense of reason against what he considers its detractors in those fields, the author elucidates the goal of reason to be an intelligible whole of necessarily related parts according to Blanshard, but notes that this whole or Absolute is not identical with values or the Good.

RECKER, Doren. There's More Than One Way to Recognize a Darwinian: Lyell's Darwinism. Phil Sci, 57(3), 459-478, S 90.

There are a number of reasons for doubting the standard view that scientific theories (understood as sets of connected statements) are the best units for investigating scientific continuity and change (that is, research programs continue as long as groups of scientists accept the central tenets of such theories). Here it is argued that one weakness of this approach is that it cannot be used to demarcate adequately scientific communities or conceptual systems (that is, it fails as a classificatory scheme). Recent alternative proposals by Philip Kitcher and David Hull are assessed in terms of their usefulness in demarcating "Darwinism" and the "Darwinians" in the first decade or so after the publication of *The Origin of Species*, focusing on the case of Charles Lyell.

RECKI, Birgit. Die Metaphysik der Kritik: Zum Verhältnis von Metaphysik und Erfahrung bei Max Horkheimer und Theodor W Adorno. Neue Hefte Phil, 30-31, 139-171, 1991.

In contradiction to their early polemics, the Frankfurt school has not succeeded in getting rid of metaphysics. Max Horkheimer obviously remained unconscious of the metaphysical extent that the project of a *critical theory of society* necessarily had to have. It was Adorno, who in a more consequent reflexion upon the *implications of critical thinking*, had to face and to admit metaphysical dimensions. The argumentation of the article is indebted to a concept, which does not restrict the notion of "metaphysics" to one of its historical impacts, but emphasizes the *structural criterion* of a *rational* and thereby *holistic reflection on reality*.

REDDING, Paul. Hermeneutic or Metaphysical Hegelianism? Kojève's Dilemma. Owl Minerva, 22(2), 175-190, Spr 91.

Alexandre Kojève pointed to the importance of the notion of recognition in Hegel's *Phenomenology of Spirit* but swung between two conflicting interpretations of this idea, resulting in a contradiction at the heart of his account of the master-slave dialetic. The most prominent interpretation takes the "desire for recognition" as an essential human trait. Read in this way Hegel becomes a metaphysical realist. On the other, contrary, interpretation, recognition is a necessary context for the existence of any intentional human subject. Here Hegel appears more like a nommetaphysical hermeneuticist. The latter interpretation is closer to the real Hegel.

REDDING, Paul. Nietzschean Perspectivism and the Logic of Practical Reason. Phil Forum, 22(1), 72-88, Fall 90.

From a comparison of the categorial structures of master and slave thinking in Nietzsche's *Genealogy of Morals*, it is argued that "perspectivism" applies primarily to practical reason and knowledge. Using the work of Pierre Bourdieu and Charles Taylor, it is shown that the masters' conceptual pairs are indexically centred on their own form of life espoused as good. Consequently, their judgements are action-guiding. The slaves invert the evaluative poles of the masters' judgements but leave their indexicality intact. *Their* judgements do not encode an image of a 'good life' to be followed, only an evil one to be avoided.

REDDY, V Ananda. Sri Aurobindo and the Process of Physical Transformation. Indian Phil Quart, 18(2), 315-334, Ap 91.

"A divine life in a divine body" is the ideal envisioned by Sri Aurobindo. The process of physical transformation has first to conquer the psychological difficulties of food, sleep and sex-impulse. Next, the principal physical organs have to be gradually replaced by the *chakras* or the Tantric centres of universal energy in our body. Ultimately, the new body would be one that is light, luminous, plastic and adaptable, capable of radiating from within the beauty and bliss of the immanent Divine Consciousness. The new body is envisaged to be not just an exceptional or individual achievement but to become the very principle of evolution which is marching toward a new species beyond man.

REDHEAD, Michael L G and CLIFTON, Robert K and BUTTERFIELD, Jeremy N. Nonlocal Influences and Possible Worlds—A Stapp in the Wrong Direction. Brit J Phil Sci, 41(1), 5-58, Mr 90.

REDHEAD, Michael L G. "Undressing Baby Bell" in *Harré and His Critics*, BHASKAR, Roy (ed), 122-128. Cambridge, Blackwell, 1990.

REDHEAD, Michael. Explanation. Philosophy, 27, 135-154, 90 Supp.

REDHEAD, Michael. The Lakatos Award Lecture: The Nature of Reality. Brit J Phil Sci, 40(4), 429-441, D 89.

REDHEAD, Michael and FRENCH, Steven. Quantum Physics and the Identity of Indiscernibles. Brit J Phil Sci, 39(2), 233-246, Je 88.

This paper is concerned with the question of whether atomic particles of the same species, i.e., with the same intrinsic state-independent properties of mass, spin, electric charge, etc, violate the Leibnizian Principle of the Identity of Indiscernibles, in the sense that, while there is more than one of them, their state-dependent properties may also all be the same. The answer depends on what exactly the state-dependent properties of atomic particles are taken to be. On the plausible interpretation that these should comprise all monadic and relational properties that can be expressed in terms of physical magnitudes associated with self-adjoint operators that can be defined for the individual particles, then the weakest form of the Principle is shown to be violated for bosons, fermions and higher-order paraparticles, treated in first quantization.

REDMOND, Walter. Relations and Sixteenth-Century Mexican Logic. Critica, 22(65), 23-41, Ag 90.

Alonso de la Vera Cruz's *Recognitio Summularum* shows how Scholastic logicians worked with patterns of categorical sentences more complex than subject-predicate. They used analytical techniques allowing them to treat relations and their quantification. Indeed, the sentence-type they identified as having a "complexively conjoined, multiple-sense" subject or predicate seems able to represent the relation as such.

REDPATH, Peter A (ed). *From Twilight to Dawn: The Cultural Vision of Jacques Maritain*. Notre Dame, Univ Notre Dame Pr, 1990.

REDPATH, Peter A. "Poetic Revenge and Modern Totalitarianism" in *From Twilight to Dawn: The Cultural Vision of Jacques Maritain*, REDPATH, Peter A (ed), 227-240. Notre Dame, Univ Notre Dame Pr, 1990.

REED, R C. A Decidable Ehrenfeucht Theory with Exactly Two Hyperarithmetic Models. Annals Pure Applied Log, 53(2), 135-168, Jl 91.

Millar showed that for each n less than ω, there is a complete decidable theory having precisely eighteen nonisomorphic countable models where some of these are decidable exactly in the hyperarithmetic set $H(n)$. By combining ideas from Millar's proof with a technique of Peretyat'kin, the author reduces the number of countable models to five. By a theorem of Millar, this is the smallest number of countable models a decidable theory can have if some of the models are not $0''$-decidable.

REED-DOWNING, Teresa. Husserl's Presuppositionless Philosophy. Res Phenomenol, 20, 136-151, 1990.

REEDER, Harry P. Never say "Never say 'Never'": A Reply to Nicholas Gier. J Brit Soc Phenomenol, 22(2), 97-98, My 91.

The article responds briefly to Nicholas Gier's critique ("Never Say Never", *JBSP*, Volume 22, May 1990) of Harry Reeder's "Wittgenstein Never Was a Phenomenologist" (*JBSP*, Volume 20, October 1989, pages 49-68). Gier cites passages in Wittgenstein's writings to support the thesis that Wittgenstein was a phenomenologist, finding in them the phenomenological themes of 'phenomenological reduction,' 'transcendental conditions for human experience,' 'intentionality,' and 'free variation as eidetic reduction.' Reeder offers an interpretation of the passages in question according to which they provide no such support.

REEDIJK, Wim M. Some Observations on the Influence of Christian Scholastic Authors on Jewish Thinkers in the 13th and 14th Century. Bijdragen, 4, 382-396, 1990.

It is a well-known fact that in the late Middle Ages Christian Scholastics were influenced by Jewish thinkers. But contrary to what is often thought, traces of Christian writings can also be found in the works of Jewish authors, like Hillel ben Samuel, Levi ben Gershon, Chasdai Crecas and Jehuda Romano. This article outlines briefly what has been said up till now on this particular subject, and illustrates by two examples, taken from Jehuda Roman's commentary on the Creation, how this author used the insights of Christian scholars, such as Thomas Aquinas.

REEVES, T V. A Theory of Probability. Brit J Phil Sci, 39(2), 161-182, Je 88.

This paper argues that probability is not an objective phenomenon that can be identified with either the configurational properties of sequences, or the dynamic properties of sources that generate sequences. Instead, it is proposed that probability is a function of subjective as well as objective conditions. This is explained by formulating a notion of probability that is a modification of Laplace's classical enunciation. This definition is then used to explain why probability is strongly associated with disordered sequences, and is also used to throw light on a number of problems in probability theory.

REGAL, Philip J. *The Anatomy of Judgment*. Minneapolis, Univ of Minn Pr, 1990.

REGAN, Thomas J. The Matrix of Personality: A Whiteheadian Corroboration of Harry Stack Sullivan's Interpersonal Theory of Psychiatry. Process Stud, 19(3), 189-198, Fall 90.

Sullivan himself, recognized the potential of Whitehead's process philosophy to serve as the conceptual ground for a theory of psychiatry. It is here shown that Whitehead's ontology is able not only to corroborate most of the central insights of Sullivan's interpersonal theory of psychiatry, but that it is capable of going beyond it. Inchoate in Whitehead's writings are shown to be distinct developmental stages which when brought together reveal a theory of personality even more comprehensive than Sullivan's.

REGAN, Tom (ed). *Earthbound: Introductory Essays in Environmental Ethics*. Prospect Heights, Waveland Pr, 1990.

REGEHLY, Thomas. Der "Atheist" und der "Theologe": Schopenhauer als Hörer Schleiermachers. Schopenhauer Jahr, 71, 7-16, 1990.

RÉGIMBALD, Manon. Vers une mise en signe de l'installation. Horiz Phil, 1(1), 123-142, 1990.

This text sets out to show a mediation of Peirce's semiotics and a contemporary art practice: installation. Peirce's phaneroscopy, wherein semiosis is found, takes into account the art object's singularity and context as well as its condition for meaning and communication. Abduction, the first mode of inference is moreover given a crucial function generating logic and creativity. Would this aesthetic turn not breach the everlasting monopoly of linguistics as the only valuable object of research while revealing in Peirce's semiotic a much larger and pertinent domain for the study of art production and interpretation?

REHG, William R. Lonergan's Performative Transcendental Argument Against Scepticism. Proc Cath Phil Ass, 63, 257-268, 1990.

This article draws on Bernard Lonergan's *Insight* for a reply to Barry Stroud's critique of anti-sceptical transcendental arguments. Because Lonergan focuses on the performances (rather than on the conceptual frameworks) involved in Cartesian sceptical arguments, he avoids the dilemma posed by Stroud. These performances commit the sceptic to a notion of objectivity that undermines—at least at a meta-level—the content of sceptical doubt.

REHG, William. Discourse and the Moral Point of View: Deriving a Dialogical Principle of Universalization. Inquiry, 34(1), 27-48, Mr 91.

Central to the discourse ethics advanced by Jürgen Habermas is a principle of universalization (U) amounting to a dialogical equivalent of Kant's Categorical Imperative. Habermas has proposed that 'U' follows by material implication from two premises: 1) what it means to discuss whether a moral norm ought to be adopted and 2) what those involved in argumentation must suppose of themselves if they are to consider a consensus they reach as rationally motivated. To date, no satisfactory derivation of 'U' from these two premises has been presented. Thus the present study attempts to show how one can, without begging the question, arrive at 'U' by assuming a suitable explications of these two premises, supplemented with a fairly innocuous assumption about the context of discourse. If the argument is sound, then 'U' brings both deontological and consequentialist intuitions together with a note of solidarity that requires an intersubjective account of insight.

REHG, William. Discourse Ethics and the Communitarian Critique of Neo-Kantianism. Phil Forum, 22(2), 120-138, Wint 90-91.

This article asks whether Jürgen Habermas's discourse ethics avoids flaws that neo-Aristotelians such as Alasdair MacIntyre attribute to neo-Kantian moral theories. The chief advance in discourse ethics is to link the validity of a moral norm to real dialogue about the foreseeable impact of the norm on the interests of those affected. A detailed examination of such a dialogical process shows that, at least in principle, discourse ethics makes rational consensus on norms possible, and in a way that promises to move the liberal-communitarian debate forward.

REICH, K Helmut. The Relation between Science and Theology: The Case for Complimentarity Revisited. Zygon, 25(4), 369-390, D 90.

Donald MacKay has suggested that the logical concept of complementarity is needed to relate scientific and theological thinking. According to Ian Barbour, this concept should only be used within, not between, disciplines. This article therefore attempts to clarify that contrast from the standpoint of cognitive process. Thinking in terms of complementarity is explicated within a structuralist-genetic, interactive-constructivist, developmental theory of the neo- and post-Piagetian kind, and its role in religious development is indicated. Adolescents' complementary views on Creation and on the corresponding scientific accounts serve as an illustration. After further analysis of parallel and circular complementarity, it is shown under which conditions complementarity of science and theology can be better justified and may be potentially more fruitful than is apparent from Barbour's or even MacKay's considerations.

REICHENBACH, Bruce R. *The Law of Karma: A Philosophical Study*. Honolulu, Univ of Hawaii Pr, 1990.

The book examines what advocates of the law of karma mean by the doctrine, various ways they interpret it, and how they see it operating. The study proceeds to investigate and critically evaluate the law of karma's connections to significant philosophical concepts like causation, freedom, God, persons, the moral law, liberation, and immortality. For example, it explores in depth the implications of the doctrine for whether we are free or fatalistically determined, whether human suffering can be reconciled with cosmic justice, the nature of the self, and the character of moral experience.

REIDENBACH, R Eric and ROBIN, Donald P. A Conceptual Model of Corporate Moral Development. J Bus Ethics, 10(4), 273-284, Ap 91.

The conceptual model presented in this article argues that corporations exhibit specific behaviors that signal their true level of moral development. Accordingly, the authors identify five levels of moral development and discuss the dynamics that move corporations from one level to another. Examples of corporate behavior which are indicative of specific stages of moral development are offered.

REIDENBACH, R Eric and ROBIN, Donald P. Epistemological Structures in Marketing: Paradigms, Metaphors, and Marketing Ethics. Bus Ethics Quart, 1(2), 185-200, Ap 91.

This article uses Arndt's depiction of marketing epistemology to suggest a possible explanation for the lack of emphasis on marketing ethics within the marketing literature. While a growing number of writers are turning their attention to the area, marketing's heavy reliance on logical empiricism has contributed to a disinclination in the development of this area. Only through recent and numerous revelations of misconduct has the discipline of marketing responded to its ethical dimensions.

REILLY, B J and KYJ, M J. Economics and Ethics. J Bus Ethics, 9(9), 691-698, S 90.

Business theory and management practices are outgrowths of basic economic principles. To evaluate the proper place of *ethics* in business, the meaning of ethics as defined by economic theory must be assessed. This paper contends that classical economic thought advocates a nonethical decision-making context and is not functional for a modern complex, interdependent environment.

REINER, Hans and ADLER, Pierre (trans) and PASKIN, David (trans). The Emergence and Original Meaning of the Name 'Metaphysics'. Grad Fac Phil J, 13(2), 23-53, 1990.

REINER, Paula. Aristotle on Personality and Some Implications for Friendship. Ancient Phil, 11(1), 67-84, Spr 91.

Aristotle intuited our distinction between character traits and personality traits, as seen in his isolation in the Eudemian Ethics of six personality traits (all means but not excellences) and in the Nicomachean Ethics of three personality traits (all connected with social interaction). This distinction paves the way for a challenge to his doctrine of the "seriously good man" (spoudaios) as a universal standard of judgment, and raises the question of how personality traits figure in Aristotle's first and best friendship, known as "character friendship."

REINES, Brandon P. On the Locus of Medical Discovery. J Med Phil, 16(2), 183-209, Ap 91.

A search for consensus about the methodology of discovery among physicians and physiologists led the author to identify a crucial anomaly of medical historiography: in general, physicians stress the significance of clinico-patholigic method, while physiologists emphasize the experimental. Hence, physicians and bench scientists might be perceived as members of epistemically distinct research traditions. However, analysis of the historical development of discoveries in medicine, exemplified by case studies in physiology, bacteriology, immunology, and therapeutics, reveals that the epistemic dichotomy is illusory. Both physicians and bench scientists discover in the same way: by identifying and explaining clinical anomalies. It is argued that the sociological role of experimentation is to dramatize clinical hypotheses and not test them in a Popperian sense.

REINIKAINEN, Pekka. Biotechnology and Warfare. Ethics Med, 7(1), 1-2, Spr 91.

REISCH, George A. Chaos, History, and Narrative. Hist Theor, 30(1), 1-20, F 91.

REISCH, George A. Did Kuhn Kill Logical Empiricism? Phil Sci, 58(2), 264-277, Je 91.

In the light of two unpublished letters from Carnap to Kuhn, this essay examines the relationship between Kuhn's *The Structure of Scientific Revolutions* and Carnap's philosophical views. Contrary to the common wisdom that Kuhn's book refuted logical empiricism, it argues that Carnap's views of revolutionary scientific change are rather similar to those detailed by Kuhn. This serves both to explain Carnap's appreciation of *The Structure of Scientific Revolutions* and to suggest that logical empiricism, insofar as that program rested on Carnap's shoulders, was not substantially upstaged by Kuhn's book.

REISER, Stanley Joel. "Hospitals as Humane Corporations" in *Integrity in Health Care Institutions: Humane Environments for Teaching, Inquiry, and Healing*, BULGER, Ruth Ellen (ed), 121-128. Iowa City, Univ of Iowa Pr, 1990.

REISER, Stanley Joel (ed) and BULGER, Ruth Ellen (ed). *Integrity in Health Care Institutions: Humane Environments for Teaching, Inquiry, and Healing*. Iowa City, Univ of Iowa Pr, 1990.

REISS, Hans (ed). *Political Writings—Kant*. New York, Cambridge Univ Pr, 1991.

REMEDIOS, F. The Foundationalist Justification of Epistemic Principles. Phil Inq, 12(1-2), 44-58, Wint-Spr 90.

RENARDEL DE LAVALETTE, Gerard R. Extended Bar Induction in Applicative Theories. Annals Pure Applied Log, 50(2), 139-189, N 90.

TAPP is a total applicative theory, conservative over intuitionistic arithmetic. In this paper, we first show that the same holds for TAPP + the choice principle EAC; then we extend TAPP with choice sequences and study the principle EBI-super-a-sub-zero (arithmetical extended bar induction of type zero). The resulting theories are used to characterise the arithmetical fragment of EL (elementary intuitionistic analysis) + EBI-super-a-sub-zero. As a digression, we use TAPP to show that P. Martin-Löf's basic extensional theory ML_0 is conservative over intuitionistic arithmetic. (edited)

RENAUD, Michel. O discurso filosófico e a unidade da verdade nas primeiras obras de Paul Ricoeur. Rev Port Filosof, 46(1), 19-48, Ja-Mr 90.

This study pays special attention to the theory of truth elaborated in Ricoeur's work from 1947 to 1960. It seeks to stress the complication of—on one hand—ontological understanding, at first influenced by Karl Jasper's thought (1947), and—on the other hand—phenomenological understanding, centered on the theory of judgement (1960). The analysis of the tension between the unity of the true and the multiplicity of philosophies leads however to the concept of truth as communication and as object of hope. It seeks then to show what founds this hope, as well as the dimension by which hope goes beyond the universe of philosophy. In conclusion, it is mentioned that the later developments of Ricoeur's philosophy (1960-1989), e.g., the hermeneutics of symbol, metaphor, and narrative, can be replaced and reread advantageously in the horizon of the tension involved in the problem of truth.

RENAUD, Michel. A essência da técnica segundo Heidegger. Rev Port Filosof, 45(3), 349-377, Jl-S 89.

This article on the essence of "Technik" according to Heidegger has three parts. In the first, Heidegger's basic ideas on "Technik" are presented in view of understanding the specific problematics that he develops. In the second, a quasi-philological analysis of the semantical derivations that provide the text with a continuity of meaning is proposed; the principle concepts of *Die Frage nach der Technik* are brought forth. Finally, there is a critical reflection concerning the implications of these concepts and concerning the level of intelligibility of Heidegger's discourse.

RENAUD, Michel. As relações entre o Deus da Razão e o Deus da Fé. Rev Port Filosof, 46(3), 309-330, Jl-S 90.

In this study dedicated to the relationship between theology and philosophy, three models of understanding are considered; these models are those of Hegel, Husserl, and Heidegger. But there is an internal limitation within each one of these models: the relation between representation and thought, the transcendental analysis of religious consciousness, and the difference between Being and being cannot provide the problem of God with a satisfactory presentation for neither philosophers nor believers. For this reason the analysis has to be reconsidered from a new perspective—that of the concept of Person and that of desimplification—after studying the results of those models.

RENAUT, Alain. "L'idée d'égalité et la notion moderne du droit" in *Égalité Uguaglianza*, FERRARI, Jean (ed), 61-74. Napoli, Liguori, 1990.

RENDTORFF, Trutz. "Conceptions of Peace" in *Celebrating Peace*, ROUNER, Leroy S (ed), 89-101. Notre Dame, Univ Notre Dame Pr, 1990.

RENICK, Timothy M. Response to Berlin and McBride. Soc Theor Pract, 16(3), 323-335, Fall 90.

From a perspective grounded in conceptions of the individual and her liberty put forth by 19th century British idealist T H Green, the essay offers an alternative to both Isaiah Berlin's concept of "negative freedom" and William McBride's Sartre-inspired conception. Through a discussion of Robert Nozick's *Anarchy, State and Utopia*, the incompatibility of "negative freedom" and political obligation is explored. Far from subsuming individual liberty, Green's vision of freedom is posited as one which both fashions obligations to society and carves out a revered place for individual choice.

RENNER, Zsuzsanna. India and the Theory of the Asiatic Mode of Production (in Hungarian). Magyar Filozof Szemle, 5-6, 441-462, 1990.

Oriental society, as it is depicted in Marx's relevant writings, is organized on two levels: despotic power 'above' and village communities 'below'. When dealing with the East, Marx's interest originally focused on the great empires of his age. Premodern Indian history had a decisive role in the formation of the theory to be called "the Asiatic mode of production". Premodern Indian state was organized on two levels; the two levels were essentially of different nature. There is no general theory including that of the Asiatic mode of production that could be extended to the whole geographical and temporal range of Indian history. (edited)

RENTTO, Juha-Pekka. What Can a Discursive Theory of Morality Learn from Aquinas? Vera Lex, 10(1), 1-4, 1990.

REPICI, Luciana. L'epiglottide nell'antichità tra medicina e filosofia. Hist Phil Life Sci, 12(1), 67-104, 1990.

In antiquity, the epiglottis and the related question whether drink enters the lung is a problem embracing both differently organized philosophical strategies and differently developed medical competences. Over the centuries, the history of a physiological question gradually turns into a debate where we find philosophers disagreeing with philosophers and physicians with physicians. A peculiar feature of this debate is that from a certain time on it involves a division between those who defend Plato's view on the subject and those who (philosophers as well as physicians) criticize it. Plato, Aristotle and Chrysippus, the Hippocratic authors and Erasistratus in the testimony of Aulus Gellius, Plutarch and indirectly also of Cicero, and then Galen and Macrobius have a special place in the development of this topic.

REQUATE, Till. Once Again Pure Exchange Economies: A Critical View Towards the Structuralistic Reconstructions by Balzer & Stegmüller. Erkenntnis, 34(1), 87-116, Ja 91.

This article mainly consists in a criticism towards the structuralistic reconstructions of exchange economies by Balzer and Stegmüller. It will be shown that Balzer's special law of market clearing is no specialization, that is, no additional axiom but that it can rather be derived within his reconstruction, if we make one additional assumption, essential concerning exchange economies, and which is usually made in the economic literature. Moreover it will be argued from an economic point of view against separating a 'law of market clearing' from 'maximizing utilities' and regarding market clearing as a special law. Finally we will propose an alternative view.

RESCHER, Nicholas. *Baffling Phenomena: And Other Studies in the Philosophy of Knowledge and Valuation*. Savage, Rowman & Littlefield, 1991.

RESCHER, Nicholas. Conceptual Idealism Revisited. Rev Metaph, 44(3), 495-523, Mr 91.

RESCHER, Nicholas. How Wide Is the Gap Between Facts and Values? Phil Phenomenol Res, 50 SUPP, 297-319, Fall 90.

RESCHER, Nicholas. *Human Interests: Reflections on Philosophical Anthropology*. Stanford, Stanford Univ Pr, 1990.

RESCHER, Nicholas. Luck. Proc Amer Phil Ass, 64(3), 5-19, N 90.

RESNICK, Larry. A Very Short Guide to Understanding Wittgenstein. Eidos, 9(1), 67-77, Je 90.

RESNICK, Stephen and AMARIGLIO, Jack and WOLFF, Richard. Division and Difference in the "Discipline" of Economics. Crit Inquiry, 17(1), 108-137, Autumn 90.

The article argues that the "discipline" of economics is an agnostic field of fundamentally different and conflicting discourses. Neoclassical, Keynesian, and Marxian schools are distinguished by the ways they understand both unity and difference in economics; key means by which these schools define and mark differences are their different uses of "scientific" epistemological positions, differences in theoretical "entry points," and diverse concepts of causality. The paper criticizes foundationalist epistemologies and reductionist forms of causal explanation, especially humanism and structuralism, in neoclassical, Keynesian, and traditional Marxian economics and offers a nonessentialist conception of knowledge and causality as an alternative.

RESNIK, Michael D. "Beliefs About Mathematical Objects" in *Physicalism in Mathematics*, IRVINE, Andrew D (ed), 41-71. Norwell, Kluwer, 1990.

An account of beliefs about mathematical objects faces a serious obstacle in beliefs *de* mathematical *res*. Mathematical examples of apparent dicto/de re contrasts are plentiful, but extant theories of *de re* belief fail to make sense of them. Mathematics yields evidence for Quine's conclusion that the dicto/de re distinction is context dependent and interest relative. Due to this, I change the focus to giving a criterion of reference applicable to mathematical terms and an account of how we came to refer to mathematical objects. I offer an immanent solution to the first and a postulational one to the second.

RESNIK, Michael D. Computation and Mathematical Empiricism. Phil Topics, 17(2), 129-144, Fall 89.

REUTER, K K and GUTE, Hans B. The Last Word on Elimination of Quantifiers in Modules. J Sym Log, 55(2), 670-673, Je 90.

Consider the structure with universe A group G, in the language where a relation symbol is introduced for every coset modulo A subgroup of a power of G; then this structure eliminates quantifiers. This result generalizes the well-known elimination by PP-formulae for Abelian groups and modules.

REY, George. Transcending Paradigms. Metaphilosophy, 21(4), 447-455, O 90.

REYES, Mario G C and TERPSTRA, David E and BOKOR, Donald W. Predictors of Ethical Decisions Regarding Insider Trading. J Bus Ethics, 10(9), 699-710, S 91.

This paper examines potential predictors of ethical decisions regarding insider trading. An interactionist perspective is taken, in which person variables, situational variables, and the interaction of these two sets of variables are viewed as influencing ethical decisions. The results of our study support such a perspective. Ethical decisions regarding insider trading appear to be a function of a complex set of interacting variables related to both the person and the situation. The implications of these findings are discussed.

REYNOLDS, Terrence. Method Divorced from Content in Theology: An Assessment of Lonergan's *Method in Theology*. Thomist, 55(2), 245-269, Ap 91.

The article examines critiques of Bernard Lonergan's *Method in Theology*, particularly of his attempt to divorce method from content in theological inquiry. Critics have argued that this approach leaves the specific roles of grace and Christian faith in the enterprise of theology ill-defined. The article suggests some misunderstanding of Lonergan by his critics and a possible rationale for his method, but concludes that the objections raised to his work are well-founded. There is, indeed, an underlying ambiguity in Lonergan's *Method* which renders his argument unconvincing.

REYNOLDS, Vernon. "Ordinary Animals, Language Animals and Verbal Tradition" in *Harré and His Critics*, BHASKAR, Roy (ed), 288-294. Cambridge, Blackwell, 1990.

RHEINWALD, Rosemarie. Minds, Machines and Gödels Theorem (in German). Erkenntnis, 34(1), 1-21, Ja 91.

Mechanism is the thesis that men can be considered as machines, that there is no essential difference between minds and machines. John Lucas has argued that it is a consequence of Gödel's theorem that mechanism is false. Men cannot be considered as machines, because the intellectual capacities of men are superior to that of any machine. Lucas claims that we can do something that no machine can do—namely to produce as true the Gödel-formula of any given machine. But no machine can prove its own Gödel-formula. In order to discuss and evaluate this argument, the author makes a distinction between *formal* and *informal* proofs, and between proofs *given by men* and proofs *given by machines*. It is argued that the informal proof capacities of machines are possibly greater and the formal proof capacities of men are possibly smaller than the antimechanist claims. So the argument from Gödel's theorem against mechanism fails. (edited)

RHENÁN SEGURA, Jorge. Las Sociedades de Pensamiento y la Revolución Francesa. Rev Filosof (Costa Rica), 27(66), 457-464, D 89.

The article shows the genesis, evolution and development of so-called "Thinking Societies" (applying the terminology of Cochin) namely the political clubs that sprang up in France in the years prior to the French Revolution (1750-1792). These societies played a role of vital importance in the development and promotion of the philosophical and political ideas of the French Revolution. These societies established their own doctrine, and decided about the ways of action to carry out their programs. They constituted important centers of schooling for the future revolutionary cadres, and parallel to this, created a broad network through which the ideas of the Revolution spread throughout the country.

RIBEIRO FERREIRA, Maria Luisa. "Pontos de vista—exercício hermenêutico sobre um excerto da *Monadologia*" in *Dinâmica do Pensar: Homenagem a Oswaldo Market*, FAC LETRAS UNIV LISBOA (ed), 111-126. Lisboa, Fac Letras U Lisboa, 1991.

Il s'agit d'un exercice herméneutique d'application de la thématique leibnizienne des "points de vue" à un texte de la *Monadologie*. Les paragraphes 65-68 sont successivement interprétés du point de vue historique, du point de vue positiviste, du point de vue logico-métaphysique, du point de vue religieux, du point de vue magico-mythique. Aucune de ces lectures est complète. Toutes ensemble elles perméttent une meilleure compréhension de la thémathique du "plein".

RIBEIRO, Renato Janine. Hobbes, Jacobo I y el derecho inglés. Rev Latin De Filosof, 16(2), 165-181, Jl 90.

RICCI, Saverio. Infiniti mondi e mondo nuovo: Conquista dell'America e critica della civilità europea in Giordano Bruno. G Crit Filosof Ital, 69(2), 204-221, My-Ag 90.

RICCIO, Stefano. Etica e diritto penale nella filosofia attualistica. Sapienza, 43(4), 411-425, O-D 90.

RICE, Hugh. Blackburn on Filling in Space. Analysis, 51(2), 106, Mr 91.

RICHARD, Arsene. Teaching Philosophy: Skills and Mentalities. Thinking, 9(2), 25-27, 1990.

This article formulates a first hypothesis: there is an underlying mental activity that is a prerequisite for the efficiency of a range of thinking skills ordinarily reported in different taxonomies, US New Jersey task force taxonomy of thinking skills. This mental activity is called intuition. If this first hypothesis is adequate, there is a needed mentality or activity on the part of the teacher to appreciate this underlying mental activity in the student. This mentality/activity is a special blend of faith and empathy.

RICHARD, Jean. Dieu tout-puissant et souffrant. Laval Theol Phil, 47(1), 39-51, F 91.

Cette étude rappelle d'abord quelques-unes des objections qu'on oppose aujourd'hui à l'idée d'une toute-puissance divine. Elle montre ensuite l'enjeu méthodologique que recouvre la question. Il s'agit de voir le rapport entre deux méthodes caractéristiques de la théologie: l'analogie et le paradoxe. L'article présente d'abord la toute-puissance divine selon la voie de l'analogie, puis la souffrance de Dieu d'après la voie du paradoxe, pour tenter finalement une synthèse de ces deux démarches avec la notion d'une toute-puissance de l'amour.

RICHARD, Lionel. Qu'est-ce que l'expressionnisme allemand? Philosophique (France), 1(90), 35-40, 1990.

RICHARD, Mark. Comments on Schiffer's *Remnants of Meaning*. Pac Phil Quart, 71(3), 223-239, S 90.

RICHARDS, Barry. "Tenses, Temporal Quantifiers and Semantic Innocence" in *Truth and Interpretation: Perspectives on the Philosophy of Donald Davidson*, LE PORE, Ernest (ed), 135-178. Cambridge, Blackwell, 1986.

RICHARDS, Edgardo. Sociedad informatizada y poder político. Rev Filosof (Costa Rica), 28(67-68), 55-57, D 90.

I propose a discussion of a new condition of production possibilities, such that to generalize from technological changes based on the intensive use of information recourses might have a relation as political regimen, and that these make a necessary society based on participation.

RICHARDS, Evelleen and SCOTT, Pam and MARTIN, Brian. Captives of Controversy: The Myth of the Neutral Social Researcher in Contemporary Scientific Controversies. Sci Tech Human Values, 15(4), 474-494, Autumn 90.

According to both traditional positivist approaches and also to the sociology of scientific knowledge, social analysts should not themselves become involved in the controversies they are investigating. But the experiences of the authors in studying contemporary scientific controversies—specifically, over the Australian Animal Health Laboratory, fluoridation, and vitamin C and cancer—show that analysts, whatever their intentions, cannot avoid being drawn into the fray. The field of controversy studies needs to address the implications of this process for both theory and practice.

RICHARDSON, Alan. How Not to Russell Carnap's *Aufbau*. Proc Phil Sci Ass, 1, 3-14, 1990.

In this paper I adduce reasons to reject the standard interpretation of Carnap's (1928) *Der logische Aufbau der Welt*. Rather than a philosophically derivative working out of Russell's External World Program, I argue that Carnap is engaged in a broadly Kantian attempt to use logic to guarantee the objectivity of scientific knowledge. This is implicit in Carnap's deferences with Russell on questions of acquaintance and its role in epistemology and in the scope and purpose of logical analysis.

RICHARDSON, Henry S. Commensurability as a Prerequisite of Rational Choice: An Examination of Sidgwick's Position. Hist Phil Quart, 8(2), 181-197, Ap 91.

To address the question whether one can choose rationally between competing ends, values, or principles without beforehand making them commensurable, this essay reconstructs Sidgwick's unusually deep and explicit argument that one cannot, which he develops in *The Methods of Ethics*. Laying out the structure of his argument, which turns on the figure of an appeal to a higher authority when norms conflict, both enables us to see how to criticize the postulates of rationality that underly it and prepares us to imagine new ways to structure rational choice without relying upon a single commensurating end or principle.

RICHARDSON, Henry S (ed) and DOUGLASS, R Bruce (ed) and MARA, Gerald M (ed). *Liberalism and the Good*. New York, Routledge, 1990.

RICHARDSON, Henry S. "The Problem of Liberalism and the Good" in *Liberalism and the Good*, DOUGLASS, R Bruce (ed), 1-28. New York, Routledge, 1990.

This essay introduces a collection of original essays that constructively explore how or whether liberal theory can coherently defend its commitment to toleration without invoking normative premises that will, in the end, displace that toleration. It sets out this dilemma, questions whether the liberal's conception of the good need be strongly metaphysical, and distinguishes different dimensions of a conception of the good. Its claim is that the liberal must take a stand in favor of some good, however political and non-metaphysical, however procedural or higher-order it may be.

RICHARDSON, Henry S. Specifying Norms as a Way to Resolve Concrete Ethical Problems. Phil Pub Affairs, 19(4), 279-310, Fall 90.

Arguing that deductivist approaches to resolving ethical problems are unworkable and that intuitive balancing models are insufficiently discursive, this article develops the idea of specification (a relation between norms) as providing a middle way. It shows that conflicts among norms can often be resolved by making them more specific. This is not mere revision, however, for the specification relation explains how the original norms are still brought to bear even though revised. It is further argued that specification is subject to rational criticism and defense and that it does not collapse back into either deductivism or intuitionism.

RICHARDSON, Robert C. The "Tally Argument" and the Validation of Psychoanalysis. Phil Sci, 57(4), 668-676, D 90.

The classic charge against Freudian theory is that the therapeutic success of psychoanalysis can be explained without appeal to the mechanisms of repression and insight. Whatever therapeutic success psychoanalysis might enjoy would then provide no support for the diagnostic claim that psychological disorders are due to repressed desires or for the therapeutic claim that the gains in psychoanalysis are due to insight into repressed causes. Adolf Grünbaum has repeated the charge in *The Foundations of Psychoanalysis* (1984), arguing that Freud's response to it in what he calls the "Tally Argument" is woefully inadequate. Grünbaum claims that Freud's defense depends on the view that *only* psychoanalytic techniques can yield therapeutic effects, and therefore that the transience of some psychoanalytic "cures," the existence of alternative treatment modalities, and the frequency of spontaneous remission undermine Freud's defense of psychoanalysis. I argue that, whatever the merits of psychoanalysis, Freud is not logically committed to any view as extreme as that attributed to him by Grünbaum; and, furthermore, Grünbaum's rendering of Freud is historically inaccurate.

RICHARDSON, Robert C and KANE, Thomas C and FONG, Daniel W. The Phenotype as the Level of Selection: Cave organisms as Model Systems. Proc Phil Sci Ass, 1, 151-164, 1990.

RICHARDSON, William J. "Heidegger and the Problem of World" in *Reconsidering Psychology: Perspectives from Continental Philosophy*, FAULCONER, James E (ed), 198-209. Pittsburgh, Duquesne Univ Pr, 1990.

RICHARDSON, William. The Subject of Hermeneutics and the Hermeneutics of the Subject. Grad Fac Phil J, 14(2)-15(1), 405-422, 1991.

RICHMOND, Stuart. Three Assumptions that Influence Art Education: A Description and a Critique. J Aes Educ, 25(2), 1-15, Sum 91.

This paper critically analyzes three assumptions that influence teaching and learing in art, namely, that art cannot be defined, that teaching is facilitating learning, and that school subjects should be integrated. The educational implications and pitfalls of each view are laid out together with alternative and more rationally defensible conceptions for curriculum planning.

RICHTER, Klaus. Moral und Biologie. Deut Z Phil, 39(2), 147-155, 1991.

RICHTER, Reed. Ideal Rationality and Handwaving. Austl J Phil, 68(2), 147-156, Je 90.

It is commonly held that one of the conditions for being an ideally rational agent (an IRA) is that the agent believe all the logical consequences of any of her beliefs. Yet there can exist peculiar circumstances in which believing the truth of some proposition P can literally cause P to become false: cases in which P is true iff it is not the case the agent believes that P. Contrary to the position of Roy A Sorensen, I argue that in such peculiar circumstances we should not apply the logical closure condition to an IRA.

RICKELS, Laurence A. "Friedrich Nichte" in *Looking After Nietzsche*, RICKELS, Laurence A (ed), 137-158. Albany, SUNY Pr, 1990.

RICKELS, Laurence A (ed). *Looking After Nietzsche*. Albany, SUNY Pr, 1990.

RICKEN, Friedo and WATKINS, Eric (trans). *Philosophy of the Ancients*. Notre Dame, Univ Notre Dame Pr, 1991.

A text discussing ancient Greek philosophy from the pre-Socratics through Plato and Aristotle to neoplatonism. (staff)

RICKETTS, Martin. The Economic Analysis of Institutions. Crit Rev, 4(1-2), 266-283, Wint-Spr 90.

This paper discusses attempts by economists to analyse institutions using individualist methodology. Game theory and transactions cost theory have proved fertile in yielding insights into the nature and structure of institutions. The example of the university is used to illustrate the applications of the economic approach to institutions. In particular, the nature of academic contracts and the nonprofit status of universities are related to the literature on contractual hazards. It is concluded that the new economic analysis of institutions can help to provide a bridge between the hitherto separate disciplines of economics and sociology.

RICOEUR, Paul. "Action, Story, and History—On Rereading 'The Human Condition'" in *The Realm of Humanitas: Responses to the Writings of Hannah Arendt*, GARNER, Reuben (ed), 149-164. New York, Lang, 1990.

RICOEUR, Paul. Éthique et Morale. Rev Port Filosof, 46(1), 5-17, Ja-Mr 90.

RICOEUR, Paul. Etica e morale: mira teleogica e prospettiva deontologica. Aquinas, 34(1), 3-14, Ja-Ap 91.

RICOEUR, Paul. John Rawls: de l'autonomie morale à la fiction de contrat social. Rev Metaph Morale, 95(3), 367-384, Jl-S 90.

RICOEUR, Paul. Narrative Identity. Phil Today, 35(1), 73-81, Spr 91.

RICOEUR, Paul. The Man as Subject of the Philosophy (in Hungarian). Magyar Filozof Szemle, 5-6, 612-625, 1990.

RIDLEY, Aaron and NEILL, Alex. Burning Passions. Analysis, 51(2), 106-108, Mr 91.

In this article we argue (against the view defended by Jerome Neu and O. H. Green, for example) that if a particular evaluative belief is held to be a conceptually necessary constituent of a given emotion, it cannot also be held to be causally efficacious in the production of that emotion.

RIDLEY, Mark. Comments on Wilkinson's Commentary. Biol Phil, 5(4), 447-450, O 90.

My original argument (Ridley 1989) was with Ghiselin (1987): Ghiselin had used the biological (reproductive) species concept in his argument for the individuality of species; I maintained that the reproductive species concept was not up to the job, and that individuality is properly a cladistic concept. Wilkinson is mainly concerned with other matters. He does suggest that individuality might also be due to "functional integration" as well as cladistic relationship; but he does not say how functional integration could be objectively defined and it has a larger-than-life subjective look to me. Subjective concepts are not much use in classification (Ghiselin 1966, 1987; Hennig 1966; Ridley 1986). I have a few things to say about Wilkinson's main concerns.

RIE, Michael A. Defining the Limits of Institutional Moral Agency in Health Care: A Response to Kevin Wildes. J Med Phil, 16(2), 221-224, Ap 91.

RIE, Michael A. The Limits of a Wish. Hastings Center Rep, 21(4), 24-27, Jl-Ag 91.

RIESBECK, Christopher K and MORPHIS, Maxine. Feminist Ethics and Case-Based Reasoning: A Marriage of Purpose. Int J Applied Phil, 5(2), 15-28, Fall 90.

By rejecting abstract, rule-based reasoning in favor of contextually sensitive reasoning, feminist ethics has been accused of retreating to intuitions. Critics maintain that rule-oriented ethical systems achieve more desirable results. Feminist ethics can strengthen its proposals by understanding their relationship to case-based reasoning (CBR), an AI model of reasoning applicable to moral decision making. While CBR is a valuable tool in rule-based arenas, it is central in case-determined fields, i.e., fields dependent on the use of precedents to define concepts and their conditions of application. Aspects of the ethics of care considered intuitive are actually case-determined.

RIGGS, Peter J. A Critique of Mellor's Argument against 'Backwards' Causation. Brit J Phil Sci, 42(1), 75-86, Mr 91.

In this paper, criticisms are made of the main tenets of Professor Mellor's argument against 'backwards' causation. He requires a closed causal chain of events if there is to be 'backwards' causation, but this condition is a metaphysical assumption which he cannot totally substantiate. Other objections to Mellor's argument concern his probabilistic analysis of causation and the use to which he puts his analysis. In particular, his use of conditional probability inequality to establish the 'direction' of causation is shown to be in error.

RILEY, Jonathan. 'One Very Simple Principle'. Utilitas, 3(1), 1-35, My 91.

An argument that Mill's famous doctrine of liberty really can be interpreted as "one very simple principle," as he says, despite a common view to the contrary. To defend the Millian doctrine, harm must be defined to exclude mere dislike or emotional distress that does not depend directly on any perceptible damage such as physical injury, loss of wealth, disappointed contractual expectations, and so on. If the meaning of harm is restricted in this way, a significant class of actions may be inferred to be harmless to other people. Mill's doctrine is that each adult "capable of rational persuasion" has an absolute moral right to choose as he likes with respect to these purely self-regarding actions.

RILEY, Patrick (ed) and BOSSUET, Jacques-Benigne. *Politics Drawn From the Very Words of Holy Scripture—Jacques-Benigne Bossuet*. New York, Cambridge Univ Pr, 1991.

RING, Jennifer. The Pariah as Hero: Hannah Arendt's Political Actor. Polit Theory, 19(3), 433-452, Ag 91.

RING, Merrill and LINVILLE, Kent. Moore's Paradox Revisited. Synthese, 87(2), 295-309, My 91.

Moore's remarking the oddness of the sentences "*p*, but I don't believe that *p*" deserves Wittgenstein's praise as the "only discovery of Moore's that greatly impressed him." For as this study shows, Moore's sentences provide a metaphysically neutral datum with which to oppose *both* Cartesian dualism and, what many contemporary philosophers take to be its corrective, physicalism. Despite all manner of philosophical temptation to think otherwise, Moore's sentences make it to see that "I believe" statements neither arise from nor advert to a state of the (mind or brain or mind/brain of the) speaker.

RIORDAN, Patrick. Reconstruction, Dialectic and Praxis. Method, 9(1), 1-22, Mr 91.

RISSER, James. Reading Nietzsche. Man World, 23(4), 361-373, O 90.

This paper explores the hermeneutical question of how one reads the texts of Nietzsche in light of Nietzsche's own comments, taken primarily from his Prefaces, about reading. The analysis shows how the question is answered from a philosophical analysis of the themes of interpretation, language, and communication, and argues for the necessity of equivocal readings of Nietzsche's texts on the basis of Nietzsche's remarks on the multiplicity of interpretation and the metaphoric nature of language.

RISTAD, Eric Sven. Computational Structure of GPSG Models. Ling Phil, 13(5), 521-587, O 90.

The primary goal of this essay is to demonstrate how considerations from computational complexity theory can inform grammatical theorizing. To this end, generalized phrase structure grammar (GPSG) linguistic theory is revised so that its power more closely matches the limited ability of an ideal speaker-hearer: GPSG Recognition is EXP-POLY time hard, while Revised GPSG Recognition is NP-complete. A second goal is to provide a theoretical framework within which to better understand the wide range of existing GPSG models, embodied in formal definitions as well as in implemented computer programs.

RITCHIE, Karen. Response to Dr Sakai's 'Psychoactive Drug Prescribing in Japan'. J Med Phil, 16(2), 159-160, Ap 91.

RITSERT, Jürgen. *Models and Concepts of Ideology*. Amsterdam, Rodopi, 1990.

The author considers theories of ideology as social science; he considers the theories of Marx, Weber, existentialism, contemporary French, and Adorno. He looks at the construction of these ideological types and offers comparisons between them. (staff)

RITSERT, Jürgen. "The Wittgenstein-Problem in Sociology or: the 'Linguistic Turn' as a Pirouette" in *The Social Horizon of Knowledge*, BUCZKOWSKI, Piotr (ed), 5-37. Amsterdam, Rodopi, 1991.

Three main types of relations between the terms "language-game", "form of life" and "society" are shown in Wittgenstein's work. Their relation to specific social ontologies in sociology is documented. The thesis is that a dialectical type of relation between "Sprachspeil" and "Lebensform" seems to be most fruitful for current sociology.

RITTER, Henning. "Die Geschichte hat kein Libretto": Zu Isaiah Berlins Begriff des Nationalismus. Deut Z Phil, 39(2), 168-179, 1991.

RITZEL, Wolfgang. Kant über den Witz und Kants Witz. Kantstudien, 82(1), 102-109, 1991.

In Kant's day and age "Witz" means: a) a talent, b) a remark which is only formulated and laughed at by someone who has this talent. For example: "It is a serious transgression to have grown old, for which one is however without exemption punished by death" (Kant). Kant attributes talent and the witty remark to a combination of understanding and judgement. He finds examples in "Tristram Shandy" and "Hudibras". If his own wit becomes sarcastic, it is aimed at his victims: scholars without any philosophy and his unjust adversaries in the learned fraternity.

RIUMIN, V A. The Humanism of Economics or Economizing on Humanism? Soviet Stud Phil, 30(1), 14-41, Sum 91.

RIVADULLA, Andrés. Mathematical Statistics and Metastatistical Analysis. Erkenntnis, 34(2), 211-236, Mr 91.

This paper deals with meta-statistical questions concerning frequentist statistics. In Sections 2 to 4 I analyse the dispute between Fisher and Neyman on the so-called logic of statistical inference, a polemic that has been concomitant of the development of mathematical statistics. My conclusion is that, whenever mathematical statistics makes it possible to draw inferences, it only uses deductive reasoning. Therefore I reject Fisher's inductive approach to the statistical estimation theory and adhere to Neyman's deductive one. In Section 5 I disapprove Hacking's evidentialists criticisms of the Neyman-Pearson's theory of statistics (NPT), as well as Hacking's interpretation of NPT as a theory of probable inference. I conclude, by claiming that Mayo's conception of the Neyman-Pearson's testing theory, as a model of learning from experience, does not purport any advantages over Neyman's behavioristic model. (edited)

RIX, Bo Andreassen. Should Ethical Concerns Regulate Science? The European Experience with the Human Genome Project. Bioethics, 5(3), 250-256, Jl 91.

RIZZACASA, Aurelio. Continuità e discontinuità tra Husserl e Heidegger: genesi e sviluppo d una polemica filosofica. Aquinas, 33(3), 541-566, S-D 90.

ROACH, Catherine. Loving Your Mother: On the Woman-Nature Relationship. Hypatia, 6(1), 46-59, Spr 91.

In this essay I explore the relation between woman and nature. In the first half, I argue that the environmental slogan "Love Your Mother" is problematical because of the way "mother" and "motherhood" function in patriarchal culture. In the essay's second half, I argue that the question, "Are women closer to nature than men?" is conceptually flawed and that the nature/culture dualism upon which it is predicated is in need of being biodegraded for the sake of environmental soundness.

ROBACK, Jennifer. Plural But Equal: Group Identity and Voluntary Integration. Soc Phil Pol, 8(2), 60-80, Spr 91.

This paper uses economic reasoning to analyze how integrated society should be. Specifically, the paper analyzes tradeoffs between two valuable goods. The paper first discusses functions that ethnic groups perform for their members. The paper then discusses the benefits of ethnic integration. The question of how integrated society should be is then answered with an analogy with decentralized market economies and centrally planned economies. Some central authority could decide the relative value of integration and separateness. The ethnic group, with support of the central government, could decide how its members should interact with outsiders. Finally, individuals may make decisions about the desirable extent of integration. The paper argues that this third process has most advantages.

ROBENSTINE, Clark. The Dead Horse Phenomenon in Educational Theory. Phil Stud Educ, /, 152-163, 1987-88.

ROBERTS, Lawrence D. Relevance as an Explanation of Communication. Ling Phil, 14(4), 453-472, Ag 91.

Sperber and Wilson in *Relevance* (1986) use a principle of relevance to explain how ostensive-inferential communication works. I argue that their examples of communication require, in addition to the principle of relevance, several other steps; these include devices for conveying particular content and two types of mutual knowledge. From these additional steps comes the positive content of messages; in contrast, the principle of relevance is purely critical in its functioning. Also, because relevance as defined by Sperber and Wilson gives no weight to the speaker's intentions, it allows interpretations of messages that are contrary to such intentions.

ROBERTS, Richard H. *Hope and Its Hieroglyph: A Critical Decipherment of Ernst Bloch's "Principle of Hope"*. Atlanta, Scholars Pr, 1990.

The philosophy of Ernst Bloch, and in particular the *Principle of Hope* has suffered a deeply problematic reception in the English-speaking world. *Hope and Its Hieroglyph* presents a critical reading of what is often regarded as an impenetrable and problematic text. Bloch's work is placed in its historical and cultural context and the inner logic of his masterpiece exposed in terms of its affinities with German idealism and Romanticism, Marburg neo-Kantianism, and Neoplatonic/German mysticism. Roberts provides an accessible and reliable introduction to Bloch in the conviction that the latter offers an emancipatory challenge of undiminished importance.

ROBERTS, Richard H. Nietzsche and the Cultural Resonance of the 'Death of God'. Hist Euro Ideas, 11, 1025-1035, 1989.

The notion of the "Death of God" is pervasive in twentieth century culture, but the degree to which this can be attributed to the influence of Nietzsche is difficult to determine, not least because of the complexity of the reception of the latter's work. A preliminary ground-clearing is provided in which the main strands and stages in the reception of Nietzsche are clarified in relation to major literary and philosophical figures.

ROBERTS, Robert C. Virtues and Rules. Phil Phenomenol Res, 51(2), 325-343, Je 91.

An ethics of virtue is sometimes regarded as opposed to an ethics of rules. This paper argues that, with an appropriate revision in our concept of a moral rule, an ethics of virtue is necessarily an ethics of rules. The concept of the grammar of a virtue is commended, as a way of thinking of the rules that govern virtues. Such rules are capable of reflecting differences between moral traditions (e.g., the differences between Christian and Aristotelian generosity), and capturing the motivational and emotive requirements for virtues, as well as the actions characteristic of them.

ROBERTS, Robert C. What is Wrong With Wicked Feelings? Amer Phil Quart, 28(1), 13-24, Ja 91.

Some feelings, considered without regard to their allied behavior, are felt to be morally reprehensible. What other beliefs might support this intuition, which seems ill supported by both deontology and consequentialism? A number of suggestions are made, centering around the insight that friendship and similar relationships depend on attitudes to which the wicked feelings are contrary. If the reprehensibleness of these feelings is not limited to cases of actual friendship or family ties, perhaps this intuition belongs to a moral view in which all humans are somehow regarded as having family-like ontological bonds with one another.

ROBERTSON, Emily. Moral Judgment. Proc Phil Educ, 46, 377-382, 1990.

ROBERTSON, John A. Comment on Hospice of Washington's Policy. Kennedy Inst Ethics J, 1(2), 139-140, Je 91.

ROBERTSON, John A. Cruzan: No Rights Violated. Hastings Center Rep, 20(5), 8-9, S-O 90.

Cruzan violates no rights because an irreversibly comatose incompetent patient is incapable of exercising choice, has no interest in living or dying and the family has no independent rights to terminate treatment of a comatose family member. Thus the desirability of withdrawing nutrition and hydration from an irreversibly comatose patient is a question separate from whether there is a constitutional right to do so.

ROBERTSON, John. Hume on Practical Reason. Proc Aris Soc, 90, 267-282, 1989-90.

Hume's arguments against practical reason in the *Treatise* include one that is very frequently misunderstood or passed over altogether. This argument assumes that practical reason would involve *a priori* causal relations between belief, desire and action, and thus be inconsistent with an empirical science of psychology. Hume's arguments also conflate basic desires with the capacity to acquire desires. His basic desires have the role in the explanation of action, and the determinacy, of relatively specific desires, and the causal independence of belief of motivational capacities. There is no reason to think anything satisfies all these conditions.

ROBIN, Donald P and REIDENBACH, R Eric. A Conceptual Model of Corporate Moral Development. J Bus Ethics, 10(4), 273-284, Ap 91.

The conceptual model presented in this article argues that corporations exhibit specific behaviors that signal their true level of moral development. Accordingly, the authors identify five levels of moral development and discuss the dynamics that move corporations from one level to another. Examples of corporate behavior which are indicative of specific stages of moral development are offered.

ROBIN, Donald P and REIDENBACH, R Eric. Epistemological Structures in Marketing: Paradigms, Metaphors, and Marketing Ethics. Bus Ethics Quart, 1(2), 185-200, Ap 91.

This article uses Arndt's depiction of marketing epistemology to suggest a possible explanation for the lack of emphasis on marketing ethics within the marketing literature. While a growing number of writers are turning their attention to the area, marketing's heavy reliance on logical empiricism has contributed to a disinclination in the development of this area. Only through recent and numerous revelations of misconduct has the discipline of marketing responded to its ethical dimensions.

ROBIN, Régine. "Le signe en défaut". Horiz Phil, 1(1), 111-121, 1990.

ROBINS, Robert H. "Leibniz and Wilhelm von Humboldt and the History of Comparative Linguistics" in *Leibniz, Humboldt, and the Origins of Comparativism*, DE MAURO, Tullio (ed), 85-102. Philadelphia, John Benjamins, 1990.

Both Leibniz and Wilhelm von Humboldt developed much time and thought to questions about language and the history of languages. Neither of them was a full-time professional linguist, but both were men of public affairs for whom linguistic studies were additional activities of the highest importance. Each in his way was typical of the age in which he lived and worked. Leibniz was especially concerned with etymology and etymological methods as a key to a knowledge of the past history and the historical relations of languages. Humboldt, though very sympathetic to contemporary Indo-European historical linguistics and Sanskritic scholarship, as himself more interested in the general linguistic question of the typological development of languages as the instruments and the manifestations of their speakers' nationhood and civilization.

ROBINSON, Daniel N. *Aristotle's Psychology*. New York, Columbia Univ Pr, 1989.

Aristotle's psychology is at once systematic and coherent and, at the same time, irksomely distributed throughout his naturalistic, ethical, political and rhetorical treatises. In the present work, an attempt is made to locate this coherent and systematic psychology, to illuminate its essentially ethological and descriptive character, and to show the extent to which it finally supports a moral vision that transcends the physical-biological domain while remaining true to what it takes to be human nature. The bearing of major concepts and theories on certain historical and current trends in psychology is briefly discussed.

ROBINSON, Don. The Infinite Apparatus in the Quantum Theory of Measurement. Proc Phil Sci Ass, 1, 251-261, 1990.

This paper is a response to Jeffrey Bub's recent proposal to solve the measurement problem in standard quantum mechanics by idealizing the measuring apparatus as consisting of an infinite number of subsystems. The author points out that this idealization could also make the measurement limitations incorporated into the Wigner-Araki-Yanase theory of measurement go to zero. It is argued that, since the apparatus consists of a finite number of subsystems, the proposed idealization would only be made by someone who has already adopted a nonliteral or nonrealistic interpretation of the quantum mechanical formalism and who would therefore not take the above-mentioned problems seriously.

ROBINSON, Don. On Crane and Mellor's Argument Against Physicalism. Mind, 100(397), 135-136, Ja 91.

This brief discussion is a response to an argument advanced by Tim Crane and D H Mellor (1990) against the supervenience physicalist. Their argument is based on a thought experiment in which the supervenience thesis is seen to fail. The present author points out that this thought experiment is formulated in terms unacceptable to certain defenders of the supervenience thesis, particularly Donald Davidson. The author reformulates the thought experiment in terms Davidson would accept and it is shown that the supervenience thesis does not obviously fail.

ROBINSON, Edmund and ROSOLINI, Giuseppe. Colimit Completions and the Effective Topos. J Sym Log, 55(2), 678-699, Je 90.

The effective topos is an extension of recursive realisability to give a model of intuitionistic Zermelo-Fraenkel set theory. It is a natural setting in which to discuss much of the recursion theory at higher types (as well as HEO models for type theories). In this paper we discuss how we can give meaning to the concept of a "recursively-indexed disjoint union of sets," and show that the effective topos can also be obtained from the classical universe of sets by freely adjoining non-empty recursively-indexed disjoint unions.

ROBINSON, Glen O. "Risk, Causation, and Harm" in *Liability and Responsibility*, FREY, R G (ed), 317-347. New York, Cambridge Univ Pr, 1991.

ROBINSON, Howard. "A Dualist Account of Embodiment" in *The Case for Dualism*, SMYTHIES, John R (ed), 43-57. Charlottesville, Univ Pr of Virginia, 1989.

ROBINSON, Jenefer. "Experiencing Art" in *XIth International Congress in Aesthetics, Nottingham 1988*, WOODFIELD, Richard (ed), 156-160. Nottingham, Nottingham Polytech, 1990.

In this paper I defend the view that our emotional experience of a literary work can constitute a way of coming to understand that work, even if it is a relatively inarticulate understanding, and further, than an articulate critical report of the work often depends upon and is colored by an actual emotional experience of the work. Thus when we give an interpretation of a work we are typically not giving a dispassionate account of the work but an account which expresses our emotional experience of the work.

ROBINSON, Paul. McDowell Against Criterial Knowledge. Ratio, 4(1), 59-75, Je 91.

John McDowell has argued that, if criteria of the kind associated with the work of Wittgenstein are defeasible, knowledge that p cannot be grounded merely in an experience of the satisfied criteria for p. This paper gives an exegesis of McDowell's argument, and then argues that, on the interpretation given, the argument relies on an assumption about empirical knowledge which is both intrinsically implausible and insufficiently supported by McDowell's collateral discussion. It is further suggested that McDowell is wrong to suggest that his argument is motivated by internalist intuitions about knowledge.

ROBINSON, William S. Rationalism, Expertise and the Dreyfuses' Critique of AI Research. S J Phil, 29(2), 271-290, Sum 91.

Hubert and Stuart Dreyfus have recently argued 1) that rationalism has failed the empirical test that pre-connectionist work in AI puts to it; and 2) that Euthyphro represents true expertise on piety. I argue that the Dreyfusian critique undercuts rationalism in one sense of the term, but in two other senses, the view remains unscathed. In so arguing, I clarify some distinctions among information processing theories, simple connectionism and other explanatory principles. I also argue that in certain cases of disagreement, typified by Socrates and Euthyphro, claims to expertise cannot provide resolution and the Socratic quest is justified.

ROBLES, José A. Hobbes, Berkeley y las ideas abstractas. Rev Filosof (Venezuela), 12, 43-54, 1989.

The aim of this paper is to show that Berkeley's views on abstraction and generality were strongly motivated by Hobbes's proposals in his 'Six Lessons to the Professors of Mathematics' (cf. Lesson 1). There is a close similitude not only of views but even in the wording of them which appear in Berkeley's PC 254, 722 where 'consider' is used as a key word, besides the use of the same examples by both philosophers. Other passages in Berkeley's PC, plus some other in his published works, help to sustain the claim of a direct influence by Hobbes on Berkeley.

ROBLES, Laureano. Unamuno y la Revolución de Octubre. El Basilisco, 6, 49-52, Jl-Ag 90.

El filósofo ruso Boris Jakovenko invitó a Unamuno a escribir en la revista *Der Russische Gedanke*. V Polonski le invitó a escribir en *Novyi Mir* (Moscú 1928, XII-23): qué autores rusos conoce; qué influjo ha ejercído la Revolución de Octubre 1917. Contesta Unamuno: "Cuando pase el tiempo" se verá que es una mancha en la historia; no es nada. Es más importante la revolución de Cronwell y la Revolución francesa. "Me repugna la concepción materialista de la historia. No es el estómago, sino la conciencia, la que creo que hace la historia. Se hace historia no para vivir sino para sobre-vivir".

ROBSON, Ann P. "Mill's Second Prize in the Lottery of Life" in *A Cultivated Mind: Essays On J S Mill Presented to John M Robson*, LAINE, Michael (ed), 215-241. Buffalo, Univ of Toronto Pr, 1991.

When John Stuart Mill was widowed in 1858, his public writings and influence might well have ended. But his step-daughter, Helen Taylor, left her stage-career and until Mill's death in 1873, she was his intellectual companion, amanuensis, housekeeper and hostess in their Blackheath and Avignon homes. It is due to her moral and practical support that Mill was able to publish his later major works, run successfully for Parliament, forward the cause of women's suffrage, pursue Governor Eyre, and found the Land Tenure Reform Association, thus greatly extending his contemporary and subsequent prestige.

ROBSON, John M (ed) and FILIPIUK, Marion (ed) and LAINE, Michael (ed) and MILL, John Stuart. *Additional Letters (Collected Works of John Stuart Mill, Volume XXXII)*. Buffalo, Univ of Toronto Pr, 1991.

ROBSON, John M (ed) and MILL, John Stuart and O'GRADY, Jean (ed). *Indexes to the Collected Works (Collected Works of John Stuart Mill, Vol XXXIII)*. Buffalo, Univ of Toronto Pr, 1991.

ROCCA, Gregory. The Distinction between *Res Significata* and *Modus Significandi* in Aquinas's Theological Epistemology. Thomist, 55(2), 173-197, Ap 91.

The article shows how the named distinction functions in Aquinas' theological epistemology of the absolute and positive predication of analogical divine names—as a kind of negative theology at the heart of analogical predication. After an historical introduction to the terminology, the article explains the three bases for Aquinas' treatment of the distinction: God's infinite modelessness versus the creature's finite mode, the peculiar human mode of understanding, and the peculiar human mode of signification. The distinction protects rather than obviates the analogicity of divine predication, and is the direct consequence of already acknowledged first-order truths about God and humans.

ROCCARO, Giuseppe. L'aporia della kìnesis in Aristotele. G Metaf, 11(3), 397-463, S-D 89.

ROCHA, Acílio Estanqueiro. Hermenêutica e Estruturalismo. Rev Port Filosof, 46(1), 87-124, Ja-Mr 90.

After presenting the presuppositions which underlie a question which is central to Ricoeur's work, "the subject as act, as instance", and which exemplify Ricoeur's way of doing philosophy, as well as presenting Lévi-Strauss's thought concerning this question, the article proposes the fundamental topics which define the controversy. These topics gravitate around the problem of the intelligibility of *sense* and the sense of *intelligibility*, of the complementary of methods, and of the semiotic and semantic levels, the latter level is established by the fullness of the sentence and of the word (mot) as operator between structure and event.

ROCHA, Filipe. Educação para valores e maturidade pessoal do educador. Rev Port Filosof, 46(2), 213-226, Ap-Je 90.

Until recently it seemed anachronical to speak of values in eduction. It was the era dominated by behaviorism. The atmosphere has however changed: a pure humanist oriented psychology is quite compatible with a pluralistic society; in both cases, a base of fundamental values is necessary for man and community. The current law dealing with foundations of the Portuguese educational system proposes values to our educators. The success of this proposal depends in great part on these same educators who give witness to certain values.

ROCHE, John F. "New Tasks for the Philosophy of Physics" in *Harré and His Critics*, BHASKAR, Roy (ed), 89-111. Cambridge, Blackwell, 1990.

ROCKEFELLER, Steven C. *John Dewey: Religious Faith and Democratic Humanism*. New York, Columbia Univ Pr, 1991.

ROCKMORE, Tom. Heidegger After Farias. Hist Phil Quart, 8(1), 81-102, Ja 91.

ROCKMORE, Tom. Herméneutique et épistémologie Gadamer entre Heidegger et Hegel. Arch Phil, 53(4), 547-557, O-D 90.

According to Gadamer, hermeneutics results from the epistemological debate and surpasses epistemology. Although it is correct to understand hermeneutics as the most recent phase of the debate, it does not bring the discussion to a close. Gadamer contributes to the problem of knowledge by drawing attention to its inseparability from hermeneutics.

ROCKMORE, Tom. Marx and Perestroika. Phil Soc Crit, 16(3), 193-206, 1990.

ROCKMORE, Tom. "Marxian Ideology and Causality" in *Perspectives on Ideas and Reality*, NYÍRI, J C (ed), 210-221. Budapest, Kiskonyvtara, 1990.

ROCKMORE, Tom. On Heidegger and National Socialism: A Triple Turn? Grad Fac Phil J, 14(2)-15(1), 423-439, 1991.

RÖD, Wolfgang. The Problem of Infinity in Kant's Works (in German). Deut Z Phil, 38(6), 497-505, 1990.

During his pre-critical period, Kant maintains a naive notion of real infinity. At the heyday of the critical period the view that infinity can only be spoken of potentially, prevails. Later, Kant admits again the idea of real infinity, probably due to ethical motives.

RODA, Roberto. Individuo y acción en el pensamiento griego. Pensamiento, 47(185), 91-95, Ja-Mr 91.

RODIS-LEWIS, Geneviève. Le premier registre de Descartes. Arch Phil, 54(3), 353-377, Jl-S 91.

H Gouthier did identify the parts of the first notebook of Descartes which had been partly copied (without their titles) by Leibniz and published by Foucher de Careil. Scientific considerations, written contrarywise, will be examined further on. As did Leibniz, we begin with personal thoughts, with their possible dating, with some problems raised, commenting what is essential in the dreams which were neglected by Leibniz.

RODRIGUEZ AMENABAR, S M. Culpabilidad, rito y ritualismo: Una aproprimación psicoanaliítica. Stromata, 46(3-4), 411-416, Jl-D 90.

RODRÍGUEZ CONSUEGRA, Francisco. La interpretación russelliana de Leibniz y el atomismo metodológico de Moore. Dianoia, 36(36), 121-156, 1990.

The main thesis of this article is that Moore's influence on the young Russell was not only philosophical, that is, concerning a particular philosophical conception, but also methodological, that is, concerning a particular way to understand what a philosopher is supposed to do. Russell's work on Leibniz and his article due to the Paris Congress, both from 1900, are the main texts studied to look for the relevant evidence, although the secondary literature and other materials—including some unpublished manuscripts—are also used.

RODRÍGUEZ CONSUEGRA, Francisco. El logicismo russelliano: su significado filosófico. Critica, 23(67), 15-39, Ap 91.

After a brief presentation of Russell's logicism, I attempt a global explanation of its philosophical significance. I reject the existence of two different kinds of logicism (Putnam) with the argument that Russell was trying to justify the existing mathematics and, at the same time, to escape from a mere formal calculus. For the same reason, the logicist definitions cannot be regarded as new axioms to be added to Peano's postulates (Reichenbach): according to Russell it is necessary to show that there is a constant meaning satisfying those postulates. The lack of a clear definition of logic in Russell (and Frege) is a consequence of his whole philosophy, therefore we must not look for it in the concept of necessity (Griffin), nor must we interpret this lack as a gap in the system (Grattan-Guinness). Russell's starting point was Moore's notion of truth as something indefinable and intuitive according to which we immediately *recognize* the true propositions. The problem of logicism is rather the deep tension between the ontological preeminence of relations (structures) and their terms (fields).

RODRÍGUEZ DUPLÁ, Leonardo. La benevolencia como categoría fundamental de la Etica eudemonista. Rev Filosof (Spain), 3, 215-222, 1990.

RODRÍGUEZ HÖLKEMEYER, Patricia. El papel de la comunicación espontánea en los procesos de evolución social. Rev Filosof (Costa Rica), 28(67-68), 47-54, D 90.

This paper proposes a methodological approach for the study of evolutionary social processes that acknowledge the autonomy of the subject, both in the cognitive process as well as in the creation of new forms of social organization. This approach highlights the positive and determining aspect—rejected by the Marxist theory of ideologies and by the classical theories of socialization—of the formidable unconscious knowledge that human experience has sedimented in social and individual memory. This perspective goes beyond the political and scientific conception that has predominated in the present century and that unites, in a selective and unidimensional manner, knowledge and power.

RODRÍGUEZ HÖLKEMEYER, Patricia. El paradigma de sistemas: posibilidades para una prácica social emancipadora. Rev Filosof (Costa Rica), 27(66), 387-398, D 89.

The author, from a system's based perspective of social evolution, points, in the first part (which appeared in the last edition of this magazine) and in this second part, to the blunders of the "cibernetic" approach, to the limitations of the Probabilistic Theory of Information, to the obsolescence of the organism as a paradigmatic unit, to the role of the dialectical contradiction and to the importance of the primary life-world structures, in explaining self-organizing processes. She draws from the socio-biological concept of "autopoiesis" a conception that brakes with the structural determinism of classical socialization theories, offering a perspective that revitalizes the individual and reassesses liberty.

RODRIGUEZ LOPEZ, Jose Luis. "Work in Organizations as Social Activity" in *Harré and His Critics*, BHASKAR, Roy (ed), 240-255. Cambridge, Blackwell, 1990.

RODRÍGUEZ VALLS, Francisco. Trinidad y ontología trascendental: Ideas en torno al libro IX del "De Trinitate" de S Agustín. Themata, 6, 137-153, 1989.

Terms of transcendental relationship (which is called *praxis* by Aristotle) come from the goal aimed with action. At the same time action is defined by its terms. In that relationship number three and number one are each other related and making reciprocally possible their existences. My paper deals with an explanation of that idea taking as its foundation book IX of Augustine's *De Trinitate*. According to this, I use as means of interpretation his analysis of relations that man's different elements have with man himself, knowledge relationship, and inner relations between God's unity and trinity.

RODRIGUEZ, Antonio J and TORRENS, Antoni. Lukasiewicz Logic and Wajsberg Algebras. Bull Sect Log, 19(2), 51-55, Je 90.

The purpose of this paper is to prove that the class of Wajsberg algebras is the equivalent variety semantics for Lukasiewicz Logic (in the sense of Blok-Pigozzi). This is obtained as a consequence of the main result of the paper which shows that in any algebra of type (2,1) the lattice of all Wajsberg implicative filters is isomorphic to the lattice of all congruence relation relative to the variety of Wajsberg algebras.

RODRÍGUEZ, Juan Acosta. El averroísmo de Juan de Sècheville. Logos (Mexico), 18(54), 9-31, S-D 90.

This work wants to show the presence of Averroes in a master of the natural philosophy in the thirteenth century. It is concluded here that Averroes is the most widely dealt with author after Aristotle and that he maintains a psychic dualism. The subject of the intellect isn't directly dealt with here, only on an occasional and collateral way. John de Secheville expresses himself very cautiously and he appears very wary. The closeness of the open conflict in the thirteenth century is guessed and it is also announced the disparity in the treatment over the same doctrine by the philosopher and by the believer.

RODRIGUEZ, M L. Lenguaje y verdad en Aristóteles. Pensamiento, 46(184), 385-402, O-D 90.

Las reflexiones de los sofistas sobre el lenguaje concluyeron en algo muy similar a lo que viera Nietzsche muchos siglos después: la imposibilidad de la verdad concebida como adecuación. Contra ellas, la teoría aristotélica de la significación, basada en la ruptura del vínculo entre *lógos* y ser que la concepción, convencionalista supone, y distinguiendo entre significación y significado, pretende instituirse como condición de posibilidad de la doctrina correspondencialista de la verdad. Porque la composición o división de términos significantes que es la proposición sí que imita, se asemeja, a la relación que las cosas mantienen entre sí.

RODRÍGUEZ, Ramón. Heidegger, pensador con biografía. Rev Filosof (Spain), 3, 211-214, 1990.

RODRÍGUEZ-CONSUEGRA, Francisco. A Global Point of View on Russell's Philosophy. Dialogos, 26(57), 173-186, Ja 91.

This is an essay-review of C Wade Savage and C Anthony Anderson (editors), *Rereading Russell: Essays in Bertrand Russell's Metaphysics and Epistemology*, Volume XII of Minnesota Studies in the Philosophy of Science, Minneapolis, University of Minnesota Press, 1989. The book is devoted to studying Russell's later philosophy, although the actual content concerns also Russell's early logical and epistemological writings. Here I study and criticize a group of contributions (mainly those by Hylton, Goldfarb, Cocchiarella, Pears and Demopoulos/Friedman) from a global and methodological approach to Russell's whole philosophy I have developed in other publications.

ROEHRSSEN, Carlo. Le critiche a Kelsen durante la Repubblica di Weimar. Riv Int Filosof Diritto, 67(2), 305-307, Ap-Je 90.

ROEPER, Peter and LEBLANC, Hugues. "Conditionals and Conditional Probabilities: Three Triviality Theorems" in *Knowledge Representation and Defeasible Reasoning*, KYBURG JR, Henry E (ed), 287-306. Norwell, Kluwer, 1990.

ROEPER, Peter and LEBLANC, Hugues and THAU, Michael and WEAVER, George. Henkin's Completeness Proof: Forty Years Later. Notre Dame J Form Log, 32(2), 212-232, Spr 91.

Provided here are two new completeness proofs for a first-order logic with denumerably many terms. The first proof, unlike Menkin's 1949 proof, does not call for the addition of extra terms; the second, especially suited for truth-value semantics, calls for the addition of denumerably many. Shown in the process is that a set of statements has a Henkin model, i.e., a model in which every member of the domain has a name, iff the set is what we call *instantially consistent* (i.e., iff *consistent in omega-logic*).

ROEPER, Peter and LEBLANC, Hugues. Indiscernibility and Identity in Probability Theory. Notre Dame J Form Log, 32(1), 1-46, Wint 91.

Specified in the paper are the circumstances under which two elements (sets, statements, etc.) are counted indiscernible under a conditional probability function or under an absolute one. The resulting notions and that of identity are then used to characterize and classify various families (some of them new) of Popper probability functions.

ROGERSON, Kenneth. Verificationism and Anti-Realism. SW Phil Rev, 7(1), 69-80, Ja 91.

This paper is an attempt to get a bit clearer on the notion of verificationism particularly as it is used in antirealist discussions. I argue that the antirealist needs two versions of verifiability—a weak one, similar to that advanced by positivists, for a criterion of meaning and a stronger one for a criterion of truth (decidability). Only if we admit this distinction can we make sense of the antirealist claim that there are some meaningful sentences that have no decidable truth value.

ROHRLICH, Fritz. Pluralistic Ontology and Theory Reduction in the Physical Sciences. Brit J Phil Sci, 39(3), 295-312, S 88.

It is demonstrated that the reduction of a physical theory S to another one, T, in the sense that S can be derived from T holds in general only for the mathematical framework. The interpretation of S and the associated central terms cannot all be derived from those of T because of the qualitative differences between the cognitive levels of S and T. Their cognitively autonomous status leads to an epistemic as well as ontological pluralism. This pluralism is consistent with the unity of nature in the sense of a substantive monism.

ROIG GIRONELLA, J. La analogía del ser en Suárez. Espiritu, 36(95), 5-47, Ja-Je 87.

ROJO, Roberto. Ideas de mundo en el *Tractatus*. Cuad Filosof, 21(34), 21-29, My 90.

This paper deals with the idea of world (Welt) in Wittgenstein's *Tractatus*. In it I hold that there are three ideas of world in that work: one, corresponding to the totality of facts; in the second place, what I call "ethical world"; finally, underlying both, a transcendental idea of world. The three ideas hold some relations among themselves. It is easier to estimate the importance of these distinctions, if we take into account the mistakes that ensue when one does not, as in Eddy Zemach's interpretation, for example. It is precisely against it that I argue in this paper.

ROLDÁN, Concha. Crusius: un jalón olvidado en la ruta hacia el criticismo. Rev Filosof (Spain), 3, 123-140, 1990.

ROLLIN, B E. "The 'Frankenstein Thing': The Moral Impact of Genetic Engineering of Agricultural Animals" in *Agricultural Bioethics: Implications of Agricultural Biotechnology*, GENDEL, Steven M (& other eds), 292-308. Ames, Iowa St Univ Pr, 1990.

ROLLIN, Bernard E. "Federal Laws and Policies Governing Animal Research: Their History, Nature, and Adequacy" in *Biomedical Ethics Reviews, 1990*, HUMBER, James M (ed), 195-227. Clifton, Humana Pr, 1991.

This article discusses the nature, history, and philosophical basis of federal legislation governing animal research. In particular, the discussion focusses on the emergence of a new ethic for the treatment of animals in society, based on the exportation of our consensus ethics for humans, *mutatis mutandis*, to sentient non-human beings. The core of this ethic involves protective fundamental aspects of animal nature or *telos* from human infringement, and encoding that protection in law. The new laws are critically assessed in reference to that moral ideal.

ROLLINS, Mark. La condición pública del lenguaje y la autoridad de la primera persona. Dianoia, 35(35), 187-202, 1989.

ROMAIN, Dianne. Feminist Reflections on Humans and Other Domestic Animals. Between Species, 6(4), 213-218, Fall 90.

ROMANYSHYN, Robert. "Life-World as Depth of Soul: Phenomenology and Psychoanalysis" in *Reconsidering Psychology: Perspectives from Continental Philosophy*, FAULCONER, James E (ed), 234-251. Pittsburgh, Duquesne Univ Pr, 1990.

Phenomenology and psychoanalysis converge in their respective criticisms of scientific psychology. While phenomenology challenges the prejudice of the objective world and opens up the world as the landscape of experience, psychoanalysis challenges the prejudices of the ego as author of experience and memory as a matter of fact. Drawing upon these criticisms, the author offers a phenomenological-depth psychology which is a therapeutics of culture.

ROMBACH, Heinrich. *Strukturanthropologie "Der menschliche Mensch"*. Freiburg, Alber, 1991.

This develops a new basis for a philosophical anthropology not in terms of "what man is", but how his essence is constructed as regards the social reality and the coming phases of mankind's history. The book can be described as the road from "critical phenomenology" to a modern critique of "postmodernity".

ROMERO BARÓ, José María. El concepto de verdad en la física moderna. Dialogo Filosof, 6(3), 335-344, S-D 90.

ROMERO, Jorge Enrique. Medio ambiente y derecho. Rev Filosof (Costa Rica), 28(67-68), 225-229, D 90.

This paper tries to state the relation between the law and the environment; taking into consideration that Costa Rica is an underdeveloped country. That is why it is so important for nations like us to have an appropriate and effective protection of our environment. The destruction of the nature will continue unless enormous political pressure appears to put a brutal stop to it.

ROMERO, Ramón. Filosofía e identidad nacional en Honduras. Rev Filosof (Costa Rica), 28(67-68), 93-97, D 90.

This short paper focuses on different problems: the potential of National Identity for the progress of a nation; the discussion about if there is or is not a Hondurean National Identity; the strategy of abortion or destruction of National Identity as an element of the American Policy in Honduras; the contribution of philosophy to the creation of a National Identity in today's Honduras.

ROMEYER DHERBEY, Gilbert. L'inquiétante étrangeté de Jules Amédée Barbey d'Aurevilly. Arch Phil, 53(4), 573-587, O-D 90.

The marvelous according to Barbey d'Aurevilly means the supernatural making a violent entry into everyday life; there is mostly a disturbing oddness where object or subject is separated from itself, essentially by time, by the past, but there is also a duality of conscience given up to pretence and falsehood until it overcomes its dualism and finds in God *the mysterious* "third" of reconciliation.

RONELL, Avital. "Namely, Eckermann" in *Looking After Nietzsche*, RICKELS, Laurence A (ed), 233-257. Albany, SUNY Pr, 1990.

ROOCHNIK, David. In Defense of Plato: A Short Polemic. Phil Rhet, 24(2), 153-158, 1991.

Brian Vickers, in his *In Defense of Rhetoric*, professes to defend rhetoric against its critics, foremost among whom is Plato. His work, therefore, includes a sustained attack on Plato, who is described as "biased to an extreme" and "rigidly authoritarian." The present paper is a polemical response to Vicker's polemical, and entirely wrong-headed, treatment of Plato.

ROOCHNIK, David. The Serious Play of Plato's *Euthydemus*. Interpretation, 18(2), 211-232, Wint 90-91.

This paper offers an analysis of Socrates' protreptic argument in the *Euthydemus*. The conclusion of the argument is, "one ought to pursue wisdom since only wisdom can generate real happiness." Unfortunately, this exhortation to philosophy has serious problems. These are explored and it is shown that in spite of its difficulties, the protreptic argument is extremely useful in understanding Socratic philosophy.

ROOCHNIK, David. *The Tragedy of Reason: Toward a Platonic Conception of Logos*. New York, Routledge, 1990.

This book is an attempt to defend Plato against his "postmodern" critics. At least since Nietzsche's *The Birth of Tragedy*, Plato has been repeatedly damned as the architect of the life-denying world of modern science and technology. In recent years, Rorty, Derrida and their many epigones have reiterated this charge. This book argues against Nietzsche's view. It argues that the Platonic conception of logos is "tragic," i.e., it is aware of its own limitations as well as its goodness.

ROONEY, Phyllis. A Different Different Voice: On the Feminist Challenge in Moral Theory. Phil Forum, 22(4), 335-361, Sum 91.

Discussions emerging out of the work on gender and moral development tend to focus on whether or how individuals of different genders are encouraged into different moral perceptions, attitudes, and judgments. Shifting the focus somewhat, I first examine what it means to say that traditional philosophical moral discourse has regularly been gendered. I then argue for an emphasis on different differences—different than those normally taken as salient in the development of discussion. I show how such an emphasis enables us to more effectively address many of the gender-related limitations that have worked their way into much of our philosophical theorizing.

ROONEY, Phyllis. Gendered Reason: Sex Metaphor and Conceptions of Reason. Hypatia, 6(2), 77-103, Sum 91.

Reason has regularly been protrayed and understood in terms of images and metaphors that involve the exclusion or denigration of some element—body, passion, nature, instinct—that is cast as "feminine." Drawing upon philosophical insight into metaphor, I examine the impact of this gendering of reason. I argue that our conceptions of mind, reason, unreason, female, and male have been distorted. The politics of "rational" discourse has been set up in ways that still subtly but powerfully inhibit the voice and agency of women.

ROOT, Michael. "Davidson and Social Science" in *Truth and Interpretation: Perspectives on the Philosophy of Donald Davidson*, LE PORE, Ernest (ed), 272-304. Cambridge, Blackwell, 1986.

ROOTES, C A. Theory of Social Movements: Theory *for* Social Movements? Phil Soc Act, 16(4), 5-17, O-D 90.

Activists sometimes argue that sociological theories of social movements are mere academic parasitism and that what is needed, if theory is needed at all, is theory *for* social movements, theory fashioned by people committed to social movements and designed to be useful to movement activists rather than to further the careers of theorists. There is, however, no inherent conflict between an interest in understanding the world and a determination to change it; it is merely that whereas theory may be comfortably remote from action, action which is not informed by theoretical understanding will often be counterproductive. The problem for the activist is to decide which of the variety of available theories is most likely to sustain effective action. The type of theory that has given theory a bad name with activists is, in general, theory that is as unhelpful to social scientific understanding as it is to action. But there are other theories, other *kinds* of theory, that are more useful on both counts.

RORTY, Amélie Oksenberg and WONG, David. "Aspects of Identity and Agency" in *Identity, Character, and Morality: Essays in Moral Psychology*, FLANAGAN, Owen (ed), 19-36. Cambridge, MIT Pr, 1990.

RORTY, Amélie Oksenberg (ed) and FLANAGAN, Owen (ed). *Identity, Character, and Morality: Essays in Moral Psychology*. Cambridge, MIT Pr, 1990.

Nineteen original essays explore the interconnections between psychology and moral theory. Topics include: Identity, Commitment and Agency; Character, Temperament, and Emotion; Moral Psychology and the Source Virtues; Rationality, Responsibility, and Morality; Virtue Theory.

RORTY, Amelie Oksenberg. King Solomon and Everyman: A Problem in Coordinating Conflicting Moral Intuitions. Amer Phil Quart, 28(3), 181-194, Jl 91.

RORTY, Amelie Oksenberg. *Mind in Action: Essays in the Philosophy of Mind*. Boston, Beacon Pr, 1991.

RORTY, Amelie Oksenberg. Varieties of Pluralism in a Polyphonic Society. Rev Metaph, 44(1), 3-20, S 90.

RORTY, Amélie. 'Pride Produces the Idea of Self': Hume on Moral Agency. Austl J Phil, 68(3), 255-269, S 90.

RORTY, Richard. *Essays on Heidegger and Others: Philosophical Papers, Volume 2*. New York, Cambridge Univ Pr, 1991.

RORTY, Richard. Nietzsche, Socrates and Pragmatism. S Afr J Phil, 10(3), 61-63, Ag 91.

Nietzsche's views of truth and knowledge are often thought to be incompatible with political liberalism. But these views are pretty much the same as those of William James and John Dewey, who were right to see no such incompatibility. The pragmatists, like Nietzsche, wanted to drop the cognitivism which has dominated western intellectual life since Plato, but, unlike Nietzsche, they wished to do so in the interests of an egalitarian society rather than in the interests of a defiant and lonely individualism.

RORTY, Richard. *Objectivity, Relativism, and Truth: Philosophical Papers, Volume 1*. New York, Cambridge Univ Pr, 1991.

RORTY, Richard. "Pragmatism, Davidson and Truth" in *Truth and Interpretation: Perspectives on the Philosophy of Donald Davidson*, LE PORE, Ernest (ed), 333-355. Cambridge, Blackwell, 1986.

RORTY, Richard. "The Priority of Democracy to Philosophy" in *Reading Rorty*, MALACHOWSKI, Alan (ed), 279-302. Cambridge, Blackwell, 1991.

RORTY, Richard. "Unger, Castoriadis, and the Romance of a National Future" in *Critique and Construction: A Symposium on Roberto Unger's "Politics"*, LOVIN, Robin W (ed), 29-45. New York, Cambridge Univ Pr, 1990.

ROS, Arno. Kants Begriff der synthetischen Urteile a priori. Kantstudien, 82(2), 146-172, 1991.

The usually raised critiques against Kant's concept of synthetic judgments a priori may be shown to be unjustified, if we take into account Kant's distinction between "making given concepts clear" and "making, i.e., construing, concepts": The first task, for Kant, must be done by means of analytic judgments, the second by synthetic a priori ones. To put it into more modern terms: Analytic judgments serve to articulate conceptual rules *within* a certain field of concepts; synthetic judgments a priori serve to articulate rules of actions which aim to *generate* a certain field of concepts.

ROSA, Joaquim Coelho. Variações sobre o *De Interpretatione*, de Aristóteles. Rev Port Filosof, 46(3), 379-390, Jl-S 90.

The ontological principle *par excellence* is the principle of non-contradiction. This principle is formulated by Aristotle in terms of modals: being is the exclusion of impossibility. However this implies that impossibility is posterior to its exclusion.

ROSALES, Amán. Hacia un desarrollo de la cultura y una cultura del desarrollo. Rev Filosof (Costa Rica), 28(67-68), 71-76, D 90.

In this paper the meaning of "culture" and "development" are going to be analyzed and debated. The close relationship between these two concepts, it is argued, can only be fully perceived through a criticism of simplicit views on the subject. These perspectives lead to misunderstandings and false expectations concerning worldwide and national development, and at the same time encourage the process of *cultural alienation* with its pernicious non-humanistic implications. The decisive consequence of the discussion is the consideration of philosophy as a theoretical activity involved in the promotion of the quality of life in a society. (edited)

ROSE, John M. "Nothing of the Origin and Destiny of Cats": The Remainder of the Logos. Between Species, 6(2), 53-62, Spr 90.

Through an exegesis of the methods for inquiring about the origins and natures of animals in Aristotle's *The Parts of Animals* and Heidegger's *Being and Time,* I show that their discussion of animals is structured and guided by the metaphor of human production. Further, their view that "animals are products which produce themselves" is the result of their notions of reason. I conclude with a consideration both of the limitations of ethics which begin with the notion of a productive agent and of the possible ethical treatment of animals which is independent of the rationale of human productivity.

ROSE, Margaret A. "Innovation and Tradition in Post-Modernism" in *XIth International Congress in Aesthetics, Nottingham 1988*, WOODFIELD, Richard (ed), 161-164. Nottingham, Nottingham Polytech, 1990.

A discussion of I—the ways in which post-modernism theories have seen themselves as 1) breaking from the traditions of modernism, and 2) introducing innovations to them; II—and of the importance of their understanding of the meaning of modernism to these procedures.

ROSE, Margaret A. Post-Modern Pastiche. Brit J Aes, 31(1), 26-38, Ja 91.

The paper is a critical survey of some recent discussions of post-modern pastiche by such as J-F Lyotard, Fredric Jameson and Charles Jencks. It argues that Jameson has projected categories used by Jean Baudrillard to describe modern art and architecture onto the post-modern and has also used buildings such as Portman's Bonaventure Hotel as examples of post-modernism where Jencks and others have shown them to be "Late-Modern." Jencks's descriptions of pastiche as a means to "double-coding" the modern with other styles in the post-modern is also discussed and the point made that while pastiche has existed as a device prior to the post-modern (contra Jameson) it can have such post-modern functions which are distinct from earlier uses of pastiche.

ROSE, Marilyn Gaddis. "Translation and Language Games" in *Hermeneutics and the Poetic Motion, Translation Perspectives V—1990*, SCHMIDT, Dennis J (ed), 57-68. Binghamton, CRIT, 1990.

The author uses passages from her English translation of Sainte-Beuve's *Volupte* to illustrate how translating functions as a language game in its Lyotard avatar. That is, the experience of the *differend* describes the experience of many translators while their brain is processing a transfer between languages.

ROSE, Rebecca Fine (trans) and WEIL, Simone and TESSIN, Timothy (trans). Essay on the Notion of Reading. Phil Invest, 13(4), 297-303, O 90.

RÖSEBERG, Ulrich. Responsibility—A Challenge in Terms of Philosophy (in German). Deut Z Phil, 38(3), 238-244, 1990.

The problem of responsibility seems to be reduced now by many authors to responsibility of scientists only. As consequence scientists are stressing the complexity of modern world and their dependence of decisions made by others. At least in the socialist countries nobody is seeing any responsibility for its own doings. The talk given on November 1st 1989 in the Plenary Session of the GDR Conference for Philosophy based on the illusion that philosophers will contribute in the process of renewing the socialism in this country.

ROSEMANN, Philipp and WELTE, Werner. *Alltagssprachliche Metakommunikation im Englischen und Deutschen*. New York, Lang, 1990.

In their truly comprehensive treatment of the phenomenon of metacommunication, the authors begin by situating the concept within the philosophical problematic of self-reflexivity, then tracing its history in ancient, mediaeval, and modern philosophy of language. Another chapter is devoted to the central importance which contemporary linguistics has invariably accorded the functions of metalanguage in communication. The syntactic, morphological, semantic, lexical, and pragmatic properties of metacommunication are given detailed scrutiny in a theoretical framework which integrates the linguistic with the philosophical viewpoint. (edited)

ROSEMONT JR, Henry (ed). *Chinese Texts and Philosophical Contexts*. La Salle, Open Court, 1991.

A festschrift devoted to the writings of Angus C Graham, the essays in this volume range from Chinese philology (2), issues of translation and interpretation (5), and problems of epistemology, choice, and relativism (3). The contributors are D C Lau, E Pulleyblank, C Harbsmeier, J Major, H Roth, D Nivison, R Ames, C Hansen, H Fingarette, and H Rosemont, Jr. The volume concludes with a 55-page series of replies to the essays by Graham. Bibliography and Index.

ROSEMONT JR, Henry. "Who Chooses?" in *Chinese Texts and Philosophical Contexts*, ROSEMONT JR, Henry (ed), 227-263. La Salle, Open Court, 1991.

In part a critique of A C Graham's *Reason and Spontaneity*, this essay argues that the concept of choice in moral theory needs revision, largely because of the untenability of the mind-body dichotomy on which the concept of choice has been based in modern Western philosophy.

ROSEN, Michael. Must We Return to Moral Realism? Inquiry, 34(2), 183-194, Je 91.

In this paper I discuss Taylor's criticism of contemporary moral philosophy and the role which this plays in his wider account of the development of Western moral consciousness, an account which I compare with Hans Blumenberg's *The Legitimacy of the Modern Age*. While I endorse Taylor's rejection of 'naturalism', I deny that this entails the rejection of non-realism and I maintain that, indeed, the non-realist conception of a social foundation for morality represents the most cogent response to the contemporary dilemmas Taylor identifies.

ROSEN, Stanley. Squaring the Hermeneutical Circle. Rev Metaph, 44(4), 707-728, Je 91.

I argue against the possibility of transcendental or ontological foundations for hermeneutics. The argument is developed from critical discussion of texts in Kant, Heidegger, and Plato.

ROSEN, Stanley. Suspicion, Deception, and Concealment. Arion, 1(2), 112-127, Spr 91.

Evidence is presented from Greek poetry, history, and philosophy to show that Nietzsche's doctrines of the mask and the veiling of sense in genesis as well as in human behavior (a doctrine that plays a central role in Heidegger) is Greek in nature, and is as old as Homer.

ROSENAU, Hartmut. Schellings metaphysikkritische Sprachphilosophie. Z Phil Forsch, 44(3), 399-424, 1990.

Usually, philosophy of language is guided by metaphysics as "first philosophy." This evaluation is the consequence of a Platonic understanding of "being," which takes it as unchangeable, everlasting, etc. But language is in time and changeable, therefore it is not of that value as metaphysics are. Schelling, in his early philosophy, shares this point of view. As soon as Schelling takes the principle of metaphysics as developing in time (theogony), "ordinary language" becomes more and more worthful to criticize traditional metaphysics. But this "linguistic turn" is not caused by antimetaphysical effects, but by still thinking metaphysically.

ROSENBAUM, Stuart E (ed) and BAIRD, Robert M (ed). *Animal Experimentation: The Moral Issue*. Buffalo, Prometheus, 1991.

This collection of sixteen essays raises and discusses the moral question: is experimentation on animals morally justified, and, if so, under what conditions? Part one introduces the issues to those unfamiliar with moral philosophy. Part two contains position statements by Peter Singer and Tom Regan, two foremost animal advocates, along with critiques of their views. Part three introduces arguments of those who support animal experimentation. Part four contains a position statement adopted by the deans of thirteen medical schools, as well as proposals for addressing the conditions of animals in experimental facilities. Part five, a concluding essay, challenges assumptions of those on both sides of the issue.

ROSENBERG, Alexander. Adequacy Criteria for a Theory of Fitness. Biol Phil, 6(1), 38-41, Ja 91.

ROSENBERG, Alexander. The Biological Justification of Ethics: A Best-Case Scenario. Soc Phil Pol, 8(1), 86-101, Autumn 90.

I argue that the only interesting role for biological theory in moral philosophy is an explanatory one: it just might explain the emergence of one necessary condition for morality—cooperation. I try to identify the many assumptions needed for even so minimal a task. I examine the conditions under which such an explanation can be parlayed into an answer to the moral skeptic's question, why should I be moral?

ROSENBLUM, Nancy. Strange Attractors: How Individualists Connect to Form Democratic Unity. Polit Theory, 18(4), 576-586, N 90.

ROSENOW, Eliyahu. Kierkegaard's Mirror. Educ Phil Theor, 22(1), 8-15, 1990.

Kierkegaard's conception of education is based on his distinction between education and instruction. He conceives education as a process of the realization of the individual's authentic selfhood, i.e., as self education. His is a radical and paradoxical individualistic philosophy, which is exclusively concerned with the manner and style of educational communication. The article discusses Kierkegaard's basic philosophical assumptions and his theoretical and practical impact on contemporary education.

ROSENTHAL, Erwin. "Scientific Philosophical and Sociopolitical Aspects of the Work of Mario Bunge" in *Studies on Mario Bunge's "Treatise"*, WEINGARTNER, Paul (ed), 549-563. Amsterdam, Rodopi, 1990.

Mario Bunge's philosophical position, which has been partially discussed here, is based on the structure of his philosophical system: positivism is rejected as it cannot, in his view, support scientific development. On the other hand the notion of an objectively existing reality is a necessary element of this system. On attempting to work out a philosophy to be made productive for scientific development, which corresponds with modern science—thus the objective compulsion to dialectics is given—in many attempts at solution the proximity to dialectical materialism is reached. At the same time, however, Mario Bunge has some reservation about materialistic dialectics and considers a profitable connection between materialism and dialectics impossible.

ROSENTHAL, Sandra B. From the Phenomenology of Time Toward Process Metaphysics: Pragmatism and Heidegger. J Speculative Phil, 5(3), 161-179, 1991.

Within classical American pragmatism, the focus on the biological context of meaning as habit had led to far-reaching misinterpretations which have contributed to the historical alienation of pragmatism and Heidegger. This essay argues that a focus on the temporally founded features of meaning as habit can at once undercut such misinterpretations and uncover deeply rooted affinities between these two positions, both in their respective understandings of time and in the way in which this draws each toward a metaphysics of process.

ROSENTHAL, Sandra B and BOURGEOIS, Patrick L. Role Taking, Corporeal Intersubjectivity, and Self: Mead and Merleau-Ponty. Phil Today, 34(2), 117-128, Sum 90.

While at first there may seem to be no common ground between the interpretations of self as developed in the pragmatic philosophy of George Herbert Mead and in the existential phenomenology of Maurice Merleau-Ponty, on closer inspection their views can be found to house a fundamental and pervasive rapport between their respective positions. This paper attempts to explain the intersubjective nature of the self and the function of role taking in the development of the personal level of intersubjectivity out of a primordial, pre-personal sociality or corporeal intersubjectivity of the lived body. From such an analysis they can be seen to share a vision of the self that provides a contemporary understanding of a concrete, reflexive individual which undercuts the problematics of the various versions of a transcendental ego or of psychical contents paralleling or replacing an objective reality, and which inextricably interweaves the sense of one's self with the sense of one's existence in an intersubjective world.

ROSENTHAL, Sandra B and BOURGEOIS, Patrick L. Scientific Time and the Temporal Sense of Human Existence: Merleau-Ponty and Mead. Res Phenomenol, 20, 152-163, 1990.

This paper attempts to show that, though Merleau-Ponty and Mead develop philosophies representing differing contexts and traditions, they are led down converging pathways in their examination of the role of the present in temporal existence. For both, lived temporality entails the human praxis which gives rise to a perceived world, and incorporates a temporally extended present within which experience opens onto past and future and to which past and future adjust. Because of this, time, for both, moves as a whole and with depth. Both look at the priority of the present in a strict and in a broad sense, and explicate the sense of a depth of the present. In so doing, they each offer a view of time which is constitutive for the very sense of human existence.

ROSIER, Irène and ROY, Bruno. Grammaire et Liturgie dans les "Sophismes" du XIIIe Siècle. Vivarium, 28(2), 118-135, N 90.

In the thirteenth century, grammatical sophismata are difficult sentences which are taken as the starting point of a discussion. A number of them are taken from religious texts and from the liturgy. Liturgical examples appear to be either grammatically incomplete sentences, which are nevertheless meaningful thanks to the ritual, or performative sentences, used not only to mean something, but to perform an action. A list of examples with references to grammatical and religious texts is appended.

ROSIER, Theo. Indirect Utilisme. Alg Ned Tijdschr Wijs, 83(1), 1-23, Ja 91.

Utilitarians are never really bothered by the criticism that the direct pursuit of happiness is self-defeating. They simply take refuge in indirect strategies. According to many critics, however, this way utilitarianism maneuvers itself into the paradoxical position that it is forced to renounce itself. What the arguments for indirectness show, these critics say, is that utilitarians should try to promote the Good by teaching themselves and others that it is not allowed to promote the Good. This criticism is analysed in connection with three common arguments for indirectness and is found wanting with respect to the first two.

ROSMINI, Antonio and WATSON, Terence (ed & trans) and CLEARY, Denis (ed & trans). *The Origin of Thought*. Durham, Rosmini, 1987.

ROSMINI, Antonio and WATSON, Terence (trans) and CLEARY, Denis (trans). *Principles of Ethics*. Durham, Rosmini, 1988.

ROSOLINI, Giuseppe and ROBINSON, Edmund. Colimit Completions and the Effective Topos. J Sym Log, 55(2), 678-699, Je 90.

The effective topos is an extension of recursive realisability to give a model of intuitionistic Zermelo-Fraenkel set theory. It is a natural setting in which to discuss much of the recursion theory at higher types (as well as HEO models for type theories). In this paper we discuss how we can give meaning to the concept of a "recursively-indexed disjoint union of sets," and show that the effective topos can also be obtained from the classical universe of sets by freely adjoining non-empty recursively-indexed disjoint unions.

ROSS, David. The Special Model Axiom in Nonstandard Analysis. J Sym Log, 55(3), 1233-1242, S 90.

ROSS, Don and LA CASSE, Chantale. Response to W J Norman's "Has Rational Economic Man a Heart". Eidos, 8(2), 235-246, D 89.

ROSS, Glenn (ed) and ROTH, Michael D (ed). *Doubting: Contemporary Perspectives on Skepticism*. Norwell, Kluwer, 1990.

Two common roads to skepticism about knowledge of the external world are: a) a low road where one redefines a key term to gain support for a controversial skeptical claim, and b) a high road where one argues that on the nonskeptic's notion of knowledge we do not have knowledge of the external world. This paper argues that there is no safe road to knowledge skepticism deriving from considerations about justification.

ROSS, Malcolm. The Hidden Order of Arts Education. Brit J Aes, 31(2), 111-121, Ap 91.

The study reported in this paper investigates the mental constructs which inform arts teachers' thinking about their own subjects and the relation of those subjects to the rest of the curriculum. The following concepts appear to dominate teachers' thinking in the arts: expression, feeling, form, creativity, communication, fun (in that order). The study reveals a consistent mental set operating to inform arts teachers' perceptions of their work. Other studies suggest, however, that this belief system does not operate in practice.

ROSS, Murray and SELMAN, Mark. Epistemology, Practical Research, and Human Subjects. Proc Phil Educ, 46, 319-331, 1990.

This paper reviews major strands of criticism by educational philosophers of process-product research in education. It argues that such criticism has been ineffective at least in part because it has focussed too narrowly on obvious epistemological deficiencies while failing to attend to the practical and political results. Foucault's notion of disciplinary power is shown to be useful in illuminating the link between the epistemic and political aspects of such programs of practical research.

ROSS, Stephen David. "Translation as Transgression" in *Hermeneutics and the Poetic Motion, Translation Perspectives V—1990*, SCHMIDT, Dennis J (ed), 25-42. Binghamton, CRIT, 1990.

Pursuing Foucault's idea of transgression and Benjamin's sense of translation, the question of translation as transgression is pursued: Translation falls at the midpoint of language's alterity, where the multiplicity of languages marks their truth and meaning. Translation can be disruptive and transgressive by first and always disrupting itself, but especially by disrupting the rule of the same that defines it.

ROSS, Steven. A Comment on the Argument Between Gewirth and his Critics. Metaphilosophy, 21(4), 405-413, O 90.

Gewirth's claim to have 'derived' rights from pre-moral descriptions of persons has been predictably criticised as either circular or not a true derivation. The author distinguishes two senses in which a 'derivation' of rights from non-controversial descriptions of persons can be claimed. Gewirth's argument cannot succeed in one of these ways, since no argument can. But modified, understood in a different way, an argument like Gewirth's can succeed. This requires sketching a different account of what a successful derivation of rights from persons can be like than the one assumed by both Gewirth and his critics.

ROSS, Steven. The Nature of Moral Facts. Phil Forum, 22(3), 243-269, Spr 91.

The author begins with the very popular version of moral realism that follows from mapping contemporary pragmatist or 'wholist' conceptions of reference on to moral language and argues this version of moral realism is trivial. The important issue is what *kind* of fact one holds a moral fact to be. Rejecting both traditional realism and projectivism, the author argues (i)moral facts are to be thought of as *constructed*, and that this conception alone generates a satisfactory account of moral-natural supervenience.

ROSSET, Clément. Problèmes de l'expression. Philosophique (France), 1(90), 3-12, 1990.

ROSSI, Arcangelo. R J Boskovic's Philosophy of Space (in Serbo-Croatian). Filozof Istraz, 32-33(5-6), 1596-1604, 1989.

In 1755 R J Boskovic raised a very important issue on the structure of physical space in contrast with I Newton's conceptions. According to it, it is not possible to put an absolute motion in evidence when it is composed by, exempli gratia, a rotation plus a common intertial motion which can sometimes overcome the first and then reduce it to a mere relative motion, while being itself undetectable. So Boskovic made explicit, for the first time, full dynamical meaning of Galilean relativity as the impossibility of detecting an absolute motion by mere dynamical means. Afterwards, R J Boskovic's conception of space is also linked to the unique force law by which he represents all the phenomena in the universe in his

Philosophiae Naturalis Theoria of 1758. Here he reduces matter to unextended point atoms acting according to their reciprocal distances. Then space is identified by Boskovic with the universal force pervading the whole universe and differentiated according to the spatial relations between point atoms, in contrast with Newton's distinction between (absolute) space, matter and force.

ROSSI, Fabio. Charles Renouvier e le scuole di morale in Francia nel XIX secolo. Riv Filosof Neo-Scolas, 82(1), 46-86, Ja-Mr 90.

ROSSI, G F. La neoscolastica italiana dalle sue prime manifestazioni all'enciclica *Aeterni Patris*. Riv Filosof Neo-Scolas, 82(2-3), 365-411, Ap-S 90.

ROSSO, Corrado. "La 'grande illusion' du XVIIIe siècle" in *Égalité Uguaglianza*, FERRARI, Jean (ed), 11-18. Napoli, Liguori, 1990.

ROSSOUW, G. A Response to Olivier's Postmodern, but Pre-South African Proposal. S Afr J Phil, 9(4), 223, N 90.

This article is a response to an article by G Olivier which appeared in the *S A Journal of Philosophy* 1990:9(2), in which he tried to utilize Rorty's concept of philosophy in order to make a philosophical contribution to the issue of socio-political dialogue in South Africa. My critique on his article was that he remained within the framework of the debate surrounding Rorty's philosophy and only makes a few rather superficial remarks concerning socio-political dialogue in South Africa. Unlike Olivier who thinks that "adaption" is perhaps too strong a word when it comes to applying Rorty's concept of philosophy to socio-political dialogue, I am convinced that that is exactly what is needed. I then indicate in which areas I think that severe adaption of Rorty is necessary as well as which aspects of the South African political scene should be taken into consideration.

ROSSOUW, H W. Remarks about the Idea of the University (in Dutch). S Afr J Phil, 10(3), 68-75, Ag 91.

In this article the author discusses several sets of conceptual factors standing in a relation of polarity to each other, which one encounters in reflecting on the idea of the university. The relations of polarity which are distinguished and analysed are those of identity and relevance, universality and particularity, elitism and egalitarianism, autonomy and limitation, and community and corporation. All these relations are characterized by a tension between, on the one hand, claims implied by the hereditary elements of the university and, on the other, claims exerted by the contemporary environment of the university.

ROTA, Gian-Carlo. The Concept of Mathematical Truth. Rev Metaph, 44(3), 483-494, Mr 91.

ROTA, GianCarlo. Mathematics and Philosophy: The Story of a Misunderstanding. Rev Metaph, 44(2), 259-271, D 90.

ROTH, Gerhard and SCHWEGLER, Helmut. Self-Organization, Emergent Properties and the Unity of the World. Philosophica, 46(2), 45-64, 1990.

ROTH, Harold. "Who Compiled the *Chuang Tzu*?" in *Chinese Texts and Philosophical Contexts*, ROSEMONT JR, Henry (ed), 79-128. La Salle, Open Court, 1991.

The *Chuang Tzu*, one of the two foundational texts of Taoist philosophy in China, is not a monolothic work, as tradition has assumed. Its contents include at least five different philosophical positions and span roughly two centuries. By analyzing the core ideas of the final or "Syncretist" section and comparing them to contemporary and earlier works (i.e., *Kuan Tzu* and *Huai-nan Tzu*), I argue that this last stratum is part of the "Huang-Lao" philosophical lineage and that the entire work was compiled within this lineage circa 130 BC at the court of Liu An, second king of Huai-nan.

ROTH, Michael D (ed) and ROSS, Glenn (ed). *Doubting: Contemporary Perspectives on Skepticism*. Norwell, Kluwer, 1990.

Two common roads to skepticism about knowledge of the external world are: a) a low road where one redefines a key term to gain support for a controversial skeptical claim, and b) a high road where one argues that on the nonskeptic's notion of knowledge we do not have knowledge of the external world. This paper argues that there is no safe road to knowledge skepticism deriving from considerations about justification.

ROTH, Michael S. The Ironist's Cage. Polit Theory, 19(3), 419-432, Ag 91.

"The Ironist's Cage" examines the privileging of irony in contemporary theory. Three examples are given: Alexandre Kojève, Michel Foucault and Jacques Derrida. Kojève is shown to have changed from being a dramatic pragmatist whose philosophy aimed at political change to being an ironic culture critic announcing the end of history. The essay points out that Foucault's ironic accounts of the vicissitudes of modernity are limited by their inability to connect criticism and legitimation. Finally, Derrida's sophisticated deconstruction, it is suggested, on a political level may only end up in an appeal to prudence.

ROTH, Patricia A and HARRISON, Janet K. Orchestrating Social Change: An Imperative in Care of the Chronically Ill. J Med Phil, 16(3), 343-359, Je 91.

The ethical challenges of caring for the chronically ill are of increasing concern to nurses as they attempt to create humanitarian environments for long-term care. This article suggests two ethical perspectives to guide the agenda of the nursing profession to achieve social change in the care of the chronically ill and aging. First, a reemphasis on the public duties of the professions is recommended which extends beyond serving the interests of the nursing profession to recognizing the need to serve the common good. Second, the limitations of the autonomy paradigm are explored and the foundation for the development of a new moral paradigm is analyzed in terms of its' potential usefulness in addressing ethical problems of chronic illness. Several initiatives that nursing must undertake to facilitate the emergence of this paradigm are proposed.

ROTH, Paul A. Truth in Interpretation: The Case of Psychoanalysis. Phil Soc Sci, 21(2), 175-195, Je 91.

This article explores and attempts to resolve some issues that arise when psychoanalytic explanations are construed as a type of historical or narrative explanation. The chief problem is this: If one rejects the claim of narratives to verisimilitude, this appears to divorce the notion of explanation from that of truth. The author examines, in particular, Donald Spence's attempt to deal with the relation of narrative explanations and truth. In his critique of Spence's distinction between narrative truth and historical truth, the author develops some suggestions regarding the role of truth in narrative explanations.

ROTH, Robert J. David Hume on Religion in England. Thought, 66(260), 51-64, Mr 91.

This paper explores David Hume's rendition of the religious influences on the history of England during the reign of the early Stuarts. His philosophical works, essays, and *The History of England* are used as source materials. The paper attempts to illustrate how his anti-Presbyterian and anti-Puritan bias colored his view of the history of England leading to the Civil War and the execution of Charles I in 1649. Along the way, his views on the Anglican and Roman Catholic Churches are also described.

ROTH, Robin A. Verily, Nietzsche's Judgment of Jesus. Phil Today, 34(4), 364-376, Wint 90.

This paper argues that there is a closer affinity between Dionysus and the Crucified than is commonly supposed. The paper explores Nietzsche's assessment of Jesus. This exploration in turn reveals what Nietzsche admires in Jesus and what he regards as tragic. It is then argued that Nietzsche attempts to overcome Jesus' failure, to develop a more worldly concept of love, and to reconcile the Crucified with Dionysus, who himself dies in order to transfigure the world.

ROTH, Robin Alice. Nietzsche's Metaperspectivism. Int Stud Phil, 22(2), 67-77, 1990.

Nietzsche's theory of perspectivism, understood as a criticism of Platonism, is frequently debated as to whether it is foundationalistic or anti-foundationalistic. This essay demonstrates that Nietzsche's theory of perspectivism entails a metaperspectivism which accounts for the semifluid direction of values and makes possible the ranking of values based on Will to Power.

ROTH, Robin Alice. Nietzsche's Use of Atheism. Int Phil Quart, 31(1), 51-64, Mr 91.

This paper seriously questions the popular interpretations of Nietzsche's alleged atheism by asking: What is the function of atheism within Nietzsche's philosophy? To answer this question the distinction between the death of God and atheism is carefully delineated. Nietzsche's relation to Schopenhauer is reviewed, and the character of the "good European" is decoded. Finally, Nietzsche's own atheistic statements are reinterpreted, demonstrating their intended iconotropy, not godlessness.

ROTHMAN, Barbara Katz. "Recreating Motherhood: Ideology and Technology in American Society" in *Beyond Baby M: Ethical Issues in New Reproductive Techniques*, BARTELS, Dianne M (ed), 9-27. Clifton, Humana Pr, 1990.

This article focuses on the meaning of pregnancy as a social relationship, emphasising the nurturance that gestation entails, and its meaning for both the woman and the fetus. The article is based on the author's recent book, *Recreating Motherhood: Ideology and Technology in a Patriarchal Society* (W W Norton, 1989).

ROTHMAN, Barbara Katz. "Surrogacy: A Question of Values" in *Beyond Baby M: Ethical Issues in New Reproductive Techniques*, BARTELS, Dianne M (ed), 235-241. Clifton, Humana Pr, 1990.

This brief essay presents an analysis of some of the underlying values used by feminists in opposition to "surrogacy" arrangements, distinguishing the position of these feminists from the religious and traditionalist opposition. The article is drawn from the author's recent book, *Recreating Motherhood: Ideology and Technology in a Patriarchal Society* (W W Norton, 1989).

ROTHWELL, Andrew (trans) and JACQUES, Francis. *Difference and Subjectivity: Dialogue and Personal Identity*. New Haven, Yale Univ Pr, 1991.

ROTT, Hans. Two Methods of Constructing Contractions and Revisions of Knowledge Systems. J Phil Log, 20(2), 149-173, My 91.

This paper investigates the formal relationship between two prominent approaches to the logic of belief change. The first one uses the idea of "relational partial meet contractions" as developed by Alchourrón, Gärdenfors and Makinson (in the *JSL* 1985), the second one uses the concept of "epistemic entrenchment" as elaborated by Gärdenfors and Makinson (in *Theoretical Aspects of Reasoning about Knowledge*, E. M. Vardi, Los Altos 1988). The two approaches are shown to be strictly equivalent via direct links between the underlying formal relations. The paper closes with observations about the application of epistemic entrenchment to simple and iterated revisions.

RÖTTGERS, Kurt. Buchphilosophie und philosophische Praxis. Deut Z Phil, 38(12), 1187-1201, 1990.

What is the praxis of philosophy? Two opposed answers to this question are examined: 1) that philosophy procedes by writing books out of books, each of them pretending to be a copy of the world, so that the universe of books depends on the universe of the real world, either as the original book or as the sphere of effects; 2) that the practice of philosophy therefore is a kind of action out from philosophy onto the world, two models (counselling and subversive intervention) and two dimensions (political and therapeutic) are critically examined with the result that the way philosophy is practical cannot be thought of as a kind of application or use in a sphere alien to it. So the model of the text (as a process in opposition to the book) is proposed as the specific kind of the philosophical proceeding which is both theoretical and practical. This proposal is finally tested confronting the problems of human sufferings and of the conditions of coherence of philosophy.

RÖTTGERS, Kurt. *Spuren der Macht*. Freiburg, Alber, 1991.

In its first part, this semiology of power—which relies on the art of interpreting vestiges or signs—deals with the historical traces of a conceptual development, from the Greek idea of dynamis to Hegel's concept of power. This yields the rehabilitation of a concept of power as model relation. The second part builds on this to examine power in the area intersected by the theory of texts, the theory of historical narratives, and the theory of action.

ROTTSCHAEFER, William A. Evolutionary Naturalistic Justifications of Morality: A Matter of Faith and Works. Biol Phil, 6(3), 341-349, Jl 91.

Robert Richards has presented a detailed defense of evolutionary ethics, a revised version of Darwin's views and a major modification of E O Wilson's. He contends that humans have evolved to seek the community welfare by acting altruistically. And since the community welfare is the highest moral good, humans ought to act altruistically. Richards asks us to take his empirical premises on faith and aims to show how they can justify an ethical conclusion. He identifies two necessary conditions for a naturalistic justification of morality (NJ): its premises 1) must be empirical and 2) concerned with morally relevant causal factors. I argue that these two conditions are insufficient. An NJ must also appeal to teleological or teleonomic laws which identify proper effects and reliable causes of these effects. So I supplement biological faith with an NJ that I believe has a better chance of working since faith without works is dead.

ROTTSCHAEFER, William A. Philosophical and Religious Implications of Cognitive Social Learning Theories of Personality. Zygon, 26(1), 137-148, Mr 91.

This paper sketches an alternative answer to James Jones's recent attempt to explore the implications of cognitive social learning theories of personality for issues in epistemology, philosophy of science, and religious studies. Since the 1960s, two cognitive revolutions have taken place in scientific psychology: the first made cognition central to theories of perception, memory, problem solving, and so on; the second made cognition central to theories of learning and behavior, among others. Cognitive social learning theories find their place in the latter revolution. Because of an ongoing naturalistic revolution in philosophy, these cognitive revolutions in psychology are having a profound effect on both descriptive and normative issues in epistemology and philosophy of science. From the naturalistic perspective, philosophy cannot adequately pursue its goals without the contributions of the empirical sciences, including psychology. The author concludes that the cognitive revolutions in psychology and the naturalistic revolution in philosophy have similar descriptive and normative import for the study of religion.

ROUNER, Leroy S (ed). *Celebrating Peace*. Notre Dame, Univ Notre Dame Pr, 1990.

ROUNER, Leroy S. *To Be at Home: Christianity, Civil Religion, and World Community*. Boston, Beacon Pr, 1991.

ROUSE, Joseph. Indeterminacy, Empirical Evidence, and Methodological Pluralism. Synthese, 86(3), 443-465, Mr 91.

Roth (1987) effectively distinguishes Quinean indeterminacy of translation from the more general underdetermination of theories by showing how indeterminacy follows directly from holism and the role of a shared environment in language learning. However, Roth is mistaken in three further consequences he draws from his interpretation of indeterminacy. Contra Roth, natural science and social science are not differentiated as offering theories about the shared environment and theories about meanings respectively; the role of the environment in language learning does not justify an empiricist sense of "objective evidence"; and his advocacy of methodological pluralism does not appropriately sustain the project of social scientific methodology in response to holism and indeterminacy.

ROUSE, Joseph. Philosophy of Science and the Persistent Narratives of Modernity. Stud Hist Phil Sci, 22(1), 141-162, Mr 91.

ROUSSEAU, Mary F. *Community: The Tie That Binds*. Lanham, Univ Pr of America, 1991.

ROVANE, Carol. "The Metaphysics of Interpretation" in *Truth and Interpretation: Perspectives on the Philosophy of Donald Davidson*, LE PORE, Ernest (ed), 417-429. Cambridge, Blackwell, 1986.

Davidson claims that theories of meaning (in his sense) have metaphysical significance, largely because interpretation is governed by the principle of charity. The paper argues (1) this significance depends on a Kantian, or antiskeptical, strategy in metaphysics; (2) while such strategies are in general worthy, Davidson's charity-based conclusions are empty; and (3) rather than look to theories of meaning per se for metaphysical insights, we should examine the metaphysical presuppositions of the concept of communication—presuppositions which govern the activity of interpretation prior to devising a theory of meaning.

ROWE, Christopher. "Ethics in Ancient Greece" in *A Companion to Ethics*, SINGER, Peter (ed), 121-132. Cambridge, Blackwell, 1991.

The purpose of the essay is to give a short summary of the main topics and arguments of the ancient Greek ethical philosophers.

ROWE, M W. The Definition of 'Art'. Phil Quart, 41(164), 271-286, Jl 91.

ROWE, M W. Goethe and Wittgenstein. Philosophy, 66(257), 283-303, Jl 91.

ROWE, M W. Why 'Art' Doesn't Have Two Senses. Brit J Aes, 31(3), 214-221, Jl 91.

ROWLANDS, Mark. Anomalism, Supervenience, and Davidson on Content-Individuation. Philosophia (Israel), 20(3), 295-310, D 90.

ROWLANDS, Mark. Towards a Reasonable Version of Methodological Solipsism. Mind Lang, 6(1), 39-57, Spr 91.

ROY, Bernard. The Outranking Approach and the Foundations of Electre Methods. Theor Decis, 31(1), 49-73, Jl 91.

In the first part of this paper, we describe the main features of real-world problems for which the outranking approach is appropriate and we present the concept of outranking relations. The second part is devoted to basic ideas and concepts used for building outranking relations. The definition of such outranking relations is given for the main "electre" methods in part three. The final part of the paper is devoted to some practical considerations.

ROY, Bruno and ROSIER, Irène. Grammaire et Liturgie dans les "Sophismes" du XIIIe Siècle. Vivarium, 28(2), 118-135, N 90.

In the thirteenth century, grammatical sophismata are difficult sentences which are taken as the starting point of a discussion. A number of them are taken from religious texts and from the liturgy. Liturgical examples appear to be either grammatically incomplete sentences, which are nevertheless meaningful thanks to the ritual, or performative sentences, used not only to mean something, but to perform an action. A list of examples with references to grammatical and religious texts is appended.

ROY, Krishna. Heideggerian Retrieval of Cartesianism. J Indian Counc Phil Res, 6(3), 37-48, My-Ag 89.

Heidegger's early writings express dissatisfaction with Cartesianism but his attitude changed later. Heidegger criticises Descartes as his interest towards the subject did not spring from the fundamental ontological function of Dasein. Due to Cartesian overemphasis on the subject, the intentionality of Dasein goes neglected. Unlike Cartesianism, self and world belong together in Dasein. Like Descartes, Heidegger was interested in science and mathematics. Referring to Cartesianism he shows how *mathesis* deals both with the nature of thing and man. In his later writings Heidegger hermeneutically discerns from this Cartesian metaphysical project the emancipation of man and reveals that the freedom that he has chosen is self-determination and the ground of all his certitudes is to be found in his self-awareness. Since Descartes we experience the dawn of humanism. Thus Heidegger remembers Descartes not only for forgetfulness of Being but also for rediscovery of man and his freedom.

ROY, Krishna. Man and Hermeneutics. J Indian Counc Phil Res, 7(3), 103-107, My-Ag 90.

ROY, Krishna. Scientific Knowledge and Human Happiness. J Indian Counc Phil Res, 5(1), 153-159, S-D 87.

Knowledge and happiness are the twin *telos* of man. Scientific knowledge has given us useful information about physical nature. But can it give information about human nature and make man free, virtuous and happy? Happiness is a state of mind but modern interpretations give more emphasis on physical and social components. Though science and technology have minimized, ignorance, poverty and discomfort man feels dehumanized, alienated, unhappy, loses individuality, spirituality and contentment. Science of medicine cures sick body but no science can cure unhappy soul or can remove the anxiety of fate, death and suffering. Not mere *techne* but *episteme* can make man happy—somatically and spiritually.

ROY, Louis. Wainwright, Maritain and Aquinas on Transcendent Experiences. Thomist, 54(4), 655-672, O 90.

The article presents the interpretative context in which each thinker belongs, and expounds how each discusses the noetic validity of transcendent experiences. The author argues that Wainwright lacks an explicit epistemology, that Maritain operates with an inadequate one, and that Aquinas uses both an epistemology and a metaphysics which enable him to locate the experience of God with regard to the various aspects of human activity. The role of love and of a person's awareness of one's feelings and acts of love are explained in some detail.

ROY, Pabitrakumar. Action and Freedom. J Indian Counc Phil Res, 7(2), 105-124, Ja-Ap 90.

ROYAL, Robert. "Creative Intuition, Great Books, and Freedom of Intellect" in *Freedom in the Modern World: Jacques Maritain, Yves R Simon, Mortimer J Adler*, TORRE, Michael D (ed), 181-195. Notre Dame, Univ Notre Dame Pr, 1989.

ROYAL, Robert. "Human Nature and Unnatural Humanisms" in *From Twilight to Dawn: The Cultural Vision of Jacques Maritain*, REDPATH, Peter A (ed), 167-200. Notre Dame, Univ Notre Dame Pr, 1990.

ROZDZENSKI, R. Heidegger und die Frage um die Quelle des Grundbegriffes der Metaphysik (in Polish). Stud Phil Christ, 27(1), 71-99, 1991.

Heidegger vertrat die Meinung, jedes Seiende werde als solches dem Menschen begrifflich ausschliesslich aufgrund der früheren Erfahrung des Seins selbst als des Nichts. Dieses Sein selbst wird dem Menschen zugänglich in der Erfahrung, die ihm die Angst gibt. Sie enthüllt ihm das Sein als solches alles Seienden in der Gestalt des Nichts. So erscheint die Erfahrung der wesentlichen Angst als ursprüngliche Quelle des Grundbegriffes der Metaphysik. (edited)

RUBA, Marek. Max Scheler: Theory of Forms of Knowledge and Perspective of Overcoming the Crisis of European Culture (in Polish). Ann Univ Mariae Curie-Phil, 11, 121-140, 1986.

The paper analyzes the diagnosis of the situation of European culture and a proposition of its therapy outlined by Max Scheler. Scheler's conception belongs to the trend opposed to scientism, yet it is highly original and relevant, not merely as a document of the history of thought. Exposing the one-sidedness of the developmental direction of European culture, as well as—for other reasons—of cultures outside Europe, it is a call to the undertaking of an intercultural dialogue (especially between the East and the West). Scheler's theory of "forms of knowledge," from whose point of view the cultural crisis is discussed, has numerous deficiencies and weaknesses, yet it also contains some penetrating and still actual thoughts. One of the components of these thoughts is a conviction that the crisis of culture is in the same extent a crisis of man, while the therapy of culture should simultaneously be a therapy of man and of the forms of knowledge through which he/she related to himself/herself and to the world.

RUBEN, David-Hillel. Singular Explanation and the Social Sciences. Philosophy, 27, 95-117, 90 Supp.

Some philosophers have argued that there is a methodological difference between the natural and social sciences, since in the latter not all full explanations essentially include at least one law or lawlike generalization. I argue against the requirement of a law, for both natural and social science. On my view, laws play an epistemic role in explanation; they provide the criteria for coming to know, of an explanation, whether it is full or complete. It may be that the social sciences, unlike the natural sciences, have little interest in discovering such full or complete explanations.

RUBEN, Peter. Die DDR und ihre Philosophen: Über Voraussetzungen einer Urteilsbildung. Deut Z Phil, 39(1), 50-58, 1991.

RUBENSTEIN, Richard L. "Totalitarianism and Population Superfluity" in *The Realm of Humanitas: Responses to the Writings of Hannah Arendt*, GARNER, Reuben (ed), 101-119. New York, Lang, 1990.

RUBIOLO, E. Aportes para el debate en torno a la teología de la libercíón. Stromata, 46(1-2), 175-186, Ja-Je 90.

RUCHLIS, Hy. *Clear Thinking: A Practical Introduction*. Buffalo, Prometheus, 1990.

The purpose of this book is to improve the practical reasoning ability of non-philosophers. The practical reasoning ability of individuals is improved by an understanding of important issues. Some of the issues included in this book are the pitfalls of informal fallacies, a readable discussion on the nature of facts, and a brief discussion of the importance of the methods of science. (staff)

RUCKER, Darnell. "The True Temper of a Teacher" in *Abeunt Studia in Mores: A Festschrift for Helga Doblin*, MERRILL, Sarah A Bishop (ed), 3-16. New York, Lang, 1990.

RUD JR, Anthony G. Comment on Romain's "Feminist Reflections on Humans and Other Domestic Animals. Between Species, 6(4), 219-220, Fall 90.

RUDDER, Charles F. Ethics and Educational Administration: Are Ethical Politics "Ethical"? Educ Theor, 41(1), 75-88, Wint 91.

RUDEBUSCH, George. Death Is One of Two Things. Ancient Phil, 11(1), 35-45, Spr 91.

Socrates' argues in the *Apology* that death is one of two things, nothingness or an afterlife of cross-examination, either of which is a gain. The argument is rarely thought convincing or even intellectually respectable. My thesis is that the argument is seriously defensible, and I defend it from the stock objections: that it is a false dilemma; that nothingness is deprivation, not gain; that the afterlife might be hell or at least different from what Socrates images; and that Socrates himself claims it is the height of ignorance to pretend to know what death is.

RUDHARDT, Jean. Dans quelle mesure et par quelles images les mythes grecs ont-ils symbolisé le néant? Rev Theol Phil, 122(3), 303-312, 1990.

La pensée traditionnelle, telle qu'elle trouve son expression dans les mythes, a-t-elle connu, a-t-elle de quelque façon symbolisé le néant? La manière dont les principaux systèmes cosmogoniques évoquent ce dont le monde est issu à l'aube des temps nous incite à répondre non à cette question. Ce n'est pas de la tradition que la pensée philosophique a reçu l'idée du néant; pour la concevoir, elle devait au contraire s'en détacher.

RÜDIGER, Wolfgang. Some Philosophical Aspects of Psychophysiology—Are There Any Elements of "Neurophilosophy"? (in German). Deut Z Phil, 38(8), 739-750, 1990.

The main concern of the article is directed towards a new way of understanding the aims of some psycho-physiologists to open a new access for creating a unified mind brain theory through a "neurophilosophical" approach in the sense of the "Neurophilosophy" of Patricia Smith Churchland or the materialistic "emergentistic monism" of Mario Bunge. Methodological problems of both behavioural neurobiology and contemporary psychology (psychology in its prescientific stage of development, in the opinion of the author) are stressed.

RÜDIGER, Wolfgang. Welchen Platz kann die Philosophie künftig in unserem Lande beanspruchen und vor welchen Aufgaben steht sie? Deut Z Phil, 38(7), 669-671, 1990.

The article is aimed at a contribution to opinions about some problems of psychophysiology from the point of view of the emergentic monism as advanced by M Bunge and H Maturana, and of "Neurophilosophy," a term that was proposed by Patricia Smith Churchland. Attempts are supported that try to elaborate a quantum theory of mental processes in order to bridge in some fashion the cleft between the psychological and neuro-physiological sides which deal with cognition. According to the experiences of the author as a neurophysiologist examples are provided that give support to monistic emergentism.

RUE, Leslie W and IBRAHIM, Nabil A and MC DOUGALL, Patricia P and GREENE, G Robert. Characteristics and Practices of "Christian-Based" Companies. J Bus Ethics, 10(2), 123-132, F 91.

There is a sizeable group of self-described "Christian" companies which have declared their belief in the successful merging of biblical principles with business activities. As these companies have become more visible, an increasing number of anecdotal newspaper and magazine articles about these companies have appeared. Surprisingly, no rigorous research had been conducted prior to our recent study. This article provides national estimates of the size and predominant characteristics of self-identified "Christian" companies. In addition, the study investigated the types of relationships these companies maintained with their employees, customers, communities, and suppliers.

RUE, Loyal D. *Amythia: Crisis in the Natural History of Western Culture*. University, Univ Alabama Pr, 1989.

This interdisciplinary work advances the thesis that Western culture is suffering from "amythia," a loss of shared orientation in nature and in history. Under the conditions of amythia cultures lack intellectual resources for achieving individual well-being and social coherence. Thus Western culture is in a state of intellectual and moral crisis, and is in need of generating a unifying myth. The book encourages new ventures in myth making, but warns that any myth attempting to address Western culture effectively must be both scientifically plausible and religiously distinctive. The proposed strategy for rescuing Western culture from further decline, therefore, is to transpose the idea of Covenant (the essence of Judaeo-Christian tradition) to new and plausible conventions of meaning.

RUEGER, Alexander. Independence from Future Theories: A Research Strategy in Quantum Theory. Proc Phil Sci Ass, 1, 203-211, 1990.

The paper argues that renormalization in quantum field theory was not a radically new—and possibly *ad hoc*—technique to save a badly flawed theory, but rather the culmination of a methodological strategy that physicists had been applying for a long time. The strategy was to obtain reliable results from unreliable theories by making the derivation of the results independent of possible future modifications of the theory. Examples of this practice include Bohr's use of the correspondence principle and Heisenberg's S-matrix theory.

RUELLAND, Jacques G. *De l'épistémologie à la politique: La philosophie de l'histoire de Karl R Popper*. Paris, Pr Univ de France, 1991.

While Karl Popper's contribution to epistemology is widely acknowledged, his position on politics appears often as its polemic extension, more or less extrinsic to his central project. This book emphasizes clearly and precisely that problematic but necessary coherence of these two dimensions. As a true re-introduction to Popper's unity of thought, this inquiry projects a new light on a strategic area of today's philosophy: the encounter point of science and political knowledge into the actual crisis of history.

RUFFINO, Marco Antonio. Context Principle, Fruitfulness of Logic and the Cognitive Value of Arithmetic in Frege. Hist Phil Log, 12(2), 185-194, 1991.

I try to reconstruct how Frege thought to reconcile the cognitive value of arithmetic with its analytical nature. There is evidence in Frege's texts that the epistemological formulation of the context principle plays a decisive role; it provides a way of obtaining concepts which are truly fruitful and whose contents cannot be grasped beforehand. Taking the definitions presented in the *Begriffsschrift*, I shall illustrate how this schema is intended to work.

RUITENBURG, Wim and BANKSTON, Paul. Notions of Relative Ubiquity for Invariant Sets of Relational Structures. J Sym Log, 55(3), 948-986, S 90.

Given a finite lexicon L of relational symbols and equality, one may view the collection of all L-structures on the set of natural numbers ω as a space in several different ways. We consider it as (i) the space of outcomes of certain infinite two-person games; (ii) a compact metric space; and (iii) a probability measure space. For each of these viewpoints, we can give a notion of relative ubiquity, or largeness, for invariant sets of structures on ω. For example, in every sense of relative ubiquity considered here, the set of dense linear orderings on ω is ubiquitous in the set of linear orderings on ω.

RUIZ ZAPATERO, Guillermo. La elusión mediante sociedades a la luz de los principios constitucionales. El Basilisco, 2, 19-26, N-D 89.

This article "Tax Avoidance Through Corporations and Constitutional Law" (A case and Dworkin's philosophy of law) considers a "hard case" recently raised in Spanish Tax Law as a "test" for Dworkin's philosophy as it is constructed in his book "Law's Empire". In our opinion, Dworkin's theory works for the best construction of this case, giving evidence that a philosophy such as "law as integrity" should be required to provide law with more solid grounds than it receives from other theories. A historical comparison is made at the beginning quoting Leibniz's Meditation on the common notion of Justice.

RUIZ, Angel. El lugar de las superestructuras y los intelectuales en la filosofía política de Gramsci. Rev Filosof (Costa Rica), 28(67-68), 59-63, D 90.

It is intended to compare methodologically the ideas of Gramsci about the status of "superstructures" and the role of the intelligence in society, with the classical Marxist theory. It is stated that though Gramsci goes beyond the Marxist intellectual framework, he does not get rid of the basic ideological premises of Marxism. This situation is considered a permanent characteristic of Gramsci's thought. Also compared are the concepts of ideology used by Marx and Gramsci.

RUIZ-PESCE, Ramón Eduardo. *Metaphysik als Metahistorik oder Hermeneutik des unreinen Denkens Die Philosophie Max Müllers*. Freiburg, Alber, 1991.

This book provides, for the first time, a systematic presentation of Max Müller's philosophy. The author comments on the "metahistorical" concept of Max Müller. He gives the reader a comprehensive view of Müller's road from classical metaphysics (Thomas Aquinas) to Heidegger, from the ontology of mind to the ontology of freedom.

RUMPEL, Roland. *Geschichte, Freiheit und Struktur*. Freiburg, Alber, 1991.

The author develops a model of structural theory of history which can be regarded as a systematic attempt to modify ancient metaphysics by using a broadened interpretation of transcendental phenomenology. This means that the basic historical pattern of occidental thought and action can be rendered perceptible as an existential form of life. This is carried out by means of the narrative reconstruction of that structure-forming achievement of free subjects which originally generates meaning.

RUNDE, Jochen. Keynesian Uncertainty and the Weight of Arguments. Econ Phil, 6(2), 275-292, O 90.

This paper examines Keynes's notion of the weight of arguments and how this is related to his views on probability and uncertainty. Section I and II, on probability and the notion of relevance respectively, introduce the concepts needed to define weight. An interpretation of weight as the degree of completeness of the information on which a probability is based is outlined in Section III. Section IV deals with the relation between weight and Keynes's views on uncertainty and confidence. Finally, in section V, some implications of weight for the subjective expected utility model are considered.

RUNDLE, Bede. *Wittgenstein and Contemporary Philosophy of Language*. Cambridge, Blackwell, 1990.

Beginning with the identification of meaning and use, a number of Wittgensteinian themes are investigated, including ostensive definition, explanations of meaning, family resemblance, intention, belief, and a cluster of topics in which truth is central. These include the possibility of a uniform account of meaning, the sentence radical, and the involvement of meaning with verification. While the argument frequently goes against Wittgenstein, the general approach is in his spirit, the aim throughout being to dispel confusions and to give an account of language as it is, not as rewritten to accord with the preconceptions of current logical theory.

RUNGGALDIER, Edmund. The Transcendental Method of Metaphysics of Coreth and Muck and Its Relation to Analytic Philosophy. Asian J Phil, 2(1), 57-69, Sum 90.

Since World War II, Innsbruck University has had a strong school of transcendental Thomists: Rahner, Coreth and Muck. Coreth considered in his interpretation of classical metaphysics Continental philosophers, whereas Muck concentrated in his analysis of metaphysical methods on analytic philosophers. The aim of the paper is to look for the usefulness of the transcendental method—the term "transcendental" is used here in the Kantian sense—in finding connections between developments in analytic philosophy on the one hand, and the concerns of classical metaphysics on the other.

RUSE, Michael. Evolutionary Ethics and the Search for Predecessors: Kant, Hume, and All the Way Back to Aristotle? Soc Phil Pol, 8(1), 59-85, Autumn 90.

I argue that ethics can be put on an evolutionary basis at least in the sense that one can explain ethics away using evolution even though one cannot justify moral claims. In this article I compare my position with the great moral philosophers of the past arguing in effect that an adequate evolutionary ethics is akin to David Hume's moral philosophy brought up to date via Charles Darwin.

RUSE, Michael. "The Significance of Evolution" in *A Companion to Ethics*, SINGER, Peter (ed), 500-510. Cambridge, Blackwell, 1991.

RUSSELL, Bruce. Truth, Justification and the Inescapability of Epistemology: Comments on Copp. S J Phil, SUPP 29, 211-215, 1990.

In this comment on David Copp's "Normativity and the Very Idea of Moral Epistemology" (same volume, pp. 189-210), I criticize his arguments for his view that moral propositions are true only if they are appropriately justified. I offer the alternative view that they are true if they either are, or are related to, propositions about what people have reason to do or subscribe to. Since these propositions have a truth-value, questions about their justification are epistemic and, if problematic, are problematic for the same reason that the justification of any philosophical claim is—it appears to be *a priori*, not empirical.

RUSSELL, Denise. Feminism and Relativism. Method Sci, 22(3), 149-158, 1989.

Two questions concerning epistemological relativism are posed: (1) If reason is relative can there be a place for feminist epistemology? (2) If we support a feminist epistemology is it necessary to reject relativism? In answering these questions an account of relativism is outlined and defended which excludes the possibility of a feminist relativism as logically incoherent but still allows feminism to have a bearing upon epistemology. Secondly, it is argued that on certain interpretations of "feminist epistemology" it is not necessary to reject relativism. There is some fear of relativism within feminist epistemology. I argue that this is unjustifiable, that relativism is a defensible position which could allow greater input for feminism within epistemology than nonrelativist views.

RUSSELL, Greg. Jeffersonian Ethics in Foreign Affairs: John Quincy Adams and the Moral Sentiments of a Realist. Interpretation, 18(2), 273-291, Wint 90-91.

John Quincy Adams joined Jefferson in affirming natural rights as the moral compass of the union. Adams's worldview was one that could rarely decouple the expression of national interest from underlying values of national purpose. He was reluctant to condone any *essential* difference between public and private moral acts. Adams's political and diplomatic career was conspicuous by his belief in a vital connection between America's commitment to mankind and clear limits to the moral authority of the nation's power in world affairs.

RUSSELL, Paul. Hume on Responsibility and Punishment. Can J Phil, 20(4), 539-563, D 90.

This paper is principally concerned with an interpretation of the nature and character of Hume's theory of punishment and a critical assessment of its contemporary interest and value. Hume's theory of punishment, I argue, rests on the foundation of a naturalistic theory of responsibility—that is, a theory which draws our attention to the role of moral sentiment in this sphere. On the basis of this naturalistic foundation Hume develops a "mixed" or teleological retributivist account of punishment. Hume's position is critically evaluated with respect to the justificatory "gap" between our moral sentiments and our retributive practices, and also with respect to retributive practices and the will.

RUSSELL, Stuart. *Do the Right Thing: Studies in Limited Rationality*. Cambridge, MIT Pr, 1991.

It is proposed that classical notions of perfect rationality, and descriptive approaches to bounded rationality, should be replaced by the notion of "bounded optimality", a property not of individual decisions but of certain "programs" within finite machines. The rich structure of actual intelligent agents results from the pressure for optimal behavior operating within systems of limited resources. New designs for new intelligent systems are outlined, and theoretical and practical tools are described for enabling programs to control their own reasoning effectively. The tools are applied to game-playing and real-time problem-solving, with surprising results.

RUSSMAN, Thomas A. "A Faith of True Proportions: Reply to Sullivan" in *Thomistic Papers, V*, RUSSMAN, Thomas A (ed), 81-90. Notre Dame, Univ Notre Dame Pr, 1990.

Dr Thomas Sullivan has argued that religious claims to certainty cannot be adequately grounded in any evidence, but must instead by grounded in a perceived moral obligation: the religious believer finds himself/herself morally obliged to accept various propositions with certainty, because such acceptance is necessary to achieve an obligatory end, i.e., happiness in Heaven. I argue that such self-induced certainty, by someone who at the same time knows that the evidence is insufficient for certainty, is psychologically incoherent and presupposes an odd view of God (a God who would oblige such a thing).

RUSSMAN, Thomas A (ed). *Thomistic Papers, V*. Notre Dame, Univ Notre Dame Pr, 1990.

A collection of six articles bearing upon the relationship between philosophical methodology and various kinds of religious questions. John Knasas asks whether Etienne Gilson theologized Thomistic metaphysics. Armand Maurer discusses Gilson's use of the history of philosophy as a series of experiments concerning the viability of various philosophical positions. Leonard Kennedy explores the historical impact of the strong notion of divine absolute power upon the methods and conclusions of both philosophy and theology. Thomas Sullivan and Thomas Russman debate the roles of evidence and choice in the progress toward certitude concerning religious propositions.

RUSSOW, Lilly-Marlene. "NIH Guidelines and Animal Welfare" in *Biomedical Ethics Reviews, 1990*, HUMBER, James M (ed), 229-252. Clifton, Humana Pr, 1991.

I argue that a full assessment of NIH Guidelines must address two questions: How well do the guidelines handle theoretical issues, and how effective are they at moving accepted scientific practice closer to a morally acceptable situation. I argue that while (especially when viewed as an evolving practice) they do surprisingly well at the second task, there are important gaps on the practical level that cannot be solved without closer and more rigorous examination of the theoretical assumptions.

RUSTERHOLTZ, Wallace P. Humanist Religion for the Troubled. Relig Hum, 25(2), 83-89, Spr 91.

RUTHERFORD, Donald P. Phenomenalism and the Reality of Body in Leibniz's Later Philosophy. Stud Leibniz, 22(1), 11-28, 1990.

I argue that phenomenalist interpretations of Leibniz's view of body should be rejected on the grounds of the strong textual evidence supporting Leibniz's commitment to the thesis that bodies are aggregates of monads. In addition, however, I reject the most common understanding of the aggregate thesis itself: that certain pluralities of monads merely give the illusion of being bodies when "misperceived" by other monads. I argue instead that the aggregate thesis must be understood as a claim about the nature or essence of body; in Leibniz's view, any body *is*, in terms of its essence, some plurality of monads.

RUTHERFORD, Donald. Leibniz's "Analysis of Multitude and Phenomena into Unities and Reality". J Hist Phil, 28(4), 525-552, O 90.

The paper examines Leibniz's thesis that monads are "in" bodies and the related claim that matter is to be conceived as an "aggregate" of monads. Based on an account of Leibniz's technical notion of "being in" (*inesse*), it is shown that his thesis turns on an a priori analysis of the nature or essence of body. To say that monads are "in" a body is just to say that necessarily if anything is a body, then its existence presupposes the existence of monads. From this follow important consequences for Leibniz's general view of the reality of matter.

RYAN, Alan. "Sense and Sensibility in Mill's Political Thought" in *A Cultivated Mind: Essays On J S Mill Presented to John M Robson*, LAINE, Michael (ed), 121-138. Buffalo, Univ of Toronto Pr, 1991.

The essay argues that Mill's *Autobiography* is of philosophical interest as a "self-subverting" text; Mill offers it as an account of his education but also implies that he never stopped being educated by Harriet Taylor. It goes on to explore this ambiguity as it appears in *Liberty* and *The Subjection of Women*.

RYBAKOV, V V. Logical Equations and Admissible Rules of Inference with Parameters in Modal Provability Logics. Stud Log, 49(2), 215-239, Je 90.

This paper concerns modal logics of provability—Gdel-Lb system *GL* and Solovay logic *S*—the smallest and the greatest representation of arithmetical theories in propositional logic respectively. We prove that the decision problem for admissibility of rules (with or without parameters) in *GL* and *S* is decidable. Then we get a positive solution to Friedman's problem for *GL* and *S*. We also show that

A V Kuznetsov's problem of the existence of finite basis for admissible rules for *GL* and *S* has a negative solution. Afterwards we give an algorithm deciding the solvability of logical equations in *GL* and *S* and constructing some solutions.

RYBAKOV, V V. "Problems of Admissibility and Substitution, Logical Equations and Restricted Theories of Free Algebras" in *Logic, Methodology and Philosophy of Science, VIII*, FENSTAD, J E (ed), 121-139. New York, Elsevier Science, 1989.

RYBAKOV, V V. Problems of Substitution and Admissibility in the Modal System Grz and in Intuitionistic Propositional Calculus. Annals Pure Applied Log, 50(1), 71-106, N 90.

Questions connected with the admissibility of rules of inference and the solvability of the substitution problem for modal and intuitionistic logic are considered in an algebraic framework. The main result is the decidability of the universal theory of the free modal algebra F_ω(Grz) extended in signature by adding constants for free generators. As corollaries we obtain: (a) there exists an algorithm for the recognition of admissibility of rules with parameters (hence also without them) in the modal system Grz, (b) the substitution problem for Grz and for the intuitionistic calculus *H* is decidable, (c) intuitionistic propositional calculus *H* is decidable with respect to admissibility (a positive solution of Friedman's problem). A semantical criterion for the admissibility of rules of inference in Grz is given.

RYCHLAK, Joseph F. Some Theoretical and Methodological Questions Concerning Harcum's Proposed Resolution of the Free Will Issue. J Mind Behav, 12(1), 135-150, Wint 91.

Questions of both a theoretical and methodological nature are raised concerning Harcum's interesting paper on the resolution of the free will issue. The theoretical questions deal with the meaning of "free" as the supposed capricious disregard of environmental circumstances, the theoretical perspective from which agency is construed, the sort of causation that is involved, the choice of a prediction model rather than a mediation model, and the role of opposition in framing alternatives. Methodological questions raised center on the role of the experimental instruction, manipulation of the independent variable, and the reliance on randomness or error variance in the validation of free will conceptions. It is concluded that Harcum's findings are consistent with human agency, but that his theoretical account requires some rethinking.

RYCKMAN, Thomas. *Conditio sine qua non? Zuordnung* in the Early Epistemologies of Cassirer and Schlick. Synthese, 88(1), 57-95, Jl 91.

In early major works, Cassirer and Schlick differently recast traditional doctrines of the concept and of the relation of concept to intuitive content along the lines of recent epistemological discussions within the exact sciences. In this, they attempted to refashion epistemology by incorporating as its basic principle the notion of functional coordination, the theoretical sciences' own methodological tool for dispensing with the imprecise and unreliable guide of intuitive evidence. Examining their respective reconstructions of the theory of knowledge provides an axis of comparison along which to locate Cassirer's Neo-Kantianism and Schlick's pre-positivist empiricism, and an immediate background of contrast to the subsequent rise of logical empiricism.

RYDER, Richard D. Souls and Sentientism. Between Species, 7(1), 1-5, Wint 91.

SAAB, Salma. La creencia y su conexión con los actos linguísticos. Dianoia, 35(35), 175-186, 1989.

It is claimed that Wittgenstein regards the relation between beliefs and actions as internal, considers that in "I believe that *p*" predominates the "expressive" use and that in this use it is equivalent to asserting *p*. These claims would make Moore's Paradox ("I believe that *p* but *p* is false") absurd rather than contradictory. Linville considers that if the Moore example is absurd, then the first conjunct must refer to the person, while we hold that for Wittgenstein it would be contradictory. We also differ from Rosenthal's interpretation whereby he connects the expressive - descriptive distinction with the assertability and truth conditions distinction.

SAARI, Heikki. Some Aspects of R G Collingwood's Doctrine of Absolute Presuppositions. Int Stud Phil, 23(1), 61-73, 1991.

In this paper I argue that Collingwood is right in maintaining that there are what he calls "absolute presuppositions" that we cannot question as long as we are committed to them: we have to presuppose them in testing and justifying ordinary empirical propositions. I demonstrate that absolute presuppositions may be true or false in the same sense in which metaphysical propositions may be true or false. However, Collingwood does not give us sufficiently distinctive criteria by which to distinguish absolute presuppositions from relative ones. I conclude that this crucial defect considerably diminishes the plausibility of his doctrine.

SABIN, James E and DANIELS, Norman. When Is Home Care Medically Necessary? Commentary. Hastings Center Rep, 21(4), 37-38, Jl-Ag 91.

SABOUK, Sava. The Substance of Aesthetic Education in the School (in Czechoslovakian). Estetika, 27(4), 248-250, 1990.

SABRE, Ru Michael. An Alternative Logical Framework for Dialectical Reasoning in the Social and Policy Sciences. Theor Decis, 30(3), 187-211, My 91.

This article provides a concise logical, and as a consequence conceptual, critique of dialectical reasoning and its place in planning and policy in the work of Richard O. Mason and Ian I. Mitroff. Based on this critique, a construct called Strategic Forum is presented as an advance of the use of dialectical reasoning in the social and policy sciences. The place of Strategic Forum within group decision support systems is discussed.

SACCHI, Dario. Divenire, principio di causalità, affermazione teologica. Riv Filosof Neo-Scolas, 81(4), 614-634, O-D 89.

SACCHI, Mario E. Los fundamentos de la especulación metafísica sobre el conocimiento. Sapientia, 46(179), 13-34, Ja-Mr 91.

SACHS, David. A Philosophical Resistance to Freud. Dialectica, 44(1-2), 203-214, 1990.

SACHS, Mendel. On the Origin of Spin in Relativity. Brit J Phil Sci, 40(3), 409-412, S 89.

The purpose of this note is to show how the concept of 'spin' in relativistic quantum mechanics, as expressed in terms of 'spinor variables', originated in the underlying symmetry of relativity theory, rather than in the quantum theory itself. The implication is that any theory of a physical system, from elementary particle physics to cosmology, that would be compatible with the symmetry requirement of the theory of relativity, must use spinor variables in its most primitive expression.

SACHWANOWICZ, Wojciech. A Note on Complete Partitions in Boolean Algebras. Z Math Log, 36(3), 229-232, 1990.

SACKS, Mark. "Through a Glass Darkly: Vagueness in the Metaphysics of the Analytic Tradition" in *The Analytic Tradition: Philosophical Quarterly Monographs, Volume 1*, BELL, David (ed), 173-196. Cambridge, Blackwell, 1990.

Two presuppositions of the Analytic tradition are identified: i) that there is a tenable dichotomy between language and the world, such that it makes sense to think of the one as a description of the other, and ii) that some such language can in principle be rendered as determinate as the world that is to be described. The centrality of these tenets is outlined, and it is argued that, in fact, results internal to that tradition suffice to undermine the assumption that these two presuppositions are jointly viable. The discussion draws on work by Wittgenstein, Quine and Goodman in particular.

SACKSTEDER, William. Hobbes' Science of Human Nature. Hobbes Stud, 3, 35-53, 1990.

Among Hobbes's doctrines concerning human nature, those regarded as scientific in his strict but minimal sense conform to prior sciences, though they are not deducible from them. Studies of mankind add peculiar material principles to formal preconditions stated elsewhere. Shared with all animal beings are competence to originate activity in sensing, endeavor, and voluntary activity. In addition, human beings proclaim against others they suppose like in kind, for which claims they ask general recognition or even moral reciprocation. Origination of one's own activity is principle to human nature, as further civil science presupposes authorizing another to speak for one's self.

SACKSTEDER, William. Least Parts and Greatest Wholes Variations on a Theme in Spinoza. Int Stud Phil, 23(1), 75-87, 1991.

Spinoza's effective definitions of part and whole are odd and obscurely placed among his writings. Yet all segments of his thought seem entangled with them and with two questions, whether least parts may be found and whether some greatest whole is controlling principle. It is argued here that for him parts are increasingly complex and least ones are inconceivable; and that a whole which can also be a principle must be simple and must never be taken as organic, composite or additive. This disposition among these notions is sketched for each of various portions of his systematic philosophy.

SADURSKI, Wojciech. *Moral Pluralism and Legal Neutrality*. Norwell, Kluwer, 1990.

How should law, in contemporary societies, respond to moral pluralism and the diversity of ethical beliefs among the members of these societies? On the one hand, law inevitably does enforce some moral values; on the other hand, there exists no moral consensus in liberal-democratic societies. This book addresses the issue in two parts. First, it describes the dimensions of the problem, and criticizes some of the currently influential legal and philosophical responses. Second, and more importantly, it outlines and defends a remedy which consists in the adoption of law's neutrality toward the competing conceptions of the good.

SAGASTUME, M and GALLI, A. Kernels in N-Normal Symmetric Heyting Algebras. J Non-Classical Log, 6(2), 5-17, N 89.

By adding a negation (satisfying double negation law) and contraposition rule to the Hilbert-Bernays positive propositional calculus, Moisil established the modal symmetric calculus. A symmetric Heyting algebra is the Lindembaum algebra of this calculus. A o-normal algebra is a symmetric Heyting algebra such that each x is greater or equal to v(x) (v(x) negation followed by pseudocomplement applied to x). We call n-normal algebra a symmetric Heyting algebra such that for each x, n+1 applications of v to x is greater or equal to n applications of v to x. We characterize simple and subdirectly irreducible n-normal algebras under certain conditions.

SAGASTUME, Marta and GALLI, Adriana C. N-Normal Factors in Finite Symmetric Heyting Algebras. J Non-Classical Log, 7(1-2), 43-50, My-N 90.

In a previous paper we defined n-normal algebras as a subvariety of the variety of symmetric Heyting algebras. We proved that every finite symmetric Heyting algebra is n-normal for some *n* greater than or less than 0 or it contains a "cyclic" element. In this communication we characterize the n-formal finite algebras by the property that every boolean element is strongly boolean. This characterization enables us to obtain a decomposition of a finite symmetric Heyting algebra as a product of two algebras: one n-normal and the other one cyclic without normal factors.

SAGATOVSKII, V N. Dialogue or Mutual Accusations? Soviet Stud Phil, 29(3), 62-68, Wint 90-91.

The purpose of the article is to make a transition from mutual accusations to a dialogue in argument about the destiny of socialism. The author enters into a dispute with participants of the discussion: A Butenko and A Tsipko. A Butenko does not accuse Marx of not having an answer about a substitution of private interest and private property as a stimulus and an organizational principle of production. A Tsipko justly criticizes Marxism but he does not see how we can oppose totalitarism except to return to standards of an industrial civilization. We need a third way to come to a developed harmony between the liberty of individuality and a unity with a whole of a culture and nature instead of an antinomy. (edited)

SAHA, Sukharanjan. Gangesa and Transfer of Meaning. J Indian Counc Phil Res, 7(1), 57-98, S-D 89.

In this paper Sukharanjan Saha first discusses the views about metaphors held by Panini, Patanjali, Gautama and Vatsyayana. They hold that metaphors involve transfer of meaning. He then explains Gangesa's proposal for extension of the hypothesis of transfer of meaning for solving some tricky problems regarding the meanings of (i) conjugational inflections, (ii) compound words and (iii) self-referring expressions. Saha, however, differs from Gangesa and offers alternative solutions to such problems. He ends with a Davidson-like thesis that metaphorical sentences are to be understood in their literal meaning as false.

SAHA, Sukharanjan. In Search of a Theory of Truth in Nyāya. J Indian Counc Phil Res, 5(3), 19-34, My-Ag 88.

In contemporary Western philosophy knowledge has been analysed in terms of the independent concepts of belief, justification and truth and theories of justification (of the test of truth) and of truth (of the nature of truth) have been separately developed. Analogues of these have been shown in Nyaya by treating *pramlOa* as equivalent to knowledge, *pramlOana* to justification and *pramlOatva* to truth. After comparing certain traditional counterexamples to Gettier-like cases, Nyaya theory of justification has been shown to be only a variety of coherentism and Gangesa's definition of *pramlOatva* has been interpreted as offering a most general definition of truth.

SAHA, Sukharanjan. Thought and Language. J Indian Counc Phil Res, 8(1), 17-56, S-D 90.

SAHU, Neelamani. On 'This is Red and This is Blue': *Tractatus* 6.3751. J Indian Counc Phil Res, 6(1), 1-19, S-D 88.

SAINATI, Vittorio. La teoria aristotelica dell'apodissi. Teoria, 10(2), 3-47, 1990.

SAINSBURY, Mark. Is There Higher-Order Vagueness? Phil Quart, 41(163), 167-182, Ap 91.

I argue against a standard conception of classification, according to which concepts classify by drawing boundaries. This conception cannot properly account for "higher-order vagueness." I discuss in detail claims by Crispin Wright about "definitely," and its connection with higher-order vagueness. Contrary to Wright, I argue that the line between definite cases of *red* and borderline ones is not sharp. I suggest a new conception of classification: many concepts classify without drawing boundaries; they are *boundaryless*. Within this picture, there are no orders of vagueness, though the phenomena which suggest the description "higher-order vagueness" are real enough.

SAINSBURY, Mark. *Logical Forms: An Introduction to Philosophical Logic*. Cambridge, Blackwell, 1991.

This book sets out both to explain the detailed problems involved in finding the logical form of natural language sentences, and also the theoretical underpinnings of the project of formalization. The formalizing languages are those of propositional and predicate logic, with an indication of some variants (e.g., binary quantifiers, substitutional quantifiers, free logic), and a chapter devoted to the formalization of modal notions. The book is designed as a student text, and contains 168 exercises. It could be used either on its own in a second year course, or as an adjunct to an elementary formal logic course.

SAINT SERNIN, Bertrand. Les représentations de l'action. Bull Soc Fr Phil, 85(2), 5-78, Ap-Je 91.

SAINT-RAYMOND, Jean and LOUVEAU, Alain. On the Quasi-Ordering of Borel Linear Orders Under Embeddability. J Sym Log, 55(2), 537-560, Je 90.

We provide partial answers to the following problem: Is the class of Borel linear orders well-quasi-ordered under embeddability? We show that it is indeed the case for those Borel orders which are embeddable in R^{ω}, with the lexicographic ordering. For Borel orders embeddable in R^2, our proof works in ZFC, but it uses projective determinacy for Borel orders embeddable in some R^n, $n < \omega$, and hyperprojective determinacy for the general case.

SAISON, Maryvonne. "La 'présence' de l'acteur au théâtre" in *XIth International Congress in Aesthetics, Nottingham 1988*, WOODFIELD, Richard (ed), 165-167. Nottingham, Nottingham Polytech, 1990.

SAITTA, Dean J. "Dialectics, Critical Inquiry, and Archaeology" in *Critical Traditions in Contemporary Archaeology*, PINSKY, Valerie (ed), 38-43. New York, Cambridge Univ Pr, 1990.

This article discusses the organizing principles and practical implications of a Marxian theory of knowledge. It outlines the basic epistemological principles of Marxian science, and discusses what these come to in an archaeological context. The article also counterposes the Marxian approach with other post-empiricist philosophies emerging in archaeology. It aims to stimulate further discussion, clarification, and enrichment of a Marxian approach, and throw into sharper relief its differences with non-Marxian modes of thought.

SAKAI, Akio. Psychoactive Drug Prescribing in Japan: Epistemological and Bioethical Considerations. J Med Phil, 16(2), 139-153, Ap 91.

Today in Japan psychoactive drugs are widely prescribed for various psychiatric disorders including so-called 'functional' disorders. They are undoubtedly effective in relieving various psychological and behavioral symptoms. However, Japan has yet to address some basic questions regarding this use. Though the increased risk of the inappropriate use of these drugs - the non-therapeutic uses, and their over-prescription - has been indicated in other industrialized countries, it has not yet been fully recognized and adequately discussed in Japan. (edited)

SALA, J F A. Conocimiento metodico y no metodico; so pretexto de una incursion acerca de la dialectica segun platon. Rev Filosof (Mexico), 23(68), 220-229, My-Ag 90.

SALAMUN, Kurt (ed). *Moral und Politik aus der Sicht des Kritischen Rationalismus*. Amsterdam, Rodopi, 1991.

This book presents a collection of articles concerning basic ethical implications and political theses of Karl R Popper's philosophy called "Critical Rationalism". Some topics which are analyzed by authors like Hans Albert, Volker Gadenne, Dariusz Aleksandrowicz, Lothar Schäfer, Fred Eidlin, Andreas Pickel, Joshihisa Hagiwara, Gerard Radnitzky are: Popper's conception of freedom, his ethos of enlightenment, the concept of an open society, of democracy, of sovereignty, Popper's and Friedrich V Hayek's conception of liberalism, etc.

SALANSKIS, Jean-Michel. Die Wissenschaft denkt nicht. Rev Metaph Morale, 96(2), 207-231, Ap-Je 91.

This article purports to examine Heidegger's phrase with due seriousness, and in the final analysis, to refute it. First of all, the phrase is considered in relation to the well-known Heideggerian oppositions of fundamental versus regional ontology and of metaphysics versus thought. The conclusion is that these opposition provide no justification for the virulence of Heidegger's formulation. We, therefore, proceed to a close examination of Heidegger's conception of hermeneutics (referring both to *Sein und Zeit* and to later writings). We show that as soon as Heidegger rejects the possibility of a *formal hermeneutics* science is *a priori* excluded from his positive standard of thought. In fact, the exclusion of science stands from a more global rejection of any *literal* mode of hermeneutics; in our view this rejection provides a key to an understanding of Heidegger's historical connection with Nazism.

SALAZAR, Christine (trans) and VON ENGELHARDT, Dietrich. "Historical Consciousness in the German Romantic *Naturforschung*" in *Romanticism and the Sciences*, CUNNINGHAM, Andrew (ed), 55-68. New York, Cambridge Univ Pr, 1990.

SALKEVER, Stephen G. "'Lopp'd and Bound': How Liberal Theory Obscures the Goods of Liberal Practices" in *Liberalism and the Good*, DOUGLASS, R Bruce (ed), 167-202. New York, Routledge, 1990.

The essay aims to show that impersonalist liberal political theory, from Locke to Rawls, tends to obscure theoretical consideration of the liberal conceptions of the human good that are implicit—and hotly contested—in certain liberal practices. As examples, debates within the American practices of liberal education and constitutional law are considered. The way the good appears in these and similar practices is important, since it is within them that liberal democratic authority resides. Platonic and Aristotelian modes of theorizing are better equipped to understand this central aspect of liberalism than are liberal theories.

SALLIS, John. *Echoes: After Heidegger*. Bloomington, Indiana Univ Pr, 1990.

This book mobilizes the figure of echo, used by Heidegger to characterize originary thinking, as the motif around which to organize a radical reading of Heidegger's most important texts. It focuses on the shifts and turns that come into play at the limit of Heidegger's work and that effectively transform the Heideggerian project. Among the themes are the determination of thinking at the end of philosophy; originary; ecstatic time; the sense of the sensible; the involvement of imagination in the question of Being; death as radical alterity; the sacrifice of understanding in thinking the political; the reconstitution of mimesis; the translation of ecstasy.

SALLIS, John. Nature' Song. Rev Int Phil, 45(176), 3-9, 1991.

This paper is an analysis of Kant's discussion of the songs of birds in the *Critique of Judgment*, section 42.

SALLIS, John. Response: "The Rooting and Uprooting of Reason: On *Spacings* by John Sallis". Phil Today, 35(2), 209-211, Sum 91.

SALMAN, Charles. The Wisdom of Plato's Aristophanes. Interpretation, 18(2), 233-250, Wint 90-91.

SALMERÓN, Fernando. Introducción a la filosofía de Gaos. Dianoia, 36(36), 1-16, 1990.

Written as a prologue to José Gaos's book, *Del Hombre*, (part of *Obras Completas*), this essay explains the structure of this book and of *De la Filosofía* in order to show that together they compound an elaborate system based on the phenomenological method, taking a philosophy of language as the point of departure. The system deals with the categories of ontology and traditional metaphysics, the nature of the subject and its rationality, and concludes with a discussion of practical reason and an explanation of philosophy by means of the moral constitution of man. The study identifies Gaos's sources and the stages of his philosophical development.

SALMON, J Warren and WHITE, William and FEINGLASS, Joe. The Futures of Physicians: Agency and Autonomy Reconsidered. Theor Med, 11(4), 261-274, D 90.

The corporatization of US health care has directed cost containment efforts toward scrutinizing the clinical decisions of physicians. This stimulated a variety of new utilization management interventions, particularly in hospital and managed care settings. Recent changes in fee-for-service medicine and physicians' traditional agency relationships with patients, purchasers, and insurers are examined here. New information systems monitoring of physician ordering behavior has already begun to impact on physician autonomy and the relationship of physicians to provider organizations in both for-profit and 'not-for-profit' sectors. As managed care practice settings proliferate, serious ethical questions will be raised about agency relationships with patients. This article examines health system dynamics altering the historical agency relationship between the physician and patient and eroding the traditional autonomy of the medical profession in the United States. The corporatization of medicine and the accompanying information systems monitoring of physician productivity is seen to account of such change, now posing serious ethical dilemmas.

SALMON, Merrilee H. "Efficient Explanations and Efficient Behaviour" in *Critical Traditions in Contemporary Archaeology*, PINSKY, Valerie (ed), 10-13. New York, Cambridge Univ Pr, 1990.

This paper exposes some ambiguity in the concept of efficiency as it is used by archaeologists in evaluating explanations of human behavior. The maxim that, *ceteris paribus*, simpler (more efficient) *explanations* are to be preferred to complex explanations of the same phenomena is confused with an injunction to prefer explanations in which the *behavior* attributed to humans in a given context is most efficient with respect to some particular goal, usually the acquisition of energy. I argue that it is reasonable for archaeologists to formulate testable hypotheses concerning specific types of efficient behavior, but that no "principle of efficiency" provides a definitive answer to questions about what sort of behavior is responsible for material residues.

SALMON, Merrilee H. On the Possibility of Lawful Explanation in Archaeology. Critica, 22(66), 87-114, D 90.

Recognizing the fundamental importance of functional ascription in archaeology, this paper addresses three questions: 1) Has the presence of an item in the archaeological record been *explained* when its function is identified? 2) If so, are such explanations dependent on laws? 3) If the answer to the second question is positive, what can we say about the laws? These issues are examined in the context of the philosophical perspective adopted by the so-called new archaeology, which relies strongly on Hempel's models of confirmation and explanation, and also the contrasting "contextual" perspective of post-processual archaeology.

SALMON, Nathan. How *Not* to Become a Millian Heir. Phil Stud, 62(2), 165-177, My 91.

The author rebuts critics who argue within the framework of Millianism that "Hesperus is Phosphorus" is a posteriori. One critic's argument is based on a confusion between a piece of discourse and its subject matter. Another's is based instead on a misunderstanding of the distinction between a priori and a posteriori knowledge. The notion of apriority does not demarcate a kind of knowledge automatically attained once certain conditions are fulfilled, but characterizes a kind of knowledge in terms of necessary conditions. A pair of relativized notions that are more discriminating than the traditional notions of apriority and aposteriority are proposed.

SALMON, Nathan. "Illogical Belief" in *Philosophical Perspectives, 3: Philosophy of Mind and Action Theory, 1989*, TOMBERLIN, James E (ed), 243-285. Atascadero, Ridgeview, 1989.

The theory of content developed in the author's *Frege's Puzzle* is defended against related objections made by Saul Kripke and by Stephen Schiffer. It is shown how in special cases, a rational and reflective believer may be in no position to infer trivial logical consequences of his beliefs (that Clark Kent is not Superman, that London is not Londres, etc.). Ramifications are explored for both the de-dicto and the de-re modes, and for iterated contexts. It is shown furthermore that the author's Gricean strategy does not require that speakers recognize the literal truth of withheld propositional-attitude attributions.

SALMON, Nathan. The Pragmatic Fallacy. Phil Stud, 63(1), 83-97, Jl 91.

It is argued that language theorists have reached erroneous conclusions by citing what are essentially pragmatic phenomena (e.g., speaker assertion) as evidence for what are essentially semantic conclusions (semantic content). The Pragmatic Fallacy is illustrated by responding to arguments favoring the thesis that Donnellan's referential-attributive distinction has semantic significance. It is argued that a modal variant of the most controversial aspect of Donnellan's account—the idea that a referential use of a definite description "the such-and-such" may semantically refer to someone or something that is not a such-and-such—rufutes the thesis of semantic significance.

SALMON, Nathan. "Tense and Singular Propositions" in *Themes From Kaplan*, ALMOG, Joseph (ed), 331-392. New York, Oxford Univ Pr, 1989.

"The Doubly Modified Naive Theory" of temporal operators is proposed. Content is doubly indexed to times as well as to contexts, thereby accommodating the eternalness of information. Evidence for this theory refutes both Frege's rival theory and Kaplan's. Double indexing yields a heretofore unrecognized semantic value, "content base," which is noneternal and the proper object of temporal operators. Kaplan's three-tiered semantic structure is replaced with a four-tiered one. A new definition of indexicality is given. It is argued that the content of a predicate is a temporally indexed attribute or concept. A theory of pure tenses is offered.

SALMON, Wesley C. Causal Propensities: Statistical Causality versus Aleatory Causality. Topoi, 9(2), 95-100, S 90.

SALMON, Wesley C. "Rationality and Objectivity in Science, *or* Tom Kuhn Meets Tom Bayes" in *Scientific Theories*, SAVAGE, C Wade (ed), 175-204. Minneapolis, Univ of Minn Pr, 1990.

SALMON, Wesley C. Scientific Explanation: Causation *and* Unification. Critica, 22(66), 3-24, D 90.

SALMON, Wesley. Philosophy and the Rise of Modern Science. Teach Phil, 13(3), 233-239, S 90.

SAMONÀ, Leonardo. L' "altro inizio" della filosofia: I *Beiträge zur Philosophie* di Heidegger. G Metaf, 12(1), 67-111, Ja-Ap 90.

SANABRIA, José Rubén. Metafisica todavia? (conclusión). Rev Filosof (Mexico), 23(68), 243-260, My-Ag 90.

En la conclusión de *Metafísica todavía?* se mencionan los recientes intentos de fundar una metafísica "científica" en oposición a la metafísica tradicional. Sin embargo, estos intentos no satisfacen las exigencias de la inteligencia humana. Por eso planteo un intento de metafísica reflexiva que tiene inicio en la experiencia personal. La metafísica tradicional es abstracta y vacía; nuestro mundo quiere una metafísica existencial que proporcione al filósofo un fundamento de su existencia y de los entes circundantes.

SANCHEZ, Karen L. The 'Teacher as Midwife': New Wine in Old Skins? Phil Stud Educ, /, 72-82, 1989.

SÁNCHEZ, Manuel Esteban. Todos contra la Sociobiología. El Basilisco, 4, 89-90, Mr-Ap 90.

The purpose of this brief article is to satirize the negative opinion that some learned and intellectual people (most of them Spanish) have about Sociobiology as applied to human being. The main question is "Why is there such resistance to extend evolution to the last consequences in a coherent way following the sociobiological interpretation of it?" This question summarizes the philosophical, scientific and ethical reasons dealt with in my doctoral thesis "Sociobiology and Human Nature" and applied in my book *Implications of Sociobiology for Human Sciences*.

SANCHEZ, Pedro and KARNI, Reuven and TUMMALA, V M Rao. A Comparative Study of Multiattribute Decision Making Methodologies. Theor Decis, 29(3), 203-222, N 90.

Three "real life" cases are considered in this paper to apply and compare the ranking obtained by the Analytic Hierarchy Process (AHP) and other Multicriteria Decision Making (MCDM) techniques such as Simple Additive Weighting (SAW), ELECTRE and Weighted Linear Assignment Method (WLAM). The results indicated that the AHP, SAW, and ELECTRE rankings do not differ significantly, however, the WLAM tends to exhibit more disagreement. However, because of the limited nature of this study, we do not suggest this as a general conclusion.

SANCHEZ-GONZALEZ, Miguel A. Medicine in John Locke's Philosophy. J Med Phil, 15(6), 675-695, D 90.

John Locke's philosophy was deeply affected by medicine of his times. It was specially influenced by the medical thought and practice of Thomas Sydenham. Locke was a personal friend of Sydenham, expressed an avid interest in his work and shared his views and methods. The influence of Sydenham's medicine can be seen in the following areas of Locke's philosophy: his "plain historical method"; the emphasis on observation and sensory experience instead of seeking the essence of things; the rejection of hypotheses and principles; the refusal of research into final causes and inner mechanisms; the ideal of irrefutable evidence and skepticism on the possibilities of certainty in science. The science which for Locke held the highest paradigmatic value in his theory of knowledge was precisely medicine. To a great extent, Locke's *Essay on Human Understanding* can be understood as an attempt to justify, substantiate, and promote Sydenham's medical method. This method, generalized, was then proposed as an instrument for the elaboration of all natural sciences.

SANCHEZ-PUENTES, Ricardo. Educational Research in Mexico. Proc Phil Educ, 46, 51-61, 1990.

SANCIPRIANO, Mario. Pensiero e trascendenza. Aquinas, 33(3), 669-673, S-D 90.

SANDELANDS, Lloyd E. What is so Practical about Theory? Lewin Revisited. J Theor Soc Behav, 20(3), 235-262, S 90.

This article finds that Kurt Lewin's famous epigram that there is nothing so practical as a good theory admits no simple interpretation, and certainly not the literal one too often given or implied, i.e., that theory can be applied to practice and used to guide it. Theory and practice are logically incommensurable and therefore not intertranslatable. However, practice can develop differently in the presence of a theory, such as when a theory calls attention to particular actions and thereby leads a person to emphasize or avoid them in practice. And theory can supply the confidence needed to act, and through action practice can be refined. Thus, even if literally untrue, Lewin's epigram nevertheless can create conditions in which it will be seen as true.

SANDERMANN, Edmund. *Die Moral der Vernunft Tanszendentale Handlungs-und Legitimationstheorie in der Philosophie Kants*. Freiburg, Alber, 1991.

It is not just since the work of Rorty that Kant's writings have been chiefly as a philosophy of mind which conceived the mind as a reflector of reality and centers on the theory of consciousness. This viewpoint fails to perceive that the critical philosophy of reason is paradigmatically oriented to the idea of the capacities of knowledge, insights and norms for being communicated and passed on. The paradigm of one's communicative commitment of oneself in the course of contradiction-free argumentation functions in this book as the basis for a transcendental deduction of "experience" and "freedom", as well as the basis for a transcendental theory of grounding of norms. Using a genetic reconstruction of Kant's theory of law, this transcendental legitimating conception is here outlined.

SANDERS, James and MC PECK, John. Teaching Johnny to Think. Proc Phil Educ, 46, 403-409, 1990.

SANDKÜHLER, Hans Jörg. Critical Marxism as an Historical Process of Society and Science (in German). Deut Z Phil, 38(6), 560-574, 1990.

SANDKÜHLER, Hans Jörg. Ka-Meh und das alte Neue—über epistemische Krise und Emanzipation. Deut Z Phil, 39(2), 113-123, 1991.

SANDKÜHLER, Hans Jörg. Wissen und Emanzipation. Deut Z Phil, 39(3), 327-331, 1991.

SANDOE, Peter. Amoralism—On the Limits of Moral Thinking. Theoria, 55(3), 191-204, 1989.

SANDOZ, Ellis (ed) and VOEGELIN, Eric. *Published Essays, 1966-1985 (The Collected Works of Eric Voegelin, Volume 12)*. Baton Rouge, Louisiana St Univ Pr, 1990.

SANDU, Gabriel and HINTIKKA, Jaakko. "Informational Independence as a Semantical Phenomenon" in *Logic, Methodology and Philosophy of Science, VIII*, FENSTAD, J E (ed), 571-589. New York, Elsevier Science, 1989.

Insofar as a formal or natural language can be treated game-theoretically, the notion of informational independence (II), in the sense of game theory, applies to its different ingredients. A notation is proposed for II and the most salient facts about it are noted. Even though II is not indicated syntactically in English, it is the gist of such varied phenomena as the *de dicto* vs. *de re* distinction, complex questions, negation-raising, branching quantifiers, actuality operators, etc. It is therefore an extremely important component of the overall semantics of natural languages, both for philosophical and for linguistic purposes.

SANDU, Gabriel and HINTIKKA, Jaakko. Metaphor and the Varieties of Lexical Meaning. Dialectica, 44(1-2), 55-77, 1990.

The "meaning lines" connecting the references of an expression in different situations or scenarios ("worlds") are usually "drawn" with the help of both similarity and continuity. In metaphoric use, emphasis shifts predominantly on suitable similarity considerations; in metonymic use, it shifts on continuity considerations. Even though metaphoric meaning lines are nonstandard, they have to be "anchored" to a literal reference of the expression in some situation or world (not necessarily in the actual one). Hence metaphor is not a matter of truth or of a special kind of language act (use of sentences).

SANDU, Gabriel and KUOKKANEN, Martti. On Social Rights. Ratio Juris, 3(1), 89-94, Mr 90.

In this paper we analyze the concept of social right which denotes rights such as: right to adequate nutrition, right to an education, etc. This type of right has not been analyzed in the traditional theory, nor does it find a place in the Hohfeldean typology. Our main claim is that social rights are strong protective permissions. The notion of protected permission is analyzed with the help of two other notions: absence of prohibition and forbearance of interference.

SANFORD, David H. The Inductive Support of Inductive Rules: Themes from Max Black. Dialectica, 44(1-2), 23-41, 1990.

Overall, Max Black's defense of the inductive support of inductive rules succeeds. Circularity is best explained in terms of epistemic conditions of inference. When an inference is circular, another inference token of the same type may, because of a difference of surrounding circumstances, not be circular. Black's inductive arguments in support of inductive rules fit this pattern: a token circular in some circumstances may be noncircular in other circumstances.

SANGUINETI, Juan J. Decir lo mismo (Frege y Santo Tomás). Sapientia, 45(175), 31-38, Ja-Mr 90.

The article studies the semantical problem of "saying the same thing" with the aid of some reflections about language in Frege and Aquinas. Particular emphasis is given to the contrast between the Fregean account on eternal truth (concerning temporal facts) and Saint Thomas's thesis that the truth of a temporal fact is a temporal truth. These divergent technical solutions rest upon two different ontologies.

SANKEY, Howard. Incommensurability and the Indeterminacy of Translation. Austl J Phil, 69(2), 219-223, Je 91.

In this paper it is argued that the concept of translation failure involved in Kuhn's thesis of incommensurability is distinct from that of translational indeterminacy in Quine's sense. At most, Kuhnian incommensurability constitutes a weak form of indeterminacy, quite distinct from Quine's. There remains, however, a convergence between the two views of translation, namely, that there is no single adequate translation between languages.

SANKEY, Howard. Translation Failure Between Theories. Stud Hist Phil Sci, 22(2), 223-236, Je 91.

The paper argues for translation failure between the vocabulary of some scientific theories. The semantic approach adopted is a causal theory of reference, modified to allow a role for descriptions in determining the reference of terms used by theories, and reference fixation subsequent to initial baptisms. It is argued that the reference of terms used by one theory may be unable to be determined in the same set of ways in another theory. They therefore fail to be translatable into the latter. The view allows for commonality of reference, so the resulting translation failure is consistent with comparison of the content of theories.

SANKOWSKI, Edward. Poetry and Autonomy. J Aes Educ, 25(2), 67-79, Sum 91.

SANKOWSKI, Edward. Two Forms of Moral Responsibility. Phil Topics, 18(1), 123-141, Spr 90.

SANTA CRUZ, María Isabel. División y dialéctica en el *Fedro*. Rev Latin De Filosof, 16(2), 149-164, Jl 90.

This paper considers the Platonic characterization of dialectic in the *Phaedrus*, in connection with the definition found at the *Sophist* 253b-254a and in the *Philebus*, and anticipated briefly in the *Republic* V. It is the intellectual skill which enables to discern *kat' eide*, i.e., precisely grasping similarities at the same time as differences. Collection and division are simultaneous and complementary operations. They allow to detect similarities and differences, which are the result of the interweaving of sameness and otherness, one and many, limited and unlimited.

SANTAMBROGIO, Marco. Meinongian Theories of Generality. Nous, 24(5), 647-673, D 90.

It is not widely appreciated that Meinong's non-existent objects are closely related with Twardowski's general objects and Locke's general abstract triangle. The latter is usually thought to be an incoherent notion. In order to disprove that, a formal semantics for such objects is outlined. The adequacy conditions it satisfies are discussed in detail. It is argued that general objects are needed, e.g., in order to account for such uses of definite descriptions as in 'The whale is a mammal'. The central section of the paper is devoted to discussing which notion of reference is appropriate for general objects.

SÂNTEAN, Lila and CALUDE, Cristian. On a Theorem of Günter Asser. Z Math Log, 36(2), 143-147, 1990.

Our purpose is to present two natural characterizations of the class of unary primitive-recursive string-functions (over a fixed alphabet) as Robinson algebras.

SANTILLI, Paul C. Socrates and Asclepius: The Final Words. Int Stud Phil, 22(3), 29-39, 1990.

Many commentators take Nietzsche's ironic comment that death is a cure for the ills of life to be the most plausible reading of Socrates' reference to a debt to Asclepius at the conclusion of the *Phaedo*. I offer an interpretation of this which challenges this view. In particular, I examine Plato's references to Asclepius in the *Republic*, which have generally been ignored by commentators, and set Socrates' final words in the context of these references and of the *Phaedo* as a whole. These words will be shown to be consistent with a view of philosophical discourse, prevalent in the Phaedo, as engaged in a context with other forms of discourse, a contest which improves and heals the soul.

SANTONI, Ronald E. The Nurture of War: "Just War" Theory's Contribution. Phil Today, 35(1), 82-92, Spr 91.

SANTORO, Liberato and CASALE, Giuseppe. Hegel, Croce, Gentile: On the Idea of the "Ethical State". Phil Stud (Ireland), 32, 113-125, 1988-90.

The essay outlines the central tenets of Hegel's conception of the "Ethical State" and rejects the naive interpretations of Hegel's philosophy as advocating a totalitarian State. The dispute between Gentile and Croce is, then, seen as resulting fundamentally from the respective reading of Hegel by the two Italian philosophers. Gentile is inclined to identify ethics and politics, while Croce sees ethics and politics as distinct. In the light of Hegel's philosophy, Gentile-logically more coherent-privileges the sphere of "Objective Spirit"; Croce-more pragmatic-favours individual freedom and hence, "Subjective Spirit."

SANTOS, José Trindade. "A noção de experiência nos diálogos platónicos" in *Dinâmica do Pensar: Homenagem a Oswaldo Market*, FAC LETRAS UNIV LISBOA (ed), 243-253. Lisboa, Fac Letras U Lisboa, 1991.

Though concept of 'experience' is not to be found in the platonic dialogues, the notion undergoes a development from which its future history will be dependent. In the elenctic works, within the opposition *epistêmê-doxa*, it points to the pretense knowledge of the sophists. In the hypothetical ones it stands for the interplay of the senses with the first step in *anamnêsis*. In the critical ones it follows either the elaboration of sense material, or the setting of objective paradigms establishing the possibility of true opinion. In all these it remains a key notion for the understanding of Plato's theory of knowledge.

SANTOS, M C A dos. The Heraclitus' Lesson (in Portuguese). Trans/Form/Acao, 13, 1-9, 1990.

Heraclitus is known in the history of thought, for his doctrine of universal mobilism. The enigmatic proposition "everything flows nothing remains unchanged" lies at the core of Western metaphysics: it inspired Plato's Theory of the Two Worlds—which puts forward a radical separation between that which moves and which doesn't—and also the platonic view of the last Dialogues, which includes motion among the attributes of being. In view of these influences and in order to understand well the genesis of Western philosophy, it seems to us that it would be important to reflect a bit more on the essence of Heraclitus' becoming.

SAPADIN, Eugene. Choosing Religious Languages: A Note on Two 'Proofs' of God's Existence. Dialogos, 26(58), 163-169, Jl 91.

SAPIRE, David. General Causation. Synthese, 86(3), 321-347, Mr 91.

This paper outlines a general theory of efficient causation, a theory that deals in a unified way with traditional or deterministic, indeterministic, probabilistic, and other causal concepts. Theorists like Lewis, Salmon, and Suppes have attempted to broaden our causal perspective by reductively analysing causal notions in other terms. By contrast, the present theory rests in the first place on a non-reductive analysis of traditional causal concepts—into formal or structural components, on the one hand, and a physical or metaphysical component, on the other. The analyzans is then generalised. The theory also affords a more general propensity notion than is standard, one that helps solve major problems facing propensity interpretations of probability.

SAPONTZIS, Steve F. "'Ought' Does Imply 'Can'". S J Phil, 29(3), 383-393, Fall 91.

SAPONTZIS, Steve F. Reply to Weir: Unnecessary Fear, Nutrition, and Vegetarianism. Between Species, 7(1), 27-32, Wint 91.

This paper defends arguments for vegetarianism based on moral injunctions against unnecessary pain against criticisms that 1) they equivocate about "vegetarian," "adequate for human nutrition," and "unnecessary for nutrition," 2) animals can be raised humanely and slaughtered mercifully, and 3) the *prima facie* obligation not to inflict pain is overridden by the nutritional risk of vegetarianism.

SARABIA, Jaime. Sobre tópicos y términos primitivos de la intensión. Rev Filosof (Spain), 4, 5-30, 1990.

SARAIVA, Maria Manuela. "Imaginação e imaginário: Para além de Husserl" in *Dinâmica do Pensar: Homenagem a Oswaldo Market*, FAC LETRAS UNIV LISBOA (ed), 255-265. Lisboa, Fac Letras U Lisboa, 1991.

On entreprend d'abord une révesion de la théorie husserlienne de l'imagination dans le but de montrer que l'imagination n'étant pas l'objet d'une étude systématique se trouve dans le cadre de l'analyse de l'intentionalité. Husserl y définit son status phénoménologique par les trois concepts d'intuition, de présentification et de neutralisation. Limitée toutefois au primat de l'intuition sensible et ne prenant pas compte de la conscience symbolique, la théorie husserlienne s'avère assez pauvre, en comparaison avec la méthode suivie par Gilbert Durand d'une recherche de l'imaginaire en tant que structure anthropologique des peuples.

SARAYDAR, Edward. Productivity and X-Efficiency: A Reply to Singh and Frantz. Econ Phil, 7(1), 91-92, Ap 91.

In a comment on my article "The Conflation of Productivity and Efficiency in Economics and Economic History," Harinder Singh and Roger Frantz have pointed out that in his work on X-Efficiency, Harvey Leibenstein does recognize that there is a difference between productivity and welfare. However, Leibenstein continually emphasizes terms like efficiency, maximization, and optimization. These terms, when applied to some of the comparative outcomes he explores, are meaningless or ludicrous unless the significant differences in environment within which the outcomes emerge are taken into account, and the cost of moving from a "less efficient" to a "more efficient" environment becomes part of the analysis.

SARBIN, Theodore R. Toward the Obsolescence of the Schizophrenia Hypothesis. J Mind Behav, 11(3-4), 259-283, Sum-Autumn 90.

The disease construction of schizophrenia is no longer tenable. That construction originated during a period of rapid growth of biological science based on mechanistic principles. Crude diagnostic measures failed to differentiate absurd, unwanted conduct due to biological conditions from atypical conduct directed to solving existential or identity problems. The patient came to be regarded as an object without agency or goals. In spite of enormous research funding, no biological or psychological marker has been discovered that would differentiate diagnosed schizophrenics from normals without creating unacceptable proportions of false positives and false negatives. The failure of eight decades of research to produce a reliable marker leads to the conclusion that schizophrenia is an obsolescent hypothesis and should be abandoned. (edited)

SARKAR, Sahotra. On the Possibility of Directed Mutations in Bacteria: Statistical Analyses and Reductionist Strategies. Proc Phil Sci Ass, 1, 111-124, 1990.

SARKER, Sunil Kumar. The Marxian Ethics. J Indian Counc Phil Res, 7(3), 59-66, My-Ag 90.

The Marxian ethics is rooted in economics and so it involves naturalistic fallacy. It is avowedly partisan, relativistic and 'revolutionary' and yet admits of some eternal moral ideals. Marx says that the societal linear historical-economic progression towards communism and moral advancement are positively correlated. This is wrong. Marx says that there will be no question of morality in the communist society. This is pure fantasy.

SARMA, Rajendra Nath. The Theory of Triple Perception. J Indian Counc Phil Res, 7(2), 145-147, Ja-Ap 90.

The theory of triple perception (Triputīpratyaksavāda) advocated by the Prābhākara School of Pūrvamimāmsā aims at giving a peculiar explanation of perception for which three factors, viz. Meya (the apprehended object), Mātā (the apprehending person), and Miti (the apprehension) are needed. These three factors (Triputī) are revealed in each and every apprehension or cognition. It may be concluded that in each act of perception (Pratyaksa), the idea of each of these factors enters as its constituent parts and so this theory is acceptable at all.

SAROT, Marcel. Auschwitz, Morality and the Suffering of God. Mod Theol, 7(2), 135-152, Ja 91.

In the present paper I comment on the use Christian theodicists make of the idea of a suffering God. I argue, especially, (1) that Elie Wiesel's story of God on the gallows cannot with integrity be interpreted as suggesting a suffering of God, not to speak of a *theologia crucis*; (2) that Christian theodicists should be reticent in using stories from Auschwitz to illustrate the horrors of (innocent and severe) suffering; and (3) that, even though the claim that theodicy requires a suffering God is true, this does not provide an independent argument in favor of the suffering of God.

SAROT, Marcel. Patripassianism, Theopaschitism and the Suffering of God. Relig Stud, 26(3), 363-375, S 90.

SARTORELLI, Joseph. McGinn on Concept Scepticism and Kripke's Sceptical Argument. Analysis, 51(2), 79-84, Mr 91.

In *Wittgenstein on Meaning*, Colin McGinn argues that the skeptical argument that Kripke distills from Wittgenstein's rule-following considerations generates at most what might be called meaning skepticism (the non-factuality view of meaning), and not concept skepticism (the non-factuality view of concepts). If correct, this would mean the skeptical reasoning is far less significant than Kripke thinks. Others have seemed to agree with McGinn. I argue that McGinn is wrong here—that, in fact, Kripke's skeptical reasoning has a straightforward extension to concepts. Whether the reasoning succeeds, however, is another matter, which I do not address here.

SARTRE, Jean-Paul and HOARE, Quintin (trans). *Critique of Dialectical Reason, Volume 2: Jean-Paul Sartre*. New York, Verso, 1990.

SARTWELL, Crispin. Doubt and Faith: Santayana and Kierkegaard on Fundamental Belief. Trans Peirce Soc, 27(2), 179-195, Spr 91.

This paper argues that Kierkegaard and Santayana converged on a critique of Cartesian epistemology and universal doubt, a critique based on the notion of faith. It further argues that this critique remains cogent.

SARTWELL, Crispin. Knowledge is Merely True Belief. Amer Phil Quart, 28(2), 157-165, Ap 91.

SARTWELL, Crispin. Natural Generativity and Imitation. Brit J Aes, 31(1), 58-67, Ja 91.

This paper provides an account of resemblance in terms of shared properties. It then describes imitation as the intentional construction of a situation in which one item comes to resemble another. Finally, it argues that it is a necessary condition of pictorial representation that the picture be an imitation of the object it represents. The paper makes use of Flint Schier's book *Deeper Into Pictures*.

SASAKI, Katsumi and HOSOI, Tsutomu. Finite Logics and the Simple Substitution Property. Bull Sect Log, 19(3), 74-78, O 90.

A notion called the simple substitution property is defined and it is proved that all the intermediate logics defined by finite models enjoy the property. The property is useful and important for the mechanical theorem prover because it provides a mechanical strategy about substituting the variables in the axioms.

SASAKI, Katsumi. The Simple Substitution Property of Gödel's Intermediate Propositional Logics S_n's. Stud Log, 49(4), 471-481, D 90.

A notion called the simple substitution property is defined. And we give the sets of axioms with the property for the logics S_n's defined by linear models. The property is useful and important for the mechanical theorem prover because it provides a mechanical strategy about substituting the variables in the axioms.

SASAKI, Kenichi. "Communication esthetique comme bonheur" in *XIth International Congress in Aesthetics, Nottingham 1988*, WOODFIELD, Richard (ed), 168-171. Nottingham, Nottingham Polytech, 1990.

I aim to reveal the base of aesthetic experience at 18th century. It was the period of transition from the objective poetics to the subjective aesthetics. People were interested in the felt qualities of a work of art; they underlined the subtle and indescribable aspects of art. The result was the aesthetics of illusion, not in a simple sense of realism. It permits us to enter physically into the "fictive" world in the art and to make communion with the people depicted there. And this experience of communion brought a happiness—new ethical ideal in this period. It's this happiness which constituted the real end of the illusionism.

SASS, Hans-Martin. "Professional Organizations and Professional Ethics: A European View" in *Ethics, Trust, and the Professions: Philosophical and Cultural Aspects*, PELLEGRINO, Edmund D (ed), 263-284. Washington, Georgetown Univ Pr, 1991.

Professional organizations play an important role in shaping the ethical dimensions of the professional—lay into—action. Codes of professional conduct have to address virtues and principles towards the individual client, society and the profession. The development of a communication-in-trust relationship is mandatory for the development of a moral covenant between clients and providers.

SASSEVILLE, Michel. Chapter One of *Harry Stottlemeier's Discovery*: An Integrative Crucible of Critical and Creative Thinking. Thinking, 9(2), 28-30, 1990.

SASSOWER, Raphael and OGAZ, Charla Phyllis. Philosophical Hierarchies and Lyotard's Dichotomies. Phil Today, 35(2), 153-160, Sum 91.

This essay illustrates through Lyotard's work that dichotomies may be unavoidable. However, the consequence of their use turns them into ordered hierarchies, regardless of the intentions of those using them. And hierarchies are to be avoided, because their establishment is never perceived as a mere heuristic; instead, they influence public behavior.

SAUTET, Marc. Ghost Story (in German). Deut Z Phil, 38(11), 1027-1034, 1990.

Nietzsche's thought is like a ghost that is waiting for us to liberate it. It won't stop haunting us until we have understood the terrors that assailed Nietzsche during his lifetime. In two nighttime visits, the ghost reveals what was terrifying the philosopher at the time he published his first texts: in the period from *The Birth of Tragedy* (1871) to *Richard Wagner in Bayreuth* (1876). Despite appearances, his fears were perfectly justified: Nietzsche was afraid that the triumph of economic liberalism would imprison Germany—and all of Europe—in this alternative: imperialism or socialism.

SAVA, Gabriella. "Sigma": conoscenza e metodo. Il Protag, 6(13-16), 181-203, Ja 88-D 89.

SAVAGE, C Wade (ed). *Scientific Theories*. Minneapolis, Univ of Minn Pr, 1990.

A first group of essays in *Scientific Theories* treats issues arising in biomedicine, economics, neuropsychology, psychoanalysis, and physics: nonepistemic factors in theory development, the nature of experimental science, realist and natural theorizing, the semantic conception of theories, and epistemic foundationalism. Holistic methods, theory choice, the use of old evidence, and the nature of ad hoc theories are considered in a second group, informed by a probabilistic viewpoint. The final selections treat issues centered around reason, revolution, and realism: semantic incommensurability of theories, underdetermination, rationality of theory acceptance, historical arguments for realism, and improvements in empiricism.

SAVELLOS, Elias E. On Defining Identity. Notre Dame J Form Log, 31(3), 476-484, Sum 90.

I argue that identity must be viewed as an indefinable, primitive notion. I first show that the popular attempts to define identity do not successfully escape the charge of circularity. I then argue that this is no accident. Any attempt to define identity is bound to be circular, since the intelligible understanding of the definition of identity *must* make recourse to the intelligible understanding of identity itself.

SAVIGNANO, Armando. La diffusione del pensiero spagnolo contemporaneo nell'Italia di oggi. Aquinas, 34(1), 103-124, Ja-Ap 91.

SAVIGNY, Eike V. The Last Word on *Philosophical Investigations* 43a. Austl J Phil, 68(2), 241-243, Je 90.

As painstaking exegesis reveals, Wittgenstein's famous dictum, in *PI* 43a, that "the meaning of a word is its use in the language," is nothing but a suggestion to reformulate 43b for an obvious therapeutical purpose. In this passage, there is no statement of a conception of meaning, and all inquiries as to the limits of such a conception are out of place.

SAVIGNY, Eike V. Self-Conscious Individual versus Social Soul: The Rationale of Wittgenstein's Discussion of Rule Following. Phil Phenomenol Res, 51(1), 67-84, Mr 91.

Careful examination of linguistic details of crucial P. I. passages and of their contexts warrants five conclusions: 1) critique of rules is restricted to the efficiency, for an agent's being guided, of his awareness of *expressions* of rules. 2) This critique rests on Wittgenstein's rejection of a basic role of autonomously enacted rules. 3) Adapting, replacing dominating as a conception of rule following, makes the latter a perfectly normal social fact about single individuals (comparable to the fact of being famous). 4) Meaning and, by parity of reasoning, any psychological fact, is thus a perfectly normal social fact about single individuals. 5) Thus man, by virtue of having a soul, is a social animal for purely conceptual reasons.

SAVILE, Anthony. "Truth, Understanding and the Artist's Vision" in *XIth International Congress in Aesthetics, Nottingham 1988*, WOODFIELD, Richard (ed), 172-175. Nottingham, Nottingham Polytech, 1990.

SAVITT, Steven F. Epistemological Time Asymmetry. Proc Phil Sci Ass, 1, 317-324, 1990.

Hans Reichenbach in *The Direction of Time* assumed that we know more about the past than the future and argued that the second law of thermodynamics explained this epistemological time asymmetry. In a recent book, *Asymmetries in Time*, Paul Horwich attempts to present a systematic account of various temporal asymmetries, including a neo-Reichenbachian account of the epistemological time asymmetry, that claims to remedy the most serious deficiency in Reichenbach's own account. I argue that Horwich's view does represent an advance on Reichenbach's but that when understood in the way I suggest, his account of the epistemological time asymmetry fails to vindicate his own main point, "...that our special knowledge of the past derives from the fork asymmetry," and therefore compromises his systematic account of temporal asymmetries within the context of an isotropic time.

SAVORELLI, Alessandro. Gentile e gli 'epigoni" dell'hegelismo napoletano: il carteggio con Sebastiano Maturi. G Crit Filosof Ital, 68(3), 403-412, S-D 89.

SAWAI, Yoshitsugu. Rāmānuja's Hermeneutics of the *Upanisads* in Comparison with Sankara's Interpretation. J Indian Phil, 19(1), 89-98, Mr 91.

SAX, Benjamin C. Foucault, Nietzsche, History: Two Modes of the Genealogical Method. Hist Euro Ideas, 11, 769-781, 1989.

SAX, Benjamin C. On the Genealogical Method: Nietzsche and Foucault. Int Stud Phil, 22(2), 129-141, 1990.

SAXE FERNÁNDEZ, Eduardo E. Filosofía y teoría general de sistemas en el pensamiento de A Rapoport. Rev Filosof (Costa Rica), 27(66), 439-444, D 89.

We offer an interpretation of A Rapoport's conceptualization of General System Theory (GST), as a basis for philosophy. The main concepts of GST are discussed, including the role of mathematics, and how the notions of organismic system introduces the discussion of ethics.

SAYERS, Sean. Gorz on Work and Liberation. Rad Phil, 58, 16-19, Sum 91.

This article gives an account and criticisms of the ideas on work contained in A Gorz's, *Critique of Economic Reason* (1989). It criticizes Gorz's argument that there is a clear distinction between activities to which economic (market) rationality is and is not applicable. Gorz's view that economic relations are destructive of the domestic sphere and caring work is criticized; and his criticisms of the welfare state are discussed. His account of economic activity as purely alienated instrumental activity is questioned. Gorz's strategy of restricting the economic and public sphere in order to defend the private and personal sphere is thus criticized.

SAYERS, Sean (ed) and OSBORNE, Peter (ed). *Socialism, Feminism and Philosophy: A Radical Philosophy Reader*. New York, Routledge, 1990.

This is an anthology of articles from *Radical Philosophy*, 1985-1990. It covers topics which are central to current controversies on the left. The first section contains articles on philosophical issues of feminism with a particular focus on moral questions (contributors: C J Arthur, J Grimshaw, P Johnson, S Parsons, R Poole). The second section deals with controversies in socialist and Marxist philosophy, including analytical Marxism (R Harris, J McCarney, J Ree, S Sayers). The final section contains articles discussing concepts of nature and human nature, particularly in relation to environmental issues (T Benton, R Keat, V Plumwood).

SAYRE, Patricia. The Task of a Theory of Meaning. Metaphilosophy, 21(4), 348-366, O 90.

The paper examines Quine's and Dummett's most fundamental assumptions about the theory of meaning. The upshot is to endorse Dummett's general vision of the task of such a theory over Quine's. Unlike Quine, Dummett views the theory of meaning as a distinctly philosophical enterprise. The reasons for adopting this view over Quine's naturalism have to do with taking language seriously as a social art and thus gaining a proper understanding of the relationship between idiolects and shared languages.

SAYRE-MC CORD, Geoffrey. Being a Realist about Relativism (In Ethics). Phil Stud, 61(1-2), 155-176, F 91.

How should a moral realist respond to the (seemingly) abundant evidence diversity provides for relativism? Many think there is only one reasonable response: abandon moral realism. Against them, I argue that moral realists can stand their ground in the face of moral diversity without relying on excessively optimistic arguments or unrealistic assumptions. In the process, I defend two theses: (i) that, far from being incompatible with moral realism, many plausible versions of relativism are *versions* of moral realism; and (ii) the best interpretation of the argument from diversity to relativism tells not at all against realist versions of relativism.

SAYRE-MC CORD, Geoffrey. "Functional Explanations and Reasons as Causes" in *Philosophical Perspectives, 3: Philosophy of Mind and Action Theory, 1989*, TOMBERLIN, James E (ed), 137-164. Atascadero, Ridgeview, 1989.

Many argue that if there is a conceptual connection between a person's reasons for acting, and his or her action, then 1) reasons cannot cause action (the Anti-Causal Thesis), and 2) action explanations must be fundamentally different from those in the physical sciences (the Explanatory Dualism Thesis). Both theses are commonly attacked; yet with flawed arguments. After criticizing these standard attacks, I defend a quasi-functionalist theory of beliefs and desires that, in its own and different way, serves to undermine both the Anti-Causal and the Explanatory Dualism Theses.

SAYWARD, Charles and HUGLY, Philip. Moral Relativism and Deontic Logic. Synthese, 85(1), 139-152, O 90.

If a native of India asserts "Killing cattle is wrong" and a Nebraskan asserts "Killing cattle is not wrong," and both judgments agree with their respective moralities and both moralities are internally consistent, then the moral relativist says both judgments are fully correct. At this point relativism bifurcates. One branch which we call content relativism denies that the two people are contradicting each other. The second branch which we call truth value relativism affirms that the two judgments are contradictory. Truth value relativism appears to be logically incoherent. We defend truth value relativism against this sort of charge of logical incoherence by showing it can be accommodated by the existing semantical metatheories of deontic logic. Having done this we go on to argue that truth value relativism is the best version of relativism. (edited)

SAYWARD, Charles and HUGLY, Philip. Offices and God. Sophia (Australia), 29(3), 29-34, O 90.

In "Existence and God" (*Journal of Philosophy*, Vol. 76, 403-420) Pavel Tichy presents an interpretation of Anselm's *Prosologian III* argument and raises doubts about one of the premises. It is argued here that the argument Tichy raises doubts about is not Anselm's.

SAYWARD, Charles and HUGLY, Philip. Quine's Relativism. Ratio, 3(2), 142-149, D 90.

A doctrine that occurs intermittently in Quine's work is that there is no extra-theoretic truth. It is argued that on its best interpretation the doctrine is inconsistent with three other doctrines accepted by Quine: bivalence, mathematical Platonism, and the disquotational account of truth.

SCAHILL, John. The Bright Side of Textbook Controversies. Phil Stud Educ, /, 90-96, 1989.

SCAHILL, John. Civic Education for Teachers. Phil Stud Educ, /, 173-184, 1987-88.

SCALTSAS, Theodore. Is a Whole Identical to its Parts? Mind, 99(396), 583-598, O 90.

My concern is to offer an account of substantial unity, namely, of why and how all the parts, constituents, aspects, of a substance make up a single whole rather than a plurality of many. I argue that the Aristotelian *substantial composition* offers such an account; I compare and contrast it to David Armstrong's account of the unity of classes and substances. I show that David Lewis's objections to substantial composition can be answered. Finally, I argue that Lewis's *mereological composition* cannot account for our metaphysical intuitions about substances, and further, that despite his aversion to it, his account commits him to a type of substantial composition.

SCALTSAS, Theodore. Parallel Governing. J Applied Phil, 7(2), 153-158, O 90.

Parallel processing systems can carry out computational tasks which would be impossible to be carried out by sequential systems. Cognitive psychologists are discovering that brains do not operate on a sequential ordering of tasks, but along parallel processing models. Sequential ordering is abandoned in the new generation computers, which are being designed on evolving parallel processing models. My proposal consists in applying the parallel processing principles to the state, creating a 'parallel governing' model for the decision-making procedures at the political level, in place of the present sequentially ordered procedures. I describe the main principles of current parallel processing models, and use them towards the creation of a parallel governing system. (edited)

SCANNONE, J C. La cuestión del Método de una filosofía latinoamericana. Stromata, 46(1-2), 75-81, Ja-Je 90.

El artículo explicita el método practicado por filósofos latinoamericanos actuales, en cuya reflexión interactúan las que Ricoeur llama "vía corta" de la fenomenología y analítica existencial, y la "vía larga" de la reflexión hermenéutica concreta a partir de símbolos culturales y acontecimientos históricos, sirviéndose de las ciencias humanas y sociales, pero enraizándose en la sabiduría popular. No son suficientes los métodos descriptivos o analíticos, el trascendental y el dialéctico, aunque constituyan momentos necesarios del método buscado. Este es el "analéctico", que los incluye y transforma.

SCANNONE, J C. Cuestiones actuales de epistemología teológica: Aportes de la teología de la liberación. Stromata, 46(3-4), 293-336, Jl-D 90.

El artículo estudia dos contribuciones de la teología de la liberación a la epistemología teológica. El primero se refiere a la autocomprensión de la teología como intelección de la caridad, más que sólo de la fe, basándose en una recta comprensión de la primacía de la praxis con respecto a la reflexión teológica. El segundo aporte está íntimamente relacionado con el anterior: se refiere al mundo de los pobres y la opción preferencial por ellos como lugar hermenéutico de la teología. Además estudia la interrelación entre los niveles teológico, filosófico y científico-social de esa hermenéutica.

SCANNONE, J C. Nueva modernidad adveniente y cultura emergente en América Latina. Stromata, 47(1-2), 145-192, Ja-Je 91.

La primera parte estudia las formas sucesivas de racionalidad en las distintas etapas de la modernidad (analítico-sinstrumental, sistemática, comunicativa) y la postmodernidad, confrontándolas con la racionalidad sapiencial latinoamericana. La segunda parte, de índole pastoral, señala, junto a la cultura moderna y postmoderna adveniente, la cultura popular emergente en América Latina (v.g. neocomunitarismo de base) y el intento de síntesis entre ambas. La tercera parte lo muestra en la problemática del trabajo (introducción de nuevas tecnologías y economía popular de solidaridad).

SCAPPARONE, Elisabetta and PIEROZZI, Letizia. Il volgarizzamento del "De Rerum natura" di Bernardino Telesio a opera di Francesco Martelli. G Crit Filosof Ital, 69(2), 160-181, My-Ag 90.

SCARAMUZZA, Gabriele and SCHUHMANN, Karl. Ein Husserlmanuskript über Ästhetik. Husserl Stud, 7(3), 165-177, 1990.

SCEDROV, Andre and MILLER, Dale and NADATHUR, Gopalan and PFENNING, Frank. Uniform Proofs as a Foundation for Logic Programming. Annals Pure Applied Log, 51(1-2), 125-157, Mr 91.

SCHACHT, Richard. Hegel, Marx, Nietzsche, and the Future of Self-Alienation. Amer Phil Quart, 28(2), 125-135, Ap 91.

SCHACHT, Richard. Nietzsche as Colleague. Int Stud Phil, 22(2), 59-66, 1990.

SCHACHT, Richard. Nietzsche on Human Nature. Hist Euro Ideas, 11, 883-892, 1989.

SCHACHT, Richard. Philosophical Anthropology: What, Why and How. Phil Phenomenol Res, 50 SUPP, 155-176, Fall 90.

SCHAFFER, Simon. "Genius in Romantic Natural Philosophy" in *Romanticism and the Sciences*, CUNNINGHAM, Andrew (ed), 82-99. New York, Cambridge Univ Pr, 1990.

SCHALL, James V. "Calvary or the Slaughter-house" in *From Twilight to Dawn: The Cultural Vision of Jacques Maritain*, REDPATH, Peter A (ed), 1-14. Notre Dame, Univ Notre Dame Pr, 1990.

The French philosopher, Jacques Maritain, was concerned in his political philosophy to understand the origins of 20th century ideology, which has caused so much destruction to mankind in this era. The question arises whether, with the demise of the political forms of 20th century ideology whether there remains within democracy itself the same intellectual premises. Hence the question arises whether the theory of autonomous man is adequate for the confrontation of true human dignity. Maritain remarked that Nietzsche did not understand that the choice for man was either "Calvary or the Slaughterhouse." By this he meant to suggest that reason and revelation eventually have to meet if only for the sake of reason.

SCHALLER, Walter E. Punishment and the Utilitarian Criterion of Right and Wrong. S J Phil, 29(1), 109-126, Spr 91.

Recent interpretations of Mill's *Utilitarianism* focus on his claim that "the real turning point of the distinction between morality and simple expediency" is that people ought to be punished for wrong actions. Since internal sanctions may be nonmoral (e.g., regret, shame) as well as moral, one must know whether a given action is morally wrong before one can determine whether a moral or a nonmoral sanction is appropriate. It is therefore question-begging to seek to distinguish wrong actions from merely inexpedient actions by saying that only in the case of the former is a moral sanction appropriate.

SCHALOW, Frank. The Anomaly of World: From Scheler to Heidegger. Man World, 24(1), 75-87, Ja 91.

This paper seeks to show that Heidegger's development of a concept of world stems as much from a critique of Scheler as from Husserl. It is argued that Heidegger's notion of world is patterned after human finitude, while Scheler's view of the same includes a relation between man's limitations and his latent affinity with the Divine as infinite. By showing how Heidegger redefines man's relation to the whole in terms of finitude, it is revealed how he arrives at a concept of Being-in-the-world that alleviates the difficulties associated with Scheler's more anomalous concept of world.

SCHALOW, Frank. Heidegger and the Temporal Constitution of the *A Priori*. SW Phil Rev, 7(1), 173-182, Ja 91.

This paper challenges the traditional notion that the a priori is of an atemporal or eternal character. By appealing to Heidegger's notion of ecstatic temporality, it is shown that the sense of the "earlier" implied in the a priori reflects the projective structure of understanding. Insofar as human understanding is finite and determined by time, it is seen that the a priori is essentially temporal as well.

SCHALOW, Frank. Is There a "Meaning" of Being? Against the Deconstructionist Reading of Heidegger. Phil Today, 34(2), 152-162, Sum 90.

This paper argues that the deconstructionist reading of Heidegger does not take fully into account the subtleties of his account of temporality. These subtleties include the mutually effacing character of being and temporality which allows for the event of disclosure to happen. The paper concludes that Heidegger's version of temporality can be upheld without conflating it with a view of time defined merely as flux.

SCHALOW, Frank. Temporality Revisited: Kierkegaard and the Transitive Character of Time. Auslegung, 17(1), 15-25, Wint 91.

The paper reexamines Kierkegaard's interpretation of time by showing how time is a prefigurement of a higher state of selfhood. While the self is to be conceived in the trajectory of its elevation toward the Divine, selfhood is really possible only because it can mark the convergence of all dimensions of time, future, present, and past. The self constitutes the development whereby each dimension of time arises through its collective relation to every other, encased within eternity. The paper thus reinterprets Kierkegaard's view of time in a way which diverges from the more explicitly ontological focus of either existentialism or hermeneutics.

SCHANTZ, Richard. *Der sinnliche Gehalt der Wahrnehmung*. Munchen, Philosophia, 1990.

This book is a defence of the adverbial analysis of the sensory content of perception. Various versions of the sense-data theory such as representative realism and phenomenalism are criticized. Moreover, the author attacks Armstrong's and Pitcher's attempt to reduce perception to various modes of belief. Finally, it is shown that, contrary to what Sellars believes, the adverbial theory is compatible with scientific realism.

SCHARFF, Robert C. Habermas on Heidegger's *Being and Time*. Int Phil Quart, 31(2), 189-201, Je 91.

SCHARLEMANN, Robert P. *Inscriptions and Reflections: Essays in Philosophical Theology*. Charlottesville, Univ Pr of Virginia, 1989.

In these essays, the author treats some of the questions arising for theology out of post-Kantian thought, especially idealism and existentialism. He develops a concept of theology as an "afterthinking" (*metanoesis*) of ontology and science. The essays are divided into three sections, those having to do with questions of principle, those involving interpretations of contemporary science and culture, and those related to the problem of pluralism. According to the author, the task of theology is to "inscribe the name 'God' upon any name, the tale 'God is' upon any event, and the judgment 'God is God' upon any identity."

SCHATZKI, Theodore R. Elements of a Wittgensteinian Philosophy of the Human Sciences. Synthese, 87(2), 311-329, My 91.

In this paper, a Wittgensteinian account of the human sciences is constructed around the notions of the surface of human life and of surface phenomena as expressions. I begin by explaining Wittgenstein's idea that the goal of interpretive social science is to make actions and practices seem natural. I then explicate his notions of the surface of life and of surface phenomena as expressions by reviewing his analysis of mental state language. Finally, I critically examine three ideas: (a) that the goal of interpretive inquiry is realized through a descriptive, context-constructing method that enables investigators to grasp the instincts, mental states, and experiences ("Geist") expressed in surface phenomena; (b) that uncovering rules plays a minor role in this enterprise; and (c) that surface phenomena not only can be made natural but also have causes and are subject to causal explanation.

SCHECHTMAN, Marya. Personal Concern and the Extension of Consciousness. Logos (USA), 11, 33-46, 1990.

Psychological accounts of personal identity have been accused of being unable to justify the special concern which we feel for ourselves. I argue that this inability rests not on peculiarities of the psychological continuity theory but on a view of consciousness as instantaneous that is shared by both psychological continuity theorists and those who object to these theories. I claim that numerical identity of consciousness is required to make sense not only of self-concern, but of anticipation and compensation as well. Neither psychological continuity theorists nor their opponents can give adequate support for these fundamental features of persons, because neither has a conception of consciousness that allows for its real persistence over time. What we learn from the special concern objection, then, is that our current conception of consciousness is incoherent, and that we need to form a new one before we can get further on the derivative problems.

SCHECTER, Darrow. Gramsci, Gentile and the Theory of the Ethical State in Italy. Hist Polit Thought, 11(3), 491-508, Autumn 90.

SCHECTER, Darrow. Two Views of the Revolution: Gramsci and Sorel, 1916-1920. Hist Euro Ideas, 12(5), 637-653, 1990.

SCHEDLER, George. Does Strict Judicial Scrutiny Involve the *Tu Quoque* Fallacy? Law Phil, 9(3), 269-283, Ag 90.

To protect what it deems "fundamental rights," the Supreme Court "strictly scrutinizes" legislation that impinges on these rights. The Court views such legislation as a means to some end the legislation seeks to accomplish. The Court requires that the statute be neither "overinclusive" nor "underinclusive"; the legislation may not affect more people than necessary to achieve its end, nor is the statue permitted to leave some people out in achieving its end. The author argues that when legislation imposes burdens, its underinclusiveness is irrelevant, and that when it dispenses rewards its overinclusiveness is irrelevant, because those affected by the statute are *ex hypothesi* deserving. One commits the *tu quoque* fallacy when one tries to infer that those affected by the law are undeserving from the fact that some deserving individuals were not affected by the statute. (edited)

SCHEER, Richard K. Wittgenstein's Indeterminism. Philosophy, 66(255), 5-23, Ja 91.

SCHEFFCZYK, Leo (ed). *Evolution: Probleme und neue Aspekte ihrer Theorie*. Freiburg, Alber, 1991.

The paradigm of the historicity of all life is a central component of contemporary thought. Almost unopposed, the idea of evolution is accepted as a dominant part of this paradigm. Nonetheless it functions as more than an explanatory model for accounting for the world. It is connected too with the idea of progress—the expectation of more perfect realities in the future. The orientation to the future which is to be found in modern thought and feeling is related towards the appearance of a new philosophy and theology of hope, clearly bound up with the concept of evolutionary processuality. In this volume, six different specialists concern themselves with central scientific, philosophical and theological themes in this complex of problems.

SCHEFFLER, Israel. *In Praise of the Cognitive Emotions*. New York, Routledge, 1991.

This book includes fourteen papers applying philosophical thinking to various educational themes. With one exception, all were written during the 1970's and 1980's. The book defends rationality as a unifying focus for education, identifying rationality as the capacity to grasp principles and purposes, and to evaluate them in the light of reasons that might be put forward for and against them. The papers include a critique of computer applications to education, a discussion of strategic rationality in understanding mathematics, and a defence of the intimate connections between cognition and emotion.

SCHEIBE, Erhard. Predication and Physical Law. Topoi, 10(1), 3-12, Mr 91.

SCHEID, Don E. Davis and the Unfair-Advantage Theory of Punishment: A Critique. Phil Topics, 18(1), 143-170, Spr 90.

Unfair-advantage theory maintains that punishment is justified in so far as it cancels out the advantage one gains over law-abiding citizens when one commits a crime. This article presents detailed criticisms of the version of unfair-advantage theory held by Michael Davis. It also offers criticism of the theory in general, including a discussion of possible meanings of 'unfair advantage' and a discussion of levels of precision required in matching scales of punishments to scales of crimes. The conclusion is that the concept of unfair advantage is too vague and ambiguous to be of any help in guaging punishments for various crimes.

SCHEINES, Richard and SPIRTES, Peter and GLYMOUR, Clark. "The Tetrad Project" in *Acting and Reflecting: The Interdisciplinary Turn in Philosophy*, SIEG, Wilfried (ed), 183-207. Norwell, Kluwer, 1990.

SCHEIT, Herbert. *Wahrheit—Diskurs—Demokratie: Studien zur "Konsensustheorie der Wahrheit"*. Freiburg, Alber, 1991.

The author presents a systematic discussion in a critical context of the "Consensus Theory of Truth" made known through Habermas. The book intends to verify the applicability of the theory of consensus to a theory of democracy based on normative and legitimate foundations.

SCHEMAN, Naomi. The Unavoidability of Gender. J Soc Phil, 21(2-3), 34-39, Fall-Wint 90.

SCHERVISH, M J and SEIDENFELD, Teddy. "Decisions Without Ordering" in *Acting and Reflecting: The Interdisciplinary Turn in Philosophy*, SIEG, Wilfried (ed), 143-170. Norwell, Kluwer, 1990.

We review the axiomatic foundations of subjective utility theory with a view toward understanding the implications of each axiom. We consider three different approaches, namely, the construction of utilities in the presence of canonical probabilities, the construction of probabilities in the presence of utilities, and the simultaneous construction of both probabilities and utilities. We focus attention on the axioms of independence and weak ordering. The independence axiom is seen to be necessary in order to prevent a form of Dutch Book in sequential problems. (edited)

SCHERVISH, M J and SEIDENFELD, Teddy and KADANE, J B. When Fair Betting Odds are Not Degrees of Belief. Proc Phil Sci Ass, 1, 517-524, 1990.

The "Dutch Book" argument, tracing back to Ramsey and to deFinetti, offers prudential grounds for action in conformity with personal probability. Under several structural assumptions about combinations of stakes (that is, assumptions about the combination of wagers), your betting policy is *coherent* only if your *fair odds* are probabilities. The central question posed here is the following one: Besides providing an operational test of coherent betting, does the "Book" argument also provide for adequate measurement (*elicitation*) of the agents degrees of beliefs? That is, are an agent's fair odds also his/her personal probabilities for those events? We argue the answer is "No!" The problem is caused by the possibility of state dependent utilities.

SCHIAPPA, Edward. Did Plato Coin *Rhētorikē*? Amer J Philo, 111(4), 457-470, Wint 90.

This essay argues that the Greek word for rhetoric may have been coined by Plato in the process of composing *Gorgias* around 385 BC. The word is not found in any text prior to Plato. Its absence is particularly noteworthy in fifth-century texts where one would expect to find it if "rhetoric" had been a term in general or specialized usage. Plato has a documented penchant for coining new words denoting arts, particularly verbal arts, and he may have coined the word in order to distinguish his pedagogy from that of his rival Isocrates.

SCHIAPPA, Edward. History and Neo-Sophistic Criticism: A Reply to Poulakos. Phil Rhet, 23(4), 307-315, 1990.

The note defends an article published in the previous issue against a response by Poulakos. Even if historical accounts are a form of "interpretation" influenced by one's pre-understanding, as Poulakos argues, one need not conclude that all interpretations are equally useful. Poulakos's previous works acknowledge the difference between historical and rational reconstruction, and he offers no reason for not keeping the two approaches distinct. The note points out that Poulakos is largely unresponsive to the particulars of the critique of his "Sophistic Definition of Rhetoric." The philological evidence concerning the coining of *rhêtorikê* is reviewed and Poulakos's counterexamples are refuted.

SCHIAPPA, Edward. Neo-Sophistic Rhetorical Criticism or the Historical Reconstruction of Sophistic Doctrines? Phil Rhet, 23(3), 192-217, 1990.

A distinction should be made between the historical reconstruction of Sophists' doctrines and the reinterpretation of sophistic ideas as part of contemporary, "neo-sophistic" theory and criticism. Because the two approaches differ in *goals* and *methods*, studies that do not keep the approaches distinct may suffer from a lack of conceptual clarity. This essay describes each approach, demonstrates through a critique of John Poulakos' "Sophistic Definition of Rhetoric" how future scholarship concerning the Sophists can profit by acknowledging the differences between the two approaches, and suggests directions for future historical reconstructions of sophistic doctrines.

SCHICK JR, Theodore W. How is Philosophy Possible? Int Phil Quart, 31(2), 203-212, Je 91.

It has recently been claimed that traditional philosophical theorizing is impossible, for it attempts to describe the world from a "God's eye" point of view. According to these authors, the only legitimate function of philosophy is to compare and contrast cultural traditions. I argue that these alternatives are not exhaustive. There is another conception of the philosophical enterprise, viz., that of explaining possibilities, which avoids the absolution of the former and the relativism of the latter.

SCHIEDERMAYER, David L and LA PUMA, John. The Clinical Ethicist at the Bedside. Theor Med, 12(2), 141-149, Je 91.

In this paper we attempt to show how the goal of resolving moral problems in a patient's care can best be achieved by working at the bedside. The skills of the clinical ethics consultant include the ability to delineate and resolve ethical problems in a particular patient's case and to teach other health professionals to build their own frameworks for clinical ethical decision making. When the clinical situation requires it, clinical ethics consultants can and should assist primary physicians with case management. (edited)

SCHIFFER, Stephen. *Ceteris Paribus* Laws. Mind, 100(397), 1-17, Ja 91.

SCHIFFER, Stephen. "Fodor's Character" in *Information, Semantics and Epistemology*, VILLANUEVA, Enrique (ed), 77-101. Cambridge, Blackwell, 1990.

SCHIFFER, Stephen. Meaning and Value. J Phil, 87(11), 602-614, N 90.

SCHIFFER, Stephen. "The Mode-of-Presentation Problem" in *Propositional Attitudes: The Role of Content in Logic, Language, and Mind*, ANDERSON, C Anthony (ed), 249-268. Stanford, CSLI, 1990.

SCHIFFER, Stephen. "Physicalism" in *Philosophical Perspectives, 4: Action Theory and Philosophy of Mind, 1990*, TOMBERLIN, James E (ed), 153-185. Atascadero, Ridgeview, 1990.

SCHIFFER, Stephen. The Relational Theory of Belief (A Reply to Richard). Pac Phil Quart, 71(3), 240-245, S 90.

SCHIRN, Matthias. Kants Theorie der geometrischen Erkenntnis und die nichteuklikische Geometrie. Kantstudien, 82(1), 1-28, 1991.

SCHIRN, Matthias. Sobre la semántica de los nombres propios. Dialogos, 25(56), 7-35, Jl 90.

SCHLAGEL, Richard H. Fine's "Shaky Game" (and Why Noa is No Ark for Science). Phil Sci, 58(2), 307-323, Je 91.

SCHLANGER, Judith. "L'histoire de la pensée scientifique et les autres histoires intellectuelles" in *Études sur/Studies on Hélène Metzger*, FREUDENTHAL, Gad , 189-194. Leiden, Brill, 1990.

SCHLECHTA, Karl. Theory Revision and Probability. Notre Dame J Form Log, 32(2), 307-319, Spr 91.

The problem of Theory Revision is to "add" a formula to a theory, while preserving consistency and making only minimal changes to the original theory. A natural way to uniquely determine the process is by imposing an order of "epistemic entrenchment" on the formulas, as done by Gärdenfors and Makinson. We improve their results as follows: we define orders which generate unique revision processes too, but in addition, 1) have nice logical properties, 2) are independent of the theory considered, and are thus well suited for iterated revision and computational purposes, and 3) have a natural probabilistic construction. Finally, we show that the completeness problems of Theory Revision carry over to a certain extent to an approach based on revising axiom systems.

SCHLEE, Edward E. The Value of Perfect Information in Non-linear Utility Theory. Theor Decis, 30(2), 127-131, Mr 91.

Wakker (1988) has recently shown that, in contrast to an expected utility maximizer, the value of information will sometimes be negative for an agent who violates the independence axiom of expected utility theory. We demonstrate, however, that the value of *perfect* information will always be nonnegative if the agent satisfies a weak dominance axiom. This result thus mitigates to some degree the normative objection to nonlinear utility theory implicit in Wakker's finding.

SCHLEGEL, Friedrich and FIRCHOW, Peter (trans). *Philosophical Fragments*. Minneapolis, Univ of Minn Pr, 1991.

SCHLESINGER, George N. The Credibility of Extraordinary Events. Analysis, 51(3), 120-126, Je 91.

The study of probability statements concerning extraordinary events yields some unexpected results, e.g., that sometimes the unconditional support for a hypothesis by a very trustworthy witness may *lower* that hypothesis's probability! Also it forces to revise Hume's claims concerning the probability of miracle stories.

SCHLESINGER, George N. Location and Range. Brit J Phil Sci, 41(2), 245-260, Je 90.

SCHLESINGER, George N. *The Sweep of Probability*. Notre Dame, Univ Notre Dame Pr, 1991.

The book engages the reader in contemporary debates about a variety of issues associated with the notion of probability without requiring any technical knowledge. By discussing a wide variety of topics illustrates that elementary probability belongs to one of those rare intellectual ventures where the returns are disproportionately high to the initial investment of effort. After introducing such elementary material as Bayes's Theorem, the work examines confirmation; prediction and retrodiction; randomness and patter repetition; relevance; reliablity of witness and of symptons; the logic of obligations; the anthropic principle, and other philosophical ideas where probability plays an essential role.

SCHLESINGER, George N. What are Discernible? Method Sci, 24(1), 23-31, 1991.

SCHLIWA, Harald and ZEDDIES, Helmut. Die Rolle des Individuums und seine Beteiligung an gesellschaftlichen Prozessen. Deut Z Phil, 39(1), 71-79, 1991.

SCHMAUS, Warren. Whither Social Epistemology? A Reply to Fuller. Phil Soc Sci, 21(2), 196-202, Je 91.

Since the publication of *Social Epistemology* (1988), Fuller has changed his conception of this discipline. He now argues that normative lessons for science policy are to be learned from cognitive psychology rather than the history of science, citing the appearance of intellectual dissension among historians, their emphasis on intellectual biography, and psychologists' use of experimental controls. I argue that these reasons are not sufficient to rule out a pluralistic approach that allows different and even opposing schools of historians, psychologists, and others to contribute to the study of science and the formulation of science policy.

SCHMERL, James H. Conductive $\aleph_0$-Categorical Theories. J Sym Log, 55(3), 1130-1137, S 90.

SCHMID, Wilhelm. Ethics in Current Affairs: The Theme of the Enlightenment in Michel Foucault (in German). Deut Z Phil, 38(10), 903-912, 1990.

SCHMIDINGER, H M. La disputa sulle origini della neoscolastica italiana: Salvatore Roselli, Vincenzo Buzzetti e Gaetano Sanseverino. Riv Filosof Neo-Scolas, 82(2-3), 353-364, Ap-S 90.

SCHMIDT, Dennis J. Changing the Subject: Heidegger, "the" National and Epochal. Grad Fac Phil J, 14(2)-15(1), 441-464, 1991.

This article asks about Heidegger's claims that the end of the western metaphysical tradition bears some special relation to the idea of nationality, specifically German nationality. Special attention is given to Heidegger's texts from the 1930s, as well as to interpretations of these issues by both Habermas and Lacoue-Labarthe.

SCHMIDT, Dennis J and GADAMER, Hans-Georg. "Culture and the Word" in *Hermeneutics and the Poetic Motion, Translation Perspectives V—1990*, SCHMIDT, Dennis J (ed), 11-23. Binghamton, CRIT, 1990.

SCHMIDT, Dennis J (ed). *Hermeneutics and the Poetic Motion, Translation Perspectives V—1990*. Binghamton, CRIT, 1990.

A collection of essays that address philosophical and literary critical issues in the idea of translation. Topics include translatability, the relation of culture to language, language and limits. Wittgenstein, Heidegger, Gadamer and Lyotard are among the philosophers whose work is discussed.

SCHMIDT, Hartwig. The Perversion of Emancipation into Repression (in German). Deut Z Phil, 38(8), 759-770, 1990.

SCHMIDT, Johannes. *Gerechtigkeit, Wohlfahrt und Rationalität*. Freiburg, Alber, 1991.

This book examines some notable formal approaches used in recent welfare economics, social choice theory and ethics, for justifying principles of distributive justice. At the outset the limitations of Paretian welfare economics are discussed, with an analysis of social welfare functions of the Arrow and Bergson-Samuelson types respectively. The core of the study deals critically with a variety of axiomatic and decision-theoretical arguments proposed by Fleming, Harsanyi, Rawls and a number of social choice theorists (d'Aspremont, Deschamps, Gevers, Hammond, Masin, Roberts, Sen, Strasnik) to justify a utilitarian, or rather an egalitarian, solution to distribution problems. It is shown that none of these arguments does in fact achieve its methodological aim to derive a unique principle of justice from weak ethical premises alone.

SCHMIDT, Lawrence K. "The Exemplary Status of Translating" in *Hermeneutics and the Poetic Motion, Translation Perspectives V—1990*, SCHMIDT, Dennis J (ed), 83-92. Binghamton, CRIT, 1990.

SCHMIDTZ, David. *The Limits of Government: An Essay on the Public Goods Arguments*. Boulder, Westview Pr, 1991.

Government involvement is widely held to be necessary for the provision of public goods—goods that demand collective action and that benefit even those who do not contribute. Chapters on property and on the right to punish explore how institutions can be defended as solutions to public goods problems. A chapter describing a noncoercive solution of the Prisoner's Dilemma leads into a chapter on the moral and strategic complexities of public goods problems that are not Prisoner's Dilemmas. I present experimental data on patterns of voluntary contribution. Finally, I consider questions about when we are morally obligated to help produce public goods and when others are permitted to force us to help.

SCHMIDTZ, David. When is Original Appropriation *Required*? Monist, 73(4), 504-518, O 90.

All property eventually traces its existence (as property) to appropriations of previously unowned goods, which suggests that whether property can be justified depends on whether original appropriation can be justified. The Lockean Proviso is generally understood to be a test that, in a world of scarcity, original appropriation cannot possibly pass. But I argue that, under conditions of scarcity, if we want enough and as good to be left for future generations, we must above all protect them from present-day commons tragedies, which means that leaving resources in the commons is out of the question. Thus, the Lockean Proviso, far from ruling out original appropriation, actually requires it.

SCHMIED-KOWARZIK, Wolfdietrich. *Franz Rosenzweig: Existentielles Denken und gelebte Bewährung*. Freiburg, Alber, 1991.

In this study the author introduces Franz Rosenzweig's existentialist philosophy and makes his existentialist problematics accessible to contemporary minds. He approaches Rosenzweig's "new thinking" most particularly from the point of view of its development in the context of discourse with his friends Hans Ehrenberg, Eugen Rosenstock and Martin Buber.

SCHMINKE, Marshall and LEMKE, Dwight K. Ethics in Declining Organizations. Bus Ethics Quart, 1(3), 235-248, Jl 91.

This paper explores the relationship between declining organizations and unethical behavior. Data form a four month long management simulation indicate that declining organizations demonstrate a greater propensity for unethical activities than do more successful companies. The results indicate that: 1) organizations in decline are more likely to be involved in unethical activities; 2) the more severe the decline is, the more unethical the behavior is likely to be; and 3) it is organizational decline and not initial propensities toward unethical conduct that explains the unethical behavior. The paper also discusses the implications of these findings and outlines future streams of research.

SCHMITT, Charles B. "Some Considerations on the Study of the History of Seventeenth-Century Science" in *Études sur/Studies on Hélène Metzger*, FREUDENTHAL, Gad , 23-33. Leiden, Brill, 1990.

SCHMITT, Frederick. Social Epistemology and Social Cognitive Psychology. Soc Epistem, 5(2), 111-120, Ap-Je 91.

SCHMITZ, Heinz-Gerd. Moral oder Klugheit? Überlegungen zur Gestalt der Autonomie des Politischen im Denken Kants. Kantstudien, 81(4), 413-434, 1990.

Kant's political philosophy seems to be dominated by the categorical imperative to oppose every approach, which maintains nonethical prudence to be the substantial political capacity. But, eventually, Kant cannot ignore the fundamental differences between the world of politics and the realm of ethics. So he replaces the categorical imperative by the demand that every political action must be publishable. Thereby, he dismisses the ethical supervision of politics and silently admits prudence as the sole political wisdom. This change of attitude is indicated by the difference of morality and legality.

SCHMITZ, Kenneth L. "Is Liberalism Good Enough?" in *Liberalism and the Good*, DOUGLASS, R Bruce (ed), 86-104. New York, Routledge, 1990.

SCHMITZ, Phyllis J and KOSHUTA, Monica A and LYNN, Joanne. Development of an Institutional Policy on Artificial Hydration and Nutrition. Kennedy Inst Ethics J, 1(2), 133-139, Je 91.

The issues involved in deciding whether to use artificial methods of delivering hydration and nutrition are often very difficult for patients, families, and health care providers. Once private and personal matters, these decisions now frequently involve the judicial system. Five years ago, Hospice of Washington recognized the need for a written policy and wrote the one published here. Its goal is to respect individual preferences and family concerns while addressing the nutrition and hydration needs of dying patients. The policy sets parameters on the issue, provides basic information, and encourages crafting the most fitting resolution to each situation.

SCHNEEWIND, J B. MacIntyre and the Indispensability of Tradition. Phil Phenomenol Res, 51(1), 165-168, Mr 91.

Agreeing with MacIntyre's claim in *Whose Justice? Which Rationality?* that inquiry is situated in a matrix of unquestioned assumptions, I argue that this does not force us to conclude, as he thinks it does, that inquiry must utilize the assumptions of some definite historical tradition of thought.

SCHNEEWIND, J B. "Modern Moral Philosophy" in *A Companion to Ethics*, SINGER, Peter (ed), 147-157. Cambridge, Blackwell, 1991.

In this survey of the history of moral philosophy from the seventeenth century to the present, I argue that by the end of the eighteenth century moral philosophy emerged from a less differentiated practical philosophy. Its development both reflected and assisted the rise of broad social concern with individual autonomy. After sketching the main schools of thought up to Reid, Bentham and Kant, I outline some main nineteenth century reactions to their views and briefly discuss later developments. With autonomy now not problematic, attention is shifting, I suggest, away from general theory and toward particular issues.

SCHNEEWIND, J B (ed). *Moral Philosophy from Montaigne to Kant: An Anthology, Volume I & II*. New York, Cambridge Univ Pr, 1990.

Here are selections from thirty-two writers on moral philosophy from the late sixteenth to the late eighteenth century. All the familiar moral philosophers from Descartes and Hobbes through Kant and Reid are represented, along with many minor writers whose work they often knew. Among the less commonly studied writers represented are Grotius, Pufendorf, Malebranche, Helvetius, and Holback; selections from Wolff, Nicole and Crusius are translated for the first time. The editor provides an introductory overview, and separate introductions, notes, and bibliographies for each author. The work is designed as a textbook for courses in the history of ethics, either beginning or advanced.

SCHNEEWIND, J B. Natural Law, Skepticism, and Methods of Ethics. J Hist Ideas, 52(2), 289-308, Ap-Je 91.

The assumption that everyone is equally able to think appropriately about morality was not generally accepted in the seventeenth century. Natural law theorists rejected it, but some, moved by the religious belief that God would not hold us accountable unless we could know what we ought to do, altered the position. Montaigne's sceptical view that each can find within the self a ruling pattern for testing intentions provided a model for moral thinking developed in different ways by later thinkers, such as Hume and Kant.

SCHNEIDER, Herbert W. Education and the Cultivation of Reflection. Thinking, 4(2), 4-9, 1982.

SCHNEIDERMAN, Lawrence J. Still Saving the Life of Ethics. Hastings Center Rep, 20(6), 22-24, N-D 90.

SCHNEIDERS, Werner. Aufklärung und Reform. Deut Z Phil, 38(12), 1135-1151, 1990.

SCHNER, George. Hume's *Dialogues* and the Redefinition of the Philosophy of Religion. Thomist, 55(1), 83-101, Ja 91.

This essay asks: in what does the work of the philosophy of religion consist? To answer the question it considers Hume's *Dialogues* for their content and structure, with emphasis on Hume's notion of the "common life" and his proposal of a succession of metaphors for the construal of god, self, and world. Interpretations of the *Dialogues* are dependent upon differing models of religion and doctrine, and Hume's own placement of the discussion in the context of education and the "common life" suggests a new reading of his text and new possibilities for the philosophy of religion.

SCHOEDINGER, Andrew B (ed). *Introduction to Metaphysics: The Fundamental Questions*. Buffalo, Prometheus, 1991.

This anthology is designed to introduce undergraduate students to the problems of metaphysics. Historical as well as contemporary readings concern the problems of universals, causation, personal identity, free will and agency and artificial intelligence. There is a total of 35 readings. Each part is preceded by an introduction by the editor. Among authors included are Abelard, Aristotle, Berkeley, Butler, Hume, Carnap, Chisholm, Ducasse, Melden, Pears, Quinton, Putnam, Shoemaker, Strawson and Scriven.

SCHOEMAN, Ferdinand. Are Kantian Duties Categorical? Hist Phil Quart, 8(1), 59-63, Ja 91.

The type of imperatives for action that are derivable from use of Kant's categorical imperative are not and cannot be of the form that Kant argues imperatives must have to qualify as moral imperatives.

SCHOEMAN, Ferdinand. Psychology and Standards of Reasonable Expectation. Pub Affairs Quart, 4(4), 387-402, O 90.

SCHOEN, Edward L. David Hume and the Mysterious Shroud of Turin. Relig Stud, 27(2), 209-222, Je 91.

Contrary to Hume's contention, there is no essential connection between miracles and violations of natural laws. Not only may violations of natural law be utterly nonmiraculous, miracles may occur in complete conformity with such laws. Furthermore, a proper understanding of miracles in terms of divine agency places them into an epistemic context where the growth of science does not directly threaten their possibility.

SCHOEN, Edward L. The Roles of Predictions in Science and Religion. Int J Phil Relig, 29(1), 1-31, F 91.

The evidential role of predictions in the sciences has long been recognized. Less often noticed is the variety of ways that predictions function nonevidentially in the sciences. By delineating these nonevidential roles, it is possible to find similar functions for predictions in assorted religious contexts. Furthermore, once the exact nature of the evidential role of scientific predictions is understood clearly, parallel religious functions for predictions can be found.

SCHOENFELDT, Lyle F and MC DONALD, Don M and YOUNGBLOOD, Stuart A. The Teaching of Business Ethics: A Survey of AACSB Member Schools. J Bus Ethics, 10(3), 237-241, Mr 91.

This report presents the findings of a survey of business ethics education undertaken in the Fall of 1988. The respondents were the deans of colleges and universities associated with the AACSB. Ethics, as a curriculum topic, received significant coverage at over 90 percent of the institutions, with 53 percent indicating interest in increasing coverage of the subject. The tabulations of this survey may prove useful to schools seeking to compare or develop their emphases in business ethics.

SCHOFIELD, Malcolm. "Heraclitus' Theory of Soul and Its Antecedents" in *Psychology (Companions to Ancient Thought: 2)*, EVERSON, Stephen (ed), 13-34. New York, Cambridge Univ Pr, 1991.

This article offers an account of what project Heraclitus was engaged upon in his aphorisms on and relating to soul. It focuses particularly on his method and its epistemological presuppositions. All the relevant fragments are quoted in English and discussed in the light of the best recent scholarship on Heraclitus. The article is designed to introduce the general philosophical reader—from undergraduate on—to the subject.

SCHOLLMEIER, Paul. Practical Intuition and Rhetorical Example. Phil Rhet, 24(2), 95-104, 1991.

Assume that we have a faculty of theoretical intuition, through which we intuit theoretical principles, and a faculty of practical intuition, through which we intuit practical principles. Could we justify or verify our theoretical and practical intuitions in the same way? Despite recent attempts to do so, one would think not. For we assume that we have two different faculties grasping principles of different kinds. We would thus ask what method or technique we could use to justify or to verify our practical principles. Aristotle suggests that an art of discourse and an inductive technique might serve to justify practical intuitions about our ends. The art is rhetoric and the technique argument by example. After all, rhetoric is an art concerned with discourse of a practical kind, and example is an argument of an inductive sort.

SCHÖNE-SEIFERT, Bettina. Philosophische Uberlegungen zu "Menschenwürde" und Fortpflanzungs-Medizin. Z Phil Forsch, 44(3), 442-473, 1990.

SCHONSHECK, Jonathan. Deconstructing Community Self-Paternalism. Law Phil, 10(1), 29-49, F 91.

Typically the justification of criminal statutes is based on "liberty-limiting principles" - e.g., the Harm Principle, the Offense Principle, Legal Paternalism, Legal Moralism, etc. Two philosophers of the criminal law, however - Richard J Arneson and Cass R Sunstein - take an entirely different tack. Both countenance the use of the crimianl law to foreclose one's future options, seeking to preserve one's "true self" from the temptations of one's baser desires. (For reasons which become clear, I call this "community self-paternalism"). In this paper, I take a careful look at "community self-paternalism"; scrutiny reveals that this proposed justification of criminalization is quite different from its initial appearance. Revealing its true character dispels much of its initial appeal. I then argue for its rejection; of necessity, "community self-paternalism" treats some individuals as means merely, and not as ends in themselves.

SCHONSHECK, Jonathan. Drawing the Cave and Teaching the Divided Line. Teach Phil, 13(4), 373-377, D 90.

Plato's "Allegory of the Cave" is a powerful teaching tool. Yet few texts provide a drawing of the Cave; those which do typically portray only the Cave's interior. If one also draws the outside realm (in accord with Plato's instructions), the drawing will portray not only the division between the Sensible World and the Intelligible World, but also all four "levels of reality" specified by another Platonic image, the Divided Line. Indeed, the *proportions* of the Cave's regions can be made identical to the proportions of the Divided Line. Thus the Cave becomes the Divided Line "writ sideways," and the two images become mutually illuminating.

SCHONSHECK, Jonathan. Nuclear Stalemate: A Superior Escape from the Dilemmas of Deterrence. Phil Pub Affairs, 20(1), 35-51, Wint 91.

Timothy van Gelder has recently argued that, in order to escape from the well-known "dilemmas of deterrence," the US ought to minimize both the scope of its deterrent threats, and the nuclear weapons stockpile backing those threats. On the contrary, I argue, a superior escape from the dilemmas of deterrence requires expanding the scope of one's deterrent threats, and possessing the weapons needed to make those threats credible. If pursued by both superpowers, this strategy would result in "nuclear stalemate," a version of nuclear deterrence both safer and more stable than the version van Gelder advocates.

SCHONSHECK, Jonathan. "On the Implications of Sociobiology for Nuclear Weapons Policy" in *Issues in War and Peace: Philosophical Inquiries*, KUNKEL, Joseph (ed), 55-68. Wolfeboro, Longwood, 1989.

Peter Singer (*The Expanding Circle*) accepts the essentials of neo-Darwinian biology ("sociobiology"); so do I. Singer sees rosy implications: selection pressures will yield an "expanding circle" of morality that will include *all* humans. I disagree, endorsing the work of Shaw and Wong: "in-group amity" reinforces, and is reinforced by, "out-group enmity." The pressures of kin and group selection will lead to mutually suspecious and hostile groups; we should expect "tribalism" and ethnic violence to persist, and perhaps to escalate. Since these hostile groups might be nation-states with nuclear weapons, there will be a continuing strategic role for nuclear deterrent threats.

SCHOPEN, Gregory. The Buddha as an Owner of Property and Permanent Resident in Medieval Indian Monasteries. J Indian Phil, 18(3), 181-217, S 90.

SCHRADER, David E. The Antinomy of Divine Necessity. Int J Phil Relig, 30(1), 45-59, Ag 91.

In this paper I argue that divine necessity should not be understood as logical necessity. Whatever legitimate explanatory power the hypothesis of divine necessity possesses, and whatever other good purposes are served by our taking God's existence to be necessary are served equally well by a notion of divine necessity a bit more modest than logical necessity. Moreover, such a more modest notion of divine necessity, unlike the notion of divine necessity as logical necessity, does not run afoul of any kind of natural notions about the infinite variability of the domains of other possible worlds.

SCHRADER, Malcolm E. Reward, Punishment, and the Strategy of Evolution. Relig Hum, 24(4), 178-184, Autumn 90.

A scheme is proposed for a hereafter with an automatic system which rewards contributions to humanity and cannot act as an "opiate of the people." Contributions may be on a micro or macro scale, e.g., to individuals (including self), small groups, large groups, or humanity as a whole. With respect to population control, the system encourages procreation of lives that have a good chance of being happy. It is shown that this type of solution to the reward and punishment problem can also arise from a search for purpose in group oriented evolutionary strategy.

SCHRAG, Calvin O. "Explanation and Understanding in the Science of Human Behavior" in *Reconsidering Psychology: Perspectives from Continental Philosophy*, FAULCONER, James E (ed), 61-74. Pittsburgh, Duquesne Univ Pr, 1990.

The essay demonstrates a complimentarity of explanation and understanding as these two procedures are illustrated in the doing of a science of human behavior. Although the author recognizes that there is a distinction of some consequence between the data of the social and the natural sciences, he argues that interpretation is at work in both of the scientific endeavors. The central point is that interpretation binds or integrates explanation and understanding differently in a science of human behavior than is the case in the projects of a natural science.

SCHRAG, Calvin O. "Rationality between Modernity and Postmodernity" in *Life-World and Politics: Between Modernity and Postmodernity*, WHITE, Stephen K (ed), 81-106. Notre Dame, Univ Notre Dame Pr, 1989.

In this essay the author develops a new notion of rationality (which he has come to call "transveral rationality") that passes between the modernist claims for universality and the postmodernist celebration of incommensurable particulars. This new notion of rationality enables one to avoid the pretentious claims for universal, ahistorical foundations without succumbing to a postmodern historicism and relativism. Transversality makes possible a *transcultural understanding and communication* that effects a passage between ahistorical knowledge and a relativizing historicism.

SCHRAG, Francis. Discretion, Punishment, and Juvenile Justice. Crim Just Ethics, 10(1), 3-7, Wint-Spr 91.

SCHRECK, P A. Cartesian Scepticism and Relevant Alternatives. Eidos, 8(2), 125-137, D 89.

In recent years many philosphers, such as Dretske, Goldman, and Stine, have attempted to refute scepticism by arguing that the sceptic makes unnecessary demands on the cognizer. These philosophers argue that the hypothetical situations upon which sceptical arguments are based need not be considered and that only relevant alternatives to knowledge need be taken into account. This essay seeks to refute these arguments by demonstrating that they all ultimately beg the question against the sceptic.

SCHRECK, P A. Locke's Account of Personal Identity. Gnosis, 3(3), 89-100, D 90.

One of the most prominent theories of personal identity is that of Locke, who equates personal identity with identity of consciousness. This essay seeks to critically examine Locke's theory in light of certain objections which have been made to it. The conclusion reached is that Locke's account is inadequate because it ignores any physical criteria of personal identity, and such criteria cannot be ignored. Although no set of criteria are established in this essay, a combination of physical and non-physical criteria are indicated as being defensible.

SCHREITER, Jörg. Hermeneutics (in Hungarian). Magyar Filozof Szemle, 5-6, 574-592, 1990.

Hermeneutik ist Deutungslehre, Lehre vom Verstehen. Vielmehr hatte die Anwendung hermeneutischer Verfahren häufig das (beabsichtigte) Ergebnis, mit Hilfe anerkannter Autoritäten der Vergangenheit (Gelehrter, Gesetzgeber usw.) auf das gesellschaftliche Bewusstsein späterer Epochen einzuwirken, um nicht nur auf geistige, sondern auch auf politische, ökonomische, juristische usw. Prozesse Einfluss zu nehmen. (edited)

SCHRENK, Lawrence P. A Middle Platonic Reading of Plato's Theory of Recollection. Ancient Phil, 11(1), 103-110, Spr 91.

This study traces the changing interpretation of Platonic recollection by examining its role in one middle Platonic thinker, Albinus (c. first century A.D.), who devotes an extended section of his *Didaskalikos* (chapter 25, 3) to this subject. He develops a most thorough and innovative interpretation of Platonic recollection, for he integrates the Platonic theory of recollection with an Aristotelian philosophy of science: he uses recollection to establish first principles which ground a demonstrative science.

SCHREURS, Nico. "Keine festbegrenzte und Wahrhaft anschauliche Vorstelling". Frei Z Phil Theol, 38(1-2), 27-56, 1991.

In Schleiermacher's 'Glaubenslehre' the doctrine of the Last Things is part of the doctrine of the Church, the part namely in which the totally new life of the Church at the end of time is described. Schleiermacher's endeavour to find one all-encompassing image for these, as he calls them, 'prophetic doctrines' fails. This is due to the fact that at the same time he wants to visualise the continuation of individuals after death. It is argued that Schleiermachers naturalistic vision on religion which does not allow for divine initiative in history is the main obstacle why his doctrine of the Last Things remains unsatisfactory.

SCHRIFT, Alan D. Nietzsche and the Critique of Oppositional Thinking. Hist Euro Ideas, 11, 783-790, 1989.

The critique of binary, oppositional thinking is one of the themes dominating contemporary philosophy. In attempting to think beyond traditional oppositions (truth/error, good/evil), I argue that Nietzsche's genealogical method stands as a model for several postmodern thinkers. Nietzsche's genealogical account of will to power is shown to avoid the inevitable hierarchization accompanying oppositional thinking. The value of his pluralistic account, and the view of language on which it is based, emerge most clearly in Nietzsche's deconstructive critique of authority and in the ways his attempt to think difference differently are appropriated by, among others, Derrida and Foucault.

SCHRIFT, Alan D. *Nietzsche and the Question of Interpretation*. New York, Routledge, 1990.

The book offers detailed expositions of Nietzsche's views on language, metaphor, rhetoric, perspectivism, philology, truth and genealogy, showing the methodological implications of his remarks for hermeneutics and questions of textuality. It provides a critical analysis of Heidegger's Nietzsche-Interpretation as dogmatic and Nietzsche's French reception as relativistic. Arguing that Nietzsche anticipated the hermeneutic dilemma of dogmatism and relativism, I propose a pluralistic alternative. By examining the tension between perspectivism and philology and showing how it animated Nietzsche's own genealogical interpretations, I display genealogy as a practice which can accept multiple interpretations without relinquishing the ability to judge some as better than others.

SCHRÖDER, Richard. Fundamental Question of Philosophy: Remarks on the Pending Philosophical Reappraisal of the Past in the GDR (in German). Deut Z Phil, 38(11), 1064-1082, 1990.

Der Marxismus-Leninismus behauptet, es gebe nur eine "Grundfrage der Philosophie", namlich die Frage: "Was ist das Primare, die Materie oder das Bewusstsein?" Der Aufsatz analysiert die Widersprüche und semantischen Absurditäten der offiziellen Fassung dieser Lehre (I) und gibt eine kurze Dogmengeschichte dieser Lehre, in der sich Fragestellungen unverinerht verschoben haben (II).

SCHRÖDER, Richard. The Philosophy of Responsibility (in German). Deut Z Phil, 38(6), 551-559, 1990.

Der Beitrag stellt das Denken Georg Pichts (1913-1982) vor, dessen Gesamtausgabe seit 1985 erscheint. Picht geht der Frage nach, warum die von Wissenschaft und Technik gestaltete Welt nicht, wie einst erwartet, die Welt der befreiten, sondern die der zuhöchst gefährdeten Menschheit geworden ist. Und befragt mit diesem Interesse die Geschichte des europäischen Denkens. "Verantwortung" ist für ihn der Leitbegriff einer Philosophie, die an der Zukunft der Menschheit ihre Orientierung hat. Und die neuzeitliche Orientierung am Subjektbegriff überwindet, die nach Picht ein versteckter Theomorphismus ist.

SCHUBERT, Lenhart. "Monotonic Solution of The Frame Problem in The Situation Calculus" in *Knowledge Representation and Defeasible Reasoning*, KYBURG JR, Henry E (ed), 23-67. Norwell, Kluwer, 1990.

McCarthy and Hayes concluded (ca. 1969) that axiomatizing dynamic worlds required huge numbers of "frame axioms" specifying what *doesn't* change in the course of any given action. Many nonmonotonic and procedural remedies for this difficulty have been proposed since then. This paper proposes a monotonic approach based on "explanation closure axioms." These attribute changes to the occurrence of certain actions, and hence rule out changes not attributable to the actions that actually occurred. Such axioms are succinct, independently motivated, and justify the application of efficient STRIPS-like (but monotonic) methods of inferring change and nonchange.

SCHUELER, G F. Anti-Realism and Skepticism in Ethics. Iyyun, 40(1), 3-18, Ja 91.

This paper examines a feature of the project of replacing the 'philosophical picture' which distinguishes descriptive concepts from concepts which we merely project onto reality (i.e., the picture that makes anti-realism in ethics plausible) with some form of 'internal realism' which denies this distinction. It is argued that such a change would have no effect at all on ethical skepticism. Genuine ethical skeptics suspect that only ones own interests and conerns give one any reason to act and that ethical considerations, just by themselves, do not. This suspicion is not allayed by making 'cause' as much a projection as 'fair'.

SCHUHMANN, Karl and SCARAMUZZA, Gabriele. Ein Husserlmanuskript über Ästhetik. Husserl Stud, 7(3), 165-177, 1990.

SCHUHMANN, Karl and SMITH, Barry. Elements of Speech Act Theory in the Work of Thomas Reid. Hist Phil Quart, 7(1), 47-66, Ja 90.

The account of social acts sketched by Thomas Reid is shown to constitute an anticipation of the theory of speech acts standardly associated with Austin and Searle. Reid's ideas are compared also with that other (and in many ways more important) pre-Austinian speech act theory worked out by the phenomenologist Adolf Reinach in his monograph on the act of promising of 1913.

SCHUHMANN, Karl. Herbert Spiegelberg 1904-1990. Husserl Stud, 7(2), 123-127, 1990.

SCHUHMANN, Karl. Husserl's Concept of Philosophy. J Brit Soc Phenomenol, 21(3), 274-283, O 90.

SCHUHMANN, Karl. Husserl's Yearbook. Phil Phenomenol Res, 50 SUPP, 1-25, Fall 90.

SCHULMAN, J Neil. Informational Property: Logorights. J Soc Biol Struct, 13(2), 93-117, My 90.

"Informational Property: Logorights" is not, specifically, about copyright, patent, or "intellectual" property rights. It is a theoretical base for a new concept of "informational" property, not based on copyright and patent laws, but on a natural-rights approach to property rights. The concept of the logoright is based on the right to the "material identity" of a property being one of the exploitable aspects of a created artifact, and a protectable property right thereby. In other words, I'm saying that there are property rights in information based on natural rights, regardless of whether political bodies recognize these rights in constitutions, treaties, or legislation.

SCHULTE, Christoph. Philosophy of History is Heternomous Philosophy (in German). Deut Z Phil, 38(9), 809-817, 1990.

SCHULTE, Joachim. "Wittgenstein's Notion of Secondary Meaning and Davidson's Account of Metaphor—A Comparison" in *The Mind of Donald Davidson*, BRANDL, Johannes (ed), 141-148. Amsterdam, Rodopi, 1989.

There are similarities between Davidson's theory of meaning and that of Wittgenstein's *Tractatus*. But in Wittgenstein's later work the relation between meaning and use is seen in a completely different way and not in the least similar to Davidson's conception. In spite of this divergence, however, certain parallels exist between Wittgenstein's treatment of expressions which can be said to have secondary meanings and Davidson's notion of the metaphorical use of certain expressions.

SCHULTHESS, Daniel. Obligation and Knowledge (in French). Rev Theol Phil, 123(1), 1-15, 1991.

Knowledge is required in the actual exercise of practical reason: knowledge of one's obligations (according to the deontological orientation in practical philosophy), knowledge of one's action, knowledge of the situations in which one is involved. Requirements relative to such knowledge can be articulated in what is called here 'second-order obligations'. The paper's aim is to show the role of these obligations and to inquire into the link they establish between practical and theoretical reason.

SCHULTZ, Frederick M. The Problematics of "Clarity" in Research of Teaching: A Response to Walden Crabtree. Phil Stud Educ, /, 82-88, 1986.

SCHULZ, Larry J and CUNNINGHAM, Thomas J. On the Concept of Freedom in the *I Ching*: A Deconstructionist View of Self-Cultivation. J Chin Phil, 17(3), 301-313, S 90.

SCHULZ, Larry J. Structural Motifs in the Arrangement of the 64 *Gua* in the *Zhouyi*. J Chin Phil, 17(3), 345-358, S 90.

SCHULZ, Richard M and BRUSHWOOD, David B. The Pharmacist's Role in Patient Care. Hastings Center Rep, 21(1), 12-17, Ja-F 91.

This article examines patient advocacy as a new role for pharmacists. As advocates, pharmacists would assist patients in drug use decisions while respecting patients' rights to make decisions. The role of patient advocate is contrasted with the existing distributive and clinical roles of pharmacists. The article discusses potential problems with pharmacists as patient advocates, such as interprofessional conflict and inadequate training. The authors conclude that the public would be well served by pharmacists who are patient advocates, and that legal scholars, ethicists, and health care analysts should seriously consider adopting policies that encourage such an expansion.

SCHUMACHER, Paul J. Art for Existence's Sake: A Heideggerian Revision. J Aes Educ, 24(2), 83-89, Sum 90.

The mnemonic slogan "Art for Art's Sake" comes closer to literary truth when a simple term is substituted: "Existence's Sake." For art is one of the most effective revealers of the truth of Existence, what Heidegger calls "the Being of beings." Art is a unitary process in which three factors are operative. The *artist* creates an as-if universe revealing the real world. The *artwork* itself, where the author's insights and the reader's expectations meet, floodlights the self and others, time, place, and language. The *audience* discovers meaning as it becomes existentially involved—acquiring correct seeing rather than correct facts.

SCHUMM, George and SHAPIRO, Stewart. Expressive Completeness and Decidability. Notre Dame J Form Log, 31(4), 576-579, Fall 90.

Under what conditions is the expressive completeness of a set of connectives decidable? The answer is shown to depend crucially upon how the set is encoded as input to a Turing machine.

SCHUPP, F and HEINEKAMP, A. Lógica y metafísica de Leibniz: Principales líneas de interpretación durante el siglo XX. Dialogo Filosof, 7(1), 4-31, Ja-Ap 91.

SCHÜRMANN, Reiner. Ultimate Double Binds. Grad Fac Phil J, 14(2)-15(1), 213-236, 1991.

SCHURZ, Gerhard. How Far Can Hume's Is-Ought Thesis Be Generalized? J Phil Log, 20(1), 37-95, F 91.

The *special Hume thesis SH* says that no contingent normative conclusion is deducible from a consistent descriptive premise set. To solve Prior's paradox, the *generalized Hume thesis GH* is developed, saying that every deduction of a *mixed* conclusion from a consistent descriptive premise set is *completely ought-irrelevant*. It is proved that GH holds in a logic L in the class of *normal alethic-deontic modal predicate logics*, iff L is axiomatizable without *is-ought bridge principles*, iff L is characterizable by *is-ought separated* Kripke frames. In contrast, SH holds only in a much narrower class of logics; nontrivial counterexamples can be found.

SCHÜSSLER, Ingeborg. Troeltsch and Nietzsche: Critical Reflections on Ernst Troeltsch's Portrayal of Nietzsche (in German). Deut Z Phil, 38(11), 1035-1046, 1990.

For Troeltsch, Nietzsche is a representative not only of "philosophy of history," but also and overall—according to the reception of Nietzsche at his time—of irrationalism and atheism. The relation of Troeltsch towards Nietzsche is not that of objective discussion, but polemics. Why is this so? Research, which doesn't consider Nietzsche by Troeltsch, but Troeltsch by Nietzsche, discovers that the position of Troeltsch is that of a *nihilism*, refusing to recognize itself. Nietzsche undermines the philosophical fundamentals of Troeltsch. Therefore Troeltsch avoids an objective discussion with him.

SCHÜSSLER, Werner. Le pouvoir, existential de l'être humain. Laval Theol Phil, 47(1), 23-37, F 91.

Le pouvoir est devenu suspect en notre temps. Parmi les chrétiens tout spécialement, s'est propagé un rejet de principe de tout utilisation du pouvoir, au sens d'une non-violence inconditionnelle. Et pourtant ces mêmes chréitiens appellent Dieu "tout-puissant" dans le Credo. Cet article cherche à montrer les malentendus qui entourent la notion de pouvoir, ainsi qu'à faire voir le pouvoir comme un existential de l'être humain. Mais en même temps, les considerérations qui suivent veulent, à partir du problème du pouvoir, ouvrir un nouvel accès à la réalité humaine.

SCHUTTE, Ofelia M. The Master-Slave Dialectic in Latin America: The Social Criticism of Zea, Freire, and Roig. Owl Minerva, 22(1), 5-18, Fall 90.

The purpose of the article is to offer some readings of the Hegelian dialectic between master and slave, as the latter topic has been interpreted by three Latin American social critics in philosophy. A critical discussion is given of perspectives by the Mexican Leopoldo Zea, the Brazilian Paulo Freire, and the Argentine Arturo A Roig. The essay relates Hegel's ideas to Zea's philosophy of history, Freire's philosophy of education, and Roig's philosophy of Latin American culture. The question of the point of departure for a specifically Latin American philosophy is also discussed.

SCHUTTE, Ofelia. Irigaray on Subjectivity. Hypatia, 6(2), 64-76, Sum 91.

In *Speculum of the Other Women (1974)*, Luce Irigaray argues that "any theory of the subject has always been appropriated by the masculine." This paper offers an analysis of Irigarary's critique of subjectivity and examines the psychological mechanism referred to as "the phallic economy of castration." A different way of conceiving the relation between subject and object is explored by imagining a new subject of desire.

SCHUTTE, Ofelia. Origins and Tendencies of the Philosophy of Liberation in Latin American Thought: A Critique of Dussel's Ethics. Phil Forum, 22(3), 270-295, Spr 91.

A historical overview of the origins of liberation philosophy in Argentina in the early 1970s is followed by an analysis of some conceptual characteristics of the movement. The political ambiguity of using the concept "people" as subject of liberation is noted, especially in the context of distinguishing between right-wing theories of national popular liberation and Marxism. A critique of Enrique Dussel's absolutist use of the concept of otherness (alterity) in liberation ethics is offered. Also considered are the culturalist approach of Juan Carlos Scannone, S J and the historicist orientation of Horacio Cerutti Guldberg.

SCHWARTZ, Howard S. Narcissim Project and Corporate Decay: The Case of General Motors. Bus Ethics Quart, 1(3), 249-268, Jl 91.

Organizational participants learn that "getting ahead" in organizational life comes from dramatizing a fantasy about the organization's perfection. The fantasy is the return to narcissim. Since the return to narcissim is impossible, orienting the organization to the dramatization of this fantasy means that the organization loses touch with reality. The result is organizational decay—a condition of systemic ineffectiveness. Organizational decay may be compared with the consequences of *hubris*. (edited)

SCHWARTZ, Justin. Reduction, Elimination, and the Mental. Phil Sci, 58(2), 203-220, Je 91.

The antireductionist arguments of many philosophers (e.g., Baker, Fodor and Davidson) are motivated by a worry that successful reduction would eliminate rather than conserve the mental. This worry derives from a misunderstanding of the empiricist account of reduction, which, although it does not underwrite "cognitive suicide," should be rejected for its positivist baggage. Philosophy of psychology needs more detailed attention to issues in natural science which serve as analogies for reduction of the mental. I consider a range of central cases, including water and H_2O, genes and DNA, and common sense and scientific solidity. The last case is illuminated by Eddington's Two Tables paradox, a resolution which suggests the plasticity of the mental under reduction. If reduction of the mental is like any of these cases, it is neither empiricist nor eliminative.

SCHWARTZ, Peter Hammond. Rejoinder to Springborg's "His Majesty Is a Baby?" A Critical Response to Peter Hammond Schwartz. Polit Theory, 18(4), 686-689, N 90.

SCHWARTZ, Stephen P and THROOP, William. Intuitionism and Vagueness. Erkenntnis, 34(3), 347-356, My 91.

Putnam has argued that vagueness is a reason to abandon realism in favor of anti-realism. Realists are faced with vagueness generated problems, such as the sorites paradox, which anti-realists can avoid. Putnam claims that intuitionist logic can serve as an anti-realist logic for vague terms and offers a solution to the sorites paradox. We argue that intuitionist logic is at best a formal "solution" to the paradox and is not a genuine solution. Furthermore, versions of the sorites do still arise in intuitionist logic. Vagueness is a serious problem for both the realist and the anti-realist.

SCHWARTZ, Thomas. "Impressions of Philosophy" in *Acting and Reflecting: The Interdisciplinary Turn in Philosophy*, SIEG, Wilfried (ed), 31-37. Norwell, Kluwer, 1990.

SCHWARZ, Dov. Al-Kindi's Psychology (in Hebrew). Iyyun, 40(2), 197-216, Ap 91.

SCHWARZE, M G and LEWIN, R A and MIKENBERG, I F. Algebraization of Paraconsistent Logic P^1. J Non-Classical Log, 7(1-2), 79-88, My-N 90.

Using techniques developed by Blok and Pigozzi, we prove that paraconsistent logic P1, introduced by Sette, is algebraizable.

SCHWEGLER, Helmut and ROTH, Gerhard. Self-Organization, Emergent Properties and the Unity of the World. Philosophica, 46(2), 45-64, 1990.

SCHWEICKART, David. The Politics and Morality of Unequal Exchange: Emmanuel and Roemer, Analysis and Synthesis. Econ Phil, 7(1), 13-36, Ap 91.

Arghiri Emmanuel, using a modified Marxian economics, has argued that unequal exchange accounts for an alliance of First World capitalists and workers against those of the Third World. John Roemer, using neoclassical, general-equilibrium theory, has shown that free trade can be exploitative. I compare and contrast these two approaches, then offer a model that synthesizes the two so as to make transparent what really happens (in terms of labor, money and material) when there is an "unequal exchange" between countries. I conclude that (under certain conditions) workers of the First World benefit from unequal exchange even though they do not exploit their Third World counterparts.

SCHWEIDLER, Walter. Human Rights and Freedom: Is Kant Relevant to the Current Discussion? Listening, 26(2), 121-133, Spr 91.

The article intends to show the relevance of the Kantian model of philosophy for questions of justification of the concept of human rights. Practical philosophy in the Kantian sense is a reconstruction of the rationality of human institutions and communication. The task of philosophy is not to derive human rights from any higher principles but to show them as necessary presuppositions for any justification of human conduct. Kant's result is the thesis that there is only one basic human right, namely freedom. Not questions of political application but this highly theoretical train of thought and his general model of philosophy are the reasons for Kant's liberal understanding of human rights.

SCHWEIZER, Paul. Blind Grasping and Fregean Senses. Phil Stud, 62(3), 263-287, Je 91.

The paper addresses the widely held belief that Frege's philosophy of language is an exemplary instance of the 'traditional theory' of meaning and reference, and hence that Frege is committed to the view that some aspect of the language user's psychological state is responsible for determining reference. It is argued that Frege's staunch semantical realism precludes any such intimate link between mind and meaning, and hence that Frege's theory is immune to both Putnam's Twin Earth argument and to Kripke's critique of descriptive theories of reference.

SCHWOERER, Lois G. Locke, Lockean Ideas, and the Glorious Revolution. J Hist Ideas, 51(4), 531-548, O-D 90.

SCHWYZER, Hubert. *The Unity of Understanding: A Study in Kantian Problems*. New York, Clarendon/Oxford Pr, 1990.

This book is about Kant's account of human understanding—of our capacity to form concepts of, and to be conscious of, things in the world. It argues that the conditions which Kant lays down for understanding—conditions about the autonomy of thought, and about the relation of concepts to objects and of language to experience—cannot be satisfied within his overall picture of understanding as *representing something to oneself*. If Kant's conditions are to be satisfied, understanding must be seen not as a capacity for mental representation, for having ideas, but rather as a capacity for action.

SCIACCA, Fabrizio. Intorno all'autofondazione delle norme: Ragione formale e principio razionale tra logica e diritto. Riv Int Filosof Diritto, 67(1), 120-126, Ja-Mr 90.

SCOLNICOV, Samuel (trans). Lucian: The Sale of Lives (in Hebrew). Iyyun, 39(4), 423-439, O 90.

SCOLNICOV, Samuel. On Taking Socratic Irony Seriously (in Hebrew). Iyyun, 40(2), 137-149, Ap 91.

SCOTT, Charles E. "Foucault and the Question of Humanism" in *The Question of Humanism: Challenges and Possibilities*, GOICOECHEA, David (ed), 205-213. Buffalo, Prometheus, 1991.

SCOTT, Charles E. Genealogy and *Différance*. Res Phenomenol, 20, 55-66, 1990.

The article is a comparative study of genealogical thought in the work of Foucault and Derrida. It considers Derrida's use of *non-historical* to describe *differance* and the historical space which determines this description.

SCOTT, Charles E. Heidegger and Psychoanalysis: The Seminars in Zollikon. Heidegger Stud, 6, 131-141, 1990.

SCOTT, Charles E. "Postmodern Language" in *Postmodernism—Philosophy and the Arts (Continental Philosophy III)*, SILVERMAN, Hugh J (ed), 33-52. New York, Routledge, 1990.

SCOTT, Charles E. The Question of Ethics in Foucault's Thought. J Brit Soc Phenomenol, 22(1), 33-43, Ja 91.

SCOTT, Charles E. *The Question of Ethics*. Bloomington, Indiana Univ Pr, 1990.

The book advances the broad claim that ethics as a way of judging and thinking has come into question as philosophers have confronted suffering and conflicts that arise from our traditional systems of value. The question of ethics arises from 19th century European thought and finds its most effective early expression in Nietzsche's writings. The book shows how the self-overcoming movement of Nietzsche's thought recoils on its own values and, in the context of the ascetic ideal, prevents the formation of normative ethics. After tracing a movement in Foucault's work on the formation of ethical subjectivity similar to that found in Nietzsche's thought the book turns to Heidegger whose writing both develops the question of ethics and betrays it.

SCOTT, Charles. Heidegger's Rector's Address: A Loss of the Question of Ethics. Grad Fac Phil J, 14(2)-15(1), 237-264, 1991.

The article is a close reading of Heidegger's 1933 Rector's Address which shows the manner in which he abandons the question of ethics and adopts with certainty an ethical position. Had he maintained the question of ethics which characterizes his previous work, Heidegger could have avoided many of the dangers that characterized his ethical position.

SCOTT, Dana S. "The Computational Conception of Mind" in *Acting and Reflecting: The Interdisciplinary Turn in Philosophy*, SIEG, Wilfried (ed), 39. Norwell, Kluwer, 1990.

SCOTT, Joan W. The Evidence of Experience. Crit Inquiry, 17(4), 773-797, Sum 91.

SCOTT, Pam and RICHARDS, Evelleen and MARTIN, Brian. Captives of Controversy: The Myth of the Neutral Social Researcher in Contemporary Scientific Controversies. Sci Tech Human Values, 15(4), 474-494, Autumn 90.

According to both traditional positivist approaches and also to the sociology of scientific knowledge, social analysts should not themselves become involved in the controversies they are investigating. But the experiences of the authors in studying contemporary scientific controversies—specifically, over the Australian Animal Health Laboratory, fluoridation, and vitamin C and cancer—show that analysts, whatever their intentions, cannot avoid being drawn into the fray. The field of controversy studies needs to address the implications of this process for both theory and practice.

SCOTTI, Nicoletta. Aspetti di attualità teoretica del pensiero procliano negli studi di Werner Beierwaltes. Riv Filosof Neo-Scolas, 82(1), 120-145, Ja-Mr 90.

Werner Beierwaltes, the well-known German scholar of oveoplatonism and of its "Wirkungsgeschichte," has developed some new important aspects in the study of Proclus. The present study tries to give an account of these novelties, through an analysis of all Beierwaltes' writings about these subjects. The analysis is divided in three main points: 1) the proper meaning of an historical research, 2) the relation between Hegel and Proclus, 3) the absolute transcendence of the One: 4) the complex structure of the second hypothesis, 5) knowledge as the best human way to reach God.

SCRUTON, Roger. "Aesthetic Experience and Culture" in *XIth International Congress in Aesthetics, Nottingham 1988*, WOODFIELD, Richard (ed), 176-179. Nottingham, Nottingham Polytech, 1990.

The article explores the connection between culture (in the anthropologist's sense) and religion, and between religious and aesthetic experience. He argues for a revised version of Kant's theory, that aesthetic and religious experience are closely connected.

SCRUTON, Roger. "The Left Establishment" in *Perspectives on Ideas and Reality*, NYÍRI, J C (ed), 41-54. Budapest, Kiskonyvtara, 1990.

Why do most academics and schoolteachers tend to the left? Various explanation are tried. A case is made for 'public choice' theory and the idea of 'rest-seeking' through ideological conformity. This too is not entirely plausible. Reflections on the 'clerk' and his changed position in the modern world.

SCULL, Andrew. Deinstitutionalization: Cycles of Despair. J Mind Behav, 11(3-4), 301-311, Sum-Autumn 90.

Examining the period from the rise of the asylum in the nineteenth century through the current debates about the failures of deinstitutionalization, this paper provides a critical perspective on the history of Anglo-American responses to chronic mental disability. It concludes with a pessimistic assessment of the prospects for the future evolution of public policy in this area.

SEAGER, William. Disjunctive Laws and Supervenience. Analysis, 51(2), 93-98, Mr 91.

SEAGER, William. The Logic of Lost Lingens. J Phil Log, 19(4), 407-428, N 90.

SEARLE, John R. Intentionalistic Explanations in the Social Sciences. Phil Soc Sci, 21(3), 332-344, S 91.

The dispute between the empiricist and interpretivist conceptions of the social sciences is properly conceived not as a matter of reduction or covering laws. Features specific to the social sciences include the following. Explanations of human behavior make reference to intentional causation; social phenomena are permeated with mental components and are self-referential; social science explanations have not been as successful as those in natural science because a social phenomenon exists only if people believe it exists. Elements of an apparatus necessary to analyze this problematic social ontology are given and include self-referentiality, constitutive rules, collective intentionality, linguistic permeation of the facts, systematic interrelationships among social facts, and primacy of acts over objects.

SEARLE, John R. Is the Brain a Digital Computer? Proc Amer Phil Ass, 64(3), 21-37, N 90.

SECORD, Paul F. "'Subjects' versus 'Persons' in Social Psychological Research" in *Harré and His Critics*, BHASKAR, Roy (ed), 165-188. Cambridge, Blackwell, 1990.

SEDGWICK, Sally. On Lying and the Role of Content in Kant's Ethics. Kantstudien, 82(1), 42-62, 1991.

Kant's 1797 essay *On a Supposed Right to Tell Lies from Benevolent Motives* is notorious for the obstacles it presents to those both sympathetic to his formalist project in moral philosophy and concerned to argue against critics that it does not yield a cold-hearted rigorism. In this paper the author relies on a clarification of structural features of his moral theory and of the objectives of the lying essay in particular in attempt to cast its apparent rigorism in a more acceptable light. It is argued that the heavy-handed stance Kant takes in the lying essay must be understood in the context of a discussion that is distinct from the standpoint of applied practical philosophy, and that a more plausible position on lying emerges once it is understood in this way.

SEDZIWY, Stanislaw. Progress in Mathematics and Other Arts. Phil Sci (Tucson), 4, 241-245, 1990.

The note presents an opinion that the important, often overlooked reason of the rapid development and changes of contemporary mathematics lies in the fact that mathematics like other sciences or arts became a commodity and in consequence is subordinated to the rules of the market. This fact has not only profound consequences on mathematics itself but it also drastically changed the attitude of scientists to the research work. It may be well to realize that the exaggerated activity does not necessarily mean the progress, very often it produces only a "noise" in science.

SEEL, Gerhard. Thèses sur le rôle de l'interprétation dans l'art. Diotima, 18, 25-26, 1990.

SEERVELD, Calvin. Footprints in the Snow. Phil Reform, 56(1), 1-34, 1991.

SEESE, D. The Structure of the Models of Decidable Monadic Theories of Graphs. Annals Pure Applied Log, 53(2), 169-195, Jl 91.

In this article the structure of the models of decidable (weak) monadic theories of planar graphs is investigated. It is shown that if the (weak) monadic theory of a class *K* of planar graphs is decidable, then the tree-width in the sense of Robertson and Seymour (1984) of the elements of *K* is universally bounded and there is a class *T* of trees such that the (weak) monadic theory of *K* is interpretable in the (weak) monadic theory of *T*.

SEGAL, Gabriel and SOBER, Elliott. The Causal Efficacy of Content. Phil Stud, 63(1), 1-30, Jl 91.

SEGAL, Robert A. Misconceptions of the Social Sciences. Zygon, 25(3), 263-278, S 90.

Scholars in religious studies, or "religionists," often mischaracterize the social-scientific study of religion. They assume that a social-scientific analysis of the origin, function, meaning, or truth of religion either opposes or disregards the believer's analysis, which religionists profess to present and defend. I do not argue that the social sciences analyze religion from the believer's point of view. I argue instead that a social-scientific analysis is more akin and germane to the believer's point of view than religionists assume. I single out seven mischaracterizations of the social sciences typically held by religionists.

SEGERBERG, Krister. Validity and Satisfaction in Imperative Logic. Notre Dame J Form Log, 31(2), 203-221, Spr 90.

An imperative logic is studied in which commands are treated as prescribed actions rather than as, traditionally, prescribed propositions. This approach is related to those of Jorgensen and Ross.

SEGERT, Dieter. Some Basic Problems of a Political Theory of Modern Socialism (in German). Deut Z Phil, 38(3), 230-237, 1990.

SEGURA, Carmen. El carácter inmanente del conocimiento. Themata, 6, 169-176, 1989.

SEIBT, Johanna. *Properties as Processes: A Synoptic Study of Wilfried Sellars' Nominalism*. Atascadero, Ridgeview, 1990.

Nominalists deny that abstract entities are necessary elements of philosophical theory formation. This claim must be defended on logical, semantic, epistemological, and metaphysical grounds. Amongst the many nominalist theories, ancient and contemporary, the philosophy of Wilfrid Sellars so far offers the only nominalist approach that does justice to each dimension of a nominalist stance. In a sense, the book documents the author's own initiation to Sellars's work, to nominalism, to contemporary systematic philosophy. (edited)

SEIDENFELD, Teddy and SCHERVISH, M J. "Decisions Without Ordering" in *Acting and Reflecting: The Interdisciplinary Turn in Philosophy*, SIEG, Wilfried (ed), 143-170. Norwell, Kluwer, 1990.

We review the axiomatic foundations of subjective utility theory with a view toward understanding the implications of each axiom. We consider three different approaches, namely, the construction of utilities in the presence of canonical probabilities, the construction of probabilities in the presence of utilities, and the simultaneous construction of both probabilities and utilities. We focus attention on the axioms of independence and weak ordering. The independence axiom is seen to be necessary in order to prevent a form of Dutch Book in sequential problems. (edited)

SEIDENFELD, Teddy. "Two Perspectives on Consensus for (Bayesian) Inference and Decisions" in *Knowledge Representation and Defeasible Reasoning*, KYBURG JR, Henry E (ed), 267-286. Norwell, Kluwer, 1990.

In this paper I discuss questions of consensus among Bayesian investigators, from two perspectives: (1) Inference: What are the agreements in posterior probabilities that result from increasing shared data? and (2) Decisions: What are the shared (strict) preferences of Bayesian decision makers? When do their shared preferences support coherent compromises? Concerning topic 1, I report results (obtained in collaboration with M J Schervish) about asymptotic consensus and certainty with increasing evidence. Concerning topic 2, I report results (obtained in collaboration with J B Kadane and M J Schervish) on the shared agreements of two Bayesian decision makers who have some differences in their probabilities for events *and* some differences in their utilities for outcomes. (edited)

SEIDENFELD, Teddy and SCHERVISH, M J and KADANE, J B. When Fair Betting Odds are Not Degrees of Belief. Proc Phil Sci Ass, 1, 517-524, 1990.

The "Dutch Book" argument, tracing back to Ramsey and to deFinetti, offers prudential grounds for action in conformity with personal probability. Under several structural assumptions about combinations of stakes (that is, assumptions about the combination of wagers), your betting policy is *coherent* only if your *fair odds* are probabilities. The central question posed here is the following one: Besides providing an operational test of coherent betting, does the "Book" argument also provide for adequate measurement (*elicitation*) of the agents degrees of beliefs? That is, are an agent's fair odds also his/her personal probabilities for those events? We argue the answer is "No!" The problem is caused by the possibility of state dependent utilities.

SEIDL, Horst. Sulla posizione dell'uomo nella natura. Aquinas, 33(3), 567-577, S-D 90.

SEIGFRIED, Charlene Haddock. The Pragmatist Sieve of Concepts: Description versus Interpretation. J Phil, 87(11), 585-592, N 90.

William James's writings are used to illustrate a systematic ambiguity found in pragmatism. Although sometimes treated as a debate between realist and idealist perspectives, I locate it in incompatible appeals to the immediate intuition of facts and to their irreducibly interpretive character. James intended to neutrally describe the facts of experience as a better basis for philosophic claims. But he instead demonstrated that experience is always already unified through the interests and passions of our active spontaneity. I argue that the interpretive approach better reflects the pragmatist position that we find ourselves always already within a world which we help constitute.

SEIGFRIED, Charlene Haddock. Where Are All the Pragmatist Feminists? Hypatia, 6(2), 1-20, Sum 91.

Unlike our counterparts in Europe who have rewritten their specific cultural philosophical heritage, American feminists have not yet critically reappropriated our own philosophical tradition of classical American pragmatism. The neglect is especially puzzling, given that both feminism and pragmatism explicitly acknowledge the material or cultural specificity of supposedly abstract theorizing. In this article I suggest some reasons for the neglect, call for the rediscovery of women pragmatists, reflect on a feminine side of pragmatism, and point out some common features. The aim is to encourage the further development of a feminist revisioning of pragmatism and a pragmatist version of feminism.

SEIGFRIED, Hans. Autonomy and Quantum Physics: Nietzsche, Heidegger, and Heisenberg. Phil Sci, 57(4), 619-630, D 90.

The literary and poetic turn in philosophy exudes contempt for science and hostility against technology, both allegedly justified on grounds established by Nietzsche and Heidegger. I try to show that these grounds instead call for an extremely positive assessment of science and technology. It turns out that what Nietzsche and Heidegger describe as our highest achievement, namely, human autonomy, is really made possible by modern experimental physics. And I show how this assessment is borne out by what Heisenberg describes as the lesson of quantum physics.

SEITTER, Walter. Michel Foucault: From the Humanities to Political Thought (in German). Deut Z Phil, 38(10), 922-930, 1990.

SEITZ, Brian. "The Televised and the Untelevised: Keeping an Eye On/Off the Tube" in *Postmodernism—Philosophy and the Arts (Continental Philosophy III)*, SILVERMAN, Hugh J (ed), 187-206. New York, Routledge, 1990.

SEJNOWSKI, Terrence J and CHURCHLAND, Patricia Smith. "Neural Representation and Neural Computation" in *Philosophical Perspectives, 4: Action Theory and Philosophy of Mind, 1990*, TOMBERLIN, James E (ed), 343-382. Atascadero, Ridgeview, 1990.

SEKIGUCHI, Hiroshi. M Heideggers Auslegung von Sophokles' "Oedipus Tyrannus" (in Japanese). Bigaku, 41(3), 12-22, Wint 90.

Heideggers Auseinandersetzung mit dem griechischen Denken besteht immer darin, die im griechischen Denken gestiftete Anfänglichkeit wieder zurückzunehmen. Das gilt auch von seiner Auslegung von Sophokles' "Oedipus Tyrannus". Wir stellen hier heraus, was die von Heidegger in diester Tragödiendichtung gefundene Anfänglichkeit ist. (edited)

SELBACH, Ralf. Eine bisher unbeachtete Quelle des "Streits der Fakultäten". Kantstudien, 82(1), 96-101, 1991.

In the 'Streit der Fakultaeten' Immanuel Kant follows the early enlightenment concept of the three Superior Faculties which have to be useful and deal with the main human matters. In Kant's unprinted preliminary studies the Faculty of Philosophy is connected with the idea of utility as well, but not in the printed text. In 1798 the 'Philosophical Faculty' is introduced as being responsible for the 'Wahrheit'. This key word as well as the torsion of the metaphor of the 'ancilla theologiae' Kant found in Christian Wolff whom he remembered when he got in trouble with the censorship too.

SELBY, G Raymond. 'Too Busy for Ethics'. Ethics Med, 7(1), 8-10, Spr 91.

SELF, Donnie J and JECKER, Nancy S. Separating Care and Cure: An Analysis of Historical and Contemporary Images of Nursing and Medicine. J Med Phil, 16(3), 285-306, Je 91.

This paper provides a philosophical critique of professional stereotypes in medicine. In the course of this critique, we also offer a detailed analysis of the concept of care in health care. The paper first considers possible explanations for the traditional stereotype that caring is a province of nurses and women, while curing is an arena suited for physicians and men. It then dispels this stereotype and fine tunes the concept of care. A distinction between 'caring for' and 'caring about' is made, and concomitant notions of parentalism are elaborated. Finally, the paper illustrates, through the use of cases, diverse models of caring. Our discussion reveals the complexity of care and the alternative modes of caring in health care.

SELF, Donnie J and SKEEL, Joy D. A Study of the Foundations of Ethical Decision Making of Clinical Medical Ethicists. Theor Med, 12(2), 117-127, Je 91.

A study of clinical medical ethicists were conducted to determine the various philosophical positions they hold with respect to ethical decision making in medicine and their various positions' relationship to the subjective-objective controversy in value theory. The study revealed that most clinical medical ethicists tend to be objectivists in value theory. In addition, the study revealed that most clinical medical ethicists are consistent in the philosophical foundations of their ethical decision making. (edited)

SELLERY, J'Nan Morse. "The Necessity for Symbol and Myth: A Literary Amplification" in *Archetypal Process: Self and Divine in Whitehead, Jung, and Hillman*, GRIFFIN, David Ray (ed), 93-103. Evanston, Northwestern Univ Pr, 1989.

SELLS, Peter. Disjoint Reference into NP. Ling Phil, 14(2), 151-169, Ap 91.

SELMAN, Mark and ROSS, Murray. Epistemology, Practical Research, and Human Subjects. Proc Phil Educ, 46, 319-331, 1990.

This paper reviews major strands of criticism by educational philosophers of process-product research in education. It argues that such criticism has been ineffective at least in part because it has focussed too narrowly on obvious epistemological deficiencies while failing to attend to the practical and political results. Foucault's notion of disciplinary power is shown to be useful in illuminating the link between the epistemic and political aspects of such programs of practical research.

SEN, Pranab Kumar. Truths without Facts. J Indian Counc Phil Res, 5(3), 43-53, My-Ag 88.

The purpose of the paper is to show the continuity between traditional researches on truth and the recent theories on the subject by arguing that the classical correspondence theory itself finds its most defensible form in Tarski's definition of truth in terms of satisfaction. The reason why it is the most defensible form of the theory is that, *first*, it need not postulate facts as a kind of veil hanging between sentences and things, and *second*, it need not deny the reality of facts altogether, although this has been done by those who define truth by satisfaction.

SEN, Sanat Kumar. Choiceless Awareness. J Indian Counc Phil Res, 7(1), 43-55, S-D 89.

SEN, Sanat Kumar. Knowledge as Bondage: An Unconventional Approach. J Indian Counc Phil Res, 6(1), 61-66, S-D 88.

SENCERZ, Stefan. Descartes on Sensations and 'Animal Minds'. Phil Papers, 19(2), 119-141, Ag 90.

SENCHUK, Dennis M. Behavior, Biology, and Information Theory. Proc Phil Sci Ass, 1, 141-150, 1990.

SENCHUK, Dennis M. Consciousness Naturalized: Supervenience Without Physical Determinism. Amer Phil Quart, 28(1), 37-47, Ja 91.

This article defends the anti-compatibilistic contention that consciousness originates actions not fully predetermined by a closed system of physical laws. Without running afoul of the compellingly anti-Cartesian proposal that consciousness "supervenes" on physical reality, the paper endorses a dual-aspect theory of emergent conscious flexibility *as tied to* higher-level physical indeterminacy. The possibility of emergent macro-level physical indeterminacy is urged in direct opposition to a rational reconstruction of the strongest grounds for asserting physical determinism. This possibility does not depend upon irremediably random micro-level indeterminacy and seems to allow for more meaningful freedom of action than conceived of by compatibilists.

SENDLEWSKI, Andrzej. Nelson Algebras Through Heyting Ones[1]:1. Stud Log, 49(1), 105-126, Mr 90.

SENESE, Guy B. Warnings on Resistance and the Language of Possibility: Gramsci and a Pedagogy from the Surreal. Educ Theor, 41(1), 13-22, Wint 91.

SENI, Dan Alexander. "The Sociotechnology of Sociotechnical Systems: Elements of a Theory of Plans" in *Studies on Mario Bunge's "Treatise"*, WEINGARTNER, Paul (ed), 431-452. Amsterdam, Rodopi, 1990.

The essay links three concepts: technology, sociotechnology and sociotechnical system. Based on Bunge's *Treatise*, we sketch out a framework for foundations of technology and sociotechnology as fields of practical knowledge. Technology differs from scientific research in that all technologies deal with plans as the core conceptual object. Plans are to technology what theories are to science. A distinction between active and passive social system is proposed, the latter being able to make and use plans. Finally some principles of sociotechnical methodology are proposed.

SENNETT, James F. The Free Will Defense and Determinism. Faith Phil, 8(3), 340-353, Jl 91.

Edward Wierenga has argued that the free will defense (FWD) is compatible with compatibilism (*Faith and Philosophy*, April 1988). I maintain that Wierenga is mistaken. I distinguish between the *conceptual* doctrine of compatibilism and the *metaphysical* doctrine of soft determinism, and offer arguments that the FWD fails if either doctrine is true. Finally, I reconstruct Wierenga's argument and argue that it fails because either it is equivocal or it contains a false premise.

SENNETT, James F. Universe Indexed Properties and the Fate of the Ontological Argument. Relig Stud, 27(1), 65-79, Mr 91.

I begin this paper by defending Alvin Plantinga against a charge from John Mackie that his use of "world indexed properties" in his modal ontological argument renders it unsound. Plantinga does not use world indexed properties, but what are better thought of as "universe indexed properties." These *are* modally improper. I argue that there is no non-question-begging reason to accept them, and good reason to reject them. Therefore, Plantinga's argument fails. Furthermore, I argue that any form of the ontological argument must commit to universe indexed properties and is therefore equally flawed.

SEPÄNMAA, Yrö. "Anti-Art and Anti-Criticism—The Killers of Art or its Rescuers?" in *XIth International Congress in Aesthetics, Nottingham 1988*, WOODFIELD, Richard (ed), 180-183. Nottingham, Nottingham Polytech, 1990.

SEREQUEBERHAN, Tsenay. The African Liberation Struggle: A Hermeneutic Exploration of an African Historical-Political Horizon. Ultim Real Mean, 14(1), 46-52, Mr 91.

SEREQUEBERHAN, Tsenay. *African Philosophy: The Essential Readings*. New York, Paragon House, 1991.

SEREQUEBERHAN, Tsenay. Karl Marx and African Emancipatory Thought: A Critique of Marx's Euro-centric Metaphysics. Praxis Int, 10(1-2), 161-181, Ap-Jl 90.

SERRA, Richard. Art and Censorship. Crit Inquiry, 17(3), 574-581, Spr 91.

SERRANO RAMÍREZ, Jose M. Ibn 'Arabi o la renovación espiritual del sufismo. Themata, 6, 177-196, 1989.

SERRANO, Augusto. Las dos grandes paradojas? Rev Filosof (Costa Rica), 28(67-68), 5-16, D 90.

Our epoch has two problems which are extensive to discuss, although without practical or theoretical solution. Then, the two subjects of transcendental importance are the relationship between the individual and the state, and the relationship between society and nature. We try to find an ontology which articulates a common answer as a solution for both subjects.

SERRÁO, Adriana Veríssimo. "A imortalidade do escritor—Filosofia do pensar e da morte no jovem Feuerbach" in *Dinâmica do Pensar: Homenagem a Oswaldo Market*, FAC LETRAS UNIV LISBOA (ed), 267-281. Lisboa, Fac Letras U Lisboa, 1991.

Obwohl die meisten Interpreten "Abälard und Héloise. Der Schriftsteller und der Mensch" als einen bloss autobiographischen oder literarischen Aufsatz betrachten, urteilt Feuerbach selbst er bedeute zwei wesentliche Veränderungen in der Entwicklung seines eigenen frühen Denkens. In Beziehung auf seine "Dissertation" und auf die "Gedanken über Tod und Unsterblichkeit" beweise der Aufsatz einerseits die Verwandlung einer panteistischen Auffassung der Identität in eine differnzierte "politeistische", andererseits ein neues Verständnis des Verhältnisses zwischen Denken und Sinnlichkeit. Um zu untersuchen, ob in dem Aufsatz eine wirkliche Veränderung stattfindet, werden die Kritik der persönlichen Unsterblichkeit, die Frage nach dem Sinn des Todes und des Lebens und die Konzeption des Denkens zwischen 1828 and 1834 analysiert.

SERVERAT, Vincent. L'"irrisio fidei" chez Raymond Lulle et S Thomas D'Aquin. Rev Thomiste, 90(3), 436-448, Jl-S 90.

SESSIONS, Robert. "Working in America": A New Approach for the Humanities. Teach Phil, 13(4), 331-344, D 90.

This is a description of an introductory interdisciplinary humanities course on work. Through a variety of humanities writings and visual material, students are asked to think about the many modes and meanings of human labor, and by introducing them to descriptions and images of working from the past and from other cultures they are encouraged to think imaginatively about the future of working. The central thesis of this course is that we must not (and no longer need to) ignore our selves as we work: work can be a context wherein we create and better our selves.

SESSIONS, Robert. Deep Ecology versus Ecofeminism: Healthy Differences or Incompatible Philosophies? Hypatia, 6(1), 90-107, Spr 91.

Deep ecology and ecofeminism are contemporary environmental philosophies that share the desire to supplant the predominant Western anthropocentric environmental frameworks. Recently thinkers from these movements have focused their critiques on each other, and substantial differences have emerged. This essay explores central aspects of this debate to ascertain whether either philosophy has been undermined in the process and whether there are any indications that they are compatible despite their differences.

SESSIONS, W L. The Authorship of Faith. Relig Stud, 27(1), 81-97, Mr 91.

There seem to be equally good religious reasons for thinking of the act(s) of faith *both* as agent-caused or "authored" essentially and completely by God and as authored partially though essentially by a human person. To resolve this paradox, I criticize inadequate views and explore something I call "Perspectivalism," which holds that both kinds of authorship-claim are valid but only from different perspectives or points of view. Some complications of Perspectivalism are examined, particularly the class between first- and third-person points of view, as well as the point of view of inquiry into the authorship problem.

SESSIONS, William Lad. A Dialogic Interpretation of Hume's *Dialogues*. Hume Stud, 17(1), 15-39, Ap 91.

Standard interpretations of Hume's *Dialogues* consider only the propositions and arguments expressed by Philo, Cleanthes, and Demea, appeal to some external hermeneutical context, and focus solely on theism or theological beliefs. A dialogic interpretation views the literary form as contributory and indeed essential to the philosophical message: action and rhetoric matter as much as propositional content; the hermeneutic is internally generated; and the subject-matter truly encompasses all of "natural religion," not just natural theology. Such an interpretation can make better sense out of the whole of Hume's most artful work, particularly the problematic Dialogue XII.

SESSIONS, William Lad. Plantinga's Box. Faith Phil, 8(1), 51-66, Ja 91.

Plantinga's Box is an (imaginary) epistemic engine that can alter a person's cognitive condition in various ways. Its present use is to conduct a thought-experiment exploring some questions of religious pluralism as they arise for someone who believes that his or her Christian beliefs are properly basic. The central questions are these: would it be wrong for a 'properly basic Christian' to use the Box to acquire some properly basic *non*-Christian religious beliefs? Are there good reasons for such a person to use the Box for this purpose? Various considerations pro and con are sifted; the result points toward interreligious dialogue and inquiry.

SETTE, A M and DA COSTA, Newton C A. Remarks on Analogy. Teoria, 10(2), 49-58, 1990.

We study analogy as akind of inductive reasoning, that is, a kind of non-demonstrative inference. It is examined in connection with other forms of inductive inference, and we also delineate how it can be mathematized from the point of view of category theory.

SETTLE, Tom. Swann versus Popper on Induction: An Arbitration. Brit J Phil Sci, 41(3), 401-405, S 90.

SETTLE, Tom. Van Rooijen and Mayr versus Popper: Is the Universe Causally Closed? Brit J Phil Sci, 40(3), 389-403, S 89.

SEUNG, T K. Virtues and Values: A Platonic Account. Soc Theor Pract, 17(2), 207-249, Sum 91.

This article is a critical survey of two attempts for the revival of virtue ethics: Alasdair MacIntyre's *After Virtue* and Edmund Pincoff's *Quandaries and Virtues*. In the first half of the essay, the author outlines MacIntyre's theory of social and individual virtues, and explains its difficulties. Though MacIntyre tries to combat normative skepticism and liberal individualism, he is too infected by these contemporary ideologies to provide the ontological foundation for his own theory of virtue. For the ontological foundation of Pinchoff's theory, the author appeals to Platonic Forms as the ultimate source of all virtues and values.

SÈVE, René. L'institution juridique: imposition et interprétation. Rev Metaph Morale, 95(3), 311-337, Jl-S 90.

In the first part of this paper, the author studies the birth, during the 17th century, of modern legal ontology in a wider philosophy context criticizing Aristotelian physics. In the second part, from the extensions of this modern legal ontology into Kelsen work, the author shows the deadlocks to which it is confronted and proposes an alternative ontology of law, centered on the notion of auto-interpretation.

SEVENHUIJSEN, Selma. The Morality of Feminism. Hypatia, 6(2), 173-191, Sum 91.

Inaugural lecture as Professor of Women's Studies in the Social Science Faculty at the University of Utrecht.

SEYMOUR, Daniel. Remnants of Schiffer's Principle [P]. Analysis, 51(1), 40-43, Ja 91.

Stephen Schiffer's excellent book *Remnants of Meaning* contains several arguments against Davidson's paratactic theory of indirect discourse. One such argument relies upon a principle about the function of singular terms in content sentences which states that if such a term refers to a certain entity, then the attribution sentence is true only if the attributee also referred to that entity. The purpose of the paper is to argue that the principle is false by presenting two different types of counterexample. I conclude by noting that the examples do not present a difficulty for the paratactic theory.

SEYMOUR, Michel. Wittgenstein et l'institution du langage. Lekton, 1(1), 63-101, 1990.

I argue in favour of Kripke's interpretation of Wittgenstein's conception of meaning, understanding and rule-following and discuss Colin McGinn's criticisms. I argue that, given a fairly intuitive notion of understanding which is perfectly compatible with the text, paragraph 201 of the *Investigations* turns out to agree with the idea that Wittgenstein provides a sceptical solution and not, as McGinn and others would put it, a *reductio ad absurdum* of the paradox. Simultaneously, I also try to show that Kripke is correct in his interpretation of Wittgenstein's notion of meaning as being essentially community relative.

SFEKAS, Stanley. Ousia, Substratum, and Matter. Phil Inq, 13(1-2), 38-47, Wint-Spr 91.

SFENDONI-MENTZOU, D. "Popper's Propensities: An Ontological Interpretation of Probability" in *Imre Lakatos and Theories of Scientific Change*, GAVROGLU, Kostas (ed), 441-455. Norwell, Kluwer, 1989.

The purpose of this paper is to shed light on the *ontological features* of Popper's propensity interpretation of probability and show that they are intimately related both to Peircean *Tychism* and the Aristotelian category of '*potentia*'. The interest is thus focused on that aspect of propensity related to Popper's metaphysical and cosmological interpretation of the dynamic character of a changing physical reality. In this respect it is argued—contrary to Popper's own claim—that *propensity* interpreted as *potentiality* bears the stamp both of Peircean scientific metaphysics and Aristotelian ontology.

SFENDONI-MENTZOU, Demetra. Towards a Potential-Pragmatic Account of Peirce's Theory of Truth. Trans Peirce Soc, 27(1), 27-77, Wint 91.

The purpose of this essay is to establish the thesis that the idea of potentiality can serve as an explanatory basis for a unifying account of C S Peirce's theory of truth. In this respect, interest is focused on *Thirdness* and in particular on the triadic relation of *reality-generality-law*, with the purpose of showing how they can function through the idea of *potentiality*. On the basis of this analysis, it is argued that Peirce's *Truth* has an essentially ontological character, enjoying, at the same time, the status neither of an *ideal* nor of a *transcendental* but of a *potential* being.

SHAFFER, Elinor S. "Romantic Philosophy and Organization of the Disciplines: the Founding of the Humboldt University of Berlin" in *Romanticism and the Sciences*, CUNNINGHAM, Andrew (ed), 38-54. New York, Cambridge Univ Pr, 1990.

SHAFRITZ, Jay M (ed) and MADSEN, Peter (ed). *Essentials of Business Ethics*. New York, Penguin Books, 1990.

This is a collection of essays and articles that address the most essential issues, problems and dilemmas in business ethics. It includes work from Peter Druker, Ralph Nader, Milton Friedman, Laura Nash, Patricia Werhane, Norman Bowie, Manuel Velasquez and other leading ethicists. It treats such essential issues as: defining business ethics, employee rights, management ethics, corporate social responsibility, environmental ethics and multinational ethics.

SHAFU, Xiao. Tang Junyi's Philosophical View of History and His Explanation of the Philosophy of Wang Chuanshan. Chin Stud Phil, 22(3), 55-85, Spr 91.

It points out that the inclination of Tang Junyi's philosophical thought is from the establishing of the moral ego to the explaining of the humanistic spirit and to the philosophical distillating of the culture value; interprets Tang's view of philosophical history that affirms the divergences and contradictories of the various schools are compatible with each other; so that we can see the mutual penetration of contradictories and the wisdom of philosophy lasts forever; then comments on Tang's explanations of Wang Chuanshan's philosophy, in which I stress Tang's understanding of that Chuanshan's doctrine, to sum up, is the philosophy of the history.

SHAH, K J. Indian Thought Is a Systematic Body of Thought. J Indian Counc Phil Res, 7(3), 146-150, My-Ag 90.

SHAH, K J. Philosophy, Religion, Morality, Spirituality: Some Issues. J Indian Counc Phil Res, 7(2), 1-12, Ja-Ap 90.

SHAIDA, S A. Public and Private Morality. J Indian Counc Phil Res, 6(1), 111-119, S-D 88.

SHAKED, Moshe and GOLDMAN, Alvin I. An Economic Model of Scientific Activity and Truth Acquisition. Phil Stud, 63(1), 31-55, Jl 91.

SHALOM, Albert. L'identité personnelle et la source des concepts. Rev Metaph Morale, 96(2), 233-260, Ap-Je 91.

If "mind" or "language" are autonomous realities or processes, then there is no possibility of validly referring to the physical world as the independent reality we know it to be. It is therefore necessary to start with the inference that "mind" or "language" are capacities which emerge in the course of the physical growth of the body. Conversely, the language referring to the physical world seems to have nothing in common with the language referring to personal experience of the physical world. The purpose of this paper is to argue that this problem can only be overcome by the appropriate elucidation of the nature of the human being—and it attempts a sketch of such an elucidation.

SHALOM, Albert. Temporality and the Concept of Being. Rev Metaph, 44(2), 307-333, D 90.

The ambiguity of the word "being" is due to its abstract generality. For that reason, any attempt to elucidate what the word might plausibly refer to requires the prior analysis of abstract generality or conceptualization: the concept of being is a function of the being of concepts. Concepts are analysed as designatory powers emerging in the course of evolution. The designatory powers of sensing and of conceptualizing are analysed as functions of temporal internalizations. The conclusion is that the being of concepts is reference to intelligibility, and the concept of being refers to the source of this capacity itself, traditionally called "God."

SHANKER, S G (ed). *Gödel's Theorem in Focus*. New York, Routledge, 1988.

SHANKS, Niall. Probabilistic Physics and the Metaphysics of Time. S Afr J Phil, 10(2), 37-44, My 91.

The concern of this article is with the philosophical implications of the stochastic retreat from determinism in the physical sciences. In particular, what are the ontological consequences, if any of the use of stochastic equations of motion in the treatment of the behaviour of physical systems? It is argued here that this question cannot be settled merely by inspecting the character of the equations themselves. It turns out that the issue of the ontological significance of dynamical indeterminism is a matter which is inextricably intertwined with some basic matters in the metaphysics of time.

SHANNON, Benny. Remarks on the Modularity of Mind. Brit J Phil Sci, 39(3), 331-352, S 88.

Jerry Fodor's *The Modularity of Mind* is discussed. In this book the concept of modularity of cognitive processes is introduced and a picture of mind is proposed according to which the peripheral input systems are modular whereas the central processes are not. The present paper examines this vies from both a methodological and a substantive perspective. Methodologically, a contrast between considerations of principle and of fact is made and implications for the nature of cognitive theory are discussed. Substantively, constraints on information flow are examined as they appear in various aspects of psychological phenomenology, and central processes in particular. It is suggested that the notion of modularity as *structural* and fixed be replaced by one which is *dynamic*, context-dependent. This modification, it is argued, is productive for the characterization of the workings of the mind, and it defines new questions for investigations.

SHANNON, G. Equivalent Versions of a Weak Form of the Axiom of Choice. Notre Dame J Form Log, 29(4), 569-573, Fall 88.

The Axiom of Choice for countable families of finite sets is shown to be equivalent to the statement that for any countable family of finite sets there exists a countable subfamily for which a choice function exists; and to the statement that if a quasi-order (Q,less than or equal to) contains incompatible subsets of arbitrarily large finite cardinality and if Q is a countable union of finite sets, then Q contains a countable incompatible subset. Some related results are also given.

SHANNON, Gary P. Provable Forms of Martin's Axiom. Notre Dame J Form Log, 31(3), 382-388, Sum 90.

It is shown that if Martin's Axiom (MA) is restricted to well-orderable sets, and if the countable antichain condition is replaced by either a finite antichain condition or a finite "Q-strong antichain" condition, then the resulting statements are forms of MA provable in ZF. Variations of these weak forms of MA are shown to be equivalent to the Axiom of Choice and some of its weak forms.

SHAPIRO, Daniel. Free Speech, Free Exchange, and Rawlsian Liberalism. Soc Theor Pract, 17(1), 47-68, Spr 91.

I argue that Rawlsian liberal arguments for the basic right to freedom of speech—in particular, the right to freedom of commercial speech—support a basic right to freedom of exchange, (where this is understood narrowly as a right to exchange at mutually agreed upon prices and perhaps quantities). Rawlsian liberalism must accordingly condemn wage, price, and rent controls as unjust. Thus I undermine a central claim of Rawlsian liberalism, that there are no property rights listed in the first principle of justice other than the right to hold and have exclusive use of personal property.

SHAPIRO, Gary. "Subversion of System/Systems of Subversion" in *Writing the Politics of Difference*, SILVERMAN, Hugh J (ed), 1-11. Albany, SUNY Pr, 1991.

SHAPIRO, Ian. J G A Pocock's Republicanism and Political Theory: A Critique and Reinterpretation. Crit Rev, 4(3), 433-471, Sum 90.

A growing sense of the exhaustion of both liberalism and Marxism has fueled a revival of interest in civic republicanism among historians, political theorists, and social commentators. This turn is evaluated via an examination of the normative implications of J G A Pocock's account of civic republicanism. Arguing that what is at issue between liberals and republicans has been misunderstood by both sides in the debate, the author shows that the turn to republicanism fails to address the most vexing problems liberalism confronts in the modern world, and that it is and has been compatible with much of what critics of liberalism dislike. He argues, further, that the civic republican view involves an instrumental attitude to outsiders that cannot be justified in today's world and has other unattractive dimensions of which too little account has been taken by defenders and detractors alike.

SHAPIRO, Ian. Resources, Capacities, and Ownership: The Workmanship Ideal and Distributive Justice. Polit Theory, 19(1), 47-72, F 91.

An exploration of the Lockean claim that we own what we make in virtue of our individual ownership of our productive capacities. Rejecting Locke's theological justification for this view, the author considers and rejects Marxist and neoclassical secular justifications of it. He also rejects suggestions by Rawls and Dworkin that we abandon the self-ownership view entirely, arguing instead for a consequentialist justification of the workmanship ideal, tempered by other demands of social justice and democratic politics.

SHAPIRO, Michael J. Political Economy and Mimetic Desire: A Postmodernist Reading of "Babette's Feast". Hist Euro Ideas, 13(3), 239-251, 1991.

SHAPIRO, Michael J. "Weighing Anchor: Postmodern Journeys from the Life-World" in *Life-World and Politics: Between Modernity and Postmodernity*, WHITE, Stephen K (ed), 139-165. Notre Dame, Univ Notre Dame Pr, 1989.

This is first a contrast between Foucault's genealogical approach to conversations and the more hermeneutic approaches of Habermas and Rorty. There is then a reading of Michel Tournier's *Vendredi* to illustrate the advantages of a more postmodern, distancing reading of the Robinson Crusoe story.

SHAPIRO, Stewart and SCHUMM, George. Expressive Completeness and Decidability. Notre Dame J Form Log, 31(4), 576-579, Fall 90.

Under what conditions is the expressive completeness of a set of connectives decidable? The answer is shown to depend crucially upon how the set is encoded as input to a Turing machine.

SHAPIRO, Stewart. Structure and Ontology. Phil Topics, 17(2), 145-171, Fall 89.

The slogan of structuralism is "mathematics is the science of structure". The view is a form or variation of realism. It holds that the subject matter of a branch of mathematics like arithmetic is not a collection of independently existing objects, the natural numbers, but rather a structure, or a class of related structures. The purpose of this article is to articulate and defend the view, and to discuss its ramifications for ontology and, to a lesser extent, its potential for overcoming epistemological difficulties associated with realism. One result is that the adoption of structuralism has interesting consequences for the basic questions of ontology. Structuralism has something to say about what an *object* is and what identity is, at least in mathematics.

SHARMA, Arvind. *A Hindu Perspective on the Philosophy of Religion*. New York, St Martin's Pr, 1990.

The book presents material drawn from Hindu philosophy which sheds light on the discussion of such time-honoured topics in the philosophy of religion as grounds for belief and disbelief in God, revelation, problem of evil, religious language, verification and falsification, etc.

SHARMA, Arvind. Karma and Rebirth in *Alberuni's India*. Asian Phil, 1(1), 77-91, 1991.

Alberuni regards belief in karma and reincarnation as the hallmark of Hinduism. This paper summarizes his treatment of the Hindu doctrine, highlights the significant elements in his treatment of it; identifies the points where he goes beyond its more usual understanding in his treatment and concludes with a consideration of the comparisons suggested by him between the Hindu doctrine and Islamic ideas.

SHARMA, Arvind. Karma and Reincarnation in Advaita Vedānta. J Indian Phil, 18(3), 219-236, S 90.

The paper examines the extent to which the existence of reincarnation can be established by traditional or modern epistemology as employed in the context of Advaita Vedānta. It takes into account some modern criticisms of the doctrine and also suggests that the idea of *samsāra* may be an extension of the "flow of thoughts" which characterizes normal existence.

SHARMA, Arvind. Philosophy and the Sociology of Knowledge: An Investigation into the Nature of Orthodoxy (Astikya) in Hindu Thought. J Indian Counc Phil Res, 6(3), 23-35, My-Ag 89.

It is generally believed that the acceptance of Vedic authority is the test of orthodoxy in Hinduism. The nature of Hinduism, however, is such that in it communal identification precedes doctrinal definition, which explains why the above-mentioned criterion is difficult to uphold with philosophical or historical consistency. Sociology provides the right clue for understanding this aspect of Hindu philosophy.

SHARMA, Arvind. Ramana Maharsi on the Theories of Creation in Advaita Vedānta. J Indian Counc Phil Res, 8(1), 77-92, S-D 90.

Advaita Vedanta has been typically concerned with theories of causation rather than creation, even to the extent of regarding the accounts of creation somewhat "out of joint". This paper presents and analyzes the implications of the theories of creation in Advaita as developed by Ramana Maharsi (1879-1950).

SHARMA, K N. Search for Indian Traditional Paradigm of Society. J Indian Counc Phil Res, 6(3), 131-144, My-Ag 89.

SHARP, Ann Margaret. The Community of Inquiry Education for Democracy. Thinking, 9(2), 31-37, 1990.

SHARPE, Kevin J. Relating Science and Theology with Complementarity: A Caution. Zygon, 26(2), 309-315, Je 91.

I examine Helmut Reich's recent (*Zygon*, December 1990) discussion of the complementarity model for relating science and theology and find it confusing. On the one hand, his complementarity purports to make science and theology relevant for each other. It even requires we solve their conflicts. On the other hand, it discourages the overlap of scientific and theological knowledge and thus the direct resolution of their conflicts.

SHARPE, R A. Authenticity Again. Brit J Aes, 31(2), 163-166, Ap 91.

In reply to James Young I argue that there are two reasons for advocating authentic performance. The first is that internal relations within the work be better brought out. The second is that the strangeness of other cultures is understood when we avoid translating their artefacts into the terms of our own culture and practices and that this strangeness is an important feature of the artistic experience.

SHARPLES, R W. Accessible Hellenistic Philosophy. J Hellen Stud, 110, 199-202, 1990.

An assessment of A A Long and D N Sedley, *The Hellenistic Philosophers*, Cambridge 1987. Consideration of its use in teaching, and of the interpretations advanced concerning Epicurus, especially social and theological doctrines and denial of reductionism; Stoicism, especially on freedom; and Scepticism, especially Carneades.

SHATZ, Marshall (ed) and BAKUNIN,. *Statism and Anarchy*. New York, Cambridge Univ Pr, 1991.

SHAUB, Michael K and WAPLES, Elain. Establishing an Ethic of Accounting: A Response to Westra's Call for Government Employment of Auditors. J Bus Ethics, 10(5), 385-393, My 91.

The central question in Westra's (1986) search for an ethic of accounting concerns to whom the accountant owes loyal agency: to the client or to the public interest. The authors argue that the accountant's master has already been defined as the public interest. An ethic of accounting is identified through analysis of the accountant's master and through examination of the accountant's ethical obligations under the Code of Professional Conduct (AICPA, 1988). Potential conflicts between professional and organizational loyalties are analyzed with respect to the real-life problem used by Westra to support her argument. Finally, the implications of government employment of auditors are discussed.

SHAVER, Robert. Emile's Education. J Phil Educ, 24(2), 245-255, Wint 90.

In the *Second Discourse*, Rousseau presents the problem of "life in others," wherein one's desire for opinion dominates one's other desires. I give an interpretation of *Emile* which makes it, like the more political works, a solution to this problem. I close with brief suggestions as to how the solution in *Emile* is limited.

SHAVER, Robert. Leviathan, King of the Proud. Hobbes Stud, 3, 54-74, 1990.

It is often argued that Hobbes portrays economic men, men whose desire for honour and glory is merely derivative from asocial concerns, and that his arguments for conflict in the state of nature are most helpfully modelled by game-theoretic tools such as the prisoner's dilemma. I argue instead that the desire for honour and glory, along with weakness of will, is basic to Hobbesian men, to their conflict, and to the solution Hobbes offers them.

SHAW, Bill. Shareholder Authorized Inside Trading: A Legal and Moral Analysis. J Bus Ethics, 9(12), 913-928, D 90.

This article evaluates inside trading from a legal and a moral perspective. From both of these points of view, the practice of inside trading is fraudulent whether it occurs in the traditional format or in the variation known as "misappropriation." Fraud is a legal tort and a moral wrong consisting of a breach of duty that intentionally causes harm to persons that the insider can reasonably foresee. In defense against allegations of fraudulent inside trading, the defendant may argue that one or more elements of fraud are not evident, or, if the elements are clear, that the fraud was a justified means of avoiding some worse evil or of achieving some greater good. The article concludes that inside trading, under circumstances approved by shareholders, is neither fraudulent nor unfair.

SHAW, J L. Descriptions: Contemporary Philosophy and the Nyāya. Log Anal, 31(121-122), 153-187, Mr-Je 88.

SHAW, J L. Universal Sentences: Russell, Wittgenstein, Prior, and the Nyāya. J Indian Phil, 19(2), 103-119, Je 91.

The aim of this paper is to discuss i) whether the following sentences have the same meaning, ii) whether they have the same truth-value, iii) whether there is some assertion common to all of them, and iv) if there is some such assertion, whether it can be defined. 1) All men are mortal, 2) whoever is a man is mortal, 3) wherever there is humanity, then there is mortality, 4) if anyone is a man, then he is mortal, 5) if humanity is present somewhere, then mortality is also present there.

SHAW, Martin. "War and the Nation-State in Social Theory" in *Social Theory of Modern Societies: Anthony Giddens and His Critics*, HELD, David (ed), 129-146. New York, Cambridge Univ Pr, 1990.

This chapter summarises and criticises Anthony Giddens's theory of the state, in *The Nation-State and Violence* (1985) and other writings, in the light of historical evidence and sociological theory. It argues that while Giddens's historical account is problematic, his basic argument concerning the specialisation of violence in the 'outward pointing' military function is of central importance to sociology.

SHAW, William H. *Business Ethics*. Belmont, Wadsworth, 1991.

SHEA, William R. "Tackling the Mind" in *Studies on Mario Bunge's "Treatise"*, WEINGARTNER, Paul (ed), 205-214. Amsterdam, Rodopi, 1990.

SHEAR, Jonathan. Mystical Experience, Hermeneutics, and Rationality. Int Phil Quart, 30(4), 391-401, D 90.

Hermeneutical thinkers such as Steven Katz argue that mystical experiences cannot be understood independently of their embedding conceptual contexts, and that the traditional attempt to identify and examine culture-independent "core" types is therefore misguided. Evaluation of these arguments in light of (i) the content of culture-invariant descriptions of the qualityless "introvertive" mystical experience (the "purest" mystical experience) and (ii) objective research on empirical correlates of this experience, however, falsifies Katz's claims of the necessary culture-dependence of mystical experiences in general and this experience in particular. The traditional objective approach, supplemented by current scientific research, remains the most rational, empirical one.

SHEARMUR, Jeremy. Common Sense and the Foundations of Economic Theory: Duhem versus Robbins. Phil Soc Sci, 21(1), 64-71, Mr 91.

The author argues against Lionel Robbins that it is incorrect to think that the premises of a theoretical social science can be drawn directly from common-sense knowledge. For the theorist needs to select, from this material, what is relevant, how it is to be conceptualized, and what simplifications might be required in the construction of explanatory models. He gets no help in these decisions from common-sense knowledge. Further, insofar as his theoretical social science makes use of mathematics, Pierre Duhem's argument, from *The Aim and Structure of Physical Theory*, about the difference between practical and theoretical facts also applies.

SHEARMUR, Jeremy. From Dialogue Rights to Property Rights. Crit Rev, 4(1-2), 106-132, Wint-Spr 90.

The author raises problems concerning F A Hayek's indirect utilitarian arguments for a Kantian-like conception of individual rights and of a liberal legal order. He suggests an alternative rationale for such ideas, drawn from a nonfoundationalist conception of argument about matters of fact and of the validity of ethical claims. These he develops with reference to Karl Popper. He further argues that limitations upon what can be achieved through dialogue provide a rationale for property rights, *qua* means through which judgment may be externalized and learning may take place. The result, however, combines Hayekian ideas with the idea of a (nonpolitical) public forum.

SHEARMUR, Jeremy. From Intersubjectivity through Epistemology to Property: Rejoinder to Michelman. Crit Rev, 4(1-2), 144-154, Wint-Spr 90.

Response to Michelman's critique of author's "From Dialogue Rights to Property Rights." Argues that intersubjectivity is not, on its own, sufficient to provide a rationale for individual rights. Rather, this requires a (nonfoundationalist) epistemology. But does the author's earlier argument offer a rationale for someone's according rights to a second person in some culture remote from his own, when he has already accorded rights to one such person and has no reason to suppose that the second person has any distinctive epistemological contribution to make? Author suggests tentative response using Popper's ideas about the self as a cultural object.

SHEHTMAN, Valentin. Modal Counterparts of Medvedev Logic of Finite Problems Are Not Finitely Axiomatizable. Stud Log, 49(3), 365-385, S 90.

We consider modal logics whose intermediate fragments lie between the logic of infinite problems and the Medvedev logic of finite problems. There is continuum of such logics. We prove that none of them is finitely axiomatizable. The proof is based on methods from and makes use of some graph-theoretic constructions (operations on coverings, and colourings).

SHELAH, S and GOLDSTERN, M. Ramsey Ultrafilters and the Reaping Number—Con($r < u$). Annals Pure Applied Log, 49(2), 121-142, O 90.

We show that it is consistent that the reaping number r is less than u, the size of the smallest base for an ultrafilter. To show that our forcing preserves certain ultrafilters, we prove a general partition theorem involving Ramsey ideals.

SHELAH, Saharon and JUDAH, Haim and WOODIN, W H. The Borel Conjecture. Annals Pure Applied Log, 50(3), 255-269, D 90.

SHELAH, Saharon and JECH, Thomas. Full Reflection of Stationary Sets Below $\aleph_\omega$. J Sym Log, 55(2), 822-830, Je 90.

SHELAH, Saharon and JUDAH, Haim. The Kunen-Miller Chart (Lebesgue Measure, the Baire Property, Laver Reals and Preservation Theorems for Forcing). J Sym Log, 55(3), 909-927, S 90.

SHELDON, Mark. HIV and the Obligation to Treat. Theor Med, 11(3), 201-212, S 90.

The paper is an attempt to review the basis for the claim that physicians have a professional obligation to treat AIDS patients. Considered are the historical record, two professional codes of ethics, and several recent articles. The paper concludes that the arguments considered, which attempt to support the claim that physicians have an obligation to treat, fail. It is suggested, rather, that common humanity, which physicians share with those who suffer from AIDS, ought to be the basis for engaging in the care of AIDS patients.

SHELL, Marc. Marranos (Pigs), or from Coexistence to Toleration. Crit Inquiry, 17(2), 306-335, Wint 91.

SHENG, C L. New Naturalism and Other Ethical Theories. J Value Inq, 25(2), 177-188, Ap 91.

In this essay I point out that the new naturalism recently advocated by Michael Ruse and Edward O Wilson, to the extreme, is close to determinism, and I show that even hard determinism is unable to exempt an agent from the job of free and autonomous decision-making. I further show that although naturalism is an important part of the foundation of an ethical theory, itself alone is inadequate as a comprehensive ethical theory. To be comprehensive, naturalism has to go in conjunction with another compatible theory. Finally I show that naturalism is incompatible with deontologism, but is compatible with utilitarianism.

SHERMAN, Nancy. "The Place of Emotions in Kantian Morality" in *Identity, Character, and Morality: Essays in Moral Psychology*, FLANAGAN, Owen (ed), 149-170. Cambridge, MIT Pr, 1990.

In this work I explore the various roles emotion plays in the Kantian account of acting from duty. I suggest that Kant did not view the pathological emotions as necessarily beyond control or cultivation and that we can distinguish several interrelated claims regarding their supportive role in the expression of moral character. In concluding I assess these various claims with regard to the question of how heteronomous Kant's moral theory becomes once we give ample room to the emotions. It may be that moral anthropology needs to be the accepted focus of Kantian ethics, or if it is already, that its boundary with an autonomous ethics be more sharply defined.

SHERNOCK, Stan K. The Effects of Patrol Officers' Defensiveness Toward the Outside World on Their Ethical Orientations. Crim Just Ethics, 9(2), 24-42, Sum-Fall 90.

This paper, based on a survey of 177 patrol officers in eleven departments in four states, examines how officers' alienation and concerns for infringements on their authority affect three separate orientations toward ethical conduct: (1) the comparative value placed on ethical conduct *vis-à-vis* other police values; (2) attitude toward the unethical conduct of other officers; and (3) general attitude toward ethically questionable police practices in pursuit of morally good ends. The study concludes that the continued police alienation from and suspicion of the public and outside world undermines the service ideal underlying a professional code of ethics, and that greater police governance over police matters would certainly not insure the type of self-regulation required by a code of ethics.

SHERRY, David. The Inconspicious Role of Paraphrase. Hist Phil Log, 12(2), 151-166, 1991.

In formal logic there is a premium on clever paraphrase, for it subsumes troublesome inferences under a familiar theory. (A paradigm is Davidson's analysis *1967* of inferences like 'He buttered his toast with a knife; so, he buttered his toast'.) But the need for paraphrase in formal logic runs deeper than the odd recalcitrant inference, and thus, I shall argue, commits logicians to some interesting consequences. First, the thesis that arguments are valid in virtue of their form must be severely qualified. And second, it is misleading to view a formal logical theory as a standard for justifying and criticizing inference. The latter point depends on the nature and role of paraphrase, which permits a range of conflicting logical theories. Conflicting logical theories arise from the conflicting goals of logical theorists and the promiscuous nature of paraphrase makes reconciliation impossible.

SHERRY, David. The Logic of Impossible Quantities. Stud Hist Phil Sci, 22(1), 37-62, Mr 91.

In a ground-breaking essay Nagel contended that the controversy over impossible numbers influenced the development of modern logic. I maintain that Nagel was correct in outline only. He overlooked the fact that the controversy engendered a new account of reasoning, one in which the concept of a well-made language played a decisive role. Focusing on the new account of reasoning changes the story considerably and reveals important but unnoticed similarities between the development of algebraic logic and quantificational logic.

SHERWIN, Byron L. *In Partnership with God: Contemporary Jewish Law and Ethics*. Syracuse, Syracuse Univ Pr, 1990.

The book offers a novel agenda and methodology for contemporary Jewish scholarship and applies them to a variety of theological, ethical, and legal issues, including medical ethics, euthanasia, philanthropy, repentance, parent-child relations, religious majority, and the creation of new life forms. This wide-ranging collection of essays provides an excellent integration of biblical, rabbinic, and mystical thinking on the subjects under discussion. The author presents contexts for current grapping with age-old issues in dealing with a wide variety of contemporary issues from a classical Judaic perspective.

SHEVCHENKO, V N. The Social Philosophy of Marxism: The Founders and the Present Day. Soviet Stud Phil, 29(2), 48-91, Fall 90.

SHEVTSOVA, Maria. "Dialogism in the Novel and Bakhtin's Theory of Culture" in *XIth International Congress in Aesthetics, Nottingham 1988*, WOODFIELD, Richard (ed), 184-189. Nottingham, Nottingham Polytech, 1990.

SHIEBER, Stuart M and DALRYMPLE, Mary and PEREIRA, Fernando C N. Ellipsis and Higher-Order Unification. Ling Phil, 14(4), 399-452, Ag 91.

We present a new method for characterizing the interpretive possibilities generated by elliptical constructions in natural language. Unlike previous analyses, which postulate ambiguity of interpretation or derivation in the full clause source of the ellipsis, our analysis requires no such hidden ambiguity. Further, the analysis follows relatively directly form an abstract statement of the ellipsis interpretation problem. It predicts correctly a wide range of interactions between ellipsis and other semantic phenomena such as quantifier scope and bound anaphora. Finally, although the analysis itself is stated nonprocedurally, it admits of a direct computational method for generating interpretations.

SHIELDS, Christopher. The Generation of Form in Aristotle. Hist Phil Quart, 7(4), 367-390, O 90.

I assess Aristotle's account of the generation of form, and sketch its ramifications for hylomorphism. Most of my analysis of Aristotle's position concentrates on the important argument of *Metaphysics* vii 8, the central passage in which he takes up this issue in a self-conscious way. One upshot of this analysis is that the standard interpretation, according to which forms come to be without undergoing a process of generation, has slim textual basis and in some ways distorts Aristotle's conception of the generation of form.

SHILS, Edward. "Intellectuals and Responsibility" in *The Political Responsibility of Intellectuals*, MACLEAN, Ian (ed), 257-306. New York, Cambridge Univ Pr, 1990.

SHIN, Hyung Song. A Reconstruction of Jeffrey's Notion of Ratifiability in Terms of Counterfactual Beliefs. Theor Decis, 31(1), 21-47, Jl 91.

We formalize Jeffrey's (1983) notion of ratifiability and show that the resulting formal structure can be obtained more directly by means of a theory of counterfactual beliefs. One implication is that, under the appropriate formalizations, together with certain restrictions on beliefs, Bayesian decision theory and causal decision theory coincide.

SHINOHARA, Motoaki. La communication de l'art (in Japanese). Bigaku, 41(4), 1-10, Spr 91.

Dans le monde de l'art, il y a plusieurs entretés: surtout, *entre* l'auteur et l'oeuvre, et *entre* l'oeuvre et le récepteur. Ces entretés se superposent aux entretés temporelles. Or, ces entretés sont possédées de l'excès. L'excès passé s'actualise dans la citation, l'excès présent donne lieu à la communication entre les sens, et l'excès futur s'actualise comme la pluralité de l'interprétation. Le modèle de communication proposé ici contient ces quatre types: uni-communication, bi-communication, anti-communication et hétéro-communication. Dans le monde de l'art, la communication de l'excès concerne hétéro-communication. (edited)

SHIRLEY, Edward S. Why the Problem of the External World is a Pseudo-Problem: Santayana and Danto. J Speculative Phil, 4(4), 298-309, 1990.

SHIRLEY, Edward. Hume's Ethics: Acts, Rules, Dispositions and Utility. SW Phil Rev, 7(1), 129-139, Ja 91.

Hume can be considered as an early utilitarian or as a forerunner of utilitarianism. I argue that his version is superior to others in that by making the unit of evaluation a *disposition*, rather than an act or rule, he escapes the problems of both act-utilitarianism and rule-utilitarianism. He also meets the objections of intuitionists such as W D Ross and others, and satisfies the intuitive Kantian requirement of universalizability. I also meet an objection to Hume's making the disposition, rather than the act or rule, the unit of evaluation.

SHIVE, Kenneth D. Moral Philosophy at West Point in the Nineteenth Century. Teach Phil, 13(4), 345-357, D 90.

SHKLAR, Judith N. Emerson and the Inhibitions of Democracy. Polit Theory, 18(4), 601-614, N 90.

SHKLAR, Judith. "American Citizenship: The Quest for Inclusion" in *The Tanner Lectures on Human Values, Volume XI*, PETERSON, Grethe B (ed), 385-439. Salt Lake City, Univ of Utah Pr, 1990.

SHOEMAKER, Sydney. "First-Person Access" in *Philosophical Perspectives, 4: Action Theory and Philosophy of Mind, 1990*, TOMBERLIN, James E (ed), 187-214. Atascadero, Ridgeview, 1990.

SHOEMAKER, Sydney. Qualities and Qualia: What's in the Mind? Phil Phenomenol Res, 50 SUPP, 109-131, Fall 90.

SHOENFIELD, J R. Non-Bounding Construction. Annals Pure Applied Log, 50(2), 191-205, N 90.

SHOOMAN, A P. *The Metaphysics of Religious Belief*. Brookfield, Gower, 1990.

This book generates the central concepts of religious belief from the concept of the miraculous. Our concept of God as Creator, pervading rather than invading the world, provides the foundation for the meaning of a believer's life. Losing a sense of the miraculous constitutes a pattern of atheism consistent with belief that there is a God. Individual miracles may involve the inexplicable, but not the contradictory. Nor do they need explanation; already presupposing religious belief, they cannot serve to prove it. In his account of Creation, the seemingly incompatible demands of scientific theory and religious belief are reconciled.

SHOPE, Robert K. Firth's Critique of Epistemological Rule-Utilitarianism. Phil Phenomenol Res, 51(1), 129-135, Mr 91.

SHORE, Richard A and HAUGHT, Christine Ann. Undecidability and Initial Segments of the (R.E.) TT-Degrees. J Sym Log, 55(3), 987-1006, S 90.

SHORT, David S. Embryo Research and Abortion—the Arguments that Swayed Parliament. Ethics Med, 7(1), 6-7, Spr 91.

In April 1990, the British Parliament spent two days debating a Human Fertilization and Embryology Bill, covering the areas of embryo experimentation and abortion. This debate threw up all the most weighty arguments on both sides. In this article, these arguments are catalogued and commented on briefly.

SHOTTER, John. "Rom Harré: Realism and the Turn to Social Constructionism" in *Harré and His Critics*, BHASKAR, Roy (ed), 206-223. Cambridge, Blackwell, 1990.

SHOTTER, John. Wittgenstein and Psychology. Philosophy, 28, 193-208, 90 Supp.

SHRADER-FRECHETTE, Kristin. Biological Holism and the Evolution of Ethics. Between Species, 6(4), 185-192, Fall 90.

Following Leopold, Callicott defends a wholistic environmental ethics that locates ultimate value in the biotic community. Emphasizing altruism and feelings as the originators of morality, however, Callicott's wholistic ethics faces at least three problems. 1) There is no biologically coherent notion of "community" robust enough to ground his ethics. 2) How can humans be required to safeguard biological communities when nature does not? 3) In basing his ethics on natural selection, Callicott has removed their normative force.

SHRADER-FRECHETTE, Kristin. Biology and Ethics: Callicott Reconsidered. Between Species, 6(4), 195-196, Fall 90.

In his wholistic environmental ethics, Callicott errs because he claims that evolution and natural selection provide the foundation of land ethics, yet he denies that he has an evolutionary ethics and that his ethics is non-normative in an ethical sense. I argue that genuine environmental ethics must be normative in an ethical sense and that its roots lie in metaphysics and ethical theory, not merely natural selection.

SHRADER-FRECHETTE, Kristin. Island Biogeography, Species-Area Curves, and Statistical Errors: Applied Biology and Scientific Rationality. Proc Phil Sci Ass, 1, 447-456, 1990.

Using a recent case study from island biogeography concerning tropical rates of deforestation, the essay argues that there are different types of rationality appropriate to science and applied science. Therefore, in cases of applied science (like conservation biology), the more conservative course of action is for scientists to risk type-I statistical error. The essay argues further that, on grounds of scientific rationality, Kangas, Simberloff, and others were correct in risking type-II error, but that, on grounds of decision-theoretic rationality, Noss, Waide, and others were correct in risking type-I error.

SHRADER-FRECHETTE, Kristin. "Scientific Method and the Objectivity of Epistemic Value Judgments" in *Logic, Methodology and Philosophy of Science, VIII*, FENSTAD, J E (ed), 373-389. New York, Elsevier Science, 1989.

This essay argues that we can talk about "best explanations" in science. Defending a position midway between the anarchists like Feyerabend and the logical empiricists like Carnap, the essay argues for a position called "hierarchical naturalism." In doing so, it argues for a universal criterion of theory choice in science, explanatory power as tested by prediction. The essay also argues that the logical empiricists were wrong about the epistemic value judgments used in science; that most criteria for theory choice are situation-specific; and that scientific objectivity is guaranteed by the possibility of intelligible debate and criticism. The essay uses a case study from hydrogeology to illustrate and defend each of these points.

SHUKLA, Pandit Badrinath and LATH, Mukund (trans). Dehātmavāda or the Body as Soul: Exploration of a Possibility within Nyāya Thought. J Indian Counc Phil Res, 5(3), 1-17, My-Ag 88.

SHUN, Kwong-Loi. Mencius and the Mind-Dependence of Morality: An Analysis of Meng Tzu 6A: 4-5. J Chin Phil, 18(2), 169-193, Je 91.

The paper argues for a certain interpretation of passages 6A:4-5 of the *Meng Tzu*. According to this interpretation, Mencius holds that rightness (*yi*) is internal in the sense that what is right is so in virtue of certain features of the mind (*hsin*).

SHUN, Kwong-Loi. Mencius' Criticism of Mohism: An Analysis of *Meng Tzu* 3A:5. Phil East West, 41(2), 203-214, Ap 91.

The paper defends a certain interpretation of the debate between Mencius and the Mohist Yi Chih in *Mencius* 3A:5. On this interpretation, Mencius criticized the Mohist assumption that being moral requires one's first acquiring a conception of the moral way of life from something independent of the emotional resources of the mind, and then putting that conception into practice by cultivating the necessary emotional dispositions. According to Mencius, the moral way of life has "one root"-both the validity of the moral way of life and the emotional dispositions required for living it have a common source in certain pre-dispositions of the mind.

SHUN, Kwong-Loi. The Self in Confucian Ethics. J Chin Phil, 18(1), 25-35, Mr 91.

SHUSTERMAN, Richard. "Analytic and Pragmatist Aesthetics" in *XIth International Congress in Aesthetics, Nottingham 1988*, WOODFIELD, Richard (ed), 190-194. Nottingham, Nottingham Polytech, 1990.

This paper compares analytic aesthetics and Dewey's pragmatist aesthetics on the following issues: naturalism, disinterestedness, the socio-political context of art and art theory, the role of theory and evaluation, the cultural centrality of art and aesthetics, and the importance of aesthetic experiences.. The paper argues that pragmatism offers a better direction for aesthetic theory and one which converges with important themes in contemporary continental aesthetics.

SHUSTERMAN, Richard. Form and Funk: The Aesthetic Challenge of Popular Art. Brit J Aes, 31(3), 203-213, Jl 91.

After examining the reasons why philosophical defenses of popular art are so rare and difficult, this paper examines and refutes three of the major indictments of popular art: that it requires and induces mindless passivity, that it lacks any satisfying form, and that it does not deserve aesthetic legitimacy because it displays no artistic autonomy or resistance. Rock music is the popular art which the paper mostly discusses.

SHUTTE, Augustine. Umuntu Ngumuntu Ngabantu: An African Concept of Humanity. Phil Theol, 5(1), 39-54, Fall 90.

The worldwide struggle for justice and peace between the developed and the undeveloped nations is also a struggle between different conceptions of humanity. This article outlines and defends two African concepts that could provide a deeper, more human, conception of humanity than those currently dominant in American, European or Russian thinking. The notion of *umuntu ngumuntu ngabantu* stresses the peculiarly intersubjective character of personal life, while the notion of *seriti* presents us with an idea of power or energy that overcomes the dualism of mind and matter without being materialistic. The article finally indicates the relevance of such a conception of humanity for the struggle against apartheid in South Africa.

SICHER, Efraim. The Last Utopia: Entropy and Revolution in the Poetics of Evgeny Zamjatin. Hist Euro Ideas, 13(3), 225-237, 1991.

SICHOL, Marcia W. *The Making of a Nuclear Peace: The Task of Today's Just War Theorists*. Washington, Georgetown Univ Pr, 1990.

The author focusses on the issues of proportionality and noncombatant immunity of contemporary just war theories in grappling with the question of nuclear war/peace. (staff)

SIEBERS, Tobin. Kant and the Origins of Totalitarianism. Phil Lit, 15(1), 19-39, Ap 91.

Opposed to the modernist view that Kant's philosophy contributed to the rise of totalitarianism in Germany, this essay argues that his ethics achieve their greatest influence as a response to the horrors of totalitarianism. Kant's "On a Supposed

Right to Tell Lies from Benevolent Motives" makes sense only in a totalitarian context, and its argument leaps beyond its own epoch to expose the mechanisms of terror employed by coercive modern regimes. The use of Kant found in J. P. Sartre's "The Wall" and Hannah Arendt's work further demonstrate his relevance for modern ethics.

SIEBERT, Donald T. *The Moral Animus of David Hume*. Cranbury, Univ of Delaware Pr, 1990.

Hume is not often viewed as a moralist because in recent times his more purely philosophical texts like the *Treatise*, the *Enquiries*, and the *Dialogues* have been the ones most closely studied. However, by turning to other works on which he expected much of his reputation and achievement to rest such as his essays, autobiography, and the long and important *History of England*, this study demonstrates that Hume cultivates a moral stance involving emotional involvement (feeling or sensibility), worldliness and materialism, and toleration, all of which qualities free human beings from what Hume regards as cruel, solipsistic spiritualism.

SIEBERT, Rudolf J. Announcement of the Endless in Horkheimer, Adorno and Habermas (in Serbo-Croatian). Filozof Istraz, 34(1), 77-88, 1990.

Die Absicht dieser Arbeit ist zu zeigen, dass das Zentralthema der grossen philosophischen Tradition, die sich in ihrer Entwicklung von Kant, über Schelling bis Hegel erstreckt—traditionelle Einheit, moderne Uneinheit sowie Möglichkeit der küntgigen Einheit des Unendlichen und Endlichen, des Absoluten und Relativen, des Universalen und Partikularen, von Gott und Geschichte—in unterschiedlicher Gestalt auch für die Kritische Theorie von M Horkheimer über Th. W Adorno und W Benjamin bis J Habermas eine Relevante Frage Uleibt.

SIEG, Wilfried (ed). *Acting and Reflecting: The Interdisciplinary Turn in Philosophy*. Norwell, Kluwer, 1990.

This collection of essays (with contributions by, among others, P Suppes, T Schwartz, H A Simon, C Glymour, D Hausman, T Seidenfeld, I Levi) has a programmatic intent, namely, to strengthen and invigorate a tradition in philosophy that joins theoretical analysis and reflection with substantive work in a discipline.

SIEG, Wilfried. "Reflections on Hilbert's Program" in *Acting and Reflecting: The Interdisciplinary Turn in Philosophy*, SIEG, Wilfried (ed), 171-182. Norwell, Kluwer, 1990.

This paper gives a brief description of Hilbert's program and its modification due to Bernays. Then it discusses the impact and philosophical significance of recent work in proof theory for the modified Hilbert Program.

SIEG, Wilfried. Relative Consistency and Accessible Domains. Synthese, 84(2), 259-297, Ag 90.

The paper has three tightly connected strands: (1) a careful description of foundational studies in the second half of the 19th century (in particular, the work of Dedekind, Kronecker, and Hilbert); (2) a detailed analysis of Hilbert's Program that is viewed as an attempt to mediate between classical, set theoretic and constructive mathematics via structural reductions; (3) an argument that mathematical work on a modified Hilbert Program has a significant bearing on the reflective examination of the nature of mathematics, and that it points to two most important aspects of mathematical experience.

SIEGEL, Harvey. Fostering the Disposition to be Rational. Proc Phil Educ, 46, 27-31, 1990.

SIEGEL, Harvey and ERWIN, Edward. Is Confirmation Differential? Brit J Phil Sci, 40(1), 105-119, Mr 89.

SIEGEL, Harvey. Must Thinking Be Critical to Be Critical Thinking? Reply to Finocchiaro. Phil Soc Sci, 20(4), 453-461, D 90.

SIEGEL, Jerrold. A Unique Way of Existing: Merleau-Ponty and the Subject. J Hist Phil, 29(3), 455-480, Jl 91.

SIEGWART, Geo. Zu einem "der tiefsten philosophischen Probleme". Conceptus, 24(63), 67-80, 1990.

I am interpreting a short text by Putnam as an argumentation, further I am reasoning about the nature of interpretation. The results of this interpretation are two argumentations whose theses are equivalent under certain conditions. Reflections on interpretation leads to a distinction between three different acts of interpretation and to a formulation of rules of interpretation.

SIENA, Robertomaria. A proposito di Stato e totaliarismo nel pensiero di Marx. Sapienza, 43(3), 329-334, Jl-S 90.

SIGAD, Ran. Schopenhauer and Hegel (in Hebrew). Iyyun, 40(2), 115-135, Ap 91.

SIITONEN, Arto. "Understanding Our Actual Scheme" in *The Mind of Donald Davidson*, BRANDL, Johannes (ed), 149-156. Amsterdam, Rodopi, 1989.

There are philosophers who think that questions of fact can be distinguished from questions of interpretation of facts. Davidson calls the distinction between unconceptualized facts and interpretative schemes "the third dogma of empiricism." This points to Quine's article "Two Dogmas of Empiricism." In it, Quine challenged the distinction between synthetic and analytic statements and the possibility of reducing the meaning of all synthetic statements to immediate experience. Whereas Quine has remained faithful to empiricism, Davidson gives up empiricism. It is difficult to determine his standpoint. His remark that our actual scheme is best understood as extensional and materialistic, is rather perplexing. Is it intelligible, under Davidson's premisses, to speak of our actual scheme?

SIKIC, Zvonimir. Premiss Tree Proofs and Logic of Contradiction. Z Math Log, 36(3), 273-280, 1990.

SILBERBAUER, George. "Ethics in Small-Scale Societies" in *A Companion to Ethics*, SINGER, Peter (ed), 14-28. Cambridge, Blackwell, 1991.

The chapter examines ethical systems in a variety of small-scale societies. Reciprocity and intra-group altruism appear to be universal principles. However, each large- , or small-scale society interprets and expresses these, and its other ethical principles in terms of its own values and construction of reality. Ethical systems must, therefore, be viewed relativistically. In small-scale societies ethical positions are seldom cardinal and mutually exclusive but are integrated by negotation. Resolution of value conflicts is achieved through a calculus of countervailing principles which yields not a compromise or choice of evils, but a specific moral judgment of a particular matter. Ethics in these societies is not, therefore, simple or primitive but constitutes a sophisticated, complex system for guidance in assessing gradations of good or evil.

SILK, David. Response to Foulk's "In Defense of Cahn's Scamps". Phil Stud Educ, /, 146-151, 1987-88.

SILVA CAMARENA, Juan Manuel. Dialogo sobre humanismo y Marxismo (primera parte). Rev Filosof (Mexico), 23(68), 201-210, My-Ag 90.

SILVA CAMARENA, Juan Manuel. Entre el duelo y la melancolia. Rev Filosof (Mexico), 23(68), 147-149, My-Ag 90.

SILVA CAMARENA, Juan Manuel. Unamuno: De la decepción de la verdad, a la apología de la veracidad. Logos (Mexico), 19(55), 83-93, Ja-Ap 91.

SILVA, Catherine Young. Environmental Ethics: What? Why? How? Thinking, 9(2), 38-39, 1990.

SILVERMAN, Allan. Self-Predication and Synonymy. Ancient Phil, 10(2), 193-202, Fall 90.

In this paper I examine the status of self-predication claims in Plato by focussing on the debate between Vlastos and Nehamas. Vlastos alleges that Nehamas's analysis is equivalent to the identity interpretation offered by Cherniss and Allen. I defend a modified version of Nehamas's analysis. Completely formulated self-predications should be read as real definitions. Vlastos's argument fails, I allege, because he fails to see that in Platonic definitions the expressions flanking the 'is' are not synonymous. Since the discovery of the essence of some form marks a gain in knowledge, self-predications cannot be viewed as trivial identity statements.

SILVERMAN, Hugh J and WURZER, Wilhelm S. "Filming: Inscriptions of *Denken*" in *Postmodernism—Philosophy and the Arts (Continental Philosophy III)*, SILVERMAN, Hugh J (ed), 173-186. New York, Routledge, 1990.

SILVERMAN, Hugh J. "Merleau-Ponty and Derrida: Writing on Writing" in *Ontology and Alterity in Merleau-Ponty*, JOHNSON, Galen A (ed), 130-141. Evanston, Northwestern Univ Pr, 1991.

SILVERMAN, Hugh J (ed). *Postmodernism—Philosophy and the Arts (Continental Philosophy III)*. New York, Routledge, 1990.

SILVERMAN, Hugh J (ed). *Writing the Politics of Difference*. Albany, SUNY Pr, 1991.

SILVERS, Stuart. On Naturalizing the Semantics of Mental Representation. Brit J Phil Sci, 42(1), 49-73, Mr 91.

This paper examines recent attempts to provide an adequate natural interpretation for the representational (or intentional) properties of psychological states. Two-Factor theories (conceptual role semantics and truth condition semantics) lead to 'semantic cojunctivitis'. Fodor's causal-denotational theory (*Psychosemantics*, 1987) is supposed to correct this condition by relegating conceptual role semantics to the determination of mental state modality. Truth conditions determine content. His argument for the distinction fails. My diagnosis of Fodor's denotational theory's shortcomings focuses upon his misuse of the idea of nomologically sufficient conditions for representational content to connect his individualism and naturalism in psychology.

SIMEONOVA, Stanka. "Erweitert sich der Gegenstand der Zeitgenössischen Ästhetik?" in *XIth International Congress in Aesthetics, Nottingham 1988*, WOODFIELD, Richard (ed), 195-197. Nottingham, Nottingham Polytech, 1990.

SIMMEL, Georg and FRISBY, David (ed & trans) and BOTTOMORE, Tom (trans). *The Philosophy of Money: Georg Simmel (Second Edition)*. New York, Routledge, 1991.

SIMON, Herbert A. "Discussion: Progress in Philosophy" in *Acting and Reflecting: The Interdisciplinary Turn in Philosophy*, SIEG, Wilfried (ed), 57-62. Norwell, Kluwer, 1990.

SIMON, Herbert. "Epistemology: Formal and Empirical" in *Acting and Reflecting: The Interdisciplinary Turn in Philosophy*, SIEG, Wilfried (ed), 115-128. Norwell, Kluwer, 1990.

SIMON, William H. "Social Theory and Political Practice: Unger's Brazilian Journalism" in *Critique and Construction: A Symposium on Roberto Unger's "Politics"*, LOVIN, Robin W (ed), 296-332. New York, Cambridge Univ Pr, 1990.

SIMONE, Aldo. Dall'attualismo al tensionalismo. Filosofia, 42(1), 49-60, Ja-Ap 91.

SIMONS, Peter M. "Free Part—Whole Theory" in *Philosophical Applications of Free Logic*, LAMBERT, Karel (ed), 285-305. New York, Oxford Univ Pr, 1991.

After outlining mereology (formal part-whole theory) based on classical logic, I consider motivations for basing it on a free logic. A simple mereology is developed on the basis of a free logic, and applied to three areas of philosophical interest: 1) to the notion of implexive containment of one object in other developed in Meinong's theory of objects, where properly implexively contained objects are non-existents, 2) to the distinction between actual (existent) and potential (non-existent) parts found in Aristotle's theory of the continuum, and 3) to the notion of existent parts (e.g., Pompey) of non-existent states of affairs (e.g., that Pompey conquered Britain).

SIMONS, Peter M. Tree Proofs for Syllogistic. Stud Log, 48(4), 539-554, D 89.

This paper presents a tree method for testing the validity of inferences, including syllogisms, in a simple term logic. The method is given in the form of an algorithm and is shown to be sound and complete with respect to the obvious denotational semantics. The primitive logical constants of the system, which is indebted to the logical works of Jevons, Brentano, and Lewis Carroll, are term negation, polyadic term conjunction, and functors affirming and denying existence, and use is also made of a metalinguistic concept of formal synonymy. It is indicated briefly how the method may be extended to other systems.

SIMONS, Peter. "What Is Abstraction and What Is It Good For?" in *Physicalism in Mathematics*, IRVINE, Andrew D (ed), 17-40. Norwell, Kluwer, 1990.

Abstraction is considered as a way to reduce the tension between the prima facie ontological commitments of mathematical theories and forms of nominalism. The origins are traced to Aristotle. Different conceptions of abstraction are considered and it is argued that the abstractive move from relatively concrete to relatively more abstract terms induces a change in sense of the predicates true of them (transumptive abstraction), even when the same word is used for both.

SIMPSON, Peter. Liberalism: Political Success, Moral Failure? J Soc Phil, 21(1), 46-54, Spr 90.

Liberalism is now manifestly the most successful political system, but it was this already with Hobbes. It is successful because it offers freedom. But this freedom rests on an enforced peace that is the iron fist beneath the velvet glove. Liberalism is neutral between rival visions of the good because it attacks them all equally by forcibly denying them their wish to be the only and exclusive good. This is as true of Rawls as of Hobbes. Liberalism has thus many advantages and also many, and severe, disadvantages. Nevertheless the disadvantages can be overcome if liberalism is interpreted more strictly and minimally. I show how this can be done.

SIMPSON, Peter. Making the Citizens Good: Aristotle's City and Its Contemporary Relevance. Phil Forum, 22(2), 149-166, Wint 90-91.

Aristotle says the city must aim to make the citizens good. This description does not fit actual Greek cities. But Aristotle is not blind to the historical facts; rather he defines the city in terms of the objective requirements of human nature (as analysed in Pol I and NE X.9). The abiding facts of nature are more important than the fleeting facts of history. But Aristotle also sees the historical importance of Macedon for providing the conditions for the perfection of the city. His vision here constitutes an early model of the modern liberal democratic state.

SIMS, Pamela F. Matters of Conscience. Ethics Med, 7(1), 3-5, Spr 91.

SIMS, Ronald R and SIMS, Serbrenia J. Increasing Applied Business Ethics Courses in Business School Curricula. J Bus Ethics, 10(3), 211-219, Mr 91.

Business schools have a responsibility to incorporate applied business ethics courses as part of their undergraduate and MBA curriculum. The purpose of this article is to take a background and historical look at reasons for the new emphasis on ethical coursework in business schools. The article suggests a prescription for undergraduate and graduate education in applied business ethics and explores in detail the need to increase applied business ethics courses in business schools to enhance the ethical development of students.

SIMS, Ronald R. The Institutionalization of Organizational Ethics. J Bus Ethics, 10(7), 493-506, Jl 91.

The institutionalization of ethics is an important task for today's organizations if they are to effectively counteract the increasingly frequent occurrences of blatantly unethical and often illegal behavior within large and often highly respected organizations. This article discusses the importance of institutionalizing organizational ethics and emphasizes the importance of several variables (psychological contract, organizational commitment, and an ethically-oriented culture) to the institutionalization of ethics within any organizations.

SIMS, Serbrenia J and SIMS, Ronald R. Increasing Applied Business Ethics Courses in Business School Curricula. J Bus Ethics, 10(3), 211-219, Mr 91.

Business schools have a responsibility to incorporate applied business ethics courses as part of their undergraduate and MBA curriculum. The purpose of this article is to take a background and historical look at reasons for the new emphasis on ethical coursework in business schools. The article suggests a prescription for undergraduate and graduate education in applied business ethics and explores in detail the need to increase applied business ethics courses in business schools to enhance the ethical development of students.

SINDELAR, Dusan. The Problem of Cognition and Truth in Aesthetics (in Czechoslovakian). Estetika, 27(4), 193-206, 1990.

SINDELAR, Jan. To the History of Glory and Fall of the Book "Civilization at the Crossroads" after August 1968 (in Czechoslovakian). Filozof Cas, 38(5), 647-667, 1990.

The published material originated at the end of 1969 and in those days it was determined for the internal need of an interdisciplinary team of co-authors of the book *Civilization at the Crossroads*—a book which attracted great attention both in Czechoslovakia and abroad in its time. The end of 1969 was simultaneously a period of the devastating interference of "normalization" which began to suppress and disintegrate all critical thinking. It also began to disintegrate the authors' collective. In the introductory note which was written in the spring of 1990 the author draws attention to the fact that the book *Civilization at the Crossroads* was ambiguous in its action: it met the critical current which comprehended the need of social changes. (edited)

SINDIMA, Harvey. Bondedness, *Moyo* and *Umunthu* as the Elements of aChewa Spirituality: Organizing Logic and Principle of Life. Ultim Real Mean, 14(1), 5-20, Mr 91.

This is an exploration into aChewa organizing logic and principle of life. The aChewa consider the cosmos, nature and people as bonded in moyo (life), of which divinity is part. Umunthu, fullness of human moyo, is an equally important concept. Thus, moyo and umunthu are sacred values which form the core and symbolic framework for understanding the cosmos, nature and people. These values order society and awaken consciousness of the sacred. Bondedness of moyo and umunthu is meditated through narrative, a basic way of understanding self and the world (nature) among the aChewa.

SINGER, A E and SINGER, M S. Justice in Preferential Hiring. J Bus Ethics, 10(10), 797-803, O 91.

This paper reports studies designed to examine perceptions of preferential selection. Subjects evaluated the fairness of hypothetical cases of selection decisions based on either candidate sex or ethnic origin. A within-subjects design and a between-subjects design yielded convergent results showing that (1) preferential selection was perceived as unfair, irrespective of respondent sex or the basis for the preferential treatment (i.e., candidate sex or ethnic origin), (2) the level of perceived injustice was directly related to the discrepancy in merits between the successful minority candidate and the more qualified yet unsuccessful majority candidate, and (3) the provision of either and "ethical" or "legislative" justification for the selection decisions further exacerbated feeling of injustice. Possible interpretations for the findings and practical implications of the study were then discussed.

SINGER, Alan E and LYSONSKI, Steven and SINGER, Ming and HAYES, David. Ethical Myopia: The Case of "Framing" by Framing. J Bus Ethics, 10(1), 29-36, Ja 91.

The behavioural decision-theoretic concepts of mental accounting, framing and transaction utility have now been employed in marketing models and techniques. To date, however, there has not been any discussion of the ethical issues surrounding these significant developments. In this paper, an ethical evaluation is structured around three themes: (i) utilitarian justification, (ii) the strategic exploitation of cognitive habits, and (iii) the claim of scientific status for the techniques. Some recommendations are made for ethical practices.

SINGER, Beth J. Intersubjectivity without Subjectivism. Man World, 24(3), 321-338, Jl 91.

Elaborating concepts drawn from G H Mead and J Buchler, I challenge the phenomenological approach to the problem of intersubjectivity. Utilizing the concept of perspective, I provide an analysis of self and community and their interrelations, relating this to Mead's distinction of the 'I', the 'me', and the generalized other, and showing how the perspective of the generalized other, as a component of the 'me', transcends phenomenological subjectivity. I also show that, contrary to what he sometimes seems to imply, what Mead terms the 'me' must have an individual as well as a social component.

SINGER, Brent A. Spinoza, Heidegger, and the Ontological Argument. J Brit Soc Phenomenol, 21(3), 265-273, O 90.

SINGER, M S and SINGER, A E. Justice in Preferential Hiring. J Bus Ethics, 10(10), 797-803, O 91.

This paper reports studies designed to examine perceptions of preferential selection. Subjects evaluated the fairness of hypothetical cases of selection decisions based on either candidate sex or ethnic origin. A within-subjects design and a between-subjects design yielded convergent results showing that (1) preferential selection was perceived as unfair, irrespective of respondent sex or the basis for the preferential treatment (i.e., candidate sex or ethnic origin), (2) the level of perceived injustice was directly related to the discrepancy in merits between the successful minority candidate and the more qualified yet unsuccessful majority candidate, and (3) the provision of either and "ethical" or "legislative" justification for the selection decisions further exacerbated feeling of injustice. Possible interpretations for the findings and practical implications of the study were then discussed.

SINGER, Marcus G. Concerning F L Will's *Beyond Deduction*. Philosophy, 65(253), 371-374, Jl 90.

A response to a review, in *Philosophy* July 1989, of Frederick L Will's book *Beyond Deduction: Ampliative Aspects of Philosophical Reflection* (1988). The review is incompetent and irresponsible, apparently motivated by a need to vent spleen, and characterized by an amount of ill-feeling out of place in a scholarly journal. It is thus unfair not just to the author but to the reader. This response provides an account of what the book is about—a task failed by the reviewer—and demonstrates that it is eminently readable, well worth reading, and a work of importance that deserves a wide audience.

SINGER, Marcus G. "Value Judgments and Normative Claims" in *Key Themes in Philosophy*, GRIFFITHS, A Phillips (ed), 145-172. New York, Cambridge Univ Pr, 1989.

An account of values, value judgments, and normative claims (the generic name), how they are expressed and manifested and how they can be established. A number of important problems are dealt with along the way, and the essay as a whole provides a conspectus of moral philosophy. In the process, a number of important distinctions, too often ignored, are set out. These include distinctions between liking and approving, wanting and what is in one's interest, and preference and opinion. In a general way, yet with specificity when needed, covers the whole area of ethics, morals, and values, with some excursions into history.

SINGER, Ming and SINGER, Alan E and LYSONSKI, Steven and HAYES, David. Ethical Myopia: The Case of "Framing" by Framing. J Bus Ethics, 10(1), 29-36, Ja 91.

The behavioural decision-theoretic concepts of mental accounting, framing and transaction utility have now been employed in marketing models and techniques. To date, however, there has not been any discussion of the ethical issues surrounding these significant developments. In this paper, an ethical evaluation is structured around three themes: (i) utilitarian justification, (ii) the strategic exploitation of cognitive habits, and (iii) the claim of scientific status for the techniques. Some recommendations are made for ethical practices.

SINGER, Peter and NG, Yew-Kwang. An Argument for Utilitarianism: A Defence. Austl J Phil, 68(4), 448-454, D 90.

Our argument in favour of utilitarianism based on WMP (weak majority preference) and finite sensibility was queried by Kilpi. WMP states: For a society of n individuals choosing between two possibilities, x and y, if no individual prefers y to x, and at least n/2 individuals prefer x to y, then x increases social welfare and is socially preferable. Kilpi accepts WMP and finite sensibility but rejects the transitivity of social indifferences in the presence of imperfect individual sensibility. We defend our position by arguing that the ground for social indifference/preference is compelling and exact and hence social indifferences should be transitive. Issues of time duration and other complications are also addressed.

SINGER, Peter (ed). *A Companion to Ethics*. Cambridge, Blackwell, 1991.

Written for the general reader and student, this volume surveys the entire field of ethics. Section headings are: I) The Roots; II) The Great Ethical Traditions; III) Western Philosophical Ethics; IV) How Ought I to Live?: V) Applications; VI) The Nature of Ethics; VII) Challenge and Critique. Forty-seven different essays, each of 3000 to 6000 words, allow for a comprehensive discussion of these topics.

SINGH, Ajai R and SINGH, Shakuntala A. A Peep into Man's History: The Lessons for Today. J Indian Counc Phil Res, 7(3), 23-46, My-Ag 90.

SINGH, Dasarath and SINGH, Kameshwar. Copi's Conditional Probability Problem. J Indian Counc Phil Res, 5(3), 155-157, My-Ag 88.

The problem as Copi states it is indeterminate because the probabilities we are asked to calculate depend upon the (unspecified) rules under which Copi's game is played. Hence the correctness of one's playing Copi's game can only be formally attestable and consequently any counter-argument as such, presuming the determinateness of Copi's problem, would be prima facie unfair.

SINGH, Harinder and FRANTZ, Roger. The Conflation of Productivity and Efficiency in Economics and Economic History. Econ Phil, 7(1), 87-90, Ap 91.

SINGH, Kameshwar and SINGH, Dasarath. Copi's Conditional Probability Problem. J Indian Counc Phil Res, 5(3), 155-157, My-Ag 88.

The problem as Copi states it is indeterminate because the probabilities we are asked to calculate depend upon the (unspecified) rules under which Copi's game is played. Hence the correctness of one's playing Copi's game can only be formally attestable and consequently any counter-argument as such, presuming the determinateness of Copi's problem, would be prima facie unfair.

SINGH, Navjyoti. Phenomenology and Indian Philosophy. J Indian Counc Phil Res, 7(3), 109-132, My-Ag 90.

SINGH, Shakuntala A and SINGH, Ajai R. A Peep into Man's History: The Lessons for Today. J Indian Counc Phil Res, 7(3), 23-46, My-Ag 90.

SINGHAPAKDI, Anusorn and KRAFT, Kenneth L. The Role of Ethics and Social Responsibility in Achieving Organizational Effectiveness: Students Versus Managers. J Bus Ethics, 10(9), 679-686, S 91.

This paper investigates the differences in perceptions between business students and service-sector managers regarding the role that ethics and social responsibility serve in determining organizational effectiveness. An organizational effectiveness instrument containing business ethics and social responsibility items served as a questionnaire for a sample of 151 senior business undergraduates and 53 service-sector managers. The results indicated that while students acting as managers rate some social responsibility issues as more important than do managers, they also rate ethical conduct and a few dimensions of social responsibility lower than do managers. The findings have direct implications for both business practitioners and educators.

SINGLETON, Michael. Transcultural Dialogue and the Problem of the Concept of Ultimate Reality and Meaning. Ultim Real Mean, 13(4), 286-294, D 90.

SINNOTT-ARMSTRONG, Walter. Moral Experience and Justification. S J Phil, SUPP 29, 89-96, 1990.

Tolhurst claims that moral experience is analogous to perceptual experience and can directly justify moral beliefs. I respond by arguing that (1) moral experience has a different role in justification than perceptual experience of either colors, shapes, or things like cats or protons and that (2) moral experience alone cannot directly justify any moral belief, even prima facie. These conclusions do not exclude other important roles for moral experience and do not immediately imply moral scepticism.

SINNOTT-ARMSTRONG, Walter. On Primoratz's Definition of Terrorism. J Applied Phil, 8(1), 115-120, 1991.

In "What is Terrorism?" Igor Primoratz defines 'terrorism' as "the deliberate use of violence, or threat of its use, against innocent people, with the aim of intimidating them, or other people, into a course of action they otherwise would not take." I argue that this definition needs to be modified 1) by requiring that the harm or threat be to persons other than those intimidated, 2) by including aims which do not concern action, and 3) by distinguishing terrorists who know they are terrorists from those who do not.

SINNOTT-ARMSTRONG, Walter and FOGELIN, Robert J. *Understanding Arguments: An Introduction to Informal Logic (Fourth Edition)*. San Diego, Harcourt Brace Jov, 1991.

SINTONEN, Matti. Darwin's Long and Short Arguments. Phil Sci, 57(4), 677-689, D 90.

Doren Recker has criticized the prevailing accounts of Darwin's argument for the theory of natural selection in the *Origin of Species*. In this note I argue that Recker fails to distinguish between a deductive short argument for the principle of natural selection, and a nondeductive, long argument which aims at establishing that the principle has explanatory power in the various domains of application. I shall try to show that the semantic view of theories, especially in its structuralist form, makes it easy to distinguish between the two arguments and to explain how Darwin's long argument counts as one argument. I also raise a question about Recker's views on Darwin's mid-Victorian background, arguing that Newton's First Rule of Reasoning was not just a constraint on hypotheses involving unobservables, but a general request to keep conjecture and certainty apart.

SINTONEN, Matti. How to Put Questions to Nature. Philosophy, 27, 267-284, 90 Supp.

The paper discusses the old metaphor of inquiry as a process in which an inquirer puts questions to Nature. Apart from being a metaphor—Nature does not literally engage in dialogue—she does not understand all types of questions, most notably explanation-seeking why-questions. Furthermore, to those questions Nature does understand—she usually 'answers' 'Yes and no'. The paper argues that a sufficiently rich theory notion, such as the structuralist one, helps to bring the metaphor down to earth. Theories are devices which chop unmanageable why-questions to wh- and yes-no questions which Nature does understand.

SISTARE, C T. *Responsibility and Criminal Liability*. Norwell, Kluwer, 1989.

Where moral and political perspectives dictate that standards of criminal liability be set in accordance with determinations of individual responsibility, analysis and reform require a sound theory of responsibility as well as workable criteria for liability. This book explores problems of responsibility through a capacities model of responsibility. This model is advanced in opposition to the traditional cognitivist model dominant in Anglo-American criminal law, on grounds that the capacities model is at once superior as a conception of human agency and in providing intelligible criteria of just liability. Elements of responsibility including conduct voluntariness, knowledge, and intentionality are examined in the context of liability standards and issues. Although of special interest to legal philosophers, the book also contains much that is significant for ethics and general studies of responsible human agency.

SITTER-LIVER, Beat. Neuvermessung des Rechts- und Staatsdiskurses: Zu Otfried Höffes Theorie der Politischen Gerechtigkeit. Frei Z Phil Theol, 38(1-2), 83-109, 1991.

Otfried Höffe's "Theory of Political Justice" aims at universal validity. Three main arguments supporting this claim are scrutinized. The semantic analysis of 'just' legitimates the moral point of view (the perspective of justice) only when based on a presupposition - human dignity - that is not thoroughly discussed. This also holds for the proposed legitimation of human rights, and for the demonstration that there is not proper definition of law without reference to justice. On the other hand, a number of critiques addressed to Höffe's theory, e.g., Habermas's, are dismissed. Finally it is shown that Höffe's theory cannot yield any ecological ethics.

SIVAK, Jozef. The Concept of Sense in Merleau-Ponty (in Czechoslovakian). Filozof Cas, 38(6), 772-787, 1990.

L'article est consacré à la conception de la signification du phénoménlogue français bien connu, même dans les pays d l'Est, hormis le nôtre où l'on a commencé à l'étudier dans les années 60 pour interrompre cette étude par la suite. Il se divise en trois principales parties. Dans la première, progressive, il s'agit des points de départ (F. de Saussure, Hegel, Husserl, Heidegger) et des distinctions fondamentales (signifié, signifiant, structure, non-sens, forme) de cette conception. La deuxième partie, synthétique, concerne son fondement ontologique et la structure de celui-ci. Dans la troisième partie, l'exposé remonte aux sources de la notion de sens chez Merleau-Ponty (corps propre, expression, parole). (edited)

SKEEL, Joy D and SELF, Donnie J. A Study of the Foundations of Ethical Decision Making of Clinical Medical Ethicists. Theor Med, 12(2), 117-127, Je 91.

A study of clinical medical ethicists were conducted to determine the various philosophical positions they hold with respect to ethical decision making in medicine and their various positions' relationship to the subjective-objective controversy in value theory. The study revealed that most clinical medical ethicists tend to be objectivists in value theory. In addition, the study revealed that most clinical medical ethicists are consistent in the philosophical foundations of their ethical decision making. (edited)

SKENE, Loane. Mapping the Human Genome: Some Thoughts for Those Who Say "There Should Be A Law On It". Bioethics, 5(3), 233-249, Jl 91.

SKENE, Loane. Risk-Related Standard Inevitable in Assessing Competence—Comments on Wicclair. Bioethics, 5(2), 113-117, Ap 91.

SKIDELSKY, Robert. Response to Powell's "Theory and Practice". Philosophy, 26, 11-14, 90 Supp.

SKIDELSKY, Robert. "Response to Skidelsky's 'Theory and Practice'" in *Philosophy and Politics*, HUNT, G M K (ed), 11-14. New York, Cambridge Univ Pr, 1991.

This was a brief response to Mr Enoch Powell's claim that the main job of a politician is to preserve the status quo. I pointed out that this has not been true of politicians in general, and has not even been true of the political practice of Mr Powell.

SKIDMORE, Arthur. Why are Definitions True? SW Phil Rev, 7(1), 27-33, Ja 91.

Definitions occurring in axiomatic theories are presumably *true*, but also appear as merely *stipulated*. The paper offers a resolution of this puzzle by extending some Quinean notions concerning what makes logical truths true to cover the case of definitions.

SKILLEAS, Ole Martin. Anachronistic Themes and Literary Value: *The Tempest*. Brit J Aes, 31(2), 122-133, Ap 91.

The first part of the paper presents a present-day, anachronistic interpretation of *The Tempest*. The second part explores the basis of this reading, and with particular reference to Gadamer's hermeneutics, how the reader's situation may be a powerful influence on what he or she makes out as the theme of the work. My suggestion is that the potentialities some literary works have for 'application' to different concerns, and the 'dialogue' with the audience that this feature invites, is an important element in the value of literature.

SKILLEN, Tony. Active Citizenship as Political Obligation. Rad Phil, 58, 10-13, Sum 91.

Turning Robert Nozick's equation of redistributive taxation with forced labour on its head, the article makes a case for the latter if and only if it is in the form of community service, restrictively defined, and is liberally and democratically organized. A contrast is drawn between active citizenship and the passivity and alienation inherent in current forms of tax-sustained state welfare provision.

SKINNER, Martin (ed) and PICKERING, John (ed). *From Sentience To Symbols*. Buffalo, Univ of Toronto Pr, 1990.

Consciousness has returned as a central issue to contemporary psychology and is providing a meeting ground for all who study the mind. This collection of writings on consciousness has been selected in the expectation that readers from one discipline will be able to find bridges to others. The book covers physical, biological, cognitive, philosophical, and social aspects of consciousness which are arranged in eleven sections, each preceded by editorial introduction and discussion. Its emphasis is on tracing all stages in the emergence of consciousness. The capacity for symbolic thought, for language, and for self-awareness is so much more highly developed in human beings than in other species that it amounts to a qualitative break in the evolutionary progression of mental powers. The authors are concerned with how it is that the direct awareness of the world which human beings share with other sentient organisms has been transcended to yield the unique human mode of being in the world. A key theme is the reflextive capacity of the human mind which brings into being and is brought into being by the human social and cultural context.

SKINNER, Quentin. Who are "We"? Ambiguities of the Modern Self. Inquiry, 34(2), 133-153, Je 91.

This paper concentrates on three connected features of Taylor's argument. I begin by considering his historical sections on the formation of the modern identity, raising some doubts about the focus of his discussion and offering some specific criticisms in the case of Locke and Rousseau. Next I examine Taylor's list of the moral imperatives allegedly felt with particular force in the contemporary world. I question the extent to which the values listed by Taylor are genuinely shared, and point to a range of criticisms put forward by conservatives, Marxists, feminists, and other opponents of liberalism, all of whose doubts Taylor appears to underestimate. Finally, I address Taylor's underlying claim that a religious dimension is indispensable if our highest human potentialities are to be realized, and conclude with a critique of his theistic arguments.

SKIRBEKK, Gunnar. The World Reconsidered: A Brief *AggiornamentoF* for Leftist Intellectuals. Praxis Int, 10(3-4), 224-235, O 90-Ja 91.

SKLAR, Lawrence. "Foundational Physics and Empiricist Critique" in *Scientific Theories*, SAVAGE, C Wade (ed), 136-157. Minneapolis, Univ of Minn Pr, 1990.

Certain aspects of the empiricist "critique" of theories are contrasted with the approaches of the realist and the pragmatist. Aspects of some contemporary foundational theories in physics are then examined, with the aim of indicating why many of those concerned with the nature of these theories are drawn to the empiricist side of the debate on the nature of theories.

SKLAR, Lawrence. "Invidious Contrasts within Theory" in *Meaning and Method: Essays in Honor of Hilary Putnam*, BOOLOS, George (ed), 197-212. New York, Cambridge Univ Pr, 1990.

In recent years the tendency has been to think of all putatively referring terms of a theory as "on a par" with respect to issues of how straight - forwardly their referential role is to be understood. But for a variety of reasons the distinction between terms genuinely referential and those only apparently so can still be defended.

SKLAR, Lawrence. "Real Quantities and Their Sensible Measures" in *Philosophical Perspectives on Newtonian Science*, BRICKER, Phillip (ed), 57-75. Cambridge, MIT Pr, 1990.

Looking once again at the famous "Scholium to the Definitions" of Newton's *Principia*, it is suggested that the roots of two contemporary views of the nature of space and time (as a representational framework in which the observable phenomena can be embedded and as substantival elements in their own right) can both be found in Newton's arguments for "absolute" space and time in this section of the *Principia*.

SKLEDAR, Nikola. Possibility of Dialogic Encounter of Religious and Philosophical Humanitas (in Serbo-Croatian). Filozof Istraz, 34(1), 65-76, 1990.

The text deals with the relation and possibility of dialogic encounter (*dia-logos*, and not only *polemos*) between religious and humanistic philosophical humanity (*humanitas*). The religious humanitas is theocentric, derived from supranatural being, the creation of whom is human being, and humanity is strictly related to God's goodness and obeying God's laws. Philosophical humanitas, deriving the human being from the Being, leaves his primordial and eschatological as an unanswered question and secret, and shapes meaning and humanity as constant tasks—ideal to which as a lighthouse on an open horizon one should constantly aim. In the opinion of open-minded Marxists and critical theologians in the world and in this country, those two kinds of humanitas, Marxist humanism and Christian humanity, regardless of their differences, are not diametrically opposed, but have something mutual in the comprehension of human being, his creation of history and future. Thus, their truthful and sincere dialogue and mutual life are possible (and inevitable).

SKOBLE, Aeon James. Conflicting Views of Liberalism. Dialogue (PST), 33(2-3), 47-50, Ap 91.

The Foucault-influenced conception of liberalism that, among other things, informs the Critical Legal Studies movement is contrasted with classical liberalism. The former is shown to involve a program inadequate for the realization of its own goals. The "self-transformation ethic" championed by, e.g., Roberto Unger, would actually be better served either by welfarist liberalism or by libertarianism.

SKORPEN, Erling. Images of the Environment in Corporate America. J Bus Ethics, 10(9), 687-697, S 91.

Three nature images influence the environmental policies of major American corporations. Successively they are images of the 1) unfouled nest, 2) protected habitat, and 3) uncontaminated environment. Each contains unexpected surprises for its corporation, however. Polaroid, for example, does not foul its company precincts, but is now a Superfund "Potentially Responsible Party" for its deposited wastes in its home and neighboring states. This anomaly thus extends its unfouled-nest images to its dumpsites and beyond, but also implodes upon its workplace. Parallel extensions and inversions affect Martin Marietta's favored image of the protected habitat and Union Carbide's of the uncontaminated environment. These are shown with references to Kant and to Aristotle, but a concluding moral compares further neglect of the full consequences of such images to Dante's allegorical Circles 4 and 5 of Hell.

SKORUPSKI, John. Explanation and Understanding in Social Science. Philosophy, 27, 119-134, 90 Supp.

SKORUPSKI, John. "The Intelligibility of Scepticism" in *The Analytic Tradition: Philosophical Quarterly Monographs, Volume 1*, BELL, David (ed), 1-29. Cambridge, Blackwell, 1990.

Examines the theme that sceptical hypotheses are unintelligible as a theme in 20th century analytic philosophy, and considers the foundations in the theory of meaning which it requires.

SKOURIOTI, Athéna. L'interprétation comme art de création réitérée. Diotima, 18, 76-80, 1990.

L' interpretation de l'oeuvre d'art implique un écart par rapport à l'imitation exacte étant donné que l'interprète exprime, consciemment ou à son insu, ses sentiments intimes, à travers sa création. La nouvelle création sers la composante de plusieurs élements structuraux, de plusieurs facteurs qui interviendront à sa naissance pour lui permettre de fonctionner d'une manière dynamique et de mettre en valeur son authenticité.

SKURA, Tomasz. A Complete Syntactical Characterization of the Intuitionistic Logic. Rep Math Log, 23, 75-80, 1989.

The purpose of the work is to prove that the intuitionistic propositional logic is the unique intermediate logic with the generalized disjunction property (GDP). The proof consists in showing that the refutation rule corresponding to GDP together with the reverse modus ponens, the reverse substitution, and the constant falsity axiomatize the set of non-theorems of the intuitionistic logic.

SKURA, Tomasz. On Pure Refutation Formulations of Sentential Logics. Bull Sect Log, 19(3), 102-107, O 90.

The purpose of the paper is to give a general method of obtaining pure refutation formulations (i.e., formulations using only rules of the form: if $A_1,...,A_n$ are refutable then B is refutable) for a large class of logics (equivalential logics). There are two rules common to all such formulations: reverse substitution and a kind of replacement.

SKVORTSOV, D P and ANSHAKOV, O M and FINN, V K. On Axiomatization of Many-Valued Logics Associated with Formalization of Plausible Reasonings. Stud Log, 48(4), 423-447, D 89.

This paper studies a class of infinite-valued predicate logics. A sufficient condition for axiomatizability of logics from that class is given.

SKYRMS, Brian. *The Dynamics of Rational Deliberation*. Cambridge, Harvard Univ Pr, 1990.

This book develops a theory of rational deliberation for agents in situations of strategic interaction. Concepts of classical game theory are seen as special cases which arise in highly idealized circumstances. The theory of good habits for deliberators with bounded rationality is discussed.

SKYRMS, Brian. "The Value of Knowledge" in *Scientific Theories*, SAVAGE, C Wade (ed), 245-266. Minneapolis, Univ of Minn Pr, 1990.

The theorem that the expected utility of new evidence relevant to a decision is always positive is proved for a very general model of belief change, and its presuppositions are analyzed. An anticipation is found in an unpublished manuscript of F P Ramsey.

SLAMAN, Theodore A. The Density of Infima in the Recursively Enumerable Degrees. Annals Pure Applied Log, 52(1-2), 155-179, Ap 91.

We show that every nontrivial interval in the recursively enumerable degrees contains an incomparable pair which have an infimum in the recursively enumerable degrees.

SLANEY, John K. On the Structure of De Morgan Monoids with Corollaries on Relevant Logic and Theories. Notre Dame J Form Log, 30(1), 117-129, Wint 89.

A De Morgan monoid is said to be constant if it is generated by its identity alone. It is shown that the only nontrivial proper homomorphism from a prime De Morgan monoid to a constant one is onto the 4-element algebra C4. The only element thus mapped to the 0 of C4 is the 0 of the original. These facts are used to obtain results on De Morgan monoids with idempotent generators. The paper concludes with some applications to the relevant logic R and particularly to relevant arithmetic.

SLATER, B H. Intensional Identities. Log Anal, 31(121-122), 93-107, Mr-Je 88.

SLATER, B H. Liar Syllogisms and Related Paradoxes. Analysis, 51(3), 146-153, Je 91.

SLEEPER, R W. Commentary on "Epistemology as Hypothesis". Trans Peirce Soc, 26(4), 435-442, Fall 90.

This is a reply to the paper on Dewey's *Logic* by Hilary and Ruth Anna Putnam, "Epistemology as Hypothesis," read to the SAAP symposium at the 1989 Eastern Division meeting of the APA at Atlanta, and is published with it. I accept the Putnams's reading of Dewey's *Logic* in general, but point out that they fail to attend to the nature and importance of Dewey's realist ontology of facts and values and, hence, the role of language in the ends-means relationship involved in our transactions with the world remains somewhat obscure in their account.

SLEIGH JR, Robert C. *Leibniz and Arnauld*. New Haven, Yale Univ Pr, 1990.

SLEIGH JR, Robert C. "Leibniz on Malebranche on Causality" in *Central Themes in Early Modern Philosophy*, COVER, J A (ed), 161-193. Indianapolis, Hackett, 1990.

SLEJSKA, D. The Freedom of Values and the Value of Freedom (in Czechoslovakian). Filozof Cas, 38(3), 259-272, 1990.

The determination of values as criteria of evaluation is the result of choices which have compared a greater number of value alternatives. Particularly responsible are choices conducted between alternatives giving prominence to existing reality and critique of existing reality in the name of higher values. History is known to contain periods of gradual growth of value changes with periods marked by fundamental value decisions concerning the fate of the human species. Freedom of value-related choices inheres in that these are responsible choices, proceeding through decision making on the part of the subject. The notion of unfree value choices is a nonsense. (edited)

SLEZAK, Peter. Man Not a Subject of Science? Soc Epistem, 4(4), 327-342, O-D 90.

SLEZAK, Peter. On Rhetorical Strategies: *Verstehen Sie*? Soc Epistem, 4(4), 357-360, O-D 90.

SLEZAK, Peter. Reinterpreting Images. Analysis, 50(4), 235-243, O 90.

SLEZAK, Peter. Was Descartes a Liar? Diagonal Doubt Defended. Brit J Phil Sci, 39(3), 379-388, S 88.

I defend the claim that Descartes's *cognito* and the Liar Paradox are variants of a common underlying puzzle. Besides elegant textual virtues, my 'diagonal' reconstruction gains strength from Descartes's concern with universal features of the mind which permit deploying independent arguments to illuminate the problem. A further important feature of my reconstruction of the *cogito* is that it permits according Descartes a worthy insight, by marked contrast with the uncharitability of many analyses. Sorensen's recent criticisms raise interesting questions regarding related paradoxical Buridan sentences, but I argue that they do not threaten the aptness of my reconstruction.

SLICER, Deborah. Your Daughter or Your Dog? A Feminist Assessment of the Animal Research Issue. Hypatia, 6(1), 108-124, Spr 91.

I bring several ecofeminist critiques of deep ecology to bear on mainstream animal rights theories, especially on the rights and utilitarian treatments of the animal research issue. Throughout, I show how animal rights issues are feminists issues and clarify the relationship between ecofeminism and animal rights.

SLOTE, Michael. Ethics Without Free Will. Soc Theor Pract, 16(3), 369-383, Fall 90.

Utilitarianism can be adjusted to the denial of free will, and so too can a certain form of virtue ethics that takes its inspiration from Spinoza. Without falling into Spinoza's ethical egoism, one can speak of virtues and regard certain acts and traits as deplorable or criticizable without committing oneself to the judgments of blameworthiness that virtue ethics sees as incompatible with free will. Recent work that has called freedom into question needn't be thought of as challenging the whole idea of doing substantive ethics.

SLOTE, Michael. Response to van Inwagen's "Logic and the Free Will Problem". Soc Theor Pract, 16(3), 291-295, Fall 90.

SLOTE, Michael. "Some Advantages of Virtue Ethics" in *Identity, Character, and Morality: Essays in Moral Psychology*, FLANAGAN, Owen (ed), 429-448. Cambridge, MIT Pr, 1990.

SLURINK, Pouwel. Natuurlijke selectie, doelgerichtheid en een uitzonderlijke samenloop van omstandigheden: Een kritiek op F Soontiëns. Alg Ned Tijdschr Wijs, 83(1), 69-82, Ja 91.

In this reply to the paper of F Soontiëns on "Evolution, Teleology and Chance" (*ANTW* 82.1 (1990), 1-14), it is argued that there is an important distinction between the internal teleology or teleonomy of individual organisms and a teleology of the process of evolution. The former is based on the genetic program that makes an organism goal-directed; for the latter there is not the slightest evidence. It is argued that Dr. F Soontiëns can't make clear his concept of a teleology of the process of evolution and can even less explain why there is teleology in the first place. Contrary to Soontiëns, the author argues that the notion of chance in evolution can be made free of ambiguities by speaking about the random variation on which selection works. According to the author the process of random variation and selection explains the teleonomy of individual organisms as well as the appearance of a "teleological" process of adaptation.

SLUSSER, Gerald H. "Inspiration and Creativity: An Extension" in *Archetypal Process: Self and Divine in Whitehead, Jung, and Hillman*, GRIFFIN, David Ray (ed), 105-106. Evanston, Northwestern Univ Pr, 1989.

SLUSSER, Gerald H. "Jung and Whitehead on Self and Divine: The Necessity for Symbol and Myth" in *Archetypal Process: Self and Divine in Whitehead, Jung, and Hillman*, GRIFFIN, David Ray (ed), 77-92. Evanston, Northwestern Univ Pr, 1989.

SMALL, Ian and GUY, Josephine. Usefulness in Literary History. Brit J Aes, 31(3), 259-264, Jl 91.

This essay examines and critiques various uses of the term 'literary history' in English Studies. It identifies two basic, but opposing kinds of literary history, the 'political' and the 'aesthetic'. It then examines their relative utility (where utility is defined in terms of the specificity of the explanations which a literary history provides) and demonstrates their deficiencies on these grounds. It suggests an outline for a literary history which might combine elements of the aesthetic and the political, and yet be specific in the accounts of literary works which it provides.

SMALL, Robin. Incommensurability and Recurrence: from Oresme to Simmel. J Hist Ideas, 52(1), 121-137, Ja-Mr 91.

SMART, J J C. Explanation—Opening Address. Philosophy, 27, 1-19, 90 Supp.

Introductory talk in conference on Explanation. It is argued that the concept of explanation is a somewhat polymorphous one. Explanation of a proposition is primarily fitting it into a web of belief of oneself or of someone else. Since webs of belief vary the concept is a contextual one. The contextual account of explanation is inevitably imprecise but is briefly compared with some other accounts. There is a short discussion of work by Paul Thagard on artificial intelligence modelling of explanation.

SMART, J J C. "How to Turn the *Tractatus* Wittgenstein into (Almost) Donald Davidson" in *Truth and Interpretation: Perspectives on the Philosophy of Donald Davidson*, LE PORE, Ernest (ed), 92-100. Cambridge, Blackwell, 1986.

SMART, J J C. "Methodology and Ontology" in *Imre Lakatos and Theories of Scientific Change*, GAVROGLU, Kostas (ed), 47-57. Norwell, Kluwer, 1989.

This paper is mainly concerned with the problem of closing the gap between rationality as defined by Lakatos and like-minded philosophers and probability of truth. However it is necessary to preserve a gap between rationality and truth itself. Even Peircean ideal science could in some respects be false. The paper also considers Lakatos's conception of methodology as concerned with the demarcation between science and nonscience. It is urged that metaphysics is at the extremely conjectural end of science and that scientific plausibility is a touchstone of metaphysical truth.

SMART, Ninian. Boston University Studies in Philosophy and Religion, Volumes 1-10. Phil East West, 41(3), 387-394, Jl 91.

SMART, Ninian. "Buddhism, Sri Lanka, and the Prospects for Peace" in *Celebrating Peace*, ROUNER, Leroy S (ed), 147-161. Notre Dame, Univ Notre Dame Pr, 1990.

SMILANSKY, S. Free Will and Being a Victim. Int J Moral Soc Stud, 6(1), 19-32, Spr 91.

The core of the free will problem is the question of whether libertarian free will, the ability to do otherwise in exactly the same situation, is of great importance. Compatibilists answer that libertarian free will is unimportant. I argue that this answer is over-confident. I begin by looking at what it is to be a victim. I then construct an imaginary world where, even if people lack libertarian free will, no one can be considered a victim. Once we see the great differences between the real world and this imaginary world, however, we realize that, if there is no libertarian free will, people are very often victims in ways in which they would not be victims if they had (or could have) libertarian free will.

SMILANSKY, Saul. Utilitarianism and the 'Punishment' of the Innocent: The General Problem. Analysis, 50(4), 256-261, O 90.

Anti-utilitarians have argued about the issue of utilitarianism and the 'punishment' of the innocent by presenting extreme and peripheral examples, allowing utilitarians to disclaim the reality of the problem. Both sides have shared the opinion that in daily life utilitarianism will not entail much (if any) 'punishment' of the innocent. I argue that this is a mistake. If we consider not specific detailed examples (or the total transformation of society) but the utilitarian attractions of a limited relaxation of the rigorous criteria within the current judicial framework, the opposition between utility and justice is clear.

SMILG VIDAL, Norberto. La reivindicación de la racionalidad en K O Apel. Dialogo Filosof, 6(3), 322-334, S-D 90.

SMIRNOV, V A. "The Logical Ideas of N A Vasiliev and Modern Logic" in *Logic, Methodology and Philosophy of Science, VIII*, FENSTAD, J E (ed), 625-640. New York, Elsevier Science, 1989.

SMITH, Barry and SCHUHMANN, Karl. Elements of Speech Act Theory in the Work of Thomas Reid. Hist Phil Quart, 7(1), 47-66, Ja 90.

The account of social acts sketched by Thomas Reid is shown to constitute an anticipation of the theory of speech acts standardly associated with Austin and Searle. Reid's ideas are compared also with that other (and in many ways more important) pre-Austinian speech act theory worked out by the phenomenologist Adolf Reinach in his monograph on the act of promising of 1913.

SMITH, Barry. Textual Deference. Amer Phil Quart, 28(1), 1-12, Ja 91.

Works of philosophy written in English have spawned a massive secondary literature dealing with ideas, problems or arguments. But they have almost never given rise to works of *commentary* in the strict sense, a genre which is however a dominant literary form not only in the Confucian, Vedantic, Islamic, Jewish and Scholastic traditions, but also in relation to more recent German-language philosophy. Yet Anglo-Saxon philosophers have themselves embraced the commentary form when dealing with Greek or Latin philosophers outside their own tradition. The paper seeks to establish the reasons for this peculiar asymmetry by examining those factors which might be conducive to the growth of a commentary literature in a given culture.

SMITH, Bruce. Homer's Contest: Nietzsche on Politics and the State in Ancient Greece. Kinesis, 18(1), 37-49, Wint 90.

SMITH, Charles W. "The Realism of the Symbolic" in *Harré and His Critics*, BHASKAR, Roy (ed), 224-239. Cambridge, Blackwell, 1990.

SMITH, David Woodruff. Thoughts. Phil Papers, 19(3), 163-189, N 90.

An internalist theory of intentional content is applied to Twin-Earth thought-experiments, providing a more natural account than theories of social or relational content. The theory addresses indexical thoughts, "transcendent" thoughts about natural kinds, and the dependence of thought and content on local and global context, including physical, and social-historical conditions. The results contrast with Putnam's, Burge's, and Searle's, and address Husserlian and Heideggerian views on intentionality.

SMITH, G W. "Markets and Morals" in *Philosophy and Politics*, HUNT, G M K (ed), 15-32. New York, Cambridge Univ Pr, 1991.

In response to the charge that the liberal conception of the self is 'abstract' and 'superficial' its argued that a distinction must be made between the Hayekian view and the utilitarian tradition of market thinking, represented by Adam Smith and J S Mill. In the latter, the market is regarded as having an important moral function in creating and sustaining an 'encharactered' self, i.e., a self capable of both individual autonomy and constitutive engagement in serious moral relations of a now market kind with other market agents. This view is advanced against Marxist and communitarian interpretations of market agency, and against John Gray's charge that Mill promoted a superficial understanding of the liberal individual.

SMITH, G W. Markets and Morals. Philosophy, 26, 15-32, 90 Supp.

The argument is a response to the charge made mainly by Marxists and communitarians that the typical liberal conception of the self is 'abstract' and 'superficial', especially in its market relationships, because it detaches the subject from constitutive connections and moral relations with other market agents. The Marxian alternative is briefly considered and rejected and attention focusses upon the utilitarian tradition of the market individual, as exemplified in the thought of Adam Smith and J S Mill. It is argued that the market is regarded as having an important moral function in creating and sustaining an 'encharactered self', i.e., a self capable of both individual autonomy and constitutive engagement in serious moral relations of a nonmarket kind with other market agents. In addition, Mill's views are defended against John Gray's recent charge that Mill promotes a superficial and unconvincing understanding of the liberal individual.

SMITH, Gary (ed). *On Walter Benjamin: Critical Essays and Recollections*. Cambridge, MIT Pr, 1991.

A collection of critical essays and recollections on the life and works of Walter Benjamin. The essays cover the full range of Benjamin's interests, from Hashish to Goethe to the modern city. They include important critical essays as well as several moving evocative recollections of Benjamin. (staff)

SMITH, George H. *Atheism, Ayn Rand, and other Heresies*. Buffalo, Prometheus, 1991.

SMITH, Gerrit. Quantum Cosmology and the Beginning of the Universe. Phil Sci, 57(4), 663-667, D 90.

In this note a recently developed quantum oscillating finite space cosmological model is described. The principle novelty of the model is that there is a quantum blurring of the classical singularity between cycles, instead of a singularity free bounce. Recently, Quentin Smith (1988) has argued that present theoretical and observational evidence justifies the belief that the past history of the universe is finite. The relevance of this cosmological model to Smith's arguments is discussed.

SMITH, Huston. Response to Tyler Anderson. Phil East West, 41(3), 368-370, Jl 91.

Doubting that there is much substance to the affinities that Tyson Anderson sees between Heidegger, Wittgenstein, and Rorty (on the one hand) and Frithjof Schuon and the perennial philosophy (on the other), I propose that the latter position sees the human self as joined to the Absolute—through Atman, the *imago dei*, and the Buddha nature that even grains of sand possess—whereas the philosophers Anderson cites posit no such continuity.

SMITH, Jan M. Propositional Functions and Families of Types. Notre Dame J Form Log, 30(3), 442-458, Sum 89.

When specifying the task of a computer program, it is often natural to use recursion on a data type. In Martin-Löf's type theory, a universe must be used when defining a propositional function by recursion. Using a logical framework for type theory, formulated by Martin-Löf, an extension of type theory is proposed by which propositional functions can be directly defined without using a universe.

SMITH, Janet Farrell. "Responsibility and Future Generations: A Constructivist Model" in *Philosophy of Technology*, DURBIN, Paul T (ed), 169-186. Norwell, Kluwer, 1989.

SMITH, John E. Blanshard on Philosophical Style. Ideal Stud, 20(2), 100-111, My 90.

On Philosophical Style begins with three illustrations of failed communication—Macaulay being unable to fathom a sentence from Kant; Reichenbach making no sense out of a passage from Hegel; Russell puzzling about Dewey's notion of inquiry. Blanshard puts the onus on the writer, advising that more effort go into the ultimate refinement of ideas and not only to their first approximation. Good style makes the reader feel alive by showing the person behind the thought. Concreteness is important; excessive generality loses the main focus. Style and substance should coalesce. Ordinary versus technical language is discussed in connection with James and Whitehead. Blanshard ends with Milton's word that to write well, one "ought himself to be a true poem."

SMITH, John E. "Interpreting across Boundaries" in *Understanding the Chinese Mind: The Philosophical Roots*, ALLINSON, Robert E (ed), 26-47. New York, Oxford Univ Pr, 1989.

The aim is to analyze interpretation and understanding between different cultures. Three types of encounter are considered; *parallels* in two or more cultures; *divergences* about the same issue; *collisions* in belief—the Western idea of creation and Eastern versions of the idea that the world is eternal. Parallels point to continuities in experience across cultures; divergences provide opportunity for mutual understanding and self-criticism; collisions represent ultimate historical differences which may be understood, but not mediated.

SMITH, John Maynard. Byerly and Michod on Fitness. Biol Phil, 6(1), 37, Ja 91.

SMITH, John Maynard. Explanation in Biology. Philosophy, 27, 65-72, 90 Supp.

SMITH, Joseph Wayne. Logic, Contradiction and Quantum Theory. Gnosis, 3(3), 17-27, D 90.

SMITH, Joseph Wayne. Time, Change and Contradiction. Austl J Phil, 68(2), 178-188, Je 90.

SMITH, Michael B (ed) and JOHNSON, Galen A (ed). *Ontology and Alterity in Merleau-Ponty*. Evanston, Northwestern Univ Pr, 1991.

SMITH, Michael B. "Two Texts on Merleau-Ponty by Emmanuel Levinas" in *Ontology and Alterity in Merleau-Ponty*, JOHNSON, Galen A (ed), 53-66. Evanston, Northwestern Univ Pr, 1991.

These texts, "Intersubjectivity" and "Sensibility," appeared in 1983 and 1984, and are reprinted in *Hors Sujet* (Montpellier: Fata Morgana, 1987). They take up the problem of the perception of other people, beginning with Merleau-Ponty's reworking of Husserl's "Einfühlung." Merleau-Ponty extrapolates from the experience of the "double toucher" (my right hand touching my left) to explain how intersubjectivity arises through intercorporeal "Flesh." Levinas admires Merleau-Ponty's account, but taxes it with describing the other in terms of knowledge, hence as deficiency. Levinas would preserve alterity through recourse to proximity, infinity, involuntary responsibility, and love. The other's uniqueness is said to "shatter" totality.

SMITH, Michael and PETTIT, Philip. Backgrounding Desire. Phil Rev, 99(4), 565-592, O 90.

Assume that desire is always involved in the genesis of intentional action. Does this mean that in practical deliberation, the intentional agent takes the state of his desires into account? We argue that it does not: that while desire is always present in the background of intentioanl action, it need not figure in the foreground of deliberation. We then go on to show that this view of things—we call it 'the strict background view'—impacts on a number of current debates in moral philosophy. It undermines two well-known arguments, one in defence of cognitivism, the other in defence of utilitarianism, and it has an important significance for our understanding of autonomy, integrity and prudence.

SMITH, Michael. "Realism" in *A Companion to Ethics*, SINGER, Peter (ed), 399-410. Cambridge, Blackwell, 1991.

Moral realism is the view that morality is objective, in some sense. But it seems undeniable that morality provides us with reasons for action; and, according to the standard picture of human psychology, to have a reason for action we must have a desire. Since desires seem to be subjective, in that one person's desires may not resemble those of another, in what sense *can* morality be objective? This difficulty for moral realism is the theme of this article.

SMITH, Peter. Aesthetics and Art Education. Phil Stud Educ, /, 91-102, 1987-88.

SMITH, Phil. Response to Merkle and Pritscher. Phil Stud Educ, /, 50-54, 1987-88.

SMITH, Phillip L and BELLAND, John. Reclaiming Virtue: Philosophy in the Field of Educational Technology. J Thought, 25(1-2), 56-65, Spr-Sum 90.

SMITH, Quentin. Atheism, Theism and Big Bang Cosmology. Austl J Phil, 69(1), 48-66, Mr 91.

Although some hold God created the big bang, it is argued here that big bang cosmology is inconsistent with theism. If God had created the universe's first state, he would have ensured that it evolve into a state containing living creatures. But the big bang singularity is inherently lawless and unpredictable and is not ensured to evolve in this way. Therefore, it was not created by God. Several objections to this argument are considered and rebutted.

SMITH, Quentin. An Atheological Argument from Evil Natural Laws. Int J Phil Relig, 29(3), 159-174, Je 91.

The law of "eat or be eaten" is probably ultimately evil and therefore God probably does not exist. If God existed, he would not have created carnivores but instead have created only vegetarian animals; instead of tigers, he would have created vegetarian tiger-counterparts. The attempts of Swineburne, Hick, Schlesinger, Reichenbach and Plantinga to defuse the problem of natural evil are considered and rejected.

SMITH, Quentin. Castañeda's Quasi-Indicators and the Tensed Theory of Time. Critica, 23(67), 59-73, Ap 91.

SMITH, Quentin. Concerning the Absurdity of Life. Philosophy, 66(255), 119-121, Ja 91.

Westphal and Cherry criticize Thomas Nagel's theory of the absurd by claiming that a person who is emotionally absorbed in something is immune from the value-scepticism Nagel discusses and thus does not live an absurd life. It is argued in this paper that Westphal's and Cherry's criticism is unsuccessful since the emotionally absorbed person is psychologically but not logically immune from value-scepticism, and the latter is required to prevent a person's life from being absurd. The real problem with Nagel's theory is that it is question-begging; it assumes but does not prove values are relative.

SMITH, Quentin. Reply to Vallicella: Heidegger and Idealism. Int Phil Quart, 31(2), 231-235, Je 91.

Vallicella argued that Heidegger's idealism is incoherent but that absolute idealism is coherent. I argue the reverse. There is no contradiction in the supposition that Being is dependent upon Dasein, that entities are dependent upon Being, and therefore that all entities are dependent upon Dasein. This may be false, but it is consistent. The absolute idealism of Fichte and the like is incoherent, however, because it supposes that all human minds are but representations in the Absolute Mind, and it is impossible for a mind to be nothing but a representation in another Mind.

SMITH, Quentin. Time and Propositions. Philosophia (Israel), 20(3), 279-294, D 90.

Propositions are traditionally held to exist timelessly, but it is argued in this paper they exist in time. Something exists in time if it stands in a relation at one time and does not stand in that relation at a later time. For some proposition p, p stands in the relation of BEING BELIEVED at one time but not at a later time; thus p exists in time. This argument is generalized and some counterarguments are evaluated and rebutted.

SMITH, R U. *Oratio Placabilis Deo* Eriugena's Fragmentary Eucharistic Teaching. Dionysius, 13, 85-114, D 89.

SMITH, Robin. Predication and Deduction in Aristotle: Aspirations to Completeness. Topoi, 10(1), 43-52, Mr 91.

This paper describes the SNePS knowledge-representation and reasoning system. SNePS is an intensional, propositional, semantic-network processing system used for research in AI. We look at how predication is represented in such a system when it is used for cognitive modeling and natural-language understanding and generation. In particular, we discuss issues in the representation of fictional entities and the representation of propositions form fiction, using SNePS. We briefly survey four philosophical ontological theories of fiction and sketch an epistemological theory of fiction (implemented in SNePS) using a story operator and rules for allowing propositions to "migrate" into and out of story "spaces".

SMITH, Rogers M. *Liberalism and American Constitutional Law*. Cambridge, Harvard Univ Pr, 1990.

Doctrinal developments in four key areas of American constitutional law—due process, free speech, voting rights, and federal economic duties—reveals ongoing efforts to resolve problems in early liberal constitutional principles by grafting on elements of later political outlooks. Many doctrines have thus become fragile patchworks of conflicting political theories. Modern responses to these difficulties include neoconservative calls for return to traditional or higher law values; advocacy of purely procedural democratic values; and neo-Kantian defenses of equal concern and respect for the moral potential of all persons. None of these responses meets early liberalism's difficulties while preserving its strengths. More promising is a teleological approach that sees liberal constitutionalism as aiming to protect and enhance the powers and resources of all persons to decide reflectively how they should live and to pursue their chosen courses.

SMITH, Steven G. Homicide and Love. Phil Theol, 5(3), 259-276, Spr 91.

For perspicuous comparison and evaluation of moral positions on life-and-death issues, it is necessary to take into account the different meanings that killing and getting killed can bear in the two dimensions of dealing with persons (intention meeting intention) and handling them. A homicidal scenario in Sir Gawain and the Green Knight shows the possibility of courteous dearling coinciding with lethal handling. The extreme possibility of lovingly affirming persons while killing them, suggested by the Augustinian "kindly severity" ideal for state-sponsored punitive killing, requires the killers' affirmation of a fleshliness and fallibility shared with their victims; but love can accept killing only provisionally, since it postulates freedom from the constraints that are felt to require killing.

SMITH, Tara. Why Do I Love Thee? A Response to Nozick's Account of Romantic Love. SW Phil Rev, 7(1), 47-57, Ja 91.

This essay takes issue with the account of romantic love presented by Robert Nozick in *The Examined Life*. Nozick resists the view that love should hinge on one's beloved's specific characteristics, fearing that this perspective reduces the beloved to a mere "placeholder" for some set of desired qualities. I argue that Nozick's position rests on an artificial severing of a person from his characteristics, ambiguity about which personal traits count as "characteristics," and an unfair portrayal of what the characteristics view of love's basis entails about the nature of commitment in romantic relationships.

SMITH, Tony. A Critical Look at Arguments for Food Irradiation. Pub Affairs Quart, 3(4), 15-25, O 89.

What degree of risk is socially acceptable? What ought we to do when scientists disagree in their assessments? What social interests are served by scientific research? Food irradiation provides a paradigm case of how these sorts of questions can arise when new technologies are introduced. In this article arguments proposed by the Council for Agricultural Science and Technology in favor of food irradiation are critically evaluated.

SMITHKA, Paula. "Nuclearism and Sexism: Overcoming Their Shared Metaphysical Basis" in *Issues in War and Peace: Philosophical Inquiries*, KUNKEL, Joseph (ed), 229-254. Wolfeboro, Longwood, 1989.

This essay argues that many of the oppressive and exploitive "-isms" in contemporary society, such as sexism, nuclearism, and the exploitation of the natural environment, naturism, are the consequences of the Western world's acceptance of a fundamental metaphysical principle which I call 'dissociation'. Dissociation is the result of an individual's quest for radical autonomy which is the attempt on the part of that individual to sever his/her relationship with others and nature. The essay provides a historical account of the dissociation present in sexism, naturism, and nuclearism and further suggests a more "authochthonic" perspective, i.e., an attitude of "rootedness" as an alternative to the metaphysical problem of dissociation.

SMITHKA, Paula. "Pragmatic Pacifism: A Methodology for Gaining the Ear of the Warist" in *In the Interest of Peace: A Spectrum of Philosophical Views*, KLEIN, Kenneth H (ed), 237-246. Wolfeboro, Longwood, 1990.

In this article I maintain that better communication needs to be facilitated between pacifists and warists, if advancements are to be made in realizing a peace-culture. I argue that the position of the pragmatic pacifist (which occupies the lowest extreme of Duane Cady's pacifist continuum), rather than more radical pacifist positions, has the best chance of gaining the ear of the warist and enhancing communication between the pacifist and warist traditions. Both pragmatic pacifists and warists employ the key term 'peace' in the same way—defined as the absence of armed conflict. More radical pacifists employ 'peace' in an "idealistic" sense which tends to impede efforts for communication. Thus, it is the pragmatic pacifist position that can establish a "bridge" of communication between the pacifist and warist traditions.

SMITHURST, Michael. The Elusiveness of Human Nature. Inquiry, 33(4), 433-445, D 90.

Sociobiology uses neo-Darwinism to make wide-ranging explanatory conjectures about man and society. The 'naturalism' of such an enterprise recommends it, but a thoroughgoing and Darwinian naturalism is compatible with a rejection of sociobiological conjectures. Retention of juvenile characteristics explains various human physical features and can be used to account for the playful and curiosity-driven nature of human intelligence. The malleable and hedonistic character of human sexuality is similarly explained. It has been argued (Wallace and latterly T Nagel) that human intellectual capacity transcends what is necessary for survival and so cannot be explained by natural selection. This wrongly supposes that all characteristics explained by Darwinism are explained as specifically selected for. Fears about biologically imposed limits to human understanding misrepresent intelligence as an aggregate of specifically adjusted capacities. Conceiving human intelligence as a product of neotenization frees us from the demand to explain everything as adaptive, and if the thesis is analogical, it is but one analogical conjecture against the plethora sociobiology requires.

SMOJE, Dujka. "Ingarden et la musique: Actualité de la pensée musicale de Roman Ingarden" in *XIth International Congress in Aesthetics, Nottingham 1988*, WOODFIELD, Richard (ed), 198-202. Nottingham, Nottingham Polytech, 1990.

SMOKLER, Howard. Assessing Inductive Logics Empirically. Proc Phil Sci Ass, 1, 525-535, 1990.

SMULLYAN, Raymond M. Some New Double Induction and Superinduction Principles. Stud Log, 49(1), 23-30, Mr 90.

Some new double analogues of induction and transfinite recursion are given which yields a relatively simple proof of a result of Robert Cowen which in turn is a strengthening of an earlier result of Smullyan which in turn gives a unified approach to Zorn's Lemma, the transfinite recursion theorem and certain results about ordinal numbers

SMYTHIES, John R (ed) and BELOFF, John (ed). *The Case for Dualism*. Charlottesville, Univ Pr of Virginia, 1989.

SMYTHIES, John R. "The Mind-Body Problem" in *The Case for Dualism*, SMYTHIES, John R (ed), 81-111. Charlottesville, Univ Pr of Virginia, 1989.

SNAPPER, John. Critical Synthesis on the Uses and Justifications for the Regulations of Intellectual Property. Soc Epistem, 5(1), 78-87, Ja-Mr 91.

SNARE, Francis. *Morals, Motivation and Convention: Hume's Influential Doctrines*. New York, Cambridge Univ Pr, 1991.

SNEED, Joseph D. "Machine Models for the Growth of Knowledge: Theory Nets in Prolog" in *Imre Lakatos and Theories of Scientific Change*, GAVROGLU, Kostas (ed), 245-268. Norwell, Kluwer, 1989.

This paper sketches one way that scientific knowledge or information might be stored in a digital computer and used to model the problem-solving activity of empirical scientists. Among the types of problem-solving activity that might be modeled in this way is that which is a part of some systematically informed "research program" associated with a scientific community. The theoretical basis for this approach to representing scientific knowledge is provided by the structuralist, or model-theoretic, approach to axiomatizing scientific theories. The implementation of these ideas is envisioned to be in the programming language PROLOG.

SNOW, Nancy E. Compassion. Amer Phil Quart, 28(3), 195-205, Jl 91.

SNOWDEN, John R. Innocents and Innocence: Moral Puzzles of Professional Status and Culpable Conduct. Bus Prof Ethics J, 9(1-2), 129-139, Spr-Sum 90.

SNOWDON, P F. Personal Identity and Brain Transplants. Philosophy, 29, 109-126, 91 Supp.

Can animalism—the thesis that we are identical with animals and have their persistence conditions—reply to an objection claiming that brain transplants reveal the identity does not hold? The objection is analysed into four premises and the interim conclusion is that each is plausible. A line of reply, by K Wilkes and M Johnston, opposing the method of the objection is criticized as unsupported. The conclusion is that the best reply to the objection is to deny an intuition on which one premise relies. Whether this reply is ultimately sustainable is one very important current issue about personal identity.

SNYMAN, J J. "The Avant Garde, Institutional and Critical Theories of Art" in *XIth International Congress in Aesthetics, Nottingham 1988*, WOODFIELD, Richard (ed), 203-206. Nottingham, Nottingham Polytech, 1990.

It is argued that Dickie's institutional theory of art is a welcome reaction to the dead end into which Weitz's essay 'The Role of Theory in Aesthetics' led aesthetics, but that it is inadequate as a sociological theory of art. Its novel concept of 'status conferral' as an explanatory metaphor for the way in which at least avant garde works are produced, lacks clarity. Dickie's metaphor is amended with a theory of artistic material taken from Adorno.

SNYMAN, Johan J. The Avant Garde, Institutional and Critical Theories of Art. S Afr J Phil, 9(4), 186-190, N 90.

In this article it is argued that Dickie's institutional theory of art is a welcome reaction to the dead end into which Weitz's seminal essay 'The Role of Theory in Aesthetics' led aesthetics, but that it is inadequate as a sociological theory of art. Its very novel concept of 'status conferral' as an explanatory metaphor for the way in which at least avant garde works are produced, lacks clarity. I propose to amend Dickie's metaphor with a theory of artistic material taken from Adorno, and to reinterpret it, in order to give new explanatory force to Danto's notion of 'the artworld', to which Dickie originally appealed.

SOAMES, Scott. "Direct Reference and Propositional Attitudes" in *Themes From Kaplan*, ALMOG, Joseph (ed), 393-419. New York, Oxford Univ Pr, 1989.

It is argued that the semantic content of a sentence (the proposition it expresses) cannot be identified with the set of circumstances in which it is true, no matter how fine-grained circumstances are taken to be (possible worlds, situations, etc.). This conclusion is shown to follow from a relational analysis of propositional attitude ascriptions, plus the assumption that at least some singular terms—names, indexicals, or variables relative to assignments—are directly referential. A positive theory of structured propositions as semantic contents of sentences is developed and applied to examples that ascribe beliefs and assertions.

SOAMES, Scott. Pronouns and Propositional Attitudes. Proc Aris Soc, 90, 191-212, 1989-90.

It is argued that pronouns with singular term antecedents, such as 'he' in '*John* loves *his* mother', are neither directly referential terms that inherit reference from their antecedents, nor Fregean singular terms that inherit senses from them. Rather, they are variables bound by a predicate abstraction operator that forms an n-1 place predicate from an n-place sentence structure. Crucial evidence comes from sentences ascribing propositional attitudes. The analysis is extended to complex cases in which an occurrence of a pronoun may function both as a variable bound by a quantifier and as an abstraction-triggering antecedent of another pronoun.

SOAMES, Scott. "Semantics and Semantic Competence" in *Philosophical Perspectives, 3: Philosophy of Mind and Action Theory, 1989*, TOMBERLIN, James E (ed), 575-596. Atascadero, Ridgeview, 1989.

SOARE, Robert I and JOCKUSCH JR, Carl G. Degrees of Orderings Not Isomorphic to Recursive Linear Orderings. Annals Pure Applied Log, 52(1-2), 39-64, Ap 91.

It is shown that for every nonzero r.e. degree *c* there is a linear ordering of degree *c* which is not isomorphic to any recursive linear ordering. It follows that there is a linear ordering of low degree which is not isomorphic to any recursive linear ordering. It is shown further that there is a linear ordering *L* such that *L* is not isomorphic to any recursive linear ordering, and *L* together with its 'infinitely far apart' relation is of low degree. Finally, an analogue of the recursion theorem for recursive linear orderings is refuted.

SOBEL, Jordan Howard. Conditional Probabilities, Conditionalization, and Dutch Books. Proc Phil Sci Ass, 1, 503-515, 1990.

The formal character of conditional probabilities, and their significance for doxastic states of agents are taken up. I connect them with perceived evidential bearings. Principles suggested by this connection are considered that would, under certain conditions, equate rationally revised probabilities on new information with probabilities reached by conditionalizing on this information. And lastly, for further corroboration of the evidential view of conditional probabilities announced, the possibility of 'books' against known non-conditionalizers is explored, and the question is taken up, What, if anything, would be wrong with a person against whom a book of a certain kind could be made?

SOBEL, Jordan Howard. Constrained Maximization. Can J Phil, 21(1), 25-51, Mr 91.

After attending to difficulties of interpretation posed by David Gauthier's most careful account of constrained maximization, I show that on this account there are: prisoners's dilemmas in which constrained maximizers would interact sub-optimally just as straight-maximizers; coordination problems in which they might not be able to act at all; and prisoners's dilemmas that are quite impossible for them. There are important problem-situations for which contrained maximization, as it stands, does not afford moral solutions to replace Hobbesian political ones as Gauthier would have it do. Possible revisions are sketched that, at theoretical costs, would reduce these shortcomings.

SOBEL, Jordan Howard. Hume's Theorem on Testimony Sufficient to Establish a Miracle. Phil Quart, 41(163), 229-237, Ap 91.

"[I]t is a general maxim...' That no testimony is sufficient to establish a miracle, unless the testimony be of such a kind that its falsehood would be more miraculous, than the fact which it endeavors to establish; and even in that case there is a mutual destruction of arguments, and the superior only gives us an assurance suitable to that degree of force, which remains, after deducting the inferior.'" A Bayesian interpretation of the first half is proved as a theorem. A stronger conditional principle, and a biconditional theorem based on it, are substantiated. And a truth that the second part can express is explained.

SOBEL, Jordan Howard. Non-Dominance, Third Person and Non-Action Newcomb Problems, and Metatickles. Synthese, 86(2), 143-172, F 91.

It is plausible that Newcomb problems in which causal maximizers and evidential maximizers would do different things would not be possible for ideal maximizers who are attentive to metatickles. An objection to Eells's first argument for this makes welcome a second. Against it I argue that even ideal evidential and causal maximizers would do different things in some non-dominance Newcomb problems; and that they would hope for different things in some third-person and non-action problems, which is relevant if a good theory of rational choices of acts should fit smoothly into a good theory of rational desires for facts.

SOBEL, Jordan Howard. Some Versions of Newcomb's Problem Are Prisoners' Dilemmas. Synthese, 86(2), 197-208, F 91.

I have maintained that some but not all prisoners' dilemmas are side-by-side Newcomb problems. The present paper argues that, similarly, some but not all versions of Newcomb's Problem are prisoners' dilemmas in which Taking Two and Predicting Two make an equilibrium that is dispreferred by both the box-chooser and predictor to the outcome in which only one box is taken and this is predicted. I comment on what kinds of prisoner's dilemmas Newcomb's Problem can be, and on opportunities that results reached may open for kinds of 'cooperative reasoning' in versions of Newcomb's Problem.

SOBER, Elliott and SEGAL, Gabriel. The Causal Efficacy of Content. Phil Stud, 63(1), 1-30, Jl 91.

SOBER, Elliott. "Contrastive Empiricism" in *Scientific Theories*, SAVAGE, C Wade (ed), 392-410. Minneapolis, Univ of Minn Pr, 1990.

SOBER, Elliott. *Core Questions in Philosophy: A Text With Readings*. New York, Macmillan, 1991.

This book combines a text presentation of some central problems with an anthology of readings. The main areas are philosophy of religion (does God exist?), epistemology (knowledge and induction), philosophy of mind (mind/body problem, freedom, egoism), and ethics (meta and normative).

SOBER, Elliott. "Evolutionary Altruism and Psychological Egoism" in *Logic, Methodology and Philosophy of Science, VIII*, FENSTAD, J E (ed), 495-514. New York, Elsevier Science, 1989.

The evolutionary concepts of altruism and selfishness are quite different from the psychological concepts that go by the same names. This paper clarifies each pair. The first concerns fitness relationships among organisms in the same group and among groups themselves. The latter concerns the interaction of self-directed and other-directed motives in the production of behavior.

SOBER, Elliott. Let's Razor Ockham's Razor. Philosophy, 27, 73-93, 90 Supp.

Is parsimony an irreducible and in itself in scientific theorizing? Or, are parsimonious theories valued only because they happen in some research contexts, and for contingent and empirical reasons, to be more likely? The latter position is defended via an analysis of parsimony arguments in two recent controversies in evolutionary theory.

SOBRINHO, J Zimbarg. Definability in Self-Referential Systems. Notre Dame J Form Log, 29(4), 574-578, Fall 88.

Intended models of self-referential systems are the ones satisfying the *Definability condition*: every element of the universe is definable by a one-free-variable (typed) first-order formula. It is well known that an adequate formulation of that condition required second-order logic. Hiller formulated the following question: given a self-referential theory T, find F(T) such that: (a) every intended model of T is a model of F(T); (b) every model of F(T) is elementarily equivalent to an intended model of T; (c) F(T) is the weakest extention of T for which (a) and (b) hold. The search of F(T) for a given T is referred to as *Hiller's problem*. By restricting ourselves to models of F(T), it is possible to eliminate second-order logic from the foundations of self-referential systems, and have a first-order reduction. In case T contains the axiom of regularity, we show that T admits a solution to Hiller's problem, and it is F(T) = T + (V +OD).

SOBSTYL, Edrie and BOETZKES, Elisabeth and TURNER, Susan (Guerin). Women, Madness, and Special Defences in the Law. J Soc Phil, 21(2-3), 127-139, Fall-Wint 90.

In this article some legal/jurisprudential peculiarities of the Canadian Infanticide Statute are targeted. The Statute is unjust, since it cites mental imbalance (which ought to mitigate or excuse) as an element of the offence. This anomaly is attributed to prejudicial perceptions of women embedded in the law. Two such perceptions are traced—women as uniquely good (and thus particularly depraved in infanticide); and women as morally defective (and thus dangerous to society).

Possible options for the reform of the law are considered, and a qualified recommendation made that post-partum depression serves as a special defence for homocide, pending a thorough legal reform addressing the perception of women in the law.

SOCOSKI, Patrick M. A Comparison of John Dewey and Lawrence Kohlberg's Approach to Moral Education. Phil Stud Educ, /, 89-104, 1986.

The document evaluates the normative-ethical adequacy and the practical suitability of cognitive moral theory. It contains a lengthy review of criticism of the theory of moral development. Recommendations are made on the viability of Kohlberg's theory as a basis for moral education in public education.

SOFFER, Gail. Phenomenology and Scientific Realism: Husserl's Critique of Galileo. Rev Metaph, 44(1), 67-94, S 90.

This paper proposes a phenomenological resolution of the realism/instrumentalism debate. In the first part, I reconstruct Husserl's critique of the scientific realism characteristic of seventeenth-century thinkers such as Galileo, Descartes, and Locke. In the second part, I derive the positive Husserlian conception of the ontological status of science. Here I argue that despite certain instrumentalist-sounding passages of the *Crisis*, a consistent development of Husserl's thought does not lead to instrumentalism, but to an epistemically sophisticated version of realism, a version which dissolves the problem of the "*really* real."

SOKOLOWSKI, Robert. "The Fiduciary Relationship and the Nature of Professions" in *Ethics, Trust, and the Professions: Philosophical and Cultural Aspects*, PELLEGRINO, Edmund D (ed), 23-43. Washington, Georgetown Univ Pr, 1991.

SOLOMON, George F and LEVIN, David Michael. The Discursive Formation of the Body in the History of Medicine. J Med Phil, 15(5), 515-537, O 90.

The principal argument of the present paper is that the human body is as much a reflective formation of multiple discourses as it is an effect of natural and environmental processes. This paper examines the implications of this argument, and suggests that recognizing the body in this light can be illuminating, not only for our conception of the body, but also for our understanding of medicine. Since medicine is itself a discursive formation, a science with both a history, and a future, it is argued that much can be learned by reflecting on the progression of models, or "paradigm-shifts," in terms of which modern medicine has articulated the human body that figures at the heart of its discourse. Four historical periods of medicine will be considered, each one governed by its own distinctive paradigm. (edited)

SOLOMON, Martin K. Relativized Gödel Speed-Up and the Degree of Succinctness of Representations. Z Math Log, 36(3), 185-192, 1990.

We show that many results about the relative succinctness of different representations of languages, as well as the Gödel speed-up theorem, are exactly characterized in a measure independent manner by precisely the same theorem in terms of the condition "domain (g) - domain (f) is not recursively enumerable in a Turing degree", for appropriate functions g and f.

SOLOMON, Maynard. Beethoven's Ninth Symphony: The Sense of an Ending. Crit Inquiry, 17(2), 289-305, Wint 91.

SOLOMON, Mildred Z (and others). Toward An Expanded Vision of Clinical Ethics Education: From the Individual to the Institution. Kennedy Inst Ethics J, 1(3), 225-245, S 91.

This paper advances a new paradigm in clinical ethics education that not only emphasizes development of individual clinicians' skills, but also focuses on the institutional context within health care professionals work. This approach has been applied to the goal of improving the care provided to critically and terminally ill adults. The model has been adopted by about thirty hospitals and nursing homes; additional institutions will soon join the program, entitled Decisions Near the End of Life. Here, we describe the history and rationale for this approach, its goals, pedagogical assumptions, and design.

SOLOMON, Miriam. Extensionality, Underdetermination and Indeterminacy. Erkenntnis, 33(2), 211-221, S 90.

A development of Quine's views took place between the denial of analyticity (in "Two Dogmas") and the doctrine of indeterminacy (in *Word and Object*). Quine argues for the inscrutability of extensional as well as intensional content. The debate with Carnap in the mid-fifties pushes Quine to argue for full indeterminacy. Quine initially resists arguing for indeterminacy because the doctrine seems to lead to general skepticism, not just to skepticism about meanings. Quine draws on Tarski's work on truth to dispel the skepticism, and only then argues for indeterminacy. This shows why Tarski's work is especially important for Quine.

SOLOMON, Robert C. *The Big Questions: A Short Introduction to Philosophy (Third Edition)*. San Diego, Harcourt Brace Jov, 1990.

SOLOMON, Robert C. "Business Ethics" in *A Companion to Ethics*, SINGER, Peter (ed), 354-365. Cambridge, Blackwell, 1991.

Ethics in business occupies a peculiar position in the field of "applied" ethics. As in medicine and law, it consists of an uneasy application of some very general ethical principles to rather specific and often unique situations and crises. But business ethics is concerned with an area of human enterprise whose practicioners do not for the most part enjoy professional status and whose motives, to put it mildly, are often thought (and said) to be less than noble. Almost three millenia ago, Plato and Aristotle attacked the very idea of business. So too ever since. But philosophy has tilted again toward the 'real world,' and business ethics has found or made its place in philosophy. I briefly describe that place in this essay.

SOLOMON, Robert C. Emotions, Feelings and Contexts: A Reply to Robert Kraut. Dialogue (Canada), 29(2), 277-284, 1990.

Emotions are akin to feelings and defined in part by their contexts, but this does not imply that emotions are nothing but feelings (notably, not "cognitions") or that context as such defines emotion. Such arguments have a long if not always distinguished history, but Robert Kraut has offered the most sophisticated defense of them to date (in the *Journal of Philosophy*). I reject these arguments and counter Kraut's defense of them.

SOLOMON, Robert C. In Defense of Sentimentality. Phil Lit, 14(2), 304-323, O 90.

I defend the often-dismissed concept of "sentimentality" against a number of established and recent objections, including comments by Oscar Wilde and arguments by Tanner, Kundera, Midgley and Jefferson.

SOLOMON, Robert C (ed) and MURPHY, Mark C (ed). *What Is Justice? Classic and Contemporary Readings*. New York, Oxford Univ Pr, 1990.

An anthology of readings from a wide variety of sources on the origins of justice, social contract theory, theories of property and punishment and current theories. Authors include Plato, Aristotle, Locke, Rawls, Nozick, Jefferson, Hume, Smith, Kant, Hegel, Hayek, Camus, Walzer, Wolgast, and many others. Introductions and bibliography.

SOMERVILLE, James. "Are There Aesthetic Qualities?" in *XIth International Congress in Aesthetics, Nottingham 1988*, WOODFIELD, Richard (ed), 207-211. Nottingham, Nottingham Polytech, 1990.

The view that predicates like "graceful," "delicate," or "elegant" name aesthetic qualities is vitiated by an ambiguity. In one sense the qualities of a thing determine it as belonging to one or more kinds; but by the quality of a thing can also be meant what the thing is like. Only descriptions of what a thing is like, unmediated by descriptions of what sort of thing it is, are aesthetic descriptions. These are not universalizable. Any analogy between the dependence of the ascription of aesthetic on that of nonaesthetic terms and the relational character of sensible qualities is misconceived.

SOMERVILLE, John. "War, Omnicide, and Sanity: The Lesson of the Cuban Missile Crisis" in *Issues in War and Peace: Philosophical Inquiries*, KUNKEL, Joseph (ed), 13-20. Wolfeboro, Longwood, 1989.

SOMMARUGA, Giovanni and MONTAGNA, Franco. A Note on Some Extension Results. Stud Log, 49(4), 591-600, D 90.

In this note, a fully modal proof is given of some conservation results proved in a previous paper by arithmetic means. The proof is based on the extendability of Kripke models.

SOMMERS, Christina. Do These Feminists Like Women? J Soc Phil, 21(2-3), 66-74, Fall-Wint 90.

SOMMERS, Christina. The Feminist Revelation. Soc Phil Pol, 8(1), 141-158, Autumn 90.

Two types of feminism are distinguished. "Liberal feminism" is intellectually unpretentious: it is more liberal than feminist; it seeks for women what liberals want for everyone. "Sex/gender feminism," more popular in the academy, sees women in thrall to a patriarchy that must be "overthrown." The sex/gender system is reported to be "everywhere" in a "masculinist" culture. Sex/gender feminists routinely compare themselves to Copernicus, Darwin, etc., in revealing a new world view. The article finds that sex/gender feminism is more akin to a religious movement than to a scientific revolution. The verdict is that sex/gender feminists do far more harm than good.

SOMMERVILLE, Johann P (ed) and FILMER, Sir Robert. *Patriarcha and Other Writings: Sir Robert Filmer*. New York, Cambridge Univ Pr, 1991.

SONI, Jayandra. *Dravya, Guna* and *Paryāya* in Jaina Thought. J Indian Phil, 19(1), 75-88, Mr 91.

SONTAG, Frederick. Liberation Theology and the Interpretation of Political Violence. Thomist, 55(2), 271-292, Ap 91.

Addressing the problem of the tension between traditional Christian views that reject violence on the one hand and liberation theories that accept the necessity of violence on the other hand, the author concludes that Christians are free in the practical world. There is, however, one crucial provision: each person must accept responsibility and justify his or her actions on their own without appealing to Jesus or to religious principles to justify their public/political activity.

SONTAG, Frederick. Omnipotence Need Not Entail Omniscience. Sophia (Australia), 29(3), 35-39, O 90.

If we can separate omnipotence and omniscience, and if we do so primarily to preserve the divine contingent creative power and to make sense of our feeling for contingency in nature, what must God know in order not to seem "stupid," i.e., to know less than we know? Obviously God must know every possibility open to human option, just as divinity had to know every option open to it in order to constitute our natural order out of all that was possible. To know all in nature and in human action that is possible is of course to know certain tendencies toward actualization, certain odds (as Las Vegas would say) for various actualizations to result.

SOO, Francis. "Reflections on Chinese Language and Philosophy" in *Hermeneutics and the Poetic Motion, Translation Perspectives V—1990*, SCHMIDT, Dennis J (ed), 161-172. Binghamton, CRIT, 1990.

SOONTIENS, Frans. Crypto-theologie: hoffentlich ein Ende: Reactie op Callebaut en Wachelder. Kennis Methode, 15(2), 224-227, 1991.

SORABJI, Richard. Perceptual Content in the Stoics. Phronesis, 35(3), 307-314, 1990.

SORBI, Andrea. Embedding Brouwer Algebras in the Medvedev Lattice. Notre Dame J Form Log, 32(2), 266-275, Spr 91.

We prove various results on embedding Brouwer algebras in the Medvedev lattice.

In particular, we characterize the finite Brouwer algebras that are embeddable in the Medvedev lattice.

SORBI, Andrea. Some Remarks on the Algebraic Structure of the Medvedev Lattice. J Sym Log, 55(2), 831-853, Je 90.

With this paper the author begins a series of papers devoted to the study of the Medvedev lattice *M*. It is shown that *M* is not a Heyting algebra. The paper contains also an investigation of the algebraic structure of several sublattices of *M*, and a characterization of the countable lattices that are embeddable in *M*. Some space is devoted also to the study of some properties of the degrees of enumerability, and to the relationships between *M* and two lattices, already known in the literature, which are called here the Dyment lattice and the Mucnick lattice, respectively.

SÖRBOM, Göran. "Imitation and Art" in *XIth International Congress in Aesthetics, Nottingham 1988*, WOODFIELD, Richard (ed), 212-215. Nottingham, Nottingham Polytech, 1990.

SORELL, Tom. Self, Society, and Kantian Impersonality. Monist, 74(1), 30-42, Ja 91.

The objection that community and friendship are treated by Kantian theories with a sort of righteous absurdity or else left out of account altogether; the complaint that these deficiencies are inevitable in theories that neglect individuality and feeling and are overly impersonal—these misrepresent the moral and political theory of Kant himself, which is more defensible in relation to impersonality than neo-Kantian theories such as Rawls's.

SORELL, Tom. "The World from its Own Point of View" in *Reading Rorty*, MALACHOWSKI, Alan (ed), 11-25. Cambridge, Blackwell, 1991.

According to Rorty, the idea of the world's intrinsic nature commits us to believing in a person who made the world, or to thinking of the world itself as a person, with a point of view, and preferences about how it is described. This chapter takes issue with Rorty's claim and with his case for a culture that gets rid of divinities. In morals and politics as much as in metaphysics "dedivinization" is uncompelling.

SORENSEN, L R. Rousseau's Liberalism. Hist Polit Thought, 11(3), 443-466, Autumn 90.

SORENSEN, Roy A. '*P*, Therefore, *P*' Without Circularity. J Phil, 88(5), 245-266, My 91.

The primary thesis is that some arguments of the form 'P, therefore, P' do not beg the question. For example, the following arguments are rationally persuasive and so cannot be circular: A1. Some arguments are composed solely of existential generalizations. A2. Therefore, some arguments are composed solely of existential generalizations. B1. Some deductive arguments do not reason from general to particular. B2. Therefore, some deductive arguments do not reason from general to particular. The discussion features four species of counterexamples to the universally held principle that all 'P, therefore, P' arguments beg the question. The secondary thesis is that these cases support pragmatic accounts of circularity because they are the only ones that can be amended in a natural fashion.

SORENSEN, Roy A. Fictional Incompleteness as Vagueness. Erkenntnis, 34(1), 55-72, Ja 91.

The main goal of this paper is to show how the problem of fictional incompleteness and the problem of vagueness are bridged by a hybrid paradox. I discuss the major approaches to the standard sorites puzzle. A "fiction sorites" is then presented as a prima facie counterexample to the universally held diagnosis that sorites paradoxes arise from vagueness. I dismiss the possibility that the recalcitrant paradox could be ruled out as a pseudo-sorites on the grounds that it does not turn on vagueness. The apparent counterexample issues from hidden vagueness. Despite the difficulties, I argue that the appeal to hidden vagueness is the most promising approach in view of its advantage of reducing two mysteries to one. (edited)

SORENSEN, Roy A. Process Vagueness. Ling Phil, 13(5), 589-618, O 90.

A statement can be vague by virtue of expressing a vague proposition. For example, 'Coffee is food' expresses a vague proposition because coffee is a borderline case of 'food'. However, a statement can also be vague by virtue of indecision as to which proposition it expresses. For example, a speaker may say 'Math is irrelevant' without there being any clear answer to 'Relevant to what?' The suspicion that the utterance is meaningless is overturned by the existence of borderline relata. That is, the speaker's utterance 'Math is irrelevant' is a borderline case of 'expresses the proposition that math is irrelevant to ordinary life' and a borderline case of 'expresses the proposition that math is irrelevant to most jobs' and so on. I argue that this second type of vagueness is relevant to a wide range of issues in linguistics and philosophy: generics, stereotypes, laws, metaphor, and the standards of successful reduction.

SORGI, Giuseppe. I "systemata subordinata" e il problema della partecipazione in Hobbes. Riv Int Filosof Diritto, 66(4), 659-678, O-D 89.

The aim of this study is to analyse the areas of participation Hobbes concedes to subjects through intermediate bodies. An attentive observer of the historical and political situation in which he lived, Hobbes inserts, between the sovereign power and the subjects, a great variety of dependent systems that allow participation of an administrative, economic and occasionally also political type. These institutions, however, do not affect relations between the power and the subjects, who remain bound to the sovereign's will.

SORRELL, Martin and HALPIN, David M G. Art and Neurology: A Discussion. Brit J Aes, 31(3), 241-250, Jl 91.

SORRI, Mari and GILL, Jerry H. *A Post-Modern Epistemology*. Lewiston, Mellen Pr, 1989.

The theme of this book concerns the essentially disembodied character of human knowledge in Western philosophy. This mentalistic bias has not only characterized, but in addition distorted Western epistemological endeavor. The authors have the positive purpose of using human embodiment as crucial to knowledge in relation to experience, meaning, and knowing. (staff)

SOSA, Ernest. "'Circular' Coherence and 'Absurd' Foundations" in *Truth and Interpretation: Perspectives on the Philosophy of Donald Davidson*, LE PORE, Ernest (ed), 387-397. Cambridge, Blackwell, 1986.

Having first distinguished two branches of epistemology, the practical and the theoretical, the paper then connects the two by considering the organon explication of justification: that a belief becomes justified only through the justifying of it by use of an organon. Next it takes note of the *intellectualist* view of justification shared by Rorty and Davidson, according to which a belief acquires justification only by the support of argument or reasoning, a view that for some may derive from the organon conception of justification. Davidson's attack on foundationalism is then examined, an attack found to be based on intellectualism. Davidson defends coherentism by a double-threaded argument that intertwines assumptions about (a) the nature of belief and its content, and (b) the charity required for interpretative knowledge of other minds. What is the relevance of that double-threaded argument to holding up coherence as against its rivals, especially reliability? In conclusion that seemed surprisingly occult.

SOSA, Ernest and MILLÁN, Gustavo Ortiz (trans). Cuestiones de sobrevivencia. Critica, 22(64), 55-93, Ap 90.

SOSA, Ernest. *Knowledge in Perspective: Selected Essays in Epistemology*. New York, Cambridge Univ Pr, 1991.

What is the nature and scope of human knowledge? Chapters covering all the major topics of contemporary epistemology: the nature of propositional knowledge, externalism versus internalism, foundationalism versus coherentism, and the problem of the criterion. The collection falls into four parts: one on knowledge, one on justification, and two that present and develop a view called virtue perspectivism. All previously published essays have been revised, and new material has been added, including three new chapters.

SOSA, Ernest. "Perception and Reality" in *Information, Semantics and Epistemology*, VILLANUEVA, Enrique (ed), 209-223. Cambridge, Blackwell, 1990.

Has science unveiled reality, displaying its true noncolors? Is commonsense realism refuted, superseded by a better theory? Or are common sense and science different and incommensurable "standpoints," each with its own proper standing and validity? Alternatively, can we blend common sense and science without downgrading either, while avoiding relativism? How, in short, is our perceptual experience related to the world beyond? The discussion of qualia over the last few years is of course the most recent battleground for the physicalism/mentalism war. It is interesting how far we can go in sketching accounts of experience, or belief, and of secondary qualities while avoiding that battleground.

SOSCHINKA, Hans-Ulrich. The Process of Evolution in a Holistic World (in German). Deut Z Phil, 38(10), 975-983, 1990.

Our holistic, complex and dynamic world is seen by scientists and humanists more and more from a revolutionary view. From these points of view it is not possible to separate nature and society from each other, because they are based on equal or analogous laws. Therefore the search for the causes and driving forces of the evolution of our world must be concentrated on the network of natural, technical, human-individual and social processes. The investigation of the cultural evolution resulting from it demands the unprejudiced cooperation of scientists, technicians, sociologists and humanists. Synergetic and philosophy represent a suitable scope for a gradual research project, in the center of which the innovation events in all fields of reality are placed. On this basis we chose a starting point covering all sciences for the holistic research of the world.

SOTO BRUNA, Maria Jesus. Origen de la inversión kantiana del binomio materia-forma. Anu Filosof, 23(1), 153-161, 1990.

SOTO, José Cercós. La determinación de la esencia en X: Zubiri y Tomás de Aquino. Sapientia, 45(176), 95-104, Ap-Je 90.

SOULEZ, Philippe. Les mathématiques, la biologie et le statut scientifique de la philosophie pour Bergson. Philosophique (France), 1(91), 97-108, 1991.

The author tries to reconcile the opposite interpretations of H Gouhier and J Milet. The opposition of Descartes and C L Bernard concerns the methods not the "modalite" (way of thinking). Bergson never gave up the reference to the infinitesimal calculus and dreamed of a "mechanics of transformation."

SOULEZ, Philippe. Le partage des philosophes. Rev Metaph Morale, 95(4), 537-545, O-D 90.

This article is the first synthesis of the program "The Philosophers Facing the Wars of the Twentieth Century" (University de Paris VIII). It tries to understand why the philosopher refuses to "know" of war. The idea is that there is a double mimesis: mimesis of war in philosophy, mimesis of philosophy in war.

SPADE, Paul Vincent. Ockham, Adams and Connotation: A Critical Notice of Marilyn Adams, *William Ockham*. Phil Rev, 99(4), 593-612, O 90.

This is a critical notice of Marilyn McCord Adams's book *William Ockham* (2 vols., University of Notre Dame, 1987). The article reviews the contents of her book, and then discusses Ockham's theory of "connotation," which is important to his program of reducing the number of ontological categories. The author points out certain difficulties with this program, and is less optimistic than Adams is over its prospects for final success. The author also discusses the previously unnoticed fact that Ockham's theory of connotation is really a combination of two incompatible theories.

SPAEMANN, Robert. Universalismo o eurocentrismo. Anu Filosof, 23(1), 113-123, 1990.

The author criticized cultural relativism as a self-contradictive philosophical position. It is the same universalistic, i.e., metaphysical way of thinking which underlies not only the principles of humanity and the concept of law but also the formulation of scepticism against universalism. The only way to control the powers which made European technology the determining force of world civilization is shown by the principle of human rights which was created in that European civilization.

SPAGNOLA, Antonio G. Identity and Status of the Human Embryo. Ethics Med, 6(3), 42, Autumn 90.

SPANTIDOU, Constantina. Un cosmos interprété. Diotima, 18, 51-54, 1990.

SPARKES, A W. *Talking Philosophy: A Wordbook*. New York, Routledge, 1991.

This book is a guide to the terminology of philosophy and the language of argument written with the needs of students primarily in mind. It is neither impartial nor impersonal, but endeavours to be fair and contains wide-ranging suggestions for reading.

SPARROW, Edward G. Erasing and Redrawing the Number Line: An Exercise in Rationality. Rev Metaph, 44(2), 273-305, D 90.

This article exposes the sophistry inherent in the construction of the "number line," as this continuum is named by mathematicians, and shows how another continuum, one which preserves the properties of the old "number line" but which is based on rational foundations, namely the relations to one another of the ratios that continuous magnitudes have to one another, can be generated to replace it.

SPASSOVA, Pravda. Understanding the Message of the Work of Art. Diotima, 18, 27-29, 1990.

SPECTOR, Arnold. "T E Wilkerson on Originality in Art and Morals" in *XIth International Congress in Aesthetics, Nottingham 1988*, WOODFIELD, Richard (ed), 216-218. Nottingham, Nottingham Polytech, 1990.

SPECTOR, Raz. The Newcomb Paradox as a Poker Game (in Hebrew). Iyyun, 40(2), 187-196, Ap 91.

SPELLMAN, Lynne. Referential Opacity in Aristotle. Hist Phil Quart, 7(1), 17-31, Ja 90.

I argue for a general solution to referential opacity in Aristotle, claiming that failure of substitutivity occurs because reference has been made not to a sensible object but to a specimen of a kind, numerically the same as but not identical with that object, where a specimen of a kind has only the properties given in the definition of the kind. Thus the builder (a specimen of the kind *builder*) is the cause of the house, not Callias, even if Callias is numerically the same as the builder. By this distinction the inconsistency of *Metaphysics* Zeta (form is universal, substance is not, yet substance is form) can be overcome.

SPELMAN, Elizabeth V. "The Virtue of Feeling and the Feeling of Virtue" in *Feminist Ethics*, CARD, Claudia (ed), 213-232. Lawrence, Univ Pr of Kansas, 1991.

Much of what has been included under the rubric of "feminist ethics" has obscured the long history of some women's inhumanity to other women. I offer a few reasons for this virtual silence and then suggest ways we might explore the moral dimensions of women's treatment and mistreatment of one another.

SPENCE, Donald P. Saying Good-bye to Historical Truth. Phil Soc Sci, 21(2), 245-252, Je 91.

SPENCER, Jon Michael. The Sacred, Secular, and Profane in Augustine's World of Shadows. Bridges, 3(1-2), 41-55, Spr-Sum 91.

In his *City of God*, Augustine posits that the Cosmos (the combined eternal and temporal universe) is comprised of two kinds of moral societies whose citizenship is determined by where human loyalty and love ultimately rest. The City of God is constituted of those who live according to the spirit, and the City of Man of those who live according to the flesh. A careful examination of his thought in the *City of God* shows that Augustine actually perceived human society as being divided into three moral spheres, which we can term the sacred, secular, and profane. Doubtless he neglects to make explicit this triadic delimitation of the world, perhaps due to a dualistic worldview maintained from his Manichaean background. But it will be shown that this delimitation of the world is clearly (albeit subtly) inferred in *City of God*.

SPERRY, R W. Search for Beliefs to Live by Consistent with Science. Zygon, 26(2), 237-258, Je 91.

Instead of separating religion and science into "mutually incompatible realms," the new macromental paradigm of behavioral science permits integration of the two within a single consistent worldview. A new form of causal determinism combines conventional "bottom-up" with emergent "top-down" causation. Traditional materialist tenets are overturned, along with the science-values dichotomy, clearing the way for a science-based value/belief system. Intrinsic ethicomoral directives emerge in which a revised sense of the sacred would help protect the evolving quality of the biosphere, and the rights and welfare of future generations. Subsequent versions of today's changing worldview raise questions of which interpretation to believe. An analysis of "New Age" thinking is called for, and a brief attempt at such analysis is included.

SPICKER, Paul. Mental Handicap and Citizenship. J Applied Phil, 7(2), 139-151, O 90.

Mentally handicapped people have been taken in philosophical work as an obvious exception to the canons which are applied to other, 'rational' individuals. This paper argues that mentally handicapped people should be accorded the same rights as others. If there are human rights, then mentally handicapped people are entitled to them as humans; and if there are rights which apply in general to citizens, the same rights apply equally to mentally handicapped people. The argument for the inclusion of mentally handicapped people as citizens is first, that there is a presumption of inclusion: if citizenship is accorded to all other individuals, there is no reason why citizenship should not be accorded to mentally handicapped people on the same basis as others. Second, mentally handicapped people cannot successfully be excluded without effectively challenging the presumption of inclusion applied to other groups. Third, and perhaps most important, there are positive reasons why mentally handicapped people, as a particularly vulnerable group, need to have rights to protect them against particular abuses.

SPIRTES, Peter and SCHEINES, Richard and GLYMOUR, Clark. "The Tetrad Project" in *Acting and Reflecting: The Interdisciplinary Turn in Philosophy*, SIEG, Wilfried (ed), 183-207. Norwell, Kluwer, 1990.

SPOERL, Joseph. 'Queerness' and the Objectivity of Value: A Response to J L Mackie. Proc Cath Phil Ass, 63, 108-116, 1990.

SPOHN, Wolfgang. Direct and Indirect Causes. Topoi, 9(2), 125-145, S 90.

The paper gives an account of probabilistic causation; it may be routinely extended to deterministic causation. It proceeds from a plausible explication of direct causation. It investigates possibly, actually, and ideally relevant circumstances of direct causal relationships. It presents three crucial demands on indirect causation: structural, Markovian, and positive relevance demands. It explains why these demands are in general mutually incompatible. It proposes the transitive closure of direct causation as the weakest notion of causation and shows that it satisfies the other demands under certain conditions, an important part of which is that the actual circumstances are ideal.

SPRIGGE, T L S. The Greatest Happiness Principle. Utilitas, 3(1), 37-51, My 91.

Preference is often favoured over hedonistic utilitarianism because preferences are supposed to be empirically ascertainable as subjective experiences of pleasure and pain are not. However, a notion of preference not relating to subjective experience is irrelevant ethically, so that a reasonable preference utilitarianism still requires acts of imaginative projection into the lives of different sorts of persons such as are not empirically verifiable in some absolute sense. Hedonic measurement may be difficult but utilitarianism should be conceived rather as an indication of what matters than an attempt to make that more easily ascertainable than it is.

SPRIGGE, T L S. The Satanic Novel: A Philosophical Dialogue on Blasphemy and Censorship. Inquiry, 33(4), 377-400, D 90.

This dialogue is concerned with the problems raised by the Rushdie affair for Western intellectuals, whose thought on social issues derives either from the Christian or the Western liberal tradition. This has brought to a head the many difficulties which beset a Western European country as it develops into a multi-cultural one. Since the concern of the dialogue is with a crisis in he thinking of Western intellectuals about free speech, censorship, tolerance, etc., the four participants are university teachers of philosophy in a British university. They are Ambrose Taylor, a self-styled defender of 'British' and 'Christian' values; Archie Runciman, a progressive Christian or religious eclectic; Freddie Stuart Hill, a committed Mill type liberal; and Jenny Spring, whose liberalism is tempered by the belief that the state should take a positive role in promoting certain values. The author should not be identified with any of the speakers.

SPRING, Joel. The Politics of Knowledge. Phil Stud Educ, /, 188-203, 1987-88.

SPRINGBORG, Patricia. "His Majesty Is a Baby?" A Critical Response to Peter Hammond Schwartz. Polit Theory, 18(4), 673-685, N 90.

The argument is made that Peter H Schwartz in '"His Majesty the Baby": Narcissism and Royal Authority' (*Political Theory*, 17, 1989) mistakenly identifies traditional monarchy with infantile narcissism and modern democracy with mature individual and national egos. But extrapolation from psychoanalysis of the individual to psychogenesis of a nation is suspect and so is his interpretation of the feminization of monarchy. Evidence from ancient monarchies, especially Egypt, suggests monarchical 'gigantism' is not a function of narcissism but of regime insecurity and the uneasy role of the sacral king as intermediary between the realms of gods and people.

SPRUIT, Leen and TAMBURRINI, Guglielmo. Reasoning and Computation in Leibniz. Hist Phil Log, 12(1), 1-14, 1990.

Leibniz's overall view of the relationship between reasoning and computation is discussed on the basis of two broad claims that one finds in his writings, concerning respectively the nature of human reasoning and the possibility of replacing human thinking by a mechanical procedure. A joint examination of these claims enables one to appreciate the wide scope of Leibniz's interests for mechanical procedures, concerning a variety of philosophical themes further developed both in later logical investigations and in methodological contributions to cognitive psychology.

SQUADRITO, Kathleen. Thoughtful Brutes: The Ascription of Mental Predicates to Animals in Locke's "Essay". Dialogos, 26(58), 63-73, Jl 91.

SQUADRITO, Kathy. Commentary: Interests and Equal Moral Status. Between Species, 7(2), 78-79, Spr 91.

SQUELLA, Agustí. Legal Positivism and Democracy in the Twentieth Century. Ratio Juris, 3(3), 407-414, D 90.

In this work I try to establish what is understood by "legal positivism," then, what is believed to be "democracy," and lastly, how it can be shown that the admission of some theses of legal positivism translates into a few good reasons for defining "democracy" in a particular way, as well as for preferring democracy as a form of government.

SQUIRES, Euan J. A Comment on Maxwell's Resolution of the Wave/Particle Dilemma. Brit J Phil Sci, 40(3), 413-417, S 89.

The purpose of this article is to note that the recent proposal of Maxwell for resolving the measurement problem of quantum theory requires a more precise formulation before it can be considered as a serious model of reality.

SRINIVAS, K. Analysis as a Method in Philosophy with Special Reference to A J Ayer. Indian Phil Quart, 18(1), 111-124, Ja 91.

The analysts are far more unanimous in their claim that the subject matter of philosophy is language and its legitimate method is analysis. Thus, the function of philosophy is logical analysis of our everyday language and science. In support of this view Ayer held that a philosopher does not indulge in experimentation, neither does he patiently observe the behavior of natural phenomena, yet philosophers' statements purport to provide 'knowledge' which is different from that of scientists. The chief objective of this paper would be to show the bankruptcy of this method of analysis in obtaining 'knowledge' in any form.

SROVNAL, Jindrich. The Philosophical Invariables of Masaryk's Thinking (in Czechoslovakian). Filozof Cas, 38(4), 423-434, 1990.

The principal question of Masaryk's philosophy of life is the relation of science and faith. At the same time Masaryk is a determined opposer to any subjection of science to faith or of critical reason supported by experience to myth and revelation. In Masaryk's opinion the integration of the poles of science and faith form the basis for living morality brought into action and thus the basis for real progress, too. This is of basic importance especially in politics. The point is that science must be open to faith and not fall into a state of subjection to theology and myth. (edited)

SRZEDNICKI, J. "On Subjective Appreciation of Objective Moral Points" in *Logic and Ethics*, GEACH, Peter (ed), 255-274. Norwell, Kluwer, 1991.

STACK, George J. Emerson and Nietzsche's 'Beyond-Man'. Dialogos, 25(56), 87-101, Jl 90.

A concise account of the influence that R W Emerson's ideal of "transcendent" and "synthetic" men had on Nietzsche's image of the "beyond-man." Using characterizations of those Emerson first called "sovereign individuals" presented in his *Essays* and *The Conduct of Life*, an attempt is made to show (in some detail) how closely Nietzsche followed Emerson's model of what man can yet become. Conceptual and textual comparisons indicate that the American poet and essayist whom Nietzsche read and re-read over a 26-year period profoundly shaped his idea of a person who would affirm life while facing (with what Emerson called "sacred courage") the "negative facts" about life and existence.

STAHL, Gary. "Making the Moral World" in *The Philosophy of John William Miller*, FELL, Joseph P (ed), 111-122. Lewisburg, Bucknell Univ Pr, 1990.

STAHL, Gary. "Nuclear Space and Time" in *In the Interest of Peace: A Spectrum of Philosophical Views*, KLEIN, Kenneth H (ed), 175-184. Wolfeboro, Longwood, 1990.

STAHL, Gérold. Phrases nominales énonciatives et phrases verbales. Rev Phil Fr, 181(3), 329-334, Jl-S 91.

STAHL, Gérold. Représentation structurelle de la relation partie-tout. Rev Phil Fr, 180(3), 547-554, Jl-S 90.

STALNAKER, Robert. "Narrow Content" in *Propositional Attitudes: The Role of Content in Logic, Language, and Mind*, ANDERSON, C Anthony (ed), 131-145. Stanford, CSLI, 1990.

STALNAKER, Robert. "On What's in the Head" in *Philosophical Perspectives, 3: Philosophy of Mind and Action Theory, 1989*, TOMBERLIN, James E (ed), 287-316. Atascadero, Ridgeview, 1989.

STAMBAUGH, Joan. "The Future of Continental Philosophy" in *Writing the Politics of Difference*, SILVERMAN, Hugh J (ed), 275-282. Albany, SUNY Pr, 1991.

STAMPE, Dennis W. "Content, Context and Explanation" in *Information, Semantics and Epistemology*, VILLANUEVA, Enrique (ed), 134-152. Cambridge, Blackwell, 1990.

STAMPE, Dennis W. Representation and the Freedom of the Will. Soc Theor Pract, 16(3), 435-466, Fall 90.

STANGA, Keith G and TURPEN, Richard A. Ethical Judgments on Selected Accounting Issues: An Empirical Study. J Bus Ethics, 10(10), 739-747, O 91.

This study investigates the judgments made by accounting majors when confronted with selected ethical dilemmas that pertain to accounting practice. Drawing upon literature in philosophy and moral psychology, it then examines these judgments for potential gender differences. Five case studies, each involving a specific ethical delimma that a practicing accountant might face, were administered to 151 accounting majors (males = 67; females = 84), in four sections of intermediate accounting II at a large, state university. The results suggest that although the vast majority of participants would *not* engage in unethical behavior, a reasonable opportunity exists to improve the participants' ethical awareness. The results do not, however, support the existence of gender differences in ethical judgments.

STANOJEVIC, Miroslav. Self-Management in the Context of the Disintegration of "Reali-Existing" Socialism. Praxis Int, 10(1-2), 90-103, Ap-Jl 90.

STAPP, Henry P. Comments on 'Nonlocal Influences and Possible Worlds'. Brit J Phil Sci, 41(1), 59-72, Mr 90.

Clifton, Butterfield, and Redhead [1989] have constructed two separate arguments that bear some resemblances to a proof of mine pertaining to the nonlocal character of quantum theory. Their arguments have flaws, which they point out. I explicate my proof by explaining in detail both how it differs logically from the two arguments they have constructed, and how it avoids the pitfalls of both.

STAPP, Henry P. "Transcending Newton's Legacy" in *Some Truer Method*, DURHAM, Frank (ed), 227-245. New York, Columbia Univ Pr, 1990.

The development of the conception of science starting from the ideas of Newton, and passing to those of Einstein, Bohr, and Heisenberg is discussed, with emphasis on the key issues of absolute versus relative, epistemological versus ontological, and on how the facts of nature become fixed. Heisenberg's quantum ontology is discussed in some detail, with emphasis on its nonlocal character, the distributed character of the creative input, the occurrence and fundamental importance of two different kinds of time, and the implications of this ontology for man's conception of himself.

STAR, Susan Leigh and HORNSTEIN, Gail A. Universality Biases: *How Theories About Human Nature Succeed*. Phil Soc Sci, 20(4), 421-436, D 90.

STARK, Werner. Zum Verbleib der Königsberger Kant-Handschriften: Funde und Desiderate. Deut Z Phil, 39(3), 285-293, 1991.

Paper of the Fifth International Kant-Lectures in October 1990 (Kaliningrad/Koenigsberg, USSR). Based on archive research detailed information is given about questions concerning the delivery of Kants "Handschriftlicher Nachlass," especially in the years of 1944 and 1945. In addition a short survey is given about the history of section III in the academy-edition of "Kant's gesammelte Schriften" (Berlin 1911-1955).

STATMAN, Daniel. The Debate Over the So-Called Reality of Moral Dilemmas. Phil Papers, 19(3), 191-211, N 90.

Two main lines of argument have been offered to establish the reality of moral dilemmas: the argument from the incommensurability of values and the argument from sentiment. I seek to show that these arguments really presuppose two different concepts of moral dilemmas: (1) that dilemmas are situations with no right answer, and (2) that dilemmas are not necessarily irresolvable but are situations where ultimately the agent must do wrong. I adopt concept (2) and discuss it critically. In the last section I argue that the alleged reality should be understood not as an independent feature but as referring to the existence of (serious) moral loss, and of justified regret and guilt-feelings.

STEAD, Christopher. "Augustine's Philosophy of Being" in *The Philosophy in Christianity*, VESEY, Godfrey (ed), 71-84. New York, Cambridge Univ Pr, 1989.

STECKER, Robert and ADAMS, Fred and DREBUSHENKO, David and FULLER, Gary. Narrow Content: Fodor's Folly. Mind Lang, 5(3), 213-229, Autumn 90.

For ten years Fodor and other cognitive scientists presumed that we need narrow content (content essentially independent of one's environment) to get around Twin-Earth examples and to do psychology. We show why broad content psychology (using content essentially dependent upon one's environment) is *not really challenged* by Twin-Earth examples, despite appearances. We explain (1) why narrow content is *not content*, and why (2) even if we concoct a notion of content* for narrow content, it still will be *unable to explain* intentional behavior. Thus, we herald the demise of narrow content: one cannot use it and does not need it.

STEEL, C. Thomas Aquinas and the Renewal of Philosophy: Some Reflections on the Thomism of Mercier (in Dutch). Tijdschr Filosof, 53(1), 44-89, Mr 91.

The article is a critical examination of the particular form of Thomism developed by Désiré Mercier, the first president of the Louvain Institute of Philosophy. Mercier bases his philosophical option for Thomism on his judgment that it better than any other philosophy offers a metaphysical synthesis within which the investigations of the modern sciences can be integrated, while at the same time being in concordance with the Christian view on man and world. At the end of the paper it is argued that no intrinsic philosophical argument can be given for a normative preference for Thomas. The demand to philosophize "ad mentem Thomae" only makes sense when the relation of reason to faith is considered. (edited)

STEGER, E Ecker. *The Many Dimensions of the Human Person*. New York, Lang, 1990.

STEIGER, Kornel. Sir Karl Popper on Presocratic Philosophers (in Hungarian). Magyar Filozof Szemle, 5-6, 643-652, 1990.

STEIN, A L. Literature and Language After the Death of God. Hist Euro Ideas, 11, 791-795, 1989.

STEIN, Edith and STEIN, Waltraut (trans). *On the Problem of Empathy (Third Revised Edition)*. Norwell, Kluwer, 1989.

STEIN, Howard. Eudoxos and Dedekind: On the Ancient Greek Theory of Ratios and its Relation to Modern Mathematics. Synthese, 84(2), 163-211, Ag 90.

STEIN, Howard. "On Locke, 'the Great Huygenius, and the Incomparable Mr. Newton'" in *Philosophical Perspectives on Newtonian Science*, BRICKER, Phillip (ed), 17-47. Cambridge, MIT Pr, 1990.

STEIN, Howard. On Relativity Theory and Openness of the Future. Phil Sci, 58(2), 147-167, Je 91.

It has been repeatedly argued, most recently by Nicholas Maxwell, that the special theory of relativity is incompatible with the view that the future is in some degree undetermined; and Maxwell contends that this is a reason to reject that theory. In the present paper, an analysis is offered of the notion of indeterminateness (or "becoming") that is uniquely appropriate to the special theory of relativity, in the light of a set of natural conditions upon such a notion; and reasons are given for regarding this conception as (not just formally consistent with relativity theory, but also) philosophically reasonable. The bearings upon Maxwell's program for quantum theory are briefly considered.

STEIN, Waltraut (trans) and STEIN, Edith. *On the Problem of Empathy (Third Revised Edition)*. Norwell, Kluwer, 1989.

STEIN, William M (trans) and GABEL, Joseph and MC CRATE, James (trans). *Mannheim and Hungarian Marxism*. New Brunswick, Transaction Books, 1991.

This serves as a useful introduction to the force and character of Marxism in Central Europe. Mannheim was situated in the intellectual pitch of prewar Budapest, with its plethora of revisionist Marxists, anarchists, and intellectuals from a variety of areas who brought radical ideas into the mainstream of biological and social sciences, and which provided Budapest a special environment in which the cross-currents of Europe met. Gabel covers key figures and major concepts associated with Mannheim and the sociology of knowledge: ideology and false consciousness; the socially unattached intelligentsia; and the utopian conscience. (staff)

STEINDLER, Larry. Hungarian Philosophy: Its Ideas, an Historiographical Foundations (in Hungarian). Magyar Filozof Szemle, 3-4, 357-400, 1990.

STEINER, Daniel. "Approaching Ethical Questions: A University Perspective" in *Integrity in Health Care Institutions: Humane Environments for Teaching, Inquiry, and Healing*, BULGER, Ruth Ellen (ed), 53-67. Iowa City, Univ of Iowa Pr, 1990.

STEINHOFF, Gordon. Strawson and the Refutation of Idealism. Ideal Stud, 20(1), 61-81, Ja 90.

STEKELER-WEITHOFER, Pirmin. Willkür und Wille bei Kant. Kantstudien, 81(3), 304-320, 1990.

The essay favors a nondualistic reading of Kant's solution of the third antimony. Causal necessity as a successful form of representation of nature cannot contradict free choice. In fact, we know many schemes of possible actions, make choices between them by judging them as good or bad, and often, we succeed in realizing them. The possibility to distinguish between responsible action and mere thoughtless behaviour is the very meaning of free will. Hence Kant's way from 'you ought to do X' to 'you can do X' is no "petitio principii." No further disproof of abstract determinism is needed.

STELL, Lance K. The Noncompliant Substance Abuser: Commentary. Hastings Center Rep, 21(2), 31-32, Mr-Ap 91.

Endocarditis is a common medical complication of IV substance abuse. The recurrent bacteremias resulting from an IV substance abuser's drug seeking may destroy not only one or more of his or her native heart valves but one, two, or three prosthetic replacements as well. The question is whether non-compliant behavior can ever serve as a basis for refusing to offer additional heart valve replacements. I argue that it can.

STELLINO, Ana Isabel (trans) and KVART, Igal. Contrafácticos. Dianoia, 34(34), 93-140, 1988.

STENGEL, Barbara S. How Teachers Know. Phil Stud Educ, /, 16-30, 1989.

Thinking about teachers' knowledge is typically cast in terms of what teachers know, divided into discrete categories including subject matter knowledge, pedagogical knowledge, and knowledge about learners. This formulation of teachers' knowledge is a static one which neglects the essence of teaching as active and reflective. This paper attempts to reconceptualize teachers' ways of knowing (pedagogical, professional, cultural, and logical) as claims made on various knowledge bases in the act of teaching.

STENGER, Mary Ann. Feminism and Pluralism in Contemporary Theology. Laval Theol Phil, 46(3), 291-305, O 90.

Both the feminist critique and the pluralist critique challenge Christian theology to recognize the relativity of its concepts and symbols and the negative effects of its dominating, exclusive structures. These critiques and new theologies are analysed in relationship to the issues of absoluteness and relativity and philosophical vs. theological expressions. It is argued that there is an unresolvable tension between the absoluteness of God and the more personal relationship with God that should be addressed and maintained by both feminists and pluralists.

STENSTAD, Gail. Thinking (Beyond) Being. Heidegger Stud, 6, 143-151, 1990.

STENT, Gunther S. The Poverty of Neurophilosophy. J Med Phil, 15(5), 539-557, O 90.

The monist approach to the ancient mind-body problem styled "neurophilosophy" put forward recently by Patricia Smith Churchland on the basis of latter-day advances in the neurosciences is philosophically inadequate because it does not deal with the ethical dimension of the mind.

STEPANOVA, E A. An Examination of Marxist Doctrine in the Traditions of Russian Religious Philosophy. Soviet Stud Phil, 29(4), 6-34, Spr 91.

STEPANYANTS, Marietta. The Marxist Conception of Tradition. J Indian Counc Phil Res, 5(3), 117-123, My-Ag 88.

The purpose of the article is to overcome the simplification and distortion of Marx's concept of tradition as such which is common both for the followers and the opponents of Marxism. The analysis is focused on the attitude to the philosophical traditions of the Orient. The shortcomings of the two extreme points of view on studying and evaluating any philosophical tradition are pointed out. One is a view of an 'outsider' and the other of 'insider'. The necessity of taking into account the 'internal' and 'external' measurements of philosophical knowledge is pointed out.

STÉPHANOV, Ivan. "Le kitsch en tant que valeur communicative" in *XIth International Congress in Aesthetics, Nottingham 1988*, WOODFIELD, Richard (ed), 219-220. Nottingham, Nottingham Polytech, 1990.

STEPHENSON, Wendell. Benevolence and Resentment. Theoria, 55(1), 45-61, 1989.

Benevolence is often portrayed as the greatest virtue. Resentment is often condemned, partly because it seems to conflict with benevolence. Joseph Butler takes up the question of the seeming conflict between benevolence and resentment in two of his sermons, and attempts to resolve it. In my paper, I explicate and criticize his attempt, then provide a resolution that is close to the spirit of Butler's and also tenable. Butler's resolution is essentially utilitarian, and so is my refurbishing of it. One of the interests of the paper is in seeing how a utilitarian can successfully deal with something like resentment.

STEPHENSON, Wendell. Institutional Animal Care and Use Committees and the Moderate Position. Between Species, 7(1), 6-8, Wint 91.

STEPIEN, Teodor. First-Order Theories Without Axioms. Rep Math Log, 23, 67-70, 1989.

STEPIEN, Teodor. Single-Axiom Systems. Rep Math Log, 24, 87-96, 1990.

About sixty years ago A Tarski formulated some conditions for the so-called single-axiom systems in propositional logic. The aim of this paper is to show that Tarski's conditions are also sufficient and to generalize them. Moreover, we will show that Tarski's conditions are the sufficient conditions for the single-axiom systems in the case of the classical functional calculus with identity. On the ground of the above considerations we note that the classical functional calculus with identity can be formalized without axioms and without using of Gentzen-type rules.

STERBA, James P (ed). *Justice: Alternative Political Perspectives (Second Edition)*. Belmont, Wadsworth, 1992.

STERBA, James P. "Legitimate Defense and Strategic Defense" in *Issues in War and Peace: Philosophical Inquiries*, KUNKEL, Joseph (ed), 147-158. Wolfeboro, Longwood, 1989.

STERBA, James P. *Morality in Practice (Third Edition)*. Belmont, Wadsworth, 1990.

STERBA, James P. A Rational Choice Theory of Punishment. Phil Topics, 18(1), 171-181, Spr 90.

STERBA, James. "Peace Through Justice: A Practical Reconciliation of Opposing Conceptions of Justice" in *In the Interest of Peace: A Spectrum of Philosophical Views*, KLEIN, Kenneth H (ed), 279-288. Wolfeboro, Longwood, 1990.

STERELNY, Kim and DEVITT, Michael. "Linguistics: What's Wrong with 'The Right View'" in *Philosophical Perspectives, 3: Philosophy of Mind and Action Theory, 1989*, TOMBERLIN, James E (ed), 497-531. Atascadero, Ridgeview, 1989.

Fodor names the view that linguistics is about linguistic competence, "the Right View." On this view the grammar discovered by linguists is psychologically real. The paper finds difficulties for this idea of the grammar, particularly for the version of it that requires speakers to have propositional knowledge of the grammar. The paper urges a different view of linguistics: it is about the properties of linguistic symbols. This view is usually conflated with "the Right View." The paper offers a diagnosis of this conflation. In the course of the argument, the relevance of linguistic intuitions is examined.

STERELNY, Kim. Recent Work in the Philosophy of Biology. Phil Books, 32(1), 1-17, Ja 91.

In this paper I review and discuss the recent literature on sociobiology, adaptationism, units of selection, macroevolution and the nature of species. I argue that most human sociobiology is still seriously undercut by its implicit behaviourism. I claim that the adaptationist controversy conflates real and difficult empirical issues about the relative importance and power of natural selection with methodological disputes about appeals to the best explanation in validating adaptive scenarios value and divergent choices of rhetoric. I doubt that there is a unique best way of describing most selection processes but am rather sceptical of attempts to show that populations or species function in selection as entities in their own right; I try to show why species are unlikely to be causally robust enough to be agents in the evolutionary process. Finally, I review the "nature of species" literature, suggesting that the idea that species are individuals transforms the role of systematics from taxonomy to historical explanation.

STERELNY, Kim. *The Representational Theory of Mind: An Introduction*. Cambridge, Blackwell, 1990.

The first six chapters of this book develop and defend a Darwinized version of homuncular functionalism, a computational view of the transformation of mental representations based on the idea of a language of thought, and a theory of the nature of representation combining teleological and causal ideas. It thus defends the view that intentional psychology (suitably scrubbed) is the most abstract and general cognitive psychology rather than an enterprise of a different nature, and it defends the continuity of psychology with biology. The final four chapters consider rival hypotheses, especially the constellation of views around eliminativism in philosophy of psychology and connectionism in artificial intelligence. Neither are rejected outright, for the compatibilism of the first half is an empirical conjecture that further work may refute, but the idea that the language of thought hypothesis is unbiological, psychologically implausible and neodualist is rejected.

STERLING, Marvin C. The Ethical Thought of Martin Luther King. Quest, 5(1), 80-94, Je 91.

STERLING, Marvin C. El pensamiento filosófico de Martin Luther King, Jr. Logos (Mexico), 18(54), 115-126, S-D 90.

The aim of this paper is threefold. First, I give a brief account of King's metaphysical position. Secondly, I call attention to two important consequences which King believes to follow from this position. In the latter connection, I maintain that King was correct in regarding these two consequences to follow from his basic position, provided that we properly interpret the connected claim. And thirdly, having explicated his notion of *agape*, I conclude that some such social activism as that practiced by King becomes morally obligatory for any individual who accepts the sort of metaphysical position which King espoused.

STERN, David G. The "Middle Wittgenstein": From Logical Atomism to Practical Holism. Synthese, 87(2), 203-226, My 91.

This paper outlines the developments that led from Wittgenstein's early logical atomist view that all meaningful discourse can be analyzed into logically independent elementary propositions to his later philosophy. In 1929, he rejected logical atomism for a conception of language as composed of calculi, formal systems characterized by their constitutive rules. But by the mid-1930's he rejected the model of a calculus, emphasizing that language is action within a social and natural context, more like a game than a calculus, and that rule-governed behavior is dependent on a background of practices which cannot themselves be explicitly formulated as rules.

STERN, David G. Models of Memory: Wittgenstein and Cognitive Science. Phil Psych, 4(2), 203-218, 1991.

The model of memory as a store, from which records can be retrieved, is taken for granted by many contemporary researchers. On this view, memories are stored by memory traces, which represent the original event and provide a causal link between that episode and one's ability to remember it. I argue that this seemingly plausible model leads to an unacceptable conception of the relationship between mind and brains, and that a nonrepresentational, connectionist, model offers a promising alternative. I also offer a new reading of Wittgenstein's paradoxical remarks about thought and brain processes on which they amount to a critique of the cognitivist thesis that information stored in the brain has a linguistic structure and a particular location. On this reading, Wittgenstein's criticism foreshadows some of the most promising contemporary work on connectionist models of neural functioning.

STERN, David S. Autonomy and Political Obligation in Kant. S J Phil, 29(1), 127-148, Spr 91.

STERN, David S. Foundationalism, Holism, or Hegel? J Brit Soc Phenomenol, 22(1), 21-32, Ja 91.

STERN, David S. The Immanence of Thought: Hegel's Critique of Foundationalism. Owl Minerva, 22(1), 19-33, Fall 90.

The goal of this article is twofold: (1) to further the nonmetaphysical interpretation of Hegel's basic theses about "absolute knowledge," and (2) to criticize other proponents of such a nonmetaphysical reading (Dove, Maker, Winfield) who defend the reading by making the result of the *Phenomenology* wholly negative. I accomplish both goals by arguing that Hegel provides a complex argument against (a) every form of epistemological foundationalism, which assumes that knowledge must be secured by appeal to some sort of incorrigible given, and (b) what I term "transcendental foundationalism"—the assumption that the subject is the ground of objectivity. I then indicate how these two points determine the task and argument of the *Science of Logic*.

STERN, Kenneth. Kierkegaard on Theistic Proof. Relig Stud, 26(2), 219-226, Je 90.

Despite what many analytic philosophers say, Kierkegaard does give arguments for his view that theistic proofs are impossible. The nub of much of his view is that no argument for God can produce the kind of conviction necessary for religious belief. But is there any relation between the convincingness of an argument and the argument's logical cogency? The paper discusses this issue and concludes there is such a connection.

STERNBERG, Robert J. *Metaphors of Mind: Conceptions of the Nature of Intelligence*. New York, Cambridge Univ Pr, 1990.

STERNBERG, Robert J. *Wisdom: Its Nature, Origins, and Development*. New York, Cambridge Univ Pr, 1990.

The goal of this book is to present diverse and incisive views on the nature of wisdom. Each of the chapters considers the nature of wisdom, how it can be studied, and where available, empirical results. Contributors are Robert J Sternberg, Daniel N Robinson, Mihaly Csikszentmihalyi and Kevin Rathunde, Gisela Labouvie-Vief, Paul B Baltes and Jacqui Smith, Michael J Chandler and Stephen Holliday, Lucinda Orwoll and Marion Perlmutter, John A Meacham, Karen Strohm Kitchener and Helene G Brenner, Patricia Kennedy Arlin, Juan Pascual-Leone, Deirdre A Kramer, and in an integrative essay, James E Birren and Laurel M Fisher.

STETTER, Christian. Kant und Wittgenstein. Rev Int Phil, 45(176), 59-75, 1991.

STETTER, Christian. "Wilhelm von Humboldt und das Problem der Schrift" in *Leibniz, Humboldt, and the Origins of Comparativism*, DE MAURO, Tullio (ed), 181-197. Philadelphia, John Benjamins, 1990.

This essay compares Humboldt's view of language with that of script. It is shown in what way his conception of language follows from his idea of aesthetics derived from Kant's *Kritik der Urteilskraft*. Following Derrida, the idea of the relativity of "sprachlichte Weltansichten" (linguistic conceptions of the world) is in opposition to the tradition of logocentrism; it is based on the principle of difference. This seems to be in contradiction with Humboldt's view of the alphabetic script. It is shown however that his idea of script is compatible with that of language, and that his high esteem of the alphabetic script results from the specific historical situation at the beginning of the nineteenth century.

STEUP, M. Moral Truth and Coherence: Comments on Goldman. S J Phil, SUPP 29, 185-189, 1990.

Alan Goldman believes that moral realism—the view that there are moral facts—is false, yet he insists that there is moral knowledge. This is puzzling, for how can there be knowledge without facts? Goldman attempts to solve this puzzle by proposing a coherence theory of moral truth. I argue that his thoery is incoherent because it entails that any true moral judgment is also false, and that it commits us to relativism, which I take to be an inherently implausible view.

STEUTEL, J W. Deugden en plichtsbesef. Alg Ned Tijdschr Wijs, 83(3), 174-187, Jl 91.

According to the motivation theory of R B Brandt, moral virtues are composed of relatively permanent and stable intrinsic wants and aversions that come up to a standard level of intensity. This theory implies that cultivating these wants and aversions is the one and only aim of the virtues approach in moral education. In this paper it is argued that Brandt's explanation of the virtues is essentially incomplete. By means of several examples it is shown that possessing the wants and aversions referred to is not sufficient for being a bearer of moral virtues. A sense of duty, too, is an intrinsic component of every moral virtue. Consequently, fostering the development of a sense of duty has to be considered an all-embracing aim of the virtues approach in moral education.

STEVENSON, Mark. Ethics and Energy Supplement. J Bus Ethics, 10(8), 641-648, Ag 91.

STEWARD, Jon. Die Rolle des unglücklichen Bewusstseins in Hegels *Phänomenologie des Geistes*. Deut Z Phil, 39(1), 12-21, 1991.

The author explores a parallelism between the "Force and Understanding" and the "Unhappy Consciousness" sections of Hegel's *Phenomenology of Spirit*. The central claim is that the notion of objectivity related in the former, which involves a supersensible world inhabited by unseen forces contrasted with the fleeting world of appearances, becomes reinterpreted in the "Unhappy Consciousness" in terms of an unchangeable God behind the scenes and the transitory human subject. Thus, the notion of objectivity becomes enriched in the "Self-Consciousness" chapter to become a notion of subjectivity. This reading purportedly helps to establish the much disputed unity of the *Phenomenology*.

STEWART, David and MICKUNAS, Algis. *Exploring Phenomenology (Second Edition)*. Athens, Ohio Univ Pr, 1990.

The purpose of this book is to introduce in concise, uncluttered and straightforward terms the history, development, and contemporary status of phenomenology. The book is organized so that extensive bibliographical entries (annotated) follow each major section. The second edition updates developments in phenomenological philosophy by discussing recent trends and noting significant works that have appeared in the last fifteen years.

STEWART, David and BLOCKER, H Gene. *Fundamentals of Philosophy (Third Edition)*. New York, Macmillan, 1992.

This book contains all the resources needed for a first course in philosophy. Features are the usual topics in philosophy: metaphysics, epistemology, ethics, philosophy of religion, and social and political philosophy. In addition the third edition features a new section dealing with Eastern thought featuring philosophical themes found in such great Eastern thought systems as Hinduism, Buddhism, Confucianism, and Taoism. In addition to expository and analytical text material, the book also contains primary source readings from principal philosophers both classic and contemporary.

STEWART, Olivia (trans) and URVOY, Dominique. *Ibn Rushd: Averroes*. New York, Routledge, 1991.

Going well beyond the Eurocentrist view which sees Ibn Rushd (Averroes) as little more than an intermediary between Aristotle and the scholastics, this book explores the main elements of his thought against the historical and cultural background of Muslim Spain. It gives a full account of Ibn Rushd's most important works, including his scientific, medical and legal as well as philosophical writings. It especially shows that Ibn Rushd's work formed part of the wider movement of Almohadism, a politico-religious reform movement which had a great intellectual impact in Muslim Spain.

STEWART, Robert M and THOMAS, Lynn L. Recent Work on Ethical Relativism. Amer Phil Quart, 28(2), 85-100, Ap 91.

STEWART-ROBERTSON, Charles. The Rhythms of Gratitude: Historical Developments and Philosophical Concerns. Austl J Phil, 68(2), 189-205, Je 90.

The fortunes of "Gratitude" in eighteenth-century thought prove more ambivalent than at first suspected. The ungrateful is still soundly denounced, by the likes of Shaftesbury, Hutcheson, Kames or Beattie, as later by Sydney Smith or Thomas Brown. Society is admonished to follow a less "inhuman" path. Yet Gratitude's partiality troubled some: Godwin doubted whether partial benevolences even qualified as virtues. Many Scottish thinkers, however, made Gratitude a critical element of civil society. Ought society to be sympathetic or just in character, they questioned. As the wider ramifications were increasingly aired, so certain presuppositions concerning the grateful man were reopened.

STICH, Stephen P. "The Fragmentation of Reason": Précis of Two Chapters. Phil Phenomenol Res, 51(1), 179-183, Mr 91.

STICH, Stephen P. Causal Holism and Commonsense Psychology: A Reply to O'Brien. Phil Psych, 4(2), 179-181, 1991.

STICH, Stephen P. Evaluating Cognitive Strategies: A Reply to Cohen, Goldman, Harman, and Lycan. Phil Phenomenol Res, 51(1), 207-213, Mr 91.

STICH, Stephen and RAMSEY, William and GARON, Joseph. "Connectionism, Eliminativism and the Future of Folk Psychology" in *Philosophical Perspectives, 4: Action Theory and Philosophy of Mind, 1990*, TOMBERLIN, James E (ed), 499-533. Atascadero, Ridgeview, 1990.

STICH, Stephen. *The Fragmentation of Reason*. Cambridge, MIT Pr, 1990.

STICH, Stephen and JONES, Todd and MULAIRE, Edmond. Staving Off Catastrophe: A Critical Notice of Jerry Fodor's *Psychosemantics*. Mind Lang, 6(1), 58-82, Spr 91.

Jerry Fodor's *Psychosemantics* is a sophisticated, spackling, and innovative attempt to defend commonsense psychology from its recent detractors. The arguments that Fodor sets forth in this volume will likely begin debates that will fill the literature for years to come. In this review we give an overview of Fodor's attempt to rescue commonsense psychology from the three challenges to it that have loomed largest in the literature. We also sketch what we see as the most obvious *prima facie* problems with the course that Fodor recommends.

STIEBER, John. The Behavior of the NCAA: A Question of Ethics. J Bus Ethics, 10(6), 445-449, Je 91.

The National Collegiate Athletic Association (NCAA) is commonly viewed as a safety net for individual athletes, for universities, and for inter-collegiate sports programs. There is another view that argues the NCAA is a buyers' cartel or monopolist that engages in price-fixing for colleges and universities. The prices they fix are the wages of student athletes. It is the opinion of some that these price fixing scholarship agreements limiting the income of student athletes discriminates against a whole class of scholarship recipients. They also believe that this kind of behavior on the part of colleges and universities that make up the membership of the NCAA is highly unethical and may even be illegal. (edited)

STIEBER, John and PRIMEAUX, Patrick. Economic Efficiency: A Paradigm for Business Ethics. J Bus Ethics, 10(5), 335-339, My 91.

Current teaching, writing and thinking in business ethics reflects (more than) a tendency to subsume business into the theoretical, idealistic and impractical objectives of philosophical ethics. Professors Primeaux and Stieber argue against this tendency. They propose the basic business model of *economic efficiency* as a practical and appropriate paradigm for business ethics. Understood from a behavioral perspective, economic efficiency reflects all of the ethical considerations of the academic study of philosophical ethics, but in a much more concrete and applicable manner. In effect, they are proposing that any study of business ethics defines its starting point and focus of reference in terms of economic efficiency.

STILLINGER, Jack. "John Mill's Education: Fact, Fiction, and Myth" in *A Cultivated Mind: Essays On J S Mill Presented to John M Robson*, LAINE, Michael (ed), 19-43. Buffalo, Univ of Toronto Pr, 1991.

Numerous discrepancies between the external documentation concerning J S Mill's education and the account that he gives in his *Autobiography* suggest that we should beware of taking any statement in that work at face value. The famous "education of fear" appears to be a myth that Mill invented for rhetorical and psychological purposes, rather than biographical or philosophical. In reality, Mill's father devoted considerable time, effort, and kindliness to his son's education and, in the process, provided a model of working, reading, and writing that the son imitated all his life.

STINCHCOMBE, Arthur L. The Conditions of Fruitfulness of Theorizing About Mechanisms in Social Science. Phil Soc Sci, 21(3), 367-388, S 91.

Mechanisms in a theory are defined here as bits of theory about entities at a different level, e.g., individuals, than the main entities being theorized about, e.g., groups, which serve to make the higher-level theory more supple, more accurate, or more general. The criterion for whether it is worthwhile to theorize at lower levels is whether it makes the theory at the higher levels better, not whether lower-level theorizing is philosophically necessary. The higher-level theory can be made better by mechanisms known to be inadequate in the discipline dealing with the lower level. Conditions for the usefulness of lower-level theorizing are proposed, with many examples form various social and physical sciences.

STIPANIC, Ernest. Boskovic's Mathematical Conception of Continuity and the Differentiability of Function (in Serbo-Croatian). Filozof Istraz, 32-33(5-6), 1525-1540, 1989.

In this paper the mathematical, methodological and philosophical importance of the mathematical intuition in the discovery of mathematical truth is emphasized. The way in which this intuition is related to the strict logical demonstrability is shown. Particular cases are presented in which geometrical intuition is used. The aim of this inquiry is to "demonstrate" that the continuous function is differentiable in general. From the results of the classical mathematical analysis it follows that the continuity of function is a necessary but not sufficient condition for the differentiability of function. (edited)

STITH, Richard. Generosity: A Duty Without a Right. J Value Inq, 25(3), 203-216, Jl 91.

STÖBER, Konrad and ZIEMKE, Axel. Autopoesis—Subject—Reality (in German). Deut Z Phil, 38(11), 1083-1090, 1990.

STOCKER, Margarita. "Biblical Story and the Heroine" in *The Bible as Rhetoric: Studies in Biblical Persuasion and Credibility*, WARNER, Martin (ed), 81-102. New York, Routledge, 1990.

STOCKER, Michael. "Friendship and Duty: Some Difficult Relations" in *Identity, Character, and Morality: Essays in Moral Psychology*, FLANAGAN, Owen (ed), 219-234. Cambridge, MIT Pr, 1990.

STÖCKLER, Manfred. Emergenz Bausteine für eine Begriffsexplikation. Conceptus, 24(63), 7-24, 1990.

This essay considers requirements for the fruitful use of the concept of emergence. An explication of this equivocal concept is suggested on the basis of a pragmatically restricted reductionism. A brief history of the concept of emergence and some examples prepare the way for several important distinctions. A property of a complex system is called *emergent* when the concept of this property is not required in providing an explanatory understanding of the components of the system, but needs to be added in order to give an adequate analysis of the system.

STÖCKLER, Manfred. "Realism and Classicism, or Something More? Some Comments on Mario Bunge's Philosophy of Quantum Mechanics" in *Studies on Mario Bunge's "Treatise"*, WEINGARTNER, Paul (ed), 351-363. Amsterdam, Rodopi, 1990.

In my comment on Mario Bunge's philosophy of quantum mechanics I argue for three theses: (i) Mario Bunge was successful in showing that there is no special reason in quantum mechanics for rejecting realism; (ii) Mario Bunge's defense of realism does not include a defense of classical physics and its ontological commitments; (iii) besides realism and classicism there are problems left in quantum mechanics, especially in the theory of quantum measurement. Judging these problems to be fundamental and serious, I disagree with Mario Bunge.

STOEBER, Michael. Personal Identity and Rebirth. Relig Stud, 26(4), 493-500, D 90.

STOEGER, W R and HELLER, Michael. A Causal Interaction Constraint on the Initial Singularity? Phil Sci (Tucson), 2, 61-75, 1986.

Modern cosmology presents us with a fundamental problem, that of characterizing the "Big Bang," or "initial singularity" (IS) in a causally adequate and understandable way. The problem itself is described rigorously in terms of the causal geometry used in the theory of relativity. From the apparent isotropy and homogeneity of the observable universe it seems clear that, despite other inherent difficulties, causality demands that either the IS or a three-dimensional Cauchy surface very near it be causally self-connected, and therefore non-spacelike. Recent attractive proposals, e.g., the inflationary scenario, automatically fulfil this requirement. The indirectly related problem of synchronization by observers *within* a spacetime is also discussed.

STOILJKOVIC, Dragoslav. Attraction and Repulsion in Comprehension of Boskovic, Hegel and Engels (in Serbo-Croatian). Filozof Istraz, 32-33(5-6), 1567-1576, 1989.

Attraction and repulsion (A & R) are the essence of the matter according to the opinion of Boskovic, Hegel and Engels. A & R are forces between material particles, according to Boskovic. In Hegel's comprehensions, A & R denote aggregation and separation. According to Engels, A & R are the most fundamental modes of movement of material particles. The ostensible disagreement between Boskovic, Hegel and Engels was originated because they considered the different aspects of the same process—the differentiation of matter. In fact, their comprehensions are complementary and in agreement, since the differentiation of matter includes the movement, aggregation and forces between the particles. It was shown by author that differentiation of matter is followed by the differentiation of the movement—the new modes of movement originate as well as the old modes are awakened.

STOJANOVIC, Svetozar. Marxism, Post-Marxism and the Implosion of Communism. Praxis Int, 10(3-4), 205-212, O 90-Ja 91.

STOJANOVIC, Svetozar. Some Reflections on Post-Marxism and Post-Christianity: A Response to Professor Arthur Mc Govern. Dialec Hum, 16(3-4), 107-112, Sum-Autumn 89.

STOJKOVIC, Andrija B K. Boskovic's Philosophical Understanding of Matter (in Serbo-Croatian). Filozof Istraz, 32-33(5-6), 1585-1596, 1989.

Le'auteur définit six caractéristiques fondamentales de la détermination naturelle et scientifique de la matière par Boscovich (concernant sa structure), qui sont en général en accord avec les résultats contemporains de la science naturelle théorique. D'autre part, il définit trois caractéristiques fondamentales de la détermination philosophique de la matière par Boscovich, qui sont également proches de la philosophie contemporaine, marxiste ou non, de la physique. (edited)

STOKHOF, Martin and GROENENDIJK, Jeroen. Dynamic Predicate Logic. Ling Phil, 14(1), 39-100, F 91.

STOKS, Hans. "A Perception of Reality with an East-Nilotic People" in *I, We and Body: First Joint Symposium of Philosophers from Africa and from the Netherlands*, KIMMERLE, Heinz (ed), 79-92. Atlantic Highlands, Gruner, 1989.

This article aims at developing a philosophy of perception in confrontation with the culture of the Maasai. It tries to interpret some phenomena of that culture and to reflect on it at the same time. As a special topic the words for God (Enkai) and the tribe (Maasai) are chosen and analysed. Enkai seems to be related to the words for rain (enkai) and water or river (enkare), while the word Maasai most probably (just) means 'people'. Now when the Maasai say that God and the Maasai are equal, some interesting connotations can be found.

STOLLER, Robert J and COLBY, Kenneth M and COLBY, Peter M. Dialogues in Natural Language with GURU, a Psychologic Inference Engine. Phil Psych, 3(2-3), 171-187, 1990.

The aim of this project was to explore the possibility of constructing a psychologic inference engine that might enhance introspective self-awareness by delivering inferences about a user based on what he said in interactive dialogues about his closest opposite-sex relation. To implement this aim, we developed a computer program (GURU) with the capacity to simulate human conversation in colloquial natural language. The psychologic inferences offered represent the authors' simulations of their commonsense psychology responses to expected user-input expressions. The heuristics of the natural language processor and its relation to output responses are described in enough detail for the operations of the implementation to be understood. Evaluation of this new cognitive agent presents, we hope, puzzles for artificial intelligence and cognitive science.

STOLNITZ, Jerome. On the Historical Triviality of Art. Brit J Aes, 31(3), 195-202, Jl 91.

STOMEO, Anna. Su alcuni aspetti del neoilluminismo di L Geymonat. Il Protag, 6(13-16), 79-106, Ja 88-D 89.

STONE, Carolyn M. Autonomy, Emotions and Desires: Some Problems Concerning R F Dearden's Account of Autonomy. J Phil Educ, 24(2), 271-283, Wint 90.

Dearden's analysis of *autonomy* is criticised for emphasising the role of reflection, reasoning and judgment and giving an inadequate account of the role of emotions

AUTHOR INDEX WITH ABSTRACTS 661 STRONG, Carson

and desires. An attempt to expand Dearden's analysis to include emotions and desires fails to remedy the problem, whilst helping to pinpoint the analysis's particular deficiencies. Problems concerning the *value* of autonomy are then highlighted: it is a one-sided ideal which privileges "masculine" qualities and excludes various desirable qualities associated with "femininity." Arguments in favour of conceptualising a broader ideal for human development are outlined, with some indication of the difficulties of this task.

STONE, Jim. Could Someone Else Have Had My Headache? J Indian Counc Phil Res, 5(3), 151-155, My-Ag 88.

Fissioning cases show that a token mental state can belong to different people in different possible worlds. If one of my hemispheres is destroyed and the second (sufficient to preserve psychological connectedness) transplanted to another body, I survive in that body. That fellow's headache (H) is mine. But if the first hemisphere had instead been transplanted to another body too, I would not have survived. H would still exist, but it would not be mine. I argue that the identity of a mental state depends on the identity of the matter that realizes it, not the identity of its subject.

STONE, Lynda. Postmodern Metaphors for Teacher Education? Proc Phil Educ, 46, 315-318, 1990.

STONE, Mark A. A Kuhnian Model of Falsifiability. Brit J Phil Sci, 42(2), 177-185, Je 91.

Thomas Kuhn has argued that scientists never reject a paradigm without simultaneously accepting a new paradigm. Coupled with Kuhn's claim that it is paradigms as a whole, and not individual theories, that are accepted or rejected, this thesis is seen as one of Kuhn's main challenges to the rationality of science. I argue that Kuhn is mistaken in this claim; at least in some instances, science rejects a paradigm despite the absence of a successor. In particular, such a description best fits Kuhn's most discussed example, the Copernican Revolution. By differentiating scientific discoveries into three types, spontaneous, implicit, and directed, we see that Kuhn's thesis holds for spontaneous, implicit discoveries, but not directed discoveries. Directed discoveries must be understood by and alternative account of falsifiability, bases on argument by *reductio ad absurdum* rather than argument by *modus tollens* as traditional accounts of falsifiability would have it.

STONE, Robert V and BOWMAN, Elizabeth A. "'Making the Human' in Sartre's Unpublished Dialectical Ethics" in *Writing the Politics of Difference*, SILVERMAN, Hugh J (ed), 111-122. Albany, SUNY Pr, 1991.

STOPFORD, John. The Death of the Author (as Producer). Phil Rhet, 23(3), 184-191, 1990.

This paper compares Barthes' and Benjamin's accounts of the role and function of the politically engaged author. It concludes that Barthes' subversion of the traditional conception of the author in favor of "writing" and "intertextuality" also undermines Benjamin's conception of the author as producer.

STORCKEN, A J A and DELVER, R and MONSUUR, H. Ordering Pairwise Comparison Structures. Theor Decis, 31(1), 75-94, Jl 91.

Following an introduction to the merits of pairwise comparison methods, we present various ordering algorithms for complete binary preferential structures. These procedures generalize the well-known numbering algorithm to the intransitive case. A new form of independence of irrelevant alternatives is presented. Moreover, various other criteria and characterizations for these algorithms are presented. Aside from solving ranking problems and making explicit value criteria and structures of human preference, our algorithms are applicable to subjects such as task-sequencing and artificial intelligence projects.

STORTI, Cinzia. Francesco Bonucci, tra medicina e filosofia. Filosofia, 41(3), 345-363, S-D 90.

STOUGH, Charlotte. Two Kinds of Naming in the *Sophist*. Can J Phil, 20(3), 355-381, S 90.

STRAHLER, Arthur N. The Creationist Theory of Abrupt Appearances: A Critique. Free Inq, 11(3), 37-43, Sum 91.

A theory of abrupt appearances, or discontinuist theory, proposed by creationist attorney Wendell R Bird to explain all things in the universe, asserts that every formative event occurred instantaneously from a prior state of nonexistence or from an unknown simple, primitive state. No divine or supernatural agency is permitted. The theory fails because no knowledge of the formative process is possible. Repeated ex nihilo originations would require violation of the universal laws of thermodynamics. The theory explains nothing and describes no physical process, remaining only a gratuitous postulate of no substance.

STRAUBER, Ira. Legal Reasoning and Practical Political Education. Soc Epistem, 5(1), 38-43, Ja-Mr 91.

It is generally understood that constitutional interpretation is "a very elaborated...case of practical reasoning...[the aim of which is] to persuade and to convince those whom it addresses, that...a choice, decision, or attitude is preferable to concurrent choices, decisions, and attitudes." Of course, it remains controversial what constitutes good reasons for being persuaded that one choice is superior to another. This essay concerns the political education that American constitutional interpretation actually provides citizens about those choices. Because, by and large, the only serious contact citizens have with constitutional law is in academic environments, this essay focuses on what undergraduates learn about practical political reasoning. I contend that constitutional law has become *very* elaborated, so much so that we ought to maintain a vigilant skepticism about the compatibility between its rhetoric and the goals of liberal education.

STRAUS, Nina Pelikan. Rethinking Feminist Humanism. Phil Lit, 14(2), 284-303, O 90.

STRAUSS, Daniël F M. The Ontological Status of the Principle of the Excluded Middle. Phil Math, 6(1), 73-90, 1991.

In this article we want to investigate the ontological status of the logical principle of the excluded middle. In doing this, we are not only taking notice of "epistemic values" in contemporary philosophy of science since we are also considering issues from the foundational notion of continuity—along with the whole-part relation implied by the latter. The status of the said principle crucially depends on the interconnections between number, space and the meaning of analysis. As such it forms a part of the arithmetical analogy within the modal structure of the logical-analytical mode, intimately connected with the principles of identity and non-contradiction.

STRAUSS, Leo and BARTLETT, Robert (trans). Some Remarks on the Political Science of Maimonides and Farabi. Interpretation, 18(1), 3-30, Fall 90.

STRAWSON, Galen. *The Secret Connexion: Causation, Realism, and David Hume*. New York, Clarendon/Oxford Pr, 1989.

David Hume has been misunderstood. He does not hold that there is no such thing as causal power or causal necessity. He does not hold a regularity theory of causation. He firmly believes (without claiming to know for sure) that there is such a thing as causal power. He merely insists that we cannot know its nature. His point is merely epistemological; he is not making the ontological claim that there is definitely no such thing as causal power. Such a claim is a dogmatic metaphysical claim of just the sort he abhors; it is ruled out by his sceptical principles.

STRAWSON, P F (ed). *Philosophical Logic*. New York, Oxford Univ Pr, 1985.

STRAWSON, P F. "Two Conceptions of Philosophy" in *Perspectives on Quine*, BARRETT, Robert (ed), 310-318. Cambridge, Blackwell, 1990.

A certain austere conception, represented by the work of Quine, would admit within the sphere of serious philosophical enquiry only such objects and concepts as satisfied stringently scientific requirements of precision and clarity. A more relaxed conception would aim to elucidate the character and interconnections of the fundamental concepts or types of concept which constitute the structural framework of human thinking in general. Unsurprisingly the latter allows for a more liberal ontology than the former. The point is developed in detail for the case of properties or attributes.

STROHS, S. On the Philosophy of the Czech Avant-garde, Part II (in Czechoslovakian). Filozof Cas, 39(1), 129-157, 1991.

The overriding issue of this study is the relationship between avant-garde philosophy and Marxist philosophy, as represented on the one hand by the historic form which this relationship assumed in the interwar period and on the other hand by the shape it took on in the concepts of the 1960s, specifically in the concepts of Robert Kalivoda and Vratislav Effenberger. This study offers their detailed reconstruction. (edited)

STRÖKER, Elisabeth. Modelos de cambio científico en la filosofía actual de la ciencia. Rev Filosof (Spain), 4, 31-44, 1990.

STRÖKER, Elisabeth and JANSSEN, Paul. *Phänomenologische Philosophie*. Freiburg, Alber, 1991.

This presentation of phenomenological philosophy focusses on the fundamental impulse which is at its core a philosophical method. It presents the most important themes dealt with by significant representatives of phenomenology — especially by Brentano, Husserl, Reinach, Gurwitsch, Schütz, Scheler, Heidegger, Sartre, Merleau-Ponty, Levinas—and their schools or the general approaches to which they belonged. Here it emphasizes the phenomenological method which constitutes the unity of phenomenological philosophy.

STROLL, Avrum. Max on Moore. Dialectica, 44(1-2), 153-163, 1990.

Moore claims that he knows certain propositions to be true with certainty, but refuses to say *how* he knows, i.e., refuses to give supporting reasons for his claims. Many philosophers, including Max Black, have argued that Moore's approach simply begs the philosophical issues at stake. In contrast, the author argues that Moore's assessment of scepticism shows that it cannot be defeated by rational argumentation and therefore must be met by a rebuttive technique that does not allow the sceptical regress to begin. The outcome is at least a stalemate and in a certain sense may represent a defeat for the sceptic.

STRONG, Carson. Delivering Hydrocephalic Fetuses. Bioethics, 5(1), 1-22, Ja 91.

Fetal hydrocephalus with head enlargement near term raises ethical issues concerning the choice of delivery method. One delivery method attempts to minimize maternal risks, draining fluid from the fetal head to reduce head size and avoid caesarean section. Because such drainage almost always results in stillbirth or neonatal death, this approach frequently constitutes active killing. The alternative, caesarean section, exposes the mother to risks for a fetus who might have a poor outcome. Whose risks should be minimized, the mother's or the fetus's? Is it ethical for the physician to drain the fetal head? Factors are identified which the physician should consider in making recommendations, and a suggested approach by the physician is defended.

STRONG, Carson. Maternal Rights, Fetal Harms: Commentary. Hastings Center Rep, 21(3), 21-22, My-Je 91.

When hydrocephalus with head enlargement is detected in fetuses near term, decisions must be made concerning method of delivery. Cesarean section aims to promote fetal interests but exposes the woman to risks of surgery. Vaginal delivery with cephalocentesis avoids those risks but usually causes fetal or neonatal death. Because it is likely to constitute killing, such cephalocentesis should generally be avoided. Exceptions occur when there are other anomalies incompatible with long-term survival or highly likely to result in death or severe cognitive deficit. In the absence of such associated anomalies, refusal of cesarean section by the mother would create a dilemma. Such a case would challenge the view that forced cesarean is never justifiable, for the likely alternative is to kill a neonate or fetus with serious moral standing.

STRONG, Tracy B. Aesthetic Authority and Tradition: Nietzsche and the Greeks. Hist Euro Ideas, 11, 989-1007, 1989.

Rejecting the antiquarian understanding of Nietzsche's attitude towards the Greeks (Habermas) I show that his analysis of them is central to his understanding of modernity. They provide a model of what it would mean for something to exist authoritatively in modern times. Furthermore, there exists for Nietzsche no necessary opposition between a traditional "scholarly" approach to such matters and the more "aesthetic" one of the
h of Tragedy.

STROUD, Barry. Meaning, Understanding and Translation. Can J Phil, SUPP 16, 343-361, 1990.

STROUD, Barry. "Quine's Physicalism" in *Perspectives on Quine*, BARRETT, Robert (ed), 321-333. Cambridge, Blackwell, 1990.

STROUT, Cushing. "When the Truth Is in the Telling" in *The Philosophy of John William Miller*, FELL, Joseph P (ed), 153-164. Lewisburg, Bucknell Univ Pr, 1990.

My essay is a memoir of my intellectual engagement with my teacher in philosophy, John William Miller. His theme of the bearing of time on "all modes of learning in which there is nothing to be known apart from the telling" anticipated contemporary philosophical, historical, literary, and psychological thinking about the narrative quality of experience. Miller insisted that "the way of telling stories must also be made of nothing but experience," rather than of entities generated by concepts of God, nature, or psychology. His voluntaristic, existentialist idealism prepared me for reading Louis Mink, Paul Veyne, Erik Erikson, and Frederick Olafson.

STRUB, Christian. *Kalkulierte Absurditäten*. Freiburg, Alber, 1991.

There are two types of answers to the question of the function of metaphor, one traditional and one modern. First, metaphors are replaceable by similes. Secondly, they are not so replaceable, rather they are independent, "semantically deviant" linguistic forms "calculated absurdities," in which a decisive role is played by the tension between linguistic sense and nonsense. Starting from the tradition based on linguistic analysis, from Paul Ricoeur's teaching on metaphor and Strawson's reflections on the problem of predication, the concept of linguistic deviance is worked out and an independent theory of metaphor sketched. This theory tries to defend the "scandal of metaphor" in its entirety against contemporary views. It is also shown that both general types of answers to the problem of metaphor are intrinsically capable of providing explication, and that the progression from the traditional to the modern type of answer is not an advance in precision or rationality, but merely a reflex deriving from the change from an analogical to a postanalogical ontology.

STRUVE, Lynn A. Chen Que versus Huang Zongxi: Confucianism Faces Modern Times in the Seventeenth Century. J Chin Phil, 18(1), 5-23, Mr 91.

STRUYKER BOUDIER, C E M. Authenticity as Virtue (in Dutch). Bijdragen, 1, 70-94, 1991.

This contribution originated from a reflection on the very deep impression made by Evaristo Card. Arns OFM on many people present, when he delivered a lecture at the Catholic University of Nijmegen (1989). His personality and lively description of the activities which he and his collaborators undertook during the times of military repression in Brasil and afterwards was so authentic, that it impressed us a direct realization of the Sermon of the Mount of Jesus. In this article an account is given of this 'happening', in the wider context of an analysis of what 'authenticity' means in our modern vocabulary—a semantic analysis—and in the existential-phenomenological philosophies, that have occupied themselves with the problems of authenticity in so many ways. The (im)possibilities of authenticity are discussed in relation to what psychoanalysis, actual theories about 'mimesis' and deconstructive movements have to tell us. In what kind of language can we speak authentically about authenticity? Above all, methodological and historical difficulties and ethical and religious discourses make us think, that authenticity can be found in a fundamental openness to the Other (fellow-human being and God).

STRUYKER BOUDIER, C E M. Moraliteiten: Recente ethische publikaties in Vlaanderen en Nederland. Tijdschr Filosof, 53(1), 125-131, Mr 91.

STUHR, John J. Personalist and Pragmatist Persons. Personalist Forum, 6(2), 143-160, Fall 90.

This essay is a critical comparison of personalist and pragmatist conceptions of personhood. I begin with an examination of the shared philosophical themes and cultural contexts of personalism and pragmatism, and then show how pragmatism rejects and avoids issues central to personalism. I develop a pragmatic notion of persons as (1) natural organisms, (2) social selves, and (3) communal individuals. This makes possible a contrast of personalism's idealism of persons with pragmatism's ideal of persons, and I suggest the practical implications of this.

STUMP, Eleonore S. "Faith and Goodness" in *The Philosophy in Christianity*, VESEY, Godfrey (ed), 167-191. New York, Cambridge Univ Pr, 1989.

STURGEON, Kareen B. The Classroom as a Model of the World. Environ Ethics, 13(2), 165-173, Sum 91.

This paper explores the relationship between science and ethics and its implications for educational reform and environmental change. It is a personal account of my search to find a place for ethics in an environmental science class and how, in the process, the class itself is being transformed. I document how I have come to believe that the classroom is a model of the world: within my own development, the transformation of a course is implicated and, within the development of the course, the potential transformation of an educational system and the world is enfolded.

STURGEON, Nicholas L. Contents and Causes: A Reply to Blackburn. Phil Stud, 61(1-2), 19-37, F 91.

In response to Simon Blackburn's "Just Causes" (*Philosophical Studies* 61 (1991), 1-18), I press further two objections to his noncognitivism (or "projectivism") that I first raised in "What Difference Does It Make Whether Moral Realism is True" (*Southern Journal of Philosophy* 24, supplement (1986), 115-41). One is that it cannot regard as univocal disputes between people who differ both in their moral standards and in their attitude toward morality; the other is that it cannot accommodate moral explanations. I argue that Blackburn's new proposals are either independently implausible, or else render his projectivism more difficult to defend.

STURGEON, Scott. Truth in Epistemology. Phil Phenomenol Res, 51(1), 99-108, Mr 91.

STURLESE, Loris. Florilegi filosofici ed enciclopedie in Germania nella prima metà del Duecento. G Crit Filosof Ital, 69(3), 293-319, S-D 90.

STURLESE, Rita. Il "De imaginum, signorum et idearum compositione" di Giordano Bruno, ed il significato filosofico .... G Crit Filosof Ital, 69(2), 182-203, My-Ag 90.

STURLESE, Rita. Telesio e la cultura napoletana. G Crit Filosof Ital, 69(1), 124-129, Ja-Ap 90.

STYK, Jozef. Conception of Values in Polish Sociology (in Polish). Ann Univ Mariae Curie-Phil, 11, 59-75, 1986.

The author presents a critical survey of definitions of social value proposed by Polish sociologists. Much attention is paid especially to F Znaniecki, W I Thomas, C Znamierowski, S Ossowski, J Szczapanski, K Grzegorczyk, G Kloska, M Misztal and S Jalowiecki. An attempt is also made to trace examples of empirical applications of particular definitions in studies by various authors. The author comes to a conclusion that the conceptions functioning so far reveal a number of drawbacks. He supports a solution of E Jagiello-Lysiowa who suggests a combining of studies on values with the problems of aspirations. (edited)

SUANCES MARCOS, M. Conocimiento y comunicación: Algunas reflexiones sobre la vida social. Pensamiento, 46(184), 419-443, O-D 90.

Este trabajo aborda fundamentalmente dos puntos: los complejos proceso del conocimiento, estudiados como factores decisivos para la comunicación en los diversos grupos humanos. Por lo que respecta a la primera cuestión se analizarán, en primer término, los que pudieran denominarse supuestos básicos del conocimiento: aquellos procesos que forman la urdimbre primera del conocer: el lenguaje preverbal, el mito, la magia y el propio cuerpo; se estudian luego las formas en que se plasman esos primeros procesos y se relacionan con los supuestos básicos de la comunicación como son el líder, el ansia del grupo, etc. El segundo punto es un estudio de las diversas formas grupales en que se plasman aquellos factores, yendo desde grupos estructuralmente más simples a grupos más complejos como el social y el político.

SUAREZ, Antoine. Hydatidiform Moles and Teratomas Confirm the Human Identity of the Preimplantation Embryo. J Med Phil, 15(6), 627-635, D 90.

Results of recent research on hydatidiform moles and teratomas show that during pregnancy the embryo does not receive any message or information from the mother able to control the mechanisms of development or to produce the type of cellular differentiation necessary for building the tissues of the new human adult. Thus, the biological identity of the new human being does not depend on the sojourn in the uterus; the preimplantation embryo is the same individual of the human species as the adult, into whom the embryo can in principle develop.

SUBRAHMANIAN, V S. Mechanical Proof Procedures for Many-Valued Lattice-Based Logic Programming. J Non-Classical Log, 7(1-2), 7-41, My-N 90.

Recent results of Blair, Brown and Subrahmanian and independently, M Fitting have shown that the declarative semantics of logic programs when interpreted over sets of truth values possessing some simple lattice theoretic properties shows remarkably little change. We prove here that the operational semantics (i.e., proof procedures) for such languages also show remarkably little change. The principal result is that under a natural condition of *support* a straightforward generalization of SLD-resolution is sound and complete WRT processing of queries over these differing logics.

SUBRAMANIAM, K and BHARGAVI, V. History, Indian Science and Policy-Making: A Philosophical Review. J Indian Counc Phil Res, 8(1), 115-128, S-D 90.

SUCHTING, W A. Hegel and the Humean Problem of Induction. Stud Hist Phil Sci, 21(3), 493-510, S 90.

The paper inquires into the significance of certain parts of Hegel's *Phenomenology of Spirit* and *Science of Logic* for Hume's formulation of the problem of induction. It concludes that Hegel's own treatment of relevant questions does not develop a satisfactory account but does give important clues to us which this paper sketches. (edited)

SUCHTING, W A. On Some Unsettled Questions Touching the Character of Marxism, Especially as Philosophy. Grad Fac Phil J, 14(1), 139-207, 1991.

The paper is concerned with two main issues. First, the question of the nature of historical materialism as a theory is posed and answered in terms of a general account of theories, applying to natural scientific theories also. According to this account, a theory is ultimately a set of connected concepts and 'axioms' which generate 'laws' when applied to models (not reality itself), all of which are used to analyse (explain/predict) real situations which are also concrete/particular. Second, it is asked in what sense Marxism can be or be associated with a 'philosophy'. The nature of this form of discourse as an historical phenomenon is analysed and a view of Marxist 'philosophy' as a 'standpoint' or 'policy' is defended.

SUGUMAR, Devaki. Marcel on the Problem of Freedom. Indian Phil Quart, SUPP 17(3), 37-45, Jl 90.

Existentialism conceives freedom of man as a goal which can be realised in this life itself. Man's capacity to choose between inauthentic existence and authentic existence forms the basis for his freedom. This general stand of the existentialists gains its fuller significance in Marcel thinking with his notion of commitment to God. The social significance of Marcel's conception of freedom consists in the fact that freedom should enable one to shed down his ego-centricism and to participate in the creative life of the society. In this connection Marcel's conception of freedom and grace and the need for ontological humility of man are studied in this paper.

SUKOSD, Miklos. From Propaganda to "Oeffentlichkeit" in Eastern Europe: Four Models of the Public Space Under State Socialism. Praxis Int, 10(1-2), 39-63, Ap-Jl 90.

SULLIVAN, Mark D. Reconsidering the Wisdom of the Body. J Med Phil, 15(5), 493-514, O 90.

Claude Bernard's concept of the internal environment (*milieu intérieur*) played a crucial role in the development of experimental physiology and the specific medical therapeutics derived from it. This concept allowed the experimentalist to approach the organism as fully determined yet relatively autonomous with respect to its external environment. However, Bernard's theory of knowledge required that he find organismic functioning as the result of an external necessity. He is therefore unable to explain adequately the origin or operation of organismic autonomy. A more complete conception of biological autonomy must include a theory of knowledge that can accommodate the organism as a source of discrimination and determination. Only in this way will it be possible to see organisms as active as well as reactive, as ordering as well as ordered. This shift in perspective is crucial if medicine is to be able to characterize, for example, susceptibility to disease. A cognitive sense of the organic interior is proposed as an alternative to Bernard's internal environment.

SULLIVAN, Patrick F. On Falsificationist Interpretations of Peirce. Trans Peirce Soc, 27(2), 197-219, Spr 91.

SULLIVAN, Patrick F. Pragmatics and Pragmatism. Phil Today, 35(2), 175-184, Sum 91.

SULLIVAN, T D. Coming To Be Without a Cause. Philosophy, 65(253), 261-270, Jl 90.

Quentin Smith contends that the Hawking-Penrose singularity theorems provide warrant for the belief that the universe came to be without a cause. I argue first that if there is one extramental causal event, it is impossible for the world to have arisen without a cause, and second that Smith's argument tacitly invokes a concept of cause rejected by sensible opponents.

SULLIVAN, Thomas D. Omniscience, Immutability, and the Divine Mode of Knowing. Faith Phil, 8(1), 21-35, Ja 91.

Recent attacks on the classical doctrine that God is both omniscient and immutable reason that God's knowledge of temporal events must be adequately expressible in indexical or nonindexical propositions, and that, on either account, the doctrine is incoherent. I argue that this is a false dilemma, that Aquinas exposed it as such, and that he offered a solution to the problem seldom considered by either proponents or opponents of the classical theory. I then defend Aquinas's neglected proposal.

SULLIVAN, Thomas D. "The Problem of Certitude: Reflections on the Grammar of Assent" in *Thomistic Papers, V*, RUSSMAN, Thomas A (ed), 63-80. Notre Dame, Univ Notre Dame Pr, 1990.

Many religions require absolute adherence to their tenets even though the evidence is less than compelling that God has revealed what is to be held. Can this requirement be justified? Drawing on an unconventional reading of Newman's *Grammar of Assent*, I argue that it can.

SULLIVAN, Thomas D. "A Reply to Russman's 'A Faith of True Proportions'" in *Thomistic Papers, V*, RUSSMAN, Thomas A (ed), 91-95. Notre Dame, Univ Notre Dame Pr, 1990.

Responding to me, Fr Thomas Russman claims that unqualified adherence to religious belief is justified only if the evidence of revelation is compelling in the light of grace. I spell out several unacceptable consequences for his view.

SULLIVAN, William M. "Bringing the Good Back In" in *Liberalism and the Good*, DOUGLASS, R Bruce (ed), 148-166. New York, Routledge, 1990.

SUMARES, Manuel. Acerca de uma tese ricoeuriana. Rev Port Filosof, 46(1), 125-142, Ja-Mr 90.

No one can doubt Ricoeur's contribution to contemporary thought. However, the presence of metaphysical postulates in his work limit the potential originality of his philosophical and religious project. Through the repetition of an especially fundamental thesis, the author of this article attempts to overcome this limit.

SUMMERFIELD, Donna M. Modest A Priori Knowledge. Phil Phenomenol Res, 51(1), 39-66, Mr 91.

A priori knowledge is out of fashion these days. And yet, we really could use something like a priori knowledge. In this paper, I articulate a minimal, or modest, notion of a priori warrant which shows that there is a position to be taken between those who make extravagant claims for our non-empirical knowledge and those who deny that what is non-empirical can be knowledge at all. More specifically, my characterization of a priori justification enables us to see both how we might have a priori knowledge that is defeasible and how we might have a priori knowledge within a reliabilist framework.

SUMMERFIELD, Donna M. Wittgenstein on Logical Form and Kantian Geometry. Dialogue (Canada), 29(4), 531-550, 1990.

Wittgenstein's analogy in the *Tractatus* between logical form and Kantian geometry is explored in detail by looking at the relevant texts. I then suggest that we regard the fact that Wittgenstein develops his account of logical form by analogy with a Kantian account of geometry as evidence for the bold thesis that Wittgenstein belongs within a Kantian epistemological tradition. Finally, I supply two small pieces of the interpretive puzzle needed to support the larger thesis; first, evidence that Wittgenstein's concern with logical form involves a crutical epistemological component; second, a sketch of how Wittgenstein's account of logical and mathematical knowledge can be viewed as continuing a Kantian tradition.

SUNDSTRÖM, Per. AIDS, Myth, and Ethics. Theor Med, 12(2), 151-156, Je 91.

The present paper is a commentary on an article by Larry Churchill. Churchill has argued that the negative attitudes and adverse behavior we commonly encounter in connection with (suspected) AIDS patients may be understood in terms of a dualistic 'myth' inspiring a 'ritual' avoidance of 'dirt', of 'dirt' as something that does not belong to a 'clean' world order. The deep-seated mythical character of attitudes and behavior here makes them less accessible to the kind of rational argument commonly employed in ethics. Churchill also proposes a remedy for the (morally outrageous) dualistic mythical-ritual behavior he has focused—a remedy that may be overly intellectualistic. (edited)

SUNSTEIN, Cass R. Preferences and Politics. Phil Pub Affairs, 20(1), 3-34, Wint 91.

This essay argues against the view that political outcomes should always reflect people's preferences. It claims that sometimes citizens have considered judgments that reject their own "preferences" as expressed in markets. Moreover, preferences are a product of the status quo, which can include injustice, and political outcomes can properly overcome preferences based on injustice. Drawing on theories of liberalism and democracy, the paper argues that preferences are shifting and endogenous. These ideas are applied to such areas as environmental policy, broadcasting, campaign finance, hate speech, and pornography.

SUNSTEIN, Cass R. "Routine and Revolution" in *Critique and Construction: A Symposium on Roberto Unger's "Politics"*, LOVIN, Robin W (ed), 46-70. New York, Cambridge Univ Pr, 1990.

SUNSTEIN, Cass R. Why Markets Don't Stop Discrimination. Soc Phil Pol, 8(2), 22-37, Spr 91.

SUPEK, Ivan. Ruder Boskovic as a Humanist and Scientist (in Serbo-Croatian). Filozof Istraz, 32-33(5-6), 1463-1470, 1989.

In the article it is pointed out that Ruder Boskovic is one of the great scientists who belonged to the humanist tradition of the new era. But ideal of the humanism has been gradually abandoned due to external and internal factors which are already apparent in the work of Ruder Boskovic. However, he remained, as some other Croatian scientists and philosophers, an authentic humanist. Although he was successful in many fields of science, he is best known after his major work: *Theoria philosophiae naturalis redacta ad unicam legem virium in Natura existentium*. The primary concept of the *Theoria* is the notion of a unique force which really was a farsighted idea. If we take this concept as fundamental for Boskovic, then we also have to look at matter and space in a new light. Ruder's new ideas spread over Europe and later over all the world, fascinating the minds of many excellent researchers to this day, particularly Faraday, with whom he was the founder of the physics of field; so that we could say that Boskovic also remains the inspiration of our time.

SUPPES, Patrick. "Philosophy and the Sciences" in *Acting and Reflecting: The Interdisciplinary Turn in Philosophy*, SIEG, Wilfried (ed), 3-30. Norwell, Kluwer, 1990.

SURBER, Jere. Individual and Corporate Responsibility: Two Alternative Approaches. Bus Prof Ethics J, 2(4), 67-88, Sum 83.

SURENDONK, Timothy J. A Lemma in the Logic of Action. Notre Dame J Form Log, 31(2), 222-224, Spr 90.

In this paper, a result is proved that has two consequences for Segerberg's logic of action. First, his general frames can be replaced by full frames without change to the logic; secondly, a certain rule is proved to be sound. (edited)

SURESON, Claude. About Prikry Generic Extensions. Annals Pure Applied Log, 51(3), 247-278, Mr 91.

SURIN, Kenneth. A Certain 'Politics of Speech': 'Religious Pluralism' in the Age of the McDonald's Hamburger. Mod Theol, 7(1), 67-100, O 90.

SUTHER, Judith D. "Dogmatism and Belief in French Cultural Life in the 1930s" in *From Twilight to Dawn: The Cultural Vision of Jacques Maritain*, REDPATH, Peter A (ed), 17-25. Notre Dame, Univ Notre Dame Pr, 1990.

In the contentious arena of French intellectual life in the 1930s, various -isms co-existed uneasily: Modernism, Surrealism, Existentialism, Catholicism, among others. Not mutually exclusive in principle, the groups tended to be antagonistic to one another in practice. Further, they elevated their own beliefs to the status of dogma, so that their discourse is characterized by the language of religious conversion. Few mediating voices arose in this devisive climate. A notable exception was Jacques Maritain. Although he could be as polemical as any Frenchman, on balance his record in the decade before World War II supports the principles of tolerance and mutual understanding over in-fighting and discord.

SUTHERLAND, Christine Mason. "Love as Rhetorical Principle: The Relationship Between Content and Style in the Rhetoric of St Augustine" in *Grace, Politics and Desire: Essays on Augustine*, MEYNELL, Hugo A (ed), 139-154. Calgary, Univ Calgary Pr, 1990.

Augustine of Hippo, a professor of Rhetoric before his conversion, condemns the practice of the orators of his day of allowing style to become an end in itself, without regard for the truth of the content. This debased practice, however, does not persuade him to ignore the classical theory of rhetoric in the advice he gives to Christian teachers. Rather, he uses the unifying Christian principle of love to modify the classical theory in such a way as to accommodate it to the needs of the Christian community.

SUTHERLAND, Stewart. "History, Truth, and Narrative" in *The Bible as Rhetoric: Studies in Biblical Persuasion and Credibility*, WARNER, Martin (ed), 105-116. New York, Routledge, 1990.

SUTHERLAND, Stewart. "Hope" in *The Philosophy in Christianity*, VESEY, Godfrey (ed), 193-206. New York, Cambridge Univ Pr, 1989.

SUTNER, Klaus. The Ordertype of β-R.E. Sets. J Sym Log, 55(2), 573-576, Je 90.

Let β be an arbitrary limit ordinal. A β-r.e. set is *I*-finite iff all its β-r.e. subsets are β-recursive. The *I*-finite sets correspond to the ideal of finite sets in the lattice of r.e. sets. We give a characterization of *I*-finite sets in terms of their ordertype: a β-r.e. set is *I*-finite iff it has ordertype less than β^*, the Σ_1 projectum of β.

SUTTLE, Bruce B. Do the Right Thing. Proc Phil Educ, 46, 360-363, 1990.

In "The Teacher as Judge" Michael S Katz recommends that teachers treat students fairly. Initially, I argue that teachers' obligations far exceed being fair. On the second tier, I examine Katz's belief that teachers not treating students fairly is traceable to the absence of clarification by teachers of their responsibilities. I suggest that Katz's position entails either a denial that one can discursively justify a prospective action and yet not be motivated to act accordingly or a doubt that one can intuit correctly what ought to be done, do it and yet not be able to offer discursive justification in its support.

SUTTON, Agneta. Arguments for Abortion of Abnormal Fetuses and the Moral Status of the Developing Embryo. Ethics Med, 6(1), 5-10, Spr 90.

This paper, a chapter from *Prenatal Diagnosis: Confronting the Ethical Issues* (published by The Linacre Centre, London 1990), undermines arguments for abortion by showing that on a neo-Boethian understanding of a person as an individual with a rational nature, as distinct from a Lockean definition in terms of *presently exercisable abilities*, it follows that human life is personal from the beginning. Because at fertilization a new being comes into existence inherent in whose nature are powers and potentialities without which it would not be able to grow into a mature human person.

SUZUKI, Nobu-Yuki. An Extension of Ono's Completeness Result. Z Math Log, 36(4), 365-366, 1990.

For each positive integer n, the intermediate predicate logic complete with respect to the class of all Kripke structures having constant domain, with height at most 2 and having at most n maximal elements is axiomatized by making use of Ono's method developed in his paper "Model extension theorem and Craig's interpolation theorem for intermediate predicate logics." Reports on Mathematical Logic 15, 41-58, 1983.

SUZUKI, Nobu-Yuki. Kripke Bundles for Intermediate Predicate Logics and Kripke Frames for Intuitionistic Modal Logics. Stud Log, 49(3), 289-306, S 90.

Shehtman and Skvortsov introduced Kripke bundles as semantics of non-classical first-order predicate logics. We show the structural equivalence between Kripke bundles for intermediate predicate logics and Kripke-type frames for intuitionistic modal propositional logics. This equivalence enables us to develop the semantical study of relations between intermediate predicate logics and intuitionistic modal propositional logics. New examples of modal counterparts of intermediate predicate logics are given.

SUZUKI, Nobu-Yuki. Some Syntactical Properties of Intermediate Predicate Logics. Notre Dame J Form Log, 31(4), 549-559, Fall 90.

In a previous paper the author introduced a syntactical property, which he calls the pseudo-relevance property, for the sake of studying a certain semantical aspect. An intermediate predicate logic L is said to have the *pseudo-relevance property* if for all formulas *A* and *B* which contain no predicate variable in common, either not-*A* or *B* is provable in L whenever *A* implies *B* is provable in L. The pseudo-relevance property can be regarded as a weak version of Craig's interpolation property. From the same point of view, one can see the similarity between Hallden-completeness and the disjunction property. We treat these syntactical properties and their weak versions, and study the relationships between them.

SVATON, Vladimir. The "Presuppositions" and "Realizations" in Aesthetics of Zdenek Mathauser (in Czechoslovakian). Estetika, 27(3), 184-191, 1990.

SWAIN, Margaret S and MARUSYK, Randy W. An Alternative to Property Rights in Human Tissue. Hastings Center Rep, 20(5), 12-15, S-O 90.

This article proposes a three-tiered legal structure to resolve the ethical dilemma surrounding human tissue: the need to keep it free of property rights, yet accommodate the creation of such rights in biotechnological products. The first level continues to recognize a *persona* or the *rights of publicity* in humans. The second level classifies all tissue temporarily removed from the body as *res nullius*. The third level classifies tissue that is permanently removed from the body as *res communes*, but allows property rights to be created in products developed with the use of human tissue through the investment of labor.

SWAMIDASAN, Nalini. Prediction and Explanation in Economics. J Indian Counc Phil Res, 5(3), 91-99, My-Ag 88.

SWANDA JR, John R. Goodwill, Going Concern, Stocks and Flows: A Prescription for Moral Analysis. J Bus Ethics, 9(9), 751-759, S 90.

This paper projects the decision-making dilemma faced by managers when assessing moral consequences associated with planning proposals. A case is made for viewing the results of moral behavior as a capital asset. Accepting the idea that moral business behavior proportionally influences the firm's goodwill value, the author advances the recommendation that current US accounting practices become involved with determining the moral wellness of the firm. The suggestion is made that stocks and flows are useful concepts in the development of a financial information system that incorporates benefits associated with morally accepted behavior. As a necessary part of the going concern operational strategy, a case is made for the preservation and advancement of the firm's moral capital. Overall, the intent of this paper is to offer a proposal which links moral behavior with financial decision making.

SWANGER, David. Discipline-Based Art Education: Heat and Light. Educ Theor, 40(4), 437-442, Fall 90.

The article assesses the views of Arnstine, Broudy and Eisner on discipline-based art education and focusses, in particular, on the problem of assigning equal weight and cognitive emphasis to the four domains of DBAE: art history, art criticism, aesthetic theory and creativity. The article concludes that the role of cognition in creativity is undeniable, but significantly different from cognition in historical, critical and theoretical understanding. Future directions in art education, and DBAE in particular, need therefore a more fully developed analysis of cognition in creativity, the basis of which is suggested in the article.

SWANN, Andrew J. Popper on Induction. Brit J Phil Sci, 39(3), 367-373, S 88.

The controversy surrounding Popper's proposed solution to the problem of induction is beginning to display many of the symptoms of being interminable. for decades the discussion has continued, apparently without any progress being made. Again and again, Popperians and their critics have accused each other of 'missing the point'. The essay attempts to explain what exactly *is* 'the point' of the problem of induction, and asks whether Popper does indeed miss it. An answer is proposed, and on this basis an explanation for the puzzling interminability and emptiness of the above dialogue is put forward.

SWANTON, Christine. Weakness of Will as a Species of Executive Cowardice. Can J Phil, 21(2), 123-140, Je 91.

SWAZEY, Judith P. Are Physicians a "Delinquent Community"?: Issues in Professional Competence, Conduct, and Self-Regulation. J Bus Ethics, 10(8), 581-590, Ag 91.

This paper examines the moral responsibilities of physicians, toward themselves and their colleagues, their students and patients, and society, in terms of the nature and exercise of professional self-regulation. Some of the author's "close encounters" with cases involving research misconduct, behavioral impairment or deviance, and medical practice at "the moral margin," are described to illustrate why, in Freidson's words, physicians are a "delinquent community" with respect to the ways they meet their responsibility to govern the competence and conduct of their members.

SWEET, William. Les "droits naturels" et les "titres" selon Robert Nozick. Lekton, 1(2), 81-98, 1991.

Robert Nozick argues that the "more than minimal" state cannot be justified because it would violate natural rights and entitlements. I begin by clarifying what he means by "natural rights" and "entitlements" and by examining the relations between them. Although Nozick uses these terms almost interchangeably, a close reading reveals several differences. I suggest, therefore, that Nozick's objections against limiting natural rights do not obviously apply to entitlements. Thus, even if one accepts the basic framework of Nozick's view, there are grounds to challenge his argument against the "more than minimal" state.

SWIDERSKI, E M (trans) and BUCHHOLZ, Arnold. The On-Going Deconstruction of Marxism-Leninism. Stud Soviet Tho, 40(1-3), 231-240, 1990.

The changes in the political and cultural life of the Soviet Union had a considerable time lead over changes in the official ideology. The decisive breakthrough into the ideology was in the autumn of 1989. The traditional studies subject of "Marxist-Leninist philosophy" was reorganized into the general subject of "philosophy," the subject "History of the CPSU" into "Socio-Political History of the 20th Century." The most significant conceptual synopsis of the "perestroika ideology" is to be found in the new teaching handbook for high schools under the title "Introduction into Philosophy." The crucial innovation embodied in this work is that the chapter on the so-called "basic question of philosophy," the fundamental materialistic postulate for all hierarchical derivations of ideology and practical consequences, has been dropped. The work also reveals the unmistakable attempt to draw upon Kantian philosophy in the interpretation of fundamental philosophical questions.

SWIGGERS, Pierre. "Comparatismo e grammatica comparata: Tipologia linguistica e forma grammaticale" in *Leibniz, Humboldt, and the Origins of Comparativism*, DE MAURO, Tullio (ed), 281-299. Philadelphia, John Benjamins, 1990.

The purpose of this article is to analyse, on the conceptual level, what crucially distinguishes the period of 'pre-comparativism' from comparative grammar. The essential distinction between both types of discursive formation lies in the integration, within comparative grammar, of three fundamental notions: 1) that of 'grammatical form'; 2) that of 'linguistic type', and 3) that of 'systematic mutations'. Each of these notions is linked with different aspects of the comparative method: the notion of grammatical form is correlated with the problem of the parameter of comparison (what should be compared?), that of linguistic type is correlated with the problem of the *non sequitur* of comparisons (we can never show that two languages are not genetically related). This conceptual analysis allows one to distinguish between pre-comparativism and 20th century comparative grammar, and to point to the 'transformations' of the comparative prace, in which Humboldt had an important role (cf the notion of grammatical form/language typology), although he did not, strictly speaking contribute to the advancement of comparative grammar.

SWIJTINK, Zeno G. Theory of the Apparatus and Theory of the Phenomena: The Case of Low Dose Electron Microscopy. Proc Phil Sci Ass, 1, 573-584, 1990.

In this paper I describe in the general deterministic case the possible relations between phenomena theory and instrument theory. I give a Bayesian criterion for when an experiment is a test of the theory of the apparatus, rather than a test of the theory of the phenomena, and describe strategies used to ensure that tests of the theory of the phenomena are possible. I end by extending this framework to low dose electron microscopy which has a stochastic instrument theory and which provides an exception to a thesis by Robert Ackermann on the independence between theory and instrumentation. In low dose electron microscopic imaging of macromolecules, a change in theory may lead to a change in how the instrument behaves.

SWINBURNE, R G. "Arguments for the Existence of God" in *Key Themes in Philosophy*, GRIFFITHS, A Phillips (ed), 121-133. New York, Cambridge Univ Pr, 1989.

In an inductive argument data increase the probability of a hypothesis insofar as the hypothesis makes probable the data, the data are otherwise not likely to occur, and the hypothesis is simple. The Cosmological argument from the existence of the universe, the Teleological argument from its conformity to natural law, and other arguments from more detailed features of the universe each increase the probability that there is a God. I thus summarize in simple form the main points of my book *The Existence of God*.

SWINBURNE, Richard. "Could God Become Man?" in *The Philosophy in Christianity*, VESEY, Godfrey (ed), 53-70. New York, Cambridge Univ Pr, 1989.

Christian orthodoxy has maintained that in Jesus Christ God became man, i.e., acquired a human nature, while remaining God. Given two not unreasonable restrictions on the understanding of "man", that claim is perfectly coherent. But if the New Testament is correct in claiming that in some sense Christ was ignorant, weak, and temptable, we have to suppose that Christ has a divided mind; or, in traditional terminology, that the two natures did not totally interpenetrate.

SWINBURNE, Richard. The Limits of Explanation. Philosophy, 27, 177-193, 90 Supp.

Scientific explanation in terms of laws and initial conditions (or better, in terms of objects with powers and liabilities) is contrasted with personal explanation in terms of agents with powers and purposes. In each case the factors involved in explanation may themselves be explained, and infinite regress of explanation is logically possible. There can be no absolute explanation of phenomena, which is explanation in terms of the logically necessary; but there can be ultimate explanation which is explanation in terms of factors which themselves have no explanation. Our normal criteria of explanation suggest that the explanation of the universe lies in the action of God.

SWINBURNE, Richard. Necessary A Posteriori Truth. Amer Phil Quart, 28(2), 113-123, Ap 91.

Two sentences express the same proposition if they are synonymous; they espress the same statement if they attribute the same properties to the same objects at the same time (however objects and times are picked out). Neither propositions nor statements are necessary a posteriori. Suggested examples of the necessary a posteriori, such as "Hesperus is Phosphorus", or "water is H_2O", only appear to be such because of a confusion between proposition and statement.

SWIRYDOWICZ, Kazimierz. On Regular Modal Logics with Axiom.... Stud Log, 49(2), 171-174, Je 90.

SWOYER, Chris. Structural Representation and Surrogative Reasoning. Synthese, 87(3), 449-508, Je 91.

It is argued that a number of important, and seemingly disparate, types of representation are species of a single relation, here called *structural representation*, that can be described in detail and studied in a way that is of considerable philosophical interest. A structural representation depends on the existence of a common structure between a representation and that which it represents, and it is important because it allows us to reason directly about the representation in order to draw conclusions about the phenomenon that it depicts. The present goal is to give a general and precise account of structural representation, then to use that account to illuminate several problems of current philosophical interest - including some that do not initially seem to involve representation at all. In particular, it is argued that ontological reductions (like that of the natural numbers to sets), compositional accounts of semantics, several important sorts of mental representation, and (perhaps) possible worlds semantics for intensional logics are all species of structural representation and are fruitfully studied in the framework developed here.

SYLVAN, Richard. On Making a Coherence Theory of Truth True. Philosophica, 46(2), 77-105, 1990.

SYLVAN, Richard. Related Semantics for All Lewis, Lemmon and Feys' Modal Logics. J Non-Classical Log, 6(2), 19-40, N 89.

SYLVAN, Richard. Relevant Containment Logics and Certain Frame Problems of AI. Log Anal, 31(121-122), 11-25, Mr-Je 88.

Relevant containment logics, which combine relevant logics with content containment requirements, are motivated and explained. Semantics for some of these logics are introduced and shown to be adequate. In the light of the semantics the logical theory is improved, and other directions for elaboration are indicated. Finally, the logics are applied to one significant part of the vexatious frame problems of *AI*, and a route to implementation is suggested.

SYLVAN, Richard. Variations on da Costa *C* Systems and Dual-Intuitionistic Logics (I). Stud Log, 49(1), 47-65, Mr 90.

Da Costa's *C* systems are surveyed and motivated, and significant failings of the systems are indicated. Variations are then made on these systems in an attempt to surmount their defects and limitations. The main system to emerge from this effort, system CC_{ω}, is investigated in some detail, and "dual-intuitionistic" semantical analyses are developed for it and surrounding systems. These semantics are then adapted for the original *C* systems, first in a rather unilluminating relational fashion, subsequently in a more illuminating way through the introduction of impossible situations where *and* and *or* change roles. Finally other attempts to break out of impasses for the original and expanded *C* systems, by going inside them, are looked at, and further research directions suggested.

SYMOTIUK, Stefan. Hope: Its Essence and Forms (in Polish). Ann Univ Mariae Curie-Phil, 11, 253-274, 1986.

The study constitutes a phenomenological analysis of "hope," including its objective aspects. An opinion is formulated about the "quasi-subjective" character of the objects of hope. According to the author, the situation of a full realization of hope, as a personality-shaping factor, consists in such a type of "reflexiveness" occurring in this feeling that a subject connects his hope with an object which, in turn, places its hope in this subject. In this situation there emerges a diagnosis of "being called" for something, consolidating the fundamental line of the biography of individuals and groups. (edited)

SYMOTIUK, Stefan. Social Space as a Determinant of "Collective Thinking" (in Polish). Ann Univ Mariae Curie-Phil, 10, 99-114, 1985.

The paper concerns problems from the borders of communication theory, microsociology and epistemology. The author reverses the thesis of the so-called "sociology of knowledge," namely, that social structures determine the forms and contents of thinking. He accepts an ideal of thinking which is creative, diverse, alternative, multidirectional. He is looking for systems in which it could be realized. One of such systems is a circle as a microsocial association.

SYNAN, Edward A. "St Thomas and Medieval Humanism" in *The Question of Humanism: Challenges and Possibilities*, GOICOECHEA, David (ed), 58-69. Buffalo, Prometheus, 1991.

Because there are varieties of "humanism" Thomas Aquinas can be designated a "humanist" as legitimately as, say, Thomas More. The more conventional humanism of More was grounded on Greek and Latin literary erudition and expertise. Although competent in technical Latin writing and in mediaeval Latin versification, Aquinas possessed a minimal acquaintance with Greek. Both shared a more fundamental "humanism". This metaphysical and theological vision of the human person was a major achievement of Aquinas. He saw each human person, not merely as an individual, but as oriented by nature to community and the common good.

SYNNING, Ralph. Art Works, But How?—Kant and Aesthetics/Heidegger and Truth. Gnosis, 3(3), 29-48, D 90.

The first half of this essay is devoted to a summary account of Kant's analysis of the subject's aesthetic power of judgment in the *Critique of Judgment*. The second half of the essay explores the limitations and deficiencies of the subjectivity in this account as illuminated by Heidegger in "The Origin of the Work of Art". Moving beyond Kant, Heidegger speaks of the work-being of a work of art—a broader view of the work of art in terms of a "becoming and happening of truth" which is related to a concrete time and place, and therefore to a specific culture. The problematic relations between artistic/cultural creation, truth, and power are then briefly discussed.

SZACKI, Jerzy. "Intellectuals between Politics and Culture" in *The Political Responsibility of Intellectuals*, MACLEAN, Ian (ed), 229-246. New York, Cambridge Univ Pr, 1990.

SZALAI, Erzsebet. Elites and Systematic Change in Hungary. Praxis Int, 10(1-2), 74-79, Ap-Jl 90.

SZANIAWSKI, Klemens. "On Fair Distribution of Indivisible Goods" in *Logic and Ethics*, GEACH, Peter (ed), 275-288. Norwell, Kluwer, 1991.

SZASZ, Thomas. Law and Psychiatry: The Problems That Will Not Go Away. J Mind Behav, 11(3-4), 557-563, Sum-Autumn 90.

The practice of psychiatry rests on two pillars: mental illness and involuntary mental hospitalization. Each of these elements justifies and reinforces the other. Traditionally, psychiatric coercion was unidirectional, consisting of the forcible incarceration of the individual in an insane asylum. Today, it is bidirectional, the forcible eviction of the individual from the mental hospital (which became the home) supplementing his or her prior forcible incarceration in it. So intimate are the connections between psychiatry and coercion that noncoercive psychiatry, like noncoercive slavery, is an oxymoron.

SZCZERBA, Leslaw and KRYNICKI, Michal. On Simplicity of Formulas. Stud Log, 49(3), 401-419, S 90.

Simple formula should contain only few quantifiers. In the paper the methods to estimate quantity and quality of quantifiers needed to express a sentence equivalent to given one.

SZE-KWANG, Lao. "On Understanding Chinese Philosophy: An Inquiry and a Proposal" in *Understanding the Chinese Mind: The Philosophical Roots*, ALLINSON, Robert E (ed), 265-293. New York, Oxford Univ Pr, 1989.

This paper offers an open concept of philosophy in order to improve communication between different philosophical traditions. Emphasis is placed upon a distinction between two functions of philosophical thinking, namely, cognitive and orientative function. Difficulties of understanding a philosophical tradition usually arise when people stick to one function of philosophy and ignore the other. This is especially true when European philosophers are confronted with an orientative philosophy of Chinese tradition. To overcome such difficulties, a new concept of philosophy is needed. In addition to a description of this basic idea, the later part of this paper includes an exposition of the doctrines of Mencius and Chuang-Tze as illustrations of orientative philosophy.

SZEREDI, Peter (ed) and WARREN, David H D (ed). *Logic Programming: Proceedings of the Seventh International Conference*. Cambridge, MIT Pr, 1990.

SZÍVÓS, Mihály. "The Role of Publicity in the Disintegration of the Hegelian School" in *Perspectives on Ideas and Reality*, NYÍRI, J C (ed), 85-97. Budapest, Kiskonyvtara, 1990.

SZLEZÁK, Thomas A. Struttura e finalità dei dialoghi platonici: Che cosa significa "venire in soccorso al discorso"? Riv Filosof Neo-Scolas, 81(4), 523-542, O-D 89.

The key concept of the criticism of writing (*Phaedrus* 274 b—278 e) is "helping one's writing." An examination of Plato's use of this concept shows that it has always the same meaning: helping a logos means introducing a second logos which goes substantially beyond the conceptual framework of the first one. By saying that the true *philosophos* must be able to "help his writing" orally, Plato means that oral philosophy must go substantially beyond the philosopher's written work. It would be wrong to conceive of Plato's oral theory of principles as of a mere continuation of the dialogues on the same level.

SZUMSKI, Bonnie (ed). *The Health Crisis*. Saint Paul, Greenhaven Pr, 1989.

This book offers short articles on a variety of opposing viewpoints in the question of health and health care. Topics include AIDS, health care for the elderly, privitization of health care, and ideas on improving health. (staff)

SZYDLOWSKI, Piotr. Philosophy of Culture in the Works of Szymon Starowolski (1588-1656) (in Polish). Ann Univ Mariae Curie-Phil, 10, 177-191, 1985.

Among extensive studies on Starowolski this is the first attempt to extract his philosophy of culture from his "nonphilosophical" writings. The author presents Starowolski's ideas about man as a subject and object of philosophy of culture. Although he belonged to the Counter-Reformation camp, Starowolski did not carry out counter-Renaissance activities; he did not participate in destroying the humanistic ideals of the Polish Renaissance. On the basis of the analysis of personality patterns contained in Starowolski's *Hekatontas* (Venetiis 1625, 1627), the criteria of their selection and values represented by these patterns, as well as on the basis of the analysis of the central philosophical categories of Starowolski's anthropology, the author comes to the conclusion that philosophy of culture contained in Starowolski's writings is a Renaissance philosophy.

SZYMANEK, Krzysztof. Information Functions with Applications. Stud Log, 49(3), 387-400, S 90.

The definition and fundamental properties of information functions are presented. Information functions establish a correspondence between sets of formulas and the information contained in them. The intuitions for the notion of information stem from the conception of Bar-Hillel and Carnap. The introduced notions are applied to the logic of theory change and for proving two theorems about lattices of classical subtheories and their content.

TABORSKY, Edwina. Three Realities and Two Discourses. Method Sci, 22(3), 159-167, 1989.

The three spatial realities, Material, Group and Individual operate within two discursive time frames, Current and Temporal Discourse. Material Reality is an interaction between the individual as a physical being and the sensuousity of the environment within current time. Group reality is abstracted from sensuality and exists as social logic or long-term reason within Temporal Discourse, a time frame of past imagery and future intentionality. Individual Reality is also a current-time interaction, but with the addition of reason and understanding of the sensuous experience of Material Reality. We do not move directly from the sensuous experience of Material Reality to Individual Reality. The non-current logic of Group Reality assists the individual in moving from simple sensuous awareness to reasoned understanding.

TACELLI, Ronald K. Cook Wilson as Critic of Bradley. Hist Phil Quart, 8(2), 199-205, Ap 91.

TADD, G V. The Market for Bodily Parts: A Response to Ruth Chadwick. J Applied Phil, 8(1), 95-102, 1991.

Largely as a result of public outcry, legislation has recently been passed in the UK prohibiting the sale of bodily parts. This topic was the focus of a recent article in *Journal of Applied Philosophy* by Ruth Chadwick, which acknowledged that difficulties might exist in trying to distinguish between the selling of one's bodily organs and the selling of one's labour. The position argued for, in the ensuing discussion, is that there is no relevant moral difference between the two acts. Furthermore it contests the view that the sale of bodily organs should necessarily be prohibited. The assertion is made that the legislation does little to prevent the general exploitation of the type of person likely to be involved in such transactions, places unnecessary restrictions on the autonomy of individuals, and does nothing to promote an enhanced moral attitude by health professionals.

TAGATZ, George. "Medical Techniques for Assisted Reproduction" in *Beyond Baby M: Ethical Issues in New Reproductive Techniques*, BARTELS, Dianne M (ed), 89-110. Clifton, Humana Pr, 1990.

TAKANO, Mitio and YAMAKAMI, Tomoyuki. Classification of Intermediate Predicate Logics Under the Type of Deductive Completeness. Rep Math Log, 24, 17-23, 1990.

Deductive completeness of a logic assures the equivalence of provability and validity. Strong completeness does that of propositions with premises, while weak completeness that of propositions without any premises. So, the former imples the latter; but those logics certainly exist which are weakly complete but are not strongly complete. By introducing some notions of deductive completeness intermediary between strong completeness and weak one, we classified intermediate predicate logics under types; two logics have the same type if and only if in each of our senses, both are complete or both are not.

TAKANO, Mitio and MINARI, Pierluigi and ONO, Hiroakira. Intermediate Predicate Logics Determined by Ordinals. J Sym Log, 55(3), 1099-1124, S 90.

The paper deals with intermediate predicate logics which are semantically determined by classes of well-ordered Kripke frames with constant domain. The aim—loosely speaking—is to see whether and to what extent ordinals can be defined modulo Kripke-type semantics by sets of first-order formulas. The various results presented in the paper give partial answers to this question, both for countable and uncountable ordinals.

TAKEUTI, Gaisi and KRAJICEK, Jan and PUDLÁK, Pavel. Bounded Arithmetic and the Polynomial Hierarchy. Annals Pure Applied Log, 52(1-2), 143-153, Ap 91.

Bounded arithmetic is a fragment of Peano arithmetic with induction axioms restricted to bounded formulas only. The main problem is to show that bounded arithmetic is not finitely axiomatizable. We have proved this using the assumption that the polynomial-time hierarchy does not collapse. This assumption is a famous unproved conjecture in complexity theory.

TALBOTT, Thomas. Providence, Freedom and Human Destiny. Relig Stud, 26(2), 227-245, Je 90.

TALBOTT, W J. Two Principles of Bayesian Epistemology. Phil Stud, 62(2), 135-150, My 91.

The author argues that two principles of Bayesian epistemology, Conditionalization and Reflection, are not necessary, for epistemic rationality—not even as idealization. The author argues that the type of idealization required by these two principles is importantly different from that of other idealizing principles in the literature. The author also responds to Dutch Strategy defenses of the two principles.

TALEGÓN, César. Las proposiciones de relativo en Alberto de Sajonia. Rev Filosof (Venezuela), 13, 95-106, 1989.

TALIAFERRO, Charles. The Limits of Power. Phil Theol, 5(2), 115-124, Wint 90.

One argument that there cannot exist a being who creates all laws of nature was first outlined by J L Mackie, and further developed by Gilbert Fulmer. Fulmer's version of the argument is examined, together with a recent neo-Cartesian counterargument. The Menzel-Morris thesis holds that God's power extends to creating his own nature. I argue that Fulmer's argument is false, but that it can sustain counterarguments of the type formulated by Menzel-Morris.

TALMAGE, Catherine J L and MERCER, Mark. Meaning Holism and Interpretability. Phil Quart, 41(164), 301-315, Jl 91.

The authors argue that while meaning holism makes massive error possible, it does not, as Donald Davidson fears, threaten interpretability. Thus they hold, in opposition to Davidson, that meaning holism need not be constrained by an account of meaning according to which in the methodologically most basic cases the content of a belief is given by the cause of that belief. What ensures interpretability, they maintain, is not that speakers's beliefs are in the main true, but rather that beliefs have the contents they do because of events others can in principle identify and describe.

TALMOR, Sascha. *The Concert*: Mao's Panopticon. Hist Euro Ideas, 12(6), 843-851, 1990.

Ismaïl Kadaré's great novel *The Concert* (1989) can be seen as the imaginative equivalent of Bentham's "Panopticon," used by Foucault in *Discipline and Punish* as emblem of any repressive society. Kadaré, the eminent Albanian man of letters, presents life in China during the last years of Mao's rule as a carceral universe, where man has been forced to lose his individuality and humanity. China, Russia, and Albania are shown to be dystopias or nightmares. Like *War and Peace*, the novel is multilayered, multifaceted, and finally optimistic. Man's "singularity" will save him from submergence in the undifferentiated mass.

TAMARI, Meir. Ethical Issues in Bankruptcy: A Jewish Perspective. J Bus Ethics, 9(10), 785-789, O 90.

The ethical issues involved in bankruptcy affect the debtor, the creditor and the society in which they operate. Facing the debtor is his responsibility to pay back the loans and credit extended to him while the creditor has to decide whether or not to press his legal rights, irrespective of the consequences to the debtor. Society will have to determine to what extent, if any, it is prepared or obligated to fund the rehabilitation of the debtor and those employees, whose employment is terminated as a result of the bankruptcy. These issues will be determined according to the value structure of the particular souly in which debtor and creditor operate. This paper views the issues in a Jewish perspective. (edited)

TAMÁS, G M. "The Political Irresponsibility of Intellectuals" in *The Political Responsibility of Intellectuals*, MACLEAN, Ian (ed), 247-256. New York, Cambridge Univ Pr, 1990.

The essay tries to prove that the current radically libertarian view of the freedom of expression is irreconcilable with any strong doctrine of responsibility for public utterances, including theoretical writing. Examining briefly some disastrous consequences of philosophers and artists advocating totalitarian regimes and even genocide, the author questions the point of moral theory in view of a lack of responsibility forced upon us by our knowledge of paternalistic or authoritarian control of speech.

TAMBA, Akira. "'Tradition' et 'Innovation' dans la musique" in *XIth International Congress in Aesthetics, Nottingham 1988*, WOODFIELD, Richard (ed), 221-224. Nottingham, Nottingham Polytech, 1990.

TAMBURRINI, Guglielmo and SPRUIT, Leen. Reasoning and Computation in Leibniz. Hist Phil Log, 12(1), 1-14, 1990.

Leibniz's overall view of the relationship between reasoning and computation is discussed on the basis of two broad claims that one finds in his writings, concerning respectively the nature of human reasoning and the possibility of replacing human thinking by a mechanical procedure. A joint examination of these claims enables one to appreciate the wide scope of Leibniz's interests for mechanical procedures, concerning a variety of philosophical themes further developed both in later logical investigations and in methodological contributions to cognitive psychology.

TAMINIAUX, Jacques. Le mouvement phénoménologique. Rev Phil Louvain, 88(78), 243-254, My 90.

TAMIR, Yael. Whose Education Is It Anyway? J Phil Educ, 24(2), 161-170, Wint 90.

This paper challenges a very common and long-held assumption: the assumption that parents have a right to educate their children. I should say from the start that my main objection is to the use of the term 'right' in this context. I will argue that there can be no 'right to educate'. The refutation of possible justifications of 'a right to educate', as I shall demonstrate, does not depend on the identity of the educator, or the content of the education given. The thrust of my argument is that no person or institution, under any circumstances, has a right to educate. If this is true, then educator-centered theories cannot be justified.

TAN, Y H and JANSSEN, M C W. Why Friedman's Non-Monotonic Reasoning Defies Hempel's Covering Law Model. Synthese, 86(2), 255-284, F 91.

In this paper we will show that Hempel's covering law model can't deal very well with explanations that are based on incomplete knowledge. In particular the symmetry thesis, which is an important aspect of the covering law model, turns out to be problematic for these explanations. We will discuss an example of an electric circuit, which clearly indicates that the symmetry of explanation and prediction does not always hold. It will be argued that an alternative logic for causal explanation is needed. And we will investigate to what extent non-monotonic epistemic logic can provide such an alternative logical framework. Finally we will show that our non-monotonic logical analysis of explanation is not only suitable for simple cases such as the electric circuit, but that it also sheds new light on more controversial causal explanations such as Milton Friedman's explanation of the business cycle.

TANAKA, Kazuyuki. Weak Axioms of Determinacy and Subsystems of Analysis II. Annals Pure Applied Log, 52(1-2), 181-193, Ap 91.

TANJI, Nobuharu. Quine on Theory and Language. Brit J Phil Sci, 40(2), 233-247, Je 89.

This paper proposes an articulation and improvement of Quine's model of theories (or beliefs) and language in his later works. The compatibility between "change of theory" and "change of language" is derived from the non-transitivity of (quasi-)sameness of language. And a realistic picture of scientific change is obtained by what I call the "Principle of Compensation". That principle also gives a natural account of the "theory-ladenness of observation", which explains the reciprocal supporting of theory and observation. The privileged status of observation sentences is denied without any difficulty concerning the learnability of language.

TAO, Julia. The Chinese Moral Ethos and the Concept of Individual Rights. J Applied Phil, 7(2), 119-127, O 90.

This paper is concerned with the contrast in views between traditional mainstream Chinese philosophy and Western liberal individualism on the importance of the concept of individual rights in social and political thought. The contrast is striking because, whereas individual and political rights have long featured in public discourse in the West, in China, mainstream social and political thought has developed without a notion of individual rights. In search of the significance of this major difference, the paper traces ideas of the self in China through Confucian ethics, and compares the Confucian conception of the self with the deontological liberal conception of the subject as a bearer of rights in the West. Having established that the Chinese way of thinking about the self and about moral agency is in stark contrast to the image of the self as a bearer of rights in the deontological conception, the paper goes on to discuss the inadequacy of the moral individualism of a rights-based morality and argues for an alternative view of morality which places importance on the intrinsic value of collective goods and on membership in a society.

TAPANI KLAMI, Hannu. Non-professional Judicial Reasoning. Riv Int Filosof Diritto, 67(1), 93-114, Ja-Mr 90.

TARBOX JR, Everett J. The A/Theology of Don Cupitt: A Theological Option in Our Post-Modern Age. Relig Hum, 25(2), 72-82, Spr 91.

The article introduces American readers to the thought of Don Cupitt, Dean of Emmanuel College, Cambridge. It summarizes Cupitt's theological development in the 1970s and 1980s, focusing primarily on his shift from "theological realism" to a post-modern "anti-realism." His later position presupposes two theses: theology must be post-revelatory and post-domatic, and must be post-metaphysical. Our age has become radically post-theistic in the sense that the leading theologians have left traditional metaphysical belief in God very far behind. However, there are still possibilities for religious thought in a post-theistic age.

TASSET, José L. La ética de Adam Smith: un utilitarismo de la simpatía. Themata, 6, 197-213, 1989.

TAUER, Carol. "Essential Ethical Considerations for Public Policy on Assisted Reproduction" in *Beyond Baby M: Ethical Issues in New Reproductive Techniques*, BARTELS, Dianne M (ed), 65-86. Clifton, Humana Pr, 1990.

Government commissions have identified three basic ethical principles to guide the formation of public policy on biomedical research and medical ethics: respect for persons, well-being, and equity. In this article the three principles are applied to two types of assisted reproduction: external fertilization and contract motherhood. Because our society lacks a consensus on the moral status of early embryos, the principles do not yield clear conclusions on practices related to external fertilization. However, the principles of respect for persons and equity both support the conclusion that commercial contract motherhood should be prohibited.

TAVAKOL, R K. Fragility and Deterministic Modelling in the Exact Sciences. Brit J Phil Sci, 42(2), 147-156, Je 91.

The theoretical framework adopted in the exact sciences, for constructing and testing deterministic theories on the one hand, and modelling and analysis of observed phenomena on the other, is often implicity assumed to be that of structural stability. In view of recent developments in nonlinear dynamics, it is argued here that in general it may not be possible to assume strict determinism and structural stability simultaneously; either strict determinism holds, in which case the *fragility framework* may turn out to be the appropriate framework for the study of certain phenomena in the exact sciences, or 'structural stability' is restored at the expense of introducing stochasticity. In this sense a certain degree of *indeterminacy* may be unavoidable even at the classical level.

TAVARES DE MIRANDA, Maria. Art et mystère. Diotima, 18, 30-33, 1990.

TAVUZZI, Michael. Aquinas on Resolution in Metaphysics. Thomist, 55(2), 199-227, Ap 91.

TAYLOR, Barry. 'Just More Theory': A Manoeuvre in Putnam's Model-Theoretic Argument for Antirealism. Austl J Phil, 69(2), 152-166, Je 91.

Putnam ['Models and Reality', *Realism and Reason* (CUP 1983) 1-25] challenged the metaphysical realist to show why the Completeness Theorem, in demonstrating that the ideal theory has a model, does not guarantee that the ideal theory is *true*, contrary to realism's claim that it might be false. One response is that the Completeness-guaranteed model need not assign the 'right' referents to the ideal theory's constants. Putnam replies with the 'Just More Theory Manoeuvre', to which however David Lewis has a convincing-looking answer ['Putnam's Paradox' AJP 62 (1984) 221-36]. This paper defends the Manoeuvre against Lewis's countermove.

TAYLOR, Charles. Comments and Replies. Inquiry, 34(2), 237-254, Je 91.

TAYLOR, Charles. "Rorty in the Epistemological Tradition" in *Reading Rorty*, MALACHOWSKI, Alan (ed), 257-275. Cambridge, Blackwell, 1991.

In this article, I attempt to criticize Rorty's epistemological view, on the grounds of an ultimate incoherence which comes to light when this view is applied to itself.

TAYLOR, David. "Hysteria, Belief and Magic" in *Harré and His Critics*, BHASKAR, Roy (ed), 272-287. Cambridge, Blackwell, 1990.

TAYLOR, James E. Epistemic Justification and Psychological Realism. Synthese, 85(2), 199-230, N 90.

The main thesis of this paper is that it is not possible to determine the nature of epistemic justification apart from scientific psychological investigation. I call this view "the strong thesis of methodological psychologism." Two sub-theses provide the primary support for this claim. The first sub-thesis is that no account of epistemic justification is correct which requires for the possession of at least one justified belief a psychological capacity which humans do not have. That is, the correct account of epistemic justification must be psychologically realistic. The second sub-thesis is that it is not possible to determine whether an account of epistemic justification is psychologically realistic apart from scientific psychological investigation. After defending these sub-theses, I point out some interesting consequences of the overall thesis which present a challenge to traditional epistemology.

TAYLOR, Mark C. "Back to the Future" in *Postmodernism—Philosophy and the Arts (Continental Philosophy III)*, SILVERMAN, Hugh J (ed), 13-32. New York, Routledge, 1990.

TAYLOR, Peter J and BLUM, Ann S. Ecosystems as Circuits: Diagrams and the Limits of Physical Analogies. Biol Phil, 6(2), 275-294, Ap 91.

Diagrams refer to the phenomena overtly represented, to analogous phenomena, and to previous pictures and their graphic conventions. The diagrams of ecologists Clarke, Hutchinson, and H. T. Odum reveal their search for physical analogies, building on the success of World War II science and the promise of cybernetics. H T Odum's energy circuit diagrams reveal also his aspirations for a universal and natural mean of reducing complexity to guide the management of diverse ecological and social systems. Graphic conventions concerning framing and translation of ecological processes onto the flat printed page facilitate Odum's ability to act as if ecological relations were decomposable into systems and could be managed by analysts external to the system.

TAYLOR, Peter J and BLUM, Ann S. Pictorial Representation in Biology. Biol Phil, 6(2), 125-134, Ap 91.

This introduction provides an overview of a special issue of *Biology and Philosophy* concerning the use of diagrams in biology. The introduction, as well as the articles, aims to stimulate philosophers, historians and sociologists of science to direct their attention to the role and special characteristics of pictorial and graphic representation in biology. We emphasize the heterogeneity of practice of representation in different circumstances, historical continuities in graphic conventions, and the cross-referential character of all images—perceptual, conceptual, verbal, and graphic.

TAYLOR, Rodney. *History and the Paradoxes of Metaphysics in "Dantons Tod"*. New York, Lang, 1990.

This book focuses on the relationship between literature and philosophy as found in a major play written by the nineteenth-century German dramatist, Georg Büchner. *Dantons Tod* depicts a tragic collision of ethical and utopian *Freiheitsideale* with irrational, insuperable historical specificities. In the course of the play, Büchner's monumental characters—Danton, Payne and Robespierre—articulate varying, often contradictory, metaphysical interpretations of their historical situation. This study contains a detailed analysis of these interpretations, illuminating their sources in the philosophical systems of Spinoza and Hegel, and in the philosophical reflections of the young Feuerbach.

TAYLOR, William and KONSTANTELLOU, Eva. The Question of Responsibility in the Context of Instructional Technology. J Thought, 25(1-2), 113-125, Spr-Sum 90.

TECZA, Beata. Selected Problems of Albert Caracciolo's Philosophy of Culture (in Polish). Ann Univ Mariae Curie-Phil, 10, 193-201, 1985.

The main domains of the considerations of Albert Caracciolo, a representative of Italian existentialism, are philosophy of religion and philosophy of art. The understanding of the meanings of the central categories in his thought about art and relations pertaining among them makes it possible to grasp more exactly the construction of Caracciolo's philosophical system of art. These concepts include art, god's space, *poiesis*, poetry, music, *Augenblick*, αθανατοσ, temporality and eternity, *catharsis*, action and works as well as the sense of life. Caracciolo orders the already existing theories of art, interprets them, looking for his own answers to the problems of this domain, but he mainly poses new questions and, hence, new tasks for philosophy of culture. (edited)

TEICHMANN, Roger. The Chicken and the Egg. Mind, 100(399), 371-372, Jl 91.

The following both seem possibly true: 1) Every chicken is born of chicken; 2) Chickens have not always existed. But how can they be compatible? An answer is proposed, according to which "chicken" is a vague (Sorites) term. If chickens gradually evolved from non-chickens, no chicken was born of non-chicken, so 1) would be satisfied; 2) also. An a prion consideration in favors of theories of evolution?

TEICHMANN, Roger. Future Individuals. Phil Quart, 41(163), 194-211, Ap 91.

The impossibility of backwards causation and a causal theory of reference together imply the impossibility of reference to (wholly) future individuals. But existential claims like "Someone will be born here" seem possibly-true. The article shows how a certain substitutionalist approach to quantification can cope with these facts. An assumption about the sayability of propositions is drawn out and justified. "Future facts" are discussed. Some sentences involving "actually" and future quantification are looked at.

TEJERA, V. On the Form and Authenticity of the *Lysis*. Ancient Phil, 10(2), 173-191, Fall 90.

TELFER, Elizabeth. The Unity of Moral Virtues in Aristotle's *Nicomachean Ethics*. Proc Aris Soc, 90, 35-48, 1989-90.

Aristotle argues that if a person possesses one moral virtue he must have practical wisdom and if he has practical wisdom he must have all the moral virtues. The first claim is plausible, but the second is false: the possibility of self-control shows that practical wisdom requires not moral virtue but only "well-disposedness." The most Aristotle can claim is that practical wisdom leads us to seek moral virtues and that it is vulnerable without them. A more plausible argument for the unity of the moral virtues would rest not on the role of practical wisdom but on the need for a harmony of emotional dispositions.

TELLER, Davida Y. Simpler Arguments Might Work Better. Phil Psych, 4(1), 51-60, 1991.

The article is an invited commentary on C L Hardin's *Color for Philosophers: Unweaving the Rainbow* (1988, Hackett, Indianapolis). It is argued that the trichromacy of color vision provides an important example of successful explanation of mental (color) events on the basis of physical (physiological) events.

TELLER, Paul. Prolegomenon to a Proper Interpretation of Quantum Field Theory. Phil Sci, 57(4), 594-618, D 90.

This paper digests technical commonplaces of quantum field theory to present an informal interpretation of the theory by emphasizing its connections with the harmonic oscillator. The resulting "harmonic oscillator interpretation" enables newcomers to the subject to get some intuitive feel for the theory. The interpretation clarifies how the theory relates to observation and to quantum mechanical problems connected with observation. Finally the interpretation moves some way towards helping us see what the theory comes to physically. The paper also argues that, in important respects, interpretive problems of quantum field theory are problems we know well from conventional quantum mechanics. An important exception concerns extending the puzzles surrounding the superposition of properties in conventional quantum mechanics to an exactly parallel notion of superposition of particles. Conventional quantum mechanics seems incompatible with a classical notion of property on which all quantities always have definite values. Quantum field theory presents an exactly analogous problem with saying that the number of "particles" is always definite.

TELLER, Paul. Substance, Relations, and Arguments About the Nature of Space-Time. Phil Rev, 100(3), 363-397, Jl 91.

TEMBROWSKI, Bronislaw. *B*-Varieties with Normal Free Algebras. Stud Log, 48(4), 555-564, D 89.

TEMKIN, Jack. Wittgenstein on Criteria and Other Minds. S J Phil, 28(4), 561-593, Wint 90.

TEN, C L. "Crime and Punishment" in *A Companion to Ethics*, SINGER, Peter (ed), 366-372. Cambridge, Blackwell, 1991.

TENG, Yu-jen. Logic and the Young Child. Thinking, 9(2), 40-42, 1990.

Logic, as an ongoing research, is structured and restructured by philosophical experiences. The purpose of this paper is to explore an alternative learning process by which children can understand better first-order logic. This learning process, in the methodological considerations, will be seen as triggered by puzzlement, especially playful puzzlement, and these puzzles are to be dealt with by thought experiments, which are viewed as games of thinking about thinkings. To learn logic in this view is to learn it philosophically.

TENNANT, Neil. Truth Table Logic with a Survey of Embeddability Results. Notre Dame J Form Log, 30(3), 459-484, Sum 89.

What logic is barely justified on the basis of the 'meanings' given to the connectives by the *left-right readings* of their truth tables? We set out a system T, consisting of normal proofs constructed by means of elegantly symmetrical introduction and elimination rules. In the system T there are two requirements on applications of discharge rules. We then consider a 'Duhemian' extension T*, obtained simply by dropping one of the requirements on the discharge rules. Our main result is that T* is a double negation consistency companion to classical logic. We survey all the embeddability results using various translation mappings "downwards" into subsystems of classical, intuitionistic, minimal, and intuitionistic relevant logic. (edited)

TENT, Katrin. The Application of Montague Translations in Universal Research and Typology. Ling Phil, 13(6), 661-686, D 90.

The idea of this paper is to construct intertranslatable Montague-grammars that allow for language comparison viewing languages as functional systems. Assuming these grammars to be given for all natural languages, this yields a universal framework defining the class of possible human languages. From the correspondence between syntax and semantics it is also expected to give a structural description of the semantic universe. This approach is applied to relative clause constructions in Finnish, Japanese, English, and Indonesian.

TER HARK, M R M. The Development of Wittgenstein's Views about the Other Minds Problem. Synthese, 87(2), 227-253, My 91.

The purpose of this article is to trace the development of Wittgenstein's views about the other minds problem from his Philosophical Remarks to the Philosophical Investigations. Much use is made of unpublished manuscripts that often give much insight into the meaning of published remarks. It is shown that Wittgenstein in the early thirties endorses a form of logical behaviourism that reminds strongly of Carnaps behaviourism. His rejection of the argument by analogy provides the main reason for his behaviourism about other minds. From 1933 onwards Wittgenstein articulates a non-introspectionistic as well as a non-behaviouristic analysis of the first person. Not until 1941 does he come to realise that he still has to offer arguments that demonstrate the untenability of logical behaviourism about other minds. First a non-behaviouristic interpretation is given of his expression "Einstellung zur Seele". Second, it is shown how he even manages to solve the problem of pretending, without falling into the trap of either introspectionism or behaviourism.

TERPSTRA, David E and REYES, Mario G C and BOKOR, Donald W. Predictors of Ethical Decisions Regarding Insider Trading. J Bus Ethics, 10(9), 699-710, S 91.

This paper examines potential predictors of ethical decisions regarding insider trading. An interactionist perspective is taken, in which person variables, situational variables, and the interaction of these two sets of variables are viewed as influencing ethical decisions. The results of our study support such a perspective. Ethical decisions regarding insider trading appear to be a function of a complex set of interacting variables related to both the person and the situation. The implications of these findings are discussed.

TERSMAN, Folke. Utilitarianism and the Idea of Reflective Equilibrium. S J Phil, 29(3), 395-406, Fall 91.

TESCHNER, George and MC CLUSKY, Frank. Computer Alternatives in the History of Philosophy Classroom. Teach Phil, 13(3), 273-280, S 90.

The article describes the pedagogical and cognitive theory behind, and implementation of software that is used for teaching the history of philosophy. The software replaces traditional classroom teaching by presenting the reading assignments in a hypertext format that allows the student to receive exegetical comments on the text. Computerized questions allow for an individualized teaching and testing environment by branching the questions and providing hints and explanations. The program records student work in a database which is used for automated advising and diagnosis. The paper discusses the advantages of computer based instruction, the theory behind the design of exegetical hypertext, and the future development of such technology.

TESKE, Roland J. William of Auvergne and the Eternity of the World. Mod Sch, 67(3), 187-205, Mr 90.

This article examines the reaction of William of Auvergne to the Aristotelian claims that the world was eternal. It shows that William's position was strikingly similar to that of Robert Grosseteste on a number of points. Indeed, William's position is not merely similar to Grosseteste's, but William seems to have anticipated him on these points by almost a decade. Hence, if Grosseteste's views are later reflected in the Franciscan tradition, William's arguments are reflected there as well.

TESKE, Roland. Bradley and Lonergan's Relativist. Phil Theol, 5(2), 125-136, Wint 90.

Bernard Lonergan contrasts his account of judgment with that of the relativist. This paper points out how Lonergan's characterization of the relativist account of judgment closely resembles the account of judgment that F H Bradley had given. Furthermore, the paper points to areas of commonality between Lonergan and Bradley with regard to human knowing. Despite their similarities, however, Lonergan's account of judgment clearly distinguishes his theory of knowing from anything like Bradley's idealism.

TESSIN, Timothy (trans) and ROSE, Rebecca Fine (trans) and WEIL, Simone. Essay on the Notion of Reading. Phil Invest, 13(4), 297-303, O 90.

TESSITORE, Fulvio. Croce e la storia della cultura. Arch Stor Cult, 4, 307-309, 1991.

L' Autore ripubblica, rifacendosi alle prime edizioni, la ben nota memoria crociana del 1875 *Intorno alla storia della coltura (Kulturgeschichte)* e il saggio *Storia economico-politica e storia etico-politica* (1924). Ad essi fanno corona due brevissime note: la prima apparsa ne "La Critica" del 1928 e la seconda, assai tarda, del 1952, sulla *Storia della cultura*. La rilettura di questi testi, purrisalendo a momenti diversi della riflessione crociana, consente di cogliere la spina dorsale della concezione della storia elaborata dal filosofo lungo sessant' anni di discussioni e polemiche sul *Methodenstreit* con i principali storici tedeschi della fine dell'800 (da F Meinecke a M Weber).

THALOS, Mariam and BACCHUS, Fahiem and KYBURG JR, Henry E. Against Conditionalization. Synthese, 85(3), 475-506, D 90.

This paper presents a challenge to the doctrines of Bayesian epistemology by a critical analysis of Bayesian principles. We first examine the Dutch Book principle, pointing out that an agent with logical capabilities can avoid a Dutch even if he does not possess a unique distribution over his beliefs. We then examine a dynamic Dutch Book argument, presented by Teller, that claims to support conditioning. We argue that it provides not much more than the static Dutch Book arguments. Finally we examine van Fraassen's principle of reflection, and conclude that rather than enforcing reasonable behavior, this principle can force an agent to do what is unreasonable.

THATCHER, Ian D. Trotsky's Dialectic. Stud Soviet Tho, 41(2), 127-144, Mr 91.

The paper aims to fill the gap between the commonly held rejection of Trotsky as philosopher and justification for this view based upon a detailed examination of Trotsky's philosophical writings. After an exposition and analysis of Trotsky's various understandings of the dialectic the conclusion is drawn that the commentator searching for Trotsky's underlying philosophical method is left in a maze of possible confusions.

THAU, Michael and LEBLANC, Hugues and ROEPER, Peter and WEAVER, George. Henkin's Completeness Proof: Forty Years Later. Notre Dame J Form Log, 32(2), 212-232, Spr 91.

Provided here are two new completeness proofs for a first-order logic with denumerably many terms. The first proof, unlike Menkin's 1949 proof, does not call for the addition of extra terms; the second, especially suited for truth-value semantics, calls for the addition of denumerably many. Shown in the process is that a set of statements has a Henkin model, i.e., a model in which every member of the domain has a name, iff the set is what we call *instantially consistent* (i.e., iff *consistent in omega-logic*).

THAYER, H S. Dewey and the Theory of Knowledge. Trans Peirce Soc, 26(4), 443-458, Fall 90.

THAYER-BACON, Barbara. How the Child Reasons. Phil Stud Educ, /, 107-116, 1989.

THE ARCHBISHOP OF YORK. The Embryo Debate: The Archbishop of York's Speech to the House of Lords. Ethics Med, 6(1), 1-2, Spr 90.

THEAU, Jean. *Trois essais sur la pensée*. Ottawa, Univ of Ottawa Pr, 1990.

These three essays are respectively entitled (1) language and thought, (2) reason and time, (3) analysis and dialectic. Their common purpose is to add some technical development to a previous book, published in 1985, *Certitudes et questions de la raison philosophique*, explaining, in particular, how a kind of dialectical method can be saved in philosophy, although Hegel's major objective, i.e., the bringing forth of a new logic, does not hold. In connection with this main theme, an attempt is made to show that language and time, causality and various forms of determinism, individuality and universality are fundamentally and analytically intelligible.

THEISSEN, Gerd. Biblical Hermeneutics and the Search for Religious Truth (in French). Rev Theol Phil, 122(4), 485-503, 1990.

This article solicits from biblical hermeneutics the pain of asking again the question concerning the religious truth of texts. It tries to make its perspective explicit through the inspiration of three philosophical theories on truth: truth as correspondence, as coherence and as consensus. On this basis, the author develops an evolutionary conception of biblical religion, touching particularly upon the questions of monism and dualism, religion and science, mystic religion and charismatic religion. (edited)

THÉRIEN, Gilles. La sémiotique, les objets singuliers et la complexité. Horiz Phil, 1(2), 33-49, 1991.

THERON, Stephen. Meaning in a Realist Perspective. Thomist, 55(1), 29-51, Ja 91.

In this paper the meaning of language is identified formally (not materially but no less "strictly") with the world which we apprehend precisely *as* we apprehend it, this in turn being the *truth* of the being of the world. The natures of substances, as essences, are the units of meaning because substances are the units of being. The sense, as giving cognition of substances, are thus essential to the genesis of meanings. An account of matter is offered as basis for the individuation and change by which things elude this intelligibility by identification in language.

THIEBAUT, Carlos. *Historia del nombrar: Dos episodios de la subjetividad*. Madrid, Visor, 1990.

History of Naming is an interdisciplinary ideal reconstruction of the constitution of modern subjectivity through the analysis of the relationship of proper names and their texts. After reviewing current philosophical discussions on proper names the book constructs two ideal moments of subjectivity formation: in the "ancient way of naming" (with the emblem of Jacob's new identity as Israel), identity is dependent upon a sacred text; in modernity (with one of Goya's dark paintings as an emblem) that sacred text is substituted by autobiography in which a material, reflexive subjectivity is constructed as performative of such text (as Montaigne could exemplify).

THIEL, Rainer. Coping with Complexity—Coping with Dialectics, in Theory and Practice (in German). Deut Z Phil, 38(5), 436-442, 1990.

THIELICKE, Helmut and BROMILEY, Geoffrey W (trans). *Modern Faith and Thought*. Grand Rapids, Eerdmans, 1990.

This book is a historical review of theological philosophy, written from the perspective of issues relevant to each time period. The issues examined include subjectivity, revelation, truth, faith, and the influence of several major thinkers. (staff)

THIJSSEN, J M M H. Once Again the Ockhamist Statutes of 1339 and 1340: Some New Perspectives. Vivarium, 28(2), 136-167, N 90.

The purpose of the paper is to substantiate the claim that a reference in the Proctor's Book of the English-German Nation is a reference to the statute issued by the Faculty of Arts of the University of Paris on December 25, 1340 and not to a statute now lost. Besides, it is argued that the 1340 statute indeed was anti-Ockhamist in nature, this on the basis of an analysis of the first article, which deals with "virtue sermonis", and the fifth article, which deals with the nature of scientific knowledge.

THINÈS, Georges. *Existence et Subjectivité: Études de Psychologie Phénoménologique*. Brussels, Univ Bruxelles, 1991.

This book includes fifteen studies dealing with various topics treated within the framework of phenomenological psychology. All these problems converge on the central concept of subjectivity. The latter is discussed in the studies of Michotte on causality and in relation to Buytendijk's theory of expression. Apart from a series of chapters dealing with epistemological issues of psychology, several others tackle problems of the philosophy of poetry and music.

THIROUX, Jacques P. *Philosophy: Theory and Practice*. New York, Macmillan, 1985.

THOM, Martina. Philosophiehistorische Forschung und historischer Materialismus. Deut Z Phil, 39(2), 124-135, 1991.

THOM, Paul. The Two Barbaras. Hist Phil Log, 12(2), 135-149, 1991.

This paper examines three recent discussions of Aristotle's system of syllogisms with apodeictic and assertoric premisses. Though they contain no cross-references, and though they arrive at disparate interpretations, all three pieces share a common aid. That aim is to construct an intuitively graspable interpretation of Aristotle's modal syllogistic which is based on metaphysical considerations. I argue that none of these authors has succeeded in this; nevertheless, I share their broad aim, and attempt to show that a more satisfactory interpretation can be formulated by combining and developing elements drawn from all three.

THOMAS, Charles W. Prisoners' Rights and Correctional Privatization: A Legal and Ethical Analysis. Bus Prof Ethics J, 10(1), 3-45, Spr 91.

THOMAS, D A Lloyd. Hume and Intrinsic Value. Philosophy, 65(254), 419-437, O 90.

THOMAS, Edmund J and MILLER, Eugene G. *Writers and Philosophers: A Sourcebook of Philosophical Influences on Literature*. Westport, Greenwood Pr, 1990.

The intent of *Writers and Philosophers* is to provide philosophical resource for teachers and students of literature to help them acquire a greater understanding of the philosophical influences on more than a hundred major literary figures most commonly included in college literature textbooks. The text describes philosophical influences reflected in major literary works and includes as well references to philosophical works that have played a part in the authors' intellectual and aesthetic development. The entries are supplemented by brief bio-bibliographical profiles of major philosophers and a glossary of philosophical terms, concepts, and movements.

THOMAS, J L H. 'Why Did It Happen to Me?'. Relig Stud, 26(3), 323-334, S 90.

The question 'Why did it happen to me?', self-addressed, uncommitted, and distinct from the classical problem of evil, deserves, despite common opinion, a rational answer. None of the traditional answers to it, offered by ancient, medieval, and modern philosophers and theologians, and classified as they specify the cause or the purpose of individual suffering, appear upon scrutiny, however, to satisfy the double criterion of theoretical cogency and practical efficacy. An alternative and more promising answer may, nevertheless, be sought through recognition of the role in which one suffers, and of the consequent distinction between oneself and one's sufferings.

THOMAS, J L H. Against the Fantasts. Philosophy, 66(257), 349-367, Jl 91.

The philosophical use of fantasy, or 'fantaphilosophy', which has become fashionable among English-speaking analytical philosophers, is incoherent and morally unacceptable. First, it infringes the fundamental rational principle that no cogent argument can be based upon insecure premisses. Second, radical changes in the structure of space and time or of human personality would destroy all basis for the prediction of our response to some imagined experience. Third, such fantasies weaken the sense of individual responsibility, and are in bad taste. These general criticisms of fantaphilosophy are confirmed by an examination of four particular fantasies by Professors Strawson, Hare, Dummett, and Williams.

THOMAS, Janice. Some New Directions in the Philosophy of Mind. Heythrop J, 32(1), 72-76, Ja 91.

This is a review article about writings in Philosophy of Mind over the last three or four years and, as such, can only touch tips of a handful of icebergs. Variety of opinion; well-defended, careful, with well-chosen examples and full of imaginative and inspiring new directions, representing a broad array of disparate viewpoints, are all characteristic of the subject at this time. The article talks about writings by McGinn, Lycan, Christopher Maloney, Michael Lockwood, Harold Noonan, Davidson, Kathleen Wilkes, Peter Smith and O R Jones.

THOMAS, John C. Values, the Environment and the Creative Act. J Speculative Phil, 4(4), 323-336, 1990.

THOMAS, John E and WALUCHOW, Wilfrid J. *Well and Good: Case Studies in Biomedical Ethics (Revised Edition)*. Peterborough, Broadview Pr, 1990.

THOMAS, Laurence. American Slavery and the Holocaust: Their Ideologies Compared. Pub Affairs Quart, 5(2), 191-210, Ap 91.

THOMAS, Laurence. "Morality and Psychological Development" in *A Companion to Ethics*, SINGER, Peter (ed), 464-475. Cambridge, Blackwell, 1991.

This essay examines Kohlberg's account of moral development. I argue that the account is found wanting, especially in regards to the claim that Stage 4 constitutes a form of moral development, since it seems that both Nazi Germany and contemporary Canada (say) are at Stage 4. But if so, then in what sense do we have moral development at Stage 4. I also point out that Kohlberg fails to show that our psychological development favors a deontological morality over a teleological morality—especially utilitarianism. I conclude with a suggestion that shows the importance of an Aristotelian account of moral development.

THOMAS, Laurence. "Trust, Affirmation, and Moral Character: A Critique of Kantian Morality" in *Identity, Character, and Morality: Essays in Moral Psychology*, FLANAGAN, Owen (ed), 235-257. Cambridge, MIT Pr, 1990.

This essay aims to show the role which trust plays in having a good moral character. The essay seeks to distinguish trust from mere prediction, arguing that while having trust entails making a prediction the converse does not hold. I suggest that what often falls under the label Kantian morality fails to appreciate the difference between trust and prediction. I go on to argue that trust plays a significant affirming role in our lives. Finally, I show how the analysis of trust bears upon the "one-thought-too-many" discussion in ethics.

THOMAS, Lynn L and STEWART, Robert M. Recent Work on Ethical Relativism. Amer Phil Quart, 28(2), 85-100, Ap 91.

THOMAS, Paul. Jean-Jacques Rousseau, Sexist? Fem Stud, 17(2), 195-218, Sum 91.

THOMAS, R S D. Meanings in Ordinary Language and in Mathematics. Phil Math, 6(1), 3-38, 1991.

One purpose of the paper is to give a death-blow to the sickly notion that mathematical discourse is meaningless. In order to do this it sketches a theory of meaning for ordinary language that is intended to be of independent interest and that owes much to the recent books of George Lakoff and Mark Johnson opposing what they call objectivism. The presentation of this sketch is the other purpose of the paper. Using the notions of meaning and reference for ordinary language, the paper concludes that these do appear in mathematics and in ways that are not as different from ordinary language as is often assumed.

THOMAS, Troy. Interart Analogy: Practice and Theory in Comparing the Arts. J Aes Educ, 25(2), 17-36, Sum 91.

This paper describes the use of analogy in making comparisons between the arts. The shortcomings are demonstrated of so-called structural relationships among the arts, relationships which are in fact only varieties of analogizing in disguise. Three examples that compare literature and the visual arts from different historical periods (Renaissance, nineteenth-century Romanticism, early twentieth-century Modernism) are used to clarify the nature of interart analogy. The historical evolution of different kinds of analogy in the arts based on narratives, symbols, and signs is discussed. The usefulness of such comparisons is stressed, despite reservations that have sometimes been voiced about them.

THOMAS, V C. Husserl's Notion of Constitution in Heidegger's Treatment of Care. J Indian Counc Phil Res, 5(1), 21-27, S-D 87.

THOMASMA, David C. "Anencephalics as Organ Donors" in *Biomedical Ethics Reviews, 1989*, HUMBER, James M (ed), 25-54. Clifton, Humana Pr, 1990.

In this article I discuss what an anencephalic is and whether a newborn with such a condition can be described as "brain dead" or "brain absent." Then I discuss whether anencephaly allows us to call those newborns "human beings" or "persons." I try to define human-hood and personhood in a functional way that will permit us to deal with anencephalics as organ donors and analogous conditions in an appropriate and careful way. For this reason I distinguish euthanasia from retrieving organs, and anencephalics from a permanent vegetative state. In weighing the pros and cons in conclusion, I suggest a practical policy governing organ transplantation from anencephalics without violating major ethical principles. (edited)

THOMASMA, David C. *Euthanasia: Toward an Ethical Social Policy*. New York, Continuum, 1990.

Unlike other crucial medical-moral issues where the dividing lines of argument are sharply defined, euthanasia emerges as a controversial problem from an area which is largely gray. All facets of the ethical dilemma reflect concern for the value of life and compassion for the suffering and anguish of the disabled and dying. The authors of this book first study the kinds of euthanasia currently practiced, then philosophically analyze the concepts of justified and unjustified euthanasia, voluntary and involuntary, and active and passive. Successive chapters are devoted to the family's perspective, society's perspective, and health professionals' perspective. The final chapter details a proposal to control pain and address suffering through the principles of hospice care and the use of double-effect euthanasia. Appendices of cases are included. (edited)

THOMASMA, David C. Setting Floating Limits: Functional Status Care Categories as National Policy. Bus Prof Ethics J, 9(3-4), 133-146, Fall-Wint 90.

A proposal is made to allocate health cure on the basis of need by using medical indicators and individual function for care categories. Limitations on care interventions increase with an increase in category and decrease in function on an objective basis.

THOMASMA, David C and GRABER, Glenn C. *Theory and Practice in Medical Ethics*. New York, Continuum, 1989.

THOMASMA, David C. Why Philosophers Should Offer Ethics Consultations. Theor Med, 12(2), 129-140, Je 91.

Considerable debate has occurred about the proper role of philosophers when offering ethics consultants. Some argue that only physicians or clinical experienced personnel should offer ethics consults in the clinical setting. Others argue still further that philosophers are ill-equipped to offer such advice, since to do so rests on no social warrant, and violates the abstract and neutral nature of the discipline itself. I argue that philosophers not only can offer such consultations but ought to. I conclude with some skills that trained philosophers can bring to the consultation service, and note that all consultations are in the form of recommendations. (edited)

THOMASON, Neil. Making Student Groups Work: "To Teach is to Learn Twice". Teach Phil, 13(2), 111-125, Je 90.

Well-replicated experimental results indicate that students learn more when they work closely with each other in small groups in or out of class. I provide twelve ways of getting students to philosophize together. Given the dialectical nature of philosophical understanding, for many students it may be in such small groups that they will best feel the force of the positions, alternatives and arguments.

THOMASON, Neil. Small is Beautiful. Thinking, 9(1), 38-41, 1990.

Philosophy for Children is based on a deep, justified faith in children's ability to learn to philosophize by articulating their thoughts, listening and responding to the thoughts of others, modifying their views, and so on. But the standard discussions groups give very little time for each person to speak. Dividing the class into small groups which report their results to the class gives each child more time to philosophize and far more feedback. It also can produce more intense discussions.

THOMASON, Richmond and CARPENTER, Bob. "Inheritance Theory and Path-Based Reasoning: An Introduction" in *Knowledge Representation and Defeasible Reasoning*, KYBURG JR, Henry E (ed), 309-343. Norwell, Kluwer, 1990.

THOMASON, Steven K. Toward a Formalization of Dialectical Logic. Rep Math Log, 23, 17-23, 1989.

THOMPKINS, E F. *Sachverhalt* and *Gegenstand* are Dead. Philosophy, 66(256), 217-234, Ap 91.

It is commonly accepted that the *Tractatus* and *Philosophical Investigations* respectively represent widely divergent modes of thought. This article takes the less conventional view that partly by design but largely by default Wittgenstein reaches in the *Tractatus* a position which not merely facilitates a smooth transition to his later thinking but provides the essential foundation for it.

THOMPSON JR, George B. The Emerging Tension Between Self and Society, As Exemplified in Augustine. Listening, 25(3), 267-280, Fall 90.

This article argues that Augustine signals the beginning of the West's focus upon persons as intrinsic individuals. That beginning both emerged because of, and yet was tempered by, various massive changes that occurred during Augustine's lifetime in the Late Roman Empire. Despite his discovery of intrinsic individuality, Augustine seems to have favored community as the more fundamental category, upholding views of order that seriously limited the ability of his other insights to be developed. These insights would have allowed for a richer interpretation of self and society as mutually supportive.

THOMPSON, A Gray and DUPUIS, Adrian M. P4C as "Pre-Secondary" Philosophy. Thinking, 4(2), 33-35, 1982.

Since philosophy is taught in numerous secondary schools, it seems appropriate that it be started in elementary schools. Math, history, science, etc. are begun in elementary school and involve basic content of secondary education. The *Philosophy for Children* program provides the basis for secondary school philosophy, and in the language and "experience" of children.

THOMPSON, Audrey. The Baby with a Gun: A Feminist Inquiry Into Plausibility, Certainty and Context in Moral Education. Proc Phil Educ, 46, 239-249, 1990.

THOMPSON, Bruce R. Why is Conjunctive Simplification Invalid? Notre Dame J Form Log, 32(2), 248-254, Spr 91.

Connexive logic accepts as tautologous the principle that no statement may be directly inferred from its own denial. This principle is logically inconsistent with the principle of Conjunctive Simplification, that from '*p* and *q*' we may infer '*p*. Connexive logicians generally reject Conjunctive Simplification on the grounds that some substitution instances for '*q*' might countermand the otherwise valid inference from '*p*' to '*p*'. Under the 'subtraction' theory of negation '~*p*' would be such a substitution instance, since according to the subtraction theory of negation, nothing follows from a contradiction. However, this paper argues that logicians need not necessarily adopt the subtraction theory of negation in order to find reasons to reject Conjunctive Simplification.

THOMPSON, Dennis and GUTMANN, Amy. "Moral Conflict and Political Consensus" in *Liberalism and the Good*, DOUGLASS, R Bruce (ed), 125-147. New York, Routledge, 1990.

THOMPSON, Ian J. Real Dispositions in the Physical World. Brit J Phil Sci, 39(1), 67-79, Mr 88.

The role of dispositions in the physical world is considered. It is shown that not only can classical physics be reasonably construed as the discovery of real dispositions, but also quantum physics. This approach moreover allows a realistic understanding of quantum processes.

THOMPSON, J L. Nietzsche on Woman. Int J Moral Soc Stud, 5(3), 207-220, Autumn 90.

In his writings Nietzsche had much to say about woman, whom he took to be weak, sentimental, undisciplined, slavish, and thus rightly regarded as an object of possession by those men whom he describes as 'noble souls'. I argue that Nietzsche's views about woman and his evaluation of the feminine play an important role in his philosophical thought: that they are central to the distinction he makes between noble souls and 'herd animals' and essential to his account of how noble individuals are created. I further consider how these views should be criticised and what implications such criticism has for Nietzsche's philosophy.

THOMPSON, J L. What is the Problem Concerning Social Entities? Int J Moral Soc Stud, 6(1), 77-90, Spr 91.

The main problem in understanding the philosophical debate between methodological individualists and methodological collectivists is comprehending why it exists at all. For each position seems to be based on a truism: that social events are the result of what individuals do; that what individuals do must sometimes be explained in terms of social facts. I present a number of interpretations of methodological individualism: as a thesis about reduction, verification, conceptual requirements on social explanation. I argue that all these versions are inadequate or put unjustified restrictions on social science.

THOMPSON, Janna. Land Rights and Aboriginal Sovereignty. Austl J Phil, 68(3), 313-329, S 90.

When the British in 1788 declared eastern Australia to be under their rule, they were dispossessing the native people of the sovereignty they had exercised over their territory. I argue that attempts to justify this action from a consequentialist or natural rights position fail, and I consider whether and on what grounds reparation is now due to the descendants of the dispossessed people.

THOMPSON, John B (ed) and HELD, David (ed). *Social Theory of Modern Societies: Anthony Giddens and His Critics*. New York, Cambridge Univ Pr, 1990.

THOMPSON, John B. "The Theory of Structuration" in *Social Theory of Modern Societies: Anthony Giddens and His Critics*, HELD, David (ed), 56-76. New York, Cambridge Univ Pr, 1990.

This article is a critical assessment of the theory of structuration elaborated by Anthony Giddens. Some of the key ideas of Giddens's work are outlined, including his stratification model of action, his conception of structure as rules and resources, and his attempt to provide a coherent account of the interrelations between action and structure. It is argued that Giddens's conception of structure is unsatisfactory, since the structural features of social life cannot be adequately analysed in terms of rules and resources. Thompson also argues that Giddens's emphasis on the enabling character of structure has led him to underplay the significance of structural constraint.

THOMPSON, R J and ANDRÉKA, H and NÉMETI, I. Weak Cylindric Set Algebras and Weak Subdirect Indecomposability. J Sym Log, 55(2), 577-588, Je 90.

In this note we prove that the abstract property "weakly subdirectly indecomposable" does not characterize the class IWs_α of weak cylindric set algebras. However, we give another (similar) abstract property characterizing IWs_α. The original property does characterize the directed unions of members of IWs_α iff α is countable. Free algebras will be shown to satisfy the original property.

THOMPSON, Ross A. Child Development and Research Ethics: A Changing Calculus of Concerns. Bus Prof Ethics J, 9(1-2), 193-206, Spr-Sum 90.

The participation of children in social and behavioral research raises difficult ethical dilemmas that are sharpened by the fact that children are a heterogeneous population, varying significantly in their competencies as they mature. This paper discusses how the principles governing the ethical review of research—nonmaleficence, beneficence, respect for persons, and justice—can be more sensitively applied to children of different ages and backgrounds who consequently vary in their interests and needs as research participants. Implications for conventional ethical guidelines concerning risk assessment, the risk-benefit calculus, informed consent, defining the status of "mature minor," and other procedures are also discussed.

THOMPSON, William B. *Controlling Technology: Contemporary Issues*. Buffalo, Prometheus, 1991.

This anthology is intended as a primary source for undergraduate courses dealing with technology and human values. Approximately half the essays are by philosophers; other contributions come from a variety of disciplines. The book is organized to bring into sharp focus the conflicting arguments concerning the nature of modern technology as it bears on the quality of human lives and, more fundamentally, our prospects for survival on this planet. Is our traditional faith in the capacity of technology to progressively ameliorate the human condition justified, or is technology out of control? The basic issues are moral and political.

THOMSON, Clive (ed). *Bakhtin and the Epistemology of Discourse*. Amsterdam, Rodopi, 1991.

THOMSON, Judith Jarvis. *The Realm of Rights*. Cambridge, Harvard Univ Pr, 1990.

THORNE, Gary W A. The Structure of Philo's Commentary on the Pentateuch. Dionysius, 13, 17-50, D 89.

THORNTON, Mark. Same Human Being, Same Person? Philosophy, 66(255), 115-118, Ja 91.

A defence of John Locke's view that someone existing at one time may be the same human being but not the same person as someone existing at a later time (and vice versa) against David Wiggins's claim that this view is incoherent.

THROOP, William and SCHWARTZ, Stephen P. Intuitionism and Vagueness. Erkenntnis, 34(3), 347-356, My 91.

Putnam has argued that vagueness is a reason to abandon realism in favor of anti-realism. Realists are faced with vagueness generated problems, such as the sorites paradox, which anti-realists can avoid. Putnam claims that intuitionist logic can serve as an anti-realist logic for vague terms and offers a solution to the sorites paradox. We argue that intuitionist logic is at best a formal "solution" to the paradox and is not a genuine solution. Furthermore, versions of the sorites do still arise in intuitionist logic. Vagueness is a serious problem for both the realist and the anti-realist.

THROOP, William and DORAN, Katheryn. Putnam's Realism and Relativity: An Uneasy Balance. Erkenntnis, 34(3), 347-356, My 91.

Recently, Hilary Putnam has attempted to achieve a delicate balance between relativism and metaphysical realism. Many of Putnam's critics claim that he has either lost his balance or that he is left with an incoherent mixture of relativism and realism. We argue that there is a natural way of avoiding the apparent incoherences and sustaining the balancing act, if one acknowledges that the relativist claims are made from a detached perspective which serves very different purposes than the agent's perspective within which Putnam emphasizes his commonsense realism.

TIBBETTS, Paul. "Threading-the-Needle: The Case For and Against Common-Sense Realism". Human Stud, 13(4), 309-322, O 90.

TIDEMAN, Nicolaus and BORDES, Georges. Independence of Irrelevant Alternatives in the Theory of Voting. Theor Decis, 30(2), 163-186, Mr 91.

In social choice theory there has been, and for some authors there still is, a confusion between Arrow's *Independence of Irrelevant Alternatives (IIA) and some choice consistency* conditions. In this paper we analyze this confusion. It is often thought that Arrow himself was confused, but we show that this is not so. What happened was that Arrow had in mind a condition we call *regularity*, which implies IIA, but which he could not state formally in his model because his model was not rich enough to permit certain distinctions that would have been necessary. It is the combination of regularity and IIA that he discusses, and the origin of the confusion lies in the fact that if one uses a model that does not permit a distinction between regularity and IIA, regularity looks like a consistency condition, which it is not. We also show that the famous example that 'proves' that Arrow was confused does not prove this at all if it is correctly interpreted.

TIERNEY, Brian. Marsilius on Rights. J Hist Ideas, 52(1), 3-17, Ja-Mr 91.

Marsilius of Padua is often overlooked in modern accounts of the development of natural rights theories; all the emphasis is on his contemporary, William of Ockham. But in fact Marsilius made an important contribution in this area. He distinguished two meanings of *ius*—as objective law and subjective right. The distinction was important for Suarez and other later thinkers and Marsilius seems to have been the first to make it explicitly. Moreover he sustained the distinction through an intricate discussion of the meanings of use and dominion, the acquisition and renunciation of property rights and the fundamental right of self-preservation.

TIESZEN, Richard. Frege and Husserl on Number. Ratio, 3(2), 150-164, D 90.

In *Philosophe der Arithmetik* Husserl criticized the account of number that Frege presented in the *Grundlagen der Arithmetik*. In this paper I argue that Husserl's criticisms of Frege raise deep problems in the philosophy of mathematics concerning the status of primitive terms, definability, intensionality, and constructivity. They show Frege's philosophy of mathematics to be seriously flawed on important epistemological issues. The argument of the paper also bears directly on the debate between Dummett, Sluga, Resnik and others over the question whether Frege is best understood as a realist or as some kind of Kantian transcendental idealist.

TIETZ, Udo. Dasein—Mitsein—Sprache: Heideggers Auffassung über das "Wesen der Sprache" in "Sein und Zeit". Deut Z Phil, 38(12), 1152-1160, 1990.

TIETZ, Udo. Georg Lukács and Stalinism (in German). Deut Z Phil, 38(10), 953-963, 1990.

TIGHLMAN, B R. What is it Like to be an Aardvark? Philosophy, 66(257), 325-338, Jl 91.

Thomas Nagel's understanding of his question 'What is it like to be a bat?' lacks sense because it embodies the conceptual confusion of mental privacy. How such a question actually functions in animal research is shown in the work of Cheney and Seyfarth on the mental life of monkeys. The true importance of the 'What is it like to be a ...?' question is found in asking what it is like to be another person and in understanding other people, their problems and situations when all that is stripped of the philosophical baggage of the other minds problem.

TIGUNAIT, Pandit Rajmani. *Yoga on War and Peace*. Honesdale, Himalayan, 1991.

This work looks at causes of violence and war and why attempts at peace fail. The relationship between collective consciousness and individual attitudes is discussed, and the idea that the prospect of peace can only be found in individual hearts and minds is outlined. (staff)

TIJIATTAS, Mary. Bachelard and Scientific Realism. Phil Forum, 22(3), 203-210, Spr 91.

It is argued that Bachelard's work in the philosophy of science is not concerned only with many of the questions which characterize contemporary Anglo-American debates. Through a radical reappraisal of the functions of experimentation, it also proposes a convincing way of analyzing the relations between theories and objects, explanations and events, which avoids both relativism and a return to naive correspondence theories.

TILANDER, A. Thoughts and Theses on Causality. Method Sci, 23(1), 28-48, 1990.

TILES, J E. "Our Perception of the External World" in *Key Themes in Philosophy*, GRIFFITHS, A Phillips (ed), 15-29. New York, Cambridge Univ Pr, 1989.

TILES, Mary E. *Mathematics and the Image of Reason*. New York, Routledge, 1991.

The aim of this book is to spell out as clearly as possible how it came to be proposed that mathematics and/or mathematical reasoning reduces to logic and to set out the reasons why attempts to effect such a reduction failed. The further aim is to show how this whole episode can be interpreted as revealing important characteristics of mathematics and mathematical reasoning. In particular it is suggested that the traditional (logic-based) conception of reason as closed and complete should be replaced; this episode demonstrates that the power of mathematical reason lies in its essential lack of closure.

TILES, Mary. "Method and the Authority of Science" in *Key Themes in Philosophy*, GRIFFITHS, A Phillips (ed), 31-51. New York, Cambridge Univ Pr, 1989.

The authority accorded to science is usually justified by reference to scientific method. But what is this method? In this essay, written for a non-specialist audience, Popper's answer is considered and found wanting on three counts. (1) He substitutes the logical problem of induction for the many and various real problems of how to extrapolate from data. (2) He provides no clear basis on which science could claim superiority over everyday knowledge. (3) He does not distinguish between low level empirical generalisation and scientific theorising which has an explanatory goal. Examples suggest grounding the authority of science in a unitary scientific method is over-simplistic.

TILGHMAN, B R. *Wittgenstein, Ethics and Aesthetics: The View from Eternity*. Albany, SUNY Pr, 1991.

The book explores Wittgenstein's views about ethics and aesthetics and argues that the work of the *Philosophical Investigations* made these notions intelligible in a way that the *Tractatus* could not. Important parallels between understanding people and understanding art are pointed out. Much recent philosophy of mind depends upon dualistic assumptions that make our understanding of other people unintelligible and much recent aesthetic theory relies upon analogous assumptions that make no room for the human importance of art. Wittgenstein's philosophical methods allow us to expose the philosophical confusion that stands in the way of our seeing ourselves and the world aright.

TILLEY, John J. Agent-Action Judgements. Phil Inq, 10(1-2), 64-71, Wint-Spr 88.

TIMM, Jeffrey R. The Celebration of Emotion: Vallabha's Ontology of Affective Experience. Phil East West, 41(1), 59-75, Ja 91.

Beginning with an inquiry into the contemporary cross-cultural study of emotion, and then reviewing a medieval Indian debate on the status of renunciation, this article shows that Vallabha's renunciation of renunciation, and his valorization of emotion in the service of devotional religious expression, rests on ontological affirmations of the world (*prapañca*), God and the relationship between the two. Connecting emotion, expressed through devotional service, with Vallabha's overall theological scheme, shows how emotion may reveal the presence of God who is simultaneously immanent on all levels and whose absolute subjectivity sublimates the subject/object dualism constituting the ego's lived experience (*samsara*).

TIMMERMANS, Benoît. Kant et l'histoire de la philosophie la vision problématologique. Rev Int Phil, 44(174), 297-308, 1990.

TIMMONS, Mark. *Conduct and Character: Readings in Moral Theory*. Belmont, Wadsworth, 1990.

This anthology of classical and contemporary readings is organized according to type of moral theory with chapters on Egoism, Relativism, Divine Command Theory, Natural Law Theory, Kantian Moral Theory, Utilitarianism, and Virtue-Perfectionistic Moral Theories. The editor's introduction introduces readers to the fundamental aims, structure, and methods of evaluating moral theories.

TIMMONS, Mark. On the Epistemic Status of Considered Moral Judgments. S J Phil, SUPP 29, 97-129, 1990.

This paper considers the prospects for combining a coherentist account of the epistemic justification of moral judgments with a (naturalistic) realist construal of the truth of such judgments in light of the work of N Daniels, D O Brink, and R Boyd. It is argued that the prospects look bleak owing to the fact that the needed semantic account of moral terms and expressions (one that construes them as rigid) is implausible. The implausibility of this semantic account is revealed by a version of Putnam's Twin Earth thought experiment: Moral Twin Earth.

TIMMONS, Mark. Putnam's Moral Objectivism. Erkenntnis, 34(3), 371-399, My 91.

I explore the bearing of Putnam's internal realism on the topics of moral truth and moral justification. The first two sections of the paper provide a characterization of the sort of (nonstandard) realism in ethics Putnam's view of objectivity seems to imply. In sections three and four, I argue that although Putnam's version of moral realism can more plausibly account for facts about moral diversity than can rival forms of realism, it seems to collapse into an "anything goes" form of relativism. I then consider Putnam's prospects for responding to this "anything goes" challenge.

TIRRELL, Lynne. Reductive and Nonreductive Simile Theories of Metaphor. J Phil, 88(7), 337-358, Jl 91.

This article argues that the simile theory of metaphor is untenable. It sets out the basic tenets of the simile theory and explains why in both its reductive and nonreductive forms the simile theory fails to offer an adequate analysis of metaphor. The central arguments depend upon keeping clear the distinction between interpreting literally and interpreting metaphorically.

TIRRELL, Lynne. Seeing Metaphor as Seeing-as. Phil Invest, 14(2), 143-154, Ap 91.

Davidson suggests that metaphor is a pragmatic (not a semantic) phenomenon; it prompts its audience to see one thing as another. This paper shows why the perceptual model fails to stave off semantic analysis, and argues that the professed virtues of Davidson's position are more readily found in an account that focusses on the nature of metaphorical interpretation.

TITO, Johanna Maria. *Logic in the Husserlian Context*. Evanston, Northwestern Univ Pr, 1991.

The author explores the connections between Husserl's logic and his phenomenology. She discusses the transcendental ego as a basis for the holistic nature of life and logic in Husserl. (staff)

TODESCO, Fabio. Il polipo di Trembley (1740) e la "catena delle verità": Note di ricerca. G Crit Filosof Ital, 69(3), 342-365, S-D 90.

TODISCO, Orlando. Il doppio volto dell'ineffabile in L Wittgenstein. Sapienza, 44(1), 13-24, Ja-Mr 91.

TOFFALORI, Carlo. Stability for Pairs of Equivalence Relations. Notre Dame J Form Log, 32(1), 112-128, Wint 91.

We consider pairs of equivalence relations E_0, E_1 such that, for some nonnegative integer h, every class of the join of E_0 and E_1 contains at most h classes of either E_0 or E_1. We classify these structures under categoricity (in some infinite power), nonmultidimensionality and finite cover property.

TOGNONATO, Claudio. La dialettica come "dépasser" in Sartre. Aquinas, 33(2), 365-402, My-Ag 90.

TOKARZ, Marek. On the Logic of Conscious Belief. Stud Log, 49(3), 321-332, S 90.

We discuss a system LB of belief-logic in which so-called axioms of introspection are added to the usual ones. LB is proved to be sound and complete with respect to Boolean algebras equipped with proper filters. Completeness theorems for some modifications of LB are also proved, and interpretations in classical theories are considered.

TOLHURST, William. On the Epistemic Value of Moral Experience. S J Phil, SUPP 29, 67-87, 1990.

TOMASCHITZ, Wolfgang. Über den Versuch einer philosophiegeschichtlichen Klassifikation der Lehre Nāgārjunas. Conceptus, 24(62), 49-71, 1990.

A system of classification of philosophical positions which is proper to occidental philosophy cannot seize Nāgārjuna's proper teachings. The impracticability in this case is instructive. Some aspects of Nāgārjuna's skill in argumentation are shown while resisting any classificational grasping. With that the self-evidence of occidental philosophy gets questionable.

TOMASI, John. Plato's *Statesman* Story: The Birth of Fiction Reconceived. Phil Lit, 14(2), 348-358, O 90.

This article examines Christopher Gill's claim that Plato's Atlantis story in the *Critias* is the earliest example of narrative fiction in Plato, and indeed in all Western written culture ("Plato's Atlantis Story and the Birth of Fiction," *Philosophy and Literature* 3, 1979: 64-78). By developing epistemic criteria for distinguishing the genres of history, fiction, and fable, it is shown that the story in Plato's *Statesman* dialogue should be recognized as a still earlier instance of deliberate fiction writing.

TOMASINI BASSOLS, Alejandro. La filosofía mística de Russell y lo indecible en el *Tractatus*. Dianoia, 36(36), 157-180, 1990.

Russell and Wittgenstein had a lot to say on what the former called 'mystical philosophy'. The beliefs of mystical philosophy enumerated by Russell can be traced in the Tractatus. Unlike Wittgenstein, however, when Russell works in "technical philosophy", he restrains from saying anything whatsoever on these matters. This does not mean that he lacks a mystical philosophy, in his sense, but only that in his view it can only be elaborated in a language which, from the Tractatus point of view, is openly nonsensical.

TOMASINI, Alejandro. Historia de la filosofía: para qué? Dianoia, 34(34), 194-201, 1988.

The aim of the paper is to show the usefulness and the relevance of the history of philosophy for contemporary discussions. Some of its most conspicuous consequences are (1) it is a technical introduction to classical problems; (2) it shows how to combine an abstract approach with detailed arguments; (3) it makes clear how difficult it is to provide new insights; (4) it helps to understand both the continuity and the discontinuity of the subject matter. I consider the "historical vs. topical approach" issue and argue that there cannot be such thing as the history of philosophy.

TOMBERLIN, James E. "Belief, Nominalism, and Quantification" in *Philosophical Perspectives, 4: Action Theory and Philosophy of Mind, 1990*, TOMBERLIN, James E (ed), 573-579. Atascadero, Ridgeview, 1990.

TOMBERLIN, James E (ed). *Philosophical Perspectives, 3: Philosophy of Mind and Action Theory, 1989*. Atascadero, Ridgeview, 1989.

This volume, the third in a new series of annual topical volumes, contains twenty-two original essays by leading action theorists and philosophers of mind. Authors include Lynne Rudder Baker, Michael Bratman, Fred Dretske, Carl Ginet,

Jaegmon Kim, Robert Stalnaker, and Peter van Inwagen. Topics covered include the nature of belief, perceptual thoughts, reason and cause, individualism, freedom of will, and mental causation.

TOMBERLIN, James E (ed). *Philosophical Perspectives, 4: Action Theory and Philosophy of Mind, 1990*. Atascadero, Ridgeview, 1990.

This volume contains twenty-two original essays by leading action theorists and philosophers of mind. Authors include Bruce Anne, Ned Block, Roderick M Chisholm, John Haugeland, William G Lycan, Sydney Shoemaker, and Stephen Stich. Topics covered include functionalism, AI and connectionism, practical reason, physicalism, and the mental and subjectivity.

TOMBRAS, Spyros. Interprétation de l'art—Art de l'interprétation. Diotima, 18, 68-75, 1990.

TOMLINSON, Don E. Choosing Social Responsibility Over Law: The *Soldier of Fortune* Classified Advertising Cases. Bus Prof Ethics J, 9(1-2), 79-96, Spr-Sum 90.

TOMLINSON, Hugh (trans) and DELEUZE, Gilles and HABBERJAM, Barbara (trans). *Bergsonism*. Cambridge, MIT Pr, 1991.

TONELLA, Guido. Diagonalization and Fixed Points. Teoria, 10(2), 99-107, 1990.

TONG, Lik Kuen. The Appropriation of Significance: The Concept of *Kang-Tung*in the *I Ching*. J Chin Phil, 17(3), 315-344, S 90.

In the philosophy of the *I Ching, kang-t'ung* is the process of affective attunement and penetration which constitutes the experiential-spiritual essence of appropriation. This essay explores the meaning of *kang-t'ung*, so as to exhibit the primordial morality of the human being grounded on the pivotal role of the upright body. In so doing, it will also demonstrate how the fundamental philosophical categories of the *I Ching* are primordially interconnected by virtue of the human being's upright posturality.

TONG, Rosemarie. The Epistemology and Ethics of Consensus: Uses and Misuses of 'Ethical' Expertise. J Med Phil, 16(4), 409-426, Ag 91.

In this paper I examine the epistemology and ethics of consensus, focusing on the ways in which decision makers use/misuse ethical expertise. First, are the 'experts' really experts? Second, is the experts's authority merely epistemological or is it also ethical? Third, should the authority of expertise be limited? Persons who are ethics 'experts' must be particularly careful to practice an ethics of *persuasion* rather than an ethics of *compulsion*. Their role is not to force their *group* consensus upon decision makers's *individual* moral perceptions and deliberations; rather it is to help decision makers come to their own conclusions about what they ought to do.

TONG, Rosemarie. The Overdue Death of a Feminist Chameleon: Taking a Stand on Surrogacy Arrangements. J Soc Phil, 21(2-3), 40-56, Fall-Wint 90.

In this article, I 1) outline the arguments on behalf of the four legal remedies that have been proposed for surrogacy arrangements, and 2) comment on each of these remedies, identifying those that are most likely to best serve women's interests. Specifically, I argue that since the woman who gestates a child *is* the mother of that child, 1) commercial surrogacy should be recognized for what it is—the selling of a relationship—and dealt with accordingly; and 2) noncommercial, or altruistic surrogacy should be recognized for what it is—a form of adoption—and dealt with accordingly.

TONGS, A R. In Defence of Unrepresentative Realism. Method Sci, 24(1), 32-50, 1991.

TONOIU, Vasile. Vers une Pédagogie du Dialogue. Dialectica, 44(3-4), 255-278, 1990.

Gonseth the man, his life and his work can be interpreted organically in an instructive account of dialogue. The author treats the following topics: a) Gonseth's intimate dialogical structure, b) the fruitless dialogues in *Les mathématiques et la réalité* between the characters Perfect, Sceptic and Appropriate, and finally New Appropriate, d) his contacts with neo-scholastics at Rome, e) the explicit 'doctrine' of dialogue presented in *La loi du dialogue*. The article is also concerned with conditions for a fruitful dialogue and with obstacles that can stand in the way (in particular, the incompatibility of reference systems).

TOOLEY, Michael. Causation: Reductionism Versus Realism. Phil Phenomenol Res, 50 SUPP, 215-236, Fall 90.

My basic thesis is that reductionist accounts, both of causal laws and of causal relations, are untenable. With regard to laws, I mention a fundamental epistemological difficulty, plus the problems posed by accidental uniformities, by uninstantiated basic laws, and by probabilistic laws. With regard to causal relations, I argue, first, that reductionist approaches cannot provide a satisfactory account of the direction of causation, and secondly, that causal relations between events are not logically supervenient even upon the totality of all noncausal facts, together with all laws, both causal and noncausal, plus the direction of causation in all potential causal processes.

TOOLEY, Michael. The Nature of Causation: A Singularist Account. Can J Phil, SUPP 16, 271-322, 1990.

My basic thesis is that events can be causally related without that relation being an instance of any causal law. After setting out some arguments in support of a singularist conception of causation, I consider a crucial Humean objection, and I contend that while the argument may tell against any reductionist account, it does not refute a realist approach, according to which causal relations are neither observable nor reducible to observable properties and relations. Finally, I offer a general recipe for constructing a realist, singularist account, and a specific version that incorporates my own views on the nature of causation.

TOOMBS, S Kay. The Temporality of Illness: Four Levels of Experience. Theor Med, 11(3), 227-241, S 90.

This essay argues that, while much has been gained by medicine's focus on the spatial aspects of disease in light of developments in modern pathology, too little attention has been given to the temporal experience of illness at the subjective level of the patient. In particular, it is noted that there is a radical distinction between subjective and objective time. Whereas the patient experiences his immediate illness in terms of the ongoing flux of subjective time, the physician conceptualizes the illness as a disease state according to the measurements of objective time. A greater understanding of this disparity in temporal experiencing provides insights into the lived experience of illness and can preclude difficulties in communication between physician and patient.

TOPPER, David. The Parallel Fallacy: On Comparing Art and Science. Brit J Aes, 30(4), 311-318, O 90.

The argument is made that a proposition often found in discussions involving comparisons of art and science, from which it is usually deduced that art and science are fundamentally different, is false. The proposition is: The art work X would not exist without the artist Y, whereas the scientific theory P would exist without the scientist Q. This statement is fallacious because an art work cannot be compared with a theory. In particular, the case is made for a disjunction between theories and the artifacts (e.g., the primary sources) from which they come.

TORCHIA, N Joseph. The Significance of the Moral Concept of Virtue in St Augustine's Ethics. Mod Sch, 68(1), 1-17, N 90.

This paper examines four formulations of virtue that emerged at various stages of St. Augustine's intellectual development: (1) virtue as perfect reason; (2) virtue as perfect love; (3) virtue as good will; and (4) virtue as rightly ordered love. These formulations are linked together by means of a common theme: virtue presupposes order in regard to both reason and love. First, the virtuous individual is governed by reason and thus, able to resist the pull of corporeal inclinations and passions. Secondly, virtue entails an ordered love which renders to each good the respect it deserves in light of its place in the scale of creation.

TORELL, Kurt and POLANSKY, Ronald. Power, Liberty, and Counterfactual Conditionals in Hobbes' Thought. Hobbes Stud, 3, 3-17, 1990.

Power and liberty in Hobbes are difficult to understand in themselves and in their relationships. He identifies power with cause, and cause is said always to be actual. It seems then that power can only be actual rather than potential. But if so, how can there be dispositional properties and counterfactual conditions? Without these liberty seems impossible. To explain how Hobbes may account for potentialities, the paper distinguishes two levels of motion, observable and unobservable. In addition, it shows that liberty only applies on the level of the observable motions and therefore has a status somewhat like a secondary quality.

TORRANCE, T F. "Fundamental Issues in Theology and Science" in *Science and Religion: One World-Changing Perspectives on Reality*, FENNEMA, Jan (ed), 35-46. Norwell, Kluwer, 1990.

TORRE, Michael D (ed). *Freedom in the Modern World: Jacques Maritain, Yves R Simon, Mortimer J Adler*. Notre Dame, Univ Notre Dame Pr, 1989.

TORRE, Michael D. "The Freedoms of Man and Their Relation to God" in *Freedom in the Modern World: Jacques Maritain, Yves R Simon, Mortimer J Adler*, TORRE, Michael D (ed), 263-276. Notre Dame, Univ Notre Dame Pr, 1989.

TORRENS, Antoni. Boolean Products of CW—Algebras and Pseudo-Complementation. Rep Math Log, 23, 31-38, 1989.

We show that a W-algebra is a Boolean Product of CW-algebras if and only if its underlying lattice is pseudo-complemented. Moreover we relate these W-algebras with P-algebras, L-algebras and Heyting algebras.

TORRENS, Antoni and RODRIGUEZ, Antonio J. Lukasiewicz Logic and Wajsberg Algebras. Bull Sect Log, 19(2), 51-55, Je 90.

The purpose of this paper is to prove that the class of Wajsberg algebras is the equivalent variety semantics for Lukasiewicz Logic (in the sense of Blok-Pigozzi). This is obtained as a consequence of the main result of the paper which shows that in any algebra of type (2,1) the lattice of all Wajsberg implicative filters is isomorphic to the lattice of all congruence relation relative to the variety of Wajsberg algebras.

TOSEL, André. Libre spéculation sur le rapport du vivant et du social. Philosophique (France), 1(89), 55-68, 1989.

TOSEL, André. La loi et ses législateurs ou les avatars du théologico-politique. Philosophique (France), 1(91), 43-59, 1991.

TOSENOVSKY, Ludvik. On J L Fischer's Reflections About Categories of Dialectic Materialism (in Czechoslovakian). Filozof Cas, 38(4), 496-506, 1990.

The author begins with characterization of the main ideas of J L Fischer's "On Categories." He deduced that this renowned Czech structuralist intended to write on categories of dialectic materialism in accord with the aim he stated but, in fact, as he himself later revealed, this study rather developed the categories of his system of structural philosophy of the early 1930s and the post-war period. In Chapter 2 the author proceeds analysing, from the standpoint of his conception of Marxist philosophy, Fischer's conception of the categories, as well as his relation to logics and science. The author concludes by contemplation on J L Fischer's philosophy characterizing him as a philosopher whose work is remarkable by linking empirical attitudes with standpoints of functionalist rationalism within the specificity of Czech structuralism. (edited)

TOULMIN, Stephen. "From Leviathan to Lilliput" in *Celebrating Peace*, ROUNER, Leroy S (ed), 73-86. Notre Dame, Univ Notre Dame Pr, 1990.

TOULMIN, Stephen. "Medical Institutions and Their Moral Constraints" in *Integrity in Health Care Institutions: Humane Environments for Teaching, Inquiry, and Healing*, BULGER, Ruth Ellen (ed), 21-32. Iowa City, Univ of Iowa Pr, 1990.

TOURAILLE, Alain. Théories d'algébres de Boole munies d'idéaux distingués, II. J Sym Log, 55(3), 1192-1212, S 90.

TOWNSEND, Mike. Complexity for Type-2 Relations. Notre Dame J Form Log, 31(2), 241-262, Spr 90.

Type-2 recursion theory extends ordinary recursion theory by permitting arguments that are functions. In this paper, we consider extensions of the (relativized) polynomial hierarchy to include type-2 relations. In addition, we consider some topological notions that seem to be "naturally" associated with time and space bounded computations of oracle Turing machines, and we give topological characterizations of several classes of type-2 relations. We use these characterizations to examine certain type-2 analogues of several well-known open problems of computational complexity theory. The results suggest that topological considerations are an integral part of the study of resource bounded computations of oracle Turing machines.

TOZER, Steven. PES and School Reform. Educ Theor, 41(3), 301-310, Sum 91.

TOZZI, María Verónica. Tipos ideales en historia. Rev Filosof (Argentina), 5(1), 17-35, My 90.

This paper considers the explanations given in history, beginning with Weber's ideal types method. It follows the research of witchcraft pursuit in Europe along the XV, XVI and XVII centuries made by N Cohn. The aim of this paper is to show that the generalizations presupposed in the explanations of the several pursuits have a great explanatory value if they are considered not as a law of a *quasi-legal* sentence but as an ideal type. In this way, the interest of the historian in events and singular actions is satisfied, making possible a fruitful use in the research of other social sciences.

TRABANT, Jürgen. "Humboldt et Leibniz: Le concept intérieur de la linguistique" in *Leibniz, Humboldt, and the Origins of Comparativism*, DE MAURO, Tullio (ed), 135-156. Philadelphia, John Benjamins, 1990.

When, in 1820, Humboldt delivered his first paper on the comparative study of languages before the Prussian Academy of Sciences, it was a reply to a Leibnitian text and can be interpretated as a commentary on Leibniz's linguistic conceptions. As far as historical research (*cognatio*) is concerned, Humboldt contrasts Leibniz with a century of factual and methodological insights in comparative studies. In his major work, Humboldt tries to develop Leibniz's theorem of *mixtura* and *corruptio* as the sources of the creation of new languages. (edited)

TRACY, David. *Dialogue with the Other: The Inter-Religious Dialogue*. Grand Rapids, Eerdmans, 1991.

TRAGARDH, Lars. Swedish Model or Swedish Culture? Crit Rev, 4(4), 569-590, Fall 90.

The extent to which the "Swedish Model" is an intricate web of historically rooted socio-cultural patterns, is not well explored. A comparative historical analysis of the relationships between Swedish welfare institutions and Swedish values suggests that the Swedish Welfare State, associated with Social Democratic hegemony, was made possible by and still depends on cultural proclivities of ancient origins, perhaps most aptly described as simply "Swedish." Thus, the relevance and usefulness of the Swedish experience lies less in it being a transportable model and more in indicating the challenges posed by the complex relationship between culture and political reform.

TRAPANI JR, John G. "Maritain and Rifkin: Two Critiques" in *From Twilight to Dawn: The Cultural Vision of Jacques Maritain*, REDPATH, Peter A (ed), 215-223. Notre Dame, Univ Notre Dame Pr, 1990.

Written in honor of the 50th Anniversary of the publication of Jacques Maritain's book, *The Twilight of Civilization*, this essay contrasts the political significance of Maritain's book with the ecological significance of Jeremy Rifkin's book, *Declaration of a Heretic*. Just as Maritain identifies different political forms of government as rooted in different philosophical ideas concerning human nature, so Rifkin also claims that it is our thinking about human nature that influence our ideas concerning science and technology. Ultimately, their ideas draw basically the same fundamental conclusion: a view of human nature that is cut-off from its rootedness in the Divine is destined to serious negative consequences which are identified by this essay.

TRAU, Jane Mary. *The Co-Existence of God and Evil*. New York, Lang, 1991.

The atheist claims that proposition A, 'God exists' and proposition B, 'Evil exists' are logically inconsistent, especially in traditional Judeo-Christian context. If there is some third proposition C, consistent with A and whose conjunction with A implies B, then A and B are consistent. Proposition C, 'Evil has positive value,' is established by the theory of 'positive value,' first developed and then applied to the problem of evil. Traditional and modified versions of the doctrine of double effect show it possible that evil has positive value. C is compatible with A, and their conjunction implies B. Hence, 'God exists' and 'Evil exists' are compatible.

TRAVERSO, Patrizia. L'epocalità metafisica di Nietzsche: "Sentiero interrotto" della filosofia heideggeriana. Sapienza, 44(2), 203-215, Ap-Je 91.

TREBILCOT, Joyce. "Ethics of Method: Greasing the Machine and Telling Stories" in *Feminist Ethics*, CARD, Claudia (ed), 45-51. Lawrence, Univ Pr of Kansas, 1991.

TREMBLAY, Robert. Analyse critique de quelques modèles sémiotiques de l'idéologie (deuxième partie). Philosophiques, 17(2), 53-99, Autumn 1990.

This paper deals with the problem of analysing the question of ideology as a semiotic one. It shows the weakness of the main traditional developments on this issue. In the first part, I rejected the theories of Saussurian semioticians (Hjelmslev, Barthes and Greimas) because of their conception of language and connotation. In this second part, I analyse the sociosemiotic theories of Kristeva, Morris and Eco. In conclusion, I show the relevance of a Peircean approach of this problematic.

TRESKO, Michael. John Wyclif's Metaphysics of Scriptural Integrity in the *De Veritate Sacrae Scripturae*. Dionysius, 13, 153-196, D 89.

TRESS, Daryl Mc Gowan. Feminist Theory and Its Discontents. Interpretation, 18(2), 293-311, Wint 90-91.

TRIANA, Manuel. El hombre y el misterio del ser. Rev Filosof (Costa Rica), 28(67-68), 85-91, D 90.

After presenting some criticisms to traditional metaphysics, we present in this paper trends of Gabriel Marcel's ontology. We begin with the author's question "What am I?", and then show that the main way to the mystery of being is the demand of plenitude before the death of the ones we love.

TRIANOSKY, Gregory. "Natural Affection and Responsibility for Character: A Critique of Kantian Views of the Virtues" in *Identity, Character, and Morality: Essays in Moral Psychology*, FLANAGAN, Owen (ed), 93-109. Cambridge, MIT Pr, 1990.

Kantians characteristically claim that natural benevolent motives cannot be virtuous unless they are supplemented by an articulated awareness of the rightness or goodness of altruistic conduct. One Kantian argument in favor of this view holds that moral virtue must be to the credit of its possessor; and that natural affections per se cannot be to our credit because we are not responsible for having them. The first premise can be underminded by distinguishing credit or esteem from praise. In attacking the second premise I offer an account of responsibility for character which show that natural affections can be "up to us", even if they are neither chosen nor an outcome of our choice.

TRIANOSKY, Gregory. What is Virtue Ethics All About? Amer Phil Quart, 27(4), 335-344, O 90.

TRIGEAUD, Jean-Marc. *Philosophie Juridique Européenne*. Bordeaux, Biere, 1990.

TRIGG, Roger. "'Tales Artfully Spun'" in *The Bible as Rhetoric: Studies in Biblical Persuasion and Credibility*, WARNER, Martin (ed), 117-132. New York, Routledge, 1990.

Can what appears to be history in the New Testament be properly interpreted as something quite different, such as 'myth'? Could the Gospel writers have shared our modern understanding of historical accuracy? In fact, the idea of the difference between historical and poetic truth did not suddenly appear with the advent of modern science, but was crucial in the law court. New Testament authors were consciously on the witness-stand claiming truth and prepared for cross-examination. They believed that they were speaking of real events.

TRIGG, Roger. Wittgenstein and Social Science. Philosophy, 28, 209-222, 90 Supp.

TRINKAUS, Charles. Renaissance Ideas and the Idea of the Renaissance. J Hist Ideas, 51(4), 667-684, O-D 90.

This is a review article discussing *The Cambridge History of Renaissance Philosophy*, edited by Charles B Schmitt and Quentin Skinner, Cambridge: Cambridge University Press, 1988, and *Renaissance Humanism: Foundations, Forms and Legacy*, edited by Albert Rabil, Jr., Philadelphia: University of Pennsylvania Press, 1988, as well as other recent works in the field.

TRIPATHY, Laxman Kumar. Marxism and Social Change: Some Theoretical Reflections. J Indian Counc Phil Res, 7(3), 47-57, My-Ag 90.

TRIPLETT, Timm. Azande Logic *Verus* Western Logic? Brit J Phil Sci, 39(3), 361-366, S 88.

In *Knowledge and Social Imagery*, David Bloor suggests that logical reasoning is radically relativistic in the sense that there are incompatible ways of reasoning logically, and no culturally transcendent rules of correct logical inference exist which could allow for adjudication of these different ways of reasoning. Bloor cites an example of reasoning used by the Azande as an illustration of such logical relativism. A close analysis of this reasoning reveals that the Azande's logic is in fact impeccably Aristotelian. I argue that the conclusions Bloor can legitimately draw form his case study are not controversial and do nothing to make plausible the thesis of logical relativism.

TRIVEDI, Saam. On Metainductive Sentences. Indian Phil Quart, SUPP 17(4), 61-68, O 90.

How do we know that all inductive generalisations are probable/uncertain? We cannot know this itself through an inductive generalisation, becaue if this were so, then one would face a problematic indirect self-reference. Also, while inductive generalisations are uncertain it is certain that they are uncertain. It is a necessary truth obtained through intuitive induction.

TROISFONTAINES, Claude. Philosophie et religion. Rev Phil Louvain, 88(78), 256-270, My 90.

TROTT, Elizabeth Anne. Music, Meaning, and the Art of Elocution. J Aes Educ, 24(2), 91-98, Sum 90.

TROUT, J D. Belief Attribution in Science: Folk Psychology under Theoretical Stress. Synthese, 87(3), 379-400, Je 91.

I argue that eliminativism is untouched by this simple charge of inconsistency, and introduce a different dialectical strategy for arguing against the eliminativist. I show that neuroscientists routinely rely on folk psychological procedures of intentional state attribution in applying epistemically reliable standards of scientific evaluation. The dependence of science on folk psychology, when combined with an independently plausible explanatory constraint on reduction and an independently motivated notion of *theoretical stress*, allows us to reconstitute the charge of (neurophilic) eliminativist inconsistency in a more sophisticated form. (edited)

TROUT, J D (ed) and BOYD, Richard (ed) and GASPER, Philip (ed). *The Philosophy of Science*. Cambridge, MIT Pr, 1991.

TROUTT, Marvin D. On Some Multiattribute Value Function Generalizations of the EQQ Model in the Context of Personal Inventory Decisions. Theor Decis, 30(2), 95-107, Mr 91.

By personal inventory decisions we mean the decisions on quantity purchased which are made daily in such activities as grocery shopping. This topic has previously been introduced only at the conceptual level. Hence our main purpose is to provide a quantitative discussion. Some specific models are pursued to solution. Surprisingly, a conjoint value function aggregator leads to indifference in replenishment quantity. Contrasts to the EOQ assumptions are highlighted.

TROWITZSCH, Michael. Friedrich Schleiermacher und die Praktische Philosophie. Phil Rundsch, 37(3), 227-241, 1990.

TRUBEK, David M. "Programmatic Thought and the Critique of the Social Disciplines" in *Critique and Construction: A Symposium on Roberto Unger's "Politics"*, LOVIN, Robin W (ed), 232-241. New York, Cambridge Univ Pr, 1990.

TRUCHLINSKA, Bogumila. Bogdan Suchodolski's Philosophy of Culture (in Polish). Ann Univ Mariae Curie-Phil, 10, 203-227, 1985.

The study deals with B Suchodolski's early thought, from the two decades of the interwar period. His philosophical views about culture concentrated then on the problems of the opposition between culture and nature, the ontological status of culture, relation between subjective and objective culture, unity and variety in culture, culture understood as a way of life, as well as on methodological problems concerning the study of culture. His considerations on culture and nature reveal B Suchodolski's anti-positivistic and anti-naturalistic approach; he is for the humanistic conception of culture and man, emphasizing man's role as the subject in culture. Therefore, he also questions the traditional distinction between creators and recipients of culture while trying to endow culture with a universal dimension. Hence, Suchodolski's approach is characterized by democratism and anti-elitism. Other distinctive features of his philosophy of culture include anti-intellectualism, anti-aestheticism, ethical rigorism, and a tendency to a holistic approach to culture. (edited)

TRUNDLE JR, Robert C. The Cases *For* and *Against* Theological Approaches to Business Ethics. Laval Theol Phil, 47(2), 241-259, Je 91.

A philosophical case *against* theology might consist of a constructive dilemma: If theology embraces a rationality of business persons, then it relinquishes religious belief, and if theology does not embrace such a rationality, then it does not properly contribute to business ethics. Either the first or second antecedent obtains. Therefore, theology relinquishes religious belief or does not properly contribute to business ethics. The case *for* theology does not, as has been alleged, attack all philosophy by arguing that this dilemma dogmatically presupposes an overly rational conception of human nature. Moreover, theology's perennial effectiveness in morally evaluating business persons proceeds *pari passu* with its reflecting a moral nature of persons.

TRUNDLE, Robert. The Politics of Ethics: Socratic Questioning is Needed in the Marketplace. Bridges, 2(3-4), 127-141, Fall-Wint 90.

Truth-claims about political practices being good presuppose knowing what is good. But knowing the good, in terms of truth-claims about it, presupposes a theory of truth. And since "truth" is ascribed of statements about reality, such a theory involves a theory about reality as well. But analyses of such theories, traditionally engendered by serious political conflict, have been usurped by a "politicalization" of ethics: Ethics and the theories it presupposes are not used to assess politics but rather politics (or political commitments) are misguidedly employed to assess ethics.

TRUNDLE, Robert. The Reasonableness of Moral Reasons. Dialogos, 26(57), 137-147, Ja 91.

Moral reasons (rules) and their purposes, say P_1 and P_2, in different societies, say Θ and ς respectively, either presuppose that something is good *per se* or they do not. If they do not, then P_1 and P_2 are morally pointless. If they do, and if it is not clear whether the good *per se* is universally good, then the presupposition of $P_1(P_2)$ might be correct in Θ (ς) and incorrect in ς (Θ). This renders a relativity if not incoherence that is fostered, in recent ethical theory, by an unwarranted avoidance of any "unverifiable" universal good.

TRUSTED, Jennifer. Whose Life is it Anyway? J Applied Phil, 7(2), 223-227, O 90.

This paper addresses a current confusion in debates on the morality of experimentation on human pre-embryos: the confusion that arises from ambiguity in the sense of 'human being'. We may quite legitimately decide to apply the term 'human being' to all entities with human DNA but in that case we should not then imply that all human beings are as much objects of moral concern as the fetus or a post-parturate human being. It is argued that whatever classifying terms we use, potential entities need to be distinguished from actual entities and that the very notion of potentiality rests on this distinction. The paper does not offer an argument in favour of experimentation, rather it appeals for clear thought. Moral attitudes to experimentation of pre-embryos are varied and attempts to analyse issues through implicit appeal to emotionally ambiguous terms do not help the moral debate.

TSALIKIS, John and NWACHUKWU, Osita. A Comparison of Nigerian to American Views of Bribery and Extortion in International Commerce. J Bus Ethics, 10(2), 85-98, F 91.

This study investigates the differences in the way bribery and extortion is perceived by two different cultures—American and Nigerian. Two hundred and forty American business students and one hundred and eighty Nigerian business students were presented with three scenarious describing a businessman offering a bribe to a government official and three scenarios describing a businessman being forced by pay a bribe to an official in order to do business. The Reidenbach-Robin instrument was used to measure the ethical reactions of the two samples to these scenarios. Results indicate that ethical reactions to bribery and extortion vary by (a) the nationality of the person offering the bribe, and (b) the country where the bribe is offered. In addition, Nigerians perceived some of the scenarios as being less unethical than did Americans.

TSCHURENEV, Eva-Maria. Natural and Political Society in the Thought of Edmund Burke (in German). Deut Z Phil, 38(5), 461-469, 1990.

A fair opinion about the characteristic feature of Edmund Burke's thought cannot be formed without regarding his two earliest writings "A Philosophical Inquiry into the Origin of our Ideas on the Sublime and Beautiful" and "A Vindication of Natural Society...". The careful interpretation of the latter treatise, still today controversially reviewed, shows interesting agreements, as well as with his theses not only in the "Inquiry...", as also in the most-known "Reflections on the Revolution in France" and three further memorials against the revolution. So, for example, what concerns the idea on society and on the contract of society.

TSING, Zou and DASHENG, Gao. "Philosophy of Technology in China" in *Philosophy of Technology*, DURBIN, Paul T (ed), 133-151. Norwell, Kluwer, 1989.

TSIPKO, A. The Sources of Stalinism. Soviet Stud Phil, 29(2), 6-31, Fall 90.

TSIPKO, A. Was Marx a Socialist? Soviet Stud Phil, 30(1), 6-13, Sum 91.

TSOHATZIDIS, S L. "Illocutionary Pretence Inside and Outside Fiction" in *XIth International Congress in Aesthetics, Nottingham 1988*, WOODFIELD, Richard (ed), 225-226. Nottingham, Nottingham Polytech, 1990.

TSUI, Amy B M. Sequencing Rules and Coherence in Discourse. J Prag, 15(2), 111-129, F 91.

This paper examines sequencing rules governing conversational organization. First, it argues against Levinson's (1983) position that it is impossible to formulate sequencing rules such as the one governing an *adjacency pair* which states the expectation of a certain speech act following the occurrence of a given speech act. Levinson (1983) argues that *question* can happily be followed by a range of speech acts other than *answer*. The present paper points out that while it is true that a *question* is not necessarily followed by an *answer*; it does not follow that the rule does not apply: it states what is *expected* to occur, not what *actually* occurs (see Berry 1982). Second, the paper points out that not only is there a rule governing what is *expected* to occur, but there is also a rule governing what is *allowed* to occur if the discourse is to be coherent. (edited)

TUCHANSKA, Barbara. Marxism as the Foundation of Philosophies of Science: *The Case of G Lukács' Ontology of Social Being*. Stud Soviet Tho, 41(1), 1-17, Ja 91.

The purpose of the paper is to discuss the possibility of founding philosophy of science on Marxism. Marxism seems helpful in resolving current issues in the post-analytic philosophy of science (the problem of scientific method, incommensurability, or the question of the developmental mechanisms of science). Their resolution requires concepts referring both to psycho-social and macro-social, historical dimensions of human affairs. Certain existing Marxist philosophers of science are briefly discussed and found unsatisfactory. Then, Lukacs's ontology of social being is analyzed. The discussion concludes with the claim that Lukacs's philosophy cannot help in solving those problems.

TUCK, Richard. *Hobbes*. New York, Oxford Univ Pr, 1989.

TUCK, Richard (ed) and HOBBES, Thomas. *Leviathan: Hobbes*. New York, Cambridge Univ Pr, 1991.

TUGENDHAT, Ernst. "The Necessity for Cooperation between Philosophical and Empirical Research" in *The Moral Domain: Essays in the Ongoing Discussion between Philosophy and the Social Sciences*, WREN, Thomas E (ed), 3-14. Cambridge, MIT Pr, 1990.

TULLOCK, Gordon. The Economics of (Very) Primitive Societies. J Soc Biol Struct, 13(2), 151-162, My 90.

Most current biological work on social species depends on Hamiltonian altruism for the integration of the society. Undoubtedly, such altruism is important in some social species, but by not means all. This essay revives the older view in which the social structure depended very heavily simply on niches in which a social group could outcompete individuals. Cooperation is necessary to competitive survival and noncooperative genes are selected out by nonsurvival of the entire nest that contains them. Game theory is used to analyze different degrees of cooperation.

TULLY, James. Political Freedom. J Phil, 87(10), 517-523, O 90.

John Locke held that the institutions of government and the traditions of their interpretation derive from and rest upon the prior freedom of the people to acquire and exercise the political powers of government themselves. Locke's contemporaries denied this thesis of popular sovereignty. They argued that political powers and freedom derive from and rest upon a background structure of political institutions and traditions. Both liberals and communitarians in our current debate share this anti-Lockean premise of institutional sovereignty. The revolutions in eastern Europe suggest that Locke may have been right.

TUMMALA, V M Rao and KARNI, Reuven and SANCHEZ, Pedro. A Comparative Study of Multiattribute Decision Making Methodologies. Theor Decis, 29(3), 203-222, N 90.

Three "real life" cases are considered in this paper to apply and compare the ranking obtained by the Analytic Hierarchy Process (AHP) and other Multicriteria Decision Making (MCDM) techniques such as Simple Additive Weighting (SAW),

ELECTRE and Weighted Linear Assignment Method (WLAM). The results indicated that the AHP, SAW, and ELECTRE rankings do not differ significantly, however, the WLAM tends to exhibit more disagreement. However, because of the limited nature of this study, we do not suggest this as a general conclusion.

TUNDO, Laura. *L'Utopia di Fourier*. Bari, Dedalo, 1991.

TUNG, Shih-Ping. Decidable Fragments of Field Theories. J Sym Log, 55(3), 1007-1018, S 90.

We call an arithmetical sentence *A* a universal-existential sentence if it is logically equivalent to a sentence with a single universal quantifier and a single existential quantifier. In this paper we show that there are algorithms to decide whether or not a given such sentence is true (1) an algebraic number field, (2) every number field, (3) every field with characteristic 0, (4) every cyclic (abelian, radical) extension field over *Q*, (5) every field.

TUOMELA, Raimo. "Actions by Collectives" in *Philosophical Perspectives, 3: Philosophy of Mind and Action Theory, 1989*, TOMBERLIN, James E (ed), 471-496. Atascadero, Ridgeview, 1989.

The paper gives an analysis of the notion of an action performed by a social collective. This analysis is largely based on the relevant joint actions performed by the members of the collective. Several examples are presented in support of the view defended.

TUOMELA, Raimo. Intentional Single and Joint Action. Phil Stud, 62(3), 235-262, Je 91.

The paper presents a criticism of Bratman's recent account of the contents of endeavorings or willings and proceeds to give an analysis of intentional action-both single and joint action. Two senses of intentional action are distinguished-the core sense (related to aiming) and a wide sense (related to expected consequences the agent is concerned with). Both fully intentional and weakly intentional joint actions are analyzed and discussed.

TUOMELA, Raimo. Ruben and the Metaphysics of the Social World. Brit J Phil Sci, 40(2), 261-273, Je 89.

The paper is a critical assessment of David-Hillel Ruben's book "The Metaphysics of the Social World" (Routledge, 1985). Ruben's defense of methodological holism is criticized on several grounds. It is also argued that given a nominalist account of properties Ruben's position in fact is compatible with a kind of liberal methodological individualism.

TUOMELA, Raimo. We Will Do It: An Analysis of Group Intentions. Phil Phenomenol Res, 51(2), 249-277, Je 91.

If a person intends for his group, we may call his intention a group-intention. The main task of the present paper is to give informative truth-conditions for locutions like "We will do X", when understood as expressions of group-intention. The first part of the paper gives an account of "action-prompting" group-intentions, termed we-intentions. This account improves on the author's previous analysis of this notion and of its significance. In the rest of the paper other kinds of group-intentions, especially conditional we-intentions and "standing" group-intentions, are investigated.

TURCHETTO, Maria and ESPOSITO, Joan (trans). The Divided Machine: Capitalist Crisis and the Organization of Labor. Grad Fac Phil J, 14(1), 209-240, 1991.

TURCO, Giovanni. La fondazione dei valori nell'assiologia critica di Nicola Petruzzellis. Sapienza, 43(4), 391-399, O-D 90.

TURGEON, Wendy. Pedagogy of the Unimpressed: Philosophy for Children and the Adult Learner. Thinking, 9(3), 40, 1990.

TURIANO, Mark. Peirce's Realism, Intentionality and Final Causation. Dialogue (PST), 33(2-3), 41-45, Ap 91.

After a brief discussion of some concepts fundamental to Peirce's philosophy I go on to close relationship for Peirce between the intentionality of the sign relation and final causation, with the former being but an instance of the latter. These concepts are then related to Peirce's ontology and realism, particularly to show how Peirce regarded the latter as fundamental to all his thought.

TURK, Horst. "The Question of Translatability: Benjamin, Derrida, Quine" in *Hermeneutics and the Poetic Motion, Translation Perspectives V—1990*, SCHMIDT, Dennis J (ed), 43-56. Binghamton, CRIT, 1990.

The question of plurality of languages appears in a different light depending on whether one looks at it either from the aspect of meaning (in its sense of reference), or from the aspect of demarcation (in its sense of difference), or from the aspect of sense (in its sense of correspondence). My point of view is, that we are obliged to control human communication by nonverbal experience as well as nonverbal experience by human communication and universal concepts of human understanding by different modes of articulation as well as different modes of articulation by universal concepts of human understanding.

TURNER, Dean. *Escape from God*. Pasadena, Hope, 1991.

TURNER, Jeffrey S. To Tell a Good Tale: Kierkegaardian Reflections on Moral Narrative and Moral Truth. Man World, 24(2), 181-198, Ap 91.

In *Whose Justice? Which Rationality?* Alasdair MacIntyre lays out a "traditional conception" of moral truth which is a plausible candidate for the conception of truth underlying narrative theories of morality. But this view is unable to deal with the threat to our moral narratives found in what Kierkegaard called "the aesthetic sphere." A look at *Either/Or* establishes a fundamental kinship between MacIntyre's conception and Judge William's: both fail prey to the seductive danger of over-aestheticizing one's own tales. Hence we are left, as Kierkegaard intimated in *Either/Or*, with a *tension* between the beautiful and the good.

TURNER, Raymond. Logics of Truth. Notre Dame J Form Log, 31(2), 308-329, Spr 90.

This paper surveys three recent semantic theories of truth and compares them from the perspective of their underlying logics. In particular, the underlying logic of the Gupta-Herzberger theory is investigated, and an analysis of modal logics of truth arising from this semantic theory is given.

TURNER, Susan (Guerin) and BOETZKES, Elisabeth and SOBSTYL, Edrie. Women, Madness, and Special Defences in the Law. J Soc Phil, 21(2-3), 127-139, Fall-Wint 90.

In this article some legal/jurisprudential peculiarities of the Canadian Infanticide Statute are targeted. The Statute is unjust, since it cites mental imbalance (which ought to mitigate or excuse) as an element of the offence. This anomaly is attributed to prejudicial perceptions of women embedded in the law. Two such perceptions are traced—women as uniquely good (and thus particularly depraved in infanticide); and women as morally defective (and thus dangerous to society). Possible options for the reform of the law are considered, and a qualified recommendation made that post-partum depression serves as a special defence for homocide, pending a thorough legal reform addressing the perception of women in the law.

TURNEY, Peter. The Curve Fitting Problem: A Solution. Brit J Phil Sci, 41(4), 509-530, D 90.

Much of scientific inference involves fitting numerical data with a curve, or functional relation. The received view is that the fittest curve is the curve which best balances the conflicting demands of simplicity and accuracy, where simplicity is measured by the number of parameters in the curve. The problem with this view is that there is no commonly accepted justification for desiring simplicity. This paper presents a measure of the stability of equations. It is argued that the fittest curve is the curve which best balances stability and accuracy. The received view is defended with a proof that simplicity corresponds to stability, for linear regression equations.

TURNEY, Peter. Embeddability, Syntax, and Semantics in Accounts of Scientific Theories. J Phil Log, 19(4), 429-451, N 90.

Recently several philosophers of science have proposed what has come to be known as the *semantic* account of scientific theories. It is presented as an improvement on the positivist account, which is now called the *syntactic* account of scientific theories. Bas van Fraassen claims that the syntactic account does not give a satisfactory definition of "empirical adequacy" and "empirical equivalence." He contends that his own semantic account does define these notations acceptably, through the concept of "embeddability," a concept which he claims cannot be defined syntactically. Here, I define a syntactic relation which corresponds to the semantic relation of "embeddability." I suggest that the critical differences between the positivist account and van Fraassen's account have nothing to do with the distinction between semantics and syntax.

TURNEY, Peter. A Note on Popper's Equation of Simplicity with Falsifiability. Brit J Phil Sci, 42(1), 105-109, Mr 91.

Karl Popper equates simplicity with falsifiability. He develops his argument for this equation through a geometrical example. There is a flaw in his example, which undermines his claim that simplicity is falsifiability. I point out the flaw here.

TURPEN, Richard A and STANGA, Keith G. Ethical Judgments on Selected Accounting Issues: An Empirical Study. J Bus Ethics, 10(10), 739-747, O 91.

This study investigates the judgments made by accounting majors when confronted with selected ethical dilemmas that pertain to accounting practice. Drawing upon literature in philosophy and moral psychology, it then examines these judgments for potential gender differences. Five case studies, each involving a specific ethical delimma that a practicing accountant might face, were administered to 151 accounting majors (males = 67; females = 84), in four sections of intermediate accounting II at a large, state university. The results suggest that although the vast majority of participants would *not* engage in unethical behavior, a reasonable opportunity exists to improve the participants' ethical awareness. The results do not, however, support the existence of gender differences in ethical judgments.

TURRISI, Patricia A. Peirce's Logic of Discovery: Abduction and the Universal Categories. Trans Peirce Soc, 26(4), 465-497, Fall 90.

TURSKI, George. Emotions and Responsibility. Phil Today, 35(2), 137-152, Sum 91.

The paper addresses some of the complexities involved in the notion of being responsible for our emotions. It opens with an exposition of two influential accounts of responsibility (i.e., Aristotle's and Sartre's). Next, certain experiential and structural features of emotions and actions are examined with a view to reassessing the utility of the action-passion distinction which standardly plays a critical role in thinking about responsibility. A hermeneutic or interpretationist approach to emotions, wherein responsibility is a function of a self-transforming reflective practice, is then offered as a position valuable for the manner in which it meets the issues raised. But the exercise of reflective capacities (as well as their potential for changing ourselves) must itself be placed within a broader context of a developmental-normative theory of motivation and human nature. Nor can the function of these capacities be assessed in abstraction from a social setting.

TUSA, Carlo. Elogio critico dell'imperfezione. Riv Int Filosof Diritto, 67(1), 140-148, Ja-Mr 90.

TUSA, Carlo. La speranza nel giusnaturalismo. Riv Int Filosof Diritto, 67(2), 282-289, Ap-Je 90.

TUSHNET, Mark. Change and Continuity in the Concept of Civil Rights: Thurgood Marshall and Affirmative Action. Soc Phil Pol, 8(2), 150-171, Spr 91.

Critics sometimes contend that contemporary affirmative action programs are inconsistent with the individualist vision of earlier civil rights advocates, because the programs rely on a theory of group rights. Thurgood Marshall's work as a lawyer and Justice shows that, although individualist themes were prominent in his lawyer's work, his later support for affirmative action rests not on a group rights theory but on the ideas that courts should defer to majoritarian decisions about appropriate remedies for past discrimination, and that the goal of such remedies is improving the condition of the African-American community.

TUURI, Heikki and HYTTINEN, Tapani. Constructing Strongly Equivalent Nonisomorphic Models for Unstable Theories. Annals Pure Applied Log, 52(3), 203-248, Je 91.

TWEEDALE, Martin. Aristotle's Motionless Soul. Dialogue (Canada), 29(1), 123-132, 1990.

When Aristotle in *De Anima* I denies that the soul has motions and claims that those *pathe* which clearly are motions and which are often attributed to the soul should in fact be assigned to the composite of soul and physical organs, this should not be interpreted as implying that the soul undergoes no changes whatsoever. Aristotle allows that states and various first actualities come to be and pass away in the soul. But the soul itself is not something that admits of coming-to-be and passing-away; it has an all or nothing existence similar to that Aristotle assigns to mathematical entities.

TWENEY, Ryan D. On Bureaucracy and Science: A Response to Fuller. Phil Soc Sci, 21(2), 203-213, Je 91.

TYE, Michael. Vague Objects. Mind, 99(396), 535-557, O 90.

I believe that there are vague objects. This view apparently is not shared by very many other philosophers. It is often said that the world is perfectly precise and that vagueness resides only in language. On the face of it, this is a deeply puzzling position; for common sense has it that the world contains countries, mountains, and islands, for example, and these items certainly do not seem to be perfectly precise. I attempt to clarify the thesis that there are vague objects, as I accept it, and I defend this thesis against sorites arguments and the argument from identity.

TYMAN, Stephen. "The Problem of Evil in Proto-Ethical Idealism: J W Miller's Ethics in Historical Context" in *The Philosophy of John William Miller*, FELL, Joseph P (ed), 96-110. Lewisburg, Bucknell Univ Pr, 1990.

TYMOCZKO, Thomas. "Brains Don't Lie: They Don't Even Make Many Mistakes" in *Doubting: Contemporary Perspectives on Skepticism*, ROTH, Michael D (ed), 195-213. Norwell, Kluwer, 1990.

TYSON, Thomas. Believing that Everyone Else is Less Ethical: Implications for Work Behavior and Ethics Instruction. J Bus Ethics, 9(9), 715-721, S 90.

Studies consistently report that individuals believe they are far more ethical than coworkers, superiors, or managers in other firms. The present study confirms this finding when comparing undergraduate students' own ethical standards to their perceptions of the standards held by most managers or supervisors. By maintaining a "holier than thou" ethical perception, new and future managers might rationalize their unethical behavior as being necessary for success in an unethical world. A prisoner's dilemma type problem can be said to exist when choosing an unethical behavior becomes each player's dominant strategy and the interaction of dominant behaviors is Pareto inferior. Dispelling the "holier than thou" perception may encourage students to revise their personal behavior payoffs such that the collective benefits that emanate from ethical conduct are favored and the prisoner's dilemma problem is converted into a coordination problem.

UBEROI, J P S. The Other European Science of Nature? J Indian Counc Phil Res, 5(1), 121-132, S-D 87.

UCCIANI, Louis. Eléments pour une philosophie de l'expression. Philosophique (France), 1(90), 13-26, 1990.

Toute philosophie de y expre3ssion serait une philosophie de la force contrariée—elle pense et dit le barrage et sa brisure. Une illustration du mécanisme expressif est donnée par Schopenhauer dans son explication du sise. It proviendrait de ce qu'une limite est devenue inopérante. Or dans la perspective Schopenhauerienne, toute limite est le frit de la representation. Dès lors toute philosophie de l'expression devieut une critique de la representation.

UCCIANI, Louis. Notes sur une référence fugitive: Schopenhauer lecteur de Plotin. Philosophique (France), 1(91), 83-96, 1991.

L'utilisation de références diverses est caracteristique de l'expression de Schopenhauer. L dégage ainsi un avieère. Fond de l'histoire de la philosophie qui servirait d'attache et de référence à sa propre expression. Si Plotin en foit légitimement partie Schopenhauer ne l'abords cependant qu'avec méfiance—momieut de la rupture, le jugement sux les gnostiques. La où Plotin les combat, Schopenhauer les defend et propulse référence, au none du pessimisme contre l'optimisme.

UCCIANI, Louis. La vie, ou le point de rupture: Schopenhauer-Nietzsche. Philosophique (France), 1(89), 91-105, 1989.

Certes Nietzsche voir bien dans la vie la même desolation gu'y met Schopenhauer—mais là où Schopenhauer voit finalement dansceconstat une généralité qui s'impose à tous—nous serions tous égaox face à te souffiance, Nietzsche impose une discrimination. Sa lucidité soppose au pessimisme de Schopenhauer et finalement le piège. La demonstration parcourt la theorie Schopenhauerienne de la representation où la critique manifeste se transmue en justification.

UDOIDEM, S Iniobong. "Metaphysical Foundations of Freedom in the Social and Political Thought of Yves R Simon" in *Freedom in the Modern World: Jacques Maritain, Yves R Simon, Mortimer J Adler*, TORRE, Michael D (ed), 101-107. Notre Dame, Univ Notre Dame Pr, 1989.

The essay is an analysis of the ontological foundations of freedom. With the use of the ontological groundings such as superdetermination and autonomy, the essay argues that freedom even in the social sphere is not in any way opposed to authority, rather, that the requirements of true law and the common good, far from limiting an individual's freedom actually empowers it. The essay has helped in the clarification of the relationship between freedom and authority.

UE, Satoko. Über das Geschmacksurteil und die künstlerische Freiheit bei Kant (in Japanese). Bigaku, 41(4), 34-45, Spr 91.

Die Spontaneität im Spiel der Erkenntnisvermögen, deren Zusammenstimmung den Grund der Lust im Geschmacksurteil enthält, macht nach Kant den Begriff der Urteilskraft von einer Zweckmässigkeit der Natur zur Vermittlung der Verknüpfung der Gebiete des Naturbegriffs mit dem Freiheitsbegriff in ihren Folgen tauglich, indem diese zugleich die Empfänglichkeit des Gemüts für das moralische Gefühl fördert. (edited)

UEBEL, Thomas E. Scientific Racism in the Philosophy of Science: Some Historical Examples. Phil Forum, 22(1), 1-18, Fall 90.

The question is investigated whether scientific racism—the masking of purported racial prejudice by scientific fact—can afflict not only first-order theories but also the philosophy of science. An affirmative answer is suggested by the investigation of the biological theories of knowledge underlying the metatheories of Poincaré, Duhem and Boltzmann which reveal affinities with social/racial Darwinism.

UJLAKI, Gabriella. Historical Continuity and Discontinuity in the Philosophy of Gadamer and Foucault (in Hungarian). Magyar Filozof Szemle, 5-6, 531-573, 1990.

The subject matter of the study is to compare Gadamer's hermeneutics to Foucault's archeology of knowledge. These two authors are linked by their concerns with the problems of knowledge in history, but they take opposite standpoints. Gadamer's hermeneutics compares the knowledge of the different epochs of history with the general idea of cognition. Foucault's archeology rejects the concept of a general idea of knowledge, and takes the different epochs of history to be the most accessible framework of cognition. (edited)

ULLIAN, Joseph S. "Learning and Meaning" in *Perspectives on Quine*, BARRETT, Robert (ed), 336-346. Cambridge, Blackwell, 1990.

I state a principle about meaning that I regard as Quinian in spirit: what we can mean by our terms cannot go very much beyond what was, or might have been involved in our leaning of them. The main term examined here is 'true'. The notion of truth is compared with that of *set*; each of these is found to leave many issues in its field unsettled. It is argued that though truth-values are clear for observation sentences, they are well withheld from sentences too remote from the observational, sentences unmoored by meanings.

ULLIAN, Joseph S. Truth. J Aes Educ, 25(1), 57-65, Spr 91.

I use a Quinian attitude toward meaning to argue that in only a limited range of cases is it clear what we are saying when we call a statement *true*. I urge that neither disquotation nor other paraphrase brings truth into sharp focus. Beyond the realm of observation, truth values are not generally fixed by anything we are clear about. Perhaps the conviction that they are determined independently of us is just an illusion forced upon us by a seductive word and a misleading theory about it. My conclusions have a Goodmanian flavor.

ULRICH, Dolph. An Integer-Valued Matrix Characteristic for Implicational *S5*. Bull Sect Log, 19(3), 87-91, O 90.

UMPHREY, Stewart. *Zetetic Skepticism*. Wolfeboro, Longwood, 1990.

UN-CHOL, Shin. Panofsky, Polanyi, and Intrinsic Meaning. J Aes Educ, 24(4), 17-32, Wint 90.

The purpose of this article is to provide Polanyi's theory of tacit knowing as an epistemological justification for Panofsky's concept of meaning in general and for his concept of intrinsic meaning in particular. In his iconography, Panofsky explains three levels of meaning with intrinsic meaning at the highest level. The three levels are placed in an ascending order that recognizes the meaning of a higher level greater than those at lower levels. In this article, the greater meaning of a higher level in Panofsky's iconography is supported and justified by Polanyi's epistemology.

UNGEHEUER, Gerold (ed). *Kommunikations-Theoretische Schriften II: Symbolische Erkenntnis und Kommunikation*. Aachen, Alano, 1990.

The author's main focus of research is the problem of cognitive symbolism, which he has tried to solve through texts from Plato, Nietzsche and Frege. Attempted solutions to this essential semiotic problem have been tried throughout the history of philosophy, yet it has received little attention in our present culture and therefore it is important to acknowledge how our present philosophy is influenced by the problem of cognitive symbolism. (staff)

UPADHYAYA, K N. Sankara on Reason, Scriptural Authority and Self-Knowledge. J Indian Phil, 19(2), 121-132, Je 91.

This paper demonstrates that Sankara essentially is neither a rationalist nor a traditionalist, as he is generally regarded; he is indeed an experientialist. It is precisely because of his experiential approach that he is in a position to make a unique synthesis of both reason and scriptural authority. It has also been shown how paradoxically Sankara maintains the supremacy of knowledge while holding at the same time that all conventional means of knowledge (*pramānas*) are ultimately rooted in nescience (*avidyā*). The controversy of whether or not Self or Brahman can be an object of knowledge has also been resolved.

URBACH, Peter. "The Bayesian Alternative to the Methodology of Scientific Research Programmes" in *Imre Lakatos and Theories of Scientific Change*, GAVROGLU, Kostas (ed), 399-412. Norwell, Kluwer, 1989.

URBACH, Peter. A Reply to Mayo's Criticisms of Urbach's "Randomization and the Design of Experiments". Phil Sci, 58(1), 125-128, Mr 91.

Mayo (1987) sought to discredit Urbach's (1985) arguments against randomization as a universal requirement in clinical and agricultural trials. The present reply rebuts Mayo's criticisms.

URBACH, Peter. What is a Law of Nature? A Humean Answer. Brit J Phil Sci, 39(2), 193-209, Je 88.

URBAN, Wayne J. Is There a New Teacher Unionism? Educ Theor, 41(3), 331-339, Sum 91.

URBANAS, Alban. On the Alleged Impossibility of a Science of Accidents in Aristotle. Grad Fac Phil J, 13(2), 55-77, 1990.

URBAS, Igor. On Subsystems of the System J_1 of Arruda and Da Costa. Z Math Log, 36(2), 95-106, 1990.

Subsystems of the paraconsistent sequent-system Jl of Arruda and da Costa are obtained by varying the negation postulates. Corresponding Gentzen-style sequent-systems and axiomatics are provided for most of these subsystems and coincidence of theorems is shown by proving Cut-eliminability for the Gentzen systems.

URBAS, Igor. Paraconsistency and the J-Systems of Arruda and da Costa. Log Anal, 31(121-122), 27-44, Mr-Je 88.

Of the five J=systems of Arruda and da Costa, J5 explicitly fails to be paraconsistent in allowing arbitrary conclusions to be derived from inconsistent premises, while J2 to J4 substantively fail in allowing arbitrary implicational conclusions to be derived. Only J5 enjoys the property of intersubstitutivity of provable equivalents, and is moreover the weakest extension of any of the J-systems which enjoys this property.

URBINATI, Nadia. La filosofia civile di Pasquale Villari. G Crit Filosof Ital, 68(3), 369-402, S-D 89.

URIARTE, Jose Ramon and AIZPURUA, Jose Maria and NIETO, Jorge. Choice Procedure Consistent with Similarity Relations. Theor Decis, 29(3), 235-254, N 90.

We deal with the approach, initiated by Rubinstein, which assumes that people, when evaluating pairs of lotteries, use similarity relations. We interpret these relations as a way of modelling the imperfect powers of discrimination of the human mind and study the relationship between preferences and similarities. The class of both preferences and similarities that we deal with is larger than that considered by Rubinstein. The extension is made because we do not want to restrict ourselves to lottery spaces. Thus, under the above interpretation of a similarity, we find that some of the axioms imposed by Rubinstein are not justified if we want to consider other fields of choice theory. We show that any preference consistent with a pair of similarities is monotone on a subset of the choice space. We establish the implication upon the similarities of the requirement of making indifferent alternatives with a component which is zero. Furthermore, we show that Rubinstein's general results can also be obtained in this larger class of both preferences and similarity relations.

URPETH, James R. Need, Denial and Abandonment: Heidegger and the Turn. Phil Stud (Ireland), 32, 176-196, 1988-90.

This paper critically assesses Heidegger's thematisation of the 'turn' within the 'history of being' in terms of a contrast, derived from Nietzche, between 'incomplete' and 'affirmative' nihilism. It argues that, whilst Heidegger frequently reinforces the presence/absence opposition, there are transgressive elements within his discourse which sustain his insights into the nature of being as absential self-differing and overcome his tendency to interpret the technological world negatively. It also discusses Derrida's suspicion that Heidegger resists the necessary 'contamination of essence' and suggests that his texts often have a 'moral' character which suppresses the transvaluative potential of the question of being.

URQUHART, Alasdair. "The Logic of Physical Theory" in *Physicalism in Mathematics*, IRVINE, Andrew D (ed), 145-154. Norwell, Kluwer, 1990.

Hartry Field has proposed a programme for philosophy of science which he describes as "nominalizing physical theory." The programme consists in setting out a "nominalistic" formulation of physics, and then showing that the theory which results by the addition of mathematical postulates is a conservative extension of the original theory. The present paper discusses the various ways in which this idea can be made precise, whether the programme can be carried out, and its philosophical implications.

URVOY, Dominique and STEWART, Olivia (trans). *Ibn Rushd: Averroes*. New York, Routledge, 1991.

Going well beyond the Eurocentrist view which sees Ibn Rushd (Averroes) as little more than an intermediary between Aristotle and the scholastics, this book explores the main elements of his thought against the historical and cultural background of Muslim Spain. It gives a full account of Ibn Rushd's most important works, including his scientific, medical and legal as well as philosophical writings. It especially shows that Ibn Rushd's work formed part of the wider movement of Almohadism, a politico-religious reform movement which had a great intellectual impact in Muslim Spain.

USBERTI, Gabriele. Prior's Disease. Teoria, 10(2), 131-138, 1990.

UZGALIS, William L. Relative Identity and Locke's Principle of Individuation. Hist Phil Quart, 7(3), 283-297, Jl 90.

The aim of this paper is to refute the relative identity interpretation of II.xxvii in Locke's *Essay*. On the relative identity hypothesis, an oak and the matter which composes it, or a person and the substance which thinks in her are different descriptions of the same thing. But this leads to the conclusion that individual oaks, horses, and possibly persons come into being at different places and different times. This is a clear violation of Locke's principles of identity. There is also a new positive account of Locke's identity theory, treating oaks, horses, men and persons as modes rather than substances.

VÄÄNÄNEN, Jouko and HYTTINEN, Tapani. On Scott and Karp Trees of Uncountable Models. J Sym Log, 55(3), 897-908, S 90.

Let A and B be countable relational models. If the models are nonisomorphic, there is a unique countable ordinal x with the property that A and B are equivalent in the finite quantifier infinitary language up to quantifier-rank x but not to x + 1. Let z be the first uncountable cardinal. In the paper we consider models A and B of cardinality z and construct trees which have a similar relation to A and B as x above. It turns out that the above ordinal x has two qualities which coincide in countable models but will differ in uncountable models. Respectively, two kinds of trees emerge from x, Scott and Karp trees. We construct two models with many mutually noncomparable Scott trees.

VACCARI, Michael A. Law Without Values: Do the Unborn Have to Wait for a Consensus? Proc Cath Phil Ass, 63, 160-172, 1990.

VACEK, Edward. Contemporary Ethics and Scheler's Phenomenology of Community. Phil Today, 35(2), 161-174, Sum 91.

Contemporary ethics seeks a way of affirming both individuality and communal existence. Scheler affirmed individual autonomy, equality, and self-interest within contractual, societal relationships. But there are many forms of communal life where this analysis is inappropriate. In communal life each member shares some responsibility for the group while the group also shares responsibility for its members. These groups are real, the subjects of shared experience of a particular "world," possessing a common ethos, and with real relations to other groups and individuals. Scheler offers an alternative to those who say only groups or only individuals possess moral responsibility.

VADAKKEMURIYIL, A. Philosophers on Gender and Sexuality. J Dharma, 16(2), 106-114, Ap-Je 91.

VAGGALIS, Ted. The Justification of Justice as Fairness: A Two Stage Process. Auslegung, 17(2), 157-165, Sum 91.

VAHANIAN, G. "Creation and Big Bang: The Word as Space of Creation" in *Science and Religion: One World-Changing Perspectives on Reality*, FENNEMA, Jan (ed), 183-191. Norwell, Kluwer, 1990.

Distinguishing nature (science, cosmology) and creation (theology, eschatology), stress is placed on the fact that for biblical religion a) a creation myth is found not only in Genesis but also—among others—in the prologue of John's Gospel, and b) God is a God who speaks. Language is the medium of creation—of that which happens *once for all*, of that *before* which there is nothing. Adam is thus not the first man, but man first; Christ, second, Adam and that for which the human is second nature, is man tout court; and, finally, man, reconciled with his past and his nature, is man at last. Religion cannot dismiss science, nor can science comfort religion. For science, $E=mc^2$ is an equation; for religion, it is a metaphor. However, neither assertion would be valid if scientific language and religious language were not *compatible* with one another, rather than merely being complimentary of one another.

VAITKUS, Steven. Multiple Realities in Santayana's Last Puritan. Human Stud, 14(2-3), 159-179, Jl 91.

VAJDA, Mihaly. Failure of a Renaissance (Why It Is Impossible to Remain a Marxist in East Central Europe). Grad Fac Phil J, 14(1), 49-60, 1991.

The article tries to explain the birth of a new theoretical attitude among the former East Central European Marxists. The attitude is not simply the result of disappointment over the 'actually existing' Soviet-type socialist regimes. The Stalinist terror, the suppression of the Hungarian revolution, were more than enough to be disappointed. In the sixties, however, the idea of the *Renaissance of Marxism* came into existence: we had to begin anew, we had to do well what they had done badly. The *new theoretical reorientation* meant the questioning of Marxist aims and goals themselves, the questioning of any kind of effort to realize universal aimes instead of solving burning social problems, and the questioning of the aim of *making history*. Marx's human emancipation cannot be the continuation of political emancipation.

VAKARELOV, Dimitir. Intuitive Semantics for Some Three-Valued Logics Connected with Information, Contrariety and Subcontrariety. Stud Log, 48(4), 565-575, D 89.

Four known three-valued logics are formulated axiomatically and several completeness theorems with respect to nonstandard intuitive semantics, connected with the notions of information, contrariety and subcontrariety is given.

VALDÉS, Margarita M. Nombres y objetos en el *Tractatus*. Dianoia, 35(35), 29-42, 1989.

The article deals with the problem of whether objects in the *Tractatus* should be knowable entities or could be things transcendental to experience or any other kind of actual knowledge. A certain tension in Wittgenstein's views is shown: a) if we attend to his a priori transcendental arguments to prove the existence of names and objects, and to the positive characterization he offers of them, objects seem to be ineluctably abstract entities epistemologically transcendent; b) if, on the other hand, we attend to the *tractatusian* doctrine of what understanding the meaning of a proposition consists in, we must come to the conclusion that objects must be knowable.

VALDIVIA, Benjamín. Algunos giros en torno a san Juan de la Cruz. Logos (Mexico), 18(53), 97-107, My-Ag 90.

VALLÉE, Robert. "Eigen Elements" Emerging from the Interaction of Two Knowing and Acting Subjects. Commun Cog, 23(2-3), 183-191, 1990.

We present a model of a cybernetic system and its environment, involving the concept of general "observation operator" we have already introduced. Three channels are considered: the epistemological, decisional and action chains (the epistemological and decisional chains being equivalent to one only, the pragmatical chain). Emphasis is put upon epistemological and pragmatical subjectivities due to inverse transfers. Then, from the "epistemo-praxiological closure" of the system upon its environment, emerges eigen-behaviours in the sense of H von Foerster. This first case is equivalent to the consideration of a subject (the system) and an object. The second case, a generalization concerning two subjects, involves also eigen-elements related to the co-evolution of the two subjects, their subjectivities and the perceptions they have of each other. The possibility of a mathematical "epistemo-praxiology" is considered.

VALLENTYNE, Peter and LIPSON, Morry. Equal Opportunity and the Family. Pub Affairs Quart, 3(4), 27-45, O 89.

We build upon some work of James Fishkin concerning the incompatibility of liberal principles of equal opportunity and the principle of family autonomy (which says that the state should not interfere with how parents raise their children except in extreme cases). We formulate a principle that requires that children of the equivalent capacities have the same expectations concerning the development of skills that are generally useful (no matter what one's life plans are). This principle is incompatible with the principle of family of autonomy. We argue that liberals are deeply committed to this new principle, and that therefore they must reject the traditional family autonomy principle.

VALLENTYNE, Peter. The Problem of Unauthorized Welfare. Nous, 25(3), 295-321, Je 91.

Welfare-based theories face the problem of dealing with welfare from "suspect" sources such as malice or envy. Traditionally one of two extremes approaches has been taken: totally ignoring such welfare, or taking it at face value. I articulate and defend an intermediate approach—applicable to all welfare-based theories (not just utilitarianism)—of taking such welfare into account, but without simply treating it like "non-suspect" welfare. More specifically, I articulate four conditions of adequacy for dealing with "suspect" welfare. The root idea is that "suspect" welfare should be taken into account, but only to the extent that no one is adversely affected.

VALLICELLA, William F. Reply to Davies: Creation and Existence. Int Phil Quart, 31(2), 213-225, Je 91.

VALLICELLA, William F. Reply to Smith: The Question of Idealism. Int Phil Quart, 31(3), 343-348, S 91.

VALOIS, Raynald. Le rôle des causes comme instruments de la définition. Laval Theol Phil, 47(2), 193-201, Je 91.

À côté de la définition parfaite, par genre et différence spécifique, la logique traditionnelle connaît la définition par les quatre causes: matérielle, finale, efficiente et formelle. Le recours à ces causes est nécessaire pour définir tout ce qui n'est pas une substance, surtout les êtres artificiels. Le terme "définition" a donc d'abord un sens premier et ensuite des sens dérivés, comme l'être et l'essence se disent d'abord de la substance et ensuite des autres catégories par dérivation.

VAN ASPEREN, G M. Can Utilitarianism Be Salvaged as a Theory for Social Choice? Alg Ned Tijdschr Wijs, 83(2), 103-113, Ap 91.

The author discusses the question whether Utilitarianism can be considered as a theory for social choice or whether it should be thought of as a theory of justification. Evidence about the early Utilitarians suggests that they conceived of the theory as a decision-making theory, but for the Utilitarian philosopher only! Modern criticism of the theory that proposes to make a selection between preferences that may be admitted to the Utilitarian calculus achieve the same. The most plausible interpretation of Utilitarianism is to see it as an esoteric doctrine for the use of the Utilitarian philosopher.

VAN BALEN, G. The Darwinian Synthesis: A Critique of the Rosenberg/ Williams Argument. Brit J Phil Sci, 39(4), 441-448, D 88.

VAN BEECK, Frans Jozef. Tradition and Interpretation. Bijdragen, 3, 257-271, 1990.

Doing catholic systematic theology means: interpreting the great tradition of the undivided Church in such a way as, perhaps, to help further it. This involves presenting oneself to, and letting oneself be measured by, a formidable tribunal—one that may deeply shake the theologian's confidence. Things get even more complicated when one realizes that not even the quality of one's theological work is decisive; the examples of Augustine and Aquinas show that the tradition has been narrowed and distorted not only by mediocrity, but also by great talent. Greatness, therefore, has negative effects, too; Barth, Rahner, and Von Balthasar afford recent instances of this. All of this implies that the tradition essentially lives off a dynamic that involves oblivion and loss as well as recovery and gain. (edited)

VAN BELLINGEN, Jozef. Joseph de Maistre en de Revolutie. Tijdschr Stud Verlich Denken, 17(3-4), 265-275, 1989.

VAN BENTHEM, Johan. Language in Action. J Phil Log, 20(3), 225-263, Ag 91.

Recent logical studies of natural language have emphasized structure and flow of information. This paper surveys several models for such dynamic phenomena: families of languages, of information pieces and of procedures. The resulting landscape of logical calculi is explored, showing a great variety in options for logical constants and notion of inference. This framework brings together categorial grammar, linear logic, relevant logic, relational algebra and dynamic logic.

VAN BENTHEM, Johan. Logical Constants Across Varying Types. Notre Dame J Form Log, 30(3), 315-342, Sum 89.

We investigate the notion of "logicality" for arbitrary categories of linguistic expression, viewed as a phenomenon which they can all possess to a greater or lesser degree. Various semantic aspects of logicality are analyzed in technical detail: in particular, invariance for permutations of individual objects, and respect for Boolean structure. Moreover, we show how such properties are systematically related across different categories, using the apparatus of the typed lambda calculus.

VAN BENTHEM, Johan. Notes on Modal Definability. Notre Dame J Form Log, 30(1), 20-35, Wint 89.

This is a collection of results on modal definability of frame classes, most of them derived from a deeper analysis of so-called "ultrafilter extensions." In particular, there are applications to finite frames and to modal equivalence between frames.

VAN BRAKEL, J. Units of Measurement and Natural Kinds: Some Kripkean Considerations. Erkenntnis, 33(3), 297-317, N 90.

Kripke has argued that definitions of units of measurements provide examples of statements that are both contingent and a priori. In this paper I argue that definitions of units of measurement are intended to be stipulations of what Kripke calls "theoretical identities": a stipulation that two terms will have the same rigid designation. Hence such a definition is both a priori and necessary. The necessity arises because such definitions appeal to natural kind properties only, which on Kripke's account are necessary.

VAN CLEVE, James. "Mind-Dust or Magic? Panpsychism Versus Emergence" in *Philosophical Perspectives, 4: Action Theory and Philosophy of Mind, 1990*, TOMBERLIN, James E (ed), 215-226. Atascadero, Ridgeview, 1990.

VAN DE PITTE, Frederick P. The Dating of Rule IV-B in Descartes's *Regulae ad directionem ingenii*. J Hist Phil, 29(3), 375-395, Jl 91.

A careful analysis of Rule IV requires the acceptance of a later dating for this fragment—probably as late as 1639-1640, when the *Meditations* were uppermost in Descartes's thought. It also permits a clarification of his terminology: *Mathesis* is a science of necessary relations. *Mathesis universalis*, rather than a mere extension of *Mathesis*, is a distinct discipline which transforms systems of necessary relations into genuine *scientia* by providing the underlying conditions for the very possibility of knowledge. Thus Descartes provides not a simple mathematical method, but a very profound methodology.

VAN DE VIJVER, Gertrudis. Schematism and Schemata: Kant and the P.D.P.. Commun Cog, 23(2-3), 223-233, 1990.

The question of schematism was already controversial in the work of Kant. The use of schemata and the reference to Kantian schematism in contemporary neural network theories is still more problematic. Schematism is in both cases a problem of application: categories (in the case of Kant), or events (in the case of the parallel distributed processing approach), are interpreted on the basis of the constraining effect of schemata. Important shifts have to do with the level of manipulation, and with the role history is playing—the question of naturalism and emergence is under discussion here. Finally, the consequences for the explanatory value of the current networks are being analyzed.

VAN DER DOES, Jaap. A Generalized Quantifier Logic for Naked Infinitives. Ling Phil, 14(3), 241-294, Jl 91.

VAN DER DUSSEN, W Jan. Collingwood and the Idea of Progress. Hist Theor, 29(4), 21-41, D 90.

The concept of progress as conceived by Collingwood should be seen as an example of a philosophical concept as elaborated by him in *An Essay on Philosophical Method*. It is accordingly related to the concepts of change, process, development and evolution. One may distinguish four different positions in Collingwood's treatment of the subject: (a) it is dependent on a point of view; (b) it is meaningless; (c) it is meaningful; (d) it is necessary. With regard to the idea of progress in science a distinction should be made between the way it is used by historians and by scientists themselves.

VAN DER HOEVEN, J. Gadamer over 'Vermittlung': de Hegeliaanse draad in zijn hermeneutiek. Phil Reform, 56(1), 81-94, 1991.

VAN DER HOEVEN, J. Godsverduistering en Godsdienstfilosofie. Phil Reform, 55(2), 152-169, 1990.

VAN DER LEEUW, Karel and MOSTERT, Pieter. Philosophy in the *"Gymnasium:"* European Observations and Recommendations. Teach Phil, 13(2), 141-157, Je 90.

VAN DER MEULEN, Barend and LEYDESDORFF, Loet. Has the Study of Philosophy at Dutch Universities Changed under Economic and Political Pressures? Sci Tech Human Values, 16(3), 288-321, Sum 91.

From 1980 until 1985, the Dutch Faculties of Philosophy went through a period of transition. First, in 1982 the national government introduced a new system of financing research at the universities. This was essentially based on the natural sciences and did not match philosophers's work organization. In 1983 a drastic reduction in the budget for philosophy was proposed within the framework of a policy of introducing savings by distributing tasks among the universities. Recently, a visiting committee reported on the weak and strong areas of Dutch philosophy and proposed a policy to strenghten Dutch philosophy. This study explores the effects of the institutional reorganizations on the study of philosophy at the faculties, using scientometric methods. In addition to presenting empirical results, some methodological questions concerning the application of scientometric methods to a field of the humanities will be discussed. The number of publications went up as funding was cut back, and different subfields made different kinds of changes in orientation. The results show the relevance of publication-based data in research evaluation.

VAN DER SCHOOT, Albert. "Beautiful Things and the Aesthetic Subject" in *XIth International Congress in Aesthetics, Nottingham 1988*, WOODFIELD, Richard (ed), 227-229. Nottingham, Nottingham Polytech, 1990.

Even if one holds a *subjectivist* theory of beauty, one cannot dispose of *objective* qualities which give rise to the aesthetic experience (example: Hume). Such formally significant qualities do not just transmit aesthetic information to an otherwise passive subject, they affect the creative disposition of the aesthetic subject. Organic forms as well as geometric forms and mathematical proportions are productive as forms of forms. "Beautiful things" evoke the tension between the potential and its possible actualisation, but they do so in the form of one specific work of art, not as a theoretical survey of possibilities.

VAN DER STEEN, Wim J. Natural Selection as Natural History. Biol Phil, 6(1), 41-44, Ja 91.

In response to a target article by Byerly and Michod it is argued that the propensity interpretation of fitness represents a misguided search for generality in evolutionary theory. Evolutionary biology contains more natural history than theory in a strict sense of the term.

VAN DER VEKEN, J. "God's World and Man Becoming: How Can Science Possibly Help Us Transcend Dogmatism?" in *Science and Religion: One World-Changing Perspectives on Reality*, FENNEMA, Jan (ed), 131-137. Norwell, Kluwer, 1990.

VAN DER VLOET, J. Romano Guardini's Theological Critique of the Modern Age (in Dutch). Bijdragen, 2, 159-184, 1991.

Guardini creates a method which he calls "katholische Weltanschauung". It is essentially a theological understanding of the world. Guardini uses this method to formulate a critique of modernity. He is the first theologian to use the expression "das Ende der Neuzeit" to characterize the present situation of humanity. The problem, in Guardini's view, is that modernity effects its own end, because of its false notion of autonomy. Only the Christian faith is able to correct this false autonomy and thereby to save the world and mankind from impending decline. However, Guardini's ideas, which emphasize the responsibility of Christians for the world as the creation of God, without denying the problems that arise from the "otherness" of God and His revelation, still have contemporary significance for the theological understanding of the "signs of the times". They are, in a sense, the critical accompaniment of every theology, of every Christian interpretation of the modern world. (edited)

VAN DER WAL, G A. Kant's visie op de Franse Revolutie en op de grondslagen van het recht. Tijdschr Stud Verlich Denken, 17(3-4), 231-247, 1989.

VAN DER WILL, Wilfried. Nietzsche in America: Fashion and Fascination. Hist Euro Ideas, 11, 1015-1023, 1989.

The article begins with a consideration of Nietzsche's claims as to his own historical importance. It then proceeds to discuss Nietzsche's reception in the United States post-1945, in particular Walter Kaufmann, Arthur Danto, Richard Schact, Alexander Nehamas and, briefly, Allan Bloom. It is shown that Nietzsche is fashioned into a reasonable, liberal, East-coast fellow, the first interpreter of modernity characterized as ideological, political and ethical pluralism.

VAN DER WINDT, Henny J and HARBERS, Hans. Welke natuur is het beschermen waard? Kennis Methode, 15(1), 38-61, 1991.

The development of the Dutch nature conservation movement is described. It is shown that "nature" is a controversial and variable concept. However, not all concepts of nature could be accepted. Both the material history and the social history of nature constrain the interpretative flexibility of 'nature'. Practices of the nature conservationists pin down nature materially and on the other hand, nature is socially negotiated. Because of the unity of the conceptual, the material and the social history of nature, a constructivistic analysis of 'nature' has to be extended with other, more sociological and political approaches.

VAN DER ZWEERDE, Evert. Die Rolle der Philosophiegeschichte im "Neuen philosophischen Denken" in der UdSSR. Stud Soviet Tho, 40(1-3), 55-72, 1990.

The article aims at an understanding of the role history of philosophy (as a philosophic discipline) has played previously, and is playing presently in Soviet philosophy. Formerly this discipline formed part of the ideological legitimation of the Soviet system, but it fulfilled other functions at the same time: elevation of "philosophical culture" and technical training. Presently, this acquaintance with historical material provides a basis for attempts to reestablish the bond between Soviet philosophy and the mainstream of Western philosophy, as well as source of inspiration for those who aim at a revival of Russian *pochvennichestvo*.

VAN DOAN, Tran. Reflections on the Nature of Ideology. Asian J Phil, 2(1), 105-150, Sum 90.

RNI aims to give a clear and balanced picture of ideology in its positive and negative function: ideology as spiritual force of rallying and identifying group (class, nation), and as instrument of conservatists against social change. RNI proposes to study ideology not from its forms but from its genetical process: from the positive to the negative. It thus demands for a permanent critique but not for a radical abolition of ideology.

VAN DOREN, John. "Mr Adler and Matthew Arnold" in *Freedom in the Modern World: Jacques Maritain, Yves R Simon, Mortimer J Adler*, TORRE, Michael D (ed), 73-78. Notre Dame, Univ Notre Dame Pr, 1989.

VAN DORMAEL, Jan. The Emergence of Analogy: Analogical Reasoning as a Constraint Satisfaction Process. Philosophica, 46(2), 65-76, 1990.

The recent interest in computational investigations of analogy has seen the rise of a distinction between so-called syntactic and pragmatic approaches towards the study of analogy (Keane, 1988). This distinction is essentially a distinction concerning the type of constraints placed upon the mapping process. In this paper we will point out that the thought process under study is justified reasoning by analogy and argue that the mapping constraints are introduced to select a 'valid' analogy. Understanding analogical thinking differently, we will argue that an analogy emerges progressively in thinking about the target situation *as if* it is the base situation. Furthermore, we will point out some of the differences between the "cognitive-computational" and a "cognitive-logical" perspective on analogical thinking.

VAN EEMEREN, Frans H. A Pragma-Dialectical Perspective on Norms. Commun Cog, 24(1), 25-41, 1991.

VAN GERWEN, Jef. Au-delà de la critique communautarienne du libéralisme? D'Alasdair MacIntyre à Stanley Hauerwas. Rev Phil Louvain, 89(81), 129-143, F 91.

The article offers a brief introduction to communitarian thought for a French-speaking audience, focusing on the critique of liberalism by A MacIntyre and S Hauerwas. This critique is related to the narrative foundation of ethics. Then, the question is raised if the communitarian tradition is able to move beyond the stage of negative critique, formulating a contemporary conception of a common good. The work of Robert Bellah e.a., Habits of the Heart, may serve as a first resource for answering the latter question.

VAN HAUTE, P. Psychanalyse et existentialisme: A propos de la théorie lacanienne de la subjectivité. Man World, 23(4), 453-472, O 90.

VAN INWAGEN, Peter. Logic and the Free Will Problem. Soc Theor Pract, 16(3), 277-290, Fall 90.

This article begins with a general overview of the problem of free will and determinism. The remainder of the article is a defense of incompatibilism against the points raised by Michael Slote in his well-known 1982 paper, "Selective Necessity and the Free-Will Problem."

VAN INWAGEN, Peter. *Material Beings*. Ithaca, Cornell Univ Pr, 1991.

This book concerns the metaphysics of material objects, with special attention to the part whole relation. It is argued that only living organisms can have proper parts.

VAN INWAGEN, Peter. Response to Slote's "Ethics Without Free Will". Soc Theor Pract, 16(3), 385-395, Fall 90.

This article criticises Michael Slote's arguments (in his article in the same number of *Social Theory and Practice*) for the conclusion that ethics would still be possible on the assumption that no one was able to do otherwise.

VAN INWAGEN, Peter. "When is the Will Free?" in *Philosophical Perspectives, 3: Philosophy of Mind and Action Theory, 1989*, TOMBERLIN, James E (ed), 399-422. Atascadero, Ridgeview, 1989.

Most incompatibilists accept the following principle: If *p* and no one has any choice about whether *p*, and if (if *p* then *q*) and no one has any choice about whether (if *p* then *q*), then no one has any choice about whether *q*. I argue that anyone who accepts this principle should, independently of the question whether determinism is true, accept the thesis that there is (at most) very little that we have any choice about. I also argue that it does not follow from this conclusion that there is very little that we are morally accountable for.

VAN LAMBALGEN, Michiel. The Axiomatization of Randomness. J Sym Log, 55(3), 1143-1167, S 90.

We present a faithful axiomatization of von Mises' notion of a random sequence, using an abstract independence relation. A byproduct is a quantifier elimination theorem for Friedman's "almost all" quantifier in terms of this independence relation.

VAN LOOCKE, Philip R. The Dynamics of Concepts and Non-local Interactions. Commun Cog, 23(4), 331-344, 1990.

It is plausible that concepts can be represented as attractors. It is also plausible that the basin of attraction of a concept increases as it becomes more familiar. If a concept has to obey the constraint that it must have a certain amount of addressability, then this entails that the concepts may have to change their representation as the knowledge base becomes more familiar. In special, a "prototype" may appear between two or more neighboring concepts. However, if it is assumed that the system is described by a "local" potential, then this generation of prototypes does not agree with psychology. It is possible to include the relevant non-localities "automatically" if one makes recourse to a connectionist model.

VAN MAANEN, Jan A. Johan Jacob Ferguson, geb um 1630 im Haag(?), gest vor dem 24 November 1706, vermutlich am 6 Oktober 1691 in Amsterdam. Stud Leibniz, 22(2), 203-216, 1990.

In the period 1680-1684 Leibniz corresponded frequently about scientific subjects with Johan Jacob Ferguson, who was born c. 1630 and who died before 1707 (probably already in 1691). Biographical information about this Dutch administrator and amateur-mathematician was very scarce. The paper provides a detailed biography and a survey of Ferguson's mathematical work. He was an active mathematician, who had good knowledge of classical arithmetic and algebra. He published a textbook *Labyrinthus Algebrae* (1667), which gave some reputation amongst mathematicians. Yet he was unable to grasp the important new developments (Cartesian geometry and infinitesimal techniques).

VAN NESS, Peter H. Apology, Speculation, and Philosophy's Fate. Phil Theol, 5(1), 3-17, Fall 90.

My initial task in this essay is to identify precisely the original philosophical import of philosophical reflections about religion. Next I outline their changing natures and interrelations in the works of exemplary figures from the history of Western religious thought. Finally I argue that the relative desuetude of the traditional forms of apology and speculation is emblematic of the present faring of philosophy as a form of cultural discourse.

VAN OOSTEN, Jaap. Lifschitz' Realizability. J Sym Log, 55(2), 805-821, Je 90.

V Lifschitz defined in 1979 a variant of realizability which validates Church's thesis with uniqueness condition, but not the general form of Church's thesis. In this paper we describe an extension of intuitionistic arithmetic in which the soundness of Lifschitz' realizability can be proved, and we give an axiomatic characterization of the Lifshitz-realizable formulas relative to this extension. By a "q-variant" we obtain a new derived rule. We also show how to extend Lifschitz' realizability to second-order arithmetic. Finally we describe an analogous development of elementary analysis, with partial continuous application replacing partial recursive application.

VAN PARIJS, Philippe. Maîtrise, marché et société industrielle. Rev Phil Louvain, 89(81), 36-46, F 91.

Does the rise of industrial society increase or decrease our control over our fate? The article answers this question by highlighting two dilemmas. Firstly, a better control over nature has been-and can only be-gained at the expense of a weaker control of local communities over their fates. Secondly, there is a powerful trade off between control over our common fate understood as collective sovereignty and control over our individual lives understood as personal freedom.

VAN PARIJS, Philippe. Why Surfers Should Be Fed: The Liberal Case for an Unconditional Basic Income. Phil Pub Affairs, 20(2), 101-131, Spr 91.

Can an unconditional basic income-paid ex ante to all citizens-be justified? The article argues that it can, on the basis of the most defensible interpretation of the liberal ideas of equal respect and equal concern and of plausible empirical assumptions about the current situation of advanced capitalist societies. A key role is played in the argument by the demand that employment rents currently appropriated by those who have a job should be shared by all.

VAN PEPERSTRATEN, Frans. Verlichtingsfilosofie twee eeuwen later; J F Lyotard als postmoderne Kant. Alg Ned Tijdschr Wijs, 83(3), 188-205, Jl 91.

This article argues that, contrary to the general image of postmodernism, the postmodern thinking of J F Lyotard is coherent with the philosophy of Enlightenment. In the theory of reflective judgement in Kant's third Critique Lyotard finds the proper model to formulate relations between heterogeneous spheres, particularly between reality and ideas. On this model Lyotard grounds his critical attitude towards modern philosophies of history, in which the ultimate identity of reality and idea is central. Lyotard in fact elaborates Kant's concept of culture according to which the susceptibility for ideas has to be developed. Lyotard does not believe, however, that this susceptibility is to be subordinated to the moral subject as the one and final end of nature, but welcomes the irreducible heterogeneity of ends in language.

VAN PEURSEN, C A. Culture as an Open System. Chin Stud Phil, 22(3), 45-54, Spr 91.

In modern philosophy "culture" does not consist of objects (books, schools, etc.) but of human activities by which the surrounding world is being interpreted. "Culture" is not a noun, but a verb. A Comte as well as Hegel saw culture as a progress. But "progress" is questionable: culture can become static, losing the awareness of criteria. So there is a closed and an open culture. In 'primitive' society myth can indicate openness, magic manifests a closed culture. Modern society (sciences, daily behavior) is more 'relational': identity is nothing in itself, but only in relationship. 'Openness' here excludes isolation, mere 'revolution' and acknowledges other cultures.

VAN PEURSEN, C A. Reason and Imagination (in Dutch). S Afr J Phil, 10(3), 64-67, Ag 91.

Perhaps the most important change in recent philosophy is that "Rationality" does not function any more as an absolute standard. As Einstein, in 1905, transformed the absolute criteria of space and time into measuring-rods related to the observer, so rationality has become related to a cultural and social context. But all this is not new and does not imply a cultural relativism as post-modern thinkers pretend. There is a long history of the interaction of logic and "topica" (Cicero) converging into the "marriage of reason and imagination" (F Bacon). Modern conceptions of "model", "metaphor", "narratio" are rooted in that, too often forgotten, tradition. Degenaar is one of the contemporary philosophers who manifests a specific sensibility for the interaction of reason and imagination.

VAN RODEN ALLEN, Robert. Martin Heidegger and the Place of Language. Dialogos, 25(56), 103-121, Jl 90.

This essay is an exploration of the role and place of language in the work of Heidegger. It explores and follows the place of language from the period of *Sein und Zeit* through the later works, showing the continuity and relative consistency of Heidegger's treatment of the place of language, culminating in his view of language as providing the place for the emergence of meaning-beings, a view which later is restated in Heidegger's discussion of the fourfold and its ontological battle with or dissimulation as the technological enframing of "world."

VAN STEENBERGHEN, Fernand. La eleccion de un maestro. Rev Filosof (Mexico), 23(68), 230-242, My-Ag 90.

VAN STEENBERGHEN, Fernand. Travaux récents sur la pensée du XIIIe siècle. Rev Phil Louvain, 89(82), 302-322, My 91.

VAN STIGT, W P. *Brouwer's Intuitionism (Studies in the History and Philosophy of Mathematics, Vol 2)*. New York, Elsevier No-Holland, 1990.

Intuitionism as a foundational theory and practice of mathematics was the brainchild of L E J Brouwer (1881-1966), a brilliant mathematician—'one of the fathers of topology'—and a rebel, who had the courage to challenge the almost universal trend towards 'formalism' at the turn of the century. His Intuitionist alternative was a philosophy of mathematics and a programme of reform. This book attempts to give a comprehensive survey of Brouwer's Intuitionism; it follows the 'genetic' development of his ideas, linking the man Brouwer, his Weltanschauung, his philosophy of mathematics and his reconstruction of mathematics. Each of the six chapters concentrates on one of these aspects of development. Appendices provide original text and translations of important unpublished papers and correspondence. The book is written for the foundational specialist as well as for the general reader interested in the deeper issues of the nature of mathematics, its status and function.

VAN VELDHUIJSEN, Peter. External Creation and Eternal Production of the World According to Bonaventura (in Dutch). Bijdragen, 2, 139-158, 1991.

This article deals with three themes from Bonaventura's views on creation: 1) Eternal creation from nothing: a false notion. 2) Eternal production on the basis of eternal matter. 3) Bonaventura on Aristotle and the eternity of the world. (edited)

VAN VONDEREN, Marijke L. Role Theory: A Reconstruction. Method Sci, 22(3), 168-177, 1989.

Pleck's theory of role overload of employed wives gave rise to formulate role-theoretical propositions and to reconstruct hypotheses with reference to role-conflict resolutions. Three postulates are introduced: the incumbent of a social position will behave according to role expectations in that position; if role overload occurs it will be reduced, and means of reduction are those which result in greatest relief. Previous research helped to construct hypotheses on choices of role related actions. It is concluded that the advance made in role-theoretical research can be assigned to the development of insight into behavioral strategies towards role demands.

VAN ZANDT, David E. "Commonsense Reasoning, Social Change, and the Law" in *Critique and Construction: A Symposium on Roberto Unger's "Politics"*, LOVIN, Robin W (ed), 159-205. New York, Cambridge Univ Pr, 1990.

Conceptions of social order held by everyday members of society can act as substantial obstacles to social change. These conceptions are difficult to alter because they are formed in commonsensical theorizing, which is based in perceived experience. Rational argument is usually ineffectual in altering these conceptions. Legal rules operate in this environment: some attempt to change these conceptions by employing the coercive force of the state; others reflect and reinforce such conceptions. In the end, social change is more often brought about by force rather than by persuasion.

VAN ZUYLEKOM, Ruud M. "The Notion of Time in African Thinking: A Survey of Some Approaches" in *I, We and Body: First Joint Symposium of Philosophers from Africa and from the Netherlands*, KIMMERLE, Heinz (ed), 93-101. Atlantic Highlands, Gruner, 1989.

The qualitative opposition in time representation between the West and some traditional African societies might give a refreshing outlook on both Western and African concepts. This article intends to be a short presentation of some African concepts of time. It also contains supplementary aspects from an interview with two African philosophers.

VANDENBERG, Donald. *Education as a Human Right: A Theory of Curriculum and Pedagogy*. New York, Teachers College Pr, 1990.

VANDER NAT, Arnold and MOSER, Paul K. The Logical Status of Modal Reductionism. Log Anal, 31(121-122), 69-78, Mr-Je 88.

Represented by Carnap, Quine, Rescher, Kripke and others, modal reductionism aims to reduce all modal entities to nonmodal entities. This paper shows that the prominent versions of modal reductionism cannot provide a logical analysis of modal terms. It shows that those versions state *contingent* hypotheses concerning modal terms. The paper thus refutes an assumption common to many proponents of modal reductionism.

VANDERSPOEL, John. "The Background to Augustine's Denial of Religious Plurality" in *Grace, Politics and Desire: Essays on Augustine*, MEYNELL, Hugo A (ed), 179-193. Calgary, Univ Calgary Pr, 1990.

Written to show the background to Augustine's denial of religious plurality late in life, the article suggests that Augustine's early acceptance of plurality was Neoplatonic in origin. Careful examination of the few available sources, such as Themistius and Symmachus, indicates that religious plurality was a view originated by Porphyry. Augustine's retraction of his earlier view is an indication of his increasing ability to reject philosophical views held earlier as his maturity as a Christian thinker increased.

VANDERVEKEN, Daniel. *Meaning and Speech Acts: Volume I, Principles of Language Use*. New York, Cambridge Univ Pr, 1990.

The basic units of meaning in the use and comprehension of language are speech acts called illocutionary acts. In *Foundations of Illocutionary Logic* Searle and Vanderveken presented the first logic of speech acts. *Meaning and Speech Acts* further develops the logic of speech acts and of propositions to construct a general semantics of language that formulates recursive theories of success, satisfaction and truth. This approach unifies the semantics of truth (of Frege, Tarski and Montague) and speech act theory. It enables semantics to interpret sentences of all types expressing speech acts with any possible illocutionary force and to analyze practical inferences. Volume I explains the general principles that connect meaning, reason, thought and speech acts in semantics. It presupposes no detailed knowledge of logical formalism.

VANDERVEKEN, Daniel. *Meaning and Speech Acts: Volume II, Formal Semantics of Success and Satisfaction*. New York, Cambridge Univ Pr, 1991.

The primary units of meaning in the use of comprehension of language are speech acts. In *Foundations of Illocutionary Logic*, Searle and Vanderveken presented the first logic of a general theory of illocutionary acts. In *Meaning and Speech Acts* further develops the logics of speech acts and of propositions to construct a general semantic theory of natural language which formulates recursive definitions of success, satisfaction and truth. This new theoretical approach unifies formal semantics as developed by Frege, Tarski and Montague and speech act theory as developed by Austin and Searle. Volume II uses logics to develop a generally complete axiomatization of that universal grammar.

VANSINA, Frans. Bibliographie de Paul Ricoeur: Compléments (jusqu'en 1990). Rev Phil Louvain, 89(82), 243-288, My 91.

This article is a supplement to our book: *Paul Ricoeur: A Primary and Secondary Systematic Bibliography* (1935-1984), Leuven (Belgium), Editions Peeters, 1985. It covers the recent publications of Paul Ricoeur up to 1990. The referential system is identical with the one used in the book.

VANTERPOOL, Rudolph V. Affirmative Action Revisited: Justice and Public Policy Considerations. Pub Affairs Quart, 3(4), 47-59, O 89.

VARDI, Moshe Y. Verification of Concurrent Programs: the Automata-Theoretic Framework. Annals Pure Applied Log, 51(1-2), 79-98, Mr 91.

VARET, Gilbert. Traité de la créature. Philosophique (France), 1(89), 69-86, 1989.

VARGA VON KIBÉD, Matthias. "Some Remarks on Davidson's Theory of Truth" in *The Mind of Donald Davidson*, BRANDL, Johannes (ed), 47-64. Amsterdam, Rodopi, 1989.

Preventive solutions for the paradoxes lead to the inexpressability of the adequacy conditions for the representation of truth within the system. Davidsonian theories of truth presuppose an understood language (for the background theory) which should permit the expression of the solutional principles for the paradoxes. The suitability of languages for this aim is tested by inferential validity paradoxes. They necessitate the introduction of an inner and an outer truth predicate. For the paradoxes, two different types of circularity, often wrongly identified, have to be distinguished. For Davidsonian theories of truth, non-two-valuedness, different versions of convention T and "principled openness" of the background theory have to be postulated.

VARGA, Csaba. On Judicial Ascertainment of Facts. Ratio Juris, 4(1), 61-71, Mr 91.

VARGAS, Alberto. Ética sin raíces. Dianoia, 35(35), 117-122, 1989.

In this brief paper a suggestion is made that Wittgenstein's thinking of the "problem of life" comprises two mutually exclusive views. The first, an absolutist view, is prominent in the *Notebooks* and the last pages of the *Tractatus*; there the value of life depends on a grasp of religious or absolute value. The second constructs the value of life by taking account of cultural and historical dimensions, but as this value falls short of an absolute and unspeakable value, it prompts a "non-rooted" view of ethics.

VARGAS, Celso and MAYORGA, Alejandro. Compromiso Ontico y Teorías Científicas. Rev Filosof (Costa Rica), 28(67-68), 231-236, D 90.

Popper was the first philosopher who introduced a criterion of demarcation between science and pseudo-science in which metaphysical ideas play a central role. MSRP developed by Lakatos and associates provides us with a new perspective within Popperian's epistemology for evaluating the influence of metaphysical ideas in science. In this report we present some criteria for characterizing the metaphysical component of scientific theories and determining when a theory is more profound than others. We use strongly the procedure presented by Ramsey. (edited)

VARGAS, Celso. Teorías de verdad y teorías del significado. Rev Filosof (Costa Rica), 27(66), 445-456, D 89.

Some philosophers and linguistics have claimed that a semantics for natural languages are entirely different from a semantics for formal languages, the last expressed in terms of truth conditions. Katz's theory constitutes the basis of this argument. In this paper we show that both semantics cannot be different. We begin by imposing some conditions of adequacy, we describe Katz's theory and, finally, we evaluate it.

VARMA, Ved Prakash. A Case Against Theistic Morality. Indian Phil Quart, 17(3), 313-323, Jl 90.

VARNER, Gary E and LEMONS, John and BROWN, Donald A. Congress, Consistency, and Environmental Law. Environ Ethics, 12(4), 311-327, Wint 90.

In passing the National Environmental Policy Act of 1969 (NEPA), Congress committed the nation to an ethical principle of living in "productive and enjoyable harmony" with the natural environment. Thus understood, NEPA can be given either (1) a technology-forcing interpretation or (2) an intelligent decision-making interpretation. We argue that in its subsequent decision to site a high-level nuclear waste repository at Yucca Mountain, Nevada, Congress acted inconsistently with this principle under either interpretation. We conclude that for the foreseeable future, the only way to handle the nation's nuclear wastes consistent with the environmental goal enunciated in NEPA is to leave them in temporary surface storage facilities, prohibit the licensing of any new nuclear power plants, and take all appropriate steps to reduce the nuclear weapons industry.

VARNER, Gary E. No Holism without Pluralism. Environ Ethics, 13(2), 175-179, Sum 91.

In his recent essay on moral pluralism in environmental ethics, J Baird Callicott exaggerates the advantages of monism, ignoring the environmentally unsound implications of Leopold's holism. In addition, he fails to see that Leopold's view requires the same kind of intellectual schitzophrenia for which he criticizes the version of moral pluralism advocated by Christopher D Stone in *Earth and Other Ethics*. If it is plausible to say that holistic entities like ecosystems are directly morally considerable—and that is a very big *if*—it must be for a very different reason than is usually given for saying that individual human beings are directly morally considerable.

VARNER, Gary E. Species, Individuals, and Domestication: A Commentary on Jane Duran's "Domesticated and Then Some". Between Species, 6(4), 181-184, Fall 90.

Duran fails clearly to distinguish the question, "Do individual domesticated animals have any special moral significance in virtue of their being domesticated rather than wild?" (Q1), from the question, "Do domesticated species or breeds have any special moral significance in virtue of their being domesticated rather than wild?" (Q2). She offers six comparisons of wild and domesticated animals, writing as if these support an affirmative answer to Q2. By clarifying the (ir)relevance of each comparison to Q2, I show that, taken together, while they support an affirmative answer to Q1, they do not support an affirmative answer to Q2.

VARNIER, Giuseppe. La teoria hegeliana dell'autocoscienza e della sua razionalità. G Crit Filosof Ital, 70(1), 35-75, Ja-Ap 91.

VARZI, Achille C. Complementary Sentential Logics. Bull Sect Log, 19(4), 112-116, D 90.

We describe a simple axiomatic system by means of which exactly those sentences can be derived that are rated *non-tautologous* in classical sentential logic. Since the set of all *tautologies* is also specifiable by means of syntactic systems, the resulting picture would appear to give a fairly good account of that logic, let alone semantic considerations. The picture can then be completed by developing related systems adequate to specify the set of all *contradictions*, the set of all *non-contradictions*, the set of all *contingencies*, and the set of all *non-contingencies* respectively: systems of this kind, which provide additional examples of paraconsistent calculi with a classical background, are also presented.

VASSILIE-LEMENY, Sorin-Titus. *Pour une philosophie du sens et de la valeur*. Bordeaux, Biere, 1990.

The concepts of generosity and sacrifice are posited as a method of synthezation between the ideal and real, and between value and non-value. (staff)

VATTIMO, Gianni. "The Secularization of Philosophy" in *Writing the Politics of Difference*, SILVERMAN, Hugh J (ed), 283-290. Albany, SUNY Pr, 1991.

VATZ, Richard E and WEINBERG, Lee S. The Conceptual Bind in Defining the Volitional Component of Alcoholism. J Mind Behav, 11(3-4), 531-544, Sum-Autumn 90.

An essential element in both lay and professional definitions of alcoholism is the a priori claim that afflicted individuals lack control over their drinking and/or over their behavior while drinking. The social, legal and scientific consequences of accepting this claim are examined. Based on specific evidence drawn from recent journal articles, we argue that alcohol researchers fail to adequately engage the issue of volition and that their research designs and findings are thereby flawed.

VAUX, Kenneth. Theology as the Queen (Bee) of the Disciplines? Zygon, 25(3), 317-322, S 90.

Once Queen of the Medieval court of sciences, dethroned theology may be able in our time to play a strategic servant role in rightly humiliating, elevating, and ordering the disciplines, in gadflying like a mutant honeybee, generating surprise and serendipity through the intermediacy of social science, and in offering ethical homing direction to the disciplines in their applied endeavors.

VAYDA, Andrew P and MC CAY, Bonnie J and EGHENTER, Cristina. Concepts of Process in Social Science Explanations. Phil Soc Sci, 21(3), 318-331, S 91.

Social scientists using one or another concept of process have paid little attention to underlying issues of methodology and explanation. Commonly, the concept used is a loose one. When it is not, there often are other problems, such as errors of reification and of assuming that events sometimes connected in a sequence are invariably thus connected. While it may be useful to retain the term "process" for some sequences of intelligibly connected actions and events, causal explanation must be sought with respect to the *events* constituting processes rather than with respect to processes regarded as unitary entities.

VAZ PINTO, Maria José. "Λογοσ ε Ομονοια: algumas considerações em torno da razão sofística" in *Dinâmica do Pensar: Homenagem a Oswaldo Market*, FAC LETRAS UNIV LISBOA (ed), 167-188. Lisboa, Fac Letras U Lisboa, 1991.

Les sophistes, spécialistes des techniques du langage et de l'argumentation, ont pris part active dans le procès de la "crise du logos" en Grèce ancienne. On signale quelques éléments de continuité dans la réfléxion des sophistes et des présocratiques, en soulignant la substitution de *la* vérité, unique et absolute, par *des* vérités, fragmentaires et contingentes, et l'infléxion du logos sophistique dans le sens de la rhétorique. Les positions de Protagoras et de Gorgias répresentent la prise de conscience des limitations de la connaissance humaine et témoignent les efforts pour les surmonter en trouvant des solutions convenables pour bien agir. Tandis que Leibniz, métaphysicien et théologien, concevait le juste espoir de se trouver un jour "plus près du véritable point de vue des choses pour les trouver bonnes", les sophistes, prisonniers de leurs points de vue multiples, ne fondaient leur optimisme que sur les mondes possibles, sugérés ou créés par la puissance du logos. (edited)

VEATCH, Henry B. *Swimming Against the Current in Contemporary Philosophy: Occasional Essays and Papers*. Washington, Cath Univ Amer Pr, 1990.

A collection of papers written to return the attention of contemporary philosophers to the implications of the teachings of Aristotle and Aquinas in order to revive the realism in philosophy. Particular attention is paid to ethics, the philosophy of nature, and the philosophy of human nature. (staff)

VEATCH, Henry and RAUTENBERG, Joseph. Does the Grisez-Finnis-Boyle Moral Philosophy Rest on a Mistake? Rev Metaph, 44(4), 807-830, Je 91.

This paper has three objectives. First, it seeks to point up the contrast between two major types of ethics in the present-day: on the one hand, an ethics of what might be called a natural law; on the other hand, an ethics in which our moral obligations would seem to be derived largely from logico-linguistic considerations as to the meaning of moral words. Second, as to the moral philosophy of the "Grifinnboyle," the paper seeks to show that their ethics is to be classified as being of the second type. Finally, it having been shown that this second type of a duty-ethic, or a linguistically based ethic, is to be found wanting philosophically, the conclusion is drawn that the Grifinnboyle moral philosophy rests on a mistake. (edited)

VEATCH, Robert M and MORENO, Jonathan D. Consensus in Panels and Committees: Conceptual and Ethical Issues. J Med Phil, 16(4), 371-373, Ag 91.

VEATCH, Robert M. Consensus of Expertise: The Role of Consensus of Experts in Formulating Public Policy and Estimating Facts. J Med Phil, 16(4), 427-445, Ag 91.

For years analysts have recognized the error of assuming that experts in medical science are also experts in deciding the analysis of the use of the consensus of experts to their use in public policy groups such as NIH Consensus Development panels. After arguing that technical experts cannot be expected to be expert on public policy decisions, the author extends the criticism to the use of the consensus of experts in estimating facts to provide a basis for policy decisions. It is argued that to the extent that a) experts' views regarding a body of facts can be expected to correlate with their values relevant to those facts; and b) the values of experts differ from the values of lay people, even the estimates of the facts given by the consensus of expert panels can be expected to differ from the estimates lay people would have given had they had the relevant scientific expertise.

VEATCH, Robert M (ed) and PELLEGRINO, Edmund D (ed) and LANGAN, John P (ed). *Ethics, Trust, and the Professions: Philosophical and Cultural Aspects*. Washington, Georgetown Univ Pr, 1991.

Does the fiduciary paradigm characteristic of the traditional learned professions continue to serve as an appropriate ethical model for the professions of today? Or does the fact that professional relationships are often because strangers mitigate against the feasibility of trust and trustworthiness? The fourteen essays in the volume take their positions on each side of the question. In addition to offering an array of philosophical points of view on the ethics of professions, these essays also provide insight into the sociology of the professions and the professional role in Asian and European contexts.

VEATCH, Robert M. "Is Trust of Professionals a Coherent Concept?" in *Ethics, Trust, and the Professions: Philosophical and Cultural Aspects*, PELLEGRINO, Edmund D (ed), 159-173. Washington, Georgetown Univ Pr, 1991.

Thus, it is a mistake to assume that professionals can be trusted to know the best interest of their clients, to present facts and options to them objectively, or to manifest virtues inherent in professional roles. This does not imply that professionals are "untrustworthy" in the sense that they are lacking in dedication, integrity, or good character. It does not even imply that they are self-serving or conflicted by the demands to serve the interests of those other than their clients. Even if the professional is impeccably committed to the client, still, in theory, the professional ought not to be able to know the client's interest, ought not to be expected to manifest some set of virtues inherent in the professional role. Trust requires something far different: a commitment to the client, a confession of inability to present value-free facts, and an acknowledgment of which underlying belief system generates the set of virtues and the role conception under which the professional is operating.

VEATCH, Robert M. Should Basic Care Get Priority? Doubts about Rationing the Oregon Way. Kennedy Inst Ethics J, 1(3), 187-206, S 91.

Recognition of the need to ration care has focused attention on the concept of "basic care". It is often thought that care that is "basic" is also morally prior. This article questions that premise in light of the usual definitions of "basic". Specifically, it argues that Oregon's rationing scheme, which defines "basic" in terms of cost-effective care, fails to pay sufficient attention to important ethical principles such as justice.

VEAUTHIER, Frank W. Social Apriori of Responsibility in Scheler's Phenomenology (in Serbo-Croatian). Filozof Istraz, 34(1), 209-226, 1990.

Das Interesse des Verfassers gilt der phänolenologischen Denkeinstellung Schelers, wie er sie insbesondere in der mittleren Schaffensperiode (1904-1922), und hier wiederum in seinem Hauptwerk *Der Formalismus in der Ethik und materiale Wertethik* dargestellt und begründet hat. Das eigentliche Thema gehört dem Umfeld der Sozialphänomenologie an und bezieht sich auf solche Phänomene, die für das Leben des Menschen in Gemeinschaften von besonderer Bedeutung sind, nämlich auf die Phänomene "Verantwortung" und "Solidarität". Die These selbst lautet: Verantwortungsakte und Solidaritätsakte einer Person setzen als Apriori eine "Gesamtwelt" voraus, die von einer Gesamptperson, nicht einer Einzelperson gegeben ist. Der Autor bemüht sich ferner um die Darstellung der zweifachen Implikation, die diese These enthält, nämlich um das Apriori-Verständnis Schelers und zweitens um dessen Auffassung von der Person und die dazugehörige Akttheorie.

VECA, Salvatore. Questioni di filosofia politica. Teoria, 10(1), 29-50, 1990.

VECERKA, Kazimir. Bolzano's Contribution to Cognition and/or the Creation of Theory of Sets (in Czechoslovakian). Filozof Cas, 38(4), 522-528, 1990.

Schon etwa im Jahre 1830 hat Bolzano geschrieben (siehe die Anmerkung Nr. 1: diese Editionen sind nicht kritisch, weil sie nur die einzige gut lesbare, aber weder letzte, noch beste "Version" reproduzieren, allerdings der Begriff der Version selbst und das Nacheinanderfolgen der Versionen selbst problematisch sind), dass ein Element einer Menge (wenigstens von zwei Eiementen) nicht ein Teil ihres anderen Elementes derselben Ordnung sein kann und dass dem Element der Menge nicht (alle) Eigenschaften ideser Menge gehören können. Aus jeder dieser zwei Vorschriften folgt, dass die angeführte Menge ihr eigenes Element nicht sein kann und dass die Menge aller Mengen nicht möglich ist. (edited)

VEENHOVEN, Ruut. Is Happiness Relative? Soc Indic Res, 24(1), 1-34, F 91.

The theory that happiness is relative is based on three postulates: (1) happiness results from comparison, (2) standards of comparison adjust, (3) standards of comparison are arbitrary constructs. On the basis of these postulates the theory predicts: (a) happiness does not depend on real quality of life, (b) changes in living conditions to the good or the bad have only a shortlived effect on happiness, (c) people are happier after hard times, (d) people are typically neutral about their life. Together these inferences imply that happiness is both an evasive and an inconsequential matter, which is at odds with core beliefs in present-day welfare society. It is argued that the theory happiness-is-relative mixes up 'overall happiness' with 'contentment'. Contentment is indeed largely a matter of comparing life-as-it-is to standards of how-life-should-be. Yet overall happiness does not entirely depend on comparison. (edited)

VEJRAZKA, Michal. On the Concept of Mímésis (in Czechoslovakian). Filozof Cas, 38(4), 481-495, 1990.

The theory of reflection or rather the theory of knowledge occupies a distinguished place within the framework of the philosophical attitude to art. It is frequently regarded as a theoretical foundation for the depiction of the specific nature of art and basically as a vantage point for the solution of all theoretical problems pertaining to art. There, however, arises the question whether knowledge really constitutes a key factor within the context of art or whether it is only an accompanying aspect, albeit presumably ever present and necessary. The author of this article comes to the conclusion that the specific nature of art must be sought in the position of art within the framework of the entire process of socio-historical praxis and not only at the level of knowledge. (edited)

VELASCO, Monica A. Talking. Thinking, 9(1), 36-37, 1990.

VELASQUEZ, Manuel G. Why Corporations Are Not Morally Responsible for Anything They Do. Bus Prof Ethics J, 2(3), 1-18, Spr 83.

It is argued that entities which correctly can be said to be morally responsible for their actions must have a certain kind of unity of action and intentional consciousness. Corporations lack these features, and so cannot be said to be morally responsible for anything. The opposing view of Peter French is examined and shown to be mistaken. It is also argued that attributing moral responsibility to corporations leads to wrongful impositions of punishment on innocent parties and encourages a dangerous trend toward conceiving the corporation as a large-scale organism.

VELASSERRY, Sebastian. The Value-Ought of Self-Realization: A Phenomenological Approach. J Indian Counc Phil Res, 5(3), 71-77, My-Ag 88.

VELLEMAN, Dan. Partitioning Pairs of Countable Sets of Ordinals. J Sym Log, 55(3), 1019-1021, S 90.

VELLEMAN, J David and BOGHOSSIAN, Paul A. Physicalist Theories of Color. Phil Rev, 100(1), 67-106, Ja 91.

We argue that no known physicalist theory of color can adequately explain how colors are represented in visual experience, given certain reasonable epistemological and phenomenological constraints.

VELLEMAN, J David. Well-Being and Time. Pac Phil Quart, 72(1), 48-77, Mr 91.

I argue that how good a life one has is not a function of how well-off one is at each moment during that life. The argument yields implications about the nature of prudence, the evil of death, and the value of euthanasia.

VENCOVSKÁ, A and PARIS, J. "Inexact and Inductive Reasoning" in *Logic, Methodology and Philosophy of Science, VIII*, FENSTAD, J E (ed), 111-120. New York, Elsevier Science, 1989.

VENEMA, Yde. Expressiveness and Completeness of an Interval Tense Logic. Notre Dame J Form Log, 31(4), 529-547, Fall 90.

We present the syntax and semantics of an interval-based temporal logic which was defined by Halpern and Shoham. It is proved that this logic has a greater capacity to distinguish frames than any temporal logic based on points and we show that neither this nor any other finite set of operators can be functionally complete on the class of dense orders. In the last part of the paper we give sound and complete sets of axioms for several classes of structures. The methods employed in the paper show that it is rewarding to view intervals as points in a plane, in the style of two-dimensional modal logic.

VENTIMIGLIA, Giovanni. Le relazioni divine secondo S Tommaso d'Aquino: Riproposizione di un problema e prospettive di indagine. Riv Filosof Neo-Scolas, 82(2-3), 287-299, Ap-S 90.

VERBEEK, Bruno. Spinoza en het ontstaan van de staat. Alg Ned Tijdschr Wijs, 82(4), 252-268, O 90.

This article offers an interpretation of the way Spinoza explains the origin of the state. In this respect the TTP differs fundamentally from the TP. In the former work Spinoza uses a contract model. This raises serious problems with regard to the individual motivation to enter the state and the necessary transfer of natural right. In the TP Spinoza has to give up the contract model in favor of a "mechanistic" account of the origin of the state in order to solve these problems. I argue that the latter account is more consequent, more plausible, and has relevant features for today's political scientists and philosophers.

VERBEKE, Gerard. A Christian Philosopher in a "Broken World". Proc Cath Phil Ass, 63, 20-26, 1990.

The article concentrates on the relation between philosophy and Christianity. In the course of history Christianity decisively contributed to the building of Western thought and civilisation. This is exemplified by the positive attitude of the early Christian intellectuals as well as that of Thomas Aquinas towards Greek philosophy. In our own time Christian philosophers are invited to preserve this legacy from the past: they have to protect philosophy against a trend of indifference and distrust concerning basic metaphysical and moral issues.

VERENE, Donald Phillip. Philosophy, Argument, and Narration. Commun Cog, 24(1), 93-95, 1991.

This consider the theme that argument in philosophy does not exist in a self-supporting manner. All arguments in philosophy require a larger context in which to exist and have any importance. Arguments presuppose narrative either explicitly or implicity.

VERGARA ESTÉVEZ, Jorge. Modelos elitarios de democracia. Dianoia, 34(34), 65-92, 1988.

VERGOTE, A. From Philosophical Psychology to Philosophical Anthropology (in Dutch). Tijdschr Filosof, 52(4), 607-636, D 90.

Chr. Wolff introduced "rational psychology" as a complement to the newly created "empirical psychology." In the twentieth century, philosophical anthropology established itself as a full-blown philosophical domain only after some major changes in the history of thought. It can be defined as the elucidation and justification of human existence as we objectively observe it and subjectively live it in our life-world. As such, philosophical anthropology takes into account the insights of human sciences like anthropobiology, cultural anthropology, linguistics, psychoanalysis. This paper also discusses some major topics of philosophical anthropology. (edited)

VERGOTE, Antoine. The Body as Understood in Contemporary Thought and Biblical Categories. Phil Today, 35(1), 93-105, Spr 91.

VERMA, Roop Rekha. 'Is' Therefore 'Ought'. J Indian Counc Phil Res, 6(2), 25-30, Ja-Ap 89.

VERMAZEN, Bruce. "Testing Theories of Interpretation" in *Truth and Interpretation: Perspectives on the Philosophy of Donald Davidson*, LE PORE, Ernest (ed), 235-244. Cambridge, Blackwell, 1986.

VERNIER, Jean-Marie. Glose sur le prologue du traité "de l'âme" d'Aristote. Rev Thomiste, 91(2), 290-301, Ap-Je 91.

VERNIER, Jean-Marie. Physique aristotélicienne et métaphysique thomiste. Rev Thomiste, 91(1), 5-33, Ja-Mr 91.

VESEY, Godfrey (ed). *The Philosophy in Christianity*. New York, Cambridge Univ Pr, 1989.

In developing a theology for their religion, early Christians drew heavily on Platonism. Philo of Alexandria, for instance, used Plato's creation narative, in the Timaeus, to explain the Bible story given in Genesis. He connected Plato's philosophy of a Demiurge and a world of Forms with the biblical notion of a heavenly realm in which a wise and beneficient world-ruler dwells. The fourteen original papers in this volume are on the philosophy in Christianity. They include lectures by Norman Kretzmann, John Dillon, Maurice Wiles, Richard Swinburne, Christopher Stead, Gerald O'Daly, Keith Ward, J R Lucas, A H Armstrong and Eleonore Stump.

VESEY, Godfrey. "Responsibility and 'Free Will'" in *Key Themes in Philosophy*, GRIFFITHS, A Phillips (ed), 85-100. New York, Cambridge Univ Pr, 1989.

Philosophers talk of 'free will' with a view to justifying our engaging in the practice of treating people as responsible for what they do. But why do they feel the need for a justification? Is it because they want, also, to engage in the practice of looking for causes of everything that happens, and feel that the two practices are somehow incompatible? Why are they not content to say, with Aristotle (*Physics*, Book 8, Ch. 5) that the two practices are compatible, and hence that there is no need for justification? (The article is reprinted in G Vesey, *Inner and Outer: Essays on a Philosophical Myth*, London: Macmillan, 1991.)

VETO, Miklos. The Concept of "Foundation" in Schelling (in Hungarian). Magyar Filozof Szemle, 1-2, 129-139, 1990.

VETTER, Helmut. Lacan Between Freud and Heidegger (in Serbo-Croatian). Filozof Istraz, 32-33(5-6), 1701-1710, 1989.

Der Beitrag stellt einen Versuch an, Lacans Position als Theoretiker der Psychoanalyse im Hinblick auf eine bestimmte philosophische Tradition zu beleuchten. Höchtens mittelbar ist auch von Lacans Praxis als Analytiker die Rede, die Auseinandersetzung auf einige Autoren beschränkt. Von Freud aus findet Lacan Wege zur klassischen Philosophie nicht weniger als zur Linguistik und selbst zu den Vorsokratikern. Er meldet den Anspruch an, Freud gegen dessen Nachfolger zu lesen, mit einer neuen und erst jetzt authentischen Freud-Lektüre zu beginnen.

VICEDO, Marga. The Chromosome Theory of Mendelian Inheritance: Explanation and Realism in Theory Construction. Proc Phil Sci Ass, 1, 179-191, 1990.

VICEDO, Marga. Realism and Simplicity in the Castle-East Debate on the Stability of the Hereditary Units. Stud Hist Phil Sci, 22(2), 201-221, Je 91.

VIGEANT, Louise. Les objets de la sémiologie théâtrale: le texte et le spectacle. Horiz Phil, 1(1), 57-79, 1990.

VIGNAUX, Georges. À propos d'arguments qui s'ignorent. Lekton, 1(1), 159-185, 1990.

VIHVELIN, Kadri. Freedom, Necessity, and Laws of Nature as Relations between Universals. Austl J Phil, 68(4), 371-381, D 90.

It's often thought that the debate between compatibilists and incompatibilists is a debate about which conception of freedom is the correct one. But both sides can and should agree that we have free will only if we have the unconditional, categorical, and unimpeded ability to do otherwise. There is an argument from this premise to the conclusion that determinism is incompatible with freedom. But the argument succeeds only if a certain kind of non-Humean view of laws of nature is correct. The incompatibilist needs something like the Armstrong-Tooley-Dretske account of laws as relations between universals.

VILLANUEVA, Enrique (ed). *Information, Semantics and Epistemology*. Cambridge, Blackwell, 1990.

Information, Semantics, and Epistemology is a collection of papers dealing with philosophical and scientific aspects of information-theoretic approaches both to semantics and epistemology. A number of the papers deal with the philosophical difficulties surrounding the naturalization of information content. At the heart of this book is one of the most fundamental philosophical questions: Why is it that information that objective commodity, in the words of Frederick Dretske, cannot be accounted for in wholly naturalistic terms without countenancing strange properties or entities with suspicious identities (or with no identity at all)? Is it because there are normative features of content and these features resist naturalistic explication?

VILLORO, Luis. Sobre el conocimiento tecnológico. Rev Latin De Filosof, 16(2), 131-148, Jl 90.

VILLORO, Luis. Sobre justificación y verdad: respuesta a León Olivé. Critica, 22(65), 73-92, Ag 90.

VINEIS, Paolo. Causality Assessment in Epidemiology. Theor Med, 12(2), 171-181, Je 91.

Epidemiology relies upon a broad interpretation of determinism. This paper discusses analogies with the evolution of the concept of cause in physics, and analyzes the classical nine criteria proposed by Sir Austin Bradford Hill for causal assessment. Such criteria fall into the categories of enumerative induction, eliminative induction, deduction and analogy. All of these four categories are necessary for causal assessment and there is no natural hierarchy among them, although a 'deductive' analysis of the study design is preliminary to any assessment.

VIOLIN, Mary Ann. Pythagoras—The First Animal Rights Philosopher. Between Species, 6(3), 122-127, Sum 90.

VISION, Gerald. "Veritable Reflections" in *Reading Rorty*, MALACHOWSKI, Alan (ed), 74-100. Cambridge, Blackwell, 1991.

VISKER, Rudi. Can Genealogy Be Critical? A Somewhat Unromantic Look at Nietzsche and Foucault. Man World, 23(4), 441-452, O 90.

VISKER, Rudi. How to Get Rid of Your Expensive Philosopher of Science and Still Keep Control Over the Fuzzing Conversation of Mankind. Phil Soc Sci, 20(4), 483-507, D 90.

VITALE, Vincenzo. Grammatica e diritto: Una normatività fragile? Riv Int Filosof Diritto, 67(2), 255-281, Ap-Je 90.

VITELL, Scott J and RAWWAS, Mohammed Y A and FESTERVAND, Troy A. The Business Ethics of Pharmacists: Conflicts Practices and Beliefs. J Bus Ethics, 10(4), 295-301, Ap 91.

This paper represents the responses of 377 pharmacists to a mail survey examing their views concerning ethical conflicts and practices. Besides identifying the sources of ethical conflicts, pharmacists were asked how ethical standards have changed over the last 10 years as well as the factors influencing these changes. Conclusions and implications are outlined and future research needs are examined.

VITELL, Scott J and LUMPKIN, James R and RAWWAS, Mohammed Y A. Consumer Ethics: An Investigation of the Ethical Beliefs of Eldery Consumers. J Bus Ethics, 10(5), 365-375, My 91.

Business and especially marketing ethics have come to the forefront in recent years. While consumers have been surveyed regarding their perceptions of ethical business and marketing practices, research has been minimal with regard to their perceptions of ethical *consumer* practices. In addition, few studies have examined the ethical beliefs of elderly consumers even though they are an important and rapidly growing segment. This research investigates the relationship between Machiavellianism, ethical ideology and ethical beliefs for elderly consumers. The results indicate that elderly consumers, while generally being more ethical than young consumers, are diverse in their ethical beliefs.

VOEGELIN, Eric and SANDOZ, Ellis (ed). *Published Essays, 1966-1985 (The Collected Works of Eric Voegelin, Volume 12)*. Baton Rouge, Louisiana St Univ Pr, 1990.

VOEGELIN, Eric and HOLLWECK, Thomas A (ed) and CARINGELLA, Paul (ed). *What is History? And Other Late Unpublished Writings (The Collected Works of Eric Voegelin, Vol 28)*. Baton Rouge, Louisiana St Univ Pr, 1990.

The volume contains five previously unpublished texts by Voegelin belonging in the context of Volumes IV and V of *Order and History* as well as other later published writings. The texts comprise an analysis of the transcendental structure of history in the title-piece, the discussion of constants in the search of order in "Anxiety and Reason," a critique of certain modern notions of 'self' in "The Eclipse of Reality," an attempt to reformulate the connections between physics and myth in "The Moving Soul," and a meditation on the question of *fides quaerens intellectum* in "The Beginning and the Beyond."

VOELKE, André-Jea. La figure d'Héraclite dans la pensée du jeune Nietzsche. Frei Z Phil Theol, 37(1-2), 119-135, 1990.

VOELKE, André-Jean. Vide et non-être chez Leucippe et Démocrite. Rev Theol Phil, 122(3), 341-352, 1990.

Chez les philosophes de l'école d'Abdère l'opposition entre le plein et le vide est en même temps une opposition entre l'être et le non-être. Or, disent-ils, le vide existe, d'où il résulte que le non-être existe. Cette thèse s'exprime en particulier dans la formule de Démocrite: "le quelque chose (*den*) n'est pas plus que le rien (*mēden*)". Je chercherai à montrer que cette formule confère au "rien" une réalité équivalente à celle de l'être, ce qui permet d'attribuer une fonction causale au vide. J'envisagerai pour terminer divers aspects de cette fonction.

VOGEL, David. The Ethical Roots of Business. Bus Ethics Quart, 1(1), 101-120, Ja 91.

This paper traces the historical roots of some of our current preoccupations with the ethics of business. Its central argument is that many of the contemporary criteria that we use to evaluate the ethics of business are not new; rather, they date back several centuries. This paper illustrates this thesis by comparing historical and contemporary discussions of three sets of issues: the relationship between ethics and profits, the relationship between private gain and the public good and the tension between the results of capitalism and the intentions of businessmen. The fact that these tensions are inherent in the nature of capitalism, if not in human nature itself, does not make our contemporary concerns or standards any less valid. On the contrary, it underlies their significance. Contemporary discussions of business ethics constitute part of an ongoing moral dialogue with both deep secular and religious roots.

VOGEL, Jonathan. "Are There Counterexamples to the Closure Principle?" in *Doubting: Contemporary Perspectives on Skepticism*, ROTH, Michael D (ed), 13-27. Norwell, Kluwer, 1990.

Arguments for skepticism seem to depend upon the Closure Principle: roughly, if you know p and you know that p entails q, you know q. Fred Dretske's Zebra Case has been taken to show that the Closure Principle is invalid, but this is not so. One can, however, devise other apparent counterexamples to the principle ("Car Theft Cases") which are closely related to the Lottery Paradox. But these examples a) provide no comfort from skepticism in any case; b) may mislead us because of anomalies in our thinking about probabilities; c) really do not count against the Closure Principle after all. The problem cases do, though, raise difficulties for some relevant-alternatives theories.

VOGEL, Jonathan. Cartesian Skepticism and Inference to the Best Explanation. J Phil, 87(11), 658-666, N 90.

An important antiskeptical strategy is to try to show that we are justified in rejecting skeptical hypotheses (e.g., that one is a massively deceived brain in a vat) because those hypotheses furnish worse explanations than our commonsense view. I argue that an adroitly constructed skeptical hypothesis will survive some familiar criticisms along these lines. Nevertheless, I claim, close attention to the motivations behind skepticism points the way toward a successful argument that skeptical hypotheses are less simple than our everyday view of the world. The advantage of the latter view lies in its more straightforward accommodation of necessary truths about the spatial properties of objects.

VOICE, Paul. Rawls's Difference Principle and a Problem of Sacrifice. S Afr J Phil, 10(1), 28-31, F 91.

G A Cohen makes a distinction between the 'strict' interpretation of Rawls's difference principle and a 'misconstrued' interpretation. In this article it is argued that when understood 'strictly' the difference principle may demand sacrifices of life prospects comparable to the sacrifices Rawls finds unacceptable on a utilitarian account of justice. This problem arises once one introduces alternative economic systems which one must if the difference principle is to be properly understood. The author argues in favour of this point before attempting to meet a range of possible objections to his thesis. The results of the author's argument conflict with Rawls's main reasons for believing that the parties to the original position would opt for the difference principle before a utilitarian principle of justice.

VOIGTLÄNDER, Hanns-Dieter. Schopenhauers Wille und Platons Eros. Schopenhauer Jahr, 71, 154-168, 1990.

VOISE, Waldemar. The Drama of Galileo, The Past and the Present. Phil Sci (Tucson), 2, 105-117, 1986.

In discussion on the affair of Galileo one should take into consideration not only theoretical premises and empirical evidence but also socio-cultural factors determining different views of the universe and different standards of scientific interpretations. The latter elements played an important role in mutually exclusive assessments of the Copernican-Galilean system. In J Donne's poetry they inspired opinions on the pernicious consequences of heliocentric astronomy whereas in G Arakielowicz's arguments they were used to substantiate the consistency of this astronomy with Scripture. Similar differentiations of opinions may be found in contemporary social reception of new scientific theories.

VOIZARD, Alain. Conventions, règles et nécessité. Lekton, 1(1), 103-119, 1990.

VOJCANIN, Sava Alexander (ed). *Law, Culture, and Values: Essays in Honor of Gray L Dorsey*. New Brunswick, Transaction Books, 1990.

This is a collection of essays concerning law and its impact on values and cultures. The essays discuss Western and non-Western methods in which the law has had an impact on economics, the family, contracts, rights and crime control. It also discusses Marxism and totalitarian uses of the law to affect values. (staff)

VOKEY, Daniel. Moral Education: Realistically Speaking. Proc Phil Educ, 46, 364-376, 1990.

The paper presents an account of moral objectivity that is intended to avoid the extremes of objectivism and relativism, and sketches the implications of that account for the practice of moral education. It argues that what is lacking in "detachment/decentering" and in "constructivist" approaches to conceptualizing moral objectivity is an appreciation of the role of self-validating experiences in the development and justification of moral points of view. It recommends moral education that promotes intellectual and affective development, fosters sympathy to and critical appropriation of traditions, and attends to the concrete experience of its participants.

VOLBRECHT, Rose Mary. Friendship: Mutual Apprenticeship in Moral Development. J Value Inq, 24(4), 301-314, O 90.

VOLLMER, Gerhard. "Against Instrumentalism" in *Studies on Mario Bunge's "Treatise"*, WEINGARTNER, Paul (ed), 245-259. Amsterdam, Rodopi, 1990.

Instrumentalism doesn't care for truth or objectivity in science, but for the applicability and effectiveness of hypotheses and theories. Instrumentalism is modest, antimetaphysical, logically flawless, and empirically unrefutable. But it cannot explain why some theories work and, moreover, why others fail, neither the convergence of science nor the discovery of invariants; it cannot understand realists nor fundamental research; its heuristics is restricted to negative strategies. If modesty is a virtue, the instrumentalist should turn solipsist; if not, he should become a hypothetical realist.

VOLLMER, Gerhard. Philip Kitchers Soziobiologie-Kritik. Conceptus, 24(63), 93-102, 1990.

VOLLRATH, John. Ellis, Epistemic Values, and the Problem of Induction. Brit J Phil Sci, 42(2), 257-261, Je 91.

Brian Ellis argues that a values-based epistemology (where epistemic values, not truth, are the standards of rational justification) generates a solution to Hume's problem of induction. However, Hume's challenge to the standards of a truth-based account of rational justification apply equally well to the standards of a values-based account. Thus Ellis does not show that such an account generates a solution to Hume's problem.

VOLLRATH, John. *Science and Moral Values*. Lanham, Univ Pr of America, 1990.

This book examines behavior modification, recombinant DNA technology, experiments on humans, reproductive policies, and weapons research from the standpoints of utilitarianism, expected utility, rights and duties, justice, and moral virtues. It considers whether scientific explanations of behavior (in biology and psychology) should reduce our confidence in traditional moral beliefs. Finally, it considers whether scientific patterns of thinking should be standards for moral patterns of thinking.

VOLODIN, A. Lenin and Philosophy: Should We Not Pose This Problem Anew? Soviet Stud Phil, 30(1), 70-87, Sum 91.

VOLPI, Franco. La "riabilitazione" della δυναμιζ e dell'ενεργεια in Heidegger. Aquinas, 33(1), 3-27, Ja-Ap 90.

VON ENGELHARDT, Dietrich and SALAZAR, Christine (trans). "Historical Consciousness in the German Romantic *Naturforschung*" in *Romanticism and the Sciences*, CUNNINGHAM, Andrew (ed), 55-68. New York, Cambridge Univ Pr, 1990.

VON GLASERSFELD, Ernst. Teleology and the Concepts of Causation. Philosophica, 46(2), 17-43, 1990.

The paper suggests that the main disagreement about teleology is due to an ambiguity of the term and that one of the notions it covers is scientifically acceptable. The conceptual dichotomy goes back to Aristotle, whose categorization of 'causes' is discussed. Experiential finality is separated from metaphysical teleology, and shown to be derived from the notion of 'efficient cause'. Its use and interpretation in cybernetics is briefly sketched out.

VON PLATO, Jan. Probabilistic Causality from a Dynamical Point of View. Topoi, 9(2), 101-108, S 90.

VON PLATO, Jan. "Probability in Dynamical Systems" in *Logic, Methodology and Philosophy of Science, VIII*, FENSTAD, J E (ed), 427-443. New York, Elsevier Science, 1989.

VON SCHELLING, F W J and BEACH, Edward A (trans). On the Source of the Eternal Truths. Owl Minerva, 22(1), 55-67, Fall 90.

VON UEXKUELL, Thure. The Unity of the Natural Sciences: Comment on Portmann. J Med Phil, 15(5), 473-480, O 90.

Is Portmann's concept of inwardness objectively useful in understanding biological phenomena? If it is, it would seem that there is no unity to the physical sciences, because biology is as fundamental as physics. On the other hand, Portmann's interpretation of inwardness as a meaning or significance that we have to give our interpretation of biological phenomena suggests that it is sheerly subjective, and so should be reduced to objective correlates. This dilemma is false, however. One should realize that scientists construe physical and chemical processes as processes devoid of intrinsic meaning, just as they construe biological processes as having this meaning, which is Portmann's inwardness. From this angle we can integrate the significance of physical and biological processes in a way which does not reduce the latter to the former.

VON USLAR, Detlev. Heideggers Bedeutung für die Psychologie. Deut Z Phil, 38(12), 1161-1167, 1990.

The philosophy of Heidegger permits a new orientation of psychology. Instead of setting forth from the cartesian differentiation between cocitatio and extensio psychology should make the Being-there of man in its temporality, its being-in-the-world, its being-in-community and its being-as-a-body the basis of its reflection. The two questions "What is being?" and "What is the soul?" are closely connected. What occurs on a psychological level is seen here on the background of being-in-the-world and in connection with the relation of life history and history per se. Language, art, technology and religion are of essential significance for psychology in this context.

VON WRIGHT, G H and MC GUINNESS, B F. Unpublished Correspondence between Russell and Wittgenstein. Russell, 10(2), 101-124, Wint 90-91.

VON WRIGHT, Georg Henrik. On Law and Morality: A Dialogue. Ratio Juris, 3(3), 321-330, D 90.

The dialogue focusses on the distinctions and connections between law and morality. Morality is seen as axiological in character, whereas law is deontological. The possibility of a conceptual tie between goodness (axiology) and duty (deontology) is firmly disputed. Habermas's discursive foundation of ethics is criticized because it seems to confer on moral principles the status of *a priori* synthetic truths. Every moral idea has a cultural relativity which is not taken into account by Habermasian dialogue ethics. The moral and the legal points of view are kept separate: A law which does not satisfy the requirements of a "minimum content" of natural law is not said to be "law," but simply falling short of moral criteria. The possibility of introducing rational guarantees into moral discourse is not denied, but doubt remains as to whether there are "right answers" to moral questions.

VOS, H M. Value Concepts and Preconventional, Conventional and Postconventional Morality (in Dutch). Bijdragen, 3, 272-289, 1990.

Conventional value concepts give us a morally acceptable alternative for postconventional morality. This is important, as the ideal of a postconventional morality has proven to be unattainable. Moreover with conventional value concepts, though they are intuitionist in character themselves, we can check super-intuitionist preconventional convictions. So conventional value concepts can help us to solve the problems of preconventional and postconventional morality. Nevertheless the importance of substantial value concepts can be defended on more compelling grounds. Value concepts are composed of two components: a factual and an emotional one. 'Naturalistic' in character as they are, their informative function should be stressed and their central position in morals and ethics defended.

VREEKE, G J. Gilligan on Justice and Care: Two Interpretations. J Moral Educ, 20(1), 33-46, F 91.

This article illustrates that Gilligan's distinction between an ethic of justice and an ethic of care is interpreted in two ways. Some authors conceive this distinction in terms of content (different rules and values); while others regard the distinction as one of form (different ways of thinking). It is argued that Gilligan's views allow for both interpretations. Finally, a way to an inclusive interpretation is shown.

VUILLEMIN, Jule. Sur la méthode de Ferdinand Gonseth. Dialectica, 44(3-4), 225-228, 1990.

Agreement required in elementary geometry among three aspects distinguished by Gonseth (intuition, experience and theory) involves two hypotheses (continuity and infinity).

VYCINAS, Vincent. *The Great Goddess and the Aistian Mythical World*. New York, Lang, 1990.

WACHELDER, J and CALLEBAUT, Werner. Teleo-theologie und kein Ende: Reactie op Soontiens. Kennis Methode, 15(2), 218-223, 1991.

WACHS, Martin. Ethics and Advocacy in Forecasting for Public Policy. Bus Prof Ethics J, 9(1-2), 141-157, Spr-Sum 90.

Forecasts of the demand for and the costs of services and programs are widely used in public policymaking. Forecasts are used to evaluate alternatives, and to insure that public resource allocations will be cost effective. While it is widely understood that forecasts are executed with technical precision and objectivity, there are many examples of forecasts which are designed to advocate particular choices. Assumptions are made which lead to predetermined outcomes, and forecasts are presented as "science" when they are actually advocacy. The technical complexity of forecasting methods and the hierarchical structure of the organizations in which they are prepared encourage the political uses of forecasts. This paper provides evidence of this problem, explains why forecasts are susceptible to these kinds of abuses, and suggests some actions on the part of professionals which might support greater independence in the preparation of forecasts for policymaking.

WAGMAN, Morton. *Artificial Intelligence and Human Cognition*. New York, Praeger, 1991.

WAGNER DE CEW, Judith. Critical Legal Studies and Liberalism: Understanding the Similarities and Differences. Phil Topics, 18(1), 41-51, Spr 90.

WAGNER, Carl G. Corroboration and Conditional Positive Relevance. Phil Stud, 61(3), 295-300, Mr 91.

George Schlesinger's critique (*Phil Stud* 54 (1988), 141-152) of Jonathan Cohen's elegant probabilistic account of corroboration carelessly misstates several key inequalities occurring in Cohen's analysis, and fundamentally misconstrues the aim of that analysis. The alternative account proffered by Schlesinger amounts merely to the familiar observation that conditional positive relevance is a symmetric relation.

WAGNER, Gerhard. *Historizing contra fetishizing*—The Progress of Modern Technology in W Benjamin's Aesthetic Reflexion (in German). Deut Z Phil, 38(9), 859-865, 1990.

WAGNER, Gerhard and ZIPPRIAN, Heinz. Intersubjectivity and Critical Consciousness: Remarks on Habermas's Theory of Communicative Action. Inquiry, 34(1), 49-62, Mr 91.

The out-dated intentionalistic assumptions manifest in Habermas's *Theory of Communicative Action* undermine a solution to the problem of order in action theory beyond utilitarianism. An analysis of his intersubjectivistic conception, which is based on the theory of the speech-act, shows that the incompleteness of Habermas's linguistic turn is due to his attempt to revive the older Critical Theory's concept of critique. The claims for a scientifically well-founded revival of a universal concept of reason—which are asserted in this concept—invalidate the intersubjectivistic paradigm in action theory and therefore obstruct the way to a deindividualized formulation of the theory of social contract that avoids the paradox of utilitarian models.

WAHSNER, Renate. Ist die Naturphilosophie eine abgelegte Gestalt des modernen Geistes. Deut Z Phil, 39(2), 180-193, 1991.

It is to show that natural philosophy is not antiquated but that it is an unrenounceable part of philosophy as such still now. At this natural philosophy is neither misunderstood as a simple popularisation of natural sciences nor identified with the theory of sciences. From the examination follows that natural philosophy appears as a discarded shape of modern mind only in the case that the epistemological state of neural sciences is equated with that one of philosophy and it is not recognized that the objects of natural sciences are not the natural objects although natural objects can be recognized only through the objects of natural sciences.

WAHSNER, Renate. Ist die Naturphilosophie eine abgelegte Gestalt des modernen Geistes? Man World, 24(2), 199-218, Ap 91.

WAINWRIGHT, W J. James, Rationality and Religious Belief. Relig Stud, 27(2), 223-238, Je 91.

I argue that standard interpretations of James are mistaken. Beliefs which are expressions of our "passional nature" can be epistemically, as well as practically, rational. James' position is grounded in his conviction that the human mind is "congruent" with reality. This conviction is, in turn, supported by an argument from evolution. It can also be supported by two pragmatic arguments. I conclude with a critical discussion of James' position and a consideration of its ramifications for the philosophy of religion.

WAITHE, Mary Ellen. "Heloise" in *A History of Women Philosophers, Volume II: Medieval, Renaissance and Enlightenment, A.D. 500-1600*, WAITHE, Mary Ellen (ed), 67-83. Norwell, Kluwer, 1989.

WAITHE, Mary Ellen (ed). *A History of Women Philosophers, Volume II: Medieval, Renaissance and Enlightenment, A.D. 500-1600*. Norwell, Kluwer, 1989.

WAITHE, Mary Ellen. "Murasaki Shikibu" in *A History of Women Philosophers, Volume II: Medieval, Renaissance and Enlightenment, A.D. 500-1600*, WAITHE, Mary Ellen (ed), 1-26. Norwell, Kluwer, 1989.

WAITHE, Mary Ellen. "Oliva Sabuco de Nantes Barrera" in *A History of Women Philosophers, Volume II: Medieval, Renaissance and Enlightenment, A.D. 500-1600*, WAITHE, Mary Ellen (ed), 261-284. Norwell, Kluwer, 1989.

WAITHE, Mary Ellen. "Roswitha of Gandersheim, Christine Pisan, Margaret More Roper and Teresa of Avila" in *A History of Women Philosophers, Volume II: Medieval, Renaissance and Enlightenment, A.D. 500-1600*, WAITHE, Mary Ellen (ed), 309-317. Norwell, Kluwer, 1989.

WAKEFIELD, Jerome C. Vlastos on the Unity of Virtue: Why Pauline Predication Will Not Save the Biconditionality Thesis. Ancient Phil, 11(1), 47-65, Spr 91.

WALDENFELS, Bernhard. Between Necessity and Superabundance: Meta-economic Reflections on Marxism. Grad Fac Phil J, 14(1), 23-33, 1991.

Critique of economics in the sense of Marx presupposes that economics transgresses itself insofar as man, creating himself and his world, cannot be reduced to a mere *homo oeconomicus*. But how this transgression takes place? Is there a movement *from* necessity *to* suberabundance as Marx assumes, or is there an abiding movement which oscillated *between* necessity and suberabundance as A. Leroi-Gourhan, L. Mumford and others suggest? It will be argued that starting from man as 'defective being' Marx remains too much captive of the bourgeois society he is criticizing.

WALDENFELS, Bernhard. "Dialogue and Discourses" in *Writing the Politics of Difference*, SILVERMAN, Hugh J (ed), 165-175. Albany, SUNY Pr, 1991.

The presupposition is made that the global dialogue, oriented to an all-encompassing *logos*, is going splitted into heterogeneous discourses whose orders are limited. So the question arises how the discourses are connected in form of a transdiscoursivity. A new kind of dialogue would imply the intertwining of the own and the alien, an alterity of myself and a polyvocity of speaking. Authors of reference are Plato, Gadamer, Foucault, Merleau-Ponty, Levinas and Bakhtin.

WALDENFELS, Bernhard. Experience of the Alien in Husserl's Phenomenology. Res Phenomenol, 20, 19-33, 1990.

On the one hand Husserl defines the experience of the alien paradoxically as 'accessibility of what is unaccessible originally'. On the other hand he tries to show that the alien is constitued 'by means of the own'. But this constitution fails. As the experience of time shows I am alienated from myself from the beginning. There is no pure form of the own, and the contrast between the own, and the alien is irreducible. We can only do justice to the alien when we start from it. Before we could say what it is we have already responded to it.

WALDENFELS, Bernhard. "Experience of the Other: Between Appropriation and Disappropriation" in *Life-World and Politics: Between Modernity and Postmodernity*, WHITE, Stephen K (ed), 66-77. Notre Dame, Univ Notre Dame Pr, 1989.

The focus of this paper is on the contrast between the one and the alien, reviewed from the standpoint of a radicalised phenomenology. I start with a conceptual survey. Then I outline the attempt to overcome the contrast either by appropriation, based on egocentrism or logocentrism, or by disappropriation, tending to a dissolution of the limits between own and alien. Finally, I try to get a footing in the intertwining of own and alien beyond the alternatives of appropriation and disappropriation.

WALDENFELS, Bernhard. Vérité à Faire: Merleau-Ponty's Question Concerning Truth. Phil Today, 35(2), 185-194, Sum 91.

Questioning the origin of truth Merleau-Ponty does not stop at traditional conceptions like truth as adequacy, as consensus or as coherency. With Husserl and Heidegger he goes back to pre-predicative experience. Truth is something to be done. Merleau-Ponty explains the event of truth by referring to the paradox of creative expression. Expression is neither pure production nor pure reproduction but something which 'hits' what has to be said or done and what can be said or done in different ways. Truth seems to be a creative kind of responding to the other.

WALDSTEIN, Wolfgang. Is There a Natural Law? Vera Lex, 10(2), 1-3, 1990.

The purpose of this article is to show that there exists what is called natural law (ius naturale in ancient Roman law). From the great continuity in the concrete legal development over millennia in spite of all theoretical differences among the vast cultural variations one can conclude that this requires correspondingly an objective reality as its basis. Natural law norms can, of course, not be known by means of sense perception. Yet in their intelligible content they have at all times been known by an act of insight performed by the "intelligence common to us all" (Cicero).

WALKER, J C. Democratic and Professional Authority in Education. Proc Phil Educ, 46, 254-264, 1990.

Does the philosophical basis for the authority of educators lie in democratic or professional considerations, or both? Two current views are criticised: that of Aronowitz and Giroux, that the practice of the educational profession, and by implication professional educational authority, can be democratic; and that of Gutmann, that professional educational authority is in all cases justified by its being a necessary condition for democracy. Argument is presented for the view that although there may be democratic reasons for endorsing professional authority, it has its own independent grounds of justification in the conditions for educational practice.

WALKER, Lawrence J and MORAN, Thomas J. Moral Reasoning in a Communist Chinese Society. J Moral Educ, 20(2), 139-155, My 91.

This study examined the cross-cultural universality of Kohlberg's theory of moral reasoning development in the People's Republic of China—a culture quite different from the one out of which the theory arose. In particular, the applicability of the theory was evaluated in terms of its comprehensiveness and the validity of the moral stage model. An analysis of moral orientations provided an additional perspective on individuals' moral reasoning, in particular, in revealing group differences. Although, in general, the universal applicability of Kohlberg's approach was supported by these data, a subjective analysis of responses revealed some indigenous concepts, fundamental to Communist Chinese morality, that are not well tapped by the approach.

WALKER, R Scott (trans) and LANTÉRI-LAURA, Georges. Aphasia and Inner Language. Diogenes, 150, 24-36, Sum 90.

WALLACE, G. Terrorism and Argument from Analogy. Int J Moral Soc Stud, 6(2), 149-160, Sum 91.

In the absence of agreement about how terrorism is to be defined, what sort of case can be made out for the orthodox view that terrorism is always wrong? Conventional approaches resting either on the idea that terrorism is necessarily wrong or that it must always do more harm than good are rejected as inadequate or inconclusive. An alternative strategy is explored in which the orthodox view is tested against the strongest apologia that can be devised for acts of extreme terrorism, that is lethal attacks on innocent people. The apologia rests on an analogy between such acts and acts of warfare widely regarded as justifiable. It is argued that despite the plausibility of the apologia the orthodox view can cope with it.

WALLACE, Jim. Theorizing about Morals. Nous, 25(2), 176-183, Ap 91.

WALLACE, John and MASON, H E. "On Some Thought Experiments about Mind and Meaning" in *Propositional Attitudes: The Role of Content in Logic, Language, and Mind*, ANDERSON, C Anthony (ed), 175-199. Stanford, CSLI, 1990.

WALLACE, John. "Translation Theories and the Decipherment of Linear B" in *Truth and Interpretation: Perspectives on the Philosophy of Donald Davidson*, LE PORE, Ernest (ed), 211-234. Cambridge, Blackwell, 1986.

WALLACE, Kathleen (ed) and BUCHLER, Justus and MARSOOBIAN, Armen (ed). *Metaphysics of Natural Complexes (Second Edition)*. Albany, SUNY Pr, 1990.

WALLACE-BRODEUR, Paul H. Community Values in Vermont Health Planning. Hastings Center Rep, 20(5), 18-19, S-O 90.

WALLIS, Charles S. Stich, Content, Prediction, and Explanation in Cognitive Science. Proc Phil Sci Ass, 1, 327-340, 1990.

I consider Stich's principle of autonomy argument (*From Folk Psychology to Cognitive Science*) as an argument that computationalism is an incorrect approach to explanation and prediction in cognitive science. After considering the principle of autonomy argument in light of several computational systems and psychological examples, I conclude that the argument is unsound. I formulate my reasons for rejecting Stich's argument into the conjunction argument. Finally, I argue that the conjunction argument is sound, and that its soundness adds additional plausibility to computationalism as an explanatory schema in cognitive science.

WALLS, Jerry L. Hume on Divine Amorality. Relig Stud, 26(2), 257-266, Je 90.

When account is taken of our moral nature, I argue that Hume's claim that God is amoral must be rejected. First, I argue on intuitive grounds that if God is not good, He must be evil. Then I show that the conclusion that God is evil actually follows from Hume's own principles. In the end, we must choose between an evil deity or a perfectly good one.

WALLS, Jerry L. Why Plantinga Must Move from Defense to Theodicy. Phil Phenomenol Res, 51(2), 375-378, Je 91.

Alvin Plantinga has consistently held that his Free Will Defense, which hinges on the *possibility* that we are free in the libertarian sense, is not to be taken as a theodicy. This paper argues that it follows from Plantinga's belief that God is perfectly good, as well as essentially omnipotent and omniscient, that we are *in fact* free in the libertarian sense given the moral evil in our world. In view of this entailment, Plantinga moves from defense to theodicy.

WALLULIS, Jerald. *The Hermeneutics of Life History: Personal Achievement and History in Gadamer, Habermas, and Erikson*. Evanston, Northwestern Univ Pr, 1991.

Hans-Georg Gadamer calls individual self-awareness a "flickering in the closed circuits of historical life." This book opposes his critique of self-awareness, not his conception of historical life. His famous descriptions of history and play are compared to Erik Erikson's observations about individual mastery in play in order to make history and personal achievement more complementary and balanced in importance. The continuity manifest in Erikson's description of life history establishes a needed counterweight to the developmental theories of Jürgen Habermas; moreover, its similarity in this respect to Gadamer's description of historical life makes a "hermeneutics" of life history a positive option for philosophical hermeneutics.

WALMSLEY, Peter. *The Rhetoric of Berkeley's Philosophy*. New York, Cambridge Univ Pr, 1990.

The Rhetoric of Berkeley's Philosophy, the first book-length assessment of Berkeley as a writer, offers rhetorical and literary analyses of his four major philosophical texts, *The Principles of Human Knowledge*, *Three Dialogues*, *Alciphron* and *Siris*. The Berkeley that emerges from this study is an accomplished stylist, one who builds structures of affective imagery, who creates dramatic voices in his texts, and who masters the range of philosophical genres—the treatise, the dialogue and the essay. Above all, Berkeley's writing reflects his philosophical understanding of the pragmatic and affective ends of language.

WALRAVENS, Else. Justus Möser: De Revolutie en de grondslagen van de moderne staat. Tijdschr Stud Verlich Denken, 17(3-4), 215-229, 1989.

WALTER, Edward. The Modernity of St Thomas' Political Philosophy. Vera Lex, 10(1), 12-13, 1990.

WALTER, Edward. Presidential Campaigns, Television News and Voter Turnout. Pub Affairs Quart, 5(3), 279-300, Jl 91.

In the 1988 presidential election, voter turnout reached a 64 year low. Voter alienation is generally thought to be behind voter apathy. Television campaign coverage, which has become the primary source of political information is held to be mainly responsible because it trivializes and sensationalizes campaigns. This paper examines methods by which television news coverage can be elevated without violating the First Amendment rights of candidates. The role of the FCC is also examined.

WALTERS, Kerry S. Hell, This Isn't Necessary After All. Int J Phil Relig, 29(3), 175-186, Je 91.

WALTERS, LeRoy (ed). *Bibliography of Bioethics, Volume 16*. Washington, Kennedy Inst Ethics, 1990.

The annual *Bibliography of Bioethics* indexes the English-language literature on ethical and related public policy aspects of health care and biomedical research. It is the print counterpart of the National Library of Medicine's BIOETHICSLINE database. Volume 16 (1990) contains 2500 citations, many with abstracts, drawn from the disciplines of the health sciences, philosophy, law, the social sciences, and religion. Among the topics covered are bioethics and medical ethics in general; patients' rights and the professional patient relationship; health care and public health; new reproductive technologies; abortion; genetic intervention; human experimentation; euthanasia and withholding treatment; and animal experimentation.

WALTMAN, Jerold. Justice Powell and the Parochial Schools Case: A Case for Judicial Statesmanship. Pub Affairs Quart, 3(4), 61-78, O 89.

Judicial pragmatists are often pictured as those who consider each case individually with no overarching political theory. This stands in contrast to those who read the Constitution as containing a particular substantive model of society, such as laissez-faire economics or egalitarianism. Justice Powell is usually put in the former camp. However, a third choice is available, and using the decision regarding state financial aid to parochical schools, this essay argues that he belongs there. The formulation, labeled "judicial statesmanship" by Gary Jacobsohn, argues that the Constitution sets out only a general model of the political order but at the same time points the way toward specific values.

WALTON, Barbara J. Teaching Feminist Ethics as Male Consciousness-Raising. Proc Phil Educ, 46, 300-303, 1990.

WALTON, Clarence C (ed). *Enriching Business Ethics*. New York, Plenum Pr, 1990.

On the assumption that business ethicists need continuing updates on the more recent findings in cognate disciplines, scholars form the social sciences, biology and religion were invited to respond to this question: "what special contribution can your discipline make to business philosophers who wrestle with a complex corporate environment?" To help the reader identify major themes the author-editor wrote a prefatory note for each essay as well as a long introduction and conclusion. Widening the moralist's lens is the result.

WALTON, Clarence C. Punitive Damages: New Twists in Torts. Bus Ethics Quart, 1(3), 269-291, Jl 91.

Proposed is the novel thesis that revenues derived from punitive-damage (PD) awards in tort cases belong to the public, not to tort victims or their ambitious lawyers—as is presently the case. Justice, of course, demands that innocent victims be compensated fully for their losses. Once that is done, no extra compensation is necessary. While it is sound public policy to use PDs to discourage potential tortfeasors from carelessness, it is equally sound policy to support local communities and the volunteer organizations on which they depend. Allocating PD revenue to such purposes promotes both goals.

WALTON, Kendall L. *Mimesis as Make-Believe: On the Foundations of the Representational Arts*. Cambridge, Harvard Univ Pr, 1990.

The representational arts are understood to include both pictorial representations and literary fictions, as well as theater, film, etc. *Mimesis* pursues analogies with children's games of make-believe, and develops a comprehensive theory of make-believe which it employs to address a wide range of aesthetic issues concerning the nature and importance of representation, including the distinction between fiction and nonfiction, differences among representational media, notions of realism and points of view, emotional responses to fiction, etc. Along the way, it examines the imagination, dreams, legends and myths, irony, and some aspects of music and nonfigurative painting. It also treats the metaphysical and semantic problems concerning fictitious entities.

WALUCHOW, Wilfrid J and THOMAS, John E. *Well and Good: Case Studies in Biomedical Ethics (Revised Edition)*. Peterborough, Broadview Pr, 1990.

WALZER, Michael. "Nation and Universe" in *The Tanner Lectures on Human Values, Volume XI*, PETERSON, Grethe B (ed), 507-556. Salt Lake City, Univ of Utah Pr, 1990.

WALZER, R R (ed) and MINGAY, J M. *Aristotelis Ethica Evdemia*. New York, Oxford Univ Pr, 1991.

WAMBA-DIA-WAMBA, Ernest. Philosophy of African Intellectuals. Quest, 5(1), 4-17, Je 91.

Philosophy aims at achieving self-mastery and constraining onesidedness. African intellectuals formed in the context of a social epistemology of domination—whose central figures were the explorer, the missionary, the ethnologist and the developmental social scientist—and emphasizing imitation of western classicism, fail to theorize African self-mastery as the basis for the self-determination of African people. They thus vacillate between imitation of western classicism and ethnophilosophical romantic search for, or celebration of African identity. Intellectual creativity, to dare to think the unthinkable, is called for. The critique of Cheikh Anta Diop's monumental work may provide a stimulating beginning.

WAND, Yair and WEBER, Ron. "Mario Bunge's Ontology as a Formal Foundation for Information Systems Concepts" in *Studies on Mario Bunge's "Treatise"*, WEINGARTNER, Paul (ed), 123-150. Amsterdam, Rodopi, 1990.

For a number of years, we have been engaged in an effort to establish a theoretical foundation for the process of systems analysis and design. The main assumption underlying our approach is that an information system is a representation of a real-world system. Hence, we seek the basis of and fundamental concepts needed for the theoretical view of information systems in the domain of ontology. We used Mario Bunge's *Ontology* as our main source of constructs to model real systems and information systems. (edited)

WANGERIN, Paul T. Role Differentiation Problems in Professional Ethics. Bus Prof Ethics J, 9(1-2), 171-180, Spr-Sum 90.

The American systems of adversary justice, laissez-faire capitalism, and political pluralism all rest on the same underlying "model" for societal institutions, a model which assumes that human beings are, by nature, essentially self-interested and competitive. Because of that fact, American lawyers, business managers and political figures often encounter the same kind of ethical problems, problems often referred to as "role differentiation." Role differentiation problems arise in all three of these professions when professional standards call for self-interested and competitive conduct while generally accepted moral standards call for altruistic and cooperative conduct.

WANSING, Heinrich. A General Possible Worlds Framework for Reasoning about Knowledge and Belief. Stud Log, 49(4), 523-539, D 90.

In this paper non-normal worlds semantics is presented as a basic, general, and unifying approach to epistemic logic. The semantical framework of non-normal worlds is compared to the model theories of several logics for knowledge and belief that were recently developed in Artificial Intelligence (AI). It is shown that every model for implicit and explicit belief (Levesque), for awareness, general awareness, and local reasoning (Fagin and Halpern), and for awareness and principles (van der Hoek and Meyer) induces a non-normal worlds model validating precisely the same formulas (of the language in question).

WANSING, Heinrich and PEARCE, David. On the Methodology of Possible World Semantics, I: Correspondence Theory. Notre Dame J Form Log, 29(4), 482-496, Fall 88.

This paper discusses the constraints on possible worlds semantic modelling that have been proposed by J Van Benthem ('Logical Semantics as an Empirical Science', *Studia Logica* 42, 1983, pp. 299-313). The structure of the possible worlds programme in logical semantics is compared with that of other scientific research traditions, and some logical and methodological aspects of semantic explanation are examined in the context of the 'correspondence theory'.

WAPLES, Elain and SHAUB, Michael K. Establishing an Ethic of Accounting: A Response to Westra's Call for Government Employment of Auditors. J Bus Ethics, 10(5), 385-393, My 91.

The central question in Westra's (1986) search for an ethic of accounting concerns to whom the accountant owes loyal agency: to the client or to the public interest. The authors argue that the accountant's master has already been defined as the public interest. An ethic of accounting is identified through analysis of the accountant's master and through examination of the accountant's ethical obligations under the Code of Professional Conduct (AICPA, 1988). Potential conflicts between professional and organizational loyalties are analyzed with respect to the real-life problem used by Westra to support her argument. Finally, the implications of government employment of auditors are discussed.

WARD, Andrew. The Role of Homunculi in Psychology. Dialogos, 25(56), 157-165, Jl 90.

WARD, Bruce K. Prometheus or Cain? Albert Camus's Account of the Western Quest for Justice. Faith Phil, 8(2), 193-213, Ap 91.

The article focuses, first, on the analysis offered by Camus in his major philosophical work, *The Rebel*, of the contradiction apparent in the modern western project between the original demand for justice on earth and the later practice of injustice. The negative assessment of the Jewish-Christian notion of justice offered by Camus was a reflection, above all, of his critique of the biblical theodicy. This critique is the second, and central, focus of the article. The article ends with some critical comments concerning the viability of Camus's attempt to find in the religious vision of Athens that counterweight to modern nihilism which he did not find in Jerusalem. (edited)

WARD, Graham. Biblical Narrative and the Theology of Metonymy. Mod Theol, 7(4), 335-349, Jl 91.

WARD, Gregory L and HIRSCHBERG, Julia. A Pragmatic Analysis of Tautological Utterances. J Prag, 15(6), 507-520, Je 91.

The interpretation of tautological utterances of the form, e.g., if it rains, it rains has generally been characterized in the literature as a case of Gricean conversational implicature (Grice 1975). However, in recent years, this analysis, and indeed the entire Gricean program, has come under attack. Wirzbicka (1987) contends that tautology must be seen as a language-specific, attitudinal phenomenon, thus, in her view, vitiating Grice's universalist approach. In this paper, we take issue with this claim, pointing out certain flaws in Wierzbicka's 'radical semantics' approach to tautology. We then propose a new Gricean account of tautological utterances based upon a large corpus of naturally occurring data.

WARD, Keith. "God as Creator" in *The Philosophy in Christianity*, VESEY, Godfrey (ed), 99-118. New York, Cambridge Univ Pr, 1989.

WARDEKKER, Wim. Praktijkontwikkeling en wetenschappelijke (onderwijs)kunde: Een reactie op Boon e.a.. Kennis Methode, 15(2), 164-173, 1991.

This is a reaction to the paper by Louis Boon and others. Their view of the practical science turns out, upon closer inspection, to be ambiguous. The constructivist Agora model they propose might have become an adequate instrument for the analysis of the development of such sciences. Their policy recommendations, however, rest on a severely restricted interpretation of this model, and in fact are more consistent with the received nomological view of a division between pure and applied science. The cause of this is that they have taken the concept of praxis for granted, confusing between the praxis of a university trained professional, and praxis as a social community characterized by the transaction of meanings. Thinking consistently from this second interpretation, elaborated in educational theory, would lead to a better model and to different recommendations.

WARDY, Robert. *The Chain of Change: A Study of Aristotle's "Physics" VII*. New York, Cambridge Univ Pr, 1990.

WARGO, Robert J J. Japanese Ethics: Beyond Good and Evil. Phil East West, 40(4), 499-509, O 90.

WARMBRŌD, Ken. Behaviourism, Neuroscience and Translational Indeterminacy. Austl J Phil, 69(1), 67-81, Mr 91.

Quine's strict behavior methodology should be replaced by one which allows for the relevance of neurological information to translation. Strict behaviorism leads to an unnecessary indeterminacy concerning even simple semantic matters such as the translation of truth functions. This indeterminacy is avoidable if we adopt a linguistic methodology which is capable of exploiting neurological information. While neurological information has the capacity to eliminate the extreme indeterminacy in translation truth functions, it still cannot eliminate indeterminacy entirely. Hence, a linguistic science informed by neuroscience must still contend with the indeterminacy problem.

WARMBRŌD, Ken. Mechanism and Indeterminacy: Reply to MacIntosh. Dialogue (Canada), 29(4), 551-556, 1990.

It is argued that both neurological and behavioral data are relevant in adjudicating conditional predictions of behavior. Since conditional predictions of this sort are critical in deciding on the semantic interpretation of utterances, it follows that both neurological and behavioral data are relevant in testing semantic theories.

WARMBRŌD, Ken. The Need for Charity in Semantics. Phil Rev, 100(3), 431-458, Jl 91.

This paper develops an empirical methodology for testing semantic theories which eliminates the need for broad-scope, methodological asumptions to the effect that most informants are right most of the time. Such assumptions are both controversial and vague in terms of how they are to be applied. Under the testing paradigm developed here, charitable assumptions are normally narrow in scope, and they are justified by appeal to the observable behavior of individual informants and to the theoretical assumptions being tested. This approach allows for the possibility of informants who may be systematically and fundamentally mistaken in their beliefs.

WARNER, Martin (ed). *The Bible as Rhetoric: Studies in Biblical Persuasion and Credibility*. New York, Routledge, 1990.

Contemporary developments in philosophy and literary studies have focussed attention on the literary and rhetorical dimensions of works whose primary concern is with issues of truth and falsity; at the same time biblical scholars have been attempting to find ways forward from the established history-based procedures of biblical criticism. These pioneering interdisciplinary papers explore the ways in which the persuasive strategies employed in the biblical texts relate (both positively and negatively) to their preoccupations with religious and historical truth. They clarify what is at issue in the apparently competing claims that the Bible should be read 'as literature' and 'as scripture'.

WARNER, Martin. "The Fourth Gospel's Art of Rational Persuasion" in *The Bible as Rhetoric: Studies in Biblical Persuasion and Credibility*, WARNER, Martin (ed), 153-177. New York, Routledge, 1990.

The Fourth Gospel's avowedly rhetorical purpose is multilayered. A number of the disagreements between interpreters derive from failure to take account of this feature, which renders problematic several of the assumptions of conventional New Testament higher criticism. At its deepest structural level the Gospel is to be understood in terms of Old Testament 'Wisdom' models, but it goes beyond these in a strategy which has close affinities with Pascal's type of religious apologia and powerful claims to rationality.

WARREN, David H D (ed) and SZEREDI, Peter (ed). *Logic Programming: Proceedings of the Seventh International Conference*. Cambridge, MIT Pr, 1990.

WARREN, Karen J and CHENEY, Jim. Ecological Feminism and Ecosystem Ecology. Hypatia, 6(1), 179-197, Spr 91.

Ecological feminism is a feminism which attempts to unite the demands of the women's movement with those of the ecological movement. Ecofeminists often appeal to "ecology" in support of their claims, particulary claims about the importance of feminism to environmentalism. What is missing from the literature is any sustained attempt to show respects in which ecological feminism and the science of ecology are engaged in complementary, mutually supportive projects. In this paper we attempt to do that by showing ten important similarities which establish the need for and benefits of on-going dialogue between ecofeminists and ecosystem ecologists.

WARREN, Mary Anne. "Abortion" in *A Companion to Ethics*, SINGER, Peter (ed), 303-314. Cambridge, Blackwell, 1991.

WARREN, Paul. Explaining Historical Development: A Marxian Critique of Cohen's Historical Materialism. Clio, 20(3), 253-270, Spr 91.

In the *Grundrisse* and other places, Marx criticizes Bourgeois social and economic theory for it's "abstract individualism." This paper seeks to clarify that charge and use it to develop criticisms of G A Cohen's defense of Marx's theory of history. It is argued that these criticisms show that the "technological" version of historical materialism that Cohen defends is inadequate.

WARREN, W G. Personal Construct Theory as the Ground for a Rapproachment Between Psychology and Philosophy in Education. Educ Phil Theor, 22(1), 31-39, 1990.

WARTENBERG, Thomas E. Social Movements and Individual Identity: A Critique of Freud on the Psychology of Groups. Phil Forum, 22(4), 362-382, Sum 91.

This paper presents a critical assessment of Freud's account of the psychology of groups. It is argued that Freud's account of group psychology as regressive falsely universalizes the characteristics of certain groups, such as the army and the church, into a theory of groups *tout court*. Against this view, it is suggested that group membership can have a positive effect on the development of individuals. In particular, social movements are cited as the sorts of groups membership in which can allow individuals to attain a fuller and more complete self that they had been able to develop in their normal social roles.

WASHBURN, Jimmy. Persona y sociedad según Jacques Maritain. Rev Filosof (Costa Rica), 28(67-68), 153-157, D 90.

The exposition, continual with Jacques Maritain's thought, consists in the impartiality of the Christian philosopher about different political systems, liberal capitalistics or socialists. The social coexistence is not possible without moral values. This brings to mind that Christian thinkers can maintain a critical posture. (edited)

WASKIEWICZ, Hanna. The History of the Christian Philosophical Reflection on Peace. Dialec Hum, 16(3-4), 173-188, Sum-Autumn 89.

WASSERMANN, Gerhard D. Wittgenstein on Jews: Some Counter-Examples. Philosophy, 65(253), 355-365, Jl 90.

Wittgenstein, although of Jewish descent, was anti-Semitic, and his published anti-Semitic statements are examined and refuted. He thought that Jews could not be original and people of genius. This is refuted by listing 69 Jewish Nobel Laureates and many other counterexamples. Wittgenstein's typical empirical generalizations about Jews are of the form 'All Jews have property *X*' which leads to Hempel's paradox.

WASZKINEL, Romuald. L'inspiration aristotélicienne de la métaphysique de Bergson. Rev Phil Louvain, 89(82), 211-242, My 91.

The "durée rélle", a central point of Bergons's positive metaphysics, brings the answer to the question: what is time?: "(...) la *durée rélle* est ce que l'on a toujours appelé le *temps*, mais le temps perçu comme indivisible" (the *real existence* is that which has always been called *time*, but time perceived as indivisible) (PM, p 166, 1384). The present paper aims at showing that an appropriate reading of this answer is impossible without considering Bergson's work *Quid Aristoteles de loco senserit*. Aristotelian interpretation of movement and substance, as well as its impact upon philosophy, these are hardly few of the very important areas of Bergson's thought which converted the advocate ("convinced admirer") of Spencer's doctrine into the founder of the positive metaphysics.

WATANABE, Hiroshi. Author's Position in Interpretation of a Work of Art (in Japanese). Bigaku, 41(2), 12-23, Autumn 90.

In a work of art, its author seems to hold special position not found in usual communication. We find *his* expression in the work and learn *his* personality through the work. But usually, we don't have an actual proof about his real intention, and his image seen through the work is often inconsistent with real life of him. In this respect, we may say that the author is "imaginary." Nonetheless we often confuse this imaginary author with "real" author and so we have many "legends" about artists since 19th century. The aim of this study is to clarify the mechanism generating this confusion. (edited)

WATERS, C Kenneth. Why the Anti-Reductionist Consensus Won't Survive: The Case of Classical Mendelian Genetics. Proc Phil Sci Ass, 1, 125-139, 1990.

Philosophers now treat the relationship between classical genetics and molecular biology as a paradigm of nonreduction and this example is playing an increasingly prominent role in debates about the reducibility of theories in other sciences. This paper shows that the anti-reductionist consensus about genetics will not withstand serious scrutiny. In addition to defusing the main anti-reductionist objections, this critical analysis uncovers tell-tale signs of a significant reduction in progress. It also identifies philosophical issues relevant to gaining a better understanding of what is now happening in genetics and of what we might expect to happen in other sciences.

WATKINS, Eric (trans) and RICKEN, Friedo. *Philosophy of the Ancients*. Notre Dame, Univ Notre Dame Pr, 1991.

A text discussing ancient Greek philosophy from the pre-Socratics through Plato and Aristotle to neoplatonism. (staff)

WATKINS, John. "The Methodology of Scientific Research Programmes: A Retrospect" in *Imre Lakatos and Theories of Scientific Change*, GAVROGLU, Kostas (ed), 3-13. Norwell, Kluwer, 1989.

The questions (1) 'Which of these competing scientific theories should I accept as best?' and (2) 'Which should I work on?' should be kept separate. There is a clearcut answer to (1), namely whichever theory is best corroborated. If there is an answer to (2) it might be a refuted or inconsistent theory. Lakatos replaced these questions with ones about research programs, on the ground that they are the basic units of appraisal in science. The questions then become confounded, with unfortunate results: there is no longer a clearcut answer to (1) and inconsistencies become acceptable.

WATRAS, Joseph. Textbook Controversies and Community. Phil Stud Educ, /, 83-89, 1989.

WATSON, Gary. "On the Primacy of Character" in *Identity, Character, and Morality: Essays in Moral Psychology*, FLANAGAN, Owen (ed), 449-469. Cambridge, MIT Pr, 1990.

According to Rawls' influential classification, the primary concepts in moral theory are either the right or the good (here construed as good outcome or state of affairs). Although there has been much recent talk about an ethics of virtue, the structure of a theory of a third kind has not been clearly delineated. This essay explores the ways in which the concept of virtue might be taken as primary, as a distinct theoretical structure from both ethics of outcome and ethics of requirement.

WATSON, James R. Beyond the Real/Apparent World: From Signs to Imaging in Nietzsche. Hist Euro Ideas, 11, 1009-1014, 1989.

The imposition of authorship and responsibility upon "Nietzsche" is contrary to the voices signifying in and with the texts signed "Nietzsche." "Nietzsche," in other words, is not one but many. This plurality of authorship is in the play of becoming's innocence and, thus, beyond the domination of established and establishing (canonical) codes such as "good and evil." This play is also the movement of eternal recurrence and its dissemination of idolatrous images such as the Real. The dissemination of Real is also the dissemination of the Real/apparent hierarchy and its correlative Good/evil system of ethics.

WATSON, Phil. On Restricted Forms of Enumeration Reducibility. Annals Pure Applied Log, 49(1), 75-96, S 90.

WATSON, Richard A. *The Philosopher's Joke*. Buffalo, Prometheus, 1990.

This book contains seven related literary-philosophical essays on form and content beginning with the relation of perfection of form to truth of content in literature and ending with the unraveling of the content of life as a meaningless tale. In between are essays on hopping and skipping, meaning, seducing, dying, and dreaming. Five of the essays are exercises in the dominant styles of philosophical writing in the 1950s, 60s, 70s, 80s, and (by projection) 90s. The implied conclusion is that philosophical writing is mostly ambiguous and that philosophy is mostly about death.

WATSON, Stephen H. "*In Situ*: Beyond the Architectonics of the Modern" in *Postmodernism—Philosophy and the Arts (Continental Philosophy III)*, SILVERMAN, Hugh J (ed), 83-100. New York, Routledge, 1990.

WATSON, Stephen. "'On How We are and How We Are not to Return to the Things Themselves'" in *Ontology and Alterity in Merleau-Ponty*, JOHNSON, Galen A (ed), 45-48. Evanston, Northwestern Univ Pr, 1991.

WATSON, Terence (trans) and ROSMINI, Antonio and CLEARY, Denis (trans). *Principles of Ethics*. Durham, Rosmini, 1988.

WATSON, Terence (ed & trans) and ROSMINI, Antonio and CLEARY, Denis (ed & trans). *The Origin of Thought*. Durham, Rosmini, 1987.

WATSON, Walter. Types of Pluralism. Monist, 73(3), 350-366, Jl 90.

Four types of pluralism are distinguished: (1) perspectival pluralism, resulting from differences in the perspective of the knower, represented by Nicholas Rescher; (2) pluralism of hypotheses, resulting from different hypotheses about the one reality, represented by Stephen Pepper; (3) methodological pluralism, resulting from different formulations of a truth that transcends them all, represented by Wayne Booth; and (4) archic pluralism, resulting from the different principles by which philosophies may be constituted, represented by Richard McKeon.

WATT, D E. Not Very Likely: A Reply to Ramsey. Brit J Phil Sci, 40(2), 223-227, Je 89.

Keynes is concerned with epistemic probability—probability relative to knowledge. He thinks that some such probabilities, far from being numerical, are not even linearly ordered. Ramsey's attack on this idea is worthless. Keynes may not prove his point conclusively; however, by adapting one of his examples, such a proof can be provided. Two probabilities are exhibited such that on pain of contradiction, the first can neither be greater than, nor equal to, nor less than the second.

WATTEYNE, Nathalie. Le supplément poétique. Horiz Phil, 1(2), 137-160, 1991.

WAXMAN, Wayne. *Kant's Model of the Mind: A New Interpretation of Transcendental Idealism*. New York, Oxford Univ Pr, 1991.

The first part is concerned with the meaning of transcendental idealism and its significance for Kant's philosophy. It is claimed that Kant denies reality to space and time not simply outside sensibility but imagination as well. Only preformal sensation is transcendentally real. The second part analyses Kant's theory of perception (e.g., awareness of pain). It is claimed that Kant went further than any of his predecessors by treating imagination as essential even for sense perception. The book concludes with an analysis of the faculty endowed mind.

WAYMACK, Mark H. The Ethics of Selectively Marketing the Health Maintenance Organization. Theor Med, 11(4), 301-309, D 90.

Health Maintenance Organization (HMO) administrators have been accused of engaging in 'selective marketing'. That is, through such strategies as tailoring the benefits package of the program or advertising in styles or in media that do not appeal to certain 'undesirable' audiences, the administrator can minimize the percentage of persons in the HMO who are heavy users of health care services. By means of analyzing what 'insurance' is (philosophically) and what it means for something to be a free market commodity, the author argues that, as long as American society chooses to regard health insurance as a commodity or service of the free market, the use of such strategies is within the moral rights of health administrators. The author concludes by noting some morally undesirable results of treating health insurance as a market commodity.

WAYMACK, Mark H. Health Care as a Business: The Ethic of Hippocrates Versus the Ethic of Managed Care. Bus Prof Ethics J, 9(3-4), 69-78, Fall-Wint 90.

Waymack delineates two different "ethics," the ethic of Hippocrates and the ethic of health care as a business, specifically the ethic of "managed health care." The author then argues that there is an evident conflict in many cases between these two divergent ethics. Physicians who work in managed care are thus seen as obliged to two conflicting ethics. Until both society and the medical profession come to a new understanding of the ethical obligations of physicians, this moral conflict will remain.

WEAR, Stephen. The Irreducibly Clinical Character of Bioethics. J Med Phil, 16(1), 53-70, F 91.

Current bioethics scholarship and pedagogy suffers from an insufficient correlation with the realities and variables of clinical medicine, particularly in its dominant paradigm of patient autonomy. Reference to various basic clinical factors will be made here toward proposing certain conceptual, tactical and pedagogical modifications to this paradigm.

WEAR, Stephen. The Moral Significance of Institutional Integrity. J Med Phil, 16(2), 225-230, Ap 91.

WEAVER, George. Equational Subsystems. Rep Math Log, 23, 25-29, 1989.

We distinguish between equational subsystems and equationally equivalent subsystems in equational logic. This distinction parallels the distinction between elementary subsystems in first order logic. It is shown that there are equationally equivalent subsystems which are not equational subsystems. Those algebras which are determined by the positive diagrams of their finitely generated subsystems have the property that all their equationally equivalent subsystems are equational subsystems. It is shown that any abelian monoid satisfying the cancellation property is so determined and hence that the equational subsystem of abelian groups are exactly the equationally equivalent subsystems.

WEAVER, George and LEBLANC, Hugues and ROEPER, Peter and THAU, Michael. Henkin's Completeness Proof: Forty Years Later. Notre Dame J Form Log, 32(2), 212-232, Spr 91.

Provided here are two new completeness proofs for a first-order logic with denumerably many terms. The first proof, unlike Menkin's 1949 proof, does not call for the addition of extra terms; the second, especially suited for truth-value semantics, calls for the addition of denumerably many. Shown in the process is that a set of statements has a Henkin model, i.e., a model in which every member of the domain has a name, iff the set is what we call *instantially consistent* (i.e., iff *consistent in omega-logic*).

WEBBER, May A. No Moral Responsibility Without Alternative Possibilities. J Crit Anal, 9(1), 27-34, 1988.

WEBER, James. Adapting Kohlberg to Enhance the Assessment of Manager's Moral Reasoning. Bus Ethics Quart, 1(3), 293-318, Jl 91.

This paper presents an adaptation of Lawrence Kohlberg's Moral Judgement Interview and Standard Issue Scoring method. The adaptation emphasizes four points: 1) a mixture of less familiar and more familiar moral dilemmas, 2) followup questions which probe managers' moral reasoning by focusing upon key organizational values, 3) the flexibility of utilizing either an oral or written interview method, and 5) a simpler, yet reliable, system for scoring the managers' responses and identifying their stage of moral reasoning. An empirical investigation found that each adaptation could enhance the assessment of managers' moral reasoning.

WEBER, James and GREEN, Sharon. Principled Moral Reasoning: Is It a Viable Approach to Promote Ethical Integrity? J Bus Ethics, 10(5), 325-333, My 91.

In response to recent recommendations for the teaching of principled moral reasoning in business school curricula, this paper assesses the viability of such an approach. The results indicate that, while business students' level of moral reasoning in this sample are like most 18- to 21-year-olds, they may be incapable of grasping the concepts embodied in principled moral reasoning. Implications of these findings are discussed.

WEBER, Leonard. Consumer Sovereignty versus Informed Consent: Saying No to Requests to "Do Everything" for Dying Patients. Bus Prof Ethics J, 9(3-4), 95-102, Fall-Wint 90.

WEBER, Ron and WAND, Yair. "Mario Bunge's Ontology as a Formal Foundation for Information Systems Concepts" in *Studies on Mario Bunge's "Treatise"*, WEINGARTNER, Paul (ed), 123-150. Amsterdam, Rodopi, 1990.

For a number of years, we have been engaged in an effort to establish a theoretical foundation for the process of systems analysis and design. The main assumption underlying our approach is that an information system is a representation of a real-world system. Hence, we seek the basis of and fundamental concepts needed for the theoretical view of information systems in the domain of ontology. We used Mario Bunge's *Ontology* as our main source of constructs to model real systems and information systems. (edited)

WEBERMAN, David. *Historische Objektivitat*. New York, Lang, 1991.

Can our knowledge of human history approximate the ideal of objectivity? The author argues that, for fundamental reasons, it cannot. Drawing on the work of Gadamer, Danto and Habermas, it is shown that the description and narration of historical events are necessarily constituted by the temporal perspective and future-orientedness of the historian. This conception is not, however, subjectivist. On the contrary, subjectivist theories of history are exposed as disguised versions of objectivism. The author sketches a conception of historical knowledge which avoids the pitfalls of both extremes.

WEBSTER, Glenn and JANUSZ, Sharon. In Defence of Heidegger. Philosophy, 66(257), 380-385, Jl 91.

In his essay "Heidegger's Quest for Being", *Philosophy*, October 1989, Volume 64, Paul Edwards unfairly attacks Martin Heidegger's philosophy. Among Edward's contentions: Heidegger "was looking for the referent of 'exists'" (467). Such is not the case; although, Heidegger is most interested in existence, judging existence as marvelously mysterious. Heidegger's view of existence is not a problem. Edward's view of Heidegger's view is a problem, as the questions about being are not simple questions about a constant in symbolic logic. Symbolic logic is irrelevant to Heidegger's philosophy: symbolic logic cannot detect most of Heidegger's meanings because it is a formal language dependent on natural language.

WECKERT, J. Functionalism's Impotence. Phil Inq, 12(1-2), 32-43, Wint-Spr 90.

It is argued that as a theory of mind, functionalism is of little help. On closer examination, it collapses either into behaviourism, or into a Smartian type identity theory.

WEDEKING, Gary A. Is Mandatory Retirement Unfair Age Discrimination? Can J Phil, 20(3), 321-334, S 90.

The paper deals with two questions. One is the relatively specific issue of whether mandatory retirement is unjust discrimination against the aged. The position taken is that it is not. But in the development of this argument a principle is advanced which appears to have the consequence that nothing, or at least very few of the practices that we are intuitively inclined to regard as unfair discrimination, are discriminatory with respect to age. The second question is thus what, if anything, is to count as unjust age discrimination.

WEDEKING, Gary. Locke on Personal Identity and the Trinity Controversy of the 1690s. Dialogue (Canada), 29(2), 163-188, 1990.

The first part is an account of the Trinity Controversy, centering on the question of the identity of persons, and of the respects in which points made in the controversy, in particular the circularity objection, may have influenced Locke's formulation of his theory. The second part argues that Locke is attempting to come to grips with the circularity problem, but that his solution is ultimately a failure. The argument of II, xxvii, 13 is analyzed in detail and the form of Locke's theory of relative identity is discussed. Fundamental difficulties are found to reside in his theories of representation and agency.

WEDIN, Michael V. Collection and Division in the *Phaedrus* and *Statesman*. Phil Inq, 12(1-2), 1-21, Wint-Spr 90.

WEEKS, Ian. A Disproof of the Existence of God. Sophia (Australia), 29(3), 21-28, O 90.

WEEKS, P A D. Musical Time as a Practical Accomplishment: A Change in Tempo. Human Stud, 13(4), 323-359, O 90.

This is an ethnomethodological study (phenomenologically-derived) of the detailed practices of collective music-playing in synchrony. It contains an analysis of three rehearsals working out tempo changes in Handel's anthem, "The King Shall Rejoice"—a strategic case in that, here, an ongoing set of note-durations no longer serves as a reference-point for upcoming note 'placements'. The specific focus is on different expressions of musical time—from the verbal to the actual playing. We find that both the score and the verbalizations employ distinctive spatial analogies, and discover how the interpretations of the text become 'locally specified' moment-to-moment.

WEGEMER, Gerard. The Rhetoric of Opposition in Thomas More's *Utopia*: Giving Form to Competing Philosophies. Phil Rhet, 23(4), 288-306, 1990.

By analyzing the methods of character delineation and the rhetorical figures of interlocutors Morus and Hythlodaeus, this article demonstrates how author More dramatizes two opposing philosophies of life. Christian humanist Morus follows the conventions of a polite and truthful ethos aimed at fostering civic cooperation. Gnostic Hythlodaeus, however, uses strident *ad hominem* arguments, exaggeration, and misrepresentation aimed at a sophistic philosophy and way of life.

AUTHOR INDEX WITH ABSTRACTS 691 WEIPING, Chen

WEIDLICH, W. "Reconciling Concepts between Natural Science and Theology" in *Science and Religion: One World-Changing Perspectives on Reality*, FENNEMA, Jan (ed), 73-86. Norwell, Kluwer, 1990.

In the introduction the relation between basic theological and philosophical convictions is discussed resulting in the conclusion that only an existential but no logical decision between both is possible. New structures of natural sciences are thereupon considered; then the interdisciplinary relevant concepts of synergetics, are introduced. A synthesis between scientific and religious thought is then attempted. The article ends with a consideration of the relation between the objectifying truth of natural science and the existential truth of religious faith.

WEIL, Simone and ROSE, Rebecca Fine (trans) and TESSIN, Timothy (trans). Essay on the Notion of Reading. Phil Invest, 13(4), 297-303, O 90.

WEILER, Gershon. Philosophy in Israel (in Hungarian). Magyar Filozof Szemle, 5-6, 630-635, 1990.

WEINBERG, Lee S and VATZ, Richard E. The Conceptual Bind in Defining the Volitional Component of Alcoholism. J Mind Behav, 11(3-4), 531-544, Sum-Autumn 90.

An essential element in both lay and professional definitions of alcoholism is the a priori claim that afflicted individuals lack control over their drinking and/or over their behavior while drinking. The social, legal and scientific consequences of accepting this claim are examined. Based on specific evidence drawn from recent journal articles, we argue that alcohol researchers fail to adequately engage the issue of volition and that their research designs and findings are thereby flawed.

WEINBERGER, Ota. The Theory of Legal Dynamics Reconsidered. Ratio Juris, 4(1), 18-35, Mr 91.

The author criticizes Kelsen's distinction between static and dynamic systems of norms and his theory of legal dynamics. The author moreover presents the institutionalist conception of legal dynamics. Kelsen's concept of static systems is incompatible with normological scepticism: The deduction of rules from a basic principle depends on additional premises; even in static systems there is a kind of dynamics produced by actual facts. Kelsen's conception of legal dynamics is also incompatible with normological scepticism and with Kelsen's demand of purity of jurisprudence. In the institutionalist conception legal dynamics is rather conceived as an interplay of legal norms and facts. Empowering relations, the principle of co-validity, temporal limits of norms, derogation, legal validity and the basic norm are analysed accordingly. Appendices deal with Paulson's empowering theory of legal norm and Lippold's double-faced reconstruction of the legal order.

WEINER, Joan. *Frege in Perspective*. Ithaca, Cornell Univ Pr, 1990.

It is the thesis of this book that all of Frege's writings were meant as contributions to a unified project. The case is made through a careful reading, first, of Frege's description and motivation of his project in the beginnings of *Foundations of Arithmetic* and, second, of the ways in which Frege's later writings address tensions in this description of the project. Two important things come into clear view: first, the sense in which Frege can be viewed as a precursor of Wittgenstein and, second, the extent to which Frege's writings undermine both traditional and contemporary ways of thinking and writing about language, logic and mathematics.

WEINER, Scott E. "Inhabiting" in the *Phenomenology of Perception*. Phil Today, 34(4), 342-353, Wint 90.

Two key phenomena of Merleau-Ponty's *Phenomenology of Perception* are habit and inhabiting. Their chief characteristics, respectively, are generalizing actions and actively familiarizing. They are essentially and reciprocally related: inhabiting consists of being in habits and habitual actions are a way of inhabiting. The article focuses on three aspects of Merleau-Ponty's discussions: habit as simultaneously motor and perceptual, the interplay of sedimentation and spontaneity, and the body's inhabiting of space and incorporating of expressive spatiality. Merleau-Ponty's typist example and four examples of the author illustrate that the relationship of habit and inhabiting is a basic structure of being-in-the-world.

WEINGARD, Robert. "Realism and the Global Topology of Space-Time" in *Harré and His Critics*, BHASKAR, Roy (ed), 112-121. Cambridge, Blackwell, 1990.

In this article I discuss two senses in which the global topology of spacetime can be undetermined by evidence. In either case, I argue that, none the less, we have good reason thinking that it is an objective matter fact what the global topology of spacetime is.

WEINGARD, Robert. Some Comments Concerning Spin and Relativity. Brit J Phil Sci, 40(2), 287-288, Je 89.

I point out that since the spin of a massive particle can be understood in terms of the representations of the rotation group, it is nonrelativistic. But the existence of massless particles with just two spin states requires relativity for its explanation.

WEINGARTNER, Paul (ed) and MARCUS, Ruth Barcan (ed) and DORN, Georg (ed). *Logic, Methodology and Philosophy of Science, VII*. Amsterdam, North-Holland, 1986.

Proceedings of the invited papers of the Seventh International Congress of Logic, Methodology and Philosophy of Science, held in Salzburg, Austria in 1983. Three papers in each of the following categories were delivered: Proof Theory and Foundations of Mathematics, Model Theory and its Applications, Recursion Theory and Theory of Computation, Axiomatic Set Theory, Philosophical Logic, Methodology of Science, Foundations of Probability and Induction, Foundations and Philosophy of the Physical Sciences, Foundations and Philosophy of Biology, Foundations and Philosophy of Psychology, Foundations and Philosophy of the Social Sciences, Foundations and Philosophy of Linguistics.

WEINGARTNER, Paul. "The Non-Statement View: A Dialogue between Socrates and Theaetetus" in *Studies on Mario Bunge's "Treatise"*, WEINGARTNER, Paul (ed), 455-465. Amsterdam, Rodopi, 1990.

This is a dialogue which critically discusses the so-called *non - statement - view*. It gives first different interpretations of the claims of the *non-statement-view* and then tries to show that the view is at least partially a philosophical exaggeration.

WEINGARTNER, Paul (ed) and DORN, Georg J W (ed). *Studies on Mario Bunge's "Treatise"*. Amsterdam, Rodopi, 1990.

The studies in this volume discuss in detail Bunge's great attempt to combine specialised philosophical disciplines in a synthesis within the eight volumes of his *Treatise on Basic Philosophy*. The book contains 32 articles and Bunge's 32 replies to them, a short autobiography of Mario Bunge and a bibliography of his publications. The topics which have been dealt with mainly are Bunge's semantical realism, his systemic ontology, his concept of emergent evolution, his epistemological realism, his ethics, and—most prominently—his philosophy of science and technology. (edited)

WEINREB, Lloyd L. What Are *Civil* Rights? Soc Phil Pol, 8(2), 1-21, Spr 91.

Civil rights have a puzzling status as, on one hand, prior to and valid independently of positive law and, on the other hand, variable from one community to another. The explanation of their status is that rights resolve the antinomy of freedom and cause and account for human responsibility. Rights are what a person is due simply as a person. Having his rights, a person is *self-* determining and responsible. The origin of *civil* rights is, and can only be, the *nomos* of the community.

WEINRIB, Ernest J. "Liberty, Community, and Corrective Justice" in *Liability and Responsibility*, FREY, R G (ed), 290-316. New York, Cambridge Univ Pr, 1991.

WEINSHEIMER, Joel. *Philosophical Hermeneutics and Literary Theory*. New Haven, Yale Univ Pr, 1991.

This book situates H-G Gadamer's philosophical hermeneutics in the context of modern literary theory, broadly conceived. After sketching an overview of modern hermeneutics, it considers Gadamer's critique of semiotic linguistics, the antitheoretical aspect of his hermeneutics, his use of Kant for a philosophy of history, his theory of the classic and of the function of metaphor in understanding.

WEINSTEIN, Deena and WEINSTEIN, Michael A. Deconstruction as Symbolic Play: Simmel/Derrida. Diogenes, 150, 119-141, Sum 90.

Through a textual game of relays, the Derridian notion of play and the Simmelian concept of play-form are put into play with and against each other to create a reciprocal interpretation of each idea. Without reducing the respective texts to one another, Derridian deconstruction is interpreted, through Simmel, as the play-form of metaphysics; and Simmel's method of stalemating competing metaphysical doctrines is interpreted as a variant of deconstruction. The relay begins with a discussion of Derridian play, proceeds to the explication of Simmelian play-form, moves to the interpretation of deconstruction as the play-form of metaphysics, and concludes with the interpretation of Simmel's philosophical method as a form of deconstruction. The method of successively inscribing the baton shows unsuspected continuities between the high modernism of Simmel and the postmodernism of Derrida while highlighting their ruptures: differance/difference.

WEINSTEIN, Mark. Reason and the Child. Proc Phil Educ, 46, 159-171, 1990.

The paper presents a reconceptualization of theories of reason available within philosophy and psychology and traces some consequences for the status of children. The claim is that categorical theories of reason are less defensible than contextual ones, and therefore the particulars of children's accomplishments in relevant contexts must be more closely examined if status claims based on rational capacity are to be warranted.

WEINSTEIN, Mark. Towards a Research Agenda for Informal Logic and Critical Thinking. Inform Log, 12(3), 121-143, Fall 90.

This paper recommends that the recent concern with informal logic and critical thinking be redirected from its general philosophical focus and towards a greater appreciation of the particulars of practice in the various domains of human understanding. In order to render the recommendation plausible, the paper places such concerns within three significant contexts: the circumstances within which the field of critical thinking and informal logic first developed; some theoretic assumptions common in the field; and the educational framework within which the field's endeavors take place.

WEINSTEIN, Michael A and WEINSTEIN, Deena. Deconstruction as Symbolic Play: Simmel/Derrida. Diogenes, 150, 119-141, Sum 90.

Through a textual game of relays, the Derridian notion of play and the Simmelian concept of play-form are put into play with and against each other to create a reciprocal interpretation of each idea. Without reducing the respective texts to one another, Derridian deconstruction is interpreted, through Simmel, as the play-form of metaphysics; and Simmel's method of stalemating competing metaphysical doctrines is interpreted as a variant of deconstruction. The relay begins with a discussion of Derridian play, proceeds to the explication of Simmelian play-form, moves to the interpretation of deconstruction as the play-form of metaphysics, and concludes with the interpretation of Simmel's philosophical method as a form of deconstruction. The method of successively inscribing the baton shows unsuspected continuities between the high modernism of Simmel and the postmodernism of Derrida while highlighting their ruptures: differance/difference.

WEINSTEIN, Michael P. "Should Physicians Dispense Drugs for a Profit?" in *Biomedical Ethics Reviews, 1989*, HUMBER, James M (ed), 95-112. Clifton, Humana Pr, 1990.

WEIPING, Chen. On the "Arriving at Principles from Numbers" Method of Thought in the Late-Ming, Early-Qing Period. Chin Stud Phil, 22(2), 3-23, Wint 90-91.

Late-Ming early-Qing thought stands astride the intersection of tradition and modernity. Therefore, the discussion of the nature of late-Ming early-Qing thought is a major topic in the investigation of how China's intellectual culture made the strides from tradition to modern times. The intention of this essay is to take a snapshot of one angle of late-Ming early-Qing thought—i.e., the genesis, formation, and death in infancy of the "arriving at principles from numbers" (*you shu da li*) method of thinking—and use it to analyze specifically the nature of thought in the late-Ming early-Qing period.

WEIR, Jack. Response to Sapontzis's Reply. Between Species, 7(1), 33-35, Wint 91.

Space did not permit a thorough response to Sapontzis's attack on my article "Unnecessary Pain, Nutrition, and Vegetarianism." I do not dispute the claim that many people do well on a vegetarian diet. Rather, my argument is that nutritional factors—our biology—*plus* sociocultural ones make the vegetarian diet nonobligatory, although I still consider it praiseworthy. My concern in the article is with the argument—with conceptual distinctions, rational deliberations, and standards of evidence—not with my own virtues and fears, which Sapontzis attacks.

WEIR, Jack. Unnecessary Pain, Nutrition, and Vegetarianism. Between Species, 7(1), 13-26, Wint 91.

The vegetarian argument from unnecessary pain is analyzed as involving three sub-arguments. All three fail: 1) the Empirical Argument from Nutrition because equivocation occurs regarding what is meant by "vegetarian," "adequate for human nutrition," and "unnecessary for nutrition"; 2) the Empirical Argument from Pain because food animals can be raised humanely and killed mercifully, and because moderation in consumption and actual efforts for reform are morally acceptable responses to the current abuses; and 3) the Moral Argument from Unnecessary Pain because the *prima facie* obligation not to inflict pain is overridden by the nutritional risk of vegetarianism and by sociocultural factors beyond the individual's control.

WEISLOGEL, Eric L. The Irony of Richard Rorty and the Question of Political Judgment. Phil Today, 34(4), 303-311, Wint 90.

Richard Rorty's latest book is distinctly antiphilosophical. He claims the principles of modern metaphysics which made possible Enlightenment liberalism have ironically become an impediment to achieving its ideals. Rorty proposes removing philosophy from the political sphere and consigning it to the private realm. However, this is no solution. Modern metaphysics has an illiberal quality, but Rorty misses the fact that the essence of politics is nothing philosophical. Political struggles get resolved in action, not in thought. Rejecting a philosophical "final solution" to political struggles is not an argument to privatize philosophy. It merely points to the ongoing necessity of politics.

WEISMANN, F J. La libertad como búsqueda de la verdad en el joven Agustín. Stromata, 46(1-2), 65-73, Ja-Je 90.

WEISS, Allen S. "Lucid Intervals: Postmodernism and Photography" in *Postmodernism—Philosophy and the Arts (Continental Philosophy III)*, SILVERMAN, Hugh J (ed), 155-172. New York, Routledge, 1990.

WEISS, Paul. On the Impossibility of Artificial Intelligence. Rev Metaph, 44(2), 335-341, D 90.

WEISS, Penny. Rousseau's Political Defense of the Sex-Roled Family. Hypatia, 5(3), 90-109, Fall 90.

We argue that Rousseau's defense of the sex-roled family is not based on biological determinism or simple misogyny. Rather, his advocacy of sexual differentiation is based on his understanding of its ability to bring individuals outside of themselves into interdependent communities, and thus to counter natural independence, self-absorption and asociality, as well as social competitiveness and egoism. This political defense of the sex-roled family needs more critique by feminists.

WEISS, Thomas. Closing the Chinese Room. Ratio, 3(2), 165-181, D 90.

WEITHMAN, Paul J. The Separation of Church and State: Some Questions for Professor Audi. Phil Pub Affairs, 20(1), 52-65, Wint 91.

My article is a response to Robert Audi, "The Separation of Church and State and the Obligations of Citizenship" (*Phil Pub Affairs*, Summer 1989). Audi defends a principle of institutional neutrality, according to which churches must abstain from political action, and a principle of secular motivation, according to which citizens may defend restrictive public policies only if moved by sufficient secular reason to do so. I argue that a commitment to separation of church and state in a liberal democracy implies neither of Audi's principles.

WEITHMAN, Paul J. St Thomas on the Motives of Unjust Acts. Proc Cath Phil Ass, 63, 204-220, 1990.

Bernard Williams has argued that Aristotle takes the characteristic motive of unjust acts to be an undue *desire* for divisible goods; Williams goes on to criticize the account he finds in Aristotle. In this paper I argue that Aquinas understands the characteristic motive of unjust acts differently than does the Aristotle of Williams's interpretation. Aquinas argues that perpetrators of unjust acts typically *will* an undue share of the good in question. This is compatible with their being motivated by a wide variety of *desires* and shows what changes Aquinas introduced into Aristotelian ethics as a result of his greater emphasis on the will as the faculty associated with justice and injustice.

WELBY, Victoria. Educating for Meaning. Thinking, 4(2), 10-17, 1982.

WELLMAN, Carl. Relative Duties in the Law. Phil Topics, 18(1), 183-202, Spr 90.

The article explains the expression "a legal duty to" by identifying the party to whom that duty is owed. It examines and rejects the views that a relative duty is owed to the holder of the correlative right, the recipient of the good delivered or service rendered in the performance of the duty, the party benefitted by the performance of the duty, or the party given exclusive legal control over that duty. It concludes that a relative legal duty is owed to the party who has the legal power to initiate proceedings in the courts to enforce that duty.

WELLMER, Albrecht. *The Persistence of Modernity: Essays on Aesthetics, Ethics, and Postmodernism*. Cambridge, MIT Pr, 1991.

WELSCH, Wolfgang. *Unsere postmoderne Moderne (Second Edition)*. Weinheim, Acta Humaniora, 1988.

This book—which since its first edition has come to be regarded as a standard work—first presents a conceptual history of the expression "post-modern," followed by a survey of the discussion in various fields (literature, architecture, visual arts, sociology, philosophy, etc.). It examines the relation between post-modernity, modernity and the modern age, and interprets post-modernity as an exoteric realization of esoteric issues of 20th century modernity (especially of science and art). Radical plurality proves to be the crucial problem of postmodernity. Finally, the concept of "transversal reason" is developed as a "post-modern" form of reason which meets today's demands.

WELSCH, Wolfgang (ed). *Wege aus der Moderne*. Weinheim, Acta Humaniora, 1990.

This anthology contains classical texts (by Hassan, Fiedler, Eco, Venturi, Jencks, Klotz, Habermas, Bonito Oliva, Gehlen, Bell, Baudrillard, Kamper, Lyotard, Derrida, Vattimo, Wellmer and Sloterdijk), which have determined the course of the discussion on modernity and postmodernity since the sixties. The introduction outlines the status of the current debate, comments on the political problems and draws the contours of an aesthetic thinking for today. In addition the volume contains an extensive bibliography.

WELTE, Werner and ROSEMANN, Philipp. *Alltagssprachliche Metakommunikation im Englischen und Deutschen*. New York, Lang, 1990.

In their truly comprehensive treatment of the phenomenon of metacommunication, the authors begin by situating the concept within the philosophical problematic of self-reflexivity, then tracing its history in ancient, mediaeval, and modern philosophy of language. Another chapter is devoted to the central importance which contemporary linguistics has invariably accorded the functions of metalanguage in communication. The syntactic, morphological, semantic, lexical, and pragmatic properties of metacommunication are given detailed scrutiny in a theoretical framework which integrates the linguistic with the philosophical viewpoint. (edited)

WELTON, Donn. Husserl and the Japanese. Rev Metaph, 44(3), 575-606, Mr 91.

WENDEL, Hans Jürgen. Apriorische Einsicht und metaphysische Notwendigkeit: Eine Auseinandersetzung mit Kripkes Kant-Kritik. Kantstudien, 82(1), 63-80, 1991.

WENDELL, Susan. Oppression and Victimization; Choice and Responsibility. Hypatia, 5(3), 15-46, Fall 90.

This essay discusses a cluster of problems for feminist theory and practice which concern responsibility and choice under conditions of oppression. I characterize four major perspectives from which situations of oppression or victimization can be seen and questions about choice and responsibility answered: the perspective of the oppressor; the perspective of the victim; the perspective of the responsible actor; and the perspective of the observer/philosopher. I compare their strengths and weaknesses and discuss their compatibility.

WENDELL, Susan. Reply to Maryann Ayim's "In Praise of Clutter as a Necessary Part of the Feminist Perspective". Hypatia, 6(2), 216-217, Sum 91.

A response to Maryann Ayim's "In Praise of Clutter as a Necessary Part of the Feminist Perspective."

WENNEMANN, Daryl. Desacralization and the Disenchantment of the World. Phil Theol, 5(3), 237-250, Spr 91.

In this paper I explore Jacques Ellul's sociology of religion in terms of Weber's disenchantment thesis. In contrast to Mircea Eliade's depiction of modern persons as nonreligious, owing to scientific and technological development, Ellul argues that traditional religions have merely been replaced by new ones. This has occurred, according to Ellul, because the desacralization of one realm of experience results in the resacralization of another realm of experience.

WERDEL, A Alyce. Mandatory AIDS Testing: The Legal, Ethical and Practical Issues. Notre Dame J Law Ethics, 5(1), 155-221, Spr 90.

Many legal schemes have been proposed to control the spread of the AIDS, a disease which threatens the lives of millions of people. This article addresses one proposed scheme, mandatory AIDS testing. It analyzes (1) the practical considerations, such as economic efficiency and effectiveness, (2) the legal issues, such as equal protection, illegal searches and seizures, and cruel and unusual punishment, and (3) the ethical and philosophical issues, such as the idea of freedom and state paternalism. It concludes that the following groups should be required to undergo testing: (1) prisoners, (2) arrested prostitutes and drug users, and (3) those who attend sexually transmitted disease and drug abuse clinics.

WERHANE, Patricia H. Engineers and Management: The Challenge of the Challenger Incident. J Bus Ethics, 10(8), 605-616, Ag 91.

The Challenger incident was a result of at least four kinds of difficulties: differing perceptions and priorities of the engineers and management at Thiokol and at NASA, a preoccupation with roles and role responsibilities on the part of engineers and managers, contrasting corporate cultures at Thiokol and its parent, Morton, and a failure both by engineers and by managers to exercise individual moral responsibility. I shall argue that in the Challenger case organizational structure, corporate culture, engineering and managerial habits, and role responsibilities precipitated events contributing to the Challenger disaster. At the same time, a number of individuals at Morton Thiokol and NASA were responsible for the launch failure. Differing world views, conflicting priorities of the engineers and managers on this project, and the failure of either engineers or management to take personal moral responsibility for decision-making contributed significantly to the event.

WERHANE, Patricia H. The Ethics of Health Care as a Business. Bus Prof Ethics J, 9(3-4), 7-20, Fall-Wint 90.

The blame for the crisis in health care often falls to the alleged commodification of health care by the market. But what is wrong with the market model in health care is the exploitation of the market for the avarice of self-interests, and the extension of the market paradigm to inappropriate areas of concern. So it is not commercialization that is evil but its exploitation. Commodification of some aspects of health care does not imply either the end of good health care nor exclude provisions for the poor so long as justice, not self-interest, prevails.

WERHANE, Patricia H. Freedom, Commodification, and the Alienation of Labor in Adam Smith's "Wealth of Nations". Phil Forum, 22(4), 383-401, Sum 91.

Adam Smith's unique contribution to the analysis of labor is his thesis that economic liberty develops out of the distinction between the laborer and her labor such that the productivity of labor, but not the laborer, is treated as an exchangeable value and therefore as a commodity. The separation of the laborer from her productivity is the basis for worker freedom. But it is only when labor productivity is valued as a commodity that the laborer is consciously differentiated from her productivity, and thus it is only then that the laborer attains economic liberty.

WERHANE, Patricia H. The Indefensibility of Insider Trading. J Bus Ethics, 10(9), 729-731, S 91.

The article, "Inside Trading Revisited," has taken the stance that insider trading is neither unethical nor economically inefficient. Attacking my arguments to the contrary developed in an earlier article, 'The Ethics of Inside Trading' (*Journal of Business Ethics*, 1989) this article constructs careful arguments and even appeals to Adam Smith to justify its conclusions. In my response to this article I shall clarify my position as well as that of Smith to support my counter-contention that insider trading is both unethical and inefficient.

WERKMEISTER, W H. *Nicolai Hartmann's New Ontology*. Tallahassee, Florida St Univ Pr, 1990.

This is an integrative study of *all* of Nicolai Hartmann's publications, with special attention to his epistemology, his categorial analyses of the structure of the real world, of modalities, and the realm of spiritual reality. In all of his works Hartmann begins with the phenomena, not with metaphysical speculation, and carries his analyses out in great detail. There is nothing like it in the philosophy of the early twentieth century.

WERNER, Richard. "Nuclear Deterrence and the Limits of Moral Theory" in *Issues in War and Peace: Philosophical Inquiries*, KUNKEL, Joseph (ed), 129-138. Wolfeboro, Longwood, 1989.

WERNER, Richard. "The Rights and Wrongs of Animal Use for Human Organ Transplant" in *Biomedical Ethics Reviews, 1987*, HUMBER, James M (ed), 65-87. Clifton, Humana Pr, 1988.

WERTZ, Dorothy C and FLETCHER, John C. Privacy and Disclosure in Medical Genetics Examined in an Ethics of Care. Bioethics, 5(3), 212-232, Jl 91.

This paper examines moral reasoning of 682 geneticists from 19 nations responding to an open-ended questionnaire concerning six cases involving disclosure of 1) non-paternity to husbands; 2) test results to patients' spouses; 3) a patient's diagnosis to relatives at genetic risk; 4) ambiguous results; 5) fetal sex to parents who would abort the sex not desired; 6) patients' test results to insurers and employers. An ethics of care, based on patients' needs and providers' reponsibilities, is closer to clinicians' thinking than a "principle" approach, recommends full disclosure but recognizes the need to protect weaker members of society, especially women, and regards patients as members of communities.

WERTZ, S K. Hume and the Paradox of Taste Again. SW Phil Rev, 7(1), 141-150, Ja 91.

In this paper I examine Mary Mothersill's recent interpretation (1989) of David Hume's theory of taste. While I am in agreement with her about a paradox of taste in Hume's thought, I have a different account of it which involves less speculation and less anachronistic readings of him. What Hume did, Mothersill speculates, is to *ignore* the incoherence he had found in the neoclassical doctrine. Mothersill then develops what she calls a "subtext" from his essay. The argument of the subtext is surprising, especially in light of Hume's other writings which bear on this subject. I find evidence for her premises, but find little support for her initial conclusion. I argue that Hume *never* doubted that there were laws of taste and rules of composition. They are just immensely difficult to formulate, given the frailty of human reason and the complexity of the subject. I go on in the course of my essay to substantiate this from Hume's writings and offer my own account of the paradox of taste. (edited)

WESOLOWSKI, Mark A and MOSSHOLDER, Kevin W and GILES, William F. Information Privacy and Performance Appraisal: An Examination of Employee Perceptions and Reactions. J Bus Ethics, 10(2), 151-156, F 91.

Role-failure acts (Waters and Bird, 1989) have been described as a form of morally questionable activity involving a failure to perform the managerial role. The present study examined employee perceptions and reactions with regard to one form of role-failure act, failure to maintain adequate privacy of performance appraisal information. The study assessed employees' attitudes toward various performance appraisal facets as an invasion of privacy and determined the relationships between these privacy-related attitudes and employees' satisfaction with components of their appraisal system, the system as a whole, and their jobs. Responses that organizations might take to counteract appraisal privacy concerns were also discussed.

WESSON, Robert. *Beyond Natural Selection*. Cambridge, MIT Pr, 1991.

An approach to evolution in harmony with modern science and meaningful for the comprehension of our existence. Wesson begins with a useful description of Darwinian theory and the controversies over its application and then proceeds to show why natural selection cannot sufficiently account for the development of the multitude of modern species. He concludes his study by applying evolutionary theory to humans, summarizing the long-term trends of evolution and discussing the relationship between the way we understand evolution and the development of human values. (staff)

WEST, Charles C. Christians and Marxists in Dialogue Building Confidence in a Time of Crisis. Dialec Hum, 16(3-4), 17-31, Sum-Autumn 89.

Christian-Marxist dialogue has been called in question by those who call for negotiation between two opposing ideologies and power blocs on the one side and for cooperation in a common social struggle, on the other. But, analogies between Christianity and Marxism are so close that even through polemics they influence each other. Marxism has made a contribution to Christian self-understanding at two points: its analysis of economic power in a sinful world and its grasp of the way human consciousness is conditioned by material interests and social struggle. Here, however, sharp questions arise. How is economic power related to political and other powers and how may they be balanced in the interest of greater justice? How is nature understood? What source of truth and authority can in fact transcend human interests? What is the model of true humanity: covenantal community or solidarity in struggle?

WEST, Cornel. "Between Dewey and Gramsci: Unger's Emancipatory Experimentalism" in *Critique and Construction: A Symposium on Roberto Unger's "Politics"*, LOVIN, Robin W (ed), 256-266. New York, Cambridge Univ Pr, 1990.

WEST, Philip. "David Ferry's Paradise of Form" in *Abeunt Studia in Mores: A Festschrift for Helga Doblin*, MERRILL, Sarah A Bishop (ed), 351-362. New York, Lang, 1990.

WESTERMAN, Pauline. Natuur en cultuur: de heuristische waarde van een dichotomie. Kennis Methode, 15(1), 121-141, 1991.

Since Latour's proposal is clearly meant not only to solve the particular difficulties pertaining to social studies of science, but to provide for an answer to philosophical confusion in general, his claim that the dichotomy nature/society should be abolished, is examined by investigating the ways in which this dichotomy affected natural law theory. On the basis of an interpretation of the contradictions in Pufendorf's account of natural law, it is argued that Pufendorf struggled to reconcile two conflicting concepts of nature; the Hobbesian account of nature seems incompatible with traditional natural law doctrine. The result of this enterprise, however, contributed to a growing awareness of the artificiality of human society. Latour's account of nature as a merely passive pole, prove too simple. Finally, it is argued that the tension between nature and society helps shaping political theory as well as political discourse.

WESTERSTAHL, Dag. Aristotelian Syllogisms and Generalized Quantifiers. Stud Log, 48(4), 577-585, D 89.

The paper elaborates two points: 1) There is no principal opposition between predicate logic and adherence to subject-predicate form, 2) Aristotle's treatment of quantifiers fits well into a modern study of generalized quantifiers.

WESTFALL, Richard S. "Making a World of Precision: Newton and the Construction of a Quantitiative World View" in *Some Truer Method*, DURHAM, Frank (ed), 59-87. New York, Columbia Univ Pr, 1990.

WESTMORELAND, Robert. Prohibiting Immorality. Pub Affairs Quart, 3(4), 79-97, O 89.

Liberals since Mill have typically argued that the prohibition of nonharmful offenses is justifiable so long as they are not prohibited because they are immoral. I argue that the moral emotions involved in "profound" offenses are best construed as perceptions of the immorality of the offending conduct, and that liberals must either abandon the offense principle or liberalism.

WESTPHAL, Jonathan. *Colour: A Philosophical Introduction (Second Edition)*. Cambridge, Blackwell, 1991.

Colours are not simples, because there are no simple colours. If there were, Wittgenstein's puzzle questions on *Remarks on Colour* could not be answered; but they can. I give the answers. Since sensation requires simples as its objects, there is no colour sensation. A colour is rather a volume of colour space.

WESTPHAL, Jonathan. Universals and Creativity. Philosophy, 65(253), 255-260, Jl 90.

WESTPHAL, Merold. "Kierkegaard's Phenomenology of Faith as Suffering" in *Writing the Politics of Difference*, SILVERMAN, Hugh J (ed), 55-71. Albany, SUNY Pr, 1991.

Through his writings Kierkegaard develops a phenomenology of faith as suffering. Before he has finished he has developed an interpretation according to which Religiousness B, as described in *Concluding Unscientific Postscript*, is an immediacy from which true faith is a dying away. The pseudonymous writings thus call for their completion in Kierkegaard's "second authorship," which contains his most radical critique of the metaphysics of presence.

WESTPHAL, Merold. "Phenomenologies and Religious Truth" in *Phenomenology of the Truth Proper to Religion*, GUERRIÈRE, Daniel (ed), 105-125. Albany, SUNY Pr, 1990.

As phenomenology develops from Husserl into hermeneutical phenomenology and eventually into the hermeneutics of suspicion it fulfills its own destiny and better illuminates religion. The hermeneutical turn equips it better to understand religion's own sense of finitude, and the turn to suspicion equips it better to understand religion's own sense of its essentially praxical nature.

WESTPHAL, Merold. "Situation and Suspicion in the Thought of Merleau-Ponty" in *Ontology and Alterity in Merleau-Ponty*, JOHNSON, Galen A (ed), 158-179. Evanston, Northwestern Univ Pr, 1991.

The difference between his phenomenological ontology and his political writings that Merleau-Ponty sees in *Signs* typifies his work as a whole. His political writings presuppose and employ a full-fledged hermeneutics of suspicion for which no theoretical account can be found in his phenomenology.

WESTRA, Haijo J. "Augustine and Poetic Exegesis" in *Grace, Politics and Desire: Essays on Augustine*, MEYNELL, Hugo A (ed), 87-100. Calgary, Univ Calgary Pr, 1990.

WESTRA, L S and BOWEN, K L and BEHE, B K. Agricultural Practices, Ecology, and Ethics in the Third World. J Agr Ethics, 4(1), 60-77, 1991.

The increasing demand for horticultural products for nutritional and economic purposes by lesser developed countries (LDC's) is well-documented. Technological demands of the LDC's producing horticultural products is also increasing. Pesticide use is an integral component of most agricultural production, yet chemicals are often supplied without supplemental information vital for their safe and efficient implementation. Illiteracy rates in developing countries are high, making pesticide education even more challenging. For women, who perform a significant share of agricultural tasks, illiteracy rates are even higher than for men. The dilemma exists of how a developing country can improve its nutritional and economic situation without giving consideration to social and environmental consequences.

WESTRA, Laura. *Plotinus and Freedom: A Meditation on Enneads 6:8*. Lewiston, Mellen Pr, 1990.

Explicates and presents Plotinus's doctrine of freedom by paying respectful attention to his thought, together with its background and underlying intention. Demonstrates that the notion of freedom found in Plotinus represents an important and rich interpretation of a concept other thinkers have treated in less depth.

WETTERSTRÖM, Thomas. On Intuitions. Theoria, 55(3), 178-185, 1989.

This paper draws on a book by the same author, *Towards a Theory of Basic Ethics* (Doxa, Oxford, 1986). It is an attack on R M Hare's radical anti-intuitionism. Hare's prescriptivism is considered to be essentially correct, but it is argued that his position on "pure fanatics" in *Moral Thinking* (1981) is less tenable than his view of that issue in *Freedom and Reason* (1963). A distinction must be made between Harean *prima facie* intuitions and *basic* moral intuitions. Hare's method of moral reasoning works only to the extent that people's *basic* moral intuitions are similar, so there may be moral conflicts that cannot be solved by recourse to Harean critical thinking.

WETTSTEIN, Howard. "Cognitive Significance Without Cognitive Content" in *Themes From Kaplan*, ALMOG, Joseph (ed), 421-454. New York, Oxford Univ Pr, 1989.

I argue for important points of contact between direct reference philosophers of language and the later Wittgenstein. The deep lesson of the direct reference approach is the rejection of Cartesian-inspired ways of thinking about language. This leads to a resolution of Frege's famous puzzle about informative identities.

WETTSTEIN, Howard. Frege-Russell Semantics? Dialectica, 44(1-2), 113-135, 1990.

WETTSTEIN, Howard. *Has Semantics Rested on a Mistake?*. Stanford, Stanford Univ Pr, 1991.

WETTSTEIN, Howard (ed) and ALMOG, Joseph (ed) and PERRY, John (ed). *Themes From Kaplan*. New York, Oxford Univ Pr, 1989.

WETTSTEIN, Howard. "Turning the Tables on Frege or How is it that 'Hesperus is Hesperus' is Trivial?" in *Philosophical Perspectives, 3: Philosophy of Mind and Action Theory, 1989*, TOMBERLIN, James E (ed), 317-339. Atascadero, Ridgeview, 1989.

WETZEL, Linda. Expressions versus Numbers. Phil Topics, 17(2), 173-196, Fall 89.

Formalists see epistemological problems with numbers but not with linguistic expressions, mainly because expression types have perceptible tokens, but numbers do not. I argue that numbers have an epistemological counterpart to tokens, viz., perceptible *pluralities* that do for numbers whatever tokens do for expressions. So numbers are epistemologically no worse off than expressions, and whatever epistemological problems continue to motivate formalism carry over to expressions.

WETZEL, Manfred. Kann in O Höffes Ethik der politischen Gerechtigkeit eine ökologische Ethik aufgehoben werden? Z Phil Forsch, 44(4), 603-618, 1990.

WEYEMBERGH, Maurice. Over leesbaarheid en maakbaarheid van de geschiedenis. Tijdschr Stud Verlich Denken, 17(3-4), 205-213, 1989.

WHALEN, Joel and PITTS, Robert E and WONG, John K. Exploring the Structure of Ethical Attributions as a Component of the Consumer Decision Model. J Bus Ethics, 10(4), 285-293, Ap 91.

The managerial ethics literature is used as a base for the inclusion of Ethical Attribution, as an element in the consumer's decision process. A situational model of ethical consideration is consumer behavior is proposed and examined for Personal versis Vicarious effects. Using a path analytic approach, unique structures are reported for Personal and Vicarious situations in the evaluation of a seller's unethical behavior. An attributional paradigm is suggested to explain the results.

WHALLEY, Michael. Teaching by Questioning. Thinking, 9(2), 46-48, 1990.

WHEELER III, Samuel C. "Indeterminacy of French Interpretation: Derrida and Davidson" in *Truth and Interpretation: Perspectives on the Philosophy of Donald Davidson*, LE PORE, Ernest (ed), 477-494. Cambridge, Blackwell, 1986.

Donald Davidson and Jacques Derrida share important premises and conclusions in the philosophy of language. Frege and Husserl are analogous predecessors, to whose theories of meaning Davidson and Derrida, respectively, react by arguing that no level of representation is helpfully more revealing than words. This paper presents Derrida's thinking as a supplement to Davidson's 'Radical Interpretation', 'On the Very Idea of a Conceptual Scheme', and others. The indeterminacy of radical interpretation for Derrida follows from rejecting 'present' unmediated semantic items. That rejection turns on fundamental reflections on the way signs must function in order to be signs.

WHELAN JR, John M. Famine and Charity. S J Phil, 29(1), 149-166, Spr 91.

Conclusions: (1) No purchase of mine, no matter how frivolous, can be faulted morally for being a failure to give to a charity which provides emergency relief assistance. (2) Giving to a charity like CARE is not morally optional in the way that giving to the local symphony is. My arguments for (1) are that (a) contributing to a charity like CARE does not have the result that people won't starve who would have otherwise, and (b) the benefit produced by a frivolous purchase cannot be compared (and therefore cannot be unfavorably compared) with the benefit produced by a charitable contribution.

WHITE, Alan R. "Attempting the Impossible" in *Liability and Responsibility*, FREY, R G (ed), 65-86. New York, Cambridge Univ Pr, 1991.

Cases can be cited from the courts of various countries, some affirming and some denying that it is possible to attempt the impossible, e.g., pick an empty pocket or murder a dead person. It is argued that this confusion is due to a failure to distinguish what an attempt is aimed at and what it amounts to. Because of the element of intention in attempt, the former interpretation, which allows attempting the impossible, is to be preferred.

WHITE, F C. The Good in Plato's *Gorgias*. Phronesis, 35(2), 117-127, 1990.

In the *Gorgias* Socrates teaches that we should practise virtue and concern for others; at the same time he teaches that all actions are and should be done with an eye to the agent's good. A favoured way of fitting these two doctrines together is to take Socrates to be teaching that the practice of virtue, including concern for others, is an instrumental means to achieving one's own good. This paper argues that what Socrates teaches in the *Gorgias* is not that virtue is an instrumental means but that it is one among several intrinsic goods: it is the sovereign intrinsic good.

WHITE, Harry. The Fate of Independent Thought in Traditional China. J Chin Phil, 18(1), 53-72, Mr 91.

The conservative character of Chinese philosophy is evident even before the establishment of the empire when thinkers insisted there could be only one Way. But with the Ch'in and Han dynasties principles were defined and put into practice which would serve to eliminate independent thought throughout the realm. The tradition-bound character of Chinese thought, its repetition of past wisdom, the absence of critical and logical modes of thought, its conformity to accepted standards, resulted from the social, economic and political controls which have been in effect for thousands of years. The history and character of Chinese philosophy reveal the conditions under which an independent and thoughtful philosophy may thrive or be suppressed.

WHITE, James L. Knowledge and Deductive Closure. Synthese, 86(3), 409-423, Mr 91.

The question whether epistemological concepts are closed under deduction is an important one since many skeptical arguments depend on closure. Such skepticism can be avoided if closure is not true of knowledge (or justification). This response to skepticism is rejected by Peter Klein and others. Klein argues that closure *is* true, and that far from providing the skeptic with a powerful weapon for *undermining* our knowledge, it provides a tool for *attacking* the skeptic directly. This paper examines various arguments in favor of closure and Klein's attempted use of closure to refute skepticism. Such a refutation of skepticism is mistaken. But the closure principle is in any case false, so the skepticism that depends on it is undermined. The appeal of the closure principle derives from a failure to recognize an important feature of our epistemological concepts, namely, their context relativity.

WHITE, Patricia. Friendship and Education. J Phil Educ, 24(1), 81-91, Sum 90.

An examination of the nature of friendship, which uses Aristotle's treatment of the topic as its starting point, is followed by a discussion of suggestions which have been made for the kind of value friendship might have in human life. In the light of the preceding discussion of the nature and value of friendship, the place it might have amongst the aims of education is considered. Suggestions are made about what the school might refrain from doing, if it is to respect the value of friendship and, more tentatively, what the school might do positively about friendship.

WHITE, Patricia. Friendship and Education. Proc Phil Educ, 46, 62-73, 1990.

An examination of friendship starting from Aristotle's treatment of the topic is followed by a discussion of suggestions which have been made for the kind of value friendship might have in human life. In the light of the discussion of the nature and value of friendship its possible place amongst the aims of education is considered. Suggestions are made about what the school might *refrain* from doing, if it is to respect the value of friendship and, more tentatively, what it might do *positively* about friendship. A fuller discussion can be found in *The Journal of Philosophy of Education*, vol. 24, no. 1, 1990.

WHITE, Richard. Historical Perspectives on the Morality of Virtue. J Value Inq, 25(3), 217-231, Jl 91.

WHITE, Richard. Nietzsche contra Kant and the Problem of Autonomy. Int Stud Phil, 22(2), 3-11, 1990.

I argue that Nietzsche's philosophy is focussed upon the issue of autonomy and what it means to be a "sovereign individual." In this respect, Nietzsche is directly in the tradition of Kant who first valorized autonomy as the only proper foundation of moral life. As a "philosopher of the future," however, Nietzsche goes beyond Kant in describing as well as *provoking* the end of sovereignty.

WHITE, Ronald F. The Enforcement of Moral Obligations to Potential Fetuses: Johnson Controls versus the UAW. Bus Prof Ethics J, 9(3-4), 55-68, Fall-Wint 90.

Examines the Johnson controls case and argues that women have no moral obligations to their "passively potential fetuses." Where there is no child there can be no child abuse. Even if women did have such obligations, it would not necessarily follow that a corporation would have a duty to enforce them.

WHITE, Ronald. Dr Chipley's Warning. Phil Stud Educ, /, 115-127, 1987-88.

This examines an obscure publication written by William Stout Chipley, a mid-nineteenth-century physician and superintendent of Eastern State Hospital in Lexington, Kentucky, titled: *A Warning to Fathers, Teachers, and Young Men, in Relation to a Fruitful Cause of Insanity, and Other Serious Disorders of Youth*. Examined from the perspective popularized by Michel Foucault, it is argued that this work exemplifies both the anti-masturbation crusade and the principles of surveillance inherent to mental hospital ideology.

WHITE, Stephen K. "Introduction" in *Life-World and Politics: Between Modernity and Postmodernity*, WHITE, Stephen K (ed), 1-21. Notre Dame, Univ Notre Dame Pr, 1989.

WHITE, Stephen K (ed). *Life-World and Politics: Between Modernity and Postmodernity*. Notre Dame, Univ Notre Dame Pr, 1989.

WHITE, Stephen K. Paths to a Postmodern Ethics and Politics: A Reply to Gibbons. Polit Theory, 19(1), 103-104, F 91.

WHITE, Stephen K. "Selected Bibliography of Fred R Dallmayr" in *Life-World and Politics: Between Modernity and Postmodernity*, WHITE, Stephen K (ed), 236-242. Notre Dame, Univ Notre Dame Pr, 1989.

WHITE, Stephen L. "Rationality, Responsibility, and Pathological Indifference" in *Identity, Character, and Morality: Essays in Moral Psychology*, FLANAGAN, Owen (ed), 401-426. Cambridge, MIT Pr, 1990.

The ascription of irrationality where actions are concerned is a special case of the ascription of responsibility and blame. I argue that the attempt to justify such ascriptions on the grounds that we could have done other than we did fail and that they must be justified directly. I also argue that an appropriate justification must be internal—it must engage the motivational makeup of the subject to whom it is addressed. I apply these conclusions to some of the forms of pathological indifference discussed by Parfit, such as future-Tuesday-indifference, and argue that actions based on such dispositions need not be irrational.

WHITE, V Alan. Cohen on Einstein's Simultaneity *Gedankenexperiment*. Philosophy, 66(256), 244-245, Ap 91.

In successfully disposing of some errors that have been made concerning Einstein's relativity of simultaneity, Michael Cohen claimed that Einstein himself bungled his own famous *gedankenexperiment* on simultaneity. Cohen claims that by setting up his examples so that observers judge simultaneously by observation, Einstein mistakenly rests judgments of metrical simultaneity on mere perceptual judgments. However, Cohen did not read Einstein closely enough. Only in certain cases may these two judgments coincide: when inertial observers are located midway between simultaneously occurring events as measured in their respective inertial frames.

WHITE, William and SALMON, J Warren and FEINGLASS, Joe. The Futures of Physicians: Agency and Autonomy Reconsidered. Theor Med, 11(4), 261-274, D 90.

The corporatization of US health care has directed cost containment efforts toward scrutinizing the clinical decisions of physicians. This stimulated a variety of new utilization management interventions, particularly in hospital and managed care settings. Recent changes in fee-for-service medicine and physicians' traditional agency relationships with patients, purchasers, and insurers are examined here. New information systems monitoring of physician ordering behavior has already begun to impact on physician autonomy and the relationship of physicians to provider organizations in both for-profit and 'not-for-profit' sectors. As managed care practice settings proliferate, serious ethical questions will be raised about agency relationships with patients. This article examines health system dynamics altering the historical agency relationship between the physician and patient and eroding the traditional autonomy of the medical profession in the United States. The corporatization of medicine and the accompanying information systems monitoring of physician productivity is seen to account of such change, now posing serious ethical dilemmas.

WHITEHEAD, Margaret. Meaningful Existence, Embodiment and Physical Education. J Phil Educ, 24(1), 3-13, Sum 90.

The article argues that physical education should be respected as an important and worthwhile aspect of the curriculum. The case arises from phenomenological and existential views, that see the embodiment in its relation to the world as fundamental to meaningful existence. Merleau-Ponty's notion of operative intentionality is discussed. Hedonistic justifications for physical education are critically considered, and are seen to arise from the fulfilling experience of a close operative liaison with the world. Those advocating a predominantly intellectual curriculum are challenged to justify their position in the context of an education concerned to foster all aspects of our humanness.

WHITFORD, Margaret (trans) and IRIGARAY, Luce. "Questions to Emmanuel Levinas: On the Divinity of Love" in *Re-Reading Levinas*, BERNASCONI, Robert (ed), 109-118. Bloomington, Indiana Univ Pr, 1991.

In this paper, Irigaray discusses alterity, and specifically the alterity of sexual difference, which she finds absent in Levinas's account of otherness. She argues that without sexual difference, society and religion are ethically at fault. The divinity of love, the spiritual dimension of the carnal relationship, and the recognition of women's subjectivity, are essential for the renewal of ethics, religion and society.

WHITING, Jennifer E. Impersonal Friends. Monist, 74(1), 3-29, Ja 91.

WHITLOCK, Greg. *Returning to Sils-Maria: A Commentary to Nietzsche's "Also sprach Zarathustra"*. New York, Lang, 1990.

The author gives a detailed, running commentary on Nietzsche's *Thus Spake Zarathustra*. He portrays *Zarathustra* as an outlook of humankind's future, in a post-Christian era where man must create his own values. (staff)

WHITT, Laurie Anne. Theory Pursuit: Between Discovery and Acceptance. Proc Phil Sci Ass, 1, 467-483, 1990.

Drawing on diverse historical cases, this paper examines various aspects of a largely unexplored modality of scientific appraisal—theory pursuit. Specifically, it addresses the following issues: the epistemic and pragmatic commitments involved in theory pursuit, including how these differ from those characteristic of theory acceptance; how the research interests of scientists figure in their pursuit decisions; some of the strategies for the refinement and extension of a theory's empirical abilities which typify pursuit; and the need to distinguish between individual and community rationality in contexts of pursuit.

WHYTE, J T. The Normal Rewards of Success. Analysis, 51(2), 65-73, Mr 91.

WICCLAIR, Mark R. Patient Decision-Making Capacity and Risk. Bioethics, 5(2), 91-104, Ap 91.

It is often claimed that the standard of decision-making capacity should vary according to the *risk* to a patient. If the perceived risk to a patient is low, then a weak standard of decision-making capacity is said to be appropriate. By contrast, if the perceived risk to a patient is high, then a strong standard of decision-making capacity is said to be appropriate. Buchanan and Brock's argument for a risk-related standard of decision-making capacity are examined and criticized. Anomalies associated with a risk-related standard are discussed, and it is argues that a stronger reason for making sure that patients are capable of making decisions should not be confused with a stronger standard of decision-making capacity.

WICCLAIR, Mark R. A Response to Brock and Skene. Bioethics, 5(2), 118-122, Ap 91.

The response to Brock expands upon several points in my article, "Patient Decision-Making Capacity and Risk," including" 1) the claim that Buchanan and Brock's analysis casts doubt on their assertion that assessments of decision-making capacity should utilize a standard that is *process*-oriented, and not result oriented and 2) the claim that on Buchanan and Brock's analysis, the statement that the treatment choices of competent patients cannot be set aside for their own good is an empty tautology rather than a strong affirmation of patient self-determination. The response to Skene clarifies an apparent misunderstanding and indicates that Skene's views appear to be closer to mine than to Brock's.

WIDER, Kathleen. The Role of Subjectivity in the Realism of Thomas Nagel and Jean-Paul Sartre. J Speculative Phil, 4(4), 337-353, 1990.

Both Nagel in *The View from Nowhere* and Sartre in *Being and Nothingness* defend a form of realism. The following are the versions of realism which figure in their discussions: (1) the *existence* of things is independent of the human mind; (2) *facts* about the world are independent of the *human* mind; and (3) *facts* about the world are independent of *any* mind. I argue that the clarity with which Sartre draws the distinction between these forms of realism makes clear the ambiguity of Nagel's discussion of realism and his failure to defend his implicit commitment to the third and strongest form of realism.

WIDERKER, David. A Problem for the Eternity Solution. Int J Phil Relig, 29(2), 87-95, Ap 91.

WIDMER, Gabriel-Ph. The Questioning of Values in Theology (in French). Rev Theol Phil, 123(2), 131-146, 1991.

In order to conform to the gospel of the kingdom, the Paulinian writings radically oppose the redemptive capacity which Judaism and Hellenism see in values, particularly in "justice". Their rereading leads the theologian to harden his position on the crisis of values brought on by techno-scientific civilizations without being tempted, as were his predecessors, by the disgrace of axiological eclecticism.

WIEBE, Janyce M. References in Narrative Text. Nous, 25(4), 457-486, S 91.

WIECZOREK, Krzysztof. Prologomena to Jozef Tischner's Philosophy of Culture (in Polish). Ann Univ Mariae Curie-Phil, 10, 229-242, 1985.

The philosophy practised by Josef Tischner is primarily a philosophy of man. Systematic reflection about culture is absent in his writings. Nevertheless, in Tischner's works one may find a number of statements implying a definite way of understanding culture and assigning to culture a specific role in the life of man and society. According to Tischner, culture is a creation of works which become sources of the experiencing of values for the recipients. A fundamental and primeval man's relation to culture should be "metaphysical," in E Levinas's sense, i.e., disinterested and unreflecting admiration and approbation. The principal function of culture is the justification of the existence of man—the subject of its creation. Culture saves man from the absurdity of his own existence. Culture contains not only material products but also certain attitudes, acts and words. Apart from the general, metaphysical reflection about culture, Tischner develops several aspects concerning some of its specific domains, such as ethical culture, religious culture, and culture of labour. A characteristic feature of Tischner's philosophy of culture is its theocentrism.

WIEHL, Reiner. Die Verfehlung des Themas "Metaphysik und Erfahrung". Neue Hefte Phil, 30-31, 69-108, 1991.

WIGGERHAUS, Rolf. The Hopeless Realist (in Serbo-Croatian). Filozof Istraz, 34(1), 133-142, 1990.

Von den Linksintellektuellen der Weimarer Zeit, die zur Frankfurter Schule gehören oder ihrem Umkreis zugerechnet werden, ist Siegfried Kracauer bis heute der unbekannteste geblieben. Zur Zeit weckt er Interesse. Vielleicht beschränkt es sich auf ein Jubiliaumsdatum—er wäre am 8. Februar 1989 100 Jahre alt geworden—, vielleicht ist es aber auch der Beginn einer dauerhaften Aufmerksamkeit für diesen unakademischsten und am engsten mit dem Alltag in Berührung gekommenen unter den westlichen Marxisten. Bei vorliegender Arbeit geht es um die Erörterung einiger Grundprobleme der Philosophie Kracauers.

WIGGINS, David. Categorical Requirements: Kant and Hume on the Idea of Duty. Monist, 74(1), 83-106, Ja 91.

Notoriously, the idea of a categorical imperative includes more than one or two separable components. The author isolates those that are essential to ordinary morality, however that is non-reductively conceived. He rehearses and appraises Kant's attempt to obtain such imperatives from the formula of universal law. The most successful Kantian argument by which such imperatives might be obtained shows also how a Humean philosophy of morals might (equally well) deliver such imperatives—on a proper understanding of the role of desire in the Humanean construction.

WIJESEKERA, Duminda. Constructive Modal Logics I. Annals Pure Applied Log, 50(3), 271-301, D 90.

Constructive versions of modal logic are developed in which the possibility and necessity operators are not interdefinable. The logics do not stem from philosophical interest in constructivity, but rather are designed for computer science applications where partial, not total, knowledge of machines states is all that is available, and where concurrency is allowed. Unlike previous constructive modal logics, diamond does not distribute over disjunction, and this feature is what makes the logics suitable to model concurrency. The semantics is Kripke models of "possible worlds" with a partial order on worlds for intuitionistic partial knowledge and a second arbitrary accessibility relation on the same worlds. A cut free sequent calculus is shown to be complete with respect to the proposed semantics, whereby interpolation theorems are obtained. The basic calculus is enriched to allow the modal accessibility to be between points and sets to cover intended applications to concurrency. Topological and algebraic models are defined and shown to be complete.

WILDES, Kevin W. Institutional Integrity: Approval, Toleration and Holy War or 'Always True to You in My Fashion'. J Med Phil, 16(2), 211-220, Ap 91.

The advent of moral pluralism in the post-modern age leads to a set of issues about how pluralistic societies can function. The questions of biomedical ethics frequently highlight the larger issues of moral pluralism and social cooperation. Reflection on these issues has focuses on the decision making roles of the health care professionals, the patient, and the patient's family. One species of actor that has been neglected has been those institutions which are part of the public, secular realm and which have a particular moral heritage.

WILES, Maurice. "The Philosophy in Christianity: Arius and Athanasius" in *The Philosophy in Christianity*, VESEY, Godfrey (ed), 41-52. New York, Cambridge Univ Pr, 1989.

WILKES, K V. "Mind and Body" in *Key Themes in Philosophy*, GRIFFITHS, A Phillips (ed), 69-83. New York, Cambridge Univ Pr, 1989.

WILKES, Kathleen V. How Many Selves Make Me? Philosophy, 29, 235-243, 91 Supp.

WILKIE, A. "On the Existence of End Extensions of Models of Bounded Induction" in *Logic, Methodology and Philosophy of Science, VIII*, FENSTAD, J E (ed), 143-161. New York, Elsevier Science, 1989.

In this paper we give some partial results on the following problem: Given a countable model M of bounded induction, under what conditions does M have a proper end extension to a model of bounded induction? In particular, we give a complete solution in the case where M is closed under exponentiation.

WILKIE, Raymond. Basic Elements of the Concept of Individualism. Phil Stud Educ, /, 50-63, 1986.

WILKINSON, Mark. A Commentary on Ridley's Cladistic Solution to the Species Problem. Biol Phil, 5(4), 433-446, O 90.

The cladistic species concept proposed by Ridley (1989) rests on an undefined notion of speciation and its meaning is thus indeterminate. If the cladistic concept is made determinate through the definition of speciation, then it reduces to a form of whatever species concept is implicit in the definition of speciation and fails to be a truly alternative species concept. The cladistic formalism advocated by Ridley is designed to ensure that species are 'monophyletic', that they are objectively real entities, and that they are individuals. It is argued that species need not be monophyletic in order to be real entities, and that ancestor-descendant relations are not the only relations that confer individuality on entities. The species problem is recast in terms of a futile quest for a definition of that single kind of entity to which the term species should uniquely apply.

WILL, James E. The Dialectic of National and Universal Commitments in Christian-Marxist Dialogue. Dialec Hum, 16(3-4), 59-64, Sum-Autumn 89.

This essay is a response to Jozsef Lukacs's essay on "A Hungarian Christian-Marxist Dialogue and Its Lessons." It analyzes the dialectical tensions between generic, universal human values and those more concrete values that emerge from shared citizenship in national societies. The ecumenical movement has concretely reestablished the relation of the universal to the particular in contemporary churches. True dialogue between churches or other ideologies is a reciprocal sharing of values. Social power of any kind must not be abused to manipulate the less powerful partners. Adequate dialogue requires commitment to the project of creating a more universally human transnational society oriented toward truth.

WILLARD, Charles A. Authority. Inform Log, 12(1), 11-22, Wint 90.

The argument is in four parts: (1) public decision makers are inescapably dependent on authoritative testimony; (2) the expert disciplines are equally authority-dependent, especially when epistemic claims cross field lines; (3) authority dependence poses a dilemma: it is presumptively rational in a consensualist world to argue from and acquiesce to authority, but deference to authority closes off debate; and (4) the demand (from Habermas and others) that individuals achieve epistemic mastery of complex fields is an unsatisfactory response to the dilemma of authority-dependence: organizational and professional complexity combined with exponentially expanding literatures ensure increasing incompetence with increasing breadth.

WILLERS, Jack Conrad. Ethics in Educational Policy Analysis. Phil Stud Educ, /, 1-11, 1986.

WILLERS, Jack Conrad. The Philatelic Commemoration of American Education. Phil Stud Educ, /, 49-58, 1989.

WILLETT, Cynthia. Hegel, Antigone, and the Possibility of Ecstatic Dialogue. Phil Lit, 14(2), 268-283, O 90.

After establishing an analogy between dialectic and cathartic drama, I turn to the exemplary role that is played by Sophocles' *Antigone* in Hegel's *Phenomenology*. A reinterpretation of the play suggests that Hegel fails to see that emotional engagement in fact orients dramatic and ethical action. The resemblance between drama and dialectic suggests that desire can no more be purged from dialectic than from classical tragedy. Thus, Hegelian dialectic should be reconceived in terms of a notion of tragedy that is not cathartic but ecstatic.

WILLETT, Cynthia. "The Shadow of Hegel's *Science of Logic*" in *Essays on Hegel's Logic*, DI GIOVANNI, George (ed), 85-92. Albany, SUNY Pr, 1990.

While Hegel begins his *Logic* with being, his analysis of the transition from being to nothing suggests that the direction between being and nothing is reversible. Moreover, the completeness of the system requires that the difference between the two beginnings be mediated and cancelled in the third category, becoming. I argue, however, that there is a difference in directionality which operates between the two possible beginnings and that this difference cannot be cancelled. The undecidability between the privileging of being and the equally legitimate privileging of nothing would paralyze Hegel's system. Dialectic can advance only as a partial movement.

WILLIAMS, Arthur R. Heads, Feds, and Beds: Ethical Dilemmas in the Delivery of Medical Care. Bus Prof Ethics J, 9(3-4), 83-94, Fall-Wint 90.

WILLIAMS, Bernard. "Auto-da-Fé: Consequences of Pragmatism" in *Reading Rorty*, MALACHOWSKI, Alan (ed), 26-37. Cambridge, Blackwell, 1991.

WILLIAMS, Bernard. Reply to the President: "Ethics and the Limits of Consistency". Proc Aris Soc, 90, 167-170, 1989-90.

WILLIAMS, C J F. Knowing Good and Evil. Philosophy, 66(256), 235-240, Ap 91.

Why is eating from the tree of Knowledge of Good and Evil said to make man like God? It would be absurd to suppose that sinning made him godlike. However, it is a feature of sin that the sinner knowingly chooses what is worse when it is possible for him to choose what is better. But God in creation does just this. Since God's power and wisdom are infinite, any world he chooses to create is less good than some other world which he could have created. It is by imitating God in this way that man sins.

WILLIAMS, C J F. Myself. Ratio, 4(1), 76-89, Je 91.

The paper begins by identifying the sense of the reflexive pronoun in which it represents "I" in oratio oblique. Clauses subordinate to verbs of propositional attitude which include such pronouns are only fragments of propositions. Sentences containing the first person are synonymous with such clauses. Their use is to make it true that the speaker has ascribed to herself a one-place predicable. In important cases they are equivalent to subjectless sentences containing only a no-place predictable, and this syntactical asymmetry reflects the epistemic between first-person and other-person use. The difference between "I" and "herself" is a difference of scope.

WILLIAMS, C J F. Thoughts Which Only I Can Think. Phil Quart, 40(161), 489-495, O 90.

Dummett has an argument (against Frege) to show that "I am wounded" said by me and "You are wounded" said to me by you can express the same thought. This argument is not sound. An argument is given to support Frege's view that there are thoughts which only one person can think, making critical use of the symbolism Geach used to replace reflexive pronouns.

WILLIAMS, C J F. You and She. Analysis, 51(3), 143-146, Je 91.

Castaneda drew attention to the use of "she" in indirect speech which represents the use of "I" in direct speech. There is also a use of "she" in indirect speech which represents "you" in direct speech. Speaker's "you" is hearer's "I," so this is what we should expect: "I told you that you ought to go" corresponds to "You told me that I ought to go," and both can be represented by "He told me that I ought to go." Here, by good luck, gender differences prevent ambiguity, but a canonical language would need standard methods of disambiguation.

WILLIAMS, Howard. Nietzsche and Fascism. Hist Euro Ideas, 11, 893-899, 1989.

There is an affinity between the politics that might be derived from Nietzsche's philosophy and the politics of fascism. Nietzsche favours elitism, he is not wholly averse to the use of cruelty as a means of achieving political ends, he is prepared to break decisively with the past and recommends an anti-Christian ethos. Those things in Nietzsche's philosophy which appear to denote the arbitrariness of civilisation might be picked on by a person of a fascist disposition. What they arguably would not pick on is Nietzsche's dislike of nationalism, his scepticism about the state, and his pan-Europeanism. Also they might not find too congenial his interest in culture, his apparent love of scholarship and his plea for the uniqueness of the individual.

WILLIAMS, Patricia. Evolved Ethics Re-Examined: The Theory of Robert J Richards. Biol Phil, 5(4), 451-457, O 90.

This paper criticizes Robert J Richards's theory of evolved ethics on logical grounds. The criticism has three parts. First, I argue that his argument reaches only a hypothetical conclusion, not the categorial one he seeks. Secondly, he commits the fallacy of ambiguity. Thirdly, by his own criterion for the falsification of ethical theories, his theory is false.

WILLIAMS, Richard N. "The Metaphysic of Things and Discourse About Them" in *Reconsidering Psychology: Perspectives from Continental Philosophy*, FAULCONER, James E (ed), 136-150. Pittsburgh, Duquesne Univ Pr, 1990.

This essay argues that the problem of psychologism in the human sciences derives from a commitment on the part of those sciences to a metaphysic of things derived from a traditional reading of Aristotelian metaphysics. Psychologism has two manifestations relevant to psychology, first the reification of psychological states and the investing of them with causal power, and second the adoption of the methods and models of the natural sciences as appropriate for the human sciences. The traditional language of psychology, flowing from the metaphysic of things, renders psychological explanations psychologistic. The essay makes a distinction between metaphysical and practical discourse, and argues that psychology constitutes a practical discourse, and that practical discourse is the proper language in which to do psychology.

WILLIAMS, Richard N and FAULCONER, James E. "Reconsidering Psychology" in *Reconsidering Psychology: Perspectives from Continental Philosophy*, FAULCONER, James E (ed), 9-60. Pittsburgh, Duquesne Univ Pr, 1990.

The authors give a brief history of the concept of the self, beginning with Greek philosophy and carrying it through Kant. They discuss the work of Heidegger as a critique of as well as an alternative to the concepts of that history, and they suggest some implications for psychological theory of this alternative to and critique of the hypostatized, reified self, including the conclusion that psychological explanation must center on the temporal character of human beings rather than on a search for an atemporal principle of explanation.

WILLIAMS, Richard N (ed) and FAULCONER, James E (ed). *Reconsidering Psychology: Perspectives from Continental Philosophy*. Pittsburgh, Duquesne Univ Pr, 1990.

This collection of essays makes a case against mainstream psychology that is skeptical of the traditional metaphysics from which that psychology stems. The essays focus on problems in psychology to which the continental philosophical tradition contributes a useful aalternative. The essays take their lead from a variety of thinkers, including Hegel, Husserl, Heidegger, Sartre, Derrida, Habermas, Gadamer, and Lacan. They deal with methods and methodology as well as strictly philosophical issues and more specifically psychological questions. They are aimed at those who practice, teach, and study psychology more than they are at philosophers.

WILLIAMS, Richard N. Untangling Cause, Necessity, Temporality, and Method: Response to Chamber's Method of Corresponding Regressions. J Mind Behav, 12(1), 77-82, Wint 91.

This paper argues that while Chambers' method of corresponding regressions offers an intriguing way of analyzing empirical data much remains to be done to make the mathematical, and thus, the statistical meaning of the procedure clear and intuitive. Chambers' theoretical justification of the method and the claim that is can in some sense validate formal cause explanations as alternatives to efficient cause, mechanistic ones is rejected. Chambers has misattributed the mechanistic cast of most contemporary psychological explanations to linear temporality rather than to necessity, and has preserved such necessity in the quality of asymmetry. The paper seeks to distinguish and clarify temporality, causality, and necessity in order to be more clear about the central theoretical problem Chambers identifies. It is further argued that the current theoretical issues facing the discipline likely cannot be resolved by methodological advances.

WILLIAMS, Rowan. The Literal Sense of Scripture. Mod Theol, 7(2), 121-134, Ja 91.

WILLIAMS, Rowan. Peter Winch, *Simone Weil: The Just Balance*. Phil Invest, 14(2), 155-171, Ap 91.

WILLIAMS, Stephen. Belief, Desire and the Praxis of Reasoning. Proc Aris Soc, 90, 119-142, 1989-90.

The proponents of the thesis of the incommensurability of value sometimes seek to confirm it by using it to explain allegedly contrasting attitudes we have to conflict in theoretical and in practical reasoning. By detailing the general structures of such reasoning, I try to show that (i) the allegedly different attitudes to practical and theoretical conflict are greatly exaggerated, and (ii) we can explain facts about conflict in both sorts of reasoning by appeal to features of the psychological states which are in conflict. The structure of practical reasoning also suggests a plausible, natural modification of Davidson's account of weakness of will.

WILLIAMS, T C. *The Idea of the Miraculous: The Challenge to Science and Religion*. New York, St Martin's Pr, 1991.

WILLIAMS, T C. *The Unity of Kant's "Critique of Pure Reason": Experience, Language, and Knowledge*. Lewiston, Mellen Pr, 1987.

WILLIAMSON, A Mark. "'Why Be Moral?' and Reforming Selves". Monist, 74(1), 107-125, Ja 91.

This essay addresses an ancient question often considered unanswerable: Why should one be moral, given a guiltless disposition and assurance that one will not be caught? I present a new answer to the question and argue that the rational and self-interested person should work to alter his own and future selves such that other-interest becomes a component of self-interest. Increasingly empathic selves would then have increasingly great reason to prefer moral behavior. The theory places a special moral emphasis on *child-rearing* and provides the groundwork for a morality (one systematic with "wisdom" as "significant, empathic, empowering understanding").

WILLIAMSON, Colwyn. Attitudes Towards the Body: Philosophy and Common Sense. Phil Quart, 40(161), 466-488, O 90.

WILLIAMSON, George. Recent Canadian Work on Wittgenstein: 1980-1989. Eidos, 9(1), 79-104, Je 90.

The author undertakes to collect as much recent material as possible written on Wittgenstein by philosophers working out of Canadian universities during the years 1980-1989. The subject and arguments of each piece are briefly explained. Examined are two major collections, three important books, by J Canfield, S Shanker and J F M Hunter, and several papers (with bibliography).

WILLIAMSON, Timothy. First-Order Logics for Comparative Similarity. Notre Dame J Form Log, 29(4), 457-481, Fall 88.

Let *A* and be theories in the first-order languages whose only non-logical symbols are *S* ('*w* is as similar to *x* as *y* is') and *T* ('*w* is as similar to *x* as *y* is to *z*') respectively. *A* and correspond iff every model of *A* can be expanded to a model of and '*Sxyz* iff *Txyzy*' and *vice versa*. An example is given where has no corresponding theory *A*; this cannot arise if is axiomatizable by universal sentences. For many natural, finitely axiomatized choices of , the corresponding *A* is not finitely axiomatizable. Other topics discussed: differences between ordinal and cardinal similarity; Lewis's use of similarity in possible worlds semantics; doubts, such as Tversky's, about standard similarity axioms; Hilpinen's use of similarity to define verisimilitude; the relative conceptual basicness of three-termed and four-termed similarity.

WILLIAMSON, Timothy. *Identity and Discrimination*. Cambridge, Blackwell, 1990.

This book includes an analysis of the concept of discrimination; an account of the nontransitivity of indiscriminability in terms of epistemic logic, with applications to sorites paradoxes for phenomenal qualities and to the concept of the phenomenal character of experience; discussion of the view that vagueness is a kind of necessary ignorance; generalizations to problems about personal and species identity; temporal analogues of paradoxes of transworld identity; criticisms of the notion 'criterion of identity'.

WILLIAMSON, Timothy. On Rigidity and Persistence. Log Anal, 31(121-122), 89-91, Mr-Je 88.

This note makes a small correction to Nathan Salmon's account of rigid designators and persistent designators in *Reference and Essence*.

WILLIAMSON, Timothy. Verification, Falsification and Cancellation in KT. Notre Dame J Form Log, 31(2), 286-290, Spr 90.

The main result of this paper is that KT (=T) is closed under a cancellation principle (if *LA* is provably equivalent to *LB* and *MA* is provably equivalent to *MB* than *A* is provably equivalent to *B*). This result extends to KTG1, but it does not extend to modal systems associated with the provability interpretation of L, such as KW (=G) and KT4Grz (=S4Grz). Following Williamson, these results are applied to philosophical concerns about the proper form for theories of meaning, via the interpretation of L as some kind of verifiability. The cancellation principle can then be read as saying that verifiability conditions and falsifiability conditions jointly determine truth conditions.

WILLING, Anthony. Buridan's Divided Modal Syllogistic. Notre Dame J Form Log, 32(2), 276-289, Spr 91.

In *Jean Buridan's Logic: The Treatise on Supposition; The Treatise on Consequences*, Peter King raises a problem concerning Buridan's divided modal syllogistic. As King interprets Buridan's theory, there are two pairs of premises to which Buridan is committed to holding one of his theorems applies when, in fact, it does not appear to. I argue, however, that the source of the problem is not Buridan's theory, but King's interpretation of that theory. After drawing attention to certain respects in which King's interpretation seems to me to be mistaken, I present an alternative interpretation on which King's problem simply does not arise.

WILSON, Barrie A. *Hermeneutical Studies: Dilthey, Sophocles, and Plato*. Lewiston, Mellen Pr, 1990.

Represents a series of hermeneutic studies unified by two main concerns: (1) to sort out and reconcile the varying claims of the text and the interpreter's perspective; and (2) to urge reorientation of hermeneutic inquiry toward the study of types and patterns of interpretive arguments as reflected in sound interpretive practice.

WILSON, Edward O. Biology and the Social Sciences. Zygon, 25(3), 245-262, S 90.

The sciences may be conceptualized as a hierarchy ranked by level of organization (e.g., many-body physics ranks above particle physics). Each science serves as an *antidiscipline* for the science above it; that is, between each pair, tense but creative interplay is inevitable. Biology has advanced through such tension between its subdisciplines and now can serve as an antidiscipline for the social sciences—for anthropology, for example, by examining the connection between cultural and biological evolution; for psychology, by addressing the nature of learning and the structure of the unconscious; for economics, by examining economically irrational behavior and by comparing economic activity in humans and other species. Sociology, concerned mainly with advanced literate societies, is relatively remote from the genetic basis of human social behavior. However, moving between biological and social levels of organization generates richness and points to new and unexpected principles.

WILSON, Edward O. Scientific Humanism and Religion. Free Inq, 11(2), 20-23, 56, Spr 91.

WILSON, Edwin H. A New Humanism: A Response. Relig Hum, 25(1), 20-21, Wint 91.

WILSON, Elizabeth J and BURTON, Scot and JOHNSTON, Mark W. An Experimental Assessment of Alternative Teaching Approaches for Introductory Business Ethics. J Bus Ethics, 10(7), 507-517, Jl 91.

This study employs a pretest-posttest experiment design to extend recent research pertaining to the effects of teaching business ethics material. Results on a variety of perceptual and attitudinal measures are compared across three groups of students—one which discussed the ethicality of brief business situations (the business scenario discussion approach), one which was given a more philosophically oriented lecture (the philosophical lecture approach), and a third group which received no specific lecture or discussion pertaining to business ethics. Results showed some significant differences across the three groups and demonstrated that for a single lecture, the method used to teach ethics can differentially impact ethical attitudes and perceptions. Various demographic and background variables did not moderate the relationship between the teaching method and the dependent variables, but the sex of the student was strongly associated with the ethical attitude and perception measures.

WILSON, Fred. Hume's Critical Realism: A Reply to Livingston. J Hist Phil, 29(2), 291-296, Ap 91.

WILSON, George M. Reference and Pronominal Descriptions. J Phil, 88(7), 359-387, Jl 91.

It is well-known that pronouns sometimes occur as bound variables in English sentences, but, they also function in a manner similar to the instantial terms (parameters) of natural deduction systems. That is, although these occurrences of pronouns are not bound, they serve, in the context of a discourse, to help express relevantly *general* propositions. The article points out that definite descriptions are also used as bound variables and, more frequently, as instantial terms. In summary, a broader distinction between attributive *use* and pronominal *uses* of definite descriptions is defended, and referential use is presented as a significant aspect of the latter category. (edited)

WILSON, Gordon A. Thomas Aquinas and Henry of Ghent on the Succession of Substantial Forms and the Origin of Human Life. Proc Cath Phil Ass, 63, 117-131, 1990.

WILSON, Hugh R. Shadows on the Cave Wall: Philosophy and Visual Science. Phil Psych, 4(1), 65-78, 1991.

WILSON, Jack L. Sobre la no paradoja de un cretense. Rev Filosof (Costa Rica), 28(67-68), 171-181, D 90.

A lack of mathematical rigor in formalizing logical terms such as 'proposition' and 'sentence' leads to the mistaken postulation of a paradox where none really exists in the case of Crete's Epimenides. Saint Paul himself adds to the confusion. Herein is an attempt to show that rigorous formulation of functional relations gives proof that no paradox exists.

WILSON, Margaret D. "Descartes on the Representationality of Sensation" in *Central Themes in Early Modern Philosophy*, COVER, J A (ed), 1-22. Indianapolis, Hackett, 1990.

Difficulties in making consistent sense of Descartes's position on whether sensations (mis)represent real qualities—e.g., in connection with the issue of "material falsity" — can be mitigated by ascribing to him a hybrid conception of representation, one which includes both "referential" and "presentational" components. Interpreting his texts in terms of this proposal involves departure from the view developed in my book, *Descartes* (Routledge, 1978). Besides the "Third Meditation", "Fourth Objections and Replies", and passage from *Principles of Philosophy*, the paper deals briefly with Descartes's treatment of the passive emotions in the *Passions of the Soul* and a late letter to Chanut.

WILSON, Patrick A. What is the Explanandum of the Anthropic Principle? Amer Phil Quart, 28(2), 167-173, Ap 91.

The fundamental constants and initial conditions of the universe seem "finely tuned" for human habitation. The anthropic principle attempts to explain this fine tuning in terms of the eventual development of intelligent life. A closer look at the principle's explanandum, however, reveals that it is teleologically and anthropocentrically biased. Our ignorance of the physical requirements of nonhuman forms of life forces the principle to be more unjustifiably anthropocentric and more speculative than is commonly admitted. Leslie's, Barrow's and Tipler's attempts to avoid an overly anthropocentric anthropic principle fail to solve these problems.

WIMMER, Franz. Entwurf eines Klassifikationsschemas für philosophische Positionen. Conceptus, 24(62), 33-47, 1990.

The following proposal of classifying philosophical doctrines ("positions") tries to be independent from traditional coinings, be they found in distinctions like Eastern vs. Western, analytical vs. continental philosophy, etc. It is argued that there can be thought of philosophical positions in the light of purely systematic terms. Such an approach seems to be useful if we want to discuss philosophical traditions in a way which is as unbiased as possible. There are not given examples in this first formulation of the classification. The concepts used to classify are *ontology, epistemology*, and *moral theory* as far as the subject is concerned philosophical theories are supposed to deal with; and *material vs. immaterial* entities which are presupposed in a philosophical doctrine. By claiming or negating such entities with respect to the different fields the positions of (e.g., ontological) *realism, materialism, idealism*, or *nihilism* are founded. Logical compatibility of the possible combinations is discussed.

WINANT, Terry. "Rationality, Relativism, Feminism" in *Writing the Politics of Difference*, SILVERMAN, Hugh J (ed), 225-239. Albany, SUNY Pr, 1991.

Sexism is central to who we are and what we think about. I argue that gender relativism with respect to rationality does not entail epistemological relativism. However, I accept a kind of political gender relativism and a kind of methodological gender relativism. These are tied up with two departures from the philosophical tradition: I quit assuming that all philosophy is epistemology-centered, and I quit assuming that every inquiry that has a claim to be first philosophy must also qualify as a foundational discipline. Severing epistemological perspectivism from methodological and political relativism permits me to argue that gender theory's claim to be first philosophy is at least as strong as epistemology's.

WINCH, Peter. Certainty and Authority. Philosophy, 28, 223-237, 90 Supp.

WINCH, Peter. *The Idea of a Social Science and its Relation to Philosophy (Second Edition)*. Atlantic Highlands, Humanities Pr, 1990.

WINCH, Peter (ed) and MACLEAN, Ian (ed) and MONTEFIORE, Alan (ed). *The Political Responsibility of Intellectuals*. New York, Cambridge Univ Pr, 1990.

The many problems encountered in defining the relationship of intellectuals to the society in which they live are addressed in this book. Specialists in various disciplines from the United States, Great Britain, France, Holland, Poland and Hungary set out to explore the following issues: in what respects are intellectuals responsible for and to their societies? Should they seek to act as an independent arbiters of the values of those societies? Should they seek to give advice in the public domain, or should they withdraw from all involvement with politics? How should their preoccupation with truth and language find practical expression?

WINDHOLZ, George and LAMAL, P A. Pavlov's View on the Inheritance of Acquired Characteristics .... Synthese, 88(1), 97-111, Jl 91.

Pavlov's position on the inheritance of acquired characteristics we used to test selected theses of Laudan et al. (1986) concerning scientific change. It was determined that, despite negative experimental findings, Pavlov continued to accept the possibility of the inheritance of acquired habits. This confirms the main thesis I that, once accepted, theories persist despite negative experimental evidence. Pavlov's adherence to the concept of inheritance of acquired characteristics might possibly be explained by his early experiences. Adolescent readings of a popularized version of Darwin's theory, which included the concept of inheritance of acquired characteristics, profoundly influenced Pavlov's subsequent intellectual life. Overwhelmed by the theory, as originally presented, Pavlov was unable to alter his views in light of contrary findings.

WINFIELD, Richard Dien. "The Method of Hegel's *Science of Logic*" in *Essays on Hegel's Logic*, DI GIOVANNI, George (ed), 45-57. Albany, SUNY Pr, 1990.

The essay examines how Hegel's introductory arguments in the *Logic* reveal the convergence in logic's project of thinking valid thinking and in philosophy's search for a nonarbitrary beginning, as well as suggest how an autonomous conceptual development can resolve the quandaries of logic and of philosophy's starting point.

WINFIELD, Richard Dien. *Overcoming Foundations: Studies in Systematic Philosophy*. New York, Columbia Univ Pr, 1989.

Seeking to overcome foundations without overcoming philosophy, the book lays out the strategy for achieving autonomy of reason and valid norms of conduct without foundational appeals. First examining how a critique of foundations can be executed without making new foundational claims, the work proceeds to show how philosophy can think the truth without given conceptual schemes and how ethics can free itself of foundations by conceiving justice as a self-ordered system of institutional freedom. By so undertaking a systematic philosophy without foundations, this book offers a radical challenge to both postmodernism and traditional doctrines.

WINFIELD, Richard Dien. Rethinking Politics: Carl Schmitt vs Hegel. Owl Minerva, 22(2), 209-225, Spr 91.

Schmitt's critiques of liberalism and modern politics are evaluated in contrast to Hegel's theory of political association. The essay shows how Schmitt is wrong in rooting sovereignty in a friend-foe distinction or in the power to declare emergency situations, and how, contrary to Schmitt, democracy, parliamentarism and constitutionality are compatible so long as civil society and state are properly related.

WING, Betsy (trans) and HOLLIER, Denis. *Against Architecture: The Writings of Georges Bataille*. Cambridge, MIT Pr, 1989.

WINKLER, Kenneth P. Locke on Personal Identity. J Hist Phil, 29(2), 201-226, Ap 91.

WINKLER, Norbert. Dialectical Thinking in Metaphysics—Van Kues: Coincidental Thinking and the Problem of Idealistic Monism (in German). Deut Z Phil, 38(8), 715-723, 1990.

The paper deals with the coincidence principle of Cusanus (1402-1464) and describes its implications for his Platonic metaphysics of absolute identity. This principle criticizes not only the Aristotelian theorem of contradiction but also the Platonic tradition in the Middle Ages (Eleaticism). Cusanus transfers the notion of totality from the absolute to the Singularitas, developing a kind of monad theory.

The concept of the absolute is the point where dialectical and non-dialectical identity diverge. This philosophy of total unity is similar to that of Schelling.

WINQUIST, Charles E. "Imaginal Soul and Ideational Spirit: A Response to James Heisig" in *Archetypal Process: Self and Divine in Whitehead, Jung, and Hillman*, GRIFFIN, David Ray (ed), 203-208. Evanston, Northwestern Univ Pr, 1989.

WINSLADE, William J. When Death Is at the Door. Med Human Rev, 5(1), 53-63, Ja 91.

WINSLOW, Betty J and WINSLOW, Gerald R. Integrity and Compromise in Nursing Ethics. J Med Phil, 16(3), 307-324, Je 91.

Nurses are often caught in the middle of what appear to be intractable moral conflicts. For such time, the function and limits of moral compromise need to be explored. Compromise is compatible with moral integrity if a number of conditions are met. Among these are the sharing of a moral language, mutual respect on the part of those who differ, acknowledgement of factual and moral complexities, and recognition of limits to compromise. Nurses are in a position uniquely suited to leadership in fostering an environment that makes compromise with integrity possible.

WINSLOW, Gerald R and WINSLOW, Betty J. Integrity and Compromise in Nursing Ethics. J Med Phil, 16(3), 307-324, Je 91.

Nurses are often caught in the middle of what appear to be intractable moral conflicts. For such time, the function and limits of moral compromise need to be explored. Compromise is compatible with moral integrity if a number of conditions are met. Among these are the sharing of a moral language, mutual respect on the part of those who differ, acknowledgement of factual and moral complexities, and recognition of limits to compromise. Nurses are in a position uniquely suited to leadership in fostering an environment that makes compromise with integrity possible.

WINSTON, Morton. Ethics Committee Simulations. Teach Phil, 13(2), 127-140, Je 90.

This paper describes a case-based method of teaching medical ethics that involves the use of classroom simulation exercises in which students play the roles of members of a hypothetical hospital ethics committee. The author argues that this method can be useful in teaching students how to be more rational moral deliberators and judges because it exemplifies a form of procedural knowledge in ethics in which both critical and connected thinking skills have important functions in guiding the deliberators towards socially legitimized judgments on controversial ethical issues.

WINSTON, Morton. "Human Survival and the Limits of National Sovereignty" in *In the Interest of Peace: A Spectrum of Philosophical Views*, KLEIN, Kenneth H (ed), 303-313. Wolfeboro, Longwood, 1990.

The received concept of national sovereignty must be altered to cope with the threat to human survival posed by huge stockpiles of nuclear weapons. Modern political theory recognizes that the powers of governments are legitimately limited by duties to protect human rights. Using the theory of rights developed by Henry Shue, I argue that there are grounds for claiming there is a basic human right to be secure from nuclear war. While some progress towards implementing this right may be made by means of bilateral treaties, ultimately only the establishment of a world government can secure us against this threat.

WINTERBOURNE, A T. Construction and the Role of Schematism in Kant's Philosophy of Mathematics (also in Portuguese). Trans/Form/Acao, 13, 107-138, 1990.

WINTERS, E J. "The Limits and Possibilities of Fashion in Painting" in *XIth International Congress in Aesthetics, Nottingham 1988*, WOODFIELD, Richard (ed), 230-232. Nottingham, Nottingham Polytech, 1990.

WINTERS, Edward. Technological Progress and Architectural Response. Brit J Aes, 31(3), 251-258, Jl 91.

WIPPEL, John F. The Latin Avicenna as a Source of Thomas Aquinas's Metaphysics. Frei Z Phil Theol, 37(1-2), 51-90, 1990.

WIREDU, Kwasi. Are There Cultural Universals? Quest, 4(2), 4-19, D 90.

WIREDU, Kwasi and GARCÍA MONSIVÁIS, Blanca (trans). Existen los universales culturales? Dianoia, 34(34), 35-48, 1988.

WIRTH, Arthur G. Basal Readers—'Dominant But Dead' versus Gadamer and Language for Understanding. J Thought, 24(3-4), 4-19, Fall-Wint 89.

The aim is to show that ritualized, prescriptive use of the "Basal Texts" when combined with "high stakes" standardized testing is destructive of genuine literacy, and of learning as a meaning seeking process. I show the relationship of this kind of pedagogy to Foucault's account of "technical control" in *Discipline and Punish*. I point out how the pedagogy of the Basals violates Gadamer's view of language for hermeneutic understanding, and the right to dialogue with texts and people to reach understanding.

WISDO, David. Kierkegaard on the Limits of Christian Epistemology. Int J Phil Relig, 29(2), 97-112, Ap 91.

WISNIEWSKI, Andrzej. Implied Questions. Manuscrito, 13(2), 23-38, O 90.

The main goal of this paper is to propose a semantic definition of the notion "a question Q implies a question Q_1 on the basis of a set of declarative sentences X." The main properties of the analyzed relation are characterized. Finally, erotetic rules which can govern the process of acquiring useful premises are discussed.

WITKOWSKI, Lech. On the Phenomenon of Marginality in Epistemology: Gonseth and his Tradition. Dialectica, 44(3-4), 313-322, 1990.

Referring to my previous publications on the European philosophy of sciences (Swiss, Italian, French), this paper presents my views, as a historian of epistemology, concerning the scope of a certain programme of research into the development of the philosophy of science and reception of some of its conceptions, against limitations of Anglo-Saxon historiographic perception. Calling for a revaluation of various marginalized conceptions I oppose the hitherto dominating interpretations of epistemological novelty of Popper's conception and present my own approaches to Gonseth, Bachelard, Enriques, Brunschvicg and Piaget. I oppose also the predominant and false picture of the 1920s and 1930s in the European philosophy of science based on the exceptional authority and validity of the Vienna Circle climate. I apply the views of M Foucault and J Derrida to demonstrate the significance of studies on the cases from the margin of the history of epistemological evolution. The basic point is that some post-neopositivistic achievements in epistemology were chronologically prior to the internal evolution of neopositivism under Popperian influence.

WITTGENSTEIN, Ludwig and NYMAN, Heikki (ed). Philosophy: Sections 86-93 (pp 405-35) of the So-Called "Big Typescript" (Catalog Number 213)—Ludwig Wittgenstein. Synthese, 87(1), 3-22, Ap 91.

WOHLFART, Günter. *"Also sprach Herakleitos"*. Freiburg, Alber, 1991.

Heraclitus' Fragment B 52—"Lifetime is a child at play, playing a board game: it is government by small boys"—has not before been satisfactorily interpreted, nor has its epochal effect on Nietzsche's thought been sufficiently recognized. The first part of this book is an exhaustive interpretation of the fragment itself. The author systematically examines the origins and uses of expressions, word for word, illuminating their place in the history of philosophical concepts and problems. The second part is concerned historically with Nietzsche's understanding of Heraclitus in general, and in particular with his interpretation of Fragment B 52. Here the author reveals its central position as a key to the understanding of Nietzsche's metaphysics of the artist. The book satisfies both the criteria of exactitude of classical philology and those of professional philosophical thought.

WOJCIECHOWSKI, Jerzy A. Science and Consciousness. J Indian Counc Phil Res, 7(3), 1-11, My-Ag 90.

WOLENSKI, Jan. Deontic Logic and Possible World Semantics: A Historical Sketch. Stud Log, 49(2), 273-282, Je 90.

This paper describes and compares the first steps in modern semantic theory for deontic logic which appeared in works of Stig Kanger, Jaakko Hintikka, Richard Montague and Saul Kripke in late 50's and early 60's. Moreover, some further developments as well as systematizations are also noted.

WOLENSKI, Jan. On Comparison of Theories by Their Contents. Stud Log, 48(4), 617-622, D 89.

This paper offers a solution of paradoxes of Miller and Tichy formulated for the concept of verisimilitude. The solution consists in defining the falsity concept of theories with help of concepts of consequence operations suitable for reasonings preserving falsity, namely dCn (dual consequence operation) or Cn-1 (rejection consequence-operations).

WOLF, Edith. Aktuelle Aufgaben interdisziplinärer Bedürfnisforschung aus psychologischer Sicht. Deut Z Phil, 38(5), 474-480, 1990.

WOLF, Jean-Claude. John Stuart Mill über die Todesstrafe. Frei Z Phil Theol, 37(1-2), 105-118, 1990.

WOLF, Jean-Claude. Schopenhauers Entwurf einer asketischen Tugendethik. Conceptus, 24(62), 99-113, 1990.

Schopenhauer's ethics, not Kantian, nor utilitarian, shows a third way. He sketched an account of virtues, which is rather ascetic than Aristotelian in spirit. His two-level theory and his analysis of pity is of permanent interest for systematic ethics today. But the untenable dualism of egoism and selflessness and the ascetism in his actor-centred justification of morality do not survive critical examination.

WOLF, Jean-Claude. Utilitaristische Ethik als Antwort auf die ökologische Krise. Z Phil Forsch, 44(4), 619-634, 1990.

The prejudice, that utilitarianism is not apt to tackle with environmental problems, is ill-founded. Utilitarianism does favor rigid rules for practice (different from "new taboos") and does not imply that the end always will justify the means (many means are very costly). Morally relevant is not wilderness, but irreplacibility of (human and animal) individuals. Nonsentient beings like trees and lakes are beyond empathy and cannot have *inherent* value, but this is not to say that they are only instrumentally valuable. There are utilitarian reasons to cultivate a sense for the *intrinsic* value of natural phenomena.

WOLF, Ursula. Etwas ist in mir da—Zu Ulrich Posthast: Philosophisches Buch. Z Phil Forsch, 45(1), 93-111, Ja-Mr 91.

The article explains and criticizes what Pothast in *Philosophisches Buch* has to say on consciousness, subjectivity, self-consciousness and the nature of philosophy.

WOLF, Ursula. *Das Tier in der Moral*. Frankfurt, Klostermann, 1990.

The book has both a theoretical and a practical aim. First, it takes the issue of the moral status of animals to be a touchstone of the adequacy of moral theories; the prevailing theories are critically discussed, and a systematic point of view is developed, drawing upon Schopenhauer's ethics of compassion. Second, the author points out in which ways our treatment of animals is incoherent and unjustified, and she explains how the proposed moral standpoint requires a radical change of our practices.

WOLFF, Jonathan. *Robert Nozick: Property, Justice, and the Minimal State*. Stanford, Stanford Univ Pr, 1991.

This book is the first full-length study of Robert Nozick's political philosophy and of the debates it has engendered. The author examines the traditions that have influenced Nozick's thought and critically reconstructs the key arguments of *Anarchy, State, and Utopia*, focusing on Nozick's doctrine of rights, his derivation of the minimal state, and his Entitlement Theory of Justice. The author subjects Nozick's reasoning to rigorous scrutiny and argues that, despite the seductive simplicity of Nozick's libertarianism, it is, in the end, neither plausible nor wholly coherent.

WOLFF, Richard and AMARIGLIO, Jack and RESNICK, Stephen. Division and Difference in the "Discipline" of Economics. Crit Inquiry, 17(1), 108-137, Autumn 90.

The article argues that the "discipline" of economics is an agnostic field of fundamentally different and conflicting discourses. Neoclassical, Keynesian, and Marxian schools are distinguished by the ways they understand both unity and difference in economics; key means by which these schools define and mark differences are their different uses of "scientific" epistemological positions, differences in theoretical "entry points," and diverse concepts of causality. The paper criticizes foundationalist epistemologies and reductionist forms of causal explanation, especially humanism and structuralism, in neoclassical, Keynesian, and traditional Marxian economics and offers a nonessentialist conception of knowledge and causality as an alternative.

WOLFF, Robert Paul. Methodological Individualism and Marx: Some Remarks on Jon Elster, Game Theory, and Other Things. Can J Phil, 20(4), 469-486, D 90.

WOLFSKEEL, Cornelia. "Beatrice of Nazareth" in *A History of Women Philosophers, Volume II: Medieval, Renaissance and Enlightenment, A.D. 500-1600*, WAITHE, Mary Ellen (ed), 99-114. Norwell, Kluwer, 1989.

It is clear that Beatrice must be considered among the most important mystics of the 13th century in the low countries. Beatrice, stressing the importance of love for neighbor in the spiritual process of knowing God follows the Cistercian tradition. However, like Hadewych, she also considers reason of utmost importance in spiritual life. The strong, even exaggerated asceticism present in Beatrice's life was certainly part of the Cistercian tradition. However, her spiritual life shows a much greater attachment to reason and its facilities than was Cistercian custom. (edited)

WOLFSKEEL, Cornelia. "Birgitta of Sweden" in *A History of Women Philosophers, Volume II: Medieval, Renaissance and Enlightenment, A.D. 500-1600*, WAITHE, Mary Ellen (ed), 167-190. Norwell, Kluwer, 1989.

Birgitta Suecica addressed some of the most significant social, philosophical, theological and political issues of her day. She used her personal fortune to benefit the work off of her society. She personally founded hospitals and a double monastery, while living an ascetic life. Birgitta was a mystic who did not withdraw herself from social and political activities. She participated in the discussion of the philosophical and theological issues of her era, developing a concept of God, a concept of man, an account of political authority and, most importantly for women, a Mariology in which the mother of God is wise, active, and an ideal of womanhood. Birgitta's active Mary-picture is to be considered very special and a break-through in mediaeval theological thought. (edited)

WOLFSKEEL, Cornelia. "Catherine of Siena" in *A History of Women Philosophers, Volume II: Medieval, Renaissance and Enlightenment, A.D. 500-1600*, WAITHE, Mary Ellen (ed), 223-260. Norwell, Kluwer, 1989.

Catherine's writing demonstrates her knowledge of and mastery of many topics of religious philosophy, the nature of God, the nature of knowledge of God, the nature of the soul, the relationship of God to man, the relationship between intelligence, faith and virtue and, the religious foundation of moral action, in particular that exemplified by charity towards our neighbour. Her writing and preachings demonstrate that her involvement in Church politics was based on her philosophical and theological conviction that her knowledge imposed on her a duty to act on her beliefs, even at great personal risk. The old concept that philosophy was more than an intellectual system and necessarily implied "a way of life" was still alive in the Middle Ages. Catherine, who certainly was longing to be granted martyrdom for Christ's sake, was faithful to the old Platonic tradition of philosophy. (edited)

WOLFSKEEL, Cornelia. "Hadewych of Antwerp" in *A History of Women Philosophers, Volume II: Medieval, Renaissance and Enlightenment, A.D. 500-1600*, WAITHE, Mary Ellen (ed), 141-165. Norwell, Kluwer, 1989.

Hadewych certainly belongs amongst the great authors of Dutch mediaeval literature in the low countries. In her writings Hadewych proves herself an author of great erudition. She was gifted with a sharp intellectual mind, but she also had a very strong and passionate character as well. Her work is to be characterized as love-mysticism. The strong metaphysical and epistemological content of this love-mysticism, and the aesthetic quality of her language, makes Hadewych one of the great literary women of the Middle Ages.

WOLFSON, Susan J. Questioning "the Romantic Ideology": Wordsworth. Rev Int Phil, 44(174), 429-447, 1990.

WOLGAST, Elizabeth. Moral Pluralism. J Soc Phil, 21(2-3), 108-116, Fall-Wint 90.

WOLGAST, Elizabeth. The Virtue of a Representative. Soc Theor Pract, 17(2), 273-293, Sum 91.

WOLIN, Richard. *The Politics of Being: The Political Thought of Martin Heidegger*. New York, Columbia Univ Pr, 1990.

This book seeks to reconstruct the delicate interrelationship between philosophy and politics in Heidegger's work via a series of close readings of the philosopher's major texts. The book argues that Heidegger's "decision" for National Socialism, though hardly a necessary outgrowth of his philosophical texts, cannot be understood apart from the most fundamental categories of his philosophy. The author goes on to assert that the major themes of Heidegger's later work—the quasi-apocalyptical indictments of humanism, technology, and European nihilism—were profoundly shaped by his failure as a political actor in 1933-34. While Wolin cautions those who wish to seize on Heidegger's unsavory political allegiances as a pretext for disqualifying his thought, he nevertheless insists that since his political choices are rooted in his philosophy, we must now read the latter in a much more critical vein.

WOLIN, Sheldon S. "Democracy and the Political" in *The Realm of Humanitas: Responses to the Writings of Hannah Arendt*, GARNER, Reuben (ed), 167-186. New York, Lang, 1990.

WOLLGAST, Siegfried. Zu Grundfragen des Toleranzproblems in Vergangenheit und Gegenwart. Deut Z Phil, 38(12), 1121-1134, 1990.

Tolerance is conceived and defined as a central idea of man's theoretical thinking and practical action. Tolerance and the concept of tolerance are differentiated. The work shows how the thought of tolerance has developed since the 16th century, determining salient points. It uses freedom of worship and of conscience responsibility to work out the problem of tolerance. It discusses i.e., the relationship between tolerance, intolerance and freedom, dogmatic intolerance of Christianity, the relationships between tolerance and hypocrisy, tolerance and error, tolerance and values, limits of tolerance, tolerance and necessary government restraint, misuse of tolerance, conclusions from GDR history for tolerance.

WOLLHEIM, Richard. The Core of Aesthetics. J Aes Educ, 25(1), 37-45, Spr 91.

WOLLHEIM, Richard. Reply to the Symposiasts. J Aes Educ, 24(2), 30-36, Sum 90.

WOLNIEWICZ, Boguslaw. "Needs and Values" in *Logic and Ethics*, GEACH, Peter (ed), 289-302. Norwell, Kluwer, 1991.

WOLNIEWICZ, Boguslaw. A Question About Semilattices. Bull Sect Log, 19(3), 108, O 90.

WOLTER, Allan B and ADAMS, Marilyn McCord (ed). *The Philosophical Theology of John Duns Scotus*. Ithaca, Cornell Univ Pr, 1990.

WOLTERS, Gereon. "Phenomenalism, Relativity and Atoms: Rehabilitating Ernst Mach's Philosophy of Science" in *Logic, Methodology and Philosophy of Science, VIII*, FENSTAD, J E (ed), 641-660. New York, Elsevier Science, 1989.

The aim of this paper is to give a rehabilitation of Mach's philosophy of science. Mach is usually blamed for building on phenomenalism and for having led to the rejection of relativity theory and the existence of atoms. The paper shows (1) that Mach's phenomenalism is irrelevant to most of his philosophy of science, (2) that the texts, published under Mach's name, that reject relativity are forged, and (3) that Mach in his old age accepted the existence of atoms.

WOLTERSTORFF, Nicholas. The Assurance of Faith. Faith Phil, 7(4), 396-417, O 90.

In this paper I discuss an issue concerning how faith ought to be held. Traditionally there have been those who contended that faith should be held with full certainty, with great firmness. John Calvin is an example. John Locke offered both epistemological and pragmatic considerations in favor of the view that faith should be held with distinctly less than maximal firmness. He proposed a principle of proportionality. I assess the tenability of Locke's proposal—while also suggesting that Calvin's position is different from what on first reading it would appear to be. It is not straightforwardly in conflict with Locke's position.

WONG, David B. Commentary on Sayre-McCord's 'Being a Realist about Relativism'. Phil Stud, 61(1-2), 177-186, F 91.

WONG, David B. Is There a Distinction Between Reason and Emotion in Mencius? Phil East West, 41(1), 31-44, Ja 91.

WONG, David B. "Relativism" in *A Companion to Ethics*, SINGER, Peter (ed), 442-450. Cambridge, Blackwell, 1991.

WONG, David B. Response to Craig Ihara's Discussion. Phil East West, 41(1), 55-58, Ja 91.

WONG, David and RORTY, Amélie Oksenberg. "Aspects of Identity and Agency" in *Identity, Character, and Morality: Essays in Moral Psychology*, FLANAGAN, Owen (ed), 19-36. Cambridge, MIT Pr, 1990.

WONG, James. Getting Rule-Following Straight. Eidos, 9(1), 31-47, Je 90.

WONG, John K and WHALEN, Joel and PITTS, Robert E. Exploring the Structure of Ethical Attributions as a Component of the Consumer Decision Model. J Bus Ethics, 10(4), 285-293, Ap 91.

The managerial ethics literature is used as a base for the inclusion of Ethical Attribution, as an element in the consumer's decision process. A situational model of ethical consideration is consumer behavior is proposed and examined for Personal versis Vicarious effects. Using a path analytic approach, unique structures are reported for Personal and Vicarious situations in the evaluation of a seller's unethical behavior. An attributional paradigm is suggested to explain the results.

WONG, Kai-Yee. *A Priority* and Ways of Grasping a Proposition. Phil Stud, 62(2), 151-164, My 91.

Nathan Salmon attempts in *Frege's Puzzle* a refutation of Kripke's thesis that some identity statements with names are necessary *a posteriori*. The paper examines Salmon's view, which, it is explained, deserves serious considerations as it allegedly is derived from a semantic view (singular propositions) that the Kripkeans or the theorists of direct reference would find highly congenial. Having revealed a hidden tension between Salmon's objection and his own theory of singular propositions, the paper concludes that Salmon's attempt is futile.

WOO, Deborah. China's Importation of Western Psychiatry: Cultural Relativity and Mental Disorders. Theor Med, 12(1), 25-43, Mr 91.

This paper focuses on certain incongruities in psychiatric theory and practice in order to underscore many unresolved issues that still exist with respect to our cross-cultural understanding of 'mental illness'. Insofar as the trend has been towards standardizing methodology, taxonomies have been generated without a corresponding development in textured comparison. Originating from Western theoretical frameworks, comparative analyses have been otherwise devoid of culture-specific knowledge. The goal of this paper is to show that these categorical assumptions are still premature, and that examining the meaning of current 'rates of mental illness' in China specifically raises more questions than it answers.

WOOD, Allen. "Marx Against Morality" in *A Companion to Ethics*, SINGER, Peter (ed), 511-524. Cambridge, Blackwell, 1991.

The article's aim is to expound the views lying behind Marx's frequent attacks on morality as a basis for social criticisms and the programs, demands and motivation of the working class. It is argued both that Marx's anti-moralism is well-grounded in his materialist theory of history and that it raises significant questions about the rational viability of moral thinking even for those who do not share Marx's other views.

WOOD, David. Political Openings. Grad Fac Phil J, 14(2)-15(1), 465-478, 1991.

WOOD, David. "Translating the Differences: The Futures of Continental Philosophy" in *Writing the Politics of Difference*, SILVERMAN, Hugh J (ed), 291-296. Albany, SUNY Pr, 1991.

WOOD, Robert E. Aspects of Freedom. Phil Today, 35(1), 106-115, Spr 91.

The paper arranges the various meanings of freedom around the notion of Being as initially empty reference to the whole of what is. This reference frees and compels choice in relation to external and internal compulsions, provides for the freeing of the rational pattern of experience, and aims at a freeing of distinctively human potentialities organized around the capacity to grow in a sense of the encompassing mystery. This provides a framework for assessing institutions for the development of skills, sorting out the inhibiting and enabling character of compulsions and revulsions, and relating individuals to the free functioning of institutions.

WOOD, Robert E. Plato's Line Revisited: The Pedagogy of Complete Reflection. Rev Metaph, 44(3), 525-547, Mr 91.

Reflection begins with a visible line embodying a theorem. Reflected upon metaphorically, the Line folds back upon itself: with a mathematical knowledge on its own third level; on its fourth level insight into the difference between the visible and the intelligible and between vision and intellect; and the ground of the relation between intellect and intelligible as well as between intelligible and visible in the light of the Good as principle of the coherence of the whole. The Line is the surface of a circle that curves back upon itself when mind catches up with its own desire for the whole.

WOOD, Thomas E. *Mind Only: A Philosophical and Doctrinal Analysis of the Vijñānavāda*. Honolulu, Univ of Hawaii Pr, 1991.

This work discusses the idealism of the Vijnānavāda to other forms of idealism, both Eastern and Western, are detailed. (staff)

WOODFIELD, Richard (ed). *XIth International Congress in Aesthetics, Nottingham 1988*. Nottingham, Nottingham Polytech, 1990.

WOODIN, W H and JUDAH, Haim and SHELAH, Saharon. The Borel Conjecture. Annals Pure Applied Log, 50(3), 255-269, D 90.

WOODIN, W H and KECHRIS, Alexander S. A Strong Boundedness Theorem for Dilators. Annals Pure Applied Log, 52(1-2), 93-97, Ap 91.

WOODRUFF, Paul B. The Thought That Learning Is by Ordeal: An Original Essay. Med Human Rev, 5(1), 7-23, Ja 91.

A meditation on the famous chorus from Aeschylus's *Agamemnon*, "Zeus set mortals on the road / Firmly, to think that learning is by ordeal" (lines 176-8), I ask what sort of wisdom could be drawn from the survival of an ordeal, and conclude that learning from ordeals is essential to survival in the full sense.

WOODRUFF, Paul. Virtue Ethics and the Appeal to Human Nature. Soc Theor Pract, 17(2), 307-335, Sum 91.

After reviewing appeals to human nature in ancient ethics (Protagoras, Plato, and Aristotle), I defend the usefulness of such appeals in discussions of ethical issues against criticisms such as Bernard Williams. Observations about human nature that figure in ethics lack the authority of science, but are nevertheless valuable in fleshing out ethics, especially virtue ethics of the sort proposed by Edmond Pincoffs.

WOODS, John. Pragma-Dialectics: A Radical Departure in Fallacy Theory. Commun Cog, 24(1), 43-54, 1991.

In *Speech Acts in Argumentative Discussions* and other writings, F H van Eemeren and R Grootendorst propose a novel account of fallaciousness. Fallacies they identify as any breach of the rules of rational conflict management. It is also proposed that the new account should elucidate the "old" fallacies of what Hamblin calls the Standard Treatment. The present author finds that the idea of a violation of the procedural canon is too coarse-grained to elucidate complexities inhering in traditional fallacies. For one thing, in some contexts the *ad populum* and the *ad consequentiam* turn out to be the same fallacy.

WOODS, Richard. Meister Eckhart and the Neoplatonic Heritage: The Thinker's Way to God. Thomist, 54(4), 609-639, O 90.

Despite claims that Meister Eckhart rejected Neoplatonism, scrutiny of his sources reveals him as a profound exponent of Christian Neoplatonism among members of the Dominican School of Cologne, whose agenda was a synthesis of Platonic, Aristotelian, and Neoplatonic philosophy with Christian, Islamic, and Jewish theology. Eckhart typically adopted Neoplatonic rather than Aristotelian positions when differing from Aquinas, but also differed from classical Neoplatonism regarding the value of action vs. contemplation and in respect to the role of grace. Thus, it would be more accurate to view him as an eclectic than a Thomist or a Neoplatonist.

WOODWARD, Beverly. "Conscience, Citizenship, and the Nuclear State" in *In the Interest of Peace: A Spectrum of Philosophical Views*, KLEIN, Kenneth H (ed), 289-298. Wolfeboro, Longwood, 1990.

Current norms of citizenship arise largely from the legal provisions and historical experiences of nation-states. I argue that these norms are inadequate in face of the unprecedented problems of our era; that citizenship is not only a juridical notion, but a political and moral notion that may receive new content from the beliefs and actions of those who are citizens. I examine two groups, one in the US, the other in the USSR, that have responded in unique ways to the nuclear threat and in so doing have provided models of citizenship that transcend those currently offered by the nation-state system.

WOODWARD, James. Supervenience and Singular Causal Claims. Philosophy, 27, 211-246, 90 Supp.

WOOLCOCK, Peter G. The 'Disagreements' Approach to Inservicing Philosophy for Children. Thinking, 9(2), 43-45, 1990.

The paper argues that teachers are helped to see development and directionality in the Philosophy for Children program if they understand its teaching of reasoning skills as a way of helping children resolve factual and valuational disagreements. It is shown how improvement in each of the usual reasoning skills such as clarification of ambiguities, deduction or provision of counterexamples helps resolve disagreements of an increasingly sophisticated kind. Special emphasis is placed on showing how development in understanding such archetypically philosophical concepts as truth, knowledge, possibility, reality and goodness also helps resolve progressively more complex disagreements.

WOOLF, Patricia K. Accountability and Responsibility in Research. J Bus Ethics, 10(8), 595-600, Ag 91.

Fraud and misconduct in scientific research appears to be increasing since 1980 when several cases were disclosed. Earlier instances were handled awkwardly, but the scientific community has since mobilized and issued guidelines about responding to allegations of misconduct and about the responsible conduct of research. Scientists, editors and the institutions of science are slowly learing how to cope with this problem.

WOOLHOUSE, R S. "Spinoza and Descartes and the Existence of Extended Substance" in *Central Themes in Early Modern Philosophy*, COVER, J A (ed), 23-48. Indianapolis, Hackett, 1990.

WÖRNER, Markus Hilmar. *Das Ethische in der Rhetorik des Aristoteles*. Freiburg, Alber, 1991.

For Aristotle, rhetoric is the medium of practical and political reason. It consists in a method for discovering and convincingly presenting what is conductive (or inimical) to the good life in the city-state. At the same time, rhetoric lays bare the structure of discourse which leads to error. This book investigates the dependence of the rhetorical method on the leading concept of the good life. This yields an interconnection which has, beyond the boundaries of the polis, basic validity for political discourse.

WORRALL, John. Fix It and Be Damned: A Reply to Laudan. Brit J Phil Sci, 40(3), 376-388, S 89.

WORRALL, John. "Scientific Revolutions and Scientific Rationality: The Case of the Elderly Holdout" in *Scientific Theories*, SAVAGE, C Wade (ed), 319-354. Minneapolis, Univ of Minn Pr, 1990.

Kuhn has focussed attention on "elderly hold-outs": scientists who resisted what turned out to be a successful "scientific revolution." He claims that such scientists cannot be held to have been "illogical or unscientific"—a claim which ties in closely with his general thesis about the role of reason in theory-change. I criticize that general thesis via a detailed historical case-study (David Brewster who "held out" against Fresnel's wave theory of light). The details reveal flaws and ambiguities in Kuhn's account, and point to a more defensible treatment of the role of "reason" in scientific theory-change.

WREN, Thomas E (ed). *The Moral Domain: Essays in the Ongoing Discussion between Philosophy and the Social Sciences*. Cambridge, MIT Pr, 1990.

WREN, Thomas E. "The Possibility of Convergence between Moral Psychology and Metaethics" in *The Moral Domain: Essays in the Ongoing Discussion between Philosophy and the Social Sciences*, WREN, Thomas E (ed), 15-37. Cambridge, MIT Pr, 1990.

WRIGHT, Crispin. "Field and Fregean Platonism" in *Physicalism in Mathematics*, IRVINE, Andrew D (ed), 73-93. Norwell, Kluwer, 1990.

WRIGHT, Crispin. Scepticism and Dreaming: Imploding the Demon. Mind, 100(397), 87-116, Ja 91.

WRIGHT, Crispin. Wittgenstein on Mathematical Proof. Philosophy, 28, 79-99, 90 Supp.

WRIGHT, Edmond. Dialectical Perception: A Synthesis of Lenin and Bogdanov. Rad Phil, 43, 9-16, Sum 86.

The encounter of Lenin and Bogdanov over the problem of perception, fraught with historical implications outside philosophy, has never been carried through to a resolution of their differences. The present article first makes plain Bogdanov's thesis and Lenin's antithesis, and then attempts to show that, by means of the deliverances of New Representationalism, a synthesis of their opposing views can be arrived at which does justice to both.

WRIGHT, Erik Olin. "Models of Historical Trajectory: An Assessment of Gidden's Critique of Marxism" in *Social Theory of Modern Societies: Anthony Giddens and His Critics*, HELD, David (ed), 77-102. New York, Cambridge Univ Pr, 1990.

WRIGHT, George 702 AUTHOR INDEX WITH ABSTRACTS

This essay explores alternative ways of understanding the overall trajectory of human history as a theoretical object within social sciences. Particular attention is given to Anthony Gidden's analysis of Marxian historical materialism as 1) an evolutionary, 2) functionalist and 3) class reductionist theory of history. Each of these points is criticized. Particular attention is given to the problem of whether history can be thought to have any *directionality* in its development, and if so, what would constitute a plausible theory of the causes of that directionality. A modified version of historical materialism is proposed as satisfying the conditions for such a theory.

WRIGHT, George (trans) and HOBBES, Thomas. 1668 Appendix to Leviathan. Interpretation, 18(3), 323-413, Spr 91.

This article includes the first English translation of the Appendix which Thomas Hobbes wrote for the 1668 Latin edition of *Leviathan*, as well as an introduction and extensive notes on the text. Divided into three chapters, the Appendix contains a commentary on the Nicene Creed, legal and historical discussion of heresy, arguments as to the immortality of the soul and a response to critics of the English *Leviathan* of 1651. Hobbes also restates and develops his theory of the proposition and predication, his view of the justification of punishment and his theory of sovereignty.

WRIGHT, John P. Hume's Rejection of the Theory of Ideas. Hist Phil Quart, 8(2), 149-162, Ap 91.

The aim of the paper is to show that, correctly understood, Hume rejected the principle of ontological knowledge espoused by Descartes and his successors. It is argued that it was Kant, and not Reid, who correctly identified the theory of ideas and its role in Humean scepticism. Indeed, as Hume himself argued, Reid really accepted an innatist version of it. Hume's ontology has been misunderstood because his radical rejection of the theory of ideas has not been appreciated. In the final part of the paper Hume's own views on the nature of ideas themselves are discussed.

WRIGHT, Richard A. Clinical Judgment and Bioethics: The Decision Making Link. J Med Phil, 16(1), 71-91, F 91.

The literature on bioethics is diverse and confusing in its treatment of appropriate components for decision making. As a result, the literature on teaching bioethics is also confusing, even contradictory, in presenting an 'appropriate' framework within which learners may come to understand the nature and process of bioethics. The article sets out five decision components which are seen as common to *all* decision making. These components are then shown to have a significant influence both on bioethics decision making and on bioethics teaching. They are also shown to play a role in breaking down the separatism evidenced in contemporary bioethics literature aimed at individual professions.

WROBLEWSKI, Jerzy. Conceptions of Justification in Legal Discourse. Riv Int Filosof Diritto, 66(4), 679-705, O-D 89.

WRÓBLEWSKI, Jerzy and DASCAL, Marcelo. The Rational Law-Maker and the Pragmatics of Legal Interpretation. J Prag, 15(5), 421-444, My 91.

In so far as legal discourse in general, and legal interpretation in particular, is a communicative process, it is subject to rationality assumptions. In so far as it is a more regimented communicative process than ordinary communication, it should be expected that such assumptions play a more important and reliable role in the interpretation of legal discourse than in the interpretation of other forms of discourse. In an earlier installment of our interdisciplinary project of bringing together pragmatics and the theory of legal interpretation, we referred to the need to rely on rationality assumptions. We alluded briefly to the theoretical construct of a 'rational law-maker' as expressing this need. Given the importance of this notion, it deserves a more careful scrutiny - which we purport to provide in the present paper. We delineate a profile of the 'rational law-maker' (and of its counterpart, the 'rational law-interpreter'), and analyze their role in legal reasoning, in the determination of the meaning of legal texts, and in the ideologies of legal interpretation.

WU, Kathleen Johnson. A Basic Free Logic. Notre Dame J Form Log, 29(4), 543-552, Fall 88.

Natural deduction rules are proposed for a universally free logic without identity or the existence symbol 'E!'. Fitch's proof technique is followed with the exception of a technique called "prefixed proofs." Proofs, both main and subordinate, may be either regular or prefixed by a term. Within a prefixed proof, the prefixed term is assumed to refer to an existent. From the universally free system (*S1*), a non-universally free (*S2*) and a non-free (*S3*) system are generated. *S2* comes from adding to *S1* a rule that directly reflects the assumption that the domain is non-empty; *S3*, from allowing as theorems last items (formulas) of prefixed categorical main proofs.

WU, Kuang-Ming. *The Butterfly as Companion: Meditations on the First Three Chapters of the Chuang Tzu*. Albany, SUNY Pr, 1990.

Chuang Tzu's first three chapters are arranged into free verse (in Chinese, in the original word order) and translated, nearly word-for-word, with extensive critical glosses vis-a-vis over fifty Chinese, Japanese, and Western commentators. Then his philosophical and contemporary implications of these chapters are meditated upon. Chuang Tzu, the Taoist forerunner of Zen Buddhism, views all strivings as parodying stories and arguments with each playing off of and referring to the other. This serious, yet entertaining, translation of Chuang Tzu's text and meditation on philosophy is the most thorough to date, with all of his poetic beauty, philosophical insights, and unity.

WU, Kuang-Ming. "Chinese Aesthetics" in *Understanding the Chinese Mind: The Philosophical Roots*, ALLINSON, Robert E (ed), 236-264. New York, Oxford Univ Pr, 1989.

Beauty in China is a Yin-Yang constitutive inter-involvement of many counterpoints (contraries, contrasts) and counterparts (reciprocals, Five Elements) till the one resulted unison becomes concrete-particular and cosmic-universal, in mutual distinction and interchange. Beauty then is not a subject to be separately discussed by a pervasive attitude and atmosphere for various activities of human life—artistic, medical, martial, culinary, political, cosmic.

WU, Kuang-Ming. Non-World Making in Chuang Tzu. J Chin Phil, 18(1), 37-50, Mr 91.

Thinking is making a system of ideas, making a world of things to appear—seeing spontaneous ontological reciprocity (*ch'i*) of things (*wu*) in natural wheeling (*lun*). And Chuang Tzu's Second Chapter is titled "*Ch'i Wu Lun*." Although the human judgment of things depends on its perspective which in turn depends on the subject, *Ch'i Wu Lun* is not subjectivism, but a radical non-making of the world; the self is ontologically intervolved with things, as illuminated by Chuang Tzu's stories of "Penumbra and Shadow" and the "Butterfly Dream" which ends his Second Chapter.

WUESTE, Daniel E. Taking Role Moralities Seriously. S J Phil, 29(3), 407-417, Fall 91.

WUNENBURGER, Jean-Jacques. "L'égalité ambiguë: construction juridique ou déduction métaphysique?" in *Égalité Uguaglianza*, FERRARI, Jean (ed), 127-140. Napoli, Liguori, 1990.

La confusion habituelle de l'Idée d'égalité amène à distinguer en elle deux modes de construction conceptuelle: soit on part, dans les philosophies contractualistes libérales, de l'institution d'une liberté civile, qui entraine comme conséquence une égalité juridique, formelle et partielle des citoyens; soit on pose d'abord métaphysiquement l'égalité comme attribut générique de l'homme en tant qu'être de raison, ce qui permet ensuite de revendiquer des libertés concrètes qui débouchent sur l'anarchie ou le totalitarisme. Cette seconde voie, source de bien des désordres, peut-elle d'ailleurs être fondée indépendamment d'une transcendance religieuse?

WÜRKNER, Joachim. Arthur Schopenhauer als Staatsdenker. Schopenhauer Jahr, 71, 217-226, 1990.

WURZER, Wilhelm S and SILVERMAN, Hugh J. "Filming: Inscriptions of *Denken*" in *Postmodernism—Philosophy and the Arts (Continental Philosophy III)*, SILVERMAN, Hugh J (ed), 173-186. New York, Routledge, 1990.

WYBRANIEC-SKARDOWSKA, Urszula. On the Eliminatibility of Ideal Linguistic Entities. Stud Log, 48(4), 587-615, D 89.

With reference to Polish logico-philosophical tradition two formal theories of language syntax have been sketched and then compared with each other. The first theory is based on the assumption that the basic linguistic stratum is constituted by object-tokens (concrete objects perceived through the senses) and that the types of such objects (ideal objects) are derivative constructs. The other is founded on an opposite philosophical orientation. The two theories are equivalent. The main conclusion is that in syntactic researches it is redundant to postulate the existence of abstract linguistic entities.

WYLIE, Alison. "The Interpretive Dilemma" in *Critical Traditions in Contemporary Archaeology*, PINSKY, Valerie (ed), 18-27. New York, Cambridge Univ Pr, 1990.

In recent years both philosophers and archaeologists have debated claims about the relevance of philosophical analysis for research practice. Where archaeology is concerned, I argue that philosophical questions to do with the status of archaeological evidence and the structure of reliable interpretive inference arise directly in the context of practice; sustained discussion of them is crucial to the development of the discipline. An analysis of a dilemma lying at the programmatic core of the New Archaeology—between a demand for epistemic security and strong interpretive ambitions—illustrates this general thesis about the relationship between philosophical reflection and archaeological practice.

WYLLEMAN, A. Christelijke filosofie. Tijdschr Filosof, 53(2), 327-337, Je 91.

XIAOTONG, Fei. "Plurality and Unity in the Configuration of the Chinese People" in *The Tanner Lectures on Human Values, Volume XI*, PETERSON, Grethe B (ed), 165-221. Salt Lake City, Univ of Utah Pr, 1990.

This article provides a historical overview of the dynamic processes of fusion and fission which have formed the people of China. After early man, it examines the mutual influences and absorption of pluralistic Neolithic cultures, and the emergence of the Han nationality as a nucleus of integration. The infusion of new blood into the Han from the north, and the slow population expansion towards the south, is elaborated. It concludes that the Han became a powerful force absorbing and assimilating neighboring ethnic groups owing to their agricultural economy, and asks whether modernization will imply further assimilation of the national minorities.

XING-PEI, Fei. Artist and Peasant. Brit J Aes, 31(2), 99-102, Ap 91.

The article intends to reveal, through a description and some comments on the success story of a young Chinese artist, the close ties between Chinese art and Chinese culture and the complex feelings a modern Chinese artist has, in face with the modern industrial culture and the present Chinese politics, towards the old Chinese agricultural civilization.

XU, Ming. Some Descending Chains of Incomplete Model Logics. J Phil Log, 20(3), 265-283, Ag 91.

The purpose of this paper is to present some descending chains of incomplete modal logics. The general frame proposed by Cresswell (1987) and the irreflexive version of the recession frame proposed by Makinson (1969) are used in the proof. The logics with respect to which we construct descending chains include KW (G), K4, KB, KE, T, B, S4, S4.2, S4.3, and S5 etc. The last theorem provides us with denumerably many descending chains.

YABLO, Stephen. The Real Distinction Between Mind and Body. Can J Phil, SUPP 16, 149-201, 1990.

Descartes's "conceivability argument" for substance-dualism is defended against Arnauld's criticism that, for all he knows, Descartes can conceive himself without a body only because he underestimates his true essence; one could suggest with equal plausibility that it is only for ignorance of his essential hairiness that Descartes can conceive himself as bald. Conceivability intuitions are defeasible but special reasons are required; a model for such defeat is offered, and various potential defeaters of Descartes's intuition are considered and rejected. At best though Descartes shows the separability of mind from body, not (as he claims) their actual separateness.

YAGISAWA, Takashi. "The Reverse Frege Puzzle" in *Philosophical Perspectives, 3: Philosophy of Mind and Action Theory, 1989*, TOMBERLIN, James E (ed), 341-367. Atascadero, Ridgeview, 1989.

A careful examination of Putnam's Twin Earth argument reveals that it does not refute the thesis that meanings are "in the head" but refutes the thesis that mode of presentation determines cognitive value. I reject that truth condition determines cognitive value but do not reject that mode of presentation determines truth condition. Throughout I take the importance of idiolects seriously. This has some interesting consequences on ascriptions of attitudinal contents.

YAKHNIS, Alexander and YAKHNIS, Vladimir. Extension of Gurevich-Harrington's Restricted Memory Determinacy Theorem. Annals Pure Applied Log, 48(3), 277-297, Ag 90.

YAKHNIS, Vladimir and YAKHNIS, Alexander. Extension of Gurevich-Harrington's Restricted Memory Determinacy Theorem. Annals Pure Applied Log, 48(3), 277-297, Ag 90.

YAMAKAMI, Tomoyuki and TAKANO, Mitio. Classification of Intermediate Predicate Logics Under the Type of Deductive Completeness. Rep Math Log, 24, 17-23, 1990.

Deductive completeness of a logic assures the equivalence of provability and validity. Strong completeness does that of propositions with premises, while weak completeness that of propositions without any premises. So, the former imples the latter; but those logics certainly exist which are weakly complete but are not strongly complete. By introducing some notions of deductive completeness intermediary between strong completeness and weak one, we classified intermediate predicate logics under types; two logics have the same type if and only if in each of our senses, both are complete or both are not.

YAMAMOTO, Yutaka. A Morality Based on Trust: Some Reflections on Japanese Morality. Phil East West, 40(4), 451-469, O 90.

I propose a framework for understanding the Japanese system of values. I argue that the apparent enigmatic nature of Japanese behavior is largely due to a context dependent morality. This context dependency is, in turn, due to the fact that Japanese behavior is governed by a morality based mutual trust. I argue that many of the common virtues of this morality are functional—they function as means for initiating and preserving trust relations. And, depending on the degree to which a "presumption of trust" is entrenched in the context of a particular relationship, these virtues may be vices, and vice versa.

YANDELL, Keith E. The Nature of Faith: Religious, Monotheistic, and Christian. Faith Phil, 7(4), 451-469, O 90.

A religious tradition's rational kernel interprets the basic human situation and its attendant religious problem, and proffers a solution. Religious faith involves accepting, and living in accord with, a kernel's teachings. If the kernel is monotheistic, faith includes trust in God; if a kernel is Christian, it also involves trust in Christ. In addition, faith presupposes a certain epistemological ambiguity. There must be some evidence that the kernel is false, or at least what is such evidence unless one accepts a theory that is based only on the kernel itself.

YARBOROUGH, Mark and MARSH, Frank H. *Medicine and Money: A Study of the Role of Beneficence in Health Care Cost Containment*. Westport, Greenwood Pr, 1990.

YARBOROUGH, Mark. On the Dearth of Philosophical Contributions to Medicine. Theor Med, 11(4), 325-331, D 90.

A recent editorial in this journal calls for more philosophical work in the areas of philosophy of medical science and research methodology. The purpose of the present paper is to bring to light and discuss some obstacles and opportunities for development in these areas. In section I, barriers to increased philosophical work in medicine outside ethics are discussed. In sections II and III, additional areas in medicine ripe for philosophical work are identified and discussed: (a) improving the epistemic fitness of much current clinical reasoning, (b) defining the conditions under which greater epistemic fitness can be achieved, and (c) technology assessment.

YASUMOTO, Masahiro. Nonstandard Arithmetic of Hilbert Subsets. Annals Pure Applied Log, 52(1-2), 195-202, Ap 91.

YAVETZ, Ido. Theory and Reality in the Work of Jean Henry Fabre. Hist Phil Life Sci, 13(1), 33-72, 1991.

YEATMAN, Anna. "A Feminist Theory of Social Differentiation" in *Feminism/Postmodernism*, NICHOLSON, Linda J (ed), 281-299. New York, Routledge, 1990.

The argument has several steps: (1) Feminism is not reconcilable with sociology (or social science in general) because of its inherently patriarchal, modernist structure; (2) given feminism's rejection of the modernist dualisms, there is a strong political and intellectual affinity between it and postmodernism; (3) postmodernism signifies a politics which has both democratic and antidemocratic tendencies; (4) feminism should reject the intellectual deregulation that follows from postmodern relativism, and embark on exploring a postmodern democratic politics, which is conceived here as the project of developing a postpatriarchal culture of individualized and reflective agency.

YEZZI, Ron. "Prescribing Drugs for the Aged and Dying" in *Biomedical Ethics Reviews, 1987*, HUMBER, James M (ed), 31-57. Clifton, Humana Pr, 1988.

The paper examines four test cases involving prescribing drugs for the aged and dying, by applying five ethical principles: autonomy, avoidance of harm, sanctity of life, acceptance of death, and others' interests. The paper concludes with the statement of eight rules for prescribing drugs.

YIN, Lu-Jun. Dialogue as a Way of Being Human. Dialec Hum, 16(3-4), 91-95, Sum-Autumn 89.

YODER, John H. "The Credibility of Ecclesiastical Teaching on the Morality of War" in *Celebrating Peace*, ROUNER, Leroy S (ed), 33-51. Notre Dame, Univ Notre Dame Pr, 1990.

YOLTON, John W. *Locke and French Materialism*. New York, Clarendon/Oxford Pr, 1991.

YOLTON, John W. "Mirrors and Veils, Thoughts and Things: The Epistemological Problematic" in *Reading Rorty*, MALACHOWSKI, Alan (ed), 58-73. Cambridge, Blackwell, 1991.

YOLTON, John W. The Way of Ideas: A Retrospective. J Phil, 87(10), 510-516, O 90.

YOUNG, James O. Coherence, Anti-realism, and the Vienna Circle. Synthese, 86(3), 467-482, Mr 91.

Some members of the Vienna Circle argued for a coherence theory of truth. Their coherentism is immune to standard objections. Most versions of coherentism are unable to show why a sentence cannot be true even though it fails to cohere with a system of beliefs. That is, it seems that truth may transcend what we can be warranted in believing. If so, truth cannot consist in coherence with a system of beliefs. The Vienna Circle's coherentists held, first, that sentences are warranted by coherence with a system of beliefs. Next they drew upon their verification theory of meaning, a consequence of which is that truth cannot transcend what can be warranted. The coherence theory of knowledge and verificationism together entail that truth cannot transcend what can be warranted by coherence with a system of beliefs. The Vienna Circle's argument for coherentism is strong and anticipates contemporary anti-realism.

YOUNG, R E. Habermas's Ontology of Learning: Reconstructing Dewey. Educ Theor, 40(4), 471-482, Fall 90.

Habermas's ontological interpretation of communicative action implies a substantive connection between meaning and judgments of validity. Dewey's communication theory, derived from G H Mead, is seen to be incomplete. When Habermas's type of 'conversational' action is added, Dewey's view is able to be reconstructed. Applied to teaching, it is argued that teaching actions are communicative in Habermas's full sense of that term.

YOUNG, R V. *King Lear* and Natural Law. Vera Lex, 10(1), 9-11,13, 1990.

Written during the first decade of the seventeenth century, *King Lear* dramatizes a fundamental philosophical conflict of the modern world: the opposition between the traditional Christian and humanist understanding of natural law, exemplified by Hooker's *Ecclesiastical Polity* (1593/97), and the mechanistic version of humanity, with its implications of moral relativism, that would receive a quasi-scientific formulation in Hobbes's *Leviathan* (1650). The terrible events of Shakespeare's tragedy show the horror of a world in which responsibility is shirked, and rational norms succumb to the theory that appetite is the only moral reality.

YOUNG, Robert. "The Implications of Determinism" in *A Companion to Ethics*, SINGER, Peter (ed), 534-542. Cambridge, Blackwell, 1991.

In this essay the supposedly fearful ethical implications of the truth of determinism are considered. In particular, consideration is given to the claim that if our decisions and actions are determined we can have no practical effect on the world but, instead, are mere epiphenomena. Various responses made by those who think determinism is incompatible with our decisions and actions having a practical effect are outlined along with responses by those who believe in compatibility.

YOUNG, Robert and PARGETTER, Robert and BIGELOW, John. Land, Well-Being and Compensation. Austl J Phil, 68(3), 330-346, S 90.

YOUNG-BRUEHL, Elisabeth. *Creative Characters*. New York, Routledge, 1991.

The book provides a theory of character development, a character typology, and many biographical vignettes illustrating modes of relation between character types and forms of creativity. The book's introduction surveys recent work on creativity produced by a range of researchers, from cognitive theorists to psychoanalysts, and its early chapters also survey the history of theories of character and character development, both philosophical (starting with Plato and Aristotle) and psychological (concentrating on Freud). The principle argument, that different character types are differently creative also leads to discussions of ways in which creativity has been linked to neurosis or madness and assigned to the masculine gender.

YOUNGBLOOD, Stuart A and SCHOENFELDT, Lyle F and MC DONALD, Don M. The Teaching of Business Ethics: A Survey of AACSB Member Schools. J Bus Ethics, 10(3), 237-241, Mr 91.

This report presents the findings of a survey of business ethics education undertaken in the Fall of 1988. The respondents were the deans of colleges and universities associated with the AACSB. Ethics, as a curriculum topic, received significant coverage at over 90 percent of the institutions, with 53 percent indicating interest in increasing coverage of the subject. The tabulations of this survey may prove useful to schools seeking to compare or develop their emphases in business ethics.

YOUNT, Mark. Two Reversibilities: Merleau-Ponty and Derrida. Phil Today, 34(2), 129-140, Sum 90.

Merleau-Ponty progressively challenged fundamental assumptions of the philosophical tradition. The terminologies, strategies and theoretical structures he evolved in the process are strikingly like those since articulated by Derrida. The paper focuses on the motif of "reversibility" to argue that the structures described by Merleau-Ponty and by Derrida are not decidably different, but that the medium in which they locate that structure differs significantly. These points of coincidence and difference have broader implications for reading both authors, and for the relationship of phenomenology and deconstruction.

YTURBE, Corina. La democracia de los antiguos y la de los modernos. Dianoia, 36(36), 73-82, 1990.

YUANHUA, Wang. A Brief Discussion of One Aspect of the *Shangtong* Idea. Chin Stud Phil, 22(1), 3-10, Fall 90.

YUDIN, Boris G. "The Ethics of Science as a Form of the Cognition of Science" in *Logic, Methodology and Philosophy of Science, VIII*, FENSTAD, J E (ed), 79-90. New York, Elsevier Science, 1989.

YUJIN, Zhao. A Survey of Critical Theories of "Western Marxism". Chin Stud Phil, 22(4), 76-86, Sum 91.

YUQUAN, Tao. The Theoretical Premises of Scientific Socialism and Its Mode of Thought. Chin Stud Phil, 22(4), 28-55, Sum 91.

YUXIN, Zheng. From the Logic of Mathematical Discovery to the Methodology of Scientific Research Programmes. Brit J Phil Sci, 41(3), 377-399, S 90.

ZABLUDOWSKI, Andrzej. On Induction and Properties. Pac Phil Quart, 72(1), 78-85, Mr 91.

ZADEMACH, Wieland. A Christian Response to Professor Zagorka Golubovic. Dialec Hum, 16(3-4), 85-90, Sum-Autumn 89.

ZAGORIN, Perez. Historiography and Postmodernism: Reconsiderations. Hist Theor, 29(3), 263-274, O 90.

ZAGZEBSKI, Linda Trinkaus. *The Dilemma of Freedom and Foreknowledge*. New York, Oxford Univ Pr, 1991.

This book examines the three leading traditional solutions to the dilemma of divine foreknowledge and human free will—those arising from Boethius, from Ockham, and from Molina. Although all three solutions are rejected in their best-known forms, three new solutions are proposed, and the book concludes that divine foreknowledge is in fact compatible with human freedom. Discussions of the nature of time, the causal relation, and the logic of counterfactual conditionals are included. An appendix introduces a new foreknowledge dilemma which arises from a conflict between omniscient foreknowledge and temporal asymmetry. This new dilemma is independent of the question of free will.

ZAGZEBSKI, Linda. A New Foreknowledge Dilemma. Proc Cath Phil Ass, 63, 139-145, 1990.

This paper introduces a new foreknowledge dilemma which shows that omniscient foreknowledge conflicts with deep intuitions about temporal asymmetry, quite apart from considerations of free will. Common solutions to the traditional dilemma are briefly reviewed and it is shown that only a narrow range of solutions can handle this new dilemma.

ZAHN, Manfred. Kant's Theory of Peace and the Main Aspects of the Recent Discussion Surrounding It (in German). Deut Z Phil, 38(6), 508-520, 1990.

ZAIONC, Marek. λ-Definability on Free Algebras. Annals Pure Applied Log, 51(3), 279-300, Mr 91.

There is a natural isomorphism which identifies free algebras with nonempty second order types in typed lambda calculus. If *A* is a free algebra determined by type T then any closed lambda term of the type $T^n \to T$ defines some n-ary mapping in algebra *A*. The problem is to characterize lambda definable mappings in any free algebra. It is proved that the set of lambda definable operations is the minimal set containing constant functions, projections and closed for composition and limited recursion. This result is a generalization of the result of Schwichtenberg and Statman which characterize the lambda definable functions over natural type $(O \to O) \to (O \to O)$ as well as the result of Zaionc for a words and trees lambda definable functions.

ZALABARDO, José Luis. Reglas, comunidades y juicios. Dianoia, 35(35), 133-150, 1989.

I endorse Kripke's (Wittgenstein's) conclusion that the standard of correct application required by the notion of rule-following can only be made sense of in terms of intersubjective agreement. This is not to be taken, as Kripke does, merely as providing assertibility conditions, but rather as a genuine account of what normativity consists in. As Blackburn has pointed out, this result entails that the notion of objective judgement is dependent, in a sense, on the shared inclinations of the members of the community. But since the sceptical paradox admits of no noncommunal solution, it is the inclination-independence of the notion of objective judgment that has to be given up.

ZALBIDEA, M A and CARPINTERO, Helio and MAYOR, Luis. Condiciones del surgimiento y desarrollo de la Psicología Humanista. Rev Filosof (Spain), 3, 71-82, 1990.

American Humanistic Psychology grew in the 1950s and 1960s in the USA, in a situation of great insatisfaction and restlessness. The paper reviews the main principles of Humanistic Psychology conceived as a Third Force or a new path out of the mechanicism of behaviorism and the determinism and irrationalism of psychoanalysis. Its aims, as defined by Maslow, Bugental and Sutich and some of its American and European roots are here reviewed. Stress is also laid on the Zeitgeist and its influence upon the efforts to build a psychology based on the normal, free, creative man.

ZALCMAN, Lawrence. The Prisoner's *Other* Dilemma. Erkenntnis, 34(1), 83-85, Ja 91.

This article offers a transparent dissolution of a probabilistic "paradox" considered by Ruth Weintraub in "A Paradox of Confirmation," *Erkenntnis*, 29 (1988), 169-180.

ZALTA, Edward N. "Singular Propositions, Abstract Constituents, and Propositional Attitudes" in *Themes From Kaplan*, ALMOG, Joseph (ed), 455-479. New York, Oxford Univ Pr, 1989.

The author resolves a conflict between Frege's view that the cognitive significance of coreferential names may be distinct and Kaplan's view that since coreferential names have the same 'character', they have the same cognitive significance. A distinction is drawn between an expression's 'character' and its 'cognitive character'. The former yields the denotation of an expression relative to a context (and individual); the latter yields the abstract sense of an expression relative to a context (and individual). Though coreferential names have the same character, they may have distinct cognitive characters. Propositions involving these abstract senses play an important role in explaining de dicto belief contexts.

ZANARDO, Alberto. Axiomatization of 'Peircean' Branching-Time Logic. Stud Log, 49(2), 183-195, Je 90.

The branching-time logic called 'Peircean' by Arthur Prior is considered and given an infinite axiomatization. The axiomatization uses only the standard deduction rules for tense logic.

ZANARDO, Alberto. A Complete Deductive-System for Since-Until Branching-Time Logic. J Phil Log, 20(2), 131-148, My 91.

The result presented in the paper is a completeness theorem for a 'since-until' temporal logic augmented with an S5-modal operator. The frames for this logic are sets of branches in a tree, fulfilling suitable closure properties. Formulas are evaluated on (initial) branches and the interpretation of "necessarily A" is "A holds in all branches having the same initial point as that at hand."

ZANER, Richard M. "The Phenomenon of Trust and the Patient-Physician Relationship" in *Ethics, Trust, and the Professions: Philosophical and Cultural Aspects*, PELLEGRINO, Edmund D (ed), 45-67. Washington, Georgetown Univ Pr, 1991.

The fiduciary relation is ingredient to professional ethics. Taking the professional as primary, the relation is commonly seen as paternalistic and the client as secondary (if not ignored). The danger is that this conceives professional ethics as unilateral, whereas it is suggested that the fiduciary is a reciprocal relation. The client's perspective is therefore crucial to the understanding of professional ethics, the phenomenon of trust is as significant as professional trustworthiness. Various forms of trust are analyzed in relation to professionals as strangers possessing considerable power and to the key ideas of professional responsibility for, and responsiveness to, client vulnerability.

ZANETTI, Gianfrancesco. Vico, pensatore antimoderno: L'interpretazione di Eric Voegelin. Boll Centro Stud Vichiani, 20, 185-194, 1990.

ZANETTI, Véronique. Nomologie et anomie: lecture de deux antinomies. Rev Int Phil, 44(175), 581-603, 1990.

In this article, I analyse the logical structure of the two Kantian antinomies between determinism and freedom, mechanism and teleology. I consider the antinomy of the Critique of the Faculty of teleological judgment as being the only radical one. I show that, in reinterpreting the concept of mechanism, we get a radical opposition between mechanism and organism both at an ontological level and at the level of the reflecting judgment. The tension, like the one between freedom and determinism, finds a solution under the perspective of moral philosophy what neither satisfies, nor solves the architectonical problem.

ZANGWILL, Nick. "Two Dogmas of Kantian Aesthetics" in *XIth International Congress in Aesthetics, Nottingham 1988*, WOODFIELD, Richard (ed), 233-238. Nottingham, Nottingham Polytech, 1990.

I defend the Kantian doctrine that a judgement of taste is based on a felt response of pleasure or displeasure. The Kantian view faces various problems, which I try to meet. The most important problem is that it seems that we make judgements of taste on grounds of testimony and on inductive grounds. In these cases there is no response corresponding to the judgements that we make. I argue that it is unsatisfactory to define the problem out of existence by saying that these are not really judgements of taste. What we need is a more subtle account of the connection between response and judgement. We must embrace a holistic and indirect picture of this function. Given this, the original Kantian doctrine can stand. So I defend Kant by modifying his doctrine somewhat and by giving to a more subtle form, which nevertheless preserves the spirit of his original view.

ZANOTTI, Gabriel J. Epistemología contemporánea y filosofía cristiana. Sapientia, 46(180), 119-150, Ap-Je 91.

ZANUSO, Francesca. La via della pace: in merito ad un recente libro. Riv Int Filosof Diritto, 67(2), 290-295, Ap-Je 90.

ZASTOUPIL, Lynn. J S Mill and Indian Education. Utilitas, 3(1), 69-83, My 91.

ZATKA, V. On Husserl's Theory of the Constitution of Objectiving Meaning (in Czechoslovakian). Filozof Cas, 38(3), 333-345, 1990.

This study offers a critical analysis of Husserl's theory of meaning. The author commences by delineating the position and function of Husserl's meaning theory in the sum total of his phenomenological philosophy. He goes on to demonstrate that this theory was conceived as an integral component of Husserl's theory of knowledge. (edited)

ZDYBEL, Jolanta. Historical Relativism as a Manifestation of the Cognitive Activity of a Historian According to Collingwood (in Polish). Ann Univ Mariae Curie-Phil, 11, 177-188, 1986.

Formulating the foundations of his historiosophy, R G Collingwood described the

AUTHOR INDEX WITH ABSTRACTS 705 ZILIAN, Hans Georg

role of the historian in the process of historical cognition in the following way: equipped with an a priori historical imagination, the historian construes historical facts on the basis of an interpretation of historical documents. Thus, the historian's cognitive activity is not an attempt to reconstruct pure facts but, through asking questions, posing hypotheses, and formulating theories, it is construction of a subject. The picture of the past is conditioned by the historian's knowledge and, to some extent, by current problems which demand a solution and by a whole sphere of practical needs. The historian carries out constant relativization of the past, exposing elusive or forgotten significance of the past, and thus endowing past facts with new sense (cognitive relativism, historical relativism). That knowledge is valuable which is construed by the historian on the basis of his intuitive insight into thought.

ZECHA, Gerhard. "Which Values are Conducive to Human Survival? A Bunge-Test of Bunge-Ethics" in *Studies on Mario Bunge's "Treatise"*, WEINGARTNER, Paul (ed), 511-528. Amsterdam, Rodopi, 1990.

Mario Bunge (McGill University, Montreal) offers in his *Ethics: The Good and the Right* (Dordrecht, 1989) a naturalistic theory of values (supreme value: human survival) and a new moral code (leading principle, "Enjoy life and help others live"). It is argued in this paper that Bunge's moral code is, contrary to his own requirement, axiologically unfounded and in many a respect scientifically unsupported. It is suggested to improve his attempt (1) by opening the moral perspective towards the perfection and eternal survival of the individual, and (2) by adopting correspondingly the modified principle, "Help others live and you will enjoy life."

ZEDDIES, Helmut and SCHLIWA, Harald. Die Rolle des Individuums und seine Beteiligung an gesellschaftlichen Prozessen. Deut Z Phil, 39(1), 71-79, 1991.

ZEDLER, Beatrice H. "Marie le Jars de Gournay" in *A History of Women Philosophers, Volume II: Medieval, Renaissance and Enlightenment, A.D. 500-1600*, WAITHE, Mary Ellen (ed), 285-307. Norwell, Kluwer, 1989.

This article introduces Marie de Gournay (1565-1645), best known as the editor of Montaigne's *Essays*. After presenting her biography and taking note of her work in the field of literature (in particular, as a novelist, translator, poet and critic), it considers her contributions to philosophy. It discusses her work as editor of the *Essays* of Montaigne, as a moralist in several of her own essays, and as a feminist in her treatises, *Égalité des hommes et des femmes* and *Grief des dames*. As an independent woman with an active intellectual life, Marie de Gournay has appropriately been called "the French Minerva."

ZEHNPFENNIG, Barbara. *Reflexion und Metareflexion bei Platon und Fichte*. Freiburg, Alber, 1991.

The author proposes a method for thought within which thinking can cognize itself. The aporetic way in the Plato style suggests such a road—at the same time the schemes of thought of German Idealism are anticipated and refuted.

ZEHUA, Liu. The Contending Among the Hundred Schools of Thought During the Warring States Period. Chin Stud Phil, 22(1), 58-87, Fall 90.

ZEIS, John. A Critique of Plantinga's Theological Foundationalism. Int J Phil Relig, 28(3), 173-189, D 90.

In this paper, I argue that the foundationalist position proposed by Plantinga differs insignificantly from coherentist positions of justification.

ZEIS, John and JACOBS, Jonathan. The Unity of the Vices. Thomist, 54(4), 641-653, O 90.

The doctrine of the unity of the virtues is defended via a consideration of the unity of the vices.

ZELECHOW, Bernard. Derrida, Deconstruction and Nietzsche: The Tree of Knowledge and the Tree of Life. Hist Euro Ideas, 11, 901-905, 1989.

Deconstructionists and especially Derrida view Nietzsche as one of their own. The deconstructionists are correct insofar as Nietzsche practiced the most radical dialectical form of critique. But they also applaud Nietzsche for eschewing a positive philosophical stance. This paper argues that Nietzsche opposed an ungrounded dialectic as nihilism. For Nietzsche critique was an act of faith related to uprooting reification and idolatry in his infinite quest for existential significance.

ZELLNER, Harold. The Cogito and the Diallelus. Hist Phil Quart, 8(1), 15-25, Ja 91.

Does Descartes try to solve the Problem of the Criterion, as it appears in Sextus Empiricus? There is at least some reason to think that he does, and that the solution is supposed to be the Cogito. The Cogito shows that in at least one case knowledge can be had before the reliability of a method has been justified, and thus that one leg of the Diallelus is unreasonable. Since the discussion of scepticism is a second-order activity, Descartes the Porter can show that Descartes the Sailor can get cracking, without a vicious circularity.

ZEMACH, Eddy M. Churchland, Introspection, and Dualism. Philosophia (Israel), 20(3), 329-330, D 90.

ZEMACH, Eddy M. Vague Objects. Nous, 25(3), 323-340, Je 91.

A *Relative Identity Theory* with vague objects is presented and defended against some alleged proofs that such theory is incoherent. It is defended that no term used by finite beings can pick out a specific nonvague object, excluding all others. Thus our singular terms are either empty, or else they denote vague objects. Predicates are sortal relative to an ideology: 'F' may be a sortal relative to D but not to C (is less than) D or E (is greater than) D. Thus a sentence that includes 'the F' may be bivalent relative to D, but not to C or E; then *x* and *y* are identical in D, but only the same F in C or in E. Relative identity statements (*a* is the same F as *b*) make it possible to keep ontology stable when ideology expands.

ZENKO, Franjo. R J Boskovic's "Theoria" — A Sign Post to the Essence of the Modern Natural Science (in Serbo-Croatian). Filozof Istraz, 32-33(5-6), 1471-1478, 1989.

In diesem (in Wien am 5. März 1987 öffentlich gehaltenen) Vortrag wird die Frage erörtert, ob ein Versuch philosophie- und wissenschaftsgesichichtlich legitim sei, die in Wien (1758) verfasste *Theoria philosophiae naturalis* als eine 'Philosophy of Science' zu lesen. Die Beantwortung dieser Frage sollte zur Beleuchtung des dunklen Wesens der neuzeitlichen Wissenschaft verhelfen. Dabei wird nach dem wahren Sinn der Unterscheidung zwischen der (übergeordneten) "Theoria" und der (untergeordneten) "Philosophia naturalis" bei Boskovic gesucht. Es wird die These entwickelt, dass Boskovic, der als Jesuit im Geiste des spätscholastischen Aristotelismus erzogen, aber sehr früh der begeisterte Newtonianer geworden war, den neuzeitlichen Bruch zwischen Denken und Wissen besonders tief empfunden, aber durch sein allumfassendes System des absoluten Dynamismus genial aufgehoben hat. Dadurch sollte er einmal nicht nur als der neuzeitliche Naturphilosoph, weil seine *Theoria philosophiae naturalis* schon längst als "das Hauptwerk der Epoche" (Ernst Cassirer) anerkannt wurde, sondern als der eigentliche Denker der Neuzeit, ja, als der 'neuzeitliche Aristoteles' erkannt werden.

ZÉPHIR, Jacques J. Nature et fonction de la Mémoire dans À la recherche du temps perdu. Philosophiques, 17(2), 147-168, Autumn 1990.

In *Remembrance of Things Past*, Proust is actually searching for his own identity, his innermost, true self. In order to do this, he isolates himself from the present, with the aim of finding himself in the past. However, the "resurrection of the past," which ought to bring him the salvation so desperately sought, is not the product of voluntary memory. This form of memory, function of the objective, "quasi-depersonalized" evocation, does not have the capability of presenting the past to us again in its totality. Consequently, it could not lead him to the innermost self, of which it could give him only a factitious and truncated image. (edited)

ZEPPI, Stello. Le origini dell'ateismo antico (quinta parte). G Metaf, 11(3), 363-395, S-D 89.

ZERILLI, Linda M G. Machiavelli's Sisters: Women and "the Conversation" of Political Theory. Polit Theory, 19(2), 252-276, My 91.

ZHAI, Zhenming. The Problem of Protocol Statements and Schlick's Concept of 'Konstatierungen'. Proc Phil Sci Ass, 1, 15-23, 1990.

For Schlick, taking "protocol statement" as the key concept for understanding the process of verification may lead to a type of rationalism which logical positivists are supposed to avoid by all means, and it is affirmations, instead of protocols as usually understood, that will join experience and proposition together in the way an empiricist can see as legitimate. An affirmation's direct contact with reality verifies itself immediately, but also makes it unavailable as part of public knowledge. Thus the joy of verification in the scientist's part is the end of scientific activity.

ZHANG, Wei Rose. Alienation, Schools, and Society. Phil Stud Educ, /, 97-106, 1989.

ZHAO, Shanyang. Rhetoric as Praxis: An Alternative to the Epistemic Approach. Phil Rhet, 24(3), 255-266, 1991.

Rhetoric has been viewed as either a stylistic ornament to truth or an epistemic tool for discovering truth. In this paper, however, rhetoric is viewed as social praxis which integrates both knowing and doing in public discourse. Rhetoric is praxis because it is the advocacy of reality rather than the discovery of reality, is the actualization of ideas rather than the verification of ideas, is manipulation rather than confirmation. The mission of praxical rhetoric is to aid in the realization of humans as we work out the life contingencies in which we find ourselves.

ZIELONKA, Wojciech. Linear Axiomatics of Communicative Product-Free Lambek Calculus. Stud Log, 49(4), 515-522, D 90.

Axiomatics which do not employ rules of inference other than the cut rule are given for commutative product-free Lambek calculus in two variants: with and without the empty string. Unlike the former variant, the latter one turns out not to be finitely axiomatizable in that way.

ZIEMKE, Axel and STÖBER, Konrad. Autopoesis—Subject—Reality (in German). Deut Z Phil, 38(11), 1083-1090, 1990.

ZIFF, Paul. Time Preference. Dialectica, 44(1-2), 43-54, 1990.

ZIHLIN, Li. On the Duality of China's Traditional Mode of Thought and the Difficulty of Transforming It. Chin Stud Phil, 22(3), 20-44, Spr 91.

ZIJDERVELD, A C. Dezelfde wateren aan nieuwe oevers: Alexis de Tocqueville en de Franse Revolutie. Tijdschr Stud Verlich Denken, 17(3-4), 289-305, 1989.

ZILBER, B I. "Towards the Structural Stability Theory" in *Logic, Methodology and Philosophy of Science, VIII*, FENSTAD, J E (ed), 163-175. New York, Elsevier Science, 1989.

ZILIAN, Hans Georg. "Convention and Assertion" in *The Mind of Donald Davidson*, BRANDL, Johannes (ed), 109-119. Amsterdam, Rodopi, 1989.

Donald Davidson has shocked his readers by arguing that assertion is not a conventional activity, thus attacking what was taken to be a truism by most philosophers of language. The paper claims that Davidson's argument is seriously flawed by his failure to distinguish a number of questions which should be kept separate. Assertion is a matter of seriousness, not of sincerity; departures from seriousness are marked by techniques which are undeniably conventional. There are no parallel indicators of seriousness, i.e., there is no assertion-sign. But this necessary absence of a conventional marker of seriousness from our communicative repertoire does not imply that the activity of asserting is not conventional. Assertion differs in important ways from eating or walking; it is these differences which have led Searle, Lewis, Dummett and countless others to conceive of language as essentially conventional. The paper argues that Davidson's naturalistic challenge illuminates the (nonexisting) role of the assertion-sign, while failing to undermine the credentials of the 'truism'.

ZIMMERMAN, Dean W. Two Cartesian Arguments for the Simplicity of the Soul. Amer Phil Quart, 28(3), 217-226, Jl 91.

The most well-known arguments for the simplicity of the soul - i.e., for the thesis that the subject of psychological states must be an unextended substance - are based upon the logical possibility of disembodiment. Descartes introduced this sort of argument into modern philosophy, and a version of it has been defended recently by Richard Swinburne. Some of the underlying assumptions of both arguments are examined and defended, but a closer look reveals that each depends upon unjustified inferences from the conceivability of a certain state of affairs to the logical possibility of that state of affairs.

ZIMMERMAN, Michael J. The Range of Options. Amer Phil Quart, 27(4), 345-355, O 90.

It is argued that our options are far more restricted than is commonly thought. The argument is roughly this: whenever we act, most of our apparent options are such that we do not advert to them, yet also such that we can perform them only if we do advert to them; hence, whenever we act, most of our apparent options are not genuine options. This argument is refined and defended in detail. Its moral implications are then briefly assessed.

ZIMMERMANN, Rolf. Wertfreiheit und Ethik in den Sozial-und Naturwissenschaften. Z Phil Forsch, 44(4), 564-582, 1990.

ZIPPRIAN, Heinz and WAGNER, Gerhard. Intersubjectivity and Critical Consciousness: Remarks on Habermas's Theory of Communicative Action. Inquiry, 34(1), 49-62, Mr 91.

The out-dated intentionalistic assumptions manifest in Habermas's *Theory of Communicative Action* undermine a solution to the problem of order in action theory beyond utilitarianism. An analysis of his intersubjectivistic conception, which is based on the theory of the speech-act, shows that the incompleteness of Habermas's linguistic turn is due to his attempt to revive the older Critical Theory's concept of critique. The claims for a scientifically well-founded revival of a universal concept of reason—which are asserted in this concept—invalidate the intersubjectivistic paradigm in action theory and therefore obstruct the way to a deindividualized formulation of the theory of social contract that avoids the paradox of utilitarian models.

ZIVALJEVIC, Bosko. Some Results about Borel Sets in Descriptive Set Theory of Hyperfinite Sets. J Sym Log, 55(2), 604-614, Je 90.

ZIZEK, Slavoj. The Notion of Sublime in Kant and Hegel: A Psycho-Analytical Reading (in Serbo-Croatian). Filozof Istraz, 32-33(5-6), 1711-1720, 1989.

The Sublime (das Erhabene) is the paradoxical point of Kant's system where the gap separating phenomena from the Thing-in-Itself is surpassed: by means of its very failure to present the suprasensible Idea, the sublime phenomenon renders the dimension of the Idea. On the basis of Lacanian theoretical apparatus, the essay attempts to reconstruct a possible Hegelian criticism of this notion of Sublime: the suprasensible Idea is not "beyond" phenomena, it is *nothing but* this failure, discord, "negative self-relationship" of the phenomenon to itself. Which is why, in Hegel, the sublime object changes into an utterly worthless leftover which, by means of its very inadequacy, announces the dimension of radical negativity: "the Spirit is a bone," "the Self is Wealth." (edited)

ZIZEK, Slavoj. Why Should a Dialectician Learn to Count to Four? Rad Phil, 58, 3-9, Sum 91.

ZNEPOLSKY, Ivahilo. "Roland Barthes et Umberto Eco à la Recherche du Roman Postmoderne" in *XIth International Congress in Aesthetics, Nottingham 1988*, WOODFIELD, Richard (ed), 239-241. Nottingham, Nottingham Polytech, 1990.

ZÖHRER-ERNST, Ulla. Campanella's "Civitas Solis" Is Ruled by Love Without Emotion (in German). Deut Z Phil, 38(8), 705-714, 1990.

Campanella's utopia is—in a feminist perspective—read as a text caught between two models of 'Weltanschauung': the old magical approach which is falling apart in the Renaissance and the new, modern, mechanistic approach. The events around the fall of the Berlin Wall, in November 1989, are the philosophical starting point for a small step back into the general history of Campanella's time (the witch hunt), which is followed by a—preliminary—feminist reading of the text.

ZOLO, Danilo. Epistemologia e teoria politica. Teoria, 10(1), 51-62, 1990.

Today it is possible to identify the following six political-philosophical paradigms: (1) political science; (2) theories of rational action applied to politics; (3) neocontractualism; (4) the theory of communicative competence (Habermas); (5) theories of social complexity (Luhmann); (6) the *Rehabilitierung der praktischen Philosophie*. Political science and the theories of rational action have in common basic epistemological assumptions deduced from American standard empiricism and share a 'strong' conception of the epistemology of the social sciences. The other paradigms tend to abandon empiricist principle such as ethical noncognitivism, the separation between theoretical and prescriptive propositions, the *Wertfreiheit*, the demarcation between science and metaphysics. According to the author the empiricist view is no longer able to give epistemological foundation to the social and political sciences.

ZOLUA, Buenzey Maluenga. De l'Idéologie comme correlat des termes idéologiste et idéologue. Quest, 4(2), 62-79, D 90.

This article investigates the historical roots of the concept 'ideology' and the (in the French language) related concepts 'idéologue' and 'idéologiste'. The emergence of these concepts is related to the progressive French enlightenment intellectuals around 1800, e.g., Antoine Destutt de Tracy and Cabanais, the 'industrialists of ideas'. The article further traces the origins of the pregorative connotation of the concept of ideology and the development of the term in history. Unsatisfactory elements involved in the concept—in relation to Hegel and Marx especially—are highlighted. The author aims at revitalising the concept of ideology.

ZUBROW, Ezra. "Commentary: Common Knowledge and Archaeology" in *Critical Traditions in Contemporary Archaeology*, PINSKY, Valerie (ed), 44-50. New York, Cambridge Univ Pr, 1990.

ZUCKER, Arthur. Davy Refuted Lavoisier Not Lakatos. Brit J Phil Sci, 39(4), 537-540, D 88.

ZUIDERVAART, Lambert. *Adorno's Aesthetic Theory: The Redemption of Illusion*. Cambridge, MIT Pr, 1991.

The book uncovers the historical sources of Theodor W Adorno's *Aesthetic Theory*, explains Adorno's central ideas, and demonstrates the relevance of his aesthetics for contemporary discussions of popular art, cultural politics, and postmodernism. The first part of the book offers a brief biography, describes Adorno's debates with Benjamin, Brecht, and Lukács, and outlines his philosophical program. The second part examines how Adorno situates art in society, production, politics, and history as a paradoxical vehicle of truth. The third evaluates Adorno's contribution by confronting it with the critiques of Peter Bürger, Fredric Jameson, and Albrecht Wellmer.

ZUIDERVAART, Lambert. "Normative Aesthetics and Contemporary Art: Bürger's Critique of Adorno" in *XIth International Congress in Aesthetics, Nottingham 1988*, WOODFIELD, Richard (ed), 242-245. Nottingham, Nottingham Polytech, 1990.

What are the prospects for a philosophical critique of contemporary art? What norms can we use to evaluate the contributions of art in contemporary society? This article discusses a recent debate on such topics in German aesthetics. It introduces the approach of Theodor W Adorno's *Aesthetic Theory*, summarizes the criticisms of Adorno in Peter Bürger's *Theory of the Avant-Garde*, and examines three problems in Bürger's historicizing approach to normative aesthetics. The paper concludes by proposing the concept of "complex normativity" as an alternative basis for a philosophical critique of contemporary art.

ZUMR, J. Responsibility in the Tradition of Czech Thought (in Czechoslovakian). Filozof Cas, 39(1), 62-66, 1991.

ZÜRCHER, Erik (ed) and LANGENDORFF, T. *The Humanities in the Nineties: A View From the Netherlands*. Bristol, SWETS, 1990.

ZYCINSKI, Joseph. Falsification and Disconfirmation in Cosmology. Phil Sci (Tucson), 2, 53-60, 1986.

The epistemological specificity of relativistic cosmology is expressed in the fact that scientific investigations within this discipline are restricted to the unique physical object-the universe. Unrepeatability of events in cosmic history weakens the role of inductive methodology in cosmological research. On the other side, the methodological principles of Popperian deduction could easily transform cosmology into a set of unsubstantiated speculations, since they lead to a multiplicity of arbitrary cosmological models. Consequently, within the methodological framework of cosmology one should ascribe a special role to the criterion of empirical disconfirmation.

ZYCINSKI, Joseph. Plato's Ontology and the Role of Mathematics in the Description of Nature. Phil Sci (Tucson), 3, 37-55, 1988.

The paper attempts to answer the question: Why the language of mathematics can be effectively used to describe physical processes? After presenting examples that illustrate the astonishing effectiveness of mathematics in the growth of modern science, and after reflecting upon ontological implications of quantum field theory, we propose the hypothesis of the existence of the rationality field. This field, which constitutes the nomic structure of physical processes, explains why the abstract formulae of mathematics are appropriate for scientific theories. The hypothesis of the rationality field seems to confirm the theory of forms proposed in Plato's ontology.

ZYCINSKI, Joseph. Taking Mathematics Seriously? Brit J Phil Sci, 40(1), 77-82, Mr 89.

ZYCINSKI, Jozef. The Laws of Physics as Nomic Universals. Phil Sci (Tucson), 4, 83-110, 1990.

In the paper, the Humean and the Platonic conception of laws of nature are opposed. After presenting the principal difficulties faced by the basic versions of the Humean regularity theory, the author proposes a necessitarian approach in which the laws of nature are regarded as necessary relations between universals that are actualized in nature. In the framework presented, the basic ideas of D M Armstrong's theory of universals are developed to explain the effective role of mathematical descriptions in the research practice of modern physics. Consequently, the author argues that the essence of laws of nature cannot be reduced to observed physical regularities, because the latter presuppose the existence of hidden necessary links that constitute the order of nature, even if in a specific situation no empirical procedures reveal this order.

ZYGMUNT, Jan. Mojzesz Presburger: Life and Work. Hist Phil Log, 12(2), 211-223, 1991.

The life and work of Mojzesz Presburger (1904-1943?) are summarized in this article. Although his production in logic was small, it had considerable impact, both his own researches and his editions of lecture notes of Adjukiewicz and Lukasiewicz. In addition, the surviving records of his student time at Warsaw University provide information on a little-studied topic.

Guidance on the Use of the Book Review Index

The Book Review Index lists, in alphabetical order, the authors of books reviewed in philosophy journals. Each entry includes the author's name, the title of the book, the publisher, and the place and date of publication. Under each entry is listed the name of the reviewer, the journal in which the review appeared, along with the volume, pagination and date.

ABBRUZZESE, Salvatore. *Comunione e Liberazione*. Paris, Cerf, 1989.
Marty, Gilles-Marie. *Rev Thomiste* 91(1), 155-159 Ja-Mr 91

ABBS, Peter (ed). *The Symbolic Order: A Contemporary Reader on the Arts Debate*. London, Falmer Pr, 1989.
Simpson, Alan. *Brit J Aes* 31(2), 178-179 Ap 91

ABEL, Donald C. *Freud on Instinct and Morality*. Albany, SUNY Pr, 1989.
Meissner, W W. *Thought* 66(260), 113-114 Mr 91

ABEL, F and BONE, E and HARVEY, J C (eds). *Human Life: Its Beginning and Development*. Paris, Harmattan, 1988.
Wildes, Kevin W. *J Med Phil* 15(6), 697-698 D 90

ABEL, Richard (ed). *French Film Theory and Criticism 1907-1939: A History/Anthology*. Princeton, Princeton Univ Pr, 1988.
Neill, Alex and Ridley, Aaron. *Can Phil Rev* 10(9), 345-351 S 90

ABRAHAM, William J and HOLTZER, Steven W (eds). *The Rationality of Religious Belief*. New York, Clarendon/Oxford Pr, 1987.
Tilley, Terrence W. *Mod Theol* 7(3), 293-294 Ap 91

ACKERMANN, Robert J. *Wittgenstein's City*. Amherst, Univ of Massachusetts Pr, 1988.
Harré, Rom. *Int Stud Phil* 22(3), 83-84 1990
Simpson, Peter. *Rev Metaph* 44(2), 399-401 D 90
Summerfield, Donna M. *Phil Books* 31(4), 210-211 O 90

ADAMS, Marilyn McCord. *William Ockham, 2v*. Notre Dame, Univ of Notre Dame Pr, 1987.
Wolter, Allan B. *Int Stud Phil* 22(3), 85-87 1990
Tweedale, Martin. *Can J Phil* 21(2), 211-244 Je 91
Read, Stephen. *Phil Quart* 40(161), 537-538 O 90

ADORNO, Theodor W. *Negative Dialectics, E B Ashton (trans)*. London, Routledge, 1990.
Arthur, C J. *Rad Phil* 57, 54 Spr 91

AGACINSKI, Sylviane. *Aparté: Conceptions and Deaths of Soren Kierkegaard, Kevin Newmark (trans)*. Tallahassee, Florida State Univ Pr, 1988.
Walsh, Sylvia. *Int J Phil Relig* 29(2), 113-122 Ap 91

AGAZZI, E. *Philosophie, Science, Métaphysique, 2nd ed*. Fribourg, Univ Fribourg Suisse, 1987.
Ginebra i Molins, M Pau. *Anu Filosof* 23(1), 179-181 1990

AGAZZI, Evandro and MINAZZI, Fabio and GEYMONAT, Ludovico. *Filosofia, scienza e verità*. Milan, Rusconi, 1989.
Marsonet, Michele. *Epistemologia* 12(2), 353-356 Jl-D 89

AGAZZI, Evandro (ed). *Epistemologia: La filosofia della scienza in Italia nel '900*. Milan, Angeli, 1986.
Mercier, André. *Brit J Phil Sci* 39(3), 415-419 S 88

ALBANO, Maeve E. *Vico and Providence*. New York, Lang, 1986.
Costa, Gustavo. *Boll Centro Stud Vichiani* 20, 240-243 1990

ALBERT, Hans. *Kritik der reinen Erkenntnislehre*. Tübingen, Mohr, 1987.
Munz, Peter. *Phil Soc Sci* 21(1), 110-114 Mr 91

ALBIZU, Edgardo. *Estructuras formales de la dialéctica hegeliana*. Lima, Univ Nacional Federico Villarreal, 1984.
Zubiria, Martin. *Dialogos* 25(56), 200-202 Jl 90

ALEXANDER, J C and others (eds). *The Micro-Macro Link*. Berkeley, Univ of California Pr, 1987.
Agger, Ben. *Human Stud* 14(1), 81-98 Ja 91

ALEXANDER, Richard D. *The Biology of Moral Systems*. Hawthorne, Aldine de Gruyter, 1987.
Alcock, John. *Behavior Phil* 18(2), 89-96 Fall-Wint 90
Gupta, Mahesh. *Behavior Phil* 18(2), 97-99 Fall-Wint 90
Collier, John. *Can J Phil* 21(2), 195-210 Je 91
Irons, William. *Zygon* 26(2), 324-328 Je 91

ALEXEJEV, Sergei S. *Perestrojka und das Recht in der Sowjetunion: Fragen, Überlegungen, Prognosen*. Heidelberg, Müller Juristischer, 1988.
Incorvati, Giovanni. *Riv Int Filosof Diritto* 67(2), 320-322 Ap-Je 90

ALLEN, Jeffner and YOUNG, Iris Marion (eds). *The Thinking Muse: Feminism and Modern French Philosophy*. Bloomington, Indiana Univ Pr, 1989.
Brill, Susan. *Phil Lit* 14(2), 418-420 O 90
Soper, Kate. *J Brit Soc Phenomenol* 21(3), 305-308 O 90

ALLISON, Henry E. *Kant's Theory of Freedom*. New York, Cambridge Univ Pr, 1990.
Hudson, Hud. *Kantstudien* 82(2), 219-222 1991
O'Neill, Onora. *Mind* 100(399), 373-376 Jl 91

ALLISON, Henry E. *Kant's Transcendental Idealism: An Interpretation and Defense*. New Haven, Yale Univ Pr, 1986.
Hossenfelder, Malte. *Inquiry* 33(4), 467-479 D 90

ALMÁSI, Miklós. *The Philosophy of Appearances, András Vitányi (trans)*. Boston, Kluwer, 1989.
Butchvarov, Panayot. *Rev Metaph* 44(3), 613-614 Mr 91

ALSTON, William P. *Divine Nature and Human Language: Essays in Philosophical Theology*. Ithaca, Cornell Univ Pr, 1989.
Garthwaite, Gabrielle. *Relig Stud* 26(3), 433-435 S 90
Newman, Jay. *Can Phil Rev* 10(8), 301-303 Ag 90
Taylor, James E. *Phil Quart* 41(163), 249-251 Ap 91

ALSTON, William P. *Epistemic Justification: Essays in the Theory of Knowledge*. Ithaca, Cornell Univ Pr, 1989.
Taylor, James E. *Phil Quart* 41(163), 249-251 Ap 91

ALTER, Robert. *The Pleasures of Reading in an Ideological Age*. New York, Simon & Schuster, 1989.
Todd, D D. *Phil Lit* 14(2), 421-422 O 90

AMIN, Samir. *Eurocentrism*. New York, Monthly Review Pr, 1989.
Keita, Lansana. *Quest* 5(1), 104-113 Je 91

AMSELEK, Paul. *Science et déterminisme, éthique et liberté*. Paris, Pr Univ de France, 1988.
Bouquiaux, Laurence. *Rev Metaph Morale* 96(2), 261-268 Ap-Je 91

ANDREANI, Tony. *De la société à l'histoire*. Paris, Klincksieck, 1989.
Faes, Hubert. *Rev Phil Fr* 181(2), 258-259 Ap-Je 91

ANNAS, George J. *Judging Medicine*. Clifton, Humana Pr, 1988.
Kipnis, Kenneth. *Teach Phil* 13(2), 169-170 Je 90

ANNAS, Julia. *The Modes of Scepticism: Ancient Texts and Modern Interpretations*. Cambridge, Cambridge Univ Pr, 1985.
Olaso, Ezequiel de. *Nous* 25(1), 145-152 Mr 91

ANON. *Philosophie und Poesie: Otto Pöggeler zum 60, 2v*. Stuttgart, Frommann-Holzboog, 1988.
Druet, P-Philippe. *Int Phil Quart* 31(2), 247-248 Je 91

ANSALDO, Aurelio. *El Primer Principio del Obrar Moral y las Normas Especificas en el Pensamiento de G Grisez y J Finnis*. Vatican City, Pont U Lateranense, 1990.
May, William E. *Thomist* 55(2), 332-337 Ap 91

ANSCOMBE, G E M. *Collected Philosophical Papers, V1-3*. Oxford, Blackwell, 1981.
Brooks, David. *S Afr J Phil* 10(2), 55-59 My 91

AQUINAS, Thomas. *Somme théologique, 4v*. Paris, Cerf, 1986.
Bonino, Serge-Thomas. *Rev Theol Phil* 123(1), 93-97 1991

AQUINAS, Thomas. *Summa Theologiae: A Concise Translation, Timothy McDermott (ed)*. Westminster, Christian Classics, 1989.
Froelich, Gregory. *Thomist* 54(4), 727-730 O 90

AQVIST, Lennart. *Introduction to Deontic Logic and the Theory of Normative Systems*. Naples, Bibliopolis, 1987.
Tomberlin, James E. *Nous* 25(1), 109-116 Mr 91

ARANA CAÑEDO-ARGUELLES, J. *Apariencia y verdad*. Buenos Aires, Ed Carlos Lohle, 1990.
De Landázuri, Carlos O. *Anu Filosof* 24(1), 167-170 1991

ARDAL, Páll. *Passion and Value in Hume's Treatise (Second Edition)*. Edinburgh, Edinburgh Univ Pr, 1989.
Badía Cabrera, Miguel A. *Dialogos* 26(58), 171-180 Jl 91

ARENA, L V. *Comprensione e creatività: La filosofia di Whitehead*. Milan, Angeli, 1989.
Bosco, Nynfa. *Filosofia* 41(3), 444-446 S-D 90

ARISTOTLE and SMITH, Robin (trans). *Prior Analytics*. Indianapolis, Hackett, 1989.
Gasser, James. *Hist Phil Log* 12(2), 235-240 1991

ARMSTRONG, D M. *A Combinatorial Theory of Possibility*. New York, Cambridge Univ Pr, 1989.
Forbes, Graeme. *Phil Quart* 41(164), 350-352 Jl 91
Weissman, David. *Rev Metaph* 44(3), 614-617 Mr 91
Casey, Gerard. *Phil Stud (Ireland)* 32, 274-283 1988-90

ARMSTRONG, D M. *Universals: An Opinionated Introduction*. Boulder, Westview Pr, 1989.
Wolter, Allan B. *Rev Metaph* 44(4), 831-833 Je 91
Ellis, Brian. *Austl J Phil* 68(4), 462-463 D 90

ARMSTRONG, Nancy and TENNENHOUSE, Leonard (eds). *The Violence of Representation: Literature and the History of Violence*. London, Routledge, 1989.
Gullick, Mark. *Brit J Aes* 31(1), 87-89 Ja 91

ARNAULD, Antoine (trans). *True and False Ideas, New Objections to Descartes' "Meditations" and Descartes' Replies*. Lewiston, Mellen Pr, 1990.
Martinez, Roy. *Auslegung* 17(2), 171-174 Sum 91

ARON, Raymond. *Leçons sur l'histoire*. Paris, Ed Fallois, 1989.
Samama, Guy. *Rev Metaph Morale* 96(2), 279-284 Ap-Je 91

ARON, Raymond. *Memoirs: Fifty Years of Political Reflection*. New York, Holmes & Meier, undated.
Fink, Carole. *Hist Euro Ideas* 13(4), 490-492 1991

ARONSON, Ronald. *'Stay out of Politics'*. Chicago, Univ of Chicago Pr, 1990.
Glaser, Daryl. *Rad Phil* 58, 45-46 Sum 91

ARONSON, Ronald. *Sartre's Second Critique*. Chicago, Univ of Chicago Pr, 1987.
Anonymous. *Int Stud Phil* 22(3), 87-88 1990

ARRINGTON, Robert L. *Rationalism, Realism and Relativism*. Ithaca, Cornell Univ Pr, 1989.
Sayward, Charles. *Mind* 100(397), 137-139 Ja 91
Hughes, Gerard J. *Phil Books* 32(2), 114-116 Ap 91

ARTHUR, C J. *Dialectics of Labor: Marx and His Relation to Hegel*. New York, Blackwell, 1986.
Smith, Tony. *Owl Minerva* 22(1), 108-112 Fall 90

ASHBAUGH, Anne Freire. *Plato's Theory of Explanation: A Study of the Cosmological Account in the Timaeus*. Albany, SUNY Pr, 1988.
Burbidge, John. *Int Stud Phil* 22(3), 88-89 1990
Vernezze, Peter. *Ancient Phil* 10(2), 289-293 Fall 90
Mackenzie, Mary Margaret. *Phil Rev* 100(3), 517-519 Jl 91

ASHMORE, Robert. *Building a Moral System*. Englewood Cliffs, Prentice-Hall, 1987.
Moosa, Imtiaz. *Ideal Stud* 20(2), 178-179 My 90

ASSITER, Alison. *Pornography, Feminism and the Individual*. London, Pluto Pr, 1989.
Grimshaw, Jean. *Rad Phil* 56, 45-46 Autumn 90

ATLAS, Jay David. *Philosophy Without Ambiguity*. New York, Oxford Univ Pr, 1989.
Burton-Roberts, Noel. *Mind Lang* 6(2), 161-176 Sum 91

ATTFIELD, Robin. *A Theory of Value and Obligation*. New York, Methuen, 1987.
Brink, David O. *Phil Rev* 100(1), 140-148 Ja 91

ATTFIELD, Robin and DELL, Katharine (eds). *Values, Conflict and the Environment*. Oxford, Ian Ramsey Centre, 1989.
Walker, A D M. *J Applied Phil* 7(2), 236-238 O 90

AUDI, Robert. *Practical Reasoning*. New York, Routledge, 1989.
Vallentyne, Peter. *Mind* 100(397), 139-142 Ja 91
Day, Jane M. *Phil Books* 32(2), 96-98 Ap 91

AUGROS, R and STANCIU, G. *The New Biology: Discovering the Wisdom in Nature*. Boston, Shambhala, 1987.
Gallagher, David. *Rev Metaph* 44(2), 401-403 D 90

AUJOULAT, Noël. *Le néoplatonisme alexandrin Hiéroclès d'Alexandrie*. Leiden, Brill, 1986.
Schibli, H S. *Ancient Phil* 11(1), 210-223 Spr 91

AUSTIN, David. *What's the Meaning of 'This'?* Ithaca, Cornell Univ Pr, 1990.
Baldwin, Thomas. *Phil Quart* 41(162), 111-112 Ja 91

AUSTIN, David F (ed). *Philosophical Analysis: A Defense by Example*. Norwell, Kluwer, 1988.
Smith, Peter. *Can Phil Rev* 10(11), 437-439 N 90

AUSTIN, Norman. *Meaning and Being in Myth*. University Park, Pennsylvania State Univ Pr, 1990.
Wise, Christopher. *Phil Lit* 14(2), 436-438 O 90

AUSTIN, Scott. *Parmenides: Being, Bounds, and Logic*. New Haven, Yale Univ Pr, 1986.
Hussey, Edward. *Phil Rev* 99(4), 630-632 O 90

AVINERI, Shlomo. *Moses Hess: Prophet of Communism and Zionism*. New York, New York Univ Pr, 1985.
Jurist, Elliot L. *Owl Minerva* 22(1), 103-108 Fall 90

AVRAMIDES, Anita. *Meaning and Mind: An Examination of a Gricean Account of Language*. Cambridge, MIT Pr, 1989.
Elugardo, Reinaldo. *Can Phil Rev* 10(11), 439-441 N 90
Lycan, William G. *Mind Lang* 6(1), 83-86 Spr 91
Wieczorek, Malgorzata. *J Prag* 15(6), 599-606 Je 91. *What's the Meaning of "This"?* Ithaca, Cornell Univ Pr, 1990.
Devine, Philip E. *Rev Metaph* 44(1), 131-132 S 90

AYER, Alfred J. *Wittgenstein*. London, Weidenfeld & Nicolson, 1985.
Mies, Jürgen. *Erkenntnis* 33(2), 261-279 S 90

AZAR, Larry. *Twentieth Century in Crisis: Foundations of Totalitarianism*. Dubuque, Kendall/Hunt, 1990.
Ingardia, Richard. *Thomist* 55(1), 168-172 Ja 91

BACH, Kent. *Thought and Reference*. New York, Clarendon/Oxford Pr, 1987.
Kobes, Bernard W. *Phil Rev* 100(3), 469-471 Jl 91

BADIOU, Alain. *L'être et l'événement*. Paris, Seuil, 1988.
Gauthier, Yvon. *Dialogue (Canada)* 29(3), 471-473 1990
Allendesalazar, Mercedes. *El Basilisco* 1, 94-96 S-O 89

BAILIN, Sharon. *Achieving Extraordinary Ends*. Dordrecht, Nijhoff, 1988.
Hatcher, Donald. *Inform Log* 13(1), 53-60 Wint 91

BAIR, Deirdre. *Simone de Beauvoir: A Biography*. New York, Summit, 1990.
Henry, Patrick. *Phil Lit* 15(1), 178-180 Ap 91

BAIRD, Robert M and ROSENBAUM, Stuart E (eds). *Euthanasia: The Moral Issues*. Buffalo, Prometheus Books, 1989.
Meijburg, Herman H Van Der Kloot. *Bioethics* 5(2), 165-168 Ap 91

BAKER, G P and HACKER, P M S. *Language, Sense and Nonsense*. Oxford, Blackwell, 1984.
Kistner, Wietske. *S Afr J Phil* 9(4), 228-230 N 90

BAKER, Gordon. *Wittgenstein, Frege and the Vienna Circle*. Oxford, Blackwell, 1988.
Hylton, Peter. *J Sym Log* 55(3), 1319-1320 S 90

BAKER, Lynne Rudder. *Saving Belief: A Critique of Physicalism*. Princeton, Princeton Univ Pr, 1987.
Baker, Lynne Rudder. *Behavior Phil* 18(2), 67-68 Fall-Wint 90
Johnson, David M. *Behavior Phil* 18(2), 61-65 Fall-Wint 90
Dresser, Rebecca. *Crim Just Ethics* 10(1), 27-40 Wint-Spr 91

BAL, Mieke. *Death and Dissymmetry: The Politics of Coherence in the Book of Judges*. Chicago, Univ of Chicago Pr, 1988.
Oliver, Kelly. *Hypatia* 5(3), 169-171 Fall 90

BALABAN, Oded. *Subject and Consciousness: A Philosophical Inquiry into Self-Consciousness*. Savage, Rowman & Littlefield, 1990.
Kerby, Anthony. *Can Phil Rev* 10(10), 391-393 O 90

BALASUBRAMANYAN, R (ed & trans). *Naiskarmyasiddhi*. Madras, Madras Univ, undated.
Dravid, N S. *J Indian Counc Phil Res* 6(2), 184-186 Ja-Ap 89

BALDINI, M. *Epistemologia e padagogia dell'errore*. Brescia, La Scuola, 1987.
Rosetti, Livio. *Rev Latin De Filosof* 16(2), 244-246 Jl 90

BALDWIN, Thomas. *G E Moore*. London, Routledge, 1990.
Malcolm, Norman. *Phil Invest* 13(4), 357-366 O 90
White, Alan R. *Phil Books* 32(2), 90-91 Ap 91
Feldman, Fred. *Mind* 100(399), 376-379 Jl 91

BALL, Terence. *Transforming Political Discourse: Political Theory and Critical Conceptual History*. Oxford, Blackwell, 1988.
Herzog, Don. *Polit Theory* 19(1), 141-143 F 91

BALZER, W and HEIDELBERGER, M (eds). *Zur Logik empirischer Theorien*. Berlin, de Gruyter, 1983.
Mormann, Thomas. *Erkenntnis* 33(3), 411-419 N 90

BALZER, W and MOULINES, C U and SNEED, J D. *An Architectonic for Science: The Structuralist Program*. Boston, Reidel, 1987.
Rantala, Veikko. *Synthese* 86(2), 297-319 F 91
Stegmüller, Wolfgang. *Erkenntnis* 33(3), 399-410 N 90

BALZER, W and PEARCE, D A and SCHMIDT, H-J (eds). *Reduction in Science*. Dordrecht, Reidel, 1984.
Mormann, Thomas. *Erkenntnis* 33(3), 411-419 N 90

BALZER, Wolfgang (ed) and HAMMINGA, Bert (ed). *Philosophy of Economics*. Norwell, Kluwer, 1989.
Pitt, Joseph C. *Econ Phil* 7(1), 122-128 Ap 91

BANDMAN, Elsie L and BANDMAN, Bertram. *Critical Thinking in Nursing*. East Norwalk, Appleton & Lange, 1989.
Wright, Richard A. *Teach Phil* 13(2), 185-189 Je 90

BANNER, Michael C. *The Justification of Science and the Rationality of Religious Belief*. Oxford, Clarendon Pr, 1990.
Le Poidevin, Robin. *Phil Books* 32(2), 126-127 Ap 91

BANNET, Eve Tavor. *Structuralism and the Logic of Dissent*. Champaign, Univ of Illinois Pr, 1989.
Rapaport, Herman. *Phil Lit* 14(2), 442-444 O 90

BANU, Ion and PIATKOWSKI, Adelina. *Filosofia Greaca pina la Platon, 2v*. Bucharest, Editura stiintifica si Enciclopedica, 1984.
Banu, Ion and Piatkowski, Adelina. *Phil Inq* 10(1-2), 99-102 Wint-Spr 88

BARALE, Massimo. *Kant e il metodo della filosofia, I: Sentire e intendere*. Pisa, ETS, 1988.
Fabris, Adriano. *Teoria* 10(1), 188-191 1990

BARASH, Jeffrey A. *Martin Heidegger and the Problem of Historical Meaning*. Boston, Nijhoff, 1988.
Motzkin, Gabriel. *Rev Metaph Morale* 95(4), 561-563 O-D 90
Stack, George J. *Mod Sch* 67(4), 317-320 My 90

BARBER, Bernard. *The Logic and Limits of Trust*. New Brunswick, Rutgers Univ Pr, 1983.
Mills, David H. *Bus Prof Ethics J* 2(3), 77-78 Spr 83

BARBER, Michael D. *Social Typifications and the Elusive Other*. Cranbury, Bucknell Univ Pr, 1988.
Stohrer, Walter J. *Mod Sch* 68(3), 273-274 Mr 91

BARBOUR, Julian B. *Absolute or Relative Motion?, V1: The Discovery of Dynamics*. Cambridge, Cambridge Univ Pr, 1989.
Gaukroger, Stephen. *Phil Books* 31(4), 252-253 O 90

BARCO COLLAZOS, J L. *Platón: Teoría de las Ideas*. Malaga, Edinford, 1991.
Cruz Cruz, Juan. *Anu Filosof* 24(1), 170-172 1991

BARNARD, F M. *Self-Direction and Political Legitimacy: Rousseau and Herder*. New York, Oxford Univ Pr, 1988.
Riley, Patrick. *Polit Theory* 18(4), 693-698 N 90

BARNES, Annette. *On Interpretation*. New York, Blackwell, 1988.
Ross, Stephanie A. *Phil Rev* 100(3), 503-506 Jl 91

BARNES, Michael. *Religions in Conversation*. London, SPCK, 1989.
Chryssides, George. *Relig Stud* 26(2), 299-301 Je 90

BARRETT, Robert B and GIBSON, Roger F (eds). *Perspectives on Quine*. Oxford, Blackwell, 1990.
Heal, Jane. *Phil Books* 32(2), 102-104 Ap 91

BARRET-KRIEGEL, Blandine. *Les droits de l'homme et le droit naturel*. Paris, Pr Univ de France, 1989.
Kattan, Emmanuel. *Philosophiques* 17(2), 214-217 Autumn 1990

BARRY, Brian. *A Treatise on Social Justice: V1, Theories of Justice*. Berkeley, Univ of California Pr, 1989.
Hampton, Jean. *Polit Theory* 19(1), 112-115 F 91
Johnson, Nevil. *Philosophy* 65(253), 375-377 Jl 90

BARRY, Brian. *Democracy, Power, and Justice: Essays in Political Theory*. Oxford, Clarendon Pr, 1989.
Fullinwider, Robert K. *Phil Books* 32(2), 117-119 Ap 91

BARTH, E M and WICHE, R T P. *Problems, Functions and Semantic Roles*. Hawthorne, de Gruyter, 1986.
Bacon, John. *Iyyun* 40(3), 343-345 Jl 91
Sandri, Giorgio. *J Prag* 14(6), 945-956 D 90

BARTINE, David. *Early English Reading Theory: Origins of Current Debates*. Columbia, Univ of South Carolina Pr, 1989.
Griffin, Susan. *Phil Rhet* 24(1), 84-88 1991

BARTLEY III, William Warren. *Unfathomed Knowledge, Unmeasured Wealth*. La Salle, Open Court, 1990.
Flew, Antony. *Phil Books* 32(2), 98-100 Ap 91

BARUOH, Elaine H and D'ADAMO JR, Amadeo F and SEAGER, Joni (eds). *Embryos, Ethics, and Women's Rights: Exploring the New Reproductive Technologies*. New York, Haworth Pr, 1988.
Post, Stephen G. *J Med Human* 11(4), 200-201 Wint 90

BARWISE, Jon. *The Situation in Logic*. Stanford, CSLI, 1989.
Martin, John N. *Hist Phil Log* 12(1), 132-134 1990
Mott, Peter. *Phil Books* 31(4), 220-222 O 90

BARWISE, Jon and ETCHEMENDY, John. *The Liar*. New York, Oxford Univ Pr, 1987.
McGee, Vann. *Phil Rev* 100(3), 472-474 Jl 91
Cargile, James. *Nous* 24(5), 757-773 D 90

BASAVE FERNÁNDEZ DEL VALLE, Agustín. *Tratado de Metafísica: Teoría de la "habencia"*. Mexico, Limusa, 1982.
Forment Giralt, E. *Espiritu* 36(95), 100-102 Ja-Je 87

BASINGER, David. *Divine Power in Process Theism: A Philosophical Critique*. Albany, SUNY Pr, 1988.
Ford, Lewis S. *Faith Phil* 8(1), 124-127 Ja 91

BATTERSBY, Christine. *Gender and Genius: Towards a Feminist Aesthetics*. London, Women's Pr, 1989.
Taylor, Roger. *Brit J Aes* 31(1), 76-78 Ja 91
Easthope, Antony. *J Brit Soc Phenomenol* 21(3), 297-298 O 90
Mendus, Susan. *Philosophy* 65(254), 525-526 O 90

BATTIN, Margaret and others. *Puzzles about Art: An Aesthetics Casebook*. New York, St Martin's Pr, 1990.
Achtenberg, Deborah. *Rev Metaph* 44(4), 833-836 Je 91
Stewart, Marilyn G. *J Aes Educ* 25(2), 109-114 Sum 91

BAUMGOLD, Deborah. *Hobbes's Political Theory*. Cambridge, Cambridge Univ Pr, 1988.
Morgan, Michael L. *J Hist Phil* 28(4), 619-620 O 90

BAYER, Ronald. *Private Acts, Social Consequences*. New York, Macmillan, 1989.
Illingworth, Patricia. *Bioethics* 4(4), 340-350 O 90
Sullivan, William M. *Hastings Center Rep* 20(5), 45-46 S-O 90

BAYLES, Michael D. *Professional Ethics*. Belmont, Wadsworth, 1981.
Morris, Tim. *Bus Prof Ethics J* 2(3), 69-75 Spr 83

BAZERMAN, Charles. *Shaping Written Knowledge: The Genre and Activity of the Experimental Article in Science*. Madison, Univ Wisconsin Pr, 1988.
Overington, Michael A. *Phil Soc Sci* 21(3), 417-421 S 91
Fuller, Steve. *Sci Tech Human Values* 16(1), 122-125 Wint 91

BECHTEL, William (ed). *Integrating Scientific Disciplines*. Dordrecht, Nijhoff, 1986.
Recker, Doren. *Phil Sci* 57(3), 539-540 S 90

BECK, Lewis White. *Kant's Latin Writings: Translations, Commentaries and Notes*. New York, Lang, 1986.
Robinson, Hoke. *Ideal Stud* 20(2), 171-173 My 90

BECKER, Wolfgang. *Wahrheit und sprachliche Handlung*. Freiburg, Alber, 1988.
Sukale, Michael. *Phil Rundsch* 37(4), 271-277 1990

BEHLER, Ernst (ed). *The Philosophy of German Idealism*. New York, Continuum, 1989.
Wright, Walter. *Ideal Stud* 20(2), 173-174 My 90

BEISER, Frederick C. *The Fate of Reason: German Philosophy from Kant to Fichte*. Cambridge, Harvard Univ Pr, 1987.
Levine, Elliott M. *Hist Euro Ideas* 12(4), 543-544 1990

BELL, J M and MENDUS, Susan (eds). *Philosophy and Medical Welfare*. Cambridge, Cambridge Univ Pr, 1988.
Lesser, A H. *Phil Books* 31(4), 241-242 O 90

BELL, Linda A. *Sartre's Ethics of Ambiguity*. Tuscaloosa, Univ of Alabama Pr, 1989.
Perrett, Roy W. *Phil Lit* 14(2), 441-442 O 90

BELOFF, John. *The Relentless Question: Reflections on the Paranormal*. Jefferson, McFarland, 1990.
Gardner, Martin. *Free Inq* 11(1), 55-57 Wint 90-91

BENAKIS, L and others. *Lexicon of Presocratic Philosophy*. Athens, Research Center for Greek Philosophy, 1988.
Giannatsoulia, E. *Phil Inq* 12(1-2), 68-69 Wint-Spr 90

BENARDETE, José A. *Metaphysics: The Logical Approach*. New York, Oxford Univ Pr, 1989.
Bradshaw, D E. *Can Phil Rev* 10(12), 481-483 D 90
Carr, Brian. *Phil Books* 32(2), 104-105 Ap 91
Woods, John. *Hist Euro Ideas* 13(4), 461 1991

BENARDETE, Seth. *Socrates' Second Sailing: On Plato's Republic*. Chicago, Univ of Chicago Pr, 1989.
Halliwell, Stephen. *Ancient Phil* 11(1), 171-172 Spr 91
Corbett, S. *Can Phil Rev* 10(12), 483-486 D 90
Saxonhouse, Arlene W. *Polit Theory* 18(4), 690-693 N 90

BENHABIB, Seyla and CORNELL, Drucilla (eds). *Feminism as Critique: On the Politics of Gender*. Minneapolis, Univ of Minnesota Pr, 1987.
Metzger, Mary Janell. *Hypatia* 5(3), 118-124 Fall 90

BENITEZ, E E. *Forms in Plato's "Philebus"*. Assen, Van Gorcum, 1989.
Goldin, Owen. *Rev Metaph* 44(3), 617-618 Mr 91
Scolnicov, Samuel. *Can Phil Rev* 10(8), 303-305 Ag 90

BENJAMIN, Andrew (ed). *The Lyotard Reader*. Oxford, Blackwell, 1989.
Sonnet, Esther. *Brit J Aes* 31(2), 171-173 Ap 91

BENJAMIN, Andrew (ed). *The Problems of Modernity: Adorno and Benjamin*. New York, Routledge, 1989.
Newman, Michael. *Brit J Aes* 30(4), 390-392 O 90

BENJAMIN, Jessica. *The Bonds of Love*. New York, Pantheon, 1988.
Wallerstein, Beatrice. *Educ Stud* 21(2), 213-217 Sum 90

BENJAMIN, Martin. *Splitting the Difference: Compromise and Integrity in Ethics and Politics*. Lawrence, Univ Pr of Kansas, 1990.
Menlowe, Michael A. *Phil Books* 32(2), 119-121 Ap 91
Zwiebach, Burton. *Hastings Center Rep* 21(3), 36-37 My-Je 91

BENN, Stanley I. *A Theory of Freedom*. Cambridge, Cambridge Univ Pr, 1988.
D'Agostino, Fred. *Austl J Phil* 69(1), 103-105 Mr 91

BENTHAM, Jeremy. *A Fragment on Government, J H Burns and H L A Hart (eds)*. Cambridge, Cambridge Univ Pr, 1988.
Diamant, Alfred. *Hist Euro Ideas* 12(5), 692-694 1990

BENTHAM, Jeremy. *First Principles Preparatory to Constitutional Code, Philip Schofield (ed)*. Oxford, Clarendon Pr, 1989.
Diamant, Alfred. *Hist Euro Ideas* 12(5), 694-695 1990

BENVENUTO, Sergio. *Confini dell'interpretazione*. Castrovillari, Teda, 1988.
Polizzi, Gaspare. *Teoria* 10(1), 207-209 1990

BERGMANN, Peter. *Nietzsche: The Last Antipolitical German*. Bloomington, Indiana Univ Pr, 1987.
Dannhauser, Werner J. *Int Stud Phil* 22(2), 143-144 1990

BERMAN, David. *A History of Atheism in Britain*. New York, Croom Helm, 1988.
Akhtar, Shabbir. *Int Stud Phil* 23(1), 100-101 1991

BERNASCONI, Robert and WOOD, David (eds). *The Provocation of Levinas: Rethinking the Other*. New York, Routledge, 1988.
O'Connor, Tony. *J Brit Soc Phenomenol* 22(2), 107-108 My 91

BERNAUER, James and RASMUSSEN, David (eds). *The Final Foucault*. Cambridge, MIT Pr, 1989.
McWhorter, Ladelle. *Can Phil Rev* 10(9), 352-356 S 90

BERNSTEIN, John Andrew. *Nietzsche's Moral Philosophy*. Cranbury, Fairleigh Dickinson Univ Pr, 1987.
Joiner, E Earl. *Int J Phil Relig* 29(1), 55-56 F 91
Davey, Nicholas. *J Brit Soc Phenomenol* 21(3), 295-297 O 90

BEROFSKY, Bernard. *Freedom from Necessity: The Metaphysical Basis of Responsibility*. New York, Routledge & Kegan Paul, 1987.
Fischer, John Martin. *Phil Rev* 99(4), 649-653 O 90

BERTI, Enrico (ed). *Tradizione e attualità della filosofia pratica*. Genoa, Marietti, 1988.
Ratto, Marcello. *Teoria* 10(1), 214-216 1990

BERTI, Enrico. *Le ragioni di Aristotele*. Bari, Laterza, 1989.
Corradini, Antonella. *Riv Filosof Neo-Scolas* 81(4), 648-651 O-D 89

BERTOLINI, Piero. *L'esistere pedagogico*. Florence, Nuova Italia, 1988.
Priano, Giovanni B. *Riv Filosof Neo-Scolas* 82(1), 172-174 Ja-Mr 90

BEVIS, Em Olivia and WATSON, Jean. *Toward a Caring Curriculum: A New Pedagogy for Nursing*. New York, National League for Nursing, 1989.
Johnstone, Megan-Jane. *Bioethics* 5(1), 78-83 Ja 91

BEVIS, William W. *Mind of Winter: Wallace Stevens, Meditation, and Literature*. Pittsburgh, Univ of Pittsburgh Pr, 1988.
Wilson, Rob. *Phil East West* 41(2), 268-272 Ap 91

BEWELL, Alan. *Wordsworth and the Enlightenment: Nature, Man, and Society in the Experimental Poetry*. New Haven, Yale Univ Pr, 1989.
Siskin, Clifford. *Clio* 20(2), 202-205 Wint 91

BHUVANBHANUSURI, Acharya Vijay. *The Essentials of Bhagavan Mahāvīra's Philosophy Ganadharavāda*. Delhi, Motilal, 1989.
Pottampuzha, Paulose. *J Dharma* 15(3), 276-278 Jl-S 90

BIANCHI, Massimo Luigi. *Signatura rerum: Segni, magia e conoscenza da Paracelso a Leibniz*. Rome, Ateneo, 1987.
Findlen, Paula. *Stud Hist Phil Sci* 21(3), 511-518 S 90

BIARD, Joël. *Logique et théorie du signe au XIV siècle*. Paris, Vrin, 1989.
Counet, Jean-Michel. *Rev Phil Louvain* 88(79), 446-448 O 90

BIGELOW, John. *The Reality of Numbers: A Physicalist's Philosophy of Mathematics*. New York, Clarendon/Oxford Pr, 1988.
Jubien, Michael. *Nous* 25(4), 571-573 S 91
James, E P. *Phil Quart* 40(161), 531-533 O 90

BIRKE, Lynda and HIMMELWEIT, Susan and VINES, Gail. *Tomorrow's Child: Reproductive Technologies in the 90's*. London, Virago Pr, 1990.
Charlesworth, Max. *Bioethics* 4(4), 359-362 O 90

BISHOP, Anne H and SCUDDER JR, John R. *The Practical, Moral, and Personal Sense of Nursing: A Phenomenological Philosophy of Practice*. Albany, SUNY Pr, 1990.
Chambliss, Daniel F. *Med Human Rev* 5(1), 72-74 Ja 91

BITTNER, Rüdiger. *What Reason Demands, Theodore Talbot (trans)*. Cambridge, Cambridge Univ Pr, 1989.
Lachterman, David R. *Rev Metaph* 44(2), 403-406 D 90
Hill Jr, Thomas E. *J Phil* 88(9), 497-501 S 91

BJORK, Daniel W. *William James: The Center of His Vision*. New York, Columbia Univ Pr, 1988.
Coon, Deborah J. *Biol Phil* 5(4), 493-501 O 90

BLACK, Max. *Perplexities: Rational Choice, The Prisoner's Dilemma, Metaphor, Poetic Ambiguity, and Other Puzzles*. Ithaca, Cornell Univ Pr, 1990.
Ring, Merrill. *Can Phil Rev* 10(11), 442-443 N 90

BLAIS, Martin. *L'autre Thomas d'Aquin*. Montreal, Boréal, 1990.
Simpson, Diane. *Can Phil Rev* 10(11), 443-446 N 90

BLAKEMORE, Colin and GREENFIELD, Susan (eds). *Mindwaves*. Oxford, Blackwell, 1987.
Shanker, S G. *Human Stud* 13(4), 417-425 O 90

BLASI, Anthony J. *Moral Conflict and Christian Religion*. New York, Lang, 1988.
Williams, John R. *Heythrop J* 32(2), 278-279 Ap 91

BLOCH, Ernst. *Natural Law and Human Dignity, Dennis J Schmidt (trans)*. Cambridge, MIT Pr, 1986.
Gueguen, John A. *Vera Lex* 10(2), 17-18 1990

BLOCH, Ernst. *Thomas Müntzer als Theologe der Revolution*. Leipzig, Reclam, 1989.
Caysa, Petra. *Deut Z Phil* 38(9), 893-894 1990

BLOCH, O and BALAN, B and CARRIVE, P (eds). *Entre forme et histoire*. Paris, Méridiens-Klincksieck, 1988.
Lambert, Jacques. *Rev Phil Fr* 180(3), 575-578 Jl-S 90

BLUESTONE, Natalie Harris. *Women and the Ideal Society: Plato's "Republic" and Modern Myths of Gender*. Amherst, Univ of Massachusetts Pr, 1987.
Blundell, Mary Whitlock. *Ancient Phil* 10(2), 293-299 Fall 90

BLUM, Lawrence A and SEIDLER, Victor J. *A Truer Liberty: Simone Weil and Marxism*. New York, Routledge Chapman & Hall, 1989.
Allen, Diogenes. *Teach Phil* 13(3), 310-314 S 90

BLUNDELL, Mary Whitlock. *Helping Friends and Harming Enemies: A Study in Sophocles and Greek Ethics*. Cambridge, Cambridge Univ Pr, 1989.
Garvie, A F. *Hist Euro Ideas* 13(3), 299-300 1991

BODEN, Margaret A. *The Philosophy of Artificial Intelligence*. New York, Oxford Univ Pr, 1990.
Ravenscroft, Ian. *Austl J Phil* 69(2), 224-225 Je 91

BOEDER, H. *Das Vernunftgefüge der Moderne*. Munich, Alber, 1988.
Zubiría, Martín. *Dialogo Filosof* 7(1), 117-119 Ja-Ap 91

BOENKE, Michaela. *Transformation des Realitätsbegriffs*. Stuttgart, Frommann-Holzboog, 1990.
Braun, Hermann. *Phil Rundsch* 37(4), 298-326 1990

BOGDAN, Radu J (ed). *Jaakko Hintikka*. Dordrecht, Reidel, 1987.
Brkic, Slavko. *Filozof Istraz* 34(1), 285-288 1990

BOHING, Thomas. *Die Entfesselung des Intellekts*. New York, Lang, 1989.
Kossler, Matthias. *Schopenhauer Jahr* 71, 227-230 1990

BOISVERT, Raymond D. *Dewey's Metaphysics*. New York, Fordham Univ Pr, 1988.
Rosenthal, Sandra B. *J Hist Phil* 29(1), 147-149 Ja 91
Kulp, Christopher B. *Mod Sch* 68(3), 271-273 Mr 91

BOLAND, Lawrence A. *The Methodology of Economic Model Building*. New York, Routledge, 1989.
Griffith, William B. *Econ Phil* 7(1), 119-122 Ap 91

BONJOUR, Laurence. *The Structure of Empirical Knowledge*. Cambridge, Harvard Univ Pr, 1985.
Barthelemy, William. *Dialogue (Canada)* 29(2), 311-314 1990

BOOLOS, G S and JEFFREY, R C. *Computability and Logic*. Cambridge, Cambridge Univ Pr, 1990.
Kelly, John. *Phil Stud (Ireland)* 32, 295-296 1988-90
Hazen, A P. *Austl J Phil* 68(3), 347 S 90

BOOTH, Wayne C. *The Company We Keep: An Ethics of Fiction*. Berkeley, Univ of California Pr, 1988.
Kneupper, Charles W. *Phil Rhet* 23(3), 247-248 1990
Davenport, Edward. *Phil Soc Sci* 21(3), 401-406 S 91

BORCH-JAKOBSON, M. *Le sujet freudien*. Paris, Aubier/Flammarion, 1982.
Van Haute, Philippe. *Tijdschr Filosof* 52(3), 521-534 S 90

BORDO, Susan. *The Flight to Objectivity: Essays on Cartesianism and Culture*. Albany, SUNY Pr, 1987.
Watson, Richard A. *J Hist Phil* 29(1), 127-129 Ja 91

BORELLA, Jean. *Le mystre du signe*. Washington, Maisonneuve Pr, 1989.
Adam, Michel. *Rev Phil Fr* 181(3), 337-340 Jl-S 91

BORUAH, Bijoy H. *Fiction and Emotion: A Study in Aesthetics and the Philosophy of Mind*. Oxford, Oxford Univ Pr, 1988.
Pradhan, R C. *J Indian Counc Phil Res* 7(3), 155-158 My-Ag 90

BOS, A P. *Cosmic and Meta-Cosmic Theology in Aristotle's Lost Dialogues*. Leiden, Brill, 1989.
Wolters, A M. *Phil Reform* 55(2), 198-202 1990

BOUCHER, David. *The Social and Political Thought of R G Collingwood*. Cambridge, Cambridge Univ Pr, 1989.
Franco, Paul. *Polit Theory* 19(1), 133-137 F 91
Wilde, Lawrence. *Rad Phil* 57, 43-44 Spr 91
McFee, Graham. *Phil Books* 32(2), 94-96 Ap 91
Bellamy, Richard. *Hist Euro Ideas* 13(4), 469-470 1991

BOUCHER, David (ed). *Essays in Political Philosophy: R G Collingwood*. Oxford, Clarendon Pr, 1989.
Johnson, Peter. *Hist Polit Thought* 11(2), 355-356 Sum 90

BOULAD-AYOUB, Josiane. *Contre nous de la tyrannie: Des relations idéologiques entre Lumières et Révolutions*. Montréal, Hurtubise, 1990.
Knee, Philip. *Philosophiques* 17(2), 209-212 Autumn 1990

BOUTOT, Alain. *Heidegger*. Paris, Pr Univ de France, 1989.
Piché, Claude. *Philosophiques* 17(2), 225-227 Autumn 1990

BOUTROUX, Émile. *Leçons sur Platon*. Paris, Pr Univ de France, 1990.
Follon, Jacques. *Rev Phil Louvain* 89(82), 333-337 My 91

BOUVERESSE, Jacques. *Le pays des possibles*. Paris, Ed Minuit, 1988.
Largeault, J. *Rev Phil Fr* 181(2), 237-239 Ap-Je 91

BOWIE, Andrew. *Aesthetics and Subjectivity: From Kant to Nietzsche*. Manchester, Manchester Univ Pr, 1990.
Eagleton, Terry. *Rad Phil* 57, 37-38 Spr 91

BOWLER, Peter. *The Non-Darwinian Revolution: Reinterpreting a Historical Myth*. Baltimore, Johns Hopkins Univ Pr, 1988.
Martínez, Sergio. *Critica* 22(66), 131-135 D 90

BOYDSTON, JoAnn (ed). *The Later Works of John Dewey, 1925-1953, V10: 1934, "Art as Experience"*. Carbondale, Southern Illinois Univ Pr, 1987.
Zedler, Beatrice H. *Mod Sch* 67(3), 237-238 Mr 90

BOYDSTON, Jo Ann (ed). *The Later Works of John Dewey, 1925-1953, V15: 1942-1948*. Carbondale, Southern Illinois Univ Pr, 1989.
Kulp, Christopher B. *Trans Peirce Soc* 27(2), 250-256 Spr 91

BOYDSTON, Jo Ann (ed). *The Later Works of John Dewey, 1925-1953, V16: 1949-1952*. Carbondale, Southern Illinois Univ Pr, 1989.
Kulp, Christopher B. *Trans Peirce Soc* 27(2), 250-256 Spr 91

BOYER, Robert S and MOORE, J Strother. *A Computational Logic Handbook*. New York, Academic Pr, 1988.
Miller, Dale. *J Sym Log* 55(3), 1302-1304 S 90
Miller, Dale. *J Sym Log* 55(3), 1302-1304 S 90

BOYNE, Roy. *Foucault and Derrida: The Other Side of Reason*. London, Unwin Hyman, 1990.
Racevskis, Karlis. *Rad Phil* 57, 50-52 Spr 91

BRAATZ, Kurt. *Friedrich Nietzsche: Eine Studie zur Theorie der Offenlichen Meinung*. Berlin, de Gruyter, 1988.
Baker, Lang. *Phil Soc Sci* 21(1), 90-101 Mr 91

BRABECK, Mary (ed). *Who Cares?: Theory, Research, and Educational Implications of the Ethic of Care*. New York, Praeger, 1989.
Stone, Lynda. *Educ Stud* 21(4), 483-488 Wint 90

BRADFORD, George. *How Deep is Deep Ecology? With an Essay-Review on Woman's Freedom*. Ojai, Times Change Pr, 1989.
Watson, Richard A. *Environ Ethics* 12(4), 371-374 Wint 90

BRADFORD, George. *Return of the Son of Deep Ecology: The Ethics of Permanent Crisis and the Permanent Crisis in Ethics*. Place unknown, Fifth Estate, 1989.
Watson, Richard A. *Environ Ethics* 12(4), 371-374 Wint 90

BRAINE, David and LESSER, Harry (eds). *Ethics, Technology and Medicine*. Brookfield, Gower, 1988.
Vergum, Vangie. *Can Phil Rev* 10(10), 394-396 O 90

BRAITHWAITE, John and PETTIT, Philip. *Not Just Deserts*. Oxford, Clarendon Pr, 1990.
Noordhof, Paul. *J Applied Phil* 8(1), 127-129 1991
Lacey, Nicola. *Phil Quart* 41(164), 374-376 Jl 91
Stalley, R F. *Mind* 100(399), 379-381 Jl 91
Ten, C L. *Austl J Phil* 69(2), 225-227 Je 91

BRAKAS, George. *Aristotle's Concept of the Universal*. New York, Olms, 1988.
Preus, Anthony. *Int Stud Phil* 23(1), 101-103 1991

BRATMAN, M E. *Intention, Plans, and Practical Reason*. Cambridge, Harvard Univ Pr, 1987.
McCann, Hugh J. *Nous* 25(2), 230-233 Ap 91
Mohan, William J. *Int Stud Phil* 22(3), 89-90 1990
Velleman, J David. *Phil Rev* 100(2), 277-284 Ap 91

BREAZEALE, Daniel (ed & trans). *Fichte: Early Philosophical Writings*. Ithaca, Cornell Univ Pr, 1988.
Westphal, Merold. *Int Phil Quart* 31(1), 109-110 Mr 91

BRENKMAN, John. *Culture and Domination*. Ithaca, Cornell Univ Pr, 1987.
Murphy, John W. *Stud Soviet Tho* 41(1), 63-65 Ja 91

BRENNAN, Andrew. *Thinking about Nature: An Investigation of Nature, Value and Ecology*. New York, Routledge, 1988.
Sprigge, T L S. *Inquiry* 34(1), 107-128 Mr 91
Howarth, Jane M. *Phil Quart* 41(162), 94-97 Ja 91

BRENNAN, Andrew. *Conditions of Identity*. New York, Oxford Univ Pr, 1988.
Schlesinger, George N. *Nous* 25(4), 569-571 S 91

BRENNER, William H. *The Elements of Modern Philosophy: Descartes through Kant*. Englewood Cliffs, Prentice Hall, 1989.
Tlumak, Jeffrey. *Teach Phil* 13(3), 281-284 S 90

BRENTANO, Franz. *El Origen del Conocimiento Moral*. Madrid, RSEMAP, 1989.
Palacios, Juan Miguel. *Rev Filosof (Spain)* 4, 239-245 1990

BRICKHOUSE, Thomas C and SMITH, Nicholas D. *Socrates on Trial*. Princeton, Princeton Univ Pr, 1989.
McPherran, Mark. *Ancient Phil* 11(1), 161-169 Spr 91
Morgan, Michael L. *J Hist Phil* 29(2), 297-299 Ap 91

BRIGHT, Barry P (ed). *Theory and Practice in the Study of Adult Education—the Epistemological Debate*. London, Routledge, 1989.
Standish, Paul. *J Phil Educ* 24(2), 295-299 Wint 90

BRINK, David O. *Moral Realism and the Foundation of Ethics*. New York, Cambridge Univ Pr, 1989.
Fike Jr, Lawrence Udell. *Int Phil Quart* 31(3), 377-379 S 91

BRISSON, Luc (trans). *Platon: Phèdre*. Paris, Flammarion, 1989.
Griswold Jr, Charles L. *J Hist Phil* 29(3), 481-483 Jl 91

BRITO, Emilio. *La création selon Schelling*. Louvain, Peeters, 1987.
L130onard, André. *Rev Phil Louvain* 88(80), 616-618 N 90

BROADIE, Alexander. *Introduction to Medieval Logic*. New York, Oxford Univ Pr, 1987.
Longeway, John. *Int Stud Phil* 22(3), 90-91 1990
Kretzmann, Norman. *J Sym Log* 55(3), 1320-1322 S 90

BROADIE, Alexander. *The Tradition of Scottish Philosophy*. Edinburgh, Polygon, 1990.
MacIntyre, Alasdair. *Phil Quart* 41(163), 258-260 Ap 91

BRODSKY, Claudia J. *The Imposition of Form*. Princeton, Princeton Univ Pr, 1987.
Cebik, L B. *Int Stud Phil* 22(3), 91-92 1990

BRODY, Baruch A (ed). *Suicide and Euthanasia: Historical and Contemporary Themes*. Dordrecht, Kluwer, 1989.
Esser, P H. *Method Sci* 22(4), 243-244 1989
Mitchell, Ben. *J Med Human* 11(3), 147-149 Fall 90

BRODY, Howard. *Stories of Sickness*. New Haven, Yale Univ Pr, 1987.
Marshall, Patricia A. *Theor Med* 11(4), 347-349 D 90

BROUDY, Harry S. *The Uses of Schooling*. New York, Routledge, Chapman & Hall, 1989.
Tozer, Steven. *J Aes Educ* 24(3), 122-126 Fall 90

BROWN, Barry F. *Accidental Being: A Study in the Metaphysics of St Thomas Aquinas*. Lanham, Univ Pr of America, 1985.
Ewbank, Michael B. *Rev Metaph* 44(2), 406-409 D 90

BROWN, Geoffrey. *The Information Game: Ethical Issues in a Microchip World*. Atlantic Highlands, Humanities Pr, 1989.
Williams, Mary B. *Can Phil Rev* 10(8), 306-308 Ag 90
Belsey, Andrew. *J Applied Phil* 8(1), 132-133 1991
Kallman, Ernest A. *Bus Ethics Quart* 1(3), 319-331 Jl 91

BROWN, Harold. *Observation and Objectivity*. New York, Oxford Univ Pr, 1987.
Moser, Paul K. *Brit J Phil Sci* 39(4), 551-561 D 88
Fetzer, James H. *Nous* 25(2), 248-250 Ap 91

BROWN, Harold I. *Rationality: The Problems of Philosophy: Their Past and Present*. London, Routledge, 1988.
McKerrow, Raymie E. *Phil Rhet* 23(4), 316-320 1990

BROWN, Harvey R.(ed) and HARRÉ, Rom. *Philosophical Foundations of Quantum Field Theory*. Oxford, Clarendon Pr, 1988.
Hooker, C A. *Phil Sci* 58(2), 324-329 Je 91
Falkenburg, Brigitte. *Nous* 25(4), 580-583 S 91

BROWN, James Robert. *The Rational and the Social*. London, Routledge, 1989.
Nola, Robert. *Austl J Phil* 68(3), 347-349 S 90

BROWN, Robert (ed). *Classical Political Theories: From Plato to Marx*. New York, Macmillan, 1990.
Principe, Michael A. *Teach Phil* 13(3), 290-292 S 90

BROWN, Robert. *Analyzing Love*. New York, Cambridge Univ Pr, 1987.
Wertheimer, Roger. *Phil Phenomenol Res* 51(1), 244-245 Mr 91

BROWN, Wendy. *Manhood and Politics*. Totowa, Rowman & Littlefield, 1988.
Paris, Sherri. *Hypatia* 5(3), 175-180 Fall 90

BRÜHLMEIER, Daniel. *Die Rechts- und Staatslehre von Adam Smith und die Interessentheorie der Verfassung*. Berlin, Duncker & Humblot, 1988.
Wolf, Jean-Claude. *Frei Z Phil Theol* 37(3), 539-541 1990

BRUNDELL, Barry. *Pierre Gassendi: From Aristotelianism to a New Natural Philosophy*. Dordrecht, Reidel, 1987.
Watson, Richard A. *Int Stud Phil* 22(3), 92-93 1990

BRUNS, Gerald L. *Heidegger's Estrangements*. New Haven, Yale Univ Pr, 1989.
Findler, Richard. *Res Phenomenol* 20, 200-206 1990

BRUNS, Gerald L. *Heidegger's Language, Truth and Poetry: Estrangements in the Later Writings*. New Haven, Yale Univ Pr, 1989.
Rockmore, Tom. *Rev Metaph* 44(1), 132-134 S 90

BRYKCZYNSKA, Gosia M (ed). *Ethics in Paediatric Nursing*. London, Chapman & Hall, 1989.
Fitzpatrick, F J. *Ethics Med* 7(1), 15 Spr 91

BRYNE, Peter. *Natural Religion and the Nature of Religion*. New York, Routledge, 1989.
Baccari, Luciano. *Aquinas* 34(1), 181-184 Ja-Ap 91

BRYSON, Norman. *Looking at the Overlooked: Four Essays on Still Life Painting*. London, Reaktion Books, 1990.
Harris, Jonathan. *Brit J Aes* 31(2), 185-187 Ap 91

BUCHANAN, Allen E and BROCK, Dan W. *Deciding for Others: The Ethics of Surrogate Decision Making*. New York, Cambridge Univ Pr, 1990.
Cohen, Cynthia B. *Hastings Center Rep* 21(1), 41-43 Ja-F 91
Dworkin, Gerald. *Phil Quart* 41(162), 118-119 Ja 91

BUCHANAN, Allen. *Ethics, Efficiency and the Market*. Totowa, Rowman & Allanheld, 1985.
Schweickart, David. *Phil Rev* 100(3), 501-503 Jl 91

BUCHANAN, James H. *Patient Encounters: The Experience of Disease*. Charlottesville, Univ Pr of Virginia, 1989.
Matthews, Dale A. *Hastings Center Rep* 20(6), 40-42 N-D 90

BUCK-MORSS, Susan. *The Dialectics of Seeing: Walter Benjamin and the Arcades Project*. Cambridge, MIT Pr, 1989.
Tobin, Robert. *Phil Lit* 15(1), 149-150 Ap 91

BUCKLEY, K W. *Mechanical Man: John Broadus Watson and the Beginning of Behaviorism*. New York, Guilford Pr, 1989.
Morris, Edward K. *Phil Psych* 4(2), 294-297 1991

BUHR, Manfred. *Eingriffe, Stellungnahmen, Äusserungen*. Berlin, Akademie, 1987.
Wurzer, Wilhelm S. *Stud Soviet Tho* 40(1-3), 345-349 1990

BÜHLER, P (ed). *La narration: Quand le récit devient communication*. Cambridge, Labor et Fides, 1988.
Combet-Galland, Corina. *Rev Theol Phil* 123(2), 213-220 1991

BURCH BROWN, Frank. *Transfiguration: Poetic Metaphor and the Language of Religious Belief*. Chapel Hill, Univ of North Carolina Pr, 1983.
Hart, Richard E. *Process Stud* 19(1), 49-51 Spr 90

BURCH BROWN, Frank. *Religious Aesthetics: A Theological Study of Making and Meaning*. London, Macmillan, 1990.
McAdoo, Nick. *Brit J Aes* 31(2), 176-177 Ap 91
Hepburn, Ronald. *Phil Books* 31(4), 249-250 O 90

BURKHARDT, A (ed). *Speech Acts, Meaning and Intentions: Critical Approaches to the Philosophy of John R Searle*. Hawthorne, de Gruyter, 1990.
de Landázuri, Carlos O. *Anu Filosof* 24(1), 172-173 1991
Moriconi, Enrico. *Aquinas* 34(1), 139-142 Ja-Ap 91

BURNS, J H (ed). *The Cambridge History of Medieval Political Thought, c 350—c 1450*. Cambridge, Cambridge Univ Pr, 1988.
Haren, Michael. *Phil Stud (Ireland)* 32, 283-291 1988-90

BURUIANA, Michel (ed). *Avortement Oui/Non*. Québec, Humanitas, 1988.
Saint-Arnaud, Jocelyne. *Philosophiques* 17(2), 229-232 Autumn 1990

BURTON-ROBERTS, Noel. *The Limits to Debate*. New York, Cambridge Univ Pr, 1989.
Atlas, Jay David. *Mind Lang* 6(2), 177-192 Sum 91

BUSCH, Thomas W. *The Power of Consciousness and the Force of Circumstances in Sartre's Philosophy*. Bloomington, Indiana Univ Pr, 1990.
Alexakos, Panos D. *Thought* 66(260), 98-99 Mr 91

BUTLER, Judith. *Subjects of Desire: Hegelian Reflections in Twentieth-Century France*. New York, Columbia Univ Pr, 1987.
Aboulafia, Mitchell. *Int Stud Phil* 22(3), 93-94 1990
Mingo, Steven Reynolds. *Clio* 19(4), 389-393 Sum 90
Sills, Chip. *Owl Minerva* 22(1), 98-103 Fall 90

BUTLER, Judith. *Gender Trouble: Feminism and the Subversion of Identity*. New York, Routledge, 1990.
Card, Claudia. *Can Phil Rev* 10(9), 356-359 S 90
Nash, Margaret. *Hypatia* 5(3), 171-175 Fall 90

BYRNE, Peter (ed). *Health Rights and Resources: King's College Studies, 1987-8*. Oxford, Oxford Univ Pr, 1988.
Williams, John R. *Heythrop J* 32(2), 272-274 Ap 91

BYRNE, Peter (ed). *Medicine, Medical Ethics and the Value of Life*. Chichester, Wiley, 1990.
Kleinig, John. *Bioethics* 5(2), 158-160 Ap 91

CAHM, Caroline. *Kropotkin and the Rise of Revolutionary Anarchism, 1872-1886*. Cambridge, Cambridge Univ Pr, 1989.
Offord, Derek. *Hist Polit Thought* 11(2), 364-366 Sum 90

CAHN, Steven M. *Philosophical Explorations: Freedom, God, and Goodness*. Buffalo, Prometheus, 1989.
Yezzi, Ron. *Teach Phil* 13(2), 165-167 Je 90

CAILLÈ, Alain. *Mitologia delle scienze sociali: Braudel, Lévi-Strauss, Bourdieu, A Salsano (trans)*. Turin, Bollati Boringhieri, 1988.
Amato, Salvatore. *Riv Int Filosof Diritto* 66(4), 738-740 O-D 89

CALLAHAN, Daniel. *What Kind of Life: The Limits of Medical Progress*. New York, Simon & Schuster, 1990.
Churchill, Larry R. *Med Human Rev* 5(1), 35-38 Ja 91

CALLAN, Eamonn. *Autonomy and Schooling*. Montreal, McGill-Queen's Univ Pr, 1988.
Dearden, R F. *J Phil Educ* 24(1), 127-131 Sum 90

CALLINICOS, Alex. *Against Postmodernism*. Oxford, Polity Pr, 1990.
Lecercle, Jean-Jacques. *Rad Phil* 57, 47-48 Spr 91

CALLINICOS, Alex. *Making History: Agency, Structure and Change in Social Theory*. Cambridge, Polity Pr, 1987.
Rigby, S H. *Hist Euro Ideas* 12(6), 827-831 1990
Loone, Eero. *Hist Theor* 29(3), 331-339 O 90

CALLICOTT, J Baird. *In Defense of the Land Ethic: Essays in Environmental Philosophy*. Albany, SUNY Pr, 1989.
Bender, Frederic L. *Phil East West* 41(3), 437-441 Jl 91
Norton, Bryan G. *Environ Ethics* 13(2), 181-186 Sum 91

CAMPBELL, Keith. *Abstract Particulars*. Oxford, Blackwell, 1990.
Hale, Bob. *Mind* 100(397), 142-146 Ja 91
Lowe, E J. *Phil Quart* 41(162), 104-106 Ja 91
Forrest, Peter. *Austl J Phil* 69(1), 105-108 Mr 91

CAMENISCH, Paul. *Grounding Professional Ethics in a Pluralistic Society*. New York, Haven, 1983.
Frankel, Mark S. *Bus Prof Ethics J* 2(4), 105-111 Sum 83

CAMERON, Averil (ed). *History as Text: The Writing of Ancient History*. Chapel Hill, Univ N Carolina Pr, 1990.
Konstan, David. *Clio* 20(3), 291-294 Spr 91

CANGUILHEM, Georges and FAWCETT, Carolyn R (trans). *The Normal and the Pathological*. Cambridge, Zone Books, 1989.
Nicolson, Malcolm. *Stud Hist Phil Sci* 22(2), 347-369 Je 91

CAPALDI, Nicholas. *Hume's Place in Moral Philosophy*. New York, Lang, 1989.
Danford, John W. *Rev Metaph* 44(2), 409-411 D 90

CAPRIOLI, Adriano and VACCARO, Luciano (eds). *Agostino e la conversione cristiana*. Palermo, Augustinus, 1987.
Brinkman, B R. *Heythrop J* 32(2), 294-297 Ap 91

CAPRIOLI, Adriano and VACCARO, Luciano (eds). *Diritto, morale e consenso sociale*. Brescia, Morcelliana, 1989.
Tusa, Carlo. *Riv Int Filosof Diritto* 67(2), 328-330 Ap-Je 90

CAPUTO, John D. *Radical Hermeneutics: Repetition, Deconstruction, and the Hermeneutic Project*. Bloomington, Indiana Univ Pr, 1987.
Walsh, Sylvia. *Int J Phil Relig* 29(2), 113-122 Ap 91
Kisiel, Theodore. *Mod Sch* 67(3), 223-228 Mr 90
Risser, James. *Res Phenomenol* 20, 194-200 1990

CARABELLI, Anna. *On Keyne's Method*. New York, Macmillan, 1988.
Dow, Sheila C. *Econ Phil* 7(1), 132-139 Ap 91

CARANFA, Angelo. *Claudel: Beauty and Grace*. Lewisburg, Bucknell Univ Pr, 1989.
Stern-Gillet, Suzanne. *Brit J Aes* 31(1), 93-95 Ja 91

CARCHIA, Gianni. *Retorica del sublime*. Bari, Laterza, 1988.
Montori, Marco. *Filosofia* 41(3), 454-458 S-D 90

CARDONA, Carlos. *Etica del quehacer educativo*. Madrid, Rialp, 1990.
Aguado, Javier Fernández. *Anu Filosof* 24(1), 173-175 1991

CARE, Norman S. *On Sharing Fate*. Philadelphia, Temple Univ Pr, 1987.
Jenni, Kathie. *Nous* 24(5), 797-803 D 90

CARNOIS, Bernard. *The Coherence of Kant's Doctrine of Freedom, David Booth (trans)*. Chicago, Univ of Chicago Pr, 1987.
Sullivan, Roger J. *Int J Phil Relig* 28(2), 123 O 90

CARROLL, Noel. *Philosophical Problems of Classical Film Theory*. Princeton, Princeton Univ Pr, 1988.
Lauder, Robert E. *Thomist* 55(3), 535-538 Jl 91
Wilson, George M. *Phil Rev* 100(3), 506-510 Jl 91
Neill, Alex and Ridley, Aaron. *Can Phil Rev* 10(9), 345-351 S 90

CARROLL, Noel. *The Philosophy of Horror*. New York, Routledge, 1990.
Kitchen, Gary. *Rad Phil* 58, 44 Sum 91
Matravers, Derek. *Brit J Aes* 31(2), 174-176 Ap 91

CARROLL, Noël. *Mystifying Movies: Fads and Fallacies in Contemporary Film Theory*. New York, Columbia Univ Pr, 1988.
Devereaux, Mary. *Phil Lit* 15(1), 139-140 Ap 91
Linden, George W. *J Aes Educ* 24(3), 117-118 Fall 90
Neill, Alex and Ridley, Aaron. *Can Phil Rev* 10(9), 345-351 S 90

CARRUTHERS, P. *Tractarian Semantics: Finding Sense in Wittgenstein's Tractatus*. Oxford, Blackwell, 1989.
Coates, Paul. *Phil Books* 31(4), 211-213 O 90

CARRUTHERS, Peter. *The Metaphysics of the "Tractatus"*. Cambridge, Cambridge Univ Pr, 1990.
Moore, A W. *Philosophy* 66(255), 125-128 Ja 91
O'Grady, Paul. *Phil Stud (Ireland)* 32, 297-299 1988-90
Child, William. *Phil Quart* 41(164), 354-358 Jl 91

CARRUTHERS, Peter. *Tractarian Semantics*. Cambridge, Blackwell, 1989.
Child, William. *Phil Quart* 41(164), 354-358 Jl 91

CARTWRIGHT, Nancy. *Nature's Capacities and Their Measurement*. Oxford, Clarendon Pr, 1989.
Hoover, Kevin D. *Econ Phil* 6(2), 309-315 O 90

CARTWRIGHT, Richard. *Philosophical Essays*. Cambridge, MIT Pr, 1987.
McMichael, Alan. *Phil Rev* 100(2), 310-312 Ap 91

CASADO VELARDE, Manuel. *Lenguaje y Cultura*. Madrid, Ed Sintesis, 1988.
Nubiola, Jaime. *Anu Filosof* 24(1), 175-177 1991

CASAUBON, Juan Alfredo. *Palabras, ideas, cosas*. Buenos Aires, Ed Candil, 1984.
Sacchi, Mario Enrique. *Sapientia* 46(179), 79-80 Ja-Mr 91

CASEY, John. *Pagan Virtue: An Essay in Ethics*. Oxford, Clarendon Pr, 1990.
Walker, A D M. *Phil Quart* 41(162), 115-116 Ja 91
Lovibond, Sabina. *Philosophy* 66(256), 254-256 Ap 91

CASSIN, Barbara and NARCY, Michel. *La décision du sens*. Paris, Vrin, 1989.
Follon, Jacques. *Rev Phil Louvain* 88(79), 422-425 O 90

CASSIRER, Ernst. *L'idée de l'histoire*. Paris, Le Cerf, 1988.
Bourel, Dominique. *Arch Phil* 54(3), 519-522 Jl-S 91

CASSIRER, Heinz W. *Grace and Law: St Paul, Kant, and the Hebrew Prophets*. Grand Rapids, Eerdmans, 1988.
Blosser, Philip. *Faith Phil* 8(3), 402-405 Jl 91
Gunton, Colin. *Relig Stud* 26(4), 546-548 D 90

CASTAÑEDA, Hector-Neri. *Thinking, Language and Experience*. Minneapolis, Univ of Minnesota Pr, 1989.
Dipert, Randall R. *Rev Metaph* 44(3), 618-620 Mr 91
Noonan, Harold W. *Phil Quart* 41(162), 109-111 Ja 91
Macdonald, Cynthia. *J Brit Soc Phenomenol* 22(2), 110-111 My 91

CATON, Hiram. *The Politics of Progress*. Tallahassee, Florida St Univ Pr, 1988.
Livingston, Donald. *J Hist Phil* 29(3), 491-492 Jl 91
Richardson Jr, Robert D. *Hist Theor* 29(3), 375-383 O 90

CATTORINI, Paolo (ed). *AIDS and Professional Secrecy*. Padova, Liviana, 1989.
Mancini, Elena. *Bioethics* 5(2), 175-177 Ap 91

CAVE, Terence. *Recognitions: A Study in Poetics*. New York, Oxford Univ Pr, 1988.
Riquelme, John Paul. *Phil Lit* 15(1), 172-173 Ap 91

CAVELL, Stanley. *Themes Out of School: Effects and Causes*. Chicago, Univ of Chicago Pr, 1988.
Hertzberg, Lars. *Phil Invest* 14(1), 81-85 Ja 91

CAWS, Peter. *Structuralism: The Art of the Intelligible*. Atlantic Highlands, Humanities Pr, 1988.
Mullican, James S. *Rev Metaph* 44(2), 411-412 D 90

CAWS, Peter (ed). *The Causes of Quarrel*. Boston, Beacon Pr, 1989.
Zenzinger, Ted. *Auslegung* 17(2), 179-182 Sum 91
Lessnoff, Michael H. *Can Phil Rev* 10(10), 396-399 O 90

CAYGILL, Howard. *Art of Judgement*. Cambridge, Blackwell, 1989.
Crowther, Paul. *Brit J Aes* 31(3), 268-269 Jl 91

CELA-CONDE, Camilo J. *On Genes, Gods and Tyrants*. Norwell, Reidel, 1987.
Stack, George J. *Int Stud Phil* 23(1), 103-104 1991

CELL, Howard R. *Rousseau's Response to Hobbes*. New York, Lang, 1988.
Martinich, A P. *J Hist Phil* 29(1), 137-139 Ja 91

CENTRO FIORENTINO DI STORIA E FILOSIFIA DELLA SCIENZA. *The Leibniz Renaissance: International Workshop*. Florence, Olschki, 1989.
Parkinson, G H R. *Stud Leibniz* 22(1), 114-117 1990

CHADWICK, Whitney. *Women, Art and Society*. London, Thames & Hudson, 1990.
Mannings, David. *Brit J Aes* 31(2), 187-189 Ap 91

CHAMBERLIN, Rosemary. *Free Children and Democratic Schools: A Philosophical Study of Liberty and Education*. Lewes, Falmer Pr, 1989.
Williams, Kevin. *J Phil Educ* 24(2), 285-294 Wint 90

CHANEY, Norman. *Six Images of Human Nature*. Englewood Cliffs, Prentice Hall, 1990.
Kelly, Stewart E. *Teach Phil* 13(3), 308-310 S 90

CHANGEUX, Jean-Pierre and CONNES, Alain. *Matière à pensée*. Paris, Editions Odile Jacob, 1989.
Largeault, Jean. *Rev Phil Fr* 180(4), 680-682 O-D 90

CHARBONNEAU, Paul-Eugène. *El hombre en busca de Dios*. Barcelona, Herder, 1985.
Forment Giralt, E. *Espiritu* 35(93), 72-75 Ja-Je 86

CHARLES, D. *Aristotle's Philosophy of Action*. London, Duckworth, 1984.
Evans, J D G. *J Hellen Stud* 110, 240-241 1990

CHARLESWORTH, Max. *Life, Death, Genes and Ethics*. Sydney, ABC Books, 1989.
Oakley, Justin. *Austl J Phil* 69(1), 108-110 Mr 91
Oakley, Justin. *Bioethics* 5(2), 160-165 Ap 91

CHARLTON, William. *Weakness of Will*. Oxford, Blackwell, 1988.
Meynell, Hugo. *Heythrop J* 32(2), 285-286 Ap 91

CHATTERJEE, Margaret. *Gandhi's Religious Thought*. Notre Dame, Univ Notre Dame Pr, 1986.
Travers, David M W. *Ideal Stud* 20(2), 177-178 My 90

CHATURVEDI, Vibha. *The Problem of Personal Identity*. Delhi, Ajanta, 1988.
Bharadwaja, Vijay. *J Indian Counc Phil Res* 6(3), 161-162 My-Ag 89

CHIHARA, Charles S. *Constructibility and Mathematical Existence*. New York, Clarendon/Oxford Pr, 1990.
Potter, M D. *Phil Quart* 41(164), 345-348 Jl 91

CHINCHORE, Mangala R. *Dharmakirti's Theory of Hetu-centricity of Anumāna*. Delhi, Motilal Banarsidass, 1989.
Bharadwaja, Vijay. *Asian Phil* 1(1), 93-95 1991

CHISHOLM, R M. *Brentano and Intrinsic Value*. Cambridge, Cambridge Univ Pr, 1986.
McAlister, Linda Lopez. *Int Stud Phil* 22(3), 94-95 1990

CHITTICK, William C. *The Sufi Path of Knowledge: Ibn al-'Arabī's Metaphysics of Imagination*. Albany, SUNY Pr, 1989.
Stepaniants, Marietta. *Phil East West* 41(2), 255-258 Ap 91

CHOE, Wolhee. *Toward an Aesthetic Criticism of Technology*. New York, Lang, 1989.
Reichardt, Jasia. *Brit J Aes* 31(2), 182-183 Ap 91

CHOMSKY, Noam. *Language and Problems of Knowledge*. Cambridge, MIT Pr, 1988.
Lele, Jayant K and Singh, Rajendra. *J Prag* 15(2), 175-194 F 91

CHOMSKY, Noam. *On Power and Ideology*. Boston, South End Pr, 1987.
Lele, Jayant K and Singh, Rajendra. *J Prag* 15(2), 175-194 F 91

CHRISTIAN SR, William A. *Doctrines of Religious Communities: A Philosophical Study*. New Haven, Yale Univ Pr, 1987.
Walhout, Donald. *Int Stud Phil* 22(3), 95-96 1990

CHRISTEN, Yves. *El hombre biocultural*. Madrid, Cátedra, 1989.
Fernández Tresguerres, Alfonso. *El Basilisco* 2, 101-103 N-D 89

CHURCHLAND, Paul M. *A Neurocomputational Perspective: The Nature of Mind and the Structure of Science*. Cambridge, MIT Pr, 1989.
Foss, Jeffrey. *Can Phil Rev* 10(10), 399-402 O 90
Sharpe, R A. *Inquiry* 34(1), 91-106 Mr 91

CHURCHLAND, Paul M. *Matter and Consciousness, Rev Ed*. Cambridge, MIT Pr, 1988.
Dresser, Rebecca. *Crim Just Ethics* 10(1), 27-40 Wint-Spr 91

CHYTRY, Josef. *The Aesthetic State: A Quest in Modern German Thought*. Berkeley, Univ of California Pr, 1989.
Megill, Allan. *Hist Theor* 30(1), 70-79 F 91

CIARAMELLI, Fabio. *Transcendance et éthique: Essai sur Lévinas*. Brussels, Ousia, 1989.
Lannoy, Jean-Luc. *Rev Phil Louvain* 88(80), 597-603 N 90

CIBA FOUNDATION SYMPOSIUM. *Human Genetic Information*. Chichester, Wiley, 1990.
McKay, Susan. *Bioethics* 5(3), 269-272 Jl 91

CIGLIA, F P. *Un passo fuori dall'uomo*. Padova, Cedam, 1988.
Romano, Pasquale. *Filosofia* 42(1), 113-124 Ja-Ap 91

CILIBERTO, Michele. *Girdano Bruno*. Bari, Laterza, 1990.
Pirillo, Nestore. *Hist Phil Life Sci* 13(1), 157-160 1991

CLAEYS, Gregory. *Thomas Paine, Social and Political Thought*. London, Unwin Hyman, 1989.
Dickinson, H T. *Utilitas* 3(1), 145-148 My 91

CLAIR, André. *Éthique et humanisme*. Paris, Cerf, 1989.
Ponton, Lionel. *Laval Theol Phil* 46(3), 420-422 O 90

CLARK, Andy. *Microcognition: Philosophy, Cognitive Science and Parallel Distributed Processing*. Cambridge, MIT Pr, 1989.
Fishbein, Harold D. *Phil Psych* 4(2), 297-300 1991

CLARK, Linda L. *Social Darwinism in France*. University, Univ of Alabama Pr, 1984.
Brautigam, Jeffrey C. *Hist Phil Life Sci* 12(1), 111-116 1990

CLARK, P and WRIGHT, C (eds). *Mind, Psychoanalysis and Science*. Cambridge, Blackwell, 1988.
Binns, P. *Brit J Phil Sci* 41(4), 531-552 D 90

CLARK, Stephen R L. *Civil Peace and Sacred Order: Limits and Renewals I*. Oxford, Clarendon Pr, 1989.
Atkinson, R F. *Phil Books* 32(1), 55-56 Ja 91
Scruton, Roger. *Hist Polit Thought* 11(3), 546-547 Autumn 90

CLARKE, Desmond M. *Occult Powers and Hypotheses: Cartesian Natural Philosophy under Louis XIV*. New York, Oxford Univ Pr, 1989.
Joy, Lynn S. *J Hist Phil* 29(1), 129-131 Ja 91

CLARKE, Paul A B. *The Autonomy of Politics*. Aldershot, Avebury, 1988.
Lesser, A H. *J Brit Soc Phenomenol* 21(3), 300-301 O 90

CLAY, Marjorie and LEHRER, Keith (eds). *Knowledge and Skepticism*. Boulder, Westview Pr, 1989.
Moser, Paul K. *Can Phil Rev* 10(11), 447-449 N 90
Sorell, Tom. *Phil Books* 32(1), 32-33 Ja 91

CLEARY, John J. *Aristotle on the Many Senses of Priority*. Carbondale, Southern Illinois Univ Pr, 1988.
Elders, Leo J. *Rev Metaph* 44(1), 134-135 S 90

CLEARY, Thomas (ed & trans). *Immortal Sisters*. Boulder, Shambhala, 1989.
Wawrytko, Sandra A. *Phil East West* 41(3), 442-444 Jl 91

CLITEUR, P B. *Conservatisme en cultuurrecht*. Amsterdam, Rijksuniversiteit Leiden, 1989.
Koekkoek, A K. *Phil Reform* 55(2), 184-190 1990

COASE, Ronald Harry. *The Firm, the Market and the Law*. Chicago, Univ of Chicago Pr, 1988.
Amato, Salvatore. *Riv Int Filosof Diritto* 66(4), 740-742 O-D 89

COBB JR, John B and DALY, Herman E. *For the Common Good: Redirecting the Economy towards Community, the Environment, and a Sustainable Future*. Boston, Beacon Pr, 1989.
Gunter, Pete A Y. *Process Stud* 19(1), 56-61 Spr 90

COBY, P. *Socrates and the Sophistic Enlightenment: A Commentary on Plato's "Protagoras"*. Lewisburg, Bucknell Univ Pr, 1987.
Rowe, C J. *J Hellen Stud* 110, 225-226 1990

COCCHIARELLA, Nino B. *Logical Investigations of Predication Theory and the Problem of Universals*. Naples, Bibliopolis, 1986.
Bonevac, Daniel. *Nous* 25(2), 221-230 Ap 91

COCKS, Joan. *The Oppositional Imagination: Feminism, Critique and Political Theory*. London, Routledge, 1989.
Schmitt, Richard. *Soc Theor Pract* 17(1), 105-130 Spr 91

COCKS, R C J. *Sir Henry Maine: A Study in Victorian Jurisprudence*. Cambridge, Cambridge Univ Pr, 1988.
Feaver, George. *Utilitas* 2(2), 330-333 N 90

CODE, Lorraine. *Epistemic Responsibility*. Hanover, Univ Pr of New England, 1987.
Hoffmann, Susan-Judith. *Dialogue (Canada)* 29(3), 466-471 1990
Haack, Susan. *Can J Phil* 21(1), 91-107 Mr 91
Wylie, Alana. *Eidos* 9(1), 129-136 Je 90

COHEN, Avner and DASCAL, Marcelo (eds). *The Institution of Philosophy: A Discipline in Crisis?* La Salle, Open Court, 1989.
Long, Kenneth A. *Clio* 19(4), 400-403 Sum 90

COHEN, G A. *History, Labor and Freedom*. New York, Clarendon/Oxford Pr, 1988.
Bassols, Alejandro Tomasini. *Critica* 23(67), 88-96 Ap 91
Levine, Andrew. *J Phil* 88(5), 267-275 My 91

COHEN, L Jonathan. *The Dialogue of Reason*. New York, Clarendon Pr, 1986.
Balowitz, Victor. *Int Stud Phil* 22(3), 96-97 1990

COHEN, Ralph (ed). *The Future of Literary Theory*. New York, Routledge, 1989.
Newton, K M. *Brit J Aes* 30(4), 387-389 O 90

COHEN, Sherrill and TAUB, Nadine (eds). *Reproductive Laws for the 1990s*. Clifton, Humana Pr, 1989.
Keyserlingk, Edward W. *Bioethics* 5(3), 265-269 Jl 91

COHLER, Anne M. *Montesquieu's Comparative Politics and the Spirit of American Constitutionalism*. Lawrence, Univ Pr of Kansas, 1988.
Ellis, Harold A. *Hist Euro Ideas* 12(5), 687-690 1990

COLAPIETRO, Vincent M. *Peirce's Approach to the Self, A Semiotic Perspective on Human Subjectivity*. Albany, SUNY Pr, 1989.
Tejera, V. *Int Stud Phil* 23(1), 104-105 1991
Liszka, James Jakób. *Personalist Forum* 6(2), 183-185 Fall 90

COLES, M J. *Teaching Thinking: A Survey of Programs in Education*. Bristol, Bristol Pr, 1989.
Nisbet, John. *Thinking* 9(1), 43-44 1990

COLES, Robert. *The Call of Stories: Teaching and the Moral Imagination*. Boston, Houghton Mifflin, 1989.
Perakis, Charles R. *J Med Human* 11(3), 153-155 Fall 90

COLEMAN, Jules L. *Markets, Morals and the Law*. Cambridge, Cambridge Univ Pr, 1988.
Kavka, Gregory S. *Econ Phil* 7(1), 105-112 Ap 91

COLLARD, Andrée and CONTRUCCI, Joyce. *Rape of the Wild*. Bloomington, Indiana Univ Pr, 1988.
Gruen, Lori. *Hypatia* 6(1), 198-206 Spr 91

COLLIER, Andrew. *Scientific Realism and Socialist Thought*. Hemel Hempstead, Harvester Wheatsheaf, 1989.
MacDonald, Graham. *Phil Books* 31(4), 254-256 O 90

COLLINGWOOD, R G and BOUCHER, David (ed). *Essays in Political Philosophy*. New York, Clarendon/Oxford Pr, 1989.
Bellamy, Richard. *Hist Euro Ideas* 13(4), 469-470 1991
McFee, Graham. *Phil Books* 32(2), 94-96 Ap 91
Wilde, Lawrence. *Rad Phil* 57, 43-44 Spr 91

COLLINS, Arthur. *The Nature of Mental Things*. Notre Dame, Univ of Notre Dame Pr, 1987.
Avramides, Anita. *J Phil* 88(1), 52-56 Ja 91
Millgram, Elijah. *Mind* 100(397), 147-149 Ja 91
Shute, Sara. *Int Stud Phil* 22(3), 97-98 1990

COLOMER, Eusebi. *El pensamiento alemán de Kant a Heidegger, V1: La filosofía trascendental: Kant*. Barcelona, Herder, 1986.
Pegueroles, J. *Espiritu* 35(94), 145-148 Jl-D 86

COLOMER, Eusebi. *El pensamiento alemán de Kant a Heidegger, V2: El Idealismo: Fichte, Schelling, Hegel*. Barcelona, Herder, 1986.
Pegueroles, J. *Espiritu* 36(96), 169-171 Jl-D 87

COMBÈS, Joseph. *Études néoplatoniciennes*. Grenoble, Millon, 1989.
Counet, Jean-Michel. *Rev Phil Louvain* 88(79), 430-432 O 90

COMETTI, Jean-Pierre. *Robert Musil: De Törless À L'Homme sans qualités*. Bruxelles, Pierre Margada, 1987.
Latraverse, François. *Dialogue (Canada)* 29(4), 606-609 1990

CONDIT, Celeste Michelle. *Decoding Abortion Rhetoric: Communicating Social Change*. Champaign, Univ of Illinois Pr, 1990.
Tarvers, Josephine Koster. *Hastings Center Rep* 21(4), 41-42 Jl-Ag 91

CONDREN, Conal. *George Lawson's 'Politica' and the English Revolution*. Cambridge, Cambridge Univ Pr, 1989.
Franklin, Julian H. *Hist Polit Thought* 11(3), 536-540 Autumn 90

CONSTABLE, R L and others. *Implementing Mathematics with the Nuprl Proof Development System*. Englewood Cliffs, Prentice Hall, 1986.
Beeson, Michael J. *J Sym Log* 55(3), 1299-1302 S 90

CONWAY, Gertrude. *Wittgenstein on Foundations*. Atlantic Highlands, Humanities Pr, 1989.
Travis, Charles. *Rev Metaph* 44(1), 135-136 S 90

CONWAY, Stephen (ed). *The Correspondence of Jeremy Bentham, V9: January 1817 to June 1820*. Oxford, Clarendon Pr, 1989.
Hamburger, Joseph. *Utilitas* 3(1), 139-141 My 91

COOPER, David E. *Existentialism: A Reconstruction*. Cambridge, Blackwell, 1990.
Mays, Wolfe. *Phil Quart* 41(164), 362-363 Jl 91

COOPER, John W. *Body, Soul, and Life Everlasting*. Grand Rapids, Eerdmans, 1990.
Blosser, Philip. *Thomist* 55(3), 522-526 Jl 91

COPELAND, Warren R and HATCH, Roger D (eds). *Issues of Justice*. Macon, Mercer Univ Pr, 1988.
Murray, Leslie A. *Process Stud* 19(3), 203-206 Fall 90

COPELAND, Warren R. *Economic Justice*. Nashville, Abigndon Pr, 1988.
Murray, Leslie A. *Process Stud* 19(3), 203-206 Fall 90

COPLESTON, Frederick C. *Russian Religious Philosophy: Selected Aspects*. Notre Dame, Univ of Notre Dame Pr, 1988.
Mills, Judith M. *Int Phil Quart* 31(2), 248-250 Je 91

CORDUA, Carla. *El mundo ético: Ensayos sobre la esfera del hombre en la filosofía de Hegel*. Barcelona, Anthropos, 1989.
Casares, Ángel J. *Dialogos* 25(56), 185-190 Jl 90

CORETH, Emerich and others (eds). *Christliche Philosophie im katholischen Denken des 19 und 20 Jahrhunderts, 2v*. Graz, Styria, 1987.
Secrétan, Philibert. *Frei Z Phil Theol* 37(1-2), 282-287 1990

CORLETT, William. *Community Without Unity: A Politics of Derridian Extravagance*. Durham, Duke Univ Pr, 1989.
Jones, L Gregory. *Mod Theol* 7(4), 375-376 Jl 91

CORRINGTON, Robert S. *The Community of Interpreters*. Macon, Mercer Univ Pr, 1987.
Kort, Wesley A. *Int Stud Phil* 23(1), 106-107 1991

COTKIN, George. *William James: Public Philosopher*. Baltimore, Johns Hopkins Univ Pr, 1990.
Skrupskelis, Ignas K. *Trans Peirce Soc* 27(1), 115-120 Wint 91

COUGHLIN, Michael J. *The Vatican, the Law and the Embryo*. London, Macmillan, 1990.
Teichman, Jenny. *Philosophy* 66(257), 386-390 Jl 91

COWARD, Harold G and LIPNER, Julius J and YOUNG, Katherine K. *Hindu Ethics: Purity, Abortion, and Euthanasia*. Albany, SUNY Pr, 1989.
Crawford, Cromwell. *Phil East West* 40(4), 566-568 O 90

COXON, A H. *The Fragments of Parmenides*. Assen, Van Gorcum, 1986.
Matthen, Mohan. *Phil Rev* 100(1), 153-157 Ja 91

CRAWFORD, S Cromwell (ed). *World Religions and Global Ethics*. New York, Paragon House, 1989.
Keulman, Kenneth. *Phil East West* 41(3), 422-425 Jl 91

CREEGAN, Charles L. *Wittgenstein and Kierkegaard*. New York, Routledge, 1989.
Vardy, Peter. *Heythrop J* 32(3), 442-443 Jl 91

CRESSWELL, M J. *Structured Meanings*. Cambridge, MIT Pr, 1985.
Anderson, C Anthony. *Phil Rev* 100(3), 476-479 Jl 91

CRISTIN, Renato. *Heidegger e Leibniz: Il sentiero e la ragione*. Milan, Bompiani, 1990.
Ciaramelli, Fabio. *Rev Phil Louvain* 88(80), 624-627 N 90

CRITTENDEN, Brian. *Parents, the State and the Right to Educate*. Melbourne, Melbourne Univ Pr, 1988.
Warren, Bill. *Austl J Phil* 68(3), 349-351 S 90

CROMBIE, A C. *Historia de la Ciencia: de San Agustín a Galileo, 2v*. Madrid, Alianza, 1987.
Vitoria, M Angeles. *Anu Filosof* 23(1), 181-183 1990

CROSBY, Donald A. *The Specter of the Absurd*. Albany, SUNY Pr, 1988.
Dupré, Louis. *Faith Phil* 8(3), 408-410 Jl 91
Stack, George J. *J Hist Phil* 28(4), 627-631 O 90

CROUZEL, Henri. *Origen*. Edinburgh, T & T Clark, 1989.
Meredith, Anthony. *Heythrop J* 32(3), 406-407 Jl 91

CROWTHER, Paul. *The Kantian Sublime*. New York, Clarendon/Oxford Pr, 1989.
Kemal, Salim. *J Hist Phil* 29(3), 500-502 Jl 91
Schaper, Eva. *Phil Books* 32(2), 85-86 Ap 91
Collinson, Diané. *Brit J Aes* 30(4), 372-373 O 90
McCloskey, Mary A. *Philosophy* 65(253), 380-382 Jl 90

CRUZ CRUZ, Juan. *Antropología de la conducta alimentaria*. Pamplona, Univ de Navarra, 1990.
Zorroza, Idoya. *Anu Filosof* 23(2), 175-177 1990

CUA, A S. *Ethical Argumentation: A Study in Hsün Tzu's Moral Epistemology*. Honolulu, Univ of Hawaii Pr, 1985.
Shun, Kwong-loi. *Phil East West* 41(1), 111-117 Ja 91

CUMMINS, Robert. *Meaning and Mental Representation*. Cambridge, MIT Pr, 1989.
Antony, Louise. *Mind* 99(396), 637-642 O 90
Carruthers, Peter. *Phil Quart* 40(161), 527-530 O 90

CUNNINGHAM, Frank. *Democratic Theory and Socialism*. Cambridge, Cambridge Univ Pr, 1987.
Riemer, Neal. *Phil Soc Sci* 20(4), 515-518 D 90

CUPITT, Don. *The Long-Legged Fly*. London, SCM Pr, 1987.
Vardy, Peter. *Heythrop J* 32(1), 97 Ja 91

CURLEY, Edwin. *Behind the Geometrical Method: A Reading of Spinoza's "Ethics"*. Princeton, Princeton Univ Pr, 1988.
Steinberg, Diane. *J Hist Phil* 29(1), 135-137 Ja 91
Garrett, Don. *Phil Rev* 100(3), 512-514 Jl 91

CURRIE, Gregory. *An Ontology of Art*. Basingstoke, Macmillan, 1989.
Budd, Malcolm. *Brit J Aes* 30(4), 369-372 O 90
Hamilton, Andy. *Phil Quart* 40(161), 538-541 O 90
Barwell, Ismay. *Phil Lit* 15(1), 161-162 Ap 91

CUSHING, James T and MCMULLIN, Ernan. *Philosophical Consequences of Quantum Theory: Reflections on Bell's Theorem*. Notre Dame, Univ of Notre Dame Pr, 1989.
Stairs, Allen. *Synthese* 86(1), 99-122 Ja 91

CZEIZEL, Andrew. *The Right to Be Born Healthy*. New York, Liss, 1988.
Blasszauer, Bela. *Hastings Center Rep* 20(6), 39-40 N-D 90

D'AMICO, Robert. *Historicism and Knowledge*. London, Routledge, 1989.
Gorman, J L. *Phil Books* 31(4), 224-226 O 90
Rée, Jonathan. *Rad Phil* 56, 53-57 Autumn 90

D'ANGELO, P. *Simbolo e arte in Hegel*. Rome, Laterza, 1989.
Apa, Dorella. *Filosofia* 42(1), 141-144 Ja-Ap 91

D'HONDT, Jacques and BURBIDGE, John (trans). *Hegel in His Time*. Lewiston, Broadview Pr, 1988.
Harris, H S. *Dialogue (Canada)* 29(4), 602-603 1990

DACAL ALONSO, Jose Antonio. *Estética General*. San Andres, Ed Porrua, 1990.
García Montañez, Enrique Ignacio. *Logos (Mexico)* 19(56), 133-135 My-Ag 91

DAHL, Robert A. *Democracy and Its Critics*. New Haven, Yale Univ Pr, 1989.
Narveson, Jan. *Teach Phil* 13(4), 401-404 D 90

DALFERTH, Ingolf U. *Theology and Philosophy*. Cambridge, Blackwell, 1988.
Meynell, Hugo. *Heythrop J* 32(3), 431-432 Jl 91

DÄLLENBACH, Lucien. *The Mirror in the Text, Jeremy Whiteley and Emma Hughes (trans)*. Oxford, Polity Pr, 1989.
Bredin, Hugh. *Brit J Aes* 31(1), 85-87 Ja 91

DALLMAYR, Fred. *Margins of Political Discourse*. Albany, SUNY Pr, 1989.
Gordon, Haim. *J Brit Soc Phenomenol* 22(2), 109-110 My 91

DANAHER, William J. *Insight in Chemistry*. Lanham, Univ Pr of America, 1988.
Budenholzer, Frank. *Method* 9(1), 63-69 Mr 91

DANCY, Jonathan. *Berkeley: An Introduction*. Oxford, Blackwell, 1987.
Winkler, Kenneth P. *Phil Rev* 100(2), 329-331 Ap 91

DARROCH-LOZOWSKI, Vivian. *Notebook of Stone, From the Tibetan Tableau and Berlin*. Kapuskasing, Penumbra Pr, 1987.
Wolff, Kurt H. *Human Stud* 14(1), 99-104 Ja 91

DASGUPTA, Surendranath. *Natural Science of the Ancient Hindus*. New Delhi, Motilal, 1987.
Chandra, Pratap. *J Indian Counc Phil Res* 5(3), 170-173 My-Ag 88

DAVIDSON, Herbert A. *Proofs for Eternity, Creation and the Existence of God in Medieval Islamic and Jewish Philosophy*. New York, Oxford Univ Pr, 1987.
Kellner, Menachem. *Int Stud Phil* 22(3), 98-99 1990

DAVIDSON, Nicholas. *The Failure of Feminism*. New York, Prometheus, 1988.
Haack, Susan. *Int Stud Phil* 23(1), 107-108 1991

DAVIES, Paul. *The Cosmic Blueprint: New Discoveries in Nature's Ability to Order the Universe*. New York, Simon & Schuster, 1988.
Hallberg, Fred W. *Zygon* 25(4), 493-496 D 90

DAVIS, Caroline Franks. *The Evidential Force of Religious Experience*. Oxford, Clarendon Pr, 1989.
Devine, Philip E. *Rev Metaph* 44(2), 419-420 D 90
Owen, H P. *Relig Stud* 26(4), 544-546 D 90
Gaskin, J C A. *Phil Books* 32(2), 127-128 Ap 91

DAVIS, Donald Edward. *Ecophilosophy: A Field Guide to the Literature*. San Pedro, R & E Miles, 1989.
Banta, Erik Haugland. *Environ Ethics* 12(4), 369-370 Wint 90

DAY, J P. *Liberty and Justice*. Beckenham, Croom Helm, 1986.
Somerville, James. *J Applied Phil* 8(1), 130-131 1991

DE ARMEY, Michael H and SKOUSGAARD, Stephen (eds). *The Philosophical Psychology of William James*. Washington, University Pr of America, 1986.
Scott, Frederick J D. *Ideal Stud* 20(1), 84-85 Ja 90

DE CARDEDAL, Olegario G. *La gloria del hombre*. Madrid, Biblioteca de Autores, 1985.
Pegueroles, Juan. *Espiritu* 36(95), 98-99 Ja-Je 87

DE FINANCE, J. *L'ouverture et la norme: Questions sur l'agir humain*. Vatican City, Lib Ed Vaticana, 1989.
Pellecchia, Pasquale. *Aquinas* 34(1), 135-150 Ja-Ap 91

DE GRAZIA, Sebastian. *Machiavelli in Hell*. Princeton, Princeton Univ Pr, 1989.
Viroli, Maurizio. *Polit Theory* 19(2), 292-295 My 91

DE KONINCK, Thomas. *La question de Dieu selon Aristote et Hegel*. Paris, Pr Univ de France, 1991.
Vigneault, Gilles. *Laval Theol Phil* 47(2), 276-281 Je 91

DE MARCHI, Neil (ed). *The Popperian Legacy in Economics: Papers Presented at a Symposium in Amsterdam, December 1985*. Cambridge, Cambridge Univ Pr, 1988.
McMillan, John. *Phil Sci* 58(1), 136-138 Mr 91
Cohen, Avi J. *Phil Soc Sci* 20(4), 527-531 D 90

DE MONTICELLI, Roberta. *Il richiamo della persuasione: Lettere a Carlo Michelstaedter*. Genoa, Marietti, 1988.
La Rocca, Claudio. *Teoria* 10(1), 198-200 1990

DE RIJK, L M. *Through Language to Reality*. Northampton, Variorum, 1989.
Perreiah, Alan R. *Hist Phil Log* 12(1), 121-122 1990

DE ROMILLY, J. *La Grèce antique à la découverte de la liberté*. Paris, Fallois, 1989.
Cartledge, Paul. *Polis* 9(2), 187-197 1990

DE ROSA, Mario. *Dante e il padre ideale*. Napoli, Frederico & Ardia, 1990.
Placella, Vincenzo. *Sapienza* 44(2), 226-228 Ap-Je 91

DE SOUSA, Ronald. *The Rationality of Emotion*. Cambridge, MIT Pr, 1987.
Gordon, Robert M. *Phil Rev* 100(2), 284-288 Ap 91
Meynell, Hugo. *Heythrop J* 32(1), 105-106 Ja 91
Shaffer, Jerome. *Rev Metaph* 44(3), 624-628 Mr 91

DE WAAL, Frans. *Peacemaking among Primates*. Cambridge, Harvard Univ Pr, 1989.
Schubert, Glendon. *J Soc Biol Struct* 13(2), 163-174 My 90

DE VRIES, William A. *Hegel's Theory of Mental Activity: An Introduction to Theoretical Spirit*. Ithaca, Cornell Univ Pr, 1988.
Stern, Robert. *Bull Hegel Soc Gt Brit* 20, 42-44 Autumn-Wint 89

DEELY, John. *Basics of Semiotics*. Bloomington, Indiana Univ Pr, 1990.
Murphy, James Bernard. *Rev Metaph* 44(4), 836-837 Je 91

DEELY, John N and POWELL, Ralph Austin (eds). *Tractatus de Signis: The Semiotic of John Poinsot*. Berkeley, Univ of California Pr, 1985.
Braga, Lucia Santaella. *J Speculative Phil* 5(2), 151-159 1991

DEL CARO, Adrian. *Nietzsche Contra Nietzsche: Creativity and the Anti-Romantic*. Baton Rouge, Louisiana State Univ Pr, 1989.
Stein, Mark. *Phil Lit* 15(1), 176-178 Ap 91
Stack, George J. *Rev Metaph* 44(4), 838-839 Je 91

DEL NOCE, Augusto. *Giovanni Gentile*. Bologna, Il Mulino, 1990.
Todisco, Orlando. *Sapienza* 44(2), 224-226 Ap-Je 91

DEL PRETE, Thomas. *Thomas Merton and the Education of the Whole Person*. Birmingham, Religious Education Pr, 1990.
Wilkie, Raymond. *Educ Stud* 21(4), 489-497 Wint 90

DELAHUNTY, R J. *Spinoza*. London, Routledge, 1985.
Sell, Alan P F. *Phil Stud (Ireland)* 32, 299-301 1988-90

DELATTRE, Edwin J. *Character and Cops: Ethics in Policing*. Washington, American Enterprise Institute, 1989.
Cohen, Elliot D. *Crim Just Ethics* 9(2), 64-71 Sum-Fall 90

DELEUZE, G. *Le Pli*. Paris, Ed Minuit, 1989.
Frémont, Christiane. *Rev Metaph Morale* 96(1), 105-120 Ja-Mr 91

DEN OUDEN, Bernard and MOEN, Marcia (eds). *New Essays on Kant*. New York, Lang, 1987.
George, Rolf. *Kantstudien* 81(4), 478-483 1990
Potter, Elizabeth. *Phil Rev* 100(2), 341-344 Ap 91

DENBIGH, K G and DENBIGH, J S. *Entropy in Relation to Incomplete Knowledge*. Cambridge, Cambridge Univ Pr, 1985.
Price, Huw. *Brit J Phil Sci* 42(1), 111-144 Mr 91

DENIS, Henri. *Hegel, penseur politique*. Lausanne, Age d'Homme, 1989.
Gérard, Gilbert. *Rev Phil Louvain* 89(82), 289-297 My 91

DENNETT, Daniel C. *The Intentional Stance*. Cambridge, MIT Pr, 1987.
Dresser, Rebecca. *Crim Just Ethics* 10(1), 27-40 Wint-Spr 91

DENNETT, Daniel. *Content and Consciousness, 2nd ed*. London, Routledge & Kegan Paul, 1986.
Kelly, James S. *Ideal Stud* 20(1), 83-84 Ja 90

DENT, N J H. *Rousseau*. Oxford, Blackwell, 1989.
Cherry, Christopher. *Phil Books* 31(4), 205-207 O 90

DERRIDA, Jacques. *Writing and Difference, Alan Bass (trans)*. London, Routledge & Kegan Paul, 1978.
Gratton, Johnnie. *Phil Stud (Ireland)* 32, 291-294 1988-90

DERRIDA, Jacques. *Of Spirit: Heidegger and the Question, Geoffrey Bennington and Rachel Bowlby (trans)*. Chicago, Univ of Chicago Pr, 1989.
Burch, Robert. *Can Phil Rev* 10(10), 403-407 O 90

DERRIDA, Jacques. *The Ear of the Other*. Lincoln, Univ of Nebraska Pr, 1988.
Slinn, E Warwick. *Phil Lit* 14(2), 379-386 O 90

DERRIDA, Jacques. *Vom Geist: Heidegger und Die Frage*. Frankfurt am Main, Suhrkamp, 1988.
Tietz, Udo. *Deut Z Phil* 38(10), 1006-1007 1990

DESMOND, William (ed). *Hegel and His Critics: Philosophy in the Aftermath of Hegel*. Albany, SUNY Pr, 1989.
Locke, Patricia M. *Rev Metaph* 44(3), 623-624 Mr 91
Burbidge, John. *Owl Minerva* 22(2), 227-228 Spr 91

DESMOND, William. *Art and the Absolute: A Study of Hegel's Aesthetics*. Albany, SUNY Pr, 1986.
Kearney, Richard. *Phil Stud (Ireland)* 32, 301-305 1988-90

DESMOND, William. *Desire, Dialectic and Otherness: An Essay on Origins*. New Haven, Yale Univ Pr, 1987.
Kearney, Richard. *Phil Stud (Ireland)* 32, 301-305 1988-90

DETLEFSEN, Michael. *Hilbert's Program: An Essay on Mathematical Instrumentalism*. Boston, Reidel, 1986.
Steiner, Mark. *J Phil* 88(6), 331-336 Je 91

DEUTSCH, Kenneth L and SOFFER, Walter (eds). *The Crisis of Liberal Democracy*. Albany, SUNY Pr, 1987.
Asselin, D T. *Thomist* 55(3), 526-535 Jl 91

DEVARAJA, N K. *Humanism in Indian Thought*. New Delhi, Indus, 1988.
Roy, Krishna. *J Indian Counc Phil Res* 6(2), 186-193 Ja-Ap 89

DEVITIS, Joseph L (ed). *Women, Culture and Morality: Selected Essays*. New York, Lang, 1987.
Burstyn, Joan N. *Educ Stud* 21(2), 218-221 Sum 90

DEVRIES, Willem A. *Hegel's Theory of Mental Activity*. Ithaca, Cornell Univ Pr, 1988.
Greene, Murray. *J Hist Phil* 29(1), 142-143 Ja 91

DI FRANCESCO, M. *Introduzione a Russell*. Rome, Laterza, 1990.
Voltolini, Alberto. *Aquinas* 34(1), 151-155 Ja-Ap 91

DI GIOVANNI, George (ed). *Essays on Hegel's Logic*. Albany, SUNY Pr, 1990.
Manser, Anthony. *J Brit Soc Phenomenol* 22(2), 105-107 My 91

DIAMOND, Irene and QUINBY, Lee (eds). *Feminism and Foucault: Reflections on Resistance*. Boston, Northeastern Univ Pr, 1988.
Metzger, Mary Janell. *Hypatia* 5(3), 118-124 Fall 90

DÍAZ, José Luis. *Análisis estructural de la conducta*. Mexico, UNAM, 1985.
Hansberg, Olbeth. *Dianoia* 34(34), 304-306 1988

DICKEY, Lawrence. *Hegel: Religion, Economics, and the Politics of Spirit 1770-1807*. Cambridge, Cambridge Univ Pr, 1987.
Harris, H S. *Int J Phil Relig* 29(2), 123-125 Ap 91
Bienenstock, Myriam. *Int Stud Phil* 23(1), 109-111 1991
Beiser, Frederick. *Phil Rev* 99(4), 637-639 O 90

DICKIE, George and SCLAFANI, Richard and ROBLIN, Ronald (eds). *Aesthetics: A Critical Anthology, 2nd ed*. New York, St Martin's Pr, 1989.
Selk, Eugene E. *Teach Phil* 13(2), 170-172 Je 90

DICKIE, George. *Evaluating Art*. Philadelphia, Temple Univ Pr, 1988.
Gaskin, Richard. *Brit J Aes* 30(4), 367-368 O 90

DIETZ, Mary G (ed). *Thomas Hobbes and Political Theory*. Lawrence, Univ Pr of Kansas, 1990.
Morgan, Michael L. *Rev Metaph* 44(3), 628-630 Mr 91

DILLON, J M and LONG, A A (eds). *The Question of 'Eclecticism': Studies in Later Greek Philosophy*. Berkeley, Univ of California Pr, 1988.
Armstrong, A H. *Heythrop J* 32(2), 286-287 Ap 91

DILLON, M C. *Merleau-Ponty's Ontology*. Bloomington, Indiana Univ Pr, 1988.
Langer, Monika. *Rev Metaph* 44(1), 136-137 S 90

DILTHEY, Wilhelm. *Selected Works, V1: Introduction to the Human Sciences, R A Makkreel and F Rodi (eds)*. Princeton, Princeton Univ Pr, 1989.
Tillman, Mary Katherine. *Rev Metaph* 44(2), 412-414 D 90
Leiner, George H. *Man World* 24(3), 345-354 Jl 91

DINWIDDY, J R. *Bentham*. Oxford, Oxford Univ Pr, 1989.
Kelly, P J. *Hist Polit Thought* 11(3), 533-535 Autumn 90

DOBEL, J Patrick. *Compromise and Political Action*. Totowa, Rowman & Littlefield, 1990.
Menlowe, Michael A. *Phil Books* 32(2), 119-121 Ap 91
Lawson, Bill E. *Phil Quart* 41(164), 369-370 Jl 91
Zwiebach, Burton. *Hastings Center Rep* 21(3), 36-37 My-Je 91

DOCHERTY, Thomas. *After Theory: Postmodernism/Postmarxism*. New York, Routledge, 1990.
Ball, David. *Brit J Aes* 31(3), 282-283 Jl 91

DOMBROWSKI, Daniel A. *Hartshorne and the Metaphysics of Animal Rights*. Albany, SUNY Pr, 1988.
Brewster, Diane M. *Heythrop J* 32(2), 291 Ap 91

DONAGAN, Alan. *Choice: The Essential Element in Human Action*. New York, Routledge & Kegan Paul, 1987.
Brand, Myles. *Phil Rev* 100(1), 115-118 Ja 91
Hallett, Garth. *Heythrop J* 32(1), 103-104 Ja 91
Schultz, Janice L. *Thomist* 55(1), 160-165 Ja 91
Montmarquet, James. *Nous* 25(1), 135-136 Mr 91

DONALDSON, Thomas. *The Ethics of International Business*. New York, Oxford Univ Pr, 1989.
Bowie, Norman E. *Bus Ethics Quart* 1(2), 223-232 Ap 91

DONNELLY, Jack. *Universal Human Rights in Theory and Practice*. Ithaca, Cornell Univ Pr, 1990.
Milne, A J M. *Can Phil Rev* 10(12), 487-489 D 90

DONNELLY, John (ed). *Suicide: Right or Wrong?* Buffalo, Prometheus Pr, 1990.
Chwastiak, Lydia. *Med Human Rev* 5(1), 101-104 Ja 91

DOOB, Leonard. *Slightly beyond Scepticism*. New Haven, Yale Univ Pr, 1987.
Kultgen, John. *Int Stud Phil* 23(1), 111-112 1991

DORE, Clement. *God, Suffering, and Solipsism*. New York, St Martin's Pr, 1989.
Keller, James A. *Faith Phil* 8(3), 405-408 Jl 91

DÖRFLINGER, Bernd. *Die Realität des Schönen in Kants Theorie rein ästhetischer Urteilskraft*. Bonn, Bouvier, 1988.
Kopper, Margit. *Kantstudien* 81(4), 488-490 1990
Fricke, Christel. *Z Phil Forsch* 45(1), 151-155 Ja-Mr 91

DOSSA, Shiraz. *The Public Realm & The Public Self: The Political Theory of Hannah Arendt*. Waterloo, Wilfried Laurier Univ Pr, 1989.
Palonen, Kari. *Hist Euro Ideas* 13(4), 428-429 1991

DOTTI, Jorge Eugenio and HOLZ, Harald and RADERMACHER, Hans (eds). *Kant in der Hispanidad*. New York, Lang, 1988.
Caimi, Mario. *Kantstudien* 82(2), 224-226 1991

DOWER, Nigel (ed). *Ethics and Environmental Responsibility*. Aldershot, Gower, 1989.
Walker, A D M. *J Applied Phil* 7(2), 236-238 O 90

DRAGALIN, A G. *Mathematical Intuitionism: Introduction to Proof Theory, E Mendelson (trans)*. Providence, American Mathematical Society, 1988.
Troelstra, A S. *J Sym Log* 55(3), 1308-1309 S 90

DRANE, James F. *Becoming a Good Doctor*. Kansas City, Sheed & Ward, 1988.
Matthews, Dale A. *Hastings Center Rep* 20(6), 40-42 N-D 90

DRAY, William H. *On History and Philosophers of History*. New York, Brill, 1989.
Conkin, Paul K. *Clio* 19(4), 393-397 Sum 90
Donagan, Alan. *Hist Theor* 30(1), 90-95 F 91
Martin, Raymond. *Can Phil Rev* 10(9), 359-361 S 90

DRETSKE, Fred. *Explaining Behavior: Reasons in a World of Causes*. Cambridge, MIT Pr, 1988.
Heil, John. *Phil Psych* 3(2-3), 325-329 1990
Gjelsvik, Olav. *Inquiry* 33(3), 333-353 S 90
Horgan, Terence. *Mind Lang* 5(3), 230-234 Autumn 90

DRUART, Therese-Anne (ed). *Arabic Philosophy and the West: Continuity and Interaction*. Washington, Center for Contemporary Arab Studies, 1988.
Kemal, Salim. *Rev Metaph* 44(1), 137-139 S 90

DRURY, Shadia B. *The Political Ideas of Leo Strauss*. New York, St Martin's Pr, 1988.
Fuller, Timothy. *Polit Theory* 19(1), 137-141 F 91

DUFF, R A. *Intention, Agency and Criminal Liability*. Cambridge, Blackwell, 1990.
Kenny, Anthony. *Phil Quart* 41(164), 378-379 Jl 91

DUFOUR, Carlos A. *Die Lehre der Proprietates Terminorum*. Munchen, Philosophia, 1989.
Von H Berger, Rezensiert. *Hist Phil Log* 12(2), 241-267 1991

DUHEM, Pierre. *"Sôzein ta Phainomena": Essai sur la notion de théorie physique de Platon à Galilée*. Paris, Vrin, 1990.
Largeault, Jean. *Rev Phil Fr* 180(4), 686-687 O-D 90

DUMONT, Louis. *Essays on Individualism*. Chicago, Univ of Chicago Pr, 1986.
Merquior, J G. *Crit Rev* 4(3), 301-325 Sum 90

DUMOULIN, Bertrand. *Analyse génétique de la Métaphysique d'Aristote*. Montréal, Bellarmin, 1986.
Graham, Daniel W. *Ancient Phil* 10(2), 304-309 Fall 90
Ambühl, Hans. *Frei Z Phil Theol* 37(3), 527-532 1990
Devereux, Daniel T. *Phil Rev* 100(3), 519-521 Jl 91

DUNN, John. *Interpreting Political Responsibility*. Cambridge, Polity Pr, 1990.
Thomas, D A Lloyd. *Mind* 100(399), 381-382 Jl 91

DUNSTAN, G R and SELLER, Mary J (eds). *The Status of the Human Embryo: Perspectives from Moral Tradition*. Oxford, Oxford Univ Pr, 1988.
Sutton, Agneta. *Heythrop J* 32(2), 271-272 Ap 91

DUNSTAN, G R and SHINEBOURNE, E A (eds). *Doctors' Decisions: Ethical Conflicts in Medical Practice*. Oxford, Oxford Univ Pr, 1989.
Williams, John R. *Heythrop J* 32(2), 272-274 Ap 91

DUSSEL, Enrique. *Philosophie der Befreiung*. Berlin, Argument, 1989.
Röfke, Holger. *Deut Z Phil* 38(12), 1230-1232 1990

DUSSEL, Enrique and BARR, Robert R (trans). *Ethics and Community*. Tunbridge Wells, Burns & Oates, 1988.
Williams, John R. *Heythrop J* 32(3), 444-445 Jl 91

DWORKIN, Gerald. *The Theory and Practice of Autonomy*. New York, Cambridge Univ Pr, 1988.
Cust, Kenneth F T. *Int Phil Quart* 31(3), 372-374 S 91
Harriott, Howie H. *Quest* 5(1), 118-122 Je 91
Hull, Gerald. *Int Stud Phil* 23(1), 112-113 1991
Statman, Daniel. *Iyyun* 39(4), 461-464 O 90

DWYER, John. *Virtuous Discourse: Sensibility and Community in Late Eighteenth-Century Scotland*. Edinburgh, MacDonald, 1987.
Kenyon, Timothy. *Hist Euro Ideas* 12(5), 685-687 1990

DYKE, C. *The Evolutionary Dynamics of Complex Systems: A Study in Biosocial Complexity*. New York, Oxford Univ Pr, 1988.
Rottschaefer, William. *Behavior Phil* 18(2), 79-83 Fall-Wint 90

DYSON, Anthony and HARRIS, John (eds). *Experiments on Embryos*. London, Routledge, 1990.
Longthorn, Sheila M. *J Applied Phil* 8(1), 136-138 1991
Dawson, Karen. *Bioethics* 5(1), 74-78 Ja 91

DZIEMIDOK, B and MCCORMICK, P (eds). *On the Aesthetics of Roman Ingarden: Interpretations and Assessments*. Dordrecht, Kluwer, 1989.
Wood, Robert E. *Rev Metaph* 44(3), 630-632 Mr 91

EAGLETON, Terry (ed). *Raymond Williams: Critical Perspectives*. Oxford, Polity Pr, 1989.
Pechey, Graham. *Rad Phil* 57, 44-45 Spr 91

EAGLETON, Terry. *The Ideology of the Aesthetic*. Oxford, Blackwell, 1990.
Bowie, Andrew. *Rad Phil* 57, 36-37 Spr 91
Lyas, Colin. *Brit J Aes* 31(2), 169-171 Ap 91

EAMES, Elizabeth Ramsden. *Bertrand Russell's Dialogue with His Contemporaries*. Carbondale, Southern Illinois Univ Pr, 1989.
Noonan, Harold W. *Phil Books* 32(2), 86-88 Ap 91

EASTHOPE, Anthony. *Poetry and Phantasy*. Cambridge, Cambridge Univ Pr, 1989.
Thompson, John O. *J Brit Soc Phenomenol* 22(1), 97-99 Ja 91

EATON, Marcia Muelder. *Aesthetics and the Good Life*. Cranbury, Associated Univ Pr, 1989.
Jones, K. *Brit J Aes* 30(4), 368-369 O 90
Korsmeyer, Carolyn. *J Aes Educ* 24(4), 109-111 Wint 90

EBELING, Hans (ed). *Cartesianische Meditation, Teil 1*. Dordrecht, Kluwer, 1988.
San Martín, Javier. *Rev Filosof (Spain)* 4, 247-263 1990

ECHARRI, J. *Filosofía fenoménica de la naturaleza*. Bilbao, Univ Deusto, 1990.
de Landázuri, Carlos O. *Anu Filosof* 24(1), 177-180 1991

ECKEL, Malcolm David. *Jñānagarbha's Commentary on the Distinction Between the Two Truths*. Albany, SUNY Pr, 1987.
Lindtner, Christian. *J Indian Phil* 18(3), 249-260 S 90

ECO, Umberto. *Art and Beauty in the Middle Ages, Hugh Bredin (trans)*. New Haven, Yale Univ Pr, 1986.
Zawilla, Ronald John. *Mod Sch* 68(1), 84-86 N 90

ECO, Umberto. *The Aesthetics of Thomas Aquinas, Hugh Bredin (trans)*. Cambridge, Harvard Univ Pr, 1988.
Perreiah, Alan R. *Hist Euro Ideas* 12(6), 864-865 1990

EDEL, Abraham. *Interpreting Education*. Buffalo, Prometheus Books, 1989.
Casement, William. *Teach Phil* 13(4), 404-406 D 90

EDIE, James M. *Merleau-Ponty's Philosophy of Language*. Lanham, Univ Pr of America, 1987.
Busch, Thomas W. *Mod Sch* 68(3), 269-270 Mr 91

EDWARDS, James C. *The Authority of Language*. Gainesville, Univ S Florida Pr, 1990.
Quirk, Michael J. *Auslegung* 17(2), 174-179 Sum 91

EISENSTEIN, Zillah R. *The Female Body and the Law*. Berkeley, Univ of California Pr, 1989.
Sullivan, J P. *Phil Soc Sci* 21(2), 277-282 Je 91

ELDERS, Leo J. *Santo Tomás de Aquino hoy y otros estudios*. Buenos Aires, Sociedad Tomista Argentina, 1989.
De Gandolfi, Maricel C M. *Sapientia* 45(177), 237-239 Jl-S 90

ELDRIDGE, Richard. *On Moral Personhood: Philosophy, Literature, Criticism and Self-Understanding*. Chicago, Univ of Chicago Pr, 1990.
Davies, Stephen. *Phil Lit* 15(1), 166-167 Ap 91

ELIAS, John. *Moral Education: Secular and Religious*. Malabar, Krieger, 1989.
Wilkie, Raymond. *Educ Stud* 21(4), 489-497 Wint 90

ELLIS, Brian. *Truth and Objectivity*. Cambridge, Blackwell, 1990.
Whyte, J T. *Brit J Phil Sci* 42(2), 291-294 Je 91

ELLISTON, Frederick and BOWIE, Norman (eds). *Ethics, Public Policy, and Criminal Justice*. Cambridge, Oelgeschangler, 1982.
Potter, Roberto Hugh. *Bus Prof Ethics J* 2(3), 79-80 Spr 83

ELLUL, Jacques. *The Technological Bluff*. Grand Rapids, Eeerdmans, 1990.
Johnson, Paul J. *Sci Tech Human Values* 16(2), 258-260 Spr 91

ELSTER, Jon. *Nuts and Bolts for the Social Sciences*. Cambridge, Cambridge Univ Pr, 1989.
Humphreys, Paul. *Phil Soc Sci* 21(1), 114-121 Mr 91
Danielson, Peter. *Dialogue (Canada)* 29(4), 598-602 1990

ELSTER, Jon. *Making Sense of Marx*. Cambridge, Cambridge Univ Pr, 1985.
Fisk, Milton. *Nous* 25(2), 215-220 Ap 91

ELSTER, Jon. *Solomonic Judgements: Studies in the Limitations of Rationality*. Cambridge, Cambridge Univ Pr, 1989.
Chisholm, John E. *Phil Stud (Ireland)* 32, 305-307 1988-90

ELTON BULNES, Maria. *Amor y reflexión*. Pamplona, Eunsa, 1989.
Ortíz de Landázuri, Carlos. *Anu Filosof* 23(1), 185-186 1990

EMBREE, Lester (ed). *Worldly Phenomenology: The Continuing Influence of Alfred Schütz on North American Human Science*. Lanham, Univ Pr of America, 1988.
Thomason, Burke C. *J Brit Soc Phenomenol* 22(1), 93-94 Ja 91

EMILSSON, Eyjolfur Kjalar. *Plotinus on Sense-Perception: A Philosophical Study*. Cambridge, Cambridge Univ Pr, 1988.
Schiller, Jerome P. *J Hist Phil* 29(1), 118-119 Ja 91

ENGEL, J Ronald and ENGEL, Joan Gibb (eds). *Ethics of Environment and Development*. Tucson, Univ of Arizona Pr, 1990.
Hawkins, Ronnie. *Agr Human Values* 7(2), 109-114 Spr 90

ENGEL, Pascal. *La norme du vrai: Philosophie de la logique*. Paris, Gallimard, 1989.
Vernant, Denis. *Rev Metaph Morale* 95(4), 563-568 O-D 90

ENGELS, Eve-Marie. *Erkenntnis als Anpassung?* Frankfurt, Suhrkamp, 1989.
Irrgang, Bernhard. *Phil Rundsch* 37(4), 345-348 1990

ENGLER, Wolfgang. *Die Konstruktion von Aufrichtigkeit*. Vienna, Östereichs, 1989.
Marz, Lutz. *Deut Z Phil* 38(11), 1116-1118 1990

ERSKINE, Andrew. *The Hellenistic Stoa: Political Thought and Action*. Ithaca, Cornell Univ Pr, 1990.
Reesor, Margaret E. *Rev Metaph* 44(1), 139-140 S 90

ETCHEMENDY, John. *The Concept of Logical Consequence*. Cambridge, Harvard Univ Pr, 1990.
Tooley, Michael. *Mind* 100(399), 382-388 Jl 91

EUBEN, J Peter. *The Tragedy of Political Theory: The Road Not Taken*. Princeton, Princeton Univ Pr, 1990.
Ober, Josiah. *Polit Theory* 19(3), 477-480 Ag 91

EVANS, G R. *Augustine on Evil*. Cambridge, Cambridge Univ Pr, 1982.
Connellan, Colm. *Phil Stud (Ireland)* 32, 308-311 1988-90

EVANS, Rod and BERENT, Irwin. *Fundamentalism: Hazards and Heartbreaks*. LaSalle, Open Court, 1988.
Lowe, Scott C. *Teach Phil* 13(2), 183-185 Je 90
Foster, Stephen Paul. *Mod Sch* 68(3), 259-261 Mr 91

FABRIS, A. *Filosofia, storia, temporalità*. Pisa, ETS Ed, 1988.
Samonà, Leonardo. *G Metaf* 12(1), 163-164 Ja-Ap 90

FAGGIOTTO, A. *Introduzione alla metafisica kantiana*. Milano, Massimo, 1989.
Pellecchia, Pasquale. *Aquinas* 33(3), 689-692 S-D 90

FAGOT-LARGEAULT, Anne. *Les causes de la mort*. Paris, Inst Inter Etudes Epist, 1989.
Saint-Sernin, Bertrand. *Rev Metaph Morale* 96(1), 97-103 Ja-Mr 91

FAHRNKOPF, Robert. *Wittgenstein on Universals*. New York, Lang, 1988.
Kennick, W E. *Int Stud Phil* 23(1), 114-115 1991

FAIN, Haskell. *Normative Politics and the Community of Nations*. Philadelphia, Temple Univ Pr, 1987.
Simpson, Evan. *Nous* 25(3), 373-376 Je 91

FAIRBAIRN, Gavin (ed) and FAIRBAIRN, Susan. *Ethical Issues in Caring*. Brookfield, Gower, 1989.
Barrett, Anne. *Ethics Med* 7(2), 20 Sum 91

FARÍAS, Victor. *Heidegger y el nazismo*. Barcelona, Muchnik Ed, 1989.
Martínez, Gustavo Bueno. *El Basilisco* 1, 85-87 S-O 89

FARLEY, Wendy. *Tragic Vision and Divine Compassion*. Louisville, Knox Pr, 1990.
Phan, Peter C. *Thomist* 55(2), 327-329 Ap 91
Frey, Robert S. *Bridges* 3(1-2), 132-133 Spr-Sum 91

FARMER, David J. *Being in Time*. Lanham, Univ Pr of America, 1990.
Le Poidevin, Robin. *Mind* 100(399), 388-390 Jl 91

FARRAR, Cynthia. *The Origins of Democratic Thinking: The Invention of Politics in Classical Athens*. New York, Cambridge Univ Pr, 1988.
Carawan, Edwin M. *Ancient Phil* 10(2), 276-279 Fall 90
Rabel, Robert J. *Hist Euro Ideas* 12(4), 548-549 1990

FASCHING, Maria. *Zum Begriff der Freundschaft bei Aristotles und Kant*. Wurzburg, Konigshausen, 1990.
Woschnak, Werner. *Kantstudien* 82(1), 112-114 1991

FARTHING, John L. *Thomas Aquinas and Gabriel Biel: Interpretations of St Thomas Aquinas in German Nominalism on the Eve of the Reformation*. Durham, Duke Univ Pr, 1988.
Wawrykow, Joseph. *Thomist* 55(1), 149-156 Ja 91

FAVRAUX, Paul. *Une philosophie du Médiateur: Maurice Blondel*. Paris, Lethielleux, 1987.
Léonard, André. *Rev Phil Louvain* 88(80), 622-624 N 90

FAYE, Jan. *The Reality of the Future*. Odense, Odense Univ Pr, 1989.
Leslie, John. *Dialogue (Canada)* 29(3), 441-445 1990

FEENBERG, Andrew. *Lukacs, Marx and the Sources of Critical Theory*. New York, Oxford Univ Pr, 1986.
Fluxman, Tony. *S Afr J Phil* 9(4), 230-231 N 90

FEFERMAN, Solomon and others (eds). *Kurt Gödel: Collected Works, V2*. New York, Oxford Univ Pr, 1989.
Kreisel, G. *Notre Dame J Form Log* 31(4), 602-641 Fall 90

FEHER, Michel (ed). *Fragments for a History of the Human Body*. New York, Urzone, 1989.
Dissanayake, Wimal. *Phil East West* 41(2), 276-278 Ap 91

FEINBERG, Joel. *Offense to Others: The Moral Limits of the Criminal Law, V2*. New York, Oxford Univ Pr, 1985.
Amato, Salvatore. *Riv Int Filosof Diritto* 66(4), 742-744 O-D 89

FEKETE, John (ed). *Life After Postmodernism: Essays on Value and Culture*. New York, St Martin's Pr, 1987.
Birch, Andrea Croce. *Bridges* 2(3-4), 201-202 Fall-Wint 90

FELDMAN, Fred. *Doing the Best We Can: An Essay in Informal Deontic Logic*. Dordrecht, Reidel, 1986.
Belzer, Marvin. *Int Stud Phil* 22(3), 101-102 1990
Åqvist, Lennart. *Phil Phenomenol Res* 51(1), 215-225 Mr 91

FELMAN, Shoshana. *Jacques Lacan and the Adventure of Insight: Psychoanalysis in Contemporary Culture*. Cambridge, Harvard Univ Pr, 1987.
Furniss, Tom. *Rad Phil* 56, 61 Autumn 90

FELSKI, Rita. *Beyond Feminist Aesthetics: Feminist Literature and Social Change*. Cambridge, Harvard Univ Pr, 1989.
El Saffar, Ruth. *Phil Lit* 14(2), 407-409 O 90
Kneller, Jane. *Hypatia* 5(3), 165-168 Fall 90
Korsmeyer, Carolyn. *Can Phil Rev* 10(12), 489-492 D 90

FERRÉ, Frederick. *Philosophy of Technology*. Englewood Cliffs, Prentice Hall, 1988.
Rottschaefer, William A. *Bridges* 2(3-4), 203 Fall-Wint 90

FERRAJOLI, Luigi. *Diritto e ragione: Teoria del garantismo penale*. Bari, Laterza, 1989.
D'Agostino, Francesco. *Riv Int Filosof Diritto* 67(1), 164-166 Ja-Mr 90

FERRARI, G R F. *Listening to the Cicadas: A Study of Plato's "Phaedrus"*. Cambridge, Cambridge Univ Pr, 1987.
Griswold Jr, Charles L. *Rev Metaph* 44(2), 415-418 D 90
Rosen, Stanley. *Arion* 1(1), 187-207 Wint 90

FERREIRA, M Jamie. *Scepticism and Reasonable Doubt*. New York, Clarendon/Oxford Pr, 1986.
Pappas, George S. *Int J Phil Relig* 30(1), 63-64 Ag 91

FERRER, Urbano. *Perspectivas de la acción humana*. Barcelona, PBU, 1990.
Cruz Cruz, Juan. *Anu Filosof* 24(1), 180-182 1991

FERRER SANTOS, Urbano. *Perspectivas de la acción humana*. Barcelona, PPU, 1990.
Sánchez Alvarez-Castellanos, Juan José. *Dialogo Filosof* 7(1), 121-123 Ja-Ap 91

FERRY, Luc. *Homo Aestheticus: L'invention du goût à l'âge démocratique*. Paris, Grasset, 1990.
Foisy, Suzanne. *Philosophiques* 17(2), 189-200 Autumn 1990
Hoaru, Jacques. *Rev Phil Fr* 181(2), 249-251 Ap-Je 91

FERRY, Luc. *French Philosophy of the Sixties: An Essay in Antihumanism*. Amherst, Univ of Massachusetts Pr, 1990.
Bannet, Eve Tavor. *Phil Lit* 15(1), 163-164 Ap 91

FETZER, James (ed). *Probability and Causality*. Boston, Reidel, 1987.
Woodward, J. *Brit J Phil Sci* 41(4), 553-573 D 90

FEYERABEND, Paul. *Farewell to Reason*. London, Verso, 1987.
Lugg, Andrew. *Can J Phil* 21(1), 109-120 Mr 91
McCawley, James D. *Crit Rev* 4(3), 377-385 Sum 90
Hacking, Ian. *J Phil* 88(4), 219-223 Ap 91

FEYERABEND, Paul. *Against Method*. New York, Verso, 1988.
Hacking, Ian. *J Phil* 88(4), 219-223 Ap 91

FIELD, Hartry. *Realism, Mathematics and Modality*. Oxford, Blackwell, 1989.
Weir, Alan. *Phil Books* 32(1), 17-26 Ja 91

FIELD, Martha A. *Surrogate Motherhood: The Legal and Human Issues*. Cambridge, Harvard Univ Pr, 1988.
Ross, Judith Wilson. *Hastings Center Rep* 20(5), 46-48 S-O 90

FIELD, Stephen (trans). *Tian Wen: A Chinese Book of Origins*. New York, New Directions, 1986.
Graham, A C. *Phil East West* 41(3), 426-428 Jl 91

FINDLAY, John Niemeyer. *Wittgenstein: A Critique*. London, Routledge & Kegan Paul, 1984.
Petit, Jean-Luc. *Arch Phil* 53(4), 679-682 O-D 90

FINE, Arthur. *The Shaky Game: Einstein, Realism, and the Quantum Theory*. Chicago, Univ of Chicago Pr, 1986.
Howard, Don. *Synthese* 86(1), 123-141 Ja 91
Hughes, R I G. *J Phil* 88(5), 275-279 My 91

FINGARETTE, Herbert. *Heavy Drinking: The Myth of Alcoholism as a Disease*. Berkeley, Univ of Calif Pr, 1988.
Schoeman, Ferdinand. *Phil Rev* 100(3), 493-498 Jl 91

FINK, Eugen. *VI Cartesianische Meditation, 2v*. Dordrecht, Kluwer, 1988.
Gorner, Paul. *J Brit Soc Phenomenol* 21(3), 290-293 O 90

FINLAY, Marike. *Powermatics: A Discursive Critique of New Communications Technology*. London, Routledge & Kegan Paul, 1987.
Belsey, Andrew. *J Applied Phil* 8(1), 132-133 1991

FINOCCHIARO, M A. *Gramsci and the History of Dialectical Thought*. Cambridge, Cambridge Univ Pr, 1988.
Martin, James. *Hist Polit Thought* 11(2), 356-357 Sum 90

FINOCCHIARO, Maurice A (ed & trans). *The Galileo Affair: A Documentary History*. Berkeley, Univ of California Pr, 1989.
Sharratt, Michael. *Stud Hist Phil Sci* 21(4), 685-690 D 90

FINSTER, Reinhard and others (eds). *Leibniz Lexicon*. Hildesheim, Olms, 1988.
Parkinson, G H R. *Stud Leibniz* 22(1), 112-114 1990

FIORI, Gabriella. *Simone Weil: An Intellectual Biography, Joseph R Berrigan (trans)*. Athens, Univ of Georgia Pr, 1989.
Allen, Diogenes. *Teach Phil* 13(3), 310-314 S 90
Harwell, Margherita Pieracci. *Phil Lit* 15(1), 175-176 Ap 91

FISCHER, John Martin (ed). *God, Foreknowledge, and Freedom*. Stanford, Stanford Univ Pr, 1989.
Craig, William Lane. *Relig Stud* 27(2), 278-280 Je 91
Zagzebski, Linda. *Can Phil Rev* 10(8), 309-311 Ag 90

FISCHER, Michael. *Stanley Cavell and Literary Skepticism*. Chicago, Univ of Chicago Pr, 1989.
Duffy, Edward. *Clio* 20(1), 70-73 Fall 90

FISH, Stanley. *Doing What Comes Naturally: Change, Rhetoric, and the Practice of Theory in Literary and Legal Studies*. Durham, Duke Univ Pr, 1990.
Benton, Michael. *Brit J Aes* 30(4), 386-387 O 90
Bogue, Ronald. *Phil Lit* 14(2), 435-436 O 90

FISHER, Alec. *The Logic of Real Arguments*. Cambridge, Cambridge Univ Pr, 1988.
Lyon, Ardon. *Philosophy* 66(256), 249-252 Ap 91

FISHER, John Martin (ed). *God, Foreknowledge, and Freedom*. Stanford, Stanford Univ Pr, 1989.
Elders, Leo J. *Rev Metaph* 44(2), 418-419 D 90

FISHER, Simon. *Revelatory Positivism? Barth's Earliest Theology and the Marburg School*. New York, Oxford Univ Pr, 1988.
Long, Eugene Thomas. *Rev Metaph* 44(4), 839-840 Je 91

FITTING, Melvin. *Computability Theory, Semantics, and Logic Programming*. Oxford, Oxford Univ Pr, 1987.
Davis, Martin. *Notre Dame J Form Log* 31(3), 485-486 Sum 90

FITZPATRICK, F J. *Ethics in Nursing Practice: Basic Principles and their Application*. London, Linacre Centre, 1988.
Whyte, Dorothy A. *Ethics Med* 7(1), 16 Spr 91

FIUMARA, Gemma Corradi. *The Other Side of Language*. New York, Routledge, 1990.
Rée, Jonathan. *Rad Phil* 58, 41-42 Sum 91

FLAY, Joseph C. *Hegel's Quest for Certainty*. Albany, SUNY Pr, 1984.
O'Hagen, T. *Bull Hegel Soc Gt Brit* 20, 37-42 Autumn-Wint 89

FLETCHER, John C and QUIST, Norman and JONSEN, Albert R (eds). *Ethics Consultation in Health Care*. Ann Arbor, Health Administration Pr, 1989.
O'Connell, Laurence J. *Med Human Rev* 5(1), 68-71 Ja 91

FLETCHER, John and BENJAMIN, Andrew (eds). *Abjection, Melancholia, and Love*. New York, Routledge, 1990.
Atack, Margaret. *Rad Phil* 58, 44-45 Sum 91

FLEW, Antony and VESEY, Godfrey. *Agency and Necessity*. Cambridge, Blackwell, 1987.
Davis, Lawrence H. *Phil Rev* 100(3), 466-469 Jl 91

FLEW, Antony. *Thinking about Social Thinking: The Philosophy of Social Science*. New York, Blackwell, 1985.
Farr, Richard. *Phil Rev* 100(1), 151-153 Ja 91

FLOISTAD, Guttorm. *Contemporary Philosophy: African Philosophy*. Boston, Nijhoff, 1987.
Birt, Robert E. *Phil East West* 41(1), 95-109 Ja 91

FLORES, Albert. *Professional Ideals*. Belmont, Wadsworth, 1988.
Bishop, John D. *J Bus Ethics* 9(10), 817-820 O 90

FOCILLON, Henri. *The Life of Forms in Art, Charles B Hogan and George Kubler (trans)*. New York, Zone Books, 1989.
Wood, Robert E. *Rev Metaph* 44(3), 632-634 Mr 91

FODOR, Jerry A. *Psychosemantics: The Problem of Meaning in the Philosophy of Mind*. Cambridge, MIT Pr, 1987.
Lloyd, Dan. *Phil Rev* 100(2), 289-293 Ap 91
Garfield, Jay L. *Phil Phenomenol Res* 51(1), 235-240 Mr 91
Callaway, H G. *Erkenntnis* 33(2), 251-259 S 90

FOGELIN, Robert J. *Figuratively Speaking*. New Haven, Yale Univ Pr, 1988.
Johnson, Mark. *Int Stud Phil* 23(1), 115-116 1991

FOLEY, Richard. *The Theory of Epistemic Rationality*. Cambridge, Harvard Univ Pr, 1987.
Annis, David B. *Int Stud Phil* 22(3), 103-104 1990

FONTENELLE. *Oeuvres complètes*. Paris, Fayard, 1990.
Lombardi, Marco. *Rev Phil Fr* 181(1), 125-129 1991

FONTINELL, Eugene. *Self, God, and Immortality: A Jamesian Investigation*. Philadelphia, Temple Univ Pr, 1986.
Croce, Paul Jerome. *Int J Phil Relig* 29(3), 187-189 Je 91

FONTINELL, Eugene. *Self, God, and Immortality: A Jamesian Investigation*. Philadelphia, Temple Univ Pr, 1986.
Barry, Robert M. *Mod Sch* 68(1), 86-89 N 90

FORBES, Graeme. *Languages of Possibility*. Cambridge, Blackwell, 1989.
Kapitan, Tomis. *Hist Phil Log* 12(2), 263-266 1991
Milne, Peter. *Phil Books* 31(4), 222-224 O 90

FORBES, Ian. *Marx and the New Individual*. London, Unwin Hyman, 1990.
Corcoran, Paul E. *Hist Euro Ideas* 13(1-2), 155-157 1991

FORD, Marcus P (ed). *A Process Theory of Medicine: Interdisciplinary Essays*. Lewiston, Mellen Pr, 1987.
Potter, Robert Lyman. *Zygon* 25(3), 353-355 S 90

FORD, Norman M. *When Did I Begin?* Cambridge, Cambridge Univ Pr, 1988.
Williams, A M. *J Applied Phil* 7(2), 239-240 O 90
Reidy, Maurice. *Heythrop J* 32(3), 489-451 Jl 91

FORESTER, Tom and MORRISON, Perry. *Computer Ethics: Cautionary Tales and Ethical Dilemmas in Computing*. Cambridge, MIT Pr, 1990.
Kallman, Ernest A. *Bus Ethics Quart* 1(3), 319-331 Jl 91

FORMENT GIRALT, Eudaldo. *Filosofía del ser*. Barcelona, PPU, 1988.
Fernández Burillo, Santiago. *Espiritu* 38(99), 79-81 Ja-Je 89

FORNARO, Mauro. *Scuole di psicoanalisi: Ricerca storico-epistemologica sul pensiero di Hartmann, Klein e Lacan*. Milan, Vita e Pensiero, 1988.
De Paoli, Marco. *Filosofia* 41(3), 432-436 S-D 90

FORREST, P. *Quantum Metaphysics*. Oxford, Blackwell, 1988.
Krips, Henry. *Austl J Phil* 68(4), 463-465 D 90

FORRESTER, John. *The Seductions of Psychoanalysis: Freud, Lacan and Derrida*. Cambridge, Cambridge Univ Pr, 1990.
Macey, David. *Rad Phil* 57, 34-35 Spr 91

FORSTER, Michael N. *Hegel and Scepticism*. Cambridge, Harvard Univ Pr, 1989.
Inwood, M J. *Bull Hegel Soc Gt Brit* 20, 29-29 Autumn-Wint 89

FORUM FÜR PHILOSOPHIE, (ed). *Philosophie und Begründung*. Frankfurt am Main, Suhrkamp Taschenbuch, 1987.
Wüstehube, Axel. *Z Phil Forsch* 44(3), 495-499 1990

FORUM FÜR PHILOSOPHIE BAD, HOMBURG (ed). *Kants transzendentale Deduktion und die Möglichkeit von Transzendentalphilosophie*. Frankfurt am Main, Suhrkamp, 1988.
Mohr, Georg. *Z Phil Forsch* 45(1), 146-151 Ja-Mr 91

FOSS, Laurence and ROTHENBERG, Kenneth. *The Second Medical Revolution: From Biomedicine to Infomedicine*. Boston, Shambhala, 1988.
Potter, Robert Lyman. *Zygon* 25(3), 353-355 S 90

FOTION, N and ELFSTROM, G. *Military Ethics: Guidelines for Peace and War*. London, Routledge & Kegan Paul, 1987.
O'Connell, James. *Heythrop J* 32(1), 102-103 Ja 91

FOUCAULT, Michel. *Politics, Philosophy, Culture: Interviews and Other Writings, 1977-1984, Lawrence D Kritzman (ed)*. New York, Routledge, Chapman & Hall, 1988.
McWhorter, Ladelle. *Can Phil Rev* 10(9), 352-356 S 90

FOX, Richard G. *Gandhian Utopia*. Boston, Beacon Pr, 1989.
Chatterjee, Margaret. *Phil East West* 41(3), 428-431 Jl 91

FRANCHINI, R. *Eutanasia dei principi logici*. Napoli, Loffredo, 1989.
Reda, Clementina Gily. *Filosofia* 42(1), 144-147 Ja-Ap 91

FRANCK, Olof. *The Criteriologic Problem*. Stockholm, Almqvist & Wiksell, 1988.
Brümmer, Vincent. *Relig Stud* 26(4), 543-544 D 90

FRANCO, Paul. *The Political Philosophy of Michael Oakeshott*. New Haven, Yale Univ Pr, 1990.
Lawn, Chris. *Rad Phil* 58, 40 Sum 91

FRANK, Daniel H. *The Arguments "from the Sciences" in Aristotle's Peri Ideon*. New York, Lang, 1985.
Jost, Lawrence J. *Ancient Phil* 10(2), 312-316 Fall 90

FRANK, Manfred. *What Is Neostructuralism?, Sabine Wilke and Richard T Gray (trans)*. Minneapolis, Univ of Minnesota Pr, 1989.
Schreiner, Christopher S. *Phil Lit* 14(2), 430-432 O 90

FRANK, Philipp. *Das Kausalgesetz und seine Grenzen*. Frankfurt am Main, Suhrkamp, 1988.
Balibar, Françoise. *Rev Phil Fr* 180(4), 689-691 O-D 90

FRANKENBERRY, Nancy. *Religion and Radical Empiricism*. Albany, SUNY Pr, 1987.
Walhout, Donald. *Int Stud Phil* 22(3), 104-105 1990

FRANKLIN, Allan. *The Neglect of Experiment*. New York, Cambridge Univ Pr, 1986.
Ackermann, Robert. *Brit J Phil Sci* 40(2), 185-190 Je 89

FRANKLING, Stephen T. *Speaking From the Depths*. Grand Rapids, Eerdmans, 1990.
Beauchamp, Richard A. *J Speculative Phil* 5(3), 219-221 1991

FRASER, Nancy. *Unruly Practices*. Minneapolis, Univ of Minn Pr, 1989.
Mann, Patricia S. *Hypatia* 6(2), 225-228 Sum 91

FRAWLEY, W. *Text and Epistemology*. Norwood, Ablex, 1987.
Charolles, Michel. *J Prag* 15(3), 291-296 Mr 91

FRAZER, Nancy. *Unruly Practices: Power, Discourse and Gender in Contemporary Social Theory*. Minneapolis, Univ of Minnesota Pr, 1989.
Rabotnikof, Nora. *Dianoia* 35(35), 214-219 1989

FREDDOSO, Alfred (trans). *Luis de Molina: On Divine Foreknowledge*. Ithaca, Cornell Univ Pr, 1988.
Leftow, Brian. *Int Phil Quart* 31(3), 374-376 S 91

FREDE, Michael and PATZIG, Günther. *Aristoteles 'Metaphysik Z'*. Munchen, Beck, 1988.
Woods, Michael. *Phronesis* 36(1), 75-87 1991
Gill, Mary Louise. *J Hist Phil* 28(4), 602-605 O 90

FREEDBERG, David. *The Power of Images: Studies in the History and Theory of Response*. Chicago, Univ of Chicago Pr, 1989.
Wynyard, R N. *Brit J Aes* 30(4), 380-381 O 90

FREESE, Hans-Ludwig. *Kinder sind Philosophen*. Berlin, Quadriga, 1989.
Matthews, Gareth. *Thinking* 9(1), 42 1990

FRENCH, Robert E. *The Geometry of Vision and the Mind Body Problem*. New York, Lang, 1987.
Hilbert, David. *Phil Rev* 100(2), 293-297 Ap 91

FRESCO, M F and VAN DIJK, R J A and VIJGEBOOM, H W P. *Heideggers These vom Ende der Philosophie*. Bonn, Bouvier, 1989.
Grondin, Jean. *Arch Phil* 54(3), 495-496 Jl-S 91

FRIEDMAN, John B (ed). *John de Foxton's Liber Cosmographiae (1408), An Edition and Codicological Study*. Leiden, Brill, 1988.
Diekstra, F N M. *Vivarium* 28(1), 55-76 My 90

FRINGS, Manfred S. *Philosophy of Prediction and Capitalism*. Dordrecht, Nijhoff, 1987.
Spader, Peter H. *J Brit Soc Phenomenol* 21(3), 301-303 O 90

FROST, Mervyn. *Towards a Normative Theory of International Relations*. Cambridge, Cambridge Univ Pr, 1986.
Knowles, C. *S Afr J Phil* 10(2), 59-60 My 91

FULFORD, K W M. *Moral Theory and Medical Practice*. Cambridge, Cambridge Univ Pr, 1990.
Marshall, S E. *Phil Books* 32(1), 52-53 Ja 91
Pickering, Neil. *Phil Invest* 14(2), 179-183 Ap 91
Gillett, Grant. *Phil Quart* 41(164), 379-381 Jl 91
Prior, Patricia. *Rad Phil* 58, 34-35 Sum 91

FULLER, Steve. *Social Epistemology*. Bloomington, Indiana Univ Pr, 1988.
Schmaus, Warren. *Phil Soc Sci* 21(1), 121-125 Mr 91
D'Amico, Robert. *Can Phil Rev* 10(9), 362-365 S 90

FULLER, Steve. *Philosophy of Science and Its Discontents*. Boulder, Westview Pr, 1989.
Malone, Michael. *Can Phil Rev* 10(10), 407-410 O 90
Brown, Harold I. *Phil Soc Sci* 21(2), 283-287 Je 91

FUMENTO, Michael. *The Myth of Heterosexual AIDS*. New York, Basic Books, 1990.
Murphy, Timothy F. *Med Human Rev* 5(1), 87-92 Ja 91

FUNKE, Gerhard. *Phenomenology: Metaphysics or Method?, David J Parent (trans)*. Athens, Ohio Univ Pr, 1987.
Stewart, David. *Husserl Stud* 7(2), 145-151 1990

FURET, François. *Marx and the French Revolution, Deborah Kan Furet (trans)*. Chicago, Univ of Chicago Pr, 1989.
Lovell, David W. *Hist Euro Ideas* 12(6), 859-860 1990

FURET, François. *Marx et la révolution française*. Paris, Flammarion, 1986.
Lovell, David W. *Hist Euro Ideas* 12(6), 859-860 1990

FURLEY, David. *The Greek Cosmologists, V1: The Formation of the Atomic Theory and its Earliest Critics*. New York, Cambridge Univ Pr, 1987.
Inwood, Brad. *Ancient Phil* 10(2), 271-273 Fall 90
Gaukroger, Stephen. *Austl J Phil* 68(3), 351-352 S 90

FURLEY, David. *Cosmic Problems*. Cambridge, Cambridge Univ Pr, 1989.
Gaukroger, Stephen. *Austl J Phil* 68(3), 351-352 S 90

FÜRST, Gebhard. *Sprache als metaphorischer Prozess*. Mainz, Grünewald, 1988.
Borsche, Tilman. *Phil Rundsch* 37(4), 327-335 1990

GADAMER, Hans-Georg. *The Relevance of the Beautiful and Other Essays, Robert Bernasconi (ed), Nicholas Walker (trans)*. Cambridge, Cambridge Univ Pr, 1987.
Zuñiga, Joaquin. *Nous* 25(1), 139-142 Mr 91

GADAMER, Hans-Georg. *Elogio della teoria*. Milano, Guerini, 1989.
Giacometti, Chiara. *Filosofia* 42(1), 147-149 Ja-Ap 91

GAIER, Ulrich. *Herders Sprachphilosophie und Erkenntniskritik*. Stuttgart, Frommann-Holzboog, 1988.
Borsche, Tilman. *Phil Rundsch* 37(4), 327-335 1990

GALASSO, Giuseppe. *Croce e lo spirito del suo tempo*. Milano, Il Saggiatore, 1990.
Reda, Clementina Gily. *Filosofia* 42(1), 109-113 Ja-Ap 91

GALISON, Peter. *How Experiments End*. Chicago, Univ of Chicago Pr, 1987.
Franklin, Allan. *Brit J Phil Sci* 39(3), 411-414 S 88

GARCÍA MORENTE, Manuel. *La Filosofía de Kant*. Madrid, Espasa-Calpe, 1982.
Caimi, Mario. *Kantstudien* 81(4), 476-478 1990

GARDENFORS, Peter. *Knowledge in Flux: Modeling the Dynamics of Epistemic States*. Cambridge, MIT Pr, 1988.
Harriott, Howard H. *Hist Phil Log* 12(1), 111-120 1990
Levi, Isaac. *J Phil* 88(8), 437-444 Ag 91

GARFIELD, Jay L. *Belief in Psychology*. Cambridge, MIT Pr, 1988.
Segal, Gabriel. *Phil Rev* 100(3), 463-466 Jl 91

GARRETT, Thomas M and BAILLIE, Harold W and GARRETT, Rosellen M. *Health Care Ethics: Principles and Problems*. Englewood Cliffs, Prentice-Hall, 1989.
Purviance, Susan M. *Teach Phil* 13(4), 388-390 D 90

GARRY, Ann and PEARSALL, Marilyn (eds). *Women, Knowledge, and Reality: Exploration in Feminist Philosophy*. Winchester, Unwin Hyman, 1989.
Mallick, Krishna. *Teach Phil* 13(4), 399-401 D 90

GARVER, Eugene. *Machiavelli and the History of Prudence*. Madison, Univ of Wisconsin Pr, 1987.
Jost, Walter. *Phil Rhet* 24(1), 73-76 1991

GASCHÉ, Rodolphe. *The Tain of the Mirror: Derrida and the Philosophy of Reflection*. Cambridge, Harvard Univ Pr, 1986.
McCumber, John. *Phil Rev* 100(2), 300-303 Ap 91

GASKIN, J C A (ed). *Varieties of Unbelief: From Epicurus to Sartre*. New York, Macmillan, 1989.
Corrington, Robert S. *Teach Phil* 13(3), 298-301 S 90

GASSER, J. *Essai sur la nature et les critères de la preuve*. Cousset, Delval, 1989.
Panza, M. *Hist Phil Log* 12(1), 128-131 1990

GAUKROGER, S. *Cartesian Logic: An Essay on Descartes's Conception of Inference*. Oxford, Clarendon Pr, 1989.
Clarke, D M. *Hist Phil Log* 12(1), 122-123 1990
Watson, Richard A. *Rev Metaph* 44(1), 140-141 S 90

GAUTHIER, David. *Morals by Agreement*. New York, Oxford Univ Pr, 1986.
Donaldson, Thomas. *Mod Sch* 68(1), 93-94 N 90

GAUTHIER, David. *Moral Dealing: Contract, Ethics, and Reason*. Ithaca, Cornell Univ Pr, 1990.
Pogge, Thomas W. *Can Phil Rev* 10(12), 492-495 D 90

GAUTHIER, Pierre. *Newman et Blondel*. Paris, Cerf, 1988.
Narcisse, Gilbert. *Rev Thomiste* 90(4), 668-671 O-D 90

GAVIN, William J (ed). *Context over Foundation: Dewey and Marx*. Dordrecht, Reidel, 1988.
Gouinlock, James. *Trans Peirce Soc* 26(4), 521-530 Fall 90

GAVISON, Ruth (ed). *Issues in Contemporary Legal Philosophy: The Influence of H L A Hart*. New York, Oxford Univ Pr, 1987.
Belliotti, Raymond A. *Int Stud Phil* 22(3), 105-107 1990

GEAR, Jane. *Perception and the Evolution of Style: A New Model of Mind*. New York, Routledge, 1989.
Matravers, Derek. *Brit J Aes* 30(4), 378-380 O 90

GELDSETZER, Lutz. *Logik*. Aalen, Scientia, 1987.
Foulkes, Paul. *Z Phil Forsch* 44(4), 669-671 1990

GELLNER, Ernest. *Plough, Sword and Book*. Chicago, Univ of Chicago Pr, 1988.
Munz, Peter. *Phil Soc Sci* 21(2), 253-276 Je 91

GELLNER, Ernest. *Relativism and the Social Sciences*. Cambridge, Cambridge Univ Pr, 1985.
Flew, Antony. *Crit Rev* 4(1-2), 155-172 Wint-Spr 90

GELPI, Donald L (ed). *Beyond Individualism: Toward a Retrieval of Moral Discourse in America*. Notre Dame, Univ of Notre Dame Pr, 1989.
Barker, Jeffrey H. *Teach Phil* 13(4), 407-409 D 90

GELVEN, Michael. *Étre et temps de Heidegger: Un commentaire littéral*. Brussels, Mardaga, 1987.
Roy, Jean-Lévis. *Dialogue (Canada)* 29(3), 473-475 1990

GELVEN, Michael. *Spirit and Existence: A Philosophical Inquiry*. Notre Dame, Univ Notre Dame Pr, 1990.
Westphal, Merold. *Rev Metaph* 44(4), 840-841 Je 91

GENESERETH, Michael R. *Logical Foundations of Artificial Intelligence*. Los Altos, Morgan Kaufmann, 1987.
Martins, João P. *J Sym Log* 55(3), 1304-1307 S 90

GEORGOPOULOS, N. *Art and Emotion*. New York, Lang, 1989.
Hynes-Higman, Cecilia. *Brit J Aes* 31(3), 271-272 Jl 91

GERSH, S. *Middle Platonism and Neoplatonism*. Notre Dame, Univ Notre Dame Pr, 1986.
Ritacco de Gayoso, Graciela L. *Sapientia* 46(180), 158-160 Ap-Je 91

GERVAIS, Richard. *Dialectique et totalitarisme*. Ville LaSalle, Hurtubise, 1990.
Knee, Philip. *Laval Theol Phil* 47(1), 139-142 F 91

GHOSE, Ranjit. *Idea of a Person*. Calcutta, Punthi Pustak, 1990.
Bagchi, K. *J Indian Counc Phil Res* 8(1), 149-152 S-D 90

GIBBARD, Allan. *Wise Choices, Apt Feelings*. Cambridge, Harvard Univ Pr, 1990.
Cudd, Ann E. *Auslegung* 17(2), 167-171 Sum 91
Hubin, Donald C. *Phil Quart* 41(163), 252-256 Ap 91

GIBBINS, Peter. *Particles and Paradoxes: The Limits of Quantum Logic*. Cambridge, Cambridge Univ Pr, 1987.
Hughes, R I G. *Phil Rev* 99(4), 646-649 O 90

GIBSON JR, Roger F. *Enlightened Empiricism: An Examination of W V Quine's Theory of Knowledge*. Gainesville, Univ S Florida Pr, 1988.
Hocutt, Max. *Behavior Phil* 18(2), 69-77 Fall-Wint 90
Solomon, Miriam. *Phil Rev* 100(3), 484-487 Jl 91

GIERE, Ronald. *Explaining Science: A Cognitive Approach*. Chicago, Univ of Chicago Pr, 1988.
Kosso, Peter. *Nous* 25(3), 386-388 Je 91
Teller, Paul. *Phil Sci* 57(4), 729-731 D 90
Achinstein, Peter. *Int Stud Phil* 22(3), 107-108 1990
Kitcher, Philip. *J Phil* 88(3), 163-167 Mr 91

GIGERENZER, Gerd and others. *The Empire of Chance: How Probability Changed Science and Everyday Life*. Cambridge, Cambridge Univ Pr, 1989.
Franklin, James. *Hist Euro Ideas* 12(4), 572-573 1990

GILBERT, Margaret. *On Social Facts*. London, Routledge, Chapman & Hall, 1989.
Macdonald, Graham. *J Applied Phil* 7(2), 233-236 O 90
Fellows, Roger. *Phil Quart* 41(162), 100-104 Ja 91
Tuomela, Raimo. *Philosophia (Israel)* 20(3), 331-338 D 90

GILL, Christopher (ed). *The Person and The Human Mind*. Oxford, Clarendon Pr, 1990.
Cockburn, David. *Phil Invest* 13(4), 367-371 O 90

GILL, M L. *Aristotle on Substance: The Paradox of Unity*. Princeton, Princeton Univ Pr, 1989.
Scaltsas, Theodore. *Phil Books* 32(1), 26-28 Ja 91
Follon, Jacques. *Rev Phil Louvain* 89(82), 343-347 My 91
Hughes, G J. *Heythrop J* 32(3), 438-439 Jl 91
Gerson, Lloyd P. *Can Phil Rev* 10(10), 410-413 O 90

GILLIGAN, Carol and others. *Mapping the Moral Domain: A Contribution of Women's Thinking to Psychological Theory and Education*. Cambridge, Harvard Univ Pr, 1988.
Brabeck, Mary. *J Moral Educ* 20(1), 95-98 F 91

GILMAN, Sander L and BLAIR, Carole and PARENT, David J (eds & trans). *Friedrich Nietzsche on Rhetoric and Language*. New York, Oxford Univ Pr, 1989.
Lachterman, David R. *Phil Rhet* 23(4), 325-328 1990

GILMOUR, Peter (ed). *Philosophers of the Enlightenment*. Edinburgh, Edinburgh Univ Pr, 1990.
Gallie, Roger. *Phil Books* 32(2), 82-83 Ap 91

GILSON, Etienne. *Linguistics and Philosophy: An Essay on the Philosophical Constants of Language, John Lyon (trans)*. Notre Dame, Univ of Notre Dame Pr, 1989.
Baldner, Steven. *Can Phil Rev* 10(12), 495-498 D 90

GINET, Carl. *On Action*. New York, Cambridge Univ Pr, 1990.
Davis, Lawrence H. *Mind* 100(399), 390-394 Jl 91
Rostad, Michael. *Ratio* 4(1), 90-95 Je 91

GLAZER, Nathan. *The Limits of Social Policy*. Cambridge, Harvard Univ Pr, 1988.
Murray, Charles. *Crit Rev* 4(4), 493-504 Fall 90

GLOVER, Jonathan and others. *Ethics of New Reproductive Technologies*. DeKalb, Northern Illinois Univ Pr, 1989.
Boetzkes, Elisabeth. *Can Phil Rev* 10(8), 311-313 Ag 90

GODLOVE JR, Terry F. *Religion, Interpretation, and Diversity of Belief: The Framework Model from Kant to Durkheim to Davidson*. Cambridge, Cambridge Univ Pr, 1989.
Chisholm, John E. *Phil Stud (Ireland)* 32, 311-315 1988-90

GÖHLER, Gerhard. *Die Reduktion der Dialektik durch Marx*. Stuttgart, Klett-Cotta, 1980.
Koncz, Ilona. *Magyar Filozof Szemle* 1-2, 189-194 1990

GÓMEZ ROBLEDO, Antonio. *El pensamiento filosófico de Edith Stein*. México, UNAM, 1988.
Beuchot, Mauricio. *Dianoia* 35(35), 211-212 1989

GOLDMAN, Alan H. *Moral Knowledge*. New York, Routledge, Chapman & Hall, 1989.
Fotion, Nick. *Can Phil Rev* 10(9), 365-367 S 90

GOLDMAN, Alan H. *The Moral Foundations of Professional Ethics*. Totowa, Rowman & Littlefield, 1980.
Morris, Tim. *Bus Prof Ethics J* 2(3), 69-75 Spr 83

GOLDMAN, Alvin I. *Epistemology and Cognition*. Cambridge, Harvard Univ Pr, 1986.
Thagard, Paul. *Erkenntnis* 34(1), 117-123 Ja 91

GOLDMANN, Lucien. *Mensch, Gemeinschaft und Welt in der Philosophie Immanuel Kants*. New York, Campus, 1989.
Wenzel, Uwe Justus. *Kantstudien* 81(4), 490-492 1990

GÓMEZ PÉREZ, Rafael. *Cómo entender este fin de siglo*. Barcelona, Drac, 1988.
Fernández Burillo, S. *Espiritu* 38(100), 179-181 Jl-D 89

GÓMEZ ROBLEDO, Antonio. *Sócrates y el socratismo*. México, Fondo de Cultura Económica, 1988.
Díaz Cíntora, Salvador. *Dianoia* 34(34), 306-311 1988

GÓMEZ-HERAS, José María. *El apriori del mundo de la vida*. Barcelona, Anthropos, 1989.
Díaz, Carlos. *Dialogo Filosof* 6(3), 413-415 S-D 90

GOMEZ-LOBO, Alfonso. *Parmenides: Texto griego, traduccion y comentario*. Buenos Aires, Charcas, 1985.
Gurtler, Gary M. *Ancient Phil* 10(2), 274-276 Fall 90

GONZÁLEZ, Angel Luis. *Teología natural*. Pamplona, EUNSA, 1985.
Forment, E. *Espiritu* 35(94), 154-155 Jl-D 86

GONZÁLEZ, Juliana. *Ética y libertad*. México, UNAM, 1989.
Sagols, Lizbeth. *Dianoia* 35(35), 212-214 1989

GONZÁLEZ CARLOMAN, Antonio. *Estructura lógica de la geometría clásica del plano*. Oviedo, Univ Oviedo, 1987.
Martínez, Gustavo Bueno. *El Basilisco* 1, 91-94 S-O 89

GONZÁLEZ DEL TEJO, Carmen. *La presencia del pasado*. Oviedo, Pentalfa, 1990.
Fernández Lorenzo, Manuel. *El Basilisco* 6, 93-94 Jl-Ag 90

GOODIN, Robert E. *No Smoking: The Ethical Issues*. Chicago, Univ of Chicago Pr, 1989.
Feinberg, Joel. *Bioethics* 5(2), 150-157 Ap 91

GOODING, David and PINCH, Trevor and SCHAFFER, Simon (eds). *The Uses of Experiment: Studies in the Natural Sciences*. Cambridge, Cambridge Univ Pr, 1989.
Knight, David. *Phil Books* 31(4), 253-254 O 90
Powers, Jonathan. *Rad Phil* 56, 48-49 Autumn 90

GOODLAD, John I and SODER, Roger and SIROTNIK, Kenneth A (eds). *The Moral Dimensions of Teaching*. San Francisco, Jossey-Bass, 1990.
Pagano, Jo Anne. *J Moral Educ* 20(2), 220-221 My 91

GOODMAN, Nelson and ELGIN, Catherine Z. *Reconceptions in Philosophy and Other Arts*. Indianapolis, Hackett, 1988.
Adler, Jonathan. *J Phil* 87(12), 711-716 D 90
Arrell, Douglas. *Can Phil Rev* 10(8), 313-316 Ag 90
Warner, Martin. *J Applied Phil* 7(2), 231-233 O 90

GORDON, David. *Resurrecting Marx: The Analytical Marxists on Freedom, Exploitation, and Justice*. New Brunswick, Transaction, 1990.
Gottfried, Paul. *Rev Metaph* 44(4), 842-843 Je 91

GORDON, Robert M. *The Structure of Emotions*. New York, Cambridge Univ Pr, 1987.
De Sousa, Ronald. *Nous* 25(3), 367-373 Je 91

GORLIN, Rena A (ed). *Codes of Professional Responsibility, 2nd ed*. Washington, BNA Books, 1990.
Gaa, James C. *J Bus Ethics* 9(12), 960,970 D 90
Keith-Spiegel, Patricia. *Ethics Behavior* 1(3), 203-204 1991

GOSLING, Justin. *Weakness of the Will*. London, Routledge, 1990.
Mooney, Timothy. *Phil Stud (Ireland)* 32, 315-319 1988-90

GOTTHELF, Allan (ed). *Aristotle on Nature and Living Things: Philosophical and Historical Studies*. Pittsburgh, Mathesis, 1985.
Ereshefsky, Marc. *Phil Sci* 57(4), 724-727 D 90

GOTTHELF, Allan and LENNOX, James G (eds). *Philosophical Issues in Aristotle's Biology*. New York, Cambridge Univ Pr, 1987.
Carrick, Paul. *Int Stud Phil* 22(3), 108-109 1990

GOULD, Carol C. *Rethinking Democracy: Freedom and Social Cooperation in Politics, Economy, and Society*. Cambridge, Cambridge Univ Pr, 1988.
Schultz, David. *Int Stud Phil* 22(3), 109-110 1990

GOULET, R (ed). *Dictionnaire des Philosophes Antiques*. Paris, CNRS, 1989.
Follon, Jacques. *Rev Phil Louvain* 89(82), 322-328 My 91
Lafrance, Yvon. *Apeiron* 24(1), 71-80 Mr 91

GOULET, Richard. *La philosophie de Moïse: Essai de reconstitution d'un commentaire philosophique préphilonien du Prentateuque*. Paris, Vrin, 1987.
Bodéüs, Richard. *Dialogue (Canada)* 29(1), 146-147 1990

GOVIER, Trudy. *Problems in Argument Analysis and Evaluation*. Providence, Foris, 1987.
Allen, Derek. *Inform Log* 12(1), 43-62 Wint 90

GRABER, Glenn and THOMASMA, David. *Euthanasia*. New York, Continuum Pr, 1990.
Pence, Gregory. *Hastings Center Rep* 21(3), 34-35 My-Je 91

GRABMANN, M. *Die Geschichte der scholastischen Methode*. Berlin, Jahrhundert, 1988.
Glombik, Czeslaw. *Frei Z Phil Theol* 38(1-2), 193-204 1991

GRACIA, Jorge J E and DAVIS, Douglas. *The Metaphysics of Good and Evil According to Suarez*. Munich, Philosophia, 1989.
Aertsen, Jan A. *Rev Metaph* 44(2), 420-421 D 90

GRACIA, Jorge J E. *Individuality: An Essay on the Foundations of Metaphysics*. Albany, SUNY Pr, 1988.
Barry, Robert M. *Mod Sch* 68(1), 82-84 N 90

GRAEFE, Steffen. *Der gespaltene Eros: Platons Trieb zur "Weisheit"*. New York, Lang, 1989.
Kerkhoff, Manfred. *Dialogos* 26(58), 190-193 Jl 91

GRAHAM, A C. *Disputers of the Tao: Philosophical Argument in Ancient China*. La Salle, Open Court, 1989.
Birdwhistell, Anne D. *J Hist Phil* 29(2), 327-328 Ap 91

GRAHAM, Daniel W. *Aristotle's Two Systems*. New York, Oxford Univ Pr, 1987.
Weller, Cass. *Phil Rev* 100(2), 324-326 Ap 91

GRAHAM, George and LAFOLLETTE, Hugh (eds). *Person to Person*. Philadelphia, Temple Univ Pr, 1989.
Campbell, David M A. *Phil Books* 32(1), 53-55 Ja 91

GRAHAM, Loren R. *Science, Philosophy and Human Behaviour in the Soviet Union*. New York, Columbia Univ Pr, 1987.
Tomasini, Alejandro. *Dianoia* 35(35), 220-228 1989
Akhundov, M D. *Biol Phil* 6(3), 363-376 Jl 91

GRANFIELD, David. *The Inner Experience of Law*. Washington, Cath Univ Amer Pr, 1988.
Wintgens, Luc. *Phil Rhet* 24(3), 275-279 1991
Boyle, Joseph. *Can Phil Rev* 10(8), 316-318 Ag 90

GRANGER, G G. *Invitation à la lecture de Wittgenstein*. Aix-en-Provence, Ed ALINEA, 1990.
Bassols, Alejandro Tomasini. *Critica* 23(67), 81-87 Ap 91

GRANGER, Gilles-Gaston. *Pour la connaissance philosophique*. Paris, Jacob, 1988.
Lagueux, Maurice. *Dialogue (Canada)* 29(3), 415-440 1990

GRANT, Edward and MURDOCH, John D (eds). *Mathematics and its Application to Science and Natural Philosophy in the Middle Ages*. Cambridge, Cambridge Univ Pr, 1987.
Henry, John. *Heythrop J* 32(1), 122-123 Ja 91

GRANTHAM, S B. *Galvin's "Racing Pawns" Game and a Well-Ordering of Trees*. Providence, American Mathematical Society, 1985.
Larson, Jean A. *J Sym Log* 55(3), 1310-1311 S 90

GRASSI, Ernesto. *Renaissance Humanism: Studies in Philosophy and Poetics, Walter F Veit (trans)*. Binghamton, SUNY Pr, 1988.
Rosenfield, Lawrence W. *Phil Rhet* 23(4), 320-324 1990
Blackwell, C W T. *J Hist Phil* 29(3), 486-488 Jl 91

GRATHOFF, Richard (ed). *Philosophers in Exile, J Claude Evans (trans)*. Bloomington, Indiana Univ Pr, 1989.
Kaelin, E F. *Can Phil Rev* 10(12), 498-500 D 90

GRAUBARD, Stephen R (ed). *The Artificial Intelligence Debate: False Starts, Real Foundations*. Cambridge, MIT Pr, 1988.
Myin, Erik. *Philosophica* 46(2), 123-125 1990

GRAVE, S A. *Conscience in Newman's Thought*. New York, Clarendon/Oxford Pr, 1989.
Desmond, William. *Rev Metaph* 44(4), 843-844 Je 91

GRAY, John. *Liberalisms: Essays in Political Philosophy*. New York, Routledge, 1989.
Bellamy, Richard. *Utilitas* 3(1), 156-158 My 91

GRAYLING, A C. *Wittgenstein*. Oxford, Oxford Univ Pr, 1988.
Kerr, Fergus. *Heythrop J* 32(1), 119-120 Ja 91
Kulka, Tomas. *Iyyun* 39(4), 466-468 O 90

GREEN, Ronald M. *Religion and Moral Reason*. Oxford, Oxford Univ Pr, 1988.
Richards, Glyn. *Relig Stud* 26(3), 427-428 S 90

GREENE, Maxine. *The Dialectic of Freedom*. New York, Teachers College Pr, 1988.
Spitz, Ellen Handler. *J Aes Educ* 24(3), 120-122 Fall 90

GREENSPAN, Patricia S. *Emotions and Reasons: An Inquiry into Emotional Justification*. London, Routledge, 1988.
Roberts, Robert C. *Phil Books* 31(4), 233-235 O 90

GREISCH, Jean. *La Parole heureuse: Martin Heidegger entre les choses et les mots*. Paris, Beauchesne, 1987.
Bourke, Vernon J. *Mod Sch* 67(3), 229-231 Mr 90

GRICE, H P. *Studies in the Way of Words*. Cambridge, Harvard Univ Pr, 1989.
Chamizo Domínquez, Pedro José. *Dialogo Filosof* 6(3), 415-418 S-D 90
Avramides, Anita. *Phil Books* 31(4), 228-229 O 90
Fogelin, Robert J. *J Phil* 88(4), 213-219 Ap 91

GRIFFIN, David Ray (ed). *Spirituality and Community*. Albany, SUNY Pr, 1988.
Mooney, Regina E. *Process Stud* 19(1), 51-53 Spr 90

GRIFFIN, David Ray and SMITH, Huston. *Primordial Truth and Postmodern Theology*. Albany, SUNY Pr, 1989.
Hibbs, Thomas S. *Rev Metaph* 44(4), 844-846 Je 91

GRIFFIN, James. *Well-Being: Its Meaning, Measurement and Moral Importance*. New York, Clarendon Pr, 1987.
Scanlon, T M. *Phil Rev* 100(2), 312-315 Ap 91

GRIFFIN, Miriam and BARNES, Jonathan (eds). *Philosophia Togata: Essays on Philosophy and Roman Society*. New York, Clarendon/Oxford Pr, 1989.
Asmis, Elizabeth. *Ancient Phil* 11(1), 223-225 Spr 91

GRIFFITHS, A Phillips (ed). *Contemporary French Philosophy*. New York, Cambridge Univ Pr, 1987.
Good, Robert. *Hist Euro Ideas* 13(4), 434-435 1991

GRIFFITHS, A Phillips (ed). *Key Themes in Philosophy*. Cambridge, Cambridge Univ Pr, 1989.
Goldstein, Laurence. *Phil Books* 32(1), 30 Ja 91
Chisholm, John E. *Phil Stud (Ireland)* 32, 320-322 1988-90

GRIFFITHS, Morwenna and WHITEFORD, Margaret (eds). *Feminist Perspectives in Philosophy*. Bloomington, Indiana Univ Pr, 1988.
Chanter, Tina. *Rad Phil* 56, 50-51 Autumn 90

GRISWOLD JR, Charles L (ed). *Platonic Writings, Platonic Readings*. New York, Routledge, Chapman & Hall, 1988.
Prior, William J. *Teach Phil* 13(2), 172-175 Je 90
Tejera, Victorino. *J Hist Phil* 29(2), 299-301 Ap 91

GROGIN, R C. *The Bergsonian Controversy in France, 1900-1914*. Calgary, Univ Calgary Pr, 1988.
Sprigge, T L S. *Phil Quart* 41(164), 364-365 Jl 91

GROSZ, Elizabeth. *Sexual Subversions*. Sydney, Allen & Unwin, 1989.
Mackenzie, Catriona. *Austl J Phil* 68(4), 469-475 D 90

GROUND, Ian. *Art or Bunk*. Bristol, Bristol Classical Pr, 1989.
O'Hear, Anthony. *J Applied Phil* 7(2), 240-242 O 90
McFee, Graham. *Brit J Aes* 31(2), 173-174 Ap 91

GRUMLEY, John E. *History and Totality: Radical Historicism from Hegel to Foucault*. London, Routledge, 1989.
Rée, Jonathan. *Rad Phil* 56, 53-57 Autumn 90

GUARIGLIA, Osvaldo N. *Ideología, verdad y legitimación*. Buenos Aires, Sudamericana, 1986.
Yturbe, Corina. *Dianoia* 34(34), 311-316 1988

GULYAS, Balazsa (ed). *The Brain-Mind Problem: Philosophical and Neuro-physiological Approaches*. Assen, Van Gorcum, 1987.
Cruse, Carsten. *Theor Med* 11(4), 349-350 D 90

GUNDERSON, Keith. *Mentality and Machines*. Minneapolis, Univ of Minnesota Pr, 1985.
Shavit, Yaron. *J Prag* 14(4), 674-682 Ag 90

GUNDERSON, Martin and MAYO, David J and RHAME, Frank S. *AIDS: Testing and Privacy*. Salt Lake City, Univ of Utah Pr, 1989.
Plummer, David. *Bioethics* 5(2), 168-170 Ap 91

GUNKEL, Andreas. *Spontaneität und moralische Autonomie: Kants Philosophie der Freiheit*. Bern, Haupt, 1989.
Konhardt, Klaus. *Kantstudien* 81(3), 379-383 1990

GUNN, Giles. *The Culture of Criticism and the Criticism of Culture*. New York, Oxford Univ Pr, 1987.
Walker, Denis. *Phil Lit* 14(2), 420-421 O 90

GÜNTHER, Klaus. *Der Sinn für Angemessenheit*. Frankfurt am Main, Suhrkamp, 1988.
Brugger, Winfried. *Z Phil Forsch* 44(3), 491-495 1990

GURTLER, Gary M. *Plotinus: the Experience of Unity*. New York, Lang, 1988.
McDermott, John M. *Gregorianum* 72(2), 391-392 1991

GUSTAFSON, Donald F. *Intention and Agency*. Boston, Reidel, 1986.
Price, Marjorie. *Mod Sch* 68(1), 101-102 N 90

GUTMANN, Amy (ed). *Democracy and the Welfare State*. Princeton, Princeton Univ Pr, 1988.
Alleva, Ernie. *Econ Phil* 6(2), 322-326 O 90

GUTTING, Gary. *Michel Foucault's Archaeology of Scientific Reason*. Cambridge, Cambridge Univ Pr, 1989.
Rée, Jonathan. *Phil Books* 32(1), 28-29 Ja 91
Racevskis, Karlis. *Rad Phil* 57, 50-52 Spr 91

GUY, Alain. *Historia de la filosifía española*. Barcelona, Anthropos, 1985.
Forment Giralt, E. *Espiritu* 35(93), 79-81 Ja-Je 86

GUYER, Paul. *Kant and the Claims of Knowledge*. Cambridge, Cambridge Univ Pr, 1987.
Aquila, Richard E. *Int Stud Phil* 22(3), 110-111 1990
Irwin, T H. *Phil Rev* 100(2), 332-341 Ap 91

GYEKYE, Kwame. *An Essay on African Philosophical Thought*. Cambridge, Cambridge Univ Pr, 1987.
Birt, Robert E. *Phil East West* 41(1), 95-109 Ja 91

HAAKONSSEN, Knud (ed). *Traditions of Liberalism: Essays on John Locke, Adam Smith and John Stuart Mill*. New South Wales, Centre for Independent Studies, 1988.
Eccleshall, Robert. *Hist Polit Thought* 11(3), 544-546 Autumn 90

HAAR, Michel. *Heidegger et l'essence de l'homme*. Grenoble, Jérôme Millon, 1990.
Trotignon, Pierre. *Rev Phil Fr* 180(3), 559-561 Jl-S 90

HAASE, Wolfgang (ed). *Aufsteig und Niedergang der Römischen Welt*. Berlin, De Gruyter, 1987.
Schrenk, Lawrence P. *Rev Metaph* 44(3), 634-636 Mr 91

HABERMAS, Jürgen. *The Theory of Communicative Action, V1, Thomas McCarthy (trans)*. Boston, Beacon Pr, 1981.
Gupta, Kalyan Sen. *J Indian Counc Phil Res* 6(1), 164-170 S-D 88

HABERMAS, Jürgen. *Der Philosophische Diskurs der Moderne*. Frankfurt am Main, Suhrkamp, 1988.
Schmidt, Hartwig. *Deut Z Phil* 38(10), 1004-1006 1990

HABERMAS, Jurgen. *Moral Consciousness and Communicative Action, C Lenhardt and S-W Nicholsen (trans)*. Oxford, Polity Pr, 1990.
Kearney, Richard. *Phil Stud (Ireland)* 32, 322-326 1988-90

HABICHT, C. *Cicero the Politician*. Baltimore, Johns Hopkins Univ Pr, 1990.
Kallet-Marx, R M. *Phoenix* 45(1), 83-85 Spr 91

HACKENESCH, Christa. *Die Logik der Andersheit*. Frankfurt am Main, Athenäum, 1987.
Pavic, Zeljko. *Filozof Istraz* 34(1), 281-284 1990

HACKER, P M S. *Appearance and Reality: A Philosophical Investigation into Perception and Perceptual Qualities*. Oxford, Blackwell, 1987.
Levin, Janet. *Phil Rev* 99(4), 654-656 O 90

HACKING, Ian. *The Taming of Chance*. New York, Cambridge Univ Pr, 1980.
Torretti, Roberto. *Dialogos* 26(58), 185-187 Jl 91

HACKLER, Chris and MOSELEY, Ray and VAWTER, Dorothy E. *Advance Directives in Medicine: Studies in Health and Human Values, v2*. New York, Praeger, 1989.
Purviance, Susan M. *Phil Context* 20, 65-69 1990

HADARI, Saguiv A. *Theory in Practice: Tocqueville's New Science of Politics*. Stanford, Stanford Univ Pr, 1989.
Lakoff, Sanford. *Utilitas* 3(1), 153-156 My 91

HAEFFNER, Gerd. *The Human Situation: A Philosophical Anthropology, Erick Watkins (trans)*. Notre Dame, Univ of Notre Dame Pr, 1989.
Harvanek, Robert F. *Int Phil Quart* 30(4), 507-508 D 90

HAEFFNER, Gerd. *Antropología filosófica*. Barcelona, Herder, 1986.
Jiménez Guerrero, A. *Espiritu* 37(97), 91-94 Ja-Je 88

HAHN, Lewis E and SCHILPP, Paul Arthur (eds). *The Philosophy of W V Quine*. Peru, Open Court, 1986.
Kaminsky, Jack. *Int Stud Phil* 23(1), 116-118 1991

HAHN, Robert. *Kant's Newtonian Revolution in Philosophy*. Carbondale, Southern Illinois Univ Pr, 1988.
Brittan Jr, Gordon G. *J Hist Phil* 28(4), 622-624 O 90

HALBFASS, Wilhelm. *India and Europe: An Essay in Understanding*. Albany, SUNY Pr, 1988.
Taber, John. *Phil East West* 41(2), 229-240 Ap 91

HALL, David L and AMES, Roger T. *Thinking Through Confucius*. Albany, SUNY Pr, 1987.
Ivanhoe, Philip J. *Phil East West* 41(2), 241-254 Ap 91

HALL, John A. *Powers and Liberties*. Berkeley, Univ of California Pr, 1985.
Munz, Peter. *Phil Soc Sci* 21(2), 253-276 Je 91

HALLER, Rudolf. *Questions on Wittgenstein*. Lincoln, Univ of Nebraska Pr, 1988.
Hallett, Garth L. *Can Phil Rev* 10(12), 500-502 D 90

HALLER, Rudolf and STADLER, Friedrich (eds). *Ernst Mach: Werk und Wirkung*. Vienna, Hölder-Pichler-Tempsky, 1988.
Wittich, Dieter. *Deut Z Phil* 38(11), 1111-1113 1990

HALLER, Rudolf. *Questions on Wittgenstein*. London, Routledge, 1988.
Kerr, Fergus. *Heythrop J* 32(1), 119-120 Ja 91

HALLETT, Garth L. *Language and Truth*. New Haven, Yale Univ Pr, 1988.
Healy, Paul. *Phil Rhet* 24(1), 80-83 1991

HALLETT, Michael. *Cantorian Set Theory and Limitation of Size*. New York, Clarendon/Oxford Pr, 1984.
Dauben, Joseph W. *Brit J Phil Sci* 39(4), 541-550 D 88

HALPER, Thomas. *The Misfortunes of Others: End-Stage Renal Disease in the United Kingdom*. Cambridge, Cambridge Univ Pr, 1989.
Singer, Peter. *Bioethics* 5(1), 72-74 Ja 91

HAMLIN, Alan and PETTIT, Philip (eds). *The Good Polity: Normative Analysis of the State*. Oxford, Blackwell, 1989.
Kukathas, Chandran. *Austl J Phil* 69(1), 110-113 Mr 91

HAMLYN, D W. *In and Out of the Black Box: On the Philosophy of Cognition*. Oxford, Blackwell, 1990.
Heil, John. *Phil Quart* 41(163), 247-249 Ap 91
Moser, Paul K. *Phil Books* 32(2), 108-110 Ap 91

HAMPSHIRE, Stuart. *Innocence and Experience*. Cambridge, Harvard Univ Pr, 1989.
Luban, David. *J Phil* 88(6), 317-324 Je 91
Kerman, Deborah E. *Rev Metaph* 44(1), 141-144 S 90
Kingwell, Mark. *Int Phil Quart* 31(1), 112-114 Mr 91

HAMPTON, Jean. *Hobbes and the Social Contract Tradition*. Cambridge, Cambridge Univ Pr, 1986.
Johnson, Paul J. *Int Stud Phil* 22(3), 112 1990

HANCOCK, Ralph C. *Calvin and the Foundations of Modern Politics*. Ithaca, Cornell Univ Pr, 1989.
Andelson, Robert V. *Rev Metaph* 44(3), 636-637 Mr 91

HANFLING, Oswald. *Wittgenstein's Later Philosophy*. London, Macmillan Pr, 1989.
Gomm, R M. *Phil Invest* 14(2), 172-176 Ap 91

HANSON, Karen. *The Self Imagined: Philosophical Reflections on the Social Character of Psyche*. New York, Routledge & Kegan Paul, 1986.
Lemos, Ramon M. *Nous* 25(2), 250-253 Ap 91

HARAWAY, Donna. *Primate Visions: Gender, Race and Nature in the World of Modern Science*. New York, Routledge & Kegan Paul, 1989.
de Laet, Marianne. *Kennis Methode* 15(1), 142-147 1991

HARDIN, C L. *Color for Philosophers*. Indianapolis, Hackett, 1988.
Smith, A D. *Phil Books* 32(1), 41-43 Ja 91
McGilvray, James A. *Phil Sci* 58(2), 329-331 Je 91
Averill, Edward Wilson. *Phil Rev* 100(3), 459-463 Jl 91

HARDIN, Russell. *Morality Within the Limits of Reason*. Chicago, Univ of Chicago Pr, 1988.
Binmore, Ken. *Econ Phil* 7(1), 112-119 Ap 91
Duff, Antony. *Phil Books* 31(4), 242-245 O 90

HARDING, Sandra and HINTIKKA, Merrill B (eds). *Discovering Reality: Feminist Perspectives on Epistemology, Metaphysics, Methodology, and Philosophy of Science*. Dordrecht, Reidel, 1983.
Whitt, L A. *Phil Sci* 57(3), 542-546 S 90

HARE, William and PORTELLI, John P (eds). *Philosophy of Education: Introductory Readings*. Calgary, Detselig, 1988.
Bruneau, Sandra R. *Educ Stud* 21(4), 462-463 Wint 90

HARMAN, Gilbert. *Skepticism and the Definition of Knowledge*. New York, Garland, 1990.
Welbourne, Michael. *Phil Books* 32(2), 100-101 Ap 91

HARMAN, Lesley D. *The Modern Stranger: On Language and Membership*. Berlin, Mouton, 1988.
De Pasquale, Antonio. *Phil Soc Sci* 21(2), 298-299 Je 91

HARNEY, Maurita J. *Intentionality, Sense and the Mind*. The Hague, Nijhoff, 1984.
Buscarini, Carlos A. *Cuad Filosof* 21(34), 72-75 My 90

HARPER, Albert W J. *Essays on Kant's Third Critique*. London, Phelps, 1989.
Moitra, Shefali. *J Indian Counc Phil Res* 6(3), 163-164 My-Ag 89

HARPER, William L and SKYRMS, Brian (eds). *Causation in Decision, Belief Change, and Statistics*. Dordrecht, Kluwer, 1988.
de Swart, H C M. *Method Sci* 22(4), 245 1989

HARRIS, Errol E. *Formal, Transcendental, and Dialectical Thinking*. Albany, SUNY Pr, 1987.
Gordon, David. *Int Phil Quart* 30(4), 503-507 D 90

HARRIS, Errol E. *The Reality of Time*. Albany, SUNY Pr, 1989.
Lucas Jr, George R. *Rev Metaph* 44(1), 144-145 S 90

HARRIS, Leonard (ed). *The Philosophy of Alain Locke: Harlem Renaissance and Beyond*. Philadelphia, Temple Univ Pr, 1989.
Outlaw, Lucius. *Teach Phil* 13(4), 379-382 D 90

HARRIS, R. *Language, Saussure and Wittgenstein*. New York, Routledge, 1988.
Harré, Rom. *Int Stud Phil* 23(1), 118-119 1991

HART, W D. *The Engines of the Soul*. New York, Cambridge Univ Pr, 1988.
Boër, Steven. *Nous* 25(4), 561-566 S 91

HARTLE, Ann. *Death and the Disinterested Spectator: An Inquiry into the Nature of Philosophy*. Albany, SUNY Pr, 1986.
Clift, Wallace B. *Mod Sch* 68(2), 176-178 Ja 91

HARTNACK, Justus. *From Radical Empiricism to Absolute Idealism*. Lewiston, Mellen Pr, 1986.
Stepelevich, Lawrence S. *Int Stud Phil* 22(3), 112-113 1990

HARVEY, Peter. *An Introduction to Buddhism: Teachings, History and Practices*. Cambridge, Cambridge Univ Pr, 1990.
Keown, Damien. *Relig Stud* 27(2), 369-370 Je 91

HARVEY, Steven. *Falaquera's "Epistle of the Debate": An Introduction to Jewish Philosophy*. Cambridge, Harvard Univ Pr, 1987.
Levy, Ze'ev. *Int Stud Phil* 22(3), 113-114 1990

HASKAR, Vinit. *Civil Disobedience, Threats and Offers*. New York, Oxford Univ Pr, 1988.
Rao, K L Seshagiri. *Phil East West* 41(3), 425-426 Jl 91

HASKER, William. *God, Time, and Knowledge*. Ithaca, Cornell Univ Pr, 1989.
Fischer, John Martin. *J Phil* 88(8), 427-433 Ag 91
Flint, Thomas P. *Phil Stud* 60(1-2), 103-115 S-O 90
Hasker, William. *Phil Stud* 60(1-2), 117-126 S-O 90
Helm, Paul. *Relig Stud* 26(2), 295-296 Je 90

HASLETT, D W. *Equal Consideration: A Theory of Moral Justification*. Cranbury, Univ of Delaware Pr, 1987.
Ravizza, Mark. *Phil Rev* 100(1), 136-140 Ja 91

HAUBST, Rudolf. *Das Sehen Gottes nach Nikolaus von Kues*. Treves, Paulinus, 1989.
de Gandillac, Maurice. *Rev Metaph Morale* 96(2), 279-280 Ap-Je 91

HAUERWAS, Stanley. *Naming the Silences*. Grand Rapids, Eerdmans, 1990.
Campbell, Courtney S. *Hastings Center Rep* 21(3), 32-33 My-Je 91

HAUSMAN, Carl R. *Metaphor and Art: Interactionism and Reference in the Verbal and Non-Verbal Arts*. Cambridge, Cambridge Univ Pr, 1989.
Hagberg, Garry. *Brit J Aes* 30(4), 376-378 O 90
Hesse, Mary. *J Speculative Phil* 5(1), 77-83 1991

HAWKING, Stephen W. *A Brief History of Time: From the Big Bang to Black Holes*. New York, Bantam, 1988.
Porter, Jack Nusan. *Bridges* 2(3-4), 204-205 Fall-Wint 90

HAWKINS, John A (ed). *Explaining Language Universals*. Oxford, Blackwell, 1988.
Corbett, Greville G. *Mind Lang* 5(3), 235-244 Autumn 90

HAYLES, N Katherine. *Chaos Bound: Orderly Disorder in Contemporary Literature and Science*. Ithaca, Cornell Univ Pr, 1990.
Brady, Patrick. *Phil Lit* 14(2), 367-378 O 90

HEAL, Jane. *Fact and Meaning: Quine and Wittgenstein on Philosophy of Language*. Oxford, Blackwell, 1989.
Heil, John. *Phil Books* 31(4), 229-231 O 90
Hookway, Christopher. *Philosophy* 65(254), 532-534 O 90
Miller, Alexander. *Mind* 99(396), 642-647 O 90
Pisani, Assunta. *Sapienza* 43(4), 456-458 O-D 90

HEALEY, Richard. *The Philosophy of Quantum Mechanics*. Cambridge, Cambridge Univ Pr, 1990.
Hughes, R I G. *Phil Stud (Ireland)* 32, 326-330 1988-90

HEBBLETHWAITE, Brian. *The Ocean of Truth: A Defence of Objective Theism*. New York, Cambridge Univ Pr, 1988.
Dore, Clement. *Faith Phil* 8(2), 256-258 Ap 91

HEGEL, G.W.F. *Lectures on the Philosophy of Religion, V2: Determinate Religion, Peter C Hodgson (ed), R F Brown and others (trans)*. Berkeley, Univ of California Pr, 1987.
Harris, Errol E. *Owl Minerva* 22(1), 113-116 Fall 90

HEGEMAN, J H. *Justifying Policy: A Heuristic*. Amsterdam, Free Univ Pr, 1989.
Hiemstra, John. *Phil Reform* 56(1), 95-97 1991

HEIDEGGER, Martin. *Beiträge zur Philosophie (Vom Ereignis)*. Frankfurt, Klostermann, 1989.
Zimmerman, Michael E. *Int Phil Quart* 31(3), 369-372 S 91

HEIDEGGER, Martin. *Hegel's Phenomenology of Spirit, P Emad and K Maly (trans)*. Bloomington, Indiana Univ Pr, 1988.
Stack, George J. *J Value Inq* 25(2), 193-195 Ap 91

HEILPRIN, Laurence B. *Toward Foundations of Information Science*. White Plains, Knowledge Industry Pub, 1985.
Agassi, Joseph. *Iyyun* 40(3), 319-342 Jl 91

HEIM, Michael. *Electric Language: A Philosophical Study of Word Processing*. New Haven, Yale Univ Pr, 1987.
Miller, George David. *Man World* 24(1), 110-114 Ja 91
Phillips, Donald. *Heythrop J* 32(1), 109-110 Ja 91

HEINTEL, Erich. *Gesammelte Abhandlungen, 2v*. Stuttgart, Frommann-Holzboog, 1988.
Grim, Johannes. *Z Phil Forsch* 45(1), 155-159 Ja-Mr 91

HELLER, Agnes and FEHER, Ferenc. *The Postmodern Political Condition*. Oxford, Polity Pr, 1988.
Ansell-Pearson, Keith. *Rad Phil* 56, 51-53 Autumn 90

HELLER, Agnes. *A Philosophy of Morals*. Oxford, Blackwell, 1990.
Ansell-Pearson, Keith. *Rad Phil* 56, 51-53 Autumn 90

HELLER, Agnes. *Beyond Justice*. Oxford, Blackwell, 1989.
Ansell-Pearson, Keith. *Rad Phil* 56, 51-53 Autumn 90

HELLER, Hermann. *La sovranità ed altri scritti sulla dottrina del diritto e dello Stato*. Milan, Giuffrè, 1987.
Tusa, Carlo. *Riv Int Filosof Diritto* 66(4), 748-750 O-D 89

HELLMAN, Geoffrey. *Mathematics Without Numbers: Towards a Modal-Structural Interpretation*. Oxford, Clarendon Pr, 1989.
Moore, A W. *Phil Books* 32(1), 61-62 Ja 91

HELM, Paul. *Eternal God*. New York, Oxford Univ Pr, 1988.
Leftow, Brian. *Faith Phil* 8(3), 398-402 Jl 91

HEMPEL, Carl Gustav. *Oltre il Positismo logico*. Rome, Armando Ed, 1989.
Mura, Alberto. *Aquinas* 34(1), 148-151 Ja-Ap 91

HENDERSON, John B. *The Development and Decline of Chinese Cosmology*. New York, Columbia Univ Pr, 1984.
Black, Alison H. *Phil East West* 41(2), 272-276 Ap 91

HENDLEY, Brian P (ed). *Plato, Time, and Education: Essays in Honor of Robert S Brumbaugh*. Albany, SUNY Pr, 1987.
Heiser, John. *Mod Sch* 67(4), 306-307 My 90

HENRY, Michel. *Phénoménologie matérielle*. Paris, PUF, 1990.
Himy, Aimée. *Rev Phil Fr* 181(1), 67-71 1991

HERB, Karlfriedrich. *Rousseaus Theorie legitimer Herrschaft*. Würzburg, Königshausen & Neumann, 1989.
Talanga, Josip. *Filozof Istraz* 34(1), 277-280 1990

HERBERT, Gary B. *Thomas Hobbes: The Unity of Scientific and Moral Wisdom*. Vancouver, Univ of British Columbia Pr, 1989.
Condren, Conal. *Hist Euro Ideas* 12(4), 560-561 1990
Walton, Craig. *J Hist Phil* 29(3), 492-494 Jl 91

HERTZBERG, Lars and PIETARINEN, Juhani (eds). *Perspectives on Human Conduct*. Leiden, Brill, 1988.
Diamond, Cora. *Phil Invest* 14(1), 86-91 Ja 91

HERZOG, Don. *Happy Slaves: A Critique of Consent Theory*. Chicago, Univ of Chicago Pr, 1989.
Schultz, David. *Int Stud Phil* 22(3), 115-116 1990
Beitz, Charles R. *Polit Theory* 19(2), 303-305 My 91

HICK, John and HEMPEL, Lamont C (eds). *Gandhi's Significance for Today: The Elusive Legacy*. London, Macmillan, 1989.
Richards, Glyn. *Relig Stud* 27(2), 272-274 Je 91

HICK, John and MELTZER, Edmund S (eds). *Three Faiths—One God: A Jewish, Christian, Muslim Encounter*. London, Macmillan, 1989.
D'Costa, Gavin. *Relig Stud* 27(1), 133-135 Mr 91

HICK, John. *An Interpretation of Religion*. New Haven, Yale Univ Pr, 1989.
Hebblethwaite, Brian. *Zygon* 26(2), 328-333 Je 91
Deutsch, Eliot. *Phil East West* 40(4), 557-562 O 90

HICKMAN, Larry A. *John Dewey's Pragmatic Technology*. Bloomington, Indiana Univ Pr, 1988.
Rucker, Darnell. *Personalist Forum* 6(2), 188-190 Fall 90
Alexander, Thomas M. *J Speculative Phil* 5(2), 144-151 1991
Auxier, Randall E. *Man World* 24(3), 341-344 Jl 91

HILBERT, David R. *Color and Color Perception*. Stanford, CSLI, 1987.
Averill, Edward Wilson. *Phil Rev* 100(3), 459-463 Jl 91

HILEY, David R. *Philosophy in Question: Essays on a Pyrrhonian Theme*. Chicago, Univ of Chicago Pr, 1988.
Martinich, A P. *Int Stud Phil* 22(3), 116-117 1990
Livingston, Donald. *Man World* 23(4), 476-480 O 90
Moulder, James. *S Afr J Phil* 10(2), 59 My 91

HILMY, S Stephen. *The Later Wittgenstein: The Emergence of a New Philosophical Method*. Oxford, Blackwell, 1987.
Stern, David G. *Phil Rev* 99(4), 639-641 O 90
Kerr, Fergus. *Heythrop J* 32(1), 120-121 Ja 91

HILTON, Denis J (ed). *Contemporary Science and Natural Explanation: Commonsense Conceptions of Causality*. New York, New York Univ Pr, 1988.
Redner, Harry. *Phil Soc Sci* 21(2), 300-302 Je 91

HINCHMAN, Lewis P. *Hegel's Critique of the Enlightenment*. Gainesville, Univ of Florida Pr, 1984.
Westphal, Kenneth R. *Rev Metaph* 44(1), 146-148 S 90

HINTIKKA, Jaakko and HINTIKKA, Merrill. *The Logic of Epistemology and the Epistemology of Logic*. Norwell, Kluwer, 1989.
Lewis, H A. *Hist Phil Log* 12(2), 253-254 1991

HINTIKKA, Merrill B and HINTIKKA, Jaakko. *Investigating Wittgenstein*. Oxford, Blackwell, 1986.
Bradley, Raymond and Resnick, Lawrence. *Can J Phil* 20(3), 449-466 S 90

Mies, Jürgen. *Erkenntnis* 33(2), 261-279 S 90
Hunter, J F M. *Eidos* 9(1), 105-120 Je 90

HITT, William D. *Ethics and Leadership: Putting Theory into Practice*. Columbus, Battelle Pr, 1990.
Fraedrich, John. *J Bus Ethics* 10(5), 396-398 My 91

HOAGLAND, Sarah Lucia. *Lesbian Ethics: Toward New Value*. Palo Alto, Institute of Lesbian Studies, 1988.
Frye, Marilyn. *Hypatia* 5(3), 132-137 Fall 90
Lugones, María. *Hypatia* 5(3), 138-146 Fall 90
Van Kirk, Carol. *Hypatia* 5(3), 147-152 Fall 90

HOBBES, Thomas. *Court traité des premiers principes, Jean Bernhardt (ed & trans)*. Paris, PUF, 1988.
Tricaud, François. *Rev Phil Fr* 181(1), 96-101 1991

HODGES, Michael P. *Transcendence and Wittgenstein's "Tractatus"*. Philadelphia, Temple Univ Pr, 1990.
Schiller, Britt-Marie. *Mod Sch* 68(2), 178-179 Ja 91
Cooper, David E. *Phil Quart* 41(164), 358-360 Jl 91

HODGSON, Geoffrey. *Economics and Institutions: A Manifesto for Modern Institutional Economics*. Philadelphia, Univ of Pennsylvania Pr, 1988.
Boettke, Peter J. *Crit Rev* 4(1-2), 10-26 Wint-Spr 90

HODGSON, Peter C. *God in History: Shapes of Freedom*. Nashville, Abingdon Pr, 1989.
Williams, Robert R. *Owl Minerva* 22(2), 234-237 Spr 91

HOFFMAN, Frank J. *Rationality and Mind in Early Buddhism*. Delhi, Motilal Banarsidass, 1987.
Klostermaier, Klaus K. *Asian Phil* 1(1), 96-97 1991

HOFFMASTER, Barry and FREEDMAN, Benjamin and FRASER, Gwen (eds). *Clinical Ethics: Theory and Practice*. Clifton, Humana Pr, 1989.
Roe, Christopher J. *Bioethics* 5(2), 177-178 Ap 91

HÖFFE, Otfried. *L'État et la justice*. Paris, Vrin, 1988.
Warland, Geneviève. *Rev Phil Louvain* 88(80), 637-639 N 90

HOLBROOK, David. *Education and Philosophical Anthropology: Toward a New View of Man for the Humanities and English*. London, Associated Univ Pr, 1987.
Poole, Roger. *Heythrop J* 32(1), 111-113 Ja 91

HOLBROOK, David. *Evolution and the Humanities*. Aldershot, Gower, 1987.
Poole, Roger. *Heythrop J* 32(1), 111-113 Ja 91

HOLBROOK, David. *Further Studies in Philosophical Anthropology*. Aldershot, Avebury, 1987.
Poole, Roger. *Heythrop J* 32(1), 111-113 Ja 91

HÖLDERLIN, Friedrich. *Essays and Letters on Theory, Thomas Pfau (ed & trans)*. Albany, SUNY Pr, 1988.
Förster, Eckart. *J Hist Phil* 29(1), 139-140 Ja 91

HOLE, Robert. *Pulpits, Politics and Public Order in England 1760-1832*. Cambridge, Cambridge Univ Pr, 1989.
Canovan, Margaret. *Utilitas* 3(1), 148-150 My 91

HOLLAND, John H and others. *Induction: Processes of Inference, Learning, and Discovery*. Cambridge, MIT Pr, 1986.
Cheng, Peter C H. *Brit J Phil Sci* 42(2), 269-272 Je 91

HOLLIER, Denis. *Against Architecture: The Writings of Georges Bataille, Betsy Wing (trans)*. Cambridge, MIT Pr, 1989.
Haldane, John. *Brit J Aes* 31(2), 183-185 Ap 91

HOLMES, Jeremy and LINDLEY, Richard. *The Values of Psychotherapy*. Oxford, Oxford Univ Pr, 1989.
Fulford, K W M. *J Applied Phil* 7(2), 242-244 O 90

HÖLSCHER, Ludger. *The Reality of the Mind: Augustine's Philosophical Arguments for the Human Soul as a Spiritual Substance*. London, Routledge & Kegan Paul, 1986.
Booth, Edward. *J Brit Soc Phenomenol* 21(3), 304-305 O 90
Strasser, Michael W. *Nous* 25(2), 241-244 Ap 91

HÖLSCHER, Uvo (ed & trans). *Parmenides: Vom Wesen des Seienden*. Frankfurt am Main, Suhrkamp, 1986.
Eichler, Klaus-Dieter. *Deut Z Phil* 38(10), 1002-1004 1990

HONDERICH, Ted. *A Theory of Determinism: The Mind, Neuroscience, and Life-Hopes*. Oxford, Clarendon Pr, 1988.
Persson, Ingmar. *Theoria* 55(1), 62-76 1989

HONDERICH, Ted. *Conservatism*. London, Hamilton, 1990.
Scruton, Roger. *Phil Quart* 41(163), 256-258 Ap 91

HONNER, J. *The Description of Nature: Niels Bohr and the Philosophy of Quantum Physics*. Oxford, Clarendon Pr, 1987.
Krips, Henry. *Austl J Phil* 68(4), 463-465 D 90

HONNETH, Axel and others (eds). *Zwischenbetrachtunger: Im Prozess der Aufklärung*. Frankfurt am Main, Suhrkamp, 1989.
Matustik, Martin J. *Phil Soc Crit* 16(1), 61-79 1990

HOOKER, C A. *A Realistic Theory of Science*. Albany, SUNY Pr, 1987.
Thomson, Paul. *Nous* 24(5), 793-796 D 90

HOOKWAY, Christopher. *Quine: Language, Experience and Reality*. Stanford, Stanford Univ Pr, 1988.
Bar-On, Dorit. *Int Stud Phil* 22(3), 117-118 1990
Peña, Lorenzo. *Can Phil Rev* 10(11), 449-452 N 90
Gibson Jr, Roger F. *Brit J Phil Sci* 40(4), 557-567 D 89
Kirk, Robert. *Phil Rev* 100(3), 479-481 Jl 91

HOOPES, James. *Consciousness in New England: From Puritanism and Ideas to Psychoanalysis and Semiotic*. Baltimore, Johns Hopkins Univ Pr, 1989.
Colapietro, Vincent M. *Trans Peirce Soc* 26(4), 530-539 Fall 90

HOPE, V M. *Virtue by Consensus: The Moral Philosophy of Hutcheson, Hume, and Adam Smith*. Oxford, Clarendon Pr, 1989.
Martin, Marie. *J Hist Phil* 29(2), 314-315 Ap 91
Darwall, Stephen L. *Phil Quart* 41(162), 113-114 Ja 91

HORN, Laurence R. *A Natural History of Negation*. Chicago, Univ of Chicago Pr, 1989.
Snapper, John. *Phil Psych* 3(2-3), 319-321 1990
Helman, Glen. *Phil Rhet* 24(2), 164-168 1991

HORWICH, Paul. *Asymmetries in Time*. Cambridge, MIT Pr, 1987.
French, Steven. *Nous* 24(5), 804-806 D 90
Healey, Richard. *Phil Rev* 100(1), 125-130 Ja 91
Loizou, Andros. *Int Stud Phil* 23(1), 119-120 1991

HORWICH, Paul. *Truth*. Cambridge, Blackwell, 1990.
Hazen, A P. *Austl J Phil* 69(2), 227-228 Je 91

HÖSLE, Vittorio. *Hegels System*. Hamburg, Meiner, 1987.
Schaber, Peter. *Z Phil Forsch* 44(4), 675-679 1990
Williams, Robert R. *Int J Phil Relig* 29(2), 125-127 Ap 91

HOTTOIS, Gilbert. *Annales de l'Institut de philosophie et de sciences morales: "Philosophie et littérature"*. Bruxelles, Ed Univ Bruxelles, 1985.
La Chance, Michaël. *Dialogue (Canada)* 29(4), 615-620 1990

HOULGATE, Stephen. *Hegel, Nietzsche and the Criticism of Metaphysics*. Cambridge, Cambridge Univ Pr, undated.
Bognár, László. *Magyar Filozof Szemle* 1-2, 184-188 1990

HOWARD, Dick. *The Marxian Legacy, 2nd Edition*. Minneapolis, Univ of Minn Pr, 1988.
Murphy, John W. *Stud Soviet Tho* 41(2), 167-169 Mr 91

HOY, D Couzens (ed). *Michel Foucault: Lectures critiques*. Paris, Pr Univ de France, 1989.
Samama, Guy. *Rev Metaph Morale* 96(2), 286-288 Ap-Je 91

HOY, David Couzens (ed). *Foucault, Antonio Bonano (trans)*. Buenos Aires, Nueva Visión, 1988.
Rojas Osorio, Carlos. *Dialogos* 25(56), 204-207 Jl 90

HOYNINGEN-HUENE, Paul. *Die Wissenschaftsphilosophie Thomas S Kuhns*. Braunschweig, Vieweg, 1989.
Bartels, Andreas. *Conceptus* 24(63), 104-109 1990

HUBY, Pamela and NEAL, Gordon (eds). *The Criterion of Truth*. Liverpool, Liverpool Univ Pr, 1989.
Annas, Julia. *Polis* 9(2), 211-213 1990
Bogen, James. *Ancient Phil* 10(2), 324-327 Fall 90

HUDSON, Deal W and MANCINI, Matthew J (eds). *Understanding Maritain*. Macon, Mercer Univ Pr, 1988.
Copleston, Frederick C. *Heythrop J* 32(3), 443-444 Jl 91

HUFFMAN, William H. *Robert Fludd and the End of the Renaissance*. London, Routledge, 1988.
Moran, Bruce T. *J Hist Phil* 29(1), 123-125 Ja 91

HUGHES, R I G. *The Structure and Interpretation of Quantum Mechanics*. Cambridge, Harvard Univ Pr, 1989.
Stairs, Allen. *Synthese* 86(1), 99-122 Ja 91

HULL, David L. *Science as a Process*. Chicago, Univ of Chicago Pr, 1988.
Bechtel, William. *Phil Sci* 58(1), 138-139 Mr 91

HULL, David L. *The Metaphysics of Evolution*. Albany, SUNY Pr, 1989.
Rottschaefer, William A. *Can Phil Rev* 10(8), 319-321 Ag 90

HULL, Richard T (ed). *Ethical Issues in the New Reproductive Technologies*. Balmont, Wadsworth, 1990.
Curzer, Howard J. *Theor Med* 12(1), 91-93 Mr 91

HUMBER, James M and ALMEDER, Robert F (eds). *Biomedical Ethics Reviews 1989*. Clifton, Humana Pr, 1989.
Purviance, Susan M. *Teach Phil* 13(4), 388-390 D 90

HUMBOLDT, Wilhelm von. *On Language, Peter Heath (trans)*. Cambridge, Cambridge Univ Pr, 1988.
Klieneberger, H R. *Phil Stud (Ireland)* 32, 372-373 1988-90

HUND, John (ed). *Law and Justice in South Africa*. Pretoria, Inst of Public Interest Law & Research, 1988.
Girasa, Rosario J. *Vera Lex* 10(2), 18-19 1990

HUNDRICHS, Hubert. *Lebensprozesse und wissenschaftliches Denken*. Freiburg, Alber, 1988.
Meyer, Peter. *J Soc Biol Struct* 13(2), 175-177 My 90

HUNTINGTON JR, C W. *The Emptiness of Emptiness*. Honolulu, Univ of Hawaii Pr, 1989.
Williams, Paul. *J Indian Phil* 19(2), 191-218 Je 91

HURLEY, S L. *Natural Reasons*. New York, Oxford Univ Pr, 1989.
O'Hagan, Timothy. *Int Stud Phil* 23(1), 120-124 1991
Nerlich, Graham. *Phil Quart* 41(162), 86-93 Ja 91
Smart, J J C. *Mind* 100(397), 152-155 Ja 91
Hollis, Martin. *Philosophy* 65(254), 528-530 O 90

HURSTHOUSE, Rosalind. *Beginning Lives*. Cambridge, Blackwell, 1987.
Wildes, Kevin W. *J Med Phil* 16(3), 361-367 Je 91

HUSSERL, Edmund. *Aufsätze und Vorträge (1911-1921), Thomas Nenon and Hans Rainer Sepp (eds)*. Boston, Nijhoff, 1987.
Schuhmann, Karl. *J Brit Soc Phenomenol* 21(3), 293-295 O 90

HUSSERL, Edmund. *Aufsätze und Vorträge (1922-1937), Thomas Nenon and Hans Rainer Sepp (eds)*. Dordrecht, Kluwer, 1989.
Drummond, John J. *Rev Metaph* 44(3), 637-639 Mr 91

HUSSERL, Edmund. *La philosophie comme science rigoureuse*. Paris, Pr Univ de France, 1989.
Fisette, Denis. *Philosophiques* 17(2), 222-225 Autumn 1990

HUTCHEON, Linda. *The Politics of Postmodernism*. London, Routledge, 1989.
Stephenson, Susan. *Brit J Aes* 31(1), 91-92 Ja 91

HUTCHEON, Linda. *A Poetics of Postmodernism: History, Theory, Fiction*. New York, Routledge, 1988.
Hoeveler, Diane Long. *Hist Euro Ideas* 13(4), 447 1991

HYLTON, Peter. *Russell, Idealism and the Emergence of Analytic Philosophy*. Oxford, Clarendon Pr, 1990.
Hamilton, Andy. *Phil Books* 32(2), 88-89 Ap 91

HYMAN, John. *The Imitation of Nature*. Oxford, Blackwell, 1989.
Sibley, F N. *Phil Books* 31(4), 250-252 O 90

IACONO, Alfonso M. *L'evento e l'osservatore: Ricerche sulla storicità della conoscenza*. Bergamo, Lubrina, 1987.
Cavallo, Tommaso. *Teoria* 10(1), 211-213 1990

IANNONE, A Pablo. *Contemporary Moral Controversies in Business*. New York, Oxford Univ Pr, 1989.
Castro, Barry. *J Bus Ethics* 10(4), 254,272,294 Ap 91

IHDE, Don. *Technology and the Lifeworld*. Bloomington, Indiana Univ Pr, 1990.
Browning, Douglas. *Rev Metaph* 44(3), 639-641 Mr 91

ILLINGWORTH, Patricia. *AIDS and the Good Society*. London, Routledge, 1990.
Fauvel, John. *Rad Phil* 56, 61-62 Autumn 90
Murphy, Timothy F. *Med Human Rev* 5(1), 87-92 Ja 91
Post, Stephen G. *J Med Human* 12(1), 41-42 Spr 91

IMBACH, Ruedi and PERLER, Dominik (eds). *Nicolaus von Autrecourt, Briefe*. Hamburg, Meiner, 1988.
Thijssen, J M M H. *Vivarium* 28(1), 77-81 My 90

IMPERATO, Robert. *Merton and Walsh on the Person*. West Palm Beach, Liturgical Pub, 1987.
Bruteau, Beatrice. *Int Phil Quart* 31(3), 353-363 S 91

INEICHEN, Hans. *Einstellungssätze*. Munich, Fink, 1987.
Haefliger, Gregor. *Frei Z Phil Theol* 37(1-2), 288-292 1990

INGRAM, David. *Habermas and the Dialectic of Reason*. New Haven, Yale Univ Pr, 1987.
Seigfried, Hans. *Man World* 24(1), 114-116 Ja 91

INWOOD, Brad and GERSON, L P (trans). *Hellenistic Philosophy: Introductory Readings*. Indianapolis, Hackett, 1988.
Rabel, Robert J. *Ancient Phil* 11(1), 225-228 Spr 91

IRWIN, T H. *Aristotle's First Principles*. New York, Clarendon/Oxford Pr, 1988.
Striker, Gisela. *J Phil* 88(9), 489-496 S 91
Wardy, Robert. *Phronesis* 36(1), 88-106 1991
Bussanich, John. *J Hist Phil* 29(1), 115-116 Ja 91
Kirwan, Christopher. *J Hellen Stud* 110, 242-243 1990

IRWIN, Terence. *Classical Thought*. New York, Oxford Univ Pr, 1989.
Armstrong, A H. *Heythrop J* 32(3), 432-433 Jl 91

IRWIN, Terence. *A History of Western Philosophy, 1: Classical Thought*. New York, Oxford Univ Pr, 1989.
Frank, Daniel H. *Polis* 9(2), 214-219 1990

ISER, Wolfgang. *Prospecting: From Reader Response to Literary Anthropology*. Baltimore, Johns Hopkins Univ Pr, 1989.
Van de Pitte, Margaret M. *Can Phil Rev* 10(8), 322-325 Ag 90

JACKALL, Robert. *Moral Mazes: The World of Corporate Managers*. New York, Oxford Univ Pr, 1988.
Brooks, Leonard J. *J Bus Ethics* 10(4), 302,316,322 Ap 91

JACKENDOFF, Ray. *Semantics and Cognition*. Cambridge, MIT Pr, 1983.
Orilia, Francesco. *Nous* 25(3), 359-367 Je 91

JACKSON, F C. *Conditionals*. Oxford, Blackwell, 1987.
Humberstone, I L. *Phil Phenomenol Res* 51(1), 227-234 Mr 91
Appiah, Anthony. *Int Stud Phil* 23(1), 124-125 1991

JACKSON, Michael W. *Matters of Justice*. London, Croom Helm, 1986.
Schultz, David. *Int Stud Phil* 22(3), 118-119 1990

JACOB, André. *Encyclopédie philosophique universelle*. Paris, Pr Univ de France, 1989.
Kremer-Marietti, Angèle. *Rev Int Phil* 44(175), 621-624 1990

JACOB, Pierre (ed). *L'âge de la science*. Paris, Editions Odile Jacob, 1989.
Verley, Xavier. *Rev Phil Fr* 180(4), 693-697 O-D 90

JACOBUS, Mary and KELLER, Evelyn Fox and SHUTTLEWORTH, Sally (eds). *Body Politics: Women and the Discourses of Science*. London, Routledge, 1990.
Russell, Denise. *Phil Books* 32(2), 121-124 Ap 91

JAKOWLJEWITSCH, Dragan. *L Nelsons Rechtfertigung metaphysischer Grundsätze der theoretischen Realwissenschaft*. New York, Lang, 1988.
Bianco, Bruno. *Riv Filosof Neo-Scolas* 82(2-3), 322-336 Ap-S 90

JANAWAY, Christopher. *Self and World in Schopenhauer's Philosophy*. New York, Clarendon/Oxford Pr, 1989.
Schönfeld, Martin. *J Hist Phil* 29(3), 503-505 Jl 91

JANICAUD, Dominique. *L'ombre de cette pensée: Heidegger et la question politique*. Grenoble, Jérôme Millon, 1990.
Trotignon, Pierre. *Rev Phil Fr* 180(3), 562-564 Jl-S 90

JANOS, Andrew C. *Politics and Paradigms*. Stanford, Stanford Univ Pr, 1986.
Care, Norman S. *Nous* 24(5), 811-813 D 90

JANZ, Denis R. *Luther on Thomas Aquinas: The Angelic Doctor in the Thought of the Reformer*. Stuttgart, Steiner, 1989.
Tune, Anders S. *Thomist* 55(1), 145-148 Ja 91

JARDINE, Nicholas. *The Birth of History and Philosophy of Science: Kepler's "A Defence of Tycho against Ursus"*. Cambridge, Cambridge Univ Pr, 1988.
Finocchiaro, Maurice A. *J Hist Phil* 28(4), 614-615 O 90

JARDINE, Nicholas. *The Fortunes of Inquiry*. Oxford, Clarendon Pr, 1986.
Forster, Paul D. *Phil Sci* 57(4), 727-729 D 90

JARVIE, Ian. *Philosophy of the Film: Epistemology, Ontology, Aesthetics*. New York, Routledge & Kegan Paul, 1987.
Sparshott, Francis. *Int Stud Phil* 22(3), 120-121 1990

JASAY, Anthony de. *Social Contract, Free Ride: A Study of the Public Goods Problem*. Oxford, Clarendon Pr, 1989.
Frohlich, Norman. *Econ Phil* 6(2), 327-332 O 90

JAUSS, Hans Robert. *Question and Answer: Forms of Dialogic Understanding, Michael Hays (ed & trans)*. Minneapolis, Univ of Minnesota Pr, 1989.
Rendall, Steven. *Phil Lit* 15(1), 151-152 Ap 91

JEAUNEAU, Edouard. *Etudes érigéniennes*. Paris, Etudes Augustiniennes, 1987.
Brisson, Luc. *Rev Phil Fr* 181(1), 77-80 1991

JEANNIÈRE, Abel. *Lire Platon*. Paris, Aubier, 1990.
Follon, Jacques. *Rev Phil Louvain* 89(82), 338-341 My 91

JERVOLINO, Domenico and POOLE, Gordon (trans). *The Cogito and Hermeneutics*. Norwell, Kluwer, 1990.
Barber, Michael. *Mod Sch* 68(3), 270-271 Mr 91

JHANJI, Rekha. *The Sensuous in Art: Reflections on Indian Aesthetics*. Delhi, Motilal, 1989.
McGhee, Michael. *Brit J Aes* 31(1), 75-76 Ja 91

JHINGRAN, Saral. *Aspects of Hindu Morality*. Delhi, Motilal, 1989.
Ghose, A M. *J Indian Counc Phil Res* 7(2), 149-152 Ja-Ap 90

JOHNSON, Glenn L. *Research Methodology for Economists: Philosophy and Practice*. New York, Macmillan, 1986.
Peterson, E Wesley F. *Agr Human Values* 7(3-4), 124-127 Sum-Fall 90

JOHNSON, Harold J (ed). *The Medieval Tradition of Natural Law*. Kalamazoo, Medieval Institute, 1987.
Henle, R J and Thro, Linus J. *Mod Sch* 67(3), 238-242 Mr 90

JOHNSON, Mark. *The Body in the Mind: The Bodily Basis of Meaning, Imagination, and Reason*. Chicago, Univ of Chicago Pr, 1987.
Romaine, Suzanne. *J Prag* 14(4), 686-688 Ag 90
Kulas, Jack. *Phil Psych* 3(2-3), 321-325 1990
Laurier, Daniel. *Dialogue (Canada)* 29(3), 477-483 1990

JOHNSON, Paul. *Wittgenstein and Moral Philosophy*. New York, Routledge, 1989.
Elliott, David. *Eidos* 9(1), 121-127 Je 90

JOHNSON, Peter. *Politics, Innocence and the Limits of Goodness*. London, Routledge, 1989.
Jennings, Jeremy. *Phil Invest* 14(2), 176-179 Ap 91

JOHNSTON, Mark D. *The Spiritual Logic of Ramon Llull*. New York, Clarendon/Oxford Univ Pr, 1987.
Bennett, Beth S. *Phil Rhet* 24(1), 88-91 1991
Teske, Roland J. *Mod Sch* 67(4), 313-314 My 90

JOHNSTON, Paul. *Wittgenstein and Moral Philosophy*. New York, Routledge, 1989.
Tilghman, B R. *Teach Phil* 13(4), 394-397 D 90

JOLLEY, Nicholas. *The Light of the Soul: Theories of Ideas in Leibniz, Malebranche and Descartes*. Oxford, Clarendon Pr, 1990.
Scott, David. *Heythrop J* 32(1), 114-116 Ja 91

JONES, Greta. *Social Darwinism and English Thought: The Interaction between Biological and Social Theory*. Atlantic Highlands, Humanities Pr, 1980.
Brautigam, Jeffrey C. *Hist Phil Life Sci* 12(1), 111-116 1990

JONES, Howard. *The Epicurean Tradition*. New York, Routledge, 1989.
DeLacy, Phillip. *Ancient Phil* 11(1), 199-202 Spr 91
Follon, Jacques. *Rev Phil Louvain* 89(82), 347-352 My 91

JONES, Nicholas F. *Public Organization in Ancient Greece: A Documentary Study*. Philadelphia, American Philosophical Society, 1987.
Rhodes, P J. *Phoenix* 45(1), 71-76 Spr 91

JONES, Peter (ed). *The "Science of Man" in the Scottish Enlightenment: Hume, Reid and their Contemporaries*. Edinburgh, Edinburgh Univ Pr, 1989.
Somerville, James. *Phil Books* 32(2), 82-85 Ap 91

JONSEN, Albert R and TOULMIN, Stephen. *The Abuse of Casuistry: A History of Moral Reasoning*. Berkeley, Univ of California Pr, 1988.
Warnick, Barbara. *Phil Rhet* 24(1), 76-80 1991
Carey, Jonathan Sinclair. *Heythrop J* 32(2), 277-278 Ap 91
MacIntyre, Alasdair. *J Hist Phil* 28(4), 634-635 O 90

JONSEN, Albert R. *The New Medicine and the Old Ethics*. Cambridge, Harvard Univ Pr, 1990.
Tomlinson, Tom. *Hastings Center Rep* 21(4), 42 Jl-Ag 91

JORDAN, Mark D (trans). *On Faith: Summa Theologia 2-2, qq. 1-16 of St Thomas Aquinas*. Notre Dame, Univ of Notre Dame Pr, 1990.
Cessario, Romanus. *Thomist* 55(1), 141-144 Ja 91

JORDAN, Mark D. *Ordering Wisdom: The Hierarchy of Philosophical Discourses in Aquinas*. Notre Dame, Univ of Notre Dame Pr, 1986.
Bourke, Vernon J. *Mod Sch* 68(1), 91-93 N 90

JOSHI, Kireet. *Sri Aurobindo and the Mother*. Delhi, Motilal, 1989.
Bhatt, S R. *J Indian Counc Phil Res* 7(1), 139-144 S-D 89

JOY, Lynn Sumida. *Gassendi the Atomist: Advocate of History in an Age of Science*. Cambridge, Cambridge Univ Pr, 1987.
Menn, Stephen. *Phil Rev* 100(2), 326-329 Ap 91
Watson, Richard A. *Int Stud Phil* 22(3), 121-122 1990

JUANOLA SOLER, Narciso. *Atenea*. Madrid, Dossat, 1986.
Forment Giralt, E. *Espiritu* 37(97), 100-102 Ja-Je 88

JULLIEN, François. *Procès ou Création*. Paris, Seuil, 1989.
Mair, Victor H. *Phil East West* 41(3), 373-386 Jl 91

JULIEN, Philippe. *Le retour à Freud de Jacques Lacan*. Toulouse, Erès, 1985.
Ver Eecke, Wilfried. *Rev Metaph* 44(1), 148-149 S 90

JÜNGER, Ernst and HEIDEGGER, Martin. *Oltre la linea*. Milan, Adelphi, 1989.
Mangiagalli, Maurizio. *Aquinas* 33(1), 215-217 Ja-Ap 90

JUNGNICKEL, Christa and MCCORMMACH, Russell. *Intellectual Mastery of Nature: Theoretical Physics from Ohm to Einstein, 2v*. Chicago, Univ of Chicago Pr, 1986.
Forman, Paul. *Phil Sci* 58(1), 129-132 Mr 91

KAEHLER, Klaus Erich. *Leibniz' Position der Rationalität: Die Logik im metaphysischen Wissen der 'natürlichen Vernunft'*. Munich, Alber, 1989.
Frey, Gregor Karl. *Hist Phil Log* 12(1), 123-128 1990

KAELIN, E F and SCHRAG, C O (eds). *American Phenomenology: Origins and Developments*. Norwell, Kluwer, 1989.
Kavanaugh, John Francis. *Mod Sch* 68(3), 261-264 Mr 91

KAGAN, Shelly. *The Limits of Morality*. Oxford, Clarendon Pr, 1989.
Dancy, Jonathan. *Phil Books* 31(4), 193-200 O 90

KAIN, Philip J. *Marx's Method, Epistemology, and Humanism: A Study in the Development of His Thought*. Boston, Reidel, 1986.
Hutton, Patrick H. *Hist Euro Ideas* 12(6), 853-854 1990

KAIN, Philip J. *Marx and Ethics*. New York, Oxford Univ Pr, 1988.
Riemer, Neal. *Phil Soc Sci* 21(3), 409-412 S 91

KAL, Victor. *On Intuition and Discursive Reasoning In Aristotle*. Leiden, Brill, 1988.
McKirahan Jr, Richard D. *Ancient Phil* 11(1), 183-187 Spr 91

KAMBARTEL, Friedrich. *Philosophie der humanen Welt*. Frankfurt am Main, Suhrkamp, 1989.
Mitta, Dimitra. *Phil Inq* 12(3-4), 77-79 Sum-Fall 90

KANE, Robert and PHILLIPS, Stephen H (eds). *Hartshorne: Process Philosophy and Theology*. Albany, SUNY Pr, 1989.
Devenish, Philip E. *Process Stud* 19(1), 54-56 Spr 90

KANE, Rosalie A and CAPLAN, Arthur L (eds). *Everyday Ethics: Resolving Dilemmas in Nursing Home Life*. New York, Springer, 1990.
Glover, Jacqueline. *Theor Med* 12(1), 93-95 Mr 91

KANNICHT, Richard. *The Ancient Quarrel Between Philosophy and Poetry: Aspects of the Greek Conception of Literature*. Christchurch, Univ of Canterbury, 1988.
Wilson, Marcus. *Phil Lit* 14(2), 399-401 O 90

KANT, Immanuel. *Lezioni di filosofia della religione, Costantino Esposito (ed)*. Naples, Bibliopolis, 1988.
Fabris, Adriano. *Teoria* 10(1), 187-188 1990
Porro, Pasquale. *Rev Phil Louvain* 88(80), 608-611 N 90

KANT, Immanuel. *Scritti di filosofia della religione, Giuseppe Riconda (ed)*. Milan, Mursia, 1989.
Fabris, Adriano. *Teoria* 10(1), 187-188 1990

KANT, Immanuel and MANGANARO, Paolo (ed). *Ragione e ipocondria*. Salerno, Ed Salerno, 1989.
Colonnello, Pio. *Sapienza* 44(2), 233-235 Ap-Je 91

KAPLAN, Max. *The Arts: A Social Perspective*. Unknown, Assoc Univ Pr, 1990.
Rampley, Matthew. *Brit J Aes* 31(3), 272-274 Jl 91

KAPLAN, Stephen. *Hermeneutics, Holography and Indian Idealism*. Delhi, Motilal, 1987.
Potter, Karl H. *Phil East West* 41(1), 122-123 Ja 91

KASANMOENTALIB, Soemini. *De dans van dood en leven*. Zeist, Kerckebosch, 1989.
Hertogh, Kees. *Kennis Methode* 14(3), 309-315 1990

KASHAP, S Paul. *Spinoza and Moral Freedom*. Albany, SUNY Pr, 1987.
Cover, J A. *Phil Rev* 100(1), 160-164 Ja 91

KATZ, Jerrold J. *Cogitations*. New York, Oxford Univ Pr, 1986.
Gombay, André. *Can J Phil* 20(4), 565-575 D 90
Martinez, Roy. *Teach Phil* 13(2), 175-177 Je 90
Tiles, J E. *Phil Books* 31(4), 201-203 O 90

KAUTSKY, Karl. *The Materialist Conception of History, John M Kautsky (ed)*. New Haven, Yale Univ Pr, 1988.
Shlapentokh, Dmitry. *Hist Euro Ideas* 13(3), 282-284 1991

KAVANAUGH, Thomas M (ed). *The Limits of Theory*. Stanford, Stanford Univ Pr, 1989.
Miller, Seumas. *Phil Lit* 14(2), 423-424 O 90

KAVKA, Gregory. *Moral Paradoxes of Nuclear Deterrence*. New York, Cambridge Univ Pr, 1987.
Lee, Steven. *Phil Rev* 100(1), 148-150 Ja 91

KEARNEY, Richard. *The Wake of Imagination: Toward a Postmodern Culture*. Minneapolis, Univ of Minnesota Pr, 1988.
Bostar, Leo. *Grad Fac Phil J* 13(2), 241-246 1990
O'Leary, Joseph S. *Phil Stud (Ireland)* 32, 330-333 1988-90

KEELEY, Michael. *A Social-Contract Theory of Organizations*. Notre Dame, Univ of Notre Dame Pr, 1988.
Herman, Stewart W. *Bus Ethics Quart* 1(1), 121-132 Ja 91
Gilbert Jr, Daniel R. *J Bus Ethics* 9(10), 813-817 O 90

KEKES, John. *Moral Tradition and Individuality*. Princeton, Princeton Univ Pr, 1989.
Eldridge, Richard. *Phil Lit* 14(2), 387-394 O 90

KEKES, John. *The Examined Life*. Lewisburg, Bucknell Univ Pr, 1988.
Keenan, James F. *Int Phil Quart* 31(3), 376-377 S 91

KELLENBERGER, J. *God-Relationships With and Without God*. Basingstoke, Macmillan, 1989.
Clack, Beverley. *Relig Stud* 27(2), 281-282 Je 91

KELLNER, Douglas. *Critical Theory, Marxism and Modernity*. Cambridge, Polity Pr, 1989.
McCann, Graham. *Rad Phil* 56, 58-59 Autumn 90
Lang, Berel. *Phil Lit* 15(1), 157-159 Ap 91

KELLNER, Douglas. *Jean Baudrillard: From Marxism to Post-Modernism and Beyond*. Cambridge, Polity Pr, 1989.
McCann, Graham. *Rad Phil* 56, 58-59 Autumn 90

KELLY, Alfred. *The Descent of Darwin: The Popularization of Darwinism in Germany, 1860-1914*. Chapel Hill, Univ of North Carolina Pr, 1979.
Brautigam, Jeffrey C. *Hist Phil Life Sci* 12(1), 111-116 1990

KELSEN, Hans. *Il problema della sovranità*. Milan, Giuffrè, 1989.
Sciacca, Fabrizio. *Riv Int Filosof Diritto* 66(4), 753-756 O-D 89

KEMAL, Salim. *Kant and Fine Art: An Essay on Kant and the Philosophy of Fine Art and Culture*. New York, Clarendon/Oxford Pr, 1986.
Wood, Robert E. *Rev Metaph* 44(4), 846-848 Je 91

KEMP, T Peter and RASMUSSEN, David (eds). *The Narrative Path: The Later Works of Paul Ricoeur*. Cambridge, MIT Pr, 1989.
Rehg, Ellen. *Mod Sch* 68(2), 187-189 Ja 91

KENNEDY, Ellen and MENDUS, Susan (eds). *Women in Western Political Philosophy*. Brighton, Wheatsheaf, 1987.
Vallance, Elizabeth. *Heythrop J* 32(1), 113-114 Ja 91

KENNEDY, Leonard A (ed). *Thomistic Papers IV*. Houston, Center for Thomistic Studies, 1988.
Peterson, Michael L. *Faith Phil* 8(1), 115-120 Ja 91

KENNY, Anthony. *The Logic of Deterrence*. Chicago, Univ of Chicago Pr, 1985.
Stone, Jim. *J Indian Counc Phil Res* 5(1), 170-178 S-D 87

KENNY, Anthony. *The Metaphysics of Mind*. Oxford, Clarendon Pr, 1989.
Hannan, Barbara. *Phil Books* 32(1), 43-45 Ja 91
Hamlyn, D W. *Mind Lang* 6(1), 87-92 Spr 91

KENNY, Anthony. *The Legacy of Wittgenstein*. Oxford, Blackwell, 1984.
Mies, Jürgen. *Erkenntnis* 33(2), 261-279 S 90

KENYON, Timothy. *Utopian Communism and Political Thought in Early Modern England*. London, Pinter, 1989.
Davis, J C. *Hist Polit Thought* 11(2), 360-362 Sum 90

KERMODE, Frank. *An Appetite for Poetry*. Cambridge, Harvard Univ Pr, 1989.
Hall, Michael L. *Phil Lit* 14(2), 444-445 O 90

KERNER, George C. *Three Philosophical Moralists: Mill, Kant and Sartre*. Oxford, Clarendon Pr, 1990.
Gorman, J L. *Phil Quart* 41(162), 116-117 Ja 91
Matthews, Eric. *Phil Books* 32(2), 116-117 Ap 91

KILCULLEN, John. *Sincerity and Truth: Essays on Arnauld, Bayle and Toleration*. Oxford, Clarendon Pr, 1988.
Levi, A H T. *Heythrop J* 32(2), 287-288 Ap 91
Watson, Richard A. *Int Stud Phil* 23(1), 125-126 1991

KILDWARDBY, Robert. *On Time and Imagination*. New York, Oxford Univ Pr, 1987.
Rosemann, Philipp W. *Rev Phil Louvain* 89(82), 366-368 My 91

KIRWAN, Christopher. *Augustine*. London, Routledge, 1989.
Brinkman, B R. *Heythrop J* 32(2), 294-297 Ap 91

KIRWAN, James. *Literature, Rhetoric, Metaphysics*. New York, Routledge, 1990.
Meidner, Olga McDonald. *Brit J Aes* 31(3), 280-281 Jl 91

KITCHENER, R F. *Piaget's Theory of Knowledge: Genetic Epistemology and Scientific Reason*. New Haven, Yale Univ Pr, 1986.
Martínez Velasco, Jesús. *Anu Filosof* 23(1), 189-191 1990

KITCHING, Gavin. *Karl Marx and the Philosophy of Praxis*. New York, Routledge, 1988.
Thomas, Paul. *Hist Euro Ideas* 12(6), 855-857 1990
Murray, Patrick. *J Hist Phil* 29(2), 322-324 Ap 91
Harris, Roger. *Rad Phil* 58, 46-47 Sum 91

KITTAY, Eva. *Metaphor: Its Cognitive Force and Linguistic Structure*. New York, Oxford Univ Pr, 1987.
Ludlow, Peter. *J Phil* 88(6), 324-330 Je 91
Bergmann, Merrie. *Phil Rev* 100(1), 112-115 Ja 91

KITWOOD, Tom. *Concern for Others*. New York, Routledge, 1990.
Wright, Derek. *J Moral Educ* 20(2), 215-216 My 91

KIVY, Peter. *Music Alone: Philosophical Reflections on the Purely Musical Experience*. Ithaca, Cornell Univ Pr, 1990.
Davies, Stephen. *Can Phil Rev* 10(9), 368-372 S 90
Sharpe, R A. *Brit J Aes* 31(3), 276-277 Jl 91

KIVY, Peter. *Osmin's Rage: Philosophical Reflections on Opera, Drama, and Text*. Princeton, Princeton Univ Pr, 1988.
Howard, V A. *J Aes Educ* 25(1), 113-115 Spr 91

KLEIN, Martha. *Determinism, Blameworthiness, and Deprivation*. Oxford, Clarendon Pr, 1990.
Cockburn, David. *Phil Quart* 41(162), 120 Ja 91

KLOESEL, C J W (ed). *Writings of Charles S Peirce: A Chronological Edition, V4*. Bloomington, Indiana Univ Pr, 1986.
Colapietro, Vincent. *Man World* 24(2), 235-240 Ap 91
Benedict, George A. *Trans Peirce Soc* 26(4), 513-521 Fall 90

KLOSKO, G. *The Development of Plato's Political Theory*. New York, Methuen, 1986.
Skemp, J B. *J Hellen Stud* 110, 227-230 1990

KLUBACK, William. *The Idea of Humanity: Hermann Cohen's Legacy to Philosophy and Theology*. Lanham, Univ Pr of America, 1987.
Lichtigfeld, A. *Int Stud Phil* 22(3), 122-123 1990

KNIGHT, James W and CALLAHAN, Joan C. *Preventing Birth: Contemporary Methods and Related Moral Controversies*. Salt Lake City, Univ of Utah Pr, 1989.
Warren, Mary Anne. *Bioethics* 5(1), 86-89 Ja 91

KNOBLOCK, John. *Xunzi: A Translation and Study of the Complete Works, V1: Books 1-6*. Stanford, Stanford Univ Pr, 1988.
Cua, A S. *Phil East West* 41(2), 215-227 Ap 91

KOCH, Herbert. *Jenseits der Strafe: Überlegungen zur Kriminalitätsbewältigung*. Tübingen, Möhr, 1988.
Tusa, Carlo. *Riv Int Filosof Diritto* 66(4), 756-759 O-D 89

KOCKELMANS, Joseph L (ed). *Phenomenological Psychology: The Dutch School*. Dordrecht, Nijhoff, 1987.
Tuedio, James. *Husserl Stud* 7(3), 213-223 1990

KOHN, Alfie. *The Brighter Side of Human Nature*. New York, Basic Books, 1990.
Witherell, Carol S. *J Moral Educ* 20(2), 216-217 My 91

KOJÈVE, Alexandre. *L'idée du déterminisme dans la physique classique et dans la physique moderne*. Paris, Librairie Générale Française, 1990.
Largeault, Jean. *Rev Phil Fr* 180(4), 698-701 O-D 90

KOLAKOWSKI, Leszek. *Si Dios no existe*. Madrid, Tecnos, 1985.
Pegueroles, J. *Espiritu* 37(98), 163-165 Jl-D 88

KOLB, David. *Postmodern Sophistications: Philosophy, Architecture, and Tradition*. Chicago, Univ of Chicago Pr, 1990.
Harries, Karsten. *Rev Metaph* 44(3), 641-643 Mr 91

KOLENDA, Konstantin. *Rorty's Humanistic Pragmatism*. Gainesville, Univ of South Florida Pr, 1990.
Markham, I S. *Relig Stud* 27(1), 137-138 Mr 91
Conway, Daniel W. *Phil Lit* 15(1), 169-170 Ap 91
Novak, John M. *Free Inq* 11(3), 53-54 Sum 91

KOPPELBERG, Dirk. *Die Aufhebung der analytischen Philosophie*. Frankfurt, Suhrkamp, 1989.
Cometti, Jean-Pierre. *Rev Int Phil* 44(175), 624-626 1990
Schweizer, Herbert. *Dialectica* 45(1), 87-89 1991

KOSELLECK, Robert. *Critique and Crisis*. Cambridge, MIT Pr, 1988.
Schultz, David. *Int Stud Phil* 23(1), 126-127 1991

KOSIEK, R. *Historikerstreit und Geschichtsrevision*. Tübingen, Graver, 1987.
Ortiz de Landázuri, Carlos. *Anu Filosof* 23(2), 184-187 1990

KOTARBINSKI, Tadeusz. Wyklady z dziejów logiki. Warsaw, P W N, 1985.
Bednarz Jr, John. *J Sym Log* 55(3), 1322-1324 S 90

KRAUT, Richard. *Aristotle on the Human Good*. Princeton, Princeton Univ Pr, 1989.
Miller, Mitchell. *Polit Theory* 19(1), 109-112 F 91
Dent, N J H. *Phil Books* 32(2), 77-78 Ap 91
Evans, J D G. *Philosophy* 66(256), 246-247 Ap 91
Hughes, G J. *Heythrop J* 32(3), 438-439 Jl 91

KRELL, David and WOOD, David (eds). *Exceedingly Nietzsche: Aspects of Contemporary Nietzsche Interpretation*. London, Routledge Chapman & Hall, 1988.
Baker, Lang. *Phil Soc Sci* 21(1), 90-101 Mr 91
Davey, Nicholas. *J Brit Soc Phenomenol* 22(1), 90-91 Ja 91
Westphal, Merold. *Heythrop J* 32(2), 289 Ap 91

KRELL, David Farrell. *Intimations of Mortality: Time, Truth, and Finitude in Heidegger's Thinking of Being*. University Park, Pennsylvania State Univ Pr, 1986.
Schreiner, Christopher S. *Mod Sch* 67(4), 328-329 My 90

KRETZMANN, Norman (ed). *Meaning and Inference in Medieval Philosophy*. Boston, Kluwer, 1988.
Perler, Dominik. *Frei Z Phil Theol* 37(3), 532-538 1990

KRETZMANN, Norman and KRETZMANN, Barbara Ensign (eds). *The Sophismata of Richard Kilvington*. New York, Oxford Univ Pr, 1990.
Ashworth, E J. *Hist Phil Log* 12(2), 243-245 1991

KRIEGER, Leonard. *Time's Reasons: Philosophies of History Old and New*. Chicago, Univ of Chicago Pr, 1989.
Breisach, Ernst. *Hist Euro Ideas* 13(1-2), 149-150 1991

KRISHNA, Daya (ed). *India's Intellectual Traditions: Attempts at Conceptual Reconstructions*. New Delhi, Motilal, 1987.
Pande, G C. *J Indian Counc Phil Res* 6(2), 181-184 Ja-Ap 89

KRIPS, Henry. *The Metaphysics of Quantum Theory*. New York, Clarendon/Oxford Pr, 1987.
Halpin, John. *Phil Rev* 100(3), 490-492 Jl 91

KRITZMAN, Lawrence D (ed). *Michel Foucault: Politics, Philosophy, Culture: Interviews and Other Writings, 1977-1984*. London, Routledge, 1990.
Racevskis, Karlis. *Rad Phil* 57, 50-52 Spr 91

KUEHN, Manfred. *Scottish Common Sense in Germany, 1768-1800: A Contribution to the History of Critical Philosophy*. Montreal, McGill-Queen's Univ Pr, 1987.
Crombie, E James. *Dialogue (Canada)* 29(3), 453-460 1990

KUHSE, Helga. *The Sanctity of Life Doctrine in Medicine: A Critique*. Oxford, Clarendon Pr, 1987.
Erde, Edmund L. *J Med Human* 12(1), 37-41 Spr 91
Ewin, R E. *Austl J Phil* 68(2), 245-246 Je 90

KUIPERS, Theo A F (ed). *What is Closer-to-the-Truth? A Parade of Approaches to Truthlikeness*. Amsterdam, Rodopi, 1987.
Miller, David W. *Brit J Phil Sci* 41(2), 281-290 Je 90

KUKATHAS, Chandran. *Hayek and Modern Liberalism*. Oxford, Clarendon Pr, 1989.
Bellamy, Richard. *Hist Euro Ideas* 13(3), 310-311 1991
Gorman, J L. *Phil Books* 32(2), 124-125 Ap 91

KÜNG, Hans. *The Incarnation of God: An Introduction to Hegel's Theological Thought as Prolegomena to a Future Christology*. Edinburgh, Clark, 1987.
McDermott, Brian O. *Heythrop J* 32(1), 86-88 Ja 91

KURTZ, Paul. *Forbidden Fruit: The Ethics of Humanism*. Buffalo, Prometheus Books, 1988.
Hiorth, Finngeir. *Philosophia (Israel)* 20(3), 339-340 D 90

KYMLICKA, Will. *Liberalism, Community, and Culture*. Oxford, Clarendon Pr, 1989.
Okin, Susan Moller. *Polit Theory* 19(1), 123-129 F 91
Paul, Jeffrey. *Rev Metaph* 44(3), 643-645 Mr 91
Nickel, James W. *Can Phil Rev* 10(10), 413-415 O 90

LABRADA, María Antonia. *Belleza y racionalidad*. Pamplona, Eunsa, 1990.
Fontán del Junco, Manuel. *Anu Filosof* 24(1), 182-186 1991

LABRIOLA, Antonio. *Lettere inedite di Antonio Labriola*. Rome, Miccolis, 1983.
Barbera, Sandro. *G Crit Filosof Ital* 68(3), 419-425 S-D 89

LACEY, A R. *Bergson*. New York, Routledge, 1989.
Sprigge, T L S. *Phil Quart* 41(164), 364-365 Jl 91

LACEY, Nicola. *State Punishment: Political Principles and Community Values*. London, Routledge, 1988.
Ten, C L. *Utilitas* 2(2), 334-336 N 90

LACHTERMAN, David R. *The Ethics of Geometry: A Genealogy of Modernity*. New York, Routledge, Chapman & Hall, 1989.
Sepper, Dennis L. *Rev Metaph* 44(1), 149-151 S 90

LACOUE-LABARTHE, Philippe. *Typography: Mimesis, Philosophy, Politics*. Cambridge, Harvard Univ Pr, 1989.
Kronick, Joseph G. *Rev Metaph* 44(2), 421-422 D 90

LAFLEUR, Claude. *Quatre introductions à la philosophie au XIIIe* siècle. Paris, Vrin, 1988.
Panaccio, Claude. *Philosophiques* 17(2), 201-203 Autumn 1990

LAFRANCE, Guy (ed). *Éthique et droits fondamentaux—Ethics and Basic Rights*. Ottawa, Pr Univ d'Ottawa, 1989.
Sweet, William. *Laval Theol Phil* 46(3), 403-406 O 90

LAKOFF, George. *Women, Fire and Dangerous Things: What Categories Reveal about the Mind*. Chicago, Univ of Chicago Pr, 1987.
Hofman, Oscar. *Commun Cog* 23(4), 347-356 1990
Laurier, Daniel. *Dialogue (Canada)* 29(3), 477-483 1990

LAKS, André. *Diogène d'Apollonie: La dernière cosmologie présocratique*. Lille, Pr Univ de Lille, 1983.
Kerferd, G B. *Ancient Phil* 10(2), 269-271 Fall 90

LAMACCHIA, A. *Edith Stein: Filosofia e senso dell'essere*. Bari, Ecumenica, 1989.
D'Ambra, Michele. *Aquinas* 33(3), 683-685 S-D 90

LAMB, David. *Organ Transplants and Ethics*. New York, Routledge, 1990.
Upton, Hugh. *Phil Quart* 41(164), 381-382 Jl 91

LAMB, David. *Down the Slippery Slope: Arguing in Applied Ethics*. New York, Croom Helm, 1988.
Burgess, J A. *Austl J Phil* 69(1), 113-114 Mr 91

LAMBERTI, Jean-Claude. *Tocqueville and the Two Democracies, Arthur Goldhammer (trans)*. Cambridge, Harvard Univ Pr, 1989.
Lovell, David W. *Hist Euro Ideas* 13(3), 288-289 1991
Mitchell, Harvey. *Hist Polit Thought* 11(2), 366-368 Sum 90

LAMPERT, Laurence. *Nietzsche's Teaching: An Interpretation of "Thus Spoke Zarathustra"*. New Haven, Yale Univ Pr, 1986.
Higgins, Kathleen. *Int Stud Phil* 22(3), 124-125 1990

LANFREDINI, Roberta. *Oggetti e paradigmi: Per una concepzione interattiva della conoscenza scientifica*. Rome, Theoria, 1988.
Prodi, Enrico. *Aquinas* 34(1), 144-148 Ja-Ap 91

LANG, Berel. *Act and Idea in the Nazi Genocide*. Chicago, Univ of Chicago Pr, 1990.
Glaser, Daryl. *Rad Phil* 58, 45-46 Sum 91

LANGER, Claudia. *Reform nach Prinzipien: Untersuchungen zur politischen Theorie Immanuel Kants*. Stuttgart, Klett-Cotta, 1986.
Ludwig, B. *Kantstudien* 81(3), 383-391 1990

LANGLEY, P and SIMON, H A and BRADSHAW, G L and ZYTKOW, J M. *Scientific Discovery, Computational Explorations of the Creative Processes*. Cambridge, MIT Pr, 1987.
Balzer, W. *Erkenntnis* 34(1), 125-127 Ja 91

LANGTON, Christopher G (ed). *Artificial Life*. Redwood City, Addison-Wesley, 1989.
Dennett, Daniel C. *Biol Phil* 5(4), 489-492 O 90

LAPSLEY, Robert and WESTLAKE, Michael. *Film Theory: An Introduction*. New York, St Martin's Pr, 1988.
Neill, Alex and Ridley, Aaron. *Can Phil Rev* 10(9), 345-351 S 90

LARGIER, Niklaus. *Zeit, Zeitlichkeit, Ewigkeit*. New York, Lang, 1989.
Winkler, Norbert. *Deut Z Phil* 38(12), 1229-1230 1990

LARMORE, Charles Everett. *Le strutture della complessità morale*. Milano, Feltrinelli, 1990.
Andolfi, Ferruccio. *Aquinas* 33(3), 677-679 S-D 90

LASSMAN, Peter and VELODY, Irving and MARTINS, Herminio (eds). *Max Weber's "Science as a Vocation"*. London, Unwin Hyman, 1989.
Agassi, Joseph. *Phil Soc Sci* 21(1), 102-109 Mr 91

LATOUR, Bruno. *Science in Action*. Milton Keynes, Open Univ Pr, 1987.
Amsterdamska, Olga. *Sci Tech Human Values* 15(4), 495-504 Autumn 90

LATOUR, Bruno. *The Pasteurization of France, Alan Sheridan and John Law (trans)*. Cambridge, Harvard Univ Pr, 1988.
Schaffer, Simon. *Stud Hist Phil Sci* 22(1), 175-192 Mr 91
Sturdy, Steve. *Stud Hist Phil Sci* 22(1), 163-173 Mr 91

LATOUR, Bruno and WOOLGAR, Steve. *Laboratory Life: The Social Construction of Scientific Facts*. London, Sage, 1979.
Brown, James Robert. *Can J Phil* 21(2), 245-261 Je 91

LAUDAN, L. *Science and Values*. Berkeley, Univ of Calif Pr, 1984.
Worrall, John. *Brit J Phil Sci* 39(2), 263-275 Je 88

LAUER, Quentin. *G K Chesterton: Philosopher Without Portfolio*. Bronx, Fordham Univ Pr, 1988.
Schreiner, C S. *Mod Sch* 67(4), 316-317 My 90

LAVINE, T Z and TEJERA, V (eds). *History and Anti-History in Philosophy*. Norwell, Kluwer, 1989.
Goldstein, Leon J. *Int Stud Phil* 23(1), 129-130 1991

LAWSON, Tony and PESARAN, Hashem (eds). *Keynes' Economics: Methodological Issues*. London, Croom Helm, 1985.
Gillies, Donald. *Brit J Phil Sci* 39(1), 117-129 Mr 88

LEAK, Andrew N. *The Perverted Consciousness: Sexuality and Sartre*. New York, Macmillan, 1989.
Macey, David. *Rad Phil* 56, 62 Autumn 90

LEAMAN, Oliver. *Moses Maimonides: Arabic Thought and Culture Series*. New York, Routledge, 1990.
Netton, Ian Richard. *Asian Phil* 1(1), 100-102 1991

LEAR, Jonathan. *Aristotle: The Desire to Understand*. New York, Cambridge Univ Pr, 1988.
Friedman, Robert. *J Hist Phil* 29(2), 301-302 Ap 91
Kraut, Richard. *Phil Rev* 100(3), 522-524 Jl 91

LEE, Keekok. *Social Philosophy and Ecological Scarcity*. New York, Routledge, 1989.
Knowles, Dudley. *Phil Books* 32(1), 58-60 Ja 91
Walker, A D M. *J Applied Phil* 7(2), 236-238 O 90

LEE, Robert and MORGAN, Derek (eds). *Birthrights: Law and Ethics at the Beginning of Life*. New York, Routledge, 1989.
Campbell, A G M. *Heythrop J* 32(3), 448-449 Jl 91
Chadwick, Ruth F. *Bioethics* 4(4), 353-359 O 90
Williams, A M. *J Applied Phil* 7(2), 239-240 O 90

LEFORT, Claude. *Democracy and Political Theory*. Minneapolis, Univ of Minnesota Pr, 1988.
Gould, Carol C. *Praxis Int* 10(3-4), 337-345 O 90-Ja 91

LEGROS, Robert. *L'idée d'humanité*. Paris, Grasset & Fasquelle, 1990.
Ponton, Lionel. *Laval Theol Phil* 46(3), 419-420 O 90

LEHRER, Keith. *Thomas Reid*. New York, Routledge, 1989.
Adams, Todd L. *Rev Metaph* 44(3), 645-646 Mr 91
Craig, Edward. *Ratio* 3(2), 182-185 D 90
Wood, P B. *Mind* 100(397), 155-157 Ja 91
Haldane, John. *Philosophy* 66(256), 252-254 Ap 91

LEHRER, Keith. *Theory of Knowledge*. Boulder, Westview Pr, 1990.
Young, James O. *Can Phil Rev* 10(10), 416-418 O 90

LEIBNIZ, G W. *Philosophische Schriften, V5, Werner Wiater (ed & trans)*. Darmstadt, Wissenschaftl, 1989.
Schüssler, Werner. *Stud Leibniz* 22(1), 118-122 1990

LEININGER, Madeleine and WATSON, Jean (eds). *The Caring Imperative in Education*. New York, National League for Nursing, 1990.
Johnstone, Megan-Jane. *Bioethics* 5(1), 78-83 Ja 91

LEITES, Edmund (ed). *Conscience and Casuistry in Early Modern Europe*. Cambridge, Cambridge Univ Pr, 1988.
Burke, Peter. *Hist Euro Ideas* 12(6), 870-871 1990
Höpfl, H M. *Hist Polit Thought* 11(3), 548-549 Autumn 90
McCoog, Thomas M. *Heythrop J* 32(2), 276-277 Ap 91

LEMAN-STEFANOVIC, Ingrid. *The Event of Death: A Phenomenological Enquiry*. Boston, Nijhoff, 1987.
Barber, Michael D. *Mod Sch* 67(3), 235-236 Mr 90

LEMAY, J A Leo (ed). *Deism, Masonry, and the Enlightenment*. Newark, Univ of Delaware Pr, 1987.
Bagley, Paul J. *Rev Metaph* 44(1), 151-153 S 90

LEMBECK, Karl-Heinz. *Gegenstand Geschichte—Geschichtswissenschaftstheorie in Husserls Phänomenologie*. Norwell, Kluwer, 1988.
Dörflinger, Bernd. *Husserl Stud* 7(3), 205-212 1990

LEMPEREUR, Alain (ed). *L'homme et la rhétorique*. Paris, Méridiens Klincksieck, 1990.
Timmermans, Benoît. *Rev Int Phil* 44(173), 280-289 1990

LENNON, Kathleen. *Explaining Human Action*. London, Duckworth, 1990.
Edwards, Jim. *Phil Books* 32(2), 110-111 Ap 91
Cordua, Carla. *Dialogos* 26(58), 187-189 Jl 91

LEPENIES, Wolf. *Between Literature and Science: The Rise of Sociology*. Cambridge, Cambridge Univ Pr, 1988.
Staum, Martin S. *Phil Sci* 58(1), 135-136 Mr 91

LEPORE, Ernest and MCLAUGHLIN, Brian P (eds). *Actions and Events: Perspectives on the Philosophy of Donald Davidson*. New York, Blackwell, 1985.
Sinnott-Armstrong, Walter. *Nous* 25(1), 120-123 Mr 91

LERMOND, Lucia. *The Form of Man: Human Essence in Spinoza's "Ethic"*. Leiden, Brill, 1988.
Steinberg, Diane. *J Hist Phil* 29(1), 135-137 Ja 91

LESLIE, John (ed). *Physical Cosmology and Philosophy*. New York, Macmillan, 1990.
Birch, Andrea Croce. *Rev Metaph* 44(3), 646-647 Mr 91
Rolston III, Holmes. *Zygon* 26(2), 317-324 Je 91

LESLIE, John. *Universes*. New York, Routledge, 1989.
Clifton, Robert K. *Phil Quart* 41(164), 339-344 Jl 91
Katz, Jonathan. *Dialogue (Canada)* 29(4), 589-595 1990
Rolston III, Holmes. *Zygon* 26(2), 317-324 Je 91

LEVESQUE-LOPMAN, Louise. *Claiming Reality*. Totowa, Rowman & Littlefield, 1988.
Pilardi, Jo-Ann. *Hypatia* 6(2), 233-237 Sum 91

LEVIN, Michael. *Feminism and Freedom*. New Brunswick, Transaction, 1987.
Haack, Susan. *Int Stud Phil* 23(1), 107-108 1991

LEVIN, Michael. *Marx, Engels and Liberal Democracy*. New York, St Martin's Pr, 1989.
Seddon, Fred. *Stud Soviet Tho* 41(2), 145-146 Mr 91

LEVINAS, Emmanuel. *Nine Talmudic Readings*. Bloomington, Indiana Univ Pr, 1990.
Zev Harvey, Warren. *Iyyun* 40(3), 351-353 Jl 91

LEVINE, Michael P. *Hume and the Problem of Miracles: A Solution*. Dordrecht, Kluwer, 1989.
Corrigan, Patrick. *Rev Metaph* 44(2), 423-424 D 90

LEVINSON, Marjorie and BUTLER, Marilyn and MCGANN, Jerome and HAMILTON, Paul. *Rethinking Historicism: Criticial Readings in Romantic History*. Oxford, Blackwell, 1989.
Rée, Jonathan. *Rad Phil* 56, 53-57 Autumn 90

LEWIS, David. *Parts of Classes*. New York, Blackwell, 1991.
Simons, Peter. *Mind* 100(399), 394-397 Jl 91

LIEBERMAN, David. *The Province of Legislation Determined*. New York, Cambridge Univ Pr, 1989.
Stimson, Shannon. *Polit Theory* 19(3), 462-465 Ag 91

LIGHTMAN, Bernard. *The Origins of Agnosticism: Victorian Unbelief and the Limits of Knowledge*. Baltimore, Johns Hopkins Univ Pr, undated.
Stewart, Larry. *J Hist Phil* 29(2), 326-327 Ap 91

LIMBRICK, Elaine (ed) and THOMSON, Douglas F S (trans). *Francisco Sanches: That Nothing is Known*. Cambridge, Cambridge Univ Pr, 1988.
De Olaso, Ezequiel. *J Hist Phil* 29(1), 121-123 Ja 91

LINGIS, Alphonso. *Excesses*. Albany, SUNY Pr, 1983.
Pryor, Benjamin S. *Auslegung* 17(1), 85-90 Wint 91

LINGIS, Alphonso. *Phenomenological Explanations*. Dordrecht, Nijhoff, 1986.
Reeder, Harry P. *Int Stud Phil* 22(3), 126-127 1990

LINK-SALINGER, Ruth (ed). *Of Scholars, Savants, and their Texts: Studies in Philosophy and Religious Thought in Honor of Arthur Hyman*. New York, Lang, 1989.
Harvey, Warren Zev. *Iyyun* 40(1), 106-107 Ja 91

LINK-SALINGER, Ruth (ed). *A Straight Path: Studies in Medieval Philosophy and Culture*. Washington, Catholic Univ of America Pr, 1988.
Buijs, Joseph A. *J Hist Phil* 28(4), 609-611 O 90

LITTLE, Stephen. *Realm of the Immortals*. Bloomington, Indiana Univ Pr, 1988.
Wawrytko, Sandra A. *Phil East West* 41(3), 442-444 Jl 91

LIU, Shu-hsien and ALLINSON, R E (eds). *Harmony and Strife: Contemporary Perspectives East and West*. Hong Kong, Chinese Univ Pr, 1988.
Fu, Charles Wei-Hsun. *J Chin Phil* 18(1), 123-128 Mr 91

LIVI, Antonio. *Filosofía del senso comune, Logica della scienca & della fede*. Milan, Ares, 1990.
Vitoria, María Angeles. *Anu Filosof* 23(1), 191-194 1990

LLOYD, A C. *The Anatomy of Neoplatonism*. Oxford, Clarendon Pr, 1990.
Leslie, John. *Phil Books* 32(2), 78-80 Ap 91
O'Meara, Dominic J. *Rev Metaph* 44(4), 848-849 Je 91

LLOYD, G E R. *The Revolutions of Wisdom: Studies in the Claims and Practice of Ancient Greek Science*. Berkeley, Univ of California Pr, 1987.
Asmis, Elizabeth. *Phil Rev* 100(2), 321-324 Ap 91
Vegetti, Mario. *Phronesis* 35(3), 315-326 1990

LLOYD, Dan. *Simple Minds*. Cambridge, MIT Pr, 1989.
Gustafson, Donald. *Phil Psych* 4(2), 287-293 1991

LOCKE, John. *Questions Concerning the Law of Nature*. Ithaca, Cornell Univ Pr, 1990.
Melzer, Arthur M. *Rev Metaph* 44(4), 849-851 Je 91

LOCKE, John. *Some Thoughts Concerning Education, John W Yolton and Jean S Yolton (eds)*. Oxford, Clarendon Pr, 1989.
Stone, Harold Samuel. *Hist Euro Ideas* 12(4), 570-571 1990

LOCKWOOD, Michael. *Mind, Brain and the Quantum: The Compound 'I'*. Cambridge, Blackwell, 1989.
Earley, Joseph E. *Rev Metaph* 44(4), 851-852 Je 91
Clark, Andy. *Phil Quart* 40(161), 509-514 O 90
Lucas, J R. *Mind* 99(396), 650-652 O 90

LOHMAR, Dieter. *Phänomenologie der Mathematik*. Norwell, Kluwer, 1989.
Tieszen, Richard. *Husserl Stud* 7(3), 199-204 1990
Miller, J Philip. *Rev Metaph* 44(1), 153-155 S 90

LOIZOU, Andros. *The Reality of Time*. Brookfield, Gower, 1986.
Sklar, Lawrence. *Int Stud Phil* 22(3), 127-128 1990

LOMASKY, Loren E. *Persons, Rights and the Moral Community*. New York, Oxford Univ Pr, 1987.
O'Hagan, Timothy. *Int Stud Phil* 22(3), 128-129 1990

LONDEY, David and JOHANSON, Carmen. *The Logic of Apuleius*. Leiden, Brill, 1987.
Smith, Robin. *Ancient Phil* 11(1), 193-198 Spr 91

LOPEZ, Donald S. *A Study of Svātantrika*. Ithaca, Snow Lion, 1987.
Dreyfus, Georges. *Phil East West* 41(3), 431-437 Jl 91

LOPEZ, Donald S. *The Heart Sūtra Explained*. Albany, SUNY Pr, 1988.
Dreyfus, Georges. *Phil East West* 41(3), 431-437 Jl 91

LOPEZ QUINTAS, Alfonso. *Cuatro Filósofos en busca de Dios*. Madrid, Rialp, 1989.
Cavallé, Mónica. *Anu Filosof* 23(1), 194-198 1990

LORENZ, Gisela Helene. *Das Problem der Erklärung der Kategorien*. New York, de Gruyter, 1986.
Steinbeck, Wolfram. *Kantstudien* 81(4), 485-488 1990

LORENZEN, Paul. *Constructive Philosophy, Karl Richard Pavlovic (trans)*. Amherst, Univ of Massachusetts Pr, 1987.
Mercer, Mark. *Int Stud Phil* 22(3), 130-131 1990

LORENZO, Manuel F. *La última orilla*. Oviedo, Pentalfa, 1989.
Almanza, Marcelino Luna. *El Basilisco* 3, 89-90 Ja-F 90

LOSURDO, Domenico and SANDKÜHLER, Hans Jörg (eds). *Philosophie als Verteidigung des Ganzen der Vernunft*. Cologne, Pahl-Rugenstein, 1988.
Schirdewahn, Lars. *Deut Z Phil* 38(11), 1113-1114 1990

LOWE, E J. *Kinds of Being: A Study of Individuation, Identity and the Logic of Sortal Terms*. Oxford, Blackwell, 1989.
Englebretsen, George. *Iyyun* 40(1), 100-105 Ja 91
Noonan, Harold W. *Philosophy* 66(256), 248-249 Ap 91

LOWE, Jonathan. *Kinds of Being: A Study of Individuation, Identity and the Logic of Sortal Terms*. Oxford, Blackwell, 1989.
Snowdon, P F. *Phil Books* 32(1), 37-39 Ja 91

LOWE, Victor. *Alfred North Whitehead: The Man and His Works, V2*. Baltimore, Johns Hopkins Univ Pr, 1990.
Vitali, Theodore R. *Trans Peirce Soc* 27(2), 256-266 Spr 91
Boisvert, Raymond D. *Rev Metaph* 44(4), 852-854 Je 91

LUBAN, David. *Lawyers and Justice*. Princeton, Princeton Univ Pr, 1988.
Luizzi, Vincent. *Law Phil* 9(3), 311-317 Ag 90

LÜBBE, Hermann. *Religion nach der Aufklärung*. Graz, Styria, 1986.
Figl, Johann. *Z Phil Forsch* 45(1), 143-146 Ja-Mr 91

LUCAS JR, George R. *The Rehabilitation of Whitehead*. Albany, SUNY Pr, 1989.
Ford, Lewis S. *J Speculative Phil* 5(1), 74-77 1991
Grange, Joseph. *Rev Metaph* 44(1), 155-156 S 90
Lango, John W. *Trans Peirce Soc* 26(4), 540-550 Fall 90
Mayers, Eugene. *Personalist Forum* 6(2), 190-192 Fall 90

LUCAS, J R. *The Future*. New York, Blackwell, 1989.
Le Poidevin, Robin. *Phil Quart* 41(164), 333-339 Jl 91
Percival, Philip. *Mind* 100(397), 157-161 Ja 91
Williams, C J F. *Philosophy* 66(255), 124-125 Ja 91

LUFT, Eric von der (ed). *Schopenhauer: New Essays in Honor of His 200th Birthday*. Lewiston, Mellen Pr, 1988.
Hamlyn, D W. *Int Stud Phil* 22(3), 152-153 1990
Vater, Michael. *Int J Phil Relig* 29(1), 53-54 F 91

LUKÁCS, Georg and MARCUS, Judith and TAR, Zoltán (ed & trans). *Selected Correspondence 1902-1920, Dialogues with Weber, Simmel, Buber, Mannheim, and Others*. New York, Columbia Univ Pr, 1986.
Rockmore, Tom. *Stud Soviet Tho* 41(3), 235-237 My 91

LUNTLEY, Michael. *Language, Logic and Experience: The Case for Anti-Realism*. London, Duckworth, 1988.
Humberstone, I L. *Austl J Phil* 68(4), 465-467 D 90
Weiss, Bernhard. *Phil Quart* 40(161), 534-536 O 90

LUTZ, Catherine A. *Unnatural Emotions: Everyday Sentiments on a Micronesian Atoll and Their Challenge to Western Theory*. Chicago, Univ of Chicago Pr, 1988.
Morreall, John. *Phil East West* 41(1), 119-120 Ja 91

LYCAN, W G. *Consciousness*. Cambridge, MIT Pr, 1987.
Segal, Gabriel. *Phil Phenomenol Res* 51(1), 240-243 Mr 91

LYCAN, William G. *Consciousness*. Cambridge, MIT Pr, 1987.
Sicha, Jeffrey F. *Nous* 25(4), 553-561 S 91

LYCAN, William G. *Judgement and Justification*. New York, Cambridge Univ Pr, 1988.
Baker, Lynne Rudder. *Phil Rev* 100(3), 481-484 Jl 91

LYCOS, Kimon. *Plato on Justice and Power*. Albany, SUNY Pr, 1987.
Pappas, Nickolas. *Phil Rev* 100(3), 515-517 Jl 91

LYONS, William E. *The Disappearance of Introspection*. Cambridge, MIT Pr, 1986.
Rankin, Kenneth. *Nous* 25(4), 567-569 S 91

MACDONALD, Cynthia. *Mind-Body Identity Theories*. New York, Routledge, 1989.
Oderberg, David S. *Phil Books* 32(1), 45-47 Ja 91

MACEDO, Stephen. *Liberal Virtues*. New York, Clarendon/Oxford Pr, 1990.
Levinson, Sanford. *Mind* 100(399), 398-400 Jl 91

MACHAN, Tibor. *Individuals and Their Rights*. La Salle, Open Court, 1989.
Warner, Stuart D. *Nat Forum* 71(1), 47-48 Wint 91

MACINTYRE, Alasdair. *Three Rival Versions of Moral Enquiry: Encyclopaedia, Genealogy, and Tradition*. Notre Dame, Univ of Notre Dame Pr, 1990.
Dougherty, Jude P. *Rev Metaph* 44(2), 424-426 D 90
Griswold Jr, Charles L. *Polit Theory* 19(3), 465-470 Ag 91
Turner, Jeffrey S. *Inquiry* 34(2), 255-278 Je 91
Weston, M. *Mind* 100(399), 400-403 Jl 91

MACINTYRE, Alasdair. *Whose Justice? Which Rationality?* Notre Dame, Univ of Notre Dame Pr, 1988.
Quinn, Philip L. *Faith Phil* 8(1), 109-115 Ja 91
Wilcox, John T. *Int Stud Phil* 22(3), 131-132 1990
Fisher, Walter R. *Phil Rhet* 23(3), 242-247 1990
Iglesias, Teresa. *Phil Stud (Ireland)* 32, 333-337 1988-90
Kennedy, Terence. *Gregorianum* 72(1), 183-185 1991
Baumrin, Bernard. *Nous* 24(5), 774-782 D 90

MACINTYRE, Alasdair. *Dopo la virtù: Saggio di teoria morale*. Milan, Feltrinelli, 1988.
Vendemiati, Aldo. *Riv Filosof Neo-Scolas* 82(1), 170-172 Ja-Mr 90

MACKENZIE, Patrick T. *The Problems of Philosophers*. Buffalo, Prometheus Books, 1989.
Davie, William. *Can Phil Rev* 10(9), 373-375 S 90

MACKIE, John Leslie. *Logic and Knowledge: Selected Papers, V1, Joan Mackie and Penelope Mackie (eds)*. Oxford, Clarendon Pr, 1985.
Fries, Erich. *Phil Rundsch* 37(4), 336-345 1990

MACKIE, John Leslie. *Persons and Values: Selected Papers, V2, Joan Mackie and Penelope Mackie (eds)*. Oxford, Clarendon Pr, 1985.
Fries, Erich. *Phil Rundsch* 37(4), 336-345 1990

MACMILLAN, C J B and GARRISON, James W. *A Logical Theory of Teaching: Erotetics and Intentionality*. Boston, Kluwer, 1988.
Heslep, Robert D. *Educ Theor* 41(1), 89-97 Wint 91

MACNIVEN, Don. *Bradley's Moral Psychology*. Lewiston, Mellen Pr, 1987.
Harris, H S. *Owl Minerva* 22(1), 96-98 Fall 90

MADELL, Geoffrey. *Mind and Materialism*. New York, Columbia Univ Pr, 1988.
Schechtman, Marya. *Int Stud Phil* 23(1), 130-131 1991

MADISON, G B. *The Logic of Liberty*. Westport, Greenwood Pr, 1986.
DeCew, Judith Wagner. *Nous* 25(2), 233-238 Ap 91

MADISON, G B. *The Hermeneutics of Postmodernity: Figures and Themes*. Bloomington, Indiana Univ Pr, 1989.
Wallulis, Jerry. *Can Phil Rev* 10(9), 375-377 S 90

MAGEE, John. *Boethius on Signification and Mind*. Leiden, Brill, 1989.
Obertello, Luca. *Riv Filosof Neo-Scolas* 82(2-3), 329-332 Ap-S 90

MAH, Harold. *The End of Philosophy and the Origins of 'Ideology': Karl Marx and the Crisis of the Young Hegelians*. Berkeley, Univ of California Pr, 1987.
Sax, Benjamin C. *Hist Euro Ideas* 12(6), 837-841 1990

MAIER, Robert (ed). *Norms in Argumentation: Proceedings of the Conference on Norms*. Dordrecht, Providence, 1989.
Makau, Josina M. *Inform Log* 13(1), 45-48 Wint 91

MAINBERGER, Gonsalv K. *Rhetorica I: Reden mit Vernunft: Aristoteles, Cicero, Augustinus*. Stuttgart, Frommann-Holzboog, 1987.
Colette, Jacques. *Rev Metaph Morale* 95(4), 571-574 O-D 90

MAINBERGER, Gonsalv K. *Rhetorica II: Spiegelungen des Geistes: Sprachfiguren bei Vico und Lévi-Strauss*. Stuttgart, Frommann-Holzboog, 1987.
Colette, Jacques. *Rev Metaph Morale* 95(4), 571-574 O-D 90

MAIOCCHI, Roberto. *La "Belle Epoque" dell'atomo*. Milan, Angeli, 1988.
Palladino, Dario. *Epistemologia* 12(2), 359-362 Jl-D 89

MAKAU, Josina M. *Reasoning and Communication: Thinking Critically About Arguments*. Belmont, Wadsworth, 1990.
Rowland, Robert C. *Inform Log* 13(1), 49-51 Wint 91

MAKINDE, M Akin. *African Philosophy, Culture, and Traditional Medicine*. Athens, Ohio Univ Pr, 1988.
Birt, Robert E. *Phil East West* 41(1), 95-109 Ja 91

MAKKREEL, Rudolph A. *Imagination and Interpretation in Kant: The Hermeneutic Import of the "Critique of Judgment"*. Chicago, Univ of Chicago Pr, 1990.
Sacksteder, William. *Rev Metaph* 44(3), 647-649 Mr 91
Leaman, Oliver. *Brit J Aes* 31(3), 269-271 Jl 91

MAKKREEL, Rudolf A (ed). *Wilhelm Dilthey, Selected Works, VI: Introduction to the Human Sciences*. Princeton, Princeton Univ Pr, 1989.
Owensby, Jacob. *J Hist Phil* 29(3), 505-507 Jl 91

MALCOLM, Norman. *Nothing Is Hidden*. Oxford, Blackwell, 1986.
Mies, Jürgen. *Erkenntnis* 33(2), 261-279 S 90

MALONEY, J Christopher. *The Mundane Matter of the Mental Language*. Cambridge, Cambridge Univ Pr, 1989.
Addis, Laird. *Rev Metaph* 44(2), 426-427 D 90
Edwards, Jim. *Phil Quart* 41(162), 106-109 Ja 91

MALORNY, Heinz. *Zur Philosophie Friedrich Nietzsches*. Berlin, Akademie-Verlag, 1989.
Fromm, Eberhard. *Deut Z Phil* 38(11), 1109-1111 1990

MALUSA, Luciano. *Neotomismo e intransigentismo cattolico ai tempi del Sillabo, 2v*. Milan, IPL, 1989.
Bizzotto, Mario. *Filosofia* 41(3), 436-443 S-D 90

MALY, Kenneth and EMAD, Parvis (eds). *Heidegger on Heraclitus: A New Reading*. Lewiston, Mellen Pr, 1986.
Madigan, Arthur. *Mod Sch* 68(1), 96-98 N 90

MANDELBAUM, Maurice. *Purpose and Necessity in Social Theory*. Baltimore, Johns Hopkins Univ Pr, 1987.
Dawson, Lorne L. *Phil Soc Sci* 20(4), 522-526 D 90

MANN, Michael. *The Sources of Social Power*. New York, Cambridge Univ Pr, 1986.
Munz, Peter. *Phil Soc Sci* 21(2), 253-276 Je 91

MANNO, A G. *Lo storicismo di W Dilthey*. Naples, Loffredo, 1990.
Orlando, Pasquale. *Sapienza* 43(3), 348-350 Jl-S 90

MANSFELD, Jaap (ed & trans). *Die Vorsokratiker: Grieschisch und deutsch*. Stuttgart, Reclam, 1987.
Eichler, Klaus-Dieter. *Deut Z Phil* 38(10), 1002-1004 1990

MANSFIELD JR, Harvey C. *Taming the Prince: The Ambivalence of Modern Executive Power*. New York, Free Pr, 1989.
Morrisey, Will. *Interpretation* 18(1), 163-173 Fall 90

MAPEL, David. *Social Justice Reconsidered: The Problem of Appropriate Precision in a Theory of Justice*. Urbana, Univ of Illinois Pr, 1989.
Dreier, James. *Polit Theory* 19(1), 129-133 F 91

MARCIL-LACOSTE, Louise. *La raison en procès: Essais sur la philosophie et le sexisme*. Montreal, Hurtubise, 1987.
Allen, Prudence. *Dialogue (Canada)* 29(3), 460-461 1990

MARCIL-LACOSTE, Louise (ed). *La philosophie pour enfants: L'expérience Lipman*. Sainte-Foy, Griffon d'argile, 1990.
Richard, Arsène. *Thinking* 9(1), 47-48 1990

MARCONI, Diego. *L'Eredità di Wittgenstein*. Bari, Laterza, 1987.
Penco, Carlo. *Epistemologia* 12(2), 357-358 Jl-D 89
Simoni, Laura. *G Metaf* 11(3), 496-499 S-D 89

MARENBON, John. *Later Medieval Philosophy (1150-1350): An Introduction*. London, Routledge & Kegan Paul, 1987.
Moorhead, John. *Heythrop J* 32(1), 117-118 Ja 91

MARGOLIS, J and others (eds). *Rationality, Relativism and the Human Sciences*. Boston, Nijhoff, 1986.
Barber, Michael D. *Mod Sch* 68(2), 185-187 Ja 91

MARGOLIS, Joseph. *Pragmatism Without Foundations*. Cambridge, Blackwell, 1986.
Hare, Peter H. *Nous* 25(4), 578-580 S 91

MARGOLIS, Joseph. *Science Without Unity*. New York, Oxford Univ Pr, 1989.
Van Evra, James. *Can Phil Rev* 10(10), 418-420 O 90

MARION, Jean-Luc. *Réduction et donation: Recherches sur Husserl, Heidegger et la phénoménologie*. Paris, Pr Univ de France, 1989.
Trotignon, Pierre. *Rev Phil Fr* 180(3), 564-566 Jl-S 90

MARITAIN, Jacques and MARITAIN, Raïssa. *Oeuvres complètes, V7 & V8*. Paris, Saint-Paul, 1989.
Leroy, Marie-Vincent. *Rev Thomiste* 91(1), 152-155 Ja-Mr 91

MARTIN, Christopher (ed & trans). *The Philosophy of Thomas Aquinas: Introductory Readings*. New York, Routledge, 1988.
Lisska, Anthony J. *Teach Phil* 13(3), 295-298 S 90

MARTIN, Michael L. *Atheism: A Philosophical Justification*. Philadelphia, Temple Univ Pr, 1990.
Frey, Robert S. *Bridges* 2(3-4), 207-208 Fall-Wint 90
Grogan, Timothy William. *Free Inq* 10(4), 54-55 Fall 90

MARTIN, Raymond. *The Past Within Us: An Empirical Approach to the Philosophy of History*. Princeton, Princeton Univ Pr, 1990.
Fuller, Steve. *Can Phil Rev* 10(8), 326-328 Ag 90
McCullagh, C Behan. *Austl J Phil* 68(3), 352-354 S 90

MARTIN, Richard M. *Metaphysical Foundations: Mereology and Metalogic*. München-Wien, Philosophia, 1988.
Roetti, Jorge Alfredo. *Rev Latin De Filosof* 16(2), 246-249 Jl 90

MARTIN, Rex. *Rawls and Rights*. Lawrence, Univ of Kansas Pr, 1985.
Wilcox, John T. *Int Stud Phil* 22(3), 132 1990

MARSH, James L. *Post-Cartesian Meditations*. Bronx, Fordham Univ Pr, 1988.
Kavanaugh, John Francis. *Mod Sch* 68(3), 261-264 Mr 91

MARX, Werner. *Die Phänomenologie Edmund Husserls: Eine Einführung*. Munich, Fink, 1987.
Janssen, Paul. *Husserl Stud* 7(2), 137-145 1990

MARX, Werner. *Is There a Measure on Earth? T J Nenon and R Lilly (trans)*. Chicago, Univ of Chicago Pr, 1987.
White, Alan. *Int J Phil Relig* 28(2), 124-125 O 90

MARX, Wolfgang (ed). *Zur Selbstbegründung der Philosophie seit Kant*. Frankfurt am Main, Klostermann, 1987.
Steinbeck, Wolfram. *Kantstudien* 81(4), 493-495 1990

MARZOA, Felipe Martínez. *Desconocida rais común*. Barcelona, Visor, 1987.
Caimi, Mario. *Kantstudien* 82(2), 222-224 1991

MASON, J K. *Human Life and Medical Practice*. Edinburgh, Edinburgh Univ Pr, 1988.
Smith, James M. *Bioethics* 5(1), 83-86 Ja 91

MASON, Jeff. *Philosophical Rhetoric: The Function of Indirection in Philosophical Writing*. New York, Routledge, 1989.
Langsdorf, Lenore. *Teach Phil* 13(3), 303-306 S 90
Warner, Martin. *Phil Lit* 14(2), 426-427 O 90

MATES, Benson. *The Philosophy of Leibniz*. New York, Oxford Univ Pr, 1986.
Mondadori, Fabrizio. *Phil Rev* 99(4), 613-629 O 90

MATHIEN, Thomas. *Bibliography of Philosophy in Canada: A Research Guide*. Kingston, Frye Library of Canadian Philosophy, 1988.
Di Norcia, Vincent. *Dialogue (Canada)* 29(3), 462-466 1990

MATTHEN, Mohan and LINSKY, Bernard (eds). *Philosophy & Biology*. Calgary, Univ Calgary Pr, 1988.
Williams, Patricia. *Biol Phil* 6(3), 351-361 Jl 91

MATTHEWS, Michael R (ed). *The Scientific Background to Modern Philosophy*. Indianapolis, Hackett, 1989.
Tlumak, Jeffrey. *Teach Phil* 13(3), 281-284 S 90

MAY, William E. *Moral Absolutes: Catholic Tradition, Current Trends and the Truth*. Milwaukee, Marquette Univ Pr, 1989.
Kopfensteiner, Thomas R. *Thought* 66(260), 117-118 Mr 91

MAYER, Cornelius (ed). *Augustinus-Lexikon*. Basel, Schwabe, 1986.
Haren, Michael. *Phil Stud (Ireland)* 32, 337-338 1988-90

MAYR, Ernst. *Toward a New Philosophy of Biology: Observations of an Evolutionist*. Cambridge, Harvard Univ Pr, 1988.
Thompson, Paul. *Hist Phil Life Sci* 12(2), 277-278 1990

MAZLISH, Bruce. *The Meaning of Karl Marx*. Oxford, Oxford Univ Pr, 1988.
Duncan, Graeme. *Hist Euro Ideas* 12(6), 833-836 1990

MCALLESTER, Mary (ed). *The Philosophy and Poetics of Gaston Bachelard*. Lanham, Univ Pr of America, 1989.
Llewelyn, John. *J Brit Soc Phenomenol* 22(1), 91-93 Ja 91

MCCARTHY, George E. *Marx's Critique of Science and Positivism*. Boston, Kluwer, 1988.
Murphy, John W. *Stud Soviet Tho* 41(2), 166-167 Mr 91
Murray, Patrick. *Phil Soc Sci* 21(2), 293-297 Je 91

MCCARTHY, Michael H. *The Crisis of Philosophy*. Albany, SUNY Pr, 1990.
Meynell, Hugo. *Can Phil Rev* 10(12), 502-504 D 90

MCCAY, Bonnie M and ACHESON, James M (eds). *The Question of the Commons: The Culture and Ecology of Communal Resources*. Tucson, Univ of Arizona Pr, 1987.
Bailey, Conner and Skaldany, Mike. *Agr Human Values* 7(2), 105-106 Spr 90

MCCLOSKEY, Mary A. *Kant's Aesthetic*. London, Macmillan, 1987.
Hutchings, Patrick. *Austl J Phil* 68(4), 467-469 D 90

MCCOOL, Gerald A. *From Unity to Pluralism*. Bronx, Fordham Univ Pr, 1989.
Lauder, Robert E. *Thomist* 55(2), 301-319 Ap 91

MCCOOL, Gerald A. *Nineteenth-Century Scholasticism*. Bronx, Fordham Univ Pr, 1989.
Lauder, Robert E. *Thomist* 55(2), 301-319 Ap 91

MC CULLOCH, Gregory. *The Game of the Name*. New York, Oxford Univ Pr, 1989.
Hale, Bob. *Hist Phil Log* 12(2), 259-262 1991
Champlin, T S. *Phil Books* 31(4), 231-233 O 90
Kazez, Jean R. *Mind* 99(396), 647-650 O 90

MCCULLOUGH, H B (ed). *Political Ideologies and Political Philosophies*. Toronto, Wall & Thompson, 1989.
Principe, Michael A. *Teach Phil* 13(3), 290-292 S 90

MCCUMBER, John. *Poetic Interaction*. Chicago, Univ of Chicago Pr, 1989.
Switzer, Robert. *J Speculative Phil* 4(4), 354-360 1990

MCDANIEL, Jay B. *Earth, Sky, Gods and Mortals: Developing an Ecological Spirituality*. Mystic, Twenty-third Publications, 1990.
Tilley, Terrence W. *Process Stud* 19(2), 140-141 Sum 90

MCDANIEL, Jay B. *Of God and Pelicans: A Theology of Reverence for Life*. Louisville, Westminster/John Knox Pr, 1989.
Tilley, Terrence W. *Process Stud* 19(2), 140-141 Sum 90

MCFALL, Lynne. *Happiness*. New York, Lang, 1989.
Miller, Peter. *Can Phil Rev* 10(8), 328-330 Ag 90

MCFETRIDGE, I G and HALDANE, John and SCRUTON, Roger (eds). *Logical Necessity and Other Essays*. London, Aris Soc, 1990.
Craig, Edward. *Phil Quart* 41(164), 352-354 Jl 91

MCGINN, Colin. *Mental Content*. Oxford, Blackwell, 1989.
Schlagel, Richard H. *Rev Metaph* 44(2), 427-429 D 90
Davies, Martin. *Mind Lang* 5(3), 245-248 Autumn 90

MCGINN, Colin. *Wittgenstein on Meaning*. Oxford, Blackwell, 1984.
Mies, Jürgen. *Erkenntnis* 33(2), 261-279 S 90

MCGUINNESS, Brian. *Wittgenstein, A Life: Young Ludwig, 1889-1921*. London, Duckworth, 1988.
Kerr, Fergus. *Heythrop J* 32(2), 289-291 Ap 91

MCHUGH, Francis P. *Keyguide to Information Sources in Business Ethics*. London, Mansell, 1988.
Harrington, Scott T. *Heythrop J* 32(3), 446-447 Jl 91

MCINTYRE, John. *Faith, Theology and Imagination*. Edinburgh, Handsel Pr, 1987.
Wilson, Jonathan. *Mod Theol* 7(3), 294-296 Ap 91

MCKEON, Zahava K (ed). *Freedom and History and Other Essays: An Introduction to the Thought of Richard McKeon*. Chicago, Univ of Chicago Pr, 1990.
Betz, Joseph. *Trans Peirce Soc* 27(1), 135-140 Wint 91

MCKNIGHT, Stephen A. *Sacralizing the Secular: The Renaissance Origins of Modernity*. Baton Rouge, Louisiana State Univ Pr, 1989.
Copenhaver, Brian P. *J Hist Phil* 28(4), 611-613 O 90

MCLAUGHLIN, Robert N. *On the Logic of Ordinary Conditionals*. Albany, SUNY Pr, 1990.
Ferguson, Kenneth G. *Hist Phil Log* 12(2), 251-253 1991
Jackson, Frank. *Mind* 100(399), 403-406 Jl 91

MCLELLAN, David and SAYERS, Sean (eds). *Socialism and Morality*. London, Macmillan, 1990.
McCarney, Joseph. *Rad Phil* 57, 39-41 Spr 91

MCLELLAN, David. *Simone Weil, Utopian Pessimist*. London, Macmillan, 1989.
Rosen, F. *Hist Polit Thought* 11(2), 371-372 Sum 90

MCMAHON, Robert. *Augustine's Prayerful Ascent: An Essay on the Literary Form of the "Confessions"*. Athens, Univ of Georgia Pr, 1989.
Emmerson, Richard K. *Phil Lit* 14(2), 439-441 O 90

MCMURRIN, Sterling M. *The Tanner Lectures on Human Values*. New York, Cambridge Univ Pr, 1986.
Pierce, Christine. *Ideal Stud* 20(2), 175-177 My 90

MÉCHOULAN, Henry. *Amsterdam au temps de Spinoza*. Paris, Pr Univ de France, 1990.
Verbeek, Théo. *Rev Metaph Morale* 96(2), 285-286 Ap-Je 91

MEGILL, Allan. *Prophets of Extremity*. Berkeley, Univ of California Pr, 1985.
Grünfeld, Joseph. *Iyyun* 39(3), 359-367 Jl 90

MEIER, Heinrich. *Carl Schmitt, Leo Strauss und "Der Begriff des Politischen"*. Stuttgart, Metzler, 1988.
Kaufmann, Matthias. *Z Phil Forsch* 45(1), 160-163 Ja-Mr 91

MEIKLE, Scott. *Essentialism in the Thought of Karl Marx*. LaSalle, Open Court, 1985.
Sciabarra, Chris. *Crit Rev* 4(1-2), 61-73 Wint-Spr 90

MEILAENDER, Gilbert. *The Limits of Love: Some Theological Explorations*. University Park, Pennsylvania State Univ Pr, 1988.
Kelly, Kevin T. *Heythrop J* 32(2), 274-276 Ap 91

MELE, Alfred R. *Irrationality: An Essay on Akrasia, Self-Deception, and Self-Control*. New York, Oxford Univ Pr, 1987.
Homiak, Marcia L. *Phil Rev* 100(1), 122-125 Ja 91
Szabados, Béla. *Can J Phil* 20(3), 403-415 S 90

MELLE, Ullrich (ed). *Vorlesungen über Ethik und Wertlehre 1908-1914*. Norwell, Kluwer, 1988.
Neon, Tom. *Res Phenomenol* 20, 184-188 1990

MELLING, David J. *Understanding Plato*. New York, Oxford Univ Pr, 1987.
Brumbaugh, Robert S. *Ancient Phil* 10(2), 299-301 Fall 90

MELZER, Arthur M. *The Natural Goodness of Man: On the System of Rousseau's Thought*. Chicago, Univ of Chicago Pr, 1990.
Velkley, Richard L. *Rev Metaph* 44(4), 854-856 Je 91

MENDUS, Susan. *Toleration and the Limits of Liberalism*. London, Macmillan, 1989.
McKercher, William R. *Utilitas* 2(2), 328-330 N 90

MEYERS, Diana. *Self, Society, and Personal Choice*. New York, Columbia Univ Pr, 1989.
Murray, Malcolm. *Eidos* 8(2), 247-254 D 89
Hekman, Susan. *Hypatia* 6(2), 222-225 Sum 91
Young, Robert. *Austl J Phil* 68(3), 354-355 S 90

MEYERS, Robert G. *The Likelihood of Knowledge*. Dordrecht, Kluwer, 1988.
Moser, Paul K. *Nous* 25(1), 133-134 Mr 91

MICHELFELDER, Diane P and PALMER, Richard E (eds). *Dialogue and Deconstruction: The Gadamer-Derrida Encounter*. Albany, SUNY Pr, 1989.
Boyne, Roy. *J Brit Soc Phenomenol* 22(1), 84-86 Ja 91

MIDGLEY, Mary. *Wisdom, Information and Wonder*. New York, Routledge, 1989.
Sullivan, John. *Heythrop J* 32(3), 433-434 Jl 91
Mulvaney, Robert J. *Thinking* 9(1), 44-46 1990

MILLÁN-PUELLES, Antonio. *Teoría del objeto puro*. Madrid, Rialp, 1991.
Barrio Maestre, José María. *Anu Filosof* 24(1), 187-189 1991

MILLAS, José Ma. *Pecado y existencia cristiana*. Barcelona, Herder, 1989.
Ruiz Rodríguez, Virgilio. *Rev Filosof (Mexico)* 23(68), 267-269 My-Ag 90

MILLER, Nancy K. *Subject to Change: Reading Feminist Writing*. New York, Columbia Univ Pr, 1988.
Warhol, Robyn R. *Phil Lit* 14(2), 427-428 O 90

MILLER, Richard W. *Fact and Method*. Princeton, Princeton Univ Pr, 1988.
Kosso, Peter. *J Phil* 88(3), 159-162 Mr 91
Pompa, Leon. *Inquiry* 33(3), 355-371 S 90
Teller, Paul. *Phil Rev* 99(4), 641-646 O 90

MINAI, Asghar Talaye. *Design as Aesthetic Communication: Structuring Random-Order; Deconstruction of Formal Rationality*. New York, Lang, 1989.
Thistlewood, David. *Brit J Aes* 30(4), 381-383 O 90

MINH-HA, Trinh T. *Woman, Native, Other*. Bloomington, Indiana Univ Pr, 1989.
Boyce Davies, Carole. *Hypatia* 6(2), 220-222 Sum 91

MINOIS, Georges. *L'Église et la Science*. Paris, Fayard, 1990.
Russo, François. *Arch Phil* 54(2), 281-288 Ap-Je 91

MITIAS, Michael (ed). *Aesthetic Quality and Aesthetic Experience*. Atlanta, Rodopi, 1989.
Jobes, James. *Can Phil Rev* 10(11), 452-454 N 90

MITSIS, Phillip. *Epicurus' Ethical Theory: The Pleasures of Invulnerability*. Ithaca, Cornell Univ Pr, 1988.
Frede, Dorethea. *Amer J Philo* 111(4), 561-566 Wint 90
White, Stephen A. *J Hist Phil* 28(4), 605-607 O 90

MIZUNAMI, Akira. *The Thomistic Philosophy of Law*. Fukuoka, Kyushu Univ Pr, 1987.
Takahashi, Hiroshi. *Vera Lex* 10(1), 25-26 1990

MIZUNAMI, Akira. *The Thomistic Theory of Constitution*. Fukuoka, Kyushu Univ Pr, 1987.
Takahashi, Hiroshi. *Vera Lex* 10(1), 25-26 1990

MOHANTY, J N. *Transcendental Phenomenology: An Analytical Account*. Cambridge, Blackwell, 1989.
Aquila, Richard E. *Rev Metaph* 44(4), 856-857 Je 91

MOI, Toril. *Feminist Theory and Simone de Beauvoir*. Oxford, Blackwell, 1990.
Henry, Patrick. *Phil Lit* 15(1), 180-181 Ap 91

MOKED, Gabriel. *Particles and Ideas: Bishop Berkeley's Corpuscularian Philosophy*. Oxford, Clarendon Pr, 1988.
Falkenstein, Lorne. *Phil Sci* 58(1), 133-134 Mr 91
McKim, Robert. *J Hist Phil* 29(3), 496-498 Jl 91

MOLINA, Luis de. *On Divine Foreknowledge (Part IV of the Corcordia), Alfred J Freddoso (trans)*. Ithaca, Cornell Univ Pr, 1988.
Doyle, John P. *Mod Sch* 67(4), 308-310 My 90

MOMEYER, Richard W. *Confronting Death*. Bloomington, Indiana Univ Pr, 1988.
Grunfeld, Gershon B. *Theor Med* 11(3), 251-253 S 90

MOMMSEN, Wolfgang J. *The Political and Social Theory of Max Weber*. Chicago, Univ of Chicago Pr, 1989.
McLemore, Lelan. *Hist Theor* 30(1), 79-89 F 91

MONDIN, Battista. *L'uomo libero*. Rome, Dino, 1989.
Derisi, Octavio N. *Sapientia* 45(177), 230-234 Jl-S 90

MOORE, A W. *The Infinite*. New York, Routledge, 1990.
Linsky, Bernard. *Phil Books* 32(1), 62-64 Ja 91
Rodriguez-Consuegra, Francisco A. *Hist Phil Log* 12(1), 131-132 1990
Folina, Janet. *Phil Quart* 41(164), 348-350 Jl 91

MOORE, Brooke Noel and PARKER, Richard. *Critical Thinking: Evaluating Claims and Arguments in Everyday Life, 2nd ed*. Mountain View, Mayfield, 1989.
Parks-Clifford, J E. *Inform Log* 12(2), 113-116 Spr 90

MOORE, Kathleen Dean. *Pardons: Justice, Mercy, and the Public Interest*. New York, Oxford Univ Pr, 1989.
Duff, R A. *Crim Just Ethics* 9(2), 51-63 Sum-Fall 90

MORAN, Dermot. *The Philosophy of John Scottus Eriugena: A Study of Idealism in the Middle Ages*. Cambridge, Cambridge Univ Pr, 1989.
Carabine, Deirdre. *Phil Stud (Ireland)* 32, 339-341 1988-90
Miller, Paul J W. *J Hist Phil* 29(2), 302-303 Ap 91

MORAVCSIK, J M. *Language and Thought*. New York, Routledge, 1990.
McCulloch, Gregory. *Phil Quart* 41(163), 243-245 Ap 91

MORAVIA, S. *L'enigma della mente: Il "Mind-Body Problem" nel pensiero contemporaneo*. Rome-Bari, Laterza & Gigli, 1988.
Martínez Velasco, Jesús. *Anu Filosof* 23(1), 199-203 1990

MORONCINI, Bruno. *Il discorso e la cenere: Dieci variazioni sulla responsabilità filosofica*. Naples, Guida, 1988.
Ciaramelli, Fabio. *Rev Phil Louvain* 88(80), 628-632 N 90

MORRIS, Thomas V (ed). *The Concept of God*. New York, Oxford Univ Pr, 1987.
Leftow, Brian. *Int Phil Quart* 31(1), 114-116 Mr 91

MORRIS, Thomas V. *Anselmian Explorations: Essays in Philosophical Theology*. Notre Dame, Univ of Notre Dame Pr, 1987.
Miller, Barry. *Nous* 25(2), 238-241 Ap 91

MORRIS, Thomas V. *Divine and Human Action*. Ithaca, Cornell Univ Pr, 1988.
Wainwright, William J. *Faith Phil* 8(3), 390-398 Jl 91

MORRIS, William S. *Lectures on Contemporary Religious Thought*. Kingston, Frye, 1988.
Horne, James R. *Dialogue (Canada)* 29(3), 475-477 1990

MORRISS, Peter. *Power: A Philosophical Analysis*. Manchester, Manchester Univ Pr, 1987.
Hunter, Bruce. *Phil Books* 32(1), 56-58 Ja 91

MORSON, Gary Saul. *Hidden in Plain View: Narrative and Creative Potentials in "War and Peace"*. Stanford, Stanford Univ Pr, 1987.
Rohatyn, Dennis. *J Value Inq* 25(1), 89-93 Ja 91

MORTENSEN, Viggo and SORENSEN, Robert C (eds). *Free Will and Determinism*. Philadelphia, Coronet, 1987.
Peters, Ted. *Zygon* 26(1), 178-180 Mr 91

MOSER, Paul K. *Knowledge and Evidence*. Cambridge, Cambridge Univ Pr, 1989.
Radford, Colin. *Phil Books* 32(1), 33-37 Ja 91

MOTHERSILL, Mary. *Beauty Restored*. New York, Oxford Univ Pr, 1984.
Cohen, Ted. *J Phil* 87(12), 702-708 D 90

MOUKANOS, Demetrios D. *Ontologie der 'Mathematiks' in der Metaphysik des Aristoteles*. Athens, Potamitis, 1981.
Cleary, John J. *Ancient Phil* 10(2), 310-312 Fall 90

MOYA, Carlos J. *The Philosophy of Action: An Introduction*. Oxford, Blackwell, 1990.
Boddington, Paula. *Phil Books* 32(2), 112-113 Ap 91

MUDROCH, Vilem. *Kants Theorie der physikalischen Gesetze*. Hawthorne, de Gruyter, 1987.
De Gandt, François. *Rev Metaph Morale* 96(2), 271-273 Ap-Je 91

MUGERAUER, Robert and SEAMON, David (eds). *Dwelling, Place, and Environment: Towards a Phenomenology of Person and World*. New York, Columbia Univ Pr, 1989.
Capobianco, Richard. *Int Phil Quart* 31(1), 110-112 Mr 91

MULHALL, Stephen. *On Being in the World: Wittgenstein and Heidegger on Seeing Aspects*. London, Routledge, 1990.
Lyas, Colin. *Phil Books* 32(2), 91-93 Ap 91
Heaton, J M. *J Brit Soc Phenomenol* 22(2), 102-104 My 91

MULLER, John P and RICHARDSON, William J (eds). *The Purloined Poe: Lacan, Derrida and Psychoanalytic Readings*. Baltimore, Johns Hopkins U Pr, 1988.
Ver Eecke, Wilfried. *Rev Metaph* 44(4), 858-859 Je 91

MUNCK, Ronaldo. *The Difficult Dialogue: Marxism and Nationalism*. London, Zed Books, 1986.
Windhausen, John D. *Stud Soviet Tho* 40(1-3), 349-357 1990

MURDOCH, D. *Niels Bohr's Philosophy of Physics*. Cambridge, Cambridge Univ Pr, 1987.
Folse Jr, Henry J. *Int Stud Phil* 22(3), 133-134 1990
Forrest, Peter. *Theoria* 55(2), 133-136 1989
Krips, Henry. *Austl J Phil* 68(4), 463-465 D 90

MURRAY, Charles. *In Pursuit: Of Happiness and Good Government*. New York, Simon & Schuster, 1988.
Glazer, Nathan. *Crit Rev* 4(4), 479-491 Fall 90

MURPHY, Jeffrie G and HAMPTON, Jean. *Forgiveness and Mercy*. New York, Cambridge Univ Pr, 1988.
Duff, R A. *Crim Just Ethics* 9(2), 51-63 Sum-Fall 90

MURPHY, Nancey. *Theology in the Age of Scientific Reasoning*. Ithaca, Cornell Univ Pr, 1990.
Banner, Michael. *Relig Stud* 27(2), 270-272 Je 91

MURRAY, Patrick. *Marx's Theory of Scientific Knowledge*. Atlantic Highlands, Humanities Pr, 1988.
Duquette, David A. *J Hist Phil* 29(1), 144-145 Ja 91
McCarthy, George E. *Phil Soc Sci* 20(4), 508-512 D 90

MYERS, Gerald E. *William James: His Life and Thought*. New Haven, Yale Univ Pr, 1986.
Coon, Deborah J. *Biol Phil* 5(4), 493-501 O 90

NADLER, Steven M. *Arnauld and the Cartesian Philosophy of Ideas*. Manchester, Manchester Univ Pr, 1989.
Scott, David. *Heythrop J* 32(1), 114-116 Ja 91
Yolton, John W. *J Phil* 88(2), 109-112 F 91

NAESS, Arne. *Ecology, Community and Lifestyle: Outline of an Ecosophy, David Rothenberg (trans)*. New York, Cambridge Univ Pr, 1989.
Egerton, Frank N. *Hist Phil Life Sci* 12(2), 299-300 1990

NAGEL, T. *Una brevissima introduzione alla filosofia*. Milano, Il Saggiatore, 1989.
Messinese, Leonardo. *Aquinas* 34(1), 155-165 Ja-Ap 91

NARVESON, Jan. *The Libertarian Idea*. Philadelphia, Temple Univ Pr, 1989.
Frey, R G. *Can Phil Rev* 10(11), 455-458 N 90
Narveson, Jan. *Dialogue (Canada)* 29(2), 299-303 1990
Ripstein, Arthur. *Dialogue (Canada)* 29(2), 285-298 1990
Brown, Grant. *Can J Phil* 20(3), 417-447 S 90
Herzog, Don. *Crit Rev* 4(1-2), 74-85 Wint-Spr 90

NASH, Cristopher (ed). *Narrative in Culture: The Uses of Storytelling in the Sciences, Philosophy, and Literature*. London, Routledge, 1990.
Macey, David. *Rad Phil* 56, 57 Autumn 90

NASH, Ronald H. *Christianity and the Hellenistic World*. Exeter, Paternoster Pr, 1984.
Sell, Alan P F. *Phil Stud (Ireland)* 32, 341-342 1988-90

NATANSON, Maurice. *Anonymity: A Study in the Philosophy of Alfred Schutz*. Bloomington, Indiana Univ Pr, 1986.
Barber, Michael D. *Mod Sch* 68(1), 94-96 N 90

NAYAK, G C. *Philosophical Reflections*. Delhi, Motilal, 1987.
Upadhyaya, K N. *Phil East West* 41(1), 120-122 Ja 91

NELKIN, Dorothy and TANCREDI, Laurence. *Dangerous Diagnostics: The Social Power of Biological Information*. New York, Basic Books, 1989.
Slack, Nancy G. *Hastings Center Rep* 21(1), 38-40 Ja-F 91

NELSON, R J. *The Logic of Mind*. Boston, Kluwer, 1989.
Anonymous. *Phil Psych* 4(1), 159-162 1991

NERLICH, Graham. *Values and Valuing: Speculations on the Ethical Lives of Persons*. Oxford, Clarendon Pr, 1989.
Dent, N J H. *Philosophy* 65(254), 524-525 O 90
Dunn, Robert. *Phil Books* 31(4), 245-248 O 90

NETTON, Ian Richard. *Allāh Transcendent: Studies in the Structure and Semiotics of Islamic Philosophy, Theology and Cosmology*. New York, Routledge, 1989.
Leaman, Oliver. *Asian Phil* 1(1), 97-100 1991

NEUBERG, Leland Gerson. *Conceptual Anomalies in Economics and Statistics*. Cambridge, Cambridge Univ Pr, 1988.
Hamminga, Bert. *Erkenntnis* 34(1), 129-132 Ja 91

NEUGEBAUER, C. *Einführung in die Afrikanische Philosophie*. Munchen, Afrikanische Hoch, 1990.
Van Hensbroek, Pieter Boele. *Quest* 5(1), 114-117 Je 91

NEVILLE, Robert Cummings. *Recovery of the Measure: Interpretation and Nature*. Albany, SUNY Pr, 1989.
Beardslee, William A. *Process Stud* 19(2), 138-140 Sum 90
Wyschogrod, Edith. *J Speculative Phil* 5(3), 214-217 1991

NEWMAN, Jay. *The Journalist in Plato's Cave*. Cranbury, Fairleigh Dickinson Univ Pr, 1989.
Meyers, Christopher. *Can Phil Rev* 10(11), 458-461 N 90
White, David E. *Teach Phil* 13(4), 409-411 D 90

NEWTON, Lisa H and FORD, Maureen M (eds). *Taking Sides: Clashing Views on Controversial Issues in Business Ethics and Society*. Guilford, Dushkin, 1990.
Furman, Frida Kerner. *J Bus Ethics* 10(5), 398-399 My 91

NICHOLSON, Linda. *Gender and History: The Limits of Social Theory in the Age of the Family*. New York, Columbia Univ Pr, 1986.
Weiss, Donald D. *Int Stud Phil* 22(3), 134-135 1990

NICHOLSON, Linda (ed). *Feminism/Postmodernism*. New York, Routledge, 1990.
Nye, Andrea. *Hypatia* 6(2), 228-233 Sum 91
Russell, Denise. *Phil Books* 32(2), 121-124 Ap 91

NICHOLSON, Peter P. *The Political Philosophy of the British Idealists: Selected Studies*. Cambridge, Cambridge Univ Pr, 1990.
Smith, G W. *Polit Theory* 19(2), 306-309 My 91
Clark, Stephen. *Phil Quart* 41(164), 365-367 Jl 91

NICOLOSI, Mauro (ed). *Agostino a Milano: Il Battesimo, Agostino nelle terre di Ambrogio*. Palermo, Augustinus, 1988.
Brinkman, B R. *Heythrop J* 32(2), 294-297 Ap 91

NICOLOSI, Mauro (ed). *L'opera letteraria di Agostino fra Cassiciacum e Milano, Agostino nelle terre di Ambrogio*. Palermo, Augustinus, 1987.
Brinkman, B R. *Heythrop J* 32(2), 294-297 Ap 91

NIDERST, Alain (ed). *Fontenelle*. Paris, PUF, 1989.
Lombardi, Marco. *Rev Phil Fr* 181(1), 125-129 1991

NIELI, Russell. *Wittgenstein: From Mysticism to Ordinary Language*. Albany, SUNY Pr, 1987.
Katz, Steven T. *Int Stud Phil* 22(3), 135-136 1990

NIELSEN, Kai. *Marxism and the Moral Point of View*. Boulder, Westview Pr, 1989.
Norman, Richard. *Philosophy* 65(254), 530-532 O 90
Simpson, Evan. *Dialogue (Canada)* 29(4), 583-588 1990

NIETZSCHE, Friedrich. *Unmodern Observations*. New Haven, Yale Univ Pr, 1990.
Migotti, Mark. *Int Phil Quart* 31(3), 367-369 S 91

NIETZSCHE, Friedrich. *Daybreak: Thoughts on the Prejudices of Morality, R J Hollingdale (trans)*. Cambridge, Cambridge Univ Pr, 1982.
McBride, Joseph. *Phil Stud (Ireland)* 32, 343-344 1988-90

NIGAM, R L. *Radical Humanism of M N Roy: An Exposition of His 22 Theses*. New Delhi, Indus, 1988.
Roy, Krishna. *J Indian Counc Phil Res* 6(2), 186-193 Ja-Ap 89

NIINILUOTO, Ilkka. *Truthlikeness*. Norwell, Reidel, 1987.
Miller, David W. *Brit J Phil Sci* 41(2), 281-290 Je 90

NITECKI, Matthew H (ed). *Evolutionary Progress*. Chicago, Univ of Chicago Pr, 1988.
Greene, J C. *Biol Phil* 6(1), 99-106 Ja 91

NOCHLIN, Linda. *Women, Art, and Power and Other Essays*. London, Thames & Hudson, 1989.
Battersby, Christine. *Brit J Aes* 31(1), 78-79 Ja 91

NODDINGS, Nel. *Women and Evil*. Berkeley, Univ of California Pr, 1989.
Stone, Lynda. *Educ Stud* 21(2), 221-227 Sum 90

NOLA, Robert (ed). *Relativism and Realism in Science*. Dordrecht, Kluwer, 1988.
Forge, John. *Austl J Phil* 68(3), 355-357 S 90

NOONAN, Harold W. *Personal Identity*. London, Routledge, 1989.
Matthews, Eric. *Phil Books* 31(4), 235-237 O 90

NORDENFELT, Lennart. *On the Nature of Health: An Action-Theoretic Account*. Boston, Reidel, 1987.
Hëbert, Philip C. *Phil Soc Sci* 21(1), 126-130 Mr 91

NORMAN, J and SYLVAN, R (eds). *Directions in Relevant Logic*. Norwell, Kluwer, 1989.
Read, Stephen. *Hist Phil Log* 12(2), 254-256 1991

NORRIS, Christopher. *Derrida*. Cambridge, Harvard Univ Pr, 1987.
Lawlor, Leonard. *Int Stud Phil* 22(3), 136-137 1990
Nehamas, Alexander. *Phil Rev* 100(2), 303-306 Ap 91

NOSKE, Barbara. *Humans and Other Animals*. London, Pluto Pr, 1989.
Frith, Lucy. *Rad Phil* 58, 38-39 Sum 91

NOTTURNO, Mark A (ed). *Perspectives on Psychlogism*. New York, Brill, 1989.
Smith, Barry. *Hist Phil Log* 12(2), 249-251 1991

NOVITZ, David. *Knowledge, Fiction and Imagination*. Philadelphia, Temple Univ Pr, 1987.
Kaminsky, Alice R. *Int Stud Phil* 23(1), 131-133 1991

NOVICK, Peter. *That Noble Dream: The "Objectivity Question" and the American Historical Profession*. New York, Cambridge Univ Pr, 1988.
Stuart-Fox, Martin. *Phil Soc Sci* 21(2), 287-290 Je 91

NOZICK, Robert. *The Examined Life: Philosophical Meditations*. New York, Simon & Schuster, 1989.
Jackson, Aletheia. *Crit Rev* 4(3), 345-364 Sum 90

NUOVO, Victor. *Visionary Science: A translation of Paul Tillich's "On the Idea of a Theology of Culture" with an Interpretative Essay*. Detroit, Wayne State Univ Pr, 1987.
Thomas, J Heywood. *Mod Theol* 7(2), 196-197 Ja 91

NUSSBAUM, Martha. *The Fragility of Goodness: Luck and Ethics in Greek Tragedy and Philosophy*. Cambridge, Cambridge Univ Pr, 1986.
Bodéüs, Richard. *Dialogue (Canada)* 29(1), 144-146 1990

NYIRI, J C and SMITH, Barry. *Practical Knowledge: Outlines of a Theory of Traditions and Skills*. London, Croom Helm, 1988.
Heaton, J M. *J Brit Soc Phenomenol* 21(3), 299-300 O 90

O'DONNELL, Roderick M. *Keynes: Philosophy, Economics and Politics*. New York, Macmillan, 1988.
Dow, Sheila C. *Econ Phil* 7(1), 132-139 Ap 91

O'FARRELL, Clare. *Foucault: Historian or Philosopher?* London, Macmillan, 1989.
Racevskis, Karlis. *Rad Phil* 57, 50-52 Spr 91

O'HEAR, Anthony. *The Element of Fire*. New York, Routledge, 1988.
Meynell, Hugo. *Heythrop J* 32(3), 434-435 Jl 91
Ackermann, Robert. *Phil Books* 31(4), 216-217 O 90
Beardsmore, R W. *Phil Invest* 13(4), 371-374 O 90

O'KEEFE, Martin D. *Known from the Things that Are: Fundamental Theory of the Moral Life*. Houston, Center for Thomistic Studies, 1987.
Naus, John. *Mod Sch* 67(4), 314-315 My 90

O'LEARY, Joseph. *Questioning Back: The Overcoming of Metaphysics in Christian Tradition*. Minneapolis, Winston Pr, 1985.
O'Reilly, John. *Phil Stud (Ireland)* 32, 345-350 1988-90

O'NEILL, John. *The Communicative Body: Studies in Communicative Philosophy, Politics, and Sociology*. Evanston, Northwestern Univ Pr, 1989.
Davis, Duane H. *Can Phil Rev* 10(12), 505-508 D 90

O'MEARA, J J. *Eriugena*. Oxford, Clarendon Pr, 1988.
Moran, Dermot. *Rev Metaph* 44(1), 156-157 S 90

O'NEILL, Onora. *Constructions of Reason: Explorations of Kant's Practical Philosophy*. New York, Cambridge Univ Pr, 1989.
Cooke, Vincent M. *Int Phil Quart* 31(3), 365-367 S 91
Farrell, Daniel M. *Phil Quart* 41(164), 372-374 Jl 91

OBERER, Hariolf and SEEL, Gerhard (eds). *Kant: Analysen—Probleme—Kritik*. Würzburg, Königshausen & Neumann, 1988.
Steinbeck, Wolfram. *Kantstudien* 81(3), 375-379 1990

OBERTELLO, Luca. *Boezio e dintorni: Richerche sulla cultura altomedievale*. Firenze, Nardini Ed, 1989.
Neirotti, Piero. *Sapienza* 43(4), 445-447 O-D 90

ODIFREDDI, Piergiorgio. *Classical Recursion Theory: The Theory of Functions and Sets of Natural Numbers*. Amsterdam, North-Holland, 1989.
Hinman, Peter G. *J Sym Log* 55(3), 1307-1308 S 90

ODUM, Eugene P. *Ecology and Our Endangered Life-Support Systems*. Sunderland, Sinauer, 1989.
Lockwood, Linda G. *Environ Ethics* 12(4), 375-378 Wint 90

OELMÜLLER, Willi (ed). *Metaphysik heute?* Paderborn, Schöningh, 1987.
Schönherr, Hans-Martin. *Z Phil Forsch* 44(4), 666-669 1990

OIZERMAN, T I and BOGOMOLOV, A S. *Principles of the Theory of the Historical Process in Philosophy*. Moscow, Progress, 1987.
Adelmann, Frederick J. *Stud Soviet Tho* 41(3), 233-235 My 91

OKIN, Susan Moller. *Justice, Gender, and the Family*. New York, Basic Books, 1989.
Held, Virginia. *Polit Theory* 19(2), 299-303 My 91

OKRENT, Mark. *Heidegger's Pragmatism: Understanding, Being and the Critique of Metaphysics*. Ithaca, Cornell Univ Pr, 1988.
Protevi, John. *J Hist Phil* 28(4), 631-633 O 90

OLAFSON, Frederick A. *Heidegger and the Philosophy of Mind*. New Haven, Yale Univ Pr, 1987.
Dreyfus, Hubert L. *Phil Rev* 100(3), 524-529 Jl 91

OLDING, Alan. *Modern Biology and Natural Theology*. New York, Routledge, 1991.
Swinburne, Richard. *Mind* 100(399), 406-408 Jl 91

OLDRINI, Guido (ed). *Filosofia e coscienza nazionale in Bertrando Spaventa*. Urbino, Quattro Venti, 1988.
Zappia, Elisabetta. *G Crit Filosof Ital* 68(3), 417-419 S-D 89

OLIVE, David. *Just Rewards: The Case for Ethical Reform in Business*. Toronto, Key Porter Books, 1987.
Singh, Jang B. *J Bus Ethics* 10(5), 395-396 My 91

OLIVER, Donald W and GERSHMAN, Kathleen Waldron. *Education, Modernity, and Fractured Meaning: Toward a Process Theory of Teaching and Learning*. Albany, SUNY Pr, 1989.
Sweeney, John M. *Process Stud* 19(2), 136-138 Sum 90
Doll Jr, William E. *Educ Theor* 40(4), 509-512 Fall 90

OLSON, Kenneth R. *An Essay on Facts*. Stanford, CSLI, 1987.
Leftow, Brian. *Int Phil Quart* 30(4), 508-510 D 90

OPPENHEIM, Frank M. *Royce's Mature Philosophy of Religion*. Notre Dame, Univ of Notre Dame Pr, 1987.
MacKinnon, Barbara. *Mod Sch* 67(3), 228-229 Mr 90
Chadwick, Jonathan. *Int Stud Phil* 23(1), 133 1991

ORMISTON, Gayle L and SCHRIFT, Alan D (eds). *The Hermeneutic Tradition: From Ast to Ricoeur*. Albany, SUNY Pr, 1990.
Palmer, Richard E. *Rev Metaph* 44(3), 649-651 Mr 91

ORMISTON, Gayle L and SCHRIFT, Alan D (eds). *Transforming the Hermeneutic Context: From Nietzsche to Nancy*. Albany, SUNY Pr, 1990.
Palmer, Richard E. *Rev Metaph* 44(3), 649-651 Mr 91

ORMSBY, Eric L (ed). *Moses Maimonides and His Time*. Washington, Catholic Univ of America Pr, 1989.
Lachterman, David R. *Rev Metaph* 44(1), 157-160 S 90

ORTEGA Y GASSET, José. *Metafisica e ragione storica, Armando Savignano (ed)*. Milan, Sugarco, 1989.
Masi, Giuseppe. *Aquinas* 33(2), 450-452 My-Ag 90

OSBORNE, Catherine. *Rethinking Early Greek Philosophy: Hippolytus of Rome and the Presocratics*. Ithaca, Cornell Univ Pr, 1987.
Furley, David. *Phil Rev* 100(1), 157-160 Ja 91

OST, François and VAN DE KERCHOVE, Michel. *Jalons pour une théorie critique du droit*. Brussels, Univ Saint-Louis, 1987.
Sciacca, Fabrizio. *Riv Int Filosof Diritto* 67(2), 339-342 Ap-Je 90

OVERALL, Christine. *Ethics and Human Reproduction: A Feminist Analysis*. Winchester, Unwin Hyman, 1988.
Callahan, Joan C. *Can Phil Rev* 10(10), 421-423 O 90

PACHET, Pierre. *La Force de dormier*. Paris, Gallimard, 1988.
Minazzoli, Agnès. *Rev Metaph Morale* 96(1), 125-127 Ja-Mr 91

PAILIN, David A. *God and the Processes of Reality*. London, Routledge, 1989.
Burke, T E. *Mod Theol* 7(2), 199-200 Ja 91

PANAGIOTOU, Spiro (ed). *Justice, Law and Method in Plato and Aristotle*. South Edmonton, Academic Print, 1987.
Haggerty, William P. *Ancient Phil* 11(1), 179-181 Spr 91

PANGLE, Thomas L (ed). *The Roots of Political Philosophy: Ten Forgotten Socratic Dialogues*. Ithaca, Cornell Univ Pr, 1987.
Gueguen, John A. *Mod Sch* 67(4), 307-308 My 90

PANGLE, Thomas L. *The Spirit of Modern Republicanism: The Moral Vision of the American Founders and the Philosophy of Locke*. Chicago, Univ of Chicago Pr, 1988.
Allen, W B. *Hist Polit Thought* 11(3), 551-555 Autumn 90

PANNARALE, Luigi. *Il diritto e le aspettative*. Naples, Scientifiche Italiane, 1988.
Sarzotti, Claudio. *Riv Int Filosof Diritto* 67(1), 172-175 Ja-Mr 90

PAPERNO, Irina. *Chernyshevsky and the Age of Realism: A Study in the Semiotics of Behavior*. Stanford, Stanford Univ Pr, 1988.
Goodliffe, John. *Phil Lit* 14(2), 433-434 O 90

PAPINEAU, David. *Reality and Representation*. Oxford, Blackwell, 1987.
Rosenberg, Jay F. *Phil Rev* 100(1), 109-111 Ja 91
Georgalis, Nicholas. *Behavior Phil* 18(2), 85-88 Fall-Wint 90

PAQUET, Léonce and ROUSSEL, Michel and LAFRANCE, Yvon. *Les présocratiques: Bibliographie analytique (1879-1980)*. Paris, Belles Lettres, 1988.
Brisson, Luc. *Dialogue (Canada)* 29(1), 152-154 1990

PARKES, Graham (ed). *Heidegger and Asian Thought*. Honolulu, Univ of Hawaii Pr, 1987.
Taber, John A. *Int J Phil Relig* 29(3), 189-190 Je 91

PARRET, Herman. *Le sublime du quotidien*. Philadelphia, Benjamins, 1988.
Pezzini, Isabella. *J Prag* 15(1), 92-98 Ja 91

PARRET, Herman. *Les passions: Essai sur la mise en discours de la subjectivité*. Brussels, Mardaga, 1986.
Pezzini, Isabella. *J Prag* 15(1), 92-98 Ja 91

PARRY, David M. *Hegel's Phenomenology of the "We"*. New York, Lang, 1988.
Harris, H S. *Bull Hegel Soc Gt Brit* 20, 52-54 Autumn-Wint 89

PARTHASARATHI, G and CHATTOPADHYAYA, D P (eds). *Radhakrishnan Centenary Volume*. New York, Oxford Univ Pr, undated.
Saxena, S K. *J Indian Counc Phil Res* 8(1), 129-143 S-D 90

PATEMAN, Carole. *The Sexual Contract*. Stanford, Stanford Univ Pr, 1988.
Kymlicka, Will. *Can Phil Rev* 10(11), 461-464 N 90
Mackenzie, Catriona. *Austl J Phil* 68(4), 469-475 D 90

PATRICK, James. *The Magdalen Metaphysicals: Idealism and Orthodoxy at Oxford, 1901-1945*. Macon, Mercer Univ Pr, 1985.
Sell, Alan P F. *Phil Stud (Ireland)* 32, 350-352 1988-90

PATT, Walter. *Transzendentaler Idealismus*. New York, de Gruyter, 1987.
Steinbeck, Wolfram. *Kantstudien* 81(3), 373-375 1990

PAUL, Iain and GILLET, Grant (eds). *Knowledge of God: Calvin, Einstein and Polanyi*. Edinburgh, Scottish Academic Pr, 1987.
Meynell, Hugo. *Heythrop J* 32(1), 123-124 Ja 91
Thomas, Janice. *Heythrop J* 32(1), 104-105 Ja 91

PAULSON, Michael G. *The Possible Influence of Montaigne's "Essais" on Descartes' "Treatise on the Passions"*. Lanham, Univ Pr of America, 1988.
Steinberg, Diane. *Mod Sch* 68(1), 107-109 N 90

PAVEL, Th. *Le mirage linguistique: Essai sur la modernisation intellectuelle*. Paris, Minuit, 1989.
Largeault, Jean. *Rev Phil Fr* 180(4), 708-711 O-D 90

PEACOCK, Arthur and GILLETT, Grant (eds). *Persons and Personality*. Cambridge, Blackwell, 1987.
Buford, Thomas O. *Int J Phil Relig* 30(1), 61-62 Ag 91
Griffiths, Paul J. *Thomist* 54(4), 746-750 O 90

PEARCE, David. *Roads to Commensurability*. Norwell, Reidel, 1987.
Miller, David W. *Brit J Phil Sci* 41(2), 281-290 Je 90

PEARL, Judea. *Probabilistic Reasoning In Intelligent Systems: Networks of Plausible Inference*. San Mateo, Morgan Kaufmann, 1988.
Kyburg Jr, Henry E. *J Phil* 88(8), 433-437 Ag 91

PEARS, David. *The False Prison: A Study of the Development of Wittgenstein's Philosophy, 2v*. Oxford, Clarendon Pr, 1988.
Brown, Michael A. *Man World* 24(1), 97-103 Ja 91
Harré, Rom. *Int Stud Phil* 22(3), 137-138 1990
Kerr, Fergus. *Heythrop J* 32(1), 119-120 Ja 91
Cordua, Carla. *Dialogos* 25(56), 190-194 Jl 90

PEARS, David. *The False Prison: A Study of the Development of Wittgenstein's Philosophy, V1*. Oxford, Oxford Univ Pr, 1987.
McDonough, Richard. *Nous* 25(3), 377-380 Je 91

PEDEN, W Creighton and AXEL, Larry (eds). *God, Values, and Empiricism: Issues in Philosophical Theology*. Macon, Mercer Univ Pr, 1989.
Tarbox Jr, Everett J. *Relig Hum* 25(1), 47-48 Wint 91

PEIRCE, C S. *Naturordung und Zeichenprozess*. Frankfurt, Suhrkamp, 1991.
de Landázuri, Carlos 0. *Anu Filosof* 24(1), 189-190 1991

PENDÁS GARCÍA, Benigno. *Jeremy Bentham: Política y Derecho en los orígenes del Estado Constitucional*. Madrid, Centro de Estudios, 1988.
Colomer, Josep M. *Utilitas* 2(2), 323-325 N 90

PENELHUM, Terence. *Butler*. Boston, Routledge & Kegan Paul, 1985.
Wilcox, John T. *Int Stud Phil* 22(3), 139 1990

PENLEY, Constance (ed). *Feminism and Film Theory*. New York, Routledge, Chapman & Hall, 1988.
Neill, Alex and Ridley, Aaron. *Can Phil Rev* 10(9), 345-351 S 90

PENNER, Terry. *The Ascent from Nominalism*. Norwell, Reidel, 1987.
White, Nicholas P. *Phil Rev* 100(2), 318-321 Ap 91
Fine, Gail. *Nous* 25(1), 126-132 Mr 91

PENNISI, Antonino. *La linguistica dei mercatanti: Filosofia linguistica e filosofia civile da Vico a Cuoco*. Naples, Guida, 1987.
Formigari, Lia. *Boll Centro Stud Vichiani* 20, 243-245 1990

PENROSE, Roger. *The Emperor's New Mind: Concerning Computers, Minds, and the Laws of Physics*. New York, Oxford Univ Pr, 1989.
Hays, David G. *J Soc Biol Struct* 13(2), 179-183 My 90
Clark, Andy. *Phil Quart* 40(161), 509-514 O 90

PENZO, G. *Invito al pensiero di Nietzsche*. Milano, Mursia, 1990.
Colonnello, Pio. *Sapienza* 43(4), 459-462 O-D 90

PEPERZAK, Adriaan Theodoor. *Philosophy and Politics: A Commentary on the Preface to Hegel's Philosophy of Right, Mary Ellen Petrisko (trans)*. Boston, Nijhoff, 1987.
Gueguen, John A. *Mod Sch* 67(3), 233-235 Mr 90

PEPERZAK, Adriaan Theodoor. *System and History in Philosophy*. Albany, SUNY Pr, 1986.
Howie, John. *Ideal Stud* 20(2), 174-175 My 90

PERELMAN, Chaïm. *Rhétorique*. Liège, Univ de Bruxelles, 1989.
Gratton, Claude. *Inform Log* 12(2), 117-120 Spr 90

PERKINS, Moreland. *Sensing the World*. Indianapolis, Hackett, 1983.
Kelly, J S. *Nous* 24(5), 782-792 D 90

PETERSON, Donald. *Wittgenstein's Early Philosophy*. Brighton, Harvester Pr, 1990.
Cooper, David E. *Phil Quart* 41(164), 358-360 Jl 91
Mounce, H O. *Philosophy* 66(257), 391-392 Jl 91

PETERSON, M D and VAUGHAN, R C (eds). *The Virginia Statute for Religious Freedom: Its Evolution and Consequences in American History*. Cambridge, Cambridge Univ Pr, 1988.
Griswold Jr, Charles L. *Rev Metaph* 44(1), 160-162 S 90

PETREY, Sandy. *Realism and Revolution: Balzac, Stendhal, Zola, and the Performances of History*. Ithaca, Cornell Univ Pr, 1988.
Howard, Dick. *Phil Soc Crit* 16(1), 55-59 1990

PETRICCIANI, S. *Etica dell'argomentazione: Ragione, scienza e prassi nel pensiero di Karl-Otto Apel*. Genova, Marietti, 1988.
Celano, Bruno. *G Metaf* 11(3), 501-503 S-D 89

PHARR, Suzanne. *Homophobia: A Weapon of Sexism*. Inverness, Chardon Pr, 1988.
Card, Claudia. *Hypatia* 5(3), 110-117 Fall 90
Nash, Margaret. *Hypatia* 5(3), 171-175 Fall 90

PHELAN, Shane. *Identity Politics: Lesbian Feminism and the Limits of Community*. Philadelphia, Temple Univ Pr, 1989.
Pineau, Lois. *Can Phil Rev* 10(10), 423-427 O 90

PHILLIPS, D Z. *Faith after Foundationalism*. London, Routledge, 1988.
Vardy, Peter. *Heythrop J* 32(2), 283-285 Ap 91

PHILLIPS, D Z and WINCH, Peter (eds). *Wittgenstein: Attention to Particulars*. London, Macmillan, 1989.
Bell, Richard H. *Philosophy* 65(253), 382-384 Jl 90
Reinhardt, Lloyd. *Phil Books* 31(4), 213-216 O 90

PHILONENKO, Alexis. *Le transcendantal et la pensée moderne*. Paris, Pr Univ de France, 1990.
Dumas, Denis. *Philosophiques* 17(2), 203-209 Autumn 1990

PIKE, David. *Lukács and Brecht*. Chapel Hill, Univ of North Carolina Pr, 1988.
Demaitre, Ann. *Hist Euro Ideas* 13(1-2), 146-147 1991

PIKE, Shirley R. *Marxism and Phenomenology: Theories of Crisis and their Synthesis*. London, Croom Helm, 1986.
Smart, Barry. *J Brit Soc Phenomenol* 22(1), 96-97 Ja 91

PINCHIN, Calvin. *Issues in Philosophy*. Basingstoke, Macmillan, 1990.
Hyland, Terry. *J Phil Educ* 24(1), 140-142 Sum 90

PINCOFFS, Edmund L. *Quandaries and Virtues: Against Reductivism in Ethics*. Lawrence, Univ of Kansas Pr, 1986.
Wong, David B. *Nous* 25(1), 116-120 Mr 91

PINE, Martin L. *Pietro Pomponazzi: Radical Philosopher of the Renaissance*. Padova, Antenore, 1986.
Bourke, Vernon J. *Mod Sch* 68(1), 81-82 N 90

PINKARD, Terry. *Hegel's Dialectic: The Explanation of Possibility*. Philadelphia, Temple Univ Pr, 1988.
Donovan, John F. *Rev Metaph* 44(4), 859-861 Je 91
Houlgate, Stephen. *Bull Hegel Soc Gt Brit* 20, 1-19 Autumn-Wint 89

PIPPIN, Robert. *Hegel's Idealism: The Satisfactions of Self-Consciousness*. Cambridge, Cambridge Univ Pr, 1989.
Rosen, Stanley. *Rev Metaph* 44(1), 162-164 S 90
Siep, Ludwig. *Inquiry* 34(1), 63-76 Mr 91
Flay, Joseph C. *J Hist Phil* 29(3), 502-503 Jl 91
Zelechow, Bernard. *Hist Euro Ideas* 13(4), 467-468 1991

PIVCEVIC, Edo. *The Concept of Reality*. London, Duckworth, 1986.
Sontag, Frederick. *Int Stud Phil* 22(3), 139-140 1990

PIVCEVIC, Edo. *Change and Selves*. Oxford, Clarendon Pr, 1990.
Taylor, Dan. *Phil Books* 32(2), 105-106 Ap 91

PLACHER, William C. *Unapologetic Theology: A Christian Voice in a Pluralistic Conversation*. Louisville, Knox Pr, 1989.
Lewis, Paul. *Mod Theol* 7(4), 373-374 Jl 91

PLANT, Judith (ed). *Healing the Wounds: the Promise of Ecofeminism*. Philadelphia, New Society, 1989.
Gruen, Lori. *Hypatia* 6(1), 198-206 Spr 91

PLATO. *Early Socratic Dialogues, T J Saunders (ed)*. Harmondsworth, Penguin, 1987.
Rowe, C J. *J Hellen Stud* 110, 224-225 1990

PLATO. *Lettres, L Brisson (ed & trans)*. Paris, Flammarion, 1987.
Rowe, C J. *J Hellen Stud* 110, 224-225 1990

PLATO. *Republic 10, S Halliwell (ed & trans)*. Warminster, Aris & Phillips, 1988.
Sharples, R W. *J Hellen Stud* 110, 226-227 1990

PLOCHMANN, G K and ROBINSON, F R. *A Friendly Companion to Plato's Gorgias*. Carbondale, Southern Illinois Univ Pr, 1988.
Brickhouse, Thomas C. *Ancient Phil* 10(2), 282-285 Fall 90

POGGE, Thomas W. *Realizing Rawls*. Ithaca, Cornell Univ Pr, 1989.
Norman, W J. *Can Phil Rev* 10(11), 465-468 N 90
Schultz, Bart. *Polit Theory* 19(1), 118-123 F 91
Wolff, Robert Paul. *J Phil* 87(12), 716-720 D 90

PÖGGELER, Otto. *Martin Heidegger's Path of Thinking, Daniel Magurshak and Sigmund Barber (trans)*. Atlantic Highlands, Humanities Pr, 1987.
Kisiel, Theodore. *J Brit Soc Phenomenol* 22(1), 89-90 Ja 91
Rée, Jonathan. *Rad Phil* 56, 47-48 Autumn 90

POIS, Robert A. *National Socialism and the Religion of Nature*. New York, St Martin's Pr, 1986.
Smith, Woodruff D. *Hist Euro Ideas* 12(6), 861-863 1990

POJMAN, Louis P. *Religious Belief and the Will*. New York, Routledge & Kegan Paul, 1986.
Wolterstorff, Nicholas. *Faith Phil* 8(1), 120-123 Ja 91

POLKA, Brayton. *The Dialectic of Biblical Critique: Interpretation and Existence*. New York, St Martin's Pr, 1986.
O'Neil, Patrick M. *Auslegung* 17(1), 92-94 Wint 91

POLKINGHORNE, John. *Science and Providence: God's Interaction with the World*. Boston, Shambhala, 1989.
Eccles, John C. *Zygon* 25(4), 504-507 D 90

POLLARD, Stephen. *Philosophical Introduction to Set Theory*. Notre Dame, Univ of Notre Dame Pr, 1990.
Tiles, Mary. *Notre Dame J Form Log* 32(1), 161-166 Wint 91

POLLOCK, John. *Contemporary Theories of Knowledge*. Totowa, Rowman & Littlefield, 1986.
Moser, Paul K. *Brit J Phil Sci* 39(1), 131-140 Mr 88
Mandel, Ross. *Mod Sch* 68(1), 105-107 N 90

POLLOCK, John L. *Technical Methods in Philosophy*. Boulder, Westview Pr, 1990.
Moser, Paul K. *Can Phil Rev* 10(8), 331-332 Ag 90

POMPA, Leon. *Human Nature and Historical Knowledge: Hume, Hegel and Vico*. Cambridge, Cambridge Univ Pr, 1990.
O'Connor, B P. *Phil Stud (Ireland)* 32, 352-356 1988-90

POOLE, Roger and STRANGERUP, Henrik (eds). *A Kierkegaard Reader: Texts and Narratives*. London, Fourth Estate, 1989.
Bell, Richard H. *Hist Euro Ideas* 12(5), 697 1990

POPKIN, Richard H. *Isaac La Peyrère (1596-1676): His Life, Work, and Influence*. Leiden, Brill, 1987.
Goodman, L E. *J Hist Phil* 29(1), 131-135 Ja 91

POPKIN, Richard H. *Pascal: Selections*. New York, Macmillan, 1989.
Natoli, Charles M. *Teach Phil* 13(3), 287-290 S 90

POPKIN, Richard H (ed). *Millenarianism and Messianism in English Literature and Thought, 1650-1800*. Leiden, Brill, 1988.
Williamson, Arthur H. *J Hist Phil* 29(2), 310-312 Ap 91

POPPER, Karl R. *A World of Propensities*. Bristol, Thoemmes Antiquarian Books, 1990.
Milne, Peter. *Mind* 100(397), 161-162 Ja 91
Gillies, Donald. *Philosophy* 66(257), 392-394 Jl 91
Jarvie, I C. *Phil Soc Sci* 21(3), 407-409 S 91

PORTER, Jean. *The Recovery of Virtue: The Relevance of Aquinas for Christian Ethics*. Louisville, Westminster/John Knox Pr, 1990.
Cessario, Romanus. *Thomist* 55(1), 141-144 Ja 91

POSPIELOVSKY, Dimitry V. *A History of Soviet Atheism in Theory and Practice and the Beliver*. New York, St Martin's Pr, 1987.
Colbert, James G. *Stud Soviet Tho* 41(2), 147-150 Mr 91

POST, John F. *The Faces of Existence: An Essay in Nonreductive Metaphysics*. Ithaca, Cornell Univ Pr, 1987.
Gordon, Haim. *Int J Phil Relig* 28(2), 119-120 O 90
Steinman, Robert. *Phil Rev* 100(2), 306-309 Ap 91

POSTER, Mark. *The Mode of Information*. Oxford, Polity Pr, 1990.
Elliott, Anthony. *Rad Phil* 58, 43-44 Sum 91

POWELL, Brenda J. *The Metaphysical Quality of the Tragic: A Study of Sophocles, Giraudoux and Sartre*. New York, Lang, 1990.
Curtis, Jerry. *Phil Lit* 14(2), 438-439 O 90

POZZO, Ricardo. *Hegel: 'Introductio in philosophiam'*. Florence, Nuova Italia, 1989.
Harris, H S. *Bull Hegel Soc Gt Brit* 20, 48-50 Autumn-Wint 89

PRADO, Carlos G. *The Limits of Pragmatism*. Atlantic Highlands, Humanities Pr, 1987.
Gerwin, Martin. *Dialogue (Canada)* 29(3), 447-451 1990

PRANDI, Michele. *Sémantique du contresens*. Paris, Minuit, 1987.
Danes, Frantisek. *J Prag* 14(6), 976-984 D 90

PRECIADO, Kathleen (ed). *Retaining the Original: Multiple Originals, Copies, and Reproductions*. Hanover, Univ Pr of New England, 1989.
Gaskell, Ivan. *Brit J Aes* 31(2), 179-182 Ap 91

PRELLI, Lawrence J. *A Rhetoric of Science: Inventing Scientific Discourse*. Columbia, Univ of South Carolina Pr, 1989.
Finocchiaro, Maurice A. *Phil Rhet* 24(2), 168-173 1991

PREZIOSI, Donald. *Rethinking Art History: Meditations on a Coy Science*. New Haven, Yale Univ Pr, 1989.
Harris, Jonathan. *Brit J Aes* 30(4), 384-386 O 90

PRICE, A W. *Love and Friendship in Plato and Aristotle*. Oxford, Clarendon Pr, 1989.
Taylor, C C W. *Phil Books* 31(4), 200-201 O 90

PRICE, Huw. *Facts and the Function of Truth*. Cambridge, Blackwell, 1989.
Braddon-Mitchell, David. *Austl J Phil* 69(1), 115-119 Mr 91

PRIEST, Graham. *In Contradiction: A Study of the Transconsistent*. Dordrecht, Nijhoff, 1987.
Smith, Joel M. *Nous* 25(3), 380-383 Je 91

PRIEST, Stephen. *The British Empiricists*. London, Penguin, 1990.
Gallie, Roger. *Phil Quart* 41(163), 260-261 Ap 91

PRIMORATZ, Igor. *Justifying Legal Punishment*. Atlantic Highlands, Humanities Pr, 1989.
Noordhof, Paul. *J Applied Phil* 8(1), 127-129 1991
Flew, Antony. *Phil Quart* 41(164), 376-378 Jl 91

PRINI, P. *Storia dell'esistenzialismo*. Rome, Studium, 1989.
Dovolich, Claudia. *Aquinas* 33(1), 217-221 Ja-Ap 90

PRINI, Pietro. *L'ambiguità dell'essere*. Genova, Marietti, 1989.
Cunico, Gerardo. *Filosofia* 42(1), 133-141 Ja-Ap 91
Dell'Agnese, Bruna. *Riv Filosof Neo-Scolas* 82(2-3), 320-325 Ap-S 90

PUOLIMATKA, Tapio. *Moral Realism and Justification*. Helsinki, Finnish Academy of Science and Letters, 1989.
Blosser, Ph. *Phil Reform* 55(2), 177-183 1990

PUTHENPURACKAL, Johnson J. *Heidegger: Through Authentic Totality to Total Authenticity*. Leuven, Leuven Univ Pr, 1987.
De Marneffe, J. *J Indian Counc Phil Res* 6(1), 163-164 S-D 88

PUTNAM, Hilary. *Representation and Reality*. Cambridge, MIT Pr, 1988.
Smith, Peter. *Phil Books* 32(1), 47-50 Ja 91

QUILLIEN, Jean (ed). *Cahiers Eric Weil*. Villeneuve d'Ascq, Pr Univ Lille, 1987.
Wiel, A. *Arch Phil* 53(4), 682-685 O-D 90

QUINE, W V. *Pursuit of Truth*. Cambridge, Harvard Univ Pr, 1990.
Heal, Jane. *Philosophy* 65(253), 384-385 Jl 90
Cornelis, G C. *Philosophica* 46(2), 119-122 1990

QUINTANILLA, Miguel Àngel. *Tecnología: Un enfoque filosófico*. Madrid, Fundesco, 1989.
Pérez Ransanz, Ana Rosa. *Critica* 23(67), 75-80 Ap 91

RABB, J D (ed). *Religion and Science in Early Canada*. Kingston, Frye Library of Canadian Philosophy, 1988.
Di Norcia, Vincent. *Dialogue (Canada)* 29(3), 462-466 1990

RACHELS, James. *Created from Animals: The Moral Implications of Darwinism*. Oxford, Oxford Univ Pr, 1990.
Jamieson, Dale. *Hastings Center Rep* 21(2), 47 Mr-Ap 91
Loftin, Robert W. *J Value Inq* 25(3), 291-294 Jl 91

RADEST, Howard R. *Can We Teach Ethics?* New York, Praeger, 1989.
Cochrane, Don. *Educ Stud* 21(4), 464-466 Wint 90

RADNER, Daisie and RADNER, Michael. *Animal Consciousness*. Buffalo, Prometheus Books, 1989.
Burghardt, Gordon M. *Hastings Center Rep* 21(2), 48-50 Mr-Ap 91
Nadler, Steven. *Environ Ethics* 13(2), 187-191 Sum 91

RAGGIUNTI, Renzo. *Il linguaggio, conosciuto e ignoto*. Genova, Marietti, 1990.
Peruzzi, Alberto. *Filosofia* 42(1), 149-153 Ja-Ap 91

RAJAN, R Sundara. *Towards a Critique of Cultural Reason*. Delhi, Oxford Univ Pr, 1987.
Moitra, Shefali. *J Indian Counc Phil Res* 5(2), 171-176 Ja-Ap 88

RAJNATH (ED). *Deconstruction: A Critique*. London, Macmillan, 1989.
Pinkney, Tony. *Brit J Aes* 31(1), 84-85 Ja 91

RAMANUJA TATACHARYA, N S. *Paksata with Didhiti, Didhitiprakasika of Gadahara Bhattacharyya and Bhavabodhini*. Tirupati, Ken Sans Vidyapeetha, 1988.
Prahlada Char, D. *J Indian Counc Phil Res* 8(1), 153-155 S-D 90

RAMBERG, Bjorn T. *Donald Davidson's Philosophy of Language*. Cambridge, Blackwell, 1989.
Smith, Peter. *Phil Invest* 14(3), 280-284 Jl 91
Malpas, Jeff. *Austl J Phil* 68(4), 475-477 D 90

RAMMSTEDT, Otthein (ed). *Simmel und die frühen Soziologen*. Frankfurt am Main, Suhrkamp, 1988.
Lichtigfeld, A. *Tijdschr Filosof* 53(1), 156-158 Mr 91

RAMSLAND, Katherine M. *Engaging the Immediate: Applying Kierkegaard's Theory of Indirect Communication to the Practice of Psychotherapy*. Lewisburg, Bucknell Univ Pr, 1989.
Meissner, W W. *Thought* 66(260), 114-115 Mr 91

RANTALA, Veikko and ROWELL, Lewis and TARASTI, Eero (eds). *Essays on the Philosophy of Music: Acta Philosophica Fennica*. Helsinki, Societas Philosophica Fennica, 1988.
Davies, Stephen. *Theoria* 55(2), 137-144 1989

RAPAPORT, Herman. *Heidegger and Derrida: Reflections on Time and Language*. Lincoln, Univ of Nebraska Pr, 1989.
Cook, Deborah. *Can Phil Rev* 10(10), 427-429 O 90
Wood, David. *Rad Phil* 58, 36 Sum 91

RAPP, Friederich and WIEHL, Reiner (eds). *Whitehead's Metaphysics of Creativity*. Albany, SUNY Pr, 1990.
Hendley, Brian. *Can Phil Rev* 10(11), 468-470 N 90
Nelson, Herbert J. *Trans Peirce Soc* 27(1), 121-130 Wint 91

RASMUSSEN, David. *Reading Habermas*. Oxford, Blackwell, 1990.
Kearney, Richard. *Phil Stud (Ireland)* 32, 322-326 1988-90

RAZ, Joseph. *The Libertarian Idea*. Oxford, Clarendon Pr, 1986.
Lomasky, Loren E. *Crit Rev* 4(1-2), 86-105 Wint-Spr 90

READ, Stephen. *Relevant Logic*. Cambridge, Blackwell, 1989.
Humberstone, I L. *Austl J Phil* 69(2), 233-236 Je 91

REALE, Giovanni and ANTISERI, Dario. *Historia del pensamiento filosófico y científico, V3: Del romanticismo hasta hoy*. Barcelona, Herder, 1988.
Beuchot, Mauricio. *Rev Filosof (Mexico)* 23(68), 265-267 My-Ag 90

REALE, Giovanni. *The Schools of the Imperial Age, John R Catan (ed & trans)*. Albany, SUNY Pr, 1990.
Owens, Joseph. *Rev Metaph* 44(1), 164-166 S 90

REALE, Giovanni. *Per una nuova interpretazione di Platone*. Milan, Quinta, 1987.
Reale, Giovanni. *Espiritu* 38(100), 157-160 Jl-D 89

REARDON, Bernard M G. *Kant as Philosophical Theologian*. London, Macmillan Pr, 1988.
Baccari, Luciano. *Aquinas* 33(2), 455-457 My-Ag 90

RÉCANATI, F (ed). *Éthique et philosophie politique*. Paris, Odile Jacob, 1988.
Delruelle, Édouard. *Rev Int Phil* 44(173), 277-280 1990

RÉCANATI, François. *Meaning and Force: The Pragmatics of Performative Utterances*. Cambridge, Cambridge Univ Pr, 1987.
Harnish, Robert M. *Phil Rev* 100(2), 297-300 Ap 91
Benjamin, James. *Phil Rhet* 23(3), 248-250 1990

REDDY, William M. *Money and Liberty in Modern Europe: A Critique of Historical Understanding*. Cambridge, Cambridge Univ Pr, 1987.
Chapman, S D. *Hist Euro Ideas* 12(6), 854-855 1990

REDHEAD, Michael. *Incompleteness, Nonlocality and Realism: A Prolegomenon to the Philosophy of Quantum Mechanics*. Oxford, Clarendon Pr, 1989.
Balibar, Françoise. *Rev Phil Fr* 180(4), 712-713 O-D 90
Bub, Jeffrey. *Int Stud Phil* 22(3), 140-141 1990

REDONDI, Pietro. *Galileo Heretic, Raymond Rosenthal (trans)*. Harmondsworth, Penguin Pr, 1988.
Sharratt, Michael. *Stud Hist Phil Sci* 21(4), 685-690 D 90

REED, John R. *Victorian Will*. Athens, Swallow Pr, 1989.
Brantlinger, Patrick. *Clio* 20(1), 96-99 Fall 90

REESOR, Margaret E. *The Nature of Man in Early Stoic Philosophy*. New York, St Martin's Pr, 1989.
Gould, Josiah B. *Rev Metaph* 44(2), 429-430 D 90

REEVE, C D C. *Socrates in the Apology: An Essay on Plato's Apology of Socrates*. Indianapolis, Hackett, 1986.
Brickhouse, Thomas C. *Polis* 9(2), 198-210 1990
Uzgalis, William. *Can Phil Rev* 10(11), 471-473 N 90
Lesses, Glenn. *Rev Metaph* 44(1), 166-168 S 90
Morgan, Michael L. *J Hist Phil* 29(2), 297-299 Ap 91
Stalley, R F. *Phil Books* 32(2), 75-77 Ap 91

REEVE, C D C. *Philosopher-Kings: The Argument of Plato's Republic*. Princeton, Princeton Univ Pr, 1988.
Schiller, Jerome. *J Hist Phil* 29(3), 483-486 Jl 91
Woodruff, Paul. *Ancient Phil* 11(1), 173-178 Spr 91

REGAN, Richard J. *The Moral Dimensions of Politics*. New York, Oxford Univ Pr, 1986.
Gueguen, John A. *Mod Sch* 68(2), 175-176 Ja 91

REIMAN, Jeffrey. *Justice and Modern Philosophy*. New Haven, Yale Univ Pr, 1990.
Somerville, James. *J Applied Phil* 8(1), 130-131 1991
Wilcox, William H. *Utilitas* 3(1), 141-144 My 91

RENTTO, Juha-Pekka. *Prudentia Iuris: The Art of the Good and the Just*. Turku, Turun Yliopisto, 1988.
Holmes, Arthur F. *Vera Lex* 10(1), 21 1990

RESCHER, Nicholas. *Ethical Idealism: An Inquiry into the Nature and Function of Ideals*. Berkeley, Univ of California Pr, 1987.
Graham, George. *Mod Sch* 67(4), 325-326 My 90

RHONHEIMER, M. *Natur als Grundlage der Moral*. Innsbruck, Tyrolia, 1987.
Ferrer, Urbano. *Anu Filosof* 23(1), 204-206 1990

RICCI, S and other eds. *Gli hegeliani di Napoli*. Naples, Inst Italiano per gli Studi Filosofici, 1987.
Moretti, Mauro. *G Crit Filosof Ital* 68(3), 413-417 S-D 89

RICHARD, Mark. *Propositional Attitudes: An Essay on Thoughts and How We Ascribe Them*. New York, Cambridge Univ Pr, 1990.
Cresswell, M J. *Can Phil Rev* 10(10), 430-432 O 90
Segal, Gabriel. *Mind* 100(399), 408-410 Jl 91

RICHARDS, David A J. *Foundations of American Constitutionalism*. New York, Oxford Univ Pr, 1989.
Reck, Andrew J. *Trans Peirce Soc* 27(1), 111-114 Wint 91

RICHARDS, Robert J. *Darwin and the Emergence of Evolutionary Theories of Mind and Behavior*. Chicago, Univ of Chicago Pr, 1987.
Coon, Deborah J. *Biol Phil* 5(4), 493-501 O 90

RICHARDS, Stewart (ed). *Philosophy and Sociology of Science: An Introduction, 2nd ed*. Oxford Univ Pr, Blackwell, 1987.
Roth, Paul A. *Phil Soc Sci* 21(1), 130-132 Mr 91

RICHMAN, H P. *Dilthey Today: A Critical Appraisal of the Contemporary Relevance of His Work*. New York, Greenwood Pr, 1988.
Owensby, Jacob. *J Hist Phil* 29(2), 324-325 Ap 91

RICOEUR, Paul. *Soi-même comme un autre*. Paris, Seuil, 1990.
Stevens, Bernard. *Rev Phil Louvain* 88(80), 581-596 N 90

RICOEUR, Paul. *Time and Narrative, V1, Kathleen McLaughlin and David Pellauer (trans)*. Chicago, Univ of Chicago Pr, 1984.
Mathews, William. *Phil Stud (Ireland)* 32, 356-358 1988-90

RICOEUR, Paul and BLAMEY, Kathleen (trans) and PELLAUER, David (trans). *Time and Narrative, V3*. Chicago, Univ of Chicago Pr, 1988.
Taft, Richard. *Mod Sch* 68(3), 264-265 Mr 91

RICONDA, Giuseppe. *Schelling storico della filosofia (1794-1820)*. Milan, Mursia, 1990.
De Maria, Amalia. *Filosofia* 41(3), 446-453 S-D 90

RIGOBELLO, A. *Autenticità nella differenza*. Rome, Studium, 1989.
Russo, Antonio. *Aquinas* 33(2), 457-461 My-Ag 90

RILEY, Denise. *"Am I That Name?": Feminism and the Category of Women in History*. Minneapolis, Univ of Minneasota Pr, 1988.
du Plessis, Michael. *Phil Lit* 14(2), 432-433 O 90
Hodge, Joanna. *Rad Phil* 58, 42-43 Sum 91

RIST, John M. *The Mind of Aristotle*. Toronto, Univ of Toronto Pr, 1989.
Hughes, G J. *Heythrop J* 32(3), 438-439 Jl 91

RISTINIEMI, Jari. *Experiential Dialectics*. Stockholm, Almqvist & Wiksell, 1987.
Boozer, Jack S. *Int J Phil Relig* 28(2), 121-122 O 90

RITTER, Joachim and GRÜNDER, Karlfried (eds). *Historisches Wörterbuch der Philosophie*. Basel, Shwabe, 1989.
Danek, Jaromir. *Laval Theol Phil* 46(3), 417-418 O 90

SCHRAG, Calvin O. *Communicative Praxis and the Space of Subjectivity*. Bloomington, Indiana Univ Pr, 1986.
Stack, George J. *Mod Sch* 67(4), 310-313 My 90

SCHROEDER, W Widick and GAMWELL, Franklin I (eds). *Economic Life*. Chicago, Ctr Scientific Stud Relig, 1988.
Murray, Leslie A. *Process Stud* 19(3), 203-206 Fall 90

SCHRÖDINGER, Erwin. *L'esprit et la matière*. Paris, Seuil, 1990.
Largeault, Jean. *Rev Phil Fr* 180(4), 714-716 O-D 90

SCHÜLLER, Bruno. *L'uomo veramente uomo*. Palermo, Oftes, 1987.
Mangiameli, Agata C Amato. *Riv Int Filosof Diritto* 67(2), 347-350 Ap-Je 90

SCHUMACHER, J A. *Human Posture: The Nature of Enquiry*. Albany, SUNY Pr, 1989.
Hooker, C A. *Rev Metaph* 44(4), 862-864 Je 91

SCHURZ, G (ed). *Erklären und Verstehen in der Wissenschaft*. Munich, Oldenbourg, 1988.
Bartelborth, Thomas. *Z Phil Forsch* 44(4), 671-675 1990

SCHURZ, Robert. *Ethik nach Adorno*. Frankfurt am Main, Roter Stern, 1985.
Wischke, Mirko. *Z Phil Forsch* 44(4), 679-681 1990

SCHUURMAN, E. *Filosofie van de technische wetenschappen*. Leiden, pub unknown, 1990.
Stellingwerff, J. *Phil Reform* 55(2), 191-197 1990

SCHWEMMER, Oswald. *Handlung und Struktur*. Frankfurt am Main, Suhrkamp, 1987.
Ginev, Dimiter. *Conceptus* 24(62), 122-125 1990

SCHWYZER, Hubert. *The Unity of Understanding: A Study in Kantian Problems*. Oxford, Clarendon Pr, 1990.
Hamlyn, D W. *Phil Quart* 41(162), 112-113 Ja 91
Hanna, Robert. *Rev Metaph* 44(4), 864-865 Je 91

SCOTT, Charles E. *The Question of Ethics: Nietzsche, Foucault, Heidegger*. Bloomington, Indiana Univ Pr, 1990.
Paden, Roger. *Rev Metaph* 44(4), 865-867 Je 91

SCOTT, Charles E. *The Language of Difference*. Atlantic Highlands, Humanities Pr, 1987.
Schrift, Alan D. *Int Stud Phil* 22(3), 144-145 1990

SCOTT, William G and HART, David K. *Organizational Values in America*. New Brunswick, Transaction Books, 1989.
Hodapp, P F. *J Bus Ethics* 10(6), 450,464,470 Je 91

SEANOR, Douglas and FOTION, N (eds). *Hare and Critics: Essays on Moral Thinking*. Oxford, Clarendon Pr, 1988.
Sandoe, Peter. *Theoria* 55(3), 211-222 1989

SECKEL, Al (ed). *Bertrand Russell on Ethics, Sex and Marriage*. Buffalo, Prometheus, 1987.
Andersson, Stefan. *Russell* 10(2), 178-180 Wint 90-91

SEERY, John Evan. *Political Returns: Irony in Politics and Theory from Plato the Antinuclear Movement*. Boulder, Westview Pr, 1990.
Salkever, Stephen G. *Polit Theory* 19(2), 295-299 My 91

SEIDLER, Michael (ed & trans). *Samuel Pufendorf's "On the Natural State of Men"*. Lewiston, Mellen Pr, 1990.
Den Uyl, Douglas. *Mod Sch* 68(2), 171-172 Ja 91

SEIFERT, Josef. *Essere e Persona: Verso una fondazione fenomenologica di una metafisica classica e personalistica*. Milan, Vita e Pensiero, 1989.
Crespo, Mariano. *Dialogo Filosof* 6(3), 409-411 S-D 90

SELL, Alan P. *The Philosophy of Religion, 1875-1980*. Beckenham, Croom Helm, 1988.
Vardy, Peter. *Heythrop J* 32(2), 281-282 Ap 91

SELLARS, Wilfrid. *The Metaphysics of Epistemology: Lectures by Wilfrid Sellars, Pedro V Amaral (ed)*. Atascadero, Ridgeview, 1988.
Aune, Bruce. *Can Phil Rev* 10(11), 473-475 N 90

SELTMAN, Muriel and SELTMAN, Peter. *Piaget's Logic: A Critique of Genetic Epistemology*. London, Allen & Unwin, 1985.
Kitchener, Richard F. *Brit J Phil Sci* 42(2), 285-290 Je 91

SEN, Amartya and others. *The Standard of Living*. Cambridge, Cambridge Univ Pr, 1987.
Braybrooke, David. *Econ Phil* 6(2), 339-350 O 90
O'Riordan, William K. *Phil Stud (Ireland)* 32, 361-363 1988-90

SEPPER, Dennis L. *Goethe contra Newton: Polemics and the Project for a New Science of Color*. Cambridge, Cambridge Univ Pr, 1988.
Shapiro, Alan E. *J Hist Phil* 28(4), 621-622 O 90

SEVILLA FERNANDEZ, Jose Manuel. *Giambattista Vico: metafísica de la mente e historicismo antropológico*. Sevilla, Univ de Sevilla, 1988.
Carnevale, C M de. *Rev Filosof (Mexico)* 23(68), 269-271 My-Ag 90

SHALEV, Carmel. *Birth Power: The Case for Surrogacy*. New Haven, Yale Univ Pr, 1989.
Morgan, Gail. *Bioethics* 5(2), 170-175 Ap 91

SHALYA, Yashdev. *Sattāvisayak Anvīksā*. New Delhi, Indian Council of Philosophical Research, 1989.
Pande, G C. *J Indian Counc Phil Res* 5(3), 163-170 My-Ag 88

SHANKER, S G (ed). *Philosophy in Britain Today*. Albany, SUNY Pr, 1986.
Hestevold, H Scott. *Mod Sch* 68(2), 181-183 Ja 91

SHANLEY, Mary Lyndon. *Feminism, Marriage, and the Law in Victorian England, 1850-1895*. Princeton, Princeton Univ Pr, 1989.
Kramnick, Isaac. *Polit Theory* 19(1), 115-117 F 91

SHAPIN, Steven and SCHAFFER, Simon. *Leviathan and the Air-Pump: Hobbes, Boyle and The Experimental Life*. Princeton, Princeton Univ Pr, 1985.
James, Peter J. *Hist Phil Life Sci* 12(1), 134-136 1990
Jennings, Richard C. *Brit J Phil Sci* 39(3), 403-410 S 88

SHAPIRO, Gary. *Nietzschean Narratives*. Bloomington, Indiana Univ Pr, 1989.
Harries, Karsten. *Phil Lit* 15(1), 164-165 Ap 91

SHAPIRO, Ian. *Political Criticism*. Berkeley, Univ of Calif Pr, 1990.
Gunnell, John G. *Polit Theory* 19(3), 471-473 Ag 91

SHAPIRO, Michael J. *The Politics of Representation: Writing Practices in Biography, Photography, and Policy Analysis*. Madison, Univ of Wisconsin Pr, 1988.
Lynch, Michael. *Phil Soc Sci* 20(4), 512-515 D 90

SHARMA, Arvind. *A Hindu Perspective on the Philosophy of Religion*. New York, Macmillan, 1990.
Hudson, W D. *Asian Phil* 1(1), 95-96 1991

SHARMA, Kaushal Kishore. *A Commentary on Kant's Critique of Practical Reason*. New Delhi, Indus, 1989.
Bhatnagar, Rajendra Swaroop. *J Indian Counc Phil Res* 8(1), 144-149 S-D 90

SHARPE, R A. *Making the Human Mind*. London, Routledge, 1990.
Abrahamson, Leonard. *Phil Stud (Ireland)* 32, 364-367 1988-90

SHEA, William R and SITTER, Beat (eds). *Scientists and their Responsibilities*. Canton, Watson, 1989.
Belsey, Andrew. *J Applied Phil* 8(1), 132-133 1991

SHEPPARD, Anne. *Aesthetics: An Introduction to the Philosophy of Art*. Oxford, Oxford Univ Pr, 1987.
Meynell, Hugo. *Heythrop J* 32(1), 107-108 Ja 91

SHER, George. *Desert*. Princeton, Princeton Univ Pr, 1987.
Keshen, Richard. *Can J Phil* 20(4), 601-615 D 90

SHERMAN, Nancy. *The Fabric of Character: Aristotle's Theory of Virtue*. New York, Clarendon/Oxford Univ Pr, 1989.
Price, A W. *Ancient Phil* 10(2), 332-337 Fall 90
Hughes, G J. *Heythrop J* 32(3), 438-439 Jl 91
Mele, Alfred. *Mind* 100(399), 415-418 Jl 91

SHEROVER, Charles M. *Time, Freedom, and the Common Good*. Albany, SUNY Pr, 1989.
Hibbs, Thomas S. *Thomist* 55(2), 329-331 Ap 91
Hyland, Drew A. *Man World* 24(3), 331-336 Jl 91
Schalow, Frank. *Res Phenomenol* 20, 188-194 1990
Feder-Marcus, Maureen. *Interpretation* 18(2), 317-320 Wint 90-91
Velkley, Richard L. *Rev Metaph* 44(2), 435-437 D 90
Gier, Nicholas F. *Personalist Forum* 6(2), 195-198 Fall 90

SHEROVER, Charles M. *Heidegger, Kant and Time*. Lanham, Univ Pr of America, 1988.
Protevi, John. *J Hist Phil* 28(4), 631-633 O 90

SHIVA, Vandana. *Staying Alive: Women, Ecology and Development*. London, Zed Books, 1989.
Salleh, Ariel. *Hypatia* 6(1), 206-214 Spr 91

SHKLAR, Judith N. *The Faces of Injustice*. New Haven, Yale Univ Pr, 1990.
Keohane, Nannerl O. *Polit Theory* 19(3), 453-456 Ag 91

SHOWALTER JR, English. *The Stranger: Humanity and the Absurd*. Boston, Twayne, 1989.
Cosper, Dale. *Phil Lit* 14(2), 401-402 O 90

SHULMAN, George M. *Radicalism and Reverence: The Political Thought of Gerrard Winstanley*. Berkeley, Univ of Calif Pr, 1990.
Condren, Conal. *Polit Theory* 19(3), 473-476 Ag 91

SIDELLE, Alan. *Necessity, Essence and Individuation: A Defence of Conventionalism*. Ithaca, Cornell Univ Pr, 1989.
Armstrong, D M. *Phil Books* 32(2), 106-108 Ap 91
Mackie, Penelope. *Mind* 99(396), 635-637 O 90
Carter, William R. *Can Phil Rev* 10(11), 476-478 N 90

SIEBRAND, H J. *Spinoza and the Netherlands: An Inquiry into the Early Reception of his Philosophy of Religion*. Wolfeboro, Van Gorcum, 1988.
van Leeuwen, Evert. *Rev Metaph* 44(2), 437-438 D 90
Van der Wall, E G E. *J Hist Phil* 29(2), 308-309 Ap 91

SIEFERT, Annemarie Gethmann and PÖGGELER, Otto (eds). *Heidegger und die praktische Philosophie*. Frankfurt, Suhrkamp, 1988.
Kudrna, Jaroslav. *Filozof Cas* 39(1), 162-166 1991

SIEGEL, H. *Relativism Refuted: A Critique of Contemporary Epistemological Relativism*. Norwell, Reidel, 1987.
Nola, Robert. *Brit J Phil Sci* 40(3), 419-427 S 89

SIEGEL, Harvey. *Relativism Refuted*. Dordrecht, Reidel, 1987.
Davies, David. *Phil Sci* 57(3), 537-539 S 90

SIEGWART, Geo (ed). *Johann Heinrich Lambert: Texte zur Systematologie und zur Theorie der wissenschaftlichen Erkenntnis*. Hamburg, Meiner, 1988.
Schenk, Günter. *Deut Z Phil* 38(8), 798-800 1990

SIGMUND, Paul E (ed & trans). *St Thomas Aquinas on Ethics and Politics*. New York, Norton, 1988.
Lawler, Peter Augustine. *Vera Lex* 10(1), 21-24 1990
Lisska, Anthony J. *Teach Phil* 13(3), 295-298 S 90

SILVERMAN, Hugh J (ed). *Postmodernism: Philosophy and The Arts*. New York, Routledge, 1990.
Milne, Drew. *Rad Phil* 57, 48-49 Spr 91

SILVERMAN, Hugh J and WELTON, Don (eds). *Postmodernism and Continental Philosophy*. Albany, SUNY Pr, 1988.
Baker, Lang. *Phil Soc Sci* 21(1), 90-101 Mr 91

SILVERMAN, Hugh J. *Inscriptions, Between Phenomenology and Structuralism*. New York, Routledge, 1987.
Edie, James M. *Int Stud Phil* 23(1), 138-139 1991
Wurzer, Wilhelm S. *Man World* 23(4), 473-476 O 90

SILVERS, Stuart (ed). *Rerepresentation: Readings in the Philosophy of Mental Representation*. Dordrecht, Kluwer, 1989.
Kirk, Robert. *Phil Books* 31(4), 237-239 O 90

SIMMEL, Georg. *Gesammelte Schriften zur Religionssoziologie*. Berlin, Duncker & Humblot, 1989.
Flamarique, Lourdes. *Anu Filosof* 23(1), 207-209 1990

SIMMEL, Georg. *Schopenhauer and Nietzsche, H Loiskandl and D Weinstein and M Weinstein (trans)*. Amherst, Univ of Massachusetts Pr, 1986.
Stack, George J. *Mod Sch* 68(1), 102-105 N 90

SIMON, Josef. *Philosophie des Zeichens*. Hawthorne, de Gruyter, 1989.
Colette, Jacques. *Rev Metaph Morale* 96(2), 269-270 Ap-Je 91

SIMON, Yves R. *The Definition of Moral Virtue*. Bronx, Fordham Univ Pr, 1986.
Lee, Patrick. *Mod Sch* 68(2), 179-181 Ja 91

SIMONS, Herbert (ed). *Rhetoric in the Human Sciences*. Newbury Park, Sage, 1989.
Strauber, Ira L. *Phil Rhet* 24(3), 270-274 1991

SIMONS, Peter. *Parts: A Study in Ontology*. New York, Clarendon/Oxford Pr, 1987.
Heller, Mark. *Phil Rev* 100(3), 488-490 Jl 91
Jacquette, Dale. *Phil Sci* 57(3), 540-542 S 90
Doepke, Frederick. *Nous* 25(3), 393-396 Je 91

SIMPSON, Evan. *Good Lives and Moral Education*. New York, Lang, 1989.
Wren, Thomas E. *J Moral Educ* 20(2), 213-214 My 91

SINACEUR, M A (ed). *Aristote aujourd'hui*. Paris, UNESCO, 1988.
Dorion, Louis-André. *Dialogue (Canada)* 29(1), 141-144 1990

SINCLAIR, R K. *Democracy and Participation in Athens*. New York, Cambridge Univ Pr, 1988.
Jones, Nicholas F. *Ancient Phil* 11(1), 155-158 Spr 91

SINGH, Jaideva (trans). *A Trident of Wisdom: Translation of Parātrisikā-vivarana of Abhinavagupta*. Albany, SUNY Pr, 1989.
Wayman, Alex. *Phil East West* 41(2), 266-268 Ap 91

SINNOTT-ARMSTRONG, Walter. *Moral Dilemmas*. New York, Blackwell, 1988.
Mohan, William J. *Int Stud Phil* 23(1), 139-140 1991

SIRAISI, Nancy G. *Avicenna in Renaissance Italy: The Canon and Medical Teaching in Italian Universities after 1500*. Princeton, Princeton Univ Pr, 1987.
Dupèbe, Jean. *Hist Phil Life Sci* 12(2), 284-286 1990

SIRCELLO, Guy. *Love and Beauty*. Princeton, Princeton Univ Pr, 1989.
Williams, Clifford. *Int Phil Quart* 30(4), 501-502 D 90

SKINNER, Quentin and KESSLER, Eckhard (eds). *The Cambridge History of Renaissance Philosophy*. Cambridge Univ Pr, Cambridge, 1988.
Haren, Michael. *Phil Stud (Ireland)* 32, 367-370 1988-90

SKLAR, Lawrence. *Philosophy and Spacetime Physics*. Berkeley, Univ of Calif Pr, 1985.
Torretti, Roberto. *Nous* 25(4), 574-578 S 91

SKORUPSKI, John. *John Stuart Mill*. New York, Routledge, 1990.
Flew, Antony. *Phil Quart* 41(162), 97-100 Ja 91

SLEEPER, R W. *The Necessity of Pragmatism: John Dewey's Conception of Philosophy*. New Haven, Yale Univ Pr, 1986.
Ratner, Sidney. *J Speculative Phil* 4(3), 275-278 1990

SLEIGH JR, R C. *Leibniz and Arnauld*. New Haven, Yale Univ Pr, 1990.
Janowski, Zbigniew. *Rev Metaph* 44(4), 867-868 Je 91
Nadler, Steven. *J Hist Phil* 29(3), 494-496 Jl 91

SLOTE, Michael. *Beyond Optimizing*. Cambridge, Harvard Univ Pr, 1989.
Schotter, Andrew. *Econ Phil* 7(1), 128-132 Ap 91
Sugden, Robert. *Utilitas* 2(2), 336-338 N 90

SMART, J J C. *Essays Metaphysical and Moral: Selected Philosophical Papers*. Oxford, Blackwell, 1987.
Gasper, Philip. *Phil Rev* 99(4), 656-661 O 90

SMITH, David W. *The Circle of Acquaintance: Perception, Consciousness and Empathy*. Dordrecht, Kluwer, 1989.
Mohanty, J N. *Rev Metaph* 44(2), 439 D 90
Moser, Paul K. *Hist Euro Ideas* 12(5), 706-708 1990

SMITH, Huston. *Beyond the Post-Modern Mind*. Wheaton, Theosophical, 1989.
Bernstein, Richard J. *Rev Metaph* 44(4), 868-869 Je 91

SMITH, John H. *The Spirit and Its Letter: Traces of Rhetoric in Hegel's Philosophy of "Bildung"*. Ithaca, Cornell Univ Pr, 1988.
Sills, Chip. *J Hist Phil* 28(4), 625-627 O 90
Roth, Michael S. *Clio* 19(4), 398-400 Sum 90

SMITH, Laurence D. *Behaviorism and Logical Positivism: A Reassessment of the Alliance*. Stanford, Stanford Univ Pr, 1986.
Olby, Robert C. *Hist Phil Life Sci* 12(1), 117-122 1990
Donohue, William O. *Nous* 25(3), 383-386 Je 91

SMITH, Quentin. *The Felt Meanings of the World: A Metaphysics of Feeling*. West Lafayette, Purdue Univ Pr, 1986.
Wilshire, Bruce. *Int Phil Quart* 31(2), 237-242 Je 91

SMITH, Steven B. *Hegel's Critique of Liberalism: Rights in Context*. Chicago, Univ of Chicago Pr, 1989.
McCarthy, George. *Stud Soviet Tho* 41(1), 79-82 Ja 91

SMULLYAN, Ramond. *Juegos por siempre misteriosos*. Barcelona, Gedisa, 1988.
Legris, Javier. *Rev Filosof (Argentina)* 5(1), 49-53 My 90

SMYTH, John Vignaux. *A Question of Eros: Irony in Sterne, Kierkegaard, and Barthes*. Tallahassee, Florida State Univ Pr, 1986.
Walsh, Sylvia. *Int J Phil Relig* 29(2), 113-122 Ap 91

SMYTHIES, John R and BELOFF, John (eds). *The Case for Dualism*. Charlottesville, Univ Pr of Virginia, 1989.
Baillie, James. *Phil Books* 32(2), 113-114 Ap 91

SOBER, Elliot. *Reconstructing the Past: Parsimony, Evolution, and Inference*. Cambridge, MIT Pr, 1988.
Ravenscroft, Ian. *Austl J Phil* 68(2), 246-248 Je 90

SOBLE, Alan. *The Structure of Love*. New Haven, Yale Univ Pr, 1990.
Solomon, Robert C. *Can Phil Rev* 10(11), 478-480 N 90

SOBLE, Alan (ed). *Eros, Agape, and Philia: Readings in the Philosophy of Love*. New York, Paragon, 1989.
Johnson, Rolf. *Teach Phil* 13(4), 385-388 D 90

SOFFER, Walter. *From Science to Subjectivity: An Interpretation of Descartes' "Meditations"*. New York, Greenwood Pr, 1987.
Watson, Richard A. *J Hist Phil* 28(4), 615-617 O 90
Parkinson, G H R. *Int Stud Phil* 22(3), 145-146 1990

SOLOMON, Robert C and HIGGINS, Kathleen M (eds). *Reading Nietzsche*. New York, Oxford Univ Pr, 1989.
Atwell, John E. *Teach Phil* 13(2), 177-180 Je 90

SOPER, Kate. *Humanism and Anti-Humanism*. La Salle, Open Court, 1986.
Valone, James J. *Human Stud* 14(1), 67-79 Ja 91

SORABJI, Richard (ed). *Aristotle Transformed: The Ancient Commentators and Their Influence*. Ithaca, Cornell Univ Pr, 1990.
Konstan, David. *Can Phil Rev* 10(9), 387-389 S 90
Schrenk, Lawrence P. *Rev Metaph* 44(1), 170-171 S 90

SORENSON, Roy A. *Blindspots*. Oxford, Oxford Univ Pr, 1988.
Levin, Michael. *Nous* 25(3), 389-392 Je 91

SORGE, V. *Gnoseologia e teologia nel pensiero di Enrico di Gand*. Napoli, Loffredo, 1988.
Colonnello, Pio. *Sapienza* 43(4), 462-463 O-D 90

SOUPIOS, Michael A (ed). *European Political Theory: Plato to Machiavelli*. Lanham, Univ Pr of America, 1986.
Kelly, Eugene. *Vera Lex* 10(2), 16 1990

SPARIOUSU, Mihai J. *Dionysus Reborn: Play and the Aesthetic Dimension in Modern Philosophical and Scientific Discourse*. Ithaca, Cornell Univ Pr, 1989.
Nemoianu, Virgil. *Rev Metaph* 44(2), 439-441 D 90

SPARKS, Richard C. *To Treat or Not to Treat*. New York, Paulist Pr, 1988.
Campbell, A G M. *Heythrop J* 32(3), 447-448 Jl 91

SPARSHOTT, Francis. *Off the Ground: First Steps to a Philosophical Consideration of the Dance*. Princeton, Princeton Univ Pr, 1988.
Rée, Jonathan. *Rad Phil* 57, 38-39 Spr 91

SPELLMAN, W M. *John Locke and the Problem of Depravity*. New York, Clarendon Pr, 1988.
Reedy, Gerard. *J Hist Phil* 29(2), 306-308 Ap 91

SPELMAN, Elizabeth V. *Inessential Woman: Problems of Exclusion in Feminist Thought*. Boston, Beacon Pr, 1988.
Code, Lorraine. *Soc Theor Pract* 17(1), 85-104 Spr 91

SPERBER, Dan. *On Anthropological Knowledge: Three Essays*. New York, Cambridge Univ Pr, 1985.
Gilbert, Margaret. *Int Stud Phil* 22(3), 146-147 1990

SPERLING, Susan. *Animal Liberators: Research and Morality*. Berkeley, Univ of California Pr, 1988.
Rowan, Andrew W. *Between Species* 6(3), 140-146 Sum 90

SPINOZA, Baruch and SHIRLEY, Samuel (trans). *Tractatus theologico-politicus*. Leiden, Brill, 1989.
Bagley, Paul J. *Rev Metaph* 44(4), 870-872 Je 91

SPRIGGE, T L S. *The Rational Foundations of Ethics*. New York, Routledge & Kegan Paul, 1988.
Mohan, William J. *Int Stud Phil* 22(3), 147-148 1990

SPRINKER, Michael. *Imaginary Relations*. London, Verso, 1987.
Murphy, John W. *Stud Soviet Tho* 41(1), 65-67 Ja 91

SPRINTZEN, David. *Camus: A Critical Examination*. Philadelphia, Temple Univ Pr, 1988.
Cosper, Dale. *Phil Lit* 14(2), 402-404 O 90

STAFFORD, J Martin. *Homosexuality and Education*. Manchester, J Martin Stafford, 1988.
Jones, Reynold. *J Phil Educ* 24(1), 134-136 Sum 90

STAPLETON, Timothy J. *Husserl and Heidegger: The Question of a Phenomenological Beginning*. Albany, SUNY Pr, 1983.
Grieder, Alfons. *J Brit Soc Phenomenol* 22(2), 104-105 My 91

STAROBINSKI, Jean. *The Living Eye, Arthur Goldhammer (trans)*. Cambridge, Harvard Univ Pr, 1989.
Ball, David. *Brit J Aes* 31(1), 83-84 Ja 91

STAUTH, Georg and TURNER, Bryan S. *Nietzsche's Dance*. Oxford, Blackwell, 1988.
Golomb, Jacob. *Hist Euro Ideas* 12(4), 551-552 1990

STEINBERG, Jules. *The Obsession of Thomas Hobbes: The English Civil War in Hobbes's Political Philosophy*. New York, Lang, undated.
Johnson, Paul J. *J Hist Phil* 29(2), 305-306 Ap 91

STEINBERGER, Peter J. *Logic and Politics: Hegel's Philosophy of Right*. New Haven, Yale Univ Pr, 1988.
Fuss, Peter. *J Hist Phil* 29(2), 321-322 Ap 91
Jackson, M W. *Owl Minerva* 22(2), 229 Spr 91
Hardimon, Michael O. *Phil Rev* 100(3), 498-500 Jl 91

STERBA, James P. *How to Make People Just: A Practical Reconciliation of Alternative Conceptions of Justice*. Totowa, Rowman & Littlefield, 1988.
De George, Richard T. *Teach Phil* 13(2), 167-168 Je 90

STERN, Robert. *Hegel, Kant and the Structure of the Object*. New York, Routledge, 1990.
Buchdahl, Gerd. *Philosophy* 66(255), 129-131 Ja 91

STERNBERG, R J and WAGNER, R K (eds). *Practical Intelligence: Nature and Origins of Competence in the Everyday World*. Cambridge, Cambridge Univ Pr, 1986.
Haig, Brian D. *Educ Phil Theor* 22(1), 40-44 1990

STILLMAN, Peter G. *Hegel's Philosophy of Spirit*. Albany, SUNY Pr, 1987.
Coleman, Dorothy. *Ideal Stud* 20(2), 182-183 My 90

STOCKER, Michael. *Plural and Conflicting Values*. New York, Oxford Univ Pr, 1989.
Dunn, Robert. *Austl J Phil* 69(2), 236-241 Je 91
O'Neill, Onora. *Phil Quart* 41(164), 367-372 Jl 91
Charlton, William. *Philosophy* 65(254), 522-524 O 90

STOLL, Donald. *Philosophy and the Community of Speech*. Lanham, Univ Pr of America, 1987.
Desmond, William. *Phil Rhet* 24(3), 267-270 1991

STONE, I F. *The Trial of Socrates*. Boston, Little, Brown, 1988.
Glidden, David K. *J Hist Phil* 28(4), 601-602 O 90
Dover, K J. *J Hellen Stud* 110, 239-240 1990

STOUT, Jeffrey. *Ethics After Babel*. Boston, Beacon Pr, 1988.
Bernstein, Richard J. *Rev Metaph* 44(4), 872-874 Je 91

STOVE, D C. *The Rationality of Induction*. Oxford, Clarendon Pr, 1986.
Verley, Xavier. *Rev Phil Fr* 180(4), 716-719 O-D 90
Baccari, Luciano. *Aquinas* 33(2), 453-455 My-Ag 90

STRAUGHAN, Roger. *Beliefs, Behaviour and Education*. London, Cassell, 1989.
Haydon, Graham. *J Phil Educ* 24(2), 301-304 Wint 90

STRAWSON, Galen. *Freedom and Belief*. New York, Clarendon Pr, 1986.
White, Stephen L. *Phil Rev* 100(1), 119-122 Ja 91
Kapitan, Tomis. *Nous* 24(5), 807-810 D 90

STRAWSON, Galen. *The Secret Connexion: Causation, Realism, and David Hume*. Oxford, Clarendon Pr, 1989.
Botterill, George. *Phil Books* 31(4), 203-205 O 90

STRENSKI, Ivan. *Four Theories of Myth in Twentieth-Century History: Cassirer, Eliade, Lévi-Strauss, and Malinowski*. London, Macmillan, 1987.
Burns, R M. *Relig Stud* 26(4), 548-550 D 90

STROHMEYER, Ingeborg (ed). *Studien zur Arithmetik und Geometrie*. New York, Nijhoff, 1983.
De Gandt, François. *Rev Metaph Morale* 96(1), 130-133 Ja-Mr 91

STROLL, Avrum. *Surfaces*. Minneapolis, Univ of Minnesota Pr, 1988.
Rundle, Bede. *Int Stud Phil* 22(3), 148-149 1990

STRÖKER, Elisabeth and JANSSEN, Paul. *Phänomenologische Philosophie*. Freiburg, Alber, 1989.
Janssen, Paul. *Rev Metaph* 44(4), 874-875 Je 91

STRÖKER, Elisabeth. *Wissenschaftsphilosophische Studien*. Frankfurt, Klostermann, 1989.
Rivadulla, Andrés. *Rev Filosof (Spain)* 4, 277-280 1990

STRÖKER, Elisabeth. *Husserls transzendentale Phänomenologie*. Frankfurt am Main, Klostermann, 1987.
Mohanty, J N. *Husserl Stud* 7(2), 129-136 1990

STRÖKER, Elisabeth. *Phänomenologische Studien*. Frankfurt am Main, Klostermann, 1987.
Mohanty, J N. *Husserl Stud* 7(2), 129-136 1990

STRÖKER, Elisabeth. *The Husserlian Foundations of Science*. Lanham, Univ Pr of America, 1987.
Mohanty, J N. *Husserl Stud* 7(2), 129-136 1990

STUHR, John J. *John Dewey*. Nashville, Carmichael & Carmichael, 1991.
Sullivan, Michael. *Personalist Forum* 6(2), 185-188 Fall 90

STUMP, Eleonore (trans & ed). *Boethius's In Ciceronis Topica*. Ithaca, Cornell Univ Pr, 1988.
Davis, Scott. *Ancient Phil* 10(2), 316-319 Fall 90

STUMP, Eleonore. *Dialectic and Its Place in the Development of Medieval Logic*. Ithaca, Cornell Univ Pr, 1989.
Froelich, Gregory L. *Rev Metaph* 44(3), 654-656 Mr 91
Marsonet, Michele. *Filosofia* 42(1), 128-133 Ja-Ap 91

STURM, Douglas. *Community and Alienation*. Notre Dame, Univ Notre Dame Pr, 1988.
Murray, Leslie A. *Process Stud* 19(3), 203-206 Fall 90

SULLIVAN, Robert R. *Political Hermeneutics: The Early Thinking of Hans-Georg Gadamer*. University Park, Pennsylvania State Univ Pr, 1989.
Krajewski, Bruce. *Rev Metaph* 44(2), 441-442 D 90

SULLIVAN, Roger J. *Immanuel Kant's Moral Theory*. Cambridge, Cambridge Univ Pr, 1989.
Crowther, Paul. *Mind* 99(396), 652-654 O 90

SUNSTEIN, Cass R. *After the Rights Revolution: Reconceiving the Regulatory State*. Cambridge, Harvard Univ Pr, 1990.
Macedo, Stephen. *Polit Theory* 19(3), 456-461 Ag 91

SUTER, Ronald. *Interpreting Wittgenstein: A Cloud of Philosophy, a Drop of Grammar*. Philadelphia, Temple Univ Pr, 1990.
Hodges, Michael. *Rev Metaph* 44(3), 656-657 Mr 91

SUTHERLAND, Stewart R and ROBERTS, T A (eds). *Religion, Reason and the Self: Essays in Honour of Hywel D Lewis*. Cardiff, Univ of Wales Press, 1989.
Brown, Stuart. *Philosophy* 65(253), 379-380 Jl 90

SWAIN, Gladys. *Soggetto e follia: Pinel e la nascita della psichiatria moderna*. Turin, Centro Scientifico Torinese, 1988.
Francioni, Mario. *Filosofia* 41(3), 429-432 S-D 90

SWARTZ, Norman. *The Concept of Physical Law*. New York, Cambridge Univ Pr, 1985.
Spector, Marshall. *Int Stud Phil* 22(3), 149-150 1990

SWINBURNE, Richard. *Responsibility and Atonement*. Oxford, Clarendon Pr, 1989.
Helm, Paul. *Relig Stud* 26(3), 431-433 S 90
Turco, Giovanni. *Sapienza* 44(1), 92-94 Ja-Mr 91

SWOMLEY, John M. *Religious Liberty and the Secular State*. New York, Prometheus, 1987.
Easton, Loyd D. *Ideal Stud* 20(2), 180-181 My 90

SYCHRAVA, Juliet. *Schiller to Derrida: Idealism in Aesthetics*. Cambridge, Cambridge Univ Pr, 1989.
Pollard, David. *Brit J Aes* 31(1), 82-83 Ja 91

SYPNOWICH, Christine. *The Concept of Socialist Law*. Oxford, Clarendon Pr, 1990.
Menlowe, Michael A. *Phil Quart* 41(162), 117-118 Ja 91

SZIKLAI, László (ed). *Lukács-Aktuell*. Budapest, Akad Kiado, 1989.
Furness, Raymond. *Brit J Aes* 31(3), 271 Jl 91

SZPORLUK, Roman. *Communism and Nationalism: Karl Marx versus Friederich List*. New York, Oxford Univ Pr, 1988.
Sayers, Sean. *Hist Euro Ideas* 12(4), 552-554 1990

TACHAU, Katherine H. *Vision and Certitude in the Age of Ockham: Optics, Epistemology and the Foundations of Semantics 1250-1345*. New York, Brill, 1988.
Doyle, John P. *Mod Sch* 67(4), 320-325 My 90
Molland, A G. *Hist Phil Log* 12(1), 121 1990

TANG YI-JIE and LI ZHEN and MCLEAN, George F. *Man and Nature: The Chinese Tradition and the Future*. Lanham, Univ Pr of America, 1989.
Wen Ming-Lee. *Asian J Phil* 2(1), 157-159 Sum 90

TANNER, Kathryn. *God and Creation in Christian Theology*. Oxford, Blackwell, 1988.
Meynell, Hugo. *Heythrop J* 32(2), 270-271 Ap 91
Ford, David F. *Relig Stud* 26(4), 550-552 D 90
Marshall, Bruce D. *Thomist* 55(2), 321-326 Ap 91

TÄNNSJÖ, Torbjörn. *Conservatism For Our Time*. New York, Routledge, 1990.
Magill, Kevin. *Phil Quart* 41(164), 367-369 Jl 91

TARRANT, Harold. *Scepticism or Platonism? The Philosophy of the Fourth Academy*. New York, Cambridge Univ Pr, 1985.
Striker, Gisela. *Ancient Phil* 11(1), 202-206 Spr 91

TASIC, Milan (ed & trans). *Sv Toma Akvinski: Bice i sustina*. Belgrade, Moderna, 1990.
Talanga, Josip. *Filozof Istraz* 34(1), 259-263 1990

TASIC, Milan (trans). *Aristotel: O nastajanju i nestajanju*. Belgrade, Grafos, 1989.
Talanga, Josip. *Filozof Istraz* 34(1), 259-263 1990

TASIC, Milan (trans). *Aristotel: O nebu*. Belgrade, Moderna, 1989.
Talanga, Josip. *Filozof Istraz* 34(1), 259-263 1990

TASIC, Milan (trans). *Sveti Augustin: Ispovesti*. Belgrade, Grafos, 1989.
Talanga, Josip. *Filozof Istraz* 34(1), 259-263 1990

TAYLOR, Charles. *Sources of the Self: The Making of the Modern Identity*. Cambridge, Harvard Univ Pr, 1989.
Hittinger, Russell. *Rev Metaph* 44(1), 111-130 S 90
Shklar, Judith N. *Polit Theory* 19(1), 105-109 F 91
Schneewind, J B. *J Phil* 88(8), 422-426 Ag 91

TAYLOR, Paul. *Respect for Nature*. Princeton, Princeton Univ Pr, 1986.
Elliot, Robert. *Austl J Phil* 69(2), 241-242 Je 91
Sprigge, T L S. *Inquiry* 34(1), 107-128 Mr 91

TEICHMAN, Jenny. *Philosophy and the Mind*. Oxford, Blackwell, 1988.
Pfeifer, Karl. *Can Phil Rev* 10(8), 332-333 Ag 90

TEJERA, V. *Nietzsche and Greek Thought*. Boston, Nijhoff, 1987.
Strong, Tracy B. *Ancient Phil* 10(2), 329-331 Fall 90

TELOH, Henry. *Socratic Education in Plato's Early Dialogues*. Notre Dame, Univ of Notre Dame Pr, 1986.
Snider, Eric W. *Mod Sch* 68(1), 98-100 N 90

TEN, C L. *Crime, Guilt, and Punishment: A Philosophical Introduction*. New York, Clarendon Pr, 1987.
Bedau, Hugo Adam. *Phil Rev* 100(1), 133-136 Ja 91

TESKE, Roland J and WADE, Francis C (trans). *William of Auvergne: The Trinity, or the First Principle*. Milwaukee, Marquette Univ Pr, 1989.
Lewis, Neil. *J Hist Phil* 29(1), 120-121 Ja 91

TESÓN, Fernando R. *Humanitarian Intervention: An Inquiry into Law and Morality*. Dobbs Ferry, Transnational, 1988.
Holmes, Robert L. *Law Phil* 9(3), 319-323 Ag 90

TESSIER, Linda (ed). *Concepts of the Ultimate*. London, Macmillan, 1990.
Ward, Keith. *Relig Stud* 27(1), 136-137 Mr 91

THERON, Stephen. *Morals as Founded on Natural Law*. New York, Lang, 1987.
Simpson, Peter. *Thomist* 55(2), 293-300 Ap 91

THOM, René. *Esquisse d'une sémiophysique: Physique aristotélicienne et théorie des catastrophes*. Paris, Inter-Editions, 1988.
Espinoza, Miguel. *Dialogos* 25(56), 194-200 Jl 90

THOMAS, Geoffrey. *The Moral Philosophy of T H Green*. New York, Clarendon Pr, 1987.
Allard, James W. *Phil Rev* 100(2), 344-346 Ap 91

THOMASMA, David C and GRABER, Glenn C. *Euthanasia: Toward an Ethical Social Policy*. New York, Crossroad/Continuum, 1990.
Loewy, Erich H. *Bridges* 3(1-2), 139-143 Spr-Sum 91

THOMASMA, David. *Human Life in the Balance*. Louisville, Knox Pr, 1990.
Pence, Gregory. *Hastings Center Rep* 21(3), 34-35 My-Je 91

THOMPSON, Kristin. *Breaking the Glass Armor: Neoformalist Film Analysis*. Princeton, Princeton Univ Pr, 1988.
Neill, Alex and Ridley, Aaron. *Can Phil Rev* 10(9), 345-351 S 90

THOMPSON, Paul. *The Structure of Biological Theories*. Albany, SUNY Pr, 1989.
Sloep, Peter B and Van Der Steen, Wim J. *Biol Phil* 6(1), 93-98 Ja 91

TIESZEN, Richard L. *Mathematical Intuition: Phenomenology and Mathematical Knowledge*. Dordrecht, Kluwer, 1989.
Resnik, Michael D. *Rev Metaph* 44(2), 442-444 D 90

TIFFENEAU, Dorian (ed). *Mythes et Représentations du Temps*. Meudon, CNRS, 1985.
Garvey, J C. *J Brit Soc Phenomenol* 21(3), 303-304 O 90

TILES, J E. *Dewey*. New York, Routledge, 1988.
Sprigge, T L S. *Phil Books* 31(4), 207-210 O 90

TILES, Mary. *The Philosophy of Set Theory: An Introduction to Cantor's Paradise*. Oxford, Blackwell, 1989.
Brown, James Robert. *Dialogue (Canada)* 29(2), 314-316 1990
Hallett, Michael. *Phil Quart* 41(163), 238-242 Ap 91
Dale, A J. *Brit J Phil Sci* 41(4), 575-578 D 90

TILLERS, P and GREEN, E D (eds). *Probability and Inference in the Law of Evidence: The Uses and Limits of Bayesianism*. Dordrecht, Kluwer, 1988.
Uffink, Jos. *Method Sci* 23(1), 49-55 1990

TILLIETTE, Xavier. *Filosofi davanti a Cristo*. Brescia, Queriniana, 1989.
Pellecchia, Pasquale. *Aquinas* 33(2), 461-465 My-Ag 90

TLABA, Gabriel Masooane. *Politics and Freedom: Human Will and Action in the Thought of Hannah Arendt*. New York, Univ Pr of America, 1987.
Knauer, James T. *Int Stud Phil* 22(3), 151-152 1990

TODD, D D (ed). *The Philosophical Orations of Thomas Reid Delivered at Graduate Ceremonies in King's College, Aberdeen, 1753/56/59/62*. Carbondale, So Illinois Univ Pr, 1989.
Adams, Todd L. *J Hist Phil* 29(3), 499-500 Jl 91

TOMBERLIN, James E and VAN INWAGEN, Peter (eds). *Alvin Plantinga*. Dordrecht, Reidel, 1985.
Askew, Richard. *Int J Phil Relig* 29(1), 56-62 F 91

TOMBERLIN, James E (ed). *Philosophical Perspectives, 1: Metaphysics*. Atascadero, Ridgeview, 1987.
Horgan, Terence. *Nous* 25(1), 143-145 Mr 91

TOMBERLIN, James E (ed). *Philosophical Perspectives, 3: Philosophy of Mind and Action Theory*. Atascadero, Ridgeview, 1989.
Marshall, Graeme. *Austl J Phil* 69(1), 120-122 Mr 91

TOOLEY, Michael. *Causation: A Realist Approach*. New York, Clarendon Pr, 1987.
Shoemaker, Sydney. *Phil Rev* 99(4), 661-664 O 90
Blackwell, Richard J. *Mod Sch* 68(3), 267-269 Mr 91
Woodward, J. *Brit J Phil Sci* 41(4), 553-573 D 90

TOULMIN, Stephen. *Cosmopolis: The Hidden Agenda of Modernity*. New York, Free Pr, 1990.
Arakawa, Dianne E. *Relig Hum* 24(4), 193-194 Autumn 90
Frey, Robert S. *Bridges* 2(3-4), 212-213 Fall-Wint 90

TRAPP, Rainer W. *"Nicht-klassischer" Utilitarismus*. Frankfurt am Main, Klostermann, 1988.
Birnbacher, Dieter. *Z Phil Forsch* 44(3), 486-491 1990

TRAVIS, Charles (ed). *Meaning and Interpretation*. Oxford, Blackwell, 1986.
Child, William. *Mind* 100(397), 162-171 Ja 91

TREJO, Wonfilio. *Fenomenalismo y realismo*. México, UNAM, 1987.
Benítez, Laura. *Dianoia* 34(34), 300-304 1988
Olivé, León. *Dianoia* 34(34), 295-300 1988

TRIGEAUD, Jean-Marc. *Humanisme de la liberté et philosophie de la justice, V2*. Bordeaux, Biere, 1990.
Tusa, Carlo. *Riv Int Filosof Diritto* 67(2), 350-352 Ap-Je 90

TRIGEAUD, Jean-Marc. *Essais de philosophie du droit*. Genes, Studio Ed Cultura, 1987.
Hartney, Michael. *Dialogue (Canada)* 29(4), 604-605 1990

TRIGG, Wilson. *Origen: The Bible and Philosophy in the Third-Century Church*. London, SCM Pr, 1985.
Sell, Alan P F. *Phil Stud (Ireland)* 32, 370-371 1988-90

TRIPOLITIS, Antonia. *Origen, A Critical Reading*. New York, Lang, 1990.
Torjesen, Karen Jo. *Ancient Phil* 11(1), 209-210 Spr 91

TROELSTRA, A S and VAN DALEN, D. *Constructivism in Mathematics, V1*. Amsterdam, North-Holland, 1988.
Beeson, Michael J. *Notre Dame J Form Log* 32(2), 320-322 Spr 91

TROELSTRA, A S and VAN DALEN, D. *Constructivism in Mathematics, V2*. Amsterdam, North-Holland, 1988.
Beeson, Michael J. *Notre Dame J Form Log* 32(2), 320-322 Spr 91

TSCHIERSKE, Ulrich. *Vernunftkeritik und ästhetische Subjektivität*. Tübingen, Niemeyer, 1988.
Pott, Hans-Georg. *Phil Rundsch* 37(3), 251-255 1990

TUCK, Richard. *Hobbes*. Oxford, Oxford Univ Pr, 1989.
Solomon, Graham. *Eidos* 8(2), 209-215 D 89

TUDOR, H and TUDOR, J M (eds). *Marxism and Social Democracy: The Revisionist Debate, 1896-1898*. Cambridge, Cambridge Univ Pr, 1988.
Lloyd, Christopher. *Hist Euro Ideas* 12(6), 857-858 1990

TULLOCH, Gail. *Mill and Sexual Equality*. Hemel Hempstead, Harvester-Wheatsheaf, 1989.
Crosthwaite, Jan. *Austl J Phil* 68(3), 360-361 S 90
Mendus, Susan. *Utilitas* 2(2), 325-327 N 90

TURNER, Gerald P and MAPA, Joseph (eds). *Humanistic Health Care: Issues for Caregivers*. Ann Arbor, Health Administration Pr, 1988.
Erde, Edmund L. *J Med Human* 11(4), 199-200 Wint 90

TURNER, Graeme. *Film as Social Practice*. New York, Routledge, Chapman & Hall, 1988.
Neill, Alex and Ridley, Aaron. *Can Phil Rev* 10(9), 345-351 S 90

TYE, Michael. *The Metaphysics of Mind*. Cambridge, Cambridge Univ Pr, 1989.
Sacks, Mark. *Phil Books* 32(1), 50-52 Ja 91

TYMIENIECKA, Anna-Teresa. *Logos and Life, V2: The Three Movements of the Soul*. Dordrecht, Kluwer, 1988.
Drummond, John J. *Rev Metaph* 44(2), 444-445 D 90

TYMIENIECKA, Anna-Teresa (ed). *Analecta Husserliana, V21*. Dordrecht, Reidel, 1986.
Hutcheson, Peter. *Mod Sch* 68(2), 183-185 Ja 91

ULMER, Gregory. *Teletheory: Grammatology in the Age of Video*. New York, Routledge, 1989.
Farndale, Nigel. *Brit J Aes* 31(3), 278-280 Jl 91

ULRICH, P. *Transformation der ökonomischen Vernunft*. Bern, Haupt, 1986.
Ortiz de Landázuri, Carlos. *Anu Filosof* 23(2), 192-198 1990

UMEHARA, Takeshi. *La philosophie japonaise des enfers*. Paris, Klincksieck, 1990.
Leterrier, Sophie-Anne. *Rev Phil Fr* 181(3), 360-365 Jl-S 91

URBACH, Peter. *Francis Bacon's Philosophy of Science*. Peru, Open Court, 1987.
Kaplan, Edward. *Int Stud Phil* 23(1), 141 1991

VALLÉE, Gerard and LAWSON, J B and CHAPPEL, C G (trans). *The Spinoza Conversations between Lessing and Jacobi: Text with Excerpts from the Ensuing Controversy*. Lanham, Univ Pr of America, 1988.
Breazeale, Daniel. *J Hist Phil* 29(2), 315-317 Ap 91

VALLET DE GOYTISOLO, Juan. *Montesquieu: leyes, gobiernos y poderes*. Madrid, Civitas, 1986.
Forment, E. *Espiritu* 37(98), 183-185 Jl-D 88

VAN BEECK, Frans Jozef. *God Encountered: A Contemporary Catholic Systematic Theology*. San Francisco, Harper & Row, 1989.
Dych, William V. *Thought* 66(260), 111-112 Mr 91

VAN DER LINDEN, Harry. *Kantian Ethics and Socialism*. Indianapolis, Hackett, 1988.
Kuehn, Manfred. *J Hist Phil* 29(2), 318-321 Ap 91

VAN DOORMAN, Bespreking. *Images of Science*. Brookfield, Gower, 1989.
Zandvoort, H. *Kennis Methode* 15(2), 207-212 1991

VAN FRAASSEN, Bas. *Laws and Symmetry*. Oxford, Oxford Univ Pr, 1989.
Price, Huw and Reinhardt, Lloyd. *Mind* 100(397), 149-152 Ja 91
Fetzer, James H. *Phil Books* 32(2), 65-75 Ap 91

VAN STRAATEN, Zak (ed). *Ideological Beliefs in the Social Sciences*. Pretoria, Human Sciences Research Council, 1987.
Van Veuren, Pieter. *S Afr J Phil* 9(4), 231-232 N 90

VARDY, Peter. *The Puzzle of God*. London, Collins, 1990.
Ward, Keith. *Heythrop J* 32(2), 282-283 Ap 91

VATTANKY, John. *Gangesa's Philosophy of God*. Madras, Adyar Library & Research Centre, 1984.
Matilal, Bimal Krishna. *J Indian Counc Phil Res* 5(2), 163-166 Ja-Ap 88

VATTIMO, Gianni. *The End of Modernity: Nihilism and Hermeneutics in Post-Modern Culture, Jon R Snyder (trans)*. Baltimore, Johns Hopkins Univ Pr, 1988.
Roqué, Alicia Juarrero. *Rev Metaph* 44(3), 657-658 Mr 91

VAUX, Kenneth. *Birth Ethics: Religious and Cultural Values in the Genesis of Life*. New York, Crossroads, 1989.
Thomasma, David C. *Med Human Rev* 5(1), 39-40 Ja 91

VAZ, H C de L. *Escritos de filosofia II; ética e cultura*. São Paulo, Loyola, 1988.
Nascimento, Carlos Arthur Ribeiro do. *Trans/Form/Acao* 13, 147-149 1990

VEATCH, Henry B. *Swimming Against the Current in Contemporary Philosophy*. Washington, Catholic Univ of America Pr, 1990.
Ford, John H. *Rev Metaph* 44(1), 171-172 S 90

VEESER, H Aram (ed). *The New Historicism*. New York, Routledge, 1989.
Collins, Stephen L. *Clio* 20(1), 84-91 Fall 90

VELKLEY, Richard. *Freedom and the End of Reason: On the Moral Foundations of Kant's Critical Philosophy*. Chicago, Univ of Chicago Pr, 1990.
Yack, Bernard. *Polit Theory* 18(4), 698-701 N 90
Sherover, Charles M. *Rev Metaph* 44(3), 658-660 Mr 91

VELLEMAN, J David. *Practical Reflection*. Princeton, Princeton Univ Pr, 1989.
Jewell, Robert D. *Phil Books* 32(2), 101-102 Ap 91
Kennett, Jeanette. *Austl J Phil* 68(3), 361-363 S 90
Knowles, Dudley. *Phil Quart* 40(161), 524-527 O 90

VENDLER, Zeno. *The Matter of Minds*. Oxford, Clarendon Pr, 1984.
Beck, S. *S Afr J Phil* 9(4), 227-228 N 90

VERCELLONE, Federico. *Identità dell'antico*. Torino, Rosemberg & Sellier, 1988.
Bottani, Livio. *Filosofia* 42(1), 124-128 Ja-Ap 91

VESEY, G and FOULKES, P (eds). *Collins Dictionary of Philosophy*. London, Collins, 1990.
Teichman, Jenny. *Philosophy* 66(255), 128-129 Ja 91

VESEY, Godfrey (ed). *The Philosophy in Christianity*. Cambridge, Cambridge Univ Pr, 1990.
Burns, R M. *Relig Stud* 27(2), 274-278 Je 91
Charlton, William. *Phil Quart* 41(163), 251-252 Ap 91

VESTUTI, Guido (ed). *Il realismo politico di Ludwig von Mises e Friedrich von Hayek*. Milan, Giuffrè, 1989.
Tusa, Carlo. *Riv Int Filosof Diritto* 67(2), 352-355 Ap-Je 90

VICKERS, John M. *Chance and Structure: An Essay on the Logical Foundations of Probability*. Oxford, Clarendon Pr, 1988.
Kerszberg, Pierre. *Phil Books* 31(4), 226-228 O 90

VICO, G. *Principios de una Ciencia nueva en torno a la naturaleza común de las naciones, J M Bermudo and A Camps (trans)*. Barcelona, Orbis, 1985.
Martinez Bisbal, Josep. *Boll Centro Stud Vichiani* 20, 233-240 1990

VIETTA, Silvio. *Heideggers Kritik am Nationalsozialismus und an der Technik*. Tubingen, Niemeyer, 1989.
Tertulian, Nicolas. *Arch Phil* 54(3), 497-500 Jl-S 91

VILLEY, Michel. *Questions de Saint Thomas sur le Droit et la Politique*. Paris, Pr Univ de France, 1987.
Balekjian, Wahé H. *Vera Lex* 10(1), 24-25 1990

VINCENT, Andrew (ed). *The Philosophy of T H Green*. Aldershot, Gower, 1986.
Waszek, Norbert. *Bull Hegel Soc Gt Brit* 20, 45-47 Autumn-Wint 89

VISION, Gerald. *Modern Anti-Realism and Manufactured Truth*. London, Routledge, 1988.
Malinas, Gary. *Austl J Phil* 68(3), 364-365 S 90

VOEGELIN, Eric. *Autobiographical Reflections*. Baton Rouge, Louisiana State Univ Pr, 1989.
Mitscherling, Jeff. *Hist Euro Ideas* 12(5), 704-706 1990

VOLPI, Franco and NIDA-RÜMELIN, Julian (eds). *Lexikon der philosophischen Werke*. Stuttgart, Kröner, 1988.
Schuhmann, Karl. *Z Phil Forsch* 44(3), 502-505 1990

VOLPICELLI, Ignazio. *A Schopenhauer: La natura vivente e le sue forme*. Settimo Milanese, Marzorati, 1988.
Cavallera, Hervé A. *Filosofia* 41(3), 427-428 S-D 90

VON STADEN, Heinrich. *Herophilus: The Art of Medicine in Early Alexandria*. Cambridge, Cambridge Univ Pr, 1989.
Hankinson, R J. *Phronesis* 35(2), 194-215 1990

VON WRIGHT, G H. *A Portrait of Wittgenstein as a Young Man: From the Diary of David Hume Pinsent 1912-1914*. Oxford, Blackwell, 1990.
Iglesias, Teresa. *Phil Stud (Ireland)* 32, 374-377 1988-90

VOS, Arvin. *Aquinas, Calvin, and Contemporary Protestant Thought*. Exeter, Paternoster Pr, 1985.
Sell, Alan P F. *Phil Stud (Ireland)* 32, 377-379 1988-90

VROOM, Hendrik M. *Religions and the Truth: Philosophical Reflections and Perspectives*. Grand Rapids, Eerdmans, 1989.
Kerlin, Michael J. *Thomist* 54(4), 744-746 O 90

VYVERBERG, Henry. *Human Nature, Cultural Diversity, and the French Enlightenment*. Oxford, Oxford Univ Pr, 1989.
Mason, Haydn. *Hist Euro Ideas* 12(5), 701-702 1990

WAGNER, Richard E. *To Promise the General Welfare*. San Francisco, Pacific Res Inst, 1989.
De Jasay, Anthony. *Crit Rev* 4(4), 537-544 Fall 90

WAGNER-DÖBLER, Roland. *Das Dilemma der Technikkontrolle*. Berlin, Sigma, 1989.
Rapp, Friedrich. *Conceptus* 24(62), 119-121 1990

WAITHE, Mary Ellen (ed). *A History of Women Philosophers, V1: Ancient Women Philosophers, 600 BC—500 AD*. Boston, Nijhoff, 1987.
Zedler, Beatrice H. *Mod Sch* 67(3), 231-233 Mr 90

WAITHE, Mary Ellen (ed). *A History of Women Philosophers, V2: Medieval, Renaissance and Enlightenment Women Philosophers AD 500-1600*. Boston, Kluwer, 1989.
Allen, Prudence. *Rev Metaph* 44(3), 660-662 Mr 91
Burton, Patricia. *Mod Sch* 68(2), 172-175 Ja 91

WALBY, Christine and SYMONS, Barbara. *Who Am I? Identity, Adoption and Human Fertilisation*. London, Brit Agencies for Adoption & Fostering, 1990.
Aitken, Jan. *Bioethics* 5(2), 179-181 Ap 91

WALDRON, Jeremy. *The Right to Private Property*. Oxford, Clarendon Pr, 1988.
Narveson, Jan. *Dialogue (Canada)* 29(1), 133-139 1990
Amato, Salvatore. *Riv Int Filosof Diritto* 67(1), 180-182 Ja-Mr 90
Ryan, Alan. *J Phil* 88(3), 155-159 Mr 91

WALKER, Martin. *The Bible as Rhetoric: Studies in Biblical Persuasion and Credibility*. New York, Routledge, 1990.
Coupe, Laurence. *J Brit Soc Phenomenol* 22(2), 111-113 My 91

WALKER, Ralph C S. *The Coherence Theory of Truth*. London, Routledge, 1989.
Malinas, Gary. *Austl J Phil* 68(3), 364-365 S 90
Siegwart, Geo. *Erkenntnis* 34(2), 261-266 Mr 91

WALTON, Douglas N. *Informal Logic: A Handbook for Critical Argumentation*. Cambridge, Cambridge Univ Pr, 1989.
Casey, Gerard. *Phil Stud (Ireland)* 32, 379-380 1988-90
Martinez, Roy. *Teach Phil* 13(4), 397-399 D 90
Freeman, James B. *Inform Log* 12(2), 87-105 Spr 90

WALTON, Kendall L. *Mimesis as Make-Believe: On the Foundations of Representational Art*. Cambridge, Harvard Univ Pr, 1990.
Kolenda, Konstantin. *Rev Metaph* 44(4), 875-876 Je 91

WANG, Hao. *Reflections on Kurt Gödel*. Cambridge, MIT Pr, 1987.
Shapiro, Stewart. *Phil Rev* 100(1), 130-133 Ja 91

WARE, Robert and NIELSEN, Kai (eds). *Analyzing Marxism*. Calgary, Univ of Calgary Pr, 1989.
Smith, Tony. *Can Phil Rev* 10(8), 334-336 Ag 90

WARNER, Martin. *Philosophical Finesse: Studies in the Art of Rational Persuasion*. Oxford, Clarendon Pr, 1989.
Millar, Alan. *Phil Books* 31(4), 218-220 O 90
Walton, Douglas N. *Hist Euro Ideas* 12(5), 696-697 1990
King-Farlow, John. *Philosophy* 66(255), 122-124 Ja 91

WARNER, Martin (ed). *The Bible as Rhetoric: Studies in Biblical Persuasion and Credibility*. London, Routledge, 1990.
O'Neil, Mary Anne. *Phil Lit* 15(1), 152-153 Ap 91

WARNOCK, G J. *J L Austin*. New York, Routledge, 1989.
Champlin, T S. *Philosophy* 65(254), 526-528 O 90
Holdcroft, David. *Phil Quart* 40(161), 522-524 O 90

WARTENBERG, Thomas E. *The Forms of Power: From Domination to Transformation*. Philadelphia, Temple Univ Pr, 1990.
Schmitt, Richard. *Soc Theor Pract* 17(1), 105-130 Spr 91

WASCHKIES, Hans-Joachim. *Physik und Physikotheologie des jungen Kant*. Amsterdam, Grüner, 1987.
Steinbeck, Wolfram. *Kantstudien* 81(4), 483-485 1990

WASZEK, Norbert. *The Scottish Enlightenment and Hegel's Account of 'Civil Society'*. Norwell, Kluwer, 1988.
Kuehn, Manfred. *Can Phil Rev* 10(8), 336-338 Ag 90
Stepelevich, Lawrence S. *J Hist Phil* 29(1), 141-142 Ja 91
Drydyk, Jay. *Owl Minerva* 22(2), 230-234 Spr 91
Bienenstock, Myriam. *Int Stud Phil* 23(1), 109-111 1991

WATERFIELD, Robin (trans). *Plato: Theaetetus*. Harmondsworth, Penguin, 1987.
Benson, Hugh H. *Ancient Phil* 10(2), 285-289 Fall 90

WATSON, Jean and RAY, Marilyn A (eds). *The Ethics of Care and the Ethics of Cure: Synthesis in Chronicity*. New York, National League for Nursing, 1988.
Johnstone, Megan-Jane. *Bioethics* 5(1), 78-83 Ja 91

WATSON, Richard A. *The Breakdown of Cartesian Metaphysics*. Atlantic Highlands, Humanities Pr, 1987.
Nadler, Steven. *Int Stud Phil* 22(3), 153-154 1990

WATTS, Fraser and WILLIAMS, Mark. *The Psychology of Religious Knowing*. Cambridge, Cambridge Univ Pr, 1988.
Meynell, Hugo. *Heythrop J* 32(2), 279-280 Ap 91

WAYMACK, Mark H and TALER, George A. *Medical Ethics and the Elderly: A Case Book*. Chicago, Pluribus Pr, 1988.
Glover, Jacqueline. *Theor Med* 12(1), 93-95 Mr 91
Kohn, Martin. *J Med Human* 11(4), 201-202 Wint 90

WAYMAN, Alex. *Buddhist Insight*. Delhi, Motilal, 1984.
Sen, Prabal Kumar. *J Indian Counc Phil Res* 5(2), 166-171 Ja-Ap 88

WEBB, Eugene. *Philosophers of Consciousness*. Seattle, Univ Washington Pr, 1988.
Sullivan, John. *Heythrop J* 32(3), 437 Jl 91

WEBER, Bruce H and DEPEW, David J and SMITH, James D (eds). *Entropy, Information and Evolution: New Perspectives on Physical and Biological Evolution*. Cambridge, MIT Pr, 1988.
Rottschaefer, William. *Behavior Phil* 18(2), 79-83 Fall-Wint 90

WEBER, M Andreas. *David Hume und Edward Gibbon, Religionssoziologie in der Aufklärung*. Frankfurt am Main, Hain, 1990.
Kuehn, Manfred. *Hume Stud* 17(1), 89 Ap 91

WEDIN, Michael V. *Mind and Imagination in Aristotle*. New Haven, Yale Univ Pr, 1988.
Hughes, G J. *Heythrop J* 32(3), 438-439 Jl 91

WEIL, Simone. *Leçons de philosophie*. Paris, Plon, 1989.
Küh, Rolf. *Arch Phil* 54(3), 503-504 Jl-S 91

WEINER, Joan. *Frege in Perspective*. Ithaca, Cornell Univ Pr, 1990.
Currie, Gregory. *Mind* 100(399), 419-421 Jl 91

WEINREB, Lloyd L. *Natural Law and Justice*. Cambridge, Harvard Univ Pr, 1987.
Cvek, Peter P. *Auslegung* 17(1), 81-84 Wint 91
Hughes, G J. *Heythrop J* 32(1), 99 Ja 91

WEINSHEIMER, Joel C. *Gadamer's Hermeneutics: A Reading of "Truth and Method"*. New Haven, Yale Univ Pr, 1988.
Nuyen, A T. *Phil Soc Sci* 21(1), 133-136 Mr 91

WEIR, Robert F. *Abating Treatment with Critically Ill Patients: Ethical and Legal Limits to the Medical Prolongation of Life*. New York, Oxford Univ Pr, 1989.
Young, Robert. *Bioethics* 4(4), 351-353 O 90
Cohen, Cynthia B. *Hastings Center Rep* 21(1), 41-43 Ja-F 91

WEISS, Johannes (ed). *Max Weber Heute: Erträge und Probleme der Forschung*. Frankfurt am Main, Suhrkamp, 1989.
Gessner, Willfried. *Deut Z Phil* 39(3), 344-346 1991

WEISS, Paul. *Toward a Perfected State*. Albany, SUNY Pr, 1986.
Lilly, Reginald. *Mod Sch* 68(1), 89-91 N 90

WEISSMAN, David. *Hypothesis and the Spiral of Reflection*. Albany, SUNY Pr, 1989.
Redner, Harry. *Rev Metaph* 44(3), 662-663 Mr 91

WEISZ, George (ed). *Social Science Perspectives on Medical Ethics*. Dordrecht, Kluwer, 1990.
Bouma, Gary D. *Bioethics* 5(1), 89-90 Ja 91

WELCH, Cyril. *Linguistic Responsibility*. Victoria, Sono Nis Pr, 1988.
Grimbergen, Elizabeth. *Man World* 24(1), 103-109 Ja 91

WENZEL, Harald. *George Herbert Mead zur Einführung*. Hamburg, Junius, 1990.
Cook, Gary A. *Trans Peirce Soc* 27(2), 245-250 Spr 91

WERTHEIMER, Alan. *Coercion*. Princeton, Princeton Univ Pr, 1987.
Bickenbach, Jerome E. *Can J Phil* 20(4), 577-600 D 90

WERTZ, Dorothy C and FLETCHER, John C (eds). *Ethics and Human Genetics*. Berlin, Springer, 1989.
Singer, Peter. *Bioethics* 5(3), 257-264 Jl 91

WESSEL, Horst. *Logik*. Berlin, VEB Deutscher Verlag, 1986.
Pandit, G L. *J Indian Counc Phil Res* 7(3), 158-160 My-Ag 90

WEST, Cornel. *The American Evasion of Philosophy: A Genealogy of Pragmatism*. Madison, Univ of Wisconsin Pr, 1989.
Cascardi, Anthony J. *Phil Lit* 14(2), 413-415 O 90
Gavin, William. *Personalist Forum* 6(2), 192-195 Fall 90

WESTERINK, L G. *Prolégomènes à la philosophie de Platon*. Paris, Les Belles Lettres, 1990.
Follon, Jacques. *Rev Phil Louvain* 89(82), 358-361 My 91

WESTERN, David and PEARL, Mary (eds). *Conservation for the Twenty-first Century*. New York, Oxford Univ Pr, 1989.
Gunter, Peter A Y. *Environ Ethics* 13(1), 95-96 Spr 91

WESTPHAL, Kenneth R. *Hegel's Epistemological Realism*. Dordrecht, Kluwer, 1989.
Lamb, David. *J Brit Soc Phenomenol* 22(1), 94-95 Ja 91

WHITE, Alan R. *The Language of Imagination*. Oxford, Blackwell, 1990.
Hannay, Alastair. *Phil Quart* 41(163), 245-247 Ap 91

WHITE, David A. *Myth and Metaphysics in Plato's "Phaedo"*. Selinsgrove, Susquehanna Univ Pr, 1989.
Eckstein, Jerome. *Rev Metaph* 44(2), 445-447 D 90

WHITE, Patricia (ed). *Personal and Social Education*. London, Kogan Page, 1989.
Wilson, John. *J Phil Educ* 24(1), 132-134 Sum 90

WHITE, Stephen K. *The Recent Work of Jürgen Habermas*. New York, Cambridge Univ Pr, 1988.
Mc Carthy, Thomas. *Phil Rev* 100(3), 530-533 Jl 91

WICKERI, Philip L. *Seeking the Common Ground: Protestant Christianity, the Three-Self Movement, and China's United Front*. Maryknoll, Orbis, 1988.
Jochim, Christian. *Phil East West* 41(1), 129-130 Ja 91

WIENPAHL, Paul. *The Radical Spinoza*. New York, New York Univ Pr, 1979.
Lusthaus, Dan. *J Chin Phil* 17(3), 386-395 S 90

WIERENGA, Edward R. *The Nature of God: An Inquiry into Divine Attributes*. Ithaca, Cornell Univ Pr, 1989.
Fischer, John Martin. *J Phil* 88(8), 427-433 Ag 91

WIGGINS, David. *Needs, Values, Truth: Essays in the Philosophy of Value*. Oxford, Blackwell, 1987.
DePaul, Michael R. *Mind* 99(396), 619-633 O 90

WILCOX, John T. *The Bitterness of Job: A Philosophical Reading*. Ann Arbor, Univ of Michigan Pr, 1989.
Yogev, Michael. *Phil Lit* 14(2), 429-430 O 90

WILDBERG, C. *John Philoponus' Criticism of Aristotle's Theory of Aether*. New York, de Gruyter, 1988.
Feldman, Seymour. *J Hellen Stud* 110, 243-244 1990

WILDBERG, Christian (trans). *Philoponus: Against Aristotle, On the Eternity of the World*. Ithaca, Cornell Univ Pr, 1987.
Schrenk, Lawrence P. *Ancient Phil* 10(2), 327-329 Fall 90

WILLARD, Charles Arthur. *A Theory of Argumentation*. Tuscaloosa, Univ of Alabama Pr, 1989.
Yoos, George E. *Phil Rhet* 24(2), 174-179 1991

WILLIAM OF AUVERGNE. *The Trinity, or the First Principle, Roland J Teske and Francis C Wade (trans)*. Milwaukee, Marquette Univ Pr, 1989.
Bourke, Vernon J. *Mod Sch* 67(4), 305-306 My 90

WILLIAMS, C J F. *What is Identity?* New York, Clarendon/Oxford Pr, 1989.
Elliot, Robert. *Mind* 100(399), 421-424 Jl 91
Malatesta, Michele. *Hist Phil Log* 12(2), 256-259 1991
Frápolli, Maria J. *Phil Books* 32(1), 40-41 Ja 91
Wilson, Catherine. *Rev Metaph* 44(3), 663-664 Mr 91

WILLIAMS, Carolyn. *Transfigured World: Walter Pater's Aesthetic Historicism*. Ithaca, Cornell Univ Pr, 1989.
Moye, Richard H. *Clio* 20(2), 198-202 Wint 91

WILLIAMS, Paul. *Mahayana Buddhism: The Doctrinal Foundations*. New York, Routledge, 1989.
Corless, Roger. *Mod Theol* 7(4), 376-377 Jl 91
Harvey, Peter. *Relig Stud* 26(3), 429-431 S 90

WILLIAMS, Raymond. *The Politics of Modernism: Against the New Conformists, Tony Pinkney (ed)*. London, Verso, 1989.
Laing, Stuart. *Brit J Aes* 31(1), 89-90 Ja 91

WILLIAMS, T C. *The Idea of the Miraculous*. New York, Macmillan, 1990.
Banner, Michael. *Philosophy* 66(257), 390-391 Jl 91

WILSHIRE, Bruce. *The Moral Collapse of the University: Professionalism, Purity, and Alienation*. Albany, SUNY Pr, 1989.
Gibboney, Richard A. *Educ Theor* 41(1), 99-104 Wint 91
Thompson, Warren K. *Bridges* 3(1-2), 145-146 Spr-Sum 91
Buford, Thomas O. *J Speculative Phil* 5(3), 221-225 1991

WILSON, Catherine. *Leibniz's Metaphysics: A Historical and Comparative Study*. Princeton, Princeton Univ Pr, 1990.
McRae, Robert. *Can Phil Rev* 10(12), 508-512 D 90
Parkinson, G H R. *Philosophy* 65(253), 377-378 Jl 90

WILSON, George M. *The Intentionality of Human Action*. Stanford, Stanford Univ Pr, 1989.
Dutton, Alan. *Phil Books* 31(4), 239-241 O 90

WILSON, John and COWELL, Barbara. *Taking Education Seriously*. New York, Falmer Pr, 1989.
Bandman, Bertram. *Educ Stud* 21(4), 457-461 Wint 90

WINCH, Peter. *Simone Weil: The Just Balance*. Cambridge, Cambridge Univ Pr, 1989.
Allen, Diogenes. *Teach Phil* 13(3), 310-314 S 90

WINCH, Peter. *Trying to Make Sense*. New York, Blackwell, 1987.
Mavrodes, George I. *Int J Phil Relig* 29(3), 190-192 Je 91

WINFIELD, Richard Dien. *Reason and Justice*. Albany, SUNY Pr, 1988.
Shultz, David. *Int Stud Phil* 23(1), 142 1991

WINFIELD, Richard Dien. *Reason and Justice*. Albany, SUNY Pr, 1988.
Lucas Jr, George R. *Owl Minerva* 22(1), 81-90 Fall 90
Winfield, Richard Dien. *Owl Minerva* 22(1), 91-93 Fall 90

WINKELS, Theo. *Kants Forderung nach Konstitution einer Erziehungswissenschaft*. Munchen, Profil, 1984.
Wolandt, Barbara. *Kantstudien* 82(1), 114-118 1991

WINKLER, Kenneth P. *Berkeley: An Interpretation*. New York, Clarendon/Oxford Pr, 1989.
Dancy, Jonathan. *Phil Invest* 14(3), 284-288 Jl 91
Flage, Daniel E. *Rev Metaph* 44(2), 447-448 D 90
Welker, David. *Teach Phil* 13(3), 284-287 S 90

WINNIFRITH, Tom and BARRETT, Cyril (eds). *The Philosophy of Leisure*. London, Macmillan, 1989.
Proudfoot, Michael. *Phil Books* 31(4), 248-249 O 90

WINTERBOURNE, Anthony. *The Ideal and the Real*. Norwell, Kluwer, 1988.
Treloar, John L. *Mod Sch* 68(3), 265-267 Mr 91

WITT, Charlotte. *Substance and Essence in Aristotle: An Interpretation of Metaphysics VII-IX*. Ithaca, Cornell Univ Pr, 1989.
Seidl, Horst. *Rev Metaph* 44(1), 172-174 S 90

WITTGENSTEIN, L. *Lectures on Philosophical Psychology 1946-47, P T Geach (ed)*. Chicago, Univ of Chicago Pr, 1988.
Hunter, J F M. *Can Phil Rev* 10(8), 339-341 Ag 90

WÖHLER, Hans-Ulrich. *Geschichte der Mittelalterlichen Philosophie*. Berlin, Deutscher Verlag, 1989.
Winkler, Norbert. *Deut Z Phil* 38(11), 1107-1109 1990

WOHLMAN, Avital. *Eros and Logos*. Jerusalem, Kesset, 1990.
Lowe, Malcolm. *Iyyun* 40(3), 347-350 Jl 91

WOJICKI, Ryszard. *Theory of Logical Calculi: Basis Theory of Consequence Operations*. Dordrecht, Kluwer, 1988.
Bloom, Stephen L. *J Sym Log* 55(3), 1324-1326 S 90

WOLENSKI, Jan. *Logic and Philosophy in the Lvov-Warsaw School*. Boston, Kluwer, 1989.
Perreiah, Alan R. *J Hist Phil* 29(1), 149-150 Ja 91
Schmit, Roger. *Rev Int Phil* 44(174), 496-501 1990

WOLF-GAZO, Ernest (ed). *Process in Context: Essays in Post-Whiteheadian Perspectives*. Bern, Lang, 1988.
Corrington, Robert S. *Trans Peirce Soc* 26(4), 550-557 Fall 90

WOLGAST, Elizabeth H. *The Grammar of Justice*. Ithaca, Cornell Univ Pr, 1987.
Byrne, Edmund F. *Nous* 25(1), 137-139 Mr 91

WOLIN, Sheldon S. *The Presence of the Past: Essays on the State and the Constitution*. Baltimore, Johns Hopkins Univ Pr, 1989.
Levinson, Sanford. *Polit Theory* 18(4), 701-705 N 90

WOLTER, Allan B (ed & trans). *Duns Scotus' Political and Economic Philosophy*. Santa Barbara, Old Mission Santa Barbara, 1989.
Santogrossi, Ansgar. *Rev Metaph* 44(2), 433-435 D 90

WOLTER, Allan B and MC CORD ADAMS, Marilyn (ed). *The Philosophical Theology of John Duns Scotus*. Ithaca, Cornell Univ Pr, 1990.
Incandela, Joseph M. *Thomist* 55(3), 517-522 Jl 91

WOOD, David. *The Deconstruction of Time*. Atlantic Highlands, Humanities Pr, 1989.
Hodge, Joanna. *Rad Phil* 57, 52-53 Spr 91

WORTON, Michael and STILL, Judith (eds). *Intertextuality: Theories and Practices*. Manchester, Manchester Univ Pr, 1990.
Macey, David. *Rad Phil* 57, 53 Spr 91

WREN, Thomas E and EDELSTEIN, Wolfgang and NUNNER-WINKLER, Gertrud (eds). *Essays in the Ongoing Discussion between Philosophy and the Social Sciences*. Cambridge, MIT Pr, 1990.
Pawlikowski, John T. *Bridges* 2(3-4), 215-216 Fall-Wint 90

WRIGHT, Crispin. *Realism, Meaning and Truth*. Oxford, Blackwell, 1987.
Asher, Nicholas. *Phil Rev* 100(1), 107-109 Ja 91

WRIGHT, Richard A. *African Philosophy*. Lanham, Univ of America Pr, 1984.
Birt, Robert E. *Phil East West* 41(1), 95-109 Ja 91

WRINGE, Colin. *Understanding Educational Aims*. London, Unwin Hyman, 1988.
Gilroy, Peter. *J Phil Educ* 24(1), 136-140 Sum 90

WUNEBURGER, Jean-Jacques. *La raison contradictoire*. Paris, Albin Michel, 1990.
Largeault, Jean. *Rev Phil Fr* 180(4), 720-722 O-D 90

YOUNG, Julian. *Willing and Unwilling: A Study in the Philosophy of Arthur Schopenhauer*. Dordrecht, Nijhoff, 1987.
Loptson, Peter. *Dialogue (Canada)* 29(4), 612-615 1990

YOUNG, Paul. *The Nature of Information*. New York, Praeger, 1987.
Bigelow, John. *Austl J Phil* 68(2), 244-245 Je 90

YOUNG, Robert E. *A Critical Theory of Education: Habermas and Our Children's Future*. New York, Teachers College Pr, 1990.
Collins, Clinton. *Educ Stud* 21(4), 467-472 Wint 90

YOVEL, Yirmiyahu. *Spinoza and Other Heretics, 2v*. Princeton, Princeton Univ Pr, 1989.
James, Susan. *Phil Books* 32(2), 80-82 Ap 91

YU MINGGUANG. *Huangdi Sijing yu Huang-Lao sixiang*. Harbin, Hei Longjiang People's Pr, undated.
Peerenboom, R P. *Phil East West* 41(2), 258-261 Ap 91

YUASA YASUO. *The Body: Toward an Eastern Mind-Body Theory*. Albany, SUNY Pr, 1987.
Ludwig, Walter D. *Phil East West* 41(2), 261-264 Ap 91

ZALTA, Edward N. *Intensional Logic and the Metaphysics of Intentionality*. Cambridge, MIT Pr, 1988.
Hazen, A P. *Phil Rev* 100(3), 474-476 Jl 91

ZANER, Richard M (ed). *Death: Beyond Whole-Brain Criteria*. Norwell, Kluwer, 1988.
Griener, Glenn G. *Can Phil Rev* 10(8), 341-343 Ag 90

ZANOTTI, Gabriel J. *El Humanismo del Futuro*. Buenos Aires, Belgrano, 1989.
Derisi, Octavio N. *Sapientia* 45(176), 158-160 Ap-Je 90

ZARADER, Marlène. *La dette impensée*. Paris, Seuil, 1990.
Trotignon, Pierre. *Rev Phil Fr* 181(2), 228-229 Ap-Je 91

ZARKA, Yves Charles (ed). *Thomas Hobbes, Philosophie première, thèorie de la science et politique*. Paris, Pr Univ de France, 1990.
Costa, Margarita. *Cuad Filosof* 21(34), 57-71 My 90

ZEH, H D. *The Physical Basis of the Direction of Time*. Berlin, Springer, 1989.
Price, Huw. *Brit J Phil Sci* 42(1), 111-144 Mr 91

ZILBERMAN, David B. *The Birth of Meaning in Hindu Thought*. Boston, Reidel, 1988.
Shaw, J L. *Int Stud Phil* 23(1), 143-144 1991

ZIMMERLI, Walther Ch (ed). *Technologisches Zeitalter oder Postmoderne?* Munich, Fink, 1988.
Bast, Rainer A. *Z Phil Forsch* 45(1), 163-168 Ja-Mr 91

ZIMMERMAN, Michael E. *Heidegger's Confrontation with Modernity: Technology, Politics, Art*. Bloomington, Indiana Univ Pr, 1990.
Rée, Jonathan. *Rad Phil* 57, 45-47 Spr 91

ZIZEK, Slavoj. *The Sublime Object of Ideology*. London, Verso, 1989.
Lecercle, Jean-Jacques. *Rad Phil* 57, 33-34 Spr 91

ZOLO, Danilo. *Reflexive Epistemology: The Philosophical Legacy of Otto Neurath, David McKie (trans)*. Norwell, Kluwer, 1989.
Esser, P H. *Method Sci* 23(1), 57-60 1990